COLLINS
SPANISH - ENGLISH
ENGLISH - SPANISH
DICTIONARY

DICCIONARIO
ESPAÑOL - INGLÉS
INGLÉS - ESPAÑOL

COLLINS DICCIONARIO ESPAÑOL-INGLÉS INGLÉS-ESPAÑOL

por Colin Smith
en colaboración con
Manuel Bermejo Marcos
y Eugenio Chang-Rodríguez

Collins · London & Glasgow

COLLINS
SPANISH-ENGLISH
ENGLISH-SPANISH
DICTIONARY

by Colin Smith
in collaboration with
Manuel Bermejo Marcos
and Eugenio Chang-Rodríguez

Collins · London & Glasgow

First published 1971

© Copyright 1971 William Collins Sons & Co. Ltd.

16th Printing 1987

ISBN 0 00 433471 X
Thumb Index ISBN 0 00 433472 8

COLIN SMITH IS PROFESSOR OF SPANISH, UNIVERSITY OF
CAMBRIDGE, AND FELLOW OF ST. CATHARINE'S COLLEGE
MANUEL BERMEJO MARCOS IS SENIOR LECTURER IN SPANISH,
UNIVERSITY OF LEEDS
EUGENIO CHANG-RODRÍGUEZ IS CHAIRMAN, LATIN AMERICAN
AREA STUDIES,
QUEENS COLLEGE OF THE CITY UNIVERSITY OF NEW YORK

Collins Publishers
P.O. Box, Glasgow G4 0NB, Great Britain
100 Lesmill Road, Don Mills, Ontario M3B 2T5, Canada

Printed and bound in Spain
by Artes Gráficas Toledo, S.A.

Dep. L.: To. 828 - 1987

Contents

Materias

Preface

Given the rapidity of change in language and in its social and theoretical aspects, a new dictionary hardly needs an apology. This dictionary would be justified even if it were of the traditional type; in fact it incorporates new principles (discussed in the Introduction) which may be of interest to linguists, and whose practical application should ease the task of users at every level.

The lexicographer who attempts to equate and harmonize two great world languages must honestly recognize that both in theory and in practice his task cannot be perfectly fulfilled. The simplest word often has such a range, such semantic potentiality and such nuances that it cannot be fully defined within a single-language dictionary; it is more difficult still to translate it in a two-language dictionary of modest size.

This is, however, an optimistic undertaking. It presupposes that the two linguistic areas are in contact for reasons of trade, diplomacy, and tourism; for cultural, literary, scientific and sporting exchanges; that each has something to learn from the other and the will to do so. It presupposes free intercommunication across the frontiers and the oceans. The dictionary is a tool of understanding and it speaks for peace, tolerance and mutual respect.

I am greatly indebted to the following: Dr M. Bermejo Marcos, who read all the drafts; Prof. E. Chang-Rodríguez, who read the first part to check information about American Spanish; Mr H. B. Hall, who advised on principles at the start and read sections of the second part; and for a variety of contributions, to Mr T. C. Bookless, Prof. R. F. Brown, Dr G. A. Davies, Miss A. Johnson, Mr A. Madigan, Mr A. McCallum, Miss G. Weston, Sr J. and Sra M. del Río, Sra A. Espinosa de Walker and Sra M. J. Fernández de Wangermann. My wife helped in all the ways that wives do. To them all, my warmest thanks.

CCS

Cambridge   March 1971

Prefacio

El rápido desarrollo de las lenguas y de sus aspectos sociales y teóricos eximen al autor de la necesidad de disculparse al publicar un nuevo diccionario. Este libro se justificaría aun cuando fuera del tipo tradicional; se justifica más incorporando varios principios nuevos que pueden tener interés para los lingüistas, y cuya aplicación práctica podrá ayudar a los usuarios de todo tipo.

El lexicógrafo que se esfuerza por juntar y armonizar dos grandes idiomas mundiales tiene que reconocer honradamente que tanto en la teoría como en la práctica es imposible llevar perfectamente a cabo su cometido. La palabra más sencilla puede tener tal extensión, tanta potencialidad semántica y tantos matices que resulta imposible definirla en un libro monolingüe; es más difícil todavía traducirla en un diccionario bilingüe de tamaño modesto.

Con todo, esta empresa se funda en el optimismo. Ello supone que las dos áreas lingüísticas están en contacto por razones comerciales, diplomáticas y turísticas; para el intercambio cultural, literario, científico y deportivo; porque cada una tiene interés en aprender de la otra, y la voluntad de hacerlo. Ello supone que existe la libre comunicación a través de las fronteras y de los océanos. El diccionario sirve para la comprensión mutua y habla en pro de la paz.

Agradezco la ayuda de: Dr M. Bermejo Marcos, que leyó todos los borradores; Prof. E. Chang-Rodríguez, que leyó la 1ª parte para mejorar lo referente al español de América; Sr H. B. Hall, que me aconsejó al principio y leyó varias letras de la 2ª parte. Han contribuido también: Sr T. C. Bookless, Prof. R. F. Brown, Dr G. A. Davies, Srta A. Johnson, Sr A. Madigan, Sr A. McCallum, Srta G. Weston, Sr J. y Sra M. del Río, Sra A. Espinosa de Walker y Sra M. J. Fernández de Wangermann. Mi mujer ha prestado su ayuda en las maneras en que suelen prestarla las mujeres. Para todos, mis gracias.

Introduction

I GENERAL PRINCIPLES AND AIMS

MY PRINCIPLES IN COMPILING THIS dictionary have been carefully thought out and applied. Since they differ somewhat from those obtaining in comparable works, and in order that the user should profit fully from the book and appreciate the reasons why things are done as they are, it is worth stating these principles and explaining their application in detail.

1 Modern usage

My aim was to make a dictionary of modern current English and Spanish which, rather than taking the abstraction of one national *langue* (as it is represented, for example, in the Oxford English and Spanish Academy dictionaries) and translating it into the other, should embrace no more than the typical *parole* or personal language of the average educated English speaker of 1970, and that of the corresponding speaker of Spanish. This average educated speaker uses a relatively few dozens of absolutely basic words — verbs, nouns and prepositions — which come to his lips many times a day; he further possesses an active vocabulary of a few thousand words which he speaks on occasion, reads in novels and newspapers, hears on TV and radio, uses at his work (if not too technical) and in business correspondence, and so on. This average speaker has a family and a car, an interest in a variety of mildly scholarly subjects, an active or passive interest in a number of sports; he watches his health, follows space exploration and scientific progress in general terms, travels abroad, grows flowers, eats with some variety, prays, votes, makes love and occasionally war. It is likely that he has some slightly specialized technical competence and the vocabulary that goes with it because of his work or his hobbies; and since the personal *parole* of one man — the compiler — may be untypical in this respect,

Introducción

PRINCIPIOS Y PROPÓSITOS EN GENERAL

LOS PRINCIPIOS EN QUE SE BASA EL diccionario han sido pensados con cierto cuidado. Son algo distintos de los que se observan en otros trabajos de este tipo; para ayudar al lector a sacar el máximo provecho de la obra, y para que comprenda su sistema y sus métodos, he creído tener la obligación de explicar estos principios y su aplicación en forma detallada.

El uso moderno

Mi propósito ha sido el de hacer un diccionario de las formas modernas y corrientes de los dos idiomas, tomando no la abstracción de una *langue* (lengua) nacional (tal como ésta se encuentra representada, por ejemplo, en los diccionarios de Oxford y de la Academia Española) y traduciéndola a la otra, sino abarcando tan sólo la *parole* (habla) típica o lenguaje personal del inglés (y norteamericano) culto medio de 1970, y del hispanohablante correspondiente. Este hablante típico dentro de su relativa cultura emplea algunas docenas de palabras verdaderamente básicas — verbos, sustantivos y preposiciones — que se le vienen a los labios muchísimas veces cada día; posee además un vocabulario activo de varios miles de palabras que emplea de vez en cuando, que lee en novelas y periódicos, que escucha por TV y por radio, que emplea en su trabajo (no siendo éste de tipo demasiado técnico) y en la correspondencia comercial, etc. Este hablante medio tiene familia y coche, tiene interés en varios temas ligeramente eruditos, y un interés activo o pasivo en los deportes; cuida su salud, presta atención en términos generales a la exploración espacial y al progreso científico, viaja por el extranjero, cultiva algunas flores, come con cierta variedad, reza, vota, hace el amor y alguna vez la guerra. Es probable que tenga conocimientos de alguna técnica especializada y del vocabulario que la acompaña, gracias a su

for dictionary purposes we put together a number of these technical *paroles*, none of them at all abstruse.

The dictionary does not claim, then, as others produced on different principles no doubt rightly do, that it contains so many tens of thousands of main entries, takes in most of *la langue*, and has almost all the words however abstruse which the user is likely to want to look up perhaps only once in a lifetime, perhaps never. I have borne our average educated man constantly in mind and freed these pages of lexicographical lumber; what remains is, I hope, fairly typical usage in the two languages.

2 Treatment of basic words

Attention has been concentrated on the relatively few basic words which are always in frequent use, each of them a small semantic world of its own and each of them constantly entering into idioms, figurative expressions, comparisons and the like. The reader may satisfy himself about this point by a glance at such English entries as *do, give, go, have, put, on, up, hand, life, time, way*, and on the Spanish side *dar, hacer, poner, a, en, mano*. Also special attention has been given to those words, mainly verbs, which in the experience of the compiler give students some difficulty in translation: *enjoy, like, fail, miss*. Since a verb is often a lifeless thing in isolation, the policy has been regularly to give the construction which it requires, sometimes by a sort of formula and sometimes by practical example early in the entry; these matters seem to me to belong in the dictionary and not to deserve relegation to a grammar book. The usual idioms and set phrases, even clichés, are included in great numbers, and there are often separate sections in which the figurative senses are explored. The major innovation in this regard is, however, the provision of abundant usage examples. Words hardly have an existence in isolation but come to life in meaningful continuous discourse, and I have provided these live contexts wherever possible; such examples have the further purpose of demonstrating the use of constructions, word-order differences in the two languages, the replacement of English passive by Spanish

trabajo o a algún pasatiempo; y puesto que la *parole* personal de un solo hombre — esto es, del autor — puede distar de ser típico en este aspecto, juntamos para los propósitos lexicográficos cierta cantidad de estas *paroles* técnicas, sin que ninguna de ellas llegue a ser realmente recóndita.

El diccionario no pretende, pues, como pretenden otros — sin duda con razón, pues están hechos sobre otros principios — abarcar tantas decenas de miles de palabras, ni incluir la mayor parte de *la langue*, ni contener casi todas las palabras por más oscuras que sean que el usuario pudiera buscar una vez en la vida, quizá nunca. He tenido siempre en cuenta nuestro hablante culto típico, y he procurado que estas páginas queden libres de palabras-trastos; confío en que lo que queda represente el verdadero uso típico de los dos idiomas.

Tratamiento de las palabras básicas

Se ha cifrado la atención en las palabras básicas — en número relativamente pequeño — que están en uso constantemente, siendo cada una de ellas un pequeño mundo semántico en sí, y entrando cada una a formar frases hechas, modismos, expresiones figuradas, comparaciones, etc. El lector se satisfará sobre este particular consultando p.ej. los artículos ingleses *do, give, go, have, put, on, up, hand, life, time, way*, y los españoles *dar, hacer, poner, a, en, mano*. Se ha prestado también atención especial a las palabras (sobre todo verbos) que mayor dificultad presentan en la traducción; p.ej. *enjoy, like, fail, miss*. Como el verbo casi no tiene vida cuando se cita aislado, cito de modo regular el régimen que cada uno pide, algunas veces mediante una especie de fórmula y otras mediante un ejemplo casi al principio del artículo; esta información me ha parecido ser propia del diccionario y no pertenecer únicamente al libro de gramática. Se incluyen en grandes cantidades los modismos y frases hechas, hasta los clichés, y a menudo se dedica un apartado especial a los sentidos figurados de las palabras. Pero en este aspecto la mayor innovación consiste en la provisión de copiosos ejemplos del uso. Las palabras apenas tienen verdadera existencia en el aislamiento, pero cobran vida en el discurso continuo que comunica algo; siempre cuando ha sido posible les he dado este contexto vivo. Los ejemplos del uso tienen también el propósito de demostrar las construcciones, las

reflexive, and so on. These usage examples have been made as lively, human and authentic as the compiler's imagination allowed.

A further point in the argument for expanding the treatment of the basic words and excluding abstruse terminology is that the former often go on presenting difficulties even to those who know the other language well. The correct use of modest monosyllabic prepositions can cause intense anxiety, whereas anyone possessing a slight acquaintance with English or Spanish can predict that the word *intramolecular* in English will be *intramolecular* in Spanish, or that the new state of *Pogolandia* in Spanish must be *Pogoland* in English.

3 Organization of the entry

Since many of the basic word entries are lengthy, much thought has been given to the problem of planning them (before anything was translated), and to their clear division into sections and subsections. This is explained in detail below. Here we may remark that although this is not unique it is at least unusual in English-Spanish lexicography, in which the tradition seems to be of a headword followed by a jumble of translations and phrases vaguely separated by commas and semicolons but not offering much guidance to the user. In addition to the subdivision of the longer entries, there is in this dictionary a constant provision of abbreviations and semantic and other indicators which should lead the user to the correct translation; the process of tracking down takes place within the one entry, and the ancient cry of "Keep checking back in the other half of the dictionary until you find the right word" need no longer be heard. Further details of this system are given below.

4 Technical terminology

In breadth of technical terminology, as explained, this dictionary does not stretch very far; basic medicine is included but not virology, automobile maintenance but not the parts of the nuclear breeder-reactor, elementary typography but not the arcane terms known only to typographers. To aid users who seek further information in such fields

diferencias en el orden de palabras en los dos idiomas, la sustitución de la voz pasiva inglesa por el verbo reflexivo español, etc. He procurado dar a estos ejemplos toda la viveza, humanidad y autenticidad que la imaginación ha permitido.

Hay otra razón para excluir las palabras recónditas y aumentar el espacio dedicado a las palabras básicas: es que éstas siguen planteando problemas aun para aquéllos que dominan bastante bien el otro idioma. El uso correcto de las preposiciones monosílabas, tan modestas, puede motivar la mayor incertidumbre, mientras el que tenga el más superficial conocimiento del inglés y del español podrá predecir que la palabra inglesa *intramolecular* será en español *intramolecular*, o bien que el nuevo estado de *Pogolandia* en español habrá forzosamente de llamarse en inglés *Pogoland*.

Organización del artículo

Debido a la gran extensión de muchos artículos sobre las palabras básicas, se ha estudiado con cuidado el problema de organizarlos (antes de empezar la traducción) y el problema de dividirlos claramente. El sistema se explica detalladamente más abajo. Aquí conviene apuntar que tal sistema aunque no es único es poco corriente en la lexicografía anglo-española, pues parece haber casi una tradición de que a la palabra cabeza de artículo le siga una masa de traducciones y de frases vagamente divididas por comas o por comas y puntos, donde apenas tiene guía el lector. En este diccionario no sólo se dividen y subdividen los artículos extensos sino también se ofrecen a cada paso abreviaturas y aclaraciones semánticas y de otros tipos cuya finalidad es guiar al lector hasta que encuentre la traducción apropiada; esta búsqueda se lleva a cabo dentro del mismo artículo, para que nadie tenga que volver a escuchar aquello tan repetido de "Siga comprobando en la otra parte del diccionario hasta dar con la palabra exacta".

Términos técnicos

Según hemos dicho, este diccionario no tiene gran alcance en lo referente a terminología técnica; se incluye la medicina elemental pero la virología no, la manutención del automóvil pero no los componentes del reactor-generador nuclear, algunas nociones de tipografía pero no las palabras raras que conocen únicamente los tipógrafos. Para

a list of bilingual technical dictionaries is given in an appendix. Two special fields call for comment: that of sport and spectacle, and that of natural history. In sport the policy has been to include a good deal of vocabulary for games which are international and therefore translatable; so there is plenty of football but not much cricket. Spaniards and Americans have, to the compiler's regretful but certain knowledge, the faintest possible interest in the latter subject; to tell them that an *over* consists of six throwings (?) of a ball from one end of the wicket would be pointless if brief, space-consuming if long, and would in any case probably never be read. Bullfighting (not a sport, of course) at first seemed to be in the same category of the non-translatable — though not by any means non-interesting — but a certain amount of vocabulary from it has been included under pressure from others. I remain doubtful whether the typical translation "a certain pass with the cape" is of very much help to the user who had already deduced as much from the context in which he heard or read the word. Obviously the person who really wants to know will turn to a full technical description by a specialist in the art. In natural history the problem is different but equally insoluble for the present. No doubt a *seagull* is a *gaviota* and this is all that some need to know, but it is not a specific term in scientific usage; if one divides up the vaguely generic notion of *seagull* one finds that there are agreed and quite widely known English terms, but that Spaniards — who are poor on such subjects — do not have a word at all, or have an official term which is simply a vulgarization of the Latin generic and specific names but has no real currency; one finds also that the dictionaries are cluttered with contradictory information. (On this and cognate problems, see K. Whinnom, *A Glossary of Spanish Bird-names*, London, Támesis, 1966.) The names of fish seem to change every 50 kilometres along the Spanish coasts, and British species may not correspond exactly to Spanish ones, let alone to those of the Americas. The same problems arise with insect names and botanical terms. Clearly the general lexicographer can do little until those who are qualified scientifically and in the two languages have produced reliable lists; such persons are rare in Britain and the US and very rare indeed on Hispanic territory. Even when such lists are available large parts of them would consist of Latin names and vernacular names

ayudar a los lectores que busquen más información sobre tales cosas doy en un apéndice una lista de diccionarios técnicos. Necesitan comentario especial dos esferas del vocabulario: la de los deportes y del espectáculo, y la de la historia natural. En cuanto al deporte, se ha incluido el vocabulario para los juegos que tienen carácter internacional, así que está bien representado el fútbol pero escasamente el críquet. El interés que muestran los hispanohablantes por el críquet es casi nulo; decirles que el *over* consiste en seis echadas (?) de una pelota desde un extremo del *wicket* (intraducible) sería inútil en forma escueta y ocuparía mucho espacio si se explicara adecuadamente, y en todo caso es probable que nadie lo vaya a leer. A primera vista me pareció que el toreo (que no es ningún deporte, desde luego) pertenecía a la misma categoría de lo intraducible, pero accediendo a los ruegos de otros he incluido cierta cantidad del léxico taurino. Sigo sin embargo dudando que la típica traducción "cierto pase con la capa" le vaya a ayudar al lector, pues éste ya lo habrá adivinado por el contexto en que ha oído o leído la palabra. El lector que realmente quiera saber irá naturalmente a una descripción técnica y completa por un especialista en el arte. En la historia natural el problema es distinto pero igualmente insoluble. Sin duda un *seagull* es una *gaviota* y con decirlo les basta a algunos lectores; pero *seagull* no es nombre específico que valga en el uso científico. Si se divide la vaga noción genérica de *seagull* nos encontramos con que en inglés existen nombres convenidos y extensamente conocidos, pero que los españoles — que no son muy fuertes en este campo — o no tienen palabra, o tienen un término oficial que no es más que una forma vulgarizada de los nombres latinos genérico y específico, y que deja de tener verdadera aceptación. También nos encontramos con que los diccionarios están llenos de información contradictoria. (Para este problema y afines, véase K. Whinnom, *A Glossary of Spanish Bird-names*, Londres, Támesis, 1966.) Los nombres de los peces parecen cambiar cada cierta distancia en la costa española, y las especies británicas pueden no cuadrar exactamente con las españolas, ni mucho menos con las de América. Surgen los mismos problemas con los nombres de insectos y con la botánica. Es evidente que el lexicógrafo general puede hacer muy poco hasta que aquellas personas

in one language only, without any possible correspondence in the other vernacular.

5 Time scale and social register

"Modern" and "current" perhaps require elucidation. The time scale has been stretched to take in some words which appear in the standard literature of the two countries likely to be read by foreigners, and which are widely known even if no longer in current use. This does not of course include words from as far back as Shakespeare and the *Celestina*. Other well-known archaisms are included and marked as such, for they occasionally appear in period plays and films, and in jocular use.

The range of social tone, of "register", represented in the two languages, is wide. High-class words proper to poetry and to literature are included and labelled accordingly. At the lower end of the scale a very great number of familiar or colloquial words and phrases are included on the grounds that they are an essential part of "usage" as defined above, and because in the general relaxation of the social formalities in our time such words are heard in ministerial broadcasts and read in newspaper leaders from which they were absent 20 years ago; the labelling of such items is rather arbitrary, and depends on the compiler's instinct rather than on any printed authority. As for slang, while it is picturesque, expressive, and close to the compiler's heart, it is by definition restricted in scope, and also transitory and unestablished, so that although it can often be translated only the more widely known words merit inclusion. Wherever possible the social tone of a word has been translated accurately, familiar by familiar and so on, sometimes with the addition of a more standard term for those who prefer safety first. Clichés of conversation, correspondence, news reports, political speeches and the like are also well represented; inclusion does not imply approval.

No great originality is claimed for the supplementary information given in preliminaries and appendices, but thought has been given to its presentation.

que estén capacitadas en cada ciencia y en los dos idiomas hayan publicado un estudio para cada especialidad; son escasas tales personas en el Reino Unido y en EE.UU., y escasísimas en territorio hispánico. Aun cuando dispongamos de tales listas, gran parte de ellas consistirán en nombres latinos y nombres vernáculos en un idioma nada más, no habiendo correspondencia posible en el otro.

La palabra en el tiempo y su tono social

El concepto de lo "moderno" y "corriente" en la lengua pide alguna aclaración. Se ha extendido la noción para abarcar las palabras que aparecen en la literatura clásica de los dos idiomas y que son bastante conocidas aunque no están todavía en uso. No se abarcan, desde luego, palabras de época tan remota como son la de Shakespeare o de la *Celestina*. Se incluyen (con la abreviatura correspondiente) los arcaísmos más conocidos, pues éstos aparecen alguna vez en dramas históricos y en películas, y en el uso humorístico.

Es muy ancha la gama de tono social, de "registro", que abarca el diccionario. Se incluyen las palabras aristocráticas propias de la poesía y de la literatura. En el otro extremo se incluyen muchísimas voces y frases familiares o coloquiales, siendo éstas parte tan esencial del "uso" tal como lo hemos definido, y también porque con la relajación progresiva de la etiqueta social en nuestros tiempos, tales palabras (desconocidas en estos contextos hace unos 20 años) se escuchan cuando los ministros hablan por radio y se leen en los artículos de fondo. En muchos casos es discutible la clasificación de estas palabras como *fam* (familiares); ello depende del instinto del autor y no de autoridad impresa. En cuanto al argot (*slang*), por más pintoresco y expresivo que sea, tiene por definición una aplicación restringida, es pasajero y carece de base fija, así que solamente las palabras más conocidas merecen ser incluidas. Siempre donde ha sido posible se ha traducido exactamente el tono social de la palabra, familiar por familiar, etc, a veces añadiéndose una voz más clásica para el uso de quien prefiera sentirse más seguro. Hay buen número de los clichés de la conversación, de la correspondencia, de los reportajes periodísticos, de los discursos políticos, etc; la mención en el diccionario no presupone la aprobación del autor.

No hay grandes novedades en las materias

preliminares ni en los apéndices, pero se ha estudiado con cuidado el problema de su redacción.

II *WHAT KIND OF ENGLISH AND WHAT KIND OF SPANISH?*

1 European and American

THE PROBLEM POSED BY THE GEOGRAPHICAL spread and the cultural breadth of these two great world languages has been mentioned in the Preface; it has greatly preoccupied the author and the publishers. At first the idea was to produce a rather severely limited dictionary by Europeans and for Europeans, concerned, that is, with British English and European Spanish; the corollary being that English and Spanish in the New World could be better handled by natives of the Americas. Two factors, one theoretical and the other very practical, led to the scope of the work being widened so as to take in American usage, though not without misgivings on the author's part. The first factor was the realization that contacts run not merely north and south but in all directions; North Americans have a great interest in Spain, trade and cultural contacts between Britain and Latin America are far from negligible. Moreover the standards of usage, pronunciation etc set by the mother countries (in the purely linguistic sense) of Britain and Spain are not without influence in the Americas. The second factor was the association of the British publishers for the purposes of this dictionary series with a United States house, which naturally meant that American speech and lexical preferences had to be taken into account. Considerable help was given by the United States house with details of American English, and the services of Professor E. Chang-Rodríguez were secured so that Latin American usage in Spanish could be properly covered. In the result the dictionary has a much more comprehensive look about it than was originally intended, and it is hoped that this consideration outweighs any mid-Atlantic anomalies.

2 "Oxford" English and "Academy" Spanish

The problem of authority in matters of language exists for English but is distressingly

II *INGLÉS Y ESPAÑOL: ¿DE QUÉ TIPO?*

Lo europeo y lo americano

SE HA ALUDIDO EN EL PREFACIO AL problema planteado por la extensión geográfica y la amplitud cultural de estos dos grandes idiomas mundiales; tal problema ha preocupado mucho al autor y a la casa editorial. En un principio pensamos hacer un diccionario de carácter muy limitado, por europeos y para europeos; esto es, tendría que ver con el inglés británico y el español europeo, entendiéndose como consecuencia que el inglés y el español de América podrían ser manejados mejor por americanos. Dos factores, teórico uno y muy práctico el otro, nos llevaron a extender el campo para abarcar lo americano, pero no sin alguna duda de parte del autor. Primero nos dimos cuenta de que los contactos no se limitan a seguir la línea norte-sur, sino que van en todas las direcciones; los norteamericanos se interesan vivamente por España, y no son de despreciar los contactos comerciales y culturales entre Gran Bretaña y la América Latina. Además no dejan de tener influencia las normas del uso, de la pronunciación, etc, establecidas por las dos madres patrias (en sentido lingüístico, nada más) de Gran Bretaña y España. Vino en segundo lugar la asociación — en lo referente a la serie de diccionarios — de la casa editorial británica con la compañía norteamericana, con la consecuencia lógica de que había que tomar en cuenta el habla norteamericana y sus preferencias léxicas. La compañía norteamericana nos prestó una ayuda eficaz en el asunto del inglés americano, y el Profesor E. Chang-Rodríguez ha mejorado mucho toda la materia hispanoamericana. Resulta así que el libro sale con aspecto mucho más completo del que en un principio se pensaba, y se espera que este hecho compense sobradamente cualquier anomalía que se pueda observar en alguna palabra a la deriva en el Atlántico.

El inglés de Oxford y el español de la Academia

Existe para el inglés el problema de la autoridad lingüística, pero es mucho más grave

acute for Spanish. In Britain the Oxford dictionaries, the works on usage of the Fowlers, Gowers, Partridge and others have always enjoyed (although they have scrupulously never claimed to possess) an enormous authority; in the United States the same may be said of Webster, Random House and others. But in all varieties of English it may be said that there is in fact no conception of a linguistic authority, at any rate not in the sense in which it exists in Hispanic countries with their ancient Academies. Words flow into English from other languages; they have no gender, their plurals are always very simply formed with -s or -es, and the English organs of speech seem to be able to get around almost any awkward consonant group or modify it to the general satisfaction; moreover in the general chaos of English spelling a few new anomalies are neither here nor there. In Spanish the scene is very different. Ancient and highly prestigious Academies attempt (indeed, are obliged by their mottoes: *Limpia, fija y da esplendor*) to apply to language a policy which we may in general call conservative and purist; they take a view of language which has never been current in Britain or the US and which, it must be said, is difficult to maintain in current linguistic theory. Quite apart from this, Spanish by its very nature is less able to accommodate loanwords and other innovations which have been pouring into it in the 1950s and 60s. It has fewer phonemes than English; it has a gender problem and much more uncertainty about plurals and spellings of foreign words than does English. Spanish informants, questioned about the pronunciation of (for example) *corner* or the plural of *club*, may emerge covered in confusion; the printed sources often disagree, and in this particular Latin American usage often differs again from that of Spain. The current very strong influence of English and French on Spanish is not of course confined to individual items of vocabulary; it extends to phrasing, to word order, to the use of the passive voice and to many other aspects of language. (Sections of the book of Emilio Lorenzo, *El español de hoy, lengua en ebullición*, Madrid, Gredos, 1966, illustrate these matters admirably.)

para el español. Esta autoridad la poseen (sin haberla reclamado nunca) en Gran Bretaña los diccionarios de Oxford y las obras de los Fowler, de Gowers y Partridge y otros, sobre el uso; y en Estados Unidos lo mismo se puede decir de Webster, de Random House etc. Sin embargo, respecto al inglés hay que reconocer que realmente no existe la autoridad lingüística, por lo menos en el sentido en que tal autoridad existe en los países hispánicos, cada uno con su venerable Academia. Las voces extranjeras entran libremente en el inglés; no tienen género, su plural se forma muy sencillamente con -s o con -es, y los órganos articulatorios ingleses parecen ser capaces de dominar cualquier grupo consonántico o bien de modificarlo para contentar a todos; además, dentro de la total confusión de la ortografía inglesa, no tienen gran importancia unas cuantas rarezas más. Todo es muy distinto en español. Las Academias viejas y prestigiosas se esfuerzan por aplicar al lenguaje unas normas que podemos en general calificar de conservadoras y casticistas; de hecho, su lema les obliga a ello (*Limpia, fija y da esplendor*). Su concepto del lenguaje no ha tenido nunca aceptación en Gran Bretaña ni en Estados Unidos, y hay que reconocer que dentro de las teorías lingüísticas actuales resulta difícil sostenerlo. Aparte de esto, el español por su misma naturaleza es menos capaz para recibir los préstamos y otras innovaciones que lo han invadido en los años 50 y 60 de este siglo. Tiene menos fonemas que el inglés; tiene el problema del género y vacila mucho en lo tocante a los plurales y a la ortografía de los extranjerismos. Rogamos a nuestros amigos españoles que nos ayuden pronunciando, p.ej., la palabra *corner* o que nos digan el plural de *club* y no logran ponerse de acuerdo; alguna autoridad impresa nos da una solución pero otra la contradice, y en este respecto el uso de Hispanoamérica a menudo difiere del de España. Hoy día la influencia del inglés y del francés sobre el español — influencia poderosísima — no se limita, desde luego, a los elementos del léxico; se extiende a la fraseología, al orden de palabras, al uso de la voz pasiva y a otros muchos aspectos del lenguaje. (Todo esto lo ilustran muy bien varios capítulos del libro de Emilio Lorenzo, *El español de hoy, lengua en ebullición*, Madrid, Gredos, 1966.)

3 Usage and authority

The consequence of all this for our purpose is that doubts arise and the need to give several alternative forms is felt. In English, since it is my native language, I can usually resolve these doubts in a friendly confrontation between my instinct and the authorities. In Spanish, even with the help of Spaniards, this is not the case. My own criterion is extremely liberal and in no way purist: if the word exists and is widely used it belongs in the dictionary in at least one of its forms; if it has various plurals and pronunciations these should be included; if for most Spaniards the English *slogan* is *un slogan* (rather than *un lema*) and the English *camping ground* or *campsite* is (via French) *un camping*, the fact must be honestly stated. To apply traditional and purist criteria to such cases and to neglect usage — that of the educated classes, not that of the least cultured in a society — would be to mislead the user; it would be to offer him a bookish fiction, a word which although "correct" has little currency, a word which might cause jocularity or eyebrow-raising. The authority which this dictionary hopes to have is that of accurate translation in terms of everyday usage, not that of acting as arbiter about what is "good English" or (still less) "good Spanish".

None the less it would be improper to disclaim all responsibility in this matter. The Spanish Academy is on the move, if rather slowly; it is admitting numerous neologisms and new senses and deciding questions of gender, spelling and definition, with skill and good sense. The results of many of its deliberations were published by the late Julio Casares in *Novedades en el Diccionario Académico*, Madrid, Aguilar, 1963, and others have continued to publish the Academy's decisions in numbers of the *Boletín de la Real Academia Española* since that year. I have taken account of these decisions by marking words with the abbreviation *Acad* in both parts of the dictionary; the entry in Part II "**film** = film *m*, filme *m* (*Acad*)" implies that the Academy has accepted the anglicism but only in the form *filme* (for excellent reasons), while from the order in which the two translations are given it may be assumed that as observed in conversation and in the press most Spaniards go on using the first form and obstinately pay little attention to the Academy's decision. Logically those neologisms and very numerous Spanish American words which do not have the Academy's sanction should have been

El uso y la autoridad

Las consecuencias de todo esto para nosotros son que surgen dudas y se siente la necesidad de ofrecer varias formas alternativas. Yo en inglés (lengua materna) puedo resolver estas dudas por lo general confrontando mi instinto con las autoridades. En español, aun contando con la ayuda de españoles, no ocurre esto. Mi propio criterio es de lo más liberal y de ningún modo casticista; si la palabra existe y tiene un uso extenso, ha de figurar en el diccionario bajo una de sus formas a lo menos; si tiene varias formas en plural y diversas maneras de pronunciarse éstas merecen ser incluidas; si para la mayor parte de los hispanohablantes el *slogan* inglés es *un slogan* (y no *un lema*) y el *camping ground* o *campsite* inglés es — a través del francés — *un camping*, hay que reconocer honradamente tal hecho. Seguir las normas tradicionales y casticistas y desatender el uso en tales casos — esto es, el uso de las personas cultas, no el de la clase menos culta de la sociedad — sería despistar al lector; sería ofrecerle una ficción libresca, una palabra que por más "correcta" que sea tiene poca aceptación, una palabra que pudiera motivar la risa o la extrañeza. Esperamos que el diccionario pueda reclamar cierta autoridad a base de ofrecer buenas traducciones dentro del uso diario, y rechazamos la idea de que pueda servir de árbitro en lo referente a cuestiones de "buen inglés" y (más todavía) de "castellano correcto".

A pesar de todo, sería cobarde desentenderse completamente de cierta responsabilidad en esta materia. La Real Academia Española trabaja, si bien con lentitud; admite muchos neologismos y significados nuevos y resuelve problemas de género, de ortografía y de definición, atinada y sensatamente. El fallecido Julio Casares publicó los resultados de sus discusiones en su libro *Novedades en el Diccionario Académico*, Madrid, Aguilar, 1963, y otros continúan esta labor en los números del *Boletín de la Real Academia Española*. He tomado en cuenta estas decisiones en las dos partes del diccionario mediante la abreviatura *Acad*; así el artículo de la segunda parte, "**film** = film *m*, filme *m* (*Acad*)" quiere decir que la Academia ha dado paso al anglicismo pero (por razones muy sólidas) únicamente bajo la forma *filme*; por otra parte se supone, dado el orden en que se imprimen las dos traducciones, que según lo observado en la conversación y en la

marked *non-Acad*, but this would have been a vast undertaking and would also have conceded more importance to the purists' views than I feel it is proper to give.

4 What is a word?

One of the very few problems which arises on the English side is the large one of what constitutes a word and, for dictionary listing purposes, a main entry or headword. My instinct was to use the hyphen freely and in many cases to run two words completely together without hyphen, since I felt that usage was tending in this direction. It followed that there could be no main entries which consisted of two or more separate words, these being placed as no more than sub-entries under the main noun. This policy had to be revised when collaboration with American colleagues began, for their practice differs from that of Britain; there are now fewer hyphens and a large number of main entries which consist of two or more words, and doubtless some anomalies have resulted in this process of achieving mid-Atlantic harmony. The numerous differences in spelling and pronunciation between Britain and the US have been more easily resolved by summarizing US habits in introductory notes and by constant statement of the differences within the entries, sometimes with cross-references.

prensa los españoles en general emplean la primera forma y se obstinan en no hacer caso de la decisión de su Academia. Sería lógico poner la tacha *non-Acad* a los numerosos neologismos y sudamericanismos que no han merecido la aprobación de la Academia, pero hacerlo así hubiera exigido un enorme esfuerzo y también hubiera concedido más importancia a la opinión casticista de la que ésta merece.

¿Qué es una palabra?

Uno de los pocos problemas que se plantea para el inglés es el de determinar lo que constituye *una* palabra, y, para el diccionario, lo que constituye una palabra cabeza de artículo. En un principio empleé extensamente el guión y en muchos casos uní dos palabras para formar otra sin guión, pues me parecía que tal era la tendencia del uso. La consecuencia de esto era que no podía haber palabra cabeza de artículo que constara de dos palabras separadas o de más, colocándose éstas en cambio dentro del artículo. Pero al iniciarse la colaboración con los colegas norteamericanos hubo que suprimir esta norma, pues la práctica norteamericana es distinta de la británica; por tanto hay ahora menos palabras con guión y muchas palabras que encabezan artículo aun constando de dos elementos o más; sin duda el cambio habrá creado algunas anomalías. Ha sido más fácil conciliar las diferencias en cuanto a la ortografía y pronunciación entre lo británico y lo norteamericano resumiendo las costumbres de Estados Unidos en una nota preliminar y mencionando constantemente las diferencias en cada artículo.

III *EXPLANATORY NOTES*

1 Alphabetical order is followed throughout. It must be remembered that *CH*, *LL* and *Ñ* are separate letters of the alphabet in Spanish; thus **achacar** comes after **acústico** and not after **acezar**.

2 Cross-references include alternative spellings, parts of irregular verbs, contracted forms, many prefixes and some suffixes, and parts of compound words.

3 Superior numbers are used to separate words of like spelling and pronunciation, eg **port¹**, **port²**.

4 Noun plurals in Spanish are indicated after the headword only when irregular (eg **crisis**, *pl* **crisis**). In all other cases the basic rules apply: if a noun ends in a vowel it takes **-s** in the plural (eg **casa-s**, **tribu-s**); if it ends in a consonant (including for this purpose **y**) it takes **-es** in the plural (eg **pared-es**, **árbol-es**). Note the following, however:

(i) Nouns that end in stressed **-í** take **-es** in the plural (eg **rubí**, **rubíes**). Exception: **esquí**, **esquís**.

(ii) Nouns that end in **-z** change this to **c** and add **-es** in the plural (eg **luz**, **luces**; **paz**, **paces**). The pronunciation is not affected.

(iii) The accent which is written on a number of endings of singular nouns is not needed in the plural (eg **nación-naciones**, **patán-patanes**, **inglés-ingleses**). Some words having no written accent in the singular need one in the plural (eg **crimen-crímenes**, **joven-jóvenes**).

(iv) There is little agreement about the plural of recent anglicisms and gallicisms, and some latinisms. Each case is treated separately in the dictionary; see eg **barman**, **chófer**, **club**.

5 Noun plurals in English are indicated after the headword only when they are truly irregular (eg **ox**, **oxen**), and in the few cases where a word in **-o** takes a plural in **-oes** (eg **potato-es**). In all other cases the basic rules apply:

(i) Most English nouns take **-s** in the plural: **bed-s**, **site-s**, **photo-s**.

(ii) Nouns that end in **-s**, **-x**, **-z**, **-sh** and some in **-ch** [tʃ] take **-es** in the plural: **boss-es**, **box-es**, **dish-es**, **patch-es**.

NOTAS EXPLICATIVAS

1 El orden alfabético queda rigurosamente establecido. Se mantiene la costumbre de considerar la *CH*, la *LL* y la *Ñ* como letras independientes.

2 Con referencias a otros artículos figuran las variantes ortográficas, las formas de los verbos irregulares, las formas contractas, muchos prefijos y algunos sufijos, y elementos de palabras compuestas.

3 Los números altos sirven para distinguir las palabras que se escriben y se pronuncian iguales, p.ej. **port¹**, **port²**.

4 Forma plural del sustantivo en español. Estas formas se hacen constar después de la voz cabeza de artículo sólo cuando son irregulares (p.ej. **crisis**, *pl* **crisis**). En los demás casos se aplican las siguientes reglas: si el sustantivo termina en vocal se añade **-s** para formar el plural (p.ej. **casa-s**, **tribu-s**); si termina en consonante (la **y** se considera como consonante en esta posición) se añade **-es** para formar el plural (p.ej. **pared-es**, **árbol-es**). Hay algunas excepciones:

(i) Los sustantivos que terminan en **-í** acentuada forman el plural añadiendo **-es** (p.ej. **rubí**, **rubíes**). Excepción: **esquí**, **esquís**.

(ii) Los sustantivos que terminan en **-z** la cambian en **c** al formarse el plural (p.ej. **luz**, **luces**; **paz**, **paces**). Esto no cambia la pronunciación.

(iii) El acento que se escribe en varias desinencias de los sustantivos en singular se suprime en el plural (p.ej. **nación-naciones**, **patán-patanes**). Algunas palabras que no llevan acento escrito en singular lo tienen en plural (p.ej. **crimen-crímenes**).

(iv) Reina bastante confusión acerca de la forma plural de los anglicismos y galicismos, y de algún latinismo, de reciente acuñación. Se trata separadamente cada caso; véase p.ej. **barman**, **chófer**, **club**.

5 Forma plural del sustantivo en inglés. Estas formas se hacen constar después de la voz cabeza de artículo sólo cuando son irregulares (p.ej. **ox**, **oxen**), y en los pocos casos donde una palabra terminada en **-o** forma el plural en **-oes** (p.ej. **potato-es**). En los demás casos se aplican las siguientes reglas:

(i) La mayor parte de los sustantivos en inglés forman el plural añadiendo **-s**: **bed-s**, **site-s**, **photo-s**.

(ii) Los sustantivos terminados en **-s**, **-x**, **-z**,

(iii) Nouns that end in **-y** not preceded by a vowel change the **-y** to **-ies** in the plural: **lady-ladies**, **berry-berries** (but **tray-s, key-s**).

6 Spanish and English verbs. All Spanish verb headwords are referred by number and letter (eg [1a], [2e]) to the table of verb paradigms on pp. 624–30. In a few cases in which verbs have slight irregularities or are defective, the fact is noted after the headword. English irregular or strong verbs have their principal parts noted in bold face after the headword; these are also listed on pp. 633–4. Minor variations of spelling are listed on p. 634.

7 Proper names occupy their alphabetical places in the main text. Current abbreviations are listed in the appendices, but a few which have assumed the character of words in their own right are included in the main text (eg **O.K.**).

8 Grammatical functions are distinguished by bold face numerals and abbreviations, eg **arder 1** *vt* . . . **2** *vi* . . . **3 arderse** *vr* . . . A separate division has been provided for *vr* in the English–Spanish, on the grounds that even though English has no strictly reflexive verbs this represents a convenience in translation and for the user.

9 The diverse meanings of the headword within each entry or grammatical function are separated by letters in bold face, **(a)** . . . **(b)** . . . Sometimes the distinctions made are rather fine but necessary both for the compiler and the user; they are practical rather than scientific in terms of semantics. A certain order is normally followed: basic and concrete senses first, figurative and familiar ones later; *SAm* and *US* senses and highly specialized applications come last.

10 Field and style labels in italics: some are abbreviations (eg *Bio, Mus, fam*), others complete words (eg *Art, Sport*); both types are in English but readily intelligible in Spanish.

11 Indicators are complete words in italics placed before the translation; they aid in meaning discrimination and help the user find

-sh y algunos en **-ch** [tʃ] forman el plural añadiendo **-es: boss-es, box-es, dish-es, patch-es.**

(iii) Los sustantivos terminados en **-y** no precedida por vocal forman el plural cambiando la **-y** en **-ies: lady-ladies, berry-berries** (pero **tray-s, key-s**).

6 Verbo español y verbo inglés. Los verbos españoles que encabezan artículo llevan una referencia por número y letra (p.ej. [1a], [2e]) al cuadro de conjugaciones en las págs. 624–30. En los casos donde el verbo es ligeramente irregular o defectivo, se nota tal hecho en el artículo. Se imprimen en negrilla inmediatamente después de la palabra cabeza de artículo el pretérito y participio de pasado de los verbos irregulares ingleses, y hay además lista de ellos en las págs. 633–4. Las ligeras variantes ortográficas de los verbos ingleses constan en las pág. 634.

7 Los nombres propios ocupan su lugar apropiado en el orden alfabético del diccionario. Las abreviaturas pasan sin embargo al apéndice, figurando entre los artículos del diccionario algunas que han adquirido carácter de palabras con derecho propio (p.ej. **O.K.**).

8 Las funciones gramaticales se señalan mediante números en negrilla y abreviaturas, p.ej. **arder 1** *vt* . . . **2** *vi* . . . **3 arderse** *vr* . . . En la Parte 2ª hay división especial para el *vr*, por el motivo de que (aunque el verbo inglés no tiene en rigor formas reflexivas) tal sistema es muy útil en la traducción y para el usuario.

9 Los diversos significados de la palabra cabeza de artículo quedan separados por letras en negrilla, **(a)** . . . **(b)** . . . Alguna vez la distinción puede parecer nimia, pero es necesaria para el autor y más para el lector; esto tiene una finalidad práctica y no pretende tener validez científica. Se ha establecido cierto orden para estas subdivisiones: primero los significados básicos y concretos, después los figurados y familiares; las acepciones *SAm* y *US* y las aplicaciones técnicas vienen en último lugar.

10 Las indicaciones de campo semántico y de tono se imprimen en cursiva. Algunas son abreviaturas (p.ej. *Bio, Mus, fam*), y otras palabras completas (p.ej. *Art, Sport*); ambas están en inglés pero serán fácilmente inteligibles en español.

11 Contribuyen a hacer las distinciones semánticas las indicaciones de palabras enteras en cursiva, colocadas delante de la traducción;

that part of the headword's range which he is seeking. They have been made as brief and typical as possible, but they cannot be comprehensive and must not be taken to constitute full definitions or exact limitations. The main types of indicator are:

(i) For a noun headword: a variety of near-synonyms, part-definitions and hints (in parentheses), eg **poke** (*push*) . . . (*with elbow*) . . . (*jab*) . . . (*with poker*) . . .

(ii) For an adjective headword: nouns (without parentheses) with which the adjective in its various applications might typically agree, eg **soft** (**b**) (*fig*) *air, sound* . . . *voice* . . . *step* . . . *water* . . .

(iii) For a transitive verb headword: nouns (without parentheses) which might typically be the objects of the verb in its various applications, eg **pluck** *fruit, flower* . . . *bird* . . . *guitar* . . .

(iv) For an intransitive or reflexive verb headword: nouns (in parentheses) which might be typical subjects of the verb, eg **rise 2** (**c**) (*of sun, moon*) . . . (*smoke etc*) . . . (*building, mountain*) . . .

Indicators are not repeated in derivatives but can be transferred by the user, eg adjective to adverb, adjective to abstract noun (*fair-fairness*).

12 The order of material within the entry or subdivision has been planned for convenience and does not follow a rigid pattern. However, a typical order for a lengthy noun entry is: (i) basic translations of the headword; (ii) phrases consisting of noun + adjective; (iii) the noun preceded by a preposition (often with verb as well); (iv) the noun with a verb. Alphabetical order is followed within each of these categories. No attempt is made to separate idioms from usage examples. In long verb entries in the English–Spanish all cases of verb + adverb and verb + preposition are collected into one subdivision placed towards the end of the entry, eg **do 1** (**e**), **play 2** (**j**) and **3** (**h**).

13 The placing of phrases in entries raises many problems. The principles generally followed are:

(i) Phrases consisting of noun + noun, verb + verb, adjective + adjective are entered under the first component, eg

se proponen llamar la atención del lector hacia la parte de la extensión de la palabra con que tiene que ver. Hemos ideado estas aclaraciones para que sean breves y típicas; pero ellas no pueden ser universales, e importa mucho que no se las considere como definiciones completas ni como limitaciones exactas. Las indicaciones son de varias clases:

(i) Para sustantivo que encabeza artículo: sinónimos aproximativos, definiciones parciales, consejos (en paréntesis), p.ej. **poke** (*push*) . . . (*with elbow*) . . . (*jab*) . . . (*with poker*) . . .

(ii) Para adjetivo que encabeza artículo: sustantivos (sin paréntesis) con los que el adjetivo en sus diversas aplicaciones pudiera concordar, p.ej. **soft** (**b**) (*fig*) *air, sound* . . . *voice* . . . *step* . . . *water* . . .

(iii) Para verbo transitivo que encabeza artículo: sustantivos (sin paréntesis) que típicamente pudieran ser los objetos del verbo, p.ej. **pluck** *fruit, flower* . . . *bird* . . . *guitar* . . .

(iv) Para verbo intransitivo o reflexivo que encabeza artículo: sustantivos (entre paréntesis) que típicamente pudieran ser los sujetos del verbo, p.ej. **rise 2** (**c**) (*of sun, moon*) . . . (*smoke etc*) . . . (*building, mountain*) . . .

Estas aclaraciones no se repiten para las palabras derivadas, pero las podrá trasladar el lector, p.ej. del adjetivo al adverbio, o del adjetivo al sustantivo abstracto (*fair-fairness*).

12 El orden de material dentro del artículo o subdivisión ha sido pensado para ayudar al lector y no sigue un sistema rígido. Sin embargo, el orden normal para un artículo sobre sustantivo es: (i) las traducciones básicas de la palabra cabeza de artículo; (ii) las frases que consisten en sustantivo con adjetivo; (iii) el sustantivo precedido por preposición (muchas veces con verbo también); (iv) el sustantivo con verbo. Dentro de cada categoría se mantiene el orden alfabético. No se separan los modismos de los ejemplos que ilustran el uso. En los artículos extensos sobre verbos en la Parte 2ª, se juntan en una subdivisión todos los casos de verbo + adverbio y de verbo + preposición, hacia el fin del artículo, p.ej. **do 1** (**e**), **play 2** (**j**) y **3** (**h**).

13 La colocación de las frases en los artículos suscita muchos problemas. En general los principios son:

(i) Las frases que consisten en sustantivo + sustantivo, verbo + verbo etc figuran en el artículo del primer elemento, p.ej.

"casa y comida" under **casa**, "black and blue" under **black**.

(ii) Phrases consisting of noun + adjective (Spanish) or adjective + noun (English) are entered under the noun component, eg "cabina electoral" under **cabina**, "black coffee" under **coffee**. It should be noted however that many such combinations in English now have a sufficiently independent existence to figure as main entries; thus **black box** and **black lead** are main entries in their alphabetical place, not sub-entries under **box** and **lead** respectively.

(iii) Phrases consisting of verb + noun are entered under the noun component, eg "abrir carrera" under **carrera**, "to show cause" under **cause**; but many phrases will be found in the verb entries as usage examples also.

(iv) Verb + adverb, verb + preposition (English) are normally entered under the verb, eg "to go in, go over, go up" under **go**; in the case of less common adverbs and prepositions the phrase may well appear under the adverb or preposition, eg "to go astern" under **astern**, the adverb hardly existing except in such phrases.

There is, however, intentional duplication of phrases. Thus "año bisiesto" belongs, by rule (ii) above, under **año**; but it is also the sole phrase under the headword **bisiesto**. In many other cases phrases are duplicated because they illustrate something about both headwords.

14 Translation by single word is obviously sufficient in many cases. Often a liberal policy has been followed in offering a number of near-synonyms separated by commas; this is especially true of the more emotive and less precise adjectives. The abbreviation (*approx*) is used where no full translation exists. Explanations in italics are given where a word has no correspondence in the other language, eg **cachetero (b)**, *cante*. For greater precision explanations in italics and in parentheses are occasionally added after the translation, eg **caló**, *camayo*.

15 The gender of every Spanish noun is given immediately after it in both parts of the dictionary.

16 Spanish feminine forms. In the English–Spanish the typical entry "**teacher** = profesor

"casa y comida" en **casa**, "black and blue" en **black**.

(ii) Las frases que consisten en sustantivo + adjetivo (español) o adjetivo + sustantivo (inglés) figuran en el artículo del elemento sustantivo, p.ej. "cabina electoral" en **cabina**, "black coffee" en **coffee**. Pero son muchas las combinaciones inglesas de adjetivo + sustantivo que han adquirido ya una existencia bastante independiente para que figuren como palabras cabezas de artículo; así encabezan artículos en su lugar alfabético correspondiente **black box** y **black lead**, y no están respectivamente en **box** y **lead**.

(iii) Las frases que consisten en verbo + sustantivo figuran en el artículo del sustantivo, p.ej. "to show cause" en **cause**, "abrir carrera" en **carrera**; pero se citan muchas frases de este tipo en los verbos, como ejemplos del uso.

(iv) Las frases de verbo + adverbio, verbo + preposición (inglés) están normalmente en el artículo del verbo, p.ej. "to go in, go over, go up" en **go**; pero en el caso de los adverbios y preposiciones menos frecuentes la frase bien puede estar en el artículo del adverbio o preposición, p.ej. "to go astern" en **astern**, pues el adverbio apenas tiene existencia fuera de tales frases.

Hay, sin embargo, muchos casos donde se duplica de propósito la frase. Así "año bisiesto" pertenece, según la regla (ii) arriba, a **año**; pero también es la única frase en **bisiesto**. En otros casos se duplican las frases por el motivo de que en ambos lugares ilustran algo.

14 La traducción por una sola palabra basta en muchos casos. Pero a menudo hemos seguido una norma liberal ofreciendo varios sinónimos o casi sinónimos, separados por comas, sobre todo para los adjetivos emotivos y por lo tanto menos precisos. Donde no existe traducción adecuada se emplea la abreviatura (*approx*). Cuando la palabra no tiene correspondencia en el otro idioma damos una explicación en cursiva, p.ej. para **cachetero (b)**, *cante*. Alguna vez se añade a la traducción, en cursiva y en paréntesis, una aclaración o precisión, p.ej. para **caló**, *camayo*.

15 El género de todo sustantivo español consta inmediatamente después de la palabra en las dos partes del diccionario.

16 Desinencias femeninas en español. En la Parte 2ª el artículo típico "**teacher** = profesor

m, ora *f* " is to be read as "= profesor *m*, profesora *f* ". Often a written accent on the masculine form is not needed in the feminine, eg "**Dane** = danés *m*, esa *f* " (to be read as "= danés *m*, danesa *f* "). The endings affected are: **-án, -ana; -és, -esa; -ón, -ona.** Where one vowel is given as the feminine ending, it replaces the -e or -o of the masculine; thus "**cook** = cocinero *m*, a *f* " is read as "= cocinero *m*, cocinera *f* ".

m, ora *f* " ha de leerse "= profesor *m*, profesora *f* ". A menudo el acento que lleva el masculino se suprime en el femenino, p.ej. "**Dane** = danés *m*, esa *f* " (ha de leerse "= danés *m*, danesa *f* "). Tales desinencias son: **-án, -ana; -és, esa; -ón, -ona.** Donde se cita una sola vocal de la forma femenina, esta vocal sustituye la -e o la -o del masculino; así "**cook** = cocinero *m*, a *f* " ha de leerse "= cocinero *m*, cocinera *f* ".

Pronunciation and orthography

Pronunciación y ortografía

I. *LA PRONUNCIACIÓN DEL INGLÉS (BRITÁNICO)*

COMO ES SABIDO, LA ORTOGRAFÍA DEL inglés se ajusta a criterios históricos y etimológicos y en muchos puntos apenas ofrece indicaciones ciertas de cómo ha de pronunciarse cada palabra. Por ello nos ha parecido aconsejable y de utilidad para los hispanohablantes dar para cada palabra inglesa una pronunciación figurada o transcripción. Al tratar de explicar en estas notas los sonidos del inglés mediante comparaciones con los sonidos del español en un espacio reducido nos damos cuenta de que realizamos una labor que no pasa de ser aproximativa. Tales comparaciones tienen una finalidad práctica y carecen del rigor científico que exigen los fonetistas especializados.

1 Sistema de signos

Se emplean los signos de la IPA (International Phonetic Association). Hemos seguido en general las transcripciones de Daniel Jones, *English Pronouncing Dictionary*, London, Dent, 13th ed., 1967. En el prólogo de esta obra el autor explica los principios que le han guiado en su trabajo.

2 Acentuación

En las transcripciones el signo ['] se coloca delante de la sílaba acentuada. El signo [ˌ] se pone delante de la sílaba que lleva el acento secundario o más ligero en las palabras largas, p.ej. *acceleration* [ækˌseləˈreiʃən]. Dos signos de acento principal [' '] indican que las dos sílabas, o bien dos de las sílabas, se acentúan igualmente, p.ej. *A 1* ['eiˈwʌn], *able-bodied* ['eiblˈbɒdid]. Las palabras compuestas que encabezan artículo, estando sus elementos separados o unidos con guión, se tratan para nuestros propósitos como unidades: p.ej. *anti-roll device* ['ænti'rəuldi'vais].

3 Signos impresos en cursiva

En la palabra *annexation* [ˌænekˈseiʃən], la [ə] en cursiva indica que este sonido puede o no pronunciarse; o porque muchos hablantes la pronuncian pero que otros muchos no la pronuncian, o bien porque es un sonido que se oye en el habla lenta y cuidada pero que no se oye en el habla corriente y en el ritmo de la frase entera.

4 Transcripciones alternativas

En los casos donde se dan dos transcripciones, ello indica que ambas pronunciaciones son igualmente aceptables en el uso de las personas cultas, p.ej. *medicine* ['medsin, 'medisin], o bien que la pronunciación varía bastante según la posición de la palabra en la frase y el contexto fonético, p.ej. *an* [æn, ən, n].

5 Véase también la nota sobre la pronunciación del inglés norteamericano.

6 El orden en que se explican los signos abajo es más o menos ortográfico y no el estrictamente fonético.

Vocales

[æ]	sonido breve, bastante abierto, parecido al de *a* en *carro*	bat	[bæt]
		apple	['æpl]
[ɑː]	sonido largo parecido al de *a* en *caro*	farm	[fɑːm]
		calm	[kɑːm]
[e]	sonido breve, bastante abierto, parecido al de *e* en *perro*	set	[set]
		less	[les]

[ə]	"vocal neutra", siempre átona; parecida a la *e* del artículo francés *le* y a la *a* final del catalán (p.ej. *casa, porta*)	above	[ə'bʌv]
		porter	['pɔːtə*]
		convey	[kən'vei]
[əː]	forma larga del anterior, en sílaba acentuada; algo parecido al sonido de *eu* en la palabra francesa *leur*	fern	[fəːn]
		work	[wəːk]
		murmur	['məːmə*]
[i]	sonido breve, abierto, parecido al de *i* en *esbirro, irreal*	tip	[tip]
		pity	['piti]
[iː]	sonido largo parecido al de *i* en *vino*	see	[siː]
		bean	[biːn]
		ceiling	['siːliŋ]
[ə]	sonido breve, bastante abierto, parecido al de *o* en *corra, torre*	rot	[rət]
		wash	[wəʃ]
[ɔː]	sonido largo, bastante cerrado, algo parecido al de *o* en *por*	ball	[bɔːl]
		board	[bɔːd]
[u]	sonido muy breve, más cerrado que la *u* en *burro*	soot	[sut]
		full	[ful]
[uː]	sonido largo, parecido al de *u* en *uno, supe*	root	[ruːt]
		fool	[fuːl]
[ʌ]	sonido abierto, breve y algo oscuro, sin correspondencia en español; se pronuncia en la parte anterior de la boca sin redondear los labios	come	[kʌm]
		rum	[rʌm]
		blood	[blʌd]
		nourish	['nʌriʃ]

Diptongos

[ai]	sonido parecido al de *ai* en *fraile, vais*	lie	[lai]
		fry	[frai]
[au]	sonido parecido al de *au* en *pausa, sauce*	sow	[sau]
		plough	[plau]
[ei]	sonido medio abierto, pero más cerrado que la *e* de *casé*; suena como si le siguiese una (i) débil, especialmente en sílaba acentuada	fate	[feit]
		say	[sei]
		waiter	['weitə*]
		straight	[streit]
[əu]	sonido que es una especie de *o* larga, sin redondear los labios ni levantar la lengua; suena como si le siguiese una [u] débil	ago	[ə'gəu]
		also	['ɔːlsəu]
		atrocious	[ə'trəuʃəs]
		note	[nəut]
[ɛə]	sonido que se encuentra únicamente delante de la *r*; el primer elemento se parece a la *e* de *perro*, pero es más abierto y breve; el segundo elemento es una forma débil de la "vocal neutra" [ə]	there	[ðɛə*]
		rare	[rɛə*]
		fair	[fɛə*]
		ne'er	[nɛə*]
[iə]	sonido cuyo primer elemento es una *i* medio abierta; el segundo elemento es una forma débil de la "vocal neutra" [ə]	here	[hiə*]
		interior	[in'tiəriə*]
		fear	[fiə*]
		beer	[biə*]
[əi]	sonido cuyo primer elemento es una *o* abierta, seguido de una *i* abierta pero débil; parecido al sonido de *oy* en *voy* o de *oi* en *coime*	toy	[təi]
		destroy	[dis'trəi]
		voice	[vəis]
[uə]	sonido cuyo primer elemento es una *u* medio larga; el segundo elemento es una forma débil de la "vocal neutra" [ə]	allure	[ə'ljuə*]
		sewer	[sjuə*]
		pure	[pjuə*]

Consonantes

[b]	como la *b* de *tumbar, umbrío*	bet	[bet]
		able	['eibl]
[d]	como la *d* de *conde, andar*	dime	[daim]
		mended	['mendid]

[f]	como la f de fofo, inflar	face	[feis]
		snaffle	['snæfl]
[g]	como la g de grande, rango	go	[gəu]
		agog	[ə'gog]
[h]	es una aspiración fuerte, algo así como la jota castellana [x]	hit	[hit]
	pero sin la aspereza gutural de aquélla	reheat	['riː'hiːt]
[j]	como la y de cuyo, reyes	you	[juː]
		pure	[pjuə*]
		million	['miljən]
[k]	como la c de cama o la k de kilómetro, pero acompañada por	catch	[kætʃ]
	una ligera aspiración inexistente en español	kiss	[kis]
		chord	[kɔːd]
		box	[bɔks]
[l]	como la l de leer, pala	lick	[lik]
		place	[pleis]
[m]	como la m de mes, comer	mummy	['mʌmi]
		roam	[rəum]
[n]	como la n de nada, hablan	nut	[nʌt]
		sunny	['sʌni]
[ŋ]	como el sonido que tiene la n en banco, rango	bank	[bæŋk]
		sinker	['siŋkə*]
		singer	['siŋə*]
[p]	como la p de palo, ropa, pero acompañada por una ligera	pope	[pəup]
	aspiración inexistente en español	pepper	['pepə*]
[r]	Es un sonido muy débil, casi semivocal, que no tiene la	rate	[reit]
	vibración fuerte que caracteriza la r española. Se articula	pear	[peə*]
	elevando la punta de la lengua hacia el paladar duro.	fair	[feə*]
	(NB—En el inglés de Inglaterra la r escrita se pronuncia	blurred	[blɜːd]
	únicamente delante de vocal; en las demás posiciones es muda.	sorrow	['sɔrəu]
	Véase la nota sobre la pronunciación del inglés norteamericano,		
	y el asterisco * abajo)		
[s]	como la s (sorda) de casa, sesión	sit	[sit]
		scent	[sent]
		cents	[sents]
		pox	[pɔks]
[t]	como la t de tela, rata, pero acompañada por una ligera	tell	[tel]
	aspiración inexistente en español	strut	[strʌt]
		matter	['mætə*]
[v]	Inexistente en español (aunque se encuentra en catalán y	vine	[vain]
	valenciano). En inglés es sonido labiodental, y se produce	river	['rivə*]
	juntando el labio inferior con los dientes superiores	cove	[kəuv]
[w]	como la u de huevo, puede	wine	[wain]
		bewail	[bi'weil]
[z]	como la s (sonora) de desde, mismo	zero	['ziərəu]
		roses	['rəuziz]
		buzzer	['bʌzə*]
[ʒ]	Inexistente en español, pero como la j de las palabras francesas	rouge	[ruːʒ]
	jour, nager, o como la g de las palabras portuguesas gente, geral	leisure	['leʒə*]
		azure	['eiʒə*]
	Este sonido aparece a menudo en el grupo [dʒ], parecido al	page	[peidʒ]
	grupo dj de la palabra francesa adjacent	edge	[edʒ]
		jail	[dʒeil]
[ʃ]	Inexistente en español, pero como la ch de las palabras	shame	[ʃeim]
	francesas chambre, fiche, o como la x de la palabra portuguesa	ocean	['əuʃən]
	roxo	ration	['ræʃən]
		sugar	['ʃugə*]

much	[mʌtʃ]
chuck	[tʃʌk]
natural	['nætʃrəl]
thin	[θin]
maths	[mæθs]
this	[ðis]
other	['ʌðə*]
breathe	[briːð]
loch	[lɔx]
bear	[bɛə*]
humour	['hjuːmə*]
after	['ɑːftə*]

Este sonido aparece a menudo en el grupo [tʃ], parecido al grupo *ch* del español *mucho, chocho*

[θ] como la *z* de *zumbar* o la *c* de *ciento*

[ð] forma sonorizada del anterior, algo parecido a la *d* de *todo, hablado*

[x] sonido que en rigor no pertenece al inglés de Inglaterra, pero que se encuentra en el inglés de Escocia y en palabras escocesas usadas en Inglaterra etc; es como la *j* de *joven, rojo*

[*] El asterisco en las transcripciones indica que la *r* escrita en posición final de palabra se pronuncia en el inglés británico en muchos casos cuando la palabra siguiente empieza con vocal. En algún dialecto inglés y sobre todo en los Estados Unidos esta *r* se pronuncia siempre, así cuando la palabra se pronuncia aislada como cuando la siguen otras (empezando con vocal o sin ella)

Sonidos extranjeros

El grado de corrección con que el inglés pronuncia las palabras extranjeras que acaban de incorporarse al idioma depende — como en español — del nivel cultural del hablante y de los conocimientos que pueda tener del idioma de donde se ha tomado la palabra. Las transcripciones que damos de tales palabras representan una pronunciación más bien culta. En las transcripciones la tilde [~] indica que la vocal tiene timbre nasal (en muchas palabras de origen francés). En las pocas palabras tomadas del alemán aparece a veces la [x], para cuya explicación véase el cuadro de las consonantes.

Las letras del alfabeto inglés

Cuando se citan una a una, o cuando se deletrea una palabra para mayor claridad, o cuando se identifica un avión etc por una letra y su nombre, las letras suenan así:

a	[ei]	j	[dʒei]	s	[es]
b	[biː]	k	[kei]	t	[tiː]
c	[siː]	l	[el]	u	[juː]
d	[diː]	m	[em]	v	[viː]
e	[iː]	n	[en]	w	['dʌbljuː]
f	[ef]	o	[əu]	x	[eks]
g	[dʒiː]	p	[piː]	y	[wai]
h	[eitʃ]	q	[kjuː]	z	[zed] *(en US* [ziː]*)*
i	[ai]	r	[ɑː*]		

II. *LA PRONUNCIACIÓN DEL INGLÉS NORTEAMERICANO*

Sería sin duda deseable dar aquí un resumen de las diferencias más notables que existen entre el inglés de Inglaterra y el de las regiones del Reino Unido — Escocia, Gales, Irlanda del Norte — y el de los principales países extranjeros y continentes donde se ha arraigado este idioma: Irlanda, Estados Unidos y el Canadá, las Antillas, Australia y Nueva Zelanda, Sudáfrica y los países sucesores de las antiguas colonias en el Este y Oeste de África, la India, etc. Para tal labor no disponemos ni del espacio ni mucho menos de los conocimientos necesarios. Siendo este diccionario un trabajo angloamericano, sin embargo, y considerando el predominio actual de los Estados Unidos en tantas esferas (entre ellas la lingüística), es de todos modos imprescindible apuntar algunas de las múltiples diferencias que existen entre el inglés de Inglaterra y el hablado en Estados Unidos.

Empleamos las abreviaturas *Brit* (British) y *US* (United States).

1 Acentuación

Las palabras que tienen dos sílabas o más después del acento principal llevan en *US* un acento secundario que no tienen en *Brit*, p.ej. *dictionary* [*US* 'dikʃəˌneri = *Brit* 'dikʃənri], *secretary* [*US* 'sekrəˌteri = *Brit* 'sekrətri]. En algunos casos se acentúa en *US* una sílaba distinta de la que lleva el acento en *Brit*: p.ej. *primarily* [*US* prai'mærili = *Brit* 'praimərili]. Este cambio de acento se percibe ahora también, por influencia norteamericana, en el inglés de Inglaterra.

2 Entonación

El inglés de *US* se habla con un ritmo más lento y en un tono más monótono que en Inglaterra, debido en parte al alargamiento de las vocales que se apunta abajo.

3 Sonidos

Muchas de las vocales breves acentuadas en *Brit* se alargan mucho en *US*, y alguna vocal inacentuada en *Brit* se oye con más claridad en *US*, p.ej. *rapid* [*US* 'ræːpid = *Brit* 'ræpid], *capital* [*US* 'kæːbidəl = *Brit* 'kæpitl].

Peculiaridad muy notable del inglés en *US* es la nasalización de las vocales antes y después de las consonantes nasales [m, n, ŋ].

En las vocales individuales también hay diferencias. El sonido [ɑː] en *Brit* en muchas palabras se pronuncia en *US* como [æ] o bien [æː], p.ej. *grass* [*US* græs o græːs = *Brit* grɑːs], *answer* [*US* 'ænsər o 'æːnsər = *Brit* 'ɑːnsə*]. El sonido [ə] en *Brit* se pronuncia en *US* casi como una [ɑ] oscura, p.ej. *dollar* [*US* 'dɑlər = *Brit* 'dɔlə*], *hot* [*US* hɑt = *Brit* hɔt], *topic* [*US* 'tɑpik = *Brit* 'tɔpik]. El diptongo que se pronuncia en *Brit* [juː] en sílaba acentuada se pronuncia en la mayor parte de *US* sin [j], p.ej. *Tuesday* [*US* 'tuːzdi = *Brit* 'tjuːzdi], *student* [*US* 'stuːdənt = *Brit* 'stjuːdənt]; pero muchas palabras de este tipo se pronuncian en *US* igual que en *Brit*, p.ej. *music, pure, fuel.* En último lugar entre las vocales, se nota que la sílaba final *-ile* que se pronuncia en *Brit* [ail] es a menudo en *US* [əl] o bien [il], p.ej. *missile* [*US* 'misəl, 'misil = *Brit* 'misail]. Existen otras diferencias en la pronunciación de las vocales de palabras individuales, p.ej. *tomato*, pero éstas se tratan individualmente en el texto del diccionario.

En cuanto a las consonantes, destacamos dos diferencias. La consonante sorda [t] entre vocales suele sonorizarse bastante en *US*, p.ej. *united* [*US* ju'naidid = *Brit* juː'naitid], o sufre lenición [t]. La *r* escrita en posición final después de vocal o entre vocal y consonante es por la mayor parte muda en *Brit*, pero se pronuncia a menudo en *US*, p.ej. *where* [*US* wɛər = *Brit* wɛə*], *sister* [*US* 'sistər = *Brit* 'sistə*]. Hemos tomado esto en cuenta en las transcripciones en el texto del diccionario. También en posición final de sílaba (no sólo de palabra) se nota esta pronunciación de la *r* escrita: *burden* [*US* 'bəːrdn = *Brit* 'bəːdn], *jersey* [*US* 'dʒəːrzi = *Brit* 'dʒəːzi].

Conviene advertir que aun dentro del inglés de Estados Unidos hay notables diferencias regionales; la lengua de Nueva Inglaterra difiere bastante de la del Sur, la del Mediooeste no es la de California, etc. Los datos que constan arriba no son más que indicaciones muy someras.

III. *THE PRONUNCIATION OF EUROPEAN SPANISH*

1 Except for a very few anomalies such as the writing of silent *h* and the existence of the two symbols *b* and *v* for the same sound, the pronunciation of Spanish is so well represented by normal orthography that it would be a waste of space to give a phonetic transcription for every Spanish word in Part I as is done for English in Part II. The general introduction given below should suffice. However, a transcription in IPA (International Phonetic Association) symbols is given for those few Spanish words in which spelling and pronunciation are not in accord, such as *reloj* [re'lo], and for those numerous anglicisms and gallicisms which retain an un-Spanish spelling or which have unexpected and unpredictable pronunciations even for those acquainted with the original languages. In some cases alternative pronunciations are given, an indication that cultured Spanish usage has not yet fixed firmly on one.

In this section the pronunciation described is that of educated Castilian, and little account is taken of that of the Spanish regions, even though some (notably Andalusia) have considerable cultural strength and a pronunciation which is socially acceptable throughout Spain. The pronunciation of Spanish in America is treated in a separate section.

It must be noted that in this attempt to describe the sounds of Spanish in terms of English, and in a limited space, one is conscious of making no more than approximations. Such comparisons have a practical end and inevitably lack the scientific exactness which trained phoneticians require.

2 Accentuation of Spanish words

For Spanish, unlike English, simple rules can be devised and stated which will enable the stress to be placed correctly on each word at sight:

(a) If the word ends in a vowel, or in *n* or *s*

(often the signs of the plural of verbs and nouns respectively), the penultimate syllable is stressed: *zapato, zapatos, divide, dividen, dividieron, antiviviseccionista, telefonea, historia, diluviaba* (such words are called *palabras llanas* or *graves*).

(b) If the word ends in a consonant other than *n* or *s*, the last syllable is stressed: *verdad, practicar, decibel, virrey, coñac, pesadez* (such words are called *palabras agudas*).

(c) If the word is to be stressed in some way contrary to rules (a) and (b), an acute accent is written over the vowel to be stressed: *hablará, guaraní, rubí, esté, rococó; máquina, métodos, viéndolo, paralítico, húngaro* (words of this latter type are called *palabras esdrújulas*). With only two exceptions, the same syllable is stressed in the singular and plural forms of each word, but an accent may have to be added or suppressed in the plural: *crimen, crímenes; nación, naciones*. The two exceptions are *carácter, caracteres*, and *régimen, regímenes*. Only in a few verbal forms can the stress fall further back than on the antepenultimate syllable: *cántamelo, prohíbaselo*.

3 Diphthongs, hiatus and syllable division

It will have been noted in **2 (a)** above, in cases like *telefonea* and *historia*, that not all vowels count equally for the purposes of syllable division and stress. The convention is that *a, e* and *o* are "strong" vowels, and *i, u* "weak". Four rules then apply:

(a) A combination of weak + strong forms a diphthong (one syllable), the stress falling on the stronger element: *baila, cierra, puesto, peine, causa*.

(b) A combination of weak + weak forms a diphthong (one syllable), the stress falling on the second element: *ruido, fuimos, viuda*.
(c) Two strong vowels remain in hiatus as two distinct syllables, the stress falling according to rules (a) and (b) in section 2; *ma/es/tro* (three syllables in all), *con/tra/er* (three syllables in all), *cre/er* (two syllables).
(d) Any word having a vowel combination whose parts are not stressed according to rules (a) to (c) bears an acute accent on the stressed part: *creído, período, baúl, ríe, tío*.
Note — in those cases where IPA transcriptions are given for Spanish words, the stress mark ['] is inserted in the same way as explained for English, above, section 2.

The Spanish letters and their sounds

Note — the order in which the explanations are set out is that of the alphabet and not that of the phonetic system. The system of transcription adopted is a fairly "broad" one; a more exact or "narrow" system would involve, for example, division of the vowel [e] according to quality and length, and the use of two symbols instead of one [e, ɛ].

Vowels

Spanish vowels are clearly and rather sharply pronounced, and single vowels are free from the tendency to diphthongize which is noticeable in English (eg *side* [said], *know* [nəu]). Moreover when they are in unstressed positions they are relaxed only slightly, again in striking contrast to English (compare English *natural* ['nætʃrəl] with Spanish *natural* [natu'ral]). Stressed vowels are somewhat more open and short before *rr* (compare *carro* with *caro, perro* with *pero*).

(NOTE: Examples are pronounced as in British English.)

a	[a]	Not so short as *a* in English *pat, patter*, nor so long as in English *rather, bar*	pata amara
e	[e]	In an open syllable (one which ends in the vowel) like *e* in English *they*, but without the sound of the *y*. In a closed syllable (one which ends in a consonant) is a shorter sound, like the *e* in English *set, wet*	me pelo sangre peldaño
i	[i]	Not so short as *i* in English *bit, tip*, nor so long as in English *machine*	iris filo
o	[o]	In an open syllable (one which ends in the vowel) like *o* in English *note*, but without the sound of [u] which ends the vowel in this word. In a closed syllable (one which ends in a consonant) is a shorter sound, though not quite so short as in English *pot, cot*	poco cosa bomba conté

u	[u]	Like *u* in English *rule* or *oo* in *food*. Silent after *q* and in the groups *gue*, *gui*, unless marked by a diaeresis (*argüir*, *fragüe*, *antigüedad*)	luna pula
y	[i]	As a vowel — that is in the conjunction *y* "and", and at the end of a word such as *ley*, *voy* — is pronounced like *i*.	

Diphthongs
(See also section 3 above)

ai, ay	[ai]	like *i* in English *side*	baile estay
au	[au]	like *ou* in English *sound*	áureo causa
ei, ey	[ei]	like *ey* in English *they*	reina rey
eu	[eu]	like the vowel sounds in English *may-you*, without the sound of the *y*	deuda feudo
oi, oy	[oi]	like *oy* in English *boy*	oiga soy

Semiconsonants

These are two, and appear in a variety of combinations as the first element; not all the combinations are listed here.

i, y	[j]	like *y* in English *yes*, *yacht* (See also the note under *y* in the list of consonants)	bien hielo yunta apoyo
u	[w]	like *w* in English *well*	huevo fuente agua guardar

Consonants

b, v		These two letters have the same value in Spanish. There are two distinct pronunciations depending on position and context:	
	[b]	At the start of the breath-group and after written *m* and *n* (pronounced [m]) the sound is plosive like English *b*	bomba boda enviar
	[β]	In all other positions the sound is a bilabial fricative (unknown in English) in which the lips do not quite meet	haba severo yo voy de Vigo
c		There are two different values:	
	[k]	*c* before *a*, *o*, *u* or a consonant is like English *k* in *keep*, but without the slight aspiration which accompanies it	calco acto cuco
	[θ]	*c* before *e*, *i* is like English *th* in *thin*. In parts of Andalusia and in *SAm* this is pronounced like English voiceless *s* in *same*, a phenomenon known as *seseo*	celda hacer cinco cecear
		Note — in words like *acción*, *sección* both types of *c*-sound are heard [kθ]	
ch	[tʃ]	like English *ch* in *church*	mucho chocho
d		There are three different values depending on position and context:	

	[d]	At the start of the breath-group and after *l, n* the sound is plosive like English *d*	dama aldea andar
	[ð]	Between vowels and after consonants other than *l, n* the sound is relaxed and approaches English voiced *th* [ð] in *this*; in parts of Spain and in uneducated speech it is further relaxed and even disappears, particularly in the *-ado* ending In the final position, the second type of [ð] is further relaxed or altogether omitted (though purists condemn this as a vulgar error). In eastern parts of Spain, however, this final *-d* may be heard as a [t]	pide cada pardo sidra verdad usted Madrid callad
f	[f]	like English *f* in *for*	fama fofo
g		There are three different values depending on position and context:	
	[x]	Before *e, i* it is the same as the Spanish *j* (below)	Gijón general
	[g]	At the start of the breath-group and after *n*, the sound is that of the English *g* in *get*	gloria rango pingüe
	[ɣ]	In other positions the sound is as in the second type above, but is fricative not plosive, there being no more than a close approximation of the vocal organs	haga agosto la guerra
		Note — in the group *gue, gui* the *u* is silent (*guerra, guindar*) except when marked by a diaeresis (*antigüedad, argüir*). In the group *gua* all the letters are sounded (*guardia, guapo*)	
h		always silent, a written convention only	honor hombre rehacer
j	[x]	a strong guttural sound not found in the English of England, but like the *ch* of Scots *loch*, Welsh *bach*, or German *Aachen*, *Achtung*; it is silent at the end of a word (*reloj*)	jota jején baraja
k	[k]	like English *k* in *kick*, but without the slight aspiration which accompanies it	kilogramo
l	[l]	like English *l* in *love*	lelo panal
ll	[ʎ]	approximating to English *lli* in *million*; in parts of Spain and most of *SAm* is pronounced as [j] and in other parts as [ʒ]; the pronunciation as [j] is condemned in Spain as a vulgar error but is extending rapidly even in Castile	calle ella lluvia millón
m	[m]	like English *m* in *made*	mano mamar
n	[n]	like English *n* in *none*; but before written *v* is pronounced as *m*, the group making [mb] (eg *enviar, sin valor*)	nadie pan pino
ñ	[ɲ]	approximating to English *ni* [nj] in *onion*	uña ñoño
p	[p]	like English *p* in *put*, but without the slight aspiration which accompanies it; it is often silent in *septiembre, séptimo*	padre papa
q	[k]	like English *k* in *kick*, but without the slight aspiration which accompanies it; it is always written in combination with *u*, which is silent	que quinqué busqué quiosco
r	[r]	a single trill or vibration stronger than any *r* in the English of England, but like the *r* in Scots; it is more relaxed in the final	coro quiere

		position and is indeed silent in parts of Spain and *SAm*; pronounced like *rr* at the start of a word and also after *l, n, s*	rápido real
rr	[rr]	strongly trilled in a way that does not exist in English (except in parodies of Scots)	torre arre burra irreal
s		Two pronunciations:	
	[s]	Except in the instances mentioned next, is a voiceless *s* like *s* in English *same*	casa Isabel soso
	[z]	Before a voiced consonant (*b, d, g, l, m, n*) is in most speakers a voiced *s* like *s* in English *rose, phase*	desde asgo mismo asno
t	[t]	like English *t* in *tame*, but without the slight aspiration which accompanies it	título patata
v		(*see* b)	
w		found in a few recent loanwords only; usually pronounced like Spanish *b, v* or like an English *v*, or kept as English *w*	wáter week-end wolframio
x		There are several possible pronunciations:	
	[ks]	Between vowels, *x* is pronounced like English *x* in box [ks], or	máximo
	[gs]	like *gs* in *big stick* [gs]	examen
	[s]	In a few words the *x* is pronounced between vowels like English *s* by many (but not all) speakers	exacto auxilio
	[s]	Before a consonant *x* is pronounced like English *s* in *same* by many (but not all) speakers	extra sexto
y	[j]	as a consonant or semiconsonant, is pronounced like *y* in English *yes, youth*; in emphatic speech in Spain and *SAm* this is heard as a voiced palatal plosive rather like the *j* in English *jam* [dʒ]; in *RPl, Chi* etc this *y* is pronounced like the *s* in English *leisure* [ʒ]	mayo yo mayor ya
z	[θ]	like English *th* in *thin*; in parts of Andalusia and in *SAm* this is pronounced like English voiceless *s* in *same*, a phenomenon known as *seseo*	zapato zopenco zumbar luz

Additional notes on pronunciation

1 The letter *b* is usually not pronounced in groups with *s* such as *obscuro, substituir*, and such words are now often written (with the Academy's sanction) *oscuro, sustituir etc*; they are so printed in this dictionary. A tendency to drop the *b* in pronouncing other similar groups is also noticeable, for example in *subjuntivo*, but in these cases the *b* is still always written.

2 With one exception there are no real double consonants in Spanish speech; *cc* in words like *acción* is two separate sounds [kθ], while *ll* and *rr* have their own values (see the table above).

The exception is the *-nn-* group found in learned words having the Latin prefix *in-*, eg *innato*, or occasionally *con-, sin-*, as in *connatural, sinnúmero*. In these cases the *n* is pronounced double [nn].

3 Final *-s* of the definite and indefinite articles, plural, and of plural adjectives, is usually silent when the following noun starts with *r-*: eg *unos rábanos* [uno'rraβanos], *los romanos, varias razones, dos ratas* [do'rratas].

4 Foreign sounds in Spanish hardly warrant separate treatment for our purposes; whereas the cultured Briton makes some attempt to maintain at least a vaguely French sound when he pronounces English loanwords from

French, with nasal vowels and so on, the cultured Spaniard for the most part and certainly his less cultured compatriot adapts the sounds (but often not the spelling) of loanwords taken from French or English to suit his native speech habits. This is best studied in the transcriptions of individual items in the main text of the dictionary; see for example *chalet, gag, jazz, shock.*

5 No old-established Spanish word begins with what is called "impure *s*", that is, *s* plus a consonant as an initial group. When Spaniards have to pronounce a foreign name having such a group they inevitably precede it with an *e-* sound, so that *Smith* is [ez'miθ] or [ez'mis]. Very recent anglicisms tend to be written in Spanish as *slip, slogan* and so on, but must be pronounced [ez'lip], [ez'loɣan]; those that are slightly better established are written *esnob, esprinter* etc, and then present no problem in pronunciation.

6 See also section VI of this Introduction, on "Spanish orthography and the *Nuevas Normas*".

The letters of the Spanish alphabet

When the letters are cited one by one, or when a word is spelled out for greater clarity, or when an aircraft is identified by a letter and a name, and so on, the names of the letters used are:

a	[a]	j	['xota]	r	['ere]
b	[be]	k	[ka]	rr	['erre]
c	[θe]	l	['ele]	s	['ese]
ch	[tʃe]	ll	['eʎe]	t	[te]
d	[de]	m	['eme]	u	[u]
e	[e]	n	['ene]	v	['uβe]
f	['efe]	ñ	['eɲe]	x	['ekis]
g	[xe]	o	[o]	y	[i'vrjeʋa]
h	['atʃe]	p	[pe]	z	['θeta] or
i	[i]	q	[ku]		['θeða]

The letters are of the feminine gender: "mayo se escribe con una *m* minúscula", "¿esto es una *c* o una *t*?". One says "una *a*" and "la *a*", "una *h*" and "la *h*" (not applying the rule as in *un ave, el agua*).

IV. *THE PRONUNCIATION OF SPANISH IN AMERICA*

To generalize briefly about the vast area over which Spanish ranges in the New World is difficult; the following notes are very tentative. The upland regions (settled by Castilians from the *meseta*) tend to be linguistically conserva-tive and to have more Castilian features; the lowland and coastal regions share many of the features of Andalusian speech. Among the vowels there is little to note. Among the consonants:

1 The Castilian [θ] sound — in writing *c* or *z* — is pronounced as various kinds of *s* [s] throughout America, a phenomenon known as *seseo*.

2 At the end of a syllable and a word, *s* is a slight aspiration, eg *las dos* [lah'doh], *mosca* ['mohka]; but in parts of the Andean region, in upland Mexico and in Peru the [s] is maintained as in Castilian.

3 Castilian written *ll* [ʎ] is pronounced in three different ways in regions of America. It survives as [ʎ] in part of Colombia, all Peru, Bolivia, N. Chile and Paraguay; in Argentina, Uruguay, upland Ecuador and part of Mexico it is pronounced [ʒ]; and in the remaining areas it is pronounced [j]. When this last kind [j] is in contact with the vowels *e* and *i* it disappears altogether and one finds in uneducated writing such forms as *gaína* (for *gallina*) and *biete* (for *billete*).

4 In vulgar speech in all parts there is much confusion of *l* and *r*: *clin* (for *crin*), *carma* (for *calma*) etc.

5 Written *h* is silent in Castilian, but in parts of Mexico and Peru this *h* is aspirated at the start of a word (when it derives from Latin initial *f-*), so that in uneducated writing one finds such forms as *jarto* (for *harto*) and *jablar* (for *hablar*). Compare *halar/jalar* and other cases in the text of the dictionary.

V. *LA ORTOGRAFÍA DEL INGLÉS*

El extranjero, mientras lucha con las muchas confusiones y rarezas de la ortografía inglesa, se consuela recordando que los propios niños ingleses, y muchas personas mayores, sostienen la misma lucha. El inglés ha de ser el único idioma para el que ha valido la pena — la cosa estuvo de moda hacia unos 20 años — organizar certámenes ortográficos, en los que se pedía que los concursantes deletreasen palabras como *parallel, precede* y *proceed* y *supersede, sylph* y *Ralph*. Ha habido muchas tentativas de reforma — siendo quizá la más conocida la de G. B. Shaw — pero ninguna se ha llevado a la práctica; las reformas norteamericanas (véase abajo) son útiles pero afectan sólo una pequeña parte del problema.

1 En general se aplica el sistema en todo su rigor y las dudas y desviaciones permitidas son escasísimas. Es lícito escribir algunas palabras con o sin *e* muda, como *blond(e)*, *judg(e)ment*; varía la vocal en *enquiry-inquiry*, *encrust-incrust*, y la consonante en muchas palabras terminadas en *-ise*, *-ize* (pero siempre *advertise*, *chastise*). En casos como *spirt–spurt* se hace generalmente una distinción de sentido. Son toleradas *grandad* y *granddad*, *mummie* y *mummy*, *nappie* y *nappy*. Las variantes más importantes constan en el texto del diccionario.

2 En las novelas en que se presenta la vida de la clase baja urbana (p.ej. de los *Cockneys* de Londres) o de gente del campo, el autor puede representar su habla — con sus incorrecciones y barbarismos, según el criterio casticista — con formas como las siguientes:

'e	= he	Oim	= I'm
'ere	= here	roit	= right
'ope	= hope	Lunnun	= London
'ed	= head	bruvver	= brother
et	= ate	Fursday	= Thursday
'arf	= half	dook	= duke
yer	= your	dunno	= don't know

La *-d* final tras *n* se suprime a menudo en este lenguaje, p.ej. *an'* = *and*, y la *-g* final se suprime en la desinencia *-ing*, p.ej. *boozin'* = *boozing*. Como curiosidad apuntamos que este último fenómeno se da también en representaciones del habla de las familias aristocráticas, de los militares viejos etc: *huntin'*, *shootin'* and *fishin'*. Nótese el modo de emplear la comilla (') para indicar la supresión de una letra. Tales cambios en la escritura pueden representar una diferencia no de clase sino de región, p.ej. en escocés *awa'* = away, y en el inglés de las Antillas *dis* = *this*.

3 Se observan a veces deformaciones hechas con intención humorística (*luv* = *love*, *Injun* = *Indian*) o con afán de ultramodernidad (*nite* = *night*) o como truco publicitario en el comercio (*sox* = *socks*) o como parte de la jerga de un grupo social (*showbiz* = *show business*).

4 Son mucho más importantes las diferencias ortográficas entre el inglés británico (*Brit*) y el norteamericano (*US*):

(a) La *u* que se escribe en *Brit* en las palabras terminadas en *-our* y derivadas del latín, se suprime en *US*: *US* color = *Brit* colour, *US* labor = *Brit* labour. (Esto no afecta los monosílabos como *dour*, *flour*, *sour*, donde no hay diferencia). También en *US* se suprime la *u* del grupo *ou* [əu] en el interior de la palabra: *US* mold = *Brit* mould, *US* smolder = *Brit* smoulder.

(b) Muchas palabras que en *Brit* terminan en *-re* se escriben en *US* *-er*: *US* center = *Brit* centre, *US* meter = *Brit* metre, *US* theater = *Brit* theatre. (Pero no existe diferencia en *acre*, *lucre*, *massacre*).

(c) Ciertas vocales finales, que no tienen valor en la pronunciación, se escriben en *Brit* pero se suprimen en *US*: *US* catalog = *Brit* catalogue, *US* prolog = *Brit* prologue, *US* program = *Brit* programme, *US* kilogram = *Brit* kilogramme.

(d) En *US* se suele simplificar los diptongos de origen griego y latino *ae*, *oe*, escribiendo sencillamente *e*: *US* anemia = *Brit* anaemia, *US* anesthesia = *Brit* anaesthesia. En *US* se duda entre *subpoena* y *subpena*; en *Brit* se mantiene siempre el primero.

(e) En algunos casos las palabras que en *Brit* terminan en *-ence* se escriben *-ense* en *US*: *US* defense = *Brit* defence, *US* offense = *Brit* offence.

(f) Algunas consonantes que en *Brit* se escriben dobles se escriben en *US* sencillas: *US* wagon = *Brit* waggon (pero *wagon* se admite también en Inglaterra), y sobre todo en formas verbales: *US* kidnaped = *Brit* kidnapped, *US* worshiped = *Brit* worshipped. El caso de *l*, *ll* intervocálicas ofrece más complejidades. Alguna vez lo que se escribe con *ll* en Brit se encuentra con una *l* en *US*: así *US* councilor = *Brit* councillor, *US* traveler = *Brit* traveller. Por el contrario, en posición final de sílaba o de palabra la *l* en *Brit* es a menudo *ll* en *US*: así *US* enroll, enrolls = *Brit* enrol, enrols, *US* skillful = *Brit* skilful.

(g) En *US* se modifica algún otro grupo ortográfico del inglés, pero sólo en la escritura de tono familiar: *US* tho = *Brit* though, *US* thru = *Brit* through. También son más corrientes en *US* las formas como *Peterboro* (o bien *Peterboro'*), aunque éstas no son desconocidas en *Brit*.

(h) Viene luego una serie de palabras aisladas que se escriben de modo diferente:

US	Brit	US	Brit
ax	axe	mustache	moustache
check	cheque	pajamas	pyjamas
cozy	cosy	plow	plough
gray	grey	skeptic	sceptic
gypsy	gipsy	tire	tyre
hello	hullo		

En otros casos se duda bastante; en *US* hay lucha entre *rime, rhyme,* mientras en *Brit* se escribe únicamente el segundo; en *US* hay lucha entre *tiro, tyro,* mientras en *Brit* se escribe siempre el segundo.

Conviene notar que mientras la influencia del inglés norteamericano se percibe a cada paso en el inglés británico en cuanto al léxico, a la fraseología y a la sintaxis, ésta parece no haber afectado para nada la ortografía del inglés en el Reino Unido.

5 Las mayúsculas se emplean más en inglés que en español. Se emplean como en español al principio de la palabra en los siguientes casos: en la primera palabra de la frase; en los nombres propios de toda clase; en los nombres, sobrenombres y pronombres posesivos de Dios, Cristo, Nuestra Señora etc; en las graduaciones y títulos de las autoridades del estado, del ejército, de la iglesia, de las profesiones etc.

Las mayúsculas se emplean en inglés en los siguientes casos donde se escribe minúscula en español:

(a) Los nombres de los días y meses: *Monday, Tuesday, April, May.*

(b) El pronombre personal de sujeto, primera persona: *I (yo).* Pero el pronombre de segunda persona se escribe en inglés con minúscula: *you (Vd, Vds).*

(c) Los nombres de los habitantes de los países y provincias, los adjetivos derivados de éstos y los nombres de los idiomas: *I like the French, two Frenchwomen, French cheese, to talk French, a text in old Aragonese.* Se emplea la mayúscula también en los nombres y adjetivos derivados de otras clases de nombres propios: *a Darwinian explanation, the Bevanites, two well-known Gongorists, a Beatle haircut, the Alphonsine school.* Sin embargo el adjetivo de nacionalidad puede escribirse con minúscula en algún caso cuando se refiere a una cosa corriente u objeto conocido de todos, p.ej. *a french window, french beans, german measles* (en este diccionario hemos preferido escribir algunas de estas palabras con mayúscula).

(d) En los sustantivos y adjetivos principales en los títulos de libros, artículos, películas etc: *The Third Man, Gone with the Wind, The Potato in Hungarian Folklore.*

6 La puntuación en inglés. Los signos y el modo de emplearlos son como en español con las siguientes excepciones:

(a) Los signos de admiración y de interrogación (¡¿) no se emplean en inglés en principio de frase.

(b) En inglés se emplea menos la doble raya (— ... —) con función parentética; se prefiere en muchos casos el paréntesis (. . .).

(c) La raya (—) que sirve a menudo en español para introducir el diálogo y la oración directa, y a veces también para cerrarlos, se sustituye en inglés por las comillas (". . ."). Conviene apuntar que éstas se emplean obligatoriamente al terminar la cita u oración directa y no sólo para introducirla. Los signos « » del español se escriben siempre como comillas (". . .") en inglés.

7 La división de la palabra en inglés. Las reglas para dividir una palabra en final de renglón son menos estrictas en inglés que en español. En general se prefiere cortar la palabra tras vocal, *hori-zontal, vindi-cation,* pero se prefiere mantener como unidades ciertos sufijos comunes, *vindica-tion, glamor-ous.* De acuerdo con esto se divide la palabra dejando separadâ la desinencia *-ing,* p.ej. *sicken-ing,* pero si ésta está precedida por un grupo de consonantes, una de ellas va unida al *-ing,* p.ej. *tick-ling, ramb-ling.* Se divide el grupo de dos consonantes iguales: *pat-ter, yel-low, disap-pear,* y los demás grupos consonánticos de acuerdo con los elementos separables que forman la palabra: *dis-count, per-turb;* son admisibles *be-tween, bet-ween* y *atmo-sphere, atmos-phere.*

VI. *SPANISH ORTHOGRAPHY AND THE NUEVAS NORMAS*

The system of spelling in Spanish is extremely logical and apart from a few small anomalies it presents no problems. The more important of the Academy's *Nuevas Normas* of 1959 are appended for information and to help maintain the unity of the system. An excellent book for those in doubt is Manuel Seco's *Diccionario de dudas y dificultades de la lengua española,* Madrid, Aguilar, 2nd ed., 1964.

1 Spelling reform in Spanish to correct the few remaining anomalies is rarely attempted. Some favour always writing *j* (not a mixture of *g* and *j*) for the [x] sound: *jeneral, Jibraltar* — quite logically, since *jirafa, jícara* and *jirón,* and many others, are so spelled by everybody. Poetic texts of Juan Ramón Jiménez are always printed with such spellings.

2 The Academy's *Nuevas Normas* are (as currently noted in 1970) being obeyed only in part by private individuals and printers. The recommended spelling of the rare words beginning in *mn-* and rather frequent words in *ps-* with *m, s* respectively is taking a long time to establish itself; we have preferred in the dictionary to give such words as *ps-* in both parts, but with a cross-reference from *s-* in the Spanish-English, in accordance with our principle of following usage rather than rules. (Note that the element *seudo-* is well established, however, and has virtually ousted *pseudo-*.)

3 Novels representing the life of the lower urban classes, peasants and the regions are numerous and often important. In them the author may portray their speech (phonetically substandard on the purists' criteria) by such forms as:

señá *for* señora	pá *for* para
usté *for* usted	ná *for* nada
verdá *for* verdad	tó *for* todo
pué *for* puede	güevo *for* huevo
	agüela *for* abuela

4 Those who read familiar letters from less well-educated Spaniards may welcome a note on the kind of error which often appears in such documents (and is not wholly unknown in public notices and in print). The errors depend on the few anomalies of the official spelling system. Great confusion reigns over *b, v*; one finds *boy* for *voy*, *escrivir* for *escribir*, *tranbía* for *tranvía*, and even *vrabo* for *bravo*. *H* being silent is often omitted: *acer, reacer, ombre*; but equally it is often added where it does not belong, *hera* for *era*, *honce* for *once* and so on. Since written *ll* [ʎ] is often regionally and vulgarly pronounced [j], one sometimes finds *ll* written by hypercorrection in place of *y*: *cullo* for *cuyo*, *rallo* for *rayo*.

5 Much of the above applies also to Spanish in America, partly because of error and partly because it reflects pronunciation there (see the previous section). The confusion between written *ll* and *y* goes further than in Spain, eg with *llapa–yapa*; the same is true of initial *h-* and *j-*, eg *halar–jalar*, and of *gua-* and *hua-*, eg *guaca–huaca*; we have tried to provide cross-references to these variants in the dictionary. Forms such as *güevo* (for *huevo*) and *güeno* (for *bueno*) are common too. Newspapers and even books are more carelessly printed in parts of America than they are in Spain; examples noted recently from Central America include *excabar* (for *excavar*), *haya* (for *aya*), *desabitada* (for *deshabitada*); while because the regular *seseo* equates Castilian [θ] with [s] in America, one finds in print *capas* (for *capaz*), *saga* (for *zaga*), and by hypercorrection *sociego* (for *sosiego*) and *discución* (for *discusión*).

6 Use of capitals in Spanish. Capital letters are used to begin words as in English in the following cases: for the first word in the sentence; for proper names of every kind; for the names, bynames and possessive pronouns of God, Christ, the Virgin Mary etc; for ranks and authorities in the state, army, church, the professions etc.

Usage differs from English in the following cases:

(a) The names of the days and months do not have capitals in Spanish: *lunes, martes, abril, mayo.*

(b) The first person subject pronoun does not have a capital unless it begins the sentence: *yo.* In Spanish it is usual to write the abbreviations *Vd, Vds* with capitals, but *usted, ustedes* in their extended form.

(c) Capitals are used for the names of countries and provinces etc, but not for the names of their inhabitants, for the adjectives relating to them or for their languages: *Francia*, but *un francés, una francesa, el vino francés, hablar francés*. The same is true of adjectives and nouns formed from other types of proper names: *la teoría darviniana, los estudios cervantinos, el conocido gongorista, la escuela alfonsí.*

(d) In the titles of books, articles, films etc the capital is used only at the start of the first word, unless later words are proper names: *El tercer hombre, Lo que el viento se llevó, La patata en el folklore húngaro* (but *Boletín de la Real Academia Española, Por tierras de Ruritanià*).

(e) A very few words which do not have capitals in English often have them in Spanish: *el Estado, la Iglesia* and such. This is not obligatory and may depend on the amount of respect being shown.

7 Spanish punctuation. This is as in English except for the following features:

(a) Exclamation and question marks are placed inverted (¡¿) at the start of the exclamation or question as well as at the end. Note that this does not always coincide with the start of the sentence: eg *Pues ¿vamos o no vamos?; Son trece en total, ¿verdad?*

(b) The long dash (—, called a *raya*) is often used in Spanish where English would put parentheses.

(c) The same dash is much used to introduce dialogue or direct speech; sometimes at the start and at the end of the quotation, but sometimes only at the start.

(d) The inverted commas ('') with which English encloses passages of direct speech and uses for a variety of other purposes are often represented in Spanish by « ».

8 Word division in Spanish. There are rules, rather different from those of English, about how a word may be divided in writing at the end of a line. The main points are:

(a) A single consonant between vowels is grouped with the second of them: *pa-lo*, *Barcelo-na*.

(b) In a group of two consonants between vowels, the first is grouped with the preceding vowel and the second with the following vowel: *in-nato*, *des-mochar*, *paten-te*. But groups having *l* or *r* as the second element are considered as units and join the following vowel only: *re-probar*, *de-clarar*.

(c) A group consisting of consonant + *h* may be split: *ex-hibición*, *Al-hambra*.

(d) It must be remembered that *ch*, *ll* and *rr* are considered as individual letters and must therefore never be split: *aprove-char*, *aga-lla*, *contra-rrevolucionario*.

(e) In a group of three consonants, the first two join the preceding vowel and the third joins the following vowel: *trans-porte*, *cons-tante*. Exception: if the third consonant in the group is *l* or *r*, only the first consonant joins the preceding vowel while the second and third join the following vowel: *som-bra*, *des-preciar*, *con-clave*.

(f) Two vowels should never be separated, whether they form one syllable or not: *rui-do*, *maes-tro*, *pro-veer*.

(g) Where it can be clearly recognized that a word consists of two or more words having an independent existence of their own, the long word may be divided in ways that contravene the foregoing rules: *latino-americano*, *re-examinar*, *vos-otros*. The same applies to some prefixes: *des-animar*, *ex-ánime*.

9 Use of the hyphen (-, called a *guión*) in Spanish. Strictly speaking this should only be used in Spanish in the cases mentioned in Nos. 22 and 23 of the *Nuevas Normas*, quoted below. Compound words with or without a hyphen in English should be written as single words without hyphen in Spanish; a hotplate is *un calientaplatos* and a windscreen wiper is *un limpiaparabrisas*, while a Latin American is *un hispanoamericano* or *un latinoamericano*. None the less in the dictionary we have used the hyphen in a few Spanish words which have been regularly noted in that form in print.

THE NUEVAS NORMAS

Their full title is *Nuevas Normas de prosodia y ortografía de la Academia Española;* they were promulgated as being *de aplicación preceptiva* from 1 January 1959. Here a selection is made of the more important sections of the 25 which make up the full text; it has seemed best to retain the Spanish of the original to avoid all risk of misinterpreting the Academy's wishes:

4 Se autoriza la simplificación de los grupos iniciales en las palabras que empiezan con *ps-*, *mn-*, *gn-*: *sicología, nemotecnia, nomo*. Las formas tradicionales, *psicología, mnemotecnia, gnomo*, se conservan en el Diccionario y en ellas se da la definición correspondiente.

5 Se autoriza el empleo de las formas contractas *remplazo, remplazar, rembolso, rembolsar*, que se remiten en el Diccionario a las formas con doble *e*.

6 Cuando un vocablo simple entre a formar parte de un compuesto como primer elemento del mismo, se escribirá sin el acento ortográfico que como simple le habría correspondido: *decimoséptimo, asimismo, rioplatense, piamadre*.

7 Se exceptúan de esta regla los adverbios en *-mente*, porque en ellos se dan realmente dos acentos prosódicos, uno en el adjetivo y otro en el nombre *mente*. La pronunciación de estos adverbios con un solo acento, como voces llanas, ha de tenerse por incorrecta. Se pronunciará, pues, y se escribirá el adverbio marcando en el adjetivo el acento que debiera llevar como simple: *ágilmente, cortésmente, lícitamente*.

8 Los compuestos de verbo con enclítico más complemento (tipo *sabelotodo*) se escribirán sin el acento que solía ponerse en el verbo.

9 En los compuestos de dos o más adjetivos unidos con guión, cada elemento conservará su acentuación prosódica y la ortográfica si le correspondiere: *hispano-belga, anglo-soviético, cántabro-astur, histórico-crítico-bibliográfico*.

13 La combinación *ui* se considerará, para la práctica de la escritura, como diptongo en todos los casos. Sólo llevará acento ortográfico cuando lo pida el apartado *e*) del número 539 de la *Gramática*; y el acento se marcará, como allí se indica, en la segunda de las débiles, es decir, en la *i*: *casuístico, benjuí*; pero *casuista*, voz llana, se escribirá sin tilde.

14 Los vocablos agudos terminados en *-ay, -ey, -oy, -uy* se escribirán sin tilde: *taray, virrey, convoy, maguey, Uruguay*.

15 Los monosílabos *fue, fui, dio, vio*, se escribirán sin tilde.

16 Los pronombres *éste, ése, aquél*, con sus femeninos y plurales, llevarán normalmente tilde, pero será lícito prescindir de ella cuando no exista riesgo de anfibología.

17 La partícula *aun* llevará tilde (*aún*) y se pronunciará como bisílaba cuando pueda sustituirse por *todavía* sin alterar el sentido de la frase: *aún está enfermo; está enfermo aún*. En los demás casos, es decir, con el significado de *hasta, también, inclusive* (o *siquiera*, con negación), se escribirá sin tilde: *aun los sordos han de oírme; ni hizo nada por él ni aun lo intentó*.

18 La palabra *solo*, en función adverbial, podrá llevar acento ortográfico si con ello se ha de evitar una anfibología.

19 Se suprimirá la tilde en *Feijoo, Campoo* y demás paroxítonos terminados en *oo*.

20 Los nombres propios extranjeros se escribirán, en general, sin ponerles ningún acento que no tengan en el idioma a que pertenecen; pero podrán acentuarse a la española cuando lo permitan su pronunciación y grafía originales. Si se trata de nombres geográficos ya incorporados a nuestra lengua o adaptados a su fonética, tales nombres no se han de considerar extranjeros y habrán de acentuarse gráficamente de conformidad con las reglas generales.

21 El uso de la diéresis solo será preceptivo para indicar que ha de pronunciarse la *u* en las combinaciones *gue, gui*: *pingüe, pingüino*. Queda a salvo el uso discrecional de este signo cuando, por licencia poética o con otro propósito, interese indicar una pronunciación determinada.

22 Cuando los gentilicios de dos pueblos o territorios formen un compuesto aplicable a una tercera entidad geográfica o política en la que se han fundido los caracteres de ambos pueblos o territorios, dicho compuesto se escribirá sin separación de sus elementos: *hispanoamericano, checoslovaco*. En los demás casos, es decir, cuando no hay fusión sino oposición o contraste entre los elementos componentes, se unirán éstos con guión: *franco-prusiano, germano-soviético*.

23 Los compuestos de nueva formación en que entren dos adjetivos, el primero de los cuales conserva invariable la terminación masculina singular, mientras el segundo concuerda en género y número con el nombre correspondiente, se escribirán uniendo con guión dichos adjetivos: *tratado teórico-práctico lección teórico-práctica, cuerpos técnico-administrativos*.

25 Se declara que la *h* muda colocada entre dos vocales no impide que estas formen diptongo: *de-sahu-cio, sahu-me-rio*. En consecuencia, cuando alguna de dichas vocales, por virtud de la regla general, haya de ir acentuada, se pondrá el acento ortográfico como si no existiese la *h*: *vahído, búho, rehúso*.

(Note — In the above, for example 13, the Academy uses the word *tilde* to mean "acute accent").

Works of Reference

Obras de consulta

1 DICTIONARIES OF SPANISH

María Moliner, *Diccionario de uso del español*
2 vols., Madrid, 1966 & 1967

S. Gili Gaya, *Vox: Diccionario general ilustrado de la lengua española*, 2nd ed., Barcelona, 1961

Real Academia Española: *Diccionario de la lengua española*, Madrid, 19th ed., 1970. See also: J. Casares, *Novedades en el Diccionario académico*, Madrid, 1963, and regular articles in *Boletín de la Real Academia Española* on new decisions of the Academy.

J. Corominas, *Diccionario crítico etimológico de la lengua castellana*, 4 vols., Berne, 1954–7 (also *Breve diccionario* . . . , Madrid, 1961)

M. Alonso Pedras, *Enciclopedia del idioma. Diccionario histórico y moderno de la lengua española* (Siglos XII–XX), 3 vols., Madrid, 1968

2 ON SPANISH GRAMMAR, USAGE, etc

Dictionaries

M. Seco, *Diccionario de dudas y dificultades de la lengua española*, 5th ed., Madrid, 1967

R. J. Alfaro, *Diccionario de anglicismos*, Madrid, 1964

S. Gili Gaya, *Diccionario Vox de sinónimos*, 3rd ed., Barcelona, 1968

J. Casares, *Diccionario ideológico de la lengua española*, 2nd ed., Barcelona, 1963

M. Alonso, *Ciencia del lenguaje y arte del estilo*, 6th ed., Madrid, 1964

A. Bryson Gerrard, *Beyond the Dictionary in Spanish*, 2nd ed., London, 1972

Grammar

L. C. Harmer & F. J. Norton, *A Manual of Modern Spanish*, 2nd ed., London, 1957

M. Alonso, *Gramática del español contemporáneo*, Madrid, 1968

S. Fernández Ramírez, *Gramática española*, I, Madrid, 1951

S. Gili Gaya, *Curso superior de sintaxis española*, 8th ed., Madrid, 1961

Pronunciation

T. Navarro Tomás, *Manual de pronunciación española*, 14th ed., New York, 1968

E. Alarcos Llorach, *Fonología española*, 4th ed., Madrid, 1968

Colloquial

W. Beinhauer, *Spanische Umgangssprache*, 2nd ed., Bonn, 1958; translated as *El español coloquial*, 2nd ed., Madrid, 1968

E. Lorenzo, *El español de hoy, lengua en ebullición*, 2nd ed., Madrid, 1971

M. Muñoz Cortés, *El español vulgar*, Madrid, 1958

R. Carnicer, *Sobre el lenguaje de hoy*, Barcelona, 1969

3 AMERICAN SPANISH

A. Malaret, *Diccionario de americanismos*, 3rd ed., Buenos Aires, 1946

A. Malaret, *Lexicón de fauna y flora*, Bogotá, 1970

M. A. Morínigo, *Diccionario manual de americanismos*, Buenos Aires, 1966

C. E. Kany, *American–Spanish Euphemisms*, Berkeley & Los Angeles, 1960

C. E. Kany, *American–Spanish Semantics*, Berkeley & Los Angeles, 1960 (Spanish translation, *Semántica hispanoamericana*, Madrid, 1969)

A. Alonso, *Estudios lingüísticos hispanoamericanos*, 2nd ed., Madrid, 1961

A. Aguero Chaves, *El español en América*, San José de Costa Rica, 1960

A. Rosenblat, *El castellano de España y el castellano de América. Unidad y diferenciación*, Caracas, 1962

J. L. Lope Blanch, *El español de América*, Madrid, 1968

D. L. Canfield, *La pronunciación del español en América. Ensayo histórico-descriptivo*, Bogotá, 1962

4 DICTIONARIES OF THE ENGLISH LANGUAGE

British

Oxford English Dictionary, Oxford University Press, London, 1928

Shorter Oxford English Dictionary, Oxford University Press, 3rd ed., London, 1944

Concise Oxford Dictionary of Current English (ed. Fowler), Oxford University Press, 5th ed., London, 1964

The Advanced Learner's Dictionary of Current English, Oxford University Press, 2nd ed., London, 1963

New English Dictionary, Collins, Glasgow, 1956

Chambers's Twentieth Century Dictionary, Chambers, revised ed., Edinburgh, 1972

Penguin English Dictionary, Penguin Books, revised ed., Harmondsworth: Middx, 1969

American

Random House Dictionary of the English Language, Random House, New York, 1967

Random House Dictionary of the English Language, College Edition, Random House, New York, 1968

Webster's Third New International Dictionary, Merriam, Springfield: Mass., 1961

Webster's New Collegiate Dictionary, Merriam, Springfield: Mass., 1973

American Heritage Dictionary of the English Language, American Heritage with Houghton Mifflin, New York, 1969

5 ON ENGLISH GRAMMAR, USAGE, etc

British

O. Jespersen, *Essentials of English Grammar*, Allen & Unwin, London, 1933

H. W. Fowler, ed. Sir E. Gowers, *Dictionary of Modern English Usage*, Oxford University Press, 2nd ed., London, 1965

E. Partridge, *Usage and Abusage*, Penguin Books, Harmondsworth: Middx, 1963

The Oxford Dictionary of English Etymology, Oxford University Press, London, 1966

P. M. Roget, ed. D. C. Browning, *Thesaurus of English Words and Phrases*, Dent, London, 1952

D. Jones, *English Pronouncing Dictionary*, J. M. Dent & Sons Ltd, 13th ed., London, 1967

American

Wilson Follett, *Modern American Usage*, Longmans, London, 1966

B. & C. Evans, *Dictionary of Contemporary American Usage*, Random House, New York, 1957

6 BILINGUAL TECHNICAL DICTIONARIES

General: L. B. Sell, *Comprehensive Technical Dictionary, English–Spanish*, I, New York, 1944; II, 1959

Castilla: *Diccionario politécnico de las lenguas española e inglesa*, 3rd ed., Madrid, 1965 (also as *Castilla's Spanish & English, English & Spanish Technical Dictionary*, London, 1958)

Duden español: Diccionario por la imagen, 2nd ed., London, 1963 (in Spanish, but with indices in both English and Spanish)

Many of the multilingual technical dictionaries published between 1962 and 1969 by the Elsevier Publishing Co. (London, Amsterdam, New York) have Spanish sections, eg on Aeronautics, Electronics, High Vacuum Science, Industrial Chemistry, Medicine, Metallurgy, Nautical affairs, Pharmaceutical Science, Physics

Accountancy: Mancera Hermanos (publishers), *Diccionario de contabilidad español–inglés, inglés–español*, Mexico, 1943

Aeronautics: J. Klein Serrallés, *English–Spanish & Spanish–English Dictionary of Aeronautical Terms*, New York—London, 1944

Chemistry etc: M. Goldberg, *English–Spanish Chemical & Medical Dictionary*, New York, 1947; *Spanish–English Chemical and Medical Dictionary*, New York, 1952

Commerce: C. Reyes Orozco, *Spanish–English & English–Spanish Commercial Dictionary*, Oxford, 1969

Communications: R. L. Freeman, *English–Spanish and Spanish–English Dictionary of Communications and Electronic Terms*, Cambridge, 1971

Electronics: H. Piraux, *Diccionario inglés–español de la terminología relativa a electrotecnia y electrónica*, Madrid, 1966

Law: L. A. Robb, *Dictionary of Legal Terms, Spanish–English & English–Spanish*, 3rd printing, New York, 1966

Librarianship: D. Rubio & M. C. Sullivan, *A Glossary of Technical Library and Allied Terms in Spanish & English*, Washington, 1936

Medicine: F. Ruiz Torres, *Diccionario inglés–español y español–inglés de medicina*, 3rd ed., Madrid, 1965

A

a *prep* **(a)** *(place = direction)* to; **ir a Madrid** to go to Madrid; **llegar a Madrid** to arrive in Madrid; to reach Madrid; **llegar al teatro** to arrive at the theatre; **ir al parque** to go to the park; **ir a casa** to go home; **subir a un avión** to get into a plane; **subir a un tren** to get into a train, to get on a train; **mirar al norte** to look northwards; **de cara al norte** facing north; **torcer a la derecha** to turn (to the) right; **caer al mar** to fall into the sea.

(b) *(place = distance)* **está a 7 km de aquí** it is 7 km (away) from here.

(c) *(place = position)* at; **al lado de** at the side of; **a la puerta** at the door; **estar a la mesa** to be at table; **estaba sentado a su mesa de trabajo** he was sitting at his desk; **a retaguardia** in the rear; **a orillas de** on the banks of; **al margen** in the margin.

(d) *(time)* at; **a las 8** at 8 o'clock; **¿a qué hora?** at what time?; **a mediodía** at noon; **a la noche** at nightfall; **a la mañana siguiente** the following morning; **a 3 de junio** on the third of June; **a los 55 años** at 55, at the age of 55; **al año de esto** after a year of this; **a los pocos días** within a few days, after a few days, a few days later; **a los 18 minutos** *(of game)* in the 18th minute; **"Cervantes a los 400 años"** *(title of article)* "Cervantes after 400 years", "Cervantes 400 years on".

(e) *(manner)* **a la americana** in the American fashion, (in) the American way; **a caballo** on horseback; **a escape** at full speed; **a oscuras** in the dark, in darkness; **a petición de** at the request of; **a pie** on foot; **a solicitud** on request; **tres a tres** three at a time, in threes, by threes; **beber algo a sorbos** to drink something in sips; **mirarse a los ojos** to look into each other's eyes.

(f) *(means, instrument)* **a lápiz** in pencil; **cocina a gas** gas stove; **a puñetazos** with (blows of) one's fists; **a mano** by hand; **bordado a mano** hand-embroidered; **girar algo a mano** to turn something by hand; **despertarse al menor ruido** to wake at the least sound.

(g) *(rate)* **poco a poco** little by little; **palmo a palmo** inch by inch; **a un precio elevado** at a high price; **a 30 ptas el kilo** at 30 pesetas a kilo, for 30 pesetas a kilo; **al 5 por ciento** at 5% *(per cent)*; **a 50 km por hora** at 50 km an hour; **a 5 veces al año** 5 times a year.

(h) *(dative)* to; **se lo di a él** I gave it to him; **le di dos a Pepe** I gave two to Joe, I gave Joe two.

(i) *(dative of separation)* **se lo compré a él** I bought it from him.

(j) *(with personal object: not translated)* **le vi al jefe** I saw the boss.

(k) *(construction with certain verbs)* to; **empezó a cantar** he began to sing; **voy a verle** I'm going to see him; **sabe a queso** it tastes of cheese; **huele a vino** it smells of wine.

(l) *(al + infin)* **al verle** on seeing him; when I saw him; *see also* **al**.

(m) *(a + infin)* **asuntos a tratar** agenda, items to be discussed; **el criterio a adoptar** the criterion to be adopted.

(n) *(if)* **a no ser esto así** if this were not so; **a saberlo ellos** if they had known; **a decir verdad** ... to tell the truth ...

abacería *nf* grocer's (shop), grocery store.

abacero *nm* grocer, provision merchant.

ábaco *nm* abacus.

abacorar [1a] *vt* **(a)** *(PR, Ven etc)* to harass, plague, bother; to catch, surprise.

(b) *(Cu)* to undertake boldly.

(c) *(Cu: Comm)* to monopolize, to corner (the market in).

abad *nm* abbot.

abadejo *nm* *(Fish: sea)* cod, codfish, *(freshwater)* ling; *(Ent)* Spanish fly, cantharides.

abadengo **1** *adj* abbatial, of an abbot. **2** *nm* abbacy.

abadesa *nf* **(a)** abbess. **(b)** *(SAm)* madame, brothel keeper.

abadía *nf* **(a)** abbey. **(b)** *(office, rank)* abbacy.

abajadero *nm* slope, incline.

abajeño *(SAm)* **1** *adj* lowland *(attr)*, of the lowland(s), from the lowland(s). **2** *nm*, **abajeña** *nf* lowlander.

abajera *nf* *(Arg)* saddlecloth.

abajero *adj* *(SAm)* lower, under.

abajino *(Chi)* **1** *adj* northern. **2** *nm*, **abajina** *nf* northerner.

abajo **1** *adv* *(position)* down, below, down below, underneath, *(in house)* downstairs; *(direction)* down, downwards, *(in house)* downstairs; **¡— el gobierno!** down with the Government!; **aquí —** down here; here below; **desde —** from below; **hacia —** down, downwards; **más —** lower down, further down; **cuesta —** downhill; **río —** downstream; **del rey —** from the king down.

2 — de *prep* below, under.

3 de — adj: **la parte de —** the lower part, the underside; **el piso de —** the downstairs flat; the floor below, the next floor down; **los de —** the underdogs, the downtrodden, the under-privileged.

abalanzar [1f] **1** *vt* **(a)** to weigh; to balance.

(b) to hurl, throw; to impel.

2 abalanzarse *vr* **(a)** to spring forward, rush forward, dash forward; **— a** *danger* to rush thoughtlessly into; **— sobre** to spring at, rush at, hurl oneself on; to pounce on.

(b) *(Arg: horse)* to rear up.

abaldonar [1a] *vt* to degrade, debase; to affront.

abalorio *nm* glass bead; beads, beadwork; **no vale un —** it's worthless.

abanderado *nm* standard bearer.

abanderar [1a] *vt* *(Naut)* to register.

abanderizar [1f] **1** *vt* to organize into bands. **2 abanderizarse** *vr* to band together, to join a band.

abandonado *adj* abandoned; *place etc* abandoned, deserted, godforsaken; *building* deserted, derelict; *appearance* neglected; forlorn; slovenly, uncared-for; *(morally)* profligate.

abandonamiento *nm see* **abandono**.

abandonar [1a] **1** *vt place etc* to leave; *helpless person* to leave, abandon; to desert, forsake; to flee from; *object* to leave behind; *attempt, habit* to drop, give up; to renounce, relinquish; **— una empresa** to give up an attempt; **abandonaron a sus hijos** they deserted their children; **cuando abandonó la casa** when he left the house; **tuvo que — el cargo** he had to give up the post.

2 *vi* to give up; *(Sport)* to withdraw, scratch, retire.

3 abandonarse *vr* **(a)** to give in, give up; to lose heart, get discouraged; to let oneself go, get slovenly, get slack; **no se abandone** don't let yourself go.

(b) **— a** to give oneself over to, yield to, indulge in an excess of.

abandonismo *nm* defeatism.

abandonista **1** *adj* defeatist. **2** *nmf* defeatist.

abandono *nm* **(a)** *(act)* abandonment; dereliction; desertion; giving up, renunciation, relinquishment; *(Sport)* withdrawal, retirement; **ganar por —** to win by default, win thanks to an opponent's withdrawal.

(b) *(state)* moral abandon; profligacy; forlornness; neglect, slovenliness; abandoned state; indulgence *(a* in); **darse al —** to go morally downhill, indulge one's vices; **viven en el mayor —** they live in utter degradation.

abanicada *nf* fanning, fanning action.

abanicar [1g] **1** *vt* to fan. **2 abanicarse** *vr* to fan oneself.

abanicazo *nm* tap with a fan.

abanico *nm* fan; fan-shaped object; (*fam*) sword; (*window*) fanlight; (*Naut*) derrick; **— de chimenea** fire screen; **— eléctrico** electric fan; **extender las cartas en —** to fan out one's cards; **con hojas en —** with leaves arranged like a fan.

abaniquear [1a] (*SAm*) **1** *vt* to fan. **2 abaniquearse** *vr* to fan oneself.

abaniqueo *nm* fanning, fanning movement; (*with hands*) gesticulation.

abaniquero *nm* fan maker; dealer in fans.

abaratamiento *nm* cheapening, reduction in price; greater cheapness.

abaratar [1a] **1** *vt article* to make cheaper, reduce the price of; *price* lower. **2** *vi and* **abaratarse** *vr* to get cheaper, come down.

abarca *nf* sandal.

abarcar [1g] *vt* to include, embrace, take in; to contain, comprise; to extend to; *work* to undertake, take on; (*Mex*) to monopolize, corner (the market in); **el capítulo abarca 3 siglos** the chapter covers 3 centuries, the chapter deals with 3 centuries; **sus conocimientos abarcan todo el campo de . . .** his knowledge ranges over the whole field of . . .

abarquillar [1a] **1** *vt* to curl up, roll up; to wrinkle. **2 abarquillarse** to curl up, roll up; to crinkle.

abarraganarse [1a] *vr* to live together (as man and wife).

abarrancadero *nm* tight spot, jam.

abarrancar [1g] **1** *vt* to make cracks in, open up fissures in.

    2 abarrancarse *vr* **(a)** to fall into a ditch (*or* pit etc).

    (b) to get stopped up.

    (c) (*Naut*) to run aground; (*fig*) to get into a jam.

abarrotar [1a] **1** *vt* **(a)** to bar, fasten with bars.

    (b) (*Naut*) to stow, pack tightly; (*Comm*) to overstock; (*fig*) to overstock, overfill; **abarrotado de** filled to bursting with, stuffed full of.

    2 abarrotarse *vr* (*SAm*) to become a glut on the market.

abarrote *nm* **(a)** (*Naut*) packing. **(b) —s** (*SAm*) groceries; **tienda de —s** grocer's (shop), grocery store.

abarrotería *nf* (*Mex*) grocer's (shop), grocery store; (*SAm*) ironmonger's (shop), hardware store (*US*).

abarrotero *nm* grocer.

abastardar [1a] **1** *vt* to degrade, debase. **2** *vi* to degenerate.

abastar [1a] *vt* to supply.

abastecedor *nm*, **abastecedora** *nf* supplier; purveyor.

abastecer [2d] *vt* to supply, provide (*de* with).

abastecimiento *nm* (*act*) supplying, provision; provisioning, catering; (*quantity*) supply, provision; provisions; **— de agua** water supply.

abastero *nm* (*SAm*) cattle dealer; provision merchant; (*Chi*) wholesale butcher.

abasto *nm* supply; provisioning; **dar — a** to supply; **dar — a un pedido** to fill an order, meet an order.

abatanado *adj* skilled, skilful.

abatanar [1a] *vt cloth* to beat, full; (*fig*) to beat.

abatatarse [1a] *vr* (*RPl*) to be shy, be bashful.

abatí *nm* (*SAm*) maize, corn (*US*).

abatible *adj*: **asiento —** tip-up seat; **mesa de alas —s** gate-leg(ged) table, table with flaps.

abatido *adj* depressed, dejected, downcast, crestfallen; (*morally*) low, contemptible, despicable; (*Comm, Fin*) depreciated; **estar — por el dolor** to be prostrate with pain; **estar muy —** to be very depressed.

abatimiento *nm* (*act*) demolition, knocking down; (*state*) depression, dejection; (*moral*) contemptible nature, despicable character.

abatir [3a] **1** *vt* **(a)** *house etc* to demolish, knock down; to dismantle; *tent* to take down; *tree* to cut down, fell; *plane* to shoot down; *bird* to shoot, bring down; *flag* to lower, strike; *person* to knock down; (*of illness, pain etc*) to prostrate, lay low.

    (b) (*fig*) to depress, sadden, discourage; to humble, humiliate.

    2 abatirse *vr* **(a)** to drop, fall; (*bird, plane*) to swoop, dive; **— sobre** to swoop on, pounce on.

    (b) (*fig*) to be depressed, get discouraged.

abdicación *nf* abdication.

abdicar [1g] **1** *vt* to renounce, relinquish; **— la corona** to give up the crown.

    2 *vi* to abdicate; **— de algo** to renounce something,

relinquish something; **— en uno** to abdicate in favour of someone.

abdomen *nm* abdomen.

abdominal *adj* abdominal.

abducción *nf* (*Med*) abduction.

abductor *nm* (*Anat*) abductor.

abecé *nm* ABC, alphabet; (*fig*) rudiments, basic elements.

abecedario *nm* alphabet; (*book*) primer, spelling book.

abedul *nm* birch; **— plateado** silver birch.

abeja *nf* bee; **— machiega, — maestra, — reina** queen bee; **— macho** drone; **— obrera** worker.

abejar *nm* apiary.

abejarrón *nm* bumblebee.

abejaruco *nm* bee-eater.

abejón *nm* drone.

abejonear [1a] (*SD*) **1** *vt* (*fig*) to whisper (*a* to). **2** *vi* to hum.

abejorro *nm* bumblebee; (*beetle*) cockchafer.

abellacado *adj* villainous.

aberenjenado *adj* violet-coloured.

aberración *nf* (*all senses*) aberration.

aberrante *adj* (*all senses*) aberrant.

aberrar [1a] *vi* to be mistaken, err.

abertura *nf* opening; gap, hole, aperture; crack, cleft, slit; fissure; (*Geog*) cove; wide valley, gap; (*fig*) openness.

abetal *nm* fir wood.

abeto *nm* (*tree*) fir; (*fruit*) fircone; **— blanco** silver fir; **— falso, — del norte, — rojo** spruce.

abiertamente *adv* openly.

abiertazo *adj* (*Guat*) generous, open-handed.

abierto 1 *ptp of* **abrir.**

    2 *adj* open; opened; *city, face, field, letter, competition etc* open; *character* open, frank; (*SAm*) generous; (*SAm*) conceited; **la puerta estaba abierta** the door was open, the door stood open; **muy abierto** wide open; **una brecha muy abierta** a gaping hole, a wide gap; **es una carrera muy abierta** it's a very open race, the race is wide open; **dejar un grifo —** to leave a tap running.

abigarrado *adj* variegated, many-coloured, of many colours; *animal* piebald, brindled; *scene* motley, vivid, colourful; *speech etc* disjointed, uneven.

abigarramiento *nm* variegation; many colours; motley colouring; vividness, colourfulness.

abigarrar [1a] *vt* to variegate; to paint (*etc*) in a variety of colours.

abintestato *adj* intestate.

abiselar [1a] *vt* to bevel.

Abisinia *f* Abyssinia.

abisinio 1 *adj* Abyssinian. **2** *nm*, **abisinia** *nf* Abyssinian.

abismal *adj* abysmal.

abismar [1a] **1** *vt* to cast down, humble; to spoil, ruin; **— a uno en la tristeza** to plunge someone into sadness.

    2 abismarse *vr* **(a)** (*SAm*) to be amazed.

    (b) — en to plunge into; to sink into; **— en el dolor** to abandon oneself to one's grief; to be plunged into sadness; **estar abismado en** to be lost in, be sunk in.

abismo *nm* abyss (*also fig*), chasm; (*of wave*) trough; (*Rel*) hell; **desde los —s de la Edad Media** from the dark depths of the Middle Ages; **estar en el borde del —** to be on the brink of ruin (*or* failure, disaster etc).

abjurar [1a] **1** *vt* to abjure, forswear. **2** *vi*: **— de** to abjure, forswear.

ablactación *nf* weaning.

ablactar [1a] *vt* to wean.

ablandabrevas *nmf*, **ablandahigos** *nmf* (*fam*) good-for-nothing.

ablandamiento *nm* softening; softening up; mitigation; soothing; moderation.

ablandar [1a] **1** *vt* to soften; (*Mil etc*) to soften up; (*Aut*) to run in; *bowels* to loosen; *harshness* to mitigate, temper; *harsh person* to soothe, mollify, appease.

    2 *vi* (*of cold*) to become less severe; (*of wind*) to moderate.

    3 ablandarse *vr* to soften, soften up, get soft(er); (*cold*) to become less severe, (*wind*) moderate, (*elements*) decrease in force; (*person*) to relent, become less harsh, (*with age*) mellow.

ablande *nm* (*Aut*) running-in.

ablativo *nm* ablative; **— absoluto** ablative absolute.

ablución *nf* ablution.

abnegación *nf* self-denial, abnegation; unselfishness.

abnegado *adj* self-denying, self-sacrificing; unselfish.

abnegarse [1h *and* 1k] *vr* to deny oneself, go without, act unselfishly.

abobado adj silly; stupid-looking, bewildered; **mirar** — to look bewildered.

abobamiento nm silliness, stupidity; bewilderment.

abobar [1a] **1** vt to make stupid; to daze, bewilder. **2 abobarse** vr to get stupid.

abocado adj wine smooth, pleasant.

abocar [1g] **1** vt to seize (or catch) in one's mouth; to bring nearer, bring up; wine to pour out, decant; **verse abocado a un peligro** to see danger looming ahead, to see trouble coming closer.
2 vi (Naut) to enter a river, enter a channel.
3 abocarse vr to approach; — **con uno** to meet someone, have an interview with someone.

abocinado adj trumpet-shaped.

abocinar [1a] **1** vt to shape like a trumpet; (Sew) to flare. **2 abocinarse** vr (fam) to fall flat on one's face.

abochornar [1a] **1** vt to make flushed, overheat; to shame, embarrass.
2 abochornarse vr to get flushed, get overheated; (Bot) to wilt; — **de** to feel ashamed at, get embarrassed about.

abofetear [1a] vt to slap, hit (in the face).

abogacía nf legal profession, the law.

abogaderas nfpl, **abogaderías** nfpl (SAm) specious arguments.

abogado nm lawyer; solicitor, barrister, attorney-at-law (US); counsel; — **del diablo** devil's advocate; — **defensor** defending counsel; — **de secano** shady solicitor; barrack-room lawyer; — **charlatán**, — **trampista** shady solicitor; **ejercer de** — to practise law, be a lawyer; **recibirse de** — to qualify as a solicitor; to be called to the bar.

abogar [1h] vi to plead; — **por** to plead for, defend; (fig) to advocate, champion, back.

abolengo nm ancestry, lineage; inheritance.

abolición nf abolition, abolishment.

abolicionista nmf abolitionist.

abolir [3a; defective] vt to abolish; to cancel, annul, revoke.

abolsado adj full of pockets, baggy.

abolsarse [1a] vr to form pockets, be baggy.

abolladura nf dent; hump; bruise; (Art) embossing.

abollar [1a] **1** vt to dent; to raise a bump on; to bruise; (Art) to emboss, do repoussé work on. **2 abollarse** vr to get dented; to get bruised.

abollonar [1a] vt metal to emboss.

abombado adj **(a)** convex; domed. **(b) estar** — (SAm: fam) to be bewildered; to be silly; to be tight.

abombar [1a] **1** vt **(a)** to make convex; to cause to bulge.
(b) (fam) to deafen; to confuse, bewilder; to stun.
2 abombarse vr (SAm) **(a)** to rot, decompose, to smell bad.
(b) (fam) to get tight.

abominable adj abominable.

abominablemente adv abominably.

abominación nf abomination; loathing, detestation; execration.

abominar **1** vt and **2** vi: — **de** to loathe, detest, abominate.

abonable adj payable; due.

abonado **1** adj reliable, trustworthy; **estar** — **a** + infin to be ready to + infin; to be inclined to + infin; **es** — **para ello** he is perfectly capable of (doing) it.
2 nm, **abonada** nf subscriber; (Theat etc) season-ticket holder; (Rail) season-ticket holder, commuter.

aborigen adj and nm aboriginal; **aborígenes** nmpl aborigines.

aborrascarse [1g] vr to get stormy.

aborrecer [2d] vt to hate, loathe, detest; to bore; nest, offspring to desert, abandon.

aborrecible adj hateful, loathsome, detestable; abhorrent.

aborrecido adj hated, loathed; boring.

aborrecimiento nm hatred, loathing, detestation; abhorrence, boredom.

aborregado adj: **cielo** — mackerel sky.

abortar [1a] **1** vt to abort, cause to miscarry; **hacerse** — to have an abortion, to have oneself aborted.
2 vi **(a)** (Med) (accidentally) to have a miscarriage; (deliberately) to abort; **hacer** — **a una mujer** to procure an abortion for a woman.
(b) (fig) to miscarry, fail, go awry.

abortista nmf abortionist.

abortivo adj abortive.

aborto nm **(a)** (Med: accidental) miscarriage;

(deliberate) abortion; (Law) (criminal) abortion; — **ilegal** illegal abortion; — **provocado** abortion.
(b) (Bio) monster, unnatural creature.
(c) (fig) miscarriage, failure.

abortón nm (Vet) abortion.

abotagarse [1h] vr to swell up, become bloated.

abotonador nm buttonhook.

abotonar [1a] **1** vt to button up, do up. **2** vi (Bot) to bud. **3 abotonarse** vr (fig) to well up, rise.

abovedado **1** adj vaulted; domed, arched. **2** nm vaulting.

abovedar [1a] vt to vault, arch.

aboyar [1a] vt (Naut) to buoy, mark with buoys.

abozalar [1a] vt to muzzle.

abra nf (Geog) cave, small bay, inlet; dale, gorge, (Geol) fissure; (RPl) clearing.

abracadabra nf abracadabra; hocus-pocus.

Abraham, Abrahán m Abraham.

abrasado adj burnt, burnt up; **estar** — to burn with shame; **estar** — **en cólera** to be in a raging temper.

abrasador adj burning, scorching; (fig) withering.

abrasar [1a] **1** vt **(a)** to burn, burn up; plants (of sun) to dry up, parch, (of wind) sear, (of frost) cut, nip.
(b) (fig) to squander, waste; to fill with shame.
2 abrasarse vr to burn (up); to catch fire; (of earth etc) to be parched; — **de amores** to burn with love, be violently in love; — **de calor** to be dying of the heat; — **de sed** to have a raging thirst.

abrasión nf graze, abrasion.

abrasivo **1** adj abrasive. **2** nm abrasive.

abrazadera nf bracket; clasp, brace; (Typ) bracket; — **para papeles** paper clip.

abrazar [1f] **1** vt to embrace; to clasp, hug, take in one's arms; (fig) to include, comprise, take in; opportunity to seize; business to take charge of; faith to adopt, embrace; doctrine to espouse; profession to adopt, enter, take up.
2 abrazarse to embrace (each other); — **a** person to embrace; to cling to, clutch.

abrazo nm embrace, hug; **un** — (afectuoso, cordial etc) (ending letter) with best wishes, with kind regards, yours.

abrecartas nm, pl **abrecartas** letter opener, paper knife.

ábrego nm south-west wind.

abrelatas nm, pl **abrelatas** tin opener, can opener.

abrevadero nm watering place, drinking trough.

abrevar [1a] **1** vt animal to water, give a drink to; land to water, irrigate; skins to soak; surface (for painting) to size.
2 abrevarse vr (of animal) to drink, quench its thirst; — **en sangre** (fig) to wallow in blood.

abreviación nf abbreviation; abridgement, shortening; reduction.

abreviadamente adv briefly, succinctly; in an abridged form.

abreviado adj brief; short, shortened; abridged; **la palabra es forma abreviada de** ... the word is a shortened form of ..., the word is short for ...

abreviar [1b] **1** vt word etc to abbreviate; text to abridge, reduce; speech, stay, period to shorten, cut short; event to hasten; date to advance, bring forward.
2 vi to be quick; to get on quickly; **bueno, para** — well, to cut a long story short.

abreviatura nf abbreviation; contraction.

abridor nm: — **de latas** tin opener, can opener.

abrigada nf, **abrigadero** nm shelter, windbreak.

abrigado adj sheltered, protected; cosy.

abrigar [1h] **1** vt **(a)** to shelter, protect (de against, from); (of coat etc) to keep warm, protect, cover; to help, support.
(b) (fig) doubt to retain, entertain; hope to cherish, nurse; opinion to hold; suspicion to harbour.
2 abrigarse vr to take shelter (de from), protect oneself; (with clothes) to cover up (warmly), wrap oneself up; (Col) to warm oneself.

abrigo nm **(a)** (in general) shelter; protection; help, support; (of clothes) covering, protection; **al** — **de** sheltered from, protected from; **ropa de mucho** — heavy clothing, warm clothes.
(b) (Naut) harbour, haven.
(c) — **antiaéreo** air-raid shelter.
(d) coat, overcoat, outer coat; — **de pieles** fur coat; — **de visón** mink coat.

abril nm April; **en el** — **de la vida** in the springtime of one's life; **una joven de 20** —**es** a girl of 20 (summers); **estar hecho un** — to be all dressed up, be dressed to kill.

abrileño adj April (attr).

abrillantar [1a] *vt stone* to cut into facets; to polish, burnish, brighten; (*fig*) to enhance, add lustre to.

abrir [3a; *ptp* **abierto**] **1** *vt* (*general sense*) to open; to open up; (*Med*) to cut open, open up; *map etc* to open out, spread out, extend; *book* to open; *path, road* to clear, make, open up; *woodland* (*SAm*) to clear; *ditch, foundation* to dig; *hole* to make, bore; *well* to sink; *plate* to engrave; *tap etc* to turn on; *account* to open; *negotiations* to open, start; *market* to open up; *appetite* to whet, stimulate; *list* to head; *procession* to head, lead; — **una puerta con llave** to unlock a door; — **algo cortándolo** to cut something open; — **una información** (*Law*) to begin proceedings; **volver a** — **un pleito** (*Law*) to reopen a case; **en un** — **y cerrar de ojos** in the twinkling of an eye.

2 *vi* (**a**) to open; (*flower*) to open, unfold.
(**b**) (*Bridge*) to open; — **de 3 a un palo** to open 3 in a suit; — **de corazones** to open (with a bid in) hearts.

3 abrirse *vt* (*general sense*) to open; to open out, unfold, spread (out); to expand; (*SAm*) to run away, shove off; — **a uno**, — **con uno** to unbosom oneself to someone, confide in someone.

abrita *nf* (*CR*) short dry spell.

abrochador *nm* buttonhook; (*SAm*) stapler, stapling machine.

abrochar [1a] *vt* to button (up); to do up, fasten (up); to clasp, buckle; (*SAm*) *papers* to staple (together).

abrogación *nf* abrogation, repeal.

abrogar [1h] *vt* to abrogate, repeal.

abrojo *nm* (*Bot*) thistle, thorn, caltrop; (*Mil*) caltrop; —**s** (*Naut*) submerged rocks.

abroncar [1g] *vt* (*fam*) to shame, make ashamed; to ridicule; to bore; to annoy.

abroquelarse [1a] *vr*: — **con**, — **de** to shield oneself with.

abrumador *adj* crushing, burdensome; exhausting; tiresome; *majority* vast, overwhelming; *superiority* crushing, overwhelming; **el trabajo es** — the work is killing; **es una responsabilidad abrumadora** it is a heavy responsibility.

abrumadoramente *adv* crushingly; vastly, overwhelmingly.

abrumar [1a] **1** *vt* to crush, overwhelm; to oppress, weigh down; to wear out, exhaust; — **a uno de trabajo** to swamp someone with work.
2 abrumarse *vr* to get foggy, get misty.

abrupto *adj slope* steep, abrupt; *ground* rough, rugged.

abrutado *adj* brutish, brutalized.

absceso *nm* abscess.

abscisión *nf* incision.

absenta *nf* absinth(e).

absentismo *nf* absenteeism; absentee landlordism.

absentista *nmf* absentee; absentee landlord.

ábside *nm* apse.

absintio *nm* absinth(e).

absolución *nf* (*Eccl*) absolution; (*Law*) acquittal; pardon.

absoluta *nf* (**a**) dogmatic statement, authoritative assertion.
(**b**) (*Mil*) discharge; **tomar la** — to take one's discharge, leave the service.

absolutamente *adv* (**a**) absolutely, completely; positively; — **nada** nothing at all; **es** — **imposible** it's absolutely impossible.
(**b**) (*in neg sense*) not at all, by no means; "**¿así que no viene nadie?**" . . . "**—**" "so nobody is coming?" . . . "nobody at all".

absolutismo *nm* absolutism.

absolutista **1** *adj* absolutist, absolute. **2** *nmf* absolutist.

absoluto *adj* (**a**) absolute (*also Philos, Pol*); utter, complete, absolute; *faith* complete, implicit; *temperament* domineering, tyrannical; **lo** — the absolute.
(**b**) (*in neg sense*) **en** — nothing at all, by no means; **¡en** —**!** certainly not!, not at all!; **not a bit of it!**; **no sabía nada en** — **de eso** I knew nothing at all about it; **no tenía miedo en** — he wasn't a bit afraid; **está prohibido en** — it is absolutely forbidden.

absolutorio *adj* (*Law*): **fallo** — verdict of acquittal, verdict of not guilty.

absolver [2h; *ptp* **absuelto**] *vt* to absolve; (*Law*) to acquit, clear (*de una acusación* of a charge); to release (*de un empeño* from an obligation).

absorbencia *nf* absorbency.

absorbente **1** *adj* (**a**) (*Chem etc*) absorbent.
(**b**) (*fig*) interesting, absorbing; *task* demanding; *love etc* possessive, tyrannical.
2 *nm*: — **higiénico** sanitary towel, sanitary napkin (*US*).

absorber [2a] **1** *vt* to absorb; to soak up; *knowledge etc* to absorb, take in, acquire; *capital, resources* to use up; *energies* to take up; *attention* to command; *reader etc* to absorb, engross.
2 absorberse *vr*: — **en** to become absorbed in, become engrossed in.

absorción *nf* absorption (*also fig*).

absorto *adj* absorbed; **estar** — to be entranced; to be amazed; **estar** — (**en meditación**) to be lost in thought; **estar** — **en un proyecto** to be engrossed in a scheme, be intent on a scheme.

abstemio 1 *adj* abstemious; (*completely*) teetotal.
2 *nm* abstainer; teetotaller.

abstención *nf* abstention; non-participation.

abstencionismo *nm* non-participation, refusal to take part, opting out.

abstencionista *nmf* non-participant, person who opts out.

abstenerse [2l] *vr* to abstain; to refrain; — **de** + *infin* to abstain from + *ger*, refrain from + *ger*, forbear to + *infin*.

abstinencia *nf* abstinence; abstemiousness; (*Eccl*) fast, fasting; restraint, forbearance.

abstinente *adj* abstemious.

abstracción *nf* (**a**) abstraction; absent-mindedness; engrossment in something else; reverie.
(**b**) — **hecha de ese libro** leaving that book aside, with the exception of that book.

abstracto *adj* abstract; **en** — in the abstract.

abstraer [2p] **1** *vt* to abstract; to remove, consider separately.
2 *vi*: — **de** to leave aside, exclude.
3 abstraerse *vr* to be absorbed, be lost in thought; to be preoccupied.

abstraído *adj* withdrawn, absent-minded; preoccupied.

abstruso *adj* abstruse.

absuelto *ptp* of **absolver**.

absurdamente *adv* absurdly.

absurdidad *nf* absurdity.

absurdo 1 *adj* absurd, ridiculous, preposterous; farcical; **teatro de lo** — theatre of the absurd; **es** — **que** . . . it is absurd that . . .
2 *nm* absurdity; farce.

abubilla *nf* hoopoe.

abuchear [1a] *vt* to boo, hoot at; to howl down, jeer at; **ser abucheado** (*Theat etc*) to get hissed at, get the bird (*sl*).

abucheo *nm* booing, hooting; jeering; **ganarse un** — (*Theat etc*) to get hissed at, get the bird (*sl*).

abuela *nf* grandmother; (*fig*) old woman, old lady; **¡cuéntaselo a tu abuela!** go tell that to the marines!; **¡no tienes abuela!** (*fam*) come off it!, tell us another!

abuelita *nf* (**a**) (*fam*) grandma, granny (*fam*).
(**b**) (*Chi*) bonnet; (*Col*) cradle.

abuelo *nm* grandfather; (*fig*) old man; ancestor, forbear; —**s** grandparents.

abulense 1 *adj* of Ávila. **2** *nmf* native (*or* inhabitant) of Ávila; **los** —**s** the people of Ávila.

abulia *nf* lack of willpower, spinelessness.

abúlico *adj* lacking in willpower, weakwilled, spineless.

abultado *adj* bulky, large, massive; unwieldy; (*fig*) exaggerated.

abultamiento *nm* bulkiness, (large) size; swelling, increase; exaggeration; increased importance.

abultar [1a] **1** *vt* to enlarge; to make bulky; to swell, increase; (*fig*) to exaggerate.
2 *vi* to be bulky, be big; (*fig*) to increase in importance, loom large.

abundamiento *nm* abundance, plenty; **a mayor** — furthermore; with still more justification.

abundancia *nf* abundance, plenty; **en** — in abundance, in plenty.

abundante *adj* abundant, plentiful; *crop etc* heavy, copious; *supply etc* generous; — **en** abounding in; productive of.

abundantemente *adv* abundantly; in abundance, in plenty.

abundar [1a] *vi* to abound, be plentiful; — **de**, — **en** to abound in, abound with, be rich in; — **en dinero** to be well supplied with money; — **en la opinión de uno** to share someone's opinion (*or* view) wholeheartedly.

abur *interj* (*fam*) so long!

aburilar [1a] *vt* to engrave.

aburrición *nf* (*SAm*) see **aburrimiento**.

aburridamente *adv* tediously, annoyingly; in a boring manner.

aburrido *adj* (*with* ser) boring, tedious, dull; monotonous, humdrum; (*with* estar) bored.

aburridón *adj* (*Col*) rather boring.

aburrimiento *nm* boredom, tedium, monotony.

aburrir[1] [3a] **1** *vt* to bore; to tire, weary. **2 aburrirse** *vr* to be bored, get bored (con, de, por with); — **como una almeja** (*or* ostra) to be bored stiff.

aburrir[2] [3a] *vt* (*fam*) money to blue (*fam*); time to spend, waste.

abusado *interj* (*Mex: fam*) **1** *interj* look out!, careful! **2** *adj* brilliant.

abusar [1a] *vi* to go too far, exceed one's rights, take advantage; — **de** *friendship* to presume upon, take unfair advantage of; *friend* to impose upon, make unfair demands on; *authority, hospitality* to abuse; *confidence* to betray; *money* to misuse, misapply.

abusión *nf* abuse; superstition.

abusivamente *adv* improperly; corruptly.

abusivo *adj* improper; corrupt.

abuso *nm* abuse; imposition, unfair demand; betrayal; misuse; misapplication; — **de confianza** betrayal of trust, breach of faith.

abusón *adj* (*fam*) bigheaded (*sl*), uppish (*fam*); abusive; **eres un** — you're too big for your boots.

abyección *nf* wretchedness, abjectness; degradation; servility.

abyecto *adj* wretched, abject; degraded; servile.

acá *adv* **(a)** (*place*) here; over here, round here; — **y allá**, — **y acullá** here and there; hither and thither; **pasearse de** — **para allá** to walk up and down, walk to and fro; **tráelo más** — move it this way, bring it closer; **está muy** — it's right here; **¡ven** —!, **¡vente para** —! come over here!
    (b) (*time*) at this time, now; **de ayer** — since yesterday; **¿de cuándo** — **sabes tú el francés?** since when do you know French?; **de** — **a poco** of late.

acabado 1 *adj* **(a)** finished, complete; perfect; *product* finished; (*fig*) consummate, masterly, polished.
    (b) old, worn out; (*Med*) ruined in health, wrecked; (*SAm*) thin.
    (c) él, — **de llegar** . . . he, immediately after his arrival . . .
    2 *n* **(a)** (*Tech*) finish; **buen** — high finish; — **brillo** gloss finish; — **satinado** matt finish.
    (b) —s waste, waste products.

acabador *nm* (*Tech*) finisher.

acabamiento *nm* finishing, completion; end; death.

acabalar [1a] *vt* to complete.

acaballar [1a] *vt* mare to cover.

acabar [1a] **1** *vt* to finish, complete, conclude; to round off, put the finishing touches to; to kill, kill off, destroy; (*SAm*) to speak ill of.
    2 *vi* **(a)** to finish, end, come to an end; to die; **y no acaba** and there's no sign of it coming to an end; **es cosa de nunca** — there's no end to it; — **mal** to come to a sticky end; **la palabra acaba con Z, la palabra acaba por Z** the word ends in a Z; **el palo acaba en punta** the stick ends in a point, the stick comes to a point.
    (b) — **con** to put an end to, make an end of; to destroy, finish off, put paid to; *abuse* to stop, put an end to; *resources* to exhaust, use up; **esto acabará conmigo** this will be the end of me.
    (c) — **de** + *infin* to have just + *ptp*; **acabo de verle** I have just seen him; **acababa de hacerlo** I had just done it; **cuando acabó de escribirlo** when he finished writing it; **cuando acabemos de pagarlo** when we finish paying for it.
    (d) — + *ger*, — **por** + *infin* to end up by + *ger*, finish up by + *ger*.
    3 acabarse *vr* **(a)** to finish, stop, come to an end; to die; (*fig: esp SAm*) to wear oneself out; to be all over (and done with); (*stock*) to run out, be exhausted, (*supply*) fail; **¡se acabó!** it's all over!; it's all up!; **todo se acabó para él** (*fam*) he's had it (*fam*); **el acabóse** (*as n*) the end, the payoff (*fam*).
    (b) (*with indirect pers pron*) **se me acabó el tabaco** I ran out of cigarettes; **se nos acabará la gasolina** we shall soon be out of petrol; **se me acaba la paciencia** my patience is exhausted.

acabildar [1a] *vt* to get together, organize into a group.

acacia *nf* acacia; — **falsa** locust tree.

acachetear [1a] *vt* to slap, punch.

academia *nf* academy; learned society; (*private*) school; — **de baile** dancing academy; — **de comercio** business school; — **de conductores** driving school; — **gastronómica** domestic science college; — **militar** military academy; — **de música** school of music, conservatoire; **la Real A**— the Spanish Academy; **la Real A**— **de la Historia** the Spanish Academy of History.

académico 1 *adj* academic (*also fig*). **2** *nm* academician, member (of an academy); fellow (of a learned society).

acaecer [2d] *vi* to happen, occur; to befall.

acaecimiento *nm* happening, occurrence.

acalenturarse [1a] *vr* to get feverish.

acaloradamente *adv* (*fig*) heatedly, excitedly.

acalorado *adj* heated, hot; tired; (*fig*) *argument*, *words* heated, excited; *supporter* passionate.

acaloramiento *nm* ardour, heat; vehemence, passion; anger.

acalorar [1a] **1** *vt* to make hot, warm up; to overheat; to tire; (*fig*) *mind* to inflame, excite; *passions* to inflame; *audience* to excite, work up; *ambition etc* to stir up, encourage.
    2 acalorarse *vr* to get hot, become overheated; (*fig: person*) to get excited, get worked up; to get angry, get het up (*fam; por* about); (*argument*) to become heated.

acallar [1a] *vt* to silence, quieten, hush; (*fig*) *person* to assuage, pacify; *criticism, doubt* to silence.

acamar [1a] *vt* crop etc to beat down, lay.

acampada *nf* camp.

acampador *nm*, **acampadora** *nf* camper.

acampanado *adj* bell-shaped.

acampar [1a] **1** *vi* to camp; to encamp. **2 acamparse** *vr* to camp.

acampeador *nm*, **acampeadora** *nf* camper.

acampo *nm* common pasture.

acanalado *adj* grooved, furrowed; striated; fluted; *iron* corrugated.

acanaladura *nf* groove, furrow; striation; fluting (*also Archit*); corrugation.

acanalar [1a] *vt* to groove, furrow; to flute; to corrugate.

acanallado *adj* disreputable, low.

acantilado 1 *adj* *cliff* steep, sheer; *coast* (*above water*) rocky, (*below water*) shelving. **2** *nm* cliff.

acanto *nm* acanthus.

acantonamiento *nm* cantonment; billeting, quartering.

acantonar [1a] *vt* to billet, quarter (*en* on).

acaparador 1 *adj* acquisitive; **instintos** —**es** acquisitive instincts; **tendencia acaparadora** monopolizing tendency.
    2 *nm* monopolizer, monopolist; profiteer; hoarder.

acaparamiento *nm* monopolizing; cornering the market (*de* in); hoarding.

acaparar [1a] *vt* (*Comm*) to monopolize; to corner, corner the market in; *food etc* to hoard; (*fig*) to hog, keep for oneself; *interest* to hold, absorb; **los turistas acaparan los cafés** the tourists monopolize the cafés, the tourists take over the cafés; **ella acapara la atención** she occupies everyone's attention.

acápite *nm* (*SAm*) paragraph; (*SAm*) subheading, caption; **punto** — full stop, new paragraph.

acaracolado *adj* spiral, winding, twisting.

acaramelado *adj* toffee-flavoured; toffee-coloured; (*fig*) sugary, over-sweet; **estar** — (*lover*) to be engrossed in another person.

acar(e)ar [1a] *vt persons* to bring face to face; *danger etc* to face, face up to; to confront.

acardenalar [1a] **1** *vt* to bruise. **2 acardenalarse** *vr* to get bruised, go black and blue.

acariciador *adj* caressing.

acariciar [1b] *vt* **(a)** to caress, fondle, stroke; *animal* to pat, stroke; to brush, touch lightly.
    (b) (*fig*) *hope* to cherish, cling to; *plan* to have in mind.

ácaro *nm* (*Zool*) mite.

acarraladura *nf* (*Chi, Per*) run, ladder (*in stocking*).

acarreadizo *adj* transportable, that can be transported.

acarrear [1a] *vt* **(a)** to transport, haul, cart, carry; (*of person*) to lug about, lug along; (*of river*) to carry along, bring down.
    (b) (*fig*) to cause, occasion, bring in its train (*or* wake); **ello le acarreó muchos disgustos** it brought him lots of troubles; **acarreó la caída del gobierno** it led to the fall of the government.

acarreo *nm* transport, haulage, cartage, carriage; **gastos de** —, **precio de** — transport charges, haulage.

acarreto *nm* (*Mex, PR*) *see* **acarreo**.

acartonado *adj* wizened; shrivelled.

acartonarse [1a] *vr* to get like cardboard; (*fig*) to become wizened; to shrivel up.
acaserarse [1a] *vr* (*Cu, Chi, Per*) to become attached; to become a regular customer (*of a shop*).
acaso 1 *adv* (a) perhaps, maybe; by chance; **por si —** just in case.
    (b) (*SAm*) ¿— yo lo sé? how would I know?
    2 *nm* chance, accident, coincidence; **al —** at random.
acatamiento *nm* respect (*a* for); awe, reverence; deference.
acatar [1a] *vt* to respect; to hold in awe, revere; to defer to, treat with deference; *law* to obey, respect, observe.
acatarrarse [1a] *vr* to catch (a) cold; (*Per: fam*) to get boozed.
acato *nm* see **acatamiento.**
acaudalado *adj* well-off, affluent.
acaudalar [1a] *vt* to acquire, accumulate; (*pej*) to hoard.
acaudillar [1a] *vt* to lead, command, head.
acceder [2a] *vi* to accede, agree (*a* to); **— a +** *infin* to agree to + *infin*.
accesibilidad *nf* accessibility (*to* a).
accesible *adj* accessible; approachable; **— a** open to, accessible to.
accesión *nf* (a) assent (*a* to); acquiescence (*a* in).
    (b) accessory.
    (c) access, entry.
    (d) (*Med*) attack; onset.
accésit *nm, pl* **accésits** consolation prize, second prize.
acceso *nm* (a) entry, admittance, access; "**— prohibido**", "**prohibido el —**" "no admittance"; **de fácil —** of easy access, easy to approach.
    (b) way, approach, access; (*Aer*) approach; **—s** approaches.
    (c) (*Med*) attack, fit; (*of anger etc*) fit, outburst, explosion; (*of generosity*) fit, surge.
accesoria *nf* annex, outbuilding.
accesorio 1 *adj* accessory; dependent, subordinate; incidental.
    2 *nm* accessory, attachment, extra; **—s** (*Tech*) accessories, (*Aut*) spare parts, (*Theat*) properties.
accidentado 1 *adj surface* uneven; *horizon etc* broken, uneven; *terrain* hilly; rough, rugged; *life* stormy, troubled, eventful; *record* variable, up-and-down; *journey* eventful; (*in mind*) agitated, upset; (*Med*) in a faint, in a fit; (*SAm: euph*) hunchbacked.
    2 *nm* injured person; (*SAm: euph*) hunchback.
accidental *adj* accidental; unintentional; incidental.
accidentalmente *adv* accidentally, by chance; unintentionally.
accidentarse [1a] *vr* to have an accident; (*Med*) to faint.
accidente *nm* (a) accident; mishap, misadventure; **por —** by accident, by chance; **— de carretera** road accident; **— de circulación** traffic accident; **— de trabajo** industrial accident; **una vida sin —s** an uneventful life; **hay —s que no se pueden prever** accidents will happen; **sufrir un —** to have an accident, meet with an accident.
    (b) (*Med*) faint, swoon.
    (c) (*Gram*) accidence.
    (d) **—s** (*of surface*) unevenness; (*of terrain*) hilliness; roughness, ruggedness.
acción *nf* (a) (*in general*) action; act, deed;' **buena —** good deed, kind act; **mala —** evil deed, unkind thing (to do); **hombre de —** man of action; **— de gracias** thanksgiving; **mecanismo de — retardada** delayed-action mechanism; **por — química** by chemical action; **dejar sin —** to put out of action; **unir la — a la palabra** to suit the deed to the word.
    (b) (*of hand*) movement, gesture.
    (c) (*Mil*) action, engagement; **entrar en —** to go into action.
    (d) (*Theat*) action, plot, story line; **— aparte** by-play.
    (e) (*Law*) action, lawsuit; **ejercitar una —** to bring an action.
    (f) (*Comm, Fin*) share; **acciones** stock(s), shares; **— liberada** paid-up share; **— ordinaria** ordinary share, common stock (*US*); **— preferente** preference share, preferred stock (*US*); **— primitiva** ordinary share, common stock (*US*).
accionado *nm* (*Mech*) action.
accionar [1a] **1** *vt* (*Mech*) to work, drive, propel. **2** *vi* to gesticulate; to wave one's hands about.
accionista *nmf* shareholder, stockholder.
acebo *nm* holly, holly tree.
acebuche *nm* wild olive tree; olive wood.
acecinar [1a] **1** *vt meat* to salt, cure. **2 acecinarse** *vr* to get very thin.

acechadera *nf* ambush; hiding place; (*Hunting*) hide.
acechador *nm,* **acechadora** *nf* spy, watcher, observer.
acechar [1a] *vt* to spy on, watch, observe; to lie in wait for; (*Hunting*) to stalk; **— la ocasión** to wait one's chance.
acecho *nm* spying, watching; ambush; **estar al —,** **estar en —** to lie in wait, be on the watch; **cazar al —** to stalk.
acechón *adj* (*fam*) spying, prying; **hacer la acechona** to spy, pry.
acedar [1a] **1** *vt* to turn sour, make bitter; (*fig*) to sour, embitter; to vex.
    2 **acedarse** *vr* to turn sour; (*Bot*) to wither, yellow.
acedera *nf* sorrel.
acedía *nf* acidity, sourness; (*Med*) heartburn; (*fig*) sourness, unpleasantness, asperity.
acedo *adj* acid, sour; (*fig*) sour, unpleasant, disagreeable.
aceitar [1a] *vt* to oil, lubricate.
aceite *nm* oil; (*in Spain etc, freq*) olive oil; (*perfume*) essence; **— alcanforado** camphorated oil; **— de algodón** cottonseed oil; **— de almendra** almond oil; **— de ballena** whale oil; **— combustible** fuel oil; **— de hígado de bacalao** cod-liver oil; **— de linaza** linseed oil; **— lubricante** lubricating oil; **— de ricino** castor oil; **— vegetal** vegetable oil.
aceitera *nf* oilcan.
aceitero 1 *adj* oil (*attr*). **2** *nm* oil merchant.
aceitón *nm* thick oil, dirty oil.
aceitoso *adj* oily.
aceituna *nf* olive; **— rellena** stuffed olive.
aceitunado *adj* olive, olive-coloured, olive-skinned.
aceitunero *m* dealer in olives.
aceituno 1 *adj* (*SAm*) olive, olive-coloured. **2** *nm* olive tree.
aceleración *nf* acceleration (*also Mech*); speeding up, hastening.
acelerada *nf* acceleration, speed-up.
aceleradamente *adv* quickly, speedily.
acelerador *nm* accelerator.
acelerar [1a] **1** *vt* to accelerate (*also Mech*); to speed up, hasten, expedite; *pace* to quicken; **— la marcha** to go faster, accelerate.
    2 **acelerarse** *vr* to hurry, hasten.
acelga *nf* chard, saltwort.
acémila *nf* beast of burden, mule.
acemilero *nm* muleteer.
acendrado *adj* pure, unblemished, refined.
acendrar [1a] *vt* to purify; (*Tech, Lit etc*) to refine.
acensuar [1d] *vt* to tax.
acento *nm* accent; stress, emphasis; tone, inflection; (*poet*) voice, words; **— agudo** acute accent; **— ortográfico** written accent; **— tónico** tonic accent; **con fuerte — andaluz** with a strong Andalusian accent; **en — de cierto asombro** in a somewhat surprised tone; **el — cae en la segunda sílaba** the stress falls on the second syllable.
acentor *nm:* **— común** hedgesparrow, dunnock.
acentuación *nf* accentuation.
acentuar [1e] **1** *vt* to accent, stress; to emphasize; (*fig*) to accentuate.
    2 **acentuarse** *vr* to become more noticeable, be accentuated.
aceña *nf* water mill.
aceñero *nm* miller.
acepción *nf* (a) sense, meaning. (b) preference; **sin — de persona** without respect of persons, without partiality of any kind.
acepilladora *nf* planer, planing machine.
acepilladura *nf* wood shaving.
acepillar [1a] *vt* to brush; (*Tech*) to plane, shave.
aceptabilidad *nf* acceptability.
aceptable *adj* acceptable.
aceptación *nf* acceptance; approval, approbation; popularity, standing; (*Comm*) acceptance; **mandar algo a la —** to send something on approval; **este producto tendrá una — enorme** this product will get a big welcome, this product is sure to be very popular.
aceptar [1a] **1** *vt* to accept; to approve; *work* to accept, take on, undertake, agree to do; *facts* to accept, face.
    2 *vi:* **— a +** *infin* to agree to + *infin*.
acepto *adj* acceptable, agreeable (*a, de* to), welcomed (*a, de* by).
acequia *nf* irrigation ditch, irrigation channel; (*SAm*) stream.
acera *nf* pavement, sidewalk (*US*); row (*of houses*); (*Rail*) platform, bay.

acerado adj (Tech) steel (attr), steely; steel-tipped; (fig) sharp, cutting, biting.
acerar [1a] **1** vt (Tech) to make into steel; to put a steel tip (etc) on; (fig) to harden; to make sharp, make biting.
  2 acerarse vr to toughen oneself, steel oneself.
acerbamente adv (fig) harshly, scathingly.
acerbidad nf acerbity; sourness; harshness.
acerbo adj taste sharp, bitter, sour; (fig) harsh, scathing.
acerca de prep about, on, concerning.
acercamiento nm (a) approach, bringing near, drawing near. (b) (fig) reconciliation; (Pol) rapprochement.
acercar [1g] **1** vt to bring near(er); to bring over; — algo al oído to put something to one's ear.
  2 acercarse vr (a) to approach, come near, draw near; — a to approach; to come close to; (fig) to approach, verge on; — a uno to go up to someone, come up to someone; (SAm) to approach someone, open negotiations with someone.
  (b) (fig: lovers) to be reconciled, achieve a reconciliation; (Pol) to make a rapprochement.
ácere nm maple.
acería nf steelworks, steel mill.
acerico nm small cushion; (Sew) pincushion.
acero nm steel (also fig); — bruto crude steel; — colado, — fundido cast steel; — inoxidable stainless steel; — al manganeso manganese steel; tener buenos —s to have guts; to be ravenously hungry.
acerola nf haw.
acerolo nm hawthorn.
acérrimo adj (fig) supporter etc very strong, staunch, out-and-out.
acerrojar [1a] vt to lock, bolt.
acertado adj guess, solution correct, right; successful; reply sensible, wise, sound; idea bright, good; plan well-conceived; remark apt, fitting, well-aimed; eso no me parece muy — that doesn't seem right to me; en eso no anduvo muy — that was not very sensible of him.
acertante nmf (in solving problem etc) solver; (in football) forecaster; hubo 9 —s there were 9 successful solvers (or forecasters).
acertar [1k] **1** vt target to hit; solution to get, get right, guess correctly; lost thing to find, succeed in tracing; result to achieve, succeed in reaching; a ver si lo acertamos esta vez let's see if we can get it right this time; lo has acertado you've guessed it, that's right; no aciertas el modo de hacerlo you don't manage to find the proper way to do it.
  2 vi (a) to hit the mark; (fig) to hit the nail on the head; to be right, get it right; to guess right; to manage it, be successful.
  (b) — a + infin to happen to + infin; to manage to + infin, succeed in + ger.
  (c) — con algo to happen on something, hit on something; to find something (without trouble).
  (d) (Bo:) to flourish, do well.
acertijo nm riddle, puzzle.
acervo nm heap, pile; — común undivided estate.
acetato nm acetate.
acético adj acetic.
acetilénico adj acetylene (attr).
acetileno nm acetylene.
acetona nf acetone.
acetre nm small pail; (Eccl) holy-water stoup.
acezar [1f] vi to puff, pant.
aciago adj ill-fated, ill-omened, fateful.
aciano nm cornflower.
acíbar nm aloes; (fig) sorrow, bitterness.
acibarar [1a] vt to add bitter aloes to, make bitter; (fig) to embitter; — la vida a uno to make someone's life a misery.
acicalado adj metal polished, bright and clean; person smart, neat, spruce; (pej) dapper, overdressed.
acicalar [1a] **1** vt metal to polish, burnish, clean; person etc to dress up, bedeck, adorn.
  2 acicalarse vr to smarten oneself up, spruce oneself up; to get dressed up.
acicate nm spur; (fig) spur, incentive.
acidez nf acidity.
acidia nf indolence, laziness, sloth.
acidificar [1g] **1** vt to acidify. **2 acidificarse** vr to acidify.
ácido 1 adj sharp, sour, acid.
  2 n acid; — carbólico carbolic acid; — carbónico carbonic acid; — cianhídrico hydrocyanic acid; — clorhídrico hydrochloric acid; — nítrico nitric acid; — oxálico oxalic acid; — sulfúrico sulphuric acid; — úrico uric acid.
acídulo adj acidulous.

acierto nm (a) success; good shot, hit; good guess; sensible choice, wise move; fue un — suyo it was a sensible choice on his part.
  (b) (quality) skill, ability; aptness, wisdom; discretion; obrar con — to act sensibly; el periódico que con todo — dirige X the paper which X edits so well.
aciguatarse [1a] vr (Ant, Mex) to become stupid.
acitrón nm candied citron.
aclamación nf acclamation; applause, acclaim; entre las —es del público amid the applause of the audience; elegir a uno por — to elect someone by acclamation.
aclamar [1a] vt to acclaim; to applaud; — a uno por jefe to acclaim someone (as) leader, hail someone as leader.
aclaración nf (a) rinse, rinsing. (b) clarification, explanation, elucidation. (c) (Meteorol) brightening, clearing up.
aclarar [1a] **1** vt (a) clothes to rinse; liquid etc to thin, thin down; wood to clear, thin (out); see voz.
  (b) (fig) problem to clarify, cast light on, explain; doubt to resolve, remove.
  2 vi (Meteorol) to brighten, clear, clear up.
aclaratorio adj explanatory; illuminating.
aclimatación nf acclimatization, acclimation (US).
aclimatizar [1f] **1** vt to acclimatize, acclimate (US).
  2 aclimatizarse vr to acclimatize oneself, get acclimatized, acclimate (US), get acclimated (US).
acné nm acne.
—aco, —aca n and adj suffix (pej), eg libraco boring book, worthless book.
acobardar [1a] **1** vt to daunt, intimidate, cow, unnerve.
  2 acobardarse vr to be frightened, get frightened; to flinch, shrink back (ante from, at).
acobrado adj copper-coloured, coppery.
acocear [1a] vt to kick; (fig) to ill-treat, trample on; to insult.
acocharse [1a] vr to squat, crouch.
acochinar [1a] vt (sl) to bump off (sl).
acodado adj bent; elbowed.
acodalar [1a] vt to shore up, prop up.
acodar [1a] **1** vt arm to lean, rest; vine etc to layer.
  2 acodarse vr: — en to lean on; acodado en leaning on, resting on.
acodiciarse [1b] vr: — a to covet.
acodo nm (Agr) layer.
acogedizo adj gathered at random.
acogedor adj welcoming, friendly, hospitable, warm; room snug, cosy; un ambiente — a friendly atmosphere.
acoger [2c] **1** vt visitor etc to welcome, receive; refugee to take in, give refuge to; fugitive to harbour; idea to receive; new word, fact etc to accept, admit.
  2 acogerse vr to take refuge; — a (fig) pretext to take refuge in; means to resort to; promise to avail oneself of; — a la ley to have recourse to the law.
acogida nf welcome, reception; acceptance, admittance; shelter, refuge, asylum; (of waters) meeting place; dar — a to accept; tener buena — to be welcomed, be well received; ¿qué — tuvo la idea? how was the idea received?
acogollar [1a] (Agr) **1** vt to cover up, protect. **2** vi to sprout.
acogotar [1a] vt to fell, kill (with a blow on the neck); to knock down, lay out.
acohombrar [1a] vt (Agr) to earth up.
acojinar [1a] vt (Tech) to cushion.
acolada nf accolade.
acolchado adj quilted, padded.
acolchar [1a] vt to quilt, pad.
acólito nm (Eccl) acolyte, server, altar boy; (fig) acolyte, minion.
acollador nm (Naut) lanyard.
acollar [1m] vt (Agr) to earth up; (Naut) to caulk.
acollarar [1a] vt to yoke, harness; to tie by the neck; dog etc to put a collar on; (of woman: Arg, Chi) to get one's claws into, take firm charge of.
acomedido adj (SAm) helpful, obliging.
acometedor adj energetic, enterprising.
acometer [2a] vt (a) (violently) to attack; to set upon, rush on, assail.
  (b) task to undertake, attempt.
  (c) (of sleep etc) to overcome; (of fear) to seize, take hold of; (of doubt) to assail; (of illness) to attack; le acometieron dudas he was assailed by doubts, he began to have doubts.
acometida nf (a) attack, assault. (b) (Elec etc) connection.
acometimiento nm attack.

acometividad *nf* (a) energy, enterprise. (b) aggressiveness; (*Arg*) touchiness; **mostrar —** to show fight.

acomodable *adj* adaptable; suitable.

acomodación *nf* accommodation; adaptation.

acomodadizo *adj* accommodating, obliging; acquiescent; (*pej*) pliable, easy-going.

acomodado *adj* (a) suitable, fit; *price* moderate; *article* moderately-priced. (b) *person, family etc* well-to-do, wealthy, well-off.

acomodador *nm* (*Theat etc*) usher.

acomodadora *nf* (*Theat etc*) usherette.

acomodamiento *nm* (*quality*) suitability, convenience; (*act*) transaction, agreement.

acomodar [1a] **1** *vt* (a) to adjust, accommodate, adapt (*a* to); **— a uno con algo** to supply someone with something.

(b) to fit in, find room for, accommodate; *person* to take in, lodge.

(c) to suit, adapt (*a* to); *colours* to match; **¿puede —me esta lana?** can you match this wool for me?; **— un ejemplo a un caso** to apply an example to a case in point.

(d) to repair, adjust, put right.

(e) *enemies, points of view* to reconcile.

(f) *servant etc* to place; *worker* to give a job to, take on; *friend* (*Arg, Mex*) to fix up a job for (by improper means); (*Theat*) to show to a seat; *visitor* to make comfortable, make feel at home.

2 *vi* to suit, fit; to be suitable.

3 acomodarse *vr* (a) to comply, conform; to adapt oneself.

(b) (*in a place*) to install oneself, settle down; **¡acomódese a su gusto!** make yourself comfortable!, make yourself at home!

(c) (*Arg, Chi*) to get oneself a soft job, get a job by influence; (*fig, fam*) to marry a fortune.

(d) **— a** to adapt oneself to; to settle down to; to comply with, conform with; **— a + infin** to settle down to + *infin*.

(e) **— con** to reconcile oneself to; to come to an agreement with; to comply with, conform with.

(f) **— de** to provide oneself with.

acomodaticio *adj see* **acomodadizo**.

acomodo *nm* (a) arrangement; agreement, understanding; (*pej*) secret arrangement, secret deal.

(b) *post, job*; (*SAm: pej*) soft job, job obtained by influence.

(c) (*SAm*) bribe.

acompañado *adj* (a) **estar —, ir —** to go accompanied, go with someone.

(b) *place* busy, frequented.

(c) **con falda acompañada** with skirt to match, with a skirt of the same colour (*or* pattern *etc*).

acompañamiento *nm* (a) accompaniment; **sin —** unaccompanied, alone.

(b) (*person*) escort; (*persons*) retinue; (*SAm*) funeral procession, wedding party *etc*; (*Theat*) extras.

(c) (*Mus*) accompaniment; **con — de piano** with piano accompaniment; **cantar sin —** to sing unaccompanied.

acompañanta *nf* female companion, chaperon; (*Mus*) accompanist.

acompañante *nm* companion; escort; (*Mus*) accompanist.

acompañar [1a] **1** *vt* (a) to accompany, go with, (*formally*) attend; *woman* to escort, *young woman* chaperon; **prefiero que no me acompañen** I prefer to go alone; **¿quieres que te acompañe?** do you want me to come with you?; **— a uno a la puerta** to see someone to the door, see someone out; **seguir acompañando a uno** to keep with someone, stay with someone, not leave someone.

(b) (*Mus*) to accompany (*a, con* on).

(c) (*in letter*) to enclose, attach.

(d) **— lo que se ha dicho con** (*or* de) **pruebas** to support what one has said with evidence.

(e) **— a uno en** to join someone in; **le acompaño en el sentimiento** please accept my condolences, I sympathize with you (in your loss).

2 acompañarse *vr* (*Mus*) to accompany oneself (*con, de* on).

acompasado *adj* rhythmic, regular, measured; (*in speech*) slow; (*in pace*) slow, deliberate, leisurely.

acompasar [1a] *vt* (a) (*Math*) to measure with a compass.

(b) (*Mus etc*) to mark the rhythm of; **— la dicción** to speak with a marked rhythm.

acomunarse [1a] *vr* to join forces.

aconchar [1a] **1** *vt* (a) to push to safety.

(b) (*Naut*) to beach, run aground; (*of wind*) to drive ashore.

(c) (*Mex: fam*) to tell off.

2 aconcharse *vr* (a) (*Naut*) to keel over; to run aground.

(b) (*Chi: of dregs*) to settle.

acondicionado *adj*: **bien —** *person* genial, affable, nice; *thing* in good condition; **mal —** *person* bad-tempered, difficult; *thing* in bad condition.

acondicionador *nm*: **— de aire** air conditioner.

acondicionamiento *nm* conditioning; **— de aire** air conditioning.

acondicionar [1a] *vt* (a) to arrange, prepare, make suitable; (*Tech*) to condition. (b) to air-condition.

acongojado *adj* distressed, anguished.

acongojar [1a] **1** *vt* to distress, grieve. **2 acongojarse** *vr* to become distressed, get upset; **¡no te acongojes!** don't get upset!, don't worry!

acónito *nm* (*Bot*) aconite, monkshood.

aconsejable *adj* advisable; sensible, politic; **nada —,** **poco —** inadvisable; **eso no es —** that is not advisable; **no sería — que Vd + subj** you would be ill-advised to + *infin*.

aconsejado *adj* (*Arg*): **bien —** sensible; **mal —** ill-advised.

aconsejar [1a] **1** *vt* (a) to advise, counsel; **— a uno hacer algo** to advise someone to do something.

(b) *caution etc* to advise, recommend; *virtue* to preach.

2 aconsejarse *vr* to seek advice, take advice; **— con, — de** to consult; **— mejor** to think better of it.

aconsonantar [1a] *vti* to rhyme (*con* with).

acontecedero *adj* which could happen, possible.

acontecer [2d] *vi* to happen, occur.

acontecimiento *nm* event, happening, occurrence; (*in dramatists' parlance etc*) happening; **fue realmente un —** it was an event of some importance.

acopiar [1b] *vt* to gather (together), collect; (*Comm*) to buy up, get a monopoly of; *honey* to collect, hive.

acopio *nm* (a) (*act*) gathering, collecting. (b) (*quantity*) collection; store, stock; (*of timber etc*) stack; (*RPl*) abundance.

acoplado *nm* (a) (*SAm*) trailer. (b) (*RPl*) hanger-on; gatecrasher.

acoplamiento *nm* (*Mech*) coupling; joint; (*Elec*) connection; hookup; (*of spacecraft*) link-up; **— de manguito** sleeve coupling; **— en serie** series connection; **— universal** universal joint.

acoplar [1a] **1** *vt* (*Tech*) to couple; join, fit together; (*Elec*) to connect, join up; *oxen* to yoke, hitch; *breeding animals* to mate, pair; (*SAm Rail*) to couple (up); *opinions* to reconcile.

2 acoplarse *vr* (a) (*Zool*) to mate, pair.

(b) (*fam*) to make it up, be reconciled.

acoquinamiento *nm* intimidation.

acoquinar [1a] **1** *vt* to scare, intimidate, cow. **2 acoquinarse** *vr* to get scared, allow oneself to be intimidated.

acorar [1a] *vt* to distress, afflict; (*SAm*) to intimidate.

acorazado 1 *adj* (a) armour-plated; ironclad; armoured.

(b) (*fig*) forbidding.

2 *nm* battleship; **— de bolsillo** pocket battleship.

acorazar [1f] **1** *vt* to armour-plate, armour. **2 acorazarse** *vr* (*fig*) to steel oneself, arm oneself (*contra* against).

acorazonado *adj* heart-shaped.

acorchado *adj* spongy, cork-like.

acorcharse [1a] *vr* to become spongy, become like cork; to wither, shrivel.

acordada *nf* (*Law*) decree.

acordadamente *adv* unanimously, by common consent.

acordado *adj* agreed; **lo —** that which has been agreed (upon).

acordar [1m] **1** *vt* (a) to decide, resolve, agree on; **— que + subj** to resolve that . . .; to resolve to + *infin*.

(b) (*Chi, Per, RPl*) to grant, accord.

(c) *opinions* to reconcile; (*Mus*) to tune; (*Art*) to blend, harmonize.

(d) **— algo a uno** to remind someone of something.

2 *vi* to agree; to correspond.

3 acordarse *vr* (a) to agree, come to an agreement (*con* with); **se acordó hacerlo** it was agreed to do it; **se ha acordado que . . .** it has been agreed that . . .

(b) to remember, recall, recollect; **no me acuerdo** I don't remember; **si mal no me acuerdo** if my memory serves me right; — **de algo** to remember something; **¿te acuerdas de mí?** do you remember me?; **no se acuerda ni del santo de su nombre** he hardly remembers his own name.

acorde 1 *adj* (a) **estar —s** to be agreed, be in agreement.

(b) (*Mus*) harmonious; (*with* estar) in tune, in harmony.

2 *nm* (*Mus*) chord; **a los —s de la marcha nupcial** to the strains of the wedding march.

acordeón *nm* accordion.

acordeonista *nmf* accordionist.

acordeón-piano *nm* piano-accordion.

acordonado *adj surface etc* ribbed; *place* cordoned-off; *coin, edge* milled.

acordonamiento *nm* ribbing; milling.

acordonar [1a] *vt* (a) to tie up, tie with string; *corset etc* to lace up.

(b) *place* to cordon off, surround with a cordon; (*of police etc*) to surround.

(c) *coin, edge* to mill.

acornar [1m] *vt*, **acornear** [1a] *vt* to butt; to gore.

acorralar [1a] *vt animals* to round up, pen, corral; *dangerous animal* to corner, bring to bay; *person* to corner; (*fig*) to intimidate.

acorrer [2a] **1** *vt* to help, go to the aid of. **2** *vi* to run up; — **a uno** to hasten to someone.

acortamiento *nm* shortening; reduction.

acortar [1a] **1** *vt* to shorten, cut down, reduce; *sail, step* to shorten; *story* to cut short, abbreviate; (*SAm*) to tone down.

2 acortarse *vr* (*fig*) to be slow; to be shy, falter.

acosar [1a] *vt* to pursue relentlessly; (*fig*) to hound; to harass, badger; to obsess; — **a uno a preguntas** to pester someone with questions.

acosijar [1a] *vt* (*Mex*) = **acosar.**

acoso *nm* relentless pursuit; (*fig*) hounding, harassing.

acostar [1m] **1** *vt* (a) to lay down.

(b) to put to bed.

(c) (*Naut*) to bring alongside.

2 acostarse *vr* to lie down; to go to bed; (*SAm*) to be confined, give birth; **estar acostado** to be lying down; to be in bed; **nos acostamos tarde** we go to bed late; **A se acostó con B** A went to bed with B, A slept with B; **ella se acuesta con cualquiera** she sleeps around; **es hora de acostarse** it's bedtime.

acostumbrado *adj* usual, customary, habitual.

acostumbrar [1a] **1** *vt*: — **a uno a algo** to get someone used to something; — **a uno a las dificultades** to inure someone to hardships; — **a uno a hacer algo** to accustom someone to doing something; to get someone used to doing something.

2 *vi*: — + *infin*, — **a** + *infin* to be accustomed to + *infin*, be in the habit of + *ger*.

3 acostumbrarse *vr* (a) — **a algo** to accustom oneself to something, get accustomed to something; to get used to something; to get the feel of something; **estar acostumbrado a algo** to be accustomed to something, be used to something; **está acostumbrado a verlas venir** he's not easily fooled.

(b) (*SAm*) **aquí eso no se acostumbra** that isn't customary here; **ya no se acostumbra la chistera** top hats are not worn now, top hats are no longer in fashion.

acotación *nf* (a) boundary mark; (*Geog*) elevation mark. (b) marginal note; (*Theat*) stage direction.

acotar [1a] *vt* (a) *ground* to survey, mark out; to limit, set bounds to; *game reserve etc* to fence in, protect, preserve.

(b) *trees* to lop.

(c) *page* to annotate; *map* to mark elevations on.

(d) (*fig*) to accept, adopt; to choose; to vouch for; to check, verify.

acotillo *nm* sledgehammer.

acoyundar [1a] *vt* to yoke.

acre[1] *adj taste* sharp, bitter, tart; *smell* acrid, pungent; *temperament* sour; *criticism etc* biting, mordant.

acre[2] *nm* (*measure*) acre.

acrecencia *nf* (*Law*) accretion; = **acrecentamiento.**

acrecentamiento *nm* increase, growth.

acrecentar [1k] **1** *vt* to increase, augment; *person etc* to advance, promote; to further the interests of.

2 acrecentarse *vr* to increase, grow.

acrecer [2d] *vt* to increase.

acreditación *nf* accreditation.

acreditado *adj* accredited; reputable, highly-esteemed; influential; **nuestro representante —** our accredited representative, our official agent; **una casa acreditada** a reputable firm.

acreditar [1a] **1** *vt* to do credit to, add to the reputation of; to vouch for, guarantee; to prove; to sanction, authorize; (*Comm*) to credit; — **a un embajador cerca de uno** to accredit an ambassador to someone; **y virtudes que le acreditan** and qualities which do him credit.

2 acreditarse *vr* to justify oneself, prove one's worth; — **de** to get a reputation for.

acreedor 1 *adj*: — **a** worthy of, deserving of. **2** *nm*, **acreedora** *nf* creditor; — **hipotecario** mortgagee.

acrecencia *nf* (*Col, Per*) credit balance; balance owing.

acremente *adv* sharply, bitterly; pungently; bitingly.

acribar [1a] *vt* to sift, riddle.

acribillado *adj surface* pitted, pockmarked; — **a** riddled with, peppered with; — **de** filled with; honeycombed with.

acribillar [1a] *vt* (a) — **a balazos** to riddle with bullets, pepper with shots; — **a puñaladas** to cover with stab wounds.

(b) (*fig*) to pester, badger; — **a uno a preguntas** to pester someone with questions.

acridio *nm* (*Arg, Mex*) locust.

acriminación *nf* incrimination; accusation.

acriminador 1 *adj* incriminating. **2** *nm*, **acriminadora** *nf* accuser.

acriminar [1a] *vt* to incriminate; to accuse.

acrimonia *nf* sharpness; acridness, pungency; sourness; (*fig*) acrimony.

acrimonioso *adj* acrimonious.

acriollarse [1a] *vr* (*SAm*) to get used to Latin-American ways; (*pej*) to go native.

acrisolado *adj* pure; tried, tested; unquestionable; **una fe acrisolada** a pure faith; **el patriotismo más —** the noblest kind of patriotism.

acrisolar [1a] *vt* (*Tech*) to purify, refine; (*fig*) to purify, purge; to bring out, clarify; *truth etc* to prove, reveal.

acristianar [1a] *vt* to christianize; *child* to baptize.

acritud *nf* = **acrimonia.**

acrobacia *nf* acrobatics; — **aérea** aerobatics.

acrobático *adj* acrobatic.

Acrópolis *nf* Acropolis.

acróstico 1 *adj* acrostic. **2** *nm* acrostic.

acta *nf* (a) (*of meeting*) minutes, record; (*published, of society*) transactions; (*Pol*) certificate of election; (*SAm: Parl*) act, law; — **de bautismo** certificate of baptism; — **de defunción** death certificate; — **matrimonial** marriage certificate; — **notarial** affidavit; **levantar —** to take the minutes; to draw up a formal statement; **levantar — de** to take the minutes of, minute; **tomar —** (*Arg*) to take note; **tomar — de algo** (*Arg*) to bear something in mind.

(b) **—s** (*of meeting*) minutes, record; **—s de un santo** life of a saint; **—s de los mártires** lives of the martyrs.

actinia *nf* sea anemone.

actínico *adj* actinic.

actitud *nf* (a) (*of body*) posture, position, attitude, pose.

(b) (*fig*) attitude; position; outlook; **la — del gobierno** the government's attitude, the government's position; **adoptar una — firme** to take a firm stand, put one's foot down; **estar en — de** + *infin* to be getting ready to + *infin*, threaten to + *infin*.

activamente *adv* actively.

activar [1a] *vt* to activate; *work* to expedite, speed up, hurry along; *fire* to brighten up.

actividad *nf* (a) activity; liveliness; promptness; movement, bustle; **estar en —** to be active, be in operation, (*volcano*) be active, be in eruption; **estar en plena —** to be in full swing.

(b) **—es** activities; **sus —es políticas** his political activities.

activista *nmf* activist.

activo 1 *adj* active; lively; prompt; energetic; busy; (*Gram*) active.

2 *nm* (a) (*Comm*) assets; — **y pasivo** assets and liabilities; — **de la quiebra** bankrupt's estate.

(b) **estar en —** to be on active service; to be on the active list (*also fig*).

acto *nm* act; action, deed; ceremony, function; (*Theat*) act; **A—s de los Apóstoles** Acts (of the Apostles); — **de fe** act of faith; — **inaugural** opening ceremony; — **reflejo** reflex action; — **continuo**, — **seguido** next, forthwith, immediately after; — **seguido de** immediately after; **en el —** immediately; on the spot, there and then; **celebrar un —** to hold a function; **hacer — de presencia** to attend (formally), be present; (*hum*) to show up, put in an appearance.

actor *nm* (*Theat*) actor; (*fig*) protagonist; (*Law*) plaintiff; — **cinematográfico** film actor.

actora *adj*: **parte** — (*Law*) prosecution; plaintiff.

actriz *nf* actress; **primera** — leading lady.

actuación *nf* (**a**) action; performance, conduct, benaviour; (*Theat*) performance; (*Sport*) performance; (*SAm*) role.

(**b**) **—es** (*Law*) legal proceedings.

actual *adj* present; present-day; current; *question* current, topical; **el 6 del** — the 6th day of this month; **el rey** — the present king.

actualidad *nf* (**a**) present, present time; **en la** — at present, at the present time; nowadays.

(**b**) present importance, current importance; **cuestión de palpitante** — highly important current issue; highly topical question; **ser de gran** — to be current, be alive; to have great contemporary importance; **perder (su)** — to lose interest, get stale.

(**c**) **—es** current events; contemporary issues; (*Cine*) newsreel.

actualización *nf* modernization, bringing up to date.

actualizador *adj* influence etc modernizing.

actualizar [1f] *vt* to bring up to date, update, modernize.

actualmente *adv* at present; now, nowadays; at the moment; — **está fuera** he's away at the moment; **los 50** — **en servicio** the 50 at present in service.

actuar [1e] **1** *vt* to work, actuate, operate; to set in motion.

2 *vi* (*Mech*) to work, operate, function; (*of person*) to act, perform; — **de** to act as; — **sobre** to act on; **actuó bien el árbitro Sr X** Mr X refereed well; **actúa de manera rara** he's acting strangely.

actuarial *adj* actuarial.

actuario *nm* (*Law*) clerk; (*Comm, Fin*) actuary (*also* — **de seguros**).

acuadrillar [1a] **1** *vt* to form into a band; (*Chi*) to set upon. **2 acuadrillarse** *vr* to band together.

acuarela *nf* watercolour.

acuarelista *nmf* watercolourist.

acuario *nm* aquarium.

acuartelado *adj* (*Her*) quartered.

acuartelamiento *nm* (*Mil*) quartering, billeting; (*Her*) quartering.

acuartelar [1a] **1** *vt* (*Mil*) to quarter, billet. **2 acuartelarse** *vr* to withdraw to barracks.

acuático *adj* aquatic, water (*attr*).

acuátil *adj* aquatic, water (*attr*).

acuatinta *nf* aquatint.

acuatizaje *nm* (*SAm: Aer*) landing (on the sea).

acuatizar [1f] *vi* (*SAm: Aer*) to come down on the water, land on the sea.

acucia *nf* diligence, keenness; haste; keen desire, longing.

acuciadamente *adv* diligently, keenly; hastily; longingly.

acuciador *adj*, **acuciante** *adj* pressing.

acuciar [1b] *vt* (**a**) to urge on, goad, prod; to hasten; to harass; to mob; (*of problem etc*) to press, worry. (**b**) to desire keenly, long for.

acucioso *adj* diligent, zealous, keen; eager.

acuclillarse [1a] *vr* to squat down.

acuchamarse [1a] *vr* (*Ven*) to get depressed.

acuchillado *adj* (**a**) *garment* slashed. (**b**) wary, schooled by bitter experience.

acuchillar [1a] **1** *vt* (**a**) to cut, slash, hack; (*Sew*) to slash; *person* to stab (to death), knife.

(**b**) (*Tech*) to plane down, smooth.

2 acuchillarse *vr*: **se acuchillaron** they fought with knives, they slashed at each other.

acuchucar [1g] *vt* (*Chi*) to crush, flatten; to crumple.

acudir [3a] *vi* (**a**) to come, come along, come up; to turn up, present oneself; — **a la puerta** to come (*or* go) to the door, answer the door; — **a una cita** to keep an appointment, turn up for an appointment; — **a una llamada** to answer a call; **pero no acudió** but he didn't come, but he didn't turn up.

(**b**) to come (*or* go) to the rescue, go to help.

(**c**) — **a** (*fig*) to call on, turn to, have recourse to; — **al médico** to consult one's doctor; — **a uno a pedir socorro** to turn to someone for help; **tendremos que** — **a otra solución** we shall have to seek another solution.

(**d**) (*Agr*) to produce, yield.

(**e**) (*horse*) to answer, obey.

acueducto *nm* aqueduct.

ácueo *adj* aqueous.

acuerdo *nm* (**a**) (*in general*) agreement, accord; (*treaty etc*) agreement, pact; understanding; — **verbal** verbal agreement; gentleman's agreement; **¡de —!** I agree!, agreed!; yes of course!; **de** — **con**

in accordance with; **de** — **con el artículo 2 del código** under article 2 of the code, as laid down in article 2 of the code; **de común** — with one accord, unanimously; **estar de** — (*person*) to agree, be in agreement (*con* with); (*things*) to agree, correspond; **esto está de** — **con lo que me dijo** this is in line with what he told me; **llegar a un** — to reach agreement, come to an understanding (*con* with); **ponerse de** — to reach agreement, agree.

(**b**) (*Parl etc*) resolution; **tomar un** — to pass a resolution.

(**c**) (*Art*) harmony, blend.

(**d**) (*Arg*) meeting (of a deliberative assembly).

(**e**) memory, recollection.

(**f**) sense, right mind; **estar en su** — to be in one's right mind; **volver en su** — to come to one's senses.

acuidad *nf* acuity.

acuilmarse [1a] *vr* (*CAm*) to get depressed.

acuitadamente *adv* sorrowfully, with regret.

acuitar [1a] **1** *vt* to afflict, distress, grieve. **2 acuitarse** *vr* to grieve, be grieved (*por* at, by).

acular [1a] *vt* (*fam*) (**a**) *horses etc* to back (*a* against, into). (**b**) to corner, force into a corner.

acullá *adv* over there, yonder.

acullicar [1g] *vi* (*Bol, Chi, Per*) to chew coca leaves.

acumuchar [1a] *vt* (*Chi*) to pile up, accumulate.

acumulación *nf* (*act*) accumulation; (*quantity*) accumulation; pile, stock, hoard.

acumulador 1 *adj* accumulative. **2** *nm* accumulator, storage battery.

acumular [1a] **1** *vt* to accumulate; to amass, gather, collect; to pile (up), hoard; — **vapor** to get steam up.

2 acumularse *vr* (**a**) to accumulate, gather, pile up.

(**b**) (*RPl*) (*of persons*) to gather, collect, come together.

acumulativo *adj* accumulative.

acunar [1a] *vt* to rock (to sleep).

acuñación *nf* coining, minting; wedging.

acuñar [1a] *vt* *money* to coin, mint; *medal* to strike; *wheel etc* to wedge.

acuosidad *nf* wateriness; juiciness.

acuoso *adj* watery; *fruit* juicy, runny.

acupuntura *nf* acupuncture.

acurrucarse [1g] *vr* to squat, crouch; to huddle up, curl up.

acusación *nf* accusation; (*Law*) accusation, charge, indictment; **negar la** — to deny the charge, plead not guilty.

acusado 1 *adj* (**a**) (*Law etc*) accused.

(**b**) marked, pronounced; *characteristic, feature, personality* strong; *contrast* marked, striking.

2 *nm*, **acusada** *nf* accused, defendant.

acusador 1 *adj* accusing, reproachful. **2** *nm*, **acusadora** *nf* accuser.

acusar [1a] **1** *vt* (**a**) (*Law etc*) to accuse (*de* of), charge (*de* with), indict (*de* on a charge of); **¿me acusas a mí?** are you accusing me?; — **a uno de haber hecho algo** to accuse someone of having done something.

(**b**) to denounce; *suspect* to point to, proclaim the guilt of.

(**c**) to show, reveal; *emotion etc* to register, show, betray; **su rostro acusó extrañeza** his face registered surprise; **su silencio acusa cierta cobardía** his silence betrays a certain cowardice.

(**d**) *cards* to declare, lay down.

(**e**) *receipt* to acknowledge.

2 acusarse *vr* (**a**) to confess; — **de negligente** to confess one's negligence, confess to being negligent; — **de un crimen** to confess to a crime; — **de haberlo hecho** to confess to having done it.

(**b**) to become more marked, get stronger; **esta tendencia se acusa cada vez más** this tendency is becoming ever more marked, this tendency gets stronger all the time.

acusativo *nm* accusative.

acusatorio *adj* accusatory, accusing.

acuse *nm*: — **de recibo** acknowledgement of receipt.

acusete *nm* (*Arg, Per*) telltale, sneak.

acusón (*fam*) **1** *adj* telltale, sneaking. **2** *nm*, **acusona** *nf* telltale, sneak; gossip.

acústica *nf* acoustics.

acústico 1 *adj* acoustic. **2** *nm* hearing aid.

achacar [1g] *vt*: — **algo a una causa** to attribute something to a cause, put something down to a cause; — **la culpa a uno** to lay the blame on someone.

achacoso *adj* sickly, ailing.

achaflanar [1a] *vt* to chamfer, bevel.

achancharse [1a] *vr* (*Col, Ec, Per*) to get lazy; to get fat.

achantarse [1a] *vr* (a) to hide away. (b) (*fig*) to give in, comply; to sing small; — **por las buenas** to be easily intimidated.

achaparrado *adj* dwarf, stunted; *person* stocky, thickset, stumpy.

achaque *nm* (a) (*Med*) sickliness, infirmity, weakness; ailment, malady; (*fam*) period, monthlies; —**s mañaneros** morning sickness.
(b) defect, fault, weakness.
(c) matter, subject; **en — de** in the matter of, on the subject of.
(d) pretext; **con — de** under the pretext of.

achares *mpl* (*fam*) jealousy; **dar — a uno** to make someone jealous.

achatamiento *nm* (a) flattening. (b) (*Arg, Mex*) loss of moral (*or* intellectual) fibre.

achatar [1a] **1** *vt* to flatten.
2 achatarse *vr* (a) to get flat.
(b) (*Arg, Mex*) to grow weak, decline.
(c) **quedar achatado** (*Arg, Mex*) to be put to shame.

achicado *adj* childish, childlike.

achicador *nm* scoop, baler.

achicar [1g] **1** *vt* (a) to make smaller; to dwarf; (*Sew*) to shorten, take in; to minimize, diminish the importance of.
(b) (*Naut etc*) to scoop, bale (out).
(c) (*fig*) to humiliate; to intimidate, browbeat.
(d) (*Col*) to kill.
2 achicarse *vr* (a) to get smaller; to shrink.
(b) (*fig*) to humble oneself, eat humble pie.
(c) (*SAm*) to minimize one's importance, pretend to be less important than one is.

achicoria *nf* chicory.

achicharradero *nm* place of oppressive heat, inferno.

achicharrante *adj*: **calor —** sweltering heat.

achicharrar [1a] **1** *vt* (a) to scorch, overheat; (*Cook*) to fry crisp, (*in error*) overcook, burn, scorch; **el sol achicharraba la ciudad** the sun was roasting the city.
(b) (*fam*) to bother, plague.
(c) (*SAm*) to flatten, crush.
2 achicharrarse *vr* to scorch, get burnt.

achicharronar [1a] *vt* (*SAm*) to flatten, crush.

achichiguar [1i] *vt* (*Mex*) to act as nursemaid to; (*fig*) to cosset, spoil; (*Agr*) to shade.

achiguarse [1i] *vr* (*Arg*) to get fat; (*of wall etc*) to bulge, sag.

achimero *nm* (*Guat, Salv*) pedlar, peddler (*US*), hawker.

achimes *nmpl* (*Guat, Salv*) cheap goods, trinkets.

achín *nm* (*CAm*) pedlar, peddler (*US*), hawker.

achinado *adj* (a) (*RPl*) having Indian features, having an Indian appearance; (*fig*) coarse, common.
(b) (*Ant, Per*) having Mongoloid features, having a Chinese appearance.

achinar [1a] **1** *vt* (*fam*) to scare. **2 achinarse** *vr* (*RPl*) to coarsen, get common.

achiquillado *adj* (*Mex*) childish.

achiquitar [1a] *vt* (*SAm*) to make smaller, reduce in size.

achispado *adj* (*fam*) tight.

achisparse [1a] *vr* (*fam*) to get tight.

—acho, —acha *n and adj suffix* (*pej*) eg **hombracho** hulking great brute, big tough fellow; *see* **ricacho** *etc*.

achocar [1g] *vt* (a) to throw against a wall, dash against a wall.
(b) to hit, bash (*fam*).
(c) (*fam*) to hoard, stash away (*fam*).

achocolatado *adj* (*SAm*) (a) chocolate (*attr*); like chocolate. (b) dark brown, chocolate-coloured, tan.

achocharse [1a] *vr* to get doddery, begin to dodder.

acholado *adj* (*SAm*) (a) racially mixed, part-Indian.
(b) (*fig*) scared, cowed.

acholarse [1a] *vr* (*SAm*) (a) to have (*or* adopt) half-breed ways.
(b) to get scared, be cowed; to be abashed, become shy.

—achón, —achona *n and adj suffix* (*pej*) see **—acho**; see **bonachón** *etc*.

achubascarse [1g] *vr* (*of sky*) to become threatening, cloud over.

achucutado *adj* (*SAm*) depressed, sad-looking; abashed, ashamed.

achucutarse [1a] *vr* (*SAm*) to get depressed, look sad; to be abashed, feel ashamed.

achucuyarse [1a] *vr* (*CAm*) = **achucutarse**.

achuchado *adj* (*RPl*): **estar —** to have malaria; to catch a chill, be feverish; (*fig*) to be scared.

achuchar [1a] *vt* (a) to crush, squeeze flat.
(b) *person* to shove, jostle.
(c) *dog* to urge on; **— un perro contra uno** to set a dog on someone.

achucharse [1a] *vr* (*RPl*) to catch malaria; to catch a chill, get feverish; (*fig*) to be scared.

achuchón *nm* (a) squeeze; shove, push. (b) **tener un —** (*Med*) to be ill, be poorly.

achulado *adj*, **achulapado** *adj* (a) jaunty, cocky (*fam*). (b) common, uncouth.

achumado *adj* (*SAm*) drunk.

achumarse [1a] *vr* (*SAm*) to get drunk.

achunchar [1a] (*SAm*) **1** *vt* (a) to shame, cause to blush.
(b) to scare.
2 achuncharse *vr* (a) to feel ashamed, blush.
(b) to get scared.

achuntar [1a] *vt* to do properly, get right, do at the right time.

achupalla *nf* (*SAm*) pineapple.

achura *nf* (*SAm*) guts, offal.

achurar [1a] **1** *vt* (*SAm*) *animal* to gut; *person* to kill, wound.
2 *vi* (*SAm*) to benefit from a share-out, get something free.

adagio *nm* adage, proverb; (*Mus*) adagio.

adalid *nm* leader, champion.

adamado *adj man* effeminate, soft; *woman* elegant, chic, (*pej*) flashy.

adamascado *adj* damask.

adamascar [1g] *vt* to damask.

Adán *m* Adam.

adán *nm* slovenly fellow; lazy chap; **estar hecho un —** to go about in rags, be terribly shabby.

adaptabilidad *nf* adaptability; versatility.

adaptable *adj* adaptable; versatile.

adaptación *nf* adaptation.

adaptador *nm* (*Elec, Radio*) adapter.

adaptar [1a] **1** *vt* to adapt; to fit, make suitable (*para* for); to adjust. **2 adaptarse** *vr* to adapt oneself (*a* to).

adaraja *nf* (*Archit*) toothing.

adarga *nf* (oval) shield.

adarme *nm* whit, jot; **ni un —** not a whit; **sin un — de educación** without the least bit of good manners; **por —s** in driblets.

adecentar [1a] **1** *vt* to tidy up, make decent. **2 adecentarse** *vr* to tidy oneself up.

adecuación *nf* adaptation; adequacy, fitness, suitability.

adecuadamente *adv* adequately, fitly, suitably.

adecuado *adj* adequate; fit, suitable (*para* for); appropriate; **los documentos —s** the appropriate documents, the relevant papers; **el hombre — para el puesto** the right man for the job.

adecuar [1d] *vt* to adapt, fit, make suitable.

adefesiero *adj* (*Chi, Ec, Per*) nonsensical, ridiculous.

adefesio *nm* (a) piece of nonsense, absurdity; **hablar —s** to talk nonsense.
(b) (*person*) queer bird, ridiculous person; (*in appearance*) scarecrow, fright; **ella estaba hecha un —** she did look a fright.
(c) outlandish dress, ridiculous attire.

adefesioso *adj* (*Ec*) nonsensical, ridiculous.

adehala *nf* gratuity, tip; (*on pay*) bonus.

adela *nf* (*CAm*) bittersweet.

adelaida *nf* (*Mex*) fuchsia.

adelantado 1 *adj* (a) advanced.
(b) well advanced, ahead of one's age, precocious; **estar —** (*watch*) to be fast.
(c) **pagar por —** to pay in advance.
(d) (*pej*) bold, forward.
2 *nm* (*Hist*) governor (of a frontier province), captain-general.

adelantamiento *nm* advance; advancement, furtherance, promotion; progress; (*Aut*) overtaking.

adelantar [1a] **1** *vt* (a) to move forward, move on, advance; *ball* (*Sport*) to pass on, pass forward.
(b) *pace* to speed up, quicken; *plan, work* to speed up, hurry along.
(c) *sum, money* to advance, pay in advance; to lend.
(d) *clock* to put on, put forward.
(e) *competitor* to get ahead of, outstrip; (*Aut*) to overtake, pass; **no le gusta dejarse —** he doesn't like being overtaken; **estamos a punto de ser adelantados** we are about to be overtaken.
(f) (*fig*) to advance, further, promote; **— una idea** to put forward an idea.
2 *vi* (a) to go ahead, get on, make headway; to

improve, progress; **el enfermo adelanta** the patient is improving.
  (b) (*Aut*) to overtake; **"prohibido —"** "no overtaking".
  (c) (*of clock*) to be fast, gain; **mi reloj adelanta 5 minutos** my watch is 5 minutes fast.
  3 adelantarse *vr* **(a)** to go forward, go ahead; to improve, progress.
  (b) (*of watch*) to be fast, gain.
  (c) **— a uno** to get ahead of someone, outstrip someone; (*fig*) to steal a march on someone, beat someone to it; (*Aut*) to overtake someone, (*pej*) cut in on someone.
  (d) **— a los deseos de uno** to anticipate someone's wishes.
adelante *adv* **(a)** (*of place*) forward(s), onward(s); ahead; **más —** further on; **por el camino —** further along the road; **ir —** to go on, go forward; *see* **sacar (r)** *etc*.
  (b) (*of quantity*) **de 100 ptas en —** from 100 ptas up.
  (c) (*of time*) **en —, de aquí en —, de hoy en —** in future, from now on, henceforth; **más —** later, afterwards.
  (d) **¡—!** (*interj: to speaker*) go on!, go ahead!, carry on!; (*answering knock etc*) come in!; (*Mil etc*) forward!; (*RPl*) bravo!, that's the way!; **¡— con los faroles!** press on regardless! (*fam*), (*SAm*) if they don't like it they can lump it!
adelanto *nm* **(a)** (*in general*) advancement, progress.
  (b) advance, improvement; **con todos los —s modernos** with all the modern improvements; **los —s de la ciencia** the advances of science.
  (c) (*Comm etc*) advance; loan.
adelfa *nf* rosebay, oleander.
adelgazador *adj* slimming.
adelgazamiento *nm* slimming.
adelgazar [1f] **1** *vt* to make thin, make slender; *stick* to pare, whittle; *person, figure* to slim, reduce, slenderize (*US*); (*fig*) to purify, refine; *voice* to raise the pitch of; *understanding* to sharpen.
  2 *vi* to grow thin, lose weight; (*intentionally*) to slim, reduce, lose weight; (*fig*) to split hairs.
  3 adelgazarse *vr* to grow thin.
ademán *nm* **(a)** (*of hand*) gesture, movement, motion; (*of body; also Art*) posture, attitude, position; **en — de + infin** as if to **+ infin**, getting ready to **+ infin**; **hacer — de + infin** to make as if to **+ infin**, make a move to **+ infin**; **hacer —es** to gesture, make signs.
  (b) **—es** manners.
además 1 *adv* besides; moreover, furthermore; also; **y — la pegó** and he also beat her; **creo — que . . .** moreover I think that . . .
  2 — de *prep* besides, in addition to; not to mention . . .; **— de eso** moreover.
Adén *m* Aden.
adenoideo *adj* adenoidal.
adentellar [1a] *vt* to sink one's teeth into.
adentrarse [1a] *vr:* **— en** to go into, get into, get inside; to penetrate into; **— en la selva** to go deep(er) into the forest; **— en el ritmo de la marcha** to fall into step.
adentro 1 *adv* **= dentro; mar —** out at sea, out to sea; **tierra —** inland; **¡—!** (*fam*) come in!
  2 *nm* **(a)** (*Arg*) indoors, inside of the house.
  (b) **—s** innermost being, innermost thoughts; **dijo para sus —s** he said to himself.
adepto *nm* follower, supporter; (*of magic etc*) adept, initiate.
aderezado *adj* favourable, suitable.
aderezar [1f] **1** *vt* to prepare, get ready, dress; *person* to make beautiful, dress up, deck; *object* to embellish, adorn; *food* to prepare, (*with condiments*) to season, garnish; *salad* to dress; *drinks* to prepare, mix; *wines* to blend; *machine etc* to repair; *cloth* to gum, size.
  2 aderezarse *vr* to dress up, get ready.
aderezo *nm* **(a)** (*act*) preparation; dressing; embellishment; seasoning; mixing; blending; repair.
  (b) (*Cook*) seasoning, dressing; (*on dress*) adornment; set of jewels; **— de casa** household equipment; **— de diamantes** set of diamonds; **— de mesa** dinner service; **dar el — definitivo a algo** to put the finishing touch to something.
adeudado *adj* in debt.
adeudar [1a] **1** *vt money* to owe; *taxes etc* to be liable for; **— una suma en una cuenta** to charge a sum to an account, debit an account for a sum.
  2 *vi* to become related by marriage.
  3 adeudarse *vr* to run into debt.

adeudo *nm* debit, indebtedness; customs duty; debit, charge.
adeveras (*SAm*): **de — adv = de veras**.
adherencia *nf* adherence, adhesion; (*fig*) bond, connection; (*Aut*) road holding, road-holding qualities; **tener —s** to have connections.
adherente 1 *adj:* **— a** adhering to. **2** *nm* adherent, follower.
adherido *nm*, **adherida** *nf* adherent, follower.
adherir(se) [3i] *vi and vr* to adhere, stick (*a* to); **— a** (*fig*) to adhere to, espouse, follow.
adhesión *nf* adhesion; (*fig*) adherence, support.
adhesividad *nf* adhesiveness.
adhesivo 1 *adj* adhesive, sticky. **2** *nm* adhesive.
adicción *nf* (*SAm*) (alcoholic) addiction.
adición *nf* addition; (*Math*) addition; adding up; (*RPl*) bill, check (*US*).
adicional *adj* additional, extra, supplementary.
adicionar [1a] *vt* to add (*a* to); (*Math*) to add, add up.
adicto 1 *adj* **(a)** **—** devoted to, attached to; **las personas adictas a él** those who follow him, his supporters.
  (b) (*pej*) **—** a given to, addicted to.
  2 *nm*, **adicta** *nf* supporter, follower; (*RPl: pej*) addict.
adiestrado *adj* trained.
adiestramiento *nm* training; drilling; practice.
adiestrar [1a] **1** *vt* to train, teach, coach, drill; to guide, lead.
  2 adiestrarse *vr* to practise, train oneself; **— a + infin** to train oneself to **+ infin**; to teach oneself to **+ infin**.
adifés *adv* (*Guat*) with difficulty; (*Ven*) on purpose.
adinerado *adj* wealthy, moneyed, well-off.
adiós 1 *interj* good-bye!; (*on passing in street*) hullo! **2** *nm* good-bye, farewell; **ir a decir — a uno** to go to say good-bye to someone.
adiosito *interj* (*fam, esp SAm*) bye-bye!, cheerio!
adiposidad *nf*, **adiposis** *nf* adiposity.
adiposo *adj* adipose, fat.
aditamento *nm* addition.
aditivo *nm* additive.
adivinación *nf* prophecy, divination; guessing; solving; **por —** by guesswork; **— de pensamientos** thought reading.
adivinador *nm*, **adivinadora** *nf* diviner.
adivinanza *nf* riddle, conundrum.
adivinar [1a] *vt* to prophesy, foretell, guess; *riddle, puzzle* to solve; *thoughts* to read; **adivina quién te dio** it's anyone's guess who did it.
adivino 1 *nm*, **adivina** *nf* fortuneteller. **2** *nm* (*Zool*) praying mantis.
adjetivar [1a] *vt* **(a)** to modify; to use adjectivally, use attributively. **(b)** (*fig*) to apply epithets to.
adjetivo 1 *adj* adjectival. **2** *nm* adjective.
adjudicación *nf* award; (*at auction*) knocking down, sale.
adjudicar [1g] **1** *vt* to award, adjudge (*a* to); **— algo a uno en 500 ptas** (*at auction*) to knock something down to someone for 500 ptas; **— algo al mejor postor** to knock something down to the highest bidder.
  2 adjudicarse *vr:* **— algo** to appropriate something.
adjuntar [1a] *vt* to append, attach; (*in letter*) to enclose; **adjuntamos factura** we enclose our account.
adjunto 1 *adj* **(a)** joined on; attached (*a* to); (*in letter*) attached, enclosed; **remitir algo —** to enclose something.
  (b) *person* assistant; *see* **profesor**.
  2 *nm* **(a)** addition, adjunct; (*in letter*) enclosure.
  (b) (*person*) assistant.
adminículo *nm* accessory, gadget; **—s emergency kit**.
administración *nf* administration; management; running; headquarters, central office; (*Arg Pol*) administration; (*Cu, PR: Eccl*) extreme unction; **en — in trust; obras en —** books handled by us, books for which we are agents; **A— de Correos** General Post Office; **— militar** commissariat.
administrador *nm*, **administradora** *nf* administrator; manager; (*of estate*) steward, factor (*Scot*), (land) agent; bailiff; **— de aduanas** chief customs officer, collector of customs; **— de correos** postmaster; **— de fincas** land agent; **es buena administradora** (*at home*) she manages well, she's a good manager.
administrar [1a] *vt* to administer; to manage; to run; *justice, sacrament* to administer; (*Cu, PR, CAm: Eccl*) to administer extreme unction to.
administrativo *adj* administrative; managerial.
admirable *adj* admirable.

admiración nf (a) admiration; **mi — per ti** my admiration for you. (b) wonder, wonderment; **esto llenó a todos de —** this filled everyone with wonderment.

admirador nm, **admiradora** nf admirer.

admirar [1a] 1 vt (a) to admire; to respect, look up to. (b) to astonish, surprise, cause to marvel; **esto admiró a todos** this astonished everyone, this filled everyone with amazement; **me admira su declaración** your statement amazes me, I am amazed at what you say.
2 **admirarse** vr to be astonished, be surprised, marvel (de at); **se admiró de saberlo** he was amazed to hear it.

admirativo adj admiring, full of admiration.

admisibilidad nf admissibility.

admisible adj admissible; excuse etc plausible, credible, legitimate; **eso no es —** that cannot be allowed.

admisión nf admission (a to); acceptance; (Mech) intake, inlet; **— de aire** (Mech) air intake.

admitido adj (SAm) accepted, allowed, agreed.

admitir [3a] vt to admit (a to, en into); to accept, allow; to recognize; doubts to leave room for; improvement etc to allow, be susceptible of; **esto no admite demora** this allows no delay; **no admite otra explicación** it allows no other explanation; **¿admite la Academia la palabra?** does the Academy accept the word?; **hay que — que ...** (angl) it must be admitted that ..., it must be confessed that ...; **"no se admiten propinas"** "no tipping", "tipping not allowed".

admonición nf warning.

admonitorio adj sign, voice etc warning.

adobado nm pickled meat, pickled pork.

adobar [1a] vt to prepare, dress; to cook; meat to pickle; hides to tan, dress; lamp to trim.

adobe nm (a) adobe, sun-dried brick. (b) (Arg: hum) big foot.

adobera nf (a) mould for making adobes; (Chi, Mex) brick-shaped cheese, cheese mould. (b) (Arg: hum) big foot.

adobo nm (a) (act) preparation, dressing; cooking; pickling; tanning. (b) pickle, sauce; tanning mixture.

adocenado adj common, ordinary.

adoctrinamiento nm indoctrination.

adoctrinar [1a] vt to indoctrinate (en with).

adolecer [2d] vi to be ill, fall ill; **— de** (Med) to be ill with, fall ill with; (fig) to suffer from.

adolescencia nf adolescence.

adolescente 1 adj adolescent. 2 nmf adolescent.

Adolfo m Adolphus, Adolf.

adonde conj where.

adónde 1 adv interrog where? 2 conj where.

Adonis m Adonis.

adopción nf adoption.

adoptado (Mex) 1 adj adopted. 2 nm, **adoptada** nf adopted child.

adoptar [1a] vt (all senses) to adopt.

adoptivo adj adoptive; child adopted; **patria adoptiva** country of adoption.

adoquín nm (a) paving stone, wooden paving block. (b) (fam) idiot, clod.

adoquinado nm paving.

adoquinar [1a] vt to pave.

adorable adj adorable.

adoración nf adoration; worship; **A— de los Reyes** Epiphany; **una mirada llena de —** an adoring look.

adorar [1a] vt to adore; to worship.

adormecedor adj that sends one to sleep, soporific; lulling, dreamy.

adormecer [1d] 1 vt to make sleepy, send to sleep; (fig) to calm, lull.
2 **adormecerse** vr (a) to become sleepy, get drowsy; to fall asleep, go to sleep; (of limb) to go numb, go to sleep. (b) **— en** (fig) to persist in, go on with.

adormecido adj sleepy, drowsy; languorous; limb numb; (fig) inactive.

adormecimiento nm sleepiness, drowsiness; numbness.

adormidera nf poppy.

adormilarse [1a] vr, **adormitarse** [1a] vr to doze.

adornar [1a] vt to adorn (de with); to decorate, embellish, bedeck; (Sew) to trim (de with); food to garnish (de with); person to endow, bless (de with); **le adornan mil virtudes** he is blessed with every virtue.

adornista nm decorator.

adorno nm adornment; decoration, embellishment; (Sew) trimming; (Cook) garnishment; **es el principal**

— de su ciudad he is the chief adornment of his city, he is the city's chief claim to fame.

adosar [1a] vt (a) **— algo a una pared** to lean something against a wall; to place something with its back against a wall. (b) (SAm) to join firmly; to attach, enclose (with a letter).

adquirido adj: **mal —** ill-gotten.

adquirir [3I] vt to acquire; to obtain; to buy, purchase; habit to get into, form.

adquisición nf acquisition; purchase.

adquisitivo adj acquisitive; **poder —** purchasing power.

adquisividad nf acquisitiveness.

adrede adv on purpose, purposely.

adrenalina nf adrenalin.

Adriano m Hadrian.

Adriático m: **(Mar) —** Adriatic (Sea).

adscribir [3a; ptp **adscrito**] vt: **— a** to appoint to, assign to; **estuvo adscrito al servicio de ...** he was attached to ..., he was in the service of ...

aduana nf customs; customs house; customs duty; **libre de —** duty-free; **pasar por la —** to go through the customs.

aduanero 1 adj customs (attr). 2 nm customs officer, customs inspector.

aducir [3d] vt to adduce, bring forward; to offer as proof; proof to provide, furnish.

adueñarse [1a] vr: **— de** to take possession of.

adujar [1a] vt (Naut) to coil.

adulación nf flattery, adulation.

adulador 1 adj flattering, fawning. 2 nm, **aduladora** nf flatterer.

adular [1a] vt to flatter.

adulate adj, nm (SAm) = **adulón**.

adulón 1 adj fawning, cringing, soapy. 2 nm, **adulona** nf toady, creep (sl).

adulonería nf (SAm) (a) flattering, fawning. (b) fawning nature, soapiness.

adúltera nf adulteress.

adulteración nf adulteration.

adulterado adj adulterated.

adulterar [1a] 1 vt to adulterate. 2 vi to commit adultery.

adulterino adj adulterous; coin etc spurious, counterfeit.

adulterio nm adultery.

adúltero 1 adj adulterous. 2 nm adulterer.

adulto 1 adj adult, grown-up. 2 nm, **adulta** nf adult, grown-up.

adunar [1a] vt to join, unite.

adunco adj bent, curved.

adustez nf austerity, severity; grimness, sternness; sullenness.

adusto adj (a) scorching hot. (b) austere, severe; grim, stern; sullen.

advenedizo 1 adj foreign, from outside; newly arrived; (pej) upstart. 2 nm, **advenidiza** nf foreigner, outsider; newcomer; (pej) upstart.

advenimiento nm advent, arrival; **— al trono** accession to the throne.

adventicio adj adventitious.

adverbial adj adverbial.

adverbio nm adverb.

adversario nm, **adversaria** nf adversary, opponent.

adversidad nf adversity; setback, mishap.

adverso adj side opposite, facing; result etc adverse, untoward; luck bad.

advertencia nf warning; piece of advice; reminder; (in book) preface, foreword.

advertido adj sharp, wide-awake.

advertir [3i] 1 vt (a) to notice, observe; to become aware of; **— que ...** to observe that ... (b) to point out, draw attention to. (c) to advise; to warn; to caution; **— que ...** to advise that ..., recommend that ...
2 vi: **— en** to notice, observe, become aware of; to take notice of, bear in mind.

Adviento nm Advent.

advocación nf (Eccl) name, dedication; **una iglesia bajo la — de San Felipe** a church dedicated to St Philip.

advocar [1g] vt (SAm) to advocate.

adyacencia nf (RPI) nearness, proximity.

adyacente adj adjacent.

aechaduras nfpl chaff.

aeración nf aeration.

aéreo adj aerial; air (attr); railway etc overhead, elevated.

aero ... aero ...

aeroclub nm flying club.

aerochati nf (fam) air hostess.

aerodeslizador *nm,* **aerodeslizante** *nm* hovercraft.
aerodinámica *nf* aerodynamics.
aerodinámico *adj* aerodynamic; (*in design, lines*) streamlined.
aerodinamizar [1f] *vt* to streamline.
aeródromo *nm* aerodrome, airdrome (*US*), airfield.
aerofaro *nm* (*Aer*) beacon.
aerofoto *nf* aerial photograph.
aerograma *nm* aerogram.
aerolito *nm* meteorite.
aeromodelismo *nm* aeromodelling, making model aeroplanes.
aeromodelo *nm* model aeroplane.
aeromotor *nm* aero-engine.
aeromoza *nf* (*SAm*) air hostess, stewardess.
aeronauta *nm* aeronaut.
aeronáutica *nf* aeronautics.
aeronáutico *adj* aeronautical.
aeronaval *adj* air-sea; **base** — air-sea base.
aeronave *nf* airship; **— del espacio, — espacial** spaceship; **— supersónica** supersonic airliner.
aeropuerto *nm* airport.
aerosol *nm* aerosol.
aeróstato *nm* balloon, acrostat.
aerotransportado *adj* airborne.
aerovía *nf* airway.
afabilidad *nf* affability, good nature, geniality; pleasantness, niceness.
afable *adj* affable, good-natured, genial; easy, pleasant, nice.
afablemente *adv* affably; pleasantly.
afamado *adj* famous, noted (*por* for).
afamar [1a] **1** *vt* to make famous. **2 afamarse** *vr* to become famous, make a reputation.
afán *nm* (**a**) hard work, industry; exertion, toil.
(**b**) anxiety; solicitude.
(**c**) desire, urge; zeal, eagerness; **el — de** the desire for, the urge for; **— de estudios** studiousness, keenness to study; **— de lucro** profit motive; **— de superación** urge to improve, will to do better; **— de victoria** urge to win; **con —** zealously, keenly.
afanador *nm* (*Arg*) thief; (*Mex*) menial worker.
afanar [1a] **1** *vt* (**a**) to press, harass, bother.
(**b**) (*CAm*) to earn.
(**c**) (*fam*) to pinch (*fam*), swipe (*sl*).
2 afanarse *vr* (**a**) to toil, labour (*en* at); to strive hard, exert oneself, go all out; **— por +** *infin* to strive to + *infin*; to toil to + *infin*.
(**b**) (*Col*) to get angry.
afanoso *adj* work hard, heavy, laborious; *task* tough, uphill; *person's temperament* industrious; solicitous; *activity, search* feverish, hectic.
afarolado *adj* (*SAm*) excited, worked up; angry.
afarolarse [1a] *vr* (*SAm*) to get excited, get worked up; to get angry.
afasia *nf* aphasia.
afásico *adj* mute, dumb.
afeamiento *nm* (**a**) defacing, disfigurement. (**b**) condemnation, censure.
afear [1a] *vt* (**a**) to make ugly, deface, spoil, disfigure; **los errores que afean el texto** the mistakes which disfigure the text.
(**b**) (*fig*) to condemn, censure, decry.
afección *nf* (**a**) affection, fondness; inclination; **—es del alma** emotions; emotional disorders.
(**b**) (*Med*) trouble, disease; **— cardíaca** heart trouble, heart disease; **— hepática** liver complaint.
afeccionarse [1a] *vr* (*RPl*): **— a** to take a liking to, become fond of.
afectación *nf* affectation.
afectadamente *adv* affectedly.
afectado *adj* (**a**) affected; stilted, precious.
(**b**) (*Med*) **estar — del corazón** to have heart trouble; **estar — (del pecho)** (*Mex*) to be consumptive; **estar —** (*Arg*) to be hurt; to be ill.
afectar [1a] **1** *vt* (**a**) to affect, have an effect on; **nos afecta gravemente** it seriously affects us; **por lo que afecta a esto** with regard to this.
(**b**) (*emotionally*) to affect, move.
(**c**) to affect, pretend, feign; to put on a show of; **— ignorancia** to feign ignorance.
(**d**) (*Law*) to tie up, encumber.
(**e**) (*SAm*) to hurt, injure, damage.
(**f**) (*SAm*) *shape etc* to take, assume.
(**g**) (*SAm*) *funds* to destine, set aside (*a* for), devote (*a* to).
2 afectarse *vr* (*SAm*) to fall ill, catch a disease.
afectísimo *adj* affectionate; **suyo —** yours truly.
afectivo *adj* affective.
afecto 1 *adj* (**a**) affectionate; **— a** attached to, fond of; inclined towards.
(**b**) **— a** (*Law*) subject to, liable for.

(**c**) **— de** afflicted with.
2 *nm* (**a**) affection, fondness (*a* for), attachment (*a* to).
(**b**) feeling, emotion; moral instinct.
afectuosamente *adv* affectionately.
afectuosidad *nf* affection.
afectuoso *adj* affectionate.
afeitada *nf,* **afeitado** *nm* shave; shaving.
afeitadora *nf* electric razor, electric shaver.
afeitar [1a] **1** *vt* (**a**) *beard* to shave; *plant, tail* to trim; **¡que te afeiten!** (*fam*) get your head seen to! (*fam*).
(**b**) (*of woman*) to make up, paint, apply cosmetics to.
2 afeitarse *vr* (**a**) to shave, have a shave.
(**b**) to make oneself up, put one's make-up on.
afeite *nm* make-up, cosmetic(s), rouge.
afelpado *adj* plush, velvety.
afeminación *nf* effeminacy.
afeminado 1 *adj* effeminate. **2** *nm* effeminate person.
afeminamiento *nm* effeminacy.
afeminarse [1a] *vr* to become effeminate.
aferrado *adj* stubborn; **seguir — a** to remain firm in, stick to, stand by.
aferrar [1k] **1** *vt* to grasp, seize, grapple; (*Naut*) *ship* to moor, *sail etc* furl.
2 aferrarse *vr* (**a**) (*Naut*) to grapple; to anchor, moor; (*2 persons*) to grapple (together).
(**b**) **— a, — en** (*fig*) to stick to, stand by; **— a un principio** to stick to a principle; **— a una esperanza** to clutch at a hope, cling to a hope; **— a su opinión** to remain firm in one's opinion, stick to one's view.
afestonado *adj* festooned.
afgano 1 *adj* Afghan. **2** *nm,* **afgana** *nf* Afghan.
Afganistán *m* Afghanistan.
afianzamiento *nm* (**a**) strengthening, fastening, securing. (**b**) (*Fin etc*) guarantee, security; (*Law*) surety, bond.
afianzar [1f] **1** *vt* (**a**) to strengthen, fasten, secure; to support, prop up; (*fig*) to support, back.
(**b**) to guarantee, vouch for; to stand surety for.
2 afianzarse *vr* to steady oneself; (*fig*) to become strong, become established; **— a** to catch hold of, hold fast to; **la reacción se afianzó después de la guerra** the reaction set in after the war.
afición *nf* (**a**) fondness, liking (*a* for); taste (*a* for), inclination (*a* towards); **cobrar — a, tomar — a** to acquire a liking for, take a liking to; **tener — a** to like, be fond of.
(**b**) hobby, pastime; interest; **¿qué —es tiene?** what are his interests?; **pinta por —** he paints as a hobby.
(**c**) **la —** (*Sport etc*) the fans, the sporting public; **aquí hay mucha —** there is a large public for it here, support is strong here, the fans are terribly keen here.
aficionado 1 *adj* (**a**) keen, enthusiastic; **es muy —** he's very keen.
(**b**) **— a** keen on, fond of; with a taste for; **ser** (*or estar*) **muy — a** to be very keen on, be very fond of.
(**c**) *player etc* amateur.
2 *nm,* **aficionada** *nf* (*in general*) enthusiast; (*not professional*) amateur; (*as spectator etc: Sport*) fan, follower, supporter, (*Cine, Theat*) fan; **gritaban los —s** the fans were shouting; **todos los —s a la música** all music lovers; **la cantante y sus —s** the singer and her fans; **función de —s** amateur performance; **partido de —s** amateur game; **somos simples —s** we're just amateurs; **tenis para —s** amateur tennis.
aficionar [1a] **1** *vt:* **— a uno a algo** to make someone keen on something, make someone like something.
2 aficionarse *vr:* **— a algo** to get fond of something, take a liking to something, take to something; **to become a follower (or fan) of something; — a +** *infin* to get fond of + *ger,* take to + *ger.*
afiche *nm* (*Per, RPl*) poster.
áfido *nm* aphid.
afiebrado *adj* feverish.
afijo *nm* affix.
afiladera *nf* grindstone, whetstone.
afilado *adj* *edge* sharp; *point* tapering, sharp.
afilador *nm* (**a**) (*person*) knife-grinder; (*Tech*) steel, sharpener; strop, razor strop; **— de lápices** pencil sharpener. (**b**) (*RPl*) suitor, lover.
afiladora *nf* (*RPl*) flirtatious girl.
afiladura *nf* sharpening.
afilalápices *nm, pl* **afilalápices** pencil sharpener.
afilar [1a] **1** *vt* (**a**) to sharpen, put an edge on; to put a point on; to whet, grind; *razor* to strop.
(**b**) (*RPl*) to court.

2 afilarse *vr* (a) to get sharp; (*of features*) to sharpen, grow thin, get peaked; (*of fingers*) to taper. (b) (*Bol*) to get ready; to get ready to tell someone off.

afiliación *nf* affiliation.

afiliado 1 *adj* affiliated (*a* to), member . . .; (*Comm*) subsidiary; los países —s the member countries. **2** *nm*, **afiliada** *nf* (*Per, RPl*) member.

afiliarse [1b] *vr*: — **a** to affiliate to, join.

afiligranado *adj* filigreed; (*fig*) delicate, fine.

afilón *nm* strop, whetstone, steel.

afilorar [1a] *vt* (*Cu, PR*) to adorn.

afín 1 *adj* (a) bordering, adjacent. (b) related, similar, allied; *person* related. **2** *nmf* relation by marriage.

afinación *nf* refining, polishing; completion; (*Mus*) tuning.

afinado *adj* finished, polished; (*Mus*) in tune.

afinador *nm* (*Mus*) tuning key; (*person*) tuner; — **de pianos** piano tuner.

afinar [1a] **1** *vt* to perfect, put the finishing touch to, complete; to refine, polish; (*Tech*) to purify, refine; (*Mus*) to tune.
    2 *vi* to sing in tune, play in tune.

afincado *nm* (*Arg*) farmer.

afincarse [1g] *vr* to establish oneself, settle (in a town etc).

afinidad *nf* affinity (*also Chem*); relationship, similarity, kinship (*con* with); **por** — by marriage.

afirmación *nf* affirmation.

afirmado *nm* (*Arg*) paving, paved surface; (*Aut*) road surface.

afirmar [1a] **1** *vt* (a) to make firm, steady, secure, strengthen.
    (b) to affirm, assert, state; *loyalty etc* to declare, protest; — **que** . . . to affirm that . . ., state that . . .
    (c) (*Chi, Mex*) *blow* to deal, give.
    2 afirmarse *vr* (a) to steady oneself; — **en los estribos** to settle one's feet firmly in the stirrups.
    (b) — **en lo dicho** to repeat what one has said, maintain one's opinion.

afirmativamente *adv* affirmatively; **contestar** — to answer in the affirmative.

afirmativo *adj* affirmative, positive.

aflautado *adj* *voice* high, fluty.

aflicción *nf* affliction; grief, sorrow.

aflictivo *adj*, **afligente** *adj* (*SAm*) distressing, grievous.

afligido 1 *adj* grieving, sorrowing, heartbroken; — **por** stricken with; los —s **padres** the bereaved parents.
    2 *nm*: los —s the afflicted; (*at a death*) the bereaved.

afligir [3e] **1** *vt* to afflict; to grieve, pain, distress.
    2 afligirse *vr* to grieve (*con, de, por* about, at); **no te aflijas** don't grieve over it; **no te aflijas tanto** you must not let it affect you like this.

aflojamiento *nm* slackening; loosening; relaxation; abatement, weakening.

aflojar [1a] **1** *vt* (a) *nut, rope, step etc* to slacken; *knot etc* to loosen, undo; *pressure* to relax; *grip* to loosen, ease, let go; *brake* to release, take off; *bowels* to ease.
    (b) (*SAm*) *money* to fork out (*fam*), pay up.
    2 *vi* to slacken; to relent, let up; (*of fever etc*) to abate, weaken; (*of devotion*) to grow cool; (*of application etc*) to get slack.
    3 aflojarse *vr* to slacken (off, up); to come loose, work loose; (*fever, heat*) to abate; (*devotion*) to cool (off), diminish; (*interest*) to flag; (*price*) to go down, weaken.

afloramiento *nm* outcrop.

aflorar [1a] *vi* to crop out, outcrop, appear on the surface.

afluencia *nf* (a) inflow, influx, flow; (*of people etc*) rush; crowd, jam; (*at meeting*) attendance, number present; **la** — **de turistas** the influx of tourists; **la** — **de coches al estadio** the flow of cars towards the stadium; **tan grande fue la** — so great was the rush.
    (b) abundance, plenty.
    (c) eloquence, fluency.

afluente 1 *adj* (a) flowing, inflowing. (b) eloquent, fluent. **2** *nm* (*Geog*) tributary.

afluir [3g] *vi* to flow (*a* into); (*persons*) to flow, flock (*a* into, to).

aflujo *nm* (*Med*) afflux, congestion; (*Mech*) inflow, influx, inlet.

aflús *adj* (*SAm: sl*) broke (*fam*), cleaned out (*sl*).

afoetear [1a] *vt* (*Col Per, PR*) to whip, beat.

afónico *adj* (a) hoarse, voiceless; **estar** — to be hoarse, have lost one's voice. (b) *letter* silent, mute.

aforador *nm* gauger.

aforar [1a] *vt* (*Tech*) to gauge; (*fig*) to appraise, value.

aforismo *nm* aphorism.

aforístico *adj* aphoristic.

aforo *nm* (a) (*Tech*) gauging; (*fig*) appraisal, valuation.
    (b) (*Theat etc*) capacity; **el teatro tiene un** — **de 2.000** the theatre has a capacity of 2,000, the theatre can seat 2,000.

aforrar [1a] **1** *vt* to line. **2 aforrarse** *vr* (a) to wrap up warm, put on warm underclothes. (b) (*fam*) to stuff oneself, tuck it away (*fam*).

afortunadamente *adv* fortunately, luckily.

afortunado *adj* fortunate, lucky.

afrailado *adj* (*SAm*) parsonical, churchy (*fam*).

afrancesado 1 *adj* francophile; (*pej*) frenchified; (*Pol*) pro-French, supporting the French.
    2 *nm*, **afrancesada** *nf* francophile; (*pej*) frenchified person; (*Pol*) pro-French person, French sympathizer.

afrancesamiento *nm* (*feeling*) francophilism, pro-French feeling; (*process*) gallicization, frenchification.

afrancesarse [1a] *vr* to go French, become gallicized, acquire French habits; to become a francophile.

afrecho *nm* bran; (*SAm*) sawdust; — **remojado** mash.

afrenta *nf* affront, insult, outrage.

afrentar [1a] **1** *vt* to affront, insult, outrage; to dishonour. **2 afrentarse** *vr* to be ashamed (*de* of).

afrentoso *adj* insulting, outrageous.

África *f* Africa; — **del Norte** North Africa; — **del Sur** South Africa.

africaans *nm* Afrikaans.

africander *nm* Afrikander.

africano 1 *adj* African. **2** *nm*, **africana** *nf* African.

afrijolar [1a] *vt* (*Col*): — **una tarea a uno** to give someone an unpleasant job to do.

afroasiático *adj* Afro-Asian.

afrodisíaco 1 *adj* aphrodisiac. **2** *nm* aphrodisiac.

Afrodita *f* Aphrodite.

afronegrismo *nm* (*SAm*) word borrowed from an African language.

afrontar [1a] *vt* (a) *two persons etc* to bring face to face. (b) *danger, problem etc* to confront, face; to face up to.

aftosa *nf* foot-and-mouth (disease).

afuera 1 *adv* out, outside; ¡—! out of the way!, clear the way!; **de** — from outside; **por** — on the outside.
    2 — **de** *prep* (*SAm*) outside.
    3 —s *nfpl* outskirts, outer suburbs, outlying areas.

afuetear [1a] *vt* (*SAm*) to whip, beat.

afufa *nf* (*fam*) flight, escape; **tomar las** —s to beat it (*fam*).

afufar [1a] *vi* (*fam*) and **afufarse** *vr* to beat it (*fam*), get out quick.

afufón *nm* (*fam*) flight, escape.

afusilar [1a] *vt* (*SAm*) to shoot.

afutrarse [1a] *vr* (*Chi*) to dress up.

agachada *nf* (*fam*) trick, dodge.

agachadiza *nf* (*Orn*) snipe; **hacer la** — to duck, try not to be seen.

agachar [1a] **1** *vt* *head* to bend, bow; *hat* to slouch, pull down.
    2 agacharse *vr* (a) to stoop, crouch, get down; to squat; to duck; to cower.
    (b) (*fig*) to go into hiding, lie low.
    (c) (*SAm*) to give in, submit.
    (d) (*Mex*) — **algo** to keep quiet about something out of spite.
    (e) (*Col, Mex*) — **con algo** to make away with something, pocket something.

agache *nm* (*Col*) fib, tale; **andar de** — to be on the run.

agachón *nm* (*Mex*) cuckold.

agalbanado *adj* lazy, shiftless.

agalla *nf* (a) (*Bot*) gall; — **de roble** oak apple.
    (b) (*Fish*) gill.
    (c) (*Col*) greed.
    (d) —s (*Anat*) tonsils; (*Med*) tonsillitis.
    (e) —s (*fam*) pluck, guts; **es hombre de** —s he's got guts; **tener (muchas)** —s to have pluck, have guts.
    (f) (*SAm*) **tener** —s to be greedy; to be mean; to have lots of cheek.

agalludo *adj* (*SAm*) daring, bold; mean, stingy; (*Col*) greedy.

ágape *nm* (*Hist*) love feast; banquet, feast.

agarrada *nf* quarrel; scrap, brawl; (*Sport*) tackle.

agarradera *nf* (*SAm*), **agarradero** *nm* (a) handle, grip; lug.
    (b) —s pull, influence; **tener buenas** —s to have friends in the right places, have pull.

agarrado *adj* mean, stingy.

agarrador *adj* (*Chi, Ec, Per*) *liquor* strong.

agarrafar [1a] *vt* to grab hold of.
agarrar [1a] **1** *vt* **(a)** to grasp, grip, seize, catch hold of; to grab, clutch.
  (b) (*fam*) to get, wangle (*fam*).
  (c) (*Comm*) to corner the market in, pile up stocks of.
  (d) (*SAm: a substitute for* coger *in many meanings, eg*) — **un autobús** to catch a bus, — **una flor** to pick a flower, — **un resfriado** to catch a cold.
  2 *vi* **(a)** to take hold (*de* of); to take root; (*of paint etc*) to stick.
  (b) (*SAm*) — **para** to strike out for.
  3 agarrarse *vr* **(a)** (*two persons*) to grab one another, grapple with each other; (*Bol*) to fight it out; **se agarraron a tiros** they fought it out with guns.
  (b) to hold on; **¡agárrate bien!** hold on!, hold tight!; — **a**, — **de** to hold on to, grip, seize; — **al camino** (*Aut*) to hold the road.
  (c) se le agarró la fiebre the fever took hold of him; **se le agarró un fuerte catarro** he got a severe cold.
  (d) — **la con uno** (*SAm*) to pick on someone; to be spiteful to someone.
agarre *nm* (*SAm*) grasp, hold; (*Col*) handle; (*fig*) guts, toughness.
agarrete *adj* (*Bol*) mean, stingy.
agarro *nm* grasp, hold, clutch.
agarroch(e)ar [1a] *vt* (*Taur*) to prick with a pike.
agarrón *nm* (*SAm*) **(a)** jerk, pull, tug. **(b)** = **agarrada**.
agarroso *adj* (*CAm*) sharp, acrid, bitter.
agarrotamiento *nm* tightening; strangling; (*Aut*) seizing up.
agarrotar [1a] **1** *vt bundle etc* to tie tight; *person* to squeeze tight, press tightly; *criminal* to garrotte; **esta corbata me agarrota** this tie is strangling me.
  2 agarrotarse *vr* (*Med*) to stiffen, get numb; (*Aut etc*) to seize up.
agasajado *nm*, **agasajada** *nf* chief guest, guest of honour.
agasajar [1a] *vt* to treat well, fête, give a royal welcome to; to entertain royally, wine and dine.
agasajo *nm* good treatment, kindness; royal welcome, lavish hospitality, entertainment.
ágata *nf* agate.
agatas *adv* (*RPl*) **(a)** with great difficulty. **(b)** hardly, scarcely.
agauchado *adj* (*RPl*) like a *gaucho*, countrified.
agaucharse [1a] *vr* (*RPl*) to adopt the ways of the *gaucho*.
agave *nf* agave, American aloe.
agavilladora *nf* binder, reaper.
agavillar [1a] **1** *vt* to bind (in sheaves). **2 agavillarse** *vr* to gang up, band together.
agazapar [1a] **1** *vt* (*fam*) to grab, grab hold of, nab. **2 agazaparse** *vr* to hide; to crouch down, duck (down).
agencia *nf* agency; office, bureau; (*Chi*) pawnshop; — **de colocaciones** employment agency; — **de información**, — **de noticias**, — **de prensa** news agency; — **de patentes** patents office; — **de publicidad** advertising agency; — **de transportes** carriers, removal business; — **de turismo**, — **de viajes** travel agency, tourist office.
agenciar [1b] **1** *vt* to bring about, effect, engineer; to obtain, procure (*a uno* for someone); (*pej*) to wangle (*fam*), fiddle (*fam*); *deal* to negotiate.
  2 agenciarse *vr* to manage, get along.
agenciero *nm* (*Arg*) agent, representative; (*Chi*) pawnbroker.
agencioso *adj* active, diligent.
agenda *nf* diary, notebook.
agente *nm* **(a)** agent; policeman; (*SAm*) public service employee, worker in a nationalized industry; — **de bolsa** stockbroker; — **especial** special agent; — **extranjero** foreign agent; — **femenino** policewoman; — **inmobiliario** estate agent; — **literario** literary agent; — **marítimo** shipping agent; — **de negocios** business agent, broker; — **del orden (público)**, — **de policía** policeman; — **provocador** agent provocateur; — **de publicidad** (*Comm*) advertising agent; (*Theat etc*) publicity agent; — **secreto** secret agent; — **de seguros** (*SAm*) insurance agent; — **de transportes** carrier; — **de turismo** travel agent, courier; — **único** sole agent; — **viajero** (*SAm*) commercial traveller, salesman.
  (b) (*Chem*) agent; — **químico** chemical agent.
agible *adj* feasible, workable.
agigantado *adj* gigantic, huge; *see* **paso**.
agigantar [1a] **1** *vt* to enlarge, increase greatly; — **algo** to make something seem huge.

  2 agigantarse *vr* to become huge; to seem huge; (*of crisis etc*) to get much bigger.
ágil *adj* agile, nimble, quick.
agilidad *nf* agility, nimbleness, quickness.
agilitar [1a] **1** *vt* to make agile; (*fig*) to help, make it easy for; (*SAm*) to activate. **2 agilitarse** *vr* to limber up.
ágilmente *adv* nimbly, quickly.
agio *nm* agio; speculation.
agiotaje *nm* (stock)jobbery, jobbing; speculation.
agiotista *nm* (stock)jobber; speculator.
agitación *nf* **(a)** waving, flapping, shaking, stirring; (*Naut*) roughness. **(b)** (*fig*) agitation (*also Pol*); bustle, stir, movement; excitement.
agitado *adj* **(a)** *water* rough, choppy; *air* bumpy. **(b)** (*fig*) agitated; upset, anxious; excited.
agitador *nm* **(a)** (*Mech*) agitator, shaker. **(b)** (*person*) agitator.
agitanado *adj* gipsy-like.
agitar [1a] **1** *vt* **(a)** *arm, flag etc* to wave; *wing* to flap; *weapon* to shake, brandish; *bottle etc* to shake; *liquid* (*with hand*) to shake, (*with spoon etc*) to stir, stir round, stir up; **agitaba un pañuelo** she was waving her handkerchief; **agítese antes de usar** shake (*or* stir) well before using.
  (b) (*fig*) to stir up; to excite, rouse; to worry, upset, make anxious.
  2 agitarse *vr* **(a)** to wave, wave to and fro; to flutter, flap; to shake; (*sea*) to get rough.
  (b) to get excited, get worked up; to get worried, get upset, upset oneself.
aglomeración *nf* agglomeration; mass; — **de tráfico** traffic jam.
aglomerado *adj* massed together, in a mass; **viven** —**s** they live crowded together, they live on top of each other.
aglomerar [1a] **1** *vt* to agglomerate, crowd together. **2 aglomerarse** *vr* to agglomerate, form a mass; to crowd together.
aglutinación *nf* agglutination.
aglutinante *adj* agglutinative.
aglutinar [1a] **1** *vt* to agglutinate. **2 aglutinarse** *vr* to agglutinate.
agnosticismo *nm* agnosticism.
agnóstico 1 *adj* agnostic. **2** *nm*, **agnóstica** *nf* agnostic.
agobiador *adj*, **agobiante** *adj burden, heat etc* oppressive; *grief etc* unbearable; *responsibility*, *work* overwhelming; *poverty* grinding.
agobiar [1b] **1** *vt* to weigh down, bow down; to oppress, burden, overwhelm; **sentirse agobiado por** to feel oneself weighed down by; to be overwhelmed by; **está agobiado de trabajo** he is overburdened with work.
  2 agobiarse *vr*: — **con**, — **de** to be weighed down with, bow beneath.
agobio *nm* burden, weight; oppression; (*Med*) nervous strain, anxiety.
agolpamiento *nm* throng, crush, rush, crowd.
agolparse [1a] *vr* to throng, rush, crowd together; to bunch together; (*of troubles etc*) to come all together, come one on top of another; (*of tears*) to come in a flood; — **en torno a uno** to crowd round someone.
agonía *nf* **(a)** agony; death agony, death throes; **acortar la** — **a un animal** to put an animal out of its misery; **la época está en su** — the period is in its death throes.
  (b) (*fig*) anguish, agony, torment.
  (c) (*fig*) desire, yearning.
agónico *adj* (*fig*) agonizing.
agonizante 1 *adj* dying. **2** *nmf* dying person.
agonizar [1f] **1** *vt* (*fam*) to bother, pester. **2** *vi* (*also* **estar agonizando**) to be dying, be in one's death agony.
agonizos *nmpl* (*Mex*) worries, troubles.
agora *adv* (*arch and SAm*) = **ahora**.
agorar [1n] *vt* to predict, prophesy.
agorero 1 *adj* prophetic; ominous; **ave agorera** bird of ill omen. **2** *nm*, **agorera** *nf* soothsayer, fortuneteller.
agostar [1a] **1** *vt* to parch, burn up; (*fig*) to wither, kill before time. **2 agostarse** *vr* to dry up, shrivel; (*fig*) to die, fade away.
agosto *nm* August; (*fig*) harvest; **hacer su** — to feather one's nest, make one's pile.
agotado *adj*: **estar** — (*person*) to be exhausted, be worn out; (*stock, supply*) to be finished, be exhausted, (*Comm*) be sold out; (*book*) to be out of print; (*battery*) to be flat, be run down.
agotador *adj* exhausting.
agotamiento *nm* exhaustion; depletion, draining; (*Med*) exhaustion; — **nervioso** nervous strain.

agotar [1a] **1** *vt* to exhaust, use up, finish; to deplete, drain, empty; *patience* to exhaust; *person* to exhaust, tire out; (*Med*) to exhaust.

2 agotarse *vr* to become exhausted; to be finished, be used up; to give out, run out; (*book*) to go out of print; (*person*) to exhaust oneself, wear oneself out.

agraceño *adj* tart, sour.

agraciado *adj* (**a**) graceful; nice, attractive. (**b**) lucky; **salir** — to be lucky, be the winner; **estar** — de to be blessed with.

agraciar [1b] *vt* (**a**) to grace, adorn; to make more attractive.

(**b**) *prisoner* to pardon.

(**c**) — **a uno con algo** to bestow something on someone, reward someone with something.

agradabilísimo *adj* most pleasant, very nice indeed.

agradable *adj* pleasant, agreeable, nice; enjoyable; **es un sitio** — it's a nice place; **el cadáver no era muy** — **para la vista** the body was not a pretty sight; **ser** — **al gusto** to be nice, be tasty.

agradablemente *adv* pleasantly, agreeably; enjoyably.

agradar [1a] **1** *vt* to please, be pleasing to, be to the liking of; **esto no me agrada** I don't like this.

2 *vi* to please; **su presencia siempre agrada** it's always pleasant to have you with us, your presence is always welcome.

3 agradarse *vr* (**a**) to be pleased (*de* at, with).

(**b**) (*2 persons*) to like each other.

agradecer [2d] **1** *vt person* to thank; *favour, gift etc* to be grateful for; **agradezco tu ayuda** I am grateful for your help, thanks for your help; **se lo agradezco** I am grateful to you, I am much obliged to you; **un favor que él no agradecería nunca lo bastante** a favour he can never thank you enough for; **agradecería que no lo hiciera** I should be glad if you would not do it, I should be obliged if you could avoid doing it; **eso no lo tiene que** — **a nadie** he has nobody to thank for that, he owes nobody thanks for that.

2 agradecerse *vr*: **¡se agradece!** much obliged!, thanks very much!; **una copita de jerez siempre se agradece** a glass of sherry is always welcome.

agradecido *adj* grateful; appreciative; **muy** — thanks a lot, thanks for everything; **me miró agradecida** she looked at me gratefully; **estamos muy** —**s** we are very grateful.

agradecimiento *nm* gratitude, thanks; appreciation.

agrado *nm* (**a**) affability. (**b**) taste, liking; **ser del** — **de uno** to be to someone's liking.

agrandar [1a] **1** *vt* to make bigger, enlarge, expand; *difficulty etc* to exaggerate, magnify. **2 agrandarse** *vr* to get bigger.

agranijado *adj* pimply.

agrario *adj* agrarian; land (*attr*); **política agraria** farming policy, agricultural policy; **reforma agraria** land reform.

agravación *nf*, **agravamiento** *nm* aggravation, worsening; increase; (*Med*) decline, change for the worse.

agravante **1** *adj* aggravating. **2** *nf* additional burden; unfortunate circumstances; **con la** — **de que . . .** with the further difficulty that . . .

agravar [1a] **1** *vt* to weigh down, make heavier; *penalty, tax etc* to increase; *pain* to make worse; *situation* to aggravate, make worse; *people* to oppress, burden (*con* with).

2 agravarse *vr* to worsen, get worse; to get more difficult.

agraviar [1b] **1** *vt* to wrong; to offend, insult. **2 agraviarse** *vr* to be offended, take offence (*de, por* at).

agravio *nm* wrong, injury; offence, insult; (*Law*) grievance, injustice; —**s de hecho** assault and battery.

agravión *adj* (*Chi*) touchy, quick to take offence.

agravioso *adj* offensive, insulting.

agraz *nm* (**a**) sour grape; sour grape juice; **en** — prematurely, before time. (**b**) (*fig*) bitterness, ill-feeling.

agrazar [1f] **1** *vt* (**a**) to embitter. (**b**) to vex, annoy. **2** *vi* to taste sour, have a sharp taste.

agrazón *nf* (**a**) wild grape; gooseberry bush. (**b**) (*fig*) vexation, annoyance.

agredir [3a; *defective*] *vt* to attack, assault, set upon.

agregado *nm* (**a**) aggregate.

(**b**) (*Tech*) concrete block.

(**c**) (*person*) attaché; — **cultural** cultural attaché; — **militar** military attaché.

(**d**) (*SAm*) person newly added to a group, thing newly added to a collection; (*RPl*) tenant; (*Col, Ven*) tenant farmer paying rent in kind; (*PR*) day labourer.

agregar [1h] *vt* (**a**) to add (*a* to); to join (*a* to). (**b**) to gather, collect. (**c**) *person* to appoint, attach (*a* to, to the staff of).

agremiar [1b] **1** *vt* to form into a union, unionize. **2 agremiarse** *vr* to form a union.

agresión *nf* aggression; (*on a person etc*) attack, assault; **pacto de no** — non-aggression pact; **rechazar una** — to stop aggression.

agresivamente *adv* aggressively.

agresividad *nf* aggressiveness.

agresivo *adj* aggressive.

agresor *nm*, **agresora** *nf* aggressor; attacker, assailant.

agreste *adj* (**a**) rural, country (*attr*). (**b**) *flower, landscape etc* wild. (**c**) (*fig*) rough, uncouth.

agrete *adj* sourish.

agriado *adj* (*Arg*) (**a**) sour, sharp. (**b**) (*fig*) sour, resentful; cross.

agriar [1b *or* 1c] **1** *vt* (**a**) to sour, turn sour. (**b**) (*fig*) to sour; to vex, annoy. **2 agriarse** *vr* (**a**) to turn sour. (**b**) (*fig*) to get cross, get exasperated.

agrícola *adj* agricultural, farming (*attr*).

agricultor **1** *adj* agricultural, farming (*attr*). **2** *nm*, **agricultora** *nf* farmer.

agricultura *nf* agriculture, farming.

agricultural *adj* (*SAm*) agricultural, farming (*attr*).

agridulce *adj* bittersweet.

agriera *nf* (*SAm*) heartburn.

agrietar [1a] **1** *vt* to crack, crack open; to make cracks in, *hands* chap.

2 agrietarse *vr* to crack; to fissure; to get cracked, get covered in cracks; (*hands*) to get chapped.

agrifolio *nm* holly.

agrimensor *nm* surveyor.

agrimensura *nf* surveying.

agringado *adj* (*SAm*) like a *gringo*, who imitates a *gringo* (see *gringo*).

agringarse [1h] *vr* to act like a *gringo*, adopt the ways of the *gringo* (see *gringo*).

agrio **1** *adj* (**a**) *taste* sour, tart, bitter; (*fig*) sharp, sour, disagreeable.

(**b**) *path etc* rough, uneven; *material* brittle; *colour* garish.

2 *nm* sour juice; —**s** citrus fruits.

agriura *nf* (*SAm*) sourness, tartness.

agronomía *nf* agronomy, agriculture.

agrónomo **1** *adj* agricultural, farming (*attr*). **2** *nm* agronomist, agricultural expert.

agropecuario *adj* farming (*attr*), stockbreeding (*attr*); **riqueza agropecuaria** agricultural wealth; **política agropecuaria** farming policy.

agrupación *nf* (**a**) group, association; gathering; union; (*Mus*) group, ensemble. (**b**) (*act*) grouping; gathering; coming together.

agrupar [1a] **1** *vt* to group (together); to gather, assemble; to crowd together.

2 agruparse *vr* to form a group; to gather, come together; to crowd together, cluster, bunch together (*en torno a* round).

agrura *nf* sourness, tartness.

agua *nf* (**a**) water; fluid, liquid; rain; (*Naut*) wake; (*Naut*) leak; (*Archit*) slope of a roof, pitch; **¡hombre al** —! man overboard!

(**b**) (*with adj etc*) — **para beber** drinking water; — **bendita** holy water; — **blanda** soft water; — **de colonia** eau de-cologne; — **corriente** running water; — **destilada** distilled water; — **dulce** fresh water; **pez de** — **dulce** freshwater fish; — **dura** hard water; — **de espliego** lavender water; — **gruesa** (*SAm*) hard water; — **hirviendo** boiling water; — **llovediza**, — **(de) lluvia** rainwater; — **del mar** seawater; — **de pantoque** bilge water; — **pesada** heavy water; — **potable** drinking water; — **salada** salt water; — **de seltz** seltzer (water); — **de Vichy** Vichy water.

(**c**) (*with verb*) **¡—, que se quema la casa!** I'm dying for a drink!; **¡— va!** look out!, timber!; **sin decir** — **va** without any warning; — **pasada no mueve molino** it's no good crying over spilt milk; **bailar el** — **a uno** to dance attendance on someone; **bañarse en** — **de rosas** to see the world through rose-coloured spectacles; **coger** — **en cesto** to labour in vain; **echar un barco al** — to launch a boat; **echar (or llevar) el** — **a su molino** to bring the conversation round to one's own interests; to be on the make; **echarse al** — to dive in, (*fig*) take the plunge; **hacer** — (*Naut*) to leak, take in water; **se me hace la boca** — my mouth is watering; **se le hace** — **en la boca** it melts in one's mouth; **pescar en** — **turbia** to fish in troubled waters; **quedar en** — **de borrajas** to fail, come to nothing; **retener el** — to hold water; **tomar** — (*Rail*) to take on water.

(d) (*comparisons*) **como** — like water; freely, in abundance; **estar como** — **en banasta** (*or* **hornero** *etc*) to be unsteady, be unsafe; **estar como el** — **de un lago** to be calm; **ser como el** — **por San Juan** to be harmful, be unwelcome; **venir como** — **de mayo** to be a godsend, be very welcome.

(e) —**s** waters; (*Naut*) tide; (*Med*) water, urine; (*of jewel*) water, sparkle; **las** —**s del Tajo** the waters of the Tagus; —**s abajo** downstream, down-river (*de* from); —**s arriba** upstream, up-river (*de* from); —**s de consumo** water supply, drinking water; —**s corrientes** (*RPl*) running water; —**s jurisdiccionales**, —**s territoriales** territorial waters; —**s mayores** excrement, faeces; —**s menores** water, urine; —**s minerales** mineral waters; —**s residuales** sewage; **hacer** — to make water, relieve oneself; **estar** (*or* **nadar**) **entre dos** —**s** to be undecided, sit on the fence; **tomar las** —**s** to take the waters.

aguacate *nm* (a) avocado pear; avocado pear tree. (b) (*CAm: fam*) idiot, fool.

aguacatero *nm* (*Mex*) avocado pear tree.

aguacero *nm* (heavy) shower, downpour.

aguacil *nm* (*RPl*) dragonfly.

aguacha *nf* foul water, stagnant water.

aguachacha *nf* (*CAm*) weak drink, nasty drink.

aguachado *adj* (*Chi*) tame.

aguachento *adj* (*Per*, *RPl*: *Bot*) watery.

aguachinado *adj* (*Ven*) watery.

aguachirle *nf* (a) weak drink, nasty drink; slops, dishwater. (b) trifle, mere nothing.

aguachoso *adj* (*Col*, *PR*) watery.

aguada *nf* (a) (*Agr*) watering place. (b) (*Naut*) water supply. (c) (*Min*) flood, flooding. (d) water-colour, wash.

aguado *adj* watery, watered-down, thin.

aguador *nm* water carrier, water seller.

aguaducho *nm* freshet.

aguafiestas *nmf*, *pl* **aguafiestas** spoilsport, killjoy.

aguafortista *nmf* etcher.

aguafuerte *nf* etching; **grabar algo al** — to etch something.

aguafuertista *nmf* etcher.

aguaitar [1a] *vt* (*Arg*, *Cu*, *Per*: *angl*) to spy on; to lie in wait for; (*Col*, *PR*) to wait for; (*Chi etc*) to look, see.

aguaje *nm* (a) tide, spring tide; current; wake. (b) water supply; (*Agr*) watering place. (c) (*Col*, *Ec*, *Guat*) downpour. (d) (*Guat*, *Hond*) dressing-down.

aguajirarse [1a] *vr* (*Cu*, *PR*) to become countrified, acquire peasant's habits (*etc*).

aguamanil *nm* ewer, water jug; washstand.

aguamar *nm* jellyfish.

aguamarina *nf* aquamarine.

aguamarse [1a] *vr* (*Col*) to get scared, be intimidated.

aguamiel *nf* mead; sugared water.

aguanieve *nf* sleet.

aguanoso *adj* (a) wet, watery; *ground* waterlogged. (b) (*Mex*) *person* wet (*fam*).

aguantable *adj* bearable, tolerable.

aguantaderas *nfpl* (*SAm*): **tener** — to be tolerant, put up with a lot.

aguantador *adj* (*SAm*) = **aguantón**.

aguantar [1a] **1** *vt* (a) to bear, endure, stand, put up with; *insult etc* to swallow; *storm* to weather; *examination* to bear, stand up to; *pain* to endure, bear; **no aguanto más** I'm not putting up with this, I can't bear it any more. (b) *roof etc* to hold up, sustain; *breath* to hold.

2 *vi* to last, hold out; **aguanta mucho** he's very patient, he has lots of endurance.

3 aguantarse *vr* to restrain oneself, hold oneself back, sit tight; to put up with it.

aguante *nm* patience; endurance, fortitude.

aguantón *adj* (*Mex*, *PR*) long-suffering, extremely patient.

aguar [1i] *vt* (a) to water (down). (b) (*fig*) to spoil, mar; *see* **fiesta**. (c) (*Chi*, *CAm*) *cattle* to water.

aguardada *nf* wait, waiting.

aguardadero *nm* (*Hunting*) hide.

aguardar [1a] **1** *vt* to wait for, await; to expect. **2** *vi* to wait; **aguarde Vd** (*in narrative*) that's what I'm trying to tell you, I'm coming to that.

aguardentera *nf* liquor bottle, flask.

aguardentería *nf* (*SAm*) liquor store.

aguardentoso *adj* alcoholic; *voice* fruity, beery.

aguardiente *nm* brandy, liquor; — **de caña** rum; — **de cerezas** cherry brandy; — **de manzana** applejack.

aguardientoso *adj* (*SAm*) = **aguardentoso**.

aguardo *nm* (*Hunting*) hide.

aguarrás *nm* turpentine.

aguate *nm* (*Mex*) prickle, spine.

aguatero *nm* (*SAm*) water carrier, water seller.

aguatocha *nf* pump.

aguatoso *adj* (*Mex*) prickly.

aguaturma *nf* Jerusalem artichoke.

aguayo *nm* (*Bol*) many-coloured woollen cloth (*for adornment, or carried as shoulder bag*).

aguaza *nf* sap.

aguazal *nm* puddle; fen, swamp.

aguazar [1f] **1** *vt* to flood, waterlog. **2 aguazarse** *vr* to flood, become waterlogged.

agudeza *nf* (a) acuteness, sharpness; keenness. (b) wit, wittiness. (c) (*una* —) witticism, witty saying.

agudización *nf* sharpening; worsening.

agudizar [1f] **1** *vt* to sharpen, make more acute.

2 agudizarse *vr* to sharpen, become more acute, worsen; **el problema se agudiza** the problem is becoming more acute; **la competencia se agudiza** competition is intensifying.

agudo *adj* (a) sharp, pointed; *angle* acute. (b) *illness*, *pain* acute. (c) (*Mus*) *note* high, high-pitched; shrill; *sound* piercing; (*Gram*) *accent* acute. (d) *mind*, *sense* sharp, keen, acute, penetrating; *remark* smart, clever; *criticism* penetrating, trenchant; *wit* ready, lively; *question* acute, searching; *taste etc* sharp, pungent. (e) witty.

agüera *nf* irrigation ditch.

agüero *nm* omen, sign; prediction, forecast; **de buen** — lucky, propitious; **ser de buen** — to augur well; **de mal** — ill-omened; **pájaro de mal** — bird of ill omen.

agüeitar [1a] (*SAm*) = **aguaitar**.

aguerrido *adj* hardened, veteran.

aguerrir [3a; *defective*] *vt* to inure, harden.

aguijada *nf*, **aguijadera** *nf* goad.

aguijar [1a] **1** *vt* to goad; (*fig*) to urge on, spur on, goad. **2** *vi* to hurry along, make haste.

aguijón *nm* goad; (*Zool*) sting; (*Bot*) prickle, spine, sting; (*fig*) spur, stimulus, incitement; **dar coces contra el** — to kick against the pricks.

aguijonazo *nm* prick (with a goad), jab; (*Zool*, *Bot*) sting.

aguijonear [1a] *vt* = **aguijar**.

águila *nf* (a) (*Orn*) eagle; — **pescadora** osprey; — **real** golden eagle; — **ratonera** buzzard. (b) (*fig*) **ser un** — to be a genius, be terribly clever. (c) (*Chi*) cheat, swindler.

aguileña *nf* columbine.

aguileño *adj* *nose* aquiline; *face* sharp-featured; *person* hawk-nosed.

aguilera *nf* eagle's nest, eyrie.

aguililla *nm*, **aguililla** *nf* (*SAm*) fast horse.

aguilón *nm* (*Orn*) large eagle; (*of crane*) jib; (*Archit*) gable, gable-end; (*Col*, *Ec*) large heavy horse.

aguilucho *nm* (*Orn*) eaglet, young eagle; harrier; (*SAm*) hawk, falcon.

aguinaldo *nm* Christmas box, New Year gift; tip; (*SAm*) Christmas carol.

aguita *nf* (*Per*) money.

aguja *nf* (a) (*Sew etc*) needle; bodkin; hatpin; — **de arria** (*SAm*) pack needle; — **capotera** darning needle; — **de gancho** crochet hook; — **de hacer calceta** knitting needle; — **hipodérmica** hypodermic needle; — **magnética**, — **de marear** compass (needle); — **de media** knitting needle; — **de zurcir** darning needle; **buscar una** — **en un pajar** to look for a needle in a haystack. (b) (*of watch*) hand; (*of dial*) pointer, hand. (c) (*Mil*) firing pin. (d) (*Bot*) — **de pino** pine needle. (e) (*SAm*) fence post. (f) (*Archit*) spire, steeple. (g) —**s** (*Anat*) ribs. (h) —**s** (*Rail*) points. (i) (*Fish*) marlin.

agujazo *nm* prick, jab.

agujereado *adj* full of holes, pierced with holes; perforated; leaky.

agujerear [1a] *vt* to make holes in, pierce; to perforate.

agujero *nm* (a) hole; — **de hombre** manhole; **hacer un** — **en**, **practicar un** — **en** to make a hole in. (b) (*Sew*) needle case; pincushion.

agujetas *nfpl* (a) (*Med*) stitch; stiffness. (b) (*Mex*) shoelaces.

agujón *nm* hatpin.

agur *interj* (*fam*) so long!

agusanado *adj* maggoty, wormy.

agusanarse [1a] *vr* to get maggoty.

Agustín *m* Augustine.

agustiniano, **agustino 1** *adj* Augustinian. **2** *nm*, **agustiniana** *nf*, **agustina** *nf* Augustinian.

aguzamiento *nm* sharpening.

aguzanieves *nf, pl* **aguzanieves** wagtail.

aguzar [1f] *vt* (a) to sharpen.

(b) (*fig*) to incite, stir up; *appetite* to whet; — **las orejas** to prick up one's ears; — **la vista** to look sharp, look more carefully.

ah *interj* ah!; ha! ¡— **del barco!** ship ahoy!

ahechaduras *nfpl* chaff.

ahechar [1a] *vt* to sift; to winnow.

aherrojar [1a] *vt* to put in irons, fetter, shackle; (*fig*) to oppress.

aherrumbrarse [1a] *vr* to rust, get rusty; to take on the taste (*or* colour) of iron.

ahí *adv* there; ¿de —? well?; what next?, (*iro*) so what?; **de — que...** and **so...**, with the result that...; **de — se deduce que...** from that it follows that...; **por —** that way; over there; **200 pesos o por —** 200 pesos or thereabouts; **está por —** it's round here somewhere, (*of person*) he's roundabout somewhere, he's knocking around somewhere; **¡hasta — podíamos llegar!** so it has come to this!; **ir por —** (*euph*) to get around, keep dubious company; **¡— va!** there it goes!, there he goes!; (*in surprise*) goodness me!; (*in derision*) get along with you!, tell us another!

ahijada *nf* goddaughter; (*fig*) protégée.

ahijado *nm* godson; (*fig*) protégé.

ahijar [1a] *vt person* to adopt; *animal* to adopt, mother; (*fig*) — **algo a uno** to impute something to someone; to attribute something to someone.

ahijuna *interj* (Arg, Urug) son of a bitch!

ahilar [1a] **1** *vt* to line up. **2** *vi* to go in single file. **3 ahilarse** *vr* (Med) to faint with hunger; (Bot) to grow poorly; (*of wine etc*) to turn sour, go off.

ahincadamente *adv* hard, earnestly; emphatically.

ahincado *adj* earnest; emphatic.

ahincar [1g] **1** *vt* to press, urge. **2 ahincarse** *vr* to hurry up, make haste.

ahinco *nm* earnestness, intentness; emphasis; **con —** hard, earnestly; eagerly.

ahitar [1a] **1** *vt* to cloy, surfeit. **2 ahitarse** *vr* to stuff oneself (*de* with), give oneself a surfeit (*de* of); (Med) give oneself indigestion.

ahito 1 *adj* (a) gorged, surfeited, satiated.(b) (*fig*) **estar — de** to be fed up with. **2** *nm* surfeit, satiety; (Med) indigestion.

ahogadero *nm* (a) throatband; headstall, halter; hangman's rope. (b) (*fig*) **esto es un —** it's stifling in here.

ahogado 1 *adj* (a) drowned; suffocated; **perecer —** to drown; to suffocate.

(b) *room* close, stifling.

(c) *emotion* pent-up; *shout* muffled, half-smothered.

(d) **estar —, verse —** to be in a tight spot.

2 *nm,* **ahogada** *nf* drowned person.

3 *nm* (SAm) sauce.

ahogar [1h] **1** *vt* (a) to drown; to suffocate; to smother; *fire* to put out; *bill* (Parl), *plan etc* to kill.

(b) *plant* to soak.

(c) *cry, sob etc* to choke back, stifle, hold in.

(d) (*fig*) to afflict, oppress, crush.

2 ahogarse *vr* (*accidentally*) to drown; to suffocate; (*as suicide*) to drown oneself.

ahogo *nm* (a) **perecer por —** to drown.

(b) (Med) shortness of breath, tightness of the chest.

(c) (*fig*) distress, affliction.

(d) (Fin) embarrassment, financial difficulty; economic stringency.

ahoguío *nm* (Med) = **ahogo** (b).

ahondar [1a] **1** *vt* (a) to deepen, make deeper, dig out.

(b) (*fig*) to penetrate, go deeply into, probe; to study thoroughly.

2 *vi:* — **en** to go deeply into, study thoroughly. **3 ahondarse** *vr* to go (*or* sink) in more deeply.

ahora 1 *adv* now; just now; a moment ago; in a little while, very soon; **desde —** from now on; **hasta —** up till now; as yet; hitherto; **¡hasta —!** see you soon!; **por —** for the present, for the moment; — **mismito,** — **poco** (*fam*) just a moment ago; — **mismo** right now, this very minute; at this very moment.

2 *conj* now; now then, well now; on the other hand; — **bien** now then, well now; — **pues** well then; — **...** — whether ... or.

ahorcado *nm,* **ahorcada** *nf* hanged person.

ahorcadura *nf* hanging.

ahorcajarse [1a] *vr* to sit astride; — **en** to sit astride, straddle.

ahorcar [1g] **1** *vt* to hang; *see* **hábito** *etc.* **2 ahorcarse** *vr* to hang oneself.

ahorita *adv* (*esp* SAm) right now, this very minute.

ahormar [1a] *vt* (a) to fit, adjust (*a* to); to shape, mould; *shoes* to break in, stretch; *character* to mould.

(b) (*fig*) — **a uno** to make someone see sense.

ahorquillado *adj* forked.

ahorquillar [1a] **1** *vt* (a) to prop up. (b) to shape like a fork. **2 ahorquillarse** *vr* to fork, become forked.

ahorrador *adj* = **ahorrativo.**

ahorrar [1a] **1** *vt money* to save; to put by; *trouble* to save, avoid; *danger* to avoid; *slave* to free.

2 ahorrarse *vr* (a) — **molestias** to save oneself trouble, to spare oneself effort; **no —las con nadie** to be afraid of nobody.

(b) (Arg, CAm, Ven: Agr) to abort; (CR: *crop*) to fail; (Ec) to shirk, refuse to work.

ahorrativo *adj* thrifty; (*pej*) tight, stingy.

ahorro *nm* (*act*) economy, saving; (*quality*) thrift; **—s** savings.

ahoyar [1a] *vt* to dig holes in.

ahuchar[1] [1a] *vt* to hoard, put by.

ahuchar[2] [1a] *vt* (Col, Mex) = **azuzar.**

ahuecar [1g] **1** *vt* (a) to hollow (out), make a hollow in.

(b) to loosen, soften; to fluff out.

(c) *voice* to deepen, make pompous, give a solemn tone to.

(d) *see* **ala** (g).

2 *vi* **¡ahueca!** (*fam*) beat it! (*fam*).

3 ahuecarse *vr* (*fam*) to give oneself airs.

ahuesarse [1a] *vt* (Chi, Per) (a) (*goods*) to become obsolete; to get spoiled. (b) (*person*) to get thin.

ahuizote *nm* (CAm, Mex) troublesome sort.

ahulado *nm* (CAm, Mex) oilskin; **—s** rubber shoes.

ahumado 1 *adj* (a) *bacon etc* smoked; *flavour, surface, window etc* smoky. (b) (*fam*) tight. **2** *nm* (a) smoking, curing. (b) (*fam*) drunk (*fam*).

ahumar 1 *vt* (a) *bacon etc* to smoke, cure.

(b) *surface etc* to make smoky; *room* to make smoky, fill with smoke.

(c) to smoke out.

2 *vi* to smoke, give out smoke.

3 ahumarse *vr* (a) (*food*) to acquire a burnt taste.

(b) (*room*) to be smoky, get smoked up.

(c) (*fam*) to get tight.

ahusado *adj* tapering, spindle-shaped.

ahusarse [1a] *vr* to taper.

ahuyentar [1a] **1** *vt* (a) to drive away, frighten away; to put to flight; to keep off.

(b) *doubts etc* to banish, dispel.

2 ahuyentarse *vr* to run away; (Mex) to stay away.

aijuna (Arg, Urug) = **ahijuna.**

aindiado *adj* (SAm) Indian-like, Indianized.

airadamente *adv* angrily.

airado *adj* (a) angry; wild, violent. (b) *life* immoral, depraved.

airar [1a] **1** *vt* to anger. **2 airarse** *vr* to get angry (*de, por* at).

aire *nm* (a) air; wind; draught; — **colado** cold draught; — **comprimido** compressed air; — **detonante** firedamp; — **líquido** liquid air; — **puro** clean air; — **viciado** stale air, foul air, fug; **—s de cambio** (Pol) winds of change; **con — acondicionado** air-conditioned, with air conditioning; **al — libre** in the open air, outdoors, (*as adj*) open-air, outdoor; **azotar el —** to waste one's efforts; **beber los —s por** to sigh for, yearn for; to be madly in love with; **cambiar de —(s)** to have a change of air; **cortarlas en el —** to be very sharp; **darse —** to fan oneself; **echar al —** to bare, uncover; **estar en el —** (*fig*) to be in the wind; (Radio) to be on the air; **hacer — a uno** to fan someone; **hacerse — to** fan oneself; **lanzar algo al —** to throw something up; **mudarse a cualquier —** to be fickle; **ofenderse del —** to be terribly touchy; **tomar el —** to go for a stroll; **¡vete a tomar el —!** (*fam*) get lost! (*fam*); **¿qué —s te traen por aquí?** what brings you here?; **volar por los —s** to fly through the air.

(b) (*fig*) air, mien, appearance; **darse —s** to give oneself airs; **darse —s de** to boast of being; **no te des esos —s de suficiencia conmigo** don't get on your high horse with me; **tener — de salud** to look healthy.

(c) (*fig*) resemblance; — **de familia** family likeness; **darse un — a** to resemble; **tener — de** to look like, resemble.

(d) (*fig*) humour, mood; **dar buen — al dinero** to spend money freely; **estar de buen —** to be in a

good mood; **estar de mal —** to be in a bad mood; **seguir el — a uno** to humour someone, follow someone's whim.
   (e) (*fig*) air; elegance, gracefulness.
   (f) (*Mus*) tune, air.
   (g) (*Med: Arg, Par*) stiff neck; (*Par*) paralysis.
aireación *nf* ventilation.
airear [1a] **1** *vt* (a) to air, ventilate; *clothes* to air.
   (b) (*fig*) *idea, question* to air; **— la atmósfera** to clear the air, let in fresh air.
   2 airearse *vr* to take the air; (*Med*) to catch a chill.
airosamente *adv* gracefully, elegantly; jauntily; successfully.
airosidad *nf* grace, elegance; jauntiness.
airoso *adj* (a) airy; *room* draughty; *open place* windy; *weather* windy, blowy.
   (b) (*fig*) graceful, elegant; jaunty; successful; **quedar —, salir —** to be successful, acquit oneself well, come out with flying colours.
aislación *nf* insulation; **— de sonido** soundproofing.
aislacionismo *nm* isolationism.
aislacionista 1 *adj* isolationist. **2** *nmf* isolationist.
aislado *adj* (a) isolated; cut off, shut off (*de* from); lonely; **"con inodoro —"** "with separate WC". (b) (*Elec etc*) insulated.
aislador 1 *adj* (*Elec*) insulating. **2** *nm* (*Elec*) insulator, non-conductor.
aislamiento *nm* (a) isolation; loneliness. (b) (*Elec etc*) insulation; insulating material.
aislante *nm* (*Elec*) insulator.
aislar [1a] **1** *vt* (a) to isolate; to separate, detach; to cut off, shut off.
   (b) (*Elec etc*) to insulate.
   2 aislarse *vr* to isolate oneself, cut oneself off (*de* from); to live in isolation, live in seclusion.
ajá *interj* fine!, splendid!
ajamonarse [1a] *vr* (*fam*) to get plump, run to fat.
ajar[1] *nm* garlic field, garlic patch.
ajar[2] [1a] **1** *vt* (a) to crumple, crush, mess up; to ruffle, rumple; to tamper with, spoil.
   (b) (*fig*) to abuse, disparage.
   2 ajarse *vr* to get crumpled, get messed up; (*Bot*) to wither, fade.
ajarafe *nm* (*Geog*) tableland; (*Archit*) terrace, flat roof.
ajardinar [1a] *vt* to landscape.
ajedrea *nf* (*Bot*) savory.
ajedrecista *nmf* chessplayer.
ajedrez *nm* chess; **un —** a chess set, a set of chessmen.
ajedrezado *adj* chequered.
ajenjo *nm* (*Bot*) wormwood; (*as drink*) absinth(e).
ajeno *adj* (a) somebody else's, other people's; **un coche —** somebody else's car, a car belonging to somebody else; **no meterse en lo —** not to interfere with the affairs of others.
   (b) outside; alien, foreign (*a* to); inconsistent (*a* with); inappropriate (*a, de* for, to); **ser — a la muerte de uno** to have no part in someone's death; **por razones ajenas a mi voluntad** for reasons beyond my control; **eso está — a nuestro control** that is outside our control.
   (c) **— de cuidados** free from care, without a care.
   (d) uninformed, ignorant (*de* of).
   (e) **estar — de sí** to remain detached.
ajetreado *adj* life busy, tiring.
ajetrearse [1a] *vr* to bustle about, be busy; to fuss; to tire oneself out; to work hard, slave away.
ajetreo *nm* bustle; fuss; drudgery, hard work; **es un continuo —** it's all bustle, there's constant coming and going.
ají *nm*, *pl* **ajíes** *or* **ajises** (*SAm*) chili, red pepper; chili sauce; **estar hecho un —** (*SAm*) to be hopping mad, go up the wall (*fam*).
ajiaceite *nm* sauce of garlic and olive oil.
ajiaco *nm* (*Cu*) chili stew; **meterse el —** (*fam*) to eat.
ajibararse [1a] *vr* (*PR*) **= aguajirarse.**
ajigolones *nmpl* (*CAm, Mex*) troubles, difficulties.
ajilar [1a] *vi* (*CAm, Mex*) to set out for a place; to go, leave; (*Cu*) to walk quickly.
ajilimoje *nm*, **ajilimójili** *nm* sauce of garlic and pepper; **—s** (*fam*) bits and pieces, things, odds and ends.
ajiseco *nm* (*Per*) mildly hot red pepper.
ajises *nmpl* (*SAm*: *fam*) of **ají**.
ajo *nm* (a) garlic; clove of garlic; garlic sauce.
   (b) (*fig*) shady deal, secret affair; swearword, rude word; **harto de —** ill-bred, common; (*tieso*) **como un —** high and mighty, stuck-up (*fam*); **andar** (*or* **estar**) **en el —** to be mixed up in it, be concerned in a shady affair; to be in on the secret; **echar** (*or*

soltar) **—s y cebollas** to swear horribly, let fly; **revolver el —** to stir up trouble.
ajobar [1a] *vt* to carry on one's back, hump.
ajobo *nm* load; (*fig*) burden.
ajochar [1a] *vt* (*Col, Per*) **= azuzar.**
ajonje *nm*, **ajonjo** *nm* birdlime.
ajorca *nf* bracelet, bangle.
ajornalar [1a] *vt* to employ by the day.
ajotar 1 *vt* (*CAm*) **= azuzar**; (*Cu*) to scorn, reject; to rebuff. **2 ajotarse** *vr* (*Mex*) to become effeminate.
ajoto *nm* (*Cu*) rebuff.
ajuar *nm* household furnishings; trousseau; (*Hist*) dowry, bridal portion; **— de niño** layette.
ajuarar *nm* room etc to furnish, fit up.
ajuchar [1a] *vt* (*CAm, Mex*) **= azuzar.**
ajuiciado *adj* sensible.
ajuiciar [1b] *vt* to bring to one's senses.
ajumado 1 *adj* (*fam*) tight. **2** *nm* (*fam*) drunk (*fam*).
ajumarse [1a] *vr* (*fam*) to get tight.
ajuntarse [1a] *vr* (*Col*) to live together, live in sin.
ajustado *adj* (a) right, fitting. (b) *dress* tight, close-fitting; clinging; **muy —** stretched tight, skintight; too tight.
ajustador *nm* (a) tight waistcoat. (b) (*Tech*) fitter.
ajustamiento *nm* (*Fin*) settlement.
ajustar [1a] **1** *vt* (a) (*Tech etc*) to fit (*a* to, into); to fasten, engage.
   (b) *machine etc* to adjust, regulate; (*fig*) to adjust, adapt (*a* to); *abuse, error* to put right.
   (c) *bargain* to strike; *agreement* to make; *marriage* to arrange; *differences* to settle, reconcile, adjust.
   (d) *account* to settle (*also fig*).
   (e) *price* to fix.
   (f) *servant* to hire, engage.
   (g) (*Typ*) to make up.
   (h) **— un golpe a uno** (*Bol*) to give someone a blow.
   2 *vi* to fit; **— bien** to fit well, be a good fit.
   3 ajustarse *vr* (a) to fit (*a* into).
   (b) (*fig*) to adjust oneself, get adjusted (*a* to); to conform (*a* to), comply (*a* with); **— a las reglas** to abide by the rules.
   (c) (*fig*) to come to an agreement (*con* with).
ajuste *nm* (a) (*Tech etc*) fitting; adjustment; (*Sew*) fit, fitting; **mal —** maladjustment.
   (b) settlement (*also Fin*); reconciliation; compromise.
   (c) hiring, engagement; contract of employment.
   (d) (*Typ*) making up.
   (e) (*Law*) retaining fee; (*on wages*) bonus; **— por aumento del costo de la vida** cost-of-living bonus.
ajusticiar [1b] *vt* to execute.
al = a + el; **al entrar** on entering; **al entrar yo** when I came in; on coming in, I . . .; **al verlo yo** when I saw it; on seeing it, I . . .
ala *nf* (a) (*Orn, Ent, Zool and in many fig senses*) wing; **de cuatro —s** four-winged; **de —s azules** blue-winged.
   (b) (*Aer*) wing; **con —s en delta** delta-winged; **con —s en flecha** swept-wing, with swept-back wings.
   (c) (*of hat*) brim; (*Archit*) eaves; wing; (*Anat: of heart*) auricle; (*fam: Mex, Chi*) arm; (*of propeller*) blade; (*of table*) leaf, flap.
   (d) (*Pol*) wing; **el — izquierda del partido** the left wing of the party.
   (e) (*Mil*) wing, flank.
   (f) (*Sport: part of field*) wing; (*position, player*) wing-half; **medio —** half-back.
   (g) (*phrases*) **ser como — de mosca** to be paper-thin, be transparent; **ahuecar el —** (*fam*) to beat it (*fam*); to keep out of the way; **arrastrar el —** to be courting; to be depressed; **se le cayeron las —s del corazón** his heart fell; **andar con el —** caída to be downcast; **cortar las —s a uno** to clip someone's wings, put someone on a tight rein; **dar —s a uno** to encourage someone, embolden someone; **tomar —s** to get cheeky; **volar con las propias —s** to stand on one's own two feet; **en —s de la fantasía** on (the) wings of fantasy.
Alá *m* Allah.
alabador *adj* approving, eulogistic.
alabamiento *nm* praise.
alabancioso *adj* boastful.
alabanza *nf* praise (*a* of); eulogy; **—s** praise, praises; **en — de** in praise of; **digno de toda —** thoroughly praiseworthy, highly commendable; **cantar las —s de uno** to sing someone's praises.

alabar [1a] **1** *vt* to praise. **2 alabarse** *vr* (a) to boast; — de to boast of being. (b) to be pleased, be satisfied.

alabarda *nf* (*Hist*) halberd.

alabardero *nm* (*Hist*) halberdier; (*Theat*) paid applauder, member of the claque.

alabastrado *adj*, **alabastrino** *adj* alabastrine, alabaster (*attr*).

alabastro *nm* alabaster.

álabe *nm* (*Mech*) wooden cog, tooth; (*of waterwheel*) paddle, bucket; (*Bot*) drooping branch.

alabear [1a] **1** *vt* to warp. **2 alabearse** *vr* to warp.

alabeo *nm* warp, warping; **tomar** — to warp.

alacena *nf* cupboard, closet (*US*).

alacrán *nm* scorpion; (*Arg*) gossip, scandalmonger.

alacranear [1a] *vi* (*Arg*) to gossip, spread scandal.

alacraneo *nm* (*Arg*) gossip, scandal; scandalmongering.

alacridad *nf* alacrity, readiness; **con** — with alacrity, readily.

alada *nf* flutter, fluttering.

Aladino *m* Aladdin.

alado *adj* winged, with wings; (*fig*) winged, swift.

alafre (*Ven*) **1** *adj* wretched, vile. **2** *nm* wretch.

alagartado *adj* motley, variegated.

alambicado *adj* (a) distilled. (b) (*fig*) given sparingly, given grudgingly. (c) (*fig*) *style* subtle, precious, refined; (*pej*) affected.

alambicamiento *nm* (a) distilling. (b) (*fig*) subtlety, preciosity; (*pej*) affectation.

alambicar [1g] *vt* (a) to distil. (b) (*fig*) *style* to subtilize, polish; (*pej*) to overrefine, exaggerate. (c) (*fig*) to scrutinize, investigate.

alambique *nm* still; **dar algo por** — to give something sparingly; **pasar algo por** — to go through something with a toothcomb.

alambiquería *nf* (*Cu*) distillery.

alambiquero *nm* (*Cu*) distiller.

alambrada *nf* wire netting; wire fence, barbed-wire fence; (*Mil*) barbed-wire entanglement.

alambrado *nm* wire netting; wire fence; (*Elec*) wiring, wiring system.

alambrar [1a] *vt* to wire; (*SAm*) to fence with wire.

alambre *nm* wire (*also Elec*); — **cargado** live wire; — **de espino**, — **espinoso**, — **de púas** barbed wire; — **forrado** covered wire; — **de tierra** earth wire, ground wire (*US*); **estar hecho un** — to be as thin as a rake.

alambrera *nf* wire screen; wire cover; fireguard.

alambrista *nmf* tightrope walker.

alambrito *nm* (*SAm*) tall thin person.

alameda *nf* poplar grove; (*as street*) avenue, boulevard, tree-lined walk.

álamo *nm* poplar; — **blanco** white poplar; — **de Italia** Lombardy poplar; — **negro** black poplar; — **temblón** aspen.

alamparse [1a] *vr*: — **por** to crave, have a craving for.

alancear [1a] *vt* to spear.

alano[1] *nm* mastiff, wolfhound.

alano[2] **1.** *adj* of the Alani. **2** —**s** *nmpl* Alani.

alar *nm* overhanging roof, eaves; (*SAm*) pavement, sidewalk (*US*); —**es** (*sl*) trousers, pants.

alarde *nm* (*Mil*) review; (*fig*) show, display, parade; (*Sport*) supreme effort, sprint, dash; —**s** (*Arg*, *Per*) boasts; **hacer** — **de** to make a show of, make a parade of; to boast of.

alardeado *adj* vaunted, much boasted-of.

alardear [1a] *vi* to boast, brag.

alardeo *nm* boasting, bragging.

alargadera *nf* (*Chem*) adapter; (*Tech*) extension.

alargamiento *nm* lengthening, prolongation, extension; increase.

alargar [1h] **1** *vt* (a) to lengthen, prolong, extend; *dress* to lengthen, let down; *neck* to stretch, crane; *hand* to put out, stretch out; *speech*, *tale* to spin out. (b) *rope* to pay out. (c) to reach for; to hand, pass (*a* to). (d) *wages etc* to increase, raise. (e) *step* to hasten. **2 alargarse** *vr* (a) to lengthen, get longer, extend; (*of days*) to get longer, draw out; (*of speech etc*) to drag out. (b) — **en** to expatiate on, enlarge upon; se **alargó en la charla** he spun his talk out, he took his time in the talk. (c) to go away, withdraw.

alarido *nm* shriek, yell; **dar** —**s** to shriek, yell.

alarife *nmf* (*Arg*) clever sort, crafty person; (*f*) loose woman.

alarma *nf* alarm; — **aérea** air-raid warning; **falsa** — false alarm; — **de incendios** fire alarm; — **de ladrones** burglar alarm; **con creciente** — with growing alarm, with growing concern; **voz de** — warning note; **timbre de** — alarm bell; **dar la** — to raise the alarm.

alarmante *adj* alarming.

alarmantemente *adv* alarmingly.

alarmar [1a] **1** *vt* to alarm; (*Mil etc*) to alert, rouse, call to arms. **2 alarmarse** *vr* to get alarmed, be alarmed; ¡no te alarmes! don't be alarmed!, there's nothing to worry about!

alarmista 1 *adj* alarmist, alarming. **2** *nmf* alarmist.

alavés 1 *adj* of Álava. **2** *nm*, **alavesa** *nf* native (*or* inhabitant) of Álava; **los** —**es** the people of Álava.

alazán 1 *adj* *horse* sorrel. **2** *nm* sorrel (horse).

alba *nf* (a) dawn, daybreak; **al** — at dawn; **al romper el** — at daybreak. (b) (*Eccl*) alb.

albacea *nmf* executor, (*f*) executrix.

albaceteño 1 *adj* of Albacete. **2** *nm*, **albaceteña** *nf* native (*or* inhabitant) of Albacete; **los** —**s** the people of Albacete.

albahaca *nf* basil.

albanega *nf* hairnet.

albanés 1 *adj* Albanian. **2** *nm*, **albanesa** *nf* Albanian. **3** *nm* (*language*) Albanian.

Albania *f* Albania.

albañal *nm* drain, sewer; (*Agr*) dung heap.

albañil *nm* bricklayer, mason.

albañilería *nf* brickwork, masonry; bricklaying, building.

albaquía *nf* balance due, remainder.

albar *adj* white.

albarán *nm* (*Comm*) delivery note, invoice; white cloth (*in a window*, = "to let" sign).

albarda *nf* packsaddle; (*SAm*) saddle; — **sobre** — piling it on, with a lot of unnecessary repetition; ¡como ahora lleven —**s**! (*fam*) not on your life!

albardar [1a] *vt* to saddle, put a packsaddle on.

albardear [1a] *vt* (*fam*, *CAm*) to bother, vex.

albardilla *nf* (a) small saddle; cushion, pad. (b) (*Archit*) coping. (c) (*Cook*) lard; batter.

albareque *nm* dragnet, trawl.

albaricoque *nm* apricot.

albaricoquero *nm* apricot tree.

albatros *nm*, *pl* **albatros** albatross.

albayalde *nm* white lead.

albazo *nm* (*Ec*, *Mex*: *Mil*) dawn raid; (*Arg*) dawn visit.

albeador *nm* (*Arg*) early riser.

albear [1a] *vi* (*Arg*) to get up at dawn, get up early.

albedrío *nm* free will; whim, fancy; pleasure; **al** — **de uno** at one's pleasure, just as one likes, to suit oneself.

albéitar *nm* veterinary surgeon, veterinarian (*US*).

albeitería *nf* veterinary medicine.

alberca *nf* cistern, tank, reservoir; (*SAm*) swimming pool.

albérchigo *nm* (clingstone) peach; (clingstone) peach tree.

albergar [1h] **1** *vt* to shelter, give shelter to; to lodge, put up. **2 albergarse** *vr* to shelter; to lodge, stay.

albergue *nm* shelter, refuge; lodging; (*Zool*) lair, den; (*Mountaineering*) refuge, mountain hut; — **de carretera** roadhouse; — **para jóvenes** youth hostel; **dar** — **a uno** to give someone lodging, take someone in.

albero 1 *adj* white. **2** *nm* (a) pipeclay. (b) dishcloth, tea towel.

Alberto *m* Albert.

albillo *adj* white.

albina *nf* salt lake, salt marsh.

albinismo *nm* albinism.

albino 1 *adj* albino. **2** *nm*, **albina** *nf* albino.

Albión *f* Albion.

albis: quedarse en — not to know a thing, not have a clue.

albo *adj* (*lit*) white.

albogue *nm* rustic flute, shepherd's flute; bagpipes; —**s** cymbals.

albóndiga *nf* rissole, meatball.

albondigón *nm* hamburger.

albor *nm* (a) whiteness. (b) dawn, dawn light; — **de la vida** childhood, youth; —**es** dawn; **a los** —**es** at dawn.

alborada *nf* dawn; (*Mil*) reveille; (*Poet*, *Mus*) aubade, dawn song.

alborear [1a] *vi* to dawn.

albornoz *nm* (a) burnous(e). (b) bathing wrap, bathrobe.

alborotadamente *adv* excitedly; noisily, roughly; riotously.

alborotadizo *adj* turbulent; excitable, nervy, jumpy.

alborotado *adj* (a) agitated, excited; noisy, rough; mutinous, riotous. (b) hasty, rash.

alborotador 1 *adj* turbulent, rebellious; boisterous, noisy; mischief-making.
   2 *nm*, **alborotadora** *nf* agitator, troublemaker; mischief-maker; rioter.

alborotar [1a] **1** *vt* (a) to disturb, agitate, stir up; to incite to rebel.
   (b) to excite, arouse the curiosity of.
   2 *vi* to make a racket, make a row.
   3 alborotarse *vr* (*person*) to get excited, get worked up; (*mob etc*) to riot, become violent; (*sea*) to get rough; (*CAm*) to become amorous; (*Chi, RPl: horse*) to rear up.

alboroto *nm* (a) disturbance, racket, row, uproar; brawl; riot. (b) scare, shock, alarm. (c) —s (*CAm, Col*) popcorn.

alborotoso (*Ant, Col, Per*) **1** *adj* troublesome, rebellious. **2** *nm*, **alborotosa** *nf* troublemaker.

alborozado *adj* jubilant, overjoyed.

alborozar [1f] **1** *vt* to gladden, fill with joy. **2 alborozarse** *vr* to be overjoyed, rejoice.

alborozo *nm* joy, merriment.

albricias *nfpl* (a) reward (to someone bringing good news); **en — de** as a token of. (b) (*as interj*) good news!, listen to this!; congratulations!

álbum *nm*, *pl* **álbums** *or* **álbumes** album; **— de recortes** scrapbook; **— de sellos** stamp album.

albumen *nm* white of egg; (*Bot*) albumen.

albúmina *nf* (*Chem*) albumin.

albuminoso *adj* albuminous.

albur *nm* (a) (*Fish*) dace. (b) chance, risk; (*Mex*) pun; (*PR*) lie.

albura *nf* whiteness; white of egg.

alburear [1a] **1** *vt* (*CR*) to disturb, upset. **2** *vi* (a) (*Col*) to make money, get rich; (*Cu*) to line one's pockets. (b) (*Mex*) to pun, make a pun.

alca *nf* razorbill.

alcabala *nf* (*Hist*) sales tax.

alcachofa *nf* artichoke.

alcahueta *nf* procuress; go-between; gossip.

alcahuete *nm* (a) procurer, pimp; go-between; front man, receiver (of stolen goods). (b) (*Theat*) drop-curtain.

alcahuetear [1a] *vi* to procure, pimp; to act as a go-between; to act as front man, be a receiver (of stolen goods).

alcahuetería *nf* procuring, pimping; —s pimping.

alcaide *nm* (*Hist: of castle, prison*) governor; warder, jailer.

alcaidía *nf* (*Hist*) governorship.

alcalde *nm* mayor; (*SAm*) procurer, pimp; **ser el — Ronquillo** to be completely hoarse; **tener el padre —** to have influence.

alcaldear [1a] *vi* (*fam*) to lord it, be bossy.

alcaldesa *nf* mayoress.

alcaldía *nf* mayoralty, office of mayor; mayor's office.

álcali *nm* alkali.

alcalino *adj* alkaline.

alcaloide *nm* alkaloid.

alcamonías *fpl* (a) aromatic seeds (for seasoning). (b) (*fam*) pimping.

alcance *nm* (a) reach; **estar al — de uno** to be within one's reach, (*fig*) be within one's powers; **el que está más al —** the one which is nearest, the one which is most readily accessible; **estar fuera del — de uno** to be out of one's reach, be beyond one's reach, (*fig*) to be over one's head, be inaccessible; **poner el coche al — de todos** to put the car within the reach of everybody, make the car accessible to all; **al — del oído** within earshot; **al — de la voz** within call.
   (b) (*Mil etc*) range; (*fig*) scope; grasp; importance, significance; **al — within** range; **de gran —** (*Mil*) long-range, (*fig*) far-reaching.
   (c) chase, pursuit; **dar — a** to catch up (with), overtake; **seguir el — a** (*Mil*) to pursue; **andar** (*or* **ir**) **a los —s de uno** to press close on someone, be on someone's tracks; **andar** (*or* **ir**) **en los —s a uno** to spy on someone.
   (d) (*Fin*) adverse balance, deficit.
   (e) (*Typ*) stop-press (news).
   (f) intelligence, capacity; **de cortos —s** of limited intelligence, not very bright.
   (g) **buzón de —** late-collection postbox.

alcancía *nf* moneybox; (*Arg, Eccl*) collection box, poorbox.

alcancil *nm* (*Arg*) procurer, pimp.

alcándara *nf* clothes rack; (*Orn*) perch.

alcandora *nf* beacon.

alcanfor *nm* camphor; (*SAm*) procurer, pimp.

alcanforado 1 *adj* camphorated. **2** *nm* (*SAm*) procurer, pimp.

alcanforar [1a] **1** *vt* to camphorate. **2 alcanforarse** *vr* (*CAm, Col, Ven*) to disappear, vanish away.

alcantarilla *nf* sewer, drain; culvert, conduit; (*Mex, Ven*) public fountain.

alcantarillado *nm* sewer system, drains.

alcantarillar [1a] *vt* to lay sewers in, provide drains for.

alcanzadizo *adj* easy to reach, easily reachable, accessible.

alcanzado *adj* hard up, broke (*fam*).

alcanzar [1f] **1** *vt* (a) to catch, catch up (with); to overtake; **train, post** to catch; **cuando le alcancé** when I caught up with him; **no nos alcanzarán nunca** they'll never catch us.
   (b) (*of bullet etc*) to hit, strike; **un obús alcanzó la lancha** the launch was hit by a shell; **el presidente fue alcanzado por 2 balas** the president was struck by 2 bullets.
   (c) to reach; to amount to; **la producción ha alcanzado las 20 toneladas** production has reached 20 tons; **el libro ha alcanzado 20 ediciones** the book has run into 20 editions; **las montañas alcanzan los 5.000 m** the mountains rise to 5,000 m.
   (d) (*of senses*) to reach to, perceive, take in.
   (e) to live into the period of, live on into the time of.
   (f) to grasp, catch hold of; *job* to get, obtain.
   (g) *problem* to grasp, understand.
   (h) (*Bol, Col, Per, RPl*) to pass, hand over, put within reach.
   2 *vi* (a) to reach, extend (*a, hasta* to, as far as); **— para todos** to be enough (for everybody), go round.
   (b) **— a + infin** to manage to + *infin*; **no alcanzo a ver cómo . . .** I can't see how . . .; **no alcanza a hacerlo** he can't manage to do it.

alcaparra *nf* (*Bot*) caper.

alcaraván *nm* stone-curlew.

alcaravea *nf* caraway.

alcarreño 1 *adj* of La Alcarria. **2** *nm*, **alcarreña** *nf* native (*or* inhabitant) of La Alcarria; **los —s** the people of La Alcarria.

alcatraz *nm* gannet, solan goose.

alcaudón *nm* shrike.

alcayata *nf* meat hook, spike; (*Tech*) tenterhook.

alcazaba *nf* citadel, castle.

alcázar *nm* fortress, citadel; royal palace; (*Naut*) quarter-deck.

alcazuz *nm* liquorice.

alce[1] *nm* (*Zool*) elk, moose; **— de América** moose.

alce[2] *nm* (*Cards*) cut; **no dar — a uno** (*Arg*) to give someone no respite; to give someone no chance to do something.

alción *nm* kingfisher, (*classical*) halcyon.

alcista (*Comm, Fin*) **1** *adj*: **mercado —** bull market, rising market; **la tendencia —** the upward tendency, the upward trend. **2** *nm* bull, speculator.

alcoba *nf* (a) bedroom; **— de huéspedes** spare room, guest bedroom. (b) suite of bedroom furniture.

alcohol *nm* alcohol; **— absoluto** absolute alcohol, pure alcohol; **— desnaturalizado, — metilado, metílico, — de quemar** methylated spirit; **lámpara de —** spirit lamp.

alcohólico 1 *adj* alcoholic; **no — ** *drink* non-alcoholic, soft. **2** *nm*, **alcohólica** *nf* alcoholic.

alcoholismo *nm* alcoholism.

alcoholista *nmf* (*Arg*) drunk (*fam*), alcoholic.

alcoholizado *nm*, **alcoholizada** *nf* alcoholic; **morir —** to die of alcoholism.

alcoholizar [1f] **1** *vt* to alcoholize. **2 alcoholizarse** *vr* (*Arg*) to drink heavily.

alcor *nm* hill.

Alcorán *nm* Koran.

alcornoque *nm* (a) cork tree, cork oak. (b) (*fam*) idiot.

alcorza *nf* (*Cook*) icing, sugar paste; (*Arg*) crybaby, sensitive soul.

alcorzar [1f] *vt* (*Cook*) to ice.

alcotán *nm* (*Orn*) lanner, hobby.

alcotana *nf* pickaxe, mattock.

alcubilla *nf* cistern, reservoir.

alcucero *adj* sweet-toothed; (*fig*) greedy.

alcurnia *nf* ancestry, lineage; **de noble —** of noble family, of noble birth.

alcuza *nf* olive-oil bottle; (*SAm*) cruet, cruet stand.

alcuzcuz *nm* couscous.

aldaba *nf* (door) knocker; bolt, latch, crossbar; hitching ring; **tener buenas —s** to have influence, have friends in the right places.

aldabada nf knock (on the door); **dar —s en to** knock at.
aldabilla nf latch.
aldabón nm large (door) knocker; handle.
aldabonazo nm bang, loud knock (on the door); **dar —s en to** bang at.
aldea nf (small) village, hamlet.
aldeano 1 adj village (attr); (fig) rustic, rude; **gente aldeana** country people, village people.
2 nm, **aldeana** nf villager; **los —s** the villagers, the village people.
aldehuela nf hamlet.
aldeorrio nm backward little place, rural backwater.
alderredor adv = **alrededor**.
aleación nf alloy.
alear[1] [1a] vt (Tech) to alloy.
alear[2] [1a] vi to flutter, flap (its wings); to move one's arms up and down; (Med) to convalesce, recuperate.
aleatorio adj accidental, fortuitous; uncertain.
alebrarse [1k] vr to lie flat, squat; (fig) to cower.
aleccionador adj instructive, enlightening.
aleccionamiento nm instruction, enlightenment; training.
aleccionar [1a] vt to instruct, enlighten, teach a lesson to; to train.
alechado adj (SAm) milky, like milk; mixed with milk.
alechugado adj pleated; frilled, frilly; curled, curly.
alechugar [1h] vt to fold, pleat; to frill; to curl.
aledaño 1 adj adjoining, bordering. 2 nm boundary, limit; **—s** outskirts.
alegación nf allegation; (Arg, Mex, PR) argument.
alegar [1h] **1** vt (a) to allege; **— que . . . to** allege that . . .; to claim that . . ., plead that . . . (also Law).
(b) difficulties etc to plead; authority to quote, bring up, state; reason to put forward, adduce.
(c) (SAm) to argue against, dispute.
2 vi (SAm) to argue.
alegato nm (a) allegation, claim. (b) (Law) bill (of indictment); plea, argument.
alegoría nf allegory.
alegóricamente adv allegorically.
alegórico adj allegoric(al).
alegorizar [1f] vt to allegorize.
alegrador 1 adj cheering. 2 nm spill.
alegrar [1a] **1** vt (a) to cheer (up), gladden; to make merry, make happy; **esta noticia alegró a todos** this news cheered everyone up, this news made everyone happy.
(b) to enliven, cheer up, brighten up; fire to stir up, make brighter.
(c) bull to excite, stir up.
(d) (Naut) rope to slacken.
2 **alegrarse** vr (a) (state) to be glad, be happy, rejoice; **me alegro muchísimo** I'm delighted; **—con, — de, — por** to be glad about, rejoice at; **— de + infin** to be glad to + infin, be happy to + infin; **me alegro de saberlo** I am glad to hear it; **me alegro de que lo hayas hecho** I am glad you've done it.
(b) (act) to cheer up (de at); **con esto empezó a —** at this he began to cheer up.
(c) (fam) to get merry (fam), get tight.
alegre adj (a) person (state) happy, merry, glad; (temperament) cheerful, gay, sunny; face etc happy; music etc merry, gay, cheerful; news good, cheering; colour bright, gay; day, period happy; (of weather) cheerful, bright, pleasant; **— de corazón** light-hearted.
(b) bold, reckless.
(c) joke risqué, blue.
(d) life fast, immoral.
(e) (fam) **estar —** to be merry, be tight.
alegremente adv happily, merrily; cheerfully, gaily; brightly; recklessly.
alegría nf (a) happiness, joy; gladness; cheerfulness; gaiety, merriment; brightness; **¡qué —!** how marvellous!, that's splendid!; **— vital** joie de vivre; **saltar de —** to jump with joy, jump for joy.
(b) **—s** public rejoicings, festivities.
alegrón nm (a) (of fire) sudden blaze, flare-up.
(b) (fig) sudden joy.
alegrona nf (SAm) prostitute.
alejamiento nm (a) (act) removal; withdrawal; estrangement. (b) (state) distance, remoteness; aloofness.
alejar [1a] **1** vt (a) to remove, move away (de from), move to a distance; danger to remove; **conviene — tales libros de los niños** such books should be kept

away from children, such books should be kept out of children's hands.
(b) (fig) to cause a rift between, separate, estrange.
2 **alejarse** vr to move away, go away (de from); to move to a distance; (of danger) to recede; **alejémonos un poco más** let's go a bit further away.
Alejandría Alexandria.
alejandrino nm alexandrine.
Alejandro m Alexander; **— Magno** Alexander the Great.
alelado adj stupefied, bewildered; foolish, stupid.
alelamiento nm bewilderment; foolishness, stupidity.
alelar [1a] **1** vt to stupefy; to bewilder. 2 **alelarse** vr to be stupefied, be bewildered; to look foolish, gape stupidly.
aleluya 1 nm or f hallelujah.
2 nm Easter time.
3 nf Easter print; (fam: Poet) doggerel; (fam: Art) daub, bad painting; (SAm) frivolous excuse; (Bol) spoiled child; thing that one loves excessively; **estar de —** to rejoice.
alemán 1 adj German. 2 nm, **alemana** nf German. 3 nm (language) German.
Alemania f Germany.
alentada nf big breath, deep breath.
alentado adj brave; proud, haughty; (Arg) strong, vigorous.
alentador adj encouraging.
alentar [1k] **1** vt (a) to encourage, cheer, inspire; resistance to stiffen, bolster up; spirits to raise, buoy up; **— a uno a hacer algo** to encourage someone to do something; to inspire someone to do something.
(b) (Col, Ec) to clap, applaud.
2 **alentarse** vr (a) to take heart, cheer up.
(b) (Med) to get well.
(c) (CAm, Col) to give birth (de to).
alerce nm larch, larch tree.
alergia nf allergy.
alérgico adj allergic (a to).
alero nm (Archit) eaves; gable-end; (Aut) mudguard, fender (US), wing.
alerón nm aileron.
alerta 1 interj watch out!
2 adv and adj alert, watchful; **estar —, estar ojo —** to be on the alert, stand by, watch out; **todos los servicios de auxilio están —** all the rescue services are on the alert.
3 nm alert.
aleta nf (Orn etc) wing, small wing; (Aut) wing, mudguard, fin; (of propeller) blade; (of fish) fin; (of seal) flipper; (sl: hand) mitt, flipper (sl).
aletargado adj drowsy, lethargic; benumbed.
aletargamiento nm drowsiness, lethargy; numbness.
aletargar [1h] **1** vt to make drowsy, make lethargic; to numb.
2 **aletargarse** vr to grow drowsy, become lethargic; to get numb.
aletazo nm wingbeat, flap (of the wing); movement of the fin.
aletear [1a] vi to flutter, flap its wings; to move its fins.
aleteo nm fluttering, flapping (of the wings); movements of the fins; (fig) palpitation.
aleudar [1a] **1** vt to leaven, ferment with yeast.
2 **aleudarse** vr to rise.
aleve adj treacherous.
alevín nm fish nursery, fish-breeding station.
alevino nm (Arg) young fish, fry (for restocking rivers etc).
alevosía nf treachery.
alevoso 1 adj treacherous. 2 nm traitor.
alfa[1] nf (letter) alpha.
alfa[2] nf (SAm) lucerne, alfalfa.
alfabéticamente adv alphabetically.
alfabético adj alphabetic(al).
alfabetización nf teaching people to read and write; **campaña de —** literacy campaign, drive to teach people to read and write.
alfabetizado adj literate, that can read and write.
alfabetizar [1f] vt (a) to alphabetize, arrange alphabetically. (b) person to make literate, teach to read and write.
alfabeto nm alphabet; **— Morse** Morse code.
alfajor nm (a) (Arg, Per) a kind of pastry. (b) (RPl) = **facón**.
alfalfa nf lucerne, alfalfa.
alfandoque nm (a) (Ant, CAm, Mex) a kind of pastry. (b) (CAm, Col) maraca-like instrument. (c) (Col, Per) toffee-like almond paste.
alfanje nm cutlass; (Fish) swordfish.
alfaque nm (Naut) bar, bank, shoal.

alfar *nm* (a) pottery, potter's workshop. (b) clay.
alfarería *nf* pottery; pottery shop.
alfarero *nm* potter.
alfarjía *nf* door frame, window frame; batten.
alféizar *nm* (*Archit*) splay, embrasure; sill, window-sill, ledge.
alfeñicado *adj* weakly, delicate.
alfeñicarse [1g] *vr* (*fam*) (a) to get terribly thin, look frail.
  (b) to act affectedly, be overnice; to be very prim and proper.
alfeñique *nm* (a) toffee-like paste, almond-flavoured sugar paste.
  (b) (*fam*) delicate person; mollycoddle, sissy; very thin person.
  (c) affectation; primness; excessive delicacy.
alferecía *nf* epilepsy.
alférez *nm* (*Mil*) second lieutenant, subaltern; (*SAm: Eccl*) official standard bearer (in processions); — **de fragata** (*Naut*) midshipman; — **de navío** (*Naut*) sub-lieutenant.
alfil *nm* (*Chess*) bishop.
alfiler *nm* pin; brooch, clip; —**es** pin money, dress allowance; — **de corbata** tiepin; — **de gancho** (*Arg*) safety pin; — **de seguridad** safety pin; — **de sombrero** hatpin; **aquí ya no cabe ni un** — you can't squeeze anything else in; **pedir para** —**es** to ask for a tip; **prendido con** —**es** shaky, hardly hanging together; **vestido con 25** —**es** dressed up to the nines.
alfilerar [1a] *vt* to pin together, pin up.
alfilerazo *nm* pinprick (*also fig*).
alfilerillo *nm* (*Arg, Chi, Per*) grass, green pasture.
alfiletero *nm* needle case; pincushion.
alfolí *nm* granary; salt warehouse.
alfombra *nf* carpet; rug, mat; — **de baño** bathmat.
alfombrado *nm* carpeting.
alfombrar [1a] *vt* to carpet (*also fig*).
alfombrero *nm* carpet maker.
alfombrilla *nf* (a) rug, mat. (b) (*Med*) German measles; (*Cu*) rash; (*Mex*) smallpox.
alfonsí *adj* Alphonsine (*esp re Alfonso X, 1252-84*).
alfonsino *adj* Alphonsine (*esp re recent kings of Spain named Alfonso*).
Alfonso *m* Alphonso; — **el Sabio** Alphonso the Wise (1252-84).
alforfón *nm* buckwheat.
alforja *nf* saddlebag; knapsack; —**s** (*fig*) provisions (for a journey); **pasarse a la otra** — (*Arg, Chi*) to get too familiar; **sacar los pies de las** —**s** to go off on a different tack.
alforjudo *adj* (*Chi*) silly, stupid.
alforza *nf* pleat, tuck; (*fig*) slash, scar.
alforzar [1f] *vt* (*Sew*) to pleat, tuck.
Alfredo *m* Alfred.
alga *nf* seaweed, alga.
algaida *nf* (*Bot*) bush, undergrowth; (*Geog*) dune.
algalia *nf* civet.
algarabía *nf* (a) Arabic.
  (b) (*fig, fam*) gibberish; gabble; din, hullabaloo (*fam*).
  (c) (*Bot*) cornflower.
algarada *nf* outcry; **hacer una** —, **levantar una** — to kick up a tremendous fuss.
algarroba *nf* carob, carob bean.
algarrobo *nm* carob tree, locust tree.
algazara *nf* din, clamour, uproar.
álgebra *nf* algebra.
algebraico *adj* algebraic.
algecireño 1 *adj* of Algeciras. 2 *nm*, **algecireña** *nf* native (*or* inhabitant) of Algeciras; **los** —**s** the people of Algeciras.
álgido *adj* icy, cold, chilly; (*fig*) point *etc* culminating, decisive; most intense.
algo 1 *pron* (a) something; **habrá** — **para ti** there will be something for you; **esto es** — **nuevo** this is something new; — **es** — something is better than nothing; **eso ya es** — that's something; **¡por** — **será!** there must be a reason behind it, he (*etc*) can't have done it for no reason at all; **tomar** — to have a drink.
  (b) (*in interrog and neg sentences*) anything; **¿pasa** —? is anything the matter?; **¿hay** — **para mí?** is there anything for me?
  2 *adv* rather, somewhat, a bit; **es** — **difícil** it's rather hard, it's a bit awkward.
  3 *nm* (*Col*) snack, something to eat.
algodón *nm* cotton; wadding; (*Med*) swab; (*Bot*) cotton plant; — **hidrófilo** cotton wool, absorbent cotton (*US*); — **pólvora** guncotton; — **en rama** raw cotton, cotton wool; **se crió entre** —**es** he was always pampered; he was brought up in luxury.

algodonal *nm* cotton plantation.
algodonar [1a] *vt* to stuff with cotton wool, wad.
algodoncillo *nm* milkweed.
algodonero 1 *adj* cotton (*attr*). 2 *nm* (a) cotton grower; cotton dealer. (b) (*Bot*) cotton plant.
algodonosa *nf* cotton grass.
algodonoso *adj* cottony.
alguacil *nm* (*Hist*) governor; bailiff, constable; (*Taur*) mounted official.
alguien *pron* someone, somebody; anybody; **si** — **viene** if somebody comes, if anybody comes; **¿viste a** —? did you see anybody?; **para** — **que conozca la materia** for anyone who is familiar with the subject.
alguito (*SAm*) = **algo**.
alguno 1 *adj* (**algún** *before m sing noun*) (a) (*before n*) some, any; **algún obispo lo dijo** some bishop said so; **algún coche lo tiene ya** some cars already have it; **hubo algunas dificultades** there were some difficulties; there were a few difficulties; **algún libro que otro** some book or other; **leo algún libro que otro** I read an occasional book, I read a book from time to time; **por alguna que otra razón** for some reason or other.
  (b) (*preceded by negative, after n*) no, not . . . any; **no tiene talento** — he has no talent, he hasn't any talent, he has no talent at all; **sin interés** — without the slightest interest.
  2 *pron* (a) some; one; someone, somebody; — **es bueno** some are good, an occasional one is good; — **de ellos** one of them; — **que otro** one or two, an occasional one; — **dijo que** . . . someone said that . . .; **busco** — **que me ayude** I'm looking for someone to help me.
  (b) —**s** some; a few; —**s son buenos** some are good; **vimos** —**s** we saw some; we saw a few; —**s hay que** . . . there are some who . . .
alhaja *nf* (a) jewel, gem; precious object, treasure; fine piece (*of furniture*).
  (b) (*fig: person*) treasure, gem; **¡buena** —! (*iro*) what a rogue!
alhajado *adj* (*Col*) wealthy.
alhajar [1a] *vt* room to furnish, appoint (*in delicate taste*).
alhajera *nf* (*Arg*) jewel box.
alharaca *nf* fuss; **hacer** —**s** to make a fuss, make a great song and dance about something.
alharaquiento *adj* demonstrative, highly emotional.
alhelí *nm* wallflower, stock.
alheña *nf* (a) (*Bot*) privet; privet flower; (*dye*) henna. (b) blight, mildew.
alheñar [1a] 1 *vt* (a) to dye with henna. (b) to blight, cover with mildew. 2 **alheñarse** *vr* to become mildewed, get covered in mildew.
alhóndiga *nf* corn exchange.
alhucema *nf* lavender.
aliacán *nm* jaundice.
aliado 1 *adj* allied. 2 *nm*, **aliada** *nf* ally; **los A**—**s** the Allies.
alianza *nf* (a) alliance; **A**— (*Bib*) Covenant; **A**— **para el Progreso** Alliance for Progress; **Santa A**— Holy Alliance. (b) engagement ring, wedding ring.
aliar [1c] 1 *vt* to ally, bring into an alliance. 2 **aliarse** *vr* to ally oneself; to become allied, form an alliance.
alias 1 *adv* alias. 2 *nm* alias.
alicaído *adj* (*Med*) drooping, weak; (*fig*) downcast, depressed.
alicantina *nf* trick, ruse.
alicantino 1 *adj* of Alicante. 2 *nm*, **alicantina** *nf* native (*or* inhabitant) of Alicante; **los** —**s** the people of Alicante.
alicates *nmpl* pliers, pincers.
Alicia *f* Alice; "— **en el país de las maravillas**" "Alice in Wonderland"; "— **en el país del espejo**" "Alice through the Looking-glass".
aliciente *nm* incentive, inducement; lure; attraction; **ofrecer un** — to hold out an inducement; **ofrece el** — **de** . . . it holds out the attraction of . . .
alicorarse [1a] *vr* (*Col*) to get boozed.
alicrejo *nm* (*CAm*) spider-like creature; (*hum*) old horse, nag.
alicurco *adj* (*Chi*) sly, sharp.
alienación *nf* alienation; (*Med*) alienation, mental derangement.
alienado 1 *adj* insane, mentally ill. 2 *nm*, **alienada** *nf* lunatic, mad person.
alienar [1a] *vt see* **enajenar**.
alienista *nmf* specialist in mental illness, psychiatrist.
aliento *nm* (a) (*un* —) breath; (*in general*) breathing, respiration; — **fétido** bad breath; **de un** — in one breath, (*fig*) in one go; **aguantar el** —, **contener el** — to hold one's breath; **dar los últimos** —**s** to

breathe one's last; **estar sin —** to be out of breath; **le huele mal el —** his breath smells; **tomar —** to take breath.

(**b**) (*fig*) courage, spirit; strength; **cobrar —** to take heart; **dar — a uno** to encourage someone, give someone courage.

alifafe *nm* (*fam*) ailment.

aligación *nf* alloy; (*fig*) bond, tie.

aligeramiento *nm* lightening; easing, alleviation.

aligerar [1a] **1** *vt* to lighten; to ease, relieve, alleviate; to shorten; *pace* to quicken.

2 aligerarse *vr* to get lighter; **— de ropa** to put on lighter clothing.

aligustre *nm* privet.

alijar[1] [1a] *vt* (*Tech*) to sandpaper.

alijar[2] [1a] *vt* to lighten; *ship* to unload; *contraband* to land, smuggle ashore.

alijo *nm* (**a**) lightening; unloading. (**b**) contraband, collection of smuggled goods; **— de armas** consignment of smuggled arms, cache of arms.

alilaya 1 *nf* (*Col, Cu*) flimsy excuse. **2** *nmf* (*Mex*) cunning person, sharp individual; troublemaker.

alimaña *nf* (destructive, objectionable) animal; **—s** (*freq*) vermin, pests.

alimañero *nm* (*fam*) bug-hunter (*fam*); vermin officer, pest controller.

alimentación *nf* (**a**) feeding, nourishment; food; (*fig*) nurture, fostering; **el coste de la —** the cost of food; **la — de los niños** the feeding of children, the nourishment of children; **— insuficiente** malnutrition, undernourishment.

(**b**) (*Tech*) feed; supply; **bomba de —** feed pump.

alimentador *nm* (*Tech*) feed, feeder.

alimentar [1a] **1** *vt* (**a**) to feed, (*more generally*) nourish.

(**b**) (*fig*) *family* to maintain, support; to bring up, nurture; *hope* to nourish, encourage; to cherish; *feeling* to foster; *passion* to feed, add fuel to.

(**c**) (*Tech*) to feed; *furnace* to feed, stoke (**de** with); **— una máquina de algo** to feed something into a machine.

2 alimentarse *vr* to feed (**con, de** on).

alimenticio *adj* (**a**) nourishing, nutritive. (**b**) food (*attr*); **artículos —s** foodstuffs; **valor —** food value, nutritional value.

alimentista *nmf* pensioner.

alimento *nm* (**a**) food; nourishment. (**b**) (*fig*) encouragement, support; incentive; (*of passion*) fuel. (**c**) **—s** (*Law*) alimony.

alimentoso *adj* nourishing.

alindado *adj* foppish, dandified.

alindar[1] [1a] *vt* to embellish, make pretty, make look nice; *person* to doll up, prettify.

alindar[2] [1a] **1** *vt land* to mark off, mark out. **2** *vi* to adjoin, be adjacent.

alinderar [1a] *vt* (*Chi, Hond*) to mark out the boundaries of, set up the boundary marks of.

alineación *nf* (**a**) (*Tech*) alignment; **estar fuera de —** to be out of alignment, be out of true. (**b**) (*Sport etc*) line-up.

alineado *adj*: **está — con el partido** he is in line with the party; **las naciones no alineadas** the uncommitted nations.

alineamiento *nm* = **alineación**.

alinear [1a] **1** *vt* to align; to line up, put into line; (*Mil*) to form up; (*fig*) to bring into line (**con** with).

2 alinearse *vr* to line up; (*Mil*) to fall in, form up; **se alinearon a lo largo de la calle** they lined up along the street.

aliñador *nm* (*Chi*) bonesetter.

aliñar [1a] *vt* (**a**) to adorn, embellish. (**b**) to prepare; (*Cook*) to dress, season. (**c**) (*Chi*) *bone* to set.

aliño *nm* (**a**) adornment, embellishment; preparation. (**b**) (*Cook*) dressing, seasoning.

alionar [1a] *vt* (*Arg, Chi*) to stir up.

alionín *nm* blue tit.

alipego *nm* (*CAm*) extra, bonus (*added as part of a sale*); (*fam*) gatecrasher, intruder, person who comes uninvited.

aliquebrado *adj* crestfallen.

alisador *nm* (*person*) polisher; (*tool*) smoothing blade, smoothing tool.

alisadura *nf* smoothing, polishing; **—s** cuttings, shavings.

alisar[1] [1a] *vt* to smooth (down); to polish, burnish; *hair* to smooth, sleek; (*Tech*) to polish, finish, surface.

alisar[2] *nm*, **aliseda** *nf* alder grove.

alisios *nmpl* (*also* **vientos —**) trade winds.

aliso *nm* alder, alder tree.

alistamiento *nm* enrolment; (*Mil*) enlistment, recruitment.

alistar [1a] **1** *vt* (**a**) to list, put on a list; *member* to enrol; (*Mil*) to enlist.

(**b**) to prepare, make ready; (*Naut*) to clear for action.

2 alistarse *vr* (**a**) to enrol; (*Mil*) to enlist, join up. (**b**) (*SAm*) to get dressed, get ready (to go out).

aliteración *nf* alliteration.

aliterado *adj* alliterative.

alitranca *nf* (*Chi, Per*) brake, braking device.

aliviadero *nm* overflow channel (*on dam*).

aliviar [1b] **1** *vt* (**a**) to lighten; to ease, relieve; to make more bearable; to soothe; **— a uno de algo** to relieve someone of something.

(**b**) to speed up; *pace* to quicken.

2 aliviarse *vr* (**a**) (*of pain*) to diminish, become more bearable; (*of patient*) to gain relief; to get better, recover; **¡que se alivie!** get better soon!

(**b**) (*fig*) to unburden oneself (*de* of).

alivio *nm* alleviation, relief, easing; mitigation; improvement; (*Med*) relief; **— de luto** half-mourning; **¡que siga el —!** I hope you continue to improve!

aljaba *nf* (**a**) quiver. (**b**) (*Arg*) fuchsia.

aljama *nf* (*Hist*) (**a**) Moorish quarter; Jewish quarter, ghetto. (**b**) mosque; synagogue. (**c**) gathering of Moors or Jews.

aljamía *nf* Spanish written in Arabic characters (14th-16th centuries).

aljamiado *adj*: **texto —** text of Spanish written in Arabic characters.

aljibe *nm* (**a**) cistern, tank; (*Naut*) water tender; (*Aut*) oil tanker; (*Col*) well. (**b**) (*Per*) dungeon, underground prison.

aljofaina *nf* washbasin, washbowl.

aljófar *nm* pearl; (*fig*) pearl of moisture; dewdrop.

aljofarar [1a] *vt* to bedew, cover with pearls of moisture.

aljofifa *nf* floorcloth.

aljofifar [1a] *vt* to wash, mop, mop up.

alma *nf* (**a**) soul; spirit; **¡hijo de mi —!** my precious child!

(**b**) (*phrases with verb*) **le arrancó el —** he was deeply shocked; **se le cayó el — a los pies** he was deeply moved; he became very disheartened; **se echó el — a las espaldas** he wasn't in the least worried; **entregar el —** to give up the ghost; **estar con el — en la boca** to be scared to death; **hablar al —** to speak most earnestly; **se le fue el — tras la muñeca** she fell for the doll, she would have sold her soul for the doll; **me llegó al —** it affected me deeply, it really struck home; **se le cayó el — al suelo, se le partió el —** she was heartbroken; **rendir el —** to give up the ghost; **romper el — a uno** (*fam*) to do someone in (*sl*); **rompe el — verlo** it breaks one's heart to see it; **lo siento en el —** I am truly sorry; **tener el — en un hilo** to have one's heart in one's mouth; **tener el — en su almario** to keep things to oneself; **tener mucha —**, **tener el — bien puesta** to be undaunted; **no tener —** to be pitiless; **le volvió el — al cuerpo** he calmed down; he recovered his composure.

(**c**) (*fam, comparisons*) **estar como — en pena** to suffer, be terribly sad; **estar como un — perdida** to be completely undecided; **ir como — que lleva el diablo** to go at breakneck speed.

(**d**) soul, person, inhabitant; **un pueblo de 2 mil —s** a village of 2,000 souls, a village of 2,000 inhabitants; **¡— mía!** my precious!, darling!; **— bendita** simple soul; **— de caballo** twister (*fam*); **— de Caín, — de Judas** fiend, devil; **¡— de cántaro!** you idiot!; **— de Dios** good soul; **ni — nacida, ni — viviente** not a single living soul.

(**e**) soul, moving spirit, leading spirit; (*of matter*) crux, heart, vital part; **él es el — del movimiento** he is the leading spirit of the movement; **es el — de la fiesta** he's the life and soul of the party.

(**f**) **con el —, con toda el —** with all one's heart, heart and soul; **lo haré con toda mi —** I'll do it with all my heart.

(**g**) (*Bol*) corpse.

(**h**) (*Bot*) pith; (*Tech*) core, heart; (*of cable*) core; (*of rope*) central strand; (*of gun*) bore.

almacén *nm* (**a**) warehouse, store; depository; **— de depósito** bonded warehouse; **tener algo en —** to have something in store, (*Comm*) to stock something.

(**b**) (*Mech, Mil etc*) magazine.

(**c**) shop, store; (*SAm*) *esp* grocer's (shop), grocery store; (**grandes**) **—es** department store; **A—es Pérez** Pérez Department Store.

almacenaje *nm* (**a**) storage, storing; **— frigorífico** cold storage. (**b**) storage charge, storage fee.

almacenar [1a] *vt* (**a**) to store, put into storage, keep in store; to stock up (with).
(**b**) (*fig*) to keep, collect, (*pej*) hoard; — **odio** to store up hatred.

almacenero *nm* storekeeper, warehouseman; (*SAm*) shopkeeper, *esp* grocer, grocer's assistant.

almacenista *nm* warehouse owner; (*SAm*) wholesale grocer.

almáciga *nf*, **almácigo** *nm* (*SAm*) plantation, nursery.

almádena *nf* sledgehammer, large hammer.

almadía *nf* raft.

almadiarse [1c] *vr* (*SAm*) to be sick, vomit.

almadraba *nf* tunny fishing; tunny fishery; tunny net(s).

almadreña *nf* wooden shoe, clog.

almagre *nm* red ochre.

almajara *nf* (*Agr*) hotbed, forcing frame.

alma máter *nf* alma mater.

almanaque *nm* almanac; **hacer** —**s** to muse; **echar a uno vendiendo** —**s** (*Arg*, *Bol*) to send someone away with a flea in his ear.

almariarse [1c] *vr* (*Arg*, *Guat*) to be sick, vomit.

almazara *nf* oil mill, oil press.

almeja *nf* shellfish, clam (*US*).

almenado *adj* battlemented, with battlements.

almenara *nf* beacon; chandelier.

almenas *nfpl* battlements.

almendra *nf* (**a**) (*Bot*) almond; — **amarga** bitter almond; — **garapiñada** praline, sugar almond; — **tostada** burnt almond.
(**b**) (*Bot*) kernel, stone.
(**c**) cut-glass drop (of chandelier *etc*).

almendrada *nf* almond milk shake, drink made with milk and almonds.

almendrado 1 *adj* almond-shaped, pear-shaped; **de ojos** —**s** almond-eyed. 2 *nm* macaroon.

almendral *nm* almond orchard.

almendrera *nf* almond tree.

almendrillo *nm* (*SAm*) almond tree.

almendro *nm* almond tree.

almendruco *nm* green almond.

almeriense 1 *adj* of Almería. 2 *nmf* native (*or* inhabitant) of Almería; **los** —**s** the people of Almería.

almete *nm* (*Hist*) helmet.

almiar *nm* haycock, hayrick.

almíbar *nm* syrup; **estar hecho un** — to be all sweet and kind, (*pej*) to overdo the sweetness.

almibarado *adj* syrupy; (*fig*) honeyed, over-sweet; **style**, **tone** sugary.

almibarar [1a] *vt* to preserve (*or* serve) in syrup; — **las palabras** to use honeyed words, overdo the sweetness.

almidón *nm* starch.

almidonado *adj* starched; (*fig*) stiff, starchy; dapper, spruce.

almidonar [1a] *vt* to starch; **los prefiero sin** — I prefer them unstarched.

almilla *nf* (**a**) bodice; undervest. (**b**) (*Tech*) tenon. (**c**) (*Cook*) breast of pork.

alminar *nm* minaret.

almirantazgo *nm* admiralty.

almirante *nm* admiral.

almirez *nm* mortar.

almizcle *nm* musk.

almizcleño *adj* musky.

almizclera *nf* muskrat, musquash.

almizclero *nm* musk deer.

almo *adj* (*poet*) nourishing; sacred, venerable.

almocafre *nm* weeding hoe.

almodrote *nm* cheese and garlic sauce; (*fig*) hotchpotch.

almofrés *nm*, **almofrez** *nm* (*SAm*) sleeping bag.

almohada *nf* pillow; bolster; cushion; pillowcase; — **neumática** air cushion; **aconsejarse con la** —, **consultar algo con la** — to sleep on something, think something over carefully.

almohade 1 *adj* Almohad(e). 2 —**s** *nmpl* Almohades.

almohadilla *nf* small cushion, small pillow; (*SAm*) holder (for iron *etc*); (*Sew*) pincushion; (*Tech*) pad, cushion; — **de entintar** inkpad.

almohadillado 1 *adj* padded; stuffed; *stone* dressed. 2 *nm* ashlar; dressed stone.

almohadón *nm* large pillow, bolster; (*Eccl*) hassock.

almohaza *nf* currycomb.

almohazar [1f] *vt horse* to brush down, groom; *skin* to dress.

almoneda *nf* auction; clearance sale.

almoned(e)ar [1a] *vt* to auction.

almorávide 1 *adj* Almoravid(e). 2 —**s** *nmpl* Almoravides.

almorranas *nfpl* (*Med*) piles.

almorzar [1f *and* 1m] 1 *vt* to have for lunch, lunch on; (*arch*, *and parts of SAm*) to have for second breakfast, breakfast late on.
2 *vi* to lunch, have lunch; (*arch*, *and parts of SAm*) to breakfast late, have second breakfast; **vengo almorzado** I've had lunch.

almuecín *nm*, **almuédano** *nm* muezzin.

almuercería *nf* (*Mex*) lunch counter, popular restaurant.

almuerzo *nm* (**a**) lunch, (*more formally*) luncheon; wedding breakfast; (*arch*, *and parts of SAm*) late breakfast, second breakfast.
(**b**) dinner service.

alnado *nm*, **alnada** *nf* stepchild.

aló *interj* (*Per*: *Tel*) hullo?

alocado 1 *adj* crazy, mad, wild; distracted. 2 *nm*, **alocada** *nf* madcap.

alocución *nf* allocution.

áloe *nm* (*Bot*) aloe; (*Pharm*) aloes.

alojado *nm* (*SAm*) guest, lodger.

alojamiento *nm* lodging(s); housing; (*Mil*: *act*) billeting, (*house*) billet, quarters; **buscarse** — to look for lodgings.

alojar [1a] 1 *vt* to lodge, accommodate, house; (*Mil*) to billet, quarter.
2 **alojarse** *vr* to lodge, be lodged; to stay; (*Mil*) to be billeted, be quartered; — **en** to lodge at, put up at; **la bala se alojó en el pulmón** the bullet lodged in the lung.

alón 1 *adj* (*SAm*) large-winged; *hat* broad-brimmed. 2 *nm* wing (of chicken *etc*).

alondra *nf* lark, skylark.

alongar [1m] 1 *vt* = **alargar**. 2 **alongarse** *vr* to move away.

alopecia *nf* alopecia.

alpaca *nf* alpaca.

alpargata *nf* rope-soled sandal, canvas sandal.

alpargatilla *nmf* crafty person.

alpende *nm* shed, lean-to.

Alpes *mpl* Alps.

alpestre *adj* Alpine; (*fig*) mountainous, rough, wild.

alpinismo *nm* mountaineering, climbing.

alpinista *nmf* mountaineer, climber.

alpino *adj* Alpine.

alpiste *nm* (**a**) birdseed, canary seed. (**b**) (*SAm*: *sl*) brass (*sl*); (*RPl*: *sl*) drink, booze.

alquería *nf* farmhouse, farmstead.

alquiladizo 1 *adj* (**a**) for rent, for hire, that can be rented (*or* hired). (**b**) (*pej*) hireling. 2 *nm*, **alquiladiza** *nf* hireling.

alquilado *nm*, **alquilada** *nf* (*PR*) servant.

alquilador *nm*, **alquiladora** *nf* renter, hirer; tenant, lessee.

alquilar [1a] 1 *vt* (**a**) (*subject: owner*) *house* to rent (out), let; *car*, *coach etc* to hire (out); *garage*, *TV* to rent (out).
(**b**) (*subject: renter etc*) *house* to rent; *car*, *coach etc* to hire; *garage*, *TV* to rent; "**por —**" "to let", "for rent" (*US*).
2 **alquilarse** *vr* (**a**) (*house*) to be let (en at, for); "**se alquila**" (*advert*) "to let", "for rent" (*US*); **aquí no se alquila casa alguna** there is no house to let here.
(**b**) (*taxi etc*) to be on hire, be out for hire.
(**c**) (*person*) to hire oneself out; (*PR*) to go into service.

alquiler *nm* (**a**) (*act*) letting, renting; hire, hiring; **de** — for hire, on hire.
(**b**) (*price*) rent, rental; hire charge; **control de** —**es** rent control; **exento de** —**es** rent-free; **pagar el** — to pay the rent; **subir el** — **a uno** to raise someone's rent.

alquimia *nf* alchemy.

alquimista *nm* alchemist.

alquitara *nf* still.

alquitarar [1a] *vt* to distil.

alquitrán *nm* tar; — **de hulla**, — **mineral** coal tar.

alquitranado 1 *adj* tarred, tarry. 2 *nm* tarmac; tarpaulin.

alquitranar [1a] *vt* to tar.

alrededor 1 *adv* around, about; **todo** — all around.
2 — **de** *prep* (**a**) around, about; **todo** — **de la iglesia** all around the church; **mirar** — **de sí** to look about one.
(**b**) (*fig*) about, in the region of; — **de 200** about 200.
3 *nm*: **mirar a su** — to look about one; —**es** surroundings, neighbourhood; (*of town*) outskirts, environs; (*of scene*, *place*) setting; **en los** —**es de Londres** in the outskirts of London; in the area round London.

Alsacia *f* Alsace.

Alsacia-Lorena f Alsace-Lorraine.
alsaciano 1 adj Alsatian. **2** nm, **alsaciana** nf Alsatian.
alta nf (Med) (certificate of) discharge from hospital; **dar a uno de** — to discharge someone from hospital, (Mil) to pass someone (as) fit; **darse de** — to join, become a member; (Med) to return to duty.
altamente adv highly, extremely.
altanería nf (a) haughtiness, disdain, arrogance. (b) hawking, falconry. (c) (Meteorol) upper air.
altanero adj (a) haughty, disdainful, arrogant. (b) bird high-flying.
altar nm altar; — **mayor** high altar; **conducir a una al** — to lead someone to the altar; **quedarse para adornar** —es to be on the shelf.
altavoz nm (Radio) loudspeaker; (Elec) amplifier.
altea nf mallow.
altear [1a] vt (RPl) to order to stop, command to halt.
alterabilidad nf changeability.
alteración nf (a) alteration, change.
   (b) upset, disturbance; (Med) irregularity of the pulse; — **del orden público** breach of the peace.
   (c) strong feeling, agitation.
   (d) quarrel, dispute.
alterado adj agitated, upset, disturbed; angry; (Med) upset, disordered.
alterar [1a] **1** vt (a) to alter, change; to change for the worse.
   (b) to upset, disturb; to cause a commotion in; peace, silence etc to disturb.
   (c) to stir up, excite, agitate; to irritate, anger.
   2 alterarse vr (a) to alter, change.
   (b) (food) to go bad, go off; (milk etc) to go sour.
   (c) (voice) to falter.
   (d) to get upset, become agitated, become disturbed; to get angry; **siguió sin** — he went on unabashed, he went on unmoved; **¡no te alteres!** don't upset yourself!, keep calm!; — **por algo** to get angry (or excited etc) about something.
altercación nf, **altercado** nm argument, altercation.
altercar [1g] vi to argue, quarrel, wrangle.
álter ego nm alter ego.
alternación nf alternation.
alternadamente adv alternately.
alternado adj alternate.
alternador nm (Elec) alternator.
alternante adj alternating.
alternar [1a] **1** vt to alternate; to vary.
   2 vi (a) to alternate (con with); (Tech) to alternate, reciprocate; to take turns, change about; to vary; **alternar a los mandos** to take turns at the controls.
   (b) to mix, take part in the social round; (sl) to go on a pub crawl (fam), go boozing; — **con un grupo** to mix with a group, go around with a group; — **con la gente bien** to hobnob with top people, to move in elevated circles; **tiene pocas ganas de** — he doesn't want to mix, he is disinclined to be sociable; — **de igual a igual** to be on an equal footing.
alternativa nf (a) alternative, option, choice; **no tener** — to have no alternative.
   (b) alternation; shift work, work done in relays; — **de cosechas** crop rotation.
   (c) ceremony by which a novice becomes a fully-qualified bullfighter; **tomar la** — to become a fully-qualified bullfighter.
   (d) —s ups and downs, vicissitudes, fluctuations; **las** —s **de la política** the ups and downs of politics.
alternativamente adv alternately.
alternativo adj alternating (also Elec); alternative, alternate.
alterno adj (Bot, Math etc) alternate.
altero nm (Mex), **alterón** nm (Col) heap, pile.
alteza nf (a) height.
   (b) sublimity; — **de miras** high-mindedness.
   (c) A— (title) Highness; **Su A—** Real His (or Her) Royal Highness; **sí, A—** yes, your Highness.
altibajos nmpl ups and downs (also fig).
altilocuencia nf grandiloquence.
altilocuente adj, **altílocuo** adj grandiloquent.
altillo nm (a) small hill, hillock. (b) (SAm) attic.
altimático adj: **cabina altimática** pressurized cabin.
altímetro nm altimeter.
altinal nm (Mex) pillar, column.
altiplanicie nf, **altiplano** nm (SAm) high plateau.
altísimo adj very high; **el A—** the Almighty, the Most High.
altisonante adj, **altísono** adj high-flown, high-sounding.
altitud nf height; (Aer, Geog) altitude, elevation; **a una** — **de** at a height of.
altivamente adv haughtily, arrogantly.
altivarse [1a] vr to give oneself airs.
altivez nf haughtiness, arrogance.

altivo adj haughty, arrogant.
alto¹ 1 adj (a) high; person tall; building, tree, rock high, tall; command, official, price, relief, treachery etc high; chamber (Pol), class, storey upper; **el muro tiene 5 metros de** — the wall is 5 metres high; **él tiene 1,80 de** — he is 1.80 m tall; **lanzar algo de lo** — to throw something down (from above); **desde lo** — **del árbol** from the top of the tree; **estar en** (lo) — to be up high, be high up, be up on top; **estar en lo** — **de la escalera** to be at the top of the stairs; **pasó por lo** — it passed overhead.
   (b) (Geog) upper; **el A— Rin** the Upper Rhine; **el A— Volta** Upper Volta.
   (c) **estar** — (river) to be in spate, to be swollen; (sea) to be rough.
   (d) (fig) sublime, lofty, elevated; high; **un** — **sentido del deber** a high sense of duty; **pensamientos** —s lofty thoughts, noble thoughts.
   (e) hour late, advanced; **en las altas horas** in the small hours, late at night.
   (f) sound high, loud; **en alta voz** loud(ly), in a loud voice.
   (g) (Mus) note sharp; instrument, voice alto.
   (h) (Hist, Ling) high; — **antiguo alemán** Old High German; **la alta Edad Media** the high Middle Ages.
   2 adv (a) high, high up; on high; **lanzar algo** — to throw something high.
   (b) sound loud, loudly; **hablar** — to speak loudly, (fig) to speak out (frankly); **gritar** — to shout out loud; **poner la radio más** — to turn the radio up; **¡más** —, **por favor!** louder, please!
   3 nm (a) (Geog) hill, height.
   (b) (Archit) upper floor, upstairs flat.
   (c) (SAm) pile, stock.
   (d) (Mus) alto.
   (e) —s **y bajos** ups and downs.
   (f) **pasar por** — to overlook, forget, omit; to pass over, ignore.
alto² 1 nm halt (also Mil); stop; pause; **dar el** — **a uno** to order someone to halt, challenge someone; **hacer** — to halt (also Mil), stop, pause.
   2 interj halt! (also Mil), stop!; **¡— ahí!** halt!; **¡— el fuego!** cease fire!
altoparlante nm (esp SAm) loudspeaker.
altozanero nm (Col) porter.
altozano nm (a) small hill, hillock; (of town) hill part, upper part. (b) (Col, Ven) paved terrace.
altramuz nm lupin.
altruismo nm altruism, unselfishness.
altruista 1 adj altruistic, unselfish. **2** nmf altruist, unselfish person.
altura nf (a) height; altitude; (of water) depth; — **de caída** (of waterfall etc) fall; — **de la vegetación** timber line; **a una** — **de 600 m** at a height of 600 m; **sentí un dolor a la** — **de los riñones** I felt a pain in the kidney region, I felt a pain in the area of the kidneys; **tiene 5 m de** — it is 5 m high; **él tiene 1,80 m de** — he is 1.80 m tall; **ganar** —, **tomar** — (Aer) to climb, gain height.
   (b) (fig) **estar a la** — **de una tarea** to be up to a task, be equal to a task; **estar a la** — **de las circunstancias** to rise to the occasion; **estar a la** — **del tiempo** to be abreast of the times; **poner a uno a la** — **del betún** (fam) to make someone feel the lowest of the low.
   (c) (Geog) latitude; **a la** — **de** on the same latitude as; **a la** — **de Cádiz** off Cadiz; opposite Cadiz.
   (d) (Naut) high seas, open sea; **barco de** — seagoing vessel; **pesca de** — deep-sea fishing.
   (e) (Mus) pitch.
   (f) (fig) sublimity, loftiness; **ha sido un partido de gran** — it has been a match of real class, it has been a really excellent game.
   (g) —s (Geog) heights (Rel) heaven; **a estas** —s (fig) at this point, at this stage; at this (late) hour; **estar en las** —s to be on high.
alubia nf French bean, kidney bean.
alucinación nf hallucination, delusion.
alucinado adj deluded.
alucinador adj hallucinatory, deceptive.
alucinar [1a] **1** vt to hallucinate, delude, deceive; (fig) to fascinate. **2 alucinarse** vr to be hallucinated, be deluded; to delude oneself.
alud nm avalanche.
aludido adj aforesaid, above-mentioned, this . . . that has been mentioned; **darse por** — to take the hint.
aludir [3a] vi: — **a** to allude to, mention.
aluego adv etc (SAm) = **luego**.
alujado adj (Guat, Mex) bright, shining.

alujar [1a] *vt* (*Guat, Mex*) to polish, shine.
alumbrado 1 *adj* (*sl*) lit up (*sl*).
  2 *nm* lighting, lighting system, illumination;
— **eléctrico** electric lighting; — **fluorescente**
fluorescent lighting; — **de gas** gas lighting; —
público street lighting.
  3 *nm*, **alumbrada** *nf* illuminist; **los A—s** the
Illuminati.
alumbramiento *nm* (a) (*Elec etc*) lighting, illumination. (b) (*Med*) childbirth; **tener un feliz —** to have
a safe delivery, come safely through childbirth.
alumbrar [1a] **1** *vt* (a) to light (up), illuminate, shed
light on.
  (b) *person* to light the way for, show a light to.
  (c) *blind man* to give sight to, restore the sight
of.
  (d) (*fig*) to enlighten.
  (e) (*fig*) *water* to find, strike, cause to flow.
  2 *vi* (a) to give light, shed light; **esto alumbra bien**
this gives a good light.
  (b) (*Med*) to give birth, have a baby.
  3 alumbrarse *vr* (*sl*) to get lit up (*sl*).
alumbre *nm* alum.
aluminio *nm* aluminium, aluminum (*US*).
alumnado *nm* student body; (*SAm*) college, school.
alumno *nm*, **alumna** *nf* (a) (*of school*) pupil, (*Univ*)
student; — **externo** day pupil; — **interno** boarder;
antiguo — (*of school*) old boy, former pupil, (*Univ*)
old student, former student, alumnus (*US*).
  (b) (*Law*) ward, foster child.
alunarse [1a] *vr* (*CAm*) to get saddlesore (*of horse*).
alunizaje *nm* landing on the moon.
alunizar [1f] *vi* to land on the moon.
alusión *nf* allusion, mention, reference; **hacer — a**
to allude to, mention, refer to; to hint at.
alusivo *adj* allusive.
aluvial *adj* alluvial.
aluvión *nf* (a) (*Geol*) alluvium; **tierras de —** alluvial
soil(s).
  (b) (*fig*) flood; — **de improperios** shower of
insults; torrent of abuse; **llegan en incontenible —**
they come in an unstoppable flood.
álveo *nm* riverbed, streambed.
alveolar *adj* alveolar.
alvéolo *nm* (*Anat*) alveolus; socket; (*of honeycomb*)
cell; (*fig*) network, honeycomb.
alverja *nf* vetch.
alza *nf* (a) (*in price, temperature etc*) rise; **al —** *price*
rising; **jugar al —** (*Fin*) to speculate on a rising
market; **cotizarse en —, estar en —** (*Fin*) to rise,
advance; **estar en —** (*SAm*) to enhance one's
standing, go up in the world.
  (b) (*Mil*) sight; **—s** sights; **—s fijas** fixed sights;
—s graduables adjustable sights.
alzada *nf* (*of horse*) height; (*Archit*) elevation,
side view; (*Law*) appeal.
alzado 1 *adj* (a) raised, elevated.
  (b) *price* fixed; *bankruptcy* fraudulent; **por un
tanto —** for a lump sum.
  (c) (*SAm*) proud, haughty, insolent; (*SAm*)
animal shy, wild; (*Pol*) mutinous; (*Col*) drunk;
estar — (*RPI*) to be on heat.
  2 *nm* (*Typ*) gathering.
alzamiento *nm* (a) lifting, raising; (*in price*) rise,
increase; (*at auction*) higher bid, raise.
  (b) — **de bienes** fraudulent bankruptcy.
  (c) (*Pol*) rising, revolt.
alzaprima *nf* (a) lever, crowbar; wedge. (b) (*Mus*)
bridge. (c) (*Arg, Par*) heavy trolley, flat truck.
alzaprimar [1a] *vt* to lever up, raise with a lever;
(*fig*) to arouse, stir up.
alzar [1f] **1** *vt* (a) to lift (up), raise (up); to hoist (up);
(*Eccl*) *host* to elevate; *building* to raise; *crop* to get
in, gather in; (*Typ*) to gather; *tablecloth* to remove,
put away; *ban, excommunication, restriction* to lift.
  (b) to remove; to steal; to hide.
  2 alzarse *vr* (a) (*person*) to rise, get up, stand up;
(*price, temperature etc*) to rise.
  (b) (*Pol*) to rise, revolt.
  (c) (*Fin*) to go fraudulently bankrupt.
  (d) — **algo** (*SAm*), — **con algo** to steal something,
make off with something; — **con el premio** to
carry off the prize.
  (e) (*Col*) to get drunk.
  (f) (*SAm: of animal*) to run away, go wild.
alzaválvulas *nm*, *pl* **alzaválvulas** (*Mech*) tappet.
alzo *nm* (*Guat*) theft.
allá *adv* (a) (*place*) there, over there; to that place;
— **arriba** up there; — **en Sevilla** down (there) in
Seville; **más —** further away, further over; further
on; **más — de** beyond; **más — de los límites**
outside the limits; **cualquier número más — de 7**

any number higher than 7; **no sabe contar más —
de 10** she can't count above (*or* beyond) 10; **el más
—** the (great) beyond; **por —** thereabouts; **vamos
—** let's go there; **¡— voy!** I'm coming!; **¿quién va
—?** (*Mil*) who goes there?; — **lo veremos** (*fig*)
we'll see when we get there, we'll sort that one out
later.
  (b) — **tú** that's up to you, that's your concern,
that's for you to decide (*etc*); **¡— él!** (*more violently*)
that's his funeral!; — **cada uno** that's the concern
of each one of us, that's for the individual to decide.
  (c) (*time*) — **en 1600** (way) back in 1600, as long
ago as 1600; — **en mi niñez** in my childhood days;
— **por el año 60** around about 1960 (*etc*).
allacito *adv* (*SAm*) = **allá**.
allanamiento *nm* (a) levelling, flattening; smoothing;
razing.
  (b) removal.
  (c) pacification.
  (d) (*Law etc*) submission (*a* to).
  (e) — **de morada** housebreaking, breaking and
entering, burglary.
allanar [1a] **1** *vt* (a) to level (out), flatten, make
even; to smooth (down); to raze, level to the
ground.
  (b) *difficulty etc* to remove, smooth away, iron
out.
  (c) *country* to pacify, subdue.
  (d) *house* to force an entry into, break into,
burgle.
  2 allanarse *vr* (a) to level out, level off.
  (b) (*building*) to fall down, tumble down.
  (c) (*fig*) to submit, give way; — **a** to accept,
conform to; **se allana a todo** he agrees to everything.
allegadizo *adj* gathered at random, put together
unselectively.
allegado 1 *adj* (a) near, close; allied; **según fuentes
allegadas al ministro** according to sources close to
the minister.
  (b) *person* closely related, near; **los más —s y
queridos** one's nearest and dearest; **las personas
allegadas a . . .** those attached to . . .
  2 *nm*, **allegada** *nf* (a) relation, relative.
  (b) follower.
allegar [1h] **1** *vt* (a) to gather (together), collect.
  (b) — **una cosa a otra** to put something near
something else.
  (c) to add.
  2 allegarse *vr* (a) to arrive, approach; — **a uno**
to go up to someone.
  (b) (*fig*) — **a una opinión** to adopt a view,
agree with an opinion; — **a una secta** to become
attached to a sect.
allende (*lit*) **1** *adv* on the other side.
  2 (*also* — **de**) *prep* beyond; — **los mares** beyond
the seas; — **los Pirineos** beyond the Pyrenees, on
the other side of the Pyrenees, over the Pyrenees;
— **de eso** besides that.
allí *adv* there; — **arriba** up there; — **dentro** in there;
— **de** — from there; **de — a poco** shortly afterwards;
hasta — as far as that, up to that point; **por —**
over there, round there; (*down*) that way.
allicito *adv* (*SAm*) = **allí**.
ama *nf* (a) lady of the house, mistress; — **de casa**
housewife; **¿está el —?** is the lady in?
  (b) owner, proprietress; landlady; — **de cura**
priest's housekeeper; — **de gobierno, — de llaves**
housekeeper, (*of school etc*) matron, bursar.
  (c) foster mother; — **de brazos** (*SAm*), — **de cría,**
— **de leche** wet-nurse; — **seca** nurse, nursemaid.
amabilidad *nf* kindness; niceness; **tuvo la — de
+ infin** he was kind enough to + *infin*, he was
good enough to + *infin*; **tenga la — de + infin**
please be so kind as to + *infin*.
amable *adj* kind; nice; lovable; **es Vd muy —** you
are very kind; **ser — con uno** to be kind to someone,
be good to someone; **¡qué — ha sido Vd en traerlo!**
how kind of you to bring it!
amablemente *adv* kindly; **muy — me ayudó** he very
kindly helped me.
amachambrarse [1a] *vr* (*Chi*) *etc* = **amachinarse**.
amachinarse [1a] *vr* (*SAm*) to set up house together;
— **con uno** to become someone's mistress; **estar
(*or* vivir) amachinado con** to live in sin with, be
the lover of.
amacho *adj* (*Arg, CAm*) outstanding; strong,
vigorous.
amado 1 *adj* dear, beloved. **2** *nm*, **amada** *nf* lover,
sweetheart.
amador 1 *adj* loving, fond. **2** *nm*, **amadora** *nf* lover.
amadrigar [1h] **1** *vt* to receive with open arms.
  2 amadrigarse *vr* (*animal*) to go into its hole,

burrow; (*person, fig*) to go into retirement, hide oneself away; to withdraw into one's shell.

amaestrado *adj* (**a**) *animal* trained; performing. (**b**) *plan* well-contrived, artful.

amaestramiento *nm* training; drill.

amaestrar [1a] *vt person* to train, coach; *animal* to train; *horse* to break in.

amagar [1h] **1** *vt* to threaten, portend; to show signs of.
2 *vi* to threaten, be impending; to be in the offing; (*Med*) to show the first signs; (*Fencing, Mil*) to feint; — **a** + *infin* to threaten; to + *infin*, show signs of + *ger*.
3 amagarse *vr* (**a**) (*RPl*) to adopt a threatening posture, shape up.
(**b**) (*fam*) to hide.

amago *nm* (**a**) threat; threatening posture, threatening gesture. (**b**) sign, symptom. (**c**) (*Fencing, Mil*) feint.

amainar [1a] **1** *vt sail* to take in, shorten; *fury etc* to calm.
2 *vi and* **amainarse** *vr* (*anger, wind etc*) to abate, moderate; (*effort etc*) to lessen, slacken; to relax.

amaine *nm* (**a**) shortening. (**b**) abatement, moderation; lessening, slackening; relaxation.

amaitinar [1a] *vt* to spy on.

amaizado *adj* (*Col*) rich.

amalaya *interj* (*SAm*) = **ojalá**.

amalayar [1a] *vt* (*CAm, Col, Mex*) to covet, long for; — + *infin* to long to + *infin*.

Amalia *f* Amelia.

amalgama *nf* amalgam.

amalgamación *nf* amalgamation.

amalgamar [1a] **1** *vt* to amalgamate; to combine, mix, blend. **2 amalgamarse** *vr* to amalgamate.

amamantar [1a] *vt* to suckle, nurse.

amancebamiento *nm* illicit union, cohabitation.

amancebarse [1a] *vr* to live together, live in sin (*also* **estar amancebados, vivir amancebados**).

amancillar [1a] *vt* to stain; (*fig*) to stain; tarnish, dishonour.

amanecer 1 *nm* dawn, daybreak; **al** — at dawn.
2 [2d] *vi* (**a**) to dawn, begin to get light.
(**b**) to appear; begin to show.
(**c**) (*person*) **amaneció en el bosque** he found himself at dawn in the wood, he woke up in the wood; **amaneció acatarrado** he woke up with a cold; **amaneció rey** he woke up to find himself king.
(**d**) (*SAm*) — **bailando** to stay up all night dancing; — **cansado** to be tired after staying awake all night.

amanecida *nf* dawn, daybreak.

amanerado *adj* mannered, affected; (*SAm*) extra polite, excessively polite.

amaneramiento *nm* affectation; (*Lit etc*) mannerism (of style).

amanerarse [1a] *vr* to become affected, fall into affectation.

amanezca *nf* (*Mex, SD*) dawn; breakfast.

amanezquera *nf* (*Mex, PR*) early morning.

amanojar [1a] *vt* to gather by the handful, gather in bunches.

amansa *nf* (*Chi*) taming; breaking-in.

amansado *adj* tame.

amansador *nm* tamer; (*Mex*) horse breaker.

amansadora *nf* (*Arg*) waiting room (*in public building*).

amansamiento *nm* (**a**) taming; breaking-in; soothing. (**b**) tameness.

amansar [1a] **1** *vt animal* to tame; *horse* to break in; *person* to tame, subdue; *passion etc* to soothe, appease.
2 amansarse *vr* (*person*) to calm down; (*passion etc*) to moderate, abate.

amanse *nm* (*Col, Ec, Mex*) taming; breaking-in.

amante 1 *adj* loving, fond; **nación** — **de la paz** peace-loving nation.
2 *nm* lover; — **s** lovers.
3 *nf* lover, mistress; **él tuvo muchas —s** he had many mistresses; **tiene una — en Madrid** he has a mistress in Madrid.

amanuense *nm* amanuensis; scribe, copyist; secretary.

amañado *adj* (**a**) skilful, clever. (**b**) (*pej*) fake, faked; fixed, rigged.

amañador *adj* (*Col, Ec, PR, Ven*) having a pleasant climate.

amañar [1a] **1** *vt* (**a**) to do skilfully, perform cleverly.
(**b**) (*pej*) to alter; play about with, tamper with; *photo etc* to fake; *game, jury* to fix; *accounts* to cook; *excuse* to cook up; *election* to rig, rig the results of.
2 amañarse *vr* (**a**) to be skilful, be expert; to become expert, get the hang of it; (*Arg*) to make

shift to sort out one's problems; (*Mex, Ven*) to get into bad habits (*of animals*); — **a** + *infin* to settle down to + *infin*; — **con** to get along with.
(**b**) (*Col, Ec, PR, Ven*) to become accustomed to a place (*or person etc*); **ya se amaña en Quito** he's settling down in Quito, he's beginning to feel at home in Quito.

amaño *nm* (**a**) skill, expertness, cleverness; **tener — para** to have an aptitude for.
(**b**) —**s** (*Tech*) tools; (*fig*) tricks, cunning ways; guile; (*Arg*) tortuous means.

amapola *nf* poppy; **ponerse como una** — to blush like a beetroot.

amar [1a] *vt* to love.

amaraje *nm* (*Aer*) landing (on the sea); splashdown, touchdown; — **forzoso** ditching.

amarar [1a] *vi* (*Aer*) to land (on the sea); (*of space capsule*) to touch down, come down, splash down; (*to avoid accident*) to ditch.

amarchantarse [1a] *vr* (*SAm*): — **en** to become a customer of, to deal regularly with.

amargado *adj* bitter, embittered.

amargamente *adv* bitterly.

amargar [1h] **1** *vt* to make bitter, sour; (*fig*) *person, relationship* to embitter; *occasion* to spoil, upset.
2 *vi* to be bitter, taste bitter.
3 amargarse *vr* (**a**) to get bitter.
(**b**) (*person*) to get bitter, become embittered.

amargo 1 *adj* (**a**) bitter; sharp, tart; **más** — **que tueras** terribly bitter.
(**b**) (*fig*) bitter, embittered.
(**c**) (*Arg*) cowardly; (*Ven*) unhelpful, offhand.
2 (**a**) *nm* bitterness; sharpness, tartness.
(**b**) *nm*, **amarga** *nf* (*Arg*) sharp-tempered person; shirker, poor worker.
(**c**) —**s** *mpl* bitters.

amargón *nm* dandelion.

amargor *nm*, **amargura** *nf* (**a**) bitterness; sharpness, tartness. (**b**) (*fig*) bitterness; grief, distress.

amaricado (*fam*) **1** *adj* effeminate, queer (*fam*). **2** *nm* nancy boy (*fam*), queer (*fam*).

Amarilis *f* Amaryllis.

amarillear [1a] *vi* (**a**) to be yellowish; to show yellow.
(**b**) to yellow, go yellow.

amarillecer [2d] *vi* to yellow, turn yellow.

amarillejo *adj* yellowish.

amarillento *adj* yellowish; *complexion* pale, sallow.

amarillez *nf* yellow, yellowness; paleness, sallowness.

amarillo 1 *adj* yellow; *traffic light* amber. **2** *nm* (**a**) yellow. (**b**) (*PR, SD*) ripe banana. (**c**) (*Pol*) strikebreaker.

amarilloso *adj* (*Arg*) yellowish.

amarra *nf* (**a**) (*Naut*) cable, hawser; mooring line, painter; (*SAm*) rope, line, cord.
(**b**) —**s** (*Naut*) moorings; **cortar las** —**s, romper las** —**s** to break loose, cut adrift; **echar las** —**s** to moor.
(**c**) —**s** (*fig*) protection; **tener buenas** —**s** to have good connections, have influence.

amarradera *nf* (*Col*) mooring; (*Mex*) rope, line, cord.

amarradero *nm* post, bollard; moorings; berth, mooring.

amarrado *adj* (*SAm*) mean, stingy.

amarradura *nf* mooring.

amarraje *nm* mooring charges.

amarrar [1a] **1** *vt* to fasten, hitch, tie up; (*Naut*) *boat* to moor, tie up; *rope* to lash, belay; (*SAm*) to tie; *cards* to stack.
2 *vi* (*fam*) to get down to it in earnest.
3 amarrarse *vr*: —**la** (*CAm, Col, Pan*) to get drunk.

amarre *nm* (**a**) (*act*) fastening, tying; mooring; lashing. (**b**) mooring line, painter; mooring cable; — **de seguridad** (*Mountaineering*) tie, safety rope.

amarrete (*SAm*) **1** *adj* mean, stingy. **2** *nm*, **amarreta** *nf* miser, mean person.

amarro *nm* (*Bol*) knotted string, knotted rope; mass of knots; bundle, packet; — **de cigarrillos** packet of cigarettes.

amarrocar [1g] *vt* (*Arg*) to manage to save with difficulty.

amarroso *adj* (*CR, Salv*) *fruit* acrid, sharp.

amartelado *adj* lovesick; **andar** — **con, estar** — **con** to be in love with, be infatuated with; **andan muy** —**s** they're deeply in love.

amartelamiento *nm* lovesick state, utter absorption in love, infatuation.

amartelar [1a] **1** *vt* (**a**) to make jealous, torment with jealousy. (**b**) *heart* to win, conquer. **2 amartelarse** *vr* to fall in love (*de* with).

amartillar [1a] *vt* to hammer; *gun* to cock.

amasadera *nf* kneading trough.

amasado adj (Cu) (a) doughy, of bread-like consistency. (b) person fat.

amasador nm baker.

amasadora nf kneading machine.

amasadura nf (a) kneading. (b) batch.

amasamiento nm kneading; (Med) massage.

amasandería nf (Col, Chi, Ven) bakery, baker's shop.

amasandero nm (Col, Chi, Ven) baker, bakery worker.

amasar [1a] vt dough to knead; flour, plaster etc to mix, prepare; potatoes to mash; meal to prepare; (Med) to massage; (fig, fam) to cook up, concoct, fix.

amasiato nm (CR, Mex, Per) illicit union, stable union of an unmarried couple.

amasijo nm (a) (act) kneading; mixing; mashing; (fig) cooking-up, concoction.
(b) (material) mixture, mash, batch (of dough etc); (fig) hotchpotch, medley.
(c) task.
(d) plot, scheme.
(e) (Ven) wheat bread; — de palos beating, beating-up.

amasio nm, **amasia** nf (CR, Mex) lover, partner in an illicit union.

amateur 1 adj amateur. 2 nmf amateur.

amateurismo nm amateurism.

amatista nf amethyst.

amatorio adj amatory; verse etc love (attr).

amanta nm (Bol, Per) village elder.

amayorado adj (Bol) child precocious.

amazacotado adj heavy, clumsy, awkward; shapeless, formless; (Lit etc) ponderous, stodgy.

amazona nf (Hist) amazon; horsewoman, rider, equestrienne; (pej) horsy woman.

Amazonas m Amazon.

amazónico adj Amazon (attr).

ambages nmpl circumlocutions, roundabout style; sin — in plain language, without beating about the bush.

ambagioso adj involved, circuitous, roundabout.

ámbar nm amber; — gris ambergris.

ambareado adj (Per) hair chestnut, auburn.

ambarino adj amber.

Amberes Antwerp.

ambición nf ambition; (pej) ambitiousness, self-seeking, egotism.

ambicionar [1a] vt to aspire to, seek, strive after; (pej) to be out for, covet; — ser algo to have an ambition to be something, be out to become something; no ambiciona nada he seeks nothing for himself.

ambiciosamente adv ambitiously.

ambicioso 1 adj (a) ambitious.
(b) (pej) pretentious, grandiose; person over-ambitious; overweening, proud, self-seeking.
2 nm, ambiciosa nf ambitious person; careerist, pushful sort; — de figurar social climber.

ambidextro adj ambidextrous.

ambientación nf (a) orientation. (b) (Cine, Lit etc) setting.

ambiental adj environmental, relating to one's environment; tienen un descontento — they are discontented with their surroundings.

ambientar [1a] 1 vt (a) to give an atmosphere to, add colour to; ambienta el escenario con bailes folklóricos he enlivens the scene with folk dances.
(b) (Lit etc) to set; la novela está ambientada en una sociedad de ... the novel is set in a society of ...
(c) to orientate, direct.
2 ambientarse vr to orientate oneself, get a sense of direction; procuraré ambientarme I'll try to get myself sorted out, I'll try to get the feel of the thing.

ambiente 1 adj ambient, surrounding.
2 nm (a) atmosphere.
(b) (fig) atmosphere; milieu, environment, surroundings; climate; (Bio) environment; no me gusta el — I don't like the atmosphere; se crió en un — de violencia he grew up in an atmosphere of violence; voy a cambiar de — I'm going to move to new surroundings.
(c) (RPI) room, unit of living space.

ambigú nm buffet supper, cold supper.

ambiguamente adv ambiguously.

ambigüedad nf ambiguity.

ambiguo adj ambiguous; doubtful, uncertain; non-committal, equivocal; gender common.

ambilado adj (Ven): estar — to be open-mouthed, look foolish; to be distracted.

ámbito nm (a) compass, ambit, field; boundary, limit; dentro del — de within the limits of; en todo el —

nacional over the whole nation, throughout the country; en el — nacional y extranjero at home and abroad.
(b) (fig) scope, sphere, range; — de acción field of activity; buscar mayor — to look for greater scope.

ambivalencia nf ambivalence.

ambivalente adj ambivalent.

ambo nm (Arg) two-piece suit.

ambos adj and pron both; — a dos both (of them), both together.

ambrosia nf ambrosia.

Ambrosio m Ambrose.

ambucia nf (Chi) greed, greediness.

ambuciento adj (Chi) greedy.

ambulancia nf ambulance; (Mil) field hospital; — de correos post-office coach.

ambulanciero nm ambulance man.

ambulante adj walking; roving; musician etc itinerant; actor, performer strolling; salesman, exhibition etc travelling.

ambulatorio nm national health clinic, social welfare clinic.

ameba nf amoeba.

amedrentar [1a] 1 vt to scare, frighten; to intimidate.
2 amedrentarse vr to get scared.

amejorar [1a] vt (SAm) = mejorar.

amelcocharse [1a] vr (Cu) to fall in love; (Mex) to simper, act affectedly, be prim.

amelonado adj (a) melon-shaped. (b) estar — (fam) to be lovesick.

amén 1 nm amen; decir — a todo to agree to everything; en un decir — in a trice.
2 interj amen!
3 — de prep (a) except for, aside from. (b) in addition to, besides; not to mention ...
4 — de que conj in spite of the fact that ...

amenaza nf threat, menace.

amenazador adj, **amenazante** adj threatening, menacing.

amenazar [1f] 1 vt to threaten, menace; — violencia to threaten violence; — a uno de muerte to threaten someone with death; una especie amenazada de extinción a species threatened with extinction.
2 vi to threaten; to loom, impend; — + infin, — con + infin to threaten to + infin.

amenguar [1i] vt (a) to lessen, diminish. (b) (fig) to belittle; to dishonour.

amenidad nf pleasantness, agreeableness; grace, elegance.

amenizar [1f] vt to make pleasant, make more agreeable; to add charm to; conversation to enliven, make more entertaining; style to brighten up.

ameno adj pleasant, agreeable, nice; style graceful, elegant; book pleasant, readable; es un sitio — it's a nice spot; prefiero una lectura más amena I prefer lighter reading; la vida aquí es más amena life is pleasanter here.

amento nm catkin.

América f America (depending on context, may mean the whole continent, the United States, or Latin America); — Central Central America; — Latina Latin America; — del Norte North America; — del Sur South America; hacer la — (Arg: of foreigner) to make a fortune.

americana nf coat, jacket; — de sport sports jacket.

americanismo nm (Ling) americanism; (SAm: Pol) Yankee imperialism; (Ant, Mex, Ven) liking for North American ways (etc).

americanista nmf americanist, specialist in American matters; (Ant, CAm, Mex, Ven) person with a liking for North American ways (etc).

americanizar [1f] 1 vt to americanize. 2 americanizarse vr to become americanized; (CAm, Mex) to adopt North American ways.

americano 1 adj American (depending on context, may refer to the whole continent, the United States, or Latin America). 2 nm, americana nf American.

ameritado adj (Mex) worthy.

ameritar [1a] vt (SAm) to deserve.

amerizaje nm landing (on the sea); splashdown, touchdown.

amerizar [1f] vi (Aer) to land (on the sea); (of space capsule) to touch down, come down, splash down.

amestizado adj like a half-breed.

ametrallador nm machine gunner.

ametralladora nf machine-gun.

ametrallar [1a] vt to machine-gun.

amianto nm asbestos.

amiba nf, **amibo** nm amoeba.

amiga nf friend; girlfriend, sweetheart; (pej) mistress.

amigable *adj* friendly, amicable; (*fig*) harmonious.

amigablemente *adv* amicably.

amigacho *nm* (*fam*, *pej*) buddy (*esp US*), bachelor friend; **ha salido con los —s** he's out with the boys; **esos —s tuyos** those coarse friends of yours.

amigarse [1h] *vr* to get friendly; (*pej*) to set up house together, live in sin.

amigazo *nm* (*Arg*: *fam*) buddy (*esp US*), close friend.

amígdala *nf* tonsil.

amigdalitis *nf* tonsillitis.

amigdalotomía *nf* tonsillectomy.

amigo 1 *adj* friendly; **ser — de** (*fig*) to be fond of, be given to; **A es muy — de B** A is a close friend of B; **son muy —s** they are close friends.
  2 *nm* friend; boyfriend, sweetheart; (*pej*) lover; **pero ¡—!** but my dear sir!, (*informally*) look here, old chap!; **— de lo ajeno** thief; **— del alma, — de confianza, — íntimo** intimate friend, close friend; **— por correspondencia** penfriend; **— en la prosperidad** fair-weather friend; **hacerse —s** to become friends; **hacerse — de** to make friends with, become a friend of.

amigote *nm* (*fam*) old pal (*fam*), old buddy (*esp US*); (*Arg*: *pej*) buddy.

amiguero *adj* (*SAm*) friendly.

amiguita *nf* girlfriend; mistress, lover.

amiláceo *adj* starchy.

amilanar [1a] **1** *vt* to scare, intimidate. **2 amilanarse** *vr* to get scared, be intimidated.

aminorar [1a] *vt* to lessen, diminish; *expenses etc* to cut down, reduce; *speed* to reduce, slacken.

amistad *nf* (a) friendship; friendly relationship, friendly connection; **estrechar — con** to get friendly with; **hacer las —es** to make it up; **romper las —es** to fall out, break up a friendship.
  (b) **—es** friends, acquaintances; **invitar a las —es** to invite one's friends.

amistar [1a] **1** *vt* to bring together, make friends of; to bring about a reconciliation between, heal a breach between.
  2 amistarse *vr* to become friends, establish a friendship; to make it up; **— con** to make friends with.

amistosamente *adv* amicably; in a friendly way (*or* tone *etc*).

amistoso *adj* friendly, amicable.

amnesia *nf* amnesia; loss of memory; **— temporal** blackout.

amnistía *nf* amnesty.

amnistiar [1c] *vt* to amnesty, grant an amnesty to.

amo *nm* (a) master; head of the family; **— de casa** householder; **¿está el —?** is the master in? (b) owner; proprietor. (c) boss, employer; overseer; **ser el —** to be the boss; **ser el — en un juego** to be the best at a game.

amoblado 1 *adj* furnished. **2** *nm* (*CAm*) furniture, furnishings.

amoblar [1m] *vt* to furnish.

amodorramiento *nm* sleepiness, drowsiness.

amodorrarse [1a] *vr* to get sleepy, get drowsy; to fall into a stupor; to go to sleep.

amohinar [1a] **1** *vt* to vex, annoy. **2 amohinarse** *vr* to get annoyed; to sulk.

amohosado *adj* (*Chi*, *RPl*) rusty.

amojonar [1a] *vt* to mark out, mark the boundary of.

amojosado *adj* (*Chi*, *RPl*) rusty.

amoladera *nf* whetstone, grindstone.

amolado *adj* (*Arg*, *Urug*) bothered, irritated; (*Mex*, *Per*) offended; (*Mex*, *Per*) bothersome, annoying; (*Mex*, *Per*) evil, wicked; (*Bol*) damaged, ruined.

amolador 1 *adj* boring, tedious. **2** *nm* knife-grinder.

amoladura *nf* grinding, sharpening.

amolar [1m] **1** *vt* (a) to grind, sharpen. (b) to bore; to pester, annoy, irritate. (c) to damage, ruin.
  2 amolarse *vr* (*Arg*, *Mex*, *Urug*) to get cross, take offence.

amoldar [1a] **1** *vt* to mould (*also fig*; *a, según* on); to fashion; to adapt, adjust (*a* to). **2 amoldarse** *vr* to adapt oneself, adjust oneself (*a* to).

amonarse [1a] *vr* (*fam*) to get tight.

amondongado *adj* fat, flabby.

amonedación *nf* coining, minting.

amonedado *adj* (*Mex*, *PR*) rich.

amonedar [1a] *vt* to coin, mint.

amonestación *nf* (a) warning; piece of advice; (*Law*) caution. (b) (*Eccl*) marriage banns; **correr las —es** to publish the banns.

amonestador *adj* warning, cautionary.

amonestar [1a] *vt* (a) to warn; to advise, remind; to reprove, admonish. (b) (*Eccl*) to publish the banns

amoníaco 1 *adj* ammoniac(al). **2** *nm* ammonia; **— líquido** liquid ammonia.

amontarse [1a] *vr* (*CAm*, *Col*, *Mex*) to revert to scrub, go back to a wild state.

amontillado *nm* amontillado (*pale dry sherry*).

amontonadamente *adv* in heaps; in confusion.

amontonado *adj* heaped (up), piled up; **viven —s** they live on top of each other, they live in very crowded conditions.

amontonamiento *nm* heaping, piling up; banking, drifting; hoarding; accumulation; crowding; (*Aut*) traffic jam.

amontonar [1a] **1** *vt* (a) to heap (up), pile (up); *snow, clouds etc* to bank (up); to gather, collect, accumulate; to hoard, store away; **viene amontonando fichas** he's been collecting data in large quantities; **— alabanzas sobre uno** to heap praises on someone.
  (b) (*Ec*) to insult.
  2 amontonarse *vr* (a) to pile up, get piled up; (*of snow*) to drift, bank up; (*of clouds*) to gather, pile up; to accumulate, collect; (*of people*) to crowd together, huddle together; to come thronging; **la gente se amontonó en la salida** people crowded into the exit, people jammed the exit; **se amontonaron los coches** the cars got jammed.
  (b) (*fam*) to fly off the handle (*fam*), go up in smoke (*fam*).

amor *nm* (a) love (*a* for, *de* of); **— cortés** courtly love; **— fracasado** disappointment in love, unhappy love affair; **— interesado** cupboard love; **— maternal** mother love; **— propio** amour propre, self-respect, pride; **es cuestión de — propio** it's a matter of pride; **picar a uno en el — propio** to wound someone's pride; **— a primera vista** love at first sight; **por el — de** for the love of; **por the sake of; por (el) — de Dios** for God's sake; **casarse por — to** marry for love; **lo hizo por —** he did it for love; **matrimonio sin —** loveless marriage; **hacer el —** to make love; **hacer el — a** to court; to make love to.
  (b) (*person*) love, lover; **mi —, — mío** my love; **primer —** first love; **buscar un nuevo —** to look for a new love; **tiene un — en la ciudad** he's carrying on an affair in town.
  (c) **ir al — del agua** to go with the current; **estar al — de la lumbre** to be close to the fire, be by the fireside.
  (d) **—es** love affair, romance; **los mil —es de don Juan** Don Juan's numberless affairs; **¡con mil —es!** I'd love to!, I should be only too glad!; **requebrar a una de —es** to court someone.

amoral *adj* amoral.

amoratado *adj* purple, purplish; livid; blue (with cold); (*SAm*) bruised.

amoratarse [1a] *vr* (*SAm*) to turn purple; to get bruised.

amorcillo *nm* (a) flirtation, light-hearted affair. (b) Cupid.

amordazar ([1f] *vt* *person* to gag; *dog etc* to muzzle; (*fig*) to gag, silence.

amorfo *adj* amorphous, formless, shapeless.

amorío *nm* (*also* **—s**) love affair, romance.

amorochado *adj* (*SAm*) = **morocho 1** (a).

amorosamente *adv* lovingly, affectionately; amorously; caressingly.

amoroso *adj* (a) loving, affectionate, tender; amorous; *letter etc* love (*attr*), of love; **en tono —** in an affectionate tone; in a caressing tone; **empezar a sentirse —** to begin to feel amorous.
  (b) (*fig*) *land* workable; *metal* malleable; *weather* mild.

amorrar [1a] *vi* to hang one's head; (*fig*) to be sullen, sulk; (*Naut*) to pitch, dip the bows under.

amortajar [1a] *vt* to shroud.

amortecer [2d] **1** *vt* *noise* to deaden, muffle; *fire* to damp down; (*Mus*) to tone down; *passion* to curb, control.
  2 *vi* to become muffled, die away; (*Med*) to faint, swoon.

amortecido *adj*: **caer —** to fall in a swoon, faint away.

amortecimiento *nm* deadening, muffling; toning down; controlling; (*Med*) fainting.

amortiguación *nf* = **amortiguamiento**.

amortiguador 1 *adj* deadening, muffling; softening.
  2 *nm* damper, muffler; (*Mech*) shock absorber, cushion; (*Rail*) buffer; (*Aut*) bumper; (*Elec*) damper; **— de luz** dimmer; **— de ruido** muffler, silencer.

amortiguamiento *nm* deadening, muffling; cushioning; absorption; softening, toning down; damping; dimming.

amortiguar [1i] **1** vt noise to deaden, muffle; blow to cushion; shock to absorb; effect to cushion, diminish, reduce the force of; fire to damp down; colour to soften, tone down; (Elec) to damp; light to dim.
2 amortiguarse vr (Arg) (a) (Bot) to wither. **(b)** (fig) to get depressed.

amortizable adj (Fin) redeemable.

amortización nf (Law) amortization; (Fin) redemption; paying-off, repayment; (of post) suppression, abolition.

amortizar [1f] vt (Law) to amortize; (Fin) bonds etc to redeem; loan, mortgage to pay off, repay; to refund; post to suppress, abolish; — algo por desvalorización to write something off.

amoscarse [1g] vr to get cross, get peeved (fam).

amostazar [1f] **1** vt to make cross, peeve (fam).
2 amostazarse vr (a) to get cross, get peeved (fam). **(b)** (SAm) to blush, feel embarrassed.

amotinado 1 adj riotous, violent, mutinous. **2** nm rioter; rebel, mutineer.

amotinador adj and nm =amotinado.

amotinamiento nm (civil) riot; (Pol) rising, insurrection; (Mil, Naut) mutiny.

amotinar [1a] **1** vt to stir up, incite to riot (or mutiny etc). **2 amotinarse** vr to riot; to rise up, revolt, rebel; to mutiny.

amover [2h] vt to dismiss, remove (from office).

amovible adj part removable, detachable; employee temporary.

amparador 1 adj helping, protecting, protective. **2** nm, **amparadora** nf protector.

amparar [1a] **1** vt to protect (de from), shelter, help; — a los pobres to help the poor; le ampara el ministro the minister protects him.
2 ampararse vr (a) to seek protection, seek help; — a to have recourse to; — con, — de to seek the protection of.
(b) to protect oneself, defend oneself; to shelter.

amparo nm help; favour, protection; refuge, shelter; defence.

ampáyar nm, **ampáyer** nm (SAm: angl) referee, umpire.

ampe interj (Bol) please!

amperímetro nm ammeter.

amperio nm ampère, amp.

ampliación nf enlargement, extension; (Phot) enlargement; expansion; amplification.

ampliadora nf (Phot) enlarger.

ampliamente adv amply; extensively; **satisfará** — **la demanda** it will more than meet the demand.

ampliar [1c] vt to enlarge, extend; (Phot) to enlarge; trade etc to expand; sound to amplify; powers to extend, widen; statement to amplify, elaborate.

amplificación nf amplification; (SAm: Phot) enlargement.

amplificador nm (Radio) amplifier.

amplificar [1g] vt to amplify; (SAm: Phot) to enlarge.

amplio adj **(a)** spacious, wide; extensive; roomy; skirt etc full.
(b) broad, extensive, ample; powers ample, wide; sketch etc bold.

amplitud nf spaciousness, extent; roominess, fullness; amplitude.

ampo nm dazzling whiteness; snowflake; **como el** — **de la nieve** as white as the driven snow.

ampolla nf bubble; (Med) blister; flask, decanter, (Med) ampoule.

ampollarse [1a] vr to blister, form blisters.

ampolleta nf phial, small bottle; hourglass, sandglass; (of thermometer, also Elec) bulb.

ampón adj bulky; person stout, tubby.

ampulosamente adv bombastically, pompously.

ampulosidad nf bombast, pomposity.

ampuloso adj bombastic, pompous.

amputación nf amputation.

amputar [1a] vt to amputate, cut off.

amuchachado adj boyish.

amuchar [1a] vt (Arg, Bol, Chi) to increase, multiply.

amueblado 1 adj furnished (con, de with). **2** nm (Arg: euph) brothel.

amueblar [1a] vt to furnish (de with).

amuinar [1a] (Mex) **1** vt to make cross, irritate. **2 amuinarse** vr to get cross.

amujerado adj effeminate.

amularse [1a] (Mex) vr (person) to get stubborn; (Comm) to be unsaleable, become a glut on the market.

amulatado adj mulatto-like.

amuleto nm amulet, charm.

amunicionar [1a] vt to supply with ammunition.

amuñecado adj doll-like.

amura nf (Naut) **(a)** beam, breadth. **(b)** tack; **cambiar de** — to go about.

amurallado adj city walled.

amurallar [1a] vt to wall, wall in.

amurar [1a] vi (Naut) to tack.

amurrarse [1a] vr (SAm) to get depressed.

amurruñarse [1a] vr (Ven) to curl up; to nestle; to cuddle up, get close.

amusgar [1h] **1** vt ears to lay back, throw back; eyes to screw up, narrow. **2** vi (Arg, Hond) to yield, bow down. **3 amusgarse** vr (Hond) to feel ashamed.

Ana f Ann(e).

anacarado adj pearly, mother-of-pearl (attr).

anacardo nm cashew (nut).

anaconda nf anaconda.

anacoreta nmf anchorite.

Anacreonte m Anacreon.

anacrónico adj anachronistic.

anacronismo nm **(a)** anachronism. **(b)** out-of-date thing, piece of bric-à-brac.

anacuá nm (RPl) the devil.

ánade nm duck; — **real** mallard.

anadear [1a] vi to waddle.

anadeo nm waddle, waddling.

anadón nm duckling.

anagrama nm anagram.

anal adj anal.

analcohólico adj drink non-alcoholic, soft.

analérgico adj non-allergic.

anales nmpl annals.

analfabetismo nm illiteracy.

analfabeto 1 adj illiterate. **2** nm, **analfabeta** nf illiterate (person).

analgesia nf analgesia.

analgésico 1 adj analgesic. **2** nm analgesic.

análisis nm, pl **análisis** analysis; (explanatory) breakdown; — **de mercados** market research; — **de sangre** blood test.

analista nm (Chem) analyst; (of local history etc) chronicler, annalist; (in newspaper) columnist, commentator.

analítico adj analytic(al).

analizador nm analyst.

analizar [1f] vt to analyse; (Gram) to parse.

analogía nf analogy; similarity; **por** — **con** on the analogy of.

analógico adj analogical.

análogo 1 adj analogous, similar (a to). **2** nm analogue; **añadir frutas o** — add fruit or something of the kind, add fruit or something similar.

ananá(s) nm, **ananasa** nf (Col) pineapple.

anapesto nm anapaest.

anaquel nm shelf.

anaquelería nf shelves, shelving.

anaranjado 1 adj orange(-coloured). **2** nm orange (colour).

anarquía nf anarchy.

anárquico adj anarchic(al).

anarquismo nm anarchism.

anarquista 1 adj anarchist(ic). **2** nmf anarchist.

anarquizar [1f] vt (SAm) to produce anarchy in, cause utter disorder in; to sow the seeds of rebellion among.

anatema nm anathema.

anatematizar [1f] vt (Eccl) to anathematize; (fig) to curse, condemn.

anatomía nf anatomy.

anatómico adj anatomical.

anatomizar [1f] vt to anatomize; (Art) muscles etc to bring out, emphasize; (fig) to anatomize, dissect.

anca nf haunch; rump, croup; —s (fam) bottom, behind (fam); **llevar a uno a las** —s, **llevar a uno en** —(s) (SAm) to carry someone on horseback behind one, to let someone ride pillion; **esto lleva el desastre en** —(s) (SAm, fig) this brings disaster in its wake; **no sufre** —s (fam) he can't take a joke.

ancestral adj ancestral.

ancestro nm (SAm) **(a)** ancestor. **(b)** ancestry.

anciana nf old woman, old lady.

ancianidad nf old age.

anciano 1 adj old, aged. **2** nm old man; (Eccl) elder.

ancla nf anchor; — **de la esperanza**, — **de salvación** (fig) sheet anchor; **echar** —s to cast anchor, drop anchor; **estar al** — to be (or lie, ride) at anchor; **levar** —s to weigh anchor.

ancladero nm anchorage.

anclar [1a] vi to anchor, drop anchor.

ancón nm (Naut) cove; (Col, Mex) corner; (Col) gap between two hills.

áncora nf anchor.

anchamente adv widely.

ancheta *nf* (a) (*Comm*) small lot of goods; (*Cu, Ven*) small piece of business, small-time affair.

(b) gain, profit; (*Mex, Per*) bargain, profitable deal; chance to make easy money.

(c) (*Arg, Bol*) jumble of meaningless words; pointless remark; (*Col*) nonsense, piece of nonsense; (*Cu, Ven*) joke, hoax.

ancho 1 *adj* (a) wide, broad; too wide; — **de 4 cm, 4 cm de** — 4 cm wide, 4 cm in width.

(b) (*Sew*) big; loose, loose-fitting; *skirt* full; **me viene algo** — it's on the big side for me; **le viene muy** — **el cargo** the job is too much for him, he's not up to the job.

(c) (*fig*) liberal, broad-minded; *life* fast; — **de conciencia** not overscrupulous; **ponerse** — to be smug, get conceited; **quedarse tan** — to go on as if nothing had happened, remain completely unmoved.

(d) **estar a sus anchas** to be at one's ease, be comfortable; **aquí estoy a mis anchas** I feel at home here; **ponerse a sus anchas** to make oneself comfortable, spread oneself.

2 *nm* width, breadth; (*Rail*) gauge; — **normal** standard gauge.

anchoa *nf* anchovy.

anchura *nf* width, breadth; wideness; (*Sew*) bigness, looseness, fullness; (*fig*) freedom; ease, comfort; — **de conciencia** lack of scruple.

anchuroso *adj* wide, broad; spacious.

andadas *nfpl* (*Hunting*) tracks; **volver a las** — to backslide, revert to one's old ways.

andaderas *nfpl* go-cart, child's trolley.

andadero *adj* passable, easy to traverse.

andado *adj* worn, well-trodden; common, ordinary; *clothing* old, worn.

andador 1 *adj* (a) fast-walking; **es** — he's a good walker.

(b) (*Arg*) *horse* well-paced, long-striding.

(c) fond of travelling, fond of gadding about.

2 *nm*, **andadora** *nf* walker; gadabout.

3 —**es** *nmpl* leading strings.

4 andadora *nf* (*Mex*) prostitute.

andalón *adj* (*Mex*) *horse* well-paced, long-striding.

andadura *nf* walking; pace, gait, walk; (*of horse*) pace.

Andalucía *f* Andalusia.

andalucismo *nm* andalusianism, word (*or phrase etc*) peculiar to Andalusia.

andaluz 1 *adj* Andalusian. **2** *nm*, **andaluza** *nf* Andalusian. **3** *nm* (*dialect*) Andalusian.

andaluzada *nf* (*fam*) tall story, piece of Andalusian boastfulness.

andamiada *nf*, **andamiaje** *nm* scaffolding, staging.

andamio *nm* scaffold; stage, stand; — **óseo** skeleton, bone framework.

andana *nf* row, line; **llamarse** — to go back on one's word; to wash one's hands of a matter.

andanada *nf* (a) (*Mil*) broadside; (*firework*) big rocket; (*fig*) reprimand, telling-off; **por** —**s** (*Arg*) in abundance, to excess; **soltar una** — to say something unexpected, drop a bomb; **soltar la** — **a uno** to give someone a telling-off.

(b) covered grandstand; (*Taur*) section of cheap seats.

(c) (*of bricks etc*) layer, row.

andante 1 *adj* walking; *knight etc* errant. **2** *nm* (*Mus*) andante.

andanza *nf* fortune, fate; —**s** deeds, adventures.

andar [1q] **1** *vt* (a) *distance* to go, cover, travel; *road etc* to travel, go along, walk.

(b) (*CAm*) to wear; to carry, use, have; **yo no ando reloj** I don't wear a watch, I don't carry a watch.

2 *vi* (a) to go, walk; to move; to go about, travel; (*horse*) to walk, amble; — **a caballo** to ride, go on horseback; — **tras uno** to go after someone; to pursue someone; — **tras una chica** to court a girl; — **tras algo** to yearn for something, have a keen desire for something; **venimos andando** we walked, we came on foot.

(b) (*of clock*) to go; (*Mech*) to go, run, work; **el reloj anda bien** the clock keeps good time; **el reloj no anda** the clock won't go; **¿cómo anda esto?** how are things going?

(c) to be; **anda por aquí** it's around here somewhere; — **alegre** to be cheerful, feel cheerful; **hay que** — **con cuidado** one must go carefully; **anda enfermo** he's ill; **andamos mal de dinero** we're badly off for money; **¿cómo andas de tabaco?** how are you off for cigarettes?

(d) **anda en los 50** he's about 50.

(e) — **en** to tamper with, mess about with; **han**

andado en el armario they've messed up the cupboard.

(f) — **en to** be engaged in; — **en pleitos** to be engaged in lawsuits, be tied up in lawsuits.

(g) (*of time*) to pass, elapse.

(h) **¡anda!** get along with you!, well!, go on!; come on!; **¡anda, anda!** don't be silly!; **¡andando!** and that's it!, now we can get on with it!

(i) **anda que te anda** never letting up for a moment, without stopping at all.

(j) — **haciendo algo** to be doing something, be in the course of doing something.

3 andarse *vr often = vi*: (a) to go off, go away.

(b) — **con** to use, make use of, employ; — **en** to indulge in; **Juanito se anda por el abecedario** Johnny is beginning to read.

(c) **todo se andará** all in good time, it will all come right in the end.

4 *nm* walk; gait, pace; **a largo** — in due course; **a más** —, **a todo** — at full speed, as quickly as possible; **a mejor** — at best; **a peor** — at worst; **estar a un** — to be on the same footing.

andariego *adj* wandering, roving; fond of travelling; restless.

andarín *nm* walker; **es muy** — he is a great walker.

andarivel *nm* (a) cableway, cable ferry; (*Naut etc*) handrope; (*Arg*) rope bridge, temporary footbridge; (*Arg*) lane (*in a swimming pool*). (b) (*Col*) adornments, trinkets.

andas *nfpl* stretcher; litter, sedan chair; portable platform; bier; **llevar a uno en** — (*fig*) to overpraise someone; to rate someone excessively high.

ándele *interj* (*Mex*) come on!

andén *nm* (*Rail*) platform; (*Aut*) hard shoulder (*of a motorway*); (*Guat, Hond*) pavement, footpath, sidewalk (*US*); (*Naut*) quayside; (*Arg, Bol, Per: Agr*) terrace; — **de vacío** (*Rail*) arrival platform.

Andes *mpl* Andes.

andinismo *nm* (*SAm*) mountaineering, climbing; **hacer** — to go mountaineering, go climbing.

andinista *nmf* (*SAm*) mountaineer, climber.

andino *adj* Andean, of the Andes.

andito *nm* balcony, upper walk.

andolina *nf* swallow.

andón *adj* (*SAm*) = **andador**.

andonear [1a] *vi* (*Ven*) to amble along.

andorga *nf* (*fam*) belly.

andorina *nf* swallow.

Andorra *f* Andorra.

andorrano 1 *adj* Andorran. **2** *nm*, **andorrana** *nf* Andorran.

andorrear [1a] *vi* (*fam*) to bustle about, fuss around; to gad about, move about a lot.

andorrero 1 *adj* bustling, busy. **2** *nm*, **andorrera** *nf* busy sort, gadabout.

andrajo *nm* (a) rag, tatter; —**s** rags, tatters; **estar en** —**s** to be in rags. (b) rascal, good-for-nothing; trifle, mere nothing.

andrajoso *adj* ragged, in tatters.

Andrés *m* Andrew.

andrómina *nf* (*fam*) fib, tale; piece of humbug; trick.

andullo *nm* (*Arg, Cu, Mex*) plug of chewing tobacco.

andurrial *nm* (*Arg, Ec, Per*) muddy place, quagmire; —**es** out-of-the way place, the wilds; **en esos** —**es** in that godforsaken spot, in that remote area.

anea *nf* bulrush; reedmace.

aneblar [1k] **1** *vt* to cover with mist (*or cloud*); (*fig*) to obscure, darken, cast a cloud over. **2 aneblarse** *vr* to get misty, get cloudy; to get dark.

anécdota *nf* anecdote, story.

anecdótico *adj* anecdotal; **contenido** — story content; **valor** — story value, value as a story.

anega *nf* (*Arg*) = **fanega**.

anegación *nf* drowning; flooding.

anegadizo *adj* *land* subject to flooding, frequently flooded; *substance* heavier than water.

anegar [1h] **1** *vt* (a) to drown. (b) to flood; (*fig*) to overwhelm, destroy.

2 anegarse *vr* (a) to drown. (b) to flood, be flooded; — **en llanto** to dissolve into tears. (c) (*Naut*) to sink, founder.

anejo 1 *adj* attached; dependent; — **a** attached to; joined on to. **2** *nm* (*Archit*) annexe, outbuilding; (*Lit, Typ*) supplement.

anemia *nf* anaemia.

anémico *adj* anaemic.

anemómetro *nm* anemometer; (*Aer*) wind gauge; — **registrador** airspeed indicator.

anémona *nf*, **anémone** *nf* anemone; — **de mar** sea anemone.

aneroide *adj* aneroid.

anestesia *nf* anaesthesia.

anestesiar [1b] *vt* to anaesthetize, give an anaesthetic to.

anestésico 1 *adj* anaesthetic. **2** *nm* anaesthetic.

anestesista *nmf* anaesthetist.

anexar [1a] *vt* (a) (*Pol*) to annex. (b) *document etc* to attach, append; to enclose.

anexión *nf*, **anexionamiento** *nm* (*Arg, Chi*) annexation.

anexo 1 *adj* attached; dependent (*also Eccl*); **llevar algo** —, **tener algo** — to have something attached. **2** *nm* (*Archit*) annexe, outbuilding; (*Eccl*) dependency; (*in letter*) enclosure, enclosed document.

anfibio 1 *adj* amphibious; amphibian (*also Aer etc*). **2** *nm* amphibian; **los anfibios** (*as class*) the amphibia.

anfiteatro *nm* amphitheatre; (*Theat*) dress circle; — **anatómico** dissecting room.

Anfitrión *m* Amphitryon.

anfitrión *nm* host.

anfitriona *nf* hostess.

ánfora *nf* amphora; (*Bol, Guat, Mex, Per*) ballot box.

anfractuosidad *nf* roughness, unevenness; bend; turning; (*Anat*) fold, convolution; —**es** (*SAm*) rough places, up-and-down parts.

anfractuoso *adj* (*SAm*) rough, uneven, up-and-down.

angarilla *nf* (*SAm*), **angarillas** *nfpl* handbarrow; panniers, packs; (*Cook*) cruet, cruet stand.

angarrio *adj* (*Col, Ven*) terribly thin.

angas: por — **o por mangas** (*Mex*) for some reason or other; (*Per*) willy-nilly.

ángel *nm* (a) angel; — **caído** fallen angel; — **custodio**, — **de la guarda** guardian angel.
(b) **tener** — to have charm, be very charming; **tener mal** — to be a nasty piece of work; to have an unfortunate effect (on people *etc*).

angélica *nf* angelica.

angelical *adj*, **angélico** *adj* angelic(al).

angelito *nm* little angel; (*SAm*) dead child; ¡—! (*Arg, Mex*) you're not that innocent!, tell us another!; ¡no seas —! (*Arg*) don't be so silly!

angelón *nm*:— **de retablo** fat old thing.

angelote *nm* chubby child.

ángelus *nm* angelus.

angina *nf* angina, quinsy; (*Mex*) tonsil; — **de pecho** angina pectoris; **tener** —**s** to have a sore throat.

anglicanismo *nm* Anglicanism.

anglicano 1 *adj* Anglican. **2** *nm*, **anglicana** *nf* Anglican.

anglicismo *nm* anglicism.

anglicista *nmf* anglicist.

anglo ... anglo ...

anglocatolicismo *nm* Anglo-Catholicism.

anglocatólico 1 *adj* Anglo-Catholic. **2** *nm*, **anglocatólica** *nf* Anglo-Catholic.

anglófilo *nm*, **anglófila** *nf* anglophile.

anglófobo *nm*, **anglófoba** *nf* anglophobe.

angloindio 1 *adj* Anglo-Indian. **2** *nm*, **angloindia** *nf* Anglo-Indian.

anglosajón 1 *adj* Anglo-Saxon. **2** *nm*, **anglosajona** *nf* Anglo-Saxon. **3** *nm* (*language*) Anglo-Saxon.

angora *nmf* angora.

angorina *nf* artificial angora.

angostar [1a] **1** *vt* to narrow. **2 angostarse** *vr* to narrow, get narrow(er).

angosto *adj* narrow.

angostura *nf* (a) narrowness. (b) (*Naut*) narrows, strait; (*Geog*) narrow passage, narrow defile, narrow place.

angra *nf* cove, creek.

anguila *nf* eel; —**s** (*Naut*) slipway.

angular *adj* angular; *see* **piedra**.

Angulema Angoulême.

ángulo *nm* angle (*also Math*); corner; bend, turning; (*Mech*) knee, bend; — **agudo** acute angle; — **alterno** alternate angle; — **obtuso** obtuse angle; — **recto** right angle; **de** — **recto**, **en** — **recto** right-angled; — **del ojo** corner of one's eye; — **de subida** (*Aer*) angle of climb; **de gran** —, **de ancho** lens *etc* wide-angle; **en** — at an angle; **está inclinado a un** — **de 45 grados** it is leaning at an angle of 45°; **formar** — **con** to be at an angle to.

anguloso *adj* angular, sharp; tortuous, full of bends.

angurria *nf* (*Arg, Col*) (a) desperate hunger, greed; **comer con** — to eat greedily. (b) meanness, stinginess.

angurriento *adj*, **angurrioso** *adj* (*Arg, Col*) (a) greedy. (b) mean, stingy.

angustia *nf* anguish, distress; — **vital** (*Med*) anxiety state.

angustiado *adj* (a) anguished, distressed. (b) grasping, mean.

angustiar [1b] **1** *vt* to distress, grieve, cause anguish to.

2 angustiarse *vr* to be distressed, grieve, feel anguish (*por* at, on account of); to worry, get worried.

angustiosamente *adv* in an anguished tone (*etc*); anxiously; distressingly.

angustioso *adj* distressed, anguished; anxious; distressing, agonizing; heartbreaking.

anhá *interj* (*Arg*) = **anjá**.

anhelación *nf* (a) panting. (b) longing, yearning.

anhelante *adj* (a) *breathing* panting. (b) (*fig*) eager; longing, yearning.

anhelar [1a] **1** *vt* to be eager for; to long for, yearn for, crave.
2 *vi* (a) (*Med*) to gasp, pant.
(b) (*fig*) — + *infin* to be eager to + *infin*, long to + *infin*, yearn to + *infin*; — **por algo** to long for something, hanker after something; — **por** + *infin* to aspire to + *infin*.

anhelo *nm* eagerness; longing, yearning, desire (*de, por* for); **con** — longingly, yearningly; **tener** —**s de** to be eager for, long for.

anheloso *adj* (a) (*Med*) gasping, panting; *breathing* heavy, difficult. (b) (*fig*) eager, anxious.

Aníbal *m* Hannibal.

anidar [1a] **1** *vt* to take in, shelter. **2** *vi* (*Orn*) to nest, make its nest; (*fig*) to live, make one's home.

anieblar [1a] = **aneblar**.

aniego *nm* (*Chi*), **aniegue** *nm* (*Mex*) flood.

anilina *nf* aniline.

anilla *nf* curtain ring; small ring; cigar band; (*Orn*) ring; —**s** (*Sport*) rings.

anillado *adj* ringed; ring-shaped.

anillar [1a] *vt* to make into a ring, make rings in; to fasten with a ring; (*Orn*) to ring.

anillejo *nm*, **anillete** *nm* small ring, ringlet.

anillo *nm* ring (*also Astron, Mech*); cigar band; — **de boda** wedding ring; — **de compromiso**, **de prometida** engagement ring; — **pastoral** bishop's ring; **no creo que se me caigan los** —**s por eso** I don't feel it's in any way beneath my dignity; **venir como** — **al dedo** to be just right, meet the case perfectly; to come just at the right time.

ánima *nf* (a) (*Rel*) soul; — **bendita**, — **en pena**, — **del purgatorio** soul in purgatory; **las** —**s** (*Eccl*) angelus, sunset bell. (b) (*Mil*) bore.

animación *nf* liveliness, life; bustle, movement, animation; sprightliness; **había poca** — there wasn't much life about it; **una escena llena de** — a scene full of life.

animadamente *adv* in lively fashion, gaily; animatedly; in sprightly fashion; merrily.

animado *adj* (a) lively, gay: bustling, busy, animated; sprightly; merry, in high spirits. (b) well-attended, popular. (c) (*Zool*) animate. (d) (*SAm: Med*) better, improving.

animador *nm* (*SAm*) compère, master of ceremonies; cheer leader.

animadora *nf* night-club singer, crooner; (*SAm*) cheer leader.

animadversión *nf* ill will, antagonism; animadversion.

animal 1 *adj* (a) animal. (b) (*fig*) stupid.
2 *nm* (a) animal.
(b) (*fig*) fool, idiot; (*fig*) beast, brute; ¡—! you brute!; **el** — **de Juan** that beast of a John; ¡qué — **de policía!** what a beast of a policeman!; ¡no seas —! don't be beastly!, don't be horrid!

animalada *nf* (a) (*SAm*) group of animals, herd of animals.
(b) (*fig*) foolishness, stupidity; silly thing (to do *or* say *etc*); coarse thing, piece of disgraceful conduct; **hacer una** — to do something silly; to do something disgraceful.

animalaje *nm* (*RPl*) group of animals, herd of animals.

animalejo *nm* odd-looking creature, nasty animal.

animalidad *nf* animality.

animalizarse [1f] *vr* (*SAm*) to become brutalized.

animalote *nm* big animal.

animalucho *nm* ugly brute.

animar [1a] **1** *vt* (a) (*Bio*) to animate, give life to.
(b) *discussion, meeting etc* to enliven, liven up, add interest to; *room, fire, scene, view etc* to brighten up; *dull thing* to stimulate, give new life to, ginger up.
(c) *person* to cheer up; to encourage, put new heart into; — **a uno a hacer algo** to encourage someone to do something.
2 animarse *vr* (a) to become more lively, liven up, acquire new life; to brighten up.
(b) (*person*) to brighten up, cheer up, feel encouraged, take heart; to make up one's mind,

decide; **¡anímate!** cheer up!, buck up!; make up your mind!; **¿te animas?** are you game?; **— a hacer algo** to make up one's mind to do something, resolve to do something.

ánimo nm **(a)** mind; soul, spirit.

(b) courage, pluck; nerve; energy; **caer(se) de —** to lose heart, get disheartened; **cobrar —** to take heart, pluck up courage; **dar —(s) a, infundir — a** to encourage; **dilatar el — a uno** to put heart into someone.

(c) intention, purpose; **con — de +** infin with the intention of + ger, with the idea of + ger; **estar con — de +** infin to feel like + ger; **hacer — de +** infin to intend to + infin, mean to + infin; **tener —s para algo** to be in the mood for something, feel like something.

(d) ¡—! interj cheer up!; (Sport) come on!, go it!

animosamente adv bravely; with spirit, in lively fashion.

animosidad nf **(a)** courage, nerve. **(b)** animosity, ill will.

animoso adj brave; spirited, lively.

aniñado adj childlike; (pej) childish, puerile.

aniñarse [1a] vr to become childish; to act childishly.

aniquilación nf, **aniquilamiento** nm annihilation, destruction.

aniquilar [1a] **1** vt to annihilate, destroy, obliterate, wipe out.

2 aniquilarse vr **(a)** to be annihilated, be wiped out.

(b) (fig) to deteriorate, decline; (Med) to waste away; (of fortune etc) to disappear, be frittered away.

anís nm **(a)** (Bot) anise, aniseed. **(b)** (drink) anis, anisette; **estar hecho un —** (Bol, Ec, Per) to be dressed up to the nines; **llegar a los anises** to turn up late. **(c)** (Col) strength, energy.

anisado adj flavoured with aniseed.

aniseros nmpl (Col: sl): **entregar los —** to kick the bucket (sl); **vaciar los — a uno** to bump someone off (sl).

anisete nm anisette.

anivelar [1a] vt (Arg) **=nivelar.**

aniversario nm anniversary.

anjá interj (Ant, Mex, RPl) yes of course!; so that's it!; whatever next!

Anjeo m Anjou.

ano nm anus.

anoche adv last night; **antes de —** the night before last.

anochecedor nm, **anochecedora** nf late bird, person who keeps late hours.

anochecer 1 [2d] vi **(a)** to get dark.

(b) (person) to arrive at nightfall; **anochecimos en Toledo** we got to Toledo as night was falling.

2 nm nightfall, dusk; **al —** at nightfall; **antes del —** by nightfall, before nightfall.

anochecida nf nightfall, dusk.

anodino 1 adj anodyne; (fig) anodyne, harmless, inoffensive; dull. **2** nm anodyne.

ánodo nm anode.

anomalía nf anomaly.

anómalo adj anomalous.

anonadación nm, **anonadamiento** nm **(a)** annihilation, destruction. **(b)** discouragement, despair; humiliation.

anonadar [1a] **1** vt **(a)** to annihilate, destroy; to overwhelm. **(b)** to discourage, depress; to humiliate.

2 anonadarse vr **(a)** to be crushed, be overwhelmed.

(b) to get discouraged; to be humiliated.

anónimamente adv anonymously.

anonimato nm anonymity.

anónimo 1 adj anonymous; nameless; (Comm, Fin) company limited.

2 nm **(a)** anonymity; **conservar el —** to preserve one's anonymity.

(b) anonymous person, unknown person.

(c) anonymous letter; anonymous document, unsigned literary work.

anorak nm anorak.

anormal adj abnormal; irregular, unusual; child subnormal, mentally handicapped.

anormalidad nf abnormality; irregularity; unusual nature; subnormality, mental handicap.

anormalmente adv abnormally, unusually.

anotación nf annotation; note, record, observation; (SAm: Sport) score.

anotador nm annotator; (SAm) scorecard.

anotadora nf (Cine) script girl, continuity girl.

anotar [1a] vt to annotate; to note (down), jot down,

take down; to register, record; (Comm) order to note, book; (SAm: Sport) to score.

anquilostoma nm hookworm.

ánsar nm goose.

ansarino nm gosling.

Anselmo m Anselm.

ansia nf **(a)** anxiety, worry; fear, anguish. **(b)** yearning, longing (de for). **(c)** (Med) anxiety, nervous tension. **(d) —s** (Med) nausea, sick feeling.

ansiado adj longed-for; **el momento tan — the** moment which we (etc) had so much longed for.

ansiar [1b] **1** vt to long for, yearn for; to covet, crave; **— + infin** to long to + infin, yearn to + infin.

2 vi: **— por una** to be madly in love with someone.

ansiedad nf **(a)** anxiety, worry; solicitude; suspense. **(b)** (Med) anxiety, nervous tension.

ansina adv (SAm) **= así.**

ansioso adj **(a)** anxious, uneasy, worried; solicitous; **esperamos —s** we waited anxiously; **— de algo, — por algo** eager for something, avid for something; greedy for something. **(b)** (Med) anxious, nervously tense; sick, queasy.

anta nm elk, moose; (SAm) tapir.

antagónico adj antagonistic; opposed, contrasting.

antagonismo nm antagonism.

antagonista nmf antagonist, opponent.

antañazo adv a long time ago.

antaño adv last year; long ago, formerly.

antañón adj ancient, very old, of long ago.

antañoso adj (Bol) ancient, very old.

antarca nf (Arg, Bol) on one's back.

antártico 1 adj Antarctic. **2** nm: **el A—** the Antarctic.

Antártida f Antarctica.

ante[1] nm **(a)** (Zool) elk, moose; buffalo; (Mex) tapir. **(b)** buckskin, suède.

ante[2] prep person before, in the presence of; enemy, danger etc in the face of; difficulty faced with; matter with regard to; **— esta posibilidad** in view of this possibility; **— tantas posibilidades** faced with so many possibilities; **estamos — un gran porvenir** we have a great future before us.

anteado adj buff-coloured, fawn.

anteanoche adv the night before last.

anteayer adv the day before yesterday.

antebrazo nm forearm.

anteburro nm (SAm) tapir.

antecámara nf anteroom, antechamber; lobby.

antecedente 1 adj previous, preceding, foregoing; **visto lo —** in view of the foregoing.

2 nm **(a)** (Math, Philos, Gram) antecedent. **(b) —s** record, history, background; **¿cuáles son sus —s?** what's his history?, what's his background like?; **—s penales** criminal record; **un hombre sin —s** a man with a clean record; **estar en —s** to know all about it, be well informed; **poner a uno en —s** to put someone in the picture, give someone the latest information.

anteceder [2a] vt to precede, go before.

antecesor 1 adj previous, former. **2** nm, **antecesora** nf predecessor; ancestor, forbear.

antecomedor nm (SAm) room adjoining the dining room.

antecocina nf scullery.

antedatar [1a] vt to antedate.

antedicho adj aforesaid, aforementioned.

antediluviano adj antediluvian.

anteiglesia nf (Eccl) porch.

antejuela nf (CAm) **=lentejuela.**

antelación nf precedence, priority; **con —** in advance, in good time, beforehand; **con mucha —** long in advance, long beforehand.

antelina nf suède, artificial buckskin.

antellevar [1a] vt (Mex: Aut) to run down, knock down.

antellevón nm (Mex: Aut) accident.

antemano: de — adv in advance, beforehand.

antena nf **(a)** (Zool) feeler, antenna. **(b)** (Naut) lateen yard. **(c)** (Radio etc) aerial, antenna; **— direccional** directional aerial; **— encerrada** built-in aerial; **— interior** indoor aerial.

antenatal adj antenatal, prenatal.

antenombre nm title.

anteojera nf **(a)** spectacle case. **(b) —s** blinkers.

anteojero nm spectacle maker, optician.

anteojo nm **(a)** eyeglass, spyglass, (small) telescope; **— de larga vista** telescope; **— binóculo** binoculars, field glasses; **— prismático** prism binoculars; **— de teatro** opera glasses. **(b) —s** spectacles, glasses; (Aut, Tech etc) goggles; (horse's) blinkers; **—s ahumados** smoked glasses; —s **de concha** horn-rimmed spectacles; —s **para el sol** sunglasses.

antepagar [1h] *vt* to prepay, pay ·beforehand.

antepasado 1 *adj* previous, immediately past, before last. **2** *nm* ancestor, forbear; **mis** —s my forbears, my forefathers.

antepecho *nm* (*of bridge etc*) rail, guardrail, parapet; (*of window*) ledge, sill; (*Mil*) parapet, breastwork.

antepenúltimo *adj* last but two, antepenultimate.

anteponer [2r] **1** *vt* (a) to place in front (*a* of). (b) (*fig*) to prefer (*a* to).
  2 anteponerse *vr* (a) to be in front, come in between (*a* of). (b) **— a** (*fig*) to overcome.

anteportal *nm* porch.

anteproyecto *nm* preliminary sketch, preliminary plan; (*esp fig*) blueprint.

antepuerto *nm* outer harbour.

antequerano 1 *adj* of Antequera. **2** *nm*, **antequerana** *nf* native (*or* inhabitant) of Antequera; **los** —s the people of Antequera.

antera *nf* anther.

anterior *adj* (a) *leg, part etc* front, fore, anterior; **en la parte — del coche** on the front part of the car.
  (b) (*in order*) preceding, previous, former; (*Gram*) anterior; aforementioned; **cada uno mejor que el** — each one better than the last; **se había olvidado de todo lo** — he had forgotten all that had happened previously.
  (c) (*in time*) former; previous (*a* to), earlier (*a* than); **un texto — a 1140** a text earlier than 1140; **el día** — the previous day, the day before.

anterioridad *nf* precedence, priority; (*in rank*) seniority; **con** — previously, beforehand; **con — a esto** prior to this, before this.

anteriormente *adv* previously, before.

antes 1 *adv* (a) before; first; once, previously, formerly; sooner, before now; **3 días** — 3 days before, 3 days earlier; **no quiso venir** — he didn't want to come any earlier; **conviene cazar — la liebre** first catch your hare; **la planta existió aquí** — the plant occurred here formerly, the plant used to grow here; **lo vio — que yo** he saw it before I did; **— hoy que mañana** the sooner the better; **lo — posible, cuanto** — as soon as possible; as quickly as possible; **mucho** — long before; **poco** — shortly before, a short time previously.
  (b) sooner, rather; **— (bien)** rather, on the contrary; **— muerto que esclavo** better dead than enslaved; **preferimos ir en tren — que en avión** we prefer to go by train rather than by plane; **no cederemos: — lo destruimos todo** we shall never give up: rather than that we shall destroy everything.
  2 — de *prep* before; previous to; **— de 1900** before 1900; up to 1900; **— de hacerlo** before doing it; **— de terminado el discurso** before the speech was over.
  3 — (de) que *conj* before; **— de que te vayas** before you go.

antesala *nf* anteroom, antechamber; lobby; **estamos en la — de** (*fig*) we are on the verge of, we are on the threshold of; **hacer** — to wait to be received, wait to go in to see somebody, (*fig*) cool one's heels.

antesalazo *nm* (*Mex*) long wait (*before being admitted to someone's presence*).

anti... anti...; un...; non-...

antiácido 1 *adj* antacid. **2** *nm* antacid.

antiadherente *adj* non-stick.

antiaéreo 1 *adj* anti-aircraft. **2** *nm* (*SAm*) anti-aircraft gun.

antialcohólico (*SAm*) **1** *adj* teetotal. **2** *nm*, anti-alcohólica *nf* teetotaller.

antiamericano *adj* anti-American; un-American.

antibiótico 1 *adj* antibiotic. **2** *nm* antibiotic.

anticiclón *nm* anticyclone.

anticipación *nf* anticipation; foretaste; (*Comm, Fin*) advance; **hacer algo con** — to do something in good time; **reservar con** — to book in advance, book early; **llegar con bastante** — to arrive early, arrive in good time; **llegar con 10 minutos de** — to come 10 minutes early.

anticipadamente *adv* in advance, beforehand; **le doy las gracias** — I thank you in advance.

anticipado *adj* future, prospective; *payment etc* advance; **anticipadas gracias** thanks in advance.

anticipar [1a] **1** *vt* (a) *date, event* to bring forward, advance; to hasten (the date of); **anticiparon las vacaciones** they took their holiday early.
  (b) *money* to advance, lend, loan.
  (c) **— algo con placer** to look forward to something; **— las gracias a uno** to thank someone in advance.

(d) (*SAm: angl*) to anticipate, foresee; **— que ...** to anticipate that ...
  2 anticiparse *vr* (a) (*event*) to take place early, happen before the expected time.
  (b) **— a un acontecimiento** to anticipate an event, forestall an event; **— a uno** to beat someone to it, steal a march on someone; **Vd se ha anticipado a mis deseos** you have anticipated my wishes; **— a hacer algo** to do something ahead of time, do something before the proper time.

anticipo *nm* (a) anticipation, foretaste; **fue el — del fin para toda una época** it was the beginning of the end for a whole epoch; **esto es sólo un** — this is just a foretaste.
  (b) (*Comm, Fin*) advance, loan; advance payment.
  (c) (*Law*) retaining fee.

anticlerical 1 *adj* anticlerical. **2** *nmf* anticlerical.

anticlericalismo *nm* anticlericalism.

anticlinal *nm* (*SAm*) watershed; (*Geol*) anticline.

anticoagulante 1 *adj* anticoagulant. **2** *nm* anticoagulant.

anticoncepcional *adj* birth-control (*attr*), family-planning (*attr*), contraceptive.

anticonceptivo 1 *adj* birth-control (*attr*), family-planning (*attr*), contraceptive; **métodos** —s birth-control methods, contraceptive devices; **píldora anticonceptiva** contraceptive pill.
  2 *nm* contraceptive.

anticongelante 1 *adj* antifreeze. **2** *nm* antifreeze (solution).

anticorrosivo *adj* anticorrosive, antirust.

anticonstitucional *adj* unconstitutional.

anticristo *nm* Antichrist.

anticuado *adj* antiquated, old-fashioned, out-of-date; obsolete.

anticuario 1 *adj* antiquarian. **2** *nm* (*scholar etc*) antiquarian, antiquary; (*Comm*) antique dealer.

anticuarse [1d] *vr* to become antiquated, get out of date; to become obsolete.

anticucho *nm* (*Per*) delicacy eaten as an aperitif at the bar counter.

anticuerpo *nm* antibody.

antideportividad *nf* unsporting attitude, unsportsmanlike behaviour.

antideportivo *adj* unsporting, unsportsmanlike.

antiderrapante *adj* (*Aut*) non-skid.

antideslizante 1 *adj* non-slipping; (*Aut*) non-skid. **2** *nm* (*SAm*) non-skid tyre.

antideslumbrante *adj* anti-dazzle, anti-glare.

antidetonante *adj* (*Aut*) antiknock.

antídoto *nm* antidote (*contra, de* against, for, to).

antidumping *adj*: **medidas —** (*Comm: angl*) anti-dumping measures, measures against dumping.

antieconómico *adj* uneconomic(al); wasteful.

antiestético *adj* unsightly, ugly, offensive.

antifascismo *nm* antifascism.

antifascista 1 *adj* antifascist. **2** *nmf* antifascist.

antifatiga *adj*: **píldora —** anti-fatigue pill, pep pill (*fam*).

antifaz *nm* mask; veil.

antífona *nf* antiphony; anthem.

antifranquista 1 *adj* anti-Franco. **2** *nmf* opponent of Franco, person opposed to Franco.

antifriccional *adj* antifriction.

antifrís *nm* (*SAm: angl*) antifreeze (solution).

antigás *adj*: **careta —** gasmask.

Antígona *f* Antigone.

antigualla *nf* antique; (*pej*) old thing, relic, out-of-date object (*or* custom *etc*); old story; (*person*) has-been, back number; —s (*pej*) old things, junk.

antiguamente *adv* formerly, once; in ancient times, long ago.

antigüedad *nf* (a) antiquity; **los artistas de la** — the artists of antiquity, the artists of the ancient world; **remota** — high antiquity.
  (b) antiquity, age.
  (c) antique; —es antiques; antiquities; **tienda de** —es antique shop.
  (d) (*in rank*) seniority.

antiguo 1 *adj* (a) old; ancient; *car etc* vintage, classic; **a la antigua** in the ancient manner, in the old-fashioned way; **de** — from time immemorial, since ancient times; **en lo** — in olden times, in ancient times.
  (b) former, old, one-time; **un — alumno mío** an old pupil of mine; **— primer ministro** former prime minister.
  (c) **más —** (*in rank*) senior; **socio más —** senior partner; **es más — que yo** he is senior to me, he is my senior.
  2 —s *nmpl* the ancients.

antihigiénico *adj* unhygienic, insanitary.

antihistamínico 1 *adj* antihistamine. **2** *nm* antihistamine.

antilogaritmo *nm* antilogarithm.

antílope *nm* antelope.

antillanismo *nm* word (*or* phrase *etc*) peculiar to the Antilles.

antillano 1 *adj* of the Antilles, West Indian. **2** *nm*, **antillana** *nf* native (*or* inhabitant) of the Antilles, West Indian; **los —s** the West Indians.

Antillas *fpl* Antilles, West Indies.

antimacasar *nm* antimacassar.

antimisil *adj* antimissile; **misil —** antimissile missile.

antimonio *nm* antimony.

antimonopolios *adj invar*: **ley —** anti-trust law.

antinatural *adj* unnatural.

Antioquía *f* Antioch.

antioxidante *adj* antirust.

antipara *nf* screen.

antiparras *nfpl* (*fam*) glasses, specs (*fam*).

antipatía *nf* antipathy (*hacia* towards, *entre* between), dislike (*hacia* for); unfriendliness (*hacia* towards).

antipático *adj* disagreeable, unpleasant, antipathetic; uncongenial; **es un tipo —** he's a disagreeable sort; **me es muy —** I don't like him at all; **es de lo más —** he's horrible; **en un ambiente —** in an uncongenial atmosphere, in an unfriendly environment.

antipatizar [1f] *vi* (*SAm*) to feel unfriendly; **— con uno** to dislike someone.

antipatriótico *adj* unpatriotic.

antípodas *nfpl* antipodes.

antipolilla *adj invar* mothproof.

antiproyectil *adj* antimissile.

antiquista (*Mex*) **1** *adj* antiquarian. **2** *nm* antiquarian.

antirresbaladizo *adj* (*Aut*) non-skid.

antirrino *nm* antirrhinum.

antisemita *nmf* anti-semite.

antisemítico *adj* anti-semitic.

antisemitismo *nm* anti-semitism.

antiséptico 1 *adj* antiseptic. **2** *nm* antiseptic.

antisocial *adj* antisocial.

antisudoral (*SAm*) **1** *adj* deodorant. **2** *nm* deodorant.

antitanque *adj* antitank.

antítesis *nf*, *pl* **antítesis** antithesis.

antitético *adj* antithetic(al).

antiviviseccionista *nmf* antivivisectionist.

antojadizo *adj* capricious; given to sudden fancies, unpredictable.

antojado *adj* eager, desirous.

antojarse [1a] *vr* (**a**) **— algo** to take a fancy to, want.
  (**b**) **— que ...** to imagine that ..., fancy that ..., have the feeling that ...; **se me antoja que no estará** I have the feeling that he won't be in.
  (**c**) **— + infin** to have a mind to **+** *infin*; **se me antoja comprarlo** I have a mind to buy it, I fancy buying it; **no se le antojó decir otra cosa** it didn't occur to him to say anything else; **no se le antoja ir** he doesn't feel like going; **¿cómo se le antoja esto?** how does this seem to you?

antojitos *nmpl* (*Arg*) sweets, candy (*US*); (*Mex*) savouries.

antojo *nm* (**a**) caprice, whim, passing fancy, notion; **hacer a su —** to do as one pleases; **¿cuál es su —?** what's your idea?; **no morirse de —** (*RPl*) to be very unwilling.
  (**b**) (*of pregnant woman*) craving; **tener —s** (*RPl*) to have cravings, be pregnant.
  (**c**) (*Anat*) birthmark, mole.

antología *nf* anthology.

antónimo *nm* antonym.

Antonio *m* Anthony.

antonomasia *nf* antonomasia; **por —** par excellence.

antorcha *nf* torch; (*fig*) torch, lamp; **— a soplete** blowlamp.

antracita *nf* anthracite.

ántrax *nm* anthrax.

antro *nm* cavern; **— de corrupción** (*fig*) den of iniquity.

antropofagia *nf* cannibalism.

antropófago 1 *adj* man-eating, anthropophagous; cannibalistic. **2** *nm* cannibal; **—s** anthropophagi.

antropoide *adj* anthropoid.

antropoideo *nm* anthropoid.

antropomorfismo *nm* anthropomorphism.

antropología *nf* anthropology; **— social** social anthropology.

antropológico *adj* anthropological.

antropólogo *nm* anthropologist.

antruejo *nm* carnival.

antucá *nm* (*Arg*) sunshade, parasol.

antuviada *nf* sudden blow, bump.

antuviado *adj* (*Mex*) precocious.

antuvión *nm* sudden blow, bump; **de —** suddenly, unexpectedly.

anual 1 *adj* annual. **2** *nm* (*Bot*) annual.

anualidad *nf* (**a**) (*Fin*) annuity; annual payment. (**b**) annual occurrence.

anualmente *adv* annually, yearly.

anuario *nm* yearbook; annual; trade directory; reference book, handbook.

anubarrado *adj* cloudy, overcast.

anublar 1 *vt* (**a**) to cloud (over); to dim, darken, obscure.
  (**b**) (*Bot*) to blight; to wither, dry up.
  2 anublarse *vr* (**a**) to cloud over, become cloudy, become overcast; to darken, get dark.
  (**b**) (*Bot*) to wither, dry up; (*fig*) to fade away.

anudar [1a] **1** *vt* to knot, tie; to join, link, unite; *story* to resume, take up again; *voice* to choke, strangle.
  2 anudarse *vr* (**a**) to get into knots, get tied up.
  (**b**) (*Bot*) to remain stunted.
  (**c**) **se me anudó la voz (en la garganta)** I got a lump in my throat.

anulación *nf* annulment, cancellation; revocation, repeal.

anular[1] [1a] *vt* to annul, cancel; *decision etc* to overrule, override; *law* to revoke, repeal; *effect* to nullify; cancel out; *goal* to disallow; (*Math*) to cancel out; *person* to deprive of authority, remove from office.

anular[2] **1** *adj* ring-shaped, annular; **dedo — =2** *nm* ring finger.

anunciación *nf* announcement; **A—** (*Rel*) Annunciation; **(día de) la A—** the Annunciation, Lady Day (25 *March*).

anunciador *nm* announcer; (*Theat*) compère; (*Mex: Radio*) announcer.

anunciante *nmf* (*Comm*) advertiser.

anunciar [1b] **1** *vt* to announce; to proclaim; to forebode, foreshadow; *toast* to propose; (*Comm*) to advertise.
  2 anunciarse *vr*: **el festival se anuncia animado** the festival looks like being lively, everything points to the festival being a lively one; **la cosecha se anuncia buena** the crop promises to be a good one.

anuncio *nm* (**a**) announcement; sign, omen; notice.
  (**b**) (*Comm etc*) advertisement; placard, poster; (*Theat etc*) bill; **—s económicos, —s por palabras** classified advertisements, small advertisements; **— luminoso** illuminated sign.

anuo *adj* annual.

anverso *nm* obverse.

anzuelo *nm* hook, fish hook; (*fig*) bait, lure; **echar el —** to offer a bait, offer an inducement; **picar en el —, tragar el —** to swallow the bait.

añada *nf* (*Agr*) (**a**) year, season. (**b**) piece of field, strip.

añadido *nm* false hair, switch, hairpiece.

añadidura *nf* addition, extra, thing added; (*Comm*) extra measure, extra weight; **dar algo de —** to give something extra; **con algo de —** with something else, with something into the bargain; **por —** besides, in addition; on top of all that.

añadir [3a] *vt* to add (*a* to); to increase; *charm, interest etc* to add, lend (*a* to).

añagaza *nf* (*Hunting*) lure, decoy; (*fig*) lure, bait, inducement.

añal 1 *adj* (**a**) *event* yearly, annual. (**b**) (*Agr*) yearold. **2** *nm* year-old animal, yearling.

añangá *nm* (*RPl*) the devil.

añango *adj* (*Ec*) child sickly.

añañay *interj* (*Chi*) jolly good! (*fam*).

añascar [1g] *vt* to scrape together, get together bit by bit.

añaz *nm* (*Per*) skunk.

añejar [1a] **1** *vt* to age. **2 añejarse** *vr* to age, get old; (*of wine*) to-age, improve with age, mellow; (*pej*) to get stale, go musty.

añejo *adj* old; *wine* mellow, mature; (*pej*) stale, musty.

añicos *nmpl* bits, pieces, fragments; splinters; **hacer un papel —** to tear a piece of paper into little bits; **hacer un vaso —** to smash a glass, shatter a glass; **hacerse —** to shatter, smash to pieces; **hacerse —** (*fig*) to wear oneself out.

añil *nm* (*Bot*) indigo; (*dye*) indigo, indigo blue; (*for washing*) blue, bluing.

añilar [1a] *vt* to dye indigo; *washing* to blue.

añinos *nmpl* lamb's wool.

año *nm* (**a**) year; **— bisiesto** leap year; **— civil, — común** calendar year; **el — 66 de Cristo** 66 A.D.; **— económico** fiscal year; **— escolar** school year; **— de gracia** year of grace; **— lectivo** school year; **— luz**

light-year; **100 —s luz** 100 light-years; **A— Nuevo** New Year; **¡feliz — nuevo!** happy new year!; **día de A— Nuevo** New Year's Day; **— de nuestra salud** year of Our Lord; **el — verde** (SAm) never; **¡mal — para él!** good riddance to him!, and the best of luck! (iro); **hace —s** years ago; **esperamos —s y —s** we waited years and years; **5 toneladas al — 5** tons a year; **al — de casado** a year after his marriage, after he had been married a year; **una cosa del — uno** (or **catapún, de la pera**) an antiquated thing, a totally obsolete thing; **estar de buen —** to look well-fed, be in good shape; **en el — 1980** in 1980; **en los —s 60 y 70** in the sixties and seventies; **en estos últimos —s** in recent years, of late years; **en el — de la nana** (or **nanita, polca**) in the year dot, way back; **por los —s de 1950** about 1950; **¡por muchos —s!** (toast) here's health!, (birthday) many happy returns!, (introduction) how do you do?

(**b**) **—s** (of person) age, years; **cumplir los 21 —s** to reach 21, have one's 21st birthday; **cumplir —s** to have a birthday; **¿cuántos —s tienes?** how old are you?; **tengo 9 —s** I'm 9; **con los —s que yo tengo** at my age; (**nunca**) **en los —s que tengo** never before, never in my life; **de pocos —s** young, small; **entrado en —s** elderly, advanced in years.

añojal nm fallow, fallow land.
añojo nm, **añoja** nf yearling.
añoranza nf longing, yearning (de for); hankering (de after); nostalgia (de for); sense of loss, regret (de for).
añorar [1a] **1** vt to long for, yearn for, pine for, hanker after; dead person to grieve for; loss to mourn. **2** vi to yearn, pine, grieve; to feel nostalgia, be homesick.
añoso adj aged, full of years.
añublar(se) [1a] =**anublar(se)**.
añublo nm blight, mildew.
añudar [1a] =**anudar**.
añusgar [1h] **1** vi to choke. **2 añusgarse** vr to get cross.
aojada nf (Col) skylight.
aojar [1a] vt to put the evil eye on; to bewitch.
aojo nm evil eye, hoodoo; sorcery, witchcraft.
aorta nf aorta.
aovado adj oval, egg-shaped.
aovar [1a] vi to lay eggs.
aovillarse [1a] vr to roll oneself into a ball, curl up.
apa interj (Mex) goodness me!
apabullar [1a] vt to crush, flatten, squash (also fig).
apacentadero nm pasture, pasture land.
apacentar [1k] **1** vt (**a**) (Agr) to pasture, graze, feed. (**b**) (fig) disciples etc to teach, minister to; intellect to feed, give food for thought to, nourish; passions to gratify, pander to; desires to satisfy, minister to. **2 apacentarse** vr (**a**) (Agr) to graze, feed. (**b**) (fig) to feed (con, de on).
apacibilidad nf gentleness, mildness; even temper, peaceable nature; calmness, quietness.
apacible adj gentle, mild; temperament gentle, even, peaceable; weather mild, calm, quiet; wind gentle.
apaciblemente adv gently, mildly; peaceably.
apaciguamiento nm appeasement (also Pol), pacifying, calming.
apaciguar [1i] **1** vt to pacify, appease, mollify; to calm down; (Pol) to appease. **2 apaciguarse** vr to calm down, quieten down.
apachar [1a] vt (Per) to steal.
apache nm Apache (Indian); (fig) thief, crook, bandit.
apacheta nf (Arg, Bol, Chi, Per: Rel) holy place, wayside shrine; pile, heap; (Arg: Pol) lobby, pressure group; ring, gang; (Arg: Comm) fortune, ill-gotten gains; **hacer la —** (fam) to make one's pile (fam).
apachurrar [1a] vt (SAm) to smash, crush, mash, squash.
apadrinamiento nm sponsorship; patronage; (fig) backing, support.
apadrinar [1a] vt enterprise to sponsor, back; artist etc to be a patron to; (Eccl) child to act as godfather to, bridegroom be best man for; duellist to act as second to; (fig) to back, support, favour.
apagadizo adj slow to burn, difficult to ignite.
apagado adj (**a**) volcano extinct; lime slaked; **estar — fire** etc to be out. (**b**) sound muted, muffled, dull; voice quiet, timid. (**c**) colour dull, lustreless, lifeless; person, temperament listless, spiritless, colourless.
apagador nm (**a**) extinguisher. (**b**) (Mech) silencer, muffler; (Mus) damper.
apagafuego nm fire extinguisher.

apagar [1h] **1** vt (**a**) fire to put out, extinguish, quench; light to put out, turn off, switch off; radio etc to switch off; firearm (Ec, Ven) to empty, discharge; lime to slake; thirst to quench, slake. (**b**) sound to silence, muffle, deaden; (Mus) to mute, damp. (**c**) colour to dull, tone down, soften. (**d**) affection, pain etc to kill; rage etc to calm, soothe.
2 apagarse vr (**a**) (fire) to go out; (light) to go out, be put out; (volcano) to become extinct. (**b**) (sound) to die away, cease. (**c**) (rage etc) to calm down, subside.
apagón nm (Mil) blackout; (Elec) power cut, electricity failure.
apagoso adj (SAm) =**apagadizo**.
apajarado adj (Chi, RPl) silly, scatterbrained.
apalabrar [1a] **1** vt (**a**) to agree to; **estar apalabrado** to be committed, have given one's word. (**b**) to bespeak; to engage. **2 apalabrarse** vr to come to an agreement (con with).
apalabrear [1a] (SAm) =**apalabrar**.
Apalaches mpl: **Montes —** Appalachians.
apalancamiento nm leverage.
apalancar [1g] vt to lever up, move (or lift etc) with a crowbar.
apalé interj (Mex) (**a**) goodness me! (**b**) look out!
apaleada nf (Arg, Mex: Agr) winnowing.
apaleamiento nm beating, thrashing.
apalear [1a] vt animal, person to beat, thrash; carpet to beat; (Agr) to winnow; **— oro, — plata** to be rolling in money.
apaleo nm (Agr) winnowing.
apallar [1a] vt (Bol) to harvest.
apamparse [1a] vr (Arg) to get confused, get bewildered.
apanalado adj honeycombed.
apancle nm (Mex) irrigation ditch.
apandar [1a] vt (sl) to swipe (sl), knock off (sl).
apandillar [1a] **1** vt to form into a gang. **2 apandillarse** vr to gang up, form a gang, band together.
apandorgarse [1h] vr (Per) to lose heart, get scared.
apaniguarse [1i] vr (Col, PR, Ven) to gang up, get together.
apantallado adj (Mex) much-impressed; openmouthed, full of wonder.
apantallar [1a] vt (Mex) to impress; to show off to; to fill with wonder.
apantanar [1a] vt to flood, make boggy, make swampy.
apañado adj (**a**) skilful, clever, handy. (**b**) suitable (para for). (**c**) (fam) **estar — to** be tight; **¡estás —!** you've had it! (fam).
apañador nm (Sport) catcher.
apañar [1a] **1** vt (**a**) to take hold of, grasp, seize; to pick up; (pej) to steal. (**b**) to dress, dress up; to wrap up; to mend, patch up. (**c**) (Arg) crime to conceal, criminal to harbour. (**d**) (Mex) to forgive, excuse. **2 apañarse** vr (**a**) to be skilful, be clever; **— para + infin** to contrive to + infin, manage to + infin; **—las por su cuenta** to fend for oneself, get along without help. (**b**) (Arg) **— algo** to manage to get something, get hold of something.
apaño nm (**a**) patch, mend. (**b**) skill, knack, dexterity; craft, guile. (**c**) **esto no tiene —** there's no answer to this one.
apañuscar [1g] vt (fam) (**a**) to rumple, crush. (**b**) to pinch (fam), swipe (sl). (**c**) (SAm) to join together.
apayado adj (Chi) shy, scared.
aparador nm sideboard; showcase; shop window; (Tech) workshop; **estar de —** to be dressed up to receive visitors.
aparadorista nmf (Mex) window dresser.
aparar [1a] vt to prepare, prepare; hands, apron etc to stretch out (to catch something); (Agr) to weed, clean.
apararse [1a] vr: **se aparata** it's brewing up for a storm, there's a storm coming.
aparato nm (**a**) (Chem, Phys etc) apparatus, piece of apparatus; (Mech) machine; device; piece of equipment; (Radio, TV) set, receiver; (Tel) instrument, handset; (Aer) machine; (domestic) appliance; (Phot) apparatus, piece of equipment; (Med) bandage; (Theat) properties; (Anat) system; **— de afeitar** safety razor; **— antirrobo** anti-theft device; **— auditivo** hearing aid; **— crítico** (Lit) critical apparatus; **— eléctrico** (Meteorol) display of lightning, electrical storm; **— fotográfico** camera; **— lector de microfilms** microfilm reader; **—s de mando**

(Aer etc) controls; — del oído hearing aid; — de relojería clockwork mechanism; — respiratorio respiratory system; —s sanitarios bathroom fittings; — para sordos hearing aid; — de televisión television set; — tomavistas cine-camera; — de uso doméstico domestic appliance.

(b) display, show, ostentation; sin — unostentatiously, without ceremony, without fuss.

(c) signs, symptoms; (Med) symptoms; (Psych) syndrome.

aparatosamente adv showily, ostentatiously; pretentiously; in a spectacular way.

aparatosidad nf showiness, ostentation; pretentiousness; spectacular character.

aparatoso adj showy, ostentatious; exaggerated, pretentious; fall, function etc spectacular.

aparcamento nm (CAm, PR), **aparcamiento** nm parking; car park, parking lot (US), parking place; "fácil — de coches" "good parking".

aparcar [1g] vti (Aut) to park.

aparcería nf (Comm) partnership; (Arg) comradeship, friendship.

aparcero nm (Comm) co-owner, partner; sharecropper; (Arg) comrade, friend.

apareamiento nm (a) matching; levelling. (b) mating, pairing.

aparear [1a] 1 vt (a) to pair, match; to level up. (b) animals to mate, pair. 2 **aparearse** vr (a) to form a pair, go together. (b) (animals) to mate, pair.

aparecer [2d] vi and **aparecerse** vr to appear; to show up, turn up; to come into sight; to loom up; (ghost) to appear, walk; apareció borracho he turned up drunk; allí aparecen fantasmas the place is haunted; no ha aparecido el libro ese that book still hasn't shown up; Nuestra Señora se apareció a Bernadette Our Lady appeared to Bernadette.

aparecido nm ghost.

aparejado adj fit, suitable, ready (para for).

aparejador nm foreman, overseer; (Archit) architect's assistant; quantity surveyor; (Naut) rigger.

aparejar [1a] 1 vt to prepare, get ready; horse to saddle, harness; (Naut) to fit out, rig out; (before painting) to size, prime; (Meteorol) to threaten.

2 **aparejarse** vr (a) to get ready; to equip oneself. (b) (CAm, PR) to mate, pair.

aparejo nm (a) preparation.

(b) gear, equipment, tackle.

(c) (Naut) rigging; rig, type of rig.

(d) lifting gear, tackle, block and tackle; (Naut) tackle, derrick.

(e) (Fishing) tackle; — de anzuelos set of hooks.

(f) (Archit) bond, bonding.

(g) harness; (CAm, Mex) saddle; (Per) woman's saddle.

(h) sizing, priming.

(i) —s gear, equipment, tools, kit.

aparentar [1a] vt (a) to feign, affect.

(b) age to look, seem to be; ella no aparenta la edad que tiene she doesn't look her age.

(c) — + infin to feign to + infin, make as if to + infin.

aparente adj (a) apparent, seeming. (b) visible, evident; outward. (c) fit, suitable, proper; (pej) plausible.

aparentemente adv (a) seemingly. (b) visibly, outwardly.

aparición nf (a) appearance; publication; un libro de próxima — a book soon to be published, a forthcoming book. (b) apparition, spectre.

apariencia nf (a) appearance, aspect, look(s).

(b) outward appearance, semblance; en — outwardly, seemingly; por todas las —s to all appearances; juzgar por las —s to judge by appearances; cubrir —s, salvar las —s to keep up appearances, save one's face.

(c) probability.

aparragado (RPl) 1 adj stunted, dwarfish. 2 nm dwarf.

aparragarse [1h] vr (CR) to roll up, curl up; (Chi) to squat, crouch (down); (Chi, Hond, Mex, Par) to remain stunted, stay small.

apartadero nm (Aut) lay-by; (Rail) siding.

apartadijo nm (a) small portion, bit. (b) =apartadizo 2.

apartadizo 1 adj unsociable. 2 nm recess, alcove, nook.

apartado 1 adj separated; remote, isolated, out-of-the-way.

2 nm (a) spare room; side room.

(b) (also — de correos) post-office box; box number.

(c) (Typ) paragraph, section, heading.

apartamento nm apartment, flat.

apartamiento nm (a) separation; withdrawal. (b) seclusion, remoteness, isolation; secluded spot, remote area.

apartar [1a] 1 vt to separate, divide, take away (de from); to remove, move away, put aside; (Min) to extract; (SAm: Agr) cattle to separate, sort out, cut out; (Post) to sort; (Rail) to shunt; (Law) to set aside, waive; — a uno para decirle algo to take someone aside to tell him something; — a uno de un propósito to dissuade someone from an intention; lograron — la discusión de ese punto they managed to turn the discussion away from that point; el ministro le apartó del mando the minister removed him from the command; — un pensamiento de sí to put a thought out of one's mind; apartó el plato con la mano he pushed his plate aside; ¿no podemos —lo un poco más? can't we move it a bit further away?

2 **apartarse** vr (a) (two persons) to part, separate; (two things) to become separated.

(b) to move away, withdraw, retire (de from); to keep away (de from), stand aside; — de un camino to turn off a road; to stray from a path; nos hemos apartado bastante de la ruta we've got rather a long way off the route; el cohete se está apartando de la trayectoria the rocket is deviating from the trajectory.

(c) (Law) to withdraw from a suit.

aparte 1 adv apart, aside; separately, besides; (Theat) aside; tendremos que considerar eso — we shall have to consider that separately; poner algo — to put something aside, put something on one side; eso — apart from that.

2 — de prep apart from; — de eso apart from that.

3 nm (a) (Theat) aside.

(b) (Typ) (new) paragraph; "(punto y) —" (in dictating) "new paragraph".

(c) (SAm: Agr) separation, sorting out.

apasionadamente adv (a) passionately; intensely; fervently. (b) in a biassed way, partially.

apasionado 1 adj (a) passionate; impassioned, intense, emotional; fervent, enthusiastic; — a, — por passionately fond of, passionately attached to.

(b) biassed, partial, prejudiced.

2 nm, **apasionada** nf admirer, devotee; los —s de Góngora devotees of Góngora, Góngora enthusiasts.

apasionamiento nm (a) passion, enthusiasm; vehemence, intensity; great fondness (de, por for).

(b) bias, partiality, prejudice.

apasionante adj exciting, thrilling.

apasionar [1a] 1 vt (a) to fill with passion; to stir deeply, make a strong appeal to; lover to stir, arouse; me apasionan las gambas I adore prawns, I can't resist prawns; es una lectura que apasiona it's stirring stuff to read; es un estudio que apasiona it's a fascinating study.

(b) to afflict, torment.

2 **apasionarse** vr (a) to get excited, be roused, work oneself up; — de, — por person to fall madly in love with; thing to get mad about, enthuse over, become enthusiastic about.

(b) to become biassed, give way to prejudice.

apatía nf apathy; (Med) listlessness.

apático adj apathetic; (Med) listless.

apátrida 1 adj stateless; (Arg) unpatriotic. 2 nmf (Arg) unpatriotic person.

apatronarse [1a] vr (Chi, Per): — de (of girl) to find a protector in, become the mistress of.

apatuscar [1g] vt (fam) to do hurriedly, make a botch of.

apatusco nm (a) frills, adornments. (b) (Ven) trick, pretence, intrigue.

apeadero nmf (a) mounting block, step. (b) halt, stopping place; (Rail) halt, wayside station. (c) temporary quarters, temporary lodging, pied-à-terre.

apear [1a] 1 vt (a) person to help down, help to alight (de from); object to take down, get down (de from); tree to fell.

(b) horse to hobble; wheel to chock, scotch.

(c) (Archit) to prop up.

(d) (Surveying) to survey, measure; to mark the boundaries of.

(e) problem to solve, work out; difficulty to overcome.

(f) — a uno de su opinión to make someone give up his view, persuade someone that his opinion is wrong; — a uno de un propósito to wean someone away from an intention, make someone give up his plan.

(g) — el tratamiento a uno to drop someone's title, address someone without formality.

(h) (*CAm*) to dismiss, sack (*fam*); (*Col*) to kill; (*CR*) to dress down, tell off.

2 apearse *vr* **(a)** to dismount; to get down, get out, alight (*de* from); (*Rail*) to get off, get out. **(b)** — **en** to stay at, put up at. **(c)** *see* **burro.** **(d)** — **de algo** (*Bol*) to get rid of something. **(e) no** — **la** (*Nic*) to be drunk all the time.

apechugar [1h] **1** *vt* (*Arg*) to face resolutely up to; (*Chi, PR*) to lay hold of, seize; (*Ec*) to shake violently. **2** *vi*: — **con** to put up with, swallow.

apedazar [1f] *vt* **(a)** to mend, patch. **(b)** to tear to pieces, cut into pieces.

apedrear [1a] **1** *vt* **(a)** to stone, pelt with stones. **2** *vi* **(a)** to hail; to rattle like hail, patter. **(b)** (*Mex*) to smell. **2 apedrearse** *vr* to be damaged by hail.

apedreo *nm* stoning, stone throwing; hail; damage by hail.

apegadamente *adv* devotedly.

apegado *adj*: — **a** attached to, devoted to, fond of.

apegarse [1h] *vr*: — **a** to become attached to, grow fond of.

apego *nm*: — **a** attachment to, devotion to, fondness for.

apelación *nf* **(a)** (*Law*) appeal; **sin** — without appeal, final; **interponer** — to give notice of appeal; **presentar su** — to present one's appeal; **ver una** — to consider an appeal. **(b)** (*fig*) help, remedy; **no hay** —, **esto no tiene** — it's a hopeless case.

apelante *nmf* appellant.

apelar [1a] *vi* (*Law*) to appeal (*de* against); — **a** (*fig*) to resort to, have recourse to, call on.

apelativo *nm* (*Gram*) appellative; (*SAm*) surname.

apeldar [1a] *vt* (*fam*): —**las** to beat it (*fam*).

apelmazado *adj mass* compact, compressed, solid; *liquid* thick, lumpy; *writing* clumsy.

apelmazar [1f] **1** *vt* to compress, squeeze together. **2 apelmazarse** *vr* to cake, solidify; to get lumpy.

apelotonar [1a] **1** *vt* to roll into a ball. **2 apelotonarse** *vr* (*animal etc*) to roll up, curl up; (*people*) to mass, crowd together.

apellidar [1a] **1** *vt* **(a)** to name, surname, call. **(b)** — **a uno por rey** to proclaim someone king. **2 apellidarse** *vr* to be called, call oneself, have as a surname; ¿**cómo se apellida Vd?** what is your name?

apellido *nm* name; surname, family name; nickname; — **de soltera** maiden name.

apenar [1a] **1** *vt* to grieve, trouble; to cause pain to. **2 apenarse** *vr* **(a)** to grieve, sorrow, distress oneself; — **de algo**, — **por algo** to grieve about something, distress oneself on account of something. **(b)** (*Col, Mex*) to blush, feel embarrassed, feel shy.

apenas 1 *adv* hardly, scarcely; — **nadie** hardly anybody; — **si pude levantarme** I could hardly get up. **2** *conj*: — **hube llegado cuando . . .** no sooner had I arrived than . . ., I had only just arrived when . . .

apendectomía *nf* appendectomy.

apendejarse [1a] *vr* (*Ant*) to get silly; to lose one's nerve.

apéndice *nm* (*Anat*) appendix; (*fig*) appendage; (*Lit etc*) appendix, supplement; (*Law*) schedule.

apendicitis *nf* appendicitis.

Apeninos *mpl* Apennines.

apensionado *adj* (*Arg, Chi, Mex*) depressed, sad; (*Col*) worried.

apeñuscarse [1g] *vr* (*RPl*) to crowd together, crowd round.

apeo *nm* **(a)** survey. **(b)** prop, support; scaffolding.

aperar [1a] **1** *vt* **(a)** (*Agr*) to make, repair, fit up. **(b)** (*Arg*) *horse* to harness; — **a uno de herramientas** to provide someone with tools. **2 aperarse** *vr*: — **de algo** (*Arg*) to equip oneself, provide oneself with the necessary tools (*etc*); **estar bien aperado para** to be well equipped for.

apercibimiento *nm* **(a)** preparation; provision. **(b)** warning, notice. **(c)** (*Law*) summons.

apercibir [3a] **1** *vt* **(a)** to prepare, make ready; to furnish, provide; **con los fusiles apercibidos** with rifles at the ready. **(b)** to warn, advise. **(c)** (*Law*) to summon, serve a summons on. **(d)** (*SAm*) to notice, observe, see. **2 apercibirse** *vr* to prepare oneself, get ready (*para* for); — **de** to provide oneself with; — **de** (*Arg*) to notice, perceive.

apercollar [1m] *vt* **(a)** to seize by the neck. **(b)** to fell, kill (with a blow on the neck).

aperchar [1a] *vt* (*Chi, Guat*) to pile up, stack up.

apergaminado *adj* parchment-like; *skin etc* dried up, wrinkled; *face* wizened.

apergaminarse [1a] *vr* to get like parchment; (*skin etc*) to dry up, get yellow and wrinkled.

aperital *nm* (*Arg*) =**aperitivo.**

aperitivo *nm* appetizer; (*drink*) aperitif.

apero *nm* tools, gear; equipment; (*Agr*) implement; (*SAm*) riding outfit; (*Ven*) saddle; (*Mex*) ploughing team, draught animals; —**s** (*Agr*) implements, dead stock, farm equipment.

aperreado *adj* (*Mex, Par*) wretched, lousy (*fam*).

aperreador *adj* bothersome, tiresome.

aperrear [1a] **1** *vt* **(a)** to set the dogs on. **(b)** (*fig*) to harass, plague; to wear out, tire out. **2 aperrearse** *vr* to get harassed; to slave away, overwork.

aperreo *nm* harassment, worry; toil, overwork.

apersogar [1h] *vt* to tether, tie up; (*Ven*) to string up.

apersonado *adj*: **bien** — presentable, nice-looking; **mal** — unattractive, unprepossessing.

apersonarse [1a] *vr* to appear in person; (*Comm*) to have a business interview; (*Law*) to appear.

apertura *nf* (in *most senses*) opening; (*of a will*) reading.

apesadumbrado *adj* grieved, sad, distressed.

apesadumbrar [1a] **1** *vt* to grieve, sadden, distress. **2 apesadumbrarse** *vr* to grieve, be grieved, distress oneself (*con, de* about, at).

apesarar(se) [1a] =**apesadumbrar(se).**

apescollar [1m] *vt* (*Chi*) to seize by the neck.

apesgar [1h] *vt* to weigh down, overburden.

apestado *adj* **(a)** (*SAm*) pestilential; (*Med*) infected with the plague. **(b) estar** — **de** to be infested with, be full of.

apestar [1a] **1** *vt* **(a)** (*Med*) to infect (with the plague). **(b)** (*fig*) to corrupt, spoil, vitiate; (*fam*) to plague, harass; (*fam*) to sicken, nauseate. **(c)** to stink out. **2** *vi* to stink (*a* of). **3 apestarse** *vr* (*Med*) to catch the plague; (*SAm*; *Bot*) to be blighted; (*Col, Per*) to catch a cold.

apestillar [1a] *vt* (*Arg, Chi*) **(a)** to catch. **(b)** to tell off, reprimand.

apestoso *adj* **(a)** stinking; *smell* awful, pestilential. **(b)** (*fam*) annoying; sickening, nauseating.

apetecer [2d] **1** *vt* **(a)** to crave, long for, yearn for. **(b)** to appeal to, attract, take one's fancy; **me apetece un helado** I feel like an ice cream, I could manage an ice cream, the idea of an ice cream appeals to me; **me apetece ir** I should like to go; ¿**te apetece?** how about it? **2** *vi* to attract, have an appeal, be welcome; **la idea no apetece** the idea has no appeal; **un vaso de jerez siempre apetece** a glass of sherry is always welcome.

apetecible *adj* attractive, tempting, desirable.

apetencia *nf* hunger, appetite; (*fig*) hunger, craving, desire (*de* for); inclination.

apetite *nm* appetizer; (*fig*) incentive.

apetito *nm* **(a)** appetite (*de* for); **abrir el** — to whet one's appetite. **(b)** (*fig*) desire, relish (*de* for).

apetitoso *adj* **(a)** appetizing; tasty, tempting; (*fig*) tempting, attractive. **(b)** *person* fond of good food.

apiadar [1a] **1** *vt* to move to pity. **2 apiadarse** *vr*: — **de** to take pity on, express pity for.

apicararse [1a] *vr* to go to the bad, pick up dishonest ways.

ápice *nm* **(a)** apex, top. **(b)** (*fig*) crux, knotty point (*of problem*); **estar en los** —**s de** to be well up in, know all about. **(c)** (*fig*) whit, iota; **ni** — not a whit; **no ceder un** — not to yield an inch.

apicultor *nm* beekeeper, apiarist.

apicultura *nf* beekeeping, apiculture.

apilar [1a] **1** *vt* to pile up, heap up. **2 apilarse** *vr* to pile up.

apilonar [1a] *vt* (*SAm*) =**apilar.**

apimplado *adj* (*SAm*) tight.

apiñado *adj* **(a)** crowded, packed, congested (*de* with). **(b)** cone-shaped, pyramidal.

apiñadura *nf*, **apiñamiento** *nm* crowding, congestion; crowd, squash, jam.

apiñar [1a] **1** *vt* to crowd together, bunch together; to pack in, press together, squeeze together; to overcrowd, congest. **2 apiñarse** *vr* to crowd together, press together; to be packed tight, be squashed together; **la multitud se apiñaba alrededor de él** the crowd pressed round him.

apio *nm* celery.

apio-nabo *nm* celeriac.

apiolar [1a] *vt* (*sl*) **(a)** to nab, nick (*sl*). **(b)** to do in (*sl*), bump off (*sl*).

apiparse [1a] vr (fam) to stuff oneself, guzzle.
apir(i) nm (SAm) mineworker.
apirularse [1a] vr (Chi) to dress up to the nines.
apisonadora nf steamroller, road roller.
apisonar [1a] vt to roll, roll flat; to tamp down, ram down.
apitonar [1a] 1 vt eggshell to crack, pierce, break through. 2 vi (of horns) to sprout, begin to show; (of animal) to begin to grow horns. 3 **apitonarse** vr (fam) to have a slanging match (fam).
apizarrado adj slaty, slate-coloured.
aplacar [1g] vt to appease, placate; to soothe, calm down; hunger etc to satisfy.
aplanacalles nm, pl **aplanacalles** (SAm) idler, layabout.
aplanador nm: — de calles idler, layabout.
aplanamiento nm smoothing, levelling, flattening.
aplanar [1a] 1 vt (a) to smooth, level, make even; to roll flat, flatten; clothing (Bol) to iron; — las calles (SAm) to loaf, hang about in the street.
(b) (fam) to knock out, bowl over with surprise.
2 **aplanarse** vr (a) (Archit) to collapse, cave in, fall down.
(b) (fam) to get discouraged.
aplanchar [1a] vt (SAm) =**planchar**.
aplastante adj overwhelming, crushing.
aplastar [1a] 1 vt (a) to flatten (out), squash, crush (flat).
(b) (fig) enemy etc to crush, overwhelm; (fam) person to floor, flatten, leave speechless.
2 **aplastarse** vr (a) to flatten oneself; se aplastó contra la pared he flattened himself against the wall.
(b) (Archit etc) to collapse.
(c) (Arg) to get scared; to get discouraged.
(d) (Arg) to get tired out, become utterly exhausted.
(e) (Arg: of athlete, horse) to blow up.
aplatanado adj (a) estar — to have gone native.
(b) (fig) lumpish, lacking all ambition.
aplatarse [1a] vr (Cu) to get rich.
aplaudir [3a] vt to applaud, cheer, clap; (fig) to applaud, approve.
aplauso nm applause; (fig) approval, acclaim; —s applause, cheering, clapping.
aplazamiento nm (a) postponement; adjournment.
(b) summons, summoning.
aplazar [1f] vt (a) to postpone, put off, defer; to adjourn, hold over; se ha aplazado la decisión por tiempo indefinido the decision has been postponed indefinitely.
(b) to set a time for, set a date for; meeting to summon, convene.
aplebeyado adj coarse, coarsened.
aplebeyar [1a] 1 vt to coarsen, degrade. 2 **aplebeyarse** vr to become coarse; to lower oneself, demean oneself.
aplicabilidad nf applicability.
aplicable adj applicable (a to).
aplicación nf (a) application (also Med); enviar su — (SAm) to send in one's application. (b) industry, studiousness, application; le falta — he doesn't work hard enough, he lacks steadiness.
aplicar [1g] 1 vt (in many senses) to apply (a to); effort, money etc to devote, assign (a to), earmark (a for); men, resources to assign (a, para to); crime etc to attribute, impute (a to); — sanciones to impose sanctions; — a uno a una carrera to enter someone for a profession, put someone in for a profession; — el oído a una puerta to put one's ear to a door.
2 **aplicarse** vr (a) — algo to attribute something to oneself, claim something for oneself.
(b) — a to apply to, be applicable to, be relevant to.
(c) — a (person) to apply oneself to, devote oneself to, give one's mind to; — a + infin to devote oneself to + ger.
aplique nm wall lamp.
aplomar [1a] 1 vt (a) (Archit etc) to plumb, test with a plumbline; to make perpendicular, make straight.
(b) (Chi) to embarrass.
2 **aplomarse** vr (a) to collapse, cave in, fall down.
(b) (Chi) to get embarrassed.
aplomo nm self-possession, assurance, aplomb; gravity, seriousness; (pej) nerve, cheek; ¡qué —! what a nerve!; dijo con el mayor — he said with the utmost assurance; perder su — to get worried, get rattled.
apocado adj (a) diffident, timid; spiritless, spineless.
(b) common, lowly.
Apocalipsis nm Apocalypse.
apocalíptico adj apocalyptic; style obscure, enigmatic.

apocamiento nm (a) diffidence, timidity; spinelessness. (b) depression, depressed state. (c) lowliness.
apocar [1g] 1 vt (a) to make smaller, diminish, reduce; (fig) to limit, restrict.
(b) to belittle, run down; to humiliate.
2 **apocarse** vr to feel small, feel humiliated; to humble oneself.
apocopar [1a] vt to apocopate, shorten.
apócope nf (Gram) apocope; Doro es — de Dorotea Doro is a shortened form of Dorotea, Doro is short for Dorotea.
apócrifo adj apocryphal.
apochongarse [1h] vr (RPl) to get scared.
apodar [1a] vt to nickname, dub, call; to label.
apoderado nm agent, representative; (Law) proxy, attorney.
apoderar [1a] 1 vt (a) to authorize, empower. (b) (Law) to grant power of attorney to. 2 **apoderarse** vr: — de to get hold of, seize, take possession of.
apodo nm nickname; label.
apogeo nm (Astron) apogee; (fig) peak, summit, top; estar en el — de su fama to be at the height of one's fame.
apolillado adj moth-eaten.
apolilladura nf moth-hole.
apolillar [ia] 1 vi (RPl: sl) to sleep. 2 **apolillarse** vr to get moth-eaten.
apolismado adj (Col, Mex, PR) sickly, weak; (CR) lazy; (Mex, Ven) worried, depressed; (PR) stupid.
apolismar [1a] 1 vt (SAm) to mangle, make a mess of, spoil.
2 vi (CR) to laze about, idle.
3 **apolismarse** vr (SAm) to fall ill, decline, weaken; to get worried, get depressed; to lose heart.
Apolo m Apollo.
apologética nf apologetics.
apología nf defence; eulogy; (SAm: angl) apology.
apologista nmf apologist.
apoltronado adj lazy, idle.
apoltronarse [1a] vr to get lazy; to laze, loaf around, idle.
apolvillarse [1a] vr (Chi: Agr) to be blighted.
apoplejía nf apoplexy, stroke.
apoplético adj apoplectic.
apoquinar [1a] vt (fam) money to fork out (fam), lash out (fam).
aporcar [1g] vt (Agr) to earth up.
aporrar [1a] 1 vi (fam) to dry up (fam), get stuck (in a speech etc). 2 **aporrarse** vr (fam) to become a bore, become a nuisance.
aporreado adj life etc wretched, miserable; person rascally.
aporrear [1a] 1 vt (a) person to beat, bash (fam), club; to beat up.
(b) door, keys, table etc to thump (on), pound (on), bang away at.
(c) (SAm) to crush completely (in an argument).
(d) (fig) to bother, pester.
2 **aporrearse** vr to slave away, slog, toil.
aporreo nm (a) beating; beating-up. (b) thumping, pounding, banging. (c) bother, nuisance.
aportación nf contribution; —es de la mujer dowry.
aportar[1] [1a] 1 vt (a) to bring; to furnish, contribute; evidence etc to bring forward, adduce; (Law) to bring as a dowry.
2 **aportarse** vr (SAm) to come, arrive, show up.
aportar[2] [1a] vi (a) (Naut) to reach port, come into harbour. (b) to come out at an unexpected place.
aporte nm (SAm) contribution.
aportillar [1a] 1 vt to break down, break open; wall to breach. 2 **aportillarse** vr to collapse, tumble down.
aposentar [1a] 1 vt to lodge, put up. 2 **aposentarse** vr to lodge, put up (en at).
aposento nm room; lodging; (Cu, PR) main bedroom.
aposesionarse [1a] vr: — de to take possession of.
aposición nf apposition; en — in apposition.
apósito nm (Med) application, poultice; — femenino sanitary towel, sanitary napkin (US).
aposta adv, **apostadamente** adv on purpose.
apostadero nm (Mil) station, post; (Naut) naval station.
apostador nm better, backer; — profesional bookmaker.
apostar[1] [1a] vt to station, post.
apostar[2] [1m] 1 vt (a) money to lay, stake, bet (a on).
(b) —las a uno, —las con uno to compete with someone.
2 vi to bet (a, por on; a que that); apuesto a que sí I bet it is.
3 **apostarse** vr to compete (con with), be rivals,

vie; **—las a uno, —las con uno** to compete with someone.

apostasía *nf* apostasy.

apóstata *nmf* apostate.

apostatar [1a] *vi* (*Eccl*) to apostatize (*de* from); (*fig*) to change sides.

apostema *nf* abscess.

apostilla *nf* note, comment.

apostillar [1a] *vt* to add notes to, annotate; (*fig*) to add, chime in with; *comment* to echo; **"Sí", apostilló una voz** "Yes", a voice added.

apóstol *nm* apostle.

apostólico *adj* apostolic.

apostrofar [1a] *vt* (a) to apostrophize, address. (b) to insult; to tell off, reprimand; to shout at.

apóstrofe *gen m* (a) apostrophe. (b) taunt, insult; rebuke, reprimand.

apóstrofo *nm* (*Gram*) apostrophe.

apostura *nf* (a) neatness, elegance; (*hum*) nattiness. (b) good looks.

apotegma *nm* apothegm, maxim.

apoteósico *adj* (*fig*) *success etc* huge, tremendous.

apoteosis *nf* apotheosis.

apoyabrazos *nm, pl* **apoyabrazos** armrest.

apoyador *nm* support, bracket.

apoyapié *nm* footrest.

apoyar [1a] **1** *vt* (a) *elbow, head etc* to lean, rest (*en, sobre* on); (*Archit, Tech*) to hold up, support; to prop up; **— una escalera contra una pared** to lean a ladder against a wall.

(b) (*fig*) *person* to support, back; to stand by; (*pej*) to abet; *motion* to second, support; *principle* to uphold; *theory etc* to bear out, confirm, support; **apoya su argumento en los siguientes hechos** he bases his argument on the following facts; **no apoyamos más al gobierno** we no longer support the government.

2 *vi*: **— en** to rest on, be supported by.

3 apoyarse *vr*: **— en** (a) *base* to rest on, be supported by; *building* to abut on to; *shoulder, stick etc* to lean on; **— contra una pared** to lean against a wall.

(b) (*fig*) *person* to rely on; to lean on; *argument, evidence etc* to base oneself on.

apoyo *nm* (a) support; prop; bracket. (b) (*fig*) support, backing; help; approval, favour; **contamos con su —** we rely on your support.

apozarse [1f] *vr* (*Col, Chi*) to form a pool.

apreciable *adj* (a) appreciable, considerable; noticeable; measurable; **una cantidad —** an appreciable quantity; **— al oído** audible.

(b) (*fig*) worthy, estimable, esteemed; **los —s esposos** the esteemed couple.

apreciación *nf* appreciation, appraisal; (*Comm, Fin*) valuation; estimate; **según nuestra —** according to our estimation; **— del trabajo** job evaluation.

apreciado *adj* worthy, estimable, esteemed.

apreciar [1b] *vt* (a) (*Comm, Fin etc*) to value, assess, estimate (*en* at); to evaluate.

(b) (*fig*) to esteem, value (*por* for); **— algo en mucho** to value something highly; **— en poco** to set little value on, attach little value to.

(c) (*Art, Mus etc*) to appreciate.

apreciativo *adj*: **una mirada apreciativa** an appraising look, a look of appraisal.

aprecio *nm* (a) (*Comm, Fin etc*) valuation, appraisal; estimate.

(b) (*fig*) appreciation; esteem, regard; **tener a uno en gran —** to hold someone in high regard; **en señal de mi —** as a token of my esteem; **no hacer — de algo** (*Mex*) to pay no attention to something.

aprehender [2a] *vt* (a) *person* to apprehend, detain; *goods* to seize. (b) (*Philos*) to understand; to conceive, think.

aprehensible *adj* understandable; conceivable; **una idea difícilmente —** an idea which is difficult to pin down, an idea not readily understood.

aprehensión *nf* (a) apprehension, detention, capture; seizure. (b) (*Philos*) understanding; conception, perception.

apremiador *adj*, **apremiante** *adj* urgent, pressing, compelling.

apremiar [1b] **1** *vt* (a) to urge (on), press; to force, compel; **— a uno a hacer algo, — a uno para que haga algo** to press someone to do something.

(b) to hurry (along).

(c) to oppress.

2 *vi* to press, be urgent; **el tiempo apremia** time presses; **apremiaba repararlo** it was an urgent task to repair it, it was urgent to get it repaired.

apremio *nm* (a) urgency, pressure; compulsion; **por — de tiempo** because time is pressing; **por — de**

trabajo because of pressure of work; **— de pago** demand for payment, demand note; **procedimiento de —** compulsory procedure.

(b) (*Law*) writ, judgement; summons; judicial constraint.

(c) oppression.

aprender [2a] *vti* to learn; **— a hacer algo** to learn to do something.

aprendiz *nm*, **aprendiza** *nf* (a) learner; beginner, novice; **— de conductor** (*Aut*) learner, learner-driver.

(b) (*in a craft*) apprentice; (*Comm etc*) trainee; **— de comercio** business trainee; **estar de — con uno** to be apprenticed to someone; **poner a A de — con B** to apprentice A to B.

aprendizaje *nm* apprenticeship; (*Comm etc*) training period, period as a trainee; **hacer su —** to serve one's apprenticeship; **pagar su —** (*fam*) to learn the hard way.

aprensar [1a] *vt* (a) (*Tech*) to press, crush. (b) (*fig*) to oppress, crush; to distress.

aprensión *nf* apprehension, fear, worry; nervousness; (*Med*) hypochondria, fear of being ill; odd idea, strange notion, idle fancy; squeamishness.

aprensivo *adj* apprehensive, worried; nervous, timid; (*Med*) hypochondriac, fearful of being ill; squeamish.

apresador *nm*, **apresadora** *nf* captor.

apresamiento *nm* seizure; capture.

apresar [1a] *vt* (a) to seize, clutch, grab, grasp. (b) *person, ship* to capture. (c) (*Law*) to seize.

aprestado *adj* ready; **estar — para + infin** to be ready to + *infin*; (*fig*) to be calculated to + *infin*.

aprestar [1a] **1** *vt* to prepare, get ready, make ready; *cloth* to size; (*for painting*) to prime, size.

2 aprestarse *vr* to prepare, get ready; **— a + infin, — para + infin** to get ready to + *infin*.

apresto *nm* (a) preparation. (b) outfit, equipment, kit. (c) priming, sizing. (d) size.

apresuradamente *adv* hurriedly, hastily.

apresurado *adj* hurried, hasty; quick; precipitate.

apresuramiento *nm* hurry, haste, precipitation.

apresurar [1a] **1** *vt* to hurry (along); to hustle; to speed up, accelerate, expedite.

2 apresurarse *vr* to hurry, hasten, make haste; **— a + infin, — por + infin** to hasten to + *infin*; **me apresuré a sugerir que . . .** I hastened to suggest that . . ., I hastily suggested that . . .

apretadamente *adv* tightly; densely, solidly.

apretadera *nf* (a) strap, rope. (b) **—s** (*fam*) pressure, insistence.

apretado (a) *knot, screw, dress etc* tight.

(b) dense, thick, compact, solid; *writing* cramped; *room, space* full, chock-a-block; **estaba — a presión** it was full to bursting.

(c) difficult, dangerous; **es un caso —** it's a tricky business; **estar — to be in a difficult situation**, (*Med*) be in a bad way; **estar — de dinero** to be short of money.

(d) (*fam*) tight-fisted, stingy.

(e) (*Mex*) conceited.

apretador *nm* (*Tech*) wedge.

apretapapel *nm* (*Arg*) paperweight.

apretar [1k] **1** *vt* (a) *belt, nut, screw* to tighten (up); *hand* to clasp, grip, (*in greeting*) shake; *fist* to clench; *teeth* to grit, set; *button, pedal, trigger etc* to press, press down; (*of dress*) to be too tight for; (*of shoe*) to pinch; *person* to hug, squeeze; **— a uno entre los brazos** to hug someone in one's arms; **— a uno contra la pared** to pin someone against the wall.

(b) *contents* to pack in, pack tight; to press together, squeeze together.

(c) *discipline* to tighten up; *attack* (*Mil*) to press, intensify; *pace* to quicken.

(d) to afflict, distress, trouble; to beset; (*Med*) to distress.

(e) to harass, pester (*por* for).

2 *vi* (a) (*of dress*) to be too tight; (*of shoe*) to pinch, hurt.

(b) to get worse, get more severe; **cuando el calor aprieta** when the heat becomes excessive; **allí donde más aprieta el calor** out there where the heat is at its worst.

(c) to insist, exert pressure.

(d) **— con el enemigo** to close with the enemy, to close in on the enemy.

(e) (*SAm*) to make an extra effort; to hurry.

(f) **— a correr** to run faster, run harder; **— a nevar** to snow more heavily.

(g) **¡aprieta!** nonsense!; good grief!

3 apretarse *vr* (a) to narrow, get narrower.

(**b**) to crowd together, squeeze up; to huddle together.

(**c**) to grieve, be distressed.

apretarropa nm (Arg) clothes peg.

apretón nm (**a**) squeeze, pressure; hug; — **de manos** handshake; **se dieron un** — **de manos** they shook hands.

(**b**) press, crush, jam; **el** — **en el metro** the crush in the underground.

(**c**) difficulty, jam, fix; **estar en un** — to be in a fix, be in a quandary.

(**d**) dash, sprint, short run.

apretujar [1a] vt to press hard, squeeze hard; to hug; **estar apretujado entre dos personas** to be crushed between two people, be sandwiched between two people.

apretujón nm (**a**) hard squeeze; big hug. (**b**) press, crush, jam.

apretura nf (**a**)=apretón, apretujón (**a**) and (**b**). (**b**)=apretón (**c**).

aprieto nm=apretón (**a**) and (**b**); (fig) difficulty, jam, fix; distress; **estar en un** —, **verse en un** — to be in a jam; **poner a uno en un** — to put someone in a fix; **ayudar a uno a salir de un** — to help someone out of trouble.

apriorístico adj aprioristic.

aprisa adv quickly, hurriedly.

aprisco nm sheepfold.

aprisionar [1a] vt to imprison; to bind, tie; to shackle (also fig).

aprobación nf (**a**) approval; consent; **dar su** — to give one's consent, approve. (**b**) (Univ etc) pass mark.

aprobado 1 adj approved; worthy, excellent. 2 nm (Univ etc) pass, pass mark; pass certificate.

aprobar [1m] 1 vt to approve, approve of, consent to, endorse; (Parl) bill to pass; report to approve, adopt; (Univ) candidate, exam, subject to pass.

2 vi (Univ) to pass; **aprobé en francés** I passed in French.

aprobatorio adj: **una mirada aprobatoria** an approving look.

aproches nmpl (Mil) approaches; (SAm) approach road, means of access (de to); neighbourhood.

aprontamiento nm quick delivery, rapid service.

aprontar [1a] vt to get ready quickly, prepare without delay; goods, money to deliver at once, hand over immediately; (Cu, PR) money to advance.

apronte nm (RPl) (**a**) (Sport) heat, preliminary race.
(**b**) —s preparations; **irse en los** —s to waste one's energy on unnecessary preliminaries.

apropiación nf appropriation; adaptation, application; giving, gift; — **ilícita** illegal seizure, misappropriation.

apropiadamente adv appropriately, fittingly.

apropiado adj appropriate (a, para to), suitable, fitting (a, para for).

apropiar [1b] 1 vt (**a**) to adapt, fit (a to), make suitable (a for); to apply (a to).
(**b**) — **algo a uno** to give something to someone; (SAm) to assign something to someone, award something to someone.

2 **apropiarse** vr: — (de) algo to appropriate something.

apropincuarse [1d] vr (hum) to approach.

aprovechable adj available, that can be used; useful, serviceable.

aprovechadamente adv profitably.

aprovechado 1 adj (**a**) industrious, diligent, hardworking; resourceful.
(**b**) thrifty, economical.
(**c**) (pej) unscrupulous, selfish; grasping.
(**d**) time etc well-spent.

2 nm, **aprovechada** nf selfish person, person who has an eye to the main chance.

aprovechamiento nm (**a**) use, development; exploitation; — **de recursos naturales** exploitation of natural resources. (**b**) progress, improvement.

aprovechar [1a] 1 vt to make (good) use of, use, utilize; to develop, exploit; offer etc to take up, take advantage of; experience, teaching to profit by, profit from; chance to seize, avail oneself of, take; possibilities to make the most of; (pej) to exploit, make unfair use of, get the benefit of.

2 vi (**a**) to be of use, be useful, be profitable; **eso aprovecha poco** that is no use, that is of no avail; **no** — **para nada** to be completely useless; — **a uno** to be of use to someone, profit someone, be beneficial to someone; ¡**que aproveche!** phrase used to those at table, hoping they will enjoy their meal.
(**b**) to progress, improve; — **en los estudios** to make progress in one's work.

3 **aprovecharse** vr: — **de** = 1 vt.

aprovisionamiento nm supply, supplying; **Ministerio de A**—s Ministry of Supply.

aprovisionar [1a] vt to supply.

aproximación nf (**a**) approximation (a to; also Math). (**b**) nearness, closeness. (**c**) approach (a to); (Pol) rapprochement. (**d**) (in lottery) consolation prize.

aproximadamente adv approximately.

aproximado adj approximate; estimate, guess rough.

aproximar [1a] 1 vt to bring near(er), bring up, draw up (a to); — **una silla** to bring a chair nearer, bring a chair over.

2 **aproximarse** vr (**a**) to come near, come closer, approach; — **a** to near, approach; **el tren se aproximaba a su destino** the train was nearing its destination.
(**b**) — **a** (fig) to approach, approximate to.

aproximativo adj approximate; estimate, guess rough.

aptitud nf (**a**) suitability, fitness (para for). (**b**) aptitude, ability; — **para los negocios** business sense, business talent; **carece de** — he hasn't got the talent; **demostrar tener** —es to show one's ability, show promise.

apto adj suitable, fit; **ser** — **a aprender, ser** — **para aprender** to be quick to learn; — **para desarrollar** suitable for developing; **no es** — **para conducir** he's not fit to drive; **película no apta para menores** film not suitable for juveniles; — **para el servicio** fit for military service.

apuesta nf bet, wager.

apuesto adj (**a**) neat, elegant, spruce; (hum) dapper, natty. (**b**) handsome, nice-looking.

Apuleyo m Apuleius.

apunarse [1a] vr (Arg, Bol, Per) to get mountain sickness.

apuntación nf note; (Mus) notation.

apuntado adj (**a**) pointed, sharp. (**b**) (Chi: fam) merry, tight.

apuntador nm (Theat) prompter.

apuntalamiento nm propping-up, underpinning.

apuntalar [1a] vt (Archit) to prop up, shore up, underpin; (Mech) to strut.

apuntamiento nm (**a**) aiming, pointing. (**b**) note. (**c**) judicial report.

apuntar [1a] 1 vt (**a**) rifle etc to aim, level, point (a at); large gun to train (a on); — **a un blanco** to aim at a target; — **a uno con el revólver** to point a pistol at someone, cover someone with a pistol, (in robbery etc) hold someone up with a pistol.
(**b**) to point at, point to; to point out; to hint at; — **que** . . . to point out that . . .; to hint that . . .
(**c**) to note, note down, make (or take) a note of; (Sport) points to score; (in ledger etc) to enter, set down; to record; to sketch, outline; — **una cantidad en la cuenta de uno** to charge a sum to someone's account.
(**d**) tool to sharpen, put a point on.
(**e**) (Sew) to patch, mend, darn; to tack down; to fasten temporarily.
(**f**) (Cards) money to stake, put up.
(**g**) (Theat) to prompt.

2 vi (**a**) (of beard etc) to begin to show, appear; (of day) to dawn, break; (SAm: Bot) to sprout, show; **el maíz apunta bien este año** (SAm) the corn looks well this year, the corn is coming on nicely this year.
(**b**) (Theat) to prompt.
(**c**) — **y no dar** to fail to keep one's word.

3 **apuntarse** vr (**a**) — **un tanto** to score a point; (fig) to stay one up; — **una victoria** to score a win, chalk up a win.
(**b**) to turn sour.
(**c**) (fam) to get tight.

apunte nm (**a**) note; jotting; memorandum; (Comm) entry; (Art) sketch; (Arg: Comm) list of debts, note of money owing; "**A**—**s sobre el unicornio**" "Notes on the Unicorn"; **llevar el** — (Arg) to pay attention, take notice; (of woman) to begin to take an interest, accept someone's advances; **sacar** —s to take notes.
(**b**) (Theat) cue; prompter; prompt copy, prompt book.
(**c**) (Cards) stake.

apuñalar [1a] vt, **apuñalear** [1a] vt (Arg, Chi, PR) to stab; to knife; — **a uno por la espalda** (fig) to stab someone in the back; — **a uno con la mirada** to look daggers at someone.

apuñar [1a] vt to seize (in one's fist); (Arg) to knead (with the fists).

apuñear [1a] vt, **apuñetear** [1a] vt to punch, strike.

apuradamente adv (**a**) precisely, exactly. (**b**) with difficulty.

apurado adj (**a**) needy, hard up.
(**b**) difficult; dangerous; **estar** —, **estar en una**

situación apurada to be in a jam, be in a tight spot; to feel embarrassed.
(c) exhausted.
(d) precise, exact.
(e) (*SAm*) hurried, rushed; **estar — to be in a hurry; hacer algo a la apurada** (*Arg*) to do something in a hurried way, make a botch of something.
apurar [1a] **1** *vt* (a) (*Tech*) to purify, refine.
(b) *liquid* to drain, drink up; *vessel* to drain; *supply etc* to use up, exhaust, finish off; *process to* finish, conclude.
(c) *facts* to check on, verify; *subject* to study minutely, make a thorough investigation of; *mystery* to clear up, fathom, get to the bottom of.
(d) to annoy, bother; to make impatient; to embarrass.
(e) (*esp SAm*) to hurry, press, urge on.
2 apurarse *vr* (a) to worry, fret, upset oneself (*por* about, over); **ella se apura por poca cosa** she upsets herself for no reason; **¡no te apures!** don't worry!
(b) to make an effort, go hard at it, exert oneself; **— por hacer algo** to strive to do something.
(c) (*esp SAm*) to hurry, hurry up; **¡apúrate!** come along!, get moving!
apuro *nm* (a) want, financial need; hardship, distress; **pasar —s** to suffer hardship(s); **verse en —s** to be in trouble, be in distress.
(b) fix, jam, difficulty, tight spot; **colocar a uno en —s** to put someone on the spot; **estar en —s, estar en el mayor —** to be in a jam; **me da un —** I'd hate to, it would be terribly awkward; **sacar a uno de —** to get someone out of a jam.
(c) (*SAm*) haste, urgency.
apurón *nm* (*SAm*) great haste, great urgency; (*Chi*) impatience; **andar a los apurones** (*Arg*) to rush things, do things hastily and badly.
apurruñar [1a] *vt* (*Cu, Ven*) to mess up, maltreat, handle roughly.
aquejar [1a] *vt* (a) to distress, grieve, afflict; to worry, harass; to weary.
(b) (*Med*) to ail, afflict; **le aqueja una grave enfermedad** he suffers from a serious disease, he is afflicted with a serious disease.
aquel *dem adj m,* **aquella** *f* that (*remote from speaker and listener, in time etc*); **aquellos** *mpl,* **aquellas** *fpl* those.
aquél 1 *dem pron m,* **aquélla** *f* that (*remote from speaker and listener, in time etc*); **aquéllos** *mpl,* **aquéllas** *fpl* those; that one, those (ones); **éstos son negros mientras aquéllos son blancos** the latter are black whereas the former (or the others, the earlier ones) are white; **aquél que yo quiero** the one I love; **aquél que está en el escaparate** the one that's in the window; **todo aquél que . . .** each one who . . .
2 *nm* (*fam*) (a) charm; sex appeal; **tiene mucho —** she's got it, she certainly has sex appeal.
(b) **esto tiene su —** this has its awkward points.
aquelarre *nm* witches' sabbath.
aquello *dem pron* ("*neuter*") that; that affair, that business, that matter; **— no tiene importancia** that's not important; **no me gusta —** I don't care for that; **¡no se te olvide —!** see you don't forget what I told you about (*or* what I told you to do *etc*)!; **— de mi hermano** that business about my brother; **— fue de miedo** that was awful, wasn't that awful?
aquerenciarse [1b] *vr:* **— a un lugar** (*animal*) to become fond of a place, become attached to a place.
aqueridarse [1a] *vr* (*PR*) to set up house together, move in together.
aquí *adv* (a) (*place*) here; **— dentro** in here; **— mismo** right here, on this very spot; **a 2 km de —** 2 km from here; **andar de — para allá** to walk up and down, walk to and fro; **hasta —** so far, as far as here; **venga por —** come this way; **no pasó por —** he didn't come this way; **vive por — (cerca)** he lives round here, he lives hereabouts.
(b) (*time*) **de — en adelante** from now on, henceforth; **de — a un mes** in a month's time; a month from now; **hasta —** up till now.
(c) **de — que . . . and so . . .,** hence . . ., that's why . . .
aquiescencia *nf* acquiescence.
aquietar [1a] *vt* to quieten (down), calm (down); to pacify; *fears* to calm, allay.
aquilatar [1a] **1** *vt* (a) *metal* to assay. (b) (*fig*) to weigh up, test, examine. **2 aquilatarse** *vr* (*Arg*) to improve.
Aquiles *m* Achilles.
aquilón *nm* (*poet*) north wind; north.
Aquino *m* Aquinas.
Aquisgrán Aachen, Aix-la-Chappelle.

aquisito *adv* (*SAm*) = **aquí.**
aquistar [1a] *vt* to win, gain, acquire.
Aquitania *f* Aquitaine.
ara[1] *nf* altar; altar stone; **en —s de** on the altars of, in honour of.
ara[2] *nm* (*SAm*) parrot.
árabe 1 *adj* Arab, Arabian, Arabic; **lengua —** Arabic; **palabra —** Arabic word; **estilo —** (*Archit*) Mauresque.
2 *nmf* Arab; (*Mex*) hawker, street vendor.
3 *nm* (*language*) Arabic.
arabesco 1 *adj* Arabic; *style* arabesque. **2** *nm* arabesque.
Arabia *f* Arabia; **— Saudita** Saudi Arabia.
arábigo 1 *adj* Arab, Arabian, Arabic; *numeral* Arabic. **2** *nm* Arabic; **está en —** (*fig*) it's Greek to me; **hablar en —** (*fig*) to talk double Dutch.
arabista *nmf* Arabist.
arabizar [1f] *vt* to arabize.
arable *adj* (*esp SAm*) arable.
arácnido *nm* arachnid.
arada *nf* (a) ploughing. (b) ploughed land. (c) day's ploughing, area of land that can be ploughed in one day.
arado *nm* (a) plough. (b) ploughshare. (c) (*Col*) ploughland, tilled land; orchard.
arador *nm* ploughman.
Aragón *m* Aragon.
aragonés 1 *adj* Aragonese. **2** *nm,* **aragonesa** *nf* Aragonese. **3** *nm* (*dialect*) Aragonese.
aragonesismo *nm* aragonesism, word (or phrase *etc*) peculiar to Aragon.
araguato 1 *adj* (*Col, Ven*) dark tawny-coloured. **2** *nm* (*Col, Mex, Ven*) *large monkey of the genus* Mycetes.
arambel *nm* rag, shred, tatter.
arana *nf* trick, swindle; lie.
araná *nm* (*Ven*) straw hat.
arancel *nm* tariff, duty; **— protector** protective tariff.
arancelario *adj* tariff (*attr*), customs (*attr*); **barrera arancelaria** tariff wall; **protección arancelaria** tariff protection.
arándano *nm* bilberry, whortleberry; **— agrio, — encarnado** cranberry.
arandela *nf* (a) (*Tech*) washer. (b) candle stand. (c) (*Mex, Per*) frill, flounce. (d) **—s** (*Col*) frills, buttons and bows. (e) **—s** (*Col*) teacakes, buns.
araña *nf* (a) (*Zool*) spider; **matar la —** (*fig*) to take the edge off one's appetite.
(b) (*also* **— de luces**) chandelier; **— de mesa** candelabrum.
(c) (*fam*) resourceful person, calculating person; (*SAm*) prostitute.
(d) (*Ant, Arg, Chi, Mex*) light two-wheeled carriage.
arañar [1a] *vt* (a) to scratch. (b) to scrape together; **pasó los exámenes arañando** (*Arg*) he just scraped through the exams.
arañazo *nm,* **arañón** *nm* scratch.
arao *nm* guillemot.
arar [1a] *vt* to plough; to till, cultivate.
araucano 1 *adj* Araucanian. **2** *nm,* **araucana** *nf* Araucanian, Araucan.
arbitrador *nm,* **arbitradora** *nf* arbiter, arbitrator.
arbitraje *nm* (a) arbitration; **— industrial** industrial arbitration. (b) (*Comm*) arbitrage.
arbitral *adj* arbitral; of a referee (*or* an umpire); **una decisión —** a referee's ruling.
arbitrar [1a] **1** *vt* (a) *dispute* to arbitrate in; (*Sport*) *tennis etc* to umpire, boxing, football *etc* to referee.
(b) to contrive, find; to bring together; to summon up one's resources for; *funds* to raise, collect.
2 *vi* (a) to arbitrate; (*Sport*) to umpire, referee; **— en una disputa** to arbitrate in a dispute; **— entre A y B** to arbitrate between A and B.
(b) (*Philos*) to act freely, judge freely.
3 arbitrarse *vr* to get along, manage.
arbitrariamente *adv* arbitrarily.
arbitrariedad *nf* (a) arbitrariness, arbitrary nature. (b) arbitrary act, outrage; (*Law*) illegal act.
arbitrario *adj* arbitrary.
arbitrio *nm* (a) free will.
(b) means, expedient.
(c) (*Law*) adjudication, decision; choice; **al — de** at the discretion of; **dejar algo al — de uno** to leave something to someone's discretion.
(d) **—s** (*Fin*) excise taxes.
arbitrismo *nm* = **arbitrariedad.**
arbitrista *nmf* idealist, utopian; armchair politician.
árbitro *nm* arbiter, arbitrator; (*Sport: at tennis etc*) umpire, (*at boxing, football etc*) referee.

árbol nm (a) (Bot) tree; — **frutal** fruit tree; — **de Navidad**, — **navideño** Christmas tree; — **genealógico** family tree; **estar en un** — to be up (in) a tree; **estar en el** — (Bol) to be in a powerful position.

(b) (Mech) axle, shaft; spindle; — **del cigüeñal** crankshaft; — **de levas** camshaft; — **motor** drive, driving shaft; — **de transmisión** transmission shaft.

(c) (Naut) mast; — **mayor** mainmast.

arbolado 1 adj (a) wooded, tree-covered; lined with trees. (b) (Naut) with a mast, masted. **2** nm woodland.

arboladura nf masts and spars, rigging.

arbolar [1a] **1** vt to put up, place upright (a against); flag to hoist, raise; ship to fit with masts. **2 arbolarse** vr (horse) to rear up, get up on its hind legs.

arboleda nf grove, plantation, coppice.

arboledo nm woodland.

arbolejo nm small tree.

arbóreo adj (a) (Zool) arboreal, tree (attr). (b) tree-like, tree-shaped.

arbotante nm flying buttress.

arbusto nm shrub, bush.

arca nf (a) chest, box, coffer; (also —s) safe, strong-room; — **de hierro** strongbox; **ser como un** — **abierta** to be a dreadful gossip; **ser como un** — **cerrada** to know how to keep a secret.

(b) **A**— **de la Alianza** Ark of the Covenant; **A**— **de Noé** Noah's Ark.

(c) tank, reservoir; — **de agua** water tower.

(d) (Agr) hutch.

arcabucero nm (Hist) harquebusier.

arcabuco nm thick forest, impenetrable vegetation.

arcabuz nm (Hist) harquebus.

arcada nf (a) (Archit) arcade, series of arches. (b) (of bridge) arch, span; **de una sola** — single-span. (c) —s (Med) retching.

árcade 1 adj Arcadian. **2** nmf Arcadian.

Arcadia f Arcady.

arcádico adj, **arcadio** adj Arcadian.

arcaduz nm (a) pipe, conduit; (of water wheel) bucket. (b) (fig) channel, way, means.

arcaico adj archaic.

arcaísmo nm archaism.

arcaizante adj archaic; region, speech conservative, conserving many archaisms; person fond of archaisms; style old-fashioned.

arcángel nm archangel.

arcano 1 adj arcane, recondite, enigmatic. **2** nm secret, mystery.

arcar [1g] =**arquear**.

arce nm maple, maple tree.

arcediano nm archdeacon.

arcén nm (a) border, edge, brim; (of wall) curb, curb-stone. (b) (Aut) lay-by; — **de servicio** service area.

arcilla nf clay; — **de alfarería**, — **figulina** potter's clay; — **cocida** baked clay.

arcilloso adj clayey, argillaceous.

arcipreste nm archpriest.

arco nm (a) (Archit) arch; archway; — **de herradura** horseshoe arch, Moorish arch; — **ojival** pointed arch; — **redondo** round arch; — **triunfal** triumphal arch.

(b) (Anat) arch.

(c) (Geom) arc.

(d) (Elec) arc; spotlight; — **voltaico** arc lamp.

(e) (Mus) bow; — **de violín** violin bow, fiddlestick (hum).

(f) (Mil) bow; — **y flechas** bow and arrows.

(g) (of cask) hoop.

(h) — **iris** rainbow.

arcón nm large chest; bin, bunker.

archi . . . arch . . .; in humorous compounds, eg **archifresco** as fresh as one can get; **un niño archimalo** a terribly naughty child; **un hombre archiestúpido** an utterly stupid man.

archiconocido adj extremely well-known.

archidiácono nm archdeacon.

archidiócesis nf, pl **archidiócesis** archdiocese.

archiduque nm archduke.

archiduquesa nf archduchess.

archienemigo nm arch-enemy.

archimillonario nm, **archimillionaria** nf multi-millionaire.

archipámpano nm (hum) bigwig, tycoon; panjandrum; **el** — **de Sevilla** the Great Panjandrum.

archipiélago nm archipelago; (fig) labyrinth, maze.

archirredicho adj terribly affected.

archisabido adj extremely well-known; **un hecho** — a perfectly well-known fact; **eso lo tenemos** — we know that perfectly well, that is common knowledge.

architonto 1 adj utterly silly. **2** nm, **architonta** nf utter fool, complete idiot.

archivado adj (SAm) out-of-date, old-fashioned.

archivador nm (a) filing clerk. (b) filing cabinet.

archivar [1a] vt (a) to file, file away; to store away; to place in the archives.

(b) (fam) to hide away, pigeonhole, shelve.

(c) (SAm) to withdraw from circulation, take out of use.

(d) (Chi, Mex) to jail.

archivero nm, **archivera** nf filing clerk; archivist, keeper (of archives), record officer; registrar.

archivo nm (a) archive(s); registry; **A**— **Nacional** Public Record Office.

(b) —s files; archives, records, muniments; —s **policíacos** police files; **buscaremos en los** —s we'll look in the files.

(c) (Col) office.

(d) (Chi, Mex) jail.

Ardenas mpl Ardennes.

ardedor adj (Cu, Mex) quick-burning, easy to light.

ardentía nf (Med) heartburn; (Naut) phosphorescence.

arder [2a] **1** vt (a) to burn.

(b) (SAm: Med) to sting, hurt.

2 vi (a) to burn; to blaze; — **sin llama** to smoulder.

(b) (of manure etc) to ferment; (of corn: Agr) to heat up.

(c) to glow, shine, blaze; to flash.

(d) (fig) — **de amor**, — **en amor** to burn with love; — **en guerra** to be ablaze with war.

3 arderse vr to burn away, burn up; (of corn etc) to parch, burn up.

ardid nm ruse, device, stratagem; —es tricks, wiles.

ardido adj (a) brave, bold, daring. (b) (SAm) cross, angry.

ardiente adj (a) burning. (b) glowing, shining, blazing; colour bright, glowing; flower bright red. (c) fever, interest, wish etc burning; love ardent, passionate; supporter fervent, passionate.

ardientemente adv ardently, fervently, passionately.

ardiles adj invar hot-tempered, peppery.

ardiloso adj (Arg, Col) tricky, wily; (Chi) loose-tongued.

ardilla nf (a) squirrel; — **listada** chipmunk; — **de tierra** gopher; **andar como una** — to be always on the go.

(b) (SAm) clever businessman; (pej) untrustworthy person.

ardimiento[1] nm burning.

ardimiento[2] nm courage, dash.

ardita nf (Arg, Col, Ven) =**ardilla**.

ardite nm: **no me importa un** — I don't give a damn; **no vale un** — it's not worth a brass farthing.

ardor nm (a) heat, warmth.

(b) (Med) — **de estómago** heartburn.

(c) (fig) ardour, eagerness, zeal; courage, dash; (of argument) heat, warmth; **en el** — **de la batalla** in the heat of battle.

ardoroso adj (a) hot, burning; **en lo más** — **del estío** in the hottest part of the summer. (b) (fig) fiery, fervent, ardent.

arduamente adv arduously.

arduidad nf arduousness.

arduo adj arduous, hard, tough.

área nf (a) area. (b) (Math) are, square decameter. (c) (Sport) — **de castigo**, — **de penálty** penalty area; — **de gol**, — **de meta** goal area.

arena nf (a) sand; grit, gravel; —s **movedizas** quick-sands, shifting sands; —s **de oro** (fig) fine gold, gold dust; **sembrar en** — (fig) to labour in vain.

(b) (Med) —s stones, gravel.

(c) arena.

arenal nm (a) sandy spot, sandy ground. (b) sandpit; (Golf) bunker. (c) (Naut) sands, quicksand.

arenar [1a] vt (a) to sand, sprinkle with sand. (b) (Tech) to sand, polish with sand, rub with sand.

arenga nf (a) harangue, speech; (fam) sermon. (b) (Chi) argument, quarrel.

arengar [1h] vt to harangue.

arenguear [1a] vi (Chi) to argue, quarrel.

arenillas nfpl (Med) stones, gravel.

arenisca nf sandstone; grit.

arenisco adj sandy; gravelly, gritty.

arenoso adj sandy.

arenque nm herring.

areómetro nm hydrometer.

arepa nf (SAm) corn griddle-cake.

arequipa nf (Col) rice pudding.

arete nm earring.

argalia nf catheter.

argamandijo nm (fam) set of tools, tackle.

argamasa nf mortar, plaster.

argamasar [1a] vt (a) mortar to mix. (b) to mortar, plaster.

árgana nf crane.

árganas nfpl (esp RPl) wicker baskets, panniers (carried by horse).

Argel Algiers.

Argelia f Algeria.

argelino 1 adj Algerian. **2** nm, **argelina** nf Algerian.

argén nm (Her) argent.

argentado adj silvered; (fig) silvery.

argentar [1a] vt to silver.

argénteo adj (a) (Tech) silver-plated. (b) (poet) silver, silvery.

argentería nf silver (or gold) embroidery, silver (or gold) filigree.

Argentina: la — the Argentine.

argentinismo nm argentinism, word (or phrase etc) peculiar to Argentina.

argentino[1] adj silvery.

argentino[2] **1** adj Argentinian. **2** nm, **argentina** nf Argentinian.

argento nm (poet) silver; — **vivo** quicksilver.

argo nm argon.

argolla nf (a) (large) ring; hitching ring; door-knocker; serviette ring; (SAm) engagement ring, wedding ring. (b) (Sport) croquet.

argollar [1a] **1** vt (Col) pig to ring; (Mex) to hitch to a ring; — **a uno** (Mex) to have a hold over someone (because of a service rendered). **2 argollarse** vr (Col) to get engaged.

argón nm argon.

argonauta nm Argonaut.

Argos m Argus.

argot [ar'go] nm, pl **argots** [ar'go] slang.

argucia nf subtlety, sophistry, hair-splitting.

argüir [3g] **1** vt (a) to argue, contend; to indicate, point to, imply; to infer, deduce; **de ahí arguyo su buena calidad** I deduce its good quality from that; **esto arguye su poco cuidado** this indicates his lack of care; **esto le arguye de poco escrupuloso** this demonstrates his lack of scruple. (b) to reproach; **me argüian con vehemencia** they vehemently reproached me; — **a uno (de) su crueldad** to reproach someone for his cruelty. **2** vi to argue (contra against, with).

argumentación nf argumentation; line of argument.

argumentador adj argumentative.

argumentar [1a] vti to argue; — **que . . .** to argue that . . ., contend that . . .

argumento nm (a) argument (also Law); line of argument; reasoning, thinking. (b) (Lit, Theat) plot; — **de la obra** (as preface) summary of the plot, summary of the story, outline. (c) (SAm) argument, discussion, quarrel.

aria nf aria.

arica nf (Ven) wild bee.

aridecer [2d] **1** vt to dry up, make arid. **2** vi and **aridecerse** vr to dry up, become arid.

aridez nf aridity, dryness (also fig).

árido 1 adj arid, dry (also fig). **2** —**s** nmpl (Comm) dry goods; (Agr) dry grains, hard grains; **medida para** —**s** dry measure.

ariete nm battering ram.

arigua nf (Ven) wild bee.

arillo nm earring.

ario 1 adj Aryan. **2** nm, **aria** nf Aryan.

ariscar [1g] **1** vt (Guat, Mex, PR) animal to make shy, make vicious; person to make suspicious. **2 ariscarse** vr (Guat, PR) to run away.

arisco adj animal shy; wild, temperamental, vicious; person surly; unsociable, unapproachable.

arista nf (Bot) beard, awn; (Geom) edge; (Archit) arris; (Mountaineering) arête.

aristocracia nf aristocracy.

aristócrata nmf aristocrat.

aristocrático adj aristocratic.

Aristófanes m Aristophanes.

aristón nm (a) (Archit) edge, corner. (b) (Mus) pianola.

Aristóteles m Aristotle.

aristotélico adj Aristotelian.

aritmética nf arithmetic.

aritmético 1 adj arithmetical. **2** nm arithmetician.

Arlequín m Harlequin.

arlequín nm (fig) buffoon; Neapolitan ice cream.

arlequinada nf harlequinade; (piece of) buffoonery.

arlequinesco adj (fig) grotesque, ridiculous.

Arlés Arles.

arma nf (a) arm, weapon; — **arrojadiza** missile; — **atómica** atomic weapon; — **blanca** steel blade, knife, sword; —**s cortas** small arms; — **de fuego**

firearm, gun; — **de infantería** infantry weapon; — **negra** fencing foil; **¡a las** —**s!** to arms!; **¡**—**s al hombro!** shoulder arms!; **alzarse en** —**s** to rise up in arms, rebel; **¡descansen** —**s!** order arms!; **estar sobre las** —**s** to be under arms; to stand by; **pasar a uno por las** —**s** to shoot someone, execute someone; **¡presenten** —**s!** present arms!; **rendir las** —**s** to lay down one's arms; **tocar (al)** — to sound the call to arms; **tomar las** —**s** to take up arms; **es de** —**s tomar** it's a matter for concern, it's a dangerous business; **volver el** — **contra uno** to turn the tables on someone. (b) arm, branch, service. (c) —**s** (Her) arms.

armada nf (a) fleet; navy; armada; **la A**— **Invencible** the Armada (1588); **la A**— **Británica** the British Navy; **un oficial de la** — a naval officer. (b) (Chi, RPl) noose, lasso.

armadanzas nmf, pl **armadanzas** (fam) = **danzante.**

armadía nf = **almadía.**

armadijo nm trap, snare.

armadillo nm armadillo.

armado adj (a) armed; — **hasta los dientes** armed to the teeth; **ir** — to go armed. (b) (Mech) mounted, assembled. (c) (Tech) concrete reinforced.

armador nm (a) (Naut) shipowner; (Hist) privateer. (b) (Mech) fitter, assembler.

armadura nf (a) (Mil, Hist) armour; **una** — a suit of armour. (b) (Tech) frame, framework; (of glasses) frame; (Anat) skeleton; (Bot, Elec, Zool) armature; — **de la cama** bedstead. (c) (Mus) key signature.

Armagedón m Armageddon.

armamento nm (a) armament; —**s** armaments, arms. (b) (Naut) fitting-out.

armar [1a] **1** vt (a) to arm (con, de with). (b) bayonet to fix; bow to bend; gun etc to load; trap to set. (c) to prepare, arrange, get ready; (Mech) to assemble, put together; to set up; to mount; tent to pitch, set up; (Archit) to set (en, sobre on). (d) (Naut) to fit out, equip; to put into commission. (e) concrete to reinforce; (Sew) to stiffen. (f) — **a uno caballero** to knight someone, dub someone knight. (g) lawsuit to bring; row to cause, make, start, stir up; —**la** to start a row, make trouble. **2 armarse** vr (a) to arm oneself (con, de with); — **de valor** to gather up one's courage; — **de paciencia** to arm oneself with patience, resolve to be patient. (b) to prepare, get ready; see **Dios** etc. (c) (CAm, Cu, Mex, PR, Ven) to be obstinate; to refuse point blank; (Arg, Mex: of animal) to balk, shy. (d) (SAm) to be lucky, have a stroke of luck; to make lots of money, get rich. (e) **¡te vas a** —**!** (Arg: iro) you'll never manage it!

armario nm cupboard; — **(para libros)** bookcase; — **(ropero)** wardrobe; — **botiquín** medicine chest.

armatoste nm (a) unwieldy piece of furniture (etc), large useless object; (Mech) contraption; (Aut) grid (sl), crock, jalopy. (b) (person) useless great object, clumsy sort.

armazón nf (m in parts of SAm) frame, framework; (Aer, Aut) body, chassis; (Archit) shell, skeleton; (of piece of furniture) frame; (Arg, Chi, Par, Per) shelves, shelving.

armella nf eyebolt.

Armenia f Armenia.

armenio 1 adj Armenian. **2** nm, **armenia** nf Armenian.

armería nf (a) military museum, museum of arms; armoury. (b) gunsmith's (shop), gun shop. (c) art of the gunsmith.

armero nm (a) gunsmith, armourer. (b) gun rack; stand for weapons.

armiño nm (Zool) stoat; (fur, Her) ermine.

armisticio nm armistice.

armón nm (also — **de artillería**) gun carriage, limber.

armonía nf harmony; **en** — in harmony (con with), in keeping (con with).

armónica nf harmonica, mouth organ.

armónicamente adv harmonically; harmoniously.

armónico 1 adj harmonic; harmonious. **2** nm (Mus, Phys) harmonic.

armonio nm harmonium.

armoniosamente adv harmoniously; tunefully.

armonioso adj harmonious; tuneful.

armonizar [1f] **1** vt to harmonize; (fig) to harmonize, bring into harmony; differences to reconcile.
2 vi to harmonize (con with); (fig) — **con** to harmonize with, blend with, be in keeping with; — **con** (of colours) to blend with, tone in with.
arnaco nm (Col) useless object, piece of lumber.
arnero nm (SAm) sieve.
arnés nm (**a**) (Mil, Hist) armour. (**b**) —**es** harness, trappings; (fig) gear, tackle, outfit.
aro nm ring, hoop; rim; (Sport) quoit; (SAm) earring; — **de émbolo** piston ring; — **de rueda** rim of a wheel; (**juego de**) —**s** quoits; **entrar por el** — (fam) to have no option.
aroma nm aroma, scent, fragrance; (of wine) bouquet.
aromático adj aromatic, sweet-scented.
aromatizar [1f] vt to scent, give fragrance to; (Cook) to spice, flavour with herbs.
arpa nf harp; **tocar el** — (fam) to be a thief, live by thieving.
arpado adj jagged, toothed, serrated.
arpar[1] [1a] vt to scratch, claw (at); to tear, tear to pieces.
arpar[2] [1a] vt (SAm: fam) to steal, pinch (fam).
arpeo nm grappling iron.
arpero nm (Mex, Par) thief.
arpía nf (Myth) harpy; (fig) shrew, bag (sl), hag.
arpicordio nm harpsichord.
arpillera nf sacking, sackcloth.
arpir nm (Arg, Bol, Chi) mineworker.
arpista nmf harpist; (Arg) thief.
arpón nm harpoon; gaff.
arponar [1a] vt, **arponear** [1a] vt to harpoon; to gaff.
arquear [1a] **1** vt (**a**) to arch; to bend. (**b**) wool to beat. (**c**) (Naut) to gauge; (SAm: Comm) to check, check the contents of.
2 vi (Med) to retch.
3 arquearse vr to arch; to bend; (of surface) to camber.
arqueo nm (**a**) (Archit etc) arching. (**b**) (Naut) tonnage, burden; capacity; (Comm) checking; — **bruto** gross tonnage.
arqueología nf archaeology.
arqueológico adj archaeological.
arqueólogo nm archaeologist.
arquería nf arcade, series of arches.
arquero nm (**a**) (Mil) bowman, archer. (**b**) (Comm) cashier. (**c**) (SAm: Sport) goalkeeper.
arquetipo nm archetype.
Arquímedes m Archimedes.
arquimesa nf desk, escritoire.
arquitecto nm architect; — **de jardines** landscape gardener.
arquitectónico adj architectural.
arquitectura nf architecture.
arrabal nm suburb; (SAm) slums, slum quarter; —**es** outskirts, outlying area.
arrabalero 1 adj (**a**) suburban; (pej) of (or from) the poorer quarters.
(**b**) (fig) common, coarse.
2 nm, **arrabalera** nf (**a**) suburbanite, (pej) person from the poorer quarters.
(**b**) (fig) common sort, coarse person.
arracacha nf (Col) idiocy, silliness.
arracacho nm (Col) idiot.
arracada nf pendant earring.
arracimado adj clustered, clustering.
arracimarse [1a] vr to cluster together, hang in bunches.
arraigadamente adv firmly, securely.
arraigado adj firmly rooted, well-rooted, deep-rooted; (fig) established, ingrained; person landed, property-owning.
arraigar [1h] **1** vt (**a**) (fig) to establish; to strengthen (en in).
(**b**) (SAm: Law) to restrict the free movement of.
2 vi (Bot) to take root, strike root.
3 vi and **arraigarse** vr (Bot) to take root; (of customs etc) to take root, establish itself, take a hold; (of person) to settle, establish oneself; to acquire property; **la costumbre se arraigó en él** the habit grew on him.
arraigo nm (**a**) (Bot) rooting; **de fácil** — easily-rooted.
(**b**) property, land, real estate; **hombre de** — man of property.
(**c**) (fig) settling, establishment.
(**d**) (fig) hold, influence; **tener** — to have influence.
arralar [1a] vt (Mex) trees to thin out.
arrancaclavos nm, pl **arrancaclavos** claw hammer, nail extractor.

arrancada nf sudden start; sudden acceleration; jerk, jolt; sudden charge.
arrancadero nm starting point.
arrancado adj (fam) broke (fam), penniless.
arrancador nm (Aut) starter.
arrancamiento nm pulling out, extraction; snatching.
arrancar [1g] **1** vt (**a**) plant etc to pull up, root out; tooth to extract, pull; metal to win, extract; hair etc to pluck out; button etc to tear off, tear away; paper etc to tear out, rip out; phlegm to bring up; sigh to fetch.
(**b**) to snatch, snatch away (**a**, **de** from); to wrench, wrest (**a**, **de** from); **le arrancó el bolso** he snatched her handbag; **el viento lo arrancó de mis manos** the wind snatched it from my hands; **lograron** —**le el cuchillo** they managed to wrest the knife from him.
(**c**) — **a uno de una fiesta** to tear someone away from a party; **nos vimos materialmente arrancados de nuestras camas por el estruendo** we were literally shot out of bed by the noise; — **a uno de un vicio** to wean someone away from a bad habit.
(**d**) support to win, get; victory to snatch, wrest (**a** from); — **una promesa a uno** to force a promise out of someone, extort a promise from someone; — **información a uno** to worm information out of someone, extract information from someone.
(**e**) (Aut etc) to start.
2 vi (**a**) to start, set off; (Aut) to start; (Naut) to set sail; to pick up speed, accelerate; (fam) to leave, clear out; — **a correr** to start running, break into a run.
(**b**) (Arg) to start off vigorously, start in high spirits.
(**c**) — **de** (Archit: of arch etc) to spring from.
(**d**) — **de** (fig) to come from, spring from, originate in; to go back to; **esto arranca del siglo XV** this goes back to the 15th century, this began in the 15th century; **todo arranca de aquello** it all starts with that.
3 arrancarse vr (Cu, Ec, Mex: sl) to peg out (sl).
arrancón nm (Mex) =**arrancada**.
arranchar [1a] **1** vt (**a**) sails to brace.
(**b**) coast to skirt, sail close to.
(**c**) to snatch away (**a** from).
2 arrancharse vr (**a**) to gather together; to eat together.
(**b**) (Mex, Ven) to settle down temporarily, make the best of it.
arranque nm (**a**) sudden start, jerk, jolt; wrench.
(**b**) start; — **automático** (Aut) self-starter, starting motor.
(**c**) (Anat, Archit) starting point.
(**d**) (fig) impulse; (emotional) outburst; — **de cólera** fit of anger, outburst of bad temper; **en un** — impulsively.
(**e**) (fig) sally, witty remark.
(**f**) (SAm) state of being utterly broke (fam), poverty.
(**g**) **no servir ni para el** — (Mex) to be utterly useless.
arranquera nf, **arranquitis** nf (Ant, Col, Guat) = **arranque** (**f**).
arrapiezo nm (**a**) rag, tatter. (**b**) whippersnapper.
arras nfpl (**a**) pledge, security, deposit. (**b**) (Hist) 13 coins given by bridegroom to bride.
arrasar [1a] **1** vt (**a**) to level, flatten; to raze to the ground, demolish.
(**b**) to fill up, fill to the brim.
2 vi (Meteorol) to clear.
3 arrasarse vr (Meteorol) to clear; **se le arrasaron los ojos de** (or **en**) **lágrimas** her eyes filled with tears.
arrastradizo adj dangling, trailing.
arrastrado 1 adj (**a**) **llevar algo** — to drag something along.
(**b**) poor, wretched, miserable; vile; **andar** — to have a wretched life.
(**c**) wily, rascally.
(**d**) (SAm) cringing, servile.
2 nm rogue, rascal.
arrastradora nf (Per) prostitute.
arrastrar [1a] **1** vt (**a**) to drag, drag along, haul, pull; to drag down.
(**b**) dress etc to trail along the ground.
(**c**) — **los pies** to drag one's feet, shuffle along.
(**d**) (of water, wind etc) to carry away, carry down, wash along.
(**e**) (of feelings etc) to carry away; supporters etc to win over, carry with one; affection, loyalty to

command, draw, win; **no te dejes — por esa idea** don't get carried away by that idea, don't run away with that idea.

(**f**) to drag down, degrade, debase.

2 *vi* to drag, trail along the ground, hang down; (*Bot*) to trail.

3 arrastrarse *vr* (**a**) to crawl, creep; to drag oneself along; **se arrastró hasta la puerta** he dragged himself to the door.

(**b**) to drag, trail along the ground, hang down.

(**c**) (*of time, entertainment etc*) to drag.

(**d**) to grovel, fawn, creep (*sl*).

arrastre *nm* (**a**) drag, dragging, pulling; haulage; (*Aer*) drag.

(**b**) (*Sport*) crawl; **— de espaldas** backstroke.

(**c**) (*Ant, RPl*) influence; **tener mucho —** (*Arg*) to have a lot of influence, have a wide following.

(**d**) **estar para el —** to be finished, be done for.

arrayán *nm* myrtle.

arre *interj* get up!, gee up!

arreada *nf* (*Arg*) roundup.

arreado *adj* (*Chi, Mex, Per*) slow-moving, ponderous.

arreador *nm* (**a**) foreman; muleteer. (**b**) (*Arg, Par*) long whip.

arrear [1a] **1** *vt* (**a**) *cattle etc* to drive, urge on. (**b**) to harness. (**c**) (*CAm, Mex, RPl*) to steal, *cattle* rustle.

2 *vi* to hurry along; **¡arrea!** get moving!, (*fig*) get away!, nonsense!

arrebañaduras *nfpl* scrapings, remains.

arrebañar [1a] *vt* to scrape together; *meal* to eat up, clear up.

arrebatadamente *adv* suddenly, violently; headlong; rashly; **hablar —** to speak in a rush.

arrebatadizo *adj* excitable, hot-tempered.

arrebatado *adj* (**a**) hasty, sudden, violent. (**b**) rash, impetuous. (**c**) rapt, bemused; ecstatic. (**d**) *face* flushed.

arrebatamiento *nm* (**a**) snatching (away); seizure; abduction. (**b**) (*fig*) captivation; ecstasy, rapture; excitement; anger.

arrebatar [1a] **1** *vt* (**a**) to snatch, snatch away (*a* from); to seize; to wrench, wrest (*a* from); *page, part etc* to tear off, rip off; *person* to carry away, carry off, abduct; **le arrebató el revólver** he snatched the pistol from him; **nos arrebataron la victoria** they wrested victory from us; **— la vida a uno** to take someone's life.

(**b**) (*fig*) to move deeply, stir; to captivate, enrapture.

(**c**) (*Agr*) to parch.

2 arrebatarse *vr* (**a**) to get carried away; to get excited; **— de cólera** to be overcome with anger; **se dejó — por su entusiasmo** he got carried away by his enthusiasm.

(**b**) (*Cook*) to burn, overcook.

arrebatiña *nf* scramble, rush, scrimmage.

arrebato *nm* (**a**) fit of rage, fury. (**b**) ecstasy, rapture; **en un — de entusiasmo** in a sudden fit of enthusiasm.

arrebiatarse [1a] *vr* (*Guat*) to begin resolutely; (*Mex*) to agree automatically (with someone's opinion).

arrebol *nm* rouge; (*of sky*) red flush, red glow; **—es** red clouds.

arrebolar [1a] **1** *vt* to redden. **2 arrebolarse** *vr* (**a**) to apply rouge, rouge oneself. (**b**) to redden, flush.

arrebozar [1f] **1** *vt* to muffle (up). **2 arrebozarse** *vr* (**a**) to muffle up, muffle one's face. (**b**) (*Ent*) to swarm.

arrebujar [1a] **1** *vt* (**a**) to jumble together, jumble up. (**b**) to wrap up, cover. **2 arrebujarse** *vr* to wrap oneself up (*con* in, with).

arreciar [1b] **1** *vi* to grow worse, get more severe; to increase in intensity; (*of wind*) to get stronger.

2 arreciarse *vr* (**a**) = *vi*. (**b**) (*Med*) to get stronger, pick up.

arrecife *nm* causeway; (*Naut*) reef; **— de coral** coral reef.

arrechada *nf* (*CAm, Mex*) = **arrechera.**

arrechar [1a] *vi* (**a**) (*CAm*) to show energy, begin to make an effort. (**b**) (*CAm, Mex*) to be in the mood, feel randy.

arrechera *nf* (**a**) (*Arg: Zool*) heat, mating urge; (*Mex*) randiness, lechery. (**b**) (*Mex*) whim, fancy.

arrecho *adj* (**a**) (*CAm*) vigorous; energetic; brave. (**b**) (*SAm*) randy, lecherous; **estar —** (*Zool*) to be on heat; (*person*) to be in the mood, feel randy.

arrechucho *nm* (**a**) sudden impulse; fit, outburst; unforeseen difficulty, new trouble.

(**b**) (*Med*) queer turn, sudden indisposition; **dar a uno el —** to have a queer turn, be taken ill suddenly.

arredo *adv* (*CAm, Mex*): **¡— vaya!** get lost! (*fam*).

arredrar [1a] **1** *vt* (**a**) to drive back; to remove, separate.

(**b**) to scare, daunt.

2 arredrarse *vr* (**a**) to draw back, move away (*de* from).

(**b**) to get scared, lose heart; **— ante algo** to shrink away from something; **sin —** unmoved, nothing daunted.

arregazado *adj* *dress etc* tucked up; *nose* turned up, snub.

arregazar [1f] *vt* to tuck up.

arregionado *adj* (*Col, Mex*) ill-tempered, sharp; (*Col*) impulsive; (*Col*) sulky; (*Ec*) cross, angry; (*Ven*) worthy, highly-esteemed.

arregladamente *adv* regularly, in an orderly way; sensibly, reasonably.

arreglado *adj* (**a**) neat, orderly, proper; moderate, sensible, reasonable; **una vida arreglada** a well-regulated life, a sensible life, a well-adjusted life; **conducta arreglada** good behaviour, orderly behaviour; **un precio —** a reasonable price.

(**b**) **— a** in accordance with, adjusted to.

arreglar [1a] **1** *vt* (**a**) to arrange; to settle; to adjust (*a* to), regulate; *appointment, date, meeting etc* to arrange, fix up; *problem* to put right; *abuse* to correct; *dispute* to settle, put right; (*Arg, Mex*) *debt* to settle; (*SAm*) *animal* to castrate; **yo lo arreglaré** I'll see to it, I'll arrange it; **todavía no se ha arreglado nada** nothing has been fixed up yet.

(**b**) (*Mech etc*) to fix, mend, repair.

(**c**) *appearance, hair, room etc* to tidy up, smarten up, do; **voy a que me arreglen el pelo** I'm going to have my hair done.

(**d**) (*Mus*) to arrange.

2 arreglarse *vr* (**a**) to come to terms (*a, con* with), reach an understanding; **— a** to conform to, adjust oneself to; **por fin se arreglaron** eventually they reached an agreement.

(**b**) **— el pelo** to have one's hair done; **to do one's hair**, tidy one's hair.

(**c**) (*of problem etc*) to work out, be solved, be all right; **por fin el asunto se arregló** everything was finally fixed up; **todo se arreglará** things will work out, everything will be all right.

(**d**) (*SAm*) to have a stroke of luck; (*of lovers*) to click (*fam*), hit it off.

(**e**) **—las** to get by, manage; **—las para + infin** to manage to + infin; **¿cómo se las arreglan Vds?** how do you manage?; **hay que —las** you've got to get organized; it's up to you to see to it.

arreglo *nm* (**a**) (*act*) arrangement, settlement; adjustment; regulation; **esto no tiene —** there's no way of sorting this out, there's no solution to this.

(**b**) rule, order; orderliness; **vivir con —** to live an orderly life.

(**c**) agreement, understanding; compromise; **con — a** according to, in accordance with; **llegar a un —** to reach a settlement, reach a compromise.

(**d**) (*Mus*) setting, arrangement.

(**e**) (*euph*) liaison, understanding.

arregostarse [1a] *vr*: **— a** to take a fancy to.

arregosto *nm* fancy, taste (*de* for).

arrejuntarse [1a] *vr* (*Mex*) to set up house together, live in sin.

arrellanarse [1a] *vr*, **arrellenarse** [1a] *vr* (**a**) to lounge, sprawl, loll; **— en el asiento** to settle oneself comfortably in one's chair, (*pej*) to sit sprawled in one's chair.

(**b**) (*fig*) to be happy in one's work.

arremangado *adj* turned up, tucked up; *nose* turned up, snub.

arremangar [1h] **1** *vt* *sleeve etc* to turn up, tuck up, roll up; *skirt* to tuck up. **2 arremangarse** *vr* (**a**) to roll up one's sleeves (*etc*). (**b**) (*fig*) to take a firm line.

arrematar [1a] *vt* (*fam*) to finish, complete.

arremeter [2a] **1** *vt* (**a**) to attack, assail.

(**b**) *horse* to spur on, spur forward.

2 *vi* (**a**) to rush forth, attack; **— a uno, — contra uno** to rush at someone, attack someone, launch oneself at someone.

(**b**) to offend good taste, shock the eye.

arremetida *nf* (**a**) attack, assault; onrush; push; lunge. (**b**) (*of horse*) sudden start.

arremolinarse [1a] *vr* (*people*) to crowd around, mill around, swirl; (*water*) to swirl, eddy; (*dancers, dust etc*) to swirl, whirl.

arrempujar [1a] *vt* = **empujar; rempujar.**

arrendable *adj*: *casa* **—** house available for letting, house to let. ◁

arrendador *nm*, **arrendadora** *nf* (**a**) landlord, landlady; lessor. (**b**) tenant.

arrendajo *nm* jay.

arrendamiento nm (a) (act) letting, leasing; hiring; farming out; **tomar una casa en —** to rent a house. (b) rent, rental; lease; hiring fee. (c) contract, agreement.

arrendar[1] [1k] vt (a) (subject: owner) house to let, lease; machine etc to hire out; tax to farm out. (b) (subject: tenant etc) house to rent, lease; machine etc to hire.

arrendar[2] [1k] vt horse to tie, tether (by the reins).

arrendatario nm, **arrendataria** nf tenant; lessee, leaseholder; hirer; tax farmer.

arreo nm (a) adornment, dress; piece of harness. (b) —s harness, trappings; (fig) gear, equipment. (c) (SAm: Agr) drove (of cattle).

arrepentidamente adv regretfully, repentantly.

arrepentido 1 adj regretful, repentant, sorry; **estar — de algo** to regret something, be sorry about something; **se mostró muy —** he seemed very repentant. 2 nm, **arrepentida** nf (Eccl) penitent.

arrepentimiento nm regret, repentance, sorrow; (Eccl) repentance.

arrepentirse [3i] vr to repent, be repentant; **— de algo** to regret something, repent of something; **se arrepintió de haberlo dicho** he regretted having said it; **no me arrepiento de nada** I regret nothing.

arrequín nm (a) (SAm) faithful follower; helper, assistant. (b) (SAm: Agr) leading animal (of a mule train).

arrequives nmpl (a) finery, best clothes; frills, trimmings. (b) circumstances.

arrestado adj bold, daring.

arrestar [1a] 1 vt to arrest; to imprison; **— en el cuartel** (Mil) to confine to barracks. 2 **arrestarse** vr: **— a algo** to rush boldly into something; **— a todo** to be afraid of nothing.

arresto nm (a) arrest; imprisonment; (Mil) detention, confinement; **— domiciliario** house arrest; **estar bajo —** to be under arrest. (b) (fig) boldness, daring; enterprise; **tener —s to** be bold, be daring.

arrevesado adj (SAm)=**enrevesado**.

arria nf (SAm) mule train, train of pack animals; drove.

arriada nf flood.

arrianismo nm Arianism.

arriano 1 adj Arian. 2 nm, **arriana** nf Arian.

arriar [1c] 1 vt (a) to flood. (b) (Naut) flag to lower, strike; sail to haul down; rope to loosen; to pay out; (fam) to let go. 2 **arriarse** vr to flood, become flooded.

arriate nm (a) (Hort) bed, border; trellis. (b) road, causeway.

arriba 1 adv (a) (position) above; overhead; on top; high, on high; (Naut) aloft; (in house) upstairs; (direction) up, upwards; **"este lado —"** "this side up"; **lo — escrito** what has been said above; **la persona — mencionada** the aforementioned person; **de — abajo** from top to bottom, from head to foot; from beginning to end; **desde —** from (up) above; **hacia —** up, upwards; **está más —** it's higher up; it's further up; **por la calle —** up the street; **de 10 dólares para —** from 10 dollars upwards; **de la cintura (para) —** from the waist up; see **agua** (e), **cuesta, río** etc. (b) **de — adj:** **la parte de —** the upper part, the top side; **los de —** those above; those at the top; those on top. 2 interj: **¡—!** up you get!; **¡— España!** Spain for ever!, long live Spain!; **¡— Toboso!** (Sport etc) up with Toboso! 3 **— de** prep above; higher than, further up than; **el río — de la ciudad** the river above the town.

arribada nf (a) (Naut and fig) arrival, entry into harbour; **— forzosa** emergency call, unscheduled stop; **entrar de —** to put into port. (b) (Arg) brusque reply, rude answer.

arribaje nm (Naut) arrival, entry into harbour.

arribar [1a] vi (a) to arrive; (Naut) to put into port, make an emergency call; **— a** to reach. (b) (Med, Fin) to recover, improve. (c) **— a + infin** to manage to + infin.

arribeño nm, **arribeña** nf (a) (SAm) highlander, inlander. (b) (Arg, Par) stranger, person passing through.

arribista nmf upstart, parvenu, arriviste; social climber.

arribo nm arrival; **hacer su —** to arrive.

arriendo nm=**arrendamiento**.

arriero nm muleteer; (CR) carrier.

arriesgadamente adv riskily, dangerously; daringly; boldly; rashly.

arriesgado adj (a) act risky, dangerous, hazardous; daring; **unas ideas arriesgadas** some dangerous ideas; **me parece arriesgado prometerlo** it would be rash to promise it. (b) person bold, daring; rash, foolhardy.

arriesgar [1h] 1 vt life etc to risk, hazard; to endanger; guess to hazard, venture; chances to endanger, jeopardize; money to stake. 2 **arriesgarse** vr to take a risk, expose oneself to danger; to put one's life (or chances etc) in danger; **— a hacer algo** to dare to do something, risk doing something; **— en una empresa** to venture upon an enterprise.

arrimadero nm support.

arrimadillo nm wainscot.

arrimadizo 1 adj (fig) parasitic, sycophantic. 2 nm, **arrimadiza** nf parasite, hanger-on, sycophant.

arrimado 1 adj imitation etc close. 2 nm (Arg, Cu, Mex, Par) unwelcome guest, parasite; newcomer (to a group); (pej) lover.

arrimar [1a] 1 vt (a) to bring close, move up, draw up (a to); **hay que —lo todavía más** you'll have to bring it closer still; **lo arrimamos a la ventana** we put it against the window; **arrimó el oído a la puerta** he put his ear to the door; **— la escalera a una pared** to put (or lean, place) the ladder up against a wall; **las espuelas a un caballo** to dig one's spurs into a horse; **— un golpe a uno** to give someone a blow. (b) to put away, lay aside, shelve; to move out of the way; to get rid of; person to ignore, push aside; **el plan quedó arrimado** the plan was shelved; **— los libros** (fig) to lay aside one's books, give up studying. (c) (Naut) cargo to stow. (d) (Mex) child to beat, punish. (e) (Arg) **— la culpa a uno** to lay the blame on someone; see **hombro** etc. 2 **arrimarse** vr (a) to come close, come closer; to gather, come together. (b) **— a** to come close(r), to get near(er) to; to lean against, lean on; to cuddle up to, snuggle up to; **se arrimó a la lumbre** she huddled over the fire; **arrímate a mí** lean on me; cuddle up to me. (c) **— a** (fig) to join, keep company with; to seek the protection of; **arrímate a los buenos** choose your friends among good people; cultivate the virtuous. (d) (SAm) to move in together, set up house together.

arrimo nm (a) support; (Cu, PR) partition, dividing wall. (b) (fig) support, help, protection. (c) (fig) attachment.

arrimón nm loafer, idler; sponger (fam); **estar de — to** hang about, loaf around.

arrinconado adj (fig) forgotten, neglected; remote.

arrinconar [1a] 1 vt (a) to put in a corner; enemy etc to corner. (b) (fig) to lay aside, put away; to get rid of; to shelve; person to push aside, push into the background, ignore. 2 **arrinconarse** vr to retire, withdraw from the world.

arriscadamente adv boldly, resolutely.

arriscado adj (a) (Geog) craggy. (b) (fig) bold, resolute; spirited. (c) (fig) brisk, agile.

arriscamiento nm boldness, resolution.

arriscar[1] [1g] 1 vt to risk. 2 **arriscarse** vr to take a risk.

arriscar[2] [1g] 1 vt (Col, Chi, Mex) to turn up, fold up; to tuck up. 2 vi (Col) to draw oneself up, straighten up. 3 **arriscarse** vr (a) to get conceited. (b) (Per, Salv) to dress up to the nines.

arrivista=**arribista**.

arrizar [1f] vt (Naut) to reef; to fasten, lash down.

arroba nf (a) measure of weight = 11,502 kg (25 lbs). (b) a variable liquid measure.

arrobador adj entrancing, enchanting.

arrobamiento nm ecstasy, rapture, bliss; trance; **salir de su —** to emerge from one's state of bliss.

arrobar [1a] 1 vt to entrance, enchant. 2 **arrobarse** vr to become entranced, go into ecstasies, be enraptured; (of spiritualist) to go into a trance.

arrobo nm=**arrobamiento**.

arrochalarse [1a] vr (Col, Ven: of cattle) to take a liking to a place; (of dog etc) to refuse to go out; (of horse) to balk, shy.

arrodajarse [1a] vr (CAm) to sit down cross-legged.

arrodillarse [1a] vr to kneel, kneel down, go down on one's knees; **estar arrodillado** to kneel, be kneeling (down), be on one's knees.

arrogancia *nf* arrogance; pride.
arrogante *adj* arrogant, haughty; proud; brave.
arrogantemente *adv* arrogantly, haughtily; proudly; bravely.
arrogarse [1h] *vr*: — **algo** to arrogate something to oneself.
arrojadamente *adv* daringly, dashingly; rashly.
arrojadizo *adj* for throwing, that can be thrown; **arma arrojadiza** missile.
arrojado *adj* (*fig*) daring, dashing; rash.
arrojallamas *nm*, *pl* **arrojallamas** flamethrower.
arrojar [1a] **1** *vt* (**a**) to throw, fling, hurl, cast; (*Sport*) *ball* to bowl, pitch; *weight* to put; (*Fish*) to cast; — **algo de sí** to cast something from one, fling something aside.
　(**b**) *smoke etc* to give out, send out, emit; *light* to give, shed; *flowers*, *shoots* to put out; *person* to throw out, turn out; (*esp SAm*) to bring up, vomit; **este estudio arroja alguna luz sobre el tema** this study throws some light on the subject.
　(**c**) (*Comm*, *Fin*, *Math*) to give, produce, yield; *result*, *statistics* to show; **este negocio arroja déficit** this business shows an unfavourable balance.
　2 arrojarse *vr* (**a**) to throw oneself, hurl oneself (*a* into, on; *por* out of, through); — **al agua** to jump into the water; — **por una ventana** to throw oneself out of a window.
　(**b**) — **a**, — **en** (*fig*) to rush into, fling oneself into, plunge into.
arrojo *nm* daring, dash, fearlessness; rashness; **con** — boldly, fearlessly.
arrollador *adj* (*fig*) sweeping, overwhelming, crushing, devastating; **por una mayoría arrolladora** by an overwhelming majority; **es una pasión arrolladora** it is a consuming passion; **un ataque** — a crushing attack.
arrollar[1] [1a] *vt* (**a**) to roll up; (*Elec*, *Tech etc*) to coil, wind.
　(**b**) (*of water etc*) to sweep away, wash away; *enemy* to throw back, rout; (*Sport*) *opponent* to overwhelm, crush; (*Aut*, *Rail etc*) to run over, knock down; **arrollaron a sus rivales** they crushed their rivals.
　(**c**) (*fig*) *person* to dumbfound, leave speechless.
arrollar[2] [1a] *vt* (*SAm*) =**arrullar**.
arromar [1a] *vt* to blunt, dull.
arropar [1a] **1** *vt* (**a**) to cover; to wrap up (with clothes); to tuck up (in bed). (**b**) (*fig*) to protect.
　2 arroparse *vr* to wrap oneself up; to tuck oneself up (*or* in); ¡**arrópate bien!** wrap up warm!
arrope *nm* syrup; grape syrup, honey syrup.
arrorró *nm* (*SAm*) lullaby.
arrostrado *adj*: **bien** — nice-looking; **mal** — ill-favoured, ugly.
arrostrar [1a] **1** *vt* to face; to face up to, brave, defy; — **las consecuencias** to face the consequences; — **un peligro** to face a danger resolutely, face up to a danger.
　2 *vi*: — **a algo** to show a liking for something; — **con** = *vt*.
　3 arrostrarse *vr* to rush into the fight, throw oneself into the fray.
arroyada *nf* (**a**) gully, stream bed. (**b**) flood, flooding.
arroyo *nm* (**a**) stream, brook; watercourse; (*SAm*) river.
　(**b**) gutter; **estar en el** — (*woman*) to be on the streets; **poner a uno en el** — to turn someone out of the house; **ser del** — to be an orphan, be a foundling.
arroyuelo *nm* small stream, brook.
arroz *nm* rice; — **con leche** rice pudding; **hubo** — **y gallo muerto** (*fam*) it was a slap-up do (*fam*).
arrozal *nm* ricefield.
arruga *nf* (**a**) wrinkle, line; crease, fold; ruck. (**b**) (*Per: fam*) trick, wheeze (*fam*); debt.
arrugado *adj* *face etc* wrinkled, lined; *paper etc* creased; *dress etc* rucked up, crumpled.
arrugar [1h] **1** *vt* *face etc* to wrinkle, line; *brow* to knit, pucker up; *paper etc* to crease; to crumple, screw up; *dress etc* to ruck up, crumple; — **la cara** to screw up one's face; — **la frente** to knit one's brow, frown. {
　2 arrugarse *vr* (**a**) to wrinkle (up), get wrinkled; to crease, get creased; to ruck up, get crumpled; (*Bot*) to shrivel up.
　(**b**) (*Mex*) to get scared.
arrugue *nm* (*Ven*) =**arruga**.
arruinado *adj* (**a**) ruined. (**b**) (*Arg*, *Mex*, *Par*) decayed; small, stunted; (*Par*) wretched.
arruinamiento *nm* ruin, ruination.
arruinar [1a] **1** *vt* to ruin; to wreck, destroy; (*SAm*) to deflower.
　2 arruinarse *vr* to be ruined (*also Fin*); to go to rack and ruin; (*Archit etc*) to fall into ruins, fall down.

arrullar [1a] **1** *vt* to lull to sleep, rock to sleep; (*fam*) to whisper endearments to, say sweet nothings to. **2** *vi* to coo.
　3 arrullarse *vr* to bill and coo, whisper endearments; to flirt.
arrullo *nm* (*Orn*) cooing; (*fig*) billing and cooing; (*Mus*) lullaby.
arrumaco *nm* (**a**) caress. (**b**) eccentric item of dress (*or* adornment). (**c**) piece of flattery. (**d**) —s show of affection, endearments.
arrumaje *nm* (*Naut*) stowage; ballast.
arrumar [1a] **1** *vt* (*Naut*) to stow. **2 arrumarse** *vr* (*Naut*) to become overcast.
arrumbar[1] [1a] *vt* (**a**) to put aside, put on one side, discard; to neglect, forget. (**b**) *person* to silence, floor (*in an argument*); to remove (*from a post*).
arrumbar[2] [1a] (*Naut*) **1** *vi* to take one's bearings. **2 arrumbarse** *vr* (**a**) to be seasick. (**b**) (*Chi*, *Col*) to rust; to turn sour.
arruncharse [1a] *vr* (*Col*) to curl up, roll up.
arrurrú *nm* (*Bol*) lullaby.
arrurruz *nm* arrowroot.
arrutanado *adj* (*Col*) plump.
arsenal *nm* (*Naut*) navy yard, naval dockyard; (*Mil*) arsenal; (*fig*) storehouse, mine.
arsénico *nm* arsenic.
arte *m and f* (gen *m* in *sing*, *f* in *pl*) (**a**) art; —s (*Univ*) arts; **bellas** —s fine arts; —s **gráficas** graphic arts; —s **liberales** liberal arts; **por** — **de magia** (as if) by magic; — **mecánico** mechanical skill, manual skill; —s **y oficios** arts and crafts; — **poética** poetics; — **de los trucos** conjuring; — **de vivir** art of living.
　(**b**) (*Lit*) — **mayor** Spanish verse of 8 lines each of 12 syllables (15th century); — **menor** Spanish verse usually of 4 lines each of 6 or 8 syllables.
　(**c**) craft, skill; knack.
　(**d**) craftiness, cunning; trick; **malas** —s trickery, guile; **por malas** —s by trickery.
　(**e**) workmanship; artistry.
　(**f**) **no tener** — **ni parte en algo** to have nothing whatsoever to do with a matter.
artefacto *nm* (**a**) (*Tech*) appliance, device, contrivance; —s **de alumbrado** light fittings, light fixtures (*US*); — **nuclear** nuclear device.
　(**b**) (*esp archaeological*) artefact.
　(**c**) (*Aut: fam*) old crock, jalopy.
artejo *nm* knuckle, joint.
arteramente *adv* cunningly, artfully.
artería *nf* cunning, artfulness.
arteria *nf* artery (*also fig*); (*Elec*) feeder; **la** — **principal de una ciudad** the main artery of a city, the main thoroughfare of a town.
arterial *adj* arterial.
arteriosclerosis *nf* arteriosclerosis.
artero *adj* cunning, artful.
artesa *nf* trough, kneading trough.
artesanal *adj* craft (*attr*); **industria** — craft industry.
artesanía *nf* craftsmanship; handicraft, skill; **obra de** — piece of craftsmanship; **zapatos de** — craft shoes, handmade shoes.
artesano *nm* craftsman.
artesiano *adj*: **pozo** — artesian well.
artesón *nm* (**a**) kitchen tub. (**b**) (*Archit*) panel; coffer, caisson; moulding (*of ceiling*). (**c**) (*Ec*, *Mex*) vault; arcade, series of arches; flat roof, terrace.
artesonado *nm* (**a**) (*on walls*) panelling; — **de nogal** walnut panelling. (**b**) coffered ceiling; stuccoed ceiling, moulded ceiling.
artesonar [1a] *vt* (**a**) to panel. (**b**) to stucco, mould.
ártico *adj* Arctic; **el Á**— the Arctic.
articulación *nf* (**a**) (*Anat*) articulation; joint. (**b**) (*Mech*) joint; — **esférica** ball-and-socket joint; — **universal** universal joint. (**c**) (*Ling*) articulation.
articuladamente *adv* distinctly, articulately.
articulado *adj* (**a**) articulate. (**b**) (*Anat*, *Mech*) articulated, jointed.
articular [1a] **1** *vt* (**a**) to articulate; (*Mech*) to articulate, join together, join up.
　(**b**) (*Law*) to article.
　(**c**) (*Chi*, *Col*) to tell off, dress down.
　2 *vi* (*Chi*) to quarrel, squabble; to grumble.
articulista *nmf* columnist, feature writer, contributor (to a paper).
artículo *nm* (**a**) article, thing; commodity; —s (*Comm etc*) commodities, goods; —s **alimenticios** foodstuffs; — **de comercio** commodity; —s **de consumo** consumer goods; —s **de marca** branded goods; —s **de primera necesidad** basic commodities, essentials; —s **de plata** silverware; —s **de tocador** toilet articles, toiletries.
　(**b**) (*in newspaper etc*) article; feature, report,

study; (in learned journal) article, paper; (in reference book) entry, article; (in bill, document) article, section, item; — **de fondo** leading article, leader, editorial.
   (c) (Gram) article; — **definido** definite article; **indefinido** indefinite article.
   (d) (Anat) articulation, joint.
artifice nm artist, craftsman; maker; inventor; (fig) architect; **el — de la victoria** the architect of (the) victory.
artificial adj artificial.
artificialmente adv artificially.
artificio nm (a) art, craft, skill; (pej) artifice. (b) workmanship, craftsmanship. (c) contrivance, device, appliance. (d) cunning, sly trick.
artificiosamente adv (a) skilfully, ingeniously; artistically. (b) cunningly, artfully.
artificioso adj (a) skilful, ingenious; artistic. (b) cunning, artful.
artilugio nm (a) gadget, contraption. (b) gimmick, stunt. (c) thingummy (fam), whatsit (fam).
artillería nf artillery; — **antiaérea** anti-aircraft guns; — **de campaña** field guns; — **pesada** heavy artillery.
artillero nm (Mil) artilleryman, gunner; (Aer, Naut) gunner.
artimaña nf (a) trap, snare. (b) (fig) cunning.
artista nmf (Art) artist; (Theat etc) artist, artiste; — **de cine** film actor, film actress; — **de teatro** artist, artiste; — **de variedades** variety artist(e).
artísticamente adv artistically.
artístico adj artistic.
artrítico adj arthritic.
artritis nf arthritis; — **reumatoidea** rheumatoid arthritis.
artrópodos nmpl arthropods.
Arturo m Arthur.
Artús m: **el Rey —** King Arthur.
aruñar [1a] vt (Arg, Ven) =**arañar**.
aruñón nm (a) (Col) thief, pickpocket. (b) (Mex) =**arañazo**.
arveja nf (a) vetch. (b) (Bol, Col, Chi) pea.
arzobispado nm archbishopric.
arzobispo nm archbishop.
arzón nm saddle tree; — **delantero** saddlebow.
as nm (a) (Cards) ace; (in dice) one; — **de espadas** ace of spades.
   (b) (fam) ace, wizard (fam); — **del fútbol** wizard footballer, star player; — **del tenis** star tennis player; — **del volante** champion driver, speed king; **es un —** he's a wizard, he's the tops.
   (c) (fig: Tennis) ace, ace service.
asa[1] nf handle; grip; (fig) lever, pretext; **ser muy del —** (fam) to be well in.
asa[2] nf (Bot) juice.
asadero adj roasting, for roasting.
asado 1 adj (a) roast, roasted; **carne asada** roast meat; — **al horno** baked; — **a la parrilla** broiled; **bien —** well done; **poco —** underdone.
   (b) (SAm) cross, angry.
   (c) (Ven) **estar —** to be broke (fam).
   2 n roast, roast meat, joint.
asador nm (a) spit. (b) (mechanical) roasting jack; — **a rotación** rotary spit.
asaduras nfpl (a) entrails, offal; (Cook) chitterlings; **echar las —** to make a tremendous effort, bust a gut (fam). (b) sluggishness, laziness; **tiene —** he's terribly lazy.
asaetear [1a] vt (a) to shoot, hit (with an arrow). (b) (fig) to bother, pester.
asalariado 1 adj paid; wage-earning. 2 nm, **asalariada** nf (a) wage earner; employee. (b) (pej) hireling; **es — de Eslobodia** he's in the pay of Slobodia.
asalariar [1b] vt to take on, employ, hire.
asaltabancos nm, pl **asaltabancos** bank robber.
asaltador nm, **asaltante** nmf attacker, assailant; raider.
asaltar [1a] vt (a) person to attack, assail; to rush; (Mil) to storm; bank, shop etc to break into, raid; (during riot etc) to loot, sack; **le asaltaron 4 bandidos** he was held up by 4 bandits; **anoche fue asaltada la joyería** the jeweller's was raided last night, last night there was a break-in at the jeweller's.
   (b) (of disaster, death) to fall upon, surprise, overtake.
   (c) (fig: of doubt) to assail, afflict; (of thought) to cross one's mind; **le asaltó una idea** he was struck by an idea, he suddenly had an idea.
asalto nm (a) attack, assault; **tomar por —** to take by storm. (b) (Boxing, Fencing) round; — **de armas** fencing bout. (c) (Arg, Cu, Mex) unexpected visit.
asamblea nf assembly; meeting; congress, conference; **llamar a —** (Mil: Hist) to assemble, muster.

asambleísta nmf member of an assembly; conference member.
asapán nm (Mex) flying squirrel.
asar [1a] 1 vt (a) to roast; — **al horno** to bake; — **a la parrilla** to broil.
   (b) (fig) to pester, plague (con with).
   2 **asarse** vr (fig) to be terribly hot, roast; **me aso de calor** I'm roasting; **aquí se asa uno vivo** it's boiling hot here, the heat is killing here.
asaz adv (arch, lit) very, exceedingly; **una tarea — difícil** an exceedingly difficult task.
asbesto nm asbestos.
ascendencia nf (a) ancestry, descent, origin; **de remota — normanda** of remote Norman ancestry. (b) (SAm) ascendancy.
ascendente adj ascending, upward; **en una curva —** in an upward curve; **la carrera — del pistón** the up-stroke of the piston; **el tren —** the up train.
ascender [2g] 1 vt to promote; **fue ascendido a teniente** he was promoted (to) lieutenant, he was raised to the rank of lieutenant.
   2 vi (a) to ascend, rise, go up.
   (b) to be promoted (a to), go up; **Málaga asciende a primera división** Málaga goes up to the first division.
   (c) — **a** (Comm etc) to amount to, add up to, total.
ascendiente 1 adj = **ascendente**. 2 nmf ancestor. 3 nm ascendancy, influence, power (sobre over).
ascensión nf (a) ascent. (b) promotion (a to, to the rank of). (c) (Eccl) **la A—** the Ascension; **Día de la A—** Ascension Day.
ascensional adj curve, movement etc upward; (Astron) ascendant, rising.
ascensionista nmf balloonist.
ascenso nm promotion (a to, to the rank of).
ascensor nm lift, elevator (US); (Tech) elevator.
ascensorista nmf lift attendant, elevator operator (US).
asceta nmf ascetic.
ascético adj ascetic.
ascetismo nm asceticism.
asco nm (a) (feeling) loathing, disgust, revulsion; **¡qué —!** how awful!, how revolting!; **coger — a algo** to get sick of something; **dar — a uno** to sicken someone, disgust someone; **me das —** you disgust me; **me dan — las aceitunas** I loathe olives, olives revolt me; **hacer —s de algo** to turn up one's nose at something.
   (b) (object etc) loathsome thing, disgusting thing, abomination; **es un —** it's disgusting; **estar hecho un —** to be filthy; **poner a uno de —** (Mex) to call someone nasty names.
ascua nf live coal, ember; **¡—s!** ouch!; **arrimar el — a su sardina** to look after number one, put one's own interests first; **estar como — de oro** to be shining bright; **estar en —s** to be on tenterhooks; **tener a uno sobre —s** to keep someone on tenterhooks; **sacar el — con la mano del gato** (or **con mano ajena**) to get someone else to do the dirty work.
aseadamente adv cleanly, neatly, tidily; smartly.
aseado adj clean, neat, tidy; smart.
aseador nm: — **de calzado** (Mex) bootblack.
asear [1a] 1 vt (a) to adorn, embellish. (b) to clean up, tidy up; to smarten up. 2 **asearse** vr to tidy oneself up; to smarten oneself up.
asechanza nf trap, snare (also fig).
asechar [1a] vt to waylay, ambush; (fig) to set a trap for.
asediador nm besieger.
asediar [1b] vt (a) (Mil) to besiege, lay siege to; to blockade. (b) (fig) to bother, pester; (of lover) to chase, lay siege to.
asedio nm (a) (Mil) siege; blockade. (b) (Fin etc) run; — **de un banco** run on a bank.
asegún adv, prep (SAm: fam) = **según**.
asegurable adv insurable.
aseguración nf insurance.
asegurado 1 adj insured. 2 nm, **asegurada** nf the insured, the insured person.
asegurador nm (a) fastener. (b) (person) insurer; underwriter.
asegurar [1a] 1 vt (a) to secure, fasten, fix; to make firm, settle securely; — **algo con pernos** to secure something with bolts.
   (b) place etc to make secure, strengthen the defences of (contra against).
   (c) rights to safeguard, guarantee, assure.
   (d) to assure, affirm; **le aseguro que ...** I assure you that ...; **aseguró que ...** he affirmed that ..., he confirmed that ...; **se lo aseguro** I assure you, I promise you; take my word for it; **ella le aseguró de su inocencia** she assured him of her innocence.

(e) (*Comm, Fin*) to insure; — **algo contra incendios** to insure something against fire.

2 asegurarse *vr* (a) to make oneself secure (*de* from).

(b) to make sure (*de* of); **para asegurarnos del todo** in order to make quite sure.

(c) (*Comm, Fin*) to insure oneself.

asemejar [1a] **1** *vt* (a) to make alike, make similar; to copy. (b) to liken, compare (*a* to). **2 asemejarse** *vr* to be alike, be similar; — a to be like, resemble.

asendereado *adj* (a) *path* beaten, well-trodden. (b) *life* wretched, full of hardships.

asenderear [1a] *vt*: — **a uno** to chase someone relentlessly.

asenso *nm* (a) assent; **dar su** — to assent. (b) credence; **dar** — **a** to give credence to.

asentada *nf* sitting; **de una** — at one sitting.

asentaderas *nfpl* (*fam*) behind (*fam*), bottom.

asentado *adj* established, settled, permanent.

asentador *nm* razor strop.

asentar [1k] **1** *vt* (a) *person* to seat, sit down; *object* to place, fix, set; *tent* to pitch; *city etc* to found; *foundations* to make firm; *valve* to seat.

(b) *earth* to level, tamp down, firm.

(c) *blow* to give, fetch.

(d) *knife etc* to sharpen, hone.

(e) (*fig*) to settle, establish, consolidate; *principle* to lay down, establish; *impression* to fix in the mind; *opinion* to affirm, assert.

(f) to note down, set down, put in writing; (*Comm*) *order* to enter, book; *ledger* to enter up; — **algo al debe de uno** to debit something to someone; — **algo al haber de uno** to credit something to someone.

2 *vi* to be suitable, suit.

3 asentarse *vr* (a) to sit down, seat oneself; (*bird*) to alight, settle; (*liquid*) to settle; (*Archit*) to settle, sink, subside.

(b) (*fig*) to settle, establish oneself.

asentimiento *nm* assent.

asentir [3i] *vi* (a) to assent, agree; — **con la cabeza** to nod (one's head).

(b) — **a** to agree to, consent to; *request* to approve, grant; *arrangement* to accept; — **a la verdad de algo** to recognize the truth of something.

asentista *nm* contractor, supplier.

aseñorado *adj* lordly; dressed like a gentleman, behaving like a gentleman.

aseo *nm* (a) cleanliness, neatness, tidiness.(b) — **s** (*euph*) cloakroom, toilet, powder room, rest room (US).

aséptico *adj* aseptic; germ-free, free from infection.

asequible *adj* obtainable, available; *aim* attainable; *plan* feasible; *price* reasonable, within reach.

aserradero *nm* sawmill.

aserrador *nm* sawyer.

aserradora *nf* power saw.

aserradura *nf* saw cut; —**s** sawdust.

aserrar [1k] *vt* to saw, saw through; to saw up.

aserrín *nm* sawdust.

aserruchar [1a] *vt* (*SAm*) =**aserrar.**

aserto *nm* assertion.

asesina *nf* murderess.

asesinar [1a] *vt* (a) to murder; (*Pol*) to assassinate. (b) (*fig*) to pester, plague to death.

asesinato *nm* murder; (*Pol*) assassination; — **legal** judicial murder.

asesino **1** *adj* murderous. **2** *nm* (a) murderer, killer; (*Pol*) assassin. (b) (*fig*) thug, cut-throat; ¡—! you brute!; — **de carretera** roadhog.

asesor *nm*, **asesora** *nf* adviser, consultant.

asesoramiento *nm* advice.

asesorar [1a] **1** *vt* (a) to advise, give legal (*or* professional) advice to.

(b) to act as consultant to.

2 asesorarse *vr* (a) — **con,** — **de** to take advice from, consult.

(b) — **de una situación** to take stock of a situation.

asesorato *nm* (*SAm*) (a) advising. (b) consultant's office.

asesoría *nf* (a) advising; task of advising. (b) adviser's fee. (c) consultant's office.

asestar [1a] *vt* (a) *weapon* to aim (*a* at, in the direction of); to fire, shoot. (b) *blow* to deal, give, strike.

aseveración *nf* asseveration, assertion, contention.

aseveradamente *adv* positively.

aseverar [1a] *vt* to asseverate, assert.

asexual *adj* asexual.

asfaltado **1** *adj* asphalt, asphalted. **2** *nm* (a) asphalting. (b) asphalt, asphalt pavement, asphalt surface (*etc*).

asfaltar [1a] *vt* to asphalt.

asfalto *nm* asphalt.

asfixia *nf* suffocation, asphyxiation, (*Med*) asphyxia.

asfixiador *adj*, **asfixiante** *adj* suffocating, asphyxiating; *calor* — suffocating heat; *gas* — poison gas.

asfixiar [1b] **1** *vt* to asphyxiate; to suffocate; (*Mil*) to gas. **2 asfixiarse** *vr* to be asphyxiated, suffocate.

asgo *see* **asir.**

así **1** *adv* (a) so, in this way, thus; by this means, thereby; **lo hizo** — he did it like this, he did it this way; ¡—! that's right!, that's the way!; — —, — **asá,** — **asado** so-so, fair, middling; — **que asá** it makes no odds; — **como** —, — **que** — anyway; **20 dólares o** — **20** dollars or so, 20 dollars or thereabouts; **y** — **en adelante, y** — **sucesivamente** and so on; — **que** — **, so** ..., therefore ...; — **nada más** just like that, if you please; — **pues** ... **and so** ..., **so then**...; — **y todo even so;** — **es que no fuimos** so we didn't go, that's why we didn't go; **¿no es** —? is it not so?, isn't it?; ¡— **sea!** so be it!

(b) (*in comparisons*) — **A como B** both A and B, A as well as B; — **como Vd sabe ruso yo sé chino** in the same way as you know Russian I know Chinese.

(c) — **de pobre que** ... **so poor that** ...; **un baúl** — **de grande** a trunk this big, a trunk as big as this; **estaba** — **de gordo** he was that fat.

2 *adj*: **un hombre** — such a man, a man like that; **todos tenemos épocas** — we all have spells like that, we all have spells of that sort; — **es la vida** such is life, that's life; **los franceses son** — the French are like that, that's the way the French are.

3 *conj* (a) — **como,** — **que** ... **as soon as** ...; **no sooner than** ...

(b) (*SAm*) — **se esté muriendo de dolor** even though he's dying of pain, in spite of the fact that he's dying of pain.

Asia *nf* Asia; — **Menor** Asia Minor.

asiático **1** *adj* Asian, Asiatic. **2** *nm*, **asiática** *nf* Asian, Asiatic.

asidero *nm* (a) hold, grasp.

(b) handle, holder.

(c) (*fig*) pretext, excuse; lever.

(d) (*Arg*) basis, support; **eso no tiene** — that is not reasonable, that has no firm basis.

asiduamente *adv* assiduously; frequently, regularly.

asiduidad *nf* assiduousness; regularity.

asiduo **1** *adj* assiduous; frequent, regular, persistent; **parroquiano** — regular customer; **como** — **lector de su periódico** as a regular (*or* constant) reader of your newspaper.

2 *nm*, **asidua** *nf* regular customer (*etc*), habitué; **era un** — **del café** he was an habitué of the café; **es un** — **del museo** he is a frequent visitor to the museum.

asiento *nm* (a) seat, chair; place; — **de atrás,** — **trasero** rear seat; **pillion seat;** — **delantero** front seat; — **expulsor,** — **proyectable** (*Aer*) ejector seat; — **reservado** reserved seat; **no ha calentado el** — he hasn't stayed long; **tomar** — to take a seat.

(b) site, location.

(c) (*Anat*) bottom.

(d) (*Mech*) seating; — **de válvula** valve seating.

(e) sediment.

(f) (*Naut*) trim.

(g) (*Archit*) settling; **hacer** — to settle, sink.

(h) settling, settlement, establishment; **estar de** — to be settled (in a place); **vivir de** — **con uno** (*Ec, Per*) to live in sin with someone.

(i) (*Mex*) mining area, mining town.

(j) (*Comm*) contract, trading agreement.

(k) (*in ledger etc*) entry.

(l) stability; good sense, judgement; **hombre de** — sensible man.

(m) —**s** (*Anat*) bottom, buttocks.

asignación *nf* (a) (*act*) assignment; allocation; appointment; determination. (b) share, portion; (*Fin*) allowance, salary.

asignado *nm* (*Ec: Agr*) wages paid in kind.

asignar [1a] *vt* to assign; to allot, apportion; *person* to appoint; *task* to assign, set; *causes* to determine.

asignatario *nm*, **asignataria** *nf* (*Cu, Chi*) heir, legatee.

asignatura *nf* (*Univ etc*) subject, course; **aprobar una** — to pass (in) a subject.

asilado *nm*, **asilada** *nf* inmate.

asilar [1a] **1** *vt* (a) to take in, give shelter to; (*SAm*) to give political asylum to.

(b) to put into a home (*or* institution).

2 asilarse *vr* (a) to take refuge (*en* in); (*SAm*) to seek political asylum.

(b) to enter a home (*or* institution).

asilo nm (a) asylum; sanctuary; (fig) shelter, refuge; **derecho de —** right of sanctuary; **pedir (el) — político** to ask for political asylum.

(b) home, institution; **— de ancianos** old people's home; **— para desamparados** workhouse; **— de huérfanos** orphanage; **— de locos** lunatic asylum; **— de niños expósitos** foundling hospital; **— de pobres** poorhouse.

asimétrico adj assymetric(al).

asimiento nm (a) seizing, grasping; hold. (b) (fig) attachment, affection.

asimilación nf assimilation.

asimilado nm (SAm) professional person attached to the army.

asimilar [1a] **1** vt to assimilate. **2 asimilarse** vr (a) to assimilate, become assimilated. (b) **— a** to resemble.

asimismo adv likewise, in like manner, in the same way.

asir [3a; but present like **salir**] **1** vt to seize, grasp, catch, take hold of (con with, de by); **ir asidos del brazo** to walk along arm-in-arm.

2 vi (Bot) to take root.

3 asirse vr to take hold; (2 persons) to fight, grapple, lay hold of one another; **— a, —** de to seize, take hold of; to clutch on to; **— de** (fig) to avail oneself of, take advantage of; **— con uno** to grapple with someone.

Asiria f Assyria.

asirio 1 adj Assyrian. **2** nm, **asiria** nf Assyrian.

asisito adv (Bol etc) = **así**.

asistencia nf (a) attendance, presence (a at).

(b) help, assistance; domestic help, service; (Med) care, attendance; nursing; **— médica** medical care, medical attendance; **— pública** (RPl) state medical service; public health authority; **— social** welfare, welfare work, social work.

(c) (Mex) sitting room.

(d) (Col, Mex) boarding house.

(e) **—s** (Fin) allowance, maintenance.

asistenta nf assistant; charwoman, daily help; (Col, Mex) boarding-house keeper, landlady; **— social** social worker.

asistente nm (a) assistant; (Mil) orderly, batman; (Col) servant; (Col, Mex) boarding-house keeper, landlord; **— social** social worker.

(b) **los —s** those present, the people present.

asistido nm, **asistida** nf (Col, Mex) boarder, lodger, resident.

asistir [3a] **1** vt (a) to attend; to serve, wait on.

(b) to help, assist; (Med) to attend, care for; **el médico que le asiste** the doctor who attends him, the doctor in whose care he is; **— un parto** to deliver a baby.

(c) (SAm: Law) to represent, appear for.

(d) **le asiste la razón** he has right on his side.

2 vi (a) to be present (a at), attend; event, process, scene to witness, be a witness of; **no asistió a la clase** he did not attend the class, he did not come to the class; **¿vas a —?** are you going?; **asistieron unas 200 personas** some 200 people were present.

(b) (Cards) to follow suit.

asma nf asthma.

asmático 1 adj asthmatic. **2** nm, **asmática** nf asthmatic.

asna nf female donkey.

asnada nf silly thing.

asnal adj asinine, silly; beastly.

asnería nf silly thing.

asno nm (a) donkey. (b) (fig) ass, fathead (fam); **¡soy un —!** I'm an ass!

asociación nf association; society; (Comm, Fin) partnership; **— aduanera** customs union; **— obrera** trade union; **por — de ideas** by association of ideas.

asociado 1 adj associated; member etc associate. **2** nm associate; member; (Comm, Fin) partner.

asociar [1b] **1** vt to associate (a, con with); efforts, resources etc to pool, put together; (Comm, Fin) to take into partnership.

2 asociarse vr to associate; (Comm, Fin) to become partners, form a partnership; **— con uno** to team up with someone, join forces with someone.

asocio nm (SAm): **en —** in association (de with).

asolanar [1a] vt, **asolar**[1] [1a] vt to dry up, parch.

asolar[2] [1a] **1** vt to raze (to the ground), lay flat, destroy; to lay waste. **2 asolarse** vr (liquid) to settle.

asoleada nf (Col, Chi, Guat) sunstroke.

asoleado adj (CAm) (a) person stupid. (b) animal tired out.

asoleadura nf (Arg) sunstroke.

asolear [1a] **1** vt to put in the sun, keep in the sun; to dry in the sun.

2 asolearse vr (a) to sun oneself, bask in the sun; to get sunburnt.

(b) (Arg, Mex) to get sunstroke.

(c) (CAm) to get stupid.

asoleo nm (Mex) sunstroke.

asomada nf (a) brief appearance. (b) glimpse, sudden view.

asomadero nm (Col) viewpoint, vantage point.

asomar [1a] **1** vt to show, put out, stick out; **— la cabeza** to put one's head out (a la ventana of the window); **— la cara** to show one's face (also fig); **asomó un pie** she stuck a foot out.

2 vi to begin to show, appear, become visible; **asoman ya las nuevas plantas** the new plants are beginning to show; **asomó el buque en la niebla** the ship loomed up out of the fog.

3 asomarse vr (a) (object) to show, appear, stick out; (of coast, in fog etc) to loom up; **se asomaba el árbol por encima de la tapia** the tree showed above the wall.

(b) (person) to show up, show oneself; **— a, —** por to show oneself at, lean out of, look out of; **ella estaba asomada a la ventana** she was leaning out of the window; **¡asómate!** put your head out!; **— a ver algo** to take a look at something; to peep in at something.

(c) (fam) to get tight.

asombradizo adj easily alarmed.

asombrador adj amazing, astonishing.

asombrar [1a] **1** vt (a) to amaze, astonish; to frighten.

(b) to shade, cast a shadow on; colour to darken.

2 asombrarse vr (a) to be amazed, be astonished (de at); to be shocked (de at); to take fright; **— de saber algo** to be surprised to learn something.

(b) (CR) to faint.

asombro nm (a) amazement, astonishment, surprise; fear, fright.

(b) wonder; **es el — del siglo** it is the wonder of the century.

(c) (fam) spook (fam).

asombrosamente adv amazingly, astonishingly.

asombroso adj amazing, astonishing.

asomo nm (a) appearance.

(b) hint, sign, indication, trace; **ante cualquier — de discrepancia** at the slightest hint of disagreement; **sin — de violencia** without a trace of violence; **ni por —** by no means, not by a long shot.

asonada nf mob, rabble.

asonancia nf (a) (Lit) assonance. (b) (fig) harmony; correspondence, connection; **no tener — con** to bear no relation to.

asonantar [1a] vti to assonate (con with).

asonante 1 adj assonant. **2** nf (in general) assonance; (word) assonant.

asonar [1m] vi to assonate, be in assonance.

asordar [1a] vt to deafen.

asorocharse [1a] vr (Bol, Chi, Ec, Per) to get mountain sickness.

asosegar [1h and 1k] = **sosegar**.

aspa nf cross, X-shaped figure (or design etc); (Archit) crosspiece; (of mill) sail, arm; (Tech) reel, winding frame; (Arg, Ven) horn.

aspadera nf reel, winder.

aspado adj cross-shaped, X-shaped; person with arms outstretched; **estar — en algo** to be all trussed up in something.

aspador nm reel, winder.

aspamentero adj (etc) (Arg, Mex) = **aspaventero** (etc).

aspar [1a] **1** vt (a) (Tech) to reel, wind.

(b) (fig) to vex, annoy; **¡que te aspen!** (fam) get lost! (fam); **lo hago aunque me aspen** wild horses wouldn't stop me doing it.

2 asparse vr (a) to writhe.

(b) to do one's utmost, go all out (por algo to get something).

aspaventero 1 adj excitable, emotional, given to exaggerated displays of feeling; fussy. **2** nm, **aspaventera** nf excitable person; fussy person.

aspaviento nm exaggerated display of feeling; fulsome expression of feeling; fuss, to-do (fam); **—s** exaggerated gestures; **hacer —s** to make a great fuss.

aspecto nm (a) look, appearance; looks; aspect; (Archit, Geog etc) aspect; **— exterior** outward appearance; **un hombre de — feroz** a man with a fierce look, a fierce-looking man.

(b) (fig) aspect; side; **a(l) primer —** at first sight; **bajo ese —** from that point of view; **estudiar una cuestión bajo todos sus —s** to study all aspects of a question; **ver sólo un — de la cuestión** to see only one side to the question.

ásperamente *adv* roughly; harshly, gruffly; **dijo — he** said in a harsh tone.

aspereza *nf* roughness; ruggedness; sourness, bitterness; toughness; harshness; surliness; **contestar con — to answer with asperity, answer harshly.

asperges *nm* (a) sprinkling; **quedarse** — to come away empty-handed. (b) (*Eccl*) aspergillum; hyssop.

asperillo *nm* slight sour (*or* bitter) taste.

asperjar [1a] *vt* to sprinkle; (*Eccl*) to sprinkle with holy water.

áspero *adj* (a) (*to the touch*) rough; *edge* uneven, jagged, rough; *terrain* rough, rugged.
　(b) (*to the taste*) sour, tart, bitter.
　(c) *climate* hard, tough; *treatment* rough.
　(d) *voice* harsh, rough; rasping; *manner* harsh; surly, gruff; *temperament* sour; *argument etc* bad-tempered.

asperón *nm* sandstone, grit; (*Tech*) grindstone.

aspersión *nf* sprinkling; (*Agr, Hort*) spray, spraying; **riego por** — watering by spray, watering by sprinklers.

áspid *nm* asp.

aspidistra *nf* aspidistra.

aspillera *nf* (*Mil*) loophole.

aspiración *nf* (a) breath; breathing in, inhalation; (*Ling*) aspiration; (*Mus*) short pause. (b) (*Mech*) air intake. (c) **aspiraciones** (*SAm*) aspirations.

aspirada *nf* aspirate.

aspirado *adj* aspirate.

aspirador 1 *adj*: **bomba aspiradora** suction pump. 2 *nm* (*also* — **de polvo**) vacuum cleaner.

aspiradora *nf* vacuum cleaner.

aspirante 1 *adj*: **bomba** — suction pump. 2 *nmf* aspirant; candidate, applicant (*a* for); — **a cabo** private first class; — **de marina** midshipman.

aspirar [1a] **1** *vt* (a) to breathe in, inhale; to suck in, suck up; (*Tech*) to suck in, take in.
　(b) (*Ling*) to aspirate.
　2 *vi*: — **a algo** to aspire to something; **no aspiro a tanto** I do not aim so high; **A aspiró a la mano de B** A sought B's hand in marriage; — **a hacer algo** to aspire to do something, aim to do something, seek to do something; **el que no sepa eso no aspire a aprobar** whoever doesn't know that can have no hope of passing.

aspirina *nf* aspirin.

aspudo *adj* (*Arg*) big-horned.

asquear [1a] **1** *vt* to loathe, find nauseating. **2** *vi and* **asquearse** *vr* to be nauseated, feel disgusted.

asquerosamente *adv* disgustingly, sickeningly; awfully (*fam*).

asqueroso *adj* (a) disgusting, loathsome, sickening; (*fig, fam*) awful (*fam*), lousy, vile (*fam*). (b) squeamish.

asquiento *adj* (*Col, Ec*) =**asqueroso**.

asta *nf* lance, spear; shaft; handle; flagstaff, flagpole; (*Zool*) horn, antler; **a media** — at half mast; **dejar a uno en las —s del toro** to leave someone in a jam.

astabandera *nf* (*SAm*) flagstaff, flagpole.

ástaco *nm* crayfish.

astado 1 *adj* horned. **2** *nm* bull.

astear [1a] *vt* (*Chi*) to gore.

aster *nf* aster.

asterisco *nm* asterisk; **señalar con un —, poner — a** to asterisk.

asteroide *nm* asteroid.

astigmático *adj* astigmatic.

astigmatismo *nm* astigmatism.

astil *nm* (*of tool*) handle, haft; (*of arrow*) shaft; (*of balance*) beam.

astilla *nf* splinter, chip; **—s** (*for fire*) firewood, kindling; **hacer algo —s** to smash something into little pieces, smash something to matchwood; **hacerse —s** to shatter into little pieces.

astillar [1a] **1** *vt* to splinter, chip; to shatter. **2** **astillarse** *vr* to splinter; to shatter.

astillero *nm* shipyard, dockyard.

astracán *nm* astrakhan.

astrágalo *nm* (*Archit, Mil*) astragal; (*Anat*) astragalus.

astral *adj* astral, of the stars.

astreñir [3h and 3i] =**astringir**.

astrilla *nf* (*RPl*) =**astilla**.

astringente 1 *adj* astringent, binding. **2** *nm* astringent.

astringir [3e] *vt* (a) (*Anat*) to constrict, contract; (*Med*) to bind. (b) (*fig*) to bind, compel.

astro *nm* (a) (*Astron*) star, heavenly body. (b) (*fig*) star, leading light; (*Cine*) star.

astrofísica *nf* astrophysics.

astrología *nf* astrology.

astrológico *adj* astrological.

astrólogo *nm* astrologer.

astronauta *nmf* astronaut.

astronáutica *nf* astronautics.

astronave *nf* spaceship.

astronomía *nf* astronomy.

astronómico *adj* astronomical.

astrónomo *nm* astronomer.

astroso *adj* (a) dirty, untidy, shabby. (b) ill-fated, unfortunate. (c) contemptible.

astucia *nf* (a) (*quality*) astuteness, cleverness; (*pej*) guile, cunning. (b) **una** — a clever trick, a piece of cunning.

astur 1 *adj* Asturian. **2** *nm* Asturian.

asturiano 1 *adj* Asturian. **2** *nm*, **asturiana** *nf* Asturian. **3** *nm* (*dialect*) Asturian.

astutamente *adv* astutely, cleverly, smartly; (*pej*) craftily, cunningly.

astuto *adj* astute, clever, smart; (*pej*) crafty, cunning.

asueto *nm* time off, break, short holiday; **día de** — day off; **tarde de** — afternoon off, (*School*) half-holiday; **tomarse un — de fin de semana** to take a weekend break, take the weekend off.

asumir [3a] *vt* (a) *responsibility etc* to assume, take on; *command, leadership* to take over; *attitude* to strike, adopt. (b) (*SAm*: *angl*) to assume, suppose; to take for granted; — **que . . .** to assume that . . .

asunción *nf* assumption; **A—** (*Eccl*) Assumption.

asunto *nm* (a) matter, subject; topic; affair, business; (*Lit*) theme, subject; plot; **¡— concluido!** that's an end of the matter!; **el — está concluido** the matter is closed; — **de honor** affair of honour; **—s exteriores** foreign affairs; **Ministerio de A—s Exteriores** Foreign Ministry, Foreign Office, State Department (*US*); **Ministro de A—s Indígenas** Minister for Native Affairs; **—s a tratar** agenda, items to be discussed; **es un — de faldas** it concerns the women, (*hum*) cherchez la femme (*hum*); **es un — triste** it's a bad business; **ir al** — to get down to business; **entrometerse en un** — to meddle in an affair.
　(b) (*Ven*) study, attention.
　(c) (*Arg*) **¿a —de qué lo hiciste?** why did you do it?

asurar [1a] *vt* (a) (*Cook etc*) to burn; (*Agr*) to burn up, parch. (b) (*fig*) to worry.

asurcar [1g] *vt* =**surcar**.

asustadizo *adj* easily frightened; nervy, jumpy; *animal* shy, skittish.

asustar [1a] **1** *vt* to frighten, scare; to alarm, startle. **2 asustarse** *vr* to be frightened, get scared; to get alarmed, be startled; — **de algo** to be frightened at something, get alarmed about something; — **de + infin** to be afraid to + *infin*; **¡no te asustes!** don't be alarmed!

asusto *nm* (*Col*) =**susto**.

atabacado *adj* (a) tobacco-coloured. (b) (*Arg*) **con aliento** — with tobacco-laden breath, with breath smelling of tobacco.

atabal *nm* kettledrum.

atabalear [1a] *vi* (*of horse*) to stamp; (*with fingers*) to drum.

atacable *adj* attackable, assailable.

atacado *adj* (a) fainthearted; dithery, irresolute. (b) mean, stingy.

atacador 1 *nm* (*Mil*) ramrod. **2** *nm*, **atacadora** *nf* attacker, assailant.

atacadura *nf* fastener, fastening.

atacante *nmf* attacker, assailant.

atacar [1g] *vt* (a) (*Mil etc*) to attack; to assail, assault; *theory etc* to attack, impugn; (*in argument*) to attack, set about, go for; to press hard.
　(b) (*Chem, Med etc*) to attack.
　(c) to attach, fasten; to button up, do up; to sew on.
　(d) *bag etc* to stuff, pack; (*Mil, Min*) to ram home, tamp; to wad, plug.

ataché *nm* (*CAm, PR*) paper clip.

ataderas *nfpl* (*fam*) garters.

atadero *nm* rope, cord; fastening; place for tying; (*Mex*) garter; **eso no tiene** — you can't make head or tail of it, there's nothing to latch on to.

atadijo *nm* loose bundle.

atado 1 *adj* (a) tied. (b) (*fig*) shy, inhibited; irresolute. **2** *nm* bundle; bunch; — **de cigarrillos** (*RPl*) packet of cigarettes.

atadora *nf* (*Agr*) binder.

atadura *nf* (a) (*act*) tying, fastening. (b) string, cord, rope; (*Naut*) lashing; (*Agr*) rope, tether; (*fig*) bond, tie.

atafagar [1h] *vt* (a) to stupefy, suffocate. (b) to pester the life out of.

ataguía *nf* cofferdam, caisson.

atajar [1a] 1 *vt* (a) to stop, intercept; to head off, cut off; (*SAm*) to catch, catch in flight; (*Sport*) to tackle; (*Archit*) to partition off; — **a uno** (*SAm*) to hold someone back (to stop a fight); — **un golpe** (*SAm*) to parry a blow.
(b) *discussion* to cut short; *speech etc* to interrupt, break into; *process* to end, stop, call a halt to; *abuse* to put a stop to; **este mal hay que** —**lo** we must put an end to this evil.
2 *vi* to take a short cut (*por* by way of, across); (*Aut*) to cut corners.
3 **atajarse** *vr* to feel ashamed of oneself; to be overcome by confusion, be all of a dither; (*RPl*) to keep one's temper.

atajo *nm* (a) short cut; **echar por el** — to take the easiest way out, seek a quick solution; **no hay** — **sin trabajo** short cuts don't help in the long run. (b) interception; (*Sport*) tackle.

atalaya 1 *nf* (a) watchtower; observation point, observation post. (b) (*fig*) vantage point. 2 *nm* look-out, observer, sentinel.

atalayador *nm*, **atalayadora** *nf* look-out; (*fig*) snooper, spy.

atalayar [1a] *vt* to watch, observe; to watch over, guard; (*pej*) to spy on.

atañer [2f; *defective: used mostly in 3rd person present tense*] *vi*: — **a** to concern, have to do with; **en lo que atañe a eso** with regard to that, as to that; **eso no me atañe** it's no concern of mine.

atapuzar [1f] (*Ven*) 1 *vt* to fill, stop up. 2 **atapuzarse** *vr* to stuff oneself.

ataque *nm* (a) (*Mil etc*) attack (*a*, *contra* on); (*Aer*) attack, raid; — **aéreo** air raid, air attack; — **fingido** sham attack; — **de flanco** flank attack; — **de frente** frontal attack; — **por sorpresa** surprise attack; **dejarse expuesto al** — to leave oneself open to attack; **lanzar un** — to launch an attack; **volver al** — to return to the attack.
(b) (*Med etc*) attack (*de* of), fit; — **cardíaco**, — **al corazón** heart attack; — **fulminante** stroke, seizure.

atar [1a] 1 *vt* (a) to tie, tie up; to bind; to fasten; (*Agr*) *animal* to tether; *sheaf* to bind; — **corto a uno** (*fig*) to keep someone on a close rein; — **la lengua a uno** (*fig*) to silence someone; — **las manos a uno** (*fig*) to stop someone acting; **verse atado de pies y manos** (*fig*) to be tied hand and foot.
(b) to stop; to paralyze, root to the spot.
2 *vi*: **ni ata ni desata** this is nonsense, this is getting us nowhere.
3 **atarse** *vr* (a) to stick, get stuck; — **en una dificultad** to get tied up in a difficulty.
(b) to be embarrassed, get embarrassed.
(c) — **a la letra** to stick to the literal meaning; — **a una opinión** to stick to one's opinion.

ataracea *nf* = **taracea**.

atarantar [1a] 1 *vt* to stun, daze; **quedó atarantado** he was stunned, he was unconscious.
(b) (*fig*) to stun, dumbfound.
2 **atarantarse** *vr* (a) to be stunned, be dumbfounded.
(b) (*Chi, Col, Mex, Per*) to hurry, dash, rush.
(c) (*Mex*) to stuff oneself.
(d) (*Guat, Mex*) to get drunk.

atardecer 1 [2d] *vi* to get dark; **atardecía** it was getting dark, night was falling.
2 *nm* late afternoon; dusk, evening; **al** — at dusk.

atareado *adj* busy, rushed; **andar muy** — to be very busy.

atarear [1a] 1 *vt* to give a job to, assign a task to.
2 **atarearse** *vr* to work hard, keep busy; to be busy (*con*, *en* with); — **a hacer algo** to be busy doing something.

atarjea *nf* sewage pipe, culvert.

atarragarse [1h] *vr* (*Mex, Ven*) to stuff oneself, overeat.

atarugar [1h] 1 *vt* (a) to fasten (with a peg *or* wedge), to peg, wedge.
(b) *hole* to plug, stop, bung up.
(c) to stuff, fill (*de* with).
(d) — **a uno** (*fam*) to shut someone up.
2 **atarugarse** *vr* (a) to swallow the wrong way, choke.
(b) (*fig*) to get confused, be in a daze.
(c) (*fam*) to stuff oneself, overeat.

atascadero *nm* (a) mire, bog, muddy place. (b) (*fig*) stumbling block, obstacle; dead end.

atascar [1g] 1 *vt* *leak* to stop; *hole* to block, plug, stop up; *pipe etc* to clog, clog up, obstruct; *process* to hinder.

2 **atascarse** *vr* (a) (*cart etc*) to get stuck (in the mud), get bogged down; (*Aut*) to get into a jam; (*engine*) to stall; **quedó atascado a mitad de la escalada** he got stuck halfway up the climb; **el carro se atascó en el barro** the cart got stuck in the mud.
(b) (*fig*) to get bogged down (*en un problema* in a problem); (*in speech*) to get stuck, dry up (*fam*).
(c) (*of pipe etc*) to clog, get clogged up, get stopped up; (*SAm*: *Med*) to have an internal blockage.

atasco *nm* obstruction, blockage; (*Aut*) traffic jam.

ataúd *nm* coffin; bier.

ataujía *nf* (a) (*Tech*) damascene, damascene work.
(b) (*CR, Guat*) conduit, drain.

ataviar [1c] 1 *vt* to deck, array (*con*, *de* in); to dress up, get up (*con*, *de* in). 2 **ataviarse** *vr* to dress up, get oneself up (*con*, *de* in).

atávico *adj* atavistic.

atavío *nm* attire, dress; (*hum*) rig, getup; —**s** finery.

atavismo *nm* atavism.

atediante *adj* boring, wearisome.

atediar [1b] 1 *vt* to bore, weary. 2 **atediarse** *vr* to get bored.

ateísmo *nm* atheism.

ateísta *adj* atheistic.

atejonarse [1a] *vr* (*Mex*) (a) to curl up. (b) to grow cunning.

atelaje *nm* (a) team (of horses). (b) harness; (*fam*) trousseau.

atembado *adj* (*Col*) silly, stupid; lacking in willpower.

atemorizar [1f] 1 *vt* to frighten, scare. 2 **atemorizarse** *vr* to get scared (*de*, *por* at).

atemperar [1a] *vt* (a) to temper, moderate. (b) to adjust, accommodate (*a* to).

Atenas Athens.

atención *nf* (a) attention; care, heed; ¡—! attention!; (*as warning*) look out!, careful!; (*written on wrapping etc*) "with care"; ¡— **a los pies!** mind your feet!; "¡—! **frenos potentes**" "Beware!: powerful brakes"; "¡— **a los precios!**" (*Comm*) "look at our prices!"; **llamar la** — to attract attention, catch the eye; **llamar la** — **de uno** to attract someone's attention, catch someone's eye; **llamar la** — **de uno sobre un detalle** to draw someone's attention to a detail; **prestar** — to pay attention, listen (*a* to).
(b) kindness, civility; —**es** attentions, courtesies.
(c) —**es** affairs; duties, responsibilities.
(d) **en** — **a esto** in view of this, having regard to this.

atencioso *adj* (*SAm*) = **atento**.

atender [2g] 1 *vt* (a) to attend to, pay attention to; *advice, warning etc* to heed; (*Mech*) to service, maintain; *child, patient etc* to look after, care for; *request* to comply with; (*SAm*) *customer, inquirer etc* to give full satisfaction to; — **sus compromisos** to meet one's obligations; — **una orden** (*Comm*) to attend to an order; — **un giro** (*Comm*) to honour a draft.
(b) (*SAm*) to attend, be present at.
2 *vi* (a) — **a** to attend to, pay attention to; *details* to take note of; — **a un caso urgente** to see about an urgent matter.
(b) — **por** to answer to the name of.

atenerse [2l] *vr*: — **a** (a) *rule* to abide by, obey; *truth, opinion* to hold to; *promise* to stand by, adhere to, keep to.
(b) to rely on; **saber a qué** — to know what to expect; **lo hizo atendiéndose a que . . .** he did it knowing that . . ., he did it taking into account the fact that . . .

ateniense 1 *adj* Athenian. 2 *nmf* Athenian.

atentado 1 *adj* prudent, cautious; moderate.
2 *nm* illegal act, offence; outrage, crime; assault; attempt (*a, contra la vida de uno* on someone's life); — **terrorista** terrorist outrage; — **contra la honra** indecent assault.

atentamente *adv* (a) attentively. (b) politely; thoughtfully, kindly; **le saluda** — yours faithfully.

atentar [1a] 1 *vt* *act* to do illegally; *crime* to attempt, try to commit.
2 *vi*: — **a**, — **contra** to commit an outrage against; — **contra la honra de una** to make an indecent assault on someone; — **contra la vida de uno** to make an attempt on someone's life.

atento *adj* (a) attentive (*a* to), observant, watchful (*a* of); **ser** — **a los peligros** to be mindful of the dangers.
(b) polite; thoughtful, kind; obliging; **ser** — **con**

uno to be kind to someone, be considerate towards someone.
   (c) su atenta (carta) (*Comm*) your esteemed letter.
   (d) — **a** *as prep* in view of, in consideration of; — **a que . . . as** *conj* considering that . . ., in view of the fact that . . .

atenuación *nf* attenuation; lessening, diminution; (*Law*) extenuation.

atenuante 1 *adj* extenuating; **circunstancias —s** extenuating circumstances. **2** *nm* (*SAm*) excuse, plea.

atenuar [1e] **1** *vt* to attenuate; *crime etc* to extenuate; *importance* to lessen, minimize; *impression etc* to tone down. **2 atenuarse** *vr* to weaken.

ateo 1 *adj* atheistic. **2** *nm*, **atea** *nf* atheist.

ateperetarse [1a] *vr* (*CAm, Mex*) to get confused, get bewildered.

aterciopelado *adj* velvet (*attr*), velvety.

aterido *adj* numb, stiff with cold.

aterirse [3a; *defective, used only in infin and ptp*] *vr* to get numb, get stiff with cold.

aterrada *nf* (*Naut*) landfall.

aterrador *adj* frightening, terrifying; appalling.

aterraje *nm* (*Aer*) landing.

aterrar¹ [1k] **1** *vt* **(a)** to pull down, demolish, destroy.
   (b) to cover with earth; (*Agr*) to earth up.
   (c) (*CAm, Mex*) to choke, obstruct.
   2 *vi* (*Aer*) to land.
   3 aterrarse *vr* (*Naut*) to stand inshore; **navegar aterrado** to sail inshore.

aterrar² [1a] **1** *vt* to terrify, frighten; to appal. **2 aterrarse** *vr* to be terrified, be frightened (*de* at); to be appalled (*de* about, by); to panic.

aterrizaje *nm* (*Aer*) landing; — **duro** hard landing; — **forzoso** emergency landing, forced landing; — **de panza,** — **a vientre** pancake landing; — **suave** soft landing; — **violento** crash landing.

aterrizar [1f] *vi* (*Aer*) to land; (*person*) to get out (of an aeroplane).

aterronarse [1a] *vr* to get lumpy; to cake, harden.

aterrorizar [1f] *vt* to terrify; (*Mil, Pol etc*) to terrorize.

atesar [1k] *vt* = **atiesar.**

atesorar [1a] *vt* to hoard, store up, accumulate; *virtues etc* to possess.

atestación *nf* attestation.

atestado¹ *nm* (*Law*) affidavit, statement.

atestado² *adj* obstinate, stubborn.

atestado³ packed, cram-full; — **de** packed with, crammed with, full of; well-stocked with.

atestar¹ [1a] *vt* (*Law*) to attest, testify to; (*fig*) to attest, vouch for; **una palabra no atestada** an unattested word, an unrecorded word.

atestar² [1k] **1** *vt* to pack, cram, stuff (*de* with); to fill up (*de* with); to crowd; — **una de frutas** to stuff someone with fruit. **2 atestarse** *vr* to stuff oneself.

atestiguación *nf* **(a)** attestation. **(b)** deposition, testimony.

atestiguar [1i] *vt* (*Law*) to testify to, bear witness to, give evidence of; (*fig*) to attest, vouch for.

atezado *adj* **(a)** tanned; swarthy. **(b)** black, blackened.

atezar [1f] **1** *vt* **(a)** to tan, burn. **(b)** to blacken, turn black. **2 atezarse** *vr* to get tanned.

atiborrado *adj*: — **de** full of, stuffed with, crammed with.

atiborrar [1a] **1** *vt* to fill, stuff (*de* with); — **a un niño de dulces** to stuff a child with sweets. **2 atiborrarse** *vr* to stuff oneself (*de* with).

ático *nm* attic.

atiesar [1a] **1** *vt* to stiffen; to tighten, tighten up; to tauten, stretch taut.
   2 atiesarse *vr* to get stiff, stiffen (up); to tighten, to tauten; (*of building material etc*) to bind.

atiforrarse [1a] *vr* (*fam*) = **atiborrarse.**

atigrado 1 *adj* striped, marked like a tiger; *cat* tabby. **2** *nm* tabby.

atigronarse [1a] *vr* (*Ven*) to get strong.

Atila *m* Attila.

atildado *adj* neat, elegant, stylish.

atildar [1a] **1** *vt* **(a)** (*Typ*) to put a tilde (~) over, mark with a tilde.
   (b) to tidy, clean (up); to improve the looks of; to put right.
   (c) to criticize, find fault with.
   2 atildarse *vr* to spruce oneself up, titivate.

atinadamente *adv* correctly; sensibly; pertinently; **según dijo** — as he rightly said.

atinado *adj* accurate, correct; wise, sensible, judicious; pertinent; penetrating; **unas observaciones atinadas** some pertinent remarks; **una decisión poco atinada** a rather unwise decision.

atinar [1a] **1** *vt answer etc* to hit upon, find; to guess right; to succeed in finding.

2 *vi* **(a)** to guess right; to be right, do the right thing; **siempre atina** he always gets it right, he never misses.
   (b) — **al blanco** to hit the target, (*fig*) hit the mark; — **a,** — **con,** — **en** *answer etc* to hit upon, find, succeed in finding.
   (c) — **a hacer algo** to succeed in doing something, manage to do something.

atingencia *nf* (*SAm*) **(a)** connection, bearing, relationship. **(b)** obligation.

atingido *adj* (*Chi, Ec, Per*) distressed, downcast; feeble, weak; timid. **(b)** (*Bol*) penniless. **(c)** (*Mex*) sly.

atingir [3c] *vt* **(a)** (*SAm*) to concern, bear on, relate to. **(b)** (*Per*) to oppress.

atiparse [1a] *vr* (*fam*) to eat oneself sick, guzzle.

atiplado *adj voice* treble.

atiplarse [1a] *vr* to talk in a high (*or* squeaky) voice.

atipujarse [1a] *vr* (*CAm, Mex*) to stuff oneself.

atirantar [1a] **1** *vt* **(a)** (*SAm*) to tighten, tauten; to stretch. **(b)** (*Arg, Bol, Mex*) to spreadeagle, stretch out on the ground.
   2 atirantarse *vr* (*Mex: sl*) to peg out (*sl*).

atisba *nm* (*Col*) watchman, look-out; spy.

atisbadero *nm* peephole.

atisbador *nm*, **atisbadora** *nf* observer; watcher; spy.

atisbar [1a] *vt* to spy on, watch; to peep at; — **a uno a través de una grieta** to peep at someone through a crack.

atisbo *nm* **(a)** spying; watching; look, peep. **(b)** (*fig*) inkling, slight sign, first indication.

atizadero *nm* **(a)** poker. **(b)** (*fig*) spark, stimulus.

atizador *nm* **(a)** poker. **(b)** (*fig*) — **de la guerra** warmonger.

atizar [1f] **1** *vt* **(a)** *fire* to poke, stir; *furnace* to stoke; *candle* to snuff, trim.
   (b) (*fig*) *trouble* to stir up; *passion* to fan, rouse.
   (c) (*fam*) *blow, kick* to give.
   2 *vi* (*sl*): ¡atiza! gosh! (*sl*).
   3 atizarse *vr* (*SAm: fam*) to smoke marijuana, smoke pot (*sl*).

atizonar [1a] *vt* (*Bot*) to blight, smut.

Atlante *m* Atlas.

Atlántico *m* Atlantic (Ocean).

Atlántida *f* Atlantis.

atlas *nm* atlas.

atleta *nmf* athlete.

atlético *adj* athletic.

atletismo *nm* athletics.

atmósfera *nf* **(a)** (*Phys and fig*) atmosphere; **mala** — (*Radio*) atmospherics.
   (b) (*fig*) atmosphere; sphere (of influence); feeling (about *or* towards a person); **Juan tiene buena** — (*SAm*) John enjoys considerable social standing, John stands well with everybody.

atmosférico *adj* atmospheric.

atoc *nm* (*Ec, Per*) fox.

atocar [1g] *vt* (*SAm*) = **tocar.**

atocinado *adj* (*fam*) fat, well-upholstered (*fam*).

atocinar [1a] **1** *vt* **(a)** *pig* to cut up; to make into bacon; *meat* to cure. **(b)** (*sl*) to do in (*sl*), carve up.
   2 atocinarse *vr* (*fam*) to get het up (*fam*); to fall madly in love.

atocle *nm* (*Mex*) sandy soil rich in humus.

atocha *nf* esparto.

atochal *nm*, **atochar** *nm* esparto field.

atol *nm* (*SAm*) soft drink made of maize flour.

atolada *nm* (*Salv*) party.

atole *nm* (*Mex*) = **atol.**

atoleada *nf* (*Guat, Hond*) party.

atolería *nf* (*SAm*) stall (*etc*) where *atol* is sold.

atolón *nm* atoll.

atolondrado *adj* scatterbrained; silly; bewildered; stunned, amazed; thoughtless, reckless.

atolondramiento *nm* silliness; bewilderment; stunned state, amazement; thoughtlessness, recklessness.

atolondrar [1a] **1** *vt* to bewilder; to stun, amaze. **2 atolondrarse** *vr* to be bewildered; to be stunned, be amazed.

atolladero *nm* **(a)** muddy place; mire, morass.
   (b) (*fig*) awkward spot, jam; embarrassing situation; **estar en un** — to be in a jam; **sacar a uno del** — to get someone out of a fix; **salir del** — to get out of a jam.

atollar(se) [1a] *vi and vr* **(a)** to get stuck in the mud, get bogged down. **(b)** (*fig*) to get into a jam, get stuck.

atomía *nf* (*SAm*) **(a)** evil deed, savage act. **(b)** **decir —s** to say dreadful things (*a uno* to someone).

atómico *adj* atomic.

atomizador *nm* atomizer; spray, scent spray.

atomizar [1f] *vt* to atomize; to spray.

átomo *nm* atom; (*fig*) atom, particle, speck; **— de vida** spark of life; **ni un — de** not a trace of.

atonal *adj* atonal.

atónito *adj* amazed, astounded (**con**, **de**, **por** at, by); **me miró —** he looked at me in amazement.

átono *adj* atonic, unstressed.

atontadamente *adv* in a bewildered way; foolishly, silly.

atontado *adj* (a) stunned, bewildered. (b) silly, dim-witted (*fam*).

atontar [1a] **1** *vt* (a) to stun, stupefy. (b) (*fig*) to stun, bewilder. **2 atontarse** *vr* to get bewildered, get confused.

atorar[1] [1a] **1** *vt* (a) to stop up, choke, obstruct. (b) (*Mex*, *PR*) to stop, bring to a halt; to block the progress of.
    2 atorarse *vr* to choke, swallow the wrong way.

atorarse[2] [1a] *vr* (*Arg*) to get wild, get fierce.

atormentador 1 *adj* tormenting. **2** *nm*, **atormentadora** *nf* tormentor.

atormentar [1a] **1** *vt* to torture; (*fig*) to torture, torment; to plague, harass; to tantalize. **2 atormentarse** *vr* to torment oneself.

atornillador *nm* (*SAm*) screwdriver.

atornillar [1a] *vt* (a) to screw on; to screw up; to screw down; to screw together. (b) (*SAm*) to bore; to bother, annoy.

atoro *nm* (*SAm*) destruction; (*fig*) trouble, distress.

atorozarse [1f] *vr* (*CAm*) to choke, swallow the wrong way.

atorrante *nm* (*Bol*, *Chi*, *RPl*) tramp, loafer, bum (US).

atorrantear [1a] *vi* (*Arg*) to live as a tramp, be on the bum (US).

atortolar [1a] *vt* (*fam*) to rattle, scare; to shatter, flabbergast.

atortujar [1a] **1** *vt* to squeeze flat. **2 atortujarse** *vr* (*Hond*, *Ven*) to be shattered, be flabbergasted.

atorunado *adj* (*Arg*) bull-like; (*Chi*) chunky (*fam*), thick-necked.

atorzonarse [1a] *vr* (*Col*, *Mex*) to stuff oneself.

atosigar [1h] **1** *vt* (a) to poison. (b) (*fig*) to plague, harass; to rush, put the pressure on. **2 atosigarse** *vr* to be in a rush, get rushed.

atrabancar [1g] **1** *vt* to rush, hurry over. **2 atrabancarse** *vr* to be in a fix, get into a jam.

atrabiliario *adj* bad-tempered, difficult, moody.

atrabilis *nf* (*fig*) bad temper, difficult temperament, moodiness.

atracadero *nm* berth, wharf, landing place.

atracado *adj* (*Chi*, *Guat*) mean, stingy.

atracador *nm* holdup man, bandit, gangster.

atracar [1g] **1** *vt* (a) to hold up; to attack, waylay. (b) (*Naut*) to tie up, moor, bring alongside. (c) to stuff, cram (with food).
    2 *vi* (*Naut*) to tie up, moor, come alongside; **— al muelle**, **— en el muelle** to tie up at the quay, berth at the quay.
    3 atracarse *vr* (a) to cram, stuff oneself (**de** with). (b) (*Arg*, *PR*) to approach, come near, come up; **— a** to approach, go up to. (c) (*Cu*, *PR*) to brawl, fight.

atracción *nf* (a) attraction; (*of person*) attractiveness, appeal, charm; **— sexual** sexual attraction, (*of person*) sex appeal. (b) amusement; **atracciones** (*Theat*) attractions, entertainment, floor show.

atraco *nm* holdup, robbery; **— a mano armada** armed robbery; **¡es un —!** (*fig*) it's sheer robbery!

atracón *nm* (*fam*) blow-out (*sl*); **darse un —** to stuff oneself; **darse un — de** to stuff oneself with, make a pig of oneself over.

atractivamente *adv* attractively.

atractivo 1 *adj* attractive. **2** *nm* attraction; attractiveness, appeal, charm.

atraer [2p] *vt* to attract; to draw; to lure; *attention* to attract, engage; *imagination* to appeal to; *support* to attract, win, draw; **dejarse — por** to allow oneself to be drawn towards; **con su propósito de —se a la juventud** with his aim of winning over young people.

atragantarse [1a] *vr* (a) to choke (**con** on), swallow the wrong way. (b) (*fig*) to get mixed up, lose the thread of what one is saying. (c) (*fig*) **Pepe se me ha atragantado** Joe sticks in my gullet, I can't bear Joe.

atraillar [1a] *vt* to put on a leash.

atramparse [1a] *vr* (a) to fall into a trap; (*fig*) to get stuck, get oneself into a jam. (b) (*pipe*) to clog, get blocked up; (*catch*) to stick, catch, jam.

atrancar [1g] **1** *vt* *door* to bar, bolt; *pipe* to clog, block up; (*Arg*, *Chi*) to constipate.

2 *vi* to stride along, take big steps; (*fig*) to skip a lot (*in reading*).

3 atrancarse *vr* (a) to get stuck, get bogged down (**en** in); (*fig*) to get stuck. (b) (*Arg*, *Chi*) to get constipated. (c) (*Mex*) to dig one's heels in, be stubborn.

atranco *nm* = **atascadero**.

atrapar [1a] *vt* (a) to trap; to catch, nab, overtake; *job* to get, land; *cold* to catch; **quedaron atrapados en la montaña** they were trapped on the mountainside. (b) (*fig*) to take in, deceive.

atraque *nm* (a) (*Naut*) mooring place, berth. (b) (*in space exploration*) link-up, docking.

atrás *adv* (a) (*place*) **¡—!** back!, get back!; **estar —** to be behind; to be in the rear; **está más —** it's further back; **ir (hacia) —** to go back, go backwards; to go to the rear; **rueda de —** rear wheel, back wheel. (b) (*time*) previously; **días —** days ago, days before; **4 meses —** 4 months back; **más —** earlier, longer ago; **desde muy —** for a very long time.

atrasado 1 *adj* (a) slow, late, behind (time); *payment* overdue; (*Typ*) *number* back (*attr*); **andar —**, **estar — (watch)** to be slow; **estar un poco — (person)** to be a bit behind; **estar — en los pagos** to be behind, be in arrears; **estar — de noticias** to be behind the times, lack up-to-date information; **estar — de medios** to be short of resources. (b) *country* backward; underdeveloped; *pupil etc* slow, backward. (c) (*Fin*) poor, needy. (d) (*Med etc: RPl*) ill; (*Col*) thin.
    2 *nm*: **es un —** he's behind the times.

atrasar [1a] **1** *vt* to slow down, slow up, retard; to delay; *clock* to put back. (b) (*Per*) to cuckold, deceive.
    2 *vi* (*watch*) to lose, be slow; **mi reloj atrasa 8 minutos** my watch is 8 minutes slow.
    3 atrasarse *vr* (a) to be behind; to lag, stay back, remain behind; to be slow, be late; (*clock*) to lose, be slow; **— en los pagos** to be in arrears. (b) (*Arg*, *Col*, *Urug*) to suffer a setback; (*Chi*) to hurt oneself (*de in*), (*of woman*) be pregnant.

atraso *nm* (a) delay, time lag; (*of watch*) slowness; (*of country etc*) backwardness; **el tren lleva —** the train is late; **salir del —** to catch up, make up lost time; **llegar con 20 minutos de —** to arrive 20 minutes late. (b) **—s** (*Comm*, *Fin*) arrears; (*of orders etc*) backlog, quantity pending; (*Col*, *PR*) setback; **cobrar —s** to collect arrears.

atravesada *nf* (*SAm*) crossing, passage.

atravesado *adj* (a) crossed, laid across, oblique. (b) squinting, cross-eyed. (c) *dog etc* mongrel, crossbred. (d) wicked, evil; treacherous.

atravesar [1k] **1** *vt* (*of person*) to cross, cross over, go across, go over; to pass through; *rapids etc* to negotiate; *period* to go through, pass through; **atravesamos un momento difícil** we are going through a difficult time. (b) (*of bullet, sword*) to pierce, go through, transfix; **— a uno con una espada** to run someone through with a sword; **la bala atravesó el metal** the bullet passed through the metal. (c) (*of bridge etc*) to cross, span, bridge. (d) *object* to lay across, put across; to put crosswise, put obliquely; **— un tronco en el camino** to lay a trunk across the road. (e) *money* to bet, lay, stake. (f) (*SAm*: *Comm*) to monopolize, corner (the market in). (g) **le tengo atravesado** he sticks in my gullet, I can't stand him.
    2 atravesarse *vr* (a) (*obstacle*) to come in between; to interfere; to arise, spring up; (*bone etc*) to stick in one's throat. (b) **— en una conversación** to butt into a conversation; **— en un negocio** to meddle in an affair. (c) **se me atraviesa el tipo ese** I can't stand that fellow. (d) (*of 2 persons*) to wrangle, bicker, get across each other.

atrayente *adj* attractive.

atrechar [1a] *vi* (*PR*) to take a short cut.

atrecho *nm* (*PR*) short cut.

atreguar [1i] **1** *vt* to grant a truce to. **2 atreguarse** *vr* to agree to a truce.

atrenzo *nm* (*SAm*) trouble, difficulty.

atreverse [2a] *vr* (a) to dare; **no me atrevo**, **no me atrevería** I wouldn't dare; **¿te atreves?** are you game?, will you?; **— a hacer algo** to dare to do something, venture to do something; **— a una**

empresa to undertake a task, dare to undertake a task; — **con un rival** to take on a rival, (venture to) compete with a rival; **me atrevo con una tarta** I could manage a cake.
(**b**) — **con uno,** — **contra uno** to be insolent to someone.

atrevidamente *adv* (**a**) boldly, daringly. (**b**) insolently, disrespectfully, impudently.

atrevido *adj* (**a**) bold, daring. (**b**) (*pej*) insolent, disrespectful; impudent, forward; *joke etc* daring, risqué.

atrevimiento *nm* (**a**) boldness, daring, audacity. (**b**) insolence; impudence, forwardness.

atribución *nf* (**a**) attribution. (**b**) (*of post*) powers, authority, functions.

atribuible *adj* attributable (*a* to); **obras** —**s a Góngora** works which are attributed to Góngora, works not certainly by Góngora.

atribuir [3g] **1** *vt* (**a**) — **a** to attribute to; to put down to; to ascribe to, impute to.
(**b**) **las funciones atribuidas a mi cargo** the powers conferred on me by my post, the authority which goes with the post I hold.
2 atribuirse *vr*: — **algo** to assume something, claim something for oneself; to arrogate something to oneself.

atribular [1a] **1** *vt* to grieve, afflict. **2 atribularse** *vr* to grieve, be distressed.

atributivo *adj* attributive.

atributo *nm* attribute; emblem, sign of authority.

atril *nm* (*Eccl etc*) lectern; bookrest, reading desk; (*Mus*) music stand, (*conductor's*) rostrum.

atrincar [1g] *vt* (*SAm*) to tie up tightly, truss up.

atrincherar [1a] **1** *vt* to surround with a trench, dig a trench in, fortify with trenches.
2 atrincherarse *vr* to entrench (oneself), dig in; **están muy fuertemente atrincherados** (*fig*) they are very strongly entrenched.

atrio *nm* (*Hist*) atrium, inner courtyard; (*Eccl*) vestibule, porch.

atrocidad *nf* (**a**) atrocity, outrage.
(**b**) silly remark, foolish thing (to do); **decir** —**es** to say silly things.
(**c**) (*fam*) enormity, crime; ¡**qué** —! how dreadful!; **la comedia es una** — the play is awful (*fam*); **como me fastidian hago** —**es** if they upset me I'll do something dreadful; **me gustan los helados una** — I'm awfully fond of ice cream (*fam*).

atrochar [1a] *vi* to go by the byways; to take a short cut.

atrofia *nf* atrophy.

atrofiar [1b] **1** *vt* to atrophy. **2 atrofiarse** *vr* to atrophy.

atrojarse [1a] *vr* (*Cu*) to get tired, feel weak; (*Mex*) to get bewildered.

atronadamente *adv* recklessly, thoughtlessly.

atronado *adj* reckless, thoughtless.

atronador *adj* deafening; *applause* thunderous.

atronamiento *nm* (*fig*) bewilderment, confusion, stunned state.

atronar [1m] *vt* (**a**) to deafen. (**b**) to stun, daze; to fell with a blow on the neck. (**c**) (*fig*) to stun; to bewilder, confuse.

atropellada *nf* (*Arg*) attack, onrush.

atropelladamente *adv* *run etc* pell-mell, helter-skelter; *decide* hastily; *talk* incoherently, in a rushed way.

atropellado *adj* *act* hasty, precipitate, impetuous; *manner* brusque, abrupt; violent.

atropellaplatos *nmf*, *pl* **atropellaplatos** (*fam*) clumsy sort.

atropellar [1a] **1** *vt* (**a**) to trample underfoot; to knock down; to push violently past; (*Aut etc*) to knock down, run over, run down; *public figure, hero* to mob, overwhelm.
(**b**) (*fig*) *work* to do hurriedly, hurry over; *rights* to disregard; *opposition, others' views* to ride rough-shod over; *inferior* to bully, oppress; *feelings* to insult, outrage; *constitution* to violate.
(**c**) (*SAm*) to make love to; to seduce, dishonour.
2 *vi*: — **por** (**a**) to push one's way violently through.
(**b**) (*fig*) to disregard, ride roughshod over; **atropella por todo** he doesn't respect anything, he doesn't give a damn for anybody.
3 atropellarse *vr* to act hastily, do things thoughtlessly.

atropello *nm* (**a**) accident; knocking down, running over.
(**b**) (*fig*) outrage (*de* upon); abuse (*de* of); disregard (*de* for); **los** —**s del dictador** the crimes of the dictator, the outrages of the dictator.

atroz *adj* (**a**) atrocious; cruel, inhuman; outrageous.
(**b**) (*fam*) huge, terrific (*fam*); dreadful, awful (*fam*).

atrozmente *adv* (**a**) atrociously; cruelly; outrageously.
(**b**) (*fam*) dreadfully.

atuendo *nm* (**a**) attire; (*hum*) rig, getup. (**b**) pomp, show.

atufado *adj* (**a**) (*Arg*) cross, angry. (**b**) (*Cu, Guat*) proud, vain.

atufar [1a] **1** *vt* (**a**) to overcome (with smell *or* fumes).
(**b**) (*fig*) to irritate, vex.
2 atufarse *vr* (**a**) (*food*) to get smelly; (*wine*) to turn sour.
(**b**) (*person*) to be overcome (with smell *or* fumes).
(**c**) (*fig*) to get cross (*con, de, por* at, with; *also* *Arg*); (*Ec*) to get bewildered; (*Cu, Guat*) to be proud, get vain.

atufo *nm* irritation.

atún *nm* (**a**) tunny, tuna. (**b**) (*sl*) nitwit (*sl*).

aturar [1a] *vt* to close up tight.

aturdidamente *adv* (**a**) thoughtlessly, recklessly. (**b**) in a bewildered way.

aturdido *adj* (**a**) thoughtless, reckless. (**b**) bewildered, dazed.

aturdidura *nf* (*Chi*), **aturdimiento** *nm* (**a**) stunned state, dazed condition; bewilderment, confusion; amazement. (**b**) thoughtlessness, recklessness.

aturdir [3a] **1** *vt* (**a**) (*physically: with blow*) to stun, daze; (*of noise*) to deafen; (*of drug, wine etc*) to stupefy, fuddle; (*of movement*) to make giddy.
(**b**) (*fig*) to stun, dumbfound; to bewilder, confuse, perplex; **la noticia nos aturdió** the news stunned us.
2 aturdirse *vr* to be stunned; to get bewildered, get confused.

aturrullado *adj* bewildered, perplexed; flustered.

aturrullar [1a] **1** *vt* to bewilder, perplex; to fluster.
2 aturrullarse *vr* to get bewildered; to get flustered, get het up (*fam*); **no te aturrulles cuando surja una dificultad** don't get flustered when something awkward comes up.

atusar [1a] **1** *vt* to trim; to comb, smooth. **2 atusarse** *vr* (*fig*) to overdress, dress in great style.

audacia *nf* boldness, audacity.

audaz *adj* bold, audacious.

audazmente *adv* boldly, audaciously.

audibilidad *nf* audibility.

audible *adj* audible.

audición *nf* (**a**) hearing. (**b**) audition; **dar** — **a uno** to audition someone, give someone an audition; **le hicieron una** — **para el papel** they gave him an audition for the part.
(**c**) (*Mus*) concert; — **radiofónica** radio concert.
(**d**) (*SAm: Comm, Fin*) audit.

audiencia *nf* (**a**) audience, hearing; formal interview; **recibir a uno en** — to grant someone an audience, receive someone in audience.
(**b**) audience chamber; (*Law*) high court.
(**c**) (*SAm: angl*) audience.

audífono *nm* hearing aid, deaf-aid; (*SAm: Tel*) earpiece, receiver.

audiofrecuencia *nf* audio-frequency.

audiovisual *adj* audio-visual.

auditar [1a] *vt* (*CAm, Mex: angl*) to audit.

auditivo **1** *adj* auditory, hearing (*attr*). **2** *nm* (*Tel*) earpiece, receiver.

audito *nm* (*CAm, Mex: angl*) audit.

auditor *nm* (**a**) (*also* — **de guerra**) judge-advocate.
(**b**) (*SAm: Comm: angl*) auditor. (**c**) (*Mex: Rail*) ticket inspector.

auditorio *nm* (**a**) audience. (**b**) auditorium, hall.

auge *nm* peak, summit, zenith; (*Astron*) apogee; increase (*de* of); period of increase, period of prosperity; (*Comm*) boom (*de* in); **estar en** — to thrive, run at a high level, do well; (*Comm*) to boom.

Augias *m*: **establos de** — Augean Stables.

augurar [1a] *vt* (*of thing*) to augur, portend; (*of person*) to predict; — **que . . .** to predict that . . .

augurio *nm* (**a**) augury; omen, portent; prediction; **consultar los** —**s** to take the auguries.
(**b**) —**s** (*fig*) best wishes; **con nuestros** —**s para . . .** with our best wishes for . . .; **mensaje de buenos** —**s** goodwill message.

augustal *adj* Augustan.

Augusto *m* Augustus.

augusto *adj* august.

aula *nf* (*School*) classroom; (*Univ*) lecture room; — **magna** assembly hall, main hall.

aulaga *nf* furze, gorse.

áulico **1** *adj* court (*attr*), courtly. **2** *nm* courtier.

aullar [1a] *vi* to howl, to yell.

aullido *nm*, **aúllo** *nm* howl; yell; **dar aullidos to** howl, yell.

aumentador *nm* (*Elec*) booster.

aumentar [1a] **1** *vt* to increase, add to, augment; *price* to increase, raise, put up; *production* to increase, step up; (*Elec*) to boost, step up; (*Opt*) to magnify; (*Phot*) to enlarge; (*Radio*) to amplify; *details, impression etc* to magnify, exaggerate; **esto viene a aumentar el número de . . .** this helps to swell the numbers of . . .

2 *vi* and **aumentarse** *vr* to increase, be on the increase; to multiply; to rise, go up; (*of value*) to appreciate.

aumentativo 1 *adj* augmentative. **2** *nm* augmentative.

aumento *nm* (**a**) increase; (*in price*) increase, rise; (*in value*) appreciation; (*Opt*) magnification; (*Phot*) enlargement; (*Radio*) amplification; **— de población** population increase; **— de precio** rise in price; **eso le valió un —** that got him a rise (in salary); **ir en —** to increase, be on the increase; to prosper, do well; **una población que va en continuo —** an ever-growing population; **los sucesos se producen con —** things are happening at an ever-increasing rate.

(**b**) (*Guat, Mex*) postscript.

aun *adv* even; **— los que tienen dinero** even those who have money; **ni — si me lo regalas** not even if you give it to me; **— así, — siendo esto así** even so; **— cuando** although, even though; **más —** even more.

aún *adv* still, yet; **— está aquí** he's still here; **no lo sabemos** we still don't know, we don't know yet; **¿no ha venido —?** hasn't he come yet?

aunar [1a] **1** *vt* to join, unite, combine. **2 aunarse** *vr* to unite, combine.

aunque *conj* though, although, even though; **— llueva vendremos** we'll come even if it rains; **es guapa — algo bajita** she's pretty but rather short, she's pretty even if she is on the short side; **— no me creas** even though you may not believe me; **— más . . .** however much . . ., no matter how much . . .

aúpa 1 *interj* (*fam*) up!, up you get!; up with it! (*etc*); **¡— Toboso!** up Toboso!

2 *as adj* (*fam*): **una función de —** a slap-up do (*fam*), a posh affair (*fam*); **una paliza de —** a thrashing and a half; **una tormenta de —** a real storm, the father and mother of a storm.

aupar [1a] *vt* (*fam*) *person* to help up, get up; *trousers etc* to hitch up, hoist up; (*fig*) to boost, praise up.

aura *nf* (**a**) gentle breeze, sweet breeze. (**b**) (*fig*) popularity, popular favour.

aural *adj* aural.

áureo *adj* (*lit*) golden.

aureola *nf*, **auréola** *nf* halo, aureole.

aureolar [1a] *vt* (*esp SAm*) *person* to honour, pay tribute to, extol; *reputation etc* to enhance, add lustre to.

aurícula *nf* (*Anat*) auricle.

auricular 1 *adj* auricular, aural, of the ear. **2** *nm* (**a**) (*Anat*) little finger. (**b**) (*Tel*) earpiece, receiver; **—es** headphones, earphones.

aurora *nf* (*lit*) dawn (*also fig*); **— boreal(is)** aurora borealis, northern lights.

auscultación *nf* sounding, auscultation.

auscultar [1a] *vt* (*Med*) *chest etc* to sound, auscultate.

ausencia *nf* absence; **en — del gato se divierten los ratones** when the cat's away the mice will play; **condenar a uno en su —** to sentence someone in his absence; **hacer buenas —s de uno** to speak kindly of someone in his absence, remember someone with affection; **tener buenas —s** to have a good reputation; *see* **brillar.**

ausentarse [1a] *vr* to go away, absent oneself (*de* from); to stay away (*de* from).

ausente 1 *adj* absent (*de* from); **estar — de** to be absent from, be missing from; **estar — de su casa** to be away from home.

2 *nmf* absentee; (*Law*) missing person.

auspiciar [1b] *vt* (*SAm*) (**a**) to support, foster; to sponsor. (**b**) to give one's good wishes to, wish success to.

auspicios *nmpl* (*esp SAm*) auspices; protection, patronage; sponsorship; **bajo los — de** under the auspices of; under the patronage of, sponsored by.

auspicioso *adj* (*SAm*) auspicious.

austeramente *adv* austerely; sternly, severely.

austeridad *nf* austerity; sternness, severity.

austero *adj* austere; stern, severe.

austral *adj* southern.

Australia *f* Australia.

australiano 1 *adj* Australian. **2** *nm*, **australiana** *nf* Australian.

Austria *f* Austria.

austriaco, austríaco 1 *adj* Austrian. **2** *nm*, **austriaca, austríaca** *nf* Austrian.

austro *nm* (*lit*) south; south wind.

autazo *nm* (*SAm*) theft of a car.

auténtica *nf* certificate, certification; authorized copy.

auténticamente *adv* authentically; genuinely, really.

autenticar [1g] *vt* to authenticate.

autenticidad *nf* authenticity; genuineness.

auténtico *adj* authentic; genuine, real; **un — espíritu de servicio** a true spirit of service; **es un — campeón** he's a real champion; **éste es copia y no el —** this one is a copy and not the real one; **días de — calor** days of real heat.

autentificar [1g] *vt* to authenticate.

autería *nf* (*Arg*) evil omen, bad sign; witchcraft.

autero[1] *nm* (*SAm*) car thief.

autero[2] *nm*, **autera** *nf* (*Arg*) alarmist, pessimist, defeatist; person who brings bad luck.

autillo *nm* tawny owl.

autismo *nm* autism.

autístico *adj* autistic.

auto[1] *nm* (*Aut*) car, automobile (*US*).

auto[2] *nm* (**a**) (*Law*) edict, judicial decree; writ, order; document; **— de ejecución** writ of execution; **— de prisión** warrant for arrest.

(**b**) **—s** documents, proceedings, court record; **estar en —s** to be in the know; **poner a uno en —s** to put someone in the picture.

(**c**) (*Eccl and Theat*) mystery play, religious play, allegory; **— del nacimiento** nativity play; **— sacramental** eucharistic play.

(**d**) (*Eccl*) **— de fe** auto-da-fé; **hacer un — de fe de** (*fig*) to burn.

auto . . . auto . . ., self . . .

autoacusación *nf* self-accusation.

autoacusarse [1a] *vr* to accuse oneself.

autoadhesivo *adj* self-adhesive.

autoadulación *nf* self-praise.

autobiografía *nf* autobiography.

autobiográfico *adj* autobiographic(al).

autobomba *nf* fire engine.

autobombearse [1a] *vr* to blow one's own trumpet, shoot a line (*fam*).

autobombo *nm* self-advertisement, self-glorification; **hacer —** to blow one's own trumpet.

autobote *nm* motorboat.

autobús *nm* bus, omnibus; motor coach; **— de dos pisos** double-decker bus.

autocamión *nm* motor lorry, motor truck (*US*).

autocar *nm* coach, motor coach.

autoclave *nm* pressure cooker; (*Med*) sterilizing apparatus.

autoconfesión *nf* self-confession.

autoconfesarse [1a] *vr* to make a self-confession.

autoconservación *nf* self-preservation.

autocracia *nf* autocracy.

autócrata *nmf* autocrat.

autocrático *adj* autocratic.

autocremarse [1a] *vr* (*Buddhist etc*) to set fire to oneself, burn oneself (to death).

autocrítica *nf* self-criticism, self-examination.

autóctono *adj* autochthonous, original, native, indigenous.

auto-cuba *nm* tank wagon.

auto-choque *nm* bumper car, dodgem.

autodegradación *nf* self-abasement.

autodeterminación *nf* self-determination.

autodidacta *adj*, **autodidacto** *adj* self-educated, self-taught.

autodisciplina *nf* self-discipline.

autodominio *nm* self-control.

autoengaño *nm* self-deception.

autoescuela *nf* driving school.

autoexpresión *nf* self-expression.

autógena *nf* welding.

autogiro *nm* autogiro.

autogobierno *nm* self-government.

autogol *nm* own goal, goal scored by a player against his own side.

autógrafo 1 *adj* autograph. **2** *nm* autograph.

automación *nf* automation.

autómata *nm* automaton, robot; (*fig*) automaton; puppet.

automáticamente *adv* automatically.

automático 1 *adj* automatic; self-acting. **2** *nm* (*Arg*) self-service restaurant.

automatización *nf* automation.

automatizar [1f] *vt* to automate.

automedonte *nm* (*hum and SAm*) coachman; driver.

automotor 1 *adj* (*f*: **automotriz**) self-propelled. **2** *nm* (*Rail*) Diesel train; (*SAm*) self-propelled vehicle.

automóvil 1 *adj* self-propelled.
2 *nm* car, motorcar, automobile (US); — **de carreras** racing car; — **de choque** bumper car, dodgem; **ir en** — to go by car, travel by car.
automovilismo *nm* (a) motoring; — **deportivo** motor racing. (b) car industry, automobile industry (US).
automovilista 1 *adj* car (attr), automobile (attr: US), motoring (attr). **2** *nm* motorist, driver.
automovilístico *adj* = **automovilista 1; accidente** — car accident.
autonomía *nf* (a) (Pol) autonomy; self-government; home rule.
(b) (Aer, Naut) range; **un avión de gran** — a long-range aircraft; **el avión tiene una** — **de 5.000 km** the aircraft has a range of 5,000 km.
autónomo *adj* autonomous; self-governing; independent.
autopista *nf* motorway; highway, turnpike (US); — **de peaje** toll road, turnpike road (US); — **perimetral** ring road, bypass.
autopolinización *nf* self-pollination.
autoprofesor *nm* teaching machine.
autopropulsado *adj* self-propelled.
autopropulsión *nf* self-propulsion.
autopsia *nf* post mortem, autopsy.
autopublicidad *nf* self-advertisement; **hacer** — to indulge in self-advertisement.
autor *nm*, **autora** *nf* (Lit) author, writer; (of idea) creator, originator, inventor; (of crime) perpetrator (de of), person responsible (de for), person concerned (de in).
autoría *nf* authorship.
autoridad *nf* (a) authority; jurisdiction.
(b) pomp, show, ostentation.
(c) (person) authority; **las** —**es** the authorities; —**es aduaneras** customs authorities; — **de sanidad** health authorities; **¡abran a la** —**!** open up (to the police)!; **presentarse a la** — to give oneself up (to the police).
autoritario 1 *adj* authoritarian; peremptory; dogmatic. **2** *nm*, **autoritaria** *nf* authoritarian.
autoritarismo *nm* authoritarianism.
autorización *nf* authorization; permission, licence; **tener la** — **de uno para** + *infin* to have someone's authorization to + *infin*.
autorizadamente *adv* officially, authoritatively; in the approved fashion.
autorizado *adj* authorized, official; authoritative; approved; **la persona autorizada** the officially designated person, the approved person.
autorizar [1f] *vt* to authorize, empower; to approve, license; to justify, give (or lend) authority to; — **a uno para** + *infin* to authorize someone to + *infin*, empower someone to + *infin*; **el futuro no autoriza optimismo alguno** the future does not justify (or warrant) the slightest optimism.
autorradio *nf* car radio.
autorretrato *nm* self-portrait.
autozuelo *nm* scribbler, hack, penpusher.
autoservicio *nm* self-service restaurant.
autostárter *nm* (Aut) self-starter.
autostop *nm* hitch-hiking; **hacer** — to hitch-hike; **fuimos haciendo** — **de Irún a Burgos** we hitch-hiked from Irún to Burgos, we got a lift from Irún to Burgos.
autostopista *nmf* hitch-hiker.
autosuficiencia *nf* (Econ) self-sufficiency.
autosuficiente *adj* (Econ) self-sufficient.
autosugestión *nf* autosuggestion.
autotanque *nm* tank lorry, tanker, tank truck (US).
autovía *nf* motorway; highway; turnpike (US); — **de acceso** main approach road.
autovivienda *nf* caravan, trailer.
Auvernia *f* Auvergne.
auxiliar 1 *adj* auxiliary; assistant. **2** *nmf* assistant; auxiliary; assistant teacher. **3** *vt* [1b] to help, assist; to bring aid to; *dying person* to attend.
auxilio *nm* help, aid, assistance; relief; — **social** social work, welfare (work); welfare service; **primeros** —**s** (Med) first aid; **acudir en** — **de uno** to come to someone's aid.
avahar [1a] **1** *vt* to blow on, warm with one's breath. **2** *vi* and **avaharse** *vr* to steam, give off steam, give off vapour.
aval *nm* (Comm) endorsement.
avalancha *nf* avalanche.
avalar [1a] *vt* (Comm) to endorse; (fig) *decision etc* to endorse; *person* to answer for.
avalentado *adj*, **avalentonado** *adj* boastful, bullying, arrogant.

avalorar [1a] *vt* (a) to estimate, appraise. (b) (fig) to encourage.
avaluación *nf* valuation, appraisal.
avaluar [1e] *vt* to value, appraise.
avalúo *nm* valuation, appraisal.
avancarga: cañón de — muzzle loader.
avance *nm* (a) (Mil and fig) advance; (in price) rise, advance; **en** — in advance.
(b) (Arg: Mil) attack, raid.
(c) (Comm, Fin) advance, advance payment; (Comm) estimate.
(d) (Comm) balance; balance sheet.
(e) (Elec) lead; (Mech) feed.
(f) (Cine) trailer; preview; —**s** (Mex) trailer.
(g) (CAm, Mex) theft; (Mil) looting, sacking.
(h) (Arg) tempting offer, gesture (made to secure someone's goodwill); (Mex) friendly advance, friendly gesture.
avante *adv* (esp SAm) forward; (Naut) forward, ahead; **¡**—**!** forward!; **todo** — (Naut) full steam ahead; **salir** — to get ahead, get on in the world.
avanzada *nf* (Mil) (a) outpost. (b) advance party, advance guard.
avanzadilla *nf* (Mil) scout, patrol; advance party.
avanzado *adj* advanced; *ideas, tendency* advanced, avant-garde, progressive; *design etc* advanced; *hour* late; *cheekbone etc* prominent; **de edad avanzada,** — **de edad** advanced in years; **a una hora avanzada** at a late hour.
avanzar [1f] **1** *vt* (a) to advance, move forward.
(b) *money* to advance.
(c) to promote.
(d) *proposal* to advance, put forward.
(e) (Ant) to vomit, bring up.
2 *vi* and **avanzarse** *vr* (a) to advance (also Mil), move on, push on; to go forward.
(b) (of plan etc) to go forward, progress, advance.
(c) (of night, winter etc) to advance, draw on, draw to a close.
(d) — **algo** (CAm, Mex) to steal something.
avanzo *nm* (Comm) (a) balance; balance sheet. (b) estimate.
avaricia *nf* miserliness, avarice; greed, greediness.
avariciosamente *adv* avariciously; greedily.
avaricioso *adj*, **avariento** *adj* miserly, avaricious; greedy.
avariosis *nf* (SAm) syphilis.
avaro 1 *adj* miserly, mean; **ser** — **de alabanzas** to be sparing in one's praise, be mean with one's praises; **ser** — **de palabras** to be a person of few words. **2** *nm*, **avara** *nf* miser, mean person.
avasallador *adj* overwhelming; domineering.
avasallamiento *nm* subjugation.
avasallar [1a] **1** *vt* to subdue, subjugate; to dominate; to enslave. **2** **avasallarse** *vr* to submit, yield.
avatar *nm* change, transformation.
ave *nf* bird; — **acuática,** — **acuátil** water bird; — **canora,** — **cantora** songbird; — **de corral** chicken, fowl; —**s de corral** fowls, poultry; — **marina** sea bird; — **negra** (Arg) crooked lawyer; — **de paso** bird of passage (also fig), migrant; — **de presa,** — **de rapiña** bird of prey; — **zancuda** wader, wading bird.
avecinarse [1a] *vr* to approach, come near.
avecindarse [1a] *vr* to take up one's residence, settle.
avechuco *nm* (fam) ragamuffin, ne'er-do-well.
avefría *nf* lapwing.
avejentar [1a] *vi* and **avejentarse** *vr* to age (before one's time).
avejigar [1h] **1** *vt* to blister. **2** **avejigarse** *vr* to blister.
avellana *nf* (a) hazelnut. (b) (Per) firecracker.
avellanado *adj* (a) *colour* nutbrown. (b) *skin etc* shrivelled, wizened.
avellanar 1 *nm* hazel wood, hazel plantation. **2** [1a] *vt* (Tech) to countersink. **3** **avellanarse** *vr* to shrivel up.
avellanedo *nm* hazel wood, hazel plantation.
avellanero *nm*, **avellano** *nm* hazel, nut tree.
avemaría *nf* (a) (Eccl) Ave Maria, Hail Mary. (b) **al** — at dusk; **en un** — (fam) in a twinkling; **saber algo como el** — (fam) to know something inside out.
avena *nf* oats; — **loca,** — **morisca,** — **silvestre** wild oats.
avenado *adj* half-crazy, rather mad.
avenal *nm* oatfield.
avenamiento *nm* draining, drainage.
avenar [1a] *vt* *land* to drain.
avenencia *nf* agreement; compromise; (Comm) bargain, deal.
avenida *nf* (a) avenue. (b) (of river) flood, spate; (fig) gathering.
avenir [3a] **1** *vt* to reconcile, bring together.
2 **avenirse** *vr* (a) (of 2 persons: act) to come to an

agreement, be reconciled; to reach a compromise; (*state*) to be on good terms, get on well together; **no se avienen** they don't get on, they don't agree.

(b) — **con algo** to be in agreement with something, conform to something; to resign oneself to something, come to terms with something; — **con uno** to reach an agreement with someone; **¡allá te las avengas!** (*fam*) that's your look-out!, that's up to you!

(c) — **a hacer algo** to agree to do something.

aventador *nm* (*for fire*) fan, blower; (*Agr*) winnowing fork.

aventadora *nf* winnowing machine.

aventajadamente *adv* outstandingly, extremely well.

aventajado *adj* outstanding, excellent, superior; — **de estatura** exceptionally tall, having the advantage of great height.

aventajar [1a] **1** *vt* **(a)** to surpass, beat, excel; to outstrip; — **con mucho a uno** to beat someone easily, be far better than someone.

(b) to improve, better.

(c) to prefer.

2 aventajarse *vr* to get ahead; — **a** to surpass, beat, excel; to get the advantage of.

aventar [1k] **1** *vt* **(a)** *fire* to fan, blow (on); *corn* to winnow.

(b) to cast to the winds; (*of wind*) to blow away; (*Cu: Agr*) to dry in the wind; (*fam*) to chuck out, throw out.

2 aventarse *vr* **(a)** to fill with air, swell up.

(b) (*fam*) to beat it (*fam*).

aventura *nf* **(a)** adventure; bold venture, daring enterprise; (*pej*) escapade; — **sentimental** love affair, affair of the heart.

(b) chance, contingency; **a la** — at random.

(c) risk, danger, hazard.

aventurado *adj* risky, hazardous.

aventurar [1a] **1** *vt* to venture, risk; *capital* to risk, stake.

2 aventurarse *vr* to dare, take a chance, risk it; — **a** + *infin* to venture to + *infin*, dare to + *infin*, risk + *ger*.

aventurera *nf* adventuress.

aventurero 1 *adj* adventurous; enterprising. **2** *nm* adventurer; (*Mil*) mercenary, soldier of fortune; (*pej*) social climber.

avergonzado *adj expression* shamefaced; embarrassed; **estar** — to be ashamed (*de, por* about, at).

avergonzar [1f *and* 1m] **1** *vt* to shame, put to shame; to abash, embarrass.

2 avergonzarse *vr* to be ashamed; to be embarrassed, look embarrassed; — **de,** — **por** to be ashamed about (*or* at, of); to be embarrassed about; — **de** + *infin* to be ashamed to + *infin*; **se avergonzó de haberlo dicho** he was ashamed at having said it.

avería¹ *nf* (*Orn*) aviary; flock of birds.

avería² *nf* **(a)** (*Comm etc*) damage; (*Mech*) breakdown, fault, failure; **el coche tiene una** — the car has had a breakdown, there's something wrong with the car.

(b) (*Arg*) **hombre de** — tough guy, man accustomed to doing as he pleases; dangerous criminal.

avería³ *nf* (*Naut*) average; — **gruesa** general average.

averiado *adj fruit etc* damaged, spoiled; (*Mech*) broken down, faulty; **los faros están** —**s** the lights have failed, there's something wrong with the lights.

averiar [1c] **1** *vt* to damage, spoil; (*Mech*) to cause a breakdown in, cause a failure in; to damage.

2 averiarse *vr* **(a)** to get damaged; (*Mech*) to have a breakdown, have a failure, fail; **se averió el arranque** the self-starter failed, the self-starter went wrong.

(b) (*Mex*) to lose one's virginity.

averiguable *adj* ascertainable.

averiguación *nf* **(a)** ascertainment, discovery; establishment; investigation; inquiry. **(b)** (*CAm, Mex*) quarrel.

averiguadamente *adv* certainly.

averiguado *adj* certain, established; **es un hecho** — it is an established fact.

averiguador *nm*, **averiguadora** *nf* investigator; inquirer.

averiguar [1i] **1** *vt* to find out, ascertain, discover; to look up; to investigate, inquire into, find out about; — **las señas de uno** to find out someone's address; **hay que** — **esto en la biblioteca** this must be looked up in the library, you'll have to check this in the library; **eso es todo lo que se pudo** — that is all that could be discovered.

2 *vi* (*CAm, Mex*) to quarrel, use bad language.

3 averiguarse *vr* **(a)** — **con uno** (*fam*) to tie someone down; to get along with someone.

(b) (*CAm, Mex*) — **con uno** to quarrel with someone, use bad language to someone.

averigüetas *nmf, pl* **averigüetas** (*Col, Mex*) snooper, busybody.

averrugado *adj* warty.

aversión *nf* aversion (*hacia algo, por algo* to something; *a uno* for someone); distaste, disgust, loathing; **cobrar** — **a** to take a strong dislike to.

avestruz *nm* **(a)** (*Orn*) ostrich; — **de la pampa** rhea.

(b) (*SAm: fam*) dimwit (*fam*), idiot.

avetado *adj* veined, grained, streaked.

avetoro *nm* bittern.

avezado *adj* accustomed; inured, experienced; **los ya** —**s en estos menesteres** those already experienced in such matters.

avezar [1f] **1** *vt* to accustom, inure (*a* to). **2 avezarse** *vr* to get used (to it); to become accustomed; — **a algo** to get used to something, get hardened to something.

aviación *nf* **(a)** aviation. **(b)** air force; flying corps; **la** — **francesa** the French air force.

aviado *adj:* **estar** — **(a)** (*Arg*) to be well off, have all one needs; to be properly equipped (*with tools etc*).

(b) (*Arg, Mex*) to be dreaming, be in the moon.

(c) (*fam*) to be in a mess; **¡**—**s estamos!** what a mess we're in!

aviador¹ *nm* (*Aer*) airman, aviator, flyer; (*Mil*) airman, member of the air force.

aviador² *nm* (*Cu, Chi, Per*) businessman who finances mining enterprises; moneylender, financier.

aviadora *nf* aviator, woman pilot.

aviar [1c] **1** *vt* **(a)** to get ready, prepare, fit out; to tidy up; to equip, supply, provide (*de* with); (*Cu, Chi, Per*) to advance money to; to lend equipment to, provide with equipment; to provide with food for a journey.

(b) — **a uno** (*fam*) to hurry someone up, get someone moving.

(c) (*prov, SAm: Agr*) to castrate.

(d) dejar a uno aviado to leave someone in the lurch.

2 *vi* (*fam*) to hurry up, get a move on; **¡vamos aviando!** let's get a move on!

3 aviarse *vr* to get ready; — **para hacer algo** to get ready to do something.

avícola *adj* chicken (*attr*), poultry (*attr*); **granja** — chicken farm, poultry farm.

avicultor *nm* chicken farmer, poultry farmer; bird fancier.

avicultura *nf* chicken farming, poultry farming; bird fancying.

ávidamente *adv* avidly, eagerly; (*pej*) greedily.

avidez *nf* avidity, eagerness (*de* for); (*pej*) greed, greediness (*de* for); **con** — eagerly; greedily.

ávido *adj* avid, eager (*de* for); (*pej*) greedy (*de* for); — **de sangre** bloodthirsty.

avieso 1 *adj* distorted, crooked; sinister; perverse, wicked; spiteful. **2** *nm* (*Col*) abortion.

avilantarse [1a] *vr* to be insolent.

avilantez *nf* insolence.

avilesino 1 *adj* of Avilés. **2** *nm,* **avilesina** *nf* native (*or* inhabitant) of Avilés; **los** —**s** the people of Avilés.

avilanado *adj* boorish, uncouth.

avinagrado *adj* sour, acid; (*fig*) sour, jaundiced, crabbed.

avinagrar [1a] **1** *vt* to sour. **2 avinagrarse** *vr* to turn sour.

Aviñón Avignon.

avío *nm* **(a)** preparation, provision.

(b) (*Cu, Chi, Per*) loan (of money *or* of equipment); provisions for a journey.

(c) hacer su — (*fam*) to make one's pile (*fam*); (*iro*) to make a mess of things.

(d) ¡al —**!** get cracking! (*fam*), get on with it!

(e) —**s** gear, tackle, kit.

avión *nm* **(a)** (*Aer*) aeroplane, plane, aircraft, airplane (*US*); — **de caza,** — **de combate** fighter, pursuit plane; — **a** (*or* **de**) **chorro,** — **de propulsión a chorro,** — **a** (*or* **de**) **reacción** jet plane; — **de despegue vertical** vertical takeoff plane; — **de pasajeros** passenger aircraft; **por** — (*Post*) by airmail; **enviar artículos por** — to send goods by plane; **ir en** — to go by plane, go by air.

(b) (*Orn*) martin.

avionazo *nm* plane crash, accident to an aircraft.

avionero *nm* (*Arg, Par, Per*) airman, aircraftman.

avioneta *nf* light aircraft.

avisadamente *adv* sensibly, wisely.

avisado *adj* sensible, wise; **mal** — rash, ill-advised.

avisador 1 *nm*, **avisadora** *nf* **(a)** informant; (*pej*) informer. **(b)** (*Cine, Theat*) programme seller. **2** *nm* electric bell; — **de incendios** fire alarm.

avisar [1a] *vt* (a) to inform, notify, tell; — **a uno con una semana de anticipación** to let someone know a week in advance, give someone a week's notice; **¿por qué no me avisó?** why didn't you let me know?; **en cuanto ella llegue me avisas** tell me the moment she comes; **lo hizo sin** — he did it without warning.
(b) to warn; to admonish; to advise.

aviso *nm* (a) piece of information, tip; advice, piece of advice; notice; warning; admonishment; (*Comm, Fin*) demand, demand note; — **escrito** written notice, notice in writing; **con 15 días de** — at a fortnight's notice; **con poco tiempo de** — at short notice, with little warning; — **previo de despido** prior notice of discharge; **sin previo** — without warning, without notice; **hasta nuevo** — until further notice; **salvo** — **en contrario** unless otherwise informed; **según (su)** — (*Comm*) as per order, as you ordered; **mandar** — to send word.
(b) (*CAm*) advertisement; **"—s económicos"** "classified advertisements"; — **mural** poster, wall poster.
(c) caution; discretion, prudence; **estar sobre** — to be on the alert, be on the look-out.

avispa *nf* (a) wasp. (b) (*fam*) sly sort, wily bird (*fam*); (*Mex*) thief.

avispado *adj* sharp, clever, wide-awake; (*pej*) sly, wily.

avispar [1a] **1** *vt horse* to spur on, urge on; (*fig*) to stir up, prod, ginger up. **2 avisparse** *vr* to fret, worry; (*Mex*) to become alarmed.

avispero *nm* (a) wasps' nest. (b) (*Med*) carbuncle.
(c) (*fam*) mess; (*Arg*) noisy gathering, bear garden.

avispón *nm* hornet.

avistar [1a] **1** *vt* to sight, make out, glimpse. **2 avistarse** *vr* to have an interview (*con* with).

avituallar [1a] *vt* to victual, provision, supply with food.

avivar [1a] **1** *vt fire* to stoke (up); *colour, light* to brighten, make brighter; *pain* to intensify; *passion* to inflame; *dispute* to add fuel to; *interest* to stimulate, arouse; to revive; *effect* to enhance, heighten; *combatants* to urge on.
2 avivarse *vr* to revive, acquire new life; to cheer up, become brighter.

avizor 1 *adj*: **estar ojo** — to be on the alert, be vigilant. **2** *nm* watcher.

avizorar [1a] *vt* to watch, spy on.

avorazado *adj* (*Mex*) greedy; inconsiderate.

avutarda *nf* great bustard.

axial *adj* axial.

axila *nf* axilla, armpit.

axioma *nm* axiom.

axiomático *adj* axiomatic.

axis *nm*, *pl* **axis** (*Anat*) axis.

ay 1 *interj* (a) (*of physical pain*) ow!, ouch!
(b) (*of distress, grief*) oh!, oh dear!, (*more rhetorically*) alas!; ¡ — **de mí!** poor me!; it's very hard (on me)!; **whatever shall I do?**; (*very rhetorically*) woe is me!; ¡ — **del que lo haga!** woe betide the man who does it!
(c) (*of surprise, wonderment*) oh!, goodness!
2 *nm* sigh; moan, groan, cry; **un** — **desgarrador a** heartrending cry.

aya *nf* governess; child's nurse.

Áyax *m* Ajax.

ayer 1 *adv* yesterday; (*fig*) formerly, in the past; ·— **no más, no más que** — only yesterday; — **por la mañana** yesterday morning.
2 *nm* yesterday, past; **el** — **madrileño** Madrid in the past, old Madrid.

ayllu *nm* (*Bol, Per*) lineage, family; tribe (of Indians).

ayo *nm* tutor.

ayote *nm* (*CAm, Mex*) pumpkin; (*hum*) head; **dar** —**s a** to jilt.

ayotoste *nm* armadillo.

ayuda 1 *nf* (a) help, aid, assistance; —**s audiovisuales** audiovisual aids; — **económica** economic aid; —**s a la navegación** aids to navigation, navigational aids; — **visual** visual aid.
(b) (*Med*) enema; (*SAm*) laxative.
2 *nm* page; — **de cámara** valet.

ayudado *nm* (*Taur*) *a kind of pass with the cape.*

ayudador *nm*, **ayudadora** *nf* helper.

ayudante *nm*, **ayudanta** *nf* helper, assistant; (*Mil*) adjutant; (*Tech*) mate; technician; (*School, Univ*) assistant; — **de electricista** electrician's mate; — **de laboratorio** laboratory assistant; — **de dirección** (*Theat etc*) production assistant.

ayudar [1a] *vt* to help, aid, assist; to help out; to be of use to, serve; — **a uno a hacer algo** to help someone to do something; to help in doing something; — **a uno a bajar** to help someone down, help someone

---

out; me ayuda muchísimo he's a great help (to me), he helps me a lot.

ayunar [1a] *vi* to fast (*a* on); (*fig*) to go without.

ayunas *nfpl*: **salir en** — to go out without any breakfast; **estar (or quedarse) en** — to know nothing about it, be completely in the dark; to miss the point.

ayuno 1 *adj* (a) fasting. (b) **estar** — = **estar** *etc* **en ayunas. 2** *nm* fast; fasting; abstinence; **estar** *etc* **en** — =**estar en ayunas.**

ayuntamiento *nm* (a) town council, city council, corporation, municipal government.
(b) town hall, city hall.
(c) (*also* — **sexual**) sexual intercourse; **tener** — **con** to have intercourse with.

ayuntar [1a] *vt* (a) (*Naut*) to splice. (b) (*Col: Agr*) to yoke, yoke together.

azabachado *adj* jet, jet-black.

azabache *nm* (*Miner*) jet; —**s** jet trinkets.

azacán *nm*, **azacana** *nf* drudge, slave; **estar hecho un** — to be worked to death.

azacanarse [1a] *vr* to drudge, slave away.

azada *nf* hoe.

azadón *nm* large hoe, mattock.

azadonar [1a] *vt* to hoe.

azafata *nf* (a) (*Aer*) air hostess, stewardess. (b) (*Chi*) =**azafate**. (c) (*Hist*) lady-in-waiting; handmaiden.

azafate *nm* flat basket, tray.

azafrán *nm* (*Bot*) saffron, crocus; (*Cook*) saffron.

azafranado *adj* saffron, saffron-coloured.

azafranar [1a] *vt* (*Cook*) to saffron.

azagaya *nf* assegai, javelin.

azahar *nm* orange blossom.

azalea *nf* azalea.

azar *nm* (a) chance, fate; **al** — at random; **por** — accidentally, by chance; **juego de** — game of chance.
(b) misfortune, accident, piece of bad luck.

azararse [1a] *vr* (a) to go wrong, go awry. (b) = **azorarse**.

azarear [1a] *vt and* **azarearse** *vr* =**azorar(se)**.

azarosamente *adv* hazardously; eventfully.

azaroso *adj* (a) risky, hazardous, chancy; *life* eventful; full of ups and downs. (b) unlucky, ill-omened.

ázimo *adj bread* unleavened.

—azo, —aza *n and adj suffix* (a) (*augmentative*) **golpazo** heavy blow; **librazo** big book; **melenaza** long unkempt hair; **multaza** heavy fine.
(b) (*blow*) **paraguazo** blow with an umbrella; **espadazo** sword thrust, slash with a sword.
(c) (*sound*) **trompetazo** trumpet blast; **telefonazo** telephone call; **dar un timbrazo** to ring the bell.
(d) (*pej*) **animalazo** nasty creature; **mujeraza** shrew, bitch, horrid woman.

azogado 1 *adj* restless, fidgety; **temblar como un** — to shake like a leaf, tremble all over. **2** *nm* silvering (of a mirror).

azogar [1h] **1** *vt* to coat with quicksilver; *mirror* to silver. **2 azogarse** *vr* to be restless, be fidgety; to get agitated.

azogue *nm* mercury, quicksilver; **ser un** — to be always on the go; **tener** — to be restless, be fidgety.

azolve *nm* (*Mex*) sediment, deposit.

azonzado *adj* (*Arg*) silly, stupid.

azor *nm* goshawk.

azorado *adj* (a) alarmed, upset. (b) embarrassed, flustered. (c) excited.

azoramiento *nm* (a) alarm. (b) embarrassment, confusion; fluster. (c) excitement.

azorar [1a] **1** *vt* (a) to alarm, disturb, upset; to rattle.
(b) to embarrass, fluster.
(c) to excite; to urge on, egg on.
2 azorarse *vr* (a) to get alarmed, get upset; to get rattled.
(b) to be embarrassed, get flustered.

Azores *fpl* Azores.

azoro *nm* (a) (*esp SAm*) =**azoramiento**. (b) (*CAm*) ghost.

azorrillarse [1a] *vr* (*Mex*) to hide away, crouch out of sight.

azotacalles *nm*, *pl* **azotacalles** idler, loafer.

azotaina *nf* beating, spanking.

azotamiento *nm* whipping, flogging.

azotar [1a] *vt* (a) to whip, flog, beat; to scourge; *child* to thrash, spank; (' *gr etc*) to beat; *branches etc* to jar, shake; (*of rain, sea*) to lash, beat, beat down upon; **un viento huracanado azota la costa a** hurricane is lashing the coast.
(b) — **las calles** to loaf around the streets.

azotazo *nm* stroke, lash; spank.

azote *nm* (a) whip, lash, scourge.
(b) stroke, lash; spank; **ser condenado a 100** —**s**

to be sentenced to 100 lashes; **—s y galeras** monotonous fare, the same old stuff.
(c) (*fig*) scourge; calamity; **Atila, el — de Dios** Attila, the Scourge of God.

azotea *nf* flat roof, terrace roof; (*Arg*, *Per*) adobe house.

azotera *nf* (*SAm*) beating, thrashing.

azteca 1 *adj* Aztec. **2** *nmf* Aztec.

azúcar *nm* (*and sometimes f*) sugar; **— blanco, — extrafino, — fina** castor sugar; **— candi** sugar candy, rock candy; **— de cortadillo, — en terrón** lump sugar; **— morena, — negra, — terciada** brown sugar.

azucarado *adj* sugary, sweet (*also fig*).

azucarar [1a] *vt* (a) to sugar, add sugar to; to ice with sugar, coat with sugar. (b) (*fig*) to soften, mitigate; *person* to sweeten.

azucarero 1 *adj* sugar (*attr*). **2** *nm* sugar basin, sugar bowl.

azucarería *nf* sugar refinery.

azucena *nf* white lily, Madonna lily; **— atigrada** tiger lily.

azud *nm*, **azuda** *nf* waterwheel; dam (for irrigation), mill dam.

azuela *nf* adze.

azufre *nm* sulphur; brimstone.

azufroso *adj* sulphurous.

azul 1 *adj* blue.
2 *nm* blue; blueness; **— celeste** sky blue; **— de cobalto** cobalt blue; **— eléctrico** electric blue; **— de mar, — marino** navy blue; **— de Prusia** Prussian blue; **— de ultramar** ultramarine blue.

azulado *adj* blue, bluish.

azular [1a] **1** *vt* to colour blue, dye blue. **2 azularse** *vr* to turn blue.

azulear [1a] *vi* to be bluish, have a blue tinge; to show blue.

azulejar [1a] *vt* to tile.

azulejo *nm* (a) tile, glazed tile, ornamental tile. (b) (*Cu*, *Mex*: *sl*) copper (*sl*).

azulenco *adj* bluish.

azulgrana *adj invar* blue-and-scarlet.

azulina *nf* cornflower.

azulino *adj* bluish.

azuloso *adj* (*SAm*) bluish.

azumagarse [1h] *vr* (*Chi*) to rust, get rusty.

azumbrado *adj* (*fam*) sozzled (*fam*).

azumbre *nm liquid measure* =2.016 *litres*.

azur *nm* (*Her*) azure.

azurumbado *adj* (*CAm*) silly, stupid; (*Guat*) drunk.

azuzar [1f] *vt* (a) **— a los perros a uno** to set the dogs on someone, urge the dogs to attack someone. (b) (*fig*) to egg on, urge on. (c) (*fig*) to irritate.

B

baba *nf* spittle, saliva, slobber; (*Bio*) mucus; (*of slug etc*) slime, slimy secretion; **se le caía la —** (*fig*) he was thrilled to bits, he was delighted; **se le está cayendo la —** (*fig*) he's getting soft; **echar —** to drool, slobber; **echar — contra uno** to say nasty things about someone.
babador *nm* bib.
babasfrías *nm*, *pl* **babasfrías** (*Col, Mex*) fool.
babaza *nf* (a) slime, mucus. (b) (*Zool*) slug.
babear [1a] **1** *vi* (a) to drool, slobber.
    (b) (*fig*) to be sloppy, drool (over women).
    2 babearse *vr* (a) (*RPl*) to feel flattered, bask in adulation.
    (b) (*Mex*) **— por algo** to yearn for something, drool over something.
Babel *m or f* Babel; **Torre de —** Tower of Babel.
babel *m or f* bedlam; confusion, mess.
babeo *nm* drooling, slobbering.
babero *nm* bib.
Babia: estar en — to be daydreaming, have one's mind somewhere else.
babieca **1** *adj* (*fam*) simple-minded, stupid. **2** *nmf* (*fam*) idiot, dolt.
Babilonia *f* Babylon, Babylonia.
babilonia[1] *nf* bedlam.
babilónico *adj* Babylonian.
babilonio **1** *adj* Babylonian. **2** *nm*, **babilonia**[2] *nf* Babylonian.
babilla *nf* (*Vet*) stifle.
bable *nm* Asturian dialect.
babor *nm* port, port side, larboard; **a —** on the port side; **la mar a —** the sea to port; **¡tierra a —!** land to port!; **poner el timón a —, virar a —** to turn to port, port the helm; **de —** port (*attr*).
babosa *nf* slug.
babosada *nf* (*SAm*) stupid things; useless person, useless thing.
babosear [1a] **1** *vt* (a) to drool over, slobber over.
    (b) (*fig*) to drool over; (*CAm*) to insult; (*Mex*) **muchos han baboseado este problema** many have taken a superficial look at this problem.
    2 *vi* to drool.
baboseo *nm* (a) drooling, slobbering. (b) calf love, youthful infatuation.
baboso *adj* (a) drooling, slobbering; slimy.
    (b) (*fig*) sloppy (about women); mushy, foolishly sentimental; fawning; snivelling; dirty; (*SAm*) silly; (*CAm*) rotten (*fam*), caddish.
babucha *nf* slipper; (*Cu*) child's bodice; (*SD*) blouse; **—s** (*Cu*) rompers; **llevar algo a —** (*RPl*) to carry something on one's back.
babuino *nm* baboon.
babujal *nm* (*Cu*) witch, sorcerer.
baby ['beβi] *nmf* (*SAm: angl*) baby; (*Aut*) small car, mini; **— fútbol** miniature football, junior football.
baca *nf* (*of bus, coach*) top; rainproof cover. (b) (*on car etc*) luggage rack, carrier.
bacalao *nm* (a) cod, codfish; **cortar el —** (*fam*) to be the boss, have the final say.
    (b) **ser un —** (*fam*) to be as thin as a rake.
    (c) (*sl*) wet fish (*sl*), drip (*fam*); (*Chi*) miser, mean sort.
bacán *nm* (*RPl*) wealthy man; sugar daddy; showily-dressed man.
bacanal **1** *adj* bacchanalian. **2** *nf* (*also* **—es**) bacchanalia; (*fig*) bacchanalia, orgy.
bacanería *nf* (*RPl*) elegance; display of wealth, ostentation.
bacante *nf* bacchante; (*fig*) drunken and noisy woman.
bacar(r)á *nm* baccarat.
bacenica *nf* (*SAm*) = **bacinica**.

bacía *nf* basin, vessel; barber's bowl, shaving bowl.
bacilar *adj* bacillary.
bacilo *nm* bacillus, germ.
bacín *nm* (a) chamberpot; poorbox; beggar's bowl.
    (b) wretch, cur.
bacineta *nf* small chamberpot; beggar's bowl.
bacinica *nf* small chamberpot.
Baco *m* Bacchus.
bacteria *nf* bacterium, germ; **—s** bacteria, germs.
bacteriano *adj* bacterial.
bactericida **1** *adj* germ-killing. **2** *nm* germicide, germ killer.
bactérico *adj* bacterial.
bacteriología *nf* bacteriology.
bacteriológico *adj* bacteriological.
bacteriólogo *nm* bacteriologist.
báculo *nm* (a) stick, staff; **— pastoral** crozier, bishop's staff.
    (b) (*fig*) prop, support, staff; **ser el — de la vejez de uno** to be someone's comfort in old age.
bacha[1] *nf* (*Mex*) remnant, remains; fag end, cigar stub; **—s** dregs.
bacha[2] *nf* (*Ant*) spree (*fam*), merry outing.
bachata *nf* (*Ant*) spree (*fam*), merry outing.
bachatear [1a] *vi* (*Ant*) to go on a spree (*fam*), go out for a good time.
bachatero *nm* (*Ant*) reveller, carouser.
bache *nm* rut, hole, pothole; (*fig*) bad patch, bad spot, rut; (*Econ etc*) slump; **— de aire** (*Aer*) air pocket; **— económico** slump, economic depression; **salir del —** to get out of the rut, get moving again; **salvar el —** (*fig*) to get the worst over, be over the worst.
bachicha *nm* (*Chi, RPl: pej*), **bachiche** *nm* (*Arg, Ec, Per: pej*) Italian, wop (*sl*).
bachiller **1** *adj* garrulous, talkative.
    2 *nmf* (*School*) pupil who has passed the school-leaving examination or holds a certificate of higher education (*see* **bachillerato**); (*Univ: Hist*) bachelor.
    3 *nm* (*fig*) windbag.
    4 bachillera *nf* (a) bluestocking.
    (b) cunning woman, scheming woman.
bachillerato *nm* (*School*) school-leaving examination, baccalaureate; (*Univ: Hist*) bachelor's degree; **— comercial** certificate in business studies; **— elemental** lower examination (= 'O' level); **— laboral** certificate in agricultural (*or* technical) studies; **— del magisterio** certificate for students proceeding to teacher-training; **— superior** higher certificate (= 'A' level).
bachillerear [1a] *vi* (*fam*) to talk a lot, prattle away.
bachillería *nf* (*fam*) (a) talk, prattle. (b) piece of nonsense, silly thing; nonsense.
bachos *nmpl* (*Per*) fibs, tales.
badajada *nf* (a) stroke (of a bell), chime. (b) piece of idle talk, piece of gossip.
badajazo *nm* stroke (of a bell), chime.
badajo *nm* (a) clapper (of a bell). (b) (*fam*) chatterbox.
badajocense **1** *adj* of Badajoz. **2** *nmf* native (*or* inhabitant) of Badajoz; **los —s** the people of Badajoz.
badajoceño = **badajocense**.
badana *nf* dressed sheepskin; **zurrar** (*or* **sobar**) **la — a uno** (*fam*) to tan someone's hide (*fam*), (*fig*) haul someone over the coals.
badaza *nf* (*Cu*) strap (for standing passenger).
badil *nm*, **badila** *nf* fire shovel.
badilejo *nm* (*Col, Per*) builder's trowel.
badulaque *nm* (a) idiot, nincompoop. (b) (*SAm*) rogue.
badulaquear [1a] *vi* (a) to be an idiot, act like an idiot. (b) (*SAm*) to be a rogue, be dishonest, act like a rogue.

bagaje nm (a) (Mil) baggage; equipment; (SAm) luggage, baggage (US). (b) beast of burden.

bagatela nf trinket, knick-knack; trifle, mere nothing, bagatelle; ¡una —! a mere trifle!; son —s those are trivialities, those are things of no importance.

bagayo nm (Arg) (a) bundle of clothing and possessions, tramp's bundle; heavy burden, awkward burden; loot (from a crime).
(b) (fig) useless person, tedious person.

bagazo nm (a) chaff, husks; pulp; (SAm) husks of sugar cane. (b) (fig) useless person.

bagre 1 adj (a) (Bol, Col) vulgar, coarse, loud.
(b) (CAm) clever, sharp.
2 nm (a) (SAm) catfish.
(b) (SAm) unpleasant person, sly sort; ugly woman; (CR) whore.

bagrero adj (Ec, Per) fond of ugly women.

bagual 1 adj (Arg, Bol) (a) wild, untamed.
(b) person rough, loutish, rude.
2 nm (a) (Bol, Chi, RPl) wild horse, untamed horse; ganar los —es (Urug) to escape, get to safety.
(b) (Chi) rough sort, lout.

bagualada nf (RPl) (a) herd of wild horses. (b) (fig) stupid thing, piece of nonsense.

bagualón adj (Arg) half-tamed.

bah interj (scorn) bah!, that's nothing!, pooh!; (disbelief) hum!, never!

Bahama: Islas fpl —, also **Las Bahamas** Bahamas.

baharí nf sparrowhawk.

bahía nf (Geog) bay.

bahorrina nf (a) dirt, filth; slops. (b) (fig) riffraff, scum.

bailable 1 adj: música — dance music, music that you can dance to. 2 nm dance, dance number; ballet.

bailada nf (SAm) dance, dancing.

bailadero nm dance hall; dance floor.

bailador 1 adj dancing. 2 nm, **bailadora** nf dancer.

bailar [1a] 1 vt to dance: top etc to spin.
2 vi to dance; (of top) to spin, spin round; (fig) to dance, jump about; — al son que tocan to toe the line; to adapt oneself to circumstances; éste es otro que bien baila here's another one (of the same kind); ¿quieres —? shall we dance?; sacar a una a — to invite someone to dance, take someone out to dance.
3 **bailarse** vr: — a uno (Mex: sl) to do someone in (sl).

bailarín nm (professional) dancer; ballet dancer.

bailarina nf (professional) dancer; dancing-girl; ballet dancer, ballerina.

baile nm (a) dance; dancing, the dance; (Theat) dance, ballet; — clásico ballet; — folklórico, popular, — regional traditional dance; — de salón, — de sociedad ballroom dance; — de San Vito St Vitus's dance.
(b) dance, (more formal) ball; — de candil, — de medio pelo (SAm) village dance, hop (fam); — de contribución (Ant, CAm) public dance; — de etiqueta ball, dress ball, formal dance; — de fantasía (SAm), — de máscaras masked ball; — de trajes fancy-dress ball.

bailecito nm (SAm) traditional dance.

bailón adj fond of dancing, that dances a lot.

bailongo nm (SAm) village dance, low-class dance, hop (fam).

bailotear [1a] vi (pej) to dance about, hop around.

baivel nm bevel.

baja nf (a) (in price, temperature etc) drop, fall; — repentina (Econ) slump, recession; una baja de 5 por ciento a fall of 5%; una baja de temperatura a drop in temperature; jugar a la — (Fin) to speculate on a fall in prices; dar —, ir de — to decline, lose value; seguir en — to go from bad to worse.
(b) (Mil) casualty; (in post) vacancy; (to journal) cancelled subscription; las —s son grandes the casualties are heavy, there are heavy casualties; dar a uno de — to mark someone absent; to strike off someone, eliminate someone (from a list); dar de — a un soldado to discharge a soldier; dar de — a un empleado to give notice to an employee; dar de — a un miembro to expel a member, remove someone from the list of members; darse de — to drop out, withdraw, retire; to go sick; to give up one's job, leave one's post; to cease to subscribe, give up one's membership.
(c) (Cu) weak point; coger la — a uno to find someone's weak spot.

bajá nm pasha.

bajada nf (a) slope. (b) descent, going down; durante la — as we (etc) went down, on the way down.

bajamar nf low tide, low water.

bajante nm drainpipe.

bajar [1a] 1 vt (a) object to lower, let down; to bring down, carry down; luggage etc to take down, get down; person to help down, help out; to lead down; — el telón to lower the curtain; — los equipajes al taxi to take the luggage down to the taxi; ¿me ayuda a — esta maleta? would you help me to get this case down?
(b) arm, eyes etc to drop, lower; head to bow, bend.
(c) price to reduce, lower; gas, radio etc to turn down; voice to lower.
(d) slope, stairs to come down, go down, descend.
(e) (fig) to humble, humiliate.
(f) (Ant: sl) to pay up, cough up (sl).
(g) (Col: sl) to do in (sl).
2 vi (a) to come down, go down, descend.
(b) (from vehicle) to get off, get out; — de to get off, get out of.
(c) (of price, temperature, water etc) to fall; la venta no ha bajado nunca de mil sales have never been less than a thousand, sales have never fallen below a thousand.
3 **bajarse** vr (a) to bend down, stoop; — a recoger algo to bend down to pick something up.
(b) (from vehicle) to get off, get out; — de to get off, get out of.
(c) (fig) to lower oneself, humble oneself; — a hacer algo vil to lower oneself to do something mean.
(d) (RPl) to stay, put up (en in, at).

bajareque nm (a) (SAm) mud wall; (Cu, Mex, Ven) mud hut, shack. (b) (Pan) fine drizzle.

bajel nm (lit) vessel, ship.

bajera nf (a) (CAm, Col, Ven) lower leaves of the tobacco plant; inferior tobacco. (b) (fig) insignificant person, nobody. (c) (RPl) horse blanket.

bajero adj lower, under-...; falda bajera underskirt.

bajetón adj (Ant, Col, Ec) short, small.

bajeza nf (a) lowliness; vileness, baseness, meanness.
(b) (una —) mean thing, vile deed.

bajío nm (a) (Naut) shoal, sandbank; shallows.
(b) (SAm) lowland; (Mex: also —s) flat arable land on a high plateau.

bajista 1 adj (Fin): tendencia — tendency to lower prices. 2 nm (Fin) bear.

bajo 1 adj (a) low; person short, small (also — de cuerpo, — de estatura); part, side lower, under; floor lower, ground (attr); land low, low-lying; water shallow; con la cabeza baja with bowed head, with head lowered; con los ojos —s with downcast eyes, with lowered eyes; en la parte baja de la ciudad in the lower part of the town.
(b) sound faint, soft; voice low, (in tone) deep; en voz baja in an undertone, in a low voice; decir algo por lo — to say something in an undertone; hacer algo por lo — to do something secretly.
(c) colour dull; pale.
(d) metal base (also — de ley).
(e) — latín Low Latin.
(f) birth low, humble; chamber (Pol), class lower; condition lowly; task menial; quarter of town poorer, working-class (and see barrio).
(g) (pej) common, ordinary; quality low, poor; (morally) vile, base, mean.
2 nm (a) deep place, depth; hollow.
(b) (Naut) = bajío.
(c) (Sew) hemline; —s de la falda lower part of the skirt; —s del pantalón trouser turn-ups, pants cuffs (US).
(d) (Archit: esp SAm) —s ground floor, ground-floor flat (or rooms).
(e) (Mus) bass; — profundo basso profundo.
3 adv (a) down; below.
(b) play, sing quietly; speak low, in a low voice; ¡más —, por favor! quieter, please!
4 prep (a) under, underneath, below.
(b) (fig) under; — Napoleón under Napoleon; — el reinado de in the reign of.
(c) see condición, juramento etc.

bajón nm (a) decline, fall, drop; (Med) decline, worsening; (Comm, Fin) sharp fall in price; slump; — en la moral slump in morale; dar un — to fall away sharply, slump, go rapidly downhill; en 3 meses ha pegado un — de 5 años in 3 months he seems to have aged 5 years.
(b) (Mus) bassoon.

bajorrelieve nm bas-relief.

bajura nf (a) lowness; shortness, smallness, small size. (b) (PR) lowland. (c) pesca en — shallow-water fishing, coastal fishing.

bala nf (a) (Mil) bullet, shot; — de cañón cannon-ball; — fría spent bullet; — perdida stray shot; — trazadora tracer bullet; como una — like a shot;

ni a — (*SAm*) by no means, not on any account; **ser un(a)** — (**perdida**) to be no good, be a rotter; **no le entra** — (*Chi*) he's never ill, he's terribly tough; he is unyielding.
(**b**) (*Comm*) bale; — **de algodón** bale of cotton, cotton bale.

balaca *nf* (*SAm*) boast, piece of boasting, brag; (*Col*) show, pomp.

balacada *nf* (*Arg*) = **balaca**.

balacear [1a] *vt* (*CAm, Mex*) to shoot, shoot at.

balacera *nf* (*CAm, Mex*) exchange of shots, shooting affray.

balada *nf* (*Lit*) ballad; (*Mus*) ballad, ballade.

baladí *adj* trivial, paltry, worthless; trashy.

baladrar [1a] *vi* to scream, howl; to shout.

baladre *nm* oleander, rosebay.

baladrero *adj* loud, noisy.

baladro *nm* scream, howl; shout.

baladrón 1 *adj* boastful. **2** *nm* braggart, bully.

baladronada *nf* boast, brag; bravado, piece of bravado.

baladronear [1a] *vi* to boast, brag; to indulge in bravado.

bálago *nm* (**a**) thatch. (**b**) (*Prov*) soapsuds, lather; soap bubble.

balance *nm* (**a**) to-and-fro motion, oscillation; rocking, swinging; (*Naut*) roll, rolling.
(**b**) (*fig*) hesitation, vacillation.
(**c**) (*Cu*) rocking chair.
(**d**) (*Comm*) balance; balance sheet; stocktaking; — **de situación** (*Arg, Cu*) balance sheet; **hacer** — to strike a balance; to take an inventory; (*fig*) to take stock (of one's situation).
(**e**) — **de pagos** *etc see* **balanza** (**c**).
(**f**) (*Col*) affair, matter; deal.

balanceado *nm* (*Boxing*) swing.

balancear [1a] **1** *vt* to balance. **2** *vi and* **balancearse** *vr* (**a**) to move to and fro, oscillate; to rock, swing; (*Naut*) to roll. (**b**) (*fig*) to hesitate, vacillate, waver.

balanceo *nm* = **balance** (**a**) *and* (**b**).

balancín *nm* balance beam; (*Mech*) rocker, rocker arm; (*of cart, coach*) swingletree; (*Naut*) outrigger; (*of tightrope walker*) balancing pole; (*for carrying loads*) yoke; seesaw; child's rocking toy.

balandra *nf* sloop.

balandrán *nm* cassock.

balandrista *nm* yachtsman; sailing enthusiast.

balandro *nm* yacht; sloop; model yacht.

balanza *nf* (**a**) balance (*esp Chem*), scales, weighing machine; (*Astron*) **B**— Scales; — **de cocina** kitchen scales; — **de cruz** grocer's scales; — **de laboratorio**, — **de precisión** precision balance; — **romana** steelyard; **estar en la** — to be in the balance.
(**b**) (*fig*) judgement; comparison.
(**c**) (*Comm, Pol etc*) balance; — **comercial**, — **de comercio** balance of trade; — **de pagos** balance of payments; — **de poder(es)**, — **política** balance of power.

balaquear [1a] *vi* (*Arg, Bol, Urug*) to boast.

balar [1a] *vi* to bleat, baa.

balastar [1a] *vt* (*Rail*) to ballast.

balasto *nm*, **balastro** *nm* (*Arg, Mex*) ballast.

balaustrada *nf* balustrade; bannisters.

balaustre *nm* baluster; banister.

balay *nm* (*SAm*) wicker basket.

balazo *nm* shot; bullet wound; **matar a uno de un** — to shoot someone dead.

balboa *nf standard monetary unit of Panama*.

balbucear [1a] *vti*, **balbucir** [3f; *defective*; *only forms used are those having* i *in the ending*] *vti* to stammer, stutter; (*of baby*) to lisp, make its first sounds; to babble.

balbuceo *nm* stammering, stuttering; babbling.

balbuciente *adj* stammering, stuttering; babbling.

Balcanes *mpl* Balkans.

balcánico *adj* Balkan.

balcarrias *nfpl*, **balcarrotas** *nfpl* (*Col, Ec*) sideburns; (*Mex*) shaggy locks of hair.

balcón *nm* balcony; railing; (*fig*) vantage point.

balconeador *nm* onlooker, observer.

balconear [1a] **1** *vt* (*Arg*) to watch closely (from a balcony); *game etc* to watch. **2** *vi* (*Guat: of lovers*) to talk at the window.

balconero *nm* cat burglar.

baldada *nf* (*Arg*) bucketful.

baldado 1 *adj* crippled, disabled. **2** *nm*, **baldada** *nf* cripple, disabled person.

baldaquín *nm* canopy, tester.

baldar [1a] *vt* (**a**) to cripple, maim, disable. (**b**) (*fig*) to put out, inconvenience; (*Cards*) to trump.

balde¹ *nm* bucket, pail.

balde² *nm* (**a**) **obtener algo de** — to get something free, get something for nothing; **vender algo medio de** — to sell something for a song; **había muchos de** — there were a lot left over; **estar de** — (*person*) to be de trop, be unwanted, be in the way; (*Arg, Col, Par*) to be idle, be out of work.
(**b**) **¡no de** —**!** (*CAm*) goodness!, I never noticed!
(**c**) **en** — in vain, to no purpose.

baldear [1a] *vt* (**a**) to wash, wash down, swill with water. (**b**) (*Naut*) to bale out.

baldío 1 *adj* land uncultivated; waste. (**b**) lazy, idle. (**c**) vain, useless. **2** *nm* uncultivated land; waste land; uncultivated common land.

baldón *nm* affront, insult; blot, stain, disgrace.

baldonar [1a] *vt* to insult; to blot, disgrace.

baldosa *nf* floor tile; paving stone; (*SAm*) tombstone.

baldosado *nm* tiled floor, tiling; paving (of flagstones).

baldosar [1a] *vt floor* to tile; *path etc* to pave (with flagstones).

balduque *nm* (official) red tape.

baleado *nm* (*CAm, Mex*): **el** — the person shot.

balear¹ [1a] **1** *vt* (*CAm, Mex*) (**a**) to shoot (at). (**b**) to cheat, swindle. **2** **balearse** *vr* (*CAm, Mex*) to exchange shots, shoot at each other.

balear² **1** *adj* Balearic, of the Balearic Isles. **2** *nmf* native (*or* inhabitant) of the Balearic Isles; **los** —**es** the people of the Balearic Isles.

Baleares *fpl*, *also* **Islas Baleares** *fpl* Balearics, Balearic Islands.

baleárico *adj* Balearic, of the Balearic Isles.

baleo *nm* (*CAm, Mex*) shooting.

balero *nm* (*SAm*) cup-and-ball toy; (*Mex*) ball bearing; (*Arg: sl*) head.

balido *nm* bleat, bleating, baa.

balín *nm* small bullet, pellet; —**es** buckshot.

balística *nf* ballistics.

balístico *adj* ballistic.

balita *nf* (**a**) small bullet, pellet. (**b**) (*RPl*) marble.

baliza *nf* (*Naut*) (lighted) buoy, marker; (*Aer*) beacon, marker.

balneario 1 *adj* thermal, medicinal; spa (*attr*), health (*attr*). **2** *nm* spa, health resort.

balompédico *adj* football (*attr*).

balompié *nm* football.

balón *nm* (**a**) (large) ball, football; (*Chem etc*) bag (for gas); (*Meteorol*) balloon; — **neumático** (*Aut*) low-pressure tyre; — **volea** volleyball. (**b**) (*Comm*) (large) bale.

baloncesto *nm* basketball.

balonmanear [1a] *vi* (*Sport*) to handle, handle the ball.

balonmano *nm* handball.

balonvolea *nf* volleyball.

balota *nf* ballot.

balotaje *nm* (*Mex*) balloting, voting; counting of votes.

balotar [1a] *vi* to ballot, vote.

balsa¹ *nf* (**a**) (*Bot*) balsa; balsa wood. (**b**) (*Naut*) raft; ferry; — **salvavidas** life-saving raft; — **neumática** (*Aer etc*) rubber dinghy, rubber float.

balsa² *nf* pool, pond; (*Mex*) overgrown marshy place; **el pueblo es una** — **de aceite** the village is as quiet as the grave.

balsadera *nf*, **balsadero** *nm* ferry.

balsámico *adj* balsamic, balmy; (*fig*) balmy, soothing, healing.

bálsamo *nm* balsam, balm; (*fig*) balm, comfort.

balsar *nm* (*Col, Ven*) overgrown marshy place.

balsear [1a] *vt* (**a**) *river* to cross by ferry, cross on a raft. (**b**) *persons, goods* to ferry across.

balsero *nm* ferryman.

balsón¹ *nm* (*Mex*) swamp, bog.

balsón² *adj* (*Ec*) fat, flabby.

balsoso *adj* (*Ec*) soft, spongy.

Baltasar *m* Balthasar; (*Bib*) Belshazzar; *see* **cena**.

Báltico: Mar *m* — Baltic Sea.

baluarte *nm* bastion; (*fig*) bastion, bulwark.

balumba *nf* (**a**) (great) bulk, mass. (**b**) pile, heap. (**c**) (*SAm*) noise, uproar.

balumbo *nm* bulky thing, cumbersome object.

balumoso *adj* (*CAm, Ec, Mex*) bulky, cumbersome.

ballena *nf* (**a**) (*Zool*) whale; **parece una** — (*fam*) she's as fat as a cow (*fam*). (**b**) whalebone; (*of corset*) bone, stay.

ballenera *nf* whaler, whaling ship.

ballenero 1 *adj* whaling (*attr*); **industria ballenera** whaling industry. **2** *nm* (**a**) (*person*) whaler. (**b**) whaler, whaling ship.

ballesta *nf* (**a**) (*Hist*) crossbow. (**b**) (*Aut, Rail etc*) spring; —**s** springs, suspension.

ballestero *nm* (*Hist*) crossbowman.

ballestrinque *nm* clove hitch.
ballet [ba'le] *nm*, *pl* **ballets** [ba'le] ballet.
bamba[1] *nf* (*CAm*, *Ven*) one-peso silver coin.
bamba[2] *nmf* (*SD*) negro, negress.
bamba[3] *nf* (a) (*Col*, *Ec*) bole, swelling (on tree trunk). (b) (*Ec*) fat, flabbiness.
bambalear [1a] = **bambolear**.
bambalinas *nfpl* (*Theat*) flies.
bambalúa *nm* (*SAm*) clumsy fellow, lout.
bambarria *nmf* (*fam*) idiot, fool.
bambolear [1a] *vi and* **bambolearse** *vr* to swing, sway; (*in walking*) to sway, roll, reel; (*of furniture*) to wobble, be unsteady; (*of train etc*) to sway.
bamboleo *nm* swinging, swaying; rolling, reeling; wobbling, unsteadiness.
bambolla *nf* (*fam*) show, ostentation; sham.
bambollero *adj* (*fam*) showy, flashy; sham, bogus.
bambú *nm* bamboo.
bambudal *nm* (*Ec*) bamboo grove.
bamburrete *nm* (*Ven*) fool.
banal *adj* banal; trivial, ordinary; *person* ordinary, commonplace; superficial.
banalidad *nf* (a) banality; triviality, ordinariness; superficiality.
(b) banality, trivial thing; **intercambiar —es con uno** to exchange trivialities with someone, swap small talk with someone.
banana *nf* (*esp SAm*) banana; banana tree.
bananal *nm* (*SAm*) banana plantation.
bananero 1 *adj* (*SAm*) banana (*attr*); **compañía bananera** banana company; **plantación bananera** banana plantation. **2** *nm* banana tree.
banano *nm* (*SAm*) banana; banana tree.
banasta *nf* large basket, hamper.
banasto *nm* large round basket.
banca *nf* (a) bench; stand, stall.
(b) (*Comm*, *Fin*) banking; **horas de —** banking hours.
(c) (*in games*) bank; **hacer saltar la —** to break the bank; **tener la —** to be banker, hold the bank.
(d) (*RPl*) pull, influence; **tener (gran) —** to have pull.
bancada *nf* stone bench; (*Mech*) bench, bed, bed-plate; (*Naut*) thwart, seat.
bancal *nm* (*Agr*) patch, plot, bed; terrace.
bancario *adj* bank (*attr*), banking (*attr*); financial.
bancarrota *nf* (*esp* fraudulent) bankruptcy; failure; **declararse en —**, **hacer —** to go bankrupt.
banco *nm* (a) bench, seat; (*in school*) form; (*Naut*) thwart, seat; (*Tech*) bench.
(b) (*Geog*: *Naut*) bank, shoal; (*Ec*) deposit of alluvial soil; (*Ven*) raised ground; (*Geol*) stratum, layer; **— de arena** sandbank; **— de hielo** iceberg; **— de nieve** snowdrift.
(c) (*Fish*) shoal, school.
(d) (*Comm*, *Fin*) bank; **— de ahorros** savings bank; **— de crédito** credit bank; **— fideicomisario** trust company; **— de liquidación** clearing house; **— de sangre** blood bank; **B— Mundial** World Bank.
banda *nf* (a) band, strip; ribbon; (*item of dress*) sash, band; (*Billiards*) cushion; (*of land*) strip, ribbon; zone; (*of running track*) lane; (*Radio*) band; **— de dibujos** comic strip; **— magnética** magnetic tape; **— de rodamiento** (*Aut*) tread; **— de sonido, — sonora** (*Cine*) sound track.
(b) (*of sea etc*) side, edge; (*of ship*) side; **la B— Oriental** Uruguay; **de la — de acá** on this side; **cerrarse a la —** to stand firm, be adamant; to refuse to say anything; **dar un barco a la —** to careen a ship; **irse a la —** (*Naut*) to list.
(c) (*persons*) band; gang; troop; party; (*Orn*) flock; covey.
(d) (*Mus*) band, (*esp*) brass band.
bandada *nf* (a) (*of birds*) flock; flight, covey; (*of fish*) shoal. (b) (*SAm*) = **banda** (c).
bandear [1a] **1** *vt* (a) (*CAm*) to pursue, chase; (*Guat*) to court.
(b) (*CAm*) to wound severely; (*Urug*) to hurt (with a remark).
(c) (*RPl*) to cross, go right across.
2 bandearse *vr* (a) to move to and fro; (*Mex*) to move to the other side of a boat.
(b) (*Arg: Pol*) to change parties, join the bandwagon.
(c) (*Mex*) to vacillate, go one way and then another.
(d) to shift for oneself, manage.
bandeja *nf* tray, salver; (*SAm*) large serving dish, bowl; **— del cárter** (*Aut*) sump; **servir algo a uno en — (de plata)** (*fig*) to hand something to someone on a plate; **te lo han servido en —** they've made it very easy for you.

bandera *nf* (a) flag; banner, standard; (*Mil*) colours; **— de conveniencia** flag of convenience; **— de esquina** corner flag; **— de parlamento** flag of truce, white flag; **— de popa** ensign; **— de proa** jack; **— roja** red flag; **arriar la —** (*Naut*) to strike one's colours; **dar algo a uno** to give someone pride of place; **hacer algo a —s desplegadas** to do something openly; **venir a —s desplegadas** to come out with flying colours.
(b) **de —** (*fam*) terrific (*fam*), marvellous.
bandería *nf* faction.
banderilla *nf* (a) (*Taur*) banderilla (*barbed dart with banderole*); **— de fuego** banderilla with attached firecracker; **poner una — a uno, poner —s a uno** to taunt someone, provoke someone, make someone cross.
(b) (*SAm*) swindle.
banderillear [1a] *vt* (*Taur*) to thrust the banderillas into (the neck of).
banderillero *nm* (*Taur*) banderillero, bullfighter who uses the banderillas.
bandería *nm* little flag, pennant; (*Rail*) signal flag; (*Mil*) recruiting post.
banderita *nf* little flag; flag sold for charity; **día de la —** flag day.
banderola *nf* (a) banderole; signalling flag; (*Mil*) pennant, pennon; **— de esquina** corner flag. (b) female bandit, moll (*sl*). (c) (*RPl*) transom.
bandidaje *nm* banditry.
bandido *nm* (a) bandit; outlaw; desperado. (b) (*fam*) rogue, rascal; ¡—! you rogue!, you beast!
banditismo *nm* banditry.
bando *nm* (a) edict, proclamation; **—s** (*Eccl*) banns.
(b) faction, party; side; (*at games*) side; **pasar al otro —** to change sides.
bandola *nf* (*Mus*) mandolin; (*Per*) bullfighter's cape; (*Ven*) knotted whip.
bandolera *nf* bandoleer.
bandolerismo *nm* brigandage, banditry.
bandolero *nm* brigand, bandit; (*Hist*) highwayman.
bandolina *nf* (*CAm*, *Chi*, *Mex*, *Per*) mandolin.
bandoneón *nm* (*SAm*) large accordion.
bandullo *nm* (*fam*) belly, guts; **llenarse el —** to stuff oneself.
bandurria *nf* bandurria (*Spanish instrument of the lute type*).
bangaña *nf*, **bangaño** *nm* (*SAm*) calabash, gourd; vessel made from a gourd.
banjo *nm* banjo.
banquear [1a] *vt* (*Col*) to level, flatten out.
banqueo *nm* terraces, terracing.
banqueta *nf* (a) stool; low bench; **— de piano** piano stool. (b) (*CAm*, *Mex*) pavement, sidewalk (*US*). (c) (*PR*, *SD*) crowbar.
banquetazo *nm* (*fam*) spread (*fam*), blow-out (*sl*).
banquete *nm* banquet, feast; formal dinner; dinner party; **— anual** annual dinner; **— de boda** wedding breakfast; **— de gala** state banquet.
banquetear [1a] *vti* to banquet, feast.
banquillo *nm* bench; footstool; (*Law*) prisoner's seat, (*approx*) dock.
banquisa *nf* ice field, ice floe.
Bantam *nf* (a) **gallina de —** bantam; **b— (SAm)** bantam. (b) (*SAm*) **b—** (*fig*) small restless person.
banyo *nm* (*SAm*) banjo.
bañada *nf* (*SAm*) bath, dip, swim; coat (of paint).
bañadera *nf* (*Arg*) bathtub; (*hum*) open bus.
bañado *nm* (*Bol*, *RPl*) swamp, marshland; flash, temporary pool.
bañador 1 *nm* (a) (*Tech*) tub, trough. (b) bathing costume, swimsuit. **2** *nm*, **bañadora** *nf* bather, swimmer.
bañar [1a] **1** *vt* (a) to bathe, immerse, dip; (*in bath*) to bath, bathe (*US*); (*Med*) to bathe (**con, de in, with**); (*Tech*) to dip; to coat; cover (**de with**).
(b) (*of sea*) to bathe, wash.
(c) (*of light etc*) to bathe, suffuse, flood (**de with**).
(d) (*fig*) to bathe (**con, de, en in**); see **agua**.
2 bañarse *vr* (a) (*in bath*) to bath, bath oneself, take a bath, bathe (*US*); (*in sea*) to bathe, swim; **ir a —** to go for a bathe, have a bathe, go bathing, go swimming (*US*); **"prohibido —"** "no bathing", "no swimming" (*US*).
(b) (*of fish*) to leap, jump.
bañera *nf* bath, bathtub.
bañista *nmf* (a) bather. (b) person taking the waters at a spa, patient at a spa.
baño *nm* (a) (*act*) bath; (*in general*) bathing; **tomar un —** to bath, bathe (*US*), take a bath.
(b) (*vessel etc*) bath, bathtub; (*Tech*) bath; (*SD*) cool place; (*Col*: *euph*) toilet; **— de asiento** hip bath; **— de ducha** shower bath; **—s de mar** sea

bathing; — **ruso** (*Chi, RPl*) steam bath; — **de sangre** (*fig*) blood bath; — **de sol** sun bath; — **turco** Turkish bath; — **de vapor** steam bath; **dar un — a uno** (*fig*) to teach someone a lesson.

(c) —s (*Med*) baths; spa; **ir a —s** to take the waters.

(d) (*Art*) wash; (*Cook*) coating, covering.

bao nm (*Naut*) beam.

baptista nmf Baptist; **la Iglesia Baptista** the Baptist church.

baque nm bump, bang, thud.

baqueano nm etc see **baquiano**.

baquelita nf bakelite.

baqueta nf (a) (*Mil*) ramrod.

(b) (*Mus*) drumstick.

(c) **correr —s, pasar por —s** to run the gauntlet; **mandar a** — to rule tyrannically; **tratar a uno a (la)** — to treat someone harshly.

baqueteado adj experienced; **estar** — to be inured to it, be used to it; **ser un** — to know one's way around.

baquetear [1a] vt to annoy, bother.

baqueteo nm: **es un** — it's an imposition, it's an awful bind (*sl*).

baquetudo adj (*Cu*) sluggish, slow.

baquía nf (a) (*SAm*) intimate knowledge of a region, local expertise. (b) (*Arg, Col*) expertise, dexterity, skill.

baquiano 1 adj (a) (*SAm*) familiar with a region.

(b) (*Arg, Col*) expert, skilful; **para hacerse** — **hay que perderse alguna vez** (*Arg, Urug*) one learns the hard way.

2 nm (a) (*SAm*) pathfinder, guide; local expert, person with an intimate knowledge of a region; (*Naut*) pilot.

(b) (*Arg, Col*) expert.

báquico adj Bacchic; bacchanalian.

bar nm bar; snack bar.

barahúnda nf uproar, hubbub; racket, din.

baraja nf (a) pack of cards; (*Mex*) cards; **jugar a (or con) dos —s** to play a double game. (b) (*fig*) confusion, mix-up.

barajadura nf shuffle, shuffling.

barajar [1a] 1 vt (a) *cards* to shuffle.

(b) (*fig*) to jumble up, mix up, shuffle round; (*Urug*) to pass round, hand round; (*Chi, Mex*) *affair* to entangle, confuse, delay.

(c) (*RPl*) to catch (in the air); — **algo en el aire** (*fig*) to see the point of something, perceive the hidden intention with which something is said.

2 vi to quarrel, squabble.

3 **barajarse** vr (a) (*Par*) to fight, brawl.

(b) to get jumbled up, get mixed up.

barajo interj (*SAm: euph*) = **carajo**.

barajuste nm (*Ven*) stampede, rush.

baranda nf rail, railing; (*Billiards*) cushion.

barandal nm, **barandilla** nf rail, railing, handrail; bannisters; balustrade; (*Col*) altar rail; (*Mex*) plank bridge.

barata[1] nf (a) (*Col, Mex*) sale, bargain sale.

(b) (*Col, Mex*) bargain counter; cut-price store.

(c) (*Ec*): **a la** — in confusion, in disorder; **tratar a uno a la** — to treat someone with scorn.

barata[2] nf (*Chi*) cockroach.

baratear [1a] vt to sell cheaply; to sell at a loss.

baratero 1 adj (a) cheap; who sells cheap; **tienda baratera** shop offering bargains, cut-price store.

(b) (*Chi*) haggling.

2 nm (a) person who extracts money from winning gamblers.

(b) (*SAm*) shopkeeper offering bargains, cut-price merchant.

(c) (*Chi*) haggler.

baratez nf (*Cu*), **baratía** nf (*Col*) cheapness.

baratija nf trinket; (*Comm*) cheap novelty; (*fig*) trifle; —s (*Comm*) cheap goods, inexpensive articles; —s (*pej*) trash, junk.

baratillero nm seller of cheap goods.

baratillo nm (a) secondhand goods; cheap goods.

(b) secondhand shop, junkshop; bargain counter.

(c) bargain sale; **cosa de** — (*fig*) tawdry thing, gimcrack article.

barato 1 adj cheap; inexpensive, economical; **obtener algo de** — to get something free; **dar algo de** — (*fig*) to concede something, grant something (for the sake of argument); **echar a —, meter a —** to heckle, barrack, interrupt noisily.

2 adv cheap, cheaply; inexpensively.

3 nm (a) bargain sale.

(b) money extracted from winning gamblers; **cobrar el** — (*fig*) to be a bully, wield power by intimidation.

baratón 1 adj (*Col, Guat, Mex*) *argument* weak, feeble; *remark* well-worn, commonplace. 2 nm (*CAm*) long-handled spade.

baratura nf cheapness; inexpensiveness.

baraúnda nf = **barahúnda**.

barba 1 nf (a) chin.

(b) beard, whiskers (*also* —s); — **cerrada, — bien poblada** thick beard, big beard; —s **de chivo** goatee; — **honrada** distinguished personage; **a — regalada** abundantly, fully; **robar algo en las —s de uno** to steal something from under someone's nose; **2 naranjas por** — 2 oranges apiece, 2 oranges per head; **¡por las —s de Mahoma!** well I'm damned!; **colgar —s al santo** to give someone his due; **hacer la** — to shave, have a shave; **hacer la — a uno** to shave someone; (*fig*) to pester someone, annoy someone; (*fig*) to fawn on someone, flatter someone; **llevar** — to have a beard; **llevar a uno por la** — to lead someone by the nose; **mentir por la** — to tell a barefaced lie; **subirse a las —s de uno** to be disrespectful to someone; **tener pocas —s** to be young, be inexperienced; **tirarse de las —s** to rage, tear one's hair.

(c) (*Orn*) wattle.

(d) (*Bot*) beard.

2 nm (*Theat*) old man's part; performer of old men's parts; (*in melodrama*) villain.

Barba Azul m Bluebeard.

barbacana nf barbican.

barbacoa nf (a) (*SAm*) barbecue; (*Ant, CAm, Mex, Ven*) barbecued meat, meat.

(b) (*SAm*) bed made with a hurdle supported on sticks.

(c) (*Col*) rack for kitchen utensils.

(d) (*Per*) loft.

(e) (*Bol*) tap dance.

Barbada f: **la —, las —s** Barbados.

barbado 1 adj bearded, with a beard. 2 nm (a) man with a beard; full-grown man. (b) (*Bot*) seedling; **plantar de** — to transplant, plant out.

Barbados m Barbados.

barbar [1a] vi (a) to grow a beard. (b) (*Bot*) to strike root.

Bárbara f Barbara.

bárbaramente adv (a) barbarously; cruelly, savagely.

(b) (*fam*) tremendously (*fam*).

barbáricamente adv barbarically.

barbárico adj barbaric.

barbaridad nf (a) barbarity; barbarism; (*fig*) atrocity, outrage, barbarous act; **es capaz de hacer cualquier** — he's capable of committing some terrible thing.

(b) (*fig, fam*) **¡qué —!** how awful! (*fam*), shocking!

(c) —es (*fam*) awful things (*fam*), terrible things, naughty things; nonsense; **decir —es** to say awful things; to talk nonsense.

(d) **una** — (*fam*) a huge amount (*de* of); **había una — de gente** there were lots of people; **comimos una** — we ate an awful lot (*fam*); **cuesta una** — it costs a fortune; **sabe una — de cosas** he knows a tremendous amount.

(e) **una** — (*fam: as adv*) a lot, lots; **nos gustó una** — we liked it a lot; **me quiere una** — he's terribly fond of me, he likes me awfully (*fam*); **nos divertimos una** — we had a tremendous time, we had a lot of fun; **habló una** — he talked his head off; **se nota una** — it sticks out a mile.

barbarie nf (a) barbarism, barbarousness. (b) barbarity, cruelty, savagery.

barbarismo nm (a) (*Gram*) barbarism. (b) = **barbarie**.

bárbaro 1 adj (a) (*Hist*) barbarian, barbarous.

(b) (*fig*) barbarous, cruel, savage; rough, uncouth; bold, daring.

(c) (*fam*) tremendous (*fam*), terrific (*fam*), smashing (*sl*); **¡qué —!** how marvellous!, terrific!; **un éxito** — a tremendous success; **es un tío** — he's a splendid chap; **hace un frío** — it's terribly cold.

2 adv (*fam*) marvellously; terrifically (*fam*); **lo pasamos** — we had a tremendous time; **ella canta** — she sings marvellously.

3 nm, **bárbara** nf (a) barbarian.

(b) rough sort, uncouth person; **come como un** — he eats enormously; **gritó como un** — he gave a tremendous shout, he shouted like mad.

barbarote nm (*fam*) brute, savage.

barbear [1a] 1 vt (*SAm*) (a) to shave.

(b) (*Guat, Mex*) to fawn on, flatter.

(c) (*Guat, Mex*) to annoy, bore.

(d) (*Col, Cu, Guat, Mex, Ven*) *cattle* to throw, fell (by twisting the head of).

(e) to reach with one's chin, come up to, be as tall as.
2 vi: — **con** = vt (e).
barbechar [1a] vt (a) to leave fallow. (b) to plough for sowing.
barbechera nf fallow, fallow land.
barbecho nm (a) fallow, fallow land; **estar en** — (Arg: fig) to be in preparation, be on its way; **firmar como en un** — to sign a blank cheque. (b) ploughed land ready for sowing. (c) first ploughing.
barbería nf (a) barber's (shop). (b) hairdressing.
barbero nm (a) barber, hairdresser. (b) (Guat, Mex) flatterer.
barbeta nmf (Chi) fool.
barbetear [1a] vt (Mex) cattle to throw, fell (by twisting the head of), throw to the ground.
barbicano adj grey-bearded, white-bearded.
barbihecho adj freshly shaven.
barbijo nm (a) (Bol, RPl) chinstrap; (Arg, Per, PR) headscarf (knotted under the chin). (b) (Arg, Bol) scar.
barbilampiño 1 adj (a) smooth-faced, beardless. (b) (fig) inexperienced. **2** nm (fig) novice, greenhorn.
barbilindo adj dapper, spruce; (pej) dandified, foppish.
barbilla nf (tip of the) chin.
barbillear [1a] vt (fam) to chuck under the chin.
barbiponiente adj (a) beginning to grow a beard, with a youthful beard. (b) (fig) raw, inexperienced, green.
barbiquejo nm (a) = **barbijo** (a). (b) (Cu, Ec) hatter. (c) (Cu, PR) horse's bit.
barbiturato nm barbiturate.
barbo nm barbel; — **de mar** red mullet.
barbón nm (a) bearded man, man with a (big) beard; (fig) greybeard, old hand. (b) (Zool) billy goat.
barbot(e)ar [1a] vti to mutter, mumble.
barboteo nm mutter, muttering, mumbling.
barbudo adj bearded; having a big beard, long-bearded.
barbulla nf clamour, hullabaloo (fam).
barbullar [1a] vi to jabber away, talk noisily.
barca nf boat, small boat; — **de pasaje** ferry; — **de pesca**, — **pesquera** fishing boat; **como** — **sin remos** irresolute(ly), lacking a firm purpose.
barcada nf (a) boatload. (b) boat trip; crossing (by ferry).
barcarola nf barcarole.
barcaza nf barge, lighter; punt; ferry; — **de desembarco** (Mil) landing craft.
barcelonés 1 adj of Barcelona. **2** nm, **barcelonesa** nf native (or inhabitant) of Barcelona; **los** —**es** the people of Barcelona.
barcia nf chaff.
barco nm boat; ship, vessel; — **almirante** flagship; — **cablero** cable ship; — **carbonero**, — **minero** collier; — **de carga** cargo boat; — **de guerra** warship; — **meteorológico** weather ship; — **náufrago** wreck; — **patrullero** patrol boat; — **de vela** sailing ship; — **vivienda** houseboat; **abandonar el** — to abandon ship; **ir en** — to go by boat, go by ship; **como** — **sin timón** irresolute(ly), lacking a firm purpose.
barchilón nm, **barchilona** nf (Ec, Per) nurse, hospital aide; (Arg, Bol, Per) quack doctor, quack surgeon.
barda nf thatch (on a wall); —**s** top of a wall, walls.
bardal nm thatched wall.
bardana nf burdock.
bardar [1a] vt to thatch.
bardino adj reddish-grey.
bardo nm bard.
barillero nm (Mex) hawker, street vendor.
bario nm barium.
barítono nm baritone.
barjuleta nf knapsack; toolbag.
barloventear [1a] vi (a) (Naut) to tack; to beat to windward. (b) (fig) to wander about.
Barlovento: Islas fpl **de** — Windward Isles.
barlovento nm windward; **a** — to windward; **de** — windward (attr); **ganar el** —**a** to get to windward of.
barman nm, pl **barmans, bármanes, barmen** (angl) barman, bartender.
barniz nm (a) varnish; (Aer) dope; (on pottery) glaze; gloss, polish; — **para las uñas** nail varnish, nail polish; **dar de** — **a** to varnish. (b) (fig) gloss, veneer; smattering, superficial knowledge.
barnizado nm varnish, varnishing.
barnizar [1f] vt to varnish; to glaze; to polish, put a gloss on.

barométrico adj barometric.
barómetro nm barometer; — **aneroide** aneroid barometer.
barón nm baron.
baronesa nf baroness.
baronet nm baronet.
baronía nf barony.
baronial adj baronial.
barquero nm boatman; ferryman, waterman.
barquía nf skiff, rowing boat.
barquilla nf (a) (Aer: of balloon) basket; (of airship) gondola, nacelle, car. (b) (Naut) log. (c) (Ant) ice-cream cornet, cone.
barquillo nm horn, rolled wafer; ice-cream cornet, cone.
barquinazo nm tumble, hard fall; spill; (Aut etc) bump, jolt; (Col) sudden start.
barra[1] nf (a) (in general) bar; rail, railing; (Mech) rod; lever; (of bread) large roll, small loaf; (of soap) bar, stick; (of metal) bar, ingot; (**la bandera de) las** —**s y estrellas** the Stars and Stripes; — **de carmín**, — **de labios** lipstick; — **de cortina** curtain rod; — **espaciadora** spacing bar; —**s paralelas** parallel bars; **a** —**s derechas** honestly; **no pararse en** —**s** to stick at nothing. (b) (Her) stripe, bar. (c) (Naut) bar, sandbank. (d) (Law) bar, rail; (approx) dock; **llevar a uno a la** — to bring someone to justice. (e) (SAm: Law, Parl etc) public, members of the public; (Chi) spectators, audience; **había mucha** — there was a big audience. (f) (Arg) band, gang. (g) (Mex, RPl, Ven) river mouth, estuary.
barra[2] nf (Mex: Law) the Bar, the legal profession.
Barrabás m Barrabas; **ser un** — to be wicked, (child) be mischievous, be naughty.
barrabasada nf mischief; inconsiderate action; thoughtless thing.
barraca[1] nf (a) hut, cabin; workmen's hut; (Valencia) thatched farmhouse. (b) (at fair) booth, stall; — **de tiro al blanco** shooting gallery. (c) (SAm) large storage shed; (Ec) market stall. (d) **creerse algo a la** — to believe something implicitly.
barraca[2] nf (SAm: Mil) barracks.
barracón nm (a) big hut; (Cu) farmworkers' living quarters. (b) (at fair) large booth, stall; side show; — **de espejos**, — **de la risa** hall of mirrors.
barragana nf official mistress, concubine.
barranca nf gully, ravine.
barrancal nm place full of ravines.
barranco nm (a) gully, ravine. (b) (SAm) cliff; steep riverbank. (c) (fig) difficulty, obstacle.
barrar[1] [1a] vt to daub, smear (de with).
barrar[2] [1a], **barrear** [1a] vt to barricade; to bar, fasten with a bar.
barreal nm (Arg) heavy clay land; (CAm) mudhole, miry place.
barrecalles nm, pl **barrecalles** street-sweeping machine.
barredera nf street sweeper; — **de alfombras** carpet sweeper.
barredura nf (a) sweep, sweeping. (b) —**s** sweepings; rubbish, refuse.
barreminas nm, pl **barreminas** minesweeper.
barrena nf (a) drill, augur; bit; rock drill, mining drill; — **de mano**, — **pequeña** gimlet. (b) (Aer) spin; **entrar en** — to go into a spin.
barrenado adj (fam): **estar** — to be dotty (fam).
barrenar [1a] vt (a) to drill, drill through, bore; rock to blast; ship to scuttle. (b) (fig) to foil, frustrate; (fam) to make a mess of; (Law) to violate, infringe.
barrendero nm, **barrendera** nf sweeper.
barrenillo nm (a) (Zool) borer. (b) (Cu) foolish persistence; (Mex) constant worry; mania, pet idea.
barreno nm (a) (Tech) large drill, borer. (b) bore, borehole; (Min) blasthole; **dar** — **a un barco, poner un** — **a un barco** to scuttle a ship. (c) (fig) vanity, pride. (d) (Chi, Mex) constant worry; mania, pet idea.
barreño nm washing-up bowl, large pan.
barrer [1a] **1** vt (a) to sweep; to sweep clean, sweep out, sweep away. (b) (Mil, Naut) to sweep, rake (with gunfire). (c) (fig) to sweep aside, sweep away; (Col) to beat, overwhelm; **los candidatos del partido barrieron a sus adversarios** the party's candidates swept aside their rivals.

2 *vi* (a) (*RPl*) **comprar algo al —** to buy something all together, buy something without choosing properly.
(**b**) (*fam*) **— hacia dentro** to look after number one.
3 barrerse *vr* (*Mex: of horse*) to shy, start.
barrera[1] *nf* (a) barrier; rail, bar; (*Mil etc*) barricade; (*Rail*) crossing gate; (*Taur*) barrier, fence round the inside of the bullring; first row of seats; **— de contención** containing wall; **— de color** colour bar; **— coralina** coral reef; **— de portazgo** tollgate, turnpike; **— racial** racial bar, colour bar; **— del sonido** sound barrier.
(**b**) (*Mil: also* **— de fuego**) barrage; **— de fuego móvil** creeping barrage.
(**c**) (*fig*) barrier, bar; obstacle; hindrance.
barrera[2] *nf* claypit.
barrero 1 *adj* (*RPl*) *horse* that likes heavy going. **2** *nm* muddy ground; (*Bol, RPl*) salt marsh.
barretina *nf* Catalan cap.
barriada *nf* quarter, district; (*SAm esp*) slum quarter.
barrial *nm* (*Mex*) heavy clay land; (*SAm*) mudhole, miry place.
barrica *nf* large barrel.
barricada *nf* barricade.
barrida *nf* (*SAm*) sweep, sweeping; sweep, raid (by the police).
barrido *nm* sweep, sweeping; **vale tanto para un — como para un fregado** he can turn his hand to anything.
barriga *nf* (a) belly; paunch, guts; **hacer una — a una** (*fam*) to get a girl in the family way; **llenarse la —** to stuff oneself.
(**b**) (*of vessel*) belly, rounded part; (*in wall*) bulge.
barrigón 1 *adj* fat, potbellied. **2** *nm*, **barrigona** *nf* (*Ant, Col*) child.
barrigudo *adj* fat, potbellied.
barriguera *nf* (*horse's*) girth.
barril *nm* (a) barrel; cask, keg; **cerveza de —** draught beer, beer on draught; **comer del —** (*Col*) to eat poor-quality food.
(**b**) (*SAm*) hexagonal kite.
barrilería *nf* cooperage.
barrilero *nm* cooper.
barrilete 1 *nm* (a) keg, cask.
(**b**) (*Tech*) dog, clamp.
(**c**) (*of revolver*) chamber.
(**d**) (*Mex: Law*) junior barrister.
2 *nf* (*Arg*) restless woman.
barrio *nm* quarter, district, area (of a town); suburb; **el otro —** (*fam*) the other world; **mandar a uno al otro —** (*sl*) to do someone in (*sl*); **— bajos** poorer quarter, working-class district, (*pej*) slums, slum area; **— comercial** business quarter; shopping district; **— exterior** outer suburb; **— latino** Latin quarter; **— de tolerancia** (*Col*) red-light district.
**barrisco: a — ** *adv* jumbled together, in confusion; indiscriminately.
barritar [1a] *vi* (*elephant*) to trumpet.
barrizal *nm* muddy place, mire.
barro *nm* (a) mud.
(**b**) clay, potter's clay; **vasija de —** earthen vessel, earthenware vessel.
(**c**) earthenware pot; mug (for beer *etc*); **—s** earthenware, crockery.
(**d**) (*sl*) dough (*sl*), brass (*sl*); **tener — a mano** to be in the money.
(**e**) (*RPl*) bloomer (*fam*), clanger (*sl*); **hacer un —** to drop a clanger.
(**f**) (*Anat*) pimple.
barroco 1 *adj* (*Art etc*) baroque; (*Lit*) mannered, full of conceits, complicated; (*pej*) extravagant, excessively ornate, in bad taste.
2 *nm* baroque (style); baroque period.
barroquismo *nm* baroque (style); baroque taste; (*pej*) extravagance, excessive ornateness, bad taste.
barroso *adj* (a) muddy. (**b**) mud-coloured; *cow* reddish, brownish, (*Guat*) off-white. (**c**) (*Anat*) pimply.
barrote *nm* heavy bar, thick bar; crosspiece; rung.
barruntar [1a] *vt* to guess, conjecture; to suspect.
barrunte *nm* sign, indication.
barrunto *nm* (a) guess, conjecture; sign, indication; suspicion; foreboding. (**b**) (*Mex, PR*) north wind which brings rain.
barsa *adj and nmf* = **barcelonés**.
bartola *nf*: **echarse** (*or* **tenderse, tumbarse**) **a la —** to be lazy, take it easy; to do nothing.
bartolear [1a] *vi* (*Chi*) to be lazy, take it easy.

bartolina *nf* (*Ant, CAm, Mex*) jail.
Bartolo *m* (*fam*) = **Bartolomé**.
Bartolomé *m* Bartholomew.
bartulear [1a] *vi* (*Chi*) to think hard, rack one's brains.
bártulos *nmpl* things, belongings, gear (*fam*); goods; (*Tech*) tools; **liar los —** to pack up one's belongings; **preparar los —** to get ready (to go).
barullento *adj* (*RPl*) noisy, rowdy.
barullo *nm* (a) row, uproar, din. (**b**) **a —** in abundance, in great quantities.
barzón *nm* saunter, stroll; **dar —es** to stroll around.
barzonear [1a] *vi* to stroll around, wander about.
basa *nf* (a) (*Archit*) base (of a column). (**b**) (*fig*) basis, foundation.
basalta *nf* basalt.
basamento *nm* (*Archit*) base.
basar [1a] **1** *vt* to base; (*fig*) to base, found, ground (*sobre* on). **2 basarse** *vr*: **— en** (a) to be based on, rest on. (**b**) (*fig*) to base oneself on, rely on.
basca *nf* (*freq* **—s**) (a) (*Med*) nausea, queasy feeling, sick feeling; **dar —s a uno** to make someone feel sick, turn someone's stomach; **le entraron —s, tuvo una —** he felt nauseated, he felt sick.
(**b**) (*fig*) fit of rage, tantrum.
bascosidad *nf* (a) filth, dirt. (**b**) (*Ec*) obscenity.
bascoso *adj* (a) squeamish, easily upset; (*Med*) queasy. (**b**) (*Col, Ec*) nauseating, sick-making (*fam*); obscene; *person* vile, disgusting.
báscula *nf* (platform) scales, weighing machine; **— de baño** bathroom scales; **— de puente** weighbridge.
basculable *adj* (*Aut etc*) *light* directional, with swinging beam.
basculante *nm* tip-up lorry, dump truck (*US*).
báscula-puente *nf* weighbridge.
bascular [1a] *vi* to tilt, tip up; to seesaw; to rock to and fro; (*Pol etc*) to swing.
base 1 *nf* (a) (*Archit*) base; (*Tech*) base, mounting, bed; (*Surveying*) base, base line.
(**b**) (*Mil*) base; **— aérea** air base; **— aeronaval** air-sea base; **— avanzada** forward base; **— naval** naval base.
(**c**) (*Baseball*) base.
(**d**) (*fig*) basis, foundation; **a — de** on the basis of; by means of; **a — de no hacer nada** by doing nothing; with the idea of not doing anything; **a — de 50 toneladas al año** on a basis of 50 tons a year, at 50 tons a year; **partir de una — falsa** to start from a false assumption.
2 *adj, attr* basic, base (*attr*); **color —** basic colour; **salario —** basic wage, wage taken as a base.
baseball ['beisβol] *nm* (*SAm: angl*) baseball.
baseballista *nm* (*SAm*) baseball player.
basebolero 1 *adj* (*Ant*) baseball (*attr*). **2** *nm* (*Ant*) baseball player.
básico *adj* basic (*also Chem*).
Basilea Basle, Basel, Bâle.
basílica *nf* (*Hist*) basilica; basilica, large church.
basilisco *nm* (*Myth*) basilisk; (*Mex*) iguana; **estar hecho un —** to be terribly angry; **ponerse como un —** to get terribly angry.
basquear [1a] *vi* to be nauseated, feel sick; **hacer — a uno** to make someone feel sick, turn someone's stomach.
básquetbol *nm* (*SAm: angl*) basketball.
basquetbolero 1 *adj* (*SAm*) basketball (*attr*). **2** *nm*, **basquetbolera** *nf* (*SAm*) basketball player.
basquetbolístico *adj* (*SAm*) basketball (*attr*).
basquiña *nf* skirt.
basta *nf* tacking stitch.
bastante 1 *adj* enough, sufficient (*para* for; *para +* *infin* to + *infin*); (*SAm*) too much, more than enough.
2 *adv* (a) enough, sufficiently; **— grande** big enough, sufficiently large; **es — alto (como) para alcanzarlo** he's tall enough to reach it.
(**b**) (*partly pej*) **— bueno** fairly good, quite good, rather good, goodish.
bastantemente *adv* sufficiently.
bastar [1a] **1** *vti* to be enough, be sufficient, suffice; **¡basta!** that's enough!, that will do!, stop now!; **¡basta ya!** that's quite enough of that!; **basta y sobra** that's more than enough; **eso me basta** that's enough for me; **basta decir que . . .** suffice it to say that . . .; **nos basta saber que . . .** it is enough for us to know that . . .; **— a + *infin*, — para + *infin*** to be enough to + *infin*, be sufficient to + *infin*.
2 bastarse *vr*: **— a sí mismo** to be self-sufficient.
bastardear [1a] **1** *vt* to debase; to adulterate. **2** *vi* (*Bot*) to degenerate; (*fig*) to degenerate, fall away (*de* from).

bastardía *nf* (a) bastardy. (b) (*fig*) meanness, baseness; wicked thing.
bastardilla *nf* (*also* **letra —**) italic type, italics; **en —** in italics; **poner en —** to italicize.
bastardo 1 *adj* (a) bastard. (b) (*fig*) mean, base. (c) (*fig*) *style* hybrid, mixed. **2** *nm*, **bastarda** *nf* bastard.
bastear [1a] *vt* to tack, stitch loosely.
bastidor *nm* (a) (*Tech, Sew etc*) frame, framework; (*of window*) frame, case; (*for canvas*) stretcher; (*of vehicle*) chassis; (*Col, Chi*) lattice window; (*Ant*) metal bedstead.
  (b) (*Theat*) wing; **entre —es** behind the scenes (*also fig*); **estar entre —es** to be offstage; **dirigirlo entre —es** to pull strings, work the oracle.
bastilla *nf* hem.
bastillar [1a] *vt* to hem.
bastimentar [1a] *vt* to supply, provision.
bastimento *nm* (a) supply (of provisions). (b) (*Naut*) vessel.
bastión *nm* bastion.
basto[1] **1** *adj* coarse, rough; rude, uncouth. **2** *nm* packsaddle; (*SAm: also* **—s**) soft leather pad (*used under the saddle*).
basto[2] *nm* (*Cards*) ace of clubs; **—s** clubs.
bastón *nm* stick; staff; walking stick; truncheon; (*Mil etc*) baton; (*Her*) vertical bar, pallet; (*fig*) control, command; **— alpino, — de alpinista, — de montaña** alpenstock; **— de estoque** swordstick; **— de mando** baton, sign of authority; **empuñar el — to take command; meter el —** to intervene.
bastonazo *nm* blow with a stick; beating, caning.
bastonear [1a] *vt* to beat (with a stick), hit (with a stick).
bastonero *nm* (a) master of ceremonies. (b) (*Ven*) scoundrel, tough (*fam*).
bastón-taburete *nm* shooting stick.
basura *nf* (a) rubbish, refuse; litter; dust; (*Agr*) dung, manure.
  (b) (*fig*) trash, rubbish; **la novela es una —** the novel is rubbish; **él es una —** he's a shocker, he's a rotter.
basural *nm* (*SAm*) rubbish dump.
basurear [1a] *vt* (*RPl*) (a) to push someone along. (b) (*fig*) to humiliate someone.
basurero *nm* (a) dustman, garbage man (*US*); scavenger. (b) rubbish dump; (*Agr*) dung heap.
basuriento *adj* (*Arg, Chi, Col*) dirty, full of rubbish.
Basutolandia *f* Basutoland.
bata *nf* dressing gown; housecoat; negligée; smock (*of pregnant woman*); (*Chem, Med, Tech etc*) white coat, laboratory coat.
batacazo *nm* (a) bump, thump; heavy fall. (b) (*SAm*) = **batatazo**.
bataclán *nm* (*SAm*) burlesque show (*US*), striptease show.
bataclana *nf* (*SAm*) striptease girl, stripper.
batahola *nf* (*fam*) din, hullabaloo (*fam*), rumpus (*fam*).
bataholear [1a] *vi*, **batajolear** [1a] *vi* (*Col*) to make a rumpus, brawl; to be mischievous, play pranks.
batalla *nf* (a) (*Mil*) battle; (*fig*) battle, fight, struggle; (*fig*) inner struggle, agitation (of mind); **— campal** pitched battle; **la — de Inglaterra** the Battle of Britain (1940); **tazas de —** ordinary cups, cups not kept for best; **librar —** to do battle; **trabar —** to join battle.
  (b) (*Art*) battle piece, battle scene.
  (c) (*Aut etc*) wheelbase.
batallador 1 *adj* battling, fighting; warlike. **2** *nm* battler, fighter; (*Sport*) fencer.
batallar [1a] *vi* (a) to battle, fight, struggle (*con* with, against; *por* about, over); (*Sport*) to fence. (b) (*fig*) to waver, vacillate.
batallón 1 *adj*: **cuestión batallona** vexed question. **2** *nm* battalion.
batán *nm* (a) fulling mill; fulling hammer. (b) (*Chi*) dyeworks. (c) (*Col*) thickness (*of cloth*).
batanar [1a] *vt* (a) (*Tech*) to full. (b) (*fam*) to beat, thrash.
batanear [1a] *vt* (*fam*) to beat, thrash; to shake.
batanero *nm* fuller.
bantanga *nf* outrigger.
bataola *nf* = **batahola**.
batata 1 *nf* (a) (*SAm: Bot*) sweet potato, yam.
  (b) (*Ant, Col, Ven*) calf of the leg.
  (c) (*RPl*) bashfulness, embarrassment.
  2 *adj* (a) (*RPl*) bashful, shy, embarrassed.
  (b) (*PR, Urug*) simple, gullible.
  (c) (*PR*) chubby, plump; squat.
batatar *nm* (*SAm*) sweet-potato field.
batatazo *nm* (a) (*fam*) stroke of luck, fluke; (*SAm*) unexpected win (*by a racehorse*). (b) = **batacazo**.

batayola *nf* (*Naut*) rail.
bate *nm* (*esp SAm: angl*) (baseball) bat.
batea *nf* (a) tray; deep trough; (*Min*) washing pan. (b) (*Rail*) flat car, low wagon. (c) (*Naut*) flat-bottomed boat, punt.
bateador *nm* (*esp SAm: angl*) batter.
batear [1a] **1** *vt* (*esp SAm: angl*) to hit. **2** *vi* (*esp SAm: angl*) to bat.
batel *nm* small boat, skiff.
batelero *nm* boatman.
batelón *nm* (*Bol, Col, Ec, Per*) canoe.
batería *nf* (a) (*Mil, Elec, for hens*) battery; (*of lights*) bank, battery, set; (*Theat*) footlights; (*Mus*) percussion, drums; **— de cocina** kitchen utensils, pots and pans; **— seca** dry battery; **aparcar en —** (*Aut*) to park square on to the kerb.
  (b) (*Col*) round of drinks.
  (c) (*SAm: Baseball*) hit, stroke.
  (d) (*Mex*) **dar — a** to make trouble for, make a lot of work for.
batey *nm* (*Ant*) clearing in front of a country house, forecourt.
batiburrillo *nm* hotchpotch.
baticola *nf* (*Bol*) loincloth; (*Par*) nappy, diaper (*US*).
batida *nf* (a) (*Hunting*) drive; beat, beating; (*Mil*) reconnaissance; (*Arg, Per*) raid (by the police); (*fig*) search; combing; (*Per*) chase.
  (b) (*Per, PR*) beating, thrashing.
batido 1 *adj* (a) *path* well-trodden, beaten. (b) *silk* shot, chatoyant. **2** *nm* (*Cook*) batter; **— (de leche)** milk shake.
batidor *nm* (a) (*Hunting, Tech*) beater; (*Mil*) scout. (b) (*tool*) beater; comb; (*Cook*) beater, whisk, mixer; (*CAm, Mex*) wooden bowl, mixing bowl.
batidora *nf* (*Cook*) beater, whisk, mixer; (*Tech*) beater; **— eléctrica** electric mixer.
batiente *nm* (a) jamb (*of door*); frame, case (*of window*); leaf, panel (*of door*); **— oscilante** swing door. (b) (*Mus*) damper. (c) (*Naut*) open coastline.
batifondo *nm* (*RPl*) uproar, tumult.
batín *nm* (man's) dressing gown; smoking jacket.
batintín *nm* gong.
batir [3a] **1** *vt* (a) to beat; to hammer, pound (on); *drum, metal* to beat; *coin* to mint; *wings* to beat, flap; *hands* to clap; *hair* to comb.
  (b) *house* to knock down; *wall etc* (*Mil*) to batter down; *tent* to take down; *privilege* to do away with.
  (c) (*of sea*) to beat on, dash against; (*of sun*) to beat down on.
  (d) (*Cook*) to beat, mix, whisk; to stir, churn; *butter* to cream; *cream* to whip.
  (e) (*Hunting*) to beat; to comb, search; (*Mil*) to reconnoitre.
  (f) *adversary, enemy* to beat, defeat; *record* to beat.
  (g) (*Chi, Guat, Per*) *clothes* to rinse.
  (h) (*Arg*) to inform on, inform against.
  2 *vi* (*Med*) to beat violently.
  3 batirse *vr* to fight, have a fight; **— con uno** to fight someone; **— en duelo** to fight a duel.
batista *nf* cambric, batiste.
bato *nm* simpleton.
batracio *nm* batrachian.
batucar [1g] *vt* to shake, shake up.
Batuecas: las — backward region of Extremadura, equivalent to the backwoods, the hillbilly country.
batueco *adj* (*fam*) stupid, silly.
batuque *nm* (*RPl*) rumpus (*fam*), set-to (*fam*).
batuquear [1a] *vt* (*Guat*) to tell off. (b) to pester, annoy.
baturrillo *nm* hotchpotch.
baturro 1 *adj* uncouth, rough. **2** *nm*, **baturra** *nf* Aragonese peasant.
batuta *nf* (*Mus*) baton; (*SD*) power, control; **llevar la —** (*fig*) to be the boss, be firmly in command.
baúl *nm* (a) trunk; **— armario, — ropero** wardrobe trunk; **— camarote** cabin trunk; **— mundo** large trunk, Saratoga trunk; **— de viaje** portmanteau.
  (b) (*Aut*) boot, trunk (*US*).
  (c) (*fam*) belly, corporation (*fam*).
bauprés *nm* bowsprit.
bausa *nf* (*Mex, Per*) laziness, idleness.
bausán *nm* dummy; (*fig*) simpleton.
bausano *nm* (*Salv*) idler, lazy person.
bauseador *nm* (*Per*) idler, lazy person.
bautismal *adj* baptismal.
bautismo *nm* (a) baptism, christening; **— de fuego** baptism of fire. (b) **romper el — a uno** (*fam*) to smash someone's head.
Bautista *m*: **el —, San Juan —** St John the Baptist.

bautizar [1f] *vt* (**a**) to baptise, christen; **le bautizaron con el nombre de Wamba** he was baptized Wamba.
(**b**) (*fig*) to christen, name, give a name to.
(**c**) (*fam*) *wine* to water, dilute; *person* to drench, soak.
bautizo *nm* (**a**) baptism, christening. (**b**) christening party.
bauxita *nf* bauxite.
bávaro 1 *adj* Bavarian. 2 *nm*, **bávara** *nf* Bavarian.
Baviera *f* Bavaria.
baya *nf* berry.
bayajá *nm* (*Ant*) headscarf.
bayeta *nf* (**a**) baize. (**b**) floorcloth, cleaning rag. (**c**) (*Col*) nappy, diaper (*US*).
bayetón *nm* (**a**) thick woollen cloth. (**b**) (*Col*) long poncho.
bayo 1 *adj* bay. 2 *nm* bay (horse).
Bayona Bayonne.
bayoneta *nf* (**a**) bayonet; **con —s caladas** with fixed bayonets. (**b**) (*Ant, Arg, Col*) yucca.
bayonetazo *nm* bayonet thrust; bayonet wound.
bayonetear [1a] *vt* (*SAm*) to bayonet.
bayoya *nm* (*PR, SD*) row, uproar, tumult; confusion; bear garden.
bayunca *nf* (*CAm*) bar, saloon.
bayunco 1 *adj* (*CAm*) silly, stupid; shy. 2 *nm* (*Guat*) uncouth peasant; *name applied by Guatemalans to other Central Americans.*
baza *nf* (**a**) (*Cards*) trick; **— de honor** honours trick; **hacer 3 —s** to make 3 tricks.
(**b**) (*fig*) **hacer —** to get on; **meter —** to butt in; **meter — en** to interfere in; **no dejar meter — a nadie** not to let someone get a word in edgeways; **sentar —** to intervene decisively; to speak up dogmatically.
bazar *nm* bazaar; (*SAm*) bazaar, charity fair.
bazo 1 *adj* yellowish-brown. 2 *nm* (*Anat*) spleen.
bazofia *nf* (**a**) left-overs, scraps of food; pigswill. (**b**) (*fig*) pigswill, hogwash (*US*); vile thing, filthy thing.
bazuca *nf* bazooka.
bazucar [1g] *vt*, **bazuquear** [1a] *vt* to stir; to shake, jolt.
bazuqueo *nm* stirring; shaking, jolting; **— gástrico** rumblings in the stomach.
be[1]: **por —** in detail, down to the last detail; **esto tiene las tres —s** this is really very nice, this is just perfect.
be[2] *nm* baa.
beata *nf* (**a**) (*Eccl*) lay sister; sister of charity.
(**b**) devout woman; woman who lives in pious retirement; (*pej*) excessively pious woman, sanctimonious woman, goody-goody (*fam*).
beatería *nf* affected piety; cant, sanctimoniousness.
beatificación *nf* beatification.
beatificar [1g] *vt* to beatify.
beatífico *adj* beatific.
beatitud *nf* beatitude, blessedness; **su B—** His Holiness.
beatnik ['bitnik] *nm, pl* **beatniks** ['bitnik] (*angl*) beatnik.
beato 1 *adj* (**a**) happy, blessed.
(**b**) (*Eccl*) blessed.
(**c**) devout, pious; (*pej*) sanctimonious, canting, hypocritical.
2 *nm* (**a**) lay brother.
(**b**) devout man, pious person.
Beatriz *f* Beatrice.
bebé *nm* baby.
bebecina *nf* (*Col*) drunkenness; drinking spree (*fam*).
bebedera *nf* (*Col, Guat, Mex*) habitual drunkenness, constant drinking.
bebedero 1 *adj* drinkable, good to drink.
2 *nm* (**a**) drinking trough.
(**b**) spout (*of jar*).
(**c**) (*Per*) establishment selling alcoholic drinks.
bebedizo 1 *adj* drinkable. 2 *nm* (*Med*) potion; (*Hist*) love potion, philtre.
bebedor 1 *adj* hard-drinking, bibulous, given to drinking. 2 *nm*, **bebedora** *nf* drinker; (*pej*) hard drinker, toper.
bebendurria *nf* (*Arg*) drinking party. (**b**) (*Col, Mex*) drunkenness; drinking spree (*fam*).
beber 1 *nm* drink, drinking.
2 [2a] *vti* (**a**) to drink; to drink up; (*fig*) to drink in, absorb, imbibe; **— de** to drink from, drink out of; **— con la lengua** to lap up; **— a sorbos** to sip; **— mucho, — a pote** to drink a lot, be a heavy drinker; **se lo bebió todo** he drank it all up.
(**b**) (*Mex*) to have breakfast.
beberaje *nm* (*RPl*) drink (*esp alcoholic*).
beberrón *adj and nm*, **beberrona** *nf* = **bebedor**.

bebestibles *nmpl* (*SAm*) drinks.
bebezón *nf* (**a**) (*Col, Cu, Guat, Ven*) drink (*esp alcoholic*). (**b**) (*Col, Cu*) drunkenness; drinking spree.
bebible *adj* drinkable, good to drink.
bebida *nf* (**a**) drink; beverage.
(**b**) (alcoholic) drink; **— alcohólica** alcoholic drink, liquor; **dado a la —** given to drink, hard-drinking; **darse a la —** to take to drink; **tener mala — (SAm)** to get violent with drink.
bebido *adj* tipsy, merry (*fam*).
bebistrajo *nm* (*fam*) nasty drink, filthy drink.
beca *nf* (**a**) scholarship, grant; fellowship; award.
(**b**) sash, hood.
becado 1 *adj* (*SAm*) *student* who holds a scholarship. 2 *nm*, **becada** *nf* (*SAm*) scholarship holder.
becario *nm*, **becaria** *nf* scholarship holder; scholar, fellow.
becerrada *nf* (*Taur*) fight with young bulls.
becerrillo *nm* calfskin.
becerro *nm* (**a**) yearling calf, bullock; **— de oro** golden calf. (**b**) calfskin. (**c**) (*Eccl: Hist*) cartulary, record book.
becuadro *nm* (*Mus*) natural sign.
Beda *m* Bede.
bedel *nm* (*Univ: approx*) head porter.
bedoya *nm* (*Col*) idiot.
beduino 1 *adj* Bedouin. 2 *nm*, **beduina** *nf* Bedouin.
befa *nf* jeer, taunt.
befar [1a] *vt* to scoff at, jeer at, taunt.
befo 1 *adj* (**a**) thick-lipped. (**b**) knock-kneed. 2 *nm* lip.
begonia *nf* begonia.
behaviorismo *nm* behaviourism.
beige [beis] 1 *adj* beige. 2 *nm* beige.
béisbol *nm* (*angl*) baseball.
beisbolero 1 *adj* (*SAm*) baseball (*attr*). 2 *nm* (*SAm*) baseball player.
beisbolista *nm* (*SAm*) baseball player.
bejuco *nm* (*SAm*) liana; **no sacar — (Ven)** to fail to get what one wanted. (**b**) (*Ec, Guat, Per, PR*) whip.
bejuqueada *nf* (*Ec, Guat, Mex, Per, PR*) beating, thrashing.
bejuquear [1a] *vt* (*Ec, Guat, Mex, Per, PR*) to beat, thrash.
bejuquero *nm* (*Col*) confused situation, mess.
bejuquillo *nm* (**a**) (*Ant, Mex*) (variety of) liana. (**b**) (*Col*) vanilla.
bejuquiza *nf* (*Ec*) beating, thrashing.
Belcebú *m* Beelzebub.
beldad *nf* (**a**) beauty. (**b**) (*person*) beauty, belle.
beldar [1k] *vt* to winnow (with a fork).
belduque *nm* (*SAm*) steel, blade.
Belén Bethlehem.
belén *nm* (**a**) nativity scene, crib.
(**b**) (*fig*) confusion, bedlam; madhouse; risky venture; **meterse en belenes** (*Arg, Mex*) to get involved in other people's troubles.
beleño *nm* henbane.
belfo = **befo**.
belga 1 *adj* Belgian. 2 *nmf* Belgian.
Bélgica *f* Belgium.
bélgico *adj* Belgian.
Belgrado Belgrade.
belicismo *nm* warmongering, militarism.
belicista 1 *adj* warmongering, militaristic, warminded. 2 *nmf* warmonger.
bélico *adj* (**a**) warlike, martial. (**b**) *material etc* war (*attr*).
belicoso *adj* warlike; bellicose, aggressive; militant.
beligerancia *nf* belligerency; militancy, warlike spirit.
beligerante 1 *adj* belligerent; militant, warlike; **no —** non-belligerent. 2 *nmf* belligerent; **no — non-**belligerent.
belinún *nm* (*RPl*) simpleton.
belitre *nm* (**a**) rogue, scoundrel. (**b**) (*CAm, Per*) shrewd child; restless child.
beliz *nm* (*Mex*) valise.
bellaco 1 *adj* wicked; cunning, sly; (*Mex, RPl*) *horse* vicious, hard to control; (*Ec, Pan*) brave. 2 *nm* scoundrel, rogue, villain.
belladona *nf* deadly nightshade.
bellamente *adv* beautifully; finely.
bellaqueada *nf* (*RPl*) bucking, rearing; shy.
bellaquear [1a] *vi* (**a**) to cheat, be crooked. (**b**) (*Bol, RPl*) to rear up, balk; to shy; (*fig*) to dig one's heels in, be stubborn.
bellaquería *nf* (**a**) (*act*) dirty trick, wicked thing. (**b**) wickedness; cunning, slyness.
belleza *nf* (**a**) beauty, loveliness; **las —s de Mallorca** the beauties of Majorca. (**b**) (*person*) beauty, beautiful woman (*etc*); lovely thing.

bello adj beautiful, lovely; fine; noble; art fine; sex fair, gentle.

bellota nf (a) (Bot) acorn. (b) (Anat: fam) Adam's apple. (c) perfume-box. (d) — **de mar**, — **marina** sea urchin.

bemba nf (SAm) (Negro's) thick lips.

bembo adj, **bembón** adj, **bembudo** adj (SAm) thick-lipped.

bemol nm (Mus) flat; **esto tiene muchos** (or **tres**) —**es** (fam) this is a tough one, this bristles with difficulties.

bencedrina nf Benzedrine.

benceno nm benzene.

bencina nf benzine.

bendecir [approx 3p] vt to bless; to consecrate; to praise, call down a blessing on; — **la comida**, — **la mesa** to say grace.

bendición nf (a) blessing, benediction; — **de la mesa** grace; —**es nupciales** wedding ceremony; **echar la** — to give one's blessing (a to; also fig); **tuvo que echar la** — **a eso** (fam) he had to say good-bye to that, he had to give up all hope of (finding) that; **será mejor echar la** — **a eso** (fam) it will be best to have nothing more to do with it. (b) . . . **que es una** — . . . and it's just marvellous; **llovió que era una** — you should have seen how it rained, it just did rain; **lo hace que es una** — he does it splendidly, he does it with the greatest ease.

bendito 1 adj (a) blessed, holy; saintly; water holy.
(b) (fig) blessed.
(c) happy; lucky.
(d) simple, simple-minded.
(e) (in compliments) ¡—**s los ojos que te ven!** lucky eyes to be looking at you!; ¡**bendita la madre que te parió!** what a daughter for a mother to have!
2 nm (a) saint.
(b) simple soul, good soul; **es un** — he's a good kind person, he's sweet; **dormir como un** — to sleep peacefully, be fast asleep.
(c) (Arg) prayer.
(d) (Arg) wayside shrine; native hut.

benedícite nm grace.

benedictino 1 adj Benedictine. 2 nm (Eccl, liqueur) Benedictine; **es obra de** —**s** it's a huge task, it's a long job.

Benedicto m Benedict.

beneficencia nf (a) beneficence, doing good.
(b) charity; charitable organization; social welfare; **vivir a cargo de la** — to live on charity, live on public welfare.

beneficiado nm (Eccl) incumbent, beneficiary.

beneficial adj: **terreno** — (Eccl) glebe, glebe land.

beneficiar [1b] 1 vt (a) to benefit, be of benefit to.
(b) (Arg) land to cultivate; mine to exploit, work; mineral to process, treat, smelt; (Guat: Agr) to process.
(c) (SAm: Agr) animal to slaughter; to castrate; (Guat) person to shoot.
(d) (Comm) to sell at a discount.
(e) (fam) job to buy one's way into.
2 vi to be of benefit.
3 **beneficiarse** vr (a) to benefit, profit; — **de** to benefit from, take advantage of.
(b) — **a uno** (Guat) to shoot someone.

beneficiario nm, **beneficiaria** nf beneficiary.

beneficio nm (a) benefit, profit, gain, advantage; **a** — **de** for the benefit of; **en** — **propio** to one's own advantage; **en su propio** —, **no** . . . **in your own interests, do not** . . .
(b) benefaction.
(c) (Theat) benefit, benefit performance.
(d) (Eccl) living, benefice.
(e) (Comm, Fin) profit; — **bruto** gross profit; —**s excesivos** excess profits; — **líquido**, — **neto** net profit.
(f) (Agr, Min) yield.
(g) (Agr) cultivation; (Min) exploitation; (Min) processing, treatment, smelting.
(h) (SAm) slaughter, slaughtering.
(i) (Chi: Agr) manure.
(j) (CAm) slaughterhouse; coffee plantation; sugar mill.

beneficioso adj beneficial, profitable, useful.

benéfico adj (a) beneficent, charitable, kind (a to; para, con towards). (b) work etc charitable; **función benéfica** charity performance; **obra benéfica** charity.

benemérito adj (a) worthy, meritorious; notable; distinguished; **el** — **hispanista** the distinguished hispanist.
(b) **un** — **de la patria** a national hero; **la Benemérita** the Civil Guard, (loosely) the police.

beneplácito nm approval, consent; **dar su** — to give one's consent.

benevolencia nf benevolence, kindness, kindliness; geniality.

benevolente adj, **benévolo** adj benevolent, kind, kindly; genial; — **con** well-disposed towards, kind to.

Bengala f Bengal.

bengala nf flare; — **iluminadora** star shell, flare.

benignamente adv kindly, benignly; graciously, gently; mildly.

benignidad nf kindness, kindliness; graciousness, gentleness; mildness.

benigno adj kind, kindly, benign; gracious; gentle; climate mild; (Med) attack, case mild; tumour benign, non-malignant.

Benito m Benedict.

benito = **benedictino**.

Benjamín m Benjamin.

benjamín nm (also **benjasmín** nm, Arg, Chi) baby of the family, youngest child; favourite child.

beodez nf drunkenness.

beodo 1 adj drunk. 2 nm drunk (fam), drunkard.

beorí nm American tapir.

beque 1 adj (CR) stammering. 2 nmf (CR) stammerer.

bequista nmf (CAm, Cu) = **becario**.

berbén nm (Mex) scurvy.

berberecho nm cockle.

berberí adj and nmf = **bereber**.

Berbería f Barbary.

berberisco adj Berber.

berbiquí nm carpenter's brace; — **y barrena** brace and bit.

bereber 1 adj Berber. 2 nmf Berber.

berengo nm (Mex) idiot.

berenjena nf aubergine, eggplant.

berenjenal nm (a) aubergine bed. (b) (fig) mess, trouble; **en buen** — **nos hemos metido** we've got ourselves into a fine mess.

bergante nm scoundrel, rascal.

bergantín nm brig.

Beri: andar (or **ir**) **con las de** — to have a violent temper; to have evil intentions.

berilo nm (Min) beryl.

Berlín Berlin.

berlinés 1 adj Berlin (attr). 2 nm, **berlinesa** nf Berliner.

berma nf berm, ledge.

bermejo adj (a) red, bright red; reddish; cat ginger; (Cu, Mex) cow light brown. (b) (SD) splendid, excellent; only, sole.

bermellón nm vermilion.

Bermudas fpl, also **Islas** fpl **Bermuda** Bermuda.

Berna Berne.

bernardina nf (fam) yarn, tall story.

Bernardo m Bernard.

berrear [1a] vi (a) (Zool) to bellow, low; (child) to howl; (Mus: hum) to bawl, sing off key. (b) (fig) to fly off the handle (fam).

berrenchín nm (fam) rage, tantrum (fam).

berretín nm (Arg) mania; pigheadedness.

berrido nm (Zool) bellow, bellowing; lowing; (of child) howl; (Mus: hum) bawl, bawling; screech.

berrinche nm (a) (fam) rage, tantrum (fam). (b) (SAm) smell of urine.

berrinchudo adj (a) (fam) cross, bad-tempered. (b) (Mex) person randy; animal on heat.

berro nm watercress.

berza nf cabbage; — **lombarda** red cabbage; **mezclar** —**s con capachos** (fam) to get things in a shocking mess.

berzal nm cabbage patch.

besamanos nm, pl **besamanos** royal audience, levée.

besana nf (Cu, Mex) land to be ploughed.

besar [1a] vt (a) to kiss; — **la mano**, — **los pies** (fig) to pay one's humble respects (a to).
(b) (fig) to graze, touch.
2 **besarse** vr (a) to kiss, kiss one another.
(b) (fig) to touch, knock against each other; to bump heads.

beso nm (a) kiss; **dar un** — **volado a**, **echar** (or **tirar**) **un** — **a** to blow a kiss to. (b) bump, collision.

besotear [1a] vt (Mex) = **besuquear**.

bestia 1 nf (Zool) beast, animal, (esp) horse, mule; — **de carga** beast of burden; — **negra** (fig) bête noire, pet aversion; — **de tiro** draught animal.
2 nmf idiot, ignoramus; boor; beast, brute; ¡—! you idiot!, you brute!; ¡**no seas** —! don't be an idiot!
3 adj (fam) stupid; **Juan es muy** — John is a bit stupid; **el muy** — the great idiot; **ese tío** — that beastly fellow.

bestial *adj* (a) beastly, bestial. (b) (*fam*) terrific (*fam*); tremendous (*fam*), marvellous; smashing (*sl*), super (*fam*).

bestialidad *nf* (a) beastliness, bestiality. (b) (*fig*) stupidity; silly thing, piece of stupidity. (c) (*sl*) **una — de gente** lots and lots of people.

besucar [1g] *vt* = **besuquear**.

besucón *adj* free with kisses, fond of kissing.

besugo *nm* (a) sea bream; **con ojos de —** with bulging eyes; with eyes like a spaniel's. (b) (*fam*) idiot.

besuguera *nf* (a) (*Naut*) fishing boat. (b) (*Cook*) fish pan.

besuquear [1a] **1** *vt* to cover with kisses, keep on kissing. **2 besuquearse** *vr* to kiss (each other) a lot; to pet, neck (*fam*).

besuqueo *nm* kissing; petting, necking (*fam*).

betabel *nm* (*Mex*) sugar beet.

betarraga *nf*, **betarrata** *nf* sugar beet.

betel *nm* betel.

Bética *f* (*lit*) Andalusia.

bético *adj* (*lit*) Andalusian.

betonera *nf* (*Chi*) concrete mixer.

betún *nm* (a) (*Chem*) bitumen. (b) shoe polish, blacking; **dar de — a** to polish, black; **darse —** (*fam*) to swank (*fam*), show off.

betunero *nm* bootblack.

bezo *nm* thick lip; (*Med*) proud flesh.

bezudo *adj* thick-lipped.

bi . . . bi . . .

biaba *nf* (*RPl*) punch, slap; **dar la — a** to beat up; to defeat, crush.

bianual 1 *adj* (*Bot*) biennial. **2** *nm* (*Bot*) biennial.

biberón *nm* feeding bottle.

Biblia *nf* Bible; **la Santa B—** the Holy Bible; **saber la —** (*fig*) to know everything.

bíblico *adj* Biblical.

bibliobús *nm* travelling library, library van.

bibliófilo *nm* bibliophile.

bibliografía *nf* bibliography.

bibliográfico *adj* bibliographic(al).

bibliógrafo *nm* bibliographer.

bibliomanía *nf* bibliomania.

bibliorato *nm* (*RPl*) book file, box file.

biblioteca *nf* (a) library; **— circulante** lending library; circulating library; **— de consulta** reference library; **— pública** public library; **— universitaria** university library. (b) bookcase, bookshelves.

bibliotecario *nm*, **bibliotecaria** *nf* librarian.

bicamaral *adj*, **bicameral** *adj* (*Pol*) two-chamber, bicameral.

bicarbonato *nm*: **— sódico, — de sosa** bicarbonate of soda; baking soda.

bicentenario *nm* bicentenary.

biceps *nm*, *pl* **biceps** biceps.

bici *nf* (*fam*) bike (*fam*).

bicicleta *nf* bicycle, cycle; **andar en —, ir en —** to cycle; to ride a bicycle.

bicoca *nf* (a) trifle, mere nothing. (b) (*Arg, Bol, Chi*) biretta. (c) (*Bol, Chi*) slap, punch on the head.

bicolor *adj* two-colour, in two colours, (*Aut*) two-tone.

bicúspide *adj* bicuspid.

bicha *nf* (a) (*euph*) snake; (*fig*) bogy. (b) (*CAm*) child, little girl. (c) (*Per*) large cooking pot.

bichadero *nm* (*RPl*) watchtower, observation post.

bichará *nm* (*RPl*) poncho (with black and white stripes).

biche 1 *adj* (*Arg*) weak; of unhealthy colour; (*Col*) stunted, immature. **2** *nm* (*Per*) large cooking pot.

bicheadero *nm* (*Arg*) = **bichadero**.

bichear [1a] *vt* (*RPl*) to observe, watch closely; to spy on.

bicherío *nm* (*SAm*) small animals (collectively); insects, bugs, creepy-crawlies (*fam*).

bichero *nm* boat hook; (*Fish*) gaff.

bicho *nm* (a) (*Zool etc*) small animal; (unpleasant) insect, bug, creepy-crawly (*fam*); (*Cu, RPl*) maggot, grub; (*Col*) fowl pest; (*SAm*) odd-looking creature; (*Taur*) bull; **—s** (*freq*) vermin, pests, bugs.
(b) (*person*) odd-looking person, queer fish (*also* **— raro**); **mal —** rogue, villain; **es un mal —** he's a nasty piece of work, he's a rotter; **todo — viviente** every living soul, every man-jack of them.
(c) (*pej*) brat; (*CAm*) child, little boy.
(d) (*SAm*) **de puro —** out of sheer spite; **tener —** to be terribly thirsty.

bichoco *adj* (*Arg, Bol, Chi, Urug*) old, useless; unfit to work.

bidé *nm* (*Acad*), **bidet** [bi'ðe] *nm* bidet.

bidel *nm* (*SAm*) small bathtub.

bidón *nm* drum; can, tin.

biela *nf* connecting rod.

bielástico *adj* with two-way stretch.

bielda *nf* winnowing fork, (kind of) pitchfork.

bieldar [1a] *vt* to winnow (with a fork).

bieldo *nm* winnowing rake.

bien 1 *adv* (a) well; properly, right; successfully; **hacer algo —** to do something well, do something properly; **contestar —** to answer right, answer correctly; **lo sé muy —** I know that perfectly well; **no veo muy —** I can't see all that well; **— que** **mal** one way or another, by hook or by crook; **de — en —, de — en mejor** better and better; **aquí se está —** it's nice here; **¿estás —?** are you all right?, are you comfortable?; **¿está — que . . .?** is it right that . . .?; **hacer — en +** *infin* to be right to **+** *infin*, do well to **+** *infin*; **tener a — +** *infin* to see fit to **+** *infin*, deign to **+** *infin*; to think it proper to **+** *infin*.
(b) willingly, gladly, readily; **yo — iría, pero . . .** I'd gladly go, but . . .
(c) very, much, quite, a good deal, fully; **un cuarto — caliente** a nice warm room; **eso es — tonto** that's pretty silly; **un coche — caro** a very expensive car; **— temprano** very early, pretty early, quite early; **había — 8 toneladas** there were fully (*or* easily, at least) 8 tons.
(d) easily; **— se ve que . . .** one can easily see that . . ., it is easy to see that . . .; **— es verdad que . . .** it is of course true that . . .
(e) **— por avión, — en tren** either by air or by train; **— se levantó, — se sentó** whether he stood up or sat down.
(f) **— (así) como** just as, just like; **más — rather; más — bajo que alto** rather short, on the short side; **o — or else**; **pues — well**, well then.
(g) *as interj etc* **¡—!** yes!, all right!; O.K.!; jolly good!; well done!; **¡muy —!** (*approving speech etc*) hear hear!; **¡hizo muy —!** and he was quite right too!; **¡muy — (por) usted!** good for you!

2 *conj* (a) **— que, si —** although, even though.
(b) **no — llegó, empezó a llover** no sooner had he arrived than it started to rain, as soon as he arrived it started to rain.

3 *nm* (a) good; advantage, benefit, profit; **hombre de —** honest man, good man; **el — público** the common good; **sumo — highest good; en — de** for the good of, for the benefit of; **hacer — to** do good; to be honest, lead an honest life; **hacer algo para el — de** to do something for the well-being of.
(b) **mi —** my dear, my darling.
(c) **—es** goods; property, possessions; riches, wealth; **—es de capital** capital goods; **—es de consumo** consumer goods; **—es de consumo duraderos** consumer durables; **—es de equipo** capital goods; **—es dotales** dowry; **—es heredables** hereditament; **—es inmuebles, —es raíces** real estate, landed property; **—es de inversión** capital goods; **—es mostrencos** unclaimed property, ownerless property; **—es muebles** personal property, goods and chattels; **—es públicos** government property, state property; **—es relictos** estate, inheritance; **—es semovientes** livestock; **—es de la tierra** produce; **—es vinculados** entail.
(d) **decir mil —es de uno** to speak highly of someone, talk in glowing terms of someone.

bienal 1 *adj* biennial. **2** *nf* biennial exhibition, biennial show (*esp Aut*); **la — de París** the Paris motor show.

bienandante *adj* happy; prosperous.

bienandanza *nf* happiness; prosperity.

bienaventuradamente *adv* happily.

bienaventurado *adj* (a) happy, fortunate; (*Eccl*) blessed. (b) simple, naïve.

bienaventuranza *nf* (a) (*Eccl*) blessedness, (eternal) bliss; **las —s** the Beatitudes. (b) happiness; well-being, prosperity.

bienestar *nm* well-being, welfare; comfort.

bienhablado *adj* nicely-spoken, well-spoken.

bienhadado *adj* lucky.

bienhechor 1 *adj* beneficent, beneficial. **2** *nm* benefactor.

bienhechora *nf* benefactress.

bienhechuría *nf* (*Cu, Ven*) improvements in real estate.

bienintencionado *adj* well-meaning.

bienio *nm* two years, two-year period.

bienoliente *adj* sweet-smelling, fragrant.

bienquerencia *nf* affection; goodwill.

bienquerer 1 [2u] *vt* to like, be fond of. **2** *nm* affection; goodwill.

bienquistar [1a] **1** *vt* to bring together, reconcile. **2 bienquistarse** *vr* to become reconciled; **— con uno** to gain someone's esteem.

bienquisto *adj* well-liked, well-thought-of (*con, de, por by*).

bienvenida *nf* (a) welcome; greeting; **dar la — a uno** to welcome someone, make someone welcome. (b) safe arrival.

bienvenido *adj* welcome; ¡—! welcome!; ¡—s a bordo! welcome on board!

bienvivir [3a] *vi* to live in comfort; to live decently, lead a decent life.

bifásico *adj* (*Elec*) two-phase.

bife[1] *nm* (*SAm: angl*) steak, beefsteak.

bife[2] *nm* (*RPl*) slap, punch.

bifocal *adj* bifocal.

biftec *nm* (*angl*) steak, beefsteak.

bifurcación *nf* fork; junction; branch.

bifurcado *adj* forked.

bifurcarse [1g] *vr* to fork, branch, bifurcate; to branch off; to diverge.

bigamia *nf* bigamy.

bígamo 1 *adj* bigamous. **2** *nm*, **bígama** *nf* bigamist.

bigardear [1a] *vi* (*fam*) to loaf around.

bigardo *nm* loafer, idler.

bigarro *nm* winkle.

bigornia *nf* (double-headed) anvil.

bigote *nm* (*also* **—s**) moustache; (*of cat etc*) whiskers; **—s de foca** walrus moustache; **es de —** (*fam*) it's terrific (*fam*), it's marvellous.

bigotudo *adj* with a big moustache.

bigudí *nm* hair-curler.

bijirita *nf* (*Cu*) (a) kite. (b) **empinar la —** to booze, drink a lot; to make money by dubious methods.

bikini *nm* bikini.

bilateral *adj* bilateral.

bilbaíno 1 *adj* of Bilbao. **2** *nm*, **bilbaína** *nf* native (*or* inhabitant) of Bilbao; **los —s** the people of Bilbao.

bilbilitano 1 *adj* of Calatayud. **2** *nm*, **bilbilitana** *nf* native (*or* inhabitant) of Calatayud; **los —s** the people of Calatayud.

biliar *adj* bile (*attr*), gall (*attr*).

bilingüe *adj* bilingual.

bilingüismo *nm* bilingualism.

bilioso *adj* (a) bilious. (b) (*fig*) bilious, peevish.

bilis *nf* (a) bile. (b) (*fig*) bile, spleen; **descargar la —** to vent one's spleen (*contra* on); **se le exalta la —** he gets very cross; **eso me revuelve la —** it makes my blood boil.

bilongo *nm* (*Cu*) evil influence, evil eye; **tener —** to bristle with difficulties.

bilonguear [1a] *vt* (*Cu*) to bewitch, cast the evil eye on.

billar *nm* (a) billiards; **— automático, — romano** pin table. (b) billiard room; billiard table.

billete *nm* (a) (*Rail etc*) ticket; **— de abono** season ticket, commutation ticket (*US Rail*); **— de andén** platform ticket; **— de favor** complimentary ticket; **— de ida y vuelta** return ticket, round-trip ticket (*US*); **— kilométrico** runabout ticket, mileage book; **medio —** half fare; **— sencillo** single ticket, one-way ticket (*US*); **pagar el —** to pay one's fare, buy one's ticket; **sacar un —** to get a ticket. (b) (*Fin*) banknote, note, bill (*US*); **— de banco** banknote; **un — de 5 libras** a five-pound note; **un — de 100 dólares** a 100-dollar bill. (c) note, short letter; **— amoroso** love letter, billet-doux.

billetera *nf*, **billetero** *nm* wallet, notecase, billfold (*US*).

billón *nm* billion (*Brit*), trillion (*US*).

bimba[1] *nf* top hat.

bimba[2] *nf* (*Mex*) drunkenness; drinking spree (*fam*).

bimbalete *nm* (*Mex*) swing, seesaw.

bimensual *adj* twice-monthly; bimonthly.

bimensuario 1 *adj* twice-monthly. **2** *nm* publication appearing twice monthly.

bimestral *adj* bimonthly, two-monthly.

bimestre 1 *adj* bimonthly, two-monthly. **2** *nm* (a) period of two months. (b) bimonthly payment.

bimotor 1 *adj* twin-engined. **2** *nm* twin-engined plane.

binadera *nf*, **binador** *nm* weeding hoe.

binar [1a] *vt* to hoe, dig over.

binario *adj* binary; (*Mus*) time two-four.

bincha *nf* (*Per, RPl*) hairband.

binóculo *nm* (*also* **—s**) binoculars, field glasses; opera glasses; pince-nez.

binomio *nm* binomial.

biofísica *nf* biophysics.

biografía *nf* biography, life.

biográfico *adj* biographic(al).

biógrafo *nm* biographer.

biología *nf* biology.

biológico *adj* biological.

biólogo *nm* biologist.

biombo *nm* folding screen.

biopsia *nf* biopsy.

bioquímica *nf* biochemistry.

bioquímico 1 *adj* biochemical. **2** *nm* biochemist.

bióxido *nm* dioxide; **— de carbono** carbon dioxide.

bipartido *adj*, **bipartito** *adj* bipartite.

bípedo *nm* biped.

biplano *nm* biplane.

biplaza *nm* (*Aer*) two-seater.

birimbao *nm* Jew's-harp.

birlar [1a] *vt* (a) to knock down with one blow, kill with one shot. (b) (*fam*) person to swindle out of, do out of; thing to pinch (*fam*); **Juan le birló la novia** John pinched his girl; **le birlaron el empleo** he was done out of the job.

birlocha *nf* paper kite.

birlibirloque: por arte de — by magic, as if by magic.

birlonga: hacer algo a la — to do something carelessly, do something sloppily.

Birmania *f* Burma.

birmano 1 *adj* Burmese. **2** *nm*, **birmana** *nf* Burmese.

birome *nf* (*Arg*) propelling pencil.

birreactor 1 *adj* twin-jet. **2** *nm* twin-jet (plane).

birreta *nf* (*Eccl*) biretta, cardinal's hat; (*Univ*) doctor's hat.

birrete *nm* (*Eccl*) biretta, cardinal's hat; (*Univ*) cap, square (*fam*), mortarboard; (*Law*) judge's cap.

biri *nm* (*Col*) snake.

birria *nf* (*fam*) (a) monstrosity, ugly old thing; wretched piece of work; rubbish, trash; useless object; **la novela es una —** the novel is rubbish; **entre tanta —** among so much trash. (b) (*Arg, Mex*) tasteless drink. (c) (*Col*) set idea, mania; obstinacy. (d) (*SAm*) **jugar de —** to play half-heartedly.

bis 1 *adv* twice; ¡—! (*Theat*) encore! **2** *nm* (*Theat*) encore.

bisabuela *nf* great-grandmother.

bisabuelo *nm* great-grandfather; **—s** great-grandparents.

bisagra *nf* hinge; (*fam: of hips*) waggle, wiggle.

bisar [1a] **1** *vt* (a) to give as an encore, repeat. (b) (*RPl*) to encore, demand as an encore. **2** *vi* to give an encore.

bisbisar [1a] *vt* to mutter, mumble.

bisbiseo *nm* mutter, muttering, mumbling.

bisbita *nf* pipit.

biscúter *nm* bubble car.

bisecar [1g] *vt* to bisect.

bisel *nm* bevel, bevel edge.

biselado *adj* bevel (*attr*), bevelled.

biselar [1a] *vt* to bevel.

bisemanal *adj* twice-weekly, bi-weekly.

bisexual *adj* bisexual.

bisiesto *adj*: **año —** leap year.

bisílabo *adj* two-syllabled.

bismuto *nm* bismuth.

bisnieta *nf* great-granddaughter.

bisnieto *nm* great-grandson; **—s** great-grandchildren.

bisojo *adj* cross-eyed, squinting.

bisonte *nm* bison.

bisoñada *nf* naïve remark, naïve thing to do.

bisoñé *nm* wig, toupée.

bisoño 1 *adj* green, inexperienced; *recruit* raw. **2** *nm* greenhorn; (*Mil*) raw recruit, rookie (*fam*).

bisté *nm*, **bistec** *nm*, **bisteck** *nm*, **bisteque** *nm* (*angl*) steak, beefsteak.

bistongo *adj* (*Ant, CAm, Mex*) spoiled, overindulged.

bisturí *nm* scalpel.

bisunto *adj* greasy, grubby.

bisutería *nf* imitation jewellery, paste.

bitácora *nf* binnacle.

bitongo *adj*: **niño —** young man about town, elegant youth; good-for-nothing.

bitoque *nm* bung, spigot; (*CAm*) drain; (*SAm*) injection tube (*of a syringe*); (*RPl*) tap; (*Par*) bump, swelling.

bituminoso *adj* bituminous.

bivalvo *adj* bivalve; **molusco —** bivalve.

bivio *nm* (*SAm*) road junction.

Bizancio Byzantium.

bizantino 1 *adj* (a) Byzantine. (b) (*fig*) decadent. (c) (*fig*) *discussion* idle, pointless; over-subtle, Jesuitical. **2** *nm*, **bizantina** *nf* Byzantine.

bizarramente *adv* (a) gallantly, bravely; dashingly. (b) generously, splendidly.

bizarría *nf* (a) gallantry, bravery; dash, verve. (b) generosity.

bizarro *adj* (a) gallant, brave; dashing. (b) generous, splendid.

bizbirindo *adj* (*Mex*) lively, bright.

bizcar [1g] **1** *vt eye* to wink. **2** *vi* to squint, look cross-eyed.

bizco 1 *adj* cross-eyed, squinting; **mirada bizca** squint, cross-eyed look; **dejar a uno** — to impress someone strongly, leave someone open-mouthed (with wonder); **ponerse** — to squint, look cross-eyed; **quedarse** — to be very impressed, be dumb-founded.
2 *adv*: **mirar** — to squint, look cross-eyed.

bizcochera *nf* biscuit barrel, biscuit tin.

bizcocho *nm* (a) (*Cook*) sponge, sponge cake; sponge finger; (*Naut*) hardtack, ship's biscuit; **embarcarse con poco** — to set out unprepared.
(b) (*Ceramics*) bisque, biscuit ware.

bizcorneado *adj* (*SD*) = **bizco**.

bizcornear [1a] *vi* (*Cu, PR*) to squint, look cross-eyed.

bizcorneto *adj* (*Col, Mex*) = **bizco**.

bizma *nf* poultice.

bizmar [1a] *vt* to poultice.

biznieto *nm* (*etc*) = **bisnieto** (*etc*).

bizquear [1a] *vi* to squint, look cross-eyed.

bizquera *nf* (*Col, PR*) squint.

blanca *nf* (a) white woman.
(b) (*Hist*) *old Spanish copper coin*; **estar sin —, quedarse sin** — to be broke (*fam*).
(c) (*Mus*) minim.
(d) **las —s** (*Chess*) white, the white pieces.

Blancanieves *f* Snow White.

blanco 1 *adj* (a) white; *bread, hair, wine* white; *skin* white, light; *complexion* fair; **la raza blanca** the white race; **más — que el jazmín** (*or* **la nieve** *etc*) whiter than white, as white as snow; **más — que el papel** (*or* **la cera** *etc*) as white as a sheet; **deja la ropa más que blanca** it makes clothes whiter than white.
(b) *page, space* blank.
(c) *verse* blank.
(d) (*fam*) yellow, cowardly.
2 *nm* (a) white; whiteness; **— de España** whiting; **— del huevo** white of egg; **— del ojo** white of the eye; **— de plomo** white lead; **calentar al** — to make white-hot; **poner los ojos en** — to roll one's eyes; to look ecstatic; **poner lo — negro** to make out that white is black.
(b) white man, white person; **los —s** the whites.
(c) (*Zool*) white spot, white patch.
(d) interval, gap.
(e) blank, blank space; **con 2 páginas en** — with two blank pages; **cheque en** — blank cheque; **dejar un** — to leave a space; **dejar algo en** — to leave something blank; **firmar en** — to sign a blank cheque; **votar en** — to return a blank voting paper, spoil one's vote.
(f) blank, blank form.
(g) (*Mil and fig*) target; **ser el — de las burlas** to be the target for jokes, be the object of ridicule; **dar en el** — to hit the mark; **hacer** — to hit the target, strike home; **hacer — en** to hit, strike.
(h) **dejar a uno en** — to disappoint someone; **pasar la noche en** — to have a sleepless night; **quedarse en** — to fail to see the point, not understand a word; to be disappointed.
3 *attr*: **el vehículo** — the target vehicle.

blancor *nm* whiteness.

blancote 1 *adj* (a) sickly white, unhealthily white.
(b) (*fam*) yellow, cowardly. **2** *nm* (*fam*) coward.

blancura *nf* whiteness.

blancuzco *adj* whitish.

blandamente *adv* softly; mildly, gently; tenderly; indulgently.

blandear[1] [1a] *vt* = **blandir**.

blandear[2] [1a] **1** *vt* (*fig*) to convince, persuade.
2 *vi and* **blandearse** *vr* to soften, yield, give way; **— con uno** to humour someone.

blandengue (*fam*) **1** *adj* soft, weak. **2** *nm* soft sort, softie.

blandir [3a; *defective*] **1** *vt* to brandish, flourish, wave about. **2** *vi and* **blandirse** *vr* to wave to and fro, swing.

blando *adj* (a) *material, water etc* soft; *paste etc* smooth; *flesh* (*pej*) flabby, slack; **— al tacto** soft to the touch; **— de boca** *horse* tender-mouthed.
(b) *manner etc* mild, gentle, bland; *climate* mild; *look* tender; *words* bland; **— de corazón** sentimental, tender-hearted.

(c) (*in character*) soft, delicate; sensual; (*towards others*) soft, indulgent.
(d) cowardly.

blandón *nm* (*Eccl*) wax taper; large candlestick.

blanducho *adj* soft, softish; *flesh* (*pej*) flabby, slack.

blandujo *adj* softish.

blandura *nf* (a) softness; smoothness; mildness; gentleness; blandness; tenderness.
(b) moral softness, effeminacy.
(c) blandishment, flattering words; **—s** endearments, sweet nothings.

blanduzco *adj* softish.

blanqueada *nf* (*SAm*) whitening; whitewashing.

blanqueador *nm*, **blanqueadora** *nf* bleacher.

blanquear [1a] **1** *vt* to whiten; to whitewash; *cloth* to bleach; *metal* to blanch. **2** *vi* to turn white, whiten; to show white.

blanquecer [2d] *vt* = **blanquear 1**.

blanquecino *adj* whitish.

blanqueo *nm* whitening; whitewashing; bleaching.

blanquiazul *adj* white-and-blue.

blanquillo 1 *adj* whitish; *bread etc* white. **2** *nm* (*CAm, Mex*: *euph*) egg; (*Chi, Per*) white peach; (*Ant, Chi*) whitefish.

blanquimiento *nm* bleach, bleaching solution.

blanquín *nm* (*Cu*: *euph*): **— de gallina** hen's egg.

blanquinegro *adj* white-and-black.

blanquirrojo *adj* white-and-red.

blasfemador 1 *adj* blasphemous, blaspheming. **2** *nm*, **blasfemadora** *nf* blasphemer.

blasfemamente *adv* blasphemously.

blasfemar [1a] *vi* (*Eccl*) to blaspheme (**contra** against); (*fig*) to curse, swear; **— de** to curse, swear about (*or* at).

blasfemia *nf* (a) (*Eccl*) blasphemy; insult. (b) swearword, curse, oath.

blasfemo = **blasfemador**.

blasón *nm* (a) coat of arms, escutcheon; armorial bearings. (b) heraldry. (c) (*fig*) honour, glory.

blasonar [1a] **1** *vt* to emblazon; (*fig*) to praise, extol. **2** *vi* to boast, brag; **— de** to boast about; to boast of being.

bleck *nm* (*RPl*: *angl*) pitch, tar.

bledo *nm*: (**no**) **me importa un —, no se me da un —** I don't care two hoots (*de* about).

bleque *nm* (*RPl*: *angl*) pitch, tar.

blindado *adj* (*Mil*) armoured, armour-plated; (*Mech*) shielded, protected, encased.

blindaje *nm* (*Mil*) armour, armour plating; (*Tech*) shield, protective plating, casing.

blindar [1a] *vt* (*Mil*) to armour, armour-plate; (*Tech*) to shield.

bloc *nm*, *pl* **blocs** pad, writing pad; calendar pad; (*School*) exercise book; **— de dibujos** sketching pad; **— de notas** pad for notes; (reporter's) notebook; **— de taquigrafía** shorthand book.

blocaje *nm* (*Sport*) tackle.

blocao *nm* blockhouse; pillbox.

blocar [1g] *vt* (*Sport*) to tackle.

blof *nm* (*SAm*) bluff; **hacer un — a uno** to bluff someone.

blofear [1a] (*SAm*: *angl*) **1** *vt* to bluff, impress. **2** *vi* to boast, brag.

blofero *adj* (*SAm*) boastful.

blofista *nmf* (*SAm*) boaster, braggart; bluffer.

blonda *nf* (a) blond lace. (b) (*Arg*) curl.

blondo *adj* (a) blond(e); fair, light; flaxen. (b) (*SAm*) soft, smooth, silken; (*Guat*) lank; (*Arg, Mex*) curly.

bloque *nm* (a) (*in most senses*) block; **— de casas** block of houses; **— de hormigón** block of concrete; **— de sellos** block of stamps; **— de cilindros** cylinder block; **— de papel** = **bloc**.
(b) (*Pol*) bloc, group; **el — comunista** the communist bloc.
(c) block, blockage, obstruction.
(d) **en** — en bloc.

bloquear [1a] *vt* (a) to block, obstruct; **— una ley en la cámara** to block a bill in parliament; **los manifestantes bloquearon las calles** the demonstrators blocked the streets.
(b) (*Mech*) to block, jam; **el mecanismo está bloqueado** the mechanism is jammed, the mechanism is stuck.
(c) to cut off; **la inundación bloqueó el pueblo** the flood cut off the village; **quedaron bloqueados por la nieve** they were cut off by the snow.
(d) (*Aut*) to brake, pull up.
(e) (*Mil*) to blockade.
(f) (*Comm, Fin*) to freeze, block; **fondos bloqueados** frozen assets.

bloqueo nm (a) (Mil) blockade; **burlar el —, forzar el —** to run the blockade.
(b) (Comm, Fin) freezing, blocking; squeeze; **— de fondos** freezing of assets.
blufar [1a] (etc) = **blofear** (etc).
blusa nf blouse; jumper; overalls; smock.
boa nf boa.
boardilla nf = **buhardilla**.
boato nm show, showiness, ostentation; pomp, pageantry.
bob nm (angl) bobsleigh.
bobada nf silly thing, stupid thing; **esto es una —** this is nonsense; **decir —s** to say silly things, talk nonsense; **¡no digas —s!** come off it!
bobalías nmf, pl **bobalías** nitwit, dolt.
bobalicón 1 adj very silly, utterly stupid. **2** nm, **bobalicona** nf nitwit, clot.
bobamente adv stupidly; naïvely.
bobático adj silly, half-witted.
bobear [1a] vi to fool about, do silly things; to talk nonsense, say silly things.
bobelas nmf, pl **bobelas** (fam) idiot, chump (fam).
bobera nf = **bobada, bobería**.
boberá nmf (Cu) fool.
bobería nf (a) silliness, idiocy. (b) = **bobada**.
bobeta 1 adj (RPl) silly, idiotic. **2** nmf (RPl; also **—s** Col) fool.
bobicomio nm (Col) lunatic asylum.
bóbilis adv (also **de —**) free, for nothing; without effort, without lifting a finger.
bobina nf (Tech) bobbin, spool; (Phot) spool, reel; (of tape) reel; (Aut, Elec) coil; **— de encendido** ignition coil.
bobinado nm (Elec) winding.
bobinadora nf winder, winding machine.
bobinar [1a] vt to wind.
bobo 1 adj silly, stupid; simple; naïve; **estar (or andar) — con algo** to be crazy about something.
2 nm, **boba** nf idiot, fool; greenhorn; (Theat) clown, funny man; **a los —s se les aparece la madre de Dios** fortune favours fools.
boboliche nm (Per) fool.
boca nf (a) (Anat) mouth; **— de dragón** (Bot) snapdragon; **— de escorpión** (fig) wicked tongue; **a —** verbally, by word of mouth; **a pedir de —** as much as one wishes, to one's heart's content; **todo salió a pedir de —** it all turned out perfectly; **en — de** (SAm) according to; **— abajo** face downward; **— arriba** face upward; **abrir tanta —** (Mex, Per, PR) to stand amazed; **andar en — de la gente** to be talked about; **la cosa anda de — en —** the story is going the rounds; **ella anda de — en —** she is the subject of gossip, people are talking about her; **buscar la — a uno** (try to) draw someone out; **calentarse la —** to talk a lot; to get worked up; **¡cállate la —!** (fam) shut up!; **decir algo con la — chica** (or **pequeña**) to say one thing but mean another; **no decir esta — es mía** not to open one's mouth; **lo hizo sin decir esta — es mía** he did it without a word to anybody; **hablar por — de ganso** to talk through one's hat; **esto hace — (CAm)** this gives me an appetite; **se me hace la — agua** my mouth is watering; **meter a uno en la — del lobo** to put someone on the spot; **meterse en la — del lobo** to put one's head in the lion's mouth; **quedarse con la — abierta** to be dumbfounded; **tapar la — a uno** to shut someone's mouth; **torcer la —** to make a wry face; to sneer.
(b) (fig) mouth, entrance, opening; approach; **— de agua, — de riego** hydrant; **— del estómago** pit of the stomach; **a — de invierno** at the start of winter; **a — de jarro** drink excessively, immoderately; **fire** (Mil) at close range; **— de metro** tube station entrance, subway entrance (US); **— de mina** pithead, mine entrance; **— de río** river mouth, mouth of a river.
(c) (of gun) muzzle, mouth; **a — de cañón** at close range.
(d) (of lobster etc) pincer; (of tool) cutting edge.
(e) (of barrel) bunghole.
(f) (Guat) delicacy (or snack) taken between glasses of spirits.
(g) (of wine) flavour, taste; **tener buena —** to have a good flavour.
bocabajo nm (Ant) beating.
bocabierta adj (Mex, Per) silly, stupid.
bocacalle nf entrance to a street; intersection; **la primera —** the first turning.
Bocacio m Boccaccio.
bocacha nf (a) (fam) bigmouth (sl). (b) (Mil: Hist) blunderbuss.
bocacho adj (Arg) big-mouthed (also fig).

bocadear [1a] vt to divide into pieces.
bocadillo nm snack; large sandwich, meat (or cheese etc) roll; **tomar un —** to have a snack, have a bite to eat.
bocadito nm (a) small bite, morsel, bit; **a —s** piecemeal. (b) (Cu) cigarette wrapped in tobacco leaf.
bocado nm (a) mouthful; morsel, bite; **no hay para un —** that's not nearly enough; **no he pasado (or probado) — en todo el día** I've not had a bite to eat all day; **no tener para un —** to be completely penniless; **tomar un —** to have a bite to eat; **— exquisito, — regalado** titbit; **— sin hueso** sinecure, soft job.
(b) bit; bridle.
(c) **— de Adán** Adam's apple.
bocajarro: a — adv (Mil) at close range; **decir algo a —** to say something straight out.
bocal nm (a) pitcher, jar. (b) (Mus) mouthpiece.
(c) (Min) pithead, mine entrance.
bocallave nf keyhole.
bocamanga nf (a) cuff, wristband. (b) (Mex) hole for the head (in a cape).
bocamina nf pithead, mine entrance.
bocana nf (SAm) mouth (of a river).
bocanada nf (a) (of wine etc) mouthful, swallow.
(b) (of smoke, wind) puff; (of bad breath) gust, blast.
(c) **echar —s** to boast, brag.
(d) **— de gente** crush of people.
bocaracá nm (CAm) snake.
bocarada nf (SAm) = **bocanada**.
bocatero nm, **bocatera** nf (Cu, Ven) great talker, braggart.
bocatoma nf (SAm) water intake, inlet pipe.
bocazas nmf, pl **bocazas** (fam) bigmouth (sl); **¡—!** (as insult) bigmouth! (sl).
bocera nf smear on the lips.
boceras nmf, pl **boceras** (fam) idiot, fool.
boceto nm sketch, outline; design; model, mock-up.
bocina nf (Mus) trumpet; (Aut, of gramophone) horn; megaphone; speaking trumpet; (SAm) ear trumpet; (Mex: Tel) mouthpiece; **— de niebla** foghorn; **tocar la —** (Aut) to sound one's horn.
bocinar [1a] vi (Aut) to sound one's horn, blow the horn, hoot.
bocinazo nm (Aut) hoot, toot, blast (of the horn).
bocinero nm hornblower.
bocio nm goitre.
bock nm, pl **bocks** [bok] beer glass, tankard.
bocón 1 adj (a) big-mouthed.
(b) (fig) boastful, big-mouthed (sl); (Chi, Cu) loud-mouthed; backbiting, gossipy; (Mex) indiscreet.
2 nm braggart; **¡—!** (as insult) bigmouth! (sl).
bocoy nm hogshead, large cask.
bocha nf (a) bowl; **juego de las —s** bowls. (b) (RPl: sl) nut (sl).
bochar [1a] vt (a) (Mex, Ven) to rebuff, reject; **— a uno** to give someone a dressing-down. (b) (Arg: sl) to plough (sl).
boche[1] nm Boche.
boche[2] nm (a) (Chi) husks, chaff.
(b) (PR, SD, Ven) telling off, dressing-down.
(c) (Mex, Ven) snub; **dar — a uno** to snub someone, slight someone.
(d) (Mex) **llevarse un —** to have an unpleasant encounter.
(e) (Bol, Chi, Ec, Per) uproar, din; (Chi, Per) brawl.
bochinche nm (a) uproar, din; riot; commotion.
(b) (Col, PR) piece of gossip, tale, lie.
(c) (Mex) dance, party.
(d) (Mex) low-class bar; seedy general stores.
bochinchear [1a] vi (SAm) to make a commotion.
bochinchero 1 adj (SAm) rowdy, brawling. **2** nm (SAm) rowdy, brawler.
bochinchoso adj (a) (Col, Mex, Pan, PR) gossiping, telltale, lying. (b) (Col, Per) rowdy, brawling.
bochorno nm (a) (Meteorol) sultry weather, oppressive weather; stifling atmosphere; sultriness; hot summer breeze.
(b) (Med) queer turn; hot flush; blush.
(c) (fig) embarrassment, flush, (feeling of) shame; stigma, dishonour; **¡qué —!** how embarrassing!
bochornoso adj (a) (Meteorol) sultry, oppressive; thundery; stuffy, stifling.
(b) (fig) embarrassing; humiliating, shameful, degrading; **es un espectáculo —** it is a degrading spectacle, it is a shameful sight.
boda nf (also **—s**) wedding, marriage; wedding reception; **—s de diamante** diamond wedding,

(*of club etc*) diamond jubilee; —**s de oro** golden wedding, (*of club etc*) golden jubilee; —**s de plata** silver wedding, (*of club etc*) silver jubilee; — **de negros** rowdy party.

bodega *nf* wine cellar; pantry; storeroom, warehouse; (*Naut*) hold; (*esp SAm*) bar, tavern; restaurant; (*Cu, Per, Ven*) grocery store, general store.

bodegón *nm* (a) cheap restaurant, dive (*fam*). (b) (*Art*) still life.

bodeguero 1 *adj* (*Cu*) coarse, common. **2** *nm* cellarman; owner of a *bodega*; (*Cu, Per, Ven*) grocer.

bodijo *nm* (*fam*) quiet wedding; (*pej*) misalliance, unequal match.

bodolle *nm* (*Arg*) large pruning knife, billhook.

bodoque *nm* (a) small ball, pellet.
(b) lump; (*Mex: Med*) lump, swelling; (*CAm, Mex*) bunch, ball.
(c) (*Mex*) badly-made thing.
(d) (*fam*) dimwit (*fam*).

bodorrio *nm* (a) = bodijo. (b) (*Mex*) rowdy party.

bodrio *nm* (*Arg*) (a) mix-up, confusion. (b) badly-made thing.

bóor 1 *adj* Boer. **2** *nmf*, *pl* **bóers** Boer.

bofe *nm* (*Zool*) lung; —**s** lungs, lights; **echar el** —, **echar los** —**s** to slog, slave; **echar los** —**s por algo** to go all out for something.

bofetada *nf* slap in the face (*also fig*); cuff, punch; **dar de** —**s a uno** to hit someone, punch someone.

bofetón *nm* punch (in the face), hard slap.

bofia *nf* (*sl*): **la** — the cops (*sl*).

boga¹ *nf* vogue, fashion; popularity; **la** — **de la minifalda** the fashion for the miniskirt, the popularity of the miniskirt; **estar en** — to be in fashion, be in vogue.

boga² *nf* (*Rail etc*) bogey.

boga³ 1 *nmf* rower. **2** *nf* rowing.

bogada *nf* stroke (of an oar).

bogador *nm*, **bogadora** *nf*, **bogante** *nmf* rower, boater.

bogar [1h] *vi* to row; to sail.

bogavante *nm* (a) (*Naut*) stroke, first rower. (b) (*Zool*) lobster.

bogotano 1 *adj* of Bogotá. **2** *nm*, **bogotana** *nf* native (*or* inhabitant) of Bogotá; **los** —**s** the people of Bogotá.

bogotazo *nm* (*Col*) ruin, destruction, pillage.

bohardilla *nf* = buhardilla.

Bohemia *f* Bohemia.

bohémico *adj* (*Geog*) Bohemian.

bohemio (*fig*), **bohemo** (*Geog*) **1** *adj* Bohemian. **2** *nm*, **bohemia** *nf*, **bohema** *nf* Bohemian.

bohío *nm* (*SAm*) hut, shack.

boicot *nm*, *pl* **boicots** boycott.

boicotear [1a] *vt* to boycott.

boicoteo *nm* boycott, boycotting.

boicotero *nm* (*SAm*) boycott.

boina *nf* beret.

boj *nm* box; boxwood.

bojote *nm* (a) (*SAm*) bundle, package. (b) (*Guat*) irregular portion; oddly-shaped piece. (c) (*SAm: fig*) un — de a lot of, a great many of.

bojotear [1a] *vt* (*Ven*) to bundle up, tie up.

bol *nm* (a) bowl; punch bowl; (*SAm*) finger bowl. (b) (*Sport*) ninepin.

bola *nf* (a) ball; marble; (*Naut*) signal (with discs); (*Chi: sl*) nut (*sl*); —**s** (*Mech*) ball bearings; —**s** (*SAm: Hunting*) bolas; — **de billar** billiard ball; **estar como** — **de billar** to be as bald as a coot; — **de contar** abacus bead; — **de cristal** crystal ball; — **de entintar** inking pad; — **del mundo** globe; — **de naftalina** mothball; — **de nieve** snowball; — **de tempestad**, — **de tormenta** (*Naut*) storm signal; **juego de (las)** —**s** American skittles; **¡dale** —**!** what, again!; come off it!; **dejar que ruede la** — to let things take their course; **escurrir la** — to take French leave; **poner** —**s a** (*Col*) to pay attention to; **tragar la** — (*fig*) to rise to the bait, swallow the bait.
(b) (*Cards*) slam, grand slam; **media** — small slam.
(c) shoe polish, blacking.
(d) fib, tale.
(e) (*Mex*) row, hubbub; brawl; noisy party.
(f) (*Mex*) crowd (of people).

bolacear [1a] *vi* (*Arg*) to talk nonsense.

bolada *nf* (a) throw (of a ball); (*Billiards etc*) stroke. (b) (*RPl*) — **de aficionado** intervention (by a third party). (c) (*SAm*) piece of luck, lucky break; (*Comm*) bargain, lucky piece of business. (d) (*Cu, Guat, Mex*) fib, tale. (e) (*Chi*) titbit, delicacy.

bolado *nm* (a) (*CAm, Chi, Mex*) affair, deal; (*Mex*) love affair, flirtation.
(b) (*CAm: Billiards*) clever stroke.
(c) (*CAm*) fib, tale; rumour, piece of gossip.

bolardo *nm* bollard.

bolate *nm* (*Col*) confusion, mess.

bolazo *nm* (a) (*RPl*) silly remark, piece of nonsense; false news; fib, tale. (b) (*Mex*) **de** — at random; hastily.

bolchevique 1 *adj* Bolshevik. **2** *nmf* Bolshevik.

bolchevismo *nm* Bolshevism.

bolchevista 1 *adj* Bolshevist. **2** *nmf* Bolshevist.

boleada¹ *nf* (*Arg*) hunt, hunting expedition (with *bolas*).

boleada² *nf* (*Mex*) shoeshine.

boleado¹ *adj* (*Arg*): **estar** — to have lost one's touch, be in a mess; to fail to do what needs to be done.

boleado² *nm* (*Mex*) shoeshine.

boleador *nm* (*Mex*) bootblack.

boleadoras *nfpl* (*Chi, RPl*) bolas, lasso with balls.

bolear¹ [1a] **1** *vt* (a) to throw.
(b) (*SAm*) to hunt; to catch with *bolas*; (*Bol, RPl: fig*) to play a mean trick on; to floor, flummox.
(c) (*SAm*) to vote against, blackball; to sack (*fam*), fire (*fam*); (*Univ etc*) to fail.
2 *vi* (a) to play for fun, knock the balls about.
(b) (*fam*) to tell fibs.
(c) to boast.
3 bolearse *vr* (a) (*RPl: horse*) to rear and fall on its back; (*Aut*) to overturn.
(b) (*RPl*) to get confused, get bewildered; to get embarrassed.

bolear² [1a] *vt* (*Mex*) *shoes* to shine, polish.

boleco *adj* (*CAm*) drunk.

bolera *nf* bowling alley, skittle alley.

bolero¹ *nm* (a) (*dance, jacket*) bolero. (b) (*CAm, Mex*) top hat.

bolero² *nm* (*Mex*) bootblack.

boleta *nf* (a) pass, permit; authorization; ticket; (*Arg*) first draft of a deed; (*Bol, Chi*) draft of a legal document; (*Col, Cu, Chi, Ec, Per, PR*) legal document; (*Mex, Per, PR*) ballot, voting paper.
(b) (*Mil*) billet.
(c) small packet of tobacco.

boletería *nf* (a) (*SAm*) ticket agency; (*Rail etc*) booking office; (*Theat*) box office. (b) (*SAm: Sport*) gate, takings.

boletero *nm* (*SAm*) ticket clerk, ticket seller.

boletín *nm* bulletin; (*Lit*) bulletin, journal, review; (*Theat etc*) ticket; (*Cu: Rail*) ticket; (*Mil*) pay warrant; (*Mil*) billet; (*School*) report; — **de inscripción** registration form; — **meteorológico** weather report, weather forecast; — **naviero** shipping register; — **de noticias** news bulletin; — **oficial** official gazette; — **de pedido** application form; — **de precios** price list; — **de prensa** press release.

boleto *nm* (a) (*SAm*) ticket; — **de ida y vuelta**, — **de viaje redondo** return ticket, round-trip ticket (*US*); *and compare* billete.
(b) (*in football pool*) coupon; — **de apuestas** betting slip.

bolichada *nf* lucky break, stroke of luck; **de una** — at one go.

boliche¹ *nm* (a) (*in bowls*) jack.
(b) (*game*) bowls; bowling; skittles.
(c) bowling green; bowling alley.
(d) cup-and-ball toy.
(e) small dragnet.
(f) small furnace, smelting furnace.
(g) (*PR*) poor-quality tobacco.

boliche² *nm* (*Bol, Chi, Per, RPl*) small grocery store; (*Arg*) cheap snack bar; (*Per*) low-class bakery; (*Chi*) gambling den.

boliche³ *nm* (*SAm: fam*) Bolivian.

bolichero¹ *nm* (*RPl*) grocer, shopkeeper; small-time dealer.

bolichero² *nm* (*in games*) ballboy.

bólido *nm* (a) meteorite. (b) (*Aut*) racing car, hot-rod (*US sl*).

bolígrafo *nm* ball-point pen.

bolilla *nf* (*Arg*) marble; (*Arg: Univ*) (piece of paper bearing) examination question.

bolillo *nm* (a) bobbin (for lacemaking). (b) (*SAm: Mus*) drumstick. (c) (*Mex*) bread roll; —**s** toffee bars.

bolina *nf* (a) (*Naut*) bowline; **de** — close-hauled; **navegar de** — to sail close to the wind. (b) (*fam*) racket, row, uproar.

bolista *nm* (*Mex*) troublemaker; unruly element.

bolita *nf* small ball; pellet; (*Cook*) small meatball; (*Arg, Chi*) marble; (*Chi*) ballot.

bolívar nm standard monetary unit of Venezuela.
Bolivia f Bolivia.
bolivianismo nm bolivianism, word (or phrase etc) peculiar to Bolivia.
boliviano 1 adj Bolivian. **2** nm, **boliviana** nf Bolivian.
bolo[1] nm **(a)** ninepin, skittle; (juego de) —s ninepins, skittles, tenpin bowling; **andar en** — (Col) to be naked; **ir en** — (Cu) to run along; **tumbar** — (Col) to do well, bring it off; **echar a rodar los** —s (fig) to create a disturbance.
  (b) (Med) large pill.
  (c) (Ant, Mex) one-peso coin.
  (d) (Cards) slam.
  (e) (Mex) invitation card to a christening.
bolo[2] adj (CAm) drunk.
bolón nm **(a)** (Arg, Chi) pebble, stone (used in building); (SD) marble. **(b)** (Cu, Mex) mob, disorderly crowd.
Bolonia Bologna.
bolonio nm, **bolonia** nf (fam) dunce, ignoramus.
bolsa nf **(a)** bag; pouch; handbag; purse; (SAm) sack; (CAm, Mex, Per) pocket; — **de agua caliente** hot-water bottle; — **de baño** beach bag; — **de la compra** shopping bag; — **de herramientas** toolbag; — **de papel** paper bag; — **para tabaco** tobacco pouch; **¡la — o la vida!** your money or your life!; **no abre fácilmente la** — he's pretty mean; **hacer algo de** — (Chi) to do something at someone else's expense; **hacer algo** — (Arg, Chi) to tear something to pieces; **volver a uno** — (Mex) to swindle someone.
  (b) (Sew: in dress etc) bag; **hacer** — to bag, pucker up.
  (c) (Mil) pocket.
  (d) (Geol) pocket; (Aer) — **de aire** air pocket.
  (e) (Anat, Zool) cavity, sac; pouch; —s **de los ojos** bags under the eyes.
  (f) (Comm, Fin) stock exchange; stock market; — **de granos** corn exchange; — **negra** (SAm) black market; "**B— de la propiedad**" (section of newspaper) "Property Mart", "Property for Sale"; — **de trabajo** labour exchange, employment bureau; **precio en la** — price on the stock exchange; **jugar a la** — to speculate, play the market.
bolsear [1a] vi (CAm, Mex) to pick pockets.
bolsicón nm (Col, Ec) thick flannel skirt.
bolsicona nf (Col, Ec) peasant woman.
bolsillo nm **(a)** pocket; purse, moneybag, pocketbook; **guardar algo en el** — to put something in one's pocket, pocket something; **meterse a uno en el** — to win someone over, have someone eating out of one's hand; **rascarse el** — to pay up, fork out (fam); **tentarse el** — (fig) to feel in one's pocket, consider one's financial circumstances.
  (b) **de** — pocket (attr), pocket-size; **edición de** — pocket edition; **acorazado de** — pocket battleship.
bolsín nm street market, kerbside market.
bolsiquear [1a] vt (Chi) to search someone's pockets; to pick someone's pockets.
bolsista nm **(a)** stockbroker. **(b)** (CAm, Mex) pickpocket.
bolso nm bag, purse; — **de mano**, — **de mujer** handbag, purse (US); — **de viaje** travelling bag; **hacer** — (of sail) to fill, belly out.
bolsón 1 nm **(a)** (Per) handbag, purse (US).
  (b) (Bol) lump of ore.
  (c) (Mex) lagoon.
  (d) (Arg, Col, Ec) fool.
  2 adj **(a)** (Arg, Col, Ec) silly.
  (b) (Mex, SD) lazy.
bolsonada nf (Arg, Col, Ec) silly thing, foolish act.
bollería nf baker's (shop), bakery, pastry shop.
bollero nm baker, pastrycook.
bollo nm **(a)** (Cook) bread roll; bun; **perdonar el** — **por el coscorrón** to realize that the disadvantages outweigh the advantages; **no pela** — (Ven) he never gets it wrong.
  (b) dent; (Med) bump, lump; (Sew) puff.
  (c) confusion; mix-up; **armar** — to make a fuss; **meter a uno en el** — to get someone into trouble.
  (d) (Arg, Hond) punch.
  (e) —s (Col) troubles, difficulties.
bollón nm (ornamented) stud; button earring.
bomba 1 nf **(a)** (Mil etc) bomb; shell; charge; — **atómica** atomic bomb; — **de hidrógeno** H-bomb; — **de humo** smoke bomb; — **incendiaria** incendiary bomb; — **lacrimógena** tear-gas bomb; — **de mano** grenade, hand grenade; — **de profundidad** depth charge; — **de relojería**, — **de retardo** time bomb; — **revientamanzanas**, — **vuelamanzanas** blockbuster; — **volante** flying bomb; **a prueba de** —s bombproof, shellproof;

atacar con —s, **lanzar** —s **sobre** to bomb, drop bombs on; **caer como una** — to fall like a bombshell; **estar a tres** —s to be very cross; **estar echando** —s to be boiling hot.
  (b) (fig) surprise; surprising item of news; **¡—!** attention please!; **es la** — **del año** it's the surprise of the year.
  (c) (Tech) pump; (Mus) slide; — **de aire** air pump; — **de alimentación** feed pump; — **aspirante**, — **de succión** suction pump; — **de engrase** grease gun; — **de gasolina** (in engine) fuel pump, (at garage) petrol pump, gas pump (US); — **impulsora** force pump; — **de inyección** (de combustible) fuel pump; — **de incendios** fire engine; **dar a la** — to pump, work the pump.
  (d) (of lamp) glass, globe.
  (e) (Col) soap bubble.
  (f) (PR) big drum; dance accompanied by a drum.
  (g) (Ec, Ven) balloon; (Cu, Mex, RPl) round kite.
  (h) (Cu, Mex) top hat.
  (i) (Chi, Guat, Hond, Per) drinking spree (fam); drunkenness; **estar en** — (esp SAm) to be drunk.
  (j) (Ant, Col, Guat, Per) false piece of news; lie, tale.
  2 adj **(a)** **noticia** — (fam) shattering piece of news.
  (b) (Per: fam) **estar** — to be utterly useless.
  3 adv (fam): **pasarlo** — to have a grand time, have a whale of a time.
bombacha nf (Col, RPl), **bombache** nm (Cu), **bombacho** nm (Mex) baggy trousers, peasant trousers.
bombacho adj (SAm) wide, loose-fitting.
bombardear [1a] vt (Mil) to bombard, shell; (Aer) to bomb, raid; (Phys) to bombard; (fig) to bombard (de with).
bombardeo nm bombardment (also fig), shelling; bombing; raid; — **aéreo** air raid, air attack (contra, de on); — **en picado** dive bombing.
bombardero 1 adj bombing. **2** nm (Aer) bomber.
bombardino nm (Mus) tuba.
bombasí nm fustian.
bombástico adj (SAm) bombastic; (Cu) complimentary, eulogistic.
bombeador nm (RPl: Aer) bomber.
bombear [1a] **1** vt **(a)** (Mil) to shell.
  (b) liquid to pump; to pump out, pump up.
  (c) (Sew) to pad.
  (d) (fig) to praise up, inflate the reputation of.
  (e) (Arg) plan to defeat, sink, wreck; (RPl: Univ) to fail, plough (sl); (Col) to sack, fire (fam).
  (f) (Arg, Bol, Per) to spy on; to spy out, reconnoitre.
  (g) (Guat) to steal.
  2 vi (SD) to get drunk.
  3 bombearse vr (Archit) to camber; (of wood etc) to warp, bulge.
bombeo nm camber; warping, bulging; crown (of the road).
bombero nm **(a)** fireman; —s, **cuerpo de** —s fire brigade. **(b)** (Arg) spy, scout; guard.
bombilla nf lamp glass, chimney (of a lamp); (Elec) bulb; (SAm) small tube for drinking maté; (Mex) ladle; — **de flash**, — **fusible** (Phot) flash bulb.
bombillo nm (Ant, CAm, Col: Elec) bulb.
bombín nm bowler hat.
bombo 1 adj **(a)** dumbfounded, stunned.
  (b) (Cu) lukewarm; tasteless, insipid; person dull, silly.
  (c) (Mex) meat tainted, bad.
  2 nm **(a)** (Mus) big drum, bass drum; (Tech) drum; (PR) dance accompanied by a drum; **hacer algo a** — **y platillos** to make a great song and dance about something; **tengo la cabeza hecha un** — I've got a splitting headache; I'm all muddled.
  (b) (PR, SD) bowler hat.
  (c) (Naut) barge, lighter.
  (d) (fam) exaggerated praise; (Theat etc) ballyhoo (fam), big write-up; **dar** — **a uno** to give someone exaggerated praise, write someone up in a big way; to boost someone; **darse el** — **mutuo** to indulge in mutual backslapping.
  (e) **irse al** — (RPl) to come to grief, fail; **mandar a uno al** — (Arg: sl) to knock someone off (sl); **poner a uno** — (Mex) to insult someone; to hit someone.
bombón nm **(a)** sweet, candy (US); chocolate. **(b)** (fam) beauty, gem; (girl) peach (fam), smasher (sl).
bombona nf carboy.

bombonera nf (a) sweet box; sweet tin. (b) (fam) cosy little place.

bombonería nf sweetshop, confectioner's (shop).

bómper nm (SAm: Aut: angl) bumper.

bonachón adj good-natured, kindly; easy-going; (pej) simple, naïve.

bonaerense 1 adj of Buenos Aires. **2** nmf native (or inhabitant) of Buenos Aires; **los —s** the people of Buenos Aires.

bonancible adj (Meteorol) fair, calm, settled.

bonanza nf (a) (Naut) fair weather, calm conditions; **ir en —** (Naut) to have fair weather, (fig) go well, prosper.
(b) (Min) rich pocket (or vein) of ore, bonanza.
(c) (fig) prosperity, boom, bonanza; **estar en —** (Comm) to be booming.

bonazo adj = **buenazo**.

bonche nm (SAm: angl) bunch; mob, group; gang.

bondad nf goodness; kindness, helpfulness; **tener la — de + infin** to be so kind as to + infin, be good enough to + infin; **tenga la — de no fumar** please do not smoke, please be so kind as not to smoke; **tuvo la — de prestárnoslo** he very kindly lent it to us.

bondadosamente adv kindly; good-naturedly.

bondadoso adj kind, good; kindly, kind-hearted, good-natured.

bondi nm (Arg) tram.

bonete nm (Eccl) hat, biretta; (Univ) cap, mortar-board; **¡—!** (Guat, Mex: fam) not on your life!; **a tente —** doggedly, insistently.

bonetería nf (Chi, Mex, RPl) clothier's (shop), clothing store.

bóngalo nm, **bongaló** nm (angl) bungalow.

bongo nm (SAm) flat boat, small barge; (Col) small punt.

bongó nm (Cu) African-type drum.

boniata 1 adj (SAm) edible, non-poisonous. **2** nf (Cu) edible yucca.

boniato nm (Ant, RPl) sweet potato, yam.

bonificación nf (a) rise, increase; (esp Agr) improvement. (b) (Comm) allowance, discount.

bonificar [1g] **1** vt (a) (Agr, Comm) to improve. (b) (Comm) to allow, discount. **2 bonificarse** vr to improve.

bonísimo adj superl of **bueno**.

bonitamente adv (a) nicely, neatly; craftily. (b) slowly, little by little.

bonito¹ 1 adj (a) pretty; nice, nice-looking.
(b) pretty good, passable; **una bonita cantidad** a nice little sum; **¡qué —!** very nice too! (also iro).
2 adv (RPl: fam) well, nicely; **ella canta —** she sings nicely.

bonito² nm (Fish) striped tunny, bonito.

bonitura nf (SAm) beauty, attractiveness.

bono nm (a) voucher, certificate; **— de billetes de metro** booklet of metro tickets. (b) (Fin) bond; **— del estado** government bond.

boñiga nf cow dung, turd.

boqueada nf gasp; **dar la última —** to breathe one's last, be at one's last gasp; **dar las —s** to be dying.

boquear [1a] **1** vt to say, utter, pronounce.
2 vi (a) to gape, gasp.
(b) to be at one's last gasp; (fig) to be in its final stages; (of supply) to be very nearly exhausted.

boquera nf (a) (Agr) sluice. (b) (Med) lip sore, mouth ulcer. (c) **—s** (fam) hunger.

boquerel nm nozzle.

boqueriento adj (Chi) (a) suffering from lip sores. (b) (fig) vile, worthless.

boquerón nm (a) wide opening, big hole. (b) (Fish) (kind of) anchovy.

boquete nm gap, opening; hole, breach.

boquetear [1a] vt (Mex) to burgle, burglarize (US), break into.

boquiabierto adj open-mouthed; **estar —** to stand open-mouthed, stand gaping (in astonishment); to stand aghast.

boquiancho adj wide-mouthed.

boquiblando adj horse tender-mouthed.

boquifresco adj (fam) outspoken; cheeky.

boquilla nf (a) (Mus) mouthpiece; (of hose etc) nozzle; (of gas) burner; (of pipe) stem; cigarette holder; **— de filtro** filter tip.
(b) (Ec) rumour, piece of gossip.
(c) **promesa de —** insincere promise, promise not meant to be kept.

boquillazo nm (Per) piece of news given verbally.

boquillero adj (Ant) (a) talkative. (b) insincere, free with false promises.

boquirroto adj talkative, garrulous.

boquirrubio adj (a) talkative. (b) glib; indiscreet, loose-tongued. (c) simple, naïve.

boquituerto adj wry-mouthed.

boquiverde adj (fam) foulmouthed.

boraciar [1b] vi (RPl) to boast.

bórax nm borax.

borboll(e)ar [1a] vi (a) to bubble, boil up. (b) (fig) to splutter.

borbollón nm bubbling, boiling; gushing, welling up; **hablar a —es** to talk in a torrent; to splutter; **reírse a —es** to bubble with laughter; **salir a —es** (water) to come out in a torrent, come out with a rush, gush forth.

borbollonear [1a] vi = **borboll(e)ar**.

Borbón Bourbon.

borbónico adj Bourbon.

borbotar [1a] vi to bubble; to boil (up), boil over; to gush forth, well up.

borbotón nm = **borbollón**.

borceguí nm high shoe, laced boot; half boot; (baby's) bootee.

borda nf (a) (Naut) gunwale, rail; **motor de fuera de —** outboard motor; **echar (or tirar) algo por la —** to throw something overboard (also fig).
(b) (Naut) mainsail.
(c) hut.

bordada nf (Naut) tack; **dar —s** (Naut) to tack; (fig) to keep on going to and fro.

bordado nm embroidery, needlework.

bordadora nf needlewoman.

bordadura nf embroidery, needlework.

bordalesa nf (RPl) wine barrel holding 225 litres.

bordante nmf (Ant, Mex, PR) lodger.

bordar [1a] vt to embroider (also fig).

borde nm (a) edge, border; (of road etc) side; (of vessel) brim, rim, lip; (of window) ledge; (Sew) edge, hem, selvage; (Naut) board; **— de la acera** kerb; **— de ataque** (Aer) leading edge; **— del camino, — de la carretera** roadside, verge; **— del mar** seaside, seashore; **— de salida** (Aer) trailing edge; **al — de** at the edge of, on the border of, at the side of.
(b) (fig) **estar al — de una crisis nerviosa** to be on the verge of a nervous breakdown; **estar en el mismo — del desastre** to be on the very brink of disaster.

bordear [1a] **1** vt (a) to skirt, go along (or round) the edge of; to flank.
(b) **— un asunto** (Arg) to skirt round a (tricky) subject, avoid mentioning a subject.
(c) (Arg) to border, line; **el camino está bordeado de árboles** the road is lined (or fringed) with trees.
2 vi (Naut) to tack.

bordejada nf (RPl, Ven: Naut) tack.

bordej(e)ar [1a] vi (RPl, Ven: Naut) to tack.

bordillo nm kerb.

bordin nm (Ant, Mex, Per: angl) boarding house.

bordinguero nm, **bordinguera** nf (Ant, Mex, Per: angl) boarding-house keeper, landlord, landlady.

bordo nm (a) (Naut) side, board; **a —** on board; **estar a — del barco** to be on board (the) ship; **ir a —** to go on board; **al —** alongside; **buque de alto —** big ship, seagoing vessel; **personaje de alto —** distinguished person, influential person.
(b) (Naut) tack; **dar —s** to tack.
(c) (Arg, Guat, Mex) roughly-built dam; (Arg, Guat) raised ground.

bordón nm (a) pilgrim's staff; (fig) guide, helping hand.
(b) (Mus) bass string; bass stop, bourdon; (Poet) refrain; (fig) pet word, pet phrase.
(c) (Col, Pan) (youngest) child.

bordona nf (RPl) sixth string of the guitar; **—s** three bass strings of the guitar.

bordoncillo nm pet word, pet phrase.

bordonear [1a] **1** vt (Arg: Mus) to strum. **2** vi (Per, Ven) to hum, buzz.

bordoneo nm (RPl: Mus) strumming.

boreal adj northern.

Borgoña f Burgundy.

borgoña nm (also **vino de —**) burgundy.

bórico adj boric.

boricua 1 adj Puerto Rican. **2** nmf Puerto Rican.

boriqueño 1 adj Puerto Rican. **2** nm, **boriqueña** nf Puerto Rican.

borla nf tassel, pompon; tuft; (Univ) tassel on doctor's cap; **— (de empolvarse)** powder puff; **tomar la —** (Univ) to get one's doctorate.

borlete nm (Mex) row, fuss, uproar.

borne nm (Elec) terminal.

borneadizo adj easily warped, flexible.

bornear [1a] **1** *vt* (a) to twist, bend.
    (b) (*Archit*) to hoist into place; to put in place, align.
    (c) (*Mex*) *ball* to spin, turn.
    2 *vi* (*Naut*) to swing at anchor.
    3 bornearse *vr* to warp, bulge.
borneo *nm* (a) twisting, bending. (b) alignment. (c) swinging at anchor.
borona *nf* (a) maize, corn (*US*); millet. (b) maize bread, corn bread (*US*); (*CAm, Col, SD, Ven*) crumb.
borra *nf* (a) thick wool, coarse wool, flock; stuffing.
    (b) fluff; (*Bot*) down; — **de algodón** cotton waste; — **de seda** floss silk.
    (c) sediment, lees.
    (d) (*fam*) empty talk; trash, rubbish.
borrachear [1a] *vi* to booze, get drunk.
borrachera *nf* (a) drunkenness, drunken state; **despejarse la** —, **espabilarse la** —, **quitarse la** — to sober up, get rid of one's hangover; **pegarse una** —, **ponerse una** — (*Mex*) to get drunk.
    (b) spree (*fam*), binge (*sl*), drinking expedition; **tomar una** — to go on a binge.
borrachería *nf* binge (*sl*), party.
borrachez *nf* drunkenness, drunken state.
borrachín *nm* drunkard, sot, toper.
borracho 1 *adj* (a) (*temporarily*) drunk, intoxicated; (*by habit*) drunken, hard-drinking, fond of the bottle; **estar** — **como un tronco** (*or* **una uva**), **estar más** — **que una cuba** to be as drunk as a lord.
    (b) (*fig*) drunk, blind, wild (*de ira etc* with rage etc).
    (c) *cake* tipsy; (*in colour*) violet; (*SAm*) *fruit* overripe; having a winey taste.
    2 *nm*, **borracha** *nf* drunkard, drunk (*fam*).
borrador *nm* (a) first draft, preliminary sketch, rough copy.
    (b) book for rough work, scribbling pad, scratch pad (*US*); (*Comm*) daybook.
    (c) rubber, eraser; duster.
borradura *nf* erasure, crossing-out.
borraja *nf* borage.
borrajear [1a] *vti* to scribble, scrawl; to doodle.
borrar [1a] *vt* (a) to erase, rub out; to cross out; to wipe out; (*fig*) *memory etc* to erase, efface, wipe away; — **a uno de una lista** to cross someone off a list, delete someone from a list.
    (b) to blot, smear; (*Phot etc*) to blur.
borrasca *nf* (a) (*Meteorol*) storm; squall; **tras la** — **viene el buen tiempo** (*fig*) every cloud has a silver lining.
    (b) (*fig*) peril, hazard; setback.
    (c) (*fam*) orgy, spree (*fam*).
borrascoso *adj* (a) *weather* stormy; *wind* squally, gusty. (b) (*fig*) stormy, tempestuous.
borrasquero *adj* riotous, wild.
borregaje *nm* (*Arg*) flock of lambs.
borrego 1 *nm*, **borrega** *nf* (a) lamb, yearling lamb; **no hay tales** —**s** there isn't any such thing.
    (b) (*fig*) simpleton.
    2 *nm* (*Cu, Mex*) tale, hoax, false news.
    3 —**s** *nmpl* (*prov: Naut*) white horses, foamy crests of waves.
borreguillo *nm* fleecy clouds.
borrica *nf* (a) she-donkey; (b) (*fam*) stupid woman.
borricada *nf* silly thing, piece of nonsense.
borrico *nm* (a) donkey (*also fig*). (b) (*Tech*) sawhorse.
borricón *nm* (*fam*), **borricote** *nm* (*fam*) poor devil.
borriqueño *adj* asinine, foolish.
borriquete *nm* (*Art*) easel; (*Tech*) sawhorse.
borrón *nm* (a) blot, smudge, stain; (*fig*) blemish; stain, stigma; slur; **estos** —**es** (*Lit*) these humble jottings.
    (b) (*Lit*) rough draft, preliminary sketch; (*Art*) sketch.
borronear [1a] (a) = **borrajear**. (b) to make a rough draft of.
borroso *adj* (a) blurred, indistinct, fuzzy; smudgy; (*Art*) woolly. (b) *liquid* muddy, thick.
borruca *nf* (*fam*) row, din.
borujo *nm* lump, pressed mass, packed mass.
borujón *nm* (*Med*) bump, lump; bundle.
borujoso *adj* lumpy.
boruquear [1a] *vt* (*Mex*) to stir up, mess up.
bos *nm* (*Mex: fam*) bus.
boscaje *nm* thicket, grove, small wood; (*Art*) woodland scene.
Bosco *m*: **el** — Bosch.
boscoso *adj* wooded.
Bósforo *m* Bosphorus.
bosorola *nf* (*CR, Mex*) sediment, dregs.

bosque *nm* wood, woodland, forest; woods.
bosquecillo *nm* copse, small wood.
bosquejar [1a] *vt* (*Art*) to sketch, make a sketch of, draw in outline; to model in rough; (*Tech*) to design; (*fig*) to sketch, outline; *plan etc* to draft.
bosquejo *nm* sketch, outline; rough model; draft.
bosquimano *nm* (*Africa*) bushman.
bosta *nf* dung, droppings; manure.
bostezar [1f] *vi* to yawn.
bostezo *nm* yawn.
bota *nf* (a) boot; —**s de campaña** top boots; —**s de esquí** ski boots; —**s de fútbol** football boots; —**s de goma** gumboots; —**s de montar** riding boots; **morir con las** —**s puestas** to die in harness; **ponerse las** —**s** (*fam*) to strike it rich (*fam*), make one's pile (*fam*); to enjoy oneself immensely.
    (b) leather wine bottle.
    (c) *liquid measure* = 516 *litres*; large barrel.
botada *nf* (*SAm*) throw, throwing; throwing away; sacking (*fam*); loss; (*Ant, Mex*) lift.
botadero *nm* (*Col, Mex*) ford; (*Per*) rubbish dump.
botado 1 *adj* (a) cheeky.
    (b) (*CAm*) spendthrift.
    (c) (*Ec*) resigned; ready for anything, resolute.
    (d) (*Mex: Comm*) very cheap, dirt-cheap.
    (e) (*SAm*) **niño** — = **2** *nm*, **botada** *nf* (*SAm*) abandoned child, foundling.
botador *nm* (a) (*Naut*) (punt) pole. (b) nail-puller, claw-hammer. (c) (*SAm*) spendthrift.
botadura *nf* (a) (*Naut*) launching. (b) (*SAm*) = **botada**.
botafuego *nm* (*fam*) quick-tempered person.
botalodo *nm* (*Per, PR*) mudguard.
botalón *nm* (a) (*Naut*) boom, outrigger; — **de foque** jib-boom.
    (b) (*Arg, Per*) beam, long timber, prop; (*Col, Ven*) post, stake; (*Col, Ven*) tethering post.
botánica *nf* botany.
botánico 1 *adj* botanical. **2** *nm*, **botánica** *nf* botanist.
botanista *nmf* botanist.
botar [1a] **1** *vt* (a) to throw, fling, hurl; *ball* to bowl, pitch.
    (b) (*Naut*) to launch (*also* — **al agua**).
    (c) (*Naut*) *rudder* to put over.
    (d) (*SAm*) to throw away, chuck out; *person* to fire (*fam*), sack (*fam*); *fortune* to fritter away, squander; **le botaron de su trabajo** they sacked him from his job.
    (e) (*SAm*) to lose.
    2 *vi* (*ball*) to bounce; (*Aut etc*) to bump, bounce, jolt; (*horse*) to buck, rear; **está que bota** he's hopping mad.
    3 botarse *vr* (*Chi*) (a) to change jobs.
    (b) **se bota a experto** he gives himself the airs of an expert, he claims to be an expert.
botaratada *nf* wild thing; wild scheme, nonsensical idea.
botarate *nm* (a) madcap, wild fellow. (b) idiot. (c) (*SAm*) spendthrift.
botarel *nm* buttress.
botarga *nf* motley, clown's outfit.
botavara *nf* (a) (*Naut*) boom, sprit. (b) (*PR, RPl*) pole (*of a cart*).
bote[1] *nm* (a) thrust, lunge, blow.
    (b) (*of ball*) bounce; (*Aut etc*) bump, bounce, jolt; (*of horse*) buck; **de** — **y voleo** instantly; **dar un** — to jump; **dar** —**s** (*Aut etc*) to bump, bounce; **pegar un** — to jump, start (with surprise).
    (c) **estar de** — **en** — to be packed, be jammed full, be crowded out.
bote[2] *nm* (a) can, tin, canister; pot, jar; pool (*of waiters' tips*).
    (b) (*Cards*) jackpot.
    (c) (*Aut: fam*) grid (*sl*), jalop(p)y; (*CAm, Mex: fam*) jail.
    (d) **chupar del** — to curry favour, creep (*sl*); **darse el** — to run off with something; **pegarse el** — **con uno** to get on like a house on fire with someone.
bote[3] *nm* (*Naut*) boat; — **de botador**, — **de pértiga** punt; — **de carrera**, — **de un remero** skiff, sculling boat; — **de a ocho** racing eight; — **de paso** ferryboat; — **de paseo** rowing boat; — **patrullero** patrol boat; — **de remos** rowing boat; — **de salvamento**, — **salvavidas** lifeboat.
botella *nf* (a) bottle; — **de Leiden** Leyden jar; — **termos** vacuum flask, thermos, vacuum bottle (*US*); **cerveza de** —, **cerveza en** —**s** bottled beer.
    (b) (*Cu*) sinecure, soft job, plum (given for political services).
botepronto *nm* (*Sport*) half-volley.
botería *nf* (*Arg, Chi*) shoeshop.

botica nf chemist's (shop), pharmacy, drugstore (US); de todo como en — everything under the sun.
boticario nm chemist, druggist, (Hist) apothecary.
botija 1 nf (a) earthenware jug; (fam) fat person; estar como una —, estar hecho una — to be as fat as a sow; poner a uno como — verde (Col, Cu, Guat, PR) to insult someone.
(b) (Ant, CAm, Ven) buried treasure.
2 nmf (Urug) baby, child.
botijo nm earthenware jug (with spout and handle); see **tren**.
botijón adj (Mex) potbellied.
botijuela nf (SAm) (a) earthenware jug. (b) buried treasure.
botillería nf refreshment stall.
botín[1] nm (Mil etc) booty, plunder, loot.
botín[2] nm (a) half boot; legging, spat. (b) (Chi) sock.
botina nf high shoe; (baby's) bootee.
botiquín nm (a) medicine chest; (also — de emergencia) first-aid kit. (b) (Ven) retail wine store.
boto[1] adj dull, blunt; (fig) dull, dim.
boto[2] nm leather wine bottle.
botón nm (a) (Sew) button; — (de camisa) stud; ¡ni un —! (fam) not a sausage! (fam).
(b) (Elec etc) button; (Tech) button, knob; (Radio) knob; — (de puerta) doorknob, doorhandle; — de contacto, — de presión push-button; — de arranque (Aut etc) starter, starting switch; empujar (or presionar etc) el — to press the button.
(c) (Fencing: of foil) tip.
(d) (Bot) bud; (woman: fam) peach (fam), smasher (sl).
(e) (Bot) — de oro buttercup, kingcup.
botonadura nf (set of) buttons; con — doble double-breasted.
botonar [1a] (SAm) 1 vt to button (up). 2 vi to bud.
botones nm, pl **botones** buttons; bellboy, bellhop (US).
botulismo nm food poisoning; botulism.
bóveda nf vault; dome; cave, cavern; — celeste vault of heaven, sky, firmament; — craneal cranial cavity.
bovedillas nfpl: subirse a las — (fam) to go up the wall (fam).
bovino adj bovine.
box[1] [boks] nm, pl **boxes** [boks] (angl-gall) (horse's) stall; (in motor racing) pit; (CAm, PR) post-office box.
box[2] [boks] nm (SAm: angl-gall) boxing.
boxeador nm boxer.
boxear [1a] vi to box.
boxeo nm boxing.
bóxer nm boxer (dog).
boxístico adj (SAm) boxing (attr).
boya nf (Naut) buoy; (Fish) float.
boyada nf drove of oxen.
boyante adj (Naut) buoyant, light in the water; (fig) buoyant, prosperous.
boyar [1a] vi to float.
boyé nm (RPl) snake.
boyera nf, **boyeriza** nf ox stable.
boyero nm (a) oxherd, drover. (b) cattle dog. (c) (Ec) goad, spike.
bozada nf (Col) halter.
bozal 1 adj (a) new, raw, green; animal wild, untamed.
(b) stupid.
(c) (SAm) Negro pure.
(d) (SAm) speaking broken Spanish.
2 nm muzzle; (SAm) halter, headstall.
bozo nm (a) down (on the upper lip), youthful whiskers. (b) mouth, lips. (c) halter, headstall.
bracamonte nm (Col) ghost.
bracear [1a] 1 vt (a) (Naut) to measure in fathoms.
(b) furnace to tap.
2 vi to swing one's arms; to swim, (esp) crawl; (fig) to wrestle, struggle.
bracero nm (a) labourer, navvy; farmhand, farm labourer. (b) ir de — to walk arm-in-arm.
bracete: ir de — to walk arm-in-arm.
bracmán nm, **bracmana** nf Brahman, Brahmin.
braco 1 adj pug-nosed. 2 nm (also perro —) setter.
braga nf (a) (Naut, Tech) sling, rope (for hoisting).
(b) nappy, diaper (US); —s (man's) breeches; (woman's) panties; calzar las —s (of a woman) to wear the pants, be the boss.
bragado adj energetic, tough; (pej) wicked, vicious.
bragadura nf (Anat, Sew) crotch.
bragazas nm, pl **bragazas** henpecked husband.
braguero nm (Med) truss.
bragueta nf (Sew) fly, flies; (boy's) short trousers; gran — (Col) womanizer; estar como — de fraile (RPl) to be very solemn.

braguetazo nm (Per, PR, RPl) marriage for money.
braguetero 1 adj (a) lecherous.
(b) (Chi, Guat, Per, PR) who marries for money; (Per, PR) who lives on his wife's earnings.
2 nm lecher.
braguillas nm, pl **braguillas** brat.
braguitas nfpl panties.
brama nf (Zool) rut, rutting season.
bramadero nm (SAm) tethering post.
bramante nm twine, string.
bramar vi (a) (Zool) to roar, bellow. (b) (fig: of person) to roar; to rage, bluster; (of wind, storm) to howl, roar; (of sea) to roar, thunder.
bramido nm roar, bellow; howl, howling.
branquia nf gills.
brasa nf live coal, hot coal; estar en —s to be on tenterhooks; estar hecho una — to be very flushed.
brasero nm brazier; (Hist) stake; (SAm) hearth, fireplace; (Col) large bonfire.
Brasil: el — Brazil.
brasileño 1 adj Brazilian. 2 nm, **brasileña** nf Brazilian.
brava nf (a) a la — (Ant, Mex) necessarily; by force. (b) dar una — (Cu) to sponge; dar una — a to intimidate.
bravata nf threat; boast, brag, piece of bravado; echar —s to boast, talk big; to bluster.
braveador 1 adj blustering, bullying. 2 nm bully.
bravear [1a] vi to boast, talk big; to bluster.
bravera nf vent, chimney.
bravero (Cu) 1 adj blustering, bullying. 2 nm bully.
braveza nf (a) ferocity, savageness; (of the elements) fury, violence. (b) bravery.
bravío 1 adj (a) (Zool) fierce, ferocious, savage; wild; untamed; (Bot) wild.
(b) (fig) uncouth, coarse.
2 nm fierceness, savageness.
bravo 1 adj (a) brave; tough, spirited, pugnacious.
(b) fine, excellent; sumptuous.
(c) animal fierce, ferocious; sea rough, stormy; landscape rugged, rough, wild; person angry, wild; bad-tempered.
(d) boastful, swaggering.
(e) (Arg) taste hot, strong.
2 interj bravo!, splendid!, well done!
3 nm thug.
bravucón 1 adj boastful, swaggering. 2 nm boaster, braggart.
bravuconada nf (a) bluster, boastfulness. (b) boast, brag.
bravura nf (a) fierceness, ferocity. (b) bravery. (c) = bravata. (d) (Mus) bravura.
braza nf (a) (Naut: approx) fathom. (b) (Naut) brace. (c) = brazada.
brazada nf (a) movement of the arms; a una — at arm's length.
(b) (of oar) stroke.
(c) (Swimming) stroke, style; — de espalda backstroke; — de mariposa butterfly-stroke; — de pecho breast-stroke.
(d) armful.
(e) (SAm: Naut, approx) fathom.
brazado nm armful.
brazal nm (a) armband. (b) (Agr) irrigation channel.
brazalete nm (a) (jewel) bracelet, wristlet. (b) armlet, armband.
brazo nm (a) arm; (Zool) foreleg; (Tech: of chair etc) arm; bracket; (Bot) limb, branch; — derecho (fig) right-hand man; — de dirección steering arm; — de lámpara lamp bracket; — de lámpara de gas gas bracket; — de mar arm of the sea, sound; estar (or ir) hecho un — de mar to be dressed up to the nines; — de río branch of a river; — secular secular arm; — de toma de sonido pickup arm; ir asidos (or cogidos) del —, ir del — (SAm) to walk arm-in-arm; coger a uno por el — to seize someone by the arm; cruzarse de —s to fold one's arms; estarse con los —s cruzados (fig) to sit back and do nothing; dar el — a uno (fig) to give someone a helping hand; no dar su — a torcer to stand fast, not give way easily; luchar a — partido to fight hand-to-hand, (fig) fight bitterly; mover algo a — to move something by hand, manhandle something; recibir a uno con los —s abiertos to receive someone with open arms.
(b) (fig) energy, enterprise; courage.
(c) —s (fig) hands, workers; backers, protectors.
brazuelo nm (Zool) shoulder.
brea nf tar, pitch.
brear [1a] vt (a) to abuse, ill-treat; — a uno a golpes to beat someone up. (b) to make fun of, tease.

brebaje nm (Pharm) potion, mixture; (hum) nasty drink, brew, concoction.
brecina nf (Bot) heath.
breck nm (RPl) = **breque** (b).
brécoles nmpl broccoli.
brecha nf (Mil) breach; gap, opening; (fig) breach, gap; (Med) gash, head wound; **abrir — en una muralla** to breach a wall; **batir en —** (Mil) to breach, (fig) get the better of; **hacer — en** (fig) to make an impression on.
brega nf (a) struggle; **andar a la —** to slog away, toil hard.
  (b) quarrel, scrap (fam), row.
  (c) trick, practical joke; **dar — a** to play a trick on.
bregar [1h] vi (a) to struggle, fight (con against, with; also fig).
  (b) to quarrel, scrap (fam).
  (c) to slog away, toil hard; **tendremos que hacerlo bregando** we shall have to do it by sheer hard work.
bren nm bran.
breña nf, **breñal** nm scrub, rough ground; bramble patch.
breñoso adj rough, scrubby; brambly.
breque nm (angl) (a) (SAm: Hist) break. (b) (Ec, Per, RPl: Rail) luggage van, baggage car (US). (c) (SAm: Mech) brake.
brequear [1a] vti (SAm: angl) to brake.
brequero nm (CAm, Mex, Per: angl) brakeman.
Bretaña f Brittany.
brete nm (a) fetters, shackles.
  (b) (fig) tight spot, jam; predicament; **estar en un —** to be in a jam; **poner a uno en un —** to put someone on the spot.
  (c) (PR) love affair.
bretón 1 adj Breton. **2** nm, **bretona** nf Breton.
bretones nmpl Brussels sprouts.
breva nf (a) (Bot) early fig, (black) fig.
  (b) flat cigar; (PR, RPl) good-quality cigar; (CAm, Cu, Mex, Pan, Per) chewing tobacco.
  (c) **¡no caerá esa —!** no such luck!; **pelar la —** (RPl) to steal; **poner a uno como una —** to beat someone black and blue.
  (d) (fam) **es una —** it's a cinch (sl), it's a pushover (fam); **para él es una —** it's chicken feed to him.
breve 1 adj short, brief; (in style) terse, concise; **en —** shortly, before long, very soon; concisely.
  2 nm (Eccl) papal brief.
  3 nf (Mus) breve.
brevedad nf shortness, brevity; terseness, conciseness; **con la mayor —** as soon as possible, at one's earliest convenience; with all possible speed; **bueno, para mayor — . . .** well, to be brief . . .; **llamado por —** called for short.
brevemente adv briefly, concisely.
brevería nf (Typ) note, short news item; snippet; **"Breverías"** (newspaper heading) "News in Brief", "From All Quarters".
brevete nm note, memorandum; (Per) driving licence.
breviario nm (Eccl) breviary; compendium, brief treatise; bedside companion.
brezal nm moor, moorland, heath.
brezar [1f] vt to rock, lull (in a cradle).
brezo nm heather.
briaga nf (Mex) drunkenness.
briago adj (Mex) drunk.
briba nf vagabond's life, idle life; **andar** (or **vivir**) **a la —** to loaf around, be on the bum (US).
bribón 1 adj (a) idle; lazy.
  (b) dishonest, rascally.
  2 nm (a) vagabond, vagrant; loafer.
  (b) rascal, rogue.
bribona nf rascal, rogue; bitch; **¡—!** you bitch!
bribonada nf dirty trick, piece of mischief.
bribonear [1a] vi (a) to idle, loaf around. (b) to be a rogue, play dirty tricks.
bribonería nf (a) vagabond's life, idle life. (b) roguery.
bribonesco adj rascally, knavish.
bricbarca nf large sailing ship.
brida nf (a) bridle; rein; **ir a toda —** to go at top speed; **tener a uno a — corta** to keep someone on a tight rein, keep someone under strict control. (b) (Tech) clamp; flange; collar; (Rail) fishplate.
bridge [briʒ] nm (Cards: angl) bridge.
bridgista [briʒista] nmf bridge player.
bridgístico [briʒistiko] adj bridge (attr); **el mundo —** the bridge world.
bridón nm snaffle; (Mil) bridoon.

brigada 1 nf (a) (Mil) brigade.
  (b) (of workers etc) brigade, squad, gang.
  (c) (of police etc) squad; **— fluvial** river police; **— móvil** flying squad; **— sanitaria** sanitation department.
  2 nm (Mil: approx) staff-sergeant, sergeant-major.
brigadier nm brigadier(-general).
brigán nm (Guat, SD, Ven) brigand, bandit; (SD) rogue.
brigandaje nm (Ven) brigandage, banditry.
brigantino 1 adj of Corunna. **2** nm, **brigantina** nf native (or inhabitant) of Corunna; **los —s** the people of Corunna.
Brígida f Bridget.
Briján: saber más que — to be very smart, know the lot.
brillante 1 adj (a) brilliant, bright, shining; jewel bright, sparkling; scene brilliant, glittering, splendid; surface shining; glossy; conversation, wit sparkling, scintillating; company brilliant.
  (b) (fig) brilliant.
  2 nm brilliant, diamond.
brillantemente adv (a) brilliantly; brightly. (b) (fig) brilliantly.
brillantez nf (a) brilliance, brightness; splendour.
  (b) (fig) brilliance.
brillantina nf brilliantine, hair cream.
brillar [1a] vi (a) to shine; to sparkle, glitter, gleam, glisten.
  (b) (fig: in smiling) to beam; (with happiness etc) to glow, light up.
  (c) (fig: in studies etc) to shine; **— por su ausencia** to be conspicuous by one's absence.
brillazón nf (Arg) mirage.
brillo nm (a) brilliance; brightness, shine; sparkle, glitter; glow; (of surface) lustre, sheen, gloss; radiance; **sacar — a** to polish, shine.
  (b) (fig) splendour, lustre, brilliance.
brilloso adj (Arg, Per, PR, SD) = **brillante** (a).
brin nm fine canvas, duck.
brincar [1g] **1** vt (a) child to jump up and down, bounce, dandle.
  (b) passage to skip, miss out.
  2 vi (a) to skip, hop, jump, leap about; (of lambs etc) to skip about, gambol.
  (b) (fig: also **— de cólera**) to fly into a rage, work oneself up; **está que brinca** he's hopping mad.
  3 brincarse vr: **— a uno** (Col: sl) to bump someone off (sl).
brinco nm hop, jump, leap, skip; **a —s** by fits and starts; **de un —** at one bound; **de un —** (SAm), **en un —** (Col etc) in a trice; **dar —s** to hop, jump etc; **quitar los —s a uno** (Col, Ven) to take someone down a peg.
brindar [1a] **1** vt (a) to offer, present, afford; **— a uno con algo** to offer something to someone; **le brinda la ocasión** it offers (or affords) him the opportunity; **los árboles brindaban sombra** the trees afforded shade.
  (b) (Taur) bull to dedicate (a to).
  (c) **— a uno a hacer algo** to invite someone to do something.
  2 vi: **— a, — por** to drink to, drink a toast to, toast; **¡brindemos por la unidad!** here's to unity!, let's drink to unity!
  3 brindarse vr: **— a + infin** to offer to + infin.
brindis nm, pl **brindis** toast; (Taur) (ceremony of) dedication.
brío nm (also **—s**) spirit, dash, verve; determination; resolution; elegance; jauntiness; **es hombre de —s** he's a man of spirit, he's a man of mettle; **cortar los —s a uno** to clip someone's wings.
briosamente adv with spirit, dashingly, with verve; resolutely; elegantly; jauntily.
brioso adj spirited, dashing, full of verve; determined, resolute; elegant; jaunty.
briqueta nf briquette.
brisa nf breeze.
brisera nf (SAm), **brisero** nm (SAm) windshield (for a lamp etc).
británico 1 adj British. **2** nm, **británica** nf British person, Britisher (US); **los —** the British.
britano 1 adj (esp Hist) British. **2** nm, **britana** nf (in formal usage, Hist and poet etc) Briton.
brizna nf (a) strand, thread, filament; (of grass) blade, wisp; (of bean) string.
  (b) chip, piece, fragment.
  (c) (Ven) drizzle.
briznar [1a] vi (Ven) to drizzle.
broca nf (Sew) reel, bobbin. (b) (Mech) drill, bit. (c) (of shoe) tack.
brocado nm brocade.

brocal nm rim, mouth; (of well) curb, parapet; cigarette holder; (Mex) kerb.

brocha 1 nf (a) brush, large paintbrush; — **de afeitar** shaving brush; **de** — **gorda** crudely painted, (fig) slapdash, crude, badly done.

(b) (CAm) creep (sl), toady.

2 adj (CAm) meddling; creeping (sl), servile; **hacerse** — (Guat) to play the fool.

brochada nf, **brochazo** nm brush-stroke; dab, splash (of paint).

broche nm clip, clasp, fastener; brooch; (of book) clasp, hasp; (Chi, Per, PR) paper clip.

brocheta nf skewer.

brochón nm whitewash brush.

broma nf (a) (in general) fun, gaiety, merriment; **tomar algo a** — to take something as a joke; **estar de** — to be in a joking mood, be in a mood for fun; **en** — in fun, as a joke; **ni en** — never, not on any account; **lo decía en** — I was only joking, I said it as a joke.

(b) (una —) joke; hoax, leg-pull, prank; — **estudiantil** student rag; — **pesada** practical joke, hoax; (pej) poor sort of joke, unfunny joke; **pero, aparte de** —**s** . . . but joking apart . . .; **entre** —**s y veras** half-joking(ly); **no es ninguna** — this is serious; **fue una** — **nada más** it was just a joke; **¡déjate de** —**s!** quit fooling!, joke over!; **no está para** —**s** he's in no mood for jokes; **¡para** —**s estoy!** (iro) a fine time for joking!; **gastar una** — **a uno** to play a joke on someone.

(c) (Arg, PR) disappointment; vexation, annoyance.

(d) (Zool) shipworm.

bromazo nm unpleasant joke, stupid practical joke.

bromear [1a] vi and **bromearse** vr to joke, crack jokes (fam), rag; **se estaban bromeando** they were ragging each other, they were pulling each other's legs; **creía que bromeaba** I thought he was joking.

bromista 1 adj fond of joking, full of fun; **es muy** — he's full of jokes, he's a great one for jokes.

2 nmf joker, wag; practical joker, leg-puller; **lo ha hecho algún** — some joker did this.

bromuro nm bromide.

bronca nf (a) row, scrap (fam), set-to (fam); **armar una** — to kick up a row; make a great fuss; **se armó una tremenda** — there was an almighty row (fam); **dar una** — **a uno** (Theat, Taur etc) to hiss someone, give someone the bird (sl).

(b) ticking-off; **nos echó una** — **fenomenal** he gave us a severe ticking-off, he came down on us like a ton of bricks.

(c) poor sort of joke, unfunny hoax.

broncamente adv roughly, harshly; rudely.

bronce nm (a) bronze; — **de campana** bell metal; — **de cañón** gunmetal; — **dorado** ormolu.

(b) (Art) bronze (statue).

(c) copper coin.

bronceado 1 adj (a) bronze, bronze-coloured.

(b) tanned, sunburnt.

2 nm (a) (Tech) bronzing, bronze finish.

(b) tan, sun tan.

broncear [1a] **1** vt (a) (Tech) to bronze. (b) to tan, bronze, brown. **2 broncearse** vr to bronze, brown, get a sun tan.

bronco adj (a) surface rough, coarse, unpolished.

(b) metal brittle.

(c) voice gruff, rough, harsh; (Mus) rough, rasping, harsh; manner gruff, rude; surly.

(d) horse wild, untamed.

bronquedad nf (a) roughness, coarseness. (b) brittleness. (c) gruffness, harshness; roughness.

bronquial adj bronchial.

bronquina nf = **bronca** (a).

bronquinoso adj (Ven) quarrelsome, brawling.

bronquios nmpl bronchial tubes.

bronquitis nf bronchitis.

broquel nm shield (also fig), buckler.

broquelarse [1a] vr to shield oneself.

broqueta nf skewer.

brota nf bud, shoot.

brotar [1a] **1** vt (of earth) to bring forth; (of plant) to sprout, put out; (fig) to sprout; to pour out.

2 vi (a) (Bot) to sprout, bud, shoot.

(b) (of water) to spring up, gush forth, flow; (of tears) to well up, start to flow; (of river) to rise.

(c) (Med) to break out, appear, show.

(d) to appear, spring up; **han brotado las manifestaciones** demonstrations have occurred; there have been outbreaks of rioting; **como princesa brotada de un cuento de hadas** like a princess out of a fairy tale.

brote nm (a) (Bot) bud, shoot.

(b) (Med) outbreak, appearance; rash, pimples; **un** — **de sarampión** an outbreak of measles.

(c) (fig) outbreak, rash; **un** — **huelguístico** an outbreak (or rash, wave) of strikes.

(d) (fig) origin; germ, genesis.

broza nf (a) dead leaves, dead wood; chaff; brushwood. (b) (fig) rubbish, trash. (c) painter's brush.

bruces: caer de — to fall headlong, fall flat; **estar de** — to lie face downwards, lie flat on one's stomach.

bruja 1 nf (a) witch; sorceress.

(b) (fam) hag, old witch, shrew.

(c) (Arg, Cu, PR) spook (fam), ghost; whore.

2 adj (Cu, Mex, PR): **estar** — (fam) to be broke (fam).

Brujas Bruges.

brujear [1a] **1** vt (Ven) to hunt. **2** vi (a) to practise witchcraft, be a witch. (b) (Mex, PR) to go on a spree (fam).

brujería nf (a) witchcraft, sorcery, (black) magic.

(b) (PR) poverty.

brujo nm sorcerer; wizard, magician; (SAm) medicine man.

brújula nf (a) compass; magnetic needle; — **de bolsillo** pocket compass; **perder la** — to lose one's bearings, (fig) lose one's touch.

(b) (fig) guide.

brujulear [1a] **1** vt cards to uncover (gradually); (fam) to guess.

2 vi (fam) (a) to manage, get along, keep going.

(b) (Per, PR) to go on the booze.

brulote nm (Bol, Chi) rude word, dirty word; (RPl) offensive remark; (RPl) scorching article.

bruma nf mist, fog; (Naut) sea mist; — **del alba** morning mist.

brumoso adj misty, foggy.

bruno adj dark brown.

bruñido 1 adj polished, burnished. **2** nm (a) (act) polish, polishing. (b) polish, shine, gloss. (c) — **de zapato** shoe polish.

bruñidor nm, **bruñidora** nf polisher, burnisher.

bruñir [3h] **1** vt (a) to polish, burnish, shine.

(b) (fam) to paint, make up.

(c) (CAm) to bother, pester.

2 bruñirse vr (fam) to paint oneself, make oneself up.

bruscamente adv (a) suddenly, brusquely, sharply.

(b) sharply, abruptly.

brusco adj (a) attack etc sudden; movement sudden, brusque; bend sharp; fall (in temperature etc) sharp, sudden; change sudden, marked, violent.

(b) (of manner) brusque, sharp, abrupt.

Bruselas Brussels.

bruselas nfpl tweezers; **unas** — a pair of tweezers.

brusquedad nf (a) suddenness; sharpness. (b) brusqueness, sharpness, abruptness; **hablar con** — to speak sharply.

brutal 1 adj (a) brutal; brutish, beastly. (b) (fam) terrific (fam), tremendous (fam). **2** nm brute, beast.

brutalidad nf (a) brutality; brutishness, beastliness.

(b) (una —) brutal act, piece of brutality, crime.

(c) stupidity.

(d) (fam) **me gusta una** — I like it tremendously (fam).

brutalizar [1f] **1** vt to brutalize, treat brutally; woman to rape. **2 brutalizarse** vr to become brutalized.

brutalmente adv brutally.

bruteza nf (a) brutality. (b) coarseness, roughness.

Bruto m Brutus.

bruto 1 adj (a) brute, brutish; bestial.

(b) stupid, ignorant; coarse, rough, uncouth; **Pepe es muy** — Joe is pretty rough, Joe is terribly uncouth; **¡no seas** —! don't be an idiot!

(c) diamond etc (also **en** —) uncut, rough, unpolished; **en** — material rough, raw, unworked; in a rough state; **hierro (en)** — crude iron, pig iron; **a la bruta** (SAm), **a lo** — (SAm) roughly, crudely.

(d) **beber en** — (PR, SD) to drink to excess; **pegar a uno en** — (PR, SD) to beat someone mercilessly.

(e) gross; **peso** — gross weight; **producto** — gross (national) product.

(f) (Chi) poor-quality, inferior.

2 nm (a) brute, beast; **¡**—**!** you beast!

(b) idiot.

bruza nf coarse brush, scrubbing brush; horse brush.

bu nm (fam) bogeyman; **hacer el** — **a uno** to scare someone.

búa nf pimple.

buba nf, **bubo** nm tumour, bubo.

bubónico adj: **peste bubónica** bubonic plague.

bubute nm (Ven) beetle.
bucal adj oral, of the mouth; **por vía —** through the mouth, by mouth.
bucanero nm buccaneer.
bucarán nm buckram.
búcaro nm (a) (fragrant) clay. (b) vase.
buccino nm whelk.
buceador nm underwater swimmer, skin diver.
bucear [1a] vi (a) to dive; to swim under water; to work as a diver. (b) (fig) to delve, explore, look below the surface.
buceo nm diving; underwater swimming, skin diving.
bucle nm (a) curl, ringlet. (b) (fig) curve, bend, loop; (Aer) loop.
bucólica nf (a) pastoral poem, bucolic; **las B—s** the Bucolics. (b) (fam) meal.
bucólico adj pastoral, bucolic.
buchaca nf (CAm, Mex, Ven) saddlebag; billiard pocket.
buchada nf mouthful.
buche nm (a) (Orn) crop; (Zool) maw; (fam) guts, belly; **llenar el —** (fam) to fill one's belly.
(b) (fig) inner thoughts; bosom; **sacar el —** (fam) to show off; **sacar a uno** (fam) to make someone talk.
(c) mouthful; (Ec) shot (of drink).
(d) (Sew) bag; wrinkle, pucker; **hacer —** to be baggy, wrinkle up.
(e) (Ec) top hat.
(f) (Guat, Mex) goitre.
(g) (Cu) despicable person.
buché nm (Pan) rustic, peasant.
Buda m Buddha.
budín nm (a) pudding; mould, pie. (b) (Per) brothel.
budismo nm Buddhism.
budista 1 adj Buddhist. 2 nmf Buddhist.
buenamente adv (a) easily, freely, without difficulty. (b) willingly; voluntarily.
buenamoza nf (Col: euph) jaundice.
buenaventura nf (a) good luck. (b) fortune; **decir** (or **echar**) **la — a uno** to tell someone's fortune.
buenazo 1 adj kindly, good-natured; long-suffering. 2 nm good-natured person; **ser un —** to be (too) kind-hearted, be easily imposed upon.
bueno 1 adj (**buen** before m sing noun) (a) (general sense) good; weather fine, good, fair; constitution strong, sound; doctrine right, sound; society good, polite; **sé —** be good; **los —s** good people, decent people; **el — de Manolo** good old Manolo; **lo — es que...** the best thing about it is that..., the best part is that...; the funny thing is that...; **—fuera que...** it would be fine if...; **¡— está!** that's enough!, that'll do!
(b) kind, good, nice; **fue muy — conmigo** he was very nice to me; **es Vd muy —** you are very kind.
(c) fit, proper, suitable; **en el momento — at the** right moment, at the proper time; **por buen camino** along the right road (and see **camino**); **ser — para** to be suitable for, be good for; **— de comer** good to eat, nice to eat; fit to eat.
(d) (Med) **estar — to** be well; **no estar — de la cabeza** to be weak in the head.
(e) (iro) fine, pretty; **¡buen conductor!** a fine driver you are!; **¡ésa sí que es buena!** that's a good one!; **le dio un tortazo de los —s** he gave him a real bash (fam), he really did bash him (fam).
(f) (fam) attractive; **está buena** she's hot stuff (sl), she's quite a girl; **¡estaba buenísima!** she looked a real treat!
(g) **¿adónde —?** where are you off to?; **¿de dónde —?** where did you spring from?; **¡cuánto — por aquí!** hullo there!; it's good to see you!
(h) (phrases with **buenas**) **¡buenas!** hullo!; **de buenas a primeras** straight away, from the very start; suddenly, without warning; **decir una noticia a uno de buenas a primeras** to spring a piece of news on someone; **estar de buenas** to be in a good mood; **por las buenas** gladly, willingly; **por las buenas o por las malas** willy-nilly, by hook or by crook, by fair means or foul.
(i) (Bol, Chi, RPl) **estar en la buena** to be in a good mood; to be in luck.
2 adv, as interj etc; **¡—!** right!, all right!, O.K.!; (iro) come off it!, so you say!; **—, resulta que...** well, it happens that...; **—, ¿y qué?** well, so what?
buey nm (a) (Zool) ox; bullock, steer; **— almizclado** musk ox; **— giboso** zebu; **— marino** manatee, sea cow; **— del Tibet** yak.
(b) (fig: Mex) cuckold; (PR) big sum of money; **— corneta** (Chi, RPl) one-horned ox; (RPl) busybody; **nunca falta un — corneta** (Bol, RPl) there's always

someone in the group you can't trust; **— muerto** (PR) bargain; bargain sale; **— suelto** freelance, free agent; bachelor; **chinches** (etc) **como —es** enormous bedbugs (etc), bedbugs (etc) the size of buffaloes; **es un — para el trabajo** he's a tremendous worker; **hablar de —es perdidos** (RPl) to waste one's-breath on silly subjects; **pegar —es** (CAm) to go to sleep; **poner los —es antes que el carro** to put the cart before the horse; **saber con los —es que ara** (PR, RPl) to know whom one can trust; **sacar el — de la barranca** (Mex, PR) to bring off something difficult; **cuando vuelen los —es** when pigs learn to fly.
bufa 1 adj (Cu, Mex) tight, drunk. 2 nf (a) (fam) wind, fart (tabu). (b) (Cu, Mex) drunkenness.
búfalo nm buffalo.
bufanda nf scarf, muffler.
bufar [1a] vi to snort; (of cat) to spit; **— de ira to** snort with rage.
bufeo nm (Ant, Hond, Mex) tunny.
bufet [bu'fe] nm (SAm) (a) sideboard. (b) buffet supper, cold supper. (c) dining room (of an hotel); restaurant.
bufete nm (a) desk. (b) (Law) lawyer's office; **abrir —, establecer su —** to set up in legal practice.
bufido nm snort (also fig).
bufo[1] 1 adj comic, farcical; slapstick, knockabout; opera comic.
2 nm (a) clown, funny man; (Mus) buffo singer.
(b) (Arg) queer (fam), homosexual.
bufo[2] adj (Ven) spongy.
bufón 1 adj funny, comical; clownish. 2 nm funny man, buffoon, clown; (Hist) jester.
bufonada nf (a) buffoonery, clowning. (b) (una —) joke, jest; piece of buffoonery; (Theat) comic piece.
bufonearse [1a] vr to joke, jest; to clown, play the fool.
bufonesco adj funny, comical; clownish.
bugle nm bugle.
bugui-bugui nm boogie-woogie.
buharda nf, **buhardilla** nf (a) dormer window; skylight. (b) garret, loft.
búho nm (a) (Orn) (long-eared) owl. (b) (fig) unsociable person, hermit.
buhonería nf (a) peddling, hawking. (b) pedlar's wares, hawker's wares.
buhonero nm pedlar, peddler (US), hawker.
buido adj (a) sharp, pointed. (b) fluted, grooved.
buitre nm vulture.
buitrear [1a] 1 vt (a) (SAm) to kill. (b) (Chi, Per) to bring up, vomit. 2 vi (Chi, Per) to be sick, vomit.
buitrón nm fish trap (of wicker).
buje nm axle box, bushing.
bujería nf trinket, knick-knack.
bujía nf (a) candle; candlestick. (b) (Elec) candle power. (c) (Aut etc) sparking plug, spark plug (US) (also **— de encendido**).
bula nf (a) (papal) bull; **no poder con la —** (fam) to have no strength left for anything; **no me vale la — de Meco** I'm done for.
bulbo nm (Anat, Bot, Med) bulb; (Mex: Radio) valve, tube (US); (Arg: Elec) bulb.
bulboso adj bulbous.
bule nm (Mex) gourd; water pitcher.
bulevar nm boulevard, avenue.
Bulgaria f Bulgaria.
búlgaro 1 adj Bulgarian. 2 nm, **búlgara** nf Bulgarian. 3 nm (language) Bulgarian.
bulo nm hoax, false report.
bulón nm bolt; spring pin.
bulto nm (a) size, bulk, bulkiness, volume, massiveness; **de —** obvious, striking; **de gran —** (Comm) bulky; **de mucho —** heavy, sizeable, massive, (fig) important; **de poco —** small, that does not take up much room, (fig) unimportant; **hacer —** to take up space, (fig) be of little real use.
(b) shape, form; vague shape, indistinct shape; **a —** roughly, broadly; in the mass; **hacer algo a —** to do something roughly; **decir algo a —** to come right out with something, blurt something out; **ir al —, tirar al —** to come straight to the point; **buscar el — a uno** to steal up behind someone, (fig) harass someone; **escurrir el —** to dodge, duck out of it, shy away, (fig) dodge the issue; **menear el — a uno** to thrash someone.
(c) package, bundle; bale; bulky object; piece of luggage; (SAm) briefcase, bag; **—s de mano** hand-luggage.
(d) (Med) lump, swelling.
(e) (Art) bust, statue.
bululú nm (PR, Ven) excitement, disturbance.

bulla *nf* (a) noise, uproar; racket; bustle; fuss, confusion; (*SAm*) quarrel, brawl; **armar —, meter — to kick up a row; meter algo a —** to throw something into confusion.
(b) crowd, mob.
(c) **ser el hombre de la —** (*Cu*) to be the man of the moment.

bullaje *nm* noisy crowd, mob.
bullanga *nf* disturbance, riot.
bullanguero 1 *adj* riotous, rowdy. **2** *nm*, **bullanguera** *nf* noisy person; rioter, troublemaker.
bullaranga *nf* (*SAm*) noise, row; riot.
bullebulle *nmf* busybody; mischief-maker; fusspot.
bullero *adj* (*SAm*) = **bullicioso**.
bullicio *nm* uproar, din, racket, hubbub; bustle, bustling movement, bustling activity; confusion; disturbance, riot.
bulliciosamente *adv* noisily; boisterously; busily; restlessly; riotously.
bullicioso *adj* noisy, rowdy; boisterous; busy, bustling, full of movement; active; restless; turbulent, riotous.
bullir [3h] **1** *vt* to move, stir; **no bulló pie ni mano** he did not stir hand or foot.
2 *vi* (a) to boil; to bubble, bubble up; **el agua bullía ligeramente** the water rippled slightly.
(b) to move, stir, budge; to move about; to bustle about; **no bullía** he didn't move, he never stirred.
(c) (*of insects*) to swarm; **— de** (*fig*), **— en** to teem with, swarm with, seethe with; **bullía de indignación** he was seething with indignation; **la ciudad bullía de actividad** the town was humming with activity; **Londres está que bulle de juventud** London is bursting with young people.
3 bullirse *vr* to move, stir, budge.
bumerang [bume'ran] *nm, pl* **bumerangs** [bume'ran] (*angl*) boomerang.
bunga *nf* (*Cu*) lie.
bungalow ['bongalo, bunga'lo] *nm, pl* **bungalows** ['bongalo, bunga'lo] (*angl*) bungalow.
bungo *nm* (*CAm*) = **bongo**.
bunker ['bunker] *nm, pl* **bunkers** ['bunker] (*Golf: angl*) bunker.
buñolería *nf* bakery where *buñuelos* are made; shop where *buñuelos* are sold.
buñuelo *nm* (a) (*approx*) doughnut, fritter. (b) (*fam*) botched job, mess.
buque *nm* (a) ship, vessel, boat; **— de abastecimiento** supply ship; **— almirante** flagship; **— de carga, — carguero** freighter; **— costero** coaster; **— de desembarco** landing craft; **— fanal, — faro** lightship; **— de guerra** warship; **— man-of-war; — hospital** hospital ship; **— insignia** flagship; **— de línea** liner, (*Hist*) ship of the line; **— mercante** merchantman, merchant ship; **— minador** minelayer; **— nodriza** depot ship, mother ship; **— de pasajeros** passenger ship; **— portatrén** train ferry; **— de vapor** steamer, steamship; **— de vela, — velero** sailing ship; **ir en — to** go by ship, go by sea.
(b) capacity, tonnage.
(c) hull.
buque-escuela *nm* training ship.
buraco *nm* (*RPl*) hole.
burata *nf* (*Ven*) money.
burbuja *nf* bubble; **hacer —s** to bubble.
burbujeante *adj* bubbly, fizzy; bubbling.
burbujear [1a] *vi* to bubble; to form bubbles.
burbujeo *nm* bubbling.
burdégano *nm* hinny.
burdel *nm* brothel.
Burdeos Bordeaux.
burdeos 1 *nm* Bordeaux (wine) (*also* **vino de —**). **2** *adj* maroon, dark red.
burdo *adj* coarse, rough; (*fig*) lie *etc* clumsy.
burear [1a] (*Col*) **1** *vt* to fool, hoax. **2** *vi* to have a good time.
bureo *nm* entertainment, amusement; spree (*fam*); **ir de —** to have a good time, go on a spree.
bureta *nf* burette.
burgalés 1 *adj* of Burgos. **2** *nm*, **burgalesa** *nf* native (*or* inhabitant) of Burgos; **los —es** the people of Burgos.
burgués 1 *adj* middle-class, bourgeois (*also pej*); town (*attr*). **2** *nm*, **burguesa** *nf* member of the middle-class, bourgeois; townsman, townswoman.
burguesía *nf* middle-class, bourgeoisie; **alta —** upper middle-class.
buril *nm* burin, engraver's chisel.
burilar [1a] *vt* to engrave; to chisel.

burla *nf* (a) gibe, taunt, jeer; **—s** mockery, ridicule; **hacer — de** to make fun of, mock; **hace — de todo** he mocks everything.
(b) joke; **—s** joking, fun; **de —s** in fun; **—s aparte** joking aside; **— burlando** with one's tongue in one's cheek; unawares, without noticing it; on the quiet; **gastar —s con uno** to make fun of someone.
(c) trick; hoax, practical joke; **fue una — cruel** it was a cruel sort of joke.
burladero *nm* (*Aut*) street island, refuge; (*Taur*) covert; (*Rail etc*) recess (*in a tunnel*).
burlador 1 *adj* mocking. **2** *nm* (a) scoffer, mocker. (b) practical joker, hoaxer, leg-puller. (c) seducer, libertine.
burlar [1a] **1** *vt* (a) to deceive, take in, hoax, trick; *enemy etc* to outwit, outmanoeuvre; *blockade* to run; *vigilance* to defeat.
(b) *ambition, plan etc* to frustrate; *hopes* to cheat, disappoint.
(c) *woman* to seduce, deceive.
2 *vi and* **burlarse** *vr* (a) to joke, banter; to scoff; **yo no me burlo** I'm not joking, I'm in earnest.
(b) **—se de** to mock, ridicule, scoff at; to make fun of.
burlería *nf* (a) mockery; fun. (b) trick, deceit; illusion. (c) tall story, fairy tale.
burlesco *adj* (a) funny, comic. (b) (*Lit etc*) mock, burlesque.
burlete *nm* weather-strip, draught excluder.
burlisto *adj* (*Arg, Hond, Mex*) = **burlón**.
burlón 1 *adj* mocking; joking, teasing, bantering; *laughter etc* mocking, sardonic; **dijo —** he said banteringly.
2 *nm*, **burlona** *nf* (a) joker, wag, leg-puller. (b) (*pej*) mocker, scoffer.
buró *nm* bureau, (roll-top) desk.
burocracia *nf* public service, civil service; (*pej*) bureaucracy; officialdom.
burócrata *nmf* civil servant, administrative official, official of the public service; (*pej*) bureaucrat.
burocrático *adj* official; civil service (*attr*); (*pej*) bureaucratic.
burra *nf* (a) (she-)donkey. (b) (*fig*) stupid woman; hard-working woman, drudge, slave.
burrada *nf* (a) drove of donkeys.
(b) (*fig*) silly thing, stupid act (*or* saying *etc*); **decir —s** to talk nonsense, say silly things.
(c) **una — de cosas** (*fam*) a whole heap of things, heaps of things.
burrajo *adj* (*Mex*) stupid.
burrero *nm* (a) (*Mex*) owner (*or* driver) of donkeys.
(b) (*Guat*) large herd of donkeys. (c) (*Ven*) coarse individual.
burro 1 *nm* (a) donkey; (*fig*) ass, idiot; (*RPl: hum*) racehorse; old horse, nag; losing horse (*in a race*); **— de agua** (*Ant, Mex*) big wave; **— de carga** (*fig*) glutton for work, hard worker, (*pej*) slave, drudge; **— cargado de letras** pompous ass; **apearse de su —** to back down, think better of it; **no apearse de su —** to stick to one's guns, persist in one's error; **caer —s apàrejados** (*SD*) to rain cats and dogs; **caerse del —** to realize one's mistake; **poner a uno a caer de un —** to beat someone black and blue; **esto comió — ** (*Urug*) it got lost, it vanished; **no ver tres en un —** (*etc*) to be as blind as a bat; **ver —s negros** (*Chi*) to see stars; to get a sharp pain.
(b) (*Tech*) sawhorse; (*Ant, Mex*) stepladder; (*Col, PR*) swing.
2 *adj* stupid.
bursátil *adj* stock-exchange (*attr*), stock-market (*attr*).
bursitis *nf* bursitis.
burujaca *nf* (*Arg, Hond, Par*) saddlebag.
burundanga *nf* (*Cu*) worthless object; piece of junk; **de —** worthless.
burujo *nm* = **borujo**.
bus *nm* (*SAm*) bus.
busaca *nf* (*Col, Ven*) saddlebag; (*Ven*) satchel.
busca *nf* search, hunt (*de* for); pursuit; **en — de** in search of.
buscabulla *nm* (*Cu, Mex*) brawler, troublemaker.
buscada *nf* = **busca**.
buscador *nm*, **buscadora** *nf* searcher, seeker; **— de oro** gold prospector.
buscahuella *nm* (*Aut*) spotlight.
buscaniguas *nm, pl* **buscaniguas** (*CAm, Col*) squib, cracker.
buscapié *nm* hint; feeler.
buscapiés *nm, pl* **buscapiés** squib, cracker.
buscapleitos *nmf, pl* **buscapleitos** (*SAm*) troublemaker.

buscar [1g] **1** *vt* **(a)** to look for, search for, seek; to hunt for, have a look for; *enemy* to seek out; *trouble* to be asking for, look for; *benefit, profit etc* to seek, be out for; **ir a —** to go and look for; to bring, fetch; **ven a —me a la oficina** come and find me at the office, come and pick me up at the office; **nadie nos buscará aquí** nobody will look for us here; **tengo que — la referencia** I have to look the reference up.
  (b) (*SAm*) to ask for, call.
  (c) (*Mex*) to provoke.
  2 *vi* to look, search, hunt; **buscó en el bolsillo** he felt in his pocket, he hunted in his pocket.
  (b) — + *infin* (*CAm*) to seek to + *infin*, try to + *infin*.
  3 buscarse *vr* **(a)** "se busca coche", "búscase coche" (*advert*) "car wanted".
  (b) —la (*fam*) to manage, get along; to be looking for trouble, ask for it; **se la buscó** he brought it on himself.
  (c) —las (*fam*) to fend for oneself.

buscarruidos *nm, pl* **buscarruidos** rowdy, trouble-maker.

buscas *nfpl* (*Ant, Mex, Per*) perks (*sl*), profits on the side.

buscavidas *nmf, pl* **buscavidas** **(a)** snooper, meddler, busybody.
  (b) hustler; (*pej*) social climber, go-getter.

buscón 1 *adj* thieving, crooked. **2** *nm* petty thief, small-time crook; rogue.

buscona *nf* whore.

busilis *nm* (*fam*) **(a)** difficulty, snag; **ahí esta el —** there's the snag, that's the rub.
  (b) core (of the problem); **dar en el —** to put one's finger on the spot.

búsqueda *nf* = **busca**.

busto *nm* bust.

butaca *nf* armchair, easy chair; (*Theat*) stall.

butacón *nm* large armchair.

butano *nm* butane, butane gas (*also* **gas —**).

butaque *nm* (*SAm*) small armchair.

buten: de — (*fam*) terrific (*fam*), tremendous (*fam*).

butifarra *nf* **(a)** Catalan sausage.
  (b) (*fam*) badly-fitting stocking.
  (c) (*Per*) big meat-and-salad sandwich.
  (d) (*RPl*) **tomar a uno para la —** to make a laughing stock of someone.

butiondo *adj* lewd, lustful.

butuco *adj* (*CAm*) short, squat.

buz *nm* respectful kiss, formal kiss; **hacer el —** to bow and scrape.

buzamiento *nm* (*Geol*) dip.

buzar [1f] *vi* (*Geol*) to dip.

buzo *nm* diver.

buzón *nm* **(a)** letterbox, pillar box, mailbox (*US*); **— de alcance** late-collection postbox; **echar una carta al —** to post a letter.
  (b) canal, conduit.
  (c) stopper; lid, cover.

buzonero *nm* (*SAm*) postal employee (*who collects from letterboxes*).

C

ca *interj* not a bit of it!, no, indeed!, oh no!
cabal 1 *adj* exact; right, proper; finished, complete, consummate, full; *effort etc* thorough, all-out.
   2 *adv* exactly; ¡—! perfectly correct!, right!
   3—es *nmpl:* **estar en sus —es** to be in one's right mind; **hacer algo por sus —es** to do something properly; to do things in the right order.
cábala *nf* **(a)** cab(b)ala; *(fig)* cabal, intrigue. **(b)** **—s** guess, supposition.
cabalgada *nf (Hist)* troop of riders; cavalry raid.
cabalgador *nm* rider, horseman.
cabalgadura *nf* mount, horse; beast of burden.
cabalgar [1h] **1** *vt* **(a)** *(of person)* to ride.
   (b) *(of stallion)* to cover, serve.
   2 *vi* to ride; to go riding; **— en mula** to ride (on) a mule; **— sin montura** to ride bareback.
cabalgata *nf* ride; cavalcade, mounted procession.
cabalista *nm* schemer, intriguer.
cabalístico *adj* cabalistic; *(fig)* occult, mysterious.
cabalmente *adv* exactly; properly; completely, fully; thoroughly.
caballa *nf* mackerel.
caballada *nf* **(a)** drove of horses, team of horses. **(b)** *(SAm)* stupid action, blunder.
caballar *adj* horse *(attr)*, equine; **cara —** horse-face; **ganado —** horses.
caballazo *nm (SAm)* collision between two horsemen, accident involving a horse.
caballejo *nm* **(a)** pony. **(b)** *(pej)* old horse, poor horse, nag.
caballerango *nm (Mex)* head groom.
caballerear [1a] *vi* to give oneself the airs of a gentleman.
caballeresco *adj* **(a)** *(Hist)* knightly, chivalric; **literatura caballeresca** chivalresque literature, books of chivalry; **orden caballeresca** order of chivalry.
   (b) *sentiment* fine, noble, chivalrous; *treatment etc* chivalrous; *character* gentlemanly, noble.
caballerete *nm* dandy, fop, dude (US).
caballería *nf* **(a)** mount; steed; horse, mule *(etc)*; **— de carga** beast of burden.
   (b) *(Mil)* cavalry; **— ligera** light horse, light cavalry.
   (c) *(fam: pej)* brute, beast; ¡—! you beast!
   (d) *(Hist)* chivalry, knighthood; order of chivalry, military order; **— andante** knight-errantry.
   (e) **andarse en —s** to overdo the compliments.
   (f) *(Ant, CAm, Chi, Mex) a land measurement of varying sizes.*
caballericero *nm (CAm, Cu)* head groom.
caballeriza *nf* **(a)** stable; stud, horse-breeding establishment; **— de alquiler** livery stable. **(b)** stable hands, grooms.
caballerizo *nm* groom, stableman; **— mayor del rey** *(Hist)* master of the king's horse; **— del rey** equerry.
caballero 1 *n* **(a)** rider, horseman.
   (b) gentleman; **cosas indignas de un —** things unworthy of a gentleman; **— de industria** swindler, adventurer, gentleman crook; **— solitario** lone wolf; **de — a —** as one gentleman to another; **ser cumplido —, ser todo un —** to be a real gentleman; **es un mal —** he's no gentleman.
   (c) *(Hist)* knight; noble, nobleman; **— andante** knight-errant; **los —s de Malta** the Knights of Malta; **— de Santiago** Knight of (the Order of) Santiago; **el C— de la Rosa** *(title)* Rosenkavalier; **el C— de la Triste Figura** the Knight of the Doleful Countenance *(Don Quixote)*; **armar — a uno** to knight someone, dub someone knight.
   (d) *(in direct address: often iro)* sir; **¿quién es Vd,...?** who are you, sir?
   2 *adj:* **iba — en una mula** he was riding a mule,

he was mounted on a mule; **estar — en su opinión** to stick firmly to one's opinion.
caballerosamente *adv* like a gentleman; chivalrously.
caballerosidad *nf* gentlemanliness; chivalry.
caballeroso *adj* gentlemanly; chivalrous; **poco —** ungentlemanly.
caballerote *nm (pej)* so-called gentleman, gentleman unworthy of the name.
caballete *nm (Agr)* ridge; *(Archit: of roof)* ridge, *(of chimney)* cap; *(Art)* easel; *(Tech)* trestle; *(Anat)* bridge (of the nose); **— de aserrar** sawhorse; **— para bicicleta** bicycle clamp, bicycle rest; **— de pintor** painter's easel.
caballista *nm* horseman.
caballito *nm* **(a)** little horse, pony; **— de niño** rocking horse, hobby-horse; **— del diablo** dragonfly; **— de mar, — marino** sea horse.
   (b) **—s** *(at fair)* merry-go-round.
caballo *nm* **(a)** horse; **— de aros** vaulting horse; **— de balancín** rocking horse; **— de batalla** *(fig)* forte, speciality; *(in controversy)* main point, central issue; **es su — de batalla** it's a constant theme of his; **— de blanco** *(Fin)* backer; **— de buena boca** *(fig)* obliging chap; **— castrado** gelding; **— de carga** packhorse; **— de carrera(s)** racehorse; **— de caza** hunter; **— entero** stallion; **— de guerra** warhorse, charger; **— mecedor** rocking horse; **— padre** stallion; **— de tiro** cart-horse, draught horse; **— de Troya** Trojan horse; **— de vaivén** rocking horse; **a —** on horseback; **andar** *(or* **ir, montar)* a —** to ride, go on horseback; **estar a — de** **algo** to be astride something, be on something; **subir a —** to mount, get on one's horse; **ir a mata —** to go at breakneck speed; **a — regalado no le mires el diente** don't look a gift horse in the mouth; **como — desbocado** *(fig)* rashly, hastily; **estar como el — de Don Quijote** to be terribly thin, be starving; **tropas de a —** mounted troops; **es de a —** *(SAm)* he's a good rider.
   (b) *(Chess)* knight; *(Cards)* queen.
   (c) *(Tech)* sawhorse.
   (d) **— de fuerza, — de vapor** horsepower; **un motor de 18 —s** an 18 horsepower engine; **¿cuántos —s tiene este coche?** what horsepower is this car?
caballón *nm (Agr)* ridge.
caballuno *adj* horse-like, horsy.
cabanga *nf (CAm)* nostalgia, homesickness; blues.
cabaña *nf* **(a)** hut, cabin, hovel, shack; **— de madera** log cabin.
   (b) *(Billiards)* balk.
   (c) *(Agr)* flock, large flock; **la — española** the total number of sheep (and goats) in Spain, the Spanish sheep (and goat) population.
   (d) *(RPl)* cattle-breeding ranch.
cabañero *nm* shepherd.
cabañuelas *nfpl (SAm)* (fanciful) weather predictions; *(Bol)* first summer rains; *(Mex)* winter rains.
cabaré *nm* cabaret.
cabaret [kaβa're] *nm, pl* **cabarets** [kaβa're] cabaret, floor show; night club; **— de desnudo** nude show, striptease show, strip club.
cabaretera *nf* cabaret dancer, cabaret entertainer; night-club hostess.
cabás *nm* satchel.
cabe *nm:* **— de pala** windfall, lucky break; **dar un — a** to harm, do harm to; **dar un — al bolsillo** to make a hole in one's pocket.
cabeceada *nf (SAm)* nod, shake of the head.
cabecear [1a] **1** *vt* **(a)** *(Sew)* to bind (the edge of).
   (b) *wine* to strengthen; *wines* to blend.
   (c) *(Sport)* to head.
   2 *vi* **(a)** *(in sleep)* to nod; *(negation)* to shake one's head; *(of horse)* to toss its head.

(b) (*Naut*) to pitch; (*Aut etc*) to lurch, sway; (*of cargo, load*) to slip.

cabeceo *nm* **(a)** nod, nodding; shake of the head; toss of the head. **(b)** (*Naut*) pitching; (*Aut etc*) lurch, lurching, swaying; slipping.

cabecera *nf* **(a)** (*of bed, table, bridge, etc*) head; seat of honour; (*of room*) upper end, far end; — de río headwaters of a river.

(b) (*of bed*) headboard; pillow, bolster; (*fig*) bedside; **libro de** — bedside book; **médico de** — family doctor; **estar a la** — **de uno** to be at someone's bedside; to nurse someone.

(c) (*Typ*) headline; headpiece, title; vignette; (*of document*) heading.

(d) (*Pol*) administrative centre, chief town, capital.

cabeciduro *adj* (*Col*) stubborn, pigheaded.

cabecilla **1** *nmf* hothead, wrong-headed person. **2** *nm* ringleader; rebel leader.

cabellera *nf* **(a)** hair, head of hair; wig, false hair, switch, hairpiece. **(b)** scalp. **(c)** (*Astron*) tail.

cabello *nm* **(a)** hair; (*also* —s) hair, head of hair; locks; — de Venus (*Bot*) maidenhair; **estar en** — to have one's hair down; **estar en** —s to be bareheaded; **estar pendiente de un** — to hang by a thread; **asirse de un** — to latch on to any excuse; **mesarse los** —s to tear one's hair; **un dato traído por los** —s an irrelevant fact, a piece of information wholly off the point; **una comparación traída por los** —s a far-fetched simile.

(b) (*Per*) —s de ángel thin vermicelli.

cabelludo *adj* hairy, shaggy; (*Bot*) fibrous; *see* **cuero**.

caber [2m] *vi* **(a)** to go, fit (*en* in, into); to be contained (*en* in); to have enough room; **no cabe el libro** the book won't go in, there's no room for the book; **caben 3 más** there's room for 3 more, we (*etc*) can get 3 more in; **en esta maleta no cabe** it won't go into this case, there's no room for it in this case, this case won't take it; **en este depósito caben 20 litros** this tank holds 20 litres; **¿cabe uno más?** is there room for one more?, can you get one more in?; **¿cabemos todos?** is there room for us all?; **eso no cabe por esta puerta** that won't go through this door.

(b) (*Math*) **¿cuántas veces cabe 5 en 20?** how many times does 5 go into 20?

(c) (*fig*) to be possible; **los compro todos y más, si cabe** I'll buy them all and more, if (that is) possible; **no cabe en él hacerlo** it is not in him to do it; **todo cabe en ese chico** that lad is capable of any mischief, anything might be expected from that lad.

(d) (*fig*) **no cabe más** (*fig*) that's the lot, that's the limit; **no** — **en sí** to be bursting, be beside oneself; (*pej*) to be swollen-headed; **no** — **en sí de contento** to be overjoyed, be overwhelmed with joy; **no cabe perdón** it's inexcusable; **cabe preguntar si . . .** one may ask whether . . ., it is proper to ask if . . .

(e) (*fig*) — **a uno** to happen to someone, befall someone; to fall to one's lot; **le cupieron 120 pesetas** his share was 120 pesetas, he got 120 pesetas (as his share); *see* **duda, suerte** *etc*.

cabestrar [1a] *vt* to halter, put a halter on.

cabestrillo *nm* (*Med*) sling; **con el brazo en** — with one's arm in a sling.

cabestro *nm* **(a)** halter; **llevar a uno del** — (*fig*) to lead someone by the nose. **(b)** leading ox, bell-ox.

cabetes *nmpl* (*Mex*) shoelaces.

cabeza *nf* **(a)** (*Anat and in many fig senses*) head; (*of bridge, nail, rocket, table, etc*) head; — **atómica** atomic warhead; — **de biela** (*Mech*) big end; — **de chorlito** (*fam*) scatterbrain, dimwit (*fam*); — **de dragón** (*Bot*) snapdragon; — **explosiva,** — **de guerra** warhead; — **hueca,** — **sin seso** idiot; — **pelada** (*Hist: Brit*) Roundhead; — **de playa** beachhead; — **de puente** bridgehead; — **de turco** scapegoat, whipping boy, fall guy (*US*); **estar de** — to be on end; **caer de** — to fall head first, fall headlong; **ir de** — (*fam*) to be snowed under; **meterse de** — **en algo** to plunge into something; **5 dólares por** — 5 dollars a head, 5 dollars per person; **por encima de la** — over one's head, overhead; **ganar por una** — (*escasa*) to win by a (short) head; **un melocotón como mi** — a peach as big as a football; **alzar** (*or* **levantar**) **la** — (*Comm etc*) to get on one's feet again, (*Med*) be up and about, be improving; **andar en** — (*SAm*) to go bareheaded; **asentir con la** — to nod (one's head); **calentarse la** — to get tired out; **me duele la** — my head aches, I've got a headache; **escarmentar en** — **ajena** to learn by someone else's mistakes; **no estar bueno de la** — to be weak in the head; **se me fue la** — I felt giddy; **se me fue de la** — it went right out of my mind;

jugarse la — to risk one's life; **lavarse la** — to wash one's hair; **por fin se lo metimos en la** — we finally got it into his head (*que* that); **esa melodía la tengo metida en la** — I've got that tune on the brain; **mover la** — **afirmativamente** to nod (one's head); **mover la** — **negativamente** to shake one's head; **jamás se me pasó por la** — it never entered my head; **perder la** — to lose one's head; **poner la** — **de uno a precio** to put a price on someone's head; **quitar algo de la** — **a uno** to get something out of someone's head; **ella me ha quitado la** — I'm crazy about her; **me está rodando la** — I feel giddy; **romper la** — **a uno** to give someone a beating; **romperse la** — to rack one's brains; **le saca la** — **a su hermano** he is taller by a head than his brother; **sentar la** — to settle down; to come to one's senses; **el vino se me subió a la** — the wine went to my head; **no tener** — **para las alturas** to have no head for heights; **tener la** — **como un bombo** to have a splitting headache; to be all muddled; **estar tocado de la** — to be weak in the head; **traer de** — **a uno** to upset someone, bother someone; **volver la** — to look round, turn one's head.

(b) (*person*) head; chief, leader; — **de familia** head of the household.

(c) (*of hill*) top, summit; (*of league, list, etc*) head, top; **ir a la** — **de la lista** to be at the top of the list; **ir en** — to be in the lead; **tomar la** — to take the lead.

(d) (*of river*) head, headwaters.

(e) (*Pol*) main town, chief centre, capital; — **de partido** county town, administrative centre.

(f) (*Bot*) — **de ajo** bulb of garlic; — **de plátanos** (*Ec, Per*) bunch of bananas.

(g) (*fig*) origin, beginning.

cabezada *nf* **(a)** butt; blow on the head.

(b) nod; shake of the head; **dar** —s to nod (sleepily); **darse de** —s to rack one's brains.

(c) (*Naut*) pitch, pitching; **dar** —s to pitch.

(d) head stall; (*of boot*) instep; (*Ec: of shoe*) vamp; (*Arg, Ec, Per*) saddle tree.

(e) (*Arg, Cub, Mex*) headwaters.

cabezal *nm* bolster, (cylindrical) pillow; (*Med*) pad, compress; — **explosivo** warhead.

cabezazo *nm* butt; (*Sport*) header.

cabezo *nm* hillock, small hill; (*Naut*) reef.

cabezón **1** *adj* = **cabezudo.**

2 *nm* **(a)** big head. **(b)** (*Sew*) hole for the head. **(c)** collar band; **llevar a uno de los** —es to force someone to go. **(d)** —es (*Col*) rapids, whirlpool.

cabezota **1** *nf* big head. **2** *nmf* (*fam*) pigheaded person.

cabezudo **1** *adj* **(a)** bigheaded, with a big head. **(b)** (*fig*) pigheaded. **(c)** wine heady. **2** *nm* carnival figure with an enormous head.

cabezuela *nf* (*Bot*) head.

cabida *nf* **(a)** space, room; capacity (*also Naut*); (*of land*) extent, area; **con** — **para 50 personas** with space for 50 people; **dar** — **a** to make room for, leave space for; **hay que dar** — **a los imponderables** one must leave room for (*or* allow for) the imponderables; **tener** — **para** to have room for, hold.

(b) (*fig*) influence; **tener** — **con uno** to have influence with someone.

cabildear [1a] *vi* to lobby; (*pej*) to intrigue.

cabildeo *nm* lobbying; (*pej*) intriguing, intrigues.

cabildero *nm* lobbyist, member of a pressure group; (*pej*) intriguer.

cabildo *nm* **(a)** (*Eccl*) chapter; (*Pol*) town council. **(b)** chapter meeting; (*Cu*) gathering of Negroes; (*Cu*) riotous assembly.

cabilla *nf* (*Naut*) belaying pin.

cabillo *nm* end; (*Bot*) stalk, stem.

cabina *nf* (*of lorry, Naut etc*) cabin; (*Aer*) cabin, cockpit; (*Cine*) projection room; — **altimática,** — **a presión** pressurized cabin; — **del conductor** driver's cabin; — **electoral** voting booth; — **de teléfono,** — **telefónica** telephone box, telephone kiosk.

cabinera *nf* (*Col*) air hostess, stewardess.

cabio *nm* joist, rafter; lintel.

cabizbajo *adj* crestfallen, dejected, downcast.

cable *nm* (*Naut etc*) cable, rope, hawser; (*measure*) cable length; (*Tel*) cable; (*Elec*) cable, wire, lead; — **aéreo** overhead cable; — **de remolque** towline, towrope; **echar un** — **a uno** to give someone a helping hand, help someone out of a jam.

cablegrafiar [1c] *vi* to cable.

cablegrama *nm* cable, cablegram.

cablero *nm* cable ship.

cablista *adj* (*SAm*) sly, cunning.

cabo nm **(a)** end, extremity; **de — a —, de — a rabo** from beginning to end; **leer un libro de — a —** to read a book from cover to cover.

(b) (of time, process) end; termination, conclusion; **al —** finally, in the end; **al — de 3 meses** at the end of 3 months, after (the lapse of) 3 months; **dar — a** to finish off; **dar — de** to put an end to; **estar al —** to be nearing one's end; **estar al — de la calle** (fig) to know what's going on, know what's what; **llevar a —** to carry out, execute, carry through; to implement; to transact; **ponerse al — de un asunto** to get to the point of a matter.

(c) end, bit; stub, stump, butt; **— de lápiz** stub of a pencil; **— de vela** stump of a candle.

(d) strand; (Tech) thread; (of stocking) denier; (Naut) rope, cable; **— de desgarre** (Aer) ripcord; **— suelto** loose end; **atar —s** to tie up the loose ends; to put two and two together; **no dejar ningún — abierto** to leave no stone unturned.

(e) handle, haft.

(f) (Geog) cape, point; **C— de Buena Esperanza** Cape of Good Hope; **C— de Hornos** Cape Horn; **Islas de C— Verde** Cape Verde Islands.

(g) (person) chief, head; (Mil) corporal; (Rowing) stroke; **— de escuadra** corporal; **ser como — de escuadra** to be despotic, be brutal; **— de mar** petty officer.

(h) **—s** (Sew) accessories; (fig) odds and ends.
cabotaje nm coasting trade, coastal traffic.
cabra nf **(a)** (Zool) (she-) goat, nanny goat; **— montés** wild goat. **(b)** (Col, Cu, SD, Ven) trick, swindle; loaded dice. **(c)** (Chi) light carriage; sawhorse.
cabrahigo nm wild fig.
cabrearse [1a] vr (fam) to get livid (fam).
cabreriza nf goat shed, goat house.
cabrerizo 1 adj goatish; goat (attr). 2 nm goatherd.
cabrero 1 adj (Arg) bad-tempered; **ponerse —** to fly off the handle (fam). 2 nm goatherd.
cabrestante nm capstan, winch.
cabria nf hoist, derrick.
cabrio = cabio.
cabrío 1 adj goatish; **macho —** he-goat, billy goat. 2 nm herd of goats.
cabriola nf **(a)** caper; gambol; hop, skip, prance; **hacer —s** to caper about, prance around. **(b)** (Cu, PR) prank, piece of mischief.
cabriolar [1a] vi to caper (about); to gambol; to skip, prance (around), frisk about.
cabriolé nm cab, cabriolet.
cabriolear [1a] vi = **cabriolar.**
cabritilla nf kid, kidskin.
cabrito nm **(a)** kid; **a —** astride. **(b)** **—s** (Chi) popcorn.
cabro nm **(a)** (SAm) he-goat, billy goat. **(b)** (Chi) small child; boy; lover, sweetheart.
cabrón nm **(a)** cuckold, complaisant husband.

(b) (as term of abuse: tabu) **¡—!** you bastard!, (hum) you old bastard!; **el muy — le robó el coche** the bastard stole his car; **el tío — ese** that bastard. **(c)** (SAm) brothel keeper; (Chi, Per) pimp; (Arg, Guat) traitor.
cabronada nf (fam) **(a)** dirty trick; **hacer una — a uno** to play a dirty trick on someone. **(b)** tough job, fag.
cabronazo nm (fam) rotter, villain.
cabruno adj goatish; goat (attr).
cábula nf **(a)** (Arg, Per) amulet. **(b)** (Arg) cabal, intrigue. **(c)** (Ant, CAm, Col, Per) trick, stratagem.
cabulero (Ant, CAm, Col, Per) 1 adj tricky, cunning, scheming. 2 nm trickster, schemer.
cabuya nf (SAm) agave, pita; pita fibre, pita hemp; rope, cord (of pita or in general); **ponerse en la —** to cotton on (fam); **verse a uno las —s** to see what someone is up to, see the trick.
caca nf (tabu) shit (tabu), dirt; (fig) dirt, filth; **¡—!** don't touch!
cacada nf (tabu) shit (tabu).
cacahual nm cacao plantation.
cacahuete nm peanut, monkey nut; (plant) ground-nut.
cacao nm (SAm) (tree, seed) cacao; (powder, drink) cocoa; chocolate; **pedir —** (fig) to give in, ask for mercy; **no valer un —** to be worthless, be insignificant.
cacaotal nm (SAm) cacao plantation.
cacaraña nf pit, pockmark.
cacarañado adj pitted, pockmarked.
cacarañar [1a] vt (Mex) to scratch, pinch; to pit, scar, pockmark.
cacarear [1a] 1 vt to boast about, exaggerate, make

much of; **ese triunfo tan cacareado** that triumph that was so much talked of, that much trumpeted triumph, that vaunted triumph.
2 vi to crow; to cackle.
cacareo nm crowing, cackling; (fig) crowing, boasting, trumpeting.
cacarizo adj (Mex) pitted, pockmarked.
cacastle nm (CAm, Mex) skeleton.
cacatúa nf cockatoo.
cacera nf ditch, irrigation channel.
cacereño 1 adj of Cáceres. 2 nm, **cacereña** nf native (or inhabitant) of Cáceres; **los —s** the people of Cáceres.
cacería nf **(a)** (in general) hunting, shooting.

(b) (persons) hunt, shoot, shooting party; **— de zorros** fox hunt; **organizar una —** to organize a hunt.

(c) bag, total of animals (etc) bagged.

(d) (Art) hunting scene.
cacerola nf pan, saucepan; casserole.
cacica nf (SAm) woman chief; chief's wife.
cacimba nf **(a)** (Ant, Arg, Per) well; (Cu) hollow of tree where rain water is collected; (Col) outdoor privy. **(b)** (Mex, Ven) small barn.
cacique nm (SAm) chief, headman, local ruler; (Pol) local boss, party boss; (fig) petty tyrant, despot; (Chi) person who lives idly in luxury.
caciquismo nm (Pol) (system of) dominance by the local boss; petty tyranny, despotism.
cacle nm (Cu) slipper; (Mex) rough leather sandal.
caco nm **(a)** pickpocket, thief. **(b)** coward.
cacofonía nf cacophony.
cacto nm cactus.
cacumen nm acumen, brains, insight.
cacha nf **(a)** handle; **hasta las —s** up to the hilt, completely.

(b) (Col) horn.

(c) (Bol, Col) metal spur attached to the leg of a fighting cock.

(d) (Bol) large chest.
cachaciento adj (Chi, Guat, RPl) = **cachazudo.**
cachaco nm **(a)** (Col, Ec, Ven) fop, dandy. **(b)** (Per) copper (sl), cop (sl).
cachada nf **(a)** (SAm: Taur) butt, thrust; goring. **(b)** (Arg) joke, leg-pull.
cachador adj (Arg) given to leg-pulling.
cachafaz adj (Chi, RPl) rascally; crafty; bold, cheeky.
cachalote nm sperm whale.
cachaña nf (Chi) **(a)** small parrot. **(b)** hoax, leg-pull; mockery, derision. **(c)** arrogance. **(d)** stupidity. **(e)** rush, scramble (for something).
cachañar vt (Chi) = **cachar¹; — a uno** to pull someone's leg.
cachar¹ [1a] vt **(a)** to smash, break, break in pieces; to split; (Agr) to plough up.

(b) (Bol, CAm, Col) to butt, gore.

(c) (Arg, CAm, Ec, Urug) to scoff at, deride, ridicule.

(d) (Chi, Per: tabu) to screw (tabu).
cachar² [1a] vt **(a)** (Arg) bus etc to catch.

(b) (CAm) to get, obtain; (CAm, Urug) to steal; (Chi, Mex, RPl) to surprise, catch in the act; (Chi) meaning etc to penetrate.
cacharpas nfpl (SAm) useless objects, lumber, junk.
cacharpaya nf (Arg, Bol, Per) farewell banquet, farewell party; (Arg) farewell; minor festivity.
cacharrear [1a] vt (CAm, PR) to put into jail.
cacharrería nf **(a)** crockery shop. **(b)** crockery, pots.
cacharro nm **(a)** earthenware pot, crock; **—s** earthenware, crockery, pots, coarse pottery.

(b) piece of pottery, potsherd.

(c) useless object, piece of junk; (Aut etc) old crock, jalop(p)y, grid (sl).

(d) (CAm, PR) jail.
cachaza nf **(a)** slowness; calmness, phlegm. **(b)** (SAm) rum.
cachazo nm (SAm) butt, thrust, goring.
cachazudo 1 adj slow; calm, phlegmatic. 2 nm slow sort; phlegmatic person.
cachear [1a] vt **(a)** (SAm) to butt, gore. **(b)** (Arg) to punch, slap. **(c)** to search, frisk (for weapons).
Cachemira f Kashmir.
cacheo nm searching, frisking (for weapons).
cachería nf **(a)** (Bol, Guat, Salv) small business, sideline. **(b)** (RPl) bad taste, slovenliness (in dress).
cachero 1 adj **(a)** (CR, Ven) lying, untrustworthy. **(b)** (CAm) active, busy. 2 nm (SAm) sodomite.
cachetada nf (SAm) slap, box on the ear; beating.
cachetazo nm **(a)** (Col, Guat, PR) slap, box on the ear. **(b)** (Guat) swig (fam).

cachete nm (a) (fat) cheek; (Med) swollen cheek. (b) punch in the face, slap. (c) dagger. (d) (CR, Guat) favour.

cacheteada nf (Arg) slap, box on the ear.

cachetear [1a] vt (Arg, Per) to slap, box on the ear.

cachetero nm (a) dagger. (b) (Taur) bullfighter who finishes the bull off with a dagger.

cachetina nf fist fight, punch-up (fam).

cachetón adj (a) plump-cheeked, fat-faced. (b) (Mex) impudent, barefaced; (Chi) proud. (c) (CR) attractive, congenial.

cachicán 1 adj sly, crafty. 2 nm (a) (Agr) foreman, gaffer. (b) (pej) sly sort.

cachicano nm (Col, Ven) armadillo.

cachicuerno adj weapon with a horn handle.

cachiflén nm squib, cracker.

cachifo nm (Col, CR, Ven) boy, young schoolboy.

cachigordo adj squat, chunky (fam).

cachimba nf (a) (SAm) pipe. (b) (SAm) empty cartridge. (c) (RPl) shallow well, hole dug in the beach for drinking water. (d) (Cu) loose woman.

cachimbo nm (a) (SAm) pipe; **chupar** — (PR, Ven) to smoke a pipe; (hum: of child) to suck its thumb. (b) (Cu) small sugar mill. (c) (Cu) poor man. (d) (Per: Univ) freshman.

cachipolla nf mayfly.

cachiporra nf truncheon; club, big stick, cosh.

cachiporrazo nm blow with a truncheon (etc).

cachirula nf (Col) lace mantilla.

cachivache nm (a) pot, utensil. (b) worthless person, useless fellow. (c) —s pots and pans, kitchen utensils; (fig) trash, junk, lumber.

cacho[1] 1 adj bent, crooked. 2 nm (a) crumb; bit, small piece, slice; ¡— de gloria! my precious!; ¡— de ladrón! you thief! (b) (SAm) horn; —s (fig) (number of) cattle; **hombre de muchos** —s man of great wealth in cattle. (c) (Ec, Per, RPl) dice box, dice, set of dice; **jugar al** — to play dice. (d) (Chi) drinking vessel (made of horn); **empinar el** — to drink a lot. (e) (RPl) bunch of bananas. (f) (Chi) unsaleable goods, unsold merchandise. (g) (Col, CR, Ec, Par, Ven) anecdote, joke; prank; hoax; (Ven) mockery, derision. (h) (phrases) **echar** — **a uno** (Col) to excel someone; **estar fuera de** — to be in safe keeping; **raspar el** — **a uno** (Chi) to tell someone off; ¡—s **para arriba!** (Chi) that's marvellous!, splendid!

cacho[2] nm (Fish) chub.

cachón[1] adj (Mex) long-horned.

cachón[2] nm wave, breaker; small waterfall.

cachondearse [1a] vr (fam) to take things as a joke; — **de uno** to mock at someone, tease someone, ridicule someone.

cachondeo nm (fam) farce, poor show (fam), mess; ¡esto es un —! what a mess!, what a farce this is!

cachondez nf (a) heat, rut, readiness to mate. (b) sexiness; randiness.

cachondo adj (a) (Zool) on heat, in rut. (b) (of human) **ser** — to be sexy; **estar** — to feel randy, be in the mood.

cachorro nm, **cachorra** nf (a) pup, puppy; cub. (b) (Cu, PR, Ven) uncouth person; ¡—! you brute!

cachudo 1 adj (a) (Ec, Mex) horned, with horns. (b) (Col) wealthy. (c) (Chi) suspicious, distrustful; cunning. (d) (Mex) grim-faced. 2 nm: **el** — the devil, the horned one.

cachuela nf (a) stew, fricassee. (b) (Bol, Per) rapids.

cachupín nm, **cachupina** nf (SAm: pej) Spanish settler (in America).

cada adj invar each; (followed by numeral) every; — **día** each day, every day; — **uno** each one, every one; — **3 meses** every 3 months; — **y cuando** every now and then; — **y cuando que** ... whenever ...; as soon as ...; — **y siempre que** ... as soon as ...; — **cierta distancia por la carretera** every so often along the road, at intervals along the road; — **cierto tiempo** every so often; ¿— **cuánto?** how often?

cadalso nm scaffold; (Tech) stand, platform.

cadarzo nm floss, floss silk.

cadáver nm body, dead body, corpse, cadaver (US); (of animal) body, carcass; **ingresó** — he was dead on arrival (at hospital).

cadavérico adj cadaverous; ghastly, deathly pale.

cadena nf (a) (in most senses) (fig) bond, link; series, sequence; — **antideslizante** tyre chain; — **de fabricación** production line; — **de hoteles** chain of hotels; — **de montaje** assembly line; — **de montañas** range of mountains; — **de oruga** caterpillar track; — **de reloj** watch chain; — **sin fin** endless chain; **reacción en** — chain reaction. (b) (Law: Hist) chain gang. (c) (Law) — **perpetua** life imprisonment. (d) (Archit) pier, buttress.

cadencia nf cadence, rhythm; measure; (Mus: piece) cadenza.

cadencioso adj rhythmic(al), cadenced.

cadeneta nf (Sew) chain stitch; — **de papel** paper chain.

cadenilla nf, **cadenita** nf small chain; necklace.

cadera nf hip.

cadetada nf thoughtless action, irresponsible act.

cadete nm cadet.

cadi nm (angl: Golf) caddie.

Cádiz Cadiz.

cadmio nm cadmium.

caducar [1g] vi (a) (person) to become senile; to dodder, be in one's dotage. (b) to get out of date; to fall into disuse; (Comm, Law) to expire, lapse; **el abono ha caducado** the season ticket has expired.

caducidad nf lapse, lapsing, expiry.

caduco adj (a) person senile, very old, decrepit; worn out. (b) (Bot) deciduous. (c) pleasure etc fleeting, perishable. (d) (Comm, Law) lapsed, expired, invalid; **quedar** — to lapse.

caduquez nf senility, decrepitude.

caedizo 1 adj about to fall; weak; (Bot) deciduous. 2 nm (Col) shed; sloping roof.

caer [2o] 1 vt (fam) to drop, let fall; liquid to spill; house etc to knock down; (of horse etc) to throw.
2 vi and (in some senses) **caerse** vr (a) (general sense) to fall; to fall down; to tumble (down), collapse; to fall off, fall out; (Aer) to crash, come down; (of curtain etc) to hang; (of hair, branch) to hang down; — **al suelo** to fall to the ground; **el edificio se está cayendo** the building is falling down; — **sobre** (fig) to fall on, pounce on; to descend upon; **cayó un rayo en la torre** the tower was struck by lightning; **estar al** — to be about to fall, (fig) be about to happen, be due to happen; **dejar** — to drop, let fall; **dejarse** — to let oneself go, let oneself fall; **hacer** — to knock down, knock off, cause to fall; **se me cayó el guante** I dropped my glove, my glove fell off; **Eslobodia nunca cayó tan bajo** Slobodia never fell so low; — **en cama**, — **enfermo** to fall ill; — **en un error** to fall into error; — **redondo** to fall in a heap; —**se de miedo** to be terrified; —**se de tonto** (etc) to be very silly (etc); **se cae de viejo** he's so old he can hardly walk; **eso cae de suyo** that's obvious, that goes without saying.
(b) to fall (in battle); (Mil: of town) to fall, be captured; **ha caído el gobierno** the government has fallen; — **como chinches**, — **como moscas** to die like flies.
(c) (of level, price, temperature etc) to fall, go down; to diminish; (of conversation) to flag; (of custom etc) to lapse.
(d) (of sun, wind) to go down.
(e) (of day) to decline, draw to its close; (of night) to fall, close in; **al** — **de la noche** at nightfall.
(f) (of colour) to fade.
(g) (of place) to fall, lie, be located; **cae en el segundo tomo** it comes in the second volume; **eso cae más hacia el este** that lies further to the east.
(h) (of windows etc) — **a**, — **hacia** to look over, look out on, look towards.
(i) (of date, event) to fall; **el aniversario cae en martes** the anniversary falls on a Tuesday.
(j) (Comm, Fin) to fall due.
(k) (of inheritance) — **a** to fall to, come to, fall to the lot of; see **suerte**.
(l) to realize; **no caigo** I don't get it; **ya caigo** I see, now I understand; — **en que** ... to realize that ...; see **cuenta**.
(m) (of dress) — **bien a uno** (of clothes) to suit someone, look well on someone; **el traje le caía mal** the suit did not fit him, the suit was not right for him.
(n) (of impression) **A no le cayó bien a B** A did not make a good impression on B; A was not well received by B; **no les caí** (CAm) I didn't hit it off with them, I didn't get on well with them, they didn't take to me.
(o) (RPl) to come, arrive, drop in; **él suele** — **por aquí** he usually comes here.

café nm (a) (drink, berry, plant) coffee; **—helado** iced coffee; **— instantáneo** instant coffee; **— con leche** white coffee, coffee with milk; **— molido** ground coffee; **— negro** (SAm), **— solo** black coffee; **— tostado** roasted coffee; **estar de mal —** (CAm) to be out of sorts.
(b) café; coffee house; restaurant, bar; **— cantante** low night club.
(c) (RPl) ticking-off.
cafeína nf caffein(e).
cafetal nm (a) coffee plantation. (b) (Guat) coffee tree.
cafetalero (SAm) 1 adj coffee (attr), coffee-growing (attr); **industria cafetalera** coffee industry. 2 nm coffee grower.
cafetalista nm (SAm) coffee grower.
cafetear [1a] vt (RPl) to tick off.
cafetera nf (a) coffee pot; **— automática** electric kettle; **— filtradora** percolator. (b) (fam) old car, old crock, jalop(p)y.
cafetería nf café, coffee house; (Rail) buffet, refreshment room; (Ant, Col, Chi) retail coffee shop.
cafetero (SAm) 1 adj coffee (attr); **industria cafetera** coffee industry. 2 nm café proprietor, café owner; coffee grower; coffee merchant.
cafetín nm low-class bar, small café.
cafeto nm (SAm) coffee tree.
cafetucho nm seedy little café.
caficultor nm (CAm) coffee grower.
caficultura nf (CAm) coffee growing.
cáfila nf group, flock, large number; **una — de disparates** a string of inanities.
cafre 1 adj (a) Kaffir. (b) (fig) cruel, savage; uncouth. 2 nmf Kaffir; **como —s** (fig) like savages, like beasts.
caga(a)ceite nm missel thrush.
cagada nf (a) (tabu) shit (tabu); **ser como —s de hormiga** (or **ratones** etc: hum) to be wholly unimportant; to be chicken feed.
(b) (fig) shocking blunder, stupid thing (to do).
cagadero nm (tabu) bog (sl), lavatory.
cagado adj (tabu) yellow, funky ((fam)).
cagajón nm horse dung, mule dung.
cagalera nf (tabu) runs (fam), diarrhoea; **¡brava —!** (iro) what a mess!
cagar [1h] (tabu) 1 vt (a) to shit (tabu).
(b) clothing to dirty, to soil.
(c) (fig) to bungle, make a mess of, mess up. 2 vi to shit (tabu), have a shit (tabu).
3 **cagarse** vr (a) = vi.
(b) **¡me cago!, me cago en la mar!** (etc) well I'm damned!; damn it!
cagarruta nf sheep dirt, goat dirt.
cagatintas nm, pl **cagatintas** penpusher, quill driver; (Col) miser.
cagón adj (tabu) = cagado.
cahuin nm (Chi) (a) drunkenness, drunken state. (b) rowdy gathering.
caída nf (a) fall; tumble, spill; falling, falling-out; (fig) fall, collapse, downfall; (Theat) flop, failure; **la C—** (Rel) the Fall; **la — del gobierno** the fall of the government; **la — del imperio** the collapse of the empire; **la — de los dientes** the falling-out of one's teeth, the loss of one's teeth; **— de agua** waterfall; **— de cabeza** fall headfirst, header; **a la — del sol** at sunset; **a la — de la tarde** in the evening; **sufrir una —** to have a fall, have a tumble.
(b) (of level, price etc) fall, drop (de 5 grados de 5 degrees; de la temperatura in temperature); decline, diminution.
(c) (of ground) drop, fall, slope; (Geol) dip; (of shoulders) slope.
(d) (of curtain etc) fold(s); (of dress) set, hang.
(e) **— radiactiva** radioactive fallout.
(f) **—s** (Tech) shoddy.
(g) **—s** (fam) witty remarks; **¡qué —s tiene!** isn't he witty?
caído 1 adj (a) fallen; head etc drooping; collar turndown; flower etc languid, limp, drooping.
(b) (fig) crestfallen, dejected.
(c) **— de color** pale.
2 **—s** nmpl: **los —s** the fallen; **los —s por España** those who fell for Spain; **monumento a los —s** war memorial.
caigo etc see **caer**.
caimacán nm (Col) important person, big shot (fam); ace, star, expert.
caimán nm (SAm) alligator, caiman; (Bol) iguana.
(b) (Mex: Mech) wrench. (c) (Ec) lazy fellow.
caimanear [1a] (SAm) 1 vt to swindle. 2 vi to hunt alligators.
caimiento nm (a) fall, falling; (Med) decline. (b) dejection; limpness.

Caín m Cain; **pasar las de —** to have a ghastly time (fam); **venir con las de —** to have evil intentions.
cairel nm wig; fringe.
cairelar [1a] vt to trim, fringe.
Cairo: **el —** Cairo.
caita 1 adj invar (Chi) wild, shy; unsociable. 2 nm (Chi) migratory agricultural worker.
caite nm (CAm) rough leather sandal.
caitearse [1a] vr (CAm): **—las** to run away, beat it (fam).
caja nf (a) box; chest; case, crate; coffin, casket (US); **— de colores** paintbox; **— del cuerpo** chest, thorax; **— de herramientas** toolbox, tool chest; **— de música** musical box; **— de sorpresa** jack-in-the-box; **— del tambor**, **— del tímpano** (Anat) eardrum; **un cuarto como — de muerto** a poky little room; **no entrar en —** to be of no advantage, (person) to be a square peg in a round hole, fail to adapt oneself.
(b) (Mech) case, casing, housing; (of vehicle) body; **— de cambios** gearbox; **— del cigüeñal** crankcase; **— de eje** axle box; **— de engranajes** gearbox; **— de fuego** (Rail) fire box; **— de sebo** grease cup; **— de velocidades** gearbox.
(c) (Elec) box; **— de empalmes** junction box; **— de fusibles** fuse box.
(d) (Archit: of staircase) well; (of lift) well, shaft; **— de registro** manhole.
(e) **— (de fusil)** stock.
(f) (Bot) seed case, capsule.
(g) (Comm, Fin) cashbox, safe; cashier's desk, cashdesk; cashier's office; **— de alquiler** safe-deposit box; **— de caudales** strongbox, safe; **— fuerte** strongroom, bank vault; strongbox; **— de (gastos) menores** petty cash; **— registradora** cash register, till; **metálico en —** cash in hand; **hacer —** to make up the accounts for the day; **ingresar en —** (person) to pay in, (cash) be paid in.
(h) (Fin) fund; **— de ahorros** savings bank; **— postal de ahorros** post office savings bank; **— de construcciones** building society; **— de jubilaciones** pension fund; **— de reclutamiento** recruiting office; **— de resistencia** (Pol) strike fund.
(i) (Mus) drum; **despedir** (or **echar**) **a uno con —s destempladas** to send someone packing, send someone away with a flea in his ear.
(j) (Mus) (of piano etc) case; (o violin etc) body, case; (Radio) cabinet; **— de resonancia** soundbox; (fig) sounding board.
(k) (Typ) case; **— alta** upper case; **— baja** lower case.
(l) (Chi) (dry) riverbed.
cajero nm, **cajera** nf cashier; (bank) teller.
cajeta nf (a) small box; (CAm, Chi, Ec, Mex, Ven) small round box of jelly (or of candy etc); (CAm, Chi, Ec, Mex, Ven) jelly, candy, sweet; (Cu, PR) tobacco pouch, cigar case.
(b) (CR, Ec, Per) lip (of animal).
(c) **de —** (CAm, Mex: iro) first-rate, marvellous.
cajete nm (Mex) pan, casserole.
cajetilla 1 nf small box; **— de cigarrillos** packet of cigarettes, pack of cigarettes (US).
2 nm (RPl) toff (fam), dude (US); city slicker (US); effeminate person.
cajista nm compositor, typesetter.
cajita nf small box; **— de cerillas** box of matches, matchbox.
cajón nm (a) big box, case; crate; chest; **— de embalaje** packing case.
(b) (Chi, Per, RPl) coffin, casket (US).
(c) drawer; locker; (Comm) till; **— de sastre** (fig) odds and ends; ragbag; (person) muddle-headed sort; **estar como — de sastre** to be in utter disorder, be in a terrible mess.
(d) (Comm) stall, booth; (Mex) grocer's shop; **— de ropa** (Mex) dry-goods store.
(e) (Tech) **— hidráulico**, **— de suspensión** caisson.
(f) (Chi, Guat, RPl, Ven) ravine.
(g) **eso es de —** that's a matter of course, that goes without saying; that's the usual thing.
cal nf lime; **— apagada**, **— muerta** slaked lime; **— viva** quicklime; **cerrar algo a — y canto** to shut something firmly (or securely); **de — y canto** firm, strong, tough.
cala[1] nf (Geog) cove; creek, inlet; fishing ground; (Naut) hold; **— de construcción** slipway.
cala[2] nf (of fruit) sample slice; (Med) suppository; (Surg) probe; **hacer — y cata** to test for quality.
calabacear [1a] vt (Univ) candidate to fail, plough (sl); subject to fail in, plough in (sl); lover to jilt.
calabacera nf pumpkin (plant), gourd.

calabacín *nm* (a) (*Bot*) marrow. (b) (*fig*) dolt.
calabaza *nf* (a) (*Bot*) pumpkin; gourd, calabash.
(b) (*fig*) dolt.
(c) **dar —s a** *a candidate* to fail, plough (*sl*); *lover* to
jilt; to snub, offend; **llevarse —s, recibir —s**
(*Univ*) to fail, plough (*sl*); (*lover*) to be jilted; **salir —**
to be a flop (*fam*), prove a miserable failure.
calabazada *nf* butt, knock (with the head); blow on
the head.
calabazo *nm* bump on the head.
calabozo *nm* (a) pumpkin, gourd. (b) (*Ant*) drum.
calabobos *nm* drizzle.
calabozo *nm* prison; prison cell; (*esp Hist*) dungeon;
(*Mil sl*) glasshouse (*sl*).
calabrote *nm* (*Naut*) cable, hawser.
calache *nm* (*CAm*) thing, thingummyjig (*fam*).
calada *nf* (a) soaking. (b) (*of net*) lowering. (c) (*fam*)
ticking-off; **dar una — a uno** to tick someone off,
haul someone over the coals.
calado 1 *adj*: **estar — (hasta los huesos)** to be soaked
(to the skin).
2 *nm* (a) (*Tech*) fretwork; (*Sew*) openwork.
(b) (*Naut*) depth of water; (*of ship*) draught;
en iguales —s on an even keel.
calafate *nm* caulker; shipwright.
calafatear [1a] *vt* (*Naut*) to caulk; to plug (up).
calaguritano 1 *adj* of Calahorra. **2** *nm,* **calaguritana**
nf native (*or* inhabitant) of Calahorra; **los —s** the
people of Calahorra.
calamaco *adj* (*Arg*) *poncho* red; (*Arg, PR*) *poncho*
old, faded; poor-quality.
calamar *nm* squid.
calambre *nm* (*also* —s) cramp; **— de los escribientes**
writer's cramp.
calambur *nm* (*SAm*) pun.
calamidad *nf* calamity, disaster; **es una — (fam:**
event etc) it's a great pity; it's a nuisance; (*person*)
he's utterly useless, he's a dead loss; **estar hecho**
una — to be in a very bad way; **¡vaya —!** what
bad luck!
calamina *nf* calamine.
calamitosamente *adv* calamitously, disastrously.
calamitoso *adj* calamitous, disastrous.
cálamo *nm* (*Bot*) stem, stalk; (*Mus*) reed; (*Mus,*
Hist) flute; (*poet*) pen; **empuñar el —** to take up
one's pen; **menear —** to wield a pen.
calamocano *adj* (*fam*) merry (*fam*), tipsy.
calamoco *nm* icicle.
calamorra *nf* (*sl*) nut (*sl*), head.
calamorrada *nf* (*fam*) butt; bump on the head.
calandraco *adj* (*Arg, Col*) annoying, tedious;
scatterbrained.
calandria¹ *nf* (*Orn*) calandra lark.
calandria² *nf* mangle; (*Tech*) calender.
calaña *nf* model, pattern; (*fig*) nature, kind, stamp.
calañés *nm* (*Andalusia*) hat with a turned-up brim.
calar¹ 1 *adj* calcareous, lime (*attr*). **2** *nm* limestone
quarry.
calar² [1a] 1 *vt* (a) *person* to soak, drench; *material*
to soak, drench; *material* to soak into, saturate,
permeate.
(b) to penetrate, perforate, pierce, go through.
(c) (*Tech*) *metal* to do fretwork on; (*Sew*) to do
openwork on.
(d) *person* to size up; *intention* to see through;
secret to penetrate; **¡nos ha calado!** he's rumbled us!
(*fam*); **a ésos los tengo muy calados** I've got them
thoroughly weighed up (*or* sized up).
(e) *bayonet* to fix; *mast* to fix, step.
(f) *bridge* to lower, let down; *net, sail* to lower.
(g) *fruit* to cut a sample slice of; (*Arg, Mex,*
PR) *corn* to take a sample of.
(h) (*Col*) to crush, flatten, sit on.
2 *vi* (a) (*of liquid*) to sink in, soak in; (*of shoe*)
to leak, let in the water.
(b) (*Naut*) to draw; **el buque cala 12 metros**
the ship draws 12 metres, the ship has a draught of
12 metres.
(c) (*Mech*) to stop, stall.
3 calarse *vr* (a) to get soaked, get drenched
(*hasta los huesos* to the skin).
(b) to get in, squeeze in; to sneak in.
(c) (*Orn*) to swoop (down) (*sobre* on).
(d) **— el sombrero** to pull one's hat down; to put
one's hat on firmly; **— las gafas** to stick one's
glasses on; to push one's glasses back.
calatear [1a] *vt* (*Per*) to undress.
calato *adj* (*Per*) naked; (*fig*) penniless, broke (*fam*).
calavera 1 *nf* (a) (*Anat*) skull; **estar como — de**
muerto to be as bald as a coot.
(b) (*Mex: Aut*) rear light.

2 *nm* gay dog; madcap; (*pej*) rake, roué; (*pej*)
rotter, cad, heel (*sl*).
calaverada *nf* madcap escapade, foolhardy act.
calaverear [1a] *vi* to be a gay dog, live it up; to have
one's fling; (*pej*) to lead a wild life, live recklessly.
calca *nf* (*Per*) barn, granary.
calcado *nm* tracing.
calcañal *nm,* **calcañar** *nm,* **calcaño** *nm* heel.
calcar [1g] *vt* (a) to trace, make a tracing of. (b) **—**
A en B to model A on B, base A on B; (*pej*) to copy
A slavishly from B.
calcáreo *adj* calcareous, lime (*attr*).
calce *nm* (a) (steel) tyre; wedge, shim; iron tip; (*Ec*)
filling (*of a tooth*).
(b) (*CAm, Mex, PR*) foot, lower margin (of a
document).
(c) (*Arg*) chance, opportunity.
calcés *nm* masthead.
calceta *nf* (a) (knee-length) stocking. (b) fetter,
shackle. (c) **hacer —** to knit.
calcetería *nf* (a) hosiery. (b) hosier's (shop).
calcetero *nm,* **calcetera** *nf* hosier.
calcetín *nm* sock.
calcificar [1g] **1** *vt* to calcify. **2 calcificarse** *vr* to
calcify.
calcina *nf* concrete.
calcinación *nf* calcination.
calcinar [1a] **1** *vt* (a) to calcine; to burn, reduce to
ashes, blacken; **las ruinas calcinadas del edificio**
the blackened ruins of the building.
(b) (*fam*) to bother, annoy.
2 calcinarse *vr* to calcine.
calcio *nm* calcium.
calco *nm* (a) tracing.
(b) (*Ling*) calque (*de* on), semantic borrowing
(*de* from); **la palabra es — del inglés** the word is a
calque on English, the (sense of the) word is
borrowed from English.
calcomanía *nf* transfer.
calculable *adj* calculable.
calculador *adj* (a) calculating. (b) (*Chi, PR*) selfish,
mercenary.
calculadora *nf* calculating machine, computer.
calcular [1a] *vt* (a) to calculate, compute; to add up,
work out. (b) **— que . . .** to reckon that . . .; to
anticipate that . . ., expect that . . .
cálculo *nm* (a) calculation; reckoning; estimate;
conjecture; (*Math*) calculus; **— de costo** costing;
— diferencial differential calculus; **libro de —s**
hechos ready reckoner; **— mental** mental arithmetic;
según mis —s according to my calculations, by my
reckoning; **obrar con mucho —** to act cautiously.
(b) (*Med*) stone, gallstone.
Calcuta Calcutta.
calcha *nf* (a) (*Arg*) clothing, bedding; harness. (b)
(*Chi*) fetlock; fringe (of hair); tatters, strands.
calchona *nf* (*Chi*) ghost, bogey; (*fig*) hag.
calchudo *adj* (*Chi*) shrewd, cunning.
caldas *nfpl* hot springs, hot mineral baths.
caldeamiento *nm* warming, heating.
caldear [1a] **1** *vt* to warm (up), heat (up); (*Tech*) to
weld; **estar caldeado** to be very hot. **2 caldearse** *vr*
to get very hot, get overheated.
caldeo *nm* warming, heating; (*Tech*) welding.
caldera *nf* (*Tech*) boiler; boiling-pan; (*RPl*) pot;
kettle, teapot; (*Ec*) crater; **las —s de Pedro Botero**
hell.
calderero *nm* boilermaker; coppersmith; **— re-**
mendón tinker.
caldereta *nf* (a) small boiler. (b) (*Eccl*) holy-water
vessel. (c) (*Cook*) fish stew; lamb stew.
calderilla *nf* (a) (*Eccl*) holy-water vessel. (b) (*Fin*)
small change, coppers; **en —** in coppers.
caldero *nm* small boiler, copper; (*Tech*) drum, boiler.
calderón *nm* (a) large boiler, cauldron. (b) (*Naut*)
hold. (c) (*Typ*) paragraph sign, section mark; (*Mus*)
pause (sign).
caldo *nm* (a) broth, bouillon; gravy; consommé, clear
soup; dressing, sauce; **— de carne** beef tea; **— de**
cultivo (*Bio*) culture medium; **— de pollo** chicken
broth; **hacer el —** gordo to take advantage of a
situation; **hacer el — gordo a uno** to play into
someone's hands, make it easy for someone.
(b) **—s** (*Comm*) oil, wine, cider (and other vegetable juices); **los —s jerezanos** the wines of Jerez,
sherries.
cale *nm* slap, smack.
calefacción *nf* heating; **— central** central heating;
sistema de — heating (system).
calefaccionar [1a] *vt* to heat.
calefón *nm* (*Arg*) coal-fired boiler.
cale(i)doscopio *nm* kaleidoscope.

calembé *nm* (*Cu*, *Ven*) loincloth; underpants; (*Ven*) ragged clothes, shabby clothing.

calendario *nm* calendar; — **de pared** wall calendar; — **de taco** tear-off calendar; **hacer** —s to muse, dream.

caléndula *nf* marigold.

calentador *nm* heater; — **de cama** (*Hist*) warming pan; — **eléctrico** electric fire; — **a gas** gas heater, (*for bath*) geyser, water heater; — **de inmersión** immersion heater.

calentamiento *nm* heating, warming.

calentar [1k] **1** *vt* (**a**) furnace, *water etc* to heat (up); *body*, *chair*, *food*, *room etc* to warm (up); — **al blanco** to make white-hot; — **al rojo** to make red-hot.
  (**b**) *business etc* to hurry on, speed up, get moving.
  (**c**) (*Arg*, *Mex*, *Ven*) to provoke, irritate.
  (**d**) (*fam*) to warm (*fam*), tan (*fam*).
  2 calentarse *vr* (**a**) to heat up, warm up, get hot, get warm; (*at fire*) to warm oneself.
  (**b**) (*fig: of argument*) to get heated; (*of person*) to get heated, get het up, get excited (*por* about).
  (**c**) (*Zool*) to be on heat; (*Arg*, *Mex*, *Ven*) to get randy, feel in the mood.
  (**d**) (*Arg*, *Mex*, *Per*, *Ven*) to get cross.

calentón *nm* (**a**) (*Mex*) water heater. (**b**) (*Arg*, *Per*) randy person. (**c**) (*Arg*, *Per*) **tener un** — to feel randy, be in the mood.

calentura *nf* (**a**) (*Med*) fever, (high) temperature; **estar con** —, **tener** — to be feverish, have a temperature.
  (**b**) (*Chi*) tuberculosis.
  (**c**) (*Per*, *RPl*) randiness, sexual desire.
  (**d**) (*Col*) fit of anger, tantrum.

calenturiento *adj* (**a**) (*Med*) feverish. (**b**) (*Chi*) consumptive, tubercular.

calenturón *nm* high fever.

calenturoso *adj* (*Med*) feverish.

calera *nf* limestone quarry; lime kiln.

calero 1 *adj* lime (*attr*). **2** *nm* lime kiln.

calesa *nf* chaise, buggy.

calesera *nf* Andalusian jacket.

calesín *nm* gig, fly.

calesita *nf* (*Arg*, *Per*) merry-go-round.

caleta *nf* (**a**) (*Geog*) cove, small bay, inlet. (**b**) (*Col*, *Ec*) coasting vessel.

caletero *nm* (*Ven*) docker, port worker.

caletre *nm* (*fam*) gumption (*fam*), brains.

calibrador *nm* gauge; calliper(s); — **de alambre** wire gauge.

calibrar [1a] *vt* to calibrate; to gauge, measure.

calibre *nm* (**a**) calibre; (*Mil*) calibre, bore; (*Rail*) gauge; (*of wire*, *pipe etc*) diameter; (*fig*) calibre; **de grueso** — large-bore. (**b**) = **calibrador**.

calicanto *nm* (*Arg*, *PR*) stone wall; jetty.

calicó *nm* calico.

caliche *nm* (**a**) (*Bol*, *Chi*, *Per*) saltpetre; ground rich in saltpetre. (**b**) (*Arg*) crust of whitewash which flakes from a wall.

calidad *nf* (**a**) quality; grade; **de** — of quality; **de mala** — of bad quality, bad-quality, low-quality.
  (**b**) position, capacity; **en** — **de** in the capacity of.
  (**c**) (*in contract*) stipulation, term; **a** — **de que . . .** provided that . . .
  (**d**) rank, importance, quality.
  (**e**) —**es** (moral) qualities; gifts.

cálido *adj* climate, country hot; (*fig*) blanket, applause, colour etc warm.

calidoscópico *adj* kaleidoscopic.

calidoscopio *nm* kaleidoscope.

calienta-camas *nm*, *pl* **calienta-camas** electric blanket.

calientapiés *nm*, *pl* **calientapiés** hot-water bottle; foot warmer.

calienta-platos *nm*, *pl* **calienta-platos** hotplate.

caliente *adj* (**a**) warm, hot.
  (**b**) (*fig*) fiery, spirited; *argument* heated; *battle* raging.
  (**c**) **estar** — (*Zool*) to be on heat; (*SAm*) to feel randy, be in the mood.
  (**d**) **en** — at once, immediately; (*Tech*) hot; **montar algo en** — (*Tech*) to assemble something while it is hot, shrink something on.

califa *nm* caliph.

califato *nm* caliphate.

calificación *nf* (**a**) qualification; assessment; decription, label. (**b**) rating, standing; grade, mark; — **de sobresaliente** first-class mark.

calificado *adj* (**a**) qualified, competent; *worker* skilled. (**b**) well-known, eminent; *proof etc* undisputed; *theft* proven, manifest.

calificar [1g] **1** *vt* (**a**) to qualify (*also Gram*).
  (**b**) to assess; to rate; *exam* to grade, mark; *script* to correct.
  (**c**) — **a uno** to distinguish someone, give someone his standing (*or* fame); to ennoble someone.
  (**d**) — **a uno de tonto** to call someone silly, describe someone as silly, label someone silly.
  2 calificarse *vr* (*SAm: Pol*) to register as a voter.

calificativo 1 *adj* qualifying. **2** *nm* qualifier, epithet.

California *f* California.

california *nf* (**a**) (*Arg*) horse race. (**b**) (*Arg*) wire-stretcher. (**c**) (*PR*) 20-dollar gold coin.

californiano, **californio 1** *adj* Californian. **2** *nm*, **californiana**, **california** *nf* Californian.

calígine *nf* (*poet*) mist, darkness.

caliginoso *adj* (*poet*) misty, dark.

caligrafía *nf* calligraphy, penmanship.

caligráfico *adj* calligraphic.

calilla *nf* (*CAm*, *Mex*) (**a**) bore, tedious person. (**b**) nuisance. (**c**) hoax.

calina *nf* haze, mist.

calinoso *adj* hazy, misty.

calipso *nm* calypso.

calistenia *nf* cal(l)isthenics.

cáliz *nm* (**a**) (*Bot*) calyx. (**b**) (*Eccl*) chalice, communion cup; (*poet*) cup, goblet; — **de amargura**, — **de dolor** cup of sorrow, cup of bitterness.

caliza *nf* limestone.

calizo *adj* lime (*attr*); ground limy.

calma *nf* (**a**) (*Meteorol*, *Naut*) calm, calm weather; — **chicha** dead calm; **estar en** — to be calm.
  (**b**) (*Comm*, *Fin*) calm, inactivity, lull (*de* in); cessation, suspension (*de* of); **estar en** — (*market*) to be steady.
  (**c**) (of *temperament*) calm, calmness; (*pej*) slowness, phlegm, laziness; **¡—!**, **¡con** —! calm down!, don't get so worked up!, take your time!; **hacer algo con** — to do something calmly; **tomarlo con** — to take things gently; **perder la** — to get ruffled, lose one's composure.

calmante 1 *adj* soothing, sedative. **2** *nm* sedative, tranquillizer.

calmar [1a] **1** *vt* to calm; *person* to calm (down), quieten (down), soothe; *nerves* to soothe, steady; *pain* to relieve.
  2 *vi* (of *mind etc*) to abate, fall calm.
  3 calmarse *vr* to calm down, calm oneself; **¡cálmese!** calm down!, don't get so worked up!

calmazo *nm* dead calm.

calmoso *adj* (**a**) calm, quiet. (**b**) (*pej*) slow, sluggish; lazy.

caló *nm* gipsy slang; underworld slang; low-class speech of Madrid (*equivalent to* Cockney).

calofriarse [1c] *vr* see **escalofriarse**.

calofrío *nm* see **escalofrío**.

calor *nm* (**a**) heat (*also Phys*, *Tech etc*); warmth; **un** — **agradable** a pleasant warmth; **un** — **excesivo** an excessive heat; — **blanco** white heat; — **rojo** red heat; **¡qué** —! isn't it hot!, how hot it is!; **entrar en** — to get warm, begin to feel warm; (*before game*, *with exercises*) to warm up; **hace** — it's hot; **hace mucho** — it's very hot; **tener** — to be hot, feel hot.
  (**b**) (*fig: of argument*) warmth, heat; (*of battle*) heat; (*of welcome etc*) warmth; (*of feelings*) ardour, fervour; excitement, passion.

caloría *nf* calorie.

calórico *adj* caloric.

calorífero 1 *adj* heat-producing, heat-giving. **2** *nm* heating system; furnace, stove; heater, radiator; — **mural** wall radiator.

calorífico *adj* calorific.

calorifugar [1h] *vt* boiler, *pipe* to lag.

calorífugo *adj* heat-resistant, non-conducting; fireproof.

calote *nm* (*RPl*) fraud, swindle.

calotear [1a] (*RPl*) to swindle, cheat.

calta *nf* marsh marigold (*also* — **palustre**).

caluma *nf* (*Per*) gap, pass (*in the Andes*).

calumnia *nf* calumny; (*Law*) slander (*de* of), (*written*) libel (*de* on).

calumniador *nm*, **calumniadora** *nf* slanderer, libeller.

calumniar [1b] *vt* to slander, libel.

calumnioso *adj* slanderous, libellous.

calurosamente *adv* (*fig*) warmly, enthusiastically, heartily.

caluroso *adj* (**a**) warm, hot. (**b**) (*fig*) warm, enthusiastic, hearty.

calva *nf* (*on head*) bald patch; (*on dress*) bare spot, worn place; (*in wood etc*) clearing.

Calvario *nm* (a) (*Eccl*) Calvary; Stations of the Cross. (b) c— (*fig*) cross, heavy burden; series of disasters; string of debts.

calvatrueno *nm* (*fam*) (a) bald pate. (b) wild fellow, madcap.

calvero *nm* (a) glade, clearing. (b) chalkpit, marlpit.

calvicie *nf* baldness; — **precoz** premature baldness.

calvinismo *nm* Calvinism.

calvinista 1 *adj* Calvinistic. 2 *nmf* Calvinist.

calvo 1 *adj* (a) *head*, *man* bald; *patch* bald, hairless; **quedarse** — to go bald. (b) *ground* bare, barren; *garment* threadbare. 2 *nm* bald man.

calza *nf* (a) wedge; scotch, chock; **poner** — **a** to wedge, scotch.
    (b) (*fam*) stocking; —s hose; breeches; tights; **estar en —s prietas** to be in a fix.
    (c) (*Ec, Col, Pan, Nic: of tooth*) filling.

calzada *nf* roadway, highway; causeway; (*up to house*) drive; (*SD*) pavement, sidewalk (*US*); — **romana** Roman road.

calzado 1 *adj* shod, wearing shoes; — **de shod** with, wearing; **conviene ir** — it's better to wear shoes, one has to wear something on one's feet.
    2 *nm* footwear.

calzador *nm* shoehorn.

calzar [1f] 1 *vt* (a) *shoes, spurs etc* to put on; to wear; **calzaba zapatos verdes** she was wearing green shoes, she had green shoes on; **¿qué número calza Vd?** what size do you wear (*or* take)?; **el que primero llega, ése la calza** first come first served.
    (b) *person* to put shoes on; to provide with footwear, supply with shoes; **me ayudó a —me las botas** he helped me to put my boots on.
    (c) (*of firearm*) to carry, take.
    (d) *wheel etc* to wedge, scotch, chock; to put a wedge in (*or* under *etc*), put chocks under; to block; to secure.
    (e) (*Ec, Col, Pan, Nic*) *tooth* to fill.
    (f) to tip, put an iron tip on.
    2 *vi* (a) **calza bien** he wears good shoes.
    (b) (*fig*) **calza poco, no calza mucho** he's pretty dim.
    3 **calzarse** *vr* (a) — **los zapatos** to put on one's shoes; **¿qué zapatos calzaba?** what shoes was he wearing?
    (b) — **un empleo** to get a job; — **a uno** to keep someone under one's thumb.

calzo *nm* wedge, scotch, chock; shim; (*Mech*) shoe; (*Naut*) skid, chock.

calzón *nm* (*also* —**es**) (a) (*man's*) breeches; shorts; (*SAm*) trousers, pants (*US*); — **de baño** bathing trunks; **amarrarse los —es** (*SAm*) to act resolutely, button down to the job; **hablar a — quitado** to speak with excessive frankness; to ride roughshod over people; (*Mex*) to talk energetically, talk without stopping; **ponerse los —es** (*of woman: fig*) to wear the trousers.
    (b) (*woman's*) shorts; (*Arg*) pants, drawers, knickers; —**es blancos** pants; — **de baño** pants part of two-piece swimsuit.

calzonario *nm* (*SAm*) pants, knickers.

calzonazos *nm*, *pl* **calzonazos** (*fam*) stupid fellow, weak-willed fellow; henpecked husband.

calzoncillos *nmpl* pants, underpants (*US*), shorts (*US*).

calzoneras *nfpl* (*Mex, PR*) trousers buttoned down the sides.

calzonudo 1 *adj* (*CAm, Per, RPl*) stupid, weak-willed; henpecked; (*Mex*) energetic; bold, brave. 2 *nm* (*Mex*) Indian.

callada: a la —, de — on the quiet, secretly; **dar la — por respuesta** to say nothing.

calladamente *adv* quietly, silently; secretly.

callado *adj* (a) (*by temperament*) quiet, reserved, reticent.
    (b) quiet, silent; **todo estaba muy —** everything was very quiet; **tener algo —** to keep quiet about something, keep something secret; **¡qué — se lo tenía Vd!** you kept pretty quiet about it!; **pagar para tener — a uno** to pay to keep someone quiet.

callampa *nf* (*Chi*) mushroom; (*fam*) umbrella; —**s** (*fam*) big ears.

callana *nf* (*SAm*) flat earthenware pan; (*Chi: hum*) pocket watch.

callandico *adv*, **callandito** *adv* softly, very quietly; stealthily.

callar [1a] 1 *vt secret* to keep; *fact, passage etc* to pass over in silence, say nothing about, not mention; to keep back, keep to oneself, keep secret; *shameful matter* to keep quiet about, hush up; *see* **pico**.
    2 *vi and* **callarse** *vr* to keep quiet, be silent, remain silent; (*of noise*) to stop; to stop talking (*or* playing *etc*); to become quiet; (*of sea, wind*) to become still, be hushed; **¡calla!, ¡cállate!, ¡cállese!** (*order*) shut up!, be quiet!, hold your tongue!; **calla, calle** (*giving agreement*) say no more, enough said; **¡calla!** (*fig*) you don't mean to say!, well!; **hacer — a uno** to make someone be quiet, make someone stop talking (*etc*); (*energetically*) to shut someone up; **¿quieres —?** you've said enough, that's enough now; **sería mejor —se** it would be best to say nothing.

calle *nf* (a) street, road; — **abajo** down the street; — **arriba** up the street; — **de la amargura** (*fig*) difficult situation, jam; — **de dirección única,** — **de un sentido** (*Mex*) one-way street; — **mayor** high street, main street; —**s exclusivas para el tránsito de peatones** pedestrian precinct; **dejar a uno en la —** to put someone out of a job; **echar por la — de en medio** to push on, press on regardless (*fam*); **echarse a la —** to go out into the street; (*of mob*) to turn out, riot, demonstrate; **poner a uno (de patitas) en la —** to kick someone out, chuck someone out; to put someone out of a job; **quedarse en la —** not to have a penny to one's name; *see* **aplanar, rondar** *etc*.
    (b) passage, way; room; **¡—!** make way!; **abrir —, hacer —** to make way, clear the way.
    (c) (*Sport*) lane; (*Golf*) fairway.

calleja *nf* = **callejuela**.

callejear [1a] *vi* to wander about the streets, stroll around; (*pej*) to loaf, hang about idly.

callejero *adj* (a) street (*attr*); **accidente —** street accident; **disturbios —s** trouble in the streets, rioting in the streets.
    (b) *person* fond of walking about the streets, fond of gadding about.

callejón *nm* alley, alleyway, passage; (*Col*) main street; (*Taur*) space between inner and outer barriers; — **sin salida** cul-de-sac; blind alley (*also fig*); **las negociaciones están en un — sin salida** the negotiations are at an impasse, the negotiations are deadlocked.

callejuela *nf* (a) narrow street, side street; alley, passage. (b) (*fig*) subterfuge; way out (of the difficulty).

callicida *nm* corn cure.

callista *nmf* chiropodist.

callo *nm* (a) corn; callus, callosity; **criar —s** to be callous, have no feelings. (b) —**s** (*Cook*) tripe; —**s al ajo** tripe with garlic.

callosidad *nf* callosity, hard patch (*on hand etc*), rough place.

calloso *adj* horny, hard, rough.

cama *nf* (a) bed; bedstead; couch; — **de campaña** campbed; — **de columnas,** — **imperial** fourposter bed; —**s gemelas** twin beds; — **de matrimonio** double bed; **media —,** — **de monja,** — **de soltero** single bed; — **en petaca** apple-pie bed; —, **plegable,** — **de tijera** folding bed, campbed; — **turca** divan bed, day bed; — **de viento** (*Col, Hond*) cot; **caer en (la) —** to fall ill; **estar en —** (*Med*), **guardar —** to be ill in bed, be confined to bed; **hacer la —** to make the bed; **hacer** (*or* **poner**) **la — a uno** (*fig*) to work harm for someone behind his back; **quien mala — hace en ella se yace** having made your bed you must lie on it; **ir a la —** to go to bed; **levantarse por los pies de la —** to get out of bed on the wrong side.
    (b) (*for animal*) bed, bedding, litter.
    (c) (*Zool*) den, lair.
    (d) (*of cart*) floor.
    (e) (*Geol*) layer, stratum; (*Cook*) layer.

camachuelo *nm* bullfinch.

camada *nf* (a) (*Zool*) litter, brood; (*persons*) gang, band; *see* **lobo**. (b) (*Geol*) layer; (*Archit*) course.

camafeo *nm* cameo.

camagua *nf* (*CAm*) ripening maize, ripening corn (*US*); (*Mex*) unripened maize.

camal *nm* (a) halter. (b) meat hook; (*Bol, Per*) slaughterhouse.

camaleón *nm* chameleon.

camalote *nm* (*SAm*) *an aquatic plant* (*which forms floating islands*).

camamila *nf* camomile.

camándula *nf* rosary; **tener muchas —s** (*fam*) to be full of tricks, be a sly sort.

camandulear [1a] *vi* to be a hypocrite, be falsely devout; (*SAm*) to intrigue; to bumble, avoid taking decisions.

camandulería *nf* prudery, priggishness; hypocrisy, false devotion.

camandulero 1 *adj* prudish, priggish; hypocritical, falsely devout; sly, tricky; (*SAm*) intriguing; bumbling.
2 *nm* prude, prig; hypocrite; sly sort, tricky person; (*SAm*) intriguer; bumbler.
cámara 1 *nf* (a) room, hall; — **acorazada** strongroom, vault; — **ardiente**, — **mortuoria** funeral chamber; — **frigorífica** cold-storage room; **música de** — chamber music.
(b) royal chamber; **médico de** — royal doctor; **gentilhombre de** — gentleman-in-waiting.
(c) (*Naut*) stateroom, cabin; saloon; wardroom; — **de cartas** chartroom; — **de motores** engine room.
(d) (*Agr*) granary.
(e) (*Pol etc*) chamber, house; — **alta** upper house; — **baja** lower house; — **de comercio** chamber of commerce; — **de compensación** (*Fin*) clearing house; **C**— **de los Comunes** House of Commons; **C**— **de los Lores** House of Lords; **C**— **de Representantes** House of Representatives.
(f) (*Mech, Phys*) chamber; — **de aire** air chamber; — **de combustión** combustion chamber; — **de compresión** compression chamber; — **de gas** (*airship*) gasbag, (*Nazi etc*) gas chamber; — **de oxígeno** oxygen tent; — **de vacío** vacuum chamber.
(g) (*Aut etc: also* — **de aire**, — **neumática**) tyre, inner tube; **sin** — **tyre** solid.
(h) (*Mil*) breech, chamber.
(i) (*Anat*) cavity.
(j) (*Phot: also* — **fotográfica**) camera; — **de cine**, — **cinematográfica**, — **filmadora** cine-camera, film camera; **a** — **lenta** in slow motion; — **oscura** camera obscura; — **de televisión**, — **televisora** television camera.
(k) —**s** (*Med*) diarrhoea; stool; **tener** —**s en la lengua** (*fam*) to gossip a lot, tell tales (out of school).
2 *nm* cameraman.
camarada *nm* comrade, companion; chum, pal, mate; (*Pol*) comrade.
camaradería *nf* comradeship; companionship; matiness; (*Sport*) team spirit.
camarera *nf* (*in restaurant*) waitress; (*in hotel*) maid, chambermaid; (*in house*) parlourmaid; lady's maid; (*Naut*) stewardess.
camarero *nm* (*in restaurant*) waiter; (*Naut*) steward; — **mayor** (*Hist*) royal chamberlain; — **principal** head waiter.
camareta *nf* (*Naut*) cabin; messroom; — **alta** deck-house.
camarico *nm* (*Chi*) (a) favourite place. (b) love affair.
camarilla *nf* (a) small room. (b) clique, coterie; (*Pol*) lobby; (*Pol*) caucus (*of party*).
camarín *nm* (a) (*Theat*) dressing room; boudoir; side room; lift car, elevator car (*US*).
(b) (*Eccl*) niche for an image; small room where images are dressed (*behind the altar*).
camarón *nm* (a) (*Zool*) shrimp, prawn. (b) (*CR*) tip, gratuity. (c) (*Per*) turncoat; **hacer** — to change sides.
camaronear [1a] *vi* (a) (*Mex*) to go shrimping. (b) (*Per: Pol*) to change sides.
camaronero *nm* (*Per*) kingfisher.
camarote *nm* (*Naut*) cabin, stateroom; — **de lujo** first-class cabin.
camarotero *nm* (*SAm*) steward, cabin servant.
camastro *nm* rickety old bed; (*Naut*) bunk.
camastrón *adj* (*fam*) sly, untrustworthy.
camayo *nm* (*Per*) foreman (*of a country estate*).
cambado *adj* (*Arg, Col, Ven*) bow-legged.
cambalache *nm* (a) swap, exchange. (b) (*SAm*) secondhand shop.
cambalach(e)ar [1a] *vt* to swap, exchange.
cambar [1a] *vt* (*Arg, Ven*) = **combar**.
cámbaro *nm* crab.
cambiable *adj* (a) changeable; variable. (b) exchangeable.
cambiadiscos *nm, pl* **cambiadiscos** record changer.
cambiador *nm* (a) barterer; moneychanger; (*Chi, Mex, Per: Rail*) switchman. (b) — **de discos** record changer.
cambiante 1 *adj* (a) changing; variable.
(b) (*pej*) fickle, temperamental.
2 *nm* (a) moneychanger.
(b) iridescent fabric.
(c) —**s** changing colours, iridescence.
cambiar [1b] **1** *vt* (a) to change, alter, convert, turn (*en into*).
(b) to change, exchange (*con, por* for); — **libras en francos**, — **libras por francos** to change pounds

into francs; — **saludos** to exchange greetings; — **sellos** to exchange stamps, swap stamps.
(c) (*of place*) to shift, move; **¿lo cambiamos a otro sitio?** shall we move it somewhere else?
2 *vi* (a) to change, alter; — **a un nuevo sistema** to change (*or* switch) to a new system; **no ha cambiado nada** nothing has changed; **entonces, la cosa cambia** that alters matters; **está muy cambiado** he's changed a lot, he has greatly altered.
(b) — **de** to change; — **de dueño** to change hands; — **de idea** to change one's mind; — **de ropa** to change one's clothes; — **de color** to change colour; — **de sitio** to shift, move; — **de sitio con uno** to change places with someone; **cambiamos de sombrero** we exchanged hats.
(c) (*of wind*) to veer, change round.
3 cambiarse *vr* (a) to change; (*of wind*) to veer, change round.
(b) — **en** to change into, be changed into.
cambiavía *nm* (*Cu, Mex, PR: Rail*) (a) switchman. (b) switch, points.
cambiazo *nm* (*Comm: fam*) switch; **dar el** — to switch the goods.
cambio *nm* (a) change, alteration; changeover; substitution; (*in policy etc*) change, switch, shift; (*of tide*) turn; (*of place*) shift, move (*a* to); **ha habido muchos** —**s** there have been many changes; **el** — **se efectuó en 1970** the changeover took place in 1970; — **de decoración** (*Theat*) change of scenery; — **de domicilio** change of address; — **de guardia** changing of the guard; — **de marchas**, — **de velocidades** gear-change, gear-lever, gearshift (*US*); **con** — **de marchas automático** with automatic gearbox; — **de la marea** turn of the tide; — **de tiempo** change in the weather; — **de vía** (*Rail*) points.
(b) (*Fin*) change, small change; **¿tienes** — **encima?** have you any change on you?
(c) exchange; barter; **libre** — free trade; "**admitimos su coche usado a** —" "we take your old car in part exchange"; **a** — **de** in exchange for, in return for; **a las primeras de** — (*fig*) at the very start; at first sight; **en** — in exchange; on the other hand; instead.
(d) (*Fin*) rate of exchange; **al** — **de** at the rate of.
cambista *nm* moneychanger.
Camboya *f* Cambodia.
camboyano 1 *adj* Cambodian. **2** *nm*, **camboyana** *nf* Cambodian.
cambrona *nf* (*Arg*) tough cotton cloth.
cambucho *nm* (*Chi*) paper cone; paper basket for dirty clothes; straw wrapping of a bottle; poky little room, hovel.
cambujo *adj* (*CAm, Mex*) *animal* black; *person* dark, swarthy.
cambullón *nm* (*Col, Chi, Per*) swindle; plot, intrigue; swap, exchange.
cambur *nm* (*Ven*) banana; (*hum*) public office, sinecure.
cambuto *adj* (*Per*) small, squat; chubby.
camelar [1a] *vt* (a) *woman* to flirt with. (b) to cajole, blarney. (c) (*Mex*) to look into, look towards (*etc*); to spy on.
camelia *nf* camellia.
camelo *nm* (a) flirtation.
(b) joke, hoax; cock-and-bull story; humbug; blarney; **dar** — **a uno** to make fun of someone; **me huele a** — it smells fishy (*fam*), there's something funny going on here.
camello *nm* camel.
camellón *nm* drinking trough; (*Agr*) ridge (*between furrows*).
cameraman *nm, pl* **cameramans** *or* **cameramen** (*angl*) cameraman.
camerino *nm* (*Theat*) dressing room.
camero *adj* (a) bed (*attr*); for a big bed, for a double bed. (b) (*Cu: fam*) big.
Camerón *nm* Cameroon.
camilucho *nm* (*Arg, Mex*) Indian day labourer.
camilla *nf* sofa, couch; cot; table with a heater underneath; (*Med*) stretcher.
camillero *nm* stretcher-bearer.
caminante *nm* traveller, wayfarer; walker.
caminar [1a] **1** *vt distance* to cover, travel, do.
2 *vi* to walk, go; to travel, journey; (*of river etc*) to go, move, flow; (*fig*) to act, move, go; — **derecho** to behave properly; — **con pena** to trudge along, move with difficulty.
caminata *nf* long walk; hike, ramble; excursion, outing, jaunt.

caminero 1 adj road (attr); see **peón. 2** nm (SAm) road builder.

caminito nm: **— de rosas** (fig) primrose path.

camino nm (a) road; track, path; trail; **— de acceso, — de entrada** approach road; **—** forestal forest track; **— francés** (Hist), **— de Santiago** pilgrims' road to Santiago de Compostela; **C— de Santiago** (Astron) Milky Way; **— de herradura** bridle path; **— real** highroad (also fig); **— de sirga** towpath; **— trillado** well-trodden path, ·(fig) beaten track; **tener el — trillado** (fig) to have the ground prepared for one; **— vecinal** country road, lane, by-road; **C—s, Canales y Puertos** (Univ course) Civil Engineering.

(b) (of direction, distance etc: also fig) way, road (de to), route; journey; (fig) way, path, course; **el — a seguir** the route to follow; **el — de La Paz** the way to La Paz; the La Paz road; **es el — del desastre** that is the road to disaster, that way lies disaster; **el — de en medio** (fig) the middle way, the way of compromise; **— de Lima** on the way to Lima; **vamos — de la muerte** death awaits us all; **a medio —** halfway (there); **de —** on the way, (fig) in passing; **en el —** on the way, en route; **está en — de desaparecer** it's on its way out; **después de 3 horas de —** after travelling for 3 hours; **nos quedan 20 kms de —** we still have 20 kms to go; **es mucho —** it's a long way; **¿cuánto — hay de aquí a San José?** how far is it from here to San José?; **por buen —** along the right road; **ir por buen —** (fig) to be on the right track; **¿vamos por buen —?** are we on the right road?; **traer a uno por buen —** (fig) to put someone on the right road; to disabuse someone; **allanar el —** to smooth the way (a uno for someone); **echar — adelante** to strike out; **errar el —** to lose one's way; **llevar a uno por mal —** (fig) to lead someone astray; **partir el — con uno** to meet someone halfway; **ponerse en —** to set out, set forth, start.

(c) (Arg, Per, Urug) runner, strip of carpet (or matting etc); **— de mesa** table runner.

camión nm (Aut) lorry, truck (esp US); van; heavy wagon, dray; (Mex) bus; **— y acoplado** lorry and trailer; **— de agua** water cart, water wagon; **— de la basura** dustcart, refuse lorry; **— blindado** troop carrier; **— de bomberos** fire engine; **— frigorífico** refrigerator lorry; **— ganadero** cattle truck; **— de mudanzas** removal van; **— de riego** water cart, water wagon.

camionaje nm haulage, cartage.

camionero nm lorry driver, truckdriver (US), teamster (US).

camioneta nf van, light truck.

camionista nm = **camionero**.

camion-tanque nm, pl **camiones-tanque** (Aut) tanker.

camisa nf (a) (man's) shirt; **—** (de mujer, de señora) chemise, slip; (SAm) garment, article of clothing; **¡—!** (Ven) not on your life! **— de deporte** sports shirt, vest; **— de dormir** nightdress; **— de fuerza** straitjacket; **—T** T-shirt; **estar en — (mangas de —)** to be in one's shirt-sleeves; **dejar a una en —** (fig) to leave a girl without a dowry; **dejar a uno sin —** to leave someone destitute; **no le llegaba la — al cuerpo** he was simply terrified; **meterse en — de once varas** to interfere in other people's affairs.

(b) (Bot) skin; (Zool: of snake) slough.

(c) (Mech) jacket; case, casing; sleeve; **— de agua** water jacket; **— de gas** gas mantle.

(d) folder (for papers); (Typ) jacket, dust jacket, wrapper.

camisería nf outfitter's (shop).

camisero nm shirt maker; outfitter.

camiseta nf vest, undershirt (US); (Sport) singlet, vest.

camisilla nf (Par, PR) = **camiseta**.

camisolín nm stiff shirt front, dickey.

camisón nm (also **— de noche**) nightdress, nightgown; (man's) nightgown.

camítico adj Hamitic.

camomila nf camomile.

camita nf small bed, cot.

camón nm big bed; (Archit) oriel window; **— de vidrios** glass partition.

camorra nf (fam) row, set-to (fam); **armar — to** kick up a row; **buscar —** to go looking for trouble.

camorrear [1a] vi (Guat, RPl) to start a row, brawl.

camorrero nm = **camorrista**.

camorrista 1 adj quarrelsome, rowdy, brawling. **2** nmf quarrelsome person, rowdy element, hooligan.

camote nm (a) (SAm: Bot) sweet potato; (Mex) tuber, bulb.

(b) (CAm, Chi) bump, swelling, weal.

(c) (Chi) large stone.

(d) (Chi) bore, tedious person.

(e) (Guat) calf of the leg.

(f) (Guat) nuisance, bother.

(g) (SAm) love; passionate friendship, crush (fam); lovesickness; **tener un —** to be in love.

(h) (Chi, Per) lover, sweetheart.

(i) (Chi) fib.

(j) (Mex) rascal.

(k) (Arg, Ec) fool.

camotear [1a] **1** vt (a) (Arg) to rob, fleece; to take for a ride (fam).

(b) (Guat) to annoy.

2 vi (a) (Mex) to wander about aimlessly.

(b) (Guat) to be trying, cause trouble.

campal adj: **batalla —** pitched battle.

campamento nm camp; encampment; **— para prisioneros** prison camp; **— de trabajo** labour camp; **— de veraneo** holiday camp.

campana nf (a) bell; **a — herida, a — tañida, a toque de —** to the sound of bells; **echar las —s a vuelo** to peal the bells; (fig) to rejoice, celebrate (prematurely); **oír —s y no saber dónde** to get hold of the wrong end of the stick; **tañer las —s, tocar las —s** to peal the bells.

(b) bell-shaped object; **— de bucear, — de buzo** diving bell; **— de cristal** bell glass, glass cover.

(c) (Col, Per, RPl) thieves' look-out man.

campanada nf (a) stroke, peal (of a bell); (sound of) ringing.

(b) (fig) scandal, sensation, commotion; **dar una —** to make a big stir, cause a great surprise.

campanario nm (a) belfry, bell tower, church tower.

(b) **de —** (pej) mean, narrow-minded; **espíritu de —** parochial spirit, parish-pump attitude.

campanazo nm (a) = **campanada**. (b) (Col) warning.

campaneado adj (fig) much talked-of.

campanear [1a] vi (a) to ring the bells. (b) (Col, Per, RPl: of thief) to keep watch.

campaneo nm bell ringing, pealing, chimes.

campanero nm (Tech) bell founder; (Mus) bell ringer.

campanilla nf (a) small bell, handbell, electric bell; **de muchas —s** (fam) big, grand; high-class.

(b) bubble.

(c) (Anat) uvula.

(d) (Sew) tassel.

(e) (Bot) bell flower; **— azul** harebell; **— blanca, — de febrero** snowdrop.

campanillazo nm loud ring, sudden ring.

campanillear [1a] vi to ring, tinkle.

campanilleo nm ringing, tinkling.

campante adj (a) outstanding.

(b) (pej) self-satisfied, smug; **siguió tan —** he went on cheerfully, he went on as if nothing had happened; **allí estaba tan —** there he was as large as life, there he sat (etc) as cool as a cucumber.

campanudo adj (a) bell-shaped; skirt wide, spreading.

(b) style high-flown, bombastic, sonorous; speaker pompous, windy; **dijo —** he said pompously.

campánula nf bell flower, campanula; **— azul** bluebell.

campaña nf (a) countryside; level country, plain; **batir la —, correr la —** to reconnoitre.

(b) (Mil, Pol and fig) campaign; (Comm) sales drive; **de —** (Mil) field (attr), campaign (attr); **hacer — to campaign; hacer — en contra de** to campaign against; **hacer — a favor de** (or **en pro de**) to campaign for.

(c) (Naut) cruise, expedition, trip.

(d) (Agr etc) season.

campañol nm vole.

campar [1a] vi (a) (Mil etc) to camp. (b) to stand out, excel; see **respeto**.

campear [1a] vi (a) (Agr: of animals) to go to graze, go out to pasture; (of man) to work in the fields.

(b) (Bot) to show green.

(c) (Mil) to reconnoitre; (SAm) to scour the countryside.

(d) (Col) to make one's way through.

(e) (Col) to bluster.

campechana nf (a) (Ven) hammock. (b) (Cu, Mex) cocktail. (c) (Ven) whore.

campechanería nf, **campechanía** nf frankness, openness; heartiness, cheerfulness, geniality; fellow feeling; generosity.

campechano adj frank, open; good-hearted, hearty, cheerful, genial; comradely; generous.

campeón *nm*, **campeona** *nf* champion; **— de venta** bestseller, bestselling article.

campeonato *nm* championship; **de —** (*fig*) absolute, out-and-out.

campera *nf* (*Arg*) windjammer (*jacket*).

campero 1 *adj* (a) unsheltered, (out) in the open; open-air (*attr*); **ganado —** stock that sleeps out in the open.
(b) (*RPl*) knowledgeable about the countryside; expert in farming matters; *animal* trained to travel in difficult country.
2 *nm* (*Col*) jeep, land rover.

camperuso (*Ven*) **1** *adj* rural, rustic. **2** *nm* peasant.

campesina *nf* peasant (woman).

campesinado *nm* (*CAm*) peasantry, peasants.

campesino 1 *adj* (a) country (*attr*), rural (*attr*); (*pej*) rustic. (b) (*Zool*) field (*attr*). **2** *nm* peasant; countryman; farmer; (*pej*) peasant.

campestre *adj* (a) country (*attr*), rural; **en lo más — del campo** deep in the countryside, in the heart of the country. (b) (*Bot*) wild.

camping ['kampin] *nm*, *pl* **campings** ['kampin] (*angl*) (a) camping; **hacer —** to go camping. (b) camping site, camping ground.

campiña *nf* countryside, open country; flat stretch of farmland, large area of cultivated land.

campirano *nm* (*SAm*) (a) peasant; (*pej*) rustic, country bumpkin.
(b) expert in farming matters; guide, pathfinder; skilled horseman; stockbreeding expert.

campiruso (*Ven*) = **camperuso**.

campista[1] *nmf* camper.

campista[2] **1** *adj* (*CAm, PR, Ven*) rural, country (*attr*). **2** *nm* (a) (*CAm*) herdsman. (b) (*Mex, PR*) countryman.

campisto 1 *adj* (*CAm, PR, Ven*) rural, country (*attr*). **2** *nm* (*CR*) peasant.

campo *nm* (a) country, countryside; **— abierto, — raso** open country; **a — raso** in the open; **ir a — traviesa, ir — travieso** to go across country, take a cross-country route; **ir al —** to go into the country; **¿te gusta el —?** do you like the country(side)?; **el — está espléndido** the countryside looks lovely.
(b) (*Agr; also Mil, Phys, etc*) field; (*Sport*) field, ground, pitch; **— de aterrizaje** landing field; **— aurífero** goldfield; **— de aviación** airfield; **— de batalla** battlefield; **— de deportes** sports ground, playing field; recreation ground; **— de ejercicios** (*Mil*) drilling ground; **C—s Elíseos** Elysian Fields; **— de fútbol** football ground, football pitch; **— de golf** golf course, golf links; **— de instrucción** (*Mil*) drilling ground; **— de juego** playground; **— magnético** magnetic field; **— de minas** minefield; **— petrolífero** oilfield; **— santo** cemetery, churchyard; **— de tiro** firing range; **— visual** field of vision; **trabajo de —, trabajo en el propio —** fieldwork; **abandonar el —** to give something up as a bad job, chuck it up; **batir el —, reconocer el —** to reconnoitre; **dejar el — libre** to leave the field open (*para* for); **se le halló el — orégano** (*Arg*) it all turned out nicely for him; **quedar en el —** to fall in battle; to be killed in a duel.
(c) (*Col*) farm, ranch; farmhouse; (*Arg*) land too poor to support stock; (*Chi, Per*) mining concession.
(d) (*Art*) ground, background; (*Her*) field.
(e) (*Mil*) camp; **— de concentración** concentration camp; **— de internamiento** internment camp; **— de trabajo** labour camp; **levantar el —** to strike camp; (*fig*) to give up.
(f) (*in games*) side.
(g) (*fig*) scope; range, sphere; **el — de aplicación del invento** the scope of the invention, the range of application of the invention; **hay — para más** there is scope for more; **dar — a** to give free range to, allow ample scope for.

camposanto *nm* cemetery, churchyard.

campus *nm*, *pl* **campus** (*SAm Univ*) campus.

campusano *nm*, **campus(i)o** *nm* (*CR etc*) peasant.

camuesa *nf* pippin.

camueso *nm* (a) pippin tree. (b) (*fam*) dolt, blockhead.

camuflado *adj* camouflaged.

camuflaje *nm* camouflage.

camuflar [1a] *vt* to camouflage; (*SAm: fig*) to hide, disguise, cover up.

can *nm* (a) (*Zool: arch or hum*) dog, hound (*hum*). (b) (*Mil*) trigger. (c) (*Archit*) corbel.

cana[1] *nf* (*also —s*) white hair, grey hair; **echar una — al aire** to let one's hair down, cut loose; **faltar a las —s** to show a lack of respect for one's elders; **peina —s** he's getting on.

cana[2] *nf* (*SAm*) jail; police, policeman.

canaca *nmf* (a) (*Chi, Ec, Per*) Chinese. (b) (*Chi*) brothel keeper; brothel.

canaco *adj* (*Chi, Ec*) pale, yellow.

Canadá: el — Canada.

canadiense 1 *adj* Canadian. **2** *nmf* Canadian.

canal[1] *nm* (a) (*Naut*) canal; waterway; **C— de Panamá** Panama Canal; **C— de Suez** Suez Canal; **— de navegación** ship canal; **— de riego** irrigation channel.
(b) (*Naut: within river etc*) deep channel; navigation channel.
(c) (*Geog*) channel, straight; **C— de la Mancha** English Channel.
(d) (*Anat*) canal, duct, tract.
(e) (*TV*) channel.

canal[2] *nf* (a) conduit, pipe; underground watercourse; **— de desagüe** (*Per*) sewer; **— de humo** (*Mex*) flue.
(b) (*Archit*) gutter, guttering; spout; drainpipe.
(c) (*Archit*) groove.
(d) (*Geog*) narrow valley.
(e) dressed carcass; **abrir en —** to cut down the middle, slit open.

canaladura *nf* = **acanaladura**.

canalera *nf* (*Archit*) guttering.

canaleta *nf* (*Arg*) pipe, conduit.

canalete *nm* paddle.

canalización *nf* (a) canalization, channelling. (b) (*Tech*) piping; (*Elec*) wiring; (*of gas etc*) mains; (*SAm*) sewerage system, drainage.

canalizar [1f] *vt river etc* to canalize; to confine between banks, rebuild the banks (*or* course) of; *waters* to harness; to pipe; *irrigation water* to channel; (*fig*) *interests etc* to channel, direct.

canalizo *nm* navigable channel.

canalón *nm* (a) (*Archit*) gutter, guttering; spout; drainpipe. (b) shovel hat. (c) **—es** (*Cook*) ravioli.

canalla 1 *nf* rabble, mob, riffraff. **2** *nm* swine, rotter, blackguard; **¡—!** you swine!

canallada *nf*, **canallería** *nf* (*PR, SD*) dirty trick, mean thing (to do), despicable act; nasty remark, vile thing (to say).

canallesco *adj* mean, rotten (*fam*), despicable; **diversión canallesca** low form of amusement .

canana *nf* (a) cartridge belt. (b) (*SAm*) goitre. (c) (*SD*) mean trick, low prank. (d) **—s** (*Col*) handcuffs.

canapé *nm* (a) sofa, settee, couch. (b) (*Cook*) canapé.

canaquear [1a] *vi* (*Chi*) to go whoring.

canar [1a] *vi* (*Col*) to go grey.

Canarias *fpl*, *also* **Islas** *fpl* **Canarias** Canaries, Canary Isles.

canario[1] **1** *adj* of the Canary Isles. **2** *nm*, **canaria** *nf* native (*or* inhabitant) of the Canary Isles; **los —s** the people of the Canary Isles.

canario[2] *nm* (a) (*Orn*) canary. (b) (*SAm*) yellow.

canario[3] *interj* well I'm blowed!

canasta *nf* (a) (round) basket; hamper; crate; **— para desperdicios** wastepaper basket. (b) (*Cards*) canasta.

canastero *nm* basket maker.

canastilla *nf* small basket; (baby's) layette; (*Per, PR, RPl: bride's*) trousseau, (*hum*) bottom drawer, hope chest (*US*); (*Mex*) bucket; **— de la costura** sewing basket.

canastillo *nm* wicker tray, small basket.

canasto *nm* (a) large basket; hamper; crate. (b) (*Col*) servant. (c) (*interj*) good heavens!

cáncamo *nm* (*Naut*) eyebolt; **— de argolla** ringbolt.

cancamurria *nf* (*fam*) blues, gloom.

cancamusa *nf* (*fam*) trick; **armar una — a uno** to throw sand in someone's eyes.

cancán *nm* cancan.

cáncana *nf* (*Chi*) spit, jack; (*Chi*) candlestick; (*Col*) thin person.

cancanear [1a] *vi* (a) to loiter, loaf about.
(b) (*RPl*) to dance the cancan.
(c) (*CAm, Col, Mex*) to express oneself with difficulty; to stammer; to read haltingly, read without understanding.

cancaneo *nm* (*CAm, Col, Mex*) faltering, stammering.

cáncano *nm* (*fam*) louse; **andar como — loco** to go round in circles.

cancel *nm* windproof door, storm door; (*SAm*) folding screen; (*SAm*) partition, thin wall.

cancela *nf* lattice gate, wrought-iron gate; outer door, outer gate.

cancelación *nf* cancellation.

cancelar [1a] *vt* to cancel; *debt* to write off, wipe out; *decision* to cancel, annul; (*fig*) to dispel, banish (from one's mind); to do away with.

cancelaría *nf* papal chancery.

cáncer nm (a) (Med) cancer; — **de pulmón** lung cancer. (b) **C—** (Astron) Cancer.

cancerado adj cancerous; (fig) corrupt.

cancerarse [1a] vr (a) (Med) to become cancerous; (person) to get cancer, have cancer. (b) (fig) to become corrupt.

canceroso adj cancerous.

canciller nm chancellor.

cancilleresco adj (a) style etc of the chancellery. (b) (fig) formal, ceremonious; ruled by protocol.

canción nf song; (Lit) lyric, song; — **amatoria** love song; — **cuartelera** barrack-room ballad; — **de cuna** lullaby, cradle song; — **infantil** nursery rhyme; ¡**siempre la misma** —! the same old story!; **volvemos a la misma** — here we go again, you're harping on the same old theme.

cancionero nm (Mus) song book, collection of songs; (Lit) anthology, collection of verse.

cancionista nmf (a) songwriter. (b) ballad singer; singer, vocalist, crooner.

canco nm (a) (Chi) earthen jug; flowerpot; chamber-pot. (b) —**s** (Bol, Chi) buttocks; hips.

cancro nm (Bot) canker; (Med) cancer.

cancha[1] nf (in some senses, esp SAm) field, ground, open space, tract of level ground; cockpit; (Bol, Urug) wide part of a river; (Urug) path, road; ¡—! gangway! — **de aterrizaje** landing ground; — **de carreras** racecourse; racetrack; — **de fútbol** football ground; — **de pelota** pelota court; — **de tenis** tennis court; **abrir** —, **hacer** — to make way, make room; **estar en su** — (Chi, RPl) to be in one's element; **la** — **se ven los pingos** deeds speak louder than words; **tener** — (Arg) to be experienced.

cancha[2] nf (Col, Per) toasted maize, popcorn; toasted beans.

canchar [1a] vt (Arg, Per) to toast.

canche adj (a) (Guat) blond(e). (b) (Col) poorly seasoned, tasteless.

canchero nm, **canchera** nf (a) experienced person; (Sport) experienced player. (b) (Chi) layabout, loafer; (Per) grasping priest.

candado nm (a) padlock; (of book) clasp; **poner algo bajo siete** —**s** to lock something safely away. (b) (Col) goatee beard.

candanga nm: **el** — (Mex) the devil.

candar [1a] vt to lock; to lock up, put away.

cande adj: **azúcar** — sugar candy, rock candy.

candeal 1 adj: **pan** — white bread. **2** nm (Arg, Per) egg flip.

candela nf (a) candle; candlestick; (Phys) candle power; **en** — (Naut) vertical; **arrimar** — **a uno** (fam) to give someone a tanning (fam); **estar con la** — **en la mano** (fig) to be at death's door.
  (b) (esp SAm) fire; (for cigarette) light; **dar** — to be a nuisance, be trying; **echar** — (of eyes etc) to sparkle; **pegar** — **a**, **prender** — **a** to set fire to, set alight.

candelabro nm candelabra; candlestick.

Candelaria nf Candlemas.

candelaria nf (Bot) mullein.

candelero nm (a) candlestick; oil lamp; **estar en (el)** — (of person) to be high up, be in a position of authority; (of event) to be under way, be in progress; **poner a uno en (el)** — to give someone a high post. (b) (Naut) stanchion.

candelilla nf (a) small candle. (b) (Bot) catkin. (c) (SAm) glow-worm; (Arg, Chi) will-o'-the-wisp; (Ec) lively child. (d) (Arg, Cu: Sew) hem, border.

candelizo nm icicle.

candelo adj (Col) reddish-blond(e).

candente adj (a) red-hot, white-hot; glowing, burning. (b) (fig) question burning; atmosphere etc charged, electric.

candi adj: **azúcar** — sugar candy, rock candy.

candidato nm (a) candidate (a for); applicant (a for). (b) (Arg: sl) sucker (sl).

candidatura nf candidature.

candidez nf (a) simplicity, ingenousness, innocence; naïveté; stupidity. (b) (**una** —) silly remark.

cándido adj (a) simple, ingenuous, innocent; naïve; (pej) stupid. (b) (poet) snow-white.

candil nm (a) oil lamp, kitchen lamp, (Mex) chandelier; **arder en un** — (fig: of wine) to be very strong; (of subject etc) to be pretty strong stuff. (b) (Zool) tine, point, small horn.

candileja nf oil reservoir of a lamp; small oil lamp; —**s** (Theat) footlights.

candinga[1] nf (Chi) impertinence, insistence.

candinga[2] nm: **el** — (Mex) the devil.

candiota nf wine cask.

candiotero nm cooper.

candonga nf (fam) blarney, flattery; trick; playful trick, hoax, practical joke; teasing; **dar** — **a uno** to tease someone, kid someone (fam).

candongas nfpl (Col, Ec) earrings.

candongo (fam) adj 1 smooth, oily; sly, crafty; lazy. 2 nm creep (sl), toady, flatterer, sly sort; shirker, idler, lazy blighter (sl).

candonguear [1a] (fam) 1 vt to tease, kid (fam). 2 vi to shirk, dodge work.

candonguero adj (fam) = **candongo 1**.

candor nm (a) innocence, guilelessness, simplicity; frankness, candidness. (b) (poet) pure whiteness.

candorosamente adv innocently, guilelessly, simply; frankly, candidly.

candoroso adj innocent, guileless, simple; confession etc frank, candid.

candungo nm (Per) idiot.

caneca nf (a) (Arg) wooden vessel, bucket; (Cu) hot-water bottle; wine bottle (with a spout); (Mex) glazed earthenware bottle.
  (b) (Cu, Ec, Mex) liquid measure = 24.42 litres.

caneco adj (Bol, Ven) tipsy.

canela nf (a) (Bot, Cook) cinnamon; — **de la China** cassia. (b) (fig) lovely thing, exquisite object; see **flor**. (c) (Ant) mulatto girl. (d) interj (euph) good gracious!

canelero nm cinnamon tree.

canelo 1 adj cinnamon, cinnamon-coloured. **2** nm cinnamon tree.

canelón nm (a) = **canalón**. (b) icicle. (c) rolled fringe (of hair); (Guat, Ven) corkscrew curl.

canesú nm (a) (Sew) yoke. (b) underbodice, camisole.

caney nm (a) (Col, Cu, Ven) log cabin, hut; (Ant: Hist) chief's house; (Col, Ven) large shed. (b) (Cu) river bend.

canfín nm (SAm) petroleum.

cangallar [1a] vt (Bol, Chi) to steal.

cangilón nm (a) pitcher; metal tankard; (of water-wheel) bucket, scoop; (Col) drum. (b) (SAm) cart track, rut; (Ec) mudhole, miry place.

cangrejo nm (a) — **(de mar)** crab; — **(de río)** crayfish. (b) (Naut) gaff. (c) (Ec) idiot; (Per) rogue, crafty person.

cangro nm (SAm) cancer.

canguelo nm (fam) funk (fam).

canguro nm kangaroo.

caníbal 1 adj cannibal; cannibalistic, man-eating; (fig) fierce, savage. **2** nm cannibal.

canibalismo nm cannibalism; (fig) fierceness, savageness.

canica nf marble; (game) marbles.

canicie nf (of hair) greyness, whiteness.

canícula nf dog days, midsummer heat; **C—** Dog Star, Sirius.

canicular 1 adj: **calores** —**es** midsummer heat. **2** —**es** nmpl dog days.

caniche nm poodle.

canijo adj weak, frail, sickly.

canilla nf (a) (Anat) long bone (of arm or leg); shin, shinbone; (esp SAm) shank, thin leg; — **de la pierna** shinbone, tibia; — **del brazo** armbone, ulna. (b) (Tech) bobbin, reel, spool. (c) tap; (of cask) spout, cock, tap. (d) (of cloth) rib. (e) (PR) cowardice. (f) (Mex) strength; **a** — by force; against all opposition, against the odds; **tener** — to have great physical strength.

canillento adj (Per) long-legged.

canillera nf (SAm) fear, cowardice.

canillita nm (SAm) newsvendor, newspaper boy.

canillón adj (SAm), **canilludo** adj (SAm) long-legged.

canina nf dog dirt.

caninez nf ravenous hunger.

canino 1 adj (a) canine; dog (attr). (b) **hambre canina** ravenous hunger. **2** nm canine (tooth).

canje nm exchange.

canjear [1a] vt to exchange; to swap; to change over, interchange.

cano adj (a) grey-haired, white-haired, white-headed; **quedar** — to go grey. (b) (poet) snow-white. (c) (fig) venerable; (pej) hoary, ancient.

canoa nf (a) canoe; boat, launch; — **automóvil** motor boat, launch. (b) (SAm) conduit, pipe; feeding trough; chicken coop, dovecot.

canódromo nm dog track.

canoero nm (SAm), **canoísta** nmf canoeist.

canon nm (a) (Eccl, Mus, Art) canon; (Fin) tax, levy; (Agr) rent; — **de tránsito** (Aut etc) toll. (b) —**es** (Eccl) canon law.

canonical *adj* canonical; (*fig*) life easy.
canonicato *nm* (*Eccl*) canonry; (*fam*) sinecure, cushy job (*sl*).
canónico *adj* canonical; **derecho** — canon law.
canóniga *nf* (*fam*) nap before lunch; **coger una** — (*fam*) to have one over the eight.
canónigo *nm* canon.
canonista *nm* canon lawyer, expert in canon law.
canonización *nf* canonization.
canonizar [1f] **1** *vt* to canonize; (*fig*) to consecrate; to applaud, extol, show approval of.
canonjía *nf* (*Eccl*) canonry; (*fam*) sinecure, cushy job.
canoro *adj* melodious, sweet, tuneful; **ave canora** songbird.
canoso *adj* grey-haired, white-haired; *beard* grizzled, hoary.
canotaje *nm* boating.
cansadamente *adv* (**a**) wearily, in a tired way. (**b**) tediously, boringly; tiresomely.
cansado *adj* (**a**) tired, weary (**de** of); *eyes* tired, strained; *pen etc* well-worn, no longer new; **con voz cansada** in a weary voice; **estar** — to be tired; **estoy** — **de hacerlo** I'm tired of doing it, I'm sick of doing it.
 (**b**) tedious, boring; tiresome, trying.
 (**c**) **a las cansadas** (*PR, RPl*) after much delay, after a long wait.
cansador *adj* (*Arg*) tiring, wearisome.
cansancio *nm* tiredness, weariness; (*Med*) fatigue, exhaustion; **estar muerto de** — to be dead tired, be dog-tired.
cansar [1a] **1** *vt* to tire, tire out, weary; (*Med*) to fatigue, exhaust; *eyes* to tire, strain, try; *patience* to try, wear out; (*Agr*) *soil* to exhaust; *appetite* to jade; (*fig*) to bore; to badger, bother (**con** with).
 2 *vi* (**a**) to tire. (**b**) to be trying, be tiresome.
 3 cansarse *vr* to tire, get tired, grow weary (**con, de** of); to get bored (**con, de** with); to tire oneself out; — **de hacer algo** to get tired of doing something, get bored with doing something.
cansera *nf* (*fam*) bother.
cantable *adj* suitable for singing, to be sung, cantabile; melodious.
Cantabria *f* Cantabria.
cantábrico *adj* Cantabrian; **Mar C**— Bay of Biscay.
cantadera *nf* (*SAm*) loud singing, prolonged singing.
cantador *nm*, **cantadora** *nf* folksinger, singer of popular songs.
cantal *nm* (**a**) boulder; stone block. (**b**) stony ground.
cantaletear [1a] *vt* (*SAm*) (**a**) to repeat ad nauseam, say over and over. (**b**) to laugh at, make fun of.
cantalupa *nf* (*CAm*), **cantalupo** *nm* cantaloupe.
cantante 1 *adj* singing. **2** *nmf* (professional) singer, vocalist; — **de ópera** opera singer.
cantar [1a] **1** *vt* to sing; to chant; to sing about, sing of, sing the praises of; *mass* to sing, say; — **las claras** to speak out, speak frankly, (*pej*) be cheeky.
 2 *vi* (**a**) (*Mus*) to sing; to chant; (*of insect etc*) to chirp; (*of machine, wheel, etc*) to creak, squeak, grind; — **a dos voces** to sing a duet.
 (**b**) (*fam*) to squeal (*sl*), blab, spill the beans (*sl*); — **de plano** (*fam*) to tell all one knows, make a full confession.
 (**c**) (*Arg, PR, Urug*) to ask a high price, over-charge.
 (**d**) (*Cu*) to smell bad.
 3 *nm* (**a**) singing; chanting.
 (**b**) song; poem (set to music); epic poem; **C**— **de los C**—**es** Song of Songs; — **de gesta** epic poem; **C**— **de mio Cid** Poem of the Cid; **eso es otro** — that's another story.
cántara *nf* (**a**) large pitcher. (**b**) *liquid measure* = 16.13 litres.
cantarería *nf* (**a**) pottery shop, earthenware shop. (**b**) pottery.
cantarero *nm* potter, dealer in earthenware.
cantárida *nf* (*also* **polvo de** —) Spanish fly, (*Pharm*) cantharides.
cantarín 1 *adj person* fond of singing; *stream* tinkling, musical; *tone* singsong, lilting. **2** *nm*, **cantarina** *nf* singer.
cántaro *nm* pitcher, jug; jugful; **a** —**s** in plenty; **llover a** —**s** to rain cats and dogs, rain in torrents.
cantata *nf* cantata.
cante *nm*: — **flamenco**, — **jondo** Andalusian gipsy singing.
cantera *nf* (**a**) quarry, pit; — **de arena** sandpit; — **de piedra** stone quarry. (**b**) (*fig*) talent, genius.
cantería *nf* (**a**) quarrying, stone cutting. (**b**) masonry, stonework. (**c**) piece of masonry, stone.

cantero *nm* (**a**) quarryman; stonemason.
 (**b**) end, extremity; — **de pan** crust of bread.
 (**c**) (*RPl*) bed, plot (*of vegetables*); flower bed; (*Mex, Per*) plot of sugar cane.
cántico *nm* (*Eccl*) canticle; (*fig*) song.
cantidad *nf* quantity; amount, number; (*of money*) amount, sum; — **alzada** lump sum; — **de movimiento** (*Phys*) momentum; **en** — in quantity; — **de**, (**una**) **gran** — **de** a great quantity of, lots of; **tengo una** — **de cosas que hacer** I've lots of things to do, I've masses of things to do.
cantil *nm* shelf, ledge (*on rock*); coastal shelf; cliff.
cantilena *nf* ballad, song, chant; **la misma** — (*fig*) the same old stuff.
cantimplora *nf* water bottle, canteen; decanter; (*Tech*) syphon; (*Col*) powder flask; **¡**—**!** (*Cu, Per*) not on your life!
cantina *nf* (**a**) (*Rail*) buffet, refreshment room; (*Mil etc*) canteen; snack bar; (*SAm*) bar, saloon; (*Arg*) cheap restaurant.
 (**b**) wine cellar.
 (**c**) lunch box; (*Col*) milk churn; —**s** (*Mex*) saddlebags.
cantinela *nf* = **cantilena**.
cantinero *nm* barman, publican.
cantinflismo *nm* (*Mex*) unintelligible chatter.
cantío *nm* (*Cu, PR*) folksong, popular song.
cantiral *nm* stony ground, stony place.
canto[1] *nm* (*Mus*) (**a**) (*art and in general*) singing; chanting.
 (**b**) (*act in general*) singing; **el** — **de los pájaros** the singing of the birds.
 (**c**) (*piece*) song; — **llano** plainsong; **al** — **del gallo** at cockcrow, at daybreak.
 (**d**) (*Poet*) song, lyric; (*section of epic etc*) canto.
canto[2] *nm* (**a**) edge; rim, border; (*of knife*) back; end, point; corner; (*of bread*) crust; **ni un** — **de uña** absolutely nothing; **estar de** — to be on edge, be edgeways; to be on end; **le faltó el** — **de un duro** he had a narrow shave; **tener 3 cm de** — to be 3 cm thick.
 (**b**) stone, pebble; rock; (*also* — **rodado**) boulder.
cantón[1] *nm* corner; (*Her, Pol*) canton; (*Mil*) cantonment.
cantón[2] *nm* (*Sew*) cotton material.
cantonada *nf*: **dar** — **a uno** to dodge someone, shake someone off.
cantonal *adj* cantonal.
cantonear [1a] *vi* to loaf around.
cantonera *nf* (**a**) corner shelf; corner bracket, angle iron; corner table; corner cupboard; (*of book etc*) corner band.
 (**b**) (*fam*) streetwalker.
cantonero *nm* loafer, idler, good-for-nothing.
cantonés 1 *adj* Cantonese. **2** *nm*, **cantonesa** *nf* Cantonese. **3** *nm* (*dialect*) Cantonese.
cantor 1 *adj* singing, that sings; **ave cantora** songbird.
 2 *nm*, **cantora** *nf* singer; (*Orn*) songbird.
Cantorberi, Cantórbery Canterbury.
cantorral *nm* stony ground, stony place.
cantuja *nf* (*Per*) underworld slang.
canturía *nf* singing, vocal music; singing exercise; (*pej*) monotonous singing, droning.
canturrear [1a] *vti* to hum, croon, sing softly; to drone.
canturreo *nm* humming, crooning, soft singing; droning.
canutero *nm* (*SAm*) barrel (*of pen*).
canuto *nm* = **cañuto**.
canzonetista *nf* singer, vocalist.
caña *nf* (**a**) (*Bot: species*) reed.
 (**b**) (*Bot: part*) stem, stalk, cane; — **de azúcar**, — **dulce**, — **melar** sugar cane; — **de pescar** fishing rod; (*tabu, hum*) prick (*tabu*); — **del timón** tiller, helm; **las** —**s se vuelven lanzas** a joke can easily turn into something unpleasant.
 (**c**) (*Anat*) long bone (*of arm or leg*), (*esp*) shinbone; (*of boot, stocking*) leg; (*of anchor, column, horse*) shank.
 (**d**) tall wineglass, long glass; — **de cerveza** glass of beer; beer glass; "**¡dos** —**s!**" (*in bar*) "two beers please".
 (**e**) (*SAm*) sugar cane; rum, brandy.
 (**f**) (*Min*) gallery.
 (**g**) (*Ven*) swig (*fam*), drink.
 (**h**) (*Col, Ec, Ven*) false piece of news; (*Col, Ven*) piece of bluff, piece of bluster.
cañada *nf* (**a**) gully, ravine; glen. (**b**) cattle track, drover's road. (**c**) (*SAm*) stream.
cañadón *nm* (*Arg*) low-lying part of a field.
cañamar *nm* hemp field.

cañamargal nm (SAm) sugar-cane plantation.
cañamazo nm (coarse) canvas; burlap.
cañamelar nm sugar-cane plantation.
cañameno adj hempen.
cañamero adj hemp (attr).
cañamiel nf sugar cane.
cáñamo nm (Bot) hemp; hempen cloth; (CAm, Chi, SD) hempen cord; — **agranado** dressed hemp; — **indio** (CAm) Indian hemp, marijuana.
cañamón nm hemp seed; —**es** birdseed.
cañavera nf reed grass.
cañaveral nm reedbed; (Agr) sugar-cane plantation.
cañengo adj, **cañengue** adj (Col, Cu) weak, sickly; skinny.
cañería nf pipe, piece of piping, length of piping; pipeline, conduit; drain; (Mus) organ pipes; — **maestra** (**de gas**) (gas) main.
cañero 1 adj (a) (SAm) sugar-cane (attr); **machete** — sugar-cane knife.
 (b) (Col, Ec, Ven) lying, boastful.
 2 nm (a) (Tech) plumber.
 (b) (SAm: Agr) owner (or manager) of a sugar-cane plantation.
 (c) (Col, Ec, Ven) liar, bluffer, boaster.
cañete nm small pipe.
cañista nm plumber.
cañiza nf coarse linen.
cañizal nm, **cañizar** nm reedbed.
cañizo nm (Agr) hurdle (for drying fruit etc).
caño nm (a) tube, pipe; (Mus) pipe; (of fountain) jet, spout; (Archit) gutter; drain, (open) sewer.
 (b) gallery.
 (c) wine cellar.
 (d) (Naut) navigation channel, deep channel; (Col, Ven) deep navigable river.
cañón 1 nm (a) tube, pipe; (Mus) pipe, organ pipe; (of chimney) flue; shaft, stack; (of column, lift, elevator) shaft; (of staircase) well; (of gun, pen) barrel; (of pipe) stem; (Mountaineering) chimney; **escopeta de dos** —**es** double-barrelled gun; — **rayado** rifled barrel; **ni a** — **rayado** (Chi, Per, PR) by no means, not at all.
 (b) (Mil) gun; (esp Hist) cannon; — **de agua** water cannon; — **antiaéreo** anti-aircraft gun; — **antitanque** anti-tank gun; — **de avancarga** muzzle loader; — **de campaña** field gun.
 (c) (of feather) quill.
 (d) (Geog) canyon, gorge.
 (e) (Col: Bot) trunk.
 (f) (Mex, Per) path (in mountain country).
 2 as adj (fam) fabulous (fam), marvellous; ¡el hombre está —! he's fabulous!; ¡la función estaba —! the show was great! (fam); **una noticia** — a stunning piece of news.
cañonazo nm (a) gunshot; (Hist) cannon shot; —**s** gunfire, shellfire; **salva de 21** —**s** 21-gun salute; — **de advertencia** (Naut) warning shot, shot across the bows.
 (b) (fig) bolt from the blue, unexpected piece of news.
cañonear [1a] vt to shell, bombard.
cañoneo nm shelling, shellfire, gunfire; bombardment, cannonade.
cañonera nf (a) (Mil: Hist) embrasure. (b) (Naut: also **lancha** —) gunboat. (c) (SAm) holster.
cañonero nm gunboat.
cañoso adj reedy.
cañusero nm (Col) owner of a sugar-cane plantation.
cañutero nm pincushion.
cañuto nm (a) small tube, small container. (b) (Bot) internode. (c) (fam) telltale.
caoba nf mahogany.
caolín nm kaolin.
caos nm chaos.
caótico adj chaotic.
capa nf (a) cloak, cape; (Eccl: also — **pluvial**) cope; — **aguadera** waterproof cloak; — **del cielo** canopy of heaven; — **de ladrones** (fig) fence; — **rota** (fig) secret emissary; — **torera** bullfighter's cape; **abrirse de** — to pluck up courage; **andar de** — **caída** to be in a bad way, be on the decline; **echar una** — **a uno** to cover up for someone; **echar la** — **al toro** to make a final desperate effort; **hacer de su** — **un sayo** to do what one likes with one's own things, act freely; **de** — **y espada** cloak-and-dagger (attr).
 (b) (fig) cloak, pretence; mask, disguise; **so** — **de** under the pretext of, in the guise of.
 (c) (Geol) layer, bed, stratum; (Meteorol, Anat etc) layer; (of smoke) pall; (of dust) layer, film; (of snow) layer, covering, mantle; (Cook) coating; (of paint) coat; **primera** — undercoat, first coat; —**s sociales**

social layers, social levels; **madera de tres** —**s** three-ply wood.
 (d) (Naut) **estar a la** —, **ponerse a la** — to lie to.
capacidad nf (a) capacity (also Comm, Phys, Tech etc); capaciousness, size; **una sala con** — **para 900** a hall with room for 900, a hall that can hold 900; **un avión con** — **para 20 plazas** a 20-seater plane; — **adquisitiva**, — **de compra** purchasing power; — **de arrastre** (of speaker etc) drawing power, power of attraction; — **de carga** carrying capacity; — **financiera** financial standing; — **de ganancia** earning power; — **de repercusión** resilience; — **útil** effective capacity.
 (b) (fig) (mental) capacity, ability, capability; talent; competence, efficiency; **tener** — **para** to have an aptitude for, have talent for; **no tiene** — **para los negocios** he has no business sense.
 (c) (SAm) able person, talented person.
capacitación nf capacitation; (Tech etc) training.
capacitado adj qualified; **estar** — **para** + infin to be qualified to + infin.
capacitar [1a] **1** vt (a) — **a uno para algo** to fit someone for something, qualify someone for something; (Tech) to train someone for something; — **a uno para** + infin to enable someone to + infin.
 (b) (Chi) — **a uno para hacer algo** to empower (or authorize) someone to do something.
 2 capacitarse vr: — **para algo** to fit oneself for something, qualify for something.
capacha nf (a) basket, frail. (b) (Arg, Bol, Chi) jail; **caer en la** — (Arg) to fall into the trap.
capacheca nf (Chi, Per) street-vendor's barrow (or stall).
capacho nm (a) wicker basket, big basket; (Tech) hod; (Per) saddlebag. (b) (Bol, Ec, RPl) old hat. (c) (Ec) jail.
capadura nf castration.
capar [1a] vt (a) to castrate, geld.
 (b) (fig) to reduce, cut down, curtail.
 (c) (Ant, Mex: Agr) to cut back, prune.
 (d) (Bol, Ven) food to start on, begin to eat.
caparazón nm (a) (Hist) caparison; horse blanket; nosebag. (b) (Zool) shell.
caparrón nm bud.
caparrosa nf vitriol; — **azul** copper sulphate, blue vitriol.
capataz nm foreman, overseer.
capaz adj (a) (of size) capacious, roomy, large; — **de**, — **para** with a capacity of, with room for, that holds; **un coche** — **para 4 personas** a car with room for 4 people.
 (b) (of ability) able, capable; efficient, competent; fit; ⟨Law⟩ competent; **ser** — **de algo** to be capable of something; **ser** — **de hacer algo** to be capable of doing something, be up to doing something; to be competent to do something; **es** — **de cualquier tontería** he is capable of any stupidity, one might expect any idiocy from him; **¡sería** —**!** one could well believe it of him, I'm not surprised; — **de funcionar** (Tech) operational, in working order; **ser** — **para un trabajo** to be qualified for a job, be up to a job.
 (c) (Mex) **es** — **que venga** he'll probably come.
capazo nm large basket; (child's) carrycot.
capcioso adj wily, deceitful.
capeador nm bullfighter who uses the cape.
capear [1a] **1** vt (a) (Taur) to play with the cape, wave the cape at; (fig) to take in, deceive.
 (b) (Naut and fig) storm to ride out, weather.
 2 vi (Naut) to ride out the storm; to lie to.
capelo nm (a) (Eccl) cardinal's hat; (fig) cardinalate. (b) (Arg, Mex) bell glass, glass cover. (c) (SAm: Univ) — **de doctor** doctor's short cape.
capellada nf toecap; patch (on shoe).
capellán nm chaplain; priest, clergyman; — **castrense**, — **de ejército** army chaplain.
capellanía nf chaplaincy.
capellina nf (Med) head bandage.
capero nm hallstand, hatstand.
Caperucita Roja f (Little) Red Riding Hood.
caperuza nf (pointed) hood; (Mech) hood, cowling; — **de chimenea** chimney cowl.
capi[1] nm (fam) = **capitán**.
capi[2] nf (Bol) white maize flower; (Chi) unripe pod.
capia nf (Arg, Bol) white maize flower; (Arg, Col) variety of maize bearing soft sweet grain.
capiango nm (Arg) clever thief.
capicúa nf reversible number, symmetrical number (eg 12321); palindrome.
capigorra nm, **capigorrista** nm, **capigorrón** nm idler, loafer.

capilar 1 *adj* capillary; hair (*attr*); **tubo —** capillary. **2** *nm* capillary.

capilaridad *nf* capillarity.

capilla *nf* (a) (*Eccl*) chapel; **— ardiente** funeral chapel; **— mayor** choir, chancel; **— de la Virgen** Lady Chapel; **estar en (la) —** (*fig*) to be awaiting execution; to be in great danger; to be in suspense, be on tenterhooks.
(b) (*Mus*) choir.
(c) (*Typ*) proof sheet; **estar en —s** to be in proof.
(d) cowl; (*Tech*) hood, cowl.

capiller(o) *nm* churchwarden; sexton.

capillo *nm* (a) baby's bonnet; (*falcon's*) hood. (b) (*Bot, Zool*) = **capullo**.

capirotazo *nm* flip, flick.

capirote *nm* (a) (*Hist, Univ, also falcon's*) hood. (b) flip, flick. (c) **tonto de —** prize idiot, utter fool.

capirucho *nm* hood.

capisayo *nm* (*Col*) vest, undershirt (*US*).

capitación *nf* poll tax, capitation.

capital 1 *adj* (*in many senses*) capital; *city, crime, capital; enemy, sin* mortal; *feature* main, chief, principal; *point* essential, fundamental; *importance* capital, supreme, paramount; *letter* (*SAm*) capital; **lo —** the main thing, the essential point.
2 *nm* (*Fin*) capital; capital sum; **— activo** working capital, (*Col, Chi*) capital assets; **— de explotación** working capital; **— físico** (*Chi*) capital assets; **— social** share capital; **inversión de —es** capital investment.
3 *nf* (*Pol: of country*) capital, capital city; (*of region*) chief town, centre; **— de provincia** provincial capital, administrative centre of the province.

capitalino (*SAm*) **1** *adj* of the capital. **2** *nm*, **capitalina** *nf* native (*or* inhabitant) of the capital; **los —s** the people of the capital.

capitalismo *nm* capitalism.

capitalista 1 *adj* capitalist(ic). **2** *nmf* capitalist.

capitalización *nf* capitalization; compounding.

capitalizar [1f] *vt* to capitalize; *interest* to compound.

capitán *nm* (*Mil, Naut, Sport etc*) captain; leader, chief, commander; **— de corbeta** lieutenant-commander; **— de fragata** commander; **— general (de ejército)** (*approx*) field marshal; **— general (de armada)** chief of naval operations; **— de navío** captain; **— del puerto** harbour master.

capitana *nf* flagship.

capitanear [1a] *vt* *team* to captain; *expedition, rising etc* to lead, head, command.

capitanía *nf* (a) captaincy; rank of captain. (b) **— del puerto** harbour master's office. (c) harbour dues.

capitel *nm* (*Archit*) capital.

capitolio *nm* capitol; large edifice, imposing building; statehouse, parliament building; **C—** Capitol; **subir al —** (*fam*) to get to the top.

capitoné *nm* (a) removal van, furniture van. (b) (*Arg*) quilt, quilted blanket.

capitonear [1a] *vt* (*Arg*) to quilt.

capitoste *nm* (*pej*) chief, boss; petty tyrant.

capitulación *nf* (a) (*Mil*) capitulation, surrender; **— sin condiciones** unconditional surrender.
(b) agreement, pact; **—es (de boda, matrimoniales)** marriage settlement.

capitular¹ *adj* (*Eccl*) chapter (*attr*); **sala —** chapter house, meeting room.

capitular² [1a] **1** *vt* (a) *terms* to agree to, agree on.
(b) (*Law*) to charge (*de* with), impeach.
2 *vi* (a) to come to terms, make an agreement (*con* with); **— con** (*pej*) to compound with.
(b) (*Mil*) to capitulate, surrender.

capitulear [1a] *vi* (*Chi, Per: Parl*) to lobby.

capituleo *nm* (*Chi, Per: Parl*) lobbying.

capítulo *nm* (a) (*Lit, Typ*) chapter.
(b) reproof, reprimand; **— de culpas** charge.
(c) subject, matter; point; **ganar —** to make one's point.
(d) **—s matrimoniales** marriage contract, marriage settlement.
(e) meeting (*of a council*); (*Eccl*) chapter; **llamar a uno a —** to take someone to task, call someone to account.
(f) (*Eccl*) chapter house.

capó *nm* (*Aut*) bonnet, hood (*US*).

capoc *nm* kapok.

capón¹ *nm* rap on the head.

capón² 1 *adj* castrated. **2** *nm* capon; eunuch; (*RPl*) (*any*) castrated animal.

caponera *nf* (*Agr*) chicken coop, fattening pen; (*fig*) place of easy living, open house; (*sl*) clink (*sl*).

caporal *nm* chief, leader, (*Mex*) foreman, head man.

capot [ka'po] *nm* (*Aut*) = **capó**.

capota *nf* (a) (*woman's*) bonnet. (b) (*of carriage, pram*) hood; (*Aer*) cowling; (*Aut*) hood, top (*US*); **— plegable** folding hood, folding top (*US*).

capotaje *nm* somersault; overturning; (*Aer*) loop; (*Aer*) nose dive.

capotar [1a] *vi* (*Aut etc*) to turn over, turn turtle; to somersault; (*Aer*) to nose-dive.

capote *nm* (a) long cloak, cloak with sleeves; (*also* **— de brega**) bullfighter's cloak; (*Mil*) greatcoat; **— de monte** poncho; **a mi —, para mi —** to my way of thinking; **de — (Mex)** on the sly, in an underhand way; **darse — (Mex)** to give up one's job; to acknowledge defeat; **decir para su —** to say to oneself; **echar un — a uno** to give someone a helping hand.
(b) frown, scowl; (*Meteorol*) mass of dark clouds.
(c) (*Cards*) slam.
(d) (*Arg: Cards*) **quedar —** not to win a single point, be whitewashed.
(e) (*Chi, Mex*) beating.

capotear [1a] *vt* (a) *person* to deceive, bamboozle. (b) *difficulty etc* to shirk, duck, dodge. (c) (*Arg: Cards*) to win all the tricks against, whitewash.

capotera *nf* (a) (*CAm, Chi, Mex*) clothes rack. (b) (*Col, Cu, Ven: of horseman*) canvas bag.

capotudo *adj* frowning, scowling.

Capricornio *m* Capricorn.

capricho *nm* (a) whim, caprice, (*passing*) fancy; keen desire, sudden urge (*de* for); (*pej*) craze, fad, silly notion; **por puro —** just to please oneself, out of sheer cussedness; **es un — nada más** it's just a passing whim; **fue un — suyo** it was one of his silly notions; **tiene sus —s** he has his little whims, he has his moods.
(b) (*in general*) whimsicality, fancifulness.
(c) (*Anat*) birthmark.
(d) (*Mus*) caprice, capriccio.

caprichosamente *adv* capriciously.

caprichoso *adj* capricious; full of whims, having odd fancies; full of one's own pet notions; *idea, novel, etc* fanciful, whimsical; (*pej*) wilful; moody, temperamental; wayward.

caprichudo *adj* stubborn, obstinate, unyielding (*about one's odd ideas*).

cápsula *nf* (*Aer, Anat, Bot, Pharm etc*) capsule; (*of bottle*) cap; (*of cartridge*) case; (*SD*) cartridge; **— espacial** space capsule; **— fulminante** percussion cap.

capsular *adj* capsular; **en forma —** in capsule form.

captafaros *nm*, *pl* **captafaros** (*also* **placa de —**) reflector.

captar [1a] *vt* (a) to captivate; *support* to win, gain, attract; *confidence etc* to win, get; *will* to gain control over; *attention etc* to get, secure; *person* to win over.
(b) *waters* to collect; to dam, harness.
(c) (*Radio*) *station* to tune in to; *signal* to get, pick up.

captura *nf* capture; seizure; arrest.

capturar [1a] *vt* to capture; to seize; to arrest.

capucha *nf* (a) hood; (*Eccl*) hood, cowl. (b) (*Ling*) circumflex accent.

capuchina *nf* (a) (*Eccl*) Capuchin sister. (b) (*Bot*) nasturtium.

capuchino *nm* (a) (*Eccl*) Capuchin. (b) (*SAm*) Capuchin monkey. (c) coffee with a little milk.

capucho *nm* cowl, hood.

capuchón *nm* (a) lady's hooded cloak. (b) (*Phot*) hood. (c) (*Aut etc*) valve cap. (d) (*of pen*) top, cap.

capujar [1a] *vt* (*Arg*) to catch in the air; to snatch; to say what someone else was about to say.

capullo *nm* (a) (*Zool*) cocoon. (b) (*Bot*) bud, flower bud; (*of acorn*) cup; **— de rosa** rosebud. (c) (*Anat*) prepuce.

caqui¹ *nm* khaki.

caqui² *nm* (*Chi*) date plum; (*fig*) red.

caquino *nm*: **reírse a —s, reírse a — suelto** (*Mex*) to laugh uproariously.

cara *nf* (a) (*Anat*) face; **— cortada** (*as nickname*) scarface; **— de cuchillo** hatchet face; **— a —** face to face; **a — descubierta** openly; **de —** opposite, facing; **de — al norte** facing north; **mirar a uno a la —** to look someone in the face; **los banqueros sin —** the faceless bankers; **asomar la —** to show one's face (*also fig*); **se le caía la — de vergüenza** he blushed with shame; **cruzar la — a uno** to slash someone across the face; **dar la —** to face the consequences of what one has done; **dar la — por otro** to answer for someone else; **dar — a —** to face up to; **decir algo en (*or* por) la — de uno** to say something to someone's face; **echar algo en — a uno** to reproach someone for something, cast

something in someone's teeth; **to allude to some-**
thing; **entrar** (*or* **pasar**) **por la —** to gatecrash;
hacer a dos —s to engage in double-dealing; **hacer
— a** to face; *enemy etc* to face up to, stand up to;
huir la — a uno to avoid meeting someone; **lavar
la — a uno** to lick someone's boots; **no mirar la —
a uno** (*fig*) to be at daggers drawn with someone;
sacar la — por uno to stick up for someone; **nos
veremos las —s** (*as threat*) we'll meet again, we'll
see; **no volver la — atrás** not to flinch.

   (b) (*as adv*) **— adelante** forwards; facing forwards;
— atrás backwards; facing backwards; **— al sol**
facing the sun.

   (c) look, appearance; **tener — de** to look like;
tener — de querer + *infin* to look as if one would
like to + *infin*; **tener — de aburrirse** to look
bored; **tener buena —** to look nice, (*Med*) look well;
tener mala — to look bad, (*Med*) look ill; **— de
acelga** pale look; **— de aleluya** cheerful look; **tener
— de pocos amigos** to look black, have a hangdog
look; **— de corcho** cheeky look; **— dura** shamelessness; cheek, nerve; **¡qué — más dura!** what a
nerve!; **— de hereje** ugly face; hangdog look; **— de
(justo) juez** stern face, grim-looking face; **mala —**
wry face, grimace; **poner mala —** to pout, grimace,
make a (wry) face; **tener — de monja boba** to look
all innocent; **tener — de palo** to have a wooden
expression; **— de pascua(s)** smiling face; **tener — de
pascua(s)** to look pretty pleased; **tener — de
roñoso** to look mean; **— de viernes** sad look; **—
de vinagre** sour expression.

   (d) boldness, nerve; **tener — para** + *infin* to
have the nerve to + *infin*.

   (e) (*of object*) face; outside, surface; (*Archit*) face,
façade, front; (*Geom*) face; (*of cloth etc*) face, right
side, finished side; (*of slice, record etc*) side; (*of
coin*) face, obverse, (*in tossing up*) heads; **— o cruz**
heads or tails; **echar** (*or* **jugar, sortear**) **algo a — o
cruz** to toss up for something; **—, yo gano; cruz,
Vd pierde** heads I win, tails you lose.

cárabe *nm* amber.
carabela *nf* caravel.
carabina *nf* (a) (*Mil*) carbine, rifle; **ser la — de
Ambrosio** (*fam*) to be a dead loss.

   (b) (*fam*) chaperon; **hacer de —, ir de —** to go as
chaperon; to play gooseberry.
carabinero *nm* carabineer, rifleman; revenue guard.
cárabo *nm* tawny owl.
caracol *nm* (a) (*Zool*) snail; snail shell, sea shell.

   (b) (*of hair*) curl.

   (c) (*in shape*) spiral; **escalera de —** spiral
staircase, winding staircase; **subir en —** (*of smoke
etc*) to spiral up, corkscrew up; **hacer —es** (*person*)
to weave about, zigzag; (*pej*) to reel, stagger; (*horse*)
to prance about.

   (d) **¡—es!** (*euph*) good heavens!
caracolear [1a] *vi* (*of horse*) to prance about.
carácter *nm, pl* **caracteres** (a) character; nature,
kind, condition; **de medio —** of an ill-defined
nature; **de — totalmente distinto** of quite a
different kind.

   (b) (*of person*) character; **una persona de — a**
person of character; **de — duro** hard-natured;
no tiene — he lacks firmness, he's a weak character.

   (c) (*SAm: Lit, Theat*) character, personage.

   (d) (*Bio*) character; feature, characteristic; **—
adquirido** acquired characteristic; **— hereditario**
inherited characteristic.

   (e) (*Typ*) character; **— de letra** handwriting;
—es de imprenta type, typeface; **escribir en —es
de imprenta** to write in block letters.
característica *nf* (a) characteristic; trait, quality,
attribute. (b) (*Theat*) character actress.
característicamente *adv* characteristically.
característico 1 *adj* characteristic, typical (*de* of).
2 *nm* (*Theat*) character actor.
caracterizado *adj* distinguished, of note; special,
peculiar, having special characteristics, typical.
caracterizar [1f] **1** *vt* (a) to characterize; to typify;
to distinguish, set apart.

   (b) to confer (a) distinction on, confer an honour
on.

   (c) (*Theat*) *role* to play with great effect.

   2 caracterizarse *vr* (*Theat*) to make up, dress
for the part.
caracú *nm* (*SAm*) bone marrow.
caracha *nf* (*SAm*) mange, itch; scab.
carachento *adj*, **carachoso** *adj* (*SAm*) mangy,
scabby.
caracho *adj* violet-coloured.
caradura 1 *nmf* rotter, cad, shameless person; **¡—!**
you swine! **2** *nf see* **cara** (c).

carajear [1a] *vt* (*Arg*) to insult, swear at.
carajiento *adj* (*Ec*) foul-mouthed.
carajo *nm* (*tabu*) prick (*tabu*); **¡—!** hell!, damn it all!;
¡vete al —! go to hell!
caramba *interj* (*fam*) well!, good gracious!; very odd!,
how strange!; hang it all!; **¡— con...!** to hell with...!
carámbano *nm* icicle.
carambola *nf* (*Billiards*) cannon; (*fig*) trick, ruse;
por — by a lucky chance; indirectly, in a roundabout way.
caramelear [1a] *vt* (*Col*) to pull the wool over the
eyes of, deceive.
caramelo *nm* sweet, toffee; caramel; **— americano**
candyfloss, cotton candy (*US*).
caramillo *nm* (a) (*Mus*) flageolet; recorder; rustic
pipe.

   (b) untidy heap.

   (c) piece of gossip; intrigue; **armar un —** to make
mischief, start a gossiping campaign.
caramilloso *adj* fussy.
caranchear [1a] *vt* (*Arg*) to provoke.
carancho *nm* (*Per*) owl; (*RPl*) vulture.
caranga *nf* (*Ec, Guat, Hond*), **carángano** *nm* (*Col,
CR, Cu, Ec, Per*) louse.
carantamaula *nf* (*fam*) ugly mug (*sl*), ugly person.
carantoña *nf* (*fam*) (a) ugly mug (*sl*).

   (b) **ella es una —** she's mutton dressed up as
lamb, she's tarted herself up to look younger.

   (c) **—s** caresses; petting, fondling; **hacer —s a uno**
to make faces at someone; to make sheep's eyes at
someone.
carapacho *nm* shell, carapace; **meterse en su —** to
go into one's shell.
caraqueño 1 *adj* of Caracas. **2** *nm,* **caraqueña** *nf*
native (*or* inhabitant) of Caracas; **los —s** the people
of Caracas.
carátula *nf* (a) mask; **la —** (*fig: Theat*) the stage,
the theatre. (b) (*Guat, Mex*) face, dial. (c) (*SAm:
Typ*) title page.
caravana *nf* (a) (*Hist*) caravan; (*fig*) group, band;
(*fig*) crowd of trippers, group of picnickers; (*of
cars*) stream, long succession, queue.

   (b) (*Aut: angl*) caravan, trailer.

   (c) (*Cu*) bird trap.

   (d) (*SAm*) exaggerated bow; courtesy, compliment; **bailar** (*or* **correr, hacer**) **la — a uno** to
overdo the courtesies; to pay exaggerated compliments to someone.

   (e) **—s** (*SAm*) long earrings.
caravan(s)era *nf*, **caravasar** *nm* caravanserai.
caray *interj* (*sl*) gosh! (*sl*), good heavens!; well I'm
blowed!
carbohidrato *nm* carbohydrate.
carbólico *adj* carbolic.
carbón *nm* (a) (*Min*) coal; **— bituminoso** soft coal;
— de leña, — vegetal charcoal; **— menudo** small
coal, slack; **— de piedra** coal.

   (b) (*Typ: also* **papel —**) carbon paper, carbon;
copia al — carbon copy.

   (c) (*Elec*) carbon.

   (d) (*Agr*) smut.
carbonada *nf* (*Chi, Per, RPl*) meat stew.
carbonato *nm* carbonate; **— de calcio** calcium
carbonate; **— sódico** sodium carbonate.
carboncillo *nm* (*Art*) charcoal; (*Min*) small coal,
slack; (*Aut*) carbon.
carbonear [1a] *vt* (a) to make charcoal of. (b) (*Chi*)
to spur on, encourage.
carbonera *nf* (a) coalmine. (b) coal tip, coal heap.
(c) coal bin, coal bunker. (d) charcoal kiln.
carbonería *nf* coalyard.
carbonero 1 *adj* coal (*attr*); charcoal (*attr*); **barco —**
collier; **estación carbonera** coaling station.
2 *nm* (a) coal merchant; charcoal burner.

   (b) (*Naut*) collier, coal ship.

   (c) (*Orn*) coal tit.
carbónico 1 *adj* carbonic. **2** *nm* (*Arg*) carbon paper,
carbon.
carbonífero *adj* carboniferous.
carbonilla *nf* (a) small coal, coaldust; cinder. (b)
(*Aut*) carbon.
carbonización *nf* (*Chem*) carbonization; charring.
carbonizar [1f] **1** *vt* (*Chem*) to carbonize; to char;
wood to make charcoal of; **quedar carbonizado** to
be charred, be burnt to a cinder; (*Elec*) to be electro-
cuted; (*of building*) to be burnt down, be reduced
to ashes.

   2 carbonizarse *vr* (*Chem*) to carbonize; **= quedar
carbonizado**.
carbono *nm* (*Chem*) carbon.
carbonoso *adj* carbonaceous.
carborundo *nm* carborundum.

carbunclo *nm* (*Min*), **carbunco** *nm* (*Med*) carbuncle.
carburador *nm* carburettor.
carburante *nm* fuel.
carburo *nm* carbide.
carca *adj invar* (*sl*) square (*fam*).
carcaj *nm* quiver; (*Mex*) rifle case, pistol holster.
carcajada *nf* (loud) laugh, peal of laughter, guffaw; **hubo** —**s** there was loud laughter; **reírse a** —**s** to laugh heartily, roar with laughter; **soltar la** — to burst out laughing.
carcajear [1a] *vi and* **carcajearse** *vr* to roar with laughter, have a good laugh (*de at*).
carcamal *nm* (*fam*) old crock, wreck; **es un** — he's a wreck.
carcamán *nm* (a) (*Naut*) tub, hulk; (*Per, PR*) old crock, wreck. (b) (*Cu, Per, RPl*) low-class foreign immigrant. (c) (*Arg: Pol*) diehard, reactionary.
carcancha *nf* (*Mex*) bus.
carcasa *nf* (*Aut etc*) chassis, grid; (*of tyre*) carcass.
carcayú *nm* wolverine.
cárcel *nf* (a) prison, jail; — **modelo** model prison; **poner en la** — to jail, send to jail, put in prison. (b) (*Tech*) clamp.
carcelario *adj* prison (*attr*).
carcelería *nf* imprisonment, detention.
carcelero 1 *adj* prison (*attr*). 2 *nm* warder, jailer.
carcinogénico *adj* carcinogenic.
carcinoma *nm* carcinoma.
carcoma *nf* (a) (*Ent*) deathwatch beetle; woodworm. (b) (*fig*) anxiety, perpetual worry; (*person*) spend-thrift.
carcomer [2a] 1 *vt* (a) to bore into, eat into, eat away. (b) (*fig*) *health etc* to undermine; *fortune* to eat into, eat away.
  2 **carcomerse** *vr* (a) to get worm-eaten. (b) (*fig*) to decay, waste away; to be eaten away.
carcomido *adj* worm-eaten, wormy, infested with woodworm; rotten; (*fig*) rotten, decayed.
carcoso *adj* (*Ec*) dirty.
carda *nf* (a) (*Bot*) teasel; (*Tech*) teasel, card (*for combing wool*). (b) (*act*) carding. (c) (*fam*) reprimand; **dar una** — **a uno** to rap someone over the knuckles.
cardamomo *nm* cardamom.
cardar [1a] *vt* (a) (*Tech*) to card, comb. (b) (*fam; also* — **la lana a**) to tell off, rap over the knuckles.
cardenal *nm* (a) (*Eccl*) cardinal. (b) (*Med*) bruise, mark, weal. (c) (*Chi*) geranium.
cardenalato *nm* cardinalate.
cardencha *nf* (*Bot, Tech*) teasel.
cardenillo *nm* verdigris.
cárdeno *adj* purple, violet; livid; *water* opalescent.
cardíaco 1 *adj* cardiac, heart (*attr*). 2 *nm*, **cardíaca** *nf* heart case, sufferer from a heart complaint.
cardinal *adj* (*all senses*) cardinal.
cardiología *nf* cardiology.
cardiológico *adj* cardiological.
cardiólogo *nm* cardiologist.
cardo *nm* thistle.
cardume(n) *nm* (a) (*Fish*) shoal. (b) (*Chi, Per, RPl*) great number, mass; **un** — **de gente** a lot of people, a crowd of people.
carear [1a] 1 *vt persons* to bring face to face; *texts* to compare, collate, check against each other.
  2 *vi*: — **a** to face towards, look on to.
  3 **carearse** *vr* (a) to come face to face, come together, meet.
  (b) — **con** to face, face up to.
carecer [2d] *vi* (a) — **de** to lack, be in need of, be without, want for; **carece de talento** he lacks talent, he has no talent; **no carecemos de dinero** we don't lack money, we're not short of money; **eso carece de sentido** that doesn't make sense; **aquí se carece de todo** here there is a great need of everything.
  (b) (*Urug*) **carece hacerlo** it is necessary to do it; **carece no dejarla** we must not allow her to.
carecimiento *nm* lack, need.
carena *nf* (a) careening; **dar** — **a** to career. (b) (*fam*) ragging; **dar** — **a uno** to rag someone, tease some-one.
carenar [1a] *vt* to careen.
carencia *nf* lack (*de of*), shortage (*de of*), need (*de for*); scarcity; (*Med etc*) deficiency.
carencial *adj*: **mal** — deficiency disease.
carente *adj*: — **de** lacking (in), devoid of.
carentón *adj* (*Arg*) large-faced.
careo *nm* confrontation, meeting (face to face); comparison, collation.
carero *adj* expensive, dear, pricey (*fam*).
carestía *nf* scarcity, shortage, dearth; famine; (*Comm*) high price(s), high cost; — **de la vida** high cost of living; **época de** — period of shortage, lean period, bad time.

careta *nf* mask; (*Min etc*) breathing apparatus, respirator; — **antigás** gasmask; — **de esgrima** fencing mask; **quitar la** — **a uno** to unmask someone.
carey *nm* tortoiseshell; (*Zool*) turtle.
carga *nf* (a) load; cargo, freight; burden, weight; **la** — **fiscal** the tax burden; **a** —**s** in plenty, in abundance, galore; **en plena** — under full load; **bestia de** — beast of burden; **buque de** — freighter; **tomar** — to load up, (*Naut*) take on cargo.
  (b) (*Elec*) charge; load; — **máxima** peak load; **hilo con** — live wire.
  (c) (*Mech*) load; — **fija**, — **muerta** dead load; — **de fractura**, — **de rotura** breaking load; — **de pago**, — **útil** payload.
  (d) (*Mil; also of shell, furnace, etc*) charge; — **explosiva** explosive charge; — **de pólvora** (*Min*) blasting powder; — **de profundidad** depth charge.
  (e) (*Fin*) tax, charge, duty.
  (f) duty, obligation, charge; onus, responsibility; — **de familia** dependent relative; — **personal** personal commitments; **echar la** — **a uno** to put the blame on someone, put the onus on someone; **echarse con la** — (*fam*) to throw up the sponge; **llevar la** — (*fam*) to carry the can (*sl*).
  (g) (*Mil*) charge, attack; (*Sport*) charge, tackle; — **a la bayoneta** bayonet charge; — **de caballería** cavalry charge; **tocar a** — to sound the charge; **volver a la** — (*fig*) to return to the charge, return to the attack.
  (h) (*act*) loading; (*Elec, Mil*) loading; charging; **andén de** — loading platform; **"permitido** — **y descarga"** (*sign*) "loading and unloading".
cargada *nf* (a) (*Arg*) unpleasant practical joke.
  (b) (*Mex*) = **carga** (h).
  (c) (*Mex*) **ir a la** — to bet on the most heavily-backed card; (*fig*) to jump on the bandwagon.
cargaderas *nfpl* (*Col*) braces, suspenders (*US*).
cargadero *nm* (a) loading point; (*Rail*) goods platform, loading bay. (b) (*Archit*) lintel.
cargado *adj and ptp* (a) loaded, with a load, under load; *dice* loaded; (*esp fig*) laden, burdened, weighed down (*de with*); **estar** — (**de vino**) to be drunk; **estar** — **de años** to be very old, be weighed down with age; **estar cargada** (*fam*) to be in the family way; **ser** — **de espaldas** to be round-shouldered, have a stoop; **un árbol** — **de fruto** a tree laden with fruit.
  (b) (*Elec*) live, charged, hot.
  (c) (*Mil*) — (**con bala**) live.
  (d) *coffee, tea* strong.
  (e) *sky* overcast; *atmosphere* heavy, sultry, close.
cargador *nm* (a) (*person*) loader; (*Naut*) docker, stevedore; (*of furnace*) stoker.
  (b) (*Tech: of gun*) chamber; (*of pen*) filler; (*Mil: Hist*) ramrod; — **de acumuladores**, — **de baterías** battery charger.
  (c) —**es** (*Col*) braces, suspenders (*US*).
cargadora *nf* (*Col, Ven*) nursemaid.
cargamento *nm* (a) (*act*) loading. (b) load; (*Naut*) cargo; shipment; — **de retorno** return cargo.
cargante *adj* boring, tiresome, annoying; *task* irksome, tedious; *child* trying.
cargar [1h] 1 *vt* (a) to load (*de with; a, en on*); to overload, burden, weigh down (*de with*); *dice* to load; *imagination, mind etc* to fill (*de with*); — **a uno de deudas** to encumber someone with debts; — **a uno de nuevas obligaciones** to burden someone with new duties.
  (b) (*Elec*) to charge.
  (c) *furnace* to stoke, charge.
  (d) to increase the weight of, cause to bear down more heavily; *see* **mano**.
  (e) *tax* to impose, lay (*sobre on*); to increase.
  (f) (*Comm, Fin*) to charge, debit (*en cuenta a* to, to the account of); — **de menos a uno** to under-charge someone.
  (g) to impute, ascribe (*a* to); *blame* to lay (*a* on); *responsibility* to entrust (*a* to), place (*a* on).
  (h) (*Law*) to charge, accuse; — **a uno de poco escrupuloso** to accuse someone of being unscrupu-lous, charge someone with being unscrupulous.
  (i) (*Mil*) to charge, attack.
  (j) (*Mil*) *gun* to load.
  (k) (*Naut*) *sail* to take in.
  (l) (*Univ: sl*) to plough (*sl*), fail.
  (m) (*SAm*) to carry, have, use; — **anteojos** to wear glasses; — **revólver** to pack a gun (*sl*); **carga siempre mucho dinero** he always carries a lot of money, he always has a lot of money on him.
  (n) (*Chi, Per: of dog etc*) to attack, go for.

(o) (*fam*) to bore; to annoy, vex; **esto me carga** this annoys me, I find this annoying.

2 *vi* **(a)** to load, load up; to take on a load; (*Naut*) to take on (a) cargo; — (**demasiado, mucho**) to overeat, drink too much.

(b) — **con** *object, weight* to pick up, carry away, take away; *burden* (*fig*) to shoulder, take upon oneself; *responsibility* to assume, take on; *blame* to bear.

(c) (*Ling: of accent*) to fall (**en, sobre** on).

(d) to lean, tip, incline.

(e) — **en,** — **sobre** to lean on, lean against; (*Archit etc*) to rest on, be supported by.

(f) — **sobre uno** to urge someone, press someone; to importune someone.

(g) to pester, be annoying.

(h) (*Meteorol*) to turn, veer (**a** to, **hacia** towards).

(i) (*of people*) to crowd together.

3 cargarse *vr* **(a)** — **algo** to take something on oneself; — **de algo** to be full of something, be loaded with something; to fill oneself up with something, (*fig*) get one's fill of something; — **de hijos** to overburden oneself with children; — **de años** to get very old; **el árbol se carga de manzanas** the tree produces apples in abundance.

(b) = *vi* **(d)** and **(e)**.

(c) (*Elec*) to become charged, become live.

(d) (*Meteorol: of sky*) to become overcast; (*of atmosphere*) to become heavy, become oppressive.

(e) (*fam*) to get cross; to get bored.

(f) —**la** (*fam*) to get into hot water.

(g) — **a uno** (*fam*) to bump someone off (*sl*), do someone in (*sl*); **¡algún día me lo cargaré!** I'll get him one day!

cargazón *nf* **(a)** load; (*Naut*) cargo, shipment; (*fig*) dead weight, useless mass.

(b) (*Med*) heaviness (*of stomach etc*).

(c) (*Meteorol*) mass of heavy cloud.

(d) — **de espaldas** stoop.

(e) (*Arg, Chi*) abundance of fruit (*on tree*).

cargo *nm* **(a)** load, weight, burden.

(b) (*fig*) burden; — **de conciencia** burden on one's conscience; remorse, guilty feeling.

(c) (*Comm*) charge, debit; **una cantidad en** — **a uno** a sum to be charged to someone; **ser en** — **a uno** to be indebted to someone; **girar a** — **de, librar a** — **de** to draw on.

(d) post, office; (*Theat and fig*) role, part; — **estelar** star role; **un** — **casi sin responsabilidades** a post almost without duties; **desempeñar un** — to fill an office; **vestir el** — to look the part, dress the part.

(e) duty, obligation, responsibility; charge, care; **a** — **de** in the charge of; **tener algo a su** — to have something in one's charge, be in charge of something; **hacerse** — **de** to take charge of; to see about; to realize, understand; **el ejército se hizo** — **del poder** the army took over power; **apenas si pude hacerme** — **de ello** I could scarcely grasp what was going on; **parecía no hacerse** — **de la dificultad** he seemed not to understand the difficulty.

(f) (*Law*) charge, reproach, accusation; **hacer a uno** — **de algo** to charge somebody with something.

cargosear [1a] *vt* (*Chi, Per, RPl*) to pester, keep on at, annoy.

cargoso *adj* (*Chi, RPl*) troublesome, annoying; burdensome.

carguera *nf* (*Col, Ven*) nursemaid.

carguero *nm* **(a)** (*Naut*) freighter, cargo boat; (*Aer*) freight plane, transport plane; — **militar** air-force transport plane.

(b) (*Arg, Col, Per*) beast of burden.

carguío *nm* load; cargo, freight.

cariacontecido *adj* crestfallen, down in the mouth, woebegone.

cariado *adj tooth* bad, rotten, decayed, carious.

cariadura *nf* (*Med*) caries, decay.

cariancho *adj* broad-faced.

cariar [1b] **1** *vt* to cause to decay, cause decay in. **2 cariarse** *vr* to decay, become decayed.

cariátide *nf* caryatid.

caribe 1 *adj* **(a)** (*Geog etc*) Caribbean; **Mar C—** Caribbean Sea.

(b) (*SAm*) cannibalistic; (*fig*) savage, cruel; (*Ant*) furious, bad-tempered; **ponerse** — to get furious.

(c) (*Ant*) *flavour* hot, strong.

2 *nmf* Carib, inhabitant of the Caribbean area.

3 *nm* (*SAm*) cannibal; (*Ant: fig*) savage, brute.

caribú *nm* caribou.

caricato *nm* (*Mex*) = **caricatura**.

caricatura *nf* caricature (*also fig*); cartoon.

caricaturista *nmf* caricaturist; cartoonist.

caricaturesco *adj* absurd, ridiculous.

caricaturizar [1f] *vt* to caricature.

caricia *nf* **(a)** caress; pat, stroke; **hacer** —**s** to caress, fondle, stroke.

(b) (*fig*) endearment.

caricioso *adj* caressing, affectionate.

caridad *nf* charity; charitableness; **la** — **empieza en uno mismo** charity begins at home; **hacer** — **a uno** to give alms to someone.

caries *nf, pl* **caries** **(a)** (*Med*) dental decay, caries.

(b) (*Agr*) blight.

carigordo *adj* fat-faced.

carilampiño *adj* clean-shaven; smooth-faced, beardless.

carilargo *adj* long-faced.

carilla *nf* **(a)** mask. **(b)** (*Typ*) page.

carillero *adj* round-faced, full-faced.

carillón *nm* carillon.

carimbo *nm* (*SAm: Hist*) branding iron (*also Bol: Agr*).

cariño *nm* **(a)** affection, love (**a, por** for); fondness, liking (**a, por** for); tenderness; **sentir** — **por, tener** — **a** to like, be fond of; **por el** — **que te tengo** because I'm fond of you; **tomar** — **a** to take a liking to, get fond of.

(b) (*SAm*) caress, stroke; gift, token (of affection).

(c) —**s** endearments; show of affection.

cariñosamente *adv* affectionately, lovingly, fondly; tenderly.

cariñoso *adj* affectionate, loving, fond; tender.

carioca *adj* (*SAm*) of Rio de Janeiro.

cariparejo *adj* poker-faced.

carirraído *adj* brazen, shameless.

carirredondo *adj* round-faced.

carisellazo *nm* (*Col*) toss of a coin; **echar un** — to toss up.

carisma *nm* charisma.

carita *nf* little face; **de** — (*Col*) first-class; jolly good (*fam*); **dar** (*or* **hacer**) — (*Mex: of a woman*) to smile back, accept a man's advances; **hacer** —**s** (*Col*) to make faces.

caritativamente *adv* charitably.

caritativo *adj* charitable (**con, para** to).

cariz *nm* look, aspect; outlook; (*Meteorol*) look of the sky; **mal** — scowl; **poner mal** — to scowl; **esto va tomando mal** — this business is beginning to look bad, I don't like the look of this.

carlanca *nf* **(a)** (*Col, CR*) shackle, fetter.

(b) (*Chi, Hond*) tedious person; boredom; annoyance, vexation.

(c) —**s** tricks, cunning; **tener muchas** —**s** to be full of tricks.

carlinga *nf* (*Aer*) cockpit, cabin.

carlismo *nm* Carlism.

carlista 1 *adj* Carlist. **2** *nmf* Carlist.

Carlitos *m* (*pet name for* **Carlos**) Charlie.

Carlomagno *m* Charlemagne.

Carlos *m* Charles.

Carlota *f* Charlotte.

carlota *nf* (*Cook*) charlotte.

carmelita[1] (*Eccl*) **1** *adj* Carmelite. **2** *nmf* Carmelite; — **descalzo** discalced Carmelite.

carmelita[2] *adj*, **carmelito** *adj* (*esp SAm*) light brown, tan.

carmelitano *adj* Carmelite.

carmen[1] *nm* (*Granada*) country house, villa.

carmen[2] *nm* (*Lit*) song, poem.

Carmen *nm* (*Eccl*) Carmelite Order.

carmenar [1a] *vt* **(a)** (*Tech*) *wool* to card, teasel; *silk etc* to unravel; *hair* to disentangle; — **el pelo a uno** (*fam*) to pull someone's hair.

(b) (*fam*) to fleece, swindle.

carmesí 1 *adj* crimson. **2** *nm* crimson.

carmín *nm* **(a)** carmine; rouge. **(b)** (*Bot*) dog rose.

carminativo 1 *adj* carminative. **2** *nm* carminative.

carmíneo *adj* carmine, crimson.

carnada *nf* bait, lure. bait.

carnal *adj* **(a)** carnal, of the flesh. **(b)** (*of relation*) full, blood; **hermano** — full brother; **primo** — first cousin; **tío** — real uncle.

carnalidad *nf* lust, carnality.

carnaval *nm* carnival (*also fig*); (*Eccl*) Shrovetide; **martes de** — Shrove Tuesday.

carne *nf* **(a)** (*Anat*) flesh; — **de gallina** (*fig*) gooseflesh; **me pone la** — **de gallina** it gives me gooseflesh, (*fig*) it gives me the creeps; **de** — **y hueso** of flesh and blood; **de abundantes** —**s, de muchas** —**s** fat; **de pocas** —**s** thin; **en** — **viva on the raw**; **en** —**s naked**, with nothing on; **se me abrieron las** —**s** I was terrified; **cobrar** (*or* **criar, echar**) —**s** to put on weight; **perder** —**s** to lose weight.

(b) (*Cook*) meat; **— adobada** salt meat; **— asada** roast meat; **— de cañón** cannon fodder; **— de carnero** mutton; **— de cerdo** pork; **— concentrada** meat extract; **— congelada** frozen meat, chilled meat; **— de cordero** lamb, mutton; **— fiambre** cold meat; **— de horca** good-for-nothing, gallows bird; **— magra**, **— mollar** lean meat; **— de oveja**, **— ovina** mutton, lamb; **— picada** mince, minced meat; **— porcina** pork; **— de res** (*SAm*) beef; **— de ternera** veal; **— de vaca** beef; **— de venado** venison; **no ser ni — ni pescado** to be neither one thing nor the other, be nondescript; **poner toda la — en el asador** to go the whole hog, stake one's all.

(c) (*Bot*) flesh, fleshy part, pulp; (*SAm*) heart, hardest part (*of timber*); **— de membrillo** quince jelly.

(d) (*Eccl etc*) flesh, carnality.

carné *nm* (*Acad*) = **carnet**.

carneada *nf* (*Arg*) slaughter(ing).

carnear [1a] *vt* **(a)** (*Chi, RPl*) *animal* to slaughter (and dress); (*fig*) to murder, butcher.
(b) (*Chi*) to deceive, take in (*fam*).

carnerada *nf* flock of sheep.

carnerear [1a] *vi* (*RPl*) to blackleg, be a strike-breaker.

carnerero *nm* shepherd.

carnero *nm* (*Zool*) sheep, ram; **— marino** seal; **— de la tierra** (*SAm*) llama, alpaca; **— de simiente** breeding ram; **no hay tales —s** there's no such thing; it's nothing of the sort; **cantar para el —** (*Arg*) to kick the bucket (*sl*).
(b) (*Cook*) mutton.
(c) sheepskin.
(d) (*Chi, RPl*) weak-willed person; blackleg, strikebreaker.
(e) (*Chi*) **botarse** (*or* **echarse**) **al —** to chuck it all up, do nothing.

carnestolendas *nfpl* Shrovetide.

carnet [kar'ne] *nm*, *pl* **carnets** [kar'ne] (*gall*) notebook; bank book; (*tourist's*) travel voucher; **— de conducir**, **— de conductor**, **— de chófer** driving licence; **— de identidad** identity card; **— de socio** membership card.

carnicería *nf* **(a)** butcher's (shop); meat market; slaughterhouse.
(b) (*fig*) slaughter, carnage; **— en las carreteras** slaughter on the roads; **hacer una — de** to massacre, slaughter.

carnicero 1 *adj* **(a)** (*Zool*) carnivorous, flesh-eating; (*Orn*) of prey; *person* (*fam*) fond of meat.
(b) (*fig*) savage, cruel, bloodthirsty.
2 *nm* **(a)** butcher (*also fig*).
(b) (*Zool*) carnivore.

cárnico *adj* meat (*attr*); **industria cárnica** meat industry.

carnívoro 1 *adj* carnivorous, flesh-eating. **2** *nm* carnivore.

carnosidad *nf* **(a)** fleshiness; corpulence, obesity. **(b)** (*Med*) proud flesh.

carnoso *adj* beefy, fat.

carnudo *adj* fleshy.

caro 1 *adj* **(a)** dear, beloved; **las cosas que nos son tan caras** the things which are so dear to us.
(b) (*Comm*) dear, expensive; **un coche carísimo** a terribly expensive car.
2 *adv* dear, dearly; **le costó muy —** it cost him dear; **eso sale bastante —** that comes rather expensive; **vender —** to sell at a high price.

carocas *nfpl* wheedling, cajolery; **hacer —s** to put it on, give oneself airs.

caroleno *nm* (*Mex*) back slang.

Carolina[1] *f* Caroline.

Carolina[2] *f* (*Geog*): **— del Norte** North Carolina; **— del Sur** South Carolina.

carolingio *adj* Carolingian.

carón *adj* (*SAm*) broad-faced.

carona *nf* **(a)** saddle padding; *part of horse's back where the saddle rests*. **(b)** (*Arg*) bed.

caroso *adj* (*Per*) blond, fair; faded.

carótida *nf* carotid (artery).

carozo *nm* **(a)** cob of maize, corncob (*US*). **(b)** (*SAm*) stone, core (*of fruit*).

carpa[1] *nf* (*Fish*) carp; **— dorada** goldfish.

carpa[2] *nf* (*SAm*) tent; awning; market stall, open-air shop.

carpanta *nf* (*fam*) ravenous hunger.

Cárpatos: Montes *mpl* **—** Carpathians.

carpeta *nf* **(a)** folder, file; portfolio; briefcase; **cerrar la —** to close the file (*in an investigation*).
(b) table cover (*also* **— de mesa**).
(c) (*Ant, Arg, Per*) table, desk.

carpetazo *nm*: **dar —** a to shelve, put on one side, do nothing about.

carpetero *nm* filing cabinet.

carpetovetónico *adj* terribly Spanish, Spanish to the core.

carpidor *nm*, *also* **carpidora** *nf* (*SAm*) weeding hoe.

carpintear [1a] *vi* **(a)** to carpenter; to do woodwork (*as a hobby*).
(b) (*Col, RPl*) to insist; to make disagreeable noises.

carpintería *nf* **(a)** carpentry, joinery, woodwork.
(b) carpenter's shop.

carpintero *nm* **(a)** (*Tech*) carpenter; woodworker; **— de blanco** joiner; **— de carretas**, **— de prieto** cartwright, wheelwright; **— de buque**, **— de ribera** ship's carpenter, shipwright.
(b) (*Orn*) woodpecker.
(c) (*SAm*) annoying person.

carpir [3a] *vt* (*SAm*) to weed, hoe.

carraca *nf* **(a)** (*Naut: Hist*) carrack; (*pej*) tub, old hulk.
(b) (*Mus, Sport*) rattle.
(c) (*Tech*) ratchet brace.
(d) (*PR, Ven: Aut*) old crock.

carraco 1 *adj* feeble, decrepit. **2** *nm* (*Aut etc*) old crock.

carrada *nf* (*RPl*) = **carretada**.

carral *nm* barrel, vat.

carralero *nm* cooper.

carrasca *nf* kermes oak.

carraspear [1a] *vi* to be hoarse, have a frog in one's throat; to clear one's throat, hawk.

carraspera *nf* hoarseness, frog in the throat.

carrasposo *adj* **(a)** hoarse, having a sore throat. **(b)** (*SAm*) rough, harsh.

carrera *nf* **(a)** (*act*) run; running; chase, rush; **a — (abierta)**, **a — tendida** at full speed, all out; **a la —** at full speed; hastily; **de —** hastily; rashly, without thinking; easily; **partir de —** to proceed rashly; **dar — libre a** to give free rein to; **no poder hacer — con uno** to make no headway with someone, be unable to get someone to see reason; **— de aterrizaje** (*Aer*) landing run; **— del oro** goldrush.
(b) (*Sport: Baseball etc*) run.
(c) (*Sport: contest*) race; **—s** races, racing; **de —(s)** racing (*attr*), race (*attr*); **caballo de —(s)** racehorse; **coche de —s** racing car; **— de armamentos** arms race; **— de caballos** horse race; **— por carretera** road race; **— contra el reloj** (*fig*) race against the clock; **— corta** dash, short run, sprint; **— de fondo** long-distance race; **— lisa** flat race; **— hacia la luna** race for the moon, race to get to the moon; **— de Maratón** marathon; **— de obstáculos** obstacle race; **— pedestre** walking race; **— de relevos** relay race; **— de resistencia** endurance race, long-distance race; **— de sacos** sackrace; **— de vallas** hurdle race, hurdles, (*horses*) steeplechase; **abrir —** to set the pace, be the pacemaker.
(d) row, line; (*Archit: of bricks etc*) course; track; avenue, boulevard; (*in hair*) parting; (*in stocking*) run, ladder; (*Astron*) course; **la — del sol** the course of the sun.
(e) (*Archit*) beam, girder, joist.
(f) (*Mus*) run.
(g) (*Naut*) run, route.
(h) (*Mech: of piston*) stroke; (*of valve*) lift; **— ascendente** upstroke; **— descendente** downstroke.
(i) (*fig*) career; profession; **diplomático de —** career diplomat; **dar — a uno** to give someone his education, pay for someone's professional studies; to put someone to a career; **hacer —** to get on in one's career; to get on in the world, make headway; **no tiene —** he has no profession, he doesn't do anything serious in life.
(j) (*Univ*) course, studies; **cuando termine la —** when he finishes his course, when he qualifies.
(k) course of human life.

carrerista 1 *adj* fond of racing; (*pej*) horsy. **2** *nmf* racing man, racing woman, racegoer; (*professional*) punter. **3** *nf* (*fam*) streetwalker.

carrero *nm* carter, cart driver.

carreta *nf* **(a)** (long narrow) wagon, low cart; **— de mano** = **carretilla**; **— de bueyes** oxcart.
(b) (*Col*) wheel.
(c) **hacer la —** to purr.

carretada *nf* cart load; (*fig*) cart load, great quality; **a —s** in loads, galore.

carretaje *nm* cartage, haulage.

carrete *nm* reel, spool; (*Sew*) reel, bobbin; (*Elec*) coil, (*Phot*) spool; (*Fish*) reel; (*of cycle*) hub; **— de encendido** (*Aut*) ignition coil; **— de inducción** (*Elec*) induction coil.

carretear [1a] **1** vt (a) load to cart, haul. (b) cart to drive; (Aer) to taxi. **2** vi (Aer) to taxi.

carretel nm reel, spool, bobbin.

carretela nf (Hist) coach, carriage; calash; (CAm, Mex) cart.

carretera nf (main) road, highway; **de** — road (attr); **por** — by road; — **de acceso** approach road; — **de circunvalación** bypass, ring road; — **nacional** motorway, major route; — **de primer orden** first-class road.

carretero 1 adj vehicle (attr), for vehicles. **2** nm carter; cartwright, wheelwright; **jurar como un** — to swear like a trooper.

carretilla nf (a) truck, trolley; (also — **de mano**) handcart, barrow; (Agr, Hort) wheelbarrow; (child's) go-cart; (shopper's) trolley; — **eléctrica** electric truck; — **de horquilla** fork-lift truck.
 (b) squib, cracker.
 (c) (Chi, RPl) jaw, jawbone.
 (d) (Col) lot, series.
 (e) **aprender algo de** — to learn something mechanically; **saber algo de** — to know something by heart.

carretón nm small cart; wagon, dray; — **de remolque** trailer.

carricoche nm covered wagon, (gipsy) caravan; (fam) crock.

carricuba nf water cart.

carriel nm (CAm, Ec, Ven) briefcase, attaché case.

carril nm (a) rut, track; cart track, lane; (of motorway) lane; (Agr) furrow; **entrar en (el)** — (fig) to get on the right track.
 (b) (Rail) rail; (Chi, PR) train; — **de toma** third rail.

carrilano nm (Chi) (a) robber, holdup man. (b) (Rail) railwayman.

carrilera nf (a) rut, track. (b) (Cu: Rail) siding.

carrilero nm (Per) railwayman.

carrillera nf (a) (Zool) jaw. (b) chinstrap.

carrillo nm (a) cheek; jowl; **comer a dos** —s to eat greedily, stuff oneself, (fig) to have the best of both worlds.
 (b) (Tech) pulley.

carrindanga nf (RPl) old car, broken-down cart (etc).

carriola nf truckle bed.

carrito nm tea trolley, serving-trolley.

carrizal nm reedbed.

carrizo nm (a) reed. (b) —s (Ec, Mex) thin legs; **hacer** — (Col) to cross one's legs.

carro nm (a) cart, wagon; (Hist: also — **de guerra**) chariot; (SAm) (any) vehicle, (esp) car, automobile; (Mil) tank; (SAm: Rail) car, truck, coach; — **alegórico** float (in a procession); — **aljibe** water cart; — **blindado** armoured car; — **de combate** tank; — **correo** (SAm: Rail) mail van; — **cuba** tank truck; — **fuerte** heavy trolley; — **fúnebre** hearse; — **de mudanzas** removal van; — **de riego** water cart; — **tranvía**, — **urbano** (SAm) tramcar, streetcar (US); **aguantar** —s **y carretas** to put up with anything, remain undismayed; **arrimarse al** — **del que manda** to climb on the bandwagon; **enganchar el** — **a los bueyes** to put the cart before the horse; **¡pare Vd el** —! hold your horses!; **tirar del** — (fig) to do all the donkey work; **untar el** — **a uno** to grease someone's palm.
 (b) (quantity) cartload.
 (c) (of typewriter) carriage.

carrocería nf (a) coachbuilder's; carriage repair shop. (b) (Aut etc) bodywork, coachwork.

carrocero nm coachbuilder, carriage builder.

carrocha nf (Ent) eggs.

carromato nm covered wagon, (gipsy) caravan.

carroña nf carrion.

carroño adj (a) rotten, putrid, foul. (b) (Col) cowardly.

carroza nf (a) (state) coach, carriage; (in procession) float; — **fúnebre** hearse. (b) (Naut) awning.

carruaje nm carriage; vehicle.

carrusel nm (gall) merry-go-round, roundabout.

carta nf (a) (Post etc) letter; — **abierta** open letter; — **adjunta** covering letter; — **aérea** air letter; — **de ajuste** (TV) test card; — **de amor**, — **amorosa** love letter; — **certificada** registered letter; —'**de crédito** letter of credit; — **de emplazamiento** (Law) summons; — **particular**, — **privada** private letter, personal letter; — **pastoral** pastoral letter; — **de pedido** (Comm) order; — **de pésame** letter of condolence; — **de porte** bill of lading; — **postal** (SAm) postcard; — **de recomendación** letter of introduction (para to); — **de solicitud** application;

— **urgente** special-delivery letter; **echar una** — **al correo** to post a letter.
 (b) (Law) document, deed; (Hist: of town etc) charter; — **blanca** carte blanche; **dar** — **blanca a uno** to give someone carte blanche; **tener** — **blanca** to have a free hand; — **de ciudadanía**, — **de naturaleza** naturalization papers; **adquirir** — **de naturaleza** (fig) to come to seem native, be thoroughly accepted; — **ejecutoria**, — **de hidalguía** (Hist) letters patent (of nobility); **C**— **Magna** (Brit) Magna Carta; — **de pago** receipt, discharge in full; — **partida por abc** indenture; — **de privilegio** charter; — **de venta** bill of sale; **a** — **cabal** thoroughly, in every respect; loyally; **¡**— **canta!** there it is in black and white!
 (c) (Geog) map (also — **geográfica**); — **de marear**, — **marítima** chart; — **meteorológica** weather map.
 (d) (Cards) card, playing card; — **de figura** court card, picture card; **a** —s **vistas** openly, honestly; with inside information; **echar las** —s to tell someone's fortune (with cards); **enseñar las** —s (fig) to show one's hand; **poner las** —s **boca arriba**, **poner las** —s **sobre la mesa** to put one's cards on the table; **no saber a qué** — **quedarse** not to know what to think, be undecided; **tener** —s **en un asunto** to intervene in a matter, come in on an affair.
 (e) (Cook) menu; — **de vinos** wine list; **a la** — à la carte.

cartabón nm (carpenter's) square, bevel; (draughtsman's) triangle; (Mil, surveyor's) quadrant.

cartagenero 1 adj of Cartagena. **2** nm, **cartagenera** nf native (or inhabitant) of Cartagena; **los** —s the people of Cartagena.

cartaginés 1 adj Carthaginian. **2** nm, **cartaginesa** nf Carthaginian.

Cartago f Carthage.

cartapacio nm notebook; folder, briefcase; (School) satchel.

carta-tarjeta nf, pl **cartas-tarjeta** letter-card.

cartear [1a] **1** vi (Cards) to play low. **2 cartearse** vr to correspond (con with); **se cartearon durante 2 años** they wrote to each other for 2 years.

cartel nm (a) poster, placard; (Theat etc) bill; (School) wall chart; — **de escaparate** window card; **torero de** — star bullfighter; **tener** — (fam) to be a hit, be all the rage; "**se prohibe fijar** —**es**" "post no bills".
 (b) (Comm, Fin: angl) cartel, trust.

cartela nf (a) slip of paper, bit of card. (b) (Archit) console; corbel; tablet.

cartelera nf hoarding, billboard; notice board; (in newspaper) list of plays, theatre section; **mantenerse en la** —, **seguir en la** — to run, be on; **se mantuvo en la** — **durante 3 años** it ran for 3 years.

cartelero nm billsticker, billposter.

cartelón nm large notice; sign; banner.

carteo nm correspondence, exchange of letters.

cárter nm (Mech) housing, case; — **del cigüeñal** crankcase.

cartera nf (a) wallet, pocketbook; letterfile, portfolio, briefcase; (Sew) pocket flap; (SAm) handbag, purse (US); (on motorcycle) pannier bag; — **de bolsillo** wallet; — **de herramientas** toolbag; — **de mano** briefcase.
 (b) (Pol) portfolio, ministerial post; **ministro sin** — minister without portfolio.
 (c) (Fin) portfolio, holdings; **efectos en** — holdings, stocks.

carterero nm (Chi) pickpocket; bagsnatcher.

carterista nm pickpocket.

carterita nf: — **de fósforos** folder of matches.

cartero nm postman, mailman (US).

cartesiano 1 adj Cartesian. **2** nm Cartesian.

cartilaginoso adj cartilaginous.

cartílago nm cartilage.

cartilla nf (a) (School) primer, first reader; spelling book; **cantar (or leer) la** — **a uno** to give someone a severe ticking off; **no saber la** — not to know a single thing.
 (b) — **de ahorros** savings bank book, deposit book; — **de identidad** identity card; — **de racionamiento** ration book.
 (c) (Eccl) certificate of ordination; liturgical calendar.

cartografía nf cartography, mapmaking.

cartógrafo nm cartographer, mapmaker.

cartomancia nf fortunetelling (with cards).

cartón nm (a) (material) cardboard, pasteboard; (of book) board; — **alquitranado** tar paper; — **de**

encuadernar millboard; **— ondulado** corrugated cardboard; **— piedra** papier mâché.
(b) (*Art*) cartoon.
(c) (*container*) (cardboard) box, carton.
(d) (*SAm: Typ: angl*) cartoon; comic strip, strip cartoon.
cartoné *nm* (*Typ*): **en —** (bound) in boards.
cartuchera *nf* cartridge belt.
cartucho *nm* (a) (*Mil*) cartridge; cartridge case; **— sin bala, — en blanco** blank cartridge; **luchar hasta quemar el último —** to fight on to the last ditch.
(b) paper cone, paper cornet; (*of coins*) roll; (*SAm*) cornucopia.
Cartuja *nf* (*Eccl*) Carthusian order.
cartuja *nf* Carthusian monastery.
cartujano 1 *adj* Carthusian. **2** *nm* Carthusian.
cartujo *nm* Carthusian.
cartulario *nm* cartulary.
cartulina *nf* fine cardboard, pasteboard.
carura *nf* (*CAm, Ec, RPl*) (a) high price, expensiveness. (b) expensive thing.
casa *nf* (a) house; flat, apartment; building; **— de alquiler** block of flats, apartment block; **— de asistencia** (*Col, Mex*) boarding house; **— de azotea** penthouse; **— de baños** bathhouse; **—s baratas** low-cost housing; **— de bebidas** bar, saloon; **— de bombas** pumphouse; **— de campo** country house; **— de citas, — pública, — de putas** (*fam*), **— de tolerancia, — de vicio** brothel; **— consistorial** town hall; civic centre; **— de corrección** reformatory, remand home; **— de correos** post office; **— de departamentos** (*SAm*) apartment house (US); **— embrujada, — de fantasmas** haunted house; **— de fieras** zoo, menagerie; **— de guarda** lodge; **— de huéspedes** boarding house; **— de juego** gambling house; **— de labor, — de labranza** farm, farmhouse; **— de locos, — de orates** asylum; **— de maternidad** maternity hospital; **— de muñecas** doll's house; **— de pisos** block of flats; **— religiosa** monastery; convent; **— de salud** sanatorium, private hospital; **— de socorro** first-aid post; **— de vecindad** block of tenements, apartment house (US).
(b) (*with personal connotations*) home; residence, house; household; **— y comida** board and lodging; **¿dónde tiene Vd su —?** where is your home?; **— mortuoria** house of mourning, home of the deceased; **— paterna** parents' home; **— solariega** family seat, ancestral home; **es una — alegre** it's a happy home, it's a happy household; **ir a —** to go home; **ir hacia —** to head for home, go homewards; **ir a — de Juan** to go to John's house, go to John's place, go to John's; **salir de —** to leave home; **ir de — en —** to go from house to house; **estar en —** to be at home, be in; **¿está la señora en —?** is the lady in?, is the lady at home?; **están en — de los abuelos** they're at their grandparents'; **estar fuera de —** to be out, be away from home; **voy para —** I'm off home; **estar por la —** to be about the house; **de —** home (*attr*), household (*attr*); sport, clothing indoor; animal pet, family (*attr*); **estar de —** to be in one's ordinary clothes.
(c) (*home: phrases with verb*) **abandonar la —** to leave home, move out; **echar la — por la ventana** to go to enormous expense; to roll out the red carpet for someone; **franquear la — a uno** to open one's house to someone; **hacer —** to get rich; **llevar la —** to keep house, run the house; (*fam*) to wear the trousers; **cada uno manda en su —** one's home is one's castle; **poner —** to set up house; **sentirse como en su —** to feel at home; **no tener — ni hogar** to be homeless.
(d) (*courtesy formulae*) **Vd está en su —, aquí tiene Vd su —** you're always very welcome.
(e) (*Comm, Fin*) firm, business house (*also* **— de comercio**); **— armadora** shipbuilding company; **— de banca, — bancaria** banking house; **— central** head office; **— editorial** publishing house; **— de empeños** pawnshop; **— matriz** head office; parent company; **— de (la) moneda** mint.
(f) house, line, family; **— real** royal house; **la — de Borbón** the house of Bourbon.
(g) (*in games*) square.
casabe *nm* (*SAm*) cassava.
Casa *nf* **Blanca** White House.
casaca *nf* (a) dress coat; **— de montar** riding coat; **cambiar de —, volver la —** to turn one's coat, be a turncoat.
(b) (*fam*) wedding, marriage.
casación *nf* cessation, annulment.
casacón *nm* greatcoat.

casa-cuna *nf, pl* **casas-cuna** day nursery, crèche.
casada *nf* married woman.
casadero *adj* marriageable, of an age to be married.
casado 1 *adj* married; **mal —** unhappily married; **— y arrepentido** if you marry in haste you repent at leisure; **estar —** to be married (*con* to); **estar — a media carta** to live in sin.
2 *nm* (a) married man; **los —s** married men; married people; **los recién —s** the newlyweds.
(b) (*Typ*) imposition.
(c) (*SAm*) two separate varieties of food eaten together.
casal *nm* (a) country house; farmhouse; ancestral home. (b) (*RPl*) married couple; (*Zool*) pair.
casamata *nf* casemate.
casamentero *nm*, **casamentera** *nf* matchmaker.
casamiento *nm* marriage, wedding (ceremony); **— por amor** love match; **— de conveniencia** marriage of convenience; **— a la fuerza** forced marriage, shotgun marriage; **prometer a una joven en —** to betroth a girl (*con* to).
Casandra *f* Cassandra.
casapuerta *nf* entrance hall, vestibule.
casar[1] *nm* hamlet.
casar[2] [1a] **1** *vt* (a) (*subject: priest*) to marry, join in marriage, join in wedlock.
(b) (*subject: father*) to marry (off), give in marriage (*con* to).
(c) (*fig*) to pair, couple; to match; (*Typ*) to impose.
(d) (*Law*) to quash, annul.
2 *vi* (a) = *vr*.
(b) (*fig*) to match, harmonize.
3 casarse *vr* (a) to marry, get married; **A se casó con B** A married B; **¿cuándo te vas a casar?** when are you getting married?; **volver a —, — en segundas nupcias** to marry again (*and see* **nupcias**).
(b) (*fig*) to match, harmonize.
casatienda *nf* shop with dwelling accommodation, shop with flat over.
casca *nf* (a) bark (for tanning). (b) grape skins.
cascabel *nm* (little) bell; **de — gordo** pretentious; **ser un —** (*fam*) to be a scatterbrain; **echar (or soltar) el —** to drop a hint; **poner el — al gato** to bell the cat.
cascabela *nf* (*CAm*) rattlesnake.
cascabelear [1a] **1** *vt* to take in (*fam*), raise the hopes of, beguile.
2 *vi* (a) (*SAm*) to jingle, tinkle.
(b) (*fig*) to act recklessly, behave frivolously, be inconsiderate.
(c) (*Chi*) to growl, grumble.
cascabeleo *nm* jingle, jingling, tinkling.
cascabelero 1 *adj* (*fam*) scatterbrained. **2** *nm*, **cascabelera** *nf* (*fam*) scatterbrain.
cascabillo *nm* (a) little bell. (b) (*Bot: of grain*) husk, chaff; (*of acorn*) cup.
cascada *nf* waterfall; cascade.
cascado *adj* (a) broken (down); person infirm, decrepit, worn out. (b) voice weak, unmelodious, cracked; piano etc tinny.
cascajo *nm* (a) (piece of) gravel; (*Archit etc*) rubble; (*of pots etc*) fragments, sherds.
(b) junk, rubbish, lumber; **estar hecho un —** (*fam*) to be a wreck.
cascajoso *adj* gritty, gravelly.
cascanueces *nm, pl* **cascanueces** nutcracker; **un —** a pair of nutcrackers.
cascar [1g] **1** *vt* (a) to crack, split, break (open); to crunch; nut to crack.
(b) (*fig*) health to shatter, undermine.
(c) (*fam*) to bash (*fam*), slosh (*fam*); (*Sport*) to beat hollow, wipe the floor with (*fam*).
2 *vi* (a) to chatter, talk too much.
(b) (*sl*) to kick the bucket (*sl*).
3 cascarse *vr* (a) to crack, split, break (open).
(b) (*of health*) to crack up; (*of voice*) to break, crack.
cáscara *nf* (a) (*of egg, nut, ruined building*) shell; (*of grain*) husk; (*of fruit*) rind, peel, skin; (*of tree*) bark; **— de huevo** eggshell; **— de limón** lemon peel; **— sagrada** (*Pharm*) cascara; **patatas cocidas con —** potatoes in their jackets; **ser de la — amarga** to be wild, be mischievous, (*Pol*) have radical ideas; **dar —s de novillo a** (*SAm*) to thrash.
(b) **¡—s!** (*euph*) well I'm blowed!
(c) **—s** (*Col, Per: sl*) clothes.
cascarazo *nm* (a) (*Col, PR*) punch; (*Col*) lash. (b) (*PR*) swig of liquor (*fam*).
cascarear [1a] *vt* (*CAm, Col*) to bash (*fam*), slosh (*fam*).

cascarilla 1 *adj* (*Arg, Cu, PR*) touchy, peppery. **2** *nf* (a) (*Arg, Cu, PR*) quick-tempered person. (b) (*Per, RPl*) medicinal herb; dried cacao leaves (*used as tea*).

cascarón *nm* (broken) eggshell; (*Mex, PR*) eggshell filled with confetti.

cascarrabias *nmf, pl* **cascarrabias** (*fam*) quick-tempered person, irritable sort.

cascarria *nf* (*Arg*) filth, grease; (*Agr*) sheep droppings.

cascarriento *adj* (*Arg*) filthy, greasy.

cascarrón *adj* (*fam*) gruff, abrupt, rough.

cascarudo 1 *adj* thick-shelled, thickskinned. **2** *nm* (*Arg*) beetles (*collectively*).

casco *nm* (a) (*Mil etc*) helmet; (*part of hat*) crown; **— de acero** steel helmet; **— de corcho** sun helmet; **— protector** crash helmet; **— sideral** space helmet. (b) (*Anat*) skull; (*fam*) brains, head, nut (*sl*); **alegre de —s, ligero de —s** scatterbrained, frivolous; **romper los —s a uno** to bash someone's head in (*fam*); **romperse los —s** to rack one's brains; **sentar los —s** to quieten down, settle down, learn to behave oneself; **tener los —s a la jineta** to be scatterbrained. (c) (*of pot*) fragment, sherd; (*Mex*) returnable soft drink bottle. (d) (*of onion*) skin, coat. (e) cask, barrel. (f) (*Naut*) hull; (*pej*) old hulk. (g) (*Zool*) hoof. (h) (*Mech*) casing. (i) (*of city*) inner part, central area; (*Mex: Agr*) compound, main buildings and surrounding land; (*Arg: of estate*) part, section. (j) (*Per*) chest, breast. (k) (*Arg, Cu, Mex: of fruit*) quarter, segment.

cascote *nm* (piece of) rubble, (piece of) debris.

cascundear [1a] *vt* (*CAm*) to beat, thrash.

cáseo 1 *adj* cheesy. **2** *nm* curd.

caseoso *adj* cheesy.

casera *nf* landlady (*owner*); housekeeper; *see also* **casero 2.**

casería *nf* (a) country house. (b) (*SAm*) customers, clientèle.

caserío *nm* (a) country house. (b) hamlet, settlement, group of dwellings.

casero 1 *adj* (a) domestic, household (*attr*); bread etc home-made; *cloth* homespun; *remedy* household; *dress* house (*attr*), indoor, ordinary; *gathering*, *party* family (*attr*). (b) *person* home-loving. **2** *nm* (a) landlord (*owner*); caretaker; porter, concierge, janitor (*US*); tenant, occupier; (*Comm*) house agent. (b) (*also* **casera** *nf*) stay-at-home, home-lover. (c) (*SAm: also* **casera** *nf*) customer, client; (*Cu, Chi, Ec, Per*) hawker, huckster.

caserón *nm* large (ramshackle) house, barracks (of a place).

caseta *nf* (*in market*) stall, stand, booth; (*at exhibition*) stand; (*at fair*) sideshow, booth; (*Sport*) pavilion; (*at swimming pool*) cubicle, changing room; (*on beach*) bathing hut; (*in country*) cottage; **— de perro** kennel, doghouse (*US*); **— del timón** (*Naut*) wheelhouse.

casi *adv* almost, nearly; **— —** very nearly, as near as makes no difference; **está — terminado** it's almost finished, it's well-nigh finished; **— nada** next to nothing; **— nunca** almost never, hardly ever; **300 o —** some 300, 300 or thereabouts.

casilla *nf* (a) (*Archit*) hut, cabin, shed; keeper's lodge; (*in market etc*) booth, stall; (*Rail*) platelayer's hut, guard's hut. (b) (*Aut, Rail: of engine*) cab. (c) (*Theat*) box office. (d) pigeonhole; (*of box etc*) compartment; (*of paper*) ruled column, section; (*Chess etc*) square; (*Bol, Chi, Per, Urug*) post office box (number). (e) (*Ec*) lavatory. (f) (*Cu*) bird trap. (g) **sacar a uno de sus —s** to shake someone up, shake someone out of his complacency; to make someone cross, get someone worked up; **salir de sus —s** to fly off the handle (*fam*).

casillero *nm* (set of) pigeonholes.

casimba *nf* (*SAm*) = **cacimba.**

casimir *nm* cashmere.

casimiro *adj* (*SAm*) cross-eyed.

casinista *nm* clubman.

casino *nm* club; social club, political club; casino.

Casio *m* Cassius.

casita *nf* small house; cottage.

caso *nm* (a) (*Gram*) case. (b) (*Med*) case; **es un — perdido** (*hum*) he's a dead loss, he's a disaster. (c) (*in experiment etc*) case, subject; **soy un — difícil** I'm a difficult subject. (d) case, instance; event, happening; circumstances; **— de autos** (*Law*) case in hand; **— fortuito** (*Law*) act of God; unforeseen circumstance; **el — Hess** the Hess affair, the Hess case; **el — Romeo-Julieta** the Romeo and Juliet affair; the trouble between Romeo and Juliet; **en el — de Eslobodia** in the case of Slobodia; **en — de** in the event of; **— que venga, en (el) — de que venga** in case he should come, should he come, in the event of his coming; **y en el — contrario** and if not, and if it should not be so; **en el mejor de los —s** at best; **en tal —** in such a case; **en todo —** in any case, at all events; **en último —** as a last resort, in the last resort; **y en su — también otros** and where appropriate, others also; **según el —** as the case may be; **según lo requiera el —** as the case may require; **dado el — que ...** supposing (that) ...; **el — es que ...** the fact is that ...; **creerse en el — de + infin** to think fit to + *infin*; **hablar al —** to speak to the point; **hacer al —, venir al —** to be relevant; **no hacer al —, no venir al —** to be beside the point; **pongamos por — que ...** let us suppose that ...; **pongamos por — a X** let us take X as an example; **servir para el —** to serve one's purpose; **¡vamos al —!** let's get to the point!; let's get down to business!; **verse en el — de + infin** to be compelled to + *infin*. (e) notice; **hacer — a** to heed, notice; **no me hacen —** they don't pay me any attention; **¡no haga Vd —!** take no notice!, don't worry!; **maldito el — que me hace** a fat lot of notice he takes of me; **hacer — de** to pay attention to; to take into account; **sin hacer — de eso** regardless of that; **hacer — omiso de** to ignore, fail to mention, deliberately pass over.

casorio *nm* (*fam*) hasty marriage, unwise marriage.

caspa *nf* dandruff, scurf.

Caspio: Mar m — Caspian Sea.

caspiroleta *nf* (*Col, Cu, Chi, Ec, Per*) eggnog.

cáspita *interj* my goodness!; come off it!

casquete *nm* skullcap; (*Mil*) helmet; (*Mech*) cap; **— de hielo** icecap; **— polar** polar cap.

casquijo *nm* gravel.

casquillo *nm* (a) tip, cap; (*of stick*) ferrule, tip; (*Mech*) sleeve, bushing; (*Mil*) cartridge case. (b) (*SAm*) horseshoe.

casquinona *nf* (*Col*) beer bottle; beer.

casquivano *adj* scatterbrained.

casta *nf* (a) caste; breed, race; (*fig*) class; quality; **de —** of quality, of breeding; **carecer de —** to lack breeding, have no class; **eso le viene de —** that comes naturally to him. (b) (*Mex: Typ*) fount.

castamente *adv* chastely, purely.

castaña *nf* (a) chestnut; **— del Brasil, — de Pará** Brazil nut; **— de Indias** horse chestnut; **dar (or meter) la — a uno** to swindle someone, make a fool out of someone; **pelar la —** (*of lovers*) to do their courting; to chat, talk sweet nothings; **sacar a uno las —s del fuego** to pull someone's chestnuts out of the fire for him. (b) (*of hair*) bun, chignon.

castañar *nm* chestnut grove.

castañazo *nm* (*RPl*) bash (*fam*), punch.

castañero *nm*, **castañera** *nf* chestnut seller.

castañeta *nf* (a) snap (of the fingers). (b) **—s** (*Mus*) castanets.

castañetazo *nm* snap, crack, click.

castañetear [1a] **1** *vt* (a) *fingers* to snap. (b) (*Mus*) to play on the castanets. **2** *vi* (a) (*of fingers*) to snap; to click; (*of plates etc*) to clatter; (*of teeth*) to chatter, rattle; (*of bones*) to crack; (*of knees*) to knock together; **— con los dedos** to snap one's fingers. (b) (*Mus*) to play the castanets.

castañeteo *nm* (a) snap(ping); click(ing); clatter(ing); chatter(ing); rattling; crack(ing); knocking. (b) (*Mus*) sound of the castanets.

castaño 1 *adj* chestnut(-coloured), brown. **2** *nm* chestnut tree; **— de Indias** horse chestnut tree; **esto pasa de — oscuro** this is really too much, this is beyond a joke.

castañuelas *nfpl* castanets; **estar como unas —s** to be very merry, be in high spirits.

castañuelo *adj* chestnut(-coloured), brown.

castellanizar [1f] *vt* to hispanicize, give a Spanish form to.

castellano 1 *adj* Castilian; Spanish. **2** *nm*, **castellana** *nf* Castilian; Spaniard. **3** *nm* (*language*) Castilian, Spanish.

castellonense 1 *adj* of Castellón de la Plana. **2** *nmf* native (*or* inhabitant) of Castellón de la Plana; **los —s** the people of Castellón de la Plana.

castellonés *adj, n* = **castellonense**.

casticidad *nf* (**a**) (*Ling*) purity, correctness. (**b**) (*Bio*) purity of breed(ing); racial purity. (**c**) traditional character; authenticity, genuineness.

casticismo *nm* (**a**) (*Ling*) purity, correctness. (**b**) traditionalism; = **casticidad** (**c**).

casticista 1 *adj* purist. **2** *nmf* purist.

castidad *nf* chastity, purity.

castigador *nm* (**a**) punisher. (**b**) ladykiller; (*pej*) seducer, libertine.

castigar [1h] *vt* (**a**) to punish (*de*, *por* for); (*Sport*) to penalize (*por* for).
(**b**) (*fig*) to castigate; *flesh* to mortify; (*of disease etc*) to afflict, affect; (*emotionally*) to afflict, grieve; (*physically*) to strain, use hard; **— mucho a un caballo** to ride a horse hard.
(**c**) (*fig*) *style etc* to refine; *text* to correct, revise.
(**d**) (*Comm*) to write down.
(**e**) (*Mex: Mech*) to tighten up.

castigo *nm* (**a**) punishment; (*Sport etc*) penalty; fine. (**b**) (*fig*) castigation; mortification, affliction. (**c**) (*fig*) refinement; correction, revision.

Castilla *nf* Castile; **— la Nueva** New Castile; **— la Vieja** Old Castile; **¡ancha es —!** it takes all sorts!

castilla *nf* (*Arg, Par, Mex*) (**a**) (*language*) Castilian, Spanish; **hablar la —** to speak Spanish. (**b**) (*Hist*) **de —** from Castile, from Spain, from the home country.

castillejo *nm* (**a**) (*Archit*) scaffolding. (**b**) (*child's*) go-cart; playpen.

castillo *nm* castle; (*of elephant*) howdah; **—s en el aire** castles in the air; **— de fuego** firework set piece; **— de naipes** house of cards; **— de proa** forecastle.

castizo *adj* (**a**) (*Ling*) pure, correct. (**b**) (*Bio*) purebred, pedigree; racially pure; pure-blooded; untainted. (**c**) (*fig*) traditional; pure, authentic; genuine; **es un tipo —** (*fam*) he's one of the best.

casto *adj* chaste, pure.

castor *nm* beaver.

castoreño *nm* beaver (*hat*); (*Taur*) picador's hat.

castoreo *nm* (*Pharm*) castor.

castra *nf* (*Bot*) pruning; pruning season.

castración *nf* (**a**) castration, gelding. (**b**) (*Bot*) pruning. (**c**) extraction of honeycombs.

castrado 1 *adj* castrated. **2** *nm* eunuch.

castrar [1a] *vt* (**a**) to castrate, geld; *cat etc* to doctor (*euph*).
(**b**) (*Bot*) to prune, cut back.
(**c**) *hives* to extract honeycombs from.
(**d**) (*fig*) to mutilate, impair, weaken.

castrense *adj* army (*attr*), military; **las glorias —s** military glories.

casual *adj* (**a**) fortuitous, accidental, chance. (**b**) incidental. (**c**) (*Gram*) case (*attr*); **desinencia —** case ending.

casualidad *nf* (**a**) chance, accident; coincidence; **fue una pura —** it was sheer coincidence, it was entirely a matter of chance; **por —** by chance; **¿tienes por — una pluma?** do you have a pen, by any chance?, do you happen to have a pen? **me encontraba allí por —** I happened to be there, I chanced to be there; **un día entró por —** one day he dropped in; **da la — que . . .** it (so) happens that . . .; **dio la — que . . .** it happened that . . ., luck had it that . . .; **¡qué —!** what a coincidence!; **¡qué — verle aquí!** what a coincidence meeting you here!, fancy meeting you here!
(**b**) **—es** (*CAm: angl*) casualties.

casualmente *adv* by chance, by accident, fortuitously; **— le vi ayer** I happened to see him yesterday, as it happens I saw him yesterday.

casuario *nm* cassowary.

casuca *nf*, **casucha** *nf* hovel, shack; slum.

casuista *nmf* casuist.

casuística *nf* casuistry.

casulla *nf* chasuble.

cata[1] *nf* (**a**) (*in general*) tasting, testing, sampling; blending.
(**b**) taste, sample.
(**c**) (*SAm*) trial excavation, test bore; prospecting.
(**d**) **ir en — de algo** (*fam*) to go looking for something.

cata[2] *nf* (*Bol, Chi, Mex, RPl*) parrot.

catabre *nm* (*Col, Ven*) gourd; basket.

catacaldos *nm, pl* **catacaldos** (**a**) rolling stone; quitter, person who starts things but gives up easily; (*Art etc*) dilettante.
(**b**) busybody, meddler.

cataclismo *nm* cataclysm.

catacumbas *nfpl* catacombs.

catador *nm* (*of tea, wine etc*) taster, blender, sampler; (*fig*) connoisseur.

catadura[1] *nf* tasting, sampling, blending.

catadura[2] *nf* (*fam*) mug (*sl*), looks, face.

catafalco *nm* catafalque.

catajarria *nf* (*Ven*) string, line, series.

catalán 1 *adj* Catalan, Catalonian. **2** *nm*, **catalana** *nf* Catalan, Catalonian. **3** *nm* (*language*) Catalan.

catalanismo *nm* (**a**) (*Pol*) movement for Catalan autonomy. (**b**) (*Ling*) catalanism, word (*or* phrase *etc*) borrowed from Catalan.

catalanista 1 *adj* that supports (*etc*) Catalan autonomy; **el movimiento —** the movement for Catalan autonomy; **la familia es muy —** the family strongly supports Catalan autonomy.
2 *nmf* supporter (*etc*) of Catalan autonomy, Catalan nationalist, Catalan separatist.

catalejo *nm* spyglass, telescope.

catalepsia *nf* catalepsy.

cataléptico 1 *adj* cataleptic. **2** *nm*, **cataléptica** *nf* cataleptic.

Catalina *f* Catherine.

catalinaria *nf* cabal, conspiracy.

catalizador *nm* catalyst.

catalogación *nf* cataloguing.

catalogar [1h] *vt* to catalogue.

catálogo *nm* catalogue.

Cataluña *f* Catalonia.

catamarán *nm* catamaran.

cataplasma *nf* (**a**) (*Med*) poultice. (**b**) (*fam*) bore.

cataplum *interj* bang!, crash!

catapulta *nf* catapult.

catapún *adj* **una cosa del año —** an antiquated thing, a totally obsolete thing.

catar [1a] *vt* (**a**) to taste, sample, try; (*fig*) to examine, inspect, have a look at; (*fig*) to esteem.
(**b**) to look at; to look out for; **¡cata!, ¡cátale!** just look at him!; **¡cátate eso!** you just think!
(**c**) *hives* to extract honeycombs from.

catarata *nf* (**a**) (*Geog*) waterfall, falls; cataract; **C—s de Niágara** Niagara Falls; **C—s de Victoria** Victoria Falls.
(**b**) (*Med*) cataract.

catarral *adj* catarrhal.

catarriento *adj* (*SAm*) = **catarroso**.

catarro *nm* cold; catarrh; **— crónico del pecho** chest trouble; **coger un —** to catch a cold.

catarroso *adj* subject to colds; having catarrh, suffering from catarrh.

catarsis *nf* catharsis.

catártico *adj* cathartic.

catasalsas *nm, pl* **catasalsas** = **catacaldos**.

catástrofe *nf* catastrophe.

catastrófico *adj* catastrophic.

catatán *nm* (*Chi*) punishment.

catauro *nm* (*Cu*) basket.

catavinos *nm, pl* **catavinos** wine taster, wine sampler; (*fam*) boozer.

cate *nm* (*sl*) punch, bash (*fam*); **dar — a uno** (*Univ*) to plough someone (*sl*).

catear [1a] *vt* (**a**) to investigate; to try, sample.
(**b**) (*Univ: sl*) to plough (*sl*).
(**c**) (*Arg, Chi, Mex: Min*) *land* to make test borings in, explore, prospect.
(**d**) (*Mex: of police*) to search, make a search in.

catecismo *nm* catechism.

catecúmeno *nm*, **catecúmena** *nf* catechumen; (*fig*) convent.

cátedra 1 *nf* (**a**) (*Univ*) chair, professorship; lectureship; (*School*) senior teaching post (*in a grammar school*); **— del Espíritu Santo** (*Eccl*) pulpit; **explicar una —** to hold a chair (*de* of); **hacer oposiciones para una —, opositar a una —** to try to win a chair (*etc*) by public competitive examination; **sentar — sobre un argumento** to take one's stand on an argument.
(**b**) (*Univ, School*) subject.
(**c**) lecture room.
(**d**) group of students, class.
(**e**) (*Cu, Ven*) wonder, marvel; **es —, está la —** it's marvellous.
2 *adj* (*Cu, Ven*) wonderful, marvellous, excellent.

catedral *nf* cathedral.

catedrática nf (a) (Univ) woman professor, woman lecturer; professor's wife. (b) — **de instituto** grammar-school teacher.

catedrático nm (a) (Univ) professor, lecturer. (b) — **de instituto** grammar-school teacher.

categoría nf category; class, group; rank, standing; quality; prestige; **de** — important; distinguished, high-ranking, prominent; **es hombre de cierta** — he is a man of some standing; **de baja** — of low quality; of low rank; **de segunda** — (pej) second-rate; **no tiene** — he has no standing; **tiene** — **de ministro** he has the rank of minister.

categóricamente adv categorically.

categórico adj categorical; lie downright, outright; order strict, express.

catenaria nf (Rail, Elec) overhead power cable.

catequizar [1f] vt (a) (Eccl) to catechize, instruct in Christian doctrine. (b) (fam) to win over, talk round.

caterva nf host, throng, crowd; **venir en** — to come in a throng, come thronging.

catéter nm catheter.

catimbao nm (a) (Chi, Per) clown, carnival clown. (b) (Per) short fat man.

catinga nf (a) (Bol, RPl) body odour; (of animals etc) strong smell. (b) (Chi: in sailors' parlance) soldier.

catingoso adj (Arg, Bol), **catingudo** adj (Bol, RPl) smelly, having a nasty smell.

catire adj (SAm), **catiro** adj (SAm) blond, fair; reddish, red-haired.

catita nf (SAm) parrot.

catitear [1a] vi (Arg) to dodder, shake with old age.

catisumba(da) nf (CAm) lot, great number; **una** — **de** a lot of.

catoche nm (Mex) bad mood, bad temper.

catódico adj cathodic, cathode (attr).

cátodo nm cathode.

catolicismo nm (Roman) Catholicism.

católico 1 adj (a) (Eccl) (Roman) Catholic; **no** — non-Catholic.
(b) (fig) doctrine true, infallible; certain; (fam) right, as it should be; **no estar muy** — not to be quite right, be none too good, have something up (with it); (Med) to be under the weather.
2 nm, **católica** nf Catholic; **no** — non-Catholic.

Catón m Cato.

catorce adj fourteen.

catorceno adj fourteenth.

catorro nm (Mex) punch, blow.

catre nm (a) cot; (Chi, Per) bedstead; — **de tijera**, — **de viento** (Mex, Per, Ven) campbed, folding bed. (b) (Arg) — **de balsa** raft.

catrecillo nm campstool, folding seat.

catrera nf (Arg) bunk, bed.

catrín nm (CAm, Mex) toff (fam), dude (US).

Catulo m Catullus.

caucasiano (Geog), **caucásico** (by race) 1 adj Caucasian. 2 nm, **caucasiana** nf, **caucásica** nf Caucasian.

Cáucaso m Caucasus.

cauce nm riverbed; (Agr) irrigation channel.

caución nf (a) caution, wariness. (b) (Law) pledge, security, bond; bail; **admitir a uno a** — to grant someone bail.

caucionar [1a] vt (a) to prevent, guard against. (b) (Law) to bail, go bail for.

cauch nm (CAm, PR: angl) couch.

cauchal nm rubber plantation.

cauchar 1 nm (Col, Ec) rubber plantation. 2 vi (Col, Ec) to extract rubber from trees.

cauchera nf (a) rubber plant, rubber tree. (b) (Col, Ec, Per) rubber plantation.

cauchero 1 adj rubber (attr); **industria cauchera** rubber industry. 2 nm (SAm) worker in a rubber plantation, rubber worker.

caucho[1] nm (a) rubber; — **esponjoso** foam rubber; — **natural** natural rubber; — **sintético** synthetic rubber.
(b) raincoat, mac; (Col) waterproof blanket; (Col) rubber shoe; (Ven) tyre.

caucho[2] nm (PR: angl) couch.

caudal[1] nm (a) (of river) volume, flow.
(b) plenty, abundance, wealth; (of person etc) fortune, wealth; property; — **social** assets of a partnership.

caudal[2] adj caudal.

caudaloso adj (a) river large, carrying much water. (b) copious, abundant; person etc wealthy, rich.

caudillaje nm (a) leadership; **bajo el** — **de** under the leadership of. (b) (SAm: pej) tyranny, rule by political bosses.

caudillo nm (a) leader, chief; head of state; **el C—** (Spain) the Leader, the Head of State. (b) (SAm: pej) tyrant, political boss.

caula nf (CAm, Chi) plot, intrigue, cabal.

cauri nm cowrie.

causa[1] nf (a) cause; reason, motive; (for complaint) grounds; **veamos qué** — **tiene esto** let us see what is the reason for this; — **final** final cause; — **primera** first cause; **a** — **de**, **por** — **de** on account of, because of, owing to; **por mí** — for my sake; **por poca** —, **sin** — for no good reason.
(b) (Pol etc) cause; **hacer** — **común con** to make common cause with.
(c) (Law) lawsuit; case, trial; prosecution; **instruir** — to take legal proceedings.

causa[2] nf (a) (Chi) snack, bite between meals; light meal, picnic lunch. (b) (Per) potato salad.

causal 1 adj causal. 2 nf reason, grounds.

causalidad nf causality; causation.

causante 1 adj causing, originating; **el coche** — **del accidente** the car which caused the accident, the car responsible for the accident.
2 nmf (a) causer, originator.
(b) (Mex) taxpayer.
3 nf (SAm) cause.

causar [1a] vt to cause; expense, work to create, entail, make; impression to create, make; anger, protest to provoke; — **risa a uno** to make someone laugh.

causear [1a] vi (Chi) to have a snack, have a bite between meals; to have a light meal, have a picnic lunch.

causeo nm (Chi) = **causa**[2].

causativo adj causative.

cáustico adj caustic (also fig).

cautamente adv cautiously, warily, carefully.

cautela nf (a) caution, cautiousness, wariness; **con mucha** — very cautiously; **tener la** — **de** + infin to take the precaution of + ger. (b) (pej) cunning.

cautelar [1a] 1 vt to prevent, guard against. 2 **cautelarse** vr to be on one's guard (de against).

cautelosamente adv (a) cautiously, warily, carefully. (b) (pej) cunningly, craftily.

cauteloso adj (a) cautious, wary, careful. (b) (pej) cunning, crafty.

cauterio nm (a) cautery, cauterization. (b) (fig) eradication.

cauterizar [1f] vt (a) to cauterize. (b) (fig) to eradicate.

cautivar [1a] vt (a) (Mil etc) to capture, take prisoner. (b) (fig) to charm, captivate, win over; to enthrall; heart to steal, captivate.

cautiverio nm, **cautividad** nf captivity; (fig) bondage, serfdom.

cautivo 1 adj captive. 2 nm, **cautiva** nf captive.

cauto adj cautious, wary, careful.

cava nf cultivation, digging and hoeing.

cavador nm digger; excavator; — **de oro** gold digger.

cavadura nf digging, excavation.

cavar [1a] 1 vt hole to dig; well to sink; (Agr) to dig over, hoe, fork over.
2 vi (a) to dig; (of wound) to go deep.
(b) (fig) to delve (en into), go deeply (en into); to meditate profoundly (en on).

cavazón nf digging, excavation.

caverna nf cave, cavern.

cavernícola 1 adj (a) cave-dwelling, cave (attr); **hombre** — caveman.
(b) (Pol: fam) reactionary.
2 nmf (a) cave dweller.
(b) (Pol: fam) reactionary, backwoodsman.

cavernoso adj (a) cavernous; cave (attr); mountain full of caves, honeycombed with caves. (b) sound, voice hollow.

caviar nm caviar(e).

cavidad nf cavity; hollow, space; — **nasal** nasal cavity.

cavilación nf (a) deep thought, rumination. (b) (unfounded) suspicion, apprehension.

cavilar [1a] vt to ponder, consider closely; to brood over, be obsessed with.

cavilosear [1a] vi (PR) to harbour illusions; (PR) to cavil; (CAm) to gossip.

cavilosidad nf (unfounded) suspicion, apprehension.

caviloso adj (a) brooding, obsessed; suspicious, mistrustful.
(b) (CAm) gossipy, backbiting.
(c) (Col) quarrelsome, touchy, belligerent.

cayado nm staff, stick; (Agr) crook; (Eccl) crozier.

cayo nm (Ant) islet, reef, key; **C— Hueso** Key West.

cayubro adj (Col) reddish-blond, red-haired.

cayuca nf (Cu, PR) head, bean (sl).

cayuco *nm* (*Cu, PR, Ven*) dugout canoe.

caz *nm* millrace.

caza 1 *nf* (a) (*in general*) hunting; shooting, sport; (*una* —) hunt; shoot; chase, pursuit; — **furtiva** poaching, illegal hunting; — **de grillos** fool's errand, wild-goose chase; — **del hombre** manhunt; — **con hurón** ferreting; — **del jabalí** boar hunt(ing); — **con papelillos** paper chase; — **de patos** duck shoot(ing); — **submarina** underwater fishing; — **del tesoro** treasure hunt; — **del zorro** foxhunt(ing); **andar a** (**la**) — **de** to go hunting for; **dar** — to give chase, go in pursuit; **dar** — **a** to hunt, chase, go after; to hunt down; **dar** — **a un empleo** to hunt for a job; **ir a la** —, **ir de** — to go hunting, go (out) shooting.

(b) game; — **mayor** big game; — **menor** small game; **levantar la** — to put up the game, (*fig*) start the ball rolling.

2 *nm* (*Aer*) fighter, fighter-plane; — **de escolta** escort fighter; — **nocturno** night-fighter.

cazabe *nm* (*Ant*) = **casabe**.

caza-bombardero *nm* fighter-bomber.

cazaclavos *nm, pl* **cazaclavos** claw-hammer, nail-puller.

cazadero *nm* hunting ground.

cazador *nm* (a) hunter; huntsman; — **de alforja**, — **de pieles** trapper; — **de cabezas** headhunter; — **furtivo** poacher; — **de zorros** foxhunter, huntsman.

(b) (*Mil*) chasseur.

cazadora *nf* (a) huntress. (b) hunting jacket; — **de piel** leather jacket.

cazagenios *nm, pl* **cazagenios** talent scout, talent spotter.

cazamoscas *nm, pl* **cazamoscas** (*Orn*) flycatcher.

cazar [1f] *vt* (a) to hunt; to chase, pursue; to go after; (*esp fig*) to hunt down, track down, run to earth; **le cacé por fin en la tienda** I eventually ran him down in the shop.

(b) to catch; *total, game etc* to bag; *job etc* to land, get; (*pej*) to get hold of by trickery, wangle (*fam*); *person* to win over (by flattery); (*pej*) to take in (*fam*); **—las al vuelo** to be pretty sharp.

(c) to catch out.

cazasubmarinos *nm, pl* **cazasubmarinos** submarine chaser.

cazatalentos *nm, pl* **cazatalentos** talent scout, talent spotter.

cazcalear [1a] *vi* (*fam*) to fuss around, buzz about.

cazcarrias *nfpl* splashes of mud on one's clothes.

cazcarriento *adj* splashed with mud, mud-stained.

cazo *nm* (a) saucepan; — **de cola** gluepot; — **eléctrico** electric kettle. (b) ladle, dipper.

cazolero *nm* = **cominero**.

cazoleta *nf* (a) (small) pan; (*of pipe*) bowl; (*of shield*) boss. (b) (*of sword*) guard. (c) (*Mech*) housing.

cazón *nm* dogfish.

cazonete *nm* (*Naut*) toggle.

cazuela *nf* (a) (*Cook*) pan, casserole; (*meal*) casserole; (*SAm*) chicken stew. (b) (*Theat*) gallery, gods.

cazumbrón *nm* cooper.

cazurro *adj* surly, sullen.

cazuz *nm* ivy.

ce[1] *interj* hey!

ce[2] *nf* name of the letter c; — **por** be down to the tiniest detail, leaving nothing whatsoever out; **por** — **o por be** somehow or other.

ceba *nf* (a) (*Agr*) fattening. (b) (*of gun*) charge, priming. (c) (*of furnace*) stoking.

cebada *nf* barley; — **perlada** pearl barley.

cebadal *nm* barley field.

cebadera *nf* (a) nosebag. (b) (*Tech*) hopper.

cebadero *nm* (a) barley dealer.

(b) leading mule (*of a team*).

(c) feeding place.

(d) (*Tech*) mouth for charging a furnace.

cebado *adj* (*SAm*) *animal* man-eating.

cebadura *nf* (a) (*Agr*) fattening.

(b) (*of gun*) priming; (*of furnace*) stoking.

(c) (*Arg*) brewing, making (*of maté*).

(d) (*Arg: of coffee, maté*) grounds, dregs.

cebar [1a] **1** *vt* (a) (*Agr*) to fatten (up), feed (up) (**con** on).

(b) *fire, furnace* to feed, stoke (up); *gun, lamp, pump* to prime; *firework* to light, set off.

(c) *hook, line, trap* to bait.

(d) *passions etc* to feed, nourish; *anger* to inflame; *hope* to stimulate.

(e) (*SAm*) *maté* to make, brew, prepare and serve.

2 *vi* (*of nut etc*) to grip, catch, go on; (*of nail*) to go in.

3 cebarse *vr* (a) (*CR, Mex: of shot, firework*) to fail to go off.

(b) — **en** to vent one's fury on; to batten on, prey upon; (*of plague etc*) to rage among; (*of fire*) to devour, rage in.

(c) — **un estudio** to devote oneself to a study, become absorbed in a study.

(d) — **en la sangre** to gloat over the blood(shed), revel in the blood(shed).

cebellina *nf* (*Zool*) sable.

cebiche *nm* (*Per*) fish marinaded with lime juice.

cebo *nm* (a) (*Agr*) feed, food.

(b) (*of gun*) charge, priming; (*Tech*) fuel, oven load.

(c) (*Fish*) bait; (*fig*) bait, lure, incentive; — **vivo** live bait.

cebolla *nf* (a) onion; (*of tulip etc*) bulb; — **escalonia** shallot. (b) (*SAm: hum*) watch.

cebollana *nf* chive.

cebollino *nm* young onion, spring onion, onion for transplanting; onion seed; chive.

cebollita 1 *nf*: — **perla** small onion, cocktail onion. **2** *nm* (*Arg*) young boy, lad.

cebollón *nm* (*Chi, RPl*) old bachelor.

cebollona *nf* (*Chi, RPl*) old maid.

cebón 1 *adj* fat, fattened. **2** *nm* fattened animal.

ceboruco *nm* (*Cu*) reef; (*Mex*) rough rocky place; (*PR*) brush, scrub(land).

cebra *nf* zebra.

cebú *nm* zebu.

ceca *nf*: **andar** (*or* **ir**) **de la** — **a la Meca** to go hither and thither, chase about all over the place.

cecear [1a] *vi* to lisp; *to pronounce* [s] *as* [θ].

ceceo *nm* lisp; *pronunciation of* [s] *as* [θ].

ceceoso *adj* lisping, having a lisp.

Cecilia *f* Cecily.

Cecilio *m* Cecil.

cecina *nf* dried meat, smoked meat; corned beef; **estar como una** — to be terribly thin.

cedazo *nm* sieve.

ceder [2a] **1** *vt* to hand over, give up; to yield (up); to part with; *territory* to cede; *property* to transfer, make over; (*Sport*) *ball* to pass; see **paso** *etc*.

2 *vi* (a) to give in, yield (*a* to); **no ceden fácilmente a las innovaciones** they do not give in (*or* give way) easily to innovations; **no cede a nadie en experiencia** he is inferior to none in experience; — **de una pretensión** to give up a claim, renounce a claim.

(b) to diminish, decline, go down; (*of fever, wind etc*) to abate.

(c) (*of floor, rope etc*) to give, give way, sag.

cedilla *nf* cedilla.

cedizo *adj* *meat* high, tainted.

cedro *nm* cedar.

cédula *nf* certificate, document; form, blank, (slip of) paper; (official) order, decree; (*Comm*) warrant; — **de aduana** customs permit; — **en blanco** blank cheque; — **de cambio** bill of exchange; — **personal**, — **de vecindad** identity card; — **real** royal letter patent; **dar** — **a uno** to license someone.

cefalea *nf* severe headache, migraine.

cefálico *adj* cephalic.

céfiro *nm* zephyr.

cegador *adj* blinding; **brillo** — blinding glare.

cegajoso *adj* weepy, bleary-eyed.

cegar [1h *and* 1k] **1** *vt* (a) *person* to blind, make blind.

(b) (*fig*) *passage, pipe* to block up, stop up; *hole* to fill up; *door, window* to wall up.

2 *vi* to go blind, become blind(ed).

3 cegarse *vr* (*fig*) to become blinded (**de** by).

cegato *adj* short-sighted.

cegatón *adj* (*SAm*) short-sighted.

cegatoso *adj* = **cegajoso**.

ceguedad *nf*, **ceguera** *nf* blindness (*also fig*); — **para los colores** colour blindness; — **nocturna** night blindness.

Ceilán *m* Ceylon.

ceilanés 1 *adj* Ceylonese. **2** *nm*, **celanesa** *nf* Ceylonese.

ceja *nf* (a) (*Anat*) eyebrow; **arquear las** —**s** to raise one's eyebrows; **fruncir las** —**s** to knit one's brows, frown; **meterse algo entre** — **y** — to get something firmly into one's head; **quemarse las** —**s** to burn the midnight oil; **tener a uno entre** — **y** — to look askance at someone; to have a grudge against someone; **tomar a uno entre** — **y** — to take a dislike to someone.

(b) (*fig: Tech*) rim, flange; (*Sew*) edging; (*Archit*) projection; (*of hill*) brow, crown; (*Meteorol*) cloudcap; (*Mus*) bridge; (*SAm*) edge of a wood; belt of trees, copse.

cejar [1a] *vi* to move back, go back; (*fig*) to give way, back down; (*in argument etc*) to climb down; (*in effort*) to relax, slacken, weaken; **no —** to keep it up, keep going, hold out; **sin —** unflinchingly, undaunted; **no — en sus esfuerzos** to keep up one's efforts; **no — en su trabajo** to keep on with one's work.

cejijunto *adj* with bushy eyebrows; having brows that meet; (*fig*) scowling, frowning.

cejudo *adj* black-browed, with bushy eyebrows.

celada *nf* (a) ambush, trap; (*fig*) trick, ruse; **caer en la —** to fall into the trap. (b) (*Mil: Hist*) helmet; (*Her*) helmet, sallet.

celador *nm* (*of building etc*) watchman, guard; (*of library, museum*) attendant; (*at exam*) invigilator; (*Tech*) maintenance man; (*Elec*) linesman; (*Aut*) parking attendant; (*CAm, Mex*) prison warder.

celadora *nf* (*of library, museum*) attendant.

celaje *nm* (a) sky with clouds of varied hue; (*Naut*) clouds; **—s** sunset clouds, sky with scudding clouds. (b) (*CAm*) cloud painting; cloud effect. (c) (*Archit*) skylight. (d) (*fig*) (promising) sign, token. (e) (*Per, PR, SD*) ghost; **como un —** like lightning, in a flash.

celar[1] [1a] **1** *vt* to watch over, keep a watchful eye on, keep a check on; **— las leyes** to see that the laws are kept; **— la justicia** to see that justice is done.
2 *vi*: **— por, — sobre** to watch over.

celar[2] [1a] *vt* to conceal, cover, hide.

celda *nf* cell; **— de aislamiento (para furiosos)** padded cell; **— de castigo** solitary confinement cell.

celdilla *nf* (*of beehive*) cell; cavity, hollow; pigeon-hole; (*Archit*) niche.

cele *adj* (*CAm*) light green.

celebérrimo *adj superl of* **célebre**.

celebración *nf* (a) celebration; holding; conclusion; solemnization. (b) praise; applause; welcome; preaching.

celebrante *nm* (*Eccl*) celebrant, officiating priest.

celebrar [1a] **1** *vt* (a) *anniversary, happy event etc* to celebrate; *meeting* to hold; *interview, talks* to have, hold (*con* with); *treaty* to conclude (*con* with); *feast, festivity* to keep, celebrate; *marriage* to perform, solemnize; *mass* to say.
(b) to praise; to applaud, welcome; *advantages* to preach, dwell on; *joke* to laugh at, find amusing; **— + *infin*** to be glad to + *infin*, be delighted to + *infin*; **lo celebro** I'm very glad; **lo celebro mucho por él** I'm very glad for his sake.
2 *vi* (a) (*Eccl*) to say mass.
(b) to be glad, be delighted.
(c) (*Cu*) to fall in love.
3 celebrarse *vr* (*of feast day etc*) to fall, occur, be celebrated; (*of meeting*) to be held, take place.

célebre *adj* (a) famous, celebrated, noted (*por* for); remarkable.
(b) *person* witty, facetious; *event* funny, amusing; **es — ¿no?** he's a scream, isn't he? **¡fue —!** it was killing!
(c) (*CAm, Col, Ven*) charming, pretty, lovely.

celebridad *nf* (a) (*in general*) celebrity, fame. (b) (*person*) celebrity. (c) celebration(s); festivity; pageant.

célere *adj* rapid, swift.

celeridad *nf* speed, swiftness; **con —** quickly, speedily, promptly.

celeste *adj* celestial, heavenly; (*Astron*) heavenly; (*colour*) sky blue.

celestial *adj* (a) celestial, heavenly. (b) (*fig*) heavenly, delightful. (c) (*fam*) silly.

celestina *nf* bawd, procuress; (*of brothel*) madame.

celibato *nm* (a) celibacy. (b) (*fam*) bachelor.

célibe **1** *adj* single, unmarried; celibate. **2** *nmf* unmarried person, bachelor, spinster; celibate.

célico *adj* heavenly, celestial.

celidonia *nf* celandine.

celo *nm* (a) zeal, fervour, ardour; conscientiousness; (*Rel*) religious fervour, piety; (*pej*) envy, mistrust.
(b) (*Zool*) rut, heat; **caer en —** to come into rut, come into season; **estar en —** to be on heat, be in rut, be in season; *see* **época**.
(c) **—s** jealousy; **dar —s** to give grounds for jealousy; **dar —s a uno, infundir —s a uno** to make someone jealous; **tener —s de uno** to be jealous of someone.

celofán *nm* cellophane.

celosamente *adv* (a) zealously; eagerly; fervently; (b) (*pej*) suspiciously, distrustfully. (c) jealously.

celosía *nf* (a) lattice (window); blind, shutter. (b) jealousy.

celoso *adj* (a) zealous (*de* for), keen (*de* about, on); eager; fervent.
(b) (*pej*) suspicious, distrustful.
(c) jealous (*de* of).
(d) (*Mech etc*) highly sensitive; *firearm* (*SAm*) delicate, liable to go off; *boat* (*Ec*) unsteady, easily upset.

celta **1** *adj* Celtic. **2** *nmf* Celt. **3** *nm* (*language*) Celtic.

Celtiberia *f* Celtiberia.

celtibérico, celtíbero **1** *adj* Celtiberian. **2** *nm,* **celtibérica** *nf,* **celtíbera** *nf* Celtiberian.

céltico *adj* Celtic.

célula *nf* cell; **— fotoeléctrica** photoelectric cell; **— germen** germ cell; **— nerviosa** nerve cell; **— sanguínea** blood cell.

celular *adj* cellular; cell (*attr*); *see* **coche** *etc*.

celuloide *nm* celluloid.

celulosa *nf* celulose.

cellisca *nf* sleet; sleet storm.

cellisquear [1a] *vi* to sleet.

cementación *nf* (*Tech*) case-hardening, cementation.

cementar [1a] *vt* (*Tech*) to case-harden, cement.

cementerio *nm* cemetery, graveyard; **— de coches** used-car dump.

cementista *nm* cement worker.

cemento *nm* (*Anat, Tech*) cement; concrete; **— armado, — reforzado** (*Col*) reinforced concrete.

cemita *nf* (*SAm*) white bread roll.

cena *nf* supper; evening meal; (*formal etc*) dinner; **la C—, la Última C—** the Last Supper; **C— de Baltasar** Belshazzar's Feast.

cenáculo *nm* group, coterie; literary group, cenacle.

cenador *nm* arbour; pavilion; summerhouse.

cenaduría *nf* (*Mex*) eating house, restaurant.

cenagal *nm* bog, quagmire, morass; (*fig*) nasty affair, sticky business.

cenagoso *adj* muddy, boggy.

cena-homenaje *nf,* *pl* **cenas-homenaje** formal dinner, celebratory dinner; **ofrecer una — a uno** to hold a dinner for someone.

cenancle *nm* (*Mex*) maize cob, corncob (US).

cenar [1a] **1** *vt* to have for supper (*etc*), sup on, sup off.
2 *vi* to have one's supper, have dinner, dine; **invitar a uno a —** to invite someone to dinner; **vengo cenado** I've had dinner (*etc*).

cenceño *adj* thin, skinny.

cencerrada *nf* tin-pan serenade (*given to a widow or widower who remarries*); rowdy music, noise, din.

cencerrear [1a] *vi* to jangle; (*of machine etc*) to rattle, clatter; (*of door, wagon etc*) to creak; (*Mus*) to play terribly, make a dreadful noise.

cencerreo *nm* jangle; rattle, clatter; creak; (*Mus*) dreadful noise.

cencerro *nm* cowbell; **a —s tapados** stealthily, on the sly; **llevar el —** to be the leader.

cendal *nm* gauze; fine silk stuff, sendal.

cenefa *nf* (*Sew*) edging, trimming, border; (*Archit*) border.

cenicero *nm* ashtray; ash pan; ash pit, ash tip.

Cenicienta: la — Cinderella.

ceniciento *adj* ashen, ash-coloured.

cenit *nm* zenith.

ceniza *nf* ash, ashes; cinder; **—s** (*of person*) ashes, mortal remains; **huir de las —s y dar en las brasas** to jump out of the frying pan into the fire; **reducir algo a —s** to reduce something to ashes.

cenizo **1** *adj* ashen, ash-coloured.
2 *nm* (a) (*Bot*) goosefoot.
(b) jinx (*fam*), hoodoo; **es un avión —** it's a plane with a jinx on it; **entrar el — en casa** to have a spell of bad luck.
(c) (*person*) bringer of bad luck; wet blanket.

cenojil *nm* garter.

cenotafio *nm* cenotaph.

cenote *nm* (*CAm, Mex*) freshwater deposit deep in a cave; cavern where an underground river appears at the surface.

censal *adj* = **censual**.

censar [1a] *vt* (*Arg*) to take a census of.

censo *nm* (a) (*of population*) census; **— de tráfico** traffic census, traffic count; **levantar el — de** to take a census of.
(b) (*Fin*) tax; (annual) ground rent; mortgage; leasehold.
(c) (*Pol*) **— electoral** electoral roll, (*fig*) electorate.
(d) **ser un —** (*fam*) to be a constant source of trouble.

censor nm (a) (*Pol*) censor.
(b) (*Univ*) proctor.
(c) (*Comm, Fin*) — de cuentas auditor; — jurado de cuentas chartered accountant.
(d) (*fig*) critic.
censual adj (a) census (*attr*), relating to a census.
(b) tax (*attr*), mortage (*attr*) etc. (c) electoral, relating to the electoral roll.
censura nf (a) (*Pol*) censorship; censoring; someter a la — to censor.
(b) censor's office.
(c) censure, stricture, criticism; blame, reproach; (*Lit etc*) criticism, judgement; —s (*fam*) gossip, idle talk; digno de — censurable, blameworthy.
(d) (*Comm, Fin*) — de cuentas auditing.
censurable adj censurable, reprehensible, blameworthy.
censurar [1a] vt (a) (*Pol*) to censor. (b) to censure, condemn, criticize, blame, reproach; to find fault with; (*Lit etc*) to criticize, judge, review.
censurista 1 adj censorious. 2 nmf critic, faultfinder.
centaura nf centaury.
centauro nm centaur.
centavo 1 adj hundredth. 2 nm (a) hundredth (part).
(b) (*Fin*) cent.
centella nf spark (*also fig*); flash of lightning.
centelleante adj (a) sparkling; gleaming, glinting, twinkling; flashing. (b) (*fig*) sparkling.
centell(e)ar [1a] vi (a) to sparkle; to gleam, glint, glitter; (*of star*) to twinkle; (*of lightning*) to flash.
(b) (*fig*) to sparkle.
centelleo nm sparkle, sparkling; gleam(ing); glinting; flashing.
centena nf hundred.
centenada nf hundred.
centenal[1] nm, **centenar**[1] nm hundred; a —es by the hundred, by hundreds.
centenal[2] nm, **centenar**[2] nm (*Agr*) rye field.
centenario 1 adj centenary, centennial. 2 nm centenary, centennial. 3 nm, **centenaria** nf (*person*) centenarian.
centeno nm rye.
centésima nf hundredth (part).
centesimal adj centesimal.
centésimo 1 adj hundredth. 2 nm hundredth (part).
centigrado adj centigrade.
centigramo nm centigram.
centilitro nm centilitre.
centímetro nm centimetre.
céntimo 1 adj hundredth.
2 nm hundredth part (*esp* of a peseta), cent; no tiene un — he hasn't a penny, he hasn't a bean (*fam*); no vale un — it's worthless.
centinela nmf sentry, guard, sentinel; look-out man; estar de — to be on guard, do sentry duty; hacer — (*fig*) to keep watch, be on the look-out.
centiplicado adj hundredfold.
centolla nf (large) crab.
centón nm (a) (*Sew*) patchwork quilt, crazy quilt.
(b) (*Lit*) cento. (c) (*fam*) — de conocimientos walking encyclopaedia.
central 1 adj central; middle.
2 nf (*Comm*) head office, headquarters; (*Tech*) plant, station; (*Tel*) exchange; — azucarera (*Cu, PR*) sugar mill; — de correos head post office, main post office; — depuradora waterworks; — eléctrica, — de energía power station; — telefónica, — de teléfonos telephone exchange; — de teléfonos automática automatic telephone exchange; — de teléfonos manual (*or* con servicio a mano) manual telephone exchange.
centralismo nm centralism, tendency to concentrate power in the centre.
centralista 1 adj centralist, centralizing, tending to concentrate power in the centre.
2 nmf centralist, believer in the concentration of power in the centre.
3 nm (*Cu, PR*) sugarmill owner.
centralita nf (*Tel*) switchboard.
centralización nf centralization.
centralizar [1f] vt to centralize.
centrar [1a] vt to centre.
céntrico adj central, middle; es muy — it's very central, it's very convenient; ocupar una situación céntrica to occupy a central position (*also fig*).
centrífuga nf centrifuge.
centrifugar [1h] vt to centrifuge.
centrífugo adj centrifugal.
centrípeto adj centripetal.
centro nm (a) centre, middle; (*Math*) centre; (*of activity*) centre, hub; (*of fire*) seat; — de atracción centre of attraction, main attraction; — demo-

gráfico, — de población centre of population; — docente teaching institution; — de fricción trouble spot; — de gravedad centre of gravity; — de interés centre of interest, main point of interest; — de intrigas centre of intrigue; — de mesa centrepiece; — neurálgico nerve centre (*also fig*); — de rastreo (*Astron*) tracking centre; — social community centre; estar en su — (*fig*) to be in one's element; ir al — (*of town*) to go into the centre, go up to the centre, to go up to town.
(b) (*fig*) goal, purpose, objective.
(c) (*Sport*) centre; delantero — centre-forward; medio — centre-half.
(d) (*CAm*) trousers and waistcoat; (*Cu*) suit (*trousers, waistcoat and shirt*); (*Bol, Cu, Mex*) underskirt; (*Ec*) thick flannel skirt.
Centroamérica f Central America.
centroamericano 1 adj Central American. 2 nm, **centroamericana** nf Central American.
Centroeuropa nf Central Europe.
centuplicar [1g] vt to multiply a hundredfold, centuple.
centuplo 1 adj hundredfold, centuple. 2 nm centuple.
centuria nf century.
centurión nm centurion.
cénzalo nm mosquito; daddy-long-legs.
ceñido adj (a) dress tight, tight-fitting, close-fitting, clinging; narrow-waisted; curve tight.
(b) (*fig*) sparing, frugal, thrifty; moderate; — y corto straight to the point.
ceñidor nm sash, girdle.
ceñiglo nm goosefoot.
ceñir [3h and 3l] 1 vt (a) to girdle, encircle, surround; (*Mil*) to besiege; la muralla ciñe la ciudad the wall surrounds the city; — una ciudad con una muralla to encircle a city with a wall, throw a wall round a city.
(b) to fasten round one's waist; sword to gird on; belt etc to put on.
(c) brow to bind, encircle, wreathe (con, de with).
(d) to wear, carry; — espada to wear a sword.
(e) to fit tight; to tighten (up), draw in; el vestido ciñe bien el cuerpo the dress fits well; habrá que ceñirlo más we shall have to draw it in.
(f) (*fig*) to shorten, cut down, condense.
2 ceñirse vr (a) — algo to put something on; se ciñó la espada he put his sword on; — la corona to take the crown.
(b) to reduce expenditure, tighten one's belt; (*in speaking*) to limit oneself, be brief; — a un tema to limit oneself to a subject, concentrate on a subject; — al asunto to stick to the matter in hand.
ceño nm (a) frown, scowl; arrugar el —, fruncir el — to frown, knit one's brows; mirar con — (*vt*) to frown at, scowl at, give black looks to, (*vi*) to frown, scowl, look black.
(b) (*Meteorol*) threatening appearance.
ceñudo adj person frowning, grim; look black, grim.
cepa nf (a) (*Bot*) stump; (*of vine*) stock; vine; (*Zool: of horn, tail*) root; (*Archit*) pier.
(b) (*fig*) stock; de buena — (*person*) of good stock, (*thing*) of high quality; de buena — castellana of good Castilian stock.
(c) (*Mex*) large pit, ditch, foundation trench.
cepillado nm brush (*act*); se elimina con un suave — it goes away with a gentle brush.
cepillar [1a] vt (a) to brush; (*Tech*) to plane (down).
(b) (*Univ: sl*) to plough (*sl*). (c) (*SAm*) to flatter, butter up (*fam*).
cepillo nm (a) brush; — de dientes toothbrush; — para el pelo hairbrush; — de (*or* para) la ropa clothesbrush; — para las uñas nailbrush; — para el suelo scrubbing brush.
(b) (*Tech*) plane.
(c) (*Eccl*) poorbox, alms box.
(d) (*SAm*) flatterer, creep (*sl*).
cepo nm (a) (*Bot*) branch, bough.
(b) (*Hunting*) trap, snare; (*Mil*) mantrap; stocks.
(c) (*Mech*) reel; (*of anvil, anchor*) stock.
(d) (*Eccl*) poorbox, alms box.
cequión nm (*Chi*) large irrigation channel.
cera nf (a) wax; — de abejas beeswax; — de lustrar wax polish; — de los oídos earwax; — para suelos floor polish.
(b) —s honeycomb.
(c) (*Col, Ec, Mex*) candle.
cerafolio nm chervil.
cerámica nf (a) (*Art*) ceramics, pottery. (b) (*objects*) pottery (*also* —s).
cerámico adj ceramic.

ceramista *nmf* potter.
cerbatana *nf* (*Mil etc*) blowpipe; (*toy*) peashooter; (*Med*) ear trumpet.
cerca[1] *nf* fence, wall; — **viva** hedge.
cerca[2] **1** *adv* near, nearby, close; **de** — closely; (*Mil*) at close range; **examinar algo de** — to examine something closely; **aquí** — near here; **por aquí** — nearby, hereabouts, somewhere round here.
  2 — **de** *prep* (a) (*of place*) near, close to; in the neighbourhood of; **estar** — **de** + *infin* to be near + *ger*, be on the point of + *ger*.
  (b) (*of quantity*) nearly, about; (*of time*) nearly; **hay** — **de 8 toneladas** there are about 8 tons; **son** — **de las 6** it's nearly 6 o'clock.
  (c) (*Pol*) to; **embajador** — **de la corte de Ruritania** ambassador to the court of Ruritania.
  3 *nm* (a) **tiene buen** — it looks all right close up.
  (b) (*Art*) —**s** objects in the foreground.
cercado *nm* (a) enclosure; enclosed garden, fenced field, orchard; — **de reunión** (*Racing*) paddock.
  (b) fence, wall.
  (c) (*Bol*) village common land.
  (d) (*Per*) *territorial division consisting of a state capital and surrounding towns.*
cercanía *nf* (a) nearness, closeness, proximity.
  (b) —**s** neighbourhood, vicinity; surroundings.
  (c) —**s** (*of town*) outskirts, outer suburbs, outlying areas; **tren de** —**s** suburban train.
cercano *adj* near, close; nearby, neighbouring, next; *relative* close; *death, doom* approaching; — **a** near to, close to.
Cercano Oriente *m* Near East.
cercar [1g] *vt* (a) to fence in, wall in, hedge; to enclose; to encircle, surround, ring (**de** with); (*of mountains, enemy etc*) to hem in.
  (b) (*Mil*) *town* to surround, besiege; *troops* to surround, cut off, encircle.
cercén: a — *adv* (a) (*Bot*) close to the root; **cortar algo a** — (*fig*) to nip something in the bud. (b) entirely, completely.
cercenar [1a] *vt* (a) to clip; to cut the edge off, trim the edges of; *end* to cut off, slice off; *limb* to cut off, amputate; *coin* to clip.
  (b) (*fig*) *expenses* to cut down, reduce; *passage etc* to shorten, cut down; to delete, cut out.
cerceta *nf* teal.
cerciorar [1a] **1** *vt* to inform, assure. **2 cerciorarse** *vr* to find out; to make sure; — **de** to find out about, ascertain; to make sure of.
cerco *nm* (a) (*Agr etc*) enclosure; (*SAm*) fence, hedge; (*Per*) small walled property; **saltar el** — (*Arg: Pol*) to change sides, jump on the bandwagon.
  (b) (*Tech: of wheel*) rim; (*of barrel*) hoop; (*Archit*) casing, frame.
  (c) (*Astron, Meteorol*) halo.
  (d) social group, circle.
  (e) (*Mil*) siege; **alzar** (*or* **levantar**) **el** — to raise the siege; **poner** — **a** to lay siege to.
cercón *adv* (*SAm*) rather close.
cerda *nf* (a) (*Zool*) pig, sow. (b) bristle; horsehair; (*Hunting*) snare, noose.
cerdear [1a] *vi* (a) (*Mus*) to scratch, rasp, grate. (b) (*fam*) to hedge, jib, hold back.
Cerdeña *f* Sardinia.
cerdito *nm*, **cerdita** *nf* piglet.
cerdo *nm* (a) (*Zool*) pig; — **padre** boar; — **salvaje** wild pig.
  (b) (*Zool*) — **marino** porpoise.
  (c) (*Cook*) pork.
  (d) (*fig*) dirty person, slovenly fellow.
cerdoso *adj animal* shaggy, hairy, bristly; *chin* bristly, stubbly.
cereal 1 *adj* cereal; grain (*attr*). **2** *nm* cereal; —**es** cereals, grain; —**es** (*Cook*) cereals, cornflakes.
cerebelo *nm* cerebellum.
cerebral *adj* cerebral, brain (*attr*).
cerebro *nm* brain; cerebrum; (*fig*) brains, intelligence; — **electrónico** electronic brain; **estrujar el** — to rack one's brains.
ceremonia *nf* (a) (*act*) ceremony; (*Eccl*) ceremony, service; **hacer** —**s** to stand on ceremony.
  (b) (*quality*) ceremony, ceremoniousness; formality; pomp; **falta de** — informality; **reunión de** — formal meeting, ceremonial meeting; **reunirse de** — to meet with all due ceremony; **por** — as a matter of form; **hablar sin** — to speak informally; **hacer algo sin** — to do something without fuss.
ceremonial 1 *adj* ceremonial. **2** *nm* ceremonial.
ceremoniosamente *adv* ceremoniously; formally; stiffly, with an excess of politeness.

ceremonioso *adj* ceremonious; *person, dress, greeting, visit etc* formal; (*pej*) stiff, over-polite.
céreo *adj* wax (*attr*), waxen.
cerería *nf* wax-chandler's shop.
cerero *nm* wax chandler.
cereza *nf* cherry; **un suéter rojo** — a cherry-red jumper; — **silvestre** wild cherry.
cerezal *nm* cherry orchard.
cerezo *nm* cherry tree; cherry wood.
cerilla *nf* (a) match; wax taper. (b) (*Anat*) earwax.
cerillera *nf*, **cerillero** *nm* (*SAm*) matchbox.
cerillo *nm* (*Mex*) match.
cernedor *nm* sieve.
cernejas *nfpl* fetlock.
cerner [2g] **1** *vt* (a) to sift, sieve.
  (b) (*fig*) to scan, watch.
  2 *vi* (a) (*Bot*) to bud, blossom.
  (b) (*Meteorol*) to drizzle.
  3 cernerse *vr* (a) to hover; to soar; — **sobre** to be poised over, hang over; — **sobre** (*fig*) to threaten, hang over.
  (b) (*of person*) to waddle.
cernícalo *nm* (a) (*Orn*) kestrel. (b) (*fam*) lout, dolt.
  (c) **coger un** — (*fam*) to get tight.
cernidillo *nm* (a) waddle, rolling gait. (b) (*Meteorol*) drizzle.
cernido *nm* (a) sifting; sifted flour. (b) (*Col*) drizzle.
cernidor *nm* sieve.
cernidura *nf* sifting.
cero *nm* nothing; nought; (*Phys etc*) zero; (*Sport*) **por 3 goles a** — by 3 goals to nil, by 3 goals to nought; (*Tennis*) **estamos a 40 contra** — the game stands at 40-love; — **absoluto** absolute zero; **8 grados bajo** — 8 degrees below zero, 8 degrees below freezing, 8 degrees of frost; **es un** — **a la izquierda** he's a nonentity, he's a nobody; **tendremos que partir nuevamente de** — (*fig*) we shall have to start from scratch again.
ceroso *adj* (a) waxen; waxy, waxlike. (b) (*Mex*) egg lightly boiled.
cerote *nm* (a) (shoemaker's) wax.
  (b) (*fam*) panic, funk (*fam*).
  (c) (*CR, Mex*) piece of human excrement; **estar hecho un** — (*Col, Per*), **tener** — (*Arg, Mex*) to have got one's clothes dirty.
cerotear [1a] **1** *vt thread* to wax. **2** *vi* (*Chi: of candle*) to drip.
cerquillo *nm* (a) fringe of hair round the tonsure; (*Arg, Mex*) fringe, curls. (b) (*Tech*) seam, welt.
cerquita *adv* quite near, close by.
cerradero 1 *adj device* locking, fastening; **caja** *f* **cerradera** box that can be locked, box with a lock.
  2 *nm* locking device; clasp, fastener; (*of lock*) strike, keeper; (*of purse*) purse strings.
cerrado *adj* (a) closed, shut; locked; *fist* clenched; "— **por obras**" "closed for repairs (or alterations)"; **aquí huele a** — it smells stuffy in here, it's thick in here.
  (b) *subject* obscure, incomprehensible.
  (c) (*Meteorol*) *sky* cloudy, overcast; *atmosphere* heavy; *night* dark, black.
  (d) *curve* sharp, tight.
  (e) *beard* thick, full.
  (f) *person* quiet, reserved, uncommunicative; (*pej*) secretive; — **de mollera** dense, dim; pig-headed.
  (g) *person* (*pej*) typical, all-too-typical; **es un eslobodio** — he's a typical Slobodian, he has all the worst features of the Slobodian.
  (h) (*Ling*) vowel close.
  (i) (*Ling*) *person* with a broad accent; *accent* broad, marked, strong; *speech* thick, broad; **habló con** — **acento gallego** he spoke with a strong Galician accent.
  (j) (*Arg, Per*) pigheaded.
cerradura *nf* (a) (*act*) closing, shutting; locking.
  (b) lock; — **de combinación** combination lock; — **de golpe**, — **de muelle** spring lock; — **de seguridad** safety lock.
cerraja *nf* (a) lock. (b) (*Bot*) sow-thistle.
cerrajería *nf* (a) locksmith's craft (*or* trade). (b) locksmith's (shop).
cerrajero *nm* locksmith.
cerrar [1k] **1** *vt* (a) *box, eyes, mouth etc* to close, shut; *door* to lock (up); to bolt; *fist* to clench, close; *letter* to seal; *ranks* to close; — **algo con llave** to lock something.
  (b) *hole, opening, pipe etc* to block (up), stop (up), close, obstruct; *harbour, pass* to close; **han cerrado la frontera** they have closed the frontier;

la carretera está cerrada por la nieve the road is blocked by snow. **(c)** *ground, area* to enclose, close off, fence (in), wall (in). **(d)** *tap, gas, water etc* to turn off. **(e)** *(Elec) circuit* to make, close, complete. **(f)** *shop, business* to shut, close; *(permanently)* to shut up; *factory* to close (down). **(g)** *procession* to bring up the rear of; **— la marcha** to come last, bring up the rear. **(h)** *account, debate, story* to close; *programme* to end, be the final item in. **(i)** *bargain* to seal, strike.

2 *vi* **(a)** to close, shut; **la puerta cierra mal** the door doesn't close properly; **cerramos a las 9** we close at 9; **dejar una puerta sin —** to leave a door open. **(b)** *(of night)* to come down, set in; *(of winter)* to close in. **(c) — con uno** to close with someone, grapple with someone; **— con el enemigo** to come to close quarters with the enemy.

3 cerrarse *vr* **(a)** to close, shut; *(of wound)* to close up, heal; *(Mil)* to close ranks. **(b)** *(Meteorol)* to cloud over, become overcast. **(c) — en +** *infin* to persist in **+** *ger*, go on stubbornly **+** *ger*.

cerrazón *nf* **(a)** *(Meteorol)* threatening sky, storm clouds. **(b)** *(RPl)* fog, mist. **(c)** *(Col: of mountain range)* spur.

cerrero *adj* **(a)** *animal* wild; untamed, unbroken; *person* rough, uncouth. **(b)** *(Col, Cu, Ven)* unsweetened; bitter; *bread etc* ordinary.

cerril *adj* **(a)** *ground* rough; mountainous. **(b)** = **cerrero (a)**.

cerrillar [1a] *vt coin* to mill.

cerro *nm* **(a)** hill; **andar** (*or* **echarse, ir**) **por los —s de Úbeda** to wander from the point, get off the track; to talk a lot of rubbish. **(b)** *(Zool)* neck; backbone, back; **en —** bareback. **(c)** *(Tech)* bunch of cleaned hemp (*or* flax). **(d)** *(Col)* lot, heap; **un — de** a lot of.

cerrojazo *nm* bolting; **dar —** to slam the bolt; *(fig)* to come to an end unexpectedly; **dar — a uno** *(sl)* to give someone the mitten *(sl)*.

cerrojo *nm* bolt, latch; *(Sport: also* **táctica de —**) stonewalling, negative play; **echar el —** to bolt the door.

certamen *nm* competition, contest; **— de belleza** beauty contest.

certeramente *adv* accurately, unerringly.

certero *adj* **(a)** accurate, sure, certain. **(b)** *shot* accurate, well-aimed; telling; *aim* excellent; *marksman* sure, good, crack. **(c)** well-informed.

certeza *nf* certainty; **tener la — de que . . .** to know for certain that . . ., have the certain knowledge that . . .

certidumbre *nf* certainty; conviction.

certificable *adj* certifiable.

certificación *nf* certification; *(Post)* registration; *(Law)* affidavit.

certificado 1 *adj* certified; *(Post)* registered. **2** *nm* **(a)** certificate; **— de aptitud** testimonial; **— de ciudadanía** naturalization papers; **— médico** medical certificate; **— de vacuna** vaccination certificate. **(b)** *(Post)* registered packet, registered item.

certificar [1g] *vt* **(a)** to certify; to guarantee, vouch for; **— que . . .** to certify that . . . **(b)** *(Post)* to register.

certitud *nf* certainty, certitude.

cerúleo *adj* sky blue.

cerumen *nm* earwax.

cerval *adj* deer *(attr)*, deer-like.

cervantino *adj* Cervantine; of Cervantes; peculiar to Cervantes; like (that of) Cervantes; **los estudios —s** Cervantes studies, studies of Cervantes; **el estilo —** the Cervantine style.

cervantista *nmf* Cervantes scholar, specialist in Cervantes.

cervato *nm* fawn.

cervecería *nf* **(a)** brewery. **(b)** bar, public house.

cervecero *nm* brewer.

cerveza *nf* beer; **— de barril, —** (**servida**) **al grifo** draught beer, beer on draught; **— de botella, — en botellas, — embotellada** bottled beer; **— clara** light beer; **— estilo Pilsen** lager; **— negra** dark beer.

cervical *adj* neck *(attr)*, cervical; *(relating to part of the womb)* cervical.

cerviz *nf* **(a)** neck, nape of the neck; **de dura —** stubborn, headstrong, wild; **bajar** (*or* **doblar**) **la**

— to submit, bow down; **levantar la —** to lift one's head up (again). **(b)** *(part of the womb)* cervix.

cervuno *adj* deer-like; deer-coloured.

cesación *nf* cessation; suspension, stoppage; **— del fuego** ceasefire.

cesante 1 *adj* out of a job, out of office; discharged; retired; on half-pay. **2** *nm* civil servant who has been compulsorily retired, dismissed public employee.

cesantía *nf* **(a)** state of being a *cesante*. **(b)** retirement pension, half-pay, redundancy compensation.

César *m* Caesar.

cesar [1a] **1** *vt* **(a)** to cease, stop; *payment, work* to stop, suspend. **(b)** *(SAm)* to sack *(fam)*, fire *(fam)*; **le cesaron en el trabajo** they sacked him from his work. **2** *vi* **(a)** to cease, stop; to desist; **— de hacer algo** to stop doing something, leave off doing something; **no cesa de hablar** she never stops talking; **sin —** ceaselessly, incessantly. **(b)** *(of employee)* to leave, quit; to retire; **— en el trabajo** to give up one's work, retire from work.

cesáreo *adj* **(a)** Caesarean; imperial. **(b)** *(Med)* **operación cesárea** Caesarean operation.

cese *nm* **(a)** cessation; suspension, stoppage; **— de alarma** *(Mil)* all-clear signal; **— de fuego, — de hostilidades** ceasefire; **— de pagos** suspension of payments, stoppage of payments; **— temporal de los bombardeos** temporary halt to the bombing. **(b)** *(of civil servant)* dismissal, compulsory retirement; *(of worker)* sacking *(fam)*, firing *(fam)*; **dar el — a uno** to sack someone *(fam)*.

cesión *nf* **(a)** *(Pol etc)* cession. **(b)** *(Law)* cession, granting, transfer; **— de bienes** surrender of property.

cesionario *nm*, **cesionaria** *nf* grantee, assign.

cesionista *nmf* grantor, assignor.

césped *nm* **(a)** grass, lawn, (stretch of) turf; *(for games)* pitch; *(for bowls)* green. **(b)** turf, sod.

cesta *nf* basket; *(pelota)* long wicker racquet; **— para compras** shopping basket; **— de costura** sewing basket; **— para papeles, — de los papeles (rotos)** wastepaper basket; **llevar la —** *(fam)* to go along as chaperon; to play gooseberry.

cestada *nf* basketful.

cestería *nf* **(a)** basketmaking. **(b)** wickerwork, basketwork; **silla de —** wicker(work) chair. **(c)** basket shop.

cestero *nm*, **cestera** *nf* basketmaker; basket seller.

cestillo *nm* small basket; *(of balloon)* basket; **— del polen** *(of bee)* pollen sac.

cesto *nm* **(a)** (large) basket; hamper; **— de la colada** clothes basket; **— para papeles, — de los papeles (rotos)** wastepaper basket. **(b) estar hecho un —** to be very drowsy; to be fuddled with drink; **estar metido en un —** to be a spoiled child. **(c)** *(fam)* idiot.

cesura *nf* caesura.

cetáceo 1 *adj* cetacean. **2** *nm* cetacean.

cetorrino *nm* basking shark.

cetrería *nf* falconry, hawking.

cetrero *nm* **(a)** falconer. **(b)** *(Eccl)* verger.

cetrino *adj* greenish-yellow; *face, complexion* sallow; *(fig)* melancholy, jaundiced.

cetro *nm* sceptre; *(fig)* sway, power, dominion; **empuñar el —** to ascend the throne, begin to reign.

cía *nf* hip bone.

cianhídrico *adj* hydrocyanic.

cianotipia *nf*, **cianotipo** *nm* blueprint.

cianuro *nm* cyanide; **— potásico, — de potasio** potassium cyanide.

ciar [1c] *vi* **(a)** to go backwards; *(Naut)* to go astern, back water. **(b)** *(fig)* to back down, back out.

ciática *nf* sciatica.

ciático *adj* sciatic.

cibernética *nf* cybernetics.

cicatear [1a] *vi* to be stingy, be mean.

cicatería *nf* stinginess, meanness.

cicatero 1 *adj* stingy, mean. **2** *nm*, **cicatera** *nf* miser, skinflint; *(fam)* pickpocket.

cicatriz *nf* scar (*also fig*).

cicatrización *nf* healing.

cicatrizar [1f] **1** *vt* to heal. **2 cicatrizarse** *vr* to heal (up), form a scar.

Cicerón *m* Cicero.

cicerone *nm* guide, cicerone.

ciceroniano *adj* Ciceronian.

ciclamen *nm*, **ciclamino** cyclamen.

cíclico *adj* cyclic(al).

ciclismo *nm* cycling; (*Sport*) cycle racing.
ciclista *nmf* cyclist.
ciclo *nm* cycle; (*Lit*) cycle; (*of lectures etc*) course, series, programme; (*School*) term; (*SAm: Univ*) year, course.
ciclo-cross *nm* cyclo-cross.
ciclomoto(r) *nm* moped, autocycle.
ciclón *nm* cyclone.
cíclope *m* Cyclops.
ciclorama *nm* cyclorama.
ciclotrón *nm* cyclotron.
—cico,—cica (*in some combinations* **—ecico,—ecica**) *suffix: see* **—ito.**
cicuta *nf* hemlock.
cidra *nf* citron.
cidracayote *nm* (*SAm*) gourd, calabash.
cidro *nm* citron (tree).
ciega *nf* blind woman.
ciego 1 *adj* (a) blind; blinded; **a ciegas** blindly; **andar a ciegas, caminar a ciegas** to grope one's way; **volar a ciegas** to fly blind; **jugar a la ciega** (*Chess*) to play blindfold; **quedar —** to go blind; **quedó — después de la explosión** he was blinded in the accident; **más — que un topo** as blind as a bat; **tan — el uno como el otro** it's a case of the blind leading the blind.
(b) (*fig*) blind; **—, — para** blind to; **— de ira** blind with rage; **con una fe ciega** with a blind faith, with an unquestioning faith; **a ciegas** blindly; heedlessly, thoughtlessly.
(c) (*Archit*) blind; *pipe etc* blocked, stopped up, choked.
2 *nm* (a) blind man, blind person; **los —s** the blind, blind people.
(b) (*RPl: Cards*) player who holds bad cards.
(c) (*Cu*) meadow enclosed by forest.
cielo *nm* (a) sky; (*Astron*) sky, heavens, firmament; **— aborregado** mackerel sky; **— encopetado** overcast sky; **— máximo** (*Aer*) ceiling; **a — abierto, a — raso** in the open air; **mina a — abierto** opencast mine; **a — descubierto** in the open; **se le juntaron el — con la tierra** he had terrible trouble, he was in an awful mess; (*SAm*) **he lost his nerve; mover — y tierra** to move heaven and earth; **querer tapar el — con las manos** (*SAm*) to try to hide something obvious; **se vino el — abajo** it rained cats and dogs, the heavens opened.
(b) (*Archit: also* **— raso**) ceiling; (*of mouth*) roof; (*of bed*) canopy; (*CAm: Aut*) roof.
(c) (*Rel*) heaven; **¡—s!** good heavens!; **esto clama al —** this cries out to heaven (to be reformed *etc*); **ganar el —** to win salvation; **ganar el — con rosario ajeno** to use other people's efforts to one's own advantage; **ir al —** to go to heaven; **poner a uno en el —** (*or* **en los cielos,** *SAm*) **por los cielos**) to praise someone to the skies; **tomar el — con las manos** to be asking for trouble, be over-optimistic; **ver el — abierto** to see one's way out of a difficulty; *see* **llover.**
(d) (*term of endearment*) my love, sweetheart.
ciempiés *nm, pl* **ciempiés** centipede.
cien[1] *adj* (*apocopated form of* **ciento,** *before n*) (a) a hundred; **— mil** a hundred thousand; **las últimas — páginas** the last hundred pages.
(b) **10 por —** ten per cent; **— por —** (*fig*) a hundred per cent (*also fig*); **es español — por —** he's Spanish through and through, he's Spanish to the core; **lo apoyo — por —** I support it a hundred per cent, I support it wholeheartedly.
cien[2] *nm* (*RPl*) lavatory.
ciénaga *nf* marsh, bog, swamp.
ciencia *nf* science; (*older sense*) knowledge, learning, scholarship, erudition; **hombre de —** scientist; **— del hogar** domestic science, home economics (US); **—s naturales** natural sciences; **—s ocultas** occult sciences; **a — y paciencia de uno** with someone's knowledge and agreement, with someone's connivance; **saber algo a — cierta** to know something for certain (*or* for a fact).
ciencia-ficción *nf* science fiction.
cieno *nm* mud, mire, silt, ooze; slime.
cienoso *adj* muddy, miry; slimy.
científicamente *adv* scientifically.
científico 1 *adj* scientific. **2** *nm* scientist.
cientista *nmf* (*SAm*) scientist.
ciento *adj and nm* hundred, (one) hundred; **— veinte** a hundred and twenty; **en su año —** in its hundredth year; **15 por —** 15 per cent; **hay un 5 por — de descuento** there is a 5 per cent discount; **por —s** in hundreds, by the hundred; **de — en boca** tiny, insignificant; **dar — y raya al más pintado** be a match for anyone; **había — y la** madre there were far too many; and even that was still too many; **pero por allí pasan de — a viento** but hardly anybody comes that way.
cierne *nm* blossoming, budding; **en —(s)** (*Bot*) in blossom; (*fig*) in its infancy; **es un ajedrecista en —s** he's a budding chessplayer, he's a future chess champion.
cierre *nm* (a) (*act*) closing, shutting; locking; (*Radio, TV*) close-down; (*of factory*) shutdown; **— de los dueños, — patronal** lockout.
(b) closing device, locking device; snap fastener; (*of dress*) fastener; (*of belt*) buckle, clasp; (*of book*) clasp; (*of door*) catch; (*of shop*) shutter, blind; (*Aut*) choke; **— de cremallera, — relámpago** (*Per, RPl*) zip fastener, zipper; **— hidráulico** water seal; **— metálico** roll shutter, metal blind.
(c) **de —** closing; **precios de —** (*Fin*) closing prices.
cierro *nm* (a) = **cierre.** (b) (*Chi*) wall; envelope.
ciertamente *adv* certainly, surely; **no era — de los más inteligentes** he was certainly not one of the brightest.
cierto *adj* (a) sure, certain; *promise etc* positive, definite; **¡—!** certainly!; **por —** certainly; by the way; **por — que no era el único** and moreover he was not the only one, and what is more he wasn't the only one; **no, por —** certainly not; **¡sí, por —!** yes of course!; **es —** it is true; that's it; **¿es — eso?** it that really so?; **es — que...** it is certain that..., it is true that...; **lo — es que** the fact is that...; **lo único — es que...** the only sure thing is that...; **estar —** to be sure; **¿estás —?** are you sure?; **estar — de +** *infin* to be certain to + *infin*; **estar en lo —** to be right; **saber algo de —** to know something for certain.
(b) a certain; **—s** some, certain; **— día de mayo** one day in May; **cierta persona que yo conozco** a certain person I know; *see* **cada** *etc*.
cierva *nf* hind.
ciervo *nm* deer; stag; **— común** red deer; **— volante** stag beetle.
cierzo *nm* north wind.
cifra *nf* (a) number, numeral; **— arábiga** Arabic numeral; **— romana** Roman numeral; **escribirlo en —s y palabras** to write it down in figures and in words.
(b) number, quantity, amount; sum; **— global** lump sum; **la — de este año es elevada** the quantity this year is large; **la — de los muertos** the number of dead.
(c) code, cipher; **en —** in code; (*fig*) mysteriously, enigmatically.
(d) abbreviation; monogram; abridgement, summary; **en —** in brief, briefly, concisely; in a shortened form.
cifradamente *adv* (a) in code. (b) in brief, in a shortened form.
cifrado *adj* coded, in code.
cifrar [1a] *vt* (a) *message* to code, write in code; (*fig*) to abridge, summarize; to abbreviate. (b) *hope* to place, concentrate (*en* on).
cigarra *nf* cicada.
cigarral *nm* (*Toledo*) country house on the banks of the *Tagus*.
cigarrera *nf* (a) cigar case. (b) cigar maker; cigar seller.
cigarrería *nf* (*SAm*) tobacconist's (shop); tobacco factory.
cigarrero *nm* cigar maker; cigar seller.
cigarrillo *nm* cigarette.
cigarro *nm* cigar (*also —* **puro**); cigarette (*also —* **de papel**); **— habano** Havana cigar.
cigoto *nm* zygote.
ciguato *adj* (a) (*Ant, Mex*) simple, stupid. (b) (*Mex, Ven*) pale, anaemic.
cigüeña *nf* (a) (*Orn*) stork. (b) (*Mech*) crank, handle; winch, capstan. (c) (*CAm*) barrel organ. (d) (*Ant*) railway barrow.
cigüeñal *nm* crankshaft.
cija *nf* barn; hayloft.
cilampa *nf* (*CAm*) drizzle.
cilampear [1a] *vi* (*CAm*) to drizzle.
cilantro *nm* (*Bot, Cook*) coriander.
cilicio *nm* hair shirt.
cilindrada *nf* cylinder capacity.
cilindradora *nf* steamroller, road roller.
cilindrar [1a] *vt* to roll, roll flat.
cilíndrico *adj* cylindrical.
cilindro *nm* (*Math, Tech*) cylinder; (*of typewriter*) roller; (*Mex*) barrel organ; **— de caminos, — compresor** steamroller, road roller.
cilla *nf* (a) tithe barn, granary. (b) tithe.

cima *nf* (*of tree*) top; (*of mountain*) top, peak, summit; (*fig*) summit, height; (*fig*) completion; **dar — a** to complete, crown with success, carry out successfully.

cimarra *nf*: **hacer —** (*Arg, Chi*) to play truant.

cimarrón 1 *adj* (**a**) (*SAm: Bot, Zool*) wild; (*fig*) rough, uncouth; lazy; **negro —** (*Hist*) runaway slave, fugitive slave.
(**b**) (*RPl*) maté bitter, unsweetened.
2 *nm* (*RPl*) (**a**) unsweetened maté.
(**b**) wild dog; prairie dog.

cimarronear [1a] *vi* (**a**) (*SAm: of slave*) to run away.
(**b**) (*RPl*) to drink unsweetened maté.

cimba *nf* (*Bol*) plaited rope of hard leather; (*Per*) pigtail; (*Per*) hairband; (*Per*) rope ladder.

címbalo *nm* cymbal.

cimbel *nm* decoy (*also fig*).

cimbor(r)io *nm* (*Archit*) dome; base of a dome; (*Min*) roof.

cimbrear [1a] **1** *vt* (**a**) to brandish; to shake, swish, swing; to bend.
(**b**) **— a uno to** thrash someone; **le cimbreó de un porrazo** he clouted him with his stick.
2 *vi* to swerve, change direction unexpectedly.
3 cimbrearse *vr* to sway, swing, to shake; to bend; **— al viento** to sway in the wind.

cimbreño *adj* pliant, flexible; *figure* willowy, lithe.

cimbreo *nm* swaying, swinging; shaking; bending.

cimbrón *nm* (*Arg, Col, CR*) shudder of pain; strong nervous convulsion; (*Ec*) stab of pain; (*Chi, Mex*) blow with the flat of a sword; (*Arg, Col, CR, Mex*) swish (*of lasso etc*); (*Arg, Col, CR, Mex*) violent jerk, strong tug; (*Arg*) vibration.

cimbronada *nf* (*Arg, Col, Mex*), **cimbronazo** *nm* (*Arg, Col, Mex*) = **cimbrón**; (*Ven*) earthquake.

cimentación *nf* (**a**) foundation. (**b**) laying of foundations.

cimentar [1k] *vt* (**a**) (*Archit*) to lay the foundations of (*or* for); (*fig*) to found, establish. (**b**) (*fig*) to strengthen, cement.

cimera *nf* crest (*also Her*).

cimero *adj* top, topmost, uppermost.

cimiento *nm* foundation, groundwork; (*fig*) basis, source; **—s** (*Archit*) foundations; **abrir los —s** to dig the foundations; **echar los —s de** to lay the foundations for.

cimitarra *nf* scimitar.

cimpa *nf* (*Bol, Per*) = **cimba**.

cinabrio *nm* cinnabar.

cinc *nm* zinc.

cincel *nm* chisel.

cincelador *nm* (**a**) sculptor; engraver; stone cutter. (**b**) (chipping) chisel.

cincelar [1a] *vt* to chisel; to carve, engrave, cut.

cinco 1 *adj* five; (*date*) fifth; **las —** five o'clock; **estar sin —** (*fam*) to be broke (*fam*); **no estar en sus —** (*fam*) to be off one's rocker (*sl*); **le dije cuántas son —** I told him a thing or two; **saber cuántas son —** to know what's what, know a thing or two; **tener los —** **muy listos** (*fam*) to be light-fingered; **¡vengan esos —!** shake (on it)!
2 *nm* (**a**) five.
(**b**) (*CAm, Col, Ven*) 5-stringed guitar.
(**c**) (*Mex*) bottom, backside (*fam*).

cincoenrama *nf* cinquefoil.

cincuenta *adj* fifty; fiftieth.

cincuentavo 1 *adj* fiftieth. **2** *nm* fiftieth.

cincuentena *nf* fifty, group of about fifty.

cincuenteno *adj* fiftieth.

cincuentón 1 *adj* fifty-year old, fiftyish. **2** *nm*, **cincuentona** *nf* person of about fifty.

cincha *nf* (**a**) girth, saddle strap; **a revienta —s** at breakneck speed; hurriedly; (*SAm*) reluctantly.
(**b**) (*Sew: for chairs etc*) webbing.
(**c**) (*Col*) **tener —** to have a strain of Negro (*or* Indian) blood.

cinchada *nf* (*Mex, RPl*) tug-of-war.

cinchar [1a] *vt* to girth, secure the girth of; (*Tech*) to band, hoop, secure with hoops.

cincho *nm* sash, belt, girdle; iron hoop, metal band; (*CAm, Mex, PR*) = **cincha** (**a**).

cinchona *nf* (*SAm*) quinine bark.

cine *nm* (**a**) (*in general, as art*) cinema; film(s), movies (*US*); **el — español actual** the present-day Spanish cinema; **— en colores** colour films; **— hablado, — sonoro** talkies; **— mudo** silent films; **hacer —** to make films, be engaged in film work, be working for the cinema.
(**b**) (*building*) cinema, movie theatre (*US*), picture house (*US*); **ir al —** to go to the cinema, go to the pictures, go to the movies (*US*).

cine-club *nm*, *pl* **cine-clubs** [*pronunciation: see* **club**] cine club, film club.

cinema *nm* cinema.

cinemateca *nf* film library, film archive.

cinematografía *nf* films, film-making, cinematography.

cinematografiar [1a] *vt* to film.

cinematográfico *adj* cine- . . ., film (*attr*); cinematographic.

cinematógrafo *nm* (**a**) cinema. (**b**) cine projector, film projector.

cinematurgo *nm* scriptwriter, scenarist.

cineración *nf* incineration.

cinerama *nm* cinerama.

cinerario *adj* (**a**) cinerary. (**b**) = **ceniciento**.

cinéreo *adj* ashy; ash-grey, ashen.

cinética *nf* kinetics.

cinético *adj* kinetic.

cingalés 1 *adj* Singhalese. **2** *nm*, **cingalesa** *nf* Singhalese.

cíngaro 1 *adj* gipsy. **2** *nm* gipsy.

cinguería *nf* (*Arg*) sheet-metal work; sheet-metal shop.

cinguero *nm* (*Arg*) sheet-metal worker.

cínicamente *adv* (**a**) cynically. (**b**) brazenly, shamelessly, impudently; in an unprincipled way.

cínico 1 *adj* (**a**) cynical. (**b**) brazen, shameless, impudent; unprincipled. **2** *nm* (**a**) cynic. (**b**) brazen individual; unprincipled person, humbug.

cinismo *nm* (**a**) cynicism. (**b**) brazenness, shamelessness, effrontery, impudence; lack of principle, humbug; **¡qué —!** what humbug!

cinta *nf* (**a**) band, strip; tape; (*Sew*) ribbon, tape; (*Cine*) film; reel; **— adhesiva** adhesive tape; **— aisladora, — aislante** insulating tape; **— de cotizaciones, — de teleimpresor** ticker tape; **— de freno** brake lining; **— de goma** rubber band; **— de llegada** (*Sport*) (finishing) tape; **— para máquina de escribir** typewriter ribbon; **— magnética, — magnetofónica** magnetic tape, recording tape; **— de corto metraje** short (film); **— de largo metraje** full-length film; **— métrica** tape measure; **— de pelo** hairband; **— simbólica** ceremonial tape; **— transportadora, — de transporte** conveyor belt.
(**b**) (*Archit*) fillet, scroll.
(**c**) (*of pavement*) kerb.
(**d**) (*SAm*) tin, can.
(**e**) (*Mex*) **—s** shoelaces.

cinteado *adj* beribboned.

cintero *nm* (**a**) (*woman's*) girdle. (**b**) rope.

cintillo *nm* (**a**) hatband. (**b**) small ring with jewels. (**c**) (*PR*) kerb.

cinto *nm* (*Mil*) belt, girdle, sash; **armas de —** side arms.

cintura *nf* (**a**) (*Anat*) waist; waistline; **— de avispa** wasp waist; **de la — (para) arriba** from the waist up; **tener poca —** to have a slim waist.
(**b**) girdle; **meter a uno en —** to bring (*or* keep) someone under control, keep someone under; to make someone see reason.

cinturilla *nf* waistband.

cinturón *nm* (**a**) belt; girdle; **— de salvamento, salvavidas** lifebelt; **— de seguridad** safety belt; **apretarse el —** (*fig*) to tighten one's belt.
(**b**) (*fig*) belt, zone; **el — industrial de Madrid** the Madrid industrial belt; **— verde** green belt.

cipayo *nm* (**a**) sepoy. (**b**) (*Arg*) politician in the service of foreign commerce.

cipe *nm* sickly child.

cipo *nm* memorial stone; milestone, signpost.

cipote 1 *adj* (**a**) (*Col, Ven*) stupid.
(**b**) (*Guat*) plump, chubby.
2 *nm* (**a**) (*CAm, Ven*) lad, youngster; urchin.
(**b**) (*Nic*) Indian club.
(**c**) (*CAm*) chump (*fam*), blockhead.
(**d**) (*Col*) **— de chica** smashing girl (*sl*); **— de película** splendid film.
(**e**) (*esp RPl, Ven: tabu*) prick (*tabu*).

ciprés *nm* cypress (tree).

cipresal *nm* cypress grove.

circo *nm* (**a**) circus, amphitheatre. (**b**) (*show*) circus. (**c**) (*Mex*) acrobatic troupe.

circuir [3g] *vt* to encircle, surround.

circuito *nm* circuit; circumference, distance round (*the outside*); (*Elec etc*) circuit; (*Sport*) lap; **— en bucle** loop; **— cerrado** closed circuit, loop; **— cerrado de TV, — interno de TV, TV por — cerrado** closed-circuit TV; **corto —** short circuit.

circulación *nf* (**a**) circulation (*also Fin, Med*); (*fig*) circulation; propagation; **— fiduciaria** paper money, paper currency; **— sanguínea, — de la sangre**

circulation of the blood; **estar fuera de —** to be out of circulation, be no longer current; **poner algo en —** to issue something, put something into circulation.

(**b**) (*Aut*) traffic; movement of traffic; **— rodada** vehicular traffic, wheeled traffic; **"cerrado a la — rodada" "**closed to vehicles**"; la — es por la derecha** they drive on the right; **calle de gran —** busy street, street much used by traffic.

circulante *adj library* lending, circulating.

circular 1 *adj* circular, round; *ticket* return, round-trip (*US: attr*); *trip* round; *letter* circular.

2 *nf* circular.

3 *vt* to circulate; to pass round, send round; to put into circulation.

4 *vi* (**a**) to circulate (*also Fin, Med*); (*Fin*) to be in circulation; **hacer — una carta** to circulate a letter, send round a letter.

(**b**) (*of persons*) to move about, walk around (*por* in); **¡circulen!** move along!; **hacer — a la gente** to move people along.

(**c**) (*Aut*) to drive; **— por la izquierda** (*in nation*) to drive on the left, (*in street etc*) to keep to the left; **hacer — los coches** to keep the cars moving.

(**d**) (*of transport*) to run; **no circula los domingos** it does not run on Sundays; **circula entre A y B** it runs between A and B, it operates between A and B.

circulatorio *adj* circulatory.

círculo *nm* (**a**) (*Math etc*) circle; **— máximo** great circle; **C— Polar Antártico** Antarctic Circle; **C— Polar Ártico** Arctic Circle; **— vicioso** vicious circle (*also fig*).

(**b**) circle, ring, band.

(**c**) (*of people*) circle, club, group; clubhouse; (*Per, RPl*) social gathering; (*Pol*) political group, faction.

(**d**) (*fig*) scope, compass, extent.

circun . . . circum . . .

circuncidar [1a] *vt* (**a**) to circumcise. (**b**) (*fig*) to curtail; to moderate.

circuncisión *nf* circumcision.

circunciso *adj* circumcised.

circundante *adj* surrounding.

circundar [1a] *vt* to surround.

circunferencia *nf* circumference.

circunflejo *nm* circumflex.

circunlocución *nf*, **circunloquio** *nm* circumlocution, roundabout expression.

circunnavegación *nf* circumnavigation.

circunnavegar [1a] *vt* to sail round, circumnavigate.

circunscribir [3a: *ptp* **circunscrito**] **1** *vt* to circumscribe; (*fig*) to circumscribe, limit, restrict (*a* to).

2 circunscribirse *vr* (*fig*) to be limited, be confined (*a* to).

circunscripción *nf* (*of territory*) division, subdivision; (*Parl*) constituency, electoral district.

circunspección *nf* circumspection, caution, prudence.

circunspecto *adj* circumspect, cautious, prudent; deliberate; *words* carefully chosen, guarded.

circunstancia *nf* circumstance; **—s agravantes** aggravating circumstances; **—s atenuantes** extenuating circumstances; **en las —s** in (*or* under) the circumstances; **en las —s actuales** in the present state of things, under present conditions; **las —s cambian los casos** circumstances alter cases; *see* **altura.**

circunstanciado *adj* detailed, circumstantial.

circunstancial *adj* (**a**) circumstantial. (**b**) *arrangement etc* makeshift, emergency (*attr*).

circunstante 1 *adj* (**a**) surrounding. (**b**) *person* present. **2** *nmf* onlooker, bystander; **los —s** those present.

circunvalación *nf*: **carretera de —** bypass, ring road.

circunvecino *adj* adjacent, neighbouring, surrounding.

cirial *nm* (*Eccl*) processional candlestick.

cirio *nm* (*Eccl*) (wax) candle.

cirquero *nm* (*Mex*) circus performer, acrobat; circus impresario.

cirro *nm* cirrus.

cirrosis *nf* cirrhosis.

ciruela *nf* plum; **— claudia, — verdal** greengage; **— damascena** damson; **— pasa** prune.

ciruelo *nm* (**a**) (*Bot*) plum tree. (**b**) (*fam*) dolt, idiot.

cirugía *nf* surgery; **— estética, — plástica** plastic surgery.

cirujano *nm* surgeon.

ciscar [1g] **1** *vt* (**a**) to dirty, soil, mess up.

(**b**) (*Cu, Mex*) to put to shame.

(**c**) (*Cu, Mex*) to upset, needle (*fam*).

2 ciscarse *vr* (**a**) to soil oneself; **¡me cisco en todo!** (*euph*) blast it!

(**b**) (*Cu, Mex*) to feel ashamed.

(**c**) (*Cu, Mex*) to get upset, take offence, get needled (*fam*).

cisco *nm* (**a**) coaldust, slack; **estar hecho —** (*fam*) to be a wreck, be all in.

(**b**) (*fam*) row, shindy; **armar un —, meter —** to kick up a row, make trouble.

ciscón *adj* (*Cu, Mex*) easily offended.

cisma *nm* (**a**) (*Eccl*) schism; (*Pol etc*) split; (*fig*) discord, disagreement. (**b**) (*Col*) prudery, overniceness. (**c**) (*Col*) gossip.

cismático *adj* (**a**) (*Eccl*) schismatic(al); (*fig*) trouble-making, fractious, dissident. (**b**) (*Col*) prudish, overnice; finicky. (**c**) (*Col*) gossipy.

cisne *nm* (**a**) (*Orn*) swan. (**b**) (*RPl*) powder puff.

Císter *nm* Cistercian Order.

cisterciense 1 *adj* Cistercian. **2** *nm* Cistercian.

cisterna *nf* cistern; tank; reservoir.

cistitis *nf* cystitis.

cita *nf* (**a**) appointment, engagement; meeting; place of meeting, rendez-vous; (*of lovers*) meeting, (*with girlfriend*) date; **— espacial** rendez-vous in space, space link-up; **acudir a una —** to keep an appointment, turn up for an appointment; **se dieron (una) cita para las 8** they agreed to meet at 8; **faltar a una —** to miss an appointment, break an appointment, not turn up for a date; **tener una — con uno** to have an appointment with someone, have a date with someone.

(**b**) (*Lit etc*) quotation (*de* from); reference; (*act*) citation; **con largas —s probatorias** with long quotations in support.

citable *adj* quotable.

citación *nf* (**a**) (*Lit etc*) quotation. (**b**) (*Law*) summons, citation; **— a licitadores** invitation to bidders, invitation of tenders.

citado *adj* aforementioned; **en el — país** in the aforementioned country, in this country; in the country in question.

citar [1a] **1** *vt* (**a**) to make an appointment with; to make a date with; **la cité para las 9** I arranged to meet her at 9; **la cité para delante de Correos** I arranged to meet her in front of the post office.

(**b**) (*Law*) to call, summon; **tiene facultades para — testigos** he has the power to call witnesses.

(**c**) (*Taur*) to incite, provoke, stir up; to call out to.

(**d**) (*Lit etc*) to quote, cite (*de* from).

2 citarse *vr*: **— con uno** to arrange to meet someone (*para las 7* at 7); **citémonos para delante del estadio** let's meet outside the stadium.

cítara *nf* zither.

-cito, -cita *suffix* (*in some combinations* **-ecito, -ecita**): *see* **-ito.**

citrato *nm* citrate.

cítrico *adj* citric.

citrón *nm* lemon.

ciudad *nf* city, town; **C— del Cabo** Cape Town; **C— Eterna** Eternal City (*Rome*); **C— Imperial** (*Spanish Hist*) Toledo; **C— del Vaticano** Vatican City; **es el mejor café de la —** it's the best café in town; **hoy vamos a la —** we're going to (*or* into, up to) town today.

ciudadanía *nf* (**a**) citizens, citizenry.

(**b**) citizenship; **— de honor** freedom of a city; **derechos de —** citizen's rights, rights of citizenship.

ciudadano 1 *adj* civic, city (*attr*); **el orgullo —** civic pride.

2 *nm*, **ciudadana** *nf* (**a**) city dweller, townsman.

(**b**) (*Pol etc*) citizen; **—s** townsfolk, townspeople; inhabitants; **— de honor** freeman of city; **— del mundo** citizen of the world; **—s de segunda clase** second-class citizens, under-privileged persons.

ciudadela *nf* (**a**) citadel, fortress. (**b**) (*SAm*) tenement block.

civeta *nf* civet cat.

civeto *nm* civet.

cívico 1 *adj* civic; domestic; (*fig*) public-spirited, patriotic. **2** *nm* (*SAm*) policeman.

civil 1 *adj* (**a**) (*Pol etc*) civil; **derechos —es** civil rights; **guerra —** civil war; **casarse por lo —** to have a civil wedding, get married in a registry office (*or equivalent*).

(**b**) (*Mil*) **población —** civil population, civilian population.

(**c**) (*fig*) civil, courteous, polite.

2 *nm* (**a**) policeman.

(**b**) (*in Mil parlance*) civilian.

civilidad *nf* civility, courtesy, politeness.

civilización *nf* civilization.
civilizador *adj* influence etc civilizing.
civilizar [1f] **1** *vt* to civilize. **2 civilizarse** *vr* to become civilized.
civilmente *adv* civilly, courteously, politely.
civismo *nm* public spirit; community spirit; patriotism.
cizalla *nf* (a) (*also* —s) wire cutters, metal shears. (b) —s shavings, metal clippings.
cizaña *nf* (a) (*Bot*) darnel; (*Bib*) tares. (b) (*fig*) discord; **sembrar** — to sow discord (*entre* among). (c) (*fig*) vice, corruption, harmful influence.
cizañar [1a] *vt* to sow discord among.
cizañero *nm*, **cizañera** *nf* troublemaker, mischief-maker.
clac *nm*, *pl* **claques** (*gall*) (a) collapsible opera hat; cocked hat. (b) = **claque.**
clamar [1a] **1** *vt* to clamour for, cry out for; to appeal earnestly for.
 2 *vi* to cry out, clamour; — **contra** to cry out against, protest vociferously against; — **por** to clamour for, demand vociferously; **esto clama al cielo** this cries out to heaven (to be reformed *etc*).
clamor *nm* (a) cry, shout; noise, clamour. (b) (*of bell*) tolling, knell. (c) (*fig*) clamour, outcry, protest.
clamorear [1a] **1** *vt* = **clamar 1. 2** *vi* (*of bell*) to toll.
clamoreo *nm* (a) clamour(ing), (prolonged) shouting. (b) (*fig*) sustained outcry, vociferous protests; —s **de protesta** vigorous protests.
clamorosamente *adv* noisily, loudly, clamorously.
clamoroso *adj* (a) noisy, loud, clamorous; screaming, shrieking. (b) (*fig*) *success* resounding, enormous.
clan *nm* clan; (*fig*) faction, group.
clandestinamente *adv* secretly, clandestinely; by stealth, stealthily.
clandestinidad *nf* secrecy; secret nature; **en la** — in secrecy.
clandestinista *nm* (*SAm*) bootlegger.
clandestino *adj* secret, clandestine; stealthy; (*Pol*) *activity etc* clandestine, underground; *agent* secret, undercover; *marriage* secret; runaway.
claque *nf* (*gall*) claque.
clara *nf* (a) white of an egg. (b) bald spot; (*in cloth*) bare patch, thin place. (c) (*Meteorol*) bright interval.
claraboya *nf* skylight.
claramente *adv* (a) brightly; clearly. (b) (*fig*) clearly, plainly.
clarea *nf* mulled wine.
clarear [1a] **1** *vt* (a) to brighten; to light up; *colour* to make lighter.
 (b) (*fig*) to clarify, make clear(er).
 (c) (*Mex*) — **a uno** to shoot someone through.
 2 *vi* (a) (*Meteorol*) to clear up, brighten up.
 (b) (*of day*) to dawn, break; to grow light.
 3 clarearse *vr* (a) (*cloth*) to be transparent, let the light through.
 (b) (*fam*) to give the game away.
clarete *nm* claret; rosé, light red wine.
claridad *nf* (a) brightness; light.
 (b) clearness, clarity; **lo explicó todo con mucha** — he explained it all very clearly.
 (c) —**es** sharp remarks, unpleasant remarks; home truths.
claridoso *adj* (*CAm, Mex*) blunt, plain-spoken.
clarificación *nf* (a) illumination, lighting (up). (b) (*fig*) clarification.
clarificar [1g] *vt* (a) to illuminate, light (up); to brighten.
 (b) *liquid* to clarify; to refine, purify.
 (c) *wood* to clear, thin out.
 (d) (*fig*) to clarify.
clarín *nm* bugle, trumpet; (*esp fig*) clarion.
clarinada *nf* (*fam*) uncalled-for remark.
clarinazo *nm* (*fig*) trumpet call.
clarinete *nm* clarinet.
clarión *nm* chalk, white crayon.
clarividencia *nf* (a) clairvoyance. (b) (*fig*) far-sightedness; discernment; intuition.
clarividente 1 *adj* far-sighted, far-seeing; discerning; gifted with intuition. **2** *nmf* clairvoyant(e).
claro 1 *adj* (a) *day, light, eyes etc* bright; *room* light, bright, well-lit.
 (b) *water* clear, transparent; *glass* clear.
 (c) *beer, colour* light; **verde** — light green; **una tela verde** — a light-green cloth.
 (d) *outline, writing etc* clear, distinct; bold; **tan** — **como la luz del día** as plain as a pikestaff; **más** — **que el sol** as clear as daylight.
 (e) (*in consistency*) *liquid* thin; *tea etc* weak; *hair* thin, sparse.
 (f) *sound, voice* clear.

 (g) *explanation, language, proof etc* clear; plain, evident; **todo queda muy** — it's all very clear; ¡—! naturally!, of course!; ¡**pues** —! I quite agree with you!; ¡— **que sí!** yes of course!; ¡— **que no!** of course not!; — **que no es verdad** of course it isn't true; **está** — **que** . . . it is plain that . . ., it is obvious that . . .; **a las claras** clearly, plainly; openly.
 (h) (*fig*) famous, illustrious; noble.
 2 *adv* clearly; **hablar** — (*fig*) to speak plainly, speak bluntly.
 3 *nm* (a) **poner algo en** — to explain something, clear up something, clarify something; (*SAm*) to copy something out; **no sacamos nada en** — we couldn't get anything definite; there were no concrete decisions.
 (b) **pasar la noche en** — to have a sleepless night.
 (c) **de** — **en** — obviously, plainly; from dusk to dawn.
 (d) opening; gap, break, space; (*in wood*) opening, clearing, glade; (*in traffic etc*) gap, break.
 (e) (*Archit*) light, window; skylight.
 (f) (*Art*) highlight; light tone.
 (g) (*Naut*) break in the clouds; (*CAm*) bright interval.
 (h) (*Cu*) guava jelly; (*Ven*) sugar-cane brandy.
claroscuro *nm* chiaroscuro.
clase 1 *nf* (a) (*in general*) class; kind, sort; **con toda** — **de** with all kinds of, with every sort of, with all manner of; **gente de toda** — people of every kind, all sorts of people; **de esta** — of this kind; **de otra** — of another sort; **de una misma** — of the same kind; **de primera** — first-class; **os deseo toda** — **de felicidades** I wish you every kind of happiness.
 (b) (*transport, vehicles*) class; **primera** — first class; — **de cámara,** — **intermedia** (*Naut*) cabin class; — **turista** tourist class.
 (c) (*School*) class; (*Univ*) lecture, class; — **de geografía** geography class, geography lesson; — **de conducción** driving lesson; **dar** —**s** to teach; **ella da** —**s de italiano** she gives Italian lessons; **faltar a** — to miss class, not go to class; **fumarse la** —, **soplarse la** — to play truant.
 (d) (*School*) classroom, (*Univ*) lecture room.
 (e) (*Pol*) class; — **alta** upper class; — **baja** lower class(es); — **media** middle class(es); — **obrera** working class; **de la** — **obrera** working-class (*attr*); **las** —**s poseyentes** the property-owning classes; **las** —**s pudientes** the well-to-do, the moneyed classes; **ser de la** — (*Ant: euph*) to belong to the black race, be a half-breed.
 (f) (*Mil*) —**s de tropa** non-commissioned officers.
 2 *adj* (*Col, Per*) first-rate, classy (*fam*); handsome.
clasicismo *nm* classicism.
clásico 1 *adj* (a) classical.
 (b) (*fig*) classic; outstanding, remarkable; *car etc* vintage; *institution* traditional, typical; *custom* time-honoured; **le dio el** — **saludo** he gave him the time-honoured salute; **es la clásica plazuela española** it is a typical Spanish square.
 2 *nm* (a) classic.
 (b) (*person*) classicist.
clasificable *adj* classifiable.
clasificación *nf* classification; (*Sport*) table, league; (*Naut*) rating; — **nacional del disco** (*equivalent to*) top twenty, record hit parade.
clasificador *nm* (a) classifier. (b) filing cabinet; — **de cartas** letter file.
clasificar [1g] **1** *vt* to classify (*en la B* under B); to grade, rate, class; *letters* to sort.
 2 clasificarse *vr* (a) (*Sport*) to win a place; to occupy a position; **Meca se clasificó después de la Ceca** Meca came after Ceca, Meca finished after Ceca; **¿dónde se clasificó el equipo local?** where did the home team come?
 (b) (*Sport*) to qualify; **no se clasificó el equipo para la final** the team did not qualify for the final.
clasista *adj* (*Pol*) class (*attr*).
claudia *nf* greengage.
claudicar [1g] *vi* (a) to limp. (b) (*fig*) to act deceitfully; to bungle it; to waver, stall. (c) (*fig*) to give way, abandon one's principles, back down.
claustro *nm* (a) (*Eccl etc*) cloister. (b) (*Univ*) staff, faculty (*US*); (*as assembly*) senate. (c) (*Anat*) — **materno** womb.
claustrofobia *nf* claustrophobia.
cláusula *nf* clause.
clausura *nf* (a) closing, closure; formal closing, closing ceremony. (b) (*Eccl*) monastic life; **convento de** — enclosed convent.

clausurar [1a] *vt* (a) to close, bring to a close; (*Parl etc*) to adjourn. (b) (*SAm*) *house etc* to close (up).

clava *nf* club, cudgel.

clavado *adj* (a) nailed; stuck fast, firmly fixed; **quedó — en la pared** it stuck in the wall, it remained fixed in the wall; **el reloj estaba — en las 7** the watch was stopped at 7. (b) studded with nails. (c) *dress* just right, exactly fitting. (d) **dejar a uno —** to leave someone speechless; **quedó —** he was dumbfounded. (e) **a las 5 clavadas** at 5 sharp, at 5 on the dot. (f) **es Domingo —** he's the living image of Domingo. (g) **¡—!** exactly!, precisely!

clavar [1a] **1** *vt* (a) *nail* to knock in, drive in, bang in; to fasten, fix; to pin; *boards etc* to nail together, nail up; *dagger, knife etc* to stick, thrust (*en* into), bury (*en* in); *gun* to spike; **— un anuncio a** (*or* **en**) **la puerta** to nail an announcement to the door. (b) *jewel* to set, mount. (c) *eyes, gaze* to fix (*en* on), rivet (*en* to). (d) (*fam*) to cheat, twist (*fam*); **me clavaron 50 dólares** they stung me for 50 dollars (*fam*). **2 clavarse** *vr* (a) (*of nail etc*) to penetrate, go in. (b) **— una astilla en el dedo** to get a splinter in one's finger; **— una espina** to prick oneself on a thorn; **se clavó el cuchillo en el pecho** he thrust the knife into his chest. (c) (*fig*) to be mistaken. (d) **—la** (*CAm*) to get drunk. (e) (*Mex*) **— algo** to steal something, pinch something (*fam*).

clave 1 *nf* (a) (*to code, classification etc*) key; **la — del problema** the key to the problem. (b) (*Chess*) key move. (c) (*Mus*) clef; **— de fa** bass clef; **— de sol** treble clef. (d) (*Archit*) keystone. **2** *nm* (*Mus*) harpsichord. **3** *adj, attr* key (*attr*); **cuestión —** key question; **posición —** key position.

clavecín *nm* spinet.

clavel *nm* carnation; **— de poeta, — de ramillete, — de San Isidro** sweet william.

clavelón *nm* marigold.

clavellina *nf* pink.

clavero[1] *nm* (*Bot*) clove tree.

clavero[2] *nm* keeper of the keys; treasurer, cashier.

claveteado *nm* studs, studding.

clavetear [1a] *vt* (a) *door etc* to stud, decorate with studs. (b) *shoelace etc* to put a metal tip on. (c) (*fig*) *deal etc* to clinch, close, wind up.

clavicémbalo *nm*, **clavicordio** *nm* clavichord.

clavícula *nf* collar bone, clavicle.

clavija *nf* peg, dowel, pin; (*Mus*) peg; (*Elec*) plug; **— hendida, — de dos patas** cotter pin; **apretar las —s a uno** to put the screws on someone (*fam*).

clavijero *nm* set of pegs, row of pegs; clothes rack.

clavillo *nm* (a) (*also* **clavito** *nm*) small nail, brad, tack, pin. (b) (*Bot*) clove.

clavo *nm* (a) (*Tech*) nail; tack; stud; spike; **— romano** brass-headed nail; **— de rosca** screw; **de — pasado** obvious, undeniable; easy; outworn, out-of-date; **verdad de — pasado** platitude, truism; **dar en el —** (*fig*) to hit the nail on the head; **remachar el —** (*fig*) to make matters worse; to add completely superfluous reasons. (b) (*Bot*) clove. (c) (*Med*) corn. (d) (*Med*) sharp pain; (*fig*) anguish, acute distress. (e) (*Hond, Mex*) rich vein of ore. (f) (*Arg, Bol*) unpleasant thing; nasty situation; (*Comm*) unsaleable article, drug on the market.

claxon *nm, pl* **claxons** ['klakson] (*Aut*) horn, hooter; **tocar el —** to sound one's horn, hoot.

claxonar [1a] *vi* (*Aut*) to sound one's horn, hoot.

claxonazo *nm* (*Aut*) hoot, toot (on the horn).

clemátide *nf* clematis.

clemencia *nf* mercy, clemency; leniency.

clemente *adj* merciful, clement; lenient.

cleptomanía *nf* kleptomania.

cleptómano *nm*, **cleptómana** *nf* kleptomaniac.

clerecía *nf* (a) priesthood. (b) (*persons*) clergy.

clergyman [klerxi'man] *nm* (*Eccl*) modernized form of priest's attire (*adopted in Spain 1966*).

clerical 1 *adj* clerical. **2** *nm* (*CAm, Pan, PR*) clergyman.

clericalismo *nm* clericalism.

clericato *nm*, **clericatura** *nf* priesthood.

clericó *nm* (*RPl: angl*) fruit cup.

clérigo *nm* (*Catholic*) priest; (*Anglican*) clergyman, priest; (*other*) minister.

clero *nm* clergy.

cliché *nm* (a) (*Typ*) stencil. (b) (*Lit*) cliché; *see* **clisé.**

cliente *nmf* (*Comm*) client, customer; (*Law*) client; (*Med*) patient.

clientela *nf* (*Comm*) clients, clientèle, customers; (*Med*) practice; patients.

clima *nm* climate.

climatérico *adj* climacteric.

climático *adj* climatic.

climatología *nf* climatology.

clímax ['klimas] *nm, pl* **clímax** (*all senses*) climax.

clinch [klinʃ] *nm* (*SAm: angl*), **clincha** *nf* (*angl*) clinch.

clínica *nf* (a) clinic; private hospital, nursing home; teaching hospital; **— de reposo** convalescent home. (b) clinical training.

clínico *adj* clinical.

clip *nm, pl* **clips** [klis] (*angl*) paper clip; trouser clip; (*jewel*) clip; (*SAm*) earring.

clíper *nm* (*Naut: angl*) clipper.

clisar [1a] *vt* to stereotype, stencil.

clisé *nm* (*Typ*) cliché, stereotype plate; stencil, skin; (*Phot*) plate.

clisos *nmpl* (*sl*) eyes, peepers (*sl*).

clo *nm* cluck; **hacer —** to cluck.

cloaca *nf* sewer (*also fig*); drain.

cloquear [1a] *vi* to cluck.

cloqueo *nm* clucking.

cloral *nm* chloral.

clorhídrico *adj* hydrochloric.

clorinar [1a] *vt* to chlorinate.

cloro *nm* chlorine.

clorofila *nf* chlorophyl(l).

cloroformar [1a] *vt* (*Arg, Chi, Mex, PR*), **cloroformizar** [1f] *vt* to chloroform.

cloroformo *nm* chloroform.

cloruro *nm* chloride; **— de cal** chloride of lime.

clown [klawn] *nm, pl* **clowns** [klawn] (*angl*) clown.

club [klu *or* kluβ] *nm, pl* **clubs** [klus *or* kluβs] *and* **clubes** (*SAm*) (a) club; **— campestre** country club; **— nocturno** night club. (b) (*Aut*) saloon car, sedan (*US*).

clueca *nf* broody hen.

clueco *adj* (a) hen broody. (b) (*Arg*) sickly, unwell. (c) (*Ant*) stuck-up (*fam*).

cluniacense 1 *adj* Cluniac. **2** *nm* Cluniac.

co . . . co . . .

coa *nf* (a) (*Cu, Mex, Pan, Ven*) pointed stick used in digging (*or* sowing). (b) (*Chi*) underworld slang.

coacción *nf* coercion, compulsion; duress.

coaccionar [1a] *vt* to coerce, compel, put great pressure on.

coactivo *adj* coercive; compelling.

coadjutor *nm*, **coadjutora** *nf* assistant, coadjutor.

coadjuvar [1a] *vt* to help, assist; to help in, contribute to.

coagulación *nf* coagulation; clotting; curdling.

coagulante *nm* coagulant.

coagular [1a] **1** *vt* to coagulate; to clot, congeal; *milk* to curdle. **2 coagularse** *vr* to coagulate; to clot, congeal; to curdle.

coágulo *nm* coagulated mass; clot; congealed lump.

coalición *nf* coalition; **gobierno de —** coalition government.

coartada *nf* alibi.

coartar [1a] *vt* to limit, restrict.

coautor *nm*, **coautora** *nf* co-author.

coba *nf* (*fam*) (a) fib; neat trick. (b) soft soap (*sl*); cajolery; **dar — a uno** to soap someone up (*sl*), soft-soap someone (*sl*), play up to someone; to bamboozle someone (*fam*).

cobalto *nm* cobalt.

cobarde 1 *adj* cowardly; fainthearted, timid. **2** *nmf* coward.

cobardear [1a] *vi* to be a coward, show cowardice, act in a cowardly way.

cobardía *nf* cowardliness; faintheartedness, timidity.

cobardón *nm* shameful coward, great coward.

cobaya *nf*, **cobayo** *nm* guinea pig.

cobertera *nf* (a) lid, cover; watchcase. (b) (*Bot*) white water lily. (c) procuress.

cobertizo *nm* shed, outhouse, lean-to; shelter; covered passage; **— de aviación** hangar; **— de coche** carport.

cobertor *nm* bedspread, coverlet.

cobertura *nf* (a) cover, covering. (b) bedspread. (c) **— del seguro** insurance cover.

cobija *nf* (a) (*Archit*) coping tile, imbrex. (b) (*SAm*) poncho, blanket; **—s** bedclothes. (c) (*Cu, PR*) roof (of palm leaves).

cobijar [1a] **1** *vt* **(a)** to cover (up), close in. **(b)** to protect, shelter; to take in, give shelter to, (*pej*) harbour. **(c)** (*Ant, Ec*) to thatch, roof. **2 cobijarse** *vr* to take shelter.

cobijo *nm* **(a)** shelter, lodging. **(b)** (*fig*) cover.

cobista (*fam*) **1** *adj* soapy, smarmy (*fam*). **2** *nm* soapy individual, smarmy sort (*fam*).

cobo *nm* (*Ant*) **(a)** (*Zool*) sea snail. **(b)** unsociable person, shy person.

cobra[1] *nf* (*Zool*) cobra.

cobra[2] *nf* (*Hunting*) retrieval.

cobrable *adj*, **cobradero** *adj* **(a)** retrievable. **(b)** (*Comm*) *price* chargeable; *sum* recoverable.

cobrador *nm* **(a)** (*Comm*) collector. **(b)** (*of bus etc*) conductor. **(c)** (*dog*) retriever.

cobradora *nf* conductress, clippie (*fam*).

cobranza *nf* **(a)** = **cobro**. **(b)** (*Hunting*) retrieval.

cobrar [1a] **1** *vt* **(a)** *lost object* to recover; (*Hunting*) to retrieve, fetch, bring back; *rope* to take in, pull in; *blow* to receive.
(b) *price* to charge; **cobran 200 dólares por componerlo** they charge 200 dollars to repair it; **¿cuánto me va Vd a —?** what are you doing to charge me?; **me han cobrado demasiado** they've charged me too much, they've overcharged me.
(c) *sum* to collect, receive; *cheque* to cash; *salary, wages* to earn; to draw, get, collect; **¿cuánto cobras al año?** how much do you get a year?, how much do they pay you a year?; **fue a la oficina a — el sueldo** he went to the office to get his wages; **cantidades por —** sums payable, sums due; **cuenta por —** unpaid bill.
(d) (*SAm*) **— a uno** to press someone for payment.
(e) *flesh* to put on.
(f) *credit, fame etc* to get, acquire, gain; *courage* to summon up, muster; *strength* to gather; **— cariño a uno** to take a liking to someone, grow fond of someone; **— fama de** to acquire a reputation as (*or* for being).
2 *vi* **(a)** (*Fin*) to draw one's pay, get one's wages; to collect one's salary; **cobra los viernes** he gets paid on Fridays; **te pagaré en cuanto cobre** I'll pay you when I get my wages.
(b) **— al número llamado** (*Tel*) to reverse the charges.
(c) (*fam*) **¡vas a —!** you'll cop it! (*sl*).
3 cobrarse *vr* **(a)** (*Med*) to recover, get well; to come to.
(b) **— de una pérdida** to make up for a loss.

cobre *nm* **(a)** copper.
(b) (*Cook*) copper pans, kitchen utensils.
(c) (*Mus*) brass (*also* —s); **batir(se) el —** to work hard, work with a will; to hustle; (*in argument*) to get worked up; **batirse el — por** + *infin* to go all out to + *infin*.
(d) (*SAm*) cent, small copper coin; **enseñar el —** (*Col, Mex*) to show one's nasty side.

cobreado *adj* copperplated.

cobreño *adj* copper (*attr*), coppery.

cobrero *nm* coppersmith.

cobrizo *adj* coppery.

cobro *nm* **(a)** recovery, retrieval.
(b) (*Fin*) collection; payment; **cargo por —** collection charge; **deuda de — difícil** debt that is hard to collect; **— a la entrega** collect on delivery; **poner al** (*or* en) **—** to make payable; *bill* to send out.
(c) *safe place*; **poner algo en —** to put something in a safe place, put something out of harm's way; **ponerse en —** to take refuge, get to safety.

coca[1] *nf* (*fam*) **(a)** head, nut (*sl*). **(b)** rap on the nut. **(c)** (*of hair*) bun, coil. **(d)** (*in rope*) kink.

coca[2] *nf* **(a)** (*SAm: Bot*) coca; coca tea. **(b)** (*Mex*) **de —** free, gratis; vainly.

coca[3] *nf* (*SD, Ven*) bogeyman.

cocacolo *nm*, **cocacola** *nf* (*Col*) frivolous teenager, idle young person.

cocacho *nm* (*Arg, Bol*) tap on the head.

cocaína *nf* cocaine.

cocal *nm* (*Per, PR, Ven*) coca plantation.

cocción *nf* (*Cook*) cooking; (*Tech*) baking, firing.

cocear [1a] *vti* to kick (*also fig*).

cocer [2b *and* 2h] **1** *vt* **(a)** (*Cook*) to cook; to boil; to bake.
(b) (*Tech*) *bricks etc* to bake, fire.
2 *vi* **(a)** to cook; to boil; to bubble, seethe; (*of wine*) to ferment.
3 cocerse *vr* (*fig*) to suffer intensely, be in great pain.

cocido 1 *adj* **(a)** boiled, cooked; **bien —** well done.

(b) skilled, experienced; **estar — en** to be skilled at, be expert at.
2 *nm* stew (*in Spain: of meat, bacon, chickpeas etc*); **— irlandés** Irish stew; **ganarse el —** to earn one's living; to eke out a living.

cociente *nm* quotient; **— intelectual** intelligence quotient, IQ.

cocina *nf* **(a)** (*room*) kitchen; **de —** kitchen (*attr*).
(b) stove, cooker; **— económica** cooker, range, boiler; **— eléctrica** electric cooker; **— a gas, — de gas** gas stove, gas cooker; **— de petróleo** oil stove.
(c) (*art*) cooking, cookery; cuisine; **— casera** plain cooking, homely cooking; **la — valenciana** Valencian cooking, the Valencian cuisine; **libro de —** cookery book, cookbook (*US*).

cocinar [1a] **1** *vt* to cook. **2** *vi* **(a)** to cook, do the cooking. **(b)** (*fig*) to meddle.

cocinero *nm*, **cocinera** *nf* cook.

cocinilla *nf* **(a)** small kitchen, kitchenette. **(b)** small cooker; spirit stove; chafing dish.

cocker ['kokeɹ] *nm* (*angl*) cocker (spaniel).

cocktel *nm*, *pl* **cocktels** *or* **cóckteles** (*angl*) = **cóctel**.

coco[1] *nm* (*Med*) coccus; (*Ent*) grub, maggot.

coco[2] *nm* **(a)** bogeyman; **parece un —** he's an ugly devil.
(b) face, grimace; **hacer —s a uno** to make faces at someone, (*lovers*) make eyes at someone; **to coax someone, wheedle someone.**

coco[3] **1** *nm* **(a)** (*Bot*) coconut; coconut palm.
(b) (*hum*) nut (*sl*), noddle (*fam*).
(c) (*SAm*) cup (*etc*) made from a coconut shell.
(d) (*Col, Ec*) derby hat.
(e) (*Per, Urug*) percale.
2 *adj* (*Ant*) **(a)** hard, strong.
(b) obstinate.

cococha *nf* (*of cod etc*) barbel.

cocodrilo *nm* crocodile.

cocoliche *nm* (*RPl*) macaronic slang of Italian immigrants; Italian.

cocoliste *nm* (*Mex*) infectious disease; sunstroke.

cócona *nf* (*Cu*) tip.

coconote *nm* (*Mex*) child; chubby child; squat person.

cócora *nmf* **(a)** (*fam*) bore. **(b)** (*Arg*) conceited person.

cocoroco *adj* (*Chi*) vain, stuck-up (*fam*); brazen.

cocoso *adj* maggoty, worm-eaten.

cocotal *nm* coconut grove, coconut plantation.

cocotero *nm* coconut palm.

coctel *nm*, **cóctel** ['koktel *or* 'kotel] *nm*, *pl* **coctels** *or* **cócteles** (*angl*) **(a)** cocktail.
(b) cocktail party; **ofrecer un — en honor de uno** to hold a cocktail party in someone's honour.

coctelera *nf* cocktail shaker.

cocuyo *nm* (*SAm*) firefly.

cocha *nf* (*Chi, Ec*) pool; swamp; lagoon.

cochambre *nm* muck, filth; litter; filthy thing, disgusting object; (*fig*) muck, rubbish.

cochambroso *adj* filthy, nauseating, stinking; (*fig*) vile.

cochayuyo *nm* (*Bol, Chi, Per*) seaweed.

coche[1] *nm* **(a)** (*Aut*) car, motorcar, automobile (*US*); **— ambulancia** ambulance; **— de alquiler** taxi, cab; hire car; **— blindado** armoured car; **— de bomberos** fire engine; **— de carreras** racing car; **— celular** Black Maria, prison van; **—s de choque** dodgem cars; **— deportivo** sports car; **— de época** vintage car; **— fúnebre** hearse; **— de punto** taxi; **— de turismo** saloon car, sedan (*US*); tourer; **ir en —** to go by car; to drive, motor; **ir en el — de San Fernando** to go on Shank's pony, ride Shank's mare.
(b) (*Rail*) coach, car, carriage; **— directo** through carriage; **— de equipajes** luggage van, baggage car (*US*); **— de viajeros** passenger coach.
(c) (*Hist*) coach, carriage.

coche[2] *nm* (*CAm, Mex*) pig, hog; **— de monte** wild pig.

coche-cabina *nm*, *pl* **coches-cabina** bubble car.

coche-cama *nm*, *pl* **coches-cama** sleeping car, sleeper.

cochecillo *nm* small carriage (*etc*); **— de inválido** invalid carriage.

cochecito *nm* **(a)** pram, perambulator, baby carriage (*US*); **— de niño** go-cart. **(b)** (*Aut*) bubble car.

coche-comedor *nm*, *pl* **coches-comedor** dining car, restaurant car.

coche-correo *nm*, *pl* **coches-correo** (*Rail*) mail van, mobile sorting office.

coche-cuba *nm*, *pl* **coches-cuba** tank lorry, water wagon.

coche-habitación *nm*, *pl* **coches-habitación** caravan, trailer.

coche-patrulla *nm*, *pl* **coches-patrulla** patrol car.

cochera *nf* **(a)** coach house; — **de alquiler** livery stable. **(b)** (*Aut*) garage, carport. **(c)** — **de tranvías** tram shed, tram depot.

cocherada *nf* (*Mex*) coarse expression.

coche-restaurante *nm*, *pl* **coches-restaurante** dining car, restaurant car.

cochero 1 *adj*: **puerta cochera** carriage entrance. **2** *nm* coachman; — **de punto** cabman, cabby (*fam*; **hablar (en)** — (*Mex*) to use coarse language.

cocherón *nm* (*Rail*) engine shed, locomotive depot.

coche-salón *nm*, *pl* **coches-salón** (*Rail*) saloon coach.

coches-tope *nmpl* dodgem cars.

coche-vivienda *nm*, *pl* **coches-vivienda** caravan, trailer.

cochina *nf* sow.

cochinada *nf* **(a)** filth, filthiness.
(b) filthy object, dirty thing.
(c) (*fig*) beastly thing (to do); filthy act, filthy word; dirty trick; **eso fue una** — that was a beastly thing to do; **hacer una** — **a uno** to play a dirty trick on someone.

cochinear [1a] *vi* (*fam*) to talk smut, tell dirty stories, wallow in filth.

cochinería *nf* = **cochinada**.

cochinilla *nf* **(a)** (*Zool*) woodlouse. **(b)** (*Ent, colouring*) cochineal. **(c) de** — (*Cu, Mex*) trivial.

cochinillo *nm* piglet, sucking-pig.

cochino 1 *adj* **(a)** filthy, dirty.
(b) (*fig*) filthy, rotten, measly (*fam*); **esta vida cochina** this wretched life.
2 *nm* **(a)** pig; — **de leche** sucking-pig; — **montés** wild pig.
(b) (*fig*) hog; swine; filthy person; **realmente es un** — he really is a swine.

cochiquera *nf*, **cochitril** *nm* pigsty (*also fig*).

cochoso *adj* (*Col, Ec*) filthy.

cochura *nf* **(a)** (*act*) = **cocción**. **(b)** batch of loaves (*or* cakes, bricks *etc*).

codal *nm* **(a)** (*Bot*) vine shoot. **(b)** (*Archit*) strut, prop.

codaste *nm* stern post.

codazo *nm* **(a)** jab, poke, nudge (with one's elbow). **(b)** (*Mex*) tip, hint.

codeador *adj* (*Chi, Ec, Per*) bothersome, demanding.

codear [1a] *vt* **(a)** to elbow, nudge, jostle.
(b) (*Chi, Ec, Per*) — **a uno** to make insistent requests to someone, keep dropping hints to someone.
2 *vi* **(a)** to elbow, jostle; **abrirse paso codeando** to elbow one's way through.
(b) (*Chi, Ec, Per*) to beg persistently, sponge.
3 codearse *vr*: — **con** to hobnob with, rub shoulders with.

codeína *nf* codeine.

codeo *nm* (*Chi, Ec, Per*) sponging (*fam*).

codeso *nm* laburnum.

códice *nm* manuscript, codex.

codicia *nf* greed, covetousness; — **de** greed for, lust for.

codiciable *adj* covetable, desirable; enviable.

codiciado *adj* widely desired; much in demand; sought-after, coveted; **obtuvo el** — **título** he won the coveted title.

codiciar [1b] *vt* to covet.

codicilo *nm* codicil.

codiciosamente *adv* greedily, covetously.

codicioso *adj* greedy, covetous; **ser** — **de** to be greedy for, covet; **estoy** — **de verte** I am very eager to see you.

codificación *nf* codification.

codificar [1g] *vt* to codify.

código *nm* **(a)** (*Law etc*) code; law, statute; rules, set of rules; — **de (la) circulación** highway code; — **de leyes** law code, statute book; — **militar** articles of war; — **penal** penal code.
(b) (*Tel etc*) code; **mensaje en** — message in code, coded message; — **de señales** signal code.

codillo *nm* (*Zool*) knee; (*Bot*) stump; (*Tech*) elbow (joint), bend; angle iron.

codo *nm* **(a)** (*Anat*) elbow, (*Zool*) knee; **comerse los** —**s de hambre** to be utterly destitute; **dar con el** — **a uno, dar de(l)** — **a uno** to nudge someone; **empinar el** — to booze, drink; **hablar por los** —**s to** talk too much, talk 19 to the dozen; **llevar a uno** — **con** — to frogmarch someone along, drag someone along with his hands tied behind his back; (*fig*) to arrest someone; **mentir por los** —**s** to tell huge lies; **morderse el** — (*Mex, RPl*) to restrain oneself; **ser del** —, **ser duro de** — (*CAm*) to be a tight-wad.
(b) (*Tech*) elbow (joint), bend; angle iron.
(c) (*fig*) elbow grease; **hacer más** —**s** to put more

elbow grease into it; **sacó la oposición a base de** —**s** he won the post by sheer hard work.

codorniz *nf* quail.

coeducación *nf* coeducation.

coeducacional *adj* coeducational.

coeficiente *nm* coefficient; — **de inteligencia** intelligence quotient, IQ.

coercer [2b] *vt* to coerce, constrain; to restrain.

coerción *nf* coercion, constraint; restraint.

coercitivo *adj* coercive.

coetáneo 1 *adj* contemporary (*con* with). **2** *nm*, **coetánea** *nf* contemporary.

coevo *adj* coeval.

coexistencia *nf* coexistence; — **pacífica** peaceful coexistence.

coexistente *adj* coexistent.

coexistir [3a] *vi* to coexist (*con* with).

cofa *nf* (*Naut*) top; — **mayor** maintop.

cofia *nf* (*of nurse, servant etc*) cap, white cap; (*arch*) coif; bonnet.

cofrade *nm* member (of a brotherhood), brother.

cofradía *nf* brotherhood, fraternity; guild, association; (*of thieves etc*) gang.

cofre *nm* chest; case (for jewels *etc*).

cofrecito *nm* casket.

cogedero 1 *adj* fruit ripe, ready to be picked. **2** *nm* handle.

cogedor *nm* small shovel, ash shovel; dustpan.

coger [2c] **1** *vt* **(a)** *handle, object etc* to take hold of, catch hold of; to seize, grasp; to hold on to; *ball etc* to catch; *fallen object* to pick up; *dress etc* to gather up, hold up; *book etc* to pick up, take up; *tool* (*fig*) to hold, use; — **a uno de la mano** to take someone by the hand; **ir cogidos de la mano** to go hand-in-hand, (*lovers*) to go along holding hands; **no ha cogido un fusil en la vida** he's never held a gun in his life.
(b) to take, pinch (*fam*); **me coge siempre las cerillas** he always takes my matches; **en la aduana le cogieron una radio** they found a radio on him in the customs, they confiscated a radio from him in the customs.
(c) *flower, fruit etc* to pick, pluck; to harvest; to gather, collect.
(d) *person etc* to catch; (*Law*) to arrest; (*Mil*) to take prisoner; *prisoner* to take, capture; *animal* to catch, capture, trap; *fish* to catch; *runner etc* to catch (up with); **¡por fin te he cogido!** caught you at last!; — **un buen marido** to catch oneself (*or* get, acquire) a good husband; — **a uno en una mentira** to catch someone in a lie; **la noche nos cogió todavía en el mar** the night caught us still at sea; **la guerra nos cogió en Francia** the war caught us in France; **antes que nos coja la noche** before night overtakes us (*or* comes down on us); — **a uno en la hora tonta**, — **a uno detrás de la puerta** to catch someone at a disadvantage; *see also* **desprevenido** *etc*.
(e) (*of bull*) to gore; to toss; (*of car*) to knock down, run over.
(f) — **los dedos en la puerta** to catch one's fingers in the door.
(g) *tip etc* to take, accept; *work* to take on; *news etc* to take, receive; **cogió la noticia sin interés** he received the news without interest.
(h) *course, period, work etc* to begin on; **cogí la conferencia a mitad** I joined the discussion halfway through.
(i) to get, obtain, acquire; **he cogido el billete del avión** I've got my air ticket; **cógeme un puesto en la cola** get me a place in the queue; **acabo de** — **una cocinera nueva** I've got a new cook.
(j) *disease, cold etc* to catch; *dust* to gather, collect; *habit* to get, get into, catch, acquire; **el niño cogió sarampión** the child got (*or* caught) measles; **los perros cogen pulgas** dogs get fleas; **ha cogido la manía de las quinielas** he's caught the pools craze.
(k) (*of emotion*) to take; — **cariño a** to take a liking to; — **celos a** to become jealous of; — **aversión a** to take a strong dislike to.
(l) *sense, meaning* to get, understand; *spoken words* to catch; *radio* to pick up, get; *expression* to pick up; *accent* to catch, acquire; *technique* to pick up, learn; **con esta radio cogemos Praga** with this set we can get Prague.
(m) *notes etc* to take down; **le cogieron el discurso taquigráficamente** they took his speech down in shorthand.
(n) to choose, pick; **has cogido un mal momento** you've picked a bad time.
(o) *means of transport* to take, catch, go by; **vamos a** — **el tren** let's take the train.

(p) (*of container*) to hold, take; *area* to cover, extend over, take up.

(q) (*Arg, Bol, Cu, Mex, Par, Urug:* tabu) to lay (*tabu*), screw (*tabu*).

2 *vi* **(a)** (*Bot*) to take, strike.

(b) to fit, go, have room; **aquí no coge** it doesn't fit in here, there's no room for it here.

3 cogerse *vr* **(a)** to catch; **— los dedos en la puerta** to catch one's fingers in the door; **— a uno** to cling tight to someone, press close against someone.

(b) **— algo** to steal something, pinch something (*fam*).

(c) **— con uno** (*PR, SD*) to get on (well) with someone; **— en algo** to get involved in something; to get used to something.

cogestión *nf* co-partnership (*in industry etc*).

cogida *nf* **(a)** (*Agr*) gathering, picking; harvesting; (*of fish*) catch. **(b)** (*Taur*) goring, tossing; **tener una —** to be gored, be tossed.

cogido *nm* (*Sew*) fold, gather, tuck.

cogienda *nf* **(a)** (*Col, Ven*) = **cogida (a)**; (*Mil*) forced enlistment. **(b)** (*Arg, Mex:* tabu) screwing (*tabu*).

cognado 1 *adj* cognate. **2** *nm* cognate.

cognición *nf* cognition.

cogollo *nm* **(a)** (*of plant*) shoot, sprout; (*of lettuce, cabbage*) heart; (*of tree*) top; (*SAm*) top of sugar cane.

(b) (*fig*) best part, cream; **el — de la sociedad** the cream of society.

(c) (*fig*) centre, core, nucleus.

cogotazo *nm* blow on the back of the neck; (*Boxing etc*) rabbit punch.

cogote *nm* back of the neck, nape; **de — (***RPl*) **animal** fat; **carne de — (***Chi, RPl*) trash; **ponérselas en el — (***CAm*) to beat it (*fam*).

cogotudo *adj* (*Chi, Per, RPl*) well heeled (*sl*), moneyed; (*SD*) powerful in politics.

cogulla *nf* cowl.

cohabitación *nf* cohabitation.

cohabitar [1a] *vi* to live together, cohabit (*also pej*).

cohechar [1a] *vt* to bribe, offer a bribe to.

cohecho *nm* bribe, bribery.

coheredera *nf* coheiress.

coheredero *nm* coheir, joint heir.

coherencia *nf* coherence; (*Phys etc*) cohesion.

coherente *adj* coherent.

cohesión *nf* cohesion.

cohesivo *adj* cohesive.

cohete *nm* **(a)** rocket; **— espacial** (space) rocket; **— luminoso, — de señales** flare, star shell, distress signal.

(b) (*CAm, Mex*) pistol; (*Mex*) blasting fuse; (*Mex*) blast hole; **—s** (*Mex*) fireworks (*in general*).

(c) (*Bol, RPl*) **al —** in vain; without rhyme or reason.

cohetería *nf* rocketry.

cohibición *nf* restraint; inhibition.

cohibido *adj* restrained, restricted; (*in temperament*) inhibited, full of inhibitions; shy, timid, self-conscious; ill at ease; **sentirse —** to feel shy, feel embarrassed.

cohibir [3a] **1** *vt* to restrain, check, restrict; to inhibit; to make uneasy, make shy, embarrass.

2 cohibirse *vr* to feel inhibited; to get uneasy, to become shy, feel embarrassed.

cohombro *nm* cucumber.

cohonestar [1a] *vt* **(a)** to explain away, whitewash, make appear reasonable. **(b)** *two qualities etc* to blend, harmonize.

cohorte *nf* cohort.

coima *nf* **(a)** concubine. **(b)** (*of gambling operator*) rake-off (*fam*). **(c)** (*Chi, Per, RPl*) bribe.

coime *nm* **(a)** pimp, ponce. **(b)** gambling operator. **(c)** (*Col*) waiter.

coimero *adj* (*Chi, Per, RPl*) easily bribed, given to taking bribes.

coincidencia *nf* **(a)** coincidence. **(b)** agreement; **en — con** in agreement with.

coincidente *adj* coincidental.

coincidir [3a] *vi* **(a)** to coincide (*con* with). **(b)** to coincide, agree; **todos coinciden en que...** everybody agrees that...

coito *nm* intercourse, coitus.

cojear [1a] *vi* **(a)** (*person*) to limp, hobble (along); to be lame (*de* in); (*furniture*) to wobble, rock, be rocky; **cojean del mismo pie** they both have the same faults; **sabemos de qué pie cojea** we know his weak spots (*or* weaknesses).

(b) (*fig*) to slip up, be at fault (*de* in); to deviate from virtue.

cojera *nf* lameness; limp.

cojijo *nm* **(a)** bug, small insect. **(b)** (*fig*) peeve (*fam*), grudge, grumble.

cojijoso *adj* peevish, cross, grumpy.

cojín *nm* cushion.

cojinete *nm* **(a)** small cushion, pad.

(b) (*Mech*) **— a bolas, — de bolas** ball bearing; **— de rodillos** roller bearing.

(c) (*Rail etc*) chair.

(d) **—s** (*Col, Mex, Ven*) saddlebags.

cojinillos *nmpl* (*CAm, Mex*) saddlebags.

cojo 1 *adj* **(a)** *person* lame; crippled; limping; *furniture* wobbly, rocky; **— de un pie** lame in one foot.

(b) (*fig*) lame, weak, shaky; **así el verso queda —** so the line is defective; **la frase está coja** the sentence is incomplete.

2 *nm*, **coja** *nf* lame person, cripple.

cojón *nm* (*tabu*) ball (*tabu*), testicle; **¡—es!** balls!; **¡hace falta tener —es!** you've got to have guts; **es un tipo sin —es** he's a gutless individual.

cojonudo *adj* **(a)** marvellous, splendid; **¡qué —!** great stuff! (*fam*). **(b)** (*SAm*) brave, bold. **(c)** (*SAm*) lazy, slow, stupid.

cojudo *adj* **(a)** (*Agr*) *animal* entire, not castrated; used for stud purposes. **(b)** (*Bol, Chi, Ec, Urug*) simple-minded, gullible; **hacerse el —** to act dumb.

cok [kok] *nm*, **coke** ['koke] *nm* (*SAm:* angl) coke.

col *nf* cabbage; **— de bruselas** (Brussels) sprouts; **— rizada** kale; **— roja** red cabbage; **— de Saboya** savoy; **entre — y —, lechuga** a change is a good thing, variety is the spice of life.

cola[1] *nf* **(a)** (*Aer, Astron, Orn, Zool*) tail.

(b) (*of coat*) tail; (*of dress*) train.

(c) (*position*) end, last place, bottom; tail end; end seat; **estar a la — de la clase** to be (at the) bottom of the class; **venir a la —** to come last, come at the back; **estar arrimado a la — (***Pol*) to be a reactionary; **vagón de —** last truck, rear coach.

(d) (*of cars, people etc*) queue, line; **hacer —** to queue (up), line up; **¡a la —!, ¡haga Vd—!** get in the queue!

(e) (*Tech*) **— de milano, — de pato** dovetail.

(f) (*fig*) **tener —, traer —** to have grave consequences.

cola[2] *nf* glue, gum; (*for painting*) size; **— de pescado** fish glue; isinglass; **— de retal** size; **pintura a la —** distemper; (*Art*) tempera; **comer — (***RPl*) to have a setback; **eso no pega ni con —** that has nothing whatsoever to do with it; that's utter rubbish.

colaboración *nf* **(a)** collaboration; **escrito en —** written in collaboration.

(b) (*to journal etc*) contribution (*a, en* to); (*to conference*) paper, communication.

colaboracionismo *nm* (*Pol: pej*) collaboration.

colaboracionista *nmf* (*Pol: pej*) collaborator, collaborationist.

colaborador *nm*, **colaboradora** *nf* collaborator, helper, co-worker; (*Lit etc*) contributor.

colaborar [1a] *vi* **(a)** to collaborate; to help, assist; **— con uno en un trabajo** to collaborate with someone on a piece of work.

(b) (*Lit etc*) **— a, — en** to contribute (articles) to, write for.

colación *nf* **(a)** collation, comparison; **sacar a —** to mention, bring up; to air; (*pej*) to drag in, drag up; **traer algo a —** to adduce something as proof.

(b) (*Cook*) collation (*also Eccl*); light meal, snack; buffet meal; reception, wedding breakfast; (*SAm*) sweet.

colacionar [1a] *vt* to collate, compare.

colada *nf* **(a)** wash, washing; **día de —** washing day; **tender la —** to hang out the washing. **(b)** bleach, lye. **(c)** (*Agr*) sheep run, cattle run; (*Geog*) defile.

coladera *nf* **(a)** strainer; colander. **(b)** (*Mex*) sewer.

coladero *nm*, **colador** *nm* strainer; colander.

colado *adj* **(a)** *metal* cast. **(b)** *aire* — draught. **(c)** (*fam*) **estar —** to be in love.

coladura *nf* **(a)** (*act*) straining. **(b)** **—s** grounds, dregs. **(c)** (*fam*) absurdity, piece of nonsense; blunder.

colapso *nm* **(a)** (*Med*) collapse; breakdown; **— nervioso** nervous breakdown. **(b)** (*fig*) collapse; breakdown; stoppage; ruin, destruction.

colar [1m] **1** *vt* **(a)** *coffee, vegetables etc* to strain (off); to filter; *metal* to cast, pour.

(b) *clothes* to bleach.

(c) **— algo por un sitio** to slip something through a place, squeeze something past a place; **— unos géneros por la aduana** to slip goods through the customs.

(d) **— algo a uno** to foist something off on someone, palm something off on someone; **— una moneda** to pass a (false) coin; **— una noticia a uno**

to make someone believe a (false) piece of news; **¡a mí no me la cuelas!** I'm not going to swallow that!, don't give me that stuff!

(e) (*Mex*) to drive, bore; *shaft* to sink.

2 *vi* (a) (*of liquid*) to ooze, seep (through), filter (through), percolate; (*of air*) to get in (*por* through).

(b) to pass; **esa noticia es demasiado sospechosa para** — that news item is too suspect to pass.

(c) (*fam*) to booze, tipple.

3 colarse *vr* (a) to slip in, slip past, squeeze in; (*at meeting etc*) to slip in, sneak in, get in unobserved; (*at party*) to gatecrash; **la moto se cuela por entre la circulación** the motorcycle slips through the traffic; **se ha colado algún indeseable** some undesirable has slipped in.

(b) to blunder, slip up; to put one's foot in it.

colateral *adj* collateral.

colca *nf* (*Per*) barn, granary; cotton store; attic food store.

colcrén *nm* (*angl*) cold cream.

colcha *nf* bedspread, counterpane.

colchón *nm* mattress; **— de aire** airbed; (*Tech*) air cushion; **— de muelles** spring mattress, interior sprung mattress; **— neumático** airbed; **— de plumas** feather bed.

cole *nm* (*fam*) = **colegio**.

colear [1a] **1** *vt* (a) (*Taur*) *bull* to grab by the tail, hold on to the tail of; (*Arg, Col, Mex, Ven*) to throw by twisting its tail.

(b) (*Col, Ven*) to vex, nag, harass; (*Guat*) to tail, follow.

2 *vi* (a) **el perro colea** the dog wags its tail.

(b) (*fig*) **el asunto todavía colea** the affair is still not settled; **estar vivito y coleando** to be still hale and hearty.

(c) (*CAm, PR*) **colea en los 50** he's close on 50, he's knocking on 50 (*fam*).

colección *nf* collection.

coleccionador *nm*, **coleccionadora** *nf* collector.

coleccionar [1a] *vti* to collect.

coleccionista *nmf* collector.

colecta *nf* (a) collection (for charity). (b) (*Eccl*) collect.

colectar [1a] *vt taxes etc* to collect.

colecticio *adj* (a) (*Mil*) raw, untrained. (b) **tomo —** omnibus edition, collected works.

colectivamente *adv* collectively.

colectivero *nm* (*Arg*) bus driver.

colectividad *nf* (a) sum total, whole; unit, group, community; **la —** social society, the whole community. (b) (*Pol*) collective ownership.

colectivizar [1f] *vt* to collectivize.

colectivo 1 *adj* collective (*also Gram*); **acción colectiva** joint action, group action, communal action. **2** *nm* (*Bol, RPl*) (small) bus.

colector *nm* (a) (*person*) collector. (b) (*Elec*) collector; (*Mech*) sump; trap, container; sewer.

colega *nm* colleague.

colegial 1 *adj* (a) school (*attr*), college (*attr*). (b) (*Eccl*) collegiate. (c) (*Mex*) raw, inexperienced. **2** *nm* schoolboy; (*fig*) inexperienced person, callow youth.

colegiala *nf* schoolgirl.

colegiata *nf* collegiate church.

colegio *nm* (a) independent secondary school, private (*or* fee-paying) high school; **— de párvulos** kindergarten, primary school; **— integrado** comprehensive school; **— de internos** boarding school; **— de pago** fee-paying school; **ir al —** to go to school.

(b) (*Univ*) college; **— mayor** (*Hist*) college (*eg of Salamanca or Oxford*), (*modern*) hall of residence.

(c) (*other*) **— de abogados** bar association; **C— de cardenales** College of Cardinals; **— electoral** electoral college.

colegir [3c *and* 3l] *vt* (a) to collect, gather. (b) to infer, gather, conclude (*de* from); **de lo cual colijo que . . .** from which I gather that . . .

coleóptero *nm* beetle.

cólera 1 *nf* (a) anger, rage; **descargar la — en** to vent one's anger on; **montar en —** to get angry. (b) (*Anat*) bile. **2** *nm* (*Med*) cholera.

colérico *adj* angry, furious, irate; (*by nature*) irascible, bad-tempered.

coleta *nf* (a) pigtail; **gente de —** bullfighters, bullfighting people; **cortarse la —** to quit the ring, give up bullfighting; (*fig*) to quit, give it all up, retire. (b) (*fam*) postscript, afterthought.

coletazo *nm* (a) (*Zool etc*) lash, blow with the tail. (b) (*of vehicle*) sway, swaying movement; **dar —s** to sway about.

(c) (*fig*) sting in the tail; unexpected after-effect.

coletero *nm* wren.

coleto *nm* (a) (*Hist*) doublet, jerkin.

(b) (*fam*) body; oneself; **decir para su —** to say to oneself; **echarse algo al —** to eat something right up; to drink something down; **echarse un libro al —** to read a book right through, devour a book.

colgadero *nm* hook, hanger, peg.

colgadizo 1 *adj* hanging, loose. **2** *nm* lean-to shed; (*Ant*) flat roof.

colgado *adj and ptp* (a) uncertain, doubtful.

(b) **dejar — a uno** to let someone down, fail someone; **quedarse —** to be disappointed; **antes le veré — que . . .** I'll see him damned before . . .

colgadura *nf* (*also* **—s**) hangings, drapery; tapestry; **—s de cama** bed hangings, bed curtains.

colgajo *nm* (a) rag, tatter, shred. (b) (*Bot*) bunch. (c) (*Med*) flap of flesh.

colgante 1 *adj* hanging; droopy, floppy; dangling; **puente —** suspension bridge; **con la lengua —** with his tongue hanging out.

2 *nm* (a) drop, pendant, earring; (*Arg, Par, PR*) watch chain.

(b) (*Archit*) festoon.

(c) **—s** fringe.

(d) **—s** (*tabu*) balls (*tabu*).

colgar [1h *and* 1m] **1** *vt* (a) *picture etc* to hang (up) (*de* from, *en* on); *person* to hang; *flag, washing etc* to hang out.

(b) *wall* to decorate with hangings, drape (*de* with).

(c) to attribute, impute (*a* to); **— la culpa a uno** to pin the blame on someone.

(d) (*Univ sl*) to plough (*sl*).

2 *vi* to hang, be suspended (*de* on, from); (*of ears etc*) to hang down, droop, dangle; (*Tel*) to hang up, ring off.

colibrí *nm* hummingbird.

cólico *nm* colic.

colicuar [1d] **1** *vt* to melt, dissolve; to fuse. **2 colicuarse** *vr* to melt, dissolve, liquefy.

coliflor *nf* cauliflower.

coligado 1 *adj:* **estar coligados** to be allied, be in league. **2** *nm* ally, confederate.

coligarse [1h] *vr* to unite, join together, make common cause (*con* with).

colilla *nf* fag end; butt, stub.

colimbo *nm* grebe.

colín *nm* (*Ant*) machete, cane knife.

colina *nf* hill.

colindante *adj* adjacent, adjoining, neighbouring.

colindar [1a] *vi* to adjoin, be adjacent; **— con** to adjoin, be adjacent to, border on.

colirrojo *nm* redstart.

colís *nm* (*Col*) machete, cane knife.

Coliseo *nm* Coliseum.

colisión *nf* (a) (*Aut etc*) collision; crash, smash; **— de frente** head-on collision. (b) (*fig*) clash.

colitis *nf* colitis.

colmado 1 *adj* abundant, copious; full (*de* of), overflowing (*de* with); heaped (*de* with); **una cucharada colmada** one heaped spoonful; **una tarde colmada de incidentes** an afternoon (more than) full of incident.

2 *nm* cheap seafood restaurant; (*Catalonia*) grocer's shop; (*Andalusia*) retail wine shop.

colmar [1a] *vt* (a) to fill to the brim, fill right up, fill to overflowing (*with* de); to heap (*de* with).

(b) (*fig*) *hopes etc* to fulfill, more than satisfy, realize completely.

(c) (*fig*) **— a uno de honores** to shower honours upon someone; **— a uno de alabanzas** to heap praises on someone; **— a uno de favores** to lavish favours on someone, overwhelm someone with favours.

colmena *nf* (a) beehive; (*fig*) hive. (b) (*Mex*) bee; bees.

colmenar *nm* apiary.

colmenero *nm* beekeeper.

colmillo *nm* (a) (*Anat*) eye tooth, canine (tooth); (*Zool*) fang; (*of walrus, elephant etc*) tusk.

(b) (*fig*) **enseñar los —s** to show one's teeth; **escupir por el —** to talk big, brag; **tener el — torcido** to be an old fox; **¡ya tengo —s!** (*Mex*) you can't fool me!

colmillón *nm* (*SAm*) greed.

colmilludo *adj* (a) having big teeth (*or* fangs *etc*). (b) (*fig*) sharp, alert.

colmo *nm* (*fig*) height, summit, extreme; **el — de la elegancia** the height of elegance; **el — de lo absurdo** the height of absurdity; **a — in** plenty, in abundance; **con —** heaped, to overflowing; **para — de desgracias** to make matters worse, to cap it all;

¡es el —! it's the limit!, it's the last straw!; **sería el —
si . . .** it would be the end if . . .
colocación *nf* (a) (*act*) placing; positioning; (*Comm*)
investment. (b) job, place, situation; **no encuentro
— I** can't find a job. (c) place, position.
colocado *adj*: **apostar para —** to back (a horse) for
a place.
colocar [1g] **1** *vt* (a) to place, put, position; to arrange;
troops etc to position, station; **— la quilla de un
buque** to lay down a ship's keel; **— un satélite en
órbita** to put (*or* place) a satellite in orbit.
(b) *person* to place (in a job), find a post for.
(c) (*Comm, Fin*) *goods, order* to place; *money* to
place, invest; *loan* to float.
(d) **— una historia a uno** to bore someone with
the same old story; **— una responsabilidad a uno**
to saddle someone with a responsibility.
2 colocarse *vr* (a) to place oneself, station oneself.
(b) (*Sport*) to be placed, get a place; **el equipo se
ha colocado en quinto lugar** the team has climbed
to fifth position.
(c) (*person*) to get a job.
colocho (*CAm*) **1** *adj* curly(-haired). **2 —s** *nmpl*
curls; wood shavings.
colodrillo *nm* back of the neck.
colofón *nm* colophon.
colofonia *nf* rosin, colophony.
colombianismo *nm* colombianism, word (*or* phrase
etc) peculiar to Colombia.
colombiano 1 *adj* Colombian. **2** *nm*, **colombiana** *nf*
Colombian.
colombino *adj* of Columbus, relating to Columbus.
Colón *m* Columbus.
colon *nm* (*Anat*) colon.
Colonia Cologne.
colonia[1] *nf* (a) (*Bio, Pol etc*) colony; (*of town*) suburb,
estate; **— escolar** summer camp for schoolchildren;
— obrera working-class housing scheme; **— penal**
penal settlement; **— veraniega** holiday camp; **las
antiguas —s españolas** the former Spanish colonies.
(b) silk ribbon.
(c) (*PR, SD*) sugar-cane plantation.
colonia[2] *nf* eau-de-Cologne.
coloniaje *nm* (*SAm*) colonial period; system of
colonial government; (*pej*) slavery, slave status.
colonial *adj* colonial; *food, product* overseas (*attr*),
imported.
colonialismo *nm* colonialism.
colonialista 1 *adj* colonialist. **2** *nmf* colonialist.
colonización *nf* colonization; settlement.
colonizador 1 *adj* colonizing. **2** *nm* colonist, colonizer,
settler; pioneer.
colonizar [1f] *vt* to colonize; to settle.
colono *nm* (a) (*Pol*) colonist, settler; colonial. (b) (*Agr*)
tenant farmer. (c) (*PR, SD*) sugar planter.
coloquial *adj* colloquial, familiar.
coloquio *nm* conversation, talk; conference;
(*scientific etc*) colloquium; (*Lit*) dialogue.
color *nm* (a) (*in general*) colour; hue, shade; (*fig*)
colour, colouring; **a —, en —es** film in colour, colour
(*attr*); **a todo —** in full colour; **gente de —** (*euph*)
coloured people (*euph*); **zapatos de —** brown shoes;
subido de — rude, rude, scabrous; **so — de** under
pretext of; **el suceso tuvo —es trágicos** the event
had its tragic aspect, the event had a sad side to it;
— base basic colour; **— local** local colour; **—
muerto, — quebrado** dull colour; **— sólido** fast
colour; **un vestido de — malva** a mauve(-coloured)
dress; **un vino — fresa** a strawberry-coloured wine;
verlo todo — de rosa to see everything through
rose-coloured spectacles, be ridiculously optimistic;
cambiar de —, mudar de — to change colour;
ponerse de mil —es to colour up; **sacar los —es a
uno** to make someone blush; **le salieron los —es**
she blushed.
(b) (*Art*) colour, paint; (*Tech*) dye, colouring
matter; rouge.
(c) **—es** (*Mil*) colours; **los —es nacionales** the
national colours, the national flag.
coloración *nf* coloration, colouring; (*Zool etc*)
coloration, markings.
colorado 1 *adj* (a) coloured, (*esp*) red; *complexion*
rosy, ruddy; **poner — a uno** to make someone
blush; **ponerse —** to blush.
(b) (*fig*) *joke* blue, rude, scabrous; *argument*
plausible.
2 *nm* (*Cu*) scarlet fever.
coloradote *adj* red-faced, ruddy.
colorante 1 *adj* colouring. **2** *nm* colouring (matter).
colorar [1a] *vt* to colour; to dye, tint, stain; **— algo de
amarillo** to colour (*or* dye *etc*) something yellow.

colorear [1a] **1** *vt* (a) =**colorar**. (b) (*fig*) to excuse;
to put in a favourable light; to gloss over, white-
wash. **2** *vi* to redden, show red.
colorete *nm* rouge.
colorido *nm* colour(ing).
colorín 1 *adj* (*Chi*) reddish blond(e).
2 *nm* (a) bright colour; **tener muchos —es** to
have vivid colours; **¡qué —es tiene el niño!** what rosy
cheeks the little fellow has!
(b) (*Orn*) linnet.
(c) (*Med*) measles.
colorir [3a; *defective*] **1** *vt* (a) to colour. (b) (*fig*) =
colorear. **2** *vi* to take on a colour, colour up.
colosal *adj* colossal.
coloso *nm* colossus.
coludo *adj* (*Chi, RPl*) long-tailed.
Columbina *f* Columbine.
columbrar [1a] *vt* (a) to glimpse, spy, make out.
(b) (*fig*) to guess.
columna *nf* (a) (*Archit*) column; pillar.
(b) (*Mil*) column; **— blindada** armoured column;
quinta — fifth column; **— volante** flying column.
(c) (*Anat*) **— vertebral** spine, spinal column.
(d) (*Mech*) column; **— de dirección** steering
column.
(e) (*Typ*) column.
(f) (*fig*) pillar, support; **una — de la religión** a
pillar of religion.
columnata *nf* colonnade.
columnista *nmf* columnist.
columpiar [1b] **1** *vt* to swing. **2 columpiarse** *vr* (a)
to swing; (*body etc*) to sway; to waddle; to swagger
(along). (b) (*fig*) to swing to and fro, seesaw.
columpio *nm* swing; (*SAm*) rocking chair; **—
basculante, — de tabla** seesaw.
colusión *nf* collusion.
colza *nf* (*Bot*) rape, colza.
collado *nm* (a) hill, height; hillock. (b) mountain pass.
collage [ko'laːʒ] *nm* (*Art*) collage.
collalba *nf* (*Orn*) wheatear.
collar *nm* (a) necklace; chain (of office); (dog)
collar; (*Orn, Zool etc*) collar, ruff; **— de perlas** pearl
necklace.
(b) (*Mech*) collar, ring.
(c) **— de fuerza** stranglehold.
colleja *nf* dandelion.
collera *nf* (a) horse collar. (b) (*SAm*) **—s** cufflinks.
collín *nm* (*CAm*), **collines** *nm* (*Ec*) cane knife,
machete.
coma[1] *nm* (*Med*) coma.
coma[2] *nf* (*Typ*) comma; **sin faltar una —** right down
to the last detail, with complete accuracy.
comadre *nf* (a) godmother *or* mother (*with respect to
each other*).
(b) neighbour; friend, crony; village woman,
peasant woman; gossip; **un grupo de —s** a group of
gossips, a gathering of gossipy women.
(c) (*Med*) midwife.
(d) (*pej*) go-between, procuress.
(e) (*fam*) pansy (*fam*).
(f) (*prov*) *in direct address between women, not
translated*.
comadrear [1a] *vi* to gossip.
comadreja *nf* weasel.
comadreo *nm*, **comadrería** *nf* gossip; gossiping,
chattering.
comadrona *nf* midwife.
comal *nm* (*CAm, Mex*) flat earthenware pan, frying
pan.
comandancia *nf* (a) command. (b) rank of major.
(c) commander's headquarters (*or* office). (d) area
under a commander's jurisdiction.
comandante *nm* (a) commandant, commander; **—
en jefe** commander-in-chief. (b) (*rank*) major.
comandar [1a] *vt* to command, lead.
comandita *nf* sleeping partnership, silent partnership (*US*).
comanditario *adj*: **socio —** sleeping partner, silent
partner (*US*).
comando *nm* (a) (*Mil*) command; (*Tech*) control; **— a
distancia** remote control. (b) (*angl*) commando
(*group and individual*). (c) duffel coat.
comarca *nf* region, area, part.
comarcal *adj* road local; *radio station* local, regional.
comarcano *adj* neighbouring, bordering.
comarcar [1g] *vi* to border (*con* on), be adjacent
(*con* to).
comatoso *adj* comatose.
comba *nf* (a) bend; bulge, warp, sag. (b) skipping
rope; **dar a la —** to turn the skipping rope; **saltar a
la —** to skip. (c) (*game*) skipping.
combadura *nf* (*on road*) curve, camber; =**comba** (a).

combar [1a] **1** *vt* to bend, curve. **2 combarse** *vr* to bend, curve; to bulge, warp; to sag.

combate *nm* fight, combat, engagement; (*fig*) battle, struggle; **— naval** naval battle, sea fight; **— singular** single combat; **estar fuera de —** to be out of action (*also fig*); (*Boxing*) to be knocked out; **poner a uno fuera de —** to put someone out of action, (*Boxing*) to knock someone out; **ganar por fuera de —** to win by a knockout.

combatiente *nm* combatant; **no —** non-combatant.

combatir [1a] **1** *vt* (a) (*Mil*) to attack; (*fig*) *tendency, proposal etc* to combat, fight, oppose; *mind* to assail, harass.

(b) (*of waves, wind*) to beat upon.

2 *vi and* **combatirse** *vr* to fight, struggle (*con, contra* against).

combatividad *nf* fighting spirit, fight; (*pej*) aggressiveness.

combativo *adj* full of fight, spirited; (*pej*) aggressive.

combés *nm* (*Naut*) waist.

combi *nf* (*fam*), **combinable** *nf* multi-purpose van.

combinación *nf* (a) (*act etc*) combination.

(b) (*Chem*) compound; (*drink*) cocktail.

(c) (*Rail etc*) connection; **hacer — con** to connect with.

(d) (*Math, Pools etc*) permutation; **— métrica** (*Lit*) stanza form, rhyme scheme.

(e) arrangement, setup, scheme; plan; (*pej*) cunning scheme, deep-laid plan.

(f) (*Sew*) slip.

combinado *nm* cocktail.

combinar [1a] **1** *vt* to combine; to join, unite, put together; *colours etc* to blend, mix, match; *scheme* to devise, work out.

2 combinarse *vr* to combine; (*persons*) to get together, join together (*para* + *infin* to + *infin*); (*pej*) to form a ring, gang up, conspire.

combo 1 *adj* bent; bulging; warped. **2** *nm* (a) (*SAm*) sledgehammer. (b) (*Chi, Per*) slap, punch.

combustible 1 *adj* combustible. **2** *nm* fuel, combustible.

combustión *nf* combustion; **— espontánea** spontaneous combustion.

comebolas *nm, pl* **comebolas** (*Cu*) simple soul, gullible individual.

comedero 1 *adj* eatable, edible.

2 *nm* (a) (*Agr*) trough, manger.

(b) dining room.

(c) (*fam*) food, grub (*sl*); **limpiar a uno el —** to deprive someone of his bread and butter.

(d) (*Ant*) brothel.

(e) (*Col*) haunt, hangout (*fam*).

comedia *nf* (a) (*modern*) comedy; (*Hist*) play, drama, *comedia*; **alta —** high comedy; **— en un acto** one-act play; **— de costumbres** comedy of manners; **— de capa y espada** cloak-and-dagger play; **— de enredos** comedy of intrigue.

(b) (*fig*) farce; pretence; **hacer la —** to make believe, pretend.

comedianta *nf* (a) (comic) actress, comedienne. (b) (*pej*) hypocrite.

comediante *nm* (a) (comic) actor. (b) (*pej*) hypocrite.

comedidamente *adv* moderately; courteously; (*SAm*) obligingly.

comedido *adj* moderate, restrained; courteous; (*SAm*) obliging.

comedimiento *nm* moderation, restraint; courtesy; (*SAm*) helpfulness.

comedirse [3l] *vr* (a) to behave moderately, be restrained, restrain oneself; to be courteous, answer (*etc*) politely; **— en las palabras** to choose one's words carefully.

(b) (*SAm*) **— a** + *infin* to offer to + *infin*, volunteer to + *infin*.

comedón *nm* blackhead.

comedor 1 *adj* greedy, gluttonous.

2 *nm* (a) dining room; restaurant; **— de beneficencia** soup kitchen.

(b) dining-room suite.

3 *nm*, **comedora** *nf* glutton; **ser buen —** to have a good appetite; **ser mal —** to have a poor appetite, not eat much.

comefuego *nm* (*Circus*) fire eater.

comegente *nm* (*Ec, PR*) glutton.

comején *nm* (a) (*Ent*) termite, white ant. (b) (*Col*) glutton. (c) (*Ec, Per*) worry, gnawing anxiety.

comelitona *nf* (*Mex*)=**comilona**.

comelón *adj* (*SAm*)=**comilón**.

comelona *nf* (*SAm*)=**comilona**.

comendador *nm* knight commander (*of a military order*).

comendatorio *adj*: **carta comendatoria** letter of recommendation.

comensal *nmf* (a) companion at table; fellow diner; **habrá 13 —es** there will be 13 to dinner; **me lo dijo mi —** the man sitting next to me at dinner told me so.

(b) (*Col*) (*at hotel*) guest.

comentador *nm* commentator.

comentar [1a] *vt* to comment on; *theory etc* to expound; (*fam*) to discuss; to criticize, gossip about.

comentario *nm* (a) comment, remark, observation; **y ahora sin más —** . . . and now without further ado . . .

(b) (*Lit*) commentary.

(c) **—s** gossip, (nasty) talk, tittle-tattle; **dar lugar a —s** to cause gossip; **hacer —s** to gossip, pass (nasty) remarks.

comentarista *nm* commentator (*also Radio*); **— deportivo** sports commentator.

cumento *nm* comment; (*Lit*) commentary; (*fig*) lie, pretence.

comenzar [1f *and* 1k] *vti* to begin, start, commence; **— protestando** to begin by protesting; **— a hacer algo** to begin to do something, start to do something, start doing something; **— con** to begin with; **— por** to begin with; **— por** + *infin* to begin by + *ger*.

comer [2a] **1** *vt* (a) to eat; **sin —lo ni beberlo** (*fig*) without having (had) anything to do with it.

(b) to eat (*or* have) for lunch; **hoy comimos truchas** today we had trout for lunch.

(c) (*Chem*) to eat away, eat into, corrode; (*of sea etc*) to swallow up, erode; **me come la pierna** my leg itches; **esto come las existencias** this devours (*or* uses up) the stocks.

(d) *colour* to fade; **— los colores a uno** to take away someone's colours.

(e) (*fig*) **le come la envidia** she is eaten up with envy.

(f) (*Chess etc*) to take, capture.

2 *vi* (a) to eat; **— de** to eat, partake of, have some of; **— como una vaca** to eat like a horse; **no — ni dejar —** to be a dog in the manger; *see* **dar**.

(b) to have a meal, eat; (*esp*) to have lunch, (*in some regions*) to dine, have supper.

(c) (*fig*) **¡pero — y callar!** but I'd better say no more!; **el mismo que come y viste** the very same; **este pescado es de buen —** this fish is good eating; **Juan es de buen —** John eats anything, John has a hearty appetite; **no tienen qué —** they don't have enough to live on.

3 comerse *vr* (a) to eat up; **se lo comió todo** he ate it all up.

(b) (*fig*) *resources etc* to consume, devour, eat up.

(c) (*fig*) *passage etc* to skip; *consonant* to swallow, slur.

(d) (*idioms*) **— a uno por pies** to take someone in completely; **se comen unos a otros** they're at daggers drawn; *see* **vista** *etc*.

comerciable *adj* (a) (*Comm*) marketable, saleable.

(b) (*fig*) sociable.

comercial 1 *adj* commercial; business (*attr*), trading (*attr*); **barrio —** business quarter, shopping district; **centro —** business centre. **2** *nm* (*TV: angl*) commercial.

comercialización *nf* (a) commercialization. (b) marketing.

comercializar [1f] *vt* (a) (*in general*) to commercialize. (b) *product* to market.

comerciante *nm* trader, dealer, merchant; **— al por mayor** wholesaler; **— al por menor** retailer.

comerciar [1b] *vi* (*of two persons*) to have dealings; (*of two countries*) to trade; **— con** (*also* **— en**) *goods* to deal in, handle; *person* to do business with, have dealings with, *country* trade with.

comercio *nm* (a) (*in general*) commerce; trade; business; **— de, — en** trade in, traffic in; dealings in; **el —** Spanish trade; **— de esclavos** slave trade; **— de exportación** export trade; **— exterior** foreign trade, overseas trade; **— de importación** import trade; **— interior** home trade.

(b) (*persons etc collectively*) business interests, business world; big business.

(c) shop, store (*US*).

(d) (*fig*) intercourse; dealings, contacts (*con* with); **— sexual** sexual intercourse; **— social** social intercourse, social contacts.

comestible 1 *adj* eatable; *fungus etc* edible.

2 *nm* (a) foodstuff, comestible; **—s** foods, foodstuffs.

(b) (*Comm*) **—s** groceries, provisions; **tienda de —s** grocer's (shop), grocery (*US*).

cometa[1] *nm* (*Astron*) comet.

cometa[2] *nf* kite.

cometer [2a] vt (a) crime etc to commit; error to make, commit. (b) task etc to entrust, commit (a to). (c) (Ling) to use, employ.

cometido nm task, assignment; commitment.

comezón nf (a) itch, itching; (of heat etc) tingle, tingling sensation; **siento — en el brazo** my arm itches; my arm tingles. (b) (fig) itch (por for); **sentir — de + infin** to feel an itch to + infin.

comi nf (fam) = **comisaría** (a).

comible adj eatable, fit to eat.

cómica nf (comic) actress; comedienne.

comicastro nm ham (actor) (sl).

comicidad nf humour, comedy, comicalness.

comicios nmpl elections, voting.

cómico 1 adj (a) comic(al), funny, amusing. (b) (Theat) comedy (attr); **autor —** playwright. **2** nm (comic) actor; comedian.

comida nf (a) (in general) food.
(b) (act) eating; meal, (esp) lunch, dinner; **bendecir la —** to say grace.
(c) (in lodging etc) board, keep; **— y casa** board and lodging.

comidilla nf (a) hobby, special interest. (b) **ser la — de la ciudad** (etc) to be the talk of the town.

comido adj and ptp (a) **estar —** to have had lunch (etc); **venir —** to come after lunch (etc). (b) **es — por servido** it doesn't pay, it's not worth while.

comience nm (Col) = **comienzo**.

comienzo nm beginning, start; (of plan etc) birth, inception; (Med etc) onset; **al —** at the start, at first; **en los —s de este siglo** at the beginning of this century; **dar — a un acto** to begin a ceremony; **dar — a una carrera** to start a race (off).

comilón 1 adj fond of one's food, having a good appetite; (pej) greedy. **2** nm big eater, person with a good appetite; (pej) glutton, pig.

comilona nf (fam) spread (fam), blow-out (sl), feast.

comillas nfpl quotation marks, inverted commas; **en —, entre —** in inverted commas.

cominero 1 adj fussy. **2** nm fusspot (fam), fussy person.

comino nm cumin, cumin seed; **no vale un —** it's not worth tuppence; **no se me da un —, (no) me importa un —** I don't care two hoots (de about).

comisaría nf (a) police station. (b) (Mil) commissariat.

comisariato nm commissariat.

comisario nm commissary (also Mil); (Pol) commissar; **— de policía** police superintendent, commissioner of police.

comiscar [1g] vt to nibble from time to time (at).

comisión nf (a) assignment, task, commission; mission.
(b) (Parl etc) committee; board, commission; (Comm, Fin) board; **— mixta** joint committee; **— permanente** standing committee; **— planificadora** planning board.
(c) (Comm) commission; **— porcentual** percentage commission (sobre on); **— sobre las ventas** sales commission; **a —** on a commission basis.
(d) (act) commission; **pecado de —** sin of commission.

comisionado nm commissioner; (Parl etc) committee member; (Comm, Fin) board member.

comisionar [1a] vt to commission.

comisionista nm commission agent, man working on a commission basis.

comiso nm (Law) (a) seizure, confiscation. (b) confiscated goods.

comisquear [1a] vt = **comiscar**.

comistrajo nm bad meal, awful food; (fig) mess, hotchpotch.

comisura nf join; corner, angle; **— de los labios** corner of the mouth.

comité nm committee; **C— de No Intervención** Non-Intervention Committee.

comitiva nf suite, retinue; train; procession; **— fúnebre** cortège, funeral procession.

como 1 adv as, like; such as; as it were; about, approximately; **es — un pez** it's like a fish; **hay peces, — truchas y salmones** there are fish, such as trout and salmon; **juega — yo** he plays like I do; **toca — canta** she plays in much the same way as she sings, her singing is like her playing; **asistió — espectador** he attended as a spectator; **lo dice — juez** he says it (in his capacity) as a judge; **— éste hay pocos** there are few like this; **vale más — poeta** he is better as a poet; **libre — estaba** free as he was; **la manera — sucedió** the way (in which) it happened; **había — cincuenta** there were about fifty; **sentía una — tristeza** she felt a sort of sadness; **fue así —**

comenzó la cosa it was thus that the thing began, the thing started in that way; **tuvo resultados — no se habían conocido antes** it had results such as had never been known before; **pues tocar, — tocar, no sabe** if you mean really play, well, she doesn't; she doesn't actually play.

2 conj (a) (+ indic) as, since; **— no tenía dinero** as (or since, because) I had no money; **— que . . . because . . . , since . . .**
(b) (+ indic) as soon as; **— nos vio lanzó un grito** as soon as he saw us he shouted.
(c) (+ subj) **si . . .** as if . . .
(d) (+ subj) if, unless; provided that; **— no lo haga en seguida** unless he does it at once; **— sea** as the case may be; **— no sea para + infin** unless it be to + infin, except to + infin; see **así, pronto, querer** etc.

cómo 1 adv interrog how?; why?, how is it that . . .?; **¿— lo hace?** how does he do it?; **¿— son?** what are they like?, what do they look like?; **¿— están mis nietos?** how are my grandchildren?; **¿— está Vd?** how are you?; **¿— es de alto?** how tall is it?, what height is it?; **¿a — son las peras?** how much are the pears?; **¿— así?, ¿— eso?** how can that be?, how come?; **¿— no?** why not?; what do you mean?; **no sé — hacerlo** I don't know how to do it; **no veo —** I don't see how; **no había — alcanzarlo** there was no way of reaching it.
2 interj etc: **¿—?** I beg your pardon?, what?, eh?; (surprise) what was that?; (anger) how dare you!; **¡—!, ¡— no!** of course!
3 nm: **el por qué y el — de** the whys and wherefores of.

cómoda nf chest of drawers; bureau.

cómodamente adv comfortably; conveniently.

comodidad nf (a) comfort; comfortableness; convenience; **pensar en su propia —** to consider one's own convenience; **venga a su —** come at your convenience.
(b) **—es** comforts, amenities, pleasant things; **—es de la vida** good things of life; **vivir con —es** to live in easy circumstances.
(c) **—es** (CAm: angl, Comm) commodities, goods.

comodín 1 adj (Col, Mex, Per, PR) = **comodón**. **2** nm (a) (Cards) joker. (b) (Mech etc) useful gadget. (c) useful lever, standby.

cómodo adj (a) chair etc comfortable; room comfortable; cosy, snug, comfy (fam); object convenient, handy; arrangement convenient; job, task agreeable.
(b) person comfortable; **así estarás más —** you'll be more comfortable this way; **ponerse —** to make oneself comfortable.

comodón adj comfort-loving; easy-going, liking a quiet life; **es muy —** he'll do anything for a quiet life.

comodonería nf love of comfort; liking for a quiet life.

comodoro nm commodore.

comoquiera conj (lit): **— que** (a) (+ indic) since, in view of the fact that. (b) (+ subj) in whatever way; **— que sea eso** however that may be, in whatever way that may be.

compacidad nf compactness.

compactación nf compacting, compression.

compactar [1a] vt to compact, press together (or down etc), compress.

compacto adj compact; dense; lines, threads, type etc close.

compadecer [2d] **1** vt to pity, be sorry for; to sympathize with. **2 compadecerse** vr: **— con** to harmonize with, blend with; to agree with, fit, square with; **— de** = vt.

compadrada nf (RPl) brag, boast; threat; piece of effrontery.

compadrazgo nm status of the godfather.

compadre nm (a) godfather or father (with respect to each other). (b) (fam) friend, pal (fam), buddy (esp US); (prov: in direct address) friend. (c) (RPl) braggart; swank (fam), show-off (fam); bully.

compadrear [1a] vi (a) (fam) to be pals (fam). (b) (RPl) to brag; to swank (fam), show off; to adopt a bullying attitude.

compadrito nm (SAm) = **compadre** (c).

compaginar [1a] **1** vt (a) to arrange, put in order.
(b) (Typ) to make up.
(c) **— A con B** to reconcile A with B, bring A into line with B, adjust A and B.
2 compaginarse vr to agree, tally; **— con** to agree with, tally with, square with; (colours) to blend with; **no se compagina esa conducta con su carácter** such conduct does not fit in with (or square with) his character.

compañerismo nm comradeship, fellowship; companionship; (Sport etc) team spirit.

compañero nm, **compañera** nf (a) companion; partner (also Cards); mate; — **de armas** comrade-in-arms; — **de baile** dancing partner; — **de cama** bedfellow; — **de clase** schoolmate, classmate; — **de cuarto** roommate; — **de infortunio** companion in misfortune; — **de juego** playmate; — **de rancho** messmate; — **de viaje** fellow traveller (also fig); **es un — divertido** he's good company.

(b) **dos calcetines que no son —s** two socks which do not match, two socks which do not make up a pair; **¿dónde está el — de éste?** where is the one that goes with this?, where is the other one (of the pair)?

compañía nf (a) (in general) company; **hacer — a uno** to keep someone company; **andar en malas —s, frecuentar malas —s** to keep bad company, have unsavoury companions.

(b) (Comm, Eccl, Theat etc) company; **C— de Jesús** Society of Jesus; **Pérez y C—** Perez and Company (abbr: and Co.); — **inversionista** investment trust; — **naviera** shipping company; — **de seguros** insurance company; — **tenedora** holding company.

comparable adj comparable (a, con to, with).

comparación nf (a) comparison; **en — con** in comparison with, beside; **es superior a toda —, no tiene —** it is beyond compare, it is incomparable. (b) (Lit) simile.

comparado adj (a) — **con** compared with, in comparison with, beside. (b) **study etc** comparative.

comparar [1a] vt to compare (a, con to, with); to liken (con to).

comparativo 1 adj comparative. 2 nm (Gram) comparative.

comparecencia nf (Law) appearance (in court); **su no —** his non-appearance.

comparecer [2d] vi (Law) to appear (in court); — **ante un juez** to appear before a judge.

comparecencia nf (Chi, RPl) =comparecencia.

comparendo nm (Law) summons; subpoena.

comparsa 1 nf group, procession; masquerade. 2 nmf (Theat) extra, supernumerary.

comparsería nf (Theat) extras, supernumeraries.

compartimiento nm (a) (act) division, sharing; distribution.

(b) (Naut, Rail etc) compartment; — **de bombas** (Aer) bomb bay; — **estanco** watertight compartment.

compartir [3a] vi to divide (up), share (out); **opinion, responsibility etc** to share (con with); **no comparto ese criterio** I do not share that view.

compás nm (a) (Mus) measure, time; beat, rhythm; bar; — **de 2 por 4 2/4** time; — **de vals** waltz time; **a — in** time; **al — de la música** in time to the music; **martillar a — to** hammer rhythmically; **fuera de — off** beat; **llevar el — to** beat time, keep time; **perder el — to** lose the beat; **entraron a los —es de un vals** they came in to the strains of a waltz. (b) (Math etc) compasses, pair of compasses.

(c) (Naut etc) compass.

compasado adj measured, moderate.

compasar [1a] =acompasar.

compasión nf pity, compassion; sympathy; **¡por —!** for pity's sake!; **mover a uno a —** to move someone to pity; **tener — de** to feel sorry for, take pity on; **tener pronta —** to be quick to pity, be easily moved to pity.

compasivamente adv compassionately; pityingly; sympathetically, understandingly.

compasivo adj compassionate, full of pity; sympathetic, understanding.

compatibilidad nf compatibility.

compatible adj compatible (con with).

compatriota nmf compatriot, fellow countryman, fellow countrywoman.

compeler [2a] vt to compel; — **a uno a + infin** to compel someone to + infin.

compendiar [1b] vt to abridge, condense, summarize.

compendio nm abridgement, condensed version; summary, abstract; compendium; **en — briefly**, in brief.

compendiosamente adv briefly, succinctly.

compendioso adj condensed, abridged; brief, succinct.

compenetración nf (fig) mutual understanding, fellow feeling, natural sympathy; mutual influence.

compenetrarse [1a] vr (a) (Chem etc) to interpenetrate, fuse.

(b) (fig) to (come to) share each other's feelings; to undergo mutual influence; — **de** to share the feeling of; to enter into the spirit of; to absorb, take in, become permeated by, undergo the pervasive influence of.

compensación nf (a) compensation; (Law) redress, compensation; **en — in** exchange, as compensation. (b) (Fin) clearing; **cámara de — clearing** house.

compensador adj compensating, compensatory.

compensar [1a] vt **person** to compensate (de for); **loss** to compensate for, make up (for); **mistake etc** to redeem, make amends for; (Mech etc) to balance, adjust, equalize; **le compensaron con 10 dólares por los cristales rotos** they gave him 10 dollars' compensation for the broken windows.

compensatorio adj compensatory.

competencia nf (a) competition (also Comm); rivalry; competitiveness; — **desleal** unfair competition; **a — vying** with each other, as rivals; **en — con** in competition with; **estar en — to** be in competition; **hacer — con** to compete against.

(b) competence (also Law); aptitude; adequacy; suitability.

(c) domain, field, province; **y otras cosas de su —** and other things which concern him, and other things for which he is responsible; **no es de mi —** that is not my responsibility; that is not (in) my field.

competente adj (a) (Law) competent; proper, appropriate; **esto se elevará al ministerio — this** will be sent to the appropriate ministry.

(b) competent; fit, adequate, suitable; **ser — para un cargo** to be suitable for a post.

(c) **sum etc** adequate, proper.

competentemente adv (a) appropriately. (b) competently; adequately, suitably.

competer [2a] vi: — **a** to be the responsibility of, fall to; **le compete castigarlos** it is his job to punish them, it is up to him to punish them.

competición nf competition (also Sport); contest.

competidor 1 adj competing, rival. 2 nm, **competidora** nf competitor (also Comm); rival (a for); opponent.

competir [3l] vi (a) to compete (also Comm, Sport; con against, with; en in; para for).

(b) — **con** (fig) to rival, vie with; **los dos cuadros compiten en belleza** the two pictures vie with each other in beauty; **en cuanto a resistencia A no compite con B** A cannot compete with B for stamina.

competitivo adj (Comm etc) competitive.

compilación nf compilation.

compilador nm, **compiladora** nf compiler.

compilar [1a] vt to compile.

compinche nm pal (fam), chum, buddy (esp US).

complacencia nf (a) pleasure, satisfaction.

(b) willingness; **lo hizo con — he** did it gladly.

(c) indulgence, indulgent attitude; **tiene excesivas —s con los empleados** he is too indulgent towards his employees.

(d) (SAm: angl) complacency.

complacer [2x] 1 vt **person** to please; **client etc** to help, oblige; **despot** to humour; **wish etc** to gratify, indulge; **nos complace que sea así** we are glad it is so; **¿en qué puedo —le?** (Comm etc) can I help you?, what can I do for you?

2 **complacerse** vr: — **en + infin** to be pleased (or glad) to + infin; to take pleasure in + ger; **el Banco se complace en comunicar a su clientela que . . .** the Bank is glad to tell its clients that . . .

complacido adj pleased, satisfied; **me miró complacida** she gave me a grateful look; **quedamos —s de la visita** we were pleased with our visit.

complaciente adj (a) **person** kind, obliging, helpful; **look etc** cheerful; **ser — con** to be helpful to, be well-disposed towards. (b) **husband** complaisant.

complejidad nf complexity.

complejo 1 adj complex. 2 nm (a) (Psych) complex; — **de Edipo** Oedipus complex; — **de inferioridad** inferiority complex. (b) (Tech) complex; — **industrial** industrial complex.

complementar [1a] vt to complement; to complete, make up, round off.

complementario adj complementary.

complemento nm (a) (Math etc) complement.

(b) (Gram) complement, object; — **directo** direct object; — **indirecto** indirect object.

(c) essential part, natural concomitant; **el vino es un — de la buena comida** wine is an essential concomitant to good food.

(d) culmination; rounding-off, perfection; **sería el — de su felicidad** it would complete her happiness, it would be a crowning happiness to her.

(e) —s (Aut etc) accessories.

completamente adv completely.

completar [1a] *vt* to complete; to round off, make up; to perfect; *loss* to make good; (*angl*) to complete, finish.

completas *nfpl* (*Eccl*) compline.

completo 1 *adj* (a) complete; perfect, rounded, finished; *search etc* thorough; *board, charge* inclusive, all-in; **por** — completely, utterly; **fue un** — **fracaso** it was a complete (*or* total, utter) failure.
(b) (*vehicle etc*) full.
2 *nm*: **en la sesión estuvo el** — all members were present at the meeting.

complexión *nf* (a) constitution, make-up; temperament. (b) (*SAm: angl*) complexion.

complexionado *adj*: **bien** — strong, tough, robust; **mal** — weak, frail.

complexional *adj* constitutional; temperamental.

complicación *nf* complication, complexity; **una persona sin** — an uncomplicated person; **han surgido** —**es** complications have arisen.

complicado *adj* complicated, complex; *fracture etc* complex; *decoration etc* elaborate; *method* complicated, involved, intricate.

complicar [1g] **1** *vt* (a) to complicate.
(b) *person* to involve (**en** in).
2 complicarse *vr* (a) to get complicated.
(b) — **en un asunto** to get involved (*or* entangled) in a matter.

cómplice *nmf* accomplice.

complicidad *nf* complicity, involvement (**en** in).

complot [kom'plo] *nm, pl* **complots** [kom'plo] plot; conspiracy; intrigue.

complutense *adj* of Alcalá de Henares.

componenda *nf* (a) compromise; (provisional) settlement, (temporary) arrangement. (b) (*pej*) shady deal.

componente 1 *adj* component, constituent. **2** *nm* (*Chem etc*) component; (*of drink etc*) ingredient.

componer [2r] **1** *vt* (a) *collection etc* to make up, put together, compose.
(b) (*of elements*) to compose, constitute, make up; *number* to make up; **componen el jurado 12 personas** 12 persons make up the jury, the jury consists of 12 persons.
(c) (*Lit, Mus etc*) to compose, write.
(d) (*Typ*) to make up, set up (in type), compose.
(e) (*Cook*) to prepare; *salad etc* to garnish, season; *wine* to strengthen.
(f) *broken object* to mend, repair, fix; to overhaul; (*SAm*) *bones* to set; (*Med*) *stomach etc* to settle; to strengthen; *spirit* to quieten, soothe; *abuse* to set to rights, correct.
(g) *quarrel* to settle, compose, resolve; *differences* to reconcile; *persons* to reconcile.
(h) to arrange; to tidy up, polish up, adorn; *person* to dress up, deck out.
(i) (*Chi, Mex, RPl*) to castrate.
(j) (*Col*) to bewitch.
2 componerse *vr* (a) — **de** to consist of, be composed of, be made up of; **se compone de 6 partes** it consists of 6 parts.
(b) (*woman etc*) to dress up; to tidy oneself up; to make up.
(c) — **con uno** to come to terms with someone, reach an agreement with someone.
(d) —**las** to manage, get along; to find a way; —**las para** + *infin* to manage to + *infin*, contrive to + *infin*.

componible *adj* (a) repairable; worth mending. (b) reconcilable; capable of settlement.

comportable *adj* bearable.

comportamentista *adj* (*Bio etc*) behavioural.

comportamiento *nm* behaviour, conduct; (*Mech etc*) performance.

comportar [1a] **1** *vt* (a) to bear, endure, put up with.
(b) to involve, carry with it; **ello no comporta obligación alguna** it carries no obligation.
(c) (*Col, RPl*) to entail, cause, be the cause of.
2 comportarse *vr* to behave; to comport oneself, conduct oneself; — **como es debido** to behave properly.

comporte *nm* (a) = **comportamiento**. (b) bearing, carriage.

composición *nf* (a) (in several senses, also *Lit, Mus*) composition.
(b) (*of quarrel*) settlement; (*of persons*) reconciliation.
(c) arrangement.
(d) agreement.
(e) (*quality*) composure.

compositor *nm*, **compositora** *nf* (*Mus*) composer.

compostelano 1 *adj* of Santiago de Compostela.
2 *nm*, **compostelana** *nf* native (*or* inhabitant) of

Santiago de Compostela; **los** —**s** the people of Santiago de Compostela.

compostura *nf* (a) composition; structure; make-up.
(b) (*Mech etc*) mending, repair, repairing; overhauling; **estar en** — to be undergoing repairs.
(c) (*Cook*) condiment, seasoning.
(d) arrangement; tidying, polishing, adornment.
(e) arrangement, agreement; settlement.
(f) (*quality*) composure; discretion, good sense; sedateness, modesty.

compota *nf* compote, preserve; (*with meat etc*) sauce; — **de frutas** stewed fruit.

compra *nf* (a) (*act*) purchase, buying; — **al contado** cash purchase; — **a plazos** hire purchase; **ir de** —**s** to go shopping, shop.
(b) (*article*) purchase; —**s** purchases, shopping.

comprador *nm*, **compradora** *nf* buyer, purchaser; (*in shop*) shopper, customer.

comprar [1a] *vt* (a) to buy, purchase (**a**, **de** from); — **al contado** to pay cash for; — **al fiado** to buy on credit; — **a plazos** to buy on hire purchase, pay for in instalments.
(b) (*fig*) to buy off, bribe; to win over, secure the allegiance of.

compraventa *nf* (a) buying and selling, dealing. (b) (*Law*) contract of sale.

comprender [2a] *vti* (a) to comprise, include; to take in; to extend to; to consist of; **servicio no comprendido** service not included; **todo comprendido** everything included, all in.
(b) to understand; to see; — **que** ... to understand that ..., see that ...; to realize that ...; **¿comprendes?** see?, understand?; **¡comprendido!** all right!, sure!; agreed!; **¡ya comprendo!** I see!, now I get it!; **no comprendo cómo** I don't see how; **comprendo su actitud** I understand his attitude; **cuando comprendió que no iba a ayudarle** when he realized (*or* saw) I was not going to help him; **compréndase bien que** ... let it be clearly understood that ...; **compréndanme Vds** let's be clear about this; **hacerse** — to make oneself understood.

comprensible *adj* understandable, comprehensible (*para* to); **no es** — **que** ... it is incomprehensible that ..., I (*etc*) cannot understand how ...

comprensión *nf* (a) comprehensiveness, inclusiveness; inclusion.
(b) (*act, faculty*) understanding, comprehension; grasp.
(c) (*emotion*) understanding (attitude); sympathy, tolerance, kindness.

comprensivo *adj* (a) comprehensive, inclusive; all-embracing; **un bloque** — **de 50 viviendas** a block containing 50 flats.
(b) *person, attitude* understanding; sympathetic, tolerant, kindly.

compresa *nf* compress; — **higiénica** sanitary towel, sanitary napkin (US).

compresibilidad *nf* compressibility.

compresible *adj* compressible.

compresión *nf* compression.

compresor *nm* compressor.

comprimible *adj* compressible.

comprimido 1 *adj* compressed. **2** *nm* (*Med*) pill, tablet; — **para dormir** sleeping pill.

comprimir [3a] **1** *vt* (a) to compress (*also Tech*; **en** into); to squeeze (down *etc*), press (down *etc*); to condense.
(b) (*fig*) to control, restrain; *tears* to keep back.
2 comprimirse *vr* (*fig*) to control oneself, contain oneself; **tuve que comprimirme para no reír** I had to keep myself from laughing; **tendremos que comprimirnos** (*Fin*) we shall have to restrict ourselves.

comprobable *adj* provable, demonstrable; **un alegato fácilmente** — an allegation which is easy to check.

comprobación *nf* checking, verification; proof; **en** — **de ello** in proof whereof, as proof of what I (*etc*) say; **de difícil** — hard to check, difficult to prove.

comprobador *nm*: — **de lámparas** valve tester.

comprobante 1 *adj*: **documento** — supporting document; **documentos** —**s de ello** documents in proof thereof.
2 *nm* proof; (*Comm*) receipt, voucher.

comprobar [1m] *vt* (a) to check, verify; to prove; to confirm, show; — **que** ... to check that ...; to show that ..., establish that ...; — **si** ... to check whether ...
(b) (*Mech etc*) to check, test, overhaul.

comprometedor *adj* compromising.

comprometer [2a] **1** *vt* (a) *person* to compromise; to embarrass, put in an awkward situation; *suspect etc* to involve, implicate; **aquellas cartas le comprometieron** those letters compromised him.

(**b**) to risk; to endanger, imperil, jeopardize; — **la reputación** to risk one's reputation; — **la neutralidad del país** to imperil one's country's neutrality.

(**c**) — **a uno a algo** to hold someone to something, pin someone down to something; — **a uno a** + *infin* to force someone to + *infin*, make someone feel obliged to + *infin*.

(**d**) (*Comm, Law*) to agree formally to; *room, seats etc* to book, reserve.

2 comprometerse *vr* (**a**) to compromise oneself; to get involved (**en** in).

(**b**) — **a** + *infin* to undertake to + *infin*, promise to + *infin*, engage to + *infin*; **se compromete a todo** he'll say yes to anything.

comprometido *adj* (**a**) *situation etc* awkward, embarrassing.

(**b**) *writer etc* engaged; committed; **no** — uncommitted; *country* non-aligned.

(**c**) **estar** — to be engaged; to be involved; to be at stake; **estar** — **para** + *infin* to be engaged to + *infin*.

compromiso *nm* (**a**) obligation; commitment; undertaking, pledge, promise; engagement, date; **por** — out of a sense of duty; **libre de** —, **sin** — (*Comm*) without obligation; **adquirir un** — **de** + *infin* to commit oneself to + *infin*, take on an obligation for + *ger*; **atender** (*or* **cumplir**) **sus** —**s** to meet one's obligations; **hacer honor a sus** —**s** to honour one's pledges; **tener muchos** —**s** to have many commitments; **¿tienes** — **para esta noche?** have you anything on this evening?, are you booked up tonight?

(**b**) agreement; — **matrimonial** engagement (to marry); — **verbal** verbal agreement, gentlemen's agreement.

(**c**) awkward situation, jam, fix; predicament; **estar en un fuerte** — to be in a real jam; **poner a uno en un** — to place someone in an embarrassing situation; **poner a uno en el** — **de** + *infin* to put someone in the position of + *ger*; **salir de un** — to get out of a jam.

compuerta *nf* sluice, floodgate; (*in door etc*) hatch.

compuesto 1 *ptp of* **componer**; **estar** — **de** to be composed of, consist of, be made up of.

2 *adj* (**a**) (*Chem, Ling, Math, interest etc*) compound; *flower, material* composite.

(**b**) *person etc* elegant, dressed up; tidy, neat.

(**c**) (*fig*) composed, calm.

3 *nm* compound (*also Chem*); preparation; composite material; — **químico** chemical compound.

compulsa *nf* (**a**) (*act*) checking, comparison. (**b**) (*Law*) attested copy, certified true copy.

compulsar [1a] *vt* (**a**) to collate, compare. (**b**) (*Law*) to make an attested copy of.

compulsión *nf* compulsion.

compulsivo *adj* compulsory; compulsive.

compulsorio *adj* (*SAm: angl*) compulsory.

compunción *nf* compunction, regret; pity; sorrow.

compungido *adj* remorseful, contrite, sorry.

compungimiento *nm* remorse, contrition.

compungir [3c] **1** *vt* to make remorseful, arouse feelings of contrition in.

2 compungirse *vr* to feel remorseful (*por* about, because of), feel sorry (*por* for).

compurgar [1h] *vt* (*Mex, Per, RPl*) *offence* to purge.

computación *nf* = **cómputo**.

computador *nm*, **computadora** *nf* computer; — **digital** digital computer.

computar [1a] *vt* to calculate, compute, reckon (*en* at).

cómputo *nm* calculation, computation, reckoning; **según nuestros** —**s** according to our calculations.

comulgante *nmf* communicant.

comulgar [1h] **1** *vt* to administer communion to. **2** *vi* to take communion, receive communion.

comulgatorio *nm* communion rail, altar rail.

común 1 *adj* (**a**) common (*a* to); joint; public, belonging to all, held in common; *gender, grave etc* common; **los intereses** —**es** common interests; **de** — **con** in common with; **A no tiene nada de** — **con B** A has nothing in common with B; **en** — in common; joint (*attr*), mutual; **hacer algo en** — to do something jointly (*or* together).

(**b**) *distribution etc* common; *custom, opinion* common, widespread, general; **es costumbre muy** — it is a very widespread custom; **la planta es** — **en la provincia** the plant is common in the province.

(**c**) *quality* common, ordinary; **fuera de lo** — out of the ordinary; **por lo** — generally.

2 *nm* (**a**) **el** — the community, the people (at large); **bienes del** — communal property, public property.

(**b**) **el** — **de las gentes** most people, the common run of people.

(**c**) toilet.

(**d**) **los C**—**s** (*Brit: Pol*) the Commons.

comuna *nf* (**a**) commune. (**b**) (*Arg, Chi, Guat, Per*) municipality.

comunal *adj* communal; community (*attr*).

comunalmente *adv* communally; as a community.

comunicable *adj* (**a**) communicable, that can be communicated. (**b**) *person* approachable; sociable.

comunicación *nf* (**a**) communication; contact; **las** —**es están rotas** communications are broken; **no hemos tenido más** — **con él** we have had no further contact with him, we have heard nothing further from him.

(**b**) message; report; (*to conference etc*) paper.

(**c**) (*Tel*) connection, contact; **póngame en** — **con el Sr Q** please give me Mr Q's number.

comunicado *nm* communiqué.

comunicar [1g] **1** *vt* (**a**) *information* to communicate, tell, pass on (*a* to); *news* to convey, tell (*a* to); *message* to give, pass (*a* to); *disease etc* to carry; to give (*a* to); *custom* to transmit, pass on; *bequest etc* to pass on (*a* to), bestow (*a* on); *fear etc* to communicate (*a* to); **nos comunicó su miedo** he affected us with his fear, his fear infected us.

(**b**) *two rooms etc* to connect, join, open a way between.

2 *vi* (**a**) to send a report (*de* from); **comunican desde Lisboa que . . .** it is reported from Lisbon that . . .

(**b**) (*Tel*) **estar comunicando** to be engaged.

(**c**) (*Archit*) — **con** to connect with; to open into.

3 comunicarse *vr* (**a**) (*persons*) to communicate (with each other); to be in touch, correspond; **nos comunicamos nuestras impresiones** we exchanged impressions.

(**b**) to pass, be transmitted; **el miedo se comunicó a todos** the fear affected everybody.

(**c**) (*Archit*) to be connected, lead into each other, intercommunicate.

comunicativo *adj* (**a**) communicative; approachable, sociable. (**b**) *laughter etc* infectious.

comunidad *nf* community; society, corporation; (*Eccl*) community; **C**— **Europea del Carbón y del Acero** European Coal and Steel Community (*or* Pool); **C**— **Británica de Naciones** British Commonwealth; **de** — (*Law*) jointly.

comunión *nf* communion.

comunismo *nm* communism.

comunista 1 *adj* communist(ic). **2** *nmf* communist.

comunizar [1f] *vt* to communize.

comúnmente *adv* commonly; usually, generally; frequently.

con 1 *prep* (**a**) (*general sense*) with; **atado** — **cuerda** tied with string; — **su ayuda** with his help; **andar** — **muletas** to walk on (*or* with) crutches; **me escribo** — **ella** I write to her; **¡—** **lo difícil que es todo esto!** what with all this being so difficult!

(**b**) in spite of; — **tantas dificultades, no se descorazonó** in spite of all the difficulties he was not discouraged; — **ser su madre, le odia** even though she is his mother she hates him.

(**c**) (*also* **para** —) to, towards; **amable** — **todos** kind to everybody; **ser insolente** — **el jefe** to be disrespectful to the boss.

(**d**) (+ *infin*) — **llegar tan tarde** (by) arriving so late; — **confesarlo se libró del castigo** by owning up he escaped punishment; — **decirle que no voy** when I tell you I'm not going; — **llegar a las 6 estará bien** if you come at 6 it will be all right.

2 — **que** *conj* and so, so then; whereupon; **¿—** **que Vd es el jefe?** so you're the boss?; — **que fuimos a la cama** and so we went to bed.

conato *nm* attempt; endeavour, effort (*de* + *infin* to + *infin*); — **de robo** attempted robbery; **hacer un** — **de** + *infin* to make an attempt to + *infin*; **poner** — **en algo** to put everything into a task.

concatenación *nf* concatenation, linking; — **de circunstancias** chain of circumstances.

concatenar [1a] *vt* to link together, concatenate.

concavidad *nf* concavity, hollow, cavity.

cóncavo 1 *adj* concave; hollow. **2** *nm* hollow, cavity.

concebible *adj* conceivable, thinkable; **no es** — **que . . .** it is unthinkable that . . .

concebir [3l] **1** *vt* (**a**) to conceive; to imagine; to understand; — **esperanzas** to nourish hopes; to become hopeful; — **una antipatía hacia** (*or* **por**) to take a

dislike to; **no concibo que** ... I cannot understand how (or why) ...
  2 vi (Bio) to conceive, become pregnant.
conceder [2a] vt to concede, grant; to confer, bestow (a on); attention etc to pay; discount to allow; prize to award (a to); honour to confer (a on); — **que** ... to concede that ..., admit that ...
concejal nm town councillor.
concejil adj relating to a town council; municipal, public.
concejo nm council; — **municipal** town council.
concentración nf (all senses) concentration.
concentrado 1 adj concentrated. 2 nm extract, concentrate; — **de carne** meat extract.
concentrar [1a] 1 vt (all senses) to concentrate (en un lugar in a place, en una escena on a scene).
  2 **concentrarse** vr (a) (Mil etc) to concentrate, be concentrated.
  (b) (fig) — **a** + infin to concentrate on + ger; **el interés se concentra en esta lucha** the interest is centred on this fight.
concéntrico adj concentric.
concepción nf (a) (Bio etc) conception; **la Purísima C—** the Immaculate Conception. (b) (faculty) understanding. (c) conception, idea.
conceptismo nm witty, allusive and involved style (esp 17th century).
conceptista 1 adj witty, allusive and involved. 2 nmf writer in the style of conceptismo.
concepto nm (a) concept, conception; idea, notion; thought; **un — grandioso** a bold conception, a bold plan; **formarse un — de algo** to get an idea of something.
  (b) view, opinion; judgement; **en mi —** in my view; **formarse un — de uno** to form an opinion of someone; **¿qué — has formado de él?** what do you think of him?; **tener buen — de uno, tener en buen — a uno** to think highly of someone.
  (c) (of account etc) heading, section; **bajo todos (los) —s, por todos —s** from every point of view; in every way, in every respect; **en — de, por — de** as, by way of; under the heading of; **se le pagó esa cantidad por — de derechos** he was paid that amount as royalties; **por ningún —** in no way.
  (d) (Lit) conceit.
conceptual adj conceptual.
conceptuar [1e] vt to think, judge, deem; **le conceptúo poco apto para eso** I think him unsuited for that; **— a uno de** (or **como, por**) to regard someone as, deem someone to be ...; **no está bien conceptuado actualmente** he is not well thought of at present.
conceptuosamente adv wittily; (pej) over-elaborately, in a mannered way.
conceptuoso adj witty, full of conceits; (pej) over-elaborate, mannered.
concerniente adj: — **a** concerning, relating to; **en lo — a** with regard to, as for.
concertadamente adv methodically, systematically; in an orderly fashion; harmoniously.
concertado 1 adj methodical, systematic; orderly; harmonious. 2 nm, **concertada** nf (CR, Cu, Ven) servant.
concertar [1k] 1 vt (a) (Mus) to harmonize, bring into harmony; to tune (up).
  (b) efforts to coordinate; differences to adjust, bring into line, reconcile; persons to achieve agreement between; to reconcile; — **a varias personas para que** ... to get various people to agree to + infin.
  (c) to agree to; agreement, treaty to conclude (con with); deal to arrange, fix up; price to agree, fix (en at); — **una venta en 20 dólares** to agree to sell something for 20 dollars, agree to a sale price of 20 dollars; **hemos concertado el piso en mil pesetas** we have agreed to rent the flat for 1000 pesetas; — **hacer algo** to agree to do something.
  2 vi (a) (Mus) to harmonize, be in tune.
  (b) (fig) to agree (also Gram).
  3 **concertarse** vr (a) (Mus etc) to harmonize.
  (b) (persons) to reach agreement, come to terms; — **para** + infin (pej) to conspire together to + infin.
concertina nf concertina.
concertino nm first violin, leader (of the orchestra), concertmaster (US).
concertista nmf soloist, solo performer.
concesión nf concession; grant(ing); allowance; award; (Comm) concession.
concesionario nm concessionaire, licensee.
concesivo adj concessive.
conciencia nf (a) conscience; moral sense; conscientiousness; **a —** conscientiously; **hecho a —** solidly

built, well built; **en —** with a clear conscience; honestly, in truth; **con — limpia** with a clear conscience; **ancho de —** not overscrupulous; **anchura de —** lack of scruple; **libertad de —** freedom of worship; **hombre sin —** unscrupulous person; **empezó a acusarle la —** his conscience began to prick him; **tener la — tranquila** to have a clear conscience.
  (b) knowledge, awareness, consciousness; **a — de que** ... fully aware that ..., in the certain knowledge that ...; **tener plena — de** to be fully aware of; **tomar — de** to become aware of.
concienzudamente adv conscientiously, painstakingly, thoroughly.
concienzudo adj conscientious, painstaking, thorough.
concierto nm (a) concert, agreement; order; harmony; **de — con** in concert with; **quedar de acerca de** to be in agreement with regard to.
  (b) (Mus) concert; — **sinfónico** symphony concert.
  (c) (Mus) concerto.
conciliable adj reconcilable; **dos opiniones no fácilmente —s** two opinions which it is not easy to reconcile.
conciliación nf (a) conciliation; reconciliation. (b) affinity, similarity.
conciliador 1 adj conciliatory. 2 nm conciliator.
conciliar[1] [1b] 1 vt (a) enemies etc to reconcile; attitudes etc to harmonize, bring into line, blend.
  (b) respect etc to win, gain; — **el sueño** to get to sleep.
  2 **conciliarse** vr: — **algo** to win something, gain something.
conciliar[2] 1 adj (Eccl) of a council, council (attr). 2 nm council member.
conciliatorio adj conciliatory; propitiatory.
concilio n (Eccl) council; **el Segundo C— Vaticano** the Second Vatican Council.
concisamente adv concisely, briefly, tersely.
concisión nf concision, conciseness, brevity.
conciso adj concise, brief, terse.
concitar [1a] vt to stir up, incite (contra against).
conciudadano nm, **conciudadana** nf fellow citizen.
cónclave nm conclave.
concluir [3g] 1 vt (a) to conclude, finish.
  (b) to infer, deduce; consequence etc to reach, arrive at.
  (c) person to convince; to crush, silence.
  (d) — **a uno de ignorante** to judge someone to be ignorant.
  2 vi to end, conclude, finish; — **de** + infin to finish + ger; — **por** + infin to end up by + ger; — **con, en, por** (of word etc) to end in; **todo ha concluido** it's all over; **¡vamos a — de una vez!** let's get it over!
  3 **concluirse** vr to end, conclude.
conclusión nf (all senses) conclusion; **en —** in conclusion, lastly, finally; **llegar a la — de que** ... to come to the conclusion that ...
concluyente adj conclusive; decisive; unanswerable.
concluyentemente adv conclusively; decisively; unanswerably.
concomitante adj concomitant.
concordancia nf (a) concordance; harmony. (b) (Gram) concord, agreement. (c) (Mus) harmony. (d) —s (Lit) concordance.
concordante adj concordant.
concordar [1m] 1 vt to reconcile; to bring into line; (Gram) to make agree.
  2 vi to agree (con with), tally (con with), correspond (con to); (Gram) to agree; **esto no concuerda con los hechos** this does not square with (or fit in with) the facts; **los dos concuerdan en sus gustos** the two agree in their tastes, the two have the same tastes.
concordato nm concordat.
concorde adj: **estar —s** to be agreed, be in agreement; **estar — en** + infin to agree to + infin; **poner a dos personas —s** to bring about agreement between two people.
concordia nf (a) concord, harmony, agreement; conformity. (b) double finger-ring.
concreción nf concretion; (Med) stone.
concretamente adv particularly, specifically; exactly; to be exact; **se refirió — a dos** he referred specifically to two; **no es — una fiesta** it's not exactly a party; — **eran 39** to be exact there were 39.
concretar [1a] 1 vt to make concrete, make (more) specific; to express in concrete terms; to pinpoint, put one's finger on; to reduce to essentials, boil

down; **concreta sus esperanzas a ganar el premio** he is concentrating all his hopes on winning the prize; **concretemos, para** — let us be more specific, let's come down to details.

2 concretarse *vr* (a) to become (more) definite; — a to come down specifically to.

(b) — **a** + *infin* to limit oneself to + *ger*, confine oneself to + *ger*; to concentrate on + *ger*.

concreto 1 *adj* (a) concrete; definite, actual, particular, specific; **en este caso** — in this particular instance; **no me dijo ninguna hora concreta** he didn't tell me any definite (*or* particular) time; **en** — to sum up; exactly, specifically; to be exact; **en** — **había 7** there were 7 to be exact; **no hay nada en** — there's nothing you can put your finger on, there's nothing definite.

2 *nm* (a) concretion.

(b) (*SAm: angl*) concrete.

concubina *nf* concubine.

concubinato *nm* concubinage.

concúbito *nm* copulation.

concupiscencia *nf* (a) greed, acquisitiveness. **(b)** lustfulness, concupiscence.

concupiscente *adj* (a) greedy, acquisitive. **(b)** lewd, lustful, concupiscent.

concurrencia *nf* (a) (*of events etc*) concurrence.

(b) crowd, gathering, assembly; spectators, public, audience; attendance, turnout; **había una numerosa** — there was a big attendance, there was a large crowd (present).

(c) (*Comm*) competition.

concurrente 1 *adj* (a) *event etc* concurrent.

(b) (*Comm etc*) competing.

2 *nm* (a) person present, person attending; — **al cine** cinemagoer, moviegoer (*US*); **los** — **s** those present, those in the audience (*etc*).

(b) competitor.

concurrido *adj place* crowded; much frequented; *street* busy, crowded; *show* popular, well-attended, full (of people).

concurrir [3a] *vi* (a) (*of roads etc*) to meet, come together (**en** at).

(b) (*of people*) to meet, gather, assemble (*a* at, **en** in); — **a un baile** to go to a dance, attend a dance; — **a las urnas** to go to the polls; **concurren a la misma tertulia** they go to the same group.

(c) (*of people: pej*) to conspire, come together (*para* + *infin* to + *infin*).

(d) to contribute; — **a la derrota** to contribute to the defeat; — **al éxito de una empresa** to contribute to the success of an enterprise; — **con su dinero** to contribute one's money; — **en una empresa** to cooperate in an undertaking.

(e) (*of qualities etc*) to be found, be present; **concurren en ella muchas buenas cualidades** she has many good qualities.

(f) — **en una opinión** to concur in an opinion, agree with an opinion.

(g) (*of events*) to coincide (**con** with).

(h) (*Comm*) to compete; — **a un mercado** to compete in a market.

(i) (*Sport etc*) to compete (*a* in), take part (*a* in).

concursado *nm* (*Law*) insolvent debtor, bankrupt.

concursante *nmf* competitor, contestant, participant.

concursar [1a] **1** *vt* (a) (*Law*) to declare insolvent, declare bankrupt.

(b) to compete in, compete for; **va a** — **la vacante** he is going to compete for (*or* apply for) the vacancy.

2 *vi* to compete, participate.

concurso *nm* (a) = **concurrencia**.

(b) — **de acreedores** (*Law*) meeting of creditors.

(c) (*of events*) coincidence, concurrence.

(d) help, collaboration; cooperation; **con el** — **de** with the help of; **prestar su** — to help, collaborate.

(e) (*Sport etc*) competition, contest; meeting, match, tournament; show; (*for post*) examination, open competition; — **de belleza** beauty contest; — **hípico** horse show, show-jumping contest; — **de pastoreo** sheepdog trials; — **radiofónico** radio quiz (show); **precios sin** — **s** competitive prices; unbeatable prices; **ganar un puesto por** — to win a post in open competition.

concusión *nf* (a) (*Med*) concussion. **(b)** (*Fin*) extortion.

concusionario *nm* extortioner.

Concha *f pet name for* **María de la Concepción**.

concha *nf* (a) (*Zool*) shell; shellfish; tortoiseshell; **meterse en su** — to retire into one's shell; **tener muchas** — **s** to be very sharp, be a sly one.

(b) (*of china*) flake, chip.

(c) (*Theat*) prompt box.

(d) (*Col, Ec, Per, PR*) nerve, cheek.

(e) (*Col*) sloth, sluggishness.

(f) (*Anat: euph*) = **coño**.

conchabado *nm*, **conchabada** *nf* (*SAm*) servant.

conchabar [1a] **1** *vt* (a) to mix, blend.

(b) (*SAm*) *servant* to hire, engage, employ.

(c) (*Chi, Ec*) to barter.

2 conchabarse *vr* (a) to gang up (*contra* on), plot, conspire (*para* + *infin* to + *infin*).

(b) (*SAm*) to hire oneself out, get a job (as a servant).

conchabo *nm* (a) (*SAm*) hiring, engagement; **oficina de** — (*Arg*) domestic employment agency. **(b)** (*Chi*) barter(ing).

Conchita *f* = **Concha**.

conchito *nm* (*Chi, Per*) youngest child (of a family).

concho[1] *nm* (*SD*) taxi.

concho[2] *nm* (*CR*) peasant; (*pej*) rustic, country bumpkin.

concho[3] **1** *adj* (*Ec, Per*) dark reddish-brown.

2 *nm* (*SAm: also* —**s**) dregs, sediment; residue; left-overs; **hasta el** — to the very end; **irse al** — (*Chi*) to sink.

concho[4] *nm* (*Chi, Per*) = **conchito**.

concho[5] *nm* (*Anat: euph*) = **coño**.

conchudo 1 *adj* (*Arg, Col, SD*) sluggish.

2 *nm*, **conchuda** *nf* (a) (*Ec, Mex, Per*) shameless person.

(b) (*PR*) stubborn individual; fearless person.

condado *nm* county; (*Hist*) earldom.

conde *nm* earl, count; **el C**— **Fernán González** Count Fernán González.

condecoración *nf* decoration, medal; badge; insignia.

condecorar [1a] *vt* to decorate (**con** with).

condena *nf* (*Law*) sentence; conviction; term (*of imprisonment*); — **a perpetuidad**, — **de reclusión perpetua** life sentence, sentence of life imprisonment; **el año pasado hubo X** —**s por embriaguez** last year there were X convictions for drunkenness; **cumplir una** — to serve a sentence.

condenable *adj* condemnable; blameworthy.

condenación *nf* (a) condemnation; (*Eccl*) damnation; (*Law*) = **condena**. **(b)** ¡—! damn!, damnation!

condenadamente *adv* (*fam*): **una mujer** — **lista** a darned clever woman (*fam*); **es un trabajo** — **duro** it's darned hard work (*fam*).

condenado 1 *adj* (a) condemned; (*Law*) condemned, convicted; (*Eccl*) damned.

(b) (*fig*) doomed; **el buque** — the doomed vessel; **una especie condenada a la extinción** a species doomed to extinction; **instituciones condenadas a desaparecer** institutions doomed to disappear.

(c) (*fam*) *child* mischievous, naughty.

(d) (*fam*) damned, flaming (*fam*), ruddy (*euph*); **aquel** — **teléfono** that ruddy telephone.

(e) (*Chi*) clever; sharp.

2 *nm*, **condenada** *nf* (a) (*Law*) convicted person, criminal; **el** — **a muerte** the condemned man.

(b) (*Eccl*) damned soul.

(c) (*fam*) **el** — **de mi tío** that ruddy uncle of mine (*euph*).

condenar [1a] **1** *vt* (a) to condemn.

(b) (*Law*) to condemn, convict, sentence; to find guilty; — **a uno a 3 meses de cárcel** to sentence someone to 3 months in jail, give someone a 3-month prison sentence; — **a uno a una multa** to sentence someone to pay a fine; — **a uno a presidio** to sentence someone to hard labour; **le condenaron por ladrón** they found him guilty of robbery.

(c) (*Eccl*) to damn.

(d) (*Archit*) to block up, wall up.

(e) (*fam*) to vex, annoy.

2 condenarse *vr* (a) to confess (one's guilt), own up; to blame oneself.

(b) (*Eccl*) to be damned.

(c) (*fam*) to get cross, get worked up.

condensación *nf* condensation.

condensado *adj* condensed.

condensador *nm* condenser.

condensar [1a] *vt* to condense. **2 condensarse** *vr* to condense, become condensed.

condesa *nf* countess.

condescendencia *nf* helpfulness, willingness (to help); affability; acquiescence (*a* in); **aceptar algo por** — to accept something so as not to hurt feelings.

condescender [2g] *vi* to acquiesce, comply, agree, say yes; — **a algo** to consent to, say yes to; — **a los ruegos de uno** to agree to someone's requests; — **en** + *infin* to agree to + *infin*.

condescendiente *adj* helpful, willing (to help); kind; affable; acquiescent.

condición *nf* (a) nature, condition; temperament, character; **la — humana** the human condition; **de — perversa** of a perverse nature; **de — cruel** cruel-natured.

(b) social class, rank; status, position; **persona de —** person of rank; **de humilde —** of lowly origin; **una boda de personas de distinta —** a wedding between people of different social scale.

(c) **—es** qualities; **de excelentes —es** of splendid qualities; **ella no tiene —es para pintora** she is not cut out to be a painter.

(d) **—es** condition, state; **—es de trabajo** working conditions; **— de vida, —es vitales** living conditions; **nuestras —es económicas** our economic circumstances; **el coche está en malas —es** the car is in a bad state; **no está en (buenas) —es** it's not in a fit state; **no está en —es para + infin** it is not fit to + *infin*; **no estamos en —es para + infin** we are not in a position to + *infin*.

(e) condition; term, provision, stipulation; **las —es del contrato** the terms of the contract; **— sine qua non** essential condition; **a — de que . . .** on condition that . . ., provided that . . .; **con esta —** on this condition; **ayuda sin —es** help with no strings attached; **rendición sin —es** unconditional surrender; **rendirse sin —es** to surrender unconditionally.

condicionado *adj* conditioned.

condicional *adj* conditional (*also Gram*).

condicionalmente *adv* conditionally.

condicionar [1a] *vt* to condition; to determine; to prepare.

condigno *adj* proper, corresponding.

condimentar [1a] to flavour, season; to spice.

condimento *nm* seasoning, flavouring; dressing.

condiscípulo *nm*, **condiscípula** *nf* fellow pupil, fellow student.

condolencia *nf* condolence, sympathy.

condolerse [2h] *vr*: **— de, — por** to sympathize with, feel sorry for.

condominio *nm* (a) (*Law*) joint ownership; (*Pol*) condominium. (b) (*Mex*) flat, apartment (*US*) (*owned by the occupant*).

condonar [1a] *vt act* to condone; *punishment* to remit; *debt* to cancel, forgive; *criminal* to reprieve.

cóndor *nm* condor.

conducción *nf* (a) (*act*) leading; guiding; management; transport(ation); conveyance; piping; (*Phys*) conduction.

(b) (*Aut*) drive; driving; **— a derecha** right-hand drive; **coche de — interior** saloon car; **— descuidada** reckless driving.

(c) (*Tech*) pipe; intake; outlet; **— de agua** water pipe; **— principal de agua** water main; **— principal de gas** gas main.

(d) (*Comm*) agreement (on transport charges).

conducente *adj*: **— a** conducive to, leading to.

conducir [3o] **1** *vt* (a) *liquid etc* to take, convey; to pass; *load* to take, transport, convey; **los cables conducen la electricidad** the cables carry the electricity.

(b) (*Aut etc*) to drive; to steer; **— por la derecha** to drive on the right.

(c) *person* to take, lead (*a* to); to guide, conduct (*a* to); **me condujeron por un pasillo** they led me along a passage.

(d) *business, matter* to direct, manage, conduct; *army, group, revolt etc* to lead.

2 *vi* (a) (*Aut*) to drive; **aprender a —** to learn to drive.

(b) **— a** (*fig*) to lead to; **esto ha de — al desastre** this is bound to lead to disaster; **¿a qué conduce? what's the point?; no conduce a ninguna parte** this is getting us nowhere.

3 conducirse *vr* to behave, conduct oneself.

conducta *nf* (a) (*of person*) conduct, behaviour; **mala —** misconduct, misbehaviour; **cambiar de —** to mend one's ways.

(b) (*of business etc*) direction, management.

conductibilidad *nf* (*Phys*) conductivity.

conducto *nm* (a) (*for water etc*) pipe, tube, conduit; (*Anat*) duct, canal; (*Elec*) lead, cable, flex; **—s** (*Aut*) leads; **— alimenticio** alimentary canal; **— biliar, — bile duct; — de desagüe** drain; **— de humo** flue; **— lacrimal** tear duct.

(b) (*fig*) agency; channel; (*person*) agent, intermediary; **por — de** through, by means of.

conductor 1 *adj* (a) leading, guiding.

(b) (*Phys*) conductive.

2 *nm* (*Phys*) conductor; (*Elec*) lead; **no — non-conductor**.

3 *nm*, **conductora** *nf* (a) leader; guide; (*Sport*) leader.

(b) (*Aut*) driver; motorist; **aprendiz de —, — novato** learner, learner-driver.

(c) (*SAm: Mus: angl*) conductor; (*of bus etc*) conductor, conductress.

condueño *nm*, **condueña** *nf* joint owner, part owner, co-owner.

condumio *nm* (*fam*) food, grub (*sl*).

conectado *adj* (*Elec etc*) connected; **estar —** to be on, (*of wire etc*) to be live.

conectar [1a] **1** *vt* (a) (*Tech*) to connect (up); (*Elec, TV etc*) to connect (up); to switch on, plug in; **— un aparato a tierra** (*or con masa*) to earth a piece of apparatus, ground a piece of apparatus (*US*).

(b) (*SAm*) **— a uno con otra persona** to put someone in touch with somebody else; **yo les puedo —** I can put you in touch (with each other).

2 *vi* (*SAm: angl*): **este asunto conecta con lo otro** this business links up with the other.

conectivo *adj* connective.

coneja *nf* doe rabbit.

conejar *nm* warren, burrow; (*fig*) warren.

conejera *nf* (a) warren, burrow; rabbit hutch. (b) (*fam*) den, dive (*fam*).

conejillo *nm* young rabbit; bunny; **— de Indias** guinea-pig.

conejo 1 *adj* (*CAm*) flat, unsweetened; bitter, sour.

2 *nm* (a) (*Zool*) rabbit; **— casero** tame rabbit; **— de Noruega** lemming.

(b) (*RPl*) biceps.

(c) (*Guat*) detective.

(d) (*Anat: euph*) = **coño**.

conejuna *nf* rabbit fur, coney.

conexión *nf* (a) (*Tech*) connection; plug; coupling; joint. (b) (*fig*) connection; relationship.

conexionarse [1a] *vr* to get in touch; to make connections, establish contacts.

conexo *adj* connected, related.

confabulación *nf* plot; intrigue; dubious scheme; (*Comm*) ring.

confabularse [1a] *vr* to plot, conspire, scheme (*para + infin* to + *infin*); (*Comm*) to form a ring.

confección *nf* (a) (*act*) making; making-up, preparation; **— de vestidos** dressmaking.

(b) (*art*) workmanship, work; **traje de alta —** ready-to-wear suit.

(c) manufactured article, made-up article; (*Pharm*) concoction, preparation; (*Sew*) ready-made garment (*or suit etc*); **es una — Pérez** it's a Pérez creation, it's a Pérez product.

confeccionado *adj* (*Sew*) ready-made, ready-to-wear; **— a la medida** made to measure.

confeccionar [1a] *vt list etc* to make out; *account* to prepare, write up; (*Sew*) to make (up); (*Pharm*) to concoct, make up.

confederación *nf* confederation, confederacy, league.

confederado 1 *adj* confederate. **2** *nm* confederate.

confederarse [1a] *vr* to confederate, form a confederation.

conferencia *nf* (a) (*Pol etc*) conference, meeting; **— (en la) cumbre** summit conference; **— de desarme** disarmament conference; **— de prensa** press conference.

(b) lecture, address; **dar una —** to give a lecture.

(c) (*Tel*) call; **— de cobro revertido** reversed-charge call; **— interurbana, — de larga distancia** long-distance call, trunk call; **— de persona a persona** personal call.

conferenciante *nmf* lecturer.

conferenciar [1b] *vti* to confer (*con* with); to be in conference.

conferencista *nmf* (*SAm*) lecturer.

conferir [3i] *vt* (a) *prize* to award (*a* to); *honour* to grant (*a* to), confer (*a* on), bestow (*a* on).

(b) (*fig*) *quality* to lend, give (*a* to); **los cuadros confieren dignidad al cuarto** the pictures give the room dignity.

(c) *documents etc* to compare (*con* with).

confesante *nm* (*Hist*) penitent.

confesar [1k] **1** *vt* (a) to confess, admit, acknowledge, own up to; (*Eccl*) *sin* to confess.

(b) (*Eccl*) *sinner* to confess, hear the confession of.

2 *vi and* **confesarse** *vr* to confess, own up; (*Eccl*) to confess (*a, con* to), make one's confession; **— de sus pecados** to confess one's sins.

confesión *nf* (*all senses*) confession.

confesional *adj* confessional.

confes(i)onario *nm* confessional.

confeso 1 adj (a) confessed. (b) (Hist) Jew converted.
2 nm (Hist) converted Jew; (Eccl) lay-brother.
confesor nm confessor.
confeti nm (also —s) confetti.
confiabilidad nf reliability, trustworthiness.
confiable adj reliable, trustworthy.
confiadamente adv (a) trustingly. (b) confidently; self-confidently; hopefully. (c) conceitedly.
confiado adj (a) trusting; unsuspecting, gullible.
(b) confident; — **en sí mismo** self-confident, self-reliant; **estar muy** — to be excessively hopeful, nourish false hopes.
(c) (pej) vain, conceited, presumptuous.
confianza nf (a) trust (en in); reliance (en on); trustfulness; **margen de** — credibility gap; **persona de (toda)** — reliable person, trustworthy person; **puesto de** — responsible post, post of responsibility; **decir algo en** — to say something in confidence; **dicho sea en** — let it be said in confidence (or strictly between ourselves); **defraudar la** — **de uno** to let someone down; **poner su** — **en** to put one's trust in.
(b) confidence; — **en sí mismo** self-confidence; **con toda** — with complete confidence; **estar lleno de** — to be full of confidence; **infundir** — **a uno** to give someone confidence.
(c) (pej) vanity, conceit; presumption.
(d) intimacy, familiarity (con with); **amigo de** — close friend, intimate friend; **reunión de** — intimate gathering, informal gathering; **en tono de** — in a confidential tone; **tener** — **con uno** to be on close terms with someone; **tratar a uno con** — to treat someone without formality, not stand on ceremony with someone; **os ruego tratarme con toda** — I ask you to treat me as one of yourselves.
(e) —**s** confidences; (pej) familiarities; **se toma demasiadas** —**s** he is too familiar, he's too fresh, he takes too many liberties.
confianzudo adj (a) overfamiliar, fresh. (b) (SAm) meddlesome.
confiar [1c] **1** vt: — **algo a uno**, — **algo en uno** to entrust something to someone, commit something to the care of someone; — **algo al azar** to leave something to chance.
2 vi to trust, be trusting; — **en** to trust, trust in; to rely on, count on; — **en el éxito de algo** to feel confident about the success of something; **confiemos en Dios** let us trust in God; — **en que . . .** to trust that . . .; to expect that . . .
3 **confiarse** vr (a) — **a algo** to entrust oneself to something.
(b) — **a uno** (fig) to open one's heart to someone.
confidencia nf confidence, secret; confidential remark; (to police) tip-off; **hacer** —**s a uno** to tell secrets to someone, confide in someone.
confidencial adj confidential.
confidencialmente adv confidentially.
confidente nm, **confidenta** nf (a) confidant(e); intimate friend. (b) informer; secret agent.
configuración nf shape, configuration; **la** — **del futuro** the shape of things to come; **la** — **del terreno** the lie of the land.
configurar [1a] vt to shape, form, fashion.
confín nm limit, boundary; horizon; —**es** confines, limits (also fig); remote part, outermost parts, edges.
confinado adj air thick.
confinar [1a] **1** vt to confine (a, en in); to banish, exile (a to); to arrest; to shut away.
2 vi: — **con** to border on (also fig).
3 **confinarse** vr to shut oneself away.
confirmación nf confirmation (also Eccl).
confirmar [1a] vt to confirm (also Eccl); to corroborate; to endorse, bear out, prove; — **a uno de** (or **como**, **por**) to confirm someone as; **la excepción confirma la regla** the exception proves the rule.
confirmatorio adj confirmatory.
confiscación nf confiscation.
confiscar [1g] vt to confiscate.
confisgado adj (CAm) rascally.
confitar [1a] vt to preserve (in syrup); to candy; to sweeten (also fig).
confite nm sweet, candy (US).
confitería nf (a) confectionery, sweets, candies (US); (b) confectioner's (shop), sweetshop, candy store (US).
confitero nm, **confitera** nf confectioner.
confitura nf preserve; crystallized fruit; jam.
conflagración nf conflagration; (fig) flare-up, outbreak; — **bélica** outbreak of war.
conflictivo adj: **la edad conflictiva** the age of conflict.

conflicto nm (a) (Mil) conflict; struggle; (fig) clash; — **de intereses** clash of interests; — **laboral** labour dispute.
(b) (fig) difficulty, fix, jam; **estar en un** — to be in a jam.
confluencia nf confluence.
confluente adj confluent.
confluir [3g] vi (of rivers etc) to meet, join, come together; (of people etc) to gather, come together; to mass.
conformación nf shape, form, structure.
conformado adj (a) **bien** — well-made, well-shaped.
(b) patient, resigned, long-suffering.
conformar [1a] **1** vt to shape, fashion; to adjust (a to), adapt (a to), bring into line (a with); **enemies to** reconcile.
2 vi to agree (con with).
3 **conformarse** vr to conform; to resign oneself; — **con original** to conform to, agree with; **rule** to comply with, abide by, observe; **policy etc** to adjust to, conform to, fall into line with; **unpleasant situation** to resign oneself to, accept; **se conforma con cualquier cosa** he agrees to anything; he puts up with anything; **no me conformo con hacerlo así** I do not agree to doing it your way.
conforme 1 adj (a) alike, similar; **son muy** —**s en todo** they are very similar in every respect, they agree well enough.
(b) consistent (a with); **un premio** — **a sus méritos** a prize consistent with his merits, a reward in accordance with his merits.
(c) (of persons etc) agreed, in agreement; ¡—(s)! agreed!, all right!; **estar** —**s** to be agreed; **estamos** —**s en el precio** we are agreed about the price; **estamos** —**s en que . . .** we agree that . . .; **declararse** — **con algo** to consent to something, acquiesce in something; **por fin se mostró** — finally he agreed.
(d) (of persons etc) satisfied, content (con with); resigned (con to); **no se quedó** — **con la propina** he was not satisfied with the tip.
2 prep: — **a** in conformity with, in accordance with; in keeping with; — **a la muestra** as per sample; **lo hicieron** — **a sus instrucciones** they acted according to their instructions.
3 conj as; in proportion as; **todo sigue** — **estaba** everything is as it was; — **lo iban sacando** (in proportion) as they were taking it out; — **. . . así . . . as . . . so . . .**
4 nm agreement; **dar el** — to agree, give one's agreement.
conformidad nf (a) similarity; correspondence; uniformity (entre between).
(b) agreement; approval, consent; **de** — by common consent; **de** — **con** in accordance with; **en** — accordingly; **en** — **con** in compliance with; **no** — nonconformity; disagreement; **dar su** — to consent, give one's approval.
(c) resignation (con to); forbearance; **soportar algo con** — to bear something with resignation, resign oneself to putting up with something.
confort [kon'foɹ(t)] nm, pl **conforts** [kon'foɹ(t)] (gall) comfort; "**todo** —" (adverts) "all mod cons".
confortable adj comfortable.
confortablemente adv comfortably.
confortante adj (a) comforting. (b) (Med) invigorating, tonic.
confortar [1a] vt (a) to comfort, console; to encourage. (b) (Med etc) to strengthen, invigorate, act as a tonic to.
confortativo 1 adj (a) comforting, consoling; encouraging.
(b) (Med etc) invigorating, tonic.
2 nm (a) comfort, consolation; encouragement.
(b) (Med etc) tonic, restorative.
confraternidad nf fraternity, brotherhood.
confraternizar [1f] vi (SAm) to fraternize (con with).
confrontación nf (a) confrontation; — **nuclear** nuclear confrontation. (b) comparison.
confrontar [1a] **1** vt (a) danger etc to confront, face; to face up to.
(b) two persons to bring face to face; — **a uno con otro** to confront somebody with someone else.
(c) texts to compare, collate.
2 vi to border (con on).
3 **confrontarse** vr: — **con** to confront, face.
Confucio m Confucius.
confundible adj: **fácilmente** — easily mistaken (con for), easily confused (con with).
confundir [3a] **1** vt (a) outline etc to blur, confuse.
(b) to mistake (con for), confuse (con with), mix up (con with); person to confuse, muddle; **confundimos el camino** we mistook our way, we got

our route wrong; **ha confundido todos los sellos** he has mixed up (or jumbled up) all the stamps.

(c) *substances* to mix, mingle (*con* with).

(d) *opponent* to confound; to confuse, put off; to bewilder, perplex; — **a uno con atenciones** to bewilder (or overwhelm) someone with kindness.

(e) *accuser* to put to shame, humble.

(f) to lose; **me has confundido ese libro otra vez** you've lost that book of mine again.

2 confundirse *vr* (a) (*outline etc*) to become blurred, become confused.

(b) to get confused, get in a muddle; to get bewildered; to make a mistake; **Vd se ha confundido de número** (*Tel*) you have the wrong number.

(c) to feel humbled, feel ashamed.

(d) to mix; to blend, fuse; **se confundió con la multitud** he became lost in the crowd, he disappeared in the crowd; **los policías se confundieron con los manifestantes** the police mingled with the demonstrators.

confusamente *adv remember etc* confusedly; vaguely, hazily; *retreat* in confusion, in disorder.

confusión *nf* (*all senses*) confusion; **no hagamos —es** let's be clear about this, let's get this straight.

confusionismo *nf* confusion; uncertainty; confused state; **sembrar el — y desconcierto** to spread alarm and despondency.

confuso *adj* (*in most senses*) confused; mixed up, jumbled up, in disorder; *memory* confused, vague, hazy; *image* blurred, cloudy; **estar —** (*person*) to be confused, be bewildered; to be embarrassed.

confutar [1a] *vt* to confute.

conga *nf* (*SAm: Mus*) conga.

congal *nm* (*Mex*) brothel.

congelación *nf* (a) freezing; congealing. (b) (*Med*) frostbite. (c) (*Fin etc*) freeze, freezing; **— de créditos** credit freeze; **— de salarios** wage freeze.

congelado *adj* (a) *meat etc* frozen, chilled; *fat* congealed. (b) (*Med*) frostbitten. (c) (*Fin etc*) frozen, blocked.

congelador *nm* freezer; freezing unit.

congeladora *nf* deep freeze.

congelar [1a] **1** *vt* (a) *meat, water etc* to freeze; *blood, fat* to congeal.

(b) (*Med*) to freeze, affect with frostbite.

(c) (*Fin etc*) to freeze, block.

2 congelarse *vr* (a) to freeze, become frozen; to congeal.

(b) (*Med*) to get frostbitten.

congénere *nm* fellow, person (*etc*) of the same sort; **el criminal y sus —es** the criminal and others like him, the criminal and people of that sort.

congeniar [1b] *vi* to get on (well; *con* with).

congenital *adj* (*SAm: angl*), **congénito** *adj* congenital.

congestión *nf* (*all senses*) congestion.

congestionado *adj* (a) congested. (b) (*Med*) congested, (*esp*) chesty; *face* flushed, red.

congestionar [1a] **1** *vt* to congest, produce congestion in.

2 congestionarse *vr* to become congested; **se le congestionó la cara** his face became flushed, he got red in the face.

conglomeración *nf* conglomeration.

conglomerado *nm* (*Geol, Tech*) conglomerate; (*fig*) conglomeration.

conglomerar [1a] **1** *vt* to conglomerate. **2 conglomerarse** *vr* to conglomerate.

Congo: **el —** the Congo; **¡vete al —!** (*fam*) get lost! (*fam*).

congo *nm* (*SAm*) Negro.

congoja *nf* anguish, distress, grief.

congola *nf* (*Col, Ec*) pipe.

congoleño 1 *adj* Congolese. **2** *nm*, **congoleña** *nf* Congolese.

congolés = **congoleño**.

congosto *nm* narrow pass, canyon.

congraciador *adj* ingratiating.

congraciamiento *nm* ingratiation; winning over.

congraciante *adj* ingratiating.

congraciar [1b] **1** *vt* to win over. **2 congraciarse** *vr* to ingratiate oneself (*con* with).

congratulaciones *nfpl* congratulations.

congratular [1a] **1** *vt* to congratulate (*por* on).

2 congratularse *vr* to congratulate oneself, be pleased; **de eso nos congratulamos** on that we congratulate ourselves, we are glad about that.

congregación *nf* gathering, assembly; brotherhood, guild; (*Eccl*) congregation; **— de los fieles** Christendom.

congregacionalista *adj* congregational.

congresal *nmf* (*SAm*) = **congresista**.

congresional *adj* congressional

congresista *nmf* delegate, member (of a congress).

congreso *nm* congress; assembly, convention; conference; **C—** (*Pol*) Congress (*US*).

congrio *nm* conger (eel).

congruencia *nf* (a) congruence (*also Math*), congruity. (b) suitability.

congruente *adj*, **congruo** *adj* (a) congruent (*also Math*), congruous (*con* with); in keeping (*con* with); related (*con* to). (b) suitable, fitting.

cónico *adj* conical; *section etc* (*Math*) conic.

conífera *nf* conifer.

conífero *adj* coniferous.

conjetura *nf* guess, conjecture, surmise; **por —** by guesswork; **son meras —s** it's just guesswork.

conjeturable *adj* that can be guessed at; **es — que ...** one may conjecture that ...

conjetural *adj* conjectural.

conjeturar [1a] *vt* to guess (at), conjecture, surmise (*de, por* from; *que* that).

conjugación *nf* conjugation.

conjugar [1h] **1** *vt* (a) (*Gram*) to conjugate.

(b) to combine, bring together, fit together, blend; **la obra conjuga cualidades y defectos** the work has both qualities and defects; **es difícil — los deseos de los dos** it is difficult to fit their two wishes together.

2 conjugarse *vr* (a) (*Gram*) to be conjugated.

(b) to fit together, blend; to be as one, become indistinguishable.

conjunción *nf* (*all senses*) conjunction.

conjuntivitis *nf* conjunctivitis.

conjuntivo *adj* conjunctive.

conjuntamente *adv* jointly, together; **— con** together with.

conjunto 1 *adj* (a) *effort etc* joint; united.

(b) *subject etc* allied, related.

2 *nm* (a) whole; **en —** as a whole, altogether; **en su —** in its entirety; **foto de —** group photo; **impresión de —** overall impression; **vista de —** all-embracing view; **formar un —** to form a whole.

(b) (*Sew*) ensemble; costume.

(c) (*Mus: chamber etc*) ensemble; (*pop*) group; **los Beatles formaron su —** the Beatles formed their group.

(d) (*Theat*) chorus.

(e) (*Mech*) unit, assembly.

conjura *nf*, **conjuración** *nf* plot, conspiracy.

conjurado *nm*, **conjurada** *nf* plotter, conspirator.

conjurar [1a] **1** *vt* (a) *devil* to exorcise.

(b) *danger* to stave off, ward off.

(c) *thought etc* to rid oneself of, get rid of.

(d) *person* to entreat, beseech.

2 *vi and* **conjurarse** *vr* to plot, conspire (together).

conjuro *nm* (a) incantation, conjuration, exorcism; spell; **al — de sus palabras** under the magical effect of his words. (b) entreaty.

conllevar [1a] *vt* (a) *infirmity etc* to bear, suffer (patiently), live with.

(b) *person* to bear, put up with.

(c) **— las penas de otro** to help someone else to bear his troubles.

(d) (*fig*) **— a uno** to hedge with someone, jolly someone along with empty promises.

conmemoración *nf* commemoration.

conmemorar [1a] *vt* to commemorate.

conmemorativo 1 *adj* commemorative; memorial (*attr*). **2** *nm* (*Post*) commemorative.

conmigo *pron* with me; with myself.

conmilitón *nm* fellow soldier.

conminar [1a] *vt* (a) to threaten (*con* with). (b) **— a uno a hacer algo** to warn someone (officially) to do something, instruct someone to do something.

conminatorio *adj* threatening, warning.

conmiseración *nf* pity, sympathy; commiseration.

conmoción *nf* (a) (*Geol*) shock; tremor, earthquake.

(b) (*Med*) **— cerebral** concussion.

(c) (*fig*) shock; commotion, disturbance; upheaval; **una — social** a social upheaval; **producir una — desagradable a uno** to give someone a nasty shock.

conmovedor *adj* touching, moving; poignant; exciting, stirring; disturbing.

conmover [2h] **1** *vt* (a) *building etc* to shake, disturb.

(b) (*fig*) to move, touch, stir, affect; to disturb, upset.

2 conmoverse *vr* (a) to shake, be shaken.

(b) (*fig*) to be moved, be stirred.

conmuta *nf* (*Chi, Ec, Per*) change, alteration.

conmutador *nm* (*Elec*) switch.

conmutar [1a] *vt* (a) to exchange (*con, por* for); to convert (*en* into). (b) (*Law*) to commute (*en, por* to).

connatural *adj* innate, inherent.

connaturalizarse [1f] *vr* to become accustomed (*con* to); to become acclimatized, become acclimated (*US*) (*con* to).

connivencia *nf* collusion; connivance; **estar en — con** to be in collusion with.

connotación *nf* (a) connotation. (b) distant relationship.

connotado *adj* (*SAm*) notable, famous; outstanding.

connotar [1a] *vt* to connote.

cono *nm* (*all senses*) cone.

conocedor 1 *adj* expert, knowledgeable; **muy — de** very knowledgeable about.
  2 *nm*, **conocedora** *nf* expert (*de* in), judge (*de* of); connoisseur (*de* of); **es buen — de ganado** he's a good judge of cattle.

conocencia *nf* (*esp SAm*) girlfriend, sweetheart.

conocer [2d] **1** *vt* (a) to know; to know about, understand; (*for first time*) to meet, get to know; **— a uno de vista** to know someone by sight; **le conozco ligeramente** I know him slightly; **conozco las dificultades** I know the difficulties; **la conocí en Sevilla** I met her in Seville; **vengo a — Portugal** I have come to get to know Portugal; **conoce su oficio** he knows his job; **no conoce gran cosa de ciencias** he doesn't know much about science; **le conozco de haber trabajado juntos** I know him from having worked with him; **dar a —** to introduce, present; *report etc* to release (to the press *etc*), (*improperly*) leak; **darse a —** to make a name for oneself; to make one's debut; **darse a — a uno** to make oneself known to someone.
  (b) to know, tell, recognize, distinguish (*en, por* by); **— a uno por su modo de andar** to know someone by (*or* from) his walk; **él conoce cuáles son buenos** he knows (*or* can tell) which ones are good; **conocieron el peligro** they recognized the danger; **¿de qué le conoces?** how do you recognize him?; **no me conoce de nada** he doesn't know me from Adam.
  2 *vi* (a) **— de** to know about.
  (b) (*Law*) **— de** (*or* **en**) **una causa** to try a case.
  3 conocerse *vr* (a) (*person*) to know oneself; to attain self-knowledge.
  (b) (2 *persons*) to know each other; to get to know each other, meet, get acquainted; **se conocieron en un baile** they met at a dance.
  (c) **se conoce que . . .** it is clear that . . .; it is known that . . .; it is established that . . .; it is recognized that . . .

conocible *adj* knowable.

conocido 1 *adj* known; well-known, (*pej*) notorious; famous, noted (*por* for); **un médico — a** well-known doctor, a prominent doctor; **un hecho conocidísimo** a very well-known fact.
  2 *nm*, **conocida** *nf* acquaintance.

conocimiento *nm* (a) knowledge; **hablar con — de causa** to know what one is talking about; **obrar con — de causa** to know what one is up to; **hacer — de un hecho** to learn a fact; **hacer — de un tema** to learn about a subject, become acquainted with a subject; **ha llegado a mi — que . . .** it has come to my notice that . . .; **poner algo en — a uno** to inform someone of something; to bring something to someone's attention; **tener — de** to know about, have knowledge of; **al tenerse — del suceso** as soon as the event became known; **venir en — de** to learn of, hear about.
  (b) **—s** knowledge (*de* of); information (*de* about); **—s elementales** basic knowledge; **mis pocos —s de filosofía** my small knowledge of philosophy.
  (c) **—s** (*persons*) acquaintances.
  (d) good sense, understanding; **los niños no tienen — children** have no sense.
  (e) (*Med*) consciousness; **estar sin —** to be unconscious; **perder el —** to lose consciousness; **recobrar el —** to regain consciousness.
  (f) (*Naut*) bill of lading.

conorte *nm* (*SAm*) comfort.

conque 1 *conj see* **con 2**. **2** *nm* (a) (*fam*) condition, reservation; **—s** ifs and buts. (b) (*also* **conqué**: *SAm*) wherewithal, money, means.

conquense 1 *adj* of Cuenca. **2** *nmf* native (*or* inhabitant) of Cuenca; **los —s** the people of Cuenca.

conquibus *nm* (*fam*) wherewithal, money, means.

conquista *nf* conquest (*also fig*); **ir de — (***fig***)** to be dressed up to kill.

conquistador 1 *adj* conquering. **2** *nm* (a) conqueror; (*16th century*) conquistador. (b) (*fam*) wolf (*fam*), ladykiller.

conquistar [1a] *vt* (a) to conquer (*a* from); to overcome.
  (b) (*fig*) *post etc* to win; *market* to win, open up;

person to win round, win over; *woman* to win, succeed in attracting.

consabido *adj* (a) well-known, familiar; usual; old, oft-repeated, timeworn. (b) above-mentioned.

consagración *nf* consecration, dedication.

consagrado *adj* (a) consecrated (*a* to); dedicated (*a* to).
  (b) (*fig*) time-honoured, hallowed, ritual, traditional; **según la expresión consagrada** in the time-honoured phrase.

consagrar [1a] **1** *vt* (a) (*Rel*) to consecrate, hallow; to dedicate (*a* to); *emperor* to deify.
  (b) (*fig*) *life, time, effort etc* to devote, dedicate (*a* to); put in (*a* at); *monument, plaque* to put up, dedicate (*a* to).
  (c) to confirm; **este triunfo le consagra como un cirujano excepcional** this success confirms him as (*or* shows him to be) a really exceptional surgeon.
  2 consagrarse *vr*: **— a** to devote oneself to.

consanguíneo *adj* related by blood, consanguineous.

consanguinidad *nf* blood relationship, consanguinity.

consciente 1 *adj* (a) conscious; **estar — de** to be conscious of, be aware of.
  (b) (*Med*) **estar —** to be conscious.
  (c) (*Law*) fully responsible for one's actions, aware of what one is doing.
  2 *nm* conscious, conscious mind.

conscientemente *adv* consciously.

conscripción *nf* (*SAm*) conscription.

conscripto *nm* (*SAm*) conscript.

consecución *nf* obtaining, acquisition; attainment; **de difícil —** hard to obtain, difficult to get hold of; **les ayudó en la — de trabajo** he helped them in obtaining work; **para la — de estos objetos** for the attainment of these aims.

consecuencia *nf* (a) consequence; outcome, result; conclusion; **a — de eso, en — de eso** as a result of that, as a consequence of that; **como —, en —** in consequence, accordingly; **aceptar las —s** to take the consequences; **¡pues aténgase a las —s!** then you'd better watch out!; **saqué la — de que . . .** I gathered that . . .; I drew the conclusion that . . .; **no tuvo —s** it had no ill effects, nothing bad happened as a result; **traer algo a —** to bring something up.
  (b) importance; **de —** of importance, of some weight; **ser de —** to be important.
  (c) consistency; **obrar con —** to act consistently.

consecuente *adj* (a) consistent (*con* with). (b) (*Philos*) consequent.

consecuentemente *adv* consistently.

consecutivo *adj* (*Gram etc*) consecutive.

conseguible *adj* obtainable; attainable.

conseguir [3d *and* 3l] *vt* (a) to get, obtain, secure; to bring about; **— + infin** to succeed in + *ger*, manage to + *infin*; **— que uno haga algo** to manage to make someone do something, get someone to do something.
  (b) *aim etc* to attain, achieve.

conseja *nf* story, tale, legend; old wives' tale.

consejero *nm*, **consejera** *nf* adviser; consultant; member (of a board *etc*); (*Pol*) councillor; **— de publicidad** advertising consultant.

consejo *nm* (a) **un —** a piece of advice; a hint; **su —** his advice, his counsel; **agradezco el —** I am grateful for your advice; **pedir — a uno** to ask someone for advice, ask someone's advice; **— pericial** expert advice; **—s** advice.
  (b) (*Pol etc*) council; (*Comm*) board; (*Law*) tribunal; court; **— de administración** board of directors; **— de disciplina** disciplinary board; **— de ministros** cabinet; cabinet meeting; **— privado** privy council; **— de guerra** court-martial; **— de guerra sumarísimo** drumhead court-martial.

consenso *nm* accord; assent; consensus.

consentido *adj* (a) *child* spoiled, pampered. (b) *husband* complaisant.

consentidor *adj* *mother etc* indulgent; weak, compliant; *husband* complaisant.

consentimiento *nm* consent.

consentir [3i] **1** *vt* (a) to consent to; to allow, permit; to tolerate; **— a uno + infin, — que uno + subj** to allow someone to + *infin*; **aquí no consienten hablar** they don't let you speak here; **¡eso no se puede —!** we can't have (*or* allow) that!
  (b) to admit; to bear, put up with, wear (*fam*); **la plataforma no consiente más peso** the platform will not bear any more weight; **el abrigo consiente un arreglo más** the overcoat will bear repairing once more.
  (c) *child* to pamper, spoil.
  2 *vi* (a) to agree, consent, say yes (*en* to); to give

in; — **en hacer algo** to agree to + *infin*, consent to + *infin*.
　(b) — **con** to pamper, spoil.
3 consentirse *vr* to break, give (way); to split, crack (up *etc*).
conserje *nm* porter; doorman; caretaker.
conserjería *nf* porter's office.
conserva *nf* (a) (*act*) preserving.
　(b) preserved foods; preserve(s); jam; pickle; —**s alimenticias** tinned foods, canned goods; —**s de carne** canned meat; potted meat; **en** — preserved; pickled; tinned, canned.
　(c) (*Naut*) convoy; **navegar en (la)** — to sail in convoy.
conservación *nf* conservation; preservation; (*Archit etc*) maintenance, upkeep; — **refrigerada** cold storage; — **de suelos** soil conservation; **gastos de** — upkeep costs, maintenance expenses; **instinto de** — instinct of self-preservation.
conservador 1 *adj* (a) preservative.
　(b) (*Pol*) conservative.
2 *nm*, **conservadora** *nf* (a) (*Pol*) conservative.
　(b) (*of museum*) curator, keeper; — **adjunto** assistant keeper.
conservadurismo *nm* (*Pol etc*) conservatism.
conservar [1a] **1** *vt* (a) *food etc* to preserve; *meat* to tin, can; *resources* to conserve; (*Archit etc*) to preserve.
　(b) *person, life* to preserve, save.
　(c) *custom* to keep up, maintain, retain; *estate etc* to keep up; *colour, secret, friends etc* to keep; "**conserve su derecha**" "keep to the right"; **conservo varias cartas suyas** I have a few letters of his; **conserva todavía la señal** he still has (*or* bears) the mark.
2 conservarse *vr* (a) to survive, remain, still exist; to be retained, be kept; to last out.
　(b) (*person*) to keep (well); to take good care of oneself; — **con** (*or* **en**) **salud** to keep well; ¡**consérvese bien!** look after yourself!, I hope you keep well!
conservatismo *nm* conservatism.
conservativo *adj* preservative.
conservatorio *nm* (a) (*Mus*) conservatoire. (b) (*Chi*) greenhouse. (c) (*Arg*) private school.
conservero *adj* canning (*attr*); **la industria conservera** the canning industry.
considerable *adj* considerable; substantial; sizeable.
consideración *nf* (a) (*act*) consideration; thought; reflexion; **está en** — it is under consideration; **tomar en** — to take into account, take into consideration.
　(b) consideration; respect, regard; **en** — **a** considering, in consideration of; **por** — **a** out of regard for; **sin** — **a** irrespective of; without regard to; **hablar sin** — to speak disrespectfully; **tratar a uno sin** — to treat someone without consideration; **no le tengan Vds ninguna** — don't give him any special treatment.
　(c) respect, esteem; **tengo una gran** — **por él** I hold him in high esteem.
　(d) —**es** kindness; **tener** —**es con uno** to be kind to someone.
　(e) importance; **una casa de cierta** — a sizeable house; **una herida de** — a serious wound; **de poca** — unimportant, of no account.
consideradamente *adv* considerately, kindly, thoughtfully.
considerado *adj* (a) respected, esteemed; **mal** — unworthy. (b) considerate, kind (*con* to), thoughtful.
considerar [1a] *vt* (a) to consider; to think about, reflect on; — **que** . . . to consider that . . ., think that . . .
　(b) to take into account; **considera que** . . . bear in mind that . . ., don't forget that . . .
　(c) to consider; to think, deem; **lo considero imposible** I consider it (to be) impossible; **le consideran como loco** they think him mad; **le consideran como futuro rey** they consider him to be a future king.
　(d) to esteem, respect; — **poco a** to scorn, despise.
　(e) to be kind to, show consideration for.
consigna *nf* (a) order, instruction; (*Mil*) watchword; (*of campaign etc*) watchword, slogan, motto; catchword; —**s de un vuelo** (*Mil etc*) operating instructions for a flight, operational orders for a flight.
　(b) (*Rail etc*) cloakroom, left-luggage office, checkroom (*US*).
consignación *nf* (a) consignment, shipment. (b) (*Fin*) appropriation; earmarked sum.
consignador *nm* consignor.

consignar [1a] *vt* (a) (*Comm*) to send, dispatch, remit (*a* to); to consign (*a* to); to deposit (*a* with).
　(b) (*Fin*) to assign (*para* to, for).
　(c) *detail, fact* to record, register; to put, set down, state; **olvidé** — **mi nombre** I forgot to write my name in, I forgot to state my name; **el hecho no quedó consignado en ningún libro** the fact was not recorded (*or* set down) in any book.
consignatario *nm* (*Comm*) consignee; (*Comm*) agent; (*Law*) assign(ee); (*of letter etc*) recipient, addressee.
consigo *pron* with him, with her; with you; with one(self) *etc*; **no lleva nada** — he wasn't taking anything with him; **hablaba** — she was talking to herself; *see* **dar** *etc*.
consiguiente *adj* consequent (*a* upon); resulting; **por** — and so, therefore, consequently.
consistencia *nf* consistence, consistency.
consistente *adj* (a) *conduct, theory etc* consistent; *person* (*SAm*: *angl*) consistent; *reason etc* sound, valid.
　(b) *material* solid, firm, tough, durable; *paste etc* stiff, thick; substantial.
　(c) — **en** consisting of.
consistir [3a] *vi*: — **en** (*SAm*: — **de**, *angl*) (a) to consist of; to be made of, be composed of; **¿en qué consiste?** what does it consist of?
　(b) (*of cause etc*) to lie in, be due to; **no consiste en eso la dificultad** the difficulty does not lie in that; **su atractivo consiste en su naturalidad** her charm lies in her naturalness; **si en mí solo consistiese** if it lay with me alone, if it depended entirely on me.
consistorial *adj* (*Eccl*) consistorial; *see* **casa**.
consistorio *nm* (*Eccl*) consistory; (*Pol*) town council.
consocio *nm* fellow member; (*Comm*) co-partner, associate.
consola *nf* console table; (*Archit, Mus*) console.
consolación *nf* consolation.
consolador 1 *adj* consoling, comforting. **2** *nm*, **consoladora** *nf* consoler, comforter.
consolar [1m] **1** *vt* to console, comfort; **me consuela de no haber ido** it consoles me for not having gone.
　2 consolarse *vr* to console oneself; to find consolation (*con* in), take comfort (*con* from).
consolatorio *adj* consolatory.
consolidación *nf* consolidation.
consolidados *nmpl* (*Fin*) consols.
consolidar [1a] *vt* to consolidate, strengthen; *wall etc* to shore up; *debt* to fund.
consomé *nm* consommé, clear soup.
consonancia *nf* (a) consonance, harmony; **en** — **con** in accordance with, in harmony with. (b) (*Lit*) consonance, rhyme.
consonante 1 *adj* (a) consonant, harmonious; consistent.
　(b) (*Ling*) consonantal.
　(c) (*Lit*) rhyming.
　2 *nm* (*Lit*) rhyme, rhyming word.
　3 *nf* (*Ling*) consonant.
consonántico *adj* consonantal.
consonar [1m] *vi* (a) (*Mus and fig*) to be in harmony, harmonize. (b) (*Lit*) to rhyme (*con* with).
consorcio *nm* (a) (*Comm*) consortium; association; partnership; syndicate. (b) (*of circumstances etc*) conjunction.
consorte *nmf* (a) consort, spouse; **príncipe** — prince consort. (b) (*fig*) partner, companion. (c) (*Law*) —**s** colitigants; (*pej*) partners in crime, accomplices.
conspicuo *adj* eminent, famous.
conspiración *nf* conspiracy.
conspirador *nm*, **conspiradora** *nf* conspirator.
conspirar [1a] *vi* to conspire, plot (*con* with, *contra* against); — **a** + *infin* to conspire to + *infin* (*also fig*).
constancia *nf* (a) constancy; steadiness; firmness, steadfastness; loyalty.
　(b) certainty; proof, evidence; **no hay** — **de ello** there is no certainty of it; there is no record of it, it is not recorded; **dejar** — **de algo** to place something on record; to show evidence of something.
　(c) (*SAm*) documentary proof, written evidence.
constante 1 *adj* (a) *wind, effort etc* constant; unchanging; steady; *person* firm, steadfast; *friend* loyal, faithful, staunch.
　(b) constant; continual; unending.
　2 *nf* (*Math and fig*) constant.
constantemente *adv* constantly.
Constantinopla Constantinople.
Constanza *f* Constance.
constar [1a] *vi* (a) — **de** to be clear from, be evident from; **consta que** . . . it is clear that . . ., it is a fact that . . .; it is known that . . .; **me consta que** . . . I know for sure that . . ., I have evidence that . . .;

conste que yo no lo aprobé let it be clearly understood that I did not approve it; consta por . . . as is shown by . . .

(b) to be on record, exist in recorded form; "no consta" (of book) "not available"; no consta en el catálogo it is not listed in the catalogue, it does not figure in the catalogue; en el carnet no consta su edad his age is not stated on the licence; hacer — to record; to certify; hacer — que . . . to reveal that . . .

(c) — de to consist of, be composed of.

constatar [1a] vt (gall) to confirm; to show, prove, check (que that).

constelación nf constellation.

constelado adj starry, full of stars; (fig) bespangled (de with).

consternación nf consternation, dismay.

consternado adj: estar —, quedarse — to be dismayed, be shattered; to be aghast; dejar — =consternar.

consternar [1a] 1 vt to dismay, shatter, shock. 2 consternarse vr to be dismayed, be shattered; to be aghast.

constipación nf=constipado 2.

constipado 1 adj: estar — to have a cold. 2 nm (Med) cold, catarrh; coger un — to catch a cold.

constiparse [1a] vr to catch a cold.

constitución nf (all senses) constitution.

constitucional 1 adj constitutional. 2 nmf constitutionalist.

constitucionalmente adv constitutionally.

constituir [3g] 1 vt (a) family, whole etc to constitute, form, make up; lo constituyen 12 miembros it consists of 12 members, it is made up of 12 members; esa industria constituye su principal riqueza that industry constitutes (or is, forms) its chief wealth.

(b) (equivalence) to be; eso no constituye estorbo that isn't an obstacle; that doesn't amount to an obstacle; para mí constituye un placer for me it is a pleasure.

(c) body, committee etc to constitute, create, set up, establish; school etc to found; scholarship etc to institute, endow.

(d) — una nación en república to make a country into a republic; — una ciudad en capital to make a city the capital; — a uno en árbitro to set someone up as arbiter; — heredero a uno to make someone one's heir; — algo en principio to erect something into a principle, set something up as a principle.

(e) — a uno en una obligación to force someone into an obligation.

2 constituirse vr (a) — en (or por) algo to set oneself up as something, make oneself into something.

(b) — en un lugar to present oneself at a place, appear in person in a place, (in orders) report at a place.

constitutivo 1 adj constitutive; (Parl, Pol etc) constituent. 2 nm constituent.

constituyente adj (Pol) constituent.

constreñir [3h and 3l] vt (a) initiative, movement etc to restrict.

(b) — a uno a hacer algo to compel (or force, constrain) someone to do something.

(c) (Med) artery to constrict; person, bowels to constipate.

constricción nf constriction.

construcción nf (a) construction'; building; structure; — de buques, — naval shipbuilding; — de carreteras road building; en —, en vía de — under construction, in course of construction.

(b) (Gram) construction.

constructivamente adv constructively.

constructivo adj constructive.

constructor 1 adj building, construction (attr). 2 nm builder (also fig); — de buques, — naval shipbuilder; — cinematográfico designer of film sets.

construir [3g] vt (a) to construct; to build, erect, put up. (b) (Gram) to construe.

consuelda nf comfrey.

consuelo nm consolation, solace, comfort; llorar sin — to weep inconsolably; premio de — consolation prize.

consuetudinario adj (a) habitual, customary; drunkard hardened, confirmed. (b) derecho — common law.

cónsul nm consul.

consulado nm (post) consulship; (office) consulate.

consular adj consular.

consulta nf (a) (act) consultation.

(b) (Med) consulting room.

(c) (Med) examination; horas de — surgery hours;

la — es de 5 a 8 the surgery is from 5 to 8; el doctor no pasa — a domicilio the doctor does not make home visits.

(d) (Hist) opinion.

(e) libro de —, obra de — reference book, work of reference.

consultación nf consultation.

consultar [1a] vt (a) person to consult (acerca de, sobre about, on); — a un médico to consult a doctor, see a doctor.

(b) matter to discuss, raise, take up (con with); lo consultaré con mi abogado I will take the matter up with my lawyer.

(c) book to consult, look up; reference, word to look up; to hunt up, chase up.

consultivo adj consultative.

consultor nm consultant.

consultorio nm information bureau; (Med) surgery, consulting room; (of magazine) problem page.

consumación nf consummation; end; extinction.

consumado adj consummate, perfect; accomplished (en in); rogue etc thorough, out-and-out.

consumar [1a] vt (a) to complete, accomplish, carry out; crime to commit; raid, robbery to carry out; deal to close, complete; marriage to consummate; (Law) sentence to carry out.

(b) (CAm, Col) to submerge.

consumición nf (a) consumption. (b) (in restaurant etc) meal.

consumido adj (a) person skinny, wasted; fruit etc shrunken. (b) (fig) timid; fretful, easily upset; tener — a uno to keep someone in a nervous state.

consumidor nm consumer.

consumir [3a] 1 vt (a) food to consume, eat; product to use, consume; fuel to burn, use, consume; (in restaurant etc) to take, have.

(b) material to wear away; patience to wear down; liquid content to dry up; person to waste away, exhaust the energies of, wear out.

(c) (fig) le consumen los celos he is eaten up with jealousy; ese deseo le consume that desire is burning him up; me consume su terquedad his obstinacy is getting on my nerves.

2 consumirse vr (a) (fruit etc) to shrink, shrivel (up), lose its substance; (person) to waste away; (soup etc) to boil down.

(b) (by fire) to burn out, be consumed, be devoured.

(c) (person: fig) to burn oneself out; to pine away, mope (de because of); — de envidia to be eaten up with jealousy; — de rabia to fume with rage; me consumo de verle así it vexes me to see him like that.

consumo nm, consunción nf (all senses) consumption.

consuno: de — adv with one accord.

consustancial adj consubstantial; ser — con to be inseparable from, be all of a piece with.

contabilidad nf accounting, book-keeping; (as profession) accountancy.

contabilizadora nf accounting machine, adding machine.

contabilizar [1f] vt to enter in the accounts.

contable 1 adj countable. 2 nm accountant, book-keeper; — automático adding machine.

contacto nm (a) contact (also fig); touch; estar en — con to be in touch with; entrar en — con to come into contact with; poner a A en — con B to put A in touch with B; ponerse en — con to get into touch with, contact; lo hizo el municipio en — con el gobierno the city did it in collaboration with the government.

(b) (SAm) switch, contact breaker.

contado 1 adj (a) tiene los días —s his days are numbered.

(b) —s few, scarce; rare; en contadas ocasiones on rare occasions; contadas veces seldom, rarely; son —s los que . . . there are few who . . .; pero son contadísimos los que pueden but those who can are very few and far between.

2 nm (a) (Comm) al —, de — (SAm) for cash, cash down; pago al — cash payment.

(b) por de — naturally, of course; tomar algo por de — to take something for granted.

(c) (Col) instalment.

contador nm (a) (Math) abacus, counting frame.

(b) (of café) counter.

(c) (Comm) accountant, book-keeper; cashier; (Law) receiver, official auditor; (Ec) pawnbroker, moneylender; — de navío purser.

(d) (Tech) meter; — de aparcamiento parking meter; — de electricidad electricity meter; — de gas gas meter; — Geiger Geiger counter; — de revoluciones tachometer; — de taxi taximeter.

contaduría *nf* (a) (*as profession*) accountancy.
(b) accountant's office; cashier's office; (*Theat*)
box office; (*Ec*) pawnbroker's, pawnshop.
contagiar [1b] **1** *vt* (a) *disease* to pass on, transmit,
give (*a* to); to spread; *person* to infect (*con* with).
(b) (*fig*) to infect, contaminate (*con* with); to
corrupt.
2 contagiarse *vr* (a) to become infected; — **de** to
become infected with, catch.
(b) (*fig*) — **de** to become infected with, be tainted
with.
contagio *nm* infection, contagion; (*fig*) contagion,
corruption; taint.
contagioso *adj disease* contagious, infectious, catching; *person* infected, infectious; (*fig*) catching;
corrupting.
contaminación *nf* (a) contamination; (*of text*) corruption; (*lit*) influence; — **del aire** air pollution. (b)
(*fig*) taint, infection; defilement.
contaminar [1a] **1** *vt* (a) to contaminate; *air, water*
to pollute; *dress* to soil; *text* to corrupt; (*lit*) to
influence.
(b) (*fig*) to taint, infect; to defile; (*Eccl*) to
profane.
2 contaminarse *vr* to be(come) contaminated
(*con, de* with, by).
contante *adj*: **dinero** — (**y sonante**) cash, ready
money.
contar [1m] **1** *vt* (a) (*Math*) to count; to number off;
money etc to count (up); to include, count in;
cuenta 18 años she is 18; — **con los dedos** to count
on one's fingers; **hay 9 kms a — desde aquí** it's 9
kms starting from here.
(b) to count, reckon, consider; **al niño le
cuentan por medio** they count the child as half; **le
cuento entre mis amigos** I reckon him among my
friends; **sin** — not counting, not including; except for;
not to mention; **sin — con que . . .** leaving aside the
fact that . . .
(c) to remember, bear in mind; **cuenta que es
más fuerte que tú** don't forget he's stronger than
you are.
(d) *story etc* to tell; **es muy largo de** — it's a
long story; **¡cuéntaselo a tu abuela!** (*etc*) go tell that
to the marines!; **¡a quien se lo cuentas!** you're
telling me!
2 *vi* (a) (*Math*) to count, count up; **hay que** —
mucho para llegar al final del mes we have to go
carefully (*or* watch it) in order to get to the end of
the month; **cuenta por dos** he counts for (*or* as) two.
(b) (*fig*) to count; **esos puntos no cuentan** those
points don't count; **no cuenta para nada** he doesn't
count at all.
(c) — **con** to rely on, count on, depend on; to
have; **cuenta conmigo** trust me, you can rely on me;
contaban por segura su ayuda they were relying
absolutely on his help, they thought he was sure to
help them; **cuenta con varias ventajas** it has a
number of advantages; **no contábamos con eso** we
had not bargained for that, that was unexpected.
3 contarse *vr* (a) to be counted; to be included, to
figure (*entre* among); **se le cuenta entre los más
famosos** he is reckoned among the most famous;
me cuento entre sus admiradores I count myself
among his admirers.
(b) (*story*) to be told; **cuéntase que . . .** it is said
that . . ., it is related that . . .; **¿qué te cuentas?** (*fam*)
how's things? (*fam*).
contemplación *nf* (a) contemplation; meditation;
reflexion.
(b) — **es** indulgence; leniency, gentle treatment;
no andarse con — es not to stand on ceremony;
tener demasiadas — es con uno to be too indulgent
towards someone, be too soft on someone;
tratar a uno con — es to treat someone leniently; to
handle someone with kid gloves; **no me vengas con
— es** don't come to me with excuses; **sin — es**
without ceremony; without any explanation.
contemplar [1a] **1** *vt* (a) to look at, gaze at, watch,
contemplate; (*fig*) to contemplate.
(b) *person* to show (*extra*) consideration for,
treat (*too*) indulgently, be (*too*) lenient with.
2 *vi* (*Rel*) to meditate.
contemplativo *adj* contemplative.
contemporáneo 1 *adj* contemporary; contemporaneous. **2** *nm*, **contemporánea** *nf* contemporary.
contemporizador 1 *adj* excessively compliant;
lacking firm principles. **2** *nm* timeserver, compro-
miser; person who lacks firm principles.
contemporizar [1f] *vi* to be compliant, show oneself
ready to compromise; (*pej*) to lack firm principles;
to temporize; — **con uno** to hedge with someone.

contención *nf* (a) (*Mil etc*) containing, containment.
(b) contention; rivalry. (c) (*Law*) suit.
contencioso *adj* (a) contentious; *person* argumentative, captious. (b) (*Law*) litigious.
contender [2g] *vi* to contend (*con* with, *sobre* over);
to compete, be rivals (*en* in); (*Mil etc*) to fight; — **en
unas oposiciones** to take part in a competitive
examination.
contendiente *nm* contestant, contender.
contener [2l] **1** *vt* (a) *contents* to hold, contain.
(b) (*Mil etc*) to contain; *mob* to hold back; *rebels*
to keep down, hold down; *horse* to hold back,
restrain; *breath* to hold; *emotion* to keep back, choke
back, bottle up; *anger* to contain; *yawn, laughter* to
smother; *tendency* to check, restrain, curb.
(c) (*Chi*) to mean.
2 contenerse *vr* to control oneself, restrain
oneself, hold oneself in check.
contenido 1 *adj* (a) *person* restrained, controlled;
moderate; equable. (b) *emotion* suppressed. **2** *nm*
contents; content.
contenta *nf* (*Comm*) endorsement; (*Mil*) good-
conduct certificate; (*Law*) release, acknowledgement.
contentadizo *adj* (*also* **bien** —) easy to please; **mal**
— hard to please.
contentamente *adv* contentedly.
contentamiento *nm* contentment, satisfaction.
contentar [1a] **1** *vt* (a) to satisfy, content; to please,
make happy.
(b) (*Comm*) to endorse.
(c) (*SAm*) to reconcile.
2 contentarse *vr* (a) — **con** to be contented with,
be satisfied with; — **con** + *infin* to content oneself
with + *ger*; **se contenta con cualquier cosita** he's
satisfied with anything, any little thing keeps him
happy.
(b) (*SAm*) to be reconciled (*con* with).
contento 1 *adj* contented, satisfied; pleased; glad,
happy; **estar** — **con** (*or* **de**) to be satisfied with, be
happy about, be content with; **están — s con el
coche** they are pleased with the car; **no está** — **en
su trabajo** he's not happy in his work; **viven muy
— s** they live very happily; **¿estás — ?** are you happy?;
estar tan — **como unas castañuelas** to be as happy
as a lark; **para dejar** (*or* **poner, tener**) **a uno** — in
order to keep someone happy; **estar** (*or* **quedar**) —
de + *infin* to be content to + *infin*; **estaría tan** —
de + *infin* I would as soon + *infin*.
2 *nm* contentment; joy, happiness; **a** — to one's
satisfaction; **no caber en sí de** — to be overjoyed,
be overwhelmed with joy.
contentura *nf* (*Ant, Pan*) = **contento 2**.
contera *nf* (a) (*metal*) tip, end; ferrule. (b) (*fig*) small
extra, small addition. (c) **por** — to crown it all, as a
final blow.
contertuliano *nm*, **contertuliana** *nf*, **contertulio**
nm, **contertulia** *nf* fellow member (*of a social set*);
patron, regular guest (*of hotel*); — **s de café** café companions, people who regularly meet in a café,
members of the same coffee set.
contesta *nf* (a) (*SAm*) answer. (b) (*Mex, Pan*) talk,
chat. (c) (*Mex*) declaration of love.
contestable *adj* questionable, debatable.
contestación *nf* answer, reply; — **a la demanda** (*Law*)
defence plea; **mala** — sharp retort, piece of backchat; **dejar una carta sin** — to leave a letter unanswered.
contestador *adj* (*SAm*) cheeky, saucy.
contestar [1a] **1** *vti* (a) to answer, reply; (*pej*) to
answer back; — **una pregunta** (*Univ etc*) to answer a
question; — **una carta** to reply to a letter; — **el
teléfono** to answer the telephone; — **a un saludo** to
return a greeting, respond to a greeting; **contestó que
sí** he replied that it was (*or* he would *etc*); **abstenerse
de** — to make no reply; **un 7 por 100 se abstuvo de**
— (*in poll*) there were 7% "don't knows".
(b) (*Law*) to corroborate, confirm.
2 *vi* (*Mex*) to chat, talk; to argue.
contesto *nm* (*Mex, Per, RPl*) answer, reply.
contexto *nm* (a) (*Lit etc*) context. (b) (*Tech*) web,
tangle.
contextura *nf* (a) contexture. (b) (*Anat*) build,
physique; constitution; make-up.
contienda *nf* contest; struggle, fight.
contigo *pron* with you; (*arch, to* God) with thee.
contigüidad *nf* nearness, closeness, contiguity.
contiguo *adj* next; adjacent (*a* to); contiguous (*a* to),
adjoining; **en un cuarto** — in an adjoining room.
continencia *nf* continence.
continental *adj* continental.

continente 1 *adj* continent.
  2 *nm* **(a)** (*Geog*) continent; **el — norteamericano** the North-American continent.
    (b) container.
    (c) (*fig*) air, mien, bearing; **de — distinguido** with an air of distinction; **de — duro** harsh-looking.
contingencia *nf* contingency; risk; hazard, danger.
contingente 1 *adj* contingent. **2** *nm* **(a)** (*Mil etc*) contingent. **(b)** = **contingencia**. **(c)** (*Comm etc*) quota; **— de importación** import quota.
continuación *nf* continuation; sequel; **a —** then, next; immediately after; later (on), subsequently; **según lo expuesto a —** as set out below, as follows; **a — de** after, following.
continuamente *adv* continuously; continually, constantly.
continuar [1e] **1** *vt* to continue, go on with; to resume; to carry on (with); *road etc* to continue, prolong, extend.
  2 *vi* **(a)** to continue; to go on, carry on; **"continuará"** (*serial*) "to be continued"; — **hablando** to continue talking, continue to talk, go on talking; **continúa lloviendo** it's still raining; **la puerta continúa cerrada** the door is still shut; **continuaba en Noruega** he was still in Norway; he remained in Norway; **— con su trabajo** to continue (*or* go on) with one's work; **— con salud** to keep in good health; **— en su puesto** to stay at one's job, carry on with one's work.
    (b) (*of route etc*) to continue; **la carretera continúa más allá de la frontera** the road continues (on) beyond the frontier; **— con** (*also* **—se con**) to adjoin; to link up with, connect with.
continuidad *nf* continuity.
continuo 1 *adj* **(a)** (*in space, time; of series*) continuous; (*Tech*) *belt etc* endless; *see* **acto, sesión**.
    (b) (*of action*) continual, constant; **sus continuas quejas** his continual complaints.
    (c) a la continua, (de) — continually.
  2 *nm* continuum.
contonearse [1a] *vr* (*man*) to swagger, strut; (*woman*) to swing one's hips, walk with a waggle; to walk affectedly, show off as one walks.
contoneo *nm* swagger, strut; hip-swinging, waggle; affected gait.
contorcerse [2b *and* 2h] *vr* to writhe, twist.
contorno *nm* **(a)** outline (*also Art*); (*Geog*) contour; perimeter; form, shape; **en — round** about, all around.
    (b) measurement round, distance round; **— de un árbol** girth of a tree, distance round a tree's trunk; **el — de cintura es de 22 pulgadas** her waist measurement is 22 inches.
    (c) —s environs, neighbourhood, surrounding area; **Caracas y sus —s** Caracas and its environs.
contorsión *nf* contortion.
contorsionarse [1a] *vr* to contort oneself.
contorsionista *nmf* contortionist.
contra 1 *adv* **(a)** against; **puntos en —** points against; **hablar en —** to speak against; **votar en —** to vote against; **opinar en —** to disagree, take the contrary view.
    (b) de — (*SAm*) extra, over and above.
  2 *prep* against; (*of view etc*) opposite, facing; (*Comm: of draft*) on; **apoyar algo — la pared** to lean something against the wall; **en — de** against; **hablar en — de un proyecto** to speak against a plan; **en — de lo que habíamos pensado** contrary to what we had thought; **ir en — de algo** to go against something, run counter to something.
  3 *nm* con; *see* **pro**.
  4 *nf* **(a)** (*Fencing*) counter.
    (b) trouble, snag; inconvenience.
    (c) hacer la — to be consistently obstructive, persist in taking an opposite view; **llevar la — a uno** to oppose someone, contradict someone.
    (d) (*SAm*) antidote.
    (e) (*Cu, Mex, PR*) extra, bonus.
contra ... counter- ..., **contra** ...; cross- ...; *eg* **contramanifestación** counter-demonstration; **contrapropaganda** counter-propaganda.
contraalmirante *nm* rear admiral.
contraatacar [1g] *vti* to counter-attack.
contraataque *nm* counter-attack.
contrabajo *nm* double bass.
contrabalancear [1a] *vt* to counterbalance.
contrabalanza *nf* counterbalance.
contrabandear [1a] *vi* to smuggle, live by smuggling.
contrabandista *nmf* smuggler; **— de armas** gun-runner.
contrabando *nm* **(a)** (*act*) smuggling; **— de armas** gun-running.
    (b) contraband, smuggled goods; prohibited

article, banned item; **géneros de —** smuggled goods; **amores de —** (*fig*) clandestine love affair; **pasar** (*or* **introducir**) **algo de —** to smuggle something in, get something in illegally.
contrabordo *nm* (*Mex*) kerb.
contracción *nf* **(a)** contraction; shrinkage; wasting. **(b)** (*Col*) diligence, industry.
contracifra *nf* key (to a code).
contracorriente 1 *nf* cross-current; undercurrent. **2** *adv:* **estar —, ir —** to go against the tide (*fig*), go against current tendencies.
contráctil *adj* contractile.
contractual *adj* contractual.
contrachapado 1 *adj:* **madera *f* contrachapada** = **2** *nm* plywood.
contradecir [3p] *vt* to contradict.
contradicción *nf* contradiction; (*fig*) incompatibility; **espíritu de —** contrariness; **A y B están en —** A and B stand in contradiction to each other.
contradictorio *adj* contradictory.
contraempuje *nm* counter-thrust.
contraer [2p] **1** *vt* **(a)** *material, substance etc* to contract; to shrink; to make smaller (*or* tighter *etc*); *script, speech* to condense, shorten; **— la frente** to wrinkle one's brow; **la humedad contrae las cuerdas** the damp makes the ropes tauten.
    (b) *debt, obligation etc* to contract; *habit* to acquire, pick up, get into; *disease* to contract, catch; **— matrimonio** to marry (**con una** someone); **— parentesco con** to become related to.
    (c) to restrict, limit (**a** to); **contrae su teoría a ciertos puntos** he limits his theory to certain points.
  2 contraerse *vr* **(a)** to contract; to shrink; to get smaller; to tighten, tauten.
    (b) — a to limit oneself to.
contraespionaje *nm* counter-espionage.
contraexplosión *nf* (*Aut etc*) backfire.
contrafallar [1a] *vt* to overtrump.
contrafuerte *nm* (*Archit*) buttress; (*Mil*) outwork; (*Geog*) spur; foothill; (*of shoe*) stiffener.
contragambito *nm* counter-gambit.
contragolpe *nm* counter-blow; (*fig*) backlash, reaction, kickback.
contrahacer [2s] *vt* to copy, imitate; *coin* to counterfeit; *document, proof* to forge, fake; *book* to pirate; *person* to mimic, impersonate, do an impression of.
contrahaz *nm* (*of cloth*) wrong side.
contrahecho *adj* **(a)** counterfeit; fake, faked, forged; spurious, pirated. **(b)** (*Anat*) hunchbacked, deformed.
contrahechura *nf* counterfeit; forgery; fake; pirated edition, spurious edition.
contraído *adj* **(a)** contracted; shrunken, wasted. **(b)** (*Col*) diligent, industrious.
contrainteligencia *nf* counter-intelligence.
contrainterrogatorio *nm* (*Law*) cross-examination, cross-questioning.
contrairritante *nm* counterirritant.
contralto 1 *adj* contralto. **2** *nm* counter tenor. **3** *nf* contralto.
contraluz *nf* view against the light; **a —** against the light.
contramaestre *nm* (*Naut*) warrant officer; boatswain; (*Tech*) foreman.
contramandar [1a] *vt* to countermand.
contramandato *nm* counter-order.
contramarcha *nf* **(a)** (*Mil*) countermarch. **(b)** (*Aut etc*) reverse; **dar —** **(a)** to reverse, (*fig*) go into reverse.
contramarchar [1a] *vi* to countermarch.
contramatar [1a] **1** *vt* (*SAm*): **— a uno** to hurt someone by banging him into something.
  2 contramatarse *vr* **(a)** (*SAm*) to crash into something, collide with something.
    (b) (*Mex*) **— de + *infin*** to repent of + *ger*.
contramedia *nf* counter-measure.
contranatural *adj* unnatural.
contraofensiva *nf* counter-offensive.
contraoferta *nf* counter-offer.
contraorden *nf* counter-order.
contrapartida *nf* **(a)** (*Comm, Fin: in account*) balancing entry. **(b)** (*fig*) compensation; counter-weight; **como — de** as compensation for; as a counterweight to.
contrapelo: a — *adv* **(a) acariciar un gato a —** to stroke a cat up the wrong way.
    (b) a — the wrong way; against the grain; **a — de** against, counter to; **todo lo hace a —** he does everything the wrong way round; **intervino muy a —** he spoke up in a most unfortunate way, he chose quite the wrong way in which to intervene.
contrapesar [1a] *vt* to counterbalance (*con* with); (*fig*) to offset; balance, compensate for.

contrapeso nm (a) counterpoise, counterweight; (Comm) makeweight; (Circus) balancing pole. (b) (fig) counterweight. (c) (Chi) anxiety, worry.

contraponer [2r] vt (a) two colours etc to compare, set against each other.

(b) — A a B to set up A against B, put up A as a barrier against B; **a esta idea ellos contraponen su teoría de que** . . . against this idea they set up their theory that . . .

contraposición nf comparison; contrast, clash; **en —** a in contrast to.

contraproducente adj self-defeating; counter-productive; **tener un resultado —** to have a boomerang effect, boomerang.

contrapuerta nf storm door; double door; protective door.

contrapuntear [1a] vi (SAm) to sing improvised verses in competition; (fig) to compete.

contrapunteo nm (Cu, Per, PR, RPl) argument; abuse, angry words; **en —** (Per) in competition.

contrapuntístico adj contrapuntal.

contrapunto nm (a) counterpoint. (b) (SAm) poetic competition with improvised verses; **de —** in competition.

contrariar [1c] vt (a) to oppose, be opposed to, go against; to impede, thwart. (b) to vex, upset, annoy.

contrariedad nf (a) obstacle; setback, misfortune; snag, trouble.

(b) vexation, annoyance; **producir — a uno** to upset someone, cause annoyance to someone.

(c) contrary nature; opposition.

contrario 1 adj (a) (of person) opposed, different; **son —s en sus aficiones** they have opposing tastes, they differ widely in tastes.

(b) direction, side etc opposite; **en sentido —** the other way, in the other direction.

(c) sense opposite (de to); **se ha interpretado en sentido — del que realmente tiene** it has been interpreted in the opposite sense to its true one.

(d) contrary (a to); harmful, damaging, hostile (a to); **— a los intereses del país** contrary to the nation's interests.

(e) wind etc contrary; fortune adverse.

(f) (of opinion) opposed; **él es — a las reformas** he is opposed to the reforms, he is against the changes.

(g) (idioms) **al —, por el —** on the contrary; **al — de** unlike; **al — de lo que habíamos pensado** against what we had thought; **todo salió al — de lo que habíamos previsto** it all turned out differently from what we had expected; **hablar al —** to speak to the contrary, speak against; **lo —** the opposite, the reverse; **de lo —** otherwise; were it not so; **todo lo —** quite the reverse; **llevar la contraria** to maintain an opposite point of view; **llevar la contraria a uno** to oppose someone, contradict someone.

2 nm, **contraria** nf enemy, adversary; (Law, Sport etc) opponent.

3 nm obstacle, snag.

contrarreclamación nf counterclaim.

contrarreferencia nf cross-reference.

Contrarreforma nf Counter-Reformation.

contrarrestar [1a] vt (a) to counteract, offset, balance; effects to counter, counteract. (b) ball to return.

contrarrevolución nf counter-revolution.

contrasentido nm (a) contradiction; piece of nonsense; **aquí hay un —** there is a contradiction here; **pero esto hace un —** but this is a contradiction (in terms).

(b) misinterpretation; mistranslation.

contraseña nf (a) countersign, secret mark; (Mil etc) watchword, password. (b) (Theat) pass-out ticket. (c) (Arg) countersignature.

contrastar [1a] **1** vt (a) to resist.

(b) metal to assay; to hallmark; weights and measures to check; radio to monitor.

2 vi (a) to contrast, form a contrast (con with).

(b) **— a, — con, — contra** to resist; to face up to.

contraste nm (a) contrast (also TV); **en — con** in contrast to; **por — in** contrast; **hacer — con** to contrast with.

(b) assay; check; (marca del) — hallmark.

(c) inspector of weights and measures.

contratante nmf (Comm) contractor; (Law) contracting party.

contratar [1a] **1** vt goods etc to contract for; to negotiate for; to sign a contract for; work to put out to contract; lease etc to take on; person to hire, engage; player etc to sign up.

2 contratarse vr (player etc) to sign on; **— para hacer algo** to contract to do something.

contratiempo nm (a) setback, reverse; mishap, accident. (b) (Mus) a — offbeat.

contratista nmf contractor; **— de edificación** building contractor, builder.

contrato nm contract (de for).

contratuerca nf locknut.

contravención nf contravention, infringement, violation.

contraveneno nm antidote (de to).

contravenir [3s] vi: **— a** to contravene, infringe, violate.

contraventana nf shutter.

contribución nf (a) contribution; **poner a —** to make use of, put to use.

(b) (Fin) tax; **—es** taxes, taxation; **— directa** direct tax; **— municipal** rates; **exento de —es** free of tax, tax-free, tax-exempt (US); **pagar las —es** to pay one's taxes (or rates).

contribuir [3g] vti (a) to contribute (a, para to, towards); **— con una cantidad** to contribute a sum; **— al éxito de algo** to contribute to (or help towards) the success of something; **— a + infin** to help to + infin.

(b) (Fin) to pay (in taxes).

contribuyente nm contributor; (Fin) taxpayer.

contrición nf contrition.

contrincante nm opponent, rival.

contristar [1a] **1** vt to sadden. **2 contristarse** vr to grow sad, grieve.

contrito adj contrite.

control nm (a) (in general) control; **bajo —** under control; **fuera de —** out of control; **perder el —** to lose control (of oneself); **perder — de** to lose control of; **— de alquileres** rent control; **— de cambio** exchange control; **— de la circulación** traffic control; point duty; **— a distancia, — remoto** remote control; **— de (la) natalidad** birth control; **— de precios** price control; **— de sí mismo** self-control; **— de tonalidad** tone control; **— de volumen** volume control.

(b) inspection, check, checking; (Comm, Fin) audit(ing); (Aut: in rally) checkpoint; **— de frontera** frontier checkpoint; **— nuclear** nuclear inspection; **— de pasaportes** passport inspection.

controlar [1a] vt (a) to control. (b) to inspect, check; (Comm, Fin) to audit.

controversia nf controversy.

controvertible adj controversial; debatable, disputable.

controvertir [3i] **1** vt to dispute, question; to argue about. **2** vi to argue.

contubernio nm (a) ring, conspiracy; collusion. (b) cohabitation (also pej).

contumacia nf obstinacy, stubborn disobedience; perversity; (Law) contempt (of court); contumacy.

contumaz adj (a) obstinate, stubbornly disobedient; wayward, perverse; drinker etc inveterate, hardened, incorrigible; (Law) guilty of contempt (of court); contumacious.

(b) (Med) disease-carrying, germ-laden.

contumazmente adv obstinately; perversely; contumaciously.

contumelia nf contumely.

contumerioso adj (CAm) finicky; prudish.

contundente adj (a) weapon offensive, for striking a blow with; **instrumento —** blunt instrument.

(b) (fig) argument etc forceful, convincing, impressive; proof conclusive; tone forceful; defeat etc crushing, overwhelming.

contundir [3a] vt to bruise, contuse.

conturbar [1a] **1** vt to trouble, dismay, perturb. **2 conturbarse** vr to be troubled, be dismayed, become perturbed.

contusión nf bruise, bruising, contusion.

contusionar [1a] vt to bruise; to hurt, damage.

contuso adj bruised.

conuco nm (Ant, Col, Ven) smallholding, small farm.

conuquero nm (Ant, Col, Ven) smallholder, farmer.

convalecencia nf convalescence.

convalecer [2d] vi to convalesce, get better (de after), recover (de from).

convaleciente 1 adj convalescent. **2** nmf convalescent.

convección nf convection.

convecino nm, **convecina** nf (close) neighbour.

convencer [2b] vti to convince; to persuade; **¡convéncete!** believe you me!, I tell you it is so!; you'll have to get used to the idea!; **— a uno de que algo es mejor** to convince someone something is better; **— a uno para que haga algo** to persuade someone to do something; **no me convence del todo** I'm not fully convinced; **el argumento no convence** the argument does not convince (*or* is not convincing); **no me convence ese tío** I don't really trust that chap; **dejarse** — to allow oneself to be persuaded.

convencimiento *nm* (a) (*act*) convincing, persuasion.

(b) conviction, certainty; **llegar al — de** to become convinced of; **llevar algo al — de uno** to convince someone of something; **tener el — de que . . .** to be convinced that . . .

convención *nf* (*all senses*) convention.

convencional *adj* conventional.

convencionalismo *nm* conventionalism.

convencionero *adj* (*Mex, Per*) compliant, accommodating.

convenible *adj* (a) suitable; fitting; *price* fair, reasonable. (b) *person* accommodating.

conveniencia *nf* (a) suitability, fitness; usefulness, advantageousness; expediency; advisability; **a la primera** — at one's earliest opportunity, when convenient; **ser de la — de uno** to suit someone; **atender a la propia** — to think of how something will affect one.

(b) —**s** conventions (*also* —**s sociales**); proprieties, decencies.

(c) agreement.

(d) domestic post, job as a servant.

(e) —**s** (*Fin*) property; income; perquisites.

conveniente *adj* suitable; fit, fitting, proper; useful, profitable, advantageous; expedient; advisable; **nada** — *person* unsuitable; **no es** — **que . . .** it is not advisable that . . .; it is not desirable that . . .; **creer** (*or* **estimar, juzgar**) — to think fit, see fit; **juzgar** + *infin* to see fit to + *infin*, deem it wise to + *infin*.

convenio *nm* agreement, treaty, covenant; — **comercial** trade agreement; — **de préstamos y arriendos** lend-lease agreement.

convenir [3s] **1** *vi* (a) to agree (**con** with, **en** about); — (**en**) **hacer algo** to agree to do something; — (**en**) **que . . .** to agree that . . .; "**sueldo a —**" (*advert*) "salary to be agreed".

(b) to suit, be suited to; to be suitable for; to be good for; **si le conviene** if it suits you; **me conviene quedarme aquí** it is best for me to stay here; **él no te conviene para marido** he's not the husband for you; **lo que más le conviene es un reposo completo** the best thing for him is complete rest.

(c) (*impersonal*) **conviene** + *infin* it is as well to + *infin*; it is important to + *infin*; **conviene recordar que . . .** it is as well to remember that . . ., it is to be remembered that . . .; **no conviene que se publique eso** it is not desirable that that should be published; **conviene a saber** namely, that is.

2 convenirse *vr* to agree, come to an agreement (**en** on, about).

conventillo *nm* (*Bol, Chi, Per, RPl*) tenement house.

convento *nm* monastery; — (**de monjas**) convent, nunnery; (*Ec, Per*) priest's house.

conventual *adj* conventual.

convergencia *nf* (a) convergence. (b) (*fig*) common tendency, common direction; concurrence.

convergente *adj* (a) convergent, converging. (b) (*fig*) having a common tendency, tending in the same direction.

converger [2c] *vi*, **convergir** [3c] *vi* (a) to converge (**en** on).

(b) (*fig*) to have a common tendency, tend in the same direction (**con** as); to concur, be in accord (**con** with); **sus esfuerzos convergen a un fin común** their efforts have a common purpose, their efforts are directed towards the same objective.

conversa *nf* (*esp SAm*) talk, chat.

conversación *nf* conversation, talk; **cambiar de** — to change the subject; **trabar** — **con uno** to get into conversation with someone.

conversador 1 *adj* (*SAm*) talkative, garrulous. **2** *nm*, **conversadora** *nf* (a) conversationalist. (b) (*SAm*) talkative person, gossip.

conversar [1a] **1** *vt* (a) (*Chi, Ec*) to tell, relate; to report. (b) (*SD*) to chat up (*sl*). **2** *vi* (a) to talk, converse. (b) (*Mil*) to wheel.

conversata *nf* (*Chi*) talk, chat.

conversión *nf* (a) conversion. (b) (*Mil*) wheel.

converso 1 *adj* converted. **2** *nm*, **conversa** *nf* convert; (*Hist: esp*) converted Jew(ess).

conversón (*Ec, Col*) **1** *adj* talkative, gossiping. **2** *nm*, **conversona** *nf* talkative person, gossip.

conversor *nm* (*Radio*) converter.

convertibilidad *nf* convertibility.

convertible *adj* convertible.

convertidor *nm* (*Elec, Metal*) converter.

convertir [3i] **1** *vt* (a) to convert (*also Eccl*); to transform, turn (**en** into); (*Comm, Elec, Tech*) to convert; — **a uno al catolicismo** to convert someone to Catholicism.

(b) *eyes etc* to turn (**a** on).

2 convertirse *vr* to be converted, be transformed, be changed (**en** into); (*Eccl*) to be converted, convert (**a** to).

convexidad *nf* convexity.

convexo *adj* convex.

convicción *nf* conviction.

convicto 1 *adj* convicted, found guilty; condemned. **2** *nm* (*SAm: angl*) convict.

convidada *nf* round (*esp* of drinks); **dar una —, pagar una** — to stand a round.

convidado *nm*, **convidada** *nf* guest.

convidar [1a] **1** *vt* (a) to invite; — **a uno a hacer algo** to invite someone to do something; — **a uno a una cerveza** to stand someone a beer, treat someone to a beer, invite someone to have a beer; — **a uno con un café** to offer someone a cup of coffee.

(b) (*fig*) — **a** to stir to, move to; **el ambiente convida a la meditación** the setting invites one to indulge in meditation, the atmosphere is conducive to meditation.

2 convidarse *vr* (a) (*fam*) to invite oneself along.

(b) to volunteer, offer one's services.

convincente *adj* convincing.

convincentemente *adv* convincingly.

convite *nm* (a) invitation. (b) banquet, feast; treat; party; — **a escote** Dutch treat.

convivencia *nf* living together, life together, co-existence.

convivir [3a] *vi* to live together (*esp* amicably, in harmony); to share the same life, coexist; (*fig*) to exist side by side (**con** with).

convocación *nf* summoning, calling, convoking.

convocar [1g] *vt* to summon, call (together), convoke.

convocatoria *nf* (a) summons, call (to a meeting); notice of a meeting; "**C—s para hoy**" (*in press*) "Today's Meetings". (b) =**convocación**.

convólvulo *nm* convolvulus.

convoy *nm* (a) (*Naut*) convoy; (*Rail*) train; (*fam*) procession; retinue. (b) cruet, cruet stand.

convoyar [1a] **1** *vt* (a) to convoy; to guard, escort. (b) (*Chi*) to give financial backing to. **2 convoyarse** *vr* (*PR, Ven*) to connive together, plot.

convulsión *nf* convulsion.

convulsionar [1a] *vt* to convulse.

convulsivo *adj* convulsive.

convulso *adj* convulsed (**de** with).

conyugal *adj* conjugal; married.

cónyuge *nmf* spouse; partner; husband *or* wife; *see next entry*.

cónyugues *nmfpl* spouses; married couple, husband and wife.

coña *nf* (*tabu*) humour, humorous tone, joking way.

coñac [ko'na] *nm, pl* **coñacs** [ko'nas] brandy, cognac.

coñearse [1a] *vr* to speak in a joking way, adopt a humorous tone.

coñete *adj* (*Chi, Per*) mean.

coño *nm* (a) (*Anat: tabu*) cunt (*tabu*).

(b) (*fam: to person*) you idiot!; (*interj: also* ¡**qué** —!) hell!, damn it all!; well I'm damned!; (*more mildly*) well!, good heavens!

(c) (*Chi, Mex*) *pej term applied to Spaniards*.

cooperación *nf* cooperation.

cooperador 1 *adj* cooperative; collaborating, participating. **2** *nm*, **cooperadora** *nf* collaborator, co-worker.

cooperar [1a] *vi* to cooperate (**a, en** in; **con** with); — **a** + *infin* to cooperate in + *ger*; — **a un mismo fin** to work for a common aim, work together in a common cause; — **en** to collaborate in, work together on, take part (together) in; **los factores que cooperaron al fracaso** the factors which together led to failure, the factors which contributed to the failure.

cooperativa *nf* cooperative, mutual association; — **agrícola** agricultural cooperative.

cooperativo *adj* cooperative.

coordenada *nf* (*Math*) coordinate.

coordinación *nf* coordination.

coordinado *adj* coordinated; (*Mil*) *operation* combined.

coordinador *nm* coordinator.

coordinar [1a] *vt* to coordinate.

copa *nf* (a) glass; (*poet*) goblet; (*Sport etc*) cup, trophy; **llevar una — de más** to have (had) one over the eight; **tomarse unas —s** to have a drink or two.

(b) (*fig*) — **de la amargura** cup of sorrow; **apurar la** — to know the utmost depths of suffering.

(c) (*of hat*) crown; (*of tree*) top.

(d) **—s** (*Cards*) hearts; **la** — the ace of hearts.

(e) (*Col*) connoisseur, judge of wine.

copado *adj tree* thick, with dense foliage.

copal *nm* (*CAm, Mex*) resin.

copante *nm* (*Guat, Hond, Mex*) stepping stone.

copar [1a] *vt* (a) (*Mil*) to surround, cut off; (*fig*) to corner; **quedar copado en un trabajo** to get bogged down in a piece of work.

(b) (*Cards etc*) to win (all the tricks), sweep the board; (*Pol and fig*) to sweep the board, win hands down; **prize, cup** to walk off with, collar (*fam*).

coparticipe *nmf* partner; fellow participant, fellow competitor; joint owner; collaborator (*en* in).

copear [1a] *vi* (a) (*fam*) to booze, tipple; to go on a pub crawl (*fam*). (b) to sell wine (*etc*) by the glass.

Copenhague Copenhagen.

Copérnico m Copernicus.

copete *nm* (a) (*of person*) tuft (of hair), quiff; (*of horse*) forelock; (*Orn*) tuft, crest; **estar hasta el** — (*Mex, PR*) to be utterly fed up.

(b) (*fig*) pride, haughtiness; **de alto** — aristocratic; important, socially prominent; **tener mucho** — to be haughty, be stuck-up (*fam*).

copetín *nm* (*Arg, Per, Urug*) glass of spirits; cocktail, aperitif.

copetón *adj* (a) (*SAm*)=**copetudo** (a). (b) (*Col*) **estar** — to be tight. (c) (*Ven*) cowardly.

copetudo *adj* (a) tufted; crested. (b) highborn, of noble birth, blue-blooded; haughty, stuck-up (*fam*).

copia *nf* (a) copy; (*Art*) copy; replica, reproduction; duplicate; — **de calco**, — **al carbón**, — **carbónica** (*Arg*) carbon copy; — **fotostática** photostat; — **en limpio** fair copy; **sacar una** — **de** to make a copy of.

(b) abundance, plenty; **con gran** — **de** with an abundance of, with a great deal of.

copiador *nm* (a) copier, copyist. (b) copybook. (c) copying machine.

copiante *nmf* copyist.

copiar [1b] *vt* to copy (*de* from); *style etc* to imitate; *dictation* to take down.

copiloto *nm* (*Aut*) co-driver; (*Aer*) co-pilot.

copiosamente *adv* copiously, abundantly, plentifully.

copioso *adj* copious, abundant, plentiful.

copista *nmf* copyist.

copita *nf* (small) glass; (*Golf*) tee; **una** — **de jerez** a glass of sherry; **tomarse unas —s** to have a drink or two.

copla *nf* (a) (*Lit*) verse (*esp* of 4 lines); couplet; (*Mus*) popular song, folksong, ballad; **—s** verses, poetry; **—s de Calaínos** silly story (*etc*) with which someone irrelevantly interrupts; **—s de ciego** doggerel; **hacer —s** (*fam*) to write verse.

(b) (*Chi, Guat, RPl*) pipe joint.

copo *nm* (a) (*of flax etc*) tuft, small bundle; — **de algodón** cotton ball; **—s de avena** oatmeal, rolled oats; — **de nieve** snowflake.

(b) (*Col, Ven*) tree top.

(c) (*RPl*) piled-up clouds.

coproducción *nf* (*Cine etc*) joint production.

copropietario *nm*, **copropietaria** *nf* co-owner, joint owner.

copucha *nf* (*Chi*) lie, fib.

copuchar [1a] *vi* (*Chi*) to tell lies, fib.

copuchento *adj* (*Chi*) lying, untrustworthy.

copudo *adj tree* bushy, thick.

cópula *nf* (a) (*Bio*) copulation; — **carnal** copulation, sexual intercourse. (b) (*Ling*) conjunction.

copularse [1a] *vr* to copulate (*con* with).

copulativo *adj* (*Ling*) copulative.

coque *nm* (*angl*) coke.

coqueluche *nf* (*gall*) whooping cough.

coqueta 1 *adj* flirtatious, flighty, coquettish. **2** *nf* (a) flirt, coquette. (b) roll, small loaf. (c) dressing table (with a full-length mirror).

coquetear [1a] *vi* to flirt (*con* with; *also fig*).

coqueteo *nm*, **coquetería** *nf* (a) (*quality*) flirtatiousness, flightiness, coquetry; (*fig*) affection. (b) (*act*) flirtation.

coquetón 1 *adj* (a) *object* smart, natty, attractive. (b) *man* flirtatious; attractive (to women). (c) = **coqueta** 1. **2** *nm* ladykiller, wolf (*fam*).

coquitos *nmpl*: **hacer** — to make faces (*a* at).

coracha *nf* leather bag.

coraje *nm* (a) fighting spirit; toughness; courage; fortitude. (b) anger; **dar** — **a** to make angry, enrage.

corajina *nf* fit of temper, explosion of rage.

corajudo *adj* (a) spirited; tough; bold; (*Arg*) brave. (b) quick-tempered, peppery.

coral[1] (*Mus*) **1** *adj* choral. **2** *nm* chorale. **3** *nf* choir, choral group.

coral[2] *nm* (*Zool*) coral.

coralino *adj* coral (*attr*), coralline.

corambre *nf* hides, skins.

Corán m Koran.

corana *nf* (*Chi, Per*) sickle.

coránico *adj* Koranic.

coraza *nf* (a) (*Mil, Hist*) cuirass; (*fig*) breastplate, protection. (b) (*Naut*) armour-plating. (c) (*Zool*) shell. (d) (*Aut*) grille (of the radiator).

corazón *nm* (a) (*Anat and fig*) heart; **de** — willingly; **de todo** — from the heart; **de buen** — kind-hearted; **¡hijo de mi** —! my precious child!; **duro de** — hard-hearted; **sin** — heartless; **con el** — **en la mano** frankly; sincerely; **estar enfermo del** — to have heart trouble; **arrancar** (*or* **partir, romper**) **el** — **a uno** to break someone's heart; **no caber a uno el** — **en el pecho** to be bursting with joy; **le dio en el** — she had a premonition; **encoger a uno el** — to fill someone with fear (*or* dismay, pity); **llevar el** — **en la mano** to wear one's heart on one's sleeve; **meter a uno el** — **en un puño** (*or* **en la boca**) to put the wind up someone; **morir con el** — **destrozado** to die of a broken heart; **poner el** — **en algo** to set one's heart on something; **no tener** — to have no heart, be heartless; **tener el** — **para** + **infin** to have the heart to + *infin*; **no tener el** — **para algo** not to feel up to something; *see* **íntimo** *etc*.

(b) (*Bot*) core.

(c) (*Cards*) **—es** hearts.

corazonada *nf* (a) presentiment, hunch. (b) rash impulse, sudden impulse; impulsive act.

corbata *nf* tie, necktie; cravat(e); — **de lazo** bow tie.

corbatín *nm* bow tie.

corbeta *nf* corvette.

Córcega *f* Corsica.

corcel *nm* steed, charger.

corcor *nm* (*CAm, PR*) gurgle; **beber** — to swig (*fam*).

corcova *nf* (a) hump, hunchback. (b) (*Bol, Chi, Ec, Per*) prolongation of a party (*into the following day or days*).

corcovado 1 *adj* hunchbacked. **2** *nm*, **corcovada** *nf* hunchback.

corcovar [1a] *vt* to bend (over); to crook.

corcovear [1a] *vi* (a) to prance about, cut capers; to buck, plunge. (b) (*Arg, Chi, Per, PR, Urug*) to grumble, grouse (*fam*). (c) (*Mex*) to be scared.

corcovo *nm* (a) prance, caper; buck, plunge. (b) crookedness.

corcha *nf* (piece of) cork bark.

corchea *nf* (*Mus*) quaver.

corchero *adj* cork (*attr*); **industria corchera** cork industry.

corcheta *nf* (*Sew*) eye.

corchete *nm* (a) (*Sew*) snap fastener; catch, clasp; hook and eye. (b) (*Typ*) **—s** square brackets.

corcho *nm* cork; cork bark; cork mat; cork-soled clog; (*Fish*) float; — **bornizo**, — **virgen** virgin cork; **sacar el** — to draw the cork, uncork.

corchoso *adj* corklike, corky.

cordada *nf* (*Mountaineering*) team, roped team.

cordaje *nm* cordage; (*of racquet*) strings; (*Naut*) rigging.

cordel *nm* cord, line; **a** — in a straight line.

cordelería *nf* (a) cordage, ropes; (*Naut etc*) ropewalk; (*Naut*) rigging. (b) cordmaking, ropemaking.

cordelero *nm* cordmaker, ropemaker.

cordería *nf* cordage, cords, ropes.

corderillo *nm*, **corderina** *nf* lambskin.

cordero *nm*, **cordera** *nf* (a) lamb; — **asado** roast lamb; **C— de Dios** Lamb of God; **¡no hay tales —s!** it's nothing of the sort!

(b) lambskin.

(c) (*fig*) meek and mild person.

corderuna *nf* lambskin.

cordial 1 *adj* (a) cordial; heartfelt, hearty. (b) (*Pharm*) tonic, invigorating. **2** *nm* cordial; tonic.

cordialidad *nf* warmth, cordiality.

cordialmente *adv* cordially; heartily; (*ending letter*) sincerely.

cordillera *nf* range, chain (of mountains).

cordillerano *adj* (*Chi, RPl*) from the Andes, of the Andes.

Córdoba Cordova.

cordobán *nm* cordovan (leather).

cordobana: andar a la — to go around stark naked.

cordobés 1 *adj* Cordovan. **2** *nm*, **cordobesa** *nf* Cordovan.

cordón nm (a) cord, string; (Naut) strand; (of shoe) lace; (Mil) braid, lace; (Elec) flex, extension wire (US); **lana de 3 —es** 3-ply wool.
(b) (Anat) cord; **— umbilical** umbilical cord.
(c) (Archit) cordon.
(d) (Mil, of police etc) cordon; **— sanitario** sanitary cordon, cordon sanitaire.
(e) (RPl) kerb.
(f) (Chi, Per, PR) **— de cerros** chain of hills.
(g) (Per, Cu) liquor, brandy.
cordoncillo nm (of cloth) rib; (Sew) braid, piping; (of coin) milling, milled edge.
cordura nf good sense, prudence, wisdom; **con —** sensibly, prudently, wisely.
Corea f Korea; **— del Norte** North Korea; **— del Sur** South Korea.
coreano 1 adj Korean. **2** nm, **coreana** nf Korean.
corear [1a] **1** vt to say in a chorus; (Mus) to sing the chorus of, join in the chorus of. **2** vi to speak all together; (Mus) to sing all together, join in.
coreografía nf choreography.
coreógrafo nm choreographer.
coriana nf (Col) blanket.
corifeo nm (a) (Hist) coryphaeus. (b) (fig) leader, spokesman.
corindón nm corundum.
corintio adj Corinthian.
Corinto Corinth.
corista 1 nmf (Eccl) chorister. **2** nf (Theat etc) chorus girl.
cormorán nm: **— (grande)** cormorant.
cornada nf butt, thrust (with the horns), goring; **dar una — a** to gore.
cornadura nf horns; (of deer) antlers.
cornalina nf cornelian, carnelian.
cornamenta nf horns; (of deer) antlers.
cornamusa nf bagpipe; hunting horn.
córnea nf cornea.
cornear [1a] vt to butt, gore.
corneja nf crow; **— negra** carrion crow; **— calva** rook.
córneo adj horny, corneous.
córner ['korne] nm, pl **córners** ['korne or 'kornes] (Sport: angl) corner kick; **¡—!** (interj) corner!; (SAm: Sport, Boxing) corner.
cornerina nf cornelian, carnelian.
corneta 1 nf bugle; **— acústica** ear trumpet; **— de llaves** cornet; **— de monte** hunting horn. **2** nm bugler; cornet player.
cornetín nm (a) cornet. (b) cornet player.
corneto adj (a) (CAm) bow-legged. (b) (Arg, Mex, Ven) cow with a bent horn.
cornezuelo nm (Bot) ergot.
cornflaques nmpl, **cornflés** nmpl (SAm: angl) cornflakes.
cornial adj horn-shaped.
córnico 1 adj Cornish. **2** nm (language) Cornish.
corniforme adj horn-shaped.
cornisa nf cornice.
cornisamento nm entablature.
corno nm (Mus) horn; **— de caza** hunting horn; **— inglés** cor anglais.
Cornualles m Cornwall.
cornucopia nf cornucopia, horn of plenty.
cornudo 1 adj (a) horned; antlered. (b) husband cuckolded. **2** nm cuckold.
cornúpeta nm (Taur) bull.
coro nm (a) (Mus, Theat) chorus; **una chica del —** a girl from the chorus, a chorus girl; **cantar el — de** to sing the chorus of; **cantar las partes a —s** to sing the parts alternately; **decir algo a —** to say something in a chorus, say something in unison; **aprender algo de —** to learn something by heart; to learn something by rote; **hacer — de (or a) las palabras de uno** to echo someone's words.
(b) (Mus, Eccl) choir; **— celestial** celestial choir, heavenly choir; **niño de —** choirboy.
(c) (Archit) choir.
corola nf corolla.
corolario nm corollary.
corona nf (a) crown; **— de espinas** crown of thorns; **ceñirse la —** to take the crown; **perder la —** (euph) to lose one's virginity; **rey sin — de Eslobodia** uncrowned king of Slobodia.
(b) (Astron) corona; (Meteorol) halo.
(c) (of flowers) garland; chaplet; **— funeraria** wreath.
(d) (Anat) crown (of the head), top of the head; (Eccl) tonsure.
(e) (Fin) crown; **media —** half-a-crown, half-crown.

coronación nf (a) coronation. (b) (fig) crowning, completion. (c) **=coronamiento** (b). (d) (Chess) queening.
coronamiento nm (a) (fig) crowning, completion. (b) (Archit) crown, coping stone; top, ornamental finish.
coronar [1a] vt (a) to crown; **— a uno (por) rey** to crown someone king.
(b) building etc to crown (con, de with); to top, cap.
(c) (fig) to crown; to complete, round off; **— algo con éxito** to crown something with success; **para —lo** to crown it all.
(d) (Chess) to queen.
(e) (Ant, Per, RPl) to cuckold, make a cuckold of.
coronario adj coronary.
coronel nm colonel; **— de aviación** group captain, colonel (US).
coronilla nf crown, top of the head; **andar (or bailar, ir) de —** to slog away, do one's utmost (to please someone); **dar de — to bump one's head; estar hasta la —** to be utterly fed up (de with).
coronta nf (Bol, Chi, Per) corncob.
coroto nm (Ant, Col, Ec, Pan, Ven) (a) gourd, vessel. (b) thing, affair; **—s** gear (fam), things; junk.
corpacho nm, **corpanchón** nm, **corpazo** nm (fam) carcass (fam).
corpiño nm bodice.
corporación nf corporation; association; (Comm, Fin: angl) corporation, company.
corporal adj corporal, bodily; **ejercicio —** physical exercise; **higiene —** personal hygiene.
corporativo adj corporate.
corpóreo adj corporeal, bodily.
corpulencia nf burliness, heavy build; stoutness, massiveness; **cayó con toda su —** he fell with his full weight.
corpulento adj person well-built, burly, heavily-built; tree etc stout, solid, massive.
Corpus m Corpus Christi.
corpúsculo nm corpuscle.
corral nm (Agr) yard, farmyard; stockyard, cattlepen, corral (US); (child's) playpen; (Cu) small farm; **— de abasto** (RPl) slaughterhouse; **— de carbonera** coal dump, coalyard; **— de madera** timberyard; **— de vacas** (fam) slum; **— de vecindad** tenement; **hacer —es** to play truant.
corralillo nm playpen.
corralón nm large yard; (RPl) timberyard; (Per) vacant lot.
correa nf (a) strap; leather strap, thong; belt (also Tech); leash, tether; **— para pasar navaja** razor strop; **— de seguridad** safety belt; **— sin fin** endless belt; **— transportadora, — de transporte** conveyor belt; **— de ventilador** (Aut etc) fan belt; **besar la —** to eat humble pie.
(b) (quality) give, stretch, elasticity; leatheriness; **tener —** to be able to put up with a lot, know how to take it, be long-suffering.
correaje nm belts, straps; (Tech) belting.
corrección nf (a) (act) correction; adjustment.
(b) rebuke, reprimand; punishment.
(c) (quality) correctness; courtesy, politeness; good manners; properness.
correccional nm reformatory.
correcorre nm (Cu, PR) headlong rush.
correctamente adv (a) correctly; accurately; aright. (b) regularly. (c) correctly, politely; properly, fittingly.
correctivo 1 adj corrective. **2** nm corrective.
correcto adj (a) correct; accurate; right; **¡—!** right!, O.K.! (fam).
(b) features etc regular, well-formed.
(c) person correct; courteous, polite, well-mannered; conduct courteous, correct; dress proper, fitting; **estuvo muy — conmigo** he was very polite to me.
corrector nm, **correctora** nf (Typ) proofreader.
corredera nf (a) (Tech) slide; track, rail, runner; slide valve; (of fastener) zip, zipper; **puerta de —** sliding door.
(b) (Naut) log.
(c) (Tech) upper millstone.
(d) (Ent) cockroach.
(e) (Sport) racetrack.
(f) (Arg) rapids.
corredero nm (a) (Mex) racetrack. (b) (Col) old riverbed. (c) (Mex) haunt, favourite spot.
corredizo adj sliding; crane travelling; knot running, slip (attr).
corredor 1 nm (a) (Sport) runner; athlete; **— automovilista** racing driver, racing motorist; **— ciclista** racing cyclist; **— de cortas distancias**

sprinter; — **de fondo**, — **de larga distancia** long-distance runner; — **de pista** track athlete.

(b) (*Comm*) agent, broker; (*pej*) procurer, pimp; — **de bienes raíces**, — **de propiedades** (*Chi*) real-estate broker; — **de bodas** matchmaker; — **de bolsa** stockbroker; — **de casas** house agent; — **de comercio** business agent; — **de fincas rurales** land agent; — **de noticias** gossip.

2 *nm* corridor, passage; — **de popa** (*Naut*) stern gallery.

corraduría *nf* brokerage.

corregible *adj* which can be corrected.

corregidor *nm* (*Hist*) chief magistrate.

corregidora *nf* (*Hist*) wife of the chief magistrate.

corregir [3c and 3l] **1** *vt* **(a)** to correct; to put right, adjust; to revise, look over; *proofs* to correct, read.

(b) to rebuke, reprimand; to punish.

2 corregirse *vr* (*person*) to reform, mend one's ways; — **de su terquedad** to stop being obstinate.

correísta *nmf* (*Arg*) post-office employee.

correlación *nf* correlation.

correlacionar [1a] *vt* to correlate.

correlativo **1** *adj* correlative. **2** *nm* correlative.

correligionario *nm*, **correligionaria** *nf* (*Eccl*) co-religionist, person of the same faith; (*Pol*) fellow supporter, sympathizer, like-minded person.

correlón *adj* **(a)** (*Col, Guat, Ven*) running; fast, good at running. **(b)** (*Guat, Mex, Ven*) cowardly.

correntada *nf* (*Arg*) rapids, strong current.

correntilíneo *adj* (*Mex*) streamlined.

correntón **1** *adj* **(a)** busy, active; gadabout. **(b)** jokey, jolly, fond of a lark. **2** *nm* (*Col, PR*) strong current.

correntoso *adj* (*SAm*) *river* strong-flowing, rapid; in flood, in spate; *water* torrential.

correo *nm* **(a)** (*person*) courier; postman, mailman (*US*); (*Mil*) dispatch rider; (*Pol*) diplomatic courier.

(b) (*Post*) post, mail; — **aéreo** airmail; — **certificado** registered post; — **de primera clase** first-class mail; — **urgente** special delivery; **echar al** —, **poner en el** — to post, mail (*esp US*); **llevar algo al** — to take something to the post; **¿ha llegado el** —? has the post come?; **a vuelta de** — by return (of post); **por** — by post, through the post.

(c) —**s** post office; **Administración General de C**—**s** General Post Office; **ir a** —**s**, **pasar por** —**s** to go to the post office.

correosidad *nf* toughness, leatheriness; flexibility.

correoso *adj* tough, leathery; flexible.

correr [2a] **1** *vt* **(a)** *ground, distance* to traverse, cover, travel over; to pass over; **ha corrido medio mundo** he's been over half the world.

(b) (*Mil: Hist*) to overrun; to raid, invade; to lay waste.

(c) *object* to push along; *chair* to pull up, draw up; *bolt* to shoot, slide, draw; *key* to turn; *curtain, veil* to draw; *buttons etc* to move; *sail* to unfurl; *knot* to undo, untie.

(d) *horse* to race, run; *bull* to fight; *quarry* to chase, hunt, pursue.

(e) *risk* to run; *adventure* to have; *fate* to suffer, undergo.

(f) *colours* to make run.

(g) (*Comm*) to auction.

(h) *person* (*also* **dejar corrido**) to embarrass, put to shame, cover with confusion.

(i) — **la clase** (*fam*) to cut class, play hooky.

(j) —**la** (*fam*) to live it up (*fam*); to have one's fling; to go on a spree (*fam*).

(k) (*CAm, Mex, Ven*) — **a uno** to chuck someone out.

2 *vi* **(a)** to run; **corrió a decírselo** he ran to tell him, he hastened to tell him; — **a la perdición** to rush headlong to disaster; **¡no corras tanto!** don't run so hard!, not so fast!; — **a todo** — to run as hard as one can; **echar a** — to start to run, break into a run; to run off; **dejar** — **las cosas** to let things run on, let matters ride, let things take their course.

(b) (*of water, electricity etc*) to run, flow; (*of air*) to flow, go, pass; (*of tap*) to run; (*of fountain*) to play; (*of wind*) to blow; **el río corre muy crecido** the river is running very high; **corre mucho viento** it's very windy, there's a strong wind blowing; **dejar** — **la sangre** to let the blood flow.

(c) (*of time*) to pass (quickly), elapse; (*of period*) to run, extend, stretch; **el tiempo corre** time is passing, time presses; **el mes que corre** the present month, the current month; **durante lo que corre del año** during the rest of the year, for the remainder of the year.

(d) (*of money etc*) to pass, be valid, be acceptable; (*of rumour*) to circulate, go round; (*of belief*) to be commonly held.

(e) (*Geog etc*) to run; **las montañas corren del este al oeste** the mountains run from east to west.

(f) (*of salary etc*) to be payable; **su sueldo correrá desde el primer día del mes** his salary will be payable from the first of the month.

(g) — **con la casa** to run the house, manage the house; — **con los gastos** to pay (*or* meet, bear) the expenses; **él corre con eso** he is responsible for that, that is in his charge.

(h) (*Comm*) — **a**, — **por** to sell at.

3 correrse *vr* **(a)** (*object*) to slide, move along; (*ballast, cargo*) to shift; (*person*) to move (up); **se ha corrido unos centímetros el tablero** the board has moved a few centimetres; **córrete un poco hacia este lado** move a bit this way.

(b) (*person: fig*) to go too far, let oneself go; **no te vayas a** — **en la propina** don't overdo it on the tip.

(c) (*colours*) to run; (*ice etc*) to melt; (*ink*) to spread, make a blot.

(d) (*person: fig*) to get embarrassed; to become confused.

(e) — **una juerga** *etc: see* **juerga**.

(f) (*Cu, Guat, Mex, Ven*) to get scared, run away.

correría *nf* (*Mil*) raid, foray; (*fig*) trip, excursion; —**s** (*fig*) trips, travels.

correspondencia *nf* **(a)** (*in general*) correspondence.

(b) correspondence, letters; post, mail; — **entrante** incoming mail; — **particular** private correspondence; **curso por** — correspondence course; **entrar en** — **con uno** to enter into correspondence with someone; **estar en** — **con uno** to be in correspondence with someone.

(c) (*between places*) communications, contact; (*Rail etc*) connection (*con* with).

(d) agreement; harmony; gratitude; (*of affection etc*) return; **mis ofertas no tuvieron** — my offers met with no response; **yo esperaba más** — I had expected a greater response.

corresponder [2a] **1** *vi* **(a)** to correspond (*a* to, *con* with); to tally (*con* with).

(b) to be suitable, be fitting, be right; to belong; — **a** (*of colour, furniture etc*) to match; to fit, fit in with, go with; **ese libro no corresponde aquí** that book doesn't belong here; **la llave corresponde a esta cerradura** the key fits this lock; **todavía no corresponde hacerlo** it is still not the right time to do it; **el resultado no ha correspondido a nuestras esperanzas** the result did not come up to our hopes; **con una gravedad que corresponde a su importancia** with a gravity which befits its importance.

(c) — **a** to fall to the lot of, be the share of; **le dieron lo que le correspondía** they gave him his share; **correspondieron 100 ptas a cada uno** everyone got 100 ptas (as his share), each one's share amounted to 100 ptas.

(d) — **a** (*of duty etc*) to concern; to rest with, devolve upon; **"a quien corresponda"** "to whom it may concern"; **me corresponde hacerlo** it is my job to do it, it is my business to do it; **no me corresponde criticarle** it is not for me to criticize him; **me corresponde jugar a mí** it's my turn to play.

(e) to respond, reply; — **a** *affection* to return, reciprocate; *favour* to repay; — **dignamente a** to make a fitting reply to; **ella le correspondió con una corbata** she gave him a tie in return; **pero ella le correspondió con desprecio** but she responded scornfully, but all she gave in return was disdain; **nunca podré** — **a tanta generosidad** I can never adequately repay such generosity; **un amor no correspondido** an unrequited love, a love which was never returned.

(f) (*Rail etc*) to connect (*con* with).

(g) (*Archit*) to communicate (*con* with).

2 corresponderse *vr* **(a)** to correspond; to agree, be in harmony (*con* with); to have mutual affection (*etc*), have regard for one another.

(b) (*Post*) to correspond (*con* with).

correspondiente **1** *adj* corresponding (*a* to); respective. **2** *nm* (*of academy etc*) correspondent.

corresponsal *nm* (newspaper) correspondent; — **extraordinario** special correspondent; — **de guerra** war correspondent.

corretaje *nm* brokerage.

corretear [1a] **1** *vt* **(a)** (*SAm*) to pursue relentlessly, harass.

(b) (*CAm*) to scare off, get rid of.

(c) (*Arg*) to sell on someone else's behalf; to act as agent for.

(d) (*Chi*) *task* to hurry along.

2 *vi* (a) to run about, rush around.

(b) to loiter, hang about the streets.

corretero *nm*, **corretera** *nf* busy person, gadabout.

correve(i)dile *nm* (a) gossip. (b) pimp.

corrida *nf* (a) run, dash, sprint; **dar una —** to make a dash; **decir algo de —** to rattle off something from memory; **en una —** in an instant.

(b) **— de toros** bullfight.

(c) (*Mex*) **calle de una —** one-way street.

(d) (*Chi, PR, SD*) revelry, celebration.

(e) (*Chi*) row, line, file; (*Geol*) outcrop.

corrido 1 *adj* (a) **tres noches corridas** three nights running; **hasta muy corrida la noche** far into the night.

(b) *weight etc* extra (large); **un kilo —** a good kilo, a kilo and a bit more.

(c) (*Archit etc*) continuous.

(d) (*fig*) *person* abashed, sheepish; confused; embarrassed; **— de vergüenza** covered with shame.

(e) (*fig*) *person* experienced (in the wicked ways of the world), wise, sharp, knowing; **es una mujer corrida** she's a woman who has been around.

(f) *style* fluent, confident; **decir algo de —** to rattle something off; **lo sabía de —** he knew it all right through, he could say it all from memory.

(g) (*SAm*) *party* excellent, splendid.

2 *nm* (a) (*Andalusia, Col, Mex*) ballad.

(b) (*Per*) fugitive from justice.

corriente 1 *adj* (a) *water* running; *style* flowing, fluent, easy, smooth; *money etc* current, valid, accepted; *account, publication, year etc* current; *interest, news* topical; **el año —** the current year, the present year.

(b) ordinary, normal, common, everyday; standard; **— y moliente** ordinary, run-of-the-mill; **lo — es no pintarlo** the usual thing is not to paint it; **aquí es — ver eso** it's common to see that here, that is a common sight here; **es una chica —** she's an ordinary sort of girl.

(c) in order; **tiene — la documentación** his papers are in order; **todo está — para la partida** everything is fixed up for your departure.

(d) **ir** (*or* **estar**) **— en los pagos** to be up to date in one's payments.

2 *nm* (a) current month; **el 9 del corriente** the 9th of the current month, the 9th inst.

(b) **al —** punctually, on time; up-to-date.

(c) **estar al — de** to be informed about, be aware of, be well up with; **mantenerse al —** to keep up to date (**de** with); **tener a uno al — de** to keep someone informed about, keep someone in touch with; **téngame al —** keep me informed.

3 *nf* (a) (*of water*) current; stream, flow; **C— del Golfo** Gulf Stream; **— de lava** stream of lava; **— sanguínea** bloodstream; **— submarina** undercurrent.

(b) **— de aire** draught; **— de aire caliente** flow of warm air.

(c) (*Elec*) current; **— alterna** alternating current; **— directa** direct current; **el hilo está con —** the wire is live.

(d) (*of events etc*) course; tendency; drift; **dejarse llevar de la —** to drift along, follow the crowd; **las —s modernas del arte** modern trends in art; **una fuerte — innovadora** a strong innovating tendency.

corrillero *nm*, **corrillera** *nf* idler, person with time to gossip.

corrillo *nm* huddle, knot of people, small group; (*fig*) clique, coterie.

corrimiento *nm* (a) slipping, sliding; **— de tierras** landslide.

(b) (*Med*) discharge; (*Chi, PR, SD*) rheumatism; (*Per*) tooth abscess.

(c) (*fig*) embarrassment; shyness, sheepishness.

corrincho *nm* (a) mob. (b) (*Col*) uproar, row. (c) (*Ec*) excitement; haste.

corro *nm* (a) ring, circle; huddle, knot (of people); **la gente hizo —** the people formed a ring.

(b) (*children's game*) ring-a-ring-a-roses; **los niños cantan esto en —** the children sing this in a ring.

(c) circular space; **hacer —** to make room, leave a circular space.

(d) small area, part, piece (of a surface); (*Agr*) plot, small field, patch.

corroboración *nf* corroboration.

corroborar [1a] *vt* to corroborate.

corroborativo *adj* corroborative.

corroer [2a] **1** *vt* to corrode; (*Geol*) to erode; (*fig*) to

corrode, eat away, eat up; **le corroen los celos** he is eaten up with jealousy.

2 corroerse *vr* to corrode, become corroded.

corromper [2a] **1** *vt* (a) *wood etc* to rot; *food* to turn bad; to spoil, ruin, cause damage to.

(b) (*fig*) *customs, language, youth etc* to corrupt, pervert; *pleasures* to spoil; *judge, official* to bribe.

(c) *woman* to seduce, debauch, dishonour.

(d) (*fam*) to vex, annoy.

2 *vi* (*fam*) to smell bad.

3 corromperse *vr* (a) to rot; to go bad, deteriorate; to be spoiled.

(b) (*fig*) to become corrupted, become perverted.

corrompido *adj* (a) rotten, putrid. (b) (*fig*) corrupted, corrupt; depraved, degenerate, perverted.

corroncha *nf* (*CAm, Col, Ec*) crust, scale.

corroncho *adj* (a) (*Ven*) slow, sluggish. (b) (*Col*) *person* difficult, prickly.

corronchoso *adj* (*CAm, Col, Ven*) rough, coarse; scaly.

corrongo *adj* (*CR, Cu*) first-rate, splendid; charming, attractive.

corrosión *nf* corrosion; rust; (*Geol*) erosion.

corrosivo *adj* corrosive.

corrugación *nf* contraction, shrinkage.

corrupción *nf* (a) rot, decay; stink, stench.

(b) (*fig*) corruption; perversion; (*of text*) corruption; (*Law*) corruption; graft, bribery; (*Law*) seduction; **en el gobierno existe mucha —** there is a lot of corruption in the government.

corruptela *nf* (a) (*in general*) corruption. (b) (*una —*) corrupt practice, abuse.

corruptible *adj* (a) *person* corruptible, bribable. (b) *foods etc* perishable.

corrupto *adj* corrupt.

corruptor 1 *adj* corrupting. **2** *nm*, **corruptora** *nf* corrupter, perverter.

corsario *nm* privateer, corsair.

corsé *nm* corset.

corso 1 *adj* Corsican. **2** *nm*, **corsa** *nf* Corsican.

corta *nf* felling, cutting.

cortaalambres *nm*, *pl* **cortaalambres** wire cutters.

cortabolsas *nm*, *pl* **cortabolsas** pickpocket.

cortacésped *nm* lawnmower.

cortacircuitos *nm*, *pl* **cortacircuitos** circuit breaker.

cortacorriente *nm* switch.

cortada *nf* (a) (*SAm*) cut, slash; trench. (b) (*of bread etc*) slice.

cortadillo *nm* (a) small glass. (b) lump of sugar.

cortado 1 *adj* (a) cut; clipped; **— a pico** steep, sheer, precipitous.

(b) *milk* sour.

(c) *style* abrupt; disjointed.

(d) shamed, shamefaced; confused; embarrassed.

(e) **estar —** (*Chi, RPl*) to be broke (*fam*).

2 *nm* white coffee, coffee with a little milk.

cortador 1 *adj* cutting.

2 *nm* (a) cutter (*also Tech*); **— de cristal** glass cutter.

(b) (*Sew*) cutter-out.

cortadora *nf* cutter, cutting machine; slicer; **— de césped** lawnmower.

cortadura *nf* (a) (*act*) cut, cutting.

(b) cut; slash, slit; cut edge.

(c) (*Geog*) narrow pass, defile.

(d) **—s** cuttings, clippings; (*from newspaper*) cuttings.

cortafrío *nm* cold chisel.

cortahuevos *nm*, *pl* **cortahuevos** egg slicer.

cortalápices *nm*, *pl* **cortalápices** pencil sharpener.

cortante 1 *adj* (a) cutting, sharp. (b) *wind* cutting, biting; *cold* bitter. **2** *nm* cleaver, chopper; (*Arg*) scissors.

cortapapeles *nm*, *pl* **cortapapeles** paper knife; (*Tech*) paper cutter, guillotine.

cortapicos *nm*, *pl* **cortapicos** earwig.

cortapisa *nf* (a) restriction, limitation (attached to a concession), condition (attached to a gift); **sin —s** without strings attached.

(b) snag, obstacle; **se pone —s para sí mismo** he makes obstacles for himself; **hablar sin —s** to talk freely.

(c) charm, wit.

cortaplumas *nm*, *pl* **cortaplumas** penknife.

cortapuros *nm*, *pl* **cortapuros** cigar cutter.

cortar [1a] **1** *vt* (a) (*general sense*) to cut; to hack, chop, slash; *hair* to cut, clip, trim; *branch, limb etc* to cut off; *throat* to cut, slit; *tree* to cut down, fell; *meat* to carve, cut up; *cutting, drawing, dress* to cut out; **— por la mitad** to cut down the middle.

(b) (*Math*) to cut; (*Geog*) to cut, cut across; **esa**

línea corta la provincia en dos that line cuts the province in two.
(c) *ball* (*Sport*) to cut, slice, spin.
(d) *air, water etc* to cut through.
(e) *skin* (*of cold*) to chap, crack, split.
(f) *cards* to cut.
(g) *enemy, region, retreat, supply, town etc* to cut off; *bridge, road* to cut; *water etc* to cut off, turn off, shut off; (*Elec*) to switch off; *fire etc* to prevent the spread of; **la carretera está cortada** the road is cut; **quedaron cortados por la nieve** they were cut off by snow.
(h) *letter, speech etc* to cut short, stop, bring to a close; *person* to interrupt; *conversation* to interrupt, cut into, break into.
(i) *passage, detail etc* to cut out, remove, suppress.
(j) *language* to pronounce, speak; *verse* to read; **no corta bien el idioma** he does not speak the language well.
2 *vi* (a) to cut; **este cuchillo no corta** this knife doesn't cut; *see* **sano** *etc*.
(b) (*Cards*) to cut.
(c) (*of wind*) to be biting; **hace un viento que corta** there's a bitter wind.
(d) **— con el pasado** to (make a) break with the past.
3 cortarse *vr* (a) **— el pelo** to have one's hair cut.
(b) (*hands*) to get chapped; (*material*) to split, come apart.
(c) (*milk*) to curdle, turn, turn sour.
(d) (*fig*) to become embarrassed, get confused, become tongue-tied; to be daunted.
(e) (*Arg*) to become separated, get left behind; (*in deal etc*) to get left out.
(f) (*RPl*) to die.
(g) (*Mex, Per, PR*) to catch a chill, get feverish.
(h) (*Chi: horse*) to be out of breath.
cortavidrios *nm, pl* **cortavidrios** glass cutter.
corte[1] *nm* (a) (*act*) cut, cutting; (*Sew*) cutting out; (*of trees*) cutting, felling; (*Cine*) cutting; **— de pelo** haircut; **— a lo garçon** Eton crop, shingle.
(b) (*mark*) cut.
(c) (*in text*) cut, deletion; **el censor lo dejó sin —s** the censor did not cut it, the censor did not delete anything.
(d) (*Elec etc*) cut; failure; **— de corriente** power cut, power failure.
(e) (*Tech*) section; **— transversal** cross section.
(f) (*Min*) stint.
(g) (*Sew*) piece, length; **— de vestido** dress length.
(h) (*Sew*) tailoring; cut, style; **un traje de — muy moderno** a suit of very modern cut; **academia de — (y confección)** dressmaking establishment.
(i) edge (*also Typ*); **con —s dorados** with gilt edges; **dar — a** to sharpen, put an edge on.
(j) **darse —s** (*RPl*) to put on airs.
corte[2] *nf* (a) (royal) court.
(b) capital (city); **La C—** Madrid.
(c) suite, retinue.
(d) **C—s** (*Spain: Hist*) Spanish parliament; **C—s Constituyentes** constituent assembly, constitution-making body.
(e) **hacer la — a una** to woo someone, pay court to someone.
(f) (*SAm*) law court; **C— Suprema** Supreme Court.
cortedad *nf* (a) shortness, smallness; **— de vista** shortsightedness.
(b) bashfulness, timidity, shyness; diffidence.
(c) (*also* **— de alcances**) stupidity.
cortejar [1a] *vt* to court, woo (*also fig*).
cortejo *nm* (a) entourage, suite, retinue.
(b) procession; solemn gathering; **— fúnebre** funeral procession; **— nupcial** wedding procession, wedding party.
(c) wooing, courting; courtship.
(d) (*person*) lover, beau.
cortés *adj* (a) courteous, polite; gracious. (b) **amor —** courtly love.
cortesana *nf* courtesan.
cortesanía *nf* politeness; good manners.
cortesano 1 *adj* of the court; courtly; court (*attr*); **ceremonias cortesanas** court ceremony. **2** *nm* courtier.
cortesía *nf* (a) courtesy, politeness; graciousness; **visita de —** formal visit, courtesy call; **entrada de — free ticket,** complimentary ticket; **días de —** (*Comm*) days of grace; **por — as** a courtesy.

(b) social etiquette; **la — pide que . . .** etiquette demands that . . .
(c) present, gift.
(d) title.
(e) bow; curtsy; **hacer una — a** to bow to; to curtsy to.
cortésmente *adv* courteously, politely; graciously.
corteza *nf* (a) (*of tree*) bark; (*of fruit*) peel, skin, rind; (*Bot*) cortex; (*of bread*) crust; **añadir una — de limón** to add a bit of lemon peel.
(b) (*fig*) outside, outward appearance; hide, exterior.
(c) (*fig*) roughness, coarseness.
cortijo *nm* farm, farmhouse.
cortina *nf* curtain; screen, flap; **— de fuego** (*Mil*) barrage; **— de hierro** (*esp SAm*) iron curtain; **— de humo** smoke screen; **— de tienda** tent flap; **correr la —** (*fig*) to draw a veil over something; **descorrer la —** (*fig*) to draw back the veil.
cortinilla *nf* lace curtain; thin curtain.
cortisona *nf* cortisone.
corto *adj* (a) (*in space*) short, (*in time*) brief, short; (*Comm, Radio*) short; **a la corta o a la larga** sooner or later; **el vestido le ha quedado corto** the dress has got too short for her; **el niño va todavía de —** the child is still wearing short trousers (*etc*).
(b) *supply etc* scant, scanty; inadequate; defective; *ration etc* small; **— de oído** hard of hearing; **— de resuello** short of breath, short-winded; **— de vista** shortsighted; **pongamos 50 ptas y me quedo —** let's say 50 ptas and that's an underestimation; **se quedó — en la comida** she did not provide enough food, she underestimated the food that would be needed.
(c) bashful, timid, shy; socially backward; tongue-tied; **quedarse —** to say less than one should say, not say nearly enough.
(d) (*also* **— de alcances**) of limited intelligence, not very bright.
cortocircuito *nm* short-circuit; **poner(se) en — to** short-circuit.
cortometraje *nm* (*Cine*) short.
cortón *nm* (*Ent*) mole cricket.
Coruña: La — Corunna.
coruñés 1 *adj* of Corunna. **2** *nm*, **coruñesa** *nf* native (*or* inhabitant) of Corunna; **los —es** the people of Corunna.
corva *nf* back of the knee.
corvadura *nf* curve, curvature; bend.
corvejón *nm* (*of horse*) hock; (*of cock*) spur.
corveta 1 *adj* (*CAm*) bow-legged. **2** *nf* curvet, prance.
corvetear [1a] *vi* to curvet, prance.
corvo *adj* curved; bent.
corza *nf* doe.
corzo *nm* roe deer, roebuck.
cosa *nf* (a) thing; matter; **hay una — que no me gusta** there is something I don't like; **alguna — something;** **¿alguna — más?** anything else?; **20 kilos o — así** 20 kilos or thereabouts; **ni — que le parezca** nor anything else of the kind; **otra — anything else,** something else; **ésa es otra — that's another matter** (altogether); **no me queda otra — I have** no alternative; **poca — nothing much;** **es poca —, no es gran —** it's not important; it isn't up to much; **como si tal — as if nothing** (out of the ordinary) had happened; as cool as you please; **así las —s . . . at this point . . .; la — es que . . .** the trouble is that . . .; **no es — que lo dejes todo** there's no reason for you to give it all up; **no sea — que . . .** lest . . ., in case. . .; **lo que son las —s** in spite of everything; **tal como están las —s** as things stand; **¡no hay tal —!** nothing of the sort!; **¡vaya una —!** well!; **las —s van mejor** things are going better; **pasa cada —** anything can happen; **como el que no quiere la —** tentatively; unobtrusively, surreptitiously; **decir una — por otra** (*euph*) to lie; **decir cuatro —s a uno** to give someone a piece of one's mind.
(b) (*with adj etc*) **es — de nunca acabar** there's no end to it; **no es — de broma** (*or* **risa**) it's no laughing matter; **—(s) de comer** eatables, food; **es — distinta** that's another matter; **— dura, — fuerte** tough business, hard thing to bear; **—s de escribir** writing things, writing materials; **es — fácil** it's easy; **¿has visto — igual?** did you ever see the like?; **es — perdida** he's a dead loss; **— rara** strange thing; **¡(qué) — más rara!** how strange!, most odd!; **y, — rara, nadie lo vio** and, oddly enough, nobody saw it; **es — de ver** it's worth seeing, one must see it; **ésa es — vieja** that's stale, that's old history.

(c) affair, business; **ésa es — tuya** that's your affair, that's up to you.

(d) **—s** (*fig*) odd ideas, wild notions; **¡—s de España!** that's typical of Spain!, what else can you expect in Spain!; **¡—s de muchachos!** boys will be boys!; **¡son —s de Juan!** that's typical of John!, that's John all over!; **¡qué —s dices!** (*hum*) what dreadful things you say!; **¡tienes unas —s!** the things you say!

(e) **— de 8 días** about a week; **en — de 10 minutos** in about 10 minutes; **es — de unas 4 horas** it takes about 4 hours.

(f) **— que ...** (*SAm: as conj*) so that ..., in order that ...; in such a way that ...

cosaco 1 *adj* Cossack. **2** *nm*, **cosaca** *nf* (a) Cossack. (b) (*Arg*) mounted policeman.

coscacho *nm* (*Chi, Ec*) rap on the head.

coscarana *nf* cracknel.

coscoja *nf* kermes oak.

coscolino *adj* (a) (*Mex*) peevish, touchy; *child* naughty. (b) of loose morals.

coscorrón *nm* (a) bump on the head. (b) (*fig*) setback, disappointment, knock.

coscurro *nm* hard crust.

cosecha *nf* crop, harvest (*also fig*); (*act*) harvesting, gathering; (*season*) harvest, harvest time; **la — de 1972** (*wine*) the 1972 vintage; **de — propia** *vegetables etc* home-grown, home-produced; **cosas de su propia** (*fig*) things of one's own invention, things out of one's own head; **no añadas nada de tu —** don't add anything that you've made up.

cosechadora *nf* combine-harvester.

cosechar [1a] *vt* (a) to harvest, gather (in); to pick; to grow, cultivate; **aquí no cosechan sino patatas** the only thing they grow here is potatoes. (b) (*fig*) to reap, reap the reward of; *admiration etc* to win.

cosechero *nm*, **cosechera** *nf* harvester, reaper; picker.

cosechón *nm* bumper crop.

coseno *nm* cosine.

coser [2a] **1** *vt* (a) to sew (up); to stitch (up); *button etc* to sew on, stitch on; (*Med*) to stitch (up); (*Naut*) to lash. (b) (*fig*) to unite, join closely (*con* to). (c) **es cosa de — y cantar** it's straightforward; it's plain sailing; it's a cinch (*sl*). (d) **— a uno a balazos** to riddle someone with bullets; **— a uno a puñaladas** to stab someone repeatedly, carve someone up; **le encontraron cosido a puñaladas** they found him covered with stab wounds.

2 *vi* to sew.

3 coserse *vr*: **— con uno** to become closely attached to someone.

cosiaca *nf* (*SAm*) small thing, trifle.

cosido *nm* sewing, needlework.

cosignatario *nm*, **cosignataria** *nf* cosignatory.

cosijoso *adj* (a) (*CAm, Mex*) bothersome, annoying. (b) (*CAm, Mex*) peevish, irritable.

cosmético 1 *adj* cosmetic. **2** *nm* cosmetic.

cósmico *adj* cosmic.

cosmogonía *nf* cosmogony.

cosmografía *nf* cosmography.

cosmógrafo *nm* cosmographer.

cosmología *nf* cosmology.

cosmonauta *nmf* cosmonaut, spaceman, spacewoman.

cosmopolita 1 *adj* cosmopolitan. **2** *nmf* cosmopolitan.

cosmos *nm* cosmos.

coso[1] *nm* arena, enclosure, (*esp*) bullring.

coso[2] *nm* (*Ent*) deathwatch beetle, woodworm.

coso[3] *nm* (*hum*) = **cosa**.

cospel *nm* blank (for a coin).

cosquillar [1a] *vt* to tickle.

cosquillas *nfpl* tickling (sensation); ticklishness; **buscar las — a uno** to tease someone, try to stir someone up; **me hace —** it tickles; **hacer — a uno** to tickle someone; (*fig*) to tickle someone's curiosity; **siento — en el pie** my foot tickles; **tener — to** be ticklish; **no sufre —, tiene malas —** he's touchy, he can't take a joke.

cosquillear [1a] *vt* to tickle (*also fig*).

cosquilleo *nm* tickling (sensation).

cosquilloso *adj* (a) ticklish. (b) (*fig*) touchy, easily offended.

costa[1] *nf* (*Fin*) cost, price; **—s** (*Law*) costs; **a —** (*Comm*) at cost; **a — de** at the expense of; **a toda —** at any price; **a — de lo que sea** cost what it may; **condenar a uno en —s** (*Law*) to order someone to pay the costs.

costa[2] *nf* (a) (*Geog*) coast; coastline; shore, seashore; (*RPl*) riverbank, lake-side.

(b) **C— Azul** Côte d'Azur; **C— de Marfil** Ivory Coast; **C— de Oro** Gold Coast.

(c) (*Spain: tourist areas*) **C— Blanca** *coast near Almería*; **C— Brava** *coast north of Barcelona*; **C— Clara** *coast near Valencia*; **C— Dorada** *coast near Tarragona*; **C— del Sol** *coast west of Málaga*.

costado *nm* (a) (*Anat, Naut, of object*) side; (*Mil*) flank; **de — pass** sideways, *lie* on one's side; **neumáticos de — blanco** white-walled tyres. (b) (*Mex: Rail*) platform. (c) **—s** ancestors; genealogy; **español por los 4 —s** Spanish on both sides of the family, (*fig*) thoroughly Spanish, wholly Spanish, Spanish through and through; **es un gandul por los 4 —s** he's an absolute idler.

costal *nm* sack, bag; **— de huesos** (*fig*) bag of bones.

costalada *nf* violent blow.

costalar [1a] *vi* (*RPl*) to roll over; to fall on one's side (*or* back).

costalazo *nm* violent blow.

costanera *nf* (a) side, flank. (b) slope. (c) (*Arg*) jetty; paved area beside the sea (*or* river); (*Cu*) firm ground (surrounding a swamp). (d) **—s** (*Tech*) rafters.

costanero *adj* (a) sloping, steep. (b) (*Naut*) coastal.

costar [1m] *vti* (*Comm, Fin*) (a) to cost; **¿cuánto cuesta?** how much does it cost?, (*in shop*) how much is it? (b) (*fig*) to cost (dear, dearly); **cueste lo que cueste** cost what it may; **le ha costado caro** it has cost him dear; **eso me ha costado reñir con él** doing that has meant my falling out with him, I did that only at the cost of quarrelling with him; **es un trabajo que cuesta unos minutos** it's a job which takes a few minutes; *see* **trabajo** *etc*. (c) **— + infin** to find it hard to + infin, have a job to + infin; **me cuesta hablar alemán** I find it difficult to speak German, I have trouble speaking German; **me cuesta creerlo** I find that hard to believe.

Costa f Rica Costa Rica.

costarricense = costarriqueño.

costarriqueñismo *nm* word (*or* phrase *etc*) peculiar to Costa Rica.

costarriqueño 1 *adj* Costa Rican. **2** *nm*, **costarriqueña** *nf* Costa Rican.

coste *nm* cost, price; expense; *see also* **costo**.

costear[1] [1a] *vt* (*Fin*) to pay for, defray the cost of; to endow; (*Radio, TV etc*) to back, sponsor; **costea los estudios a su sobrino** he is paying for his nephew's education; **no lo podemos —** we can't afford it.

costear[2] [1a] **1** *vt* (*Naut*) to sail along the coast of; (*fig*) to skirt, go along the edge of; to pass close to. **2 costearse** *vr* (*Chi, RPl*) to have to go from place to place.

costear[3] [1a] *vt* (*Arg*) *cattle* to pasture.

costeño *adj* coastal.

costera *nf* (a) (*of packet etc*) side. (b) (*Geog*) slope. (c) (*Naut*) coast; fishing season.

costero *adj* coastal; *vessel, trade* coasting.

costilla *nf* (a) (*Naut, Anat*) rib; **— flotante** floating rib. (b) (*as meat*) chop; **— de cerdo** pork chop, pork cutlet. (c) **—s** (*fam*) back, shoulders; **todo carga sobre mis —s** I get all the burdens; **medir las —s a uno** to give someone a hiding. (d) (*hum*) wife, better half.

costilludo *adj* broad-shouldered, strapping.

costo *nm* (a) cost; **— efectivo** actual cost; **— de expedición** shipping charges; **—, seguro y flete** (*csf*) cost, insurance and freight (*cif*); **— de** (la) **vida** cost of living; **el — de salarios de la industria** the industry's wages bill. (b) (*SAm*) trouble, effort.

costosamente *adv* expensively.

costoso *adj* costly, expensive.

costra *nf* crust; (*Med*) scab.

costroso *adj* crusty; incrusted; (*Med*) scabby.

costumbre *nf* custom, habit; **—s** customs, ways, (*fig*) morals; **las —s de esta provincia** the customs of this province; **persona de buenas —s** respectable person, decent person; **de —** (*adj*) usual, (*adv*) usually; **como de —** as usual; **más que de —** more than usual; **he perdido la —** I have got out of the habit, (*Sport etc*) I'm out of practice; **tener la — de + infin, tener por — + infin** to be in the habit of + ger; **novela de —s** novel of (local) customs and manners.

costumbrismo *nm* literary genre of (local) customs and manners.

costumbrista 1 *adj novel etc* of (local) customs and manners. **2** *nmf* writer about (local) customs and manners, author with a strong regional flavour.

costura *nf* (a) (*Sew, Naut*) seam; **medias de — francesa** fully-fashioned stockings; **sentar las —s** to press the seams; **sentar las — a uno** (*hum*) to give someone a hiding.
(b) sewing; needlework; dressmaking; **alta —** haute couture, high fashion, fashion designing; **la — italiana** Italian fashions, the Italian fashion trade.

costur(e)ar [1a] *vti* (*SAm*) =**coser**.

costurera *nf* dressmaker, seamstress.

costurero *nm* (a) sewing box, sewing case; sewing room. (b) couturier, fashion designer.

cota¹ *nf* (*Hist*): **— de malla** coat of mail.

cota² *nf* (a) =**cuota**. (b) (*Geog*) height above sea level.

cotarro *nm* (*Hist*) night shelter for tramps *etc*; **alborotar el —** to stir up trouble; **andar** (*or* **ir**) **de — en —** to wander about, gad about; **dirigir el —** to be the boss.

coteja *nf* (*Bol, Ec, Pan*) equal, match.

cotejar [1a] *vt* (a) to compare, collate; to check. (b) (*Ant, Ec*) to arrange.

cotejo 1 *adj* (*SAm*) similar, same. **2** *nm* comparison, collation; check.

cotense *nm* (*Bol, Chi, Mex*), **cotensia** *nf* (*Arg, Bol*), **cotensio** *nm* (*Chi*) coarse hemp fabric.

coterna *nf* (*Col*) broad hat.

cotí *nm* ticking.

cotidiano *adj* daily.

cotiledón *nm* cotyledon.

cotilla *nmf* busybody, gossip.

cotillear [1a] *vi* to gossip.

cotilleo *nm* gossip(ing).

cotillero *nm*, **cotillera** *nf* =**cotilla**.

cotín *nm* (*Sport*) backhand shot.

cotiza *nf* (*Col, Ven*) sandal.

cotización *nf* (*Fin*) quotation, price; **— de apertura** opening price; **— de cierre, — de clausura** closing price. (b) quota. (c) (*of membership*) dues.

cotizado *adj* in demand, popular, sought-after; (*fig*) valued, esteemed.

cotizar [1f] **1** *vt* (a) (*Fin*) *share* to quote, price (*en* at).
(b) *quota* to fix; *subscription, contribution* to pay.
(c) (*Arg, PR*) to value (*en* at).
(d) (*Chi*) to share out proportionally.
(e) (*Per, PR*) to sell.
2 cotizarse *vr* (a) (*Comm, Fin*) **— a** to sell at, sell for, fetch, stand at; (*Stock Exchange*) to stand at, be quoted at; **estos tomates son los que más se cotizan** these tomatoes are the ones which fetch the highest price.
(b) (*fig*) to be valued, be esteemed; **tales conocimientos se cotizan mucho** such knowledge is highly valued.

coto¹ *nm* (a) (*Agr*) enclosure, enclosed pasture; (*Hunting*) preserve; reserve; **— cerrado** (*fig*) closed shop; **— redondo** large estate.
(b) boundary stone; (*fig*) limit; **poner — a** to put a stop to.
(c) (*Comm*) price-fixing agreement.

coto² *nm* (*SAm*) goitre.

cotón *nm* (a) cotton fabric. (b) (*SAm*) shirt; (*Mex*) vest, undervest (*US*); (*Mex*) blouse.

cotona *nf* (*SAm*) strongly-made shirt; (*Chi*) camisole; vest, undervest (*US*); (*CR, Ec, PR*) blouse; (*Mex*) leather jacket; (*PR*) child's nightdress.

cotorra *nf* (a) (*Orn*) parrot, cockatoo; magpie. (b) (*fam*) garrulous woman, chatterbox. (c) (*Mex*) chamberpot. (d) (*Mex*) taxi.

cotorrear [1a] *vi* to chatter, gabble.

cotorreo *nm* chatter, gabble.

cotorrera *nf* =**cotorra** (a) *and* (b).

cototo *nm* (*Chi*) bump, bruise (on the head).

cotudo *adj* (a) hairy, cottony. (b) (*Med*) suffering from goitre. (c) (*Ec*) stupid.

coturno *nm* buskin; **de alto —** (*fig*) lofty, elevated.

covacha *nf* (a) small cave. (b) (*Per, PR, RPl*) lumber room; (*Ant, Guat*) hut; (*Ec*) vegetable stall; (*PR*) kennel.

covadera *nf* (*Bol, Chi, Per*) guano deposit.

covín *nm*, **covín** *nm* (*Chi*) popcorn.

coxcojilla *nf* hopscotch.

coy *nm* (*Naut*) hammock; (*Col, PR*) cradle, cot.

coyote *nm* (a) (*Zool*) coyote, prairie wolf.
(b) (*Mex*) white person.
(c) (*Mex*) astute person; (*Comm, Fin*) speculator, dealer in shares (*etc*).
(d) (*Mex*) youngest child.

coyotear [1a] *vi* (*CAm, Mex*) (a) to be smart, be clever.
(b) (*Comm, Fin*) to deal (*or* speculate) in shares.

coyunda *nf* (a) (*CAm*) strap; tether, halter; lash. (b) (*hum*) yoke (of marriage).

coyuntura *nf* (a) (*Anat*) joint.
(b) (*fig*) moment, juncture, occasion; opportunity; **— crítica** critical moment; turning point; **esperar una — favorable** to await a favourable moment.

coz *nf* (a) kick; **dar coces, dar de coces a** to kick; **dar coces contra el aguijón** to kick against the pricks; **tirar coces** to lash out (*also fig*).
(b) (*of gun: movement*) kick; (*of water*) ebb, backward flow.
(c) (*of gun: part*) butt.
(d) (*fig*) insult, rude remark; **tratar a uno a coces** to be rude to someone, treat someone like dirt.

crac¹ *nm* (a) (*Comm, Fin*) failure, crash; bankruptcy; **— financiero** financial crash. (b) (*fig*) crack-up.

crac² *interj* snap!, crack!; **hizo ¡—! y se abrió** it went crack! and it opened out.

crampón *nm* crampon.

cranearse [1a] *vr* (*Chi*) to swot (*fam*), cram.

cráneo *nm* skull, cranium.

crápula *nf* drunkenness; (*fig*) dissipation.

crapuloso *adj* drunken; (*fig*) dissipated.

craque *nm* =**crac**¹.

craquear [1a] *vt* (*Tech*) to crack.

craqueo *nm* (*Tech*) cracking.

crasitud *nf* fatness.

craso *adj* (a) *person* fat. (b) *liquid* greasy, thick. (c) (*fig*) *error* gross, crass, stupid. (d) (*Arg, Ec*) *person* coarse.

cráter *nm* crater.

crayón *nm* crayon, chalk.

creación *nf* (*all senses*) creation.

creador 1 *adj* creative. **2** *nm*, **creadora** *nf* creator; inventor, originator; **el C—** the Creator.

crear [1a] *vt* to create; to make; to invent, originate; to found, establish, institute.

crece *nm or f* (*Arg, Chi*) =**crecida**.

crecer [2d] **1** *vi* (*general sense*) to grow; to increase; (*of price, river*) to rise; (*of days*) to get longer; (*of moon*) to wax; **dejar — la barba** to grow a beard, let one's beard grow.
2 crecerse *vr* (a) (*Sew*) **"se crece un punto"** "increase by one stitch".
(b) to grow bolder, acquire greater confidence; (*pej*) to get conceited, have an exaggerated sense of one's importance.

creces *nfpl* (a) increase.
(b) (*Sew*) room to let out.
(c) **con —** amply, fully; (*fig*) with a vengeance; **pagar a uno con —** to more than repay one's debt; **devolver algo con —** to return something with interest; **había cumplido su obligación con —** he had amply carried out his obligation.

crecida *nf* (*of river*) rise; spate, flood.

crecido *adj* (a) *person, plant etc* full-grown; grown up; **ya eres — para eso** you're too big for that now.
(b) *number, proportion* large.
(c) **estar —** (*river*) to be in flood.
(d) (*fig*) vain, conceited.

creciente 1 *adj* growing; increasing; rising; **luna —** crescent moon, waxing moon.
2 *nm* crescent.
3 *nf* (a) (*of river*) flood; **— del mar** high tide, flood tide.
(b) crescent moon.

crecimiento *nm* growth; increase; rise; (*Fin*) rise in value.

credenciales *nfpl* credentials.

credibilidad *nf* credibility.

crediticio *adj* (*Fin*) credit (*attr*).

crédito *nm* (a) credit; belief; credence; **dar — a** to believe (in), credit; **apenas daba — a sus oídos** he could scarcely believe his ears.
(b) (*of person*) credit; authority, standing, reputation; **persona** (**digna**) **de —** reliable person; **tiene — de muy escrupuloso** he has the reputation of being thoroughly honest.
(c) (*Comm, Fin*) credit; **a —** on credit; **abrir — a** to give credit to.

credo *nm* creed; credo; **en un —, en menos que se canta un —** in a jiffy.

credulidad *nf* credulity.

crédulo *adj* credulous.

creederas *nfpl*: **tiene buenas —** he's terribly gullible, he'll swallow anything.

creencia *nf* belief (*en* in); **en la — de que . . .** in the belief that . . .

creer [2e] **1** *vti* (a) to think, believe; **— que . . . to** think that . . ., believe that . . .; **creo que sí, lo creo** I think so; **creo que no, no creo** I don't think so; **¡ya lo creo!** I should think so!, rather!; of course!;

¡ya lo creo que está roto! I should jolly well say it's broken!; **créame** believe me, take my word for it; **no se vaya Vd a — que . . .** don't go thinking that . . .; **es difícil, no creas** it's hard enough, I'm telling you.

(b) **— en** to believe in.

(c) to think, deem, consider; **no le creo tan culpable** I don't think him so much to blame; **creo de él que es sincero** I consider him to be sincere; **lo creo de mi deber** I consider it (to be) my duty.

2 **creerse** *vr* to believe oneself (to be), consider oneself (to be); **se cree muy astuto** he thinks he's pretty clever; **¿quién se cree que es?** who do you think you are?

creíble *adj* believable, credible; **¿es — que . . .?** is it conceivable that . . .?

creído *adj* (a) (*SAm*) credulous, trusting. (b) (*Col, Chi, Ec, RPl*) vain, conceited.

crema *nf* (a) (*of milk*) cream; (*Cook*) cream; custard; **— batida** whipped cream; **un coche color —** a cream-coloured car.

(b) (*cosmetic*) cold cream, face cream; **— de afeitar** shaving cream; **— base** foundation cream; **— de belleza** beauty cream; **— dental** toothpaste; **— hidratante** moisturizing cream; **— de limpiar** cleansing cream.

(c) **— para el calzado** shoe polish.

(d) (*fig*) cream, best; **la — de la sociedad** the cream of society.

cremación *nf* cremation.

cremallera *nf* (a) (*also* **cierre de —**) zip fastener, zipper. (b) (*Tech*) rack; **— y piñón** rack and pinion.

crematorio 1 *adj:* **horno — = 2** *nm* crematorium.

crémor *nm* (*also* **— tártaro**) cream of tartar.

cremoso *adj* creamy.

crencha *nf* (*of hair*) parting.

creosota *nf* creosote.

crepitación *nf* crackling; sizzling.

crepitar [1a] *vi* (*log etc*) to crackle; (*bacon*) to sizzle.

crepuscular *adj* twilight, crepuscular; **luz —** twilight.

crepúsculo *nm* twilight, dusk.

cresa *nf* maggot.

Creso *m* Croesus.

crespo 1 *adj* (a) *hair* curly; kinky; *leaf etc* curled.

(b) *style* involved, tortuous.

(c) *person* cross, angry.

2 *nm* hair, head of hair; (*esp Arg, Chi, Cu*) curl, ringlet.

crespón *nm* crape, crêpe.

cresta *nf* (a) (*Orn*) crest, comb; tuft. (b) wig, toupée.

(c) (*of wave*) crest. (d) (*Geog*) crest, ridge; summit.

crestomatía *nf* anthology, collection of texts.

crestón *nm* (*Her*) crest.

Creta *f* Crete.

creta *nf* chalk.

cretáceo *adj* cretaceous.

cretense 1 *adj* Cretan. 2 *nmf* Cretan.

cretinez *nf* utter stupidity.

cretino 1 *adj* cretinous (*also fig*). 2 *nm,* **cretina** *nf* cretin (*also fig*).

cretona *nf* cretonne.

cretoso *adj* chalky.

creyente *nmf* believer.

creyón *nm* crayon, chalk.

cría *nf* (a) rearing, keeping, breeding; **— caballar** horse breeding; **— de ganado** cattle breeding, stock raising; **hembra de —** breeding female.

(b) baby animal, young creature; (*collectively*) young; litter, brood.

criada *nf* servant, maid; **— por horas** charwoman, cleaner; **— para todo** maid of all work, servant with general duties.

criadero *nm* (a) (*Bot*) nursery.

(b) (*Zool*) breeding ground, breeding place; **— de ostras** oyster bed; **— de peces** fish hatchery.

(c) (*Geol*) vein, seam.

criadilla *nf* (a) potato, tuber; **—s de tierra** truffles.

(b) small loaf, roll.

criado 1 *adj* bred, reared, brought up; **bien —** well-bred; **mal —** *see* **malcriado.** 2 *nm* servant.

criador *nm* breeder.

criandera *nf* (*SAm*) nursemaid, wet-nurse.

crianza *nf* (a) (*Agr etc*) rearing, keeping, breeding.

(b) (*Med*) lactation. (c) (*fig*) breeding; **mala —** bad breeding, lack of breeding; **sin —** ill-bred.

criar [1c] 1 *vt* (a) *young* to suckle, feed; **— a los pechos** to breast-feed, nurse.

(b) *plants* to grow; to tend, cultivate.

(c) *animals* to rear, raise; to keep, breed; to fatten.

(d) (*of land etc*) to bear, grow, produce; **esta tierra no cría hierba** this land does not grow grass, this soil is not suitable for grass; **los perros crían pulgas** dogs have (*or* get) fleas; **— carnes** to put on weight; **está criando pelo** he's getting some hair, his hair is growing.

(e) *children* to bring up, raise; to educate.

(f) (*fig*) *hopes etc* to foster, nourish, nurture.

2 *vi* (*of animal*) to have young, produce.

3 **criarse** *vr* to grow (up); **se criaron juntos** they were brought up together, they grew up together; **— en buena cuna** (*or* **en buenos pañales**) to be born with a silver spoon in one's mouth.

criatura *nf* (a) creature (*also fig*); being.

(b) infant, baby, small child; **¡—!** look out!; I say, do be careful!; **todavía es una —** she's still very young, she's only a child still; **¡no seas —!** be your age!; **hacer una — a una** to get a girl in the family way.

criba *nf* sieve, screen.

cribar [1a] *vt* to sieve, sift, screen.

cric *nm* (*Mech*) jack.

Crimea *f* Crimea.

crimen *nm* crime; **— de guerra** war crime.

criminal 1 *adj* criminal. 2 *nmf* criminal; **— de carretera** dangerous driver, roadhog; **— de guerra** war criminal.

criminalidad *nf* (a) criminality; guilt. (b) crime rate.

criminalista *nm* (a) criminologist. (b) criminal lawyer.

criminología *nf* criminology.

crin *nm* horsehair; (*also* **—es**) mane.

crinolina *nf* crinoline.

crinudo *adj* (*SAm*) horse long-maned.

crío *nm* (*fam*) kid (*fam*), child; (*pej*) brat.

criollaje *nm* (*SAm*) Creoles (*collectively*); peasantry.

criollo 1 *adj* (a) Creole.

(b) (*SAm*) native (to America), indigenous; national.

2 *nm,* **criolla** *nf* (a) Creole.

(b) (*SAm*) native (of America), native American.

(c) (*Col*) coward.

cripta *nf* crypt.

cripto . . . crypto . . .

criptocomunista *nmf* crypto-communist.

criptografía *nf* cryptography.

criptográfico *adj* cryptographic(al).

criptógrafo *nm* cryptographer.

criptograma *nm* cryptogram.

crisálida *nf* chrysalis.

crisalidar [1a] *vi* to pupate.

crisantemo *nm* chrysanthemum.

crisis *nf, pl* **crisis** crisis; **— económica** economic crisis; **— nerviosa** nervous breakdown; **— de la vivienda** housing shortage; **llegar a la —** to reach crisis point, come to a head.

crisma[1] *nf* (a) (*Eccl*) chrism, holy oil. (b) (*sl*) **romper la — a uno** to knock someone's block off (*sl*).

crisma[2] *nf* (*Mex*) Christmas present; *see also* **christma(s).**

crisol *nm* crucible; (*fig*) melting pot.

crispar [1a] 1 *vt* (a) *muscle* to cause to twitch (*or* contract); *nerves* to set on edge; **con el rostro crispado por la ira** with his face contorted with anger; **eso me crispa los nervios** that gets on my nerves; that jars (*or* grates) on me.

(b) (*fam*) **— a uno** to annoy someone intensely, get on someone's nerves.

2 **crisparse** *vr* to twitch, contract; (*nerves*) to get all on edge.

crispetas *nfpl* (*Col*) popcorn.

cristal *nm* (a) (*Chem*) crystal (*also fig*); **— de roca** rock crystal.

(b) glass; **un —** a pane of glass, a sheet of glass; **—es** (*freq*) window(s); **— ahumado** smoked glass; **— de aumento** lens, magnifying glass; **— cilindrado** plate glass; **—es emplomados** leaded lights; **— hilado** fibreglass; **— inastillable** splinterproof glass; **— de patente** (*Naut*) bull's-eye; **— de seguridad** safety glass; **— tallado** cut glass; **de —** glass (*attr*); **puerta de —es** glass door.

(c) glass, mirror.

cristalería *nf* (a) (*art*) glasswork; glass making. (b) (*factory*) glassworks; glassware shop. (c) glasses (*collectively*), glassware.

cristalero *nm* (*RPl*) cupboard for glassware.

cristalino *adj* (*Phys*) crystalline; (*fig*) clear, limpid, translucent.

cristalizar [1f] 1 *vti* to crystallize. 2 **cristalizarse** *vr* to crystallize.

cristalografía *nf* crystallography.

cristianamente *adv* in a Christian way; **morir** — to die as a Christian, to die like a good Christian.
cristianar [1a] *vt* to christen, baptize; *see* **trapo**.
cristiandad *nf* Christendom.
cristianismo *nm* Christianity.
cristianizar [1f] *vt* to Christianize.
cristiano 1 *adj* (a) (*Rel*) Christian.
 (b) **vino** — pure wine, unwatered wine.
 (c) (*SAm*) simple-minded.
 2 *nm*, **cristiana** *nf* Christian.
 3 *nm* (a) person, (living) soul; **eso lo sabe cualquier** — any idiot knows that.
 (b) ordinary language, (*esp*) Spanish; **hablar en** — to speak straightforwardly, make sense with what one says; (*equivalent to*) to speak the King's English.
Cristo *m* Christ; **el año 41 antes de** — 41 BC; **el año 80 después de** — 80 AD; **donde** — **dio las tres voces** at the back of beyond; in the middle of nowhere; **¡ni** — **que lo fundó!** don't you believe it!; **poner a uno como un** — to give someone a dressing-down; to heap abuse on someone.
cristo *nm* crucifix.
Cristóbal *m* Christopher.
criterio *nm* (a) criterion; yardstick, standard of judgement.
 (b) viewpoint, attitude, approach; **depende del** — **de cada uno** it depends on the individual viewpoint; **lo mira con otro** — he looks at it from a different point of view; **hace falta tener un** — **más maduro** one needs a more mature approach.
 (c) discernment, discrimination; **lo dejo a su** — I leave it to your discretion; **tiene buen** — his taste is admirable.
 (d) view, opinion; **en mi** — in my opinion; **cambiar de** — to change one's mind; **no comparto ese** — I do not share that view; **formar un** — **sobre** to form an opinion of.
crítica *nf* (a) (*in general*) criticism; — **literaria** literary criticism; — **teatral** dramatic criticism.
 (b) (*una* —) criticism; review, notice, critique; (*pej*) criticism; (*pej*) slander, gossip.
criticador 1 *adj* critical. **2** *nm*, **criticadora** *nf* critic.
criticar [1g] *vt* to criticize.
criticastro *nm* hack critic, ignorant critic.
crítico 1 *adj* critical. **2** *nm* critic.
criticón 1 *adj* hypercritical, overcritical, faultfinding. **2** *nm*, **criticona** *nf* carping critic, faultfinder.
critiquizar [1f] *vt* to be overcritical of, indulge in petty criticism of.
Croacia *f* Croatia.
croar [1a] *vi* to croak.
croasán *nm* (*gall*) croissant, breakfast roll.
croata 1 *adj* Croat(ian). **2** *nmf* Croatian.
crocitar [1a] *vi* to crow, caw.
croché *nm* (*Sew*) crochet(work); **hacer** — to crochet.
crochet [kro'tʃe] *nm* (*gall*) (a) (*Sew*) = **croché**. (b) (*Boxing*) hook.
crol *nm* (*Swimming*: *angl*) crawl.
cromado 1 *adj* chromium-plated; chrome. **2** *nm* chromium plating, chrome.
cromático *adj* chromatic.
cromo *nm* (a) (*Chem*) chromium; chrome. (b) (*also* — **recortado**) transfer.
cromosoma *nm* chromosome.
crónica *nf* (a) (*Hist*) chronicle; **C—s** (*Bible*) Chronicles; (*fig*) chronicle, account.
 (b) (*newspaper*) news report; feature, article; — **deportiva** sports page; — **literaria** literary page; — **de sociedad** society column, gossip column; "**C— de sucesos**" "News in Brief".
crónico *adj* (*Med and fig*) chronic; *vice* ingrained.
cronista *nmf* (a) (*Hist*) chronicler. (b) (*newspaper*) reporter, feature writer, columnist; — **de radio** radio commentator.
cronología *nf* chronology.
cronológicamente *adv* chronologically, in chronological order.
cronológico *adj* chronological.
cronometrador *nm* timekeeper.
cronometraje *nm* timing.
cronometrar [1a] *vt* to time.
cronómetro *nm* (*Tech etc*) chronometer; (*Sport*) stopwatch.
croquet [kro'ke] *nm* (*angl*) croquet.
croqueta *nf* croquette, (*approx*) rissole.
croquis *nm*, *pl* **croquis** sketch.
cross [kros] *nm*, *pl* **cross** (*angl*) cross-country race.
crótalo *nm* (a) (*Zool*) rattlesnake. (b) (*Mus*) —**s** castanets.
crotchet *nm see* **crochet**.
cruce *nm* (a) (*act*) crossing.
 (b) (*Math etc*) (point of) intersection.

 (c) (*Aut etc*) crossing, intersection; — **de carreteras** crossroads; — **giratorio** roundabout, traffic circle (*US*); — **a nivel** level crossing, grade crossing (*US*); — **de peatones** pedestrian crossing.
 (d) (*Tel*) crossing of lines; **hay un** — **en las líneas** the wires are crossed.
 (e) (*Bio*) cross, crossing.
 (f) (*Ling*) cross, mutual interference.
crucero *nm* (a) (*Mil*) cruiser; — **de batalla** battle cruiser; — **pesado** heavy cruiser.
 (b) (*Naut*) cruise; — **de recreo** pleasure cruise.
 (c) (*Eccl*) transept.
 (d) (*Carp*) crosspiece.
 (e) (*Aut etc*) crossroads; crossing; (*Rail*) crossing.
 (f) (*Eccl*: *person*) crossbearer.
 (g) (*Astron*) **C**— (**Austral**) Southern Cross.
cruceta *nf* (a) (*Carp etc*) crosspiece; (*Naut*) crosstree. (b) (*Mech*) universal joint, crosshead. (c) (*Chi*) turnstile.
crucial *adj* crucial.
crucificar [1g] *vt* to crucify; (*fig*) to torment, torture; to mortify.
crucifijo *nm* crucifix.
crucifixión *nf* crucifixion.
cruciforme *adj* cruciform.
crucigrama *nm* crossword.
crudelísimo *adj* (*lit*: *superl of* **cruel**) most cruel, terribly cruel.
crudeza *nf* (a) rawness; unripeness. (b) indigestibility. (c) hardness. (d) bleakness, harshness. (e) crudity, crudeness, coarseness. (f) —**s** indigestible foods.
crudo 1 *adj* (a) *meat* raw; (*Cook*) half-cooked, underdone, raw; *vegetables* green, uncooked; *fruit etc* unripe.
 (b) *foodstuffs* hard to digest.
 (c) *water* hard.
 (d) (*Tech*) untreated; *silk* raw; *linen* unbleached.
 (e) *weather* raw, bleak, harsh.
 (f) (*lit*) cruel, merciless.
 (g) *expression, subject etc* crude, coarse; overrealistic.
 (h) (*Arg, Mex*) yellowish, creamy.
 2 *nm* (*SAm*) coarse cloth, sackcloth.
cruel *adj* cruel (con, para to).
crueldad *nf* cruelty.
cruelmente *adv* cruelly.
cruento *adj* (*lit*) bloody, gory.
crujía *nf* corridor, gallery; bay; (*Med*) ward; **pasar** — to have a tough time of it.
crujido *nm* rustle; creak; crack; crunch; grinding, gnashing; chattering; crackle.
crujiente *adj* rustling; creaking; crunchy; grinding; crackling.
crujir [3a] *vi* (*of leaves, silk, paper*) to rustle; (*of wood, furniture, branch*) to creak; (*of joint, bone*) to crack; (*of gravel etc*) to crunch; (*of teeth*) to grind, gnash; to chatter; (*of burning object*) to crackle; **hacer** — **los nudillos** to crack one's knuckles.
crustáceo *nm* crustacean.
cruz *nf* (a) (*general sense*) cross; — **gamada** swastika; — **de hierro** iron cross; — **de Malta** Maltese Cross; — **de mayo** (*SAm*), **C**— **del Sur** Southern Cross; **C**— **Roja** Red Cross; **¡** — **y raya!** that's quite enough!, no more!; **en** — cross-shaped; crosswise; **con los brazos en** — with arms crossed; **por éstas que son cruces** by all that is holy; **firmar con una** — to make one's mark; **hacerse cruces** to cross oneself; (*fig*) to show one's surprise; **hacerse cruces de que** . . . to be astonished that . . .; **quedar en** — to be in an agonizing situation.
 (b) (*of sword*) hilt; (*of anchor*) crown; (*side of coin*) tails; (*Typ*) dagger; (*Zool*) withers.
 (c) (*fig*) cross, burden; **cada uno lleva su** — each of us has his cross to bear.
cruza *nf* (*Chi, RPl*) (a) (*Agr*) second ploughing. (b) (*Bio*) cross.
cruzada *nf* crusade; **La C**— (*in official Spanish usage*) the Civil War of 1936-39.
cruzadilla *nf* (*CAm*) level crossing, grade crossing (*US*).
cruzado 1 *adj* (a) *arms, cheque etc* crossed; (*placed*) crosswise. (b) (*Sew*) double-breasted. (c) (*Zool*) crossbred, hybrid. **2** *nm* (*Hist*) crusader.
cruzamiento *nm* (a) (*Bio*) crossing. (b) (*Rail*) crossover.
cruzar [1f] **1** *vt* (a) (*in most senses*) to cross; to cut across, intersect; — **un palo sobre otro** to place a stick across another; — **el lago a nado** to swim across the lake.
 (b) (*Naut*) to cruise.
 (c) (*Bio*) to cross.
 (d) *swords* to cross; *words* to have, exchange.
 (e) (*gambling*) money to put, stake.

(f) (*Agr, esp SAm*) to plough a second time.

(g) (*Chi, Ec, Per*) to fight, attack.

2 cruzarse *vr* (a) (*roads, lines etc*) to cross, cross each other; to intersect.

(b) — **de brazos** *see* **brazo**.

(c) (*persons*) to pass each other; — **con uno en la calle** to pass someone in the street.

(d) (*Chi, Ec, Per*) — **con uno** to fight someone, attack someone.

cuacar [1g] *vt* (*Col, Chi, PR*) = **cuajar; no me cuaca** I don't want to; I don't like it; it doesn't suit me.

cuácara *nf* (*Col, Ven*) frock coat; (*Chi*) workman's blouse.

cuaco *nm* (*Arg, Mex, SD*) horse.

cuacho (*CAm*) = **cuate**.

cuaderna *nf* (*Naut*) timber; rib, frame.

cuadernillo *nm* booklet; — **de sellos** book of stamps.

cuaderno *nm* notebook; (*School etc*) exercise book; folder; (*fam*) pack of cards; — **de bitácora** (*Naut*), — **de trabajo** logbook; **C—** **de Cortes** (*Hist*) official parliamentary record.

cuadra *nf* (a) (*Agr*) stable; — **de carreras** racing stable.

(b) (*of hospital etc*) ward.

(c) (*Mil*) hut.

(d) hall, large room.

(e) (*SAm*) block (of houses), city block.

(f) (*Per*) reception room.

(g) (*Ec, Ven*) small rural property (*near a town*).

(h) (*measure*: Arg, Bol, Chi) = 125.50 metres, (CAm, Col, Par, Urug, Ven) = 83.5 metres.

cuadrada *nf* (*Mus*) breve.

cuadrado 1 *adj* (a) (*Math etc*) square (*also fig*).

(b) design with squares, chequered.

(c) *person* broad, square-shouldered.

(d) (*Cu, RPl*) coarse, rude.

(e) (*Col*) graceful, elegant; generous.

2 *nm* (a) (*shape, also Math*) square.

(b) (*Math*) ruler.

(c) (*Tech*) die.

(d) (*Sew*) gusset.

(e) (*Typ*) quadrat.

(f) (*Cu, RPl*) coarse fellow, uncouth person.

Cuadragésima *nf* Quadragesima.

cuadragésimo *adj* fortieth.

cuadrangular 1 *adj* quadrangular. **2** *nm* (*Baseball*) home run.

cuadrángulo *adj* quadrangular.

cuadrante *nm* (a) (*Math, Naut*) quadrant. (b) (*of instrument, radio*) dial; (*of clock*) face; — **solar** sundial.

cuadrar [1a] **1** *vt* (a) (*Math*) to square.

(b) (*Carp etc*) to square (off), make square.

(c) *paper* = **cuadricular**.

(d) (*fig*) to please; to suit; **si le cuadra** if it suits you.

2 *vi* (a) — **con** to square with, tally with, fit, correspond to; to match; to suit, go with.

(b) (*Chi*) — + *infin* to be ready to + *infin*.

3 cuadrarse *vr* (a) to square up, square one's shoulders; (*Mil*) to stand to attention.

(b) (*fig*) to dig one's heels in, refuse to budge.

(c) — **con uno** to become very solemn towards someone, adopt a coldly official attitude towards someone.

(d) (*PR, SD*) to make one's pile (*fam*).

(e) (*Ven*) to come off well, be successful.

cuadratura *nf* quadrature.

cuadrícula *nf* squares (ruled on paper *etc*); criss-cross pattern; (*Chess*) square.

cuadriculado *adj* = **cuadricular 1**; **papel** — squared paper.

cuadricular 1 *adj* *paper* ruled in squares, divided into squares; squared; *fabric* chequered. **2** [1a] *vt* to rule squares on, divide into squares.

cuadrilátero 1 *adj* quadrilateral, four-sided. **2** *nm* (*Math, Archit*) quadrilateral; (*Boxing*) ring.

cuadrilongo 1 *adj* oblong. **2** *nm* oblong.

cuadrilla *nf* party, group; band; gang; (*Mil*) squad; (*of workmen*) gang, squad, team; shift; (*Taur*) quadrille; (*pej*) gang; — **de demolición** demolition squad; — **de noche** night shift.

cuadrillazo *nm* (Arg, Chi, Ec, Per) gang attack.

cuadrillero *nm* group leader; chief; gang leader; (*Tech*) foreman; (*pej, esp Chi, Ec*) gang member.

cuadripartido *adj* quadripartite.

cuadrito *nm* (*Cook etc*) cube; **cortar en —s** to dice.

cuadrivio *nm* quadrivium.

cuadro *nm* (a) square; — **de vidrio** pane of glass; **2 metros en —** 2 metres square; **diseño a —s** chequered pattern, check (pattern).

(b) (*Archit, Tech*) frame; — **de bicicleta** bicycle frame; — **de ventana** window frame.

(c) (*Art*) picture, painting; **dos —s de Velázquez** two Velazquez paintings.

(d) (*Theat*) scene (*also fig*); (*TV*) picture; —**s vivos** tableau; **fue un** — **desgarrador** it was a heart-breaking scene (*or* picture).

(e) (*Lit*) description, picture; — **de costumbres** description of (regional) customs, scene of local colour.

(f) (*Agr, Hort*) bed; patch; plot; — **alpino** rock garden.

(g) (*Elec etc*) panel; — **de conexión manual** (*Tel*), — **de conmutadores** (*Elec*), — **de distribución** (*Elec*) switchboard; — **de instrumentos** instrument panel; (*Aut*) dashboard; — **de mandos** control panel.

(h) (*Mil*) square (formation); **formar el** — (*fig*) to resolve to stand together.

(i) table, chart, diagram (*also* — **sinóptico**).

(j) (*persons*) cadre; staff, establishment of officials (*etc*).

(k) (*Chi*) slaughterhouse.

(l) (*Col*) blackboard.

cuadrúpedo *nm* quadruped; four-footed animal.

cuádruple *adj* quadruple; fourfold.

cuadruplicado *adj* quadruplicate; **por** — in quadruplicate.

cuadruplicar [1g] **1** *vt* to quadruple. **2 cuadruplicarse** *vr* to quadruple.

cuádruplo 1 *adj* quadruple. **2** *nm* quadruple.

cuajada *nf* curd; cottage cheese.

cuajado *adj* (a) curdled, set, coagulated, congealed.

(b) — **de** (*fig*) full of, filled with; covered with; **una situación cuajada de peligros** a situation fraught with dangers; **un texto** — **de problemas** a text bristling with problems; **una corona cuajada de joyas** a crown covered with jewels.

(c) **estar** — (*fig*) to be dumbfounded.

(d) **quedarse** — (*fig*) to fall asleep.

cuajaleche *nm* bedstraw.

cuajar [1a] **1** *vt* (a) to thicken; *milk* to curdle; *blood etc* to congeal, coagulate, clot; *fat* to congeal; *jelly etc* to set.

(b) to cover, adorn (excessively; *de* with); to fill (*de* with); **una música que cuaja el ambiente de alegría** music which fills the air with joy.

2 *vi* (a) (*of seed etc*) to set; (*of snow*) to lie; *see* **3**.

(b) (*fig*) to become set, become established; to jell; (*of plan etc*) to take shape; to come off, work; (*of result*) to materialize; (*of proposal, motion*) to be received, be acceptable; **el noviazgo no cuajó** the engagement did not work, the engagement was not a success.

(c) (*Mex*) to chatter.

3 cuajarse *vr* (a) to thicken; to curdle; to congeal, coagulate; to set.

(b) — **de** (*fig*) to fill with, fill up with; to become crowded with.

(c) (*fig*) to go fast asleep.

cuajarón *nm* clot.

cuajo *nm* (a) rennet.

(b) (*fig*) phlegm, calmness; **tiene mucho** — he's very phlegmatic.

(c) *see* **llorar**.

(d) **arrancar algo de** — to tear something out by its roots; **arrancar una puerta de** — to wrench a door out of its frame; **extirpar un vicio de** — to eradicate a vice completely.

(e) (*Mex*) chat; chatter.

(f) (*Mex*) harmless fib.

(g) (*Mex*) impossible plan.

(h) (*Mex: School*) playtime.

cual 1 *adj* (*lit*) such as, of the kind (that); (*Law*) said, aforementioned; **los cuales bienes** the said property, **which** property; **las ceremonias fueron** —**es convenían a su importancia** the ceremonies were such as befitted his importance.

2 *pron* (a) **cada** — each one; **allá cada** — every man to his own taste; **son a** — **más gandul** each is as idle as the other; **gritar a** — **más** to see who can shout the loudest; — **más,** — **menos** some more, some less.

(b) (*relative*) **el** — (*etc*) which; who; whom; **ese edificio, el** — **se construyó en el siglo XV** that building, which was built in the 15th century; **un policía, el** — **me puso una multa** a policeman, who gave me a fine.

(c) **lo** — (*relative*) which; a fact which; **se rieron mucho, lo** — **me disgustó** they laughed a lot, which upset me; **con lo** — at which, whereupon; **por lo** — (and) so, and because of this, on account of which; whereby.

3 *adv and conj*: + *noun* like, as; + *verb* (just) as;

brillaba — estrella it shone like a star; **cual . . . tal** (*or* **así**) **. . . like . . . like . . .;** (*verb*) just as **. . .,** so **. . .; — el padre, tal el hijo** like father like son; **— el otro, tal éste** this one is just like the other, this one is as bad (*etc*) as the other; **— llega el día tras la noche** just as day follows night; **— si . . . as if;** *see* **tal.**

cuál *interrog pron* which (one)?; **¿— quieres?** which (one) do you want?; **¿— es el que dices?** which one are you talking about?; **si es tan malo A, ¿— debe ser B?** if A is so bad, what must B be like?; **ignora — será el resultado** he does not know what the outcome will be.

cualidad *nf* quality; attribute, trait, characteristic; (*Philos, Phys etc*) property; **tiene buenas —es** he has good qualities.

cualificado *adj* (a) *worker* skilled, qualified; **obrero no — unskilled** worker. (b) **estar — para** + *infin* to be entitled to + *infin*. (c) *see* **calificado.**

cualitativo *adj* qualitative.

cualquier(a), *pl* **cualesquier(a) 1** *adj* (a) any; any **. . . you** care to name (*or* like to mention *etc*); **— hombre de los de aquí** any man from these parts; **en — momento** at any time; **en — sitio donde lo busques** in whatever place you look for it, whichever place you look for it in; **con — resultado que sea** with whatever result it may be.

(b) (*after noun*) any; **ella no es una mujer —** she's not just any woman, she's not just an ordinary woman.

2 *pron* (a) anybody; whoever; whichever; **te lo diría —** anyone would tell you the same; **— puede hacer eso** anybody can do that; **yo me contento con — I** am happy with any (*or* either); I don't mind either (of the two).

(b) **— que sea** whoever he is; whichever it is.

(c) **es un —** he's a nobody; **yo no me caso con un — I'm** not marrying just anybody.

cuan *adv* (*lit*): **tan estúpidos — criminales** as much criminal as they are stupid.

cuán *adv* how; **¡— agradable fue todo eso!** how delightful it all was!

cuando 1 *adv and conj* (a) (*time*) when; **— nos veamos** when we meet again; **— iba allí le veía** whenever I went there I saw him; **ven — quieras** come when(ever) you like; **me acuerdo de — . . . I** remember the time when **. . .; lo dejaremos para — estés mejor** we'll leave it until you're better.

(b) (*concessive*) if, even if, although; **— lo dice él, será verdad** if he says so, it must be true; **— no sea así** even if it is not so; **— más** at (the) most; **— menos** at least; **— no** if not, otherwise; **¡— no!** (*SAm*) of course!, I should jolly well think so! (*fam*).

(c) (*causal*) since, when; *see also* **aun, cada** *etc.*

2 *prep* at the time of; **eso fue — la guerra** that was during the war; **ocurrió — la boda** it happened at the same time as the wedding; **— niño** as a child, when I (*etc*) was a child.

cuándo *interrog adv and conj* when; **¿— lo perdiste?** when did you lose it?; **no sé — será I** don't know when it will be; **¿de — acá?** since when?; (*fig*) how come?; **¿desde — es esto así?** how long has it been like this?; **— con A, — con B** sometimes with A, sometimes with B.

cuantía *nf* quantity, amount; extent; importance; **de mayor —** first-rate; important; **de menor —, de poca —** second-rate; unimportant, of little account; **se ignora la — de las pérdidas** the extent of the losses is not known.

cuántico *adj*: **teoría cuántica** quantum theory.

cuantioso *adj* large, substantial; abundant; numerous.

cuantitativo *adj* quantitative.

cuanto 1 *adj* all that, as much as, whatever; **tiene todo —** desea he has all he wishes for; **daremos —s créditos se precisen** we will give all the credits that may be necessary, we will give whatever credits are needed; **—s hombres la ven la quieren** all the men that see her fall in love with her; **unos —s libros** a few books, some books; **—s más haya tantas más comidas habrá que preparar** the more there are the more meals will have to be cooked.

2 *pron* all that (which), as much as; **—s** all those that, as many as; **tiene — desea** he has all (that) he wants; **tome — quiera** take all you want, take as much as you want; **—s más, mejor** the more the merrier.

3 *adv and conj* (a) **en — inasmuch** as; **él, en — erudito, . . .** he, as a scholar, **. . .; en — (conj)** as soon as, immediately, directly; **en — lo supe me fui** as soon as I heard it I left; **en — a** as for, as to, with regard to; **por — and so, hence.**

(b) **— más** at least; **— más difícil parezca** the more difficult it may seem, however difficult it seems; **— más trabaja menos gana** the more he works the less he earns; **— más que resultó ser mujer** all the more so because it turned out to be a woman; *see* **antes** *etc.*

cuánto *adj, pron and adv* **1** *excl* (a) (+ *verb*) **¡— has crecido!** how you've grown!; **¡— trabajas!** how hard you work!; **¡— has gastado!** what a lot you've spent!; **¡— me alegro!** I'm so glad!

(b) (+ *noun*) **¡cuánta gente!** what a lot of people!; **¡— tiempo perdido!** what a lot of time wasted!, the time you've wasted!; *see* **bueno.**

2 *interrog* (a) (*sing*) how much? **¿— has gastado?** how much have you spent?; **¿— (tiempo)?** how long?; **¿— durará esto?** how long will this last?; **¿— hay de aquí a Bilbao?** how far is it from here to Bilbao?; **¿a — están las peras?** how much are (the) pears?; **le dije — la quería I** told her how much I loved her; *see* **cada, cinco.**

(b) **¿—s?** how many?; **¿cuántas personas había?** how many people were there?; **¿a —s estamos?** what's the date?

(c) **el señor no sé —s** Mr So-and-So; **el señor Anastasio no sé —s** Mr Anastasius Something.

cuaquerismo *nm* Quakerism.

cuáquero 1 *adj* Quaker. **2** *nm*, **cuáquera** *nf* Quaker.

cuarcita *nf* quartzite.

cuarenta *adj* forty; **ésas son otras — (Arg, Per, Urug)** that's a different story; **cantar las — a uno** to tell someone a few home truths.

cuarentena *nf* (*Med etc*) quarantine.

cuarentón 1 *adj* forty-year old, fortyish. **·2** *nm*, **cuarentona** *nf* person of about forty.

cuaresma *nf* Lent.

cuaresmal *adj* Lenten.

cuarta *nf* (a) (*Math*) quarter, fourth, fourth part.

(b) (*of hand*) span.

(c) (*Naut*) point (of the compass).

(d) (*SAm*) whip, riding crop.

(e) (*RPl*) extra pair of oxen.

(f) **andar de la — al pértigo** (*RPl*), **vivir la —** (*Chi, Mex*) to live in poverty.

cuartago *nm* pony.

cuartazos *nm, pl* **cuartazos** (*fam*) fat person, lump.

cuartear [1a] **1** *vt* **a** to quarter; to divide up, cut up.

(b) *steep road* to zigzag up.

(c) (*Naut*) *compass* to box.

(d) (*Mex, PR*) to whip, beat.

2 *vi* (a) (*Cards*) to make a fourth (player), make up a four.

(b) (*Taur*) to dodge, step aside.

3 cuartearse *vr* (a) (*surface*) to crack, split.

(b) (*Taur*) to dodge, step aside.

(c) (*Mex*) to go back on one's word, behave badly; to get scared.

(d) (*Ven*) to hedge; to change one's mind.

cuartel *nm* (a) quarter; (*of city*) quarter, district.

(b) (*Her*) quarter.

(c) (*Hort*) bed.

(d) (*Mil*) barracks; **—es** quarters; **— de bomberos** fire station; **— general** headquarters; **—es de invierno** winter quarters; **vida de —** army life, service life.

(e) **guerra sin —** war without mercy; **no dar —** to give no quarter, show no mercy; **no hubo — para los revoltosos** no mercy was shown to the rioters.

cuartelada *nf* (*pej*) military uprising, mutiny, putsch.

cuartelero *nm* (*Ec, Per*) waiter, hotel servant.

cuartería *nf* (*Cu, Chi, SD*) labourers' living quarters (*on a ranch*).

cuarterón *nm* (a) quarter pound. (b) (*Archit*) door panel. (c) (*SAm*) quadroon.

cuarteta *nf* quatrain.

cuarteto *nm* (a) (*Mus*) quartet(te). (b) (*Lit*) quatrain.

cuartilla *nf* (a) sheet (of paper); **—s** (*Typ*) manuscript, copy; notes, jottings. (b) (*of horse*) pastern. (c) fourth part (*of a measure*).

cuarto 1 *adj* fourth.

2 *nm* (a) quarter, fourth part; **abrigo tres —s** three-quarter length coat; **—s de final** quarter finals; **— de hora** quarter of an hour; **las 6 y — a** quarter past 6; **las 7 menos — a** quarter to seven; **tardó tres —s de hora** he took three-quarters of an hour; **— de luna** quarter of the moon; **— creciente** first quarter; **— menguante** last quarter; **de tres al — insignificant, worthless.**

(b) (*of meat*) joint; **—s** (*of animal*) legs, limbs; **— trasero** hindquarters, (*as meat*) rump.

(c) (*Typ*) quarto; **libro en —** quarto volume.

(d) (*Fin*) *an ancient coin*; **—s** (*fam*) money, brass (*sl*); **por 5 —s** for a song; **es hombre de** muchos —s he's a man with dough (sl); **estar sin un —, no tener un —** to be broke (fam); **dar un — al pregonero** to tell everyone one's private business.

(e) (Archit) room; rooms; small flat; **— de aseo,** — de baño bathroom; **— de desahogo,** — **trastero** lumber room; **— de descanso** rest room; **— de estar** living room; **— de juego** playroom; **— de los niños** nursery; **— oscuro** (Phot) darkroom; **poner —** to set up house; **poner — a la querida** to set one's mistress up in a little place.

(f) household, establishment of servants.
cuarzo nm quartz.
cuartones nmpl dressed timber, beams, planks.
cuás nm (Mex) bosom pal (fam).
cuasi adv (lit) = casi.
cuate (CAm, Ec, Mex) **1** adj twin. **2** nm (a) twin. (b) pal (fam), buddy (esp US). (c) double-barrelled gun.
cuaternario 1 adj quaternary. **2** nm quaternary.
cuatre(re)ar [1a] **1** vt (RPl) cattle to rustle, steal. **2** vi (RPl) to act treacherously.
cuatrero 1 adj (CAm) treacherous, disloyal. **2** nm (RPl) cattle rustler, horse thief.
cuatrillizos nmpl, **cuatrillizas** nfpl quadruplets.
cuatrimotor 1 adj four-engined. **2** nm four-engined plane.
cuatro 1 adj four; (date) fourth; **las —** four o'clock; **más de —** (fig) quite a few, rather a lot.
2 nm (a) four.
(b) (Col, PR, SD, Ven) four-stringed guitar.
(c) (Mex) trick, fraud; blunder.
cuatrocientos adj four hundred.
Cuba f Cuba.
cuba[1] nf (a) cask, barrel; tub; vat; (Rail) tank car; **— para el agua de lluvia** rainwater butt; **— de riego** water wagon, street sprinkler.
(b) (fam) pot-bellied person.
(c) (fam) drunkard, boozer; **estar hecho una —** to be as drunk as a lord.
cuba[2] nm (Col) youngest child.
cubaje nm (SAm) volume, contents.
cubanismo nm cubanism, word (or phrase etc) peculiar to Cuba.
cubano 1 adj Cuban. **2** nm, **cubana** nf Cuban.
cubero nm cooper.
cubertería nf cutlery.
cubeta nf keg, small cask; pail; (Chem, Phot) tray; (of thermometer) bulb; **— de siembra** seed box.
cubicar [1g] vt (a) (Math) to cube. (b) (Phys) to determine the volume of.
cúbico adj cubic; **metro —** cubic metre; **raíz cúbica** cube root.
cubículo nm cubicle.
cubierta nf (a) cover, covering; (Typ) cover, jacket; (Archit) roof; (Tech) casing; (Aut) bonnet, hood (US); (Aut etc) tyre, outer cover; (Post) envelope; **— de cama** coverlet; **— de lona** tarpaulin, canvas; **bajo esta —** (Post) under the same cover, enclosed herewith; **bajo — separada** (Post) under separate cover.
(b) (Naut) deck; **— de aterrizaje, — de vuelo** flight deck; **— de botes** boat deck; **— de paseo** promenade deck; **— de sol** sun deck.
(c) (Col, Ec, Mex) sheath.
(d) (fig) cover, pretext.
cubierto 1 ptp of **cubrir** and adj: (a) covered; sky overcast; **no — cheque** bad, unbacked; **poco — tyre** threadbare, worn.
(b) **la vacante está ya cubierta** the place has already been filled.
2 nm (a) **a —, bajo—** under cover; **a — de** safe from, out of the way of; **ponerse a —** to take cover, shelter (de from).
(b) place (at table); knife, fork and spoon, set of cutlery; (Cook) meal; meal at a fixed charge; **—s** cutlery; **— de 80 pesetas** 80-peseta meal; **precio del — cover** charge.
cubil nm den, lair.
cubilete nm (a) (Cook) mug, tumbler; small copper pan. (b) (in games) cup; dicebox. (c) (SAm) intrigue. (d) (SAm) top hat; bowler hat.
cubiletear [1a] vi (a) to shake the dicebox. (b) (fig) to intrigue, scheme.
cubiletero nm conjurer.
cubismo nm cubism.
cubista 1 adj cubist. **2** nmf cubist.
cubito nm (a) (child's) bucket, beach pail. (b) **— de hielo** ice cube.
cúbito nm ulna.
cubo nm (a) (Math) cube.

(b) bucket, pail; tub; **— de (la) basura** dustbin, ashcan (US); **— para el carbón** coal scuttle; **llover a —s** to rain cats and dogs, rain in torrents.
(c) (Mech) barrel, drum.
(d) (of wheel) hub.
(e) millpond.
(f) (Archit) round turret.
cubrebocas nm, pl **cubrebocas** (Med) mask.
cubrecama nf coverlet, bedspread.
cubrecorsé nm camisole.
cubremesa nf (SAm) table cover.
cubreobjetos nm, pl **cubreobjetos** (Bio etc) slide cover.
cubrerrueda nf mudguard, fender (US).
cubretetera nf tea cosy.
cubrir [3a; ptp **cubierto**] **1** vt (a) (general sense) to cover (in, over, up; con, de with); (Archit) to roof, put a roof over; fire to make up, bank up; **lo cubrieron los aguas** the waters closed over it; **el agua casi me cubría** the water almost covered me, I was almost out of my depth; **no te metas donde te cubra el agua** don't go out of your depth.
(b) (Mil) to cover; **— a uno con un revólver** to cover someone with a revolver.
(c) (of emotion etc) to cover; to hide, conceal, cloak; **cubre su tristeza con una falsa alegría** she covers up her sadness with a false cheerfulness.
(d) **— a uno de improperios** to shower insults on someone, shower someone with insults; **— a uno de alabanzas** to heap praises on someone; **— a uno de atenciones** to overwhelm someone with kindnesses; **— a uno de oprobio** to cover someone in shame; **— a uno de besos** to smother someone with kisses.
(e) friend etc to cover, protect; to cover up for.
(f) distance to cover, travel, do; **— 80 kms en una hora** to cover 80 kms in an hour.
(g) post to fill.
(h) (Bio) to cover, mate with.
(i) (Fin etc) expenses, needs to meet, cover; deficit, overdraft etc to cover; debt to repay; **esto cubre todas nuestras necesidades** this meets all our needs; **ello apenas cubre los gastos** this scarcely covers the expenses.
2 cubrirse vr (a) to cover oneself; to put on one's hat.
(b) (fig) **— de gloria** to cover oneself with glory.
(c) **— contra un riesgo** to cover (or protect) oneself against a risk; **— contra una posibilidad** to take precautions against an eventuality.
(d) (of sky) to become overcast.
cuca nf (a) (fam) tart (sl), whore. (b) **—s** sweets, candy (US); titbits; confectionery.
cucambé nm (Col, Ven) hide-and-seek.
cucaña nf (a) plum, soft job; bargain; cinch (sl), easy thing. (b) (at fair etc) greasy pole.
cucañero nm, **cucañera** nf (fam) shrewd person, fly sort; hanger-on; social climber.
cucar [1g] vt (a) to wink. (b) to deride, poke fun at. (c) (SAm) to urge on, incite, provoke.
cucaracha nf (a) (Ent) cockroach. (b) (Arg, Mex: Aut) old crock.
cucarachero nm (Col, PR) parasite, hanger-on; (Ec) flatterer, creep (sl).
cuclillas: en — squatting, crouching; **sentarse en —** to squat, sit on one's heels.
cuclillo nm (a) (Orn) cuckoo. (b) (Bot) ragged robin. (c) (fam) cuckold.
cuco 1 adj (a) shrewd; sly, crafty.
(b) pretty; cute; dainty.
2 nm (a) (Orn) cuckoo.
(b) (Ent) grub, caterpillar.
(c) (fam) gambler.
(d) (Mex) **hacer — a uno** to poke fun at someone.
cucú nm (sound) cuckoo.
cucuche (CAm): **ir a —** to ride astride.
cucufato nm (Arg, Bol, Per) hypocrite, sanctimonious person.
cucurucho nm (a) paper cone, cornet; (fig) cornucopia. (b) (Eccl etc) hooded garment; pointed hat. (c) (Ant, CAm, Col, Pan) top, summit, apex.
cuchara nf (a) spoon; scoop; ladle; (Tech) scoop; bucket; dipper; **— de café** coffee spoon, (equivalent to) teaspoon; **— de sopa, — sopera** soup spoon, (as measure) tablespoon; **militar de —** officer who has risen from the ranks; **meter su —** (in conversation) to butt in, (in matter) to meddle, shove one's oar in; **meter algo a uno con —** to have a hard job getting someone to understand something; **despacharse (or**

servirse) con la — grande (*esp SAm*) to give oneself a big helping, (*fig*) to look after number one.
  (b) (*SAm*) flat trowel; **albañil de —** skilled bricklayer.
  (c) (*CAm, Chi, PR*) pout; **hacer —** to pout.
  (d) (*Mex*) pickpocket.
cucharada *nf* spoonful; **— de café** teaspoonful; **— de sopa** tablespoonful.
cucharadita *nf* teaspoonful.
cucharear [1a] *vt* to spoon out, ladle out; (*Agr*) to pitch.
cucharetear [1a] *vi* **(a)** to stir (with a spoon). **(b)** (*fig*) to meddle.
cucharilla *nf*, **cucharita** *nf* small spoon, teaspoon (*also* **— de café**, **— de té**).
cucharón *nm* ladle; (*Tech*) scoop, bucket; **tener el — por el mango** (*fig*) to have the situation well in hand.
cuchí *nm* (*Per*) pig.
cuchichear [1a] *vi* to whisper (*a* to).
cuchicheo *nm* whispering.
cuchilla *nf* **(a)** (large, kitchen) knife; chopper, cleaver; (*Tech, also of weapon*) blade; (*of skate*) runner; scraper; (*SAm*) penknife; **— de afeitar** razor blade.
  (b) (*Geog*) ridge, crest; (*SAm*) line of low hills; (*PR*) mountain top.
cuchillada *nf* **(a)** slash, cut, gash, knife wound; **— de cien reales** long gash, severe wound; **dar —** (*fig*) to make a hit, get talked about.
  (b) (*Sew*) slash, slit.
  (c) **—s** (*fig*) fight, brawl.
cuchillazo *nm* (*SAm*)=**cuchillada (a)**.
cuchillería *nf* **(a)** cutlery. **(b)** cutler's (shop).
cuchillero 1 *adj* (*SAm*) quarrelsome, brawling; clever with a knife. **2** *nm* cutler.
cuchillo *nm* **(a)** knife; **— de caza**, **— de monte** hunting knife; **— de cocina** kitchen knife; **— del pan** breadknife; **— de trinchar** carving knife; **pasar a —** to put to the sword.
  (b) (*Archit: also* **— de armadura**) upright, support.
  (c) **— de aire** sharp draught, cold draught.
  (d) (*Mex*) surgeon.
cuchipanda *nf* (*fam*) feed (*fam*), beano (*fam*).
cuchitril *nm* **(a)** (*Agr*) pigsty. **(b)** (*fig*) hovel; pigsty; den, hole.
cucho *nm* **(a)** (*CAm*) hunchback. **(b)** (*Chi*) puss. **(c)** (*Col, Ec, Per*)=**cuchitril (b)**.
cuchuflé *nm* (*Cu*)=**cuchuflí**.
cuchufleta *nf* (*fam*) joke, crack (*fam*).
cuchuflí *nm* (*Cu*) uncomfortable place; jail.
cuchugos *nmpl* (*Col, Ec, Ven*) saddlebags.
cuchumbo *nm* (*CAm*) funnel; bucket, pail; dicebox.
cuelga *nf* **(a)** hanging (of fruit *etc* to dry); bunch (of drying fruit *etc*). **(b)** birthday present. **(c)** (*Col, Chi*) fall (in the level of a stream *etc*).
cuelgacapas *nm*, *pl* **cuelgacapas** coat hanger; hallstand.
cuellicorto *adj* short-necked.
cuellilargo *adj* long-necked.
cuello *nm* **(a)** (*Anat*) neck; **cortar el — a uno** to cut someone's throat; **erguir el —** to be haughty; **levantar el —** to get on one's feet again (*fig*).
  (b) collar; **— alto** high collar; **— blando** soft collar; **— postizo** detachable collar; **— de recambio** spare collar.
cuenca *nf* **(a)** hollow; (*Anat*) eye socket.
  (b) (*Hist*) wooden bowl.
  (c) (*Geog*) bowl, deep valley; (*of river*) basin, catchment area; **la — del Ebro** the Ebro basin; **— hullera**, **— minera** coalfield.
cuenco *nm* **(a)** hollow; (*of spoon*) bowl; **— de la mano** hollow of the hand.
  (b) earthenware bowl, wooden bowl.
cuenta *nf* **(a)** (*Math*) count, counting; calculation; (*esp fig*) reckoning; (*Boxing*) count; **— de la vieja** counting on one's fingers; **— (hacia) atrás**, **— al revés** (*rocket launch etc*) countdown; **a esa —** at that rate; **por la —** apparently, as far as one can tell; **beber más de la —** to have too much to drink, have one over the eight; **caer en la —** to catch on (*de* to), see the point (*de of*); **habida — de eso** bearing that in mind; **hacer algo con su — y razón** to be fully aware of what one is doing; **perder la — de** to lose count of; **tener** (*or* **tomar**) **en —** to bear in mind, take into account; **es otra cosa a tener en —** that's another thing to be borne in mind.
  (b) (*Comm, Fin: at bank*) account; **— de ahorros**, **— a plazo (fijo)** deposit account; **— bancaria**, **— de banco** bank account; **— corriente** current account; **— indistinta**, **— en participación** joint account; **abrir una —** to open an account; **a — on** account;

tomar un coche a — to take a car in part payment; **abonar una cantidad en — a uno** to credit a sum to someone's account; **cargar una cantidad en — a uno** to charge a sum to someone's account.
  (c) (*Comm, Fin: sent out*) account, bill; (*in restaurant etc*) bill; (*fig*) check, tally; **la — del sastre** the tailor's bill; **— de diversos** sundries account; **— de gastos** expense account; **— pendiente** unpaid bill, outstanding account; **la — es la —** business is business; **ajustar** (*or* **liquidar**) **una —** to settle an account; **echar las —s** to reckon up; **hacer las —s de la lechera** to indulge in wishful thinking, count one's chickens before they are hatched; **llevar la —** to keep an account of; **pasar la —** to send the bill; **vivir a — de** to live at the expense of.
  (d) (*fig*) account; **ajustar —s** to settle up (*con* with); **ajustar —s viejas con uno** to settle old scores with someone; **le ajusté las —s** (*fam*) I told him where to get off; **voy a ajustar —s con él** I'm going to have it out with him; **¡vamos a —s!** let's get down to business!; **tener —s pendientes con uno** to have a matter to settle with someone.
  (e) (*fig*) account; report, statement; **en resumidas —s** in short, in a nutshell; all in all; **dar — de** to give an account of, report on; **dar — a uno de sus actos** to account to someone for one's actions; **no tiene que dar —s a nadie** he's not answerable to anyone; **dar — de una botella** to finish off a bottle, put paid to a bottle; **dar buena — de sí** to give a good account of oneself; to give as good as one gets; **darse — de** to realize (*que* that); **sin darse —** without realizing it, without noticing; **exigir** (*or* **pedir**) **—s a uno** to call someone to account, bring someone to book; **rendir —s a uno** to report to someone.
  (f) (*fig*) affair, business; **ésa es — mía** that's my affair, that's up to me; **de — y riesgo de uno** at one's own risk; **por — propia, por su propia —** on one's own account, for oneself; **por mí —** in my opinion; as for me; **eso corre de** (*or* **por**) **mi —** that's my affair; **éste corre por mi —** (*drinks etc*) this one's on me; **no querer —s con uno** to want nothing to do with someone; to want no trouble with someone; *see* **apañar** *etc*.
  (g) **—s** plans; **echar —s** to reflect, take stock; **echar — de + infin** to plan to + *infin*; **le salieron fallidas las —s** his plans went wrong.
  (h) (*fig*) importance; **de (mucha) —** important; **no tiene — + infin** there is no point in + *ger*.
  (i) (*of necklace etc, also Eccl*) bead.
cuentacorrentista *nmf* depositor.
cuentagotas *nm*, *pl* **cuentagotas** (*Med*) dropper.
cuentakilómetros *nm*, *pl* **cuentakilómetros** *equivalent to* milometer; speedometer.
cuentarrevoluciones *nm*, *pl* **cuentarrevoluciones** tachometer.
cuentear [1a] **1** *vt* (*Col*) to court; to compliment. **2** *vi* (*CAm*) to gossip.
cuenterete *nm* (*CAm*) piece of gossip; tall story, tale.
cuentero *nm* (*RPl*) confidence trickster, con(fidence) man (*US*).
cuentista *nmf* **(a)** storyteller; (*Lit*) short-story writer.
  (b) gossip; talebearer.
  (c) affected person, person with a theatrical manner; conceited person, swank (*fam*).
  (d) (*RPl*) confidence trickster.
cuento¹ *nm* **(a)** story, tale; (*Lit*) short story; funny story, joke; **— de hadas** fairy tale; **— del tío** (*Chi, Per, RPl*) confidence trick, confidence game (*US*); **— de viejas** old wives' tale; **es un — largo** it's a long story; **esto es mucho —** this is terribly tedious; **es el — de nunca acabar** it's an endless business; **estar en el —** to be in the know; **ir a uno con el —** to go off and tell someone; **va de —** the story goes that..., it is said that...; **traer algo a —** to mention something, bring something up; (*pej*) to drag something in; **eso no viene a —** that's off the point, that's irrelevant; **vivir del —** to live by one's wits.
  (b) **sin —** countless.
  (c) (*pej*) story, tale, fib; pretext; **¡puro —!** a likely story!; **— chino** tall story; **¡déjese de —s!** stop beating about the bush!, get on with it!; **se me hace — (RPl)** I don't believe it.
  (d) **—s** (*fig*) trouble, difficulties; upsets; **han tenido no se qué —s entre ellos** they've had some upset among themselves; **no quiero —s con él** I don't want to have anything to do with him.
  (e) (*fam*) fuss; exaggeration; hot air, mere words; **tiene mucho —** he makes a lot of fuss (about nothing), he exaggerates everything so.
cuento² *nm* point, tip; ferrule.

cuera *nf* (a) (*SAm*) hide; leather strap. (b) (*Mex*) leather jacket. (c) (*CAm*) —s leggings. (d) (*Bol, Pan, PR*) flogging.

cuerazo *nm* (*SAm*) lash.

cuerda *nf* (a) rope; string, cord; (*for dog*) lead; (*Fish*) fishing line; (*Surveying*) measuring tape; — **arrojadiza** lasso; — **floja** tightrope; — **de plomada** plumbline; — **de salvamento**, — **salvavidas** lifeline; — **para tender la ropa** clothesline; **aflojar la** — (*fig*) to ease up; **apretar la** — (*fig*) to tighten up; **bailar en la** — **floja** to keep in with both parties; **estirar la** — (*fig*) to go too far, overdo it; **son de la misma** — they're all as bad as each other; **bajo** —, **por debajo de** — in an underhand way, by stealth, on the side.
(b) (*of watch*) spring; (*Mech*) clockwork mechanism; **dar** — **al reloj** to wind up one's watch; **dar** — **a uno** to encourage someone (to talk); **un coche de** — a clockwork car.
(c) (*Mus*) string, cord; — **de arco** bowstring; — **de tripa** catgut; **estar en su** — (*SAm*) to be in one's element; to be witty; **estar con** — (*SAm*) to be in a merry mood.
(d) (*Mus: fig*) vocal range.
(e) (*Anat*) cord; tendon; — **espinal** spinal cord; —s **vocales** vocal chords.
(f) (*Math*) chord.

cuerdamente *adv* (a) sanely. (b) wisely, sensibly, prudently.

cuerdo *adj* (a) *person* sane. (b) *act etc* wise, sensible, prudent.

cuereada *nf* (*SAm*) beating, tanning (*fam*).

cuerear [1a] *vt* (a) (*SAm*) to skin, flay. (b) (*SAm*) to whip, beat. (c) (*Cu, RPl*) to criticize mercilessly; to malign.

cuerito: de — **a** — *adv* (*SAm*) from end to end.

cueriza *nf* (*SAm*) beating, tanning (*fam*).

cuerna *nf* (a) (*Zool*) horns; antlers. (b) drinking horn. (c) (*Mus*) horn.

cuerno *nm* (a) (*in most cases*) horn; antler; — **de la abundancia** horn of plenty; **estar en los** —s (**del toro**) to be in danger; to be in a jam; **poner a uno en los** —s (**del toro**) to place someone at risk; to get someone into a fix; **poner los** —s **a uno** to cuckold someone; **ir al** — (*business*) to fall through; (*person*) to go to the dogs; ¡**vete al** —! go to hell!; **oler** (*or* **saber**) **a** — **quemado** to be suspicious; to leave a nasty taste; **esto me sabe a** — **quemado** this upsets me, this makes my blood boil.
(b) (*Cook*) roll, croissant.
(c) (*Mil*) wing.

cuero *nm* (a) (*Zool*) skin, hide; (*of rabbit etc*) pelt; (*Tech, as substance etc*) leather; — **adobado** tanned skin; — **cabelludo** scalp; — **charolado** patent leather; **andar en** —s to go about stark naked; **dejar a uno en** —s (*fig*) to rob someone of everything.
(b) wineskin; (*fam*) toper, old soak (*fam*); **estar hecho un** — to be as drunk as a lord.
(c) (*of tap*) washer.
(d) (*SAm*) whip; **arrimar** (*or* **dar** *etc*) **el** — **a uno** to give someone a beating.
(e) (*Col, Ec, PR, Ven*) whore; (*Col*) old maid; (*Cu*) old woman; (*Ec, Mex*) mistress.
(f) (*Cu, Guat*) impudence, effrontery.

cuerpear [1a] *vi* (*RPl*) to dodge.

cuerpo *nm* (a) (*Anat etc*) body; figure; build; corpse; (*Sport*) length; **combate** — **a** — hand-to-hand fight; **luchar** — **a** — to fight hand-to-hand; **de** — **entero** mirror, *picture* full-length; *rogue etc* thoroughgoing, out-and-out; true, real; **de medio** — half-length; **en** — **y alma** fully; **dar con el** — **en tierra** to fall down; **echar el** — **atrás** to lean suddenly backwards; **estar de** — **presente** to lie in state; **ganar por 4** —s to win by 4 lengths; **ganar por medio** — to win by half a length; **hacer del** — to relieve oneself; **hurtar el** — to dodge, move (one's body) out of the way; **ir a** —, **ir en** — to go without a coat; **vivir a** — **de rey** to live like a king.
(b) (*of state etc*) body; corporation; — **estatal** public body.
(c) — **de doctrina** body of teaching; — **de leyes** body of laws.
(d) (*persons*) body; brigade; force; (*Mil*) corps; — **de baile** corps de ballet; — **de bomberos** fire brigade, fire department (*US*); — **diplomático** diplomatic corps; — **de ejército** army corps; — **de intendencia** service corps; — **de sanidad** medical corps.
(e) (*Chem*) body, substance; — **compuesto** compound; — **simple** element; — **extraño** foreign body.
(f) (*Astron*) body.
(g) (*Anat: special sense*) trunk; (*fig*) main part; mass, bulk; **el** — **de un libro** the main part of a book,

the book proper; **un vino de mucho** — a full-bodied wine; **dar** — **a un líquido** to thicken a liquid; **tomar** — to swell, get bigger; (*of plan etc*) to take shape.
(h) (*of building*) wing; part; (*of furniture*) part, section.
(i) (*Sew*) bodice.
(j) (*Typ: of letter*) size; (*of paper etc*) thickness.
(k) (*Lit*) volume; **una biblioteca de 50 mil** —s a library of 50,000 books.

cuerudo *adj* (a) (*SAm*) *horse* slow, sluggish; lazy. (b) (*SAm*) *person* annoying. (c) (*Arg*) brave, tough. (d) (*CAm, Cu, PR*) impudent, shameless.

cuervo *nm* raven; — **marino** cormorant.

cuesco *nm* (a) (*Bot*) stone. (b) millstone (*of oil mill*). (c) (*fam*) punch, bash (*fam*). (d) (*tabu*) fart (*tabu*).

cuesta *nf* (a) slope; (*on road etc*) hill; — **abajo** downhill; **ir** — **abajo** (*fig*) to decline, go downhill; — **arriba** uphill; **se me hace** — **arriba** + *infin* I find it hard to + *infin*; — **de enero** period of financial stringency following Christmas spending; **hemos vencido la** — **ya** we're over the hump now; we're more than halfway.
(b) **a** —s on one's back; **echar algo a** —s to put something on one's back, (*fig*) to take on the burden of something; **lleva también eso a** —s he has the additional burden of that.

cuestación *nf* charity collection.

cuestión *nf* (a) matter, question, issue; (*Math etc*) problem; — **batallona** vexed question; — **clave** key question; — **madre** really big question; — **candente**, — **palpitante** burning question; **la cosa en** — the matter at issue, the thing in question; **en** — **de** about, concerning; **es** — **de** it is a matter of; **eso es otra** — that's another matter; **otra** — **sería si . . .** it would be different if . . .
(b) quarrel, dispute; trouble; complication; **hay** — **sobre si . . .** there's an argument about whether . . .; **la** — **es que . . .** the trouble is that . . .; **no quiero** —es **con los empleados** I don't want trouble with the staff; **no tengamos** — let's not have an argument about it, let's not have a fuss about it.

cuestionable *adj* questionable.

cuestionar [1a] **1** *vt* to question, dispute, argue about. **2** *vi* to argue.

cuestionario *nm* questionnaire; (*School, Univ etc*) question paper.

cuestor *nm* quaestor.

cuete **1** *adj* (*Mex*) drunk. **2** *nm* (a) (*Guat, Mex, Per*) pistol; = **cohete**. (b) (*Mex*) drunkenness.

cuetearse [1a] *vr* (*Col*) (a) to go off, explode. (b) (*sl*) to kick the bucket (*sl*).

cueva *nf* cave; (*for wine, in house etc*) cellar, vault; — **de ladrones** den of thieves.

cuévano *nm* pannier.

cui *nm* (*SAm*) guinea-pig.

cuica *nf* (*Ec*) earthworm.

cuico **1** *adj* (*Ec*) thin; (*Cu*) rachitic, feeble. **2** *nm* (a) (*Arg, Chi*) foreigner, outsider; (*Chi, Per, RPl*: *pej*) Bolivian; (*Cu*) Mexican. (b) (*Mex*) policeman.

cuidado *nm* (a) care, worry, concern; solicitude; **dar** — to cause concern; **estar con** — to be anxious, be worried; **estar de** — to be gravely ill, be in a bad way; **enfermar de** — to fall seriously ill; ¡**no haya** —!, ¡**pierda Vd** —! don't worry!; **eso me trae** (*or* **tiene**) **sin** — I'm not worried about that; I couldn't care less.
(b) care, carefulness; ¡—! careful!, look out!, watch out!; ¡ — **con el paquete!** careful with the parcel!; ¡ — **con el perro!** beware of the dog!; ¡ — **con los rateros!** watch out for pickpockets!; ¡ — **con perderlo!** mind you don't lose it!; **andarse con** — to go carefully, watch out; **poner mucho** — **en algo** to take great care over something; **tener** — to be careful, take care; **tener** — **con** to be careful of, watch out for, beware of; **hay que tener** — **con él** you have to handle him carefully; ¡**ten** —! careful!
(c) care; affair; business, concern; ¡**allá** —s! let others worry about that!, that's their funeral! (*fam*); "**al** — **del Sr A**" (*Post*) "care of Mr A"; **eso no es** — **mío**, **eso no corre de mi** — that's not my concern; **lo dejo a su** — I leave it to you; **está al** — **de la computadora** he's in charge of the computer; **los niños están al** — **de la abuela** the children are in their grandmother's charge.

cuidador *nm* (*Boxing*) second; (*Racing*) trainer.

cuidadora *nf* (*Mex*) nursemaid, nanny.

cuidadosamente *adv* (a) carefully. (b) anxiously; solicitously.

cuidadoso *adj* (a) careful (*con* about, with). (b) anxious, concerned (*de, por* about); solicitous (*de* for).

cuidar [1a] **1** vt **(a)** to take care of, look after; to pay attention to; **ella cuida a los niños** she looks after the children, she minds the children; **no cuidan la casa** they don't look after the house.
(b) (Med) to care for.
2 vi **(a)** — de to take care of, look after; — **de una obligación** to attend to a duty; — **de que . . .** to take care that . . ., see (to it) that . . .; **cuidó de que todo saliera bien** he ensured that everything should go smoothly; **cuide de que no pase nadie** see that nobody gets in; **que cuide que no le pase lo mismo** let him beware lest the same thing happens to him; **cuide de no caer** take care not to fail.
(b) cuida con esa gente be wary of those people.
3 cuidarse vr **(a)** to look after oneself (also Med); (pej) to look after number one; **ella ha dejado de —** she's let herself go.
(b) — de algo to worry about something; — de + infin to be careful to + infin; **no se cuida del qué dirán** she doesn't worry about what people will think.
(c) — muy bien de + infin to take good care not to + infin.

cuita nf **(a)** worry, trouble; grief, affliction; **contar sus —s a uno** to tell someone one's troubles. **(b)** (CAm) excrement; birdlime.
cuitado adj **(a)** worried, troubled; wretched. **(b)** timid.
cuja nf **(a)** bedstead. **(b)** (Hond, Mex) envelope.
cujinillos nmpl (Guat, Mex) saddlebags.
culantro nm coriander.
culata nf **(a)** (of gun) butt; (of cannon) breech; (of cylinder) head.
(b) (Zool) haunch, hindquarters.
(c) (SAm: of a house) side; rear, back.
(d) (RPl) hut, temporary shelter.
culatazo nm kick, recoil.
culebra nf **(a)** snake; — de anteojos cobra; — de cascabel rattlesnake; **hacer —** to zigzag, stagger along.
(b) (Col, Ec, Per) debt, bill.
(c) (Mex) waterspout.
culebrear [1a] vi **(a)** to wriggle (along); to zigzag; (river etc) to wind, meander. **(b)** (Ant) to stall, hedge.
culebreo nm wriggling; zigzag; winding, meandering.
culebrina nf **(a)** (Hist) culverin. **(b)** (Meteorol) forked lightning.
culeco adj **(a)** (SAm) hen broody.
(b) (SAm) person home-loving.
(c) (Per, PR, RPl) **estar —** to be very much in love.
(d) (Ant, CAm, Mex, Per) **estar — con algo** to be very pleased about something; to be very proud of something.
culero 1 adj lazy. **2** nm nappy, diaper (US).
culí nm coolie.
culibajo adj short, dumpy.
culigordo adj big-bottomed, broad in the beam (fam).
culillo nm **(a)** (Ant, Col, Pan) fear, fright. **(b)** (Cu) haste, impatience.
culinario adj culinary, cooking (attr).
culipandear [1a] vi and **culipandearse** vr (Cu, Mex, PR) to stall, hedge, make false promises.
culminación nf culmination.
culminante adj point etc highest, topmost, culminating; moment culminating; (fig) outstanding.
culminar [1a] vi to reach its highest point, reach a peak; to culminate (en in).
culo nm **(a)** (tabu in parts of SAm) bottom, backside, arse (tabu), ass (US sl); anus, arsehole (tabu); **dar a uno un puntapié en el —** to kick someone's backside, (fig) to boot someone out; **ser un — de mal asiento** to be restless, be fidgety; to chop and change, keep changing one's job (etc); **ir con el — a rastras** to be in a jam; to be broke (fam); **la ciudad va de —** the city is going downhill.
(b) (of jar etc) bottom.
culón adj = culigordo.
culpa nf **(a)** fault; blame; (Law etc) guilt; **por — de** through the fault of; through the negligence of; **no le alcanza —** no blame attaches to him; **echar la — a uno** to blame someone (de for); **tener la —** to be to blame (de for); **nadie tiene la —** nobody is to blame; **Vd tiene la —** it's your fault; **la — fue de los frenos** the brakes were to blame; **es — suya** it's his fault.
(b) sin, offence; **pagar las —s ajenas** to pay for someone else's sins.
culpabilidad nf guilt.
culpable 1 adj **(a) la persona —** the person to blame, the person at fault; (Law) the guilty person, the

culprit; **confesarse —** to plead guilty; **declarar — a uno** to find someone guilty.
(b) act to be condemned, blameworthy; **es — no hacerlo** it is criminal not to do it; **con descuido —** with culpable negligence.
2 nmf culprit; (Law etc) offender, guilty party.
culpado 1 adj guilty. **2** nm, **culpada** nf culprit; (Law) the accused.
culpar [1a] vt to blame, accuse; to condemn; — **a uno de algo** to blame someone for something; — **a uno de descuidado** to blame someone for being careless, accuse someone of carelessness.
cultamente adv in a cultured way, in a refined tone (etc); elegantly.
culteranismo nm (Lit) latinized, precious and highly metaphorical style (esp 17th century).
culterano (Lit) **1** adj latinized, precious and highly metaphorical. **2** nm writer in the style of culteranismo.
cultismo nm (Ling) learned word.
cultivable adj cultivable.
cultivador nm farmer, grower; (of specific crop) cultivator, grower; — **de vino** winegrower; — **de café** coffee grower, coffee planter.
cultivadora nf (Tech) cultivator.
cultivar [1a] vt **(a)** land to cultivate, work, till; crop etc to grow.
(b) (fig) study, art etc to cultivate; aptitude etc to develop; memory to develop, improve; friendship to cultivate.
cultivo nm **(a)** (act) cultivation, growing.
(b) crop; **el — principal de la región** the chief crop of the area; **rotación de —s** rotation of crops.
(c) (Bio) culture.
culto 1 adj **(a)** cultivated, cultured, refined; educated; elegant.
(b) (Ling) learned; **palabra culta** learned word.
2 nm worship; cult (a of); (Eccl) divine service, worship; — **a la personalidad** personality cult; **rendir — a** to worship; (fig) to pay homage to, pay tribute to.
cultura nf culture; refinement; education; elegance; — **física** physical culture; **la — popular** popular culture; **persona de —** cultured person; educated person.
cultural adj cultural.
cuma nf **(a)** (CAm) long knife, curved machete. **(b)** (Per, RPl) crone, gossip.
cumbancha nf (Ant) spree (fam), drinking bout.
cúmbila nm (Cu) pal (fam), buddy (esp US).
cumbo nm **(a)** (CAm) top hat, bowler hat. **(b)** (Guat, Hond) narrow-mouthed cup.
cumbre nf summit, top; (fig) top, height, pinnacle; **conferencia (en la) —** summit conference; **está en la — de su empresa** he is at the top of his company; **está en la — de su poderío** he is at the height of his power.
cume nm, **cumiche** nm (CAm) baby of the family.
cumpa nm (SAm) pal (fam), buddy (esp US).
cumpleañero nm, **cumpleañera** nf (SAm) person celebrating a birthday, person whose birthday it is.
cumpleaños nm, pl **cumpleaños** birthday; — **del matrimonio** (SAm) wedding anniversary.
cumplido 1 adj **(a)** complete, perfect; full; **un — caballero** a perfect gentleman, a real gentleman.
(b) (Sew etc) full, extra large.
(c) meal etc large, plentiful.
(d) courteous, correct; formal (in manner); (pej) stiff, ceremonious.
(e) tiene 60 años —s he is all of 60, he is at least 60.
2 nm compliment; courtesy; **visita de —** formal visit, courtesy call; **por —** as a compliment; out of politeness, as a matter of courtesy; **¡sin —s!** no ceremony, please!; make yourself at home!; **andarse con —s, estar de —, usar —s** to stand on ceremony, be formal; **cambiar los —s de etiqueta** to exchange formal courtesies; **he venido por —** I came out of a sense of duty.
cumplidor adj reliable, trustworthy.
cumplimentar [1a] vt **(a)** to pay one's respects to, pay a courtesy call on; to congratulate (por on). **(b)** order etc to carry out; duty to perform, do.
cumplimentero adj formal, ceremonious; effusive.
cumplimiento nm **(a)** (act) fulfilment; completion; performance; **falta de —** non-fulfilment, non-compliance; **dar — a** to fulfil. **(b)** = cumplido 2.
cumplir [3a] **1** vt **(a)** promise, wish, contract, threat etc to carry out, fulfil; stipulation to comply with; (Cards) contract to make; law etc to observe, obey; ambition to fulfil, realize.
(b) sentence to serve.

(c) *years etc* to reach, attain, complete; **hoy cumple 8 años** she's 8 today; **cuando cumpla los 21 años** when you're 21, when you reach the age of 21; **¿cuándo cumple Vd años?** when is your birthday?; **¡que los cumplas muy felices!** many happy returns (of the day)!

2 *vi* (a) (*of period*) to end, expire; (*of payment*) to fall due.

(b) (*Mil*) to finish one's military service.

(c) to do one's duty, carry out one's task, do what is required of one; **sólo por** — as a matter of form, as a mere formality.

(d) — **con** = 1(a); — **con uno** to do one's duty by someone; — **con la iglesia** to fulfil one's religious obligations; — **por uno** to act on someone's behalf.

(e) **le cumple hacerlo** it behoves him to do it, it is up to him to do it; **no le cumple** + *infin* it is not his place to + *infin*.

3 cumplirse *vr* (a) (*plan etc*) to be fulfilled, come true.

(b) (*period*) to expire, end, be up.

cumucho *nm* (*Chi*) (a) gathering, mob, crowd. (b) hut, hovel.

cumulativo *adj* cumulative.

cúmulo *nm* (a) pile, heap; accumulation; (*fig*) pile, lot. (b) (*Meteorol*) cumulus.

cumulonimbo *nm* cumulonimbus.

cuna *nf* (a) cradle; cot; — **portátil** carrycot.

(b) home, foundling hospital.

(c) (*fig*) family, stock, birth; **de** — **humilde** of humble origin; **criarse en buena** — to be born with a silver spoon in one's mouth.

(d) (*fig*) birthplace; — **del famoso poeta** the birthplace of the famous poet.

(e) —**s** (*fig*) cat's-cradle.

cundir [3a] *vi* (a) to spread; (*fig*) to spread, expand, increase; (*fig and pej*) to be rampant, be rife.

(b) (*of rice etc*) to swell, expand; to produce a good (*etc*) quantity, give good (*etc*) results; **hoy no me ha cundido el trabajo** work did not go well for me today.

cunear [1a] **1** *vt* to rock, cradle. **2 cunearse** *vr* (a) to rock, sway. (b) (*in walking*) to walk with a swing, walk with a roll.

cuneco *nm* (*Ven*) baby of the family.

cuneiforme *adj* cuneiform.

cuneta *nf* (a) ditch, gutter. (b) (*Aut*) verge, hard shoulder.

cuña *nf* (a) wedge; (*of wheel*) chock.

(b) **meter** — to sow discord.

(c) (*SAm*) big shot (*fam*), influential person.

(d) (*SAm*) lever (to obtain something), influence; **tener** —**s** (*Chi, RPl*) to have pull, have influence.

(e) (*CAm, Cu, SD*) two-seater car.

(f) (*Col: Radio*) plug (*sl*), spot, advert.

cuñada *nf* sister-in-law.

cuñado *nm* brother-in-law.

cuñete *nm* keg.

cuño *nm* (a) (*Tech*) stamp, die-stamp; **de nuevo** — (*fig*) newly-coined. (b) (*fig*) stamp, mark.

cuota *nf* (a) quota; share. (b) fee, dues; — **de enseñanza** school fees; — **de entrada** admission fee; — **del gremio** union dues; — **de socio** membership fee.

cuotidiano *adj* = cotidiano.

cupe *etc see* **caber.**

cupé *nm* (*Aut*) coupé.

Cupido *m* Cupid.

cuplé *nm* pop song, light lyric.

cupo *nm* (a) quota; share; — **de azúcar** sugar quota. (b) (*Mex*) space, room, capacity; contents.

cupón *nm* coupon; (*Comm*) trading stamp; — **de dividendos** dividend voucher; — **de respuestas internacional** international reply coupon.

cúpula *nf* (a) (*Archit*) dome, cupola. (b) (*Naut*) turret. (c) (*Bot*) husk, shell.

cuquería *nf* craftiness.

cura[1] *nm* (*Eccl*) priest; father; — **párroco** parish priest; **sí, señor** — yes, father.

cura[2] *nf* (a) (*Med*) cure, healing; treatment; remedy; **primera** — first aid; — **de reposo** rest cure; — **de urgencia** emergency treatment, first aid; **tiene** — it can be cured, it is curable; **no tiene** — (*fam*) there's no remedy, it's quite hopeless.

(b) (*Eccl*) — **de almas** cure of souls.

curable *adj* curable.

curaca *nf* (*Bol, Per*) priest's housekeeper. (b) (*Bol, Ec, Per*) Indian chief, Indian native authority.

curación *nf* cure, healing; treatment; **primera** — first aid.

curadillo *nm* (a) (*Cook*) dried cod. (b) (*Tech*) bleached linen.

curado *adj* (a) (*Tech*) cured; hardened; tanned, prepared. (b) (*Chi, Per, Urug*) drunk.

curandero *nm* quack; bonesetter.

curar [1a] **1** *vt* (a) (*Med*) *person, illness* to cure (*de* of); *wound* to treat, dress; (*with a drug etc*) to treat (*con* with).

(b) (*fig*) *wrong* to remedy, put right.

(c) *meat, fish* to cure, salt; *skin* to tan; *cloth* to bleach; *wood* to season.

2 *vi* (*Med*) to get well (*de* after), recover (*de* from).

3 curarse *vr* (a) (*Med*) to recover, get better; (*wound etc*) to heal up; to be on a cure, go for a cure.

(b) — **de** to take notice of, heed; to look after.

(c) (*Bol, Chi, Per, RPl*) to get drunk; (*Mex*) to sober up.

curativo *adj* curative.

curato *nm* curacy, parish.

curazao *nm* curaçao.

curca *nf* (*Chi, Per*) hump.

curco *adj* (*Chi, Ec, Per*) hunchbacked.

curcuncho 1 *adj* (a) (*SAm*) hunchbacked. (b) (*Bol, Ec, Per*) depressed; annoyed. **2** *nm* (*SAm*) hunchback.

curda (*fam*): **estar** —, **estar con la** — to be sozzled (*fam*).

cureña *nf* gun carriage; **a** — **rasa** out in the open.

curia *nf* (a) (*Eccl: also* — **romana**) Curia, papal Curia. (b) (*Law*) the Bar.

curiana *nf* cockroach.

curiche *nm* (*Chi*) Negro.

curiosamente *adv* (a) curiously; oddly. (b) neatly, cleanly.

curiosear [1a] **1** *vt* to glance at, look over; to look round; to nose out.

2 *vi* to look round, wander round; to poke about, nose about; (*pej*) to snoop, pry; — **por las tiendas** to wander round the shops; — **por los escaparates** to go window-shopping.

curiosidad *nf* (a) (*in general*) curiosity; (*pej*) inquisitiveness; **despertar la** — **de uno** to arouse someone's curiosity; **la** — **de noticias me llevó allí** the quest for news took me there; **tenemos** — **de saber si . . .** we are curious to know if . . .; **estar muerto de** — to be dying of curiosity.

(b) (*object*) curiosity; curio; —**es** sights, attractions; **visitar las** —**es** to see the sights.

(c) neatness, cleanliness.

(d) care(fulness), conscientiousness.

curioso 1 *adj* (a) (*of person*) curious; eager; (*pej*) inquisitive; — **de** eager for; **estar** — **por** + *infin* to be curious to + *infin*, be eager to + *infin*.

(b) *object, act etc* curious, odd; quaint; **¡qué** —**!** how curious!, how odd!

(c) neat, clean, tidy.

(d) careful, conscientious.

(e) (*fam*) queer (*fam*).

2 *nm*, **curiosa** *nf* (a) bystander, spectator, onlooker; (*pej*) busybody; **los** —**s de la literatura** those interested in literature.

(b) (*fam*) queer (*fam*).

curriculum *m* **vitae** curriculum vitae, personal and professional record.

currinche *nm* (a) (*Typ*) apprentice journalist, cub reporter. (b) (*fam*) little man, nonentity.

curro *adj* (*fam*) (a) smart; showy, flashy. (b) cocky (*fam*), brashly confident.

currutaco 1 *adj* (a) loud, showy, flashy.

(b) (*SAm*) short, squat.

2 *nm* (a) toff (*fam*), masher (*fam*), dude (*US*).

(b) insignificant little man.

(c) —**s** (*CAm*) diarrhoea.

cursante *nmf* (*SAm*) student.

cursar [1a] **1** *vt* (a) *message* to send, dispatch; *order* to send out; *application* to pass on, dispatch, deal with.

(b) *subject* to study; *course* to take, attend.

(c) *place* to frequent.

2 *vi*: **el mes que cursa** the present month.

cursi 1 *adj* in bad taste, vulgar; pretentious; loud, showy, flashy; posh, genteel, pseudo-refined; affected. **2** *nmf* = cursilón.

cursilería *nf* bad taste, vulgarity; pretentiousness; loudness, showiness, flashiness; poshness (*fam*), gentility, pseudo-refinement; affectation.

cursilón *nm*, **cursilona** *nf* common but pretentious person; flashy type; posh sort (*fam*), genteel individual; affected person.

cursillista *nmf* member (of a course).

cursillo *nm* short course; short series (of lectures).

cursiva *nf* (*Typ*) italics.

cursivo *adj* cursive; (*Typ*) italic.

curso nm (a) (of river etc) course; direction; flow; — de agua watercourse.

(b) (Astron) course.

(c) (fig) course; el — de la enfermedad the course of the disease, the progress of the disease; dejar que las cosas sigan su — to let matters take their course; en el — de la vida in the course of a lifetime; en el — de la semana in the course of the week; el proceso está en — the process is going on, the process is under way; el año en — the current year, the present year.

(d) (Law) moneda de — legal legal tender.

(e) dar — a una solicitud to deal with an application; dar — a su indignación to express one's indignation; dar — al llanto to let one's tears flow.

(f) (School, Univ: of students) year; los del segundo — those in the second year, the second years.

(g) (School, Univ: subject) course; subject; he perdido 2 —s I failed 2 subjects, I have to repeat 2 subjects; — acelerado crash course; — por correspondencia correspondence course; — de secretaria secretarial course.

(h) (Fin) price; primer — de la bolsa opening price on the stock exchange.

cursor nm (Tech) slide.

curtido 1 adj (a) leather tanned; skin hardened, leathery; face tanned, weather-beaten (also — a la intemperie).

(b) (fig) estar — en to be expert at, be skilled in; hardships to be inured to.

2 nm (a) tanning.

(b) tanned hide.

curtidor nm tanner.

curtiduría nf, **curtiembre** nf (SAm) tannery.

curtir [3a] **1** vt (a) hide to tan.

(b) face etc to tan, bronze.

(c) to harden, inure.

2 curtirse vr (a) to become tanned, become bronzed; to get weather-beaten.

(b) to become inured.

(c) (CAm, Col, Mex, SD) to get oneself dirty, dirty one's clothes.

curva nf curve; (Aut etc) curve, bend; — en herradura hairpin bend; — de nivel contour line.

curvatura nf curvature.

curvilíneo adj curved, curvilinear.

curvo adj (a) curved; crooked, bent. (b) (Col) bow-legged. (c) (PR) left-handed.

cusca nf (a) hacer la — a uno to play a dirty trick on someone; to harm someone, damage someone's interests. (b) (CAm) flirt. (c) (Mex) whore, slut.

cuscurro nm crouton.

cuscha nf (CAm) liquor, rum.

cusma nf (Col, Ec, Per) sleeveless shirt, tunic.

cúspide nm (a) (Anat) cusp. (b) (Geog) summit, peak; tip, apex. (c) (Math) apex.

custodia nf (a) care, safekeeping, custody (also Law); — preventiva protective custody; bajo la — de in the care (or custody) of. (b) (Eccl) monstrance.

custodiar [1b] vt to keep, take care of, look after; to guard, watch over.

custodio nm guardian, keeper, custodian; (of house etc) caretaker; see ángel.

cususa nf (CAm) liquor, rum.

cutacha nf = cuma.

cutama nf (a) (Arg) blanket. (b) (Chi) bag, sack.

cutáneo adj cutaneous, skin (attr).

cutaras nfpl (CR, Cu, Mex), **cutarras** nfpl (CAm, Pan) sandals, rough shoes.

cúter nm (Naut) cutter.

cutí nm ticking.

cutícula nf cuticle.

cutis nm skin, complexion.

cuto adj (a) (Bol, CAm) person maimed, crippled; toothless; object damaged, spoiled. (b) (Ec) short.

cuy nm (SAm) guinea-pig.

cuya nf (Chi, Ven) gourd, drinking vessel.

cuyano nm (Chi: pej) Argentinian.

cuyo rel adj (a) whose; of whom, of which; la señora en cuya casa nos hospedábamos the lady in whose house we were staying; el asunto —s detalles conoces the matter of which you know the details, the matter whose details you know about.

(b) en — caso in which case; por cuya razón for which reason, and for this reason.

cuz: ¡ — —! interj (to dog) here boy!

CH

chabacanear [1a] *vi* (*SAm*) to say (*or* do) coarse things.

chabacanería *nf* (**a**) (*quality*) vulgarity, bad taste; commonness; shoddiness.
   (**b**) (*una* —) coarse thing (to say), vulgar remark (*etc*); platitude; shoddy piece of work.

chabacano[1] *adj* joke, play *etc* vulgar, coarse, in bad taste; *article* cheap, common; *workmanship etc* shoddy, crude.

chabacano[2] *nm* (*Mex*) apricot.

chabola *nf* shack.

chacal *nm* jackal.

chacalín *nm*, **chacalina** *nf* (*CAm*) kid (*fam*), child.

chacanear [1a] *vt* (**a**) (*Chi*) to spur violently. (**b**) (*Chi*) to pester, annoy. (**c**) (*Bol*, *RPl*) to use daily.

chacaneo *nm* (*Bol*, *RPl*): **para el** — for daily use, ordinary.

chácara[1] *nf* (**a**) (*CAm*, *Col*, *Chi*) sore, ulcer. (**b**) (*Col*, *Pan*, *Ven*) large leather bag; (*Col*) case.

chácara[2] *nf* (*SAm*) = **chacra**.

chacarería *nf* (**a**) group of *chacras*. (**b**) (*Chi*, *Ec*, *Per*) horticulture, market gardening, truck farming (*US*); farm work.

chacarero *nm* (*SAm*) farmer, grower; market gardener, truck farmer (*US*); farm overseer; farm labourer.

chacó *nm* shako.

chacolotear [1a] *vi* to clatter.

chacoloteo *nm* clatter(ing).

chacón *nm* salamander.

chacota *nf* noisy merriment, fun (and games), high jinks; **estar de** — to be in a joking mood; **echar algo a** —, **hacer** — **de algo** to make fun of something, take something as a joke.

chacotear [1a] **1** *vi* to have fun, make merry. **2 chacotearse** *vr*: — **de algo** to make fun of something, take something as a joke.

chacotería *nf* (*RPl*) = **chacota**.

chacotero *adj*, **chacotón** *adj* (*RPl*) fond of a laugh, merry.

chacra *nf* (*SAm*) (**a**) small farm, smallholding, market garden, truck farm (*US*); country estate; cultivated land. (**b**) farmhouse. (**c**) farm produce.

chacuaco **1** *adj* (*SD*, *Urug*) coarse, rough; (*PR*) clumsy. **2** *nm* (*CAm*) roughly-made cigar; (*CAm*, *Mex*) cigar stub.

chacha *nf* maid, nursemaid.

chachacaste *nm* (*CAm*) liquor, brandy.

chachalaca *nf* (*CAm*, *Mex*) chatterbox.

chachar [1a] *vt* (*Bol*, *Ec*, *Per*) coca leaves to chew.

cháchara *nf* (**a**) chatter, idle talk, small talk; — **amorosa** sweet nothings. (**b**) (*Ec*) joke. (**c**) —**s** (*Chi*, *Mex*) things, bits and pieces; junk.

chacharachas *nfpl* (*Chi*) useless ornaments; trinkets.

chacharear [1a] **1** *vt* (*Mex*) to deal in, sell. **2** *vi* to chatter, jaw (*fam*).

chacharería *nf* (*Chi*, *Mex*) trinkets.

chacharero **1** *adj* chattering, garrulous. **2** *nm*, **chacharera** *nf* chatterbox.

chacho *nm* (**a**) boy, lad. (**b**) (*CAm*) twin. (**c**) (*Mex*) servant.

chafalonía *nf* (*Bol*, *Per*) worn-out gold jewellery.

chafalote **1** *adj* (*RPl*) common, vulgar. **2** *nm* = **chafarote**.

chafallar [1a] *vt* to botch, mend clumsily, make a mess of.

chafallo *nm* botched job.

chafar [1a] *vt* (**a**) to flatten; to crumple; to ruffle, muss up; to crease; *potatoes* (*Cook*) to mash.
   (**b**) — **a uno**, **dejar chafado a uno** to crush someone; to cut someone short, shut someone up; to take someone down a peg.
   (**c**) *deal etc* to mess up, make a hash of, spoil; **le**

chafaron el negocio they messed up the deal for him.
   (**d**) (*Chi*) *employee* to fire (*fam*).
   (**c**) (*Arg*) to hoax, deceive.

chafarote *nm* (*Hist*) cutlass; (*fam*) sword; (*SAm*) broadsword, big flat knife.

chafarrinada *nf* spot, stain.

chafarrinar [1a] *vt* to blot, stain.

chafarrinón *nm* spot, stain; **echar un** — **a** (*fig*) to smear, slander.

chafir(r)o *nm* (*CAm*, *Mex*: *angl*) knife.

chaflán *nm* bevel, chamfer.

chaflanar [1a] *vt* to bevel, chamfer.

chagra[1] **1** *nf* (*Col*, *Ec*) = **chacra**. **2** *nm* (*Ec*) peasant farmer.

chagra[2] *nf* (*Cu*) = **chaira**.

chagrén *nm* shagreen.

chagua *nf* (*Col*) gang; system of gang labour.

chaguar [1i] *vt* (*Arg*) *cow* to milk; *washing* to squeeze (dry).

cháguar *nm* (*Arg*, *Bol*, *Per*) agave fibre, hemp; rope of agave fibre.

cháguara *nf* (*Arg*, *Urug*) = **cháguar**.

chagüe *nm* (*CAm*) swamp, bog.

chagüite *nm* (*CAm*, *Mex*) swamp, flooded place; damp field; banana plantation.

chai(ne) *nm* (*Col*, *Mex*, *Pan*: *angl*) shoeshine.

chaira *nf* steel (*for sharpening*); shoemaker's knife; (*fam*) knife, razor, dagger.

chairar [1a] *vt* (*RPl*) to sharpen.

chal *nm* shawl.

chala *nf* (**a**) (*Bol*, *Chi*, *Per*, *RPl*) tender leaf of maize. (**b**) (*Arg*, *Bol*) money, dough (*sl*); **pelar la** — **a uno** to fleece someone.

chalado *adj* (*fam*) dotty (*fam*); cranky; ¡**estás** —! are you mad?; **estar** — **por una** to be crazy about someone.

chalán *nm* (**a**) dealer, huckster, (*esp*) horse dealer; (*pej*) shady businessman, shark (*fam*). (**b**) (*SAm*) horse breaker.

chalana *nf* barge, lighter, wherry.

chalanear [1a] **1** *vt* (**a**) *person* to haggle successfully with, beat down; *deal* to handle cleverly, bring off. (**b**) (*SAm*) *horse* to break in, tame. (**c**) (*Arg*) to pester. (**d**) (*CAm*) to make fun of. **2** *vi* to bargain shrewdly.

chalar [1a] (*fam*) **1** *vt* to drive crazy, drive round the bend (*sl*). **2 chalarse** *vr* to go crazy, go off one's rocker (*sl*); — **por** to be crazy about.

chalé *nm* (*Acad*) see **chalet**.

chaleco *nm* waistcoat, vest (*US*); — **salvavidas** life jacket.

chalecón *adj* (*Mex*) tricky, deceitful.

chalequear [1a] *vt* (*Mex*) to steal; (*Guat*) to get by a trick.

chalet [tʃaˈle] *nm*, *pl* **chalets** [tʃaˈles] (*angl*, *gall*) (*rural*) villa, cottage; (*seaside*) bungalow; (*mountain*) chalet; (*town*) semi-detached house, detached house (with a garden); (*Golf etc*) clubhouse.

chalina *nf* cravat(e), floppy bow tie; (*SAm*) small shawl.

chalón *nm* (*SAm*) shawl, wrap.

chalona *nf* (*SAm*) dried meat, dried mutton.

chalote *nm* shallot.

chalupa[1] *nf* launch, boat; lifeboat; (*Ec*, *Mex*, *Per*, *PR*) narrow canoe.

chalupa[2] *nf* (*Mex*) small maize cake (with chopped meat *etc*).

chalupa[3] (*sl*) **1** *adj* crazy; **volver** — **a uno** to drive someone crazy. **2** *nm* madman, crackpot.

chamaca *nf* (*Mex etc*) girl; girlfriend, sweetheart.

chamaco *nm* (*Mex etc*) boy, child; lad, young man.

chamagoso *adj* (*Mex*) filthy; vile, loathsome.

chamarasca *nf* kindling, brushwood; brush fire.

chamaril(l)ero *nm* secondhand dealer, junk dealer.
chamarra *nf* (a) sheepskin jacket; (*CAm, Ven*) blanket, cloak. (b) (*CAm: fig*) fraud, trick.
chamarrear [1a] *vt* (*CAm*) to trick, swindle.
chamarrero *nm* (*Ven*) quack doctor.
chamarro *nm* (*CAm, Chi, Mex*) coarse woollen blanket.
chamba[1] *nf* (a) (*Arg, Ec*) turf, sod.
  (b) (*Col, Ec*) pond, pool; (*Col, Ven*) ditch.
  (c) (*Guat, Mex*) work; business; occupation; (*Mex*) unproductive work; (*CAm, Mex*) cinch (*sl*); plum, sinecure, soft job.
chamba[2] *nf* fluke, lucky break; **por — by a fluke.**
chambear [1a] (*Mex*) **1** *vt* to exchange, swap, barter. **2** *vi* to work (unproductively).
chambelán *nm* chamberlain.
chambergo *nm* broad-brimmed soft hat.
chambón 1 *adj* (a) awkward, clumsy. (b) lucky. (c) slovenly. **2** *nm* clumsy but lucky player, fluky player.
chambonada *nf* (a) awkwardness, clumsiness. (b) fluke, stroke of luck, lucky shot. (c) blunder.
chambonear [1a] *vi* (*esp SAm*) to have a stroke of luck, win (*etc*) by a fluke.
chamborote *adj* (*Ec, Guat*) long-nosed.
chambra[1] *nf* housecoat; blouse; loose jacket.
chambra[2] *nf* (*Ven*) din, hubbub.
chambra[3] *nf* (*SD*) machete, broad knife.
chambrana *nf* (*Col, Ven*) row, uproar; brawl.
chamburgo *nm* (*Col*) pool, stagnant water.
chamelicos *nmpl* (*Chi, Per*) lumber, junk, old clothes; (*Col*) adornments.
chamizo *nm* (a) half-burned tree (*or log etc*). (b) thatched hut; shack, slum; (*fam*) den, joint (*sl*).
chamorro *adj* head shorn, close-cropped.
champa[1] *nf* (*SAm*) (a) sod, turf; ball of earth (*left round roots*). (b) mass of dishevelled hair, long unkempt hair. (c) (*fig*) tangled mass.
champa[2] *nf* (*CAm, Mex*) roughly-built hut.
champán *nm* champagne.
Champaña *f* Champagne.
champaña *nf* champagne.
champañazo *nm* (*Chi etc*) champagne party.
champiñón *nm* mushroom.
champú *nm* shampoo.
champudo *adj* (*SAm*) *hair* dishevelled, messy; *person* long-haired.
champurrado *nm* mixture of liquors, cocktail; (*Cu, Mex*) mixed drink (*of various ingredients*); (*fig*) mixture, mess.
champurrar [1a] *vt drinks* to mix, make a cocktail of.
champurreado *nm* (a) (*Chi, RPl*) hastily-prepared dish, hash; (*fig*) hash, botch. (b) = **champurrado**.
champurrear [1a] *vt* (*Chi, PR, RPl*) = **champurrar**; = **chapurr(e)ar**.
chamuchina *nf* (a) (*SAm*) rabble, mob; crowd of small children, mob of kids (*fam*). (b) (*Ec, Ven*) row, shindy.
chamullar [1a] *vti* (*sl*) to speak, talk; **yo también chamullo el caló** I can talk slang too; **chamullaban en árabe** they were jabbering away in Arabic.
chamuscar [1g] **1** *vt* (a) to scorch, sear, singe. (b) (*Mex*) to sell cheap. **2 chamuscarse** *vr* (a) to get scorched, singe. (b) (*Col*) to get cross, take offence.
chamusquina *nf* (a) singeing, scorching.
  (b) row, quarrel, shindy; **esto huele a — I** can see there's trouble brewing, there's something nasty coming.
  (c) (*Col, CR*) mob of kids.
chanada *nf* (*fam*) trick, swindle.
chanca *nf* (a) (*Arg, Chi, Ec, Per*) grinding, crushing. (b) (*Chi, Per*) beating.
chancaca *nf* (a) (*CAm*) maize cake, wheat cake. (b) (*Ec*) sore, ulcer. (c) (*SAm*) brown sugar, honey mass (*used in the preparation of chicha*).
chancadora *nf* (*SAm*) grinder, crusher.
chancar [1g] *vt* (a) (*SAm*) to grind, crush, triturate; (*fig*) to beat; to beat up; to ill-treat. (b) (*Chi, Ec*) to botch, bungle.
chance *nm* (*sometimes f*) (*SAm: angl*) chance; (*gall*) good luck.
chancear [1a] *vi and* **chancearse** *vr* to joke, make jokes (*de about*); to fool about, play around (*con with*); **—se de uno** to make fun of someone.
chancero *adj* joking, merry, facetious; fond of a joke.
chancillería *nf* chancery.
chancla *nf* old shoe, broken shoe; = **chancleta**.
chancleta 1 *nf* (a) slipper. (b) (*SAm*) baby girl. (c) (*Ven: Aut*) accelerator. **2** *nmf* (*fam*) good-for-nothing.
chancletero *adj* (*Ant, Col, Mex*), **chancletudo** *adj* (*Chi, Ec, Per, Ven*) common, low-class.
chanclo *nm* clog; rubber overshoe, galosh.
chancro *nm* chancre.

chancha *nf* (a) (*SAm*) sow. (b) (*Chi*) small wooden cart. (c) (*Col: hum*) mouth; (*Bol, Col, Chi*) **hacer la — to play truant.**
chanchería *nf* (*SAm*) pork-butcher's shop.
chanchero *nm* (*SAm*) pork butcher.
chanchi (*sl*) **1** *adj* marvellous, smashing (*sl*), jolly good (*fam*); **¡estás —!** I think you're marvellous! **2** *adv* marvellously, jolly well (*fam*); **me fue — I** had a smashing time (*sl*), it went like a bomb (*fam*).
chancho 1 *adj* (*SAm*) dirty, filthy.
  2 *nm* (a) (*SAm*) pig, hog; **— salvaje** wild boar.
  (b) (*SAm: Chess etc*) blocked piece.
  (c) (*Chi*) = **chancadora**.
  (d) (*SAm: fig*) **son como —s** they're very thick; **hacerse el — rengo** to pretend not to notice; **quedar como — to** come off badly.
chanchullero (*fam*) **1** *adj* crooked, bent (*fam*). **2** *nm* crook, twister (*fam*).
chanchullo (*fam*) fiddle (*fam*), wangle (*fam*); crooked deal; piece of graft, dirty business; **andar en —s** to be on the fiddle, be engaged in something shady.
chanfaina *nf* (*Bol, Col, Hond, Per*) entanglement; complication; mess.
chanfle[1] *nm* (*Arg, Urug*) policeman, bobby (*sl*), cop (*sl*).
chanfle[2] *nm* (*Mex*) = **chaflán**.
chanflón *adj* misshapen; (*fig*) crude, coarse.
changa[1] *nf* (a) (*Bol, RPl*) (portering) job; odd job, occasional job. (b) (*Bol, RPl*) tip, payment (to a porter).
changa[2] *nf* (*Ant*) joke.
changador *nm* (*Bol, RPl*) porter; odd-job man.
changango *nm* (*RPl*) (a) small guitar. (b) low-class party. (c) merriment.
changarro[1] *nm* (*fam*) old car, jalopy.
changarro[2] *nm* (*Mex*) small shop.
chango 1 *adj* (a) (*Mex*) quick, sharp; alert; **¡ponte —!** wake up!, get wise! (*fam*); watch out!
  (b) (*Ant, Mex*) mischievous, playful.
  (c) (*Mex, PR*) silly, brainless; stupidly affected.
  (d) (*Chi*) annoying.
  (e) (*Mex etc*) **la gente está changa** there are lots of people.
  2 *nm*, **changa** *nf* (a) (*Mex*) small monkey.
  (b) (*Arg, Mex, Chi*) child; young servant.
changear [1a] *vi* (*Ant, Col, Mex*) = **chancear**.
changüí *nm* (*fam*) (a) joke. (b) trick, swindle; **dar — a** to trick, swindle.
chantaje *nm* blackmail(ing).
chantajista *nmf* blackmailer.
chantar [1a] *vt* (a) *dress etc* to put on.
  (b) *object* to thrust, stick; to put.
  (c) **— algo a uno** to tell someone something to his face.
  (d) (*Per, RPl*) *object* to throw, chuck.
  (e) (*Chi, Per, RPl*) *person* to put, throw; **— a uno en la calle** to throw someone out; **— a uno en la cárcel** to put someone in jail.
  (f) (*Chi, Per, RPl*) *blow* to give.
  (g) (*Urug*) to leave in the lurch; to deceive, trick.
chantre *nm* (*Eccl*) precentor.
chanza *nf* joke; piece of tomfoolery, lark; **—s** jokes, banter; tomfoolery; **de —, en —** in fun, as a joke; **estar de — to** be joking.
chañaca *nf* (*Chi*) (a) itch, rash. (b) (*fig*) bad reputation.
chao *nm* chow.
chapa *nf* (a) (*metal*) plate, sheet; **— acanalada, — ondulada** (sheet of) corrugated iron.
  (b) (*wood*) board, panel, sheet; veneer; **madera de 3 —s** 3-ply wood.
  (c) small metal plate, disc, tally; counter; check; **— de matrícula, — de patente** (*SAm*) licence plate.
  (d) (*SAm*) lock.
  (e) rouge; flush (on the cheeks).
  (f) good sense, prudence; **hombre de — sensible** man.
chapado *adj* (a) covered (*or lined*) with sheet metal (*or veneer*); **— de roble** with an oak veneer, with an oak finish; **— de oro** gold-plated.
  (b) (*fig*) **— a la antigua** old-fashioned, of the old school.
chapalear [1a] *vi* (a) (*person*) to splash (about); (*water*) to lap. (b) (*hooves etc*) to clatter.
chapaleo *nm* (a) splash(ing); lap(ping). (b) clatter(ing).
chapar[1] [1a] *vt* (a) to plate, cover (*or line*) with sheet metal (*or veneer*); *wall* to tile. (b) *remark etc* to throw out, come out with.

chapar² [1a] vt (a) (Col, Ec, Per) to spy on. (b) (Per) to catch; to catch up with, overtake; object to seize, grasp.

chaparra nf kermes oak.

chaparrada nf=chaparrón.

chaparral nm thicket (of kermes oaks).

chaparrear [1a] vi to pour in torrents.

chaparreras nfpl (Mex) leather overalls.

chaparro 1 adj squat, short and chubby. 2 nm (a) kermes oak, dwarf oak. (b) (fig) short chubby person; (Mex) child, kid (fam).

chaparrón nm downpour, cloudburst.

chapatal nm muddy place.

chape nm (Col, Chi) tress, pigtail.

chapear [1a] vt (a)=chapar¹. (b) (SAm: Agr) to weed. (c) (Cu) — a uno to cut someone's throat.

chapeta nf=chapa (e).

chapetón (SAm) 1 adj new (in a job); awkward, unhandy. 2 nm (a) Spaniard newly arrived in America. (b) (Mex) horse brass.

chapetonada nf (a) (Chi, Per) illness caused by a change of climate.
(b) (Bol, Chi, Ec, RPl) awkwardness, clumsiness; inexperience.
(c) (SD) sudden downpour.

chapín 1 adj (SAm) with crooked legs (or feet). 2 nm (a) clog. (b) (CAm: hum) Guatemalan.

chapinada nf (CAm: hum) action typical of a Guatemalan, dirty trick.

chapisca nf (CAm) maize harvest.

chapita nf (Ec: pej) cop (sl).

chapitel nm capital; (of tower) spire.

chapo adj (Mex) stunted, dwarfed.

chapodar [1a] vt (a) tree to prune, trim. (b) (fig) to cut down, reduce.

chapola nf (Col) butterfly.

chapote nm (Ant, Guat, Mex) pitch, asphalt.

chapotear [1a] 1 vt to sponge (down); to wet, moisten. 2 vi to splash about; to paddle; to dabble (one's hands).

chapoteo nm (a) sponging; moistening. (b) splashing; paddling; dabbling.

chapucear [1a] vt (a) to botch, bungle, make a mess of. (b) (Mex) to swindle.

chapuceramente adv roughly, crudely, shoddily; amateurishly; clumsily.

chapucería nf (a) shoddiness. (b) (una —) botched job, shoddy piece of work, mess.

chapucero 1 adj object rough, crude, shoddy; work bungling, slapdash; amateurish; person clumsy, bungling.
2 nm bungler, clumsy workman (etc); bungling amateur.

chapulú nm (CAm) (a) locust. (b) (fam) child, kid (fam).

chapuro nm (CAm) asphalt.

chapurr(e)ar [1a] vt (a) drinks to mix. (b) language to speak badly; **chapurrea el italiano** he speaks broken (or bad) Italian.

chapuz nm (a) ducking; plunge, dive, dip. (b) = chapuza.

chapuza nf (a) botched job, shoddy piece of work, mess; odd job, spare-time job. (b) (Mex) trick, swindle.

chapuzar [1f] 1 vt to duck, dip, plunge. 2 vi and **chapuzarse** vr to duck, dive.

chapuzón nm (a) dip, swim; ducking; **darse un — to** go for a dip. (b) (of capsule) splashdown.

chaqué nm morning coat.

chaquet [tʃa'ke] nm, pl **chaquets** [tʃa'kes] = chaqué.

chaqueta nf jacket; — de cuero leather jacket; — de smoking dinner jacket; **cambiar la** — =chaquetear.

chaquetar [1a] vi (Mex), **chaquetear** [1a] vi to change sides, be a turncoat, turn traitor; to go back on one's word, rat (fam).

chaquete nm backgammon.

chaquetero nm (Mex, SD) turncoat.

chaquetón nm long jacket, reefer, shooting jacket.

chaquira nf small pearl; glass bead.

charada nf charade.

charaludo adj (Mex) thin.

charamusca nf (a) (SAm: also —s) firewood, kindling. (b) (Mex) candy twist. (c) (Cu, PR) noise, row.

charanga nf (a) hullabaloo (fam), merry din. (b) (Mus) brass band; band of street musicians; (Arg, Per) cavalry band. (c) (CR, Mex, Per, PR) informal dance.

charango nm (Bol, Chi, Per) a small five-stringed guitar.

charanguero adj=chapucero 1.

charca nf pond, pool.

charco nm pool, puddle; **cruzar el —, pasar el — to** cross the water, (esp) to cross the herring-pond (ie the Atlantic).

charcón adj (Bol, RPl) thin, skinny.

charla nf talk, chat; (pej) chatter; (pej) talk, gossip; — **radiofónica** radio talk; — **literaria** literary talk, informal literary lecture.

charlador 1 adj talkative; gossipy. 2 nm, **charladora** nf chatterbox; gossip.

charladuría nf (also —s) small talk, chatter, gossip.

charlar [1a] vi to chat, talk (de about); (pej) to chatter, gossip.

charlatán 1 adj talkative; gossipy.
2 nm, **charlatana** nf (a) chatterbox; gossip; bigmouth (sl), indiscreet talker.
(b) (confidence) trickster; smooth-tongued salesman, clever (but untrustworthy) salesman, showman; (Med) quack, charlatan.

charlatanear [1a] vi to chatter away, babble on; (pej) to shoot one's mouth off.

charlatanería nf (a) talkativeness, garrulity. (b) (clever) salesmanship; showmanship; quackery, charlatanism. (c) sales talk, patter; hot air.

charlatanismo nm=charlatanería.

charleta nmf (Arg) chatterbox; gossip.

charnela nf hinge.

charol nm (a) varnish; patent leather; **calzarse las de** — (RPl) to do oneself a good turn, make a packet (fam); **darse** — to swank (fam), brag. (b) (SAm) tray.

charola nf (a) (SAm) tray. (b) (CAm) —s eyes, shiners (sl).

charolado adj polished, shiny.

charolar [1a] vt to varnish, japan.

charpa nf (CAm: Mil) pistol belt, sword belt; (Med) sling.

charquear [1a] vt (SAm) (a) beef to dry, jerk. (b) person to carve up, slash, wound severely; to beat (up).

charqui nm (SAm) dried beef, jerked meat; (Chi, RPl) dried fruit, dried vegetables; **hacer — a uno** (fig) = charquear (b).

charra nf (a) (prov: Salamanca) peasant woman; (fig) low-class woman, coarse woman. (b) (Guat, Hond) broad-brimmed hat. (c) (Ec) itch, pimple.

charrada nf (a) coarse thing, piece of bad breeding; example of bad taste.
(b) flashy ornament, vulgar adornment; tastelessly decorated object.
(c) (quality) coarseness, bad breeding; bad taste; tawdriness, gaudiness.
(d) (Mus) country dance.

charral nm (CAm) scrub, scrubland.

charramasca nf (CAm) firewood, kindling.

charrán¹ nm (Orn) tern.

charrán² nm rascal, villain.

charranada nf dirty trick.

charrasca nf (Bol, Mex, RPl) knife, sharp weapon.

charrasquear [1a] vt (a) (Mex) to knife, stab. (b) (Ec, Pan, Ven) to strum.

charretera nf epaulette; shoulder flash.

charro 1 adj (a) person rustic; coarse, vulgar, ill-bred. (b) dress etc loud, gaudy; object flashy, showy; over-ornamented, decorated in bad taste.
(c) (Mex) picturesque, quaint.
(d) (Mex) skilled in horsemanship.
2 nm (a) (prov: Salamanca) peasant.
(b) (pej) rustic, boor, coarse individual; flashy sort, overdressed individual.
(c) (Mex) horseman, cowboy; typical Mexican.
(d) (Mex) wide-brimmed hat.

charrúa (SAm) 1 adj Uruguayan. 2 nmf Uruguayan.

chasca nf (SAm) mop of hair, tangled hair; tangle.

chascar [1g] 1 vt (a) tongue etc to click; fingers to snap; whip to crack; gravel etc to crunch. (b) food to swallow. 2 vi to click, snap; to crack; to crunch.

chascarrillo nm funny story.

chasco¹ adj (Arg, Bol) hair etc thick and crinkly, coarse.

chasco² nm (a) disappointment; failure, let-down; **dar un — a uno** to disappoint someone; **llevarse (un)** — to be disappointed, suffer a let-down; **¡vaya — que me llevé!** I just was sick about that!
(b) trick, joke; prank; **dar — a uno** to pull someone's leg; **dar un — a uno** to play a trick on someone.

chascón adj (Bol, Chi) (a) hair dishevelled, matted, entangled. (b) (fig) slow, clumsy.

chasis nm, pl **chasis** (Aut etc) chassis; (Phot) plateholder.

chasque nm (SAm) see chasqui.

chasquear¹ vt (a) to disappoint, let down (also **dejar chasqueado**). (b) to play a trick on, make a fool of. (c) promise to break.

chasquear² 1 vt =**chascar** 1; (Col, Pan) bit to champ. 2 vi =**chascar** 2; (of wood etc) to creak; to crack, crackle; — con la lengua to click one's tongue.

chasqui nm (SAm) messenger, courier.

chasquido nm click; snap; crack; crunch; creak, crackle.

chata nf (a) bedpan. (b) (Naut) lighter, barge, transport. (c) (RPl: Rail) flatcar. (d) (RPl: Aut) transporter.

chatarra nf scrap iron, junk; (Mil: hum) medals; vender para — to sell for scrap.

chatarrero nm scrap dealer, scrap merchant.

chateo nm (fam) pub crawl (fam), drinking expedition; ir de — to go on a pub crawl.

chati nf (sl) girl, bird (sl); ¡oye —! hey, beautiful! (fam).

chato 1 adj (a) nose flat, snub; person snub-nosed; ¡oye, chata! (fam) hey, beautiful! (fam).
(b) object flattened, blunt; boat etc flat; tower etc low, squat.
(c) (PR, RPl) ordinary, commonplace.
(d) dejar — a uno (SAm) to crush someone; to embarrass someone; (Mex) to swindle someone; quedarse — con algo to appropriate something.
2 nm wine glass; glass (of wine); tomarse unos —s to have a glass or two.

chatre nm (Chi, Ec) smartly-dressed.

chatungo adj (sl) =**chato**; ¡eh, —! (to child) hey, lad!; ¡oye, chatunga! (to girl) hey, beautiful! (fam).

chau interj (RPl) so long!

chaucha 1 adj invar (a) (Chi, Ec: Agr etc) ripening early; unripe, not fully grown; birth premature; woman who gives birth prematurely.
(b) (RPl) poor-quality; insipid, tasteless, characterless; in poor taste.
2 nf (a) (SAm) early potato, small potato; (Bol, RPl) string bean; (Per) food (in general); pelar la — (Bol, Per, RPl) to brandish (or use) one's knife.
(b) (Bol, Chi) 20-cent coin; (Bol, Chi, Per) money (in general).

chauchau nm (Chi, Per) food, chow (sl).

chauchera nf (Chi, Ec, Per) purse, pocketbook.

chauchero nm (Chi) errand boy; odd-job man; poorly-paid worker.

chauvinismo nm chauvinism.

chauvinista 1 adj chauvinist(ic). 2 nmf chauvinist.

chaval nm (fam) lad, boy, kid (fam); estar hecho un — to feel (or look) very young again; es un — he's only a kid (still).

chavala nf (fam) girl, kid (fam).

chavalo nm (CAm, Mex, Ven) street urchin.

chavalongo nm (Arg, Chi) fever; sunstroke; drowsiness, drowsy feeling.

chaveta nf cotter, cotter pin; (Mex) broad-bladed knife; perder la — (fam) to go off one's rocker (sl); to go through the roof (fam); perder la — por una to be crazy about a girl.

chavetear [1a] vt (Cu, Per) to knife.

chavo nm (fam): no tener un —, estar sin un — to be stony-broke (fam), be stone-broke (US).

chavó interj (sl) jolly good! (fam); well I'm blowed!

che interj (Bol, RPl) hey!, hi!, I say!; (Hond, Ven) who cares!, so what?

checar [1g] vt (Mex etc) =**chequear**.

checo 1 adj Czech. 2 nm, **checa** nf Czech. 3 nm (language) Czech.

checoslovaco 1 adj Czechoslovak. 2 nm, **checoslovaca** Czechoslovak.

Checoslovaquia f Czechoslovakia.

cheche nm (Cu, PR) bully, braggart.

chécheres nmpl (CAm, Col, Pan) things, gear (fam); junk, lumber.

chechón adj (Mex) child spoilt, pampered.

cheikh [tʃejk] nm sheik(h).

cheira nf =**chaira**.

chelear [1a] vt (CAm) to whiten, whitewash.

chelín nm (Fin) shilling.

chelo¹ nm (Mus: fam) 'cellist.

chelo² adj (Mex) fair, blond(e).

chepa 1 nf hump. 2 nm hunchback.

cheque nm (angl) cheque, check (US); — abierto open cheque; — en blanco blank cheque; — cruzado crossed cheque; — sin fondos, — sin provisión bad cheque; — al portador cheque payable to bearer; — de viajero traveller's cheque; pagar mediante — to pay by cheque.

chequear [1a] vt (esp SAm: angl) document, account, health etc to check; person to check (up) on; (CAm, PR, SD) cheque to issue, write; to issue a cheque for; (CAm, Col, PR) luggage to register; (Col) to note down, record, register; (Mex: Aut) to service, overhaul, check.

chequeo nm (esp SAm: angl) check; checking-up; (Med) check-up; (Aut) servicing, overhaul(ing), checking.

chequera nf (SAm) cheque book.

cherife nm (SAm: angl) sheriff (US).

cheruto nm cheroot.

cheurón nm (Her) chevron.

chévere 1 adj (Ant, Col, Mex) smashing (sl), super (fam). 2 nm (Cu, PR) bully, braggart.

chibato nm (etc) see **chivato** (etc).

chibola nf (CAm), **chibolo** nm (Col, Ec, Hond, Per) bump, swelling; wen.

chic 1 adj invar chic, smart, elegant. 2 nm elegance; composure.

chica¹ nf girl; maid, servant.

chica² nf (RPl) plug of chewing tobacco.

chicana nf (SAm: gall) chicanery.

chicanear [1a] vi (SAm: gall) to use trickery, be cunning.

chicanero adj (a) (SAm) tricky, crafty. (b) (Ec) mean.

chicle nm chewing gum; — de burbuja, — de globo bubble gum.

chiclear [1a] vi (CAm, Mex) (a) to extract gum (for chewing). (b) to chew gum.

chico 1 adj (a) small, little, tiny; dejar — a uno to put someone in the shade.
(b) (Mex: iro) big, huge.
2 nm (a) boy; child, youngster, lad; (in direct address) my boy, old boy, old man; es (un) buen — he's a good lad (or chap, fellow); los —s del equipo the chaps in the team; los —s de la oficina the fellows at the office; — de la calle street urchin; — de oficina, — para los recados office boy; como — con zapatos nuevos as happy as a sandboy; me han tomado por el — del portero they think I must know everything.
(b) (SAm: Billiards, Cards etc) game, round; first game.

chicolear [1a] 1 vi (a) (fam) to flirt, murmur sweet nothings, say nice things.
(b) (Arg) to amuse oneself, have a good time; to do childish things.
2 **chicolearse** vr (Per) to amuse oneself.

chicoleo nm (a) (fam) compliment, flirtatious remark; decir —s to say nice things.
(b) (fam) flirting; estar de — to be in a flirtatious mood.
(c) (Arg) childish thing; no andemos con —s let's be serious.

chicolero adj flirtatious.

chicoria nf chicory.

chicota nf fine girl; (pej) big girl, hefty wench.

chicotazo nm (SAm) lash, swipe.

chicote nm (a) big chap, fine lad.
(b) (Naut) piece of rope, rope end; (SAm) whip, lash.
(c) (fam) cigar; (Arg, Col, Mex, Ven) cigar stub.
(d) knotted handkerchief.

chicotear [1a] 1 vt (SAm) to whip, lash; (SAm) to beat up; (Col) to kill.
2 vi (SAm: of tail etc) to lash about.

chicha¹ nf (a) (SAm) chicha, maize liquor, corn liquor (US); — de uva (Arg, Per) unfermented grape juice; como — (Col) in plenty, in abundance; no es ni — ni limonada it's neither one thing nor the other; it's useless; it's dull, it's uninteresting; sacar la — a uno (RPl) to make the utmost use of someone; to make someone sweat.
(b) (RPl) blood.
(c) (CAm, Ec) rage, bad temper; estar de — to be in a bad mood.

chicha² nf (Per) thick-soled shoe.

chicha³ nf (fam) meat; tener poca(s) —(s) to be thin, be weak.

chícharo nm pea, chickpea.

chicharra nf (a) harvest bug, cicada; es como — en verano it's nasty, it's unpleasant; canta la — it's terribly hot.
(b) (fig) chatterbox.
(c) (Elec) bell, buzzer.
(d) (Guat, Hond, SD, Ven) crackling (of pork).

chicharrero nm oven, hothouse; (fig) suffocating heat.

chicharrón nm (a) crackling (of pork); piece of burnt meat; estar hecho un — (Cook) to be burnt to a cinder; (person) to be as red as a lobster.
(b) (fig) sunburnt person.
(c) (Cu) flatterer.

chiche 1 adj and adv (CAm) easy, simple; easily; está — it's a cinch (sl).
2 nm (a) (SAm) breast, teat.

(b) (*SAm: fig*) precious thing, delightful object; fancy jewel, trinket; small toy; trustworthy person, clever person; well-dressed person; elegant place, nice room (*etc*). **3** *nf* (*Mex*) nursemaid.

chichear [1a] *vti* to hiss.

chicheo *nm* hiss, hissing.

chichera *nf* (*CAm*) jail.

chichería *nf* chicha tavern; chicha factory.

chichero *nm* chicha vendor (*or* maker).

chichi *nf* (*Mex*) **(a)** teat. **(b)** nursemaid.

chichigua *nf* **(a)** (*CAm, Mex*) nursemaid. **(b)** (*Ant*) kite. **(c)** (*Mex*) tree that gives shade.

chicho *nm* **(a)** curl, ringlet. **(b)** curler, curling iron.

chichón¹ *adj* **(a)** (*RPl*) merry, jovial. **(b)** (*CAm*) easy, straightforward.

chichón² *nm* bump, lump, swelling.

chichonear [1a] *vi* (*RPl*) to joke.

chifa *nf* (*Per*) Chinese restaurant.

chifla *nf* hiss, hissing, whistling.

chiflado (*fam*) *adj* **1** daft, barmy (*sl*); cranky, crackpot; **estar — con, estar — por** to be crazy about. **2** *nm* crazy man, crank, crackpot.

chifladura *nf* **(a)** =chifla. **(b)** (*fam: in general*) daftness, craziness. **(c)** (*fam: una —*) whim, fad, mania; crazy idea, wild scheme; **su — es el ajedrez** his mania is chess, he is crazy about chess; **ese amor no es más que una —** what he calls love is just a stupid infatuation.

chiflar [1a] **1** *vt* **(a)** (*Theat*) to hiss, boo, whistle at; **whistle** to blow. **(b)** (*fam*) to drink, knock back (*sl*). **(c)** (*fam*) to entrance, captivate; to drive crazy; **me chifla ese conjunto** I rave about that group, I think that group is smashing (*sl*); **me chiflan los helados** I just adore ice cream; **a mí no me chiflan los eslobodios** I don't exactly go overboard for the Slobodians (*fam*); **esa chica le chifla** (*or* **tiene chiflado**) he's crazy about that girl. **2** *vi* to whistle, hiss; (*Guat, Mex: of birds*) to sing. **3 chiflarse** *vr* **(a)** (*fam*) to go barmy (*sl*), go crazy; **— con, — por** to be (*or* go) crazy about. **(b)** **—las** (*CAm*) to die.

chifle *nm* **(a)** whistle; call, bird call. **(b)** (*Hist, also Ant, Guat*) powder horn, powder flask.

chiflido *nm* whistle, shrill sound; hiss.

chiflón *nm* **(a)** (*Arg, Col, Per, Urug*) draught, blast (*of air*); (*CAm, Mex*) gale. **(b)** (*Chi, Guat, Ven*) rapids, violent current; (*CAm*) waterfall; (*Mex*) flume, race; (*Mex*) nozzle.

chifonía *nf* (*Mus*) organistrum.

Chile *m* Chile.

chile *nm* **(a)** (*Bot, Cook*) chili, red pepper. **(b)** (*CAm: fig*) lie.

chilenismo *nm* chilenism, word (*or* phrase *etc*) peculiar to Chile.

chileno, chileño 1 *adj* Chilean. **2** *nm*, **chilena** *nf*, **chileña** *nf* Chilean.

chilicote *nm* (*Arg, Bol*) cricket.

chilpayate *nm*, **chilpayata** *nf* (*Mex*) child.

chilla¹ *nf* thin board; weatherboard, clapboard (*US*).

chilla² *nf* (*Arg, Chi*) fox.

chilla³ *nf* (*Mex*) **(a)** (*Theat*) gods, gallery. **(b)** poverty; **estar en la —** to be very poor.

chilla³ *nf* (*Hunting*) call.

chillador *adj* howling, screeching, screaming; blaring; squealing; creaking.

chillante *adj* **(a)** =chillador. **(b)** (*fig*) =chillón **(b)**.

chillar [1a] **1** *vi* **(a)** (*of wild animal, cat etc*) to howl; (*of mouse*) to squeak; (*of pig*) to squeal; (*of bird*) to screech, squawk; (*of person*) to yell; to shriek, scream; (*of radio*) to blare; (*of brakes*) to screech, squeal; (*of door*) to creak; (*of frying*) to sizzle; **— a uno** to yell at someone, scream at someone. **(b)** (*of colours*) to scream, jar, be loud. **(c)** (*SAm: fig*) to shout, protest; **no — (Arg, PR)** to keep one's mouth shut, not say a word; (*Hond, PR*) to squeal, turn informer. **2 chillarse** *vr* **(a)** (*SAm*) to complain (*con* to), protest (*con* to). **(b)** (*Col, Ec, Mex, Per, PR*) to get cross; to take offence. **(c)** (*CAm*) to get embarrassed.

chillería *nf* row, hubbub.

chillido *nm* howl; squeak; squeal; screech; squawk; yell, shriek, scream; blare; creak; sizzling.

chillo *nm* **(a)** (*CAm*) debt. **(b)** (*PR*) rabble, mob. **(c)** (*Ec*) anger; loud protest.

chillón¹ *adj* **(a)** *person* loud, shrill, noisy; *sound, voice* shrill, strident; harsh; piercing. **(b)** *colour* loud, gaudy, lurid.

chillón² *nm* (*Tech*) small nail, panel pin, finishing nail (*US*).

chimal *nm* (*Mex*) dishevelled hair, mop of hair.

chimar [1a] *vt* **(a)** (*CAm*) to scratch. **(b)** (*Mex, Nic*) to annoy, bother.

chimba¹ *nf* (*Chi, Per*) opposite bank (*of a river*); (*Chi*) poor quarter (*on other side of river*); (*Per*) ford.

chimba² *nf* (*Col, Ec*) pigtail.

chimbar [1a] *vt* (*Ec, Per*) river to ford.

chimbero *adj* (*Chi*) =arrabalero.

chimbo 1 *adj* **(a)** (*Col, Ven*) worn-out, wasted, old. **(b)** (*Col*) *cheque* bad. **2** *nm* (*Col*) piece of meat.

chimenea *nf* **(a)** chimney; (*Naut etc*) funnel; smokestack; (*Min*) shaft; (*Mountaineering*) chimney; **— de aire** air shaft; **— refrigeradora** cooling tower. **(b)** (*in room*) hearth, fireplace; **— (francesa)** fireplace, mantelpiece; chimney piece.

chimiscolear [1a] *vi* (*Mex*) to gossip; to gad about.

chimiscolero *nm*, **chimiscolera** *nf* (*Mex*) gossip; gadabout.

chimpancé *nm* chimpanzee.

chimpín *nm* (*Ec*) brandy, liquor.

chimuelo *adj* (*SAm*) toothless.

China *f* China.

china¹ *nf* (*Cook etc*) china; chinaware; porcelain.

china² *nf* **(a)** (*Geol*) pebble; guessing game played with pebbles; **le tocó la —** he had bad luck; he carried the can (*sl*). **(b)** (*Col*) spinning top.

china³ *nf* **(a)** (*SAm*) (Indian) woman, (half-breed) girl; (*Bol, CAm, RPl*) nursemaid; (*Chi, Ec, Per*) servant, girl; (*SAm: pej*) mistress, concubine; (*Col*) elegant young lady. **(b)** (*Tech: SAm*) fan, blower.

china⁴ *nf* (*Ant, Mex, Ven*) orange.

chinarro *nm* large pebble, stone.

chinazo *nm* blow from a stone; **le tocó el —** he had bad luck; he carried the can (*sl*).

chinchada *nf* (*RPl*) tug-of-war.

chinchal *nm* (*Ant*) tobacco stall; small shop.

chinchar [1a] (*fam*) **1** *vt* to pester, bother, annoy; **me chincha tener que + infin** it upsets me to have to + *infin*. **2 chincharse** *vr* to get cross, get upset; ¡**chínchate!** get stuffed! (*sl*); ¡**para que te chinches!** so there!; and you can lump it!; ¡**y que se chinchen los demás!** and the rest can go chase themselves! (*fam*).

chincharrero *nm* (*Col, Ec, Per*) fishing boat.

chinche *m or f* (*Acad: f*) **(a)** (*Ent*) bug, (*esp*) bedbug; **caer** (*or* **morir**) **como —s** to die like flies. **(b)** drawing pin, thumbtack (*US*). **(c)** (*fig*) nuisance; annoying person, pest, bore; (*Col, Pan*) naughty child.

chincheta *nf* drawing pin, thumbtack (*US*).

chinchibí *nm* (*Bol, CAm, Chi: angl*), **chinchibirra** *nf* (*Arg: angl*) ginger beer.

chinchilla *nf* chinchilla.

chinchín¹ *nm* **(a)** street music, tinny music. **(b)** (*RPl*) baby's rattle.

chinchín² *nm* (*Ant, Ven*) drizzle.

chinchona *nf* quinine.

chinchorrería *nf* **(a)** fussiness; critical nature, disrespectful manner; impertinence. **(b)** piece of gossip; malicious tale.

chinchorrero *adj* **(a)** fussy (*about details*); critical, disrespectful; impertinent. **(b)** gossipy; malicious.

chinchorro *nm* **(a)** net, dragnet, trawl. **(b)** rowing boat, dinghy. **(c)** (*Ant, Col, Pan, Ven*) hammock; poor tenement; (*Ant*) little shop.

chinchoso *adj* **(a)** full of bugs. **(b)** =chinchorrero. **(c)** tiresome, annoying; boring. **(d)** (*Col, Ec, Per, PR*) touchy, irritable.

chinear [1a] **1** *vt* (*CAm*) *child* to carry in one's arms; to care for; (*pej*) to spoil. **2** *vi* (*Chi, RPl*) to have an affair with a half-breed girl.

chinela *nf* slipper, mule; clog.

chinero¹ *nm* china cupboard.

chinero² *adj* (*Chi, Ec*) fond of the (half-breed) girls.

chinesco *adj* Chinese.

chinetero *adj* (*Arg*) =chinero².

chinga *nf* **(a)** (*CAm, Ven*) fag end, cigar stub; (*fig*) drop, small amount; **una — de agua** a drop of water. **(b)** (*Ven*) drunkenness. **(c)** (*Mex*) thrashing.

chingadura *nf* (*Chi*) failure.

chingana *nf* **(a)** (*Bol, Chi, Ec, Per, RPl*) dive (*fam*), tavern, cheap dance hall. **(b)** (*Chi, RPl*) wild party.

chinganear [1a] *vi* (*Bol, Chi, Ec, Per, RPl*) to go on the town, live it up (*fam*).

chinganero (*Bol, Chi, Ec, Per, RPl*) **1** *adj* fond of living it up, wildly social. **2** *nm* owner of a *chingana*.

chingar [1h] **1** *vt* **(a)** (*CAm*) to dock, cut off the tail of. **(b)** (*Mex, Salv*) to annoy. **(c)** (*Arg*) *shot* to aim badly, miss with; *attempt* to fail in. **(d)** (*Ven*) to carry on one's shoulder. **2** *vi* **(a)** to drink too much. **(b)** (*CAm*) to joke. **3 chingarse** *vr* **(a)** (*fam*) to get sozzled (*fam*). **(b)** (*SAm*) to fail, fall through, come to nothing; **la fiesta se chingó** the party was a failure; **el cohete se chingó** the rocket failed to go off, the rocket was a dud.

chingo 1 *adj* **(a)** (*CAm, Pan*) *dress* short; *knife* blunt; *animal* docked, tailless; *person* in one's underclothes, bare. **(b)** (*Ven*) small, tiny; *nose* flat, snub. **(c)** (*Ven*) **estar — por algo** to be crazy about something. **2** *nm* **(a)** (*Col, Ec*) colt. **(b)** (*Col, Pan*) small boat. **(c)** (*CAm*) **—s** underclothes.

chingue 1 *adj* (*Chi*) stinking, repulsive. **2** *nm* (*Chi*) skunk.

chinguear [1a] *vt etc* (*CAm*) = **chingar**.

chinguirito *nm* (*Cu, Mex*) rough liquor, firewater; (*Cu, Per*) swig (of liquor: *fam*).

chinita¹ *nf* small stone, pebble; **poner —s en el camino** to lay a trail of pebbles; **poner —s a uno** (*fig*) to make trouble for someone.

chinito, chinita² *nf* **(a)** (*RPl*) servant. **(b)** (*SAm: in direct address*) dear, dearest.

chino¹ 1 *adj* Chinese. **2** *nm*, **china** *nf* Chinese; (*m also*) Chinaman. **3** *nm* (*language*) Chinese; (*fig*) Greek, double Dutch; **ni que hablara en — . . .** I couldn't have understood less even if he'd been talking Chinese.

chino² *nm* (*Geol*) pebble, stone.

chino³ 1 *adj* **(a)** (*CAm*) bald, hairless. **(b)** (*Mex*) curly, kinky. **(c)** (*CAm, Cu*) angry, furious; **estar — to be** angry; **estar — por algo** to be crazy about something. **2** *nm* **(a)** (*SAm*) half-breed; (*Arg, Chi, Par, Ven*) Indian; (*Per: also* **— cholo**) offspring of Indian and Negress; (*Cu*) offspring of mulatto and Negress; (*Col, Chi, Ec, Ven*) servant; (*Col*) street urchin; (*SAm: in direct address*) dear, dearest; **quedar como un —** (*Chi, PR, RPl*) to come off badly; **trabajar como un —** (*Chi, PR, RPl*) to work like a slave. **(b)** (*Andalusia, CR, Mex*) pig. **(c)** **—s** (*Mex*) curls. **(d)** (*Arg, CAm, Cu*) anger; **le salió el —** he got angry; **tener un —** to be angry.

chinorri *nf* (*sl*) dame (*sl*), wench, bint (*sl*).

chipe 1 *adj* (*CAm*) **(a)** weak, sickly. **(b)** whining, snivelling. **2** *nmf* (*CAm, Col, Mex*) baby, child.

chipear [1a] *vt* (*CAm*) to bother, pester.

chipi *adj etc* = **chipe**.

chipichipi *nm* (*prov, SAm*) continuous drizzle, mist.

chipión *nm* (*CAm*) telling off.

chipirón *nm* squid.

chipotear [1a] *vt* (*CAm*) to slap.

Chipre *f* Cyprus.

chipriota, chipriote 1 *adj* Cyprian, Cypriot. **2** *nmf* Cypriot.

chiquear [1a] **1** *vt* (*Cu, Mex*) to spoil, indulge; to flatter, suck up to (*fam*). **2 chiquearse** *vr* **(a)** (*Mex*) to demand flattery, expect to be flattered. **(b)** (*CAm*) to swagger along.

chiqueo *nm* **(a)** (*Cu, Mex*) piece of flattery; **—s** flattery, toadying. **(b)** (*CAm*) swagger.

chiquero *nm* pigsty; (*Taur*) bull pen; (*RPl*) hen run.

chiquilicuatro *nm* (*fam*) young rascal, whippersnapper; schemer.

chiquilín *nm* (*CAm, Mex, RPl*) tiny tot, small boy.

chiquillada *nf* childish prank; childish thing (to do); **eso son —s** that's kid's stuff, that's for children.

chiquillería *nf*: **una —** a crowd of youngsters, a mob of kids (*fam*); **llevar la —** to take the kids.

chiquillo, chiquilla *nf* kid (*fam*), youngster, child.

chiquitín 1 *adj* very small, tiny. **2** *nm*, **chiquitina** *nf* small child, tiny tot.

chiquito 1 *adj* very small, tiny. **2** *nm*, **chiquita** *nf* kid (*fam*), youngster; **andarse en chiquitas** to beat about the bush, fuss about details. **3** *nm* (*RPl*): **un —** a bit, a little; **¡espera un —!** wait a moment!

chiquitura *nf* **(a)** (*CAm, RPl*) small thing; insignificant detail. **(b)** (*CAm*) = **chiquillada**.

chira *nf* (*Col*) rag, tatter; (*CAm*) wound, sore.

chirajos *nmpl* (*CAm*) lumber, junk; (*Col*) rags, tatters.

chirajoso *adj* (*CAm*) ragged, tattered.

chircal *nm* (*Col*) brickworks, tileworks.

chiribita *nf* **(a)** spark; **echar —s, estar que echa —s** to be furious, blow one's top (*fam*); **le hacían —s los ojos** her eyes sparkled, her eyes lit up. **(b)** **—s** (*fam*) spots before the eyes. **(c)** (*Bot*) daisy.

chiribitil *nm* attic, garret; den; cubbyhole; (*pej*) slum, hole.

chirigota *nf* joke; (*person*) laughing stock; **hacer de uno una —** to make a laughing stock out of someone.

chirigotero *adj* full of jokes, facetious.

chirimbolo *nm* thingummyjig (*fam*); strange object, oddlooking implement; **—s** things, gear, equipment; lumber, junk; (*Cook*) kitchen things.

chirimía *nf* hornpipe.

chirimoya *nf* custard apple.

chirinada *nf* **(a)** (*RPl*) failure, disaster. **(b)** = **chirinola**.

chirinola *nf* **(a)** fuss, row; heated discussion; lengthy conversation, lively talk; **pasar la tarde de —** to spend the afternoon deep in conversation. **(b)** trifle, triviality, unimportant thing.

chiripa *nf* (*Billiards*) lucky break; (*fig*) lucky event, fluke, stroke of luck; **de —** (*SAm*), **por —** by a fluke, by chance.

chiripá *nm* (*Bol, Chi, RPl*) *kind of blanket worn as trousers*; **gente de —** country people, peasants.

chiripero 1 *adj* lucky, fluky. **2** *nm* lucky sort.

chirivía *nf* **(a)** (*Bot*) parsnip. **(b)** (*Orn*) wagtail.

chirivisco *nm* (*CAm*) firewood, kindling.

chirle *adj* **(a)** *soup etc* watery, wishy-washy (*fam*). **(b)** (*fig*) flat, dull, wishy-washy (*fam*); **poeta —** mere versifier, uninspired poet.

chirlo *nm* gash, slash (in the face); long scar.

chirola *nf* (*CAm, PR, SD*), **chirona** *nf* (*fam*) jug (*sl*), jail; **estar en —** to be in jug.

chiros *nmpl* (*Col*) rags, tatters.

chiroso *adj* (*CAm, Col*) ragged, tattered.

chirota *nf* (*CAm*) mannish woman; shameless woman.

chirriado *adj* (*Col*) witty; merry, jovial.

chirriar [1b] *vi* **(a)** (*of cricket etc*) to chirp, sing; (*of bird*) to chirp; to screech, squawk; (*of wheel, hinge, door*) to creak, squeak; (*of brakes*) to screech, squeal; (*of frying*) to hiss, sizzle; (*of person*) to sing (or play) out of tune. **(b)** (*Col*) to shiver (with cold *etc*). **(c)** (*Col*) to go on a spree (*fam*).

chirrido *nm* shrill sound, high-pitched unpleasant sound; chirp(ing); screech(ing), squawk(ing); creak(ing), squeak(ing); squeal(ing); sizzle, sizzling.

chirrión *nm* **(a)** tumbrel. **(b)** (*CAm, Col, Mex, Pan*) whip. **(c)** (*CAm*) string, line. **(d)** (*CAm*) chat, conversation (*esp* between lovers).

chirrionar [1a] *vt* (*Col, Mex*) to whip, lash.

chirrisco *adj* **(a)** (*CAm, Ven*) very small, tiny. **(b)** (*Mex*) rude, obscene; **viejo —** dirty old man.

chirusa *nf* (*RPl*) girl, child; low-class woman.

chis *interj* sh!

chiscón *nm* shack, hovel, slum.

chischís *nm* (*Col, Hond, Pan, PR*) drizzle.

chisgarabís *nm* (*fam*) meddler, nosey parker; good-for-nothing.

chisme *nm* **(a)** (*Tech*) gadget, contrivance, jigger (*sl*); **—s** things, gear, tackle. **(b)** (*fig*) thing, whatnot (*fam*), thingummyjig (*fam*); **dáme el — ese** give me that whatsit, please (*fam*); **—s** (*fig*) paraphernalia, things, odds and ends. **(c)** (*fig*) piece of gossip, tale; **—s** gossip, tittle-tattle, tales; **no me vengas con esos —s** don't bring those tales to me, I don't want to hear your tittle-tattle. **(d)** **es un —** he's worthless, he's a dead loss.

chismear [1a] *vi* to gossip, tell tales, spread scandal.

chismería *nf*, **chismerío** *nm* (*PR, RPl*) gossip, tittle-tattle, scandal.

chismero *adj* and *n* = **chismería**.

chismorrear [1a] *vi* = **chismear**.

chismorreo *nm* = **chismería**.

chismoso 1 *adj* gossiping, scandalmongering. **2** *nm*, **chismosa** *nf* talebearer, scandalmonger.

chispa 1 *nf* **(a)** spark (*also Elec*); (*fig*) sparkle, gleam; **echar —s** (*fig*), **estar que echa —s** (*fig*) to be hopping mad. **(b)** drop (*esp* of rain); **—s** sprinkling (of rain); **caen —s** it's damping, there are a few drops falling. **(c)** flake; small particle, (*esp*) small diamond. **(d)** (*fig*) bit, tiny amount; **ni —** not the least bit, nothing at all; **eso no tiene — de gracia** that's not in the least bit funny; **si tuviera una — de inteligencia** if he had an atom of intelligence.

(e) (*fig*) sparkle, wit; life; **el cuento tiene** — the story has some wit; **dar** —s to show oneself to be bright (*or* lively, efficient); **no da** — it's awfully dreary; he's utterly dull; **ser una** —, **tener (mucha)** — to be a lively sort.

(f) (*fam*) drunkenness; drunk (*fam*); **coger** (*or* **pillar**) **una** — to get tight; **estar con la** —, **tener la** — to be tight.

(g) (*Mex*) light two-wheeled carriage.

(h) (*Guat, Mex*) **dar** — to work, be successful, yield results.

(i) (*Col*) rumour.

2 *adj invar* (*fam*) (a) **estar** — to be tight.

(b) (*Mex*) funny, amusing.

chisparse [1a] *vr* (a) (*Col, PR*)=**achisparse.** (b) (*Guat, Mex*) to run away, slip off.

chispazo *nm* (a) spark (*also fig*); **primeros** —s (*fig*) first signs, opening shots, intimations. (b) (*fig*)= **chisme** (c).

chispeante *adj* (*fig*) sparkling, scintillating.

chispear [1a] **1** *vi* (a) to spark (*also Elec*).

(b) (*fig*) to sparkle, scintillate.

(c) (*Meteorol*) to drizzle, spot with rain.

(d) (*Col*) to gossip, spread scandal.

2 chispearse *vr* (*Arg, SD*)=**achisparse.**

chispero 1 *adj* (*Col, SD*) gossiping, scandalmongering. **2** *nm* underworld Madrid character.

chispita *f* (*fam*): **una** — **de vino** a drop of wine.

chisporrotear [1a] *vi* to throw out sparks; (*esp Cook:* *of oil etc*) to hiss, splutter; (*of bacon etc*) to sizzle; (*of burning wood*) to crackle.

chistar [1a] *vi:* **no** — not to say a word; **lo aceptó sin** — he took it without a word; **nadie chistó** nobody spoke up, nobody answered back.

chiste *nm* joke, funny story; — **goma** shaggy-dog story; — **verde** dirty story; **caer en el** — to get the point of the story, get it; **dar en el** — to guess right; **hacer** — **de algo**, **tomar algo a** — to take something as a joke; **¡aquello tiene** —! (*iro*) I suppose you think that's funny?; **no veo el** — I don't get it; what's funny about that?

chistera *nf* (a) fish basket; (*Sport*) long curved variety of pelota racquet. (b) (*fam*) top hat, topper (*fam*).

chistosamente *adv* funnily, amusingly; wittily.

chistoso 1 *adj* funny, amusing; witty. **2** *nm, chistosa nf* wit, amusing person.

chistu *nm* (Basque) flute.

chistulari *nm* (Basque) flute player, flautist.

chita[1]: **a la** — **callando** quietly; unobtrusively; (*pej*) on the quiet, on the sly.

chita[2] *nf* (a) anklebone; *boys' game played with an ankle bone*; **dar en la** — to hit the nail on the head; **no se me da una** —, (no) **me importa una** — I don't care two hoots (*de about*).

(b) (*Mex*) net bag; money; small savings.

chiticalla *nmf* (*fam*) quiet sort, clam.

chiticallando see **chita**[1].

chito, chitón *interj* sh!

chiva *nf* (a) (*Agr, Zool*) kid; (*SAm*) goat, nanny-goat; sheep.

(b) (*SAm*) goatee (beard).

(c) (*Col, Pan*) bus; car.

(d) (*CAm*) blanket, bedcover.

(c) (*PR, RPl*) naughty little girl; (*Chi, Hond*) mannish woman; (*Col, Ec, PR, SD, Urug*) immoral woman.

(f) (*Hond, RPl*) rage, tantrum (*fam*).

(g) (*Ven*) knapsack.

chivar [1a] (*prov, SAm*) **1** *vt* to annoy, upset; to swindle. **2 chivarse** *vr* (a) to get annoyed.

(b) = **chivatear** (a).

chivatazo *nm* (*fam*) tip-off; **dar** — to inform, give a tip-off.

chivatear [1a] **1** *vi* (a) (*fam*) to split (*fam; contra* on), inform (*contra* on), squeal (*sl*).

(b) (*Chi, Ec, Per*) to shout, make a hullabaloo (*fam*); to jump about; (*Ec, Per, RPl*) to indulge in horse-play, have a noisy free-for-all.

(c) (*Ven*) to create a big impression.

2 chivatearse *vr* (*Cu*) to get scared.

chivato *nm* (a) (*Agr, Zool*) kid.

(b) (*fam*) stool pigeon (*fam*), informer.

(c) (*SAm*) child, kid (*fam*).

(d) (*Col*) rascal, villain.

(e) (*Bol*) apprentice, mate.

(f) (*Ven*) outstanding individual.

(g) (*Chi*) cheap liquor, firewater.

chivearse [1a] *vr* (*Mex*) to get scared.

chivera *nf* (*CAm, Col*) goatee (beard).

chivero *nm* (a) (*Col*) busdriver. (b) (*Ec*) brawler.

(c) (*Cu, PR*) intriguer.

chivo *nm* (a) (*Agr, Zool*) kid; goat; billy goat; **esto huele a** — (*PR, RPl*) this smells suspicious.

(b) (*CAm*) dice; game of dice.

(c) (*Ant*) fraud; plot, intrigue; (*Comm*) smuggling; illegal trading; contraband, smuggled goods.

(d) (*Col, Ec, Hond, RPl, Ven*) rage, fit of anger; **comer** — (*Col, Ven*), **ponerse como** — (*Ant, CAm*) to get furious.

(e) (*Mex*) day's wages.

(f) (*Cu*) punch, blow.

(g) (*Ec, Guat*) naughty boy.

chivón (*Cu*) **1** *adj* annoying, tedious. **2** *nm*, **chivona** *nf* bore.

chocante *adj* (a) startling, striking; odd, strange; noteworthy; **es** — **que** . . . it is odd that . . ., it is surprising that . . .; it is noteworthy that . . .; **lo** — **es que** . . . the odd thing about it is that . . .

(b) shocking, scandalous.

(c) (*esp SAm*) tiresome, tedious, annoying; impertinent; (*Arg*) offensive; (*Mex*) unpleasant.

chocantería *nf* (*SAm*) (a) impertinence. (b) coarse joke.

chocar [1g] **1** *vt* (a) to shock; to startle, surprise; **me choca que no lo hayan hecho** I am surprised that they haven't done it; **ello me chocó bastante** it gave me rather a jolt; it did surprise me rather.

(b) (*Elec*) to give a shock to.

(c) *glasses* to clink; *hand* to shake; **¡chócala!** (*fam*) put it there! (*fam*), shake (on it)!; — **la mano con uno** to shake hands with someone.

2 *vi* (a) to shock; to be surprising, be startling, be odd; **no es de** — it's not all that surprising.

(b) (*Aut etc*) to collide, crash; (*of glasses*) to clink; (*of plates*) to clatter; (*Mil*) to clash; — **con** to collide with, crash into, smash against; to hit, strike; **el buque chocó con una mina** the ship struck a mine; **el balón chocó con el poste** the ball crashed into the post; **por fin chocó con el jefe** finally he fell out with (*or* clashed with) the boss; **esta teoría choca con dificultades** this theory runs into (*or* up against) difficulties.

chocarrear [1a] *vi* (a) to clown, act the fool. (b) to tell rude jokes.

chocarrería *nf* (a) (*quality*) coarseness, vulgarity; scurrility; clownishness. (b) (*una* —) coarse joke, dirty story; clownish act.

chocarrero *adj* coarse, vulgar, rude; scurrilous; clownish.

choclo[1] *nm* clog; sandal; overshoe; (*Mex*) low-heeled shoe; **meter el** — (*Mex*) to put one's foot in it.

choclo[2] *nm* (a) (*SAm*) ear of (tender) maize, cob of sweet corn; Indian maize stew.

(b) (*Chi*) —s children's arms, children's legs.

(c) (*Per*) bunch; group; **un** — **de** (*fig*) a group of, a lot of.

(d) (*Arg*) difficulty, trouble; annoyance; burden, task.

choco[1] (*Chi, Ec*) **1** *adj* curly, curly-haired. **2** *nm* poodle.

choco[2] *adj* (*Bol, Col, Ec, RPl*) dark red; chocolate-coloured; swarthy, dark.

choco[3] **1** *adj* (*CAm, Chi, Mex*) one-armed, one-legged; one-eyed; (*Chi*) tailless. **2** *nm* (a) (*Chi*) stump. (b) (*Bol*) top hat.

choco[4] *nm* (*Zool*) cuttlefish.

chocolate 1 *adj* (*SAm*) chocolate-coloured; dark red. **2** *nm* (a) chocolate; drinking chocolate, cocoa.

(b) (*SAm: hum*) blood; **sacar el** — **a uno** to make someone's nose bleed.

chocolatera *nf* (a) chocolate pot. (b) (*fam*) old thing, piece of junk; (*Aut*) old crock; (*Naut*) hulk.

chocolatería *nf* chocolate factory; *café specializing in serving drinking chocolate.*

chocolatero 1 *adj* fond of chocolate. **2** *nm* (a) (*Andalusia*) chocolate pot. (b) (*Cu, Mex*) strong northerly wind.

chocolear [1a] (*Col*) **1** *vt* to dock, cut off the tail of. **2** *vi* to get depressed.

chocha *nf* (*also* — **perdiz**) woodcock.

chochear [1a] *vi* (a) to dodder, be doddery, be senile; to be in one's dotage. (b) (*fig*) to be soft, go all sentimental.

chochera *nf*, **chochez** *nf* (a) dotage; senility; second childhood.

(b) (*una* —) silly thing; sentimental act.

(c) (*Per, RPl*) favourite, thing (*or* person) on which one dotes; **tener** — **por una** to dote on someone, be crazy about someone.

chochín *nm*, **chochita** *nf* wren.

chocho[1] *adj* (a) doddering, doddery, senile. (b) (*fig*) soft, doting, sentimental; **estar** — **por** to dote on, be soft about.

chocho[2] *nm* candy stick; **—s** sweets, candies (*US*).
chocholear [1a] *vt* (*Col*) to spoil, pamper.
chófer *nm*, **chofer** *nm* (*SAm*), *pl* **chóferes**, **chofers** (*SAm*) driver; motorist; chauffeur.
cholada *nf* (*Ec*, *Per*) action typical of a *cholo*.
cholería *nf* (*Per*), **cholerío** *nm* (*Per*) group of *cholos*.
cholo 1 *adj* (**a**) (*SAm*) half-breed, mestizo (*and see* 2).
   (**b**) (*Chi*) cowardly.
   2 *nm*, **chola** *nf* (**a**) (*SAm*) half-breed, mestizo; (*any*) dark-skinned person; (*Pan*) half-civilized Indian; (*Chi*) pure Indian from the South.
   (**b**) (*SAm*: *hum*) Peruvian.
   (**c**) (*Chi*) coward.
   (**d**) (*Ec*, *Per*, *Ven*: *in direct address*) darling, honey (*US*).
cholla *nf* (**a**) (*fam*) nut (*sl*), head; (*fig*) brains. (**b**) (*CAm*) wound, sore. (**c**) (*CAm*, *Col*) laziness, slowness.
chollo *nm* (*fam*) bargain, snip (*sl*); plum, soft job.
cholludo *adj* (*CAm*, *Col*) lazy, slow.
chamba *nf* (*Chi*) =**chamba**.
chompa *nf* (*SAm*: *angl*) jumper, sweater.
chonco (*CAm*) **1** *adj* =**choco**[3]. **2** *nm* stump.
chongo *nm* (**a**) (*Chi*) blunt knife, worn-out knife. (**b**) (*PR*, *SD*) old horse. (**c**) (*Guat*, *Mex*) **—s** pigtails, tresses; bun (*of hair*).
chontal *adj* (**a**) (*CAm*) Indian wild, uncivilized; rebellious; unruly. (**b**) (*CAm*, *Col*, *Ven*) uncivilized; rough, coarse; (*Ven*) rough-spoken.
chopa *nf* (*sl*) jacket.
chopera *nf* poplar grove.
chopo *nm* (**a**) (*Bot*) black poplar; **— de Italia**, **— lombardo** Lombardy poplar.
   (**b**) (*Mil*: *fam*) gun; **cargar con el —** (*fig*) to join up, do one's military service.
choque *nm* (**a**) impact; (*of vehicle in movement*) jolt, jar; (*of explosion*) blast, shock wave.
   (**b**) (*noise*) crash; (*of plates etc*) clatter; (*of glasses*) clink.
   (**c**) (*Aut*, *Rail etc*) crash, smash; collision; **— de frente** head-on collision; **— de trenes** rail smash, rail accident.
   (**d**) (*Elec*) shock.
   (**e**) (*Med*) shock.
   (**f**) (*Mil and fig*) clash; conflict; **entrar en —** to clash; **estar en abierto — con** to conflict openly with.
choquezuela *nf* kneecap.
chorcha *nf* (**a**) (*Mex*) group of merry people, light-hearted gathering; noisy party; **una — de amigos** a group of friends (out for a good time).
   (**b**) (*CAm*: *Orn*) crest, comb.
   (**c**) (*CAm*) goitre.
chorchero *adj* (*Mex*) merry.
chorear [1a] *vi* (*Chi*) to grumble, complain.
choreo *nm* (*Chi*) grouse (*fam*), complaint.
chorizo *nm* (**a**) (*Cook*) hard pork sausage, salami.
   (**b**) (*Circus*) balancing pole.
   (**c**) (*tabu*) prick (*tabu*).
   (**d**) (*Bol*, *RPl*) rump steak.
   (**e**) (*Bol*, *RPl*) mixture of clay and straw used in plastering.
   (**f**) (*Col*, *Ec*) idiot.
   (**g**) (*Cu*: *pej*) mulatto, Negro.
chorlitejo *nm*, **chorlito** *nm* plover.
chorlo *nm*, **chorla** *nf* (*CAm*, *Col*, *PR*) great-great-grandchild.
chorote *nm* (**a**) (*Mex*, *Ven*) drinking chocolate (with brown sugar); (*Col*) thick drinking chocolate; (*Cu*) (*any*) thick drink; (*Cu*, *PR*, *Ven*) watery drink; (*PR*) coffee.
   (**b**) (*Col*) unglazed chocolate pot.
chorra *nf* (**a**) (*sl*) luck, jam; **¡qué — tiene!** look at that for jam! (**b**) (*Chi*) underworld slang.
chorrada *nf* (**a**) (*of milk etc*) extra drop; bonus; **dar algo con —** to give something and a bit extra. (**b**) unnecessary adornment; superfluous detail.
chorrear [1a] **1** *vt* (**a**) (*Mil sl*, *also Cu*) to tick off, dress down.
   (**b**) (*Ec*) to soak.
   (**c**) (*RPl*: *sl*) to pinch (*fam*).
   2 *vi* (**a**) to gush (forth), spout (out), spirt; to drip, trickle; **— de sudor** to run with sweat; **la ropa chorrea todavía** his clothes are still wringing wet.
   (**b**) (*fig*) to trickle (in, away *etc*); **chorrean todavía las solicitudes** the applications are still trickling in.
   3 chorrearse *vr* (*Col*): **— algo** to pinch something (*fam*).
chorreo *nm* (**a**) gushing, spouting; dripping; trickling.
   (**b**) (*fig*) constant drain (on resources *etc*).
chorrera *nf* (**a**) spout; channel, runlet.
   (**b**) mark (left by dripping water *etc*).
   (**c**) (*of river*) rapids.

   (**d**) **—s** (*Sew*) frill, lace adornment.
   (**e**) (*SAm*: *fig*) string, stream, lot; **una — de a** whole string of, a lot of.
   (**f**) (*Cu*) ticking off.
   (**g**) *see* **jamón**.
chorretada *nf* (**a**) spirt, squirt, jet. (**b**) =**chorrada** (**a**).
chorrillo *nm* (*fig*) constant stream, steady trickle.
chorro *nm* (**a**) jet; spirt, squirt, stream; dribble, trickle; **beber a —** to drink a jet of wine (from a wineskin); **llover a —s** to pour; **salir a —s** to gush forth, come spirting out.
   (**b**) (*Tech*) jet, blast; (*Aer*) jet; **— de arena** sandblast; **— de vapor** steam jet; **avión a —** jet plane; **motor a —** jet engine; **con propulsión a —** jet-propelled.
   (**c**) (*fig*) stream; **un — de palabras** a stream of words, a torrent of words; **un — de voz** a verbal blast, an awfully loud voice; **a —s** in plenty, in abundance; **hablar a —s** to talk nineteen to the dozen; **soltar el —** to burst out laughing; to produce a torrent of insults (*etc*).
   (**d**) (*Bol*) strand (of a whip).
   (**e**) (*CAm*) tap, faucet.
   (**f**) (*Cu*, *PR*) ticking off.
   (**g**) (*RPl*: *sl*) thief, pickpocket.
chotacabras *nm*, *pl* **chotacabras** nightjar.
chotear [1a] **1** *vt* (**a**) (*Ant*, *CAm*, *Mex*, *Per*) to make fun of.
   (**b**) (*Col*) to spoil, pamper.
   (**c**) (*Guat*) suspect to shadow, tail.
   2 chotearse *vr* to joke, take things as a joke.
chotis *nm*, *pl* **chotis** schottische.
choto 1 *adj* (*CAm*) abundant, plentiful; **estar — de** to be full of, be loaded with; **de —** free, for nothing. **2** *nm* kid; calf.
chotuno *adj* kid, calf sucking, very young; lamb weakly; **oler a —** to smell of goat.
chova *nf* crow, rook; **— piquirroja** chough.
choza *nf* hut, shack; **— de nieve** igloo, ice house.
chozno *nm*, **chozna** *nf* great-great-grandchild.
chrisma ['krisma] *nf*, **christma(s)** ['krisma] *nm*, *pl* **christmas** ['krismas] (*angl*) Christmas card.
chubasco *nm* (**a**) (*Meteorol*) shower, squall; **— de nieve** (brief) snowstorm.
   (**b**) (*fig*) setback; series of reverses (*or* troubles *etc*); **aguantar el —** (*fig*) to weather the storm.
chubascoso *adj* squally, stormy.
chubasquero *nm* oilskins.
chucán *adj* (*CAm*) buffoonish; coarse, rude.
chúcaro *adj* (*SAm*) animal wild, untamed; person shy.
chucear [1a] *vt* (*SAm*) to prick, goad.
chuco *adj* (*CAm*, *Ec*, *Mex*) fish etc high, off.
chucruta *nf* sauerkraut.
chucha *nf* (**a**) (*Zool*) dog, bitch. (**b**) (*fam*) sweetheart. (**c**) (*Col*) opossum. (**d**) (*Col*) body odour. (**e**) (*Col*) hide-and-seek. (**f**) (*Bol*, *Per*: *tabu*) cunt (*tabu*).
chuchada *nf* (*CAm*) trick, swindle.
chuchear[1] [1a] *vt* to hunt, trap.
chuchear[2] [1a] *vi* =**cuchichear**.
chuchería *nf* (**a**) trinket, bit of jewellery, knick-knack. (**b**) titbit, dainty morsel; sweet.
chucho 1 *adj* (**a**) (*Col*) fruit soft, watery; person wrinkled.
   (**b**) (*CAm*) mean.
   2 *nm* (**a**) (*Zool*: *pej*) dog, hound, mongrel; **¡—!** down boy!
   (**b**) (*fam*) sweetheart.
   (**c**) (*Ant*: *Rail*) switch; (*Cu*: *Rail*) siding.
   (**d**) (*Ant*, *Ven*) rawhide whip.
   (**e**) (*Chi*) jail.
   (**f**) (*SAm*: *Med*) chill, fever; (*esp*) malaria.
chuchumeca *nf* (*Chi*, *Per*) whore.
chuchumeco *nm* (**a**) mean person, skinflint.
   (**b**) (*Chi*) sickly person; dwarf, runt; wastrel; (*Col*) old dodderer.
   (**c**) (*Cu*, *Per*) toff (*fam*), dude (*US*).
   (**d**) (*PR*) idiot.
chueca *nf* (**a**) (*Bot*) stump.
   (**b**) (*Anat*) rounded bone; round head of a bone.
   (**c**) (*fig*) practical joke, hoax, prank; **gastar una — a uno** to play a joke on someone.
chueco *adj* (*SAm*) knock-kneed; (*Arg*, *Per*) pigeon-toed; (*Col*) lame; (*Mex*) one-armed, one-legged; (*CAm*, *Mex*, *Ven*) crooked, twisted, bent.
chufa *nf* chufa, earth almond.
chufeta *nf* =**chufleta**.
chufla *nf* joke, merry quip; **tomar algo a —** to take something as a joke.
chuflarse [1a] *vr* to joke, make jokes; to take things as a joke.
chufleta *nf* joke, merry quip; taunt.

chufletear [1a] *vi* to joke, make jokes; to jeer, make taunting remarks.

chula *nf* (a) woman from the back streets (of Madrid), low-class woman, coarse woman. (b) loud wench, flashy female, brassy girl. (c) (*SAm*) girlfriend.

chulada *nf* (a) coarse thing; funny thing; mean trick. (b) =**chulería** (a).

chulear [1a] *vt* (*fam*) (a) to make fun of. (b) to pinch (*fam*), swipe (*sl*).

chulería *nf* (a) (*quality*) natural charm, winning ways; (*pej*) commonness, vulgarity; (*pej*) flashiness; flamboyant manner.
(b) (*la* —) the *chulos* (collectively, *as a group*).
(c) (*una* —) =**chulada** (a).

chulesco *adj* =**chulo** 1.

chuleta *nf* (a) chop, cutlet; — **de puerco** pork chop; — **de ternera** veal chop.
(b) (*Sew*) insert, piece let in; (*Carp*) filling.
(c) (*fam*) punch, bash (*fam*).
(d) (*Univ: fam*) crib (*fam*), trot (*US*).
(e) —s (*fam*) side-whiskers.

chulillo *nm* (*Per*) tradesman's assistant.

chulo 1 *adj* (a) amusing; charming, attractive, winning.
(b) (*in appearance*) smart, showy, attractive; (*pej*) flashy, vulgar, gaudy.
(c) (*of walk, air*) proud; jaunty, swaggering; **con el sombrero a lo** — with his hat at a rakish angle; **iba muy** — he walked with a swagger, he swaggered along.
(d) (*of manner*) bold, free from servility, outspoken; (*pej*) overbold, fresh; pert, saucy; brassy; **no te pongas** — **conmigo** don't get fresh with me.
(e) (*of character*) slick; rascally, villainous.
(f) (*CAm, Col, Mex*) pretty; attractive, elegant, graceful.
2 *adv* (*CAm, Mex*) well; **jugar** — to play well.
3 *nm* (a) typical working-class Madrilenian (equivalent to Cockney); common but likeable chap; easy-going sort, free-and-easy person.
(b) (*pej*) spiv (*sl*), layabout, ne'er-do-well; villain, rascal; — **de putas** pimp, pander.
(c) (*Taur*) bullfighter's assistant.
(d) (*Col*) turkey buzzard.

chulón *adj* (*CAm*) naked.

chulleco *adj* (*Chi*) twisted, crooked.

chuma *nf* (*Ec, RPl*) drunkenness.

chumacera *nf* (*Mech*) ball bearing, journal bearing; (*Naut*) rowlock, oarlock (*US*).

chumarse [1a] *vr* (*Ec, RPl*) to get drunk.

chumbar [1a] *vt* (a) (*RPl: of dog*) to attack, go for; **¡chúmbale!** at him, boy! (b) (*Bol*) to shoot. (c) (*Col*) baby to swaddle.

chumbe *nm* (*SAm*) sash.

chumbera *nf*, **chumbimba** *nf* (*SAm*) prickly pear.

chumbo[1] *nm* prickly pear (*fruit*); *see* **higo**.

chumbo[2] *nm* (*RPl*) shot, pellet.

chumeco *nm* (*CAm*) apprentice; helper, mate.

chunco *adj* (*CAm, Col*) =**choco**[3].

chuncho (*Per*) 1 *adj* savage; rustic. 2 *nm*, **chuncha** *nf* savage Indian.

chunga *nf* (*fam*) joke; fun, banter; **contar** —s to crack jokes (*fam*); **estar de** — to be in a merry mood; **decir algo de** — to say something banteringly; **tomar las cosas en** — to take things as a joke.

chungar [1h], **chunguear** [1a] *vi and* **chungarse**, **chunguearse** *vr* (*fam*) to gag, crack jokes (*fam*), be in a merry mood; to banter; — **de uno** to have a bit of fun with someone, make fun of someone.

chuño *nm* (*SAm*) (dish made with) potato starch.

chupa[1] *nf*: **poner a uno como** — **de dómine** to give someone a tremendous ticking off; to shower insults on someone; **en la prensa le pusieron como** — **de dómine** they gave him a tremendous pasting in the press (*sl*).

chupa[2] *nf* (a) (*SAm*) drunkenness. (b) (*Pan*) bag.

chupada *nf* suck; (*at pipe etc*) pull, puff; —s sucking, suction; **dar** —s **a la pipa** to puff away at one's pipe.

chupado *adj* (a) *person* skinny, gaunt; emaciated; — **de cara** with a gaunt face, lantern-jawed.
(b) *skirt* tight.
(c) **estar** — **de frío** to be pinched with cold.
(d) (*SAm*) **estar** — to be drunk.

chupador *nm* (a) teething ring; teat (*of bottle*). (b) (*SAm*) drunkard. (c) (*SAm*) smoker.

chupaflor *nm* (*CR, PR, Ven*) hummingbird.

chupalla *nf* (*Chi, Mex*) straw hat.

chupamirto *nm* (*Mex, PR*) hummingbird.

chupantina *nf* (*RPl*) boozy party.

chupar [1a] 1 *vt* (a) to suck; to suck out, suck up; to absorb, take in, take up; *drink* to sip; *essence etc* to extract; *breast, toffee etc* to suck; *pipe etc* to suck, smoke, puff at; *stamp etc* to lick, moisten (with one's tongue).
(b) (*SAm*) to smoke.
(c) (*SAm*) to drink (*esp* to excess).
(d) (*fig*) to milk; to sap; **le chupan el dinero** they are milking him (of his money); **el trabajo le chupa la salud** his work is undermining his health.
2 *vi* to suck.
3 **chuparse** *vr* (a) (*fam*) **¡chúpate eso!** put that in your pipe and smoke it! (*fam*).
(b) — **el dedo** to suck one's finger; *see also* **dedo**.
(c) (*SAm*) — **un insulto** to put up with an insult, swallow an affront.
(d) (*Med*) to waste away, decline, get thin.
(e) (*Ven*) to get scared.

chupatintas *nm*, *pl* **chupatintas** (*pej*) penpusher, scribe.

chupe *nm* (*SAm*) a typical spicy soup.

chupcta *nf* (*Naut*) roundhouse.

chupete *nm* (a) dummy, pacifier (*US*); teat (*of bottle*); (*SAm*) lollipop. (b) (*SAm*) suck. (c) **de** — *see* **rechupete**.

chupo *nm* (a) (*SAm: Med*) boil. (b) (*Col*) baby's bottle.

chupón *nm* (a) (*Bot*) sucker.
(b) (*fam*) sponger (*fam*), hanger-on, parasite; swindler.
(c) lollipop, sucking sweet; — **de caramelo** toffee apple.
(d) (*SAm*) dummy, pacifier (*US*); teething ring; baby's bottle.
(e) (*Col, PR*) puff, pull (*at pipe etc*).
(f) (*Col: Med*) boil.

churdón *nm* raspberry; raspberry cane; raspberry jam.

chureca *nf* sweet pea.

churo[1] *adj* (*Arg, Bol*) handsome, attractive.

churo[2] *nm* (a) (*Bol, Ec, Per*) coiled wind instrument. (b) (*Ec*) spiral staircase. (c) (*Ec*) curl.

churrasco *nm* (*Bol, Chi, RPl*) barbecue, barbecued meat; (*Arg*) steak, choice piece of meat.

churrasquear [1a] *vt* (*RPl*) *meat* to barbecue, roast; to prepare; *barbecued meat* to eat.

churre *nf* thick grease; filth.

churrería *nf* fritter stall.

churrero *nm*, **churrera** *nf* fritter maker, fritter seller.

churrete *nm* grease spot, dirty mark.

churretear [1a] *vt* (*SAm*) to spot, stain, dirty.

churrias *nfpl* (*Col, Guat, SD*) diarrhoea.

churriento *adj* (a) greasy; filthy. (b) (*SAm: Med*) loose.

churrigueresco *adj* (a) (*Archit*) baroque. (b) (*fig*) excessively ornate, flowery; flashy.

churro 1 *adj* *wool* coarse; *sheep* coarse-wooled.
2 *nm* (a) (*Cook*) fritter.
(b) (*fam*) botch, mess; **el dibujo ha salido un** — the sketch came out all wrong, he messed up the drawing.
(c) (*fam*) fluke.

churrullero *adj* talkative, gossipy.

churruscar [1g] 1 *vt* to fry crisp; to burn, overdo. 2 *vi* to sizzle. 3 **churruscarse** *vr* to burn, do too much, get scorched.

churrusco[1] *nm* burnt toast.

churrusco[2] *adj* (*Col, Pan*) *hair* kinky, curly.

churumbela *nf* (a) (*Mus*) flageolet. (b) (*SAm*) maté cup; (*Col, Ec*) short-stemmed pipe. (c) (*Col*) worry, care.

chus: no decir — **ni mus** not to say a word.

chuscada *nf* funny remark, joke; coarse joke.

chusco *adj* (a) funny, droll; *person* coarse but amusing; *event* oddly amusing. (b) (*Per*) *dog* mongrel; *horse etc* ordinary; *person* coarse, ill-mannered.

chuse *nm* (*Arg*) coarse woollen cloth; (*Per*) blanket.

chusma *nf* rabble, mob, riffraff.

chusmaje *nm* (*SAm*) =**chusma**.

chuspa *nf* (*SAm*) bag, pouch.

chut *nm* (*Sport: angl*) shot (at goal).

chutar [1a] *vi* (*Sport: angl*) to shoot (at goal).

chuzar [1f] *vt* (*Col*) to prick; to sting, hurt.

chuzo *nm* (a) (*Mil, Hist*) pike; spiked stick, pointed stick; prick, goad; (*Chi*) pickaxe; (*Cu, Chi, PR*) whip; (*CAm: Orn*) beak; (*CAm: of scorpion*) sting; **aunque caigan** —s whatever the weather, (*fig*) come what may; **echar** —s (*fam*) to brag; **llover a** —s to rain cats and dogs, rain in torrents. (b) (*Per*) shoe.

chuzón *adj* (a) wily, sharp, cunning. (b) witty, amusing.

chuzonada *nf* piece of tomfoolery, piece of buffoonery.

D

dable *adj* possible, feasible, practicable; **no es —hacerlo** it is not possible to do it; **en lo que sea —** as far as possible, as far as is feasible.

daca *interj* hand it over!; **en — las pajas** in a jiffy; **andar al — y toma** to be at cross-purposes.

dacrón *nm* dacron.

dactilar *adj* finger (*attr*); **huella —, impresión —** fingerprint.

dactílico *adj* dactylic.

dáctilo *nm* dactyl.

dactilografía *nf* typing.

dactilógrafo *nm*, **dactilógrafa** *nf* typist.

dadaísmo *nm* dadaism.

dadista *nm* (*Mex*) gambler.

dádiva *nf* gift, present; (*fig*) sop.

dadivosidad *nf* generosity, lavishness with gifts.

dadivoso *adj* generous, open-handed, lavish with gifts.

dado¹ *nm* (**a**) (*in games*) die; **—s dice; el — está tirado** the die is cast. (**b**) (*Archit*) dado. (**c**) (*Mech*) block.

dado² *ptp* of **dar**: (**a**) **en un caso —** in a given case; **dada su corta edad** in view of his youth; **dadas estas circunstancias** since these circumstances exist, in view of these circumstances.

(**b**) **ser — a** to be given to; **es muy — a +** *infin* he is much given to + *ger*.

(**c**) **— que . . .** (*as conj*) provided that . . ., so long as . . .; given that . . ., granted that . . .

dador *nm*, **dadora** *nf* giver, donor; (*of letter*) bearer; (*Comm*) drawer; **— de sangre** blood donor.

Dafne *f* Daphne.

dafodelo *nm* (*angl*) daffodil.

daga *nf* dagger, stiletto; (*Mex, PR*) machete.

dagazo *nm* (*Mex, PR*) stab wound.

daifa *nf* mistress, concubine; prostitute.

dalia *nf* dahlia.

Dalmacia *f* Dalmatia.

daltoniano *adj* colour-blind.

daltonismo *nm* colour blindness.

dallar [1a] *vt* to scythe, mow with a scythe.

dalle *nm* scythe.

dama *nf* (**a**) (*in general*) lady; (*noble*) lady, gentlewoman; (*pej*) mistress, lover, concubine; **el poeta y su —** the poet and his lady, the poet and his mistress; **primera —** (*Theat*) leading lady; (*Pol*) first lady (*US*), president's wife; **— de honor** (*royal*) lady-in-waiting; (*at wedding*) bridesmaid, maid of honour; **— joven** (*Theat*) ingénue; **— regidora** carnival queen.

(**b**) (*Cards, Chess*) queen; (*Draughts*) king.

(**c**) **—s** (*game*) draughts, checkers (*US*).

damajuana *nf*, **damasana** *nf* (*SAm*) demijohn.

Damasco Damascus.

damasco *nm* (**a**) damask. (**b**) (*Bot*) damson; (*SAm*) apricot.

damasquinado *adj*, **damasquino** *adj* (*Tcch*) damask; damascene.

damasquinar [1a] *vt* (*Tech*) to damask.

damesana *nf* (*SAm*) demijohn.

damisela *nf* (*Hist*) damsel; (*pej*) courtesan, prostitute.

damita *nf* (*CAm*) young lady.

damnificar [1g] *vt* to injure, harm; to disable; to harm the interests of; **los damnificados** (*in accident etc*) the victims, those affected, those who have suffered loss.

Dámocles *m* Damocles.

dancing ['dansin] *nm* (*esp SAm: angl-gall*) dance hall; night club.

dandi *nm* (*angl: Acad*), **dandy** *nm* (*angl*) dandy, fop.

danés **1** *adj* Danish. **2** *nm*, **danesa** *nf* Dane. **3** *nm* (*language*) Danish.

Daniel *m* Daniel.

danta *nf* (*CAm, Col, Mex*) tapir.

dantesco *adj* (**a**) of Dante, relating to Dante. (**b**) (*fig*) Dantesque; horrific, weird, macabre.

Danubio *nm* Danube.

danza *nf* (**a**) (*in general*) dancing; (*una —*) dance; **— de espadas** sword dance; **— de figuras** square-dance; **— guerrera** war dance; **— de la muerte** dance of death.

(**b**) (*fam*) shady affair, suspect deal; mess; **meterse en la —** to get caught up in a shady affair.

(**c**) (*fam*) row, rumpus (*fam*); **armar una —** to kick up a row.

danzante *nm*, **danzanta** *nf* (**a**) dancer. (**b**) (*fam*) hustler, live wire, person who is always on the go; (*pej*) busybody. (**c**) (*fam*) scatterbrain.

danzar [1f] **1** *vt* to dance. **2** *vi* (**a**) to dance (*also fig*). (**b**) (*fam*) to meddle; to butt in, shove one's oar in.

danzarín *nm*, **danzarina** *nf* (**a**) dancer; artistic dancer, professional dancer. (**b**) = **danzante** (**b**) and (**c**).

dañado *adj* (**a**) damaged; spoiled; bad. (**b**) (*fig*) bad, wicked, evil.

dañar [1a] **1** *vt* to damage, harm, hurt; to spoil. **2** **dañarse** *vr* to get damaged, get hurt; to spoil; to rot, go bad; (*Med*) to hurt oneself, do oneself harm.

dañinear [1a] *vt* (**a**) (*Chi*) = **dañar**. (**b**) (*Arg*) to steal.

dañino **1** *adj* harmful; damaging; injurious; **animales —s** vermin, pests, injurious creatures. **2** *nm* (*Arg*) thief.

daño *nm* (**a**) damage; hurt, harm, injury; **en — de** to the detriment of; **por mi —** to my cost; **hacer — a** to damage, harm; (*Med*) to hurt, injure; *stomach* to upset; **no hace —** it doesn't hurt; **el ajo me hace —** garlic disagrees with me; **hacerse —** to hurt oneself, do oneself an injury; **se hizo — en el pie** he hurt his foot.

(**b**) (*Med*) trouble; **los médicos no saben dónde está el —** the doctors cannot tell where the trouble is.

(**c**) (*Law*) **—s y perjuicios** damages.

(**d**) (*SAm*) witchcraft.

dañoso *adj* harmful, bad, injurious; **— para** harmful to, bad for.

dar [1r] **1** *vt* (**a**) (*general sense*) to give; *object* to give, hand, pass (*a* to); *message* to give, deliver; *notice, warning* to give; *permission* to give, grant, concede; *example* to set; *step* to take; *ride, walk* to take, go for; *blow* to give, deal, fetch, strike; *beating* to give; *cry* to give, utter; *sigh* to fetch, heave; *battle* to fight; **ir dando cuerda** to pay out a rope, let out a rope; **— los buenos días a uno** to wish (*or* bid) someone good-day; **— de comer a uno** to give someone something to eat; **nos daban garbanzos** they gave us chickpeas (to eat); **ahí me las den todas** that won't bother me, I can cope with everything; **por si vienen mal dadas** in case of emergency, (*save etc*) for a rainy day.

(**b**) *crop, profit etc* to yield, bear, produce, give; **dan un 7 por 100 de interés** they yield 7% interest, they bear interest at 7%.

(**c**) (*Cards*) to deal.

(**d**) *feeling* to give, cause, produce; *pleasure* to give; *pity* to cause, excite, arouse; **le dio un fuerte dolor de costado** he felt a sharp pain in his side.

(**e**) (*Theat etc*) to do, perform, put on.

(**f**) (*time*) to strike; **el reloj dio las 3** the clock struck 3; **han dado las 4, son las 4 dadas** it's past 4 o'clock.

(**g**) **— como, — por** to consider, regard, assume; **lo dio como cierto** he regarded it as certain, he considered it definite; **lo daba por bien empleado** he considered it well spent; **lo podremos — por terminado** we shall be able to consider it finished.

(**h**) **— de barniz a** to varnish; **— de jalbegue a** to whitewash.

(i) — **a uno de puñetazos** to punch someone.

(j) —**la de** to brag of being; to set oneself up as; **la da de poeta** he tries to make out he's a poet.

(k) **¡dale!** (*Boxing etc*) hit him!; (*in chase*) after him!; (*Sport etc*) come on!; get on with it!; (*iro*) just look at him!, what an idiot!; **¡y dale!** there he goes again!; **¡dale que dale!** you do carry one so!, stop harping on it!

(l) **lo mismo da** it's all the same, it makes no difference; **lo mismo me da** it's all the same to me; **¡qué más da!** what does it matter!; never mind!; **¡qué más da un sitio que otro!** surely one place is as good as another!

(m) *for very many phrases and idioms, see the noun entry etc*; *eg* **caza, grito, paseo, conocer, entender** etc.

2 *vi* (a) — **a** (*of window*) to look out on, look on to, overlook; (*of house*) to face, face towards; — **sobre** to overlook.

(b) — **a la bomba** to pump, work the pump.

(c) — **con** *person etc* to meet, run into, find; *idea, solution etc* to hit on; to run across; — **con algo en el suelo** to knock something to the ground, drop something; **dio con la cabeza contra la pared** he banged his head on the wall; **no doy con el nombre** I can't think of the name.

(d) — **consigo en** to end up in, land in; **dio consigo en la cárcel** he ended up in jail.

(e) — **contra** to hit (against), knock against, bang into; **el barco dio con el puente** the ship crashed into the bridge, the ship struck the bridge.

(f) — **de cabeza** to fall on one's head; — **de narices** to fall flat on one's face; — **de narices contra la puerta** to bang one's face on the door.

(g) — **en** + *infin* to take to + *ger*, get into the habit of + *ger*.

(h) — **en** *floor etc* to hit, strike; *target* to hit, land on; *solution* to hit on; *error* to fall into; *joke* to catch on to, see, get the point of; — **en ello** to see the point, get it; **el sol le daba en la cara** the sun was shining straight into her face.

(i) **le da por** + *infin* he takes it into his head to + *infin*, he decides to + *infin*; he persists in + *ger*; **le ha dado por no venir a clase** he has begun to cut classes; **al chico le daba por dormirse en clase** the boy was apt to go to sleep in class; **les dio por venir a vernos** they took it into their heads to come and see us.

(j) — **tras uno** to pursue someone vigorously, set off after someone.

(k) — **de sí** (*of cloth etc*) to give, stretch; (*Agr etc*) to bear heavily, yield well, produce a lot.

3 darse *vr* (a) to surrender, give in; to give oneself up (*a* to).

(b) — **a** to take to; to devote oneself to; (*pej*) to abandon oneself to; — **a la bebida** to take to drink; — **a creer que** . . . to take to thinking that . . .

(c) (*event*) to happen; **si se da el caso** if that happens.

(d) (*Bio etc*) to exist, occur, be found; **la planta no se da en el sur** the plant is not found in the south.

(e) (*Agr*) to grow, come up; **el cultivo se da bien este año** the crop is coming on well this year.

(f) — **por** to consider oneself (as); — **por ofendido** to take offence; — **por perdido** to give oneself up for lost; — **por vencido** to give up, acknowledge defeat.

(g) —**las de** to pose as, fancy oneself as; **nunca me las di de experto** I never claimed to be an expert.

(h) **no se me da mal** I'm not doing too badly.

(i) **no se me da un bledo** (**or higo, rábano** *etc*) I don't care two hoots (*de* about).

(j) *for many phrases and idioms, see the noun entry, eg* **prisa, tono.**

Dardanelos *mpl* Dardanelles.

dardo *nm* dart, shaft.

dares *nmpl:* — **y tomares** (*fam*) arguments, bickering; **andar en** — **y tomares con uno** to bicker with someone, squabble with someone.

Darío *m* Darius.

dársena *nf* dock; basin, inner harbour; — **de marea** tidal basin.

darviniano, darwiniano *adj* Darwinian.

darvinismo, darwinismo *nm* Darwinism.

data *nf* (a) date. (b) (*Comm*) item.

datar [1a] **1** *vt* to date, put a date on. **2** *vi:* — **de** to date from, date back to; **esto data de muy atrás** this dates back a long time, this goes a long way back.

dátil *nm* (*Bot*) date.

datilera *nf* date palm.

dativo *nm* dative.

dato *nm* fact, datum, piece of information; **un** — **interesante** an interesting fact; —**s data, facts, information; no tenemos todos los** —**s** we do not have all the facts; —**s estadísticos** statistical information, statistical data, statistics; —**s personales** personal particulars, details about oneself.

David *m* David.

de *prep* (a) (*possession*) of; **el coche** — **mi amigo** the car of my friend, my friend's car; **los coches** — **mis amigos** my friends' cars; **es** — **ellos** it's theirs; **la señora** — **Pérez** Mrs Pérez; **el interés del préstamo** the interest on the loan.

(b) (*superlative*) in; **el peor alumno** — **la clase** the worst pupil in the class; **es el coche más caro del mercado** it's the dearest car on the market.

(c) (*value*) **una moneda** — **a 5 pesos** a 5-peso coin; **un pan** — **a libra** a pound loaf.

(d) (*origin, distance*) from; **es** — **Calatayud** she's from Calatayud; **Dolores no es** — **aquí** Dolores is not from these parts; **los** — **Madrid son los mejores** those from Madrid are the best, the Madrid ones are the best; — **A a B hay 5 kms** it is 5 kms from A to B; **ir** — **A a Z** to go from A to Z; **altura del suelo** height above ground; — **puerta en puerta** from door to door; **bajar la escalera** — **4 en 4** to go down 4 stairs at a time; — **esto se deduce que** . . . from this one deduces that . . .; **tiene 3 hijos** — **su primera mujer** he has 3 children by his first wife; **el camino** — **Elche** the Elche road, the road to Elche.

(e) (*apposition*) of; **la ciudad** — **Caracas** the city of Caracas.

(f) (*partitive*) of; **uno** — **nosotros** one of us.

(g) (*numerals*) **3** — **cada 4** 3 in every 4, 3 out of every 4.

(h) (*subject*) **una clase** — **francés** a French class; **un libro** — **biología** a biology book, a book about (or on) biology; **no sé nada** — **él** I don't know anything about (or of, concerning) him; **hablaba** — **política** he was talking about politics.

(i) (*material*) of; **una cadena** — **oro** a chain of gold, a gold(en) chain.

(j) (*content*) of; **una tacita** — **café** a cup of coffee.

(k) (*age*) of; **un chico** — **15 años** a boy of 15, a 15-year old boy.

(l) (*profession*) by; **es abogado** — **profesión** he's a lawyer by profession.

(m) (*authorship*) by, of; **un libro** — **Cela** a book by Cela, a book of Cela's.

(n) (*purpose*) **goma** — **mascar** chewing gum; **máquina** — **coser** sewing machine.

(o) (*powered by*) **cocina** — **gas** gas stove; **este modelo es** — **electricidad** this model works on electricity, this is an electric model.

(p) (*manner, style*) in; **amueblado** — **roble** furnished in oak; **vestido** — **azul** dressed in blue; **pintado** — **negro** painted (in) black.

(q) (*means*) at, in, with; — **un salto** at one bound, with one jump; — **un trago** at a gulp.

(r) (*cause*) with; **estar loco** — **contento** to be crazy with joy; **saltar** — **alegría** to jump for joy; **morir** — **hambre** to die of (or from) starvation, starve to death; **estar enfermo** — **gripe** to be ill with flu; **no poder moverse** — **miedo** to be unable to move for (or with) fright; — **puro cansado** out of sheer tiredness.

(s) (*with respect to*) in; **mejor** — **salud** better in health; **paralizado** — **las dos piernas** paralysed in both legs.

(t) (*descriptive*) with; **la niña** — **pelo largo** the girl with long hair; **ese tío del sombrero** that chap with (or in) a hat.

(u) (*in the quality of*) as; — **niño** as a child; when a child; "**el gran actor, — Segismundo**" (*caption*) "the great actor as Segismundo".

(v) (*passive agent*) by; **una persona amada** — **todos** a person loved by all, a person beloved of all.

(w) (*time*) at, in, by; **a las 7** — **la mañana** at 7 o'clock, at 7 a.m.; **muy** — **mañana** very early in the morning; — **día** by day, during the day(time); — **noche** at night, by night, in the night time.

(x) (*conditional*) if; — **no poder encontrarlo** if we can't find it; — **no ser así** if it were not so, were it not so.

(y) (*after* **más, menos**) than; **más** — **7** more than 7.

(z) (*idioms*) **aquel burro** — **ministro** that ass of a minister; **el pobre** — **Pedro** poor old Peter; **el bueno** — **Juan** good old John; *for many other phrases, see noun entry etc, eg* **pie, prisa.**

dé *see* **dar.**

deambular [1a] *vi* to saunter, stroll, wander (*por* along, about in, through).

deambulatorio *nm* (*Eccl*) ambulatory.

deán nm (Eccl) dean.

debacle nf (gall: hum) débâcle, disaster.

debajo 1 adv (also por —) underneath, below; on the underside.

2 — de prep under; below, beneath; — de la mesa under the table, underneath the table; por — de under; below.

debate nm debate (also Parl); discussion, argument.

debatir[1] [3a] vt to debate (also Parl); to discuss, argue about.

debatir[2] [3a] vi and **debatirse** vr (gall) to struggle; to writhe; to flail about.

debe nm debit, debit side (of account); — y haber debit and credit; **asentar algo al — de uno** to debit something to someone.

debelador nm conqueror.

deber [2a] **1** vt to owe; **me debes 5 dólares** you owe me 5 dollars; **el respeto que todos deben a la patria** the respect which everybody owes to his country; **esto lo debe a influencia francesa** he owes this to French influence.

2 vi (a) **debo hacerlo** I must do it, I have to do it; I ought to do it; **no debes comer tanto** you shouldn't eat so much; **debiera ir** he ought to go, he should go; **deberá cambiarse cada mes** (instruction) it should be changed every month; **debíamos partir ayer** we were to have left yesterday; **he debido perderlo** I must have lost it; **hubieras debido traerlo** you ought to have brought it, you should have brought it.

(b) **debe de ser así** it must be like that; that must be it; **debe de hacer mucho frío allí** it must be pretty cold there; **debe de ser brasileño** he must be a Brazilian; **no debe de ser muy caro** it can't be very dear; **debe de haber ido** he must have gone; **debió de perderlo** he must have lost it.

3 deberse vr: — **a** to be owing to, be due to, be on account of; **se debe al mal tiempo** it's on account of the bad weather; **se debe a que no hay carbón** it is because (of the fact that) there's no coal; **puede — a que . . .** it may be because . . .; **¿a qué se debe esto?** what is the explanation of this?, why is this?

4 nm (a) duty, obligation; **últimos —es** last rites; **cumplir con un —** to perform a duty, carry out a duty.

(b) (Fin) debt.

(c) **—es** (School) homework; task, assignment.

debidamente adv properly, as one should (or as it should be etc); in due form, duly; **si te conduces —** if you behave properly; **un documento — redactado** a properly drawn document.

debido adj (a) proper, due, just; right, correct; **en debida forma** duly, in due form; **con el — respeto** with due respect; **como es —, según es —** as is (only) proper, as is right; **un padre como es — no haría eso** a true father would not do that.

(b) — **a** owing to, due to, because of; — **a ello** because of this; — **a la falta de agua** because of the water shortage; — **a que no hay plátanos** because (of the fact that) there are no bananas.

débil adj (in most senses) weak; (in body) weak, feeble, frail; health poor; character weak; effort etc feeble; half-hearted; cry faint, feeble, weak; light dim, wan, weak.

debilidad nf (a) weakness; feebleness; faintness; dimness; — **senil** senility, senile decay.

(b) (una —) weakness; **tener una — por el chocolate** to have a weakness for chocolate; **tener una — por uno** to have a soft spot for someone.

debilitación nf weakening, debilitation, enfeeblement.

debilitar [1a] **1** vt to weaken, debilitate; resistance etc to weaken, impair, lower. **2 debilitarse** vr to grow weak(er), weaken.

débilmente adv weakly; feebly; half-heartedly; faintly; dimly, wanly.

debitar [1a] vt (Comm: angl) to debit.

débito nm (Comm: angl) debit; debt.

debocar [1g] vti (SAm) to vomit.

Deborá f Deborah.

debut [de'βu] nm, **debuts** [de'βus] (gall) début.

debutanta nf, **debutante** nf (gall) débutante.

debutar [1a] vi (gall) to make one's début.

década nf decade; set of ten, series of ten.

decadencia nf decadence, decline, decay; **estar en franca —** to be in full decline.

decadente adj decadent; effete.

decaer [2o] vi to decay, decline; (of effort) to flag, weaken; (of fashion) to wane; (of business) to fall off; (in health) to decline, sink, fail; — **de ánimo** to lose heart; **ella ha decaído en belleza** her beauty is not what it was; **decayó de poderío** his power declined.

decagramo nm decagramme, decagram (US).

decaimiento nm decay; decline; weakening, weakness; warning; falling-off; — **de ánimo** discouragement, depression.

decalitro nm decalitre, decaliter (US).

decálogo nm decalogue.

decámetro nm decametre, decameter (US).

decanato nm deanship; deanery.

decano nm (a) (Univ etc) dean. (b) (in group, of press etc) doyen, senior member.

decantar[1] [1a] vt (lit) to praise, laud; **el tan decantado edificio** (iro) this building which has been so effusively praised.

decantar[2] [1a] vt wine etc to decant; to pour off; sediment to leave behind, form, deposit.

decapitar [1a] vt to behead, decapitate.

decasílabo 1 adj decasyllabic, ten-syllable. **2** nm decasyllable.

decena nf (about) ten; —**s** (Math) tens; **una — de barcos** about ten ships, some ten ships; —**s de miles de españoles** tens of thousands of Spaniards; **contar por —s** to count in tens; **vender por —s** to sell in tens.

decenal adj decennial.

decencia nf (a) decency; seemliness, decorum; respectability; modesty; **faltar a la —** to offend against decency. (b) cleanness, tidiness.

decenio nm decade.

decente adj (a) decent; seemly, proper; respectable; modest. (b) clean, tidy. (c) (Per) respectable, middle-class, white, non-Indian.

decentemente adv (a) decently; properly; respectably; modestly. (b) tidily.

decepción nf disappointment.

decepcionante adj disappointing.

decepcionar [1a] vt to disappoint.

deceso nm (SAm) decease, passing.

decibel nm, **decibelio** nm decibel.

decible adj expressible; communicable; **eso no es —** that cannot be told; that cannot be expressed.

decididamente adv decidedly.

decidido adj decided, determined; resolute; emphatic.

decidir [3a] **1** vt (a) person to decide, persuade, convince; **esto le decidió a dejarlo** this decided him to give it up; **esto por fin le decidió** this finally made his mind up (for him).

(b) outcome, question to decide, settle, resolve.

2 vi to decide (de, en about); — + infin to decide to + infin; — **en favor de uno** to decide in someone's favour; — **sobre cuál conviene más** to decide which is more suitable.

3 decidirse vr to decide, make up one's mind (a + infin to + infin).

decidor 1 adj (a) witty, amusing, racy. (b) fluent, eloquent. **2** nm (a) wit, witty talker. (b) fluent speaker, eloquent speaker.

décima nf (a) (Math) tenth; tenth part (esp of a lottery ticket). (b) (Eccl) tithe. (c) (Lit: Hist) a ten-line stanza.

decimación nf decimation.

decimal 1 adj decimal. **2** nm decimal. **3** nf: — **periódica pura** recurring decimal.

décimo 1 adj tenth. **2** nm tenth.

decimoctavo adj eighteenth.

decimocuarto adj fourteenth.

decimonónico adj (hum or pej) nineteenth-century (attr); Victorian; (fig) outdated, antiquated.

decimonono adj, **decimonoveno** adj nineteenth.

decimoquinto adj fifteenth.

decimoséptimo adj seventeenth.

decimosexto adj sixteenth.

decimotercio adj, **decimotercero** adj thirteenth.

decir 1 [3p] vti (a) (general senses) to say; to tell; (SAm) to speak; (of text) to say, read; fortune to tell; lie to tell; truth to speak, tell; mass to say; nonsense etc to talk; **no dijo nada** he said nothing; **¿quién te lo dijo?** who told you?; **dicen que . . .** they say that . . ., people say that . . .; — **a uno que se calle** to tell someone to be quiet; **nos dijo que fuéramos** he told us to go.

(b) (idioms: general) **¿digo algo?** have I said something?; **eso digo** that's what I say; that's just what I'm saying; **¡digo, digo!** hey!, say!; just listen to this!; now wait a minute!; **pero digo mal "decadent"** but I am wrong to say (or to call them etc) "decadent"; **pero dice mal** but he is wrong; **y dice bien** and he is right; **no lo digo por ti** I'm not referring to you, I'm not getting at you; — **que no** to say no; — **que sí** to say yes; — **para sí,** — **entre sí** to say to oneself; **como quien dice, como si dijéramos** so to speak; in a way, more or less; **como quien no dice nada** quite casually; as though it wasn't important; **¿cómo ha dicho Vd?** what did you say?.

pardon?; **¿decía Vd?** you were saying?; **¿cómo diríamos?** how shall I put it?; **¡lo que he dicho!** I stand by what I said!; **¡quién lo diría!** would you believe it!; did you ever? (*fam*).

(c) (*idioms with infin*) **es** — that is to say; **ya es** — that's saying a lot, that's a big claim to make; **me permito** — **que** . . . I submit that . . ., I venture to say that . . .; **querer** — to mean; **¿qué quiere** — "**spatha**"? what does "spatha" mean?; **¿qué quiere Vd** — **con eso?** what do you mean by that?; **dar que** — (**a la gente**) to make people talk, set the tongues wagging; **no sé qué** — I don't know what to say; **no hay más que** — there's no more to be said about it; **no hay que** — **que** . . ., **ni que** — **tiene que** . . . it goes without saying that . . .; **¡no hay para qué** — of course . . .; — **por** — to talk for talking's sake; **o por mejor** — or rather; **por** —**lo así** so to speak.

(d) (*idioms with future*) **dirá Vd aquel otro** you must mean that other one; **Vd dirá** it's for you to say; (*pouring drink*) how much do you like?, say when (*fam*); **ello dirá** the event will show; **el qué dirán** public opinion, what people will say; **pero no quiso por el qué dirán** but she didn't want to because of what people might say; **el maldito "qué dirán"** the curse of concern for what people will think.

(e) (*idioms with subjunctive*) **¡diga!**, **¡dígame!** (*Tel*) hullo?; **digan lo que digan** whatever they (may) say; **let them say what they please**; **digámoslo así** so to speak; for want of a better word; **¡no me digas!** you don't say!; well I'm blowed!; come off it!; **¡y que lo digas!** you can say that again!; **y no digamos de** . . . not to mention . . .; **no estuvo muy cortés, que digamos** actually he wasn't all that polite, he wasn't what you could call polite; **no es un pintor, que digamos** he's not what you could really call a painter; **es, digamos, un comerciante** he's a sort of dealer, he's a dealer . . . for want of a better word.

(f) (*idioms with ptp*) **mejor dicho** rather; **no es para dicho** it's not fit to be told; **¡lo dicho dicho!** I stand by what I said!; **¡dicho y hecho!** no sooner said than done!; **¡haberlo dicho!** you might have told me!

(g) to show, indicate, reveal; **su cara dice lo que es** his face shows him up for what he is; **una situación que tan mal dice de nuestro gobierno** a situation which shows our government up in such a bad light.

(h) (*fam*) to call; **al niño le dicen Anastasio** they call the child Anastasio.

(i) to suit; — **con** to go with, match; **el vestido le dice bien** the dress suits her (nicely); **el color dice bien con su cutis** the colour goes with (or suits, harmonizes with) her complexion.

2 decirse *vr* (a) **yo sé lo que me digo** I know what I'm talking about; I know what I'm up to.

(b) to be called, be named; **esta plaza se dice de la Revolución** this is called Revolution Square; **¿cómo se dice en inglés "cursi"?** what's the English for "cursi"?, how do you say "cursi" in English?

(c) **se dice** it is said, they say, people say; the story goes . . .; **se me ha dicho que** . . . I have been told that . . .; **no se diría eso ahora** that could not be said nowadays.

(d) **hablar portugués, lo que se dice hablar, no sé** I can't really talk Portuguese, I don't speak Portuguese at all well; **esto es lo que se dice un queso** this is a real cheese, this is what you really call a cheese.

3 *nm* saying; witty remark; **es un** — it's just a phrase; **if I may use the expression** . . .; I was only thinking aloud; **a** — **de todos** by all accounts; **al** — **de X** according to X; as X has it, as X would have it.

decisión *nf* (a) (*una* —) decision; (*Law*) judgement; **forzar una** — to force the issue; **tomar una** — to make (*or* take) a decision.

(b) (*quality*) decisiveness; determination, resolution.

decisivo *adj* decisive; *argument, consideration* overriding; *vote* casting.

declamación *nf* (a) declamation; recital, recitation; (*quality*) delivery. (b) (*pej*) ranting.

declamador *nm* (a) orator; reciter. (b) (*pej*) ranter.

declamar [1a] **1** *vt* to declaim; *verse etc* to recite. **2** *vi* (a) to speak out, hold forth (*contra* against). (b) (*pej*) to rant, carry on.

declamatorio *adj* declamatory; (*pej*) ranting.

declaración *nf* (a) declaration; pronouncement, statement; explanation; (*to girl*) proposal (of marriage); — **de derechos** (*Pol*) bill of rights; — **de ingresos**, — **de renta**, — **fiscal** (*Mex*) income tax return.

(b) (*Cards*) bid.

(c) (*Law*) statement; evidence; — **de culpabilidad** confession of guilt; — **jurada** sworn statement, affidavit; **prestar** — to make a statement; to give evidence; **tomar la** — **a uno** to take a statement from someone.

declaradamente *adv* confessedly, declaredly.

declarado *adj* confessed, declared.

declarante *nmf* (a) (*Law*) person making a statement, person giving evidence. (b) (*Cards*) bidder, declarer.

declarar [1a] **1** *vt* (a) to declare, state (*que* that); to explain, expound; (*at customs*) to declare; *war* to declare (*a* on).

(b) (*Cards*) to bid; — **2 picos** to bid 2 spades.

(c) (*Law*) to find; — **culpable a uno** to find someone guilty.

2 *vi* (a) to declare; **según él mismo declara** as he himself declares.

(b) (*Cards*) to bid, declare; **declaró menos de lo que tenía** he underbid.

(c) (*Law*) to make a statement; to testify, give evidence.

3 declararse *vr* (a) to declare oneself; to make one's opinion (*or* position *etc*) known; (*to girl*) to propose (*a* to); — **por** to come out in favour of, declare one's support for, side with.

(b) (*Law*) — **culpable** to plead guilty; — **inocente** to plead not guilty.

(c) (*epidemic, fire, war etc*) to break out.

declinable *adj* declinable.

declinación *nf* (a) decline, falling-off; decay. (b) (*Astron, Naut*) declination. (c) (*Gram*) declension.

declinar [1a] **1** *vt* (a) to decline, refuse; (*Law*) to reject.

(b) (*Gram*) to decline; to inflect.

2 *vi* (a) to decline, fall off, fall away; to decay; to deteriorate; (*of day*) to draw to a close.

(b) (*of ground*) to slope (away, down).

(c) (*Gram*) to decline.

declive *nm* (a) slope, incline, declivity; pitch; (*Rail*) gradient; **tierra en** — sloping ground, land on a slope; **estar en** — to slope.

(b) (*fig: Fin etc*) slump (*also* — **económico**).

decocción *nf* decoction.

decolorar [1a] **1** *vt* to discolour, affect the colour of.

2 decolorarse *vr* to get discoloured, lose colour.

decomisar [1a] *vt* to seize, confiscate.

decoración *nf* (a) decoration; — **de escaparate** window display; — **de escaparates** window dressing; — **del hogar**, — **de interiores** interior decorating.

(b) (*also* —**es**: *Theat*) scenery, set.

decorado *nm* (*Cine, Theat*) scenery, set.

decorador *nm*, **decoradora** *nf* decorator.

decorar[1] [1a] *vt* to decorate, adorn (*de* with).

decorar[2] [1a] *vt* to learn, memorize.

decorativo *adj* decorative, ornamental.

decoro *nm* (a) decorum, propriety, decency; proprieties; — **virginal** maidenly modesty. (b) honour, respect.

decorosamente *adv* decorously.

decoroso *adj* decorous, proper, decent; seemly; modest.

decrecer [2d] *vi* to decrease, diminish; (*of flood, water*) to go down; (*of days*) to get shorter, draw in.

decreciente *adj* decreasing, diminishing.

decrecimiento *nm*, **decremento** *nm* decrease, diminution; fall; shortening.

decrépito *adj* decrepit.

decrepitud *nf* decrepitude.

decretar [1a] *vt* (a) to decree, order, ordain; — **que** . . . to decree that . . . (b) *prize* to award (*a* to). (c) (*Mex*) *dividend* to declare.

decreto *nm* decree, order; (*Parl*) act.

decreto-ley *nm*, *pl* **decretos-leyes** bill, law.

decúbito *nm* (*Med*): — **prono** prone position; — **supino** supine position; **úlcera de** — bedsore.

decuplar [1a] *vt*, **decuplicar** [1g] *vt* to multiply tenfold, increase tenfold.

décuplo 1 *adj* tenfold. **2** *nm*: **es el** — **de lo que era** it is ten times what it was, it has increased tenfold.

decurso *nm* (*lit*): **en el** — **de los años** over the years; **en el** — **del tiempo** in the course of time.

dedada *nf* thimbleful; (*fig*) very small quantity, very modest amount; (*of jam etc*) spot, dab, drop; (*of snuff*) pinch; **dar una** — **de miel a uno** (*fig*) to give someone a slight hope.

dedal *nm* (a) thimble. (b) (*fig*) thimbleful.

dedalera *nf* foxglove.

dédalo *nm* (a) labyrinth. (b) (*fig*) tangle, mess.

dedicación *nf* (a) dedication; (*fig*) dedication, devotion (*a* to).

(b) (*Eccl*) consecration.

(c) estar en (régimen de) — exclusiva (or **plena**), **trabajar con — plena** to work full-time; "**— plena**" (advert) "full-time".

dedicar [1g] **1** vt **(a)** to dedicate (a to); (Eccl) to consecrate; book to dedicate (a to), copy to autograph, inscribe, write in.
(b) effort, time to devote, give (a to); **dedico un día a la semana a pescar** I spend one day a week fishing; **tengo que — mucho tiempo a eso** I have to give up a lot of time to that.
2 dedicarse vr: **— a** to devote oneself to; to go in for, take up; **— a** + infin to devote oneself to + ger; **se dedicó a la cerámica** he devoted himself to pottery, he took up pottery; **¿a qué se dedica Vd?** what do you do?; what's your line?, what business are you in?

dedicatoria nf inscription, dedication.
dedicatorio adj dedicatory.
dedil nm fingerstall.
dedillo nm: **saber algo al —** to have something at one's fingertips; **saber una lección al —** to have a lesson off pat; **dijo la lista al —** he rattled off the list with complete accuracy.
dedo nm **(a)** finger; **— (del pie)** toe; **— anular** ring finger; **— auricular, — meñique** little finger; **— del corazón, — cordial** middle finger; **— chico** little toe; **— gordo** big toe; **— índice** index finger, forefinger; **— pulgar** thumb; **ligero de —s** light-fingered; **comerse** (or **morderse**) **los —s** to get very impatient; **contar con los —s** to count on one's fingers; **chuparse los —s** to eat with relish; (fig) to smack one's lips; to rub one's hands; **dale un — y se toma hasta el codo** give him an inch and he'll take a yard; **entrar a —** to get in (or get a job) by pulling strings; **se le escapó de entre los —s** it slipped through his fingers; **hacer —s** (Mus) to practise, do scales; **no se mama el —** he's pretty smart; **meterse los —s en la nariz** to put one's fingers to one's nose; **meter el — en la boca a uno** to try to get someone to talk; **poner el — en** to put one's finger on, pinpoint, identify precisely; **poner el — en la llaga** to put one's finger on the spot; **señalar algo con el —** to point something out; **no se ven los —s de la mano** it's pitch-dark.
(b) (fig) spot, bit, drop; (as measure) finger; finger's breadth; **¡dos —s nada más!** (drink) just a tiny drop!; **estar a dos —s de** to be within an inch of, be within an ace of; to be on the verge of; **no tiene dos —s de frente** he's pretty dim; he's a lout.

deducción nf **(a)** deduction; inference. **(b)** (sum etc) deduction.
deducible (a) deducible, inferable (de from); **según es fácilmente —** as may readily be deduced. **(b)** (Fin etc) deductible; (for tax purposes) allowable.
deducir [3o] vt **(a)** to deduce, infer (de from); formula to deduce, derive. **(b)** sum etc to deduct; **deducidos los gastos** less charges. **(c)** (Arg) to produce.
deductivo adj deductive.
deescalación nf de-escalation.
defalcar [1g] vt =**desfalcar.**
defecación nf defecation.
defecar [1g] vi to defecate.
defección nf defection, desertion.
defectible adj fallible, imperfect; faulty.
defectivo adj defective (also Gram).
defecto nm fault, defect, flaw; (Elec, Tech) fault; (in manufacture, argument) flaw; (moral) shortcoming, failure; **— físico** physical defect; **— de fonación, — de la palabra** speech defect, impediment; **en — de** for lack of, for want of.
defectuosamente adv defectively, faultily.
defectuoso adj defective, faulty.
defender [2g] **1** vt to defend (contra against, de from); to protect; (Law) to defend; cause to champion, uphold; **para —los contra el frío** in order to protect them from the cold.
2 defenderse vr **(a)** to defend oneself (contra against, de from); **— bien** to resist firmly; to give a good account of oneself.
(b) (fig) **me defiendo en inglés** I can manage in English, I can get along in English, I can keep going in English; "**¿qué tal?**" . . . "**hombre, nos defendemos**" "how are things?" . . . "we're managing"; **— como un gato, — panza arriba** to get by but only just; to scrape through.
defendible adj defensible; that can be defended.
defensa 1 nf **(a)** defence (also Chess, Law, Sport); protection, shelter; **— contra, — de** defence against; **— pasiva** civil defence; **— en profundidad** defence in depth; **en — propia** in self-defence.
(b) (Naut) fender; (Sport) shinpad, leg pad; **— marítima** (Arg) sea wall.

(c) —s (Mil) defences, defensive works; **—s costeras** coastal defences.
2 nm (Sport) back, fullback.
defensiva nf defensive; **estar a la —** to be on the defensive.
defensivo 1 adj defensive. **2** nm defence, safeguard.
defensor nm, **defensora** nf defender; protector; (of cause) champion, upholder; (Law: also **abogado —**) defending counsel.
deferencia nf deference.
deferente adj deferential.
deferir [3l] **1** vt (Law) to refer, relegate (a to). **2** vi: **— a** to defer to.
deficiencia nf deficiency, shortcoming, defect (de in, of).
deficiente adj deficient, wanting (en in); defective.
déficit nm or **déficit** nm, pl **déficits** or **deficits** (Comm, Fin) deficit; (fig) lack, shortage; shortfall.
definible adj definable, that can be defined.
definición nf definition; **por —** by definition.
definido adj definite (also Gram); **bien —** well defined, clearly defined.
definir [3a] vt to define; to clarify, explain; to determine, establish.
definitivo adj definitive; final, ultimate; **en definitiva** definitively; finally, once and for all; in short.
deflación nf deflation.
deflacionar [1a] vt to deflate.
deflacionario adj, **deflacionista** adj deflationary.
deflector nm (Tech) baffle, baffle plate.
deformación nf deformation; (Radio etc) distortion; (Mech) strain; (of wood etc) warping.
deformar [1a] **1** vt to deform; to disfigure; (Radio etc) to distort; (Mech) to strain; wood etc to warp, push out of shape.
2 deformarse vr to become deformed; to get distorted; to warp, get out of shape, lose shape.
deforme adj deformed, misshapen; ugly; abnormal.
deformidad nf **(a)** deformity, malformation; abnormality. **(b)** (fig) (moral) shortcoming.
defraudación nf **(a)** defrauding; deceit; **— fiscal, — de impuestos** tax evasion. **(b)** dashing, disappointment.
defraudar [1a] vt **(a)** to cheat, defraud; to deceive; **— impuestos** to evade taxes, fiddle one's income tax (fam). **(b)** hopes to dash, disappoint, frustrate. **(c)** (Phys) light to intercept, cut off.
defuera adv (also **por —**) outwardly, on the outside.
defunción nf decease, demise.
degeneración nf **(a)** degeneration (en into). **(b)** (moral) degeneracy.
degenerado 1 adj degenerate. **2** nm degenerate, degenerate type.
degenerar [1a] vi to degenerate (en into); to decline, decay; to get worse, get more serious; **la manifestación degeneró en una sangrienta revuelta** the demonstration degenerated into a bloody disturbance.
deglución nf swallowing.
deglutir [3a] vti to swallow.
degollación nf throat cutting; (Law) beheading, execution; (wider sense) massacre, slaughter; **D— de los Inocentes** Massacre of the Innocents.
degolladero nm **(a)** (Anat) throat, neck, throttle.
(b) (Hist) scaffold, block (for executions); **ir al —** (fig) to expose oneself to mortal danger, (hum) put one's head in the lion's mouth, go to the chopping block.
(c) slaughterhouse.
degollador nm (Hist) executioner.
degollar [1n] vt **(a)** to cut (or slit) the throat of; (Law) to behead, decapitate; (fig) to massacre, slaughter.
(b) (fig) to destroy; play etc to murder, make nonsense of; part to make a dreadful hash of.
(c) (Sew) to cut low in the neck.
degradación nf **(a)** degradation; humiliation. **(b)** (Mil etc) demotion, reduction in rank.
degradante adj degrading.
degradar [1a] **1** vt **(a)** to degrade, debase; to humiliate. **(b)** (Mil etc) to demote, reduce in rank. **2 degradarse** vr to demean oneself.
degüello nm **(a)** =**degollación; entrar a — en una ciudad** to put the people of a city to the sword, give no quarter to the inhabitants of a town.
(b) (of weapon) shaft, neck, narrow part.
degustación nf tasting, sampling.
degustar [1a] vt to taste, sample.
dehesa nf pasture, meadow; pastureland, range.
deidad nf deity; divinity; **— pagana** pagan god, pagan deity.
deificación nf deification; apotheosis (also fig).

deificar [1g] *vt* (a) to deify; to apotheosize (*also fig*). (b) (*fig*) to exalt, over-praise, put on a pedestal.
deísmo *nm* deism.
deísta 1 *adj* deistic(al). 2 *nmf* deist.
dejación *nf* (a) (*Law*) abandonment, relinquishment. (b) (*CAm, Col*) carelessness.
dejadez *nf* (a) untidiness, slovenliness; abandon. (b) carelessness, negligence, neglect, slackness; laziness; supineness, lack of willpower.
dejado *adj* (a) untidy, slovenly; abandoned; unkempt. (b) careless, negligent, slack; lazy. (c) dejected. (d) — **de la mano de Dios** (*fig*) godforsaken; beyond all hope of redemption.
dejamiento *nm* =dejación (a); =dejadez.
dejar [1a] 1 *vt* (a) to leave; to forget, leave out; to leave, abandon, desert, forsake; *book etc* to lend; *effort, work etc* to give up, stop, abandon; *passenger* to put down, set down; to drop; (*Comm*) *balance etc* to show, leave; *profit* to produce, yield; — **aparte** to leave aside; — **atrás** to leave behind, outstrip, out-distance; (*fig*) to surpass; — **a uno muy atrás** to leave someone far behind; — **algo para mañana** to leave something till tomorrow, postpone (*or* put off) something till tomorrow; — **algo para después** to leave something till later; **lo dejamos por muy difícil** we gave it up because it was too hard; **lo dejamos por imposible** we gave it up as (being) impossible; **así que lo dejamos** so we gave it up; **¡— eso!** stop that, drop that!, chuck it!; **se lo dejo en la conserjería** I'll leave it for you at the porter's office; — **así las cosas** to leave things as they are; **dejémoslo así** let's leave it at that; **como dejo dicho** as I have said; **deja escritas 3 novelas** he left 3 novels which he had written; he left 3 finished novels; **deja mucho que desear** it leaves a lot to be desired.
(b) to let, allow; **quiero pero no me dejan** I want to but they won't let me; — **a uno** + *infin* to let someone + *infin*, allow someone to + *infin*; — **a uno entrar** to let someone in; **dejar a uno pasar** to let someone in (*or* through, past *etc*); — **a uno salir** to let someone out; — **que las cosas vayan de mal en peor** to let things go from bad to worse; — **que se enfríe** (*instruction*) let it get cold; *see* **caer, mano** *etc*.
2 *vi*: — **de** + *infin* (a) to stop + *ger*, leave off + *ger*, give up + *ger*; **dejó de cantar** she stopped singing; **cuando deje de llover** when it stops raining, when the rain stops; **no puedo** — **de fumar** I can't give up smoking; *see* **existir** *etc*.
(b) to fail to + *infin*, neglect to + *infin*; **no dejes de visitarles** don't fail to visit them, on no account neglect to pay them a visit.
(c) **no puedo** — **de asombrarme** I cannot but be amazed, I cannot help being astonished; **no puedo** — **de pensar que . . .** I can't help thinking that . . .; **no deja de ser algo raro** all the same it's rather odd; **yo había dejado de oírle tocar desde hacía 5 años** I had not heard him play for 5 years.
3 **dejarse** *vr* (a) to neglect oneself, let oneself go, get slovenly.
(b) — **de** + *infin* to allow oneself to be + *ptp*, let oneself be + *ptp*; — **persuadir** to allow oneself to be persuaded; **no se dejó engañar** he was not to be deceived; **se dejó decir que . . .** he let it slip that . . .; **se dejó oír una débil voz** a weak voice made itself heard (*or* could be heard); *see* **vencer** *etc*.
(c) — **de** + *infin* to stop + *ger*; **¡déjese de eso!** stop that!, cut it out!; *see* **broma**.
dejo *nm* (a) aftertaste, tang; **tiene un** — **raro** it leaves an odd taste. (b) (*fig*) touch, smack, tang, flavour. (c) (*Ling*) accent, trace of accent, special inflection.
del =de + el.
delación *nf* accusation; denunciation; information.
delantal *nm* apron; — **de cuero** leather apron; — **de niña** pinafore.
delante 1 *adv* (*also por* —) in front; ahead; opposite; **la parte de** — the front part; **la casa no tiene nada** — the house has nothing opposite; **estando otros** — with others present; in the presence of others; **abierto por** — open in front; **¡las damas por** —! ladies first!; **entrar al puerto (con) la popa** — to enter harbour stern first; **tenemos todavía 4 horas por** — we still have 4 hours in front of us.
2 — **de** *prep* in front of, before; ahead of.
delantera *nf* (a) front, front part; (*Theat*) front row; (*Sport*) forward line.
(b) (*fig*) advantage, lead; **llevar la** — to lead, be in the lead; **llevar la** — **a uno** to be ahead of someone; **coger la** — **a uno** to get ahead of someone; to

get a start on someone; **sacar la** — **a uno** to steal a march on someone; **tomar la** — to take the lead.
(c) —**s** overalls.
delantero 1 *adj part, row, wheel etc* front; *leg* front, fore; *line, position* (*Sport*) forward; (*in progress etc*) first, foremost.
2 *nm* (*Sport*) forward; — **centro** centre-forward; — **extremo** outside-forward, wing-forward; — **interior** inside-forward.
delatar [1a] *vt* (a) to denounce, inform against, accuse; to betray; **éste los delató a la policía** this man reported them to the police, (*pej*) this man gave them away to the police.
(b) (*fig*) to reveal, betray.
delator *nm*, **delatora** *nf* informer, accuser; betrayer.
delectación *nf* delight, delectation.
delegación *nf* (a) (*act*) delegation; — **de poderes** (*Parl*) devolution.
(b) (*body*) delegation; **la** — **fue a cumplimentar al Ministro** the delegation went to pay its respects to the minister.
(c) (*Comm etc*) local office, branch; office of a government department; police station; — **de Hacienda** local Treasury office.
delegado *nm*, **delegada** *nf* delegate; (*Comm*) agent, representative.
delegar [1h] *vt* to delegate (*a* to).
deleitable *adj* enjoyable, delightful, delectable.
deleitación *nf*, **deleitamiento** *nm* delectation.
deleitar [1a] 1 *vt* to delight, charm. 2 **deleitarse** *vr*: — **con**, — **en** to delight in, take pleasure in; — **en** + *infin* to delight in + *ger*.
deleite *nm* delight, pleasure; joy; —**s** delights.
deleitosamente *adv* delightfully; deliciously.
deleitoso *adj* delightful, pleasing; delicious.
deletéreo *adj* deleterious.
deletrear [1a] *vt* (a) to spell (out). (b) (*fig*) to decipher, interpret. (c) (*Chi*) to observe in great detail, look minutely at.
deletreo *nm* (a) spelling. (b) decipherment, interpretation.
deleznable *adj* (a) fragile, brittle; crumbly; unstable; *surface etc* slippery. (b) (*fig*) frail; *argument etc* weak; fleeting, ephemeral; insubstantial.
délfico *adj* Delphic.
delfín *nm* (*Zool*) dolphin.
Delfos Delphi.
delgadez *nf* (a) thinness; slimness. (b) delicateness; tenuousness. (c) sharpness.
delgado 1 *adj* (a) thin; *person, figure* thin; slim, slender; slight.
(b) (*fig*) delicate; light, tenuous.
(c) (*fig*) *soil* poor, exhausted.
(d) (*fig*) sharp, clever.
2 *adv*: **hilar (muy)** — to draw it fine, (*pej*) to split hairs.
deliberación *nf* deliberation.
deliberadamente *adv* deliberately.
deliberado *adj* deliberate.
deliberar [1a] 1 *vt* to debate, discuss; — + *infin* to decide to + *infin*. 2 *vi* to deliberate (*sobre* on), discuss (*si* whether).
deliberativo *adj* deliberative.
delicadamente *adj* delicately.
delicadez *nf* (a) =delicadeza. (b) weakness. (c) hypersensitiveness, touchiness, susceptibility.
delicadeza *nf* (a) delicacy; daintiness; thinness; frailness; refinement.
(b) touchiness, hypersensitiveness; fastidiousness; squeamishness; tactfulness; subtlety; **falta de** — tactlessness; **¡qué** —! how charming of you!
delicado *adj* (a) delicate; dainty; *machine etc* delicate, sensitive; *material* thin; slender, frail; *health* delicate; *colour* soft, delicate; *dish* dainty; *taste* refined, exquisite; *distinction* nice, delicate, subtle; *situation* delicate, tricky; embarrassing; *point* tender, sensitive; sore; **está** — **del estómago** he has a delicate stomach.
(b) (*of person's character*) demanding; hard to please; touchy, hypersensitive; fastidious; squeamish; (over)scrupulous; tactful, considerate; *mind* subtle; keen; **es muy** — **en el comer** he's very choosy about food (*fam*); **es muy** — **para la limpieza** he's very particular about cleanliness.
delicia *nf* delight; delightfulness; **el país es una** — the country is delightful; **tiene un jardín que es una** — he has a delightful garden; **un libro que ha hecho las** —**s de muchos niños** a book which has been the delight of many children.
delictivo *adj* act etc criminal.
delimitación *nf* delimitation.
delimitar [1a] *vt* to delimit.

delincuencia *nf* delinquency, criminality; — **juvenil**, — **de menores** juvenile delinquency; **cifras de la** — figures of crimes committed, incidence of criminality.

delincuente 1 *adj* delinquent; criminal; guilty. **2** *nmf* delinquent, criminal, offender; guilty person; — **sin antecedente penal** first offender; — **habitual** hardened criminal; — **juvenil** juvenile delinquent.

delineación *nf*, **delineamiento** *nm* delineation.

delineante *nm* draughtsman.

delinear [1a] *vt* to delineate; to outline; to draw.

delinquimiento *nm* delinquency; guilt.

delinquir [3e] *vi* to commit an offence; to offend, transgress.

deliquio *nm* swoon, fainting fit.

delirante *adj* delirious; light-headed; raving.

delirar [1a] *vi* to be delirious, rave; (*fig*) to rave, rant, talk nonsense.

delirio *nm* (**a**) (*Med and fig*) delirium; ravings, wanderings; nonsense, nonsensical talk.
  (**b**) frenzy; mania; — **de grandezas** megalomania; — **de persecución** persecution mania.
  (**c**) (*fam*) **con** — madly; **me gusta con** — I'm crazy about it; **¡fue el** —! it was great! (*fam*); **cuando acabó de hablar fue el** — when he finished speaking there were scenes of wild enthusiasm.

delírium *nm* **tremens** delirium tremens.

delito *nm* (**a**) crime, offence; — **de mayor cuantía** felony; — **de menor cuantía** misdemeanour. (**b**) (*fig*) misdeed, wicked act, offence.

delta 1 *nm* (*Geog*) delta. **2** *nf* (*letter*) delta.

deludir [3a] *vt* to delude.

delusorio *adj* delusive.

demacración *nf* emaciation.

demacrado *adj* emaciated, wasted away.

demacrarse [1a] *vr* to become emaciated, waste away.

demagogia *nf* demagogy, demagoguery.

demagógico *adj* demagogic.

demagogismo *nm* demagogy, demagoguery.

demagogo *nm* demagogue.

demanda *nf* (**a**) demand, request (*de* for); inquiry; claim; petition; — **de pago** demand for payment; — **del Santo Grial** quest for the Holy Grail; **escribir en** — **de ayuda** to write asking for help; **ir en** — **de** to go in search of, go looking for; **partir en** — **de** to go off in search of.
  (**b**) (*Theat*) call.
  (**c**) (*Comm*) demand; **hay mucha** — **de cerillas** matches are in great demand; **tener** — to be in demand; **ese producto no tiene** — there is no demand for that product.
  (**d**) (*Elec*) load; — **máxima** peak load.
  (**e**) (*Law*) action, lawsuit; **entablar** — to bring an action, take legal proceedings, sue; **presentar** — **de divorcio** to sue for divorce, take divorce proceedings.

demandado *nm*, **demandada** *nf* defendant; (*in divorce*) respondent.

demandante *nmf* claimant; (*Law*) plaintiff.

demandar [1a] *vt* (**a**) to demand, ask for, request; to claim; to petition.
  (**b**) (*Law*) to sue, file a suit against, start proceedings against; **demandó al periódico por calumnia** he sued the paper for libel; — **a uno por daños y perjuicios** to sue someone for damages; **ser demandado por libelo** to be sued for libel.

demaquillante *nm* make-up remover.

demarcación *nf* demarcation; **línea de** — demarcation line.

demarcar [1g] *vt* to demarcate.

demás 1 *adj*: **los** — **libros** the other books, the rest of the books, the remaining books; **y** — **gente de ese tipo** and other people of that sort.
  2 *pron*: **lo** — the rest (of it); **los** —, **las** — the others, the rest (of them); **por lo** — for the rest, as to the rest; otherwise; furthermore, moreover.
  3 *adv* = **además**; **por** — moreover; in vain; **y** — **etcetera**, and so on; *see* **más** (**estar de más**).

demasía *nf* (**a**) excess, surplus; superfluity; **en** — too much, excessively. (**b**) (*fig*) excess, outrage, wicked thing; wrong; affront. (**c**) (*fig*) boldness; insolence.

demasiado 1 *adj* (**a**) too much; overmuch, excessive; **eso es** — that's too much; **con** — **cuidado** with excessive care; **hace** — **calor** it's too hot; **¡esto es** —! this is too much!, that's the limit!
  (**b**) —**s** too many.
  2 *adv* too; too much, excessively; (*SAm*) a lot, a great deal; **comer** — to eat too much; **es** — **pesado para levantar** it is too heavy to lift; — **lo sé** I know it only too well.

demediar [1b] **1** *vt* to divide in half. **2** *vi* to be divided in half.

demencia *nf* madness, insanity, dementia.

dementar [1a] **1** *vt* to drive mad. **2 dementarse** *vr* to go mad, become demented.

demente 1 *adj* mad, insane, demented. **2** *nmf* mad person, lunatic.

demérito *nm* (**a**) demerit, fault; disadvantage. (**b**) unworthiness. (**c**) (*SAm*) depreciation.

demeritorio *adj* undeserving, unworthy.

democracia *nf* democracy.

demócrata *nf* democrat.

democráticamente *adv* democratically.

democrático *adj* democratic.

democratizar [1f] *vt* to democratize.

demografía *nf* demography.

demográfico *adj* demographic; population (*attr*); **la explosión demográfica** the population explosion.

demoledor *adj* (*fig*) argument *etc* powerful, overwhelming; *attack* shattering.

demoler [2h] *vt* (**a**) to demolish; pull down. (**b**) (*fig*) to demolish.

demolición *nf* demolition.

demonche *nm* (*euph*) = **demonio**.

demoníaco *adj* demoniacal, demonic.

demonio *nm* (**a**) devil; demon; evil spirit.
  (**b**) **ese** — **de sereno** that devil of a night watchman; **como el** — like the devil; **ir como el** — to go like the devil, go hell for leather; **esto pesa como el** — this is devilish heavy; **¡vete al** —! go to the devil!; **¡vaya con mil** —**s**! go to blazes!; **¡que se lo lleve el** —! to hell with it!; **the devil take it!**; **tener el** — **en el cuerpo** to be always on the go, have the devil in one; **esto sabe a** —**s** this tastes awful (*fam*); **ruido de todos los** —**s** a devil of a noise.
  (**c**) (*exclamatory etc*) **¡**—**!**, **¡qué** —! (*rage*) hell!, confound it!; (*exasperation*) hang it all!; (*surprise*) good heavens!; **what the devil . . .?**; **the devil it is!**; **¿qué** —**s será?** what the devil can that be?; **¡qué príncipe ni qué** —**s!** prince my foot!; **¿dónde** — **lo habré dejado?** where the devil can I have left it?

demontre *nm* (*euph*) = **demonio**.

demora *nf* (**a**) delay; **sin** — without delay. (**b**) (*Naut*) bearing.

demorado *adj* *effect etc* delayed.

demorar [1a] **1** *vt* to delay; to hold up, hold back.
  2 *vi* to stay on, linger on, delay, waste time.
  3 demorarse *vr* = **2**; — **en** + *infin* (*esp SAm*) to take a long time to + *infin*, be slow in + *ger*.

demorón *adj* (*Arg, Chi, Per*) = **demoroso**.

demoroso *adj* (*Chi*) slow, lazy; late, overdue; **ser** — **en** + *infin* to take a long time to + *infin*, be slow in + *ger*.

Demóstenes *m* Demosthenes.

demostrable *adj* demonstrable, that can be demonstrated.

demostración *nf* demonstration, show, display; gesture; — **de cariño** show of affection; — **de cólera** display of anger; — **comercial** commercial display, trade exhibition.

demostrar [1m] *vt* to demonstrate, show; to show off; to prove; — **cómo se hace algo** to demonstrate how something is done; — **que . . .** to show that . . ., **prove that . . .**; **Vd no puede** —**me nada** you can't prove anything against me.

demostrativo 1 *adj* demonstrative. **2** *nm* demonstrative.

demótico *adj* demotic.

demudación *nf* change, alteration.

demudado *adj* (*fig*) upset, distraught.

demudar [1a] **1** *vt* to change, alter.
  2 demudarse *vr* (**a**) to change, alter.
  (**b**) (*fig*) to change colour, change countenance; to look upset, show one's distress; **sin** — without a flicker of emotion; **continuó sin** — he went on quite unaffected (*or* unabashed).

denegación *nf* refusal; rejection; denial.

denegar [1h *and* 1k] *vt* to refuse; to reject; to deny; (*Law*) *appeal* to reject, refuse to allow.

dengoso *adj* affected; prudish; dainty, finicky.

dengue *nm* (**a**) affectation; coyness; prudery; daintiness, finickiness; **hacer** —**s** to act coyly, simper; **to be finicky**; **no me vengas con esos** —**s** I don't want to hear your silly complaints.
  (**b**) (*Med*) influenza, flu (*fam*).

denguero *adj* = **dengoso**.

denier *nm* denier.

denigrante *adj* insulting; degrading.

denigrar [1a] *vt* to denigrate, revile, run down; to insult.

denodadamente *adv* boldly, dauntlessly, intrepidly; **luchar** — to fight bravely.

denodado *adj* bold, dauntless, intrepid, brave.

denominación nf (a) (act) naming. (b) name, designation; denomination; — **social** (Mex) firm's official name.

denominado adj named, called; so-called.

denominador nm denominator; — **común** common denominator.

denominar [1a] vt to name, call, designate.

denostar [1m] vt to insult, revile, abuse; to condemn.

denotar [1a] vt to denote; to indicate, show; to express.

densamente adv densely; compactly; thickly; drily; solidly.

densidad nf density; compactness; thickness; heaviness, dryness; solidity; — **de población** density of population.

denso adj (in most senses) dense; compact; smoke, liquid etc thick; book, reading, speech heavy, dry; solid.

dentado adj having teeth; wheel cogged, toothed; edge jagged; stamp perforated; (Bot) dentate.

dentadura nf set of teeth, teeth (collectively); denture; — **artificial, — postiza** false teeth, denture(s); **tener mala —** to have bad teeth.

dental 1 adj dental. 2 nf dental.

dentar [1k] 1 vt to put teeth on, furnish with teeth; edge to make jagged; (Tech) to indent; stamp to perforate; **sello sin —** imperforate stamp. 2 vi to teethe, cut one's teeth.

dentellada nf (a) bite, nip; **partir algo a —s** to sever something with one's teeth. (b) tooth mark.

dentellar [1a] vi (of teeth) to chatter; **estaba dentellando** his teeth were chattering; **el susto le hizo —** the fright made his teeth chatter.

dentellear [1a] vt to bite, nibble (at), sink one's teeth into.

dentera nf (a) the shivers, the shudders; **dar — a uno** to set someone's teeth on edge, give someone the shivers.
(b) (fig) envy, jealousy; great desire; **dar — a uno** to make someone jealous; to make one's mouth water; **le da — que hagan fiestas al niño** it makes him jealous when they make a fuss of the baby.

dentición nf (a) (act) teething; **estar con la —** to be teething. (b) (Anat) dentition.

dentífrico 1 adj tooth (attr); **pasta dentífrica** toothpaste. 2 nm dentifrice, toothpaste.

dentina nf (of tooth) ivory.

dentista nmf dentist.

dentón adj large-toothed, buck-toothed, toothy.

dentrera nf (Col) servant.

dentro 1 adv (a) (estar) inside; indoors; feel etc inwardly, inside; **allí —** in there; **de —, desde —** from inside; **por —** inside, on the inside, in the interior.
(b) (ir) in, inside; indoors; **meter algo para —** to push something in; **vamos —** let's go in(side).
2 — **de** prep (a) (estar) in, inside, within; — **de la casa** inside the house.
(b) (meter etc) into, inside; **lo metió — del cajón** he put it into the drawer.
(c) (time) within, inside; — **de 3 meses** inside 3 months, within 3 months; — **de poco** shortly; soon after.
(d) — **de lo posible** as far as one (etc) can, as far as is possible; **eso no cabe — de lo posible** that does not come within the bounds of possibility.

dentrodera nf (Col) servant.

denudación nf denudation.

denudar [1a] vt to denude (de of); to lay bare.

denuedo nm boldness, daring; bravery.

denuesto nm insult; **llenar a uno de —s** to heap insults on someone.

denuncia nf report; denunciation; (Law etc) accusation; — **de accidente** report of an accident; — **falsa** false accusation.

denunciable adj crime indictable, punishable.

denunciación nf denunciation; accusation.

denunciador nm, **denunciadora** nf, **denunciante** nmf accuser; informer; **el — del accidente** the person who reported the accident.

denunciar [1b] vt to report (a to); to proclaim, announce; to foretell; (Law etc) to denounce (a to), accuse (a before), inform against; (pej) to betray, give away (a to); **denunciaron los precios abusivos a las autoridades** they reported the exorbitant prices to the authorities; **el accidente fue denunciado a la policía** the accident was reported to the police; **esto denunciaba la presencia del gas** this betrayed the presence of gas, this indicated the presence of gas; **lo hemos denunciado muchas veces** we have denounced this many times.

denuncio nm (SAm) = **denuncia**.

deparar [1a] vt to provide, furnish with; to present, offer; **nos deparó la ocasión para . . .** it gave us a chance to . . .; **los placeres que el viaje nos deparó** the pleasures which the trip afforded us; **pero también nos deparó la solución** but it also furnished us with the solution.

departamental adj departmental.

departamento nm (a) (in general) department, section; office; bureau; — **jurídico** legal department; — **de visados** visa section.
(b) (of box etc) compartment.
(c) (Rail etc) compartment; — **de fumadores** smoking compartment; — **de no fumadores** non-smoking compartment; — **de primera** first-class compartment.
(d) (Naut) — **de máquinas** engine room.
(e) (SAm) flat, apartment.
(f) (SAm) department, administrative district, province.

departir [1a] vi to talk, converse (con with, de about).

depauperación nf (a) impoverishment. (b) (Med) weakening, exhaustion.

depauperar [1a] vt (a) to impoverish. (b) (Med) to weaken, deplete, exhaust.

dependencia nf (a) (in general) dependence (de on); reliance (de on).
(b) relationship, kinship.
(c) (Pol etc) dependency.
(d) (Comm) section, office; branch office.
(e) (Archit) room; outbuilding, outhouse.
(f) (Comm etc) personnel, sales staff, employees.
(g) —s accessories.

dependienta nf salesgirl, saleswoman, shop assistant.

dependiente 1 adj dependent (de on). 2 nm employee; clerk; salesman, shop assistant.

depender [2a] vi to depend; — **de** to depend on; to rely on; **depende** it (all) depends; **depende de lo que haga él** it depends on what he does; **todo depende de que él esté listo** it all turns on his being ready; **no depende de mí** it does not rest with me; **todos dependemos de ti** we are all relying on you.

depilar [1a] vt to depilate, remove the hair from; eyebrows to pluck.

depilatorio 1 adj depilatory. 2 nm depilatory.

deplorable adj deplorable; lamentable, regrettable.

deplorar [1a] vt to deplore, regret; to condemn; **lo deploro mucho** I greatly deplore it, I'm extremely sorry.

deponente 1 adj (a) (Ling) deponent. (b) (Law) la **persona —** the person giving evidence. 2 nmf (Law) person giving evidence, person making a statement.

deponer [2r] 1 vt (a) to lay down; to lay aside; to remove, take down; arms to lay down.
(b) king to depose; ruler to oust, overthrow; minister to remove from office.
2 vi (a) (Law) to give evidence, make a statement.
(b) (CAm, Mex) to vomit.

deportación nf deportation.

deportar [1a] vt to deport.

deporte nm sport; game; outdoor recreation; — **acuáticos** water sports; — **de bucear** skin diving; — **hípico** horse-riding; —**s de invierno** winter sports; — **del remo** rowing; — **de la vela** sailing; **el fútbol es un —** football is a game; **es muy aficionado a los —s** he is very fond of sport.

deportista 1 adj sports (attr); sporting; **el público —** the sporting public. 2 nm sportsman; sporting man, sports fan (fam). 3 nf sportswoman.

deportividad nf sportsmanship.

deportivo 1 adj (a) club, paper etc sports (attr). (b) outlook, conduct etc sporting, sportsmanlike. 2 nm (Aut) sports car.

deposición nf (a) (act) deposition, removal. (b) assertion, affirmation; (Law) deposition, evidence, statement.

depositador nm, **depositadora** nf, **depositante** nmf (Comm, Fin) depositor.

depositar [1a] 1 vt to deposit; to place; to lay aside; to put away, store, put into store; to entrust (en to), confide (en to). 2 **depositarse** vr (liquid) to settle.

depositaría nf depository; (Fin etc) trust.

depositario nm, **depositaria** nf depository, trustee; receiver; (of secret etc) repository.

depósito nm (a) (Chem etc) deposit; sediment; (Geol, Min) deposit.
(b) (Comm, Fin) deposit; — **bancario** bank deposit; **dejar una cantidad en —** to leave a sum as a deposit.
(c) (Comm etc) store, storehouse, warehouse; depot; (for lost objects, cars etc) pound; (Mil) depot; dump; — **de aduana** customs warehouse; —

afianzado bonded warehouse; — de basura rubbish dump, tip; — de cadáveres mortuary, morgue; — de carbón coal tip; — de equipajes cloakroom; — de libros book stack; — de locomotoras engine shed; — de maderas timber yard; — de municiones ammunition dump.

(d) (for liquids) tank; cistern; reservoir; — de agua water tank, cistern; — de gasolina petrol tank; — de combustible fuel tank.

depravación nf depravity, depravation, corruption.

depravado adj depraved, corrupt.

depravar [1a] 1 vt to deprave, corrupt. 2 **depravarse** vr to become depraved.

depreciación nf depreciation.

depreciar [1b] 1 vt to depreciate, reduce the value of. 2 **depreciarse** vr to depreciate, lose value.

depredación nf depredation; outrage, excess; pillage.

depredar [1a] vt to pillage; to commit outrages against.

depresión nf (a) (Geog etc) depression; hollow; (in horizon etc) dip; (in wall) recess, niche.

(b) (act) lowering; drop, fall (de in); — del mercurio fall in temperature (or pressure).

(c) (Meteorol) depression.

(d) (Econ) depression, slump, recession.

(e) (mental) depression.

depresivo adj, **deprimente** adj depressing; depressive.

deprimido adj (all senses) depressed.

deprimir [3a] 1 vt (a) (physically) to depress, press down; to flatten.

(b) (mentally etc) to depress.

(c) level etc to lower, reduce.

(d) (fig) to humiliate; to belittle, disparage. 2 **deprimirse** vr to get depressed.

depuración nf (a) purification; cleansing. (b) (Pol etc) purge.

depurador nm purifier.

depurar [1a] vt (a) to purify; to cleanse, purge. (b) (Pol etc) to purge.

depurativo nm blood tonic.

derecha nf (a) right hand; right side, right-hand side; **estar a la** — de to be on the right of; **torcer a la** — to turn (to the) right; **conducción a** — (Aut) right-hand drive; **el poste de la** — the post on the right; **seguir por la** — to keep (to the) right.

(b) (Pol) right.

(c) a —s rightly, aright; justly; **si le entiendo a** —s if I understand you aright.

derechamente adv (a) straight, directly. (b) (fig) properly, rightly.

derechazo nm (Boxing) right; (Tennis) forehand drive; (Taur) a pass with the cape.

derechista 1 adj rightist, right-wing. 2 nmf rightist, right-winger.

derecho 1 adj (a) right; right-hand.

(b) right-handed.

(c) straight; upright, erect, standing; **más** — **que una vela** as straight as a die; **poner algo** — to stand something upright.

(d) (CAm, Col, SD, Ven) lucky.

2 adv (a) straight, directly; upright.

(b) straight, directly; **ir** — a to go straight to.

3 nm (a) right side.

(b) right; claim, title; privilege, exemption; —s **cinematográficos** film rights; —s **civiles** civil rights; — **divino** divine right; — **de paso**, — **de tránsito** right of way; — **de propiedad literaria** copyright; — **de visita** right of search; — **de votar** right to vote, franchise; **con** — rightly, justly; **con** — a with a right to, with entitlement to; **por** — propio in his own right; **según** — by right(s); "**reservados todos los** —**s**" "all rights reserved", "copyright"; ¡no hay —! it's not fair!; **tener** — a to have a right to, be entitled to; **tener** — a + infin to have a right to + infin.

(c) (Law) law; justice; **Facultad de D**— Faculty of Law; **estudiante de** — law student; **lo que manda el** — **en este caso** what justice demands in this case.

(d) (Fin) due(s); fee(s); tax(es); (on book, oil etc) royalties; (professional) fee(s); **franco de** —s duty-free; **sujeto a** —s subject to duty, dutiable; —s **de aduana**, —s **arancelarios** customs duty; —s **de autor** royalties; —s **de entrada** import duties; —s **de peaje** (Aut) toll; — **preferente** prefential duty; —s **de puerto** harbour dues.

derechura nf (a) straightness; directness; **hablar en** — to speak plainly, talk straight; **hacer algo en** — to do something right away.

(b) rightness, justice.

(c) (CAm, Per) (good) luck.

deriva nf (Naut) drift; leeway; (from course) deviation; **buque a la** — ship adrift, drifting ship; **ir a la** — to drift, be adrift.

derivación nf (a) derivation (also Ling); origin, source. (b) (Elec) shunt; **en** — shunt (attr); **hacer una** — **en un alambre** to tap a wire.

derivado 1 adj derived; derivative (also Ling). 2 nm (a) derivative (also Ling). (b) (Chem etc) by-product.

derivar[1] [1a] 1 vt to derive (de from; also Ling). 2 vi and **derivarse** vr to derive, be derived (de from).

derivar[2] [1a] vi (Naut) to drift.

derivativo 1 adj derivative. 2 nm derivative.

dermatología nf dermatology.

dermatólogo nm dermatologist.

dérmico adj skin (attr); **enfermedad dérmica** skin disease.

derogación nf repeal, abolition.

derogar [1h] vt to repeal, abolish.

derrabar [1a] vt to dock, cut off the tail of.

derramadero nm spillway.

derramamiento nm (a) spilling; shedding; overflowing; — **de sangre** bloodshed. (b) scattering, spreading. (c) (fig) wasting, lavishing.

derramar [1a] 1 vt (a) liquid to spill; to pour out, pour away; tears to weep, shed; blood to shed; light to shed, cast; — **una taza de café** to spill a cup of coffee.

(b) to scatter, spread (about); gossip, news to spread.

(c) taxes to apportion.

(d) (fig) to squander, waste; gifts etc to lavish (en on).

2 **derramarse** vr (a) to spill; to pour out, overflow, run over, flow out; (of pen, vessel) to leak; **llenar una taza hasta** — to fill a cup to overflowing.

(b) to spread, scatter, be scattered; **la multitud se derramó por todos lados** the crowd scattered in all directions.

derrame nm (a) (act) = **derramamiento**.

(b) (quantity) loss; overflow; outflow; leakage; waste.

(c) (Med) discharge; excess of liquid present in the body; — **sinovial** water on the knee.

derrapar [1a] vi (Aut) to skid; (Naut) to yaw.

derrape nm (Aut) skid; (Naut) yaw.

derredor: **al** — (**de**), **en** — (**de**) adv and prep around, about; **en su** — round about him.

derrelicto nm (Naut) derelict.

derrengado adj (a) bent, twisted, crooked. (b) crippled, lame; **estar** — (fig) to ache all over; to be footsore; **dejar** — **a uno** (fig) to wear someone out.

derrengar [1h] vt (a) to bend, twist, make crooked.

(b) — **a uno** to break someone's back, cripple someone; (fig) to wear someone out.

derrepente nm (CAm): **en un** — = **de repente**.

derretido adj (a) metal melted; molten; snow thawed.

(b) **estar** — **por una** to be crazy about someone.

derretimiento nm (a) melting; thawing. (b) (fig) squandering. (c) (fig) mad passion, burning love.

derretir [3l] 1 vt (a) metal to melt; to liquefy; ice cream etc to melt; snow to thaw.

(b) (fig) to squander, throw away.

(c) (fam) to bore to tears; to exasperate.

2 **derretirse** vr (a) to melt; to run, liquefy.

(b) (fig) to be very susceptible to love, fall in love easily; — **por una** to be crazy about someone.

(c) (fam) to get worked up, fret and fume.

derribar [1a] 1 vt (a) building to knock down, pull down, demolish; barrier to tear down; door to batter down.

(b) person to knock down; to floor, lay out; wrestler to throw, throw.

(c) (Aer) to shoot down, bring down; **fue derribado sobre el Canal** he was shot down over the Channel.

(d) (Hunting) to shoot, bag, bring down.

(e) government etc to bring down, overthrow, overturn.

(f) (fig) to humiliate.

2 **derribarse** vr (a) to fall down, collapse.

(b) (person) to throw oneself down, hurl oneself to the ground; to prostrate oneself.

derribo nm (a) knocking down, demolition. (b) (Wrestling) throw. (c) (Aer) shooting down; destruction. (d) overthrow. (e) —s rubble, debris.

derrisco nm (Cu) gorge, ravine.

derrocadero nm cliff, precipice, steep place.

derrocamiento nm (a) flinging down, throwing down. (b) demolition. (c) overthrow, toppling; ousting. (d) humbling.

derrocar [1g] 1 vt (a) object, person to fling down, hurl down.

(b) building etc to knock down, demolish.

(c) *government* to overthrow, topple; *minister etc* to oust (*de* from). **(d)** (*fig*) to humble.

2 derrocarse *vr:* — **por un precipicio** to throw oneself over a cliff.

derrochador 1 *adj* spendthrift. **2** *nm* spendthrift, wastrel.

derrochar [1a] *vt* **(a)** *money etc* to squander, waste; to lavish, pour out. **(b)** — **salud** to be bursting with health; — **mal genio** to be excessively bad-tempered.

derroche *nm* **(a)** squandering, waste; lavish expenditure; extravagance; **con un formidable — de recursos** with a lavish use of resources; **no se puede tolerar tal** — such extravagance is not to be tolerated.
(b) abundance, excess; **con un — de buen gusto** with an excess of good taste.

derrota[1] *nf* **(a)** road, route, track. **(b)** (*Naut*) course.

derrota[2] *nf* defeat; rout; débâcle, disaster; **sufrir una grave** — to suffer a serious defeat, (*in plan etc*) to suffer a grave setback.

derrotado *adj* **(a)** defeated; *team* defeated, beaten, losing. **(b)** *dress, person* shabby; **un actor** — a shabby old actor, a down-and-out actor.

derrotar [1a] *vt* **(a)** (*Mil*) to defeat; to rout, put to flight; *team etc* to defeat, beat. **(b)** *clothing* to tear, ruin; (*fig*) *health* to ruin.

derrotero *nm* **(a)** (*Naut*) course; (*fig*) course, plan of action; **tomar otro** — (*fig*) to adopt a different course. **(b)** (*Cu*) hidden treasure.

derrotismo *nm* defeatism.

derrotista 1 *adj* defeatist. **2** *nmf* defeatist.

derruir [3g] *vt* to demolish, tear down.

derrumbadero *nm* **(a)** cliff, precipice, steep place. **(b)** (*fig*) danger, hazard; pitfall.

derrumbamiento *nm* **(a)** plunge, headlong fall.
(b) demolition; collapse; fall, cave-in; — **de piedras** fall of rocks; — **de tierra** landslide.
(c) (*fig*) collapse, ruin, destruction; (*of price*) sharp fall, collapse.

derrumbar [1a] **1** *vt* **(a)** *object, person* to fling down, hurl down; to throw headlong.
(b) *building etc* to knock down, demolish.
(c) *balanced object* to upset, overturn.

2 derrumbarse *vr* **(a)** (*person etc*) to fling oneself, hurl oneself (headlong; *por* down, over); to fall headlong.
(b) (*building etc*) to collapse, fall down, tumble down; (*roof*) to fall in, cave in.
(c) (*fig: hopes etc*) to collapse, be ruined; **se han derrumbado los precios** prices have tumbled; the bottom has fallen out of the market.

derrumbe *nm* **(a)** =**derrumbadero**. **(b)** =**derrumbamiento**.

derviche *nm* dervish.

des . . . de . . ., **des . . .**; **un . . .**; *eg* **descolonización** decolonization; **desmilitarizado** demilitarized; **desempleo** unemployment; **desfavorable** unfavourable; **desgana** unwillingness.

desabastecido *adj:* **estar** — **de** to be out of (supplies of); **nos cogió** —**s de gasolina** it caught us without petrol.

desabillé *nm* deshabille.

desabollar [1a] *vt* to knock the dents out of, straighten.

desabonarse [1a] *vr* to stop subscribing.

desabono *nm* (*fig*) discredit; **hablar en — de uno** to say damaging things about someone, speak ill of someone.

desaborido *adj* **(a)** insipid, tasteless; *person* dull. **(b)** flimsy, unsubstantial.

desabotonar [1a] **1** *vt* to unbutton, undo. **2** *vi* (*Bot*) to open, blossom. **3 desabotonarse** *vr* to come undone.

desabrido *adj* **(a)** tasteless, insipid, flat.
(b) *weather* unpleasant.
(c) *person* surly, rude, disagreeable; *manner* harsh, rough; *answer etc* sharp; *debate* bitter, acrimonious.

desabrigado *adj* (*fig*) unprotected, exposed; defenceless.

desabrigar [1h] **1** *vt* **(a)** to remove the clothing of; to leave bare, uncover.
(b) (*fig*) to leave without shelter, deprive of protection.
2 desabrigarse *vr* to take off one's (outer) clothing; to leave oneself bare, uncover oneself; — **en la cama** to throw off one's bedcovers.

desabrigo *nm* **(a)** (*act*) uncovering. **(b)** (*state*) bareness; exposure; lack of clothing (*or* covers). **(c)** (*fig*) unprotectedness; poverty, destitution.

desabrimiento *nm* **(a)** tastelessness, insipidness.
(b) unpleasantness.

(c) surliness, rudeness; harshness; sharpness; acrimony; **contestar con** — to answer sharply.
(d) (*fig*) depression, lowness of spirits; uneasy feeling.

desabrir [3a] *vt* **(a)** to give a nasty taste to. **(b)** (*fig*) to embitter; to torment.

desabrochar [1a] **1** *vt* **(a)** to undo, unfasten, unbutton; *person* to loosen the clothing of.
(b) (*fig*) to penetrate, expose.
2 desabrocharse *vr* (*fig*) to unbosom oneself (*con* to).

desacatador *adj* disrespectful, insulting.

desacatar [1a] *vt* to be disrespectful to, behave insultingly towards.

desacato *nm* disrespect; insulting behaviour; (*Law etc*) contempt, act of contempt; — **a la justicia** contempt of court.

desacertadamente *adv* mistakenly, erroneously, wrongly; unwisely, injudiciously.

desacertado *adj* mistaken, erroneous, wrong; unwise, injudicious.

desacertar [1k] *vi* to be mistaken, be wrong; to get it wrong; to act unwisely.

desacierto *nm* mistake, miscalculation, error; miss; unfortunate remark (*etc*); **fue uno de muchos** —**s suyos** it was one of his many errors; **ha sido un — elegir tal sitio** it was a mistake to choose such a place.

desacomodado *adj* **(a)** unemployed, out of a job.
(b) badly off. **(c)** awkward, troublesome, inconvenient.

desacomodar [1a] **1** *vt* **(a)** *servant* to discharge. **(b)** to put out, inconvenience. **2 desacomodarse** *vr* to lose one's post.

desaconsejable *adj* inadvisable.

desaconsejado *adj* ill-advised.

desaconsejar [1a] *vt person* to dissuade, advise against; **los rigores del viaje desaconsejaron esa decisión** the rigours of the journey made that decision seem inadvisable (*or* made that decision seem wrong).

desacoplar [1a] *vt* (*Elec*) to disconnect; (*Mech*) to take apart, uncouple.

desacordar [1m] **1** *vt* to put out of tune. **2 desacordarse** *vr* **(a)** (*Mus*) to get out of tune. **(b)** to be forgetful; — **de algo** to forget something.

desacorde *adj* **(a)** (*Mus*) discordant. **(b)** (*fig*) discordant, incongruous.

desacostumbrado *adj* unusual; unaccustomed.

desacostumbrar [1a] **1** *vt:* — **a uno de** to break someone of the habit of, wean someone away from.
2 desacostumbrarse *vr:* — **de** to break oneself of the habit of.

desacreditar [1a] **1** *vt* **(a)** to discredit, damage the reputation of, bring into disrepute.
(b) to cry down, disparage, run down.
2 desacreditarse *vr* to become discredited.

desacuerdo *nm* **(a)** discord, disagreement; **amistoso** agreement to differ; **estar en** — to be out of keeping (*con* with), be at variance (*con* with); **la corbata está en — con la camisa** the tie does not go with the shirt.
(b) error, blunder.
(c) forgetfulness.

desadeudarse [1a] *vr* to get out of debt.

desadorno *nm* bareness, lack of ornamentation.

desadvertido *adj* careless.

desadvertir [3i] *vt* to fail to notice; to disregard.

desafecto 1 *adj* disaffected; hostile; **elementos** —**s al régimen** those hostile to the régime, those out of sympathy with the régime.
2 *nm* disaffection; ill-will, dislike; hostility.

desaferrar [1k] *vt* **(a)** to loosen, unfasten.
(b) — **a uno** to make someone change his mind, dissuade someone (from a strongly held opinion *etc*).
(c) (*Naut*) *anchor* to weigh.

desafiador 1 *adj* defiant; challenging. **2** *nm*, **desafiadora** *nf* challenger.

desafiante *adj* challenging; *attitude etc* defiant.

desafiar [1a] *vt* **(a)** to challenge; — **a uno a** + *infin* to challenge someone to + *infin*, dare someone to + *infin*.
(b) to defy; to face, face up to; **han desafiado todos los peligros** they have defied all the dangers.
(c) (*fig*) to challenge, compete with, measure up to.
(d) (*Mex*) to fight.

desaficionarse [1a] *vr:* — **de** to come to dislike, take a dislike to.

desafilar [1a] **1** *vt* to blunt, dull. **2 desafilarse** *vr* to get blunt.

desafinadamente *adv sing etc* out of tune, off key.

desafinado *adj:* **estar** — to be out of tune.
desafinar [1a] *vi* (a) to be (*or* play, sing) out of tune; to go out of tune. (b) (*fig*) to speak out of turn.
desafío *nm* (a) challenge; duel. (b) (*fig*) challenge; defiance; competition, rivalry; **es un** — **a todos nosotros** it is a challenge to us all.
desaforadamente *adv* (a) *behave etc* outrageously. (b) *shout* at the top of one's voice.
desaforado *adj* (a) lawless, violent, disorderly; *behaviour* outrageous; **es un** — he's a violent sort, he's dangerously excitable.
(b) great, huge; *shout* mighty, ear-splitting.
desaforarse [1m] *vr* to behave in an outrageous way, act violently; to get worked up, lose control.
desafortunado *adj* unfortunate, unlucky.
desafuero *nm* outrage, excess.
desagraciado *adj* graceless, unattractive; unsightly.
desagradable *adj* disagreeable, unpleasant; **ser** — **con uno** to be rude to someone.
desagradablemente *adv* unpleasantly.
desagradar [1a] **1** *vt* to displease; to bother, upset; **me desagrada ese olor** I don't like that smell; **me desagrada tener que hacerlo** I dislike having to do it. **2** *vi* to be unpleasant.
desagradecido *adj* ungrateful.
desagradecimiento *nm* ingratitude.
desagrado *nm* displeasure; dislike; dissatisfaction; **hacer algo con** — to do something with distaste, do something unwillingly.
desagraviar [1b] **1** *vt* (a) *person* to make amends to; to indemnify; to apologize to.
(b) *offence etc* to make amends for, put right.
2 desagraviarse *vr* to get one's own back; to exact an apology; to restore one's honour.
desagravio *nm* amends; compensation, indemnification, satisfaction; **en** — **de** as amends for.
desagregación *nf* disintegration.
desagregar [1h] **1** *vt* to disintegrate. **2 desagregarse** *vr* to disintegrate.
desaguadero *nm* drain (*also fig; de* on).
desaguar [1i] **1** *vt* (a) to drain, empty, run off. (b) (*fig*) to squander. **2** *vi* (a) to drain away, drain off. (b) (*of river*) — **en** to drain into, flow into.
desagüe *nm* (a) (*act*) drainage, draining. (b) drainage channel; drainpipe; outlet, drain; **tubo de** — drainpipe, waste pipe.
desaguisado 1 *adj* illegal. **2** *nm* offence, outrage.
desahogado 1 *adj* (a) *dress, house etc* roomy, large.
(b) *space* clear, free, unencumbered.
(c) *life, situation* comfortable; *person* comfortably off, in easy circumstances.
(d) brazen, impudent, fresh; **el tan** — **se lo comió todo** he was brazen enough to eat it all up.
2 *nm* brazen person, shameless individual.
desahogar [1h] **1** *vt* (a) *pain etc* to ease, relieve; *anger* to vent (*en* on).
(b) *person* to console.
2 desahogarse *vr* (a) to recover; to make things more comfortable for oneself; to take it easy, relax.
(b) to get out of a difficulty (*or* debt *etc*).
(c) (*emotionally*) to relieve one's feelings; to let off steam, let oneself go; to speak one's mind frankly; to confess, get something off one's chest (*fam*); — **con uno** to unbosom oneself to someone.
desahogo *nm* (a) comfort, ease; comfortable circumstances; **vivir con** — to be comfortably off.
(b) relief; recovery; **es un** — **de tantas cosas malas** it's an outlet for so many unpleasant things, it's a way of getting rid of so many bad things.
(c) freedom; (*pej*) excessive freedom, brazenness, impudence; **expresarse con cierto** — to express oneself with a certain freedom, feel free to say what one really thinks.
desahuciado *adj case* hopeless.
desahuciar [1b] **1** *vt* (a) *tenant* to evict, eject; *occupant of post* to oust, remove, get out; (*Chi*) to dismiss.
(b) to deprive of hope, kill the hopes of; *sick person* to give up hope for, declare past recovery; **con esa decisión le desahuciaron definitivamente** by that decision they finally put an end to his hopes.
2 desahuciarse *vr* to lose all hope.
desahucio *nm* eviction, ejection; (*Chi*) dismissal.
desairado *adj* (a) disregarded. (b) unsuccessful; **quedar** — to be unsuccessful, come off badly. (c) unattractive; graceless; shabby.
desairar [1a] *vt* (a) to slight, snub; to disregard; to rebuff; **lo haré por no** — I'll do it rather than cause offence. (b) (*Comm*) to dishonour; to default on.
desaire *nm* (a) slight, snub; act of disrespect; rebuff; **fue un** — **sin precedentes** it was an unprecedented

snub; **dar** (*or* **hacer**) **un** — **a uno** to rebuff someone, offend someone; **¿me va Vd a hacer ese** —**?** (*concerning invitation*) I won't take no for an answer!; **sufrir un** — to suffer a rebuff; **no lo tome Vd a** — don't be offended.
(b) unattractiveness, gracelessness, lack of charm.
desajustar [1a] **1** *vt* to disarrange, disturb the order of. **2 desajustarse** *vr* (a) to get out of order. (b) to disagree, fall out.
desajuste *nm* (a) disorder, disarrangement. (b) (*in person*) imbalance, lack of balance. (c) disagreement.
desalación *nf* desalination.
desalado *adj* hasty; impatient; eager; anxious.
desalar[1] [1a] *vt* to remove the salt from; *sea water* to desalinate.
desalar[2] [1a] **1** *vt* to clip the wings of. **2 desalarse** *vr* (a) to rush, hasten along. (b) to long, yearn; — **por** + *infin* to long to + *infin*; to be keen to + *infin*.
desalentar [1k] **1** *vt* (a) — **a uno** to make someone breathless, make someone gasp for breath.
(b) (*fig*) to discourage.
2 desalentarse *vr* to get discouraged, lose heart.
desaliento *nm* (*fig*) discouragement; depression, dejection; dismay.
desalinar [1a] *vt*, **desalinizar** [1f] *vt* to desalinate.
desalinización *nf* desalination.
desaliñado *adj* (a) slovenly, dirty, down-at-heel; shabby; untidy, unkempt, dishevelled. (b) careless, slipshod, slovenly.
desaliño *nm* (a) slovenliness, dirtiness; shabbiness; untidiness; dishevelled state. (b) carelessness.
desalmado *adj* cruel, heartless.
desalmarse [1a] *vr:* — **por** to long for, crave (for).
desalojamiento *nm* (a) ejection, ousting, removal; dislodging. (b) evacuation; abandonment; clearing.
desalojar [1a] **1** *vt* (a) *occupant* to eject, oust, remove (*from* de); to dislodge (*also Mil; de* from); to clear out.
(b) *contents, gas etc* to dislodge, remove, expel.
(c) *place* to evacuate; to abandon, move out of, move away from; — **un tribunal de público** to clear a court, to clear the public from a court; **las tropas han desalojado el pueblo** the troops have moved out of the village; **la policía desalojó el local** the police cleared people out of the place.
2 *vi* to move out.
desalquilado *adj* vacant, untenanted.
desalquilar [1a] **1** *vt* to vacate, move out of. **2 desalquilarse** *vr* to become vacant.
desalterar [1a] **1** *vt* to assuage, calm; to quieten down. **2 desalterarse** *vr* to calm down, quieten down.
desamar [1a] *vt* to cease to love; to dislike, detest.
desamarrar [1a] *vt* to untie; (*Naut*) to cast off.
desamor *nm* coldness, indifference; dislike; enmity.
desamorado *adj* cold-hearted.
desamparado *adj* (a) *child etc* helpless, defenceless; abandoned; **los niños** —**s de la ciudad** the city's waifs and strays; **sentirse** — to feel helpless.
(b) *place* exposed.
(c) *place* lonely, deserted.
desamparar [1a] *vt* (a) *person* to desert, abandon, leave helpless; to forsake. (b) *place* to leave, abandon; to leave defenceless.
desamparo *nm* (a) (*act*) desertion, abandonment. (b) (*state*) helplessness; defencelessness, lack of protection.
desamueblado *adj* unfurnished.
desamueblar [1a] *vt* to remove the furniture from, clear the furniture out of.
desandar [1q] *vt:* — **lo andado**, — **el camino** to retrace one's steps, go back the way one has come; **no se puede** — **lo andado** one cannot undo what has been done.
desangramiento *nm* bleeding; **morir de** — to bleed to death.
desangrar [1a] **1** *vt* (a) *person* to bleed; *lake* to drain. (b) (*fig*) to impoverish, bleed white. **2 desangrarse** *vr* to lose a lot of blood; to bleed to death.
desangre *nm* (*SAm*) bleeding, loss of blood.
desanidar [1a] **1** *vt* to oust, dislodge. **2** *vi* to fly, begin to fly.
desanimado *adj* (a) downhearted, dispirited, dejected. (b) dull, lifeless, flat; **fue una fiesta de lo más** — it was a terribly dull party.
desanimar [1a] **1** *vt* to discourage; to depress, sadden. **2 desanimarse** *vr* to get discouraged, lose heart.
desánimo *nm* (a) despondency, depression, dejection. (b) dullness, lifelessness.
desanudar [1a] *vt* to untie; to disentangle; — **la voz to** manage to speak again, find one's voice.
desapacible *adj* unpleasant, disagreeable; *sound* sharp, jangling; nasty; discordant; *tone* harsh,

rough; *taste* unpleasant, sharp; *discussion* bitter, bad-tempered.

desaparecer [2d] **1** *vt* to hide; to remove, take away; to cause to vanish. **2** *vi* to disappear, vanish; to drop out of sight; (*of effects*) to wear off.

desaparecido *adj* missing; extinct; **el libro** — the missing book; **número de muertos, heridos y** —s number of dead, wounded and missing; **uno de los animales** —s one of the extinct animals.

desaparejar [1a] *vt* (a) to unharness, unhitch. (b) (*Naut*) to unrig.

desaparición *nf* disappearance; extinction.

desapasionadamente *adv* dispassionately, impartially.

desapasionado *adj* dispassionate, impartial.

desapego *nm* (a) coolness, indifference (*a* towards); alienation, detachment (*a* from). (b) detachment, impartiality.

desapercibido *adj* (a) unnoticed; **marcharse** — to slip away (unseen); **pasar** — to go unnoticed. (b) unprepared.

desaplicación *nf* slackness, laziness.

desaplicado *adj* slack, lazy.

desapoderado *adj action, movement* headlong, precipitate; *passion etc* wild, violent, uncontrollable; *greed etc* excessive; *pride* overweening.

desapoderar [1a] *vt* to deprive of authority; to dispossess (*de* of).

desaprender [2a] *vt* to forget; to unlearn.

desaprensión *nf* unscrupulousness, lack of scruple.

desaprensivamente *adv* unscrupulously.

desaprensivo *adj* unscrupulous.

desapretar [1k] *vt* to loosen, slacken, undo.

desaprobación *nf* disapproval; condemnation; rejection.

desaprobar [1m] *vt* to disapprove of; to frown on, condemn; *request etc* to reject, dismiss.

desapropiarse [1b] *vr*: — **de** to divest oneself of, surrender, give up.

desaprovechado *adj* (a) unproductive, unprofitable; below expectations. (b) *student etc* slow, backward; slack.

desaprovechar [1a] **1** *vt* to fail to take advantage of, not use, waste; *opportunity* to waste, miss. **2** *vi* to lose ground, slip back.

desarbolar [1a] *vt* to dismast.

desarmador *nm* (*of gun*) hammer; (*Mex*) screwdriver.

desarmar [1a] **1** *vt* (a) (*Mil*) to disarm. (b) (*Mech*) to take apart, take to pieces, dismantle; to strip down; *oars* to ship. (c) (*fig*) *person* to disarm; *anger* to calm, appease. **2** *vi* to disarm.

desarme *nm* disarmament.

desarraigado *adj person* rootless, without roots.

desarraigar [1h] *vt* (a) to uproot, root out, dig up. (b) (*fig*) to root out, eradicate; to extirpate; *person* to uproot; to banish, expel.

desarraigo *nm* (*fig*) eradication; extirpation; uprooting; banishment, expulsion.

desarrajar [1a] *vt* (*SAm*) to break open, force the lock of.

desarrapado *adj* = **desharrapado**.

desarrebujar [1a] *vt* (a) to untangle; to uncover. (b) (*fig*) to clarify, elucidate.

desarreglado *adj* (a) (*Mech etc*) out of order; *stomach etc* upset; *room etc* untidy, in disorder. (b) *conduct* disorderly; *appearance* slovenly, untidy; (*in habits*) irregular; unsystematic; (*pej*) immoderate.

desarreglar [1a] **1** *vt* to disarrange; to disturb, mess up, upset; (*Mech*) to put out of order; **el viento le desarregló el peinado** the wind made a mess of her hairdo; **no desarregles la cama** don't mess up your bed. **2 desarreglarse** *vr* to get disarranged, get untidy; (*Mech*) to get out of order.

desarreglo *nm* disorder, confusion, chaos; untidiness; irregularity; (*Mech*) trouble; (*Med*) upset; **para evitar los** —s **estomacales** in order to avoid stomach upsets; **viven en el mayor** — they live in complete chaos.

desarrimado *nm* (*fam*) loner (*fam*), lone wolf.

desarrollado *adj* (*also* **bien** —) well-developed.

desarrollar [1a] **1** *vt* (a) *object* to unroll, unwind; to unfold, open (out). (b) *abbreviation, equation* to expand. (c) (*fig*) to develop; to evolve; *theory etc* to explain, expound. (d) (*Mech*) **el motor desarrolla 30 caballos** the engine develops 30 hp. **2 desarrollarse** *vr* (a) to unroll, unwind; to open (out).

(b) (*fig*) to develop; to evolve; to unfold; (*of event, meeting etc*) to take place; **la industria se desarrolla rápidamente** the industry is developing rapidly; **la acción se desarrolla en Roma** (*Cine etc*) the scene is set in Rome, the action takes place in Rome.

desarrollo *nm* development; evolution; unfolding; expansion; growth; ((*of game, play*) run; — **en línea** ribbon development; **durante el** — **de** in the course of; during the development of; **un país en vías de** — a developing country; **la industria está en pleno** — the industry is making rapid growth, the industry is expanding steadily; **el niño tiene mucho** — **para su edad** the child is overdeveloped for his age.

desarroparse [1a] *vr* to undress; to uncover oneself.

desarrugar [1h] *vt* to smooth (out), remove the wrinkles from.

desarticulado *adj* disjointed.

desarticular [1a] *vt* to take apart, take to pieces; to separate; *bones* to put out.

desarzonar [1a] *vt rider* to throw, unsaddle.

desaseado *adj* slovenly, dirty; untidy, unkempt, messy; shabby.

desasear [1a] *vt* to dirty, soil; to mess up.

desaseo *nm* slovenliness, dirtiness; untidiness; messiness; shabbiness.

desasimiento *nm* (a) loosening, undoing; release. (b) (*fig*) detachment (*de* from), disinterest; (*pej*) indifference (*de* to), remoteness (*de* from).

desasir [3a, *but present like* **salir**] **1** *vt* to loosen, undo, let go. **2 desasirse** *vr* (a) to extricate oneself (*de* from), get clear (*de* of). (b) — **de** to let go, give up; to rid oneself of, free oneself of; to get rid of.

desasnar [1a] *vt* to civilize, improve, knock the corners off; to make less stupid.

desasosegado *adj* uneasy, anxious; restless.

desasosegar [1h *and* 1k] **1** *vt* to disturb, perturb, make uneasy; to make restless. **2 desasosegarse** *vr* to become uneasy, get perturbed; to become restless.

desasosiego *nm* disquiet, uneasiness, anxiety; restlessness; (*Pol etc*) unrest.

desastrado *adj* (a) dirty, shabby, ragged. (b) unlucky; wretched.

desastre *nm* disaster; ¡**un** —! (*hum*) what a calamity!; how awful! (*fam*); **la boda fue un** — the wedding was a disaster; **la función fue un** — the show was a shambles.

desastroso *adj* disastrous, calamitous.

desatado *adj* (*fig*) wild, violent, uncontrolled.

desatar [1a] **1** *vt* (a) to untie, undo, unfasten; to loosen, slacken; to detach, separate; *dog* to unleash; (*Chem*) to dissolve. (b) (*fig*) *repression etc* to unleash. (c) (*fig*) *mystery* to solve, clear up, unravel. **2 desatarse** *vr* (a) to come untied, come undone, unfasten itself; to work loose; (*dog etc*) to break away, break loose. (b) — **de un compromiso** to get out of an agreement. (c) (*fig: storm etc*) to break, burst; (*riot*) to break out; (*enthusiasm*) to break all bounds; (*disaster*) to fall (*sobre* on); — **en injurias** to begin to pour out a stream of insults. (d) (*fig: person*) to get worked up, lose self-control; to talk wildly; to go too far, forget oneself.

desatascar [1g] *vt* (a) *cart etc* to pull out of the mud; — **a uno** (*fig*) to get someone out of a jam. (b) *pipe etc* to clear, free, unblock.

desatención *nf* (a) inattention; absent-mindedness. (b) discourtesy.

desatender [2g] *vt* to disregard, pay no attention to; to ignore; *duty* to neglect; *person* to slight, offend.

desatentado *adj* (a) thoughtless, rash, ill-advised; unwise, foolish. (b) excessive, extreme, out of all proportion.

desatento *adj* (a) heedless, careless; inattentive. (b) discourteous, unmannerly (*con* to).

desatierre *nm* (*SAm*) slag heap, rubbish tip.

desatinadamente *adv* foolishly; wildly, recklessly.

desatinado *adj* silly, foolish; wild, reckless.

desatinar [1a] **1** *vt* to perplex, bewilder. **2** *vi* to act foolishly; to talk nonsense, rave; to get rattled, begin to act wildly.

desatino *nm* (a) foolishness, folly, silliness; tactlessness. (b) (*act etc*) silly thing, foolish act; blunder, mistake; —s nonsense; ¡**qué** —! how silly!, what rubbish!; **un libro lleno de** —s a book stuffed with nonsense; **cometer un** — to make a blunder.

desatornillar [1a] *vt* to unscrew.

desatracar [1g] *vi* (*Naut*) to cast off.
desatraillar [1a] *vt* to unleash, let off the lead.
desatrancar [1g] *vt* (a) *door* to unbar, unbolt. (b) *pipe etc* to clear, unblock; *well* to clean out.
desatufarse [1a] *vr* (a) to get some fresh air, go out for a breather. (b) (*fig*) to calm down.
desautorizado *adj* unauthorized; unwarranted.
desautorizar [1f] *vt* (a) *person* to deprive of authority; to declare without authority. (b) *report etc* to deny, issue a denial of.
desavenencia *nf* disagreement; friction, unpleasantness; rift, quarrel.
desavenido *adj* incompatible; contrary, opposing; in disagreement; **ellos están —s** they are at odds, they disagree.
desavenir [3s] **1** *vt* to cause a rift between, make trouble between; to split, break the unity of.
  2 desavenirse *vr* to disagree (**con** with), fall out (**con** with).
desaventajado *adj* inferior; unfavourable, disadvantageous.
desayunado *ptp:* **estar —** to have had breakfast; **venir —** to come after breakfast.
desayunar [1a] *vi and* **desayunarse** *vr* to breakfast, have breakfast; **— con** to have for breakfast, breakfast on; **— de un acontecimiento** to receive the first news of an event.
desayuno *nm* breakfast.
desazón *nf* (a) tastelessness, lack of flavour.
  (b) (*of soil*) poorness.
  (c) (*Med*) discomfort, indisposition, slight trouble.
  (d) (*fig*) annoyance, displeasure; frustration; uneasiness.
desazonar [1a] **1** *vt* (a) *food* to make tasteless, take the flavour out of.
  (b) (*fig*) to annoy, upset, displease; to worry, cause anxiety to.
  2 desazonarse *vr* (a) (*Med*) to feel off-colour, be out of sorts.
  (b) (*fig*) to be annoyed; to worry, be anxious.
desbancar [1g] **1** *vt* (a) *banker* (*Cards*) to bust (*fam*), take the bank from.
  (b) (*fig*) to displace, oust; to cut out, supplant (in someone's affections).
  2 *vi* (*Cards*) to go bust (*fam*).
desbandada *nf* rush (to get away); **hubo una — general de turistas** there was a mass exodus of tourists, masses of tourists suddenly left; **cuando empezó a llover hubo una — general** when it started to rain everyone rushed for shelter; **a la —** in disorder; helter-skelter; **retirarse a la —** to retreat in disorder, make a disorderly retreat.
desbandarse [1a] *vr* (a) (*Mil*) to disband. (b) (*fig*) to flee in disorder; to go off in all directions, disperse in confusion.
desbarajustar [1a] *vt* to throw into confusion.
desbarajuste *nm* confusion, chaos, disorder.
desbaratar [1a] **1** *vt* (a) to ruin, spoil, destroy; to mess up; *plan etc* to foil, thwart, frustrate; *system* to disrupt, cause chaos in; *theory* to make nonsense of, debunk.
  (b) (*Mil*) to throw into confusion.
  (c) *fortune* to squander.
  (d) (*Mech*) to take to pieces.
  2 *vi* to rave, talk nonsense.
  3 desbaratarse *vr* (a) (*Mech*) to get out of order, develop a defect.
  (b) (*person*) to fly off the handle (*fam*), go off the deep end; to become unbalanced.
desbaratamiento *nm*, **desbarate** *nm*, **desbarato** *nm* (a) ruin, destruction, foiling, thwarting; disruption; debunking.
  (b) (*Mil*) rout.
  (c) (*Med: also* **— de vientre**) bowel upset.
  (d) squandering.
desbarbar [1a] **1** *vt* *person* to shave; *paper* to trim the edges of; *plants* to cut back, trim (off).
  2 desbarbarse *vr* to shave.
desbarrancadero *nm* (*Col, Guat, Mex, Ven*) precipice.
desbarrancar [1g] **1** *vt* (a) *ground* to level. (b) (*SAm*) to fling over a precipice. (c) (*Col, Per, PR*) to ruin.
  2 desbarrancarse *vr* (*SAm*) to fall over a precipice.
desbarrar [1a] *vi* to talk rubbish; to be very wide of the mark.
desbastar [1a] **1** *vt* (a) (*Tech*) to rough-hew; to plane (down), smooth (down).
  (b) (*fig*) to take the rough edges off; to refine, polish; *recruit etc* to knock the corners off, lick into shape.
  2 desbastarse *vr* (*fig*) to acquire some polish.

desbaste *nm* (a) (*Tech*) planing, smoothing. (b) (*fig*) polishing, refinement; licking into shape.
desbeber [2a] *vi* (*tabu*) to piss (*tabu*).
desbloquear [1a] *vt* (a) to break the blockade of. (b) (*Comm, Fin*) to unfreeze, unblock.
desbocado *adj* (a) *vessel* with a broken rim.
  (b) *gun* wide-mouthed.
  (c) *horse* runaway; *animal* escaped, stray.
  (d) *tool* worn, defective, damaged.
  (e) *person* foul-mouthed, foul-spoken.
  (f) *liquid* (*SAm*) overflowing.
desbocar [1g] **1** *vt* *vessel* to break the rim (or mouth) of.
  2 *vi:* **— en** (*of river*) to run into, flow into; (*of street*) to open into, come out into.
  3 desbocarse *vr* (a) (*horse*) to bolt, run away.
  (b) (*person*) to start to swear, let out a stream of insults.
desbordamiento *nm* (a) overflowing, flooding; spilling. (b) (*fig*) eruption, outburst; **un tremendo — de entusiasmo** a great upsurge of enthusiasm.
desbordar [1a] **1** *vt* to pass, go beyond; to exceed, surpass; **desbordaron las líneas enemigas** they burst through the enemy lines; **el proyecto desborda los límites señalados** the plan goes well beyond the limits which were set; **esto desborda mi tolerancia** this exceeds my capacity for tolerance.
  2 *vi and* **desbordarse** *vr* (a) (*of river*) to overflow, flood, burst its banks; (*of liquid*) to overflow, spill (over).
  (b) (*of enthusiasm etc*) to erupt, burst forth.
  (c) (*of person*) to give free rein to one's feelings; (*pej*) to fly off the handle (*fam*), lose one's self-control; **—(se) de alegría** to be bursting with happiness.
desborde *nm* (*Arg*) = **desbordamiento**.
desbravador *nm* horse-breaker.
desbravar [1a] **1** *vt* to break in, tame.
  2 *vi and* **desbravarse** *vr* (a) (*of animal*) to get less wild, grow less fierce.
  (b) (*of current etc*) to lose its strength, diminish in force.
  (c) (*of liquor*) to lose its strength.
desbrozar [1f] *vt* *passage etc* to clear (*of rubbish*); *land* to clear of scrub, clear the undergrowth from.
descabalgar [1h] *vi* to dismount.
descabellado *adj* (*fig*) wild, crazy, preposterous.
descabellar [1a] *vt* (a) *person* to dishevel; to ruffle, rumple. (b) *bull* to kill with a thrust in the neck, administer the coup de grâce to.
descabello *nm* (*Taur*) final thrust, coup de grâce.
descabezado *adj* (a) headless. (b) (*fig*) wild, crazy, light-headed.
descabezar [1f] **1** *vt* (a) *person etc* to behead, cut the head off; *tree* to lop, poll, cut the top off; *plant* to top.
  (b) (*fig*) *difficulty* to begin to get over, get over the worst part of, surmount.
  2 descabezarse *vr* (a) (*Bot*) to shed the grain.
  (b) (*person*) to rack one's brains.
descachalambrarse [1a] *vr* (*Col, Ec, Per*) to dress carelessly.
descachar [1a] *vt* (*Col, Chi, Ven*) to de-horn.
descacharrado *adj* (*CAm*) dirty, slovenly.
descalabrado *adj:* **salir —** to come out the loser (*de* in), come off badly.
descalabrar [1a] **1** *vt* (a) to smash, damage; *person* to hit, hurt, (*esp*) to hit on the head; (*Naut*) to cripple, disable.
  (b) (*fig*) to harm, damage, injure; to attack the character of.
  2 descalabrarse *vr* to hurt one's head, give oneself a bang on the head.
descalabro *nm* blow, setback; disaster, misfortune; damage; (*Mil*) defeat; **— electoral** electoral setback, disaster at the polls.
descalificación *nf* disqualification.
descalificar [1g] *vt* to disqualify.
descalzar [1f] **1** *vt* (a) *shoe* to take off.
  (b) **— a uno** to take off someone's shoes (*etc*); **A no vale para — a B** A can't hold a candle to B.
  (c) *wheel* to remove the chocks from.
  (d) (*fig*) to dig under, undermine.
  2 descalzarse *vr* (a) to take off one's shoes (*etc*); **— los guantes** to take off one's gloves.
  (b) (*of horse*) to cast a shoe.
descalzo *adj* (a) barefoot(ed); shoeless, stockingless; **estar —, estar con los pies —s** to be barefooted, have one's shoes off, have no shoes (*etc*) on; **ir —** to go barefooted.
  (b) (*Eccl*) discalced.
  (c) (*fig*) destitute.
descamarse [1a] *vr* to flake off, scale off.

descaminado adj (a) **andar** —, **ir** — to be on the wrong road.
(b) (fig) mistaken; misguided; ill-advised; **ir** — to be on the wrong track; **andar** — **en** to be mistaken in (or about); **en eso no anda Vd muy** — you're not far wrong there.
descaminar [1a] **1** vt (a) to misdirect, give wrong directions to, put on the wrong road; (fig) to mislead, lead astray.
(b) goods to seize as contraband.
(c) (SAm) to hold up.
2 descaminarse vr (a) to get lost, go the wrong way; (fig) to go astray.
(b) to run off the road.
descamisado 1 adj (fig) ragged, shabby; wretched.
2 nm ragamuffin; down-and-out; poor devil, wretch.
descamisar [1a] vt (a) to strip the shirt off. (b) (Col, Guat, Per) fruit etc to remove the outer covering of; (fig) to ruin; (at cards etc) to fleece.
descampado nm open space, piece of empty ground; **comer al** — to eat in the open air; **vivir en** — to live in open country; **se fue a vivir en** — he went off to live in the wilds.
descansadero nm stopping place, resting place.
descansado adj (a) rested, refreshed. (b) restful; life etc tranquil, unworried, free from care.
descansapié nm pedal, footrest.
descansar [1a] **1** vt (a) to rest, support, lean (sobre on).
(b) to rest; **esto descansa la vista más** this rests one's eyes better.
(c) to help, give a hand to.
(d) — **sus penas en uno** to tell one's troubles to someone, confide in someone about one's troubles.
2 vi (a) (of person) to rest; to take a rest, have a break (de from); to sleep, lie down; (of corpse) to lie, rest; **necesito** — **un rato** I need to rest a bit; **podemos** — **aquí** we can rest here; — **en paz** to rest in peace; **no descansé en todo el día** I didn't have a moment's rest all day; **¡descanse Vd!** don't worry!; **¡que Vd descanse!**, **¡descanse bien!** sleep well!
(b) (Agr) to lie fallow.
(c) — **en** (Archit) to rest on, be supported by.
(d) — **en** (fig) to rely on; to trust in; **el argumento descansa sobre los siguientes hechos** the argument is based on the following facts.
3 descansarse vr: — **en uno** to rely on someone, count on someone; to confide in someone.
descansillo nm (Archit) landing.
descanso nm (a) (in general) rest; repose; (from pain etc) relief; (period) rest, break; **tomarse unos días de** — to take a few days' rest; **trabajar sin** — to work without a break; **es un** — **saber que no estás solo** it's a relief to know you are not alone.
(b) (Sport) interval, half-time; (Theat) interval.
(c) (Tech) rest, support; bench; bracket; — **de cabeza** headrest.
(d) (Archit) landing.
descañonar [1a] vt (a) fowl to pluck. (b) face to shave against the grain. (c) (Cards: fam) to fleece, clean out (sl).
descapachar [1a] vt (Col) maize to husk.
descapiruzar [1f] vt (Col) to rumple the hair of.
descapotable (Aut) **1** adj convertible. **2** nm convertible.
descapsulador nm bottle opener.
descaradamente adv shamelessly, brazenly; cheekily, saucily; blatantly.
descarado adj shameless, brazen, barefaced; cheeky, saucy; blatant.
descararse [1a] vr to behave impudently, be insolent, be cheeky (con to); — **a pedir algo** to have the nerve to ask for something.
descarbonizar [1f] vt, **descarburar** [1a] vt to decarbonize.
descarga nf (a) (Naut etc) unloading; clearing; — **de aduana** customs clearance.
(b) (Mil) firing, discharge; — **(cerrada)** volley; **como una** — suddenly, unexpectedly.
(c) (Elec) discharge.
descargadero nm wharf.
descargado adj empty, unloaded; battery flat.
descargador nm docker.
descargar [1h] **1** vt (a) boat, cart etc to unload; to empty.
(b) gun to fire, discharge, shoot; to unload; — **un golpe en uno** to let fly a blow at someone, deal someone a blow; — **golpes sobre la mesa** to beat the table, rain blows on the table; — **un golpe contra la censura** to strike a blow against the censorship.

(c) (Elec) to discharge; battery to flatten, exhaust.
(d) bowels to evacuate.
(e) (of cloud) hail etc to send down, let fall.
(f) anger etc to vent (en, sobre on).
(g) conscience to ease, relieve; heart to unburden.
(h) (Comm) draft to take up.
(i) person to relieve, release (de una obligación from an obligation); to free (de una deuda from a debt); (Law etc) to clear, acquit (de of).
2 vi (a) — **en** (of river) to run into, flow into; (of street) to open into, come out into.
(b) (Elec) to discharge.
(c) (of storm) to burst, break.
3 descargarse vr (a) to unburden oneself, disburden oneself; — **de algo** to get rid of something; — **con** (or **en**) **uno de algo** to unload something on to someone.
(b) (Law etc) to clear oneself, vindicate oneself (de of).
(c) to resign.
descargo nm (a) unloading; emptying.
(b) (of debt) discharge.
(c) (Comm) receipt, voucher.
(d) — **de una obligación** release from an obligation; — **de una acusación** acquittal on a charge.
(e) (Law: also —**s, pliego de** —**s**) evidence, depositions (in favour of the defendant); (fig) excuses, piece of special pleading; **testigo de** — witness for the defence.
descargue nm unloading; emptying.
descarnado adj thin, lean, scrawny; emaciated; cadaverous; (fig) bare.
descarnador nm dental scraper; cuticle remover.
descarnar [1a] **1** vt (a) bone to remove the flesh from; hide to scrape the flesh from.
(b) (fig) to eat away, corrode, wear down.
2 descarnarse vr to lose flesh, get thin.
descaro nm shamelessness, brazenness; cheek, sauce, nerve; blatancy; **tuvo 'el** — **de decirme que . . .** he had the nerve to tell me that . . .; **¡qué** —**!** what cheek!, what a nerve!
descarriar [1c] **1** vt (a) to misdirect, put on the wrong road.
(b) (fig) to lead astray.
(c) animal to separate from the herd, single out.
2 descarriarse vr (a) to lose one's way; (animal) to stray, get separated (from the herd).
(b) (fig) to err, go astray.
descarrilamiento nm derailment.
descarrilar [1a] vi (also **descarrilarse** vr (SAm)) (a) (Rail) to be derailed, run off the rails, jump the track.
(b) (fig) to get off the track, wander from the point.
descarrilo nm derailment.
descartar [1a] **1** vt to discard (also Cards); to put aside, lay aside; to reject; possibility etc to rule out.
2 descartarse vr (a) (Cards) to discard.
(b) — **de** to excuse oneself from; to shun, shirk, evade.
descarte nm (a) (Cards) discard. (b) discarding, rejection, ruling out. (c) (fig) excuse; shirking, evasion.
descasar [1a] vt (a) to annul the marriage of. (b) (fig) to separate; to disarrange, upset the arrangement of.
descascar [1g] **1** vt to peel; to shell; to remove the bark from. **2 descascarse** vr (a) to smash to pieces, come apart. (b) (fam) to chatter.
descascarar [1a] **1** vt (a) to peel; to shell, take the shell off.
(b) (Col) to flay, skin.
(c) (Col) to dishonour.
2 descascararse vr to peel (off), scale (off); to chip off.
descastado adj (a) that has lost caste, untouchable; word etc improper. (b) alienated from one's family; cold, indifferent (to affection).
descaudalado adj penniless.
descendedero nm ramp.
descendencia nf (a) descent, origin. (b) offspring, descendants; **morir sin dejar** — to die without issue, leave no children.
descendente adj descending, downward; downward-sloping; quantity diminishing; **tren** — down train.
descender [2g] **1** vt (a) to lower, let down; luggage etc to get down, lift down, take down.
(b) stairs etc to go down, descend.
2 vi (a) to descend, come down, go down.
(b) (of fever, temperature, water level etc) to drop, fall, go down (en un 5 por cien by 5%).
(c) (of liquid) to run, flow.

(d) (*of curtain etc*) to hang.

(e) (*of person, strength*) to fail, get weak, decay; **— de** (*or* **en**) **energía** to suffer a loss of energy.

(f) **— a** (*fig*) to stoop to, lower oneself to.

(g) **— de** to descend from, be descended from; to be derived from; **— de linaje de reyes** to come from a line of kings; **la tribu desciende de la región central** the tribe comes from the central region; the tribe originated in the central region; **de esa palabra descienden otras muchas** many other words derive from that one.

descendiente *nmf* descendant.

descendimiento *nm* descent; lowering; **el D— de la Cruz** the Descent from the Cross.

descenso *nm* **(a)** (*act*) descent; going down; (*of fever, temperature etc*) drop, fall; (*of production*) downturn; (*Sport*) relegation; (*in quality*) decline, falling-off; **las cifras han experimentado un brusco —** the figures show a sharp fall; **hay un — de calidad** there is a falling-off in quality.

(b) (*Min etc*) collapse, subsidence.

(c) (*Med*) rupture; **— del útero** prolapse, fallen womb.

(d) (*place*) slope, drop, descent; **el — hacia el río** the descent to the river, the slope down to the river.

descentrado *adj* **(a)** off centre.

(b) (*fig*) out of focus; wrongly adjusted; **parece que el problema está —** the problem seems to be out of focus, it seems that the question has not been properly stated; **todavía está algo —** he is still somewhat out of touch, he is still not properly adjusted (to the situation).

descentralización *nf* decentralization.

descentralizar [1f] *vt* to decentralize.

desceñir [3h *and* 3l] *vt* to loosen; to undo, unfasten.

descepar [1a] *vt* **(a)** (*Agr*) to uproot, pull up by the roots. **(b)** (*fig*) to extirpate, eradicate.

descercar [1g] *vt* **(a)** to remove the fence round. **(b)** (*Mil*) city to relieve, raise the siege of.

descerco *nm* (*Mil*) relief.

descerrajado *adj* (*fam*) **(a)** raving mad, unhinged. **(b)** wicked.

descerrajar [1a] *vt* **(a)** to force the lock of; to break open, force. **(b)** *shot* to let off, fire (*a* at).

descervigar [1h] *vt* **(a)** to break the neck of. **(b)** (*fig*) to humiliate.

descifrable *adj* decipherable.

descifrador *nm* decipherer; decoder; **el — del misterio** the man who solved the mystery.

descifrar [1a] *vt* *writing* to decipher, (manage to) read; *message* to decode; *problem* to puzzle out, figure out; *mystery* to solve, crack.

descinchar [1a] *vt* *horse* to loosen the girths of.

desclasificación *nf* disqualification.

desclasificar [1g] *vt* (*Sport*) to disqualify.

desclavar [1a] *vt* to pull out the nails from, unnail.

descobijar [1a] *vt* to uncover, leave exposed.

descocado *adj* (*fam*) =**descarado**; *girl* brazen, forward.

descocarse [1g] *vr* (*fam*) =**descararse**.

descoco *nm* =**descaro**.

descochollado *adj* (*Chi*) **(a)** ragged, shabby. **(b)** wicked. **(c)** ill-tempered.

descoger [2c] *vt* to spread out, unfold.

descolada *nf* (*Mex*) snub, rebuff.

descolar [1a] *vt* **(a)** to dock, cut the tail off. **(b)** (*CAm*) to fire, sack. **(c)** (*Mex*) to snub, slight.

descolgar [1h *and* 1m] **1** *vt* to take down, get down; to unhook; to lower, let down; *telephone* to pick up.

2 descolgarse *vr* **(a)** to let oneself down (*con* by, *de* from), lower oneself; to come down, descend, climb down; **— por una pared** to climb down a wall.

(b) (*fig: person*) to turn up unexpectedly; (*Meteorol*) to come on suddenly, set in unexpectedly.

(c) **— con una estupidez** to come out with a silly remark, blurt out something silly.

descolocado *adj* *servant* out of work, unplaced.

descolón *nm* (*Mex*) snub, rebuff.

descolonización *nf* decolonization.

descoloramiento *nm* discolo(u)ration.

descolorar [1a] *vt* =**decolorar**.

descolorido *adj* **(a)** discoloured, faded; pale. **(b)** (*fig*) colourless.

descollante *adj* outstanding.

descollar [1m] *vi* to stand out, be outstanding; **descuella entre los demás** he stands out among the others; **la obra que más descuella de las suyas** his most outstanding work; **la iglesia descuella sobre los demás edificios** the church stands out above (*or* towers over) the other buildings.

descombrar [1a] *vt* to clear (of obstacles), disencumber.

descomedidamente *adv* **(a)** excessively. **(b)** rudely, insolently, disrespectfully.

descomedido *adj* **(a)** excessive, immoderate. **(b)** *person* rude, insolent, disrespectful (*con* to, towards).

descomedimiento *nm* rudeness, insolence, disrespect.

descomedirse [3l] *vr* to be rude, be disrespectful (*con* to, towards).

descompaginar [1a] *vt* to disarrange, disorganize, mess up.

descompasado *adj* excessive, out of all proportion; **a una hora descompasada** at an unearthly hour; **de tamaño —** of disproportionate size, extra big.

descompasarse [1a] *vr* =**descomedirse**.

descompletar [1a] *vt* (*SAm*) to make incomplete, impair the completeness of; *set* to break, ruin.

descomponer [2r] **1** *vt* **(a)** to separate into its constituent parts; (*Chem*) to separate into its elements; *unit, mass etc* to split up, break down; *argument* to break down, analyse, reduce to a series of points; (*Math*) to break down.

(b) *decaying matter* to rot, decompose.

(c) (*Mech*) to break; to put out of order; to tamper with, mess up; *features* to distort; *stomach etc* to upset; **— el peinado a una** to disarrange someone's hair.

(d) *order etc* to disarrange, disturb, upset; *calm* to ruffle, disturb; **— los planes de uno** to upset someone's plans, mess up someone's plans.

(e) *person* to shake up, give a jolt to; to put out; to anger, provoke.

(f) *two persons* to cause a rift between, set at odds.

2 descomponerse *vr* **(a)** to rot, decompose.

(b) (*Mech*) to break down, get out of order, develop a fault; (*stomach*) to get upset; (*weather*) to break up, change for the worse; **— el brazo** (*Col*) to put one's arm out of joint.

(c) to lose one's temper, get worked up; **— con uno** to fall out with someone.

descomposición *nf* **(a)** splitting up, breakdown; (*Chem*) decomposition; **— estadística** statistical breakdown.

(b) rotting, decomposition.

(c) (*Med*) **— de vientre** stomach upset, diarrhoea.

(d) (*fig*) discomposure.

descompostura *nf* **(a)** (*Mech etc*) breakdown, fault, trouble; bad working order; disorder; disorganization; untidiness, slovenliness.

(b) (*fig*) discomposure.

(c) (*fig*) brazenness, forwardness.

(d) (*Col*) dislocation.

descompresión *nf* decompression.

descompuesto *adj* **(a)** (*Mech etc*) broken, out of order, faulty; *face, features* twisted, distorted; *system etc* disordered, disorganized, chaotic; *room* untidy; *appearance* slovenly.

(b) (*fig*) angry; **ponerse —** to get angry, get worked up, lose one's composure.

(c) (*fig*) brazen, forward; rude.

(d) (*SAm*) *estar —* to be tipsy.

descomunal *adj* huge, enormous, colossal.

desconcentración *nf* decentralization, breaking-up.

desconcentrar [1a] *vt* *industry etc* to decentralize, break up, distribute over a wider area.

desconceptuado *adj* discredited; not well thought-of, ill-reputed.

desconcertado *adj* (*fig*): *estar —*, *quedar —* to be disconcerted, be taken aback; to be bewildered.

desconcertador *adj*, **desconcertante** *adj* disconcerting, upsetting; embarrassing; baffling, bewildering, puzzling.

desconcertar [1k] **1** *vt* **(a)** (*Mech etc*) to put out of order, damage; (*Anat*) to dislocate; *order* to disarrange, disturb; *plan* to upset, dislocate, throw out of gear.

(b) *person* to disconcert, upset, put out; to embarrass; (*of problem etc*) to baffle, bewilder, puzzle; **le desconcertó encontrarme allí** it disconcerted him to find me there; **la noticia desconcertó a todos** the news upset everybody.

2 desconcertarse *vr* **(a)** (*Mech etc*) to get out of order, develop a fault; (*Anat*) to get out of joint, be dislocated.

(b) (*person*) to be disconcerted, be upset, be put out; to get embarrassed; to be bewildered; **siguió sin —** he went on quite unruffled; **esto basta para que se desconcierte el más sosegado** this would get even the calmest of men worked up.

desconcierto *nm* **(a)** (*Mech etc*) disorder, trouble; damage; disarrangement, disturbance, chaos.

(b) (*fig*) uneasiness, uncertainty; embarrassment;

bewilderment; **contribuye al — de la juventud** it increases young people's bewilderment; **sembrar el — en el partido** to sow confusion in the party, create discord in the party; **hay un — fundamental** there is a basic disagreement.
desconchabar [1a] *vt* (*SAm*) to dislocate.
desconchar [1a] **1** *vt* to strip off, peel off; to chip off. **2 desconcharse** *vr* to peel off, flake off; to chip.
desconectar [1a] *vt* (*Mech*) to disconnect; to uncouple; (*Elec*) to disconnect; to switch off, turn off.
desconfiado *adj* distrustful, suspicious (*de* of).
desconfianza *nf* distrust, mistrust, lack of confidence; **voto de —** vote of no confidence.
desconfiar [1c] *vi* to be distrustful; to lack confidence; **— de** to distrust, mistrust, suspect; to have no confidence in; **desconfío de ello** I doubt it; **desconfíe de las imitaciones** (*Comm*) beware of imitations; **desconfía de sus posibilidades** he has no faith in his potentiality; **desconfío de que llegue a tiempo** I doubt if he will get here in time, I cannot be sure that he will arrive in time.
desconformar [1a] *vi and* **desconformarse** *vr* (a) to disagree, dissent.
(b) **se desconforman** they do not get on well together; they are not suited to each other.
desconforme *adj* = **disconforme.**
descongelar [1a] *vt refrigerator* to defrost.
descongestión *nf* (*of city overcrowding, traffic pressure etc*) relief, relieving; **una política de —** a policy of relieving population pressure in the cities.
descongestionar [1a] *vt head* to clear; *town etc* to make less crowded, relieve the population pressure in; *street* to relieve the traffic problems of, make less crowded.
desconocer [2d] *vt* (a) not to know, be ignorant of, be unfamiliar with; to be unaware of; to fail to remember; **desconocen los principios fundamentales** they are ignorant of the basic principles; **no desconozco que . . .** I am not unaware that . . .
(b) not to recognize; to pretend not to know; to ignore, disregard.
(c) to disown, repudiate; **pero el poeta desconoció la obra** but the poet disowned the work.
desconocido 1 *adj* (a) unknown, not known (*de*, *para* to); strange, unfamiliar; unrecognized; **lo —** the unknown; **por razones desconocidas** for reasons which are not known (*to us etc*); **el triunfo de un atleta —** the success of an unknown athlete.
(b) much changed; **está —** he is much altered, he is hardly recognizable.
(c) ungrateful.
2 *nm*, **desconocida** *nf* stranger; unknown person.
desconocimiento *nm* (a) ignorance. (b) disregard, repudiation. (c) ingratitude.
desconsideración *nf* inconsiderateness, thoughtlessness.
desconsideradamente *adv* inconsiderately, thoughtlessly.
desconsiderado *adj* inconsiderate, thoughtless.
desconsoladamente *adv* disconsolately.
desconsolado *adj* disconsolate; *face* sad, woebegone.
desconsolador *adj* distressing, grievous.
desconsolar [1m] **1** *vt* to distress, grieve. **2 desconsolarse** *vr* to be grieved; to despair, lose hope.
desconsuelo *nm* affliction, distress, grief; sadness; despair; **con —** sadly, despairingly.
descontado *adj*: **por —** of course, naturally; **eso lo podemos dar por —** we can take that for granted, we can assume that; we can rely on that.
descontaminación *nf* decontamination.
descontaminar [1a] *vt* to decontaminate.
descontar [1m] *vt* (a) to take away; (*Comm*) to discount, deduct. (b) to discount; to assume, take for granted.
descontentadizo *adj* hard to please; restless, unsettled.
descontentar [1a] *vt* to displease.
descontento 1 *adj* dissatisfied, discontented (*de* with); disgruntled (*de* about, at); **estar — de** to be dissatisfied with, be unhappy about.
2 *nm* (a) dissatisfaction, displeasure; disgruntlement.
(b) (*Pol etc*) discontent, unrest; **hay mucho —** there is a lot of unrest.
descontinuación *nf* discontinuation.
descontinuar [1e] *vt* to discontinue.
descontrolado *adj* (*SAm*) upset, irritated; uncontrolled.
desconvenir [3s] *vi* (a) (*persons*) to disagree (*con* with).
(b) to be incongruous; not to fit, not match; to differ (*con* from).

(c) to be inconvenient; to be unsuitable.
descorazonador *adj* discouraging, disheartening.
descorazonamiento *nm* discouragement; dejection, depression.
descorazonar [1a] **1** *vt* to discourage, dishearten. **2 descorazonarse** *vr* to get discouraged, lose heart.
descorchador *nm* corkscrew.
descorchar [1a] *vt* (a) *tree* to remove the bark from; to strip. (b) *bottle* to uncork, draw the cork of, open. (c) *chest etc* to force, break open.
descornar [1m] **1** *vt* to de-horn, poll. **2 descornarse** *vr* (*fig*) to slog away, work like a slave; to rack one's brains.
descorrer [2a] *vt curtain, bolt* to draw back.
descortés *adj* discourteous, rude, impolite.
descortesía *nf* discourtesy, rudeness, impoliteness.
descortésmente *adv* discourteously, rudely, impolitely.
descortezar [1f] *vt* (a) *tree* to strip the bark from, remove the bark of; *bread* to cut the crust off; *fruit etc* to peel.
(b) (*fig*) to polish up a bit, knock the corners off.
descoser [2a] **1** *vt* (a) (*Sew*) to unstitch, unpick; to rip, tear.
(b) to separate, part; *see* **labio.**
2 descoserse *vr* (a) to come apart (at the seam), burst, tear.
(b) (*fam*) to blurt out a secret, let the cat out of the bag.
(c) (*tabu*) to fart (*tabu*).
(d) **— de risa** to split one's sides with laughing, die of laughing.
descosido 1 *adj* (a) (*Sew*) unstitched, torn; shabby.
(b) (*fig*) *narrative etc* disconnected, disjointed, chaotic.
(c) *person, speech etc* wild, immoderate; talkative; big-mouthed (*sl*), indiscreet, blabbing.
2 *nm* (a) (*Sew*) open seam; rip, tear.
(b) **obrar como un —** to act wildly; **beber como un —** to drink an awful lot; **comer como un —** to eat to excess, stuff oneself; **gastar como un —** to spend money wildly; **estudiar** (*etc*) **como un —** to study (*etc*) like mad.
descoyuntado *adj* (a) (*Anat*) dislocated, out of joint. (b) *narrative etc* incoherent, disjointed, chaotic.
descoyuntar [1a] **1** *vt* (a) (*Anat*) to dislocate, put out of joint.
(b) *person* (*fig*) to tire out; to bother; to weary, annoy.
(c) *facts etc* to twist, force the sense of, adapt improperly.
2 descoyuntarse *vr* (a) (*Anat*) **— un hueso** to put a bone out of joint; **los huesos se descoyuntaron** the bones became dislocated.
(b) **— de risa** to split one's sides with laughing, die of laughing; **— a cortesías** to overdo the courtesies, be exaggeratedly polite.
descrecer [2d] *vi* to decrease.
descrédito *nm* discredit; disrepute; **caer en —** to fall into disrepute; **ir en — de** to be to the discredit of, damage the reputation of.
descreencia *nf* (*esp SAm*) unbelief.
descreer [2e] **1** *vt* (a) to disbelieve; to place no faith in. (b) to deny due credit to. **2** *vi* (*Rel*) to lose one's faith.
descreído 1 *adj* unbelieving; (*pej*) godless. **2** *nm*, **descreída** *nf* unbeliever.
descreimiento *nm* unbelief.
descremar [1a] *vt* (*SAm*) *milk* to skim.
descrestar [1a] *vt* (a) to cut the comb of. (b) (*fam*) to swindle, cheat.
describir [3a; *ptp* **descrito**] *vt* (*all senses*) to describe.
descripción *nf* description; **supera a toda —** it is beyond description, it is indescribable.
descriptible *adj* describable.
descriptivo *adj* descriptive.
descrismar [1a] **1** *vt*: **— a uno** to bash someone on the head (*fam*); **¡o eso o te descrismo!** either that or I'll bash you! (*fam*).
2 descrismarse *vr* (a) to slave away; to rack one's brains.
(b) (*fam*) to blow one's top (*fam*).
descrito *ptp of* **describir**; **no es para — it is indescribable, it beggars description.
descuajar [1a] *vt* (a) *solid mass* to melt, dissolve.
(b) (*Bot*) to uproot, pull up by the root; *object* to pull out, tear from its place.
(c) (*fig*) to eradicate.
(d) (*fig*) to dishearten.
descuajaringarse [1h] *vr* (a) (*Anat*) to come apart; to do oneself an injury; **— de risa** to split one's sides

with laughing, die of laughing; **es para — it's enough to make you die of laughing.**
(b) *(SAm)* to fall to bits.
descuartizar [1f] *vt* (a) *animal* to carve up, cut up.
(b) *person (Hist)* to quarter; *(fig)* to tear apart; **ni que me descuarticen** not even if they tear me apart.
descubierta 1 *nm (Mil)* scout. **2** *nf* (a) *(Mil)* reconnoitring, patrolling. (b) **a la —** openly; in the open.
descubierto 1 *ptp of* **descubrir.**
2 *adj* (a) *situation* open, exposed; *(Mil)* under fire; *body* bare, uncovered; *head* bare; *person* bareheaded, hatless; *car* open; *field* open, bare, treeless.
(b) **al —** in the open; exposed; in full view; **poner algo al —** to lay something bare, expose something to view; **quedar al —** to be exposed; to be manifest, be obvious.
3 *nm (Comm: in account)* deficit, shortage; *(on loan)* overdraft; **a —** short; *loan etc* unbacked; **vender al —** to sell short; **estar en —** to be overdrawn; **girar en —** to overdraw.
descubridero *nm* look-out post.
descubridor *nm* (a) discoverer. (b) *(Mil)* scout.
descubrimiento *nm* discovery; detection; disclosure, revelation; unveiling.
descubrir [3a; *ptp* **descubierto**] **1** *vt* (a) to discover; to find, detect, spot; to bring to light; to unearth, uncover; *oil etc* to find, strike; *answer etc* to discover, ascertain, learn.
(b) to see, make out, glimpse; **apenas lo descubría entre las nubes** I could just see it among the clouds.
(c) *statue, plaque etc* to unveil.
(d) to expose to view; to show, reveal, disclose; **— el estómago** to uncover one's stomach, bare one's stomach; **— la cabeza** to bare one's head; **— sus intenciones** to reveal one's intentions; **— su pecho a uno** to unbosom oneself to someone; **le descubrió su escritura** his writing gave him away, his writing betrayed him; **fue la criada la que les descubrió a la policía** it was the servant who gave them away to the police.
2 descubrirse *vr* (a) to reveal oneself, show oneself; to disclose one's whereabouts.
(b) to take off one's hat; to raise one's hat (in greeting).
(c) **— a uno, — con uno** to confess to someone, unbosom oneself to someone.
descuento *nm* discount; rebate, reduction; **a — below par; al —, con — at a discount; — por pago al contado** discount for cash payment.
descuerar [1a] *vt (Chi)* (a) to flay, skin. (b) *(fig)* to defame.
descuernar [1a] *vt (Col, Cu, Guat, PR)* to de-horn.
descuidadamente *adv* (a) carelessly; slackly, negligently; forgetfully. (b) untidily; in a slovenly way.
descuidado *adj* (a) careless; slack, negligent; forgetful.
(b) *appearance etc* untidy, slovenly; unkempt.
(c) unprepared; off guard; **coger** *(or* **pillar** *etc)* **a uno —** to catch someone off his guard, catch someone at a careless moment.
(d) easy in one's mind, without worries; **puedes estar —** you needn't worry.
(e) neglected; **con aspecto de niños —s** with the look of neglected children.
descuidar [1a] **1** *vt* to neglect; to disregard; to overlook; **ha descuidado mucho su negocio** he has neglected his business a lot.
2 *vi and* **descuidarse** *vr* (a) to be careless, be negligent; to get careless; to feel safe, drop one's guard; **en cuanto me descuide él me lo roba** the moment I drop my guard *(or* cease to watch out) he'll steal it from me; **a poco que uno se descuide le cobran el doble** you've got to watch them all the time or they'll charge you double.
(b) not to worry; **¡descuida!** don't worry!, it's all right!, you can forget about that!; **—se de algo** not to bother about something; **—se de hacer algo** not to bother to do something.
(c) to let oneself go, stop taking care of oneself.
descuidero *nm* sneak thief.
descuido *nm* (a) *(in general)* carelessness; slackness; negligence; forgetfulness; **al — nonchalantly; con — thoughtlessly, without thinking.**
(b) *(of appearance)* untidiness, slovenliness.
(c) *(un—)* oversight; mistake, slip; **en un — (SAm)** when least expected; **por — by an oversight, inadvertently.**
deschachar [1a] *vt (CAm)* to sack *(fam),* fire *(fam).*
deschalar [1a] *vt (Arg, Per) maize* to husk.
deschapar [1a] *vt (SAm) lock* to break.

desde 1 *prep* (a) *(place etc)* from; **— Burgos hay 30 km** it's 30 km from Burgos; **— abajo** from below; **— arriba** from (up) above; **— lejos** from afar, from a long way off; **— A hasta M** from A to M.
(b) *(time)* from; since; **— ahora** from now on; **— entonces** since then; **— el siglo XV para acá** from the 15th century onward; **— 1960 no existe** it ceased to exist in 1960, it went out of existence in 1960; **— el martes** since Tuesday, after Tuesday; **— el 4 hasta el 16** from the 4th to the 16th; **llueve — hace 3 días** it's been raining for 3 days; **— hace 2 años no le vemos** we haven't seen him for 2 years, we haven't seen him these last 2 years; **¿— cuándo es esto así?** how long has it been like this?
(c) **— niño** since childhood, since I *(etc)* was a child.
2 — que *conj* since; **— que llovió** since it rained; **— que puedo recordar** ever since I can remember, **(for)** as long as I can remember.
desdecir [3p] **1** *vi:* **— de** (a) to be unworthy of, be below the standard set by; to be unbecoming to; **desdice de su patria** he is unworthy of his country; **esta novela no desdice de las otras** this novel is well up to the standard of the others, this novel is not inferior to the others.
(b) to clash with, not match, not suit; **la corbata desdice del traje** the tie does not go with the suit.
2 desdecirse *vr* to retract, withdraw; to go back on what one has said; **— de algo** to go back on something, take back something one has said; **— de una promesa** to go back on a promise.
desdén *nm* scorn, disdain; **al — carelessly, nonchalantly.**
desdentado *adj* toothless.
desdeñable *adj* contemptible; **una cantidad nada — a** far from negligible amount.
desdeñar [1a] **1** *vt* to scorn, disdain; to turn up one's nose at; to despise. **2 desdeñarse** *vr:* **— de + *infin*** to scorn to + *infin,* not deign to + *infin.*
desdeñosamente *adv* scornfully, disdainfully; contemptuously.
desdeñoso *adj* scornful, disdainful; contemptuous.
desdibujado *adj* blurred; unclear; faded.
desdibujar [1a] **1** *vt* to blur (the outlines of).
2 desdibujarse *vr* to blur, get blurred, fade (away); **el recuerdo se ha desdibujado** the memory has become blurred.
desdicha *nf* (a) *(in general)* unhappiness, wretchedness; misfortune; misery. (b) *(una —)* misfortune, calamity.
desdichadamente *adv* unhappily; unluckily, unfortunately.
desdichado 1 *adj* (a) unhappy; unlucky; unfortunate; wretched; **¡qué — soy!** how wretched I am!
(b) unlucky, ill-fated; **fue un día —** it was an unlucky day.
2 *nm* poor devil, wretch.
desdinerar [1a] **1** *vt* to impoverish. **2 desdinerarse** *vr* (a) to cough up *(sl),* fork out *(fam).*
desdoblado *adj (fig)* personality split.
desdoblar [1a] *vt* (a) to unfold, spread out; *wire etc* to untwist, straighten; to take apart.
(b) *(Chem)* to break down *(en* into).
(c) *(fig)* to double, make two of; to split; **— un cargo** to split the functions of a post.
desdorar [1a] *vt* to tarnish *(also fig).*
desdoro *nm (fig)* blot, blemish, stigma, dishonour; **consideran un — trabajar** they think it dishonourable to work; **es un — para todos** it is a blot on us all; **hablar en — de uno** to speak disparagingly of someone, discredit someone by what one says.
deseable *adj* desirable.
desear [1a] *vt* to want, desire, wish (for); **os deseo toda clase de éxito** I wish you every success; **¿qué desea la señora?** *(Comm etc)* what can I do for you, madam?; **desearía más tiempo** I should like more time; **estoy deseando que esto termine** I wish this would end; **— + *infin*** to want to + *infin,* wish to + *infin; see* **dejar.**
desecación *nf* desiccation.
desecar [1g] **1** *vt* to dry up, desiccate; *land* to drain. **2 desecarse** *vr* to dry up.
desecha *nf (Col)* = **desecho.**
desechar [1a] *vt* (a) *rubbish* to throw out; *useless object* to scrap, get rid of, jettison; *clothing* to cast off.
(b) *advice, fear, scruple* to cast aside; *claim, offer* to reject; *idea, plan* to drop, discard.
(c) to underrate, underestimate; to think little of.
(d) to censure, reprove.
(e) *key* to turn.
desecho *nm* (a) *(also* **—s**) residue; waste, rubbish; scrap, junk; *(of butcher)* offal; *(of corn)* chaff; **— de**

hierro, hierro de — scrap iron; **producto de** — waste product; **vestidos de** — cast-off clothing.
(b) **el — de la sociedad** the scum of society, the dregs of society.
(c) **ese tío es un** — that fellow is a disaster, that chap is a dead loss.
(d) contempt, scorn; low opinion.
(e) (Cu) superior-quality tobacco.
(f) (SAm) short cut; detour; path, temporary road.

desellar [1a] vt to unseal, open.

desembalaje nm unpacking.

desembalar [1a] vt to unpack.

desembanastar [1a] **1** vt (a) to unpack; to take out (of a basket); (fam) sword to draw. (b) (fig) secret to blurt out.
2 desembanastarse vt (a) (animal) to break out. (b) to alight.

desembarazado adj (a) way etc clear, free, open; unburdened, light. (b) (fig) free and easy, free of commitments; **— de trabas** free, unrestrained.

desembarazar [1f] **1** vt (a) road etc to clear, free (de of); **— un cuarto de trastos** to clear a room of furniture.
(b) place to vacate, leave free, leave empty.
(c) **— a uno de algo** to rid someone of something.
(d) (Chi, Ec, Per, PR) to give birth to.
2 desembarazarse vr: **— de algo** to get rid of something, free oneself of something.

desembarazo nm (a) (act) clearing, freezing; disencumbrance; unburdening.
(b) (Chi, Ec, Per, PR) birth, delivery.
(c) (state) freedom; ease, naturalness; lack of restraint; **hablar con** — to talk easily, talk freely.

desembarcadero nm quay, landing stage, pier.

desembarcar [1g] **1** vt persons to land, put ashore; goods to land, unload.
2 vi and **desembarcarse** vr (a) to land, go ashore, disembark.
(b) (esp SAm) to alight (de from), get out (de of).
(c) **estar para** — (fam) to be about to give birth.

desembarco nm (Archit, Naut) landing.

desembargar [1h] vt to free; to remove the embargo on, remove the impediments from.

desembarque nm landing; unloading.

desembarrancar [1g] vt boat to refloat, get off.

desembarrar [1a] vt to clear of mud, remove the silt from.

desembaular [1a] vt (a) to unpack; to take out, get out (of a trunk); (fig) to empty. (b) (fig) to unburden oneself of.

desembocadero nm, **desembocadura** nf outlet, exit; (of river) mouth; (of drain) outfall; (of street) opening, end.

desembocar [1a] vi: **— en** (a) (of river) to flow into, run into, empty into; (of street) to meet, join, run into, lead into.
(b) (fig) to end in, result in, produce; **esto desembocó en una tragedia** this ended in tragedy, this led to tragedy.

desembolsar [1a] vt to pay out.

desembolso nm payment; disbursement; outlay, expenditure; **— inicial** deposit, down payment; **cubrir —s** to cover expenses.

desembozar [1f] vt to unmask (also fig), uncover.

desembragar [1h] **1** vt (Mech) to disengage, disconnect; clutch to release, let out. **2** vi (Aut) to declutch, let out the clutch.

desembrague nm disengagement; (Aut: act) declutching; (part) clutch release.

desembravecer [2d] vt to tame; (fig) to calm, pacify.

desembriagar [1h] **1** vt to sober up. **2 desembriagarse** vr to sober up.

desembrollar [1a] vt to unravel, disentangle.

desembuchar [1a] **1** vt to disgorge; (fig) to tell, reveal, let out.
2 vi (fig) to reveal a secret, spill the beans (sl); ¡**desembucha!** out with it!
3 desembucharse vr (Chi) to be sick.

desemejante adj dissimilar, unlike; **A es — de B** A is unlike B, A is different from B.

desemejanza nf dissimilarity.

desemejar [1a] **1** vt to alter (the appearance of), change (for the worse); to disfigure. **2** vi to be dissimilar, look different, not look alike.

desempacar [1g] vt to unpack.

desempacharse [1a] vr (a) **se desempachó** he got over his sick feeling; his stomach settled down (after its upset).
(b) (fig) to cease to feel shy, stop feeling awkward.

desempacho nm ease, confidence; unconcern; (pej) forwardness.

desempañar [1a] vt glass to clean, de-mist.

desempapelar [1a] vt parcel to unwrap; wall to remove the paper from.

desempaquetar [1a] vt to unpack, unwrap.

desempatar [1a] vi: volvieron a jugar para — they held a play-off (to resolve the earlier tie).

desempate nm play-off (to resolve an earlier tie).

desempedrar [1k] vt street to take up the paving stones of; **ir desempedrando la calle** (fig) to dash along the street.

desempeñar [1a] **1** vt (a) pawned property to redeem, recover, get out of pawn.
(b) **— a uno** to get someone out of debt, pay someone's debts; (fig) to get someone out of a jam.
(c) post to hold, fill, occupy; duty to perform, discharge; (Theat and fig) role to play.
2 desempeñarse vr to get out of debt; (fig) to get oneself out of a jam.

desempeño nm (a) redeeming, redemption.
(b) payment.
(c) occupation; performance, discharge; (Theat and fig) performance, acting, showing; **un — meritorio** a worthy performance.

desempleado 1 adj unemployed, out of work. **2** nm unemployed man.

desempleo nm unemployment.

desempolvar [1a] vt to dust, remove the dust from.

desencadenar [1a] **1** vt (a) to unchain; to unleash, let loose.
(b) (fig) to unleash; to cause, start, set off.
2 desencadenarse vr (a) to break loose, free oneself.
(b) (fig: storm etc) to burst; (war) to break out; **se desencadenaron los aplausos** a storm of clapping broke out; **se desencadenó una violenta reacción** a violent reaction was produced.

desencajado adj face twisted, contorted; eyes wild.

desencajar [1a] **1** vt (a) to throw out of joint; (Anat) to dislocate.
(b) (Mech) to disconnect, disengage, put out of gear.
2 desencajarse vr (face) to become distorted (with fear); (eyes) to look wild.

desencajonar [1a] vt to unpack.

desencallar [1a] vt boat to refloat, get off.

desencantar [1a] vt to disillusion, disenchant.

desencanto nm disillusion(ment), disenchantment.

desencoger [2c] **1** vt to spread out; to smooth out, straighten out. **2 desencogerse** vr to lose one's timidity.

desenconar [1a] **1** vt (a) inflammation to reduce.
(b) (fig) to calm down, soothe.
2 desenconarse vr (a) to grow less.
(b) (fig: hatred) to die down, abate; (person) to calm down.

desencorvar [1a] vt to unbend, straighten (out).

desenchufar [1a] vt to disconnect, unplug.

desendeudar [1a] vi (SAm) to pay one's debts, get out of the red.

desenfadaderas nfpl: **tener buenas** — to be unflappable, be slow to anger; to be good at getting out of jams.

desenfadado adj (a) character, manner etc free, uninhibited; free-and-easy; carefree; unabashed; (pej) forward, disrespectful; dress etc casual, unconventional.
(b) space free, unencumbered; ample.

desenfadar [1a] vt to pacify, calm down. **2 desenfadarse** vr to calm down.

desenfado nm freedom, lack of inhibition; free-and-easy manner; (pej) forwardness, disrespect.

desenfocado adj out of focus.

desenfrenadamente adv wildly, in an uncontrolled way; immoderately; licentiously.

desenfrenado adj wild, uncontrolled; immoderate; unbridled, licentious.

desenfrenarse [1a] vr (a) (person etc) to give free rein to one's passions, let one's feelings run wild, lose all self-control; (crowd) to run riot, rampage.
(b) (storm etc) to burst; to rage.

desenfreno nm wildness; lack of self-control; lack of moderation; licentiousness.

desenganchar [1a] vt to unhook, undo, unfasten; (Rail) to uncouple; (Mech) to disengage; horse to unhitch.

desengañado adj (a) disillusioned. (b) (Chi, Ec) terribly ugly.

desengañar [1a] **1** vt to disillusion; to disabuse (de about, of); **es mejor no —la** it is best not to disillusion her; it is best not to destroy her hopes.

2 desengañarse vr (a) to become disillusioned (de about).
(b) to see the light, come down to earth, see things as they really are; ¡desengáñate! don't you believe it!, don't go deceiving yourself!
desengaño nm (a) disillusion(ment); disappointment; sufrir un — amoroso to be disappointed in love, have an unhappy love affair; le enseñarán los —s the disillusioning experiences (of life) will teach you. (b) admonition, reproof; home truth.
desengranar [1a] vt to disengage.
desengrasar [1a] vt to degrease, remove the grease from; to scour.
desenjaular [1a] vt (a) to take out of a cage; to release from a cage. (b) (fam) to let out of jail.
desenlace nm outcome; (Lit) ending; dénouement; — fatal, — trágico tragic ending; el libro tiene un — feliz the book has a happy ending.
desenlatar [1a] vt (SAm) canned goods to open.
desenlazar [1f] 1 vt (a) to untie, unlace, undo. (b) (fig) problem to solve; plot to unravel.
2 desenlazarse vr (a) to come undone.
(b) (Lit) to end, turn out.
desenmarañar [1a] vt to disentangle, unravel (also fig).
desenmascarar [1a] vt (fig) to unmask, expose.
desenojar [1a] vt to soothe, appease, calm down.
desenredar [1a] 1 vt to unravel; to straighten out; to resolve, clear up.
2 desenredarse vr (fig) to get out of a jam; — de to get out of, extricate oneself from.
desenredo nm (a) unravelling, disentanglement. (b) (Lit) dénouement.
desenrollar [1a] 1 vt to unroll, unwind. **2 desenrollarse** vr to unroll, unwind; to get unrolled.
desenroscar [1g] vt (SAm) to unscrew.
desensibilizar [1f] vt to desensitize.
desensillar [1a] vt to unsaddle.
desentenderse [2g] vr: — de (a) to affect ignorance of, pretend not to know about.
(b) to wash one's hands of; to repudiate; to have nothing to do with; se ha desentendido de todo eso he has ceased to take any part in that, he has withdrawn completely from that.
desentendido adj: hacerse el — to pay no attention; to pretend not to be interested (or to hear etc); no te hagas el — don't pretend you haven't heard.
desenterrar [1k] vt (a) corpse to exhume, disinter. (b) (fig) to unearth, dig up, rake up.
desentonado adj (a) (Mus) out of tune. (b) colour clashing, not matching.
desentonar [1a] 1 vi (a) (Mus) to be out of tune.
(b) (fig) to be out of tune (con with); (of colours) to clash (con with), not match.
2 desentonarse vr (fig) to behave rudely, speak disrespectfully, raise one's voice angrily.
desentono nm (fig) rudeness, disrespect; rude (or angry) tone of voice.
desentorpecer [2d] vt (a) limb etc to stretch, loosen up. (b) person (fam) to polish up.
desentramparse [1a] vr to get out of the red.
desentrañar [1a] vt (a) to disembowel; to eviscerate. (b) (fig) mystery to puzzle out, get to the bottom of, unravel; meaning to puzzle out, work out.
desentrenado adj out of practice; off form.
desentumecer [2d] vt to free from numbness, restore the feeling to, get the feeling back into; limb to stretch; muscles (Sport) to loosen up.
desenvainar [1a] vt (a) sword to draw, unsheathe; peas to shell; claws to show, put out. (b) (fig) to show, reveal, expose.
desenvoltura nf ease, naturalness; confidence; free-and-easy manner; (of speech) fluency, facility; (pej) forwardness, brazenness.
desenvolver [2h; ptp **desenvuelto**] vt (a) packet etc to unwrap; roll to unwind, unroll; wool etc to disentangle, unravel.
(b) theory etc to develop; to expound, explain, set out.
desenvolvimiento nm development; exposition.
desenvuelto adj easy, natural; confident; free-and-easy; speech fluent, easy; (pej) forward, brazen.
desenyugar [1h] vt (SAm), **desenyuntar** [1a] vt (SAm) to unyoke.
deseo nm wish, desire; el — de the desire for; el — de + infin the desire to + infin; — de saber thirst for knowledge; buen — good intentions; arder en —s de algo to yearn for something; se cumplieron sus —s his wishes were fulfilled; tener — de, venir en — de to want, yearn for.
deseoso adj: ser — de + infin to be anxious to + infin, be eager to + infin.

desequilibrado adj (a) unbalanced; badly balanced, out of true; one-sided, lop-sided. (b) (Med) (mentally) unbalanced.
desequilibrar [1a] vt to unbalance; to overbalance, throw off balance.
desequilibrio nm (a) disequilibrium; unbalance, lack of balance; (fig) imbalance. (b) (Med) unbalanced mental condition, instability, psychological disorder.
deserción nf desertion; defection.
desertar [1a] 1 vt (a) to desert; home to desert, abandon, quit.
(b) (Law) right of appeal to forfeit, give up.
2 vi: — de (Mil etc) to desert; — de su hogar to abandon one's home, leave home; — de sus deberes to neglect one's duties; — de una tertulia to stop going to a gathering.
desertor nm deserter.
deservicio nm disservice.
desescalada nf de-escalation.
desescalar [1a] vti to de-escalate.
desescarchador nm (Mech) defroster.
desescombrar [1a] vt to clear up, clear of rubbish (or debris etc).
desescombro nm clearing-up.
desespañolizar [1f] vt to weaken the Spanish nature of; person to cause to become less Spanish, wean away from Spanish habits (etc).
desesperación nf (a) despair, desperation; con — despairingly.
(b) fury; nadar con — to swim furiously.
(c) infuriating thing; es una — it's maddening; it's unbearable; es una — tener que . . . it's infuriating to have to . . .
desesperadamente adv desperately, despairingly; hopelessly.
desesperado 1 adj (a) desperate, despairing; in despair; hopeless; estar — de to have despaired of, have no hope of.
(b) effort etc furious, frenzied.
2 nm: como un — like mad.
3 nf: hacer algo a la desesperada to do something as a last hope, try a final desperate solution.
desesperante adj maddening, infuriating.
desesperanzar [1f] 1 vt to deprive of hope. **2 desesperanzarse** vr to lose hope, despair.
desesperar [1a] 1 vt to deprive of hope, drive to despair; (fam) to drive to distraction, drive crazy.
2 vi to despair (de of), lose hope; — de + infin to give up all hope of + ger.
3 desesperarse vr to despair, lose hope; to get desperate.
desespero nm (esp SAm) despair, desperation.
desestancar [1g] vt product to remove the state monopoly from, allow a free market in.
desestimar [1a] vt (a) to have a low opinion of; to scorn, belittle, disparage. (b) claim, motion etc to reject.
desfachatado adj brazen, impudent, barefaced; cheeky.
desfachatez nf brazenness, impudence; cheek, nerve.
desfalcador nm embezzler.
desfalcar [1g] vt to embezzle.
desfalco nm embezzlement.
desfallecer [2d] 1 vt to weaken. **2** vi to get weak, weaken; to faint; (of voice) to fail, falter; — de ánimo to lose heart.
desfallecido adj weak; faint.
desfallecimiento nm weakness; faintness.
desfasado adj: estar — to be out of step (fig; de with); (Mech) to be out of phase, be badly adjusted.
desfasar [1a] vt to phase out.
desfavorable adj unfavourable.
desfavorablemente adv unfavourably.
desfavorecer [2d] vt (a) to cease to favour, withdraw support from. (b) (of clothes) to be unbecoming to, not suit, not look well on.
desfiguración nf, **desfiguramiento** nm disfigurement, disfiguration; defacement; alteration; distortion, misrepresentation; (Phot etc) blurring; (Radio) distortion.
desfigurado adj disfigured; deformed; meaning etc distorted, twisted; outline (also Phot) blurred; (Radio) distorted.
desfigurar [1a] vt face to disfigure; body to deform; picture etc to deface; outline (also Phot) to blur; voice to alter, disguise; meaning to distort, twist; to cloud; event to misrepresent, distort the truth of, alter the details of; una cicatriz le desfigura la cara a scar disfigures his face; la niebla lo desfigura todo the fog alters everything, the fog makes everything look strange.
desfiladero nm defile, pass; gorge.

desfilar [1a] *vi* to parade; to march past; to file by, file out (*etc*), file past; **desfilaron ante el general** they paraded before the general, they marched past the general.

desfile *nm* procession; (*Mil*) parade, march-past; — **de modelos** fashion show, fashion parade; — **naval** naval review; — **de la victoria** victory parade.

desfloración *nf* (a) deflowering, defloration. (b) tarnishing, messing-up, destruction of the fine appearance of.

desflorar [1a] *vt* (a) *woman* to deflower.
(b) to tarnish, mess up, destroy the fine appearance of.
(c) — **un asunto** to touch briefly on a matter, treat a matter no more than superficially.

desfogar [1h] **1** *vt* (*fig*) to vent (*con*, *en* on).
2 *vi* (*Naut*: *of storm*) to burst.
3 desfogarse *vr* (*fig*) to vent one's anger; to let oneself go, let off steam.

desfogue *nm* (*fig*) venting.

desfondar [1a] *vt* (a) to knock the bottom out of, stave in (*also Naut*). (b) (*Agr*) to plough deeply.

desfortalecer [2d] *vt* to dismantle the fortifications of).

desgaire *nm* (a) (*of dress etc*) slovenliness, carelessness.
(b) (*of manner*) nonchalance, affected carelessness; scornful attitude, disdain.
(c) **vestido al** — dressed in a slovenly way; **hacer algo al** — to do something with a scornful air; **mirar a uno al** — to sneer at someone, look scornfully at someone.

desgajar [1a] **1** *vt* (a) to tear off, break off, split off.
(b) — **a uno de** to tear someone away from.
2 desgajarse *vr* (a) to come off, break off, split away.
(b) — **de** (*person*) to tear oneself away from.

desgalichado *adj* *movement etc* clumsy, awkward; *dress* shabby, slovenly, sloppy; *person* down-at-heel, unprepossessing.

desgana *nf* (a) lack of appetite, loss of appetite.
(b) (*fig*) unwillingness, disinclination, reluctance; **su — para hacerlo** his unwillingness to do it; **hacer algo a** — to do something reluctantly.
(c) (*Med*) weakness, faintness.

desganado *adj*: **estar** —, **sentirse** — to have no appetite, not be hungry.

desganarse [1a] *vr* (a) to lose one's appetite. (b) (*fig*) to lose interest, get bored, get fed up.

desgañitarse [1a] *vr* to bawl, shout; to scream oneself hoarse.

desgarbado *adj* (in *movement*) clumsy, ungainly, gawky; graceless; (in *appearance*) slovenly, uncouth.

desgarrado *adj* (a) torn; tattered, in tatters. (b) (*fig*) shameless, barefaced, brazen. (c) (*fig*) vicious, licentious.

desgarrador *adj* heartbreaking, heartrending; uncontrollable; *cry* piercing.

desgarrar [1a] *vt* (a) to tear, rip (up), rend. (b) (*fig*) to shatter, crush; *heart* to break. (c) (*SAm*) *phlegm* to cough up.

desgarro *nm* (a) tear, rip, rent. (b) (*fig*) impudence, brazenness, effrontery; (*woman's*) forwardness. (c) (*fig*) boastfulness. (d) (*SAm*) phlegm.

desgarrón *nm* big tear.

desgastar [1a] **1** *vt* (a) to wear away, wear down; (*Geol*) to erode, weather; *rope etc* to chafe, fray; *metal* to corrode, eat away, eat into; — **la ropa** to wear one's clothes out.
(b) (*fig*) to spoil, ruin.
2 desgastarse *vr* (a) to wear away; to erode; to chafe, fray; to corrode; to get worn out.
(b) (*Med*) to get weak, decline; to wear oneself out.

desgaste *nm* (a) wear; wear and tear; erosion; chafing; fraying; corrosion; **aumenta el — del motor** it increases wear on the engine; **debido al — de su ropa** because his clothes were so worn.
(b) waste, loss; slow wasting; (*Mil*) attrition; (*Med*) weakening, decline; — **económico** drain on one's resources; **guerra de** — war of attrition.

desglobar [1a] *vt* *figures etc* to break down, analyse, split up.

desglosar [1a] *vt* to separate, remove, detach.

desgobernado *adj* uncontrollable, undisciplined; *child* wild.

desgobernar [1k] *vt* (a) (*Pol*) to misgovern, misrule; *affair* to mismanage, handle badly, make a mess of. (b) (*Anat*) to dislocate.

desgobierno *nm* (a) misgovernment, misrule; mismanagement, bad handling. (b) dislocation.

desgolletar [1a] *vt* *bottle* to knock the neck off.

desgoznar [1a] **1** *vt* (a) to take off its hinges, unhinge.
(b) to take the hinges off.
2 desgoznarse *vr* (a) (*person*) to get wild, lose control; to go off the rails.
(b) (*of plan etc*) to be thrown out of gear.

desgracia *nf* (a) misfortune; mishap; accident; (piece of) bad luck; setback; **por** — unfortunately; **¡qué** —! what a misfortune!; what bad luck!; **estar en** — to be unfortunate, suffer constant setbacks; **en el accidente no hay que lamentar —s personales** there were no casualties in the accident; **la familia ha tenido una serie de —s** the family has had a series of misfortunes.
(b) disgrace; disfavour; **caer en (la)** — to fall into disgrace.

desgraciadamente *adv* unfortunately, unluckily; **¡—!** more's the pity!, alas!

desgraciado 1 *adj* (a) unlucky, unfortunate; luckless, hapless; wretched; unhappy, miserable; **una elección desgraciada** an unfortunate choice; — **en sus amores** unlucky in love; — **en el juego** unlucky at cards; **era — en su matrimonio** he was unhappy in his marriage; **una vida desgraciada** a wretched life, a life of misery; **¡qué — estoy!** how wretched I am!
(b) ill-fated, unlucky; **ese día** — that ill-fated day.
(c) *appearance* graceless, ugly, lacking charm.
(d) unpleasant.
2 *nm*, **desgraciada** *nf* wretch, poor devil, unfortunate; **lo tiene aquel** — that wretched creature has got it.

desgraciar [1b] **1** *vt* (a) to spoil, ruin (the appearance of).
(b) to displease.
2 desgraciarse *vr* (a) to spoil, be ruined, suffer damage; (*plan etc*) to fall through, collapse, fail to mature.
(b) — **con uno** to fall out with someone; to lose someone's favour.

desgranar [1a] **1** *vt* (a) to remove the grain (*or* pips *etc*) from; *corn* to thresh; *peas* to shell; — **un racimo** to pick the grapes from a bunch.
(b) — **las cuentas del rosario** to tell one's beads.
(c) — **imprecaciones** to produce a rapid series of imprecations; — **mentiras** to come out with a string of lies.
2 desgranarse *vr* (a) (*Bot*) to fall; (*corn*) to shed its grain, (*other plant*) to drop its seeds.
(b) (*of beads*) to come apart.

desgrasar [1a] *vt* = **desengrasar**.

desgravar [1a] *vt* *product* to reduce the tax (*or* duty *etc*) on.

desgreñado *adj* dishevelled, tousled.

desgreñar [1a] *vt* to dishevel, rumple, tousle.

desgreño *nm* (*Col, Chi, RPl*) dishevelment; (*fig*) disorder, disarray; (*fig*) carelessness.

desguarnecer [2d] *vt* (a) (*Tech*) to strip down; to remove the accessories (*or* trimmings *etc*) from; — **un barco de velas** to remove the sails from a boat.
(b) *horse* to unharness.
(c) (*Mil*) *town* to abandon, remove the garrison from; *fortress* to dismantle (the fortifications of).

desguarnecido *adj* (a) bare, shorn of trimmings (*etc*). (b) *city* undefended, unprotected; *flank* exposed.

desguazar [1f] *vt* (a) *timber* to dress, rough-hew. (b) *ship* to break up.

deshabitado *adj* uninhabited; deserted; empty, vacant.

deshabitar [1a] *vt* to move out of, leave empty; to desert, quit.

deshabituarse [1e] *vr* to lose the habit, get out of the habit.

deshacer [2s] **1** *vt* to undo, unmake; to spoil, ruin, damage, destroy; (*Mech etc*) to take apart; to pull to pieces; *carcass, joint* to cut up, carve up; *ship* to break up; *bed* to unmake, pull to pieces; *parcel* to undo, unpack, unwrap; *trunk* to unpack; *knot* to undo, untie; *seam* to unpick; *metal etc* to wear down; *ice etc* to melt, dissolve; *eyesight* to harm, damage; *person, economy etc* to shatter; *enemy* to shatter, rout, put to flight; *opponent* to defeat; *treaty etc* to break, violate; *wrong* to right; — **algo en agua** to dissolve something in water; **la lluvia deshizo el techo** the rain damaged the roof; — **un brazo contra algo** to hurt one's arm on something.
2 deshacerse *vr* (a) to come undone; to be spoiled, get damaged; to come apart; to fall to pieces; to break up; to come untied; to melt, dissolve; to be shattered, disintegrate; to vanish; **se deshizo la pierna al caer** he hurt his leg when he

fell; **se deshizo como el humo** it vanished into thin air, it vanished like smoke; **cuando se deshizo la reunión** when the meeting broke up.
(b) (*Med*) to get weak, grow feeble; to waste away.
(c) (*emotionally*) to grieve; to pine; to get impatient, get worked up.
(d) — **de algo** to get rid of something; (*Comm etc*) to dump something, unload something; **no quiero deshacerme de eso** I don't want to part with that; **logramos deshacernos de él** we managed to get rid of him.
(e) — **en lágrimas** to burst into tears; — **en elogios de uno** to shower praises on someone; — **en cumplidos** to pay lavish compliments, come out with extravagant courtesies; to overdo the politeness.
(f) — **por los melocotones** to be crazy about peaches, adore peaches; — **por hacer algo** to strive to do something, struggle to do something; — **por complacer a uno** to do one's utmost to please someone.
desharrapado *adj* ragged, tattered, shabby.
deshebillar [1a] *vt* to unbuckle.
deshebrar [1a] *vt* to unthread.
deshechizar [1f] *vt* to remove the spell from, disenchant.
deshecho 1 *adj* (a) undone; untied; broken, smashed, in pieces; shattered; **tener un brazo** — to have a badly injured arm; **estar** — (*fam*) to be worn out.
(b) (*Med*) *person* weak, emaciated; *health* broken.
(c) (*fig*) *storm* violent.
(d) (*Arg*) untidy.
2 *nm* (*Col, Chi, Ven*) short cut.
deshelador *nm* (*Aer*) de-icer.
deshelar [1k] **1** *vt* to thaw, melt; (*Tech*) to defrost; (*Aer*) to de-ice. **2** *vi and* **deshelarse** *vr* to thaw, melt; (*Meteorol*) to thaw.
desherbaje *nm* weeding.
desherbar [1k] *vt* to weed.
desheredar [1a] *vt* to disinherit.
desherrarse [1k] *vr* (*horse*) to cast a shoe.
deshidratación *nf* dehydration.
deshidratado *adj* dehydrated.
deshidratar [1a] *vt* to dehydrate.
deshielo *nm* thaw.
deshilachado *adj* shabby; worn, frayed.
deshilachar [1a] **1** *vt* to pull threads out of; to wear, fray. **2 deshilacharse** *vr* to get worn, fray.
deshilada *nf*: **a la** — (a) (*Mil*) in single file. (b) (*fig*) secretly, stealthily.
deshilado *nm* (*Sew*) openwork.
deshilar [1a] **1** *vt* (*Sew*) to unravel; *meat* to shred. **2** *vi* to get thin. **3 deshilarse** *vr* to get worn, fray, come apart.
deshilvanado *adj* (*fig*) disjointed, disconnected, incoherent.
deshilvanar [1a] *vt* (*Sew*) to untack, take the stitches out of.
deshinchar [1a] **1** *vt* (a) *tyre* to deflate, let down; *swelling* to reduce (the swelling of).
(b) (*fig*) *anger* to give vent to.
2 deshincharse *vr* (a) (*tyre*) to go flat; (*swelling*) to go down.
(b) (*fig*) to get down off one's high horse.
deshipotecar [1g] *vt property* to pay off the mortgage on.
deshojado *adj branch etc* leafless; *flower* stripped of its petals.
deshojar [1a] **1** *vt tree* to strip the leaves off, (*Chem*) to defoliate; *flower* to pull the petals off; (*SAm*) *maize* to husk; *fruit* to peel; *book* to tear the pages out of.
2 deshojarse *vr* to lose its leaves (*etc*).
deshollejar [1a] *vt grapes etc* to peel, skin.
deshollinador *nm* (chimney) sweep.
deshollinar [1a] *vt* (a) to sweep. (b) (*fig*) to take a close look at.
deshonestamente *adv* indecently, lewdly.
deshonestidad *nf* indecency, impropriety, lewdness.
deshonesto *adj* indecent, improper, lewd.
deshonor *nm* (a) dishonour, disgrace. (b) (*un* —) insult, affront (*de* to); **no es un** — **trabajar** it is no disgrace to work.
deshonorar [1a] *vt* (a) to dishonour, disgrace; to be unworthy of. (b) to spoil, disfigure. (c) to dismiss, deprive of office (*or* title *etc*).
deshonra *nf* (a) dishonour, disgrace; shame; **lo tiene a** — he thinks it shameful, he considers it beneath him; **tienen a** — **trabajar** they think it beneath them to work.
(b) shameful act.

deshonrabuenos *nmf*, *pl* **deshonrabuenos** (a) slanderer. (b) black sheep (of the family).
deshonrar [1a] *vt* (a) to dishonour, disgrace, bring disgrace on. (b) to insult. (c) *woman* to seduce, ruin.
deshonroso *adj* dishonourable, disgraceful, ignominious.
deshora: a — *adv* at the wrong time; at an inconvenient time; **llegar a** — to come unexpectedly; **acostarse a** — to go to bed at some unearthly hour; **hacer algo a** — to do something at the wrong moment, mistime something.
deshuesar [1a] *vt meat* to bone; *fruit* to stone.
deshumanizar [1f] *vt* to dehumanize.
deshumedecerse [2d] *vr* to dry up, lose its moisture.
desiderátum *nm*, *pl* **desiderátums** desideratum.
desidia *nf* (a) laziness, idleness. (b) neglect; slovenliness, carelessness.
desidioso *adj* (a) lazy, idle. (b) neglected; slovenly, careless.
desierto 1 *adj* (a) *island, region etc* desert; *landscape* empty, bleak, desolate; *house etc* empty, deserted; **la calle estaba desierta** the street was deserted.
(b) **declarar** — **un premio** to declare that a prize will not be awarded (for lack of good candidates *etc*); **declarar desiertas unas oposiciones** to declare a competition void.
2 *nm* desert; wilderness; **clamar en el** — to cry in the wilderness.
designación *nf* (a) (*act*) designation, appointment. (b) designation, name.
designar [1a] *vt* to designate, appoint, name; to select; *date, place etc* to name, fix, decide on.
designio *nm* plan, design.
desigual *adj* (a) unequal, different; *struggle etc* unequal; *treatment* unfair, inequitable.
(b) *weather etc* variable, changeable; *character* unpredictable.
(c) *ground, writing etc* uneven; irregular; *edge* rough.
desigualdad *nf* (a) inequality. (b) variableness, changeableness; unpredictability. (c) unevenness; irregularity; roughness.
desilusión *nf* disillusion(ment), disappointment; **caer en la** — to get disillusioned; **sufrir una** — to suffer a disappointment.
desilusionante *adj* disillusioning, disappointing.
desilusionar [1a] **1** *vt* to disillusion; to disappoint, let down.
2 desilusionarse *vr* to get disillusioned, lose one's illusions; to be disappointed; to have one's hopes destroyed.
desinencia *nf* (*Ling*) ending.
desinfección *nf* disinfection.
desinfectante *nm* disinfectant.
desinfectar [1a] *vt* to disinfect.
desinfestar [1a] *vt* to decontaminate.
desinflación *nf* disinflation, deflation.
desinflacionar [1a] *vt* (*Comm, Fin*) to deflate.
desinflacionista *adj* disinflationary, deflationary.
desinflar [1a] *vt* to deflate, let the air out of.
desinsectación *nf* protection against insect pests; **la** — **de un jardín** the campaign to free a garden of insect pests.
desintegración *nf* disintegration; — **nuclear** nuclear fission; **la** — **del átomo** the smashing of the atom.
desintegrar [1a] **1** *vt* to disintegrate; *atom* to split, smash. **2 desintegrarse** *vr* to disintegrate; to split, be smashed.
desinterés *nm* disinterestedness, impartiality; unselfishness.
desinteresado *adj* disinterested, impartial; unselfish.
desintoxicar [1g] **1** *vt* to sober up. **2 desintoxicarse** *vr* to sober up.
desistimiento *nm* (a) desisting. (b) (*Law*) waiving of a right.
desistir [3a] *vi* (a) to stop, desist; — **de algo** to desist from something; — **de** + *infin* to desist from + *ger*, stop + *ger*.
(b) (*Law*) to waive a right; — **de un derecho** to waive a right.
desjarretar [1a] *vt animal* to hamstring; (*Med*) to weaken, debilitate.
desjuntar [1a] *vt* to separate, take apart; to divide.
deslavado *adj* (a) half-washed. (b) (*fig*) brazen, barefaced. (c) = **deslavazado**.
deslavar [1a] *vt* (a) to half-wash, wash superficially; to wash away. (b) to weaken; to fade.
deslavazado *adj* (a) soft, weak, limp; drooping; *person* limp. (b) faded, washed-out, pale; (*fig*) colourless. (c) (*fig*) *speech etc* disjointed, incoherent.

desleal *adj* disloyal (*a*, *con* to); *competition* (Comm) unfair.
deslealmente *adv* disloyally; unfairly.
deslealtad *nf* disloyalty; unfairness.
deslechar [1a] *vt* to milk.
desleído *adj* (a) dissolved; diluted. (b) (*fig*) *idea etc* weak, woolly.
desleír [3m] **1** *vt* to dissolve; to dilute, thin; to make weaker. **2 desleírse** *vr* to dissolve; to become diluted; to get weaker.
deslenguado *adj* foul-mouthed.
deslenguarse [1i] *vr* to shoot one's mouth off, talk too much, be too free in what one says; to speak insolently; to pour out obscenities.
desliar [1c] **1** *vt* to untie, undo. **2 desliarse** *vr* to come undone.
desligado *adj* (a) loose, free; unfastened. (b) (*fig*) separate, detached; **vive — de todo** he lives detached from everything, he lives in a world of his own.
desligamiento *nm* (*fig*) detachment (*de* from).
desligar [1h] **1** *vt* (a) to untie, undo, unfasten; to unbind; to extricate (*de* from).
(b) (*fig*) to separate, detach; to consider separately; **— el primer aspecto del segundo** to separate the first aspect from the second.
(c) (*fig*) *matter* to unravel, disentangle, clarify.
(d) *person* to absolve, free (*de* from); to excuse, exempt (*de* from); **— a uno de una promesa** to release someone from a promise.
2 desligarse *vr* to come undone, get unfastened; (*person*) to extricate oneself (*de* from).
deslindar [1a] *vt* (a) to mark out, fix the limits (*or* boundaries) of. (b) (*fig*) to define.
deslinde *nm* (a) demarcation, fixing of limits (*or* boundaries). (b) definition.
desliz *nm* (a) slip, slide; (Aut) skid.
(b) (*fig*) slip; lapse; indiscretion; **— de lengua** slip of the tongue; **los deslices de la juventud** the indiscretions of youth, the minor sins of youth.
deslizadero *nm* (a) slide; slippery spot. (b) (Tech) chute, slide.
deslizadizo *adj* slippery.
deslizador *nm* (a) (*child's*) scooter. (b) (Naut) small speedboat. (c) (Aer) glider; **— acuático** hovercraft.
(d) (*of skate etc*) runner, skid.
deslizamiento *nm* slide, sliding, slipping; (Aut) skid; **— (suave)** glide; **— de tierra** landslide.
deslizar [1f] **1** *vt* (a) to slide, slip (*en* into, *por* along, through); **— una mesa por el suelo** to slide a table along the floor.
(b) **— una propina a uno** to slip someone a tip; **— una observación** to slip a remark in; to let slip a remark.
2 deslizarse *vr* (a) (*accidentally*) to slip (*en* on, up on), slide (*por* along); (Aut) to skid.
(b) (*secret*) to slip out; (*error*) to slip in, creep in; **aquí se ha deslizado un error** an error has crept in here.
(c) (*of movement*, *snake etc*) to slide, glide, slither; (*boat*) to glide; (*water*) to go (gently), pass, flow gently; (*time*) to pass, glide past; (*person*) to slip away, slip off; to slip in; **— en un cuarto** to slip into a room; **— en una fiesta** to slip unnoticed into a party; **— fuera de un agujero** to wriggle out of a hole; **el agua se desliza mansamente** the water flows along gently; **la anguila se deslizaba entre mis manos** the eel slipped away between my fingers.
(d) (*person*: *fig*) to slip up, blunder; to go wrong morally, get into bad ways, backslide.
deslomar [1a] **1** *vt* to break the back of; (*fig*) to wear out, exhaust utterly; **— a uno a garrotazos** to beat someone mercilessly.
2 deslomarse *vr* (*fig*) to get worn out; to work one's guts out.
deslucido *adj* (a) tarnished; worn out, old and useless.
(b) flat, dull, lifeless; undistinguished, characterless; **hizo un papel —** he was dull in the part; **el jugador estuvo muy —** the player was far from his best form, he played in a very lifeless way.
(c) graceless, inelegant, awkward.
(d) fruitless, unsuccessful; **quedar —** to be unsuccessful.
deslucimiento *nm* (a) tarnished state; useless condition.
(b) flatness, dullness, lifelessness; lack of character.
(c) gracelessness, inelegance.
(d) failure, lack of success.
deslucir [3f] **1** *vt* (a) to tarnish; to damage, spoil, ruin; to impair the splendour of, diminish the attractiveness of, dull; **la lluvia deslució el acto** the rain ruined the ceremony.
(b) to discredit, damage the standing of.

2 deslucirse *vr* (*fig*) to fail, be unsuccessful; to do badly.
deslumbrador *adj* (a) dazzling, brilliant; glaring. (b) (*fig*) dazzling; puzzling, confusing, bewildering.
deslumbramiento *nm* (a) glare, dazzle; brilliance. (b) (*fig*) confusion; bewilderment.
deslumbrante *adj* dazzling.
deslumbrar [1a] *vt* (a) to dazzle; to blind.
(b) (*fig*) to dazzle; to puzzle, confuse, bewilder; to daze; **deslumbró a todos con su oratoria** he captivated everyone with his oratory, he gave a dazzling oratorical display.
deslustrado *adj* (a) *glass* frosted, ground; *pottery* unglazed. (b) (*esp fig*) dull, lustreless; tarnished.
deslustrar [1a] *vt* (a) *glass* to frost. (b) (*esp fig*) to dull, tarnish (the brilliance of), dim (the lustre of).
(c) (*fig*) *reputation etc* to sully, stain, tarnish.
deslustre *nm* (a) frosting. (b) tarnishing; dullness, dimness. (c) (*fig*) stigma, stain; disgrace.
deslustroso *adj* (a) unbecoming, unsuitable. (b) (*fig*) disgraceful.
desmadejamiento *nm* enervation, weakness.
desmadejar [1a] *vt* to enervate, weaken, take it out of.
desmalezar [1f] *vt* (SAm) to weed.
desmallar [1a] **1** *vt* *stitches* to pull out; *stocking* to make a ladder (*or* run) in. **2 desmallarse** *vr* (*stocking*) to ladder.
desmamar [1a] *vt* to wean.
desmán[1] *nm* excess, outrage; piece of bad behaviour; abuse (of authority); **cometer un —** to commit an outrage (*contra* on).
desmán[2] *nm* (Zool) muskrat.
desmanchar [1a] **1** *vt* (SAm) to clean, remove the spots (*or* stains etc) from.
2 desmancharse *vr* (CAm, Col, Ec, Per) (a) to hurry out; to withdraw.
(b) (Agr) to stray from the herd.
desmandado *adj* (a) unruly, unbridled; wild; uncontrollable, out of hand; obstreperous. (b) *animal* stray; *horse* runaway.
desmandarse [1a] *vr* (a) to get out of hand, run wild, go out of control; to be obstreperous, behave badly; to be insolent.
(b) (*animal*) to stray (from the herd); (*horse*) to bolt, run away.
desmanotado *adj* clumsy, awkward.
desmantelamiento *nm* (a) (*act*) dismantling; abandonment. (b) (*state*) dilapidation.
desmantelar [1a] **1** *vt* (Mil etc) to dismantle, raze; *scaffold etc* to take down; *walls* to strip; *house etc* to strip of its contents, leave bare; (Naut) to unmast, unrig; (*fig*) to abandon, forsake.
2 desmantelarse *vr* (*house etc*) to fall into disrepair, become dilapidated.
desmaña *nf* clumsiness, awkwardness; slowness, helplessness; unpractical nature.
desmañado *adj* clumsy, awkward; slow, helpless; unpractical.
desmarcado *adj* (Sport) unmarked.
desmayado *adj* (a) (Med) unconscious. (b) (*fig*) weak, faint; languid; *character etc* dull, lacklustre, colourless. (c) *colour* pale, dull.
desmayar [1a] **1** *vi* (*of person*) to lose heart, get discouraged, get depressed; (*of effort etc*) to falter, flag.
2 desmayarse *vr* (a) (Med) to faint (away), swoon.
(b) (*plant etc*) to droop low, trail.
desmayo *nm* (a) (Med: *act*) faint, fainting fit, swoon; (*state*) unconsciousness; **sufrir un —** to have a fainting fit, faint.
(b) (*of voice*) faltering, flagging; (*of spirit*) dejection, depression; (*of body in general*) languidness, limpness, limp feeling, listlessness; **tenía un — 'en todo el cuerpo** he felt limp all over; **las ramas caen con —** the branches droop low, the branches trail; **hablar con —** to talk in a small voice, speak falteringly.
desmedido *adj* excessive, disproportionate, out of all proportion; *ambition*, *pride* boundless, overweening; *grief etc* exaggerated.
desmedirse [3l] *vr* to forget oneself, go too far.
desmedrado *adj* (a) impaired; reduced; in decline. (b) (Med) run down; weak, emaciated; ill-looking.
desmedrar [1a] **1** *vt* (a) to impair; to reduce; to spoil, ruin, affect badly.
(b) (*fig*) to disparage, belittle.
2 *vi and* **desmedrarse** *vr* (a) to fall off, decline; to go downhill; to deteriorate.
(b) (Med) to get weak; to get thin; (*child*) to be sickly, waste away; (Bot) to grow poorly, do badly.
desmedro *nm* (a) impairment; reduction; decline, deterioration.. (b) (Med) weakness, emaciation, thinness. (c) disparagement, belittling.

desmejora nf, **desmejoramiento** nm = desmedro (a) and (b).

desmejorado adj: **queda muy desmejorada** she's lost her looks, she's not as attractive as she used to be; (Med) she's not looking at all well.

desmejorar [1a] **1** vt (a) to impair, spoil, damage; to cause to deteriorate.
(b) (Med) to weaken, affect the health of.
2 desmejorarse vr (a) to be impaired, be spoiled; to decline, deteriorate, go downhill.
(b) (person) to lose one's looks, look less attractive; (Med) to lose one's health, suffer, waste away.

desmelenado adj dishevelled, tousled.

desmelenar [1a] vt to dishevel, tousle the hair of.

desmembración nf dismemberment, break-up.

desmembrar [1k] vt to dismember, separate, break up.

desmemoria nf poor memory, forgetfulness.

desmemoriado adj forgetful, absent-minded.

desmemoriarse [1b] vr to grow forgetful, become absent-minded.

desmentida nf denial; **dar una — a** to deny, give the lie to.

desmentimiento nm denial; refutation.

desmentir [3i] **1** vt accusation to deny, refute, give the lie to; rumour to deny, scotch, scout; theory etc to refute, explode; to contradict; character, origins etc to belie, not fit in with, be unworthy of; — **rotundamente una acusación** to deny a charge flatly.
2 vi to be out of line, not fit; — **de** to belie, clash with, be unworthy of.
3 desmentirse vr to contradict oneself; to go back on one's word.

desmenuzable adj crumbly, crumbling; flaky; friable.

desmenuzar [1f] **1** vt (a) bread etc to crumble (up), break into small pieces; meat to chop, shred, mince; cheese to shred.
(b) (fig) to examine minutely, take a close look at.
2 desmenuzarse vr to crumble (up), break up.

desmerecer [2d] **1** vt to be unworthy of.
2 vi (a) to deteriorate, go off, be less good; to lose value.
(b) — **de** to compare unfavourably with, not be comparable to, not live up to; **ésta no desmerece de sus otras películas** this is in no way inferior to his other films, this is every bit as good as his earlier films.

desmesura nf (a) excess, enormity; disproportion; extra size. (b) lack of moderation.

desmesuradamente adv disproportionately, excessively; enormously; **abrir — la boca** to open one's mouth extra wide.

desmesurado adj (a) disproportionate, excessive, inordinate; enormous; ambition etc boundless; (in measurement) extra big, unduly large, much too big.
(b) insolent, impudent.

desmesurarse [1a] vr to become insolent, forget oneself, lose all restraint.

desmigajar [1a] vt, **desmigar** [1h] vt to crumble.

desmilitarización nf demilitarization.

desmilitarizado adj demilitarized.

desmilitarizar [1f] vt to demilitarize.

desmirriado adj weak, sickly; thin, weedy.

desmochar [1a] vt tree to lop, cut off the top of; to pollard; horns to cut off the points of; text etc to cut, hack about, mutilate.

desmoche nm (a) lopping, pollarding.
(b) (fig) general slaughter, mowing down, mass removal; **hubo un — en el primer examen** there was a mass slaughter of candidates in the first exam.

desmocho nm lopped branches, cuttings.

desmolado adj toothless.

desmonetizar [1f] vt (a) to demonetize; to convert into gold. (b) (Arg) to devalue.

desmontable 1 adj detachable; sectional, in sections, which takes apart; collapsible; that takes down. **2** nm tyre lever.

desmontaje nm dismantling, stripping down; demolition.

desmontar [1a] **1** vt (a) (Mech) to dismantle, strip down; to take apart, take to pieces; (Archit) to knock down, demolish; shotgun to uncock; enemy guns to silence, knock out; sail to take down.
(b) ground to level; to clear of trees (etc); trees to fell; rubbish to clear away.
(c) rider to throw, unseat, unhorse; — **a uno de un vehículo** to help someone down from a vehicle.
2 vi and **desmontarse** vr to dismount, alight (de from).

desmonte nm (a) (act) levelling; clearing; clearing away, removal; **los trabajos exigirán el — de X metros cúbicos** the work will necessitate the removal of X cubic metres.
(b) levelled ground; heap of soil extracted.
(c) (Rail) cutting, cut (US).
(d) felled timber.

desmoralizador adj demoralizing.

desmoralizar [1f] vt army etc to demoralize; customs etc to corrupt.

desmoronadizo adj crumbling; rickety; dilapidated.

desmoronado adj tumbledown, ruinous, dilapidated.

desmoronamiento nm crumbling, dilapidation, decay; collapse (also fig).

desmoronar [1a] **1** vt to wear away, destroy little by little; (fig) to erode, affect, make inroads into.
2 desmoronarse vr (Geol etc) to crumble, fall apart; (house etc) to get dilapidated, become ruinous, fall into disrepair; (part of masonry) to fall, come down, collapse; (fig) to decline, decay.

desmovilización nf demobilization.

desmovilizar [1f] vt to demobilize.

desmultiplicar [1g] vt (Mech) to gear down.

desnacionalización nf denationalization.

desnacionalizado adj (a) industry etc denationalized.
(b) person stateless.

desnacionalizar [1f] vt to denationalize.

desnarigada nf (hum): **la —** the skull.

desnatar [1a] vt milk to skim, take the cream off; other liquid to remove the top of, remove the scum from; (fig) to take the cream off; **leche sin —** whole milk.

desnaturalizado adj (a) (Chem) denatured. (b) person etc unnatural; cruel, inhuman.

desnaturalizar [1f] **1** vt (a) (Chem) to denature.
(b) (fig) to denaturalize, alter the fundamental nature of; to pervert, corrupt; text etc to distort; sense to misrepresent, twist.
2 desnaturalizarse vr to give up one's nationality; to become stateless.

desnivel nm (a) unevenness; high ground, low ground.
(b) (fig) inequality, difference, gap; lack of adjustment (entre between).

desnivelado adj (a) uneven. (b) (fig) unbalanced, badly adjusted, unequal.

desnivelar [1a] vt (a) to make uneven. (b) (fig) to unbalance, upset the balance of, create imbalance in.

desnucar [1g] **1** vt to break the neck of; to fell, poleaxe. **2 desnucarse** vr to break one's neck.

desnuclearizado adj: **región desnuclearizada** nuclear-free area.

desnudar [1a] **1** vt (a) to strip (also Bot and fig; de of); person to strip, undress; arm etc to bare; sword to draw; (Geol) to denude; object, statue etc to lay bare, uncover, remove the coverings from.
(b) (fig) to ruin, break; gambler to fleece.
2 desnudarse vr (a) (person) to undress, get undressed; to strip (off); — **hasta la cintura** to strip to the waist.
(b) — **de algo** to get rid of something, cast something aside; **el árbol se está desnudando de sus hojas** the tree is shedding (or losing) its leaves.

desnudez nf (a) nudity, nakedness. (b) (fig) bareness.

desnudismo nm nudism.

desnudista nmf nudist.

desnudo 1 adj (a) body naked, nude; unclothed, bare; arm, tree etc bare; landscape bare, flat, featureless; **en las paredes desnudas** on the bare walls; **la ciudad quedó desnuda como la palma de la mano** the town was left as flat as a pancake (after bombing etc); **cavar con las manos desnudas** to dig with one's bare hands.
(b) (fig) bare, unadorned; truth naked, plain, unvarnished; **estar — de** to be devoid of, be bereft of, be without.
(c) (fig) penniless; **y ahora están —s** and now all they've got is what they stand up in; **quedarse —** to be ruined, be bankrupt.
2 nm (a) (Art etc) nude; **la retrató al —** he painted her in the nude.
(b) **poner algo al —** (fig) to lay something bare.

desnutrición nf malnutrition, undernourishment.

desnutrido adj undernourished.

desobedecer [2d] vti to disobey.

desobediencia nf disobedience.

desobediente adj disobedient.

desobstruir [3g] vt to unblock, unstop, clear.

desocupación nf (a) leisure; (pej) idleness. (b) (Econ) unemployment.

desocupado adj (a) space, seat etc empty, vacant, unoccupied.
(b) time spare, free; leisure (attr).

(c) person free, not busy; at leisure; (pej) idle; (Econ) unemployed.

desocupar [1a] **1** vt **(a)** house etc to vacate, move out of; to leave empty; container to empty.
(b) contents to remove, take out.
2 vi (tabu) to shit (tabu).
3 desocuparse vr **(a)** — **de un puesto** to give up one's job.
(b) (Arg, Chi, Ven) to give birth.

desodorante nm deodorant.

desodorizar [1f] vt to deodorize.

desoír [3q] vt to ignore, disregard; to turn a deaf ear to.

desojarse [1a] vr to strain one's eyes.

desolación nf **(a)** desolation. **(b)** (fig) grief, distress.

desolado adj **(a)** desolate. **(b)** (fig) sad, distressed, disconsolate; **estoy** — **por aquello** I'm terribly grieved about that.

desolador adj distressing, grievous.

desolar [1a] **1** vt to lay waste, ruin, desolate. **2 desolarse** vr to grieve, be distressed, be disconsolate.

desolladero nm **(a)** slaughterhouse. **(b)** (fam) talking-shop, place for gossip; gambling joint (sl).

desollado adj (fam) brazen, barefaced.

desollador nm (fig) extortioner, robber.

desolladura nf **(a)** skinning, flaying. **(b)** (Med) graze, abrasion; bruise. **(c)** (fig) extortion, piece of robbery.

desollar [1m] vt **(a)** to skin, flay.
(b) — **vivo a uno** (fig) to fleece someone, make someone pay through the nose; to flay someone verbally, criticize someone unmercifully.

desopinar [1a] vt to denigrate.

desorbitado adj **(a)** disproportionate, excessive; claim etc exaggerated. **(b)** **con los ojos** —**s** wide-eyed, pop-eyed, with bulging eyes.

desorbitar [1a] **1** vt **(a)** to carry to extremes; to exaggerate.
(b) — **un asunto** to misinterpret a matter, get a matter out of perspective, take an unbalanced view of a matter.
2 desorbitarse vr (person) to go to extremes, lose one's sense of proportion; (matter etc) to get out of hand.

desorden nm **(a)** disorder; confusion; turmoil; disarray; (Pol) disorder; **en** — in confusion, in disorder; **poner las cosas en** — to upset things, confuse things.
(b) (un —) mess, litter, confusion.
(c) (fig) irregular life; loose living.
(d) —**es** (of youth etc) excesses.

desordenadamente adv **(a)** untidily; in disorder, in a mess. **(b)** in a disorderly fashion; irregularly; unmethodically; wildly; lawlessly.

desordenado adj **(a)** room etc untidy, in disorder; objects disordered, confused, in a mess.
(b) behaviour disorderly; life irregular; character unmethodical; child etc wild, unruly; country lawless.

desordenar [1a] vt **(a)** to disarrange, mess up; to throw into confusion. **(b)** (Mech etc) to put out of order.

desorejado adj **(a)** (Col, Chi, PR) without handles.
(b) (Bol, Per) hard of hearing.
(c) (fig) abject, degraded; dissolute.
(d) (Cu) lavish; wasteful.
(e) (Guat) silly.

desorganización nf disorganization, disruption.

desorganizar [1f] vt to disorganize, disrupt.

desorientar [1a] **1** vt: — **a uno (a)** to make someone lose his way.
(b) (fig) to lead someone astray; to confuse someone, bewilder someone, put someone off.
2 desorientarse vr **(a)** to lose one's way, lose one's bearings.
(b) (fig) to go wrong, go astray, get off the track; to get confused.

desovar [1m] vi (Fish) to spawn; (insect, amphibian etc) to lay eggs.

desove nm spawning; egg-laying.

desovillar [1a] vt **(a)** wool to unravel, unwind; to disentangle. **(b)** (fig) to unravel, clarify.

desoxidar [1a] vt to deoxidize.

despabiladeras nfpl snuffers; **unas** — a pair of snuffers.

despabilado adj **(a)** wide-awake. **(b)** (fig) wide-awake; alert, watchful; quick, sharp.

despabilar [1a] **1** vt **(a)** candle to snuff; lamp, wick to trim.
(b) (fig) wits to sharpen; person to wake up; to sharpen the wits of, liven up, brighten up.
(c) (fig) fortune to squander rapidly; meal to dispatch; business to get through quickly.

(d) (fam) to pinch (fam).
(e) (sl) — **a uno** to do someone in (sl).
2 vi and **despabilarse** vr **(a)** to wake up; (fig) to look lively, get a move on; **¡despabílate!** get a move on!, jump to it!
(b) (Cu, Chi, Guat) to vanish, disappear suddenly.

despacio 1 adv **(a)** slowly; gently; gradually; **¡**—**!** gently!, not so fast!, easy there!
(b) (SAm) softly, in a low voice.
2 nm (SAm) **(a)** delay; slowness.
(b) delaying tactic.

despaciosamente adv (SAm) slowly.

despacioso adj slow, deliberate; sluggish; phlegmatic.

despacito adv **(a)** very slowly, very gently. **(b)** softly.

despachaderas nfpl **(a)** surly retort, unfriendly answer.
(b) resourcefulness, quickness of mind; business sense, practical know-how; **tener buenas** — to be practical, be on the ball; to be good at getting rid of fools.
(c) brazenness, insolence.

despachado adj **(a)** resourceful, quick; businesslike; practical; **ir bien** — **de** to be well off for, be well provided with. **(b)** brazen, insolent.

despachador nm, **despachadora** nf dispatcher, sender.

despachante nm (Arg) clerk; =**despachador**.

despachar [1a] **1** vt **(a)** task to complete; business to do, complete, dispatch, settle, transact; correspondence to deal with, attend to; theme etc to deal with; to polish off, knock off; — **asuntos con el gerente** to do business with the manager, settle matters with the manager; **medio capítulo llevo despachado ya** I've already knocked off half a chapter.
(b) (fam) food etc to dispatch, put away, knock off (fam); drink to knock back (sl).
(c) ticket etc to issue.
(d) goods, person to send, dispatch (a to).
(e) to expedite, hurry along.
(f) person to send away, send off; to send packing; employee to fire (fam), sack (fam).
(g) (fam) to kill, do in (sl).
(h) (Comm) goods to sell, deal in; customer to attend to; **en seguida le despacho** I'll attend to you at once.
2 vi **(a)** (Comm) to do business; to serve; **no despacha los domingos** he doesn't do business on Sundays, he's not in on Sundays; **¿quién despacha?** is anybody serving?
(b) to finish things off, get things settled, come to a decision; **¡despacha de una vez!** settle it once and for all!, make up your mind!
(c) to hurry up, get on with it; **¡despacha!** get on with it!
3 despacharse vr **(a)** to finish off; **me despacho a las 5** I finish at 5, I knock off at 5; — **de algo** to finish something off; to get rid of something, get clear of something.
(b) to hurry (up).
(c) — **a su gusto con uno** to say what one really thinks to someone, speak very plainly to someone.
(d) — **con el cucharón** (fam) to help oneself to the biggest (or best) portion.

despachero nm (Chi) shopkeeper.

despacho nm **(a)** (act) dispatch; sending (out); (of business) dispatch, handling, settling.
(b) (quality) resourcefulness, quickness of mind; business sense; promptness, energy, efficiency; **tener buen** — to be very efficient, be on top of one's job.
(c) (Comm) sale (of goods); **géneros sin** — unsaleable goods; **tener buen** — to find a ready sale, be in good demand.
(d) message; (Mil, diplomatic) dispatch; — **telegráfico** telegram.
(e) (Comm, Pol etc) office; (in house) study; — **de billetes,** — **de boletos** (SAm) booking office; — **de localidades** box office; — **de telégrafos** telegraph office.
(f) (Comm) shop; depot; (Chi) general stores; small village shop.
(g) set of office furniture.
(h) (Mil) — **de oficial** commission.

despachurrar [1a] vt **(a)** material to squash, crush; to squelch; (Cook) to mash.
(b) account, story to mangle, make a dreadful mess of.
(c) person (in argument etc) to crush, flatten, floor.

despampanante adj (fam) stunning, shattering.

despampanar [1a] **1** vt **(a)** vine to prune, trim.
(b) (fam) to shatter, stun, bowl over.

2 *vi* (*fam*) to blow one's top (*fam*), give vent to one's feelings; to speak out freely.

3 despampanarse *vr* (*fam*) to give oneself a nasty knock.

despancar [1g] *vt* (*Bol, Per*) *maize* to husk.

desparejado *adj*, **desparejo** *adj*: **son** —s they're odd, they don't match.

desparpajar [1a] **1** *vt* (a) to take apart carelessly; to botch, bungle, spoil, mess up.
 (b) (*CAm, Mex*) to scatter, disperse.
 2 *vi* to talk wildly, rant, rave.
 3 desparpajarse *vr* (a) =*vi*.
 (b) (*Hond, PR*) to wake up.

desparpajo *nm* (a) ease of manner, self-confidence; naturalness; charm; (*pej*) glibness; (*pej*) nerve, pertness, impudence.
 (b) savoir-faire, practical know-how; sharpness, quickness of mind; presence of mind.
 (c) (*CAm*) disorder, muddle.
 (d) (*Col*) flippant remark.

desparramado *adj* scattered; wide, open.

desparramar [1a] **1** *vt* (a) to scatter, spread (*por* over); *liquid etc* to spill; *parts* to separate.
 (b) *fortune* to squander; *attention* to spread too widely, fail to concentrate.
 2 desparramarse *vr* (a) to scatter, spread out; to spill, be spilt; (*of animals*) to bolt, stampede.
 (b) (*fam*) to have a whale of a time.

desparramo *nm* (a) (*Cu, Chi, RPl*) scattering, spreading; dispersal; spilling; disorderly flight, rush, stampede. (b) (*Chi*) confusion, disorder.

despatarrado *adj*: **quedar** — (a) to have one's legs wide apart.|(b) (*fig*) to be dumbfounded; to be scared to death.

despatarrar [1a] **1** *vt* (*fig*) to amaze, dumbfound; to scare to death.
 2 despatarrarse *vr* (a) to open one's legs wide; (*on floor etc*) to do the splits; to fall with one's legs spread wide.
 (b) (*fig*) to be amazed, be dumbfounded; to be scared to death.

despatriar [1b] *vt* (*Col, Per, PR*) to exile.

despavorido *adj*: **estar** — to be utterly terrified.

despe *nf* (*fam*) tag, "he"; **dar la** — to play tag.

despeado *adj* footsore, weary.

despearse [1a] *vr* to get footsore, get utterly weary.

despectivamente *adv* contemptuously, scornfully; in derogatory terms; (*Ling*) pejoratively.

despectivo *adj* contemptuous, scornful; derogatory; (*Ling*) pejorative.

despechado *adj* angry, indignant; spiteful.

despechar [1a] **1** *vt* (a) to anger, enrage; to spite; to drive to despair.
 (b) (*Chi, Hond, PR*) to wean.
 2 despecharse *vr* to get angry; to fret; to despair.

despecho *nm* (a) spite, rancour; despair; **de puro** —, **por** — out of (sheer) spite.
 (b) **a** — **de** in spite of, despite; in defiance of.
 (c) (*Chi, Hond, PR*) weaning.

despechugado *adj person* with one's collar open, with one's shirt front undone; *shirt* open-necked, open at the neck.

despechugarse [1h] *vr* to open one's collar, unbutton one's shirt at the neck; to unbutton one's shirt down the front.

despedazar [1f] *vt* (a) to tear apart, tear to pieces; to cut into bits; to lacerate, mangle, cut to shreds. (b) (*fig*) *heart* to break; *honour* to hurt.

despedida *nf* (a) farewell; leave-taking; send-off; (*from job*) dismissal, sacking (*fam*); **cena de** — farewell dinner; **función de** — (*Theat*) farewell performance; **regalo de** — parting gift.
 (b) farewell ceremony.
 (c) (*Lit etc*) closing couplet; (*in letter*) closing formula, closing phrases.

despedir [3l] **1** *vt* (a) *guest, friend* to see off; to see out; to say goodbye to; *client etc* to show out; **fuimos a** —**le a la estación** we went to see him off at the station.
 (b) *workman etc* to dismiss, sack (*fam*), discharge; *bore* to get rid of, send away; *tenant* to evict; to give notice to.
 (c) — **algo de sí** to get rid of something; — **un pensamiento de sí** to put a thought out of one's mind, banish a thought from one's mind.
 (d) *object* to hurl, fling; to project; *arrow etc* to fire; *missile* to launch; *jet etc* to send up; *rider* to throw; *smell etc* to give off, give out, emit, throw off; *heat* to give out; *juice etc* to release, allow to come out; — **el espíritu** to give up the ghost.
 2 despedirse *vr* to say goodbye, take one's leave; to give up one's job, leave (one's work); **se despi-**

dieron they said goodbye to each other; — **de uno** to say goodbye to someone, take one's leave of someone; (*at station etc*) to see someone off; **¡ya puedes despedirte de ese dinero!** you can say goodbye to that money!

despegado 1 *adj* (a) detached, loose. (b) *person* cold, indifferent, unconcerned. **2** *nm*: **es un** — he has cut himself off from his family, he has kept no roots.

despegar [1h] **1** *vt* to unglue, unstick; to detach, loosen; *envelope* to open; **sin** — **los labios** without uttering a word.
 2 *vi* (*Aer*) to take off.
 3 despegarse *vr* (a) to come loose, come unstuck; to come apart.
 (b) (*person*) to become alienated, become detached (*de* from); — **de los amigos** to break with one's friends; — **del mundo** to withdraw from the world, renounce worldly things.
 (c) (*fam*) — **con** not to go well with.

despego *nm* =**desapego**.

despegue *nm* (*Aer*) takeoff; — **corto** short takeoff; — **vertical** vertical takeoff.

despeinado *adj* dishevelled, tousled; unkempt.

despeinar [1a] *vt hair, person* to tousle, ruffle; *hairdo* to mess up, muss.

despejado *adj* (a) *way, space* clear, free, unobstructed, open; *brow* clear; *room etc* unencumbered, spacious.
 (b) *sky* cloudless, clear.
 (c) (*person: estar*) wide-awake; (*Med*) free of fever; lucid.
 (d) (*person: ser*) sharp, bright, smart.

despejar [1a] **1** *vt* (a) *space etc* to clear, disencumber, free from obstructions; **los bomberos despejaron el teatro** the firemen cleared the theatre (of people); **los guardias obligaron a** — **el tribunal** the police ordered the court to be cleared, the police ordered people to leave the court; **¡despejen!** move along!; everybody out!
 (b) (*Sport*) *ball* to clear.
 (c) *mystery* to clear up, clarify, resolve; (*Math*) *unknown quantity* to find.
 2 *vi* (a) (*Sport*) to clear (the ball).
 (b) (*Meteorol*) to clear.
 3 despejarse *vr* (a) (*Meteorol*) to clear, clear up; (*of mystery etc*) to become clearer.
 (b) (*person*) to liven oneself up; to feel better, feel brighter; to clear one's head.
 (c) (*person*) to relax, amuse oneself.
 (d) (*person: in temperament*) to become more free and easy.

despeje *nm* (*Sport*) clearance.

despejo *nm* brightness; self-confidence, ease of manner; fluency.

despeluchado *adj* dishevelled, tousled.

despeluchar [1a] *vt* to dishevel, tousle.

despeluzar [1f] **1** *vt* (a) *hair* to dishevel, tousle, rumple.
 (b) — **a uno** (*fig*) to horrify someone, make someone's hair stand on end.
 (c) (*Cu*) to ruin, leave penniless.
 2 despeluzarse *vr* (a) (*hair*) to stand on end.
 (b) (*person*) to be horrified.

despellejar [1a] *vt* (a) to skin, flay. (b) (*fig*) to flay, criticize unmercifully. (c) (*fam*) — **a uno** to fleece someone.

despenar [1a] *vt* (*sl*) to bump off (*sl*).

despendedor *adj* extravagant.

despensa *nf* (a) pantry, larder; food store; (*Naut*) storeroom. (b) stock of food.

despensero *nm* butler, steward; (*Naut*) storekeeper.

despeñadero *nm* (a) (*Geog*) cliff, precipice. (b) (*fig*) risky enterprise.

despeñadizo *adj* dangerously steep, sheer, precipitous.

despeñar [1a] **1** *vt* to fling down, hurl from a height, throw over a cliff.
 2 despeñarse *vr* (a) to hurl oneself down, throw oneself over a cliff; to fall headlong.
 (b) — **en el vicio** to plunge into vice.

despeño *nm* (*fig*) failure, collapse.

despepitar [1a] **1** *vt* to remove the pips (*etc*) from.
 2 despepitarse *vr* (a) to bawl, shriek (one's head off), shout oneself hoarse; to rave, act wildly.
 (b) — **por algo** to long for something, be crazy about something; — **por** + *infin* to long to + *infin*.

despercudir [3a] *vt* (a) to clean, wash. (b) (*SAm: fig*) *person* to liven up, wake up, ginger up.

desperdiciado *adj* wasteful.

desperdiciador 1 *adj* spendthrift. **2** *nm* spendthrift.

desperdiciar [1b] *vt* to waste, squander, fritter away; *time* to waste; *chance* to throw away.

desperdicio nm (a) waste; wasting; squandering.
(b) —s rubbish, refuse; scraps, left-overs; (Bio, Tech) waste products; —s de algodón cotton waste; —s de cocina kitchen scraps; —s de hierro scrap iron, junk.
(c) el cerdo es un animal que no tiene — nothing from a pig is wasted, everything from a pig can be used; el muchacho no tiene — he's a fine lad.

desperdigar [1h] 1 vt to scatter, separate, disperse; energy etc to spread too widely, dissipate. 2 desperdigarse vr to scatter, separate.

desperezarse [1f] vr to stretch (oneself).

desperfecto nm flaw, blemish, imperfection; slight damage; sufrió algunos —s en el accidente it suffered slight damage in the accident.

despernado adj footsore, weary.

despersonalizar [1f] vt to depersonalize.

despertador nm (a) alarm clock; — de viaje travelling clock. (b) (person) knocker-up. (c) (fig) warning.

despertamiento nm awakening; (fig) awakening, revival, rebirth.

despertar [1k] 1 vt (a) person etc to wake (up), awaken.
(b) (fig) hopes etc to awaken, raise, arouse; memory to awaken, revive, recall; feeling to arouse, stir up.
2 vi and **despertarse** vr to wake up, awaken; — a la realidad to wake up to reality.
3 nm: el — religioso the religious awakening; el — de la primavera the awakening of spring.

despestañarse [1a] vr (a) to strain one's eyes. (b) (fig) to burn the midnight oil.

despiadadamente adv cruelly; mercilessly, relentlessly; heartlessly.

despiadado adj cruel; merciless, relentless; heartless.

despicarse [1g] vr to get even, get one's revenge.

despichar [1a] 1 vt (Col, Chi, Ven) to crush, smash. 2 vi (sl) to kick the bucket (sl).

despido nm dismissal, sacking (fam).

despiece nm (of carcass) quartering, carving-up.

despierto adj (a) awake. (b) (fig) wide-awake; sharp; alert, watchful.

despilfarrado adj (a) extravagant, wasteful, spendthrift. (b) ragged, shabby.

despilfarrador 1 adj=despilfarrado. 2 nm spendthrift.

despilfarrar [1a] vt to waste, squander.

despilfarro nm (a) (act) wasting, squandering. (b) (quality) extravagance, wastefulness. (c) shabbiness, slovenliness, ragged state.

despintar [1a] 1 vt (a) to take the paint off.
(b) (fig) story etc to alter, distort; to spoil.
(c) (Col, Chi, PR) no — a uno not to let someone out of one's sight.
2 vi: A no despinta de B A is not unworthy of B, A is in no way inferior to B.
3 despintarse vr (a) to wash off; to fade, lose its colour.
(b) no se me despinta que . . . I never forget that . . .; I remember vividly that . . .

despiojar [1a] vt (a) to delouse. (b) — a uno (fig) to rescue someone from the gutter.

despique nm satisfaction, revenge.

despistado 1 adj (a) (ser) vague, absent-minded; unpractical; hopeless.
(b) (estar) confused, out of touch, all at sea; off the beam (fam); ando muy — con todo esto I'm terribly muddled about all this.
2 nm, despistada nf absent-minded person, vague individual; unpractical type; es un — he's hopeless, he's a dream.

despistar [1a] 1 vt (a) (Hunting) to throw off the track (or scent).
(b) (fig) to put off the scent; to mislead, muddle; esa pregunta está hecha para — that question is designed to put people off.
2 despistarse vr (fig) to go wrong, take the wrong route (or turning etc); to get confused.

despiste nm (a) (Aut etc) swerve.
(b) mistake, slip.
(c) absent-mindedness; muddle, confusion, bewilderment; ¡qué — tienes! you're a bright one!, what a clot you are!; tiene un terrible — he's terribly absent-minded; he's hopelessly unpractical; he's hopeless, he's a dream.

desplacer 1 [2x] vt to displease. 2 nm displeasure.

desplantador nm trowel.

desplantar [1a] vt (a) plant to pull up, uproot, take up. (b) object to move out of vertical, tilt.

desplante nm (a) incorrect position (of the body); irregular posture.
(b) bold statement, outspoken remark; (pej)

impudent remark (etc); dar un — to interrupt someone rudely.

desplazado 1 adj (a) displaced, wrongly placed, off-centre.
(b) person badly adjusted; out of one's depth, out of one's element; (Pol) displaced; sentirse un poco — to feel rather out of place.
2 nm, desplazada nf misfit; ill-adjusted person; outsider; (Pol) displaced person.

desplazamiento nm (a) displacement, movement; — de tierras landslip.
(b) (Naut) displacement.
(c) journey, trip.
(d) (of opinion, votes etc) shift, swing.

desplazar [1f] 1 vt (a) object to displace, move.
(b) (Naut, Phys) to displace.
(c) person etc to displace, supplant, take the place of.
2 desplazarse vr (a) (object) to move, shift.
(b) (person, vehicle) to go, travel; tiene que — todos los días 25 kms he has to travel 25 kms every day; el avión se desplaza a más de 1500 mph the aircraft travels at more than 1500 mph.
(c) (opinion, votes etc) to shift, swing; se ha desplazado un 4 por 100 de los votos there has been a swing of 4% in the voting.

desplegar [1h and 1k] 1 vt (a) to unfold, open (out), spread (out); wings to spread, open; sails to unfurl; (Mil) to deploy; sin — los labios without uttering a word.
(b) (fig) energy etc to put forth, use, display; resources to deploy.
(c) (fig) mystery to clarify, elucidate.
2 desplegarse vr (flower etc) to open (out), unfold; to spread (out); (Mil) to deploy.

despliegue nm (a) unfolding, opening; (Mil) deployment. (b) (fig) display, manifestation, show, exhibition.

desplomarse [1a] vr (a) to lean, tilt, get out of vertical; to bulge, warp.
(b) to collapse, tumble down, come crashing down; to topple over; (prices etc) to slump, tumble; (government, system) to collapse; (Aer) to make a pancake landing; (person) to collapse, crumple up; se ha desplomado el techo the ceiling has fallen in, the ceiling has collapsed; ¡se desploma el cielo! it's incredible!

desplome nm (a) (act) leaning, tilting; fall, collapse; slump; (Aer) pancake landing.
(b) (Archit, Geol etc) overhang, projecting part; (Mountaineering) overhang.

desplomo nm=desplome (b).

desplumar [1a] 1 vt (a) to pluck. (b) (fig) to fleece, skin. 2 desplumarse vr to moult.

despoblación nf depopulation; — rural, — del campo rural depopulation, drift from the land.

despoblado 1 adj unpopulated, deserted; (fig) desolate. 2 nm deserted spot, uninhabited place; wilderness.

despoblar [1m] vt to depopulate; to reduce the population of, clear people out of; to lay waste; — una zona de árboles to clear an area of trees.

despojar [1a] 1 vt: — de to strip of, clear of, leave bare of; (fig) to divest of, denude of; (Law) to dispossess of, deprive of; habían despojado la casa de muebles they had stripped the house of furniture, they had cleared all the furniture out of the house; verse despojado de su autoridad to find oneself stripped of one's authority.
2 despojarse vr to undress; — de to take off, remove, strip off; leaves etc to shed; powers etc to divest oneself of, relinquish, give up; prejudice etc to get rid of, free oneself from.

despojo nm (a) (act) spoliation, despoilment; plundering.
(b) (Mil etc) plunder, loot, spoils.
(c) —s waste, left-overs, scraps; (of animal) offal; (Archit) rubble; secondhand building materials, usable waste; (Geol) debris; —s de hierro scrap iron; —s mortales mortal remains.

despolvorear [1a] vt to dust.

desportilladura nf chip; nick.

desportillar [1a] 1 vt to chip, nick. 2 desportillarse vr to chip, chip off.

desposado adj newly-wed, recently married; los —s the bridal couple, the newly-weds.

desposar [1a] 1 vt (of priest) couple to marry.
2 desposarse vr (a) (one person) to become engaged (con to); to get married (con to).
(b) (two persons) to get engaged; to marry, get married.

desposeer [2e] **1** *vt* to dispossess (*de* of); to oust (*de un puesto* from a post); — **a uno de su autoridad** to remove someone's authority, strip someone of his authority.

2 desposeerse *vr:* — **de algo** to give something up, relinquish something, divest oneself of something.

desposeído *nm*, **desposeída** *nf:* **los** —**s** the deprived, those in want, the have-nots.

desposeimiento *nm* dispossession; ousting.

desposorios *nmpl* engagement, betrothal; marriage (ceremony).

déspota *nm* despot.

despóticamente *adv* despotically.

despótico *adj* despotic.

despotismo *nm* despotism.

despotricar [1g] *vi* to rave, rant, carry on (*contra* about).

despreciable *adj* (*morally*) despicable, contemptible; (*in quality*) worthless, trashy, valueless; (*in quantity*) negligible; **una suma nada** — a far from negligible amount.

despreciar [1b] **1** *vt* to scorn, despise, look down on; to spurn, reject; to slight; to underestimate, underrate; — **los peligros** to scorn the dangers; — **una oferta** to reject an offer; **no hay que** — **tal posibilidad** one should not underestimate such a possibility.

2 despreciarse *vr:* — **de** + *infin* to think it beneath oneself to + *infin*, not deign to + *infin*.

despreciativamente *adv* scornfully, contemptuously; in a derogatory way; cynically.

despreciativo *adj* scornful, contemptuous; *remark etc* derogatory; cynical.

desprecio *nm* (a) scorn, contempt, disdain; disparaging attitude; cynicism; **lo miró con** — he looked at it contemptuously.

(b) slight, snub; **le hicieron el** — **de no acudir** they snubbed him by not coming.

desprender [2a] **1** *vt* (a) to unfasten, loosen, detach, separate.

(b) *gas etc* to give off; *skin etc* to shed.

2 desprenderse *vr* (a) (*part*) to become detached, work loose, fall off; to fly off.

(b) — **de un estorbo** to extricate oneself from a difficulty, get free of a difficulty; **la serpiente se desprende de la piel** the snake sheds its skin.

(c) — **de algo** to give something up, part with something; to get rid of something; to deprive oneself of something; **se desprendió de sus joyas** she parted with her jewels; **tendremos que desprendernos del coche** we shall have to get rid of the car; **se desprendió de su autoridad** he relinquished his authority.

(d) (*gas etc*) to be given off, issue; **de la pared se desprende humedad** there is damp coming from the wall.

(e) (*meaning etc*) — **de** to follow from; to be implied by; to be clear from; **se desprende que . . .** one gathers that . . .; **se desprende de esta declaración que . . .** it is clear from this statement that . . .; **por fin se desprendió que . . .** finally it transpired that . . .

desprendido *adj* (a) *part* loose, detached; unfastened.

(b) (*fig*) disinterested; generous.

desprendimiento *nm* (a) loosening, detachment; unfastening; — **de tierras** landslide.

(b) (*of gas etc*) release, emission; (*of skin etc*) shedding.

(c) (*fig*) disinterestedness; generosity.

despreocupación *nf* (a) unconcern; carefree nature; nonchalance, casualness.

(b) unconventional outlook (*or* style *etc*); (*pej*) sloppiness, slovenliness.

(c) impartiality.

(d) indifference, apathy; broad-mindedness.

(e) looseness.

despreocupado *adj* (a) unworried, unconcerned; carefree; nonchalant, casual; free-and-easy.

(b) (*in dress etc*) unconventional, casual; (*pej*) careless, sloppy, slovenly.

(c) (*in judgement*) unbiassed, impartial.

(d) (*Rel*) indifferent, apathetic; broad-minded.

(e) *woman* loose.

despreocupamiento *nm* lack of interest, apathy.

desprestigiar [1b] **1** *vt* to disparage, run down; to discredit; to cheapen. **2 desprestigiarse** *vr* to lose (one's) prestige; to lose caste; to cheapen oneself.

desprestigio *nm* disparagement; discredit; loss of prestige (*or* caste, standing); unpopularity; **esas cosas que van en** — **nuestro** those things which are to our discredit, those things which harm our reputation.

desprevención *nf* unreadiness, unpreparedness; lack of foresight.

desprevenido *adj* unready, unprepared; **coger a uno** — to catch someone unawares, catch someone off his guard, take someone by surprise.

desproporción *nf* disproportion, lack of proportion.

desproporcionadamente *adv* disproportionately.

desproporcionado *adj* disproportionate, out of proportion.

despropósito *nm* absurdity, silly thing (to say), piece of nonsense; —**s** nonsense.

desprovisto *adj:* — **de** devoid of, bereft of, without; **estar** — **de** to lack, be lacking in, be devoid of; **estar** — **de medios** to be without means; **un libro no** — **de méritos** a book not without merit.

después 1 *adv* (a) (*time*) afterwards, later; since, since then; next; **un año** — a year later; **años** — years later; **¿qué pasó** —? what happened then?; **poco** — soon after, shortly after.

(b) (*order*) next, after; **¿y** —? and what comes next?; **nuestra casa viene** — and then our house is next.

2 — **de** *prep* (a) (*time*) after; since; — **de esa fecha** (*past*) since that date, (*future*) from that date, after that date; — **de verlo** after seeing it; **no** — **de 1980** not later than 1980; — **de descubierta la isla** after the discovery of the island, after the island had been discovered.

(b) (*order*) next (to); **mi nombre está** — **del tuyo** my name comes next to yours; my name comes after yours; **es el primero** — **de éste** it's the next one after this.

3 — (**de**) **que** *conj* after; — (**de**) **que lo escribí** after (*or* since) I wrote it, after writing it.

despuntado *adj* blunt.

despuntar [1a] **1** *vt* to blunt, dull (the point *or* edge of).

2 *vi* (a) (*Bot*) to sprout, bud, begin to show.

(b) (*of dawn*) to break, appear; (*of day*) to dawn.

(c) (*of person etc*) to excel, stand out; to shine, sparkle; to show intelligence; — **de agudo** to have a sparkling wit; **despunta en matemáticas** he shines at maths; **despunta por su talento** her talent shines out, her talent is outstanding.

desquiciar [1b] *vt* (a) *door* to unhinge, take off its hinges.

(b) (*fig*) to upset, disturb, turn upside down, make a mess of.

(c) *person* (*mentally*) to disturb, upset; to unhinge, affect seriously, unbalance; to anger, provoke.

(d) *person* (*from post*) to oust, lever out.

desquicio *nm* (*Arg*, *Guat*) confusion, disorder.

desquitarse [1a] *vr* to obtain satisfaction; (*Comm*, *Fin*) to recover a debt, get one's money back; (*fig*) to get even (*con* with), get one's own back (*con* on); — **de una pérdida** to make up for a loss, compensate oneself for a loss; — **de una mala pasada** to get one's own back for a dirty trick (played on one).

desquite *nm* satisfaction; compensation for a loss, recovery of a debt; revenge, retaliation; (*Sport*, *also* **partido de** —) return match; **tomar el** — to have one's revenge, get one's own back; **tomar el** — **de algo** to make up for something.

desratizar [1f] *vt* to clear of rats.

desrazonable *adj* unreasonable.

desrielar [1a] *vt* (*SAm*) to derail.

destacable *adj*, **destacado** *adj* notable, outstanding, distinguished.

destacamento *nm* (*Mil*) detachment.

destacar [1g] **1** *vt* (a) (*Art etc*) to make stand out; (*fig*) to emphasize, show up, point out; bring out; to throw into relief; **quiero** — **que . . .** I wish to emphasize that . . .; **sirve para** — **su belleza** it serves to enhance her beauty, it serves to show up her beauty.

(b) (*Mil*) to detach, detail.

2 *vi and* **destacarse** *vr* (a) to stand out; —**se contra**, —**se en**, —**se sobre** to stand out against, be outlined against, be silhouetted against.

(b) (*fig*) to stand out, be outstanding, be exceptional.

destajar [1a] *vt* (a) (*Cards*) to cut. (b) (*Col*, *Ec*, *Guat*, *Mex*) *carcass* to cut up. (c) *work etc* to contract for, make arrangements about; to do as piecework.

destajero *nm*, **destajista** *nm* pieceworker.

destajo *nm* (*in general*) piecework; contract work; (*un* —) job; stint; **a** — by the job; (*fig*) eagerly, keenly; energetically; (*Chi*) by guesswork; **trabajar a** — to do piecework, be on piecework; **trabajo a** — piecework; **hablar a** — (*fam*) to talk nineteen to the dozen.

destapar [1a] **1** vt to uncover; bottle to open, uncork; box to open, take the lid off; vessel to take the lid off, raise the lid of; (fig) to reveal, uncover.
   2 destaparse vr **(a)** to get uncovered.
   (b) (fig) to cause surprise, do something unexpected; to show oneself in one's true character; **se destapó metiéndose monja** she astounded everyone by becoming a nun.
   (c) (fig) — **con uno** to unbosom oneself to someone.
destaponar [1a] vt to uncork.
destartalado adj room etc untidy, in disorder; house etc large and rambling; ruinous, tumbledown, dilapidated; vehicle etc rickety, shaky.
destazar [1f] vt to cut up.
destechar [1a] vt to unroof.
destejar [1a] vt **(a)** to remove the tiles from. **(b)** (fig) to leave unprotected.
destejer [2d] vt **(a)** to undo, unravel; to take the stitches out of. **(b)** (fig) to upset; to interfere with the progress of; see **tejer**.
destellante nm (Aut) indicator, winking light.
destellar [1a] vi to sparkle, flash; to glint, gleam; (Aut: of light) to wink.
destello nm **(a)** sparkle; flash; glint, gleam; wink(ing). **(b)** (Tech) signal light, winking light.
   (c) (fig) atom, particle; **no tiene un — de verdad** there's not an atom of truth in it.
   (d) —**s** (fig) glimmer; **tiene a veces —s de inteligencia** he sometimes shows a glimmer (or glimmerings) of intelligence.
destemplado adj **(a)** (Mus) instrument out of tune; voice harsh, unpleasant.
   (b) (Art) inharmonious, badly blended, ill-matched.
   (c) pulse irregular.
   (d) (Med) indisposed, out of sorts; feverish.
   (e) character, gesture etc ill-tempered; attitude ill-judged, intemperate, harsh.
   (f) (Meteorol) unpleasant.
destemplanza nf **(a)** (Mus) tunelessness; harshness, unpleasantness.
   (b) lack of harmony.
   (c) irregularity.
   (d) (Med) indisposition; feverish condition.
   (e) intemperance, harshness.
   (f) (Meteorol) unpleasantness, inclemency.
   (g) (una —) sharp remark, harsh comment.
destemplar [1a] **1** vt **(a)** (Mus) to untune, put out of tune, upset the pitch of.
   (b) (fig) to upset, disturb (the order of); to disconcert.
   2 destemplarse vr **(a)** (Mus) to get out of tune, lose its pitch.
   (b) (fig) to get out of order; (person) to get upset, get worked up; (pulse) to become irregular; (Med) to become indisposed, get out of sorts.
   (c) (SAm) **con eso me destemplo** that sets my teeth on edge, that gives me the shivers.
destemple nm (in most senses) = **destemplanza**; (of metal) lack of temper, poorly-tempered nature.
desteñido adj faded, discoloured.
desteñir [3l] **1** vt to fade, discolour, take the colour out of.
   2 vi and **desteñirse** vr **(a)** to fade, lose colour, discolour.
   (b) (of colours in fabric) to run; "**esta tela no destiñe**" "this fabric will not run".
desternillarse [1a] vr: — **de risa** to split one's sides with laughing, die of laughing.
desterrado nm, **desterrada** nf exile; outlaw; (esp fig) outcast.
desterrar [1k] vt **(a)** to exile, banish.
   (b) (fig) to banish; to dismiss, put aside; — **una sospecha** to banish a suspicion from one's mind; — **el uso de las armas de fuego** to banish firearms, prohibit the use of firearms.
   (c) (Agr, Min) to remove the soil from.
destetar [1a] **1** vt to wean. **2 destetarse** vr **(a)** to be weaned; — **con el vino** (fig) to have been brought up on wine. **(b)** to break oneself of a (bad) habit.
destete nm weaning.
destiempo nm: **a — at** the wrong time, at an inopportune moment.
destierro nm **(a)** exile; banishment; **vivir en el — to** live in exile. **(b)** (fig) wilderness; remote spot.
destilación nf distillation.
destiladera nf still, distilling vessel; (SAm) filter.
destilador nm **(a)** still. **(b)** (person) distiller.
destilar [1a] **1** vt **(a)** alcohol to distil; blood etc to exude, ooze.
   (b) (fig) to exude, ooze; to reveal; **la carta**

destilaba odio the letter exuded hatred; **es una orden que destila crueldad** it is an order which is steeped in cruelty.
   2 vi to drip, fall (drop by drop); to ooze (out); to filter through.
destilatorio nm still.
destilería nf distillery; — **de petróleo** oil refinery.
destinar [1a] vt **(a)** to destine (a, para for, to); to assign (a to); to design (a for); to intend, mean (a, para for); funds etc to set aside, earmark (a for); **me habían destinado una habitación elegante** they had assigned me an elegant room; **le destinan al sacerdocio** they intend him for the priesthood; **fabricantes de aviones destinados a Eslobodia** makers of aircraft destined for (or for use in) Slobodia; **una carta que viene destinada a Vd** a letter for you, a letter addressed to you; **ir destinado a** (Naut etc) to be bound for; **estar destinado a** + infin to be destined to + infin.
   (b) person to appoint, assign (a to); (Mil etc) to post (a to); **le han destinado a Lima** they have appointed him to Lima.
destinatario nm, **destinataria** nf addressee.
destino nm **(a)** destiny, fate; **es mi — no encontrarlo** I am fated not to find it; **el — lo quiso así** it was destiny, fate willed it thus.
   (b) (of traveller, ship etc) destination; **van con — a Londres** they are going to London, (Naut) they are bound for London; **salir con — a** to leave for; **¿cuál es el — de este cuadro?** what is the destination of this picture?, where is this picture for?
   (c) job, post, position; — **público** public appointment; **buscarse un — de sereno** to look for a job as night watchman.
   (d) use, utility; **dar — a algo** to put something to good use, find a use for something.
destitución nf dismissal, removal.
destituido adj: — **de** devoid of, bereft of, lacking (in).
destituir [3g] vt **(a)** person to dismiss, remove, sack (fam; de from); to remove from office; **le destituyeron por inmoral** they sacked him for immorality.
   (b) — **a uno de algo** to deprive someone of something.
destorcer [2b and 2h] **1** vt string etc to untwist, take the twists out of; rod etc to straighten. **2 destorcerse** vr (Naut) to get off course.
destornillado adj (fam) crazy, potty (fam).
destornillador nm screwdriver.
destornillar [1a] **1** vt to unscrew. **2 destornillarse** vr **(a)** (fig) to behave wildly; (fam) to go crazy. **(b)** (SAm) = **desternillarse**.
destrabar [1a] vt to loosen, detach; prisoner etc to unfetter, take the shackles off.
destraillar [1a] vt to let off the leash, unleash.
destral nm hatchet.
destreza nf skill, dexterity; cleverness; handiness.
destripacuentos nm, pl **destripacuentos** interrupter, person who butts in.
destripador nm: **Juanito el D— Jack** the Ripper.
destripar [1a] vt **(a)** animal to gut, draw, paunch; person to disembowel; to cut open the belly of, slash the stomach of.
   (b) (fig) to mangle, crush; story to spoil (by interrupting and telling its ending).
destripaterrones nm, pl **destripaterrones** poor labourer; (fig) clodhopper.
destronamiento nm dethronement; (fig) overthrow.
destronar [1a] vt to dethrone; (fig) to overthrow.
destroncar [1g] vt **(a)** tree to chop off, lop (the top off); (Chi, Mex) plant to cut off at ground level; to uproot.
   (b) person to maim; (fig) to tire out, exhaust; steed to wear out.
   (c) (fig) plans etc to ruin; development to harm, damage, dislocate; speech etc to interrupt.
destrozado adj smashed, shattered, ruined.
destrozar [1f] vt **(a)** to smash, shatter, ruin; to break up, break to pieces; to destroy; clothing, shoes to ruin; (Mil) army, enemy to smash; flesh to mangle, lacerate, tear; nerves to shatter; resources etc to squander, dissipate.
   (b) (fig) person to ruin; to shatter; life etc to ruin; heart to break; — **la armonía** to ruin the harmony; — **a uno en una discusión** to crush someone in an argument; **le ha destrozado el que no quisiera casarse con él** he was shattered when she wouldn't marry him, her refusal to marry him broke him up.
destrozo nm destruction; (of army) smashing, annihilation, rout; (of persons) massacre; —**s** damage, havoc, ravages; **causar —s en** to create havoc in, cause great damage to, ravage.

destrozón *adj*: **un niño** — a child who is hard on his clothes; **la criada es muy destrozona** the servant is a terrible one for breaking things.
destrucción *nf* destruction.
destructible *adj* destructible.
destructivo *adj* destructive.
destructor 1 *adj* destructive. 2 *nm* (*Naut*) destroyer.
destruible *adj* destructible.
destruir [3g] 1 *vt* to destroy; to ruin, wreck; to damage; *balance etc* to destroy, upset; *resources* to squander; *plans* to ruin.
   2 **destruirse** *vr* (*Math*) to cancel (each other) out.
desudar [1a] *vt* to wipe the sweat off.
desuellacaras *nm*, *pl* **desuellacaras** (*fam*) (a) clumsy barber. (b) rogue, villain.
desuello *nm* (a) skinning, flaying. (b) brazenness, insolence. (c) (*fam*) extortion; **¡es un —!** it's daylight robbery!
desuncir [3b] *vt* to unyoke.
desunión *nf* (a) separation; disconnection. (b) disunity; rift.
desunir [3a] *vt* (a) to separate, sever, detach; (*Tech*) to disconnect, disengage, uncouple. (b) (*fig*) to cause a rift between.
desuñarse [1a] *vr* (a) to work one's fingers to the bone (*por* + *infin* to + *infin*). (b) (*fig*) to be constantly involved in wicked things.
desurbanización *nf* relief of city overcrowding, dispersal of city population(s) (to satellite towns).
desusado *adj* (a) obsolete, antiquated, out of date.
   (b) **esa palabra está desusada de los buenos escritores** that word is no longer in use among good writers.
   (c) (*fig*) unwonted, unusual.
desusar [1a] 1 *vt* to stop using, discontinue the use of, give up. 2 **desusarse** *vr* to go out of use, become obsolete.
desuso *nm* disuse; desuetude; **caer en** — to fall into disuse, become obsolete; **una expresión caída en** — an obsolete expression; **dejar algo en** — to cease to use something, discontinue the use of something.
desvaído *adj* (a) *colour* pale, dull, washed-out.
   (b) *outline* ill-defined, vague, blurred.
   (c) *person* (*in character*) weak, characterless; *personality* flat, dull.
   (d) (*in stature*) gaunt.
desvainar [1a] *vt peas etc* to shell.
desvalido *adj* helpless; destitute; (*Pol*) underprivileged; **los —s** the helpless, (*Pol*) the underprivileged; **niños —s** waifs and strays, abandoned children.
desvalijamiento *nm* robbing, robbery; rifling; burgling.
desvalijar [1a] *vt* to rob, plunder; *drawer, case etc* to rifle; *shop* to burgle, burglarize (*US*), break into, rob.
desvalorar [1a] *vt* to devaluate; *currency* to devalue.
desvalorización *nf* devaluation.
desvalorizar [1f] *vt* to devalue.
desván *nm* loft, attic; garret.
desvanecer [2d] 1 *vt* (a) to cause to vanish, make disappear.
   (b) *doubt etc* to dispel; *thought, memory* to banish, dismiss.
   (c) *colours* to tone down; *outline* to blur; (*Phot*) to mask.
   2 **desvanecerse** *vr* (a) to vanish, disappear.
   (b) (*doubt etc*) to vanish, be dispelled.
   (c) (*Chem etc*) to evaporate; to dissolve, melt away, disappear.
   (d) (*Med*) to faint (away).
   (e) (*sound, also Radio*) to fade (away), fade out.
desvanecido *adj* (a) (*Med*) faint; giddy, dizzy; **caer** — to fall in a faint. (b) (*fig*) vain; proud, haughty.
desvanecimiento *nm* (a) vanishing, disappearance; dissipation, dispelling.
   (b) blurring; (*Phot*) masking.
   (c) evaporation; melting.
   (d) (*Med*) fainting fit, swoon; dizzy spell, attack of giddiness.
   (e) (*Radio etc*) fading.
   (f) (*fig*) vanity; pride, haughtiness.
desvarar [1a] *vt* to refloat.
desvariar [1c] *vi* (a) (*Med*) to be delirious. (b) (*fig*) to rave, talk nonsense.
desvarío *nm* (*Med*) (a) delirium; raving. (b) (*fig*) absurdity; extravagant notion, strange notion; whim; **—s** ravings, ramblings.
desvelado *adj* (a) sleepless, wakeful; **estar** — to be awake, be unable to get to sleep. (b) (*fig*) watchful, vigilant.
desvelar [1a] 1 *vt* to keep awake; **el café me desvela** coffee keeps me awake.

   2 **desvelarse** *vr* (a) to stay awake, keep awake; to go without sleep, have a sleepless night.
   (b) (*fig*) to be watchful, be vigilant, keep one's eyes open; — **por algo** to be anxious about something, be much concerned about something; to take great care over something; — **por** + *infin* to do everything possible to + *infin*; **se desvela porque no nos falte nada** she works hard so that we should not go short of anything.
desvelo *nm* (a) lack of sleep; sleeplessness, insomnia.
   (b) (*fig*) watchfulness, vigilance.
   (c) **—s** *pl* (*fig*) anxiety, care, concern; effort, hard work; **gracias a sus —s** thanks to his efforts.
desvencijado *adj* ramshackle, rickety, broken-down.
desvencijar [1a] 1 *vt* (a) to break; to loosen, weaken.
   (b) *person* to weaken, exhaust.
   2 **desvencijarse** *vr* (a) to come apart, fall to pieces, break; to become disjointed.
   (b) (*Med*) to rupture oneself.
desventaja *nf* disadvantage; handicap, liability; **estar en** — **con respecto a otros** to be in a disadvantageous position compared with others.
desventajosamente *adv* disadvantageously, unfavourably.
desventajoso *adj* disadvantageous, unfavourable.
desventura *nf* misfortune.
desventuradamente *adv* unfortunately.
desventurado 1 *adj* (a) unfortunate, unlucky; ill-fated.
   (b) miserable, wretched; unhappy; **¡qué — estoy!** how wretched I am!
   (c) timid, shy.
   (d) mean.
   2 *nm*, **desventurada** *nf* wretch, unfortunate; **algún** — some poor devil.
desvergonzado 1 *adj* shameless; impudent, brazen; unblushing. 2 *nm*, **desvergonzada** *nf* shameless person.
desvergonzarse [1f *and* 1m] *vr* (a) to lose all sense of shame.
   (b) to be impudent, be insolent (*con* to); to behave in a shameless way (*con* to).
   (c) — **a pedir algo** to have the nerve to ask for something, dare to ask for something.
desvergüenza *nf* shamelessness; brazenness, effrontery, impudence; **esto es una** — this is disgraceful, this is shameful; **¡qué —!** how shocking!; what a nerve!, the effrontery of it!; **tener la** — **de** + *infin* to have the impudence (*or* nerve) to + *infin*.
desvestir [3l] 1 *vt* to undress. 2 **desvestirse** *vr* to undress.
desviación *nf* (a) (*act*) deviation (*from* de); deflection (*de* from), departure (*de* from); (*Mech, Phys, of compass*) deviation; — **normal** standard deviation; **es una** — **de sus principios** it is a deviation (*or* departure) from his principles.
   (b) (*Pol, Psych*) deviation.
   (c) (*Aut etc*) detour; diversion; bypass, ring road; — **de la circulación** traffic diversion.
desviacionismo *nm* deviationism.
desviacionista 1 *adj* deviationist. 2 *nmf* deviationist.
desviadero *nm* (*Rail*) siding.
desviado *adj* (a) oblique; deflected. (b) *place* remote, off the beaten track; — **de** remote from, away from.
desviar [1c] 1 *vt* (a) (*in physical sense*) to turn aside; to deflect, divert (*de* from); *arrow etc* to deflect; *ball* to deflect, glance; *blow, thrust* to parry, ward off, deflect; *question* to parry; *eyes* to avert, turn away; (*Aut*) to divert, re-route (*por* through); (*Rail*) to switch (into a siding), shunt aside; — **el cauce de un río** to alter the course of a river.
   (b) (*fig*) to turn aside (*de* from); **le desviaron de su propósito** they dissuaded him from his intention; — **a uno de su vocación** to turn someone from his (true) vocation; — **a uno de su pensamiento** to sidetrack someone from his theme; — **a uno de las malas compañías** to wean someone away from evil company; — **a uno del buen camino** (*fig*) to lead someone astray.
   2 **desviarse** *vr* (*person etc*) to turn aside, turn away, deviate (*de* from); (*road*) to branch off, leave; (*Naut*) to sheer off; (*Naut*) to go off course; (*Aut*) to turn off; to swerve; — **de un tema** to digress from a theme; to wander from the point.
desvincularse [1a] *vr*: — **con** to break one's links with, sever one's connections with; to get free of.
desvío *nm* (a) (*act*) deflection, deviation (*de* from); (*Aut etc*) swerve.
   (b) (*Aut etc*) detour, diversion; bypass; (*Rail*) siding.
   (c) (*fig*) coldness, indifference; dislike.
desvirgar [1h] *vt* to deflower.

desvirtuar [1e] **1** *vt* to impair, spoil; to detract from, adversely affect the quality of; to counteract, cancel, nullify the effect of.
2 desvirtuarse *vr* to spoil, go off, decline in quality.
desvivirse [3a] *vr*: — **por algo** to crave something, yearn for something, long for something; to be crazy about something; — **por los amigos** to do one's utmost for one's friends, live only to help one's friends; — **por** + *infin* to be very eager to + *infin*; to do one's best to + *infin*, go out of one's way to + *infin*; **se desvivió por ayudarme** he leant over backwards to help me.
desyerbar [1a] *vt* =**desherbar**.
desyerba *nf*, **desyerbo** *nm* (*SAm*) weeding.
detalladamente *adv* in detail, with full particulars; at great length.
detallado *adj* detailed; circumstantial; *knowledge* detailed, intimate.
dctallar [1a] *vt* (**a**) to detail, list in detail, specify, itemize. (**b**) *story etc* to tell in detail. (**c**) (*Comm*) to sell retail.
detalle *nm* (**a**) detail, particular; item; **al** — in detail; **con todo** —, **con todos los** —**s** in detail, with full details; with full particulars; **en** — in detail; **hasta en sus menores** —**es** down to the last detail; **para más** —**s vea . . .** for further details see . . .; **no pierde** — he misses nothing, he doesn't miss a trick; **me observaba sin perder** — he was watching me very closely, he watched my every move.
(**b**) (*fig*) token (of appreciation), gesture; **¡qué** —! how sweet of you!, what a nice gesture!; **tiene muchos** —**s** he is very considerate; **es el primer** — **que te veo en mucho tiempo** it's the first sign of consideration I've had from you for a long time.
(**c**) (*Comm*) **al** — retail (*adj, adv*); **vender al** — to sell retail; **comercio al** — retail trade.
detallista 1 *adj* retail; **comercio** — retail trade. **2** *nmf* retailer, retail trader.
detección *nf* detection.
detectar [1a] *vt* to detect.
detective *nm* (*angl*) detective; — **de la casa** house detective; — **privado** private detective.
detectivesco *adj* detective (*attr*); **dotes detectivescas** gifts as a detective.
detector *nm* (*Naut, Tech etc*) detector; — **de mentiras** lie detector; — **de minas** mine detector.
detención *nf* (**a**) stopping; stoppage, holdup; delay; — **de juego** (*Sport*) stoppage of play; **una** — **de 15 minutos** a 15-minute delay.
(**b**) (*Law*) arrest, detention; — **ilegal** unlawful detention; — **en masa** mass arrest.
(**c**) =**detenimiento**.
detener [2l] **1** *vt* (**a**) *person, ball, vehicle, charge, epidemic etc* to stop; to hold up, check, delay; — **el progreso de** to hold up the progress of; **no quiero** —**le** I don't want to delay you; **me detuvo en la calle** he stopped me in the street, he accosted me in the street.
(**b**) to keep, hold back, retain; *breath* to hold.
(**c**) (*Law*) to arrest, detain.
2 detenerse *vr* to stop; to pause; to delay, linger; **se detuvo a mirarlo** he stopped to look at it; **¡no te detengas!** don't hang about!, don't delay!; **se detiene mucho en eso** he's taking a long time over that.
detenidamente *adv* carefully, thoroughly; at great length.
detenido 1 *adj* (**a**) (*Law*) arrested, under arrest.
(**b**) *story etc* detailed; *examination* lengthy, thorough; careful; (*pej*) slow, dilatory.
(**c**) (*fig*) timid.
(**d**) (*fig*) mean, niggardly.
2 *nm*, **detenida** *nf* person under arrest.
detenimiento *nm* care, thoroughness; **con** — carefully, thoroughly.
detentar [1a] *vt* (**a**) (*Sport etc*) *record, title* to hold. (**b**) (*pej*) *title* to hold unlawfully; *post etc* to occupy unlawfully.
detentor *nm* (*Sport*) holder; — **de marca** record holder; — **de trofeo** cup holder, champion.
detergente 1 *adj* detergent. **2** *nm* detergent.
deterger [2c] *vt* to clean, clean of grease; *wound* to clean; (*Cook etc*) to clean with detergent.
deteriorado *adj* spoiled, damaged; worn; *goods* shopsoiled, damaged.
deteriorar [1a] **1** *vt* to spoil, damage; to impair; (*Mech etc*) to cause wear on, cause wear and tear to.
2 deteriorarse *vr* to deteriorate, spoil; to get damaged; (*Mech etc*) to wear, get worn.
deterioro *nm* deterioration; impairment; damage; (*Mech etc*) wear, wear and tear; **en caso de** — **de las**

mercancías should the goods be imperfect in any way; **sin** — **de sus derechos** without any loss of rights, without any impairment of his rights.
determinable *adj* determinable; **fácilmente** — easy to determine.
determinación *nf* (**a**) (*act*) determination; decision; **tomar una** — to take a decision. (**b**) (*quality*) determination, resolution.
determinado *adj* (**a**) fixed, set, certain; **un día** — on a certain day; on a given day; **hay** —**s límites** there are fixed limits; **no hay ningún tema** — there is no particular theme, there is no set subject.
(**b**) (*Math*) determinate; (*Ling*) *article* definite.
(**c**) *person* determined, resolute; purposeful.
determinante 1 *adj* determinant. **2** *nm* determinant.
determinar [1a] **1** *vt* (**a**) to determine, fix, settle; *date, price etc* to fix; *damages, tax etc* to determine, assess; *course* to fix, decide, shape; — **el peso de algo** to determine (*or calculate*, work out, fix) the weight of something; **el reglamento determina que . . .** the rule lays it down that . . ., the rule states that . . .
(**b**) to cause, bring about; **aquello determinó la caída del gobierno** that brought about the fall of the government.
(**c**) *person* to decide, make up the mind of; **esto le determinó** this decided him; — **a uno a hacer algo** to determine someone to do something, lead someone to do something.
2 determinarse *vr* to decide, make up one's mind; **¿te has determinado?** have you made up your mind?; — **a hacer algo** to decide to do something, determine to do something; **no se determina a marcharse** he can't make up his mind to go.
determinismo *nm* determinism.
detersión *nf* cleaning (of grease); cleansing.
detestable *adj* detestable; odious, hateful; damnable.
detestablemente *adv* detestably.
detestación *nf* detestation, hatred, loathing.
detestar [1a] *vt* to detest, hate, loathe.
detonación *nf* detonation; report, explosion, bang.
detonador *nm* detonator.
detonante *adj* (*fig*) stunning, shattering.
detonar [1a] *vi* to detonate, explode, go off.
detracción *nf* disparagement; knocking (*sl*); slander; vilification.
detractor 1 *adj* disparaging; slanderous. **2** *nm*, **detractora** *nf* detractor, (*Pol etc*) knocker (*sl*); slanderer.
detraer [2p] *vt* (**a**) to remove, separate, take away. (**b**) to turn aside. (**c**) to disparage, (*Pol etc*) knock (*sl*); to slander; to vilify.
detrás 1 *adv* behind; at the back, in the rear; — **la foto lleva una dedicatoria** the photo has a dedication on the back; **salir de** — to come out from behind; **por** — behind; **atacar a uno por** — to attack someone from behind; **los coches de** — the cars at the back, the cars in the rear.
2 — **de** *prep* behind, back of (*US*); **por** — **de uno** (*fig*) behind someone's back; **salir de** — **de un árbol** to come out from behind a tree.
detrimento *nm* (*to object*) harm, damage; (*to interests etc*) detriment; **en** — **de** to the detriment of; **lo hizo sin** — **de su dignidad** he did it without detriment to (*or* loss of) his dignity.
detrito *nm*, **detritus** *nm* (*Geol etc*) detritus; debris.
deuda *nf* (**a**) (*in general*) indebtedness, debt; **estar en** — to be in debt, owe (*por* for); **estar en** — **con uno** to be in debt to someone, (*fig*) to be indebted to someone.
(**b**) (*una* —) debt; — **a largo plazo** long-term debt; —**s activas** (*Fin*) assets; —**s pasivas** liabilities; — **exterior** foreign debt; — **incobrable** bad debt; — **pública** national debt; **una** — **de gratitud** a debt of gratitude; **contraer** —**s** to contract debts, get into debt; **estar lleno de** —**s** to be heavily in debt, be burdened with debts.
(**c**) (*Eccl*) sin; **perdónanos nuestras** —**s** forgive us our trespasses.
deudo *nm* relative.
deudor 1 *adj* (**a**) *saldo* — debit balance, adverse balance.
(**b**) **le soy muy** — I am greatly indebted to you.
2 *nm*, **deudora** *nf* debtor; — **moroso** slow payer, defaulter.
deuterio *nm* deuterium.
devalar [1a] *vi* (*Naut*) to drift off course.
devaluación *nf* (*Fin*) devaluation.
devaluar [1e] *vt* (*Fin*) to devalue.
devanadera *nf* (*Sew*) reel, spool; winding frame.
devanado *nm* (*Elec*) winding.
devanador *nm* (*Sew*) reel, spool, bobbin.

devanar [1a] **1** *vt* to wind; (*of insect, spider*) to spin.
2 devanarse *vr* **(a)** — los sesos to rack one's brains.
(b) (*Cu, Guat, Mex*) — de dolor to double up with pain; — de risa to double up with laughter.
devanear [1a] *vi* to rave, talk nonsense.
devaneo *nm* **(a)** (*Med*) delirium; (*fig*) ravings, nonsense, absurd talk. **(b)** time-wasting pastime, idle pursuit. **(c)** affair, flirtation.
devastación *nf* devastation.
devastador *adj* devastating (*also fig*).
devastar [1a] *vt* to devastate.
devengar [1h] *vt wages* to earn; to draw, receive; *interest* to earn, bear; **interés devengado** accrued interest, earned interest.
devenir 1 [3s] *vi* to become, evolve into; — en to become, turn into, change into.
2 *nm* evolution, process of development, (slow) change, transformation; **una nación en perpetuo** — a nation in a constant process of development, a nation which is changing all the time.
devoción *nf* **(a)** (*Rel etc*) devotion; devoutness, piety; **con** — devoutly; piously; **la** — a esta imagen the cult of this image, the veneration from of this image.
(b) (*in general*) devotion (*a* to); attachment (*a* to); liking, affection (*a* for); **sienten** — por su general they feel devotion to their general, they are devoted to their general; **estar a la** — de uno to be completely under someone's thumb; **tener gran** — a uno to be wholly devoted to someone; **tener por** — + *infin* to be in the habit of + *ger*.
(c) (*Eccl*) devotion, prayer; religious observance; *see* **santo**.
devocionario *nm* prayer book.
devolución *nf* return; (*Sport*) return; (*Comm*) repayment, refund; (*Fin*) drawback; **pidió la** — de los libros he asked for the books to be given back, he asked for the return of the books.
devolver [2h; *ptp* **devuelto**] **1** *vt* **(a)** to return; to give back, send back; to hand back; *ball, blow* to return; (*Comm*) to repay, refund; (*fam*) to throw up, vomit; *favour etc* to return; — una carta al remitente to return a letter to the sender; — un florero a su sitio to put a vase back in its place; — mal por bien to return ill for good; **el espejo devuelve la imagen the¦mirror** sends back (*or* reflects) the image; — la salud a uno to give someone back his health, restore someone to health.
(b) to restore; **han devuelto el castillo a su antiguo esplendor** they have restored the castle to its former glory.
2 devolverse *vr* (*SAm*) to return, come back, go back.
devorador *adj* devouring; **fuego** — all-consuming fire; **hambre devoradora** ravenous hunger.
devorar [1a] *vt* **(a)** to devour; to eat up, gobble up.
(b) (*fig*) to devour; to consume, use up; **todo lo devoró el fuego** the fire consumed everything; **devora las novelas de amores** she laps up love stories, she devours love stories; **le devoran los celos** he is consumed with jealousy; **los chicos devoran el calzado** the kids are terribly hard on their shoes.
devotamente *adv* devoutly.
devoto 1 *adj* **(a)** (*Rel*) devout; pious; **ser muy** — de un santo to have a special devotion to a saint; **ser** — de la Virgen del puño to be tight-fisted.
(b) (*Rel*) **obra devota** devotional work, work of devotion.
(c) devout; devoted; **su** — amigo your devoted friend; **es** — de ese café he is much attached to that café.
2 *nm,* **devota** *nf* **(a)** (*Rel*) devout person; (*in church*) worshipper; **los** —s the faithful, (*in church*) the worshippers, the congregation.
(b) (*fig*) devotee, votary; admirer; **la estrella y sus** —s the star and her admirers (*or* fans: *fam*); **los** —s del ajedrez devotees of chess.
deyección *nf* (*also* —es) excrement, (*Med*) motion; (*Geol*) debris.
dextrosa *nf* dextrose.
di *etc see* **dar.**
día *nm* **(a)** day; **el** — 2 de mayo (on) the second of May; **ocho** —s week; **quince** —s fortnight; **cuatro** —s (*fig*) a couple of days; **¿qué** — es? what's the date today?; **hace buen** — it's a fine day, it's fine today; **¡buenos** —s! good morning!, good day!; **dar los buenos** —s a uno to wish (*or* bid) someone good day; **dar los** —s a uno to wish someone many happy returns of the day (*birthday or saint's day*); — y noche night and day; **no tener más que el** — y la noche to be utterly poor.
(b) (*expressions with article, adj etc*) el — de hoy today; **el** — de mañana tomorrow; (*fig*) at some future date; **el mejor** — some fine day; **el** — menos pensado when you least expect it; **un** — de éstos one of these days; **un** — sí y otro no, — (de) por medio (*SAm*) every other day; on alternate days; — tras — day after day; **algún** — some day, sometime; **cada** — each day, every day; **¡cualquier** —! (*iro*) not on your life!; **cualquier** — viene (*iro*) some fine day he'll turn up; **otro** — some other day, some other time; **dejémoslo para otro** — let's leave it for the moment; **¡tal** — hará un año! a fat lot I care!; **todos los** —s every day, daily; **no es cosa de todos los** —s it's not an everyday thing; **todo el santo** — the whole livelong day; the whole blessed day; *see* **hoy.**
(c) (*expressions with prep*) a —s at times, once in a while; **a los pocos** —s within a few days, after a few days, a few days later; **al otro** — (on) the following day; **al** — siguiente on the following day; **7 veces al** — 7 times a day, 7 times daily; **estar al** — to be up to date; (*in fashion etc*) to be with it (*fam*); **quien quiera estar al** — en estos estudios, lea . . . if anybody wants to keep up to date in these matters, he should read . . .; **poner al** — diary to enter up, write up; *ledger* to write up; **vivir al** — to live from hand to mouth; **de** — en — from day to day; **ese problema es ya** — s that's an old problem; **pollitos de un** — day-old chicks; **los estilos del** — fashionable styles, up-to-date styles, with-it styles (*fam*); **en** —s de Dios (*or* del mundo, de la vida) never; **en los** —s de Victoria in Victoria's day, in Victoria's times; **en su** — in due time; **¡hasta otro** —! so long!
(d) (*forms with adj etc*) — de asueto day off; — de ayuno fast day; — de la banderita flag day; — de boda wedding day; — feriado holiday, day off; — festivo, — de fiesta holiday; —s de gracia (*Comm*) days of grace, days (allowed) to pay; — hábil working day; — inhábil non-working day; — de inocentes *equivalent to* All Fools' Day (*in Britain and US, 1 April; in Spain, 28 December*); — del Juicio (Final) Judgement Day; **estaremos aquí hasta el** — del Juicio we'll be here till Kingdom come; — laborable working day, weekday; — lectivo (*School*) working day, class day, teaching day; — libre free day, day off; — malo, — nulo off day; — de paga payday; **D** — de la Raza Columbus Day (12 October); **D** — de Reyes Epiphany (6 January, *on which the Magi bring presents to Spanish children*); — señalado special day, red-letter day; — de trabajo, — útil working day, weekday; — de tribunales court day; — de vigilia day of abstinence; *see* **anunciación, año** *etc.*
(e) daytime; daylight; **antes del** — before dawn; **de** — by day, during the day(time); **en pleno** — in broad daylight.
diabetes *nf* diabetes.
diabético 1 *adj* diabetic. **2** *nm,* **diabética** *nf* diabetic.
diabla *nf,* **diablesa** *nf* she-devil; **a la diabla** carelessly, any old how.
diablillo *nm* (*fam*) imp, monkey.
diablo *nm* **(a)** devil; fiend; **ése es el** — that's the devil of it; **ahí será el** — there'll be the devil to pay; **donde el** — perdió el poncho (*Arg, Chi*) in some godforsaken spot.
(b) (*fig*) devil; fiend; **pobre** — poor devil; **algún pobre** — de cartero some poor devil of a postman; *for numerous fig phrases, see* **demonio.**
(c) —s azules (*SAm: angl*) blue devils, delirium tremens.
(d) (*Chi*) heavy oxcart.
diablura *nf* devilry, devilment; prank; —s mischief, monkey tricks.
diabólicamente *adv* diabolically, fiendishly.
diabólico *adj* diabolical, devilish, fiendish.
diaconato *nm* (*post*) deaconry.
diaconía *nf* (*area, house*) deaconry.
diaconisa *nf* deaconess.
diácono *nm* deacon.
diacrítico *adj* diacritic(al); **signo** — diacritic, diacritical mark.
diacrónico *adj* diachronic.
diacho *nm* (*fam: euph*) = **diablo.**
diadema *nf* diadem; crown; (*jewel*) tiara.
diafanidad *nf* transparency; filminess; sheerness; limpidity.
diáfano *adj* diaphanous, transparent; filmy; sheer; *water* limpid, crystal-clear.
diafragma *nm* diaphragm.
diagnosis *nf, pl* **diagnosis** diagnosis.
diagnosticar [1g] *vt* to diagnose.
diagnóstico 1 *adj* diagnostic. **2** *nm* diagnosis.

diagonal 1 *adj* diagonal. **2** *nf* diagonal.
diagonalmente *adv* diagonally.
diagrama *nm* diagram.
dialectal *adj* dialectal, dialect (*attr*); **es palabra —** it's a dialect word.
dialectalismo *nm* (a) dialectal nature, dialectalism; **un texto lleno de —** a text of a strongly dialectal character.
(b) dialectalism, dialect word (or phrase *etc*).
dialéctico *adj* dialectical.
dialecto *nm* dialect.
dialogar [1h] **1** *vt* to set down (or compose *etc*) as a dialogue, write in dialogue form. **2** *vi* to talk, converse; **— con** (*Pol etc*) to engage in a dialogue with.
diálogo *nm* dialogue.
diamante *nm* (a) diamond; **— en bruto** uncut diamond; **— falso** paste; **— de imitación** imitation diamond. (b) **—s** (*Cards*) diamonds.
diamantífero *adj* diamond-bearing.
diamantino *adj* diamond-like, adamantine; glittering.
diamantista *nm* diamond cutter; diamond merchant.
diametral *adj* diametrical.
diametralmente *adv* diametrically; **— opuesto a** diametrically opposed to.
diámetro *nm* diameter; **— de giro** (*Aut*) turning circle; **faros de gran —** wide-angle headlights.
Diana *f* Diana.
diana *nf* (a) (*Mil*) reveille. (b) (of *target*) centre, bull's-eye; **dar en la —**, **hacer —** to get a bull's-eye.
diantre *nm* (*fam*: *euph*)=**diablo**; **¡—!** oh hell!; **los había como un —** (*Chi*) there were a devil of a lot of them.
diapasón *nm* (a) (*Mus*) diapason; range, scale.
(b) (of *violin etc*) finger board.
(c) **— normal** tuning-fork.
(d) (*fig*: of *voice*) tone; **bajar el —** to lower one's voice; **subir el —** to raise one's voice.
diapositiva *nf* (*Phot*) slide, transparency; (of *glass*) lantern slide.
diariamente *adv* daily, every day.
diario 1 *adj* daily; everyday; day-to-day.
2 *adv* (*SAm*) daily, every day.
3 *nm* (a) newspaper, daily; diary; (*Comm*) daybook; **— de a bordo**, **— de navegación** (*Naut*) logbook; **— hablado** (*Radio etc*) news, news bulletin; **— dominical** Sunday paper; **— matinal**, **— de la mañana** morning paper; **— de la noche**, **— vespertino** evening paper; **— de sesiones** (*Parl*) parliamentary report, report of proceedings in Parliament.
(b) (*Fin*) daily expenses.
(c) **a —** daily; **de —**, **para —** for everyday use; **nuestro mantel de —** our tablecloth for everyday (use), our ordinary tablecloth.
diarismo *nm* (*SAm*) journalism.
diarista *nmf* (a) diarist. (b) (*SAm*) newspaper owner (or publisher).
diarrea *nf* diarrhoea.
diarrucho *nm* (*SAm*: *fam*) rag (*fam*).
diatónico *adj* diatonic.
diatriba *nf* diatribe, tirade.
dibujante *nm* (a) (*Art*) sketcher; cartoonist. (b) (*Tech*) draughtsman; designer.
dibujar [1a] **1** *vt* (a) (*Art*) to draw, sketch.
(b) (*Tech*) to design.
(c) (*fig*) to sketch (in words), describe, depict.
2 dibujarse *vr* (a) to be outlined (*contra* against); to loom, show up.
(b) (of *emotion etc*) to show, appear; **el sufrimiento se dibujaba en su cara** suffering showed in his face.
dibujo *nm* (a) (*art in general*) drawing; sketching; art of design.
(b) (**un —**) drawing, sketch; (*Tech*) design; pattern; (*in newspaper etc*) cartoon; caricature; **— animado**, **—s animados** (*Cine*) cartoon (film); **— al carbón** charcoal drawing; **— del natural** drawing from life; **— (hecho) a pulso** freehand drawing; **un papel con — a rayas** a wallpaper with a striped pattern; **sedas con —s de última novedad** silks with the latest patterns (or designs).
(c) (*fig*) description, depiction.
dicción *nf* (a) (*in general*) diction; style. (b) (*una —*) word; expression.
diccionario *nm* dictionary; **— de bolsillo** pocket dictionary; **— bilingüe** bilingual dictionary; **— geográfico** gazetteer.
diccionarista *nmf* lexicographer, dictionary maker.
diciembre *nm* December.
dicotomía *nf* dichotomy.
dictado *nm* (a) dictation; **escribir al —** to take

dictation; **escribir algo al —** to take something down (as it is dictated).
(b) **—s** (*fig*) dictates; **los —s de la conciencia** the dictates of conscience.
(c) honorific title, title of honour.
dictador *nm* dictator.
dictadura *nf* dictatorship.
dictáfono *nm* Dictaphone.
dictamen *nm* opinion, dictum; judgement; report; (*Law*) legal opinion; **— contable** (*Mex*) auditor's report; **— facultativo** (*Med*) medical report; **emitir un —** to issue a report; **tomar — de** to consult with.
dictaminar [1a] **1** *vt* judgement to pass. **2** *vi* to pass judgement, give an opinion (*en* on).
dictar [1a] **1** *vt* (a) *letter etc* to dictate (*a* to).
(b) *judgement* to pass, pronounce; *decree etc* to issue.
(c) to suggest, say, dictate; **lo que dicta el sentido común** what common sense suggests.
(d) (*SAm*) *class* to give; *lecture* to deliver.
2 *vi*: **— a su secretaria** to dictate to one's secretary.
dictatorial *adj*, **dictatorio** *adj* dictatorial.
dicterio *nm* insult, taunt.
dicha *nf* (a) happiness; **para completar su —** to complete her happiness.
(b) (*una —*) happy thing, happy event; **es una — poder . . . it** is a happy thing to be able to . . .
(c) luck, good luck; **por —** by chance, fortunately.
dicharachero 1 *adj* witty, racy, sparkling; slangy; (*pej*) coarse.
2 *nm* witty person, racy talker, sparkling conversationalist; slangy sort; (*pej*) coarse individual.
dicharacho *nm* coarse remark, rude thing (to say).
dicho 1 *ptp* of **decir**.
2 *adj* said; above-mentioned, aforementioned; **—s animales** the said animals; **en — país** in this country, in this same country; **las avispas propiamente dichas** true wasps, wasps in the strict sense; *see also* **decir 2** (f).
3 *nm* saying, proverb; tag; bright remark, witty observation; insult; **— gordo** rude remark; **del — al hecho hay gran trecho** talking is not the same as actually doing; there's many a slip 'twixt cup and lip; **es un —** it's just a saying; **tomarse los —s** to exchange promises of marriage.
dichosamente *adv* luckily, fortunately.
dichoso *adj* (a) happy; **hacer — a uno** to make someone happy; **me siento — de + infin** I feel privileged to + *infin*.
(b) lucky, fortunate.
(c) (*fam*) blessed; **¡aquel — coche!** that blessed car!
didáctico *adj* didactic.
diecinueve *adj* nineteen; (*date*) nineteenth.
diecinueveavo *adj* ninteenth.
dieciochavo *adj*, **dieciocheno** *adj* eighteenth.
dieciochesco *adj* eighteenth-century (*attr*).
dieciocho *adj* eighteen; (*date*) eighteenth.
dieciséis *adj* sixteen; (*date*) sixteenth.
dieciseisavo 1 *adj* sixteenth. **2** *nm* sixteenth (part).
diecisiete *adj* seventeen; (*date*) seventeenth.
diecisieteavo *adj* seventeenth.
Diego *m* James.
diente *nm* (a) (*Anat*) tooth; (*Zool*) tusk; fang; **— canino** canine (tooth); **— cariado** decayed tooth, bad tooth; **— incisivo** incisor; **— de leche** milk tooth; **— molar** molar; **—s postizos** false teeth; **de —s afuera** (*fig*) as mere lip service, without meaning it; **más cerca están mis —s que mis parientes** charity begins at home; **daba — con —** his teeth were chattering; he was trembling like a leaf, he was all of a shiver; **enseñar los —s** (*fig*) to show one's claws, turn nasty; **estar a —** to be ravenous; **hablar entre —s** to mumble, mutter; **hincar el — en** to sink one's teeth into, bite into; **hincar el — en uno** (*fig*) to get one's knife into someone; **nunca pude hincar el — a ese libro** I could never get my teeth into that book; **pelar el —** (*SAm*) to smile affectedly; to flirt; (*CAm*) to laugh a lot; **tener buen —** to be a hearty eater.
(b) (*Mech*) cog; (of *buckle*) tongue; (of *comb*, *saw etc*) tooth.
(c) (*Bot*) **— de ajo** clove of garlic; **— de león** dandelion.
diéresis *nf* diaeresis.
Diesel: motor m — Diesel engine.
dieseléctrico *adj* diesel-electric.
diestra *nf* right hand.
diestramente *adv* (a) skilfully; dexterously; deftly.
(b) shrewdly; (*pej*) cunningly.

diestro 1 *adj* (a) (*not left*) right; (*Her*) dexter; **a — y siniestro** wildly, at random, all over the place; **repartir golpes a — y siniestro** to lash out wildly, throw out punches right and left.
(b) skilful; dexterous; handy, deft.
(c) shrewd, clever; (*pej*) cunning.
2 *nm* (a) (*Taur*) matador, bullfighter.
(b) expert swordsman; expert fencer.
(c) bridle.
dieta *nf* (a) (*Med*) diet; **— láctea** milk diet; **estar a —** to diet, be on a diet. (b) (*Pol*) diet, assembly. (c) **—s** subsistence allowance, expense allowance.
dietética *nf* dietetics.
dietético 1 *adj* dietetic, dietary. **2** *nm* dietician.
dietista *nmf* dietician.
diez¹ 1 *adj* ten; (*date*) tenth; **las —** ten o'clock; **hacer las — de últimas** to scoop the pool, sweep the board; (*fig*) to queer one's own pitch, damage one's own cause.
2 *nm* ten.
diez² *nm euph for* **Dios**, *in many fam phrases*.
diezmar [1a] *vt* to decimate (*also fig*).
diezmillo *nm* (*Mex*) =**solomillo**.
diezmo *nm* tithe.
difamación *nf* slander, defamation (*de* of); libel (*de* on).
difamador 1 *adj* slanderous, defamatory, libellous. **2** *nm*, **difamadora** *nf* slanderer, defamer; scandalmonger.
difamar [1a] *vt* to slander, defame; (*in writing esp*) to libel; (*fig*) to slander, malign.
difamatorio *adj* slanderous, defamatory, libellous.
diferencia *nf* (*all senses*) difference; **— de edades** difference in ages; **a — de** unlike; in contrast to; as distinguished from; **con corta —, con poca —** more or less; **hacer — entre** to make a distinction between; **partir la —** to split the difference; **partir la — con uno** (*fig*) to meet someone halfway, agree to compromise; **— va de A a Z** there's a big difference between A and Z; **no veo — de A a Z** I see no difference between A and Z; I see nothing to choose between A and Z.
diferencial 1 *adj* differential (*also Math*); distinctive; *duty etc* discriminatory. **2** *nm* (*Math*) differential. **3** *nm* (*also sometimes f*) (*Aut*) differential.
diferenciar [1b] **1** *vt* (a) to differentiate between; to make a difference between; **— A de B** to separate A from B, distinguish between A and B.
(b) (*Math*) to differentiate.
(c) to vary (the use of), alter the function of.
2 *vi* to differ (*de* from), be in disagreement (*de* with; *en* about, over).
3 diferenciarse *vr* (a) to differ, be different (*de* from); to be distinctive, be distinguished; **no se diferencian en nada** they do not differ at all; **se diferencian en que . . .** they differ in that . . .
(b) to distinguish oneself.
diferente *adj* (a) different; **— de algo** different from something, unlike something. (b) **—s** several, various; **por —s razones** for various reasons.
diferentemente *adv* differently.
diferir [3i] **1** *vt* (a) to defer, postpone, put off; to hold over; (*Law*) *judgement* to reserve.
(b) *period, turn* to prolong, extend.
2 *vi* to differ, be different (*de* from, *en* in).
difícil *adj* (a) difficult, hard; awkward; **— de vencer** hard to beat, difficult to overcome; **es — que . . .** it is unlikely that . . ., it is doubtful whether . . .; **encuentro — decidir** I find it hard to decide, I find difficulty in deciding; **se hizo un silencio —** there was an awkward (*or* embarrassing) silence.
(b) (*in character*) difficult; **es un hombre —** he's a difficult man.
(c) (*fam*) face odd, ugly.
difícilmente *adv* with difficulty; hardly; **— se podrá hacer** it can hardly be done; **aquí — va a haber para todos** there's hardly going to be enough of this for everybody.
dificultad *nf* difficulty; trouble; objection; **sin — alguna** without the least difficulty; **la — es que . . .** the difficulty is that . . ., the trouble is that . . .; **no hay — para aceptar que . . .** there is no difficulty about accepting that . . .; **ha tenido —es con la policía** he's been in trouble with the police; **tuvieron algunas —es para llegar a casa** they had some trouble getting home; **poner —es** to raise objections; to create obstacles; **me pusieron —es para darme el pasaporte** they created obstacles to giving me a passport, they made it awkward for me to get a passport.
dificultar [1a] *vt* (a) *way etc* to obstruct, impede, hinder; to put obstacles in the way of; to interfere

with, hold up; to render difficult; **las restricciones dificultan el comercio** the restrictions hinder trade, the restrictions make trade difficult.
(b) **— que +** *subj* to make it unlikely that . . .; (*person*) to think it unlikely that . . .
dificultoso *adj* (a) difficult, hard; awkward, troublesome. (b) (*fam*) face odd, ugly. (c) *person* difficult, awkward, full of silly objections.
difracción *nf* diffraction.
difractar [1a] *vt* to diffract.
difteria *nf* diphtheria.
difundir [3a] **1** *vt* to diffuse; to spread, disseminate; to divulge, circulate; *gas etc* to give off, give out, emit; **— una noticia** to spread a piece of news, divulge a piece of news; **— la alegría** to spread happiness, radiate happiness.
2 difundirse *vr* to spread (out); to become diffused.
difunto 1 *adj* dead, deceased; **el — ministro** the late minister.
2 *nm*, **difunta** *nf* (a) deceased person; **la familia del —** the family of the deceased; **Día de D—s** All Souls' Day.
(b) corpse.
difusión *nf* (a) (*act*) diffusion; spread(ing), dissemination; divulging, circulation. (b) (*quality*) diffuseness.
difuso *adj* (a) *light* diffused; *knowledge etc* widespread, widely extended. (b) *style etc* diffuse, wordy, discursive.
digerible *adj* digestible.
digerir [3i] *vt* (a) *food* to digest; to swallow.
(b) (*Chem*) to digest, absorb, dissolve.
(c) (*fig*) *opinions etc* to digest, absorb, assimilate; to ponder, think over; (*in negative phrases*) to swallow, stomach; **no puedo — a ese tío** I can't stand that chap.
digestible *adj* digestible.
digestión *nf* digestion.
digestivo *adj* digestive.
digesto *m* (*Law etc*) digest.
digitación *nf* (*Mus*) fingering.
digital 1 *adj* digital; finger (*attr*); **impresión —** fingerprint. **2** *nf* (*Bot*) foxglove; (*drug*) digitalis.
dígito *nm* (*Math etc*) digit.
dignación *nf* condescension.
dignamente *adv* (a) worthily; fittingly, properly, appropriately. (b) honourably. (c) with dignity, in a dignified way. (d) decently.
dignarse [1a] *vr*: **— +** *infin* (a) to deign to + *infin*, condescend to + *infin*.
(b) (*formulae*) please . . ., *eg* **dígnese venir a esta oficina** please (be so good as to) come to this office.
dignatario *nm* dignitary.
dignidad *nf* (a) (*quality*) dignity; honour; self-respect; **herir la — de uno** to offend someone's self-respect.
(b) post, office; rank; **tiene — de ministro** he has the rank of a minister.
(c) (*person*) dignitary, worthy.
dignificar [1g] *vt* to dignify.
digno *adj* (a) worthy; fitting; proper, appropriate; **— de worthy of, deserving; — de elogio** praiseworthy; **— de toda alabanza** thoroughly praiseworthy, highly commendable; **— de mención** worth a mention, worth mentioning; **un — castigo** a fitting punishment; **es — de nuestra admiración** it deserves our admiration; **es — de verse** it is worth seeing.
(b) *person etc* worthy, upright, honourable.
(c) (*in manner, appearance*) dignified.
(d) decent; **viviendas dignas para los obreros** decent homes for the workers.
digresión *nf* digression.
dije¹ *etc see* **decir**.
dije² *nm* (a) medallion, locket; amulet, charm; (*pej*) trinket. (b) (*fig*) gem, treasure, person of sterling qualities.
dilación *nf* delay; **sin —** without delay, forthwith; **esto no admite —** this must suffer no delay, this is most urgent.
dilapidación *nf* squandering, waste.
dilapidar [1a] *vt* to squander, waste.
dilatación *nf* (a) dilation; expansion (*also Phys*), enlargement, widening, stretching; protraction, prolongation. (b) (*fig*) calm, calm dignity.
dilatado *adj* dilated; vast, extensive, spacious; numerous; long drawn-out; long-winded, discursive.
dilatar [1a] **1** *vt* (a) (*in space*) to dilate; to expand (*also Phys*), enlarge, widen; to stretch, extend; *fame etc* to spread.
(b) (*in time*) to protract, prolong, stretch out.
(c) to delay, put off.

2 dilatarse vr (a) to dilate; to expand (also Phys); to stretch, extend; to spread; **la llanura se dilata hasta el horizonte** the plain spreads (or extends, rolls) right to the horizon; **el valle se dilata en aquella parte** the valley widens (or spreads out) at that point.
(b) to be long-winded, be discursive; — **en**, — **sobre** to expatiate on; to linger over, take one's time over.
(c) (SAm) to delay, be slow; (train etc) to be late; — **en** + infin to take a long time to + infin, be slow to + infin.

dilativo adj dilatory.

dilatorias nfpl procrastination; delaying tactics; **andar en** — **con uno, traer a uno en** — to use delaying tactics with someone, hedge with someone; **no me venga Vd con** — don't hedge with me.

dilección nf affection.

dilema nm dilemma; **estar en un** — to be in a dilemma.

diletante nmf dilettante.

diligencia nf (a) (quality) diligence, care; assiduity; speed, dispatch.
(b) piece of business; errand, job, mission; **hacer** —**s** to do business; **hacer una** — to run an errand, go on an errand; (fam: tabu) to do one's business (fam); **hacer las** —**s de costumbre** to take the usual steps; **practicar sus** —**s** to make every possible effort, do one's utmost (para + infin to + infin).
(c) (Law) —**s** formalities; inquiries; steps (of an investigation etc); —**s judiciales** judicial proceedings; —**s previas** inquest.
(d) (Hist) stagecoach.

diligenciar [1b] vt matter to see about, deal with; to further, get moving.

diligente adj diligent; industrious, assiduous; quick, speedy, prompt; **un alumno poco** — a slack pupil, a lazy pupil.

diligentemente adv diligently; industriously; assiduously; speedily.

dilucidar [1a] vt to elucidate, explain, clarify; case, mystery etc to solve, clear up.

dilución nf dilution.

diluido adj dilute; diluted, weak; watered down.

diluir [3g] vt to dilute; to water down, weaken; (fig) to water down.

diluviar [1b] vi to pour with rain, rain in torrents.

diluvio nm deluge, flood (also fig); **el D—** the Flood; **un** — **de cartas** a deluge of letters; **¡fue el** —**!** it was chaos!; **¡esto es el** —**!** what a mess!

dimanar [1a] vi: — **de** to arise from, spring from, stem from.

dimensión nf (a) dimension (also fig); **de grandes** —**es** of great size, of large dimensions.
(b) (fig: of personal quality) stature, standing; **un matemático de** — **universal** a mathematician of world stature.

dimes nmpl: — **y diretes** bickering, squabbling; gossip; petty intrigue; **andar en** — **y diretes con uno** to bicker (or squabble) with someone.

diminuendo nm (Mus) diminuendo.

diminutivo 1 adj diminutive. **2** nm diminutive.

diminuto adj (a) tiny, minute, exceedingly small; miniature. (b) defective, imperfect.

dimisión nf resignation; **presentar la** — to send in (or tender, submit) one's resignation.

dimitente 1 adj resigning, outgoing, retiring; **el presidente** — the outgoing chairman, the retiring chairman. **2** nmf person resigning.

dimitir [3a] **1** vt to resign; to give up, relinquish; — **la jefatura del partido** to resign (from) the party leadership. **2** vi to resign (de from).

din nm (sl) dough (sl); **el** — **y el don** money and rank, dough and dukedom.

Dinamarca f Denmark.

dinamarqués = danés.

dinámica nf (la —) dynamics; (una —) dynamic.

dinámico adj dynamic.

dinamita nf dynamite.

dinamitar [1a] vt to dynamite.

dinamitazo nm dynamite explosion; dynamiting.

dínamo nf, **dinamo** nf (often m in SAm) dynamo.

dinastía nf dynasty.

dinástico adj dynastic.

dinerada nf, **dineral** nm fortune, mint of money; **habrá costado un** — it must have cost a fortune.

dinerario adj money (attr), financial.

dinerillos nmpl (fam): **tiene sus** — she's got a bit of money (put by).

dinero nm money; (of country, period etc) currency, coinage, money; **persona de** — moneyed person, wealthy person; **es hombre de** — he is a man of means; **¿cuánto es en** — **americano?** how much is

that in American money?; — **contante** cash; — **contante y sonante** cash, ready money; — **de curso legal** legal tender; — **en caja** cash in hand; — **por callar** hush money; **los** —**s del sacristán cantando se vienen y cantando se van** easy come easy go; **el** — **malo echa fuera al bueno** bad money drives out good; **el** — **lo puede todo, el** — **puede mucho** money can do anything, money talks; **andar mal de** — to be badly off, be in financial difficulties; **el negocio no da** — the business does not pay, the business is not profitable, the business is not a paying proposition; **ganar** — **a espuertas** (or **a porrillo**) to make money hand over fist.

dinosaurio nm dinosaur.

dintel nm lintel; (SAm) threshold.

diñar [1a] vt (fam) to give; —**la** to kick the bucket (sl); —**sela a uno** to swindle someone.

diocesano adj diocesan.

diócesi(s) nf, pl **diócesis** diocese.

Dionisio m Denis; (classical) Dionysius.

Dios m (a) God; — **delante** with God's help; — **mediante** God willing, D.V.; **a** — **gracias** thank heaven; **a la buena de** — at random; thoughtlessly, without preparation; trusting to luck; any old how; **a la de** — **(es Cristo)** rashly; **una de** — **es Cristo** an almighty row; **armar la de** — **es Cristo** to raise hell, cause a tremendous fuss; **esto clama a** — this cries out to heaven (to be reformed etc); — **los cría y ellos se juntan** birds of a feather flock together; **dar a** — **lo que es de** — **y al César lo que es del César** render unto Caesar that which is Caesar's and unto God that which is God's; **lo hace como** — **le da a entender** he does it as best he can, he does it according to his lights; **como** — **manda** as is proper; properly, well; **donde** — **pasó de largo a** **godforsaken spot; cuando** — **quiera** all in God's good time; **a** — **rogando y con el mazo dando** God helps those who help themselves; — **sabe** God knows; **sólo** — **sabe** God alone knows; **sabe** — **que no quería ofender** God knows I did not intend to cause offence; **vaya con** — good-bye, (formally) may God be with you, (iro) and good riddance, and the best of luck; **le vino** — **a ver** he struck lucky, he had a stroke of luck.
(b) (exclamatory) **¡**— **mío!** good gracious!, good heavens!; well!; **¡por** —**!** for God's sake!; **¡**— **le ampare!**, **¡**— **le asista!**, — **te la depare buena!** (iro) I hope it keeps fine for you!, and the best of luck!; **¡**— **le ayude!** (on sneezing) bless you!; **¡**— **te bendiga!** God bless you!; **¡**— **me libre!** Heaven forbid!; **¡líbreme** — **de ...!** Heaven forbid that I ...!; **¡plegue a** —**!** please God!; **¡no lo quiera** —**!** God forbid!; **¡válgame** —**!** bless my soul!; **¡vive** —**!** good God!

dios nm god; idol; **los** —**es paganos** the pagan gods.

diosa nf goddess.

diploma nm diploma.

diplomacia nf diplomacy.

diplomado 1 adj qualified, trained, having a diploma. **2** nm, **diplomada** nf qualified person, holder of a diploma.

diplomarse [1a] vr (SAm) to graduate (from college etc).

diplomática nf (a) (Hist, Law) diplomatic. (b) (Pol) diplomatic corps; diplomatic career, (career in the) foreign service.

diplomáticamente adv diplomatically.

diplomático 1 adj diplomatic. **2** nm diplomat; (fig) diplomatist.

dipsomanía nf dipsomania.

dipsomaníaco nm, **dipsomaníaca** nf, **dipsómano** nm, **dipsómana** nf dipsomaniac.

díptero nm fly.

diptongar [1h] vti to diphthongize.

diptongo nm diphthong.

diputación nf (a) deputation, delegation; committee; — **permanente** (Parl) standing committee.
(b) — **provincial** equivalent to county council; county council offices.

diputado nmf delegate, representative; (Parl) deputy, member of parliament, representative (US); — **a Cortes** (Spain) parliamentary deputy, member of the Spanish Cortes; **el** — **por Guadalajara** the member for Guadalajara; — **provincial** equivalent to member of a county council.

diputar [1a] vt to delegate, depute; to empower.

dique nm (a) dike, sea wall; jetty, mole; breakwater; dam; dock; — **de contención** dam; — **flotante** floating dock; — **seco** dry dock; **entrar en** —, **hacer** — to dock.
(b) (fig) check; barrier; **es un** — **contra la expansión** it is a barrier to expansion; **poner un** — **a** to check, restrain.

diré *etc see* **decir.**

dirección *nf* (a) (*general sense*) direction; way; (*fig*) course, trend; — **del viento** wind direction; con — **norte** in a northerly direction; **con — a, en — a, en la — de** in the direction of; towards; **"— prohibida"** (*Aut*) "no entry", "no thoroughfare"; **calle de — obligatoria, calle de — única** one-way street; **calle de 2 —es** street with two-way traffic; con**mutador de 2 —es** two-way switch; **cambiar de —** to change direction; **¿podría Vd indicarme la — de ...?** could you please direct me to ...?; **salir con — a** to leave for, depart for; to go off in the direction of; **salir con — desconocida** to leave for an unknown destination.

(b) (*act*) direction; guidance; control; (*Comm etc*) management; (*Pol*) leadership; **bajo la — de** under the direction of; **asumir la —, tomar la —** to take (over) control.

(c) (*persons*) management; board of directors; (*Pol*) leadership; **habrá cambios en la — del partido** there will be changes in the party leadership, there will be changes among the party's top men.

(d) (*post*) directorship; post of manager; (*of newspaper*) editorship; (*Mus*) conductorship.

(e) (*Aut etc*) steering; — **asistida** power steering; **de —** steering (*attr*).

(f) (*head*) office, administrative office; **D— General de Turismo** State Tourist Office; **D— General de Seguridad** State Security Office (*or* Service).

(g) (*Post*) address; — **del remitente** return address; **ponga claramente su —** write your address clearly.

direccional *adj* directional.
directa *nf* (*Aut*) top gear.
directamente *adv* (*all senses*) directly.
directiva *nf* board of directors; governing body.
directivo 1 *adj board etc* managing, governing; *function* managerial, administrative; *class* managerial, executive.

2 *nm* (*Comm etc*) manager, executive; **un congreso de los —s de la industria** a conference of executives from the industry.

directo 1 *adj* (a) direct; straight; immediate; *action, manner, translation etc* direct.

(b) (*Rail etc*) through, non-stop.

(c) (*TV*) *programme, shot* live; **transmitir en —** to broadcast live.

2 *nm* (*Boxing*) straight punch; (*Tennis*) forehand shot (*or drive etc*).

director 1 *adj* leading; controlling; guiding; = **directivo.**

2 *nm* director; (*Comm etc*) director; manager, executive; (*Mus*) conductor; (*School*) headmaster; principal; (*of training college etc*) principal; (*Univ: of college*) master, (*of residence*) warden; (*of prison*) governor; (*of newspaper*) editor; — **de escena** stage manager; — **espiritual** father confessor; — **de funeraria** undertaker, funeral director, mortician (*US*); — **gerente** managing director; — **de hotel** hotel manager; — **de orquesta** conductor; — **de personal** personnel manager.

directora *nf* manageress (*see also* **director**); (*School*) headmistress; principal; (*Univ: of college*) mistress, (*of residence*) warden.

directorial *adj* (*Comm etc*) managing, executive; *clase* — managers, management, executive class.

directorio *nm* (a) directive, instructions.

(b) (*persons*) directors, board of directors, directorate.

(c) (*book*) directory; — **de teléfonos** (*Mex*) telephone directory.

dirigencia *nf* (*Pol etc*) leadership.

dirigente 1 *adj* leading. 2 *nm* (*Pol etc*) leader; — **de la oposición** leader of the opposition; **los —s del partido** the party leaders.

dirigible 1 *adj* (*Aer*) dirigible; (*Naut*) navigable. 2 *nm* dirigible.

dirigido *adj missile* guided.

dirigir [3c] **1** *vt* (a) (*general sense*) to direct (*a, hacia* at, to, towards); *accusation* to level (*a* at), make (*a* against); *letter, protest, question, remark* to address (*a* to); *order* to place (*a* with); *book* to dedicate (*a* to); *look* to direct (*a* towards), turn (*a* on); *hose* to play, turn (*a* on); *gun, telescope etc* to aim, point (*a* at).

(b) (*Comm etc*) *business* to manage; to run, operate; *expedition, party, revolt* to lead, head; *newspaper, series etc* to edit; *thesis, work etc* to direct, supervise.

(c) *person* to direct; to guide, advise (*en* about,

in); *course of action* to direct, shape; *efforts* to direct (*a* towards), concentrate (*a* on).

(d) (*Aut, Naut*) to steer; (*Aut*) to drive.

(e) (*Mus*) to conduct.

(f) (*Cine, Theat*) to produce, direct.

2 **dirigirse** *vr*: — **a** (a) to go to, make one's way to; to head for; to turn towards; (*Naut etc*) to steer for, head for; — **hacia** to head for.

(b) (*fig*) to speak to, address; to approach; — **a uno solicitando algo** to apply to someone for something; **se dirigió a mí en la calle** he spoke to me in the street; he accosted me in the street; "**diríjase a ...**" (*adverts*) "apply to ...", "write to ..."

dirigismo *nm* management, control; — **estatal** state control.

dirimente *adj argument etc* decisive; *vote* casting; *opinion, decision* (*in competition etc*) final.

dirimir [3a] *vt* (a) *contract, marriage etc* to dissolve, annul, declare void. (b) *dispute* to settle.

discernidor *adj* discerning, discriminating.

discernimiento *nm* discernment, discrimination; judgement; **edad de —** years of discretion.

discernir [3i] **1** *vt* (a) to discern, distinguish; — **A de B** to distinguish A from B.

(b) (*Law*) *guardian* to appoint.

(c) (*esp SAm: gall*) *prize etc* to award (*a* to); confer (*a* on).

2 *vi*: — **entre** to distinguish between, discriminate between.

disciplina *nf* (a) (*in most senses*) discipline. (b) *whip*; **—s** lashes.

disciplinar [1a] *vt* (a) to discipline. (b) to school, train; (*Mil*) to drill, train. (c) to whip, scourge.

disciplinario *adj* disciplinary.

discipulado *nm* (a) (*Rel*) discipleship. (b) group of pupils, body of students.

discípulo *nm*, **discípula** *nf* (a) (*Eccl, Philos etc*) disciple; follower. (b) (*School*) pupil, student.

disco *nm* (a) disk, disc; (*Sport*) discus; (*Rail*) signal; (*Tel*) dial; (*Mus etc*) gramophone record, phonograph record (*US*); — **de duración extendida** extended-play record (*EP*); — **de larga duración, — microsurco** long-playing record (*LP*); — **giratorio** (gramophone) turntable; — **de marcar** (*Tel*) dial; — **volante** flying saucer.

(b) (*fam*) boring affair; boring speech; tedious tale; **es un —** it's a bore, it's so boring; **nos soltó el — una vez más** he told us the whole dreary tale again.

discóbolo *nm* discus thrower.

discográfico *adj* record (*attr*); **el momento — actual** the present state of the record industry.

díscolo *adj* uncontrollable, unruly; rebellious; *child* mischievous.

disconforme *adj* differing; **estar —** to be in disagreement (*con* with), not agree.

disconformidad *nf* disagreement.

discontinuidad *nf* lack of continuity.

discontinuo *adj* discontinuous.

discordancia *nf* discord (*also fig*).

discordante *adj* discordant (*also fig*).

discordar [1m] *vi* (a) (*Mus*) to be out of tune. (b) (*persons etc*) to disagree (*de* with), differ (*de* from); (*of opinions, colours etc*) to clash.

discorde *adj* (a) (*Mus*) *sound* discordant, unharmonious; *instrument* out of tune.

(b) (*fig*) discordant, differing; clashing; **estar —s** (*persons*) to disagree, be in disagreement (*de* with).

discordia *nf* discord, disagreement.

discoteca *nf* record library, record collection; discothèque.

discreción *nf* (a) discretion, tact, good sense; discrimination; prudence; wisdom, sagacity, shrewdness.

(b) secrecy.

(c) wit; witticism.

(d) **a —** at one's discretion; **añadir azúcar a —** (*Cook*) add sugar to taste; **comer a —** to eat as much as one likes; **con vino a —** with as much wine as one wants; **¡a —!** (*Mil*) stand easy!; **rendirse a —** (*Mil*) to surrender unconditionally.

discrecional *adj* discretionary; optional, not prescribed, within one's judgement; **parada —** request stop.

discrepancia *nf* discrepancy; divergence; (*between persons etc*) disagreement.

discrepante *adj* divergent; dissenting; **hubo varias voces —s** there were some dissenting voices, some were not in agreement.

discrepar [1a] *vi* to differ (*de* from), disagree (*de* with); **discrepamos en varios puntos** we disagree on a number of points; **discrepo de esa opinión** I disagree with that view.

discretamente *adv* (a) discreetly, tactfully, sensibly; with discrimination; prudently, shrewdly. (b) soberly; quietly; unobtrusively.

discretear [1a] *vi* to try to be clever, be frightfully witty.

discreto *adj* (a) (*of person, character etc*) discreet, tactful, sensible; discriminating; prudent, wise, sagacious, shrewd.
(b) *dress etc* sober, sensible; *colour* quiet, sober; *position etc* unobtrusive; *hint, reminder* discreet, gentle, tactful.
(c) fair, middling, reasonable; **de inteligencia discreta** of reasonable intelligence, reasonably intelligent; **¡le daremos un plazo —** we'll allow him a reasonable time.
(d) (*Phys etc*) discreet.

discriminación *nf* discrimination (*contra* against); **— racial** racial discrimination.

discriminar [1a] *vi* to discriminate (*contra* against).

discriminatorio *adj* discriminatory.

disculpa *nf* excuse; plea; apology.

disculpable *adj* excusable, pardonable.

disculpar [1a] **1** *vt* to excuse, pardon, forgive; to exonerate (*de culpa* from blame); **disculpa el que venga tarde** forgive me for coming late; **le disculpan sus pocos años** his youth is an excuse, his youth provides an excuse; **te ruego —me con el anfitrión** please make my apologies to the host.
2 disculparse *vr* to excuse oneself (*de* from); to apologize (*por* + *infin* for + *ger*); **— con uno por haber hecho algo** to apologize to someone for having done something.

discurrir [3a] **1** *vt* to invent, think up, contrive; **esos chicos no discurren nada bueno** these lads must be cooking up something nasty, these lads are up to no good.
2 *vi* (a) to roam, wander (*por* about, along).
(b) (*river*) to flow.
(c) (*time*) to pass, flow by; (*life, period, meeting*) to go, pass, be spent; **la sesión discurrió sin novedad** the meeting went off quietly; **el verano discurrió sin grandes calores** the summer passed without great heat.
(d) to think, reason, meditate (*en* about, on); to speak, discourse (*sobre* about, on).
(e) **— poco** to do little, produce little, be inactive; **discurre menos que un mosquito** he doesn't do a stroke.

discursear [1a] *vi* to speechify.

discurso *nm* (a) speech, address, discourse; **— de clausura** closing speech; **— político** political speech; **pronunciar un —, dictar un —** (*SAm*) to make (*or* deliver) a speech.
(b) (*written*) treatise.
(c) (*in general*) speech, faculty of speech.
(d) (*mental*) reasoning power, mental powers.
(e) (*of time*) period; passing, passage; **en el — del tiempo** with the passage of time; **en el — de 4 generaciones** in the space of 4 generations.

discusión *nf* discussion; argument; **eso no admite —** there can be no argument about that; **estar en —** to be under discussion.

discutible *adj* debatable, arguable; **es — si . . .** it is debatable whether . . .; **de mérito algo —** of somewhat dubious worth.

discutido *adj* much-discussed; controversial.

discutidor *adj* argumentative, disputatious.

discutir [3a] **1** *vt* to discuss, debate, talk over; to argue about; to contradict, argue against, object to; **— a uno lo que uno está diciendo** to contradict what someone is saying.
2 *vi* to discuss, talk; to argue (*de, sobre* about, over); **— de política** to argue about politics, talk politics; **¡no discutas!** don't argue!

disecar [1g] *vt* (a) (*Med and fig*) to dissect. (b) (*for museum etc*) *animal* to stuff; *plant* to preserve, mount.

disección *nf* (a) dissection. (b) stuffing; preservation, mounting.

diseminación *nf* dissemination, spread(ing), scattering; **— nuclear** spread of nuclear weapons.

diseminar [1a] *vt* to disseminate, spread, scatter.

disensión *nf* dissension.

disentería *nf* dysentery.

disentimiento *nm* dissent, disagreement.

discutir [3l] *vi* to dissent (*de* from), disagree (*de* with).

diseñador *nm* (*Tech etc*) designer.

diseñar [1a] *vt* (*Tech etc*) to design; (*Art*) to draw, sketch; to outline.

diseño *nm* (*Tech etc*) design; (*Art*) drawing, sketch; (*Sew etc*) pattern, design; (*in words*) sketch, outline.

disertación *nf* dissertation, disquisition, discourse.

disertar [1a] *vi* to speak, discourse; **— acerca de, — sobre** to discourse upon, expound on, speak about; **— largamente** to speak at length.

disfavor *nm* disfavour.

disforme *adj* ill-proportioned, badly-proportioned; monstrous, huge; ugly.

disfraz *nm* (a) disguise; mask; fancy dress; (*Mil*) camouflage; (*fig*) pretext, blind (*de* for); **baile de disfraces** fancy dress ball; **bajo el — de** in the guise of; under the cloak of.
(b) (*fam*) **ser un —** to be out of place; to look all wrong.

disfrazado *adj*: **— de** disguised as; in the guise of; **ir — de duque** to be made up like a duke; to masquerade as a duke.

disfrazar [1f] **1** *vt* to disguise; to cover up, mask, conceal, cloak; (*Mil*) to camouflage; **— a uno de lavandera** to disguise someone as a washerwoman, make someone up as a washerwoman.
2 disfrazarse *vr*: **— de** to disguise oneself as, make oneself up as.

disfrutar [1a] **1** *vt* to enjoy; to make use of, have the benefit of.
2 *vi* (a) to enjoy oneself, have a good time; **¡cómo disfruto!** I'm enjoying this!, this is the life!; **— con algo** to enjoy something, benefit from something; **siempre disfruto con los libros así** I always enjoy books of that sort.
(b) **— de** to enjoy; to have, possess; **— de buena salud** to enjoy good health; **disfruta de las rentas de su finca** he enjoys (*or* has) the income from his estate.

disfrute *nm* enjoyment; use; possession.

disfuerzo *nm* (*Per*) (a) impudence, effrontery. (b) prudishness. (c) **—s** threats, bravado.

disgregación *nf* disintegration; break(ing)-up; separation; severance.

disgregar [1h] **1** *vt* to disintegrate; to break up; to separate (*de* from); to sever (*de* from). **2 disgregarse** *vr* to disintegrate; to break up (*en* into).

disgustar [1a] **1** *vt* to annoy, upset, displease; to offend; **es un olor que me disgusta** it's a smell which upsets me; **me disgusta tener que repetirlo** it annoys me to have to repeat it, I don't like having to repeat it; **comprendí que le disgustaba mi presencia** I realized that my presence annoyed him; **estaba muy disgustado con el asunto** he was very upset about the affair.
2 disgustarse *vr* (a) to be annoyed, get upset (*con, de* about); to be displeased, be offended, feel hurt (*con, de* about); **— de algo** to get bored with something, get fed up with something.
(b) (*2 persons*) to fall out; **— con uno** to fall out with someone.

disgusto *nm* (a) (*feeling*) annoyance, displeasure; vexation; grief, chagrin, sorrow; repugnance; boredom; **a —** unwillingly, against one's will.
(b) (*act*) trouble, bother, difficulty; unpleasant experience; misfortune; blow, shock; **reírse de los —s del prójimo** to laugh at a fellow man's troubles (*or* misfortunes); **me causó un gran —** it was a great blow to me; it upset me very much; **han de sobrevenir —s** there's trouble ahead; **matar a uno a —s** to wear someone out with burdens, heap troubles on someone.
(c) quarrel, upset; **tener un — con uno** to have a quarrel with someone, fall out with someone.

disidencia *nf* dissidence, disagreement; (*Eccl*) dissent.

disidente 1 *adj* dissident; dissenting. **2** *nmf* dissident person (*or* element *etc*); (*Eccl*) dissenter, nonconformist.

disidir [3a] *vi* to dissent.

disílabo 1 *adj* disyllabic. **2** *nm* disyllable.

disimulación *nf* dissimulation; furtiveness; cunning.

disimuladamente *adv* furtively; cunningly, slyly; covertly.

disimulado *adj* furtive; underhand; cunning, sly; covert; **hacerse el —** to dissemble; to pretend not to notice (*etc*); **hacer la disimulada** to feign ignorance.

disimular [1a] **1** *vt* (a) to hide; (*fig*) to hide, cloak, disguise; *emotion, intention etc* to conceal.
(b) to excuse; to condone, overlook; to tolerate; *offence etc* to pass off; *person etc* to be lenient to, behave tolerantly towards; **le ruego — la indiscreción** please pardon the liberty; **disimule mi atrevimiento** forgive me if I have been too bold.
2 *vi* to dissemble, pretend.

disimulo *nm* (a) dissimulation; furtiveness; craftiness; **con —** cunningly, craftily. (b) indulgence, tolerance.

disipación *nf* (*all senses*) dissipation.

disipado *adj* (a) dissipated; rakish, raffish. (b) extravagant, spendthrift.

disipador nm spendthrift.
disipar [1a] **1** vt (a) mist etc to drive away, cause to disappear, dispel.
   (b) doubt etc to dispel, remove; hope to destroy.
   (c) money to squander, fritter away (en on).
  2 disiparse vr (a) (smoke etc) to vanish; to evaporate.
   (b) (doubt etc) to be dispelled, vanish.
dislate nm absurdity, silly thing; —s nonsense.
dislocación nf dislocation; (Med) dislocation, sprain; (Geol) slip, fault.
dislocar [1g] vt to dislocate; to sprain.
disloque nm (fam): **es el** — it's the limit, it's the last straw; **fue el** — (of humour etc) it was the great moment, it was the crowning touch.
disminución nf diminution, decrease (de of), fall (de in); **proceso de** — **de réditos** law of diminishing returns; **continuar sin** — to continue unchecked, continue unabated; **ir en** — to diminish, be on the decrease.
disminuir [3g] vti to diminish, decrease, lessen.
disociación nf dissociation.
disociar [1b] **1** vt to dissociate, separate (de from).
  2 disociarse vr to dissociate oneself (de from).
disoluble adj dissoluble, dissolvable.
disolución nf (a) (act) dissolution (also Parl). (b) (Chem) solution. (c) (Comm) liquidation. (d) (moral) dissoluteness, dissipation.
disoluto adj dissolute, dissipated.
disolvente nm solvent.
disolver [2h; ptp **disuelto**] **1** vt (a) to dissolve; to melt (down).
   (b) contract, marriage to dissolve; (Parl) to dissolve; meeting, riot etc to break up.
  2 disolverse vr (a) to dissolve, melt.
   (b) (Comm) to be dissolved, go into liquidation; (Parl) to dissolve.
disonancia nf (a) (Mus) dissonance. (b) (fig) discord, disharmony; **hacer** — **con** to be out of harmony with.
disonante adj (a) (Mus) dissonant, discordant. (b) (fig) discordant.
disonar [1m] vi (a) (Mus) to be discordant, be out of harmony, be out of tune; to sound wrong.
   (b) (fig) to lack harmony; to disagree; — **con** to be out of keeping with, clash with.
dísono adj discordant.
dispar adj unlike, different, disparate.
disparada nf (SAm) sudden flight, stampede, wild rush; **ir a la** — to go at full speed; **irse a la** — to be off like a shot; **de una** — (Arg) in a trice, instantly; **tomar la** — (Arg) to beat it (fam).
disparadero nm trigger, trigger mechanism; **poner a uno en el** — to drive someone to distraction, make someone resort to violence.
disparado adj: **entrar** — to shoot in; **salir** — to shoot out, be off like a shot; **ir** — to go like mad, go hell for leather.
disparador 1 adj (Mex) lavish. **2** nm (Mil etc) trigger; (Phot, Tech) release; (of watch) escapement; — **atómico** aerosol, spray; — **de bombas** bomb release.
disparar [1a] **1** vt gun, rocket etc to shoot, fire; stone to throw, hurl, let fly (contra at); (Sport) ball to shoot (a at, en into).
  2 vi (a) to shoot, fire; **¡disparad!** fire!; — **a una distancia de 5 metros** to fire at a range of 5 metres.
   (b) =**disparatar**.
   (c) (Mex) to spend lavishly.
  3 dispararse vr (a) (gun etc) to go off; (catch etc) to be released.
   (b) (person) to rush off, dash away; see **disparado**.
   (c) (horse etc) to bolt.
   (d) (emotionally) to lose control, blow one's top (fam).
disparatadamente adv absurdly, nonsensically.
disparatado adj absurd, crazy, nonsensical.
disparatar [1a] vi to talk nonsense; to do something silly, blunder.
disparate nm (a) foolish remark, silly idea; absurd thing (to do); blunder, crass mistake; —s nonsense; **¡qué** —! what rubbish!, how absurd!; **hiciste un** — **protestando** it was silly of you to complain.
   (b) **reírse un** — to laugh a lot; **costar un** — to cost a fortune.
disparidad nf disparity.
disparo nm (a) shot; report; (of rocket) firing; (Sport) shot; —s shots, shooting, exchange of shots; — **inicial** (of rocket) blast-off.
   (b) (Mech) release, trip.
   (c) (fig) =**disparate**.
dispendio nm waste; extravagance.
dispendioso adj expensive.

dispensa nf exemption, excusal (de from); (Eccl) dispensation.
dispensable adj dispensable.
dispensación nf dispensation.
dispensador nm dispenser.
dispensar [1a] **1** vt (a) to dispense; to give out, distribute; honour to give, grant; attention to pay; aid to give; welcome etc to give, accord.
   (b) to excuse, exempt (de from); person, fault etc to excuse, pardon; **¡Vd dispense!**, **¡dispénseme Vd!** I beg your pardon!, do forgive me!; — **a uno de una obligación** to excuse someone (from) an obligation; **me dispensaron la multa, me dispensaron del pago de la multa** they excused me (from payment of) the fine; — **a uno de** + infin to excuse someone from + ger, relieve someone of the need to + infin; — **que uno** + subj to excuse someone for + ger; **así el cuerpo queda dispensado de ese esfuerzo** thus the body is freed from that effort (or relieved of that effort).
  2 dispensarse vr: **no puedo dispensarme de** + infin I cannot help + ger, I cannot refrain from + ger.
dispensario nm dispensary; clinic; — **de alimentos** soup kitchen.
dispepsia nf dyspepsia.
dispéptico adj dyspeptic.
dispersar [1a] vt to disperse, scatter; (Mil) to rout; riot etc to break up, disperse. **2 dispersarse** vr to disperse, scatter; to break up.
dispersión nf dispersion, dispersal; (Phys) dispersion.
disperso adj scattered; dispersed; sparse; (Mil) separated, straggling.
displicencia nf (a) peevishness, bad temper. (b) lack of enthusiasm; indifference.
displicente adj (a) disagreeable, peevish, bad-tempered; fretful. (b) unenthusiastic, lukewarm; indifferent.
disponer [2r] **1** vt (a) to arrange, dispose; to lay out; to put in order; to line up.
   (b) to prepare, get ready.
   (c) to order, decide; (Med) to order; — **que** ... **to order that** ..., arrange that ..., provide that ...; **la ley dispone que** ... the law provides that ...
  2 vi: — **de** to have, own; to have available, have at one's disposal; to make use of, avail oneself of; **dispone de 2 coches** he has 2 cars; **disponemos de poco tiempo** we have very little time (at our disposal).
   (b) to dispose of (as one wishes); **no puede** — **de esos bienes** she cannot dispose of those properties.
  3 disponerse vr: — **a** + infin, — **para** + infin to prepare to + infin, get ready to + infin.
disponibilidad nf (a) availability. (b) —**es** resources, means.
disponible adj available; on hand, spare.
disposición nf (a) arrangement, disposition; order; layout (also Archit).
   (b) order; provision, disposition; stipulation; **según las** —**es del código** according to the provisions of the statute; **última** — last will and testament.
   (c) —**es** preparations (para for); steps, measures; **tomar sus** —**es** to make one's preparations, take steps.
   (d) disposal; **a la** — **de** at the disposal of; **a la** — **de Vd, a su** — at your service; **tener algo a su** — to have something at one's disposal, have something available; **poner algo a la** — **de uno** to put something at someone's disposal.
   (e) position; **estar en** — **de** + infin to be in a position to + infin.
   (f) disposition, temperament; aptitude (para for); turn of mind; — **de ánimo** attitude of mind; **no tener** — **para** to have no aptitude for.
dispositivo nm device, mechanism; appliance; contrivance; gadget; — **de arranque** starting mechanism; — **de seguridad** safety catch, safety device.
dispuesto adj and ptp (a) arranged, disposed; — **según ciertos principios** arranged according to certain principles; **bien** — (Archit) well designed, well laid out.
   (b) (person) **bien** — well-disposed (hacia towards); **mal** — ill-disposed; (Med) ill, indisposed.
   (c) **estar** — **a** + infin, to be prepared to + infin; **estar poco** — **a** + infin to be reluctant to + infin.
   (d) bright, clever, go-ahead.
   (e) **bien** — handsome.
disputa nf dispute; argument; controversy; **los asuntos en** — the matters in dispute, the matters at issue; **sin** — undoubted(ly), beyond dispute.
disputable adj disputable, debatable.

disputador 1 *adj* disputatious. **2** *nm* disputant.
disputar [1a] **1** *vt* (a) *matter* to dispute, question, challenge; to debate.
    (b) *possession* to fight for, contend for.
    2 *vi* (a) to debate, argue (*con* with; *de, sobre* about).
    (b) — **con uno por un premio** to contend with someone for a prize.
    3 disputarse *vr:* — **un premio** to contend for a prize; — **la posesión de** to fight over (*or* for) the possession of.
disquero *adj* record (*attr*).
disquisición *nf* (a) disquisition. (b) —**es** comments on the side, marginal reflections.
distancia *nf* distance; (*of time etc*) interval; gap, difference, disparity; — **de despegue** (*Aer*) length of takeoff; — **focal** focal distance; — **de parada** braking distance; — **del suelo**, — **sobre el suelo** (*Aut etc*) height off the ground, clearance; **a** — at a distance; **a gran** —, **a larga** — long-distance (*attr*); **mantener a uno a** — to keep someone at a distance, keep someone at arm's length; **mantenerse a** — to keep one's distance, (*fig*) to hold back, remain aloof; **cada cierta** — every so often, at intervals; **guardar las** —**s** to keep one's distance, maintain proper (social) distinctions.
distanciado *adj* (a) remote (*de* from); widely separated, isolated.
    (b) (*fig*) far apart; **estamos algo** —**s** we are not particularly close; **ella está distanciada de su familia** she has grown apart from her family, she has no close ties with her family; **estamos** —**s en ideas** our ideas are poles apart.
distanciamiento *nm* (a) (*act*) spacing out. (b) (*state*) remoteness, isolation; (*fig*) distance, lack of close links (*entre* between).
distanciar [1b] **1** *vt* (a) *objects* to space out, separate; to put further apart.
    (b) *rival* to outdistance.
    (c) *persons* to cause a rift between.
    2 distanciarse *vr* (a) — **de un rival** to get ahead of a rival.
    (b) (*two persons*) to fall out, become estranged; to become (more) remote from each other.
distante *adj* (a) distant; far-off, remote; — **de 10 kms** 10 kms away. (b) (*fig*) distant.
distar [1a] *vi* (a) **dista 5 kms de aquí** it is 5 kms from here; **dista mucho** it's a long way away; **¿dista mucho?** is it far?, how far is it?
    (b) **dista mucho de la verdad** it's very far from the truth, it's a long way off the truth; **disto mucho de aprobarlo** I am far from approving of it.
distender [2g] *vt* to distend; to stretch.
distensión *nf* distension; stretching; (*Med*) strain; — **muscular** muscular strain.
dístico *nm* distich.
distinción *nf* (a) distinction, difference; distinctness, differentness; **a** — **de** unlike, in contrast to; **sin** — indiscriminately; all together, mixed; **obrar sin** — to act arbitrarily, act blindly; **sin** — **de personas** without respect to persons, without regard for the differences (of rank *etc*) between people; **sin** — **de edades** irrespective of differences of age; **hacer una** — **entre** to make a distinction between, differentiate between; **hacer** — **con uno** to show someone special consideration.
    (b) clarity, distinctness.
    (c) distinction, honour; — **honorífica** honour.
    (d) elegance, refinement.
distingo *nm* reservation; subtle distinction; (petty) objection; **aquí hago un** — here I must make a reservation.
distinguible *adj* distinguishable.
distinguido *adj* (a) distinguished; prominent, well-known. (b) elegant, refined; gentlemanly, ladylike; cultured.
distinguir [3d] **1** *vt* (a) to distinguish, discern, make out; to recognize.
    (b) to distinguish (*de* from, *entre* between), tell (*de* from); **no distingo cuál es el mío** I can't tell which is mine; **lo sabría** — **entre cien iguales** I would know mine among a hundred similar ones.
    (c) to distinguish, separate, single out; **aquí distingo dos aspectos** here I distinguish two aspects.
    (d) to mark, stamp, distinguish; **lo distinguen con una señal especial** they mark it with a special sign.
    (e) to single out, mark out (for special treatment); to honour, bestow an honour on; *friend etc* to have a special regard for; **me distingue con su amistad** he honours me with his friendship.
    2 *vi:* **no** — to have no critical sense, be undis-

criminating; **es un hombre que sabe** — he is a discerning (*or* discriminating) person.
    3 distinguirse *vr* (a) (*fig*) to be distinguished (*de* from), differ (*de* from).
    (b) (*fig*) to distinguish oneself.
distintivo 1 *adj* distinctive; *mark etc* distinguishing. **2** *nm* badge, emblem; (*fig*) distinguishing mark, characteristic, typical feature.
distinto *adj* (a) *outline etc* clear, distinct, plain; well-defined.
    (b) different, distinct (*a, de* from); **son muy** —**s** they are very different.
    (c) —**s** several, various; **hay distintas opiniones sobre eso** there are various opinions about that.
distorsión *nf* (a) (*Anat*) torsion, twisting. (b) (*Radio etc*) distortion.
distracción *nf* (a) distraction; amusement, relaxation; hobby, pastime; **es mi** — **favorita** it's my favourite amusement; **lo hace como** — **nada más** he only does it as a hobby.
    (b) absence of mind, forgetfulness; heedlessness; **por** — through sheer forgetfulness, absent-mindedly.
    (c) slip, blunder, oversight; **fue una** — **mía** it was an oversight on my part.
    (d) (*Fin*) embezzlement.
distraer [2p] **1** *vt* (a) to distract, divert, lead away (*de* from); (*morally*) to lead astray; — **a uno para robarle algo** to distract someone's attention so as to steal something from him; — **a uno de su dolor** to take someone's mind off his grief; — **a uno de su pensamiento** to divert someone from his train of thought.
    (b) to amuse, relax, entertain; **la música me distrae** music relaxes me, I find music relaxing.
    (c) (*Fin*) to embezzle, divert to one's own use.
    2 *vi* to be relaxing; **el pescar distrae** fishing is a relaxation.
    3 distraerse *vr* (a) to amuse oneself, entertain oneself; to relax; **me distraigo pescando** I relax when I fish, I find fishing relaxing; **no me opongo a que se distraiga honestamente** I don't mind her having a little innocent amusement.
    (b) to be (*or* get) absent-minded; to cease to pay attention; **me distraje un momento** I allowed my attention to wander for a moment; — **de** to forget about, be inattentive to.
distraídamente *adv* (a) absent-mindedly; unobservantly; (*pej*) inattentively; slackly. (b) idly, casually.
distraído 1 *adj* (a) *person's character* absent-minded; vague, dreamy, unpractical; unobservant; (*pej*) inattentive; slack, lackadaisical; **iba yo algo** — I was rather absorbed in other things, I was not taking much notice.
    (b) *look, manner etc* absent-minded; idle, casual; **con aire** — idly, casually, in a casual manner; **me miró distraída** she gave me a casual glance.
    (c) *game etc* amusing, entertaining.
    (d) *life* dissolute.
    (e) (*Chi, Mex*) slovenly, untidy, shabby.
    2 *nm:* **hacerse el** — to pretend not to notice; to pretend not to be interested.
distribución *nf* (a) (*act*) distribution; giving-out; sending out; (*Post*) sorting; delivery; — **de premios** prize giving.
    (b) (*statistical etc*) distribution; incidence; **la** — **de los impuestos** the incidence of taxes.
    (c) (*state*) distribution, arrangement; (*Archit*) layout, ground plan.
    (d) (*Pol*) deal; **Nueva D**— New Deal; **D**— **Equitativa** Fair Deal (*esp US Pol*).
    (e) (*Mech*) timing gears.
distribuido *adj:* **una casa bien distribuida** a well-designed house.
distribuidor *nm* (a) (*person*) distributor; (*Post*) sorter; (*Comm*) dealer, agent, stockist; **su** — **habitual** your regular dealer.
    (b) — **automático** (automatic) vending machine, slot machine.
    (c) (*Aut*) distributor.
distribuidora *nf* (*Tech*) spreader.
distribuir [3g] *vt* (a) to distribute; to hand out; to give out; to send out, send round; *letters* to sort; *letters, milk etc* to deliver; *duties etc* to allocate; *prizes* to give out, award; (*Tech*) to spread; *cargo etc* to stow, arrange; *weight* to distribute (equally *etc*).
    (b) (*Archit*) to design, plan, lay out.
distributivo *adj* distributive.
distrito *nm* district, region, zone; administrative area; (*Law*) circuit; — **electoral** constituency, ward, electoral area; precinct (*US*); — **postal** postal district.

distrofia *nf*: — **muscular** (progressive) muscular dystrophy.

disturbio *nm* (a) disturbance; riot, commotion; **los —s** the disturbances, the troubles. (b) (*Tech*) disturbance; — **aerodinámico** (*Aer*) wash, slipstream.

disuadir [3a] *vt* to dissuade, deter, discourage (*de* from); — **a uno de** + *infin* to dissuade someone from + *ger*.

disuasión *nf* dissuasion; (*Mil etc*) deterrent.

disuasivo *adj* discouraging; dissuasive; (*Mil*) deterrent.

disuasorio *adj* (*Mil*) deterrent; *see* **fuerza.**

disyuntiva *nf* dilemma; crisis.

disyuntivo *adj* disjunctive.

disyuntor *nm* (*Elec*) circuit breaker.

dita[1] *nf* (a) surety; security, bond. (b) (*Andalusia*) loan at a high rate of interest; (*SAm*) small debt.

dita[2] *nf* (*PR*) dish, cup, pot.

ditirambo *nm* dithyramb.

diurético 1 *adj* diuretic. **2** *nm* diuretic.

diurno *adj* diurnal, day (*attr*).

diva *nf* prima donna.

divagación *nf* digression; —**es** wanderings, ramblings.

divagador *adj* rambling, discursive.

divagar [1h] *vi* to digress; to wander, ramble; ¡**no —**! get on with it!, come to the point!

diván *nm* divan.

divergencia *nf* divergence.

divergente *adj* divergent; contrary, opposite.

divergir [3c] *vi* (a) to diverge. (b) (*of views etc*) to differ, be opposed, clash; (*of persons*) to differ, disagree.

diversidad *nf* diversity, variety.

diversificación *nf* diversification.

diversificar [1g] *vt* to diversify.

diversión *nf* (a) amusement, entertainment; recreation; hobby, pastime; —**es de salón** parlour games, indoor games. (b) (*Mil*) diversion.

diverso *adj* **1** (a) diverse.
(b) different (*de* from); other; **se trata de — asunto** it's about a different (*or* another) matter.
(c) —**s** several, various; some; sundry; **está en —s libros** it figures in several books.
2 —**s** *nmpl* (*Comm*) sundries, miscellaneous items.

divertido *adj* (a) entertaining, amusing; funny; enjoyable; *party etc* gay, merry; *joke* funny; *person* funny, amusing, witty.
(b) (*iro*) **estar —** to be in for a good time; ¡**estamos —s!** how terribly amusing! (I don't think); **la que se case con él estará divertida** the girl who marries him is much to be pitied.
(c) (*SAm*) **estar —** to be tight.

divertimiento *nm* (a) amusement, entertainment.
(b) diversion (*also* (*Mil*).

divertir [3i] **1** *vt* (a) to amuse, entertain.
(b) to divert, distract (the attention of).
2 divertirse *vr* to amuse oneself; to have a good time; **la juventud moderna no quiere más que —** all modern youth wants to do is have a good time; — **haciendo algo** to amuse oneself doing something; — **con el amor de una** to toy with someone's affections; ¡**que se diviertan!** have a good time!

dividendo *nm* dividend.

dividir [3a] *vt* to divide (up); to split (up), separate; to share out, distribute; — **12 entre 4** to divide 12 among 4; — **12 por 4** (*Math*) to divide 12 by 4; — **algo en 5 partes** to divide something into 5 parts; — **algo por mitad** to divide something into two, halve something; — **algo por la mitad** to divide something down the middle.

divieso *nm* (*Med*) boil.

divinamente *adv* divinely (*also fig*).

divinidad *nf* (a) divinity.
(b) divinity; godhead; deity; — **marina** sea god; — **pagana** pagan god(dess), pagan divinity; **la D—** the Deity.
(c) (*fig*) goddess, beauty, beautiful woman; precious thing, lovely object.

divinizar [1f] *vt* to deify; (*fig*) to exalt, extol.

divino *adj* divine (*also fig*).

divisa *nf* (a) emblem, badge; (*Her*) device, motto.
(b) —**s** (*Fin*) foreign exchange; **control de —s** exchange control.

divisar [1a] *vt* to make out, spy, descry.

divisible *adj* divisible.

división *nf* (*Math, Mil etc*) division; (*Pol*: *of party*) split; (*of country*) partition.

divisional *adj* (*Mil*) divisional.

divisivo *adj* divisive.

divisor *nm* (*Math*) divisor; **máximo común —** highest common factor.

divisoria *nf* dividing line; (*Geog*) divide; — **de aguas** watershed; — **continental** continental divide.

divisorio *adj* dividing; divisive; **línea divisoria de las aguas** watershed.

divorciado 1 *adj* (a) divorced. (b) (*fig*) **las opiniones están divorciadas** opinions are divided. **2** *nm*, **divorciada** *nf* divorcee.

divorciar [1b] **1** *vt* (a) to divorce. (b) (*fig*) to divorce, separate (*de* from). **2 divorciarse** to get divorced, get a divorce (*de* from).

divorcio *nm* (a) divorce. (b) (*fig*) separation; division, split; **existe un — entre A y B** there is a wide division between A and B.

divulgación *nf* spreading, circulation; popularizing; (*pej*) disclosure.

divulgar [1h] **1** *vt* to spread, circulate, publish; to popularize; (*pej*) to divulge, disclose, let out.
2 divulgarse *vr* (*secret*) to leak out; (*rumour etc*) to get about, become known.

diz (*arch form of* **dice**; *SAm*): — **que...** they say that ..., it is said that ...

dobladillar [1a] *vt* to hem.

dobladillo *nm* hem; (*of trousers*) turn-up(s), cuff(s) (*US*).

doblado *adj* (a) (*Sew etc*) double; doubled over, folded. (b) (*Anat*) stocky, thickset. (c) *surface* rough. (d) (*fig*) sly, deceitful.

dobladura *nf* fold, crease.

doblaje *nm* (*Cine*) dubbing.

doblamiento *nm* folding, creasing.

doblar [1a] **1** *vt* (a) (*general sense*) to double; — **el sueldo a uno** to double someone's salary; **te doblo la edad** I'm twice your age.
(b) *material, paper etc* to fold (up, over), crease; **hem** to turn up; *page* to turn down; *head, knee, pipe etc* to bend; (*Mex*) to shoot down; — **a uno a palos** to give someone a beating.
(c) *corner* to turn, round, go round; *cape* (*Naut*) to round; (*Aut*: *gall*) to overtake.
(d) *film* to dub.
(e) (*Theat*) — **dos papeles** to take two parts; — **a uno** to understudy (for) someone.
(f) (*Bridge*) to double; *stake, money* (*in quiz game*) to double.
2 *vi* (a) to turn (*a la izquierda* to the left).
(b) (*of bell*) to toll (*a muerto, por uno* for a death).
(c) (*Theat etc*) to stand in (*a* for).
3 doblarse *vr* (a) (*in quantity etc*) to double.
(b) to fold (up), crease; to bend, buckle.
(c) (*fig*) to give in, yield (*a* to).

doble 1 *adj* (a) double; *door, flower, meaning etc* double; *control, nationality etc* dual; *bottom* false; *material* double, extra thick; *string* thick, stout; — **o nada** double or quits.
(b) (*fig*) insincere; two-faced, deceitful.
2 *nm* (a) double (quantity); **el —** twice the quantity, twice the amount; twice as much; **hoy gana el —** today he earns double, todays he earns twice as much; **su sueldo es el — del mío** his salary is twice mine; **un — de whiskey** a double whisky; **un — de cerveza** a big glass of beer.
(b) (*Sew etc*) fold, crease.
(c) (*of bell*) toll, tolling; knell.
(d) —**s** (*Tennis*) doubles; —**s (de) damas** ladies' doubles; —**s de caballeros**, —**s masculinos** men's doubles; —**s mixtos** mixed doubles.
(e) (*Bridge*) double; — **de castigo** penalty double; — **de llamada** asking double.
3 *nmf* (*Cine*) double, stand-in; **ser el — de uno** (*fig*) to be someone's double.

doblegar [1h] **1** *vt* (a) to fold, crease; to bend.
(b) *weapon* to brandish.
(c) (*fig*) to persuade, sway; — **a uno** to force someone to abandon his course (*or* change his ways *etc*), make someone give in.
2 doblegarse *vr* (*fig*) to yield, give in.

doblemente *adv* (a) doubly. (b) insincerely; deceitfully.

doblez 1 *nm* fold, crease; hem; (*of trousers*) turn-up(s), cuff(s) (*US*). **2** *nf* insincerity; double-dealing, deceitfulness, duplicity.

doblón *nm* (*Hist*) doubloon; — **de a ocho** piece of eight.

dócar *nm* dogcart.

doce 1 *adj* twelve; (*date*) twelfth; **las —** twelve o'clock. **2** *nm* twelve.

docena *nf* dozen; — **del fraile** baker's dozen; **a —s** by the dozen, in great numbers; **por —(s)** by the dozen, in dozens.

doceno *adj* twelfth.

docente *adj* educational; teaching (*attr*); **centro —** teaching institution; **personal —** teaching staff.

dócil *adj* docile; obedient; gentle, mild.

docilidad *nf* docility; obedience; gentleness; mildness.

dócilmente *adv* in a docile way; obediently; gently, mildly.

doctamente *adv* learnedly.

docto 1 *adj* learned, erudite; scholarly. **2** *nm* scholar; learned person.

doctor *nm* (*Med, Univ*) doctor; (*Eccl*) father, saint; **— en derecho** doctor of laws; **—es tiene la Iglesia** there are plenty of people well able to pass an opinion (on that).

doctora *nf* (*Med*) woman doctor; (*Univ*) doctor; (*fam*) bluestocking.

doctorado *nm* doctorate.

doctoral *adj* doctoral.

doctorar [1a] **1** *vt* to confer a doctor's degree on. **2 doctorarse** *vr* to take one's doctor's degree (*or* doctorate).

doctrina *nf* doctrine; learning; teaching; (*School*) catechism, religious instruction; **no saber la —** to know nothing at all.

doctrinal *adj* doctrinal.

doctrinar [1a] *vt* to teach.

doctrinario 1 *adj* doctrinaire. **2** *nm*, **doctrinaria** *nf* doctrinaire.

doctrinero *nm* (*SAm*) parish priest (*among Indians*).

documentación *nf* (a) documentation. (b) papers, documents; **— del barco** ship's papers; **la —, por favor** your papers, please.

documental 1 *adj* documentary. **2** *nm* (*Cine etc*) documentary.

documentar [1a] *vt* to document, establish with documentary evidence.

documento *nm* document; paper; record; certificate; (*Law*) exhibit; **—s del coche** papers relating to a car; **— justificativo** voucher, certificate; supporting document; **— nacional de identidad** identity card; **— secretísimo** top-secret document; **los —s, por favor** your papers, please.

dodo *nm*, **dodó** *nm* dodo.

dogal *nm* halter; hangman's noose; **estar con el — al cuello** (*or* **a la garganta**) to be in an awful jam.

dogma *nm* dogma.

dogmáticamente *adv* dogmatically.

dogmático *adj* dogmatic.

dogmatismo *nm* dogmatism.

dogmatizador *nm* dogmatist.

dogmatizar [1f] *vi* to dogmatize.

dogo *nm* (*angl*) bulldog.

doguillo *nm*, **doguino** *nm* small bulldog.

dola *nf* (*fam*) **=pídola.**

dolamas *nfpl*, **dolames** *nfpl* (*Vet*) hidden defects (*of a horse*); (*SAm*) chronic complaint, constant indisposition.

dólar *nm* dollar.

dolencia *nf* ailment, complaint, affliction; ache; (*fig*) ailment, ill; **la — de la economía** the ills of the economy.

doler [2i] **1** *vti* (a) (*Med*) to hurt, pain; to ache; **me duele el brazo** my arm hurts, my arm aches; **me duele el estómago** I have a pain in my stomach, my stomach aches, I've got stomach ache; **¿dónde te duele?** where does it hurt (you)?; **¿duele mucho?** does it hurt much?; **no me ha dolido nada** it didn't hurt at all.

(b) (*fig*) to grieve, distress; **le duele aún la pérdida** the loss still grieves him, he still feels the loss; **no me duele el dinero** I don't mind about the money, the money doesn't bother me; **a cualquiera le dolería verlo** it would grieve anyone to see it; **¡ahí (le) duele!** that's the whole point!, you've put your finger on it!

2 dolerse *vr* (a) to grieve (*de* about, for), feel sorry (*de* about, for); **— de** to regret; to repent (of); *person* to feel sorry for, pity; **¡duélete de mí!** pity me!; show some sympathy for me!; **se duele de que no le visitéis** he resents the fact that you don't go to see him; **— de los pecados** to repent (of) one's sins.

(b) to complain; to moan, groan; **lo sufre todo sin —** he puts up with everything without complaining.

loliente 1 *adj* (a) (*Med*) suffering, ill; aching.

(b) sad, sorrowful; (*in bereavement*) grieving, mourning; **la familia —** the bereaved family, the sorrowing relatives.

2 *nmf* (a) (*Med*) sufferer, sick person; patient.

(b) bereaved person; (*at funeral*) mourner.

dolo *nm* fraud, deceit; **sin —** openly, honestly.

dolomita *nf* dolomite.

dolor *nm* (a) pain; ache; pang; **— de cabeza** headache; **con — de mi corazón** with an ache in my heart; **— de estómago** stomach ache; **— de muelas** toothache; **— de oídos** earache; **—es del parto** labour pains; **— sordo** dull ache; **estar con mucho —, tener mucho —** to be in great pain; **estar con —es** (*woman*) to feel the labour pains beginning.

(b) (*fig*) grief, sorrow; affliction, distress; regret; **le causa mucho —** it causes him great distress, it is a great grief to him; **con — te lo digo** it grieves me to say it to you; **es un —** it's a shame, it's a pity.

dolorido *adj* (a) (*Med*) sore, tender, aching; **la parte dolorida** the part which hurts, the part where the pain is.

(b) (*fig*) *person* distressed; grieving, grief-stricken.

(c) *tone* plaintive, sad, pained.

dolorosa *nf* (*hum*) bill, check (*US*) (*in a restaurant*).

dolorosamente *adv* (a) (*Med*) painfully. (b) (*fig*) painfully, grievously, distressingly.

doloroso *adj* (a) (*Med*) painful. (b) (*fig*) painful, grievous, distressing.

doloso *adj* fraudulent, deceitful.

doma *nf*=**domadura.**

domable *adj* tamable; controllable.

domador *nm*, **domadora** *nf* trainer; tamer; **— de caballos** horse-breaker.

domadura *nf* (a) taming; training; breaking-in. (b) (*fig*) mastering, controlling.

domar [1a] *vt* (a) to tame; to train; *horse etc* to break in. (b) (*fig*) to master, control; to repress.

domeñar [1a] *vt*=**domar.**

domesticación *nf* domestication; taming.

domesticado *adj* tame; pet; **un tejón —** a tame badger, a pet badger.

domesticar [1g] **1** *vt* to tame, domesticate; to make a pet of. **2 domesticarse** *vr* to become tame, become domesticated.

domesticidad *nf* (a) domesticity, homeliness; homely atmosphere.

(b) (*of animal*) (state of being in) captivity; **el lobo no vive bien en —** the wolf does not live happily in captivity, the wolf does not take to captivity.

doméstico 1 *adj* (a) *life etc* domestic; home (*attr*), family (*attr*); **economía doméstica** home economy, housekeeping, home economics (*US*); **gastos —s** household expenses, housekeeping expenditure; **faenas domésticas** household jobs.

(b) *animal* tame, pet.

2 *nm*, **doméstica** *nf* servant, domestic.

Domiciano *m* Domitian.

domiciliar [1b] **1** *vt* (a) to domicile, establish; to house. (b) (*Mex*) *letter* to address. **2 domiciliarse** *vr* to establish oneself, take up (one's) residence.

domiciliario *adj* domiciliary; house (*attr*); **arresto —** house arrest.

domicilio *nm* home; (*in official parlance*) domicile, residence, abode; **— particular** private residence; **— social** (*Comm*) head office; **a —** (*Sport*) at home; **servicio a —** delivery service; **sin — fijo** of no fixed abode.

dominación *nf* (a) domination; dominance; rule, sway. (b) (*Mil*) high ground, commanding position.

dominador *adj* (a) dominating, controlling. (b) *character* domineering.

dominante *adj* (a) dominant (*also Mus*), predominant; **la tendencia —** the dominant tendency, the ruling tendency; **el viento —** the prevailing wind; **la consideración —** the overriding consideration.

(b) *character* domineering; masterful; *love etc* possessive.

dominar [1a] **1** *vt* (a) to dominate; to rule (over), hold sway over; *person* to overpower; *boat, horse etc* to control, bring under control; *epidemic, fire* to check, bring under control; *revolt* to put down, suppress, subdue; *passion* to control, master; *grief etc* to get over; **le domina la envidia** he is ruled by envy, his ruling passion is envy.

(b) *language* to know well, be fluent in, have a good command of; **domina 7 idiomas** he knows 7 languages well.

(c) (*of building etc*) to dominate, tower above (*or* over), look down on.

2 *vi* (*of building etc*) to dominate; (*of colour, feature etc*) to stand out; (*of opinion, wind, tendency etc*) to predominate, prevail.

3 dominarse *vr* to control oneself.

dómine *nm* (*Hist*) schoolmaster; (*hum*) pedant.

domingo *nm* Sunday; **D— de Cuasimodo** Low Sunday; **D— de Ramos** Palm Sunday; **D— de Resurrección** Easter Sunday; **hacer —** to take a day off, make a day into a holiday.

dominguejo *nm* (a) (*Chi*, *Per*) scarecrow. (b) (*Ven*) poor devil.

dominguero *adj* Sunday (*attr*).

Dominica *f* Dominica.

dominical *adj* Sunday (*attr*); **periódico** — Sunday newspaper.

dominicanismo *nm* word (*or* phrase *etc*) peculiar to the Dominican Republic.

dominicano 1 *adj* (*Eccl and Pol*) Dominican. **2** *nm* (*Eccl*) Dominican. **3** *nm*, **dominicana** *nf* (*Pol*) Dominican.

dominico *nm* (*Eccl*), **domínico** *nm* (*SAm*) Dominican.

dominio *nm* (a) dominion; power, sway, authority (*sobre* over); ascendancy, supremacy; hold, grip (*de* on); (*of language*) command (*de* of), fluency (*de* in); — **público** public property, national property; **ser del** — **público** (*of news etc*) to be widely known, be common knowledge; — **de** (*or* **sobre**) **sí mismo** self-control.
(b) (*land*) domain; (*Pol*) dominion.

dominó *nm* domino; **un** — a domino; a set of dominoes; **juego de** — dominoes.

don[1] *nm* courtesy title equivalent to Mr, used before Christian name: on envelopes = Esquire; in other cases not directly translated, *eg* **soy alumno de don Ramón** I am one of Menéndez Pidal's students; **el rey don Pedro** King Peter; see also **Juan**.

don[2] *nm* (a) gift; present.
(b) (*in fairy tale*) wish; **el hada le concedió 3** —**es** the fairy gave him 3 wishes.
(c) (*fig*) gift; knack; aptitude, talent (*de* for); **tiene un** — **especial** he has a special gift; — **de acierto** happy knack (of doing things well); intuition; — **de gentes** personal charm, human touch; **tener** — **de gentes** to have a way with people, have the human touch, know how to handle people; — **de lenguas** gift for languages; — **de mando** (qualities of) leadership, (*Mil*) generalship; — **de palabra** gift of the gab (*fam*).

dona *nf* (*Chi*) gift; legacy; —**s** (*Mex*) trousseau.

donación *nf* donation; (*Law*) gift.

donada *nf* lay sister.

donado *nm* lay brother.

donador *nm*, **donadora** *nf* donor; — **de sangre** blood donor.

donaire *nm* (a) charm, wit, cleverness. (b) grace(fulness); elegance. (c) (*un* —) witticism; **tiene muchos** —**s** he's terribly witty.

donante *nmf* donor; — **de sangre** blood donor.

donar [1a] *vt* to donate; to grant, bestow.

donativo *nm* donation, contribution.

doncel *nm* (*Hist*) page; young nobleman, young squire.

doncella *nf* (a) maid, lady's maid, maidservant. (b) virgin; (*Hist and lit*) maid, maiden.

doncellez *nf* (a) (*state*) virginity, maidenhood. (b) (*Anat*) maidenhead.

donde 1 *rel adv* (a) where; (*fig*) wherein; in which; **el sitio** — **lo encontré** the place where I found it; **a** — to where, to which; **fue a** — **estaban** he went to (the place) where they were; **es a** — **vamos nosotros** that's where we're going; **de** — from where; from which, out of which; **el país de** — **vienen** the country they come from; **la caja de** — **lo sacó** the box from which he took it, the box he took it out of; **en** — where; in which; **por** — through which; (*fig*) whereby; **no hay por** — **cogerle** there's no way to catch him, he has no weak spots.
(b) (*Chi*) as, since.
2 *prep* (a) **es allí** — **el farol** it's where the lamppost is, it's over there by the lamppost.
(b) (*SAm*) at the house (*etc*) of; **están cenando** — **mi madre** they are dining at my mother's (house).

dónde *interrog adv* (a) where?; **¿** — **lo dejaste?** where did you leave it?; **¿a** — **vás?** where are you going (to)?; **¿de** — **vienes?** where have you come from?; **¿en** —? where?; **¿por** —? where?, whereabouts?; **which way?**; why?, for what reason?; **¿por** — **se va al estadio?** which way to the stadium?, how do I get to the stadium?
(b) (*indirect*) where; **no sé** — **lo puse** I don't know where I put it.
(c) (*SAm*) how?

dondequiera 1 *adv* anywhere; **por** — everywhere, all over the place. **2** *conj* anywhere, wherever; — **que lo busques** wherever you look for it.

donosamente *adv* (*lit*) wittily, amusingly.

donoso *adj* (*lit*) witty, amusing; (*iro*) fine; **¡donosa idea!** (*iro*) highly amusing I'm sure!

donostiarra 1 *adj* of San Sebastián. **2** *nmf* native (*or* inhabitant) of San Sebastián; **los** —**s** the people of San Sebastián.

Don Quijote *m* Don Quixote.

doña *nf* courtesy title, used before Christian names; not translated.

dopar [1a] *vt* (*angl*) to dope, drug.

doping ['dopin] *nm* (*angl*) doping, drugging.

dopingar [1h] *vt* (*angl*) to dope, drug.

doquier *adv* (*arch or lit*) = **dondequiera**; **por** — all over, everywhere; all over the place.

dorado 1 *adj* golden; (*Tech*) gilt, gilded; gold-plated. **2** *nm* (a) (*Tech*) gilding, gilt. (b) (*Fish*) dorado; goldfish.

doradura *nf* gilding.

dorar [1a] *vt* (a) (*Tech*) to gild; (*Cook*) to brown, cook lightly. (b) (*fig*) to gild; to palliate, make more palatable, put a gloss on; — **la píldora** to gild the pill.

dormida *nf* (*SAm*) sleep.

dormidera *nf* (a) (*opium*) poppy. (b) **tener buenas** —**s** to get off to sleep easily.

dormidero *nm* (*SAm*: *of cattle*) sleeping place; (*of hens*) roost.

dormilón 1 *adj* sleepy; much given to sleeping. **2** *nm*, **dormilona** *nf* sleepyhead; (*pej*) sleepy sort, lazy sort, lie-a-bed. **3 dormilona** *nf* deckchair, reclining chair.

dormir [3k] **1** *vt* (a) — **la siesta** to have one's afternoon nap, have a doze.
(b) —**la** (*fam*) to sleep it off; — **la mona** (*fam*) to sleep off a hangover.
(c) — **a uno** to send someone to sleep, make someone go to sleep; **Delius me duerme de maravilla** Delius is marvellous for sending me to sleep.
2 *vi* to sleep; to stay overnight, spend the night; — **como un lirón** (*or* **tronco**, **poste** *etc*) to sleep like a log; — **como un santo** (*or* **bendito**) to sleep peacefully, be fast asleep; — **a pierna suelta** (*or* **tendida**) to sleep soundly, sleep the sleep of the just; — **con una** to sleep with someone; **quedarse dormido** to go to sleep, drop off; **durmiendo se me pasó la hora** the time went by while I slept, I overslept.
3 dormirse *vr* (a) to go to sleep, fall asleep.
(b) (*limb*) to go to sleep, get numb.

dormirela *nf* (*fam*) nap, snooze.

dormirlas *nm* hide-and-seek.

dormitar [1a] *vi* to doze, snooze.

dormitorio *nm* bedroom; (*of school etc*) dormitory.

dornillo *nm* wooden bowl; (*Agr*) small trough.

Dorotea *f* Dorothy.

dorsal *adj* dorsal; back (*attr*).

dorso *nm* back (*also fig*); **escribir algo al** — to write something on the back; **"véase al** —**"** "see other side"; **"please turn over"** (*PTO*).

dos 1 *adj* (a) two; (*date*) second; **las** — two o'clock; — **a** — two against two; — **por** — **son 4** two times two makes 4; **a cada** — **por tres** in rapid succession, continually; intermittently; **de** — **en** — in twos, two by two; **cortar algo en** — to cut something in(to) two; **como ése no hay** — they don't come any better than that.
(b) **los** — the two of them, both (of them); **es para los** — it's for both of you; **para entre los** — (strictly) between you and me.
2 *nm* two; **estamos a** — (*Tennis*) the score is deuce; **en un** — **por tres** in no time at all.

doscientos *adj* two hundred.

dosel *nm* canopy.

doselera *nf* valance.

dosificación *nf* dosage.

dosificar [1g] *vt* medicine to measure out, put up in doses; ingredients to measure out, mix in proportion.

dosis *nf*, *pl* **dosis** (a) dose; dosage, amount, quantity; injection, shot. (b) (*fig*) dose; admixture; **con buena** — **de vanidad** with a good proportion of vanity.

dos piezas *nm*, *pl* **dos piezas** two-piece.

dotación *nf* (a) (*act*, *money*) endowment.
(b) staff, establishment, personnel; (*Naut*) crew, complement; **una** — **del parque de bomberos** a squad of firemen; **la** — **es insuficiente** the staff is inadequate, we are under-staffed.

dotado *adj* (a) person gifted; **los niños excepcionalmente** —**s** exceptionally gifted children; **bien** — highly talented, well-equipped for life.
(b) — **de** person endowed with; machine *etc* equipped with, fitted with, possessing.

dotar [1a] *vt* (a) woman to endow (**con** with), give a dowry to; **la dotó muy bien** he gave her a good dowry; **la dotó con** (*or* **en**) **un millón** he gave her a million as a dowry.
(b) (*fig*) to endow (**con**, **de** with); **la naturaleza le dotó de buenas cualidades** nature endowed him with good qualities.
(c) foundation *etc* to endow; to provide funds for, assign money to; to fix a salary for; to provide staff (*etc*) for; **son necesarias X pesetas para** — **estos**

puestos de enseñanza X pesetas are needed to pay for these teaching posts; **la Academia ha dotado 2 premios** the Academy has established (*or* set aside funds for) 2 prizes.

(d) (*Mech etc*) to supply, fit, provide (*de* with); — **un avión de todos los adelantos modernos** to equip a plane with all the latest devices.

(e) *ship etc* to man (*de* with); *laboratory, office etc* to staff (*de* with).

dote *n gen f* (a) dowry, marriage portion; **con un millón de** — with a dowry of a million.

(b) (*fig*) —**s** gifts, talents, aptitude; **tiene excelentes** —**s** she has great gifts; —**s de adherencia** (*Aut*) road-holding qualities; —**s de mando** (qualities of) leadership.

doy *see* **dar.**

dozavo 1 *adj* twelfth. **2** *nm* twelfth (part); **en** — (*Typ*) in duodecimo.

dracma *nf* (a) (*Pharm*) drachm, dram. (b) (*coin*) drachma.

draconiano *adj* draconian.

draga *nf* dredge; (*boat*) dredger.

dragado *nm* dredging.

dragaminas *nm, pl* **dragaminas** minesweeper.

dragar [1h] *vt* to dredge; *mines* to sweep.

dragomán *nm* dragoman.

dragón *nm* (a) dragon. (b) (*Mil*) dragoon. (c) (*Bot*) snapdragon.

dragona *nf* (a) (*Mil*) shoulder knot. (b) (*Chi, Mex, Per*) guard (*of sword*). (c) (*Mex*) hooded cloak.

dragoncillo *nm* (*Bot*) tarragon.

dragonear [1a] **1** *vt* (*RPl*) to court, woo. **2** *vi* (*SAm*) to boast, brag; — **de** to boast of being; (*Chi*) to pretend to be, pass oneself off as.

drama *nm* drama (*also fig*).

dramática *nf* drama, dramatic art.

dramáticamente *adv* dramatically.

dramático *adj* **1** dramatic (*also fig*). **2** *nm* dramatist; (tragic) actor.

dramatizar [1f] *vt* to dramatize.

dramaturgo *nm* dramatist, playwright.

drásticamente *adv* drastically.

drasticidad *nf* drastic nature, drastic character.

drástico *adj* drastic.

drenaje *nm* (*esp Agr, Med*) drainage.

drenar [1a] *vt* to drain.

Dresde Dresden.

dribl(e)ar [1a] *vti* (*Sport: angl*) to dribble; — **a uno** to dribble past someone.

drible *nm* (*Sport: angl*) dribble.

dril *nm* duck, drill.

driza *nf* halyard.

droga *nf* (a) (*Med, Pharm*) drug; medicine; (*pej*) drug; (*Horseracing etc*) dope; — **milagrosa** wonder drug; **el peligro de las** —**s** the drug menace.

(b) (*fam*) trick, hoax; stratagem; fib.

(c) (*fam*) nuisance; **es (mucha)** — it's a dreadful nuisance.

(d) (*Arg, Chi, Mex, Per*) debt; bad debt; **hacer** — to refuse to pay up.

(e) (*Cu*) drug on the market, unsaleable article.

(f) (*CAm, Cu*) **mandar a uno a la** — to tell someone to go to hell.

drogadicto *nm*, **drogadicta** *nf* (*CAm, Mex*) drug addict.

drogado *nm* (*Sport*) doping.

drogar [1h] **1** *vt* to drug; (*Sport*) to dope. **2 drogarse** *vr* to drug oneself, take drugs.

droguería *nf* druggist's (shop).

droguero *nm* (a) druggist. (b) (*fam*) cheat, crook; (*Arg, Chi, Mex, Per*) slow payer, defaulter.

droguista *nm* =**droguero.**

drogui *nm* (*RPl*) (a) liquor, alcohol. (b) drunkard.

dromedario *nm* dromedary.

dromeo *nm* emu.

druida *nm* druid.

dual *adj* dual (*also Gram*).

dualidad *nf* (a) duality. (b) (*Chi*) tied vote, indecisive election.

dualismo *nm* dualism.

dubletón *nm* (*Bridge: angl*) doubleton.

Dublín Dublin.

ducado *nm* (a) duchy, dukedom. (b) (*Fin*) ducat.

ducal *adj* ducal.

duco *nm* thick paint, lacquer; **pintar al** — to lacquer, spray (with paint).

ducentésimo *adj* two hundredth.

dúctil *adj* (a) ductile, soft. (b) (*fig*) flexible, yielding; easy to handle.

ductilidad *nf* ductility, softness.

ducha *nf* shower, shower bath; (*Med*) douche; **tomarse una** — to have a shower, shower oneself;

dar una — de agua fría a un proyecto (*fig*) to pour cold water on a plan.

duchar [1a] **1** *vt* (*Med*) to douche. **2 ducharse** *vr* to have a shower, shower oneself.

ducho *adj*: — **en** well versed in, experienced in; skilled at, adept at.

duda *nf* doubt; misgiving; indecision; suspense; **fuera de toda** — beyond all doubt; **sin** — no doubt, doubtless; undoubtedly; **¡sin** —**!** of course!; **le acometieron** —**s** he was assailed by doubts, he began to have doubts; **ello constituye una** — **importante** this is a big question mark, it's a big if; **no cabe** — there is no doubt about it; **no cabe** — **de que . . .** there can be no doubt that . . .; **¿qué** — **cabe** (*or* **coge**)? is something bothering you?; **no le quepa** — make no mistake about it, get this straight; **para desvanecer toda** — in order to dispel all uncertainty; **queda la** — **en pie** the doubt remains; **surge una** — a question arises; **estar en** — to be in doubt; **poner algo en** — to cast doubt on something, call something in question.

dudar [1a] **1** *vt* to doubt; **no lo dudo** I don't doubt it.

2 *vi* to doubt, be in doubt; — **acerca de** to be uncertain about; — **de** to doubt; to question; to mistrust; **no dudo de su talento** I don't question his talent; — **en** + *infin* to hesitate to + *infin*; — **entre A y B** to hesitate between A and B; — **que . . .**, — **si . . .** to doubt whether; **dudo que sea capaz de hacerlo** I doubt whether he will be capable of doing it.

dudosamente *adv* doubtfully, uncertainly; — **eficaz** of doubtful efficacy.

dudoso *adj* (a) doubtful, dubious, uncertain; *point* debatable; *result* unclear, indecisive.

(b) hesitant, undecided.

(c) (*of moral quality*) dubious, suspect.

duela *nf* stave.

duelista *nm* duellist.

duelo[1] *nm* (*Mil*) duel; **batirse en** — to fight a duel.

duelo[2] *nm* (a) grief, sorrow; bereavement; —**s** sufferings, hardships; **sin** — unrestrainedly; **gastar sin** — to spend lavishly; **pegar a uno sin** — to beat someone mercilessly.

(b) (*period, dress etc*) mourning; (*persons*) mourners, party of mourners.

duende *nm* (a) imp, goblin, elf; ghost; mischievous child; prankster. (b) **tener** — to have it, to have magic, be out of this world.

duendecillo *nm* (*Aer etc*) gremlin (*sl*), jinx (*US fam*).

dueña *nf* (a) owner, proprietress; landlady; — **de la casa** mistress of the house, lady of the house.

(b) (*Hist*) lady; matron; duenna, companion, governess.

(c) (*fig*) mistress; **la marina era** — **de los mares** the navy was mistress of the seas.

dueño *nm* owner, proprietor; landlord; master; employer; **organismo de los** —**s** (*Comm etc*) employers' organization; **ser** — **de** to own, be the owner of, possess; **ser** — **del baile, ser** — **de la situación** to be the master of the situation, have the situation in hand; **ser** — **de sí mismo** to be self-possessed, have self-control; **ser muy** — **de sí** to be very much in control of oneself; **es Vd muy** —, **es Vd** — **de mi casa** you're very welcome; **ser** — **de** + *infin* to be free to + *infin*; **cambiar de** — to change hands; **hacerse** — **de** to take over, take possession of; to acquire.

duermevela *nf* (*fam*) nap, snooze.

Duero m Douro.

dula *nf* common land, common pasture.

dulcamara *nf* nightshade.

dulce 1 *adj* (in most senses) sweet; *water* fresh; *metal* soft; *voice, sound* soft; *character* gentle, sweet, mild; *climate* mild; **un instrumento** — a sweet-sounding instrument; a mellow instrument; **con el acento** — **del país** with the soft accent of the region; **más** — **que el almíbar** (*or* **azúcar** *etc*) sweeter than honey.

2 *adv* gently, softly; **habla muy** — she speaks very softly.

3 *nm* (a) sweet, candy (*US*); —**s** sweets; — **de almíbar** preserved fruit; **melocotón en** — preserved peaches; **a nadie le amarga un** — nobody says no to a bit of luck.

(b) (*CAm, Col, Ven*) brown sugar.

dulcémele *nm* dulcimer.

dulcemente *adv* sweetly; softly; gently, mildly.

dulcería *nf* confectioner's, sweetshop, candy store (*US*).

dulcificar [1g] **1** *vt* (a) to sweeten.

(b) (*fig*) to soften, make more gentle; to make more pleasant, make more tolerable.

2 dulcificarse *vr* (*weather*) to turn mild.

dulzarrón *adj* (a) sickly-sweet, too sugary. (b) (*fig*) cloying, sickening.

dulzura *nf* sweetness; softness; gentleness; mildness; **con —** sweetly, softly.

dumping ['dumpin] *nm* (*Comm: angl*) dumping; **hacer —** to dump goods.

dunas *nfpl* dunes.

dundeco *adj* (*CAm, Col*) silly, stupid.

dundera *nf* (*CAm, Col*) silliness, stupidity.

dundo *adj* (*CAm, Col*) =**dundeco.**

Dunquerque Dunkirk.

dúo *nm* duet, duo.

duodecimal *adj* duodecimal.

duodécimo *adj* twelfth.

duodeno *nm* duodenum.

duplicación *nf* duplication.

duplicado 1 *adj* duplicate; **número 14 —** (*abbr* **dpdo**) No. 14ᴬ. **2** *nm* duplicate; **por —** in duplicate.

duplicar [1g] **1** *vt* to duplicate; to repeat; *number, quantity* to double.

   2 duplicarse *vr* to double; **la cifra antigua se ha duplicado** the old number has doubled.

duplicidad *nf* duplicity, deceitfulness.

duplo *adj* double; **12 es — de 6** 12 is twice 6.

duque *nm* duke.

duquesa *nf* duchess.

durabilidad *nf* durability.

durable *adj* durable, lasting.

duración *nf* duration; period, length of time; (*Aut, Mech etc*) life; **— media de la vida** average life span; **de larga —** *illness etc* long-lasting, lengthy; *record* long-playing.

duradero *adj* (a) *cloth, dress etc* hard-wearing, tough, durable. (b) *effects etc* lasting, permanent.

duramente *adv* (*fig*) harshly; cruelly, callously.

durante *prep* during; **— todo el reinado** during the whole reign, right through the reign; **— muchos años** for many years; **habló — una hora** he spoke for an hour.

durar [1a] *vi* (*of period etc*) to last, go on for, continue; (*of effect, memory etc*) to survive, endure, remain; to survive; (*of clothing etc*) to last, wear (well).

duraznero *nm* peach tree.

durazno *nm* peach; peach tree.

Durero *m* Dürer.

dureza *nf* (a) hardness, toughness; stiffness.
   (b) harshness; callousness; roughness.
   (c) **— de oído** hardness of hearing; **— de vientre** constipation.
   (d) (*Med*) hard patch, callosity.

durmiente 1 *adj* sleeping. **2** *nmf* (a) sleeper; **la bella D—** (**del Bosque**) Sleeping Beauty. **3** *nm* (*Rail*) sleeper, tie (*US*).

duro 1 *adj* (a) (*general sense*) hard; tough; *bread* stale, old; *meat, vegetables etc* tough; *collar* stiff; *door, joint, mechanism* stiff; *punch* hard, heavy; *light, sound, water* hard; **más — que una piedra** (*etc*) as hard as nails; **más — que un mendrugo** as tough as old boots; **tomar las duras con las maduras** to take the rough with the smooth.
   (b) *character, climate, test etc* tough; *attitude, policy* tough, harsh, hard; cruel, callous; *play* rough; *style etc* harsh; **ser — con uno** to be tough with (or on) someone, adopt a tough attitude to someone.
   (c) **— de mollera** dense, dim; pigheaded; **— de oído** hard of hearing, (*Mus*) tone-deaf; **es muy — de pelar** (*or* **roer**) it's a tough job, it's a hard nut to crack.
   (d) (*Mex, Urug*) **estar —** to be drunk.
   2 *adv* (*SAm*) hard.
   3 *nm Spanish coin*, =5 *pesetas*; **estar sin un —** to be broke (*fam*).

dux *nm* doge.

E

e *conj* (*before words beginning with* **i**— *and* **hi**—, *but not* **hie**—) *and; see also* **y.**

ea *interj* hey!; come on!; ¡— **pues!** well then!; let's see!

ebanista *nm* cabinetmaker, carpenter.

ebanistería *nf* (**a**) cabinetmaking; woodwork, carpentry. (**b**) cabinetmaker's (shop), carpenter's (shop).

ébano *nm* ebony.

ebonita *nf* ebonite.

ebriedad *nf* intoxication.

ebrio *adj* (**a**) intoxicated, drunk. (**b**) (*fig*) blind (*de* with); — **de algería** drunk with happiness, beside oneself with joy.

ebullición *nf* (**a**) boiling; **punto de** — boiling point; **entrar en** — to begin to boil, come to the boil. (**b**) (*fig*) movement, activity; state of flux; ferment; **la juventud está en** — youth is in a state of ferment.

eclecticismo *nm* eclecticism.

ecléctico 1 *adj* eclectic. 2 *nm,* **ecléctica** *nf* eclectic.

eclesiástico 1 *adj* ecclesiastic(al); church (*attr*). 2 *nm* clergyman, priest, ecclesiastic.

eclipsar [1a] *vt* to eclipse; (*fig*) to eclipse, outshine, overshadow.

eclipse *nm* eclipse *nm* (*also fig*).

eclisa *nf* (*Rail*) fishplate.

eclosión *nf* bloom, blooming; **hacer** — (*fig*) to bloom, blossom (forth).

eco *nm* (**a**) echo; **hacer** — to echo, awaken an echo. (**b**) (*fig*) echo; response; **despertar un** —, **encontrar un** — to produce a response (*en* from), awaken an echo (*en* in); **la llamada no encontró** — the call produced no response, the call had no effect; **hacer** — to fit, correspond; to make an impression; **hacerse** — **de una opinión** to echo an opinion; **tener** — to catch on, arouse interest.

ecología *nf* ecology.

ecológico *adj* ecological.

ecólogo *nm* ecologist.

economato *nm* cooperative store; cut-price store; company store; (*Mil: equivalent to*) NAAFI shop, PX (US).

econometría *nf* econometrics.

economía *nf* (**a**) economy; **la** — **ruritana** the Ruritanian economy; — **dirigida** planned economy; — **de pleno empleo,** — **de empleo completo** full-employment economy; — **doméstica** home economy, housekeeping, home economics (*US*); — **política** political economy; economics. (**b**) (*una* —) economy, saving; **hacer** —**s** to make economies, economize, save. (**c**) (*quality*) economy, thrift, thriftiness.

económicamente *adv* economically.

económico *adj* (**a**) economic; *year etc* fiscal, financial; **la situación económica** the economic position; the state of the economy; **estudio** — economic study. (**b**) *person* economical, thrifty; (*pej*) miserly. (**c**) (*Comm, Fin*) economical, inexpensive; cheap; **edición económica** cheap edition, popular edition.

economista *nmf* economist.

economizar [1f] 1 *vt* to economize (on), save; — **tiempo** to save time. 2 *vi* to economize, save; to save up; (*pej*) to be miserly, skimp, pinch.

ecónomo *nm* trustee, guardian; ecclesiastical administrator.

ectoplasma *nm* ectoplasm.

ecuación *nf* equation; — **cuadrática,** — **de segundo grado** quadratic equation.

ecuador *nm* equator.

Ecuador: el — Ecuador.

ecuánime *adj character* level-headed, equable; *mood, state* calm, composed; *judgement etc* impartial.

ecuanimidad *nf* level-headedness; calmness, composure; impartiality.

ecuatoreñismo *nm* word (*or* phrase *etc*) peculiar to Ecuador.

ecuatorial *adj* equatorial.

ecuatoriano 1 *adj* Ecuador(i)an. 2 *nm,* **ecuatoriana** *nf* Ecuador(i)an.

ecuestre *adj* equestrian.

ecuménico *adj* (o)ecumenical.

eczema *nm* (*Acad: f*) eczema.

echacuervos *nm, pl* **echacuervos** (**a**) pimp. (**b**) cheat, impostor.

echada *nf* (**a**) throw, cast; pitch, shy; (*of coin etc*) toss. (**b**) (*Mex*) boast; bluff.

echadizo 1 *adj* (**a**) *person* spying, sent to spy. (**b**) *propaganda* secretly spread; *letter* circulated in a clandestine way. (**c**) *material* waste. 2 *nm* spy.

echado *adj and ptp* (**a**) **estar** — to lie, be lying (down). (**b**) thrown; thrown away. (**c**) (*CAm, PR*) well-placed, in a good position. (**d**) (*CR*) lazy. (**e**) (*Arg, Per*) — **para atrás** boastful; swanky (*fam*).

echador (*Cu, Mex, SD*) 1 *adj* boastful, bragging. 2 *nm* boaster, braggart.

echadora *nf:* — **de cartas** fortuneteller.

echamiento *nm* throwing etc (*see* **echada**).

echar [1a] 1 *vt* (**a**) to throw; to cast, fling, pitch, toss; *anchor, hook* to cast; *coin* to toss; *look* to cast, give; *lots* to cast, draw; *dice* to throw. (**b**) (*Cook etc*) to put in, add; — **un poco de azúcar al líquido** add a little sugar to the liquid; — **carbón a la lumbre** to put coal on the fire. (**c**) *wine etc* to pour out; *food* to serve (out); **échame agua** give me some water, pour me some water. (**d**) to emit, send forth, discharge; *gas* to give off, give out; *blood* to lose, shed; *cards* to deal; *curses* to mutter. (**e**) *person* to eject, throw out, chuck out; to turn out; *employee* to dismiss, fire (*fam*); (*from club etc*) to expel; *rubbish* to throw away, throw out; (*Naut*) to jettison; *skin* to slough; — **algo de sí** to throw something off, get rid of something; **cuando protesté me echaron** when I protested they threw me out; **¡que le echen fuera!** chuck him out! (**f**) *hair etc* to grow, begin to grow, begin to have; *teeth* to cut; (*Bot*) *leaves etc* to put forth, sprout. (**g**) *key* to turn; *bolt* to shoot; *catch* to slide, work. (**h**) to move, push; — **a uno a un lado** to push someone aside; — **atrás a la multitud** to push the crowd back; — **el cuerpo atrás** to lean suddenly backwards. (**i**) — **abajo** to demolish, pull down; (*fig*) to overthrow. (**j**) *speech* to give, make, deliver; *reprimand* to give; *decree* to issue. (**k**) *letter* to post, put in the post, mail. (**l**) *tax* to lay, impose (*a* on). (**m**) to attribute, ascribe (*a* to); (*pej*) to impute (*a* to); *blame* to lay (*a* on). (**n**) (*Arg, PR*) *animal* to urge on. (**o**) (*other idiomatic uses*) *account* to make up, balance; *brake* to apply, put on; *cigarette* to have, smoke; *fortune* to tell; *foundations* to lay; *root* to strike; *game* to have, play; *play* to put on, perform. (**p**) — **la de** to pose as, give oneself the airs of, claim to be. (**q**) (*Chi*) — **las** to run away; *for many phrases, see the noun entry.*

2 *vi* (**a**) — **por una dirección** to go in a direction, turn in a direction; — **por una calle** to go down a street; **echemos por aquí** let's go this way. (**b**) — **a** + *infin* to begin to + *infin*, start to

+ *ger*; — **a reír** to start laughing, burst out laughing; — **a correr** to start to run, break into a run; to run off; *see* ver *etc*.

3 echarse *vr* (a) — **un pitillo** to have a smoke; — **una novia** to get oneself a girlfriend; — **una siestecita** to have a doze.

(b) to throw oneself, fling oneself; — **atrás** to throw oneself back(wards); — **en brazos de uno** to throw oneself into someone's arms; — **por un precipicio** to throw oneself over a cliff; — **sobre uno** to hurl oneself at someone, rush at someone; to fall on someone.

(c) to lie down; to stretch out; **se echó en el suelo** he lay down on the floor.

(d) — **a** + *infin* = 2 (b).

(e) —**las de** = 1 (p).

echarpe *nm* (*gall*) scarf, sash.

echazón *nf* (a) (*act*) throwing. (b) (*Naut*) jettison, jetsam.

echón *nm* (*Mex, Ven*) braggart, swank (*fam*), poseur.

echona *nf* (*Arg, Chi*) small sickle, reaping hook.

edad *nf* (a) (*of person*) age; **¿qué — tiene?** what age is he?, how old is he?; **a la — de 8 años, en — de 8 años** at the age of 8; **de —** elderly; **de corta —** young, of tender years; **de — madura, de mediana —** middle-aged; **avanzado de —, de —** avanzada advanced in years; **a una — avanzada** at an advanced age, late in life; **mayor —** majority; **ser mayor de —** to be of age, be adult; **llegar a mayor —,** **cumplir la mayoría de —** to come of age; **menor —** minority; **ser menor de —** to be under age; **el instrumento es como una guitarra menor de —** the instrument is like a young (*or* undersized, underdeveloped) guitar; **— adulta** adult age; manhood, womanhood; **llegar a la — adulta** to reach manhood (*etc*); **la — ingrata** the awkward age (*13–16*); **la — del pavo, la — del chivateo** (*SAm*) the tender years, the green years; the awkward age; **— tierna** tender years; **— viril** manhood; prime of life; **— crítica** change of life; **— escolar** school age; **ella no aparenta la — que tiene** she doesn't look her age; **¿qué — le das?** how old do you think she is?

(b) (*Hist*) age, period; **E—es Bárbaras** Dark Ages; **E— de Bronce** Bronze Age; **E— de Hierro** Iron Age; **E— Media** Middle Ages; **E— de Piedra** Stone Age.

edecán *nm* aide-de-camp.

Edén *m* Eden, Paradise; **es un e—** it's a garden of Eden, it's an earthly paradise.

edible *adj* (*SAm*) edible.

edición *nf* (a) (*act*) publication, issue; publishing.

(b) edition; — **aérea** airmail edition; — **de bolsillo** pocket edition; — **económica** cheap edition, popular edition; — **extraordinaria** special edition; late-night final; — **de la mañana** morning edition; — **príncipe** first edition; — **semanal** weekly edition; **en — de** edited by; **"al cerrar la —"** (*Typ*) "stop-press"; **ser la segunda — de uno** to be the very image of someone.

(c) (*Comm*) **E—es Ramírez** Ramirez Publications.

edicto *nm* edict, proclamation.

edificación *nf* (a) (*Archit*) construction, building. (b) (*fig*) edification.

edificante *adj* (a) edifying; improving; uplifting, ennobling; **una escena poco —** an unedifying spectacle. (b) (*Chi*) scandalous; dishonest.

edificar [1g] *vt* (a) (*Archit*) to build, construct. (b) (*fig*) to edify; to improve; to uplift, ennoble.

edificio *nm* building; edifice; (*fig*) edifice, structure.

Edimburgo Edinburgh.

Edipo *m* Oedipus.

editar [1a] *vt* (a) to publish. (b) to edit, correct.

editor 1 *adj* publishing (*attr*); **casa editora** publishing house. **2** *nm* (a) publisher. (b) editor, corrector. (c) (*SAm: angl*) newspaper editor.

editorial 1 *adj* (a) publishing (*attr*); **casa —** publishing house. (b) *function, policy etc* editorial. **2** *nm* leading article, editorial. **3** *nf* publishing house.

editorialista *nm* leader-writer.

edredón *nm* eiderdown; feather pillow.

eduardiano *adj* Edwardian.

Eduardo *m* Edward.

educable *adj* educable, teachable.

educación *nf* (a) education; training; upbringing; — **física** physical education; — **de la voz** elocution lessons; **Ministro de E— Nacional** Minister of Education.

(b) (good) manners, (good) breeding; politeness, civility; **mala —** bad manners, incivility; **es de mala — escupir** it's bad manners to spit, it's ill-mannered to spit; **es de mala — comportarse así** it's rude to behave like that; **es una persona sin —** he's a badly-bred person, he's an ill-mannered

individual; **¡qué falta de —!** how rude!; **¡habla con más —!** don't be so rude!, be more civil!; **no tener —** to lack breeding, lack good manners.

educacional *adj* educational.

educacionista *nmf* education(al)ist.

educado *adj* well-mannered, polite; nicely behaved; cultivated, cultured; **mal —** ill-mannered, unmannerly; rude.

educador *nm*, **educadora** *nf* educator, teacher.

educando *nm*, **educanda** *nf* pupil.

educar [1g] *vt* to educate; to train; to raise, bring up; *voice* to train.

educativo *adj* educative.

educción *nf* (a) deduction, inference. (b) (*Tech*) exhaust.

edulcoración *nf* (*Pharm*) sweetening.

edulcorado *adj* (*fig*) *person* sweet, charming.

edulcorar [1a] *vt* (*Pharm*) to sweeten.

efectismo *nm* straining after effect; sensationalism.

efectista 1 *adj* strained; sensational. **2** *nmf* strainer after effect; sensationalist.

efectivamente *adv* really; in fact; (*as reply*) exactly, precisely, just so; sure enough.

efectivo 1 *adj* (a) effective; **hacer algo —** to make something effective, carry something out; to put something into effect; **hacer — un cheque** to cash a cheque.

(b) actual, real; **el poder — está en manos de X** the real power is in X's hands.

(c) *employment* regular, permanent.

2 *nm* (a) cash; specie; **con 50 libras en —** with £50 in cash; **y 3 premios en — and 3 cash prizes; — en caja, — en existencia** cash in hand.

(b) —**s** (*Mil etc*) forces, troops; establishment.

efecto *nm* (a) effect; —**s sonoros** sound effects; — **útil** (*Mech*) efficiency, output; **hacer — (of medicine)** to take effect; **hacer —, surtir —** to have the desired effect; to work; to tell (*en on*); (*of idea etc*) to get across, have an impact; **poner en —** to put into effect, carry out; **tener —** to take effect; (*of event etc*) to take place; **en —** in effect; in fact, really; (*as reply*) yes indeed, precisely.

(b) result; **tener por —** to have as a result (*or* consequence).

(c) purpose, end; **a este —, a tal —** to this end; **a cuyo —** to which end; **a —s de + *infin*** with a view to + *ger*, with the object of + *ger*; **construido al —** (specially) built for the purpose.

(d) effect, impression, impact; **hacer —** to make an impression.

(e) (*on ball*) spin; **dar — a una pelota** to put some spin on a ball; **lanzar una pelota con —** to throw a ball so that it spins (*or* swerves).

(f) —**s** (*Fin*) bills, securities; —**s a cobrar** bills receivable; —**s a pagar** bills payable.

(g) —**s** effects, goods; things; (*Fin*) assets; (*Comm*) goods, articles, merchandise; —**s de consumo** consumer goods; —**s de escritorio** writing materials.

efectuación *nf* accomplishment; bringing about.

efectuar [1e] *vt* to effect, carry out, bring about; *plan, repair* to carry out; *recovery, tour, visit, stop, trick* (*Cards*) etc to make; *census* to take.

efervescencia *nf* (a) effervescence; fizziness; **entrar en —, estar en —** to effervesce. (b) (*fig*) commotion, agitation; high spirits, effervescence.

efervescente *adj* (a) effervescent; fizzy, bubbly. (b) (*fig*) effervescent; high-spirited, bubbling.

eficacia *nf* (a) efficacy, effectiveness. (b) efficiency.

eficaz *adj* (a) efficacious, effective; telling. (b) efficient.

eficazmente *adv* (a) efficaciously, effectively; tellingly. (b) efficiently.

eficiencia *nf* efficiency.

eficiente *adj* efficient.

eficientemente *adv* efficiently.

efigie *nf* effigy; **quemar a uno en —** to burn someone in effigy.

efímera *nf* mayfly.

efímero *adj* ephemeral, fleeting, short-lived.

eflorescente *adj* efflorescent.

efluente *adj* effluent.

efugio *nm* subterfuge, evasion.

efusión *nf* (a) outpouring; shedding; — **de sangre** bloodshed, shedding of blood.

(b) (*fig*) effusion, outpouring; warmth, effusiveness; (*pej*) gush, gushing manner; **con —** effusively.

efusivo *adj* effusive; *thanks* effusive, warm; *manner* effusive, (*pej*) gushing; **mis más efusivas gracias** my warmest thanks.

Egeo: Mar *m* **— Aegean Sea.**

égida *nf* (a) aegis, protection; **bajo la — de** under the aegis of. **(b)** rule, domination; **bajo la — de Stalin** under Stalin's rule.

egipcio 1 *adj* Egyptian. 2 *nm*, **egipcia** *nf* Egyptian. **Egipto** *m* Egypt.

egiptología *nf* Egyptology.

eglantina *nf* eglantine.

eglefino *nm* haddock.

égloga *nf* eclogue.

egocéntrico *adj* egocentric(al), self-centred.

egoísmo *nm* egoism; selfishness.

egoísta 1 *adj* egoistical; selfish. 2 *nmf* egoist, selfish person.

egolatría *nf* self-worship.

egotismo *nm* egotism.

egotista 1 *adj* egotistic(al). 2 *nmf* egotist.

egregio *adj* eminent, distinguished.

egresado *nm*, **egresada** *nf* (*SAm*) graduate.

egresar [1a] *vi* (*SAm*) **(a)** to go out, go away, leave; **— de** to go away from, leave; to emerge from. **(b)** (*Univ*) to graduate, take one's degree.

egreso *nm* (*SAm*) **(a)** departure, leaving, going away. **(b)** (*Univ*) graduation.

eh *interj* hey!, hi!; I say!

eider *nm* eider, eider duck.

Eire *m* Eire.

eje *nm* **(a)** (*Geog*, *Math*) axis; **partir a uno por el —** (*fam*) to muck up someone's plans; to do someone a mischief.
   (b) (*Mech: of wheel*) axle; **— delantero** front axle; **— trasero** rear axle; **untar el —** (*fam*) to grease someone's palm.
   (c) (*Mech: of machine*) shaft, spindle; **— de balancín** rocker shaft; **— del cigüeñal** crankshaft; **— de la hélice** propeller shaft; **— de impulsión**, **— motor** drive shaft.
   (d) (*Pol*) axis; **las fuerzas del E—** the Axis forces.
   (e) (*fig*) hinge, hub; essential part, crux, core; central idea, main idea.

ejecución *nf* **(a)** execution, performance, carrying out; fulfilment; enforcement; **poner en —** to carry out, carry into effect.
   (b) (*Law*) attachment, distraint.
   (c) (*Mus*) performance, rendition.
   (d) (*killing*) execution.

ejecutable *adj* feasible, practicable.

ejecutante *nmf* (*Mus*) performer.

ejecutar [1a] *vt* **(a)** *order etc* to execute, carry out; *wishes* to perform, fulfil; *deed* to execute.
   (b) (*Law*) to attach, distrain on.
   (c) (*Mus*) to perform, render, play.
   (d) (*kill*) to execute.

ejecutivo 1 *adj* **(a)** *function, power* executive.
   (b) *demand etc* pressing, insistent; *response* prompt.
   2 *nm* **(a)** (*Pol*) executive.
   (b) (*SAm: Comm*) board member, executive (*US*).

ejecutor *nm* (*also* **— testamentario**) executor.

ejecutoria *nf* **(a)** letters patent of nobility; (*fig*) pedigree. **(b)** (*Law*) final judgement.

ejem *interj* hem!

ejemplar 1 *adj* exemplary; model.
   2 *nm* **(a)** example; (*Zool etc*) specimen, example; (*of book*) copy; (*of journal*) number, issue; **— gratuito**, **— de regalo** complimentary copy, free copy.
   (b) example, model, precedent; **sin —** unprecedented.

ejemplaridad *nf* exemplariness.

ejemplarizador *adj* (*SAm*) exemplary.

ejemplarizar [1f] *vt* (*esp SAm*) to set an example to; to exemplify, demonstrate by example, set an example of.

ejemplificar [1g] *vt* to exemplify, illustrate, be illustrative of.

ejemplo *nm* example, instance; object lesson; precedent, parallel; **por —** for example, for instance; **sin —** unprecedented, unparalleled; **dar —** to set an example; **tomar algo por —** to take something as an example.

ejercer [2b] 1 *vt* to exercise; *influence* to exert, use, bring to bear; *power* to exercise, wield; *profession* to practise; *business etc* to manage, conduct, run; *functions* to perform.
   2 *vi* to practise (*de* as); to be in office, hold office.

ejercicio *nm* **(a)** exercise; practice; drill; (*Mil*) exercise, drill, training; **— acrobático** (*Aer*) stunt; **— antiaéreo** air-raid drill; **— de castigo** (*School*) imposition; **— de defensa contra incendios** fire drill; **—s gimnásticos** gymnastic exercises; **hacer —s** to do exercises; to take exercise; (*Mil*) to drill, train.
   (b) (*of office*) tenure.
   (c) (*Comm, Fin*) fiscal year; financial year;

business year; **durante el — actual** during the current financial year.

ejercitar [1a] 1 *vt* to exercise; *profession* to practise; *troops* to drill, train. 2 **ejercitarse** *vr* to exercise; to practise; (*Mil*) to drill, train.

ejército *nm* army; **— de ocupación** army of occupation; **— permanente** standing army; **E— de Salvación** Salvation Army; **estar en el —** to be in the army.

ejido *nm* common.

—ejo, —eja *n and adj suffix* (*pej*), eg **animalejo** odd-looking creature, nasty animal; **caballejo** old horse, poor horse, nag; **discursejo** tedious speech, rotten speech; **palabreja** strange word; nasty-sounding word.

ejote *nm* (*CAm*, *Mex*) string bean.

el[1] *def art m*, **la** *f* the; *not translated in such cases as* **La India** India; **en el México de hoy** in present-day Mexico; **me gusta el fútbol** I like football; **está en la cárcel** he's in jail; **el General Prim** General Prim; **¿qué manda la señora?** what would madam like?; **a las ocho** at eight o'clock; **a los quince días** after a fortnight.

el[2] *dem pron*; **mi libro y — de Vd** my book and yours; **este jugador y — de la camisa azul** this player and the one in the blue shirt; **— de Pepe es mejor** Joe's is better; **y — de todos los demás** and that of everybody else, and everybody else's.

el[3]: **— que** *rel pron* (*also* **la que, los que, las que**) he who, whoever; the one(s) that; **el que quiera, que lo haga** whoever wants to can get on with it; **los que hacen eso son tontos** those who do so are foolish; **el que compramos no vale** the one we bought is no good; **a los que mencionamos añádase éste** add this one to the ones we mentioned.

él *pers pron m* **(a)** (*subject: person*) he, (*thing*) it.
   (b) (*after prep: person*) him, (*thing*) it; **esto es para —** this is for him; **vamos sin —** let's go without him.
   (c) (*after de: person*) his, (*thing*) its; **mis libros y los de —** my books and his; **todo eso es de él** all that is his, all that belongs to him.

elaboración *nf* elaboration; manufacture, production; working; working-out.

elaborar [1a] *vt* to elaborate; to make, manufacture, produce; to prepare; *metal, wood etc* to work; *plan etc* to work on, work out.

elación *nf* **(a)** haughtiness, pride. **(b)** generosity. **(c)** (*of style*) pomposity. **(d)** (*SAm: angl*) elation.

elasticidad *nf* **(a)** elasticity; spring, sponginess; give. **(b)** (*fig*) elasticity; (*moral*) resilience.

elástico 1 *adj* **(a)** elastic; flexible; *surface etc* springy. **(b)** (*fig*) elastic; (*morally*) resilient. 2 *nm* elastic.

elección *nf* **(a)** choice, selection; option; **una — acertada** a sensible choice; **su patria de —** his chosen country.
   (b) (*Pol etc*) election (*a* for); **— complementaria**, **—es parciales** by-election; **—es generales** general election.

eleccionario *adj* (*SAm*) electoral, election (*attr*).

electivo *adj* elective.

electo *adj* elect; **el presidente —** the president-elect.

elector *nm*, **electora** *nf* elector; voter.

electorado *nm* electorate; voters.

electoral *adj* electoral; **potencia —** voting power, power in terms of votes.

electricidad *nf* electricity; **— estática** static electricity.

electricista *nm* electrician.

eléctrico *adj* electric(al).

electrificación *nf* electrification.

electrificar [1g] *vt* to electrify.

electrizante *adj* (*fig*) electrifying.

electrizar [1f] *vt* to electrify (*also fig*).

electro . . . . electro . . .

electrocardiograma *nm* electrocardiogram.

electrocución *nf* electrocution.

electrocutar [1a] *vt* to electrocute.

electrochapado *adj* electroplated.

electrodinámica *nf* electrodynamics.

electrodo *nm* electrode.

electroimán *nm* electromagnet.

electrólisis *nf* electrolysis.

electromagnético *adj* electromagnetic.

electromotor *nm* electric motor.

electrón *nm* electron.

electrónica *nf* electronics.

electrónico *adj* electronic; electron (*attr*).

electrotecnia *nf* electrical engineering.

electrotermo *nm* immersion heater.

elefante *nm*, **elefanta** *nf* elephant; **— blanco** (*SAm: angl*) white elephant.

elefantino *adj* elephantine.

elegancia *nf* elegance; gracefulness; stylishness, smartness; tastefulness; polish.

elegante *adj* elegant; graceful; *dress, party, shop etc* stylish, fashionable, smart; *society* fashionable, elegant; *decoration etc* tasteful; *phrase etc* elegant, well-turned, polished; **no es — escupir** it's rude to spit, it's not nice to spit.

elegantemente *adv* elegantly; gracefully; stylishly, fashionably, smartly; tastefully; in a polished way.

elegantoso *adj* (*SAm*)=**elegante**.

elegía *nf* elegy.

elegíaco *adj* elegiac.

elegibilidad *nf* eligibility.

elegible *adj* eligible.

elegido *adj* (a) chosen, selected. (b) (*Pol etc*) elect, elected.

elegir [3c *and* 3l] *vt* (a) to choose, select; to opt for; **café con bizcochos a —** coffee with a choice of cakes; **a — entre 5 tipos** there are 5 sorts to choose from; **hablará en francés o italiano, a —** he will talk in French or Italian, as you (*etc*) prefer; **le toca a Vd —** the choice is yours, it's up to you to choose.
(b) (*Pol etc*) to elect.

elementado *adj* (*Col, Chi*) bewildered; silly, stupid.

elemental *adj* elementary; elemental; **eso es —** that's elementary.

elementarse [1a] *vr* (*Chi*) to get bewildered.

elemento *nm* (a) element; **los cuatro —s** the four elements; **estar en su —** to be in one's element.
(b) (*Chem etc*) element; (*fig*) ingredient, constituent (part); (*in situation*) element, factor; **—s material,** ingredients.
(c) (*Elec*) element; (*of battery*) cell.
(d) (*SAm*) person, individual; **vino a verle un —** someone came to see you; **dos —s distinguidos** two distinguished individuals.
(e) (*Chi, Per, PR, SD*) dimwit (*fam*), ass.
(f) (*PR, SD*) odd person, eccentric.
(g) (*Spain: pej*) undesirable person, suspicious individual.
(h) **—s** (*of a subject*) elements, rudiments, first principles.

Elena *f* Helen.

elenco *nm* catalogue, list; (*Theat: esp SAm*) cast.

elevación *nf* (a) (*act*) elevation (*a* to), raising, lifting; (*Eccl*) elevation; (*in price, rate etc*) rise.
(b) (*Geog etc*) elevation, height, altitude.
(c) (*of mind, style etc*) elevation; (*of person*) exaltation, loftiness; (*pej*) conceit, pride.
(d) rapture.

elevadamente *adv* loftily, sublimely.

elevado **1** *adj* (a) elevated, raised; high, lofty; *building* high, tall; *price, rate etc* high; *post* exalted, high; **a precios elevadísimos** at terribly high prices.
(b) *thought, style etc* elevated, lofty, noble; grand, sublime; **de pensamientos —s** of noble thoughts, high-minded.
2 *nm* (*Cu*) overhead railway.

elevador *nm* elevator, hoist; (*SAm*) lift, elevator (*US*); **— de granos** (grain) elevator.

elevar [1a] **1** *vt* (a) to raise, lift (up), elevate; *price, rate* to raise, put up; *production* to step up; (*Elec*) to boost; (*Math*) to raise (*a una potencia* to a power); *person* to promote; to exalt; *style* to raise the tone of; **— los pensamientos a Dios** to raise one's thoughts to God.
(b) *report etc* to present, submit (*a* to); **el comité elevará un informe al ministro** the committee will report to the minister.
2 elevarse *vr* (a) to rise, go up; (*of building etc*) to rise, soar, tower; **la cantidad se eleva a . . .** the quantity amounts to . . .; **los precios se han elevado mucho** prices have risen a lot.
(b) to be transported, go into a rapture.
(c) (*pej*) to get conceited, become overbearing.

elidir [3a] **1** *vt* to elide. **2 elidirse** *vr* to elide, be elided.

eliminación *nf* elimination; removal; **— progresiva** (*Sport*) knockout.

eliminar [1a] **1** *vt* to eliminate; to remove; *need etc* to remove, obviate; *waste products* to get rid of; (*Sport*) to eliminate, knock out.
2 eliminarse *vr* (*Mex*) to go away.

eliminatoria *nf* (*Sport*) heat, preliminary round, qualifying round; knockout competition.

elipse *nf* ellipse.

elipsis *nf, pl* elipsis ellipsis.

elíptico *adj* elliptic(al).

Eliseo *m* Elysium.

elisión *nf* elision.

elite [e'lite] *nf* (*gall*) élite.

elixir *nm* elixir.

elocución *nf* elocution.

elocuencia *nf* eloquence.

elocuente *adj* eloquent; (*fig*) telling; significant; **un dato —** a significant fact, a fact which speaks for itself.

elocuentemente *adv* eloquently.

elogiable *adj* praiseworthy.

elogiar [1b] *vt* to praise, eulogize.

elogio *nm* praise, eulogy; tribute; **queda por encima de todo —** it's beyond praise; **hacer — de** to praise, extol; **to pay (a) tribute to; hizo un caluroso — del héroe** he paid a warm tribute to the hero, he was warm in his praise of the hero.

elogiosamente *adv* eulogistically; very favourably, with warm approval; **comentó — sus cualidades** he spoke very favourably of his qualities.

elogioso *adj* eulogistic; highly favourable, warmly approving; **en términos —s** in highly favourable terms.

elotada *nf* (*CAm, Mex*) (a) ears of green maize (collectively). (b) meal at which elotes are eaten.

elote *nm* (*CAm, Mex*) ear of green maize; sweet corn; **coger a uno asando —s** to catch someone red-handed.

elotear [1a] *vi* (*CAm, Mex: of maize*) to come into ear.

elucidación *nf* elucidation.

elucidar [1a] *vt* to elucidate.

eludible *adj* avoidable.

eludir [3a] *vt* to elude, evade, avoid, escape.

elusivo *adj* (*SAm*) evasive, tricky.

ella *pers pron f* (a) (*subject: person*) she, (*thing*) it.
(b) (*after prep: person*) she, (*thing*) it; **estuve con —** I was with her; **no podemos sin —** without her we can't.
(c) (*after de: person*) hers, (*thing*) its; **mi sombrero y el de —** my hat and hers; **nada de esto es de —** none of this is hers, none of this belongs to her.

ellas see **ellos**.

ello "*neuter*" *pron* (a) it; this business, that whole affair; **— es difícil** it's awkward; **— no me gusta** I don't like it; **todo — se acabó** the whole thing is over and done with; **no tiene fuerzas para —** he is not strong enough for it.
(b) (*idioms*) **— es que . . .** the fact is that . . .; **por — no quiero** that's why I don't want to; **es por — que . . .** (*SAm*) that is why . . .; **luego será —** there'll be trouble later; **— dirá** the event will show; **¡a por —!** here goes!; **¡aquí fue —!** and then it started, and that was it.

ellos *pers pron mpl*, **ellas** *pers pron fpl* (a) (*subject*) they. (b) (*after prep*) them. (c) (*after de*) theirs; *see* **él, ella** *for usage examples.*

emanación *nf* emanation; smell, effluvium.

emanar [1a] *vi:* **— de** to emanate from, come from, originate in.

emancipación *nf* emancipation; freeing.

emancipado *adj* emancipated; independent, free.

emancipar [1a] **1** *vt* to emancipate; to free.
2 emanciparse *vr* to become emancipated (*de* from); to become independent (*de* of); to free oneself (*de* from).

emascular [1a] *vt* to castrate; (*fig*) to emasculate.

embadurnar [1a] *vt* to daub, bedaub, smear (*de* with).

embaidor *nm* cheat, swindler.

embaimiento *nm* imposture, trick, swindle; deceit.

embaír [3a: *defective*] *vt* to swindle, cheat.

embajada *nf* (a) embassy. (b) ambassadorship. (c) (*fig*) errand, message.

embajador *nm* ambassador (*en* in, *cerca de* to); **— itinerante** roving ambassador, ambassador at large.

embajadora *nf* (woman) ambassador; ambassador's wife.

embalador *nm*, **embaladora** *nf* packer.

embaladura *nf* (*SAm*), **embalaje** *nm* packing.

embalar [1a] **1** *vt* to pack, parcel up, wrap; *heavy goods* to crate, bale.
2 *vi* (a) (*Sport*) to sprint, make a dash; (*Aut*) to step on it.
(b) (*PR, SD*) to run off, escape.
3 embalarse *vr* (*SAm: Aut*) to coast at high speed.

embaldosado *nm* tiled floor.

embaldosar [1a] *vt* to tile, pave with tiles.

embalsadero *nm* boggy place.

embalsado *nm* (*Arg*) mass of floating water weeds.

embalsamar [1a] *vt* to embalm.

embalsar [1a] **1** *vt* (a) *water* to dam, dam up; to retain, collect; **este mes se han embalsado X m³** this month reservoir stocks have gone up by X cubic metres.
(b) (*Naut*) to sling, hoist.
2 *vi* (*Col*) to cross a river (*etc*).

embalse nm dam; reservoir.
embanastar [1a] vt to put into a basket; (fig) to jam in, overcrowd.
embancarse [1g] vr (Chi, Ec) to silt up, become blocked by silt.
embanderar [1a] vt to deck with flags; **embanderado** beflagged, decked with flags.
embarazada 1 adj pregnant; **dejar — a una** to get a girl pregnant, put a girl in the family way. **2** nf pregnant woman, expectant mother.
embarazar [1f] vt (a) to obstruct, hamper, hinder. (b) woman to make pregnant, get with child, put in the family way.
embarazo nm (a) obstacle, obstruction, hindrance. (b) pregnancy; **durante el —** during pregnancy.
embarazosamente adv awkwardly, inconveniently; embarrassingly.
embarazoso adj awkward, inconvenient, troublesome; embarrassing.
embarcación nf (a) boat, craft, (small) vessel; **— de arrastre** trawler; **— de cabotaje** coasting vessel; **— pesquera** fishing boat; **— de recreo** pleasure boat; **— de vela** sailing boat. (b) (act) embarkation.
embarcadero nm (a) pier, landing stage, jetty. (b) (SAm: Rail) goods station; loading platform; (Arg) cattle pen (attached to a railway station).
embarcar [1g] **1** vt (a) persons to embark, put on board; cargo to ship, get on board, stow. (b) (fig) **— a uno en una empresa** to launch someone on an enterprise. (c) (Arg, Mex, Per, PR) **— a uno** to persuade someone dishonestly to undertake a dubious enterprise.
2 embarcarse vr (a) to embark, go on board; (of sailor) to sign on; **— para** to sail for. (b) (SAm: Rail etc) to get on, get in; **se embarcó en el autobús** he got on the bus, he boarded the bus. (c) (fig) **— en un asunto** to get involved in a matter.
embarco nm embarcation.
embargar [1h] vt (a) to impede, hinder; to restrain, put a check on. (b) senses to blunt, confuse, paralyse, overpower. (c) (Law) to seize, impound, distrain upon.
embargo nm (a) (Law) seizure, distraint; (Comm etc) embargo; **sin —** still, however, none the less; **sin — de** notwithstanding, in spite of. (b) (Med) indigestion.
embarnizar [1f] vt to varnish.
embarque nm shipment, loading.
embarrada nf (SAm) blunder.
embarradura nf smear, daub.
embarrancar [1g] **1** vti (a) (Naut) to run aground. (b) (Aut etc) to run into a ditch.
2 embarrancarse vr (a) to run aground. (b) to run into a ditch; to get stuck.
embarrar [1a] **1** vt (a) to smear, bedaub (de with); to splash with mud. (b) (SAm) wall to cover with mud; to plaster. (c) (CAm, Mex) **— a uno** to involve someone in a shady affair. (d) (Cu, Chi, PR, RPl) **— a uno** to smear someone, damage someone's standing.
2 embarrarse vr (Ven: of child) to dirty oneself.
embarrialarse [1a] vr (a) (CAm, Ven) to get covered with mud. (b) (CAm: Aut) to get stuck.
embarullador adj bungling.
embarullar [1a] vt to bungle, mess up.
embastar [1a] vt to stitch, tack.
embaste nm stitching, tacking.
embate nm (a) (Mil etc) sudden attack; brunt of the attack. (b) (of waves) dashing, breaking, beating; violence. (c) (fig) **—s de la fortuna** blows of fate.
embaucador nm, **embaucadora** nf trickster, swindler; impostor; humbug.
embaucamiento nm swindle, swindling; humbug.
embaucar [1g] vt to trick, swindle; to fool, lead up the garden path.
embaular vt (a) to pack (into a trunk). (b) (fam) food to tuck away (fam), stuff oneself with.
embazar [1f] **1** vt (a) to dye brown. (b) (fig) to astound, amaze. (c) (fig) to hinder.
2 vi to be dumbfounded, stand amazed.
3 embazarse vr to get tired, get bored; to have had enough.
embebecer [2d] **1** vt to entertain, amuse; to fascinate.
2 embebecerse vr to be fascinated, be lost in wonder; to be dumbfounded.
embebecimiento nm (a) absorption, fascination; enchantment. (b) astonishment, wonderment.

embeber [2a] **1** vt (a) to absorb, soak up; to saturate. (b) (Sew) to take in, gather in. (c) (fig) to imbibe; to insert, introduce (en into); to contain, incorporate, comprise.
2 vi (of cloth) to shrink.
3 embeberse vr (a) to be absorbed, become engrossed (en in), to be enraptured, be enchanted (en with). (b) **— de** to imbibe, soak oneself in, become well versed in.
embelecar [1g] vt to deceive, cheat.
embeleco nm, **embelequería** nf (Col, Chi, PR) deceit, fraud.
embelequero adj (a) (SAm) given to making a great fuss, highly emotional. (b) (Col, Cu, PR) shifty.
embelesado adj spellbound, enraptured.
embelesador adj enchanting, entrancing.
embelesar [1a] **1** vt to enchant, entrance, enrapture.
2 embelesarse vr to be enchanted, be enraptured.
embeleso nm (a) enchantment, rapture, delight. (b) (endearment) sweetheart, my love.
embellecedor nm (Aut) hub cap.
embellecer [2d] vt to embellish, beautify.
embellecimiento nm embellishment.
embestida nf (a) assault, onrush, onslaught; (of bull etc) charge, rush. (b) (fig) importunate demand.
embestir [3l] **1** vt (a) to assault, attack, assail; to rush at (or upon); (of bull etc) to charge. (b) (fig) **— a uno** to pester someone for a loan.
2 vi to attack; to rush, charge; **— con, — contra** to rush upon; (of bull etc) to charge down on.
embetunar [1a] vt to impregnate with pitch; shoes to black.
embicar [1g] vt (a) (Chi, RPl) boat to head straight for land. (b) (Cu) to insert. (c) (Mex) to turn upside down, upturn.
embicharse [1a] vr (Arg) to become wormy; (Bot) to get maggoty.
embiste nm (Ven) =**embestida**.
emblandecer [2d] **1** vt to soften; (fig) to mollify. **2 emblandecerse** vr to soften, get soft; (fig) to relent.
emblanquecer [2d] **1** vt to whiten; to bleach. **2 emblanquecerse** vr to whiten, turn white; to bleach.
emblema nm emblem.
emblemático adj emblematic.
embobamiento nm amazement; fascination.
embobar [1a] **1** vt to amuse, entertain; to amaze; to fascinate; **esa niña me emboba** that girl is driving me crazy.
2 embobarse vr to be amazed, stand agape (con, de, en at); to be fascinated (con, de, en by); **reírse embobado** to laugh like mad.
embobecer [2d] **1** vt to make silly.
2 embobecerse vr to get silly.
embocadura nf (a) narrow entrance; (of river) mouth; (Naut) passage, narrows. (b) (Mus) mouthpiece; (of cigarette etc) tip; (of bridle) bit. (c) (of wine) taste, flavour. (d) (Theat) proscenium arch.
embocar [1g] vt (a) **— algo** to put something into someone's mouth; **— una cosa en un agujero** to insert something into a hole; **— la comida** to cram one's food, wolf one's food. (b) **— un negocio** to undertake a piece of business. (c) **— algo a uno** (fig) to put one over on someone, hoax someone with something.
embochinchar [1a] vt (SAm) to throw into confusion, create chaos in.
embolado nm (a) bull with wooden balls on its horns. (b) (Theat) bit part, minor role. (c) (fam) trick.
embolador nm (SAm) bootblack.
embolar [1a] **1** vt (a) bull's horns to tip with wooden balls. (b) (SAm) shoes to black, shine. (c) (CAm, Mex) to make drunk.
embolia nf (Med) clot; embolism; **— cerebral** clot on the brain.
embolismar [1a] vt to gossip about; to make mischief for.
embolismo nm (a) muddle, mess, confusion. (b) gossip. (c) hoax, trick.
émbolo nm plunger; (Mech) piston.
embolsar [1a] vt, **embolsicar** [1g] vt (SAm) to pocket, put into one's pocket; money, proceeds etc to pocket, collect, take in.
embonar [1a] vt (a) (Cu, Chi, Mex) land to manure. (b) (fig) to improve. (c) (Naut) to sheathe; (Ec, Mex) to join (the ends of). (d) (Cu, Ec, Mex) **le embona el sombrero** the hat suits him, the hat looks well on him.

emboque *nm* (*fam*) trick, hoax.
emboquillado *adj* cigarette tipped.
emboquillar [1a] *vt* (**a**) *cigarette* to tip. (**b**) (*Arg, Chi: Archit*) to point, repoint.
emborrachar [1a] **1** *vt* to intoxicate, make drunk; to get drunk. **2 emborracharse** *vr* to get drunk (*con, de* on).
emborrar [1a] *vt* (**a**) to stuff, pad, wad (*de* with). (**b**) (*fam*) *food* to cram, wolf.
emborrascarse [1g] *vr* (**a**) to get stormy. (**b**) (*fig*) to get cross, get worked up. (**c**) (*Comm: of business*) to fail. (**d**) (*Arg, Hond, Mex: of lode*) to peter out.
emborronar [1a] **1** *vt* to blot, make blots on; to scribble on. **2** *vi* to make blots; to scribble.
emboscada *nf* ambush; **tender una — a** to lay an ambush for.
emboscarse [1g] *vr* to lie in ambush; to hide away (in the woods); **estaban emboscados cerca del camino** they were in ambush near the road.
embotado *adj* dull, blunt (*also fig*).
embotamiento *nm* (**a**) (*act*) dulling, blunting (*also fig*). (**b**) (*state*) dullness, bluntness (*also fig*).
embotar [1a] *vt* (**a**) to dull, blunt. (**b**) (*fig*) to dull, blunt; to weaken, enervate.
embotellado 1 *adj* bottled; *speech etc* prepared (beforehand). **2** *nm* bottling.
embotellador *nm* bottler.
embotellamiento *nm* (**a**) (*Aut*) traffic jam. (**b**) (*place*) bottleneck (*also fig*).
embotellar [1a] **1** *vt* (**a**) to bottle. (**b**) (*Mil etc*) to bottle up. (**c**) (*Ant*) *speech* to prepare beforehand, memorize. **2 embotellarse** *vr* (**a**) (*Aut*) to get into a jam, get jammed. (**b**) (*Ant*) to learn a speech off by heart.
emboticarse [1g] *vr* (*Chi, Mex*) to stuff oneself with medicines.
embotijar [1a] **1** *vt* to put into jars; to keep in jars. **2 embotijarse** *vr* (*fig*) to fly into a passion.
embovedar [1a] *vt* to arch, vault.
embozadamente *adv* covertly, stealthily.
embozado *adj* (**a**) muffled up (to the eyes). (**b**) (*fig*) covert, stealthy.
embozalar [1a] *vt* (*Arg*) to muzzle.
embozar [1f] **1** *vt* (**a**) to muffle (up), wrap (up). (**b**) (*fig*) to cloak, disguise, conceal. **2 embozarse** *vr* to muffle oneself up (*con, de* in).
embozo *nm* (**a**) muffler; mask, covering of the face; **quitarse el — (***fig***)** to drop the mask, end the playacting. (**b**) turned-down bedclothes. (**c**) (*fig*) cunning; concealment; **sin —** frankly, openly.
embragar [1h] **1** *vt* (*Aut, Mech*) to engage; *parts to* connect, couple; (*Naut*) to sling. **2** *vi* (*Aut etc*) to put the clutch in.
embrague *nm* (*Aut, Mech*) clutch.
embravecer [2d] **1** *vt* to enrage, infuriate. **2** *vi* (*Bot*) to flourish, grow strongly. **3 embravecerse** *vr* (**a**) (*of sea*) to get rough. (**b**) (*of person*) to get furious.
embravecido *adj* (**a**) *sea* rough; *wind etc* wild. (**b**) *person* furious, enraged.
embravecimiento *nm* rage, fury.
embrear [1a] *vt* to tar, cover with tar; to cover with pitch; **— y emplumar a uno** to tar and feather someone.
embretar [1a] *vt* (*SAm*) *animals* to pen, corral.
embriagador *adj* intoxicating; *wine etc* heady, strong.
embriagar [1h] **1** *vt* (**a**) to make drunk, intoxicate; to get drunk. (**b**) (*fig*) to enrapture, delight. **2 †embriagarse** *vr* to get drunk.
embriaguez *nf* (**a**) drunkenness, intoxication. (**b**) (*fig*) rapture, delight.
embridar [1a] *vt* (**a**) to bridle, put a bridle on. (**b**) (*fig*) to check, restrain.
embrión *nm* embryo; **en —** in embryo.
embrionario *adj* embryonic.
embrocación *nf* embrocation.
embrocar [1g] **1** *vt* (**a**) (*Sew*) *thread* to wind (on to a bobbin); *shoes* to tack. (**b**) *liquid* to pour from one container into another. (**c**) to turn upside down, invert. **2 embrocarse** *vr* (*Mex*): **— un vestido** to put a dress on over one's head.
embrollar [1a] **1** *vt matter* to muddle, confuse, complicate; to mess up; *persons* to involve, embroil (*en* in.) **2 embrollarse** *vr* to get into a muddle, get into a mess; **— en un asunto** to get involved in a matter.

embrollista *nm* (*Chi, Guat, Per*) = **embrollón**.
embrollo *nm* muddle, tangle, confusion; fix, jam, entanglement; (*pej*) fraud, trick.
embrollón *nm*, **embrollona** *nf* troublemaker, mischief-maker.
embromado *adj* (*SAm*): **estar — to be in a fix**; to be having a tough time; (*Med*) to be in a bad way; (*Fin*) to be in financial trouble.
embromar [1a] **1** *vt* (**a**) to tease, make fun of, rag. (**b**) to wheedle, cajole. (**c**) to hoodwink. (**d**) (*SAm*) to annoy, vex; to harm, set back (*in health etc*), affect badly. **2 embromarse** *vr* (*SAm*) to get cross; to get bored.
embrujado *adj person* bewitched; *house, place* haunted; **una casa embrujada** a haunted house.
embrujar [1a] *vt person* to bewitch, put a spell on; *house, place* to haunt; **la casa está embrujada** the house is haunted.
embrutecer [2d] **1** *vt* to brutalize, deprave; to coarsen. **2 embrutecerse** *vr* to become brutalized, get depraved; to coarsen.
embuchacarse [1g] *vr* (*CAm, Mex*): **— algo** to pocket something; (*fig*) to pocket something, appropriate something.
embuchado *nm* (**a**) (*Cook*) sausage. (**b**) (*fam*) pretext, blind.
embuchar [1a] *vt* (**a**) (*Cook*) to stuff with minced meat. (**b**) (*fam*) *food* to wolf, bolt.
embudar [1a] *vt* (**a**) (*Tech*) to fit with a funnel, put a funnel into. (**b**) (*fig*) to trick.
embudo *nm* (**a**) funnel; (*Col, Mex*) hopper. (**b**) (*fig*) trick, fraud.
embullar [1a] (*CAm, Col, Cu, PR, Ven*) **1** *vt* (**a**) to excite, disturb. (**b**) *enemy* to put to flight. **2 embullarse** *vr* (**a**) to get excited, get worked up; to become tense. (**b**) to revel, have a good time.
embullo *nm* (*Ant, CAm*) noise, excitement, bustle; revelry.
emburujar [1a] **1** *vt* (**a**) to jumble together, jumble up; to pile up; *thread etc* to tangle up. (**b**) (*Col*) to bewilder. **2 emburujarse** *vr* (*Col, Mex, PR, Ven*) to wrap oneself up.
emburujo *nm* (*Ant*) ruse, trick.
embuste *nm* (**a**) trick, fraud, imposture; lie, (*hum*) fib, story. (**b**) **—s** trinkets.
embustería *nf* trickery, deceit; lying.
embustero 1 *adj* (**a**) deceitful, rascally. (**b**) (*Chi*) **persona embustera** person who cannot spell properly. (**c**) (*Guat*) haughty. **2** *nm*, **embustera** *nf* cheat; impostor; liar, (*hum*) fibber, storyteller; hypocrite; **¡—!** (*affectionately*) you rascal!
embutido *nm* (**a**) (*Cook*) sausage. (**b**) (*Tech*) inlay, inlaid work, marquetry. (**c**) (*Mex, RPl, Ven*) strip of lace.
embutir [3a] **1** *vt* (**a**) to insert (*en* into); to pack tight, stuff, cram (*de* with, *en* into); (*fam*) *food* to cram, scoff (*fam*); **— algo a uno** to make someone swallow something; **ella estuvo embutida en un vestido apretadísimo** she had been poured into a terribly close-fitting dress. (**b**) (*Tech*) to inlay; *metal* to hammer, work. **2 embutirse** *vr* (*fam*) to stuff oneself (*de* with).
emergencia *nf* (**a**) emergence; appearance. (**b**) emergency; **de —** emergency (*attr*).
emergente *adj* (**a**) resultant, consequent. (**b**) *nation* emergent.
emerger [2c] *vi* to emerge; to appear; (*of submarine*) to surface.
emeritense 1 *adj* of Mérida. **2** *nmf* native (*or* inhabitant) of Mérida; **los —s** the people of Mérida.
emérito *adj* emeritus, retired.
emético 1 *adj* emetic. **2** *nm* emetic.
emigración *nf* emigration; migration.
emigrado *nm*, **emigrada** *nf* emigrant; (*Pol etc*) emigré(e).
emigrante 1 *adj* emigrant. **2** *nmf* emigrant.
emigrar [1a] *vi* to emigrate; to migrate.
Emilia *f* Emily.
emilianense *adj* of San Millán de la Cogolla (*Riojan monastery*).
eminencia *nf* (**a**) (*Geog*) height, eminence; loftiness. (**b**) (*fig*) eminence; prominence. (**c**) (*in titles*) **Su E— His Eminence**; **Vuestra E— Your Eminence**.
eminente *adj* (**a**) high, lofty. (**b**) (*fig*) eminent, distinguished; prominent.

eminentemente *adv* eminently, especially.
emir *nm* emir.
emisario *nm* emissary.
emisión *nf* (a) emission; (*Fin etc*) issue.
(b) (*Radio, TV*) broadcasting; broadcast, programme; — **deportiva** sports programme; — **publicitaria** commercial, advertising spot.
emisor *nm* transmitter; — **de radar** radar station.
emisora *nf* radio station; broadcasting station; — **de onda corta** shortwave radio station.
emisor-receptor *nm* walkie-talkie, transmitting and receiving set, transceiver.
emitir [3a] *vt* (a) *sound, smell etc* to emit, give off, give out.
(b) *money, stamps, bonds etc* to issue; *forged money* to utter; *loan* to float, launch.
(c) *opinion* to express; *vote* to give, cast.
(d) (*Radio, TV*) to broadcast; *signal* to send out.
emoción *nf* (a) emotion; feeling; **sentir una honda** — to feel a deep emotion; **nos comunica una — de nostalgia** it gives us a nostalgic feeling.
(b) excitement; thrill; tension, suspense; **¡qué —!** how exciting!; **al abrirlo sentí gran** — I felt very excited on opening it; **la — de la película no disminuye** the excitement (*or* tension) of the film does not flag.
emocionado *adj* deeply moved, deeply stirred.
emocional *adj* emotional.
emocionante *adj* exciting, thrilling; touching, moving; stirring.
emocionar [1a] **1** *vt* to excite, thrill; to touch, move; to stir.
2 emocionarse *vr* to get excited, be thrilled; to be moved; to be stirred; **¡no te emociones tanto!** don't get so excited!, don't get so worked up!
emolumento *nm* emolument.
emotivo *adj* emotive.
empacada *nf* (*SAm*) (a) balk, shy. (b) (*fig*) obstinacy.
empacadizo *adj* (*Arg*) easily packed.
empacadora *nf* (*Agr*) baler, baling machine.
empacar [1g] **1** *vt* (a) to bale, crate, pack up; (*Agr*) to bale. (b) (*Mex, Per*) to package.
2 empacarse *vr* (a) to get rattled, get confused. (b) (*SAm: horse*) to balk, shy; (*fig*) to be obstinate, get stubborn.
empachado *adj* (a) clogged; (*Naut*) overloaded; *stomach* upset, uncomfortable. (b) embarrassed. (c) awkward, clumsy.
empachar [1a] **1** *vt* (a) to stop up, clog; (*Naut*) to overload; (*Med*) *stomach* to upset, make uncomfortable; *person* to give indigestion to.
(b) to impede, hinder; to embarrass.
2 empacharse *vr* (a) to get stopped up, get clogged; (*Med*) to get indigestion, have indigestion.
(b) to get embarrassed, feel awkward; to become bashful.
empacho *nm* (a) hindrance, obstacle.
(b) (*Med*) surfeited feeling, indigestion.
(c) (*fig*) embarrassment; awkwardness, awkward feeling; bashfulness; **sin** — without ceremony; unconcernedly; **no tener — en** + *infin* to have no objection to + *ger*.
empachoso *adj* (a) *food* cloying, indigestible. (b) (*fig*) embarrassing.
empadronamiento *nm* (a) census; register. (b) (*act*) census-taking; registration.
empadronar [1a] *vt* to take a census of; to register, enter on a register.
empajar [1a] *vt* to cover (*or* fill *etc*) with straw; (*Col, Chi*) to thatch.
empalagar [1h] **1** *vt* (a) *food* to pall on, surfeit, cloy. (b) (*fig*) to pall on, bore; to sicken. **2** *vi* to pall. **3 empalagarse** *vr* to get surfeited (*de* with).
empalago *nm* (a) cloying, palling. (b) boredom; disgust.
empalagoso *adj* (a) cloying; sickeningly sweet, overrich. (b) (*fig*) boring, wearisome; trying.
empalar [1a] **1** *vt* to impale. **2 empalarse** *vr* (*Chi, Per*) to dig one's heels in.
empalizada *nf* fence (*of palings*); (*Mil etc*) palisade, stockade.
empalmar [1a] **1** *vt* (a) to join, connect; *ropes* to splice. (b) (*fig*) to combine, put together.
2 *vi* (*Rail etc: of lines*) to join, meet, come together; (*of trains*) to connect (*con* with).
empalme *nm* (a) (*Tech*) joint, connection, union; splice. (b) combination. (c) (*of lines, roads*) junction; (*of trains*) connection.
empamparse [1a] *vr* (*SAm*) (a) to get lost on the pampas; to get disorientated, lose one's way. (b) to be amazed, stand agape.

empanada *nf* (a) (meat) pie, patty; (kind of) shepherd's pie. (b) fraud, piece of shady business.
empanado *adj* (*Cook*) done (*or* rolled *etc*) in breadcrumbs.
empanar [1a] *vt* (a) (*Cook*) to do (*or* roll *etc*) in breadcrumbs; to roll in pastry. (b) (*Arg*) to sow with wheat.
empantanado *adj* flooded, swampy.
empantanar [1a] **1** *vt* (a) to flood, swamp.
(b) (*fig*) to obstruct; to bog down.
2 empantanarse *vr* (a) to be flooded, get swamped.
(b) (*fig*) to be obstructed, be held up; — **en un asunto** to get bogged down in a matter.
empañado *adj* *window etc* misty, steamy, steamed-up; *outline* dim, blurred; *surface* tarnished; *voice* faint, unsteady; *honour* tarnished.
empañar [1a] **1** *vt* (a) *baby* to swaddle, wrap up.
(b) *window etc* to mist, steam up; *outline* to dim, blur; *surface, honour* to tarnish.
2 empañarse *vr* (a) to film over, get misty; to cloud over; (*voice*) to falter.
(b) (*fig*) to become sad, get gloomy.
empañetar [1a] *vt* (*SAm*) to plaster; to whitewash.
empapar [1a] **1** *vt* (a) to soak, saturate, drench; to steep (*also fig*; *de, en* in).
(b) to soak up, absorb.
2 empaparse *vr* (a) to soak.
(b) — **de** to soak up, soak in.
(c) — **de, — en** (*fig*) to steep oneself in; to become imbued with.
empapelado *nm* papering, paperhanging.
empapelador *nm* paperhanger.
empapelar [1a] *vt* *object* to wrap in paper; *box* to paper, line with paper; *room, wall* to paper.
empaque *nm* (a) packing. (b) (*fam*) look, appearance; manner. (c) (*fig*) solemnness, pomposity. (d) (*SAm*) nerve, effrontery.
empaquetador *nm*, **empaquetadora** *nf* packer.
empaquetadura *nf* packing; filling; (*Mech*) gasket.
empaquetar [1a] *vt* to pack; to pack up, parcel up; (*Comm*) to package.
emparamarse [1a] *vr* (*Bol, Ec, Col, Ven*) to get soaked; to get numb with cold, die of cold.
emparedado *nm* sandwich.
emparedar [1a] *vt* to immure, confine.
emparejar [1a] **1** *vt* (a) to pair, match. (b) to level, make level; to make flush; to even up. **2** *vi* (a) to catch up (*con* with), come abreast (*con* of). (b) to be even (*con* with). **3 emparejarse** *vr* to match.
emparentado *adj* related by marriage (*con* to).
emparentar [1k] *vi* to become related by marriage (*con* to); — **con una familia** to marry into a family.
emparrado *nm* trained vine; vine arbour.
emparrandarse [1a] *vr* (*SAm*) to go on a binge (*sl*).
empastado *adj* (a) (*Typ*) clothbound, bound. (b) *tooth* filled.
empastar [1a] **1** *vt* (a) to paste.
(b) (*Typ*) to bind in stiff covers, bind in cloth.
(c) *tooth* to fill, stop.
(d) (*SAm*) to convert into pasture land.
2 empastarse *vr* (*Arg, Chi: of cattle*) to get blown.
empaste *nm* filling.
empatar [1a] **1** *vt* (a) (*SAm*) to join, connect, tie firmly together.
(b) (*Ven*) to bother, harass.
(c) (*Chi*) *time* to waste.
2 *vi* (*games*) to draw, tie; (*races*) to tie, have a dead heat; (*voting*) to tie; **los equipos empataron a 2** the teams drew 2-all.
empate *nm* (a) draw, tie; dead heat; **un — a 0** a 0-0 draw, a goalless draw. (b) (*SAm*) joint, connection.
emparar [1a] *vt* (a) (*Ec*) to anger. (b) (*Per*) to make fun of. **2 empararse** *vr* (*Per*) to blush.
empavesado *nm* bunting.
empavesar [1a] *vt* to deck, adorn; *ship* to dress.
empavonar [1a] **1** *vt* (a) (*Tech*) *steel* to blue. (b) (*SAm*) to grease, cover with grease. **2 empavonarse** *vr* (*CAm*) to dress up.
empecatado *adj* (a) incorrigible; wily, fiendish. (b) ill-fated.
empecinado *adj* (*SAm*) stubborn, pigheaded.
empecinamiento *nm* (*SAm*) stubbornness, pigheadedness.
empecinarse [1a] *vr* (*SAm*) to be stubborn; — **en algo** to be stubborn about something; — **en** + *infin* to persist wilfully in + *ger*.
empedarse [1a] *vr* (*Mex, RPl*) to get drunk.
empedernido *adj* (a) *person* heartless; obdurate; *heart* flinty, stony.
(b) (*in a bad habit*) hardened, inveterate; **un fumador** — a strongly addicted smoker, a smoker

firmly set in the habit; **un pecador** — an unregenerate sinner.

empedernir [3a: *defective*] **1** *vt* to harden. **2 empedernirse** *vr* (a) to harden; to petrify. (b) (*fig*) to harden one's heart, resolve to be tough.

empedrado 1 *adj surface* paved; (*fig*) pitted (*de* with); *face* pockmarked; *colouring* dappled, flecked; *sky* cloud-flecked. **2** *nm* paving.

empedrar [1k] *vt* to pave.

empegado *nm* tarpaulin.

empeine *nm* (a) (*Anat*) groin; instep. (b) (*Bot*) cotton flower. (c) —s (*Med*) ringworm.

empelotado *adj* (a) (*Col, Cu, Chi, Mex*) naked, stripped. (b) (*Mex*) in love.

empelotar [1a] **1** *vt* (a) (*SAm*) to undress, strip to the skin.
　(b) (*SAm*) to strip down, dismantle, take to pieces.
　2 empelotarse *vr* (a) (*fam*) to get muddled.
　(b) (*fam*) to get into a row.
　(c) (*Col, Cu, Chi, Mex*) to strip naked.
　(d) (*Cu, Mex*) to fall in love (*con* with).

empelucado *adj* bewigged.

empella *nf* (a) (*shoemaker's*) vamp; uppers. (b) (*SAm*) lard.

empellar [1a] *vt* to push, shove, jostle.

empellón *nm* push, shove; **mover a** —es to shove, move by pushing; **abrirse paso a** —es to get through by shoving, push one's way rudely through, push roughly past; **dar** —es to shove, jostle.

empenachar [1a] *vt* to adorn with plumes.

empeñado *adj* (a) *valuable* pawned.
　(b) **estar** — **hasta los ojos** to be deeply in debt.
　(c) *person* determined; **estar** — **en** + *infin* to be determined to + *infin*, be completely set on + *ger*.
　(d) *argument* bitter, heated.

empeñar [1a] **1** *vt* (a) *valuable* to pawn, pledge.
　(b) *word* to pledge, give; *person* to engage, compel.
　(c) *battle* to join; *argument* to start.
　2 empeñarse *vr* (a) to bind oneself, pledge oneself.
　(b) to get into debt.
　(c) — **en algo** to insist on something; to persist in something; — **en** + *infin* to be determined to + *infin*, be set on + *ger*; to insist on + *ger*; **se empeña en que es así** he insists that it is so.
　(d) — **en una lucha** to engage in a fight; — **en una discusión** to get involved in a heated argument.
　(e) — **por uno** to intercede for someone, intervene on someone's behalf.

empeñero *nm* (*Mex*) pawnbroker, moneylender.

empeño *nm* (a) pledge.
　(b) obligation, undertaking.
　(c) determination; insistence; **su** — **en hacerlo** his determination to do it; his insistence on doing it; **con** — with determination; insistently; eagerly, keenly; **tener** — **en** + *infin* to be bent on + *ger*, be eager to + *infin*.
　(d) pawnshop; moneylender's.

empeñoso *adj* (*SAm*) persevering, diligent.

empeoramiento *nm* deterioration, worsening.

empeorar [1a] **1** *vt* to make worse, worsen; to impair.
　2 *vi and* **empeorarse** *vr* to get worse, worsen, deteriorate.

empequeñecer [2d] *vt* (a) to dwarf, make (seem) smaller. (b) (*fig*) to minimize; to belittle.

emperador *nm* (a) emperor. (b) (*Cu*) swordfish.

emperatriz *nf* empress.

emperejilarse [1a] *vr* to dress up, doll oneself up.

empericarse [1g] *vr* (a) (*Col, Ec*) to get drunk. (b) (*Cu, Mex*) to blush.

emperifollar [1a] **1** *vt* to adorn, deck; *person* to doll up. **2 emperifollarse** *vr* to dress up, doll oneself up.

empernar [1k] *vt* to bolt, secure with a bolt; to fit a bolt to.

empero *conj* (*arch and lit*) but; yet, however,

emperramiento *nm* stubbornness.

emperrarse [1a] *vr* to get stubborn, be obstinate; — **en algo** to be stubborn about something; to persist in something.

emperro *nm* (*prov, Ec*) stubbornness; fit of temper.

empertigar [1h] *vt* (*Chi*) *horse* to hitch up.

empezar [1f *and* 1k] *vti* to begin, start; — **a** + *infin* to start to + *infin*; — **por** + *inf*, — + *ger* to begin by + *ger*, start by + *ger*; **empezó diciendo que** . . . he began by saying that . . .; **bueno, para** — well, to start with.

empicotar [1a] *vt* to pillory.

empiezo *nm* (*Arg, Col, Ec, Guat*) =**comienzo**.

empilchar [1a] *vt* (*RPl*) *horse* to saddle; *person* to provide with clothing.

empilonar [1a] *vt* (*Col, Cu, PR*) to pile up.

empinada *nf* (*Aer*) steep climb, zoom upward.

empinado *adj* (a) steep; high, lofty. (b) (*fig*) proud; stiff.

empinar [1a] **1** *vt* (a) to raise, lift; to tip up; *see* **codo**.
　(b) to straighten.
　2 *vi* (*fam*) to drink, booze.
　3 empinarse *vr* (a) (*person*) to stand on tiptoe; (*horse*) to rear up; (*building*) to tower, soar; (*Aer*) to climb steeply, zoom upwards.
　(b) (*Chi, Ec*) to overeat.

empingorotado *adj* (*fam*) stuck-up (*fam*).

empipada *nf* (*Chi, Ec*) blow-out (*sl*).

empiparse [1a] *vr* (*Chi, Ec*): — **algo** to eat something right up, drink something down.

empírico 1 *adj* empiric(al). **2** *nm* empiricist.

empirismo *nm* empiricism.

empizarrado *nm* slate roof.

empizarrar [1a] *vt* to roof with slates.

emplantillar [1a] *vt* (a) (*Chi, Per, SD*) *shoes* to put insoles into. (b) (*Chi, Per*) *wall* to fill with rubble.

emplastar [1a] *vt* (a) (*Med*) to put a plaster on, poultice. (b) *face* to make up, paint. (c) *deal* to block.

emplaste *nm* (a) (*Med*) plaster, poultice. (b) (*fig*) makeshift arrangement. (c) *weakling*; misfit, useless individual. (d) (*SAm*) bore, tedious person.

emplazamiento *nm* (a) (*Law*) summons; summoning. (b) site, location; (*Mil*) (*gun*) emplacement.

emplazar [1f] *vt* (a) to summon, convene; (*Law*) to summons; to subpoena. (b) to site, locate, place; *statue etc* to set up, erect.

empleado *nm* employee; (*esp*) clerk, office worker, clerical worker; — **bancario**, — **de banco** bank clerk; — **de confianza** confidential clerk; — **de correos** post-office worker; — **de pompas fúnebres** undertaker's assistant, mortician's assistant (US); — **público** civil servant; — **de ventanilla** booking office clerk, counter clerk.

emplear [1a] **1** *vt* *tool, word etc* to use, employ; *person* to employ; to give a job to, engage, hire; *time* to occupy, spend; to put in; *money* to invest; — **mal** to misuse; **-- mal el tiempo** to waste time.
　2 emplearse *vr* to be used, be employed; — **haciendo algo** to occupy oneself doing something; **¡bien se te emplea!** it serves you right!

empleo *nm* (a) (*in general*) use, employment; occupation, spending; (*Comm*) investment; "**modo de** —" (*on label*) "instructions for use"; **el** — **de esa palabra es censurable** the use of that word is to be condemned.
　(b) employment, work; **pleno** — full employment.
　(c) job, employment, post; **buscar un** — to look for a job; **estar sin** — to be unemployed, be out of a job; "**solicitan** —" (*heading*) "situations wanted".

emplomadura *nf* leading; lead covering, lead lining; (*Arg: of tooth*) filling.

emplomar [1a] *vt* to lead; to cover (*or* line, weight *etc*) with lead; to seal with lead; (*Arg*) *tooth* to fill.

emplumar [1a] **1** *vt* (a) to adorn with feathers; (*punishment*) to tar and feather; **¡que te cmplumen!** (*fam*) get lost! (*fam*).
　(b) (*CAm, Cu*) to swindle.
　(c) (*CAm*) to beat up; to thrash.
　(d) (*Cu*) *employee* to fire (*fam*).
　(e) (*Col, Chi*) —**las** to run away.
　2 *vi* (a) to grow feathers.
　(b) (*SAm*) to run away, take to one's heels.

emplumecer [2d] *vi* to grow feathers.

empobrecer [2d] **1** *vt* to impoverish. **2 empobrecerse** *vr* to become poor, become impoverished.

empobrecimiento *nm* impoverishment.

empolvado *adj substance* powdery; *surface* dusty.

empolvar [1a] **1** *vt* *face* to powder; *surface* to cover with dust, make dusty.
　2 empolvarse *vr* (a) (*person*) to powder oneself, powder one's face, put powder on; (*surface*) to get dusty, gather dust.
　(b) (*Mex*) to get rusty, get out of practice.
　(c) (*SD*) to run away.

empollar [1a] **1** *vt* (a) to incubate, sit on; to hatch. (b) (*Univ etc: fam*) *subject* to swot up (*fam*).
　2 *vi* (a) (*of hen*) to sit, brood.
　(b) (*of insects*) to breed.
　(c) (*Univ etc: fam*) to swot (*fam*), cram.

empollón *nm*, **empollona** *nf* (*Univ etc: fam*) swot (*fam*).

emponchado *adj* (a) (*SAm*) wearing a poncho, covered with a poncho. (b) (*Arg, Per, Urug*) suspicious; crafty, hypocritical.

emponcharse [1a] *vr* (*SAm*) to put on one's poncho, wrap oneself up in one's poncho.

emponzoñamiento *nm* poisoning.

emponzoñar [1a] *vt* to poison; (*fig*) to poison; to taint, corrupt.

emporcar [1g *and* 1m] *vt* to soil, dirty, foul.

emporio *nm* emporium, mart, trading centre; (*SAm*) large department stores.

emporroso *adj* (*CAm, Ven*) annoying; wearisome.

empotrado *adj* cupboard *etc* built-in; (*Mech*) fixed, integral.

empotrar [1a] **1** *vt* to embed, fix; *cupboard etc* to build in.
  2 empotrarse *vr*: **el coche se empotró en la tienda** the car embedded itself in the shop; **los vagones se empotraron uno en otro** the carriages telescoped together.

empotrerar [1a] *vt* (a) (*SAm*) *cattle* to pasture, put out to pasture. (b) (*Arg, Cu*) *land* to convert into fenced pasture.

empozarse [1f] *vr* (*Arg, Per*) to form pools.

emprendedor 1 *adj* enterprising; go-ahead, pushful. **2** *nm* (*Fin*) entrepreneur.

emprender [1a] *vt* (a) to undertake; to take on, tackle; to begin on, embark on; — **marcha a** to set out for; — **el regreso** to go back, return; to begin the homeward journey; — **la retirada** to retreat.
  (b) —**la** to start, set out; —**la con uno** to tackle someone about a matter, have it out with someone; to have a row with someone; **la emprendieron con el árbitro a botellazos** they attacked the referee by throwing bottles at him.

empreñar [1a] **1** *vt* *woman* to make pregnant, get with child; *animal* to impregnate, mate with. **2 empreñarse** *vr* to become pregnant.

empresa *nf* (a) (*spirit etc*) enterprise; — **libre, libre** — free enterprise; — **privada** private enterprise.
  (b) (*Comm, Fin*) enterprise, undertaking, venture; company, concern; — **colectiva** joint venture; — **funeraria** undertaker's; — **particular** private company; — **de servicios públicos** public utility company.
  (c) (*esp Theat*) management; **la — lamenta que . . .** the management regrets that . . .

empresarial *adj* owners', managers'; *function, class etc* managerial.

empresario *nm* (*Tech*) manager; (*Mus, of opera etc*) impresario; (*Boxing*) promoter; (*Comm*) contractor; — **de pompas fúnebres** undertaker, mortician (*US*); — **de transporte** (*Arg*) shipping agent.

emprestar [1a] *vt* (*SAm*) to lend; to borrow.

empréstito *nm* (public) loan; — **de guerra** war loan.

empujada *nf* (*Arg, Guat, Urug, Ven*) push, shove.

empujadora-niveladora *nf* bulldozer.

empujar [1a] *vt* (a) to push, shove; to push, thrust (en into); (*Mech*) to drive, move, propel; *bicycle* to push, *wheel*; *button* to press; **"empujad"** (*on doors etc*) **"push"**; — **el botón a fondo** to press the button down hard; **¡no empujen!** stop pushing!, don't shove!
  (b) (*fam*) *person* to sack (*fam*), give the push to (*fam*).
  (c) — **algo** (*fam*) to work behind the scenes for something, intrigue to get something.

empujatierra *nf* bulldozer.

empuje *nm* (a) (*in general*) pressure; (*Mech, Phys*) thrust.
  (b) (*un* —) push, shove.
  (c) (*fig*) push, pushfulness, drive, thrustfulness; **le falta** — he hasn't got any go to him, he lacks drive; **en un espíritu de** — in a thrustful spirit.

empujón *nm* push, shove; dig, poke, jab; **abrirse paso a** —**es** to shove one's way through, get through by pushing; **avanzar a** —**es** to go forward by fits and starts, go jerkily forward; **trabajar a** —**es** to work intermittently.

empulgueras *nfpl* thumbscrew.

empuntar [1a] **1** *vt* (a) to put a point on. (b) (*Col, Ec*) —**las** to run away. **2 empuntarse** *vr* (*Ven*) to dig one's heels in.

empuñadura *nf* (a) (*of sword*) hilt; (*of tool etc*) grip, handle. (b) (*of story*) start, opening.

empuñar [1a] *vt* (a) to grasp, clutch, grip, take (firm) hold of; (*Chi*) *fist* to clench. (b) (*fig*) — **las armas** to take up arms; — **el bastón** to take command. (c) (*Bol*) to punch, hit with one's fist.

empupar [1a] *vt* (*SAm*) to pupate.

empurrarse [1a] *vr* (*CAm*) to get angry.

emú *nm* emu.

emulación *nf* emulation.

emulador 1 *adj* emulous (*de* of). **2** *nm*, **emuladora** *nf* rival.

emular [1a] **1** *vt* to emulate, rival. **2** *vi*: — **con** = *vt*.

émulo 1 *adj* emulous. **2** *nm*, **emula** *nf* rival, competitor.

emulsión *nf* emulsion.

emulsionar [1a] *vt* to emulsify.

en *prep* (a) (*place*) in; into; on, upon; at; **está — el cajón** it's in the drawer; **meter algo — el bolsillo** to put something in (*or* into) one's pocket; **no entra — el agujero** it won't go into the hole; **está — el suelo** it's on the floor; **está — Argentina** he's in Argentina; **está — Santiago** he's in Santiago; **está — algún lugar de la Mancha** he's at some place in la Mancha; — **casa** at home; **te esperé — la estación** I waited for you at the station; **trabaja — la tienda** she works in the shop; **ir de puerta — puerta** to go from door to door.
  (b) (*time*) in; on; — **1605** in 1605; — **el siglo X** in the 10th century; — **aquella ocasión** on that occasion; **lo terminaron — 3 semanas** they finished it in 3 weeks.
  (c) (*price*) at, for; **lo vendió — 5 dólares** he sold it at (*or* for) 5 dollars.
  (d) (*rate*) by; **reducir algo — una tercera parte** to reduce something by a third; **ha aumentado — un 20 por cien** it has increased by 20%.
  (e) (*means*) **le conocí — el andar** I recognized him by his walk; **ir — avión** to go by plane, go by air; **vine — el autobús** I came by bus, I came in the bus.
  (f) (*with verb*) — **viéndole se lo dije** the moment I saw him I told him; — **viéndole se lo diré** the moment I see him I'll tell him, as soon as I see him I'll tell him.

enaceitar [1a] *vt* (*RPl*) to oil.

enagua *nf* (*SAm*), **enaguas** *nfpl* petticoat; underskirt.

enaguazar [1f] *vt* to flood.

enajenación *nf*, **enajenamiento** *nm* (a) (*Law etc*) alienation; transfer; **enajenación forzosa** expropriation.
  (b) estrangement.
  (c) absentmindedness; rapture, trance; — **mental** mental derangement.

enajenar [1a] **1** *vt* (a) (*Law etc*) *property* to alienate, transfer; *rights* to dispose of.
  (b) *person* to alienate, estrange.
  (c) (*fig*) to enrapture, carry away; to drive mad. **2 enajenarse** *vr* (a) — **algo** to deprive oneself of something; — **las simpatías** to alienate people, make oneself disliked.
  (b) (*of friends*) to become estranged.
  (c) to be enraptured, get carried away.

enaltecer [2d] *vt* to exalt; to praise, extol.

enamoradizo *adj* susceptible (to women), of an amorous disposition.

enamorado *adj* (a) in love, lovesick. (b) **estar** — to be in love (*de* with). (c) (*Arg, Chi, PR*) = **enamoradizo**.

enamoramiento *nm* falling in love; infatuation.

enamorar [1a] **1** *vt* to inspire love in, win the love of; **por fin la enamoró** eventually he got her to fall in love with him.
  2 enamorarse *vr* to fall in love (*de* with).

enamoricarse [1g] *vr*, **enamoriscarse** [1g] *vr* (*SAm*) to be just a bit in love (*de* with); to become mildly infatuated (*de* with).

enancar [1g] **1** *vt* (*SAm*) to put someone on the crupper (of one's horse).
  2 *vi* (*Arg*) to follow, be a consequence (*a* of).
  3 enancarse *vr* (a) (*SAm*) to get up on the crupper, ride behind.
  (b) (*Mex: of horse*) to rear up.

enangostar [1a] **1** *vt* to narrow. **2 enangostarse** *vr* to narrow, get narrower.

enano 1 *adj* dwarf, small, tiny; stunted. **2** *nm* dwarf; midget; (*pej*) runt.

enarbolar [1a] **1** *vt* *flag etc* to hoist, raise; to hang up, hang out; *sword etc* to flourish.
  2 enarbolarse *vr* (a) (*person*) to get angry.
  (b) (*horse*) to rear up.

enarcar [1g] *vt* (a) (*Tech*) to hoop, put a hoop on.
  (b) *eyebrows* to raise, arch; *back* (*of cat*) to arch; *chest* to throw out.

enardecer [2d] **1** *vt* to fire, inflame; to fill with enthusiasm.
  2 enardecerse *vr* (a) (*Med*) to become inflamed.
  (b) (*fig*) to get excited, get enthusiastic (*por* about); to blaze, be afire (*de* with).

enarenar [1a] **1** *vt* to sand, cover with sand. **2 enarenarse** *vr* (*Naut*) to run aground.

enastado *adj* horned; antlered, with antlers.

encabalgamiento *nm* (*Lit*) enjambement.

encabestrar [1a] **1** *vt* (a) to put a halter on; to lead by a halter. (b) (*fig*) to overcome, dominate. **2 encabestrarse** *vr* (*SAm*) to dig one's heels in.

encabezado 1 *adj wine* fortified. **2** *nm* **(a)** (*Mex*) heading; headline. **(b)** (*PR*) foreman.

encabezamiento *nm* **(a)** heading; headline; rubric; caption; opening words, preamble; (*Comm*) bill head, letterhead. **(b)** roll, register.

encabezar [1f] *vt* **(a)** *movement, revolution etc* to lead, head.
(b) *list, league etc* to head, be at the top of, come first in.
(c) *paper, document* to put a heading to; *article* to head, entitle; *sketch etc* to caption.
(d) *population etc* to register (for tax purposes etc).
(e) *wine* to fortify.

encabrestarse *vr* (*SAm*) =**emperrarse**.

encabritarse [1a] *vr* (*of horse*) to rear up.

encabronar [1a] *vt* (*Col, Cu*) to make angry.

encabuyar [1a] *vt* (*Ant, Col, Ven*) to tie up (with sisal cord).

encachar [1a] **1** *vt* (*Chi*) *head* to lower. **2** *vi* (*Mex*) to get oneself a sweetheart. **3 encacharse** *vr* (*Ven*) to refuse to give way.

encachilarse [1a] *vr* (*Arg*) to get furious.

encachorrarse [1a] *vr* (*Col*) to get angry; (*Chi, PR, Ven*) to turn obstinate.

encadenación *nf*, **encadenamiento** *nm* **(a)** chaining (together). **(b)** (*fig*) linking, connection, concatenation.

encadenar [1a] *vt* **(a)** to chain (together); to put chains on, fetter, shackle. **(b)** (*fig*) to shackle, paralyse, immobilize. **(c)** (*fig*) to connect, link.

encajadura *nf* **(a)** (*act*) insertion, filling. **(b)** socket; groove; frame.

encajar [1a] **1** *vt* **(a)** to insert, fit (*en* into); to push in, thrust in, force in; *machine etc* to house, encase; *parts* to join, fit together, fit into each other.
(b) *remark etc* to get in, put in, intrude; *story* (*fam*) to come out with, choose the wrong moment to tell; *hint* to drop.
(c) — *algo a uno* to palm something off on someone, foist something off on someone; — *una historia a uno* to force someone to listen to a (disagreeable) story.
(d) *blow* (*fam*) to give, deal; **le encajó un bofetón** he gave him a punch.
(e) (*fam*) to chuck (*a* at).
2 *vi* to fit; to fit well (*or* properly); **esto no encaja bien** this doesn't fit properly.
(b) (*fig*) to fit, match, correspond; to be appropriate; **esto no encaja con lo que dijo antes** this does not square with what he said before.
3 encajarse *vr* **(a)** (*fam*) to squeeze (oneself) in; (*fig*) to intrude, gatecrash; — **en una reunión** to intrude upon a meeting; — **en una fiesta** to crash a party (*fam*).
(b) (*fam*) to butt in.
(c) — **una chaqueta** to put on a jacket.

encaje *nm* **(a)** (*act*) insertion, fitting; fitting together, joining.
(b) socket, cavity; groove; frame; (*Mech*) housing.
(c) inlay, inlaid work, mosaic; (*Sew*) lace; — **de aplicación** appliqué (work).
(d) (*Fin*) reserve, stock; — **de oro** gold reserve.

encajera *nf* lacemaker.

encajetillar [1a] *vt* (*Mex*) to pack in boxes, box.

encajonado *nm* cofferdam.

encajonar [1a] **1** *vt* **(a)** to box (up), put in a box, crate, pack (in a box); (*Mech*) to box in, encase.
(b) *river* to confine (between banks), canalize.
(c) to squeeze in, squeeze through.
2 encajonarse *vr* (*SAm: of river*) to run through a narrow place, run between steep banks.

encalabrinar [1a] **1** *vt* **(a)** (*Med*) to make dizzy, make giddy.
(b) — **a uno** to get someone worked up; to fluster someone.
(c) (*fam*) — **a una** to attract a girl, click with a girl (*fam*), get a girl to show an interest.
2 encalabrinarse *vr* (*fam*) **(a)** to get an obsession, get the bit between one's teeth; to dig one's heels in.
(b) — **de una** to get infatuated with a girl; **X anda encalabrinado con Z** X is mad keen on Z (*fam*).

encaladura *nf* **(a)** whitewash(ing). **(b)** (*Agr*) liming.

encalambrarse [1a] *vr* (*SAm*) to get cramp; to get stiff with cold.

encalamocar [1g] **1** *vt* (*Col, Ven*) **(a)** to make drunk.
(b) to confuse, bewilder.
2 encalamocarse *vr* (*Col, Ven*) **(a)** to get drunk.
(b) to get confused, get bewildered.

encalar [1a] *vt* **(a)** *wall* to whitewash. **(b)** (*Agr*) to lime.

encalatarse [1a] *vr* (*Per*) **(a)** to strip naked. **(b)** to be ruined.

encalmado *adj* **(a)** (*Naut*) becalmed. **(b)** (*Comm, Fin*) quiet, slack, dull.

encalmarse [1a] *vr* to be becalmed.

encalvecer [2d] *vi* to go bald.

encalladero *nm* shoal, sandbank.

encalladura *nf* stranding, running aground.

encallar [1a] *vi* **(a)** (*Naut*) to run aground, run ashore, get stranded (*en* on). **(b)** (*fig*) to fail; (*in negotiation etc*) to get stuck, get bogged down.

encallecido *adj* hardened.

encamar [1a] **1** *vt* **(a)** (*CAm, Mex*) to take to hospital, hospitalize.
(b) (*Cu*) *animals* to litter, bed down.
2 encamarse *vr* **(a)** to take to one's bed; — **con una** (*Arg, Per*) to go to bed with someone; **estar encamado** to be confined to bed.
(b) (*corn etc*) to be laid, be flattened.
(c) (*animal*) to crouch, hide.

encamillado *nm*, **encamillada** *nf* (*CAm, Mex*) stretcher case.

encaminar [1a] **1** *vt* **(a)** to guide, direct, set on the right road (*a* to); **pude** —**le** I was able to tell him the way to go.
(b) *vehicle, expedition etc* to route (*por via*).
(c) *attention, energies etc* to direct (*a* towards); **medidas encaminadas a corregir esto** measures designed to correct this; **el proyecto está encaminado a** + *infin* the plan is directed towards + *ger*, the plan is designed to + *infin*.
2 encaminarse *vr* **(a)** — **a** to set out for, make for, take the road to.
(b) (*fig*) — **a** to be directed towards, be intended for.

encamotado *adj* (*SAm*): **estar** — to be in love (*de* with).

encamotarse [1a] *vr* (*SAm*) to fall in love (*de* with); to become very affectionate (*de* towards).

encampanado *adj* bell-shaped.

encampanar [1a] **1** *vt* **(a)** (*Col, PR, SD, Ven*) to raise, raise on high.
(b) (*Mex, Per, PR*) to leave in the lurch, leave in a jam.
(c) (*PR, Ven*) — **a uno a** to send someone to.
2 encampanarse *vr* **(a)** (*SAm*) to boast, brag.
(b) (*Col*) to fall in love.
(c) (*Mex*) to get into a jam.
(d) (*Ven*) to go off to a remote spot.

encanalar [1a] *vt*, **encanalizar** [1f] *vt* to pipe; to channel, canalize.

encanallarse [1a] *vr* to degrade oneself; to become coarse, acquire coarse habits.

encanar [1a] *vt* (*Arg, Col, Chi*) to nick (*sl*), arrest.

encandecer [2d] *vt* to make white-hot.

encandelar [1a] *vt* (*Cu*) to annoy, irritate.

encandelillar [1a] *vt* (*SAm*) to dazzle; to bewilder.

encandellar [1a] *vt* (*Col, Per*) to kindle, light.

encandiladera *nf* procuress; madame.

encandilado *adj* high, erect.

encandiladora *nf* procuress; madame.

encandilar [1a] **1** *vt* **(a)** to dazzle.
(b) *fire* to stir, poke.
(c) (*fig*) *person* to daze, bewilder.
(d) (*fig*) *emotion* to kindle, stimulate.
(e) (*Per, PR*) to deprive of sleep.
2 encandilarse *vr* **(a)** (*eyes*) to glitter, sparkle, look unnaturally bright.
(b) (*Col, Per, PR*) to get scared; (*Mex, PR*) to get angry.

encanecer [2d] *vi and* **encanecerse** *vr* **(a)** (*of hair*) to go grey; (*of person*) to go grey, look old. **(b)** (*fig*) to go mouldy.

encanijado *adj* weak, puny.

encanijarse [1a] *vr* to grow weak, become emaciated, begin to look ill.

encanillar [1a] *vt* to wind (on to a spool).

encantado *adj* **(a)** bewitched; haunted; *spot* romantic, bewitching; *house* (*fig*) rambling.
(b) delighted, pleased, charmed; ¡—! (*at introduction*) how do you do!, pleased to meet you; **estoy** — **de conocerle** I'm delighted to meet you; **yo,** — it's all right with me.
(c) absent-minded, daydreaming; **parecer estar** — to seem to be in a trance.

encantador 1 *adj* charming, delightful, lovely, enchanting. **2** *nm*, **encantadora** *nf* magician, enchanter; — **de serpientes** snake charmer.

encantamiento *nm* enchantment.

encantar [1a] *vt* **(a)** to bewitch, cast a spell on (*or* over).
(b) to charm, delight, enchant, captivate,

fascinate; **nos encanta la casa** we are delighted with the house, we are charmed with the house; **pero pronto dejó de —nos** but we soon stopped liking it.
encanto nm (a) charm, spell, enchantment; **como por** — as if by magic; (fig) in a flash, instantly.
   (b) (fig) charm; enchantment, delight; **la playa es un** — the beach is delightful, the beach is marvellous; **el niño es un** — the child is a little treasure; **¡qué — de jardín!** what a lovely garden!
   (c) (as endearment) sweetheart, my love; **¡oye, —!** hullo gorgeous! (fam).
encantoso adj (Mex) =**encantador.**
encañada nf ravine.
encañado nm conduit, pipe.
encañar [1a] **1** vt (a) water to pipe. (b) plant to stake, prop up. (c) land to drain. (d) silk to wind (on to a spool). **2** vi (of plant) to form a stalk.
encañizado nm wire netting, protective fence.
encañonar [1a] **1** vt (a) to pipe. (b) (fam) to stick up (sl), hold up; to cover (with a gun). **2** vi (of bird) to grow feathers.
encapado adj cloaked, wearing a cloak.
encapotado adj (a) cloaked, wearing a cloak. (b) sky cloudy, overcast.
encapotar [1a] **1** vt to cover with a cloak.
   2 encapotarse vr (a) to put on one's cloak; to wrap up.
   (b) (fig) to frown.
   (c) (Meteorol) to become cloudy, cloud over, become overcast.
encapricharse [1a] vr to persist in one's foolishness; to dig one's heels in, insist on having one's way; **— por** to take a fancy to, get infatuated with.
encapuchado adj hooded.
encarado adj: **bien —** good-looking, with nice features; **mal —** ill-favoured, plain; (SAm) wicked-looking, with criminal features.
encaramar [1a] **1** vt (a) to raise, lift up.
   (b) to praise, extol.
   (c) (Col, CR) to embarrass, cause to blush.
   2 encaramarse vr (a) to perch, sit up high; **— a** to climb (up, on to), get to the top of.
   (b) (Col, CR) to get embarrassed, blush.
encarapitarse [1a] vr (Col, Ec, SD) =**encaramarse** (a).
encarar [1a] **1** vt (a) gun to aim, point.
   (b) to face; (SAm) to face up to, begin to study.
   (c) (Par) to sicken.
   2 encararse vr: **— a, — con** to face, confront, come face to face with; **tendrá que — con los electores** he will have to face the electorate; **se encaró en seguida con el problema** he immediately faced up to the problem.
encarcelación nf, **encarcelamiento** nm imprisonment.
encarcelar [1a] vt to imprison, jail.
encarecer [2d] **1** vt (a) (Comm) to put up the price of, make more expensive.
   (b) to praise, extol; person to recommend; policy etc to recommend (a to), urge (a on); difficulty etc to stress, emphasize; to exaggerate; **le encarezco que . . .** I urge you to + infin.
   2 vi and **encarecerse** vr (Comm) to get dearer, rise in price.
encarecidamente adv insistently, earnestly, strongly.
encarecimiento nm (a) rise in price, price increase.
   (b) extolling; stressing, emphasizing; exaggeration, overrating; **con —** insistently, earnestly, strongly.
encargado 1 adj: **el empleado — de estos géneros** the employee in charge of these stocks.
   2 nm, **encargada** nf agent, representative; person in charge; **— de curso** lecturer in charge; **— de mostrador** counter clerk; **— de negocios** (Pol) chargé d'affaires; (Col, Mex) agent; **— de la recepción** receptionist; **— de relaciones públicas** public relations officer; **encargada de vestuario** (Theat) wardrobe mistress.
encargar [1h] **1** vt to entrust; to charge, commission; to urge, recommend, advise; to ask for; (Comm) to order; **— algo a uno** to entrust something to someone; to put someone in charge of something; **— un deber a uno** to charge someone with a duty.
   2 encargarse vr (a) **— de algo** to take charge of something; to take something over; to look after something, see about something, attend to something; **no había queso, pues las ratas se habían encargado de ello** there was no cheese, because the rats had seen to that (or had made sure of that).
   (b) **— de + infin** to see about + infin, attend to the matter of + ger; to undertake to + infin.
encargo nm (a) assignment, job; post; charge, commission; responsibility; **tener — de + infin** to have

the job of + ger, have the responsibility of + ger.
   (b) order, request; (Comm) order (de for); **cancelar el —** de to cancel the order for, stop the delivery of.
   (c) **estar de —** (Arg, SD, Urug) to be pregnant.
encargue nm (Arg, Par) =**encargo.**
encariñado adj: **estar — con** to be fond of, be attached to.
encariñarse [1a] vr: **— con** to grow fond of, get attached to.
encarnación nf incarnation; embodiment.
encarnadino adj incarnadine, blood-red.
encarnado adj (a) incarnate. (b) red, blood-red; flesh-coloured; complexion ruddy, (pej) florid; **ponerse —** to blush red.
encarnar [1a] **1** vt (a) to embody, personify; (Theat) role to play, bring to life.
   (b) fish hook to bait.
   2 vi (a) (Rel etc) to become incarnate.
   (b) (Med) to heal (up).
   (c) (of weapon) to enter the flesh, penetrate the body.
encarnecer [2d] vi to put on flesh.
encarnizadamente adv (fig) bloodily, bitterly, fiercely.
encarnizado adj (a) wound etc red, inflamed; eye bloodshot. (b) bloody; bitter, fierce.
encarnizamiento nm rage, fury; bitterness, ferocity.
encarnizar [1f] **1** vt (fig) to enrage, infuriate; to make cruel.
   2 encarnizarse vr (a) **— en** to gorge on; to become greedy for.
   (b) (fig) to get furious; to fight fiercely; **— con, — en** to be cruel to, treat cruelly.
encaro nm (a) stare, staring, gaze. (b) aim(ing). (c) (Hist) blunderbuss.
encarpetar [1a] vt (a) to file away; to pigeonhole; (fig) plan etc to shelve, bury. (b) (SAm) motion to table, propose.
encarrilar [1a] vt (a) to put back on the rails.
   (b) (fig) to put on the right track, start off again on the right lines; to correct; to direct, guide.
   (c) **ir encarrilado** (fig) to be on the right lines, be doing nicely; (pej) to be in a rut.
encarrujar [1a] vt (RPl: Sew) to ruffle, frill.
encartuchar [1a] vt paper to make a cone of, roll up into a cone.
encartar [1a] vt (a) to enroll, register, enter (on a list); (Law) to summon; (b) criminal to outlaw.
encartonar [1a] vt to cover with cardboard; (Typ) to bind in boards.
encasar [1a] vt bone to set.
encasillado 1 adj actor type-cast. **2** nm (set of) pigeonholes.
encasillar [1a] vt (a) to pigeonhole; to sort out, classify; to file. (b) (Theat etc) to type-cast.
encasquetar [1a] **1** vt (a) hat to pull on, pull down tight, jam on. (b) **— una idea a uno** to get an idea firmly fixed in someone's mind. **2 encasquetarse** vr see vt.
encasquillador nm (SAm) blacksmith, horse-shoer.
encasquillar [1a] **1** vt (a) to put a tip on.
   (b) (SAm) horse to shoe.
   2 encasquillarse vr (a) (Cu, Ec: of bullet) to stick in the barrel.
   (b) (Ec: in speech etc) to get stuck, dry up (fam).
   (c) (Cu) to get scared.
encastillado adj (a) (Archit) castellated. (b) (fig) haughty; stubborn.
encastillar [1a] **1** vt to fortify, defend with castles. **2 encastillarse** vr (a) (Mil) to take to the hills; (Hist) to shut oneself up in a castle. (b) (fig) to refuse to yield; **— en un principio** to stick to a principle, refuse to give up a principle.
encatrado nm (Arg, Chi) hurdle.
encatrinarse [1a] vr (Mex) to dress up.
encauchado nm (Col, Ven) rubberized cloth; waterproof blanket.
encauchar [1a] vt to rubberize, waterproof.
encausar [1a] vt to prosecute, sue; to put on trial.
encauzar [1f] vt (a) to channel.
   (b) (fig) to channel, direct, guide; **las protestas se pueden — a fines buenos** the protests can be directed towards good objectives, the protests can be guided into useful channels.
encefalitis nf encephalitis; **— (letárgica)** sleeping sickness.
enceguecer [2d] (SAm) **1** vt to blind. **2** vi and **enceguecerse** vr to go blind.
encelar [1a] **1** vt to make jealous. **2 encelarse** vr to become jealous.
encenagado adj (a) muddy, mud-stained. (b) (fig) sunk in vice, depraved.

encenagarse [1h] vr (a) to get muddy. (b) (fig) to wallow in vice, get depraved.

encendedor nm (a) lighter; — de cigarrillos cigarette lighter; — a gas gas lighter; — del gas gas poker. (b) lamplighter.

encender [2g] 1 vt (a) to light; to set fire to, ignite; to kindle; match to strike, light; (Elec) light to turn on, switch on, put on; gas to light, turn on; radio to switch on, turn on.
(b) (fig) to kindle, inflame; to stir up, provoke.
(c) (Cu) to beat.
2 **encenderse** vr (a) (fire) to catch, catch fire, ignite; (flame) to burn up, flare up.
(b) (fig) to get excited; to flare up.
(c) (face) to blush, get red.

encendida nf (Cu) beating.

encendidamente adv passionately, ardently.

encendido 1 adj (a) estar — to be alight, be on fire, be burning; (light) to be on; (wire) to be live.
(b) colour glowing (de with); fiery.
(c) face red (de with); inflamed (de with).
2 nm (Aut) ignition.

encendimiento nm (a) burning; kindling. (b) (fig) passion, ardour; eagerness; intensity.

encenizar [1f] vt to cover with ashes.

encentar [1k] vt to begin to use; loaf etc to cut the first slice from.

encerado 1 adj waxed; waxy, wax-coloured. 2 nm (a) oilcloth; (Naut) tarpaulin. (b) (Med) sticking plaster. (c) (School etc) blackboard.

encerador nm, **enceradora** nf polisher, polishing machine.

encerar [1a] vt to wax; floor to wax, polish.

encercamiento nm (SAm) encirclement.

encercar [1g] vt (SAm: angl) to encircle; = cercar.

encerotar [1a] vt thread to wax.

encerradero nm fold, pen.

encerrar [1k] 1 vt (a) to shut in, shut up; to lock in, lock up; to enclose; to confine, hem in.
(b) to include, contain, comprise; el libro encierra profundas verdades the book contains deep truths.
(c) to involve, imply.
2 **encerrarse** vr to shut oneself up, lock oneself in; to go into seclusion; se encerró en su cuarto she shut herself in her room; — en el silencio to maintain a total silence.

encespedar [1a] vt to turf.

encía nf (Anat) gum.

encíclica nf encyclical.

enciclopedia nf encyclopaedia.

enciclopédico adj encyclopaedic.

encielar [1a] vt (Chi, Guat) to roof, put a roof on.

encierra nf (Chi) (a) penning (of cattle, for slaughter). (b) winter pasture.

encierre nm (Ven) penning (of cattle, for slaughter).

encierro nm (a) shutting-in. shutting-up, locking, closing; confinement.
(b) enclosure; prison, lock-up; (Agr) pen; (Taur) bull pen.
(c) (Taur) penning (of bulls), corralling.

encima 1 adj (a) (place) above, over; overhead; at the top; on top; por — over, overhead; muy por — (fig) very superficially, very hastily; póngalo — y no debajo put it over and not under, put it on top and not underneath; el avión pasó — the plane passed over.
(b) (fig) echarse algo — to take something upon oneself; quitarse algo de — to get rid of something; to cast something off, shake something off; la guerra está — war is upon us, war is imminent; no llevo tabaco — I haven't any tobacco on me, I don't carry tobacco; ¿tienes un duro —? do you have a duro about you?; ¿tienes cambio —? have you any change on you?; tienes bastante — you've got enough to worry about.
(c) (fig) besides; y otras muchas cosas — and a lot else besides, and much else in addition; de — (SAm) into the bargain; y — no me dio las gracias and on top of all that he didn't even thank me.
2 — de prep (a) (place) above, over; on; on top of; por — de over; pasó — de nuestras cabezas it passed over our heads.
(b) (fig) besides, in addition to; y luego — de todo eso and then in addition to all that, and then on top of all that.

encimar [1a] (Col, Chi, Per) 1 vt to give as a bonus, put in as an extra. 2 vi (Cards) to add a new stake.

encime nm (Col) bonus, extra.

encina nf ilex, holm oak, evergreen oak.

encinar nm holm-oak wood.

encinta adj pregnant; (Zool) with young; mujer —

pregnant woman, expectant mother; dejar a una — to get a girl with a child, put a girl in the family way.

encintado nm kerb, kerbstone.

encizañar [1a] 1 vt to sow discord among, create trouble among. 2 vi to sow discord, cause trouble.

enclaustrar [1a] vt to cloister; (fig) to hide away.

enclavar [1a] 1 vt (a) to nail; to pierce, transfix.
(b) to embed, set; building etc to set, place; las ruinas están enclavadas en un valle the ruins are set in a valley, the ruins have a valley as their setting.
(c) (fam) to swindle.
2 **enclavarse** vr to interlock.

enclave nm (Pol etc) enclave; small area, isolated area; — regional de gobierno regional seat of government.

enclavijar [1a] vt to peg, pin; to join.

enclencle adj (SAm) terribly thin.

enclenco adj (Col, PR), **enclenque** adj weak, weakly, sickly.

enclítico adj enclitic.

enclocar [1g and 1m] vi, **encloquecer** [2d] vi to go broody.

encobar [1a] vi and **encobarse** vr (of hen) to sit, brood.

encocorante adj annoying, maddening.

encocorar [1a] (fam) 1 vt to annoy, enrage, madden. 2 **encocorarse** vr (a) to get cross, get mad. (b) (Cu) to get suspicious.

encofrado nm (Tech: for concrete etc) form, plank mould.

encoger [2c] 1 vt (a) to shrink, contract, shorten.
(b) (fig) to intimidate, scare, discourage.
2 **encogerse** vr (a) to shrink, contract; to shrivel up.
(b) — de hombros to shrug one's shoulders.
(c) (fig) to cringe; to get discouraged, get disheartened; to be shy, be timid.

encogidamente adv (fig) shyly, timidly, bashfully.

encogido adj (a) shrunken; shrivelled. (b) (fig) shy, timid, bashful.

encogimiento nm (a) shrinking, contraction; shrinkage. (b) — de hombros shrug (of the shoulders). (c) (fig) shyness, timidity, bashfulness.

encogollado adj (Chi) stiff, haughty.

encogollarse [1a] vr (Chi) to get conceited, be haughty.

encohetarse [1a] vr (Bol, CR) to get furious.

encojar [1a] 1 vt to lame, cripple. 2 **encojarse** vr to go lame; (fam) to pretend to be ill.

encolar [1a] vt to glue, gum, paste; to size; to stick down, stick together.

encolerizar [1f] 1 vt to anger, provoke. 2 **encolerizarse** vr to get angry.

encomendar [1k] 1 vt to entrust, commend (a to, to the charge of). 2 **encomendarse** vr: — a to entrust oneself to, put one's trust in; to send greetings to.

encomendería nf (Per) grocery store.

encomendero nm (Per) grocer; (Cu) wholesale meat supplier.

encomiar [1b] vt to praise, extol, pay tribute to.

encomienda nf (a) (Hist) concession, holding (land and inhabitants granted to a conquistador).
(b) charge, commission.
(c) protection; patronage.
(d) praise, tribute, commendation.
(e) (SAm: Post) parcel; parcel post; — contra reembolso parcel sent cash on delivery.
(f) —s regards, respects.

encomio nm praise, eulogy, tribute.

encomioso adj (SAm) laudatory, eulogistic.

enconado adj (a) (Med) inflamed, angry; sore. (b) (fig) angry, bitter.

enconar [1a] 1 vt (a) (Med) to inflame; to make sore.
(b) (fig) to anger, irritate, provoke.
(c) (Cu, Mex) to pilfer.
2 **enconarse** vr (a) (Med) to become inflamed; to fester.
(b) (fig) to get angry, get irritated; (of grievance) to fester, rankle.

enconcharse [1a] vr (SAm) to go into one's shell; to retire into seclusion.

encono nm (a) rancour, spite(fulness); ill-feeling, bad blood. (b) (Col, Chi) inflammation, soreness.

enconoso adj (a) (Med) sensitive, subject to inflammation. (b) (fig) resentful, rancorous, malevolent. (c) (SAm) plant noxious, poisonous.

encontradizo adj met by chance; hacerse el — to contrive an apparently chance meeting, manage to bump into someone.

encontrado adj contrary, conflicting, hostile.

encontrar [1m] 1 vt (a) to find; lo encontró bastante fácil he found it pretty easy; ¿qué tal lo encuentras?

how do you find it?; **no lo encuentro en ninguna parte** I can't find it anywhere; **no sé lo que le encuentran** I don't know what they see in her.

(b) to meet, encounter, run into; **— dificultades** to encounter difficulties, run into trouble.

2 **encontrarse** vr (a) to meet, meet each other; **— con uno** to meet someone, run across someone, encounter someone; **— con un obstáculo** to run into an obstacle, encounter an obstacle; **me encontré con que no tenía gasolina** I found I was out of petrol; I was faced with the fact that I had no petrol.

(b) (vehicles etc) to crash, collide; (opinions etc) to clash, conflict, come into collision.

(c) to be, be situated, be located, stand; **se encuentra en la plaza principal** it is in the main square; **¿dónde se encuentra el cine?** where is the cinema?

(d) to find oneself, be; **se encuentra enferma** she is ill; **¿cómo te encuentras ahora?** how are you now?, how do you feel now?, how do you find yourself now?; **me encontré sin coche** I found myself without a car.

(e) **si lo haces te la encuentras** (fam) if you do that you'll have it coming to you (fam).

encontrón nm, **encontronazo** nm collision, crash, smash.

encopetado adj (a) of noble birth; blue-blooded. (b) haughty, high and mighty; conceited; important, prominent; of high social position.

encopetarse [1a] vr to get conceited, give oneself airs.

encorajar [1a] 1 vt (a) to encourage, put heart into. (b) to inflame. 2 **encorajarse** vr to fly into a rage.

encorajinar [1a] 1 vt (SAm) = **encorajar**; (Mex) to anger, irritate. 2 **encorajinarse** vr (Chi: of deal) to fail, go awry.

encorar [1m] vt to cover with leather.

encorchar [1a] vt (a) bottle to cork. (b) bees to hive.

encordado (a) nm (Arg: Mus) strings; guitar. (b) (Boxing) ring.

encordar [1m] 1 vt (a) (Mus etc) to string, fit strings to. (b) to bind, tie, lash (with ropes); to rope together. (c) space, area to rope off. 2 **encordarse** vr (mountaineers) to rope themselves together.

encordelar [1a] vt to tie (with string).

encornado adj: **un toro bien —** a bull with good horns.

encornadura nf horns.

encornar [1m] vt to gore.

encornudar [1a] vt to cuckold.

encorralar [1a] vt to pen, corral.

encorvada nf stoop, bend; **hacer la —** (fam) to malinger, pretend to be ill.

encorvado adj curved, bent; stooping; crooked.

encorvadura nf curve, curving, curvature; bend; crookedness.

encorvar [1a] 1 vt to bend, curve; to bend (down, over), stoop; to hook; to make crooked. 2 **encorvarse** vr (a) to bend (down, over), stoop. (b) to sag, warp; to buckle.

encrespado adj curly.

encrespador nm curling tongs.

encrespar [1a] 1 vt (a) hair to curl, frizzle; feathers to ruffle; water to ripple; to make rough, produce waves on. (b) (fig) to anger, irritate. 2 **encresparse** vr (a) to curl; to ripple; to get rough. (b) (fig) to get cross, get irritated.

encrestado adj haughty.

encrucijada nf crossroads; intersection, junction.

encuadernación nf (a) binding; **— en cuero, — en piel** leather binding; **— en tela** cloth binding. (b) bindery, binder's.

encuadernador nm bookbinder.

encuadernar [1a] vt to bind (en in); to cover; **libro sin —** unbound book.

encuadrar [1a] 1 vt (a) to frame, put in a frame, make a frame for. (b) to fit, insert (en into). (c) (fig) to contain, comprise. (c) (SAm) to summarize, give a synthesis of. 2 vi (Arg) to fit, square (con with).

encuadre nm (Phot etc) setting, background, frame.

encuartar [1a] (Mex) 1 vt to join, put together. 2 **encuartarse** vr (a) (animal) to shy, balk; to get caught in its straps (etc). (b) (fig) to get involved, get bogged down (en in). (c) to butt in.

encuartelar [1a] vt (SAm) = **acuartelar**.

encubierta nf fraud.

encubierto adj hidden, concealed; underhand; undercover.

encubridor 1 adj concealing. 2 nm, **encubridora** nf harbourer; receiver of stolen goods; (Law) accessory after the fact, abettor.

encubrimiento nm concealment, hiding; receiving of stolen goods; (Law) complicity, abetment.

encubrir [3a; ptp **encubierto**] vt to conceal, hide, cover (up), cloak; criminal, suspect to harbour, shelter; crime to conceal; to abet, be an accomplice in.

encucurucharse [1a] vr (CAm, Col) to get up on top, reach the top.

encuentro nm (a) meeting, encounter; **un — fortuito** a chance meeting; **su primer — con la policía** his first encounter with the police; **ir (or salir) al — de uno** to go to meet someone; **ir al — de lo desconocido** to go out to face the unknown.

(b) (Mil) encounter; skirmish, action, fight.

(c) (Sport) meeting, match, game.

(d) (Aut etc) collision, smash, crash; (of opinions etc) clash; **llevarse a uno de —** (Mex, PR) to knock someone down, (fig) to drag someone down to disaster.

encuerada nf (Cu, Mex) naked woman, nude.

encuerado adj (Cu, Mex) ragged; nude, naked.

encuerar [1a] 1 vt (Cu, Chi, Mex) (a) to strip (naked). (b) (fig) to skin, fleece. 2 **encuerarse** vr (a) (Cu, Chi, Mex) to strip off, get undressed. (b) (Ven) to live in sin.

encuerista nf (Cu, Mex) striptease artiste.

encuesta nf (a) (Law) inquiry, investigation; probe (de into); inquest (fig); **— judicial** post-mortem, coroner's inquest. (b) public-opinion poll; **E— Gallup** Gallup Poll.

encuestador nm, **encuestadora** nf pollster.

encuitarse [1a] vr (a) to grieve. (b) (Col) to get into debt.

encujado nm (Cu, PR, Ven) framework, lattice.

enculecarse [1g] vr (SAm) to go broody.

encumbrado adj (a) building etc lofty, towering, high. (b) person exalted, eminent. (c) (pej) high and mighty, haughty.

encumbramiento nm (a) (act) raising, elevation. (b) height, loftiness; exaltation, eminence. (c) (fig) haughtiness.

encumbrar [1a] 1 vt (a) to raise, elevate. (b) person to elevate, exalt (a to); (fig) to extol. 2 **encumbrarse** vr (a) (of building) to rise, soar, tower. (b) (fig) **— sobre** to tower over, be far superior to. (c) (fig: pej) to be proud, be haughty.

encurrucarse [1g] vr (SAm) = **acurrucarse**.

encurtido nm pickle.

encurtir [3a] vt to pickle.

enchapado nm plating; veneer.

enchapar [1a] vt (a) to plate, overlay (with metal); to veneer. (b) (Mex) to fit locks to.

enchaquetarse [1a] vr (a) (Col, Per, PR) to put one's jacket on. (b) (Col) to dress up.

encharcada nf pool, puddle.

encharcado adj still, stagnant.

encharcar [1g] 1 vt to swamp, flood; to cover with puddles, turn into pools. 2 **encharcarse** vr (a) (land) to swamp, get flooded, get covered with puddles. (b) (water) to form puddles, form a pool; to become stagnant. (c) (SAm) to get muddy. (d) (Arg) to get stuck in a puddle. (e) (fig) **— en los vicios** to wallow in vice.

encharralarse [1a] vr (CAm) to make an ambush, lie in ambush.

enchauchado adj (Chi) well heeled (sl).

enchicharse [1a] vr (a) (SAm) to get drunk on chicha. (b) (CAm, Col, Ec) to get angry, boil up.

enchilada nf (Guat, Mex) rolled omelette seasoned with chili.

enchilado 1 cdj (a) (CAm, Mex: Cook) seasoned with chili. (b) (Mex) bright red. 2 nm (Cu, Mex) stew with chili sauce.

enchilar [1a] 1 vt (a) (CAm, Mex: Cook) to season with chili. (b) (CR, Mex) to annoy, vex; (CR) to disappoint. 2 vi (CR, Mex) to sting, burn.

enchiloso adj (CAm, Mex) taste hot.

enchilotarse [1a] vr (Arg) to get cross.

enchinar [1a] 1 vt (Mex) to curl, frizzle. 2 **enchinarse** vr: **— el cuerpo** to get gooseflesh, to get scared.

enchinchar [1a] 1 vt (a) (Guat, Mex, SD) to put out, bother. (b) (Mex) to cause to waste time; matter to delay. 2 **enchincharse** vr (a) (Guat, Mex, Per, PR) to get infested with bugs. (b) (Arg) to get bad-tempered.

enchiquerar [1a] *vt* (*SAm*) to pen, corral.
enchisparse [1a] *vr* (*SAm*) to get tight.
enchisterado *adj* top-hatted, with a top hat on.
enchivarse [1a] *vr* (*Col, Ec*) to fly into a rage.
enchufable *adj* which plugs in, plug-in (*attr*).
enchufar [1a] *vt* (a) (*Tech etc*) to join, connect, fit together, fit in; to telescope together; (*Elec*) to plug in. (b) (*Comm, Fin*) to merge.
enchufe *nm* (a) (*Tech etc*) joint, connection; sleeve; socket.
　(b) (*Elec*) plug; point, socket.
　(c) (*fam*) connection, useful contact; **tiene un — en el ministerio** he's got a contact in the ministry, he can pull wires at the ministry; **hay que tener —s** you've got to have contacts.
　(d) (*fam*) soft job, cushy job (*sl*).
enchufismo *nm* (*fam*) (system of getting things done by) wirepulling (*fam*), use of contacts to obtain favours; old-boy network.
enchufista *nm* (*fam*) wirepuller (*fam*), contact man, man who uses the old-boy network.
ende *adv* (*arch or lit*): **por —** hence, therefore.
endeble *adj* (*Med*) feeble, weak, frail; (*fig*) feeble, flimsy.
endeblez *nf* feebleness, weakness, frailty; flimsiness.
endecasílabo 1 *adj* hendecasyllabic. **2** *nm* hendecasyllable.
endecha *nf* dirge.
endecharse [1a] *vr* to grieve, mourn.
endémico *adj* endemic; (*fig*) rife, chronic.
endemoniado (a) (possessed of the devil. (b) (*fig*) devilish, fiendish; perverse; furious, wild.
endemoniar [1b] **1** *vt* (a) to bedevil. (b) (*fam*) to provoke, anger. **2 endemoniarse** *vr* (*fam*) to get angry.
endenantes *adv* (*SAm*) a short time back.
endentadura *nf* serration, teeth.
endentar [1k] *vti* (*Mech*) to engage, mesh (*con* with).
endentecer [2d] *vi* to teethe, cut one's teeth.
enderezado *adj* appropriate; favourable, opportune.
enderezar [1f] **1** *vt* (a) to straighten, straighten out (*or* up); to unbend.
　(b) to set upright, stand vertically; (*Naut*) to right; *vehicle etc* to stand the right way up, put back on its wheels (*etc*).
　(c) (*fig*) to put in order, set to rights.
　(d) (*fig*) to direct; to manage; to address, dedicate (*a* to); **las medidas están enderezadas a** (*or* **para**) **corregirlo** the measures are designed to correct it.
　2 enderezarse *vr* (a) to straighten up, stand up straight, draw oneself up; (*Naut*) to right itself; (*Aer*) to flatten out.
　(b) **— a un lugar** to set out for a place.
　(c) **— a + *infin*** to take steps to + *infin*, prepare to + *infin*; (*of measure etc*) to be designed to + *infin*.
endespués *adv* (*Col, PR*) =**después.**
endeudarse [1a] *vr* to get into debt (*con* with), contract a debt (*con* to).
endeveras *adv* (*SAm*) =**de veras.**
endiablado *adj* (a) devilish, diabolical, fiendish.
　(b) (*hum*) impish, mischievous, wicked.
　(c) ugly.
　(d) furious, angry.
　(e) (*SAm*) *road etc* difficult, dangerous; *affair* complicated, tricky.
endiablar [1a] **1** *vt* (a) to bedevil, bewitch. (b) (*fam*) to pervert, corrupt. **2 endiablarse** *vr* to get furious.
endibia *nf* endive.
endija *nf* (*SAm*) =**rendija.**
endilgar [1a] *vr* (*fam*) (a) to send, direct; to guide.
　(b) *blow* to fetch.
　(c) **— algo a uno** to spring something on someone; to unload something on to someone; **— un sermón a uno** to give someone a lecture, ram a sermon down someone's throat.
endiñar [1a] *vt* (*fam*) *blow* to fetch.
endiosado *adj* stuck-up (*fam*), conceited; stand-offish.
endiosamiento *nm* (a) vanity, conceit; haughtiness.
　(b) absorption.
endiosar [1a] **1** *vt* to deify; (*fig*) to make a god out of.
　2 endiosarse *vr* (a) to get conceited, give oneself airs; to be stand-offish.
　(b) **— en algo** to be(come) absorbed in something.
enditarse [1a] *vr* (*Guat, Per*) to get into debt.
endocrina *nf* endocrine.
endocrino *adj* endocrine.
endogamia *nf* inbreeding; **engendrado por —** inbred.
endomingado *adj* all dressed up, in one's Sunday best.

endomingarse [1h] *vr* to dress up, put on one's Sunday best.
endosar [1a] *vt* (*CAm, Mex, PR*: *angl*) =**endosar;** (*fig*) to endorse, support, back; to confirm.
endosante *nmf* endorser.
endosar [1a] *vt* (a) *cheque etc* to endorse.
　(b) (*fam*) **— algo a uno** to lumber someone with something, make someone put up with something; to unload something on to someone.
endosatario *nm*, **endosataria** *nf* endorsee.
endoso *nm* endorsement; **sin —** unendorsed.
endriago *nm* fabulous monster, dragon.
endrogarse [1h] *vr* (*Mex, Per*) to get into debt.
endulzante *nm* (*Arg*) sweetening, sugar.
endulzar [1f] *vt* (a) to sweeten. (b) (*fig*) to sweeten; to soften, mitigate.
endurecer [2d] **1** *vt* (a) to harden, make hard; to toughen; to stiffen; *mud etc* to harden, cake, set.
　(b) (*fig*) to toughen, inure; **— a uno a los peligros** to inure someone to dangers.
　2 endurecerse *vr* (a) to harden, get hard; to stiffen; to cake, set, set firm; (*Fin*: *of price*) to harden.
　(b) (*fig*) to become cruel, become hard-hearted.
　(c) **— a los peligros** to become inured to danger, inure oneself to danger.
endurecido *adj* (a) hard; tough; stiff; *mud etc* hardened, caked, set.
　(b) (*fig*) hardy, tough; **— a** inured to, used to.
　(c) (*fig*: *pej*) cruel, callous, hard-hearted; obdurate.
endurecimiento *nm* (a) (*act*) hardening; stiffening; setting; **— de las arterias** hardening of the arteries.
　(b) (*state*) hardness; toughness; stiffness; firmness.
　(c) (*fig*) cruelty, callousness, hard-heartedness; obduracy.
enea *nf* =**anea.**
Eneas *m* Aeneas.
enebro *nm* juniper.
Eneida *f* Aeneid.
enema *nf* enema.
enemiga *nf* enmity, hostility.
enemigo 1 *adj* enemy, hostile; unfriendly; **ser — de** (*fig*) to dislike, be hostile to; (*of tendency etc*) to be inimical to; **una actitud enemiga de todo progreso** an attitude inimical to all progress.
　2 *nm*, **enemiga** *nf* enemy; foe, adversary, opponent; **el E—, el — malo** the devil; **pasarse al — to** go over to the enemy.
enemistad *nf* enmity.
enemistar [1a] **1** *vt* to make enemies of, cause a rift between, set at odds.
　2 enemistarse *vr* to become enemies; **— con uno** to become an enemy of someone; to fall out with someone, become estranged from someone.
energético *adj* (*SAm*: *angl*) =**enérgico.**
energía *nf* (a) energy; vigour, drive; push, go; **obrar con —** to act energetically; **reaccionar con —** to react vigorously.
　(b) (*Tech*) power; energy; (*Elec*) power, energy, current; **— atómica** atomic energy; **— hidráulica** water power; **— nuclear** nuclear power.
enérgicamente *adv* energetically; vigorously; forcefully; emphatically; strenuously; boldly, drastically.
enérgico *adj* energetic; *person* energetic, vigorous; (*in manner*) forceful, forthright; vital; pushful; *gesture, speech, tone etc* emphatic, forceful; *effort* determined, vigorous; *exercise* strenuous; *campaign* vigorous, forceful, high-pressure; *stroke* bold; *measure* bold, drastic; *attack etc* vigorous, strong; **ponerse — con uno** to get tough with someone.
energúmeno *nm*, **energúmena** *nf* person possessed of the devil; (*fig*) demon, wild person, madman.
enero *nm* January.
enervador *adj* enervating.
enervar [1a] *vt* to enervate.
enésimo *adj* (a) (*Math*) nth; **elevado a la enésima potencia** raised to the nth power, (*fig*) to the nth degree. (b) (*fig*) umpteenth (*fam*); **por enésima vez** for the umpteenth time.
enfadadizo *adj* irritable, crotchety.
enfadar [1a] **1** *vt* (a) to anger, irritate, annoy; to offend.
　(b) (*SAm*) to bore.
　2 enfadarse *vr* (a) to get angry, get cross, get annoyed (*con* with, *de* about, at); **no te enfades** don't be cross; don't be offended; **de nada sirve enfadarte** it's no good getting cross.
　(b) (*SAm*) to be bored, get bored.
enfado *nm* (a) annoyance, irritation, anger. (b) trouble, bother.
enfadoso *adj* annoying, vexatious; irksome, tedious.

enfajillar [1a] *vt* (CAm, Mex: *Post*) to put a wrapper on.

enfangar [1h] **1** *vt* to cover with mud. **2 enfangarse** *vr* (a) to get muddy, get covered in mud; to sink into the mud. (b) (*fig*) to dirty one's hands, get involved in dirty work; **— en los vicios** to wallow in vice.

enfardadora *nf* (*Agr etc*) baler, baling machine.

enfardar [1a] *vt* to bale.

énfasis *nm* (a) emphasis; stress; **hablar con —** to speak emphatically; to speak ponderously. (b) (*fig*) emphasis; **poner el — en** to put the emphasis on, stress.

enfático *adj* emphatic; positive; *speech* heavy, ponderous; **dijo —** he said emphatically.

enfatizar [1f] *vt* (SAm: *angl*) to emphasize, stress.

enfermar [1a] **1** *vt* to make ill, cause illness in. **2** *vi* to fall ill, be taken ill (*de* with); **— del corazón** to develop heart trouble.

enfermedad *nf* (a) illness; sickness; **durante esta —** during this illness; **una — que duró 6 meses** an illness which lasted 6 months; **ausentarse por —** to be away ill, be away sick. (b) illness, disease; complaint; (*fig*) disease, malady, ill; **una — muy peligrosa** a very dangerous disease; **— contagiosa** contagious disease; **— de la piel** skin disease, skin infection; **— profesional** occupational disease; **— del sueño** sleeping sickness; **— venérea** venereal disease; **— por virus** virus disease; **contagiar a uno con una —, pegar una — a uno** to give someone a disease.

enfermera *nf* nurse; **— ambulante** visiting nurse; **— jefa** matron.

enfermería *nf* infirmary; sanatorium; (*of school etc*) sick bay; (*Taur*) hospital, medical section.

enfermero *nm* male nurse; (*Mil*) medical orderly.

enfermizo *adj* sickly, weak, unhealthy; infirm; *mind* morbid, unhealthy.

enfermo 1 *adj* ill, sick, unwell; sickly; **— de amor** lovesick; **caer —, ponerse —** to fall ill (*de* with); **estar — de gravedad, estar — de peligro** to be seriously ill, be dangerously ill. **2** *nm*, **enferma** *nf* patient; invalid, sick person.

enfermoso *adj* (SAm) =**enfermizo**.

enfiestarse [1a] *vr* (SAm) to have a good time, make merry.

enfilada *nf* enfilade.

enfilar [1a] *vt* (a) (*Mil*) to enfilade. (b) to line up, put in a row; *beads* to thread. (c) *course* to direct, bear. (d) *street etc* to go straight along (*or* down *etc*).

enflaquecer [2d] **1** *vt* to make thin; to weaken, sap the strength of. **2** *vi and* **enflaquecerse** *vr* (a) to get thin, lose weight. (b) (*fig: effort etc*) to flag, weaken; (*person*) to lose heart.

enflaquecido *adj* thin, extenuated.

enflaquecimiento *nm* (a) loss of weight; emaciation. (b) (*fig*) weakening.

enflatarse [1a] *vr* (a) (CAm, Ven) to grow sad. (b) (Cu, Mex) to fly into a rage.

enflautada *nf* (Guat, Hond, Per) blunder.

enflautado *adj* pompous.

enflautar [1a] *vt* (Col, Guat, Mex): **— algo a uno** to unload something on to someone.

enfocar [1g] **1** *vt* (a) (*Phot etc*) to focus (*a, sobre* on). (b) *problem etc* to approach, consider, look at; to size up; **podemos — este problema de tres maneras** we can approach this problem in three ways; **no me gusta su modo de — la cuestión** I do not like his approach to the question. **2** *vi and* **enfocarse** *vr* to focus (*a, sobre* on).

enfoque *nm* (a) (*Phot etc*) focus; focusing. (b) magnification; **potencia de —** magnifying power, magnification. (c) (*fig*) grasp; approach.

enfoscar [1g] **1** *vt* to fill with mortar. **2 enfoscarse** *vr* (a) to sulk, be sullen. (b) **— en un negocio** to plunge into a deal, rush into a deal. (c) (*of sky*) to cloud over.

enfrascar [1g] **1** *vt* to bottle. **2 enfrascarse** *vr* (a) **— en un libro** to bury oneself in a book, become absorbed in a book. (b) **— en un problema** to get tangled up in a problem, get deeply involved in a problem.

enfrenar [1a] *vt* (a) *horse* to bridle; (*Mech*) to brake, slow, halt. (b) (*fig*) to curb, restrain.

enfrentar [1a] **1** *vt* (a) to put face to face. (b) to face, confront. **2** *vi* to face. **3 enfrentarse** *vr*: **— con** to face, face up to, con-

front; to stand up to; (*Sport*) to meet, play against; **hay que — con el peligro** one must face up to the danger, one must face the danger squarely.

enfrente 1 *adv* opposite; in front, facing; (*fig*) in opposition; **la casa de —** the house opposite, the house across the street. **2 — de** *prep* opposite (to), facing; (*fig*) opposed to, against.

enfriadera *nf* cooling jar; bottle cooler.

enfriadero *nm* cold storage; refrigerator.

enfriador *nm* cooler, cooling plant.

enfriamiento *nm* (a) cooling; refrigeration. (b) (*Med*) cold, chill.

enfriar [1c] **1** *vt* (a) to cool, chill; (*fig*) to cool down, take the heat out of. (b) (SAm) to kill. **2 enfriarse** *vr* (a) to cool, cool down, cool off; **déjelo hasta que se enfríe** leave it till it gets cool, leave it to cool down. (b) (*fig*) to cool off, grow cold.

enfrijolarse [1a] *vr* (Mex: *of a deal*) to get messed up.

enfullinarse [1a] *vr* (Chi) to get angry.

enfundar [1a] *vt* (a) to sheathe; to put away, put in its case. (b) to fill, stuff (*de* with).

enfurecer [2d] **1** *vt* to enrage, madden. **2 enfurecerse** *vr* (a) to get furious, fly into a rage. (b) (*of sea*) to get rough.

enfurruñarse [1a] *vr* (*fam*) (a) to get angry. (b) to sulk; to get disgruntled.

engaitar [1a] *vt* (*fam*): **— a uno** to wheedle someone, talk someone round.

engajado *adj* (Col) curly.

engalanar [1a] **1** *vt* to adorn, deck (*de* with). **2 engalanarse** *vr* to adorn oneself; to dress up, deck oneself out.

enganchar [1a] **1** *vt* (a) to hook; to hitch; to hang up; *horse* to harness; *horse, wagon, trailer* to hitch up; (*Mech*) to couple, connect; (*Rail*) to couple (up). (b) (*fig*) to inveigle, ensnare; to rope in. (c) (*Mil*) to recruit; to persuade to join up, lure into military service. **2 engancharse** *vr* (a) to get hooked up, catch (*en* on); (*Mech*) to engage (*en* with). (b) (*Mil*) to enlist, join up, sign on.

enganche *nm* (a) (*act*) hooking (up); hitching; coupling, connection. (b) (*Mech*) coupling, connection; (*Rail*) coupling. (c) (*Mil*) recruitment, enlistment; (*payment*) bounty.

engañabobos *nm, pl* **engañabobos** (a) trickster. (b) trick, trap.

engañadizo *adj* gullible.

engañador 1 *adj* deceiving, cheating; deceptive. **2** *nm*, **engañadora** *nf* cheat, deceiver, impostor.

engañapichanga *nf* (Bol, Chi, RPl) trick, fraud, hoax.

engañar [1a] **1** *vt* to deceive; to cheat, trick, swindle, fool; to mislead; to beguile, delude; *hunger* to stay; *time* to kill, while away; **a mí no me engaña nadie** you can't fool me; **logró — al inspector** he managed to trick the inspector. **2** *vi* to be deceptive; **las apariencias engañan** appearances are deceptive. **3 engañarse** *vr* to deceive oneself; to be wrong, be mistaken; to delude oneself; **en eso te engañas** you're wrong there; **se engaña con falsas esperanzas** she deludes herself with false hopes.

engañifa *nf* (*fam*) trick, swindle.

engañito *nm* (Chi) small gift, token.

engaño *nm* (a) deceit; deception; fraud, trick, swindle; sham; delusion; **— sentimental** (*Philos, Poet*) pathetic fallacy; **todo es —** it's all a sham; **aquí no hay —** there is no attempt to deceive anybody here, it's all on the level (*fam*). (b) mistake, misunderstanding; **no haya — let** there be no mistake about it; **padecer — to** labour under a misunderstanding. (c) **—s** wiles, tricks. (d) (Chi) small gift, token.

engañosamente *adv* deceitfully, dishonestly; deceptively; misleadingly, wrongly.

engañoso *adj person etc* deceitful, dishonest; *appearance* deceptive; *advice etc* misleading, wrong.

engarabitarse [1a] *vr* (a) to climb, shin up. (b) to get stiff with cold. (c) (Col) to grow weak, get thin.

engaratusar [1a] *vt* (CAm, Col, Mex) =**engatusar**.

engarce *nm* (a) setting, mount. (b) (*fig*) linking, connection. (c) (Col) row, shindy.

engaripolarse [1a] *vr* (Ven) to doll oneself up.

engarrotarse [1a] *vr* (SAm: *of limbs*) to get stiff, go numb.

engarruñarse [1a] *vr* (Col, Hond, Mex) =**engurruñarse**.

engarzar [1f] **1** *vt* (a) *jewel* to set, mount; *beads* to thread; *hair* to curl. (b) (*fig*) to link, connect. (c) (*Col*) to hook (up). **2 engarzarse** *vr* (*Chi, RPl*) to get tangled, get stuck.

engastar [1a] *vt* to set, mount.

engaste *nm* setting, mount.

engatado *adj* thievish.

engatusar [1a] *vt* to coax, wheedle, inveigle; — **a uno para que haga algo** to coax someone into doing something.

engendrar [1a] *vt* (a) (*Bio*) to beget, breed; to have as offspring. (b) (*Math*) to generate. (c) (*fig*) to breed, cause, engender.

engendro *nm* (a) (*Bio*) foetus; (*pej*) runt. (b) (*fig*) abortion, monstrosity; bungled job; idiotic scheme, impossible plan; brain-child; **el proyecto es el — del ministro** the plan is some brain-child of the minister. (c) **mal —, — del diablo** bad lot, no-good lout (*US fam*).

engerido *adj* (*Col, Ven*) weak, sickly; wretched; timid.

engerirse [3l] *vr* (*Col, Ven*) to grow sad.

engestado *adj* ugly.

engestarse [1a] *vr* (*Mex*) to make a wry face.

englobar [1a] *vt* (a) to include, comprise. (b) to lump together, put all together.

engodo *nm* (*Cu*) bait.

engolfarse [1a] *vr* (a) (*Naut*) to sail out to sea, lose sight of land. (b) — **en** (*fig*) to get deeply involved in; to plunge into, become deeply absorbed in; to launch out into.

engolondrinarse [1a] *vr* (a) to get conceited. (b) to have a flirtation.

engolosinar [1a] **1** *vt* to tempt, entice. **2 engolosinarse** *vr*: — **con** to grow fond of; to grow accustomed to.

engolletarse [1a] *vr* to give oneself airs.

engorda *nf* (a) (*Col, Chi, Mex: Agr*) fattening (up). (b) (*Chi, Mex*) fattened animals (*collectively*).

engomar [1a] *vt* to gum, glue, stick.

engordar [1a] **1** *vt* to fatten (up). **2** *vi* (a) to get fat; to fill out, put on weight; (*Agr*) to fatten. (b) (*fam*) to get rich.

engorde *nm* fattening (up).

engorrar [1a] *vt* (*Mex, PR, Ven*) to annoy.

engorro *nm* bother, nuisance.

engorroso *adj* bothersome, vexatious, trying; cumbersome, awkward.

engrampar [1a] *vt* (*SAm*) to clip together, staple.

engranaje *nm* gear; gears, gearing; mesh; gear teeth; — **de distribución** timing gear.

engranar [1a] **1** *vt* to gear; to put into gear; — **con** to gear into, engage. **2** *vi* to interlock; (*Mech*) to engage (*con una rueda* a wheel, mesh (*con* with); **A engrana con B** A is in gear with B; **A y B están engranados** A and B are in mesh. **3 engranarse** *vr* (a) (*Arg, Mex: Mech*) to seize up, get locked, jam. (b) (*Arg*) to get angry.

engrandecer [2d] *vt* (a) to enlarge, magnify. (b) (*fig*) to extol, magnify; to exalt; to exaggerate.

engrandecimiento *nm* (a) enlargement. (b) exaltation; exaggeration.

engrane *nm* (a) mesh, meshing. (b) (*Arg, Mex: Mech*) seizing, jamming.

engrasación *nf* greasing, lubrication.

engrasado *nm* greasing, lubrication.

engrasador *nm* greaser, lubricator; grease point; grease cup; — **de compresión**, — **de pistón** grease gun.

engrasamiento *nm* greasing, lubrication.

engrasar [1a] *vt* (a) (*Mech*) to grease, lubricate, oil. (b) to make greasy, stain with grease. (c) (*Agr*) to manure.

engrase *nm* greasing, lubrication.

engreído *adj* (a) vain, conceited, stuck-up (*fam*). (b) (*SAm*) affectionate; spoiled.

engreimiento *nm* vanity, conceit.

engreír [3l] **1** *vt* (a) to make vain, make conceited. (b) (*SAm*) *child* to spoil, pamper. **2 engreírse** *vr* (a) to get conceited. (b) (*SAm*) to get spoiled, be pampered. (c) (*SAm*) — **a**, — **con** to grow fond of.

engrescar [1g] *vt* (a) to goad into fighting. (b) to rouse to merriment.

engrifarse [1a] *vr* (a) (*Col*) to get haughty. (b) (*Mex*) to get cross; (*Mex: fam*) to get high on drugs.

engrillar [1a] **1** *vt* (a) to shackle. (b) (*Col, PR*) to trick. **2 engrillarse** *vr* (a) (*PR, Ven: of horse*) to lower its head. (b) (*PR, Ven*) to get conceited. (c) (*Col, Pan*) to get into debt.

engringolarse [1a] *vr* (a) (*Col*) to get excited; to become insolent. (b) (*Ec, Nic*) to get awry. (c) (*Ven*) to doll oneself up.

engrosar [1m] **1** *vt* to enlarge; *quantity* to increase, swell; to thicken. **2** *vi* to get fat. **3 engrosarse** *vr* to increase, swell, expand.

engrudar [1a] *vt* to paste.

engrudo *nm* paste.

enguacharse [1a] *vr* (*Col*) to coarsen, get coarse.

enguadar [1a] *vt* (*Cu*) = **engatusar.**

engualichar [1a] *vt* (*Arg*) (a) to bewitch; — **a uno** to give someone a potion. (b) *lover* to rule, tyrannize.

enguandos *nmpl* (*Col*) (a) useless things. (b) wiles, dodges.

enguandujar [1a] *vt* (*Col*) to cover with useless adornments.

enguantado *adj* gloved, wearing a glove.

enguantarse [1a] *vr* to put one's gloves on.

enguaracarse [1g] *vr* (*CAm*) to hide oneself away.

enguaraparse [1a] *vr* (*CAm: of sugar cane*) to ferment.

enguasimar [1a] *vt* (*Cu*) to hang.

enguijarrado *nm* cobbles.

enguijarrar [1a] *vt* to cobble.

enguirnaldar [1a] *vt* to garland, wreathe (*de, con* with); (*fig*) to wreathe.

engullir [3a *and* 3h] *vt* to gobble, bolt, gulp (down); to devour.

engurruñarse [1a] *vr* to get sad, grow gloomy.

enhebrar [1a] *vt* to thread.

enhestar [1k] **1** *vt* (a) to erect; to set upright. (b) to hoist (up), raise (on high). **2 enhestarse** *vr* (a) to straighten up, stand up straight. (b) to rise high.

enhiesto *adj* (a) erect, straight, upright. (b) raised; lofty, towering.

enhilar [1a] *vt* (a) *needle* to thread. (b) (*fig*) to arrange, put in order.

enhorabuena 1 *nf* congratulations; ¡—! congratulations!, and the best of luck!; **dar la — a uno** to congratulate someone, wish someone well. **2** *adv*: ¡—! all right!; well and good; — **que . . .** thank heavens that . . .

enhoramala *interj*: ¡—! good riddance!; ¡**vete** —! go to the devil!

enhorquetarse [1a] *vr* (*Ant, Arg, Mex, Urug*) to sit astride.

enhuerar [1a] *vt* to addle.

enigma *nm* enigma; puzzle; mystery.

enigmáticamente *adv* enigmatically.

enigmático *adj* enigmatic; puzzling; mysterious.

enjaboɹar [1a] *vt* (a) to soap; to lather. (b) (*fam*) to soap up (*sl*), soft-soap (*sl*). (c) (*fam*) to abuse.

enjaezar [1f] *vt* to harness, saddle up.

enjalbegado *nm*, **enjalbegadura** *nf* whitewashing.

enjalbegar [1h] *vt* to whitewash; *face* to paint, make up.

enjambrar [1a] **1** *vt* to hive. **2** *vi* to swarm.

enjambre *nm* swarm (*also fig*).

enjaranarse [1a] *vr* (*CAm*) to get into debt.

enjarciar [1b] *vt* (*Naut*) to rig.

enjaretado *nm* grating, grille.

enjaretar [1a] *vt* (*Arg, Mex*): — **algo a uno** to lumber someone with something.

enjaular [1a] *vt* to cage, put in a cage; to coop up, pen in; (*fam*) to jail, lock up.

enjertar [1a] *vt* = **injertar.**

enjetado *adj* (*Arg*) cross-looking.

enjetarse [1a] *vr* (*Arg, Mex*) to get cross.

enjoyado *adj* bejewelled, set with jewels.

enjoyar [1a] *vt* to adorn with jewels, set with precious stones; to set precious stones in; (*fig*) to bejewel, adorn, embellish.

enjuagadientes *nm, pl* **enjuagadientes** mouthwash.

enjuagar [1h] *vt* to rinse, rinse out; to wash out, swill out.

enjuague *nm* (a) mouthwash. (b) (*act*) rinse, rinsing; washing, swilling. (c) (*fig*) scheme, intrigue.

enjugamanos *nm, pl* **enjugamanos** towel.

enjugar [1h] *vt* (a) to wipe (off), wipe the moisture from; to dry; — **se la frente** to wipe one's brow, mop one's brow. (b) *debt, deficit* to wipe out.

enjuiciamiento *nm* (a) judgement. (b) (*Law*) — **civil** lawsuit, civil suit; — **criminal** trial, criminal prosecution.

enjuiciar [1b] *vt* **(a)** to judge, pass judgement on; to examine. **(b)** (*Law*) to indict; to prosecute, try; to sentence.

enjuncado *adj* rush-covered.

enjundia *nf* **(a)** animal fat, grease. **(b)** (*fig*) substance; strength, drive, vigour; essence, character.

enjundioso *adj* **(a)** fat. **(b)** (*fig*) substantial, solid, meaty.

enjuto *adj* **(a)** dry; dried; *see* **pie. (b)** shrivelled up; wizened. **(c)** lean, skinny, spare.

enlabiar [1b] *vt* to blarney, bamboozle (*fam*), take in.

enlabio *nm* blarney, honeyed words, plausible talk.

enlace *nm* **(a)** link, tie-up, connection; bond; relationship; (*Chem, Elec*) linkage; (*Mil etc*) liaison; (*Rail*) connection; marriage, union; meeting, rendez-vous; **el — de A con B** the marriage of A and B; **el — de las dos familias** the linking of the two families by marriage; **los buques no lograron efectuar el — en el punto indicado** the ships did not manage to rendez-vous at the spot indicated.
(b) — sindical shop steward.

enladrillado *nm* brick paving.

enladrillar [1a] *vt* to pave with bricks.

enlardar [1a] *vt* (*Cook*) to baste.

enlatado *nm* canning, tinning.

enlatar [1a] *vt* to can, tin.

enlazar [1f] **1** *vt* **(a)** to link, connect; to tie (together), bind (together); to knit together.
(b) (*SAm*) to lasso.
2 *vi* (*Rail etc*) to connect (*con* with).
3 enlazarse *vr* to link (up), be linked; to be connected; to join; to interlock; to entwine; to marry, get married; (*of families*) to become linked by marriage (*con* to).

enlistar [1a] *vt* (*Guat, Mex, PR, SD*)=**alistar.**

enlodar [1a], **enlodazar** [1f] **1** *vt* **(a)** to muddy, cover in mud. **(b)** (*fig*) to besmirch, stain; to smear, defame. **2 enlodarse** *vr*, **enlodazarse** *vr* to get muddy.

enloquecedor *adj* maddening; *headache* splitting; *pain* excruciating.

enloquecer [2d] **1** *vt* to drive mad; (*fig*) to madden, drive crazy. **2** *vi* and **enloquecerse** *vr* to go mad, go out of one's mind.

enloquecimiento *nm* madness.

enlosado *nm* flagstone pavement.

enlosar [1a] *vt* to pave (with flagstones).

enlozado *adj* (*SAm*) enamelled, glazed.

enlozar [1f] *vt* (*SAm*) to enamel, glaze.

enlucido *nm* plaster.

enlucidor *nm* plasterer.

enlucir [3f] *vt* to plaster; *metal* to polish.

enlutado *adj* in mourning, wearing mourning; *city etc* stricken.

enlutar [1a] **1** *vt* **(a)** *person* to put into mourning; to dress in mourning.
(b) *dress etc* to put crêpe on; to put a symbol of mourning on.
(c) *city, country etc* to plunge into mourning; (*fig*) to sadden, grieve; **el accidente enlutó a la ciudad entera** the accident plunged the whole town into mourning.
(d) (*fig*) to darken.
2 enlutarse *vr* to go into mourning, dress in mourning.

enmaderado *adj* timbered; boarded.

enmaderamiento *nm* timbering; boarding.

enmaderar [1a] *vt* to timber; to board (up).

enmalezarse [1f] *vr* (*Chi, Per, PR*) to get overgrown, get covered in scrub.

enmaniguarse [1i] *vr* (*Cu, PR*) **(a)** to get overgrown with trees, turn into jungle. **(b)** (*person*) to revert to rustic ways.

enmarañar [1a] **1** *vt* **(a)** to tangle (up), entangle.
(b) (*fig*) to complicate, make more involved; to make a mess of; to confuse, perplex; **sólo logró — más el asunto** he only managed to make a still worse mess of the matter, he only succeeded in complicating things further.
2 enmarañarse *vr* **(a)** to get tangled (up), become entangled.
(b) (*fig*) to get more involved; to get into a mess; to get confused; **— en un asunto** to get entangled in an affair.
(c) (*of sky*) to darken, cloud over.

enmarcar [1g] *vt* (*fig*) to provide the setting for, act as a background to.

enmarillecerse [2d] *vr* to turn yellow; to turn pale.

enmascarar [1a] **1** *vt* **(a)** to mask. **(b)** (*fig*) to mask, disguise. **2 enmascararse** *vr* **(a)** to put on a mask.
(b) (*fig*) **— de** to masquerade as.

enmendación *nf* emendation, correction.

enmendar [1k] **1** *vt* **(a)** to emend, correct; *law, constitution etc* to amend.
(b) (*morally*) to reform.
(c) *loss* to make good, compensate for.
2 enmendarse *vr* to reform, mend one's ways.

enmienda *nf* **(a)** emendation; correction; (*Law, Pol etc*) amendment; **la quinta —** the fifth amendment.
(b) reform. **(c)** compensation, indemnity.

enmohecer [2d] **1** *vt* **(a)** *metal* to rust. **(b)** (*Bot etc*) to make mouldy. **2 enmohecerse** *vr* **(a)** to rust, get rusty. **(b)** (*Bot etc*) to get mouldy.

enmohecido *adj* **(a)** rusty, rust-covered. **(b)** mouldy, mildewed.

enmonarse [1a] *vr* (*SAm*) to get tight.

enmontarse [1a] *vr* (*CAm, Col, Ven*) to get overgrown, revert to scrub.

enmudecer [2d] **1** *vt* to silence. **2 enmudecerse** *vr* to be silent; to remain silent, say nothing; to become dumb; to lose one's voice.

enmugrar [1a] *vt* (*Col, Chi, Mex*), **enmugrecer** [2d] *vt*, **enmugrentar** [1a] *vt* (*Chi*) to begrime, soil, dirty.

ennegrecer [2d] **1** *vt* to blacken; to dye black; to darken, obscure. **2** *vi* and **ennegrecerse** *vr* to turn black; to get dark, darken.

ennoblecer [2d] *vt* **(a)** to ennoble. **(b)** (*fig*) to embellish, adorn; to dignify.

ennoblecimiento *nm* ennoblement.

enojada *nf* (*Mex, PR*) (fit of) anger.

enojadizo *adj* irritable, peevish, short-tempered.

enojado *adj* angry, cross; **dijo —** he said angrily.

enojar [1a] **1** *vt* to anger; to upset, annoy, vex.
2 enojarse *vr* to get angry, lose one's temper; to get annoyed, get cross (*con, contra* with; *de* at, about); **¡no te enojes!** don't bother!, don't trouble yourself!

enojo *nm* **(a)** anger; annoyance, vexation; **decir con — to** say angrily.
(b) de prontos —s, de repentinos —s quick-tempered; **tener prontos** (*or* **repentinos**) **—s** to be quick to anger, be easily upset.
(c) —s troubles, trials.

enojón *adj* (*Chi, Ec, Mex*)=**enojadizo.**

enojoso *adj* irritating, annoying.

enorgullecer [2d] **1** *vt* to fill with pride. **2 enorgullecerse** *vr* to be proud, swell with pride; **— de** to be proud of, pride oneself on.

enorme *adj* **(a)** enormous, huge, vast; tremendous. **(b)** (*fig*) heinous, monstrous.

enormemente *adv* enormously, vastly; tremendously.

enormidad *nf* **(a)** enormousness; hugeness.
(b) (*fig: quality*) heinousness, monstrousness, enormity.
(c) (*act etc*) wicked thing, monstrous thing.
(d) (*fam*) **me gustó una —** I liked it enormously.

enqué *nm* (*Col, Ec, Ven*) container, bag.

enrabiar [1b] **1** *vt* to enrage. **2 enrabiarse** *vr* to get enraged.

enraizar [1f] *vi* to take root.

enramada *nf* **1 (a)** arbour, bower. **(b)** (*RPl*) cover (*etc*) made of branches. **2** *vi* (*RPl: Bot*) to come into leaf.

enranciarse [1b] *vr* to go rancid, get stale.

enrarecer [2d] **1** *vt* **(a)** *air etc* to rarefy.
(b) to make scarce, cause to become rare.
2 enrarecerse *vr* **(a)** to become rarefied, get thin.
(b) to become scarce, grow rare.

enrarecido *adj* rarefied.

enrarecimiento *nm* **(a)** rarefaction; thinness. **(b)** scarceness, rareness.

enrastrojarse [1a] *vr* (*SAm*) to get covered in scrub.

enrazado *adj* (*Col*) half-breed; crossbred.

enrazar [1f] *vt* (*Col*) to mix (racially); *animals* to crossbreed.

enredadera *nf* (*Bot*) climbing plant, creeper; **— (de campo)** bindweed.

enredador **1** *adj* trouble-making, mischief-making. **2** *nm*, **enredadora** *nf* gossip; busybody, meddler; troublemaker, mischief-maker.

enredar [1a] **1** *vt* **(a)** *animal etc* to net, catch in a net.
(b) *trap* to set.
(c) to intertwine, interweave; (*pej*) to entangle, tangle (up).
(d) *affair* to confuse, complicate; to make a mess of.
(e) *person* to embroil, involve, implicate (*en* in).
(f) *persons* to sow discord among (*or* between); **— a A con B** to sow discord between A and B, embroil A with B.
2 enredarse *vr* **(a)** to get entangled, get tangled (up); **— en** (*rope etc*) to catch on, (*Naut*) foul.

(b) (*affair*) to get complicated; to get into a mess.
(c) (*person*) to get entangled (*con* with), get involved (*con* with); **no se enrede Vd** don't you get mixed up in this, keep out of this mess; **se enredó con una estudiante** he got involved with a student, he had an affair with a student; — **de** (*or* **en**) **palabras** to get involved in an argument.

enredista *nmf* (*SAm*) = **enredador 2**.

enredo *nm* **(a)** tangle.
(b) (*fig*) tangle, entanglement; love affair; mess, confusion, mix-up; (*of details etc*) maze, tangle.
(c) jam, difficult situation.
(d) embroilment, involvement.
(e) (*Theat*) plot.
(f) —**s** intrigues; mischief, mischievous lies; **comedia de** —**s** comedy of intrigue.

enredoso *adj* **(a)** tangled, complicated; tricky. **(b)** (*Mex*) = **enredador 1**.

enrejado *nm* grating, grille; (*of window*) lattice; (*in garden*) trellis; (*Sew*) openwork; fence, railings; (*of cage*) bars; — **de alambre** wire netting (fence).

enrejar [1a] *vt* **(a)** to fix a grating to, put a grating on; to fence, put railings round.
(b) (*SAm*) to put a halter on.
(c) (*Mex*) to darn, patch.

enrevesado *adj* = **revesado**.

enrielar [1a] *vt* **(a)** (*Tech*) to make into ingots.
(b) (*SAm*) to lay rails on.
(c) (*SAm*) to put on the tracks, set on the rails; (*fig*) to put on the right track.

Enrique *m* Henry.

enriquecer [2d] **1** *vt* to make rich, enrich.
2 enriquecerse *vr* to get rich; to prosper; (*pej*) to enrich oneself; — **a costa ajena** to do well at other people's expense.

enriquecimiento *nm* enrichment.

enriscado *adj* craggy, rocky.

enristrar [1a] *vt* **(a)** to string, make a string of, put on a string. **(b)** (*fig*) difficulty to straighten out, iron out. **(c)** *place* to go straight to.

enrizar [1f] **1** *vt* to curl. **2 enrizarse** *vr* to curl.

enrocar [1g] *vi* (*Chess*) to castle.

enrojecer [2d] **1** *vt* to redden, turn red; *person* to make blush; *metal* to make red-hot.
2 *vi and* **enrojecerse** *vr* to blush, redden; to go red (with anger); to get red-hot.

enrojecimiento *nm* reddening; blushing, blush.

enrolar [1a] (*SAm*) **1** *vt* to enrol, sign on, sign up; (*Mil*) to enlist. **2 enrolarse** *vr* to enrol, sign on; (*Mil*) to enlist, join up.

enrollable *adj* that rolls up, roll-up (*attr*); **persiana** — slatted shutter.

enrollamiento *nm* roll; (*Elec etc*) coil.

enrollar [1a] *vt* to roll (up), wind (up); to coil.

enronquecer [2d] **1** *vt* to make hoarse. **2** *vi and* **enronquecerse** *vr* to get hoarse, grow hoarse.

enronquecido *adj* hoarse.

enroque *nm* (*Chess*) castling.

enroscado *adj* **(a)** coiled; twisted; kinky. **(b)** (*Col*) angry.

enroscadura *nf* coil; twist; kink.

enroscar [1g] **1** *vt* **(a)** to coil (round), wind; to twist, twine; to curl (up).
(b) to screw in.
(c) to wreathe (*de* in).
2 enroscarse *vr* to coil, wind; to twist, twine; to curl (up); — **alrededor de un árbol** to twine round a tree.

enrulado *adj* (*RPl*) curly; set in curls.

enrular [1a] *vt* (*Bol, RPl*) to curl.

enrumbar *vi* (*SAm*) to decide on a direction, go, set off.

ensacar [1g] *vt* to sack, bag, put into bags.

ensalada *nf* **(a)** (*Cook*) salad; — **de col** cabbage salad; — **de patatas** potato salad. **(b)** (*fig*) hotchpotch, unholy mixture; mix-up; medley; (*Aut*) traffic jam.

ensaladera *nf* salad bowl, salad dish.

ensaladilla *nf* **(a)** (Russian-type) salad. **(b)** (*Col, Ven*) lampoon, satirical verse.

ensalmado *adj* (*SAm*) magic.

ensalmador *nm* quack, bonesetter.

ensalmar [1a] *vt bone* to set; *complaint* to cure by spells, treat by quack remedies.

ensalme *nm* (*Ec*) spell, incantation.

ensalmo *nm* spell, charm, incantation; (*Med*) quack remedy, quack treatment; (**como**) **por** — as if by magic.

ensalzamiento *nm* exaltation; extolling.

ensalzar [1f] *vt* to exalt; to praise, extol.

ensamblador *nm* joiner; fitter.

ensambladura *nf* **(a)** (*in general*) joinery; assembling.
(b) (*Tech*) joint; — **de inglete** mitre joint.

ensamblaje *nm* (*Tech*) assembly; **planta de** — assembly plant.

ensamblar [1a] *vt* to join; to assemble.

ensanchador *nm* (*Tech*) stretcher.

ensanchar [1a] **1** *vt* to enlarge, widen, extend; to stretch; to expand; (*Sew*) to enlarge, let out.
2 ensancharse *vr* **(a)** to get wider, spread, expand; to stretch.
(b) (*fig*) to give oneself airs.

ensanche *nm* enlargement, widening, extension; expansion; stretch(ing); (*of town*) extension, new suburb, suburban development; (*Sew*) extra piece, room to let out.

ensangrentado *adj* bloodstained; bloody, gory.

ensangrentar [1k] **1** *vt* to stain with blood, cover in blood.
2 ensangrentarse *vr* (*fig*) to get angry; — **con**, — **contra** to be cruel to, treat cruelly, be vindictive towards.

ensañado *adj* furious; cruel, merciless.

ensañamiento *nm* rage; fury; cruelty, barbarity.

ensañar [1a] **1** *vt* to enrage. **2 ensañarse** *vr*: — **con**, — **en** to vent one's anger on; to delight in tormenting, take a sadistic pleasure in the sufferings of.

ensarnarse [1a] *vr* (*CAm, Chi, Mex*) to get mangy.

ensartador *nm* (*Arg*) roasting spit.

ensartar [1a] **1** *vt* **(a)** *beads etc* to string; *needle* to thread; *meat* to spit, broach.
(b) (*fig*) to string together; to link; *excuses etc* to reel off, trot out, rattle off.
2 ensartarse *vr* **(a)** (*Col, PR*) to get into a jam.
(b) (*Arg*) to come badly out of a deal.

ensayar [1a] **1** *vt* **(a)** to test, try, try out.
(b) *metal* to assay.
(c) (*Mus, Theat*) to rehearse.
2 ensayarse *vr* to practise; to rehearse; — **a** + *infin* to practise + *ger*.

ensaye *nm* assay.

ensayista *nmf* essayist.

ensayo *nm* **(a)** test, trial; experiment; attempt; practice, exercise; **de** — tentative; practice (*attr*); experimental; **pedido de** — (*Comm*) trial order; **viaje de** — trial run; **vuelo de** — test flight; **hacer algo a modo de** — to do something as an experiment, do something to try it out; **hacer** —**s** to practise (*en* on), train.
(b) (*of metal*) assay.
(c) (*Lit, School etc*) essay.
(d) (*Mus, Theat*) rehearsal; — **general** dress rehearsal.
(e) (*Rugby*) try.

ensebado *adj* greased, greasy.

enselvado *adj* wooded.

ensenada *nf* **(a)** inlet, cove; creek. **(b)** (*Arg*) small fenced pasture.

enseña *nf* ensign, standard; **la E**— **Blanca** (*Brit*) the White Ensign.

enseñado *adj* trained; informed; educated; **bien** — dog house-trained.

enseñanza *nf* **(a)** education; teaching; instruction, training; schooling; tuition; **primera** —, — **primaria** elementary education; **segunda** —, — **secundaria** secondary education; — **superior** higher education; — **universitaria** university education; — **de los niños atrasados** remedial teaching, teaching of backward children; — **para ambos sexos** coeducation; **la** — **es gratuita** the training is free.
(b) teaching, doctrine; **la** — **de la Iglesia** the teaching of the Church.

enseñar [1a] **1** *vt* **(a)** to teach, instruct, train; to educate; — **a uno a hacer algo** to teach someone (how) to do something, train someone to do something; to show someone how to do something.
(b) to show; to point out; **nos enseñó el museo** he showed us (over) the museum; **te enseñaré mis aguafuertes** I'll show you my etchings; **esto nos enseña las dificultades** this reveals the difficulties to us.
2 enseñarse *vr* **(a)** (*SAm*) to learn; — **a hacer algo** to learn (how) to do something.
(b) (*esp SAm*) to accustom oneself, become inured (*a* to); **no me enseño aquí** I can't get used to it here, I can't settle down here.

enseñorearse [1a] *vr* **(a)** to control oneself. **(b)** — **de** to take possession of, take over; (*fig*) to overlook, dominate.

enseres *nmpl* goods and chattels; things, gear, tackle, equipment; — **domésticos** household goods.

enseriarse [1b] *vr* (*Ant, Col, Guat, Per, Ven*) to become serious.

ensilado *nm*: — **de patatas** potato clamp.

ensiladora *nf* silo.

ensilar [1a] *vt* to store in a silo.

ensillar [1a] *vt* to saddle (up), put a saddle on.

ensimismamiento *nm* absorption; reverie, brown study.

ensimismarse [1a] *vr* (a) to be(come) lost in thought, go into a reverie, go into a brown study. (b) (*SAm*) to get conceited.

ensoberbecer [2d] **1** *vt* to make proud. **2 ensoberbecerse** *vr* (a) to become proud, become arrogant. (b) (*sea*) to get rough.

ensombrecer [2d] **1** *vt* (a) to darken, cast a shadow over. (b) (*fig*) to overshadow, put in the shade. **2 ensombrecerse** *vr* (a) to darken, get dark. (b) (*fig*) to get gloomy.

ensoñación *nf* (a) (*SAm*) fantasy, fancy, dream. (b) ¡ni por —! not a bit of it!, never!

ensoñador **1** *adj* dreamy. **2** *nm* dreamer.

ensopar [1a] (*SAm*) **1** *vt* to soak, drench, saturate; *biscuit etc* to dip, dunk. **2 ensoparse** *vr* to get soaked.

ensordecedor *adj* deafening.

ensordecer [2d] **1** *vt* to deafen; *noise* to muffle. **2** *vi* to go deaf; (*fig*) to pretend not to hear, pretend to be deaf.

ensortijar [1a] **1** *vt* (a) *hair* to curl, put curls into. (b) *nose* to ring, fix a ring in. **2 ensortijarse** *vr* to curl.

ensuciamiento *nm* soiling, dirtying.

ensuciar [1b] **1** *vt* (a) to soil, dirty; to foul; to mess up, make a mess of. (b) (*fig*) to defile, pollute. **2 ensuciarse** *vr* to get dirty; (*child*) to soil oneself; to wet the bed.

ensueño *nm* (a) dream, fantasy, illusion; reverie; **de —** dream-like; other-wordly; **una cocina de —** a dream kitchen, a kitchen of one's dreams; **mundo de —** dream world, world of fantasy. (b) **—s** visions, fantasies; ¡**ni por —s**! not a bit of it!, never!

entabicar [1g] *vt* (*SAm*) to partition off.

entablado *nm* boarding, planking; floorboard.

entabladura *nf* boarding, planking.

entablar [1a] **1** *vt* (a) to board (in, up), plank, cover with boards. (b) *chessmen* to set up; *game* to draw. (c) (*Med*) to splint, put in a splint. (d) *conversation etc* to start, strike up; *deal* to enter into; *lawsuit* to begin, file, bring; *claim* to file, put in. **2** *vi* (a) (*Chess*) to draw. (b) (*Per*) to boast. **3 entablarse** *vr* (*wind*) to settle.

entable *nm* (a) boarding, planking. (b) (*Chess*) position. (c) (*SAm*) order, arrangement, disposition. (d) (*Col*) (start of an) enterprise; (*Ec*) breaking, opening up (*of new land*).

entablillar [1a] *vt* (*Med*) to splint, put in a splint.

entablonada *nf* (*Ec*, *Per*) boast.

entalegar [1h] *vt* (a) to bag, put in a bag. (b) (*fig*) to hoard, stash away (*fam*).

entallador *nm* sculptor; engraver.

entalladura *nf* (a) sculpture, carving; engraving. (b) slot, notch, cut, groove.

entallar [1a] **1** *vt* (a) to sculpt, carve; to engrave; **— el nombre en un árbol** to carve one's name on a tree. (b) to notch, cut a slot in, cut a groove in. (c) (*Sew*) to cut, tailor. **2** *vi* to fit (well); **traje que entalla bien** a suit that fits well, a well-cut suit.

entallecer [2d] *vi and* **entallecerse** *vr* to shoot, sprout.

entapizado **1** *adj* (a) upholstered (*de* with); hung (*de* with); covered (*de* with). (b) (*Bot*) overgrown (*de* with). **2** *nm* (*Chi*, *RPl*) carpets, carpeting; (*Mex*) wall-coverings, tapestries.

entapizar [1f] *vt* (a) to upholster (*de* with, in); *wall* to hang with tapestries; *chair etc* to cover with fabric; (*RPl*) *floor* to carpet. (b) (*Bot*) to grow over, cover, spread over.

entarascar [1g] **1** *vt* to dress up, doll up. **2 entarascarse** *vr* to dress up, doll up.

entarimado *nm* floorboarding, roof boarding; inlaid floor; **— (de hojas quebradas)** parquet.

entarimar [1a] *vt* to board, plank; to put an inlaid floor on (*or* over).

entarugado *nm* block flooring, block paving.

ente *nm* (a) entity, being; **— oficial** official entity, official body. (b) (*fam*) fellow, chap (*fam*); odd sort.

entecarse [1g] *vr* (*Chi*) to be stubborn.

enteco *adj* weak, sickly, frail.

entechar [1a] *vt* (*SAm*) to roof.

entejar [1a] *vt* (*SAm*) to tile.

enteje *nm* (*SAm*) tiling.

entelerido *adj* (a) shivering with cold; shaking with fright. (b) (*SAm*) weak, sickly, frail. (c) (*SAm*) distressed, upset.

entenada *nf* stepdaughter.

entenado *nm* stepson; stepchild.

entendederas *nfpl* (*fam*) brains; **ser corto de —**, **tener malas —** to be pretty dim, be slow on the uptake.

entendedor *nm*, **entendedora** *nf* understanding person; **al buen —, pocas palabras (le bastan)** a word to the wise is sufficient; enough said!

entender [2g] **1** *vti* (a) to understand; to realize, grasp; to comprehend; ¿**entiendes**? (do you) understand?, do you get me?; **no le entiendo** I don't understand you; **lo que es —, entiendo** I understand it as far as anybody can understand it; **no entiendo palabra** it's Greek to me; **no entendió jota** (*or* **una patata** *etc*) he didn't understand a word of it; **a mi —** to my way of thinking, in my opinion; **— mal** to misunderstand; **dar a — que . . .** to give to understand that . . ., imply that . . .; **según él da a —** according to what he says, as he implies; **hacer — algo a uno** to make someone understand something, put something across to someone; **hacerse —** to make oneself understood, get across (*por* to); **lograr —** to manage to grasp; to get the hang of. (b) to intend, mean; ¿**qué entiendes con eso**? what do you mean by that? (c) to think, believe; to infer.

2 *vi* (a) **— de** to be an expert on, be good at, know all about; **— de carpintería** to know all about carpentry, be an expert carpenter; **yo no entiendo de vinos** I'm no judge of wines; **ella no entiende de coches** she's hopeless with cars. (b) **— en** to deal with, be concerned with, have to do with; to be familiar with; **— en un asunto** to have the authority to handle a matter, be in charge of an affair. (c) **— por** (*of dog*) to answer to the name of.

3 entenderse *vr* (a) to be understood; to be meant; ¿**qué se entiende por estas palabras**? what is meant by these words?; ¿**cómo se entiende que . . .**? how can one understand that . . .?, how can one grasp that . . .?; **se entiende que . . .** it is understood that . . .; **eso se entiende** that is understood. (b) to know what one is about; **yo me entiendo** I know what I'm up to; I have my reasons; **— con algo** to know how to deal with something. (c) (*of 2 persons*) to understand each other; to get along (well) together; to have a (secret) understanding; **— con uno** to come to an arrangement with someone, fix things with someone; **— con una mujer** to have an affair with a woman. (d) **eso no se entiende conmigo** that doesn't concern me, that has nothing to do with me.

entendido 1 *adj* (a) understood; agreed; ¡**—!** agreed!; **bien — que . . .** on the understanding that . . .; **no darse por —** to pretend not to understand; **tenemos — que . . .** we understand that . . .; **según tenemos —** as far as we can gather. (b) *person* expert; skilled, trained; wise; knowing; well-informed; **ser — en** to be versed in, be skilled at. **2** *nm*, **entendida** *nf* knowledgeable person; expert; connoisseur; **según el juicio de los —s** in the opinion of those who know, according to the experts; **el whisk(e)y de los —s** the connoisseur's whisky.

entendimiento *nm* (a) understanding; grasp, comprehension. (b) mind, intellect, understanding; **de — poco lucido** of limited understanding. (c) judgement.

entenebrecer [2d] **1** *vt* (a) to darken, obscure. (b) (*fig*) to fog, cloud, obscure; **esto entenebrece más el asunto** this fogs the issue still more. **2 entenebrecerse** *vr* to get dark.

enterado *adj* (a) knowledgeable; well-informed; **lo sabe cualquier persona enterada** any well-informed person knows it; **estar —** to be informed, be in the know; **estar — de** to know about, be aware of; **estar — de que . . .** to know that . . ., be aware that . . .; **no darse por —** to pretend not to understand, not take the hint. (b) (*Chi*) conceited, stuck-up (*fam*).

enteramente *adv* entirely, completely; quite.

enterar [1a] **1** *vt* (a) to inform (*de* about, of), acquaint (*de* with), tell (*de* about). (b) (*SAm*) *money* to pay, hand over; (*Arg*, *Chi*,

Mex, Per) *quantity* to make up, complete, round off.
2 *vi* (a) (SAm) to get better, get well.

(b) (Chi) to let the days go by.

3 enterarse *vr* (a) to find out, get to know; — **de**
to find out about, learn of, hear of, get to know
about; **¿se entera?** do you hear?; do you understand?, do you get it?; **¡entérate!, ¡entérese!** listen!,
get this!

(b) (SAm) to recoup one's losses.

entereza *nf* (a) entirety; completeness; perfection.

(b) (*fig*) integrity; decency, honesty; strength of
mind; fortitude; firmness.

(c) (*fig*) strictness, severity.

entérico *adj* enteric.

enteritis *nf* enteritis.

enterizo *adj* in one piece, one-piece (*attr*).

enternecedor *adj* affecting, touching, moving.

enternecer [2d] **1** *vt* to soften; to affect, touch, move
(to pity). **2 enternecerse** *vr* to relent; to be
affected, be touched, be moved (to pity).

entero 1 *adj* (a) entire, complete; whole; **la cantidad
entera** the whole sum, the complete sum; **por el
mundo** — over the whole world; **con entera satisfacción** with complete satisfaction; **por** — wholly,
completely, fully.

(b) (*Math*) whole, integral.

(c) (*Bio*) not castrated.

(d) (*fig*) upright, honest; resolute, firm.

(e) sound; robust; *cloth etc* strong, thick.

(f) (Guat, Per, SD, Ven) identical, similar.

2 *nm* (a) (*Math*) integer.

(b) (*Comm, Fin*) point; **las acciones han subido
dos** —s the shares have gone up two points.

(c) (SAm) payment.

(d) (Chi) balance.

enterradero *nm* (*Arg*) burial ground.

enterrado *adj* buried; *nail* ingrowing.

enterrador *nm* gravedigger.

enterramiento *nm* burial, interment.

enterrar [1a] *vt* (a) to bury, inter. (b) (SAm) *weapon*
to bury (*en* in), thrust (*en* into). (c) (*fig*) to bury,
forget.

enterratorio *nm* (*Chi, RPl*) Indian burial ground;
archaeological remains, site of archaeological
interest.

entesar [1k] *vt* to stretch, tauten.

entibiar [1b] **1** *vt* (a) to cool; to take the chill off. (b)
(*fig*) to cool (down). **2 entibiarse** *vr* (a) to become
lukewarm, cool down. (b) (*fig*) to cool off.

entibo *nm* (*Min*) prop.

entidad *nf* (a) entity; (*Pol etc*) body, organization;
(*Comm, Fin*) firm, concern, company. (b) **de** — of
importance, of consequence.

entierro *nm* (a) burial, interment. (b) funeral;
asistir al — to go to the funeral. (c) grave. (d) (SAm)
(buried) treasure; treasure-trove.

entintar [1a] *vt* to ink; to ink in; to stain with ink.

entizar [1f] *vt* (SAm: *Billiards*) *cue* to chalk.

entoldado *nm* awning; marquee, large tent.

entoldar [1a] **1** *vt* (a) to put an awning over, fit with
an awning.

(b) to decorate (with hangings).

2 entoldarse *vr* (a) (*Meteorol*) to cloud over,
become overcast.

(b) (*emotion, joy*) to be dimmed.

(c) (*person*) to give oneself airs.

entomología *nf* entomology.

entomólogo *nm* entomologist.

entonación *nf* (a) (*Ling*) intonation. (b) (*fig*) conceit.

entonado *adj* (a) (*Mus*) toned; harmonious; in tune.

(b) (*fig*) conceited; haughty, arrogant, stiff.

entonar [1a] **1** *vt* (a) (*Mus*) *song etc* to intone; *voice* to
modulate; to sing in tune; *note* to give, pitch, set;
organ to blow.

(b) (*fig*) *praises* to sound.

(c) (*Art, Phot*) to tone.

(d) (*Med*) to tone up.

2 *vi* (a) (*Mus*) to intone; to be in tune (*con* with).

(b) (*fig*) to be in tune (*con* with), harmonize
(*con* with).

3 entonarse *vr* to give oneself airs.

entonces *adv* (a) (*time*) then; at that time; **desde** —
since then; **en aquel** — at that time; **hasta** —
up till then; **las costumbres de** — the customs
of the time; **el** — **embajador de Eslobodia** the
then ambassador of Slobodia; **fue** — **que . . .** it was
then that . . .

(b) (*concessive*) and so; then; **pues** — well then;
¿ — **cómo no viniste?** then why didn't you come?;
¡y —**!** (*Arg, Chi*) why of course!

entonelar [1a] *vt* to put into barrels (*or* casks).

entongado *adj* (Col) cross.

entongar [1h] *vt* (a) (Cu, Mex) to pile up, make a pile
of. (b) (Col) to stun; to anger.

entono *nm* (a) (*Mus*) intoning; being in tune, singing
in tune. (b) (*fig*) conceit; haughtiness.

entontecer [2d] **1** *vt* to make silly. **2** *vi and* **entonte-
cerse** *vr* to get silly.

entorchado *nm* gold braid, silver braid; lace.

entorchar [1a] *vt* (a) to twist (up). (b) to braid.

entornado *adj* half-closed; ajar.

entornar [1a] *vt* (a) *eyes* to half-close; to screw up;
door to half-close, leave ajar. (b) to upset, tip over.

entorpecer [2d] *vt* (a) to dull, benumb, stupefy; to
make torpid, make lethargic.

(b) to obstruct, hinder; *plans etc* to set back;
traffic, movement to slow down, slow up; *work* to
hinder, delay.

entorpecimiento *nm* (a) stupefaction; numbness;
torpor, lethargy.

(b) obstruction; obstacle, drawback; delay,
slowing-up.

entrada *nf* (a) (*place*) entrance (*de* to), way in (*de*
to); gate, gateway; access; (*Min*) entrance, adit;
(*part of house*) porch, doorway; entrance hall.

(b) (*Mech*) inlet, intake; — **de aire** air intake.

(c) (*act*) entry, entrance (*en* into); admission (*en*
into); right of entry; **la** — **de las tropas en 1940** the
entry of the troops in 1940; **la** — **de turistas este
año** this year's influx of tourists; — **en escena** (*Theat*)
entrance; — **a viva fuerza** forced entry; **"— gratis"**
"admission free"; **"prohibida la —"** "no entry",
"no admission", "keep out"; **su** — **en la Academia**
his admission to the Academy; **la** — **de la palabra
en el diccionario** the admission of the word into the
dictionary, the acceptance of the word for the
dictionary; **dar** — **a** to admit; **hacer su** — to make
one's entry, make a formal entry.

(d) (*Theat etc*) ticket; — **de favor,** — **de regalo**
complimentary ticket.

(e) (*Theat etc*) house, audience; (*Sport*) gate,
crowd; — **floja** thin audience; **gran** —, — **llena** full
house; **hubo poca** — there was a small audience.

(f) (*Theat, Fin*) receipts, takings; (*Sport*) gate
money.

(g) (*of book, speech, year etc*) beginning; **la** — **de la
primavera** the start of spring; **de** — right away,
from the start.

(h) (*Cook*) entrée.

(i) (*Sport*) innings.

(j) (*Comm*) entry.

(k) (Arg, Cu, Mex) attack, onslaught; assault.

(l) (Arg, Cu, Mex) beating.

(m) (Col) down payment, deposit.

(n) —s (*Fin*) receipts, takings; income; —s
familiares family income; —s **brutas** gross receipts;
—s **y salidas** income and expenditure.

entrado *adj* (a) — **en años** elderly, advanced in years.

(b) **hasta muy entrada la noche** until late at
night; on into the small hours.

(c) (Chi) meddling, officious.

entrador *adj* (a) (SAm) brave; spirited; energetic;
enterprising.

(b) (Chi) meddling, officious.

(c) (SAm) charming, likeable, attractive.

(d) (Col, Ec, Mex, Per, Ven) amorously inclined.

(e) **entradora** (Guat, Ven) coquettish; fast, loose.

entramado *nm* (*Archit*) truss; timber framework; (*of
bridge*) framework; span.

entrambos *adj pl* (*lit*) both.

entrampar [1a] **1** *vt* (a) to trap, catch, snare; (*fig*) to
snare, trick.

(b) (*fig*) to mess up, make a mess of.

(c) (*Comm*) to burden with debts.

2 entramparse *vr* (*fig*) (a) to get into a mess, get
tangled up.

(b) (*Comm*) to get into debt.

entrante 1 *adj* (a) next, coming; **la semana** — next
week.

(b) *person* new, incoming.

2 *nm* (a) (*Geog*) inlet.

(b) **ser** — **en una casa** to have the run of a
house, have free entry to a house.

entraña *nf* (a) (*fig*) core, root, essential part; **ésta es
la verdadera** — **del problema** this is the real core of
the problem.

(b) **de mala** — malicious; evil-minded.

(c) —s (*Anat*) entrails; insides; bowels; (*fig*)
core, innermost parts; (*fig*) heart, feelings; disposition; **¡hijo de mis** —**s!** my precious child!;
arrancar las —**s a uno** (*fig*) to break someone's
heart; **dar hasta las** —**s** to give one's all; **echar las**
—**s** (*fam*) to puke; **no tener** —**s** (*fig*) to be heartless,
lack all feelings.

entrañable adj (a) close, intimate. (b) beloved, dearly loved. (c) affectionate.
entrañablemente adv love etc dearly, deeply.
entrañar [1a] **1** vt (a) to bury deep.
(b) (fig) to contain, carry within; to entail.
2 entrañarse vr (a) to become deeply attached.
(b) — en to reach to the bottom of, reach to the very heart of.
entrañudo adj (Arg) (a) brave, daring. (b) cruel, heartless.
entrar [1a] **1** vt (a) to introduce; to bring in, show in.
(b) to influence, get at.
(c) (Mil) to attack; to invade; to capture, enter.
2 vi (a) to go in, come in, enter; — a (SAm), — en to go into, come into, enter; (fig) to enter into; — bien to be fitting, be appropriate; to be relevant; — a puerto to enter port, come into port; **el enchufe entra en esa toma** the plug goes into (or fits into) that point; **el paquete no entra en el saco** the parcel won't go into the bag; — **en una profesión** to adopt a profession, take up a profession; — **en una sociedad** to join a society, become a member of a society, be admitted to a society; **el río entra en el lago** the river flows into the lake; — **en el número de** to be one of, count among, be reckoned among; — **en detalles** to go into details; **eso no entra en nuestros planes** that does not enter into our plans; **entra por una sexta parte** he gets a sixth, his share is one sixth; **le entraron deseos de** + infin he felt a sudden urge to + infin.
(b) (of year etc) to begin; (of wind, tide) to rise; **el año que entra** next year.
(c) **ese tío no me entra** I can't bear that fellow, I can't get on with that chap; **no me entra la lógica** I can't get the hang of logic.
(d) — a + infin to begin to + infin.
entrazado adj (Arg) (a) ragged, shabby; **mal** — shabby. (b) nasty-looking.
entre prep between; among, amongst; in the midst of; — **tú y yo** between the two of us; — **esto y lo otro** what with this and that; — **azul y verde** midway between blue and green, of some colour between blue and green; **había** — **todos 12 personas** there were 12 people in all (or all told); **de** — out of, from among; **por** — through; between; **decir** — **sí** to say to oneself.
entre ... **inter** ...
entreabierto adj half-open; ajar.
entreabrir [3a; ptp **entreabierto**] vt to half-open, open halfway; to leave ajar.
entreacto nm interval, entr'acte.
entreayudarse [1a] vr to help one another, be of mutual assistance.
entrecano adj greyish, greying.
entrecarril nm (Ven: Rail) gauge.
entrecejo nm space between the eyebrows; frown; **arrugar el** —, **fruncir el** — to frown, wrinkle one's brow.
entrecerrar [1k] vt (CAm, Mex) to half-close, close halfway; to leave ajar.
entrecoger [2c] vt (a) to catch, intercept; to seize. (b) (fig) to press, compel; to silence.
entrecomillado nm inverted commas.
entrecoro nm chancel.
entrecortado adj intermittent; speech faltering, hesitant, confused; **en voz entrecortada** in a faltering voice, in a voice choked with emotion.
entrecortar [1a] vt (a) to cut into, partially cut, cut halfway through.
(b) to cut off, interrupt (from time to time); voice to cause to falter, choke from time to time.
entrecruzar [1f] **1** vt (a) to interlace, interweave. (b) (Bio) to cross, interbreed. **2 entrecruzarse** vr (Bio) to interbreed.
entrecubiertas nfpl between-decks.
entrechocarse [1g] vr to collide, crash; to clash.
entredicho nm (a) prohibition, ban, interdict; (Law) injunction; **estar en** — to be under a ban, be banned; **levantar el** — **a** to raise the ban on.
(b) (Arg) disagreement, split; breaking-off of relations.
(c) (Bol) alarm bell.
entredós nm (Sew) insertion, panel.
entrefino adj medium, medium-quality.
entrefuerte adj (SAm) tobacco medium strong.
entrega nf (a) (act) delivery; handing over, surrender; (Post) post, delivery; — **contra pago**, — **contra reembolso** cash on delivery; — **en fecha futura** forward delivery; **pagadero a la** — payable on delivery; **hacer** — **de** to hand over (formally), present.

(b) (of novel etc) part, instalment; (of journal etc) part, number, fascicule.
entregar [1h] **1** vt to deliver; to hand, hand over, hand in; to surrender; to give up, part with; — **algo a un abogado** to refer something to a lawyer, place a matter in a lawyer's hands; —**la** (sl) to kick the bucket (sl); **no quiso** —**melo** he refused to hand it over to me.
2 entregarse vr (a) to surrender, give in, submit.
(b) — **a** to devote oneself to; (pej) to give oneself up to, abandon oneself to, indulge in; — **a estudiar** to devote oneself to studying.
(c) — **de** to take possession of.
entreguerras: el período de — the inter-war period, the period between the wars (ie 1918-39).
entrelazado adj entwined, interlaced; criss-crossed (de with); interlocking.
entrelazar [1f] **1** vt to entwine, interlace, interweave; to interlock. **2 entrelazarse** vr to entwine, interlace; to interlock.
entrelistado adj striped.
entrelucir [3f] vi (a) to show through. (b) to gleam, shine dimly.
entremás adv (Arg, Col, Mex, Per) moreover; especially.
entremedias 1 adv in between, halfway; in the meantime. **2** — **de** prep between; among.
entremés nm (a) (Theat: Hist) interlude, short farce. (b) (Cook) side dish; — **salado** savoury; —**es hors d'oeuvres.
entremeter [2a] vt to insert, put in; to put between.
entremeterse etc see **entrometerse** etc.
entremezclar [1a] **1** vt to intermingle; **entremezclado de** interspersed with. **2 entremezclarse** vr to intermingle.
entrenador nm (a) (Sport) trainer, coach. (b) (Aer) trainer, training plane.
entrenamiento nm training; coaching.
entrenar [1a] **1** vt (Sport) to train, coach; horse to exercise; **estar entrenado** (footballer etc) to be in training, be fit. **2 entrenarse** vr to train.
entreoír [3q] vt to half-hear, hear indistinctly.
entrepaño nm door panel; shelf.
entrepierna nf (also —**s**) crotch, crutch.
entrepuente nm between-decks; steerage.
entrerrenglonar [1a] vt to interline, write between the lines of.
entresacar [1g] vt to pick out, select; to sift; hair, plants etc to thin out.
entresemana nf midweek; (SAm) working days of the week; **de** — midweek (attr); **cualquier día de** — any day in midweek.
entresijo nm (a) (Anat) mesentery.
(b) (fig) secret, mystery; hidden aspect; difficulty, snag; **esto tiene muchos** —**s** this is very complicated, this has its ins and outs; **él tiene sus** —**s** he's a deep one.
entresuelo nm mezzanine, entresol.
entretanto 1 adj meanwhile, meantime. **2** nm meantime; **en el** — in the meantime.
entretecho nm (Chi, RPl) attic, garret.
entretejer [2a] vt to interweave; to intertwine, entwine; (fig) to interweave, insert, put in.
entretela nf (a) (Sew) interlining. (b) —**s** inmost being; heartstrings; **¡te voy a sacar las** —**s!** (fam) I'll tear your guts out! (fam).
entretelar [1a] vt to interline.
entretelones nmpl (fig) inner workings, secret goings-on.
entretención nf (SAm) entertainment, amusement.
entretener [2l] **1** vt (a) to entertain, amuse; to distract.
(b) to delay; to hold up, detain, keep waiting; to keep occupied; to keep in suspense; **nos entretuvo en conversación** he engaged us in conversation; he kept us talking; — **a los acreedores** to keep one's creditors at bay, hold off one's creditors; **pues no le entretengo más** then I won't keep you any longer.
(c) hunger to kill, stave off; pain to allay; time to while away.
(d) (Mech etc) to maintain.
2 entretenerse vr (a) to amuse oneself; to while away the time.
(b) to delay; to loiter (on the way); **¡no te entretengas!** don't hang about!, don't loiter on the way!
entretenida nf (a) mistress; kept woman.
(b) **dar (con) la** — **a uno** to hold someone off with vague promises, hedge with someone, stall someone; to keep someone talking.
entretenido adj entertaining, amusing.

entretenimiento nm (a) entertainment, amusement; diversion, distraction; recreation; **es un — nada más** it's just an amusement.

(b) (*Mech etc*) upkeep, maintenance; **sólo necesita un — mínimo** it only needs minimum maintenance.

entretiempo nm period between seasons; spring, autumn.

entrever [2v] vt (a) to glimpse, catch a glimpse of; to see indistinctly, make out something of. (b) (*fig*) to guess, suspect (something of).

entreverado adj mixed; patchy; *bacon* streaky.

entreverar [1a] **1** vt to mix, intermingle; to mix up.

2 entreverarse vr (a) to intermix, be intermingled.

(b) (*Arg*) to mix in a confused mass, mingle in confusion.

entrevero nm (a) mix-up; jumble. (b) (*Bol, Chi, Per, RPl*) confusion, disorder; brawl; (*Mil*) confused cavalry skirmish.

entrevía nf (*Rail*) gauge; **— angosta** narrow gauge; **de — angosta** narrow-gauge (*attr*); **— normal** standard gauge.

entrevista nf interview; meeting, conference; **celebrar una — con** to have an interview with, hold a meeting with.

entrevistar [1a] **1** vt to interview.

2 entrevistarse vr to have an interview, meet; **— con** to interview, meet, have an interview with; **el ministro se entrevistó con la reina ayer** the minister saw the queen yesterday.

entripado nm (*Arg*) ghastly secret; concealed anger, secret rage.

entripar [1a] **1** vt (a) (*Arg, Col, Ec*) to anger, upset. (b) (*Ant, Mex*) to soak.

2 entriparse vr (a) (*Arg, Col, Ec*) to get cross, get upset.

(b) (*Ant, Mex*) to get soaked.

entristecer [2d] **1** vt to sadden, grieve. **2 entristecerse** vr to grow sad, grieve.

entrometerse [2a] vr to meddle, interfere (*en* in, with), intrude.

entrometido 1 adj meddlesome, interfering. **2** nm, **entrometida** nf busybody, meddler; intruder.

entromparse [1a] vr (*SAm*) to get cross.

entrón adj (a) (*Col*) meddlesome. (b) (*Mex*) spirited, daring. (c) **entrona** (*Mex*) coquettish; fast, loose.

entroncar [1g] **1** vt to connect, establish a relationship between. **2** vi (a) to be related, be connected (*con* to, with). (b) (*SAm*) to connect (*con* with).

entronización nf (a) enthronement. (b) (*fig*) exaltation.

entronizar [1f] vt (a) to enthrone. (b) (*fig*) to exalt.

entronque nm (a) relationship, connection, link. (b) (*SAm*) connection; junction.

entruchada nf (a) (*fam*) trap, trick. (b) (*Chi*) violent interview, shouting match; friendly talk.

entruchar [1a] **1** vt (a) to lure, decoy, lead by the nose. **2 entrucharse** vr (*Mex*) (a) to stick one's nose into other people's affairs. (b) to get besotted with love.

entuerto nm (a) wrong, injustice. (b) **—s** (*Med*) afterpains.

entumecer [2d] **1** vt to numb, benumb. **2 entumecerse** vr (a) (*limb*) to get numb, go to sleep. (b) (*river*) to swell, rise; (*sea*) to surge.

entumecido adj numb, stiff.

entumecimiento nm numbness, stiffness.

entumido adj (a) (*SAm*) numb, stiff. (b) (*Col, Mex*) timid.

enturbiar [1b] **1** vt (a) *water* to muddy; to disturb, make cloudy.

(b) *issue* to fog, confuse; *mind, person* to derange, unhinge.

2 enturbiarse vr (a) to get muddy; to become cloudy.

(b) to get confused, become obscured; to become deranged.

entusiasmar [1a] **1** vt to fill with enthusiasm; to fire, excite; to delight, please a great deal.

2 entusiasmarse vr to get enthusiastic, get excited (*con, por* about); **— con, — por** to be keen on, rave about, be delighted with; **se ha quedado entusiasmada con el vestido** she was delighted with the dress, she raved about the dress.

entusiasmo nm enthusiasm (*por* for): excitement, keenness, zeal, zest; delight, pleasu. **—n — en-** thusiastically; keenly.

entusiasta 1 adj enthusiastic; keen (*de* on); zealous (*de* for). **2** nmf enthusiast; fan (*fam*), follower, supporter; admirer.

entusiástico adj enthusiastic.

enumeración nf enumeration; count, reckoning.

enumerar [1a] vt to enumerate; to count, reckon up.

enunciación nf enunciation; statement, declaration.

enunciar [1b] vt to enunciate; to state, declare.

enuresis nf enuresis, bedwetting.

envagonar vt (*SAm*) *goods* to load into a railway truck.

envainar [1a] **1** vt (a) to sheathe, put in a sheath; **¡enváinala!** (*sl*) shut your trap! (*sl*). (b) (*Col*) to vex, annoy. **2** vi (*Col*) to succumb. **3 envainarse** vr (*Col*) to get into trouble.

envalentonamiento nm boldness; (*pej*) Dutch courage; bravado.

envalentonar [1a] **1** vt to embolden; (*pej*) to fill with Dutch courage.

2 envalentonarse vr to take courage, become bolder; (*pej*) to strut, brag; to put on a bold front.

envanecer [2d] **1** vt to make conceited. **2 envanecerse** vr to grow vain, get conceited, give oneself airs; to swell with pride (*con, de* at).

envanecido adj conceited, stuck-up (*fam*).

envanecimiento nm conceit, vanity.

envarar [1a] **1** vt (*Col: Agr*) to stake. **2 envararse** vr (*Mex*) to be numb, become stiff.

envasar [1a] **1** vt (a) to pack, wrap; to package; to bottle; to can, tin; to barrel; to sack, bag.

(b) *wine* (*fam*) to knock back (*sl*), put away.

(c) (*esp SAm*) **— un puñal en uno** to plunge a dagger into someone, bury a dagger in someone. **2** vi (*fam*) to tipple, knock it back (*sl*).

envase nm (a) (*act*) packing, wrapping; packaging; bottling; canning.

(b) container; package, wrapping; bottle; can, tin; barrel; bag; **— de hojalata** tin can; **precio con —** price including packing; **géneros sin —** loose goods, unwrapped goods; **—s a devolver** returnable empties.

envasijar [1a] vt (*SAm*) = **envasar**.

envedijarse [1a] vr to get tangled (up).

envegarse [1h] vr (*Chi*) to get swampy, turn into a swamp.

envejecer [2d] **1** vt to age, make (seem) old.

2 vi and **envejecerse** vr (a) to age, get old, grow old; to look old; **en 2 años ha envejecido mucho** he's got very old these last two years.

(b) to become old-fashioned, become antiquated, get out-of-date.

envejecido adj old, aged; old-looking; **está muy —** he looks terribly old.

envelar [1a] vi (*Chi*) to hoist the sails; (*fig: also* **—las**) to run away.

envenenador nm, **envenenadora** nf poisoner.

envenenamiento nm poisoning.

envenenar [1a] **1** vt to poison; (*fig*) to poison, embitter. **2 envenenarse** vr to poison oneself, take poison.

enverdecer [2s] vi to turn green.

envergadura nf (a) expanse, spread, extent; (*Naut*) breadth, beam; (*Aer: also* **— de alas**) wingspan; (*Ent, Orn*) span, wingspan; (*of boxer*) reach.

(b) (*fig*) scope, compass; magnitude; **un programa de gran —** a programme of considerable scope, a far-reaching programme; **una operación de cierta —** an operation of some magnitude; an operation of some size; **la obra es de —** the plan is ambitious.

envés nm (*of cloth*) back, wrong side; (*of sword*) back, flat; (*Anat: fam*) back.

enviado nm envoy.

enviar [1b] vt to send; **— a uno a hacer algo** to send someone to do something; **— a uno a una misión** to send someone on a mission; **— por el médico** to send for the doctor, fetch the doctor.

enviciar [1b] **1** vt to corrupt; (*fig*) to vitiate.

2 enviciarse vr to get corrupted; **— con, — en** to become (unhealthily) addicted to, acquire an excessive fondness for.

envidar [1a] vti (*Cards*) to bid.

envidia nf envy, jealousy; desire; bad feeling; **es pura —** it's sheer envy; **tener — a** to envy.

envidiable adj enviable.

envidiar [1b] vt to envy; to desire, covet; **— algo a uno** to envy someone something, begrudge someone something.

envidioso adj envious, jealous; covetous.

envilecer [2d] **1** vt to debase, degrade. **2 envilecerse** vr to degrade oneself, lower oneself; to grovel, crawl.

envilecimiento nm degradation, debasement.

envinado adj (a) (*Arg*) drunk. (b) (*Mex*) wine-coloured.

envinarse [1a] vr (*Mex*) (a) to get drunk (on wine). (b) to become satiated with wine.

envío nm (a) (act) sending, dispatch; shipment; gastos de — (cost of) postage and packing, transport charges.

(b) (of goods) consignment, lot, (Naut) shipment; (of money) remittance.

envión nm push, shove.

envite nm (a) stake; side bet. (b) offer, bid; invitation. (c) push, shove; al primer — right away, from the very start.

enviudar [1a] vi to become a widow(er), be widowed; — de su primera mujer to lose one's first wife; enviudó 3 veces she lost three husbands.

envoltijo nm, **envoltorio** nm bundle, package.

envoltura nf cover; wrapper, wrapping; case, casing; sheath; (Aer, Bot etc) envelope; —s swaddling clothes.

envolvedero nm, **envolvedor** nm cover; wrapper, wrapping; envelope.

envolvente adj surrounding; movement (Mil) encircling, enveloping.

envolver [2h; ptp envuelto] 1 vt (a) (with paper etc) to wrap (up), pack (up), tie up, do up; (with clothes) to wrap, swathe, cover; to envelop, enfold; to muffle (up); envuelto en una capa wrapped in a cloak, muffled up in a cloak; dos paquetes envueltos en papel two parcels wrapped in paper; ¿quiere que se lo envuelva? shall I wrap it (up) for you?

(b) (Mil) to encircle, surround.

(c) (fig) to imply, involve, mean; person to involve, implicate (en in).

2 envolverse vr (a) to wrap oneself up (en in).

(b) (fig) to become involved (en in).

envolvimiento nm (a) wrapping; envelopment. (b) (Mil) encirclement. (c) (fig) involvement.

enyerbar [1a] 1 vt (Col, Chi, Mex) to bewitch.

2 enyerbarse vr (a) (SAm) to get covered with grass.

(b) (Cu: of deal) to fail.

(c) (Guat, Mex) to poison oneself.

(d) (Mex) to fall madly in love.

enyesado nm, **enyesadura** nf plastering.

enyesar [1a] vt (a) to plaster. (b) (Med) to put in a plaster cast.

enyugar [1h] vt to yoke.

enyuntar [1a] vt (SAm) to put together, join.

enzacatarse [1a] vr (CAm, Mex) to get covered with grass.

enzarzar [1f] 1 vt (fig) to involve (in a dispute), entangle, embroil.

2 enzarzarse vr to get involved in a dispute; to get oneself into trouble; — en una discusión to get involved in an argument.

enzima nf enzyme.

enzocar [1g] vt (Chi) to insert, put in, fit in.

enzolvar [1a] vt (Mex) to clog, stop up.

eón nm aeon.

épica nf epic.

epicentro nm epicentre.

épico adj epic.

epicureo 1 adj epicurean. 2 nm epicurean.

epicureísmo nm, **epicurismo** nm epicureanism.

epidemia nf epidemic.

epidémico adj epidemic.

epidermis nf epidermis.

Epifanía nf Epiphany.

epiglotis nf epiglottis.

epígrafe nm epigraph; inscription; title, headline; caption; motto.

epigrama nm epigram.

epigramático adj epigrammatic(al).

epilepsia nf epilepsy.

epiléptico 1 adj epileptic. 2 nm, **epiléptica** nf epileptic.

epilogar [1h] vt to sum up; to round off, provide a conclusion to.

epílogo nm epilogue.

episcopado nm (a) (office) bishopric. (b) (period) episcopate. (c) bishops (collectively), episcopacy.

episcopal adj episcopal.

episcopaliano 1 adj episcopalian. 2 nm, **episcopaliana** nf episcopalian.

episcopalista adj and nmf = episcopaliano.

episódico adj episodic.

episodio nm episode; incident; (of story etc) episode, instalment, part.

epístola nf epistle.

epistolar adj epistolary.

epistolario nm collected letters.

epitafio nm epitaph.

epíteto nm epithet.

epitomar [1a] vt to condense, abridge; to summarize.

epítome nm summary, abstract, résumé; compendium.

época nf period, time; age, epoch; spell; la — de Carlos III the age of Charles III; en la — de Carlos III in Charles III's time; en aquella — at that time, in that period; — de celo (Zool) mating season, rutting season; — de la serpiente de mar (hum) silly season; muebles de — period furniture; coche de — vintage car; una puerta victoriana de primera — an early Victorian door; con decoraciones de — with period set; anticiparse (or adelantarse) a su — to be ahead of one's time; formar —, hacer — to be epoch-making, be a landmark; el invento hace — it's an epoch-making discovery; eso hizo — en nuestra historia that was a landmark in our history; todos tenemos —s así we all go through spells like that.

epopeya nf epic (also fig).

equidad nf equity; justice, fairness, impartiality; (of price etc) reasonableness.

equidistante adj equidistant.

equilátero adj equilateral.

equilibrar [1a] 1 vt (a) to balance; to poise. (b) (fig) to balance; to adjust, redress; budget to balance.

2 equilibrarse vr to balance (oneself; en on).

equilibrio nm (a) balance, equilibrium; perder el — to lose one's balance. (b) (fig) balance; (social etc) poise; — político balance of power.

equilibrista nmf (a) tightrope walker; acrobat. (b) (SAm) politician of shifting allegiance.

equino 1 adj equine, horse (attr). 2 nm sea urchin.

equinoccio nm equinox; — otoñal autumnal equinox; — vernal vernal equinox.

equipaje nm (a) (el —) luggage, baggage (US); (un —) piece of luggage, piece of baggage (US); equipment, outfit, kit; — de mano hand luggage; facturar el — to register one's luggage; hacer el — to pack, do the packing.

(b) (Naut) crew.

equipal nm (Mex) leather chair.

equipar [1a] vt to equip, furnish, fit up (con, de with); (Naut) to fit out.

equiparable adj comparable (con to, with); applicable (con to); esa experiencia con animales no es — con la del hombre that experience with animals is not applicable to man's; los dos no son —s the two are not comparable.

equiparación nf comparison.

equiparar [1a] 1 vt to put on the same level, consider equal; to compare (con with).

2 equipararse vr: — con to be on a level with, rank equally with.

equipo nm (a) equipment; outfit, kit; gear, tackle; (industrial) plant; (of turbines etc) set; el — de la fábrica está bastante anticuado the factory plant is pretty antiquated; — de alpinismo climbing kit; — de caza hunting gear; — cinematográfico móvil mobile film unit; — de fumador smoker's outfit, smoker's accessories; — de novia trousseau; — de primeros auxilios first-aid kit; — de reparaciones repair kit; — rodante (Rail) rolling stock.

(b) (of men) team; gang; (of workers) shift; (hum) outfit; — de día day shift; — médico medical team, medical unit; no tuve nada que ver con ese — I had nothing to do with that outfit.

(c) (Sport) team; side; — de fuera away team; — de fútbol football team; los —s formaron así . . . the teams lined up as follows . . .

equis nf (a) name of the letter X; pongamos que cuesta — dólares let us suppose it costs X dollars; averiguar la — to find the value of X.

(b) (CAm, Col, Ec) estar en la — to be all skin and bones; to be broke (fam).

equitación nf (a) riding; escuela de — riding school. (b) horsemanship.

equitativamente adv equitably, fairly; reasonably.

equitativo adj equitable, fair; reasonable; trato — fair deal, square deal.

equivalencia nf equivalence.

equivalente 1 adj equivalent (a to). 2 nm equivalent.

equivaler [2a] vi to be equivalent, be equal; — a to be equivalent to, be equal to; to rank as, rank with, be on a level with.

equivocación nf mistake, error; oversight; misunderstanding; por — by mistake, in error; mistakenly; ha sido por — it was a mistake.

equivocado adj wrong, mistaken; affection, trust etc misplaced; Vd está — you are mistaken.

equivocar [1g] 1 vt to mistake; — A con B to mistake A for B; — el camino to take the wrong road, go the wrong way.

2 equivocarse vr to be wrong, be mistaken; to

make a mistake; **pero se equivocó** but he was wrong; **A puede — con B** A can be mistaken for B; **— de casa** to go to the wrong house; **— de camino** to take the wrong road; **— en una elección** to make a wrong choice, choose wrongly.

equívoco 1 *adj* equivocal, ambiguous. **2** *nm* **(a)** equivocation, ambiguity; quibble. **(b)** pun, wordplay, play on words. **(c)** ambiguous word.

equivoquista *nmf* quibbler; punster.

era[1] *etc see* ser.

era[2] *nf* era, age; **— atómica** atomic age; **— cristiana, — de Cristo** Christian era.

era[3] *nf* (*Agr*) threshing floor; (*Hort*) bed, plot, patch.

erario *nm* exchequer, treasury; public funds, public finance.

erasmismo *nm* Erasmism.

erasmista 1 *adj* Eramist. **2** *nmf* Erasmist.

Erasmo *m* Erasmus.

erección *nf* erection, raising; (*fig*) establishment, foundation.

eremita *nm* hermit; recluse.

ergio *nm* erg.

ergonómica *nf* ergonomics.

erguido *adj* **(a)** erect, straight. **(b)** (*fig*) proud.

erguir [3n] **1** *vt* **(a)** to raise, lift.
   (b) to straighten.
   2 erguirse *vr* **(a)** to straighten up, stand up straight, sit up straight.
   (b) (*fig*) to swell with pride.

erial 1 *adj* uncultivated, untilled. **2** *nm* common; uncultivated land.

Erico *m* Eric.

erigir [3c] **1** *vt* **(a)** to erect, raise, build.
   (b) (*fig*) to establish, found.
   (c) — a uno en algo to set someone up as something.
   2 erigirse *vr*: **— en algo** to set oneself up as something.

erisipela *nf* erysipelas.

erizado *adj* **(a)** bristly; **— de espinas** covered with thorns, with prickles all over. **(b) — de problemas** bristling with problems.

erizarse [1f] *vr* to bristle; to stand on end.

erizo *nm* **(a)** (*Zool*) hedgehog; **— de mar, — marino** sea urchin. **(b)** (*Bot*) burr; prickly husk. **(c)** (*fam*) surly individual, grumpy sort.

ermita *nf* hermitage.

ermitaño *nm* **(a)** hermit. **(b)** (*Zool*) hermit crab.

ermitía *nf* hermitage.

Ernesto *m* Ernest.

erogación *nf* **(a)** distribution. **(b)** (*Arg, Mex, Par*) expenditure, payment; (*Per, Ven*) contribution.

erogar [1h] *vt* **(a)** *property* to distribute. **(b)** (*Arg*) to pay; *debt* to settle; (*Chi, Ec*) to contribute; (*Mex*) to spend, lay out.

erosión *nf* (*Geol etc*) erosion; (*Med*) graze; **causar — en** to erode.

erosionar [1a] **1** *vt* to erode. **2 erosionarse** *vr* to erode, be eroded.

erosivo *adj* erosive.

erótico *adj* erotic; *verse etc* love (*attr*); **el género —** the genre of love poetry.

erotismo *nm* eroticism.

erotomanía *nf* (pathological) eroticism.

erotómano *adj* (pathological) erotic.

errabundeo *nm* wanderings.

errabundo *adj* wandering, roving.

erradamente *adj* mistakenly.

erradicación *nf* eradication.

erradicar [1g] *vt* to eradicate.

erradizo *adj* wandering, roving.

errado *adj* mistaken, wrong; wide of the mark; unwise.

errante *adj* **(a)** wandering, roving; itinerant; nomadic; *animal* lost, stray. **(b)** (*fig*) errant; **el marido —** the errant husband.

errar [11] **1** *vt* **(a)** *shot* to miss with, aim badly; *target* to miss; *vocation etc* to miss, mistake; **— el camino** to lose one's way.
   (b) *person* to fail, fail in one's duty to.
   2 *vi* **(a)** to wander, rove; to roam about.
   (b) =**3 errarse** *vr* to err, go astray, be mistaken; **— es cosa humana** to err is human.

errata *nf* misprint, erratum, printer's error; **es — por "poder"** it's a misprint for "poder".

errático *adj* erratic.

erre *nf* name of the letter R; **— que —** stubbornly, pigheadedly.

erróneamente *adv* mistakenly, erroneously; falsely.

erróneo *adj* mistaken, erroneous; false, untrue.

error *nm* error, mistake; fault; fallacy; **— de copia** clerical error; **— de imprenta, — tipográfico** misprint, printer's error; **— judicial** miscarriage of justice; **— de pluma** clerical error; **— de tecla** typing error; **por —** by mistake, in error; **caer en un —** to fall into error; **salvo — u omisión** errors and omissions excepted.

eructación *nf* belch.

eructar [1a] *vi* to belch.

eructo *nm* belch.

erudición *nf* erudition, learning, scholarship.

eruditamente *adv* learnedly.

erudito 1 *adj* erudite, learned, scholarly.
   2 *nm*, **erudita** *nf* scholar; savant; learned person; **los —s en esta materia** those who are expert in this subject, those who really know about this subject; **— a la violeta** (*pej*) pseudo-intellectual, soi-disant expert.

erupción *nf* **(a)** (*Geol*) eruption; **— solar** solar flare; **estar en —** to be erupting; **entrar en —** to erupt.
   (b) (*Med: also — cutánea*) rash, eruption.
   (c) (*fig*) eruption; outbreak, explosion; outburst.

eruptivo *adj* eruptive.

esa, ésa *etc see* ese, ése.

Esaú *m* Esau.

esbeltez *nf* slimness, slenderness; litheness, willowyness; gracefulness.

esbelto *adj* slim, slender; lithe, willowy; graceful.

esbirro *nm* henchman; (*Hist*) bailiff, constable.

esbozar [1f] *vt* to sketch, outline; **— una sonrisa** to smile wanly, force a smile.

esbozo *nm* sketch, outline.

escabechar [1a] *vt* **(a)** (*Cook*) to pickle, souse. **(b)** *hair* to dye. **(c)** (*fam*) to do in (*sl*), carve up. **(d)** (*Univ: sl*) to plough (*sl*).

escabeche *nm* **(a)** (liquid) pickle, brine. **(b)** soused fish; **estar como el —** (*of meal*) to be stone-cold.

escabel *nm* low stool, footstool.

escabiosa *nf* scabious.

escabioso *adj* scabby; mangy.

escabro *nm* (*Vet*) sheep scab, scabs; (*Bot*) scaly bark.

escabrosamente *adv* (*fig*) riskily, scabrously, salaciously.

escabrosidad *nf* **(a)** roughness, ruggedness; unevenness. **(b)** harshness. **(c)** toughness, difficulty. **(d)** riskiness, scabrous nature, salaciousness.

escabroso *adj* **(a)** *ground* rough, rugged; *surface* uneven. **(b)** (*fig*) *sound etc* harsh. **(c)** *problem etc* tough, difficult, thorny. **(d)** *joke etc* risky, risqué, blue, scabrous.

escabuche *nm* weeding hoe.

escabullarse [1a] *vr* (*SAm*), **escabullirse** [3a] *vr* to slip away, slip off, clear out; to make oneself scarce; to scamper; **— por** to slip through.

escachalandrado *adj* (*CAm, Col*) slovenly.

escafandra *nf* diving suit.

escafandrismo *nm* underwater fishing.

escala *nf* **(a)** ladder; **— de cuerda, — de viento** (*Naut*) rope ladder.
   (b) (*Math, Mus and fig*) scale; (*of colours, speeds etc*) range; **— móvil** sliding scale; **— de la popularidad** popularity chart, (*Mus*) hit parade; **— de sueldos** salary scale; **a (or en) — nacional** on a national scale; **una investigación a — nacional** a nation-wide inquiry, a countrywide investigation; **en gran(de)** — on a large scale, in a big way; **un plan en gran** — a large-scale plan; **a (or en) pequeña** — on a small scale; **reproducir según** — to reproduce to scale.
   (c) stopping place; (*Naut*) port of call; intermediate stop, stopover; **vuelo sin —s** non-stop flight; **hacer — en** to stop at, make an intermediate stop at, (*Naut*) to call at, put in at.

escalación *nf* (*Mil, Pol*) escalation.

escalada *nf* **(a)** climb; climbing, scaling; **— en rocas** rock climbing. **(b)** (*Mil, Pol*) escalation.

escalador *nm* **(a)** climber; mountaineer; **— en rocas** rock climber. **(b)** burglar, housebreaker.

escalafón *nm* **(a)** roll, list, register; list of officials, establishment.
   (b) salary scale, wage scale.
   (c) (*fig*) table, chart; **en esta industria España ocupa el tercer lugar en el — mundial** Spain occupies third place in the world table for this industry.

escalamera *nf* rowlock, oarlock (*US*).

escalamiento *nm* **(a)** climbing, scaling. **(b)** (*Mil, Pol*) escalation.

escálamo *nm* thole, tholepin.

escalante *adj* (*Mil, Pol*) escalating; **la crisis —** the escalating crisis.

escalar [1a] **1** vt (a) *mountain etc* to climb, scale.
  (b) *house* to burgle, burglarize (US), break into, force an entry into.
  2 vi (a) to climb.
  (b) (*Naut*) to call, put in (*en* at).
  (c) (*Mil, Pol*) to escalate.
Escalda m Scheldt.
escaldado adj (a) wary, fly, cautious. (b) *woman* loose.
escaldadura nf (a) scald, scalding. (b) chafing.
escaldar [1a] **1** vt (a) *person* to scald. (b) *skin* to chafe, rub. (c) *metal* to make red-hot. **2 escaldarse** vr (a) to get scalded, scald oneself. (b) to chafe.
escalera nf (a) stairs, staircase, stairway; ladder; steps, flight of steps; (*of cart, lorry*) tailboard; — **de caracol** spiral staircase, winding staircase; — **doble**, — **de mano**, — **de tijera** steps, stepladder; — **de incendios** fire escape; — **mecánica**, — **móvil**, — **rodante** escalator, moving staircase; — **de servicio** service stairs, backstairs.
  (b) (*Cards*) run, sequence.
escalerilla nf small ladder; low step; (*Naut*) gangway.
escalfador nm chafing dish.
escalfar [1a] vt *egg* to poach.
escalinata nf steps, flight of steps; outside staircase.
escalofriado adj: **estar** — to feel chilly, feel shivery, feel hot-and-cold.
escalofriante adj bloodcurdling, hair-raising; chilling, frightening.
escalofriarse [1c] vr (a) to feel chilly, get the shivers, feel hot-and-cold by turns. (b) to shiver with fright, get a cold shiver of fright.
escalofrío nm (a) (*Med*) chill, feverish chill. (b) —**s** (*fig*) shivers; shivery fright.
escalón nm (a) (*of stairway*) step, stair; (*of ladder*) rung; (*part of stair*) tread; (*of rocket*) stage; — **de hielo** ice step.
  (b) (*fig*) stage, grade; (*towards success etc*) ladder; rung, stepping stone.
  (c) (*Mil*) echelon.
escalonar [1a] vt to spread out at intervals; (*Mil etc*) to echelon; *land* to terrace, cut in a series of steps; *hours, production etc* to stagger.
escalope nm (*Cook*) escalope; — **de ternera** escalope of veal.
escalpar [1a] vt to scalp.
escalpelo nm scalpel.
escama nf (a) (*Bot, Fish etc*) scale; (*of soap etc*) flake; —**s de jabón, jabón en** —**s** soapflakes. (b) (*fig*) resentment, grudge; suspicion.
escamado adj (a) wary, fly, cautious. (b) (*Arg*) wearied, cloyed.
escamar [1a] **1** vt (a) to scale, remove the scales from.
  (b) (*fig*) to make wary, create distrust in, shake the confidence of; **eso me escama** that makes me suspicious, that sounds ominous to me.
  2 escamarse vr (a) to scale (off), flake off.
  (b) (*fig*) to get wary, become suspicious; **y luego se escamó** and after that it was a case of once bitten twice shy.
escamocha nf (*Mex*) left-overs.
escamón adj wary, distrustful; apprehensive.
escamondar [1a] vt to prune; (*fig*) to prune, trim.
escamoso adj *fish* scaly; *substance* flaky.
escamoteador nm (a) conjurer, juggler. (b) (*pej*) swindler.
escamot(e)ar [1a] vt (a) to whisk away, whisk out of sight, snatch away, make vanish; *card* to palm.
  (b) (*fam*) to lift (*fam*), swipe (*sl*).
  (c) (*fig*) *difficulty etc* to shirk, disregard.
escamoteo nm (a) sleight of hand; conjuring; palming.
  (b) (*un* —) conjuring trick.
  (c) (*fam*) lifting (*fam*), swiping (*sl*); swindling; (*un* —) swindle.
  (d) shirking.
escampar [1a] **1** vt to clear out.
  2 vi (a) (*of sky*) to clear; (*of rain*) to stop; (*of weather*) to clear up, stop raining.
  (b) (*CAm, Col, Chi, Mex, PR*) to shelter from the rain.
  (c) (*SAm: fam*) to clear off, beat it (*fam*).
escampavía nf revenue cutter.
escanciador nm wine waiter; (*Hist*) cupbearer.
escanciar [1b] **1** vt *wine* to pour (out), serve; *glass* to drain. **2** vi to drink a lot of wine, make merry on wine.
escandalizar [1f] **1** vt to scandalize, shock.
  2 vi to make a fuss, kick up a row.
  3 escandalizarse vr to be shocked (*de* at, by), be scandalized; to be offended (*de* at, by); **se escandalizó ante la pintura** he threw up his hands in horror at the picture.

escándalo nm (a) scandal; outrage; **¡qué** —**!** what a scandal!; **el** — **de los autobuses municipales** the scandal of the town's buses.
  (b) row, uproar, commotion; **armar un** — to make a scene, cause an uproar.
  (c) sense of shock; astonishment.
escandalosa nf (a) (*Naut*) topsail. (b) (*Col*) tulip.
escandalosamente adv scandalously, shockingly, outrageously; flagrantly; licentiously.
escandaloso adj scandalous, shocking, outrageous; *crime etc* flagrant; *life* scandalous; disorderly, licentious; *laughter* uproarious, hearty; *child* noisy; uncontrollable, undisciplined; *colours* (*Col*) loud.
escandallo nm (*Naut*) lead.
Escandinavia f Scandinavia.
escandinavo **1** adj Scandinavian. **2** nm, **escandinava** nf Scandinavian.
escandir vt *verse* to scan.
escansión nf scansion.
escantillón nm pattern, template.
escaño nm bench; settle; (*Parl*) seat.
escapada nf (a) escape, flight; — **en una tabla** narrow squeak, near thing; **en una** — in a jiffy.
  (b) (*Racing, Sport*) breakaway.
  (c) flying visit, quick trip; **hice una** — **a la capital** I made a flying visit to the capital.
  (d) (*pej*) escapade.
escapado adj, adv at top speed, in a rush; **irse** — to rush off, be off like a shot; **se volvió** — he rushed back; **tengo que volverme** — **a la tienda** I must get back double-quick to the shop; **lo harán** —**s** they'll do it like a shot.
escapar [1a] **1** vt *horse* to ride hard, drive hard.
  2 vi (a) to escape, flee, run away; — **a uno** to escape from someone; — **de la cárcel** to escape from prison; **escapó de mis manos** it escaped from my hands, it eluded my grasp.
  (b) (*Racing, Sport*) to break away.
  3 escaparse vr (a) (*person*) to escape, flee, run away, get away; — **con algo** to make off with something; — **de morir** to miss death narrowly; — **por un pelo**, — **en una tabla** to have a narrow escape, have a close shave.
  (b) (*gas etc*) to leak, leak out, escape.
  (c) (*detail, news etc*) **se me escapa** it eludes me, it escapes me; **se me escapa su nombre** his name escapes me; **se le escapó la fecha de la reunión** he let the date of the meeting slip out, he unintentionally revealed the date of the meeting; **ese detalle se me había escapado** that detail had escaped my notice.
escaparate nm (a) shop window; showcase, display case. (b) (*SAm*) wardrobe.
escaparatista nmf window dresser.
escapatoria nf (a) escape, flight; getaway; (*fam*) secret trip; — **del trabajo** escape from work. (b) (*fig*) way out, loophole; excuse, pretext.
escape nm (a) escape, flight, getaway; **a** — at full speed; in a great hurry; **salir a** — to rush out.
  (b) (*of gas etc*) leak, leakage, escape.
  (c) (*Tech*) exhaust; **gases de** — exhaust (fumes); **tubo de** — exhaust (pipe).
  (d) (*Mech*) escapement.
escapismo nm escapism.
escapista **1** adj escapist. **2** nmf escapist.
escápula nf scapula, shoulder blade.
escapulario nm scapular(y).
escaque nm (*of chessboard*) square; —**s** (*Hist*) chess.
escaquearse [1a] vr (*fam*) to shirk.
escara nf (*Med*) crust, slough.
escarabajas nfpl firewood, kindling.
escarabajear [1a] **1** vt (*fam*) to bother, worry. **2** vi (a) to crawl; to wriggle, squirm. (b) to scrawl, scribble.
escarabajo nm (a) (*Ent*) beetle; — **del Colorado**, — **de la patata** Colorado beetle. (b) (*Tech*) flaw. (c) (*fam*) dwarf, runt. (d) —**s** (*fam*) scrawl, scribble.
escaramujo nm (a) (*Bot*) wild rose, dog rose, briar; hip. (b) (*Zool*) goose barnacle. (c) (*Cu*) bewitchment.
escaramuza nf (a) (*Mil*) skirmish, brush. (b) (*fig*) brush; squabble.
escaramuzar [1f] vi to skirmish.
escarapela nf (a) cockade, rosette. (b) (*fam*) brawl, shindy.
escarapelar [1a] **1** vt (a) (*Col, CR, Mex, Ven*) to scrape off, scale off, chip off.
  (b) (*Col*) to crumple, rumple, muss.
  2 vi (a) to wrangle, quarrel.
  (b)=**3 escarapelarse** vr (a) (*Col, CR, Mex, Ven*) to peel off, flake off.
  (b) (*Mex, Per*) to get gooseflesh, tremble all over.
escarbadientes nm, pl **escarbadientes** toothpick.
escarbador nm scraper.

escarbar [1a] **1** *vt* (a) *ground* (*of chicken*) to scratch; *fire* to poke; *ears, teeth* to pick, clean.
    (b) (*fig*) to inquire into, investigate, delve into; (*pej*) to pry into; to rake around in (*or* among).
    2 *vi* (a) to scratch.
    (b) — **en** = **1** (b).
escarcear [1a] *vi* (*Chi, RPl, Ven*) to prance.
escarcela *nf* (a) (*Hunting*) pouch, bag. (b) — **para limosnas** collecting tin.
escarceo *nm* (a) (*of horse*) nervous movement; prance.
    (b) —**s** small waves.
    (c) —**s** (*fig*): —**s amorosos** amorous posturings, amorous attitudinizing.
escarcha *nf* frost, hoarfrost.
escarchado *adj* (a) covered in hoarfrost, frosted. (b) *fruit* crystallized.
escarchar [1a] **1** *vt* (a) to frost, cover in hoarfrost.
    (b) (*Cook*) *cake* to ice.
    (c) (*Sew*) to embroider with silver (*or* gold).
    2 *vi*: **escarcha** there is a frost, it's frosty, it's freezing.
escarchilla *nf* (*Col, Ec, Ven*) small ice particles.
escarcho *nm* roach.
escarda *nf* (a) weeding, hoeing. (b) weeding hoe.
escardador *nm* weeding hoe.
escardadura *nf* weeding, hoeing.
escardar [1a] *vt* (a) to weed, weed out. (b) (*fig*) to weed out.
escardillo *nm* weeding hoe.
escariador *nm* reamer.
escariar [1b] *vt* to ream.
escarificación *nf* (*Agr, Med*) scarification.
escarificador *nm* scarifier.
escarificar [1g] *vt* to scarify.
escarlata **1** *adj invar* scarlet. **2** *nf* (a) scarlet. (b) scarlet cloth.
escarlatina *nf* scarlet fever.
escarmenar [1a] *vt* (a) *wool* to comb. (b) (*fig*) to punish; — **algo a uno** (*fam*) to do someone out of something bit by bit.
escarmentado *adj* wary, cautious.
escarmentar [1k] **1** *vt* to punish severely, teach a lesson to.
    2 *vi* to learn one's lesson; **yo escarmenté y no lo volví a hacer** I learned my lesson and never did it again; **¡para que escarmientes!** that'll teach you!; — **en cabeza ajena** to learn by someone else's mistakes.
escarmiento *nm* punishment; lesson, warning, example; **para** — **de los malhechores** as a lesson to wrongdoers; **que esto te sirva de** — let this be a lesson (*or* warning) to you.
escarnecedor **1** *adj* mocking. **2** *nm* scoffer, mocker.
escarnecer [2d] *vt* to scoff at, mock, ridicule.
escarnio *nm* jibe, taunt; derision, ridicule.
escarola *nf* (a) (*Bot*) endive. (b) (*Mex: Sew*) ruff, flounce.
escarolar [1a] *vt* (*Sew*) to frill, flounce; to curl.
escarpa *nf* (a) slope; (*Geog, Mil*) scarp, escarpment. (b) (*Mex*) pavement.
escarpado *adj* steep, sheer; craggy.
escarpadura *nf* = **escarpa** (a).
escarpar [1a] *vt* (a) (*Geog etc*) to escarp. (b) (*Tech*) to rasp.
escarpia *nf* spike; meat hook; (*Tech*) tenterhook.
escarpín *nm* pump, slipper; extra sock, outer sock; ankle sock.
escarrancharse [1a] *vr* (*fam*) to do the splits.
escasamente *adv* (a) scantily, sparingly; meagrely. (b) scarcely, hardly, barely.
escasear [1a] **1** *vt* to be sparing with, give out in small amounts, skimp. **2** *vi* to be scarce, get scarce; to fall short; to diminish.
escasez *nf* (a) scarcity, shortage, lack; poverty, want; — **de dinero** lack of money, shortage of funds; **vivir con** — to live in poverty. (b) meanness, stinginess.
escaso *adj* (a) scarce; scant, scanty; limited; slight; *allowance* meagre, skimpy; *audience, crop* thin, sparse; *chance* slim, slender, small; *resources* slender; *money* scarce, tight; *supply* small, short, insufficient; *visibility* poor; — **de población** thinly populated; — **de recursos naturales** poor in natural resources; **andar** — **de dinero** to be short of money, be in need of money; **con escasa compasión** with scant pity; **su inteligencia es escasa** his intelligence is slight, his intelligence is limited.
    (b) bare; **hay 2 toneladas escasas** there are barely 2 tons; **tiene 15 años** —**s** he's barely 15, he's hardly 15; **ganar por una cabeza escasa** to win by a short head.
    (c) mean, stingy; sparing.

escatimar [1a] *vt* to curtail, cut down; to give grudgingly, skimp, stint; to be sparing of; **no** — **esfuerzo para** + *infin* to spare no effort to + *infin*; **no escatimaba sus alabanzas de** . . . he was unstinting in his praise of . . ., he did not stint his praise of . . .
escatimoso *adj* (a) sparing, scrimpy, mean. (b) malicious.
escatología *nf* eschatology.
escayola *nf* (*Med etc*) plaster.
escayolar [1a] *vt* to put in plaster; **con la pierna escayolada** with his leg in plaster; **tener el cuello escayolado** to have one's neck in plaster.
escena *nf* (a) (*in general*) scene; **una** — **conmovedora** a touching scene; **con** —**s de la revolución** with scenes from the revolution; — **muda** by-play; — (*Cine*) **retrospectiva** flashback.
    (b) stage; **entrar en** — to enter, come on; **poner en** — to stage, put on, perform.
    (c) scenery.
escenario *nm* (a) (*Theat*) stage; setting; scenery; **en el** — on (the) stage.
    (b) (*Cine*) scenario; continuity.
    (c) (*fig*) scene; setting; **el** — **del crimen** the scene of the crime; **fue** — **de un motín** it was the scene of a riot; **desapareció del** — **político** he disappeared from the political scene; **la ceremonia tuvo por** — **X** the ceremony was set in X, the ceremony had X as its setting.
escénico *adj* scenic.
escenografía *nf* scenography.
escenógrafo *nm* theatrical designer, designer of sets; scene painter.
escepticismo *nm* scepticism.
escéptico **1** *adj* sceptical. **2** *nm*, **escéptica** *nf* sceptic; doubter.
Escila *f* Scylla; — **y Caribdis** Scylla and Charybdis.
escindible *adj* fissionable.
escindir [3a] **1** *vt* to split; **el partido está escindido** the party is split. **2 escindirse** *vr* to split (**en** into); (*of faction*) to split off.
Escipión *m* Scipio.
escisión *nf* (a) scission; fission; split; (*Med*) excision; — **nuclear** nuclear fission. (b) (*fig*) split, division; **la** — **del partido** the split in the party.
esclarecer [2d] **1** *vt* (a) to light up, illuminate. (b) (*fig*) to explain, elucidate, shed light on. (c) (*fig*) to enlighten. (d) (*fig*) to ennoble. **2** *vi* to dawn.
esclarecido *adj* illustrious, distinguished.
esclarecimiento *nm* (a) illumination. (b) explanation, elucidation, clarification. (c) enlightenment. (d) ennoblement.
esclava *nf* (a) slave; (*fig*) slave, drudge; — **blanca** white slave. (b) slave bangle, bracelet.
esclavatura *nf* (*SAm: Hist*) (a) slaves (*collectively*). (b) period of slavery. (c) slavery.
esclavina *nf* short cloak, cape, tippet.
esclavitud *nf* slavery, servitude, bondage.
esclavizar [1f] *vt* to enslave.
esclavo *nm* slave; **ser** — **del tabaco** to be a slave to tobacco; **vender a uno como** — to sell someone into slavery.
esclerosis *nf* sclerosis.
esclusa *nf* lock, sluice; floodgate; — **de aire** airlock.
esclusero *nm* lock keeper.
escoba *nf* (a) broom; brush. (b) (*Bot*) broom.
escobada *nf* brush, sweep.
escobar [1a] *vt* to sweep, sweep out.
escobazo *nm* (a) blow with a broom. (b) quick sweep; **dar un** — to have a quick sweep-up; **echar a uno a** —**s** to kick someone out.
escobilla *nf* (a) small broom, brush; whisk. (b) (*Aut, Elec*) brush. (c) (*Bot*) teasel.
escobillar [1a] *vi* (*SAm*) to dance with quick steps.
escobillón *nm* (*Mech, Med*) swab.
escobón *nm* large broom, long-handled broom; scrubbing brush; (*Mech, Med*) swab.
escocedor *adj* (*fig*) painful, hurtful.
escocer [2b and 2h] **1** *vt* to annoy, upset.
    2 *vi* to smart, sting; to feel a burning pain; **esto escuece en la lengua, esto me escuece la lengua** it makes my tongue smart.
    3 escocerse *vr* to chafe, get chafed.
escocés **1** *adj* Scotch, Scots, Scottish. **2** *nm* Scot, Scotsman. **3** *nm* (*dialect*) Scots.
escocesa *nf* Scot, Scotswoman.
Escocia *f* Scotland.
escoda *nf* stonecutter's hammer.
escofina *nf* rasp, file.
escofinar [1a] *vt* to rasp, file.
escogedor *nm* (*Agr etc*) riddle.

escoger [2c] *vti* to choose, select, pick (out); (*Pol etc*) to elect.

escogido *adj* chosen, selected; (*in quality*) choice, select; *works* selected.

escogimiento *nm* (a) (*act*) choosing, selecting, picking. (b) selection; choice, pick.

escolar 1 *adj* scholastic; school (*attr*); año — school year. **2** *nm* schoolboy, pupil.

escolaridad *nf* schooling; — obligatoria compulsory schooling, compulsory attendance at school; el porcentaje de — es elevado the school population is high, the proportion of those in school is high.

escolástica *nf*, **escolasticismo** *nm* scholasticism.

escolástico 1 *adj* scholastic. **2** *nm* scholastic, schoolman.

escoleta *nf* (*Mex*) (a) amateur band. (b) rehearsal, practice (of an amateur band). (c) dancing lesson.

escoliar [1b] *vt text* to gloss, furnish with explanations.

escolopendra *nf* (*Zool*) centipede.

escolta *nf* escort; dar — a to escort, accompany.

escoltar [1a] *vt* to escort; to guard, protect; to attend, accompany; (*Naut*) to escort, convoy.

escollar [1a] *vi* (a) (*Arg, Per*) to hit a reef, strike a rock. (b) (*Arg, Chi: of enterprise*) to fail, come unstuck.

escollera *nf* breakwater, jetty.

escollo *nm* (a) reef, rock. (b) (*fig*) pitfall; stumbling block; hidden danger.

escombrar [1a] *vt* to clear out, clean out, clear of rubbish.

escombrera *nf* tip, dump, rubbish heap; (*Min*) slag heap.

escombro *nm* (*Fish*) mackerel.

escombros *nmpl* rubbish; debris, wreckage, rubble; (*Min*) waste, slag.

escondedero *nm* hiding place.

esconder [2a] **1** *vt* to hide, conceal (*de* from). **2** esconderse *vr* to hide (*de* from); to hide oneself, conceal oneself; to be hidden; to lurk.

escondida(s) *nf(pl)* (*SAm*) hide-and-seek; hacer algo a —s to do something secretly, do something by stealth; hacer algo a —s de uno to do something behind someone's back.

escondite *nm* (a) hiding place. (b) hide-and-seek; jugar al — con (*fig*) to play hide-and-seek with.

escondido(s) *nm(pl)* (*SAm*) hide-and-seek.

escondrijo *nm* hiding place, hideout; (*fig*) nook.

escopeta *nf* shotgun; — de aire comprimido popgun; airgun; — de dos cañones, — de tiro doble double-barrelled gun; — de viento airgun.

escopetazo *nm* (a) gunshot; gunshot wound. (b) (*fig*) bad news; blow; bombshell.

escopetear [1a] **1** *vt* (a) to shoot at (with a shotgun). (b) (*Mex*) to get at, allude offensively to. **2** *vi* (*Ven*) to answer irritably. **3** escopetearse *vr*: se escopetearon en el bosque they shot at each other in the wood; se escopetean a injurias they shower one another with insults, they heap insults upon each other.

escopeteo *nm* (a) shooting, volley of shots. (b) (*of insults etc*) shower, lively exchange.

escopetero *nm* gunsmith.

escoplear [1a] *vt* to chisel.

escoplo *nm* chisel.

escor *nm* (*SAm: angl*) score.

escora *nf* (*Naut*) (a) level line, load line. (b) prop, shore. (c) list; con una — de 30 grados with a thirty-degree list.

escorar [1a] *vi* (*Naut*) to list, heel (over); — a babor to list to port.

escorbútico *adj* scorbutic.

escorbuto *nm* scurvy.

escorchar [1a] *vt* (a) to flay, skin. (b) (*Arg*) to bother, annoy.

escoria *nf* (a) (*Metal*) slag, dross; — básica basic slag. (b) (*fig*) scum, dregs; la — de la humanidad the scum of humanity.

escorial *nm* dump, slag heap, tip; bed of lava, deposit of volcanic ash.

escorpión *nm* scorpion; E— Scorpio.

escorzar [1f] *vt* to foreshorten.

escorzo *nm* foreshortening.

escota *nf* (*Naut*) sheet.

escotado 1 *adj dress* low-cut, low-necked, cut low, décolleté. **2** *nm* = escotadura.

escotadura *nf* (a) (*Sew*) low neck(line). (b) (*Theat*) large trap door. (c) recess; notch.

escotar [1a] **1** *vt* (a) (*Sew*) to cut out, cut to fit; to cut low in front. (b) *river etc* to draw water from. **2** *vi* to pay one's share.

escote *nm* (a) (*Sew*) low neck; décolletage. (b) (*Fin*) share; ir a —, pagar a — to share the expenses, go fifty-fifty, (*on outing*) to go Dutch.

escotilla *nf* (*Naut etc*) hatch, hatchway.

escotillón *nm* trap door.

escozor *nm* (a) smart, sting; burning pain. (b) (*fig*) grief, heartache.

escriba *nm* scribe.

escribanía *nf* (a) writing desk; writing case. (b) writing materials; inkstand. (c) (*Law*) clerkship; clerk's office, (*Hist*) notary's office.

escribano *nm* (a) court clerk; lawyer's clerk; (*Hist*) notary; — municipal town clerk. (b) (*Orn*) bunting; — cerillo yellowhammer.

escribiente *nm* copyist, amanuensis; clerk; — en jefe chief clerk, head clerk.

escribir [3a; *ptp* escrito] **1** *vti* (a) to write; — a mano to write in longhand; to write out; — a máquina to type; el que esto escribe the present writer, (*to press etc*) this correspondent. (b) to spell; "voy" se escribe con "v" "voy" is spelled with a "v"; ¿cómo se escribe eso? how is that spelled?, how do you spell that? **2** escribirse *vr* to write to each other.

escrito 1 *ptp* of escribir. **2** *adj* written; said, stated; lo arriba — what has been said above. **3** *nm* writing, document; text; manuscript; (*Law*) brief; —s (*Lit etc*) writings, works; por — in writing; in black and white; acuerdo por — written agreement, agreement in writing; poner algo por — to commit something to paper; to write something down, get something down in writing; tomar algo por — to write something down.

escritor *nm*, **escritora** *nf* writer; — de material publicitario copywriter; — satírico satirist, satirical writer.

escritorio *nm* (a) desk, bureau; writing case. (b) office.

escritorzuelo *nm* hack (writer), scribbler.

escrituario *adj* scriptural.

escritura *nf* (a) (*act, art*) writing. (b) (*of nation etc*) writing, script; alphabet; (*of person*) writing, handwriting; tiene malísima — her writing is terrible; no acierto a leer su — I can't read his writing; — aérea skywriting; — corrida, — normal longhand; — china Chinese writing, Chinese script; — fonética phonetic script; — a máquina typing. (c) Sagrada E— (Holy) Scripture. (d) (*Law*) deed; document, instrument; — de aprendizaje indenture; — de propiedad title deed; — de seguro insurance certificate; — de traspaso conveyance.

escriturar [1a] *vt* (a) (*Law*) to execute by deed, formalize legally; *apprentice* to indenture. (b) (*Theat etc*) to book, engage, sign up.

escriturístico *adj* Scriptural.

escrófula *nf* scrofula.

escrofuloso *adj* scrofulous.

escroto *nm* scrotum.

escrupulizar [1f] *vt* to scruple, hesitate; no — en + *infin* not to scruple to + *infin*.

escrúpulo *nm* (a) scruple; doubt, hesitation; falta de —s unscrupulousness; sin — unscrupulous; no hizo — de + *infin* he did not scruple to + *infin*, he did not hesitate to + *infin*. (b) scrupulousness. (c) (*Pharm*) scruple.

escrupulosamente *adv* scrupulously; exactly, precisely.

escrupulosidad *nf* scrupulousness; exactness, preciseness.

escrupuloso *adj* scrupulous; exact, particular, precise.

escrutador 1 *adj look etc* searching, penetrating. **2** *nm* (*Pol*) returning officer, scrutineer; inspector of election returns; (*Parl*) teller.

escrutar [1a] *vt* (a) to scrutinize, examine. (b) *votes* to count.

escrutinio *nm* (a) scrutiny, examination, inspection. (b) (*Pol*) count, counting (of votes); voting, ballot.

escuadra *nf* (a) (*Tech*) carpenter's square, draughtsman's square; bracket, angle iron; — de delineante set square; a — square, at right angles; fuera de — out of true. (b) (*Mil*) squad; (*Naut*) squadron; (*of cars etc*) fleet; — de demolición demolition squad; — de fusilamiento firing squad. (c) (*Col*) pistol.

escuadrar [1a] *vt* (*Tech*) to square.

escuadrilla *nf* (*Aer*) wing, squadron.

escuadrón *nm* (*Aer*) squadron; (*Mil*) squadron, troop.

escualidez *nf* paleness, weakness, emaciation; skinniness, scragginess.

escuálido *adj* pale, weak, emaciated; skinny, scraggy.

escualo *nm* shark, dogfish.

escucha 1 *nf* (a) (*act*) listening; listening-in; **estar a la — to listen in; estar de — to spy, eavesdrop.
   (b) (*Eccl*) chaperon.
   2 *nm* (*Mil*) scout; (*Radio*) monitor (*person*); listener.

escuchar [1a] 1 *vt* to listen to; (*SAm*) to hear; *advice etc* to listen to, heed, pay attention to; *applause, ovation, warning etc* to receive. 2 *vi* to listen.

escucho *nm* (*Col*) whispered secret.

escuchón *adj* (*Ec*) prying, inquisitive.

escudar [1a] 1 *vt* to shield, protect, defend. 2 **escudarse** *vr* to shield oneself, protect oneself.

escudero *nm* (*Hist*) squire; page.

escudete *nm* (a) (*Her*, *Hist*) escutcheon. (b) (*Sew*) gusset. (c) (*Bot*) white water lily.

escudilla *nf* bowl, basin.

escudo *nm* shield (*also fig*); **— de armas** (*Her*) coat of arms.

escudriñar [1a] *vt* to inquire into, investigate; to examine, scan, scrutinize.

escuela *nf* (a) school; **— de artes y oficios** technical school, trade school; **— automovilista** driving school; **— de baile** school of dancing; ballet school; **— de comercio** business school, school of business studies; **— elemental**, **— primaria**, **— de primera enseñanza** primary school; **— de equitación** riding school; **— de formación profesional** polytechnic; **— de hogar** domestic science college; **— laboral** technical school; trade school; **— nocturna** night school; **— normal** training college, college of education; **— particular**, **— privada** private school; **— de párvulos** infant(s') school, kindergarten; **estar en la — to be at school; ir a la — to go to school; soplarse la — to play truant.
   (b) (*of thought etc*) school; **la — catalana** the Catalan school; **gente de la vieja — people of the old school; formarse en una — dura** to learn in a tough school.

escuelante *nm* (a) (*Mex*) schoolmaster. (b) (*Col*, *Ven*) schoolboy.

escuelero 1 *adj* (*SAm*) school (*attr*). 2 *nm* (a) (*CAm*, *Cu*, *Chi*, *Mex*, *Per*, *Urug*, *Ven*: *pej*) schoolmaster. (b) (*Col*, *Guat*, *Par*, *Ven*) schoolboy, pupil.

escuelista *nmf* (*Urug*) schoolboy, schoolgirl, pupil.

escuerzo *nm* toad.

escuetamente *adv* plainly; baldly, without frills.

escueto *adj* plain, unadorned, bare; bald.

escuincle *nm* (*Mex*) child.

esculcar [1g] *vt* (*Ant*, *CAm*, *Col*, *Mex*) to search.

esculpir [3a] *vt* to sculpture; to carve, engrave; *inscription* to cut.

escultor *nm* sculptor.

escultora *nf* sculptress.

escultura *nf* sculpture, carving; **— en madera** wood carving.

escultural *adj* sculptural; (*fig*) figure *etc* statuesque.

escupidera *nf* (a) spittoon. (b) (*SAm: euph*) chamberpot; **pedir la — to get scared; to give in, give oneself up.

escupidor *nm* (a) spitter. (b) (*Ec*, *PR*) spittoon. (c) (*Col*) round mat, doormat.

escupir [3a] *vti* (a) to spit; *food etc* to spit out; **— a uno** to spit at someone; **— a la cara a uno** to spit in someone's face; **— en el suelo** to spit on the ground.
   (b) (*fig*) *word* to spit, spit out, fling (*a at*); *flames etc* to spit, belch, give out; to throw off, fling off, cast aside; **— a** to scoff at.

escurana *nf* (*SAm*) darkness; overcast sky, threatening sky.

escurialense *adj* of (*or from*) El Escorial.

escurreplatos *nm*, *pl* **escurreplatos** plate rack.

escurribanda *nf* (*fam*) (a) (*Med*) looseness, diarrhoea. (b) (*Med: of sore*) running. (c) escape; (*fig*) loophole, way out. (d) thrashing.

escurridero *nm* draining board, drainboard (*US*).

escurridizo *adj* (a) slippery; difficult to hold; *knot* running; **hacerse — to slip away, vanish. (b) *character* slippery.

escurrido *adj* (a) narrow-hipped, slightly built; wearing a tight-fitting skirt. (b) (*Cu*, *Mex*, *Per*, *PR*) abashed, ashamed.

escurridor *nm* wringer; **— (de loza)** plate rack; (*Cook*) colander, strainer; (*Phot*) drying rack.

escurriduras *nfpl* dregs.

escurrir [3a] 1 *vt clothes* to wring (out); *plates, liquid* to drain; *substance* to press dry, squeeze dry.
   2 *vi* (a) (*of liquid*) to drip, trickle; to ooze; (*of object*) to slip, slide.
   (b) (*of surface*) to be slippery.
   3 **escurrirse** *vr* (a) (*liquid*) to drip, trickle; to ooze; (*object*) to slip, slide; **se me escurrió de entre las manos** it slipped out of my hands.
   (b) (*dishes etc*) to drain; (*Cook*) to drain, strain; **"se escurre bien"** (*recipe*) "drain well".
   (c) (*remark etc*) to slip out.
   (d) (*person etc*) to slip away, sneak off; to glide away.

escúter *nm* (*angl*) (motor) scooter.

esdrújula 1 *adj* having dactylic stress, accented on the antepenult.
   2 *nm* word having dactylic stress, word accented on the antepenult (*eg* **mísero**, miserly).

ese[1] *nf* (a) *name of the letter* S. (b) S-shaped part (*or link etc*); **hacer —s** to zigzag, twist and turn; (*of drunk*) to reel about, stagger along.

ese[2] *dem adj m*, **esa** *f* that; **esos** *dem adj mpl*, **esas** *fpl* those.

ése *dem pron m*, **ésa** *f* that; that one; the former; **ésos** *dem pron mpl*, **ésas** *fpl* those; the former; **en ésa** in your town; **ni por ésas** on no account, under no circumstances; **¡no me salgas ahora con ésas!** don't bring all that up again!; **no es una chica de ésas** she's not one of those, she's not that kind of a girl.

esencia *nf* essence; (*of problem etc*) heart, core; **en — in essence.

esencial 1 *adj* essential; chief, main; **lo — the essential thing, the main thing; **cosa no — non-essential thing, inessential. 2 *nm* essential.

esfágnea *nf* sphagnum.

esfera *nf* (a) (*Geog*, *Math etc*) sphere; globe; **— celeste** celestial sphere; **en forma de — spherical, globular.
   (b) (*Tech*) dial; (*of watch*) face.
   (c) (*fig*) sphere; plane, field; **— de acción** scope, range; **— de actividad** sphere of activity; **— de influencia** sphere of influence.

esférico *adj* spherical.

esferográfica *nf* (*Cu*) ballpoint pen.

esferoide *nm* spheroid.

esfinge *nf* (a) sphinx. (b) (*Ent*) hawk moth.

esfínter *nm* sphincter.

esforzado *adj* vigorous, energetic, strong; tough; enterprising; brave, valiant.

esforzar [1f *and* 1m] 1 *vt* (a) to strengthen; to invigorate.
   (b) to encourage, raise the spirits of.
   2 **esforzarse** *vr* to exert oneself, make an effort; to strain; **hay que — más** you must try harder, you must put more effort into it; **— en** + *infin*, **— por** + *infin* to struggle to + *infin*, strive to + *infin*.

esfuerzo *nm* (a) effort, endeavour; exertion; (*of imagination*) effort, stretch; **sin — effortlessly, without strain; **no perdonar —s para** + *infin* to spare no effort to + *infin*; **bien vale el — it's well worth the effort.
   (b) (*Mech*) stress.
   (c) courage, spirit; vigour; **con — with spirit.

esfumar [1a] 1 *vt* (*Art*) to shade (in); to tone down, soften.
   2 **esfumarse** *vr* (a) to fade away, melt away.
   (b) (*person*) to vanish, make oneself scarce.

esfumino *nm* (*Art*) stump.

esgrima *nf* (*Sport*) fencing; (*Mil: art*) swordsmanship.

esgrimidor *nm* (*Sport*) fencer; (*Mil*) swordsman.

esgrimir [3a] 1 *vt sword* to wield; to brandish; (*fig*) *argument etc* to use; to brandish, flourish, fling about. 2 *vi* to fence.

esgrimista *nmf* (*SAm*) fencer.

esguazar [1f] *vt* to ford.

esguince *nm* (a) swerve, dodge, avoiding action; **dar un — to swerve, duck, dodge.
   (b) (*Med*) sprain.
   (c) scowl, frown; scornful look.
   (d) (*of plot*, *story*) twist; **un — ingenioso** an ingenious twist.

eslabón *nm* link (*also fig*); steel; (*Naut*, *Tech*) shackle; **— giratorio** swivel; **— hipotético**, **— perdido** (*Bio and fig*) missing link.

eslabonar [1a] *vt* to link (together, up), join; (*fig*) to link, interlink, connect, knit together.

eslavo 1 *adj* Slav, Slavonic. 2 *nm*, **eslava** *nf* Slav. 3 *nm* (*language*) Slavonic.

eslinga *nf* (*Naut*: *angl*) sling.

eslingar [1h] *vt* (*Naut*) to sling.

eslip *nm*, *pl* **eslips** (*angl*) *see* **slip**.

eslogan *nm*, *pl* **eslogans** (*angl*) *see* **slogan**.

eslora nf (Naut) length; **tiene 250 m de —** she is 250 m in length.

eslovaco 1 adj Slovak(ian). **2** nm, **eslovaca** nf Slovak.

esloveno 1 adj Slovene. **2** nm, **eslovena** nf Slovene.

esmaltar [1a] vt (a) to enamel; **nails** to varnish, paint. (b) (fig) to embellish, beautify, adorn (with a variety of colours).

esmalte nm (a) (Anat, Tech) enamel; enamelwork, smalt; **— de uñas** nail varnish, nail polish. (b) (fig) lustre.

esmeradamente adv carefully, neatly; elegantly.

esmerado adj (a) work careful, neat; polished, elegant. (b) person careful, painstaking, conscientious.

esmeralda nf emerald.

esmerar [1a] **1** vt to polish, brighten up.
2 esmerarse vr to take great pains (en over), exercise great care (en in), do one's best; to shine, do well; **— en + infin** to take great pains to + infin, go to great trouble to + infin.

esmerejón nm merlin.

esmeril nm emery.

esmerilar [1a] vt to polish with emery.

esmero nm care, carefulness; neatness; polish, elegance; refinement; **con el mayor —** with the greatest care; **poner — en algo** to take great care over something.

Esmirna Smyrna.

esmirriado adj =desmirriado.

esmoladera nf grindstone.

esmoquin nm (Acad) dinner jacket, tuxedo (US).

esnob (angl) **1** adj invar person snobbish; car, restaurant etc posh (fam), de luxe, swish (sl). **2** nmf, pl **esnobs** [ez'noβ] snob.

esnobismo nm snobbery, snobbishness.

eso dem pron "neuter" that; that thing, that affair, that matter; **— no me gusta** I don't like that; **¿qué es —?** what's that?; **— de su coche** that business about his car; **— de no tener dinero el colegio** that story about the college having no money; **— de que los cerdos volarán algún día** the idea that pigs will fly one day; **¿qué es — de que . . .?** what's all this about . . .?; **¡— a ellos!** that's their look-out!; **— es** that's it, that's right; that's just it; **no es —** that's not the reason; **¡no es —!** hardly!; **nada de —** nothing of the kind, far from it; **¡nada de —!** not a bit of it!; **¿no es —?** isn't that so?; **— sí** yes; naturally, of course; **el coche es viejo, — sí** the car is certainly old, to be sure the car is old; **a — de las 2** at about 2 o'clock, round about 2; **antes de —** before that; **después de —** after that; **en —** thereupon, at that point; **por —** therefore, and so; **por — no vine** that's why I didn't come; **y — que llovía** in spite of the fact that it was raining; bearing in mind that it was raining.

esófago nm oesophagus, gullet.

Esopo m Aesop.

esotérico adj esoteric.

espabilada nf (Col) blink; **en una —** in a jiffy.

espabilar [1a] **1** vt candil to snuff; see **despabilar**.
2 vi (Col) to blink.
3 espabilarse vr to wake up; (fig) to look lively, get a move on; **¡espabílate!** get a move on!; jump to it!; **¡espabilado!** (iro) wake up!, you're a bright one!

espaciador nm spacing key, spacing bar.

espacial adj (a) (Math etc) spatial. (b) space (attr); **programa —** space programme; **viajes —es** space travel.

espaciar [1b] **1** vt to space (out; also Typ); to spread, expand; news to spread.
2 espaciarse vr (a) to expatiate, spread oneself; **— en un tema** to enlarge on a subject, expatiate on a subject. (b) to relax, take one's ease; to make merry.

espacio nm (a) (in general) space, room; distance; period, interval; **— libre** room, clear space; **— muerto** clearance; **— vital** living space, (Pol) lebensraum; **en el — de una hora** in the space of one hour; **en el — de 3 generaciones** in the space of 3 generations, over 3 generations; **por — de** during, for. (b) (Aer, Geog) space; **exploración del —** space exploration; **— estelar, — exterior, — extraterrestre** outer space. (c) delay, slowness. (d) (Typ) space; spacing; **a dos —s, a doble —** double-spaced. (e) (Mus) interval. (f) (Radio, TV) short programme, item; spot; **— publicitario** advertising spot, commercial.

espacioso adj (a) spacious, roomy, big; capacious. (b) movement slow, deliberate.

espada 1 nf (a) sword; **estar entre la — y la pared** to be between the devil and the deep blue sea; **estar hecho una —** to be as thin as a rake; **poner a — to** put to the sword. (b) **—s** (Cards) spades.
2 nm (a) swordsman; (Taur) matador. (b) (pej) bully; swashbuckler.

espadachín nm skilled swordsman; (pej) bully, thug.

espadaña nf bulrush.

espadarte nm swordfish.

espadazo nm sword thrust, slash with a sword.

espadero nm swordsmith.

espadín nm dress sword, ceremonial sword.

espadón nm (a) broadsword. (b) (hum) big shot (fam), top person; (Mil) brass hat (sl).

espaguetis nmpl spaghetti.

espalda nf (a) (also **—s**) back, shoulder(s); **a —s de uno** behind someone's back; **a —s (vueltas)** treacherously; **eso ha quedado ya a la —** that's all behind us now; **echar algo a las —s** to forget about something; **— con —** back to back; **de —s** from behind; **dar de —s** to fall on one's back; **estar de —s** to be on one's back; **de —s a la marcha** (in vehicle) facing backwards, with one's back to the engine (etc); **volverse de —s a** to turn one's back on (also fig); **fue muerto por la —** he was killed from behind; **echar algo sobre las —s** to take something on, take charge of something; **tener guardadas las —s** to have influential friends; **volver la —** to turn away; (pej) to turn tail; **volver las —s a uno** to give someone the cold shoulder, cold-shoulder someone. (b) (Ec) fate, destiny; star.

espaldar nm (a) (of chair) back. (b) (Hort) trellis, espalier. (c) **—es** wall hangings.

espaldarazo nm slap on the back; (Hist) accolade.

espaldera nf trellis, espalier.

espaldero nm (Ven) bodyguard, henchman.

espaldilla nf shoulder blade.

espantable adj =espantoso.

espantada nf (a) sudden scare, sudden fear; **dar la — a uno** to scare the wits out of someone. (b) stampede, panic.

espantadizo adj shy, timid, easily scared (off).

espantado adj frightened, scared, terrified; (SAm) ill from fright.

espantador adj (a) frightening. (b) (Arg, Col, Guat) = espantadizo.

espantajo nm (a) scarecrow. (b) (fig) scarecrow; sight, fright; bogey, bogeyman.

espantapájaros nm, pl **espantapájaros** scarecrow.

espantar [1a] **1** vt to frighten, scare; to frighten off, scare away; to appal, horrify.
2 espantarse vr (a) to get frightened, get scared (de at, of); to be appalled; to be amazed, be astonished (de at). (b) (SD) to get suspicious.

espanto nm (a) fright, terror; consternation, dismay; amazement, astonishment. (b) threat, menace. (c) (SAm) ghost. (d) (fam) **¡qué —!** how awful! (fam); goodness!; **es un coche de —** it's a smashing car (sl), it's a tremendous car (fam).

espantosamente adv frightfully; terrifyingly; shockingly; amazingly.

espantosidad nf (CAm, Col, PR) horror.

espantoso adj frightful, dreadful; terrifying; shocking; appalling; amazing.

España f Spain; **Nueva —** (Hist) New Spain (ie Mexico); **la — de pandereta** (pej) touristy Spain, pseudo-romantic Spain, picturesque Spain.

español 1 adj Spanish.
2 i.m, **española** nf Spaniard; **los —es** the Spaniards, the Spanish.
3 nm (language) Spanish; **— antiguo** Old Spanish; **— medieval** Medieval Spanish; **— moderno** Modern Spanish.

españolidad nf Spanishness.

españolísimo adj superl typically Spanish, unmistakably Spanish, Spanish to the core; terribly Spanish.

españolismo nm (a) love of Spain, love of things Spanish; tendency to adopt Spanish ways (etc). (b) Spanishness; Spanish nature, essentially Spanish character. (c) (Ling) hispanicism, word (or phrase etc) borrowed from Spanish.

españolizar [1f] **1** vt to make Spanish, hispanicize; to give a Spanish flavour (or colouring etc) to.
2 españolizarse vr to adopt Spanish ways (etc);

to acquire a Spanish flavour (etc); (pej) to affect Spanish ways; **se españolizó por completo** he became completely Spanish.
esparadrapo nm sticking plaster; adhesive tape.
esparaván nm (**a**) (Orn) sparrowhawk. (**b**) (Vet) spavin.
esparavel nm (fishing) net.
esparceta nf sainfoin.
esparcido adj (**a**) scattered. (**b**) (fig) merry, jolly, cheerful; open, frank.
esparcimiento nm (**a**) spreading, scattering. (**b**) (fig) relaxation; amusement, diversion; recreation. (**c**) (fig) cheerfulness; openness, frankness.
esparcir [3b] **1** vt (**a**) to spread, scatter; to sow; to disseminate.
    (**b**) (fig) to amuse, divert.
    2 esparcirse vr (**a**) to spread (out), scatter, be scattered.
    (**b**) (fig) to relax; to amuse oneself.
espárrago nm asparagus; **estar hecho un** — to be as thin as a rake; **¡vaya a freír** —**s!** (fam) go to hell!; **mandar a uno a freír** —**s** (fam) to tell someone to go to hell.
esparrancado adj (with legs) wide apart, (with legs) spread far apart.
esparrancarse [1g] vr to spread one's legs (wide apart); to do the splits; — **sobre algo** to straddle something.
Esparta Sparta.
espartal nm esparto field.
espartano 1 adj Spartan (also fig). **2** nm, **espartana** nf Spartan.
esparteña nf = **alpargata**.
espartillo nm (SAm) esparto (grass).
espartizal nm esparto field.
esparto nm esparto (grass); **estar como el** — to be all dried up.
espasmo nm spasm; jerk, sudden movement, fitful movement.
espasmódico adj spasmodic; jerky, fitful.
espasticidad nf spasticity.
espástico 1 adj spastic. **2** nm, **espástica** nf spastic.
espato nm (Geol) spar.
espátula nf (**a**) (Med) spatula; (Art) palette knife; (Archit) putty knife; **estar hecho una** — to be as thin as a rake. (**b**) (Orn) spoonbill.
especia nf spice.
especiado adj spiced, spicy.
especial adj special, especial; **en** — especially, particularly.
especialidad nf speciality, specialty; special branch, special field (of study etc), line; **no es de mi** — it's not in my line.
especialista nmf specialist.
especializado adj specialized; worker skilled, trained; **mano de obra especializada** skilled labour.
especializarse [1f] vr to specialize (en in).
especialmente adv (e)specially, particularly.
especiar [1b] vt to spice.
especie nf (**a**) (Bio) species.
    (**b**) kind, sort; **de otra** — of another kind.
    (**c**) matter; idea, notion; piece of news; remark; pretext; **con la** — **de que** . . . on the pretext that . . .; **corre la** — **de que** . . . there is a rumour about that . . .; **soltar la** — to mention a matter, drop a remark.
    (**d**) **en** — in kind; **pagar en** — to pay in kind.
especificación nf specification.
específicamente adv specifically.
especificar [1g] vt to specify; to particularize; to list, itemize.
específico 1 adj specific. **2** nm (Med) specific; patent medicine.
espécimen nm, pl **especímenes** or **especimens** specimen.
especioso adj specious, plausible; deceitful.
espectacular adj spectacular.
espectacularidad nf spectacular nature; showiness.
espectáculo nm spectacle; sight; (Theat etc) show; function, performance; — **de variedades** variety show; — **de luz y sonido** son et lumière show; **dar un** — to make a scene; to create a stir.
espectador nm, **espectadora** nf spectator; onlooker, looker-on; **los** —**es** the spectators; (Theat etc) the audience.
espectral adj (**a**) (Phys) spectral. (**b**) (fig) ghostly; unearthly.
espectro nm (**a**) (Phys) spectrum. (**b**) spectre, ghost; (fig) spectre; **el** — **del hambre** the spectre of famine.
espectroscopio nm spectroscope.

especulación nf (**a**) speculation; contemplation, meditation. (**b**) (Comm, Fin) speculation; venture; — **bursátil** speculation on the stock exchange.
especulador nm, **especuladora** nf speculator.
especular[1] [1a] **1** vt to examine, inspect; to speculate about, reflect on, contemplate.
    2 vi (**a**) to speculate, meditate.
    (**b**) (Comm, Fin) to speculate (en, sobre in, on).
especular[2] [1a] vt (SAm) to ruffle the hair of.
especulativo adj speculative.
espéculo nm (Med) speculum.
espejado adj glossy, bright, shining, mirror-like.
espejeante adj shining.
espejear [1a] vi to shine (like a mirror), gleam, glimmer, glint.
espejeras nfpl (Cu) chafing, chafed patch.
espejismo nm (**a**) mirage. (**b**) (fig) mirage, illusion; (piece of) wishful thinking.
espejo nm (**a**) mirror, looking-glass; — **de cuerpo entero** full-length mirror, pier glass; — **retrovisor**, — **de retrovisión** driving mirror, rear-view mirror; **mirarse al** — to look at oneself in the mirror.
    (**b**) (Zool) white patch.
    (**c**) (fig) model; **un** — **de caballería** a model of chivalry.
espejuelo nm small looking-glass; —**s** lenses, spectacles.
espeleología nf spelaeology, potholing.
espeleólogo nm spelaeologist, potholer.
espelta nf (Bot) spelt.
espeluznante adj hair-raising, horrifying, blood-curdling; lurid.
espeluzno nm (Mex) = **escalofrío**.
espera nf (**a**) wait, period of waiting; waiting; delay; **en** — **de** waiting for; expecting; **la cosa no tiene** — the matter brooks no delay, the affair is most urgent.
    (**b**) (Law) stay, respite.
    (**c**) (quality) restraint.
esperable adj to be hoped for; to be expected; **unos adelantos que hace 10 años no eran** —**s** certain advances which were not to be hoped for 10 years ago.
esperanto nm Esperanto.
esperanza nf hope; expectation; prospect; **un jugador de** —**s** a promising player, a player of promise; **¡qué** —**!** (SAm) some hope!; not on your life!; **hay pocas** —**s de que venga** there is little prospect of his coming; **no daba** —**s de permitirlo** he held out no prospect of allowing it, he gave no hope of allowing it; **tener** —**s de** to have hopes of; **tener la** — **puesta en** to pin one's faith to; to set one's heart on.
esperanzador adj hopeful, encouraging.
esperanzar [1f] vt to give hope to, buoy up with hope.
esperar [1a] **1** vt (**a**) to hope for; to expect (de of); **no esperaba yo menos, no se podía** — **menos** it was the least that could be expected; **no esperaba menos de Vd** I expected nothing less of you, I hoped for nothing less from you; — **que** + subj to hope that . . .; **espero que sea así** I hope it is so, I hope it will be so; **espero que te haya gustado** I hope you liked it; **espero que vengas** I hope you'll come.
    (**b**) to wait for, await; baby, visitors etc to expect; — **el avión** to wait for the plane; **espero la llamada en cualquier momento** I expect his call at any moment; **ir a** — **a uno** to go and meet someone; **no me esperes después de las 7** don't wait for me after 7.
    2 vi (**a**) to hope; to expect; — + infin to hope to + infin; — **a que** + subj to expect that . . ., anticipate that . . .; — **en uno** to put one's hopes (or trust) in someone; — **en Dios** to trust in God; — **desesperando** to hope against hope.
    (**b**) to wait; to stay; **esperaré aquí** I'll wait here; **¡espera un momento!** wait a moment!, just a minute!; — **que salga uno** to wait for someone to come out; — **a** (or **hasta**) **que uno haga algo** to wait for someone to do something, wait until someone does something; **hacer** — **a uno** to make someone wait, keep someone waiting; **espera y verás** wait and see.
    3 esperarse vr: **como podía** — as might have been expected, as was to be expected; **no fue tan bueno como se esperaba** it was not so good as was hoped, it did not come up to expectations; **se espera que todo esté listo** it is hoped that all will be ready.
esperma nf (**a**) sperm; — **de ballena** spermaceti. (**b**) (SAm) candle.
espermaceti nm spermaceti.
espermatozoo nm spermatozoon.
espernancarse [1g] vr = **esparrancarse**.
esperón nm (Cu) long wait.

esperpento nm (a) fright, sight; scarecrow. (b) (fig) absurdity, (piece of) nonsense. (c) macabre story, grostesque tale.

espesamente adv thickly; densely.

espesar [1a] **1** vt (a) to thicken; to make dense(r). (b) fabric to weave tighter.
2 espesarse vr to thicken, get thicker, get denser; to coagulate, solidify.

espeso adj (a) thick; dense; paste etc stiff; liquid thick, heavy. (b) dirty, untidy.

espesor nm thickness; density; (of snow) depth; **tiene medio metro de** — it is half a metre thick.

espesura nf (a) thickness; density.
(b) (Bot) thicket, overgrown place; **se refugiaron en las —s serranas** they took refuge in the mountain fastnesses.
(c) dirtiness, untidiness.

espetar [1a] **1** vt (a) to transfix, pierce, run through; meat to skewer, spit; person to run through.
(b) (fig) order to rap out; lecture, sermon to read; question to pop; — **algo a uno** to broach a subject (unexpectedly) with someone, spring something on someone.
2 espetarse vr (a) to steady oneself, settle oneself.
(b) to get on one's high horse.

espetón nm (a) skewer, spit; large pin, iron pin; poker. (b) jab, poke.

espía nmf spy.

espiantar [1a] **1** vt (Arg, Urug) to pinch (fam). **2** vi and **espiantarse** vr (Arg, Chi) to scram (sl), beat it (fam).

espiar [1c] **1** vt (a) to spy on; to watch out for. (b) (Arg, CAm) to look at, see, watch. **2** vi to spy.

espichar[1] [1a] **1** vt (a) to prick.
(b) (Chi) to hand over reluctantly, relinquish.
(c) (Chi, Per) to put a tap on.
2 vi (sl) to peg out (sl).
3 espicharse vr (a) (Col: tyre) to go flat.
(b) (Cu, Mex) to get thin.
(c) (Mex) to feel ashamed.
(d) (Guat) to get scared.

espichar[2] [1a] vi (SAm) to make a speech; to speechify.

espiche[1] nm spike; peg.

espiche[2] nm (SAm: angl) speech.

espidómetro nm (SAm: angl) speedometer.

espiga nf (a) (Bot: of grain) ear; (of flowers) spike.
(b) (Tech) spigot; tenon, dowel, peg; (of bolt etc) shaft; (of knife) tang.
(c) (of bell) clapper.
(d) (Mil) fuse.
(e) (Naut) masthead.

espigadera nf gleaner.

espigado adj (a) (Bot) ripe; ready to seed. (b) tall, lanky; grown-up.

espigador nm, **espigadora** nf gleaner.

espigar [1h] **1** vt (a) (Agr) to glean (also fig).
(b) (Tech) to pin, peg, dowel.
2 vi (a) (of wheat) to form ears, come into ear; to run to seed.
(b) =**3 espigarse** vr to get very tall, shoot up.

espigón nm (a) (Bot) ear; spike. (b) (Zool) sting. (c) (of tool) sharp point, spike. (d) (Naut) breakwater.

espigueo nm gleaning.

espiguero nm (Mex) granary.

espina nf (a) (Bot) thorn, prickle; splinter; **estar en —s** to be on tenterhooks, be all on edge; **me da mala** — it worries me, it makes me suspicious; it gives me a bad impression; **sacarse la** — (fig) to pay off an old score, get even.
(b) (fig) bone.
(c) (Anat: also — **dorsal**) spine.
(d) (fig) doubt, worry, suspicion.

espinaca nf, **espinacas** nfpl (as food) spinach.

espinal adj spinal.

espinar **1** [1a] vt (a) to prick. (b) (fig) to sting, hurt, nettle. **2** nm (a) thicket, thornbrake, thorny place. (b) (fig) difficulty.

espinazo nm spine, backbone.

espineta nf (Mus) spinet.

espinilla nf (a) (Anat) shin, shinbone. (b) (Med) blackhead.

espinillera nf shinpad, shin guard (US).

espino nm hawthorn (also — **albar**, — **blanco**); — **negro** blackthorn, sloe.

espinoso **1** adj (a) plant thorny, prickly; fish bony, spiny. (b) (fig) thorny, knotty, difficult. **2** nm stickleback.

espinudo adj (SAm) =**espinoso 1**.

espión nm spy.

espionaje nm spying, espionage; **novela de** — spy story.

espira nf (Math etc) spiral; (Zool) whorl, ring; (Elec etc) turn.

espiráculo nm blow-hole; spiracle.

espiral **1** adj spiral; winding; (Tech) helical; corkscrew (attr), corkscrew-shaped.
2 nm (of watch) hairspring.
3 nf spiral; corkscrew (shape); (Tech) whorl; (of smoke etc) spiral, wreath; **la** — **inflacionista** the inflationary spiral; **dar vueltas en** — to spiral (up etc); **el humo subía en** — the smoke went spiralling up.

espirar [1a] **1** vt to breathe out, exhale; to give off, give out. **2** vi to breathe; to breathe out, exhale.

espiritado adj (fig) like a wraith, ghost-like.

espiritifláutico adj (hum) thin, weedy.

espiritismo nm spiritualism.

espiritista **1** adj spiritualist(ic). **2** nmf spiritualist.

espiritoso adj (a) liquor spirituous. (b) person spirited, lively.

espíritu nm (a) spirit; — **de cuerpo** esprit de corps; — **de equipo** team spirit; — **guerrero**, — **de lucha** fighting spirit; **en la letra y en el** — in the letter and in the spirit; **pobre de** — poor in spirit; **levantar el** — **de uno** to raise someone's spirits.
(b) mind; intelligence; turn of mind; **con** — **amplio** with an open mind; in a generous spirit; **de** — **crítico** of a critical turn of mind; **edificar el** — **de uno** to improve someone's mind.
(c) (Rel) spirit, soul; **E— Santo** Holy Ghost; **dar el —, rendir el** — to give up the ghost.
(d) spirit, ghost; "**Un** — **burlón**" "Blithe Spirit".
(e) spirits, liquor; — **de vino** spirits of wine.

espiritual adj (a) spiritual. (b) unworldly; ghostly. (c) (Col, Chi: gall) gay, witty.

espiritualidad nf spirituality.

espiritualizar [1f] vt to spiritualize.

espiritualmente adv spiritually.

espita nf (a) tap, faucet (US); cock, spigot; **abrir la** — **de las lágrimas** (hum) to weep buckets. (b) (fam) drunkard, soak (fam).

espitar [1a] vt to tap, broach.

espleen nm (angl) =**esplín**.

espléndidamente adv (a) splendidly, magnificently, grandly. (b) lavishly; generously; "**gratificaré —**" (advert) "there will be a generous reward".

esplendidez nf (a) splendour; magnificence, grandeur; pomp. (b) lavishness; generosity.

espléndido adj (a) splendid; magnificent, grand. (b) lavish; liberal, generous.

esplendor nm splendour; magnificence, grandeur; brilliance.

esplendoroso adj magnificent; brilliant, radiant.

esplénico adj splenetic.

espliego nm lavender.

esplín nm (angl) melancholy, depression, the blues.

espolada nf (a) prick with a spur. (b) — **de vino** swig of wine.

espolazo nm prick with a spur.

espolear [1a] vt (a) horse to spur (on). (b) (fig) to spur on, stimulate; to stir up, enliven, keep on one's toes.

espoleta nf (a) (Mil) fuse. (b) (Anat) wishbone.

espolín nm fixed spur, small spur.

espolón **1** nm (a) (Zool: of cock) spur; (of horse) fetlock.
(b) (Geog) spur (of a mountain range).
(c) (Naut: of bow) stem; (as weapon) ram.
(d) (Naut) sea wall, dike; jetty; (of bridge) cutwater; (Archit) buttress.
(e) promenade.
(f) (Med: fam) chilblain.
2 adj (Col) sharp, astute.

espolvorear [1a] vt to dust, sprinkle (de with); **espolvoree X sobre la superficie** dust X on the surface, dust the surface with X.

espondeo nm spondee.

esponja nf (a) sponge; — **de baño** bath sponge; **beber como una** — to drink like a fish; **pasar la** — (fam) to scrub round it (fam), forget about it.
(b) (fam) sponger (fam).
(c) (Arg, Mex, Par) old soak (fam), toper.

esponjado adj (a) spongy; fluffy. (b) (fig) puffed up, pompous.

esponjar [1a] **1** vt to make spongy; wool etc to fluff up, make fluffy.
2 esponjarse vr (a) to become spongy; to fluff up, become fluffy.
(b) (fig) to glow with health; to look prosperous.
(c) (fig) to be puffed up, swell with conceit.

esponjosidad nf sponginess; sogginess.

esponjoso adj spongy; porous; soggy, waterlogged.

esponsales nmpl betrothal.

espontáneamente adv spontaneously.

espontanearse [1a] *vr* to own up; to speak frankly; to unbosom oneself.

espontaneidad *nf* spontaneity.

espontáneo 1 *adj* spontaneous; impromptu, unprepared. **2** *nm* (*Taur*) intruder, spectator who rushes into the ring and attempts to take part.

espora *nf* spore.

esporádicamente *adv* sporadically.

esporádico *adj* sporadic.

esportillo *nm* basket, pannier.

esportivo *adj* (*SAm*: *angl*) sporty.

esportón *nm* large basket; **a —es** in vast quantities, by the ton.

esposa *nf* (a) wife. (b) —s handcuffs; manacles; **poner las —s a uno** to handcuff someone.

esposar [1a] *vt* to handcuff.

esposo *nm* husband; **los —s** husband and wife, the couple.

esprín *nm* (*CAm*: *angl*) spring; spring mattress.

esprint *nm*, *pl* **esprints** (*angl*) sprint; sudden dash, burst of speed.

esprintar [1a] *vi* (*angl*) to sprint.

esprínter *nm* (*angl*) sprinter.

espuela *nf* (a) spur (*also fig*); **— de caballero** larkspur.
(b) (*Col*) feminine charm; coquettishness.
(c) (*Col*) skill in business, acumen.
(d) (*fam*) last drink, one for the road.

espueleado *adj* (*Col*, *PR*) tested, tried.

espuelear [1a] *vt* (a) (*SAm*) to spur, spur on. (b) (*Col*, *PR*) to test, try out.

espuelón *adj* (*Col*) sharp, astute.

espuerta *nf* basket, pannier; **a —s** in vast quantities, by the ton.

espulgar [1h] *vt* (a) to delouse, rid of fleas, get the lice (*or* fleas) out of. (b) (*fig*) to scrutinize.

espuma *nf* (*of water*) foam, spray; surf; (*on beer*) froth, head; (*of soap*) lather; floating waste, surface scum; **— de caucho**, **— de látex** foam rubber; **— de mar** (*fig*) meerschaum; **crecer como la —** to flourish like the green bay tree; **echar —** to foam, froth.

espumadera *nf*, **espumador** *nm* (*SAm*: *Cook etc*) skimmer, skimming ladle; (*of spray*) nozzle.

espumajear [1a] *vi* to foam at the mouth.

espumajo *nm* froth, foam (*at the mouth*).

espumajoso *adj* frothy, foamy.

espumar [1a] **1** *vt* to skim off. **2** *vi* to froth, foam; (*of wine*) to sparkle.

espumarajo *nm* froth, foam (*at the mouth*); **echar —s (de rabia)** to foam with rage, splutter with rage.

espumilla *nf* (*CAm*, *Ec*) meringue.

espumoso *adj* frothy, foamy; foaming; *wine* sparkling.

espurio *adj* spurious; adulterated; *child* bastard.

esputar [1a] *vti* to spit (out), hawk (up).

esputo *nm* spit, spittle, (*Med*) sputum.

esqueje *nm* (*Hort*) slip, cutting.

esquela *nf* (a) note; **— amorosa** love letter, billet doux. (b) notice, announcement; **— de defunción**, **— mortuoria** death notice, announcement of death.

esquelético *adj* skeletal.

esqueleto *nm* (a) (*Anat*) skeleton.
(b) (*fig*) skeleton; bare bones (*of a matter*); framework; (*SAm*) rough draft, outline, preliminary plan; **en —** unfinished, incomplete.
(c) (*CAm*, *Col*, *Mex*) blank, form.

esquema *nm* (a) diagram, plan; scheme; sketch, outline. (b) (*Eccl*) schema.

esquemático *adj* schematic; diagrammatic.

esquí *nm*, *pl* **esquís** (a) (*object*) ski. (b) (*sport*) skiing; **— acuático** water-skiing; surfriding; **hacer —** to go skiing.

esquiador *nm*, **esquiadora** *nf* skier.

esquiar [1c] *vi* to ski.

esquife *nm* skiff.

esquila[1] *nf* small bell, handbell; cowbell.

esquila[2] *nf* (*Agr*) shearing.

esquilador *nm* shearer.

esquilar [1a] *vt* to shear; to clip, crop.

esquileo *nm* shearing.

esquilimoso *adj* fastidious, finicky.

esquilmar [1a] *vt* (a) *crop* to harvest. (b) *soil* (*also fig*) to exhaust, impoverish. (c) (*fam*) *gambler* to skin (*fam*), fleece.

esquilmo *nm* harvest, crop; yield.

Esquilo *m* Aeschylus.

esquimal 1 *adj* Eskimo. **2** *nmf* Eskimo. **3** *nm* (*language*) Eskimo.

esquina *nf* (a) corner (*also Sport*); **doblar la —** to turn the corner; (*Chi*) to die. (b) (*SAm*) corner shop, village store.

esquinado *adj* (a) having corners; sharp-cornered.
(b) (*SAm*) *furniture* standing in a corner, corner (*attr*). (c) (*fig*) prickly; unsociable.

esquinar [1a] **1** *vt* (a) to form a corner with; to be on the corner of.
(b) *timber etc* to square (off).
(c) (*SAm*) to put in a corner.
2 *vi*: **— con** to form a corner with; to be on the corner of.
3 esquinarse *vr* (a) to quarrel (*con* with), fall out (*con* with).
(b) to sulk.

esquinazo *nm* (a) (*fam*) corner. (b) (*Arg*, *Chi*) serenade. (c) **dar — a uno** to dodge someone, give someone the slip, shake someone off.

esquirla *nf* splinter.

esquirol *nm* blackleg, scab (*fam*), strikebreaker, fink (*US*).

esquisto *nm* schist.

esquite *nm* (*CAm*, *Mex*) popcorn.

esquivada *nf* (*SAm*) dodge, evasion.

esquivar [1a] **1** *vt* to avoid, shun; to elude, dodge, side-step; **— el contacto con uno** to avoid meeting someone; **— un golpe** to dodge a blow; **— + infin** to avoid **+** *ger*, be chary of **+** *ger*, be shy of **+** *ger*.
2 esquivarse *vr* to withdraw, stand back, shy away; to dodge.

esquivez *nf* (a) shyness, reserve, aloofness; unsociability; evasiveness. (b) scorn, disdain.

esquivo *adj* (a) shy, reserved, aloof; unsociable; evasive. (b) scornful, disdainful.

esquizofrenia *nf* schizophrenia.

esquizofrénico 1 *adj* schizophrenic. **2** *nm*, **esquizofrénica** *nf* schizophrenic.

esquizoide 1 *adj* schizoid. **2** *nmf* schizoid.

esta, ésta *etc see* **este**, **éste**.

estabilidad *nf* stability.

estabilización *nf* stabilization.

estabilizador *nm* stabilizer.

estabilizar [1f] **1** *vt* to stabilize; to make stable, steady; *prices* to stabilize, peg. **2 estabilizarse** *vr* to become stable, become stabilized.

estable *adj* stable, steady; firm; regular.

establecer [2d] **1** *vt* to establish; set up, found, institute; *people* to settle; *allegation* to justify, substantiate; *record* to set (up); *residence* to take up, establish.
2 establecerse *vr* to establish oneself, settle; (*Comm*) to set up in business, start a business; to open an office, open a branch.

establecimiento *nm* (a) (*act*) establishment, setting-up, founding; institution; settlement.
(b) establishment; (*RPl*) plant, works; **— central** head office; **— comercial** commercial establishment, business house.
(c) (*Law*) statute, ordinance.

establero *nm* stableboy, groom.

establo *nm* cowshed, stall; (*esp SAm*) barn; **—s de Augias** Augean stables.

estaca *nf* (a) stake, post, paling; (*for croquet, tent*) peg; cudgel, stick.
(b) (*Agr*) cutting.
(c) (*Chi*, *Ec*, *Per*) spur.
(d) (*Arg*, *Col*, *Chi*, *Per*) mining claim, mining property.
(e) (*Mex*) wish to obtain something.
(f) (*Ven*) hint, taunt.

estacada *nf* (a) fence, fencing; (*Mil*) palisade, stockade; (*SAm*) dike; **dejar a uno en la —** (*fig*) to leave someone in the lurch; **estar** (*or* **quedar**) **en la —** to be in a jam, be left in the lurch; to fail disastrously.
(b) (*SAm*) wound, prick.

estacar [1g] **1** *vt* (a) *land*, *claim etc* to stake (out, off), mark with stakes; to fence with stakes; (*SAm*) to stretch by fastening to stakes.
(b) *animal* to tie to a post.
(c) (*Ven*) to wound, prick.
(d) (*Col*, *Ven*) to deceive.
2 estacarse *vr* (a) to stand rooted to the spot, stand stiff as a pole.
(b) (*CAm*, *Col*, *Cu*, *Ven*) **— un pie** to prick oneself in the foot, hurt one's foot.

estación *nf* (a) (*Rly*) station; **— balnearia** spa; **— ballenera** whaling station; **— de bombeo** pumping station; **— cabecera** (*Arg*), **— de cabeza**, **— terminal** terminus; **— carbonera** coaling station; **— cósmica**, **— espacial** space station; **— depuradora**, **— purificadora de aguas residuales** sewage works, sewage farm; **— emisora** broadcasting station; **— de empalme**, **— de enlace** junction; **— de ferrocarril** railway station; **— de fuerza** power station; **— de gasolina** petrol station; **— de mercancías** goods station; **— meteorológica** weather station; **— de**

rastreo, — **de seguimiento** tracking station; — **de servicio** service station; — **transformadora** substation; — **transmisora** transmitter; — **veraniega** summer resort.

(b) (*Eccl*) **E**—**es del vía Crucis** Stations of the Cross; **correr las** —**es** (*fam*) to go on a pub crawl (*fam*).

(c) season; — **de las lluvias** rainy season; — **muerta** off season, dead season.

estacional *adj* seasonal.

estacionamiento *nm* stationing, placing; (*Aut*) parking.

estacionar [1a] **1** *vt* to station, place; (*Aut*) to park. **2 estacionarse** *vr* to station oneself; (*Aut*) to park; to remain stationary.

estacionario *adj* stationary; motionless; (*Comm, Fin*) slack.

estacionómetro *nm* (*Mex*) parking meter.

estacón *nm* (*Col, Cu, Guat, Mex*) prick, jab.

estadía *nf* (a) (*Comm*) demurrage. (b) (*Naut*) stay in port; (*SAm*) stay.

estadígrafo *nm* statistician.

estadio *nm* (a) stage, phase. (b) (*Math*) furlong. (c) (*Sport*) stadium.

estadista *nm* (a) (*Pol*) statesman. (b) (*Math*) statistician.

estadística *nf* (a) statistics; official return(s). (b) (*una* —) figure, statistic.

estadístico 1 *adj* statistical. **2** *nm* statistician.

estado *nm* (a) (*in general*) state, condition; — **de ánimo** state of mind; — **de emergencia** state of emergency; — **de guerra** state of war; — **de sitio** state of siege; **estar en** — **(interesante), estar en** — **de buena esperanza** to be pregnant, be expecting, be in the family way; **estar en buen** — to be in good condition; to be in good order, be in working order; **estar en malísimo** — to be in a terrible condition. (b) status; rank, class; — **civil** marital status.

(c) (*Pol: Hist*) estate; **el cuarto** — the fourth estate; — **llano** third estate, commoners. (d) — **mayor** (*Mil*) staff; — **mayor general** general staff.

(e) (*Pol*) state; **las fuerzas del E**— the forces of the state; — **benefactor,** — **de bienestar,** — **de previsión** welfare state; — **policía** police state; — **tapón** buffer state; **hombre de** — statesman. (f) list (of employees).

(g) summary; report, statement; — **de contabilidad** (*Mex*) balance sheet; — **de cuenta(s)** statement of account.

Estados *mpl* **Unidos** United States.

estadounidense 1 *adj* United States (*attr*), American. **2** *nmf* United States citizen (*etc*), American.

estafa *nf* swindle, trick; (*Comm, Fin*) racket, ramp (*fam*), fraud.

estafador *nm* swindler, trickster; (*Comm, Fin*) swindler; racketeer.

estafar [1a] *vt* to swindle, defraud, twist (*fam*); — **algo a uno** to swindle something out of someone, defraud someone of something.

estafeta *nf* (a) post; — **diplomática** diplomatic bag. (b) (*sub*) post office. (c) (*person*) courier (*also nm*).

estafetero *nm* postmaster, post-office clerk.

estafilococo *nm* staphylococcus.

estagnación *nf* (*CAm, PR: angl*) = **estancamiento**.

estaje *nm* (*CAm*) piecework.

estajear [1a] *vt* (*CAm*) to do as piecework; to discuss rates and conditions for.

estajero *nm* (*CAm*) pieceworker.

estalactita *nf* stalactite.

estalagmita *nf* stalagmite.

estalladura *nf* bursting, explosion; eruption; shattering; crack; breaking-out, outbreak; (*Aut*) burst, blow-out.

estallar [1a] *vi* (*of shell etc*) to burst, explode, go off; (*like volcano*) to erupt; (*of tyre*) to burst; (*of glass etc*) to shatter; (*of whip*) to crack; (*of epidemic*) to break out; (*of revolt*) to break out, flare up; — **en llanto** to burst into tears; **el parabrisas estalló en pedazos** the windscreen shattered; **cuando estalló la guerra** when the war broke out; **hacer** — to set off; (*fig*) to spark off, start.

estallido *nm* explosion, report; crash, crack; (*fig*) outbreak.

estambre *nm* (a) worsted, woollen yarn. (b) (*Bot*) stamen.

Estambul Istanbul.

estamento *nm* (*Pol*) state.

estameña *nf* serge.

estampa *nf* (a) imprint; footprint, track; (*Typ*) print, engraving; (*fig*) stamp; appearance, aspect; **de** — **poco agradable** of disagreeable appearance, un-

pleasant-looking; **ser la propia** — **de uno** to be the very image of someone; **romper la** — **a uno** (*fam*) to do someone in (*sl*).

(b) printing; printing press; **dar un libro a la** — to publish a book.

estampación *nf* printing; engraving; (*Typ*) tooling.

estampado 1 *adj fabric* printed; *dress* print. **2** *nm* (a) printing; stamping. (b) print (dress), cotton print.

estampar [1a] *vt* to print, stamp; to engrave; (*Typ*) *cover* to tool; *kiss* to plant, place (*en on*); (*fig*) to stamp, imprint (*en on*); **quedaba estampado en la memoria** it was stamped on one's memory.

estampía: de — *adv* suddenly, without warning, unexpectedly.

estampida *nf* (a) (*Agr, Zool: esp SAm*) stampede. (b) **de** — *see* **estampía**. (c) = **estampido**.

estampido *nm* report; detonation; bang, boom, crash; — **sónico** sonic boom.

estampilla *nf* (a) stamp, seal; rubber stamp. (b) (*SAm: Post*) stamp.

estampillado *nm* (*SAm*) stamp duty.

estampillar [1a] *vt* to stamp, put a stamp on; to rubber-stamp.

estancado *adj* (a) *water* stagnant. (b) (*fig*) static; **estar** — to be held up, be blocked, be at a standstill; to be deadlocked.

estancamiento *nm* (a) stagnancy, stagnation. (b) (*fig*) stagnation; blockage, stoppage, suspension; deadlock.

estancar [1g] **1** *vt* (a) *water* to hold up, hold back, stem.

(b) (*fig*) *progress* to stem, block, check, hold up; *business* to stop, suspend; *negotiation* to bring to a standstill; to deadlock; (*Comm: officially*) to monopolize, establish a monopoly in; (*pej*) to corner. **2 estancarse** *vr* (a) (*of water*) to stagnate, become stagnant; to be held back.

(b) (*fig*) to stagnate.

estancia *nf* (a) stay. (b) dwelling, abode; living room. (c) (*SAm*) farm, cattle ranch; (*Cu, PR*) small farm, smallholding. (d) (*Poet*) stanza.

estanciero *nm* (*SAm*) farmer, rancher.

estanco 1 *adj* watertight.

2 *nm* state monopoly; government store where monopoly goods are sold, (*esp*) tobacconist's (shop), cigar store (*US*); (*Ec*) liquor store.

estándar (*angl*) **1** *adj* standard. **2** *nm* standard.

estandar(d)ización *nf* standardization.

estandar(d)izado *adj* standardized.

estandar(d)izar [1f] *vt* to standardize.

estandarte *nm* banner, standard; — **real** royal standard.

estánnico *adj* stannic.

estanque *nm* pool, pond, small lake; (*Agr etc*) tank, reservoir; — **de juegos,** — **para chapotear** paddling pool.

estanquero *nm* tobacconist.

estanquillo *nm* (*Mex*) booth, kiosk, stall; = **estanco**.

estante *nm* (a) shelf. (b) rack, stand; — **(para libros)** bookcase. (c) (*SAm*) prop.

estantería *nf* shelving, shelves.

estantigua *nf* apparition; (*fam*) fright, sight, scarecrow.

estantillo *nm* (*Col, Ven*) prop, support.

estañar [1a] *vt* (a) (*Tech*) to tin; to solder. (b) (*Ven*) to wound. (c) (*Ven*) *employee* to fire (*fam*).

estaño *nm* tin.

estaquear [1a] *vt* (*SAm*) *hides* to spread, stretch (with stakes).

estaquilla *nf* peg; pin; spike, long nail; tent peg.

estaquillar [1a] *vt* to pin, peg (down, out), fasten with pegs.

estar [1p] **1** *vi* (a) to be; to stand, be found; to be in, be at home; to stay, remain, keep; to be present (*en* at); **el monumento está en el mercado** the monument is (*or* stands) in the market; **¿está?** is he in?; **la señora no está** the lady is not in, the lady is not at home; **está fuera** she's away; she's out of town, she's on a trip; **¿cómo está?** how is he?; **está mucho mejor** he's much better; **"nunca habéis estado mejor"** (*slogan*) "you never had it so good"; **¿cómo estamos?** how do we stand?; (*Sport*) what's the score?; **el día que estuve a verlo** the day I went to see it.

(b) (+ *adj*) to be; **está enfermo** he is ill; **ahora está vacío** now it's empty; **¡qué elegante estás!** how smart you're looking!; **está más viejo** he looks older, he seems older.

(c) (*idiom*) **¿está Vd?** do you get it?, understand?; **¿estamos?** are we agreed?

(d) (*idiom*) to be ready; **en seguida está** it'll be ready in a moment; **dos vueltas más y ya está** two more turns and that's it, two more turns and it's done; ¡ya **estamos!** that's it!; (*angrily*) that's enough!, I'll not listen to any more!

(e) (+ *ger*) to be; **estaba corriendo** he was running; **me está molestando** he's annoying me; **está siendo preparado** it is being prepared; **nos estamos engañando** we are deceiving ourselves.

(f) (+ *ptp*) to be; **está envasado en papel** it is wrapped in paper; **para las 5 estará terminado** it will be finished for 5 o'clock.

(g) (*date*) **estamos a 5 de mayo** it is the 5th of May, today is the 5th of May; **¿a cuántos estamos?** what's the date?

(h) (*price*) — **a** to be, sell at, stand at; (*record*) to stand at; **las uvas están a 5 pesetas** grapes are at 5 pesetas; **el récord anterior estaba a** (or **en**) **33 minutos** the previous record stood at 33 minutes.

(i) — **a lo que resulte** to stand by the result.

(j) — **con la gripe** to have flu, be down with flu; **estuvo con la enfermedad durante 2 años** she suffered from the disease for 2 years.

(k) — **de vacaciones** to be (away) on holiday; — **de paseo** to be out for a walk; — **de viaje** to be travelling, be on a trip.

(l) — **de embajador** to be acting as ambassador, be acting ambassador.

(m) **estoy así de nervioso** I'm so nervous, I'm that nervous.

(n) — **en** to be the cause of; **en eso está** that's the reason, that must be the motive.

(o) — **en algo** to be involved in something, be mixed up in something.

(p) **no está en él hacerlo** it is not in his power to do it.

(q) — **en que . . .** to believe that . . ., understand that . . .; to be sure that . . .

(r) — **para** + *infin* to be about to + *infin*, be on the point of + *ger*.

(s) — **para** + *n* to be in the mood for + *n*.

(t) — **por** *policy* to be in favour of; *person* to back, support, side with.

(u) — **por** + *infin* to be half inclined to + *infin*, have half a mind to + *infin*.

(v) **está todavía por hacer** it remains to be done, it is still to be done; **la historia de aquello está por escribir** the history of that is still to be written.

(w) **está que rabia** he's hopping mad, he's furious.

(x) — **sobre sí** to be on one's guard; to be puffed up with conceit; *see* **bien, mal, más**, *and many noun entries*.

2 estarse *vr* (a) *reinforces sense of vi:* **se estaba muriendo** he was (gradually, at that moment) dying.

(b) to stay, remain; — **tranquilamente en casa** to stay quietly at home.

(c) **¡estáte quieto!** keep still!, stop fidgeting!; behave yourself!

estarcido *nm* stencil.
estarcir [3b] *vt* to stencil.
estatal *adj* state (*attr*).
estática *nf* statics.
estático *adj* static.
estatificación *nf* nationalization.
estatificado *adj* nationalized.
estatificar [1g] *vt* to nationalize.
estatización *nf* (*CAm, Chi*) nationalization.
estatizar [1f] *vt* (*CAm, Chi*) to nationalize.
estator *nm* (*Elec, Math*) stator.
estatua *nf* statue.
estatuaria *nf* statuary (*art*).
estatuario *adj* statuesque.
estatuilla *nf* statuette, figure.
estatuir [3g] *vt* (a) to establish, enact, ordain. (b) to prove. (c) to arrange.
estatura *nf* stature, height; **de regular** — of average height; **un hombre de 1,80m de** — a man 1.80m in height.
estatutario *adj* statutory.
estatuto *nm* (*Law*) statute; (*of city etc*) by-law; (*of committee*) rule, standing rule.
estay *nm* (*Naut*) stay.
este[1] (*Geog*) **1** *adj part* east, eastern; *direction* easterly; *wind* east, easterly.

2 *nm* (a) east; **en la parte del** — in the eastern part; **al** — **de Toledo** to the east of Toledo, on the east side of Toledo; **eso cae más hacia el** — that lies further (to the) east. (b) east wind.
este[2] *dem adj m*, **esta** *f* this; **estos** *dem adj mpl*, **estas** *fpl* these.
éste *dem pron m*, **ésta** *f* this; this one; the latter; **éstos** *dem pron mpl*, **éstas** *fpl* these; the latter; en

ésta in this town (from where I am writing); **jurar por éstas** to swear by all that is holy.
estearina *nf* (*Chem*) stearin; (*SAm*) candle.
esteatita *nf* soapstone.
Esteban *m* Stephen.
estela *nf* (a) (*Naut*) wake, wash; (*Aer*) trail; — **de condensación** vapour trail.
(b) (*fig*) trail; **el discurso dejó larga** — **de comentarios** the speech left a long trail of criticism.
(c) (*Archit*) stele, stela.
estelar *adj* (a) (*Astron*) stellar, sidereal. (b) (*Theat etc*) star (*attr*); **cargo** — star role; **combate** — (*Boxing*) star bout, star contest.
estemple *nm* pit prop.
esténcil *nm* (*SAm:* angl) stencil.
estenografía *nf* shorthand, stenography.
estenografiar [1c] *vt* to take down in shorthand.
estenográfico *adj* shorthand (*attr*).
estenógrafo *nm*, **estenógrafa** *nf* shorthand writer, stenographer.
estentóreo *adj* stentorian.
estepa *nf* (a) (*Geog*) steppe. (b) (*Bot*) rockrose.
estera *nf* mat, matting; — **de baño** bathmat.
esteral *nm* (*Arg, Urug*) swamp, marsh.
esterar [1a] **1** *vt* to cover with a mat, put a mat on (*or* over). **2** *vi* (*fam*) to put on one's winter clothes (ahead of time).
estercoladura *nf*, **estercolamiento** *nm* manuring; muck spreading.
estercolar [1a] *vt* to manure.
estercolero *nm* manure heap, dunghill.
estereo . . . stereo . . .
estereofonía *nf* stereophony.
estereofónico *adj* stereophonic.
estereoscópico *adj* stereoscopic.
estereoscopio *nm* stereoscope.
estereotipado *adj* stereotyped.
estereotipar [1a] *vt* to stereotype.
estereotipo *nm* stereotype.
estéril *adj* (a) sterile, barren. (b) (*fig*) *effort etc* vain, futile, unproductive.
esterilidad *nf* (a) sterility, barrenness. (b) (*fig*) futility, uselessness.
esterilización *nf* sterilization.
esterilizar [1f] *vt* to sterilize.
estérilmente *adv* (*fig*) vainly, uselessly, fruitlessly.
esterilla *nf* (a) small mat; straw mat.
(b) matting; (*SAm*) wickerwork, rush matting; **silla de** — rush chair, wicker chair; — **de alambre** wire mesh.
(c) (*Sew*) gold (*or* silver) braid.
esterlina *adj:* **libra** — pound sterling.
esternón *nm* breastbone, sternum.
estero[1] *nm* matting.
estero[2] *nm* estuary; tideland; inlet; (*RPl*) swamp, marsh; (*Chi, Ec*) brook; (*Ven*) puddle, pool; **estar en el** — (*Ven*) to be in a fix.
estertor *nm* death rattle.
estertoroso *adj* stertorous.
esteta **1** *nmf* aesthete. **2** *nm* (*fam*) pansy (*fam*), queer (*fam*).
estética *nf* aesthetics; aesthetic doctrine, aesthetic outlook.
esteticismo *nm* aestheticism.
estético *adj* aesthetic.
estetoscopio *nm* stethoscope.
esteva *nf* plough handle.
estevado *adj* bow-legged, bandy-legged.
estiaje *nm* low water.
estiba *nf* (a) (*Mil: Hist*) rammer. (b) (*Naut*) stowage; **mudar la** — to shift the cargo about.
estibador *nm* stevedore.
estibar [1a] *vt* (*Naut*) to stow, put; to house, store. (b) *wool etc* to pack tight, compress.
estiércol *nm* dung, manure; — **de caballo** horse manure.
Estigio *m* Styx.
estigio *adj* Stygian.
estigma *nm* (a) stigma; mark, brand; birthmark; —**s** (*Eccl*) stigmata. (b) (*Bot*) stigma.
estigmatizar [1f] *vt* to stigmatize.
estilar [1a] **1** *vt* (a) *document* to draw up (in due form).
(b) to use, be in the habit of using; to wear, adopt.
2 *vi and* **estilarse** *vr* to be in fashion, be used, be worn; **ya no se estila la chistera** top hats aren't in fashion anymore; — + *infin* to be customary to + *infin*.
estilete *nm* stiletto; (*of gramophone etc*) stylus.
estilista *nmf* (*Lit etc*) stylist; (*Tech*) designer.
estilística *nf* stylistics.

estilístico adj stylistic.
estilización nf (Tech) styling.
estilizado adj stylized.
estilizar [1f] vt to stylize; (Tech) to design, style.
estilo nm (a) (in general) style; manner; fashion; **el —
oscuro del escritor** the writer's obscure style; **—
directo** (Gram) direct speech; **el — de vida británico**
the British way of life; **un comedor — Luis XV** a
dining-room suite in Louis XV style; **al — de** in the
style of; after the manner of; **al — antiguo** in the old
style; **algo por el —** something of the sort, that sort
of thing; something along these lines; **los dictadores
y otros por el —** dictators and others of that sort,
dictators and suchlike; **no tenemos nada por ese —**
we have nothing in that line.
  (b) (Swimming) stroke; **— libre** freestyle; **— (de)
pecho** breast-stroke.
  (c) (pen: Tech) stylus.
  (d) (Bot) style.
estilográfica nf fountain pen.
estima nf (a) esteem, respect; **tener a uno en gran —**
to hold someone in high esteem. (b) (Naut) dead
reckoning.
estimable adj (a) estimable, esteemed; reputable; **su
— carta** (Comm) your esteemed letter. (b) quantity
etc considerable.
estimación nf (a) (act) estimation; valuation. (b)
estimate, estimation; valuation. (c) esteem, regard;
— propia self-esteem.
estimar [1a] **1** vt (a) to estimate; to appraise; to gauge,
reckon, compute; **— algo en mil pesetas** to value
something at a thousand pesetas.
  (b) **— que . . .** to think that . . ., reckon that . . .
  (c) (morally) to esteem, respect; **— a uno en
mucho** to have a high regard for someone; **— a uno
en poco** to have a low opinion of someone; **se lo
estimo mucho** I am much indebted to you for it.
  2 estimarse vr (a) to be estimated (en at), be
valued (en at).
  (b) **¡se estima!** thanks very much!, I appreciate it!
  (c) to have a good opinion of oneself.
estimulante **1** adj stimulating. **2** nm stimulant.
estimular [1a] vt to stimulate; to encourage, excite,
incite, prompt; appetite to stimulate; discussion etc
to promote; effort, industry to encourage, boost.
estímulo nm stimulus, stimulation; encouragement;
inducement, incentive.
estío nm summer.
estipendiar [1b] vt to pay a stipend to.
estipendiario **1** adj stipendiary. **2** nm stipendiary.
estipendio nm stipend; salary; fee.
estíptico **1** adj (a) styptic. (b) constipated. (c) (fig)
mean, miserly. **2** nm styptic.
estipulación nf stipulation, condition, proviso.
estipular [1a] vt to stipulate.
estirado adj (a) stretched, extended; stretched tight;
(Tech) drawn. (b) (fig) stiff, starchy; pompous;
(RPl) vain, stuck-up (fam). (c) (fig) tight-fisted.
estirador nm (Tech) stretcher.
estiraje nm stretching.
estirajar [1a] (fam) = **estirar**.
estirar [1a] **1** vt (a) to stretch, pull out, draw out; to
extend; (Tech) wire etc to draw; ears to prick up;
neck to stretch, crane; clothes to iron lightly, run the
iron over.
  (b) to overstretch, strain.
  (c) (fig) money, speech etc to spin out, stretch out.
  (d) (Arg, Bol, Chi, Per) to kill, shoot.
  (e) (Per) to flog.
  (f) (Mex, Par) to pull, tug at.
  2 estirarse vr to stretch.
estirón nm (a) pull, tug, jerk. (b) spurt, sudden
growth; **dar un —** (child) to shoot up.
estironear [1a] vt (Chi, RPl) to pull hard at, tug
sharply at.
estirpe nf stock, lineage; race; **de la — regia** of royal
stock, of the blood royal.
estítico = **estíptico**.
estitiquez nf (SAm) constipation.
estival adj summer (attr); summery.
esto dem pron "neuter" this; this thing, this affair, this
matter; **— es difícil** this is difficult; **todo — es
inútil** all this is useless; **— es, . . .** that is (to say),
. . .; **— de la boda** this business about the wedding;
antes de — before this; **con —** herewith; hereupon;
durante — in the meantime, while this was going
on; **en —** at this point; **por —** for this reason;
¿qué es —? what's all this?; **y esto ¿qué es?** whatever
is this?
estocada nf (a) stab, thrust; lunge; stab wound;
(Taur etc) death blow, (final) thrust. (b) (fig) sharp
retort.

Estocolmo Stockholm.
estofa nf (a) quilting, quilted material. (b) (fig)
quality, class; **de baja —** poor-quality, person
low-class.
estofado **1** adj (a) (Cook) stewed. (b) (Sew) quilted.
2 nm stew, hotpot.
estofar [1a] vt (a) (Cook) to stew. (b) (Sew) to quilt.
estoicismo nm stoicism.
estoico **1** adj stoic(al). **2** nm stoic.
estola nf stole.
estolidez nf stupidity.
estólido adj stupid.
estomacal **1** adj stomachic; stomach (attr); **trastorno
—** stomach upset. **2** nm stomachic.
estomagante adj (fam) upsetting, annoying.
estomagar [1h] vt (a) to give indigestion to, upset.
  (b) (fig) to upset, annoy.
estómago nm stomach; **dolor de —** stomach ache;
revolver el — a uno to revolt someone, make someone's stomach turn over; to upset someone, annoy
someone; **tener buen —** (fig) to be thick-skinned;
to have an elastic conscience, be none too scrupulous.
Estonia f Esthonia.
estonio **1** adj Esthonian. **2** nm, **estonia** nf Esthonian.
3 nm (language) Esthonian.
estopa nf tow; burlap; (Naut) oakum; (Cu) cotton
waste; **— de acero** steel wool.
estoperol nm (a) tow wick. (b) (Col, Chi) brass tack.
  (c) (Col) frying pan.
estopilla nf cheesecloth.
estoque nm (a) rapier, sword; **estar hecho un —** to be
as thin as a rake. (b) (Bot) gladiolus.
estoquear [1a] vt to stab, run through.
estorbar [1a] **1** vt to hinder, obstruct, impede, be (or
get) in the way of; to interfere with; to bother,
disturb, upset. **2** vi to be in the way.
estorbo nm hindrance, obstruction, impediment,
obstacle; drag; nuisance; **no hay — para que se haga**
there is no obstacle (or bar, impediment) to its
being done; **el mayor — es el director** the biggest
obstacle is the headmaster.
estornino nm starling.
estornudar [1a] vi to sneeze.
estornudo nm sneeze.
estoy etc see **estar**.
estrabismo nm squint, strabismus.
estrada nf (a) road, highway; **batir la —** (Mil) to
reconnoitre. (b) (Bol, Per) section of a rubber plantation (150 trees).
estrado nm stage, platform; dais; (Mus) bandstand;
(Hist) drawing room; **—s** law courts; **— del testigo**
witness stand; **citar a uno para —s** to subpoena
someone.
estrafalario adj (a) odd, outlandish, eccentric. (b)
dress slovenly, sloppy.
estragado adj ruined; corrupted, spoiled, perverted;
depraved; slovenly, careless, disorderly.
estragar [1h] vt to ruin; taste etc to corrupt, spoil,
pervert; to deprave.
estrago nm ruin, destruction; corruption, perversion;
—s havoc, destruction, ravages; **los —s del tiempo**
the ravages of time; **hacer —s en** (or **entre**) to play
havoc with, wreak havoc among.
estragón nm (Bot, Cook) tarragon.
estramador nm (Mex) comb.
estrambólico adj (SAm), **estrambótico** adj odd,
outlandish, eccentric.
estrangul nm (Mus) mouthpiece.
estrangulación nf strangulation.
estrangulador nm (a) (person) strangler. (b) (Mech)
throttle; (Aut etc) choke.
estrangulamiento nm (Aut) narrow stretch of road,
bottleneck.
estrangular [1a] vt (a) person to strangle. (b) (Med)
to strangulate. (c) (Mech) to throttle; to choke.
estraperlista **1** adj black-market (attr). **2** nm
blackmarketeer.
estraperlo nm black market; **comprar algo en el —,
comprar algo de —** to buy something on the black
market.
estrapontín nm back seat; side seat, extra seat.
Estrasburgo Strasbourg.
estratagema nf stratagem.
estratega nm strategist.
estrategia nf strategy; generalship.
estratégico adj strategic(al).
estratificación nf stratification.
estratificado adj stratified.
estratificar [1g] **1** vt to stratify. **2 estratificarse** vr
to stratify, be stratified.

estrato *nm* stratum, layer; **los —s sociales** the social strata, the social levels.

estratosfera *nf* stratosphere.

estratosférico *adj* stratospheric; **avión —** stratocruiser.

estraza *nf* rag; **papel de —** brown paper, wrapping paper.

estrechamente *adv* (a) narrowly; tightly. (b) austerely. (c) closely, intimately. (d) strictly, rigidly; meanly; narrow-mindedly.

estrechar [1a] **1** *vt* (a) to narrow; *dress* to make smaller, reduce, take in; *link etc* to tighten (up), draw tighter.

(b) to squeeze; *person* to hug, embrace, enfold in one's arms; *hand* to grasp, clasp; to shake.

(c) (*fig*) *enemy* to press hard.

(d) (*fig*) to compel, constrain, bring pressure to bear on.

2 estrecharse *vr* (a) to narrow, get narrow; to tighten, get tighter; **— en** to squeeze into.

(b) (*of two persons*) to embrace (one another), hug.

(c) **se estrecharon la mano** they shook hands.

(d) (*of link etc*) to become closer, become more intimate; **— con uno** to get very friendly with someone.

(e) **— (en los gastos)** to stint oneself, economize, cut down on expenditure.

estrechez *nf* (a) narrowness, tightness; cramped nature, smallness, lack of room.

(b) (*Fin*) want; financial stringency; **— del dinero** tightness of money, shortage of money; **estrecheces** financial difficulties, financial straits; **vivir con —** to live in straitened circumstances.

(c) closeness, intimacy.

(d) strictness, rigidity; austerity; **— de conciencia** small-mindedness; **— de miras** narrow-mindedness.

estrecho 1 *adj* (a) narrow; tight; *room* cramped, small; *skirt etc* tight; *trousers* tight, narrow, close-fitting; **estos zapatos me están muy —s** these shoes are too small for me, these shoes pinch my feet.

(b) *money etc* tight, short; *living* austere.

(c) *relationship etc* close, intimate; *link* close.

(d) *attitude, prohibition* strict, rigid; *character* austere; (*pej*) mean, mean-spirited; (*also* **— de conciencia**) small-minded; (*also* **— de miras**) narrow-minded; insular, parochial.

2 *nm* (a) (*Geog*) strait(s); narrows, channel; **E— de Gibraltar** Straits of Gibraltar.

(b) fix (*fam*), jam, predicament; **al —** by force, under compulsion; **poner a uno en el — de + infin** to force someone into a position of having to + *infin*.

estrechura *nf* (a) = **estrechez**. (b) = **estrecho 2**.

estregadera *nf* (a) scrubbing brush; floor mop. (b) door scraper, boot scraper.

estregar [1h *and* 1k] *vt* to rub; to scrape; to scrub, scour.

estrella *nf* (a) (*Astron and fig*) star; **— de Belén** star of Bethlehem; **— fija** fixed star; **— fugaz** shooting star; **— de guía** guiding star; **— de mar** starfish; **— del norte** north star; **— polar** polar star; **— de rabo** comet; **— vespertina** evening star; (**la bandera de las**) **—s y bandas**, **—s y listas** the Stars and Stripes; **creer en su buena —** to believe in one's lucky star; **nacer con —** to be born under a lucky star, be born lucky; **poner a uno sobre las —s** to praise someone to the skies; **tener (buena) —** to be lucky; **tener mala —** to be unlucky; **ver las —s** (*fig*) to see stars.

(b) (*Typ*) asterisk, star.

(c) (*Zool*) blaze, white patch.

(d) (*Mil*) star, pip.

(e) (*Cine, Theat etc*) star; **— del cine** movie star, film star; **ser la —** to be the star, be the star.

estrelladera *nf* (*Cook etc*) slice.

estrelladero *nm* egg pan.

estrellado *adj* (a) starred; star-shaped; *sky* starry, full of stars; *dress* spangled. (b) smashed, shattered. (c) (*Cook*) egg fried.

estrellamar *nf* starfish.

estrellar [1a] **1** *vt* (a) to star, spangle, cover with stars.

(b) to smash, shatter; to dash to pieces, smash to pieces; **lo estrelló contra la pared** he smashed it against the wall; **estrelló el balón en el poste** he crashed the ball into the goal-post; **la corriente amenazaba con — el barco contra las rocas** the current threatened to dash the boat on to the rocks.

(c) egg to fry.

2 estrellarse *vr* to smash, shatter, crash (*contra* against); to be dashed to pieces; **— contra** (*Aer, Aut etc*) to crash into; **— con una dificultad** to come right up against a difficulty.

estrellato *nm* stardom.

estrellón *nm* (a) (*fig*) star, large star; star firework. (b) (*fam*) stroke of luck. (c) (*esp SAm: Aer*) crash; (*Aut*) crash, smash, collision.

estremecer [2d] **1** *vt* to shake (*also fig*).

2 estremecerse *vr* (*building etc*) to shake, vibrate, tremble; (*person: with fear*) to tremble (*ante* at, *de* with); (*with horror*) to shiver, shudder (*de* with); (*with excitement*) to tingle, tremble, thrill (*de* with); (*with cold*) to shiver (*de* with).

estremecido *adj* shaking, trembling (*de* with).

estremecimiento *nm*, **estremezón** *nm* (*Col, Ven*) tremor, vibration; shiver, shudder; shaking, trembling; tingling.

estrena *nf* (a) good-luck gift, token. (b) = **estreno**.

estrenar [1a] **1** *vt* (a) to use for the first time; to wear (*or* put on *etc*) for the first time, show off for the first time.

(b) (*Cine*) film to give its première, show for the first time; to release, put on release; (*Theat*) play to perform for the first time, give a first performance to.

2 *vi* (a) (*Theat*) **aquí estrenan mucho** they stage a lot of premières here, they put on a lot of new plays here.

(b) (*Cu*) to make a down payment.

3 estrenarse *vr* (a) (*person*) to make one's début, appear for the first time.

(b) (*film*) to have its première, be shown for the first time; (*play*) to open, have its first night; to be performed for the first time.

(c) (*Comm*) to make the first sale of the day.

estrenista *nmf* (*Theat*) first-nighter.

estreno *nm* (a) first use; first appearance; **fue cuando el — del coche nuevo** it was when we went out in the new car for the first time.

(b) (*of person*) début, first appearance; **¡mal —!** what a wretched start!

(c) (*Cine*) première; release; (*Theat*) first night, first performance; **— general** general release; **riguroso —** world première.

(d) (*Cu*) down payment, deposit.

estrenque *nm* stout esparto rope.

estrenuo *adj* vigorous, energetic; enterprising.

estreñido *adj* constipated, costive.

estreñimiento *nm* constipation.

estreñir [3h *and* 3l] **1** *vt* to constipate, bind. **2 estreñirse** *vr* to get constipated.

estrepitarse [1a] *vr* (*Cu*) to kick up a fuss, make a scene.

estrépito *nm* noise, racket, row; tremendous din; fuss; **reírse con —** to laugh uproariously.

estrepitosamente *adv* noisily; loudly, deafeningly; rowdily, boisterously.

estrepitoso *adj* noisy; loud, deafening; *person, party etc* rowdy, boisterous; **con aplausos —s** with loud applause.

estreptococo *nm* streptococcus.

estreptomicina *nf* streptomycin.

estría *nf* groove; (*Archit*) flute, fluting; (*Bio etc*) striation.

estriado *adj* grooved; (*Archit*) fluted; (*Bio etc*) striate, striated.

estriar [1c] *vt* to groove, make a groove in; to flute; to striate.

estribación *nf* (*Geog etc*) spur; **—es** spurs, foothills.

estribar [1a] *vi*: **— en** to rest on, be supported by; (*fig*) to rest on, be based on; **la dificultad estriba en el texto** the difficulty lies in the text, the difficulty stems from the text; **su prosperidad estriba en esta industria** their prosperity is based on (*or* derives from) this industry.

estribera *nf* (a) stirrup. (b) (*SAm*) girth, saddle strap.

estribillo *nm* (*Lit*) refrain; (*Mus*) chorus; (*fig*) pet word, pet phrase; **¡siempre (con) el mismo —!** the same old story!

estribo *nm* (a) (*rider's*) stirrup; (*Aut etc*) running board, step, footboard; footrest; **perder los —s** (*fig*) to fly off the handle, lose one's temper; to get hot under the collar; to lose one's head.

(b) (*Tech*) brace, bracket, stay.

(c) (*Archit*) buttress; (*of bridge*) pier, support.

(d) (*Geog*) spur.

(e) (*fig*) basis, foundation.

(f) (*Bol, Ec, RPl*) **tomar algo para el —** to drink a stirrup cup; to have one for the road.

estribor *nm* starboard.

estricnina *nf* strychnine.

estricote *nm* (*Ven*) (a) disorderly life, licentious conduct. (b) **andar al —** to go hither and thither; to live in a disorderly way; to get mixed up in a brawl.

estrictamente *adv* strictly; severely.

estrictez nf (SAm) strictness; severity.
estricto adj strict; severe.
estridente adj strident, raucous, unpleasant-sounding; jangling.
estridor nm stridency; raucousness; screech; jangling sound.
estrillar [1a] vi (Per, RPl) to get cross.
estrillo nm (Per, RPl) bad temper, annoyance.
estro nm inspiration.
estrofa nf verse, stanza, strophe.
estrófico adj strophic; composed in stanzas.
estroncio nm strontium; — **90** strontium 90.
estropajo nm (a) scourer, scrubber; dishcloth; swab, mop; **poner a uno como un —** to shower insults on someone; **to make someone feel a heel; servir de —** to be exploited, be used to do the dirty work. (b) dirt, rubbish; worthless object.
estropajoso adj (a) meat etc tough, leathery, gristly. (b) speech stammering; indistinct. (c) person slovenly; mean, despicable.
estropeado adj damaged, spoiled; ruined; crumpled; torn; person maimed, crippled.
estropear [1a] **1** vt to damage, spoil; to ruin; to mess up, make a mess of; to crumple, tear; person to maim, cripple, hurt; text etc to mangle; meaning to pervert, destroy.
　2 estropearse vr to get damaged; to spoil, go bad; to deteriorate; (plan etc) to fail.
estropicio nm (fam) (a) breakage, smashing, smash-up.
　(b) harmful effects, damaging results; **ese alimento es responsable de muchos —s** that foodstuff can have very harmful effects.
　(c) (fig) rumpus (fam), row, fuss; turmoil.
estructura nf structure; frame, framework; arrangement.
estructural adj structural.
estructuralmente adv structurally.
estructurar [1a] vt to construct; to arrange, organize.
estruendo nm (a) noise, clamour, din; crash, clatter, racket; thunder. (b) (fig) uproar, turmoil, confusion. (c) (fig) pomp, ostentation.
estruendosamente adv noisily, uproariously; loudly, obstreperously.
estruendoso adj noisy; uproarious; person loud, obstreperous.
estrujadura nf squeeze, press(ing).
estrujar [1a] vt to squeeze, press, crush; to bruise, mash; (fig) to drain, bleed white.
estrujón nm squeeze, press; pressing, crushing; (Agr) final pressing of grapes; (fam) crush, jam.
Estuardo m Stuart.
estuario nm estuary.
estucar [1g] vt to stucco, plaster.
estuco nm stucco, plaster.
estuche nm (a) box, case, container; sheath; **— de afeites** vanity case; **— de aseo** toilet case; **— de cigarros** cigar case; **— de joyas** jewel box.
　(b) **ser un —** (fam) to be a real expert, be a useful chap (fam).
estudiado adj (fig) studied, elaborate; (pej) recherché.
estudiantado nm (a) (SAm) students (collectively), student body. (b) (Chi) college.
estudiante nmf student; **— de derecho** law student; **— de medicina** medical student; **— de ruso** student of Russian.
estudiantil adj student (attr); **vida —** student life; **los problemas —es** student problems, problems of students, problems relating to students.
estudiantina nf student music group, student band.
estudiantino adj student (attr); **a la estudiantina** like a student, in the manner of students.
estudiar [1b] vti to study; to work; to think about, think over, ponder; **— para abogado** to study to become a lawyer, study law; **tengo que ir a —** I must go and work; **estudia todo el día en la biblioteca** he works all day in the library; **lo estudiaré** I'll think about it.
estudio nm (a) (in general) study; research; survey; investigation; plan, design (de for); planning; **—s** schooling, education; **—s** work, studies, researches; **le pagaron los —s** they paid for his schooling, they paid for his education; **hizo sus —s en París** he studied in Paris; **se fue a Suiza para completar sus —s** she went to Switzerland to finish her education; **los —s de Menéndez Pidal sobre la épica española** Menéndez Pidal's work on Spanish epic; **los últimos —s de lingüística** the latest work in linguistics, recent research in linguistics; **publicó un — sobre Bécquer** he published a study of Bécquer; **—s del mercado, — de mercados** market research;

—s de tiempo y movimiento time and motion study; **estar en —** to be under consideration.
　(b) (room in house) study.
　(c) (Art, Cine, Radio etc) studio; **— de cine, — cinematográfico** film studio; **— radiofónico** broadcasting studio; **— de registro de sonidos** sound-recording studio; **— de televisión** television studio.
　(d) (Art) study.
　(e) (Mus) study, étude.
　(f) (Arg: lawyer's etc) office.
　(g) studiousness, diligence.
　(h) learning; **un hombre de mucho —** a man of great learning.
estudiosamente adv studiously.
estudioso 1 adj studious; bookish. **2** nm student, scholar.
estufa nf (a) stove, heater; **— eléctrica** electric fire; **— de gas** gas fire; **— de petróleo** oil stove. (b) (Agr) hothouse; **criar a uno en —** (fig) to pamper someone.
estufilla nf (a) small stove, brazier. (b) muff.
estulticia nf stupidity, foolishness.
estultificar [1g] vt (CAm): **— a uno** to make someone look stupid, make someone out to be a fool.
estulto adj stupid, foolish.
estupefacción nf stupefaction.
estupefaciente 1 adj stupifying; narcotic; **sustancia — = 2** nm narcotic, drug.
estupefacto adj astonished, speechless, thunderstruck; **me miró —** he looked at me in amazement; **dejar a uno —** to leave someone speechless.
estupendamente adv stupendously; (fam) marvellously, wonderfully, terrifically (fam).
estupendo adj stupendous; (fam) marvellous, wonderful, terrific (fam), great (fam); **¡—!** that's great!, splendid!; **tiene un coche —** he's got a marvellous car; **hay chicas estupendas** there are some smashing girls (sl); **es — para tocar la trompeta** he's great on the trumpet.
estúpidamente adv stupidly.
estupidez nf (a) stupidity, silliness. (b) stupid thing, piece of stupidity; **fue una — mía** it was a silly mistake of mine; **cometer una —** to do something silly.
estúpido adj stupid, silly.
estupor nm (a) (Med etc) stupor. (b) (fig) astonishment, amazement.
estuprar [1a] vt to rape.
estupro nm rape.
estuque nm stucco.
estuquería nf stuccoing, stucco work.
esturión nm sturgeon.
estuve etc see **estar**.
—eta n suffix diminutive: eg **avioneta** light aircraft; **camioneta** van, light truck; see **caseta** etc.
etapa nf (a) (of journey etc) stage; (Sport) stage, leg; lap; (Mil) stopping place; **a cortas —s, a pequeñas —s** in easy stages.
　(b) (of rocket) stage; **cohete de 3 —s** 3-stage rocket.
　(c) (Mil) food ration (for stage of a march).
　(d) (fig) stage, phase; **en la segunda — del plan** in the second phase of the plan; **una adquisición proyectada por —s** a phased takeover; **lo haremos por —s** we'll do it in stages, we'll do it gradually.
etcétera adv etcetera; **gatos y perros —, — cats and dogs and so on, cats and dogs and what have you.
éter nm ether.
etéreo adj ethereal (also fig).
eternamente adv eternally, everlastingly.
eternidad nf eternity.
eternizar [1f] **1** vt to etern(al)ize, perpetuate; to make everlasting; (pej) to drag out, prolong endlessly. **2 eternizarse** vr (pej) to be interminable.
eterno adj eternal, everlasting.
ética nf ethics; **— profesional** (Med etc) professional ethics.
ético[1] adj ethical.
ético[2] adj (Med) consumptive; (fig) frail.
etilo nm ethyl.
etimología nf etymology; **— doble** doublet.
etimológico adj etymological.
etíope 1 adj Ethiopian. **2** nmf Ethiopian.
Etiopía f Ethiopia.
etiquencia nf (Cu, Mex, PR: Med) consumption.
etiqueta nf (a) etiquette; formality; **—s** refinements, formalities, ceremony; **de —** formal, full-dress (attr); **baile de —** ball, dress ball, formal dance; **"vestir de —"** (on invitation) "dress: formal".
　(b) ticket, label, tag.
etiquetero adj formal, ceremonious, punctilious; stiff, prim.
étnico adj ethnic.
etnografía nf ethnography.
etnología nf ethnology.

etrusco 1 *adj* Etruscan. **2** *nm*, **etrusca** *nf* Etruscan. **3** *nm* (*language*) Etruscan.
eucalipto *nm* eucalyptus, gum tree.
Eucaristía *nf* Eucharist.
eucarístico *adj* eucharistic.
Euclides *m* Euclid.
eufemismo *nm* euphemism.
eufemístico *adj* euphemistic.
eufonía *nf* euphony.
eufónico *adj* euphonic, euphonious.
euforia *nf* euphoria; exuberance.
eufórico *adj* euphoric; exuberant.
Eufrates *m* Euphrates.
eugenesia *nf* eugenics.
Eugenio *m* Eugene.
eugenismo *nm* eugenics.
eunuco *nm* eunuch.
eurasiano 1 *adj* Eurasian. **2** *nm*, **eurasiana** *nf* Eurasian.
eureka *excl* eureka!
Eurídice *f* Eurydice.
Eurípedes *m* Euripides.
eurítmica *nf* eurhythmics.
euro *nm* (*lit*) east wind.
Europa *f* Europe.
europeidad *nf* Europeanness; Europe-mindedness; European character.
europeísta 1 *adj* pro-European; European-minded; **la tendencia — actual en Inglaterra** the present tendency in England to favour close links with Europe. **2** *nmf* pro-European; European-minded person.
europeización *nf* Europeanization.
europeizante *adj* (*SAm*)=**europeísta**.
europeizar [1f] **1** *vt* to Europeanize. **2 europeizarse** *vr* to become Europeanized.
europeo 1 *adj* European. **2** *nm*, **europea** *nf* European.
Eurovisión *f* Eurovision.
éuscaro 1 *adj* Basque. **2** *nm* (*language*) Basque.
eutanasia *nf* euthanasia, mercy killing.
Eva *f* Eve.
evacuación *nf* (a) evacuation. (b) (*Tech*) waste; exhaust.
evacuado *nm*, **evacuada** *nf* evacuee.
evacuar [1d] *vt* (a) to evacuate; to move out of, leave empty, vacate; *city, population* to evacuate; *vessel* to empty; *sore* (*Med*) to drain.
(b) **— el vientre** to have a movement of the bowels. (c) *duty* to fulfil; *consultation* to carry out, undertake; *business* to transact; *deal* to conclude.
evacuatorio *nm* public lavatory.
evadido *nm* fugitive, escaped prisoner.
evadir [3a] **1** *vt* to evade, avoid. **2 evadirse** *vr* to escape; to break out, slip away.
evaluación *nf* evaluation.
evaluar [1e] *vt* to evaluate.
evanescente *adj* evanescent.
evangélico *adj* evangelic(al).
evangelio *nm* gospel; **el E— según San Juan** the Gospel according to St John; **ser como el —** to be certain, be infallible; **dice como el —** he speaks the gospel truth.
Evangelista *adj*: **San Juan —** St John the Evangelist.
evangelista *nm* (a) gospeller; **los cuatro —s** the four evangelists. (b) (*Mex*) public writer, scribe.
evangelizador *nm* evangelist.
evangelizar [1f] *vt* to evangelize.
evaporación *nf* evaporation.
evaporar [1a] **1** *vt* to evaporate. **2 evaporarse** *vr* to evaporate; (*fig*) to vanish.
evaporizar [1f] **1** *vt* to vapourize. **2 evaporizarse** *vr* to vapourize.
evasión *nf* escape, flight; (*fig*) evasion; **— de capitales** (*Fin*) flight of capital; **— fiscal, — tributaria** tax evasion.
evasiva *nf* evasion; loophole, way out; excuse.
evasivo *adj* evasive, non-committal, ambiguous.
evento *nm* (a) unforeseen happening; contingency; eventuality; **a cualquier —** whatever happens, in any event.
(b) (*SAm*: *angl*) event; sporting fixture; social event.
eventual *adj* (a) fortuitous; possible; conditional upon circumstances. (b) *work, worker* temporary, casual; *official etc* acting; *solution* stopgap, temporary.
eventualidad *nf* eventuality; contingency; **en esa —** in that eventuality.
eventualmente *adv* (a) by chance, fortuitously. (b) possibly, depending upon circumstances.
evidencia *nf* (a) evidence, proof; **poner en —** to make clear; to show, demonstrate; **ponerse en —** to put oneself forward. (b) obviousness.

evidenciar [1b] *vt* to prove, show, demonstrate; to make evident; **— de modo inconfundible** to give clear proof of, prove unmistakably.
evidente *adj* obvious, clear, evident.
evidentemente *adv* obviously, clearly, evidently.
evitable *adj* avoidable, preventable; **un accidente fácilmente —** an accident which could easily be avoided.
evitación *nf* avoidance, prevention; **— de accidentes** accident prevention.
evitar [1a] *vt* to avoid; to prevent; *danger etc* to avoid, escape; *trouble* to save, spare; *temptation etc* to shun; **para — tales dificultades** in order to avoid such difficulties; **para — se trabajo** in order to save oneself trouble; **no lo lograrán si puedo —lo** they won't get away with that if I can help it; **— hacer algo** to avoid doing something; to be chary of doing something.
evocación *nf* evocation; invocation.
evocador *adj* evocative; reminiscent (*de* of).
evocar [1g] *vt* to evoke, call forth, conjure up; *spirits etc* to invoke, call up.
evocativo *adj* (*SAm*) evocative.
evolución *nf* (a) (*Bio*) evolution. (b) (*fig*) evolution, change, development. (c) (*Mil etc*) manoeuvre.
evolucionar [1a] *vi* (a) (*Bio*) to evolve. (b) (*fig*) to evolve, change, develop. (c) (*Mil*) to manoeuvre, wheel; (*Aer*) to manoeuvre, circle, wheel.
evolutivo *adj* evolutionary.
ex . . . ex; former, late; **ex secretario** ex-secretary, former secretary; **la ex querida de** the former mistress of, the ex-mistress of, the one-time mistress of.
exabrupto *nm* (*hum*) broadside; sudden attack.
exacción *nf* (a) (*act*) exaction, extortion. (b) (*sum etc*) demand; levy.
exacerbante *adj* (*SAm*) irritating, provoking; (*fig*) aggravating.
exacerbar [1a] *vt* to irritate, provoke; (*fig*) to aggravate, exacerbate.
exactamente *adv* exactly; accurately; precisely; punctually; correctly.
exactitud *nf* exactness; accuracy; precision; punctuality; correctness.
exacto *adj* exact; accurate; precise; punctual; right, correct; **¡—!** exactly!, quite right!; that's just what I say!; **eso no es del todo —** that's not quite right.
exageración *nf* exaggeration.
exageradamente *adv* in an exaggerated way; excessively, exorbitantly; over-demonstratively, theatrically; intensely; fulsomely; oddly.
exagerado *adj* *account, claim etc* exaggerated; highly-coloured; *price etc* excessive, exorbitant, steep; *person* over-demonstrative, theatrical, given to extravagant gestures; intense; fulsome; peculiar, odd.
exageradura *nf* (*Ven*) exaggeration.
exagerar [1a] **1** *vt* to exaggerate; to overdo, over-state, make too much of; to enlarge upon. **2** *vi* to exaggerate; (*pej*) to overdo it, overdo things.
exaltación *nf* (a) exaltation. (b) overexcitement; elation; excitability, intenseness; hotheadedness; passion, impassioned nature. (c) (*Pol*) extremism.
exaltado 1 *adj* (a) exalted.
(b) *state, mood* over-excited, worked up; elated; (*in character*) excitable, intense; hot-headed; *speech etc* impassioned.
(c) (*Pol*) extreme, far out.
2 *nm* hothead; (*Pol*) extremist, far-out person.
exaltar [1a] **1** *vt* (a) to exalt; to elevate, raise (*a* to).
(b) (*fig*) to extol, praise.
(c) to excite, carry away, work up; *emotion* to intensify; *imagination* to fire.
2 exaltarse *vr* (*person*) to get excited, get worked up; to get carried away (*con* by); (*in argument*) to get heated; (*emotion*) to run high, become very intense; **¡no te exaltes!** don't get so worked up!
exalumno *nm*, **exalumna** *nf* (*SAm*: *Univ*) graduate; former student; alumnus, alumna (*US*).
examen *nm* examination; exam (*fam*); inquiry (*de* into); inspection; **— de admisión, — de ingreso** entrance examination; **— de conductor** driving test; **— eliminatorio** qualifying examination; **— de fin de curso** final examination, finals; **— oral** oral examination; **presentarse a un —** to enter (or go in for, sit) an examination.
examinado *nm*, **examinada** *nf* examinee, candidate.
examinador *nm*, **examinadora** *nf* examiner.
examinando *nm*, **examinanda** *nf* examinee, candidate.
examinar [1a] **1** *vt* to examine (*also Med, School, Univ etc*); to test; to inspect, look through, go over; to inquire into, investigate, look into.

2 examinarse *vr* to take an examination, be examined (*en* in; *de* for the degree of); **— de doctor** to take one's doctoral examination.

exangüe *adj* bloodless; anaemic; (*fig*) weak.

exánime *adj* lifeless; (*fig*) weak, exhausted, lifeless; **caer —** to fall in a faint.

exasperación *nf* exasperation.

exasperador *adj*, **exasperante** *adj* exasperating, infuriating.

exasperar [1a] **1** *vt* to exasperate, infuriate. **2 exasperarse** *vr* to get exasperated, lose patience.

excarcelación *nf* release (from prison).

excarcelar [1a] *vt* to release (from prison).

excavación *nf* excavation.

excavador *nm* excavator, digger.

excavar [1a] *vt* to excavate, dig (out); to hollow out.

excedente 1 *adj* excess, surplus; excessive. **2** *nm* excess, surplus.

exceder [2a] **1** *vt* to exceed, surpass; to pass, outdo, excel; (*in importance etc*) to transcend.
  2 *vi:* **— de** to exceed, surpass.
  3 excederse *vr* (a) to excel oneself.
  (**b**) (*pej*) to overreach oneself; to go too far, go to extremes; **— en sus funciones** to exceed one's duty.
  (**c**) **— de** to exceed, surpass; **no — de lo corriente** to be no more than average.

excelencia *nf* (a) excellence; superiority, superior quality; **por —** par excellence. (**b**) **su E—** his Excellency; **sí, E—** yes, your Excellency.

excelente *adj* excellent; superior.

excelentemente *adv* excellently.

excelso *adj* lofty, exalted, sublime.

excentricidad *nf* eccentricity.

excéntrico 1 *adj* eccentric; erratic. **2** *nm* eccentric.

excepción *nf* exception; **— de la regla** exception to the rule; **la — confirma la regla** the exception proves the rule; **a — de** with the exception of, except for; **hacer una —** to make an exception.

excepcional *adj* exceptional.

excepcionalmente *adv* exceptionally; as an exception.

excepto *prep* except (for), excepting.

exceptuar [1e] *vt* to except, exclude, leave out of account; (*Law etc*) to exempt.

excesivamente *adv* excessively; unreasonably, unduly.

excesivo *adj* excessive; unreasonable, undue; over-, *eg* **con generosidad excesiva** over-generously, with excessive generosity.

exceso *nm* (a) excess; (*of food*) surfeit; (*Comm, Fin*) surplus; **— de equipaje** excess luggage, excess baggage (*US*); **— de peso** excess weight; **debido al — de peso** because of the extra weight; **me detuvieron por — de velocidad** they arrested me for speeding, they booked me for exceeding the speed limit; **en —, por —** excessively, to excess; **cuidadoso en —** excessively careful, too careful; **una cantidad en — de X toneladas** a quantity in excess of (*or* over) X tons; **generoso hasta el —** generous to a fault; **beber en —** to drink to excess; **llevar algo al —** to carry something to excess, overdo something.
  (**b**) (*fig*) excess; **los —s de la revolución** the excesses of the revolution.

excisión *nf* excision.

excitabilidad *nf* excitability.

excitable *adj* excitable; highly-strung, high-strung (*US*), nervy; temperamental.

excitación *nf* (a) excitement; **— loca** hysteria. (**b**) excitation.

excitante 1 *adj* (a) exciting. (**b**) (*Med*) stimulating. **2** *nm* stimulant.

excitar [1a] **1** *vt* (a) to excite; *feeling* to excite, arouse, stir up; *doubts, hopes* to raise.
  (**b**) to incite, urge on; **— al pueblo a la rebelión** to incite the populace to rebellion; **— a uno a hacer algo** to urge someone to do something.
  (**c**) (*Elec*) to excite, energize.
  2 excitarse *vr* to get excited, get worked up.

exclamación *nf* exclamation; cry.

exclamar [1a] **1** *vi* to exclaim; to cry out. **2 exclamarse** *vr* to complain (*contra* about), protest (*contra* against).

exclamativo *adj*, **exclamatorio** *adj* exclamatory.

exclaustración *nf* (*Eccl*) secularization; expulsion (*of monks or nuns*).

exclaustrada *nf* secularized nun; expelled nun; ex-nun.

exclaustrado (*Eccl*) **1** *adj* secularized; expelled (from the order). **2** *nm* secularized monk, expelled monk; ex-monk.

excluir [3g] *vt* to exclude (*from* de); to shut out; *solution* to reject; *possibility etc* to exclude, rule out, preclude.

exclusión *nf* exclusion; **con — de** excluding, to the exclusion of; **por —** as an exception.

exclusiva *nf* (a) (*Comm*) sole right, sole agency; **tener la — de un producto** to have the sole right to sell a product, be the sole agents for a product.
  (**b**) (*Journalism*) exclusive interview; exclusive news release.
  (**c**) refusal, rejection (*for a post etc*).

exclusivamente *adv* exclusively.

exclusive 1 *adv* exclusively. **2** *prep* exclusive of, not counting.

exclusividad *nf* (a) exclusiveness; clannishness; snobbery. (**b**) (*Comm*) **=exclusiva (a)**.

exclusivista *adj club etc* exclusive, select; *group* clannish; *attitude* snobbish.

exclusivo *adj* exclusive; sole; (*of working hours*) full-time.

excluyente *adj* (*SAm*) *class, club etc* exclusive.

excombatiente *nm* exserviceman, veteran (*US*).

excomulgado 1 *adj* (a) (*Eccl*) excommunicated. (**b**) (*fam*) blessed, cursed. **2** *nm*, **excomulgada** *nf* excommunicated person.

excomulgar [1h] *vt* (a) (*Eccl*) to excommunicate. (**b**) (*fig*) to ban, banish; (*fam*) to curse.

excomunión *nf* excommunication.

excoriar [1b] **1** *vt* to skin, flay; to graze, take the skin off. **2 excoriarse** *vr* to graze oneself, skin oneself.

excrecencia *nf* excrescence.

excreción *nf* excretion.

excremento *nm* excrement.

excretar [1a] *vt* to excrete.

exculpación *nf* exoneration; (*Law*) acquittal.

exculpar [1a] **1** *vt* to exonerate, exculpate; (*Law*) to acquit (*de* of). **2 exculparse** *vr* to exonerate oneself.

excursión *nf* excursion, outing, trip; (*Mil*) raid, incursion; **— campestre** picnic; **— de caza** hunting trip; **— a pie** walk, hike, ramble; **ir de —** to go (off) on a trip, go on an outing.

excursionar [1a] *vi* (*SAm*) to go on a trip, have an outing.

excursionismo *nm* going on trips; sightseeing; walking, hiking, rambling.

excursionista *nmf* tourist; tripper; sightseer; hiker, rambler.

excusa *nf* excuse; apology; **buscar —** to look for an excuse; **presentar sus —s** to make one's excuses, excuse oneself; **presentar —s de su país** to make excuses for one's country.

excusabaraja *nf* hamper, basket with a lid.

excusable *adj* excusable, pardonable.

excusado 1 *adj* (a) unnecessary, superfluous; **— es decir que...** needless to say..., I (*etc*) need scarcely say that...; **pensar en lo —** to think of something which is quite out of the question.
  (**b**) **estar — de** to be exempt from.
  (**c**) reserved, private.
  2 *nm* lavatory, toilet.

excusar [1a] **1** *vt* (a) to excuse; **— a A con B** to tell B that A begs to be excused, to present A's apologies to B.
  (**b**) to exempt (*de* from).
  (**c**) to avoid, prevent; **así excusamos disgustos** this way we avoid difficulties; **podemos — lo otro** we can forget about the rest of it, we don't have to bother with the rest.
  (**d**) **— + infin** not to have to + infin; to save the trouble of + ger; **excusamos decirle que...** we don't have to tell you that...; **por eso excuso escribirte más largo** so I can save myself the trouble of writing at greater length.
  2 excusarse *vr* to excuse oneself; to apologize (*de* for); **— de + infin** to decline to + infin; to apologize for not being able to + infin; **— de haber hecho algo** to apologize for having done something.

execrable *adj* execrable.

execración *nf* execration.

execrar [1a] *vt* to execrate, loathe, abominate.

exégesis *nf* exegesis.

exención *nf* exemption (*de* from); immunity, freedom (*de* from).

exencionar [1a] *vt* to exempt (*de* from).

exentar [1a] *vt* to exempt (*de* from); to excuse (*de* from).

exento *adj* (a) exempt (*de* from); free (*de* from, of); **— de alquileres** rent-free; **— de derechos** duty-free; **— de impuestos** tax-free, tax-exempt (*US*), free of tax; **estar — de cuidados** to be free of worries; **una expedición no exenta de peligros** an expedition not without (its) dangers.
  (**b**) *passage, place etc* clear, unobstructed, open.
  (**c**) (*Archit*) free-standing.

exequias *nfpl* funeral rites, obsequies.

éxeunt vi exeunt.

exfoliador nm (Chi, Mex) tear-off pad, loose-leaf notebook.

exhalación nf (a) exhalation; fumes, vapour. (b) (Astron) shooting star; **como una —** at top speed, like lightning.

exhalar [1a] **1** vt to exhale, breathe out; fumes etc to emit, give off, give out; sigh to breathe, heave; moan to utter. **2 exhalarse** vr to breathe hard; to hurry, run.

exhaustivo adj exhaustive.

exhausto adj exhausted.

exheredar [1a] vt to disinherit.

exhibición nf exhibition, display, show; **— de escaparate** window display; **la pobre — del equipo** the team's poor showing; **una impresionante — de fuerza** an impressive show of strength.

exhibicionismo nm exhibitionism.

exhibicionista **1** adj exhibitionist. **2** nmf exhibitionist.

exhibir [3a] **1** vt (a) to exhibit, display, show. (b) (Mex) sum to pay in cash. **2 exhibirse** vr to show oneself.

exhortación nf exhortation.

exhortar [1a] vt to exhort (a + infin to + infin).

exhorto nm (Eccl, Law) charge.

exhumar [1a] vt to exhume, disinter.

exigencia nf (a) demand, requirement; exigency; **según las —s de la situación** as the situation requires; **tener muchas —s** to be very demanding. (b) (Ven) request.

exigente adj demanding, exacting, exigent; particular; **ser — con uno** to be hard on someone; **es muy — en la limpieza** she is very particular about cleanliness.

exigir [3c] vt (a) contribution etc to exact, levy (a from). (b) to demand, require (a of, from); to call for (a from); **— el pago** to demand payment; **esto exige mucho cuidado** this needs a lot of care; **exigirá mucho dinero** it will require (or need, take) a lot of money; **ello no exige comentario** it does not call for any comment, comment on it would be superfluous; **exige mucho** he's very demanding. (c) (Ven) thing to ask for, request; person to beg, plead with, entreat.

exiguo adj meagre, small, scanty, exiguous.

exilado **1** adj exiled, in exile. **2** nm, **exilada** nf exile.

exilar [1a], **exiliar** [1b] (Acad) **1** vt to exile. **2 exilarse** vr, **exiliarse** vr to go into exile; to exile oneself.

exiliado (SAm) = **exilado**.

exilio nm exile; **estar en el —, vivir en el —** to be in exile; **gobierno en el —** government in exile.

eximio adj (a) person distinguished, eminent. (b) goods choice, select.

eximir [3a] **1** vt to exempt (de from); to free, excuse (de from); **esto me exime de toda obligación con él** this frees me from any obligation to him. **2 eximirse** vr: **— de + infin** to excuse oneself from + ger; to free oneself from having to + infin.

existencia nf (a) existence; being; life; **lucha por la —** struggle for survival; **amargar la — a uno** to make someone's life a misery; **quitarse la —** (euph) to do away with oneself, commit suicide. (b) (also **—s**: Comm) stock; goods; **nuestras —s de carbón** our coal stocks, our stock(s) of coal; **estar en —** to be in stock; **tener en —** to have in stock.

existencial adj existential.

existencialismo nm existentialism.

existencialista **1** adj existentialist. **2** nmf existentialist.

existente adj (a) existing; in being, in existence; text etc extant; surviving; **la situación —** the existing (or present) situation. (b) (Comm) in stock.

existir [3a] vi to exist, be; **dejar de —** to pass out of existence, come to an end; (of person: euph) to pass away (euph); **esta sociedad existe desde hace 90 años** the company has been in existence for 90 years, the company was founded 90 years ago; **no existe tal cosa** there's no such thing.

éxito nm (a) result, outcome; **buen —** happy outcome, success; **con buen —** successfully; **tener buen —** to succeed, be successful; **tener mal —** to have an unfortunate outcome, fail, be unsuccessful. (b) success; **con —** successfully; **tener — en** to be successful in; to make a success of; **el hombre de —** the successful man; **es una chica de mucho —** she's a girl who has lots of success (with the men). (c) (Mus, Theat and fig) success, hit; **— editorial, — de librería** bestseller; **— de taquilla** box-office success, successful play; **— clamoroso, — fulminante, — rotundo** huge success, overwhelming success; (Mus etc) hit song, smash hit.

exitosamente adv (SAm) successfully.

exitoso adj (SAm) successful.

éxodo nm exodus; **el — rural** the depopulation of the countryside, the drift from the land.

exoneración nf (a) exoneration; freeing, relief. (b) dismissal.

exonerar [1a] vt (a) to exonerate; **— a uno de un deber** to free someone from a duty, relieve someone of a duty. (b) employee to dismiss. (c) **— el vientre** to have a movement of the bowels.

exorbitancia nf exorbitance.

exorbitante adj exorbitant.

exorcismo nm exorcism.

exorcizar [1f] vt to exorcise.

exornar [1a] vt to adorn, embellish (de with).

exótico adj exotic.

exotismo nm exoticism; taste for the exotic.

expandir [3a] **1** vt (Anat) to expand; (Comm etc) to expand, enlarge; (fig) to expand, extend, spread; **— el mercado de un producto** to expand the market for a product; **— la afición a la lectura** to spread a love of reading. **2 expandirse** vr to expand; to extend, spread; **Madrid se expande** Madrid is expanding, Madrid is spreading.

expansible adj expansible; that can be expanded (or extended etc).

expansión nf (a) expansion; enlargement; extension, spread(ing); **la — económica** economic growth; **la — industrial** industrial expansion. (b) (fig) relaxation. (c) (fig) expansiveness.

expansionar [1a] **1** vt market etc to expand. **2 expansionarse** vr (a) to expand. (b) (fig) to relax. (c) (fig) to unbosom oneself, open one's heart (con to).

expansionismo nm (Pol etc) expansionism.

expansionista adj (Pol etc) expansionist.

expansivo adj (a) expansive. (b) (fig) expansive, affable; communicative.

expatriación nf expatriation; exile.

expatriado nm, **expatriada** nf expatriate; exile.

expatriarse [1b] vr to emigrate, leave one's country; (Pol etc) to go into exile.

expectación nf (a) expectation; **— de vida** expectation of life. (b) expectation, expectancy, anticipation; eagerness; excitement; **la — crece de un momento a otro** the excitement is growing every moment.

expectante adj expectant; eager; excited.

expectativa nf expectation; hope, prospect; **— de vida** expectation of life; **estar a la —** to wait and see (what will happen); **estar a la — de algo** to look out for something, be on the watch for something.

expectorar [1a] vti to expectorate.

expedición nf (a) expedition (also Geog, Mil etc); **— de salvamento** rescue expedition; **— militar** military expedition. (b) (Comm etc) shipment, shipping; **gastos de —** shipping charges. (c) (fig) speed, dispatch.

expedicionario adj expeditionary.

expedidor nm shipper, shipping agent.

expedientar [1a] vt to make a file on, draw up a dossier on; (fig) to expel.

expediente nm (a) expedient; means; device, makeshift; **recurrir al — de + infin** to resort to the device of + ger. (b) (Law) action, proceedings; records of a case; **— judicial** legal proceedings; **incoar un —** to start proceedings; **instruir un —** to collect all the documents. (c) record; dossier; file; **— policíaco** police dossier; **— académico** (School etc) student's record, pupil's record card. (d) **cubrir el —** to do just enough to keep out of trouble.

expedienteo nm (pej) bureaucracy, red tape.

expedir [3l] vt goods etc to send, ship off, forward; document to draw up; to make out, issue; order, ticket etc to issue; business to deal with, dispatch.

expeditar [1a] vt (SAm) to expedite, hurry along; to conclude.

expeditivo adj expeditious.

expedito adj (a) expeditious, prompt, speedy. (b) road, way clear, unobstructed, free; **dejar — el camino para** to clear the way for. (c) (SAm) easy.

expeler [2a] *vt* to expel, eject.
expendedor *nm* (a) (*person*) dealer, retailer; agent; tobacconist; (*Theat*) ticket agent; — **de billetes** ticket clerk, booking clerk; — **de moneda falsa** distributor of counterfeit money.
   (b) — **automático** vending machine; — **automático de bebidas** drink vending machine.
expendeduría *nf* retail shop, (*esp*) tobacconist's (shop), cigar store (US).
expender [2a] *vt* (a) *money* to expend, spend.
   (b) *counterfeit money* to utter; to pass, circulate.
   (c) *goods* to sell (retail); to be an agent for, sell on commission; to deal in.
expendición *nf*: — **de moneda falsa** uttering counterfeit money, passing false coin.
expendio *nm* (a) expense, outlay.
   (b) (*SAm*) retail store, (*esp*) tobacconist's (shop), cigar store (US), liquor store; — **de boletos** (*Mex*) ticket office.
   (c) (*act*) retailing, retail selling.
expensar [1a] *vt* (*SAm*) to defray the costs of.
expensas *nfpl* expenses; (*Law*) costs; **a** — **de** at the expense of (*also fig*); **a mis** — at my expense.
experiencia *nf* (a) experience; **una triste** — a sad experience; **aprender por la** — to learn by experience; **saber algo por** — to know something from experience.
   (b) (*scientific etc*) experiment (*en* on).
experimentación *nf* experimentation.
experimentado *adj* experienced.
experimental *adj* experimental.
experimentalmente *adv* experimentally.
experimentar [1a] **1** *vt* (a) (*Tech etc*) to test, try out; to experiment with; **el nuevo fármaco está siendo experimentado** the new drug is being tested, experiments with the new drug are going on; **están experimentando un nuevo helicóptero** they are testing a new helicopter.
   (b) *change etc* to experience, undergo, go through; *loss, decline* to suffer; *rise, increase* to show; *emotion* to feel; **las cifras han experimentado un aumento de un 5 por 100** the figures show an increase of 5%; **no experimenté ninguna sensación nueva** I felt no new sensation.
   2 *vi* to experiment (*con* with, *en* on).
experimento *nm* experiment (*con* with, *en* on); **como** — as an experiment, by way of experiment; **hacer** —**s** to experiment (*con* with, *en* on).
experticia *nf* expertise.
experto 1 *adj* expert; skilled, experienced; seasoned; knowledgeable. **2** *nm* expert.
expiación *nf* expiation, atonement.
expiar [1c] *vt* to expiate, atone for.
expiatorio *adj* expiatory.
expiración *nf* expiration.
expirar [1a] *vi* to expire.
explanación *nf* (a) (*Tech*) levelling. (b) (*fig*) explanation, elucidation.
explanada *nf* raised area, terrace, platform; levelled area; esplanade; (*Mil*) glacis; — **de ensillado** saddling enclosure.
explanar [1a] *vt* (a) (*Rail, Tech etc*) to level, grade.
   (b) (*fig*) to unfold; to explain, elucidate.
explayar [1a] **1** *vt* to extend, expand, enlarge.
   2 explayarse *vr* (a) to extend, spread; to open out, unfold.
   (b) (*fig*) to relax, take it easy; to take an outing.
   (c) (*in speech etc*) to speak at length; to spread oneself; — **a su gusto** to talk one's head off, talk to one's heart's content; — **con uno** to unbosom oneself to someone, confide in someone.
explicable *adj* explicable, explainable; **cosas no fácilmente** —**s** things not easily explained, things not easy to explain.
explicación *nf* explanation; reason (*de* for); **sin dar** —**es** without giving any reason.
explicaderas *nfpl*: **tener buenas** — to be good at explaining things (away); (*pej*) to be plausible.
explicar [1g] **1** *vt* to explain; *theory etc* to expound; *course* to lecture on, teach; *subject* to lecture in; *lecture* to give, deliver.
   2 explicarse *vr* (a) to explain (oneself); **se explica con claridad** he states things clearly; **¡explíquese Vd!** explain yourself!; **explíquese con la mayor brevedad** please be as brief as possible.
   (b) — **algo** to understand something; **no me lo explico** I can't understand it, I can't make it out.
   (c) to be explained; **esto no se explica fácilmente** this cannot be explained (away) easily.
explicativo *adj*, **explicatorio** *adj* explanatory.
explícitamente *adv* explicitly.
explícito *adj* explicit.

exploración *nf* exploration; (*Mil*) reconnaissance, scouting; (*Radar etc*) scanning; — **submarina** underwater exploration, (*as sport*) skin diving.
explorador *nm* (a) (*Geog etc*) explorer; pioneer; (*Mil*) scout; (*niño*) — (boy) scout. (b) (*Med*) probe; (*Radar etc*) scanner.
exploradora *nf* girl guide, girl scout (US).
explorar [1a] **1** *vt* (*Geog etc*) to explore; to pioneer, open up; (*Med*) to probe; (*Radar etc*) to scan. **2** *vi* to explore; (*Mil*) to scout, reconnoitre.
exploratorio *adj* exploratory.
explosión *nf* (a) explosion; blast; **motor de** — internal combustion engine; **hacer** — to explode.
   (b) (*fig*) explosion, outburst; **una** — **de cólera** an explosion of anger.
explosionar [1a] *vti* to explode.
explosiva *nf* (*Ling*) plosive (consonant).
explosivo 1 *adj* explosive (*also fig*). **2** *nm* explosive; **alto** —, — **detonante**, — **de gran potencia**, — **rompedor** high explosive.
explotación *nf* exploitation; running, operation; (*Min etc*) working; — **a cielo abierto** opencast working, opencast mining; — **forestal** forestry; **en** — in operation; **gastos de** — operating costs, operating expenses.
explotar [1a] **1** *vt* (a) to exploit; *plant etc* to run, operate; *mine, seam* to work; *resources* to exploit, tap; to harness.
   (b) (*pej*) *workers* to exploit; *situation* to exploit, make capital out of.
   (c) (*Mil etc*) to explode.
   2 *vi* (*Mil etc*) to explode; to go off; **explotaron 2 bombas** 2 bombs exploded; **cayó sin** — it fell but did not go off, it landed without going off.
exponente 1 *nmf* exponent.
   2 *nm* (a) (*Math*) index, exponent.
   (b) (*SAm*) model, (prime) example; **el tabaco cubano es** — **de calidad** Cuban tobacco is the best of its kind.
exponer [2r] **1** *vt* (a) to expose (*also Eccl, Phot*); *picture etc* to show, exhibit, put on show; *notice* to display, put up.
   (b) *life* to risk.
   (c) *child* to abandon.
   (d) *argument* to expound; *idea* to explain, unfold; *facts* to set out, set forth, state; (*Law*) *charge* to bring.
   2 exponerse *vr*: — **a** to expose oneself to, lay oneself open to; — **a** + *infin* to run the risk of + *ger*.
exportable *adj* exportable.
exportación *nf* (a) (*act*) export, exportation.
   (b) export, exported article; exports; **géneros de** — exports, exported goods; **comercio de** — export trade.
exportador *nm*, **exportadora** *nf* exporter; shipper.
exportar [1a] *vt* to export.
exposición *nf* (a) (*act*) exposing, exposure; (*Phot*) exposure; (*of picture etc*) showing; **debido a una** — **excesiva al sol** because of undue exposure to sunlight; **no se puede permitir la** — **de tal cuadro** the showing of such a picture cannot be allowed.
   (b) (*of facts etc*) statement, exposition; (*to authorities*) petition, claim.
   (c) (*Art etc*) show, exhibition; (*Comm*) show, fair; — **canina** dog show; — **de modas** fashion show; — **universal** world fair.
exposímetro *nm* (*Phot*) exposure meter.
expósito 1 *adj*: **niño** — = **2** *nm*, **expósita** *nf* foundling.
expositor *nm*, **expositora** *nf* (*Art etc*) exhibitor; (*of theory*) exponent.
exprés *nm* (*SAm*) express train.
expresado *adj* above-mentioned; **según las cifras expresadas** according to these figures, according to the figures I (*etc*) have already quoted, according to the figures given earlier.
expresamente *adv* expressly; on purpose, deliberately; clearly, plainly; **no lo dijo** — he didn't say so in so many words.
expresar [1a] **1** *vt* to express; to voice; to word, phrase, put; to state, set forth; to quote; **expresa las opiniones de todos** he is voicing the opinions of us all; **estaba expresado de otro modo** it was worded differently; **el papel no lo expresa** the paper doesn't say so; **Vd deberá** — **el número del giro postal** you should quote (*or* give, state) the number of the postal order.
   2 expresarse *vr* (a) to express oneself; **no se expresa bien** he doesn't express himself well.
   (b) to be stated; **el número no se expresa** the number is not given, the number is not stated; **como abajo se expresa** as is stated below.

expresión *nf* **(a)** expression; **esta — de nuestro agradecimiento** this expression of our gratitude.
(b) (*Ling*) expression; — **familiar** colloquialism, conversational expression; **la — es poco clara** the expression is not very clear.
(c) —**es** greetings, regards; ¡**mis —es a los amigos!** give my regards to everybody!, remember me to them!
expresionismo *nm* expressionism.
expresivamente *adv* **(a)** expressively. **(b)** tenderly, affectionately, warmly.
expresivo *adj* **(a)** expressive. **(b)** tender, affectionate, warm.
expreso 1 *adj* **(a)** express; specific, clear, exact.
(b) *train etc* fast.
2 *nm* **(a)** special messenger; **empresa de —** express company; **mandar algo por —** to send something by express (delivery).
(b) (*Rail etc*) fast train.
exprimelimones *nm*, *pl* **exprimelimones** lemon squeezer.
exprimidera *nf* squeezer.
exprimidor *nm* **(a)** squeezer; — **de limones** lemon squeezer. **(b)** (*for clothing*) wringer.
exprimir [3a] *vt* **(a)** to squeeze; to squeeze out, press out, express; *clothes* to wring out, squeeze dry; *lemon etc* to squeeze.
(b) — **a uno** (*fig*) to pick someone's brains.
exprofeso *adv* on purpose.
expropiación *nf* expropriation; commandeering.
expropiar [1b] *vt* to expropriate; to commandeer.
expuesto 1 *ptp of* **exponer**; **según lo arriba —** according to what has been stated (*or* set out, said) above.
2 *adj* **(a)** *place etc* exposed; dangerous.
(b) *picture etc* on show, on display, on view; **los artículos —s en el escaparate** the goods displayed in the window.
(c) **estar — a** to be exposed to, be open to; to be liable to.
expugnar [1a] *vt* to take by storm.
expulsanieves *nm*, *pl* **expulsanieves** snowplough.
expulsar [1a] *vt* to expel (*de* from), eject (*de* from), turn out (*de* of); *player* to send off; — **a uno a puntapiés** to kick someone out.
expulsión *nf* expulsion, ejection; (*Sport*) sending-off.
expulsor 1 *adj*: **asiento —** (*Aer*) ejector seat. **2** *nm* (*Tech*) ejector.
expurgar [1h] *vt* to expurgate.
expurgatorio *adj* expurgatory; **índice —** (*Eccl*) Index.
exquisitamente *adv* **(a)** exquisitely; deliciously, delightfully; excellently. **(b)** (*pej*) affectedly.
exquisitez *nf* **(a)** exquisiteness; excellence. **(b)** (*pej*) affectation.
exquisito *adj* **(a)** exquisite; delicious, delightful; excellent. **(b)** (*pej*) affected.
extasiar [1c] **1** *vt* to entrance, enrapture, captivate.
2 extasiarse *vr* to become entranced; to go into ecstasies, rhapsodize (*ante* over, about).
éxtasis *nm*, *pl* **éxtasis** ecstasy; rapture; (*of medium etc*) trance; **estar en el —** to be in ecstasy.
extático *adj* ecstatic, rapturous; **lo miró —** he looked at it ecstatically.
extender [2g] **1** *vt* **(a)** to extend; to enlarge, make bigger; to prolong; to stretch (out), expand; *cloth, map etc* to spread (out), open (out); to lay out; *cards* to lay down; *butter, face cream* to spread; *pile* to spread out; *war* to extend, widen, escalate; *knowledge* to extend, spread (*a* to).
(b) *document* to draw up; to write out; *cheque* to draw, make out; *receipt* to make out; *certificate* to issue.
2 extenderse *vr* **(a)** (*in space*) to extend; to stretch (out); to spread (out); to be, lie; **delante de nosotros se extendía la mar** before us the sea stretched away, the sea lay spread out before us; **sus terrenos se extienden sobre muchos kilómetros** his lands spread over many miles; **no se extiende más al oeste** it does not go any further west.
(b) (*place*: *fig*) to range, extend; **las posibilidades se extienden de A a Z** the possibilities range from A to Z.
(c) (*in time*) to extend, last (*a* to, till; *de* from).
(d) (*fig*: *custom, knowledge*) to spread, extend; (*war*) to escalate, widen, broaden; **su venganza se extendió hasta matar a las mujeres** in his vengeance he even killed the women; **la epidemia se extendió rápidamente** the epidemic spread rapidly.
(e) (*of amount*) — **a** to amount to, reach, go as high as; (*in size*) to run to; **el libro se extiende a 400 páginas** the book runs to 400 pages.
(f) (*fig*: *in speech*) to spread oneself; — **sobre un tema** to enlarge on a subject.

extendido *adj* **(a)** spread out, open; extended; *arms* outstretched, spread wide.
(b) *custom etc* widespread; prevalent, (*pej*) rife, rampant; *knowledge* widespread.
extensamente *adv* **(a)** extensively, widely. **(b)** fully, in full, with full details.
extensible *adj* extending, extensible.
extensión *nf* **(a)** (*act*) extension; stretching; spreading; — **de plazo** (*Comm*) extension.
(b) extent, size; spaciousness; **un solar de mayor —** a site of greater size, a site of larger area.
(c) (*of land, sea*) expanse, stretch; **por toda la — del paisaje** over the whole (expanse) of the countryside.
(d) (*of time*) length, duration; span.
(e) (*Mus*) range, compass.
(f) (*fig*: *of knowledge etc*) extent, range; (*of meaning*) range; (*of plan, programme*) scope.
(g) (*SAm*: *Tel*) extension.
extensivo *adj* extensive; **hacer — a** to extend to, apply to, make applicable to; **la crítica se hizo extensiva a toda la ciudad** the criticism applied to the whole city.
extenso *adj* **(a)** extensive; vast; *room etc* big, broad, spacious; *empire* far-flung.
(b) *knowledge etc* widespread; *report, story* full; **por —** in full, with full particulars, at length.
extenuación *nf* emaciation, weakness.
extenuado *adj* emaciated, wasted, weak.
extenuar [1e] **1** *vt* to emaciate, weaken. **2 extenuarse** *vr* to become emaciated, waste away; to get weak.
exterior 1 *adj* **(a)** exterior, external; outer; *appearance* outward; *room* outside, outward-facing.
(b) *relations, trade* foreign; *asuntos* —**es** foreign affairs; **comercio —** foreign trade, overseas trade.
2 *nm* **(a)** exterior, outside; outward appearance; **al —, por el —** on the outside; outwardly; **avanzar por el —** (*Racing*) to come up on the outside; **de poco agradable —** of unprepossessing appearance; **con el — pintado de azul** with the outside painted blue.
(b) foreign parts; **noticias del —** foreign news, overseas news, news from abroad; **comercio con el —** foreign trade, overseas trade.
(c) (*Sport*) wing, wing-forward, winger; — **derecho** outside-right; — **izquierdo** outside-left.
exterioridad *nf* **(a)** outward appearance, externals.
(b) —**es** (*fig*) pomp, show; formalities.
exteriorizar [1f] *vt* to express outwardly; to show, reveal.
exteriormente *adv* outwardly.
exterminar [1a] *vt* to exterminate.
exterminio *nm* extermination.
externamente *adv* externally; outwardly.
externalizar [1f] *vt* = **exteriorizar**.
externo 1 *adj* external, outside; outward. **2** *nm*, **externa** *nf* day pupil.
extinción *nf* (*all senses*) extinction.
extinguido *adj* **(a)** **estar —** (*fire*) to be out, be extinguished. **(b)** *animal, volcano* extinct.
extinguir [3d] **1** *vt* **(a)** *fire etc* to extinguish, put out; *mutiny* to put down.
(b) (*Bio*) to exterminate, wipe out.
(c) *debt etc* to wipe out.
2 extinguirse *vr* **(a)** (*fire*) to go out.
(b) (*Bio*) to die out, become extinct.
extinto *adj* **(a)** extinct. **(b)** (*Chi, Mex, RPl*: *euph*) dead, deceased.
extintor *nm* (*also* — **de incendios**) fire extinguisher.
extirpación *nf* **(a)** extirpation, eradication. **(b)** (*Med*) removal.
extirpar [1a] *vt* **(a)** to extirpate, eradicate, stamp out.
(b) (*Med*) to remove (surgically); **le extirparon el ojo derecho** they removed his right eye, he had his right eye removed.
(c) (*fam*) *person* to fire (*fam*); to get rid of.
extra¹ 1 *adj invar* extra; — **de** in addition to, on top of.
2 *nm* **(a)** (*on menu, bill*) extra; (*on pay*) bonus. **(b)** (*Typ*) extra, special edition. **3** *nmf* (*Cine*) extra.
extra² . . . extra . . .
extracción *nf* extraction; (*in lottery*) draw.
extracorto *adj* *wave* ultra-short.
extractar [1a] *vt* **(a)** to make extracts from. **(b)** to abridge, summarize.
extracto *nm* **(a)** (*Chem etc*) extract. **(b)** (*Lit*) abstract, summary.
extractor *nm* extractor.
extradición *nf* extradition; **crimen sujeto a —** extraditable offence.
extradicionar [1a] *vt* to extradite.
extraer [2p] *vt* to extract (*also Math, Med, Min*), take out, pull out.
extrafino *adj* superfine.

extrajudicial *adj* extrajudicial.
extralimitación *nf* abuse (of authority).
extralimitarse [1a] *vr* to go too far, exceed (*or* abuse) one's authority.
extramuros *adv* outside the city.
extranjería *nf* alien status.
extranjerismo *nm* foreign word (*or* phrase *etc*).
extranjerizante *adj* tending to favour foreign ways (*etc*); *word* foreign-looking, foreign-sounding.
extranjero 1 *adj* foreign; alien.
  2 *nm*, **extranjera** *nf* foreigner; alien.
  3 *nm* foreign country; foreign lands; **cosas del —** things from abroad; foreign things; **estar en el —** to be abroad, be overseas, be in foreign parts; **ir al — to go abroad; pasó 6 años en el —** he spent 6 years abroad; **no me siento a gusto en el —** I don't feel at ease abroad.
extrañamente *adv* strangely, oddly.
extrañamiento *nm* (a) estrangement (*de* from).
  (b) = **extrañeza.**
extrañar [1a] **1** *vt* **(a)** to find strange, find odd, wonder at; **extrañaba la falta de autobuses** she found the absence of buses strange; **me extrañaba que no hubieras venido** I was surprised that you should not have come; **apenas es de — que . . .** it is hardly surprising that . . .; **eso me extraña** that surprises me, that puzzles me, I find that odd; **me extraña su conducta** I am surprised at your behaviour.
  (b) (*SAm*) to miss; to feel the lack of, regret the absence of; to yearn for.
  2 extrañarse *vr* **(a)** to be amazed, be surprised (*de* at); to marvel (*de* at); **— de que . . .** to be surprised that . . .; to marvel that . . .
  (b) to refuse.
  (c) (*of friends etc*) to become estranged, grow apart.
extrañeza *nf* **(a)** strangeness, oddness, oddity.
  (b) surprise, amazement; uneasiness; **me miró con —** he looked at me in surprise.
  (c) estrangement, alienation.
extraño *adj* **(a)** strange, odd, queer; singular; **la extraña guerra** (1939) the phoney war; **es muy —** it's very odd; **¡cosa extraña!** how strange!, how odd!; **parece — que . . .** it seems strange that . . .
  (b) extraneous (*a* to); **cosas extrañas a las que tratamos** things unconnected with those we handle; **país —** foreign country.
extrañoso *adj* (*Ec*) surprised.
extraoficial *adj* unofficial; informal.
extraoficialmente *adv* unofficially; informally.
extraordinariamente *adv* extraordinarily.
extraordinario 1 *adj* extraordinary; unusual; outstanding; *edition, number, discount etc* special; *charge* extra, supplementary; **por sus servicios —s** for his outstanding services; **no tiene nada de —** there's nothing special about it.
  2 *nm* **(a)** treat; **invitar a uno a un —** to stand someone a treat.
  (b) (*on menu*) special dish, extra dish.
  (c) (*Typ*) special issue.
extraplano *nm* (*Mountaineering*) overhang.
extrarradio *nm* (*of town*) outer parts, outlying area.
extrasensorial *adj* extrasensory.
extraterrenal *adj* (*SAm*), **extraterreno** *adj* (*SAm*) unearthly, supernatural.
extraterritorial *adj* extraterritorial.
extravagancia *nf* **(a)** (*quality*) extravagance; outlandishness; oddness, strangeness.
  (b) (*una —*) whim; vagary, peculiarity; **—s** nonsense; **tiene sus —s** he has his oddities.
extravagante *adj* extravagant; outlandish, eccentric; odd, strange, nonsensical.
extravagantemente *adv* extravagantly; eccentrically; oddly, strangely; nonsensically.
extravasarse [1a] *vr* to leak out, flow out; (*blood*) to ooze out.

extraviado *adj* lost; missing; *animal* lost, stray.
extraviar [1c] **1** *vt* **(a)** *person* to mislead, misdirect; to lead astray.
  (b) *article* to lose, mislay, misplace.
  (c) *money* (*pej*) to embezzle.
  2 extraviarse *vr* **(a)** (*person*) to lose one's way, get lost; (*animal*) to stray, wander; (*letter*) to go astray, get lost in the post, miscarry.
  (b) (*morally*) to go astray, err, fall into evil ways.
extravío *nm* **(a)** loss, misplacement, mislaying; straying; wandering; (*fig*) deviation (*from* de). **(b)** (*fig: moral*) misconduct, erring, evil ways.
extremadamente *adv* extremely, exceedingly; extraordinarily.
extremado *adj* extreme; excessive; intense; extremely bad; extremely good; **frío —** extreme cold; **con extremada delicadeza** with extraordinary delicacy.
extremar [1a] **1** *vt* to carry to extremes; to force the sense of, stretch the application of; to overdo; **sin — el sentimentalismo** without overdoing the sentimentality; **el dictador extrema sus incendiarios discursos** the dictator is making even more inflammatory speeches, the dictator is being still more outrageous in his inflammatory speeches.
  2 extremarse *vr* to do one's utmost, exert oneself to the full, make every effort (*en* + *infin* to + *infin*).
extremaunción *nf* extreme unction.
extremeño 1 *adj* Extremaduran. **2** *nm*, **extremeña** *nf* Extremaduran.
extremidad *nf* **(a)** end, tip, extremity; edge, outermost part. **(b)** **—es** (*Anat*) extremities.
extremismo *nm* extremism.
extremista 1 *adj* extremist. **2** *nmf* extremist.
extremo 1 *adj* **(a)** (*of place*) extreme, last; end (*attr*); far, furthest, outer, outermost.
  (b) (*in order*) last.
  (c) (*fig*) extreme; utmost; critical, desperate; **en caso —** as a last resort, in an extreme case.
  2 *nm* **(a)** end; extremity; **— muerto** dead end; **pasar de un — a otro** to go from one end to the other, (*fig*) go from one extreme to the other.
  (b) (*fig*) highest point, highest degree; lowest point; extreme; **al — de, hasta el — de** to the point of; **con —** in the extreme; **por —** extremely; **hacer —s** to gush, behave effusively; **quedó reducido al — de ir a pie** he was reduced to (the extreme of) going on foot.
  (c) (*fig*) point, matter, question; **ese — no se tocó en la discusión** that point was not dealt with in the discussion.
  (d) (*fig*) great care.
  (e) (*Sport*) wing; (*person*) wing-forward, winger; **— derecho** outside-right; **— izquierdo** outside-left.
Extremo Oriente *m* Far East.
extremoso *adj* **(a)** *person* gushing, effusive; vehement, extreme in his (*etc*) attitudes (*or* reactions). **(b)** *landscape etc* of extremes, of violent contrasts.
extrínseco *adj* extrinsic.
extrovertido 1 *adj* extrovert; outgoing. **2** *nm*, **extrovertida** *nf* extrovert.
exuberancia *nf* **(a)** exuberance. **(b)** (*Bot*) luxuriance, lushness. **(c)** fullness, buxomness.
exuberante *adj* **(a)** exuberant. **(b)** (*Bot*) luxuriant, lush. **(c)** *figure etc* full, buxom, well-covered.
exudación *nf* exudation.
exudar [1a] **1** *vt* to exude, ooze (*de* from). **2** *vi* to exude, ooze out.
exultación *nf* exultation.
exultar [1a] *vi* to exult.
exvoto *nm* votive offering.
eyector *nm* (*Tech*) ejector.
eyaculación *nf* (*Med*) ejaculation.
eyacular [1a] *vti* (*Med*) to ejaculate.

F

fabada nf (Asturias) rich stew of beans, pork etc.

fábrica nf (a) (Tech) factory; works, plant; mill; (Col) still, distillery; **— de cerveza** brewery; **— de conservas** canning plant; **— experimental** pilot plant; **— de gas** gasworks; **— de moneda** mint; **— de papel** paper mill; **marca de —** trademark; **precio en —** price ex-factory.
(b) (act) manufacture, making.
(c) make; **de — alemana** of German make.
(d) (Archit) building, structure; fabric; masonry.

fabricación nf manufacture, making, production; make; **— de coches** car manufacture; **— de tejas** tile making; **de — casera** home-made; **de — nacional** made in Spain (or Britain etc); **de — propia** made on the premises, our own make; **— en serie** mass production; **estar en —** to be in production.

fabricante nm manufacturer; maker; factory owner, mill owner.

fabricar [1g] vt (a) to manufacture, make; to put together; (Archit) to build, construct; **— en serie** to mass-produce.
(b) (fig: pej) to fabricate, invent, devise.

fabril adj manufacturing.

fabriquero nm (a) = fabricante. (b) (Eccl) churchwarden. (c) (Mex) distillery operator (in a sugar mill).

fábula nf (a) (Lit etc) fable; myth; tale.
(b) (Lit: of play) story, plot, action.
(c) rumour; piece of gossip; fib.
(d) (person) talk of the town; laughing stock.
(e) (fam) **un negocio de —** a splendid piece of business; **es una cosa de —** it's fabulous (fam).

fabulario nm collection of fables.

fabulista nm writer of fables.

fabulosamente adv fabulously.

fabuloso adj (a) fabulous; mythical; imaginary, fictitious. (b) (fam) fabulous (fam), fantastic; **es francamente —** it's just fabulous.

facción nf (a) (Pol) faction; (pej) breakaway group; hostile group, group of troublemakers.
(b) (of face) feature; **de —es irregulares** with irregular features.
(c) (Mil) routine duty; **estar de —** to be on duty.

faccioso 1 adj factious; hostile; rebellious, seditious. 2 nm rebel; hostile person, troublemaker.

faceta nf facet (also fig).

facial adj facial; **valor —** face value.

fácil 1 adj (a) easy; simple, straightforward; **es — ver que . . .** it is easy to see that . . .; **— de hacer** easy to do.
(b) style etc easy, fluent; ready; (pej) facile, too easy; glib.
(c) person docile, compliant; **woman** easy, loose.
(d) **es — que venga** he is likely to come; **no veo muy — que . . .** I don't think it is at all likely that . . . 2 adv (fam) = fácilmente.

facilidad nf (a) ease, easiness, facility; simplicity, straightforwardness; **con la mayor —** with the greatest ease.
(b) fluency; **— de palabra** fluency in speech, readiness with which one talks.
(c) docility, compliant nature.
(d) **—es** facilities; **—es de crédito** credit facilities; **"—es de pago"** (Comm) "easy terms"; **las —es del puerto** the port facilities; **me dieron todas las —es** they gave me every facility.

facilitar [1a] vt (a) to facilitate, make easy; to expedite; to help to cause.
(b) to provide, furnish, supply; document to issue; **¿quién facilitó el dinero?** who provided the money?; **me facilitó un coche** he supplied me with a car, he provided the car.
(c) (Arg) **— algo** to make something out to be easier than it really is.

fácilmente adv easily; readily; simply, straightforwardly.

facilongo adj (Per) rather easy.

facineroso 1 adj criminal; wicked, villainous. 2 nm criminal; wicked person, criminal.

facistol 1 adj (a) (Ant, Col, Mex, Ven) insolent.
(b) (Cu, PR) full of jokes; given to practical joking.
2 nm (a) (Eccl) lectern; choir desk.
(b) (Ant, Col, Mex, Ven) insolent person; braggart.

facistolería nf (Ant, Col, Mex, Ven) insolence; boastfulness, conceit.

facón nm (RPl) long knife, gaucho knife.

facsímil 1 adj facsimile. 2 nm facsimile.

factible adj feasible; workable, practical.

facticio adj artificial, factitious.

factor nm (a) (Math) factor.
(b) factor, element; **— determinante** determining factor; **— humano** human factor; **— de seguridad** safety factor; **el — suerte** the luck factor, the element of chance; **es un nuevo — de la situación** it is a new factor in the situation.
(c) (Comm) agent, factor; commission merchant.
(d) (Rail) clerk; freight agent.

factoría nf (a) (Comm) trading post; agency. (b) (angl) factory; (Ec, Per) foundry.

factótum nm (a) factotum; jack-of-all-trades. (b) (pej) busybody.

factual adj factual; based on fact(s), consisting of facts.

factura nf (a) (Comm) bill, invoice; **— simulada** pro forma invoice; **según —** as per invoice; **pasar —, presentar —** to send an invoice. (b) (Arg) buns, cakes.

facturación nm (a) (Comm) invoicing. (b) (Rail) registration.

facturar [1a] vt (a) (Comm) to invoice. (b) (Rail) luggage to register, check (US).

facultad nf (a) faculty.
(b) power, authority; permission; **tener la — de + infin** to have the power to + infin; **tener — para + infin** to be authorized to + infin.
(c) **—es** faculties, powers; **—es del alma** mental powers.
(d) (Univ) faculty, school; **F— de Filosofía y Letras** Faculty of Arts; **F— de Derecho** Faculty of Law.
(e) (Univ: loosely) university; **está en la —** he's at the university; **quedarse a comer en la —** to lunch at the university.

facultar [1a] vt to authorize, empower; **— a uno para hacer algo** to empower someone to do something.

facultativo 1 adj (a) optional.
(b) (Univ) faculty (attr).
(c) professional; (Med) medical; **dictamen —** medical report; **prescripción facultativa** medical prescription.
2 nm doctor, practitioner.

facundia nf eloquence.

facundo adj eloquent.

facha nf (a) (fam) look, appearance; face; (person) sight, object; **— a —** face to face; **estar hecho una —** to look a sight, look terrible (fam).
(b) (Naut) **ponerse en —** to lie to.

fachada nf (a) (Archit) façade, front; (as measurement etc) frontage; **con — al parque** looking towards the park, overlooking the park; **con 15 metros de —** with a frontage of 15 metres.
(b) (Typ) frontispiece.
(c) (fig) façade, outward show; **no tiene más que —** it's all just show with him; **tener mucha —** to be all show and no substance.

fachado adj: **bien —** good-looking; **mal —** ugly, plain.

fachenda (*fam*) **1** *nf* swank (*fam*), conceit. **2** *nm* swank (*fam*), show-off (*fam*).

fachendear [1a] *vi* (*fam*) to swank (*fam*), show off.

fachendista *adj* (*fam*), **fachendón** *adj* (*fam*), **fachendoso** *adj* (*fam*) swanky (*fam*), conceited, snooty (*fam*).

fachinal *nm* (*Arg*) swamp, swampy place.

fachoso *adj* (a) (*SAm*)=**fachendista**. (b) ridiculous, odd-looking. (c) (*Arg, Per*) elegant, natty.

faena *nf* (a) task, job, piece of work; duty; (*fam*) tough job, sweat, fag; (*Mil*) fatigue; — **doméstica** housework; —**s** (*at home*) chores; **esto es una** — this is a tough one, this is a real sweat; **estar de** — to be at work; **estar en plena** — to be hard at work; **tener mucha** — to be terribly busy.
(b) (*Ant, Guat, Mex*) extra work, overtime.
(c) (*fam: also* **mala** —) dirty trick; **hacer una** — **a uno** to play a dirty trick on someone; **¡menuda** — **la que me hizo!** a fine thing he did to me!
(d) (*Taur*) play with the cape; performance; **hizo una — maravillosa** he gave a splendid performance (with the cape).
(e) (*Chi*) gang of workers; working place.

faenar [1a] (*RPl*) **1** *vi* to work, labour. **2** *vt cattle* to slaughter and dress; *wood* to cut, work.

faenero *nm* (*Chi*) farmhand, farm worker.

fafarechero 1 *adj* (*fam*) swanky (*fam*), conceited. **2** *nm* (*fam*) swank (*fam*), show-off (*fam*).

fagot *nm* bassoon; bassoonist.

failear [1a] *vt* (*CAm, RPl: angl*) to file.

fain *adj* (*CAm: angl*) fine.

fainada *nf* (*Cu*) silly thing, foolish act.

faíno *adj* (*Cu*) rude; coarse, rough.

faisán *nm* pheasant.

faite (*SAm: angl*) **1** *adj* tough, strong.
2 *nm* (a) tough man, good fighter.
(b) (*pej*) quarrelsome sort, brawler.

faitear [1a] *vi* (*SAm: angl*) to fight (with fists).

faja *nf* (a) (*of cloth*) strip, band; (*garment*) sash, belt; girdle, corset; (*Mil*) sash; (*Med*) bandage, support.
(b) (*Post*) wrapper (*also* — **postal**).
(c) (*fig*) strip, belt, zone; **una estrecha** — **de terreno** a narrow strip of land.
(d) (*Aut*) lane.
(e) (*Radio, TV*) channel.
(f) (*Archit*) band, fascia.
(g) (*Mex: Typ*) spine.

fajada *nf* (a) (*Ant*) attack, rush. (b) (*Arg*) beating. (c) (*Ven*) disappointment.

fajar [1a] **1** *vt* (a) to wrap; to swathe; to bandage; (*Post*) to wrap up, put a wrapper on.
(b) (*SAm*) to attack, lay into (*fam*); to bash (*fam*), beat; to thrash; *woman* (*fam*) to try to seduce.
(c) (*Arg, Mex*) **¡que lo fajen!** tell him to wrap up! (*sl*).
2 *vi*: — **con uno** (*fam*) to go for someone, lay into someone (*fam*).
3 fajarse *vr* (a) to put on one's belt (*or sash etc*); (*fig*) to tighten one's belt.
(b) (*SAm*) to come to blows; to fight, bash each other (*fam*); **los boxeadores se fajaron duro** the boxers really laid into each other (*fam*).

fajilla *nf* (*Arg: Post*) wrapper.

fajín *nm* (*Mil*) sash.

fajina *nf* (a) (*Agr*) shock, pile, rick.
(b) kindling, brushwood, faggots.
(c) (*Mil*) bugle call, (*esp*) call to mess.
(d) (*Arg*) task, job (to be done quickly); hard work; **tenemos mucha** — we've a lot to do, we've a tough job on here.
(e) (*Cu*) extra work, overtime.
(f) (*Arg*) **ropa de** — working clothes; **uniforme de** — ordinary uniform.

fajo *nm* (a) (*of papers*) bundle, sheaf; (*of notes*) roll, wad. (b) —**s** swaddling clothes. (c) (*Mex*) blow. (d) (*SAm*) swig (of liquor) (*fam*).

falacia *nf* (a) deceit, fraud. (b) deceitfulness.

falange *nf* (a) (*Mil*) phalanx; **F**— *Spanish fascist party*. (b) (*Anat*) phalange.

falangista 1 *adj* Falangist. **2** *nmf* Falangist.

falanjear [1a] *vt* (*sl*) to pinch (*fam*), swipe (*sl*).

falaropo *nm* phalarope.

falaz *adj person* deceitful; treacherous; *doctrine etc* fallacious; *appearance etc* deceptive, misleading.

falca *nf* (a) (*Col, Mex, Ven*) river ferryboat. (b) (*Bol*) small still.

falda *nf* (a) (*dress*) skirt; (*Sew*) flap, fold; — **escocesa** kilt; **estar cosido a las** —**s de su madre** to be tied to mother's apron strings; **estar cosido a las** —**s de su mujer** to be dominated by one's wife; **haberse criado bajo las** —**s de mamá** to have led a very sheltered life.
(b) (*Anat*) lap; **sentarse en la** — **de una** to sit on someone's lap.
(c) (*fam: person*) bird (*sl*), dame (*sl*); **ser muy aficionado a** —**s** to be fond of the ladies.
(d) (*Geog*) slope, hillside; foot, bottom (of a slope); **a la** — **de la montaña** at the foot of the mountain.

faldellín *nm* (a) short skirt; underskirt. (b) (*Ant, Ven*) christening robe.

faldero *adj*: **perro** — lapdog; **hombre** — ladies' man; **es muy** — he's a great one for the ladies.

faldicorto *adj* short-skirted.

faldillas *nfpl* coattails.

faldón *nm* (a) (*of dress*) tail, skirt; coattails; (*Sew*) flap. (b) (*Archit*) gable.

falencia *nf* (a) deceit; error, mistake. (b) (*SAm*) bankruptcy.

falena *nf* moth.

falibilidad *nf* fallibility.

falible *adj* fallible.

fálico *adj* phallic.

falo *nm* phallus.

falsamente *adv* falsely; unsoundly, mistakenly; insincerely, dishonestly.

falsario *nm*, **falsaria** *nf* (a) falsifier; liar. (b) forger, counterfeiter.

falseador *nm*, **falseadora** *nf* forger, counterfeiter.

falsear [1a] **1** *vt* to falsify; to forge, counterfeit, fake; to fiddle (with), juggle with; *lock* to pick; (*Tech*) to bevel. **2** *vi* (a) to buckle, sag, give way; (*fig*) to flag, slacken. (b) (*Mus*) to be out of tune.

falsedad *nf* (a) (*in general*) falseness; falsity; unsoundness; hollowness, insincerity; dishonesty; treachery, deceit. (b) (*una* —) falsehood.

falsete *nm* (a) (*Tech*) plug, bung. (b) (*Mus*) falsetto.

falsía *nf* falseness, duplicity.

falsificación *nf* (a) (*act*) falsification, forging. (b) (*object*) forgery; fabrication.

falsificador *nm*, **falsificadora** *nf* forger, counterfeiter.

falsificar [1g] *vt* to falsify; *coin* to counterfeit; *picture, stamp etc* to forge, fake; *election, results etc* to rig, fiddle (with), juggle with.

falso 1 *adj* (a) false; *coin* false, counterfeit, bad, dud; *picture, stamp etc* forged, fake; bogus, sham; *jewel* imitation (*attr*); *horse, mule* vicious; *statement* false; *opinion, theory* unsound; mistaken; *evidence* false, untrue; perjured; *person* hollow, insincere; dishonest; *friend* false, treacherous.
(b) **en** — falsely; without proper support; **coger a uno en** — to catch someone in a lie; **jurar en** — to commit perjury; **dar un paso en** — to step on something that is not there, trip; (*fig*) to take a false step.
2 *nm* (*CAm, Mex*) false evidence.

falta *nf* (a) lack, want, need; absence; shortage; (*Law*) default; non-, *eg* — **de asistencia** non-attendance; — **de pago** non-payment; **a** — **de** (*as prep*) failing; **a** — **de, por** — **de** for want of, for lack of; — **de dinero** shortage of money; — **de peso** short weight; — **de respeto** lack of respect, disrespect; — **de seriedad** frivolity; irresponsibility; **hacer** — to be lacking, be wanting; to be missed; **el hombre que hace** — the right man, the man we (*etc*) want; **eso me hace (mucha)** — I need it (badly); **me hizo Vd mucha** — I missed you a lot; **aquí no haces** — you are not needed here; **¡— hacía!** and about time too!; **hacer** — + *infin* to be necessary to + *infin*; **hace** — **pintarlo** somebody ought to paint it, it needs painting.
(b) failure, shortcoming; fault, mistake; misdeed; (*in manufacture etc*) flaw, defect, fault; (*Mech*) trouble; — **de ortografía** spelling mistake; — **garrafal** stupid mistake; gross blunder; **sin** — without fail; **sacar** —**s a uno** to point out someone's defects.
(c) (*Sport*) foul, infringement; (*Tennis*) fault; **cometer una** — **contra uno** to commit a foul on someone, foul someone.

faltar [1a] **1** *vt* (*Arg, Mex, Ven*) to be rude to, show disrespect for.
2 *vi* (a) to be lacking, be wanting; **le falta dinero** he lacks money, he needs money; **no le faltan buenas cualidades** he is not lacking in good qualities; **nos falta tiempo para hacerlo** we lack the time to do it, we are short of time to do it, we haven't the time to do it; **lo que falta es libros** what is lacking is books.
(b) to be absent, be missing (*de* from); **faltaron 3 de la reunión** there were 3 missing (*or* absent) from the meeting; — **a clase** to miss class, not go to class; — **a una cita** to miss an appointment, break an appointment, not turn up for a date; — **al trabajo** to stay away from work; **¿falta algo?** is

anything missing?; **faltan 9** there are 9 missing, we are 9 short; **no falta quien opina que** . . . there are some who think that . . .; **en 8 años no he faltado ni una sola vez** I've not missed once in 8 years.

(c) (*of gun, mechanism, supply etc*) to fail, go wrong, break down.

(d) — **a** *principle* to be false to; *person* to fail; to offend; — **a la decencia** to offend against decency; — **a una promesa** to break a promise, go back on one's word; — **al respeto** to be disrespectful (*a* to); — **a la verdad** to lie, be untruthful; — **en los pagos** to default on one's payments.

(e) — **en hacer algo** to fail to do something; **no faltaré en comunicárselo** I shall not fail to tell him.

(f) (*of quantity, time etc*) **faltan pocos minutos para el comienzo** it's only a few minutes to go to the start; **faltan 3 semanas para las elecciones** there are 3 weeks to go to the election, the election is 3 weeks off; **falta poco para las 8** it's nearly 8 o'clock, it's getting on for 8 o'clock; **falta poco para terminar** it's almost over; it's almost finished; **falta todavía por hacer** it remains to be done, it is still to be done.

(g) (*idioms*) ¡no faltaba más! it's the limit!; it's the last straw!; ¡lo que faltaba!, ¡es lo único que faltaba! that's the very end!

(h) (*esp SAm*) to be rude, be disrespectful.

falto *adj* (a) short, deficient, lacking; **estar — de** to be short of; *quality etc* to be wanting in, be lacking in; **estar — de personal** to be short-handed.

(b) (*morally*) poor, wretched, mean.

(c) (*Col*) fatuous, vain.

faltón *adj* (a) remiss, neglectful, unreliable (about carrying out duties); (*SAm*) slack (about work), often absent. (b) (*Andalusia, Cu*) disrespectful.

faltoso *adj* (a) (*CAm, Mex*)=**faltón** (a). (b) (*CAm, Mex*) disrespectful. (c) (*Col*) quarrelsome.

faltriquera *nf* fob, watch pocket; handbag; **rascarse la —** to dig into one's pocket (*fig*).

falúa *nf* launch; tender.

falla *nf* (a) fault, defect; failure; (*SAm*) lack, shortage; (*SAm*) failure to keep one's promises; — **en caja** cash shortage; **géneros que tienen —s** (*Comm*) defective goods, seconds.

(b) (*Geol*) fault.

(c) (*Mech*) failure, breakdown; — **de encendido** (*Aut*) ignition fault; — **de tiro** (*Mil*) misfire.

(d) (*Col: Cards*) void.

fallada *nf* (*Cards*) ruff, trumping.

fallar [1a] **1** *vt* (a) (*Cards*) to ruff, trump.

(b) (*Law*) to pronounce sentence on.

2 *vi* (a) (*of memory, crop, brakes etc*) to fail; (*of plans*) to go wrong, miscarry; (*of shot*) to miss, go astray; (*of rope, support etc*) to break, snap, give way; (*of gun*) to misfire, fail to go off; (*of motor*) to miss; — **a uno** to fail someone, let someone down; **algo le falla a X** there's something up with X; **algo falló en sus planes** something went wrong with his plans.

(b) (*Law*) to pronounce sentence, pass judgement.

(c) (*Cards*) to ruff, trump (in).

falleba *nf* bolt.

fallecer [2d] *vi* (a) to pass away, die. (b) to end, run out, expire.

fallecido 1 *adj* late. **2** *nm*, **fallecida** *nf* deceased, person who has lately died.

fallecimiento *nm* decease, demise, passing.

fallero *adj* (*Chi*) slack (about work), often absent.

fallido 1 *adj* (a) *effort etc* unsuccessful; *hope* disappointed; (*Mech, Mil etc*) dud; *debt* bad, uncollectable.

(b) (*Comm*) bankrupt.

2 *nm* bankrupt.

fallir [3a] *vi* (a) to fail. (b) to end, run out, expire.

(c) (*Ven*) to go bankrupt.

fallo 1 *adj* (a) **estar —** (*Cards*) to be out of a suit; **estar — de** (*Cards*) to be out of, have a void in; (*Mex, PR*) to lack, be without.

(b) (*Chi*) fatuous; stupid.

2 *nm* (a) (*Mech*) failure, trouble, breakdown; (*Med*) failure; (*Sport*) mistake, tactical error, mix-up; **debido a un — de los frenos** because of a brake failure; — **de corazón** heart failure.

(b) (*Cards*) void; **tener un — a corazones** to have a void in hearts.

(c) (*Law etc*) sentence, verdict; decision, ruling; findings.

falluto *adj* (*RPl*) (a) unsuccessful, failed. (b) untrustworthy.

fama *nf* (a) fame; reputation, repute; **mala —** bad reputation; notoriety; **de mala —** of ill fame; **el libro que le dio —** the book which made him famous,

the book which made his name; **tener — de gran cazador** to have the reputation of being a great hunter, be known as a great hunter; **tiene — de poco escrupuloso** he is thought to be unscrupulous.

(b) report, rumour; **corre la — de que** . . . it is rumoured that . . .

famélico *adj* starving, famished; **los —s** the starving.

familia *nf* (a) family; household; — **política** relatives by marriage, in-laws; **de buena —** of good family; **tener mucha —** to have lots of children; **ser como de la —** to be one of the family; **eso viene de —** that runs in the family.

(b) (*Ant, Col, Mex, Per*) relative.

(c) (*Typ*) fount.

familiar 1 *adj* (a) family (*attr*); **los lazos —es** the family bond, the ties of blood; **subsidio —** family allowance; **dioses —es** household gods.

(b) familiar (*a* to).

(c) homely, domestic; informal; plain, ordinary; (*Ling*) colloquial, familiar; *style* familiar.

2 *nmf* relative, relation; member of the household; intimate friend, close acquaintance.

familiaridad *nf* familiarity (*con* with); homeliness; informality; —**es** familiarities.

familiarizar [1f] **1** *vt* to familiarize, acquaint (*con* with). **2 familiarizarse** *vr*: — **con** to familiarize oneself with, make oneself familiar with, get to know.

famoso *adj* (a) famous (*por* for). (b) (*fam*) famous, great (*fam*), splendid.

fan *nmf*, *pl* **fans** (*Cine, Mus etc: angl*) fan (*fam*).

fanal *nm* (a) lighthouse; (harbour) beacon; lantern; (*Aut*) headlight. (b) bell glass; lampshade.

fanático 1 *adj* fanatical.

2 *nm* fanatic; bigot; (*Cine, Sport etc*) fan (*fam*), supporter, admirer; **es un — del aeromodelismo** he's an aeromodelling fiend (*or* enthusiast); **los —s de la estrella** the star's fans, the star's admirers.

fanatismo *nm* fanaticism; bigotry; enthusiasm.

fandango *nm* (a) (*Mus*) fandango. (b) (*fam*) row, shindy; **se armó un —** there was a great row. (c) (*SAm*) spree (*fam*), carousal.

fandanguear [1a] *vi* (*Arg*) to carouse, live it up (*fam*).

fané *adj* (*SAm: gall*) messed-up, crumpled, rumpled.

fanega *nf* (a) *grain measure* (=Spain 1.58 bushels, Mex 2.57 bushels, Arg 3.89 bushels). (b) *land measure* (=Spain 1.59 acres, Ven 1.73 acres).

fanfarrear [1a] *vi*=**fanfarronear**.

fanfarria *nf* (a) bluster, bravado, bragging. (b) (*Mus*) fanfare.

fanfarrón 1 *adj* blustering, boastful; flashy. **2** *nm* blusterer, braggart; bully; flashy type.

fanfarronada *nf* bluster, bravado, swagger; bluff.

fanfarronear [1a] *vi* to bluster, boast, swagger; to rant; to talk big (*sl*), bluff.

fanfarronería *nf* blustering, boasting, bragging; ranting; big talk, bluffing.

fangal *nm* bog; quagmire, muddy place.

fango *nm* mud, mire; slush; (*fig*) mire, dirt.

fangoso *adj* muddy, miry; slushy.

fanguero 1 *adj* (*Arg*) *animal, player* suited to heavy going. **2** *nm* (*Cu, PR, Mex*) = **fango, fangal.**

fanta-ciencia *nf* science-fiction.

fantasear [1a] *vi* to dream, let one's imagination run free.

fantaseo *nm* (*SAm*) dreaming, imagining.

fantasía *nf* (a) (*faculty*) fantasy, imagination, fancy; **es obra de la —** it is a work of the imagination; **dejar correr la —** to let one's imagination roam.

(b) (*Art, Lit etc*) fantasy; fantastic tale; work of the imagination; (*Mus*) fantasia.

(c) (*una —*) whim, fancy.

(d) (*fam*) conceit, vanity, airs.

(e) (*Comm*) **de —** fancy; **joyas de —** imitation jewellery.

(f) (*Ven*) **tocar por —** to play by ear.

fantasioso *adj* (*fam*) vain, conceited, stuck-up (*fam*); ¡fantasiosa! you vain thing!

fantasma 1 *nm* (a) ghost, phantom, apparition. (b) solemn and vain person. (c) (*TV*) ghost image. **2** *nf* bogey.

fantasmagoría *nf* phantasmagoria.

fantasmagórico *adj* phantasmagoric.

fantasmal *adj* ghostly; phantom (*attr*).

fantásticamente *adv* fantastically; weirdly; fancifully.

fantástico *adj* (a) fantastic; weird, unreal; fanciful, whimsical. (b) vain. (c) (*Arg*) capricious. (d) (*Chi*) bragging, swaggering.

fantoche *nm* (a) puppet, marionette. (b) (*fam*) mediocrity, man of straw, nonentity.

fantochesco *adj* puppet-like.

faquín *nm* porter, errand boy.

faquir *nm* fakir.
farabute *nm* (*Arg*) rogue; untrustworthy person; poor wretch.
farallón *nm* (*Geog*) steep rock, cliff; headland; (*Geol*) outcrop; (*Arg, Chi*) rocky peak.
faramalla *nf* (*fam*) (a) blarney, humbug, claptrap; trash. (b) empty show, sham. (c) (*Chi*) bragging, boasting.
faramallear [1a] *vi* (*Chi, Mex*) to brag, boast.
faramallero *adj* (*Chi, Mex*) bragging, boastful.
farándula *nf* (a) (*Theat: Hist*) troupe of strolling players.
     (b) (*fam*) humbug, claptrap; pack of lies; confidence trick, confidence game (*US*), swindle; wicked gossip.
farandulero 1 *adj* (a) (*Theat: Hist*) theatre (*attr*).
     (b) (*SAm*) = **farolero**.
     2 *nm*, **farandulera** *nf* (a) (*Theat: Hist*) strolling player.
     (b) confidence trickster, confidence man (*US*), swindler, rogue.
Faraón *m* Pharaoh.
faraónico *adj* Pharaonic.
faraute *nm* (a) (*arch*) herald. (b) (*fam*) busybody.
fardel *nm* (a) bag, knapsack; ragbag. (b) bundle.
fardo *nm* bundle; bale, pack; (*fig*) burden.
farfulla 1 *nf* (*fam*) (a) splutter, jabber. (b) = **faramalla** (a). (c) (*Chi, Ec, Per, PR*) bragging, boasting. 2 *nmf* (*fam*) jabberer, gabbler.
farfullador *adj* spluttering; jabbering; gabbling.
farfullar [1a] *vi* to splutter; to jabber, gabble.
farfullero *adj* (*Per, PR, SD*) (a) = **farfullador**. (b) = **fanfarrón**.
farináceo *adj* starchy, farinaceous.
faringe *nf* pharynx.
faringitis *nf* pharyngitis.
fariña *nf* (*Per, RPl*) manioc gratings.
farisaico *adj* Pharisaic(al), hypocritical; smug.
fariseo *nm* Pharisee, hypocrite; smug sort.
farmacéutico 1 *adj* pharmaceutical. 2 *nm* chemist, pharmacist.
farmacia *nf* (a) pharmacy. (b) chemist's (shop), drugstore (*US*); — **de guardia** all-night chemist's.
fármaco *nm* drug.
farmacológico *adj* pharmacological.
farmacología *nf* pharmacology.
farmacólogo *nm* pharmacologist.
farmacopea *nf* pharmacopoeia.
faro 1 *nm* (a) (*Naut*) lighthouse; beacon; — **aéreo** air beacon.
     (b) (*Naut*) light, lantern; (*Aut*) headlamp; headlight; — **lateral** sidelight; — **piloto**, — **trasero** rear light, tail light; — **de marcha atrás** reversing light.
     2 *as adj* (*fam*): **idea** — bright idea, brilliant idea.
farol *nm* (a) lantern, lamp; (*Rail*) headlamp; — **de calle**, — **público** street lamp; — **de viento** hurricane lamp; *see* **adelante** (d).
     (b) lamppost; (*Gymnastics*) handstand.
     (c) wrapping of cigarette packet.
     (d) — **es** (*SAm: fig*) eyes.
     (e) (*Arg, Bol*) bay window, glassed-in balcony.
     (f) (*fam*) swank (*fam*); **marcarse un** — to shoot a line (*fam*), swank, brag; **tiene mucho** — he's terribly swanky (*fam*).
farola *nf* street lamp; lamppost.
farolazo *nm* (*CAm, Mex*) swig of liquor (*fam*).
farolear [1a] *vi* (*fam*) to swank (*fam*), strut around; to brag.
farolero 1 *adj* (*fam*) vain, stuck-up (*fam*), swanky (*fam*). 2 *nm* (a) lamppost. (b) lamp maker; lamplighter. (c) (*fam*) swank (*fam*); braggart.
farolillo *nm* (a) (*Elec*) fairy light, Chinese lantern. (b) (*Bot*) Canterbury bell.
farra[1] *nf* (*Fish*) salmon trout.
farra[2] *nf* (a) (*SAm*) spree (*fam*), party, carousal. (b) (*RPl*) mockery, teasing; **tomar a uno para la** — to pull someone's leg.
fárrago *nm* medley, hotchpotch.
farrear [1a] 1 *vi* (*SAm*) to make merry, carouse. 2 **farrearse** *vr* (a) (*RPl*) — **de uno** to tease someone. (b) — **el dinero** to spend one's money on drink.
farrero 1 *adj* (*Chi, Per*) merry; fun-loving. 2 *nm*, **farrera** *nf* reveller.
farrista *adj* (*Chi, RPl*) dissipated, hard-drinking; too boisterous, too rowdy.
farruto *adj* (*Arg, Bol, Chi*) sickly, weak.
farsa *nf* (a) (*Theat*) farce; (*pej*) bad play, crude play. (b) (*fig*) humbug, sham, masquerade.
farsante *nm* (*fam*) humbug, fraud, fake.
farsear [1a] *vi* (*Arg, CAm, Chi*) to joke.

fas: por — **o por nefas** by hook or by crook, rightly or wrongly; at any cost.
fascículo *nm* fascicule, part.
fascinación *nf* fascination.
fascinador *adj* fascinating.
fascinar [1a] *vti* to fascinate; to captivate; to bewitch, cast the evil eye on.
fascismo *nm* fascism.
fascista 1 *adj* fascist. 2 *nmf* fascist.
fase *nf* (a) phase, stage; **estar fuera de** — to be out of phase. (b) (*Astron, Bio, Elec*) phase.
fastidiar [1b] 1 *vt* (a) to annoy, bother, vex; to bore; to upset, disgust, sicken, irk; **eso me fastidia terriblemente** it annoys me no end; it upsets me terribly; **¡no fastidies!** you can't mean it!, you're kidding!; **¡no me fastidies!** stop bothering me!
     (b) to harm, damage.
     2 **fastidiarse** *vr* (a) to get cross; to get bored; **¡fastídiate!** (*fam*) get lost! (*fam*); **¡que se fastidie!** (*fam*) tell him to go to blazes!
     (b) to harm oneself.
fastidio *nm* (a) annoyance, bother, nuisance; **¡qué** —**!** what a nuisance! (b) boredom. (c) disgust, repugnance.
fastidioso *adj* (a) annoying, bothersome, vexing; tedious, tiresome, boring; irksome; sickening. (b) (*SAm: angl*) fastidious.
fasto *nm* (a) pomp, pageantry. (b) —**s** (*Lit*) annals.
fastuosamente *adv* magnificently, splendidly; lavishly; pompously.
fastuoso *adj* magnificent, splendid; lavish; pompous.
fatal *adj* (a) fatal; ill-fated, disastrous.
     (b) irrevocable, unavoidable.
     (c) (*fam*) awful (*fam*), ghastly (*fam*), rotten (*fam*); **tiene un ∮inglés** — he speaks awful English; **la obra fue** — the play was rotten.
fatalidad *nf* (a) fate; fatality. (b) mischance, misfortune, ill-luck.
fatalismo *nm* fatalism.
fatalista 1 *adj* fatalistic. 2 *nmf* fatalist.
fatalizarse [1f] *vr* (a) (*Col*) to commit a grave crime. (b) (*Chi*) to suffer grave harm; (*Per*) to suffer a series of misfortunes (as a punishment for a wrong committed).
fatalmente *adv* (a) fatally; disastrously. (b) unavoidably, irremediably.
fatídicamente *adv* (a) prophetically. (b) fatefully, ominously.
fatídico *adj* (a) prophetic. (b) fateful, ominous.
fatiga *nf* (a) fatigue, weariness; — **cerebral** brain-fag, mental fatigue. (b) (*Tech*) fatigue; — **del metal** metal fatigue. (c) —**s** hardships, troubles, toils.
fatigadamente *adv* with difficulty, wearily.
fatigar [1h] 1 *vt* (a) to tire, weary, fatigue. (b) to annoy. 2 **fatigarse** *vr* to tire, get tired, grow weary; — **de andar** to wear oneself out walking.
fatigosamente *adv* painfully, with difficulty.
fatigoso *adj* (a) tiring, exhausting, fatiguing. (b) laboured, difficult; **respiración fatigosa** laboured breathing. (c) trying, tiresome.
fatuidad *nf* (a) fatuity, foolishness, inanity. (b) conceit.
fatuo *adj* (a) fatuous, foolish, inane. (b) conceited; *see* **fuego**.
fauces *nfpl* (*Anat*) fauces, gullet; (*SAm*) tusks, teeth; (*fig*) jaws, maw.
fauna *nf* fauna.
fauno *nm* faun.
Fausto *m* Faust.
fausto *nm* splendour, pomp, magnificence.
fautor *nm* accomplice, helper; instigator.
favor *nm* (a) favour, service, good turn, kindness; —**es** (*of woman*) favours; **entrada de** — complimentary ticket; **es de** — it's complimentary, it's free; **por** — please; **no es** —, **no hay** — (*in reply to "please"*) think nothing of it, it's no trouble; **haga el** — **de esperar** please wait, kindly wait; **haga el de no fumar** (*severely*) please be so good as to refrain from smoking; **¿me hace el** — **de pasar la sal?** would you please pass the salt?, would you be so kind as to pass the salt?; — **que Vd me hace** you're very kind, it's good of you; — **de venir puntualmente** (*Mex etc*) please be punctual.
     (b) favour, good graces; **estar en** — to be in favour; **gozar de** — **cerca de uno** to be in favour with someone.
     (c) protection, support; **gracias al** — **del rey** thanks to the king's protection.
     (d) (*symbol*) favour; token; gift.
     (e) **a** — **de** in favour of; on behalf of; (*Comm*) to the order of; **a** — **de la marea** helped by the tide, taking advantage of the tide; **a** — **de la noche** under the cover of night, helped by the darkness.

favorable *adj* favourable; auspicious; advantageous.
favorablemente *adv* favourably; auspiciously; advantageously.
favorecedor *adj dress etc* becoming.
favorecer [2d] *vt* (a) to favour; to help, protect; to treat favourably; (*of fortune*) to favour, smile on.
(b) (*of dress*) to become, flatter, look well on; (*of picture*) to flatter.
favorecido *adj* favoured; **trato de nación más favorecida** (*Comm*) most-favoured nation treatment.
favoritismo *nm* favouritism.
favorito 1 *adj* favourite. **2** *nm*, **favorita** *nf* favourite (*also Sport*).
faz *nf* (a) (*lit, fig*) face; front; aspect; — **a** — face to face; — **de la tierra** face of the earth. (b) (*of coin*) obverse.
fe *nf* (a) (*Rel*) faith (en in); **la** — **católica** the Catholic faith.
(b) faith, belief; reliance; **de buena** — in good faith; (*Law*) bona fide; **obrar de buena** — to act in good faith; **mala** — bad faith; **a** — **mía, por mí** — (*arch*) by my faith, upon my honour; **dar** — **a, prestar** — **a** to believe, credit, place reliance on; **tener** — **en** to have faith in, believe in.
(c) assurance; **a** — in truth; **en** — **de lo cual** in witness whereof; **dar** — **de** to testify to, bear witness to.
(d) fidelity, loyalty.
(e) certificate; — **de bautismo** certificate of baptism; — **de erratas** (*Typ*) list of errata.
fealdad *nf* ugliness, hideousness.
feamente *adj* hideously.
Febo *m* Phoebus.
febrero *nm* February.
febril *adj* (a) (*Med*) fevered, feverish. (b) (*fig*) feverish, hectic.
febrilmente *adv* (*fig*) feverishly, hectically.
fécula *nf* starch.
feculento *adj* starchy.
fecundación *nf* fertilization; — **artificial** artificial insemination.
fecundar [1a] *vt* to fertilize; — **por fertilización cruzada** to cross-fertilize.
fecundidad *nf* (a) fertility; fecundity. (b) (*fig*) fruitfulness, productiveness.
fecundizar [1f] *vt* to fertilize.
fecundo *adj* (a) fertile; fecund; prolific.
(b) (*fig*) fruitful; copious, abundant; productive; — **de palabras** fluent, eloquent; — **en** fruitful of, productive of; **una época muy fecunda en buenos poetas** a period very productive of good poets, a period in which good poets abounded; **un libro** — **en ideas** a book full of ideas.
fecha *nf* date; — **tope** closing date, last date; **de larga** — (*Fin*) long-dated; **a partir de esta** — from today, starting from today; **a 30 días** — (*Comm*) at 30 days' sight; **con** — **del 15 de agosto** dated the 15th of August; **con** — **adelantada** *cheque* postdated; **en** — **próxima** soon, at an early date; **hasta la** — to date, so far; **para estas** —**s** by this time; **por estas** —**s** now, about now; **manuscrito sin** — undated manuscript.
fechador *nm* (*Arg, Chi, Mex*) date stamp.
fechar [1a] *vt* to date.
fechoría *nf* misdeed, villainy.
federación *nf* federation.
federal *adj* federal.
federalismo *nm* federalism.
federalista *nmf* federalist.
federativo *adj* federative.
Federico *m* Frederick.
feérico *adj* fairy (*attr*).
féferes *nmpl* (*CAm, Col, Cu, Ec, Mex, SD*) junk, lumber; things (in general), thingummyjigs (*fam*).
fehaciente *adj* reliable, authentic.
feldespato *nm* felspar.
felicidad *nf* (a) happiness.
(b) good luck, good fortune; success.
(c) —**es** best wishes, congratulations; **os deseo toda clase de** —**es** I wish you every kind of happiness; **¡mis** —**es!** congratulations!
felicitación *nf* congratulation.
felicitar [1a] *vt* to congratulate (*a uno por algo* somebody on something); **¡le felicito!** congratulations!
feligrés *nm*, **feligresa** *nf* parishioner.
feligresía *nf* parish; parishioners (*collectively*).
felino *adj* feline, catlike.
Felipe *m* Philip.
feliz *adj* (a) happy; **¡** — **año nuevo!** happy new year!; **y vivieron felices** (*end of story*) and they lived happily ever after.

(b) **turn of phrase** *etc* felicitous, happy, exactly right.
(c) lucky, fortunate; successful; **la cosa tuvo un fin** — the affair had a successful outcome, the affair turned out well.
felizmente *adv* (a) happily. (b) felicitously. (c) luckily, fortunately; successfully.
felón 1 *adj* wicked, treacherous. **2** *nm* wicked person, villain.
felonía *nf* (*SAm: angl*) felony, crime.
felpa *nf* (a) plush. (b) (*fam*) hiding; dressing-down.
felpar [1a] *vt* to cover with plush; (*fig*) to carpet.
felpeada *nf* (*Arg, Mex*) dressing-down.
felpear [1a] *vt* (*Arg, Mex, Urug*) to dress down.
felpilla *nf* chenille.
felpudo 1 *adj* plush, plushy. **2** *nm* doormat.
femenil *adj* (a) feminine, womanly. (b) (*CAm, Mex*) women's (*attr*); **equipo** — women's team.
femenino 1 *adj* feminine; (*Bot*) female; **deporte** — **sport for women; equipo** — women's team; **del género** — of the feminine gender. **2** *nm* (*Gram*) feminine.
fementido *adj* treacherous, false.
feminidad *nf* femininity.
feminismo *nm* feminism.
feminista *nmf* feminist.
fémur *nm* femur.
fenecer [2d] **1** *vt* to finish, conclude, close. **2** *vi* (a) to come to an end, cease. (b) (*euph*) to pass away, die; to perish.
fenecimiento *nm* (a) end, conclusion, close. (b) (*euph*) passing, demise.
Fenicia *f* Phoenicia.
fenicio 1 *adj* Phoenician. **2** *nm*, **fenicia** *nf* Phoenician.
fénix *nm* phoenix; (*fig*) marvel; **el F**— **de los ingenios** the Prince of Wits, the genius of our times (*Lope de Vega*).
fenol *nm* phenol.
fenomenal *adj* (a) phenomenal. (b) (*fam*) tremendous (*fam*), terrific (*fam*).
fenómeno 1 *nm* phenomenon; (*fig*) freak, accident.
2 *adj* (*fam*) great (*fam*), marvellous; **una chica fenómena** a smashing girl (*sl*); **¡él estuvo** —**!** he was great!; he was the tops! (*fam*).
3 *adv* (*sl*) **lo hemos pasado** — we had a terrific time (*fam*).
feo 1 *adj* (a) *appearance* ugly; hideous, unsightly; **más** — **que Picio, más** — **que un grajo** (*etc*) as ugly as sin.
(b) *smell etc* bad, nasty; *play* dirty, foul; *weather* foul; *situation* nasty; ugly; **es una costumbre fea** it's a nasty habit; **eso es muy** — that's nasty, that's not nice; **él me puso el problema** — he made me see the difficulties of the problem; **esto se está poniendo** — this is beginning to look bad, I don't like the look of this.
(c) (*Arg, CAm, Col, Mex*) bad, foul, foulsmelling, foul-tasting.
2 *nm* insult, slight; **hacer un** — **a uno** to insult someone, offend someone; **¿me va Vd a hacer ese** —**?** (*concerning invitation*) but you can't refuse!
3 *adv* (*SAm*) bad, badly; **oler** — to smell bad, have a nasty smell; **cantar** — to sing terribly *fam*.
feón *adj* (*SAm*) ugly; **medio** — rather ugly.
feote *adj* (*fam*) terribly ugly (*fam*).
feracidad *nf* fertility.
feraz *adj* fertile.
féretro *nm* coffin; bier.
feri *nm* (*SAm*) *see* **ferryboat**.
feria *nf* (a) fair, market; agricultural show; carnival; (*SAm*) village market, weekly market; **la F**— **de Sevilla** the Seville Fair, the Seville Carnival; — **de muestras** trade show, trade exhibition.
(b) holiday; rest, rest day.
(c) (*Mex: Fin*) change; (*CAm*) tip.
feriado *adj*: **día** — holiday, day off; **día medio** — half-holiday, half-day off.
ferial *nm* fair, market; fairground.
feriante *nmf* (a) stallholder, trader; showman. (b) fair-goer.
feriar [1b] **1** *vt* (a) to buy, sell (in a market, at a fair); to trade, exchange. (b) (*Col*) to sell cheap. **2** *vi* to take time off, take a break.
ferino *adj* savage, wild; **tos** *f* **ferina** whooping cough.
fermata *nf* (*Mus*) run.
fermentación *nf* fermentation.
fermentado *adj* fermented.
fermentar [1a] *vi* to ferment; **hacer** — to ferment, cause fermentation in.
fermento *nm* (a) ferment. (b) leaven, leavening.
Fernando *m* Ferdinand; **te lo han puesto como a** — **VII** (*fam*) they've given it to you on a plate.

ferocidad *nf* fierceness, ferocity, savageness; cruelty.

feroz *adj* (a) fierce, ferocious, savage; cruel. (b) (*SAm*) ugly.

ferozmente *adv* fiercely, ferociously, savagely; cruelly.

férreo *adj* (a) iron (*also fig*); (*Chem*) ferrous; **metal no** — non-ferrous metal. (b) (*Rail*) rail (*attr*).

ferrería *nf* ironworks, foundry.

ferretería *nf* (a) ironmongery, hardware. (b) (*Comm*) ironmonger's (shop), hardware store. (c) = **ferrería**.

ferretero *nm* ironmonger, hardware dealer.

férrico *adj* ferric, ferrous; **metal no** — non-ferrous metal.

ferrobús *nm* (*Rail*) diesel car.

ferrocarril *nm* railway, railroad (*US*); — **de cremallera** rack railway; — **elevado** elevated railway, overhead railway; — **funicular** funicular (railway); — **de vía estrecha** narrow-gauge railway; — **de vía única** single-track railway; **por** — by rail, by train; **de** — railway (*attr*), railroad (*attr*: *US*), rail (*attr*).

ferrocarrilero (*SAm*) **1** *adj* railway (*attr*), railroad (*attr*: *US*), rail (*attr*). **2** *nm* railway, railroad (*US*).

ferrohormigón *nm* ferroconcrete.

ferroprusiato *nm* (*Archit, Tech*) blueprint.

ferroso *adj* ferrous; **metal no** — non-ferrous metal.

ferrotipo *nm* (*Phot*) tintype.

ferroviario 1 *adj* railway (*attr*), railroad (*attr*: *US*), rail (*attr*). **2** *nm* railwayman.

ferryboat [feri'βot] *nm* (*SAm*: *angl*) ferryboat, railway ferry, train-ferry.

fértil *adj* fertile, fruitful, productive; rich (**en** in); imagination etc fertile.

fertilidad *nf* fertility; fruitfulness; richness.

fertilizante *nm* fertilizer.

fertilizar [1f] *vt* to fertilize; to make fruitful; to enrich.

férula *nf* (a) ferule, birch, rod. (b) (*Med*) splint. (c) (*fig*) rule, domination; **vivir bajo la** — **de un tirano** to live under the harsh rule (*or* jackboot) of a tyrant.

férvido *adj* fervid, ardent.

ferviente *adj* fervent.

fervor *nm* fervour, ardour, passion.

fervorosamente *adv* fervently, ardently, passionately.

fervoroso *adj* fervent, ardent, passionate.

festejar [1a] *vt* (a) *person* to feast, wine and dine; to entertain; to fête. (b) *occasion, anniversary etc* to celebrate. (c) *woman* to woo, court. (d) (*SAm*) to thrash.

festejo *nm* (a) feast; entertainment; (*Per*) revelry. (b) celebration; —**s** public festivities, rejoicings. (c) wooing, courtship.

festín *nm* feast, banquet.

festinar [1a] *vt* (a) (*CAm*) to feast, wine and dine; to entertain. (b) (*SAm*) to mess up, ruin (by being overhasty). (c) (*SAm*) to hurry along, speed up.

festival *nm* festival.

festivamente *adj* wittily, facetiously, humorously; jovially.

festividad *nf* (a) festivity, merrymaking. (b) (*Eccl*) feast, festivity; holiday. (c) wit, humour; joviality.

festivo *adj* (a) festive, merry, gay. (b) **día** — holiday. (c) witty, facetious, humorous; jovial; (*Lit etc*) humorous, comic, burlesque.

festón *nm* (*Sew*) festoon, scallop; (*of flowers*) garland.

festonear [1a] *vt* to festoon, scallop; to garland.

fetén (*sl*) **1** *adj* smashing (*sl*), super (*fam*); **una chica** — a smashing girl. **2** *nf*: **de** — smashing, super; **ser la** — (**y la chupén**) to be smashing; to be gospel truth.

fetiche *nm* fetish; (*fig*) mumbo jumbo, rigmarole.

fetichismo *nm* fetishism.

fetichista 1 *adj* fetishist. **2** *nmf* fetishist.

fetidez *nf* smelliness, rankness.

fétido *adj* foul-smelling, stinking, rank.

feto *nm* (a) foetus. (b) (*fam*) plain girl, ugly girl.

feúcho *adj* (*fam*) horribly ugly.

feudal *adj* feudal.

feudalismo *nm* feudalism.

feudo *nm* (a) (*Hist*) fief; manor. (b) (*Law*) — **franco** freehold.

feúra *nf* (*SAm*) (a) (in general) ugliness. (b) (**una** —) ugly person, ugly thing.

fiable *adj* reliable, trustworthy.

fiado *nm* (a) **al** — on trust, (*Comm*) on credit. (b) (*Law*) **en** — on bail.

fiador *nm* (a) (*person: Law*) surety, guarantor; (*Comm*) sponsor, backer; **salir** — **por uno** to go bail for someone, stand security for someone.

(b) (*Mech*) catch, fastener, pawl, trigger; (*of gun*) safety catch; (*of lock*) tumbler; (*of window*) fastener, bolt. (c) (*fam*) bottom. (d) (*Chi, Ec, Urug*) muzzle; (*Chi, Ec*) chinstrap.

fiambre 1 *adj* (a) (*Cook*) cold, served cold. (b) (*fam*) *news etc* old, stale. **2** *nm* (a) (*Cook*) cold meat, cold food; cold lunch, buffet lunch; —**s** cold meats, cold cuts (*US*). (b) (*fam*) corpse, stiff (*sl*); **el pobre está** — the poor chap is stone dead, the poor devil is cold meat now. (c) (*fam*) (piece of) stale news. (d) (*fam*) corny joke (*fam*). (e) (*Arg*) lifeless party, cold affair.

fiambrera *nf* (a) lunch basket, dinner pail (*US*). (b) (*RPl*) meat safe; icebox.

fiambrería *nf* (*SAm*) delicatessen store.

fianza *nf* (a) surety, security, bond; deposit; — **de aduana** customs bond; — **carcelera** bail. (b) (*person*) surety, guarantor.

fiar [1c] **1** *vt* (a) to entrust, confide (*a* to). (b) (*Fin etc*) to guarantee, vouch for; to stand security for; (*Law*) to go bail for. (c) (*Comm*) to sell on credit; (*SAm*) to buy on credit. **2** *vi* to trust (**en** in); **ser de** — to be reliable, be trustworthy. **3 fiarse** *vr*: — **de uno** to trust someone; to rely on someone, depend on someone; to confide in someone; **me fié completamente de ti** I trusted in you completely; **no me fío de él** I don't trust him; **nos fiamos de Vd para conseguirlo** we rely on you to get it.

fiasco *nm* fiasco.

fíat *nm*, *pl* **fíats** fiat.

fibra *nf* (a) fibre; — **artificial** man-made fibre; — **de vidrio** fibre-glass. (b) (in *wood*) grain; (*Min*) vein. (c) (*fig*) vigour, toughness; sinews; —**s del corazón** heartstrings.

fibravidrio *nm* fibre-glass.

fibrina *nf* fibrin.

fibroso *adj* fibrous.

ficción *nf* (a) fiction; (*pej*) invention, fabrication. (b) (*SAm*: *Lit*: *angl*) fiction.

ficcioso (*Chi*) **1** *adj* bluffing; false, double-dealing. **2** *nm* bluffer; double-dealer.

ficticio *adj* fictitious; imaginary; (*pej*) fabricated.

ficha *nf* (a) (*Tel etc*) token; (in *games*) token, counter, marker; (*Poker*) chip; (*Chess etc*) piece, man; (*Comm, Fin*) tally; — **de ajedrez** chessman; — **del dominó** domino. (b) card; index card, record card, catalogue card; — **antropométrica** card recording personal particulars; — **policíaca** police record, police dossier. (c) (*Elec*) plug. (d) (*Arg, CR, PR*) 5-cent piece. (e) (*Mex*) flat bottle cap. (f) (*Col, Cu, Ec, PR: also* **mala** —) rogue, villain.

fichaje *nm* (*Sport*) signing-up.

fichar [1a] **1** *vt* (a) *card* to file, index. (b) to file the personal particulars of; **le tenemos fichado** we have his record, (*fig*) we've got him taped (*fam*), we know all about him. (c) *domino* to play. (d) (*Sport etc*) to sign up, sign on (**en un club** for a club, with a team). (e) (*Cu*) to swindle. **2** *vi* (a) (*Sport etc*) to sign up, sign on; (in *factory etc*) to clock in. (b) (*Col*) to die.

fichero *nm* card index; filing cabinet; — **fotográfico de delincuentes** photographic records of criminals, rogues' gallery.

fidedigno *adj* reliable, trustworthy.

fideicomisario 1 *adj* trust (*attr*); **banco** — trust company. **2** *nm* trustee.

fideicomiso *nm* trust.

fidelería *nf* (*SAm*) noodles factory.

fidelidad *nf* (a) fidelity, loyalty (*a* to). (b) accuracy. (c) **alta** — (*Radio*) high fidelity; **de alta** — high-fidelity (*attr*), hi-fi.

fideo *nm* (a) (*fam*) lath, skinny person. (b) —**s** (*Cook*) noodles, vermicelli, spaghetti.

fiduciario 1 *adj* fiduciary. **2** *nm* fiduciary, trustee.

fiebre *nf* (a) (*Med*) fever; — **aftosa** foot-and-mouth disease; — **amarilla** yellow fever; — **entérica** enteric fever; — **glandular** glandular fever; — **del heno** hay fever; — **palúdica** malaria; — **reumática**

rheumatic fever; — **tifoidea** typhoid; **tener** — to have fever, be in a fever.

(b) (*fig*) fever; feverish excitement, fevered atmosphere; **la — del juego** the gambling fever.

(c) (*Arg, Chi*) shrewd person; tedious person.

fiel 1 *adj* (a) faithful, loyal; honest, reliable, trustworthy; **seguir siendo — a** to remain loyal to, remain true to.

(b) *account, translation etc* accurate, exact, faithful.

2 los —es *nmpl* (*Eccl*) the faithful.

3 *nm* (a) (*person*) inspector of weights and measures.

(b) (*Tech*) needle, pointer.

fielmente *adv* (a) faithfully, loyally; reliably. (b) accurately, exactly.

fieltro *nm* (a) (*material*) felt. (b) (*object*) felt, piece of felt; felt rug; felt hat; **— de la cerveza** beer mat.

fiera *nf* (a) wild beast, wild animal; (*Taur*) bull.

(b) (*fig*) fiend; virago, dragon; **es una — para el deporte** he's a fiend for sport, he's a sports fiend; **estar hecho una —** to be wild, be furious; **ella entró hecha una —** she came in absolutely furious.

(c) **— sarda** (*Col*) expert, top man.

fierecilla *nf* (*fig*) shrew; "**La — domada**" "The Taming of the Shrew".

fiereza *nf* (a) fierceness; ferocity; cruelty, frightfulness. (b) ugliness.

fiero 1 *adj* (a) fierce, ferocious; cruel; frightful. (b) ugly. **2 —s** *nmpl* threats, boasts; **echar —s, hacer —s** to utter threats, bluster, brag.

fierro *nm* (*SAm: in general*) iron; (*Agr*) marking iron, brand; (*Arg*) knife; (*Arg: Aut*) accelerator; (*Mex*) cent; **—s** (*Mex: fig*) money.

fiesta *nf* (a) (*in house*) party, entertainment; social gathering; celebration; (*in town*) festival, fête; **—s** public festivities, public rejoicings; **— de armas** (*Hist*) tournament; **la — brava, la — nacional** bullfighting; **organizar una — en honor de uno** to give a party in someone's honour; **¡se acabó la —!** (*fig*) drop it!, that's enough of that!, joke over!; **aguar la —** to spoil the fun, be a spoilsport; **estar en —s** to be en fête; **para coronar la —, por fin de —** to round it all off, as a finishing touch; **¡tengamos la — en paz!** none of that!; cut it out!

(b) (*Eccl*) feast, feast day; holiday; **—s** holidays; **— de la banderita** flag day; **— fija, — inmoble** immovable feast; **— de guardar, — de precepto** day of obligation; **F— de la Hispanidad, F— de la Raza** Columbus Day; **— movible** movable feast, movable holiday; **— nacional** public holiday, bank holiday; **F— del Trabajo** Labour Day; **mañana es — it's a holiday tomorrow; la — del santo** the saint's feast, the saint's day; **celebrar la —, guardar la —** to observe the feast (*de of*); **hacer —** to take a day off.

(c) merrymaking, festivities, fun and games; **las —s continuaron hasta muy tarde** the festivities went on very late; **estar de —s** to be in high good humour; **no estoy para —s** I'm in no mood for jokes.

(d) **—s** endearments; soothing words, flattering words, caresses; **hacer —s a** to caress, fondle; (*of dog*) to fawn on; (*fig*) to make a great fuss of.

fiestero *adj* gay; fun-loving, pleasure-seeking; fond of parties.

fifí *nm* (*SAm*) playboy, young man about town.

fifiriche *adj* (*CAm, Mex*) weak, sickly.

figón *nm* cheap restaurant.

figulino *adj*: **arcilla figulina** potter's clay.

figura *nf* (a) (*in general, Art etc*) figure; shape, form; image; **de — entera** full-length; **— de nieve** snowman.

(b) (*person*) figure; **una — destacada** an outstanding figure; **las principales —s del partido** the chief figures in the party; **cuando uno es —** when one is a famous person; **hacer —** to cut a figure.

(c) face.

(d) (*Geom etc, Typ*) figure, drawing, diagram; **— celeste** horoscope.

(e) (*Ling*) figure; **— retórica** rhetorical figure, figure of speech.

(f) (*Theat*) character, role; **en la — de** in the role of.

(g) (*Theat*) marionette.

(h) (*Cards*) picture card, court card; (*Chess*) piece, man.

(i) (*Dancing, Skating*) figure.

(j) (*Mus*) note.

figuradamente *adv* figuratively.

figurado *adj* figurative.

figurante *nm*, **figuranta** *nf* (a) (*Theat*) extra, walker-on, super(numerary). (b) (*fig*) figurehead.

figurar [1a] **1** *vt* to figure, shape, form; to represent.

2 *vi* (a) to figure (*como* as, *entre* among), appear; **los nombres no figuran aquí** the names do not appear here.

(b) (*fig*) to show off, cut a dash; **todo se debe al afán de —** it's all due to the urge to cut a dash, it's the urge to be somebody that causes it all.

3 figurarse *vr* to suppose; to imagine, fancy; to figure (*US*); **¡figúrate!, ¡figúrese!** just think!, just imagine!; **¡figúrate lo que sería con dos!** imagine what it would be like with two of them!; **ya me lo figuraba** I thought as much; **me figuro que es caro** I fancy it's dear, I imagine it's dear; **¿qué se figuran que me preguntó ayer?** what do you think he asked me yesterday?; **no te vayas a — que . . .** don't go thinking that . . .

figurativo *adj* figurative; *art* representational.

figurín *nm* fashion plate; model; dummy; (*Theat*) design for a costume.

figurina *nf* figurine, statuette.

figurinista *nmf* (*Theat*) costume designer.

figurón *nm* (a) grotesque figure, huge figure; **— de proa** (*Naut*) figurehead. (b) (*fam*) pretentious nobody; pompous ass.

figuroso *adj* (*Chi, Mex*) showy, loud.

fija *nf* (a) (*Tech*) hinge; (*Archit*) trowel.

(b) (*Chi, Per, RPl: Racing*) favourite; **es una —** (*RPl*) it's a cert (*sl*); **ésa es la —** that's for sure; **ésta es la —** this is it, this is the real thing.

fijacarteles *nm*, *pl* **fijacarteles** billposter.

fijación *nf* (a) (*act*) fixing; securing; fastening; sticking (on); posting; establishing. (b) (*Med*) fixation.

fijador *nm* (a) (*Phot*) fixer; fixing bath. (b) **— para el pelo** hair lotion, hair cream.

fijamente *adv* firmly, steadily, securely; fixedly; **mirar — a uno** to stare at someone, look hard at someone.

fijapelo *nm* hair lotion, hair cream.

fijar [1a] **1** *vt* (a) to fix; to secure, fasten (on, down *etc*); *stamp etc* to affix, stick (on), paste on, glue on; *poster* to post, stick, put up; *hair* to set; (*Phot*) to fix; *residence* to take up, establish; *eyes* to fix (*en* on); *attention* to focus, fix (*en* on).

(b) (*fig*) to settle (on), decide, determine; *date, hour, price etc* to fix, set; **la fecha no se puede — con precisión** the date cannot exactly be determined; **hemos fijado una hora** we have fixed a time, we have agreed on a time.

2 fijarse *vr* (a) to become fixed, get set; to settle, lodge; to establish oneself.

(b) to notice, pay attention; **lo malo es que no se fija** the trouble is he doesn't pay attention; **no me había fijado** I hadn't noticed; **fíjese bien** pay close attention, watch this carefully; **¡fíjate!** fancy that!, just imagine!

(c) **— en algo** to notice something, observe something, pay attention to something; to stare at something; **— en un detalle** to seize upon a detail; **¡fíjense en los precios!** just look at these prices!; **se fijó en mí** he fixed on me at once; **— en + infin** to be intent on + *ger*.

fijasello *nm* stamp hinge.

fijativo *nm* fixative.

fijeza *nf* firmness, stability; constancy; fixity; **mirar con — a uno** to stare at someone, look hard at someone.

fijo *adj* (a) fixed; firm, steady, stable, secure; *date, star, price etc* fixed; *look* fixed, steady; **de —** certainly, for sure.

(b) *purpose etc* fixed, firm.

(c) *staff* permanent, established.

fil *nm*: **— derecho** leapfrog.

fila *nm* (a) row, line; file; (*Sport, Theat etc*) row, tier (of seats); **una — de coches** a line of cars; **— india** single file, Indian file; **una chaqueta de dos —s** a double-breasted jacket; **en —** in a row; in a line; **en — de a uno** in single file; **ponerse en —** to line up, get into line.

(b) (*Mil*) rank; **las —s** (*fig*) the ranks; **¡en —s!** fall in!; **apretar las —s** (*fig*) to close ranks; **estar en —s** to be with the colours, be on active service; **llamar a uno a —s** to call someone up, call someone to the colours; **romper —s** to fall out, dismiss; **¡rompan —s!** dismiss!; **romper las —s** to break ranks.

(c) (*fam*) dislike, antipathy.

filacteria *nf* phylactery.

Filadelfia Philadelphia.

filamento *nm* filament.

filantropía *nf* philanthropy.

filantrópico *adj* philanthropic.

filántropo *nm*, **filántropa** *nf* philanthropist.

filarmónico adj philharmonic.
filatelia nf philately, stamp collecting.
filatélico adj philatelic.
filatelista nmf philatelist, stamp collector.
filático adj (Col) horse vicious; person mischievous; crafty; rude.
filete nm (a) (Archit) fillet.
  (b) (Mech) worm; (of screw) thread; (of bridle) snaffle bit.
  (c) (Cook) (meat) fillet, tenderloin, steak; (fish) fillet; **darse el —** (fam) to neck (fam), pet.
  (d) (Sew) narrow hem.
  (e) (Typ) ornamental bar (or line).
filfa nf (fam) (a) fraud, hoax; piece of humbug. (b) fake. (c) (Mech etc) dud, useless object.
filiación nf (a) filiation; (of ideas etc) connection, relationship. (b) personal description; characteristics.
filial 1 adj filial; (Comm) subsidiary, affiliated. 2 nf (Comm) subsidiary, affiliated company.
filibusterismo nm (SAm: Pol) filibustering.
filibustero nm pirate, freebooter.
filigrana nf (a) (Tech) filigree; filigree work; (Typ) watermark. (b) (Sport etc) delicate move, clever piece of play.
filípica nf harangue, tirade, philippic.
Filipinas: las —, las Islas — the Philippines.
filipino 1 adj Philippine. 2 nm, **filipina** nf Philippine, Filipino.
filisteísmo nm Philistinism.
filisteo 1 adj Philistine. 2 nm (a) (Bib) Philistine.
  (b) (fig) big man, giant.
film nm, pl **films** [film] (angl) film; picture, movie (US).
filmación nf filming, shooting.
filmador nm film maker.
filmadora nf film studio.
filmar [1a] vt to film, shoot.
filme nm (Acad)=**film**.
fílmico adj film (attr), movie (attr: US); screen (attr); **obras teatrales y fílmicas** theatrical and screen works, works for stage and screen.
filmina nf (Phot) slide, transparency.
filmlet nm, pl **filmlets** ['filmlet] short advertising film, short commercial film.
filmografía nf study of the film; **la — de la estrella** the star's film history, the star's screen history; **la — del Oeste** the history of the Western, films (collectively) about the West.
filmología nf science of film making, art of film making.
filmoteca nf film library, film archive.
filo[1] nm (a) edge; cutting edge, blade; dividing line; ridge; **— del viento** (Naut) direction of the wind; **de dos —s** double-edged (also fig); **al — de las 12** at about 12 o'clock; **por —** exactly; **de —** (Col) resolutely; **dar (un) — a**, **sacar el — a** to sharpen, put an edge on; **dar — a** (fig: Ec) to tell off, (SD) to wound with a knife; **herir a uno por los mismos —s** to pay someone back in his own coin; **pasar al — de la espada** to put to the sword.
  (b) (CAm, Mex) hunger.
  (c) (Arg: sl) tale, hoax.
  (d) (Arg: sl) suitor; girlfriend; courtship.
filo[2] nm (Bio) phylum.
filo[3] . . . philo . . ., eg **francófilo** nm, **francófila** nf francophile.
filocomunismo nm pro-communist feeling(s); fellow-travelling.
filocomunista 1 adj pro-communist; with communist leanings, fellow-travelling. 2 nmf pro-communist; fellow traveller.
filología nf philology.
filológico adj philological.
filólogo nm philologist.
filomela nf, **filomena** nf (poet) nightingale.
filón nm (Min) seam, vein, lode; (fig) rich seam, gold mine.
filongo nm (Arg) girlfriend (of inferior social status).
filoso adj (a) (CAm, Mex, RPl) sharp. (b) (Hond) hungry.
filosofal adj: **piedra —** philosopher's stone.
filosofar [1a] vi to philosophize.
filosofía nf philosophy; **— moral** moral philosophy; **— natural** natural philosophy; **— de la vida** philosophy of life.
filosófico adj philosophic(al).
filósofo nm philosopher.
filote nm (Col) ear of green maize; maize silk; **estar en —** (child) to begin to grow hair.
filotear [1a] vi (Col: of maize) to come into ear, begin to ripen; (of child) to grow hair.

filoxera nf phylloxera.
filtración nf filtration; seepage, leakage, loss.
filtrador 1 adj filtering. 2 nm filter.
filtrar [1a] 1 vt to filter; coffee etc to strain.
  2 vi and **filtrarse** vr (a) to filter; **— por** to filter through; to percolate (through); to seep through, leak through.
  (b) (fig: of money etc) to dwindle, disappear bit by bit.
filtro nm (a) (Tech) filter; (Cook) strainer; **— de aceite** oil filter; **— de aire** air filter; **— de café** coffee strainer; **cigarrillo con —** filter-tipped cigarette.
  (b) (Hist) love potion, philtre.
filudo adj (SAm) sharp.
filum nm (Bio) phylum.
filván nm featheredge; (on paper) deckle edge; (on knife) burr.
fimbria nf (Sew) border, hem.
fin nm (a) end; ending; conclusion; **"— de la cita"** "end of quote", "unquote"; **— de fiesta** (Theat etc) grand finale; **— de semana** weekend; **a —es del mes** at (or about) the end of the month; **hacia —es del siglo** towards the end of the century; **al —** finally, in the end; **al — y al cabo** at long last; **in the end**; after all, when all is said and done; **en —, por —** finally, at last; in short; **en —** (fig) well, well then; **jen —!** so that's that!, what next?; **en — de cuentas** in the last analysis; **sin —** (adv) endlessly; (adj: also Tech) endless; **correa sin —** endless belt; **un sin — de** see **sinfín**; **dar — a un discurso** to end a speech, close a speech; **llevar algo a buen —** to carry something through to a successful conclusion; **poner — a** to stop, put a stop to.
  (b) aim, purpose, objective; scope; **los —es de este estudio** the aims of this study; the scope of this study; **a — de + infin** in order to **+ infin**, so as to **+ infin**; **a — de que . . .** in order that . . ., so that . . .; **con el — de + infin** with the purpose of **+ ger**; **con —es deshonestos** with an immoral purpose.
finado 1 adj late, deceased; **el — presidente** the late president. 2 nm, **finada** nf deceased.
final 1 adj final, last; ultimate; eventual. 2 nm end; conclusion; (Mus) finale; **al — de la calle** at the end of the street; **por —** finally. 3 nf (Sport etc) final.
finalidad nf (a) object, purpose, intention; **la — de este libro** the aim of this book; **¿qué — tendrá todo esto?** what can be the purpose of all this?; **perseguir algo como —** to set something as one's goal.
  (b) (Philos etc) finality.
finalista nmf finalist.
finalizar [1f] 1 vt (a) to end, finish.
  (b) (Law) deed to execute.
  2 vi and **finalizarse** vr to end, finish, conclude; **finalizada la ceremonia . . .** once the ceremony was finished . . .
finalmente adv finally, lastly.
finamente adv politely; elegantly; acutely, shrewdly; subtly; delicately.
finamiento nm decease, demise, passing.
financiación nf financing.
financiar [1b] vt to finance.
financiero 1 adj financial; **los medios —s** the financial means; **el mundo —** the financial world, the world of finance. 2 nm financier.
financista nm (SAm) financier; financial expert.
finanzas nfpl finances.
finar [1a] 1 vi to pass away, die. 2 **finarse** vr to long, yearn.
finca nf (a) property; land, real estate; **— raíz** (Col) real estate.
  (b) country estate, country house; (SAm) farm; small rural holding; ranch; **— azucarera** sugar plantation; **— cafetera** coffee plantation; **cazar en — ajena** to poach (on somebody else's property); **penetrar en — ajena** to trespass (on somebody else's property); **tienen una — en Guadalajara** they have a country house (or property, estate) in Guadalajara; **pasan un mes en su —** they're spending a month at their country place.
fincar [1g] 1 vt (PR) to till, cultivate. 2 vi (Col, Mex, Per, RPl) **— en** to rest on, be based on.
finchado adj (fam) stuck-up (fam), conceited.
finés = **finlandés**.
fineza nf (a) (quality) fineness, excellence; purity; select quality.
  (b) (of manner) refinement; elegance.
  (c) (act) kindness, favour; courtesy, nice thing (to say or do etc); compliment; small gift, token.
fingidamente adv feignedly; in a sham way; as a piece of make-believe.
fingido adj feigned, false; fake, sham; mock; make-believe.

fingimiento nm pretence; simulation, feigning.

fingir [3c] **1** vt to sham, fake; to invent; to simulate; — **desinterés** to feign disinterest, pretend not to be interested; — **mucha humildad** to pretend to be very humble; **lo habrán fingido** I expect they invented it, I expect they faked it up.

2 vi to pretend, feign; — **dormir** to pretend to be asleep, to feign sleep.

3 fingirse vr: — **un sabio** to pretend to be an expert; — **dormido** to pretend to be asleep.

finiquitar [1a] vt account to settle and close, balance up.

finiquito nm (Comm, Fin) settlement.

finito adj finite.

finlandés 1 adj Finnish. **2** nm, **finlandesa** nf Finn. **3** nm (language) Finnish.

Finlandia f Finland.

fino adj (a) (in quality) fine, excellent; pure; fruit, wine etc choice, quality (attr); tobacco etc select; (Min) refined; **oro** — pure gold, refined gold.

(b) thin; person (in stature) slender, slight; fabric thin, delicate, sheer; slice thin.

(c) point sharp.

(d) person (in manner) polite, well-bred, refined; manners refined, cultured; compliment etc elegant, well-turned; **ponerse** — to turn on the charm.

(e) intelligence shrewd, acute, penetrating; taste fine, discriminating; hearing sharp, acute.

(f) distinction etc fine, subtle, delicate; irony subtle.

finta nf feint; **hacer** —s to feint, spar.

fintar [1a] vi, **fintear** [1a] vi (SAm) to feint, spar.

finura nf (a) fineness, excellence; purity; choiceness, high quality.

(b) politeness, courtesy, refinement; elegance; **¡qué** —! what refinement!, how charming!

(c) shrewdness, acuteness.

(d) subtlety, delicacy.

fiñe adj (Cu) small, weak, sickly.

fiordo nm fiord.

fique nm (Col, Mex, Ven) vegetable fibre, rope, cord.

firma nf (a) signature; (act) signing; **es de mi** — I signed that; **6 novelas de su** — 6 novels of his, 6 novels which he has written.

(b) (Comm, Fin) firm, company, concern.

firmamento nm firmament.

firmante 1 adj signatory (de to). **2** nmf signatory; **el abajo** — the undersigned.

firmar [1a] vti to sign; **firmado y lacrado, firmado y sellado** signed and sealed.

firme 1 adj (a) firm; steady, secure, stable; hard; solid, compact; colour fast; resistance firm; resolute; **estar en lo** — to be in the right; to be positive; **mantenerse** — to hold one's ground, not give way.

(b) (Comm, Fin) market steady; price firm, stable.

(c) person staunch, steadfast, resolute.

(d) (Mil) **¡**—**s**! attention!; **estar en posición de** —s to stand at attention; **poner** —s **a un pelotón** to bring a squad to attention; **ponerse** —s to come to attention.

(e) **de** — firmly, strongly; steadily; **batir de** — to strike hard; **resistir de** — to resist strongly; **trabajar de** — to work hard, work solidly.

(f) (Comm) **oferta en** — firm offer; **pedido en** — firm order.

2 nm roadbed, road foundation layer; road surface; "— **ondulado**" "uneven surface"; "— **provisional**" "temporary surface"; — **del suelo** rubble filling, rubble base (of floor).

firmemente adv (a) firmly; securely, solidly. (b) staunchly, steadfastly.

firmeza nf (a) firmness; steadiness, stability; solidity, compactness. (b) (Comm, Fin) steadiness. (c) (moral) firmness; steadfastness, resolution.

firuletes nmpl (SAm) elaborate adornment, flourishes; (in dance) gyrations, contortions.

fiscal 1 adj fiscal, financial; tax (attr); **año** — fiscal year, financial year.

2 nm (Law) prosecutor, counsel for the prosecution, district attorney (US); — **general** attorney-general.

(b) (fam) busybody, meddler.

fiscalía nf office of the public prosecutor.

fiscalizar [1f] vt (a) to control, oversee, inspect (officially). (b) (fig) to criticize, find fault with. (c) (fam) to pry into, meddle with.

fisco nm treasury, exchequer; **declarar algo al** — to declare something for tax purposes.

fisga nf (a) fish spear; (Guat, Mex: Taur) banderilla. (b) (fig) banter, chaff; **hacer** — **a uno** to tease someone, banter someone.

fisgar [1h] **1** vt (a) fish to spear, harpoon. (b) (fig) to pry into, spy on. **2** vi (a) to pry, snoop, spy. (b) to mock, scoff, jeer.

fisgón (fam) **1** adj (a) snooping, prying, nosey. (b) bantering, teasing; mocking. **2** nm, **fisgona** nf (a) snooper, nosey-parker. (b) banterer, tease; mocker.

fisgonear [1a] vt (fam) to be always prying into, spy continually on.

fisgoneo nm (fam) constant prying; chronic nosiness.

física nf physics; — **nuclear** nuclear physics; — **del estado sólido** solid-state physics.

físicamente adv physically.

físico 1 adj (a) physical.

(b) (Cu, Mex, SD) finicky; prudish; affected.

2 nm (a) physicist; (Med: arch) physician.

(b) (Anat) physique; appearance, looks; **de** — **regular** ordinary-looking.

físil adj fissile.

fisiología nf physiology.

fisiológico adj physiological.

fisiólogo nm physiologist.

fisión nf fission; — **nuclear** nuclear fission.

fisionable adj fissionable.

fisioterapia nf physiotherapy.

fisioterapista nmf physiotherapist.

fiso nm (SAm: sl) clock (sl), dial (sl).

fisonomía nf physiognomy, face; features.

fistol nm (a) (Mex) tiepin. (b) (fam) crafty fellow.

fístula nf fistule.

fisura nf fissure.

flaccidez nf flaccidity; softness, flabbiness.

fláccido adj flaccid; soft, flabby.

flaco 1 adj (a) thin, skinny, lean; **ponerse** — to get thin. (b) weak, feeble; memory bad, short; point, side weak. **2** nm weakness, weak spot, failing.

flacón adj (Arg, Mex, PR) very thin.

flacuchento adj (SAm) very thin.

flacura nf (a) thinness, skinniness. (b) weakness, feebleness.

flagelación nf flagellation, whipping.

flagelar [1a] vt (a) to flagellate, whip, scourge. (b) (fig) to flay, criticize severely.

flagelo nm (a) whip, scourge. (b) (fig) scourge, calamity.

flagrante adj flagrant; **en** — in the act, red-handed.

flamante adj (a) brilliant, flaming. (b) (fig) brand-new.

flameante adj flamboyant (also Archit).

flamear [1a] vi (a) to flame, blaze (up). (b) (Naut: of sail) to flap; (of flag) to flutter.

flamenco¹ nm (Orn) flamingo.

flamenco² 1 adj (a) Flemish.

(b) Andalusian gipsy (attr); **cante** — Andalusian gipsy singing.

(c) (pej) flashy, vulgar, gaudy.

(d) **ponerse** — (fam) to get cocky (fam); to get on one's high horse.

(e) (Hond, Mex, PR) = **flaco**.

2 nm, **flamenca** nf Fleming; **los** —s the Flemings, the Flemish.

3 nm (a) Andalusian gipsy singing and dancing, flamenco.

(b) (language) Flemish.

flamenquilla nf small marigold, tagetes.

flámula nf streamer.

flan mf cream caramel, caramel custard (dessert dish).

flanco nm (a) (Anat) side, flank. (b) (Mil) flank; **coger a uno por el** — to catch someone off guard.

Flandes m Flanders.

flanquear [1a] vt (a) to flank. (b) (Mil) to outflank.

flaquear [1a] vi to weaken, grow weak; (of effort) to slacken, flag; (of timber etc) to give way; (of health) to decline, get worse; (morally) to lose heart, become dispirited.

flaquencia nf (SAm) = **flacura**.

flaqueza nf (a) thinness, leanness; weakness; feebleness, frailty; **la** — **de su memoria** his poor memory; **la** — **humana** human frailty.

(b) (una —) failing, weakness; **las** —s **de la carne** the frailties to which the flesh is heir.

flash [flas] nm, pl **flashes** or **flashs** [flas] (a) newsflash. (b) (Phot) flash, flashlight; **con** — by flashlight.

flato nm (a) flatulence, wind. (b) (CAm, Col, Mex, Ven) gloom, depression; (Col, Cu, Guat, Ven) fear, apprehension.

flatoso adj (a) flatulent, windy. (b) (Cu) gloomy, depressed; (CAm, Ven) apprehensive.

flatulencia nf flatulence.

flatulento adj flatulent.

flatuoso adj flatulent, windy.

flauta 1 *nf* flute; **estar hecho una —** to be as thin as a rake.
  2 *nm* flautist, flute player.
  3 *interj* (*Chi, Per, RPl*) gosh! (*sl*); **¡la gran —!** my God!; **¡por la —!** (*Chi*) oh dear!
flautín *nm* piccolo.
flautista *nmf* flautist, flute player; **el — de Hamelin** the Pied Piper of Hamelin.
flebitis *nf* phlebitis.
fleco *nm* fringe, fringe curls; tassel; **—s** gossamer.
flecha *nf* arrow; dart; (*Col*) sling; **— de mar** squid; **— de dirección** (*Aut*) trafficator; **como una —** like an arrow, like a shot; **con alas en —** swept-wing, with swept-back wings.
flechar [1a] *vt* (a) *bow* to draw, stretch.
  (b) to wound (*or* kill) with an arrow, shoot (with an arrow).
  (c) (*fam*) to make a hit with, (*more formally*) inspire sudden love in.
  (d) (*Arg*) to prick (*esp* with a goad); (*of the sun*) to burn, scorch.
flechazo *nm* (a) arrow shot, bowshot; arrow wound; (*Col*) slingshot.
  (b) (*fam*) love at first sight; **con nosotros fue el —** with us it was love at first sight.
  (c) (*fam*) sudden illumination, revelation; **aquello fue el —** then it hit me, that was the moment of illumination.
flechero *nm* (a) archer, bowman; arrow maker. (b) quiver.
fleje *nm* iron hoop, metal band.
flema *nf* phlegm (*also fig*).
flemático *adj* phlegmatic, matter-of-fact, unruffled.
flemón *nm* gumboil.
flemudo *adj* slow, sluggish.
flequetería *nf* (*Col*) cheating, swindling.
flequetero *adj* (*Col*) tricky, dishonest.
flequillo *nm* fringe.
Flesinga Flushing.
fleta *nf* (*Col, Cu, PR, Ven*) (a) rub, rubbing. (b) thrashing.
fletamento *nm* charter, chartering; **contrato de —** chartering agreement.
fletar [1a] **1** *vt* (a) *plane, ship* to charter; to load, freight.
  (b) (*SAm*) *vehicle etc* to hire.
  (c) (*Arg, Chi, Per*) *insults* to let fly, utter; *blow* to deal.
  (d) (*Arg*) to fire (*fam*), sack (*fam*); to chuck out, remove by force.
  2 fletarse *vr* (a) (*Col, Cu, Mex*) to get out, beat it (*fam*); to slip away, get away unseen; (*Arg*) to gatecrash.
  (b) (*CAm*) to be annoyed, get cross.
  (c) (*Cu, Mex*) **salir fletado** to be off like a shot.
  (d) (*Chi*) **"se fleta"** (*notice*) "to let".
flete *nm* (a) charter; **vuelo —** (*angl*) charter flight.
  (b) freight, cargo; **salir sin —s** (*Col, Ven*) to leave in a hurry, leave.
  (c) freightage; (*SAm*) transport charges, carriage; (*SAm*) hire, hire charge, hiring fee.
  (d) (*Bol, Col, RPl*) fast horse; racehorse; (*Chi*) old nag.
  (e) (*Per*) lover, companion.
fletera *nf* (*Cu*) prostitute.
fletero 1 *adj* (a) charter (*attr*); freight (*attr*); **avión —** (*angl*) charter plane.
  (b) (*SAm*) hired, for hire; **camión —** lorry for hire.
  2 *nm* (a) (*SAm*) owner of vehicles for hire; owner of a transport business; collector of transport charges.
  (b) (*Ec, Guat*) porter.
flexibilidad *nf* flexibility; suppleness, pliability; compliant nature.
flexible 1 *adj* flexible; soft, supple, pliable; *hat* soft; *person* compliant. **2** *nm* (a) soft hat. (b) (*Elec*) flex, cord, wire.
flexión *nf* flexion; (*Ling*) inflexion.
flexional *adj* flexional, inflected.
flirt, *pl* **flirts** [flirt] (*fam: angl*) **1** *nmf* sweetheart; boyfriend, girlfriend; **la estrella vino con su — del momento** the star came with her current boyfriend.
  2 *nm* flirtation, (light-hearted, semi-serious) affair; **A tuvo un — con B** A had a brief affair with B.
flirteador *nm*, **flirteadora** *nf* (*fam*) flirt.
flirtear [1a] *vi* (*fam*) to flirt (*con* with), have a light-hearted affair (*con* with).
flirteo *nm* (*fam*) (a) (*in general*) flirting. (b) (*un —*) flirtation, (light-hearted, semi-serious) affair.
flojamente *adv* (a) loosely, slackly; limply. (b) weakly, feebly; lightly.

flojear [1a] *vi* to weaken; to slacken, ease up.
flojedad *nf* (a) looseness, slackness; limpness.
  (b) weakness, feebleness; lightness.
  (c) limpness, flaccidity.
  (d) poor quality.
  (e) slackness, laxity, negligence.
flojel *nm* (*on cloth*) nap; (*Orn*) down.
flojera *nf* (*fam*) =**flojedad**.
flojo *adj* (a) *rope etc* loose, slack; limp; *nut etc* loose.
  (b) *effort* weak, feeble; *wind* light.
  (c) (*in consistency*) soft, limp, flaccid.
  (d) *tea, wine etc* weak; *literary work etc* poor, thin, weak, feeble.
  (e) *student etc* poor, weak; slack, lax.
  (f) *price* low, weak; *market* slack, dull.
  (g) (*SAm*) lazy; timid, cowardly.
flor 1 *nf* (a) (*Bot*) flower, blossom, bloom; **— de harina** flour; **— de mano** artificial flower; **— del sol** sunflower; **en —** in flower, in bloom; **en plena —** in full bloom; **hijos como una —** lovely children; **de —** (*Cu, PR, Ven*) very good, splendid.
  (b) (*on plum etc*) bloom.
  (c) (*in leather*) grain.
  (d) (*fig*) flower, best part, cream; **la — y nata de la sociedad** the cream of society, the pick of society; **es la — de la canela** it's the very best, it's the tops (*fam*); **en la — de la edad** in the flower of one's youth; **en la — de la vida** in the prime of life; **frenar a uno en —** to cut someone off in his prime.
  (e) surface; **a — de** level with, on a level with; flush with; **on the surface of; a — del agua** at water level, close to the surface of the water; (*of flooded boat*) awash; **tiene el humorismo a — de piel** his humour is always ready to break out, his wit is never far below the surface; **los odios salen a — de piel** hatred comes out into the open, hatred comes to the surface.
  (f) compliment, nice thing (to say); **decir (*or* echar) —es a una** to pay pretty compliments to a girl, flirt with a girl.
  (g) **—es** (*Chi*) popcorn.
  2 *adj* (*SAm*) splendid, excellent.
flora *nf* flora.
floración *nf* flowering; bloom.
floral *adj* floral.
florar [1a] *vi* to flower, bloom.
florcita *nf* (*SAm*) little flower; **andar de —** (*Arg*) to live in idleness.
floreado *adj* (a) *fabric* flowery, flowered. (b) *bread* of the finest flour, top-quality. (c) (*Mus*) elaborate, with flourishes.
florear [1a] **1** *vt* (a) to adorn with flowers, add a flowery design to.
  (b) *flour* to sift.
  (c) *cards* to stack.
  2 *vi* (a) (*SAm*) to flower, bloom.
  (b) (*Mus*) to play a flourish, play elaborate variations.
  (c) to indulge in flowery compliments, flatter.
  3 florearse *vr* (*SAm*) to show off; to perform brilliantly.
florecer [2d] *vi* (a) (*Bot*) to flower, bloom. (b) (*fig*) to flourish, thrive; to flower.
floreciente *adj* (a) (*Bot*) in flower, flowering, blooming. (b) (*fig*) flourishing, thriving.
florecimiento *nm* (a) (*Bot*) flowering, blooming. (b) flourishing, thriving; flowering.
Florencia Florence.
florentino 1 *adj* Florentine, of Florence. **2** *nm*, **florentina** *nf* Florentine.
floreo *nm* (a) (*Fencing, Mus*) flourish. (b) witty but insubstantial talk; compliment, nicely-turned phrase; **andarse con —s** to beat about the bush.
florería *nf* florist's (shop).
florero *nm* (a) florist; (street) flower seller. (b) vase; flower stand. (c) (*Art*) flower painting. (d) flatterer, specialist in elegant compliments.
florescencia *nf* florescence.
floresta *nf* (a) wood, grove; glade; beauty spot; charming rural scene; (*Col*) forest, jungle. (b) (*Lit*) anthology.
florete *nm* (*Fencing*) foil.
floretear [1a] *vt* to decorate with flowers.
floretista *nmf* (*SAm*) fencer.
floricultura *nf* flower growing.
floridano, floridense, florideño 1 *adj* Floridian (*US*). **2** *nm*, **floridana** *nf*, **florideña** *nf* Floridian (*US*).
florido *adj* (a) *field etc* flowery, full of flowers. (b) (*fig*) choice, select. (c) *style* flowery, florid.
florilegio *nm* anthology.
florín *nm* florin.
florión *nm*, **floriona** *nf* (*Col*) =**fanfarrón**.

floripón nm (SAm), **floripondio** nm (SAm) (a) big flower (in pattern, decoration etc). (b) (Lit) rhetorical flourish, extravagant figure. (c) effeminate person.

florista nmf florist.

floristería nf florist's (shop).

florón nm (a) (Bot) big flower. (b) (Archit) fleuron, rosette. (c) (Typ) tailpiece.

flota nf (a) (Naut) fleet; shipping; — **mercante** merchant marine; **la — española** the Spanish fleet. (b) (Aer) fleet (of civil airline). (c) (Bol, Col etc) long-distance bus, inter-city bus. (d) (SAm) lot, crowd, heap; **una — de** a lot of, a crowd of. (e) (Col, Pan, Ven) boast, bluff; (Ven) lie; **echar —s** (Col, Pan, Ven) to brag.

flotación nf floating, flotation; see **línea**.

flotador nm (in most senses) float; (in cistern) ball-cock.

flotante 1 adj dock, ice, population, rib etc floating; part loose, hanging loose. 2 nm (Col) braggart.

flotar [1a] vi (a) to float. (b) (of part etc) to hang, hang loose; — **al viento** (of hair etc) to stream in the wind.

flote nm: **estar a** — to be afloat; **poner a** — to float, set afloat; (also **sacar a** —) to refloat, raise; **ponerse a** — (fig) to get back on one's feet, get out of a jam; **sostenerse a** — to keep afloat.

flotear [1a] vi: — **en el aire** to hover.

flotilla nf flotilla, fleet of small ships; line of vessels being towed, string of barges.

flox [flos] nm phlox.

fluctuación nf (a) fluctuation; **las —es de la moda** the fluctuations of fashion, the ups and downs of fashion. (b) uncertainty, hesitation.

fluctuante adj fluctuating.

fluctuar [1e] vi (a) to fluctuate. (b) to waver, hesitate.

fluente adj fluid, flowing.

fluidez nf (a) fluidity. (b) (fig) fluency, smoothness.

fluido adj (fig) fluent, free-flowing, smooth.

flúido 1 adj fluid. 2 nm (a) fluid. (b) (Elec) current, power.

fluir [3g] vi to flow, run; to pass.

flujo nm (a) flow; stream; flux; (Naut) rising tide, incoming tide; — **y reflujo** ebb and flood, (fig) ebb and flow. (b) (Med) — **de sangre** flow of blood, loss of blood, haemorrhage; — **de vientre** diarrhoea.

fluminense (SAm) 1 adj of Río de Janeiro. 2 nmf native (or inhabitant) of Río de Janeiro; **los —s** the people of Río de Janeiro.

fluorescencia nf fluorescence.

fluorescente adj fluorescent.

fluorización nf fluoridation.

fluoruro nm fluoride.

flus nm (Ant, Col, Ven) suit of clothes.

fluvial adj fluvial, river (attr); fish river (attr), freshwater (attr).

flux [flus] nm, pl **flux** [flus] (a) (Cards) flush; — **real** royal flush. (b) (CAm) stroke of luck. (c) (Ant, Col, Ven) suit of clothes. (d) (Arg, Mex) **estar a —, quedarse a** — not to have a shirt to one's back; **hacer** — to squander everything without paying one's debts.

fobia nf phobia.

—fobia -phobia, eg **agorafobia** nf agoraphobia.

—fobo -phobe, eg **francófobo** nm, **francófoba** nf francophobe.

foca nf seal; — **de trompa** sea elephant.

focal adj focal.

foco nm (a) (Math, Med, Phys etc) focus; focal point, centre; (of heat, light) source; (of fire) seat; **estar fuera de** — to be out of focus. (b) (Elec) floodlight; (Theat etc) spotlight; street lamp; (SAm) electric-light bulb. (c) (fig) centre, focal point.

focha nf coot.

foche (Chi) 1 adj smelly. 2 nmf dissolute person.

fodolí adj meddlesome.

fodongo adj (Mex) filthy, slovenly.

foete nm =**fuete**.

fofadal nm (Arg) bog, quagmire.

fofo adj (a) soft, spongy; porous; fluffy. (b) (fam) fat, plump.

fogaje nm (a) (SAm) scorching heat; sultry weather. (b) (Arg, Cu, Mex) heat rash; (PR) blush. (c) (Ec) fire, blaze.

fogarada nf, **fogarata** nf (Arg), **fogata** nf blaze, bonfire.

fogón nm (a) (Cook) stove, kitchen range; (Rail) firebox; (Naut) galley. (b) (of gun, machine) vent. (c) (Arg, CAm, Chi) fire, bonfire; hearth.

fogonazo nm (a) flash, explosion. (b) (Mex) coffee with brandy added.

fogonero nm (a) (Naut) stoker. (b) (Rail) foreman, stoker. (c) (Col) chauffeur.

fogosidad nf spirit, mettle; fire, dash, verve; fieriness, friskiness.

fogoso adj spirited, mettlesome; fiery, ardent; horse fiery, frisky.

fogueado adj (a) (SAm) expert, experienced. (b) (Col) weary.

foguear [1a] vt (SAm) to fire on.

foguerear [1a] vt (Cu, Chi) brushwood to burn off; bonfire to set light to.

foguista nm (RPl) =**fogonero**.

foja nf coot.

folgo nm foot muff.

foliación nf foliation, page numbering.

foliar [1b] vt to foliate, number the pages of.

folio nm (a) folio; leaf, sheet; (Typ) running title; **al primer** — (fig) at first glance; **en** — in folio; **libro en** — folio book. (b) (Col) tip.

folklore nm (a) folklore. (b) (fam) row, shindy; **se armó un** — there was a row.

folklórico adj folklore (attr); folk (attr), popular, traditional; **es muy** — it's very quaint, it's full of local colour; it is rich in historical interest.

folklorista 1 adj folklore (attr). 2 nmf folklorist, specialist in folklore, student of folklore.

folklorizar [1f] 1 vt to give a popular (or folksy) character to. 2 **folklorizarse** vr to acquire popular (or folksy) features.

follado nm (Col) petticoat.

follaje nm (a) (Bot) foliage, leaves; (Art) leaf motif. (b) (fig) excessive ornamentation; bombast, verbiage.

follar [1m] 1 vt to blow (on) with bellows. 2 vi (tabu) =**joder**. 3 **follarse** vr (tabu) to fart silently (tabu).

folletín nm newspaper serial.

folletista nmf pamphleteer.

folleto nm pamphlet; folder, brochure, leaflet.

follín nm (Chi) bad-tempered individual.

follisca nf (Ant, CAm, Col, Ven) confusion, shindy; brawl.

follón 1 adj (a) lazy, slack. (b) arrogant, puffed-up; blustering. (c) cowardly. (d) (Guat) dress roomy, loose; (Ven) dress short. 2 nm (a) (Bot) sucker. (b) good-for-nothing, layabout; conceited person. (c) noiseless rocket; (tabu) silent fart (tabu). (d) (fam) rumpus (fam), row, shindy; (of students) rag; **hubo** (or **se armó**) **un tremendo** — there was a hell of a row. (e) (Ec) skirt, petticoat. (f) (Cu, PR) drinking bout.

follonarse [1a] vr (Chi, Mex: tabu) to fart silently (tabu).

fomentación nf (Med) fomentation, poultice.

fomentar [1a] vt (Med) (a) to foment; to warm. (b) (fig) to promote, foster, encourage, foment; revolt to foment, stir up; production etc to boost. (c) (Cu, PR) business to found, promote.

fomento nm (a) (Med) fomentation. (b) promotion, fostering, encouragement, fomentation; **Ministerio de F—** ministry responsible for public works, agriculture etc.

fonda nf (Hist) inn, tavern; small restaurant; (Rail) buffet; (Chi) refreshment stall.

fondeadero nm anchorage; berth.

fondeado adj (a) (Naut) **estar** — to be anchored, be at anchor. (b) (SAm) **estar** — to be in the money, be well heeled (sl); **quedar** — (Arg) to be broke (fam).

fondear [1a] 1 vt (a) (Naut) depth to sound; ship to search; (fig) to examine. (b) (PR) to rape. (c) (CAm) to provide with money. 2 vi to anchor, drop anchor. 3 **fondearse** vr (a) (SAm) to get rich; to save for the future. (b) (SAm) to get drunk.

fondero nm (SAm) innkeeper; restaurant owner.

fondillos nmpl (a) seat (of trousers). (b) (SAm: Anat) seat, bottom.

fondilludo nm, **fondilluda** nf (SAm) person with a large backside, big ass (US: fam).

fondista nmf innkeeper; restaurant owner.

fondo nm (a) (of box, sea etc) bottom; (of room etc) back, far end; (as measurement) depth; **doble —, — falso** false bottom; — **del mar** bottom of the sea, sea bed, sea floor; **a** — (adj) thorough, (adv) thoroughly; **una investigación a** — a thorough investigation; **conocer algo a —** to know something thoroughly; **al — de** at the bottom of; at the back of; **de —** *race* long-distance (*attr*), endurance (*attr*); **de bajo —** shallow; flat; **en el —** (*fig*) at bottom; at heart; **en el — del corazón** deep down in one's heart; **sin —** bottomless; **dar —** to anchor; **echar un buque al —** to sink a ship; to scuttle a ship; **irse al —** to sink, founder, go to the bottom; **llegar al — de un misterio** to get to the bottom of a mystery.

(**b**) (*Art*) background, ground; (*Sew*) ground; **se ve una casa en el —** there is a house in the background.

(**c**) **bajos —s sociales** lowest strata of society, dregs of society.

(**d**) (*Comm, Fin*) fund; **—s** funds; money; finance; resources; **— de amortización** sinking fund; **—s bloqueados** frozen assets; **— de huelga** strike fund; **cheque sin —s** bad cheque; **estar sin —s** to have no money, be broke; **reunir —s** to get money together.

(**e**) (*fig*) fund, supply, reservoir; **tiene un — de alegría** he has a fund of cheerfulness.

(**f**) (*fig*) nature, disposition; **de —** jovial of cheery disposition; **tener buen —** to be good-natured.

fondongo *nm* (*Cu, Mex: Anat*) bottom.
fonducha *nf* (*Per*) =**fonducho**.
fonducho *nm* cheap restaurant.
fonema *nm* phoneme.
fonémico *adj* phonemic.
fonendoscopio *nm* stethoscope.
fonética *nf* phonetics.
fonético *adj* phonetic.
fonetista *nmf* phonetician.
fónico *adj* phonic.
fono *nm* (*Chi: Tel*) earpiece.
fonocaptor *nm* (*of gramophone*) pickup.
fonógrafo *nm* (*SAm*) gramophone, phonograph (*US*).
fonología *nf* phonology.
fonológico *adj* phonological.
fontanal *nm*, **fontanar** *nm* spring.
fontanería *nf* plumbing.
fontanero *nm* plumber.
footing ['futin] *nm, pl* **footings** ['futin] (*SAm: pseudo-angl*) walk, hike.
foque *nm* jib.
foquillos *nmpl* fairy lights.
forajido *nm* outlaw, bandit; desperado.
foral *adj* relative to the *fueros*, pertaining to the privileges of a town (*or* region).
foramen *nm* (*Mex*) hole.
foráneo *adj* foreign, strange.
forastero 1 *adj* alien, strange; exotic. **2** *nm*, **forastera** *nf* stranger; outsider; visitor; person from another part.
forcej(e)ar [1a] *vi* to struggle, wrestle; to make violent efforts; to flounder about.
forcej(e)o *nm* struggle; violent efforts; floundering.
forcejudo *adv* tough, strong, powerful.
fórceps *nm, pl* **fórceps** forceps.
forcito *nm* (*SAm*) little Ford (*vehicle*).
forense 1 *adj* forensic, legal; *see* **médico. 2** *nm* pathologist.
forestación *nf* afforestation.
forestal *adj* forest (*attr*); *see* **repoblación** *etc*.
forito *nm* (*SAm*) =**fotingo**.
forja *nf* (**a**) forge; foundry. (**b**) (*act*) forging.
forjado *adj* iron wrought.
forjar [1a] *vt* (**a**) to forge, shape, beat (into shape).

(**b**) to forge, shape, make; **— un plan** to make a plan, hammer out a plan; **tratamos de — un estado moderno** we are trying to build a modern state.

(**c**) (*pej*) to invent, think up, concoct; to forge.
forma *nf* (**a**) form, shape; **de — triangular** of triangular shape, triangular in shape; **en — de U** U-shaped, shaped like a U.

(**b**) (*Tech*) mould; block, pattern; hatter's block.

(**c**) (*Sport etc*) form; (*Med*) fitness; **estar en — to be in (good) form; to be fit; estar en plena —** to be on top form, be on the top of one's form; **ponerse en — to get fit.**

(**d**) way, means, method; **la única — de hacerlo es . . .** the only way to do it is . . .; **no hubo — de convencerle** there was no means of persuading him, it was impossible to persuade him; **— de pago** (*Comm*) manner of payment, method of payment; **de esta — in this way; de — que . . .** so that . . .; in such a way that . . .; **de todas —s** at any rate, in any case, anyway; **en debida —** duly, in due form; **ver la — de + infin** to see one's way to + *infin or ger*.

(**e**) **—s** social forms, conventions; **buenas —s** good manners.

(**f**) formula; **es pura —** it's just for form's sake, it's a mere formality.

(**g**) (*Typ*) format.

formación *nf* (**a**) formation. (**b**) (*Geol*) formation. (**c**) training, education; **sin la debida — erudita** without the proper scholarly training.
formado *adj* formed; grown; **bien —** nicely-shaped, well-formed; **hombre (ya) —** grown man.
formal *adj* (**a**) (*relating to shape*) formal.

(**b**) *matter* serious; official; *promise, statement etc* formal, express, definite; *manner* serious, earnest, inspiring confidence; *person* reliable, dependable; businesslike; steady, stable; (*in age*) adult, grown-up; *child* well-behaved; **es una persona muy —** he is a perfectly reliable sort; **¿has sido —?** (*to child*) did you behave yourself?; **¡estáte —!** behave yourself!; **siempre estuvo muy — conmigo** he was always very correct towards me.

(**c**) (*Col*) affable, pleasant.

(**d**) (*SAm: angl*) *dress etc* formal.
formaldehido *nm* formaldehyde.
formaleta *nf* (*CAm, Col, Mex*) bird trap.
formalidad *nf* (**a**) form, formality; established practice; **son las —es de costumbre** these are the usual formalities; **es pura —** it's a pure formality, it's just a matter of form; **hay muchas —es** there are a lot of formalities, there's a lot of red tape.

(**b**) seriousness; formal nature, express character; earnestness; reliability, dependable nature; steadiness, stability; (*of child*) good behaviour; **hablar con — to speak in earnest; ¡niños, —!** kids, behave yourselves!; **¡señores, un poco de —!** gentlemen, let's be serious!
formalina *nf* formalin(e).
formalismo *nm* conventionalism; (*pej: bureaucratic etc*) red tape, useless formalities.
formalista *nmf* formalist.
formalizar [1f] **1** *vt* to formalize; to formulate, draw up; to put in order, give proper form to, regularize; **— sus relaciones** to become formally engaged.

2 formalizarse *vr* (**a**) to grow serious.

(**b**) to take offence.
formalote *adj* (*fam*) stiff, serious.
formar [1a] **1** *vt* (**a**) to form, shape, fashion, make; *plan etc* to make, lay; *reserve, stock* to build up.

(**b**) to form, make up, constitute; **está formado por** it is formed by, it is made up of.

(**c**) *pupil etc* to train, educate.

(**d**) (*Mil*) to form up, parade.

2 *vi* (*Mil*) to form up, fall in; (*Sport*) to line up; **¡a —!** (*Mil*) fall in!; **los equipos formaron así: . . .** the line-up of the teams was: . . .

3 formarse *vr* (**a**) to form; to take form, begin to form; to shape, develop.

(**b**) to be trained, be educated; **se formó en la escuela de Praga** he was trained in the school of Prague.

(**c**) (*Mil*) to form up, fall in, get into line; (*Sport*) to line up; **¡fórmense!** fall in line!; **el equipo se formó sin González** the team lined up without Gonzalez; the team left out Gonzalez at the start.

(**d**) **— una opinión** to form an opinion; **¿qué impresión se ha formado?** what impression have you formed?
formativo *adj* formative.
formato *nm* (*Typ*) format; (*of paper*) size; **papel (de) — holandesa** (*approx*) foolscap; **periódico de — reducido** tabloid newspaper; **¿de qué — lo quiere?** what size do you want?
fórmico *adj*: **ácido — formic** acid.
formidable *adj* (**a**) formidable, redoubtable; huge; forbidding. (**b**) (*fig*) terrific (*fam*), tremendous (*fam*); **¡—!** that's great! (*fam*), splendid!
formón *nm* chisel.
fórmula *nf* (*Chem, Math, fig*) formula; (*Med etc*) prescription; **una — para conseguir el éxito** a formula to ensure success; **por pura —** just for form's sake, purely as a matter of form.
formulación *nf* formulation.
formular [1a] *vt* to formulate; to draw up, make out; *question* to frame, pose; *protest* to make, lodge; *claim* to file, put in.
formulario *nm* formulary (*also Pharm*), collection of formulae; form, blank; **— de inscripción, — de solicitud** application form; **— de pedido** (*Comm*) order blank, order form; **llenar un —** to fill in a form.
formulismo *nm* red tape; useless formalities.
fornicación *nf* fornication.
fornicador, fornicario 1 *adj* fornicating. **2** *nm* fornicator.
fornicar [1g] *vi* to fornicate.
fornicio *nm* fornication.
fornido *adj* well-built, strapping, hefty.
fornitura *nf* (*CAm, Mex, PR: angl*) furniture.

foro *nm* (a) (*Hist*) forum. (b) (*Law*) court of justice; (*fig*) bar, legal profession. (c) (*Theat*) back of the stage, upstage area.

forrado *adj* (a) (*Sew etc*) lined; — **de nilón** lined with nylon; **un libro** — **de pergamino** a book bound in parchment; **un coche** — **de** . . . a car upholstered in . . .

(b) (*fam*) well heeled (*sl*), moneyed.

(c) (*Arg*) **estar** — to know one's stuff (*for exam*).

forraje *nm* (a) forage, fodder. (b) (*act*) foraging. (c) (*fam*) hotchpotch, mixture.

forrajear [1a] *vi* to forage.

forrar [1a] **1** *vt* (*Sew etc*) to line (*de* with); to pad; *book* to cover (*de* with), bind (*de* in); *car* to upholster; (*Tech*) to line, face, cover; *pipe*, *tank* to lag.

2 forrarse *vr* (a) to line one's pockets; to make one's pile (*fam*).

(b) to stuff oneself (*fam*).

(c) (*Guat*, *Mex*) to get in provisions for a journey.

(d) (*Arg: Univ*) to prepare oneself well for an exam.

forro *nm* (a) (*Sew*) lining; padding; (*Typ*) cover; (*Naut*) sheathing; (*Tech*) lining; facing, sheathing; (*Aut*) upholstery; **con** — **de piel** with a fur lining, fur-lined; — **de freno** (*Aut*) brake lining; **ni por el** — not by a long shot.

(b) (*Arg*) rubber sheath.

(c) (*Cu*, *Chi*) swindle, fraud.

(d) (*Chi*) aptitude.

forsitia *nf* forsythia.

fortacho *nm* (*Arg*) strongly-built car, good car; old car, old crock.

fortalecer [2d] **1** *vt* (a) to strengthen; (*Mil*) to fortify.

(b) (*morally*) to encourage; *morale* to stiffen; — **a uno en una opinión** to encourage someone in a belief.

2 fortalecerse *vr* (a) to fortify oneself (*con* with).

(b) (*of belief etc*) to become stronger.

fortalecimiento *nm* (a) strengthening; fortification, fortifying. (b) encouragement; stiffening.

fortaleza *nf* (a) (*Mil*) fortress, stronghold. (b) (*quality*) strength, toughness, vigour; (*moral*) fortitude, resolution. (c) (*Chi*, *Mex*) nasty smell.

fortificación *nf* fortification.

fortificar [1g] *vi* to fortify; (*fig*) to strengthen.

fortín *nm* (small) fort; pillbox, bunker, blockhouse.

fortísimo *adj* *superl* of **fuerte**; (*Mus*) fortissimo.

fortuitamente *adv* fortuitously; accidentally; by chance, by coincidence.

fortuito *adj* fortuitous; accidental; chance (*attr*).

fortuna *nf* (a) fortune; chance; (good) luck; **mala** — misfortune; **por** — luckily, fortunately; **tener la** — **de** + *infin* to have the good fortune to + *infin*; **probar** — to try one's luck, have a shot.

(b) (*Naut*) **correr** — to weather a storm, ride out a storm.

(c) (*Fin*) fortune; wealth.

fortunón *nm* (*fam*) vast fortune, pile (*fam*).

forzadamente *adv* forcibly, by force; **sonreír** — to force a smile; **reírse** — to laugh in a forced way.

forzado *adj* forced; compulsory; **sonrisa forzada** forced smile; *see* **trabajo**.

forzar [1f *and* 1m] *vt* (a) to force, compel, make; — **a uno a hacer algo** to force someone to do something, make someone do something.

(b) *door etc* to force, break down, break open; *lock* to force, pick; *house* to break into, enter by force, force a way into; *blockade* to run; (*Mil*) to storm, take; to force a passage through; *woman* to ravish, rape.

(c) *ears*, *eyes* to strain.

forzosamente *adv* necessarily; inescapably; compulsorily; **tiene** — **que ser así** it must necessarily be so; **tuvieron** — **que venderlo** they had no choice but to sell it.

forzoso *adj* necessary; inescapable, unavoidable; compulsory; *landing* (*Aer*), *sale etc* forced; **es** — **que** . . . it is inevitable that . . .; **le fue** — **hacerlo** he was forced to do it, he had no choice but to do it.

forzudo 1 *adj* strong, tough, brawny. **2** *nm* (*in circus*) strong man; (*pej*) thug, tough (*fam*).

fosa *nf* (a) pit; grave; — **de reparaciones** (*Aut*) inspection pit; — **séptica** septic tank; — (**sub**)**marina** deep trough in the ocean bed.

(b) (*Anat*) fossa, fosse; cavity; —**s nasales** nasal cavities.

fosar [1a] *vt* to dig a ditch (*or* trench *etc*) round.

fosfato *nm* phosphate.

fosforecer [2d] *vi* to phosphoresce, glow.

fosforera *nf* matchbox.

fosforescencia *nf* phosphorescence.

fosforescente *adj* phosphorescent.

fosfórico *adj* phosphoric.

fósforo *nm* (a) (*Chem*) phosphorus.

(b) (*esp* S *Am*) match; (*Col*) percussion cap.

(c) (*Mex*) coffee laced with brandy.

(d) (*Arg*) intelligence, wit, shrewdness.

(e) (*Nic*, *Mex*) irritable person; hothead.

fosforoso *adj* phosphorous.

fosgeno *nm* phosgene.

fósil 1 *adj* fossil, fossilized. **2** *nm* fossil.

fosilizado *adj* fossilized.

fosilizarse [1f] *vr* to fossilize, become fossilized.

foso *nm* pit, hole; ditch, trench; (*Theat*) pit; (*Mil*) moat, fosse; entrenchment, defensive ditch; — **de agua** (*Sport*) water jump; — **de reconocimiento** (*Aut*) inspection pit; **irse al** —, **venirse al** — (*Theat*) to flop (*fam*), fail.

fostró *nm* (*Mus: angl*) foxtrot; (*PR*, *Ven*) riot, brawl.

fotingo *nm* (*SAm*) cheap car; old car, old crock.

foto *nf* photo; snap, snapshot; — **de conjunto** group photo; **sacar una** —, **tomar una** — to take a photo (*de* of); **ella saca buena** — she photographs well.

fotocalco *nm* photoprint.

fotocontrol *nm* photocontrol; **resultado comprobado por** — photo finish.

fotocopia *nf* photocopy, print.

fotocopiador *nm* photocopier.

fotocopiar [1b] *vt* to photocopy.

fotocromía *nf* colour photography.

fotoeléctrico *adj* photoelectric; **célula** *f* **fotoeléctrica** photoelectric cell.

fotogénico *adj* photogenic.

fotograbado *nm* photogravure, photoengraving.

fotografía *nf* (a) (*in general*) photography; — **aérea** aerial photography; — **en colores** colour photography.

(b) (*una* —) photograph; — **en colores** colour photograph; — **al flash**, — **al magnesio** flashlight photograph; — **instantánea** snapshot; "— **de X**" (*caption*) "photographed by X"; **hacer una** — **de** to take a photograph of, photograph; *see also* **foto**.

fotografiar [1c] *vt* to photograph.

fotográficamente *adv* photographically.

fotográfico *adj* photographic.

fotógrafo *nm*, **fotógrafa** *nf* photographer; — **aficionado** amateur photographer; — **de prensa** press photographer.

fotograma *nm* (*Cine*) shot.

fotogrametría *nf*: — **aérea** aerial photography, map-making from the air.

fotómetro *nm* exposure meter, light meter, photometer.

fotón *nm* photon.

fotosíntesis *nf* photosynthesis.

fotostatar [1a] *vt* to photostat.

fotostato *nm* photostat.

fototeca *nf* collection of photographs.

fototopografía *nf* = **fotogrametría**.

fototropismo *nm* phototropism.

foul [faul] **1** *interj* (*Sport*: *angl*) foul! **2** *nm* (SAm: *angl*) foul.

fox [fos] *nm*, *pl* **fox** [fos] foxtrot.

frac *nm*, *pl* **fracs** *or* **fraques** dress coat, tails.

fracasado 1 *adj* failed; unsuccessful. **2** *nm*, **fracasada** *nf* failure, person who is a failure.

fracasar [1a] *vi* to fail, be unsuccessful; (*of plan etc*) to fail, come to grief, fall through.

fracaso *nm* failure; fiasco; collapse, breakdown; — **sentimental** disappointment in love, disastrous love affair; **el** — **de las negociaciones** the failure of the negotiations, the breakdown of the talks; **es un** — **total** it's a complete disaster.

fracción *nf* (a) (*Math*) fraction; — **decimal** fraction.

(b) fraction, part, fragment.

(c) (*Pol etc*) faction, splinter group.

(d) (*act*) division, breaking-up (*en* into).

fraccionamiento *nm* (a) division; breaking-up (*en* into). (b) (*Mex*) real-estate development.

fraccionar [1a] *vt* to divide, break up, split up (*en* into).

fraccionario *adj* fractional.

fractura *nf* fracture (*also* Med), break; — **complicada** compound fracture.

fracturar [1a] **1** *vt* to fracture, break. **2 fracturarse** *vr* to fracture, break.

fragancia *nf* fragrance, sweet smell, perfume.

fragante *adj* (a) fragrant, sweet-smelling, scented. (b) = **flagrante**.

fragata *nf* frigate.

frágil *adj* fragile, frail; (*Comm*) breakable; (*fig*) frail, delicate.

fragilidad *nf* fragility, frailty; (*fig*) frailty, delicacy.

fragmentario *adj* fragmentary.

fragmento nm fragment; piece, bit.
fragor nm din, clamour, noise; uproar; crash, clash; (of machine, river etc) roar.
fragoroso adj deafening, thunderous.
fragosidad nf (a) roughness, unevenness; difficult nature; denseness. (b) (una —) rough spot; rough road.
fragoso adj rough, uneven; terrain difficult; wood dense.
fragua nf forge.
fraguado nm (a) forging. (b) hardening, setting.
fraguar [1i] 1 vt (a) to forge. (b) (fig) to hatch, concoct; to plot. 2 vi (of cement etc) to harden, set.
fraile nm (a) friar; monk; (fam and pej, any) priest; — descalzo barefooted friar; — mendicante mendicant friar (gen Franciscan); — de misa y olla ignorant friar, simple-minded friar; — predicador friar preacher (gen Dominican).
  (b) (Cu) bagasse, residue of sugar cane.
frailecillo nm (Orn) puffin.
frailería nf friars (collectively); monks (collectively); (pej) priests.
frailesco adj, **fraileuno** adj (pej) monkish.
frambuesa nf raspberry.
frambueso nm raspberry cane.
francachela nf (fam) spread (fam), big feed (fam); spree (fam), binge (sl), jamboree (sl).
francachón adj (SAm) too direct, too outspoken, bad-mannered.
francamente adv (a) frankly, openly, forthrightly.
  (b) generously, liberally.
  (c) frankly; really, definitely; — no lo sé frankly I don't know, I really don't know; eso está — mal that is definitely wrong; es una obra — divertida it's a really funny play; estoy — harto contigo I'm frankly fed up with you, I really am fed up with you.
francés 1 adj French; a la francesa in the French manner (or style etc); despedirse a la francesa to take French leave.
  2 nm Frenchman.
  3 nm (language) French.
francesa nf Frenchwoman.
francesilla nf (a) (Bot) buttercup. (b) (Cook) roll.
Francia f France.
fráncico 1 adj Frankish. 2 nm (language) Frankish.
Francisca f Frances.
franciscano 1 adj Franciscan. 2 nm Franciscan.
Francisco m Francis.
francmasón nm (free)mason.
francmasonería nf (free)masonry.
franco[1] (Hist) 1 adj Frankish. 2 nm Frank.
franco[2] (Fin) franc.
franco[3] adj (a) frank, open, forthright, candid; seré — contigo I will be frank with you, I will be plain with you; son francas imposibilidades they are plain impossibilities, they are downright impossible; estar en franca rebeldía to be in open rebellion; estar en franca decadencia to be in full decline.
  (b) generous, liberal.
  (c) (Comm etc) free, gratis; exempt; road etc free, open; port etc free; — a bordo free on board; — de derechos duty-free; — de porte (Comm) carriage-free, (Post) post-free; — sobre vagón free on rail.
  (d) (SAm) on leave (from military service or duties).
franco ... franco ...
francocanadiense 1 adj French-Canadian. 2 nmf French-Canadian.
francófilo nm, **francófila** nf francophile.
francófobo nm, **francófoba** nf francophobe.
franco-hispano adj Franco-Spanish.
francote adj outspoken, blunt, bluff.
francotirador nm sniper, sharpshooter.
franchute nm, **franchuta** nf (fam: pej) Frenchy (fam), frog (fam).
franela nf (a) flannel. (b) (Col, Cu, PR, Ven) vest, undershirt (US).
frangollar [1a] 1 vt (a) to bungle, botch, rush. (b) (Chi, RPl) corn to grind. 2 vi (Bol) to dissemble.
frangollero adj (Arg, Bol) bungling.
frangollo nm (a) (Cook: SAm) crushed and boiled corn, wheat porridge; (Ant) sweet made from mashed bananas; (Arg, Cu, Mex, Per, PR) hastily-prepared meal.
  (b) (SAm: Orn) birdseed.
  (c) (Mex) muddle, mess; mixture.
frangollón (SAm) 1 adj bungling. 2 nm bungler.
franja nf (a) (Sew) fringe, border, trimming; braid.
  (b) fringe, strip, band; — fotoacústica sound track; — de tierra strip of land; la — de Gaza the Gaza strip.
franj(e)ar [1a] vt to fringe, trim (de with).
franqueadora nf (Post) franking machine.

franquear [1a] 1 vt (a) slave to free, liberate; taxpayer etc to free, exempt (de from).
  (b) right etc to grant, allow, concede (a to).
  (c) road, way to clear, open.
  (d) river etc to cross; obstacle to negotiate, overcome, get round.
  (e) (Post) to frank, stamp; to pay postage on; una carta franqueada a post-paid letter, a letter with the postage paid on it; una carta insuficientemente franqueada a letter with insufficient postage.
  2 **franquearse** vr (a) to give way, fall in with someone's wishes.
  (b) — a uno, — con uno to unbosom oneself to someone, have a heart-to-heart talk with someone.
franqueo nm postage; franking; con — insuficiente with insufficient postage, with postage underpaid.
franqueza nf (a) frankness, openness, forthrightness, candidness; con — frankly; lo digo con toda — I say so quite frankly. (b) generosity, liberality.
franquía nf (Naut) searoom, room to manoeuvre.
franquicia nf exemption (de from); — aduanera exemption from customs duties; — postal privilege of franking letters.
franquista 1 adj pro-Franco; tendencia — tendency to support Franco, pro-Franco tendency; es una familia muy — it is a strongly pro-Franco family, it is a family which strongly supports Franco.
  2 nmf supporter of Franco, pro-Franco person.
frasca nf (a) dry leaves, small twigs. (b) (CAm, Mex) riotous party.
frasco nm (a) flask, bottle; — de campaña (SAm) water bottle; — de perfume scent bottle; — al vacío vacuum flask.
  (b) liquid measure (Cu = 2.44 litres, Arg = 21.37 litres).
frase nf (a) (Gram) sentence; — compleja complex sentence. (b) (Ling) phrase, expression; — hecha saying, proverb; idiom; (pej) cliché, stock phrase.
fraseo nm (Mus) phrasing.
fraseología nf phraseology.
fratás nm plastering trowel.
fraterna nf (fam) ticking-off.
fraternal adj brotherly, fraternal.
fraternidad nf brotherhood, fraternity; (CAm, PR: Univ) fraternity.
fraternización nf fraternization.
fraternizar [1f] vi to fraternize.
fraterno adj brotherly, fraternal.
fratricida 1 adj fratricidal. 2 nmf fratricide (person).
fratricidio nm fratricide (act).
fraude nm (a) (quality) dishonesty, fraudulence. (b) (act) fraud, swindle; deception; por — by fraud, by false pretences.
fraudulencia nf fraudulence.
fraudulentamente adv fraudulently, by fraud; dishonestly.
fraudulento adj fraudulent; dishonest, deceitful.
fray nm (Eccl: before names) brother, friar.
frazada nf blanket.
frecuencia nf (a) frequency; con — frequently, often.
  (b) (Elec, Radio) frequency; alta — high frequency; de alta — high-frequency (attr).
frecuentador nm, **frecuentadora** nf frequenter.
frecuentar [1a] vt to frequent; to haunt.
frecuente adj frequent; common; custom etc common, usual, prevalent; (pej) rife.
frecuentemente adv frequently, often.
fregada nf (Arg, CAm, Mex) nuisance; misfortune, untoward event.
fregadera nm (SAm) nuisance, annoyance.
fregadero nm (a) (kitchen) sink. (b) scullery. (c) (CAm, Mex) constant nuisance; recurrent misfortune.
fregado 1 adj (a) (SAm) tiresome, annoying.
  (b) (SAm) affair nasty, messy, dishonest.
  (c) (SAm) silly, stupid.
  (d) (Col, Guat, Mex, Pan, Per) cunning, sly.
  (e) (Pan, Per, PR) pigheaded.
  (f) (PR) brazen, fresh.
  2 nm (a) rubbing, scrubbing, scouring; washing-up; hacer el — to do the washing-up, wash up.
  (b) mess, messy affair; nasty affair, dishonest deal.
  (c) (SAm) row, tiff; tener un — con uno to have a row with someone.
  (d) (fam) dar un — a uno to give someone a dressing down.
  (e) (Chi, Col, Per) es un — he's a dead loss.
fregador nm (a) sink. (b) dishcloth; scourer; mop.
fregadura nf (a) = fregado 2 (a). (b) (Chi) = fregada.
fregancia nf (Col) = fregada.
fregandera nf (Mex) charwoman, cleaner.
fregantina nf (Bol, Col, Chi, Per) = fregada.

fregar [1h *and* 1k] *vt* (a) to rub, scrub; to scour; *floor* to mop, scrub; *dishes* to wash (up).
(b) (*SAm*) to bother, annoy; to worry, harass; ¡no me fregue! stop bothering me!
(c) (*Cu, PR*) to thrash; (*Sport*) to beat, thrash.
fregasuelos *nm, pl* **fregasuelos** mop.
fregazón *nm* (*Chi*) =**fregada**.
fregón *adj* (a) (*Bol, CAm, Col, Ec, Mex*) trying, tiresome, annoying. (b) (*SAm*) silly, stupid. (c) (*Ec, PR*) brazen, fresh.
fregona *nf* kitchen maid, dishwasher; (*pej*) skivvy; (*PR*) shameless hussy.
freidera *nf* (*Cu*) frying pan.
freiduría *nf* (*also* — de pescado) fried-fish shop.
freír [3m; *ptp* **frito**] 1 *vt* (a) (*Cook*) to fry; (*fig: of sun*) to burn, fry; al — será el reír the proof of the pudding is in the eating.
(b) (*fig*) to annoy; to torment; to bore.
2 **freírse** *vr* (a) (*Cook*) to fry, be frying; — de calor to fry in the heat, be roasted.
(b) —la a uno (*fam*) to plan to deceive someone.
fréjol *nm* =**frijol**.
frenaje *nm* (*Aut*) braking.
frenar [1a] *vt* (a) (*Aut, Mech*) to brake; to put the brake on, apply the brake to. (b) (*fig*) to check, curb, restrain.
frenesí *nm* frenzy.
frenéticamente *adv* frantically, frenziedly; furiously, wildly.
frenético *adj* frantic, frenzied; furious, wild.
freno *nm* (a) (*Aut, Mech etc*) brake; — de aire air brake; — de mano handbrake; — de pedal footbrake; poner el —, echar los —s to put the brake(s) on, apply the brake(s); soltar el — to release the brake.
(b) (*horse's*) bit; bridle; morder (*or* tascar) el — (*fig*) to stop before going too far.
(c) (*fig*) check, curb, restraint; —s y contrapesos, —s y equilibrios (*Pol*) checks and balances; poner — a to curb, check; poner — a las malas lenguas to stop the gossip.
(d) (*Arg*) hunger.
frenología *nf* phrenology.
frenólogo *nm* phrenologist.
frentazo *nm* (*Arg, Mex*) rebuff, disappointment; pegarse un — to suffer a disappointment; to have things turn out badly for one.
frente 1 *nm* (a) front, front part; face; (*Archit*) front, face, façade; — de arranque, — de trabajo (*Min*) working face; al — in front (*de* of); al — de (*fig*) in charge of, at the head of; ¡de — (mar)! forward march!, by the right quick march!; ir de — to go forward; to face forwards; chocar de — to crash head-on; atacar de — to make a frontal attack; viajar de — a la marcha (*Rail*) to travel facing the engine; marchar 6 de — to march 6 abreast; en — opposite; in front; la casa de en — the house opposite; estar — por — de to be directly opposite; hacer — a to resist, stand up to, face; hacer — a unos grandes gastos to (have to) meet considerable expenses; hacer — a un temporal (*Naut*) to weather a storm.
(b) (*Mil*) front; — de batalla battle front, firing line; — del oeste western front; cambiar de — to wheel.
(c) (*Pol*) front; — popular popular front; hacer un — común con uno to make common cause with someone.
(d) (*Meteorol*) front; — frío cold front.
2 *nf* forehead, brow; face; — a — face to face; arrugar la— to knit one's brow, frown; llevarlo escrito en la — to make no effort to hide one's feelings.
3 *prep*: — a opposite (to), facing; in front of; (*fig*) as opposed to, as contrasted with.
freo *nm* channel, strait.
fresa *nf* (a) (*Bot*) strawberry (*esp wild*); strawberry plant. (b) (*Tech*) milling cutter; (*dentist's*) drill, bit.
fresado *nm* (*Mech*) milling.
fresadora *nf* (*Mech*) milling machine; — de roscar thread cutter.
fresal *nm* strawberry bed.
fresar [1a] *vt* (*Mech*) to mill.
fresca *nf* (a) fresh air, cool air; cool part of the day; tomar la — to get some fresh air, go out for a breath of air.
(b) (*fam*) decir cuatro —s a uno to give someone a piece of one's mind.
(c) (*fam*) shameless woman, brazen woman; ¡es una —! she's a hussy!, she's quite brazen!
frescachón *adj* (a) glowing with health, ruddy; robust. (b) *child* bouncing, healthy. (c) *woman* buxom. (d) (*Naut*) *breeze* fresh, stiff.

frescales *nm, pl* **frescales** (*fam*) rogue; brazen person, cheeky sort.
fresco 1 *adj* (a) fresh; new, recent; *bread* new; *egg* new-laid; cosas todavía frescas en la memoria things still fresh in the memory.
(b) cool; agua fresca cold water; bebida fresca cool drink, cooling drink, cold drink; hacer — (*Meteorol*) to be cool, be fresh.
(c) *cloth*, dress light, thin.
(d) *complexion* fresh, ruddy, healthy.
(e) cool, calm, unabashed; tan — quite unabashed, quite unconcerned; me lo dijo tan — he said it to me as cool as you please; estar más — que una lechuga to be as cool as a cucumber.
(f) (*fam*) cool, fresh; cheeky, saucy; bad-mannered; ¡qué —! what cheek!, what a nerve!; ponerse — con una to get fresh with a girl.
2 *nm* (a) fresh air, cool air; al — in the open air, out of doors; tomar el — to get some fresh air, go for a stroll in the open; ¡vete a tomar el —! (*fam*) get lost! (*fam*).
(b) (*Archit, Art*) fresco; pintar al — to paint in fresco.
(c) (*fam*) fresh guy (*US fam*), shameless individual; bad-mannered person; ¡Vd es un —! you've got a nerve!; mind your manners!
(d) (*SAm*) echar — a uno to tell someone a few home truths.
frescor *nm* freshness; coolness; gozar del — nocturno to enjoy the cool night air.
frescote *adj* blooming; buxom.
frescura *nf* (a) freshness; coolness; (*of complexion*) freshness.
(b) coolness, calmness, unconcern; con la mayor — with the greatest unconcern, completely unconcerned.
(c) (*fam*) cheek, sauce, nerve; ¡qué —! what a nerve!; tiene la mar de — he's got the cheek of the devil.
(d) (*fam*) impudent remark, cheeky thing (to say); me dijo unas —s he said some cheeky things to me.
fresia *nf* freesia.
fresnada *nf* ash grove.
fresno *nm* ash, ash tree.
fresón *nm* strawberry (*esp cultivated*); strawberry plant.
fresquera *nf* meat safe; icebox.
fresquería *nf* (*SAm*) refreshment stall, ice-cream parlour.
freudiano *adj* Freudian.
freza *nf* (a) (*Fish*) spawn; (*act, season*) spawning. (b) (*Zool*) dung, droppings.
frezar [1f] *vi* to spawn.
friable *adj* friable.
frialdad *nf* (a) coldness, cold, chilliness. (b) (*fig*) coldness, coolness; indifference, unconcern. (c) (*Mex*) impotence; frigidity.
fríamente *adv* (*fig*) coldly.
frica *nf* (*Chi*) beating.
fricasé *nm* fricassee.
fricativa *nf* fricative.
fricativo *adj* fricative.
fricción *nf* rub, rubbing; (*Med*) massage; (*Mech*) friction; (*fig: Pol etc*) friction, trouble.
friccionar [1a] *vt* to rub; (*Med*) to rub, massage.
friega *nf* (a) rub, rubbing; (*Med*) massage.
(b) (*SAm*) nuisance, annoyance; bother; fuss.
(c) (*Arg, Col, CR, Mex, Per, PR*) silliness, stupidity.
(d) (*Arg, Cu, Chi, Per, PR*) thrashing.
(e) (*Mex, Per*) ticking-off.
friegaplatos *nm, pl* **friegaplatos** dishwasher (*person*).
frígano *nm* caddis fly.
frigidaire *nm or f* (*SAm: angl*) refrigerator.
frigidez *nf* frigidity (*also Med*).
frígido *adj* frigid (*also Med*).
frigo *nm* (*fam*) fridge (*fam*), refrigerator.
frigocentral *nm* (*Arg*) refrigeration plant.
frigorificación *nf* (*Arg*) refrigeration.
frigorífico 1 *adj* refrigerating, cold-storage (*attr*); camión — refrigerator lorry, refrigerator truck (*US*); instalación frigorífica cold-storage plant.
2 *nm* refrigerator; (*RPl*) cold-storage plant, meat-packing depot; (*Naut*) refrigerator ship.
frijol *nm*, **frijol** *nm* (a) (*Bot*) kidney bean, French bean.
(b) —es (*SAm*) food (*in general*); meterse los —es (*Cu*) to eat, have a meal.
(c) (*Mex*) taunt; —es (*Mex*) boasts.
(d) ¡—es! (*Cu, PR*) certainly not!, rubbish!
(e) (*Mex, Per*) coward.

fringolear [1a] *vt* (*Chi*) to thrash, beat.
frío 1 *adj* (a) cold; chilly; **más — que el hielo** (*etc*) as cold as charity.
  (b) *bullet* spent.
  (c) (*fig*) cold, unconcerned, unmoved, indifferent; *reception etc* cool, frigid; **¡me deja Vd —!** you amaze me!; **eso me deja —** that leaves me cold.
  2 *nm* (a) cold; coldness; **¡qué —! isn't it cold!**, how cold it is!; **hace —** it's cold; **hace mucho —** it's very cold; **coger —** to catch cold; **pasar —** to be cold, suffer cold; **tener —** to be cold, feel cold; **no me da ni — ni calor** it's all the same to me; *see* **helador** *etc*.
  (b) (*fig*) coldness, indifference.
  (c) **—s** (*CAm, Col, Ec, Mex*) intermittent fever; malaria.
friolento *adj* person chilly, sensitive to cold, shivery.
friolera *nf* trifle, mere nothing.
friolero *adj* = **friolento**.
frisa *nf* (a) (*fabric*) frieze.
  (b) (*Bol, Chi, RPl*) nap (on cloth); (*Chi*) fluff; (*PR, SD*) blanket; **sacar a uno la —** (*Chi*) to tan someone's hide (*fam*); **sacar la — a algo** (*Chi*) to extract the maximum advantage from something.
frisar [1a] **1** *vt* cloth to frizz, rub. **2** *vi:* **— en** to border on, be close to; **frisa en los 50** she's close on 50, she's getting on for 50.
Frisia *f* Friesland.
friso *nm* frieze; wainscot, dado.
fritada *nf* fry, fried dish.
fritanga *nf* (a) (*SAm: Cook*) fried food; frying. (b) (*Chi*) kitchen; stove; (*Mex*) portable stove. (c) (*Chi*) nuisance, bother.
fritar [1a] *vt* (*Arg, CAm, Col, Ven*) to fry.
frito 1 *adj* (a) (*Cook*) fried.
  (b) **tener — a uno** (*fam*), **traer — a uno** (*fam*) to worry someone to death; to defeat someone; to make someone cross; **ese hombre me trae —** that chap bothers me all day long, that chap makes me really cross; **las matemáticas me traen —** maths is getting me down, maths just defeats me.
  (c) (*Arg, Cu*) **estar —** to be finished, be done for.
  2 *nm* (a) fry, fried dish; **—s variados** mixed grill.
  (b) (*Ven*) daily bread; food (*in general*); **ganarse el —** to earn a living.
  (c) (*Arg, Ven*) **a esa mujer le gusta el —** she's no angel (though she may try to look like one).
fritura *nf* (a) fry, fried dish. (b) fritter.
frívolamente *adv* frivolously.
frivolidad *nf* frivolity, frivolousness.
frivolité *nm* (*Sew:* gall) tatting.
frívolo *adj* frivolous.
fronda *nf* frond; **—s** fronds; foliage, leaves.
frondis *adj* (*Col*) dirty.
frondosidad *nf* leafiness; luxuriance.
frondoso *adj* leafy; luxuriant.
frontal *adj* frontal.
frontera *nf* (a) frontier, border; frontier area, borderland (*also fig*). (b) (*Archit*) façade.
fronterizo *adj* (a) frontier (*attr*); border (*attr*). (b) opposite, facing; **las casas fronterizas** the houses opposite.
frontero *adj* opposite, facing.
frontis *nm* (*Archit*) façade.
frontispicio *nm* frontispiece; (*fam*) face, clock (*sl*).
frontón *nm* (a) (*Archit*) pediment. (b) (*Sport*) pelota court; front wall of a pelota court.
frotación *nf*, **frotadura** *nf*, **frotamiento** *nm* rub, rubbing; (*Mech*) friction.
frotar [1a] **1** *vt* to rub; *match* to strike; **quitar algo frotando** to rub something off. **2 frotarse** *vr* to rub, chafe; **— las manos** to rub one's hands.
frote *nm* rub.
fructifero *adj* (a) (*Bot etc*) productive, fruit-bearing. (b) (*fig*) fruitful.
fructificación *nf* (*fig*) fruition.
fructificar [1g] *vi* (a) (*Bot*) to produce, yield a crop, bear fruit. (b) (*fig*) to yield a profit; to come to fruition.
fructuosamente *adv* fruitfully.
fructuoso *adj* fruitful.
frugal *adj* frugal; thrifty; parsimonious.
frugalidad *nf* frugality; thrift, thriftiness; parsimony.
frugalmente *adv* frugally; thriftily; parsimoniously.
fruición *nf* enjoyment; satisfaction, delight; **— maliciosa** malicious pleasure.
frunce *nm* pleat, tuck, gather, shirr.
fruncido 1 *adj* (a) contracted; (*Sew*) pleated, gathered; *brow* wrinkled, furrowed; *face* frowning.
  (b) (*Arg, Chi*) prudish, demure; affected.
  2 *nm* = **frunce**.
fruncimiento *nm* = **frunce**.
fruncir [3b] *vt* to contract, pucker; to ruffle; (*Sew*) to

pleat, gather, shirr, put a tuck in; *brow* to wrinkle, knit; *lips* to purse; *see* **ceño** *etc*.
fruslería *nf* trifle, trinket; (*fig*) trifle, small thing, triviality.
frustración *nf* frustration.
frustrar [1a] **1** *vt* to frustrate, thwart. **2 frustrarse** *vr* to be frustrated; (*of plan etc*) to fail, miscarry.
fruta *nf* (a) fruit; **—s** (*Cook*) fruit; **— prohibida** forbidden fruit; **— de sartén** fritter; **— seca** dried fruit.
  (b) (*fig*) fruit, consequence.
frutal 1 *adj* fruit-bearing, fruit (*attr*); **árbol — = 2** *nm* fruit tree.
frutar [1a] *vi* to fruit, bear fruit.
frutera *nf* fruit dish, fruit bowl.
frutería *nf* fruiterer's (shop), fruit shop.
frutero 1 *adj* fruit (*attr*); **plato —** fruit dish. **2** *nm* (a) fruiterer. (b) fruit dish, fruit bowl; basket of fruit.
fruticultura *nf* fruit growing.
frutilla *nf* (*SAm*) Indian strawberry; Chilean strawberry.
fruto *nm* (a) (*Bot*) fruit; **— del pan** breadfruit; **—s del país** (*RPl*) agricultural products; **dar —** to fruit, bear fruit.
  (b) (*fig*) fruits; result, consequence; profit, benefit; offspring, child; **— de bendición** legitimate offspring; **el — de esta unión** the offspring of this marriage; **sacar — de** to profit from, derive benefit from.
fu: ni — ni fa neither one thing nor the other.
fuácata *nf* (*Ant, Mex*): **estar en la —** to be broke (*fam*).
fucilazo *nm* (flash of) sheet lightning.
fuco *nm* wrack.
fucsia *nf* fuchsia.
fudiño *adj* (*Cu*) small, sickly.
fuego *nm* (a) fire; conflagration; **—s artificiales** fireworks; **— fatuo** will-o'-the-wisp; **apagar el —** to put out the fire; **atizar el —** to poke the fire; **encender un —** to light a fire; **se declaró el —** fire broke out; **echar — por los ojos** to glare, look daggers; **jugar con —** (*fig*) to play with fire; **matar a uno a — lento** to worry someone to death; **pegar** (*or* **prender**) **— a** to set fire to, set on fire; **poner un pueblo a — y sangre** to lay a village waste.
  (b) (*of gas stove*) burner; (*of oven, electric stove*) plate; **una cocina a gas de 4 —s** a gas cooker with 4 burners.
  (c) (*Cook*) flame, heat; **sobre un — bajo** on a low flame, on a low gas; **hervir a — lento** to simmer.
  (d) (*Naut etc*) beacon, signal fire.
  (e) (*for cigarette*) light; **¿tienes —?** have you a light?; **le pedí —** I asked him for a light.
  (f) (*Mil*) fire; firing; **¡—! fire!; ¡alto el —!** cease fire!; **— de andanada** (*Naut*) broadside; **— cruzado** crossfire; **— graneado**, **— nutrido** heavy fire; **abrir —** to open fire; **hacer —** to fire (*sobre* at, on); **romper el —** to open fire.
  (g) (*Med*) rash, skin eruption; **— pérsico** shingles.
  (h) hearth, home; **un pueblo de 50 —s** a village of 50 houses (*or* families).
  (i) (*fig*) fire, ardour, passion; **apagar los —s de uno** to damp down someone's ardour; **atizar el —** to add fuel to the flames, stir things up.
fueguino (*Arg*) **1** *adj* of Tierra del Fuego. **2** *nm*, **fueguina** *nf* native (*or* inhabitant) of Tierra del Fuego; **los —s** the people of Tierra del Fuego.
fuel-oil [fuel'oil] *nm* paraffin, kerosene.
fuelle *nm* (a) bellows; blower; **— de pie** foot pump.
  (b) (*of car, carriage*) folding hood, folding top (*US*); (*Phot*) bellows; **— quitasol** (*Phot*) hood.
  (c) (*fam*) telltale.
fuente *nf* (a) fountain, spring; **— de beber** drinking fountain; **— termal** hot spring; **— de río** source of a river; **abrir la — de las lágrimas** (*hum*) to weep buckets.
  (b) (*Cook*) large dish, bowl; serving dish.
  (c) (*fig*) source; origin; **de — desconocida** from an unknown source; **de — fidedigna** from a reliable source; **— de suministro** source of supply.
fuer: ni — de as a; in the manner of; **a — de caballero** as a gentleman; **a — de hombre honrado** as an honest man.
fuera 1 *adv* (a) outside; out; **¡—! get out!**, off with you!; chuck him out!; **"¡ruritanos —!"** (*placard etc*) "Ruritanians go home!"; **ir —** to go out, go away, go outside; **con la camisa —** with his shirt hanging out; **el perro tenía la lengua —** the dog had his tongue hanging out; **la parte de —** the outside part, the outer part; **desde —** from outside; **por — (on the) outside**; **los de —** those from outside; strangers, newcomers.
  (b) **estar —** (*of person*) to be out of town, be on

a trip; to be away; **estuvo — 8 semanas** he was away for 8 weeks.

(c) (*Sport*) **estar —** to be out, be in touch; **poner —** to put into touch; **jugar —** (*of team*) to play away (from home); **los de —, el equipo de —** the away team.

2 — de (*prep*) **(a)** outside (of); out of; **estaba — de su jaula** it was outside (*or* out of) its cage; **esperamos — de la puerta** we waited outside the door; **— de alcance** out of reach, beyond one's reach; **— de moda** out of fashion; **estar — de sí** to be beside oneself; *see* **combate** *etc.*

(b) (*fig*) in addition to, besides, beyond; **pero — de eso** but in addition to that; but aside from that; **todo — de mentir** everything short of lying.

fuera-borda *nm*, *pl* **fuera-borda; fuerabordo** *nm*, *pl* **fuerabordo** outboard engine, outboard motor; dinghy with an outboard engine.

fuereño *nm*, **fuereña** *nf* (*Mex*) outsider, stranger (*living temporarily in Mexico City*).

fuerino *nm*, **fuerina** *nf* (*Chi*) stranger, non-resident.

fuero *nm* **(a)** municipal charter; local (*or* regional *etc*) law code; (*of group*) privilege, exemption; **a — according to law; ¿con qué —?** by what right?; **de — de jure**, in law.

(b) jurisdiction, authority; **el — no alcanza a tanto** his authority does not extend that far.

fuerte 1 *adj* (*in many senses*) strong; tough, sturdy; robust; vigorous; solid; *town, defences, wind, argument, objection, belief, will etc* strong; *terrain* rough, difficult; *blow* hard, heavy; *noise* loud; *expense, rain* heavy; *meal* heavy, big; *dish* main; rich; *bend* sharp; *taste, tea, wine etc* strong; *heat, pain etc* intense, great, considerable; *crisis* grave; *exercise* strenuous; *rigour etc* excessive, extreme; **hacerse — en una colina** to entrench oneself on a hill, make a fortified position on a hill; **se hicieron —s en la casa** they prepared to defend the house; they barricaded themselves in the house; they made a stand in the house; **ser — en filosofía** to be strong in (*or* on) philosophy, be well up in philosophy.

2 *adv* strongly; *hit* hard; *play, talk* loud, loudly; **pegar — al enemigo** to hit the enemy hard; **toca muy —** she plays very loudly; **¡más —!** (*to speaker*) speak up!; **poner la radio más —** to turn the radio up; **comer —** to eat a big meal, eat too much.

3 *nm* **(a)** (*Mil*) fort, strongpoint.

(b) (*Mus*) forte.

(c) (*fig*) forte, strong point; **el canto no es mi —** singing is not my strong point.

fuertemente *adv* strongly; loudly; intensely.

fuerza *nf* **(a)** (*in many senses*) strength; toughness, sturdiness; vigour; solidity; power; intensity; **—s** (*of person*) strength; (*of argument*) force, strength, effect; **a — de** by dint of, by force of; **a viva —** by sheer strength, by main force; **entrada a viva —** forced entry; **cobrar —s** to recover one's strength; to gather strength; **hacer — de vela** (*Naut*) to crowd on sail; **restar —s a** to weaken; **no me siento con —s para eso** I don't feel up to it; **tener —s para + infin** to have the strength to + *infin*, be strong enough to + *infin*.

(b) (*Mech, Phys*) force; power; **— de arrastre** pulling power; **— ascensional** (*Naut*) buoyancy; **— de brazos** manpower; **— centrífuga** centrifugal force; **— centrípeta** centripetal force; **— de gravedad** force of gravity; **— hidráulica** water power, hydraulic power; **— motriz** motive power; **— de sustentación** (*Aer*) lift.

(c) (*Elec*) power, current, energy; **han cortado la — they've** cut off the power.

(d) force, compulsion; pressure; **— mayor** force majeure; act of God; **por — mayor** by sheer force; **a la —, por —** by force; willy-nilly, against one's will; **under pressure,** compulsively; **perforce,** of necessity; **en — de** by virtue of; **es — + infin** it is necessary to + *infin*.

(e) force, violence; **— bruta** brute force; **hacer — a una mujer** to rape a woman; **recurrir a la —** to resort to force, use violence; **rendirse a la —** to yield to violence; **sin usar —** without using force, without using violence.

(f) (*Mil*) force, forces; **—s aéreas** air force; **—s aliadas** allied forces; **—s armadas** armed forces; **— de disuasión, — disuasoria, — disuasiva** deterrent; **— expedicionaria** expeditionary force; **—s de mar y de tierra** land and sea forces; **— pública** police (force); **—s terrestres** land forces.

fuetazo *nm* (*SAm*) lash.

fuete *nm* (*SAm: gall*) whip; **dar — a** (*Ant*) to whip.

fuetear [1a] *vt* (*SAm*) to whip.

fuga¹ *nf* **(a)** flight, escape; (*of lovers*) elopement; **— de**

la cárcel escape from prison, jailbreak; **apelar a la —, darse a la —, ponerse en —** to flee, take to flight; **poner al enemigo en —** to put the enemy to flight. **(b)** (*of gas etc*) leak, escape. **(c)** (*fig*) ardour, impetuosity.

fuga² *nf* (*Mus*) fugue.

fugarse [1h] *vr* **(a)** to flee, escape (*a* to); to run away (*con* with); (*of lovers*) to elope (*con* with); **— de la ley** to abscond from justice.

(b) (*of gas etc*) to leak out, escape.

fugaz *adj* **(a)** *moment etc* fleeting, short-lived, transitory, brief. **(b)** elusive. **(c) estrella —** shooting star.

fugazmente *adv* fleetingly, briefly.

fugitivo 1 *adj* **(a)** fugitive, fleeing. **(b)** =**fugaz. 2** *nm*, **fugitiva** *nf* fugitive.

fui, fuimos *etc see* **ser**; *see* **ir.**

fuina *nf* marten.

fulana *nf* **(a) Doña F—** Mrs So-and-so, Mrs Blank. **(b)** (*fam*) tart (*sl*), whore.

fulano *nm* so-and-so, what's-his-name; **— de tal, Don F—** Mr So-and-so, Mr Blank; Joe Soap; John Doe (US); **—, zutano y mengano** Tom, Dick and Harry; **me lo dijo —** somebody told me; old what's-his-name told me; **no te vas a casar con un —** you're not going to marry just anybody; **nombramos a — y ya está** we nominate some chap and that's that.

fulcro *nm* fulcrum.

fulero *adj* **(a)** useless, sham, bogus; poor-quality, poorly made; nasty. **(b)** *person* tricky, sly. **(c)** *person* blundering, incompetent.

fulgente *adj*, **fúlgido** *adj* dazzling, bright, brilliant, radiant.

fulgor *nm* brilliance, radiance, glow; (*fig*) splendour.

fulgurante *adj* **(a)** bright, shining. **(b)** (*fig*) shattering, stunning.

fulgurar [1a] *vi* to shine, gleam, glow; to flash.

fulguroso *adj* bright, shining, gleaming; flashing.

fúlica *nf* coot.

fulmicotón *nm* guncotton.

fulminación *nf* fulmination.

fulminador *nm* fulminator (*de* against), thunderer (*de* against).

fulminante 1 *adj* **(a)** *powder* fulminating; **cápsula —** percussion cap.

(b) (*Med*) fulminant; *see* **ataque (b)**.

(c) (*fam*) *success etc* terrific (*fam*), tremendous (*fam*); **golpe —** terrific blow, smash hit; **tiro —** (*Sport*) sizzling shot.

2 *nm* **(a)** (*Arg*) match.

(b) (*SAm*) percussion cap.

fulminar [1a] **1** *vt* **(a)** to fulminate; *threats* to utter, thunder (*contra* against); **— a uno con la mirada** to look daggers at someone.

(b) to strike with lightning.

2 *vi* to fulminate, explode.

fulo *adj* **(a)** (*Pan*) blond(e), fair. **(b)** (*Arg*) furious, enraged; maddened.

fullerear [1a] *vi* (*Col*) to swank (*fam*).

fullería *nf* **(a)** cheating, cardsharping; guile, low cunning. **(b)** trick. **(c)** (*Col*) swankiness (*fam*), conceit.

fullero *nm* **(a)** cheat, cardsharper; crook; tricky individual. **(b)** (*Col*) swank (*fam*), show-off (*fam*).

fullingue *adj* (*Chi*) **(a)** *tobacco* inferior, poor-quality. **(b)** *child* small, sickly.

fumada *nf* whiff of smoke, puff of smoke.

fumadero *nm* smoking room; **— de opio** opium den.

fumador *nm*, **fumadora** *nf* smoker; **— de pipa** pipe smoker; **no —** non-smoker.

fumante *nm* (*Arg*) cigar, cigarette.

fumar [1a] **1** *vti* to smoke; **"prohibido —"** "no smoking"; **— como un carretero** to smoke like a chimney; **él fuma en pipa** he smokes a pipe; **está fumando su pipa** he is smoking his pipe; **¿puedo —?, ¿se permite —?** may I smoke?

2 fumarse *vr* (*money* to dissipate, squander; *class* to cut, miss.

(b) **—lo a uno** (*Arg, Cu, Mex*) to outdo someone; **— de uno** to trick someone, swindle someone.

fumarada *nf* **(a)** puff of smoke. **(b)** (*of tobacco*) pipeful.

fumigación *nf* fumigation.

fumigar [1h] *vt* to fumigate; **¡que te fumiguen!** (*fam*) get lost! (*fam*).

fumista *nm* (*Arg: gall*) joker, tease.

fumo *nm* (*Ven*) puff of smoke.

fumosidad *nf* smokiness.

fumoso *adj* smoky.

funámbulo *nm*, **funámbula** *nf* tightrope walker.

funcia *nf* (*CAm, Col, Chi, Ven: hum*) =**función.**

función *nf* **(a)** function; functioning, operation.

(b) (*of post*) duties; **presidente en —es** acting president; **entrar en —es** to take up one's duties; **excederse en sus —es** to exceed one's duty.

(c) (*Theat etc*) show, performance; entertainment; spectacle; **— benéfica** charity performance; **— de despedida** farewell performance; **— de la tarde** matinée; **— de títeres** puppet show; **— taquillera** box-office success, big draw; **mañana no hay —** there will be no performance tomorrow.

funcional *adj* functional.

funcionalidad *nf* functional character.

funcionamiento *nm* functioning, operation; (*Mech, Tech*) operation, working, running; performance; behaviour; **máquina en —** machine in working order; **sociedad en —** going concern; **entrar en —** to come into operation; **poner en —** to bring into operation, bring into service.

funcionar [1a] *vt* to function; (*Mech, Tech*) to go, work, run; to perform; to behave; **"funcionando"** (*in advert etc*) in working order, in running order; **"no funciona"** (*notice*) "out of order"; **hacer — una máquina** to operate a machine.

funcionario *nm* official, functionary; employee; civil servant; **— público** public official.

funda *nf* (a) case, cover, sheath; **— de almohada** pillowcase, pillowslip; **— de pistola** holster. **(b)** holdall. **(c)** (*Col*) shirt.

fundación *nf* foundation.

fundadamente *adv* with good reason, on good grounds.

fundado *adj* firm, well-founded, justified; **una pretensión mal fundada** an ill-founded claim.

fundador *nm*, **fundadora** *nf* founder.

fundamental *adj* fundamental, basic; essential.

fundamentalmente *adv* fundamentally, basically; essentially.

fundamentar [1a] *vt* **(a)** to lay the foundations of. **(b)** (*fig*) argument *etc* to base, found (*en* on).

fundamento *nm* **(a)** (*Archit etc*) foundation.
   (b) (*fig*) foundation, basis; groundwork; grounds, reason; **eso carece de —** that is groundless, that is completely unjustified; **creencia sin —** groundless belief, unfounded belief; **¿qué — tiene esta teoría?** what is the basis of this theory?, what is the basic justification for this theory?
   (c) (*moral*) reliability, trustworthiness.
   (d) (*Tech*) weft, woof.
   (e) (*Anat*) fundament.
   (f) **—s** (*fig*) fundamentals; basic essentials.

fundar [1a] **1** *vt* **(a)** to found; to institute, set up, establish; to raise, erect; (*with money*) to endow.
   (b) theory *etc* to base, found (*en* on).
   2 fundarse *vr* **(a)** to be founded, be established.
   (b) **— en** to be founded on, be based on; to base oneself on; **me fundo en los siguientes hechos** I base myself on the following facts.

fundente 1 *adj* melting. **2** *nm* (*Chem*) dissolvent; flux.

fundería *nf* foundry; **— de hierro** iron foundry.

fundición *nf* **(a)** fusing, fusion; (*Tech*) smelting, founding; melting.
   (b) (*Tech*) foundry, forge, smelting plant; **— de hierro** iron foundry.
   (c) cast iron; casting; **— de acero** steel casting.
   (d) (*Typ*) font, fount.

fundido *adj* (*SAm: Comm*) ruined, bankrupt.

fundidor *nm* smelter, founder.

fundillos *nmpl* (*SAm*) seat (*of trousers*); (*fam*) seat, bottom; (*Arg*) pants.

fundir [3a] **1** *vt* **(a)** to fuse (together); to join, unite.
   (b) (*Tech*) to melt (down), smelt; snow *etc* to melt; (*Elec*) to fuse; piece, part to found, cast; (*Comm*) to merge; **el faro está fundido** the lamp is fused, the lamp is broken.
   (c) (*SAm*) to ruin.
   2 *vi* (*Cine*) to fade (*a* to).
   3 fundirse *vr* **(a)** to fuse (together); to join, unite; (*of colours, effects etc*) to merge, blend (together).
   (b) to melt (*also fig*); (*Elec: of fuse*) to blow, burn out; **se le fundió el corazón** her heart melted.
   (c) (*SAm*) to ruin oneself; to be ruined.

fundón *nm* (*Col, Ven*) riding habit.

fúnebre *adj* **(a)** funeral (*attr*). **(b)** (*fig*) funereal; sound *etc* mournful, lugubrious.

funeral 1 *adj* funeral (*attr*). **2** *nm* funeral; **—es** funeral, obsequies.

funerala *nf*: **marchar a la —** to march with reversed arms; **ojo a la —** black eye.

funeraria *nf* undertaker's, undertaker's establishment, funeral parlor (*US*); **director de —** undertaker, funeral director, mortician (*US*).

funerario *adj*, **funéreo** *adj* funeral (*attr*); funereal.

funestamente *adv* banefully; fatally, disastrously.

funestidad *nf* (*Mex*) calamity.

funesto *adj* ill-fated, unfortunate; baneful; fatal, disastrous (*para* for).

fungir [3c] *vi* (*CAm, Mex*) to act (*de* as); (*Cu*) to substitute, stand in (*a* for).

fungoideo *adj* fungoid.

fungoso *adj* fungous.

funicular *nm* funicular (railway).

fuñido *adj* **(a)** (*Ven*) quarrelsome; unsociable. **(b)** (*Cu*) weak, sickly, feeble.

fuñingue *adj* (*Chi*) weak.

furcia *nf* (*sl*) tart (*sl*), whore.

furgón *nm* wagon, van, truck; (*Rail*) van; **— de cola** guard's van; caboose (*US*); **— de equipajes** luggage van, baggage car (*US*); **— de mudanzas** removal van.

furgonada *nf* wagonload, vanload.

furgonero *nm* carter, vanman.

furgoneta *nf* van; (*Aut*) shooting brake, station wagon (*US*).

furia *nf* fury; rage, violence; **a toda —** like fury; **a la —** (*RPl*) at top speed; **ella salió como una —, ella salió hecha una —** she went out furiously (angry).

furibundo *adj* furious; frenzied.

furiosamente *adv* furiously; violently; frantically.

furioso *adj* furious; violent; frantic, raging; **estar —** to be furious; **ponerse —** to get furious.

furor *nm* **(a)** fury, rage; frenzy; passion; **— uterino** nymphomania; **dijo con —** he said furiously.
   (b) (*fig*) rage; **hacer —** to be all the rage; **tener — por** (*SAm*) to have a passion for.

furquina *nf* (*Bol, Col*) short skirt.

furriel *nm*, **furrier** *nm* quartermaster.

furrusca *nf* (*Col*) row, brawl.

furtivamente *adv* furtively; in a clandestine way; slyly, stealthily.

furtivo *adj* furtive; clandestine; sly, stealthy; edition pirated; see **cazador**.

furuminga *nf* (*Chi*) intrigue, scheme, plot.

furúnculo *nm* (*Med*) boil.

fusa *nf* demisemiquaver.

fuselado *adj* streamlined.

fuselaje *nm* fuselage.

fusible *nm* fuse.

fusil *nm* rifle, gun; **— de juguete** popgun, toy gun.

fusilamiento *nm* shooting, execution.

fusilar [1a] *vt* to shoot, execute; (*Ven etc*) to kill (*in general*).

fusilazo *nm* rifle shot.

fusilero *nm* rifleman, fusileer.

fusión *nf* fusion; joining, uniting; (*of metal etc*) melting; (*Comm*) merger, amalgamation.

fusionamiento *nm* (*Comm*) merger, amalgamation.

fusionar [1a] **1** *vt* to fuse (together); (*Comm*) to merge, amalgamate. **2 fusionarse** *vr* to fuse; (*Comm*) to merge, amalgamate.

fusta *nf* **(a)** long whip; riding whip. **(b)** brushwood, twigs.

fustán *nm* **(a)** fustian. **(b)** (*SAm*) petticoat, underskirt; (*Ec, Per*) skirt.

fuste *nm* **(a)** wood, timber; **de —** wooden.
   (b) (*of weapon*) shaft; (*of chimney, column*) shaft; **de —** (*fig*) important, of some consequence.
   (c) saddle tree.
   (d) (*CAm, Ven: Anat*) bottom.

fustigar [1h] *vt* **(a)** to whip, lash. **(b)** (*fig*) to upbraid, lash (with one's tongue).

fútbol *nm* (*angl*) football; **— americano** American football; **— asociación** association football, soccer; **— rugby** rugby football.

futbolín *nm* table football, bar football.

futbolista *nm* footballer, football player.

futbolístico *adj* football (*attr*).

futearse [1a] *vr* (*Col: of fruit etc*) to go bad, rot.

futesa *nf* trifle, mere nothing; **—s** small talk, trivialities.

fútil *adj* trifling, trivial.

futilidad *nf* triviality, trifling nature, unimportance.

futre *nm* (*Bol, Chi, Ec, Per, RPl*) dandy, toff (*fam*), dude (*US*).

futrería *nf* (*Chi, Per*) **(a)** affected behaviour. **(b)** group of dandies, group of dudes (*US*). **(c)** dude's hangout (*US*).

futura *nf* **(a)** (*Law*) reversion. **(b)** (*fam*) fiancée.

futurismo *nm* futurism.

futurístico *adj* futuristic.

futuro 1 *adj* future; **en lo —** in (the) future.
   2 *nm* **(a)** future; **en el —** in (the) future; **en un — próximo** in the very near future, very soon.
   (b) (*Gram*) future, future tense.
   (c) (*fam*) fiancé.
   (d) **—s** (*Comm*) futures.

G

gaba nmf (Texas: pej) white American, Yankee.
gabacho 1 adj (a) (Geog) Pyrenean.
 (b) frenchified.
 (c) (Col: fam) **le salió gabacha la cosa** it came to nothing, the affair was a failure.
 2 nm, **gabacha** nf (a) (Geog) Pyrenean villager.
 (b) (pej) Frenchy (fam), froggy (fam); frenchified Spaniard; (Texas) white American, Yankee; (Mex) (any) foreigner, outsider.
gabán nm overcoat, topcoat.
gabarda nf wild rose.
gabardina[1] nf gabardine; raincoat, mackintosh.
gabardino nm, **gabardina**[2] nf (Texas: pej) white American, Yankee.
gabarra nf barge, lighter, flatboat.
gabarrero nm bargee, bargeman, lighterman.
gabarro nm (a) (in cloth) flaw, defect. (b) (Vet) pip. (c) (fig) error, slip, miscalculation; snag; annoyance.
gabela nf (a) (Hist) tax, duty; (fig) burden. (b) (Col, Ec, PR, SD, Ven) advantage, profit.
gabinete nm (a) study, library; private sitting room; boudoir; (Law, Med) office; laboratory; museum; (Art) studio; (Col) enclosed balcony; — **de consulta** consulting room; — **de lectura** reading room; — **de teléfono** (Mex) telephone booth; **estratega de** — armchair strategist.
 (b) (Pol) cabinet.
 (c) suite of office furniture.
gablete nm gable.
gacel nm, **gacela** nf gazelle.
gaceta nf (a) gazette, official journal; (SAm) newspaper. (b) (Ant) gossip; telltale.
gacetero nm (a) newswriter, journalist. (b) newspaper seller.
gacetilla nf (a) gossip column; section of local news, section of miscellaneous news items; "G—" (heading) "News in Brief".
 (b) (fam) gossip, scandalmonger; **ella es una** — **andando** (or **con dos patas**) she's a dreadful gossip.
gacetillero nm newspaper reporter; gossip columnist; (pej) hack, penny-a-liner.
gacetista nmf gossip, scandalmonger.
gacilla nf (CAm: Sew) clasp, hook and eye.
gacha f (a) thin paste; watery mass, mush; —s (as food) pap; porridge; —s **de avena** oatmeal porridge; **se ha hecho unas** —s it's got mushy, it's got soggy, (fig) she's got mushy, she's turned all sentimental.
 (b) (Col, Ven) earthenware bowl.
gachí nf, pl **gachís** (sl) dame (sl), bird (sl).
gacho adj (a) bent down, turned downward; horn down-curved; cow with down-curved horns; hat with down-turned brim; ears etc drooping, floppy; sombrero — slouch hat.
 (b) (Mex) unpleasant.
 (c) **ir a gachas** to go on all fours.
gachó nm, pl **gachós** (a) (sl) chap (fam), bloke (sl).
 (b) interj bravo!, jolly good! (fam).
gachón adj (fam) nice, charming, sweet; child spoilt.
gachumbo nm (Col, Ec) hard woody shell (of certain fruits: used to make cups etc).
gachupín nm (CAm, Mex: pej) (any) Spaniard.
gaditano 1 adj of Cadiz. **2** nm, **gaditana** nf native (or inhabitant) of Cadiz; **los** —s the people of Cadiz.
gaélico 1 adj Gaelic. **2** nm, **gaélica** nf Gael. **3** nm (language) Gaelic.
gafa nf grapple; clamp; —s glasses, spectacles; goggles; —s **ahumadas** smoked glasses; —s **sin aros** rimless glasses; — **bifocales**, —s **graduadas** bifocals; —s **de motorista** motorcyclist's goggles; —s **negras** dark glasses; —s **protectoras** protective goggles; —s **de sol**, —s **para sol** sunglasses; —s **submarinas** underwater goggles.
gafancia nf (tendency to have) constant bad luck, capacity for messing things up.

gafar [1a] vt (a) to hook, claw, latch on to. (b) (fam) to bring bad luck to, put a hoodoo on; to spoil, mess up.
gafe 1 adj (fam): **ser** — to have constant bad luck, have a great capacity for messing things up. **2** nm (fam) bad luck; hoodoo.
gafete nm clasp, hook and eye.
gafo adj (a) (SAm, Col, PR) footsore, dog-tired; (Mex) numb. (b) (Ven) unreliable.
gag [gax] nm, pl **gags** [gax] (angl: Theat etc) gag.
gago (Cu, Chi, Mex, Per, PR, Ven) **1** adj stammering. **2** nm, **gaga** nf stammerer.
gagoso adj (Col) stammering.
gaguear [1a] vi (Cu, Chi, Mex, Per, PR, Ven) to stammer, stutter.
gagueo nm (Cu, Chi, Mex, Per, PR, Ven) stammer(ing).
gaguera nf (Cu, Chi, Mex, Per, PR, Ven) stammer, speech defect.
gaita 1 nf (a) (Mus) flute, flageolet; hurdy-gurdy; — (**gallega**) bagpipe; **ser como una** — to be dissatisfied, be very demanding; **estar de** — to be merry; **templar** —s to calm someone down, smooth things out.
 (b) (fam) neck; **sacar la** — to stick one's neck out.
 (c) (Arg) bother, nuisance; tough job.
 2 nmf (SAm: hum) Galician, (any) Spaniard.
gaitero 1 adj (a) gaudy, flashy. (b) inappropriately jocular, witty in the wrong way. **2** nm (bag)piper.
gajes nmpl pay, emoluments; perquisites; —s **del oficio** (hum) occupational hazards, occupational risks.
gajo nm (a) (torn-off) branch, bough, limb; (of grapes) small cluster, bunch.
 (b) (of orange etc) slice, segment, quarter.
 (c) (of fork) point, prong; (Geog) spur.
 (d) (Col, Guat, Hond, SD) curl, ringlet.
gala nf (a) full dress; best dress; court dress; **de** — state (attr), dress (attr), full-dress (attr); gala (attr); **estar de** — to be in full dress; to be in one's best dress, be all dressed up; (town etc) to be bedecked, be in festive mood.
 (b) —s finery, trappings; jewels, adornments; regalia; fine things; —s **de novia** bridal attire.
 (c) (fig) elegance, gracefulness; pomp, display; **hacer** — **de** to display, show off; to boast of, glory in; **tener algo a** — to be proud of something; **tener a** — + infin to be proud to + infin.
 (d) (fig) cream, flower, pride, chief ornament; **es la** — **de la ciudad** it is the pride of the city.
 (e) delight; speciality, special accomplishment; **su mejor** — **está en recorrer las calles con guitarras** their special delight is to roam the streets with their guitars.
 (f) (SAm) gift, tip.
galáctico adj galactic.
galafate nm expert thief, sly thief.
galán 1 nm (a) handsome fellow, attractive young man; ladies' man; (Hist) young gentleman, courtier.
 (b) gallant, beau; suitor.
 (c) (Theat) male lead, chief male part; hero; **joven** — juvenile lead; **primer** — leading man.
 2 adv (SAm: fam) = **bien**.
galanas nfpl (CAm): **echar** — to boast, brag; **hacer** — to do naughty things, be wicked.
galanamente adv smartly, sprucely; elegantly, tastefully.
galancete nm handsome young man; (hum) dapper little man; (Theat) male juvenile lead.
galano adj (a) smart, spruce; elegant, tasteful; gaily dressed. (b) (Cu) cow mottled (with red and white patches).

galante *adj* (a) *man* gallant; charming, attentive (to women); polite, urbane. (b) *woman* flirtatious; (*pej*) wanton, free, licentious.

galantear [1a] *vt* to court, woo; to flirt with.

galantemente *adv* gallantly; charmingly, attentively; politely.

galanteo *nm* courting, courtship, wooing; flirting.

galantería *nf* (a) (*in general*) gallantry; attentiveness (to women); politeness, urbanity. (b) (*remark etc*) compliment; charming thing (to say), gallantry.

galanto *nm* (*Bot*) snowdrop.

galanura *nf* prettiness; charm; elegance, tastefulness.

galápago *nm* (a) (*Zool*) freshwater tortoise. (b) (*Agr*) mould board. (c) (*Tech*) ingot, pig. (d) light saddle; (*SAm*) sidesaddle.

Galápagos: Islas *fpl* **de (los)** — Galapagos Isles.

galardón *nm* (*lit*) reward, prize.

galardonar [1a] *vt* (*lit*) to reward, recompense (*de* with); (*Lit*) *work* to give a prize to; **obra galardonada por la Academia** work which won an Academy prize.

galaxia *nf* galaxy.

galbana *nf* sloth, laziness; shiftlessness.

galbanoso *adj* slothful, lazy; shiftless.

galembo *nm* (*Col, Ven*) turkey buzzard.

Galeno *m* Galen.

galeón *nm* galleon.

galeote *nm* galley slave.

galera *nf* (a) (*Naut*) galley; **echar a uno a** —**s** to condemn someone to the galleys. (b) (covered) wagon. (c) (*Med*) hospital ward; (*Hist*) women's prison; (*CAm, Mex*) shed; (*CR*) slaughterhouse. (d) (*SAm*) top hat; derby hat; felt hat; bowler hat. (e) (*Typ*) galley.

galerada *nf* (a) wagonload. (b) (*Typ*) galley proof.

galería *nf* (*in many senses*) gallery; passage, corridor; (*Min*) gallery; (*on beach etc*) beach hut, changing room, (*at swimming pool*) cubicle; (*on outside of house*) veranda(h); (*Art*) gallery; — **de columnas** colonnade; — **de popa** (*Naut*) stern gallery; — **secreta** secret passage; — **de tiro** shooting gallery; — **de viento** (*Aer*) wind tunnel; — **visitable** manhole.

galerita *nf* crested lark.

galerna *nf*, **galerno** *nm* violent north-west wind (*on N coast of Spain*).

galerón *nm* (*CAm*) shed; shed roof; (*Mex*) big room.

Gales *m* Wales.

galés 1 *adj* Welsh. **2** *nm* Welshman. **3** *nm* (*language*) Welsh.

galesa *nf* Welshwoman.

galga *nf* (a) (*Zool*) greyhound (bitch). (b) (*Geol*) boulder, rolling stone; (*Tech*) millstone (of an oil press). (c) (*Agr*) hub brake (on a cart).

galgo[1] *nm* greyhound; — **ruso** borzoi, Russian wolfhound; **¡échale un** —**!** good heavens!, you don't say!; **search me!** (*fam*); **¡vaya Vd a espulgar un** —**!** (*fam*) go to blazes!

galgo[2] *adj* (*Col*) sweet-toothed, fond of sweets.

galgón *adj* (*Ec*) = **galgo**[2].

galguear [1a] *vi* (*CAm, RPl*) to feel terribly hungry; to wander about looking for food.

Galia *f* Gaul.

galicano *adj* Gallic.

galiciano 1 *adj* Galician. **2** *nm*, **galiciana** *nf* Galician.

galicismo *nm* gallicism.

gálico *nm* syphilis.

galicoso 1 *adj* syphilitic. **2** *nm* syphilitic.

Galilea *f* Galilee.

galillo *nm* (*Anat*) uvula.

galimatías *nm*, *pl* **galimatías** rigmarole; gibberish, nonsense.

galo 1 *adj* Gallic. **2** *nm*, **gala** *nf* Gaul.

galocha *nf* clog, patten.

galón[1] *nm* (*Sew*) braid; (*Mil*) stripe, chevron; **quitar los** —**es a uno** to take his stripes away from someone, demote someone; **la acción le valió 2** —**es** the action got him a couple of stripes.

galón[2] *nm* (*measure*) gallon.

galonear [1a] *vt* to trim with braid.

galopada *nf* gallop.

galopante *adj* (*Med and fig*) galloping.

galopar [1a] *vi* to gallop; **echar a** — to break into a gallop.

galope *nm* gallop; **a** —, **al** — (*SAm*), **de** — at a gallop, (*fig*) in great haste, in a rush; **a** — **tendido** at full gallop; **alejarse a** — to gallop off; **desfilar a** — to gallop past; **llegar a** — to gallop up; **medio** — canter.

galopín *nm* ragamuffin, urchin, street arab; scoundrel, rogue; smart-aleck (*fam*), clever dick (*fam*); (*Naut*) cabin boy.

galpón *nm* (*SAm*) (large) shed, storehouse; (*Aut*) garage; (*Col*) tileworks, pottery.

galucha *nf* (*SAm*) short gallop; (*Cu*) start of a gallop.

galuchar [1a] *vi* (*SAm*) to gallop.

galvánico *adj* galvanic.

galvanismo *nm* galvanism.

galvanizado *adj* galvanized.

galvanizar [1f] *vt* to galvanize (*also fig*), electroplate.

gallada *nf* (*CAm, Chi, Col*) bold deed, great achievement; piece of boasting.

gallardamente *adv* gracefully, elegantly; splendidly; bravely; gallantly, dashingly; nobly.

gallardear [1a] *vi* to be elegant, be graceful, act with ease and grace; to bear oneself well.

gallardete *nm* pennant, streamer.

gallardía *nf* gracefulness, elegance; fineness, splendidness; bravery; gallantry, dash; nobleness.

gallardo *adj* graceful, elegant; fine, splendid; brave; gallant, dashing; noble.

gallareta *nf* (*SAm*) South American coot; see **pato**.

gallear [1a] **1** *vt* (*of cock*) to tread. **2** *vi* (a) to excel, stand out. (b) to put on airs, strut; to bully, chuck one's weight about; to brag; to bluster, bawl.

gallego 1 *adj* (a) Galician. (b) (*SAm: pej*) Spanish (*in general*). **2** *nm*, **gallega** *nf* (a) Galician. (b) (*SAm: pej*) (*any*) Spaniard. (c) north-west wind. **3** *nm* (*dialect*) Galician.

gallera *nf* (*SAm*) cockpit; (*Guat, Per*) coop (for gamecocks).

gallería *nf* (a) (*Cu*) place where gamecocks are raised; (*Cu*) building for cockfights; (*Guat*) cockpit. (b) (*Cu: fig*) egotism, selfishness.

gallero 1 *adj* (*SAm*) fond of cockfighting. **2** *nm* (a) (*SAm*) man in charge of gamecocks (*or* cockfighting); cockfighting enthusiast. (b) (*Chi: Rail*) pilferer.

galleta *nf* (a) (*Naut*) biscuit; wafer; (*Naut*) ship's biscuit, hardtack; (*Chi*) coarse bread; — **dulce** rusk; — **de perro** dog biscuit. (b) (*fam*) bash (*fam*), punch, slap. (c) (*Bol, RPl, Ven*) small bowl for drinking maté. (d) (*Chi*) ticking-off. (e) (*Ven*) joke; hoax, deception. (f) **colgar la** — **a uno, dar la** — **a uno** (*RPl*) to sack someone (*fam*); to jilt someone; to refuse to accept someone's advances; **hacerse una** — (*RPl*) to get muddled. (g) — **del tráfico** (*Ven*) traffic jam.

galletear [1a] *vt* (*Chi, RPl*) (a) to sack (*fam*), fire (*fam*); to tick off. (b) to bash (*fam*), punch.

galletero *nm* (a) biscuit barrel, biscuit tin. (b) (*Chi*) quick-tempered person; argumentative sort, brawler.

gallina 1 *nf* (a) hen, fowl; — **de agua** coot; — **de Bantam** bantam; — **clueca** broody hen; — **de Guinea** guinea fowl; — **ponedora** laying hen, hen in lay; **acostarse con las** —**s** to go to bed early; **estar como** — **con huevos** to be very distrustful; **estar como** — **en corral ajeno** to have no freedom of movement; to be like a fish out of water; to be timid, be shy; **¡hasta que meen las** —**s!** (*fam*) till pigs learn to fly! (*fam*); **la** — **de arriba ensucia a la de abajo** (*SAm*) the underdog always suffers. (b) **jugar a la** — **ciega** to play blind man's buff. **2** *nmf* (a) (*fam*) coward. (b) (*Ec: pej*) Peruvian.

gallinacera *nf* (*Ec, Per*) bunch of Negroes.

gallinaza *nf* hen droppings.

gallinazo *nm* (*SAm*) turkey buzzard.

gallinería *nf* (a) flock of hens; poultry shop, chicken market. (b) (*fig*) cowardice.

gallinero *nm* (a) henhouse, coop; poultry basket. (b) chicken farmer; poulterer, poultry dealer. (c) (*Theat*) gods, top gallery. (d) babel, hubbub; noisy gathering.

gallineta *nf* (*Orn*) sandpiper; (*SAm*) guinea fowl.

gallinilla *nf*: — **de Bantam** bantam.

gallipavo *nm* (a) (*Orn*) turkey. (b) (*Mus*) false note, wrong note.

gallito *nm* (a) (*Orn*) small cock. (b) (*fig*) rowdy, tough (*fam*), troublemaker; **el** — (**del mundo**) the cock-o'-the walk, the top dog. (c) (*Col*) small arrow, dart.

gallo *nm* (a) (*Orn*) cock, cockerel, rooster; — **lira** black grouse; — **montés**, — **silvestre** capercaillie; — **de combate**, — **de pelea**, — **de riña** gamecock, fighting cock; **estar como** — **en gallinero** to be much esteemed, be well thought-of; **en menos que canta un** — in an instant; **otro** — **me cantara** that would be quite a different matter; **otro** — **que cantara si . . .** things would have turned out very differently if . . .; **comer** — (*CR, Ec*) to suffer a blow;

haber comido — (*Mex*) to be in a fighting mood; **hay** — **tapado** (*SAm*) I smell a rat; **no me va nada en el** — (*Mex*) it doesn't matter to me; **levantar el** — (*Mex, PR, SD*) to pack it in; **matar a uno el** — **en la mano** to floor someone (in an argument), shut someone up.

(b) (*fam*) boss; (*SAm*) expert, master; **yo he sido** — **para eso** I was a great one at that.

(c) **alzar el** —, **levantar el** — (*fig*) to put on airs, brag; to bawl, behave noisily; **tener mucho** — to be cocky (*fam*).

(d) (*Fish*) cork float.

(e) (*Mus*) false note, wrong note; break in the voice; **soltar un** — to sing a wrong note.

(f) (*Arg, CAm, Mex, PR*) phlegm, sputum.

(g) (*Col*) small arrow, dart.

(h) (*Chi, Per*) fire engine, hose truck.

(i) (*Mex: Mus*) street serenade.

(j) (*Mex*) secondhand article, discarded object; **vestirse de** — to wear old things.

gallofero 1 *adj* idle, loafing; vagabond. **2** *nm* idler, loafer; tramp; beggar.

gallón *adj* (*Mex*) cocky (*fam*).

gallote *adj* (*CAm, Mex*) cocky (*fam*).

gama[1] *nf* (*Mus*) scale; (*fig*) range, scale, gamut; **una extensa** — **de colores** an extensive range of colours; — **de frecuencias** frequency range; — **de ondas** wave range; — **sonora** sound range.

gama[2] *nf* (*letter*) gamma.

gama[3] *nf* (*Zool*) doe (of fallow deer); **sentársele a uno la** — (*Arg*) to get discouraged.

gamba *nf* prawn; (*sl*) 100 pesetas.

gambado *adj* (*Ant*) knock-kneed.

gamberrada *nf* piece of hooliganism, loutish thing (to do).

gamberrear [1a] *vi* to go around causing trouble, act like a hooligan; to be a lout; to loaf.

gamberrismo *nm* hooliganism; loutishness.

gamberrístico *adj* loutish, ill-bred.

gamberro 1 *adj* ill-bred, loutish, rough. **2** *nm* lout, hooligan, troublemaker, roughneck (*sl*).

gambeta *nf* (of horse) prance, caper; (*Bol, Per, RPl*) dodge, avoiding action; (*fig*) dodge, pretext.

gambito *nm* gambit.

gambuza *nf* (*Naut*) store, storeroom.

gamella *nf* trough; washtub.

gamín *nm* (*Col*) street urchin.

gamo *nm* buck (of fallow deer).

gamonal *nm* (*CAm, Col, Ec, Per*) = **cacique**.

gamonalismo *nm* (*CAm, Col, Ec, Per*) = **caciquismo**.

gamuza *nf* (a) (*Zool*) chamois. (b) chamois leather, wash leather; duster.

gana *nf* desire, wish (*de* for); appetite (*de* for); inclination, longing (*de* for); **¡las** —**s!** you'll wish you had (agreed)!; **son** —**s de joder** (*or* **molestar** *etc*) they're just trying to be awkward; **es** — (*Mex, Per, PR*) it's a waste of time; — **tiene de coles quien besa al hortelano** it's just cupboard love; **con** —**s** (*CAm, PR*) really, truly; **de** — (*Ec*) unintentionally; as a joke, in fun; **de buena** — willingly, readily; **¡de buena** —**!** gladly!; **de mala** — unwillingly, reluctantly, grudgingly; **hasta las** —**s** (*Mex*) right up to the end; **comer con** — to eat heartily; **me da la** — **de** + *infin* I feel like + *ger*, I want to + *infin*, I have an inclination to + *infin*; **esto da** —**s de comerlo** it makes you want to eat it; **porque no me da la (real)** — because I don't (damned well) want to; **como te dé la** — just as you wish; **le entran** —**s de** + *infin* he begins to want to + *infin*, he feels the urge to + *infin*; **quedarse con las** —**s** to fail, be disappointed; **quitársele a uno las** —**s de** to spoil one's appetite for; **tener** —**s de** + *infin* to feel like + *ger*, have a mind to + *infin*; **tengo pocas** —**s de** + *infin* I don't much feel like + *ger*.

ganadería *nf* (a) cattle raising, stockbreeding; ranching. (b) stock farm; cattle ranch. (c) cattle, livestock; strain, breed, race (of cattle).

ganadero 1 *adj* cattle (*attr*), stock (*attr*); cattle-raising (*attr*). **2** *nm* stockbreeder, rancher (*US*); cattle dealer.

ganado *nm* (a) stock, livestock; (*esp SAm*) cattle; (*un* —) herd, flock; — **asnal** donkeys; — **caballar** horses; — **cabrío** goats; — **lanar**, — **ovejuno** sheep; — **mayor** cattle, horses and mules; — **menor** sheep, goats and pigs; — **porcino** pigs; — **vacuno** cattle.

(b) (*SAm*) **un** — **de** (*fig*) a crowd of, a mob of.

ganador 1 *adj* winning, victorious; **el equipo** — **the** winning team; **apostar a** — **y colocado** to back (a horse) each way, back for a win and a place.

2 *nm*, **ganadora** *nf* winner; (*Fin*) earner; (*fig*) gainer, one who gains.

ganancia *nf* (a) gain; increase; (*Comm, Fin*) profit; —**s** earnings; profits, winnings; —**s y pérdidas** profit and loss; — **bruta** gross profit; —**s de capital** capital gains; — **líquida** net profit; **sacar** — **de** to draw profit from. (b) (*SAm*) extra, bonus.

ganancial *adj* profit (*attr*).

ganancioso 1 *adj* (a) gainful; profitable, lucrative.

(b) winning; **salir** — to emerge the winner, come out on top; to be the gainer.

2 *nm*, **gananciosa** *nf* gainer, one who gains; winner; **en esto el** — **es él** in this he is the gainer.

ganapán *nm* (a) messenger, porter. (b) casual labourer; odd-job man. (c) lout, rough individual.

ganar [1a] **1** *vt* (a) to gain; to get, acquire, obtain; (*Comm, Fin*) to earn; *interest* to draw; *money* to earn, make; *prize* to win; **gana un sueldo** he earns a salary; **¿cuánto ganas al mes?** how much do you earn (*or* make) a month?; **tierras ganadas al mar** land reclaimed from the sea, land won from the sea.

(b) (*Sport etc*) *match, race, contest* to win; *point* to score, win; *opponent* to beat; *rival* to outstrip, surpass, leave behind; — **unas oposiciones para un puesto** to win a post by public competition; **A le ganó a B esta vez** A beat B this time; **no hay quien le gane** there's nobody who can beat him; **A le gana a B en pericia** A has more expert knowledge than B; **A le gana a B trabajando** A is a better worker than B; **A le ganó 5 duros a B** A won 5 duros from (*or* off) B.

(c) (*Mil*) *town etc* to take, capture.

(d) to reach; — **la orilla** to reach the shore; — **la orilla nadando** to swim to the shore.

(e) (*fig*) to win over; *support, supporters* to win, get; **dejarse** — **por** to allow oneself to be won over by; **no se deja** — **en ningún momento por la desesperación** he never gives way to despair.

2 *vi* (a) (*Sport etc*) to win; to gain.

(b) (*fig*) to thrive, improve, do well.

(c) (*also* **ganarse**; *SAm*) to go off; to escape, take refuge; — **a la cama** to go off to bed; — **hasta la casa** to get to the house; **se ganó en la iglesia** he took refuge in the church; **el caballo ganó para el bosque** the horse moved off towards the wood, the horse made for the wood.

ganchera *nf* (*Arg*) matchmaker.

ganchero *nm* (*Arg*) helper, assistant; (*Chi*) odd-job man.

ganchete *nm*: **mirar al** — (*Ven*) to look askance (at); **ir de** — (*SAm*) to go arm-in-arm.

ganchillo *nm* (a) small hook; (*Sew*) crochet hook. (b) crochet, crochet work; **hacer** — to crochet.

gancho *nm* (a) hook; hanger; (*Agr*) shepherd's crook; (*SAm*) hairpin; — **de carnicero** butcher's hook; **echar el** — **a** (*fig*) to hook, land, capture.

(b) (*person*) main attraction, centre of attraction; (*pej*) pimp, procurer; (*pej*) tout.

(c) (*fam*) sex appeal, charm, attractiveness; **tiene muchísimo** — she's got lots of sex appeal.

(d) (*Col, Ec*) lady's saddle.

(e) (*SAm*) help; protection; **hacer** — (*Arg, Guat*) to lend a hand.

ganchoso *adj*, **ganchudo** *adj* hooked.

gandido *adj* (*Col*) hungry; greedy.

gandinga *nf* (*Cu, PR*) (a) (*Cook*) liver stew. (b) sloth, apathy; **tener poca** — to have small sense of shame.

gandul 1 *adj* idle, lazy, slack; good-for-nothing. **2** *nm*, **gandula** *nf* idler, slacker; good-for-nothing.

gandulear [1a] *vi* to idle, loaf, slack.

gandulería *nf* idleness, loafing, slackness.

gandulitis *nf* (*hum*) congenital laziness.

gane *nm* (*CAm: Sport*) win, victory; **llevarse el** →, **lograr el** — to win.

gang [gan] *nm*, *pl* **gangs** [gan] (*angl*) gang.

ganga *nf* (a) (*Comm*) bargain; **¡una verdadera** —**!** a genuine bargain! (b) (*fig*) windfall; cinch (*sl*), gift (*fam*); **esto es una** — this is a gift. (c) (*Mex*) taunt, jeer.

ganglio *nm* ganglion; swelling.

gangosear [1a] *vi* (*Arg, Col*) = **ganguear**.

gangoseo *nm* (*Arg, Col*) = **gangueo**.

gangoso *adj* accent nasal, twanging.

gangrena *nf* gangrene.

gangrenarse [1a] *vr* to become gangrenous.

gangrenoso *adj* gangrenous.

gángster ['ganster] *nm*, *pl* **gángsters** ['ganster] (*angl*) gangster, gunman.

gangsterismo [ganste'rizmo] *nm* (*angl*) gangsterism.

ganguear [1a] *vi* to talk with a nasal accent, speak with a twang.

gangueo *nm* nasal accent, twang.

ganoso *adj* (a) anxious, keen; — **de** + *infin* anxious to + *infin*, keen to + *infin*. (b) (*Chi*) *horse* spirited, fiery.

gansa nf (a) (Orn) goose. (b) (fam) goose, silly girl.
gansada nf stupid thing (to do), piece of stupidity.
ganso nm (a) (Orn) goose, gander; — **salvaje** wild goose. (b) (fam) idiot, dimwit (fam), dolt; country bumpkin; ¡no seas —! don't be an idiot!
Gante Ghent.
ganzúa 1 nf picklock, skeleton key. 2 nmf burglar, thief; inquisitive person, smeller out of secrets.
gañán nm farmhand, labourer.
gañido nm yelp, howl; croak; wheeze.
gañir [3h] vi (of dog) to yelp, howl; (of bird) to croak; (of person) to wheeze, talk hoarsely, croak.
gañón nm (fam), **gañote** nm (fam) throat, gullet.
garabatear [1a] 1 vt to scribble, scrawl. 2 vi (a) to throw out a hook. (b) to scribble, scrawl. (c) to beat about the bush.
garabato nm (a) hook; grapple, grapnel; (Ant) long forked pole; (Naut) grappling iron; — **de carnicero** meat hook.
 (b) (in writing exercise) pothook.
 (c) (Ant) skinny person.
 (d) (Chi) coarse remark.
 (e) —s scribble, scrawl.
 (f) =**gancho** (c).
garabina nf (a) (Bol) trifle, bagatelle; cheap finery. (b) (Cu) chrysalis.
garabito nm (a) market stall. (b) (Bol) bum, tramp.
garaje nm garage; — **de varios pisos** multi-storey car park.
garajista nm garage owner; garage man, garage attendant.
garambaina nf (a) cheap finery, tawdry finery.
 (b) gaudiness.
 (c) —s (affected) grimaces; absurd mannerisms; ¡déjate de —s! stop that silly simpering!
 (d) —s scribble, scrawl.
garambetas nfpl (PR) =**garambaina** (a) and (c).
garandumba nf (Arg) (a) flatboat, flat river boat. (b) (hum) big woman.
garante 1 adj responsible. 2 nmf guarantor, surety.
garantía nf guarantee; pledge, security; undertaking; (Law) warranty; **bajo** — under guarantee; —s **constitucionales** constitutional guarantees; — **en efectivo** cash guarantee, surety; **de máxima** — absolutely guaranteed.
garantir [3a; defective] vt (a) to guarantee. (b) (Chi, Per, PR) to guarantee, assure; **le garanto** I assure you, I warrant you.
garantizado adj guaranteed.
garantizar [1f] vt to guarantee, warrant; to vouch for.
garañón nm (a) stud jackass; (SAm) stallion. (b) (Chi) brothel keeper.
garapiña nf (a) sugar icing, sugar coating. (b) (SAm) iced pineapple drink. (c) (Mex) theft.
garapiñar [1a] vt ice cream etc to freeze; cream to clot; cake to ice, coat with sugar; fruit to candy.
garapiñera nf ice-cream freezer.
garapullo nm dart, arrow; (Taur) =**banderilla**.
garata nf (PR, SD) fight, brawl, row.
garatusas nfpl: **hacer** — **a uno** to coax someone, wheedle someone.
garba nf (Agr) sheaf.
garbanzo nm (a) (Bot) chickpea; **ser el** — **negro** to be the black sheep of the family.
 (b) **de** — ordinary, unpretentious, common; **gente de** — humble folk, ordinary people.
garbear [1a] 1 vt (fam) to pinch (fam), swipe (sl). 2 vi (a) to affect elegance, make a show, show oneself off. (b) = 3 **garbearse** vr to get along, rub along (fam).
garbeo nm affected elegance, show; **darse un** —, **pegarse un** — to take an elegant stroll, walk to show oneself off.
garbera nf (Agr) stook, shock.
garbillar [1a] vt (Agr) to sift, sieve; (Min) to sift, screen, riddle.
garbillo nm sieve; screen, riddle.
garbo nm (a) grace, elegance; graceful bearing, fine carriage; jauntiness, jaunty bearing; (woman's) glamour, allure, attractiveness; **andar con** — to walk gracefully, carry oneself well; **hacer algo con** — to do something with grace and ease (or with style); ¡qué —! what a carriage!, (freq) isn't she lovely!
 (b) magnanimity, generosity.
garbosamente adv (a) gracefully, elegantly; in sprightly fashion; jauntily; alluringly, attractively; gracefully and easily, stylishly. (b) generously.
garboso adj (a) graceful, elegant; jaunty; glamorous, alluring, attractive; graceful and easy, stylish. (b) magnanimous, generous.
garceta nf egret.

gardel nm (Arg) toff (fam), masher (fam).
gardelear [1a] vi (Arg) to dress smartly.
gardenia nf gardenia.
garduña nf (Zool) marten.
garduño nm, **garduña** nf sneak thief.
garete nm: **estar al** —, **ir al** — to be adrift.
garfa nf claw.
garfada nf clawing, scratching.
garfio nm hook; gaff; (Tech) grapple, grappling iron, claw; (Mountaineering) climbing iron.
gargajear [1a] vi to spit phlegm, hawk.
gargajo nm phlegm, sputum.
garganta nf (a) (Anat) throat, gullet; neck; **le tengo atravesado en la** — he sticks in my gullet.
 (b) (Anat: of foot) instep.
 (c) (Mus) singing voice; **tener buena** — to have a good singing voice.
 (d) (of bottle) neck.
 (e) (Geog) gorge, ravine; narrow pass.
 (f) (Archit: of column etc) shaft.
gargantear [1a] vi (Mus) to warble, quaver, trill.
gargantilla nf necklace.
gárgara nf gargle, gargling; **hacer** —s to gargle; ¡vaya Vd a hacer —s! (fam) go to blazes!
gargarear [1a] vi (Chi, Guat, Per) to gargle.
gargarismo nm (a) gargle, gargling solution. (b) gargle, gargling.
gargarizar [1f] vi to gargle.
gárgol nm (Tech) groove.
gárgola nf gargoyle.
gargolet nm wren.
garguero nm gullet; windpipe.
garifo adj (a) spruce, elegant, natty. (b) (Arg, Bol) lively, merry. (c) (Col) stuck-up (fam). (d) (CR, Ec, Per) hungry, greedy.
garita nf cabin, hut, box; (Mil) sentry box; (of lorry etc) cab; (of building) porter's lodge; look-out post; (fam) water closet; (SAm: of traffic police) stand, box; — **de señales** (Rail) signal box.
garitea nf (Bol, Ec) river flatboat.
garitero nm keeper of a gaming house; gambler.
garito nm (a) gaming house, gambling den. (b) gambling profits.
garlador 1 adj garrulous. 2 nm, **garladora** nf chatterer, great talker.
garlito nm fish trap; (fig) snare, trap; **caer en el** — to fall into the trap; **coger a uno en el** — to catch someone in the act.
garlopa nf jack plane.
garnacha nf (a) (Law: Hist) gown, robe. (b) (Mex: Cook) omelette. (c) (CAm) **a la** — violently; **ni de** — (Ven) not at all, by no means.
garnucho nm (Mex) tap, rap on the nose.
Garona m Garonne.
garra nf (a) (Zool) claw; talon; (fig) hand, paw; (Mex: fig) muscular strength; **echar la** — **a uno** to arrest someone, seize someone; **estar como una** — (Arg, Col) to be terribly thin.
 (b) —s (Zool) claws, talons; (fig) jaws; (fig) clutches; (fig) grip, clutch; **caer en las** —s **de uno** to fall into someone's clutches.
 (c) (Tech) claw, tooth, hook; (Mech) clutch; — **de seguridad** safety clutch.
 (d) (fig) bite, penetration; **esa canción no tiéne** — that song has no bite to it.
 (e) (SAm) piece of (hard, wrinkled, old) leather; —s (Mex) bits, pieces, scraps; **no hay cuero sin** —s (Mex) nothing is ever perfect.
 (f) (Col) leather bag; sack.
garrafa nf carafe, decanter.
garrafal adj enormous, terrific; blunder etc monumental, terrible.
garrafón nm carboy, demijohn.
garrancha nf (fam) sword; (Col) hook.
garrapata nf (a) (Zool) tick. (b) (Mil: hum) disabled horse, useless horse.
garrapatear [1a] vi to scribble, scrawl.
garrapatero nm cowbird, buffalo bird; (SAm) tick-eater bird.
garrapato nm pothook; —s (fig) scribble, scrawl.
garrapaticida nm (SAm) insecticide, tick-killing agent.
garrear [1a] (Arg) 1 vt (a) to skin the feet of. (b) (fam) to steal. 2 vi to sponge, live at someone else's expense.
garreo nm (Arg: fam): **es de puro** — it's a cinch (sl).
garrete nm (Arg, Guat, Col, Ven) =**jarrete**.
garrido adj (a) neat, elegant, smart. (b) (arch) handsome; pretty.
garroba nf carob bean.
garrocha nf (Agr) goad; (Taur) spear; (Sport) vaulting pole.

garrón nm (Orn) spur; talon; (Zool) paw; heel; (of meat) shank; (Arg) hock; (Bot) snag, spur; **vivir de — (Arg) =garronear.**

garronear [1a] vi (Arg) to live in idleness; to sponge (fam), live at someone else's expense.

garrotazo nm blow with a stick (or club etc).

garrote nm (a) stick, club, truncheon, cudgel; **política del gran — (SAm) policy of the big stick; jugar — (Ven) to get angry.**
(b) (Med) tourniquet; (Law) garrotte; **dar — a uno** to garrotte someone.
(c) (Mex: Aut) brake; **darse — to check oneself,** hold oneself back.

garrotero 1 adj (Cu, Chi) stingy. **2** nm (a) (Mex) brakeman. (b) (Chi, Ec, Per) bully, tough (fam); brawler, troublemaker.

garrotillo nm (a) (Med) croup. (b) (Arg) very cold drizzle.

garrucha nf pulley.

garrudo adj (a) (Mex) tough, muscular. (b) (Col) cow terribly thin.

garrulería nf chatter.

garrulidad nf garrulity, talkativeness.

gárrulo adj person garrulous, chattering, talkative; bird twittering; water babbling, murmuring; wind noisy.

garúa nf (a) (SAm) drizzle. (b) (PR) row, uproar.

garuar [1e] vi (SAm) to drizzle; ¡qué le garúe fino! I wish you luck!, I hope it keeps fine for you!

garubar [1a] vi (Hond, Urug) =garuar.

garuga nf (Chi, Nic, Mex, RPl) =garúa.

garugar [1h] vi (Arg, Chi) =garuar.

garulla nf (a) loose grapes. (b) (fam) mob, rabble. (c) (fam) urchin.

garullada nf (fam) mob, rabble.

garullo nm (fam) lanky youth, gawky lad.

garza nf (also — real) heron; — imperial purple heron.

garzo adj blue, bluish; blue-eyed.

garzón nm (Chi, RPl: gall) waiter.

gas nm (a) gas; fumes; — del alumbrado coal gas; — asfixiante, — tóxico poison gas; — butano butane; —es de escape exhaust (fumes); — hilarante laughing gas; — lacrimógeno tear gas; — mostaza mustard gas; — natural natural gas; — de los pantanos marsh gas; — pobre producer gas; asfixiar con — to gas; estar — (Guat) to be in love. (b) (CAm, Mex, PR) petrol, gas (US); ir a todo — (Aut) to go full out.

gasa nf gauze; (for mourning) crêpe.

Gascuña f Gascony.

gaseosa nf aerated water, carbonated water, mineral water; (freq) pop (fam), fizz (fam), fizzy drink; — de limón fizzy lemonade.

gaseoso adj gaseous; aerated, carbonated; gassy; drink fizzy.

gásfiter nm, pl gásfiters (Chi: angl) plumber.

gasfitería nf (Chi, Ec, Per) plumber's (shop).

gasfitero nm (SAm: angl) plumber.

gasista nm gas fitter, gasman.

gasoducto nm gas pipeline.

gas-oil [ga'soil] nm (angl) diesel oil.

gasóleo nm (Acad) diesel oil.

gasolina nf (a) (Aut) petrol, motor spirit, gasoline (US), gas (US fam); — de aviación aviation spirit; — de alto octanaje high-octane petrol.
(b) (PR) petrol station, gas station (US).

gasolinera nf (a) (Naut) motorboat. (b) (Aut) petrol station, gas station (US).

gasómetro nm gasometer.

gásquet nm, pl gásquets (SAm: angl) gasket.

gastable adj expendable; dispensable.

gastado adj (a) spent; used up. (b) worn out; dress shabby, threadbare. (c) cliché etc hackneyed, trite; joke old, corny (fam).

gastador 1 adj extravagant, lavish; wasteful. **2** nm, **gastadora** nf (a) spender; (pej) spendthrift. (b) (Mil: Hist) sapper, pioneer.

gastar [1a] **1** vt (a) effort, money, time etc to spend; to expend; to lay out; **han gastado un dineral** they've spent a fortune.
(b) resources etc to use up, exhaust, consume.
(c) (pej) to waste; — una semana en hacer algo to waste a week doing something; — palabras to waste words, waste one's breath.
(d) (Mech etc) to wear away, wear down; clothes, shoes to wear out; to spoil.
(e) to have, wear, sport; to use; to show habitually; car etc to have, own, run; — barba to have a beard, wear a beard, sport a beard; antes no gastaba gafas he used not to wear glasses.
(f) joke to crack; trick to play (a on).
(g) —las (fam) to act, behave.

2 vi to spend.

3 gastarse vr to become exhausted; to run out; to wear out; to waste, go to waste, spoil.

gasto nm (a) (act) spending, expenditure.
(b) amount spent, expenditure, expense; ello supone un gran — para él it means a considerable expense for him.
(c) consumption, use.
(d) (Mech etc) wear.
(e) waste.
(f) (of gas etc) flow, rate of flow.
(g) —s (Comm, Fin) expenses; charge(s), cost(s), rate(s); —s de acarreo transport charges, haulage; —s de administración administrative costs, overheads; —s bancarios bank charges; —s de conservación, —s de mantenimiento upkeep costs, maintenance expenses; —s de correos postal charges; —s de defensa (Mil) defence costs; —s de explotación operating costs, operating expenses; —s fijos fixed charges; —s de flete freight charges; —s generales overheads; —s menores (de caja) petty cash; —s de viaje travelling expenses; cubrir —s to cover expenses; meterse en —s to go to expense, incur expense; pagar los —s to pay the expenses, foot the bill.

gastoso adj extravagant, wasteful.

gástrico adj gastric.

gastritis nf gastritis.

gastronomía nf gastronomy.

gastronómico adj gastronomic.

gastrónomo nm, **gastrónoma** nf gastronome, gourmet; gastronomist.

gata nf (a) (Zool) cat, she-cat.
(b) (fam) Madrid woman; (Mex) servant, maid.
(c) (Meteorol) hill cloud.
(d) (Chi, Per) crank, handle.
(e) a —s on all fours; (Bol, RPl) barely, hardly; with great difficulty; andar a —s to go on all fours; to creep, crawl; (of child) to crawl.
(f) echar la — (CAm), soltar la — (Col) to pilfer, steal.

gatada nf (a) movement (or act etc) typical of a cat. (b) litter of kittens. (c) scratch, clawing. (d) artful dodge, sly trick.

gateado 1 adj (a) catlike, feline.
(b) streaked, striped.
2 nm (a) crawl, crawling; climb, climbing.
(b) scratch, clawing.
(c) (Ant) hard veined wood (used in cabinet-making).

gateamiento nm =gateado 2 (a) and (b).

gatear [1a] **1** vt (a) to scratch, claw.
(b) (fam) to pinch (fam), swipe (sl).
(c) (Mex) servants to make love to; (Bol, Ec, Guat) to make love to.
2 vi (a) to climb, clamber (por up); to creep, crawl, go on all fours.
(b) (SAm) to go looking for sexual adventure.

gatera nf (a) catlover. (b) cat hole (also Naut). (c) (Bol, Ec, Per) market woman, stallholder.

gatería nf (a) cats, collection of cats. (b) gang of louts. (c) pretended humility, assumed modesty.

gatillo nm (a) (Mil) trigger; (Med) dental forceps; (Tech) clamp. (b) (Zool) nape (of the neck). (c) young thief, young pickpocket.

gatita nf (female) kitten.

gatito nm kitten; puss, pussy.

gato¹ nm (a) (Zool) cat, tomcat; — de algalia civet cat; — de Angora Angora cat; — montés wild cat; — romano tabby cat; — siamés Siamese cat; "El — con botas" "Puss in Boots"; dar a uno — por liebre to take someone in, pull the wool over someone's eyes, sell someone a pig in a poke; el — escaldado del agua fría huye once bitten twice shy; aquí hay — encerrado I smell a rat, there's something fishy here; no había más que 4 —s there was hardly anybody there; jugar al — y ratón con uno to play a cat-and-mouse game with someone; llevar el — al agua to pull off something difficult; pasar sobre algo como — sobre ascuas to tread carefully round something.
(b) (Tech: Aut etc) jack; clamp, vice, grab; (Mex) =gatillo; — de tornillo screw jack.
(c) (Fin) money bag.
(d) (fam) sneak thief, petty thief; slyboots (fam).
(e) native of Madrid.
(f) (Mex) servant.
(g) (CAm, Col, SD) fleshy part of the arm.
(h) (Mex) tip.
(i) (Ven) syphilis.
(j) (Chi) hot-water bottle.
(k) (RPl) a popular folk dance.

gato² nm (Per) open-air market, market place.

gatuno adj catlike, feline.

gatuperio nm (a) hotchpotch. (b) fraud, piece of underhand dealing.

gaucha nf (Arg) mannish woman.

gauchada nf (RPl) (a) gauchos (collectively). (b) gaucho exploit, (pej) typical gaucho trick. (c) kind deed, favour; disinterested act.

gauchaje nm (RPl) gauchos (collectively); gathering of gauchos; (pej) riffraff, rabble.

gauchear [1a] vi (RPl) (a) to live like a gaucho, observe the customs of the gauchos. (b) to be mixed up in dangerous love affairs.

gauchesco adj (RPl) gaucho (attr); like a gaucho; of the gauchos; **vida gauchesca** gaucho life.

gaucho 1 nm (a) (RPl) gaucho; cowboy, herdsman, rough rider; (Arg: hum) inhabitant of the coastal provinces.
  (b) (Chi, RPl) good rider, expert horseman.
  (c) (Ec) wide-brimmed straw hat.
2 adj (a) gaucho (attr); gaucho-like.
  (b) (SAm: pej) coarse, rough; sly, tricky.

gaudeamus nm (hum) party, beano (fam).

gaveta nf drawer, till; locker.

gavia nf (a) (Naut) (main) topsail. (b) (Orn) seagull. (c) (Agr) ditch.

gavilán nm (a) (Orn) sparrowhawk. (b) (of quill pen) nib. (c) (of sword) quillon. (d) (SAm) ingrowing nail.

gavilla nf (a) (Agr) sheaf. (b) (fam) gang, band.

gaviota nf (a) (Orn) seagull, gull. (b) (Mex: hum) airman.

gavota nf (Hist) gavotte.

gaya nf (a) (Orn) magpie. (b) (in cloth) coloured stripe.

gayo adj (a) merry, gay; **gaya ciencia** (Lit: Hist) art of poetry, art of the troubadours. (b) bright, showy.

gayola nf cage; (fam) jail.

gaza nf loop; (Naut) bend, bight.

gazafatón nm (fam) = **gazapatón**.

gazapa nf (fam) fib, lie.

gazapatón nm (fam) blunder, slip; piece of nonsense.

gazapera nf (a) rabbit hole, warren. (b) (fam) den of thieves. (c) brawl, shindy.

gazapo nm (a) (Zool) young rabbit. (b) sly fellow; (SAm) liar. (c) blunder, bloomer (fam); lie; (Typ) meaningful misprint. (d) (PR) trick.

gazmoñada nf, **gazmoñería** nf (a) hypocrisy, cant. (b) prudery, priggishness; affected demureness; sanctimoniousness.

gazmoñero adj, **gazmoño 1** adj (a) hypocritical, canting. (b) prudish, priggish; strait-laced; affectedly demure; sanctimonious.
2 nm, **gazmoñera** nf, **gazmoña** nf (a) hypocrite. (b) prude, prig; affectedly demure person; sanctimonious person.

gaznápiro nm, **gaznápira** nf dolt, simpleton.

gaznatada nf (CAm, PR) punch, slap.

gaznate nm (a) gullet; windpipe, throttle; **remojar el —** (fam) to wet one's whistle (fam), have a swig (fam). (b) (Mex) fritter.

gaznetón nm adj (CAm, Col, Mex) loud-mouthed, bawling.

gazpacho nm (a) cold soup (esp Andalusian) made of oil, vinegar, garlic, onion, cucumber etc. (b) (Hond) residue, dregs, left-overs.

gazuza nf (a) (fam) ravenous hunger. (b) (CR) din, row, merry noise. (c) (Guat) common people. (d) (Hond) wily bird.

géiser nm (Geog) geyser.

geisha ['geiʃa] nf geisha (girl).

gelatina nf gelatin(e), jelly; **— explosiva** gelignite.

gelatinoso adj gelatinous.

gelignita nf gelignite.

gema nf (a) gem, jewel. (b) (Bot) bud.

gemelo 1 adj twin; **buque —** sister ship; **hermanas gemelas** twin sisters.
2 (a) nm, **gemela** nf twin.
  (b) —s nmpl **de campo** field glasses, binoculars; —s **de teatro** opera glasses.
  (c) —s nmpl (Sew) cufflinks.
  (d) **G—s** mpl (Astron) Gemini.
  (e) nm (Naut) sister ship.

gemido nm groan, moan; wail, howl.

gemidor adj groaning, moaning; wailing, howling.

Géminis nm (Astron) Gemini.

gemiquear [1a] vi (Chi) to whine.

gemiqueo nm (Chi) whining.

gemir [3l] vi to groan, moan; to wail, howl; (of animal) to whine; (of wind etc) to moan, howl; (fig) to moan, lament; (in jail) to languish, rot; **"Sí" dijo gimiendo** "Yes" he groaned.

gen nm gene.

genciana nf gentian.

gendarme nm (SAm: gall) policeman, gendarme.

gendarmería nf (SAm: gall) police, gendarmerie.

genealogía nf genealogy; family tree; pedigree.

genealógico adj genealogical.

genealogista nmf genealogist.

generación nf (a) (act) generation.
  (b) (group) generation; **la — del '98** the '98 generation; **la — de 1927** (Lit) the 1927 generation; **las nuevas —es** the rising generation.
  (c) progeny, offspring; succession.

generador 1 adj generating. **2** nm generator.

general 1 adj general; wide, universal; common, prevailing, (pej) rife; usual; **es — por toda España** it is common throughout Spain, it exists in the whole of Spain; **de distribución —** of general distribution, generally distributed; **en —, por lo —** generally, as a general rule, in general; for the most part; **el mundo en —** the world in general, the world at large.
  2 nm general; **— de brigada** brigadier-general; **— de división** major-general.
  3 —es nfpl personal particulars.

generala nf (a) general's wife. (b) call to arms, general alert.

generalato nm generalship.

generalidad nf (a) generality; mass, majority; **la — de los hombres** the mass of ordinary people, the common run of men.
  (b) vague answer, generalization, general statement.
  (c) (Pol) **la G—** Catalan autonomous government of 1931-36.

generalísimo nm generalissimo, supreme commander; **el G— Franco** (usually called) General Franco.

generalización nf (a) generalization. (b) (of conflict) widening, escalation.

generalizar [1f] **1** vt (a) to generalize; to make more widely known, bring into general use.
  (b) (Mil) to widen, escalate, scale up.
  2 vi to generalize.
  3 generalizarse vr (a) to become general, become universal; to become widely known (or used etc).
  (b) (Mil) to widen, escalate.

generalmente adv generally.

generar [1a] vt to generate.

generativo adj generative.

genérico adj generic.

género nm (a) class, kind, type, sort; **— humano** human race, mankind; **le deseo todo — de felicidades** I wish you all the happiness in the world.
  (b) (Bio) genus.
  (c) (Art, Lit) genre; type; **— chico** (genre of) comic one-act pieces, short farces; zarzuela, Spanish operetta; **— novelístico** novel genre, fiction; **pintor de —** genre painter; **es todo un — de literatura** it is a whole type of literature.
  (d) (Gram) gender; **del — masculino** of the masculine gender.
  (e) (Comm) cloth, stuff, material; —s goods, merchandise; commodities; —s **de lino** linen goods; —s **de punto** knitwear, knitted goods; **le conozco el —** I know his sort; I know all about him, I recognize the type.

generosamente adv generously; nobly, magnanimously.

generosidad nf (a) generosity; nobility, magnanimity. (b) (Hist) nobility; valour.

generoso adj (a) generous (con, para to); noble, magnanimous.
  (b) (Hist) noble, highborn; gentlemanly; brave, valiant; **de sangre generosa** of noble blood; **en pecho —** in a noble heart.
  (c) wine rich, full-bodied.

genésico adj genetic.

génesis nf genesis.

Génesis nm (Bib) Genesis.

genética nf genetics.

genético adj genetic.

genetista nmf geneticist.

genial 1 adj (a) inspired, brilliant, of genius; **escritor —** writer of genius; **fue una idea —** it was a brilliant idea; **¡eso fue —!** it was marvellous!, it was wonderful!
  (b) pleasant, cheerful, genial.
  (c) in character, characteristic; individual; typical.
  2 nm (fam) temper, disposition.

genialidad nf (a) genius; stroke of genius, brilliant stroke, inspired move; **tiene una — para los negocios**

he has a genius for business; **eso fue una —** it was a stroke of genius; **es una — suya** it's one of his brilliant ideas.

(b) temperament.

(c) peculiarity, typical feature, characteristic; eccentricity.

genialmente *adv* (a) in an inspired way, brilliantly, with genius. (b) pleasantly, cheerfully.

genio *nm* (a) disposition, nature, character, temper; **— alegre** cheerful nature; **buen —** good nature; **de — franco** of an open nature; **mal —** bad temper; evil disposition; **de mal —** bad-tempered; ill-disposed; **estar de mal —** to be in a bad temper; **— vivo** quick temper, hot temper; **corto de —** dimwitted; spiritless, timid; **llevar el — a uno** to humour someone; not to dare to contradict someone.

(b) bad temper; **es una mujer de mucho —** she's a quick-tempered woman; **tiene —** he's temperamental; he has an uncertain temper, he's bad-tempered.

(c) genius; **¡eres un —!** you're a genius!

(d) genius, special nature, peculiarities; **esto va en contra del — de la lengua** this goes against the genius of the language.

(e) (*Myth, Rel*) spirit; genie; **— del mal** evil spirit; **— tutelar** guardian spirit.

genioso *adj* (*Col, Mex, SD*) bad-tempered.

genista *nf* broom, genista.

genital 1 *adj* genital. **2 —es** *nmpl* genitals, genital organs.

genitivo 1 *adj* generative, reproductive. **2** *nm* (*Gram*) genitive.

genocidio *nm* genocide.

Génova *f* Genoa.

genovés 1 *adj* Genoese. **2** *nm*, **genovesa** *nf* Genoese.

gental *nm* (*Col*) lot, mass; **un — de gente** a mass of people.

gente *nf* (a) people, folk; race, nation; (*Mil*) men, troops, followers, retinue; (*fam*) relatives, folks, people; **el rey y su —** the king and his retinue; **mi —** my people, my folks; **son — inculta** they're rough people; **no me gusta esa —** I don't like those people; **hay muy poca —** there are very few people; **— baja** lower classes, low-class people; **— bien** upper-class people; nice people, respectable people; (*pej*) posh people (*fam*); smart set; **— de bien** honest folk, decent people; **— de capa parda** country folk; **— de color** (*euph*) coloured people; **— de la cuchilla** butchers; **— de mar** seafaring men; **— menuda** small fry; humble folk; children, little people; **¡— de paz!** (*Mil*) friend!; **— de pelo** well-to-do people; **— de medio pelo** people of limited means; **— natural** (*CAm*) Indians, natives; **— perdida** bad people; criminals; idlers, loafers; **— de pluma** clerks, penpushers; **— principal** nobility, gentry; **— de tomuza** (*Ven*) Negroes, mulattoes; **— de trato** tradespeople; **de — en —** from generation to generation.

(b) (*SAm*) upper-class people; nice people, respectable people; **ser —** to be somebody, to have social importance.

(c) (*Mex, SD*) person; **había dos —s** there were two people, there were two persons.

gentecilla *nf* unimportant people; (*pej*) rabble, riffraff.

genterío *nm* (*CR*) = **gentío**.

gentil 1 *adj* (a) elegant, graceful, attractive; charming; pretty; courteous.

(b) (*iro*) pretty, fine; **¡— cumplido!** a fine compliment!

(c) (*Rel*) pagan, heathen; gentile.

2 *nmf* pagan, heathen; gentile.

gentileza *nf* (a) elegance, gracefulness; charm; prettiness; courtesy. (b) show, splendour, ostentation. (c) dash, gallantry.

gentilhombre *nm* (*Hist*) gentleman; **— de cámara** gentleman-in-waiting.

gentilicio *adj* national, tribal; family (*attr*); **nombre —** family name.

gentilidad *nf*, **gentilismo** *nm* heathendom; heathenism.

gentilmente *adv* (a) elegantly, gracefully, attractively; charmingly; prettily; courteously. (b) (*iro*) prettily.

gentío *nm* crowd, throng.

gentualla *nf*, **gentuza** *nf* rabble, mob; riffraff; **¡qué —!** what a shower! (*sl*).

genuflexión *nf* genuflexion.

genuflexo *adj* (*Arg*) servile, slavish.

genuinamente *adv* genuinely; really, truly.

genuino *adj* (a) genuine; real, pure, true. (b) (*Col*) smashing (*sl*), super (*fam*).

geodesia *nf* geodesy.

geodésico *adj* geodesic.

geofísica *nf* geophysics.

Geofredo *m* Geoffrey.

geografía *nf* geography.

geográfico *adj* geographical.

geógrafo *nm* geographer.

geología *nf* geology.

geológico *adj* geological.

geólogo *nm* geologist.

geometría *nf* geometry; **— del espacio** solid geometry.

geométrico *adj* geometric(al).

geopolítica *nf* geopolitics.

georgiano *adj* Georgian.

geranio *nm* geranium.

Gerardo *m* Gerald, Gerard.

gerencia *nf* (a) management. (b) managership, post of manager. (c) manager's office.

gerente *nm* manager, director; executive; **— de personal** personnel manager.

geriatra *nm* geriatric specialist.

geriatría *nf* geriatrics.

germanesco *adj* slang.

germanía *nf* thieves' slang, cant, underworld parlance.

germánico *adj* Germanic.

germano *adj* German; Germanic.

germanófilo *nm*, **germanófila** *nf* germanophile.

germanófobo *nm*, **germanófoba** *nf* germanophobe.

germen *nm* (a) (*Bio, Med*) germ; **— plasma** germ plasma. (b) (*fig*) germ, seed; source, origin; **el — de una idea** the germ of an idea.

germicida 1 *adj* germicidal. **2** *nm* germicide, germ killer.

germinación *nf* germination.

germinar [1a] *vi* to germinate; to sprout, shoot.

gerontología *nf* gerontology.

gerontólogo *nm* gerontologist.

Gertrudis *f* Gertrude.

gerundense 1 *adj* of Gerona. **2** *nmf* native (*or* inhabitant) of Gerona; **los —s** the people of Gerona.

gerundiano *adj* bombastic.

gerundiar [1b] *vi* (*of Indians*) to speak in gerunds, use the gerund a lot.

gerundino *nm* gerundive (*Latin*).

gerundio *nm* gerund; **— adjetivado** gerundive.

gervasio *nm* (*Col*) fellow, guy; shrewd fellow.

gesta *nf* (a) heroic deed, epic achievement; (b) (*Lit: Hist*) epic, epic poem; *see also* **cantar**.

gestación *nf* gestation.

Gestapo *nf* Gestapo.

gestear [1a] *vi* = **gesticular**.

gesticulación *nf* (a) gesticulation. (b) grimace, (wry) face.

gesticular [1a] *vi* (a) to gesticulate, gesture. (b) to grimace, make a face.

gestión *nf* (a) (*Comm etc*) management, conduct.

(b) negotiation.

(c) measure, step; action; effort; **—es** measures, steps; **hacer las —es necesarias para +** *infin* to take the necessary steps to + *infin*; **hacer las —es preliminares** to do the groundwork, make the first steps; **donde él tenía que realizar unas —es** where he had some business to transact; **el gobierno tendrá que hacer las primeras —es** the government will have to make the first move.

gestionar [1a] *vt* (a) to manage, conduct. (b) to negotiate (for). (c) to try to arrange, strive to bring about, (take steps to) procure, work towards, work for.

gesto *nm* (a) face; expression on one's face; **estar de buen —** to be in a good mood; **estar de mal —** to be in a bad mood; **poner mal —, torcer el —** to make a (wry) face; to scowl, look cross.

(b) grimace, (wry) face; scowl; **hacer —s** to make faces (*a* at); **hacer un —** to make a face; **hizo un — de asco** he looked disgusted; **hizo un — de extrañeza** he looked surprised.

(c) gesture; sign; **hacer —s** to make gestures (*a* to); **con un — de cansancio** with a weary gesture.

gestor 1 *adj* managing. **2** *nm* manager; promoter; business agent, representative.

gestoría *nf* agency (for undertaking business with government departments).

Getsemaní Gethsemane.

Ghana *f* Ghana.

ghaneano 1 *adj* Ghanean. **2** *nm*, **ghaneana** *nf* Ghanean.

giba *nf* (a) hump; hunchback. (b) (*fam*) nuisance, bother.

gibado adj with a hump, hunchbacked.
gibar [1a] vt (fam) to annoy, bother.
gibón nm gibbon.
giboso adj with a hump, hunchbacked.
Gibraltar m Gibraltar.
gibraltareño 1 adj of Gibraltar. 2 nm, **gibraltareña** nf native (or inhabitant) of Gibraltar; los —s the people of Gibraltar.
giganta nf (a) giantess. (b) (Bot) sunflower.
gigante 1 adj giant, gigantic. 2 nm giant.
gigantesco adj gigantic, giant.
gigantez nf gigantic stature, vast size.
gigantón nm big giant; giant carnival figure.
gigoló nm gigolo.
gijonés 1 adj of Gijón. 2 nm, **gijonesa** nf native (or inhabitant) of Gijón; los —es the people of Gijón.
Gil m Giles.
gilda nf lollipop.
gilí adj (fam) stupid, silly.
gilipollada nf (fam) silly thing.
gilipollas nmf, pl **gilipollas** (fam) idiot; ¡—! you idiot!
gilipollear [1a] vi (fam) to do silly things.
gilipollez nf (fam) stupidity, silliness.
gillet(t)e [xi'lete] nf (angl) (any) razor blade.
gimnasia nf gymnastics; physical training; — **respiratoria** deep breathing; **hacer** — to do gymnastics, do physical training.
gimnasio nm gymnasium, gym (fam).
gimnasta nmf gymnast.
gimnástica nf gymnastics.
gimnástico adj gymnastic.
gimotear [1a] vi to whine, whimper; to wail; (of child) to snivel, grizzle.
gimoteo nm whine, whining; whimpering; wailing; snivelling, grizzling.
Ginebra[1] (Geog) Geneva.
Ginebra[2] f (Hist) Guinevere.
ginebra[1] nf gin.
ginebra[2] nf (fam) bedlam, uproar, confusion.
ginecología nf gynaecology.
ginecólogo nm gynaecologist.
ginesta nf = **hiniesta**.
ginfizz [ʒin'fiθ] nm, pl **ginfizz** (angl) gin with mineral water.
Gioconda: la — (the) Mona Lisa.
gira nf (Mus, Theat etc) tour; trip; **estar en** — to be on tour; see also **jira**.
girado nm, **girada** nf (Comm) drawee.
girador nm, **giradora** nf (Comm) drawer.
giralda nf, **giraldilla** nf weathercock.
girar [1a] 1 vt (a) to turn, turn round, rotate; to twist; to spin; — **la manivela 2 veces** turn the crank twice.
(b) to swing, swivel; — **la vista** to look round.
(c) (Comm) to draw (a cargo de, contra on), issue.
2 vi (a) to turn, turn round, go round; to rotate, revolve; to spin, gyrate; to wheel; (Sport: of ball) to spin; — **hacia la derecha** to turn (to the) right, swing right; **gira a 1600 rpm** it rotates at 1600 rpm; **el satélite gira alrededor del mundo** the satellite circles the earth, the satellite revolves round the earth; **la conversación giraba en torno de las elecciones** the conversation turned on (or centred on) the election.
(b) to swing (from side to side), swivel; to hinge; to pivot; **la puerta giró sobre sus goznes** the door swung on its hinges.
(c) (Comm, Fin) to operate, do business; **la compañía gira bajo la razón social de X** the company operates under the name of X.
(d) (Comm) to draw; — **en descubierto** to overdraw.
girasol nm sunflower.
giratorio adj revolving, rotatory; gyratory; door, stage etc revolving; bridge swing (attr), swivel (attr).
giro[1] nm (a) turn; revolution, rotation; gyration; **hacer un** — to turn, make a turn; **el coche dio un** — **brusco** the car swung away suddenly.
(b) (fig: of events etc) trend, tendency, course; **tomar otro** — to change one's mind, change one's tactics; **la cosa ha tomado un** — **favorable** the affair has taken a favourable turn; **la intriga tiene un** — **inesperado** the plot has an unexpected twist in it.
(c) (Ling) turn of phrase, expression.
(d) (Comm) draft; bill of exchange; — **en descubierto** overdraft; — **postal** money order, postal order; — **a la vista** sight draft.
giro[2] adj (a) (SAm) cock with some yellow colouring.

(b) (Cu) scatterbrained, thoughtless. (c) (Guat) drunk. (d) (Mex) cocky (fam), confident.
girocompás nm gyrocompass.
Gironda m Gironde.
giroscópico adj gyroscopic.
giroscopio nm **giróscopo** nm gyroscope.
gis nm (a) chalk; (Col) slate pencil. (b) (Mex) pulque, (any) colourless drink.
gitana nf gipsy; (at fair etc) fortuneteller.
gitanada nf (a) gipsy trick, mean trick. (b) wheedling, cajolery; humbug.
gitanear [1a] vt to wheedle, cajole.
gitanería nf (a) band of gipsies; gathering of gipsies. (b) gipsy (way of) life. (c) gipsy saying. (d) (fig) wheedling, cajolery.
gitanesco adj (a) gipsy (attr); gipsy-like. (b) (pej) wily, tricky.
gitano 1 adj (a) gipsy (attr); **las costumbres gitanas** gipsy customs. (b) (fig) wheedling, cajoling; smooth, flattering. (c) (fig) wily, tricky, sly. 2 nm gipsy.
glabro adj glabrous; hairless.
glaciación nf glaciation.
glacial adj (a) glacial; wind etc icy, bitter, freezing. (b) (fig) icy, cold, stony.
glaciar nm glacier.
glacis nm, pl **glacis** glacis.
gladiador nm gladiator.
gladio nm, **gladíolo** nm gladiolus.
glándula f gland; — **cerrada**, — **de secreción interna** ductless gland; — **endocrina** endocrine gland; — **pituitaria** pituitary (gland); — **prostática** prostate (gland); — **tiroides** thyroid (gland).
glandular adj glandular.
glaseado adj glazed, glossy; glacé.
glasear [1a] vt paper etc to glaze.
glauco adj green, light-green.
glaucoma nm glaucoma.
gleba nf clod.
glicerina nf glycerin(e).
global adj global; total, complete, overall; inquiry, report etc full, searching, comprehensive; amount total, aggregate; sum lump (attr).
globo nm (a) globe, sphere; — **de luz** spherical lamp, spherical lampshade; — **del ojo**, — **ocular** eyeball; — **terráqueo** globe, schoolroom globe.
(b) (Aer) — (aerostático) balloon; — **cautivo** captive balloon; — **dirigible** dirigible; — **de protección** barrage balloon.
(c) en — as a whole, all in all; (Comm) in bulk; (fig) in broad outline only.
globosidad nf globosity.
globoso adj, **globular** adj globular, spherical.
glóbulo nm (a) globule. (b) (Anat) corpuscle; — **blanco** white corpuscle; — **rojo** red corpuscle.
gloria nf glory; (fig) glory, delight, bliss; **una vieja** — a has-been, a great figure (etc) from the past; **el día es pura** — it's a wonderful day; ¡**sí**, —! yes, my love!; ¡**por la** — **de mi madre!** by all that's holy!; **estar en su(s)** —(s) to be in one's element, be in one's glory; **saber a** — to taste heavenly; **Dios le tenga en su santa** — God rest his soul.
gloriado nm (CAm, Col, Ec) hot drink of rum, lemon and cinnamon; (Per) tea drink with brandy or rum.
gloriarse [1b] vr: — **de algo** to boast of something, be proud of something; — **en algo** to glory in something, rejoice in something.
glorieta nf (a) bower, arbour; summerhouse. (b) (Aut) roundabout, traffic circle (US); circus; intersection of streets.
glorificación nf glorification.
glorificar [1g] 1 vt to glorify, extol, praise. 2 **glorificarse** vr: — **de**, — **en** to boast of, be proud of, glory in.
gloriosamente adv gloriously.
glorioso adj (a) glorious; (Eccl) saint blessed, in glory; memory blessed; **la Gloriosa** (Eccl) the Virgin; (Hist: fam) the 1868 revolution (in Spain). (b) (pej) proud, boastful.
glosa f gloss; comment, note, annotation.
glosar [1a] vt to gloss; to comment on, annotate; (fig) to put an unfavourable interpretation on, criticize.
glosario nm glossary.
glosopeda nf foot-and-mouth disease.
glotis nf, pl **glotis** glottis.
glotón 1 adj gluttonous, greedy. 2 nm, **glotona** nf glutton. 3 nm (Zool) glutton; — **de América** wolverine.
glotonear [1a] vi to be greedy, be gluttonous, gormandize.
glotonería nf gluttony, greediness.
glucosa nf glucose, grape sugar.

gluglú nm (a) (of water) gurgle, gurgling; **hacer** — to gurgle. (b) (of turkey) gobble, gobbling; **hacer** — to gobble.

gluglutear [1a] vi (of turkey) to gobble.

gluten nm gluten.

glutinoso adj glutinous.

gneis [neis] nm gneiss.

gnomo ['nomo] nm gnome.

gobelino nm hand-woven wall tapestry.

gobernable adj (a) (Pol) governable; **un pueblo dificilmente** — a people hard to govern, an unruly people. (b) (Naut) navigable, steerable.

gobernación nf (a) (act) governing, government; **Ministerio** m **de la G**— Ministry of the Interior, Home Office (Brit), Department of the Interior (US); **Ministro** m **de la G**— Minister of the Interior, Home Secretary (Brit), Secretary of the Interior (US).
(b) governor's residence, governor's office.

gobernador 1 adj governing, ruling. 2 nm governor, ruler; — **general** governor-general.

gobernalle nm rudder, helm.

gobernanta nf (SAm: gall) governess.

gobernante 1 adj ruling, governing. 2 nmf ruler, governor; (fig) self-appointed boss (or leader etc).

gobernar [1k] 1 vt (a) (Pol) to govern, rule.
(b) (in general) to govern; to guide, direct; to control, manage, run; to handle.
(c) (Naut) to steer, sail.
2 vi (a) (Pol) to govern, rule; — **mal** to misgovern.
(b) (Naut) to handle, steer.

gobierno nm (a) (Pol) government; **el** — **español** the Spanish government; — **fantasma** shadow cabinet.
(b) (in general) guidance, direction; control, management, running; handling; — **doméstico**, — **de la casa** housekeeping, running of the household; **para su** — for your guidance; **servir de** — **a** to act as a guide to, serve as a norm for.
(c) (post) governorship.
(d) (Naut) steering; helm; **buen** — navigability, good steering qualities; **de buen** — navigable, easily steerable.
(e) **mirar contra el** — (PR, RPl) to squint.

gobio nm gudgeon.

goce nm enjoyment; possession.

gocho nm (a) (fam) pig. (b) (Col) ear; handle.

godo 1 adj Gothic.
2 nm, **goda** nf (a) (Hist) Goth.
(b) (SAm: pej) Spaniard; (Hist: early 19th century) loyalist; (modern Pol) conservative, reactionary.
(c) (Canaries) (peninsular) Spaniard.

Godofredo m Geoffrey, Godfrey.

gofio nm (Canaries, SAm) roasted maize meal mixed with sugar.

gol nm (angl) goal (score); ¡—! goal!

gola nf (a) (Anat) throat, gullet. (b) (Mil: Hist) gorget; (Sew: Hist) ruff. (c) (Archit) cyma, ogee.

goleada nf quantity of goals, avalanche of goals.

goleador nm goal scorer; **el máximo** — **de la liga** the top goal scorer in the league.

golear [1a] 1 vt to score a goal against; **Eslobodia goleó a Ruritania por 13 a 0** Slobodia overwhelmed Ruritania by 13-0; **A fue goleado por B** A had a lot of goals scored against it by B.
2 vi to score (a goal).

goleta nf schooner.

golf nm (angl) golf; golf course; — **miniatura** miniature golf (course).

golfa nf (fam) tart (sl), whore.

golfán nm waterlily.

golfante nm oaf, lout; rascal.

golfear [1a] vi to loaf, idle; to live like a street urchin.

golfería nf (a) loafers (collectively); street urchins (collectively). (b) loafing, idling; life of idleness; life in the gutter. (c) dirty trick.

golfillo nm urchin, street urchin.

golfista nmf golfer.

golfístico adj golf (attr), golfing (attr).

golfo[1] nm (Geog) (a) gulf, bay; **G**— **de Méjico** Gulf of Mexico; **G**— **Pérsico** Persian Gulf; — **de Vizcaya** Bay of Biscay.
(b) open sea.
(c) (fig) gulf, abyss.
(d) (fig) chaos, confusion.

golfo[2] nm urchin, street urchin; tramp; oaf, lout; loafer.

Goliat m Goliath.

golilla nf (a) (Sew: Hist) ruff, gorget; magistrate's collar; (Bol, RPl) neckcloth, neckerchief; **andar de** — (Bol, RPl) to be in full regalia.
(b) (SAm: Orn) collar, ruff.
(c) (Tech) flange (of a pipe).
(d) (Cu) debt.
(e) (Cu) trick, ruse.
(f) **alzar** — (Guat) to be brave; (Mex) to show fear.
(g) **de** — (Hond) free, for nothing.

golondrina nf (a) swallow; — **de mar** tern; **una** — **no hace verano** one swallow does not make a summer. (b) (Chi) furniture van.

golondrino nm (a) tramp; (Mil) deserter. (b) (Med) tumour under the armpit.

golondro nm (fam) fancy, yen (fam), longing; **andar de** —**s** to cherish foolish hopes; **campar de** — to sponge (fam), live on other people.

golosina nf (a) titbit, delicacy, dainty; sweet.
(b) bauble, trifle; useless object.
(c) desire, longing; fancy.
(d) sweet tooth, liking for sweet things; greed.

goloso adj (a) sweet-toothed, fond of dainties. (b) (pej) greedy.

golpe nm (a) blow; hit, punch, knock; smack; bump; (with oar etc) stroke; (of heart) beat, throb; (of clock etc) tick; **se dio un** — **en la cabeza** he got a bump on his head, he banged his head; **A le dio a B un** — **en el pecho** A punched B on the chest; **A dio a B un** — **con un palo** A gave B a blow with his stick, A hit B with his stick; — **aplastante** crushing blow, knockout blow; — **bien dado** hit, well-aimed blow; — **de gracia** coup de grâce (also fig); — **mortal** death blow; **dar** —**s en la puerta** to thump the door, pound (at, on) the door; **descargar** —**s sobre uno** to rain blows on someone; **darse** —**s de pecho** to beat one's breast; **no dar** — not to do a stroke, be bone-idle; ¡**qué** —! (fam) what a joke!; **a** — **dado no hay quite** (CAm) what's done cannot be undone.
(b) (Tech) stroke; — **de émbolo** piston stroke.
(c) (Sport: Boxing) blow, punch; (Football etc) kick; (Baseball, Golf, Tennis etc) hit, stroke, shot; **con un total de 280** —**s** (Golf) with a total of 280 strokes; — **de abajo arriba** (Boxing) uppercut; — **de acercamiento** (Golf) approach shot; — **de castigo** (Football etc) penalty kick; — **franco** (Football) free kick; — **franco indirecto** indirect free kick; — **de martillo** (Tennis) smash; — **de salida** (Golf) drive, drive-off; — **de voleo** volley.
(d) (fig) blow, (hard) knock, misfortune; **ha sufrido un** — **duro** he has had a hard knock.
(e) (fig) shock, clash.
(f) (fig) surprise, astonishment.
(g) (fam: of criminal) job (fam); **él preparaba su primer** — he was planning his first job; **dieron un** — **en un banco** they did a bank job.
(h) (fig) — **de agua** heavy fall of rain; — **de estado** coup d'état; — **de fortuna** stroke of luck; — **maestro** master stroke, stroke of genius; — **de mano** rising; sudden attack; — **de mar** heavy sea, surge; — **de sol** sunstroke; — **de teatro** coup de théâtre; — **de tos** fit of coughing; — **de viento** gust of wind; — **de vista** look, glance.
(i) (phrases with prep) **a** — **seguro** with an assurance of success, without any risk; **ir a** — **de calcetín** (fam) to go on Shanks' pony; **al** — (Cu) instantly; **de** — (y porrazo) suddenly, unexpectedly; **de un** — at one stroke, in one go; outright; at a stretch; **abrir una puerta de** — to fling open a door; **la puerta se abrió de** — the door flew open; **cerrar una puerta de** — to slam a door.
(j) (fig) crowd, mass; abundance; — **de gente** crowd of people.
(k) (Mech) spring lock; **de** — spring (attr), eg **pestillo de** — spring bolt.
(l) (Sew) pocket flap; (Col) facing.
(m) (Mex) sledgehammer.
(n) (Ven) swig (of liquor) (fam).

golpeador nm (Col, Chi, Guat) door knocker.

golpeadura nf = golpeo.

golpear [1a] 1 vt to strike, knock, hit; to beat, pound (on, at); to punch; to thump, bang; to tap.
2 vi to throb, tick; (Aut, Mech) to knock; **el** — **de las olas** the buffeting of the waves, the pounding of the sea.

golpecito nm (light) blow, tap, rap; **dar** —**s en** to tap (on), rap (on).

golpeo nm striking, knocking, hitting; beating, pounding; punching, thumping, banging; tapping; (Aut, Mech) knock, knocking.

golpetear [1a] vti to beat (repeatedly); to knock, hammer, drum, tap; to rattle.

golpeteo nm beating; knocking, hammering, drumming, tapping; rattling.

golpiza nf (SAm) bash (fam), bashing (fam), beating-up (fam); **dar una — a uno** to bash someone, beat someone up.

gollería nf dainty, titbit, delicacy; extra, special treat; **pedir —s** to ask too much.

golleroso adj affected; pernickety.

gollete nm throat, neck; (of bottle) neck.

goma nf (a) (in general) gum; rubber; (Sew) elastic; **— arábiga** gum arabic; **— espumosa** foam rubber; **— de mascar** chewing gum; **— de pegar** gum, glue.

(b) (una —) rubber band, elastic band; length of elastic, piece of elastic; (Aut) tyre; (fam) rubber sheath, condom; (SAm) rubber overshoe; **— de borrar** rubber, eraser; **— de borrar de máquina** typewriter rubber.

(c) **estar de —** (CAm) to have a hangover.

goma-espuma nf foam rubber.

gomal nm (Col, Ec, Per) rubber plantation.

gomero 1 adj gum (attr); rubber (attr). **2** nm (a) (Bot) gum tree; rubber tree. (b) (person) rubber planter, rubber producer; rubber-plantation worker.

gomina nf (SAm) hair lotion, hair groom (US).

gomita nf rubber band, elastic band.

gomosidad nf gumminess, stickiness.

gomoso 1 adj gummy, sticky. **2** nm (fam) toff (fam), masher (fam), dandy.

gónada nf gonad.

góndola nf (Naut) gondola; (Rail) goods wagon, freight truck (US), (Chi) bus; **— de cable** cable-car; **— del motor** (Aer) engine casing.

gondolero nm gondolier.

gong [gon] nm, pl **gongs** [gon], **gongo** nm gong.

gonorrea nf gonorrhoea.

gorda nf (fam) (a) fat woman.

(b) = **perra gorda**.

(c) **la G—** the 1868 revolution (in Spain); **se armó la —** there was a hell of a row, there was a tremendous fuss; **aquí se va a armar la —** there's going to be trouble; **ahora nos va a tocar la —** now we're for it.

(d) (Mex) thick maize omelette.

gordal 1 adj fat, big, thick. **2** nm kind of large olive.

gordiflón adj, **gordinflón** adj (fam) podgy, chubby; **¡—!** fatty! (fam).

gordo 1 adj (a) person fat; stout, plump; object big; cloth, thread etc thick, coarse, rough; event important, big; prize first, big, main; **está más — que nunca** he's fatter than ever; **en mi vida las he visto más gordas** (fig) I've never been in a tougher spot; **fue el desastre más — de su historia** it was the biggest (or worst) disaster in their history.

(b) food, matter fatty, greasy, oily.

(c) water hard.

(d) (fam) unpleasant; **ese tipo me cae —** that chap gets on my nerves, I can't bear that fellow.

2 adv (fam): **hablar —** to talk big (sl).

3 nm (a) fat man; **¡—!** fatty! (fam).

(b) (Cook) fat, suet.

(c) (fam) first prize, big prize; **ganar el —** to win the big prize; **sacarse el —** (fig) to bring home the bacon (fam).

gordolobo nm mullein.

gordura nf (a) fat, fatness; corpulence, stoutness. (b) (Cook) grease, fat. (c) (Arg, PR) cream.

gorgojo nm (a) (Ent) grub; weevil. (b) (fig) dwarf, runt.

gorgón nm (Col) concrete.

gorgoritear [1a] vi to trill, warble.

gorgorito nm trill, warble.

górgoro nm (Mex) bubble.

gorgotear [1a] vi to gurgle.

gorgoteo nm gurgle.

gorguera nf ruff; (Mil: Hist) gorget.

gori nm: **armar el —** (fam) to make a row, kick up a fuss.

gorigori nm (fam) funeral chanting, dirge; (fig) wailing, gloomy chanting.

gorila 1 nf (Zool) gorilla. **2** nm (fam) tough (fam), thug, bruiser (fam).

goriloide nm (fig) brute, thug.

gorja nf throat, gorge; **estar de —** (fam) to be very cheerful.

gorjear [1a] **1** vi to chirp, twitter, trill. **2 gorjearse** vr (of child) to crow, gurgle, burble.

gorjeo nm (a) chirping, twittering, trilling; crowing, gurgling, burbling.

gorobeto adj (Col) twisted, bent, warped.

gorra 1 nf (peaked) cap; (baby's) bonnet; (Mil) bearskin, busby; (Univ) cap; **— de montar** riding cap; **— de paño** cloth cap; **— de punto** knitted cap;

— de visera peaked cap; **— de yate** yachting cap.

2 nm (fam) cadger, sponger (fam), parasite; **andar** (or **ir, vivir**) **de —** to cadge, sponge (fam), scrounge (fam), live at someone else's expense; **colarse de —** to gatecrash; **comer de —** to scrounge a meal (fam).

gorrear [1a] **1** vt (Chi) to cuckold. **2** vi (Ec) to sponge (fam), live as a parasite.

gorrero nm (fam) = **gorra 2**.

gorriada nf (a) (number of) pigs. (b) (fig) dirty trick.

gorrinera nf pigsty.

gorrinería nf (a) dirt. (b) (fig) dirty trick.

gorrino nm, **gorrina** nf (a) small pig, sucking-pig; hog, sow. (b) (fig) dirty individual.

gorrión nm sparrow; **de —** (SD) = **de gorra**.

gorrista nmf (fam) = **gorra 2**.

gorro nm cap; (baby's, woman's) bonnet; **— de baño** bathing cap; **— de dormir** nightcap; **— de montaña** Balaclava (helmet); **— de papel** paper hat; **poner el — a uno** to embarrass someone by petting in his (etc) presence.

gorrón¹ nm (a) pebble; cobblestone. (b) (Mech) pivot, journal, gudgeon.

gorrón² nm (fam) = **gorra 2**.

gorrona nf tart (sl), whore.

gorronear [1a] vi (fam) to cadge, sponge (fam), scrounge (fam), live at someone else's expense.

gorronería nf (CAm) greedy selfishness.

gota nf (a) drop; bead; blob; **—s amargas** bitters; **— a —** drop by drop; **caer a —s** to drip; **parecerse como dos —s de agua** to be as like as two peas; **sudar la — gorda** to sweat blood; **no ver —** to see nothing.

(b) (Med) gout; **— caduca, — coral** epilepsy.

(c) **—s de leche** (fig: SAm) child welfare clinic, welfare food centre.

goteado adj speckled, spotted.

gotear [1a] vi to drip, dribble; to trickle; to leak; (o candle) to gutter; (Meteorol) to sprinkle, rain lightly.

goteo nm dripping, dribbling; trickle, trickling; leak.

gotera nf (a) drip; trickle; leak.

(b) mark left by dripping water, stain.

(c) (of canopy) valance.

(d) (Med) chronic ailment; **estar lleno de —s** to be full of aches and pains, feel a wreck.

(e) **—s** (SAm) outskirts, environs.

gotero nm (SAm: Med) dropper.

goterón nm big raindrop.

gótico 1 adj Gothic; (fig) noble, illustrious. **2** nm (language) Gothic.

gotita nf droplet; **¡una — nada más!** (on pouring drink) just a drop!; **hubo dos —s de lluvia** it rained a drop or two.

gotoso adj gouty.

gourmet [gur'me] nm, pl **gourmets** [gur'me] (gall) gourmet, connoisseur (of food).

goyesco adj (a) of Goya, pertaining to Goya. (b) Goyesque, in the style of Goya, after the manner of Goya.

gozar [1f] **1** vt (a) to enjoy; to have, possess.

(b) (arch) woman to have, enjoy, seduce.

2 vi to enjoy oneself, have a good time; **— de** to enjoy; to have, possess; **— de buena salud** to enjoy good health.

3 gozarse vr to enjoy oneself; to rejoice; **— en +** infin to enjoy **+** ger, take pleasure in **+** ger.

gozne nm hinge.

gozo nm (a) enjoyment, pleasure; delight; joy, gladness, rejoicing; **es un — para la retina** it's a joy to see, it's a sight for sore eyes; **¡mi — en el pozo!** I'm sunk!, it's all ruined!; **no caber (en sí) de —** to be beside oneself with joy, be overjoyed; **da —** escucharle it's a pleasure to listen to him.

(b) **—s** (Lit, Mus) couplets in honour of the Virgin.

gozosamente adv joyfully, delightedly.

gozoso adj glad, joyful, delighted (con, de about).

gozque nm small yapping dog.

grabación nf recording; **— en cinta, — magnetofónica** tape recording.

grabado 1 adj music etc recorded; on tape.

2 nm engraving, print; (in book) illustration, picture, print; **— al agua fuerte** etching; **— al agua tinta** aquatint; **— en cobre** copperplate; **— en madera** woodcut; **— rupestre** rock carving.

grabador nm engraver.

grabadora nf (a) (Tech) graver, cutting tool. (b) (Elec etc) recorder; **— de cinta** tape recorder.

grabadura nf (act of) engraving.

grabar [1a] *vt* (a) (*Art*) to engrave; — **al agua fuerte** to etch.

(b) (*on disc, tape*) to record.

(c) (*fig*) to engrave, impress; — **algo en el ánimo de uno** to impress something on someone's mind; **la escena está grabada en mi memoria** the scene is engraved on my memory.

gracejada *nf* (*CAm, Mex*) clownish act, stupid (and tasteless) joke.

gracejo *nm* (a) charm, grace; charming manner. (b) wit, humour; repartee. (c) (*Guat, Mex*) clown.

gracia *nf* (a) grace, gracefulness; attractiveness; **sin** — graceless, unattractive.

(b) favour, kindness; **de** — free, gratis; **hacer a uno** — **de algo** to excuse someone from something, free someone from something.

(c) graciousness.

(d) grace, good graces, favour; **caer de la** — **de uno** to lose someone's favour; **caer en** — **a uno** to find favour with someone, please someone, make a hit with someone.

(e) (*Law*) pardon, mercy.

(f) joke, witticism; **hacer una** — **a uno** to play a (practical) joke on someone.

(g) humour, funniness; wit; point (of a joke); **por** — in fun, as a joke; **¡qué** —! how funny!, (*iro*) what a nerve!, the very ideal; **coger** (*or* **pescar**) **la** — to see the point (of a joke); **dar en la** — **de** + *infin* to fall into the (amusing) habit of + *ger*; **dar en la** — **de decir algo** to mention something repeatedly, harp on something; **hacer** — **a uno** to amuse someone, strike someone as funny; **no nos hace** — we are not amused; **no me hace** — **la idea** I'm not keen on the idea; **tener** — to be funny, be amusing; **el tío tiene mucha** — **hablando** the chap talks very amusingly, the fellow is an amusing talker; **si lo haces se va la** — if you do it it breaks the spell.

(h) (*fam*) name; **¿cuál es su** —? what's your name?

(i) (*Rel*) grace; — **de Dios** (*fig*) sunshine, fresh air; **por la G— de Dios** (*on coin etc*) by the grace of God; **estar en** — (**de Dios**) to be in a state of grace.

(j) **en** — **a** for the sake of; on account of, because of; **en** — **a la brevedad** for brevity's sake, to be brief.

(k) —**s** thanks; **¡** —**s!** thanks!, thank you!; **¡muchas** —**s!**, **¡muchísimas** —**s!** many thanks!, thanks very much!; —**s a Dios** thank heaven; —**s a la ayuda de otros** thanks to the help of others; —**s a que** . . . thanks to the fact that . . . , because of the fact that . . . ; **toma eso, ¡y** —**s!** take that and be thankful!; **con anticipadas** —**s** thanking you in advance; **con repetidas** —**s** thanking you again; **dar las** —**s a uno por algo** to thank someone for something.

(l) **las G**—**s** (*Myth*) the Three Graces.

graciable *adj* (a) gracious; affable. (b) *concession etc* easily granted.

grácil *adj* graceful; slender; small, delicate; **un coche de líneas** —**es** a car of graceful lines, an elegantly designed car.

graciosamente *adv* (a) gracefully; pleasingly, elegantly. (b) graciously. (c) funnily, amusingly; wittily; comically.

graciosidad *nf* (a) grace, gracefulness; elegance; beauty. (b) graciousness. (c) funniness, amusing qualities; wittiness.

gracioso 1 *adj* (a) graceful; pleasing, elegant.

(b) gracious; **su graciosa Majestad** her gracious Majesty.

(c) funny, amusing; witty; comical; **una situación muy graciosa** a very amusing situation; **¡qué** —! how funny!, that's rich!; **es un tío de lo más** — he's a most amusing chap; **lo** — **del caso es que** . . . the funny thing about it is that . . .

(d) free.

2 *nm* (*Theat: Hist*) comic character, fool, funny man.

grada *nf* (a) step, stair; (*Eccl*) altar step; —**s** (flight of) steps.

(b) (*Sport, Theat etc*) tier, row (of seats).

(c) —**s** (*Naut*) slips, slipway; —**s de construcción** shipyard, shipbuilding yard.

(d) (*Agr*) harrow; — **de disco** disk harrow; — **de mano** hoe, cultivator.

(e) —**s** (*Chi, Per*) paved terrace (in front of a building).

gradación *nf* (a) gradation; graded series. (b) (*Rhetoric*) climax; (*Gram*) comparison.

gradar [1a] *vt* (*Agr*) to harrow; to hoe.

gradería *nf*, **graderío** *nm* (a) (flight of) steps. (b)

(*Sport, Theat etc*) tiers, rows (of seats); — **cubierta** covered stand, grandstand.

grado *nm* (a) step.

(b) degree; stage, step; measure; rate; **el** — **que ahora hemos alcanzado** the stage we have now reached; **está en el segundo** — **de elaboración** it is now in the second stage of production; — **de velocidad** (rate of) speed; **es lo mismo pero en mayor** — it's the same only more so; **de** — **en** —, **por** —**s** by degrees, gradually, step by step; **en sumo** —, **en** — **superlativo** in the highest degree; **in the extreme**; vastly.

(c) grade, quality; (*Mil*) rank; **de** — **superior** of superior quality.

(d) (*School*) class, year, grade (*US*).

(e) (*Univ*) degree; — **universitario** university degree.

(f) (*Geog, Math, Phys*) degree; — **de latitud** degree of latitude; **en un ángulo de 45** —**s** at an angle of 45 degrees; **la temperatura es de 40** —**s** the temperature is 40 degrees.

(g) (*Gram*) degree (of comparison).

(h) (*of relationship*) degree; **dentro de los** —**s prohibidos** within the prohibited degrees.

(i) willingness; **de** —, **de buen** — willingly; **de mal** —, **mal de mi** — unwillingly; **de** — **o por fuerza** willy-nilly.

(j) —**s** (*Eccl*) minor orders.

graduable *adj* adjustable, that can be adjusted.

graduación *nf* (a) gradation, grading; graduation.

(b) rating, grading; (*of drink*) alcoholic strength, proof grading; — **octánica** octane rating.

(c) (*Mil*) rank; **de alta** — of high rank, high-ranking.

graduado *nm*, **graduada** *nf* graduate.

gradual *adj* gradual.

gradualmente *adv* gradually.

graduar [1e] **1** *vt* (a) to grade, classify (*de, por* as); to appraise; to gauge, measure; (*Tech*) to calibrate; *sight* to test; *thermometer etc* to graduate.

(b) (*Univ*) to confer a degree on.

(c) (*Mil*) to confer a rank on, commission; — **a uno de capitán** to confer the rank of captain on someone.

2 graduarse *vr* (a) to graduate, take one's degree; — **de** to take the degree of.

(b) (*Mil*) to take a commission (*de* as).

grafía *nf* (*Ling*) graphy, signs representing the sound of a word; (way of) spelling; **se inclina por la** — "**jira**" he prefers the spelling "jira".

gráfica *nf* graph; diagram; — **de fiebre**, — **de temperatura** (*Med*) temperature chart.

gráficamente *adv* graphically.

gráfico 1 *adj* (a) graphic; pictorial, illustrated. (b) (*fig*) graphic, vivid, lively. **2** *nm* (*Math etc*) graph; diagram; chart; (*Rail etc*) timetable; = **gráfica**.

grafito *nm* graphite, black lead.

grafología *nf* graphology.

gragea *nf* small coloured sweets; (*Med*) sugar-coated pill.

graja *nf* rook.

grajea *nf* (*Col*) fine shot, birdshot.

grajear [1a] *vi* (*Orn*) to caw; (*of baby*) to crow, gurgle.

grajiento *adj* (*SAm*) sweaty, smelly.

grajilla *nf* jackdaw.

grajo *nm* (a) rook. (b) (*SAm*) body odour, smell of sweat; underarm odour.

grama *nf* (*esp SAm*) grass.

gramática *nf* (a) grammar. (b) — **parda** native wit, horse sense; **andar a la** — to look out for oneself.

gramatical *adj* grammatical.

gramático 1 *adj* grammatical. **2** *nm* grammarian.

gramil *nm* (*Tech*) gauge.

gramilla *nf* (*RPl*) grass.

gramillar *nm* (*RPl*) meadow, grassland.

gramo *nm* gramme, gram (*US*).

gramófono *nm* gramophone, phonograph (*US*).

gramola *nf* gramophone, phonograph (*US*); (*in cafe etc*) jukebox.

grampa *nf* (*SAm*) = **grapa**.

gran *adj* (*apocopated form*) see **grande**.

grana[1] *nf* (*Bot*) (a) small seed; **dar en** — to go to seed, run to seed. (b) seeding; seeding time.

grana[2] *nf* (*Zool etc*) cochineal; (*dye*) kermes; (*colour*) scarlet; scarlet cloth; **de** — scarlet, bright red; **ponerse como la** — to turn scarlet.

granada *nf* (a) (*Bot*) pomegranate. (b) (*Mil*) shell; grenade; — **fallida** dud shell; — **de mano** hand grenade; — **de metralla** shrapnel shell; **a prueba de** — shellproof.

granadero *nm* grenadier.

granadilla *nf* passionflower; passionfruit.

granadino 1 adj of Granada. **2** nm, **granadina** nf native (or inhabitant) of Granada; **los —s** the people of Granada.

granado[1] nm pomegranate tree.

granado[2] adj **(a)** fine, choice, select; mature; distinguished, illustrious; **lo más — de** the cream of, the pick of. **(b)** tall, full-grown.

granar [1a] vi to seed, run to seed.

granate nm garnet.

granazón nf seeding.

Gran Bretaña f Great Britain.

grande 1 adj **(a)** (in size) big, large; (in stature) big, tall; number, speed etc high, great; **en cantidades más —s** in larger quantities; **hay una diferencia no muy —** there is not a very big difference; **los zapatos le están muy —s** the shoes are too big for her; **con gran placer** with great pleasure; **¿cómo es de —?** how big is it?, what size is it?

(b) (morally etc) great; **un gran hombre** a great man; **fue una gran hazaña** it was a great achievement.

(c) grand, grandiose, impressive.

(d) en — as a whole; on a large scale, on a grand scale, in a big way; **estar en —** to be going strong; **pasarlo en —** to have a tremendous time (fam); **hacer algo en —** to do something in style, make a splash; **vivir en —** to live in style.

(e) grandísimo (hum or iro) great big, huge; **un coche —** a whacking big car (fam), a car and a half; **¡grandísimo tunante!** you awful old rogue!

2 adv (RPl) much, a lot.

3 nm **(a) los —s** the great.

(b) — (de España) grandee.

4 nf **(a)** (Arg) first prize, big prize (in the lottery). **(b)** (Chi, Col) naughty thing, misdeed.

grandemente adv greatly, extremely; **— equivocado** greatly mistaken.

grandeza nf **(a)** bigness; size, magnitude.

(b) greatness.

(c) grandness, grandiose quality, impressiveness; grandeur, magnificence.

(d) status of grandee.

(e) grandees (collectively), nobility.

grandilocuencia nf grandiloquence.

grandilocuente adj (SAm) boastful, arrogant.

grandílocuo adj grandiloquent.

grandiosidad nf = **grandeza** (c).

grandioso adj grand, impressive, magnificent; (pej) grandiose.

grandor nm size.

grandote adj great big, huge; see also **—ote.**

grandullón adj overgrown, oversized.

grandura nf (Arg) = **grandeza** (b) and (c).

granear [1a] vt **(a)** seed to sow. **(b)** (Tech) to grain, stipple.

granel nm heap of corn; **a —** in abundance; by the score, by the ton; lavishly; at random; (Comm) in bulk, loose; in quantity; **vino a —** wine in bulk, wine in the barrel.

granero nm granary, barn; (fig) granary, corn-producing area.

granetario nm precision balance.

granete nm (Tech) punch.

granilla nf grain (in cloth).

granítico adj granitic, granite (attr).

granito[1] nm (Geol) granite.

granito[2] nm (Agr etc) small grain; granule; (Med) pimple.

granizada nf **(a)** (Meteorol) hail, hailstorm. **(b)** (fig) hail; shower, volley; vast number; **una — de balas** a hail of bullets. **(c)** (Chi, Guat) iced drink.

granizado nm iced drink; **— de café** iced coffee.

granizal nm (Col, Chi, Guat, Mex) hailstorm.

granizar [1f] vi to hail; (fig) to rain, shower.

granizo nm hail.

granja nf farm; farmhouse; dairy; country house; **— avícola** chicken farm, poultry farm; **— colectiva** collective farm.

granjear [1a] **1** vt to gain, earn; to win; (Chi) to steal. **2 granjearse** vr to win for oneself, gain for oneself.

granjería nf **(a)** (Comm, Fin) profit, earnings; (Agr) farm earnings. **(b)** (Agr) farming, husbandry.

granjero nm farmer.

grano nm **(a)** (Agr, Bot) grain; seed; berry; **—s** grain, corn, cereals; **— de arroz** grain of rice; **— de trigo** grain of wheat; **— de café** coffee bean; **—s panificables** bread grains; **tomarlo con un — de sal** to take it with a pinch of salt; **ir al —** to get to the point, get down to brass tacks; **¡vamos al —!** let's get on with it!

(b) particle, grain; speck; **— de arena** grain of sand; **no es — de anís** (or **arena**) it's not just a small thing, you can't laugh this one off.

(c) (in stone, wood etc) grain; **de — fino** fine-grained; **de — gordo** coarse-grained.

(d) (Med) pimple, spot.

(e) (Pharm) grain.

granoso adj granular; granulated.

granuja 1 nf loose grapes; grape seed. **2** nm urchin, ragamuffin; rogue.

granujería nf urchins (collectively), rogues (collectively).

granujiento adj, **granujoso** adj pimply, spotty.

granulación nf granulation.

granular[1] adj granular.

granular[2] [1a] **1** vt to granulate. **2 granularse** vr **(a)** to granulate, become granulated. **(b)** (Med) to break out in pimples, become spotty.

gránulo nm granule.

granuloso adj granular.

grapa nf (for papers) staple; clip, fastener; (Mech) dog, clamp; (Archit) cramp.

grasa nf **(a)** (in general) grease; (Cook) fat; suet; **— de ballena** blubber; **— de pescado** fish oil; **— vegetal** vegetable fat.

(b) (Aut, Mech) oil; grease; **— para ejes** axle grease.

(c) (Anat) fat, fattiness; **tener mucha —** to be very fat.

(d) (Mex) shoe polish.

(e) (pej) grease, greasy dirt, filth.

(f) —s (Min) slag.

grasiento adj greasy, oily; road surface greasy, slippery; (pej) filthy.

grasilla nf (Bot) sundew.

graso 1 adj fatty; greasy; food oily. **2** nm fattiness; greasiness; oiliness.

grata nf (Comm) favour (letter).

gratamente adv pleasingly, pleasantly, agreeably; gratifyingly.

gratificación nf **(a)** (Fin etc) reward, recompense; tip; gratuity; bonus (on wages); bounty. **(b)** (angl: esp SAm) gratification, pleasure, satisfaction.

gratificador adj (SAm) gratifying; pleasurable, satisfying.

gratificar [1g] vt **(a)** (Fin etc) to reward, recompense; to tip, give a gratuity to; to give a bonus to, pay extra to; **"se gratificará"** (adverts) "a reward is offered".

(b) to gratify; to give pleasure to, satisfy; longing to gratify, indulge.

gratis adv gratis, free, for nothing; **"entrada —"** "admission free"; **de —** (SAm) gratis.

gratitud nf gratitude.

grato adj **(a)** pleasing, pleasant; agreeable; welcome, gratifying; **una decisión muy grata para todos** a very welcome decision for everybody; **recibir una impresión grata** to get a pleasing impression; **nos es — informarle que...** we are pleased to inform you that...

(b) (Bol, Chi) grateful; **le estoy — por ello** I am grateful to you for it.

gratuitamente adv **(a)** free, for nothing. **(b)** gratuitously; unfoundedly.

gratuito adj **(a)** free, free of charge. **(b)** remark etc gratuitous, uncalled-for; charge unfounded, unjustified.

gratulatorio adj congratulatory.

grava nf gravel; crushed stone; road metal.

gravamen nm burden, obligation; (Law) lien, encumbrance; (Fin) tax, impost; **libre de —** unencumbered, free from encumbrances.

gravar [1a] **1** vt to burden, encumber (de with); property (Law) to place a lien upon; (Fin) to assess for tax; **— con impuestos** to burden with taxes; **— un producto con un impuesto** to place a tax on a product.

2 gravarse vr (SAm) to get worse, become more serious.

gravativo adj burdensome.

grave adj **(a)** heavy, weighty.

(b) (fig) grave, serious; critical; important, momentous; loss etc grave, severe, grievous; **un deber muy —** a very grave duty; **la situación es —** the situation is grave (or critical); **me es muy — tener que + infin** it is very hard for me to + infin.

(c) (in character) serious, sedate, dignified; **y otros hombres —s** and other worthy men.

(d) (Med) illness, condition grave, serious; wound severe; **estar —** to be seriously ill, be critically ill.

(e) (Mus) note, pitch low, deep.

(f) (Ling) accent grave; word paroxytone, stressed on the penultimate syllable (eg padre, romance).

gravedad nf (a) (Phys) gravity.
(b) (fig) gravity, seriousness; importance; severity, grievousness.
(c) seriousness, dignity.
(d) (Med) gravity; **estar de — to be seriously ill, be dangerously ill; estar herido de — to be severely injured (or wounded); tiene heridas de — he has serious injuries; parece que la lesión es sin —** it seems that the injury is not serious.
(e) (Mus) depth.

gravemente adv gravely, seriously; critically; severely, grievously; **habló — he spoke gravely; estar — enfermo to be critically ill.**

grávido adj (a) pregnant; (Zool) with young, carrying young.
(b) (fig) full (de of), heavy (de with); **me sentí — de emociones** I was heavy with emotions, I was weighed down with emotions.

gravilla nf gravel.

gravitación nf gravitation.

gravitacional adj gravitational.

gravitar [1a] vi (a) (Phys) to gravitate (hacia towards). (b) **— sobre** to rest on; to bear down on, weigh down on; (fig) to be a burden to; to encumber.

gravitatorio adj gravitational.

gravoso adj (a) burdensome, oppressive, onerous; **ser — a** to be a burden to, weigh on.
(b) (Fin) costly, expensive; burdensome; charge extortionate.
(c) tiresome, vexatious.

graznar [1a] vi to squawk; (of crow) to caw, croak; (of goose) to cackle; (of duck) to quack; (of singer: hum) to croak.

graznido nm squawk; caw, croak; cackle; quack.

grébano nm (Arg: pej) Italian.

Grecia f Greece.

greco adj, n (lit) = **griego.**

greda nf (Geol) clay; (Tech) fuller's earth.

gredal nm claypit.

gredoso adj clayey.

gregario adj (a) gregarious; **instinto — herd instinct.**
(b) (fig) servile, slavish.

gregarismo nm gregariousness.

gregoriano adj Gregorian.

Gregorio m Gregory.

greguería nf (a) hubbub, uproar. (b) (Lit) brief, humorous and often mildly poetic comment or aphorism about life.

gremial 1 adj (a) (Hist) guild (attr). (b) (modern Pol) trade-union (attr), trades-union (attr); (SAm) trade (attr). **2** nm union member.

gremio nm (a) (Hist) guild, corporation, company. (b) (modern Pol) union; **— obrero, — de obreros** trade union, trades union.

greña nf (a) (also **—s**) shock of hair, mat (or mop) of hair, matted hair.
(b) (fig) tangle, entanglement; **andar a la — to** bicker, squabble.
(c) **en —** (Mex) silk raw; silver unpolished.

greñudo adj hair tangled, matted; person dishevelled.

gres nm (a) (Geol) potter's clay. (b) earthenware, stoneware.

gresca nf uproar, hubbub; row, shindy; **andar a la — to** row, brawl.

grey nf (Eccl) flock, congregation.

Grial nm: **Santo —** Holy Grail.

griego 1 adj Greek, Grecian.
2 nm, **griega** nf (a) Greek.
(b) (fam) cheat.
3 nm (language) (a) Greek; **— antiguo** ancient Greek.
(b) (fig) gibberish, double Dutch; **para mí es —** it's Greek to me; **hablar en — to** talk double Dutch.

grieta nf fissure, crack; chink; crevice; chasm; (on skin) chap, crack; (Pol etc) rift.

grietarse [1a] vr = **agrietarse.**

grifa nf (Mex) marijuana.

grifear [1a] vi (Mex) to smoke marijuana.

grifería[1] nf taps (collectively), faucets (collectively: US).

grifería[2] nf (Ant) Negroes (collectively).

grifo[1] nm (a) tap, faucet (US); cock; **cerveza (servida) al — draught** beer, beer on draught. (b) (Per) petrol station, gas station (US); dive (fam); drink shop.

grifo[2] **1** adj (a) (Mex) **estar — to** be drunk; to be mad; to be high on pot (sl), be under the influence of marijuana.
(b) (Col) vain, stuck-up (fam).
2 nm (Mex) (a) marijuana, pot (sl).
(b) marijuana addict, pot smoker (sl).
(c) drunkard.

grifo[3] (Ant) **1** adj (a) hair curly, kinky. (b) person (euph) coloured. **2** nm (a) kinky hair. (b) (euph) Negro, coloured person.

grifo[4] nm (Myth) griffin.

grigallo nm blackcock.

grilla nf (a) (Ent) female cricket; **¡ésa es — (y no canta)!** (fam) that's a likely story! (iro). (b) (Col, Ec, Per) annoyance, bother. (c) (Col) row, slanging match (fam).

grillera nf cage for crickets; cricket hole.

grillete nm fetter, shackle.

grillo nm (a) (Ent) cricket; **— cebollero, — real** mole cricket. (b) (Bot) shoot, sprout. (c) **—s** fetters, shackles, irons; (fig) shackles.

grima nf (a) horror, loathing, disgust; aversion, reluctance; uneasiness; annoyance, irritation, displeasure; **me da — it** gets on my nerves, it gives me the shivers; it sickens me.
(b) (Chi) bit, small particle.
(c) (Col) **en — alone; estar solo en — to** be all alone.

grimillón nm (Chi) lot, heap.

grímpola nf pennant.

gringada nf, **gringaje** nm (RPl) gringos (collectively); group of gringos.

gringo 1 adj (a) (SAm) foreign (see 2).
(b) (SAm) language foreign, unintelligible.
(c) (Per) blond(e), fair.
2 nm, **gringa** nf (a) (SAm, freq pej) foreigner (in 19th century esp Briton, Anglo-Saxon, now esp North American, Yankee; RPl freq Italian).
(b) (Chi, Per) blond(e), fair-haired person.
(c) (SAm) gibberish, unintelligible speech; **hablar en — to** talk double Dutch.

gringuería nf (SAm) group of gringos.

gripe nf influenza, flu.

gris 1 adj grey; day, weather grey, dull; **— perla** pearl-grey. **2** nm grey; **hace un — there's** a cold wind.

grisáceo adj greyish.

grisma nf (Chi, Guat, Hond) strand, shred, bit.

grisú nm firedamp.

grita nf uproar, hubbub; shouting; (Theat) catcalls, booing; **dar — a** to boo, hoot (at).

gritadera nf (SAm) loud shouting, clamour.

gritar [1a] vti to shout, yell; to scream, shriek, cry out; to hoot, boo; **¡no grites!** stop shouting!

gritería nf, **griterío** nm shouting, uproar, clamour.

grito nm (a) shout, yell; scream, shriek, cry; hoot, boo; bellow; (Zool) cry, sound; (Orn) call, cry; **a —s, a — herido, a — pelado, a voz en — at** the top of one's voice; **llorar a —s** to weep and wail; **poner el — en el cielo** to make a great fuss, scream blue murder (fam); **es el último — (gall)** it's the very latest, it's the latest craze.
(b) (SAm) proclamation; **— de independencia** proclamation of independence; **el — de Dolores the** proclamation of Mexican independence (1810).

gritón adj loud-mouthed; screaming, shouting.

gro nm grosgrain.

groenlandés 1 adj Greenland (attr). **2** nm, **groenlandesa** nf Greenlander.

Groenlandia f Greenland.

groggy ['grogi] adj, **grogui** adj (Boxing etc) groggy.

grosella nf (red)currant; **— espinosa** gooseberry; **— negra** blackcurrant; **— roja** redcurrant.

grosellero nm currant bush.

groseramente adv rudely, discourteously; coarsely, crudely, vulgarly, indelicately; roughly, loutishly; grossly, stupidly.

grosería nf (a) (in general) rudeness, discourtesy; coarseness, crudeness, vulgarity; roughness; stupidity.
(b) (remark etc) rude thing, coarse thing, vulgar remark (etc).

grosero adj rude, discourteous; coarse, crude, vulgar, indelicate; rough, loutish; error etc gross, stupid.

grosor nm thickness.

grosura nf (a) fat, suet. (b) (Med) meat diet.

grotescamente adv grotesquely; bizarrely, absurdly.

grotesco adj grotesque; bizarre, absurd.

grúa nf (Tech) crane; derrick; **— corredera, — corrediza, — móvil** travelling crane; **— de pescante** jib crane; **— (de) puente** overhead crane; **— de torre** tower crane.

gruesa nf gross, twelve dozen.

gruesamente adv (a) thickly; bulkily. (b) (Comm etc) in bulk.

grueso 1 adj (a) thick; bulky, stout, massive, solid; big, heavy; person stout, thickset; artillery, sea heavy; intestine large; chest large; trunk etc thick, massive.
(b) quality etc coarse.

2 *nm* (a) thickness; bulkiness, bulk, size; density. (b) thick part; main part, major portion; (*of crowd, troops etc*) main body, mass; **el — del pelotón** (*Racing*) the ruck of the runners; **va mezclado con el — del pasaje** he is mingling with the mass of the passengers.
(c) (*Comm*) **en —** in bulk.

grujidor *nm* glass cutter, glazier.

grulla *nf* (*Orn*) crane (*also* — **común**).

grullo 1 *adj* (a) (*fam*) uncouth, rough. (b) (*Mex*) sponging (*fam*), cadging. (c) (*Guat, Mex*) horse, mule grey.
2 *nm* (*Mex*) grey (horse); (*RPl*) big colt, large stallion.

grumete *nm* cabin boy, ship's boy.

grumo *nm* (a) clot, lump; dollop; (*of blood*) clot; — **de leche** curd. (b) (*of grapes etc*) bunch, cluster.

grumoso *adj* clotted; lumpy.

gruñido *nm* grunt, growl; snarl; (*fig*) grouse (*fam*), grumble; **dar —s** = **gruñir**.

gruñidor 1 *adj* grunting, growling; snarling; (*fig*) grumbling. **2** *nm* (*fig*) grumbler.

gruñir [3h] *vi* to grunt, growl; to snarl; (*fig*) to grouse (*fam*), grumble; (*of door etc*) to creak.

gruñón 1 *adj* grumpy, grumbling. **2** *nm* grumbler.

grupa *nf* crupper; hindquarters, rump (of horse).

grupera *nf* (*of horse*) pillion (seat); **ir en la —** to sit behind the rider, be carried on the horse's crupper.

grupo *nm* (a) group; (*of trees etc*) cluster, clump; (*Pol*) group; — **del dólar** dollar block; — **de presión** pressure group; — **sanguíneo** blood group; **discusión en —** group discussion; **reunirse en —s** to gather in groups; **reunirse en — en torno a** to gather round, cluster round.
(b) (*Elec, Tech etc*) unit, set, plant; assembly; — **compresor** compressor unit; — **dental** dentist's operating equipment; — **electrógeno,** — **generador** generating set, power plant.

gruta *nf* cavern, grotto.

gua *interj* (*SAm: distress*) oh dear!; (*surprise*)' well!; (*scorn*) get away!

gua . . .: *for some words so spelled in SAm, see also* **hua . . .**

guabiroba *nf* (*RPl*) dugout canoe.

guaca *nf* (a) (*SAm*) (*Indian*) tomb, funeral mound; buried treasure; wealth, money; (*Bol, CR, Cu, Mex, Ven*) moneybox; **hacer —** (*Bol, Col, Cu, Mex*) to make money, make one's pile (*fam*); **hacer su —** (*Cu, Chi, PR*) to make hay while the sun shines.
(b) (*Cu*) ticking-off.
(c) (*Mex*) double-barrelled shotgun.
(d) (*Ven*) large sore; **se sacó la —** he got fleeced, he was cheated.

guacal *nm* (*SAm*) wooden crate; gourd, vessel.

guacamayo 1 *adj* (*RPl*) absurdly dressed; (*PR*) flashily dressed. **2** *nm* (a) macaw. (b) (*PR*) flashily-dressed person; (*Cu: pej*) Spaniard.

guacarnaco *adj* (a) (*Col, Cu, Chi, Ec*) silly, stupid. (b) (*Chi*) long-legged.

guachafita *nf* (a) (*Col, SD, Ven*) hubbub, din; disorder. (b) (*Ven*) gambling joint (*sl*). (c) (*PR, Ven*) mockery, jeering.

guachaje *nm* (*Chi*) orphaned animal; group of calves separated from their mothers.

guachalomo *nm* (*Chi*) sirloin steak.

guachapear [1a] **1** *vt* (a) *water* to dabble in, splash about in.
(b) to botch, mess up, bungle.
(c) (*Chi*) to pinch (*fam*), borrow.
(d) (*Col*) brushwood to clear, cut.
2 *vi* to rattle, clatter, bang about.

guachar [1a] *vt* (*Mex: angl*) to watch.

guáchara *nf* (*Cu, PR*) lie.

guache *nm* (*Col, Ven*) common sort, uneducated person; (*pej*) layabout, loafer.

guachicar(ro) *nm* (*Mex: angl*) parking attendant.

guachimán *nm* (*CAm, Mex: angl*) watchman.

guachinanga *nf* (*Cu*) wooden bar (on door etc).

guachinango 1 *adj* (*Col, Cu, PR*) soapy, smooth; teasing. **2** *nm* (a) (*Cu: pej*) Mexican. (b) (*Ant*) smooth person, flatterer.

guacho 1 *adj* (*esp Chi, Per, RPl*) (a) *person* homeless, orphaned, abandoned; *animal* motherless.
(b) *shoe etc* odd.
2 *nm* (a) baby bird, chick.
(b) (*Chi, Per, RPl*) homeless child, abandoned child; orphan, foundling; illegitimate child; (*Agr*) motherless animal.
(c) (*Chi, Per, RPl*) odd one (of a pair); isolated object.

guadal *nm* (*Col, RPl*) sandy bog.

guadalajareño 1 *adj* of Guadalajara. **2** *nm,* **guadalajareña** *nf* native (*or* inhabitant) of Guadalajara; **los —s** the people of Guadalajara.

guadaloso *adj* (*RPl*) boggy.

guadamecí *nm* embossed leather.

guadaña *nf* scythe.

guadañadora *nf* mowing machine.

guadañar [1a] *vt* to scythe, mow.

guadañero *nm* mower.

guadaño *nm* (*Cu, Mex*) small harbour boat.

guagua[1] *nf* (*Cu, PR, Canaries*) bus.

guagua[2] **1** *adj* (*Ec*) small, little. **2** *nf* (*in parts also m*) (a) (*SAm*) baby. (b) trifle, small thing; **de —** (*Cu, Mex*) free, for nothing.

guaguarear [1a] *vi* (*Guat, Mex*) to burble, chatter.

guaguatear [1a] *vt* (*Chi, Guat, RPl*) *baby* to breastfeed; to carry in one's arms.

guaguatera *nf* (*RPl*) nurse.

guagüero 1 *adj* (a) (*Ant*) sponging (*fam*), parasitical. (b) (*Cu*) bus (*attr*).
2 *nm,* **guagüera** *nf* (a) (*Cu*) bus driver.
(b) (*Ant*) bargain hunter, person looking for something for nothing.

guaica *nf* (*Arg*) bead; (*Bol*) rosary beads; (*Col*) bead necklace.

guaico *nm* (*Arg, Col, Chi, Ec*) hollow, dip, depression; ravine; (*Col*) hole, pit; (*Col*) out-of-the-way place, lonely spot; (*Per*) mountain torrent; (*Per*) avalanche; (*Bol*) dung heap, rubbish tip.

guaina 1 *nf* (*Arg*) girl, young woman. **2** *nm* (*Bol, Chi*) youth, young man.

guaino *nm* (*Arg, Per*) young man; small man; (*Sport*) jockey.

guaipe *nm* (*SAm: angl*) wiper, cloth.

guáiper *nm* (*CAm: angl*) windscreen wiper, windshield wiper (*US*).

guaira *nf* (a) (*CAm*) Indian flute. (b) (*Arg, Bol, Chi, Per*) earthenware smelting furnace (*for silver ore*). (c) (*Cu, Ven*) triangular sail.

guairana *nf* (*Per*) lime kiln; = **guaira.**

guairo *nm* (*Cu, Ven*) small coastal vessel (*with 2 triangular sails*).

guajada *nf* (*Mex*) stupid thing.

guajalote (*Mex, PR*) = **guajolote.**

guaje 1 *adj* (*Hond, Mex*) silly, stupid; **hacer — a uno** to fool someone.
2 *nm* (a) (*Hond, Mex*) gourd, calabash.
(b) (*Hond, Mex*) idiot, fool.
(c) (*CAm*) old thing, piece of junk.

guajear [1a] *vi* (*Mex*) to play the fool, be silly.

guajería *nf* (*Mex*) (a) idiocy, foolishness. (b) stupid thing, foolish act.

guajero *nm,* **guajera** *nf* (*Cu*) (white) peasant; (*SD*) peasant; (*Guat*) countryman; outsider.

guajolote (*Mex*) **1** *adj* silly, stupid. **2** *nm* (a) turkey. (b) (*fam*) fool, idiot.

gualdo *adj* yellow, golden.

gualdrapa *nf* (a) (*Hist*) trappings. (b) (*fam*) tatter, ragged end.

gualdrapear [1a] *vi* (a) (*Naut: of sail*) to flap. (b) (*Cu: of horse*) to walk slowly.

gualicho *nm* (a) (*Arg, Bol, Chi*) devil, evil spirit; evil spell; hurt, harm. (b) (*Arg*) powerful talisman, good-luck charm.

Gualterio *m* Walter.

guama *nf* (a) (*CAm, Col, Ven*) lie. (b) (*Col*) big foot; big hand. (c) (*Col, Ven*) calamity, disaster, misfortune; annoyance.

guambra *nmf* (a) (*Bol*) peasant, Indian. (b) (*Col, Ec, Per*) child, baby; (*fam*) sweetheart.

guampa *nf* (*Bol, PR*) horn; drinking vessel.

guámparo *nm* (*Chi*) horn; drinking vessel.

guanacada *nmf* (*SAm*) simpleton, dimwit (*fam*); rustic.

guanaco 1 *adj* (*SAm*) simple, silly; slow.
2 *nm* (a) (*Zool*) guanaco.
(b) (*SAm*) simpleton, dimwit (*fam*); rustic.
(c) (*Guat*) Honduran; (*any*) Central American.

guanajada *nf* (*Ant*) silly thing, foolish act.

guanajo *nm,* **guanaja** *nf* (*Ant*) (a) (*Orn*) turkey. (b) (*fam*) fool, idiot.

guanay *nm* (*Chi*) oarsman; longshoreman; (*fig*) tough man.

guanear [1a] **1** *vt* (a) (*Per*) to fertilize with guano. (b) (*Bol*) to dirty, soil. **2** *vi* (*SAm: of animals*) to defecate.

guanera *nf* (*SAm*) guano deposit.

guanero *adj* (*SAm*) guano (*attr*), pertaining to guano.

guanín *nm* (*Ant, Col, Chi: Hist*) base gold.

guano[1] *nm* (*SAm*) (a) guano; artificial manure; (*Chi, Per*) dung, manure. (b) (*Cu, PR: hum*) money, brass (*sl*); **meter —** to work hard.

guano² nm (Ant) palm tree; palm leaf.
guantada nf, **guantazo** nm slap.
guante nm (a) glove; — **de boxeo** boxing glove; — **de cabritilla** kid glove; — **de goma** rubber glove; — **con puño** gauntlet; **se ajusta como un** — it fits like a glove; **me conviene como un** — it suits me down to the ground; **arrojar el** — to throw down the gauntlet; **recoger el** — to take up the challenge; **echar un** — to take a collection (a beneficio de for, on behalf of); **echar el** — **a uno** to catch hold of someone, seize someone; (fig) to catch someone out, come down on someone.
(b) (Chi) whip, cat-o'nine-tails.
(c) —s tip, commission.
guantear [1a] vt (Chi, Mex) to slap, hit.
guantelete nm gauntlet.
guantera nf (Aut) glove compartment.
guantería nf (a) glove shop; glove factory. (b) glove making.
guantero nm, **guantera** nf glover.
guantón nm (SAm) slap, hit, blow.
guañusco adj (Arg) (a) withered, faded. (b) burned, burned up.
guapear [1a] vi (fam) (a) to cut a dash, dress flashily. (b) to bluster, swagger.
guapetón 1 adj (a) good-looking, handsome; dashing. (b) (pej) flashy. 2 nm bully, roughneck (sl).
guapeza nf (a) good looks; prettiness, attractiveness. (b) smartness, elegance; (pej) flashiness. (c) boldness, dash; (pej) bravado.
guapo 1 adj (a) good-looking; girl pretty, attractive; man handsome; **¡oye, guapa!** hey, beautiful!
(b) smart, elegant, well-dressed; (pej) flashy, overdressed; **¡hombre, qué** — **estás!** how smart you're looking!
(c) bold, dashing.
2 nm (a) lover, gallant, beau.
(b) swell (fam), toff (fam); (pej) bully, tough guy (US fam); braggart.
guaposo adj (Cu) bold, dashing.
guapucha nf (Col) cheating (at cards).
guaquear [1a] vt (Cam, Col, Per) tomb to rob (in search of archaeological valuables).
guaqueo nm (CAm, Col, Per) tomb robbing.
guaquero nm (CAm, Col, Per) tomb robber.
guara nf (a) (Per) lot, heap. (b) (Arg, Chi) —s tricks, wiles.
guaraca nf (Col, Chi, Ec, Per) sling; whip; (Per) sling shot; (Chi) cosh, blunt instrument.
guaracha nf (a) (Ant) merry song, merry dance.
(b) (Ant) din, hubbub; quarrel; spree (fam), carousal.
(c) (Cu: pej) small-time band.
(d) (PR) joke.
(e) (Bol) litter, rough bed.
(f) —s (Guat) old shoes.
guarache nm (Mex) (a) sandal, light shoe. (b) (Aut) tyre patch.
guarachear [1a] vi (Ant) to revel, carouse.
guaragua nf (a) (Bol, Per) adornments; tawdry finery.
(b) (Guat, Hond) lie; hoax.
(c) (CR) liar, taleteller.
(d) (Chi, Ec, Per) rhythmical movement (of the body in dancing).
guaral nm (Col,Ven) rope, line.
guarango adj (a) (Chi, Per, RPl) rough, rude, ill-bred. (b) (Bol) ragged, dirty.
guaranguear [1a] vi (Chi, RPl) to act in an ill-bred way, be rude.
guaranguería nf (Chi, RPl) roughness, rudeness, lack of breeding.
guaranismo nm word (or expression etc) from the Guaraní language.
guarapazo nm (Col) (a) sugar-cane liquor. (b) blow, knock; hard fall.
guarapear [1a] vi and **guarapearse** vr (Per) to drink sugar-cane liquor; (SD) to drink, get drunk.
guarapo nm (SAm) sugar-cane liquor; (PR, SD) watered-down drink; (Ven) fermented pineapple juice; **menear el** — (Cu,Ven) to get things moving; **se le enfrió el** — he lost the urge.
guarapón nm (Bol, Chi, Per) broad-brimmed hat.
guarda 1 nm guard; keeper, custodian; (Arg) bus conductor, tram conductor; (Arg: Rail) guard, brakeman; — **de coto**, — **forestal**, — **jurado** gamekeeper, game warden; — **de dique** lock keeper; — **nocturno** night watchman.
2 nf (a) guard, guarding; safekeeping; custody.
(b) (of law) observance.
(c) (of lock) ward; (of sword, machine) guard; (Typ) flyleaf, endpaper.
(d) (Per, RPl: Sew) ribbing, trimming.

guarda(a)gujas nm, pl **guarda(a)gujas** (Rail) switchman.
guarda(a)almacén nm storekeeper.
guardabarrera nm (a) (Rail: person) crossing keeper.
(b) (Rail) level-crossing gate(s), grade-crossing gate(s) (US).
guardabarros nm, pl **guardabarros** mudguard, fender (US).
guardabosque(s) nm gamekeeper, game warden; ranger, forester.
guardabrisa nf (Aut) windscreen, windshield (US); (Mex) screen.
guardacabo nm (Naut) thimble.
guardacabras nm, pl **guardacabras** goatherd.
guardacalor nm cosy, cover.
guardacantón nm kerbstone; roadside post.
guardacartas nm, pl **guardacartas** letter file.
guardacenizas nm, pl **guardacenizas** ash pan.
guardacoches nm, pl **guardacoches** parking attendant.
guardacostas nm, pl **guardacostas** coastguard vessel, revenue cutter.
guardador 1 adj (a) protective.
(b) observant, watchful.
(c) (pej) mean, stingy.
2 nm (a) keeper; guardian; protector.
(b) (of laws) observer.
(c) (pej) mean person.
guardaespaldas nm, pl **guardaespaldas** bodyguard, henchman.
guardafango nm mudguard, fender (US).
guardafrenos nm, pl **guardafrenos** (Rail) guard, brakeman.
guardafuego nm fireguard; fender.
guardajoyas nm, pl **guardajoyas** jewel case.
guardalado nm railing, parapet.
guardalodos nm, pl **guardalodos** mudguard, fender (US).
guardamano nm guard (of a sword).
guardameta nm goalkeeper.
guardamuebles nm, pl **guardamuebles** furniture repository.
guardapapeles nm, pl **guardapapeles** filing cabinet.
guardapelo nm locket.
guardapolvo nm (a) dust cover, dust sheet. (b) (dress) dust coat; overalls; outdoor coat. (c) (of watch) inner lid.
guardapuerta nf outer door, storm door.
guardapuntas nm, pl **guardapuntas** top (of pencil etc).
guardar [1a] 1 vt (a) to guard; to watch over, protect, take care of, keep safe; to maintain, preserve; flock etc to watch over, tend; **¡Dios guarde a la Reina!** God save the Queen!; **Dios os guarde** (Hist) may God be with you.
(b) to keep, hold, hold on to, retain; to put away, put by, lay by, store away; to save; — **algo para sí** to keep something for oneself; **lo guardó en el bolsillo** he put it away in his pocket; **te lo puedes** — you keep it, you can keep it; **guardo los sellos para mi hermano** I save the stamps for my brother.
(c) promise, secret to keep.
(d) commandment etc to keep; law to observe, respect.
(e) respect etc to have, show (a for); malice etc to bear, have (a for, towards); see **cama, silencio** etc.
2 vi: **¡guarda!** look out!, watch out!
3 **guardarse** vr (a) to be on one's guard, look out for oneself.
(b) — **de algo** to avoid something; to look out for something; to refrain from something; to protect oneself against something; — **de** + infin to be careful not to + infin; to refrain from + ger; to avoid + ger; to guard against + ger; **guárdate de no ofenderle** take care not to upset him; **¡ya te guardarás de hacerlo!** I bet you won't!; you wouldn't dare!
(c) — **la a uno** to keep a rod in pickle for someone, have it in for someone.
guardarropa 1 nm (a) (room) cloakroom, checkroom (US). (b) (cupboard) wardrobe. 2 nmf cloakroom attendant.
guardarropía nf (Theat) wardrobe; properties, props (fam); **de** — make-believe, (pej) sham, fake.
guardatrén nm (RPl: Rail) guard, brakeman.
guardavalla nm (SAm) goalkeeper.
guardavía nm (Rail) linesman.
guardavidas nm, pl **guardavidas** (Arg) lifeguard (on beach).
guardavista nm visor, sunshade.

guardería *nf*: — **infantil** crèche, day nursery.

guardia 1 *nf* (a) (*in general*) custody, care; defence, protection; (*Mil etc*) guarding; **estar de** — to be on guard, be on duty; to keep watch; **estar en** — **contra** to be on one's guard against; **montar (la)** — to mount guard; **poner a uno en** — to put someone on his guard.
(b) (*body of men*) guard; (*Mil*) guard; police; (*Naut*) watch; — **de asalto** riot police; **G— Civil** Civil Guard; — **de corps** bodyguard; — **de cuartillo** (*Naut*) dog watch; — **de honor** guard of honour; **—s montadas** horse guards; — **municipal**, — **urbana** town police, traffic police; — **real** household troops; — **suiza** Swiss guard; **relevar la** — to change guard.
(c) (*Fencing: position*) guard; **aflojar la** — to lower one's guard (*also fig*); **estar en** — to be on guard.
2 *nm* policeman; (*Mil*) guard, guardsman; **—s de asalto** riot police, (*Mil*) shock troops; — **de la circulación**, — **de la porra**, — **de tráfico**, — **urbano** traffic policeman; — **civil** civil guard; — **forestal** game warden, ranger; — **marina** midshipman.

guardián *nm*, **guardiana** *nf* guardian, custodian, keeper; warden; watchman; (*Zool*) keeper; — **de niño(s)** baby-sitter; — **de parque** park keeper; — **de prisiones** warder.

guardiero *nm* (*Cu*) watchman (*on an estate*).

guardilla *nf* attic, garret; attic room.

guardoso *adj* careful, thrifty; (*pej*) mean.

guare *nm* (*Ec*) punt pole.

guarearse [1a] *vr* (*CAm*) to drink sugar-cane liquor.

guarecer [2d] **1** *vt* to protect, give shelter to, take in; to preserve. **2 guarecerse** *vr* to shelter, take refuge (*de* from).

guargüero *nm* (*SAm*) throat, throttle.

guari *nm* (*Chi*) throat, throttle.

guaricha *nf* (a) (*Col, Ec, Pan, Ven*) little woman; nasty woman; (*Ven*) young (Indian) woman; (*Pan*) sly old woman.
(b) (*Pan*) brass lamp.

guariche *nm* (*Col*) = **guaricha**.

guaricho *nm* (*Ven*) young farm labourer.

guarida *nf* (*Zool*) den, lair, hideout; (*fig*) refuge, shelter; cover; (*of person*) haunt, hideout.

guarismo *nm* figure, numeral; **en** — **y por extenso** in figures and in words.

guarnecer [2d] *vt* (a) to equip, provide (*de* with); to adorn, embellish, garnish (*de* with); (*Sew*) to trim, edge (*de* with); *brakes* to line; *wall* to plaster, stucco; *jewel* to set, mount; *horse* to harness; (*Tech*) to cover, protect, reinforce (*de* with).
(b) (*Mil*) to man, garrison.

guarnecido *nm* plaster, plastering.

guarnición *nf* (a) (*act*) equipment, provision; fitting; adorning, embellishing.
(b) adornment; (*Sew*) trimming, edging, binding; (*of brake*) lining; (*of wall*) plastering; (*of jewel*) setting, mount; (*of sword*) guard; (*Mech*) packing.
(c) **—es** harness; gear; (*domestic*) fittings, fixtures; **—es del alumbrado** light fittings.
(d) (*Mil*) garrison.

guarnicionar [1a] *vt* to garrison, man.

guarnicionero *nm* harness maker.

guaro *nm* (a) (*CAm*) sugar-cane liquor, rum. (b) small parrot.

guarra *nf* sow; (*fig*) slut.

guarro 1 *adj* dirty, filthy. **2** *nm* pig, hog; (*fig*) dirty person, slovenly person.

guarrusca *nf* (*Col*) machete, big knife.

guarte *interj* (*arch*) look out!, take care!

guasa *nf* (a) joke; joking, teasing, kidding; **con —, de** — jokingly, in fun.
(b) dullness, insipidness.
(c) (*Chi*) peasant woman.
(d) **armar** — to kick up a row; to cause a sensation.

guasábara *nf* (*Col, PR, SD*) uprising, riot; tumult; clamour, uproar.

guasada *nf* (*RPl*) coarseness, crudity.

guasamaco *adj* rough, coarse.

guasanga *nf* (a) (*CAm, Col, Cu, Mex*) = **guasábara**; (*Guat*) quarrel, squabble. (b) (*Guat*) joke.

guasca[1] *nf* (*SAm*) leather strap, rawhide thong; **dar** — **a** (*SAm*) to whip, flog; (*Chi, RPl*) to insist stubbornly on; (*Per*) to wind up; **¡déle** — **no más!** (*Urug*) keep at it!; **pisarse la** — (*Col, Chi, RPl*) to fall into the trap; to be too clever by half; **volverse** — (*Col*) to be full of longing.

guasca[2] *nf* (*Col*) mountain peak.

guascazo *nm* (*SAm*) lash; blow, punch.

guasearse [1a] *vr* to joke, tease, kid, rag.

guasería *nf* (*Bol, Chi, RPl*) coarseness, crudity.

guaserío *nm* (*Bol, Chi, RPl*) peasants, peasantry.

guaso 1 *adj* (*Cu, Ec, RPl*) coarse, crude, rough. **2** *nm*, **guasa** *nf* (*Bol, Chi, Per, RPl*) peasant, countryman. **3** *nm* (*Cu*) merry din; merrymaking, revels.

guasón 1 *adj* (a) witty, humorous; joking; **dijo** — he said jokingly, he said teasingly.
(b) dull, insipid; boring.
2 *nm*, **guasona** *nf* (a) wag, wit; joker, tease.
(b) tedious person, bore.

guasqueada *nf* (*Arg*) lash; whipping, flogging.

guasquear [1a] *vt* (*Col, Chi, Per, RPl*) to whip, flog.

guata[1] *nf* (a) (*Arg, Chi, Per*) paunch, belly; stomach; (*Cook*) tripe; **echar** — to get fat. (b) (*Chi*) warping, bulging.

guata[2] *nf* (a) raw cotton; padding; (*Bol*) twine, cord.
(b) (*Cu*) lie, fib.
(c) (*Ec*) inseparable friend.
(d) (*Guat*) double-barrelled shotgun.

guata[3] *nmf* (*Col*) inhabitant of the interior.

guataca 1 *nf* (a) (*Cu*) small hoe; wooden shovel; (b) (*Cu, SD*) big ear. **2** *nmf* (*Cu*) creep (*sl*), bootlicker (*fam*).

guataco *adj* (a) (*Col: pej*) Indian, native. (b) (*Cu*) rough, coarse. (c) (*Hond*) squat; thickset.

guatal *nm* (*CAm*) = **guate** (a).

guate *nm* (a) (*CAm*) maize plantation (for fodder).
(b) (*Col*) inhabitant of the interior; (*Ven*) highlander; (*Ven*) Colombian.
(c) (*Ec*) inseparable friend.

guatearse [1a] *vr* (*Chi*) to warp, bulge.

Guatemala *f* Guatemala.

guatemalteco 1 *adj* Guatemalan, of Guatemala. **2** *nm*, **guatemalteca** *nf* Guatemalan.

guatemaltequismo *nm* word (*or phrase etc*) peculiar to Guatemala.

guateque *nm* party, celebration, binge (*sl*).

guatón *adj* (*Arg, Chi, Per*) fat, paunchy, pot-bellied.

guatuso *adj* (*CAm*) blond(e), fair.

guau 1 *interj etc* bow-wow! **2** *nm* bark.

guayaba *nf* (a) (*SAm: Bot*) guava; guava jelly.
(b) (*fig and hum*: *SAm*) fib, lie; hoax; (*CAm*) worthless object; (*Ec*) ankle; (*Guat*) kiss; (*Guat, Salv: Pol*) power, presidency; **—s** (*CR*) (protruding) eyes.

guayabal *nm* grove of guava trees.

guayabear [1a] **1** *vt* (*Guat*) to kiss. **2** *vi* (a) (*CAm*) to pick guavas; to eat guavas. (b) (*PR, RPl*) to lie, tell fibs.

guayabera *nf* (*CAm, Cú, Mex*) light blouse.

guayabero *adj* (*Ant, Arg, Ec*) lying, deceitful.

guayabo *nm* (a) (*Bot*) guava tree. (b) (*Col*) grief, sorrow; nostalgia; (*fam*) hangover. (c) (*fam*) pretty girl, smasher (*sl*).

guayaca 1 *adj* (*Chi*) slow, dull; simple-minded. **2** *nf* (*SAm*) bag, purse.

guayacán *nm* lignum vitae.

Guayana *f* Guayana; (*earlier name*) Guiana; — **Británica** British Guiana; — **Francesa** French Guiana; — **Holandesa** Dutch Guiana.

guayanés 1 *adj* Guayanese. **2** *nm*, **guayanesa** *nf* Guayanese.

guayar [1a] **1** *vt* (*Ant: Cook*) to grate, break up; to scrape. **2** *vi* (*Ant*) to work hard. **3 guayarse** *vr* (*PR*) to get drunk.

guayo *nm* (*Ant: Cook*) grater; (*hum*) poor-quality band.

guayunga *nf* (*Ec*) lot, heap.

gubernamental 1 *adj* governmental; (*as faction*) loyalist. **2** *nmf* loyalist, government supporter; (*Mil*) government soldier.

gubernativo *adj* governmental.

gubia *nf* gouge.

guedeja *nf* long hair, lock; (*lion's*) mane.

güe—: *alternative spelling* (*prov, SAm*) *for some words, see* **hue—**: *eg for* **güevo** *see* **huevo**.

güegüecho 1 *adj* (a) (*CAm, Col*) silly, stupid.
(b) (*CAm, Mex: Med*) suffering from goitre.
2 *nm* (a) (*CAm, Mex: Med*) goitre.
(b) (*CAm, Mex: Orn*) wattle; turkey.

Guernesey *m* Guernsey.

güeñi *nm* (*Chi*) boy; servant; swarthy person.

güero *adj* (*CAm, Mex*) blond(e), fair.

guerra *nf* (a) war; warfare; struggle, fight, conflict; — **de agotamiento**, — **de desgaste** war of attrition; — **atómica** atomic war(fare); — **bacteriológica** germ warfare; — **civil** civil war; — **fría** cold war; — **de guerrillas** guerrilla warfare; — **a muerte** war to the knife, war to the bitter end; — **mundial** world war; — **de nervios** war of nerves; — **nuclear** nuclear war(fare); — **relámpago** blitzkrieg; — **santa** holy war, crusade; — **a tiros** shooting war, hot

war; — **de trincheras** trench warfare; **G— de los Cien Años** Hundred Years' War; **G— de los Treinta Años** Thirty Years' War; **G— de la Independencia** (*Spain, also* SAm) War of Independence; **G— de Liberación** (*Spain, 1936-39*) Civil War; **G— del Transvaal** Boer War; **Primera G— Mundial** First World War; **Segunda G— Mundial** Second World War; **de —** military; war (*attr*); **Ministerio m de G—** Ministry of War, War Office (*Brit*), War Department (*US*); **estar en —** to be at war (*con* with); **dar —** to be annoying (*a* to), be a nuisance (*a* to), make trouble (*a* for); (*of child*) to carry on, make a great fuss; **dar — a uno** to rag someone; **declarar la —** to declare war (*a* on); **hacer la —** to wage war, make war (*a* on).
 (b) billiards.

guerrear [1a] *vi* to wage war, fight; (*fig*) to put up a fight, resist.

guerrero 1 *adj* (a) fighting (*attr*); war (*attr*); **espíritu — fighting spirit.**
 (b) warring.
 (c) (*of character*) warlike, martial; **un pueblo —** a warlike people.
 2 *nm* warrior, soldier, fighter.

guerrilla *nf* (a) guerrilla band; group of partisans.
 (b) guerrilla warfare.

guerrillear [1a] *vi* to wage guerrilla warfare; to fight as a guerrilla band.

guerrillero *nm* guerrilla (fighter); partisan; irregular.

güi . . .: *for some words so spelled in* SAm *see also* **hui . . .**

guía 1 *nf* (a) (*act*) guidance, guiding; **— vocacional** vocational guidance; **para que le sirva de —** for your guidance.
 (b) (*Typ*) guide, guidebook (*de* to); handbook; directory; **— de campo** (*Bio*) field guide; **— de carga** (*Rail*) waybill; **— oficial de ferrocarriles** official railway guide, official timetable; **— telefónica,** **— de teléfonos** telephone directory; **— del turista** tourist's guide; **— del viajero** traveller's guide.
 (c) (*Mech*) guide; (*of cycle*) handlebars; (*horse*) leader, front horse; **—s** reins; **— sonora** (*Cine*) soundtrack.
 2 *nmf* (*person*) guide; leader; adviser.

guiar [1c] **1** *vt* (a) (*in general*) to guide; to lead, direct; to manage; to advise.
 (b) (*Aut etc*) to drive; (*Naut*) to steer; (*Aer*) to pilot.
 (c) (*Bot*) to train.
 2 guiarse *vr*: **— por** to be guided by, be ruled by, go by.

Guido *m* Guy.

guija *nf* pebble; (*on road*) cobble, cobblestone.

guijarral *nm* stony place; (*beach*) shingle, pebbles, pebbly part.

guijarro *nm* pebble; boulder; (*on road*) cobble, cobblestone.

guijarroso *adj* ground stony; boulder-strewn; *road* cobbled; *beach* pebbly, shingly.

guijo *nm* (a) gravel; (*for roadmaking*) granite chips; (*on beach*) shingle. (b) (*Col, Mex*) shaft of a water wheel; (*Cu, Mex*) shaft of a sugar mill.

güila *nf* (a) (*Mex*) whore. (b) (*Mex*) small paper kite. (c) (*CR*) small spinning top. (d) (*Chi*) rags, tatters.

guili *nm* (*fam*) bobby (*sl*), cop (*sl*).

güiliento *adj* (*Chi*) ragged, tattered.

güilo *adj* (*Mex*) maimed, crippled; (*fig*) weak, sickly.

guillado *adj* (*fam*) cracked, crazy; **estar — to** be cracked; to be in love.

guilladura *nf* (*fam*) craziness, light-headedness, idiotic joy.

guillame *nm* (*Tech*) rabbet plane.

guillarse [1a] *vr* (*fam*) to go crazy.

guillate *adj* (*fam*) crazy; **ella me vuelve —** she drives me crazy, I'm crazy about her.

Guillermo *m* William; **— el Conquistador** William the Conqueror.

guillotina *nf* guillotine; paper cutter; **ventana de —** sash window.

guillotinar [1a] *vt* to guillotine.

güincha *nf* (*Bol, Chi, Per*) (a) narrow strip of cloth; ribbon; hair ribbon; (*Sport*) tape. (b) measuring tape, tape measure.

güinche *nm* (*SAm: angl*) winch, hoist; crane.

güinchero *nm* (*SAm*) winch operator; crane operator.

guinda *nf* (a) mazzard cherry, morello cherry; **ponerse como una —** to turn scarlet.
 (b) (*Naut*) height of masts.
 (c) (*Cu*) guttering, spout.
 (d) (*Chi*) **eso es una —** that's simple, it's a cinch (*sl*).

guindalejo *nm* (*Col, PR*) old clothes, junk, lumber.

guindaleza *nf* hawser.

guindar [1a] **1** *vt* (a) to hoist, hang up (high); (*Ven etc*) to hang (up); *criminal* (*fam*) to hang, string up (*fam*).
 (b) (*fam*) to pinch (*fam*), swipe (*sl*).
 2 guindarse *vr* (*fam*) to hang oneself.

guindaste *nm* (*CAm*) jib crane.

guindilla *nm* (*fam*) bobby (*sl*), cop (*sl*).

guindo *nm* mazzard (*or* morello) cherry tree.

guindola *nf* lifebuoy.

Guinea *f* Guinea; **— Española** Spanish Guinea.

guinea *nf* (*coin*) guinea.

guineo¹ 1 *adj* Guinea(n), of Guinea. **2** *nm*, **guinea** *nf* Guinean.

guineo² *nm* (*SAm: Bot*) banana.

guiña *nf* (*Col, Ven*) bad luck; (*Col*) witchcraft.

guiñada *nf* (a) wink; blink, (*Aer, Naut*) yaw.

guiñapo *nm* (a) rag, tatter; **poner a uno como un — to** shower insults on someone. (b) slovenly person; ragamuffin; rogue, reprobate.

guiñar [1a] **1** *vt* to wink; to blink. **2** *vi* (a) to wink; to blink. (b) (*Aer, Naut*) to yaw.

guiño *nm* (a) wink; grimace, wry face; **hacer —s a** to wink at, (*of lovers*) to make eyes at. (b) (*Aer, Naut*) yaw.

guiñol *nm* art of the puppeteer, puppet theatre, Punch-and-Judy show.

guión *nm* (a) (*Zool, person*) leader.
 (b) (*Typ*) hyphen, dash.
 (c) (*Lit*) summary, outline; handout; explanatory text; (*Cine*) script, scenario; (*Cine*) subtitle.
 (d) royal standard; (*Eccl*) processional cross, processional banner.
 (e) (*Orn*) **— de codornices** corncrake.

guionista *nmf* (*Cine*) scriptwriter; writer of subtitles.

guipuzcoano 1 *adj* of Guipúzcoa. **2** *nm*, **guipuzcoana** *nf* native (*or* inhabitant) of Guipúzcoa; **los —s** the people of Guipúzcoa.

guiri *nm* (*Hist*) Carlist soldier.

guirigay *nm* (a) gibberish, jargon.
 (b) hubbub, uproar; chaos, confusion; **¡esto es un —!** the place is like a bear garden!; **la nación se sumirá en un espantoso —** the country will fall into dreadful anarchy.

guirizapa *nf* (*Ven*) quarrel, squabble.

guirnalda *nf* garland; (*at funeral*) wreath; (*Art*) garland, floral motif.

güiro *nm* (a) (*SAm*) bottle gourd.
 (b) (*Ant, Ven*) musical instrument made of a gourd.
 (c) (*Col, Cu, PR*) head, bean (*fam*).
 (d) (*Guat*) small baby.
 (e) (*Cu, PR*) whore.
 (f) (*Cu*) love affair.

güirro 1 *adj* (*SAm*) weak, sickly. **2** *nm* (*CR*) small baby.

guisa *nf*: **a — de** as, like, in the manner of; **de tal — in** such a way (*que* that).

guisado *nm* stew.

guisador *nm*, **guisadero** *nm* cook.

guisante *nm* pea; **— de olor** sweet pea.

guisar [1a] *vt* (a) to prepare; to arrange. (b) (*Cook*) to cook; to stew.

güisingue *nm* (*Col*) whip.

güisinguear [1a] *vt* (*Col*) to whip.

guiso *nm* (a) cooked dish; (*SAm*) stew. (b) seasoning.

guisote *nm* (*pej*) hash, poor-quality stew; concoction; grub (*sl*).

guita *nm* (a) twine; packthread. (b) (*sl*) dough (*sl*); **aflojar la —, soltar la —** to stump up (*fam*), fork out (*fam*).

guitarra *nf* guitar; **ser como — en un entierro to** be quite out of place, strike the wrong note; **chafar la — a uno** to queer someone's pitch.

guitarrear [1a] *vi* to play the guitar.

guitarrista *nmf* guitarist.

gula *nf* greed, gluttony.

guloso *adj* greedy, gluttonous.

gulusmear [1a] *vi* to nibble titbits; to sniff the cooking.

gurguciar [1b] *vt* (*CAm*) to sniff at, sniff out.

gurí *nm, pl* **gurís, guríes,** *or* **gurises** (*RPl*) Indian *or* half-breed child; boy, lad.

gurisa *nf* (*RPl*) Indian *or* half-breed child; girl, lass; young wife.

gurrí *nm* (*SAm*) wild duck.

gurrumina *nf* (a) (*Col, Ec, Guat, Mex*) bother, vexation; (*Col*) sadness.
 (b) (*Guat, Mex*) trifle, mere nothing.
 (c) (*Hond*) shrewd person.

gurrumino 1 adj (a) weak, sickly; small, puny.
  (b) husband henpecked, hag-ridden; uxorious.
  (c) (Bol) cowardly.
  (d) (Hond) clever, sharp.
  2 nm (a) henpecked husband; uxorious man.
  (b) (Mex, Salv) child.

gur(r)upié nm (a) (SAm: gall) croupier. (b) (Cu, Ec) false bidder (at auction). (c) (Cu) buddy (esp US), pal (fam). (d) (PR, Ven) servant, family retainer.

gus nm (Col) turkey buzzard.

gusanera nf (a) nest of maggots; breeding ground for maggots. (b) (fig) bunch, lot, crowd; **una — de chiquillos** a bunch of kids.

gusaniento adj maggoty, worm-eaten, grub-infested.

gusanillo nm small maggot, small worm; **me anda el —** I feel peckish; **matar el —** to have a snack, take the edge off one's appetite; to have a nip of liquor first thing in the morning.

gusano nm (a) maggot, grub, worm; (of butterfly, moth) caterpillar; **— de luz** glow-worm; **— de seda** silkworm; **— de tierra** earthworm.
  (b) (fig) worm, contemptible person; meek creature.
  (c) (Arg, Ec, Per) liquor; **matar el —** to have a drink.
  (d) (Cu: Pol) anti-Castro Cuban.

gusanoso adj = **gusaniento**.

gusgo adj (Mex) sweet-toothed.

gustación nf tasting, trying.

gustado adj (SAm) esteemed, well-liked, popular.

gustar [1a] **1** vt to taste, try, sample.
  2 vi (a) to please, be pleasing; **es una película que siempre gusta** it's a film which always pleases (or gives pleasure); **la comedia no gustó** the play was not a success, the play was not much liked; **mi número ya no gusta** my act isn't popular any more.
  (b) (with personal indirect object) **me gusta el té** I like tea; **¿te gusta Méjico?** do you like Mexico?; **no le gusta que le llamen Pepe** he doesn't like to be called Joe; **no me gusta mucho** I don't like it much, I'm not very struck (on it); **me gusta como anda** I like the way she walks.
  (c) (formal phrases) **¿gusta Vd?** would you like some?, may I offer you some?; **si Vd gusta** if you please, if you don't mind; **como Vd guste** as you wish.
  (d) **— de algo** to like something, enjoy something; **— de** + infin to like to + infin, be fond of + ger, enjoy + ger.

gustazo nm great pleasure; (pej) unhealthy pleasure, nasty pleasure.

gustillo nm suggestion, touch, tang.

gusto nm (a) taste (sense); **agregue azúcar a —** add sugar to taste.
  (b) (of food) taste, flavour; **tiene un — amargo** it has a bitter taste, it tastes bitter.
  (c) (Art etc) taste; style, fashion; **buen —** good taste; **mal —** bad taste; **de buen —** in good taste; **es de un mal — extraordinario** it is in extraordinarily bad taste; **para mi —** to my taste; **al — de hoy, según el — de hoy** in the taste of today; **ser persona de —** to be a person of taste; **sobre —s no hay disputa, de —s no hay nada escrito** there's no accounting for tastes; **tiene — para vestir** she dresses elegantly, she has taste in dresses.
  (d) pleasure; **con mucho —** with pleasure; gladly, willingly; **con sumo —** with the very greatest pleasure; **comer con —** to eat heartily; **estar a —** to be at ease, feel comfortable; **aquí me encuentro a —** I like it here, I feel at home here; **acomodarse a su —** to make oneself comfortable, make oneself at home; **sentirse mal a —** to feel ill at ease; **tengo los pies a — y calientes** my feet are nice and warm; **dar — a** to please, give pleasure to; **tener el — de** + ger to have the pleasure of + ger; **tener — en** + infin to be glad to + infin.
  (e) (introductions) **¡mucho —!**, **¡tanto —!** how do you do?; pleased to meet you; **el — es mío** how do you do?; the pleasure is mine; **tengo mucho — en presentar al Sr X** allow me to introduce Mr X; **tengo mucho — en conocerle** I'm very pleased to meet you.
  (f) liking (por for); **al — de** to the liking of; **ser del — de uno** to be to someone's liking; **tener — por** to have a liking for, have an eye for; **tomar — a** to take a liking to.
  (g) whim, fancy; **a —** at will, according to one's fancy.
  (h) (RPl: Comm) style, design, colour; range, assortment.

gustoso adj (a) tasty, savoury, nice.
  (b) pleasant.
  (c) willing, glad; **lo hizo —** he did it gladly, he did it with pleasure; **le ofrezco — una habitación de matrimonio** I am glad to be able to offer you a double room.

gutapercha nf gutta-percha.

gutifarra nf (SAm) = **butifarra**.

gutural adj guttural (also Ling); throaty.

H

ha *see* **haber.**

ha *interj* ha!

haba *nf* (broad) bean; (*of coffee etc*) bean; — **de las Indias** sweet pea; **son —s contadas** we know all about that; it's a sure thing, it's a certainty; **en todas partes cuecen —s** it's the same the whole world over.

Habana: La — Havana.

habanera *nf* (*Mus*) habanera.

habanero 1 *adj* of Havana. **2** *nm*, **habanera** *nf* native (*or* inhabitant) of Havana; **los —s** the people of Havana.

habano 1 *adj and n* = **habanero. 2** *nm* Havana cigar.

hábeas corpus *nm* habeas corpus.

haber [2k] **1** *vt* (a) (*arch*) to have, possess.

(b) (*lit*) to get; to catch, lay hands on; **lee cuantos libros puede —** he reads all the books he can lay hands on.

(c) (*Rel: formulae*) **bien haya . . .** blessed be . . .; **X, que Dios haya X**, God rest his soul.

(d) (*Law: formula*) **todos los inventos habidos y por haber** all inventions present and future, the present inventions and any others that may be made.

(e) (*lit, journalese*) **en el encuentro habido ayer** in the fight which occurred yesterday; **la baja de temperatura habida ayer** the fall in temperature recorded yesterday; **la lista de los caídos habidos** the list of casualties suffered.

2 *v aux* (a) (*used in forming compound tenses*) to have; **he comido** I have eaten; **lo hubiéramos hecho** we would have done it; **antes de —lo visto** before seeing him, before having seen him; **de —lo sabido** if I had known it.

(b) **— de +** *infin:* **he de hacerlo** I have to do it, I am to do it, I must do it; **¿qué he de hacer?** what am I to do?; **ha de llegar hoy** he is due to arrive today; **ha de haberse perdido** it must have got lost; **han de ser las 9** it must be about 9 o'clock.

3 *v impersonal* (a) (*general sense*) **hay** there is, there are; **hay calefacción** there is heating; **hay tanto que hacer** there is so much to be done; **no hay plátanos** there are no bananas, we have no bananas; **no lo hay** there isn't any; **no hubo discusión** there was no discussion; **"mejores no hay"** (*Comm: slogan*) "none better!"; **¿habrá tiempo?** will there be time?; **¿hay puros?** (*in shop*) have you any cigars?; **tomará lo que haya** he'll take whatever there is, he'll take whatever is going; **lo que hay es que . . .** what's happening is that . . ., it's like this . . .; **hay sol** the sun is shining, it is sunny; **¿qué hay?** what's up?, what's the matter?, what goes on?; **¡no hay de qué!** don't mention it!, not at all!; **¿cuánto hay de aquí a Cuzco?** how far is it from here to Cuzco?

(b) **hay que +** *infin* it is necessary to **+** *infin,* one must **+** *infin;* **hay que trabajar** one has to work, everything must work; **hay que trabajar más** (*to individual*) you must work harder; **hay que hacerlo** it has to be done; **¡había que verlo!** you should have seen it!; **hay que ser fuertes** we must be strong; **no hay que tomarlo a mal** there's no cause to take it badly, you mustn't get upset about it; **y no hay más que conformarse** there's nothing one can do but fall into line.

(c) (*expressions of time*) **3 años ha** 3 years ago; **poco tiempo ha** a short time ago.

4 haberse *vr* (a) (*arch*) to behave, comport oneself; **se ha habido con honradez** he has behaved honourably.

(b) **—las con uno** to be up against someone, have to do with someone, have to contend with someone; **tenemos que habérnoslas con un enemigo despiadado** we are up against a ruthless enemy; **¡allá te las hayas!** that's your affair!

5 *nm* income, salary; (*Comm*) assets; (*of balance sheet*) credit side; **—es** assets, property, goods; **asentar algo al — de uno, pasar algo al — de uno** to credit something to someone; **¿cuánto tenemos en el —?** how much have we on the credit side? (*also fig*).

habichuela *nf* kidney bean; **ganarse las —s** to earn one's living.

hábil *adj* (a) clever; skilful; able, capable, proficient; good, expert (*en at*); (*pej*) cunning, smart.

(b) **— para** fit for.

(c) **día —** working day.

(d) (*Law*) competent.

habilidad *nf* (a) cleverness; skill; ability, proficiency; expertness, expertise; (*pej*) cunning, smartness; **hombre de gran — política** a man of great political skill; **tener — manual** to be clever with one's hands.

(b) fitness (*para* for).

(c) (*Law*) competence.

habilidoso *adj* (*esp pej*) clever, smart.

habilitación *nf* (a) qualification, entitlement.

(b) equipment, fitting out.

(c) financing; (*Arg, Par: Agr*) credit in kind; (*Guat, Mex*) loan.

(d) (*Arg, Par*) offer of a partnership.

(e) paymaster's office.

habilitado *nm* paymaster.

habilitar [1a] *vt* (a) to qualify, entitle (*para que haga* to do); to enable (*para que haga* to do); to empower, authorize (*para que haga* to do).

(b) to equip, fit out, set up.

(c) to finance; **— a uno** (*Arg, Par: Agr*) to make someone a loan in kind (with the next crop as security), give someone credit facilities; (*Guat, Mex*) to advance money to.

(d) (*Arg, Par: Comm*) to take into partnership.

(e) (*CR: Agr*) to cover, serve.

(f) (*Cu*) to annoy, provoke.

hábilmente *adv* cleverly; skilfully; ably, proficiently, expertly; (*pej*) cunningly, smartly.

habiloso *adj* (*Chi*) = **habilidoso.**

habitabilidad *nf* habitability; (*of house*) quality, quality of the living accommodation.

habitable *adj* inhabitable, that can be lived in.

habitación *nf* (a) habitation; dwelling, abode; lodging(s), apartment; (*Bio*) habitat.

(b) (*personal, hotel etc*) room; **—es (particulares)** rooms, suite; **— de dos camas, — doble, — de matrimonio** double room; **— individual** single room; **— lacustre** lake dwelling.

habitado *adj* inhabited; lived-in; *satellite etc* manned, carrying a crew.

habitante 1 *nmf* inhabitant; resident; (*of house*) occupant, tenant; **una ciudad de 10.000 —s** a city of 10,000 inhabitants (*or* people), a city with a population of 10,000.

2 *nm* (*hum*) louse; **tener —s** to be lousy.

habitar [1a] **1** *vt* to inhabit, live in, dwell in; *house etc* to occupy, be the occupant of. **2** *vi* to live.

habitat *nm, pl* **habitats** habitat.

hábito *nm* (a) habit, custom; **una droga que conduce al — morboso** a habit-forming drug; **tener el — de +** *infin* to be in the habit of **+** *ger.*

(b) (*Eccl*) habit; **— monástico** monastic habit; **ahorcar** (*or* **colgar**) **los —s** to leave the priesthood; **tomar el —** (*man*) to take holy orders, become a monk, (*woman*) to take the veil, become a nun.

habituado *nm,* **habituada** *nf* habitué(e).

habitual 1 *adj* habitual, customary, usual; *criminal* hardened; *liar* incorrigible; *sin* besetting; **su restaurante —** one's usual restaurant; **como**

lector — de esa revista as a regular reader of your journal.
2 *nmf* (*of bar etc*) habitué(e); (*of shop*) regular customer.

habituar [1e] **1** *vt* to accustom (*a* to). **2 habituarse** *vr*: **— a** to become accustomed to, get used to.

habla *nf* (a) (*faculty in general*) speech; **dejar a uno sin —** to leave someone speechless, dumbfound someone; **estar sin —** to be speechless; **perder el —** to become speechless.
(b) (*national etc*) language; (*regional*) dialect, speech; (*of class, profession etc*) talk, speech; (*Lit*) language, style; **de — francesa** French-speaking.
(c) talk; **¡García al —!** (*Tel*) García speaking!; **estar al —** to be in contact, be in touch; (*Naut*) to be within hail; (*Tel*) to be on the line, be speaking (*con* to); **negar** (*or* **quitar**) **el — a uno** to stop speaking to someone, not be on speaking terms with someone; **ponerse al — con uno** to get into touch with someone.

hablachento *adj* (*Ven*) talkative.

hablada *nf* (a) (*Chi*) speech.
(b) (*Arg, Mex*) boast.
(c) (*Ec*) scolding, telling-off.
(d) (*Chi, Guat, Mex*) hint, innuendo; piece of gossip; **echar —s** to drop hints, make innuendoes.

habladera *nf* (a) (*SAm*) talking, noise of talking.
(b) (*Ant, CAm, Chi, Mex*) = **habladuría**.

habladero *nm* (*Chi, SD*) piece of gossip.

hablado (a) *adj and ptp* spoken; **la palabra hablada** the spoken word.
(b) *adj*: **bien —** nicely-spoken, well-spoken; **mal —** coarse, rude; foul-mouthed.

hablador 1 *adj* (a) talkative; chatty; voluble.
(b) gossipy, given to gossip.
(c) (*Mex*) boastful, bullying.
(d) (*Mex, SD*) lying; loud-mouthed.
2 *nm*, **habladora** *nf* (a) talkative person, great talker, chatterbox.
(b) gossip.

habladuría *nf* rumour; nasty remark, sarcastic remark; idle chatter, piece of gossip; **—s** gossip, scandal.

hablanchín *adj*, **hablantín** *adj* talkative, garrulous, chatty.

hablante 1 *adj* speaking. **2** *nmf* speaker.

hablantina *nf* (*Col, Ven*) gibberish, meaningless torrent; empty talk.

hablantín(so) *adj* (*Col*) = **hablador** (a) *and* (b).

hablar [1a] **1** *vt language* to speak, talk; *nonsense etc* to talk; **habla bien el portugués** he speaks good Portuguese, he speaks Portuguese well; **hablarlo todo** to talk too much, give the game away; **y no hay más que —** so there's no more to be said about it.
2 *vi* to speak, talk (*a, con* to; *de* about, of); **que hable él** let him speak, let him have his say; **¡hable!, ¡puede —!** (*Tel*) you're through!; **¿quién habla?** (*Tel*) who is it?, who's calling?; **¡ni —!** nonsense!; no fear!, not likely!; **de eso ni —** that's out of the question, that's not on; **— alto** to speak loudly, (*fig*) to speak out (frankly); **— bajo** to talk quietly, speak in a low voice; **— claro** (*fig*) to speak plainly, speak bluntly; **¡para que luego hablen de coches!** as if other cars came into it!; **— por sólo —** to talk just for talking's sake; **habla por sí mismo** it speaks for itself; **los datos hablan por sí solos** the facts speak for themselves; **el retrato está hablando** the portrait is a speaking likeness; **dar que — a la gente** to make people talk, cause people to gossip; **hacer — a uno** (*fig*) to make someone talk; **el vino hace —** wine loosens people's tongues.
3 hablarse *vr*: **"se habla inglés"** (*notice*) "English spoken here"; **en el Brasil se habla portugués** Portuguese is spoken in Brazil; **se habla de que van a comprarlo** there is talk of their buying it; **no se hablan** they are not on speaking terms, they don't speak.

hablilla *nf* rumour, story; (piece of) gossip, tittle-tattle.

habloteo *nm* incomprehensible talk.

Habsburgo Hapsburg.

hacedero *adj* practicable, feasible.

hacedor *nm*, **hacedora** *nf* maker; **el (Supremo) H—** the Maker; **el — de reyes** the kingmaker.

hacendado 1 *adj* landed, property-owning. **2** *nm* landowner, property owner; gentleman farmer; (*SAm*) rancher.

hacendario *nm* (*CAm, Mex*) treasury.

hacendista *nm* economist, financial expert.

hacendoso *adj* industrious, hard-working; busy, bustling.

hacer [2s] **1** *vt* (a) to make, create; (*Tech*) to make, manufacture; to build, construct; *dress etc* to make; *work of art* to make; to fashion; (*Lit, Mus*) to compose; *money* to make, earn; *smoke etc* to make, give off, emit, produce; *war* to fight, wage; **— algo** to have something made.
(b) to make, prepare; *bed* to make; *meal* to make, prepare, get, cook; *suitcase* to pack; *tie* to tie; *balance* (*Comm*) to strike; *bet* to lay; *objection* to make, raise; *question* to put, ask; *order* to give; *speech* to make, deliver; *visit* to pay; **— la barba a uno** to shave someone (*see also* **barba**[1]); **— el pelo a una** to do someone's hair; **— un recado** to run a message, go on an errand.
(c) to cause, make; *shadow* to cast; **el árbol hace sombra** the tree gives shade, the tree casts a shadow.
(d) *eg* **— cine** to make films, be engaged in film work, be working for the cinema; **este año hace turismo en África** this year he's gone touring (*or* as a tourist) in Africa.
(e) to do; to execute, perform, put into practice; *play* to do, perform; *wonders etc* to do, work, perform; **no sé qué —** I don't know what to do; **haga lo que quiera** do as you please; **¿qué haces ahí?** what are you doing?, what are you up to?; **¿qué le vamos a —?** what shall we do with him?, what can we do about him?; **— por —** to do something for the sake of doing it, do something even though it is not necessary; **la ha hecho buena** (*iro*) a fine mess he's made of it; *see* **bien, mal** *etc*.
(f) (*substitute verb in repetitions*) to do; **él protestó y yo hice lo mismo** he protested and I did the same; **no viene como lo solía —** he doesn't come as he used to (do).
(g) **— algo pedazos** (*etc*): *see* **pedazo** *etc*.
(h) (*Theat*) **— el malo** to play the (part of the) villain, act the villain.
(i) to imagine, think, assume; **yo le hacía más viejo** I thought he was older; **te hacíamos en el Perú** we thought you were in Peru, we assumed you were in Peru.
(j) **me hizo con dinero** he provided me with money.
(k) to accustom, inure; **— el cuerpo al frío** to inure the body to cold, get the body used to cold.
(l) (*with verb construction*) to make, force, oblige, compel; **les hice venir** I made them come; **nos hizo que fuésemos** he made us go; **yo haré que vengan** I'll see to it that they come; **hágale entrar** show him in, have him come in; **me lo hizo saber** he told me it, he informed me of it; **— construir una casa** to have a house built, get a house built; **hago lavar la ropa a mi vecina** I have a neighbour (to) wash my clothes.
(m) (*numerals*) to make (up), amount to; **6 y 3 hacen 9** 6 and 3 make 9; **éste hace 100** this one makes 100.
(n) (*with adj*) to make, turn, render, send; **el vino lo hizo borracho** the wine made him drunk; **la tinta lo hizo azul** the ink made (or turned) it blue; **esto lo hará más difícil** this will make (*or* render) it more difficult.
2 *vi* (a) to act, behave; to pretend; **— como que . . ., — como si . . .** to act as if . . .; **— uno como que no quiere** to be reluctant, seem not to want to; **— de** to act as, (*Theat*) act, play the part of; **— el muerto** to pretend to be dead (*see also* **muerto**); **— el tonto** to act the fool, play the fool.
(b) **dar que —** to cause trouble; to make work; **daban que — a la policía** they gave the police trouble, they caused trouble to the police.
(c) **— para +** *infin*, **— por +** *infin* to try to + *infin*, make an effort to + *infin*.
(d) to be important, matter; **no le hace** it doesn't matter, never mind; *see* **caso**.
(e) to be suitable, be fitting; **hace a todo** he's good for anything; **¿hace?** will it do?, is it all right?; **la llave hace a todas las puertas** the key fits (*or* does for) all the doors.
3 *v impersonal* (a) (*Meteorol*) to be; *see* **calor, frío, tiempo** *etc*.
(b) (*SAm*) **hace sed** I'm thirsty; **hace sueño** I'm sleepy.
(c) (*of time*) ago; **hace 3 años** 3 years ago; **hace 2 años que se fue** he left 2 years ago, it's 2 years since he left; **desde hace 4 años** for (the last) 4 years; **está perdido desde hace 15 días** it's been lost for a fortnight; **hace poco** a short while back, a short time ago; **no hace mucho** not long ago; *see* **tiempo** *etc*.
4 hacerse *vr* (a) to be made, be done *etc*; **se**

hará de ladrillos it will be built of brick; **todavía no se ha hecho** it still has not been done; **¡eso no se hace!** that's not done!

   (b) *(mutual)* — **cortesías** to exchange courtesies.

   (c) *(personal)* **se hizo cortar el pelo** she had her hair cut; **me hago confeccionar un traje** I'm having a suit made; — **un retrato**, — **retratar** to have one's portrait painted; — **afeitar** to have a shave, have oneself shaved.

   (d) *(with noun complement)* to become; **se hicieron amigos** they became friends; — **enfermera** to become a nurse, take up nursing, go into nursing.

   (e) *(with noun complement: idiom)* to pretend; — **el sordo** to pretend not to hear, turn a deaf ear; — **el sueco** *(fam)* to pretend not to hear *(or* understand); to act dumb, not let on *(fam)*; — **el tonto** to act the fool, play the fool.

   (f) *(with adj complement)* to become, grow; to turn (into), come to be; **esto se hace pesado** this is becoming tedious; **si las cosas se hacen difíciles** if things get difficult, if things turn awkward; — **grande** to grow tall, get tall; — **viejo** to grow old, get old; — **cristiano** to turn Christian, become a Christian, be converted to Christianity; **se me hace imposible trabajar** it's becoming impossible for me to work, I'm finding it impossible to work.

   (g) — **a** + *infin* to get used to + *ger*, become accustomed to + *ger*.

   (h) **se me hace que . . .** *(esp SAm)* I think that . . ., it seems to me that . . ., I get the impression that . . .

   (i) — **con algo** to get hold of something; to take something, appropriate something; **logró — con una copia** he managed to get hold of a copy.

   (j) — **a un lado** to stand aside *(also fig)*, move over; — **atrás** to move back, fall back; *for many phrases, see the adj or noun.*

hacia *prep* (a) *(of place)* towards, in the direction of; about, near; — **abajo** down, downwards; — **arriba** up, upwards; **ir — las montañas** to go towards the mountains; **eso está más — el este** that's further over to the east, that is more in an easterly direction; **vamos — allá** let's go in that direction, let's go over that way.

   (b) *(of time)* about; — **mediodía** about noon, towards noon.

   (c) *(of attitude)* towards; **su hostilidad — la empresa** his hostility towards the undertaking.

hacienda *nf* (a) property; country estate, large farm; *(SAm)* ranch; *(SAm)* plantation; — **de azúcar** *(PR)* sugar mill.

   (b) *(RPl)* cattle, livestock.

   (c) — **pública** public finance; **(Ministerio de) H—** Treasury, Exchequer, Ministry of Finance.

   (d) —**s** household chores.

hacina *nf* pile, heap; *(Agr)* stack, rick.

hacinamiento *nm* heaping (up); *(Agr)* stacking; *(fig)* crowding, overcrowding; accumulation.

hacinar [1a] *vt* to pile (up), heap (up); *(Agr)* to stack, put into a stack *(or* rick); *(fig)* to crowd, overcrowd; to accumulate, amass; to hoard.

hacha[1] *nf* (a) axe; chopper; hatchet; — **de armas** battle-axe.

   (b) *(fig)* genius, wizard; **¡eres un —!** you're a wizard!; **es un — para el bridge** he's a genius at bridge, he's a brilliant bridge player.

   (c) *(phrases)* **de — y tiza** *(Arg)* tough, virile, *(pej)* brawling; **de —** *(adv: Chi)* unexpectedly, without warning; **ser — para la ropa** *(Mex)* to be hard on one's clothes; **estar —** *(Mex)* to be ready.

hacha[2] *nf* torch, firebrand; large candle; **como — de muerto** *light* dim, weak.

hachador *nm (Arg, Cu, Guat, Ven)* woodman, lumberjack.

hachar [1a] *vt (SAm)* = **hachear**.

hachazo *nm* (a) axe blow, stroke with an axe; hack, cut.

   (b) *(SAm)* gash, open wound.

   (c) *(Col)* bolt, dash *(of startled horse)*.

hache *nf name of the letter* h; **llámele Vd — call it what you will; volverse —s y erres** *(Col)*, **volverse —s y cúes** *(Chi)* to come to nothing, fall through.

hachear [1a] **1** *vt* to hew, cut (down *etc)*. **2** *vi* to wield an axe.

hachero[1] *nm* woodman, lumberjack; *(Mil)* sapper.

hachero[2] *nm* torch stand.

hacheta *nf* adze; small axe, hatchet.

hachich *nm* hashish.

hacho *nm* beacon.

hachón *nm* (large) torch, firebrand.

hachuela *nf* = **hacheta**.

hada *nf* fairy; — **madrina** fairy godmother; **cuento de —s** fairy tale.

hadado *adj* fated; **bien —** lucky; **mal —** ill-fated, ill-starred.

hado *nm* fate, destiny.

haga, hago *etc: see* **hacer**.

hagiografía *nf* hagiography.

haiga *nm (fam)* big car, posh car *(fam)*.

Haití *m* Haiti.

haitiano 1 *adj* Haitian. **2** *nm*, **haitiana** *nf* Haitian.

hala *interj* (a) hi!, hoy!

   (b) come on!, let's go!

   (c) get on with it!, hurry up!

   (d) *(Naut)* heave!; *see also* **jalar**.

halaco *nm (CAm)* piece of junk, useless object.

halagar [1h] *vt* (a) to show affection to, make up to.

   (b) to please, gratify; to allure, attract; **es una perspectiva que me halaga** it's a possibility which pleases me.

   (c) to flatter; to cajole.

halago *nm* (a) *(also* —**s**) pleasure, delight; gratification; allurement, attraction; blandishment; **los —s de la vida rural** the attractions of country life, the blandishments of country life.

   (b) *(also* —**s**) flattery; cajolery.

halagüeño *adj* pleasing, gratifying, alluring, attractive; *opinion, remark* flattering (**para** to); *outlook* promising, rosy, hopeful.

halar [1a] *vt and vi* = **jalar**.

halcón *nm* falcon; — **común** peregrine; — **abejero** honey buzzard; **los —es y las palomas** *(Pol etc)* the hawks and the doves.

halconería *nf* falconry, hawking.

halconero *nm* falconer.

halda *nf* (a) skirt; **de —s o de mangas** at all costs, by hook or by crook. (b) sackcloth, coarse wrapping material.

haleche *nm* anchovy.

halibut [ali'βu] *nm*, *pl* **halibuts** [ali'βu] *(angl)* halibut.

hálito *nm* breath; vapour, exhalation; *(poet)* gentle breeze.

halitosis *nf* halitosis.

halo *nm* halo.

halógeno *nm* halogen.

halón *nm (SAm)* = **jalón** (c).

hall [xol] *nm*, *pl* **halls** [xol] *(angl)* hall; *(Theat)* foyer; *(of hotel)* lounge, foyer.

hallador *nm*, **halladora** *nf* finder.

hallar [1a] **1** *vt* to find; to discover; to locate; to find out; *approval, opposition etc* to meet with, run up against.

   2 hallarse *vr* to be; to find oneself; **se hallaba fuera** he was away at the time; **¿dónde se halla la catedral?** where is the cathedral?; **se halla sin dinero** he has no money, he finds himself out of money; — **enfermo** to be ill; — **mejor** to be better; **aquí me hallo a gusto** I'm all right here, I'm comfortable here; **no se halla bien con el nuevo jefe** he doesn't get on with the new boss; — **con un obstáculo** to encounter an obstacle, be up against an obstacle; **se halla en todo** he's mixed up in everything.

hallazgo *nm* (a) *(act)* finding, discovery.

   (b) *(object)* find, thing found; **un — interesantísimo** a most interesting find.

   (c) finder's reward; **"500 pesos de —"** *(notice)* "500 pesos reward".

hamaca *nf* hammock; *(Arg)* swing; *(Arg, Par)* reclining chair; — **plegable** deckchair.

hamacar [1g], **hamaquear** [1a] *(SAm)* **1** *vt* (a) to rock, swing.

   (b) *(Mex)* — **a uno** *(fig)* to keep someone waiting for a decision.

   (c) *(PR, Ven)* to beat, ill-treat.

   2 hamacarse, hamaquearse *vr* to rock (oneself), swing.

hambre *nf* (a) hunger; famine; starvation; — **canina** ravenous hunger; **estar con —, padecer —, pasar —** to be hungry, go hungry, starve; **entretener el —** to stave off hunger; **matar el —** to satisfy one's hunger; **morir de —** to die of *(or* from) starvation, starve to death; **hacer morir de —** to starve to death; **tener —** to be hungry; **tener mucha —** to be very hungry; **vengo con mucha —** I'm terribly hungry, I've got a vast appetite.

   (b) *(fig)* hunger, keen desire, longing (**de** for); **tener — de** to hunger for, be hungry for.

hambreado *adj (SAm)* = **hambriento**.

hambrear [1a] **1** *vt* to starve. **2** *vi* to starve, be hungry, be famished.

hambriento 1 *adj* (a) starving, hungry, famished.
(b) (*fig*) — de starved of, hungry for, longing for.
2 *nm*, **hambrienta** *nf* starving person; **los —s** the hungry, the starving.
hambruna *nf* (*Arg*, *Col*), **hambrusia** *nf* (*Mex*, *PR*) ravenous hunger; **tener —** to be ravenously hungry.
Hamburgo Hamburg.
hamburguesa *nf* hamburger.
hamo *nm* fish hook.
hampa *nf* underworld, low life, criminal classes; (*Hist*) rogue's life, vagrancy; **gente del —** people of the underworld, criminals, riffraff.
hampante *nm* criminal, underworld character.
hampesco *adj* underworld (*attr*), criminal.
hampón *nm* tough (*fam*), rowdy, thug.
hámster *nm*, *pl* **hámsters** (*angl*) hamster.
han *see* **haber**.
handicap [andiˈkap] *nm*, *pl* **handicaps** [andiˈkap] (*angl*) handicap.
handicapar [1a] *vt* (*angl*) to handicap.
hangar *nm* (*Aer*) hangar.
Hanovre *m* Hanover.
haragán 1 *adj* idle, lazy, good-for-nothing. **2** *nm*, **haragana** *nf* idler, layabout, good-for-nothing.
haraganear [1a] *vi* to idle, waste one's time; to lounge about, loaf around.
haraganería *nf* idleness, laziness.
harapiento *adj* ragged, tattered, in rags.
harapo *nm* rag, tatter; **estar hecho un —** to go about in rags; **poner a uno como un —** to shower insults on someone, make someone feel a heel.
haraposo *adj* = **harapiento**.
haraquiri *nm* hara-kiri.
harén *nm* harem.
harina *nf* (a) flour; meal; powder; **— de avena** oatmeal; **— de huesos** bone meal; **— lacteada** malted milk; **— leudante** self-raising flour; **— de maíz** cornflour, corn meal; **— de trigo** wheat-flour; **eso es — de otro costal** that's another story, that's a horse of a different colour; **estoy hecho —** I'm exhausted.
(b) (*Col*) small piece; **una — de pan** a bit of bread.
(c) (*Ant*: *hum*) money, dough (*sl*).
harinear [1a] *vi* (*SD*, *Ven*) to drizzle.
harineo *nm* (*SD*, *Ven*) drizzle.
harinero 1 *adj* flour (*attr*). **2** *nm* (a) flour merchant.
(b) flour bin.
harinoso *adj* floury.
harnear [1a] *vt* (*Col*, *Chi*, *Mex*) to sieve, sift.
harnero *nm* sieve.
harpagón *adj* (*Col*) very thin.
harpillera *nf* sacking, sackcloth.
hartar [1a] **1** *vt* (a) to satiate, surfeit, glut, more than satisfy (*con*, **de** with).
(b) (*fig*) to weary, tire.
(c) **— a uno de algo** (*fig*) to overwhelm someone with something; **— a uno de palos** to rain blows on someone.
(d) (*Guat*) to malign, slander; (*Ven*) to insult.
2 hartarse *vr* (a) to eat one's fill (*con* of), gorge (*con* on), be satiated; **comer hasta —** to eat to repletion; **— de uvas** to stuff oneself with grapes, eat too many grapes.
(b) (*fig*) to weary, get weary (*de* of); to get fed up (*de* with); **— de reír** to laugh fit to burst; **no se hartaron de reír** they couldn't stop laughing.
hartazgo *nm* surfeit, satiety; repletion; glut; **darse un —** to eat to repletion, eat one's fill, overeat; **darse un — de** to eat one's fill of; (*fig*) to overdo, have too much of.
harto 1 *adj* (a) full (*de* of), satiated (*de* with).
(b) (*fig*) **estar — de** to be fed up with, be tired of; **¡estamos —s ya!** we're fed up!, enough is enough!; **¡estoy — de decírtelo!** I'm fed up with telling you so!
2 *adv* (*lit*) enough; very, quite; **una tarea — difícil** a very difficult task, a difficult enough task.
hartón 1 *adj* (a) (*CAm*, *Mex*, *SD*) greedy, gluttonous.
(b) (*Mex*) stupid; annoying. **2** *nm* (*Col*, *Mex*, *PR*) large banana.
hartura *nf* (a) surfeit; glut; abundance, plenty; **con —** in abundance, in plenty. (b) full satisfaction (*of a desire*).
has *see* **haber**.
hasta 1 *adv* even; **y — la pegó** and he even hit her; **— en Valencia hiela a veces** even in Valencia it freezes sometimes.
2 *prep* (a) (*of place*) as far as; up to, down to; **lo llevó — la iglesia** he carried it as far as the

church; **los árboles crecen — los 4.000 metros** the trees grow up to 4,000 metres.
(b) (*of time*) till, until; as late as; up to; **se quedará — el martes** she will stay till Tuesday; **siguió en pie — el siglo pasado** it stood until (*or* up to, as late as) the last century; **no me levanto — las 9** I don't get up until (*or* before) 9 o'clock; **no iré — después de la reunión** I shan't go till after the meeting; *see* **luego**, **vista** *etc*.
3 *conj*: **— que** till, until; **— que me lo des** until you give it to me.
hastial[1] *nm* (*Archit*) gable end.
hastial[2] *nm* lout, roughneck (*sl*).
hastiar [1c] **1** *vt* to weary, bore; to sicken, disgust.
2 hastiarse *vr*: **— de** to tire of, get fed up with.
hastío *nm* weariness; boredom; disgust, loathing.
hatajo *nm* lot, collection.
hatillo *nm* = **hato**.
hato *nm* (a) clothes, set of clothing; personal effects, possessions; **— y garabato** (*Cu*, *Ec*) all that one has; **liar el —** to pack up, get ready to go; **menear el — a uno** to beat someone up; **revolver el — to stir up trouble.
(b) provisions.
(c) shepherd's hut; stopping place (*of migratory flocks etc*).
(d) (*Agr*) flock, herd; (*of people*) group, crowd, collection; (*pej*) bunch, band, gang; (*of objects*, *remarks etc*) lot, collection.
(e) (*Cu*, *Ec*, *PR*, *Ven*) cattle ranch.
Hawai: Islas *fpl* **—** Hawaii.
hawaiano 1 *adj* Hawaiian. **2** *nm*, **hawaiana** *nf* Hawaiian.
haxix [aˈtʃiʃ] *nm* hashish.
hay, **haya** *etc*: *see* **haber**.
Haya: La — The Hague.
haya *nf* beech, beech tree.
hayaca *nf* (*Ven*) mince pie.
hayal *nm*, **hayedo** *nm* beechwood.
hayuco *nm* beechnut; beechnuts, beechmast (*also* **—s**).
haz[1] *nm* (a) bundle, bunch; (*Agr*: *of corn*) sheaf, (*of straw*) truss; **haces** (*Hist*) fasces.
(b) (*of light*, *TV etc*) beam; **— de luz** beam of light, pencil of light.
haz[2] *nf* (*Anat*: *lit*) face; (*fig*) face, surface; (*of cloth*) right side; **— de la tierra** face of the earth; **de dos haces** two-faced.
haz[3] *see* **hacer**.
hazaña *nf* feat, exploit, deed, achievement; **las —s del héroe** the hero's exploits, the hero's great deeds; **sería una —** it would be a great thing to do, it would be a great achievement.
hazañería *nf* fuss, exaggerated show; histrionics.
hazañero *adj* person dramatic, histrionic, given to making a great fuss; *act* histrionic, exaggerated.
hazañoso *adj* person heroic, gallant, dauntless; *deed* heroic, doughty.
hazmerreír *nm* laughing stock, joke.
he[1] *see* **haber**.
he[2] *adv* (*lit*): **— aquí** here is, here are; this is, these are; (*more dramatically*) behold; **¡heme aquí!, ¡héteme aquí!** here I am!; **¡helo aquí!** here it is!; **¡helos allí!** there they are!; **— aquí la razón de que . . .**, **— aquí por qué . . .** that is why . . .; **— aquí los resultados** these are the results, here you have the results.
hebdomadario 1 *adj* weekly. **2** *nm* (*Typ*) weekly.
hebilla *nf* buckle, clasp.
hebra *nf* (*Sew*) thread; piece of thread, length of thread; (*Bot etc*) fibre; strand; (*of silkworm*) thread; (*of wood*) grain; (*of metal*) vein, streak; (*fig*) thread (*of the conversation*); **—s** (*poet*) hair; **ni —** (*Col*) nothing; **tabaco de —** loose tobacco; **de una —** (*Chi*, *Mex*) all at once; in one go; **pegar la —** to start a conversation; to chatter, talk nineteen to the dozen; **romperse la —** (*Mex*: *of friendship etc*) to break up, come to an end.
hebraico *adj* Hebraic.
hebreo 1 *adj* Hebrew. **2** *nm*, **hebrea** *nf* Hebrew; (*fam*, *pej*) usurer, extortioner; pawnbroker. **3** *nm* (*language*) Hebrew.
Hébridas *fpl* Hebrides.
hebroso *adj* fibrous; *meat* stringy.
hecatombe *nf* hecatomb; (*fig*) slaughter, butchery; **¡aquello fue la —!** what a disaster that was!, you should have seen it!
hectárea *nf* hectare (= *2.471 acres*).
héctico *adj* consumptive.
hectogramo *nm* hectogramme, hectogram (*US*).
hectolitro *nm* hectolitre, hectoliter (*US*).
hechicera *nf* sorceress, enchantress, witch.
hechicería *nf* (a) (*in general*) sorcery, witchcraft.
(b) (*una —*) spell. (c) (*fig*) spell, enchantment, charm.

hechicero 1 adj magic(al); bewitching, enchanting. **2** nm wizard, sorcerer, enchanter; (African etc) witch doctor.

hechizar [1f] vt (a) to bewitch, cast a spell on. (b) (fig) to charm, enchant, fascinate; (pej) to bedevil.

hechizo 1 adj (a) artificial, false, fake.
(b) detachable, removable.
(c) (Tech) manufactured.
(d) (CAm, Chi, Mex, Per) home-made, locally produced, craft (attr); (Mex, Per: pej) home-made, rough and ready.
2 nm (a) (in general) magic, witchcraft; (un —) magic spell, charm.
(b) (fig) magic, spell, enchantment; glamour; fascination; —s (of woman etc) charms.

hecho 1 ptp of **hacer** done; ¡—! agreed!, it's a deal!; **a lo — pecho** we must make the best of it now; **lo — está —** what's done cannot be undone; **bien —** well done; well made; person well-proportioned; ¡bien —! well done!; **mal —** badly done; poorly made; person ill-proportioned; **él, — un . . .** he, like a . . .; **ella, hecha una furia, se lanzó . . .** she hurled herself furiously . . ., she threw herself in a fury . . .; **estar — a** to be used to, be inured to; see **basilisco, fiera** etc.
2 adj (a) complete, finished; mature; perfect; (Sew) ready-made, ready-to-wear; made-up; phrase stock; **— y derecho** complete, right and true, as it should be in every way; **un hombre — y derecho** a real man, every inch a man.
(b) (Cook) **muy —** overdone, well-cooked; **no muy —, poco —** underdone, undercooked.
3 nm (a) deed, act, action; **— de armas** feat of arms; **H—s de los Apóstoles** Acts of the Apostles; **—s y no palabras** deeds not words.
(b) fact; factor; matter; event; **esto es un —** this is a fact; **el — es que . . .** the fact is that . . ., the position is that . . .; **volvamos al —** let's get back to the matter in hand; **de —** in fact, as a matter of fact; (Pol etc: adj and adv) **de facto; de — y de derecho** de facto and de jure; **en — de verdad** as a matter of solid fact.

hechor nm (a) (SAm) stud donkey. (b) (Chi) = **malhechor**.

hechura nf (a) (act) making, creation; **no tiene —** it can't be done.
(b) (object etc) creation, product; **somos — de Dios** we are God's handiwork.
(c) form, shape; (of person) build; (of suit) cut; **a — de** like, after the manner of; **tener —s de algo** to show an aptitude for something; **no tener uno —** (Arg, Mex) to be a dead loss.
(d) (Sew) making-up, confection; **—s** cost of making up; **de — sastre** tailor-made.
(e) (Tech) craftsmanship, workmanship; **de exquisita —** of exquisite workmanship.
(f) (fig) creature, puppet; **él es una — del ministro** he is a creature of the minister.

heder [2g] vi (a) to stink, smell, reek (a of). (b) (fig) to annoy, be unbearable.

hediondez nf (a) stink, stench. (b) stinking thing.

hediondo adj (a) stinking, foul-smelling, smelly. (b) filthy; repulsive; obscene. (c) (fig) annoying, unbearable.

hedonismo nm hedonism.

hedonista nmf hedonist.

hedor nm stink, stench, smell (a of).

hegemonía nf hegemony.

hégira nf hegira.

helada nf frost; freeze, freeze-up; **— blanca** hoar-frost.

heladera nf (RPl) refrigerator; (Mex) ice-cream dish.

heladería nf (esp SAm) ice-cream stall, ice-cream parlour.

heladero nm (Chi, RPl) ice-cream man.

helado 1 adj (a) frozen; freezing, icy; icebound.
(b) (fig) chilly, cold, disdainful.
(c) **dejar — a uno** to dumbfound someone, shatter someone; ¡me deja Vd —! you amaze me!
(d) (Ven: Cook) iced.
2 nm ice cream.

helador adj wind etc icy, freezing; **hace un frío —** it's icy cold, it's perishing cold.

heladora nf freezing unit, freezer (in refrigerator); (esp Chi, RPl) refrigerator, icebox.

helaje nm (Col) intense cold; chilly feeling.

helar [1k] **1** vt (a) (Meteorol) to freeze; to ice (up); liquid to congeal, harden; drink etc to ice, chill.
(b) (fig) to dumbfound, shatter, amaze; to discourage.
2 vi to freeze.

3 helarse vr (Meteorol) to freeze; to be frozen; (Aer, Rail etc) to ice (up), freeze up: (liquid) to congeal, harden, set.

helecho nm bracken, fern.

Helena f Helen.

helénico adj Hellenic, Greek.

heleno nm, **helena** nf Hellene, Greek.

hélice nf (a) spiral; (Anat, Elec, Math) helix. (b) (Aer) propeller, airscrew; (Naut) propeller, screw.

helicoidal adj spiral, helicoidal, helical.

helicóptero nm helicopter.

helio nm helium.

heliógrafo nm heliograph.

helioterapia nf heliotherapy, sun-ray treatment.

heliotropo nm heliotrope.

helipuerto nm heliport.

hematites nf, **hematita** nf bloodstone.

hembra nf (a) (Bot, Zool) female; (human) woman, (pej) female; **el armiño —** the female stoat, the she-stoat; **el pájaro —** the female bird, the hen bird; **una real —** a fine figure of a woman; **5 hijos, esto es 2 varones y 3 hembras** 5 children, that is 2 boys and 3 girls.
(b) (Mech) nut; **— de terraja** die.
(c) (Sew) eye.

hembraje nm (SAm) female flock, female herd; (hum) womenfolk.

hembrería nf (Mex), **hembrerío** nm (Ant, Mex: pej) group of women, crowd of women; excessive number of women.

hembrilla nf (Mech) nut; eyebolt.

hemiciclo nm semicircular theatre; (Parl) chamber; floor.

hemiplejía nf hemiplegia.

hemisferio nm hemisphere.

hemistiquio nm hemistich.

hemofilia nf haemophilia.

hemofílico 1 adj haemophilic. **2** nm, **hemofílica** nf haemophiliac, bleeder.

hemoglobina nf haemoglobin.

hemorragia nf (Med) haemorrhage; bleeding, loss of blood; (fig) drain, loss.

hemorroides nfpl haemorrhoids, piles.

henal nm hayloft.

henar nm meadow, hayfield.

henchir [3h] **1** vt to fill (up), stuff, cram (de with).
2 henchirse vr (a) to swell; (person) to stuff oneself (with food).
(b) **— de orgullo** to swell with pride.

hendedura nf crack, fissure, crevice; cleft, split, slit; (Geol) rift, fissure.

hender [2g] vt to crack; to cleave, split, slit; waves to cleave, breast; to make one's way through; (fig) to split.

hendidura nf = **hendedura**.

hendija nf (SAm) crack, crevice.

hendir [3i] vt (SAm) = **hender**.

heneador nm hay-turner; haymaker.

henequén nm (SAm) agave, henequen.

henificación nf haymaking.

henil nm hayloft.

heniquén nm (Cu, Mex) = **henequén**.

heno nm hay.

hepático adj hepatic, liver (attr).

heráldica nf heraldry.

heráldico adj heraldic.

heraldo nm herald.

herbáceo adj herbaceous.

herbaje nm (a) herbage; grass, pasture. (b) (Naut) coarse woollen cloth.

herbaj(e)ar [1a] **1** vt to graze, put out to pasture. **2** vi to graze.

herbario 1 adj herbal. **2** nm (a) herbarium, plant collection. (b) (person) herbalist; botanist.

herbazal nm grassland, pasture.

herbicida nm weed-killer; **— selectivo** selective weed-killer.

herbívoro adj herbivorous.

herbolario 1 adj (fig) crazy, cracked. **2** nm herbalist.

herborizar [1f] vi to gather herbs, pick herbs; (as collector) to botanize, collect plants.

herboso adj grassy.

hercúleo adj Herculean.

Hércules m Hercules; **h—** (in circus) strong man; **es un —** (fig) he's awfully strong.

heredable adj inheritable, that can be inherited.

heredad nf landed property; country estate, farm.

heredar [1a] vt (a) property to inherit (de from); to be heir to. (b) person to name as one's heir. (c) (SAm) to leave, bequeath (a to).

heredera nf heiress.

heredero nm heir (de to); inheritor (de of); — **forzoso** heir apparent; — **único** universal heir; **príncipe** — crown prince; — **del trono** heir to the throne.

hereditario adj hereditary.

hereje 1 adj (a) (RPl: Rel) indifferent, agnostic; lacking in respect (for traditions etc).
(b) (Ven) excessive; **un trabajo** — a heavy task.
2 nmf heretic; ¡—! (fam) you brute!

herejía nf (a) (Rel) heresy. (b) (fig) dirty trick, low deed. (c) (Ec, Mex, RPl) silly remark, stupid thing.

herencia nf inheritance, estate, legacy; (fig) heritage; (Bio) heredity.

hereque nm (Ven: Med) skin disease; (Bot) a disease of coffee.

herético adj heretical.

herida nf (a) wound, injury. (b) (fig) wound, insult, outrage; **lamer las** —s to lick one's wounds.

herido 1 adj (a) injured; (Mil etc) wounded.
(b) (fig) wounded, offended.
2 nm (a) injured man; (Mil) wounded man; **los** —s (Mil) the wounded; **el número de los** —s **en el accidente** the number of people hurt in the accident, the number of casualties in the accident.
(b) (Chi, Mex) ditch, channel.

herir [3i] vt (a) to injure, hurt; (Mil etc) to wound; — **a uno en el brazo** to wound someone in the arm.
(b) to beat, strike, hit; (Mus) to pluck, strike, play; (of sun) to strike on; to beat down on; **un sonido hirió el oído** a sound reached (or struck) my ear; **es un color que hiere la vista** it's a colour which impinges (or strikes) on the eye.
(c) (fig) heart etc to touch, move, sway.
(d) (fig) to offend, hurt.

hermafrodita 1 adj hermaphrodite. 2 nm hermaphrodite.

hermana nf (a) sister; **media** — half-sister; **prima** — first cousin; — **gemela** twin sister; — **política** sister-in-law.
(b) (Eccl) sister; — **lega** lay sister.
(c) (1 of pair) twin; other half (of pair), corresponding part.

hermanable adj (a) fraternal. (b) compatible. (c) matching, that can be matched.

hermanar [1a] vt to match, put together; to join; to relate; to harmonize, bring into harmony; (Chi) to put into pairs.

hermanastra nf stepsister.

hermanastro nm stepbrother.

hermandad nf (a) (state) brotherhood; close relationship, intimacy.
(b) (group etc) brotherhood, fraternity; sisterhood; (Hist) brotherhood.

hermano 1 adj similar; matched, matching; **ship** sister.
2 nm (a) brother; **medio** — half-brother; **primo** — first cousin; — **carnal** full brother; — **gemelo** twin brother; — **de leche** foster brother; — **político** brother-in-law; **mis** —s my brothers, my brothers and sisters.
(b) (Eccl) brother; —s brothers, brethren.
(c) (1 of pair) twin; other half (of pair), corresponding part; — **gemelo** (Naut) sister ship.
(d) (CR) ghost.

herméticamente adv hermetically.

hermético adj hermetic; airtight, watertight; (fig) theory watertight; mystery impenetrable.

hermetismo nm (fig) tight secrecy, close secrecy.

hermosamente adv beautifully; handsomely.

hermosear [1a] vt to beautify, embellish, adorn.

hermoso adj (a) beautiful, lovely; fine, splendid; man handsome; **un día** — a fine day, a lovely day; **¡qué escena más hermosa!** what a lovely scene!; **seis** —s **toros** six magnificent bulls.
(b) (SAm) large, robust; person large, impressive, stout.

hermosura nf (a) beauty, loveliness; splendour; handsomeness. (b) (person) beauty, belle.

hernia nf rupture, hernia.

Herodes m Herod.

héroe nm hero.

heroicamente adv heroically.

heroicidad nf (a) heroism. (b) (una —) heroic deed.

heroico adj heroic.

heroicocómico adj mock-heroic.

heroína[1] nf heroine.

heroína[2] nf (Pharm) heroin.

heroísmo nm heroism.

herpes nmpl or fpl (Med) herpes, shingles.

herrada nf (a) bucket. (b) (Col: Agr) branding.

herrador nm farrier, blacksmith.

herradura nf horseshoe; **curva en** — (Aut) hairpin bend; **mostrar las** —s (fig) to kick over the traces.

herraje nm (a) ironwork, iron fittings. (b) (Arg) horseshoe. (c) (Mex) silver harness fittings.

herramental nm toolkit, toolbag.

herramienta nf (a) tool; implement, appliance; set of tools; — **de filo** edge tool; — **de mano** hand tool; — **mecánica** power tool.
(b) (fam) horns (of bull); teeth.

herranza nf (Col) branding.

herrar [1k] vt (Agr) horse to shoe; cattle to brand; (Tech) to bind with iron, trim with ironwork.

herrería nf (a) smithy, forge, blacksmith's (shop).
(b) ironworks.
(c) blacksmith's trade, craft of the smith.
(d) (fig) uproar, tumult.

herrerillo nm (Orn) tit.

herrero nm blacksmith, smith; — **de grueso** foundry worker.

herrete nm metal tip, ferrule, tag; (SAm) branding-iron, brand.

herrumbre nf (a) rust; **a prueba de** — rustproof, rust-resistant. (b) (Bot) rust. (c) (fig) iron taste, taste of iron.

herrumbroso adj rusty.

hervederas nfpl (PR) heartburn, indigestion.

hervidero nm (a) (act) boiling; bubbling, seething.
(b) hot spring; bubbling spring.
(c) (fig) swarm, throng, crowd; **un** — **de gente** a swarm of people.

hervido 1 ptp and adj boiled. 2 nm (Arg, Chi, Ven) stew.

hervidor nm kettle; boiler, boiling pan.

hervir [3i] 1 vt (esp SAm) to boil; to cook.
2 vi (a) to boil; to bubble, seethe; (of sea etc) to seethe, surge; — **a fuego lento** to simmer; **dejar de** — to stop boiling, go off the boil; **empezar a** — to begin to boil, come to the boil.
(b) (fig) — **de**, — **en** to swarm with, seethe with, teem with; **la cama hervía de pulgas** the bed was swarming with fleas.

hervor nm (a) (act) boiling; seething; **alzar el** —, **levantar el** — to come to the boil.
(b) (fig) fire, fervour (of youth); passion; restlessness.

hervoroso adj (a) boiling, seething; sun burning.
(b) (fig) = **fervoroso**.

heteo 1 adj Hittite. 2 nm, **hetea** nf Hittite.

heterodoxo adj heterodox, unorthodox.

heterogéneo adj heterogeneous.

heterosexual 1 adj heterosexual. 2 nmf heterosexual.

heterosexualidad nf heterosexuality.

heticarse [1g] vr (PR, SD) to contract tuberculosis.

hético adj consumptive.

hetiquencia nf (PR) tuberculosis.

hexagonal adj hexagonal.

hexágono nm hexagon.

hexámetro nm hexameter.

hez nf (esp **heces** pl) sediment, dregs; (fig) dregs, scum; **la** — **de la sociedad** the scum of society.

hiato nm (Ling) hiatus.

hibernación nf hibernation.

hibernal adj wintry, winter (attr).

hibernar [1a] vi to hibernate.

hibridación nf hybridization.

hibridar [1a] vti to hybridize.

hibridismo nm hybridism.

híbrido 1 adj hybrid. 2 nm, **híbrida** nf hybrid.

hice etc see **hacer**.

hidalga nf noblewoman.

hidalgo 1 adj noble; illustrious; (fig) gentlemanly, honourable; generous.
2 nm (a) nobleman, hidalgo.
(b) (Mex) 10-peso gold coin.

hidalguía nf nobility; (fig) nobility, gentlemanliness, honourableness; generosity.

hidra nf hydra; **H**— (Myth) Hydra.

hidratar [1a] vt to hydrate; to moisturize.

hidrato nm hydrate; — **de carbono** carbohydrate.

hidráulica nf hydraulics.

hidráulico adj hydraulic, water (attr); **fuerza hidráulica** water power, hydraulic power.

hidro ... hydro ..., water- ...

hidroala nf hovercraft.

hidroavión nm seaplane, flying boat.

hidrocarburo nm hydrocarbon.

hidrocefalía nf (Med) hydrocephalus, water on the brain.

hidrodinámica nf hydrodynamics.

hidroeléctrico adj hydroelectric.

hidrófilo adj absorbent; (fam) bibulous, boozy.

hidrofobia nf hydrophobia; rabies.

hidrofóbico *adj*, **hidrófobo** *adj* hydrophobic.
hidrófugo *adj* damp-proof, damp-resistant, water-repellent.
hidrógeno *nm* hydrogen.
hidrografía *nf* hydrography.
hidrólisis *nf* hydrolysis.
hidrolizar [1f] **1** *vt* to hydrolyze. **2 hidrolizarse** *vr* to hydrolyze.
hidropesía *nf* dropsy.
hidrópico *adj* dropsical.
hidroplaneador *nm* glider.
hidroplano *nm* seaplane.
hidrovelero *nm* glider.
hidróxido *nm* hydroxide.
hiedra *nf* ivy.
hiel *nf* (a) (*Anat*) gall, bile; **echar la** — to overwork, sweat one's guts out.
  (b) (*fig*) gall, bitterness; **no tener** — to be very sweet-tempered.
  (c) **—es** (*fig*) troubles, upsets.
hielo *nm* (a) ice; frost; **— a la deriva**, **— flotante**, **— movedizo** drift ice; **romper el** — (*fig*) to break the ice. (b) (*fig*) coldness, indifference.
hiena *nf* hyena; **hecho una** — furious; **ponerse como una** — to get furious.
hierba *nf* grass; small plant; (*Med*) herb, medicinal plant; **—s** grass, pasture; **mala** — weed, (*fig*) evil influence; **— cara** groundsel; **— gatera** catmint; **— lombriguera** ragwort; **— mate** maté; **— mora** nightshade; **— rastrera** cotton grass; **— de San Juan** St John's-wort; **y otras —s** (*fig*) and so forth, and suchlike; **oír** (*or* **sentir, ver**) **crecer la** — to be pretty smart; **pisar mala** — to have bad luck.
hierbabuena *nf* mint.
hierra *nf* (*SAm*) branding.
hierro *nm* (a) iron; **— acanalado** corrugated iron; **— batido** wrought iron; **— bruto** crude iron, pig iron; **— colado** cast iron; **— forjado** wrought iron; **— de fundición**, **— fundido** cast iron; **— en lingotes** pig iron; **— ondulado** corrugated iron; **— viejo** scrap iron, old iron; **a — candente batir de repente** strike while the iron is hot; **como el** — like iron, tough, strong; **de —** iron (*attr*); **llevar — a Vizcaya** to carry coals to Newcastle; **machacar en — frío** to beat one's head against a wall, flog a dead horse; **el que a — mata, a — muere** those that live by the sword die by the sword; **quitar —** to minimize something, cut things down to their proper size.
  (b) iron object; tool; (*of arrow etc*) head; (*Agr*) brand, branding-iron; (*Golf*) iron; **—s** irons.
higa *nf* rude sign, obscene gesture; (*fig*) scorn, derision.
hígado *nm* (a) (*Anat*) liver; **echar los —s** to wear oneself out; **tener — de indio** (*CAm, Mex*) to be a disagreeable sort.
  (b) **—s** (*fig*) guts, pluck.
  (c) (*CAm, Mex*) **ser un** — to be tedious, be a nuisance.
higadoso *adj* (*CR, Mex*) tedious, annoying.
higiene *nf* hygiene.
higiénico *adj* hygienic; sanitary.
higienizar [1f] **1** *vt* (*SAm*) to clean up. **2 higienizarse** *vr* (*Arg*) to wash, bath.
higo *nm* (a) (*Bot*) fig, green fig; **— chumbo**, **— de tuna** prickly pear; **— paso**, **— seco** dried fig; **de —s a brevas** once in a blue moon; *see* **importar** *etc*.
  (b) (*Vet*) thrush.
higuera *nf* fig tree; **— chumba**, **— de tuna** prickly pear (cactus), Indian fig tree; **— del infierno**, **— infernal** castor-oil plant; **caer de la** — to come down to earth with a bump; **estar en la** — to be naïve; to be at a loss, not know what to do; to be day-dreaming.
higuerilla *nf* (*Mex*) castor-oil plant.
hija *nf* daughter; child; (*in direct address, usually not translated, eg*) **—**, **no te lo puedo decir** I can't tell you; **— política** daughter-in-law; **— del mar** mermaid.
hijastra *nf* stepdaughter.
hijastro *nm* stepson.
hijo *nm* (a) son; child; **—s** (*freq*) children; sons and daughters; offspring, descendants; **sin —s** childless, without children; **¿cuántos —s tiene?** how many children has she?; **Pitt — Pitt** the Younger, the younger Pitt; **Juan Pérez, — Juan Pérez** Junior; **— de bendición** legitimate child; **— de la cuna** foundling; **— de leche** foster child; **— natural** illegitimate child; **— político** son-in-law; **nombrar a uno — predilecto de la ciudad** to give someone the freedom of the city; **— pródigo** prodigal son; **cada — de vecino** everyone, every mother's son; **— de**

puta bastard, son of a bitch; **ser — de sus obras** to be a self-made man; **ser (muy) — de papá** to be daddy's boy, be a spoiled child; to have led a very sheltered life; **entró en el negocio como — de papá** he just followed his father in the business (so it was easy for him).
  (b) (*in direct address: to child*) son, sonny (*fam*), my boy; (*to adult*) man, old chap (*fam*) (*but often not translated*); **¡— de mi alma!**, **¡— de mis entrañas!** my precious child!
  (c) **hacer a una un —** to get someone with child; **hacer a uno un — macho** (*SAm*) to do someone harm.
hijuela *nf* (a) little girl; small daughter.
  (b) (*Tech etc*) accessory.
  (c) (*Law*) estate of a deceased person; share, portion, inheritance; list of bequests.
  (d) (*Arg, Chi, Per*) rural property, piece of land (*resulting from division of estate*).
  (e) (*Sew*) piece of material (*for widening a garment*).
  (f) (*Agr*) small irrigation channel.
  (g) (*Mex: Min*) seam of ore.
hijuelo *nm* (a) little boy; small son; **—s** small children, (*Zool*) young. (b) (*Bot*) shoot. (c) (*Col*) side road, minor road.
hijuna (*SAm*) *interj* you bastard!
hila *nf* (a) row, line; **a la —** in a row, in single file. (b) thin gut; **—s** (*Med*) lint. (c) (*Ven*) **irse a la —** to fail, come to nothing.
hilacha *nf* ravelled thread; shred; fibre, filament; **— de acero** steel wool; **— de vidrio** spun glass; **—s** (*Med*) lint; **mostrar la —** (*RPl*) to show oneself in one's true colours.
hilachento *adj* (*SAm*) ragged, tattered; frayed; shabby.
hilacho *nm* = **hilacha**; **—s** (*Mex*) rags, tatters; shabby clothing.
hilachudo *adj* (*Mex*) = **hilachento**.
hilada *nf* row, line; (*Archit*) course.
hilado 1 *adj and ptp* spun; **seda hilada** spun silk. **2** *nm* (a) spinning. (b) thread, yarn.
hilador *nm* spinner.
hiladora *nf* (a) (*person*) spinner. (b) (*Tech*) spinning jenny.
hilandería *nf* (a) (*craft*) spinning. (b) spinning mill; **— de algodón** cotton mill.
hilandero, **hilandera** *nf* spinner.
hilangos *nmpl* (*Col*) rags, tatters.
hilar [1a] *vt* (a) to spin (*also Zool*). (b) (*fig*) to reason, infer; **— (muy) delgado** to draw it fine, (*pej*) to split hairs.
hilaracha *nf* = **hilacha**.
hilarante *adj* hilarious; merry, mirthful; **gas —** laughing gas.
hilaridad *nf* hilarity; merriment, mirth.
hilaza *nf* yarn, coarse thread; **descubrir la —** to show oneself in one's true colours.
hilera *nf* (a) row, line; string; (*Mil etc*) rank, file; (*Archit*) course; (*Agr*) row, drill. (b) (*Sew*) fine thread.
hilo *nm* (a) (*Sew etc*) thread, yarn; (*Bot etc*) fibre, filament; **— bramante** twine; **— de perlas** string of pearls; **a — uninterruptedly**, continuously; **coser al —** to sew on the straight; **escapar con el — en una pata** (*Arg, PR, Urug*) to get oneself cleverly out of a jam; **colgar** (*or* **pender**) **de un —** to hang by a thread; **contar algo del — al ovillo** to tell something without omitting a single detail; **estar al —** to be watchful, be on the look-out; **estar hecho un —** to be as thin as a rake; **tela de —** (*Col, Ven*) cotton cloth.
  (b) (*of metal*) thin wire; (*Elec*) wire; flex; **— de tierra** earth wire, ground wire (*US*); **el — rojo** (*Tel*) the hot line.
  (c) (*of liquid*) thin line, thin stream, trickle; (*of people*) thin line; **— de humo** thin line of smoke, plume of smoke; **decir algo con un — de la voz** to say something in a barely audible voice; **irse tras el — de la gente** to follow the crowd.
  (d) (*cloth*) linen; **traje de —** linen dress.
  (e) (*fig: of conversation, speech*) thread, theme; (*of life*) course; (*of thought*) train; **coger el —** to pick up the thread; **perder el —** to lose the thread.
hilván *nm* tacking, basting; (*Chi*) basting thread; (*Ven*) hem.
hilvanar [1a] *vt* (a) (*Sew*) to tack, baste.
  (b) (*fig*) job to do hurriedly; *construction* to throw together, knock up hurriedly; **bien hilvanada** well done, well constructed.
Himalaya *m*: **el —**, **los montes —** the Himalayas.
himen *nm* hymen, maidenhead.

himeneo nm (lit) nuptials (lit), wedding.
himnario nm hymnal, hymnbook.
himno nm hymn; — **nacional** national anthem.
hincada nf (a) (Col, Cu, Per, PR, Ven) thrust. (b) (Chi, PR) genuflection. (c) (Per, PR) sharp rheumatic pain.
hincadura nf (a) thrust, thrusting, driving. (b) — **de alfiler** pinprick.
hincapié nm: **hacer** — to make a stand, take a firm stand; **hacer** — **en** to insist on; to dwell on, emphasize, make a special point of.
hincapilotes nm, pl **hincapilotes** (Arg) piledriver.
hincar [1g] 1 vt to thrust (in), drive (in), push (in); **tooth** to sink (en into); **foot** etc to set (firmly) (en on); **hincó la mirada en ella** he fixed his gaze on her, he stared at her fixedly; **hincó el bastón en el suelo** he stuck his stick in the ground, he thrust his stick into the ground; see **diente, rodilla**.
　2 **hincarse** vr: — **de rodillas** to kneel (down).
hinco nm (Chi) post, stake.
hincha 1 nf (a) ill will, animosity, bad blood; grudge; **tener** — **a uno** to have a grudge against someone; **tomar** — **a uno** to take a dislike to someone.
　(b) (person, thing) pet aversion; **es mi** — he's my pet aversion, he's one of my special dislikes.
　2 nmf (a) (Sport etc) fan (fam), supporter, rooter (US); **los** —**s del Madrid** the Madrid supporters.
　(b) (Per) pal (fam), chum.
hinchada nf (Col, RPl) mass of supporters, group of fans (fam).
hinchado [adj (a) swollen. (b) (fig) person arrogant, vain; **style** etc pompous, high-flown, windy.
hinchador nm (Chi, RPl) bore, nuisance.
hinchar [1a] 1 vt (a) to swell; to distend, enlarge; **tyre** etc to blow up, inflate, pump up.
　(b) (fig) to exaggerate.
　(c) (RPl) to annoy.
　2 vi (RPl): — **por** to shout for, root for.
　3 **hincharse** vr (a) to swell (up); to get distended; (fam) to stuff oneself (de with).
　(b) (fig) to get conceited, become vain.
　(c) — **a correr** (etc) to run (etc) hard, run (etc) about a lot; — **a reír** to laugh a lot, have a good laugh.
hinchazón nf (a) (Med etc) swelling; bump, lump.
　(b) (fig) arrogance, vanity, conceit; (of style etc) pomposity, windiness.
hindú 1 adj Hindu. 2 nm, **hindúa** nf Hindu.
hiniesta nf (Bot) broom.
hinojo[1] nm (Bot, Cook) fennel.
hinojo[2] nm (Anat: arch) knee; **de** —**s** on bended knee; **ponerse de** —**s** to kneel (down), go down on one's knees.
hipar [1a] 1 vi (a) to hiccup, hiccough.
　(b) (of dog) to pant; — **por algo** to long for something, yearn for something; — **por** + infin to long to + infin, yearn to + infin.
　(c) (fig) to be worn out, be exhausted.
　2 vi [xi'par] to whine, whimper.
hipato adj (Col) full, replete; swollen; (Col, Cu, Mex) = **jipato**.
hipear [1a] vi (Mex) = **hipar**.
hiper . . . hyper . . .
hiperacidez nf hyperacidity.
hipérbaton nm, pl **hipérbatos** hyperbaton.
hipérbola nf hyperbola.
hipérbole nf hyperbole.
hiperbólico adj hyperbolic(al), exaggerated.
hipercrítico adj hypercritical; carping, censorious.
hipersensibilidad nf hypersensitivity.
hipersensible adj hypersensitive.
hipertensión nf hypertension.
hipiar [1b] vi (Mex) = **hipar**.
hípico adj horse (attr); equine.
hipnosis nf hypnosis.
hipnótico 1 adj hypnotic. 2 nm hypnotic.
hipnotismo nm hypnotism.
hipnotista nmf hypnotist.
hipnotizador adj hypnotizing.
hipnotizar [1f] vt to hypnotize, mesmerize.
hipo nm (a) hiccup(s), hiccough(s); **quitar el** — **a uno** to cure someone's hiccups, (fig) to take someone's breath away; **tener** — to have hiccups.
　(b) (fig) longing, yearning; **tener** — **por** to long for, crave.
　(c) (fig) disgust; grudge, ill will; **tener** — **contra uno** to have a grudge against someone, have it in for someone.
hipocampo nm sea horse.
hipocondria nf hypochondria.
hipocondríaco 1 adj hypochondriac(al). 2 nm, **hipocondríaca** nf hypochondriac.

hipocorístico adj: **nombre** — pet name, affectionate form of a name (eg Jim for James).
Hipócrates m Hippocrates.
hipocresía nf hypocrisy.
hipócrita 1 adj hypocritical. 2 nmf hypocrite.
hipócritamente adv hypocritically.
hipodérmico adj hypodermic; **aguja hipodérmica** hypodermic needle.
hipódromo nm racetrack, racecourse; (Hist) hippodrome.
hipopótamo nm hippopotamus.
hiposulfito nm: — **sódico** (Phot) hypo, sodium thiosulphate.
hipoteca nf mortgage; **redimir una** — to pay off a mortgage.
hipotecar [1g] vt to mortgage.
hipotecario adj mortgage (attr).
hipotenusa nf hypotenuse.
hipótesis nf, pl **hipótesis** hypothesis, supposition.
hipotéticamente adv hypothetically.
hipotético adj hypothetic(al).
hiriente adj remark, tone wounding, cutting; contrast striking.
hirsuto adj (a) hairy, hirsute; bristly. (b) (fig) brusque, gruff, rough.
hirvición nf (Ec) abundance, multitude.
hirviendo (as adj) boiling.
hirviente adj boiling, seething.
hisca nf birdlime.
hisopear [1a] vt (Eccl) to sprinkle with holy water.
hisopo nm (a) (Eccl) sprinkler, aspergillum. (b) (Bot) hyssop. (c) (SAm) paintbrush; (Par) dishcloth.
hispalense 1 adj Sevillian. 2 nmf Sevillian.
Híspalis (lit) Seville.
hispánico adj Hispanic, Spanish.
hispanidad nf (a) Spanishness; Spanish quality, Spanish characteristics.
　(b) (Pol) Spanish world, Hispanic world; **Día de la H**— Columbus Day (12 October).
hispanismo nm (a) word (or phrase etc) peculiar to Spain; word (etc) borrowed from Spanish, hispanicism.
　(b) (Univ etc) Hispanism, Hispanic studies; **el H**— **holandés** Hispanic studies in Holland.
hispanista nmf (a) (Univ etc) hispanist, Spanish scholar, student of Spain. (b) lover of Spain; **yo soy muy** — I am a great lover of Spain.
hispanizar [1f] vt to hispanicize.
hispano 1 adj Spanish, Hispanic. 2 nm Spaniard.
hispano- . . ., **Hispano-** . . ., eg **pacto hispano-ruritano** Hispano-Ruritanian pact.
Hispanoamérica f Spanish America, Latin America.
hispanoamericano 1 adj Spanish-American, Latin-American. 2 nm, **hispanoamericana** nf Spanish-American, Latin-American.
hispanófilo nm, **hispanófila** nf hispanophile.
hispanófobo nm, **hispanófoba** nf hispanophobe.
hispanomarroquí adj Spanish-Moroccan.
histerectomía nf hysterectomy.
histeria nf hysteria.
histéricamente adv hysterically.
histérico adj hysterical; **paroxismo** — hysterics.
histerismo nm hysteria; hysterics.
histología nf histology.
historia nf (a) story; tale; —**s** (pej) tales, gossip; (Mex, RPl) confused tale; ins-and-outs; (Mex, RPl) worthless excuses; evasions; **la** — **es larga de contar** it's a long story; **dejarse de** —**s** to come to the point, stop beating about the bush; **no me vengas con** —**s** don't come telling tales to me.
　(b) history; **en toda la** — **humana** in the whole of human history; — **antigua** ancient history; — **del arte** history of art, art history; — **natural** natural history; **H**— **Sacra, H**— **Sagrada** Biblical history, (School) Scripture; — **universal** world history; **es una mujer que tiene** — she's a woman with a past; **ser de** — to be famous; (pej) to be notorious; **pasar a la** — to go down in (or to) history (como as); **picar en** — to be a serious matter.
historiador nm, **historiadora** nf historian; chronicler, recorder.
historial 1 adj historical. 2 nm record; dossier; (Med) case history; **el brillante** — **del club** the club's brilliant record.
historiar [1b] vt (a) to tell the story of; to write the history of; to record, chronicle, write up. (b) (Art etc) to paint, depict.
histórico adj historical; (esp fig) historic.
historiero adj (Arg) gossipy, intriguing.
historieta nf short story, tale; anecdote; — **muda** (Typ) strip cartoon.

historiografía *nf* historiography, writing of history.
histrión *nm* actor, player; (*pej*) playactor; buffoon.
histriónico *adj* histrionic.
histrionismo *nm* (a) (*Theat*) acting, art of acting. (b) (*fig*) histrionics. (c) actors (*collectively*), theatre people.
hita *nf* (a) (*Tech*) brad, headless nail. (b) = **hito**.
hitita 1 *adj* Hittite. 2 *nmf* Hittite. 3 *nm* (*language*) Hittite.
hito *nm* (a) boundary post, boundary mark; milestone; — **kilométrico** kilometre stone.
(b) (*fig*) landmark, milestone; **es un — en nuestra historia** it is a landmark in our history; **esto marca un — histórico** this marks a historical milestone.
(c) (*Sports*) quoits.
(d) (*Mil*) target; (*fig*) aim, goal; **a —** fixedly; **dar en el —** to hit the nail on the head; **mudar de —** to change one's methods.
(e) **mirar a uno de — en —** to look someone up and down; to stare at someone.
hocicar [1g] 1 *vt* (*of pig*) to root among; (*of person etc*) to nuzzle.
2 *vi* (a) to root; to nuzzle; **— con, — en** to put one's nose against (or into *etc*).
(b) (*Naut: of bow*) to dip.
(c) to fall on one's face.
(d) (*fig*) to run into trouble, come up against it.
hocico *nm* (a) (*Zool*) snout, muzzle, nose; (*of person*) snout (*sl*); face, mug (*sl*); **caer** (or **dar**) **de —s** to fall on one's face; **dar de —s contra algo** to bump into something, go slap into something; **cerrar el —** (*fam*) to shut one's trap (*sl*); **estar de —** to be in a bad mood; **meter el —** to meddle, shove one's nose in.
(b) (*fig*) angry face, grimace; **poner —** to show one's anger (or resentment) in one's expression.
hocicudo *adj* (*Guat, Per, PR*) disgusted, disagreeable.
hociquear [1a] *vti* = **hocicar**.
hociquera *nf* (*Cu, Per*) muzzle.
hockey ['oki *or* 'xoki] *nm* (*angl*) hockey; **— sobre patines, — sobre hielo** ice hockey.
hogaño *adv* (*arch or lit*) this year; these days, nowadays.
hogar *nm* (a) fireplace, hearth; fireside; (*Tech*) furnace; (*Rail*) firebox.
(b) (*fig*) home, house; home life, family life; **— nacional judío** Jewish national home; **los que han quedado sin —** the homeless, those left homeless; **no tienen —** they have no home.
hogareño *adj* home (*attr*), family (*attr*); fireside (*attr*); *person* home-loving, stay-at-home.
hogaza *nf* large loaf, cottage loaf.
hoguera *nf* bonfire; blaze; **la casa estaba hecha una —** the house was ablaze, the house was an inferno.
hoja *nf* (a) (*Bot*) leaf; petal; **— de parra** (*fig*) figleaf; **de — ancha** broad-leaved; **de — caduca** deciduous; **de — perenne** evergreen.
(b) (*of paper*) leaf, sheet; (*Typ*) leaf, page; (*official etc*) sheet, form, document; **— de guarda** flyleaf; **— de ruta** waybill; **— de servicios** record (of service); **— volante** leaflet, handbill, pamphlet; **doblar la —** (*fig*) to change the subject; **volver la —** to turn the page; (*fig*) to change the subject; (*fig*) to turn over a new leaf.
(c) (*of metal*) sheet; thin plate; (*of door*) leaf; (*of sword*) blade; (*of skate*) blade; (*of glass*) sheet, pane; **— de afeitar** razor blade; **— de estaño** tinfoil; **— de lata** tin, tinplate; **— plegadiza** flap (*of table etc*); **— de tocino** side of bacon, flitch.
hojalata *nf* tin, tinplate.
hojalatería *nf* (a) tinwork; sheet-metal work. (b) tinsmith's (shop).
hojalatero *nm* (*CAm, Col, Mex*) tinware.
hojalatero *nm* tinsmith.
hojalda *nf* (*SAm*), **hojaldra** *nf* (*SAm*), **hojaldre** *gen m* puff pastry.
hojarasca *nf* (a) dead leaves, fallen leaves. (b) (*fig*) rubbish, trash, worthless stuff; empty verbiage.
hojear [1a] 1 *vt* to turn the pages of, leaf through; to skim through, glance through.
2 *vi* (a) (*Mex: Bot*) to put out leaves.
(b) (*CAm, Mex: Agr*) to eat leaves.
(c) (*of surface*) to scale off, flake off.
hojerío *nm* (*CAm*) leaves, foliage.
hojoso *adj* leafy.
hojuela *nf* (a) (*Bot*) leaflet, little leaf.
(b) flake; (*of metal*) foil, thin sheet; **— de estaño** tinfoil.
(c) (*Cook*) pancake; (*SAm*) ordinary fare, daily food; (*Cu, Mex*) = **hojaldre**.

hola *interj* (*greeting*) hullo!; (*surprise*) hullo!, hey!, I say!
holán *nm* (a) cambric, fine linen. (b) (*Mex*) flounce, frill.
Holanda *f* Holland.
holandés 1 *adj* Dutch. 2 *nm* Dutchman; **los —es** the Dutch. 3 *nm* (*language*) Dutch.
holandesa *nf* Dutchwoman.
holgadamente *adv* (a) loosely, comfortably.
(b) idly; in leisurely fashion.
(c) **vivir —** to live comfortably, live in luxury, be well off.
holgado *adj* (a) *dress etc* loose, full, comfortable; roomy; baggy; **demasiado —** too big.
(b) idle, unoccupied, free; leisured.
(c) (*Fin*) comfortably off, well-to-do; **vida holgada** comfortable life, life of luxury.
holganza *nf* (a) idleness; rest; leisure, ease. (b) amusement, enjoyment.
holgar [1h *and* 1m] 1 *vi* (a) to rest, take one's ease, be at leisure; (*of worker etc*) to be idle, be out of work; (*of thing*) to lie unused.
(b) to be unnecessary, be superfluous; **huelga toda protesta** no protest is necessary, it is not necessary to protest; **huelga decir que ...** it goes without saying that ..., needless to say, ...
(c) = 2 **holgarse** *vr* to amuse oneself, enjoy oneself, have a good time; **—(se) con algo** to take pleasure in something; **—(se) con una noticia** to be pleased about a piece of news; **—(se) de que ...** to be pleased that ..., be glad that ...; **huelgo de saberlo** I'm delighted to hear it.
holgazán 1 *adj* idle, lazy, slack. 2 *nm*, **holgazana** *nf* idler, slacker, loafer; ne'er-do-well.
holgazanear [1a] *vi* to laze around, be idle, slack, loaf.
holgazanería *nf* idleness, laziness, slackness.
holgazanitis *nf* (*hum*) congenital laziness, work-shyness.
holgorio *nm* = **jolgorio**.
holgura *nf* (a) (*Sew etc*) looseness, fullness; roominess, bagginess; (*Mech*) play, free movement.
(b) freedom, leisure; ease, comfort.
(c) enjoyment; merriment, merrymaking.
(d) comfortable living, luxury; **vivir con —** to live well, live comfortably, live in luxury.
holocausto *nm* (*Rel: Hist*) holocaust, burnt offering; (*fig*) sacrifice.
hollar [1m] *vt* (a) to tread, tread on; to trample down, trample underfoot. (b) (*fig*) to trample underfoot; to humiliate, humble.
hollejo *nm* (*Bot*) skin, peel.
hollín *nm* soot.
holliniento *adj*, **hollinoso** *adj* sooty, covered in soot.
hombracho *nm*, **hombrachón** *nm* hulking great brute, big tough fellow.
hombrada *nf* (a) manly deed, brave act. (b) (*pej*) piece of bravado; show of courage.
hombradía *nf* manliness; courage, guts.
hombre 1 *nm* man; (*in general*) man, mankind; **su —** (*fam*) her man, her husband; **pobre —** poor devil; (*pej*) poor fish, weak man; slow-witted chap; **es un pobre —** he's a poor fish; **está hecho un pobre —** he's now a man to be pitied, he's a shadow of his former self; **una charla de — a —** a man-to-man talk; **el — propone, pero Dios dispone** man proposes, but God disposes; **ser muy —** to be a real man, be pretty tough; **no me fastidien, pues sé ser muy —** don't provoke me, because I can get tough; **¡— al agua!, ¡— al mar!** man overboard!; **— de armas** man-at-arms; **— de bien** honest man, good man; **— blanco** white man; paleface; **— bueno** (*Law*) arbiter; **el — de** (or **en**) **la calle** the man in the street; **— de las cavernas** caveman; **— de confianza** right-hand man; **— de estado** statesman; **el — fuerte de Ruritania** the strong man of Ruritania; **— hecho** grown man; **— de letras** man of letters; **— de mar** seafaring man, seaman; **el — masa, el — medio, el — del montón** the average man, the ordinary man, the man in the street; **— mundano** man-about-town; **— de mundo** man of the world; **— de negocios** businessman; **el abominable — de las nieves** the abominable snowman; **— de pro, — de provecho** worthy man, honest man; **— del tiempo** weather man.
2 *interj* (a) (*in ordinary address*) old chap (*fam*), my boy, man (*but often not translated*); **sí —** yes, yes of course.
(b) (*surprise*) well!, good heavens!, you don't say!
(c) (*pitying*) dear me!; yes I know!
(d) (*protesting*) come now!, but my dear fellow!, heavens man!

hombre-anuncio nm, pl **hombres-anuncio** sandwich-board man.

hombrear[1] [1a] **1** vi (a) (of youth) to play the man, act grown-up; (of man) to act tough, try to be somebody; (Mex: of woman) to be mannish, behave like a man.

(b) — **con** = 2 **hombrearse** vr: — **con uno** to try to keep up with someone, strive to equal someone.

hombrear[2] [1a] vt (a) to shoulder; to push with one's shoulder, put one's shoulder to.

(b) (Arg, Col, Mex) to help, lend a hand to, back.

hombrecillo nm (a) little man, little fellow. (b) (Bot) hop.

hombrera nf (of dress) shoulder strap; (in dress) shoulder pad; (Mil) epaulette.

hombre-rana nm, pl **hombres-rana** frogman.

hombría nf manliness; — **de bien** honesty, uprightness, worthiness.

hombro nm shoulder; — **a** —, — **con** — shoulder to shoulder; ¡**armas al** —!, ¡**sobre el** — **armas!** shoulder arms!; **arrimar el** —, **poner el** — (Arg) to put one's shoulder to the wheel, lend a hand; **cargar algo sobre los** —**s** to shoulder something; **echar algo al** — (fig) to shoulder something, take something upon oneself; **encogerse de** —**s** to shrug one's shoulders; **enderezar los** —**s** to square one's shoulders, straighten up; **mirar a uno por encima del** — to look down on someone; **sacar a uno en** —**s** to carry someone out on (their) shoulders; **el vencedor salió en** —**s** the victor was carried out shoulder-high.

hombruno adj mannish, manlike.

homenaje nm (a) (Law, Hist etc) homage; allegiance; **rendir** — **a** to do (or pay, render) homage to, swear allegiance to.

(b) (fig) tribute, testimonial; **en** — **a** in honour of; in recognition of; **rendir** — **a**, **tributar** — **a** to pay a tribute to; **una cena** — **para don XY** a dinner in honour of don XY; **partido** — benefit match.

(c) (SAm) celebration; gathering (in honour of someone).

(d) (Chi) gift, favour.

homenajeado nm, **homenajeada** nf: **el** — the person being honoured, the guest of honour.

homenajear [1a] vt (SAm) to honour, pay tribute to.

homeópata nmf homeopath.

homeopatía nf homeopathy.

homérico adj Homeric.

Homero m Homer.

homicida 1 adj murderous, homicidal. **2** nm murderer. **3** nf murderess.

homicidio nm murder, homicide; manslaughter.

homilía nf homily.

homogeneidad nf homogeneity.

homogéneo adj homogeneous.

homógrafo nm homograph.

homónimo 1 adj homonymous. **2** nm homonym; (person) namesake.

homosexual 1 adj homosexual. **2** nmf homosexual.

homosexualidad nf homosexuality.

honda nf sling; (SAm) catapult.

hondear[1] [1a] vt (Naut) (a) to sound. (b) to unload.

hondear[2] [1a] vt (SAm) to hit with a slingshot, kill with a sling; to hit with a catapult.

hondo 1 adj (a) deep; low.

(b) (Cu) river etc swollen, high.

(c) (fig) profound, deep, heartfelt; **con** — **pesar** with deep regret, with profound sorrow.

2 nm depth(s); bottom.

hondón nm (a) (of cup, valley etc) bottom; (of stirrup) footrest. (b) (of needle) eye.

hondonada nf (a) hollow, coombe; dip, depression; gully, ravine. (b) lowland.

hondura nf (a) depth; profundity. (b) depth; deep place; **meterse en** —**s** to get out of one's depth, get into deep water (also fig).

Honduras f Honduras; — **Británica** British Honduras.

hondureñismo nm word (or phrase etc) peculiar to Honduras.

hondureño 1 adj Honduran. **2** nm, **hondureña** nf Honduran.

honestamente adv (a) decently, properly, decorously.

(b) modestly; purely.

(c) fairly, justly, reasonably.

(d) honourably; (angl: esp SAm) honestly.

honestidad nf (a) decency, decorum. (b) modesty; purity, chastity. (c) fairness, justice. (d) honourableness; (angl: esp SAm) honesty.

honesto adj (a) decent, proper, decorous. (b) modest; pure, chaste. (c) fair, just, reasonable. (d) honourable; (angl: esp SAm) honest.

hongo nm (a) (Bot) fungus; (edible) mushroom; (poisonous) toadstool; **un enorme** — **de humo** an enormous mushroom of smoke; **surgen como** —**s** they grow like mushrooms.

(b) bowler, bowler hat, derby (US).

Honolulú Honolulu.

honor nm honour; (of woman) honour, virtue, good name; (fig) glory; —**es** (Mil etc) honours, honorary status (or rank); — **profesional** professional etiquette; **en** — **a la verdad** to be fair, for the sake of truth; **en** — **de uno** in someone's honour; **13 puntos de** —**es** (Cards) 13 honours points; **hacer** — **a un compromiso** to honour a pledge; **hacer** — **a su firma** to honour one's signature; **hacer los** —**es de la casa** to do the honours (of the house); **hacer los debidos** —**es a una comida** to do full justice to a meal; **sepultar a uno con todos los** —**es militares** to bury someone with full military honours; **tener al** — **de** + infin to have the honour to + infin, to be proud to + infin; **el poeta X,** — **de esta ciudad** the poet X in whom this city glories, the poet X who is this city's claim to fame.

honorable adj honourable, worthy.

honorario 1 adj honorary, honorific. **2** nm honorarium; —**s** (professional) fees, charges.

honorífico adj honourable; honorific; **mención honorífica** honourable mention.

honra nf self-esteem, sense of personal honour, dignity; (of woman) honour, virtue, good name; chastity; good name, reputation; —**s fúnebres** last honours, funeral rites; ¡**a mucha** —! I'm honoured!, delighted!; **tener algo a mucha** — to be proud of something, consider something an honour; **tener a mucha** — + infin to be proud to + infin, deem it an honour to + infin; see **atentado**.

honradamente adv honestly; honourably, uprightly.

honradez nf honesty; honourableness, uprightness, integrity.

honrado adj honest; honourable, upright; **hombre** — honest man, decent man, honourable man.

honrar [1a] **1** vt (a) to honour, revere, respect; to do honour to.

(b) (Comm etc) to honour.

2 honrarse vr: — **con algo** to be honoured by something; — **de** + infin to be honoured to + infin, deem it an honour to + infin.

honrilla nf: **por la negra** — out of concern for what people will say, out of a sense of shame; for the sake of appearances.

honrosamente adv honourably.

honroso adj honourable; respectable, reputable; **es una profesión honrosa** it is an honourable profession, it is a respectable profession.

hontanar nm spring, group of springs.

hopa[1] nf cassock.

hopa[2] interj (a) (RPl) stop it!, that hurts! (b) (Col, Guat, Mex) = **hola**.

hopear [1a] vi (Ven) to call, shout.

hopo ['xopo] nm (fox's) brush, tail.

hora nf (a) hour; (more generally) time; **media** — half an hour; **durante 2** —**s** for 2 hours; **esperamos** —**s y** —**s** we waited hours and hours; **en la** — **de su muerte** at the moment of his death, at the time of his death; ¿**a qué** —? at what time?; ¿**qué** — **es?** what is the time?, what time is it?; ¡**la** —!, ¡**es la** —! time's up!; **es** — **de** + infin it is time to + infin; **es** — **de irnos** it's time we went, it's time for us to go; ¡**ya es** — **de que . . .!** it is high time that . . .!; ¡**ya era** —! and about time too!; **éstas son las** —**s mías** this is my time, this is the time I like.

(b) (with adj or prep) **a altas** —**s, en las altas** —**s** in the small hours, late at night; **a una** — **avanzada** at a late hour; **a buena** — opportunely; ¡**a buena** —, **mangas verdes!** a fine time you choose to tell me that!, it's too late now!; **en buena** — fortunately; safely; — **de comer** mealtime; **a la** — **de comer** at lunchtime; —**s extra**, —**s extraordinarias** overtime; —**s de insolación** hours of sunshine; — **legal** official time, standard time; —**s libres** free time, spare time; **en mala** — unluckily; — **oficial** official time, standard time; —**s de oficina** business hours, office hours; **a primera** — first thing in the morning; — **punta** peak hour, rush hour; —**s punta** peak hours, rush hours; — **de recreo** playtime; —**s suplementarias** overtime; —**s de trabajo** working hours; working day; "**última** —" (Press) "stop-press"; **a última** — at the last moment; in the nick of time; at the eleventh hour; last thing at night; **noticias de última** — last-minute news; **dejar las cosas hasta última** — to leave things until the last moment; — **de verano** summertime; **a la** — punctually, on the dot; **a la** — **justa** on the stroke of time; **a estas —s** now, at this time; **fuera de —s** out of hours, out of working hours; **por —s** by the hour; **trabajar por —s** to be paid by the hour; to work part-time.

(c) (*with verb*) **dar —** to fix a time, offer an appointment; **dar la —** to strike (the hour); **poner el reloj en —** to set one's watch, put one's watch right; **tener —** to have an appointment; **no ver la — de algo** to be scarcely able to wait for something, look forward impatiently to something.

(d) **—s** (*Eccl*) book of hours; **—s canónicas** canonical hours.

horaciano *adj* Horatian.

Horacio m Horace.

horadar [1a] *vt* to bore (through), pierce, drill, perforate; to tunnel (into).

hora-hombre *nf*, *pl* **horas-hombre** man-hour.

horario 1 *adj* hourly; hour (*attr*), time (*attr*).
2 *nm* hour hand; (*Aer, Rail etc*; *also* SAm: *School*) timetable; **llegar a —** (SAm) to arrive on time, be on schedule.

horca *nf* (a) gallows, gibbet; **condenar a uno a la —** to condemn someone to the gallows.
(b) (*Agr*) pitchfork; hayfork; manure fork.
(c) (*of garlic, onions*) string.
(d) (PR, Ven) birthday present, present given on one's saint's day.

horcadura *nf* fork (of a tree).

horcajadas: a — *adv* astride.

horcajo *nm* (a) (*Agr*) yoke. (b) (*of river, tree*) fork.

horcar [1g] *vt* (SAm) = **ahorcar**.

horcón *nm* (a) (*Agr*) pitchfork. (b) (*Agr*) forked prop (*for branches of fruit trees*); (SAm) prop, support (*for beam of roof*).

horchata *nf* orgeat.

horchatería *nf* refreshment stall.

horda *nf* horde; (*fig*) gang.

hordiate *nm* barley water.

horero *nm* (Bol, Ec, Guat, Mex) hour hand.

horita *adv* (SAm) = **ahorita**.

horizontal *adj* horizontal.

horizontalmente *adv* horizontally.

horizonte *nm* horizon (*also fig*); (*also* **línea del —**) skyline.

horma *nf* (a) (*Tech*) form, mould; **— de sombrero** hat block; **— de calzado**) last, boot tree; **encontrar-(se con) la — de su zapato** to meet one's match.
(b) dry-stone wall.

hormadoras *nfpl* (Col) petticoat.

hormiga *nf* (a) ant; **— blanca** white ant; **— león** ant lion.
(b) **—s** (*Med*) itch; pins and needles.
(c) (Arg, Mex) **ser una —** to be hard-working; to be thrifty.

hormigón *nm* concrete; **— armado** reinforced concrete; **— pretensado** pre-stressed concrete.

hormigonera *nf* concrete mixer.

hormiguear [1a] *vi* (a) to itch; to have pins and needles; to have a feeling as though insects were crawling over one. (b) to swarm, teem.

hormigueo *nm* (a) itch, itching; tingling; prickly feeling, feeling as though insects were crawling over one.
(b) (*fig*) anxiety, uneasiness.
(c) swarming.

hormiguero 1 *adj* ant-eating; **oso —** anteater. 2 *nm* (a) ant-hill. (b) (*fig*) ant-hill; swarm of people, place swarming with people.

hormiguillo *nm* = **hormigueo** (a).

hormón *nm* (Acad), **hormona** *nf* hormone.

hornacina *nf* (vaulted) niche.

hornada *nf* (a) batch (of loaves etc), baking. (b) (*fig*) batch, collection, crop.

hornalla *nf* (RPI) furnace; firebox (of oven).

hornazo *nm* (a) batch (of cakes etc), baking. (b) Easter cake.

hornear [1a] **1** *vt* (SAm) to cook, bake. **2** *vi* to bake, be a baker.

hornero *nm*, **hornera** *nf* baker.

hornillo *nm* (a) (*Tech*) small furnace; (Cook) cooker, stove; portable stove; (*of pipe*) bowl; **— eléctrico** hotplate; **— de gas** gas ring.
(b) (*Mil: Hist*) mine.

horno *nm* (Cook) oven; (*Tech*) furnace; (*for pottery*) kiln; **— alto** blast furnace; **— de cal** lime kiln; **— crematorio** crematorium; **— de fundición** smelting furnace; **— de ladrillos** brick kiln; **asar al —** to bake; **el — no está para bollos** this is the wrong moment, this is a bad time to ask.

horóscopo *nm* horoscope.

horqueta *nf* (*all senses*) fork.

horquetear [1a] **1** *vt* (a) (Arg) *ears* to prick up; to listen suspiciously to.
(b) (Col, Mex, Urug) to bestride, sit astride.
2 *vi* (Col, Mex, Urug) to grow branches, put out branches.

horquilla *nf* hairpin, hairclip; (*Agr*) pitchfork; **— de cavar**) garden fork; (*of bicycle*) fork; (*Mech*) yoke; (*Tel*) rest, cradle; (*on stilt*) footrest.

horrarse [1a] *vr* (SAm: *Agr*) to abort.

horrendo *adj* horrible; hideous; dire, frightful.

hórreo *nm* (*prov*) (raised) granary.

horrible *adj* (a) horrible, dreadful, ghastly.
(b) (*fig*) dreadful, nasty, terrible (*fam*); **¡qué persona más —!** what a dreadful man!; **la película es —** the film is dreadful.

horriblemente *adv* (a) horribly, dreadfully. (b) (*fig*) dreadfully, terribly (*fam*).

horripilante *adj* hair-raising, horrifying; harrowing; grisly; creepy.

horripilar [1a] **1** *vt*: **— a uno** to make someone's hair stand on end, horrify someone, give someone the creeps.
2 horripilarse *vr* to be horrified, be terrified; **era para —** it was enough to make your hair stand on end.

horror *nm* (a) horror, dread, terror (*a* of); abhorrence (*a* of); enormity; frightfulness; **¡qué —!** how ghastly!; isn't it dreadful?; (*fam*) well!, goodness!; **la fiesta … ¡un —!** the party was ghastly! (*fam*); **tener — a algo** to have a horror of something; **tener algo en —** to detest something, loathe something.
(b) (*act*) atrocity, terrible thing.
(c) (*as adv*: *fam*) **me gusta un —** I like it awfully (*fam*); **hoy he trabajado un —** today I worked awfully hard (*fam*); **se divirtieron —es** they had a tremendous time (*fam*).

horrorizar [1f] **1** *vt* to horrify; to terrify, frighten. **2 horrorizarse** *vr* to be horrified, be aghast.

horrorosamente *adv* (a) horrifyingly; horribly, frightfully. (b) (*fig*) dreadfully, awfully (*fam*).

horroroso *adj* (a) horrifying, terrifying; horrible, frightful. (b) (*fig*) ghastly (*fam*), dreadful, awful (*fam*); hideous, ugly.

horrura *nf* filth, dirt; rubbish.

hortaliza *nf* (a) vegetable; **—s** vegetables, garden produce. (b) (Mex) vegetable garden.

hortelano *nm* gardener; market gardener, truck farmer (US).

hortensia *nf* hydrangea.

hortera 1 *nf* wooden bowl. **2** *nm* (Madrid) shop assistant, grocer's boy.

hortícola 1 *adj* horticultural; garden (*attr*). **2** *nmf* = **horticultor**.

horticultor *nm* horticulturist; gardener; nurseryman.

horticultura *nf* horticulture; gardening.

hosco *adj* (a) dark; gloomy. (b) *person* sullen; morose; grim.

hospedaje *nm* (cost of) board and lodging.

hospedar [1a] **1** *vt* to put up, lodge, give a room (*etc*) to; to receive as a guest, entertain.
2 hospedarse *vr* to stay, stop, put up, lodge (*con* with, *en* at).

hospedera *nf* hostess; innkeeper's wife.

hospedería *nf* (a) hostelry, inn. (b) guest room. (c) (*Eccl*) hospice, guest quarters.

hospedero *nm* host; innkeeper, landlord.

hospiciano *nm*, **hospiciana** *nf*, **hospiciante** *nmf* inmate of a poorhouse.

hospicio *nm* poorhouse; orphanage; (*Eccl*) hospice.

hospital *nm* hospital; infirmary; **— de aislamiento**, **— de contagiosos** isolation hospital; **— de (primera) sangre** field dressing station.

hospitalario *adj* hospitable.

hospitalidad *nf* hospitality.

hospitalizar [1f] **1** *vt* to send (*or* take) to hospital, hospitalize. **2 hospitalizarse** *vr* (SAm) to go into hospital.

hosquedad *nf* sullenness; moroseness; grimness.

hostelería *nf* hotel trade, hotel business.

hostelero *nm* innkeeper, landlord.

hostería *nf* inn, hostelry.

hostia *nf* (a) (*Eccl*) host, consecrated wafer.
(b) (*fam*) punch, bash (*fam*).
(c) **no entiendo ni —** I don't understand a word of it.
(d) **¡—!** damn it!

hostigar [1h] *vt* (a) to lash, whip, scourge. (b) (*fig*) to harass, plague, pester; to bore. (c) (SAm: *of food*) to surfeit, cloy.

hostigoso *adj* (CAm, Col, Chi, Per) *food* sickening, cloying; *person* annoying, tedious.

hostil *adj* hostile.

hostilidad *nf* (a) hostility. (b) hostile act; **romper las —es** to start hostilities.

hostilizar [1f] *vt* (*Mil*) to harry, harass, worry; (*fig*) to antagonize.

hotel *nm* (a) hotel. (b) detached house, suburban house, villa.

hotelero 1 *adj* hotel (*attr*); **la industria hotelera** the hotel trade. **2** *nm* hotelkeeper, hotel manager.

hoy 1 *adv* (a) today; now, nowadays; **la juventud de — the** youth of today; **en el correo de —** in today's post; **— día, — en día** nowadays; in this day and age; **— por —** at the present time, right now; **de — en ocho días, de — en una semana** today week, a week today; **de — en quince (días)** today fortnight, a fortnight today; **de — a mañana** any time now, when one least expects it; **está para llegar de — a mañana** it might happen any day now; **de — en adelante** from now on, henceforward; **de — no pasa que le escriba** I'll write to him this very day; **desde —** from now on, starting from now; **¡y hasta —!** and I've heard no more about it!, and that was the last I heard!; **por —** for the present.

(b) (*SAm*) now; this year.

2 *nm* present time; **el — cubano** Cuba at the present time, the present state of affairs in Cuba.

hoya *nf* (a) pit, hole; grave; **— de arena** (*Golf*) bunker. (b) (*Geog*) vale, valley; (*SAm*) riverbed, river basin. (c) (*Agr*) seedbed.

hoyada *nf* hollow, depression.

hoyador *nm* (*Col, Cu, Mex*) dibber, seed drill.

hoyanco *nm* (*Mex:Aut*) pothole.

hoyar [1a] *vt* (*Cu, Guat, Mex*) to make holes (for sowing seeds).

hoyito *nm* (*SAm*) dimple.

hoyo *nm* (a) hole, pit; hollow, cavity; grave. (b) (*Golf*) hole; **en el — 18** at the 18th hole. (c) (*Med*) pockmark. (d) (*Theat*) **irse al —** to flop (*fam*), be a disaster.

hoyuelo *nm* dimple.

hoz *nf* (a) (*Agr*) sickle. (b) (*Geog*) defile, narrow pass, gorge. (c) **de — y coz** wildly, recklessly.

hozar [1f] *vt* (*of pig*) to root in, root among.

hua . . .: *for some words so spelled in SAm, see also* **gua . . .,** *eg for* **huaico** *see* **guaico**.

huaca *nf etc see* **guaca** *etc*.

huacalón *adj* (*Mex*) (a) rough-voiced, gruff. (b) fat.

huaco *adj* (*SAm*) toothless.

huachafería *nf* (*Per*) middle-class snobs, would-be social climbers.

huachafo *nm*, **huachafa** *nf* (*Per*) middle-class snob, would-be social climber.

huacho *nm* (*Per*) section of a lottery ticket.

huahua *nf* (*Ec, Mex, Per*) = **guagua**.

huaica *nf* (*Per*) bargain sale.

huáncar *nm*, **huáncara** *nf* (*Bol, Per*) Indian drum.

huasicama *nmf* (*Ec*) Indian servant.

hube *etc see* **haber**.

hucha *nf* (a) chest, bin; moneybox. (b) (*fig*) savings; **tener una buena —** to have money laid by, have a nest egg.

hueco 1 *adj* (a) hollow; empty; (*on paper*) blank. (b) soft, spongy. (c) *voice, sound* resonant, resounding, booming. (d) *person* conceited; *style* pompous, affected.

2 *nm* hollow, cavity; hole; gap, opening; empty space; (*Archit*) recess, window space; (*of staircase*) well; (*of lift*) shaft; (*fam*) vacancy; **— de la mano** hollow of the hand; **deja un — que será difícil llenar** he leaves a gap which it will be hard to fill.

huecograbado *nm* (*Typ*) photogravure.

huelán *adj* (a) (*Chi*) immature, not fully developed; *wood* unseasoned; *herbage* withered; *corn* unripe. (b) decayed, in decline, that has come down in the world.

hueleflor *nmf* (*PR*) idiot.

hueleguisos *nm*, *pl* **hueleguisos** (*Per*) sponger (*fam*).

huelehuele *nmf* (*PR*) idiot.

huelga *nf* (a) rest, repose; leisure; idleness; recreation. (b) (*Pol etc*) strike; stoppage, walkout; **— de brazos caídos** sit-down strike; **— de hambre** hunger strike; **— patronal** lockout; **— por solidaridad** sympathy strike; **los obreros en —** the workers on strike, the striking workers; **estar en —** to be on strike; **declarar la —, declararse en —, ponerse en —** to come out on strike, go on strike; to walk out. (c) (*Mech*) play, free movement.

huelgo *nm* (a) breath; **tomar —** to take breath, pause. (b) room, space. (c) (*Mech*) play, free movement.

huelguear [1a] *vi* (*Per*) to strike, be on strike.

huelguista *nmf* striker.

huella *nf* (a) (*act*) tread, treading. (b) trace, mark, sign, imprint; footprint; footstep; (*of animal, vehicle*) track; **— dactilar, — digital** fingerprint; **sin dejar —** without leaving a trace, leaving no sign; **seguir las —s de uno** to follow in someone's footsteps. (c) (*of stair, tyre*) tread. (d) **— del sonido** (*Cine*) sound track.

huellear [1a] *vt* (*Col*) to track, follow the trail of.

huellero *adj* (*Col*): **perro —** tracking dog.

huello *nm* condition of the ground etc (for walking); **camino de buen —** good road for walking; **camino de mal —** bad road for walking, badly-surfaced road.

huérfano 1 *adj* orphan, orphaned; (*fig*) unprotected, defenceless, uncared-for; **una niña huérfana de madre** a motherless child, a child that has lost her mother.

2 *nm*, **huérfana** *nf* orphan.

huero *adj* (a) *egg* addled, rotten. (b) (*fig*) empty, sterile; rotten; dud. (c) (*Guat, Mex*) blond(e).

huerta *nf* (a) vegetable garden, kitchen garden; (large) market garden, truck farm (US). (b) (*esp Murcia, Valencia*) irrigated region, fertile irrigated area. (c) (*Ec*) cocoa plantation.

huertero *nm* (*Arg, Chi, Mex, Per*) gardener.

huerto *nm* kitchen garden, (small) market garden, truck garden (US); orchard; back garden.

huesa *nf* grave.

huesear [1a] *vi* (a) (*CAm*) to beg. (b) (*Mex*) to work.

hueserío *nm* (*Per*) unsaleable merchandise.

huesero *nm*, **huesera** *nf* (*Cu*) slum dweller.

huesillo *nm* (*Chi, Per*) sun-dried peach.

huesista *nm* (*CAm*) government employee.

hueso *nm* (a) (*Anat*) bone; **— de la alegría** funny bone; **un — duro de roer** a hard nut to crack, a tough assignment; **— de la suerte** wishbone; **sin — boneless**; **la sin —** (*fam*) the tongue; **soltar la sin — (fam*) to shoot one's mouth off (*fam*); **no dejar — sano a uno** to pull someone to pieces; **estar en los —s** to be nothing but skin and bone; **meterse a — de puerco** (*Mex*) to brag; **tener los —s molidos** to be fagged out (*fam*), ache all over.

(b) (*Bot*) stone, pit (US); core.

(c) (*Col*) unsaleable article, drug on the market.

(d) (*fig*) hard work, drudgery.

(e) (*CAm, Mex*) government job, sinecure, political plum; soft job.

(f) **ser un —** (*fig*) to be terribly strict, be an old battle-axe (*fam*).

(g) (*Ec*) mule.

(h) (*Mex*) **— colorado** strong northerly wind.

huesoso *adj* bony; bone (*attr*).

huésped *nm* (a) guest, boarder, resident. (b) host. (c) (*Hist*) innkeeper, landlord.

huéspeda *nf* (a) guest; lodger, boarder, resident. (b) hostess. (c) (*Hist*) innkeeper's wife; **no contar con la —** to fail to take something into account.

huesudo *adj* bony; big-boned, raw-boned.

hueva *nf* (*Fish*) (hard) roe; **—s** eggs, spawn.

huevada *nf* (a) (*SAm*) nest of eggs, clutch of eggs; number of eggs. (b) (*Chi, Per*) foolish remark, piece of nonsense, crazy idea.

huevera *nf* eggcup.

huevo *nm* (a) egg; **— en cáscara** boiled egg; **— crudo** raw egg; **— duro** hard-boiled egg; **— escalfado** poached egg; **— estrellado, — frito, — al plato** fried egg; **— fresco** new-laid egg; **— pasado por agua, — tibio** (*CAm, Col, Mex*) soft-boiled egg; **—s pericos** (*Col*), **— revueltos** scrambled eggs; **ser como el — de Colón** to be simple, be easy; **¡que le fríen un —!** (*fam*) get knotted! (*sl*); **pensar en los —s del gallo** (*CAm, Col*) to be in a daydream.

(b) (*tabu*) ball (*tabu*), testicle; **me costó un — **it took me a lot of trouble, it was hard work; **tener —s** to have guts, be tough.

huevón 1 *adj* (a) (*Cu, Chi, Guat, Mex, RPl*) slow; lazy; stupid, dim; cowardly. (b) (*Nic*) tough, brave.

2 *nm* (a) (*Ant, CAm, Mex*) slowness; idleness, laziness; (*Chi, Per, PR, Ven*) stupidity; (*Chi*) cowardice. (b) (*Nic*) courage, guts, toughness.

Hugo *m* Hugo.

hugonote 1 *adj* Huguenot. **2** *nm*, **hugonota** *nf* Huguenot.

hui . . .: *for some words so spelled in SAm, see also* **gui . . ., güi . . .,** *eg for* **huinche** *see* **güinche**.

huida *nf* (a) flight, escape. (b) (*of horse*) shy, bolt.

huidizo adj (a) person etc shy; elusive. (b) impression etc fleeting.

huido adj very shy, easily scared.

huile nm (Mex) roasting grill.

huilón adj (Ec, Per) elusive.

huilla nf (Ven) cork (of bottle).

huir [3g] 1 vt to run away from, flee (from), escape (from); to avoid, shun.
2 vi and **huirse** vr to run away, flee, escape; (of time) to fly; (SAm) to elope.

huira nf (Chi, Per) rope; halter, tether; **dar — a uno** to thrash someone; **sacar las —s a uno** to beat someone up.

huiro nm (Chi) seaweed.

huisachear [1a] vi (CAm, Mex) (a) to go to law, engage in litigation. (b) to practise law without a qualification.

huisachería nf (CAm, Mex) (a) lawyer's tricks, legal intricacies. (b) practice of law without a qualification.

huisachero nm (CAm, Mex) (a) shyster lawyer, unqualified lawyer. (b) (Mex) scribbler, pen-pusher.

hulado nm (CAm) oilskin, rubberized cloth.

hular nm (Mex) rubber plantation.

hule[1] nm (a) rubber. (b) oilskin, oilcloth. (c) (CAm, Mex) rubber tree.

hule[2] nm (Taur) goring; (fam) row; **habrá —** there is going to be trouble.

hulear [1a] vi (CAm) to extract rubber (from trees).

hulero 1 adj (CAm) rubber (attr). 2 nm rubber worker.

huloso adj (CAm) rubbery, elastic.

hulla nf coal, soft coal.

hullera nf colliery, coalmine.

hullero adj coal (attr).

humanar [1a] 1 vt to humanize.
2 **humanarse** vr (a) to become more human; **— a + infin** (SAm) to condescend to + infin. (b) (Eccl: of Christ) to become man.

humanidad nf (a) humanity, mankind. (b) (quality) humanity. (c) (fam) corpulence. (d) **las —es** the humanities.

humanismo nm humanism.

humanista nmf humanist.

humanístico adj humanistic.

humanitario 1 adj humanitarian; humane. 2 nm humanitarian.

humanización nf humanization.

humanizar [1f] 1 vt to humanize, make more human.
2 **humanizarse** vr to become more human.

humano 1 adj (a) human. (b) act, character etc humane. (c) **ciencias humanas** humane learning, humanistic learning, humanities. 2 nm human.

humarasca nf (CAm), **humareda** nf cloud of smoke.

humazo nm dense smoke, cloud of smoke; **dar — a uno** to smoke someone out.

humeante adj smoking, smoky; steaming.

humear [1a] 1 vt (a) (Col, Mex, Ven) to fumigate. (b) (Chi, Mex) to beat, thrash.
2 vi (a) to smoke, give out smoke; to fume, steam, give off fumes. (b) (fig: of memory etc) to be still alive. (c) (fig) to give oneself airs, be conceited.

humectador nm humidifier; humidor.

humectar [1a] vt = **humedecer**.

humedad nf humidity; damp, dampness; moisture; **a prueba de —** damp-proof; **sentir la —** (Per, Ven) to feel the consequences of one's act.

humedecer [2d] 1 vt to dampen, wet, moisten; to humidify. 2 **humedecerse** vr to get damp, get wet.

húmedo adj humid; damp, wet; moist.

humera nf (a) (PR) cloud of smoke. (b) = **jumera**.

humero nm (a) chimney, smokestack; flue. (b) (Col) cloud of smoke.

húmero nm humerus.

humildad nf (a) humbleness, humility; meekness. (b) humbleness; lowliness.

humilde adj (a) character etc humble; meek; voice small. (b) class etc low, modest; lowly, lowborn, humble; **son gente —** they are humble people, they are poor people.

humildemente adv humbly; meekly.

humillación nf humiliation; humbling.

humillante adj humiliating; humbling; degrading.

humillar [1a] 1 vt to humiliate; to humble; head to bow, bend; revolt etc to crush.
2 **humillarse** vr to humble oneself; **— a** to bow to, bow down before; to grovel to.

humo nm (a) smoke; fumes; vapour, steam; **a — de pajas** thoughtlessly, heedlessly; **quedó en — de pajas** it all came to nothing; **hacer —, echar — to** smoke; **lo que hace — es porque está ardiendo, donde se hace — es porque hay fuego** there's no smoke without fire; **hacerse —, irse todo en — to** go up in smoke; (fig) to disappear completely, vanish without trace; **irsele al — a uno** (Mex, RPl) to fall suddenly on someone, jump someone (sl); **tomar la del —** (fam) to beat it (fam).
(b) **—s** (fig) homes, hearths.
(c) **—s** (fig) conceit, airs; **bajar los —s a uno** to take someone down a peg; **tener muchos —s** to be terribly vain, have a swelled head; **tener —s para + infin** to have the nerve to + infin; **vender —s to** brag, talk big.

humor nm (a) mood, humour; temper, disposition; **buen —** good humour, good mood, high spirits; **estar de buen —** to be in a good mood; **mal —** bad mood, bad temper; **en un tono de mal —** in an ill-tempered tone; **seguir el — a uno** to humour someone, go along with someone's mood. (b) (angl) humour; humorousness.

humorada nf (a) joke, witticism, pleasantry. (b) caprice, whim.

humorado adj: **bien —** good-humoured, good-tempered; **mal —** bad-tempered, cross, peevish.

humorismo nm humour; humorousness.

humorista nmf humorist.

humorísticamente adv humorously, facetiously.

humorístico adj humorous, funny, facetious.

humoso adj smoky.

humus nm humus.

hundible adj sinkable.

hundido adj sunken; eyes deep-set, hollow.

hundimiento nm (a) sinking. (b) collapse, fall, ruin, destruction; cave-in, subsidence.

hundir [3a] 1 vt (a) to sink; to submerge, engulf. (b) building etc to ruin, destroy, cause the collapse of; plan etc to sink, ruin; (in argument) to confound.
2 **hundirse** vr (a) (Naut) to sink; (in sand, mud etc) to sink; (of swimmer etc) to plunge, go down. (b) (of building etc) to collapse, tumble (down), fall (down); (of ground) to cave in, subside. (c) (fig) to be destroyed, be ruined; to disappear, vanish; **se hundió la economía** the economy collapsed; **se hundieron los precios** prices slumped; **se hundió en el estudio de la historia** he plunged into the study of history, he became absorbed in the study of history; **se hundió en la meditación** he became lost in meditation.

húngaro 1 adj Hungarian. 2 nm, **húngara** nf Hungarian. 3 nm (language) Hungarian.

Hungría f Hungary.

huno nm Hun.

huracán nm hurricane.

huracanado adj: **viento —** hurricane wind, violent wind.

huraco nm (SAm) hole.

hurañía nf shyness; unsociableness; elusiveness.

huraño adj shy; unsociable; animal shy, elusive, wild.

hure nm (Col) large pot, vessel.

hureque nm (Col) = **huraco**.

hurgar [1h] 1 vt (a) to poke, jab; to stir (up); fire to poke, rake. (b) (SAm) = **hurguetear**. (c) (fig) to stir up, excite, provoke.
2 **hurgarse** vr (also **— las narices**) to pick one's nose.

hurgón nm (a) poker, fire rake. (b) thrust, stab (with weapon).

hurgonada nf, **hurgonazo** nm poke, jab; poking, raking.

hurgonear [la] vt fire to poke, rake (out); to thrust at, jab (at).

hurgonero nm poker, fire rake.

hurguete nm (Chi, RPl) busybody, nosey-parker.

hurguetear [la] vt (SAm) to finger, turn over, rummage (inquisitively) among; to shove one's nose into, pry into.

hurí nf houri.

hurón 1 adj (a) shy, unsociable. (b) (Chi) greedy.
2 nm (a) (Zool) ferret. (b) (fig) shy person, unsociable person. (c) (fig: pej) busybody, nosey-parker, snooper.

huronear [1a] vt (fig) to ferret out; to pry into, shove one's nose into.

huronera nf ferret hole; (fig) den, lair; hiding place.

hurra interj hurray!, hurrah!

hurtadillas: a — *adv* stealthily, by stealth, on the sly.
hurtar [la] **1** *vt* **(a)** to steal; (*Lit etc*) to plagiarize, pinch (*fam*), lift.
(b) (*of sea*) to eat away, erode, encroach on.
(c) — **el cuerpo** to dodge, move (one's body) out of the way.
2 hurtarse *vr* to withdraw; to make off; to keep out of the way.
hurto *nm* **(a)** (*act*) theft, robbery; (*in general*) thieving, robbery; — **doméstico** burglary, housebreaking; **a** — stealthily, by stealth, on the sly.
(b) thing stolen, (piece of) stolen property, loot.
húsar *nm* hussar.
husillo *nm* **(a)** (*Mech*) spindle, shaft; (*of a press etc*) screw, worm. **(b)** drain.

husma *nf* snooping, prying; **andar a la** — to go snooping around, go prying (*de* after, for).
husmear [la] **1** *vt* **(a)** to scent, get wind of, sniff out.
(b) (*fig*) to smell out; to nose into, pry into. **2** *vi* (*of meat*) to (begin to) smell high, be smelly.
husmeo *nm* **(a)** scenting. **(b)** (*fig*) smelling-out; prying, snooping.
husmo *nm* high smell, strong smell, gaminess; **estar al** — to watch one's chance.
huso *nm* **(a)** (*Tech*) spindle; bobbin; (*of lathe, windlass*) drum. **(b)** (*Chi*) kneecap.
huy *interj* (*pain*) ow!, ouch!; (*surprise*) well!; (*relief*) phew!
huyente *adj* forehead receding.
huyón (*SAm*) **1** *adj* cowardly; shy, unsociable. **2** *nm* coward; shy person, unsociable person.

I

iba *etc see* **ir.**
Iberia *f* Iberia.
ibérico *adj* Iberian.
ibero, íbero 1 *adj* Iberian. 2 *nm,* **ibera** *nf,* **íbera** *nf* Iberian.
Iberoamérica *f* Latin America.
iberoamericano 1 *adj* Latin-American. 2 *nm,* **iberoamericana** *nf* Latin-American.
íbice *nm* ibex.
ibicenco 1 *adj* of Ibiza. 2 *nm,* **ibicenca** *nf* native (*or* inhabitant) of Ibiza; **los —s** the people of Ibiza.
ibis *nf, pl* **ibis** ibis.
ibón *nm* Pyrenean lake, tarn.
iceberg *nm* [iθe'βer], *pl* **icebergs** [iθe'βer] iceberg.
—ico, —ica *n and adj etc suffix* (*regional variation; in some combinations* **—(e)cico, —(e)cica**): *see* **—ito.**
icono *nm* ikon, icon.
iconoclasta 1 *adj* iconoclastic. 2 *nmf* iconoclast.
icterícia *nf* jaundice.
id *nm* id.
ida *nf* (a) going, departure; **—s y venidas** comings and goings; **en dos —s y venidas** in an instant; **dejar las —s por las venidas** to miss the boat; **(viaje de) —** outward journey, trip out; **— y vuelta** round trip.
(b) (*Hunting*) track, trail.
(c) (*fig*) rash act; rashness, hastiness.
idea *nf* (a) idea, notion; **— faro** (*fam*), **— genial, — luminosa** bright idea, brilliant idea; **— fija** fixed idea, obsession, idée fixe; **— monstruo** (*fam*) fantastic idea; **una persona de mala —** a malicious person, an evil-minded person; **¡ni —!** I haven't a clue!, search me! (*fam*); **meterse una — en la cabeza** to get an idea into one's head; **no tengo la menor —, no tengo la más remota —** I haven't the faintest (*or* foggiest) idea; **no tenía la menor — de que** . . . I had no idea that . . .
(b) idea, opinion, estimate; **¿qué — tienes de él?** what impression do you have of him?; **darse una — de, hacerse una — de** to get an idea of, form an impression of.
(c) idea, intention; **con la — de +** *infin* with the idea of **+** *ger;* **cambiar de —, mudar de —** to change one's mind; **hace falta que cambie de —** he'll have to alter his outlook; he'll have to buck his ideas up; **llevar — de +** *infin* to have the idea of **+** *ger,* intend to **+** *infin.*
(d) ingenuity, inventiveness.
ideación *nf* conception, thinking-out.
ideal 1 *adj* ideal; **nuestra casa —** our ideal house, our dream house. 2 *nm* ideal.
idealismo *nm* idealism.
idealista 1 *adj* idealistic 2 *nmf* idealist.
idealización *nf* idealization.
idealizar [1f] *vt* to idealize.
idealmente *adv* ideally.
idear [1a] *vt* to think up; to contrive, invent, devise; to plan, design.
ideario *nm* set of ideas; ideology; ideological formation.
ideático *adj* (a) (*SAm*) eccentric, having odd ideas, full of whims. (b) (*Hond*) ingenious, full of ideas.
ídem 1 *pron* ditto, the same, idem. 2 *nm:* **ser un — de lienzo** to be another of the same sort, be tarred with the same brush.
idénticamente *adv* identically.
idéntico *adj* identical; the same, the very same.
identidad *nf* identity; sameness, similarity.
identificación *nf* identification; **— errónea** mistaken identity.
identificar [1g] 1 *vt* to identify; to recognize, spot, pick out; **víctima sin —** unidentified victim. 2 **identificarse** *vr:* **— con** to identify oneself with.

ideología *nf* ideology.
ideológico *adj* ideological.
ideólogo *nm* ideologist.
ideoso *adj* (*Arg, Bol, Mex*) full of strange notions; odd, eccentric; nervous, suspicious.
idílico *adj* idyllic.
idilio *nm* idyll.
idioma *nm* language; (*of group*) speech, idiom.
idiomático *adj* language (*attr*), linguistic; idiomatic.
idiosincrasia *nf* idiosyncrasy.
idiosincrásico *adj* idiosyncratic.
idiota 1 *adj* idiotic, stupid. 2 *nmf* idiot; **¡—!** you idiot!
idiotez *nf* idiocy.
idiotismo *nm* (a) (*Gram*) idiom, idiomatic expression. (b) ignorance.
idiotizar [1f] *vt* (*SAm*): **— a uno** to drive someone crazy.
ido 1 *adj* (*fam*) (a) (*SAm*) absent-minded.
(b) (*SAm*) potty (*fam*), barmy (*sl*); **estar — (de la cabeza)** to be crazy, be nuts.
(c) (*CAm, Mex*) tight.
2 *nmpl:* **los —s** the dead, the departed.
idólatra 1 *adj* idolatrous. 2 *nmf* idolater, (*f*) idolatress.
idolatrar [1a] *vt* to worship, adore; (*fig*) to idolize.
idolatría *nf* idolatry.
idolátrico *adj* idolatrous.
ídolo *nm* idol.
idoneidad *nf* suitability, fitness; aptitude, ability.
idóneo *adj* suitable, fit, fitting.
idus *nmpl* ides.
iglesia *nf* church; **I— Anglicana** Church of England, Anglican Church; **— catedral** cathedral; **I— Católica** Catholic Church; **— colegial** collegiate church; **— parroquial** parish church; **casarse por la —** to get married in church, have a church wedding; **casarse por detrás de la —** to set up house together, form a permanent union (without benefit of clergy); **cumplir con la —** to fulfil one's religious obligations; **llevar a una a la —** to lead someone to the altar; **¡con la — hemos topado!** now we're really up against it!
iglesiero *adj* (*SAm*) churchy (*fam*), much given to church-going.
iglú *nm* igloo.
Ignacio *m* Ignatius.
ignaro *adj* ignorant.
ígneo *adj* igneous.
ignición *nf* ignition.
ignominia *nf* ignomINY, shame, disgrace.
ignominiosamente *adv* ignominiously, shamefully.
ignominioso *adj* ignominious, shameful, disgraceful.
ignorado *adj* unknown; obscure, little-known.
ignorancia *nf* ignorance; **por —** through ignorance.
ignorante 1 *adj* ignorant; uninformed. 2 *nmf* ignoramus.
ignorar [1a] *vt* (a) not to know, be ignorant of, be unaware of; **lo ignoro en absoluto** I don't know at all, I've no idea; **ignoramos su paradero** we don't know his whereabouts; **no ignoro que** . . . I am fully aware that . . . , of course I know that . . .
(b) (*SAm: angl*) to ignore.
ignoto *adj* unknown; undiscovered.
igual 1 *adj* (a) equal (*a* to); (the) same; alike, similar; **no vi nunca cosa —** I never saw the like; **1 kilómetro es — a 1.000 metros** a kilometre is equal to 1,000 metres, a kilometre equals 1,000 metres; **A es — a B** A is like B, A is the same as B; **es —** it makes no difference, it's all the same; **me es —** it's all the same to me.
(b) even, level; uniform, constant, unvarying, unchanging; smooth; *temperature* even; *climate* equable; **ir —es** (*in race*) to be level, be even.

(c) — que (*as prep*) like, the same as; A, — que B, no sabe A, like B, doesn't know.

(d) al — que (*as prep or conj*) like, just like; while, whereas; **Chile, al — que Argentina, estima que** ... Chile, (just) like Argentina, thinks that ...

2 *nmf* equal; **al —, por —** equally, on an equal basis; **sin —** without equal, matchless; **ser el — de** to be the equal of, be a match for; **no tener —** to be unrivalled, have no equal; **alternar de — a —** to be on an equal footing; **tratar a uno de — a —** to treat someone as an equal.

3 *nm* (*Math*) equals sign, sign of equality.

iguala *nf* **(a)** equalization. **(b)** (*Comm*) agreement; agreed fee.

igualación *nf* equalization; evening up, levelling; (*Math*) equating.

igualada *nf* (*Sport*) equalizer, equalizing goal (*etc*).

igualado *adj* (*Guat, Mex*) free and easy, excessively familiar (to a superior); (*Mex, Nic*) cheeky; (*Salv*) sly.

igualar [1a] **1** *vt* **(a)** to equalize, make equal; (*Math*) to equate (*a* to); (*fig*) to compare, match (*a* with).
(b) to level, level off, level up; to even, even out; to smooth; (*fig*) to even out, adjust.
(c) (*Comm*) to agree upon.
2 *vi and* **igualarse** *vr* **(a)** to be equal; **— a, — con** to equal, be equal to, be the equal of.
(b) (*Sport*) to equalize, score the equalizer; to tie.
(c) (*Comm*) to come to an agreement.
(d) (*Guat, Mex*) to be excessively familiar (to a superior).

igualatorio *nm* (*Med*) association.

igualdad *nf* **(a)** equality; sameness; (*Math*) equality; **— de retribución** equal pay; **en — de condiciones** on the same conditions, on an equal basis.
(b) evenness, levelness; uniformity; smoothness; **— de ánimo** equanimity.

igualitariedad *nf* egalitarianism.

igualitario *adj* egalitarian.

igualmente *adv* **(a)** equally.
(b) evenly; uniformly.
(c) likewise, also.
(d) (*replying to good wishes etc*) the same to you.

iguana *nf* iguana.

ijada *nf* **(a)** flank, side, loin. **(b)** (*Med*) stitch, pain in the side; **esto tiene su —** this has its weak side.

ijadear [1a] *vi* (*Zool*) to pant.

ijar *nm* flank, side.

ilación *nf* inference; connection, relationship; sequence.

ilativo *adj* inferential; (*Gram*) illative.

ilegal *adj* illegal, unlawful.

ilegalidad *nf* illegality, unlawfulness.

ilegalmente *adv* illegally, unlawfully.

ilegible *adj* illegible, unreadable.

ilegítimamente *adv* illegitimately.

ilegitimidad *nf* illegitimacy.

ilegítimo *adj* **(a)** illegitimate; unlawful. **(b)** false, spurious.

ilerdense 1 *adj* of Lérida. **2** *nmf* native (or inhabitant) of Lérida; **los —s** the people of Lérida.

ileso *adj* unhurt, unharmed; untouched; **salió — del accidente** he came out of the accident unharmed, he got out of the accident unscathed; **los pasajeros resultaron —s** the passengers were unhurt.

iletrado *adj* uncultured, illiterate.

Ilíada *nf* Iliad.

iliberal *adj* illiberal.

ilícitamente *adv* illicitly, illegally, unlawfully.

ilicitano 1 *adj* of Elche. **2** *nm*, **ilicitana** *nf* native (or inhabitant) of Elche; **los —** the people of Elche.

ilícito *adj* illicit, illegal, unlawful.

ilimitado *adj* unlimited, limitless, unbounded.

ilógicamente *adv* illogically.

ilógico *adj* illogical.

iluminación *nf* **(a)** illumination, lighting; floodlighting; **— indirecta** indirect lighting. **(b)** (*fig*) enlightenment.

iluminado 1 *adj* illuminated, lighted, lit; **estar —** (*fam*) to be lit up (*sl*). **2** *nm*, **iluminada** *nf* visionary; illuminist; **los I—s** the Illuminati.

iluminador 1 *adj* illuminating. **2** *nm* illuminator.

iluminar [1a] *vt* **(a)** to illuminate, light, light up; to floodlight. **(b)** (*fig*) to enlighten.

ilusión *nf* **(a)** illusion; delusion; **— de óptica** optical illusion; **todo es —** it's all an illusion.
(b) (unfounded) hope, dream; piece of wishful thinking; hopefulness; **con —** hopefully; **el hombre de sus —es** the man of her dreams; **su — era comprarlo** her dream was to buy it, she dreamed of buying it; **forjarse —es, hacerse —es** to build up

(false) hopes, deceive oneself with false hopes, indulge in wishful thinking; **no te hagas —es** don't get any false ideas; **se hace la — de que** ... she fondly imagines that ... ; **tendió la mano con —** she put her hand out hopefully.
(c) excitement, thrill; eagerness; hopeful anticipation; **¡qué —!** how thrilling!, how exciting!; **comer con —** to eat eagerly; **trabajar con —** to work with a will; **el viaje me hace mucha —** I am so looking forward to the trip, I am getting very excited about the trip; **tu carta me hizo mucha —** I was thrilled to get your letter; **me hace una gran — que** ... it gives me a thrill that ...

ilusionado 1 *adj* hopeful; excited, eager; **el viaje me trae muy —** I am so looking forward to the trip, I am getting very excited about the trip.
2 *nm*, **ilusionada** *nf* hopeful; **joven —** young hopeful.

ilusionar [1a] **1** *vt* (*SAm*) to deceive; to give grounds for false hopes to, encourage falsely.
2 **ilusionarse** *vr* to have unfounded hopes, indulge in wishful thinking; **no te ilusiones** don't get any false ideas.

ilusionismo *nm* **(a)** wishful thinking. **(b)** conjuring.

ilusionista *nmf* conjurer, illusionist.

iluso 1 *adj* easily deceived; deluded. **2** *nm*, **ilusa** *nf* dreamer, visionary; **¡—!** you're hopeful!

ilusorio *adj* illusory, deceptive, unreal; empty, ineffectual.

ilustración *nf* **(a)** illustration.
(b) illustration, picture, drawing.
(c) learning, erudition; enlightenment; **la I—** the Enlightenment, the Age of Enlightenment (*18th century*).

ilustrado *adj* **(a)** illustrated. **(b)** learned, erudite; enlightened.

ilustrador 1 *adj* illustrative; enlightening. **2** *nm*, **ilustradora** *nf* illustrator.

ilustrar [1a] **1** *vt* **(a)** to illustrate.
(b) to explain, elucidate, make clear.
(c) to instruct, enlighten.
(d) to make famous, make illustrious.
2 **ilustrarse** *vr* **(a)** to acquire knowledge, become enlightened.
(b) to become famous.

ilustrativo *adj* illustrative.

ilustre *adj* illustrious, famous.

ilustrísimo *adj* most illustrious; **Su Ilustrísima** His Grace; **Vuestra Ilustrísima** Your Grace.

illanco *nm* (*Per*) slow stream, quiet-flowing stream.

—illo, —illa *n and adj etc suffix* (*in some combinations* —(e)cillo, —(e)cilla): *see* —ito.

imagen *nf* **(a)** image; (mental) picture; likeness; **ser la viva — de** to be the living image of; **hacer a uno a su —** to make somebody in one's own image.
(b) (*Eccl*) image, statue; **quedar para vestir imágenes** to be an old maid.
(c) (*TV*) picture; **— fantasma** ghost image.
(d) (*Lit*) image; **imágenes** (*collectively*) imagery.

imaginable *adj* imaginable, conceivable.

imaginación *nf* imagination; fancy; **ni por —** on no account; **no se me pasó por la — que** ... it never even occurred to me that ... ; **ella se deja llevar por la —** she lets her imagination run away with her.

imaginar [1a] **1** *vt* to imagine; to visualize; to think up, invent; **cosas que nadie imagina** things that no-one imagines; **¿quién imaginó esto?** who thought this one up?
2 *vi and* **imaginarse** *vr* to imagine, fancy, suppose; to picture (to oneself); **¡imagínate!** just imagine!, just fancy!; **imagínese que** ... suppose that ... , imagine that ... ; **me imagino que** ... I suppose that ... ; **sí, me imagino** yes, I can imagine.

imaginaria *nf* (*Mil*) guard, night guard.

imaginario *adj* imaginative.

imaginativa *nf* imagination, imaginativeness.

imaginativo *adj* imaginary, fanciful.

imaginería *nf* **(a)** (*Eccl*) images, statues. **(b)** (*Lit*) imagery.

imaginero *nm* maker (or painter) of religious images.

imán *nm* magnet (*also fig*); **— de herradura** horseshoe magnet.

iman(t)ación *nf* magnetization.

iman(t)ar [1a] *vt* to magnetize.

imbatible *adj* unbeatable.

imbatido *adj* unbeaten.

imbécil 1 *adj* **(a)** (*Med*) imbecile, feeble-minded.
(b) silly, stupid.
2 *nmf* **(a)** (*Med*) imbecile.
(b) imbecile, idiot; **¡—!** you idiot!

imbecilidad *nf* (a) (*Med*) imbecility, feeble-mindedness. (b) silliness, stupidity, idiocy; **decir —es** to say silly things.
imberbe *adj* beardless.
imbibición *nf* imbibing.
imbíbito *adj* (*Guat, Mex*) included (in the total).
imbombera *nf* (*Ven*) pernicious anaemia.
imbombo *adj* (*Ven*) anaemic.
imbornal *nm* scupper; **irse por los —es** (*SAm*) to get off the beam, wander.
imborrable *adj* ineffaceable, indelible.
imbricación *nf* (*esp SAm*) overlapping; interweaving; interdependence.
imbricar [1g] (*SAm*) **1** *vt* to overlap; to interweave. **2 imbricarse** *vr* to overlap; to be interwoven.
imbuir [3g] *vt* to imbue, infuse (*de, en* with); **imbuido de la cultura de** imbued with the culture of, full of the culture of.
imbunchar [1a] *vt* (*Chi*) (a) to bewitch. (b) to swindle, cheat.
imbunche *nm* (*Chi*) (a) spell, piece of witchcraft. (b) mess; fuss, row.
imitable *adj* imitable.
imitación *nf* (a) imitation; mimicry; **a — de** in imitation of; **desconfíe de las —es** (*Comm*) beware of imitations.
    (b) **de — imitation** (*attr*); **joyas de — imitation** jewellery.
    (c) (*Theat*) imitation, impersonation.
imitador 1 *adj* imitative. **2** *nm*, **imitadora** *nf* imitator; follower; (*Theat*) imitator, impersonator.
imitar [1a] *vt* (a) to imitate; to mimic, ape; to follow. (b) to counterfeit.
imitativo *adj* imitative.
impaciencia *nf* impatience.
impacientar [1a] **1** *vt* to make impatient; to irritate, exasperate.
    2 impacientarse *vr* to get impatient (*ante, por* about, at; *con* with), lose patience, get worked up; to fret; **— por + infin** to be impatient to + *infin*.
impaciente *adj* impatient; anxious; fretful.
impacientemente *adv* impatiently; anxiously; fretfully.
impacto *nm* impact; (*Mil*) hit; (*SAm: Boxing*) punch, blow; **— directo** (*Mil*) direct hit; **— político** political impact.
impagable *adj* unpayable.
impagado *adj* unpaid, still to be paid.
impago 1 *adj* unpaid, still to be paid. **2** *nm* non-payment.
impalpable *adj* impalpable.
impar 1 *adj* (*Math*) odd; **los números —es** the odd numbers. **2** *nm* odd number.
imparable *adj* (*Sport*) unstoppable.
imparcial *adj* impartial, unbiassed, fair.
imparcialidad *nf* impartiality, lack of bias, fairness.
imparciálmente *adv* impartially, fairly.
impartible *adj* indivisible.
impartir [3a] *vt teaching etc* to impart, give, convey; *order* to give.
impase *nm* (*Bridge*) finesse; **hacer el — a uno** to finesse against someone.
impasible *adj* impassive, unmoved.
impávidamente *adv* (a) intrepidly; dauntlessly. (b) (*SAm*) cheekily.
impavidez *nf* (a) intrepidity; dauntlessness. (b) (*SAm*) cheek, cheekiness.
impávido *adj* (a) intrepid; dauntless, undaunted. (b) (*SAm*) cheeky.
impecable *adj* impeccable, faultless.
impecablemente *adv* impeccably, faultlessly.
impedido *adj* crippled, disabled; **estar — para algo** to be unfit for something.
impedimenta *nf* (*Mil*) impedimenta.
impedimento *nm* (a) impediment (*also Law*), obstacle, hindrance. (b) disability.
impedir [3l] *vt* (a) to impede, obstruct, hinder, hamper; to deter; **— el tráfico** to block the traffic, obstruct the traffic.
    (b) to stop, prevent; to thwart; **— algo a uno** to keep someone from doing something, to make something impossible for someone; **— a uno hacer algo, — que uno haga algo** to stop someone doing something, prevent someone (from) doing something; **me veo impedido para ayudar** I find it impossible for me to help; **lo que no se puede —** what cannot be prevented.
impeditivo *adj* preventive.
impeler [2a] *vt* (a) (*Mech*) to drive, propel.
    (b) to drive, impel; to urge; **— a uno a hacer algo** to drive someone to do something; to urge someone to do something; **impelido por la necesidad** impelled by necessity.
impenetrabilidad *nf* impenetrability.
impenetrable *adj* impenetrable (*also fig*); impervious; (*fig*) obscure, incomprehensible.
impenitencia *nf* impenitence.
impenitente *adj* impenitent, unrepentant.
impensable *adj* unthinkable.
impensadamente *adv* (a) unexpectedly. (b) at random, by chance. (c) inadvertently.
impensado *adj* (a) unexpected, unforeseen. (b) random, chance (*attr*).
impepinable *adj* (*fam*) certain, inevitable.
impepinablemente *adv* (*fam*) inevitably; **— se le olvida** he's sure to forget, he always forgets.
imperante *adj* ruling (*also Comm*), prevailing.
imperar [1a] *vi* (a) to rule, reign; to be in command. (b) (*fig*) to reign, prevail; (*of price etc*) to be in force, be current.
imperativamente *adv* (a) imperatively. (b) *say etc* imperiously, in a commanding tone.
imperativo 1 *adj* (a) imperative (*also Gram*). (b) imperious, commanding. **2** *nm* imperative (mood).
imperceptible *adj* imperceptible, undiscernible.
imperceptiblemente *adv* imperceptibly.
imperdible *nm* safety pin.
imperdonable *adj* unpardonable, unforgivable, inexcusable.
imperdonablemente *adv* unpardonably, inexcusably.
imperecedero *adj* imperishable, undying.
imperfección *nf* imperfection; flaw, fault, blemish.
imperfectamente *adv* imperfectly.
imperfecto 1 *adj* (a) imperfect, faulty. (b) unfinished, incomplete. (c) (*Gram*) imperfect. **2** *nm* imperfect (tense).
imperial 1 *adj* imperial. **2** *nf* (*of bus*) top, upper deck; (*of coach*) top, roof.
imperialismo *nm* imperialism.
imperialista 1 *adj* imperialist(ic). **2** *nmf* imperialist.
imperialmente *adv* imperially.
impericia *nf* unskilfulness; lack of experience, inexperience; **a prueba de —** foolproof.
imperio *nm* (a) empire; **I— Español** Spanish Empire; **vale un —, vale siete —s** it's worth a fortune. (b) rule, authority; sway. (c) (*fig*) haughtiness, pride.
imperiosamente *adv* (a) imperiously. (b) urgently; imperatively, overridingly.
imperioso *adj* (a) imperious; lordly. (b) urgent; imperative, overriding; **necesidad imperiosa** absolute necessity, pressing need.
imperito *adj* inexpert, unskilled; inexperienced; clumsy.
impermanente *adv* impermanent.
impermeabilidad *nf* impermeability, imperviousness.
impermeabilizar [1f] *vt* to waterproof, make waterproof.
impermeable 1 *adj* impermeable, impervious (*a* to); waterproof. **2** *nm* raincoat, mackintosh, mac.
impersonal *adj* impersonal.
impersonalidad *nf* impersonality.
impersonalismo *nm* (*SAm*) disinterestedness.
impersonalmente *adv* impersonally.
impertérrito *adj* unafraid, unshaken, undaunted.
impertinencia *nf* (a) irrelevance. (b) fussiness, peevishness. (c) impertinence; intrusion.
impertinente 1 *adj* (a) irrelevant, not pertinent; uncalled for. (b) touchy, fussy; peevish. (c) impertinent; intrusive. **2 —s** *nmpl* lorgnette.
impertinentemente *adv* (a) irrelevantly. (b) impertinently.
imperturbable *adj* imperturbable; unruffled, unflappable; impassive.
imperturbablemente *adv* imperturbably; impassively.
imperturbado *adj* unperturbed.
impétigo *nm* impetigo.
impetrar [1a] *vt* to beg for, beseech.
ímpetu *nm* (a) impetus, impulse; momentum. (b) rush, onrush. (c) haste; violence; impetuosity.
impetuosamente *adv* impetuously, impulsively; violently; hastily.
impetuosidad *nf* impetuousness, impulsiveness; violence; haste, hastiness.
impetuoso *adj* *person* impetuous, impulsive; headstrong; *torrent etc* rushing, violent; *act* hasty, impetuous.
impiedad *nf* impiety, ungodliness; wickedness, cruelty; pitilessness, heartlessness.

impío adj impious, ungodly; wicked, cruel; pitiless, heartless.

implacable adj implacable, relentless, inexorable.

implacablemente adv implacably, relentlessly, inexorably.

implantación nf implantation; introduction.

implantar [1a] vt to implant; to introduce.

implementar [1a] (SAm) 1 vt to implement. 2 vi to help, give aid.

implemento nm (SAm) means; tool, implement; (Agr) implement.

implicación nf (a) contradiction (in terms). (b) involvement, implication, complicity. (c) (SAm) implication.

implicancia nf (SAm) implication.

implicar [1g] vt (a) to implicate, involve. (b) to imply; **esto no implica que . . .** this does not imply that . . . , this does not mean that . . .

implícitamente adv implicitly.

implícito adj implicit, implied.

imploración nf supplication, entreaty.

implorar [1a] vt to implore, beg.

implume adj featherless; unfledged.

impolítico adj (a) impolitic, imprudent, tactless, undiplomatic. (b) impolite.

impoluto adj unpolluted, pure.

imponderable 1 adj imponderable; inexpressible, unutterable. 2 —s nmpl imponderables.

imponencia nf (SAm) imposing character, impressiveness; stateliness, grandness.

imponente 1 adj (a) imposing, impressive; stately, grand. (b) terrific (fam), tremendous (fam), smashing (sl).
2 nmf (Comm, Fin) investor; depositor; lender.

imponer [2r] 1 vt (a) (general sense) to impose; (Eccl, Typ) to impose; obligation, penalty, silence etc to impose (a on); burden to lay, thrust (a upon); task to set; tax to put, impose (a, sobre on).
(b) obedience etc to exact (a from), demand (a from), enforce (a upon); respect to command (a from); fear etc to inspire (a in).
(c) to impute falsely (a to).
(d) to inform, instruct (en in).
(e) (Comm, Fin) to invest, deposit.
(f) (Mex) to accustom; **estoy impuesto a madrugar** I'm used to getting up early.
2 **imponerse** vr (a) — **un deber** to assume a duty, take on a duty.
(b) to assert oneself, get one's way; — **a** to dominate, impose one's authority on, exact obedience from.
(c) to prevail (a over); (of custom) to grow up; **se impondrá el buen sentido** good sense will prevail.
(d) to be necessary, to impose itself; **la conclusión se impone** the conclusion is inescapable, the conclusion imposes itself.
(e) — **de** to acquaint oneself with, inform oneself about.
(f) (Mex) to get accustomed (a + infin to + infin).

imponible adj (Fin) taxable, subject to tax; dutiable, subject to duty; **no** — free of tax, tax-free, tax-exempt (US).

impopular adj unpopular.

impopularidad nf unpopularity.

importación nf (a) importation, importing; **artículo de** — imported article; **comercio de** — import trade. (b) import; imports.

importador nm, **importadora** nf importer.

importancia nf importance; significance, weight; size, magnitude; **de cierta** — of some importance; **sin** — unimportant, insignificant, minor; **carecer de** — to be unimportant; **conceder** (or dar) **mucha** — **a** to attach great importance to, make much of, put the emphasis on; **no dar** — **a** to consider unimportant; to make light of; **darse** — to give oneself airs; **restar** — **a** to diminish the importance of; to make light of; **no tiene** — it's nothing, it's not important.

importante adj (a) important; significant, weighty, momentous; **lo** — **es . . . , lo más** — **es . . .** the main thing is . . . ; **poco** — unimportant.
(b) loss, quantity, sum considerable, sizeable.

importantizarse [1f] vr (Ven) to give oneself airs.

importar[1] [1a] vt (Comm) to import (a, en into; de from).

importar[2] [1a] 1 vt (a) (Fin) to amount to; to cost, be worth; **la cuenta importa 5 pesos** the bill amounts to 5 pesos; **el libro importa 5 dólares** the book costs 5 dollars.
(b) to involve, imply, carry with it.
2 vi to be important, be of consequence, matter;

— **a** to concern; **esto importa mucho** this is very important; **no importa** it doesn't matter; **¡no importa!** never mind!; **¿qué importa?** what does it matter?, what difference does it make?; who cares?; **no le importa** he doesn't care, it doesn't bother him; **(no) me importa un bledo** (or **higo** etc) I don't care two hoots (de about); **¿te importa prestármelo?** would you mind lending it to me?; **no le importa conducir todo el día** he doesn't mind driving all day; **"no importa precio"** (adverts) "cost no object"; **lo comprará a no importa que precio** he'll buy it at any price, he'll buy it regardless of the price; **iremos no importa el tiempo que haga** we'll go whatever the weather.

importe nm amount; value, cost; — **total** final total, grand total; **hasta el** — **de** up to the amount of; **el** — **de esta factura** the amount of this bill.

importunación nf importuning, pestering.

importunar [1a] vt to importune, bother, pester.

importunidad nf (a) importunity, pestering. (b) annoyance.

importuno adj (a) importunate, troublesome, annoying. (b) inopportune, ill-timed.

imposibilidad nf (a) impossibility. (b) **mi** — **para** + infin my inability to + infin.

imposibilitado adj (a) (Med) disabled, crippled; (Fin) helpless, without means.
(b) **estar** — **para** + infin, **verse** — **para** + infin to be unable to + infin, be prevented from + ger.

imposibilitar [1a] vt (a) to disable; to make unfit, incapacitate (para for).
(b) to make impossible, preclude, prevent; **esto me imposibilita hacerlo** this makes it impossible for me to do it, this prevents me from doing it.

imposible 1 adj (a) impossible; intolerable, unbearable; **es** — it's impossible, it's out of the question; **es** — **de toda imposibilidad** it's utterly impossible; **es** — **de predecir** it's impossible to forecast.
(b) person difficult, awkward, impossible.
(c) (SAm) slovenly, dirty, repulsive.
2 nm the impossible; impossible thing; **hacer los** —**s** to do one's utmost (para + infin to + infin).

imposición nf (a) (general sense) imposition.
(b) (Comm, Fin) tax, impost, imposition.
(c) (Typ) imposition, make-up.
(d) (Fin) deposit; **efectuar una** — to make a deposit; to deposit money.
(e) (Eccl) — **de manos** laying-on of hands.

impositiva nf (SAm) tax office.

impositivo adj (a) (SAm) tax (attr); **sistema** — taxation, tax system. (b) (Arg) authoritative, domineering; imperative.

impositor nm (Fin) depositor.

impostor nm, **impostora** nf (a) impostor, fraud. (b) slanderer.

impostura nf (a) imposture, fraud; sham. (b) aspersion, slur, slander.

impotable adj undrinkable.

impotencia nf (a) impotence, powerlessness, helplessness. (b) (Med) impotence.

impotente (a) impotent, powerless, helpless. (b) (Med) impotent.

impracticabilidad nf impracticability.

impracticable adj (a) impracticable, unworkable. (b) road impassable, unusable.

imprecación nf imprecation, curse.

imprecar [1g] vt to curse.

imprecisión nf lack of precision, vagueness.

impreciso adj imprecise, vague.

impredecible adj (CAm, Mex, PR), **impredictible** adj unpredictable.

impregnación nf impregnation.

impregnar [1a] vt to impregnate (de with); to saturate (de with); (fig) to pervade.

impremeditado adj unpremeditated.

imprenta nf (a) printing, art of printing. (b) press, printing house, printing office. (c) print, letterpress. (d) printed matter.

imprentar [1a] vt (a) (Chi: Sew) to put a permanent crease into. (b) (SAm) to mark.

imprescindible adj essential, indispensable; **cosas** —**s** essential things, things one cannot do without; **es** — **que . . .** it is essential that . . . , it is imperative that . . .

impresentable adj unpresentable.

impresión nf (a) impression; imprint; — **dactilar**, — **digital** fingerprint.
(b) (Typ) printing; print; edition, impression, issue; **quinta** — fifth impression; **una** — **de 5.000 ejemplares** an edition of 5,000 copies; — **en color(es)** colour printing.
(c) (Phot) print.

(d) (*fig*) impression; **cambiar —es** to exchange impressions, compare notes; **da la — de +** *infin* it gives the impression of + *ger*; **formarse una — de** to get an idea of; **hacer buena —** to make a good impression, impress; **no me hizo buena —** I was not impressed (with it); **¿qué — te produjo?** how did it impress you?, what impression did it make on you?; **tener la — de que . . .** to have the impression that . . .

impresionable *adj* impressionable.

impresionado *adj* (a) impressed. (b) (*Phot*) exposed; **excesivamente —** overexposed.

impresionante *adj* impressive; striking; moving, affecting.

impresionar [1a] **1** *vt* (a) *record* to cut; (*Phot*) to expose; **película sin —** unexposed film.
(b) (*fig*) to impress, strike; to move, affect; **me impresionó mucho** it greatly impressed me; **no se deja fácilmente —** he is not easily impressed.
2 *vi* to impress, make an impression; **lo hace sólo para —** he just does it to impress.
3 impresionarse *vr* to be impressed; to be moved, be affected.

impresionismo *nm* impressionism.

impresionista 1 *adj* impressionist(ic). **2** *nm* impressionist.

impreso 1 *adj* printed. **2** *nm* (a) printed paper, printed book (*etc*). (b) **— de solicitud** application form. (c) **—s** printed matter.

impresor *nm* printer.

imprevisible *adj* unforeseeable; *person* unpredictable.

imprevisión *nf* improvidence; lack of foresight; thoughtlessness.

imprevisor *adj* improvident; lacking foresight; thoughtless, happy-go-lucky.

imprevisto 1 *adj* unforeseen, unexpected. **2 —s** *nmpl* incidentals, unforeseen expenses.

imprimar [1a] *vt* (*Art*) to prime.

imprimátur *nm* imprimatur.

imprimible *adj* printable.

imprimir [3a; *ptp* **impreso**] *vt* (a) to imprint, impress, stamp (*a, en* on; *also fig*). (b) (*Typ*) to print.

improbabilidad *nf* improbability, unlikelihood.

improbable *adj* improbable, unlikely.

improbidad *nf* dishonesty.

improbo *adj* (a) dishonest, corrupt. (b) *task* arduous, thankless, tough; *effort etc* tremendous, awful, strenuous.

improcedencia *nf* (a) wrongness; inappropriateness, inapplicability. (b) (*Law*) inadmissibility.

improcedente *adj* (a) wrong, not right; inappropriate, inapplicable. (b) (*Law*) unfounded, inadmissible.

improductivo *adj* unproductive.

impronta *nf* stamp, impress, impression; (*fig*) stamp, mark.

impronunciable *adj* unpronounceable.

improperio *nm* insult, taunt.

impropiamente *adv* improperly; inappropriately, unsuitably.

impropicio *adj* inauspicious, unpropitious.

impropiedad *nf* (a) inappropriateness, unsuitability. (b) impropriety, infelicity (of language).

impropio *adj* improper (*also Math, Gram*); inappropriate, unsuitable; **— de** inappropriate for; unbecoming to; foreign to.

impróvidamente *adv* improvidently.

impróvido *adj* improvident.

improvisación *nf* improvisation; (*Mus*) extemporization, impromptu.

improvisado *adj* improvised; makeshift; (*Mus etc*) extempore, impromptu.

improvisamente *adv* unexpectedly, suddenly.

improvisar [1a] *vi* to improvise; (*Mus etc*) to extemporize.

improviso *adj* (a) unexpected, unforeseen. (b) **al —, de —** unexpectedly, suddenly; on the spur of the moment; **hablar de —** to speak extempore, speak unprepared; **tocar de —** to play impromptu.

improvisto *adj* unexpected, unforeseen; **de —** unexpectedly, suddenly.

imprudencia *nf* imprudence; rashness; indiscretion; carelessness.

imprudente *adj* unwise; imprudent; rash; indiscreet; *driver etc* rash, careless; ill-judged.

imprudentemente *adv* unwisely, imprudently; rashly; carelessly.

impublicable *adj* unprintable.

impudencia *nf* shamelessness, brazenness.

impudente *adj* shameless, brazen.

impúdicamente *adv* immodestly, shamelessly; lewdly; lecherously.

impudicia *nf* immodesty, shamelessness; lewdness; lechery.

impúdico *adj* immodest, shameless; lewd; lecherous.

impudor *nm* = **impudicia**.

impuesto 1 *ptp of* **imponer**; **estar — de, quedar — de** to be informed about; **estar — en** to be well versed in. **2** *nm* tax; duty, levy (*sobre* on); **—s** taxes, (*collectively, as system*) taxation; **sujeto a —** taxable, dutiable; **— sobre apuestas** betting tax; **— sobre los bienes heredados, — sobre herencias, — sobre las sucesiones** estate duty; **— sobre espectáculos** entertainments tax; **— de plusvalía** capital gains tax; **— sobre la propiedad** property tax; **— sobre la renta** income tax; **— del timbre** stamp duty; **— de venta** sales tax, purchase tax.

impugnar [1a] *vt* to oppose, contest, challenge; *theory etc* to impugn, refute.

impulsador *nm* (*Aer*) booster.

impulsar [1a] = **impeler**.

impulsión *nf* (a) impulsion; (*Mech*) propulsion, drive; **— por correa** belt drive; **— por reacción** jet propulsion. (b) (*fig*) impulse.

impulsividad *nf* impulsiveness.

impulsivo *adj* impulsive.

impulso *nm* (a) impulse; (*Mech*) drive, thrust; impetus, momentum.
(b) (*fig*) impulse; stimulus, urge; **los —s del corazón** the promptings of the heart; **a —s del miedo** driven on by fear; **no resisto al — de decir que . . .** I can't resist saying that . . .

impulsor 1 *adj* drive (*attr*), driving. **2** *nm* drive.

impune *adj* unpunished.

impunemente *adv* with impunity.

impunidad *nf* impunity.

impuntual *adj* unpunctual.

impuntualidad *nf* unpunctuality.

impureza *nf* (a) impurity. (b) (*fig*) unchastity, lewdness.

impurificar [1g] *vt* (a) to adulterate, make impure. (b) (*fig*) to corrupt, defile.

impuro *adj* (a) impure. (b) (*fig*) impure, unchaste, lewd.

imputable *adj*: **fracasos que son —s** a failures which can be attributed to, failures which are attributable to.

imputación *nf* imputation.

imputar [1a] *vt*: **— a** to impute to, attribute to.

—in, —ina *n and adj etc suffix* (*regional variation*): see **—ito**.

inabordable *adj* unapproachable.

inacabable *adj* endless, interminable.

inacabablemente *adv* endlessly, interminably.

inacabado *adj* unfinished.

inaccesibilidad *nf* inaccessibility.

inaccesible *adj* inaccessible.

inacción *nf* inaction; inactivity, idleness; drift.

inacentuado *adj* unaccented, unstressed.

inaceptable *adj* unacceptable.

inactividad *nf* inactivity; laziness, idleness; (*Comm, Fin*) dullness.

inactivo *adj* inactive; lazy, idle; (*Comm, Fin*) dull.

inactual *adj* (*SAm*) lacking present validity, no longer applicable; old-fashioned, out-of-date.

inadaptable *adj* unadaptable.

inadaptación *nf* maladjustment; failure of adjustment, failure to adjust (*a* to).

inadaptado 1 *adj* maladjusted, who fails to adjust (*a* to). **2** *nm*, **inadaptada** *nf* misfit; person who fails to adjust.

inadecuación *nf* inadequacy; unsuitability, inappropriateness.

inadecuado *adj* inadequate; unsuitable, inappropriate.

inadmisibilidad *nf* inadmissibility.

inadmisible *adj* inadmissible.

inadvertencia *nf* (a) inadvertence; **por —** inadvertently, through inadvertence. (b) (*una —*) oversight, slip.

inadvertidamente *adv* inadvertently.

inadvertido *adj* (a) *person* unobservant, inattentive; careless. (b) unnoticed, unobserved; **pasar —** to escape notice, slip by.

inafectado *adj* unaffected.

inagotable *adj* inexhaustible.

inaguantable *adj* intolerable, unbearable.

inaguantablemente *adv* intolerably, unbearably.

inajenable *adj* inalienable; not transferable.

inalámbrico *adj* wireless.

inalcanzable *adj* unattainable.

inalienable *adj* inalienable; not transferable.

inalterabilidad *nf* inalterability, unchangingness; immutability.

inalterable adj unalterable, unchanging; immutable; colour fast; gloss etc permanent.
inalterado adj unchanged, unaltered.
inamistoso adj (SAm) unfriendly.
inamovible adj fixed, immovable; undetachable.
inanición nf starvation, (Med) inanition; **morir de** — to die of starvation.
inanidad nf inanity.
inanimado adj inanimate.
inánime adj lifeless.
inapagable adj unquenchable; inextinguishable.
inapeable adj (a) incomprehensible. (b) obstinate, stubborn.
inapelable adj (Law) unappealable; (fig) inevitable.
inapercibido adj unperceived.
inapetencia nf lack of appetite, loss of appetite.
inaplazable adj which cannot be postponed.
inaplicable adj inapplicable, not applicable.
inaplicado adj slack, lazy.
inapreciable nf invaluable, inestimable.
inaprehensible adj indefinite, hard to pin down.
inapto adj unsuited (para to).
inarmónico adj unharmonious, unmusical.
inarrugable adj crease-resisting, which does not crease.
inarticulado adj inarticulate.
inasequible adj unattainable, out of reach; un-obtainable.
inasistencia nf absence.
inastillable adj glass unsplinterable, non-splinter.
inatacable adj unassailable.
inatención nf inattention.
inatento adj inattentive.
inaudible adj inaudible.
inaudito adj unheard-of; unprecedented; outrageous.
inauguración nf inauguration; opening; unveiling; — **privada** (Art) private view.
inaugural adj inaugural; opening; voyage etc maiden.
inaugurar [1a] vt to inaugurate; bridge, canal, exhibition etc to open (formally); statue etc to unveil.
inca nmf Inca.
incachable adj (SAm) useless.
incaico adj Inca.
incalculable adj incalculable.
incalificable adj indescribable, unspeakable.
incanato nm (Per) Inca period; reign of an Inca.
incandescencia nf incandescence; white heat; glow.
incandescente adj incandescent; white hot; glowing.
incansable adj tireless, untiring, unflagging.
incansablemente adv tirelessly, untiringly.
incapacidad nf incapacity; unfitness (para por); inadequacy, incompetence; **su** — **para** + infin his inability to + infin.
incapacitado adj incapacitated; unfitted (para for).
incapacitar [1a] vt to incapacitate, render unfit, handicap (para for); to disqualify (para for).
incapaz adj (a) incapable (de of); unfit; inadequate, incompetent; (Law) incompetent; — **de** + infin unable to + infin. (b) (Guat, Mex) child trying, difficult.
incario nm (Bol, Ec, Per) = **incanato**.
incasable adj unmarriageable.
incásico adj (SAm) Inca.
incautación nf seizure, confiscation.
incautamente adv unwarily, incautiously.
incautarse [1a] vr: — **de** to seize, confiscate, impound; to take possession of.
incauto adj unwary, incautious.
incendiar [1b] 1 vt to set on fire, set fire to, set alight; (fig) to kindle, inflame.
2 **incendiarse** vr to catch fire.
incendiario 1 adj (a) incendiary.
(b) (fig) inflammatory.
2 nm, **incendiara** nf fire-raiser, pyromaniac; incendiary; — **de la guerra** warmonger.
incendio nm fire; conflagration; — **intencionado**, — **malicioso**, — **premeditado** arson, fire-raising; **echar** (or **hablar**) —**s de uno** (Arg, Chi, Per) to speak ill of someone, curse someone; to attribute evil deeds to someone.
incensar [1k] vt (Eccl) to cense, incense; (fig) to flatter.
incensario nm censer.
incentivo nm incentive.
incertidumbre nf uncertainty, doubt.
incesable adj, **incesante** adj incessant, unceasing.
incesantemente adv incessantly, unceasingly.
incesto nm incest.
incestuoso adj incestuous.
incidencia nf (a) (Math etc) incidence. (b) incident.
incidental adj incidental.
incidente 1 adj incidental. 2 nm incident.

incidentemente adv incidentally.
incidir [3a] 1 vt (Med) to incise.
2 vi: — **en** to fall upon; to influence, affect, impinge on; — **en un error** to fall into error; **el impuesto incide más en ellos** the tax falls most heavily on them, the tax affects them worst; **la familia ha incidido fuertemente en la historia** the family has influenced history a lot, the family has made itself strongly felt in history.
incienso nm (Eccl) incense; (Bib) frankincense; (fig) flattery.
inciertamente adv uncertainly.
incierto adj uncertain, doubtful; inconstant.
incineración nf incineration; — **de cadáveres** cremation.
incinerador nm incinerator.
incinerar [1a] vt to incinerate, burn; corpse to cremate.
incipiente adj incipient.
incircunciso adj uncircumcised.
incisión nf incision.
incisivo 1 adj sharp, cutting; (fig) incisive. 2 nm incisor.
inciso nm (Gram) clause, sentence; comma.
incitación nf incitement; provocation.
incitante adj provoking, provocative, inviting.
incitar [1a] vt to incite, rouse, spur on; — **a uno a hacer algo** to urge someone to do something; — **a uno contra otro** to incite someone against another person.
incivil adj uncivil, rude.
incivilidad nf incivility, rudeness; **una** — an incivility, a piece of rudeness.
incivilizado adj uncivilized.
inclasificable adj unclassifiable, nondescript.
inclemencia nf harshness, severity, inclemency; **la** — **del tiempo** the inclemency of the weather; **dejar algo a la** — to leave something exposed to wind and weather.
inclemente adj harsh, severe, inclement.
inclinación nf (a) inclination; slope, incline; slant, pitch, tilt; (of body) stoop; — **lateral** (Aer) bank; **a una** — **de 45 grados** at an inclination of 45 degrees.
(b) bow; (of head) nod.
(c) (fig) inclination, leaning, propensity; **de malas** —**es** evilly inclined.
inclinado adj (a) inclined, sloping, leaning, slanting; plane inclined.
(b) (esp SAm: fig) **estar** — **a** + infin to be inclined to + infin.
inclinar [1a] 1 vt (a) to incline; to slope, slant, tilt; head to incline, bend, nod; to bow.
(b) (fig) — **a uno a hacer algo** to induce someone to do something; to persuade someone to do something.
2 vi: — **a uno** to take after someone, resemble someone.
3 **inclinarse** vr (a) to incline; to slope, slant, tilt, be inclined.
(b) (person) to stoop, bend; to bow; — **ante** (fig) to bow to, bow down before.
(c) — **a uno** to take after someone, resemble someone.
(d) — **a hacer algo** to be inclined to do something, tend to do something; **me inclino a decir que** . . . I am inclined to say that . . .
ínclito adj illustrious, renowned.
incluir [3g] vt to include; to comprise, contain; to incorporate; (in letter) to enclose; **todo incluido** (Comm) inclusive terms; all found, all-in.
inclusa nf foundling hospital.
inclusero nm, **inclusera** nf foundling.
inclusión nf inclusion; **con** — **de** including.
inclusivamente adv inclusive, inclusively.
inclusive 1 adv inclusive, inclusively. 2 prep including.
inclusivo adj inclusive.
incluso 1 adj included; enclosed.
2 adv (a) including.
(b) even, actually; — **la pegó** he even hit her, he actually hit her.
incoar [1a] vt to start, initiate.
incobrable adj irrecoverable; debt bad.
incógnita nf (Math) unknown quantity; (fig) unknown quantity; unknown factor; hidden motive.
incógnito 1 adj unknown. 2 nm incognito; **viajar de** — to travel incognito.
incoherencia nf incoherence; disconnectedness.
incoherente adj incoherent; disconnected.
incoloro adj colourless.
incólume adj safe; unhurt, unharmed; **salir** — **del accidente** to emerge unharmed from the accident.

incombustible *adj* incombustible, fire-resisting; fireproof.

incomible *adj* uneatable, inedible.

incómodamente *adv* inconveniently; uncomfortably.

incomodar [1a] **1** *vt* to inconvenience, trouble, put out.
　2 incomodarse *vr* **(a)** to put oneself out, take trouble; **¡no se incomode!** don't bother!, don't trouble yourself!
　　(b) to get cross, get annoyed (*con* with); **— con** to fall out with; **estar incomodado con** to be cross with; to be at odds with.

incomodidad *nf* **(a)** inconvenience; discomfort, uncomfortableness. **(b)** annoyance, annoying thing, vexation.

incomodo *nm* (*SAm*) = **incomodidad (b)**.

incómodo 1 *adj* inconvenient; uncomfortable; tiresome, annoying; **un bulto** — an awkward package, a cumbersome package; **una casa incómoda** an inconvenient house; **sentirse** — to feel uncomfortable, feel ill-at-ease; **estar — con uno** (*Arg, Chi*) to be fed up with someone, be cross with someone.
　2 *nm* = **incomodidad (b)**.

incomparable *adj* incomparable.

incomparablemente *adv* incomparably.

incomparecimiento *nm*: **pleito perdido por —** suit lost by default, undefended suit.

incompasivo *adj* unsympathetic; pitiless.

incompatibilidad *nf* incompatibility.

incompatible *adj* incompatible.

incompetencia *nf* incompetence.

incompetente *adj* incompetent.

incompletamente *adv* incompletely.

incompleto *adj* incomplete, unfinished.

incomprendido 1 *adj* *person* misunderstood; not appreciated.
　2 *nm,* **incomprendida** *nf* misunderstood person; person who is not appreciated.

incomprensibilidad *nf* incomprehensibility.

incomprensible *adj* incomprehensible.

incomprensión *nf* incomprehension, lack of understanding; lack of appreciation.

incomunicación *nf* isolation; lack of communication; (*Law*) solitary confinement.

incomunicado *adj* isolated, cut off; (*Law*) in solitary confinement, incommunicado.

incomunicar [1g] **1** *vt* to cut off the communications of, leave without communications; to cut off, isolate; (*Law*) to put into solitary confinement.
　2 incomunicarse *vr* to isolate oneself, withdraw from society.

inconcebible *adj* inconceivable, unthinkable.

inconcebiblemente *adv* inconceivably.

inconciliable *adj* irreconcilable.

inconcluso *adj* unfinished, incomplete.

inconcluyente *adj* inconclusive.

inconcuso *adj* indisputable, undeniable.

incondicional 1 *adj* **(a)** unconditional; *faith* implicit, complete, unquestioning; *support* wholehearted; *assertion* unqualified; *friend, supporter etc* staunch, stalwart.
　　(b) (*SAm*) servile, fawning.
　2 *nmf* **(a)** stalwart, staunch supporter (*etc*); (*pej*) diehard, hardliner.
　　(b) (*SAm*) toady, yes man (*sl*).

incondicionalismo *nm* (*SAm*) toadyism, servility.

incondicionalmente *adv* unconditionally, unreservedly; implicitly, unquestioningly; wholeheartedly; staunchly.

inconexión *nf* disconnectedness; incongruity.

inconexo *adj* unconnected; disconnected, disjointed; unrelated; incongruous.

inconfesable *adj* which cannot be told (*or* confessed); shameful, disgraceful.

inconfeso *adj* unconfessed.

inconformismo *nm* nonconformism.

inconformista 1 *adj* nonconformist. **2** *nmf* nonconformist.

inconfundible *adj* unmistakable.

incongruencia *nf* incongruity.

incongruente *adj,* **incongruo** *adj* incongruous.

inconmensurable *adj* immeasurable, vast; incommensurate.

inconmovible *adj* unshakeable.

inconmutable *adj* immutable.

inconocible *adj* unknowable; **lo —** the unknowable.

inconquistable *adj* unconquerable; (*fig*) inconquerable, unyielding.

insconsciencia *nf* **(a)** (*Med*) unconsciousness. **(b)** (*fig*) unawareness. **(c)** (*fig*) thoughtlessness; recklessness.

inconsciente *adj* **(a)** (*Med*) unconscious; **lo —** the unconscious; **le encontraron —** they found him unconscious.
　　(b) (*fig*) unconscious, unaware (*de* of); oblivious (*de* to); unwitting.
　　(c) (*fig*) thoughtless, reckless, carefree; **es más — que malo** he's thoughtless rather than wicked; **son gente —** they're thoughtless people.

inconscientemente *adv* **(a)** unconsciously; unawares, unwittingly. **(b)** thoughtlessly; recklessly; in a carefree manner.

inconsecuencia *nf* inconsistency; inconsequence.

inconsecuente *adj* inconsistent; inconsequent, inconsequential.

inconsideración *nf* inconsiderateness, thoughtlessness; rashness, haste.

inconsideradamente *adv* inconsiderately, thoughtlessly; rashly, hastily.

inconsiderado *adj* inconsiderate, thoughtless; rash, hasty.

inconsistencia *nf* lack of firmness; unevenness; weakness; looseness; flimsiness.

inconsistente *adj* lacking firmness, not solid; uneven; *argument* weak; *earth etc* loose; *cloth* flimsy, thin.

inconsolable *adj* inconsolable.

inconstancia *nf* inconstancy; unsteadiness; fickleness; inconsistency.

inconstante *adj* inconstant, changeable; unsteady; fickle; inconsistent.

inconstantemente *adv* inconstantly; unsteadily; in a fickle way; inconsistently.

inconstitucional *adj* unconstitutional.

inconstitucionalmente *adv* unconstitutionally.

incontable *adj* countless, innumerable.

incontenible *adj* uncontrollable, unstoppable.

incontestable *adj* unanswerable; undeniable, unchallengeable, indisputable.

incontestablemente *adv* unanswerably; undeniably, indisputably.

incontestado *adj* unanswered; unchallenged, unquestioned.

incontinencia *nf* incontinence (*also Med*).

incontinente 1 *adj* incontinent (*also Med*). **2** *adv* = **incontinenti**.

incontinenti *adv* at once, instantly, forthwith.

incontrastable *adj* *difficulty* insuperable; *argument* unanswerable; *person* unshakeable, unyielding.

incontrolable *adj* uncontrollable.

incontrolado *adj* uncontrolled.

incontrovertible *adj* incontrovertible.

inconveniencia *nf* **(a)** unsuitability, inappropriateness; inadvisability; inconvenience. **(b)** impoliteness. **(c)** silly remark, tactless remark.

inconveniente 1 *adj* **(a)** unsuitable, inappropriate; inadvisable; inconvenient.
　　(b) impolite.
　2 *nm* obstacle, difficulty; disadvantage, drawback; objection; **el — es que . . .** the trouble is that . . ., the difficulty is that . . .; **no hay — en + *infin*, no hay — para + *infin*** there is no objection to + *ger*; **poner un —** to raise an objection; **no tengo —** I have no objection, I don't mind; **¿tienes algún — en + *infin*?** do you mind + *ger*?; **no veo —** I see no objection, I see no difficulty.

inconvertibilidad *nf* inconvertibility.

inconvertible *adj* inconvertible.

incordiar [1b] *vt* (*fam*) to bother, annoy; **¡déjate de —!** stop bothering me; **¡no incordies!** stop it!, behave yourself!

incordio *nm* (*fam*) nuisance.

incorporación *nf* incorporation, embodiment.

incorporado *adj* (*Tech*) built-in; **con antena incorporada** with built-in aerial.

incorporal *adj* = **incorpóreo**.

incorporar [1a] **1** *vt* **(a)** to incorporate (*a, con, en* into, in); to embody (*a, con, en* in); to mix.
　　(b) **— a uno** to make someone sit up (in bed), help someone to sit up.
　2 incorporarse *vr* **(a)** to sit up, raise oneself; **— en la cama** to sit up in bed.
　　(b) **— a** *regiment, society etc* to join.

incorpóreo *adj* incorporeal, bodiless; intangible.

incorrección *nf* **(a)** incorrectness, inaccuracy.
　　(b) irregularity.
　　(c) discourtesy; piece of bad manners, gaffe; impropriety; **cometer una —** to commit a faux pas.

incorrectamente *adv* **(a)** incorrectly, inaccurately, wrongly. **(b)** discourteously; improperly.

incorrecto *adj* **(a)** incorrect, inaccurate, wrong.
　　(b) *features* irregular, odd.
　　(c) *conduct* discourteous, bad-mannered; improper; **ser — con una** to take liberties with someone.

incorregible adj incorrigible.
incorruptible adj incorruptible.
incorrupto adj (a) body uncorrupted. (b) (fig) pure, chaste, undefiled.
incredibilidad nf incredibility.
incredulidad nf incredulity, unbelief.
incrédulo 1 adj incredulous, unbelieving, sceptical. **2** nm, **incrédula** nf unbeliever, sceptic.
increíble adj incredible, unbelievable; **es — que . . .** it is unbelievable that . . .
increíblemente adv incredibly, unbelievably.
incremento nm increment; increase, rise, addition; **— de temperatura** rise in temperature; **tomar —** to increase.
increpación nf reprimand, rebuke.
increpar [1a] vt to reprimand, rebuke.
incriminación nf accusation; incrimination.
incriminar [1a] vt (a) to accuse; to incriminate. (b) fault etc to magnify. (c) goods etc to obtain illegally.
incruento adj bloodless.
incrúspido adj (Col, Mex, Nic) awkward, clumsy.
incrustación nf (a) incrustation; (fig) grafting. (b) (Art) inlay, inlaid work.
incrustar [1a] vt to incrust (de with); to inlay (de with); (fig) to graft (en on to), introduce (en into); **una espada incrustada de joyas** a sword encrusted with jewels; **la palabra se ha incrustado en nuestro idioma** the word has been grafted on to our language.
incubación nf incubation.
incubadora nf incubator.
incubar [1a] vt to incubate; to hatch (also fig).
íncubo nm incubus; nightmare.
incuestionable adj unquestionable, unchallengeable.
incuestionablemente adv unquestionably.
inculcar [1g] **1** vt to instil, inculcate (en in, into). **2 inculcarse** vr to be obstinate.
inculpable adj blameless, guiltless.
inculpación nf charge, accusation.
inculpar [1a] vt to charge (de with), accuse (de of); to blame (de for); **los crímenes que se le inculpan** the crimes with which he is charged.
incultamente adv in an uncultured way; uncouthly.
incultivable adj uncultivable, unworkable.
inculto adj (a) (Agr) uncultivated, unworked, untilled; **dejar un terreno —** to leave land uncultivated. (b) (fig) uncultured; uncivilized; uncouth.
incultura nf lack of culture; uncouthness.
incumbencia nf obligation, duty, concern; **no es de mi —** it is not my job, it is not my concern.
incumbir [3a] vi: **— a** to be incumbent upon; **no me incumbe a mí** it's not my job, it is no concern of mine; **le incumbe hacerlo** it is his business to do it; it behoves him to do it.
incumplido adj unfulfilled.
incumplimiento nm non-fulfilment; **— de contrato** breach of contract; **— de promesa matrimonial** breach of promise; **por —** by default.
incunable nm incunable, incunabulum; **—s** incunabula.
incurable 1 adj (Med) incurable; (fig) hopeless, irremediable. **2** nmf incurable.
incuria nf negligence; carelessness, shiftlessness; **por —** through negligence.
incurrir [3a] vi: **— en error** to fall into; crime etc to commit; debt, hatred, wrath etc to incur; disaster etc to bring on oneself, become a victim of.
incursión nf raid, incursion, attack.
indagación nf investigation, inquiry.
indagador nm, **indagadora** nf investigator (de into, of), inquirer (de into).
indagar [1h] vt to investigate, inquire into; to find out, ascertain.
indebidamente adv unduly; improperly; illegally, wrongfully.
indebido adj undue; improper; illegal, wrongful.
indecencia nf (a) indecency; obscenity. (b) filth; wretchedness. (c) indecent act.
indecente adj (a) indecent, improper; obscene. (b) filthy; miserable, wretched; low, mean; **algún empleadillo —** some wretched clerk; **un cuchitril —** a miserable pigsty of a place; **la calle está — de lodo** the street is terribly muddy; **es una persona —** he's a low sort, he's a mean character.
indecentemente adv (a) indecently, obscenely. (b) miserably, wretchedly.
indecible adj unspeakable, unutterable; indescribable; **sufrir lo —** to suffer terribly.
indeciblemente adv unspeakably, unutterably; indescribably.
indecisión nf indecision, hesitation

indeciso adj (a) undecided; hesitant, irresolute; vague. (b) result etc indecisive.
indeclinable adj (a) (Gram) indeclinable. (b) unavoidable.
indecoro nm unseemliness, indecorum; indelicacy.
indecorosamente adv indecorously, unbecomingly; indelicately.
indecoroso adj unseemly, indecorous, unbecoming; indelicate.
indefectible adj unfailing, infallible.
indefectiblemente adv unfailingly, infallibly.
indefendible adj indefensible.
indefenso adj defenceless.
indefinible adj indefinable; inexpressible.
indefinidamente adv indefinitely.
indefinido adj indefinite; undefined, vague; (Gram) indefinite; **por tiempo —** for an indefinite time, indefinitely.
indeleble adj indelible.
indemne adj undamaged; person unharmed, unhurt.
indemnidad nf indemnity.
indemnizable adj that can be indemnified, recoverable.
indemnización nf (a) (act) indemnification. (b) (payment) indemnity, compensation; **—es** (eg 1918) reparations; **— de despido** severance pay; **pagó un dólar de —** he paid a dollar in damages (or in compensation).
indemnizar [1f] vt to indemnify (de against, for), compensate (de for).
independencia nf independence.
independiente 1 adj independent; self-sufficient, self-contained; **hacerse —** to become independent. **2** nmf independent.
independientemente adv independently.
independizar [1f] **1** vt to emancipate, free; to make independent, grant independence to. **2 independizarse** vr to become free, become independent (de of).
indescifrable adj undecipherable, indecipherable; mystery impenetrable.
indescriptible adj indescribable.
indescriptiblemente adv indescribably.
indeseable 1 adj undesirable. **2** nmf undesirable (person); **es un —** he's an unsavoury sort, he's beyond the pale.
indeshilachable adj non-fraying.
indesmallable adj stocking etc ladderproof, which does not ladder, runproof.
indestructible adj indestructible.
indeterminado adj (a) indeterminate; inconclusive; (Gram) indefinite. (b) person irresolute.
India f: **la —** India; **las —s** the Indies; **—s Occidentales** West Indies; **—s Orientales** East Indies.
indiada nf (a) (SAm) group of Indians, crowd of Indians; (Arg: pej) collection of ignorant people, mob. (b) (SAm) typically Indian thing to do (or say etc).
indiana nf printed calico.
indiano 1 adj (Spanish-)American. **2** nm Spaniard returning rich from America, equivalent to nabob; **— de hilo negro** miser.
indicación nf (a) indication, sign; (Med) sign, symptom. (b) hint, suggestion; **por — de** at the suggestion of; **aprovechó la —** he took the hint; **seguiré sus —es** I will follow your suggestion, I will do what you say. (c) piece of information; (of dial, thermometer etc) reading. (d) **—es** (Comm etc) instructions, directions; **—es para el empleo** instructions for use.
indicado adj right, suitable, proper; obvious; likely; **el sitio más —** the most obvious place; **una elección indicada** an obvious choice; **es el más — para el puesto** he is the most suitable man for the job, he is the best man for the job; **tú eres el menos — para hacerlo** you're the last person to do it, you're the least suitable person to do it.
indicador nm indicator; gauge, meter, dial; hand, pointer; roadsign; **— de dirección** (Aut) indicator, trafficator; **— de velocidades** speedometer.
indicar [1g] vt (a) (Tech etc) to indicate, show; to register, record; (of thermometer etc) to read. (b) to indicate, point out, point to; to show; to suggest, hint, intimate; **me indicó que . . .** he told me that . . ., he suggested to me that . . .
indicativo 1 adj indicative (also Gram). **2** nm (a) (Gram) indicative. (b) (Radio) call sign; **— de nacionalidad** (Aut) national identification plate.

índice nm (a) (Typ etc) index; (library) catalogue; — **de materias** table of contents.
   (b) index; ratio, rate; — **de compresión** (Mech) compression ratio; — **del coste de (la) vida** cost-of-living index; — **expurgatorio** (Eccl) Index; — **de mortalidad** death rate; — **de natalidad** birth rate; — **de vida** expectation of life, life expectancy. (c) (Tech) pointer, needle, hand; (of clock) hand. (d) (Anat) index finger, forefinger. (e) (Math) index.

indiciario adj: **prueba indiciaria** circumstantial proof.

indicio nm (a) indication, sign; token; piece of evidence, clue (de to); trace, vestige; **es — de** it is an indication of, it is a sign of; **no hay el menor — de él** there isn't the faintest sign of him, there isn't the least trace of him; **dar —s de sorpresa** to show surprise, evince surprise.
   (b) **—s** (Law) evidence; **—s vehementes** circumstantial evidence.

indiferencia nf indifference; apathy, lack of interest.

indiferente adj (a) indifferent (a to), unconcerned (a about); apathetic, uninterested.
   (b) indifferent, immaterial; **me es —** it is immaterial to me, it makes no difference to me.

indiferentemente adv indifferently.

indiferentismo nm indifference; apathy; (Rel) scepticism, unbelief.

indígena 1 adj indigenous (de to), native (de to); (SAm) Indian. **2** nmf native; (SAm) Indian.

indigencia nf poverty, destitution, indigence.

indigenismo nm word (or phrase etc) borrowed from a native language.

indigente 1 adj destitute, poverty-stricken, indigent. **2** nmf poor person.

indigerible adj undigestible.

indigestar [1a] **1** vt to cause indigestion to.
   2 indigestarse vr (a) (person) to get indigestion, have indigestion.
   (b) (food) to cause indigestion, be indigestible; **esa carne se me indigestó** that meat gave me indigestion, I couldn't digest that meat.
   (c) (fig) to be insufferable; **se me indigesta ese tío** I can't stand that fellow.
   (d) (SAm) to get worried, get alarmed.

indigestible adj indigestible.

indigestión nf indigestion.

indigesto adj undigested; indigestible, hard to digest; (fig) muddled, turgid, badly thought-out.

indignación nf indignation, anger; **descargar la — sobre** to vent one's spleen on, take out one's anger on.

indignado adj indignant, angry (con, contra with; por at, about).

indignamente adv (a) unworthily. (b) contemptibly, meanly.

indignante adj outrageous, infuriating, unworthy, humiliating.

indignar [1a] **1** vt to anger, make indignant; to provoke, stir up.
   2 indignarse vr to get angry, get indignant; — **con uno** to get indignant with someone; — **por algo** to get indignant about something, get angry about something.

indignidad nf (a) unworthiness. (b) unworthy act; indignity, insult; **sufrir la — de** + infin to suffer the indignity of + ger.

indigno adj (a) unworthy (de of). (b) contemptible, mean, low.

indigo nm indigo.

indino adj (a) (CAm, Cu) cheeky. (b) (Ec, PR) mean, stingy.

indio 1 adj (a) Indian.
   (b) blue.
   2 nm, **india** nf (a) Indian (of India, of West Indies, of America).
   (b) **hacer el —** to play the fool; **le salió el —** (Arg) he behaved like the lout he is; he got angry for no reason at all; **se le subió el —** (CAm) he got angry.

indirecta nf hint; insinuation, innuendo; — **del padre Cobos** broad hint; **soltar una —** to drop a hint, make an insinuation.

indirectamente adv indirectly.

indirecto adj indirect; roundabout.

indiscernible adj indiscernible.

indisciplina nf indiscipline, lack of discipline; insubordination.

indisciplinado adj undisciplined; lax.

indiscreción nf indiscretion; tactless thing (to do), tactless remark (etc), gaffe; **. . ., si no es — . . .,** if I may say so; **cometió la — de** + infin he

committed the indiscretion of + ger, he was so tactless as to + infin.

indiscretamente adv indiscreetly; tactlessly.

indiscreto adj indiscreet; tactless.

indisculpable adj inexcusable, unforgivable.

indiscutible adj indisputable, unquestionable.

indiscutiblemente adv indisputably, unquestionably.

indisoluble adj indissoluble; inseparable.

indisolublemente adv indissolubly; inseparably.

indispensable adj indispensable, essential.

indisponer [2r] **1** vt (a) plan etc to spoil, upset.
   (b) (Med) to upset, make ill, make unfit.
   (c) — **a uno con otro** to set someone against another person, prejudice someone against another person.
   2 indisponerse vr (a) (Med) to become ill, fall ill.
   (b) — **con uno** to fall out with someone.

indisponible adj not available, unavailable.

indisposición nf (a) (Med) indisposition, slight illness. (b) disinclination, unwillingness.

indispuesto adj (a) (Med) indisposed, unwell, slightly ill; **sentirse —** to feel slightly ill, feel queer. (b) disinclined, unwilling.

indisputable adj indisputable, unquestioned; unchallenged.

indistinción nf (a) indistinctness; vagueness. (b) lack of discrimination. (c) lack of distinction, sameness, identity.

indistinguible adj indistinguishable (de from).

indistintamente adv (a) indistinctly; vaguely. (b) without distinction, indiscriminately.

indistinto adj (a) indistinct; vague; faint, dim. (b) indiscriminate.

individua nf (fam) whore.

individual 1 adj (a) individual; peculiar, special; **room** single.
   (b) (Col, Chi, Ven) alike, similar, identical; **A es — a B** A is like B, A is identical to B.
   2 nm (Sport) singles, singles match; — **femenino** women's singles; — **masculino** men's singles.

individualidad nf individuality.

individualismo nm individualism.

individualista 1 adj individualistic. **2** nmf individualist.

individualizar [1f] vt to individualize.

individualmente adv individually.

individuar [1e] vt to individualize.

individuo 1 adj individual.
   2 nm (a) individual; (pej) individual, fellow; **el — en cuestión** the person in question.
   (b) (of society) member, fellow.

indivisible adj indivisible.

indiviso adj undivided.

indo 1 adj Hindu. **2** nm, **inda** nf Hindu.

indo . . . Indo . . .

Indo m (Geog) Indus.

indócil adj unmanageable, headstrong; disobedient.

indocilidad nf unmanageableness, headstrong character; disobedience.

indocto adj ignorant, unlearned.

indoctrinar [1a] vt (SAm) to indoctrinate.

indocumentado 1 adj without identifying documents, who carries no identity papers. **2** nm person who carries no identity papers.

Indochina: **la —** Indochina.

indoeuropeo 1 adj Indo-European. **2** nm, **indoeuropea** nf Indo-European. **3** nm (language) Indo-European.

índole nf (a) nature; character, disposition. (b) class, kind, sort; **cosas de esta —** things of this kind.

indolencia nf indolence, laziness; apathy.

indolente adj indolent, lazy; apathetic.

indoloro adj painless.

indomable adj indomitable; animal untameable; (fig) unmanageable, uncontrollable.

indomado adj wild, untamed.

indomesticable adj untameable.

indómito adj = **indomable.**

Indonesia f Indonesia.

indonesio 1 adj Indonesian. **2** nm, **indonesia** nf Indonesian.

indormia nf (Col, Ven) trick, wangle (fam), wheeze (fam).

Indostán nm Hindustan.

indostanés 1 adj Hindustani. **2** nm, **indostanesa** nf Hindustani.

indostaní nm (language) Hindustani.

indostánico 1 adj Hindustani. **2** nm (language) Hindustani.

indotado adj without a dowry.

indubitable adj indubitable, undoubted.

indubitablemente adv indubitably, undoubtedly.

inducción nf (a) (*Elec, Philos*) induction; **por —** by induction, inductively. (b) inducement, persuasion.
inducido nm (*Elec*) armature.
inducir [3o] vt (a) (*Elec*) to induce; (*Philos*) to infer.
 (b) to induce, persuade; **— a uno a hacer algo** to induce someone to do something; **— a uno en el error** to lead someone into error.
inductivo adj inductive.
indudable adj undoubted, indubitable; unquestionable; **es — que . . .** there is no doubt that . . .
indudablemente adv undoubtedly, doubtless; unquestionably.
indulgencia nf (a) indulgence; forbearance; **proceder sin — contra** to proceed ruthlessly against.
 (b) (*Eccl*) indulgence; **— plenaria** plenary indulgence.
indulgente adj indulgent (con towards).
indulgentemente adv indulgently.
indultar [1a] **1** vt (a) (*Law*) to pardon, reprieve (de from).
 (b) to exempt, excuse (de from).
 2 indultarse vr (a) (*Bol*) to meddle, pry.
 (b) (*Cu*) to get oneself out of a jam.
indulto nm (a) (*Law*) pardon, reprieve. (b) exemption, excusal.
indumentaria nf (a) clothing, apparel, dress. (b) (history of) costume.
indumentario adj clothing (*attr*); **elegancia indumentaria** elegance of dress, sartorial elegance.
indumento nm clothing, apparel, dress.
industria nf (a) industry; **— algodonera** cotton industry; **— del automóvil** car industry, automobile industry (*US*); **— básica** basic industry; **— pesada** heavy industry; **— siderúrgica** iron and steel industry; **Ministro de — y Comercio** President of the Board of Trade (*Brit*), Secretary of Industry and Trade (*US*).
 (b) industry, industriousness.
 (c) ingenuity, skill, expertise; **de —** on purpose.
industrial 1 adj industrial. **2** nm industrialist, manufacturer.
industrialismo nm industrialism.
industrialista nm (*SAm*) industrialist.
industrialización nf industrialization.
industrializar [1f] **1** vt to industrialize. **2 industrializarse** vr to become industrialized.
industriarse [1b] vr to manage, find a way; **—las para + infin** to manage to + infin, contrive to + infin.
industriosamente adv (a) industriously. (b) skilfully, resourcefully.
industrioso adj (a) industrious. (b) skilful, resourceful, versatile, handy.
inédito adj (a) (*Lit*) unpublished; **un texto rigurosamente —** a text never published previously in any form.
 (b) (*fig*) new; not known hitherto, hitherto unheard of; **una experiencia inédita** a completely new experience.
ineducable adj ineducable.
ineducado adj (a) uneducated. (b) ill-bred, bad-mannered, uncouth.
inefable adj indescribable, inexpressible, ineffable.
ineficacia nf (a) ineffectiveness. (b) inefficiency.
ineficaz adj (a) ineffective, ineffectual. (b) inefficient.
ineficazmente adv (a) ineffectively, ineffectually. (b) inefficiently.
ineficiencia nf inefficiency.
ineficiente adj inefficient.
inelástico adj inelastic.
inelegancia nf inelegance, lack of elegance.
inelegante adj inelegant.
inelegantemente adv inelegantly.
inelegible adj ineligible.
ineluctable adj, **ineludible** adj unavoidable, inescapable.
inenarrable adj inexpressible.
inencogible adj unshrinkable, non-shrink, which will not shrink.
inencontrable adj unobtainable.
inepcia nf (a) ineptitude, incompetence; stupidity. (b) (*SAm*) silly thing (to say *etc*); **decir —s** to say silly things.
ineptitud nf ineptitude, incompetence.
inepto adj inept, incompetent; stupid; **— de toda ineptitud** utterly incompetent.
inequívoco adj unequivocal, unambiguous; unmistakable.
inercia nf (a) (*Phys*) inertia. (b) (*fig*) passivity; sluggishness, slowness.
inerme adj unarmed; defenceless, unprotected.

inerte adj (a) (*Phys*) inert. (b) (*fig*) passive, inactive; sluggish, slow.
Inés f Agnes.
inescrupuloso adj unscrupulous.
inescrutabilidad nf inscrutability.
inescrutable adj inscrutable.
inesperadamente adv unexpectedly; without warning, suddenly.
inesperado adj unexpected, unforeseen; sudden.
inesquivable adj unavoidable; which cannot be overlooked.
inestabilidad nf instability, unsteadiness.
inestable adj unstable, unsteady.
inestimable adj inestimable, invaluable.
inevitabilidad nf inevitability.
inevitable adj inevitable, unavoidable.
inevitablemente adv inevitably, unavoidably.
inexactitud nf inaccuracy; incorrectness, wrongness.
inexacto adj inaccurate; incorrect, untrue; **esto es —** this is not so, this is incorrect.
inexcusable adj (a) inexcusable, unforgivable. (b) essential.
inexcusablemente adv inexcusably, unforgivably.
inexhausto adj (a) unused, still to be used; unspent. (b) inexhaustible.
inexistencia nf non-existence.
inexistente adj non-existent; which no longer exists, defunct.
inexorable adj inexorable.
inexorablemente adv inexorably.
inexperiencia nf inexperience; unskilfulness, lack of skill.
inexperto adj inexperienced; unskilled, inexpert.
inexplicable adj inexplicable, unaccountable.
inexplicablemente adv inexplicably, unaccountably.
inexplicado adj unexplained.
inexplorado adj unexplored; *sea etc* uncharted.
inexplotado adj unexploited, unused.
inexpresable adj inexpressible.
inexpresivo adj inexpressive; dull, flat, wooden.
inexpuesto adj (*Phot*) unexposed.
inexpugnable adj (a) (*Mil*) impregnable. (b) (*fig*) firm, unyielding, unshakeable.
inextinguible adj inextinguishable, unquenchable.
inextirpable adj ineradicable.
inextricable adj inextricable.
infalibilidad nf infallibility; certainty.
infalible adj infallible; certain, sure; foolproof; *aim* unerring.
infaliblemente adv infallibly; surely; unerringly.
infamación nf defamation.
infamador 1 adj defamatory, slanderous. **2** nm, **infamadora** nf slanderer.
infamar [1a] vt to dishonour, discredit; to defame, slander.
infamatorio adj defamatory, slanderous.
infame 1 adj infamous, odious, vile; *task* terrible, thankless; **esto es —** this is monstrous, this is infamous. **2** nmf vile person, villain.
infamia nf infamy; disgrace.
infancia nf (a) infancy, childhood; (*fig*) infancy. (b) children.
infanta nf (a) infant. (b) (*Hist*) infanta, princess.
infante nm (a) infant. (b) (*Hist*) infante, prince; (*Mil: Hist*) infantryman.
infantería nf infantry; **— de marina** marines.
infanticida nmf infanticide (*person*), child-killer.
infanticidio nm infanticide (*act*).
infantil adj (a) infant; child's, children's; **de tamaño —** child's size; **para el uso —** for children (to use). (b) childlike, innocent; (*pej*) infantile, childish.
infanzón[1] nm, **infanzona** nf (*Hist*) member of the lowest rank of the nobility.
infanzón[2] nm (*Cu*) boast.
infatigable adj tireless, untiring.
infatigablemente adv tirelessly, untiringly.
infatuación nf vanity, conceit.
infatuar [1d] **1** vt to make conceited. **2 infatuarse** vr to get conceited (con about).
infausto adj unlucky; ill-starred, ill-fated.
infección nf infection.
infeccioso adj infectious.
infectar [1a] **1** vt (a) to infect. (b) to contaminate, corrupt; to pervert. **2 infectarse** vr to become infected (de with; *also fig*).
infecto adj infected (de with); foul; corrupt, tainted.
infecundidad nf infertility; sterility, barrenness.
infecundo adj infertile; sterile, barren; **la época infecunda de la mujer** the woman's infertile period.
infelicidad nf unhappiness; misfortune.

infeliz 1 *adj* (a) unhappy; unfortunate, miserable, wretched. (b) simple, kind-hearted, good-natured; (*pej*) gullible. (c) (*Arg, Guat, Mex*) trifling, insignificant. **2** *nmf* (a) wretch, poor devil. (b) good-natured simpleton.

infelizmente *adv* unhappily.

infelizón *nm* (*fam*), **infelizote** *nm* (*fam*) = **infeliz 2** (a).

inferencia *nf* inference; **por — by** inference.

inferior 1 *adj* (a) (*physically*) lower (*a* than); **la parte — the** lower part; **el lado — the** underside, the side underneath; **el Egipto — lower** Egypt. (b) (*in quality, rank*) inferior (*a* to), lower (*a* than); **de calidad — of** inferior quality; **no ser — a nadie** to be inferior to none; **le es — en talento** he is inferior to him in talent. (c) (*Math*) lower; **cualquier número — a 9** any number under 9, any number below 9, any number less than 9; **una cantidad — a** lesser quantity. **2** *nm* inferior, subordinate; (*pej*) underling.

inferioridad *nf* inferiority.

inferir [3i] *vt* (a) to infer, deduce; **— una cosa de** (or **por**) **otra** to infer one thing from another. (b) to lead to, cause, bring on. (c) *wound* to inflict (*a, en* on); *insult* to offer (*a* to).

infernáculo *nm* hopscotch.

infernal *adj* infernal; (*fig*) infernal, hellish, devilish; **un ruido — a** hell of a noise (*fam*), a hellish noise.

infértil *adj* infertile.

infestación *nf* infestation.

infestar [1a] *vt* (a) to infect; to infest, overrun, invade. (b) (*fig*) to harass, beset.

inficionar [1a] *vt* = **infectar.**

infidelidad *nf* (a) infidelity, unfaithfulness; **— conyugal** marital infidelity. (b) (*Eccl*) unbelief, lack of faith. (c) (*Eccl*) unbelievers, infidels.

infidencia *nf* (a) disloyalty, faithlessness; treason. (b) disloyal act; breach of trust.

infiel 1 *adj* (a) unfaithful, disloyal (*a, con, para* to); **fue — a su mujer** he was unfaithful to his wife. (b) (*Eccl*) unbelieving, infidel. (c) *account etc* inaccurate; **la memoria le fue —** his memory failed him. **2** *nmf* (*Eccl*) unbeliever, infidel.

infielmente *adv* (a) unfaithfully, disloyally. (b) inaccurately.

infiernillo *nm* (also **— de alcohol**) spirit lamp, spirit stove; **— campestre** camp stove; **— de gasolina** petrol stove.

infierno *nm* (a) hell. (b) (*fig and in phrases*) hell, inferno; hades; **¡anda al —!** go to hell!; **está en el quinto —** it's at the back of beyond, it's right off the map; **mandar a uno al quinto —** to tell someone to go to hell.

infiltración *nf* infiltration.

infiltrar [1a] **1** *vt* to infiltrate (*en* into); (*fig*) to inculcate (*en* in). **2 infiltrarse** *vr* to infiltrate (also *fig; en* into), filter (*en* in, through); to percolate.

ínfimo *adj* lowest; (*fig*) very poor, of very poor quality; vile, mean; least; **a precios —s** at very low prices, at ridiculously low prices.

infinidad *nf* (a) (*Math etc*) infinity. (b) great quantity, enormous number; **— de an** infinity of, vast numbers of; **durante una — de días** for days on end; **— de veces** times out of number; **hay — de personas que . . .** there are great numbers of people who . . .

infinitamente *adj* infinitely.

infinitesimal *adj* infinitesimal.

infinitivo 1 *adj* infinitive. **2** *nm* infinitive (mood).

infinito 1 *adj* (a) (*Math etc*) infinite. (b) (*fig*) infinite; boundless, limitless, endless; **hasta lo —** ad infinitum. **2** *adv* infinitely, immensely. **3** *nm* (*Math*) infinity; **el —** (*Philos etc*) the infinite.

infinitud *nf* infinitude.

inflación *nf* (a) inflation (also *Econ*); swelling. (b) (*fig*) pride, conceit.

inflacionismo *nm* (*Econ*) inflation, inflationism.

inflacionista *adj* inflationary, inflationist.

inflador *nm* (*SAm*) bicycle pump.

inflamable *adj* inflammable.

inflamación *nf* (a) ignition, combustion; **— espontánea** spontaneous combustion. (b) (*Med*) inflammation.

inflamar [1a] **1** *vt* (a) to set on fire, ignite. (b) (*Med*) to inflame. (c) (*fig*) to inflame, excite, arouse. **2 inflamarse** *vr* (a) to catch fire, flame up, ignite; **se inflama fácilmente** it is highly inflammable. (b) (*Med*) to become inflamed. (c) (*fig*) to become inflamed (*de, en* with), get excited.

inflamatorio *adj* inflammatory.

inflar [1a] **1** *vt* (a) to inflate, blow up, pump air into. (b) (*fig*) to inflate, exaggerate; to make conceited. **2 inflarse** *vr* (a) to swell. (b) (*fig*) to get conceited.

inflatorio *adj* inflationary.

inflexibilidad *nf* inflexibility; unyielding nature.

inflexible *adj* inflexible; unbending, unyielding; **— a los ruegos** unmoved by appeals, unresponsive to appeals; **regla —** strict rule, hard-and-fast rule.

inflexión *nf* inflexion.

infligir [3c] *vt* to inflict (*a* on).

influencia *nf* influence (*sobre* on); **bajo la — de** under the influence of.

influenciable *adj* impressionable, easily influenced.

influenciar [1b] *vt* to influence.

influenza *nf* (*esp SAm*) influenza.

influir [3g] **1** *vt* to influence; **A, influido por B . . .** A, influenced by B . . . **2** *vi* (a) to have influence, carry weight, have pull (*con* with); **es hombre que influye** he's a man of influence, he's a man who carries weight. (b) **— en, — sobre** to influence, affect, have an influence on; to have a hand in.

influjo *nm* influence (*sobre* on).

influyente *adj* influential.

información *nf* (a) (*in general*) information; news; (*Mil*) intelligence; **una —** a piece of information, a piece of news; **— secreta** secret information, classified information. (b) report, account; reference, testimonial; (*in newspaper, as heading*) section; **— de crédito** credit report; **— deportiva** sports section, sporting page; **— extranjera** news from abroad, foreign news; **— periodística** newspaper report. (c) (*Law*) legal proceedings; judicial inquiry, investigation; **abrir una —** to begin proceedings.

informador *nm*, **informadora** *nf* informant.

informal *adj* (a) irregular, incorrect; *behaviour etc* bad, unmannerly; unconventional. (b) *person* unreliable, untrustworthy; shifty; unbusinesslike, disorganized; offhand, bad-mannered; frivolous.

informalidad *nf* (a) irregularity, incorrectness; unmannerliness; unconventionality. (b) unreliability, untrustworthiness, shiftiness; unbusinesslike nature; offhandedness, bad manners; frivolity, levity.

informalmente *adv* (a) irregularly; badly; unconventionally. (b) unreliably; shiftily; in an unbusinesslike way; offhandedly; frivolously.

informante *nmf* informant.

informar [1a] **1** *vt* (a) to inform, tell (*de* of, *sobre* about). (b) to form, shape. **2** *vi* (a) to report (*acerca de, de* on); **el profesor informará de su descubrimiento** the professor will report on his discovery. (b) (*Law*) to plead. (c) (*Law*) to inform (*contra* against), lay information (*contra* against). **3 informarse** *vr* to find out, inform oneself; **— de** to find out about, acquaint oneself with, inquire into; **— sobre algo** to gather information about something.

informativo *adj* (a) informative; news (*attr*); **un folleto —** a booklet of information, an explanatory booklet. (b) *body etc* consultative, advisory.

informe[1] *adj* shapeless.

informe[2] *nm* (a) report, statement; (*Parl*) report, white paper; **el — del ministro** the minister's statement. (b) (*Mil*) briefing. (c) piece of information; **—s** information; data, particulars, references; **según mis —s** according to my information; **dar —s sobre** to give information about; **pedir —s** to ask for information, make inquiries (*a* of, *sobre* about); **tomar —s** to gather information. (d) (*Law*) plea; **— forense, — jurídico** legal speech, speech in court.

infortunado *adj* unfortunate, unlucky.

infortunio *nm* misfortune, ill luck; mishap.

infra . . . infra . . .

infracción *nf* infraction, infringement (*de* of); breach

(de of); (Aut etc) offence (de against); — de contrato breach of contract.
infractor nm offender (de against).
infraescrito 1 adj undersigned; undermentioned.
2 nm, **infraescrita** nf: el — the undersigned; (SAm: hum) the present speaker, I myself.
infraestructura nf substructure; (fig) underlying structure.
in fraganti adv: coger a uno — to catch someone red-handed.
infrahumano adj subhuman.
inframundo nm underworld.
infrangible adj unbreakable.
infranqueable adj impassable; (fig) unsurmountable.
infrarrojo adj infrared.
infrecuencia nf infrequency.
infrecuente adj infrequent.
infringir [3c] vt to infringe, break, contravene.
infructuosamente adv fruitlessly, unsuccessfully; unprofitably.
infructuoso adj fruitless, unsuccessful; unprofitable.
infulas nfpl conceit; darse — to put on airs, get on one's high horse; tener (muchas) — de to fancy oneself as.
infumable adj (a) unsmokable. (b) (Mex) unbearable, intolerable.
infundado adj unfounded, baseless.
infundia nf (SAm) = enjundia.
infundio nm (fam) fairy tale, fib.
infundir [3a] vt (a) to infuse (a, en into).
(b) (fig) to instil (a, en into); — ánimo a uno to encourage someone; — miedo a uno to scare someone, frighten someone, fill someone with fear; — un espíritu nuevo a un club to inject new life into a club, to put new life into a club.
infusión nf infusion; — de té infusion of tea.
ingeniar [1a] **1** vt to devise, think up, contrive.
2 ingeniarse vr to manage, find a way, get along; — con algo to manage with something, make do with something; — para + infin to manage to + infin, contrive to + infin (also —las).
ingeniería nf engineering.
ingeniero nm engineer (also Mil, Naut); — agrónomo agronomist, agricultural expert; — de caminos, canales y puentes civil engineer; — forestal, — de montes forestry expert; — de minas mining engineer; — naval shipbuilder, naval architect; — químico chemical engineer.
ingenio nm (a) ingenuity, inventiveness; talent; creativeness; wit, wits; aguzar el — to sharpen one's wits.
(b) clever person, talented person; (Hist) wit.
(c) (Mech) apparatus, engine, device; (Mil) device; — nuclear nuclear device.
(d) (Tech) mill, plant; — (de azúcar) sugar mill, sugar refinery; (Bol, Per) foundry, smelting plant.
ingeniosamente adv (a) ingeniously, cleverly. (b) wittily.
ingeniosidad nf (a) ingenuity, ingeniousness, cleverness, resourcefulness. (b) (una —) clever idea. (c) wittiness.
ingenioso adj (a) ingenious, clever, resourceful. (b) witty.
ingénito adj innate, inborn.
ingente adj huge, enormous.
ingenuamente adv ingenuously, naïvely; with candour; simply, unaffectedly.
ingenuidad nf ingenuousness, naïveté; candour; simplicity.
ingenuo adj ingenuous, candid; simple, unaffected.
ingerido adj (Col, Mex, Ven) ill.
ingerir [3i] vt to swallow; to ingest, consume, take in; el automovilista había ingerido 3 litros de alcohol the motorist had taken 3 litres of alcohol.
ingestión nf swallowing; ingestion.
Inglaterra f England; (often loosely used by foreigners when strict usage requires) Great Britain, United Kingdom; la batalla de — the Battle of Britain (1940).
ingle nf groin.
inglés 1 adj English; (often loosely used by foreigners when strict usage requires) British.
2 nm Englishman; Briton, Britisher (US); los —es the English, the British.
3 nm (language) English.
inglesa nf Englishwoman; Briton, Britisher (US); montar a la — to ride sidesaddle.
inglesismo nm anglicism.
inglete nm dovetail.
ingobernable adj uncontrollable, unmanageable; (Pol) ungovernable.
ingratitud nf ingratitude.

ingrato adj (a) (person) ungrateful; ¡—! you wretch!
(b) (taste) unpleasant, disagreeable; task etc thankless, unrewarding.
ingravidez nf weightlessness.
ingrávido adj weightless; very light.
ingrediente nm ingredient; —s (Arg) dish of hors d'oeuvres on the bar counter.
ingresado nm, **ingresada** nf (Univ etc) entrant, new student.
ingresar [1a] **1** vt money to deposit, pay in; — dinero en una cuenta to pay money into an account.
2 vi (a) to come in, enter; — en una sociedad to join a club, become a member of a club, be admitted to a society; — en la Academia to be admitted to the Academy, be received into the Academy; — en el ejército to join the army, join up; — en el hospital to be admitted to hospital; pero ingresó cadáver but he was dead on arrival (at hospital).
(b) (of money, profits) to come in.
3 ingresarse vr (Mex) to join, become a member; (Mex: Mil) to join up.
ingreso nm (a) entry (en into), joining; admission (en to); su — en la Academia his admission to the Academy; examen de — entrance examination.
(b) (Comm) entry; deposit; sum received.
(c) —s (Comm, Fin) income; revenue; receipts, takings; —s accesorios additional earnings, earnings on the side; fringe benefits; —s anuales annual income; —s brutos gross receipts; vivir con arreglo a los —s to live within one's income.
íngrimo adj all alone.
inguandia nf (Col) fib, tale.
inhábil adj (a) unskilful, inexpert, clumsy; incompetent. (b) unfit (para for, para + infin to + infin). (c) día — non-working day.
inhabilidad nf (a) unskilfulness; clumsiness; incompetence. (b) unfitness (para for).
inhabilitación nf (a) disqualification; see nota. (b) disablement.
inhabilitar [1a] vt (a) to disqualify (para + infin from + ger). (b) to disable; to render unfit (para for).
inhabitable adj uninhabitable.
inhabitado adj uninhabited.
inhabituado adj unaccustomed (a to).
inhalación nf inhalation.
inhalador nm (Med) inhaler.
inhalante nm inhalant.
inhalar [1a] vt to inhale.
inherente adj inherent (a in).
inhibición nf inhibition.
inhibir [3a] **1** vt to inhibit; (Law) to restrain, stay.
2 inhibirse vr to keep out (de of), to stay away (de from); to keep out of the way, lie low.
inhibitorio adj inhibitory.
inhospitalario adj inhospitable; (fig) bleak, cheerless, uninviting.
inhospitalidad nf inhospitality.
inhóspito adj inhospitable.
inhumación nf burial, inhumation.
inhumanamente adv inhumanly.
inhumanidad nf inhumanity.
inhumano adj inhuman; (Chi) dirty, disgusting.
iniciación nf initiation; beginning.
iniciado 1 adj initiate(d). **2** nm, **iniciada** nf initiate.
iniciador nm initiator, starter; pioneer.
inicial 1 adj initial. **2** nf initial.
iniciar [1b] vt (a) to initiate (en into); — a uno en un secreto to initiate someone into a secret. (b) to begin, start, initiate; to originate, set on foot; to pioneer.
iniciativa nf initiative, enterprise; lead, leadership; — privada private enterprise; bajo su — on his initiative; por — propia on one's own initiative; carecer de — to lack initiative; tomar la — to take the initiative.
inicuamente adv wickedly, iniquitously.
inicuo adj wicked, iniquitous.
inigualado adj unequalled.
inimaginable adj unimaginable, inconceivable.
inimitable adj inimitable.
ininteligente adj unintelligent.
ininteligibilidad nf unintelligibility.
ininteligible adj unintelligible.
ininterrumpidamente adv uninterruptedly; continuously, without a break; steadily.
ininterrumpido adj uninterrupted; continuous, without a break; steady; prolonged, sustained.
iniquidad nf wickedness, iniquity; injustice.

injerencia *nf* interference, meddling (*en* in).
injerir [3i] **1** *vt* (**a**) to insert, introduce (*en* into); (*Agr*) to graft (*en* on, on to). (**b**) = **ingerir**. **2 injerirse** *vr* to interfere, meddle (*en* in).
injertar [1a] *vt* (*Agr*, *Med*) to graft (*en* on, on to); (*fig*) to graft; to inject (*en* into).
injerto 1 *nm* (**a**) grafting. (**b**) (*Agr*, *Med*) graft; — **de piel** skin graft. **2** *nm*, **injerta** *nf* (*Per*) *mestizo* with Chinese blood.
injuria *nf* (**a**) insult, offence, affront (*para* to); outrage, injustice; —s insults, abuse; **llenar a uno de —s** to heap abuse on someone. (**b**) damage, harm.
injuriar [1b] *vt* (**a**) to insult, abuse, revile; to wrong. (**b**) to injure, damage, harm.
injuriosamente *adv* (**a**) insultingly, offensively; outrageously. (**b**) harmfully.
injurioso *adj* (**a**) insulting, offensive; outrageous. (**b**) harmful, damaging.
injustamente *adv* unjustly, unfairly; wrongfully.
injusticia *nf* injustice; unfairness; **una solemne —** a terrible injustice; **con —** unjustly.
injustificable *adj* unjustifiable.
injustificadamente *adv* unjustifiably.
injustificado *adj* unjustified, unwarranted.
injusto *adj* unjust, unfair; wrong, wrongful; **ser — con uno** to be unjust to someone.
inllevable *adj* unbearable, intolerable.
inmaculado *adj* immaculate.
inmadurez *nf* immaturity.
inmancable *adj* (*Col*, *PR*, *SD*) unfailing, infallible.
inmanejable *adj* unmanageable.
inmanente *adj* immanent; inherent (*a* in).
inmarcesible *adj*, **inmarchitable** *adj* imperishable, undying, unfading.
inmaterial *adj* immaterial.
inmaturo *adj* immature; unripe.
inmediaciones *nfpl* neighbourhood, surroundings, environs; immediate area; **en las — de** in the neighbourhood of.
inmediatamente *adv* immediately, at once.
inmediatez *nf* immediacy.
inmediato *adj* (**a**) (*of time*) immediate; prompt; **de —** immediately, promptly. (**b**) (*of place*) immediate, next; adjoining; **— a** close to, next to.
inmejorable *adj* unsurpassable; —s **recomendaciones** excellent references; **precios —s** unbeatable prices; **de calidad —** of the very best quality.
inmemorable *adj*, **inmemorial** *adj* immemorial.
inmensamente *adv* immensely, vastly.
inmensidad *nf* immensity, hugeness, vastness.
inmenso *adj* immense, huge, vast.
inmensurable *adj* immeasurable.
inmerecidamente *adv* undeservedly.
inmerecido *adj*, **inmérito** *adj* undeserved; uncalled-for.
inmergir [3c] *vt* to immerse.
inmersión *nf* immersion; (*by diver etc*) dive, plunge.
inmigración *nf* immigration.
inmigrado *nm*, **inmigrada** *nf* immigrant.
inmigrante 1 *adj* immigrant. **2** *nmf* immigrant.
inmigrar [1a] *vi* to immigrate.
inminencia *nf* imminence.
inminente *adj* imminent, impending.
inmiscuirse [3g] *vr* to interfere, meddle (*en* in).
inmisericorde *adj* insensitive, hard-hearted.
inmisericordioso *adj* merciless.
inmobiliaria *nf* building society.
inmobiliario *adj* real-estate (*attr*).
inmoble *adj* (**a**) immovable; motionless. (**b**) (*fig*) unmoved, unshaken.
inmoderadamente *adv* immoderately, excessively.
inmoderado *adj* immoderate, excessive.
inmodestamente *adv* immodestly.
inmodestia *nf* immodesty.
inmodesto *adj* immodest.
inmolar [1a] *vt* to immolate.
inmoral *adj* immoral; unethical.
inmoralidad *nf* immorality; unethical nature.
inmortal 1 *adj* immortal. **2** *nmf* immortal.
inmortalidad *nf* immortality.
inmortalizar [1f] *vt* to immortalize.
inmotivado *adj* motiveless, unmotivated, without motive.
inmoto *adj* unmoved.
inmovible *adj* immovable.
inmóvil *adj* (**a**) immovable; immobile; motionless, still; **quedar —** to remain (*or* be, stand *etc*) motionless; (*vehicle etc*) to remain stationary. (**b**) (*fig*) steadfast, unshaken.
inmovilidad *nf* immovability; immobility; stillness.
inmovilismo *nm* (*fig*) stagnation, deadness; do-nothing policy.

inmovilizar [1f] *vr* to immobilize; to stop, paralyse, bring to a standstill; *capital* (*Fin*) to tie up, lock up.
inmueble 1 *adj*: **bienes —s** real estate, landed property. **2** *nm* property; —s real estate, landed property.
inmundicia *nf* filth, dirt; nastiness; —s filth, rubbish.
inmundo *adj* filthy, dirty; foul, nasty.
inmune *adj* (**a**) (*Med*) immune (*contra* against, to). (**b**) (*fig*) exempt, free (*de* from).
inmunidad *nf* (**a**) immunity; — **diplomática** diplomatic immunity; — **parlamentaria** parliamentary immunity. (**b**) exemption.
inmunizar [1f] *vt* to immunize.
inmutabilidad *nf* immutability.
inmutable *adj* immutable, changeless.
inmutarse [1a] *vr* to change countenance, turn pale, lose one's self-possession; **se inmutó** his face fell, he seemed disappointed; **siguió sin —** he carried on unperturbed, he showed no sign of what he was feeling.
innato *adj* innate, inborn; inbred.
innatural *adj* unnatural.
innavegable *adj* *river etc* unnavigable; *ship* unseaworthy.
innecesariamente *adv* unnecessarily.
innecesario *adj* unnecessary.
innegable *adj* undeniable.
innoble *adj* ignoble.
innocuo *adj* innocuous, harmless.
innominado *adj* nameless, unnamed.
innovación *nf* innovation; novelty, new thing.
innovador *nm*, **innovadora** *nf* innovator.
innovar [1a] *vt* to introduce.
innumerable *adj*, **innúmero** *adj* innumerable, countless.
inobediencia *nf* disobedience.
inobediente *adj* disobedient.
inobjetable *adj* (*SAm*) unobjectionable.
inobservado *adj* unobserved.
inobservancia *nf* non-observance (*de* of); disregard (*de* for); neglect; (*of law*) violation, breaking (*de* of).
inocencia *nf* innocence.
inocentada *nf* (**a**) naïve remark, simple-minded thing; blunder. (**b**) practical joke, April Fool joke; hoax.
inocente¹ 1 *adj* (**a**) innocent (*de* of); harmless. (**b**) simple, naïve. **2** *nmf* (**a**) innocent, innocent person. (**b**) simple soul, naïve person.
inocente² nm (**a**) (*Chi*, *Ec*) avocado pear. (**b**) (*Ec*) masquerade.
inocentemente *adv* innocently.
inocentón 1 *adj* simple, naïve, gullible. **2** *nm*, **inocentona** *nf* simple soul, naïve person.
inocuidad *nf* innocuousness, harmlessness.
inoculación *nf* inoculation.
inocular [1a] *vt* (**a**) (*Med*) to inoculate (*contra* against, *de* with). (**b**) (*fig*) to corrupt, contaminate (*de* with).
inocuo *adj* = **innocuo**.
inodoro 1 *adj* odourless, having no smell. **2** *nm* lavatory, toilet.
inofensivo *adj* inoffensive, harmless.
inoficioso *adj* (*SAm*) useless.
inolvidable *adj* unforgettable.
inolvidablemente *adv* unforgettably.
inope *adj* impecunious, indigent.
inoperable *adj* (*Arg*, *Guat*, *Mex*: *Med*) inoperable.
inoperante *adj* (**a**) inoperative; unworkable. (**b**) (*SAm*) useless, fruitless, unproductive; inactive.
inopia *nf* indigence, poverty.
inopinadamente *adv* unexpectedly.
inopinado *adj* unexpected.
inoportunamente *adv* (**a**) inopportunely, at the wrong time. (**b**) inconveniently; inappropriately.
inoportunidad *nf* (**a**) inopportuneness, untimeliness. (**b**) inconvenience; inexpediency; inappropriateness.
inoportuno *adj* (**a**) inopportune, untimely, ill-timed. (**b**) inconvenient; inexpedient; inappropriate.
inorgánico *adj* inorganic.
inoxidable *adj* rustless; *steel* stainless.
inquebrantable *adj* (**a**) unbreakable. (**b**) (*fig*) unshakeable, unyielding, unswerving.
inquietador *adj* = **inquietante**.
inquietamente *adv* (**a**) anxiously, uneasily. (**b**) restlessly.
inquietante *adj* worrying, disturbing.
inquietar [1a] **1** *vt* to worry, disturb, trouble, upset; to torment. **2 inquietarse** *vr* to worry, get worried, upset oneself; **¡no te inquietes!** don't worry!

inquieto adj (a) anxious, worried, uneasy; **estar —
por** to be anxious about, be worried about. (b)
restless, unsettled.
inquietud nf (a) anxiety, worry, uneasiness, disquiet. (b) restlessness.
inquilinaje nm (Chi) = **inquilinato**; (Mex) tenants,
tenantry.
inquilinato nm (a) tenancy; (Law) lease, leasehold.
(b) rent; (**impuesto de**) — rates. (c) (Arg) tenement
house.
inquilino nm, **inquilina** nf tenant; lessee; (Chi)
tenant farmer.
inquina nf dislike, aversion; ill will, spite; **tener — a
uno** to have a grudge against someone, have one's
knife in someone.
inquiridor 1 adj inquiring. **2** nm, **inquiridora** nf
inquirer; investigator.
inquirir [3i] **1** vt to enquire into, investigate, look
into. **2** vi to inquire.
inquisición nf inquiry, investigation; **la I—** the
Inquisition.
inquisidor nm inquisitor.
inquisitorial adj inquisitorial.
insaciable adj insatiable.
insaciablemente adv insatiably.
insalubre adj unhealthy, insalubrious; insanitary.
insanable adj incurable.
insania nf insanity.
insano adj (a) insane, mad. (b) unhealthy.
insatisfacción nf dissatisfaction.
insatisfactorio adj unsatisfactory.
insatisfecho adj unsatisfied; dissatisfied.
inscribir [3a; ptp **inscrito**] **1** vt to inscribe (also
Math); to list, enter (on a list); to enrol; to register,
record. **2 inscribirse** vr to enrol, register.
inscripción nf (a) (act) inscription; enrolment;
registering, recording. (b) inscription; lettering.
insecticida nm insecticide.
insectívoro adj insectivorous.
insecto nm insect.
inseguridad nf unsafeness; insecurity; unsteadiness;
uncertainty.
inseguro adj unsafe; insecure; unsteady; uncertain.
inseminación nf insemination; — **artificial** artificial
insemination.
inseminar [1a] vt to inseminate, fertilize.
insensatez nf folly, foolishness, stupidity.
insensato adj senseless, foolish, stupid.
insensibilidad nf (a) insensitivity; lack of feeling,
callousness. (b) (Med) insensibility, unconsciousness; numbness.
insensibilizar [1f] vt to desensitize.
insensible adj (a) insensitive (a to); unfeeling,
callous. (b) imperceptible. (c) (Med) insensible,
unconscious; limb numb, without feeling.
insensiblemente adv (a) insensitively; unfeelingly.
(b) imperceptibly.
inseparable adj inseparable.
inseparablemente adv inseparably.
insepulto adj unburied; without burial.
inserción nf insertion.
insertar [1a] vt to insert.
inservible adj useless.
insidia nf snare, trap; ambush.
insidiosamente adv insidiously; treacherously.
insidioso adj insidious; treacherous.
insigne adj distinguished; notable, famous.
insignia nf (a) badge, device, emblem; decoration.
(b) flag, banner; (Naut) pennant. (c) —**s** insignia.
insignificancia nf insignificance.
insignificante adj insignificant; trivial, tiny, petty.
insinceridad nf insincerity.
insincero adj insincere.
insinuación nf insinuation.
insinuador adj insinuating.
insinuante adj (a) insinuating. (b) ingratiating. (c)
cunning, crafty.
insinuar [1e] **1** vt (a) to insinuate, hint at, imply; —
que . . . to hint that . . . , imply that . . .
(b) — **una observación** to slip in a comment.
2 insinuarse vr (a) — **con uno** to ingratiate
oneself with somebody.
(b) — **en** to worm one's way into, creep into,
slip into; — **en el ánimo de uno** to work one's way
gradually into someone's mind.
insipidez nf insipidness, tastelessness; (fig) dullness,
flatness.
insípido adj insipid, tasteless; (fig) dull, flat, tedious.
insistencia nf insistence (en on); persistence; **con
— machacona** with wearisome insistence.
insistente adj insistent; persistent.
insistentemente adv insistently; persistently.

insistir [3a] vi to insist; to persist; — **en algo** to
insist on something; to stress something, emphasize
something; — **en una idea** to press an idea; — **en
hacer algo** to insist on doing something; — **en que
se haga algo** to insist that something should be done;
— **en que algo es así** to insist that something is so.
insobornable adj incorruptible.
insociabilidad nf unsociability.
insociable adj unsociable.
insolación nf (a) (Meteorol) sunshine; **horas de —**
hours of sunshine; **la — media diaria es de . . .** the
daily sunshine average is . . .
(b) exposure (to the sun); (Med) sunstroke; **darse**
(or **coger**) **una —** to get sunstroke.
insolar [1a] **1** vt to expose to the sun, put in the sun.
2 insolarse vr (Med) to get sunstroke.
insoldable adj (fig) irremediable; unmendable.
insolencia nf (a) insolence, effrontery. (b) piece of
rudeness, rude thing.
insolentarse [1a] vr to be insolent (con to), become
insolent.
insolente adj (a) insolent, rude; unblushing. (b)
haughty, contemptuous. (c) sound harsh, grating.
insolentemente adv (a) insolently, rudely; unblushingly. (b) haughtily, contemptuously.
insólito adj unusual, unwonted.
insoluble adj insoluble.
insolvencia nf insolvency, bankruptcy.
insolvente adj insolvent, bankrupt.
insomne 1 adj sleepless. **2** nmf insomniac.
insomnio nm sleeplessness, insomnia.
insondable adj bottomless; (fig) unfathomable,
impenetrable, inscrutable.
insonorización nf soundproofing.
insonorizado adj soundproof; **estar —** to be sound-
proofed.
insonoro adj noiseless, soundless.
insoportable adj unbearable, intolerable.
insoportablemente adv unbearably, intolerably.
insoria nf (Ven) insignificance.
insoslayable adj undeniable; problem etc unavoidable, which cannot be got round.
insospechado adj unsuspected.
insostenible adj untenable.
inspección nf inspection, examination; check;
survey; — **ocular** visual examination.
inspeccionar [1a] vt to inspect, examine; to check;
to survey; to supervise.
inspector nm inspector; superintendent, supervisor.
inspectorado nm inspectorate.
inspiración nf (a) inspiration. (b) (Med) inhalation.
inspirador adj inspiring.
inspirar [1a] **1** vt (a) to inspire; — **algo a uno** to
inspire someone with something; to inspire something in someone. (b) (Med) to inhale, breathe in.
2 inspirarse vr: — **en** to be inspired by, find
inspiration in.
inspirativo adj inspiring; inspirational.
instable adj = **inestable**.
instalación nf (a) (act) installation, instalment. (b)
installation; fittings, equipment; (Tech) plant; —
de fuerza power plant; —**es portuarias** harbour
installations; — **sanitaria** sanitation, plumbing.
instalador nm installer; fitter; — **sanitario** plumber.
instalar [1a] **1** vt to install; to set up, erect, fit up,
lay on. **2 instalarse** vr to install oneself, establish
oneself, settle (down).
instancia nf (a) request; application; (Law) petition;
a — de at the request of; **pedir algo con —** to
demand something insistently, demand something
urgently. (b) application form.
instantánea nf (Phot) snap, snapshot.
instantáneamente adv instantaneously, instantly.
instantáneo adj instantaneous, instant; **café —**
instant coffee.
instante nm instant, moment; **al —** instantly, at
once; (a) **cada —** every single moment, all the time;
en un — in a flash; **por —s** incessantly, all the time;
hace un — a moment ago.
instantemente adv insistently, urgently.
instar [1a] **1** vt to urge, press; — **a uno a hacer algo,
— a uno para que haga algo** to urge someone to do
something. **2** vi to be urgent, be pressing.
instauración nf (a) restoration, renewal. (b) establishment, setting-up.
instaurar [1a] vt (a) to restore, renew. (b) to establish, set up (again).
instigación nf instigation; **a — de** at the instigation
of.
instigador nm, **instigadora** nf instigator; — **de un
delito** instigator of a crime, (Law) accessory before
the fact.

instigar [1h] *vt* to instigate; to abet; — **a uno a hacer algo** to incite someone to do something, induce someone to do something.
instilar [1a] *vt* to instil (*a, en* into).
instintivamente *adv* instinctively.
instintivo *adj* instinctive.
instinto *nm* instinct; impulse, urge; — **sexual** sexual urge, sexual desire; **por** — by instinct, instinctively.
institución *nf* (**a**) (*act*) institution, establishment. (**b**) institution; establishment; — **benéfica** charitable foundation; — **pública** public institution, public body. (**c**) —**es** (*of a study etc*) principles.
institucional *adj* institutional.
instituir [3g] *vt* to institute, establish; to found, set up.
instituto *nm* (**a**) institute, institution; **el benemérito** — the Civil Guard; — (**de segunda enseñanza**) state grammar school, high school (US); — **laboral** technical grammar school. (**b**) principle, rule; (*Eccl*) rule.
institutriz *nf* governess.
instrucción *nf* (**a**) instruction; education, teaching; (*Mil etc*) training, drill; (*Sport*) coaching, training; — **primaria** primary education; — **pública** state education.
(**b**) knowledge, learning, instruction; **tener poca** — **en** to have little knowledge of, know little about.
(**c**) (*Law*) proceedings.
(**d**) —**es** instructions, orders, direction; **de acuerdo con sus** —**es** in accordance with your instructions; —**es para el uso** directions for use.
instructivo *adj* instructive; illuminating, enlightening; *film etc* educational.
instructor *nm* instructor, teacher; (*Sport*) coach, trainer.
instructora *nf* instructress, teacher; (*Sport*) coach, trainer.
instruido *adj* well-educated; well-informed.
instruir [3g] **1** *vt* (**a**) to instruct, teach (*de, en, sobre* in, about); to educate; (*Mil etc*) to train, drill; (*Sport*) to coach, train.
(**b**) (*Law*) *case* to prepare, draw up; to investigate.
2 instruirse *vr* to learn, teach oneself (*de, en, sobre* about).
instrumentación *nf* orchestration, scoring.
instrumental 1 *adj* instrumental. **2** *nm* instruments, set of instruments.
instrumentar [1a] *vt* to score, orchestrate; **está instrumentado para** it is scored for.
instrumentista *nmf* instrumentalist; instrument maker.
instrumento *nm* (**a**) instrument; tool, implement; —**s científicos** scientific instruments; —**s de mando** (*Aer etc*) controls; — **de precisión** precision instrument; —**s quirúrgicos** surgical instruments; —**s topográficos** surveying instruments; **volar por** —**s** (*Aer*) to fly on instruments.
(**b**) (*Mus*) instrument; — **de batería,** — **de percusión** percussion instrument; — **de cuerda** stringed instrument; — **musical,** — **músico** musical instrument; — **de viento** wind instrument.
(**c**) (*fig*) instrument, tool; **fue solamente el** — **del dictador** he was merely the dictator's tool, he was just a tool in the dictator's hands.
(**d**) (*Law*) deed, legal document, instrument.
insubordinación *nf* insubordination; turbulence, unruliness.
insubordinado *adj* insubordinate; turbulent, rebellious, unruly.
insubordinar [1a] **1** *vt* to stir up, rouse to rebellion. **2 insubordinarse** *vr* to become unruly; to rebel.
insuficiencia *nf* (**a**) insufficiency, inadequacy; lack, shortage; — **de franqueo** underpaid postage; **debido a la** — **de personal** through shortage of staff.
(**b**) incompetence.
insuficiente *adj* (**a**) insufficient, inadequate. (**b**) *person* incompetent.
insuficientemente *adv* insufficiently, inadequately.
insuflar [1a] *vt* to breathe into, introduce by blowing.
insufrible *adj* unbearable, insufferable.
insufriblemente *adv* unbearably, insufferably.
insular *adj* insular.
insularidad *nf* insularity.
insulina *nf* insulin.
insulsez *nf* (**a**) tastelessness, insipidity. (**b**) (*fig*) flatness, dullness.
insulso *adj* (**a**) tasteless, insipid. (**b**) (*fig*) flat, dull.
insultante *adj* insulting; abusive.
insultar [1a] *vt* to insult.
insulto *nm* (**a**) insult (*para* to). (**b**) (*Arg, Ven*) fainting fit; (*Mex, Nic*) indigestion.
insumergible *adj* unsinkable.

insumiso *adj* unsubmissive, rebellious.
insuperable *adj* insuperable, unsurmountable; *quality* unsurpassable.
insuperado *adj* unsurpassed.
insurgente 1 *adj* insurgent. **2** *nmf* insurgent.
insurrección *nf* revolt, insurrection.
insurreccional *adj* insurrectionary.
insurreccionar [1a] **1** *vt* to rouse to revolt, incite to rebel. **2 insurreccionarse** *vr* to rebel, rise in revolt.
insurrecto 1 *adj* rebel, insurgent. **2** *nmf* rebel, insurgent.
insustancial *adj* unsubstantial.
insustituible *adj* irreplaceable.
intacto *adj* untouched; whole, intact, undamaged; pure.
intachable *adj* irreproachable; faultless, perfect, not open to criticism on any score.
intangible *adj* intangible, impalpable.
integérrimo *adj* *superl of* **íntegro**.
integración *nf* integration; — **racial** racial integration.
integrado *adj* (**a**) integrated; in one piece, all of a piece; *society* integrated; *school* comprehensive (*Brit*). (**b**) **un grupo** — **por** a group made up of, a group consisting of.
integral 1 *adj* integral; (*Mech etc*) built-in; (*Math*) integral; *bread* wholemeal. **2** *nf* (*Math*) integral; integral sign.
íntegramente *adv* (**a**) wholly, entirely, completely. (**b**) (*fig*) uprightly, with integrity.
integrante 1 *adj* integral. **2** *nmf* member; **los** —**s del conjunto** the members of the group.
integrar [1a] *vt* (**a**) to make up, compose, form; **y los que integran el otro grupo** and those who make up the other group. (**b**) (*Math and fig*) to integrate. (**c**) (*Fin*) to repay, reimburse; (*Arg, Col, Mex*) to hand over.
integridad *nf* (**a**) wholeness, completeness. (**b**) (*fig*) uprightness, integrity. (**c**) (*fig*) virginity.
íntegro *adj* (**a**) whole, entire, complete; integral; **la cantidad íntegra** the whole sum, the sum in full; **versión íntegra** (*Lit*) unabridged version; **en versión íntegra de Pérez** in Pérez's edition of the complete text.
(**b**) (*fig*) honest, upright.
integumento *nm* integument.
intelectiva *nf* intellect, mental faculty.
intelecto *nm* intellect; understanding; brains.
intelectual 1 *adj* intellectual; brain (*attr*). **2** *nmf* intellectual.
intelectualidad *nf* (**a**) intellectuality. (**b**) intelligentsia, intellectual people.
intelectualmente *adv* intellectually.
inteligencia *nf* (**a**) intelligence; mind, wits, understanding; ability; **de mediocre** — of mediocre intelligence; **una persona de fina** — a person with a sharp mind.
(**b**) understanding; **la buena** — **entre los pueblos** good understanding between peoples.
(**c**) (*SAm: Mil etc*) intelligence.
(**d**) (*pej*) secret agreement, collusion.
inteligente *adj* (**a**) intelligent; clever, brainy, talented. (**b**) skilful; skilled, trained (*en* in).
inteligentemente *adv* intelligently.
inteligibilidad *nf* intelligibility.
inteligible *adj* intelligible.
inteligiblemente *adv* intelligibly.
intemperancia *nf* intemperance, excess.
intemperante *adj* intemperate, excessive.
intemperie *nf* inclemency (of the weather); bad weather, rough weather; **estar a la** — to be out in the open, be exposed to wind and weather, be at the mercy of the elements; **aguantar la** — to put up with wind and weather; **una cara curtida a la** — a face tanned by wind and weather.
intempestivamente *adv* in an untimely way, at a bad time; unseasonably.
intempestivo *adj* untimely, ill-timed; unseasonable.
intención *nf* intention; purpose; plan; **mis** —**es** my intentions, my plans; — **delictiva** criminal intent; —**es delictivas** criminal intentions; **segunda** — duplicity, underhandedness; **con** — deliberately; **con segunda** — meaningfully; with a second meaning, implying something else; (*pej*) nastily; **con la** — **de** + *infin* with the idea of + *ger*, intending to + *infin*; **de** — on purpose; **aceptar las** —**es de uno** to accept someone's advances, respond to someone's advances; **sin hacer la menor** — **de** + *infin* without making the least move to + *infin*; **tener la** — **de** + *infin* to intend to + *infin*, mean to + *infin*.

intencionadamente *adv* (a) meaningfully; nastily. (b) deliberately.

intencionado *adj* (a) meaningful. (b) deliberate. (c) **bien** — well-meaning; **mal** — ill-disposed, hostile, unkind; malicious.

intencional *adj* intentional.

intencionalmente *adv* intentionally.

intendencia *nf* (a) management, administration. (b) manager's office. (c) (*Mil: also* **cuerpo de** —, *approx*) service corps. (d) (*Arg*) mayoralty.

intendente *nm* (a) manager. (b) — **de ejército** quartermaster general. (c) (*Arg*) mayor.

intensamente *adv* intensely; powerfully, strongly; vividly, profoundly.

intensar [1a] **1** *vt* to intensify. **2 intensarse** *vr* to intensify.

intensidad *nf* intensity; power, strength; vividness; deepness; (*Elec, Tech*) strength.

intensificación *nf* intensification.

intensificar [1g] *vt* to intensify.

intensión *nf* intensity, intenseness.

intensivamente *adv* intensively.

intensivo *adj* intensive.

intenso *adj* intense; *feeling* intense, powerful, strong; *impression* vivid, profound; *tan* deep; *colour* deep, intense; (*Elec etc*) strong.

intentar [1a] *vt* (a) to try, attempt; — **algo** to try something; — + *infin* to try to + *infin*, attempt to + *infin*, endeavour to + *infin*. (b) to mean, intend (*con* by); — + *infin* to mean to + *infin*.

intento *nm* (a) intention, intent, purpose; **al** — **de** + *infin* (*Arg, Chi*) with the aim of + *ger*; **de** — on purpose. (b) attempt; — **fracasado** failed attempt, unsuccessful attempt; **acusado de** — **de violación** charged with attempted rape.

intentona *nf* foolhardy attempt, wild attempt; (*Pol*) putsch, rising.

inter . . . inter . . .

interacción *nf* interaction, interplay.

interamericano *adj* inter-American.

interandino *adj* inter-Andean, concerning areas on both sides of the Andes.

intercalación *nf* intercalation, insertion.

intercalar [1a] *vt* to intercalate, insert.

intercambiable *adj* interchangeable.

intercambiar [1b] *vt* to change over, interchange; *publications, prisoners etc* to exchange; *stamps etc* to exchange, swap.

intercambio *nm* interchange; exchange; swap, swapping.

interceder [2a] *vi* to intercede; — **con A por B** to intercede with A on B's behalf, to plead with A for B.

interceptación *nf* interception; stoppage, holdup.

interceptar [1a] *vt* to intercept, cut off; to stop, hold up.

interceptor *nm* (a) interceptor. (b) (*Mech*) trap; separator.

intercesión *nf* intercession; mediation.

interclub *adj* (*SAm*) *game* inter-club, between two clubs.

intercomunicación *nf* intercommunication.

intercomunión *nf* intercommunion.

interconectar [1a] *vt* to interconnect.

interconfesional *adj* interdenominational.

intercontinental *adj* intercontinental.

interdecir [3p] *vt* to forbid, prohibit.

interdependencia *nf* interdependence.

interdependiente *adj* interdependent.

interdicción *nf* prohibition, interdiction.

interdicto *nm* prohibition, ban, interdict.

interés *nm* (a) interest; concern; **con gran** — with great interest; **de gran** — of great interest, very interesting; **su** — **en, su** — **por** his interest in; his concern for; **poner** — **en** to take an interest in; **sentir** — **por** to be interested in, feel an interest in; **no tiene** — it has no interest. (b) interest, share, part; — **es** interests, affairs; **los** — **es españoles en África** Spanish interests in Africa; — **es creados** vested interests; **en** — **de** in the interest of; **en** — **de la higiene** in the interest of hygiene, for the sake of cleanliness; **fomentar los** — **es de uno** to promote someone's interests; **tener** — **en** to hold a share in, have a part in. (c) (*pej*) self-interest; selfishness, egotism; **todo es cuestión de** — it's all a matter of self-interest. (d) (*Comm, Fin*) interest; **con** — **de 9 por cien, con un** — **del 9 por cien** at an interest of 9%; — **compuesto** compound interest; — **devengado** accrued interest, earned interest; — **simple** simple interest; **dar a** — to lend at interest; **devengar** — **es** to bear interest; **poner a** — to put out at interest, invest.

interesado 1 *adj* (a) interested; concerned; **estar** — **en** to be interested in, have an interest in; **la compañía está interesada en comprarlo** the company is interested in buying it. (b) biassed, prejudiced; **actuar de una manera interesada** to act in a biassed way. (c) selfish, self-seeking; having an ulterior motive; mercenary. **2** *nm,* **interesada** *nf* (a) person concerned, interested party; **los** — **s** those interested, those concerned. (b) (*in applications*) the undersigned, the applicant.

interesante *adj* interesting.

interesar [1a] **1** *vt* (a) to interest, be of interest to; to appeal to; ¿**te interesa el fútbol?** are you interested in football?; **no me interesan los toros** I'm not interested in bullfighting, bullfighting does not appeal to me; **la propuesta no nos interesa** the proposal is of no interest to us. (b) to interest (*in* en); **logré** — **le en mi idea** I succeeded in interesting him in my idea. (c) to concern, involve; **el asunto interesa a todos** the matter concerns everybody. (d) (*Med*) to affect, involve; **la lesión interesa la región lumbar** the injury affects the lumbar region. **2** *vi* to be of interest; to be important; **la idea no interesó** the idea was of no interest, the idea did not interest anybody. **3 interesarse** *vr* to be interested, take an interest (*en, por* in); — **en una empresa** to participate in an enterprise, concern oneself with an enterprise.

interestatal *adj* inter-state.

interestelar *adj* interstellar.

interferencia *nf* (a) (*Phys, Radio*) interference, (*deliberate*) jamming. (b) (*angl*) interference (*en* ✔ in); **no** — non-interference.

interferir [3i] **1** *vt* (a) (*Phys, Radio*) to interfere with, (*deliberately*) jam. (b) (*angl*) to interfere with, upset, affect; **su acción ha interferido nuestras operaciones** his action has interfered with our operations. **2** *vi* (*angl*) to interfere (*en* in, with). **3 interferirse** *vr* (*angl*) to interfere (*en* in, with); **no está en posición de** — **en el conflicto** he is in no position to interfere in the conflict.

ínterin 1 *adv* meanwhile. **2** *conj* while; until. **3** *nm* (a) interim; **en el** — in the interim, in the meantime. (b) temporary incumbency.

interinamente *adv* (a) in the interim, meanwhile. (b) temporarily, as a temporary holder of the post (*etc*), as a stopgap.

interinar [1a] *vt post* to occupy temporarily, occupy in an acting capacity.

interinato *nm* (a) (*Arg*) temporary nature (of a post). (b) (*Arg*) period of temporary occupation of a post. (c) (*Arg, Chi, Guat, Hond*) temporary post.

interino 1 *adj* (a) provisional, temporary, interim. (b) *person* acting. **2** *nm,* **interina** *nf* temporary holder of a post, acting official (*etc*); stopgap, stand-in; (*Eccl, Med*) locum, locum tenens.

interior 1 *adj* interior, inner, inside; *thoughts etc* inward, inner; *politics, trade* domestic, internal; (*Geog*) inland, *part of country* inner; **en la parte** — inside, on the inside; **pista** — (*Sport*) inside track; *see* **ropa** *etc*. **2** *nm* (a) interior, inside; inner part. (b) (*fig*) mind, soul; **en su** — in one's heart, deep inside one; **dije para mí** — I said to myself. (c) **Ministerio del I** — Ministry of the Interior, Home Office (*Brit*), Department of the Interior (*US*). (d) (*Sport*) inside-forward; — **derecho** inside-right; — **izquierdo** inside-left. (e) — **es** (*Anat*) insides.

interioridad *nf* (a) inwardness; **en su** —, **sabe que . . .** (*CAm*) in his heart he knows that . . . , deep inside himself he knows that . . . . (b) — **es** family secrets; private affairs; inner history, secret goings-on; ins and outs; **explicó las** — **es de la lucha** he explained the inner history of the struggle; **desconocen las** — **es del mercado** they don't know all the ins and outs of the market.

interiorizar [1f] (*SAm*) **1** *vt* to look into, investigate closely. **2 interiorizarse** *vr:* — **algo** to familiarize oneself with something.

interiormente *adv* internally, inwardly; **lo que pasa —** what goes on inside.

interjección *nf* interjection.

interlineado *nm* space between the lines.

interlineal *adj* interlinear.

interlinear [1a] *vt* (**a**) to interline, write (*or* print *etc*) between the lines. (**b**) (*Typ*) to space, lead.

interlocutor *nm*, **interlocutora** *nf* speaker, interlocutor; **mi —** the person I was speaking to, the person who spoke to me.

intérlope 1 *adj* interloping, intrusive; (*Mex*) fraudulent. 2 *nm* (*Comm*) interloper, unauthorized trader.

interludio *nm* interlude.

intermediario 1 *adj* (**a**) intermediary.
  (**b**) mediating.
  2 *nm*, **intermediaria** *nf* (**a**) intermediary.
  (**b**) mediator.
  3 *nm* (*Comm*) middleman.

intermedio 1 *adj* (**a**) intermediate, halfway (*entre* between).
  (**b**) intervening; **el período —** the intervening period, the period between.
  2 *nm* (**a**) interval (*also Theat*); (*Parl*) recess.
  (**b**) **por — de** (*SAm*) through, by means of.

intermezzo [inter'metso] *nm* intermezzo.

interminable *adj* endless, interminable.

interminablemente *adv* endlessly, interminably.

intermisión *nf* intermission.

intermitente 1 *adj* intermittent. 2 *nm* (*Aut*) flashing light, indicator.

internacional 1 *adj* international. 2 *nf*: **I—** International(e).

internacionalismo *nm* internationalism.

internacionalizar [1f] *vt* to internationalize.

internada *nf* (*Sport*) tackle.

internado 1 *nm*, **internada** *nf* (*Mil etc*) internee. 2 *nm* boarding school; boarding; (*pupils collectively*) boarders.

internamiento *nm* internment.

internar [1a] 1 *vt* (**a**) (*Mil*) to intern; **a uno en un manicomio** to put someone into an asylum, commit someone to an asylum.
  (**b**) to send inland.
  2 **internarse** *vr* (**a**) to advance (deeply); to penetrate; **el jugador se interna** the player goes deep into the opponent's half.
  (**b**) **— en** to go into, go deeply into, penetrate into; **se internó en el edificio** he went into the building, he disappeared into the building; **— en un país** to go into the interior of a country.
  (**c**) **— en un estudio** to go deeply into a subject, study a subject in depth.

interno 1 *adj* internal, interior; inside; **la política interna** internal politics, domestic politics; **por vía interna** (*Med*) internally. 2 *nm*, **interna** *nf* boarder.

interpelación *nf* appeal, plea.

interpelar [1a] *vt* (**a**) to implore, beseech; to beg for the aid of. (**b**) to address, speak to; (*Parl*) to ask for explanations, question formally.

interplanetario *adj* interplanetary.

interpolación *nf* interpolation.

interpolar [1a] *vt* (**a**) to interpolate. (**b**) to interrupt briefly.

interponer [2r] 1 *vt* (**a**) to interpose, put in, insert.
  (**b**) (*Law*) *appeal* to lodge, put in.
  (**c**) (*in speech*) to interpose, interject.
  2 **interponerse** *vr* to intervene.

interposición *nf* (**a**) insertion. (**b**) lodging, formulation. (**c**) interjection.

interpretación *nf* (**a**) interpretation; **mala —** misinterpretation, misunderstanding.
  (**b**) interpretation, translation.
  (**c**) (*Mus*) rendition, performance; interpretation.
  (**d**) (*Theat*) performance; playing.

interpretar [1a] *vt* (**a**) to interpret; **— mal** to misinterpret, misunderstand, miscontrue.
  (**b**) (*Ling*) to interpret, translate; **— del chino al ruso** to translate from Chinese into Russian.
  (**c**) (*Mus*) to render, perform; to interpret; (*Theat*) *play* to perform; *part* to play.

interpretativo *adj* interpretative.

intérprete *nmf* (**a**) (*Ling*) interpreter, translator. (**b**) (*Mus*) performer; exponent; artist(e).

interracial *adj* interracial.

interregno *nm* interregnum; (*SAm*) interval, intervening period.

interrelación *nf* interrelation.

interrelacionado *adj* interrelated.

interrelacionar [1a] *vt* to interrelate.

interreligioso *adj*: **contactos —s** contacts between religions.

interrogación *nf* (**a**) interrogation. (**b**) question. (**c**) question mark.

interrogador *nm*, **interrogadora** *nf* interrogator; questioner.

interrogante 1 *adj* questioning. 2 *nmf* interrogator; questioner. 3 *nf* question mark; (*fig*) question mark, query.

interrogar [1h] *vt* to question, interrogate; (*Law*) to examine.

interrogativo 1 *adj* interrogative. 2 *nm* interrogative.

interrogatorio *nm* (**a**) questioning; (*Law*) examination. (**b**) questionnaire.

interrumpir [3a] *vt speaker etc* to interrupt; *holiday etc* to interrupt, cut short; *supply* to cut off; *traffic etc* to block, hold up; (*Elec*) to switch off.

interrupción *nf* interruption; stoppage, holdup.

interruptor *nm* (*Elec*) switch; **— de dos direcciones** two-way switch.

intersecarse [1g] *vr* to intersect.

intersección *nf* intersection; (*Aut*) intersection, crossing, junction.

intersticio *nm* interstice; crack; interval, gap; (*Mech*) clearance.

intertanto (*SAm*) 1 *adv* meanwhile. 2 *conj*: **— que él llegue** until he comes, while we wait for him to come. 3 *n*: **en el —** in the meantime.

interurbano *adj* inter-city; (*Tel*) long-distance, trunk (*attr*).

intervalo *nm* (*in time*) interval; break; (*Mus*) interval; (*in space*) gap; **a —s** at intervals; intermittently; every now and then.

intervención *nf* (**a**) supervision, control.
  (**b**) (*Comm*) audit, auditing.
  (**c**) (*Med*) operation; **— quirúrgica** surgical operation.
  (**d**) (*Tel*) tapping.
  (**e**) intervention (*en* in); participation (*en* in), contribution (*en* to); **su — en la discusión** his contribution to the discussion; **la política de no —** the policy of non-intervention, the non-intervention policy.

intervenir [3s] 1 *vt* (**a**) to supervise, control.
  (**b**) (*Comm*) to audit.
  (**c**) (*Med*) to operate on.
  (**d**) (*Tel*) to tap.
  2 *vi* (**a**) to intervene (*en* in); to take part, participate (*en* in); to contribute (*en* to); **no intervino en el debate** he did not take part in the debate, he did not contribute to the debate; **él no intervino en la decisión** he did not have a hand in the decision; **una reyerta en la que intervino X** a brawl in which X was involved.
  (**b**) to intercede; to mediate; **— por uno** to intercede for someone.

interventor *nm* inspector, supervisor; (*Comm*) auditor (*also* **— de cuentas**).

interviú *nf* interview; **hacer una — a uno** to interview someone.

interviuvada *nf* series of interviews, interview session.

interviuvador *nm*, **interviuvadora** *nf* interviewer.

interviuvar [1a] *vt* to interview, have an interview with.

intestado *adj* intestate.

intestinal *adj* intestinal.

intestino 1 *adj* internal; domestic, civil. 2 *nm* intestine; gut; **— ciego** caecum; **— delgado** small intestine; **— grueso** large intestine.

intimación *nf* intimation, announcement, notification.

íntimamente *adv* intimately.

intimar [1a] 1 *vt* to intimate, announce, notify (*a* to); to order, require (*que* that).
  2 *vi and* **intimarse** *vr* to become intimate, become friendly (*con* with); **ahora intiman mucho** they're very friendly now.

intimidación *nf* intimidation.

intimidad *nf* (**a**) intimacy, familiarity; **disfrutar de la — de uno** to be on close terms with someone, enjoy someone's confidence; **entrar en — con uno** to become friendly with someone.
  (**b**) privacy, private life; **conocido en la — como X** known in private life as X; **la ceremonia se celebró en la —** the wedding took place privately, it was a quiet wedding.

intimidar [1a] 1 *vt* to intimidate, overawe; to bully, scare.
  2 **intimidarse** *vr* to be intimidated, be overawed; to get scared.

íntimo *adj* intimate; *relationship* intimate, close; *thoughts* inner, innermost; *life etc* private; **una boda**

íntima a quiet wedding, a private wedding; **es —
amigo mío** he is a close friend of mine; **en lo más
— de su corazón** in one's heart of hearts.
intitular [1a] *vt* to entitle, call.
intocable 1 *adj* untouchable. **2** *nmf* untouchable.
intolerable *adj* intolerable, unbearable.
intolerancia *nf* intolerance; narrow-mindedness,
bigotry.
intolerante *adj* intolerant (*con, para* of); narrow-
minded, bigoted (*en* about).
intonso *adj* book uncut.
intoxicación *nf* poisoning; **— alimenticia** food
poisoning.
intoxicar [1g] *vt* to poison.
intra . . . intra . . .
intradós *nm* inside surface of an arch (*or* vault); side
of a window frame.
intraducible *adj* untranslatable.
intragable *adj* unpalatable (*also fig*).
intramuros *adv* within the city, within the walls.
intranquilidad *nf* worry, uneasiness, disquiet,
anxiety.
intranquilizar [1f] **1** *vt* to worry, disquiet, make
uneasy. **2 intranquilizarse** *vr* to get worried, feel
uneasy, be anxious.
intranquilo *adj* worried, uneasy, anxious; restless.
intranscendente *adj* (*SAm*) unimportant, insignificant.
intranscribible *adj* unprintable.
intransferible *adj* untransferable, not transferable.
intransigencia *nf* intransigence; uncompromising
attitude.
intransigente *adj* intransigent; uncompromising,
unyielding; diehard.
intransitable *adj* impassable.
intransitivo *adj* intransitive.
intratable *adj* problem intractable; awkward, tough;
person unsociable; difficult, impossible; **¡son —s!**
they're impossible!
intravenoso *adj* intravenous.
intrépidamente *adv* intrepidly, dauntlessly.
intrepidez *nf* intrepidity, intrepidness.
intrépido *adj* intrepid, dauntless.
intriga *nf* intrigue; plot, scheme; (*Theat*) plot; **—
secundaria** subplot.
intrigante 1 *adj* (**a**) (*pej*) intriguing, scheming. (**b**)
(*angl*) intriguing, interesting, puzzling. **2** *nmf*
intriguer.
intrigar [1h] **1** *vt* (**a**) to intrigue, interest, puzzle.
(**b**) (*SAm*) *affair* to conduct in a surprising way.
2 *vi* to intrigue, scheme, plot.
3 intrigarse *vr* (*SAm*) to be intrigued, be puzzled.
intrincadamente *adv* (**a**) densely, impenetrably.
(**b**) (*fig*) intricately.
intrincado *adj* (**a**) dense, impenetrable; tangled.
(**b**) (*fig*) intricate; involved, complicated.
intrincar [1g] *vt* to entangle; to confuse, complicate.
intríngulis *nm* (*fam*) ulterior motive; hidden snag;
puzzle, mystery.
intrínsecamente *adv* intrinsically; inherently.
intrínseco *adj* intrinsic; inherent.
intro . . . intro . . .
introducción *nf* introduction; insertion; creation.
introducir [3o] **1** *vt* to introduce; *visitor etc* to bring
in, show in; *object* to insert, introduce, put in;
discord etc to create, sow, cause.
2 introducirse *vr* (**a**) to get in, slip in, gain
access (*en* to); (*fig*) to insinuate oneself, worm one's
way (*en* into).
(**b**) (*fig*) to interfere, meddle.
introductor *adj* introductory.
introito *nm* (*Theat*) prologue; (*Eccl*) introit.
intromisión *nf* (**a**) introduction, insertion. (**b**) (*pej*)
interference, meddling.
introspección *nf* introspection.
introspectivo *adj* introspective.
introversión *nf* introversion.
introvertido 1 *adj* introvert. **2** *nm*, **introvertida** *nf*
introvert.
intrusión *nf* intrusion; (*Law*) trespass.
intruso 1 *adj* intrusive. **2** *nm*, **intrusa** *nf* intruder,
interloper; outsider; (*at party etc*) gatecrasher;
(*Law*) trespasser.
intuición *nf* intuition; **por —** by intuition, intuitively.
intuir [3g] **1** *vt* to know by intuition.
2 intuirse *vr*: **eso se intuye** that can be guessed;
se intuye que . . . one can tell intuitively that . . .,
one can guess that . . .; **el hombre se intuye
observado** the man guesses he is being watched,
the man realizes he is under observation.
intuitivamente *adv* intuitively.

intuitivo *adj* intuitive.
intuito *nm* glance, look; **por — de** in view of.
inundación *nf* flood, flooding.
inundadizo *adj* (*SAm*) liable to flooding.
inundar [1a] *vt* to flood, inundate, swamp (*all also
fig; de, en* with); **— el mercado de un producto** to
flood the market with a product; **quedamos
inundados de ofertas** we are swamped with offers;
la lluvia inundó la campiña the rain flooded the
countryside, the rain left the countryside under
water.
inusitado *adj* (**a**) unusual, unwonted, rare. (**b**)
obsolete.
inútil *adj* useless; *attempt etc* vain, fruitless; *effort*
vain; **todo es —** nothing is any use; **es — que Vd
proteste** it is useless for you to protest, it's no good
your protesting.
inutilidad *nf* uselessness.
inutilización *nf* disablement; spoiling; (*of stamp*)
cancellation.
inutilizar [1f] **1** *vt* to make useless, render useless;
ship etc to disable, put out of action; to spoil, ruin;
effort etc to nullify; *stamp* to cancel.
2 inutilizarse *vr* to become useless; to be disabled;
to be spoiled.
inútilmente *adv* uselessly; vainly, fruitlessly.
invadeable *adj* unfordable; (*fig*) impassable; (*fig*)
unsurmountable.
invadir [3a] *vt* (**a**) to invade; to overrun; **la turba
invadió las calles** the mob poured out on to the
streets. (**b**) (*fig*) *rights etc* to encroach upon.
invalidar [1a] *vt* to invalidate, nullify.
invalidez *nf* (**a**) disablement; unfitness. (**b**) in-
validity, nullity.
inválido 1 *adj* (**a**) (*Med*) invalid, disabled; unfit.
(**b**) (*Law etc*) invalid, null and void; **declarar
inválida una elección** to declare an election invalid.
2 *nm*, **inválida** *nf* (*Med*) invalid.
3 *nm* (*Mil: Med*) disabled soldier, wounded
soldier; pensioner.
invaluable *adj* (*SAm*) invaluable.
invariable *adj* invariable.
invariablemente *adv* invariably.
invasión *nf* (**a**) invasion (*also Med*); attack. (**b**)
(*fig*) encroachment (*de* on); inroad (*de* into).
invasor 1 *adj* invading. **2** *nm*, **invasora** *nf* invader,
attacker.
invectiva *nf* invective; **una —** a piece of invective,
a tirade.
invectivar [1a] *vt* to inveigh against.
invencibilidad *nf* invincibility.
invencible *adj* invincible; *obstacle* unsurmountable,
insuperable.
invenciblemente *adv* invincibly; insuperably.
invención *nf* invention; discovery, finding; (*pej*)
fabrication; (*Poet etc*) fiction, tale, fable.
invendible *adj* unsaleable, unmarketable.
inventar [1a] *vt* to invent; to devise; (*pej*) to make up,
fabricate, concoct.
inventariar [1b] *vt* to inventory, make an inventory
of.
inventario *nm* inventory; stocktaking; **hacer — de**
to make an inventory of, take stock of.
inventiva *nf* inventiveness; ingenuity, resourcefulness.
inventivo *adj* inventive; ingenious, resourceful.
invento *nm* invention.
inventor *nm*, **inventora** *nf* inventor.
invernáculo *nm* greenhouse, hothouse; conservatory.
invernada *nf* (**a**) winter season.
(**b**) wintering; hibernation.
(**c**) (*Arg, Col, Per, Urug*) winter pasture.
(**d**) (*Ven*) heavy rainstorm.
invernadero *nm* (**a**) = **invernáculo**. (**b**) (*SAm*)
winter pasture.
invernal *adj* wintry, winter (*attr*).
invernar [1k] *vi* to winter, spend the winter; (*Zool*)
to hibernate.
invernazo *nm* (*PR, SD*) rainy season (*July to
September*).
inverne *nm* (*SAm*) winter pasturing; winter fattening.
invernizo *adj* wintry, winter (*attr*).
inverosímil *adj* unlikely, improbable; implausible.
inverosimilitud *nf* unlikeliness, improbability;
implausibility.
inversamente *adv* inversely; **e —** and vice versa.
inversión *nf* (**a**) inversion; reversal; (*Aut, Mech*)
reversing; **— de marcha** reversing, backing; **—
sexual** homosexuality.
(**b**) (*Comm, Fin*) investment (*en* in); **— de
capitales** capital investment.

inversionista *nmf* (*Comm, Fin*) investor.
inverso *adj* inverse, inverted; reverse, contrary; **a la inversa** inversely, the other way round; (*fig*) vice versa; on the contrary.
inversor *nm*, **inversora** *nf* (*SAm: Comm, Fin*) investor.
invertebrado 1 *adj* invertebrate. 2 *nm* invertebrate.
invertido 1 *adj* (a) inverted; reversed. (b) homosexual. 2 *nm* homosexual.
invertir [3i] *vt* (a) to invert, turn upside down; to reverse, put the other way round; to change over, change the order of; (*Aut, Mech*) to reverse.
(b) *effort, time* to spend, put in (*en* on); **invirtieron 5 días en el viaje** they spent 5 days on the journey. (c) (*Comm, Fin*) to invest (*en* in).
investidura *nf* investiture.
investigación *nf* (a) investigation; inquiry (*de* into); — **policíaca** police investigation.
(b) (*Univ etc*) research, research work (*de* in, into).
investigador *nm*, **investigadora** *nf* (a) investigator.
(b) (*Univ etc*) research worker, researcher.
investigar [1h] *vt* (a) to investigate; to inquire into, look into.
(b) (*Univ etc*) to do research into, do research work on.
investir [3l] *vt*: — **a uno con algo**, — **a uno de algo** to invest someone with something, confer something on someone.
inveterado *adj* inveterate; confirmed, hardened; *habit* deep-seated, well-established.
invicto *adj* unconquered, unbeaten.
invidencia *nf* sightlessness.
invierno *nm* (a) winter, wintertime. (b) (*CAm, Col, Ec, Ven*) rainy season. (c) (*Ven*) heavy shower.
inviolabilidad *nf* inviolability; — **parlamentaria** parliamentary immunity.
inviolable *adj* inviolable.
inviolado *adj* inviolate.
invisibilidad *nf* invisibility.
invisible 1 *adj* invisible. 2 *nm* (*Arg*) hairpin; (*Mex*) hairnet.
invitación *nf* invitation (*a* to).
invitado *nm*, **invitada** *nf* guest.
invitar [1a] *vt* (a) to invite; — **a uno a hacer algo** to invite someone to do something; to call on someone to do something; **hoy invito a café** today I'll buy the coffee, today I'll stand coffees all round; **dio las gracias a los que le habían invitado** he thanked his hosts.
(b) to attract, entice.
invocar [1g] *vt* (a) to invoke, call on; — **la ley to** invoke the law.
(b) to beg for, implore; — **la ayuda de** to beg for the help of.
involucrar [1a] 1 *vt*: — **algo en un discurso** to bring something irrelevant into a speech.
2 **involucrarse** *vr* (*esp SAm*) to meddle, interfere (*en* in); to get involved (*en* in); **las personas involucradas en el caso** the people involved in the affair, the persons concerned in the matter.
involuntariamente *adv* involuntarily; unintentionally.
involuntario *adj* involuntary; *offence etc* unintentional.
invulnerabilidad *nf* invulnerability.
invulnerable *adj* invulnerable.
inyectable *nm* serum, vaccine.
inyección *nf* injection, shot; **hacerse** (*or* **ponerse**) **una** — to give oneself an injection.
inyectado *adj*: **ojos** —**s** (**en sangre**) bloodshot eyes.
inyectar [1a] *vt* to inject (*en* into); — **algo en uno** to inject someone with something.
inyector *nm* injector; (*Tech*) nozzle.
ion *nm* ion.
iónico *adj* ionic.
ionizar [1f] *vt* to ionize.
ionosfera *nf* ionosphere.
iota *nf* iota.
ipecacuana *nf* ipecacuanha.
ir [3t] 1 *vi* (a) (*general sense*) to go; to move; to travel; (*on foot*) to go, walk; (*in car etc*) to go, drive; (*on cycle, horse etc*) to go, ride; — **a Quito** to go to Quito; **este camino va a Huesca** this road goes to Huesca, this is the road to Huesca; — **hacia Sevilla** to go towards Seville, go in the direction of Seville; — **hasta León** to go as far as León; **fui en coche** I went by car, I drove; **fui en tren** I went by train, I went by rail; — **despacio** to go slow(ly); — **con tiento** to go carefully, go cautiously; **vaya donde vaya, encontrará** . . . wherever you go, you will find . . .; **ya ha ido** (*fam*) you've had it (*fam*);

¡voy! I'm coming! (*answering a call*); **¡vamos!** let's go! (*see also* (k)); **¿quién va?** (*Mil etc*) who goes there?; — **por leña** to fetch wood, go and fetch wood, go for wood; **voy por el médico** I'll (go and) fetch the doctor, I'll call the doctor; — **tras una** to chase someone, chase after someone.
(b) (*idioms*) — **de mal en peor** to go from bad to worse, get worse; **esto va de veras** this is serious; I'm in earnest; **en lo que va de año** so far this year; **a eso voy** I'm coming to that; **si vamos a eso** for that matter, as for that; — **a lo suyo** to go one's own way; (*pej*) to act selfishly, think only of oneself; **va para los 40** he's going on for 40, he's knocking on 40 (*fam*); **va para viejo** he's getting old; **con éste van 30** that makes 30.
(c) (*of progress*) to go; (*Med*) to be, go, get along; **¿cómo va eso?** how are things going?; **¿cómo le va?** how goes it?; **¿cómo va el ensayo?** how are you getting on with the essay?; **no me va bien el inglés** I can't get on with English; **el enfermo va mejor** the patient is better, the patient is getting along nicely.
(d) (*of difference*) **va mucho de A a B** there's a lot of difference between A and B, A is very different from B; **¡lo que va del padre al hijo!** what a difference there is between father and son!; **de 7 a 9 van 2** 7 from 9 leaves 2.
(e) (*of intention*) **eso no va por Vd** I wasn't referring to you, that wasn't meant for you; it's not your fault.
(f) (*of concern*) **va mucho en esto** a lot depends on it; **¿qué te va en ello?** what does it matter to you?; **no le va la vida en esto** it's not as though his life depends on it.
(g) (*of betting*) **van 5 duros a que no lo haces** I bet 5 *duros* that you won't do it; **¿cuánto va?** how much do you bet?
(h) (*of career etc*) **va para ingeniero** he's going to become an engineer, he's going into engineering.
(i) (*Cards*) to lead; to go.
(j) (*of clothes*) to suit, become; **¿me va bien esto?** does this suit me?; **no le va bien el sombrero** the hat doesn't suit her.
(k) (*interj*) etc **¡vaya!** well!, there!, I say!; **¡vaya coche!** what a car!, there's a car for you!, that's some car!; **¡vaya susto que me pegué!** what a fright I got!; **¡vaya, vaya!** well I'm blowed!; come now!; **¡vamos!** well!; **vamos, no es difícil** come now, it's not difficult; **una chica, vamos, una mujer** a girl, well . . . a woman; **¡qué va!** rubbish!; nonsense!; **¡vaya por Pepe!** here's to Joe!
(l) (*in continuous tenses*) **iba anocheciendo** it was getting dark; **iban fumando** they were smoking; **voy comprendiendo que** . . . I am beginning to see that . . ., I am in the process of learning that . . .
(m) (*with ptp*) **iba cansado** he was tired; **van escritas 3 cartas** that's 3 letters I've written; **va vendido todo** everything has been sold.
(n) (*ir a* + *infin*) **voy a hacerlo** I'm going to do it; **vamos a hacerlo** we are going to do it; let's do it; **fui a verle** I went to see him, I went and saw him; **¿qué le vamos a hacer?** what can we do about him?
(o) *ir de* + *noun*: see the corresponding noun entry.
2 **irse** *vr* (a) **por aquí se va a Jaca** this is the way to Jaca; **¿por dónde se va al aeropuerto?** which way to the airport?
(b) to go away, leave, depart; **se fueron** they went, they went off, they left; **es hora de irnos** it's time we were off, it's time for us to go; **¡vete!** go away!, get out!; **¡vete ya!** off with you!; **¡no te vayas!** don't go!; **¡vámonos!** let's go!, (*Rail etc*) all aboard!; — **de algo** to discard something; **me voy de con Vd** (*CAm*) I'm leaving you.
(c) *see* **mano, pie** *etc*; to slip, lose one's balance; (*of wall etc*) to give way.
(d) (*of container*) to leak; to overflow; (*of contents*) to leak out, overflow, ooze out; to evaporate; **se fue el vino** the wine leaked out; the wine overflowed; **el neumático se va** the tyre is losing air.
(e) (*euph*) to be dying; to die; **se nos va el amo** the master is dying; **se nos fue hace 3 años** he departed from us 3 years ago, he passed away 3 years ago.
ira *nf* anger, rage, wrath (*lit*); (*of elements*) fury, violence.
iracundia *nf* ire; irascibility.
iracundo *adj* irate; irascible.
Irak: **el** — Iraq.
irakí *see* **iraquí**.

Irán: el — Iran, Persia.
iranés = **iraní.**
iraní 1 adj Iranian, Persian. **2** nmf Iranian, Persian.
iranio = **iraní.**
iraquí 1 adj Iraqui. **2** nmf Iraqui.
irascibilidad nf irascibility.
irascible adj irascible.
iridescencia nf iridescence.
iridescente adj iridescent.
iris nm rainbow; (Anat) iris.
irisación nf iridescence.
irisado adj iridescent.
irisar [1a] vi to be iridescent, iridesce.
Irlanda f Ireland; — **del Norte** Northern Ireland, Ulster.
irlandés 1 adj Irish. **2** nm Irishman; **los** —**es** the Irish. **3** nm (language) Irish.
irlandesa nf Irishwoman.
ironía nf irony; **con** — ironically.
irónicamente adv ironically.
irónico adj ironical.
ironizar [1f] vt to ridicule.
irracional 1 adj irrational; unreasoning; **ser** — brute, brute creature. **2** nm brute, brute creature.
irracionalidad nf irrationality; unreasonableness.
irracionalmente adv irrationally; unreasonably, unreasoningly.
irradiación nf irradiation.
irradiar [1b] vt to irradiate, radiate.
irrazonable adj unreasonable.
irreal adj unreal.
irrealidad nf unreality.
irrealizable adj unrealizable; unworkable; impossible to carry out; objective etc unattainable.
irrebatible adj unanswerable, irrefutable, unassailable.
irreconciliable adj irreconcilable; inconsistent, incompatible.
irreconocible adj unrecognizable.
irrecuperable adj irrecoverable, irretrievable.
irrecusable adj unimpeachable.
irredimible adj irredeemable.
irreducible adj irreducible.
irreductible adj defender etc uncompromising, unyielding.
irreembolsable adj deposit non-returnable.
irreemplazable adj irreplaceable.
irreflexión nf thoughtlessness; rashness, impetuosity.
irreflexivamente adv thoughtlessly, unthinkingly; rashly.
irreflexivo adj thoughtless, unthinking; rash, impetuous; act rash, ill-considered.
irrefrenable adj violence etc unrestrained, unbridled, uncontrollable; person irrepressible; unmanageable.
irrefutable adj irrefutable, unanswerable.
irregular adj irregular; abnormal.
irregularidad nf irregularity; abnormality.
irregularmente adv irregularly; abnormally.
irrelevante adj (SAm) irrelevant.
irreligioso adj irreligious; ungodly.
irremediable adj irremediable; incurable.
irremediablemente adv irremediably; incurably.
irremisible adj irremissible, unpardonable; loss irretrievable.
irremisiblemente adv unpardonably; — **perdido** irretrievably lost, lost beyond hope of recovery.
irremunerado adj unremunerated.
irreparable adj irreparable.
irreparablemente adv irreparably.
irreprimible adj irrepressible.
irreprochable adj irreproachable.
irresistible adj irresistible.
irresistiblemente adv irresistibly.
irresoluble adj unsolvable; unresolved.
irresolución nf irresolution, hesitation, undecidedness.
irresoluto adj (a) irresolute, hesitant, undecided. (b) problem unresolved.
irrespetuosamente adv disrespectfully.
irrespetuoso adj disrespectful.
irresponsabilidad nf irresponsibility.
irresponsable adj irresponsible.
irresuelto adj = **irresoluto** (a).
irreverencia nf irreverence; disrespect.
irreverente adj irreverent; disrespectful.
irreversible adj irreversible.
irrevocable adj irrevocable, irreversible.
irrevocablemente adv irrevocably.
irrigación nf (a) (Med) irrigation. (b) (SAm: Agr) irrigation.
irrigador nm sprinkler.

irrigar [1h] vt (Agr, Med) to irrigate.
irrisible adj laughable, absurd; price absurdly low, bargain (attr).
irrisión nf (a) derision, ridicule. (b) laughing stock.
irrisorio adj derisory, ridiculous, absurd; price absurdly low, bargain (attr).
irritabilidad nf irritability.
irritable adj irritable.
irritación nf irritation.
irritador adj irritating.
irritante 1 adj irritating. **2** nm irritant.
irritar [1a] **1** vt (a) to irritate, anger, exasperate. (b) (fig) to stir up, inflame. (c) (Med) to irritate, inflame.
2 irritarse vr to get angry, lose one's temper (de about, at, with).
irrompible adj unbreakable.
irrumpir [3a] vi: — **en** to burst into, rush into; to invade.
irrupción nf irruption; inrush; invasion.
Isaac m Isaac.
Isabel f Isabel, Elizabeth; (queens of England) Elizabeth.
isabelino adj: **la España isabelina** Isabelline Spain, the Spain of Isabel (II); **la Inglaterra isabelina** Elizabethan England, the England of Elizabeth.
Isabelita f Betty; Bess, Bessie; Liz.
Iseo f Iseult, Isolde.
—ísimo adj suffix (a) **un asunto importantísimo** a very important matter, a most important matter; **una cuestión discutidísima** a highly controversial question; **un desarrolladísimo sentido de orgullo** a very highly developed sense of pride; **es dificilísimo** it is extremely difficult; **resultó incomodísimo** it was extremely uncomfortable; **le golpeó violentísimamente** he hit him with considerable violence.
(b) (more emotionally) **es amabilísimo** he's terribly kind (fam); **¡es simpatiquísimo!** he's awfully nice! (fam); **¡es guapísima!** she is awfully pretty (fam), she just is pretty.
(c) (hum, iro) **un grandísimo libro** an enormous great book, a shockingly heavy book; **una comida costosísima** a shockingly expensive meal.
(d) **aquel españolísimo plato** that most Spanish of all dishes, that most typically Spanish dish; **la madrileñísima plaza de Santa Ana** St Anne's square which is so typical of Madrid, St Anne's square which sums up so much of Madrid.
isla nf (a) island; isle. (b) (Archit) block. (c) (Mex, PR) isolated cluster of trees, isolated patch of scrub.
Isla f: —**s Británicas** British Isles; — **de Francia** Mauritius; for other names, see the second element.
Islam m Islam.
islámico adj Islamic.
islandés 1 adj Icelandic. **2** nm, **islandesa** nf Icelander. **3** nm (language) Icelandic.
Islandia f Iceland.
islándico adj Icelandic.
isleño 1 adj island (attr). **2** nm, **isleña** nf islander.
isleta nf islet.
islote nm small island, rocky isle.
ismo nm ism.
iso . . . iso . . .
isobara nf isobar.
isoca nf (RPl) caterpillar, grub.
Isolde f Iseult, Isolde.
isósceles adj: **triángulo** — isosceles triangle.
isoterma nf isotherm.
isótopo nm isotope.
Israel m Israel.
israelí 1 adj Israeli. **2** nmf Israeli.
israelita 1 adj Israelite. **2** nmf Israelite.
istmeño 1 adj of the Isthmus, (loosely) Panamanian. **2** nm, **istmeña** nf native (or inhabitant) of the Isthmus, Panamanian.
istmo nm isthmus; neck; — **de Panamá** Isthmus of Panamá.
itacate nm (Mex) food, provisions.
Italia f Italy.
italianismo nm italianism, word (or phrase etc) borrowed from Italian.
italiano 1 adj Italian. **2** nm, **italiana** nf Italian. **3** nm (language) Italian.
ítem 1 nm item. **2** adv also, moreover.
itemizar [1f] vt (SAm) to itemize, specify; to divide into sections.
iterar [1a] vt to repeat.
itinerante adj roving, travelling; ambassador roving, at large.

itinerario *nm* itinerary, route.

—ito, —ita *n and adj etc suffix (in some combinations* **—(e)cito, —(e)cita). (a)** *(diminutive)* **un caballito** a little horse; **Juanito** Johnny; **su hijito** her small son, her baby boy; **es más bien bajita** she's rather on the short side; **es mayorcito ya** he's quite tall now; **¡un momentito!** just a moment!

(b) *(superlative)* **ahora mismito** this very instant; **estaba solito** he was completely alone; **están calentitos** they're extra hot, they're piping hot; **salimos tempranito** we left very early; **lo mejorcito que haya** the very best there is.

(c) *(emotive)* **¡pobrecito!** poor old chap! *(fam)*, poor little fellow!; **¡una limosnita!** surely you can spare a copper or two?

(d) *(suffix added from habit, without extra sense:* *esp SAm)* **allacito** = **allá**; **lueguito** = **luego**; *see* **adiosito, ahorita** *etc.*

izar [1f] *vt (Naut)* to hoist, haul up; *flag* to hoist, run up; **la bandera está izada** the flag is flying.

izcuinche *nm (Mex)* **(a)** mangy dog, mongrel. **(b)** ragged child, urchin.

izquierda *nf* **(a)** left hand; left side, left-hand side; **estar a la —— de** to be on the left of; **torcer a la ——** to turn (to the) left; **conducción por la ——** *(Aut)* left-hand drive; **el árbol de la ——** the tree on the left; **seguir por la ——** to keep (to the) left. **(b)** *(Pol)* left.

izquierdista 1 *adj* leftist, left-wing. **2** *nmf* leftist, left-winger.

izquierdo *adj* **(a)** left; left-hand. **(b)** left-handed. **(c)** *(fig)* crooked, twisted.

J

ja *interj* ha!

jaba *nf* (a) (*SAm*) stout basket, crate.
(b) (*Ven*) hollow gourd; (*fig*) poverty.
(c) (*Cu*) beggar's bag; **llevar** (*or* **tener**) **algo en** — (*fig*) to have something in the bag; **no poder ver a otro con** — **grande** to envy someone; **soltar la** — to go up in the world, acquire polish.
(d) (*SAm*) = **haba**.

jabado *adj* (*Ant, Mex, Ven*) off-white with dark spots; (*Cu*) half-bred with pretentions to be white; (*fig*) hesitant, undecided.

jabalí *nm* wild boar.

jabalina *nf* (a) (*Zool*) wild sow, female wild boar.
(b) (*Sport*) javelin.

jabato **1** *adj* (*Cu, Mex*) rough, uncouth; ill-tempered.
2 *nm* young wild boar.

jábega *nf* (a) seine; sweep net, dragnet. (b) fishing smack.

jabón *nm* (a) soap; (*un* —) piece of soap, tablet of soap; — **de afeitar** shaving soap; — **en escama** soapflakes; — **de olor**, — **de tocador** toilet soap; — **en polvo** soap powder, washing powder; — **de sastre** French chalk; **no es lo mismo** — **que hilo negro** (*Per, PR*) they're as different as chalk from cheese.
(b) (*fam*) soft soap (*sl*), flattery; **dar** — **a uno** to soft-soap someone (*sl*).
(c) (*fam*) **dar un** — **a uno** to tell someone off.
(d) (*Arg*) **hacer** — to laze around.
(e) (*Arg, Mex, PR*) fright, fear; **agarrarse un** — to have a scare.

jabonada *nf* (a) (*SAm*) = **jabonadura**. (b) (*Arg, Chi, Mex*) telling-off.

jabonado *nm* (a) soaping. (b) wash, laundry.

jabonadura *nf* (a) soaping. (b) —s lather, soapsuds.
(c) (*fam*) telling-off; **dar una** — **a uno** to tell someone off.

jabonar [1a] *vt* (a) to soap; *clothes* to wash; *beard* to soap, lather. (b) (*fam*) to tell off, dress down.

jaboncillo *nm* (piece of) toilet soap; — **de sastre** French chalk.

jabonera *nf* soapdish.

jabonería *nf* soap factory.

jabonete *nm* piece of toilet soap.

jabonoso *adj* soapy.

jabuco *nm* (*Cu*) large basket, big crate.

jaca *nf* (a) pony, small horse; (*Cu*) gelding. (b) (*Arg*) (old) fighting cock.

jacal *nm* (*Guat, Mex, Ven*) shack, hut; **al** — **viejo no le faltan goteras** old age is bound to have its problems; **no tener** — **donde meterse** to be terribly poor.

jacalear [1a] *vi* (*Mex*) to wander about gossiping.

jacalón *nm* (*Mex*) shed; tumbledown building; (*Theat*) fleapit (*fam*).

jácara *nf* (a) (*Lit: Hist*) comic ballad of low life; (*Mus: Hist*) a merry dance; band of night revellers; **estar de** — to be very merry; **tener mucha** — to have a fund of stories.
(b) (*fam*) fib, story; hoax.
(c) (*fam*) annoyance.

jacarandá *nm or f* jacaranda.

jacarandoso *adj* merry, jolly; lively; spirited, stylish.

jacaré *nm* (*SAm*) alligator.

jacarear [1a] *vi* (a) to sing in the streets at night, go serenading.
(b) (*fig*) to cause a commotion; to be rude, make offensive remarks.

jacarero *nm* amusing person, wag.

jácena *nf* girder.

jacinto *nm* (*Bot*) hyacinth; (*Min*) jacinth.

jaco *nm* small horse, young horse; (*pej*) nag, hack.

jacobino **1** *adj* Jacobin. **2** *nm*, **jacobina** *nf* Jacobin.

Jacobo m Jacob.

jactancia *nf* boasting, bragging; boastfulness.

jactanciosamente *adv* boastfully.

jactancioso *adj* boastful.

jactarse [1a] *vr* to boast, brag; — **de** to boast about, boast of; — **de** + *infin* to boast of + *ger*.

jachudo *adj* (*Ec*) strong, tough; obstinate.

jade *nm* (*Min*) jade.

jadeante *adj* panting, gasping, breathless.

jadear [1a] *vi* to pant, gasp for breath, puff and blow.

jadeo *nm* panting, gasping, puffing and blowing.

jaez *nm* (a) harness, piece of harness; **jaeces** trappings.
(b) (*fig*) kind, sort; **y gente de ese** — (*pej*) and people of that sort.

jaguar *nm* jaguar.

jagüel *nm*, **jagüey** *nm* (*SAm*) pool; tank, cistern.

jaiba **1** *nf* (a) (*SAm*) crab.
(b) (*Col*) mouth; **abrir la** — to show oneself greedy for money.
2 *nmf* (*Ant, Mex*) sly person, sharp businessman.

jáibol *nm* (*SAm: angl*) highball (*US*).

jaibón *adj* (*CAm: angl*) stuck-up (*fam*), pretentious, snobbish.

jailaif (*SAm: angl*) **1** *adj* high-life (*attr*). **2** *nf* high life.

jailoso *adj* (*Col: angl*) well-bred; (*pej*) stuck-up (*fam*), pretentious, snobbish.

Jaime m James.

jalada *nf* (*Mex*) (a) pull, tug, heave. (b) harsh remark, rebuke. (c) (*Per: Univ*) failure.

jalar [1a] **1** *vt* (a) to pull, haul; (*Naut*) to heave; (*Per etc*) to push, push at, shove.
(b) (*fam*) = **jamar**.
(c) (*Col, Ven*) to make, do, perform.
2 *vi* (a) (*SAm*) to go, go off; to clear out; — **para su casa** to go off home.
(b) (*Per: Univ*) to fail.
(c) (*CAm*) to make love; to be courting.
(d) (*Mex*) —**le a una cosa** to get fond of something, be fond of something.
3 jalarse *vr* (a) (*CAm*) to make love; to be courting.
(b) (*SAm*) to get drunk.
(c) = *vi* (a).

jalbegar [1h] *vt* to whitewash; *face* (*fam*) to make up, paint.

jalbegue *nm* whitewash; whitewashing; (*fam*) make-up, paint.

jalde *adj*, **jaldo** *adj* bright yellow.

jalea *nf* jelly; — **de guayaba** guava jelly; **estar hecho una** — (*person*) to be as sweet as can be, (*pej*) to be soapy.

jalear [1a] **1** *vt* (a) *dogs* to urge on; *dancers* to encourage (by shouting and clapping).
(b) (*Chi, Mex*) to pester; (*Mex*) to tease, mock.
2 *vi* (*Mex*) to amuse oneself noisily.

jaleo *nm* (a) spree (*fam*), binge (*sl*); **estar de** — to make merry, have a good time.
(b) row, racket, uproar; fuss; **armar un** — to kick up a row; **se armó un tremendo** — there was a hell of a row.
(c) (*Hunting*) hallooing.
(d) (*Mus*) shouting and clapping (to encourage dancers).

jalisco[1] *adj* (*Guat, Mex*) drunk.

jalisco[2] *nm* (*Guat, Mex*) straw hat.

jalón *nm* (a) stake, pole; surveying rod.
(b) (*fig*) stage.
(c) (*SAm*) pull, tug; **hacer algo de un** — (*Mex*) to do something in one go.
(d) (*Ant, CAm, Mex, Per, Ven*) distance, stretch; **hay un buen** — it's a good way.
(e) (*CAm, Mex*) swig (*fam*), drink.
(f) (*CAm*) lover, sweetheart; suitor.

jalona *nf* (*CAm*) flirt, flighty girl.

jalonar [1a] *vt* to stake out, mark out; (*fig*) to mark; **el camino está jalonado por plazas fuertes** the route is marked out by a series of strongholds, a line of strongholds marks the route.

jalonazo *nm* (*CAm, Mex*) pull, tug.

jalonear [1a] **1** *vt* (*Mex*) to pull, tug, drag. **2** *vi* (a) (*CAm, Mex*) to pull, tug. (b) (*CAm, Mex*) to haggle.

jallo *adj* (*Mex*) vain, stuck-up (*fam*); showy; quick to take offence.

Jamaica *f* Jamaica.

jamaica¹ *nf* (*CAm, Mex*) charity fair, function held to raise funds.

jamaica² *nm* (*Jamaica*) rum.

jamaicano, jamaiquino (*SAm*) **1** *adj* Jamaican. **2** *nm*, **jamaicana** *nf*, **jamaiquina** *nf* Jamaican.

jamar [1a] *vi* (*fam*) to eat to excess, stuff oneself.

jamás *adv* never; (not) ever; **¿se vio — tal cosa?** did you ever see such a thing?; **¡—!** never!; *see* **nunca** *etc*.

jamba *nf* jamb; **— de puerta** jamb, door post.

jambado *adj* (*Mex*) greedy, gluttonous; **estar —** to be feeling over-full.

jambarse [1a] *vr* (*CAm, Mex*) to overeat; to eat greedily.

jamelgo *nm* wretched horse, nag, jade.

jamón *nm* (a) ham; **— en dulce** boiled ham; **¡y un — (con chorreras)!** you're hopeful!, you want jam on it!
(b) (*sl*) **una mujer jamón** a knockout (of a woman) (*sl*); **ella es un —** she's a smasher (*sl*).
(c) (*Ven*) bargain.

jamona *nf* (*fam*) buxom (middle-aged) woman.

jampa *nf* (*Ec*) threshold.

jámparo *nm* (*Col*) canoe, small boat.

jamurar [1a] *vt* (*Col*) to rinse; to bale out.

jan *nm* (*Cu*) stout pointed stake, fencing post; **ensartarse en los —es** to get involved in an unprofitable piece of business.

jandinga *nf* (*Cu*) food.

janearse [1a] *vr* (*Cu*) (a) to leap into the saddle. (b) to stand still; to come to a complete stop.

jangada¹ *nf* (*Naut*) raft.

jangada² *nf* stupid remark; dirty trick.

Japón: el — Japan.

japonés 1 *adj* Japanese. **2** *nm*, **japonesa** *nf* Japanese. **3** *nm* (*language*) Japanese.

jaque *nm* (a) (*Chess*) check; **¡—!** (**al rey**)**!** check!; **— continuo** continuous check; **— mate** checkmate; **¡— de aquí!** get out of here!; **dar — a** to check; **dar — mate a** to checkmate, mate; **tener en —** to check; (*fig*) to hold a threat over; (*fig*) to keep in check, hold at bay.
(b) (*fam*) bully, braggart.

jaquear [1a] *vt* (*Chess*) to check; (*Mil and fig*) to harass.

jaqueca *nf* (severe) headache, migraine; **dar — a** (*fig*) to bore.

jaquetón *nm* (*fam*) bully, braggart.

jáquina *nf* (a) (*SAm*) headstall. (b) (*CAm, Mex*) drunkenness, drunken state.

jaquinón *nm* (*SAm*) headstall, halter.

jara¹ *nf* (a) (*Bot*) a species of Cistus; clump, thicket. (b) dart, arrow; (*Mex*) arrow. (c) (*Mex: sl*) **la — the cops** (*sl*).

jara² *nf* (*Bol*) halt, rest.

jarabe *nm* syrup; sweet drink; **— de arce** maple syrup; **— de pico** (*fig*) mere words, lip service; **— para la tos** cough syrup, cough mixture; **dar — a uno** (*fam*) to butter someone up (*fam*); **estar hecho un —** *see* **jalea**.

jaral *nm* (a) ground covered with *jaras*, scrub; thicket. (b) (*fig*) difficult affair, thorny question.

jaramago *nm* hedge mustard.

jaramillo *nm* (*fam*) row; **armar un —** to kick up a row.

jarana *nf* (a) spree (*fam*), binge (*sl*), carousal; rumpus (*fam*), row; **andar de —** to roister, carouse; to lark about, have a high old time; **ir de —** to go on the spree (*fam*).
(b) trick, deceit; (*SAm*) joke, practical joke, hoax; (*Col*) fib; **la — sale a la cara** (*CAm*) a hoax can have a boomerang effect.
(c) (*Mus: Bol, Per*) dance; (*Col, Ec, PR*) hop (*fam*), informal dance; (*Per*) festival of regional dances.
(d) (*Mus: Mex*) small guitar.
(e) (*Fin: CAm*) debt.

jaranear [1a] **1** *vt* (*CAm, Col*) to cheat, swindle. **2** *vi* (a) to go on a spree (*fam*); to roister, carouse; to lark about, have a high old time.

(b) (*Bol, Per, PR*) to make merry at an informal dance.
(c) (*CAm*) to get into debt.

jaranero *adj* (a) merry, roistering, rowdy. (b) (*CAm*) deceitful, tricky.

jaranista *adj* (*SAm*) = **jaranero** (a).

jarano *nm* (*Mex*) broad hat, sombrero.

jarcia *nf* (a) tackle, fishing tackle; (*Naut: also* **—s**) ropes, rigging; (*Cu, Mex*) rope (made from agave fibre).
(b) (*Guat, Mex, Nic*) agave.
(c) heap, mess.

jardín *nm* garden, flower garden; **— alpestre, — rocoso** rock garden; **— botánico** botanical garden; **— de (la) infancia** kindergarten, nursery school; **— zoológico** zoo.

jardinaje *nm* (*SAm*) gardening.

jardinera *nf* (a) (woman) gardener.
(b) window box.
(c) (*RPl*) light two-wheeled handcart, barrow.
(d) (*Col*) jacket.

jardinería *nf* gardening.

jardinero *nm* gardener.

jarea *nf* (*Mex*) hunger, keen appetite.

jarear¹ [1a] *vi* (*Bol*) to halt, stop for a rest.

jarearse² [1a] *vr* (*Mex*) (a) to be dying of hunger. (b) to flee. (c) to rock, sway.

jareta *nf* (a) (*Naut*) cable, rope. (b) (*CR, Par*) trouser flies. (c) (*Ven*) snag, setback.

jarete *nm* (*Ven*) paddle.

jarifo *adj* (*lit*) elegant, showy, spruce.

jaro *nm* arum lily.

jarope *nm* syrup; (*fam*) brew, concoction, nasty drink.

jarra *nf* jar, pitcher; (for milk) churn; (for beer) mug, tankard; **de —s, en —s** with arms akimbo.

jarrada *nf* (*SAm*) jarful, jugful.

jarrete *nm* (*Anat*) back of the knee; (horse's) hock; (*Col*) heel.

jarro *nm* jug, pitcher; **echar un — de agua fría a una idea** to pour cold water on an idea.

jarrón *nm* vase; (*Archit*) urn.

jartón *adj* (*CAm, Mex*) greedy, gluttonous.

Jartum, Jartún Khartoum.

jaspe *nm* jasper.

jaspeado *adj* mottled, speckled, marbled; streaked.

jaspear [1a] **1** *vt* to speckle, marble; to streak. **2 jaspearse** *vr* (*Ven*) to get cross.

jato *nm* (a) calf.
(b) (*PR*) stray dog, mongrel.
(c) (*Mex*) implement and load of a mule.
(d) (*Mex*) stopping place (of muleteers).
(e) (*Per*) saddle.
(f) *see* **hato**.

Jauja, jauja *nf* (a) promised land, earthly paradise; **¡esto es —!** this is the life!; **¿estamos aquí o en —?** where do you think you are?; **vivir en —** to live in luxury, have a marvellous life.
(b) (*Chi*) rumour, tale.

jaula *nf* cage; (*Min*) cage; (for packing, milk bottles etc) crate; (in asylum) cell; (*fam*) lock-up; (*Aut*) lock-up garage; (*Mex: Rail*) cattle truck; (*PR*) Black Maria, police wagon (*US*); **hacer —** (*Mex*) to dig one's heels in.

jauría *nf* pack of hounds.

Javier *m* Xavier.

jayán *nm* big strong man; (*pej*) hulking great brute.

jáyaro *adj* (*Ec*) rustic, uncouth.

jazmín *nm* jasmine; **— del Cabo, — de la India** gardenia.

jazz [jaθ *or* jas] *nm* jazz.

jazzístico [ja'θistiko] *adj* jazz (attr).

jebe *nm* (a) (*SAm: Bot*) rubber plant. (b) club, cudgel; **llevar —** to suffer a lot.

jebero *nm* (*SAm*) rubber-plantation worker.

jeep [jip] *nm* jeep.

jefa *nf* (woman) head, (woman) boss; manageress.

jefatura *nf* (a) leadership; chieftainship; **bajo la — de** under the leadership of; **dimitir la — del partido** to resign the party leadership.
(b) headquarters; central office; **— de policía** police headquarters.

jefe *nm* (a) chief, head, boss; leader; manager; (*Mil*) field officer, officer in command; **— de bomberos** fire officer; **— de camareros** head waiter; **— de cocina** chef; **— de estación** station master; **— de estado** head of state, chief of state; **— de estado mayor** chief of staff; **— de los mozos** head groom; **— de redacción** editor-in-chief; **— supremo** commander-in-chief; **— de taller** foreman; **— de tren** guard, conductor (*US*); **— de ventas** sales manager; **comandante en —** commander-in-chief; **¡sí, —!** (esp SAm) yes, boss!; **ser el —** (fig) to be the boss.

(b) (of tribe) chief.

Jehová m Jehovah.

jején nm (a) (SAm) gnat; **sabe donde el — puso el huevo** (Cu, PR) he's pretty smart.

(b) (Mex) great number, lot; **un — de cosas** a lot of things, a mass of things.

jelenque nm (Cu, Mex) brawl, squabble, set-to (fam).

jemiquear [1a] vi (Chi) = **jeremiquear**.

jengibre nm ginger.

jenízaro adj mixed, hybrid.

Jenofonte m Xenophon.

jeque nm sheik(h).

jerarca nm chief, leader; important person; (pej) big shot (fam).

jerarquía nf hierarchy; (high) rank; **una persona de —** a high-ranking person.

jerárquico adj hierarchic(al).

Jeremías m Jeremy; (Bib) Jeremiah.

jeremiquear [1a] vi (SAm) to snivel, whimper; to make repeated requests.

jerezano 1 adj of Jerez. 2 nm, **jerezana** nf native (or inhabitant) of Jerez; **los —s** the people of Jerez.

jerga[1] nf coarse cloth, sackcloth; (SAm) horse blanket; (Col) coarse cloak.

jerga[2] nf jargon; slang, cant; gibberish; **— de germanía** thieves' cant; **— publicitaria** sales talk, salesman's patter.

jergón nm palliasse, straw mattress; (fam) ill-fitting garment; (fam) awkward-looking person.

Jericó Jerico.

jerigonza nf (a)] = **jerga**[2]. (b) silly thing, piece of folly.

jeringa nf (a) syringe; **— de engrase** grease gun.

(b) (SAm) annoyance, bother; (Arg) pest, annoying person.

jeringador adj (SAm) annoying, bothersome, vexing.

jeringar [1h] vt (a) to syringe; to inject; to squirt. (b) (SAm) to annoy, bother, plague.

jeringazo nm syringing; injection; squirt.

jeringón 1 adj (SAm) = **jeringador**. 2 nm (SAm) pest, annoying person.

jeringuear [1a] vt (SAm) = **jeringar** (b).

jeringuilla nf mock orange.

jeroglífico 1 adj hieroglyphic. 2 nm hieroglyph(ic); (fig) puzzle.

Jerónimo m Jerome.

jerónimo[1] (Eccl) 1 adj Hieronymite. 2 nm Hieronymite.

jerónimo[2] (hum): **sin — de duda** without a shadow of doubt.

jersé nm, **jersei** nm, **jersey** [xer'sei] nm, pl **jerseys** [xer'seis] jersey, sweater, pullover; jumper; (SAm) knitted cloth.

Jerusalén Jerusalem.

jeruza nf (Guat, Hond: sl) clink (sl), jail.

Jesucristo m Jesus Christ.

jesuita 1 adj (Eccl) Jesuit; (fig) Jesuitic(al). 2 nm (Eccl) Jesuit; (SAm) hypocrite, sly person.

jesuítico adj Jesuitic(al).

Jesús m Jesus; **¡—!** good heavens!; (on sneezing) bless you!; **en un decir —** in an instant, before one can say Jack Robinson; **morir sin decir —** to die very suddenly.

jet [jet] nm, pl **jets** [jet] (angl) jet, jet plane.

jeta nf (a) thick lips; **poner —** to pout, make a wry face.

(b) (Zool) snout; (sl) face, mug (sl), dial (sl); **estirar la —** (Chi, RPl) to die; (Arg) to make a wry face.

(c) (fam) nerve, neck (fam); **¡qué — tienes!** you've got a nerve!

jetear [1a] vi (Arg) to eat at someone else's expense.

jetón adj (a) (SAm) thick-lipped. (b) (Chi) stupid.

jibarear [1a] vi (SD) to flirt.

jibaro 1 adj (Ant, Mex) peasant, rustic; shy; (SD) wild, untamed.

2 nm, **jíbara** nf (SD) peasant; (PR) (white) peasant, rustic.

3 nm (a) (Hond) big strong man.

(b) (Cu) wild dog.

jibia nf cuttlefish.

jicaque adj (Guat, Hond) uncouth.

jícara nf (a) small cup (for drinking-chocolate etc).

(b) (CAm, Mex) gourd, drinking vessel made from a gourd; (CAm: hum) head; bald head; face; **sacar la — a uno** to shower someone with attentions.

jicarazo nm (CAm, Mex) cupful.

jícaro nm (CAm, Mex) (a) calabash tree. (b) bowl.

jicarón adj (CR) big-headed.

jicarudo adj (Mex) broad-faced, broad-browed.

jicote nm (CAm, Mex) wasp.

jicotera nf (CAm, Mex) wasps' nest; buzzing of wasps; **armar una —** to kick up a row.

jiche nm (CAm, Mex) tendon, sinew.

jiennense 1 adj of Jaén. 2 nmf native (or inhabitant) of Jaén; **los —s** the people of Jaén.

jifero 1 adj (fam) filthy. 2 nm (a) slaughterer, butcher. (b) butcher's knife.

jifia nf swordfish.

jijene nm sandfly.

jilguero nm goldfinch.

jilibioso adj (Chi) person weepy, tearful; finicky, hard to please; horse nervous.

jilote nm (CAm, Mex) green ear of maize.

jilotear [1a] vi (CAm, Mex) to come into ear.

jimagua (Cu) 1 adj twin; identical. 2 nmf twin.

jimba nf (Ec) pigtail, tress; (Mex) bamboo, long pole of bamboo.

jimbal nm (Mex) bamboo thicket.

jimbito nm (Guat, Hond) small wasp; wasps' nest.

jimbo adj (Mex) drunk.

jinaiste nm (Mex) group of children, mob of kids.

jindama nf (sl) fear, funk (fam).

jineta nf horsewoman, rider.

jinete nm horseman, rider; (Mil) cavalryman.

jinetear [1a] 1 vt (SAm) to break in; to ride; **— la burra** (CAm) to go the whole hog, stake everything.

2 vi to ride around, show off one's horsemanship.

3 **jinetearse** vr (a) (Col, Mex) to get into the saddle, manage to stay in the saddle; (fig) to stand firm.

(b) (Col) to be vain.

jingo nm (angl) jingoist, jingo.

jingoísmo nm jingoism.

jingoísta 1 adj jingoistic. 2 nmf jingoist, jingo.

jiote nm (CAm, Mex: Med) shingles.

jipa nf (Col) straw hat.

jipatera nf (Col, Mex, PR, Ven), **jipatez** nf (Mex, PR, Ven) paleness, wanness.

jipato adj (SAm) pale, wan, anaemic; (Cu) tasteless; (Guat) drunk.

jipe nm (Mex, Per) straw hat.

jipi nm (Cu, Mex) straw hat.

jipijapa nf (SAm) fine woven straw; straw hat.

jira[1] nf (of cloth) strip.

jira[2] nf excursion, outing; picnic (also **— campestre**); **ir de —** to go on an outing, go for a picnic; see also **gira**.

jirafa nf giraffe; (of microphone etc) jib, arm, boom.

jiribilla nf (Mex) spin, turn; **tener —** (Cu) to have its awkward points; (PR) to be anxious.

jirimiquear [1a] vi (SAm) = **jeremiquear**.

jirón nm (a) rag, shred, tatter; **en —es** in shreds; **hacer algo —es** to tear something to shreds.

(b) (fig) bit, shred.

(c) (Per) avenue, boulevard.

jit nm, pl **jits** [xit] (CAm: angl) hit.

jitazo nm (Mex: angl) hit, blow; (Sport) hit, stroke.

jitomate nm (Mex) tomato.

jiu-jitsu nm jiu-jitsu.

Job m Job.

jockey ['joki] nm, pl **jockeys** ['jokis] (angl) jockey; (SAm) jockey cap.

joco adj (a) (CAm, Mex) sharp, sour, bitter. (b) (Col) hollow.

jocolote nm (Hond) hut, shanty.

jocoque nm (Mex) sour milk, sour cream.

jocosamente adv humorously, comically.

jocoserio adj seriocomic.

jocosidad nf humour; (una —) joke.

jocoso adj humorous, comic, jocular.

joda nf (SAm: tabu) (a) annoyance; bother; harm.

(b) joke; **lo dijo en —** he said it as a joke.

joder [2a] (tabu in all senses; in SAm used only in fig senses) 1 vt (a) to fuck (tabu), screw (tabu); **¡—!** (annoyance) damn it!, damnation!; (surprise) well I'm damned!

(b) (fig) to annoy, vex, upset; to harm, spoil; **esto me jode** this really feeds me up (fam), I'm fed up with this; **son ganas de —** they're just trying to be awkward; **¡no me jodas!** stop bothering me!; come off it!, tell us another!

(c) to pinch (fam), steal; **alguien le jodió el puesto** someone pinched the job from him.

2 vi to fuck (tabu), screw (tabu).

3 **joderse** vr (a) **¡que te jodas!** get stuffed! (sl); **¡hay que —!** this is the end!, to hell with it all!

(b) to fail; to get spoiled, get messed up; **se jodió todo** everything was spoiled; **se ha jodido la función** the show was a failure.

jodido adj (tabu in all senses) (a) awkward, difficult; **es un libro** — it's a very difficult book.
(b) **estoy** — I'm worn out, I'm shagged (tabu).
(c) bloody; **ni una jodida peseta** not one bloody peseta.
(d) **todo está** — it's all ruined, everything's in a mess.
(e) (SAm) person selfish; evil, wicked; awkward, prickly; soapy, oily.
jodienda nf (Arg, Chi, Mex: tabu) bother, annoyance.
jodón adj (SAm: tabu) (a) annoying; given to stupid jokes. (b) tricky, untrustworthy.
jodontón adj (tabu) randy, oversexed, wolfish (fam).
jofaina nf washbasin.
jojoto adj (Cu, PR) fruit partly spoiled; (SD) fruit undeveloped; person anaemic; (Ven) fruit, maize soft, tender.
jolgorio nm (a) fun, merriment; revelry; rowdiness.
(b) (un —) spree (fam), binge (sl); lark; **ir de** — to go on a binge.
jolín, jolines interj (fam) cor! (fam).
jolinche adj, **jolino** adj (Mex) short-tailed, bob-tailed.
jolón nm (Mex) wasp; wasps' nest.
jolongo nm (Cu) bag, bundle.
jolote nm (CAm, Mex) turkey.
joma nf (Mex) hump.
jombado adj (Mex) hunchbacked.
Jonás m Jonah.
jónico adj (Archit) Ionic.
jonja nf (Chi) imitation, mimicry.
jonjear [1a] vt (Chi) to tease, make fun of.
jonjolear [1a] vt (Col) to spoil, lavish attentions upon.
jonrón nm (SAm: Sport: angl) home run.
jonronear [1a] vi (SAm: Sport: angl) to make a home run.
jopo[1] interj get out!, be off!
jopo[2] nm = **hopo**.
jora nf (SAm) maize specially prepared for making high-grade chicha.
Jordán m Jordan (river).
Jordania f Jordan (country).
jorga nf (Ec) band of crooks, gang.
Jorge m George.
jorguín nm sorcerer, wizard.
jorguina nf sorceress, witch.
jorguinería nf sorcery, witchcraft.
jorgón nm (Ec) lot, abundance.
jornada nf (a) day's journey; stage (of a journey); **a largas** —s (Mil) by forced marches; **al fin de la** — at the end, in the end.
(b) working day; hours of work; shift; (fig) lifetime, span of life; **— de 8 horas** 8-hour day; **— legal máximo** legal working hours; **hay — limitada en la industria** there is short-time working in the industry; **trabajar en** —s **reducidas** to work short-time.
(c) (Mil) expedition; **la — de Orán** the expedition against Oran.
(d) (Theat: Hist) act.
(e) (Chi) day's wage.
jornal nm (day's) wage; day's work; **— mínimo** minimum wage; **política de** —es **y precios** prices and incomes policy; **trabajar a** — to work for a day wage, be paid by the day.
jornalero nm (day) labourer.
joro nm (Ven) small basket.
joroba 1 nf (a) hump, hunched back. (b) (fig) nuisance, bother, annoyance. 2 nm hunchback.
jorobado 1 adj hunchbacked. 2 nm, **jorobada** nf hunchback.
jorobar [1a] 1 vt to annoy, pester, bother; **esto me joroba** I'm fed up with this, this gives me the hump; **¡no me jorobes!** stop bothering me!
2 **jorobarse** vr to get cross, get worked up; to get fed up; **¡hay que** —! to hell with it!
jorobeta nf (Arg) nuisance.
jorobón adj (SAm) annoying.
joronche nm (Mex: euph) hunchback.
jorongo nm (Mex) poncho, peasant's blanket.
jorro nm (Cu, PR) poor-quality cigarette, slow-burning tobacco.
jorungo 1 adj (Cu) annoying, vexing. 2 nm (Ven) foreigner, gringo.
José m Joseph.
Josefina f Josephine.
Josué m Joshua.
jota[1] nf (a) name of the letter J.
(b) (fig) jot, iota; **no entendió** — he didn't understand a word of it; **sin faltar una** — to a T, with complete accuracy, just as it should be; **no saber** — to have no idea; not to know what it's all about.

jota[2] nf Spanish dance and tune (esp Aragonese).
jote nm (Chi) buzzard; large kite; unattractive person; (pej) priest.
joto 1 adj (Mex) effeminate. 2 nm (Col) bundle; (Mex) effeminate person.
joven 1 adj young; appearance etc youthful.
2 nm young man, youth; los —es young people, youth, the young; **¡eh, —!** I say, young man!
3 nf young woman, young lady, girl.
jovencito nm, **jovencita** nf, **jovenzuelo** nm, **jovenzuela** nf youngster.
jovial adj jolly, cheerful, jovial.
jovialidad nf jolliness, cheerfulness, joviality.
jovialmente adv in a jolly way, cheerfully, jovially.
joya nf (a) jewel, gem, piece of jewellery; **— de familia** heirloom.
(b) —s jewels, jewellery; (bride's) trousseau; **— de fantasía**, —s **de imitación** imitation jewellery.
(c) (fig) gem, treasure, precious thing; (person) gem, treasure.
joyería nf (a) jewellery, jewels. (b) jeweller's (shop).
joyero nm (a) jeweller. (b) jewel case.
juagar [1h] vt (Col, Ec) = **enjuagar**.
Juan m John; **don** — don Juan; (Mus) Don Giovanni; **San — Bautista** St John the Baptist; **un buen** — a simple soul, a good-natured fool; **— Lanas**, **— Vainas** (CAm, PR) even-tempered person, calm sort; (pej) simpleton, ninny; **— Palomo** lone wolf, independent sort; **— Zoquete** rustic, idiot.
juan nm (Bol, Mex) common soldier.
Juana f Joan, Joan, Jane; **— de Arco** Joan of Arc.
juana nf (a) (Col) whore. (b) (Mex) marijuana.
juancho nm (Col) boyfriend, lover.
juanear [1a] vt (Arg) to swindle.
juanete nm (a) bunion; prominent cheekbone. (b) (Naut) topgallant sail. (c) (Col, Hond) hip.
juanillo nm (Chi, Per) tip, gratuity.
juapao nm (Ven) beating, thrashing.
jubilación nf (a) retirement. (b) pension, retirement pension.
jubilado 1 adj (a) retired; **vivir** — to live in retirement.
(b) (Col, Cu) wise, sagacious, expert.
(c) (Col: pej) stupid; wretched.
2 nm retired person, pensioner.
jubilar [1a] 1 vt (a) person to pension off, retire.
(b) (fig) person to shunt aside, put out to grass; thing to discard, get rid of, cast aside.
2 vi to rejoice.
3 **jubilarse** vr (a) to retire, take one's pension.
(b) (CAm, Ven) to play truant.
(c) (Col, Cu, Mex) to acquire skill, gain experience.
(d) (Col) to deteriorate, go downhill; to go mad.
jubileo nm jubilee; (fam) comings and goings; **por** — once in a lifetime.
júbilo nm joy, jubilation, rejoicing; **con** — joyfully, with jubilation.
jubiloso adj jubilant.
jubón nm doublet, jerkin, close-fitting jacket; (woman's) bodice.
jud nm (CAm, Mex: Aut: angl) bonnet, hood (US).
Judá m Judah.
judaico adj Jewish, Judaic.
judaísmo nm Judaism.
Judas m Judas; (fig) traitor, betrayer.
judas nm (a) (SAm) peephole.
(b) (Mex) saint's day, name day (of person).
(c) (Chi) snooper, inspector.
(d) (CAm, Mex) naughty child.
Judea f Judea.
judería nf (a) Jewish quarter, ghetto. (b) Jewry. (c) (Guat, Mex) prank, lark.
judía nf (a) Jewess, Jewish woman.
(b) (Bot) kidney bean; **— blanca** haricot bean; **— colorada**, **— escarlata**, **— de España**, **— negra** runner bean; **— de la peladilla** Lima bean.
judiada nf (a) cruel act, cruel thing. (b) (Fin) extortion.
judicatura nf (a) judicature. (b) judgeship, office of judge.
judicial adj judicial; **recurrir a la vía** — to go to law, have recourse to the law.
judío 1 adj (a) Jewish. (b) (pej) extortionate, usurious. 2 nm Jew.
Judit f Judith.
judo nm judo.
juego[1] etc (verb) see **jugar**.
juego[2] nm (a) play, playing; sport; fun, amusement; **los niños en el** — children at play; **— duro** rough

play; — **limpio** fair play; — **sucio** foul play, dirty play; **el balón está en** — the ball is in play; **entrar en** — (*person*) to take a hand, (*factor*) come into play; **poner algo en** — to set something in motion, bring something into play; **estar fuera de** — (*person*) to be offside, (*ball*) be out, be out of play; **por** — in fun, for fun.

(**b**) (*un* —) game, sport; **es solamente un** — it's only a game; —**s atléticos** (athletic) sports; — **de azar** game of chance; — **de las bochas** bowls; — **de (las) bolas** American skittles; — **de las bolitas**, — **de las canicas** marbles; — **de bolos** ninepins, skittles, tenpin bowling; — **de cartas** card game; — **de damas** draughts, checkers (*US*); — **de destreza** game of skill; —**s infantiles** children's games; —**s malabares** juggling; — **de manos** conjuring trick; —**s de manos** conjuring; — **de naipes** card game; **J**—**s Olímpicos** Olympic Games; — **de palabras** pun, play on words; — **de prendas** (game of) forfeits; **del tejo** hopscotch.

(**c**) (complete *or* finished) game; (*Tennis*) game; (*Bridge*) rubber; —, **set y partido** game, set and match.

(**d**) (*fig*) game; **le conozco el** —, **le veo el** — I know his little game, I know what he's up to.

(**e**) gambling, gaming; **el** — **es un vicio** gambling is a vice; **lo perdió todo en el** — he lost the lot gambling; **lo que está en** — what is at stake.

(**f**) (*Mech*) play, movement; **estar en** — to be in gear, be in mesh.

(**g**) (*of light etc*) play; **el** — **de luces sobre el agua** the play of light on the water; **el** — **de los colores** the interplay of the colours.

(**h**) field, pitch, court; **en el** — **de pelota** on the pelota court.

(**i**) set; (*of dishes*) set, service; (*of furniture*) suite; (*of tools etc*) set, kit, outfit; (*of cards*) hand; pack; — **de bolas** (*Mech*) ball bearing, set of ball bearings; — **de café** coffee set; — **de campanas** peal of bells; — **de comedor** dining-room suite; — **de mesa** dinner service; **una falda a** — **con un jersey** a skirt with a jersey to match; a skirt which goes with a jersey; **con falda a** — with skirt to match; **hacen** — they match, they go well together.

juepucha *interj* (*RPl: euph*) well I'm damned!

juerga *nf* binge (*sl*), spree (*fam*), carousal; good time; **correr las grandes** —**s** to live it up (*fam*); **¡vaya que nos vamos a correr con ellas!** what a time we'll have with them!; **ir de** — to go on a spree, go out for a good time.

juerguista *nm* reveller.

jueves *nm*, *pl* **jueves** Thursday; **J**— **Santo** Maundy Thursday; **no es cosa del otro** — it's nothing to write home about.

juez *nm* (**a**) (*Law*) judge (*also fig*); — **árbitro** arbitrator, referee; — **de instrucción** examining magistrate; — **municipal** magistrate; — **de paz** justice of the peace; **parece un** — he looks terribly serious.

(**b**) (*Sport*) judge; — **de línea** linesman; — **de llegada**, — **de meta**, — **de raya** (*Arg*) judge; — **de salida** starter.

jugada *nf* (**a**) play; playing.

(**b**) piece of play; move; stroke, shot; throw; **una bonita** — a pretty piece of play, a pretty shot; **con dos** —**s más** in two more moves; **hacer una** — to make a move, make a shot (*etc*).

(**c**) (**mala**) — bad turn, dirty trick; **hacer una mala** — **a uno** to play someone a dirty trick.

(**d**) (*Mex*) dodge, duck, evasive movement.

jugado *adj* (*Col, Mex*) expert, experienced.

jugador *nm*, **jugadora** *nf* player; gambler; — **de bolsa** speculator, gambler on the stock exchange; — **de fútbol** footballer, football player; — **de manos** juggler, conjurer.

jugar [1h *and* 1o] **1** *vt* (**a**) card, trick, role *etc* to play; **¡me la han jugado!** (*fam*) they've done it on me!

(**b**) to gamble, stake; — **5 dólares a una carta** to stake (*or* put) 5 dollars on a card; **lo jugó todo** he gambled it all away.

(**c**) weapon to handle, wield.

2 *vi* (**a**) to play (*con* with, *contra* against); — **limpio** to play fair, play the game; — **sucio** to play unfairly, indulge in dirty play; **yo no juego** I don't play, I can't play; — **al tenis** to play tennis; — **al ajedrez** to play chess; **la niña juega a ser madre** the little girl plays at being mother; — **con** (*pej*) to play about with; to finger, handle, mess up; (*fig*) to toy with, trifle with; **solamente está jugando contigo** he's just trifling with you, he's just having a game with you; **un coche de** — a toy car, a model car; **de jugando** (*Arg, Guat, PR*) in fun, for fun.

(**b**) to play, make a move; **¿quién juega?** whose move is it?, whose turn is it?, who's to play next?

(**c**) to gamble; (*Fin*) to speculate, gamble; *see* **bolsa** *etc*.

(**d**) (*SAm*) to have room, move about; **la varilla juega dentro de la unión** the rod moves about inside the joint.

(**e**) to match, go together.

3 jugarse *vr* to gamble (away), risk; **se jugó 500 dólares** he staked 500 dollars; **esto es** — **la vida** this means risking one's life; — **el todo por el todo** to stake one's all, (*fig*) go to extremes, go the whole hog.

jugarreta *nf* (**a**) bad move, poor piece of play. (**b**) dirty trick; **hacer una** — **a uno** to play a dirty trick on someone.

juglar *nm* (*Hist*) minstrel, jongleur; juggler, tumbler, entertainer.

juglaresco *adj* (*Hist*): **arte** — art of the minstrel(s); **estilo** — minstrel's style, popular style.

juglaría *nf* (*Hist*) minstrelsy, art of the minstrel(s).

jugo *nm* (**a**) (*Bot etc*) juice; sap; (*of meat*) juice; gravy; — **de naranja** orange juice; — **de muñeca** (*fam*) elbow grease (*fam*).

(**b**) (*fig*) essence, substance, pith; **sacar el** — **a uno** to pick someone's brains.

jugosidad *nf* (**a**) juiciness, succulence. (**b**) (*fig*) substantial nature, pithiness.

jugoso *adj* (**a**) juicy, succulent.

(**b**) (*fig*) substantial, pithy; meaty, full of good stuff, full of solid sense; **un discurso** — a solid sort of speech, a speech full of good things.

juguete *nm* (**a**) toy; **un cañón de** — a toy gun.

(**b**) (*fig*) toy, plaything; **fue el** — **de las olas** it was the plaything of the waves.

(**c**) joke.

(**d**) (*Theat*) skit, sketch.

juguetear [1a] *vi* to play, romp, sport; — **con** to play with, sport with.

jugueteo *nm* playing, romping.

juguetería *nf* (**a**) toy trade, toy business. (**b**) toyshop.

juguetón *adj* playful, frisky, frolicsome.

juicio *nm* (**a**) (*faculty*) judgement, reason.

(**b**) sanity, reason; good sense, prudence, wisdom; **asentar el** — to come to one's senses, return to sanity; **lo dejo a su** — I leave it to your discretion, I leave it to you to decide; **estar en su** (**cabal**) — to be in one's right mind; **estar fuera de** — to be out of one's mind; **perder el** — to lose one's reason, go mad; **no tener** — to lack common sense; **¿se te ha vuelto el** —? are you mad?, have you gone out of your mind?

(**c**) opinion; — **de valor** value judgement; **a mi** — in my opinion, to my mind.

(**d**) (*Law*) trial; — **de Dios** trial by ordeal; **pedir a uno en** — to sue someone.

(**e**) (*Law*) verdict, judgement; **J**— **Final** Last Judgement; — **en rebeldía** judgement by default.

juicioso *adj* judicious, wise, prudent, sensible.

juilipío *nm* (*Per*) sparrow.

juilón *adj* (*Mex*) cowardly.

julepe *nm* (**a**) julep.

(**b**) (*fam*) telling-off, dressing-down.

(**c**) (*SAm*) scare, fright; **irse de** —, **salir de** — (*Ec*) to run away in terror.

(**d**) (*Cu, Mex, Ven*) fag, hard work; trouble.

(**e**) (*Col, Per*) **meter un** — to hurry on, speed up.

julepear [1a] **1** *vt* (**a**) (*RPl*) to scare, terrify.

(**b**) (*Mex*) to wear out, tire out.

(**c**) (*Col*) to hurry along, speed up.

2 julepearse *vr* (*RPl*) to get scared; (*Chi*) to smell danger.

julia *nf* (*Mex: sl*) Black Maria, police wagon (*US*).

Julián *m*, **Juliano** *m* Julian.

Julieta *f* Juliet.

Julio *m* Julius; — **César** Julius Caesar.

julio *nm* July.

juma *nf* (*SAm*) drunkenness, drunken state.

jumadera *nf* (*Mex*) (**a**) drunkenness, drunken state.

(**b**) = **humareda**.

jumado *adj* (*SAm*) drunk.

jumarse [1a] *vr* (*SAm*) to get drunk.

jumatán *nm* (*Cu*) habitual drunkard.

jumazo *nm* (*PR*) cigarette.

jumeado *adj* (*Per*) drunk.

jumento *nm* donkey; beast of burden; (*fig*) dolt.

jumo *adj* (*SAm*) drunk.

juncal 1 *adj* (**a**) rushy, reedy. (**b**) (*fig*) willowy, lissom. **2** *nm* = **juncar**.

juncar *nm* ground covered in rushes.

juncia *nf* sedge.

junco[1] *nm* rush, reed; (*Hond*) fine straw; — **de Indias** rattan.

junco² nm (Naut) junk.
juncoso adj (a) rushy, reedy, reed-like. (b) place covered in rushes.
jungla nf jungle.
junio nm June.
junior nm (a) (Eccl) novice monk. (b) ['junior] (Sport: angl) junior.
Juno f Juno.
junquera nf rush, bulrush.
junquillo nm (a) jonquil; reed. (b) (Cu, Mex, PR) golden necklace.
junta nf (a) meeting, assembly; session; — de acreedores meeting of creditors; — general general meeting; — general extraordinaria special general meeting; celebrar — to hold a meeting; to sit.
  (b) board, council, committee; (Comm, Fin) board; la — de la asociación the committee of the association; — directiva board of management; J— para Ampliación de Estudios Council for Research; J— Nacional del Carbón National Coal Board (Brit).
  (c) junction, (point of) union.
  (d) (Tech) joint; coupling; — cardán, — universal universal joint.
  (e) (Tech) washer, gasket.
juntadero nm (Arg) meeting place.
juntamente adv (a) hacer algo — to do something together; to do something at the same time.
  (b) A — con B A together with B; ella y yo — she and I together, she and I jointly.
juntar [1a] 1 vt (a) to join, unite; to assemble, put together; to collect, gather (together), amass; money to collect, raise.
  (b) door to half-close, leave ajar.
  2 juntarse vr (a) to join, come together; (persons) to meet, assemble, gather (together); — con uno to join someone; to meet (up with) someone; to associate with someone; se juntaron para oírle they assembled to hear him, they came together to hear him; se juntó con ellos en la estación he met them at the station, he joined them at the station.
  (b) (Zool) to mate, copulate.
  (c) (Mex: euph) to live together.
juntillo etc see pie.
junto 1 adj (a) joined, united; together; fuimos —s we went together; tenía los ojos muy —s his eyes were very close together.
  (b) (Col) —s both.
  2 adv near, close; together; (de) por —, en — in all, all together; (Comm) wholesale; demasiado — too close; muy — very close, very near; ocurrió todo — it happened all at once.
  3 prep: — a near (to), close to, next to; — con together with.
juntura nf join, junction; (Anat) joint; (Tech) seam; (Tech) joint, coupling.
jupa nf (CAm, Mex) gourd; (hum) head.
jupiarse [1b] vr (CAm) to get drunk.
Júpiter m Jupiter.
jura¹ nf oath, pledge.
jura² nm (Cu, Guat: sl) cop (sl).
juraco nm (CAm) hole.
jurado nm (a) jury; (in contest, quiz etc) panel (of judges). (b) juror, juryman; member of a panel.
juramentar [1a] 1 vt to swear in, administer the oath to. 2 juramentarse vr to be sworn in, take the oath.
juramento nm (a) oath; bajo — on oath; prestar — to take the oath (sobre on); tomar — a uno to swear someone in, administer the oath to someone.
  (b) oath, swearword, curse; decir —s a uno to swear at someone.
jurar [1a] 1 vti to swear; — decir la verdad to swear to tell the truth; le juro a Vd que . . . I swear to you

that . . .; ¡no jures! don't swear!; — en falso to commit perjury.
  2 jurarse vr: —las a uno to have it in for someone.
jurel nm (Cu) (a) fish used for food (Caranx latus). (b) fear, dread. (c) drunkenness, drunken state.
jurero nm (Chi, Ec, Per) perjurer, false witness.
jurgo nm, **jurgonera** nf (Col) = jorga.
jurídico adj juridical; legal; departamento — (Comm) legal department.
jurisdicción nf (a) jurisdiction. (b) district, administrative area.
jurisdiccional adj: aguas —es territorial waters.
jurisprudencia nf jurisprudence, (study of the) law.
jurista nmf jurist, lawyer.
jurungo nm (Ven) = jorungo.
juro nm right of perpetual ownership; pension; a — (Col, Ven), de — certainly.
justa nf joust, tournament; (fig) contest.
justamente adv (a) justly, fairly.
  (b) just, precisely, exactly; ¡—! precisely!, that's just it!; de eso se trata — that's just the point, that's exactly the point; son — las que no se venden they are precisely the ones which are not for sale.
justar [1a] vi to joust, tilt.
justicia nf (a) justice; fairness, equity, rightness; right; — poética poetic justice; de — justly, deservedly; lo estimo de — I think it right; es de — añadir que . . . it is only right to add that . . .; en — by rights; hacer — a to do justice to; hacerse — por sí mismo to take the law into one's own hands.
  (b) —s y ladrones (fam) cops and robbers (fam).
justiciable adj (a) actionable. (b) subject to review by a court; subject to arbitration.
justiciero adj (strictly) just, righteous.
justificable adj justifiable.
justificación nf justification.
justificante nm voucher.
justificar [1g] vt to justify; to verify, substantiate; suspect to clear (de of), vindicate.
justillo nm jerkin.
justipreciar [1b] vt to evaluate, appraise.
justiprecio nm evaluation, appraisal.
justo 1 adj (a) just, fair, right; una decisión justa a just decision; los —s the righteous; me parece muy — it seems perfectly fair to me; más de lo — more than is proper, more than usual.
  (b) quantity etc exact, correct; el peso — the correct weight; ¡—! that's it!, correct!, right!
  (c) dress tight; el traje me viene muy — the suit is rather tight for me, the suit is a very tight fit.
  2 adv (a) justly.
  (b) right.
  (c) tightly; vivir muy — to be hard up, have only just enough to live on.
jute nm (Guat, Hond) edible snail.
juvenil adj youthful; obra — youthful work, early work; en los años —es in one's early years, in one's youth; de aspecto — youthful in appearance.
juventud nf (a) youth; early life. (b) young people; la — de hoy young people today, today's youth; J—es Hitlerianas Hitler Youth (Movement).
juyungo nm, **juyunga** nf (Col, Ec) Negro.
juzgado nm court, tribunal.
juzgar [1h] vti to judge; — mal to misjudge; júzguelo Vd mismo see for yourself, form your own judgement; lo juzgo mi deber I consider it my duty, I deem it my duty; juzgue Vd mi sorpresa imagine my surprise; — de to judge of, pass judgement on, appraise; a — por to judge by, judging by; a — según lo que hemos visto to judge by (or from) what we have seen.
juzgón adj (Guat, Mex) hypercritical, carping, fault-finding.

K

kaki nm (SAm) = **caqui**.
karting ['kartin] nm (SAm: angl) go-kart; go-kart racing.
kayac nm, **kayak** nm kayak.
Kenia f Kenya.
kermese nf charity fair, bazaar.
kerosén nm, **kerosene** nm, **kerosín** nm (CAm), **kerosina** nf (CAm) kerosene, paraffin.
kilate nm see **quilate**.
kilo nm kilo.
kilociclo nm kilocycle.
kilogramo nm kilogramme, kilogram (US).
kilolitro nm kilolitre, kiloliter (US).
kilometraje nm distance (or rate etc) in kilometres, (equivalent to) mileage.

kilométrico 1 adj (a) kilometric; **billete** — runabout ticket, mileage book. (b) (fam) very long; **palabra kilométrica** very long word, multisyllabic word. **2** nm = **billete** —.
kilómetro nm kilometre, kilometer (US).
kilovatio nm kilowatt.
kilovatios-hora nmpl kilowatt-hours.
kimona nf (Cu, Mex), **kimono** nm (RPl) kimono.
kiwi nm kiwi.
knock-out [kaw] nm, **K.O.** [kaw] nm, (angl) knock-out; knockout blow; **dejar a uno** —, **poner a uno** — to knock someone out, give someone a knockout blow.
kodak nf, pl **kodaks** [ko'ðak] (SAm: angl) (any kind of) small camera.

L

la[1] *def art f* the (*see* **el**[1] *for usage examples*).

la[2] *pron* (*person*) her; (*corresponding to* Vd) you; (*thing*) it.

la[3] *dem pron*: **mi casa y — de Vd** my house and yours; **esta chica y — del sombrero verde** this girl and the one in the green hat; **— de Pedro es mejor** Peter's is better; **y — de todos los demás** and that of everybody else; **— de Rodríguez** Mrs Rodríguez.

la[4]: **— que** *rel pron: see* **el**[3] **que**.

laberintero *adj* (*Mex*) = **laberintoso.**

laberíntico *adj* labyrinthine; *house etc* rambling.

laberinto *nm* (**a**) labyrinth, maze; (*fig*) maze, tangle. (**b**) (*SAm*) uproar, confused shouting; row, fuss.

laberintoso *adj* (*Mex, Per*) rowdy, brawling; gossipy.

labia *nf* fluency, persuasive verbosity, blarney; (*pej*) glibness; **tener mucha — to** have the gift of the gab (*fam*), be terribly persuasive.

labial 1 *adj* labial. **2** *nf* labial.

labihendido *adj* harelipped.

labio *nm* lip; (*of vessel etc*) lip, edge, rim; (*fig*) tongue; **—s** lips, mouth; **— inferior** lower lip; **— superior** upper lip; **— leporino** harelip; **lamerse los —s** to lick one's lips; **no morderse los —s** to be outspoken, pull no punches; **no descoser los —s** to keep one's mouth shut; **sin desplegar los —s** without uttering a word.

labiolectura *nf* lip-reading.

labiosear [1a] *vt* (*CAm*) to flatter; to blarney, chat up (*sl*).

labiosidad *nf* (*CAm, Ec*) flattery.

labioso *adj* (*SAm*) talkative; flattering; persuasive, glib; sly.

labor *nf* (**a**) labour, work; (*una —*) job, task, piece of work; **— de equipo** teamwork. (**b**) (*Agr*) farm work, cultivation; ploughing. (**c**) (*Guat, Mex, Salv*) small farm, smallholding. (**d**) (*Sew*) needlework, sewing, embroidery; **una — a** piece of needlework (*etc*): **— de aguja, —es femeninas** needlework; **— de ganchillo** crochet, crocheting. (**e**) **—es** (*Min*) workings.

laborable *adj* workable; arable; *see* **día.**

laboral *adj* labour (*attr*); technical; *see* **escuela** *etc.*

laboratorio *nm* laboratory.

laborar [1a] **1** *vt* to work, till. **2** *vi* (**a**) (*CAm*) to work. (**b**) (*pej*) to scheme, plot.

laborear [1a] *vt* to work (*also Min*); (*Agr*) to work, till.

laboreo *nm* (*Agr*) working, cultivation, tilling; (*Min*) working.

laborero *nm* (**a**) (*Bol, Chi, Per*) foreman. (**b**) (*Chi*) tanner.

laboriosamente *adv* industriously; painstakingly.

laboriosidad *nf* (**a**) industry; painstaking skill. (**b**) laboriousness.

laborioso *adj* (**a**) *person* hard-working, industrious, painstaking. (**b**) *work* tough, hard, laborious.

laborismo *nm* (*SAm*) labour movement, workers' movement; (*of Brit Pol*) Labour Party, Labour Movement.

laborista 1 *adj* (**a**) (*SAm*) labour (*attr*). (**b**) (*of Brit Pol*) Labour (*attr*); **Partido L—** Labour Party; **miembro —** Labour member. **2** *nmf* (**a**) (*Guat*) small farmer, smallholder. (**b**) (*Brit Pol*) Labour Party member, supporter of the Labour Party; Labour member of parliament.

labradío *adj* arable.

labrado 1 *adj* worked; *metal* wrought; *wood etc* carved; *cloth* patterned, embroidered. **2 —s** cultivated field; **—s** cultivated land.

labrador *nm* farmer; farm labourer; ploughman; peasant; (*Mex*) lumberjack.

labradora *nf* peasant (woman).

labrantío *adj* arable.

labranza *nf* (**a**) farming; cultivation. (**b**) farm; farmland.

labrar [1a] *vt* to work; to fashion, shape; *metal* to work; *wood etc* to carve; *tree* (*Guat, Mex*) to fell and smooth; *land* to work, farm, till; *cloth* to embroider; (*fig*) to cause, bring about.

labriego *nm*, **labriega** *nf* farmhand, labourer; peasant.

laburno *nm* laburnum.

laca *nf* (**a**) (*also* **goma —**) shellac; (*varnish*) lac, lacquer; (*colour*) lake; **— de uñas, — para uñas** nail polish, nail varnish. (**b**) (*Chi*) = **lacra.**

lacayo *nm* footman; (*fig*) lackey.

laceada *nf* (*Arg*) whipping.

lacear [1a] *vt* (**a**) to beribbon, adorn with bows; to tie with a bow; *horse's load* (*Guat, Mex*) to tie on firmly, strap securely. (**b**) (*Arg*) to whip. (**c**) (*Hunting*) to snare, trap; to beat, drive.

laceración *nf* laceration; (*fig*) damage, spoiling.

lacerar [1a] *vt* to lacerate, tear, mangle; (*fig*) to damage, spoil.

lacería *nf* poverty, want; distress, wretchedness; toil.

laciar [1b] *vt* (*SAm*) *curly hair* to straighten.

Lacio *m* Latium.

lacio *adj* (*Bot*) withered, faded; *hair* lank, straight; *movement etc* limp, languid.

lacón *nm* shoulder of pork.

lacónicamente *adv* laconically, tersely.

lacónico *adj* laconic, terse.

laconismo *nm* laconic style (*or* manner *etc*), terseness.

lacra *nf* (**a**) (*Med*) mark, trace, scar; (*SAm*) sore, ulcer. (**b**) (*fig*) blot, blemish; **la prostitución es una — social** prostitution is a blot on society, prostitution is a disgrace to society.

lacrar[1] [1a] **1** *vt* (**a**) (*Med*) to injure the health of; to infect, strike (with a disease). (**b**) (*fig*) to injure, harm, cause damage (*or* loss) to. **2 lacrarse** *vr*: **— con algo** to suffer harm (*or* damage, loss *etc*) from something; **— con el trabajo excesivo** to harm oneself through overwork.

lacrar[2] [1a] *vt* to seal (*with sealing wax*).

lacre 1 *adj* (*SAm*) bright red. **2** *nm* sealing wax.

lacrimógeno *adj* (**a**) tear-producing; *gas* **—** tear gas. (**b**) (*fig*) tearful, highly sentimental; *canción* **lagrimógena, comedia lagrimógena** tear-jerker.

lacrimoso *adj* tearful, lachrymose.

lacrosse [la'kros] *nf* lacrosse.

lactación *nf*, **lactancia** *nf* lactation; nursing.

lactante *adj*: *mujer* **—** nursing mother.

lactar [1a] **1** *vt* to nurse, suckle; to feed on milk. **2** *vi* to suckle; to feed on milk.

lácteo *adj* lacteal, milk (*attr*); (*fig*) milky, lacteous.

láctico *adj* lactic.

lactosa *nf* lactose.

lacustre *adj* lake (*attr*), lacustrine; (*SAm*) marshy.

lachear [1a] *vt* (*Chi*) to court.

lacho *nm* (*Chi, Per*) lover; beau, gallant.

ladeado *adj* (**a**) tilted, leaning, inclined. (**b**) (*Arg*) slovenly. (**c**) (*Arg*) wily. (**d**) (*Arg*) *andar* **—** to be in a bad temper; **andar — con uno** to feel hostile to someone.

ladear [1a] **1** *vt* (**a**) to tilt, tip; to incline (to one side); (*Aer*) to bank, turn; *head* to tilt, put on one side. (**b**) *hill etc* to skirt, go round the side of. **2** *vi* (**a**) to tilt, tip, lean. (**b**) to turn aside, turn off. **3 ladearse** *vr* (**a**) to lean, incline (*also fig: a*

towards); (*Aer*) to bank, turn; **ladea al otro partido** he leans towards the other party.
   (**b**) — **con** to be equal to, be even with.
   (**c**) (*Chi*) to fall in love (*con* with).
ladeo *nm* (**a**) tilting, inclination, leaning; (*Aer*) banking, turning. (**b**) (*fig*) inclination.
ladera *nf* slope, hillside.
ladero 1 *adj* side (*attr*), lateral. **2** *nm* (*Arg*) helper, backer.
ladilla *nf* crab louse.
ladillento *adj* (*Guat, Mex*) lousy.
ladinazo *adj* (*Arg*) cunning, shrewd.
ladino 1 *adj* (**a**) cunning, wily; smart, shrewd.
   (**b**) (*CAm, Col, Ec, Per, RPl*) Indian Spanish-speaking.
   (**c**) (*CAm, Mex*) half-breed, mestizo; non-Indian, white, of Spanish descent.
   (**d**) (*Col, SD*) talkative, loquacious.
   (**e**) (*Mex*) voice high-pitched, fluty.
   2 *nm* (**a**) (*CAm, Col, Ec, Per, RPl*) Spanish-speaking Indian.
   (**b**) (*CAm, Mex*) half-breed, mestizo; non-Indian, white man.
   (**c**) (*Ling*) Ladin (*Rhaeto-Romance dialect*); Ladino, Sephardic (*mixed Spanish and Hebrew*).
lado *nm* (**a**) (*in most senses*) side; — **débil** weak spot; — **izquierdo** left(-hand) side; — **a** — side by side; **al** — near, at hand; **al** — **de** by the side of, beside; **estuvo a mi** — she was at my side, she was beside me; **al otro** — **de la calle** on the other side of the street, across the street; **llevar algo al otro** — **del río** to carry something across (*or* over) the river; **al** — **de aquello, esto no es nada** beside (*or* in comparison with) that, this is nothing; **la casa de al** — the house next door; **viven al** — **de nosotros** they live next door to us; **ir de un** — **a otro** to go to and fro, walk up and down; **poner algo de** — to put something sideways (*or* edgeways); **por el** — **del mar** towards the sea, on the sea side; **por el** — **de Madrid** in the direction of Madrid; **salieron corriendo cada uno por su** — they all ran off in different directions; **por todos** —**s** on all sides, all round; **por un** — **. . ., por otro . . .** on the one hand . . ., on the other . . .; **dar a uno de** — to disregard someone, be unconcerned about someone; **dejar a un** — to skip, omit, pass over; to leave aside; **echar a un** — to cast aside; **hacer** — to make room (*a* for); **hacerse a un** — to stand aside (*also fig*), move over; **mirar de (medio)** — to look askance at; to steal a glance at; **poner a un** — to put aside.
   (**b**) (*Mil*) flank.
   (**c**) (*Sport*) end; **cambiar de** — to change ends.
   (**d**) (*genealogical*) side; **por el** — **de la madre** on the mother's side.
   (**e**) (*Pol etc*) side; faction; **ponerse al** — **de uno** to side with someone.
   (**f**) favour, protection; **tener buenos** —**s** to have good connections.
ladrar [1a] *vi* to bark.
ladrería *nf* (*Col, Cu, Mex*), **ladrerío** *nm* (*Mex*) barking.
ladrido *nm* bark, barking; (*fig*) slander, scandal.
ladrillado *nm* brick floor; tile floor.
ladrillar 1 *nm* brickworks. **2** *vt* to brick, pave with bricks.
ladrillería *nf* (*SAm*) brickworks.
ladrillo *nm* brick; tile; (*of chocolate*) block; — **de fuego,** — **refractario** firebrick.
ladrón 1 *adj* thieving. **2** *nm*, **ladrona** *nf* thief; — **de corazones** ladykiller; **¡al** —! stop thief!
ladronera *nf* (**a**) den of thieves. (**b**) robbery, theft.
lagaña *nf* = **legaña.**
lagar *nm* wine press; oil press.
lagarta *nf* (**a**) lizard; **¡**—, —! look out! (**b**) (*Ent*) gipsy moth; — **falsa** lackey moth. (**c**) sly woman; **¡**—! you bitch!
lagartear [1a] *vt* (**a**) (*Chi*) to pinion. (**b**) (*Col*) to fiddle (*fam*), wangle (*fam*).
lagartera *nf* lizard hole.
lagartija *nf* (small) lizard, wall lizard.
lagartijo *nm* (*Mex*) young man-about-town, elegant idler.
lagarto *nm* (**a**) lizard: — **de Indias** alligator; **¡**—, —! look out!; (*Ec, Mex, Per*) God forbid!
   (**b**) sly fellow, fox.
   (**c**) (*Ec*) shopkeeper who charges high prices; (*Mex, Nic*) grasping sort, greedy person; (*Col*) unemployed man seeking to live at government expense; intriguer, wirepuller (*fam*).
lagartón *adj* (*Guat, Mex*) greedy; sharp, shrewd; sly.

lago *nm* lake; **los Grandes L**—**s** the Great Lakes.
lágrima *nf* tear; drop; —**s de cocodrilo** crocodile tears; —**s de San Pedro** (*Arg, Chi*) June rains; **beberse las** —**s** to hold back one's tears; **deshacerse en** —**s** to burst into tears; **llorar a** — **viva** to sob one's heart out, cry uncontrollably.
lagrimar [1a] *vi* to cry.
lagrimear [1a] *vi* (*of person*) to shed tears easily, be tearful; (*of eyes*) to water, fill with tears.
lagrimilla *nf* (*Chi*) unfermented grape juice.
lagrimoso *adj* person lachrymose, tearful; eyes watery.
laguna *nf* (**a**) (*Geog*) pool; (*near coast*) lagoon. (**b**) (*Lit etc*) gap, lacuna; (*in process*) hiatus, gap, break.
lagunajo *nm* pool, pond; puddle.
lagunato *nm* (*Cu, Hond*) = **lagunajo.**
lagunoso *adj* marshy, swampy.
laicado *nm* laity.
laical *adj* lay.
laicidad *nf* (*SAm*), **laicismo** *nm* laicism (*doctrine of the independence of the state etc from church interference*).
laicizar [1f] *vt* to laicize.
laico 1 *adj* lay. **2** *nm* layman.
laísmo *nm* use of **la** and **las** as indirect objects.
laísta 1 *adj* that uses **la** and **las** as indirect objects. **2** *nmf* user of **la** and **las** as indirect objects.
laja[1] *nf* (**a**) (*Arg, Chi, Hond*) sandstone (*easily broken into slabs*); slab, flagstone. (**b**) (*Ec*) steep ground, steep place.
laja[2] *nf* (*Col*) fine rope.
Lalo *m* (*SAm*) pet name for **Eduardo.**
lama[1] *nf* (**a**) mud, slime, ooze. (**b**) (*Bol, Col, Mex*) mould, verdigris; (*Mex*) moss; duckweed.
lama[2] *nf* (*Sew*) lamé.
lama[3] *nm* (*Rel*) lama.
lambarear [1a] *vi* (*Cu*) to wander aimlessly about.
lambeculo *nmf* (*Arg, Mex*) creep (*sl*), toady.
lambeladrillos *nm, pl* **lambeladrillos** (*Col*) hypocrite.
lambeplatos *nmf, pl* **lambeplatos** (*SAm*) (**a**) bootlicker (*fam*). (**b**) poor wretch.
lamber [2a] *vt* (*SAm*) (**a**) = **lamer.** (**b**) to fawn on, toady to, suck up to (*fam*).
lambeta *nmf* (*Arg*) creep (*sl*), toady.
lambetada *nf* (*Arg, Mex, PR*) (**a**) lick. (**b**) servile action; remark designed to flatter.
lambetazo *nm* (*SAm*) (**a**) lick. (**b**) = **lambetada.**
lambetear [1a] *vt* (*SAm*) (**a**) to lick; to lick greedily, lick noisily. (**b**) to suck up to (*fam*).
lambiche *adj* (*Mex*) = **lambiscón.**
lambida *nf* (*SAm*) lick.
lambido *adj* (*SAm*) prim, affected; vain; (*Col, Ec, Mex, PR, SD*) shameless, cynical; (*Per*) disrespectful towards women.
lambioche *adj* (*Mex*) servile, soapy, fawning.
lambiscón *adj* (*Mex, Per*) (**a**) greedy, gluttonous. (**b**) = **lambioche.** (**c**) prim, affected.
lambisconear [1a] (*Col, Mex, Per*) **1** *vt* (**a**) to lick greedily. (**b**) (*fig*) to suck up to (*fam*). **2** *vi* (*fig*) to creep (*sl*), crawl.
lambisconería *nf* (*Mex, Per*) (**a**) greediness, gluttony. (**b**) servility, soapiness. (**c**) primness, affectation.
lambisquear [1a] (*Col, Mex, Per*) = **lambisconear.**
lambón *adj* (*SAm*) = **lambioche.**
lambraña *nmf* (*Col*) wretch.
lambrijo *adj* (*Mex*) very thin.
lambrusquear [1a] *vt* (*Chi, Mex*) to lick.
lambuzo *adj* (*Col, Ec, Mex, Ven*) (**a**) greedy, gluttonous. (**b**) shameless, brazen.
lameculos *nmf, pl* **lameculos** (*fam*) bootlicker (*fam*), toady.
lamedero *nm* (*Agr*) salt lick.
lamedura *nf* lick, licking.
lamentable *adj* regrettable; lamentable; pitiful; **es** — **que . . .** it is regrettable that . . .
lamentablemente *adv* regrettably.
lamentación *nf* lamentation; sorrow; **ahora no sirven** —**es** it's no good crying over spilt milk.
lamentar [1a] **1** *vt* to be sorry about, regret; loss etc to lament, bemoan, bewail; death to mourn; — **que . . .** to be sorry that . . ., regret that . . .; **lamentamos mucho que . . .** we very much regret that . . .
   2 lamentarse *vr* to lament, wail, moan (*de, por* about, over); to mourn (*de, por* over); to complain (*de, por* about).
lamento *nm* lament; moan, wail; —**s** lamentation.
lamentoso *adj* (**a**) = **lamentable.** (**b**) plaintive.
lameplatos *nmf, pl* **lameplatos** (**a**) person who eats scraps. (**b**) (*Mex*) toady; poor wretch; worthless individual.

lamer [2a] vt to lick; (of water) to lap, lap against.
lametada nf lick; lap.
lamido adj (a) very thin; pale. (b) scrubbed. (c) prim, affected.
lámina[1] nf (of metal, glass etc) sheet; (Metal, Phot, Typ) plate; (in book etc) plate, illustration, picture; engraving; —s de acero steel in sheets, sheet steel.
lámina[2] nmf (Col) rogue, rascal.
laminadero nm: — de hierro steel rolling mill.
laminado adj (a) laminate(d). (b) (Tech) sheet (attr), rolled; **cobre** — sheet copper, rolled copper.
laminador nm rolling mill.
laminar [1a] vt to laminate; (Tech) to roll.
lamiscar [1g] vt to lick greedily, lick noisily.
lampa nf (SAm) spade, hoe.
lampalague nf (a) (Arg, Chi) boa constrictor. (b) (Chi: fig) glutton.
lámpara 1 nf lamp, light; bulb; (Radio) valve, tube (US); —s (SAm) eyes; — de alcohol spirit lamp; — de arco arc lamp; — de bolsillo torch, flashlight; — de lectura reading lamp; — de mesa table lamp; — de pared wall light; — de pie standard lamp; — de señales signalling lamp; — de soldar blowlamp, blow torch; — de techo overhead lamp; — solar ultravioleta sun-ray lamp; **atizar la** — (fam) to fill up the glasses; **quebrar la** — (Ven) to ruin everything.
2 nmf (Cu) bore; (Ven) thief, swindler.
lamparero nm lampmaker; lamplighter.
lamparilla nf (a) small lamp; nightlight. (b) (Bot) aspen.
lamparín nm (a) (Chi) candle. (b) (Per) paraffin lamp.
lamparista nm = **lamparero**.
lámparo adj (Col) penniless, broke (fam).
lamparón nm (a) (Med) scrofula. (b) large grease spot.
lampazo[1] nm (Bot) burdock.
lampazo[2] nm (a) (Naut) swab; (Arg) floor mop. (b) (Col, Ven) whipping.
lampear [1a] vt (Per) to shovel.
lampiño adj hairless; person clean-shaven.
lampión nm Chinese lantern.
lampista nm (a) = **lamparero**. (b) tinsmith.
lampón[1] adj (Col) starving, hungry.
lampón[2] nm (Ec) spade, hoe.
lamprea nf (a) (Fish) lamprey. (b) (Med) sore, ulcer.
lamprear [1a] vt (CAm) to whip.
lana[1] nf (a) wool; fleece; woollen cloth; — de acero steel wool; de —, hecho de — wool (attr), woollen; **ir por** — y volver trasquilado to get nothing for one's pains, be disappointed in one's hopes. (b) (Mex) money. (c) (Mex) lie. (d) (CAm) trickster, swindler; rotter.
lana[2] nf (CR, Guat) = **lama**[1] (b).
lanar adj wool (attr), wool-bearing; **ganado** — sheep.
lance nm (a) (of net etc) throw, cast. (b) (Fish) catch, quantity of fish caught. (c) (in games etc) stroke, move, piece of play. (d) incident, event, occurrence, episode; chance, accident; — de honor affair of honour, duel; **el libro tiene pocos** —s the book is dull, not much happens in the book; **tirarse (a) un** — (Arg, Par) to take a chance. (e) critical moment, difficult moment. (f) row, quarrel. (g) (Chi) duck, dodge; **sacar** — to dodge, duck away. (h) (Arg, Par: Archit) section, range; **casa de 3** —s house in 3 sections. (i) de — (Comm) secondhand; cheap; **libros de** — secondhand books; **comprar algo de** — to buy something secondhand, buy something cheap.
lancear [1a] vt to spear.
lancero 1 nm (Mil) lancer; —s (Mus) lancers. 2 nmf (Arg) excessively optimistic person, irresponsible person.
lanceta nf (a) (Med etc) lancet; **abrir con** — to lance. (b) (SAm) goad.
lancinante adj pain piercing.
lancinar [1a] vt to lance, pierce.
lancha[1] nf launch; (small) boat; lighter, barge; — **automóvil** motor launch, motorboat; — **cañonera** gunboat; — **de carga** lighter, barge; — **de carreras** speedboat; — **de desembarco** landing craft; — **motora** motorboat, speedboat; — **neumática** (Aer etc) rubber dinghy; — **de pesca** fishing boat; — **rápida** speedboat; — **salvavidas**, — **de socorro** lifeboat; — **torpedera** torpedo boat.
lancha[2] nf (Ec) mist, fog; (hoar)frost.
lanchaje nm (Mex) freight charge.

lanchar [1a] vi (Ec) to become overcast; to freeze.
lanchero nm boatman; lighterman, bargee.
lanchón nm lighter, barge.
landó nm landau.
landra nf: ¡mala — te coma! curse you!
lanería nf (a) woollen goods. (b) wool shop.
lanero 1 adj wool (attr); woollen; **la industria lanera** the wool industry. 2 nm (a) woolman, wool dealer. (b) wool warehouse.
lángara nmf (Mex) untrustworthy individual.
lángaro adj (a) (CAm) vagrant, wandering, idle; (Col, Mex) starving, poverty-stricken; (Mex) wicked; sly, untrustworthy. (b) (CR) lanky.
langarucho adj (CAm, Mex), **langarutano** adj (Ec) lanky.
langosta nf (a) lobster. (b) (Ent) locust.
langostera nf lobster pot.
langostín nm, **langostino** nm prawn; crayfish.
languceta adj (Chi), **languciento** adj (Chi, Mex), **langucio** adj (Chi) starving; weakly.
lánguidamente adv languidly; weakly, listlessly.
languidecer [2d] vi to languish, pine (away).
languidez nf languor, lassitude; listlessness.
lánguido adj languid; weak, listless, drooping.
languso adj (Mex) (a) sly, shrewd. (b) lanky.
lanilla nf nap (on cloth); thin flannel cloth.
lanolina nf lanolin(e).
lanoso adj woolly, fleecy.
lanudo adj (a) woolly, fleecy. (b) (Ec, Ven) rustic, uncouth.
lanza 1 nf (a) (Mil) lance, spear; **estar** — **en ristre** to be ready for action, be all set to go; **medir** —s to cross swords; **ser una** — to be pretty sharp; (Mex) to be sly, be a rogue. (b) (of wagon) pole. (c) (of hose) nozzle.
2 nm (Col, CR, Ven) swindling businessman, dishonest dealer, shark (fam).
lanzabombas nm, pl **lanzabombas** (Aer) bomb release; (Mil) trench mortar.
lanzacohetes nm, pl **lanzacohetes** rocket launcher.
lanzada nf spear thrust; spear wound.
lanzadera nf shuttle.
lanzador nm (a) thrower; (Sport) pitcher; — de cuchillos knife-thrower. (b) (Comm, Fin) promoter.
lanzaespumas nm, pl **lanzaespumas** foam extinguisher.
lanzallamas nm, pl **lanzallamas** flamethrower.
lanzamiento nm (a) throw, cast; throwing, casting, hurling; (Aer) drop (by parachute), jump, descent; — de pesos putting the weight. (b) (Naut) launch, launching. (c) (Comm, Fin) launching; promotion. (d) (Law) dispossession, eviction.
lanzaminas nm, pl **lanzaminas** minelayer.
lanzar [1f] 1 vt (a) to throw, cast, fling, hurl; (Sport) ball to pitch, bowl (a at, to); weight to put; (Aer) to drop (by parachute); (Med) to bring up, throw up, vomit; challenge to throw out, throw down. (b) cry to give, utter; look to give, cast (a at). (c) (Naut) to launch. (d) (Bot) leaves etc to put forth. (e) (Comm, Fin) to launch, promote. (f) (Law) to dispossess, evict.
2 **lanzarse** vr (a) to throw oneself, hurl oneself, fling oneself (a, en into; sobre on); to rush (sobre at, on), fly (sobre at); (Aer) to jump (by parachute), bale out; **se lanzó a la pelea** he rushed into the fray; **se lanzó al río** he jumped into the river, he dived into the river. (b) — a (fig) to launch into; to embark upon, undertake.
Lanzarote m Lancelot.
lanzatorpedos nm, pl **lanzatorpedos** torpedo tube.
laña nf clamp; rivet.
lañar [1a] vt to clamp (together); to rivet.
Laos m Laos.
laosiano 1 adj Laotian. 2 nm, **laosiana** nf Laotian.
lapa nf (a) (Zool) limpet. (b) (CAm) odd-looking person, outlandish individual; (Mex) scrounger (fam). (c) (Chi) soldiers' camp follower. (d) (Chi, Per) half gourd (used as bowl etc). (e) (Ec) large flat-topped hat.
lapalada nf (Mex) drizzle.
lape adj (Chi) (a) massed, packed tight; matted. (b) dance etc merry, lively.
lapicera nf (Chi, RPl) = **lapicero**.
lapicero nm propelling pencil; pencil-holder; (SAm) penholder, pen; (Per etc) ball-point pen.

lápida nf stone, stone tablet, memorial tablet; — **conmemorativa** commemorative tablet; — **mortuoria** headstone, gravestone; — **mural** tablet let into a wall; — **sepulcral** tombstone.

lapidar [1a] vt (a) to stone, throw stones at; to stone to death. (b) (Col, Guat, Hond, Mex, Per) gem to cut.

lapidario 1 adj lapidary. 2 nm lapidary.

lapislázuli nm lapis lazuli.

lápiz nm (a) pencil; crayon; — **de cejas** eyebrow pencil; — **labial,** — **de labios** lipstick; — **(de) plomo** lead pencil; **escribir algo a** (or **con**) — to write something in pencil; **está añadido a** — it is added in pencil; it is pencilled in.

(b) (Min) blacklead, graphite.

lapo nm (a) (sl) bash (fam), swipe; **de un** — (Col) at one go. (b) (Col, Ec, Ven) swig (fam). (c) (Ven) simple soul.

lapón nm, **lapona** nf Lapp, Laplander.

Laponia f Lapland.

lapso nm lapse; — **de tiempo** interval of time, passage of time.

lapsus nm, pl **lapsus;** — **calami** slip of the pen; — **linguae** slip of the tongue.

laqueado adj lacquered; varnished.

laquear [1a] vt to lacquer; nails to varnish.

lard(e)ar [1a] vt to lard, baste.

lardo nm lard, animal fat.

lardoso adj lardy, fatty; greasy.

lares nmpl (Hist) household gods, lares; (fig) home; **volver a los** — to return home.

largamente adv (a) for a long time; tell at length, fully; **conversamos** — we talked at length, we had a long conversation.

(b) live comfortably, at ease.

(c) reward, treat etc generously.

largar [1h] 1 vt (a) to let go, let loose, release; to loosen, slacken; rope to let out, pay out; flag, sail to unfurl; boat to launch, put out.

(b) blow to give, fetch, deal.

(c) curse etc to let fly.

(d) (Arg, Mex, Par) to throw, hurl.

(e) (Col) to give, lend.

2 **largarse** vr (a) (fam) to beat it (fam), hop it (fam); to quit; **¡lárgate!** clear off!

(b) (Naut) to set sail, start out.

(c) (SAm) to start, begin; — **a** + infin to start to + infin.

largo 1 adj (a) (of distance, measure) long; (of time) long, lengthy; — **de pelo** long-haired; — **de uñas** light-fingered, thieving; —**s años** long years, many years; **no es bastante** — it's not long enough; **es muy** — **de contar** it's a long story.

(b) (fam) **¡**— **(de aquí)!** clear off!

(c) (with de) **estar de** — to be in a long dress; **ponerse de** — to put on grown-up clothes, dress as an adult (for the first time); **pasar de** — to pass by, go by (without stopping); **dejar pasar a uno de** — to give someone a wide berth.

(d) (with lo) **a lo más** — at the most; **a lo** — put lengthways; tell at great length, lengthily; see etc in the distance, far off; **a lo** — **de** along; alongside; (of time) all through, throughout; **a lo** — **del río** along the river; **a lo** — **del túnel** throughout the tunnel.

(e) (of quantity) full, good; **tardó media hora larga** he took a good (or full) half-hour; **los aventajó en un minuto** — he beat them by a full minute; **le costó 50 dólares** —**s** it cost him all of 50 dollars, it cost him a good 50 dollars.

(f) (larga) **a la larga** in the long run; eventually, in the end; **dar largas a un asunto** to delay a matter, put off making a decision about a matter; **me dio largas con una promesa** she put me off with a promise; **saberla larga** to be shrewd; to know one's way about.

(g) generous; lavish; **tirar de** — to spend lavishly.

(h) abundant, copious; crop, harvest heavy.

(i) person sharp, shrewd; quick.

(j) (Naut) rope loose, slack.

2 nm (a) length; **el** — **de las faldas** the length of skirts; **tiene 9 metros de** — it is 9 metres long; **¿cuánto tiene de** —**?** how long is it?

(b) (Mus) largo.

lárgona nf (a) (Chi, Per) delay. (b) (Chi) **darse una** — to take a rest.

largor nm length.

largucho adj (SAm) lanky.

larguero 1 adj (a) (Arg, Chi) long, lengthy; person slow, slow-working; (Sport) trained for long-distance running.

(b) (Chi) generous; lavish; abundant, copious.

2 nm (Archit) main beam, chief support; (of door) jamb; (Sport) goal-post, crossbar; (of bed) bolster.

largueza nf generosity.

larguirucho adj lanky, gangling.

largura nf length.

largurucho adj (SAm) lanky, gangling.

lárice nm larch.

laringe nf larynx.

laringitis nf laryngitis.

larva nf larva; grub, maggot.

las def art fpl etc: see **los.**

lasca nf chip of stone.

lascadura nf (Mex) sore, abrasion.

lascar [1g] 1 vt (a) (Naut) to slacken. (b) (Mex) to graze, bruise; stone to chip, chip off. 2 vi (Mex) to chip off, flake off.

lascivamente adv lewdly, lasciviously; lustfully; (fig) playfully, wantonly.

lascivia nf lewdness, lasciviousness; lust, lustfulness; (fig) playfulness.

lascivo adj lewd, lascivious; lustful; (fig) playful, wanton.

lasitud nf lassitude, weariness.

laso adj weary; weak; limp, slack, languid.

lástima nf (a) (feeling) pity; compassion; shame; **¡qué** —**!** what a pity!, what a shame!, that's too bad!; **¡qué** — **de hombre!** isn't he pitiful?; **es una** — it's a shame; **es** — **que** ... it's a pity that ..., it's too bad that ...; **dar** — to be pitiful, rouse to pity; **eso me da mucha** — I feel very sorry about that; **es una película que da** — it's a pathetic film; (pej) it's a pathetically bad film; **todos me dan** — I feel sorry for them all.

(b) pitiful object, pitiful sight; **estar hecho una** — to be a sorry sight, be in a dreadful state.

(c) complaint.

lastimada nf (Guat, Mex) = **lastimadura.**

lastimador adj harmful, injurious.

lastimadura nf (SAm) wound, injury; bruise; sore.

lastimar [1a] 1 vt (a) to hurt, harm, injure; to wound, bruise.

(b) to offend, distress.

(c) to pity, sympathize with, feel pity for.

(d) to move to pity.

2 **lastimarse** vr (a) to hurt oneself, injure oneself; **se lastimó el brazo** he hurt his arm.

(b) — **de** to complain about.

(c) — **de** to feel sorry for, pity.

lastimero adj (a) harmful, injurious. (b) = **lastimoso.**

lastimón nm (SAm) = **lastimadura.**

lastimosamente adv pitifully, pathetically.

lastimoso adj piteous, pitiful, pathetic.

lastrar [1a] vt to ballast.

lastre nm (a) (Tech) ballast; **en** — (Naut) in ballast. (b) (fig) ballast; dead weight, useless load. (c) good sense, steadiness.

lata nf (a) (metal) tinplate; tin, can; (Col) food, daily ration; **sardinas en** — tinned sardines, canned sardines; **sonar a** — (Mus etc) to sound tinny.

(b) (fam) nuisance, bore, bind (sl); **es una** — **tener que** ... it's a nuisance having to ...; **¡vaya una** —**!, ¡qué** —**!** what a nuisance!; **dar** — (Nic, Per) to talk nonsense; **dar la** — to be a nuisance, be annoying, be boring; **dar la** — **a uno** to annoy someone.

(c) (wood) lath.

(d) **estar sin** — (fam), **estar en la(s)** —**(s)** (CAm, Col) to be penniless, be broke (fam).

(e) (CAm) whippersnapper, young rascal.

latazo nm (fam) nuisance, bore, bind (sl).

latear [1a] vi (SAm) (a) to be a nuisance, be annoying. (b) to talk a lot, chatter away pointlessly.

latente adj (a) latent. (b) (SAm) alive, intense, vigorous; memory fresh, alive.

lateral 1 adj lateral, side (attr). 2 nm (Theat) wings, side of the stage.

lateralmente adv laterally; sideways.

latería nf (CAm) tinplate; (Arg, Cu, Par) tinsmith's workshop; tinworks.

laterío nm (Mex) tinned goods, canned goods.

latero nm (SAm) (a) tinsmith. (b) bore, tedious person.

látex nm latex.

latido nm (a) (of heart) beat, beating; throb, throbbing; palpitation. (b) (of dog) bark, yelp.

latifundia nf latifundia, large estates.

latifundio nm large estate.

latifundista nm (SAm) important landowner, owner of a large estate.

latigazo nm (a) lash; crack (of a whip). (b) (fig) harsh reproof; verbal lashing. (c) (fam) swig (fam), swallow; strong nightcap.

látigo nm (a) whip; (Col, Ec, Hond, Per) lash; crack (of a whip).
(b) (Chi: Sport) finishing post, finishing line; **salir al** — to complete a task.
(c) (Arg, Per, Urug) horseman, rider.
latigudo adj (SAm) leathery.
latigueda nf (Ec, Hond, Mex, Nic) whipping, thrashing.
latiguear [1a] vt (Arg, Ec, Hond, Mex) to whip, thrash.
latiguera nf (Per) whipping, thrashing.
latín nm (a) Latin; **bajo** — Low Latin; — **clásico** Classical Latin; — **tardío** Late Latin; — **vulgar** Vulgar Latin; **saber (mucho)** — (fam) to be pretty sharp.
(b) —**es** Latin tags, learned quotations and references.
latinajo nm dog Latin, bad Latin; —s Latin tags, learned quotations and references.
latinidad nf latinity.
latinismo nm latinism.
latinista nmf latinist.
latinización nf latinization.
latinizar [1f] vti to latinize.
latino 1 adj Latin; (SAm: angl) Latin-American.
2 nm, **latina** nf Latin; (SAm: angl) Latin-American.
Latinoamérica f Latin America.
latinoamericano 1 adj Latin-American. **2** nm, **latinoamericana** nf Latin-American.
latir [3a] **1** vt (a) (Mex) **me late que todo saldrá bien** I have a feeling that all will be well, something tells me that everything will be all right.
(b) (Ven) to annoy, upset.
2 vi (a) (heart) to beat, throb, palpitate.
(b) (dog) to bark, yelp.
latitud nf (Geog and fig) latitude; breadth; area, extent.
latitudinal adj latitudinal.
lato adj broad, wide, extensive; sense broad.
latón nm (a) brass. (b) (RPl) big tin, large tin container; (Per, PR) tin bucket.
latoso adj annoying, tiresome; boring.
latrocinio nm robbery, theft.
Latvia f Latvia.
latvio 1 adj Latvian. **2** nm, **latvia** nf Latvian. **3** nm (language) Latvian, Lettish.
lauca nf (Chi) baldness, loss of hair; alopecia.
laucadura nf (Chi) baldness.
laucar [1g] vt (Chi) to fleece, shear, remove the hair (or wool) from.
lauco adj (Chi) bald, hairless.•
laucha nf (Chi, RPl) mouse; (fig) thin person, small-featured person; (Arg) dirty old man; (Col) = **baquiano**; **ser una** —, **ser una lauchita** (Chi, RPl) to be very sharp, be quick; **aguaitar la** —, **catear la** — (Chi, RPl) to await a favourable opportunity, bide one's time.
laúd nm (Mus) lute.
laudable adj laudable, praiseworthy.
laudablemente adv laudably, in a praiseworthy way.
láudano nm laudanum.
laudatorio adj laudatory.
laudo nm (Law) award, decision, finding.
laureado 1 adj honoured, distinguished, famous. **2** nm laureate.
laurear [1a] vt to crown with laurel; (fig) to honour, reward.
laurel nm laurel; (fig) laurels; honour, reward; — **rosa** rosebay, oleander; **descansar** (or **dormirse**) **sobre sus** —**es** to rest on one's laurels.
lauréola nf (a) laurel wreath, crown of laurel; halo.
(b) (Bot) daphne.
lauro nm laurel; (fig) laurels; glory, fame.
Lausana Lausanne.
lava[1] nf (Geol) lava.
lava[2] nf (Min) washing; **camisa de** — **y pon** drip-dry shirt.
lavable adj washable.
lavabo nm (a) washbasin; washstand. (b) (euph) lavatory, washroom (euph), toilet (euph).
lavacara nf (Col, Ec) washbasin.
lavacaras nmf, pl **lavacaras** (fam) toady, creep (sl).
lavacoches nm, pl **lavacoches** car wash.
lavada nf (SAm) wash, washing.
lavadedos nm, pl **lavadedos** finger bowl.
lavadero nm (a) laundry, wash house; (in river) washing place. (b) (SAm) gold-bearing sands (in river).
lavado nm (a) (act) wash, washing; — **de cabeza** shampoo; — **de cerebro** brainwashing; — **químico**, — **en seco** dry cleaning.
(b) (clothes) wash, laundry.
(c) (Art) wash.

lavador nm (a) (Arg, Par) washbasin. (b) (Guat) = **lavabo** (b).
lavadora nf (a) washing machine; — **de coches** car wash; — **de platos** dish-washer. (b) (Col, Ec) laundress, washerwoman.
lavadura nf (a) washing. (b) dirty water.
lavagallos nm (Col, Ven) poor-quality brandy, firewater.
lavaje nm (Chi, RPl) (a) = **lavadura**. (b) (Med) enema.
lavamanos nm, pl **lavamanos** washbasin.
lavanda nf lavender.
lavandera nf (a) laundress, washerwoman. (b) (Orn) wagtail.
lavandería nf laundry; — **automática** launderette.
lavandero nm launderer, laundryman.
lavándula nf lavender.
lavaojos nm, pl **lavaojos** eye bath.
lavaplatos nm, pl **lavaplatos** (a) (machine) dish-washer. (b) (Arg: person) dishwasher, washer-up.
(c) (Chi, Mex) sink.
lavar [1a] **1** vt (a) to wash; — **y marcar** hair to shampoo and set; — **en seco** to dry-clean; — **la cabeza** to wash one's hair.
(b) (fig) to wipe away; to wipe out.
2 lavarse vr to wash, have a wash; — **las manos** to wash one's hands; (fig) to wash one's hands of it.
lavativa nf (a) (Med) enema. (b) (fig) nuisance, bother, bore.
lavatorio nm (a) washstand. (b) (SAm: angl) lavatory, washroom (euph). (c) (Med) lotion.
lavavajillas nm, pl **lavavajillas** dishwasher.
lavazas nfpl dishwater, dirty water, slops.
lavoteo nm (fam) quick wash, cat-lick (fam).
laxante 1 adj laxative. **2** nm laxative.
laxar [1a] vt to ease, relax, slacken; bowels to loosen.
laxativo adj laxative.
laxitud nf laxity, slackness.
laxo adj lax, slack.
laya nf (a) spade; — **de puntas** (garden) fork. (b) (fig) kind, sort; **de esta** — of this kind.
lazada nf bow, knot.
lazar [1f] vt to lasso, rope; (Mex, Nic) = **enlazar**.
lazariento adj (Arg, Mex, Nic) leprous.
lazarillo nm blind man's guide.
lazarino 1 adj leprous. **2** nm leper.
Lázaro m Lazarus.
lazo nm (a) bow, knot; loop; lasso, lariat; — **corredizo** slipknot; — **de zapato** bootlace.
(b) (Hunting) snare, trap (also fig); **caer en el** — to fall into the trap; **tender un** — **a uno** to set a trap for someone.
(c) (Aut) hairpin bend.
(d) (fig) link, bond, tie; **los** —**s culturales entre A y B** cultural ties between A and B; **los** —**s familiares** the family bond, the ties of blood.
le personal pron (a) (acc) him; (relating to **Vd**) you; **no le veo** I don't see him; **¿le ayudo?** shall I help you?
(b) (dative) (to) him, (to) her, (to) it; (relating to **Vd**) (to) you; **le hablé** I spoke to him, I spoke to her; **quiero darle esto** I want to give you this; **le he comprado esto** I bought this for you; **uno de los mejores papeles que le hayamos visto** one of the best performances we have seen from him; **no se le conoce otra obra** no other work of his is known.
leal adj loyal, faithful, trustworthy.
lealmente adv loyally, faithfully.
lealtad nf loyalty, fidelity; trustworthiness.
Leandro m Leander.
lebrato nm leveret.
lebrel nm greyhound.
lebrón adj (Mex) (a) sharp, wide-awake. (b) boastful, insolent. (c) sly; evil-minded.
lección nf (a) lesson (also Eccl); (School) lesson, class, (Univ) lecture, class; (fig) warning, example; — **particular** private lesson; — **práctica** object lesson (de in); **dar** —**es** to teach, give lessons; **dar una** — **a uno** (fig) to teach someone a lesson; **¡que te sirva de** —! let that be a lesson to you!; **tomar** — to have a lesson.
(b) (Lit: of MS etc) reading.
leco adj (Mex) crazy, stupid.
lectivo adj school (attr); see **año, día** etc.
lector nm, **lectora** nf (a) reader. (b) (School, Univ) conversation assistant.
lectura nf reading; reading matter; **una persona de mucha** — a well-read person; **dar** — **a** to read (publicly).
lecha nf milt, (soft) roe.
lechada nf (a) whitewash; paste; grout; (in paper making) pulp. (b) (SAm) milking.

lechal 1 *adj* sucking. **2** *nm* milk (*fig*), milky juice.
lechar [1a] *vt* (a) (*SAm*) to milk; (*CAm, Col, Ec*) to give suck to, produce milk for. (b) (*CAm, Mex*) to whitewash.
lechazo *nm* young lamb.
leche *nf* (a) milk; — **condensada** condensed milk; — **desnatada** skim(med) milk; — **de magnesia** milk of magnesia; — **pasterizada** pasteurized milk; — **en polvo** powdered milk; **estar con** (*or* **tener**) **la** — **en los labios** (*fig*) to be young and inexperienced, be wet behind the ears (*fig*).
　(b) (*Bot*) milk, milky juice; (*Bol*) rubber; (*Ant*) rubber tree.
　(c) (*tabu*) semen, spunk (*tabu*); ¡—! hell!; **un tío de mala** — a nasty sort, an evil person; a disagreeable chap; **tener mala** — to be vindictive, be nasty; **hay mucha mala** — **entre ellos** there's a lot of bad blood between them; **aquí hay mucha mala** — there's a lot of ill-feeling here.
　(d) (*SAm*) good luck; **estar con** —, **estar de** —, **tener** — to be lucky.
lecheada *nf* (*Arg*) = **lechada.**
lechear [1a] *vt* (*SAm*) to milk.
lechecillas *nfpl* sweetbreads.
lechera *nf* (a) milkmaid, dairymaid. (b) milk can, milk churn. (c) (*SAm*) cow.
lechería *nf* (a) dairy, creamery; (*Col, Chi*) milking parlour. (b) (*Chi*) cows, herd. (c) (*Col, Mex, Ven*) meanness.
lecherita *nf* milk jug.
lechero 1 *adj* (a) milk (*attr*); dairy (*attr*); **producción lechera** milk production; *see* **vaca.**
　(b) (*SAm*) lucky.
　(c) (*Mex, Ven*) mean, stingy.
　(d) (*Ant*) greedy, grasping. **2** *nm* dairyman; milkman.
lechigada *nf* litter, brood; (*fig*) gang.
lecho *nm* (a) bed; couch; (*Agr*) bedding; — **mortuorio** deathbed. (b) (*of river*) bed; bottom, floor; (*Geol*) layer; — **de roca** bedrock.
lechón *nm* (a) piglet, sucking-pig. (b) (*fig*) pig, filthy person.
lechona *nf* (a) sow. (b) (*fig*) pig, sow; slob (*sl*).
lechoncillo *nm* piglet, sucking-pig.
lechoso *adj* (a) milky. (b) (*CAm, Ven*) lucky.
lechucear [1a] *vi* (*Per*) to be on night duty.
lechucero *nm* (*Ec, Per*) (a) night worker; night taxi driver. (b) night taxi.
lechudo *adj* (*SAm*) lucky.
lechuga 1 *nf* (a) lettuce; — **Cos** cos lettuce. (b) (*Sew*) frill, flounce. (c) (*Cu, PR*) banknote. **2** *nm* (*fam*) rotter, cad, heel (*sl*).
lechuguilla *nf* (*Sew*) frill, flounce, ruff.
lechuguino *nm* (a) young lettuce. (b) (*fam*) toff (*fam*), dude (*US*).
lechuza *nf* (a) (*Orn*) owl; — **común** barn owl. (b) (*Chi, Mex*) albino, light blond(e). (c) (*Cu, Mex*) whore.
leer [2e] *vti* to read; — **en la boca** to lip-read; — **entre líneas** to read between the lines; — **la mano a uno** to read someone's palm; **"al que leyere"** "to the reader".
lega *nf* lay sister.
legación *nf* legation.
legado *nm* (a) legate. (b) (*Law*) legacy, bequest.
legajar *vt* (*Col, Chi, Ec, Mex*) to file.
legajo *nm* file, bundle (of papers).
legal *adj* (a) legal, lawful; **time** standard. (b) **person** trustworthy, truthful; (*Mex*) upright. (c) (*Per*) fine, marvellous.
legalidad *nf* legality, lawfulness.
legalización *nf* legalization; authentication.
legalizar [1f] *vt* to legalize, make lawful; **document** to authenticate.
legalmente *adv* legally, lawfully.
légamo *nm* slime, mud, ooze; clay.
legamoso *adj* slimy, oozy; clayey.
legaña *nf* rheum.
legañoso *adj* bleary.
legar [1h] *vt* to bequeath (*also Law, fig*), leave (*a* to).
legatario *nm*, **legataria** *nf* legatee.
legendario *adj* legendary.
legibilidad *nf* legibility.
legible *adj* legible.
legiblemente *adv* legibly.
legión *nf* legion; **L— Extranjera** Foreign Legion; **son** — they are legion; **el autor** — (*Lit*) the author whose name is legion, the collectivity of anonymous authors (*of ballads etc*).
legionario 1 *adj* legionary. **2** *nm* legionary; legionnaire.
legislación *nf* legislation.

legislador *nm*, **legisladora** *nf* legislator.
legislar [1a] *vi* to legislate.
legislativo *adj* legislative.
legislatura *nf* (*SAm*) legislature, legislative body.
legista 1 *nm* jurist, legist. **2** *adj* (*SAm*): **médico** — forensic expert, criminal pathologist.
legítimamente *adv* legitimately, rightfully; justly; genuinely.
legitimar [1a] **1** *vt* to legitimize; to legalize. **2 legitimarse** *vr* to establish one's identity; to establish one's title (*or* claim etc).
legitimidad *nf* legitimacy; justice; authenticity.
legitimista 1 *adj* loyalist. **2** *nmf* loyalist.
legítimo *adj* legitimate, rightful; just; genuine, authentic, real.
lego 1 *adj* (a) (*Eccl*) lay; secular. (b) (*fig*) ignorant, uninformed. **2** *nm* layman; lay brother; **los** —**s** the laity.
legón *nm* hoe.
legua *nf* league; **a la** — far away, a mile away; **eso se ve a la** — you can tell it a mile away.
leguaje *nm* (a) (*Mex, Nic*) distance in leagues. (b) (*Per: Parl*) travelling expenses.
leguario *nm* (*Bol, Chi*) milestone.
leguleyo *nm* pettifogging lawyer.
legumbre *nf* vegetable.
leguminoso *adj* leguminous.
leíble *adj* legible.
Leida, Leide(n) Leyden.
leída *nf* (*SAm*) reading; **de una** — in one reading, at one go; **dar una** — a to read.
leído *adj* **person** well-read.
leísmo *nm* use of **le** instead of **lo** and **la** (direct objects).
leísta 1 *adj* that uses **le** instead of **lo** and **la** (direct objects). **2** *nmf* user of **le** instead of **lo** and **la.**
lejanía *nf* distance, remoteness; remote place.
lejas *adj pl*: **de** — **tierras** of (*or* from) some distant land.
lejano *adj* distant, remote, far off.
Lejano Oriente *m* Far East.
lejía *nf* (a) bleach; lye. (b) (*fam*) dressing-down.
lejos 1 *adv* far, far away, far off; **a lo** — in the distance, far off; **de** —, **desde** — from afar, from a long way off; **más** — further (off); **está muy** — it's a long way (away); **¿está** —**?** is it far?; **eso queda demasiado** — that's too far (away); **ir** — to go far (*also fig*); **para no ir más** — (*fig*) to take an obvious example.
　2 — **de** *prep* far from; **estoy muy** — **de pensar que . . .** I am very far from thinking that . . .
　3 *nm* distant view; appearance from a distance; glimpse; (*Art*) background; **tiene buen** — it looks all right at a distance.
lejura *nf* (*Col, Ec*) distance; —**s** (*Arg*) remote place, remote area.
lele *adj* (*CAm, Chi*), **lelo** *adj* silly, stupid.
lema *nm* motto, device; theme; (*Pol etc*) slogan, watchword.
lempira *nf* standard monetary unit of Honduras.
lempo 1 *adj* (*Col*) big, large. **2** *nm* (*Col, Ec*) bit, piece. (b) (*Col*) **un** — **de caballo** a big horse.
lémur *nm* lemur.
lencería *nf* (a) linen, drapery; (*woman's*) lingerie. (b) draper's (shop). (c) linen cupboard.
lencero *nm* draper.
lendroso *adj* lousy.
lengón *adj* (*Col, Mex*) = **lenguón.**
lengua *nf* (a) (*Anat and fig*) tongue; **mala** —, — **larga** (*SAm*), — **de trapo** (*fam*) gossip; **de** — **en** — from mouth to mouth; **andar en** —**s** to be the talk of the town; **atar la** — **a uno** (*fig*) to silence someone; **beber con la** — to lap up; **buscar la** — **a uno** to pick a quarrel with someone; **dar a la** — to chatter, talk too much; **estar con la** — **fuera** (*fig*) to be dead beat, be exhausted; **hacerse** —**s de** to praise to the skies, rave about; **írsele a uno la** — to talk too much; to let the cat out of the bag; **morderse la** — to hold one's tongue; to keep something back; **no morderse la** — not to mince one's words, not to pull one's punches; **nacer con la** — **fuera** to be born idle; **sacar la** — **a uno** (*fig*) to cock a snook at someone (*fam*); **soltar la** — (*fam*) to spill the beans (*sl*); **tirar de la** — **a uno** to draw someone out, make someone talk; to provoke someone; **se le trabó la** — he began to stammer.
　(b) (*of bell*) clapper.
　(c) (*Geog*) — **de tierra** spit of land, tongue of land.
　(d) (*Ling*) language, tongue; — **franca** lingua franca; — **madre** parent language; — **materna** mother tongue; — **moderna** modern language; — **muerta** dead language; — **viva** living language; **hablar en** — (*Per*) to speak Quichua.

lenguado nm (Fish) sole.
lenguaje nm (a) (in general) language; (faculty of) speech.
  (b) idiom, parlance, (mode of) speech; — **comercial** business language; — **periodístico** newspaper language, journalese; — **vulgar** common speech, ordinary speech; **en** — **llano** in plain English (etc).
  (c) (Lit) style, diction.
lenguaraz adj talkative; (pej) foul-mouthed.
lenguaz adj garrulous.
lengüeta nf (a) tab, small tongue; (Carp, Mus, of shoe) tongue; (Anat) epiglottis; (of balance etc) needle, pointer; (of arrow) barb.
  (b) (SAm) chatterbox; gossip.
  (c) (SAm) paper cutter.
  (d) (SAm) fringe of a petticoat.
lengüetada nf lick.
lengüetazo nm (SAm) lick; rapid movement of the tongue.
lengüetear [1a] **1** vt (SAm) to lick (with the tip of the tongue). **2** vi (SAm) to stick one's tongue out; (Ant) to jabber, chatter.
lengüeterías nfpl (SAm) gossip, tales.
lengüetero adj (Ant) garrulous; gossiping.
lengüicorto adj (fam) shy, timid.
lengüilargo adj, **lengüisucio** adj (Mex, PR) foul-mouthed.
lengüón (SAm) **1** adj garrulous; outspoken; gossiping. **2** nm gossip, talebearer.
lenidad nf lenience.
Leningrado Leningrad.
lenitivo 1 adj lenitive. **2** nm lenitive.
lenocinio nm pandering, procuring; (**casa de**) — brothel.
lentamente adv slowly.
lente nm or f lens; eyeglass; —s (Hist) spectacles; — **de aumento** magnifying glass; —s **de contacto** contact lenses.
lenteja nf lentil.
lentejuela nf spangle, sequin.
lentitud nf slowness; **con** — slowly.
lento adj slow.
leña nf (a) firewood; sticks, kindling; — **de oveja** (RPl) sheep droppings; **echar** — **al fuego** to add fuel to the flames; **llevar** — **al monte** to carry coals to Newcastle.
  (b) (fam) thrashing; **cargar de** —, **dar** — **a**, **hartar de** — to lay it on, thrash.
leñador nm woodcutter, woodman.
leñar [1a] vt (Arg, Mex), **leñatear** [1a] vt (Col) to make into firewood, cut up for firewood.
leñateo nm (CAm, Col) woodpile.
leñatero nm (RPl) woodcutter, woodman.
leñazo nm blow with a stick.
leñe nm (euph) = **leche**.
leñera nf woodshed.
leñero nm (a) dealer in wood. (b) woodshed.
leño nm (a) log; timber, wood, piece of wood. (b) (fam) blockhead.
leñoso adj woody.
León m Leon; — (**de Francia**) Lyons.
león nm lion (also fig); (SAm) puma; — **marino** sea lion; **estar hecho un** — to be furious; **ponerse como un** — to get furious.
leona nf (a) lioness. (b) (Chi) confusion, mess, mix-up.
leonado adj tawny.
leonera nf (a) lion's cage; lion's den; **parece una** — it's shockingly dirty.
  (b) (fam) gambling den, dive (fam); lumber room, attic; (Mex) bawdy house; (Arg, Ec, PR) communal prison cell; (Per) noisy gathering; (Col, Chi) underworld gathering.
leonés 1 adj Leonese. **2** nm, **leonesa** nf Leonese. **3** nm (dialect) Leonese.
leonino adj leonine.
Leonor f Eleanor.
leontina nf watch chain.
leopardo nm leopard; — **cazador** cheetah.
leopoldina nf fob, short watch chain.
Lepe: ir donde las — (Chi) to make a bloomer (in calculating) (fam); **saber más que** — to be pretty smart, have lots of savoir-faire.
leperada nf (CAm, Mex) coarse remark; dirty trick, rotten thing (to do) (fam).
lépero nm, **lépera** nf (CAm, Mex) low-class person, plebeian; (pej) rotter, heel (sl), villain; (Cu) clever person, quick-witted person.
leperusco adj (Mex) low-class, plebeian; (pej) rotten (fam), villainous.
lepidópteros nmpl lepidoptera, butterflies and moths.
lepisma nf silverfish.

leporino adj leporine; hare-like; **labio** — harelip.
lepra nf leprosy.
leprosería nf leper colony.
leproso 1 adj leprous. **2** nm, **leprosa** nf leper.
lerdear [1a] vi (Arg, CAm) to be slow (about doing things), do things unwillingly.
lerdera nf (CAm) = **lerdez**.
lerdez nf, **lerdeza** nf (CAm) slowness; heaviness, dullness; slow-wittedness; clumsiness.
lerdo adj slow; heavy, dull; slow-witted; clumsy.
lerdura nf (RPl) = **lerdez**.
leridense 1 adj of Lérida. **2** nmf native (or inhabitant) of Lérida; **los** —s the people of Lérida.
les personal pron (a) (acc) them; (relating to **Vds**) you.
  (b) (dative) (to) them; (relating to **Vds**) (to) you; for usage examples, see **le**.
lesa majestad nf lese-majesty.
lesbiana nf lesbian.
lesbianismo nm lesbianism.
lésbico adj lesbian.
lesbio adj lesbian.
lesera nf (Chi, Per) stupidity.
lesión nf wound, lesion; injury (also fig).
lesionado adj hurt, injured; player injured, unfit.
lesionar [1a] **1** vt to hurt, injure; to wound. **2 lesionarse** vr to get hurt.
lesivo adj harmful, damaging.
lesna nf awl.
leso adj (a) hurt; injured, offended.
  (b) (Bol, Chi, Per) simple, stupid; **no está para** — (Chi) he's not easily taken in; **hacer** — **a uno** (Chi) to play a trick on someone.
lesura nf (Chi) stupidity.
letal adj deadly, lethal.
letanía nf (Eccl) litany; (fig) rigmarole; long list; tedious recitation.
letárgico adj lethargic.
letargo nm lethargy.
Lete(o) m Lethe.
letón 1 adj Latvian. **2** nm, **letona** nf Latvian. **3** nm (language) Latvian, Lettish.
letra nf (a) (of alphabet) letter; — **gótica** Gothic script, black letter; — **de imprenta** print; — **inicial** initial letter; — **mayúscula** capital letter; — **minúscula** small letter; **en** —s **de molde** in print; in block letters; — **muerta** dead letter; — **negrilla** bold type, heavy type; — **versal** capital letter; — **versalita** small capital.
  (b) (fig) letter, literal meaning; **a la** — to the letter; **atarse a la** — to stick to the literal meaning.
  (c) —s piece of writing; **poner unas** (or **dos**) —s **a uno** to drop someone a line.
  (d) writing, handwriting; — **cursiva** cursive writing; **tiene buena** — he writes a good hand; **tiene malísima** — his writing is shocking.
  (e) (Comm) letter, bill, draft; — **abierta** letter of credit; — **aceptada** accepted letter; — **de cambio** bill (of exchange), draft; — **a la vista** sight draft; **pagar a** — **vista** to pay on sight.
  (f) (Mus) words, lyric.
  (g) —s (fig) letters, learning; (Univ) Arts; **bellas** —s belles lettres, literature; —s **humanas** humanities; **primeras** —s elementary education, three Rs; —s **sagradas** Scripture.
letrado 1 adj learned; (pej) pedantic. **2** nm lawyer.
letrero nm sign, notice; placard, poster; label; inscription; words, (piece of) writing.
letrina nf latrine, privy; (fig) sewer, sump, filthy place; **el río es una** — the river is an open sewer.
letrista nmf songwriter.
leucemia nf leukaemia.
leudante adj: **harina** — self-raising flour.
leudar [1a] **1** vt to leaven. **2 leudarse** vr (of bread etc) to rise.
leva nf (a) (Naut) weighing anchor.
  (b) (Mil) levy.
  (c) (Mech) lever; cam.
  (d) (CAm, Col) trick, swindle, ruse; **bajar la** — **a uno** (Bol, Chi) to do someone a mischief; **caer de** — (CAm) to play the fool; **echar** —s (Col) to boast; to bluster, utter threats; (Mex) to tell lies; **encender la** — **a uno** (Cu) to bash someone (fam); **ponerse la** — (Col) to play truant; to stay away from work; to beat it (fam).
levada nf (of horse) prance.
levadizo adj that can be raised; **puente** — drawbridge.
levadura nf yeast, leaven; — **de cerveza** brewer's yeast; — **en polvo** baking powder.
levantador nm: — **de pesos** weight lifter.
levantamiento nm (a) raising, lifting; elevation; — **de pesos** weight lifting. (b) (Pol) rising, revolt.

levantar [1a] **1** vt (a) to raise, lift (up); to elevate; fallen object to raise up, stand up; to straighten; dropped object to pick up; weight (Sport) to lift; (Archit) to raise, build, erect; bump etc (Med) to raise; army to raise, recruit; census to take; dust to raise; game to flush, put up; house to move, remove; plan, survey to make, draw up; session to adjourn; siege to raise; tone, voice to raise; **levantó la mano** he raised his hand, he put up his hand; — **los ojos** to look up, raise one's eyes; **¡no levantes la voz!** keep your voice down!; **fue imposible** —**lo** it was impossible to lift it.

(b) (fam) to lift (fam), steal.

(c) table, tablecloth to clear away; camp to strike; tent to take down.

(d) ban to raise, lift.

(e) person (fig) to uplift, hearten, cheer up; spirits to raise; (Pol) to rouse, stir up.

2 levantarse vr (a) to rise, to get up, stand up, rise to one's feet; to straighten up; — **(de la cama)** to get up, get out of bed.

(b) (of fog) to lift; (of wind etc) to rise.

(c) (on horizon etc) to stand up, stick up, stand out; **se levanta por encima de los demás edificios** it stands up higher than the other buildings.

(d) (of session) to be adjourned; to conclude, be concluded.

(e) — **con algo** to make off with something.

(f) (Pol) to rise, revolt, rebel.

levantaválvulas nm, pl **levantaválvulas** valve tappet.

Levante nm (a) Levant; el — the Levant, the (Near) East. (b) (Spain) east coast, south-east coast.

levante¹ nm (Geog) (a) east. (b) east wind.

levante² nm (a) (PR) uprising; riot.

(b) (Ven) driving of cattle.

(c) (CAm, PR) slander; **armar un** — to invent a slander.

(d) (Col) arrogance, haughtiness.

(e) (Arg) **dar** (or **pegar**) **un** — **a uno** to give someone a dressing-down.

levantino 1 adj (a) Levantine.

(b) of the eastern coast (or provinces etc) of Spain.

2 nm, **levantina** nf (a) Levantine.

(b) native (or inhabitant) of the eastern provinces of Spain; **los** —**s** the people of the east of Spain.

levantisco adj restless, turbulent.

levar [1a] **1** vt: — **anclas** to weigh anchor. **2 levarse** vr to weigh anchor, set sail.

leve adj light; slight; trivial, small, unimportant; **una herida** — **a** slight wound; **sin el más** — **optimismo** without the slightest optimism.

levedad nf lightness; (fig) levity.

levemente adv lightly; slightly.

leviatán nm leviathan.

levita¹ nf frock coat.

levita² nm Levite.

léxico 1 adj lexical. **2** nm lexicon, dictionary; vocabulary; word list.

lexicografía nf lexicography.

lexicográfico adj lexicographical.

lexicógrafo nm lexicographer.

ley nf (a) law; (Parl) act, bill, measure; (Sport etc) rule, law; — **de la calle**, — **de Lynch** mob law, lynch law; **la** — **del embudo** "might is right"; — **no escrita** unwritten law; — **marcial** martial law; — **de Moisés** the Law (Jewish); — **natural** law of nature; — **de préstamos y arriendos** Lend-Lease Act; **a** — **de** on the word of; **de acuerdo con la** —, **según la** — in accordance with the law; by law, in law; **es la** — it's the law; **su palabra es** — his word is law; **está fuera de la** — he's outside the law; **un fuera de** — an outlaw; **está por encima de la** — he's above the law; **recurrir a la** — to go to law.

(b) (fig) loyalty, devotion; **tener** — **a** to be devoted to; to have great respect for.

(c) (Metal) legal standard of fineness; **oro de** — standard gold; **bajo de** — base; **de buena** — (fig) genuine, reliable; **de mala** — (fig) base, disreputable; **en buena** — really; **entonces me toca esperar en buena** — then I really do have to wait.

leyenda nf (a) legend; **la** — **negra** the black legend.

(b) (Typ) legend, inscription; key.

leyente nmf reader.

leyista nm (Cu) pettifogging lawyer.

leyoso adj (Col) cunning, sly; sophistical.

lezna nf awl.

lía nf (SAm) plaited esparto grass.

liana nf (SAm) liana.

liar [1c] **1** vt to tie, tie up, do up; to bind; to wrap

up; cigarette to roll; (fig) to embroil, confuse; —**las** (fam) to beat it (fam); to kick the bucket (sl).

2 liarse vr (a) to get tied up; to entwine.

(b) (fig) to get involved (con with), get embroiled (con in); to get involved in a love affair (con with), form a liaison (con with).

(c) — **a** + infin (fam) to start to + infin.

libación nf libation; —**s** libations, potations.

libanés 1 adj Lebanese. **2** nm, **libanesa** nf Lebanese.

Líbano: el — the Lebanon.

libar [1a] vt to suck; to sip; to taste.

libelista nm lampoonist, writer of lampoons.

libelo nm (a) lampoon, satire (contra of). (b) (Law) petition.

libélula nf dragonfly.

liberación nf liberation; release.

liberado adj (Comm, Fin) paid-up, paid-in (US).

liberal 1 adj (a) (Pol) liberal. (b) character liberal, generous; lavish. **2** nmf liberal.

liberalidad nf liberality, generosity, lavishness.

liberalismo nm liberalism.

liberalizar [1f] vt to liberalize.

liberalmente adv liberally, generously; lavishly.

liberar [1a] vt (a) to free, liberate.

(b) (SAm) — **a uno de una obligación** to release someone from a duty; — **a uno de una contribución** to exempt someone from a tax.

Liberia f Liberia.

libertad nf liberty, freedom; licence; (undue) familiarity; "**¡—!**" (slogan) "freedom!"; — **de comercio** free trade; — **condicional**, — **vigilada** (Law) probation; **estar en** — **condicional** (or **vigilada**) to be on probation; — **de cultos** freedom of worship, religious freedom; — **de imprenta** freedom of the press; — **de** (**la**) **palabra** freedom of speech; **estar en** — to be free, be at liberty; **poner a uno en** — to set someone free, release someone, set someone at liberty; **tomarse una** — to take a liberty; **tomarse la** — **de** + infin to take the liberty of + ger, presume to + infin.

libertador 1 adj liberating. **2** nm, **libertadora** nf liberator.

libertar [1a] vt to set free, liberate, release (de from); to exempt, release (de from); to save, deliver (de from); — **a uno de la muerte** to save someone from death.

libertinaje nm licentiousness; profligacy.

libertino 1 adj (a) loose-living, rakish, profligate.

(b) (Rel Hist) freethinking. **2** nm (a) libertine, rake.

(b) (Rel Hist) freethinker.

Libia f Libya.

libídine nf libido.

libidinoso adj lustful, libidinous.

libido nf libido.

libio 1 adj Libyan. **2** nm, **libia** nf Libyan.

liborio nm (Cu): **el** — the Cuban people.

libra nf pound; — **esterlina** pound sterling.

libraco nm boring book, worthless book.

librado nm, **librada** nf (Comm) drawee.

librador nm, **libradora** nf (Comm) drawer.

libramiento nm rescue, delivery (de from).

librante nmf (Comm) drawer.

libranza nf (Comm) draft, bill of exchange; — **de correos** (SAm), — **postal** (SAm) money order.

librar [1a] **1** vt (a) to save, free, rescue, deliver (de from); (Law) to exempt, free, release (de from); — **a uno de una obligación** to free someone from an obligation; **¡Dios me libre!** Heaven forbid!; **¡líbreme Dios de . . .!** Heaven forbid that I . . .!

(b) confidence, hope to place (en in).

(c) sentence to pass; edict etc to issue.

(d) (Comm) to draw; cheque to make out; — **a cargo de** to draw on.

(e) battle to fight, wage; to join.

2 vi (a) to be delivered of a child.

(b) — **bien** to fare well, succeed; — **mal** to fare badly, fail.

3 librarse vr to free oneself, escape; — **de** to escape from, get out of, get away from; to get rid of; **de buena nos hemos librado** we did well to get out of that, we're well out of that.

libre 1 adj (a) (in most senses) free (de from, of); **¿estás** —? are you free?; **esa plaza no está** — that seat is not free; **cada cual es** — **de hacer lo que quiera** everyone is free to do as he wishes; **por fin estamos** —**s de él** at last we're rid of him; — **de derechos** free of duty, duty-free; **al aire** — in the open air.

(b) (pej) free, outspoken; licentious, loose, immoral; **de vida** — loose-living, immoral.

(c) (Sport) free, free-style; **los 200 metros** —**s** the 200 metre free-style race.

2 nm (a) (Sport) free kick.

(b) (Mex) taxi.

librea 1 *nf* livery, uniform. **2** *nm* (*Chi*) footman.
librecambio *nm* free trade.
librecambista 1 *adj* free-trade (*attr*). **2** *nm* free-trader.
librepensador *nm*, **librepensadora** *nf* freethinker.
librepensamiento *nm* freethinking.
librera *nf* (*RPl*) bookcase.
librería *nf* (a) bookshop; — **anticuaria** antiquarian bookshop; — **de ocasión,** — **de viejo** secondhand bookshop.
    (b) bookcase; (personal, private) library.
    (c) bookselling, book trade, book business.
librero *nm* (a) bookseller; — **de viejo** secondhand bookseller. (b) (*Cu, Mex, Par*) bookcase.
libresco *adj* bookish.
libreta *nf* (a) notebook; (*Comm*) account book; — **de banco,** — **de depósitos** bank book, pass book. (b) one-pound loaf.
librete *nm* booklet.
libretista *nmf* librettist.
libreto *nm* libretto.
libro *nm* book. — **de actas** minute book; — **de apuntes** notebook; — **de cabecera** bedside book; — **de caja** cashbook; — **de cálculos hechos** ready reckoner; — **de cocina** cookery book, cookbook (*US*); — **de consulta** reference book, work of reference; — **de cuentas** account book; — **de cuentos** storybook; — **de cheques** cheque book; — **diario** journal; — **de encargos** order book; — **escolar** school report; — **genealógico** (*Agr*) herd-book; — **de hojas cambiables** loose-leaf book; — **de honor** visitors' book; — **de imágenes** picture book; — **de lectura** reader; — **mayor** ledger; — **parroquial** parish register; — **de pedidos** order book; — **de reclamaciones** complaints book; **L— Rojo** (*Pol*) White Paper; — **en rústica** paperback (book); — **talonario** receipt book; book of tickets, book of counterfoils; — **de texto** textbook; — **de visitas** visitors' book; — **de vuelos** (*Aer*) logbook; **ahorcar los** —**s, arrimar los** —**s** (*fig*) to lay aside one's books, give up studying; **no estar en el** — (*Arg*), **no tener el** — (*Arg*) to be unaware of a matter; to be uninterested in a matter, have no intention of pursuing a matter; **hacer** — **nuevo** to turn over a new leaf.
librote *nm* big book, tome.
licencia *nf* (a) (*general sense*) licence, permission; **sin mi** — without my permission; **dar su** — to give one's permission, grant permission.
    (b) (*document*) licence, permit; — **de armas** gun licence; — **de caza** game licence, hunting permit; — **de conducir,** — **de conductor,** — **de manejar** (*SAm*) driving licence; — **de matrimonio** marriage licence.
    (c) (*Mil etc*) leave; — **por enfermedad** sick leave; — **sin sueldo** leave without pay, unpaid leave; **estar de** — to be on leave; **ir de** — to go on leave.
    (d) (*Mil*) discharge (*also* — **absoluta**); — **honrosa** honourable discharge.
    (e) (*moral*) licence, licentiousness; — **poética** poetic licence.
    (f) (*Univ: Hist*) degree.
licenciado *nm*, **licenciada** *nf* (a) (*Univ*) licenciate, bachelor; **L— en Filosofía y Letras** Bachelor of Arts.
    (b) (*SAm*) lawyer (*not translated as title before proper name*).
licenciar [1b] **1** *vt* (a) to license, grant a permit (*or* licence) to.
    (b) to permit, allow.
    (c) (*Mil*) to discharge.
    (d) (*Univ*) to confer a degree on.
    2 licenciarse *vr* to graduate, take one's degree.
licenciatura *nf* (a) degree, licentiate. (b) graduation.
    (c) degree course, university degree.
licencioso *adj* licentious.
liceo *nm* lyceum; (*Chi, Mex*) secondary school; (*Arg*) secondary school for girls.
licitación *nf* bidding (*at auction*).
licitador *nm* bidder; (*SAm*) auctioneer.
licitar [1a] **1** *vt* (a) to bid for. (b) (*SAm*) to sell by auction. **2** *vi* to bid.
lícito *adj* lawful, legal, licit; fair, just; permissible; **si es** — **preguntarlo** if one may ask.
licitud *nf* legality; fairness, justness; **la controversia sobre la** — **del aborto** the controversy about whether abortion should be permitted.
licor *nm* (a) (*in general*) liquid. (b) (*alcoholic*) liquor, spirits; liqueur; —**es espiritosos** hard liquor.
licorería *nf* (*SAm*) distillery.
licorero *nm* (*SAm*) distiller.
licorista *nm* distiller; dealer in liquor, seller of liquor.

licoroso *adj* wine *etc* strong, of high alchoholic content.
licuar [1d] *vt* to liquefy, turn into liquid.
licuefacción *nf* liquefaction.
líchigo *nm* (*Col*) provisions, food.
lid *nf* fight, combat; dispute, controversy; **en buena** — in (a) fair fight, (*fig*) by fair means, fairly.
líder *nm*, *pl* **liders** *or* **líderes** (*angl*) leader; (*Sport*) leader, league leader, top club (*etc*).
liderato *nm* leadership; (*Sport*) lead, leadership, top position.
lidia *nf* (a) (*Taur*) bullfight; bullfighting; **toro de** — fighting bull. (b) (*Mex, RPl*) trouble, nuisance; **dar** — to be trying, be a nuisance.
lidiadera *nf* (*Ec, Guat*) quarrel; **andar en** —**s** to quarrel, bicker.
lidiador *nm* fighter; (*Taur*) bullfighter.
lidiar [1b] **1** *vt* bull to fight. **2** *vi* to fight (*also fig*; **con,** **contra** against, **por** for).
liebre *nf* hare; (*fig*) coward; — **corrida** (*Mex*) old hand, experienced person; whore; **levantar la** — to blow the gaff.
Lieja Liège.
liencillo *nm* (*SAm*) thin cotton material.
liendre *nf* nit.
lienzo *nm* (a) linen; (*Art*) canvas; handkerchief; **un** — a piece of linen (*etc*).
    (b) (*Archit*) wall; face, front; (*SAm*) section (*of fence etc*); (*Mex*) corral, pen.
liga *nf* (a) (*Pol etc*) league.
    (b) (*Sew*) band; suspender, garter.
    (c) (*Metal*) alloy; mixture.
    (d) (*Bot*) mistletoe.
    (e) birdlime.
    (f) (*Cu, Guat, Hond, Mex*) binding; state of being bound.
    (g) (*RPl*) piece of luck.
    (h) (*Col*) theft.
    (i) (*Ec*) bosom friend.
ligado *nm* (*Mus*) slur, tie; (*Typ*) ligature.
ligadura *nf* bond, tie; (*Naut*) lashing; (*Med, Mus*) ligature.
ligamento *nm* ligament.
ligamiento *nm* bond, tie.
ligar [1h] **1** *vt* (a) to tie, bind; (*Metal*) to alloy; to mix; (*Med*) to put a ligature on, bind up; (*Mus*) to slur; (*fig*) to join, bind together; — **dos bebidas** to mix two drinks, blend two drinks; **estar ligado por contrato** a to be bound by contract to.
    (b) (*Col*) to pinch (*fam*).
    (c) (*Cu: Agr*) to contract in advance for.
    2 *vi* (a) to mix (well), blend, go well together; **ligan A y B** (*Arg, Per*) A and B get on well together.
    (b) (*Cu, Mex, PR*) to have a bit of luck, be lucky; **la cosa se ligó** (*CAm, Col*) the affair went well for him.
    (c) (*Cu, Mex, PR*) to look, stare.
    (d) (*Guat, Per, PR, SD: of wish*) to be fulfilled.
    (e) (*prov, Mex*) — **con una** to flirt with someone; to pick a girl up.
    3 ligarse *vr* (a) to unite, band together.
    (b) to bind oneself, commit oneself.
ligazón *nf* (a) (*Naut*) rib, beam. (b) (*fig*) bond, tie, union.
ligeramente *adv* (a) lightly. (b) *know etc* slightly. (c) *judge etc* hastily.
ligerear [1a] *vi* (*Chi*) to walk fast, move quickly.
ligereza *nf* (a) lightness; thinness.
    (b) swiftness, quickness, speed.
    (c) agility, nimbleness.
    (d) slightness.
    (e) superficiality, shallowness; flippancy; frivolity; **obrar con** — to act rashly, act thoughtlessly.
    (f) — **de espíritu** light-heartedness, gaiety.
    (g) (*act*) indiscretion.
ligero 1 *adj* (a) (*of weight*) light; *material* light, lightweight, thin; *meal, sleep* light; *tea* weak; — **de ropa** lightly clad, scantily clad, not wearing much; **más que un corcho** (*or* **una pluma** *etc*) as light as a feather.
    (b) (*of speed*) swift, quick, rapid; — **de dedos** light-fingered; — **de pies** light-footed; quick; **corrió** — **por el puente** she ran quickly over the bridge; **más** — **que una bala** (*or* **el viento** *etc*) as quick as a flash.
    (c) (*in movement*) agile, quick, nimble.
    (d) (*of gravity, importance*) slight; **un** — **conocimiento** a slight acquaintance, a superficial acquaintance.
    (e) (*of character*) superficial, shallow, flippant; frivolous, flighty; — **de cascos** scatterbrained, frivolous; **hacer algo a la ligera** to do something

quickly; to do something without fuss; (*pej*) to do something perfunctorily; **juzgar a la ligera** to judge hastily, jump to conclusions; **obrar de** — to act rashly, act thoughtlessly.
2 *adv* (*SAm*) lightly; quickly, swiftly.
lignito *nm* lignite.
ligón *nm* hoe.
liguero *nm* suspender belt, garter belt (*US*).
ligustro *nm* privet.
lija *nf* (a) (*Zool*) dogfish. (b) (*Tech: also* **papel de —**) sandpaper; — **esmeril** emery paper. (c) **darse** — (*Cu*) to give oneself airs.
lijar [1a] *vt* to sandpaper.
lijoso *adj* (*Cu*) vain, stuck-up (*fam*).
Lila Lille.
lila[1] *nf* (*Bot*) lilac.
lila[2] *nm* (*fam*) boob (*sl*), twit (*fam*).
lilailas *nfpl* (*fam*) tricks.
lilaya *nm* (*fam*) sissy.
lile *adj* (*Chi*) weak, weak-willed.
liliputiense 1 *adj* Lilliputian. 2 *nmf* Lilliputian.
liliquear [1a] *vi* (*Chi*) to tremble nervously, shake.
lima[1] *nf* (*Bot*) lime, sweet-lime tree.
lima[2] *nf* (*Tech*) (a) file; — **de uñas**, — **para las uñas** nail file.
 (b) (*act*) filing, polishing.
 (c) (*fig*) polish, finish; **dar la última** — **a una obra** to give a work its final polish.
limadura *nf* (a) (*act*) filing; polishing. (b) —s filings.
limar [1a] *vt* (*Tech*) to file, file down, file off; to smooth (over); (*fig*) to polish (up), put the final polish on.
limatón *nm* (*SAm*) crossbeam, roofbeam.
limaza *nf* slug.
limazo *nm* slime, sliminess.
limbo *nm* limbo; **estar en el** — to be in limbo; (*fig*) to be distracted, be bewildered.
limeño 1 *adj* of Lima. 2 *nm*, **limeña** *nf* native (*or* inhabitant) of Lima; **los** —s the people of Lima.
limero *nm* lime (tree).
limeta *nf* (a) (*Arg*) broad brow, domed forehead; bald head. (b) (*Par*) bottle.
limitación *nf* limitation; limit; — **de velocidad** speed limit; **sin** — unlimited.
limitado *adj* (a) limited (*also Comm*). (b) slow-witted, dim.
limitar [1a] 1 *vt* to limit, restrict; to cut down, reduce; — **a uno a** + *infin* to limit someone to + *ger*, restrict someone to + *infin*.
 2 *vi*: — **con** to border on, be adjacent to, be bounded by.
 3 **limitarse** *vr* to limit oneself, restrict oneself; — **a** + *infin* to limit oneself to + *infin*, confine oneself to + *infin*.
límite *nm* limit; end; (*Geog, Pol*) boundary, border; — **forestal** timber line, tree line; — **de velocidad** speed limit; **asciende a 100 como** — it goes up to 100 at the most; **se celebrará en octubre como** — it will be held in October at the latest; **sin** —s limitless; **poner un** — **a** to set a limit to; (*fig*) to draw the line at; **no tener** —s to have no limits, know no bounds.
limítrofe *adj* bordering, neighbouring.
limo *nm* slime, mud.
limón *nm* lemon; — **mejicano** lime.
limonada *nf* lemonade; — **natural** lemon juice, lemon squash.
limonado *adj* lemon, lemon-coloured.
limonar *nm* lemon grove.
limonero *nm* lemon tree.
limosina *nf* limousine.
limosna *nf* alms; charity; **¡una** —, **señor!** can't you spare something, sir?; **vivir de** — to live by begging, live on charity.
limosnear [1a] *vi* to beg, ask for alms.
limosnera *nf* collecting tin (*for charity*).
limosnero 1 *adj* charitable. 2 *nm* (a) (*Hist*) almoner. (b) (*SAm*) beggar.
limoso *adj* slimy, muddy.
limpia 1 *nf* (a) cleaning; (*CAm, Mex: Agr*) weeding, cleaning, clearing; (*fig: Pol etc*) clean-up, purge. (b) (*Col, Mex, Par*) beating.
 2 *nm* (*fam*) bootblack.
limpiabarros *nm*, *pl* **limpiabarros** scraper; doormat.
limpiabotas *nm*, *pl* **limpiabotas** bootblack.
limpiacristales *nm*, *pl* **limpiacristales** window cleaner.
limpiachimeneas *nm*, *pl* **limpiachimeneas** chimney-sweep.
limpiada *nf* (a) (*SAm*) clean, clean-up. (b) (*Arg, Par*) treeless area, bare ground; clearing in a wood.

limpiadientes *nm*, *pl* **limpiadientes** toothpick.
limpiadora *nf* cleaner.
limpiadura *nf* (a) cleaning, cleaning-up. (b) —s dirt, dust, scourings.
limpiamanos *nm*, *pl* **limpiamanos** (*CAm, Mex*) hand towel.
limpiamente *adv* cleanly; neatly; honestly; skilfully.
limpiametales *nm*, *pl* **limpiametales** metal polish.
limpiaparabrisas *nm*, *pl* **limpiaparabrisas** windscreen wiper, windshield wiper (*US*).
limpiapiés *nm*, *pl* **limpiapiés** scraper; (*Mex*) doormat.
limpiaplumas *nm*, *pl* **limpiaplumas** penwiper.
limpiar [1b] 1 *vt* (a) to clean; to cleanse; to wipe, wipe off, wipe clean; to wipe away; *shoes* to shine, polish; — **en seco** to dry-clean; — **las narices a un niño** to wipe a child's nose.
 (b) (*fig*) to cleanse, purify, clean up; (*Mil etc*) to mop up; (*of police*) to clean up; (*Bot*) to prune, cut back.
 (c) (*fam: at gambling*) to clean out (*sl*).
 (d) (*sl*) to swipe (*sl*).
 (e) (*Arg, Mex*) to hit, bash (*fam*), beat.
 2 **limpiarse** *vr* to clean oneself; to wipe oneself; — **las narices** to wipe one's nose.
limpiavía *nm* (*SAm: Rail*) cowcatcher.
límpido *adj* limpid.
limpieza *nf* (a) (*act*) clean; cleaning, cleansing; shine, shining, polishing; — **en seco** dry cleaning; — **de primavera** spring cleaning; **hacer la** — to clean (up).
 (b) (*act: fig*) cleansing, cleaning-up; (*Mil*) mopping-up; (*by police*) clean-up.
 (c) (*state*) cleanness, cleanliness; — **de sangre** purity of blood, racial purity.
 (d) (*moral quality*) purity; integrity, honesty; (*Sport etc*) fair play.
 (e) skill.
limpio 1 *adj* (a) clean; neat, tidy; *blood* pure; *water etc* pure, clean; — **de** free from, clear of; **más** — **que el oro** (*etc*) as clean as can be.
 (b) (*morally*) pure; honest; *play* fair, clean.
 (c) (*Fin*) clear, net; **50 dólares de ganancia limpia** 50 dollars of clear profit.
 (d) alone; **se defendieron a pedrada limpia** they defended themselves with stones alone; **lo hizo a clavo** — he simply nailed it together, he did it just using nails; **luchar a puñetazo** — to fight with bare fists.
 (e) **estar** — (*fam*) not to know a single thing; **quedar(se)** — (*fam*) to be cleaned out (*sl*).
 2 *adv* *play* fair, clean.
 3 *nm* (a) **en** — (*as adv*) clearly; (*Fin*) clear, net; **copia en** — fair copy; **estar** (*or* **quedar**) **en** —, **estar** — **y soplado** (*Col*) to be broke (*fam*); **poner algo en** — to make a fair copy of something; **quedó en** — **que . . . it** was clear that . . .; **sacar algo en** — to make sense of something; **no pude sacar nada en** — I couldn't make anything of it.
 (b) (*Mex*) treeless area, bare ground; clearing in a wood.
limpión *nm* (a) wipe, (quick) clean; **dar un** — **a algo** to give something a wipe.
 (b) cleaning rag, cleaning cloth; (*Col, CR, Ven*) dishcloth.
 (c) cleaner.
 (d) (*Col*) ticking-off.
limusina *nf* limousine.
lina *nf* (*Chi*) (a) coarse wool. (b) pigtail, long hair.
linaje *nm* (a) lineage, family; **de** — **de reyes** descended from royalty, of royal descent; **de** — **honrado** of decent family, of good parentage.
 (b) —s (local) nobility, noble families.
 (c) class, kind; — **humano** mankind; **de otro** — of another kind.
linajudo *adj* highborn, noble, blue-blooded.
linar *nm* flax field.
linaza *nf* linseed.
lince 1 *nm* (a) lynx; (*Mex, Salv*) wild cat.
 (b) **ser un** — (*fig*) to be very observant, be sharp-eyed; to be shrewd, be crafty.
 2 *adj*: **ojos** —s sharp eyes; **es muy** — he's very observant, he's very sharp-eyed; he's pretty shrewd.
linchamiento *nm* lynching.
linchar [1a] *vt* to lynch.
linche *nm* (*Ec*) knapsack; —s (*Mex*) saddlebags.
lindamente *adv* (a) prettily; daintily; elegantly. (b) (*iro*) well, jolly well (*fam*). (c) (*esp SAm*) excellently, marvellously, jolly well (*fam*).
lindante *adj* bordering (**con** on), adjoining, adjacent (**con** to).

lindar [1a] *vi* to adjoin, be adjacent; **— con** to border on, adjoin, be adjacent to; to extend to, be bounded by; (*Archit*) to abut on.

linde *nm or f* boundary.

lindero 1 *adj* adjoining, bordering. **2** *nm* edge, border; boundary.

lindeza *nf* **(a)** prettiness; daintiness; elegance.
(b) (*esp SAm*) niceness; excellence, high quality.
(c) witticism.
(d) **—s** pretty things; pretty ways, charming ways.
(e) **—s** (*iro*) insults, improprieties.

lindo 1 *adj* (*in all senses, more used in SAm than in Spain*) **(a)** pretty; dainty; exquisite, elegant, delicate.
(b) (*iro*) fine, pretty.
(c) nice, lovely; fine, excellent, first-rate, marvellous; **un — coche** a nice car, a fine car; **un — partido** a first-rate game; **un — concierto** a marvellous concert; **de lo —** a lot, a great deal; wonderfully, marvellously, jolly well (*fam*); **es de —** (*SAm*) it's fine, it's marvellous.
2 *adv* (*SAm*) nicely, well, marvellously; **baila —** she dances beautifully.
3 *nm* (*Hist*) fop.

lindura *nf* **(a)** (*Chi, RPl*) prettiness, loveliness; **estar hecha una —** to look very pretty.
(b) (*Chi, PR, Ven*) outstanding person; ace, champion; expert; **ella es una — en el vestir** she's an expert on clothes.

línea *nf* **(a)** (*in most senses*) line; (*Elec*) line, cable; (*Rail, Tel etc*) line; **—s** (*Mil*) lines; **— aérea** (*Aer*) airline; (*Elec*) overhead cable; **— de alto el fuego** ceasefire line; **— de banda** sideline, touchline; **— de base** (*Surveying*) base line; **— de batalla** line of battle, battle line; **— de carga** load line; **— de medio campo**, **— de centro** halfway line; **— delantera** forward line; **— derivada** (*Tel*) extension; **— divisoria** dividing line; **— férrea** railway; **— de flotación** water line; **— de fuego** firing line; **— de gol** goal line; **— lateral** sideline, touchline; **— de meta** goal line; (*in race*) finishing line; **— de montaje** assembly line; production line; **— primera —** front line; **— de puerta** goal line; **— de puntos** dotted line; **— recta** straight line; **— de saque** base line, service line; **— de alta tensión** high-tension cable; **— de tiro** line of fire; **— de toque** touchline; **— de la vida** life line; **explicar algo a grandes —s**, **explicar algo en sus —s generales** to set something out in broad outline, give the broad outline of something; **de —** (*Mil*) regular, front-line, (*Naut*) of the line; **en — in** (*a*) line, in a row; **en — recta** in a straight line; **en toda la —** all along the line; **leer entre —s** to read between the lines; **poner unas —s a uno** to drop a line to someone; **tirar una —** to draw a line.
(b) (*woman's*) figure; (*of ship etc*) lines, outline; **guardar la —** to keep one's figure (trim); **la — de 1902** the 1902 line, the fashion line of 1902.
(c) (*genealogical*) line (*also fig*); **en — directa** in an unbroken line; **es único en su —** it is unique in its line, it is the only one of its kind; **en esa — no tenemos nada** we have nothing in that line.
(d) (*moral, Pol etc*) line; **— de conducta** course of action; **— dura** (*Pol*) hard line; **— de partido** party line; **ser de (una or una sola) —** (*Arg, Chi, PR*) to be honest, be absolutely straight.

lineal *adj* linear; **dibujo —** line drawing.

lineamento *nm* lineament.

linear [1a] *vt* **(a)** to line, draw lines on. **(b)** (*Art*) to sketch, outline.

linfa *nf* lymph.

linfático *adj* lymphatic.

lingote *nm* ingot.

lingüista *nmf* linguist, language specialist, linguistician.

lingüística *nf* linguistics.

lingüístico *adj* linguistic.

linimento *nm* liniment.

lino *nm* **(a)** (*Bot*) flax. **(b)** (*Arg, PR*) linseed. **(c)** linen; canvas; **géneros de —** linen goods.

linóleo *nm* lino, linoleum.

linón *nm* lawn (*fabric*).

linotipia *nf* linotype.

linotipo *nm* (*SAm*) linotype.

linterna *nf* lantern; lamp; (*Elec*) spotlight; **—s** (*SAm*) eyes; **— eléctrica**, **— de bolsillo**, **— a pila** torch, flashlight; **— mágica** magic lantern.

linyera (*RPl*) **1** *nf* knapsack; poor man's belongings, bundle of belongings. **2** *nm* tramp, bum (*US*).

lío *nm* **(a)** bundle; package, parcel; (*Arg*) truss.
(b) (*fam*) row, fuss; mess, mix-up, confusion, muddle; jam; **ese — de los pasaportes** that fuss about the passports; **armar un —** to make a fuss,

kick up a row; to cause confusion; **se armó un tremendo —** there was an almighty row (*fam*); **hacerse un —** to get all mixed up, get into a muddle; **meterse en un —** to get into a jam.
(c) (*fam*) affair, liaison; **tener un — con una** to be having an affair with someone.
(d) (*SAm*) tale, piece of gossip; **no me venga con —s** don't come telling tales to me, I don't want to know.

Liorna Leghorn.

lioso *adj* (*Arg*) gossiping, talebearing.

lipa *nf* (*Ven*) belly.

lipe *nm* (*SAm: also* **piedra —**) vitriol; copper sulphate.

lipidia 1 *nf* **(a)** (*CAm*) poverty.
(b) (*Cu, Mex*) impertinence.
(c) (*Ec, Per*) indigestion; stomach upset.
2 *nmf* (*Cu, Mex*) annoying person, pest.

lipidiar [1b] *vt* (*Cu, Mex, PR*) to annoy, bother, pester.

lipidioso *adj* (*Cu, Mex, PR*) silly; annoying.

lipón *adj* (*Ven*) fat, pot-bellied.

liquen *nm* lichen.

líquida *nf* (*Ling*) liquid.

liquidación *nf* **(a)** (*Chem*) liquefaction.
(b) (*Comm, Fin*) liquidation; winding-up; (*of account*) settlement; **entrar en —** to go into liquidation.
(c) (*also* **venta de —**) sale, clearance sale; **vender en —** to sell up.
(d) (*Pol*) liquidation.

liquidar [1a] **1** *vt* **(a)** (*Chem*) to liquefy.
(b) (*Comm, Fin*) to liquidate; *account* to settle; *business* to wind up; *debt* to settle, pay off, clear; *stocks* to sell off, sell up.
(c) (*Pol*) to liquidate; (*SAm*) to kill, kill off.
(d) (*SAm*) to destroy, ruin, render useless.
2 liquidarse *vr* (*Chem*) to liquefy.

liquidez *nf* liquidity, fluidity.

líquido 1 *adj* **(a)** liquid; fluid.
(b) (*Ling*) liquid.
(c) (*Comm*) net; **ganancia líquida** net profit.
(d) (*SAm*) exact; accurate, right, correctly measured; **4 varas líquidas** exactly 4 yards; **una líquida vez** once only, just once.
2 *nm* **(a)** liquid; fluid.
(b) (*Comm, Fin*) net amount, net profit; **— imponible** net taxable income.

lira *nf* (*Mus*) lyre; (*Italian: Fin*) lira; (*Lit*) a 5-line stanza popular in the 16th century.

lírica *nf* lyrical poetry; **la — provenzal** the Provençal lyric, Provençal lyrical poetry.

lírico 1 *adj* **(a)** (*Lit*) lyric(al); (*Theat*) musical.
(b) (*SAm*) *person* dreamy, full of idealistic plans, given to making Utopian projects; (*Arg, Mex, Nic, Ven*) *plan* Utopian, fantastic.
2 *nm* (*Arg*) dreamer, Utopian.

lirio *nm* iris; **— de los valles** lily of the valley.

lirismo *nm* **(a)** lyricism; lyrical feeling, sentimentality, (*pej*) gush, effusiveness.
(b) (*SAm*) fantasy, dreams, Utopian ideals; dreaminess, fancifulness.

lirón *nm* dormouse; (*fig*) sleepyhead; **dormir como un —** to sleep like a log.

lirondo: *see* **mondo.**

lisamente *adv* smoothly, evenly; **lisa y llanamente** plainly, in plain language.

Lisboa Lisbon.

lisboeta 1 *adj* of Lisbon. **2** *nmf* native (*or* inhabitant) of Lisbon; **los —s** the people of Lisbon.

lisbonense, lisbonés = lisboeta.

lisiado 1 *adj* injured, hurt; lame, crippled. **2** *nm*, **lisiada** *nf* cripple; **— de guerra** wounded ex-serviceman.

lisiar [1b] *vt* to injure (permanently), hurt (seriously); to cripple, maim.

liso 1 *adj* **(a)** smooth, even; *hair* straight; *sea* calm; *race* flat; **los 400 metros —s** the 400-metre flat race.
(b) (*fig*) plain, unadorned; **— y llano** plain, simple.
(c) (*Mex, Per*) fresh, impudent; **irse —** (*Ven*) to depart without saying good-bye.
2 *nm* (*Arg*) tall beer glass.

lisol *nm* lysol.

lisonja *nf* flattery.

lisonjear [1a] *vt* **(a)** to flatter. **(b)** to please, delight.

lisonjeramente *adv* **(a)** flatteringly; gratifyingly.
(b) pleasingly, agreeably.

lisonjero 1 *adj* **(a)** flattering; gratifying. **(b)** pleasing, agreeable. **2** *nm*, **lisonjera** *nf* flatterer.

lista *nf* **(a)** list; catalogue; (*Mil*) roll; roll call; (*School*) roll, register; **— de comidas** menu; **— de**

correos poste restante; — **electoral** electoral roll, register of voters; — **de espera** waiting list; — **negra** blacklist; — **de pagos** payroll; — **de platos** menu; — **de precios** price list; — **de raya** (*Mex*) payroll; — **de tandas** duty roster, rota; — **de vinos** wine list; **pasar** — (*Mil*) to call the roll, (*School*) to call the register, call the roll.
  (b) (*of cloth*) strip; (*of paper*) slip.
  (c) **stripe; tela a** —**s** striped material.
listadillo *nm* (*Col, Mex, PR*) striped (white and blue) cotton cloth.
listado 1 *adj* striped. **2** *nm* (*Col, Per, PR, SD, Ven*) = **listadillo.**
listar [1a] *vt* to list, enter on a list.
listero *nm* (*SAm*) timekeeper, wages clerk.
listín *nm* telephone directory; (*SD*) newspaper.
listo *adj* (a) ready, prepared; **una pintura lista para usar** a ready-to-use paint; **un traje** — (*Mex*) a ready-made suit; **el avión estará** — **para volar en 6 meses** the plane will be ready to fly in 6 months; **¿estás** —**?** are you ready?; **todo está** — everything is ready, everything is in order.
  (b) **¡**—**!** (*interj: SAm*) all right!, OK!; that's the lot!, it's all over!
  (c) (*of character*) clever, smart, sharp, quick; **¡**—**!** (*iro*) wake up!, you're a bright one!; **es la mar de** — (*fam*) he's terribly clever (*fam*); **ser más** — **que el hambre** to be as smart as they come; **pasarse de** — to be too clever by half.
listón *nm* (*Sew*) ribbon; (*of wood*) strip, lath; (*Sport:* high-jump *etc*) bar; (*in vaulting*) pole; (*of metal, rubber etc*) strip; (*Archit*) fillet.
lisura *nf* (a) smoothness, evenness; straightness; calmness.
  (b) plainness; sincerity; naïvety.
  (c) (*SAm*) shamelessness, brazenness, impudence.
  (d) (*SAm*) shameless remark, impudent remark, disrespectful thing (to say); (*Per*) coarse remark, rude thing (to say *or* do).
lisurero *adj* (*Per*) fresh, brazen, impudent.
litera *nf* litter; (*in dormitory*) bunk, bunk bed; (*Naut, Rail*) bunk, berth.
literal *adj* literal.
literalmente *adv* literally (*also fig*).
literario *adj* literary.
literata *nf* woman writer, literary lady; (*pej*) bluestocking.
literato *nm* man of letters, writer; —**s** (*freq*) literati.
literatura *nf* literature.
litigación *nf* litigation.
litigante *nmf* litigant.
litigar [1h] **1** *vt* to dispute at law; to fight. **2** *vi* (*Law*) to go to law; to indulge in lawsuits; (*fig*) to argue, dispute.
litigio *nm* litigation; lawsuit; (*fig*) dispute; **en** — **at stake,** in dispute.
litigioso *adj* litigious; contentious.
litio *nm* lithium.
litisexpensas *nfpl* (*Law*) costs.
litografía *nf* (a) (*art*) lithography. (b) (*picture*) lithograph.
litografiar [1c] *vt* to lithograph.
litoral 1 *adj* coastal, littoral, seaboard (*attr*). **2** *nm* seaboard, littoral, coast.
litre *nm* (*Chi*) nausea.
litro[1] *nm* litre, liter (*US*).
litro[2] *nm* (*Chi*) coarse woollen cloth.
Lituania *f* Lithuania.
lituano 1 *adj* Lithuanian. **2** *nm*, **lituana** *nf* Lithuanian. **3** *nm* (*language*) Lithuanian.
liturgia *f* liturgy.
litúrgico *adj* liturgical.
livianamente *adv* (a) in a fickle way; frivolously; in a trivial way. (b) lewdly.
liviandad *nf* (a) fickleness; frivolity, triviality. (b) lewdness. (c) (*SAm*) lightness.
liviano 1 *adj* (a) fickle; frivolous, trivial. (b) lewd. (c) (*SAm*) light. **2** —**s** *nmpl* lights, lungs.
lividez *nf* (a) lividness. (b) (*SAm*) paleness, pallor.
livido *adj* (a) livid; black and blue. (b) (*SAm*) pale, pallid.
living ['liβin] *nm*, *pl* **livings** ['liβin] (*angl*) living room.
Livio *m* Livy.
lixiviar [1b] **1** *vt* to leach. **2 lixiviarse** *vr* to leach.
liza *nf* (*Hist*) lists; contest.
lo[1] "*neuter*" *def art* (a) — **bello** the beautiful, what is beautiful, that which is beautiful; — **difícil** what is difficult; — **difícil es que** . . . the difficult thing about it is that . . .; **quiero** — **justo** I want what is just; **defiendo** — **mío** I defend what is mine; **visto** — **ocurrido** in view of what has happened; — **insospechado del caso** what was unsuspected about the

matter; — **totalmente inesperado del descubrimiento** the completely unexpected nature of the discovery; — **mejor de la película** the best part of the film, the best thing about the film; **sufre** — **indecible** she suffers terribly.
  (b) **construido a** — **campesino** built in peasant style; **viste a** — **americano** he dresses in the American style, he dresses like an American.
  (c) **no saben** — **aburrido que es** they don't know how boring it is; **me doy cuenta de** — **amables que ellas son** I realize how kind they are.
lo[2] *pron* (*person*) him; (*thing*) it; — **tengo aquí** I have it here; — **creo** I think so; (*not translated in such cases as*) — **veo** I see, — **sé** I know; **no** — **hay** there isn't any; "**¿anarquista?**" . . . "**no** — **soy**" "an anarchist?" . . . "I'm not"; "**¿estás cansado?**" . . . "— **estoy**" "are you tired?" . . . "I am" (*or* "yes"); **guapa sí que** — **es** she's certainly very pretty, I should jolly well say she's pretty (*fam*).
lo[3] *dem pron:* — **de** that matter of, that business about; — **de ayer** what happened yesterday; — **de Suez** the Suez affair; — **de no traer dinero** that business about not having any money.
lo[4] *rel pron:* — **que** (a) what, that which; — **que digo es** . . . what I say is . . .; **toma** — **que quieras** take what(ever) you want; **con** — **que él gana** with what he earns; **¡**— **que sufre un hombre honrado!** what an honourable man has to suffer!; — **que pasa es que** . . ., — **que hay es que** . . . what's happening is that . . ., it's like this . . .; **empezó a tocar,** — **que le fastidió** she began to play, which made him cross.
  (b) (*idioms*) — **que es eso** as for that; **¡**— **que has tardado!** how late you are!; **¡**— **que cuesta vivir!** isn't living expensive!; **¡**— **que es saber lenguas!** isn't it wonderful to speak several languages!; **¡**— **que he dicho!** I stand by what I said!; **¡**— **que ves!** can't you see?, it's there for you to see!
loa *nf* (a) praise. (b) (*Theat: Hist*) prologue, playlet. (c) (*CAm, Mex*) reproof.
loable *adv* praiseworthy, commendable, laudable.
loablemente *adv* commendably.
loar [1a] *vt* to praise.
loba *nf* (a) (*Zool*) she-wolf. (b) (*Agr*) ridge (between furrows).
lobanillo *nm* wen, cyst.
lobato *nm* wolf cub.
lobelia *nf* lobelia.
lobero *adj* wolf (*attr*); **perro** — wolfhound.
lobezno *nm* wolf cub.
lobito *nm* (*RPl*) otter (*also* — **de río**).
lobo 1 *adj* (*Mex*) shrewd, cunning; (*Chi*) shy; (*SD*) green, raw.
  2 *nm* wolf; — **de mar** old salt, sea dog, (*Chi*) seal; — **marino** seal; **son** —**s de una camada** they're birds of a feather; **arrojar a uno a los** —**s** to throw someone to the wolves; **gritar ¡el** —**!** to cry wolf; **pillar un** — (*fam*) to get boozed.
  3 *nm* (*SAm*) half-breed.
lóbrego *adj* dark, murky, gloomy.
lobreguez *nf* darkness, murk(iness), gloom(iness).
lóbulo *nm* lobe.
lobuno *adj* wolf (*attr*); wolfish, wolflike.
loca *nf* (a) madwoman, lunatic. (b) (*RPl*) whore. (c) **dar** (*or* **venir**) **a uno la** — (*RPl*) to get cross, get into a temper.
local 1 *adj* local; **equipo** — home team; **los** —**es** (*Sport*) our boys, the home team.
  2 *nm* place; site, scene; rooms; premises; **en el** — on the spot; on the premises.
localidad *nf* (a) locality; location. (b) (*Theat*) seat, ticket; **sacar** —**es** to get tickets; "**no hay** —**es**" "house full", "sold out".
localización *nf* location; placing, siting; finding.
localizar [1f] *vt* (a) to locate; to place, site; to find, track down; **el sitio donde se va a** — **la nueva industria** the place where the new industry is to be sited.
  (b) to localize.
locamente *adv* madly; wildly; — **enamorado** madly in love.
locatario *nm*, **locataria** *nf* (*SAm*) tenant, lessee.
locatis *nm*, *pl* **locatis** madman, crackpot, crazy sort.
locería *nf* (*Col, Mex*) china, chinaware; (*Col*) pottery.
locero *nm* (*CAm, Col, Mex*) potter.
loción *nf* lotion; wash; — **capilar,** — **para el cabello** hair restorer; — **facial,** — **para después del afeitado** after-shave lotion.
lock-out ['lokaut] *nm*, *pl* **lock-outs** ['lokaut] (*angl*) lock-out.
loco 1 *adj* (a) mad, crazy; (*fig*) wild, mad; — **de atar,** — **rematado** (*SAm*) raving mad; — **de verano** (*Arg*) cracked, crazy; — **lindo** (*Arg*) mad in a nice sort of

way; **más — que una cabra** as mad as a hatter; **andar — con algo** to be worried to death about something; **ando — con el examen** the exam is driving me crazy; **estar — de alegría** to be mad with joy; **estar — por una chica** to be mad about a girl; **estar — por hacer algo** (*SAm*) to be mad keen to do something; **esto me tiene** (*or* **trae**) — it's driving me crazy; **volver — a uno** to drive someone mad; **volverse —** to go mad; **esto es para volverse** — it's maddening, it's enough to drive you mad; **estar para volverse —** to be at one's wit's end.
   (b) (*Mech*) loose, free.
   (c) (*fam*) huge, tremendous (*fam*); **un éxito —** a huge success; **estoy con** (*or* **tengo**) **una prisa loca** I'm in a tremendous rush; **he tenido una suerte loca** I've been fantastically lucky.
   2 *nm* madman; lunatic, maniac; **correr como un —** to run like mad; **gritar como un —** to shout like a madman.
locomoción *nf* locomotion.
locomotora *nf* (*Rail*) engine, locomotive; **— de maniobras** shunting engine, switch engine (*US*).
locomóvil *nf* traction engine.
locrear [1a] *vi* (*SAm*) to eat, to have a meal.
locro *nm* (*SAm*) meat and vegetable stew.
locuacidad *nf* loquacity, talkativeness.
locuaz *adj* loquacious, voluble, talkative.
locución *nf* expression, phrase.
locuelo *nm*, **locuela** *nf* madcap.
locura *nf* (a) madness, lunacy, insanity; **¡qué —!** it's madness!, what lunacy!; **me gusta con —** (*fam*) I'm crazy about it; **es una casa de —** (*fam*) it's a smashing house (*sl*).
   (b) (*act*) mad thing, crazy thing; **—s** folly; **es capaz de hacer cualquier —** he is capable of any madness.
locutor *nm*, **locutora** *nf* (*Radio*) announcer; commentator; (*TV*) newscaster, newsreader; (*of comedy show*) compère; (*at fashion show etc*) presenter.
locutorio *nm* (*Eccl*) parlour; (*Tel*) telephone box; **— radiofónico** studio.
locha *nf* loach.
loche *nm* (*Col*) reddish colour.
locho *adj* (*Col*) red, reddish.
lodacero *nm* (*Ec*), **lodazal** *nm* muddy place, mudhole, quagmire.
lodo *nm* mud, mire; sludge; **—s** (*Med*) mudbath.
lodoso *adj* muddy.
loga *nf* (a) (*CAm*) eulogy; **echar una — a uno** (*iro*) to tell someone off. (b) (*Chi*) ballad, short poem.
logaritmo *nm* logarithm.
logia *nf* (a) (*masonic etc*) lodge. (b) (*Archit*) loggia.
lógica *nf* logic.
lógicamente *adv* logically.
lógico 1 *adj* logical; natural, right, reasonable; **es — que . . .** it is natural that . . ., it stands to reason that . . . **2** *nm* logician.
logística *nf* logistics.
logístico *adj* logistic.
logradamente *adv* successfully.
logrado *adj* successful.
lograr [1a] *vt* (a) to get, obtain; to achieve, attain; **por fin lo logró** eventually he achieved it, eventually he managed it; **logra cuanto quiere** he gets whatever he wants; **¡no lo lograrán!** they shan't get away with it!
   (b) **— hacer algo** to manage to do something, succeed in doing something; **— que uno haga algo** to (manage to) get someone to do something, persuade someone to do something.
logrear [1a] *vi* to lend money at interest, be a moneylender.
logrero *nm* (a) moneylender, (*pej*) profiteer. (b) (*SAm*) sponger (*fam*), parasite.
logro *nm* (a) achievement, attainment; success; **uno de sus mayores —s** one of his greatest successes (*or* achievements).
   (b) (*Comm, Fin*) profit; (*pej*) usury; **a — at** (a high rate of) interest.
logroñés 1 *adj* of Logroño. **2** *nm*, **logroñesa** *nf* native (*or* inhabitant) of Logroño; **los —es** the people of Logroño.
Loira *m* Loire.
loísmo *nm* use of *lo* instead of *le* (*indirect object*).
loísta 1 *adj* that uses *lo* instead of *le* (*indirect object*). **2** *nmf* user of *lo* instead of *le*.
Lola *f*, **Lolita** *f* pet names for **María de los Dolores**.
loma *nf* hillock, low ridge; **en la — del diablo** (*Arg*) at the back of beyond.
lomada *nf* (*SAm*) =**loma**.
lombarda *nf* (*Agr*) red cabbage.
Lombardía *f* Lombardy.

lombardo 1 *adj* Lombard. **2** *nm*, **lombarda** *nf* Lombard.
lombriciento *adj* (*SAm*) suffering from worms.
lombriz *nf* worm, earthworm; **— solitaria** tapeworm.
lomería *nf*, **lomerio** *nm* (*Guat, Mex*) group of low hills, series of ridges.
lometón *nm* (*Cu, Mex*) isolated hillock.
lomillería *nf* (*RPl*) (a) harness maker's; harness shop. (b) harness, harness accessories.
lomillero *nm* (*RPl*) harness maker; harness seller.
lomillo *nm* (a) (*Sew*) cross-stitch. (b) **—s** (*SAm*) pads (of a pack saddle).
lomo *nm* (a) (*Anat*) back; (*of meat*) loin; **—s** ribs; **iba a —s de una mula** he was riding a mule, he was mounted on a mule. (b) (*Agr*) balk, ridge; (*of hill*) shoulder; (*Rail*) gradient. (c) (*of book*) spine, back.
lona *nf* canvas; sailcloth; (*Mex, RPl*) sackcloth.
loncha *nf* =**lonja**[1].
lonchar [1a] (*SAm*) **1** *vt* to have for lunch. **2** *vi* to have lunch, lunch.
lonche *nm* (*SAm: angl*) lunch, midday snack; (*Per*) tea, afternoon snack.
lonchear [1a] *vt* (*Mex*) to have for lunch.
lonchería *nf* (*SAm*) lunch counter, snack bar, restaurant.
loncho *nm* (*Col*) bit, piece, slice.
londinense 1 *adj* London (*attr*), of London. **2** *nmf* Londoner; **los —s** the people of London, (the) Londoners.
Londres London.
londri *nm* (*SAm: angl*) laundry.
loneta *nf* (*SAm*) coarse cotton cloth.
longanimidad *nf* forbearance, magnanimity.
longánimo *adj* forbearing, magnanimous.
longaniza *nf* (a) long pork sausage. (b) (*Chi*) string, series.
longevidad *nf* longevity.
longevo *adj* long-lived; **las mujeres son más longevas que los hombres** women live longer than men.
longitud *nf* (a) length; **— de onda** wavelength. (b) (*Geog*) longitude.
longitudinal *adj* longitudinal.
longitudinalmente *adv* longitudinally; lengthways.
longo *nm* (*Ec*) Indian youth.
longui(s) *nm* (*fam*): **hacerse el —** to pretend not to know; to pretend not to be interested.
lonja[1] *nf* (a) slice; (*of bacon*) rasher. (b) (*RPl*) strip of leather; tip of a whiplash; **sacar —s a uno** to thrash someone severely.
lonja[2] *nf* (*Comm*) (a) market, exchange; **— de granos** corn exchange; **— de pescado** fish market; **manipular la —** to rig the market.
   (b) grocer's (shop).
lonjear [1a] *vt* (*RPl*) *leather* to cut into strips; *person* to thrash severely.
lonjista *nm* grocer.
lontananza *nf* (*Art*) background; **en —** far away, in the distance.
loor *nm* praise.
loquear [1a] *vi* to play the fool; to make merry, have a high old time.
loqueo *nm* (*Urug*) uproar, hullaballoo (*fam*).
loquera *nf* (a) madhouse, lunatic asylum. (b) (*SAm*) madness.
loquería *nf* (*Chi, Per*) madhouse, lunatic asylum.
loquero *nm* (a) (*RPl*) nurse in an asylum. (b) (*RPl*) confusion, pandemonium.
loquira *nf* (*Col*) foolish thing, idiocy.
loquircho *adj* (*Arg*) crazy, cracked.
lor *nm* (*angl*) lord.
lora *nf* (a) (*SAm: Orn*) female parrot. (b) (*Chi, RPl*) ugly woman; chatterbox. (c) (*Col, Ec, PR, Ven*) severe wound, open wound.
Lorena *f* Lorraine.
Lorenzo *m* Laurence, Lawrence.
loro *nm* (a) parrot.
   (b) (*SAm*) chatterbox; (*Chi*) spy; thieves' lookout man.
   (c) (*Chi*) bedpan.
   (d) (*Arg, Chi*) **sacar los —s** to pick one's nose.
   (e) pointed and curved knife.
los[1] *def art mpl*, **las** *def art fpl* the (*see* **el** *for usage examples*).
los[2], **las** *pron* them; **¿los hay?** are there any?; **los hay** there are some.
los[3], **las** *dem pron*: **mis libros y los de Vd** my books and yours; **nuestros cines y los de París** our cinemas and those of Paris, our cinemas and the Paris ones; **las de Juan son verdes** John's are green; **una inocentada de las de niño pequeño** a practical joke typical of a small child, a practical joke such as a

small child might play; **un bombardeo de los de
cataclismo** a really shattering bombardment.
los[4], las: los que, las que *rel pron: see* **el que.**
losa *nf* (stone) slab, flagstone; — **sepulcral** gravestone, tombstone.
losange *nm* diamond (shape); (*Math*) rhomb; (*Her*)
lozenge; (*Sport*) diamond.
lote[1] *nm* (a) portion, share; (*Comm etc*) lot.
   (b) *land measure:* (*Mex*) = *about* 100 *hectares;*
(*Arg*) = *about* 400 *hectares.*
   (c) (*Chi*) **al** — in a rough and ready way, crudely,
without bothering much.
lote[2] *nm* (*Arg: sl*) idiot, clot (*sl*).
lotear [1a] *vt* (*Arg, Chi*) to divide into lots.
lotería *nf* lottery; **le cayó la —, le tocó la —** he won a
big prize in the lottery, (*fig*) he struck lucky, he
struck it rich.
lotero *nm*, **lotera** *nf* seller of lottery tickets.
lotificar [1g] *vt* (*Guat, Mex*), **lotizar** [1f] *vt* (*Per*) to
divide into lots.
loto *nm* lotus.
Lovaina Louvain.
loza *nf* crockery; earthenware; — **fina** china, chinaware; **hacer la —** to wash up.
lozanamente *adv* (a) luxuriantly; rankly; profusely;
vigorously; in a lively fashion, in a sprightly way.
   (b) haughtily, proudly.
lozanear [1a] *vi* (*Bot*) to flourish, do well, grow
strongly; to grow profusely; (*person*) to be full of
life, be vigorous, flourish.
lozanía *nf* (a) lushness, luxuriance; vigour; liveliness,
sprightliness. (b) haughtiness, pride.
lozano *adj* (a) (*Bot*) lush, luxuriant; rank; profuse;
person, animal vigorous, lusty; lively, sprightly.
   (b) haughty, proud.
lubricación *nf* lubrication.
lubricador 1 *adj* lubricating. **2** *nm* lubricator.
lubricante 1 *adj* lubricant, lubricating. **2** *nm* lubricant.
lubricar [1g] *vt* to lubricate, oil, grease.
lubricidad *nf* (a) slipperiness. (b) lewdness, lubricity.
lúbrico *adj* (a) slippery. (b) (*fig*) lewd, lubricious.
lubrificar [1f] *vt etc see* **lubricar** *etc.*
Lucano m Lucan.
Lucas m Luke, Lucas; (*Eccl*) Luke.
lucas *adj invar* (*Mex*) crazy, cracked.
lucense 1 *adj* of Lugo. **2** *nmf* native (*or* inhabitant) of
Lugo; **los —s** the people of Lugo.
lucera *nf* skylight.
lucerna *nf* chandelier.
lucernario *nm* skylight.
lucero *nm* (a) (*Astron*) bright star, (*esp*) Venus; —
del alba morning star; — **de la tarde,** — **vespertino**
evening star.
   (b) (*fig*) brilliance, radiance.
lucidez *nf* (a) lucidity, clarity. (b) (*Arg, Chi, Guat*)
brilliance.
lúcido *adj* lucid, clear.
lucido *adj* (a) splendid, brilliant; sumptuous, magnificent; elegant; successful.
   (b) **estar —, quedar(se) —** (*iro*) to do splendidly
(*iro*), make a mess of things; **¡estamos —s!** (*iro*) a
fine mess we're in!
luciente *adj* bright, shining, brilliant.
luciérnaga *nf* glow-worm.
Lucifer m Lucifer.
lucimiento *nm* brilliance, lustre, splendour; show,
ostentation; dash, verve; success; **hacer algo con —**
to do something outstandingly well, do something
very successfully.
lucio[1] *nm* (*Fish*) pike.
lucio[2] *adj* =**lúcido.**
lución *nm* slow-worm.
lucir [3f] **1** *vt* (a) to illuminate, light up.
   (b) to show off, display; to sport; — **las habili-
dades** to show off one's talents; **lucía traje nuevo**
he was sporting a new suit.
   2 *vi* (a) to shine; to sparkle, glitter, gleam.
   (b) (*fig*) to shine, be brilliant; to be a success;
(*in dress etc*) to look nice, cut a dash; to show off;
no lucía en los estudios he did not shine at his
studies.
   3 lucirse *vr* (a) to dress up, dress elegantly; =*vi* (b).
   (b) (*iro*) to make a fool of oneself, make a mess
of things; **¡te has lucido!** (*iro*) a fine thing you've
done! (*iro*), what a mess you've made!
lucrarse [1a] *vr* to do well out of a deal; (*pej*) to
enrich oneself, feather one's nest.
lucrativo *adj* lucrative, profitable, remunerative;
institución no lucrativa non-profitmaking institution.
Lucrecia f Lucretia.
Lucrecio m Lucretius.

lucro *nm* profit; —**s y daños** (*Fin*) profit and loss.
luctuoso *adj* mournful, sad, tragic.
lucubración *nf* lucubration.
lúcuma *nf* (*Chi*) *a pear-shaped fruit;* (*fam*) head.
Lucha f pet name for Luz, Lucía.
lucha *nf* (a) fight, struggle (*por* for); conflict; contest,
dispute; — **de clases** class war; — **contra la subversión** struggle against subversive elements; witch
hunt.
   (b) (*Sport*) — **de la cuerda** tug-of-war; — **gre-
corromana,** — **libre** wrestling.
luchador *nm* fighter; (*Sport*) wrestler.
luchar [1a] *vi* (a) to fight, struggle (*por algo* for
something; *por hacer* to do); **luchaba con los mandos**
he was struggling (*or* wrestling) with the controls;
— **con uno,** — **contra uno** to fight (against) someone.
   (b) (*Sport*) to wrestle (*con* with).
luche *nm* (*Chi*) (a) hopscotch. (b) *an edible seaweed.*
ludibrio *nm* mockery, derision.
ludir [3a] *vt* to rub (*con, contra* against).
luego *adv* then, next; presently, soon; later (on),
afterwards; (*also Mex*) at once, instantly, immediately; (*SAm*) later; (*Col, Mex, Par, Per, PR*)
sometimes, from time to time; (*Par*) already, earlier,
previously; **¿y —?** what next? what happened then?;
desde — naturally, of course; **desde — que** no of
course not; **¡hasta —!** I see you later, so long!; **¡para
— es tarde!** (*Guat, Mex*) prove it to us right now!;
— **de eso** immediately after that; — **de haberlo
dicho** immediately after saying it; — **que . . . as**
soon as . . .
lueguito *adv* (a) (*Arg, Chi, Guat, Mex, Par*) at once,
immediately. (b) (*Chi, Guat, Mex*) near; **aquí —**
right here, near here.
lúes *nf* syphilis.
luengo *adj* (*arch, lit, also SAm*) long.
lugar *nm* (a) place, spot; position; — **seguro** safe
place; **el — del crimen** the scene of the crime; **una
emisión de algún — de Europa** a broadcast from
somewhere in Europe; **en — de** instead of, in place
of; **en primer —** in the first place, firstly; for one
thing . . .; **yo en su —** if I were him; in his place,
I . . .; **estar fuera de —** to be out of place (*also fig*);
dejar a uno en mal — to let someone down, leave
someone in the lurch; **devolver un libro a su —** to
put a book back (in its place); **ocupar el — de** to
take the place of; **poner las cosas en su —** (*fig*) to
put things straight, put the record straight;
póngase en mi — put yourself in my place; **ponerse
en su —** to stand on one's dignity; **tener —** to take
place, happen, occur.
   (b) room, space; **¿hay —?** is there any room?;
hacer — para to make room for, make way for.
   (c) village, town, place.
   (d) reason (*para* for), cause; **no hay — para preocupaciones** there is no cause for concern, there is no
need for worry.
   (e) opportunity; **si se me da el —** if I have the
chance; **dar — a** to give rise to, occasion; **dejar — a**
to allow, permit of.
   (f) — **común** commonplace, cliché, platitude.
lugareño 1 *adj* village (*attr*). **2** *nm,* **lugareña** *nf*
villager.
lugarteniente *nm* deputy.
lugre *nm* lugger.
lúgubre *adj* mournful, lugubrious, dismal.
luir [3g] *vt* (*Chi*) to rumple, mess up; *pottery* to polish.
Luis m Louis.
Luisa f Louise.
Luisiana f Louisiana.
lujo *nm* (a) luxury; sumptuousness, lavishness; **de —**
de luxe, luxury (*attr*); **vivir en el —** to live in
luxury.
   (b) (*fig*) profusion, wealth, abundance; **con — de
fuerza** with an excessive show of force.
lujosamente *adv* luxuriously; sumptuously, lavishly;
ostentatiously; profusely.
lujoso *adj* luxurious; sumptuous, lavish; ostentatious;
profuse.
lujuria *nf* lust, lechery; lewdness.
lujuriante *adj* (a) luxuriant, lush. (b) lustful.
lujuriar [1b] *vi* to lust.
lujurioso *adj* lustful, lecherous; lewd, sensual.
lulo 1 *adj* (*Chi*) (a) *object* long and cylindrical; *person*
lank, slender.
   (b) *character* dull, colourless.
   2 *nm* (a) (*Chi*) cylindrical object; bundle; curl.
   (b) — **del ojo** (*Col*) eyeball.
lullir [3h] *vt* (*Col, CR, Mex*) to rub (*con, contra*
against, on).
lumbago *nm* lumbago.

lumbar *adj* lumbar.
lumbre *nf* (a) fire; **cerca de la —** near the fire, at the fireside; **echar —** to be furious.
  (b) (*for cigarette*) light; **¿tienes —?, ¿me das —?** have you got a light?
  (c) light; brightness, brilliance, splendour; **— del agua** surface of the water.
  (d) (*Archit*) light, opening (in a wall); skylight.
lumbrera *nf* (a) luminary; (*Archit*) skylight.
  (b) (*Mech*) vent, port; **— de escape** exhaust vent.
  (c) (*fig*) luminary, leading light, authority; **estaba rodeado de —s literarias** he was surrounded by leading literary figures.
  (d) (*Mex: Taur, Theat*) box.
luminar *nm* luminary; =**lumbrera** (c).
luminaria *nf* altar lamp; **—s** illuminations, lights.
lumínico *adj* light (*attr*).
luminiscenia *nf* luminescence.
luminosidad *nf* (a) brightness (*also TV*), luminosity. (b) (*fig*) brightness, brilliance.
luminoso *adj* (a) bright, luminous, shining; **sign** illuminated. (b) (*fig*) *idea* bright, brilliant.
luna *nf* (a) moon; **— creciente** crescent moon, waxing moon; **— llena** full moon; **media —** half-moon, (*fig*) crescent; **— menguante** waning moon; **— nueva** new moon; **— de miel** honeymoon; **estar de buena —** to be in a good mood; **estar de mala —** to be in a bad mood; **estar en la — de Valencia** to be wool-gathering; **eso es hablar de la —** that's nonsense; **quedarse a la — de Valencia** (*or de Paita: Chi, Ec, Per*) to be disappointed, be left in the lurch; **vivir en la —** to be completely out of touch with reality, have one's head in the clouds.
  (b) plate glass; mirror; lens.
lunar 1 *adj* lunar.
  2 *nm* (*Anat*) mole, spot; (*fig*) defect, flaw, blemish; (*moral*) stain, blot; black spot; **— postizo** beauty spot; **hay —es en la prosperidad general** there are black spots in the general prosperity.
lunarejo *adj* (*SAm*) spotty, spotty-faced.
lunático 1 *adj* lunatic. 2 *nm* lunatic.
lunch [lunʃ] *nm*, *pl* **lunchs** [lunʃ] (*angl*) lunch; midday snack; formal luncheon, luncheon party.
lunchería *nf* (*SAm: angl*) =**lonchería**.
lunes *nm*, *pl* **lunes** Monday; **hacer San L—** (*SAm*) to stay away from work on Monday; **no ocurre cada — y cada martes** it doesn't happen every day of the week.
luneta *nf* (a) lens, glass (of spectacles). (b) half-moon shape, crescent. (c) (*Theat: Hist, Mex*) stall.
lunfa *nm* (*Arg: sl*) thief.
lunfardismo *nm* (*RPl*) word (*or phrase etc*) from thieves' slang.
lunfardo *nm* (*Per, RPl*) (a) thieves' slang, language of the underworld; slang (*in general*). (b) thief.
lupa *nf* lens, magnifying glass.
lupanar *nm* brothel.
Lupe *f* pet name for **Guadalupe**.
lupia[1] *nf* (a) wen, cyst. (b) (*Col; also* **—s**) small amount of money; small change.
lupia[2] *nmf* (*Hond*) quack doctor.
lúpulo *nm* (*Bot*) hop, hops.
luquete *nm* (*Chi*) unploughed patch of land; bald patch (*on head*); grease spot (*on clothing*).
lurio *adj* (*Mex*) in love; crazy, cracked.
lusitano 1 *adj* Portuguese; (*ancient Hist*) Lusitanian. 2 *nm*, **lusitana** *nf* Portuguese; (*ancient Hist*) Lusitanian.
luso *adj* =**lusitano**.
lustrabotas *nm*, *pl* **lustrabotas** (*esp SAm*) bootblack.
lustrada *nf* (*SAm*) shoeshine.

lustrador *nm* (a) (*Tech*) polisher. (b) (*SAm*) bootblack.
lustrar [1a] *vt* to shine, polish.
lustre *nm* (a) polish, shine, gloss, lustre; **dar — a** to polish, put a shine on.
  (b) polish; **— para calzado** shoe polish; **— para metales** metal polish.
  (c) (*fig*) lustre, glory.
lustrín *nm* (a) (*Chi*) shoeshine parlour. (b) (*Ec*) = **lustrina** (a).
lustrina *nf* (a) (*Arg, Par*) shiny material of alpaca; (*Ec*) silk cloth. (b) (*Chi*) shoe polish.
lustro *nm* lustrum, period of five years.
lustroso *adj* glossy, bright, shining.
luteranismo *nm* Lutheranism.
luterano 1 *adj* Lutheran. 2 *nm*, **luterana** *nf* Lutheran.
Lutero *m* Luther.
luto *nm* (a) mourning; grief, sorrow; **medio —** half-mourning; **— riguroso** deep mourning; **estar de —, llevar —** to be in mourning (*por* for); **dejar el —** to come out of mourning.
  (b) **—s** mourning (*clothes*), crêpe.
Luxemburgo *m* Luxembourg.
luz *nf* (a) (*in general*) light; daylight; **— y sombra** light and shade; **la — del día** the light of day; **a la — del día** (*fig*) in the cold light of day; **como la — del día** as clear as daylight; **— eléctrica** electric light; **— de la luna** moonlight; **— del sol, — solar** sunlight; **a la — de una vela** by the light of a candle; **a primera —** at first light; **espectáculo de — y sonido** son et lumière show; **entre dos luces** at twilight; (*fam*) mellow, tipsy; **dar a —** to give birth; **dar a — un niño** to give birth to a child; **dar a — un libro** to publish a book; **negar la — del día a uno** to concede absolutely nothing to someone; **quitar la — a uno** to stand in someone's light; **sacar a —** to bring to light; *book* to publish; **salir a —** to come to light; (*book*) to appear, come out, be published.
  (b) (*Elec: fam*) electricity, electric current, juice (*sl*).
  (c) (*fig*) light; **a la — de** in the light of; **a la — de un nuevo descubrimiento** in the light of a new discovery; **a todas luces** anyway; evidently; by any reckoning; **arrojar — sobre** to cast (*or* shed, throw) light on; **estudiar algo a una nueva —** to study something in a new light; **tuvo una larga experiencia de estar a la — de la publicidad** he had long experience of being in the limelight, he was used to being in the public eye.
  (d) (*Elec etc*) light, lamp; **— de costado** sidelight; **— de cruce** dipped headlight; **— destelladora** winking light; **luces de detención, luces de freno** braking lights; **luces de estacionamiento** parking lights; **— intermitente** winking light; **— lateral** sidelight; **— piloto, — de situación** sidelight, parking light; **— relámpago** (*Phot*) flashlight; **— roja** red light; **luces de tráfico** traffic lights; **luces traseras** rear lights, tail lamps; **— verde** green light; **apagar la —** to switch off (*or* put off, turn off) the light; **poner la —** to switch on (*or* put on, turn on) the light; **poner una lámpara a media —** to dim a light.
  (e) (*Archit etc*) light; window, opening; (*of bridge*) space, span; (*RPl*) distance between two objects; **dar — a uno** (*RPl: Sport*) to give someone a start; **te doy 10 metros de —** I'll give you 10 metres' start.
  (f) **luces** (*fig*) enlightenment; intelligence; **corto de luces, de pocas luces** dim, stupid; **el Siglo de las Luces** the Age of Enlightenment (*18th century*).
Lyón Lyons.

LL

llacsa *nf* (*Chi*) molten metal.

llaga *nf* (a) wound; ulcer, sore; ¡por las—s! damnation! (b) (*fig*) sore, affliction, torment; **las —s de la guerra** the afflictions of war, the havoc of war.

llagar [1h] *vt* (a) to make sore; to wound, injure. (b) (*fig*) to wound, injure.

llalla *nf* (*Chi*) see **yaya**.

llama[1] *nf* (*Zool*) llama.

llama[2] *nf* (a) flame; blaze; **— piloto** pilot light (*on stove*); **arder sin —** to smoulder; **entregar algo a las —s** to commit something to the flames; **estallar en —s** to burst into flames; **salir de las —s y caer en las brasas** (*fig*) to jump out of the frying pan into the fire. (b) (*fig*) flame; passion, ardour.

llamada *nf* (a) call; (*at door*) knock, ring; (*Tel*) call; (*Mil*) call to arms; **— a larga distancia, — inter-urbana** long-distance call, trunk call; **— al orden** call to order. (b) signal, sign, gesture. (c) (*Typ*) reference mark. (d) (*Mex*) cowardliness; timidity.

llamado 1 *adj* so-called. **2** *nm* (*SAm*) = **llamada**.

llamador *nm* (a) (*person*) caller. (b) door-knocker; bell; push-button.

llamamiento *nm* call; **hacer un — a uno para que + subj** to call on someone to + *infin*.

llamar [1a] **1** *vt* (a) to call, name; **le llamaron el Gordo** they called him Fatty; **¿cómo le van a —?** what are they going to call him? (b) to call; to summon; to invoke, call upon; (*with gesture*) to beckon; (*Tel*) to call, ring up, telephone (to); **¿quién me llama?** who's asking for me?; **que me llamen a las 7** please have them call me at 7; **le llamaron a palacio** they called (*or* summoned) him to the palace; **le llaman desde París** they're calling you from Paris; **— a uno a hacer algo** to call on someone to do something. (c) to draw, attract; **attention** to attract. (d) **estar llamado a + infin** to be destined to + *infin*; **esto está llamado a ser de gran utilidad** this is destined to be very useful; **estaba llamado a fracasar** it was doomed to failure. **2** *vi* (a) to call; **¿quién llama?** (*Tel*) who's calling?, who's that?; **"llama D de Dulcinea"** (*Aer etc*) "this is D for Dulcinea (calling)"; **— por ayuda** to call for help. (b) to knock, ring; **— a la puerta** to knock at the door; **¿quién llama?** who's there? **3 llamarse** *vr* to be called, be named; **me llamo Mimi** my name is Mimi, they call me Mimi; **¿cómo te llamas?** what's your name?; **¡eso sí que se llama cantar!** that's what you really call singing!; **¡eso sí que se llama hablar!** now you're talking!, that's more like it!; **¡como me llamo Rodríguez, que lo haré!** as sure as my name's Rodríguez, I'll do it!

llamarada *nf* flare-up, sudden blaze; (*on face*) sudden flush; (*fig*) flare-up, outburst.

llamarón *nm* (*CAm, Col, Chi*) = **llamarada**.

llamativo *adj* gaudy, flashy, showy; *colour* loud; **de modo —** in such a way as to draw attention.

llame *nm* (*Chi*) bird trap.

llamear [1a] *vi* to blaze, flame, flare.

llamón *adj* (*Mex*) cowardly; timid.

llampo *nm* (*Arg, Bol, Chi*) ore, pulverized ore; pebble deposit.

llana *nf* (a) (*Geog*) plain; flat ground. (b) (*Archit*) mason's trowel.

llanada *nf* plain; flat ground.

llanamente *adv* (a) smoothly, evenly. (b) plainly, simply; clearly, straightforwardly; openly, frankly; see **lisamente**.

llanca *nf* (*Per*) earthworm.

llanero *nm*, **llanera** *nf* plainsman, plaindweller.

llaneza *nf* (*fig*) plainness, simplicity; clearness, straightforwardness; naturalness; modesty; openness, frankness; informality.

llano 1 *adj* (a) level, flat, smooth, even. (b) (*fig*) plain, simple, unadorned; clear, easy, straightforward; open, frank; **en lenguaje —** in plain language; **a la llana** simply; openly, frankly; **decir algo por lo —** to put matters bluntly, say things straight out; **de —** openly. **2** *nm* plain, flat ground.

llanque *nm* (*Per*) rustic sandal.

llanta[1] *nf* tyre (*esp SAm*); rim (*of a wheel*); (*PR*) large finger-ring; **— de oruga** caterpillar track.

llanta[2] *nf* (*Bol, Per*) sunshade, awning.

llantén *nm* plantain.

llantería *nf* (*Chi*) weeping, wailing.

llanto *nm* weeping, crying; tears; (*fig*) lamentation; (*Lit*) dirge, funeral lament; **dejar el —** to stop crying.

llanura *nf* (a) flatness, smoothness, evenness. (b) (*Geog*) plain; prairie.

llapa *nf* see **yapa**.

llapango *adj* (*Ec*) barefoot.

llauto *nm* (*Bol, Per*) headband.

llave *nf* (a) (*to door*) key; (*Tech*) key; **— de cambio** shift key; **— de contacto** (*Aut*) ignition key; **— espacial** spacing bar; **— maestra** skeleton key, master key; **¡por las —s de San Pedro!** by heaven!; **bajo —, debajo de —** under lock and key; **cerrar una puerta con —** to lock a door; **echar la —** (a) to lock up; **tener las —s de la caja** (*fig*) to hold the purse strings. (b) (*for gas, water etc*) tap, faucet (*US*); (*Elec*) switch; **— de bola, — de flotador** ballcock; **— de cierre** stopcock. (c) (*Mech*) spanner; **— ajustable** adjustable spanner; **— inglesa** wrench, monkey wrench. (d) (*Mus*) stop, key. (e) (*Wrestling*) lock. (f) (*of gun*) lock. (g) (*Arg: Archit*) beam, joist. (h) (*Mex: Taur*) —s horns.

llavero *nm* (a) key ring. (b) (*person: also —* **de cárcel**) turnkey.

llavín *nm* latchkey.

llegada *nf* arrival, coming.

llegar [1h] **1** *vt* to bring up, bring over, draw up. **2** *vi* (a) to arrive, come; **— a** to arrive at, reach; **por fin llegamos** we're here at last; **avíseme cuando llegue** tell me when he comes; **cuando llegue eso** when that happens; **le llegó el año pasado** (*SAm*) he died last year. (b) (*SAm*) to arrive, get to the top, triumph. (c) (*of extent etc*) to reach; to be enough; (*of quantity, money etc*) to amount to, equal, be equal to; **esta cuerda no llega** this rope won't reach, this rope isn't long enough; **las personas no llegan a 100** the people don't amount to 100, the people are fewer than 100; **el importe llega a 50 pesos** the total is 50 pesos; **con ese dinero no va Vd a —** you won't have enough money; **el pobrecito no llega a Navidades** the poor chap won't last out (*or* live) till Christmas; **hacer — el dinero** to make one's money last out, eke out one's money; **hacer — el sueldo** to make both ends meet (on one's salary); **este libro no me llega** this book is no help (*or* use) to me. (d) (*with following verb*) — **a + infin** to reach the point of + *ger*; to manage to + *infin*, succeed in + *ger*; **por fin llegó a hacerlo** he managed to do it eventually; **llegué a creerlo** I even believed it; **— a saber algo** to find something out; to get wind of something; **si llego a saberlo** if I had known it; **— a ser + adj or n** to become + *adj or n*; **— a**

ser el jefe to become the boss; **el país llegará a ser una nulidad** the country will become a nonentity.

3 llegarse vr to come near, draw near, approach; **llégate más a mí** come closer to me.

llenador adj (Arg, Chi) food filling, satisfying.

llenar [1a] **1** vt **(a)** to fill (de with); surface etc to cover (de with); space, time etc to fill, occupy, take up (de with); form to fill in, fill up, fill out (US).

(b) duty etc to fulfil; wish to satisfy; requirements to meet, satisfy.

(c) (fig) — **a uno de elogios** to heap praises on someone; — **a uno de insultos** to heap insults on someone, revile someone.

2 llenarse vr **(a)** to fill, fill up (de with); (fam) to stuff oneself (de with); **la superficie se llenó de polvo** the surface got covered in dust.

(b) (fig) to get cross, get annoyed.

llenazón nm (Mex) blown-out feeling, indigestion.

lleno 1 adj full (de of), filled (de with); full up; — **hasta el borde** brimful (de of); **estar — a reventar** to be full to bursting; **estar — de polvo** to be covered in dust; **estar — de sí mismo** to be full of oneself, be conceited; **de —** fully, entirely.

2 nm **(a)** abundance, plenty; perfection.

(b) (Theat) full house, sellout.

(c) (Astron) full moon.

llevadero adj bearable, tolerable.

llevar [1a] **1** vt **(a)** to carry, take, transport, convey; **¿me llevas esta carta?** will you take this letter for me?; **yo llevaba la maleta** I was carrying the case; **es muy pesado para —lo los dos** it's too heavy for the two of us to carry; — **adelante** plan etc to carry forward, go on with; — **a uno por delante** (SAm: Aut) to run someone over.

(b) clothes etc to wear; small objects to have, wear, carry (on one); arms, name, title to bear; **llevaba traje azul** he wore a blue suit; **llevaba puesto un sombrero raro** she had an odd hat on, she was wearing an odd hat; **no llevo dinero encima** (or **conmigo**) I have no money on me, I have no money about me; **lleva un rótulo que dice . . .** it has a label which says . . .; **el libro lleva el título de . . .** the book has the title of . . ., the book is entitled . . .; **el tren no lleva coche-comedor** the train has no dining car; **el avión no llevaba paracaídas** the plane had no parachutes, the plane was not carrying parachutes.

(c) (with personal object) to take (a to); to lead (a to); **este camino nos lleva a Bogotá** this road takes us to Bogotá; **le llevamos al teatro** we took him to the theatre; — **a uno de la mano** to lead someone by the hand; **¿adónde me llevan Vds?** where are you taking me?; **me llevaron de suplente** they took me along as a substitute.

(d) course, direction to follow, keep to; **¿qué dirección llevaba?** what direction was he going in?, what route was he following?

(e) to carry off, take away, cut off; **el viento llevó una rama** the wind carried a branch away; **la bala le llevó dos dedos** the shot cut off two of his fingers.

(f) prize etc to win, get, carry off; **llevó el primer premio** he carried off the first prize.

(g) price to charge; **¿cuánto me van a —?** what are you going to charge me?

(h) (Agr) to bear, produce; (Comm, Fin) to bear, carry; **no lleva fruto este año** it has no fruit this year; **los bonos llevan un 8 por cien de interés** the bonds bear interest at 8%.

(i) life to lead; — **una vida tranquila** to live a quiet life, lead a quiet life.

(j) to bear, stand, put up with; — **las desgracias con paciencia** to bear misfortunes patiently.

(k) (of time) to spend; **llevo 3 días aquí** I have been here for 3 days, I have so far spent 3 days here; **¿cuánto tiempo llevas aquí?** how long have you been here?; **el tren lleva una hora de retraso** the train is an hour late.

(l) (as v aux) **llevo 3 meses buscándolo** I have been looking for it for 3 months; **lleva conseguidas muchas victorias** he has won many victories; **llevo estudiados 3 capítulos** I have studied 3 chapters, I have covered 3 chapters; **llevaba hecha la mitad** he had done half of it.

(m) affair, negotiation etc to conduct, direct, manage; — **una finca** to manage an estate; — **los libros** (Comm) to keep the books; — **la casa** to run the house (see also **casa**).

(n) to exceed; **ella me lleva 2 años** she's 2 years older than I am; **él me lleva la cabeza** he's taller

than me by a head; **les llevamos una gran ventaja** we have a great advantage over them.

(o) (Math) to carry.

(p) — **a uno a creer que . . .** to lead someone to think that . . .; **esto me lleva a pensar que . . .** this leads me to think that . . .

(q) (idioms) **la lleva hecha** he's got it all worked out; **llevo las de perder** I'm likely to lose, I'm in a bad way; — **lo mejor** to get the best of it; — **lo peor** to get the worst of it; **no las lleva todas consigo** he's not all there; **¡la que llevaba encima aquella noche!** (fam) how drunk he was that night!

2 vi (of road) to go, lead; **esta carretera lleva a La Paz** this road goes to La Paz.

3 llevarse vr **(a)** object, person to carry off, take away, remove; **se lo llevaron al cine** they took him off to the cinema; **se llevó mi máquina** he took my camera, he went off with my camera; **los ladrones se llevaron la caja** the thieves took the safe away; **¡que se lo lleve el diablo!** to hell with it!; **el pistolero se llevó 10.000 libras** the gunman got away with £10,000.

(b) — **bien** to get on well (together); **no se lleva bien con el jefe** he doesn't get on (or along) with the boss.

(c) — **a uno por delante** (SAm) to offend someone; to ride roughshod over someone.

llimo adj (Chi) small-eared; earless.

llocalla nm (Bol) boy.

lloquena nf (Bol, Per) fish spear, harpoon.

llora nf (Ven) funeral wake.

llorado adj: **el — rey** the (late) lamented king; **un hombre no —** an unlamented man.

llorar [1a] **1** vt to weep over, weep for, cry about, to bewail, lament; loss, death to mourn.

2 vi **(a)** (of person) to cry, weep; **¡no llores!** don't cry!; — **a cuajo**, — **lágrima viva**, — **a moco y baba**, — **a moco tendido** to sob one's heart out, cry uncontrollably; — **como una fuente** (or **criatura** etc) to weep buckets.

(b) (of eyes) to water; (of tap etc) to drip.

(c) (Chi) to suit, be becoming, look nice (a on).

(d) (Per, PR, RPl) to be very unbecoming.

lloretas nmf, pl **lloretas** (Col, CR) crybaby.

lloriquear [1a] vi to snivel, whimper.

lloriqueo nm snivelling, whimpering.

llorisquear [1a] vi (PR, RPl) etc =**lloriquear** etc.

llorón 1 adj weeping, tearful; snivelling, whining; willow weeping.

2 nm, **llorona** nf tearful person, weepy sort; crybaby.

3 llorona nf (Mex) ghost, soul in torment.

4 lloronas nfpl (Col, RPl) large spurs.

lloroso adj weeping, tearful; sad.

llovedera nf (Col, Guat, Ven), **llovedero** nm (Arg) (period of) continuous rain.

llovedizo adj **(a)** roof leaky. **(b) agua llovediza** rainwater.

llover [2h] **(a)** vi to rain; **llueve, está lloviendo** it is raining; — **a cántaros**, — **a cubos**, — **a chuzos**, — **a mares**, — **a torrentes** to rain cats and dogs, rain in torrents; **como llovido (del cielo)** unexpectedly; **ser una cosa llovida del cielo** to come just right, be a godsend; **llueva o no** rain or shine, come what may; **mucho (or ya) ha llovido desde entonces** much water has flowed under the bridge since then; **¡como ahora llueve pepinos (or uvas)!** (Col) rubbish!; see **mojado**.

(b) (fig) to rain; **le llovieron regalos encima** gifts were rained on him, he was showered with gifts.

llovida nf (SAm) rain, shower.

llovido nm stowaway.

llovizna nf drizzle.

lloviznar [1a] **1** vi to drizzle. **2 lloviznarse** vr to get wet.

lloviznoso adj drizzly.

llueca nf broody hen.

lluqui adj (Ec) left-handed.

lluvia nf rain; shower; (as quantity) rainfall; (of insecticide etc) spray; (of missiles, bullets) hail, shower; (of watering can) rose; (Chi, RPl) shower, shower bath; (fig) shower, mass, abundance; **día de — rainy** day; — **fría**, — **menuda** fine rain, drizzle; —**s monzónicas** monsoon rains; — **de oro** (Bot) laburnum; — **radiactiva** radioactive fallout; — **torrencial** torrential rain; **una — de regalos** a shower of gifts; **la — cae sobre los buenos como sobre los malos** it rains on the just as well as on the unjust.

lluvioso adj rainy, wet.

M

maca[1] *nf* flaw, defect; spot; (*on fruit*) bruise, blemish, bad patch.
maca[2] *nf* (*Ant*) parrot.
macabí *nm* (**a**) (*Col*) shrewd person. (**b**) (*SD*) bandit.
macabro *adj* macabre.
macaco 1 *adj* (**a**) (*SAm*) deformed, misshapen; ugly. (**b**) (*PR*) silly.
2 *nm* (**a**) (*Zool*) macaque. (**b**) (*Ec, Mex, Pan, Per*) half-breed peasant; (*RPl: pej*) Brazilian. (**c**) (*Mex*) bogie. (**d**) (*interj: to child*) you rascal!; (*to person*) little man!
macadán *nm* macadam.
macadamizar [1f] *vt* to macadamize.
macagua *nf* (*SAm*) macaw.
macana *nf* (**a**) (*SAm*) club; cudgel, truncheon. (**b**) (*Bol, Chi, Pan, RPl*) absurdity, piece of nonsense, silly thing; doubtful thing; fib, falsehood; tale. (**c**) (*Arg*) bad job, botch. (**d**) (*Arg*) long boring conversation; ¡qué —! what a bind! (*sl*). (**e**) (*Cu*) de — undoubtedly; es de — que ... of course ...
macanazo *nm* (**a**) (*Ant*) blow (with a club). (**b**) (*Chi, RPl*) =macana (**b**); nuisance, bore.
macaneador (*RPl*) 1 *adj* deceitful; unreliable. 2 *nm*, **macaneadora** *nf* charlatan.
macanear [1a] 1 *vt* (**a**) (*Ant*) to beat, hit. (**b**) (*Col, Ven*)=**desbrozar**; =**rozar.** (**c**) (*Col, Ven*) *matter* to handle.
2 *vi* (**a**) (*Bol, Col, Chi, RPl, Ven*) to talk nonsense, say silly things; to exaggerate wildly, tell tall stories, fib. (**b**) (*Col, Hond*) to work hard.
macanero *adj* (*Bol, Chi, RPl*) given to talking nonsense, silly; given to telling tall stories.
macanudo *adj* (**a**) (*esp SAm*) smashing (*sl*), super (*fam*); first-rate; great (*fam*). (**b**) (*Chi*) big; overlarge, disproportionate. (**c**) (*Col, Ec*) strong, tough; *task* tough, difficult.
macaquear [1a] 1 *vt* (*CAm*) to steal. 2 *vi* (*Chi, RPl*) to make faces.
macarrón[1] *nm* (**a**) (*also* — de almendras) macaroon. (**b**) —es macaroni.
macarrón[2] *nm* (*Naut*) bulwark, stanchion.
macarrónico *adj* macaronic.
macarse [1g] *vr* (*fruit*) to get bruised, (begin to) rot.
macear [1a] 1 *vt* to hammer, pound. 2 *vi*=machacar 2.
maceración *nf* maceration; (*fig*) mortification.
macerar [1a] 1 *vt* to macerate; (*pej*) to mortify. 2 **macerarse** *vr* to macerate; (*fig*) to mortify oneself.
macero *nm* macebearer.
maceta 1 *adj* (**a**) (*Bol, Chi, RPl*) slow, sluggish; **ponerse** — to get old. (**b**) (*PR*) miserly.
2 *nf* (**a**) flowerpot; pot of flowers; (*Chi*) bouquet, bunch of flowers. (**b**) mallet, small hammer; stonecutter's hammer; (*RPl*) club, cudgel. (**c**) (*Mex*) head; ser duro de — (*Arg, Bol*) to be pretty thick.
macetero *nm* flowerpot stand (*or* holder); (*Arg, Chi, Per, PR*) flowerpot.
macetón *nm* tub (*for plants*).
macia *nf*= macis.
macicez *nf* massiveness; solidity; stoutness.
macilento *adj* wan, haggard; gaunt; emaciated.
macillo *nm* (*Mus*) hammer.
macis *nf* mace (*spice*).
macizamente *adj* massively; solidly; stoutly.

macizar [1f] *vt* to fill up, fill in, pack solid.
macizo 1 *adj* massive; *door, gold, tyre etc* solid; solidly made, stoutly made; *person* solid, stoutly built; de roble — of solid oak; — de gente solid with people.
2 *adv* (*CAm, Mex*) quickly, fast.
3 *nm* (**a**) mass; lump, chunk, solid piece. (**b**) (*Geog*) massif. (**c**) (*Hort*) bed, plot. (**d**) (*Aut*) solid tyre. (**e**) (*Archit*) stretch, section (of a wall).
macolla *nf* bunch, cluster.
macro ... macro ...
macró *nm* (*Per, RPl: gall*) pimp.
macrocosmo *nm* macrocosm.
macuco 1 *adj* (**a**) (*Arg, Chi, Per, Ven*) crafty, cunning. (**b**) (*Ec*) old, useless. (**c**) (*Arg, Bol, Col, Chi, Ven*) big, great; overgrown.
2 *nm* (*Arg, Bol, Col*) overgrown boy, big lad.
macuenco *adj* (**a**) (*Cu, PR*) thin, weak, feeble. (**b**) (*SD*) useless. (**c**) (*Col*) big; overgrown, extra large; (*fig*) splendid, terrific (*fam*).
mácula *nf* (**a**) (*mostly fig*) stain, spot, blemish; (*Anat*) blind spot; — solar sunspot. (**b**) trick, fraud.
macular [1a] *vt* to stain, spot.
macundales *nmpl* (*Col, Ven*), **macundos** *nmpl* (*Ven*) things, gear (*fam*), junk.
macuteno *nm* (*Mex*) pickpocket.
macuto *nm* (**a**) knapsack; satchel. (**b**) (*Cu, SD, Ven*) begging basket.
macha *nf* (*Bol, Per, SD*) mannish woman.
machaca 1 *nf* crusher, pounder. 2 *nmf* (*person*) pest, bore.
machacadora *nf* crusher, pounder.
machacar [1g] 1 *vt* (**a**) to crush, pound; to grind (up); to mash. (**b**) (*fig*) *object* to knock to bits; *enemy* to maul, crush; (*in argument*) to crush, flatten, make mincemeat of; *price* to slash.
2 *vi* (**a**) to go on, keep on; to nag; — en un asunto to keep on about a matter, harp on a matter; ¡no machaques! don't go on so!, stop harping on it!; *see* hierro. (**b**) (*Univ etc*) to swot (*fam*).
3 **machacarse** *vr* (*fam*): — el verano to spend the summer swotting (*fam*).
machacón 1 *adj* tiresome, wearisome; insistent; monotonous; con insistencia machacona with wearisome insistence.
2 *nm*, **machacona** *nf* pest, bore.
machado *nm* hatchet.
machamartillo: a — *adv*: creer a — to believe firmly, (*pej*) to believe blindly; cumplir a — to carry out a task to the letter, perform a task down to the last detail; eran cristianos a — they were absolutely convinced Christians.
machango *adj* (**a**) (*Cu*) coarse, rough. (**b**) (*Chi*) stupid; annoying, tedious.
machaquear [1a] *vti* (*Mex*)=machacar.
machaqueo *nm* crushing, pounding.
machaquería *nf* tiresomeness; insistence, harping (on a subject); monotony.
macharse [1a] *vr* (*Arg, Bol, Ec*) to get drunk.
machetazo *nm* (*SAm*) (**a**) large *machete*. (**b**) blow (*or* slash) with a *machete*.
machete *nm* (*SAm*) *machete*, cane knife, big knife.
machetear [1a] 1 *vt* (**a**) (*SAm*) *cane etc* to cut down with a *machete*; *person* to slash (*or* wound, stab *etc*) with a *machete*. (**b**) (*Col*) to sell cheap.
2 *vi* (**a**) (*Col, Mex*) to insist, be stubborn. (**b**) (*Mex*) to work; (*of student*) to plod on.

machetero nm (a) (SAm: Agr) cane cutter.
(b) (Mex) slave, drudge.
(c) (Ant) revolutionary; — **de salón** armchair radical.
(d) (Mex) plodding student.
(e) (Ven) soldier.

machi nm, **machí** nm (SAm) medicine man.

machiega nf queen bee.

machihembrado nm (Carp) dovetail (joint).

machihembrar [1a] vt to dovetail.

machina nf (a) crane, derrick; pile driver. (b) (PR) merry-go-round.

machirulo nm tomboy; mannish woman.

macho 1 adj (a) (Bio) male; **la flor** — the male flower.
(b) (fig) masculine; strong, tough; **es muy** — he's very tough.
(c) (Mech) male.
(d) (fam) stupid.
(e) (Col) big, huge, splendid, terrific (fam).
2 nm (a) (Bio) male; (Zool) mule; — **cabrío** he-goat, billy-goat; — **de varas** leading mule; (fig) person in charge.
(b) (Mech) pin, peg; (Elec) pin; plug; (Sew) hook.
(c) (Tech) sledgehammer.
(d) (Archit) buttress.
(e) (fig: person) tough guy (US fam), he-man (fam); (pej) idiot.
(f) (SAm) **parar el** — **a uno** to restrain someone; to take the wind out of someone's sails.

machón nm buttress.

machona nf (Bol, Ec, PR, RPl) mannish woman; tomboy.

machota nf (a) mannish woman. (b) (Tech) hammer, mallet; rammer. (c) **a la** — (Col, Cu) carelessly; (CAm) rudely, roughly.

machote nm (a) (fam) tough guy (US fam), he-man (fam). (b) (SAm) rough draft, sketch; model; pattern. (c) (Mex) blank form.

machucar [1g] vt (a) to pound, crush; to beat; to dent; to knock about, damage.
(b) (Med) to bruise.
(c) (Col, Mex, PR) horse to tire out (before a race).
(d) (Cu) clothes to wash badly.

machucón nm (SAm) bruise.

machucho adj (a) elderly, getting on in years. (b) prudent; sedate; wise beyond one's years. (c) (Col, Mex) cunning, sly, shrewd.

madama nf (Bol, Per, RPl) madame, brothel keeper.

madeja nf (of wool) skein, hank; (of hair) mass, mop; — **de nervios** bundle of nerves; **se está enredando la** — the affair is getting complicated, the plot thickens.

Madera Madeira.

madera[1] nm Madeira (wine).

madera[2] nf (a) wood; — (**de construcción** etc) timber; (una —) piece of wood; — **contrachapada**, — **laminada** plywood; — **de deriva** driftwood; — **dura** hardwood; — **fósil** lignite; **de** — wood, wooden; **¡toca** —**! touch wood!
(b) (Zool) horny part (of hoof).
(c) (fig) nature, temperament; aptitude; **tiene buena** — there's a lot (of good) in him, he's made of solid stuff; **tiene** — **de futbolista** he'll make a footballer, he's got football in him.

maderable adj: **árbol** — tree useful for its wood; **bosque** — wood containing useful timber.

maderaje nm, **maderamen** nm timber, wood; woodwork, timbering.

maderero nm timber merchant; lumberman.

madero nm (a) beam; log; (piece of) timber. (b) (fig) ship, vessel. (c) (fam) oaf, blockhead.

Madona f Madonna.

madrastra nf stepmother; (fig) unloving mother.

madre 1 adj (a) mother; **buque** — mother ship; **lengua** — parent language; **acequia** — main channel; **alcantarilla** — main sewer, principal sewer.
(b) (SAm) tremendous (fam), terrific (fam); **una regañada** — a tremendous dressing-down, the father and mother of a telling-off.
2 nf (a) mother; (in orphanage etc) matron; — **adoptiva** foster mother; — **política** mother-in-law; **M— de Dios** Mother of God; **¡M— de Dios!** good heavens!; **futura** — expectant mother; **su señora** — your mother; **sin** — motherless; **¡— mía!** well!; oh dear!; **ahí está la** — **del cordero** that's just the trouble.
(b) the word enters into a number of very strong insults which have no equivalents in English, eg **¡la** —**!, ¡tu** —**!; mentar la** — **a uno** to insult someone violently.

(c) (fig: of civilization etc) origin, cradle.
(d) (games) **la** — home.
(e) (Anat) womb.
(f) (of river) bed; **sacar de** — **a uno** to provoke someone, upset someone; **salirse de** — (river) to overflow, burst its banks; (person) to lose all self-control; (process etc) to go beyond its normal limits.
(g) (of wine etc) dregs, lees; sediment.
(h) (Agr) main channel, main irrigation ditch; (Tech) main sewer.
(i) (Col) dead skin, scab.

madrejón nm (Agr) watercourse.

madreperla nf mother-of-pearl; — **de río** freshwater mussel.

madreselva nf honeysuckle.

madrigal nm madrigal.

madriguera nf (a) (Zool) den; burrow. (b) (fig) den.

madrileño 1 adj of Madrid; **madrileñísimo** typical of Madrid, full of the character of Madrid; **la madrileñísima Cibeles** Cibeles Square which is so typical of Madrid, Cibeles Square which sums up so much of Madrid.
2 nm, **madrileña** nf native (or inhabitant) of Madrid; **los** —s the people of Madrid.

Madriles mpl: **Los** — (fam) Madrid.

madrina nf (a) godmother; (of enterprise etc) patron(ess), protectress; — **de boda** (approx) bridesmaid.
(b) (Archit etc) prop, shore; (Tech) brace.
(c) (Agr) leading mare.
(d) (SAm) tame animal (used in breaking in or catching others).

madroño nm strawberry tree, arbutus.

madrugada nf early morning; dawn, daybreak; **levantarse de** — to get up early; **a las 4 de la** — at 4 o'clock in the morning, at 4 a.m.

madrugador 1 adj early rising, who gets up early.
2 nm, **madrugadora** nf early riser; (fig) early bird.

madrugar [1h] **1** vt (Arg, Mex) — **a uno** to forestall someone, get in ahead of someone.
2 vi (a) to get up early; to be an early riser; **a quien madruga, Dios le ayuda** God helps those who help themselves.
(b) (fig) to get ahead; to get in first (in replying etc); (Sport) to jump the gun.

madrugón nm: **darse** (or **pegarse**) **un** — to get up terribly early.

maduración nf ripening; maturing.

madurar [1a] **1** vt (a) fruit to ripen.
(b) (fig) to mature; person to mature; to toughen (up); plan etc to think out.
2 vi (a) fruit to ripen.
(b) (fig) to mature.
3 madurarse vr to ripen.

madurez nf (a) ripeness. (b) (fig) maturity; mellowness; sageness, wisdom.

maduro 1 adj (a) fruit ripe; **poco** — unripe, underripe.
(b) (fig) mature; mellow; **de edad madura** middle-aged; **la cosa está madura para la reforma** the business is ripe for reform; **el divieso está** — the boil is about to burst.
2 nm (SAm) (ripe) banana.

maesa nf queen bee.

maestra nf (a) teacher (also fig); — **de escuela** schoolteacher. (b) (Ent) queen bee. (c) (Archit) guide line.

maestranza nf (a) arsenal, armoury; (Naut) naval dockyard. (b) staff of an arsenal (or dockyard). (c) (SAm) machine shop.

maestrazgo nm (Hist) office of grand master.

maestre nm (Hist) grand master (of a military order).

maestrear [1a] vt (a) to direct, manage. (b) (Agr) to prune.

maestría nf mastery; skill, expertise; **lo hizo con** — he did it very skilfully, he did it in a masterly fashion.

maestro 1 adj (a) masterly; skilled, expert.
(b) (Tech) main, principal; master (attr); **cloaca maestra** main sewer; **llave maestra** skeleton key, master key; **obra maestra** masterpiece; **viga maestra** main beam.
(c) (Ent) **abeja maestra** queen bee.
(d) animal trained; **halcón** — trained hawk.
2 nm (a) (in general) master; teacher; authority; — (**de escuela**) schoolteacher; (Tech) master craftsman; **el** — **de todos los medievalistas españoles** the greatest authority among the Spanish medievalists; **beber en los grandes** —s to absorb wisdom from the great teachers.
(b) (in apposition) master . . .; — **albañil** mason, skilled building craftsman; — **sastre** master tailor; **"Los** —**s cantores"** "The Mastersingers".

(c) (*Mus*) maestro; **el — Falla** the great musician (*or* composer) Falla.

(d) **— de armas, — de esgrima** fencing master; **— de ceremonias** master of ceremonies; **— de cocina** chef; **— de coros** choirmaster; **— de maquillaje** make-up expert; **— de obras** master builder; foreman.

(e) (*SAm*) skilled workman, craftsman; **— de caminos** skilled road-construction man.

mafioso *nm* (*Per, RPl*) mafioso, member of the Mafia.

Magallanes *m* Magellan.

magancear [1a] *vi* (*Col, Chi*) to idle, loaf.

magancia *nf* (*Chi*) villainy.

maganciero *adj* (*Chi*) villainous.

maganto *adj* (a) wan, wasted. (b) worried; lifeless, dull.

maganza *nf* (*Col, Ec*) idleness.

maga(n)zón *nm* (*SAm*) lazy person, idler, loafer.

Magdalena *f* Magdalen, Madeleine.

magenta *nf* magenta.

magia *nf* magic; **— negra** black magic; **por arte de —** (as if) by magic.

magiar 1 *adj* Magyar. 2 *nmf* Magyar.

mágico 1 *adj* magic, magical. 2 *nm* magician.

magín *nm* (*fam*) fancy, imagination; mind; **todo eso salió de su —** it all came out of his own head.

magisterio *nm* (a) teaching; teaching profession; **dedicarse al —** to go in for teaching; **ejerció el — durante 40 años** he taught for 40 years.
(b) teachers (*collectively*).
(c) (*fig*) pompousness, pedantry.

magistrado *nm* magistrate; judge.

magistral 1 *adj* (a) magisterial. (b) (*fig*) masterly. (c) pompous, pedantic. 2 *nm* wall clock.

magistratura *nf* magistracy; judgeship.

magnánimamente *adv* magnanimously.

magnanimidad *nf* magnanimity.

magnánimo *adj* magnanimous.

magnate *nm* magnate; tycoon; (*Hist*) baron; **los —s de la industria** the top people in industry, the big industrialists; **— de la prensa** press baron, press lord.

magnavoz *nm* (*Mex*) loudspeaker.

magnesia *nf* magnesia.

magnesio *nm* (*Chem*) magnesium; (*Phot*) flash, flashlight.

magnéticamente *adv* magnetically.

magnético *adj* magnetic.

magnetismo *nm* magnetism.

magnetizar [1f] *vt* to magnetize.

magneto *nf* magneto.

magnetofón *nm*, **magnetófono** *nm* tape recorder.

magnetofónico *adj* tape (*attr*), recording (*attr*); **cinta magnetofónica** recording tape.

magnicidio *nm* assassination (of an important person).

magníficamente *adv* splendidly, wonderfully, superbly, magnificently.

magnificar [1g] *vt* to praise, extol.

magnificencia *nf* (a) splendour, magnificence. (b) lavishness, generosity.

magnífico *adj* splendid, wonderful, superb, magnificent; **¡—!** splendid!, that's grand!; **es un muchacho —** he's a fine boy; **tenemos un — profesor** we have a splendid teacher.

magnitud *nf* magnitude (*also Astron*); **de primera —** (*Astron*) of the first magnitude.

magnolia *nf* magnolia.

mago *nm* magician, wizard; **los Reyes Magos** the Magi, the Three Wise Men.

magra *nf* (a) lean part (*of meat*). (b) slice; rasher. (c) **¡—!** (*fam*) rubbish!, not on your nelly! (*fam*).

magrez *nf* leanness.

magro *adj* (a) *person* thin, lean. (b) *meat* lean. (c) *land* poor, thin.

magrura *nf* leanness.

magua *nf* (*Ant, Ven*) disappointment; failure, setback.

maguarse [1i] *vr* (*Cu, PR, Ven*) (a) (*party etc*) to be a failure, be spoiled. (b) (*person*) to suffer a disappointment; to get depressed.

maguey *nm* (*Bot*) maguey.

maguillo *nm* wild apple tree.

magulladura *nf* bruise.

magullar [1a] *vt* to bruise; to hurt, damage; to batter, bash (*fam*); (*Per, PR*) to crumple, rumple.

magullón *nm* (*SAm*) bruise.

Maguncia Mainz.

maharajá *nm* maharajah.

Mahoma *m* Mahomet.

mahometanismo *nm* Mahommedanism.

mahometano 1 *adj* Mahommedan. 2 *nm*, **mahometana** *nf* Mahommedan.

maicena *nf* (*SAm*) cornflour, corn starch (*US*).

maicero *adj* maize (*attr*), corn (*attr*: *US*).

maitines *nmpl* matins.

maíz *nm* maize, corn (*US*), sweet corn, Indian corn; **— en la mazorca** corn on the cob.

maizal *nm* maize field, cornfield (*US*).

maja *nf* woman (*or* girl) of the people, low-class woman (*esp of Madrid*).

majada *nf* (a) sheepfold. (b) dung. (c) (*Chi, RPl*) (flock of) sheep, goats.

majaderear [1a] *vt* (*SAm*) to bother, annoy.

majadería *nf* (a) silliness; absurdity. (b) (*una —*) silly thing, absurdity; **—s** nonsense.

majadero 1 *adj* silly, stupid; rotten (*fam*), lousy (*fam*), caddish.
2 *nm* (a) idiot, fool; **— rotter**, villain, cad; **¡—!** you idiot!
(b) (*Tech*) pestle.
(c) (*Sew*) bobbin.

majador *nm* pestle.

majagranzas *adj etc* = **majadero**.

majar [1a] *vt* (a) to pound, crush, grind; to mash; (*Med*) to bruise. (b) (*fam*) to bother, pester.

majareta *adj* (*fam*) cracked, potty (*fam*).

majestad *nf* majesty; stateliness; **Su M—** His (*or* Her) Majesty; **M—, Vuestra M—** Your Majesty.

majestuosamente *adv* majestically.

majestuosidad *nf* majesty, stateliness.

majestuoso *adj* majestic, stately, imposing.

majo 1 *adj* (a) nice; pretty, attractive, handsome; lovely.
(b) smart, natty; (*pej*) flashy, gaudy.
2 *nm* (a) toff (*fam*), masher (*fam*), sport (*esp from the lower classes of Madrid, 19th century*); (*pej*) flashy sort.
(b) (*pej*) lout, bully; **echársela de —** to brag, give oneself airs.

mal 1 *adv* (a) badly; poorly; wrongly; hardly, with difficulty; **¡—!** that's bad!, oh dear!; **lo hace muy —** he does it very badly; **hace — en + infin** he is wrong to + *infin*, he is mistaken in + *ger*, it is unwise of him to + *infin*; **oigo —** I don't hear well, I have difficulty in hearing; **ahora veo bastante —** my sight is rather weak now; **huele —** it smells bad; **sabe —** it tastes nasty; **estar —** to be ill; **sentirse —** to feel ill, feel bad; **está muy — escrito** it's very badly written; **lo hice lo menos —** que pude I did it as well as I could; **me entendió —** he misunderstood me; **pero digo —** but I am wrong to say . . .; **— puedo hablar yo de este asunto** I can hardly talk about this matter, I'm hardly the right person to talk about this.
(b) (*idioms*) **— que bien** willy-nilly; rightly or wrongly; **hacer algo — que bien** to do something somehow; **ir de — en peor** to go from bad to worse, get worse; **¡menos —!** that's a relief!; **menos — que . . .** it's just as well that . . ., it's a good job that . . .

2 *conj*: **— que le pese** however much he resents it, even though he hates the idea.

3 *adj* (*apocopated form before m sing noun*) see **malo**.

4 *nm* (a) (*in general*) evil, wrong; **el bien y el —** good and evil, right and wrong; **caer en el —** to fall into evil ways; **combatir el —** to fight against evil; **echar algo a —** to despise something; to waste something, squander something; **— está en que . . .** the trouble is . . .; **estar a — con uno** to be on bad terms with someone; **no hay — que por bien no venga** it's an ill wind that blows nobody any good; **it may be a blessing in disguise; parar en — to come to a bad end.**
(b) harm, hurt, damage; misfortune; **no le deseo ningún —** I don't wish him any harm (*or* ill); **hacer — a uno** to do someone harm; **el — ya está hecho** the harm is done now; **no hay ningún —** there's no harm done; **¡— haya quien . . .!** a curse on whoever . . .!; **decir — de uno** to speak ill of someone, slander someone; **llevar** (*or* **tomar**) **algo a —** to take something amiss, be offended about something.
(c) (*Med*) disease, illness; (*fig*) suffering; **—es** (*fig*) ills; **— caduco** epilepsy; **— francés** (*Hist*) syphilis; **— de mar** seasickness; **— de ojo** evil eye; **— de la tierra** homesickness; **los —es de la economía** the things that are wrong with the economy; **dar — a uno** to make someone suffer; **darse — to** torment oneself.
(d) (*Med: SAm*) epileptic fit.

mala[1] *nf* (*Ec*) bad luck.

mala[2] *nf* (*Post*) mailbag; mail, post.

malabar *adj*: **juegos —es** juggling.

malabarismo nm (a) juggling, conjuring. (b) —s (fig) juggling; balancing act.
malabarista nmf juggler, conjurer.
Malaca f Malaya.
malacate nm winch, capstan; (Guat, Mex) spindle.
malaconsejado adj ill-advised.
malacostumbrado adj (a) having bad habits, vicious. (b) spoiled, pampered.
malacostumbrar [1a] vt (CAm): — a uno to get someone into bad habits.
malacrianza nf (SAm) = **malcriadez**.
malagradecido adj ungrateful.
malagueño 1 adj of Málaga. 2 nm, **malagueña** nf native (or inhabitant) of Málaga; los —s the people of Málaga.
malamente adj badly; poorly; wrongly; **estar — de dinero** to be badly off for money; **tenemos gasolina — para** + infin we hardly have enough petrol to + infin.
malandante adj unfortunate.
malandanza nf misfortune.
malandrín nm, **malandrina** nf (arch or hum) scoundrel, rogue.
malanga 1 adj (Cu, PR) incompetent. 2 nf (Ant, CAm, Mex) tuber resembling a sweet potato.
malapata nmf (fam) pest, nuisance; tedious individual; clumsy sort.
malaria nf malaria.
Malasia f Malaysia.
malasombra nmf (fam) = **malapata**.
malavenido adj: **estar** —s to be in disagreement, be in conflict.
malaventura nf misfortune.
malaventurado adj unfortunate.
malaya interj (SAm) damn!
Malaya f Malaya.
malayo 1 adj Malay(an). 2 nm, **malaya** nf Malay. 3 nm (language) Malay.
Malaysia f Malaysia.
malbaratar [1a] vt (Comm) to sell off cheap, sell at a loss; (fig) to squander.
malcarado adj ugly, repulsive; fierce-looking, cross-looking.
malcasado adj unhappily married; errant, unfaithful.
malcasarse [1a] vr to make an unhappy marriage.
malcomer [2a] vi to have a poor meal, eat badly.
malcontento 1 adj discontented. 2 nm, **malcontenta** nf malcontent.
malcriadez nf (SAm) bad breeding, lack of breeding.
malcriado adj rude, bad-mannered, coarse.
malcriar [1c] vt child to spoil, pamper.
maldad nf (a) evil, wickedness. (b) (una —) wicked thing.
maldecir [approx 3p] 1 vt (a) to curse.
(b) to loathe, detest.
2 vi: — **de** (a) to speak ill of; to slander; to disparage, run down.
(b) to curse, complain bitterly of.
maldiciente 1 adj that speaks ill of everything, forever criticizing; foul-mouthed. 2 nmf grumbler, complainer; malcontent; slanderer.
maldición nf curse; ¡—! curse it!, damn!; **parece que ha caído una — sobre este programa** there seems to be a curse on this programme.
maldispuesto adj ill-disposed; (Med) ill, indisposed.
maldita nf (a) tongue; **soltar la —** to talk too much; to explode angrily, blow up (fam). (b) (Cu, PR) sore, swelling; (PR, Ven) insect bite.
maldito 1 adj (a) damned (also Eccl), accursed.
(b) damned; ¡— sea! damn it!; **ese — niño** that wretched child, that blessed child; **ese — libro** that damned book; — **lo que me importa** I don't care a damn; **no le hace — el caso** he doesn't take a blind bit of notice; **no le encuentro maldita la gracia** I don't find it in the least amusing; **no sabe maldita la cosa de ello** he knows damn-all about it.
(c) wicked.
(d) (Mex) crafty.
2 nm (a) **el —** the devil.
(b) (Theat) extra.
maleabilidad nf malleability.
maleable adj malleable.
maleante 1 adj wicked; villainous, rascally; unsavoury. 2 nmf malefactor, unsavoury character, suspicious person; vagrant.
malear [1a] 1 vt to damage, spoil, harm; land to sour; (fig) to corrupt, pervert. 2 **malearse** vr to spoil, be harmed; to be corrupted.
malecón nm pier, jetty, mole.
maledicencia nf slander, scandal.

maleficiar [1b] vt (a) to bewitch, cast an evil spell on. (b) to harm, damage.
maleficio nm curse, spell; witchcraft.
maléfico adj harmful, damaging, evil.
malejo adj (fam) rather bad, pretty bad.
malentendido nm misunderstanding; **tiene que haber algún —** there must be some misunderstanding.
malestar nm (a) (Med) discomfort; indisposition. (b) (fig) uneasiness, malaise; (Pol etc) unrest.
maleta[1] adj (a) (CAm, Mex, Per, PR) naughty; mischievous; wicked. (b) (Chi, RPl) stupid; useless. (c) (Chi, RPl) sly. (d) (Arg, Mex) lazy.
maleta[2] 1 nf (a) case, suitcase; travelling bag; **hacer la —, hacer las —s** to pack (up); **ya puede preparar la —** he's on his way out, the skids are under him (fam).
(b) (Aut) boot, trunk (US).
(c) (Arg, Chi, Guat) saddlebag.
(d) (CAm, Col, Chi, Ec) bundle of clothes.
(e) (Col, Cu, PR: Anat) hump.
2 nm (fam) bungler, clumsy novice; (Taur) clumsy bullfighter; (Sport) poor player, rabbit (fam); (Theat) ham (sl).
maletera nf (a) (Col, Mex) saddlebag. (b) (Per: Aut) boot, trunk (US).
maletero nm (a) (Aut) boot, trunk (US). (b) (person) porter.
maletín nm small case, bag; satchel; — **de excursiones** picnic case; — **de grupa** (Mil) saddlebag.
maletón adj (Col) hunchbacked.
maletudo (Col, Cu, Ec, Per) 1 adj hunchbacked. 2 nm hunchback.
malevaje nm (Bol, RPl) malefactors (collectively), underworld.
malevo nm (Bol, RPl) malefactor.
malevolencia nf malevolence, malice, spite, ill will; **por —** out of spite; **sin — para nadie** with malice toward none.
malévolo adj malevolent, malicious, spiteful.
maleza nf (a) (Agr) weeds. (b) scrub; undergrowth; brushwood; thicket. (c) (Arg, Chi: Med) pus.
malezal nm (a) (Arg, Chi, PR) mass of weeds. (b) (Chi: Med) pus.
malformación nf malformation.
malgastador 1 adj spendthrift, thriftless, wasteful. 2 nm spendthrift.
malgastar [1a] vt money, resources to waste, squander; effort, time to waste; health to ruin.
malgeniado adj, **malgenio(so)** adj (SAm) bad-tempered.
maihablado adj coarse, rude; foul-mouthed.
malhadado adj ill-fated, ill-starred.
malhaya interj (SAm) damn!
malhecho nm misdeed.
malhechor nm, **malhechora** nf malefactor, criminal, wrongdoer.
malhumorado adj bad-tempered, cross, peevish.
malicia nf (a) wickedness.
(b) evil intention; spite, malice, maliciousness; **lo dijo sin —** he said it without any evil intention.
(c) (of animal) viciousness, vicious nature; (of child etc) mischief, mischievous nature.
(d) (of look, joke etc) roguishness, naughtiness, provocative nature; **contó un chiste con mucha —** he told a very naughty story; **el niño tiene demasiada — para su edad** the kid is too knowing for his age.
(e) slyness, guile.
(f) —s suspicions; **tengo mis —s** I have my suspicions.
maliciarse [1b] vr to suspect, have one's suspicions; **ya me lo maliciaba** I thought as much, it's just what I suspected.
maliciosamente adv (a) wickedly. (b) spitefully, maliciously. (c) viciously; mischievously. (d) roguishly, naughtily, provocatively. (e) slyly.
malicioso adj (a) wicked, evil.
(b) ill-intentioned; spiteful, malicious.
(c) vicious; mischievous.
(d) roguish, naughty, provocative; **una mirada maliciosa** a roguish look, a provocative glance.
(e) sly, crafty.
malignidad nf (a) (Med) malignancy. (b) evil nature, viciousness; harmfulness; malice.
maligno 1 adj (a) (Med) malignant; pernicious. (b) person evil, vicious; influence evil, pernicious, harmful; remark, attitude malicious. 2 nm: **el —** the devil.
malintencionado adj ill-disposed, hostile, unkind; malicious.
malísimamente adv very badly, dreadfully, appallingly.
malísimo adj very bad, dreadful, appalling.

malmandado *adj* disobedient; obstinate, bloody-minded (*sl*).
malmirado *adj* (a) **estar** — to be disliked. (b) thoughtless, inconsiderate.
malmodado *adj* (*Cu, Mex*) rude, rough.
malnutrido *adj* undernourished.
malo 1 *adj* (**mal** *before* m *sing noun*) (a) (*in most senses*) bad; poor; wretched, dreadful; *smell etc* bad, nasty, unpleasant; *jewel* false; *tooth, finger etc* bad, sore; *child* bad, naughty, disobedient; **este papel es — para escribir** this paper is bad for writing; **ir por mal camino** to be on the wrong road; **¡no seas —!** don't be naughty!, behave yourself!; that's a wicked thing to say!
  (b) (*Med*) **estar** — to be ill; **sentirse** — to feel ill, feel bad; **ponerse — de risa** to die of laughing.
  (c) **es muy — de vencer** he's very hard to beat; **es un animal — de domesticar** it's a difficult animal to tame.
  (d) (*idioms*) **¡—!** oh dear!, that's bad!; **lo — es que . . .** the trouble is that . . .; **a la mala** if the worst comes to the worst; (*Cu, Per, PR*) by force, forcibly; (*Chi, Mex, PR*) treacherously; **andar a malas con uno** to be on bad terms with someone; **los dos se pusieron a malas** the two fell out; **ponerse a malas con uno** to fall foul of someone, get on the wrong side of someone; **estar de malas** to be out of luck; to be in a bad mood; **venir de malas** to have evil intentions; **por las malas** by force, willy-nilly.
  2 *nm* (a) (*Rel*) **el** — the devil.
  (b) (*Theat*) villain.
  3 mala *nf* spell of bad luck.
maloca *nf* (a) (*Chi, RPl: Hist*) Indian raid. (b) (*Bol, Col*) village of uncivilized Indians.
malogrado *adj* (a) *plan etc* abortive; ill-fated; *effort etc* wasted. (b) *person* who died before his time, who died early; **el — ministro** the late-lamented minister.
malograr [1a] **1** *vt* to spoil, upset, ruin; *chance, time* to waste.
  2 malograrse *vr* (a) (*plan etc*) to fail, miscarry, come to grief.
  (b) (*person*) to die before one's time, die early, come to an untimely end.
malogro *nm* (a) failure; waste. (b) early death, untimely end.
maloliente *adj* stinking, smelly.
malón *nm* (*Chi, RPl*) (a) (*Hist*) Indian raid. (b) rowdy party. (c) dirty trick, bad turn.
malparado *adj*: **salir** — to come off badly; **salir — de** to get the worst of.
malparar [1a] *vt* to damage; to harm, impair, wreck; *person* to ill-treat.
malparir [3a] *vt* to have a miscarriage.
malparto *nm* miscarriage.
malpensado *adj* nasty, evil-minded; **¡no seas —!** don't be nasty!, don't be so horrid! (*fam*).
malquerencia *nf* dislike.
malquistar [1a] **1** *vt*: — **a dos personas** to cause a rift between two people, set one person against another; — **a A con B** to set A against B.
  2 malquistarse *vr* (a) (*person*) — **con uno** to incur the dislike of someone, become estranged from someone.
  (b) (*2 persons*) to fall out, become estranged.
malquisto *adj*: **estar** — to be disliked, be unpopular; **los dos están —s** the two are estranged.
malsano *adj* (a) *climate, atmosphere etc* unhealthy, bad. (b) (*Med*) sickly; *mind* sick, morbid.
malsín *nm* slanderer; informer, talebearer.
malsonante *adj* *word* nasty, rude, offensive.
malsufrido *adj* impatient.
Malta *f* Malta.
malta *nf* malt.
maltés 1 *adj* Maltese. **2** *nm*, **maltesa** *nf* Maltese. **3** *nm* (*language*) Maltese.
maltón *nm*, **maltoncillo** *nm* (*SAm*) young animal; child.
maltraer [2p] *vt* (a) to insult, abuse. (b) to ill-treat.
maltraído *adj* (*Arg, Bol, Chi, Per*) shabby, untidy.
maltratamiento *nm* = **maltrato**.
maltratar [1a] *vt* (a) to ill-treat, maltreat; to handle roughly, knock about, damage. (b) (*also* — **de palabra**) to abuse, insult.
maltrato *nm* (a) ill treatment, maltreatment; rough handling, damage. (b) abuse, insults.
maltrecho *adj* battered, damaged; injured; **dejar — a uno** to leave someone in a bad way.
malucho *adj* (*Med: fam*) poorly, under the weather.
malura *nf* (*Chi*) pain, discomfort; indisposition; — **de estómago** stomach ache.
malva *nf* mallow; — **loca**, — **real**, — **rósea** holly-hock; (**de**) **color de** — mauve; **ser como una** — to be very meek and mild.
malvado 1 *adj* evil, wicked, villainous. **2** *nm* villain.
malvarrosa *nf* hollyhock.
malvavisco *nm* (*Bot*) marshmallow.
malvender [2a] *vt* to sell off cheap, sell at a loss.
malversación *nf* embezzlement, misappropriation.
malversador *nm* embezzler.
malversar [1a] *vt* to embezzle, misappropriate.
Malvinas: Islas *fpl* — Falkland Isles.
malviviente *nmf* (*Mex*) = **maleante**.
malvón *nm* (*Mex, RPl*) geranium.
malla *nf* (a) mesh; network; — **de alambre** wire mesh, wire netting; **hacer** — to knit.
  (b) (*Sport*) **las** —**s** the net.
  (c) (*Hist*) chain mail.
  (d) (*Theat etc*) —**s** tights.
mallo *nm* mallet.
Mallorca *f* Majorca.
mallorquín 1 *adj* Majorcan. **2** *nm*, **mallorquina** *nf* Majorcan. **3** *nm* (*dialect of Catalán*) Majorcan.
mama *nf* mammary gland; breast; udder.
mamá *nf* (a) (*fam*) mummy (*fam*), mum (*fam*), mamma (*mainly US*), mom (*US*).
  (b) (*CAm, Mex etc*) mother; **futura** — expectant mother, mother-to-be.
mamada *nf* (a) suck; milk; feeding time. (b) (*SAm*) cinch (*sl*); soft job, plum, sinecure; bargain. (c) (*RPl*) drunkenness.
mamadera *nf* (*Ant, Arg, CAm*) rubber teat; (*SAm*) feeding bottle.
mamado *adj* (a) (*SAm*) drunk. (b) (*Cu, PR*) silly, stupid.
mamagrande *nf* (*Arg, Mex, Par*) grandmother.
mamaíta *nf* (*fam*) = **mamá** (a).
mamalón *adj* (*Ant, Ven*) idle; sponging (*fam*).
mamamama *nf* (*Per*) grandmother.
mamandurria *nf* (*SAm*) = **mamada** (b).
mamantear [1a] *vt* (*CAm, Cu, PR*) (a) to nurse, feed, suckle. (b) (*fig*) to spoil, pamper.
mamar [1a] **1** *vt* (a) *breast, milk* to suck.
  (b) (*fig*) to absorb, assimilate; to acquire in infancy.
  (c) (*fam*) *food* to wolf, bolt; *resources etc* to milk, suck dry; *funds* to pocket (illegally); **¡cómo la mamamos!** this is the life!, we never had it so good!
  2 *vi* to suck; **dar de** — **a** to feed, suckle.
  3 mamarse *vr* (a) *advantage, post etc* to wangle (*fam*), fiddle (*fam*); to land, manage to get.
  (b) — **un susto** to give oneself a scare.
  (c) — **a uno** to get the best of someone; (*Col, Chi, Mex*) to cheat someone; (*Pan*) to do someone in (*sl*).
  (d) (*esp SAm*) to get tight.
  (e) (*Col*) to go back on one's word.
mamario *adj* mammary.
mamarracha *nf*, **mamarracho** *nm* grotesque object, ridiculous sight; mess, botch; (*person*) sight, object, scarecrow; (*Art*) daub; **ella estaba hecha una** — she looked a complete mess.
mamá-señora *nf* (*Arg, Col, Cu, Nic, Par*) grandmother.
mameluca *nf* (*Chi*) whore.
mameluco *nm* (a) (*Hist*) Mameluke. (b) (*SAm*) Brazilian mestizo, half-breed. (c) (*fam*) chump (*fam*), idiot. (d) (*SAm: also* —**s**) rompers; overalls.
mamey *nm* (*SAm*) mamey, mammee.
mamífero 1 *adj* mammalian, mammal (*attr*). **2** *nm* mammal.
Mammón *m* (*Bib*) Mammon (*also fig*).
mamola *nf* chuck under the chin; **dar** (*or* **hacer**) **la — a uno** to chuck someone under the chin; (*fig*) to make a sucker out of someone (*sl*).
mamón 1 *adj* small, baby, suckling.
  2 *nm* (a) small baby, baby still at the breast.
  (b) (*Bot*) sucker, shoot.
  (c) (*Bol, RPl*) papaya tree (*or* fruit).
  (d) (*Arg, Mex, Par*) suck.
  (e) (*Guat, Hond*) club, stick.
  (f) (*Mex*) soft spongecake.
  (g) (*Cu*) tobacco from the second crop.
mamonear [1a] *vt* (a) (*Guat, Hond*) to beat. (b) (*SD*) to postpone; *time* to waste.
mamotreto *nm* (a) hefty tome, whacking great book (*fam*). (b) (*Arg, Mex*) = **armatoste**. (c) (*PR, SD*) shapeless object.
mampara *nf* screen; partition.
mamparo *nm* (*Naut*) bulkhead.
mamplora *nf* (*CAm*) queer (*fam*).
mamporro *nm* (*fam*) bash (*fam*), punch, clout; (*on falling*) bump; **atizar un — a uno** to give someone a swipe; **liarse a —s con uno** to come to blows with someone.

mampostería *nf* masonry; rubblework.

mampuesto *nm* (a) rough stone. (b) wall, parapet. (c) (*SAm*) rest (*used in aiming a gun*). (d) de — spare, emergency (*attr*), extra.

mamut *nm* mammoth.

mana *nf* (a) (*CAm, Col*) spring, fountain. (b) (*SAm*) =maná.

maná *nm* manna.

manada *nf* (a) (*Zool*) herd, flock; (*of wolves*) pack; (*of lions*) pride. (b) (*fam*) crowd, mob; a —s, en — in a mob; in crowds.

manadero *nm* shepherd, herdsman, drover.

manager ['manaʒer] *nm*, *pl* **managers** ['manaʒer] (*Sport, Theat*) manager.

manantial 1 *adj*: **agua** — running water, flowing water. 2 *nm* (a) spring, fountain; **agua de** — spring water. (b) (*fig*) source, origin; cause.

manantío *adj* running, flowing.

manar [1a] 1 *vt* to run with, flow with; — **sangre** to run with blood.

2 *vi* (a) (*of liquid*) to run, flow (**de** from, **en** with); to pour out, stream, gush forth; to well up. (b) (*fig*) to abound, be plentiful; — **de** to spring from, flow from; — **en** to flow with, abound in.

manare *nm* (*Col, Ven*) wicker basket; sieve.

manatí *nm* manatee.

manaza *nf* (a) great big hand; dirty hand. (b) **ser un** —s to be clumsy.

manazo *nm* punch, slap.

mancar [1g] *vt* (a) to maim, cripple. (b) (*Arg*) — **el tiro** to miss.

mancarrón *nm* (a) (*Arg, Urug*) worn-out horse, nag. (b) (*Arg, Chi, Per*) disabled workman. (c) (*Chi, Per*) small dam.

manceba *nf* whore; lover, mistress.

mancebía *nf* brothel.

mancebo *nm* (a) youth, young man. (b) bachelor. (c) (*Comm*) clerk; (*Pharm*) assistant, dispenser.

mancera *nf* plough handle.

mancilla *nf* stain, blemish; **sin** — unblemished, (*Rel*) immaculate, pure.

mancillar [1a] *vt* honour to stain, sully.

manco 1 *adj* (a) one-handed, one-armed; armless; crippled, maimed, disabled; — **de la izquierda** with a maimed left hand, lacking a left hand. (b) (*fig*) defective, faulty. (c) **no ser** — to be useful, be active; (*fam*) to be light-fingered, have thievish propensities; to be quite unscrupulous; A, **jugador que tampoco es** — A, who is a pretty useful player; **no ser** — **en** not to be backward in, not be lacking in skill (*etc*) in.

2 *nm*, **manca** *nf* (a) cripple, disabled person; one-armed person, one-handed person. (b) (*Chi*) old horse, nag.

mancomún: de — *adv, also* **mancomunadamente** *adv* jointly, conjointly, together; by common consent; **obrar de mancomún con uno** to act jointly with someone.

mancomunar [1a] 1 *vt* persons to unite, associate, bring together; *interests* to combine; *resources* to pool; (*Law*) to make jointly responsible.

2 **mancomunarse** *vr* to unite, merge, combine, join together.

mancomunidad *nf* union, association; pool; community; (*Pol*) commonwealth; (*Law*) joint responsibility; **la M—Británica** the British Commonwealth.

mancornar [1m] *vt* (a) *bull* to seize by the horns; to hobble. (b) (*fig*) to join, couple.

mancornas *nfpl* (*SAm*), **mancuernas** *nfpl* (*Mex*), **mancuernillas** *nfpl* (*CAm, Mex*) cufflinks.

mancha *nf* (a) (*Zool etc*) spot, mark; speckle; (*on pattern*) spot, fleck; (*of dirt*) spot, stain, mark; (*of ink etc*) blot, smudge; (*Med*) spot; bruise, mark; (*of vegetation etc*) patch, small area; (*Art*) shading, shaded area; — **solar** sunspot; —**s del sarampión** measles spots. (b) (*fig*) stain, stigma; blemish, blot; **sin** — unblemished. (c) (*Col, PR*) cloud, swarm (*of locusts etc*).

manchado *adj* skin spotty; *animal* spotted; dappled; *bird* speckled; pied; *paper etc* smudged, smudgy, covered with smudges (*etc*); **un abrigo** — **de barro** a coat stained (*or* bespattered) with mud.

manchar [1a] 1 *vt* (a) to spot, mark; to soil, dirty, stain; to smudge. (b) (*fig*) honour etc to stain, sully; *person* to soil; — **a otro** to smear someone else's reputation.

2 **mancharse** *vr* (a) to get dirty. (b) (*fig*) to stain one's reputation; to dirty one's hands, soil oneself.

manchego 1 *adj* of La Mancha. 2 *nm*, **manchega** *nf* native (*or* inhabitant) of La Mancha; **los** —s the people of La Mancha.

manchón[1] *nm* large stain, big spot (*etc*), patch; (*Bot*) patch of dense vegetation.

manchón[2] *nm* (*Arg, Chi*) muff.

Manchuria *f* Manchuria.

manchuriano 1 *adj* Manchurian. 2 *nm*, **manchuriana** *nf* Manchurian.

manda *nf* (a) bequest. (b) (*SAm*) religious vow.

mandadero *nm* messenger; errand boy, office boy.

mandado *nm* order; commission, errand, job; **muchacho de** —s errand boy, office boy; **hacer los** —s, **ir a los** —s to run errands.

mandamiento *nm* (a) order, command. (b) (*Law*) writ; warrant; — **de entrada y registro** search warrant; — **judicial** warrant; — **de venir** summons. (c) (*Eccl*) commandment; **los diez** —s the Ten Commandments.

mandar [1a] 1 *vt* (a) to order; — **que** . . . to order that . . ., give orders that . . .; — **a uno hacer algo** to order someone to do something; — **hacer un traje** to order a suit, have a suit made; — **reparar el coche** to get (*or* have) the car repaired; — **llamar a uno** to send for someone; — **salir a uno** to order someone out; **mándele sentarse** please ask him to take a seat. (b) (*Comm*) to order, ask for; **¿qué manda Vd?** what can I do for you?; **¿manda Vd algo más?** is there anything else? (c) (*Mil etc*) to lead, command; *group* to be in charge of, lead, be the leader of; *country* to rule (over). (d) to send; **le manda muchos recuerdos** he sends you warmest regards; **se lo mandaremos por correo** we'll send it to you by post, we'll post it to you. (e) to bequeath. (f) (*SAm*) to throw, hurl; to throw away. (g) (*SAm*) blow to give, strike, fetch; person to hit, punch.

2 *vi* (a) to be in charge, be in command; to be in control; **¿quién manda aquí?** who's in charge here?; **aquí mando yo** I give the orders here, I'm the boss. (b) to give the orders; **¡mande Vd!** at your service!; **¿mande?** pardon?, what did you say?; **por uno** to send for someone, fetch someone. (c) (*pej*) to be bossy, boss people about.

3 **mandarse** *vr* (a) (*Med*) to get about by oneself, manage unaided. (b) (*Archit: of rooms*) to communicate (**con** with). (c) (*Ant, Chi*) to go away, slip away; to disappear secretly. (d) (*SAm*) — **algo** to eat something up. (e) (*Arg: Mus*) — **una sinfonía** to play (*or* perform) a symphony. (f) (*SAm*) **mándese entrar** please come in; — **cambiar**, — **mudar** to go away, leave; to get out; — **con uno** to be rude to someone, be bossy to someone.

mandarín *nm* (a) mandarin; (*pej*) petty bureaucrat, jack-in-office. (b) (*SAm*) domineering person, bossy individual.

mandarina *nf* (a) (*Bot*) tangerine, mandarin (orange). (b) (*language*) Mandarin.

mandarino *nm* mandarin (orange) tree.

mandatario *nm* (a) (*Law*) agent, attorney. (b) (*SAm: Pol*) leader.

mandato *nm* (a) order; (*Law*) writ, warrant; — **judicial** (search) warrant; — **de prisión** warrant of arrest. (b) (*Law*) power of attorney. (c) (*Pol*) mandate; **territorio bajo** — mandated territory. (d) (*Pol*) term (of office); **durante su** — during his term of office. (e) (*Eccl*) maundy. (f) (*Post*) — **internacional** international money order.

mandíbula *nf* jaw (*also Tech*), mandible; **reírse a** — **batiente** to laugh one's head off.

mandil *nm* (a) (leather) apron; (*woman's*) pinafore dress. (b) (*Arg, Chi*) horse blanket.

mandilón *nm* (*fam*) coward.

mandinga 1 *adj* (a) (*CAm, RPl*) effeminate. (b) (*Arg, Ven*) impish, mischievous. 2 *nm* (a) (*SAm*) devil; goblin; evil spirit. (b) (*Col, Ec, Per, PR*) Negro.

mandioca *nf* cassava, tapioca, manioc.

mando *nm* (a) command; rule; control; authority; leadership; **alto** — high command; **un oficial al** — **de un pelotón** an officer in command of a squad; **un**

pelotón al — de un oficial a squad under the command of (or led by) an officer; **ejercer el —**, **estar al —**, **tener el —** to be in command, be in control; **entregar el —** to hand over command (or control).
(b) (in race) lead; **tomar el —** to take the lead.
(c) **—s** (persons) leaders, leadership, top people.
(d) (Mech) drive; **— a la izquierda** left-hand drive.
(e) (Mech) control; **— a distancia**, **— remoto** remote control; **— por botón** push-button control; **palanca de —** control lever.
(f) (Radio, Tech etc) **—s** controls.
(g) (Pol etc) term of office.

mandoble nm (a) two-handed blow, blow struck with two hands. (b) large sword, broadsword. (c) (fam) ticking-off.

mandolina nf mandolin(e).

mandón 1 adj bossy, domineering. **2** nm (Arg) mine foreman; (Chi: Racing) starter.

mandrágora nf mandrake.

mandria 1 adj worthless. **2** nm useless individual.

mandril[1] nm (Zool) mandrill.

mandril[2] nm (Tech) mandrel.

manducar [1g] vt (fam) to scoff (fam), stuff oneself with.

manea nf hobble.

maneador nm (Mex, RPl) hobble; (Arg) whip; (Mex) halter.

manear [1a] **1** vt to hobble. **2 manearse** vr (Col, Mex) to trip over one's own feet.

manecilla nf (a) (Tech) pointer, hand; (of watch) hand; **— grande** minute hand; **— pequeña** hour hand. (b) (of book) clasp.

maneco adj (Arg, Mex, PR) maimed; with deformed hands (or feet); knock-kneed.

manejable adj manageable; tool etc handy, easy to use; aircraft etc manoeuvrable.

manejador nm, **manejadora** nf (Mex: Aut) driver, motorist.

manejar [1a] **1** vt (a) language, tool, horse etc to handle; machine to run, work, operate; house etc to run, manage.
(b) person to manage; **ella maneja a su marido** she manages her husband, she bosses her husband about.
(c) (SAm: Aut) to drive.
2 vi (a) " **— con cuidado**" "handle with care".
(b) (SAm) to drive.
3 manejarse vr (a) to act, behave.
(b) to manage; **se maneja bien con los chiquillos** she manages all right with the kids; **¿cómo te manejas para hacer eso?** how do you manage to do that?, how do you set about doing that?; **ya se manejarán** they'll manage, they'll find a way.
(c) (Med) to get about unaided.

manejo nm (a) handling; running, working, operation; management; **— a distancia** remote control; **— doméstico**, **— de la casa** housekeeping, running the house; **una casa de fácil —** an easily-run house, a house which is easy to run; **llevar todo el — de** to be in sole charge of.
(b) confidence, ease of manner; savoir-faire, shrewdness; **no tiene bastante —** he's not sufficiently wide-awake.
(c) address, quickness, speed of action; **hay que ver el — que tiene la chica** you should see how quick the girl is.
(d) (pej) intrigue; stratagem; shady deal; **—s turbios** intrigues, underhand dealing.
(e) (SAm: Aut) driving.

manera nf (a) way, manner, fashion; **— de obrar** way of going about things; conduct; **— de ser** way of life; manner (of person); **no me gusta su —** I don't like his manner; **hay varias —s de hacerlo** there are various ways of doing it; **no hay —** there's no solution, there's nothing one can do; **no hay — con él** he's hopeless; **no hay — de + infin** there's no way of + ger; **no había — de persuadirle** there was no convincing him; **¡qué — de + infin!, ¡vaya una — de + infin!** what a way to + infin!
(b) (phrases with prep) **a la —** de in the manner of, after the fashion of; **siguen arando a la — de los abuelos** they still plough as their grandfathers did; **a mi — de ver** in my view, as I see it; **de esta —** (in) this way, like this; **¡llovía de una —!** it just was raining!, you should have seen how it rained!; **de la — que sea** in whatever way you (etc) like; however he (etc) does it; **la pegó de mala —** he hit her really hard; **le han estafado de mala —** they really have cheated him, they've properly done him down; **de la misma —** in the same way; **de otra —** otherwise, if not; **de ninguna —** by no means; **¡de ninguna —!**

certainly not!, never!; **de tal — que ...** in such a way that . . .; **to such a degree that . . .**; **de — que . . .** so that . . .; **¿de — que esto no le gusta?** so you don't like it?; **de todas —s** at any rate; **en cierta —** up to a point, to some degree; **en gran —** in great measure; greatly, extremely; **sobre —** exceedingly; for other phrases, compare modo (a) and (b).
(c) (lit) kind, sort; **es otra — de afirmación** it is another kind of affirmation; it is another method of saying yes; **que es otra — de valentía** which is another kind of courage.
(d) (Art, Lit etc) manner, style; **la segunda — de Picasso** Picasso's second manner; **las dos —s de Góngora** the two styles of Góngora.
(e) **—s** (of person) manners; **de —s muy groseras** with very rude manners; **se lo dije con buenas —s** I told him politely; **tener —s** (SAm) to have good manners, show breeding.

maneto adj (Col, Guat, Hond, PR) = **maneco**.

manflor(ita) nm (SAm) pansy (fam), queer (fam).

manga nf (a) sleeve; **— de camisa** shirtsleeve; **estar en —s de camisa** to be in one's shirtsleeves; **sin —s** sleeveless; **estar de —** to be in league; **ser de — ancha, tener — ancha** to be easy-going, be over-indulgent, be too lenient; to be broad-minded; (pej) to be not overscrupulous; **andar — por hombro** to be terribly poor; **pegar las —s** (sl) to kick the bucket (sl).
(b) (also **— de riego**) hose, hosepipe; **— de incendios** fire hose.
(c) (Cook) filter, strainer.
(d) (Aer) windsock, windgauge.
(e) portmanteau.
(f) (Meteorol) cloudburst; **— marina** waterspout; **— de viento** whirlwind.
(g) (Naut) beam, breadth.
(h) (Bridge) game; **ir a —** to go to game.
(i) (SAm) crowd, mob, swarm.
(j) (SAm: Agr) funnel, narrow entrance (to a corral etc).
(k) (CAm) poncho, coarse blanket.
(l) (Col) pasture.

mangal nm (SAm) = **manglar**.

mangana nf lasso, lariat.

manganear [1a] vt (a) to lasso. (b) (Per) to bother, annoy. (c) (Guat, Urug) to pillage, plunder; to steal.

manganeso nm manganese.

manganeta nf (SAm), **manganilla** nf (Mex) disappearing trick; (fig) swindle, dodge, racket.

mangante 1 adj brazen. **2** nm beggar, scrounger (fam); brazen individual.

mangar [1h] **1** vt (a) to plug in, fit together.
(b) (fam) to swipe (sl), pinch (fam).
(c) (fam) to beg (for), scrounge (fam).
2 vi (Arg) to live by scrounging (fam), live on graft.

mangazón adj (SAm) lazy.

manglar nm mangrove swamp.

mangle nm mangrove.

mango[1] nm (Bot) mango.

mango[2] nm handle, haft; **— de escoba** broomstick, (Aer: fam) joystick; **— de pluma** penholder.

mangón nm (Arg, Bol, Col) pasture; cattle ranch.

mangoneador nm (a) meddler, interfering sort; bossy individual. (b) (SAm) corrupt official, grafter.

mangonear [1a] **1** vt (a) person to manage, boss about.
(b) (fam) to swipe (sl), pinch (fam).
(c) (SAm) to pillage, plunder.
2 vi (a) to meddle, interfere (en in); to dabble (en in).
(b) to boss people about; to take charge and insist on doing everything oneself; to thrust oneself brazenly forward.
(c) (SAm) to graft, be on the fiddle (fam).

mangoneón, mangonero 1 adj meddlesome, interfering; bossy; brazen. **2** nm busybody; bossy individual; brazen sort.

mangosta nf mongoose.

manguear [1a] **1** vt (Arg, Chi, Mex) cattle to drive; game to beat, put up.
2 vi (a) (Col, PR, Ven) to pretend to be working.
(b) (Ant, Ven) to beckon.

manguera nf (a) hose, hosepipe; pipe, tube; **— de aspiración** suction pump; **— de incendios** fire hose.
(b) (Col) bicycle tyre.
(c) (Meteorol) waterspout.
(d) (Chi, RPl) corral, yard.

manguillo nm (Mex) penholder.

manguito nm (a) muff. (b) (Tech) sleeve; coupling; **— incandescente** gas mantle.

maní nm, pl **maníes** or **manises** (a) (SAm) peanut, groundnut plant. (b) (Cu, PR: fam) dough (sl), money. (c) (RPl) **¡—!** never!

manía nf (a) (Med) mania; — **de grandezas** megalomania; — **persecutoria** persecution mania.

(b) (fig) mania; rage, craze (de for); whim, fad; peculiarity, oddity; **la — del fútbol** the soccer craze; **la — de la minifalda** the fashion for miniskirts; **tiene —s** she's rather odd, she has her little ways; **tiene la — de +** infin she has the (odd) habit of + ger; **ha dado en la — de salir sin abrigo** she's taken to going out without a coat.

(c) (pej) dislike; spite, ill will; **tener — a uno** to dislike someone; **el maestro me tiene —** the teacher has got it in for me; **tiene — a los eslobodos** he can't stand the Slobodians.

maniabierto adj (PR, SD) lavish, generous.

maníaco 1 adj maniac(al). **2** nm, **maníaca** nf maniac; **— sexual** sex maniac.

maniacodepresivo 1 adj manic-depressive. **2** nm, **maniacodepresiva** nf manic-depressive.

maniatar [1a] vt person to tie the hands of; to handcuff; animal to hobble.

maniático 1 adj (a) maniacal.

(b) (fig) crazy; odd, eccentric, peculiar; cranky.

(c) stubborn.

2 nm, **maniática** nf (a) maniac.

(b) (fig) maniac; odd individual, eccentric, crank.

manicero nm (SAm) peanut seller.

manicomio nm lunatic asylum, mental hospital.

manicura nf manicure.

manicuro nm, **manicura** nf manicurist.

manida nf lair, den.

manido adj (a) meat high, gamy; smelly. (b) subject etc trite, stale.

manierismo nm (Art, Lit) mannerism.

manierista 1 adj mannerist. **2** nmf mannerist.

manifestación nf (a) (of emotion etc) manifestation; show; sign; **una gran — de entusiasmo** a great show of enthusiasm.

(b) (of policy etc) statement, declaration.

(c) (Pol) demonstration; mass meeting; riot.

manifestante nmf demonstrator; rioter.

manifestar [1k] **1** vt (a) emotion etc to show, manifest, demonstrate, reveal.

(b) policy etc to state, declare; to express.

2 manifestarse vr (a) (emotion etc) to show, be manifest; to become apparent; **— en** to be evident in (or from), be revealed by, be shown by.

(b) (Pol) to demonstrate; to hold a mass meeting; to riot.

manifiesto 1 adj clear, manifest; evident, obvious; error glaring, obvious; truth manifest; **poner algo de —** to make something clear; to disclose something, reveal something; **quiero poner de — que . . .** I wish to state that . . .; **quedar —** to be plain, be clear.

2 nm (a) (Naut) manifest.

(b) (Pol) manifesto.

manigua nf (Ant, Mex) swampy scrubland, jungle; (fig) countryside; **irse a la —** to take to the hills (in revolt).

manigual nm (Ant) = **manigua**.

manigueta nf (a) handle, haft; crank; (RPl: Aut) starting handle. (b) hobble.

manija nf (a) handle. (b) (Mech) clamp, collar; (Rail) coupling. (c) (Agr) hobble.

manilargo adj (a) open-handed. (b) (SAm) light-fingered, thievish.

manilense 1 adj of Manila. **2** nmf native (or inhabitant) of Manila; **los —s** the people of Manila.

manileño = **manilense**.

manilla nf (a) bracelet; **—s (de hierro)** handcuffs, manacles. (b) (of watch) hand.

manillar nm handlebar(s).

maniobra nf (a) (act) handling; manoeuvring; operation, control; (Rail) shunting; **hacer —s** to manoeuvre (Rail) to shunt.

(b) (Naut) seamanship, (art of) navigation; handling.

(c) (Naut) gear, rigging.

(d) **—s** (Mil) manoeuvres.

(e) (fig) manoeuvre, move; (pej) trick, stratagem; **mediante una hábil —** by a clever move; **es una — para expulsar al jefe** it's a manoeuvre to get rid of the chief.

maniobrabilidad nf manoeuvrability; handling qualities.

maniobrable adj manoeuvrable; easy to handle.

maniobrar [1a] **1** vt to handle, operate; to manoeuvre; (Rail) to shunt. **2** vi to manoeuvre (also fig).

maniota nf hobble.

manipulación nf manipulation.

manipulador 1 nm, **manipuladora** nf manipulator; handler. **2** nm (Elec, Tel) key, tapper.

manipular [1a] **1** vt to manipulate; to handle. **2** vi: **— con, — en** to manipulate.

maniquí 1 nm (a) (tailor's) dummy, manikin; (Fencing etc) dummy figure. (b) (fig) puppet. **2** nf mannequin, model.

manirroto 1 adj lavish, extravagant, prodigal. **2** nm spendthrift.

manisero nm (SAm) = **manicero**.

manita nf little hand; **—s de cerdo** (etc) trotters; **—s de plata** (or de oro) delicate hands, artistic hands, talented hands; **echar una — a uno** to lend someone a hand; **hacer —s** (of lovers) to hold hands (con with).

manito[1] nm (SAm) = **hermanito (hermano)**; (in direct address) mate (fam), chum.

manito[2] nm (SAm) = **manita**.

manivacío adj empty-handed.

manivela nf crank; **— de arranque** starting handle.

manjar nm (tasty) dish, special dish; **— blanco** blancmange; **— delicado, — exquisito** tasty morsel; **— espiritual** food for the mind, spiritual sustenance.

mano[1] nf (a) (Anat) hand; (Zool) foot, forefoot, paw; (elephant's) trunk; (of bird) foot, (of hawk) claws, talons.

(b) (in fig phrases, mostly) hand; **— derecha** (fig) right-hand man; **—s muertas** (Law) mortmain; **— de santo** sure remedy; **última —** final touch, finishing touch; **¡—s a la obra!** to work!, let's get on with it!; **¡—s quietas!** hands off!, keep your hands to yourself!; **¡qué —!** (SAm) what luck!; what a surprise!; how ghastly! (fam), how horrid! (fam).

(c) (phrases with prep) **a —** by hand; **bordado a —** hand-embroidered; **hecho a —** handmade; **escribir a —** to write in longhand, write out; **girar una manivela a —** to turn a crank by hand; **mandar algo a —** to send something by hand; **estar a (la) —** to be at hand, be on hand, be handy; to be within one's grasp; **¡eso está a la —!** that's obvious!; **a — airada** violently; **robo a — armada** armed robbery; **a — salva** without risk; **estar (or quedar) a — (**SAm) to be quits, be even; **a —s llenas** lavishly, generously; **dirigir una carta a —s de uno** to send a letter care of (c/o) someone; **morir a —s de** to die at the hands of; **llegó a mis —s** it reached me, it came into my hands; **llegar a las —s** to come to blows; **si a — viene** when it comes to the point; yet; **¡arriba las —s!** hands up!; **bajo —** in secret, behind the scenes; in an underhand way; **coger a uno con las —s en la masa** to catch someone red-handed, catch someone in the act; **de —** hand (attr), eg **equipaje de —** hand-luggage; **los dos iban de la —** the two were walking hand-in-hand; **llevar a uno de la —** to lead someone by the hand; **de buena —** on good authority; **de primera —** (at) first-hand; **de segunda —** (at) secondhand; **de —s de** at the hands of; **recibir algo de —s de uno** to receive something from someone; **de —s a boca** unexpectedly, suddenly; **vivir de la — a la boca** to live from hand to mouth; **dar de — to** stop working; **darse de —s con uno** to come across someone; **dejar a uno de la —** to abandon someone; **no pude dejar el libro de la —** I couldn't put the book down; **ponerse de —s** (horse) to rear (up); **en —s de** in the hands of, into the hands of; **ha hecho cuanto ha estado en su —** he has done all in his power (para + infin to + infin); **traer un asunto entre —s** to have a matter in hand; to have a matter on one's hands; **¡fuera las —s!** hands off!, keep your hands to yourself!; **ganar por la — a uno** to beat someone to it; **tomarse la justicia por su —** to take justice into one's own hands; **estar — sobre —** to be idle, be out of work.

(d) (phrases with verb) **alzar la — a** (or contra) to raise one's hand against; **cargar la —** to overdo it; to press too hard, be too exacting; (Comm) to overcharge; (Cook) to put too much spice (etc) in; **darse las —s** to join hands; to shake hands; **déle la — y se tomará el pie** give him an inch and he'll take a yard; **echar una — to** lend a hand (a to); **echar — a** to lay hands on; **echar — de** to make use of; to resort to; **estrechar la — a uno** to shake someone's hand; **hacerse la —, hacerse las —s** to get one's hand in; **se le fue la —** his hand slipped (also fig); **meter — a uno** to bring someone to book; **meter — a una** to make a pass at a girl; **no hay quien le meta —** there's nobody to touch him; **pasar la — a uno** (SAm) to flatter someone, suck up to someone (fam); **sentar la — a uno** to beat someone, (fig) to bring someone to heel; (Comm) to overcharge someone; **tener buena —** to be lucky; to have the knack; **tener mala —** to be clumsy, be awkward; **tener — con** to have a way with; **tener — para** to be clever at; **tener las —s largas** to be light-fingered; **untar la — a uno** to grease someone's palm; **¡venga esa —!** shake!, put it there!

(e) (*Sport*) handling, handball; **¡—!** handball!

(f) (*of watch*) hand.

(g) (*of paint*) coat; (*of soap*) wash, soaping; **dar una — de jabón a la ropa** to give the clothes a soaping.

(h) (*Cards etc*) hand; round; game; **echar una — de mus** to have a game (*or* hand) of *mus*; **ser —, tener la —** to lead; **soy —** it's my lead.

(i) (*Mus*) scale.

(j) **— de almirez** pestle.

(k) lot, series; (*CAm, Chi, Ec, Mex*) group of 5 (*or* 4, 6) things of the same kind; (*SAm: of bananas*) bunch, hand; **una — de bofetadas** a series of punches; **una — de papel** a quire of paper.

(l) **— de obra** labour, manpower; labour force; **— de obra especializada** skilled labour.

(m) **—s** (*fig*) hands, workmen; **contratar —s** to sign up workmen.

(n) (*SAm*) misfortune, mishap; unexpected event.

mano² *nm* (*SAm*)=**hermano**; (*in direct address*) mate (*fam*), chum.

manojo *nm* handful, bunch; (*fam*) bunch; (*Cu, PR*) bundle of raw tobacco (*about 2 lbs*); **— de hierba** tuft of grass; **— de llaves** bunch of keys; **— de pillos** bunch of rogues.

manoletina *nf* (*Taur*) *a kind of pass with the cape*.

Manolo *m* *pet name for* **Manuel**.

manolo *nm* toff (*fam*), masher (*fam*) (*esp Madrid equivalent of* cockney).

manómetro *nm* (pressure) gauge; **— de aceite** oil gauge; **— de combustible** fuel gauge.

manopla *nf* (a) flannel, face flannel. (b) (*Hist, Tech etc*) gauntlet. (c) (*Chi, PR*) knuckleduster.

manoseado *adj* (*fig*) hackneyed, well-worn.

manosear [1a] *vt* (a) to handle, finger, touch; to rumple, mess up; to paw; to fiddle with, mess about with; (*SAm*) to caress, fondle, feel (sexually).

(b) *theme etc* to overwork, repeat.

manoseo *nm* (a) handling, fingering, touching; rumpling; pawing; (*SAm*) caressing, fondling. (b) overworking, repetition.

manotada *nf* (a) slap, smack. (b) (*Col, Chi, Mex*) handful, fistful.

manotazo *nm* slap, smack.

manoteador *nm* (*Arg, Mex*) (a) bag-snatcher. (b) gesticulator.

manotear [1a] **1** *vt* to slap, smack, cuff. **2** *vi* to gesticulate, move (*or* use) one's hands.

manoteo *nm* gesticulation.

manque *conj* (*SAm: fam*)=**aunque**.

manquear [1a] *vi* to be maimed, be crippled; to pretend to be crippled; (*Mex, RPl*) to limp.

manquedad *nf*, **manquera** *nf* (a) disablement, crippled state, bodily incapacity. (b) (*fig*) defect.

mansalino *adj* (*Chi*) huge; extraordinary.

mansalva: a — without risk, without any danger; **le dispararon a —** they shot him with complete certainty of hitting him; **estar a — de** to be safe from.

mansamente *adv* gently, mildly, meekly.

mansarda *nf* (*Arg, Chi, Mex*) attic.

mansedumbre *nf* (a) gentleness, meekness. (b) tameness.

mansión *nf* (*esp SAm: angl*) mansion.

manso *adj* (a) gentle, mild, meek. (b) *animal* tame.

manta *nf* (a) blanket; shawl; **— eléctrica** electric blanket; **— de viaje** travelling rug; **a — (de Dios)** plentifully, abundantly; **liarse la — a la cabeza** to decide to go the whole hog; to press on regardless; **tirar de la —** to let the cat out of the bag, give the game away.

(b) (*Col, Mex, Ven*) coarse cotton cloth; (*Chi, Ec*) poncho.

(c) (*fam*) hiding.

mantear [1a] *vt* (a) to toss in a blanket. (b) (*Arg, PR*) to ill-treat, abuse. (c) (*Mex, PR*) to set on, beat up.

manteca *nf* (a) (animal) fat; (*SAm*) butter; **— de cacahuete** peanut butter; **— de cacao** cocoa butter; **— de cerdo** lard; **— de vaca** butter; **— vegetal** vegetable fat.

(b) (*Col*) servant, girl.

mantecado *nm* (*approx*) ice cream.

mantecón *nm* (*fam*) milksop, mollycoddle.

mantecoso *adj* fat, greasy; buttery.

mantel *nm* tablecloth; (*Eccl*) altar cloth; **levantar los —es** to clear the table; **poner los —es** to lay the table.

mantelería *nf* table linen.

mantelillo *nm* table runner.

mantención *nf* (*SAm*)=**manutención**.

mantenedor *nm* (*of contest*) chairman, president; **— de la familia** breadwinner.

mantener [2l] **1** *vt* (a) (*Archit, Tech etc*) to hold up, support; **— algo en equilibrio** to keep something balanced.

(b) *idea, opinion* to support, defend, maintain; *person* to sustain, support.

(c) *fire etc* to keep in, keep going; (*of food*) to sustain; **le mantiene la esperanza** he is sustained by hope, hope keeps him going.

(d) (*Fin*) to maintain, support.

(e) (*Mech etc*) to maintain, service.

(f) *custom, discipline, relations etc* to keep up, maintain.

(g) **— + adj** to keep + *adj*; **— la comida caliente** to keep the food hot; **"Mantenga limpia España"** "Keep Spain clean".

2 mantenerse *vr* (a) **se mantiene todavía en pie** it is still standing.

(b) **— firme** to hold one's ground, not give way; **— en vigor** to stand, remain in force; **— en un puesto** to stay in one's job, keep one's post; **— en contacto con** to keep up one's contacts with.

(c) to sustain oneself, subsist, keep going (*con, de on*); **se mantiene con leche** she keeps going on milk.

mantenido *nm* (*Guat, Mex*) pimp; kept man, gigolo; sponger (*fam*), parasite.

mantenimiento *nm* maintenance; upkeep; support, sustenance.

mantequera *nf* (a) churn. (b) butter dish.

mantequería *nf* dairy, creamery; grocer's (shop).

mantequilla *nf* butter.

mantequillera *nf* (*SAm*) butter dish.

mantilla *nf* (a) mantilla; **— de blonda, — de encajes** lace mantilla.

(b) **—s** baby clothes; **estar en —s** (*person*) to be terribly innocent; (*plan*) to be in the very early stages, be in its infancy; **dejar a uno en —s** to leave someone helpless.

mantillo *nm* humus, mould.

mantillón *nm* (*CAm, Mex*) coloured horse blanket.

mantis *nf, pl* **mantis** mantis; **— religiosa** praying mantis.

manto *nm* (a) cloak; (*Eccl, Law etc*) robe, gown.

(b) (*Zool*) mantle.

(c) (*Archit: also* **— de chimenea**) mantel.

(d) (*Min*) layer, stratum.

(e) (*fig*) cloak, mantle.

mantón *nm* shawl.

mantudo *adj* (a) *bird* with drooping wings. (b) (*CAm*) masked, in disguise.

manuable *adj* handy, easy to handle.

manual 1 *adj* (a) manual, hand (*attr*); **habilidad —** manual skill; **tener habilidad —** to be clever with one's hands; **obrero —** manual worker, worker who uses his hands; **trabajo —** manual labour.

(b)=**manuable**.

2 *nm* manual, handbook, guide.

manualmente *adv* manually, by hand.

manubrio *nm* (a) handle, crank; winch. (b) (*SAm*) handlebar(s). (c) (*Mus*) barrel organ.

manudo *adj* (*SAm*) with big hands.

Manuel *m* Emmanuel.

manufactura *nf* (a) (*act, product*) manufacture. (b) factory.

manufacturar [1a] *vt* to manufacture.

manufacturero 1 *adj* manufacturing. **2** *nm* (*SAm*) manufacturer.

manuscrito 1 *adj* handwritten, manuscript. **2** *nm* manuscript.

manutención *nf* (a) maintenance; support; keep, board. (b) (*Mech etc*) maintenance.

manyar [1a] *vti* (*Chi, PR, RPl*) to eat.

manzana *nf* (a) apple; **— de la discordia** (*fig*) apple of discord, bone of contention; **— silvestre** wild apple, crab apple.

(b) (*SAm: Anat*) **— de Adán** Adam's apple.

(c) (*Archit: esp SAm*) block.

(d) (*Arg*) *land measure,*=2.5 *acres*; (*CAm*) *land measure,*=1.75 *acres*.

manzanal *nm* (a) apple orchard. (b) apple tree.

manzanar *nm* apple orchard.

manzanilla *nf* (a) (*Bot*) camomile; camomile tea. (b) *a variety of small olive*. (c) manzanilla (*a very dry sherry-type wine*).

manzano *nm* apple tree.

maña *nf* (a) (*in general*) skill, dexterity; ingenuity; (*pej*) craft, guile; **con —** craftily, slyly; **darse — para + infin** to contrive to + *infin*.

(b) (*una —*) trick, knack; (**malas**) **—s** evil ways, bad habits, vices; (*of child etc*) naughty ways; **tiene**

— **para hacerlo** he's got the knack of doing it; **es una — para conseguir algo** it's a trick (or ruse) to get something.

(c) (Col) idleness; **hacer —** to kill time.

mañana 1 adv (a) tomorrow; **— por la —** tomorrow morning; **¡hasta —!** see you tomorrow!; **pasado —** the day after tomorrow; **— temprano** early tomorrow.

(b) later, some other time; in time to come; **vuelva Vd —** come back later.

2 nm future; **el — es incierto** the future is uncertain.

3 nf (a) morning; tomorrow; **a la —** in the morning; **a la — siguiente** (on) the following morning, the morning after; **a las 7 de la —** at 7 o'clock, at 7 a.m.; **de —, por la —** in the morning; **muy de —** very early in the morning; **— es otro día** there's a new day tomorrow.

(b) (SAm) **tomar la —** to take a shot of liquor before breakfast.

mañanero 1 adj early-rising, who gets up early. 2 nm, **mañanera** nf early riser.

mañanita nf (a) early morning; **de —** very early in the morning, at the crack of dawn. (b) bed jacket.

mañear [1a] 1 vt to manage cleverly, contrive skilfully. 2 vi to act shrewdly, go about things cunningly; (pej) to get up to one's tricks.

mañero adj (a) = **mañoso** (a). (b) (RPl) animal vicious; obstinate; shy, nervous.

mañosamente adv cleverly, ingeniously, skilfully; (pej) craftily.

mañosear [1a] vi (Arg, Col, Chi, Ven)=**mañear** 2; (Arg, Mex: of child) to be difficult (esp about food).

mañoso adj (a) clever, ingenious, skilful; (pej) sharp, crafty, wily.

(b) (Col) lazy, indolent.

(c) (Arg, CAm, Mex, Per) animal vicious; obstinate; shy, nervous; (Arg, Mex) child difficult (esp about food).

mapa nm map; **— geológico** geological map; **— meteorológico** weather map; **— mural** wall map; **— en relieve** relief map.

mapache nm rac(c)oon.

mapamundi nm globe; world map.

mapeango adj, **mapiango** adj (Cu, Mex) useless, incompetent.

mapurito nm (CAm) skunk.

maque nm lacquer.

maquear [1a] vt to lacquer.

maqueta nf model, scale model, mock-up, maquette.

maquiavélico adj Machiavellian.

Maquiavelo m Machiavelli.

maquillador nm, **maquilladora** nf (Theat etc) make-up assistant.

maquillaje nm make-up; (act) making-up.

maquillar [1a] 1 vt to make up. 2 **maquillarse** vr to make up.

máquina nf (a) machine; (Rail) engine, locomotive; (Phot) camera; (fam) bike (fam); (Cu) car; taxi; **— de afeitar** (safety) razor; **— de afeitar eléctrica** electric razor, shaver; **— de calcular, — computadora** computer; **— de contabilidad, — de sumar** adding machine; **— copiadora** copier, copying machine; **— de coser** sewing machine; **— de direcciones** Addressograph (Protected Trade Name); **— de discos** juke box; **— electrónica, — tragaperras** fruit machine, one-armed bandit; (Comm) slot machine; (Mus) juke box; **— de escribir** typewriter; **— fotográfica** camera; **— herramienta** machine tool; **— de lavar** washing machine; **— de matasellar** franking machine; **— para hacer punto, — de tricotar** knitting machine; **— registradora** (SAm) cash register; **— de vapor** steam engine; **hecho a —** machine-made; script typed; **acabar a —, coser** (etc) **a —** to machine; **escribir a —** to type; **entrar en —** to go to press.

(b) (Archit) imposing building; edifice; structure.

(c) (fig) machinery, workings; scheme of things.

(d) (fig) plan, project.

maquinación nf machination, scheme, plot.

maquinador nm, **maquinadora** nf schemer, plotter.

maquinal adj (fig) mechanical, automatic.

maquinalmente adv (fig) mechanically, automatically.

maquinar [1a] vti to plot, machinate.

maquinaria nf (a) machinery; plant; **— agrícola** agricultural machinery, farm implements. (b) (of watch etc) mechanism, works.

maquinilla nf small machine; winch; (for hair) clippers; **— de afeitar** (safety) razor; **— eléctrica** electric razor, shaver; **— para liar cigarrillos** cigarette(-rolling) machine.

maquinista nm (Rail) engine driver, engineer (US); (Naut etc) engineer; (Tech) operator, machinist.

maquinístico adj (fig) mechanical; materialistic.

mar[1] nm and f (a) sea; ocean; tide; **— de fondo** groundswell; **— gruesa** heavy sea; **— llena** high tide; **— adentro, — afuera** out at sea, out to sea; **caer al —** to fall into the sea, (from ship) to fall overboard; **de alta —** boat seagoing, ocean-going; fishing deep-water (attr); **en alta —** on the high seas; **por —** by sea, by boat; **arar en el —** to labour in vain; **echar a la —** to launch; **es hablar de la —** its all very vague; it's just a dream; **hacerse a la —** to put to sea; to stand out to sea.

(b) **M— Adriático** Adriatic Sea; **M— de las Antillas, M— Caribe** Caribbean Sea; **M— Báltico** Baltic Sea; **M— Caspio** Caspian Sea; **M— Mediterráneo** Mediterranean Sea; **M— Muerto** Dead Sea; **M— Negro** Black Sea; **M— del Norte** North Sea; **M— Rojo** Red Sea.

(c) **un — de confusiones** a sea of confusion, a welter of confusion; **hay un — de diferencia** there's a world of difference.

(d) **estar hecho un — de lágrimas, llorar a —es** to weep floods; **llover a —es** to rain cats and dogs, rain in torrents.

(e) (fam) **la —** (as adv) a lot; **la — de cosas** lots of things, no end of things, ever so many things; **es la — de tonto** he's no end of a fool; **es la — de guapa** she's awfully pretty (fam); **está la — de contento** he's terribly happy (fam).

mar[2] nf: euph for **madre** (in obscene expressions).

mar[3] interj (Mil) march!; see **frente** etc.

maraca nf (a) (SAm) maraca, rattle. (b) (Chi) whore. (c) (Col, PR, Ven) useless person.

maraña nf (a) (Bot) thicket; tangle of plants. (b) (of threads etc) tangle. (c) (fig) mess, tangle; jungle; puzzle. (d) (fam) trick, ruse. (e) (Col) small tip.

marañero 1 adj scheming. 2 nm schemer.

marañón nm (Bot) cashew.

maraquear [1a] vt (SAm) to shake, rattle.

marasmo nm (a) (Med) wasting; atrophy. (b) (fig) paralysis, stagnation.

maravedí nm, pl **maravedíes** or **maravedises** old Spanish coin.

maravilla nf (a) marvel, wonder; wonderment; **las siete —s del mundo** the seven wonders of the world; **hacer —s** to work wonders; **ir a —, ir a las mil —s** to go wonderfully well, go extremely well; to go swimmingly; **lo hace a —** he does it perfectly, he does it splendidly; **por —** for a wonder; by chance; very seldom.

(b) (Bot) marigold.

maravillar [1a] 1 vt to astonish, amaze. 2 **maravillarse** vr to be astonished, be amazed (con, de at); **— con, — de** to wonder at, marvel at.

maravillosamente adv wonderfully, marvellously.

maravilloso adj wonderful, marvellous.

marbete nm (a) label; tag, ticket, docket; **— engomado** sticker. (b) (Sew) edge, border.

marca 1 nf (a) mark; stamp; name tab; (of foot) footprint, footmark; (in paper) watermark; (Comm) trademark; (Comm) make, brand; **— de agua, — transparente** watermark; **— de fábrica** trademark; **— de ley** hallmark; **— registrada** registered trademark; **de —** excellent, outstanding; **de — mayor** absolutely outstanding; really big; **coches de 3 —s distintas** cars of 3 different makes; **productos de varias —s** various brands of products.

(b) (Naut) seamark; marker, buoy; landmark.

(c) (Sport) record; **batir la —, mejorar la —** to break the record; **establecer una —** to set up a record.

(d) (Cards) bid.

(e) (tool) stamp.

(f) (Hist) march, frontier area; **la M— Hispánica** the Spanish March (Catalonia).

2 nm (Rowing) stroke.

marcable adj (Cards) biddable.

marcación nf (Naut) bearing.

marcadamente adv markedly.

marcado 1 adj marked, strong, pronounced; distinct; **con — acento argentino** with a marked Argentinian accent. 2 nm hairnet.

marcador nm (a) marker (also Billiards); bookmark; **— de caminos** roadsign. (b) (Sport) scoreboard; (person) scorer.

marcar [1g] 1 vt (a) (general sense) to mark (de with); to brand, stamp (de with); ground etc to mark off, mark out; clothing to put one's name on, embroider a name on.

(b) (fig) to mark, indicate, point to; (of dial, thermometer etc) to show, register, record, read, say;

las agujas **marcan las 2** the hands point to 2 o'clock; **el tanteador marca 3 goles** the scoreboard shows 3 goals; **mi reloj marca la hora exacta** my watch keeps exact time.

(c) *numbers etc* to keep a tally (*or* score) of, record; *score* (*Sport*) to keep.

(d) (*Mus etc*) *pace, step* to mark; *time* to beat, keep.

(e) (*Tel*) to dial.

(f) (*Cards*) to bid.

(g) (*Sport*) *goal, point* to score (*also fig*); **— un tanto en la discusión** to score a point in the argument.

(h) *task* to assign, set; *policy* to lay down.

(i) (*Comm*) to put a price on.

(j) *hair* to set.

2 *vi* (a) (*Sport*) to score.

(b) (*Tel*) to dial.

3 marcarse *vr* (a) (*Naut*) to take one's bearings.

(b) (*Sport*) to score.

(c) (*fam*) to make one's mark, stand out; **— con relieve** to stand out in relief.

Marcial *m* Martial.

marcial *adj law etc* martial; *bearing, discipline* military.

marciano 1 *adj* Martian. **2** *nm*, **marciana** *nf* Martian.

marco *nm* (a) (*Art, Archit, of mirror etc*) frame; **— de chimenea** mantelpiece; **— para cuadro** picture frame; **— de ventana** window frame; **poner — a un cuadro** to frame a picture.

(b) (*Sport*) goal-posts.

(c) (*fig*) setting; **el paisaje ofreció un bello — para la fiesta** the countryside made a splendid setting for the festivity.

(d) (*fig: of scheme etc*) framework.

(e) (*Fin*) mark.

(f) (*of weights etc*) standard.

márcola *nf* (*prov*) pruning hook.

Marcos *m* Mark.

marcha *nf* (a) (*Mil etc*) march; **— forzada** forced march; **— del hambre** hunger march; **a largas —s** speedily; **a —s forzadas** (*fig*) with all speed, as a matter of great urgency; **abrir la —** to come first, be at the head of the procession (*etc*); **cerrar la —** to come last, bring up the rear; **¡en —!** (*Mil*) forward march!; (*fig*) let's go!, (*to someone else*) get going!, get moving!; (*fig*) here goes!; **España es país en —** Spain is a country on the move; **estar en —** to be in motion, be going; (*Naut*) to be under way; (*fig*) to be on the move; **poner en —** to start; (*fig*) to get going, set in motion, set on foot; **ponerse en —** to start, get going.

(b) (*Sport*) walk; **— atlética, — de competición** walk, walking race.

(c) (*of vehicle*) speed; **"— moderada"** (*Aut*) "drive slowly"; **moderar la — de un coche** to slow a car down, reduce the speed of a car; **a toda —** at full speed, at top speed; (*fig*) at full blast, full-blast.

(d) (*Mech*) running, working, functioning, operation; **estar en —** to be working; to be in working order.

(e) (*Aut, Mech*) gear; speed; **primera —** first gear, bottom gear; **— directa** top gear; **— atrás** reverse gear; **dar — atrás, poner en — atrás, invertir la —** to reverse, put into reverse; **el coche tiene cinco —s** the car has five gears.

(f) (*Mus*) march; **— fúnebre** funeral march, dead march; **— lenta** slow march; **— nupcial** wedding march.

(g) (*fig*) progress; march; trend, course; (*of hurricane*) path, track; **la — de los acontecimientos** the march of events, the course of events; **coger la — de algo** to get into the way (*or* habit) of something, get the hang of something.

(h) (*Cu, PR: of horse*) walk, walking pace.

(i) (*Mex: Aut*) self-starter.

marchantaje *nm* (*SAm*) clients, clientèle.

marchante *nm*, **marchanta** *nf* (a) dealer, merchant; (*SAm*) pedlar. (b) (*SAm*) client, customer. (c) (*Ant*) trickster.

marchantía *nf* (*CAm, PR, Ven*) clients, clientèle.

marchar [1a] **1** *vi* (a) to go; to move, travel; (*Mil*) to march.

(b) =**marcharse**.

(c) (*Mech etc*) to go; to run, function, work; (*of train etc*) to run; **el motor no marcha** the engine isn't working, the engine won't work; **el motor marcha mal** the engine is running badly; **— en vacío** to tick over; **el reloj marcha atrasado** the watch is slow.

(d) (*fig*) to go, proceed; **todo marcha bien** everything is going well; **el proyecto marcha bien** the plan is coming along nicely; **el negocio no marcha** the business is getting nowhere, the deal is making no progress.

(e) (*Cu, Chi, PR: of horse*) to walk.

2 marcharse *vr* to go (away), leave; **— a otro sitio** to go somewhere else, leave for another place; **— de la capital** to leave the capital; **¿os marcháis?** are you leaving?, must you go?; **con permiso me marcho** if you don't mind I must go.

marchitar [1a] **1** *vt* to wither, fade, shrivel, dry up.

2 marchitarse *vr* (a) (*Bot*) to wither, fade, shrivel up.

(b) (*fig*) to languish, fade away; to go into a decline.

marchitez *nf* withered state, faded condition.

marchito *adj* (a) withered, faded. (b) (*fig*) faded; in decline.

marea *nf* (a) tide; **— alta** high tide, high water; **— baja** low tide, low water; **— creciente** rising tide; **— menguante** ebb tide; **— muerta** neap tide; **— viva** spring tide.

(b) (*fig*) tide; **la — de la rebelión** the tide of revolt.

(c) light sea breeze.

(d) drizzle; (*Chi*) sea mist.

mareado *adj*: **estar —** (a) to feel sick; to feel dizzy; (*Naut*) to be (*or* feel) seasick. (b) (*fam*) to be a bit drunk.

mareaje *nm* (a) navigation, seamanship. (b) ship's course.

marear [1a] **1** *vt* (a) (*Naut*) to sail, navigate.

(b) (*Med*) **— a uno** to make someone feel sick; to make someone seasick; to make someone feel dizzy.

(c) (*fig*) to annoy, upset, disturb; to burden with (useless) things to do.

(d) (*Mex, PR*) to cheat.

2 marearse *vr* (a) (*Med*) to feel sick; to be (*or* get, feel) seasick; to feel dizzy, feel giddy; to feel faint.

(b) **no te marees con esto** don't bother your head about this.

(c) (*fam*) to get a bit drunk.

(d) (*Arg, Cu, PR: cloth*) to fade.

marejada *nf* (a) (*Naut*) swell, heavy sea, surge. (b) (*fig*) undercurrent (*of unrest etc*).

maremagno *nm*, **maremágnum** *nm* (*fig*) ocean, abundance; (*fig*) noisy confusion.

maremoto *nm* tidal wave.

mareo *nm* (a) (*Med*) sick feeling; travel sickness, seasickness; dizziness, giddiness.

(b) (*fig*) irritation; confusion; nervy state; boredom.

(c) nuisance, bore; **es un — tener que . . .** it is a nuisance having to . . .; **¡qué — de hombre!** what a bore that man is!

marfil *nm* (a) ivory. (b) (*SAm*) fine-toothed comb.

marfileño *adj* ivory, like ivory.

marga *nf* marl, loam.

margal *nm* marly patch; marlpit.

margarina *nf* margarine.

Margarita *f* Margaret.

margarita *nf* (a) (*Zool*) pearl; **echar —s a los cerdos** to cast pearls before swine. (b) (*Zool*) winkle. (c) (*Bot*) daisy.

margen 1 *nm* (a) border, edge, fringe; (*of paper, Typ*) margin; **al —** in the margin.

(b) (*Lit*) marginal note.

(c) (*fig*) margin; gap, space; leeway; **— de beneficio, — de ganancia** profit margin; **— de confianza** credibility gap; **— de error** margin of (*or* for) error; **— de seguridad** safety margin; **hay un — de aproximación de 8 días** we allow a week each way; **le digo el número con un — de unos 20** I'm telling you the number, give or take about 20.

(d) (*fig*) **dejar a uno al —** to leave someone out (in the cold); **mantenerse al —** to keep out, stand aside.

(e) (*fig*) occasion, opportunity; **dar — para** to give an opportunity for.

2 *nf* (*of river etc*) bank.

marginal *adj* marginal.

marginar [1a] *vt* (a) *page* to leave margins on. (b) *text* to add marginal notes to, write marginal notes against.

margoso *adj* marly, loamy.

margullo *nm* (*Cu, Ven*) shoot, runner.

Mari *f pet name for* **María**.

María *f* Mary; **— Antonieta** Marie Antoinette; **— Estuardo** Mary Stuart; **— la Sangrienta** Bloody Mary.

marial *adj*, **mariano** *adj* Marian.

marica 1 nf (Orn) magpie. **2** nm (fam) weak character; milksop, sissy, mollycoddle; (fam) = **maricón**.

Maricastaña: en los días de —, en tiempos de — way back, long ago; in the good old days.

maricón nm (fam) queer (fam), pansy (fam).

maridaje nm (a) conjugal life, marriage ties. (b) (fig) marriage, close association, intimate connection. (c) (pej) collusion.

marido nm husband.

marijuana nf (also **mariguana**, **marihuana**) marijuana, cannabis, Indian hemp.

marimacha nf (Per) = **marimacho**.

marimacho nm (fam) mannish woman.

marimba nf (a) (Mus) kind of drum; (SAm) marimba, kind of xylophone; (Arg, PR) tuneless instrument. (b) (RPl) beating. (c) (Col) large goitre.

marimoña nf buttercup.

marimorena nf fuss, row, shindy; **armar una —** to kick up a row.

marina nf (a) (Geog) coast, coastal area. (b) seamanship; navigation; **término de —** term from navigation, nautical term. (c) ships; **— (de guerra)** navy; **la — española** the Spanish navy, the Spanish fleet; **— mercante** merchant navy; **servir en la —** to serve in the navy. (d) (Art) sea piece, seascape.

marinar [1a] vt (Cook) to marinade, marinate.

marinería nf (a) seamanship. (b) ship's crew; seamen, sailors (collectively).

marinero 1 adj (a) = **marino**. (b) people sea (attr), seafaring. (c) ship seaworthy. (d) **a la marinera, a lo —** in a seamanlike way; sailor-fashion.
2 nm sailor, seaman; mariner, seafarer; **— de agua dulce** landlubber; **— de cubierta** deckhand; **— de primera** able seaman.

marinesco adj seamanly; **a la marinesca** in a seaman-like way; sailor-fashion.

marino 1 adj sea (attr), marine; **pez —** sea fish; **fauna marina** marine life, sea creatures. **2** nm sailor, seaman.

mariolatría nf mariolatry.

marioneta nf marionette, puppet; (fig) puppet; **régimen —** puppet régime.

mariposa nf (a) (Ent) butterfly; **— (nocturna)** moth; **— de la col** cabbage-white butterfly; **— cabeza de muerte, — de calavera** death's head moth. (b) (Swimming) butterfly stroke; **100 metros —** 100 metres butterfly. (c) (Col, Hond) toy windmill. (d) (Col) blind man's bluff.

mariposear [1a] vi (a) to flutter about, flit to and fro. (b) (fig) to be fickle, act capriciously; to flirt; **— alrededor de uno** to dance attendance on someone, be constantly fluttering round someone.

mariposilla nf small moth, (esp) clothes moth.

mariposón nm (a) flirt, wolf (fam). (b) (Per) queer (fam), pansy (fam).

Mariquita f pet name for **María**.

mariquita 1 nf (a) (Ent) ladybird. (b) (Orn) parakeet. **2** nm = **marica 2**.

marisabidilla nf (fam) bluestocking; know-all.

mariscal nm (Hist) blacksmith, farrier; (Hist) major-general; **— de campo** field marshal.

mariscos nmpl shellfish, seafood.

marisma nf marsh, swamp; mud flats.

marisquería nf shellfish bar, seafood restaurant.

marital adj marital.

maritatas nfpl (Andalusia, SAm), **maritates** nmpl (CAm, Mex) gear, tackle, tools; (pej) things, junk.

marítimo adj maritime; marine, sea (attr); agent etc shipping (attr); **ciudad marítima** seaside town, coastal town; **ruta marítima** ocean route, seaway, route by sea; **seguro —** marine insurance.

maritornes nf, pl **maritornes** sluttish servant; wench, tart (sl).

marjal nm marsh, fen, bog.

marmita nf (a) (Cook) pot; (Mil) mess tin. (b) (Geol) **— de gigante** pothole.

marmitón nm kitchen boy, scullion.

mármol nm marble.

marmolejo nm small marble column.

marmóreo adj marble; marmoreal.

marmosete nm (Typ) tailpiece, vignette.

marmota nf (a) (Zool) marmot; **— de Alemania** hamster; **— de América** woodchuck; **dormir como una —** to sleep like a log. (b) (fig) sleepyhead.

maroma nf (a) rope. (b) (SAm) tightrope; acrobatic performance; (SD) circus. (c) (SAm) **—s** acrobatics, acrobatic stunts; **hacer —s = maromear**.

maromear [1a] vi (SAm) (a) to walk (on) a tightrope; to do acrobatic stunts. (b) (fig) to change one's political allegiance, climb on the bandwaggon; to keep in with all parties, do a political balancing act.

maromero nm (SAm) (a) tightrope walker, acrobat. (b) (fig) clever politician, politician who manages to be on good terms with all parties.

marqués nm marquis.

marquesa nf marchioness.

marquesina nf glass canopy, porch; glass roof, cantilever roof; (Rail) roof, cab (of locomotive).

marquetería nf marquetry, inlaid work.

marrajo 1 adj bull vicious, dangerous; person sly. **2** nm (a) shark. (b) (Mex) skinflint.

marramizar [1f] vi (of cat) to howl, caterwaul.

marrana nf (a) (Zool) sow. (b) (fam) slut.

marranada nf, **marranería** nf (a) filthiness. (b) (una —) filthy act; dirty trick, vile deed.

marrano 1 adj filthy, dirty. **2** nm (a) (Zool) pig, boar. (b) (fam) swine; dirty pig. (c) (Hist) Jew, converted Jew.

marrar [1a] **1** vt: **— el tiro** to miss; **— el golpe** to miss (with a blow). **2** vi (a) to miss; (fig) to miss the mark. (b) (fig) to fail, miscarry, go astray; **no me marra una** everything's going well for me.

marras adv (a) **de —** old; long-standing; well-known, that you (etc) know all about; in question, aforementioned; **es el problema de —** it's the same old problem; **volver a lo de —** to go back over the same old stuff. (b) (Bol, Ec) **hace — que no le veo** it's ages since I saw him.

marrazo nm mattock; short machete; (Mex) bayonet.

marrón 1 adj chestnut, brown; maroon. **2** nm (a) chestnut (colour); maroon. (b) (Cook) marron glacé. (c) (SAm) (descendant of) fugitive Negro slave. (d) (Col) curlpaper.

marroncito nm (Ven) coffee with milk.

marroquí 1 adj Moroccan. **2** nmf Moroccan. **3** nm (Tech) morocco (leather).

marrubio nm (Bot) horehound.

marrueco = marroquí 1 and **2**.

Marruecos m Morocco; **el — Español** Spanish Morocco.

marrullería nf (a) (quality) smoothness, glibness, plausibility. (b) (una —) plausible excuse; **—s** smooth approach, cajolery, wheedling.

marrullero 1 adj smooth, glib, plausible; cajoling, wheedling. **2** nm smooth type, plausible individual.

Marsella Marseille.

Marsellesa nf Marseillaise.

marsopa nf porpoise.

marsupial 1 adj marsupial. **2** nm marsupial.

marta nf (pine) marten; (fur) sable; **— cebellina** sable.

martajar [1a] vt (SAm) (a) maize to pound, grind. (b) **— el español** to speak broken Spanish.

Marte m Mars.

martellina nf sledgehammer.

martes nm, pl **martes** Tuesday; **— de carnaval, — de carnestolandas** Shrove Tuesday.

martillada nf hammer blow, blow with a hammer.

martillar [1a] vt (a) to hammer; to pound. (b) (fig) to worry, torment.

martillazo nm (heavy) blow with a hammer; **a —s** by hammering; **formar algo a —s** to hammer something out (or into shape).

martillear [1a] **1** vt = **martillar**. **2** vi (of engine) to knock.

martilleo nm hammering; pounding.

martillero nm (SAm) auctioneer.

martillo nm (a) hammer; (of chairman etc) gavel; **— de madera** mallet; **— mecánico** power hammer; **— de orejas, — sacaclavos** claw-hammer; **— picador** pneumatic drill. (b) (Comm) auction room. (c) (Archit) projecting part, house (etc) that sticks out from the row; (SAm) wing (of a building). (d) (fig: person) hammer, scourge.

Martín m Martin; **San — St Martin**, (as festivity) Martinmas, (Agr) season for slaughtering pigs; **a cada puerco le llega su San —** everything has to come to an end sometime; see **veranillo**.

martín nm: **— pescador** kingfisher.

martinete nm drop hammer; pile driver; (Mus) hammer.

martingala nf (fam) knack, trick; (pej: SAm) trick, cunning device, fiddle (fam).

Martinica f Martinique.

mártir nmf martyr.

martirio nm (a) (Eccl) martyrdom. (b) (fig) torture, torment.

martirizador adj (fig) agonizing, excruciating.

martirizar [1f] vt (Eccl) (a) to martyr. (b) (fig) to torture, torment.

martirologio nm martyrology.

Marucha f, **Maruja** f pet names for **María**.

marusa nf (Ven) knapsack, bag.

maruto nm (Ven) (a) (Anat) navel. (b) (Med) wart; bruise, welt.

marxismo nm Marxism.

marxista 1 adj Marxist. 2 nmf Marxist.

marzal adj March (attr), of March.

marzo nm March.

más 1 adv and adj (a) (basic comparisons: comp) more, (superl) most; A es — difícil que B A is more difficult than B, A is harder than B; ella es la — guapa de todas she is the prettiest of all; él es el — inteligente he is the most intelligent (one); es el que — sabe — he's the one who knows most; tiene — dinero que yo he has more money than I (do); un libro de lo — divertido a most amusing book, a highly amusing book; es de lo — verde it's as dirty as can be, it's as dirty as they come; un hombre de lo — desaprensivo a completely unscrupulous man.
(b) (examples of use with certain verbs) **correr** — to run faster; **durar** — to last longer; **trabajar** — to work harder; **ha viajado** — he has travelled more (widely); — **quiero** + infin I would rather + infin, I would prefer to + infin.
(c) (idiomatic use with adjs) **¡qué perro — feo!** what an ugly dog!; **¡ya verán qué cena — rica!** you wait and see what a splendid supper it will be!; **¡es — bueno!** (fam) he's so kind!, he's ever so kind!
(d) (comparisons of quality and quantity) — **de**, — **de lo que**, — **que** more than; — **de 10** more than 10; **con — dinero de lo que creíamos** with more money than we thought; **no veo — solución que de** . . . I see no other solution than to . . . (or but to); **se trata de voluntad — que de fuerza** it's more a question of will power than of strength, it's a matter of will power rather than of strength; **se estima en — de mil** it is reckoned at more than a thousand; **no — que ayer** only yesterday; **hace no — de 3 semanas** 3 weeks ago, no longer than 3 weeks ago; **nadie lo sabe — que yo** nobody knows it better than I do.
(e) (other uses, and idioms with prep) — **y** — more and more; — **o menos** more or less; **el que — y el que menos** every single one; **the whole lot; los — most people; los — de** most of, the majority of; **es** — . . . furthermore. . .; **a — in** addition, besides; **a — de** in addition to, besides; **a lo — at** most, at the most; **a las 8 a — tardar** at 8 o'clock at the latest; **está nevando a — y mejor** it really is snowing, it's snowing harder than ever; **como el que — as** well as anyone, as well as the next man; **llevaba 3 de — he** was carrying 3 too many; **trae una manta de — bring** an extra blanket; **estar de — to be** unnecessary, be superfluous; **aquí yo estoy de — I'm** not needed here, I'm de trop here, I'm in the way here; **está de — decir que** . . . it is unnecessary to say that . . .; **de — en — more** and more; **hasta no — to** the utmost, to the limit; **nada — nothing** else; **¡nada —! that's all!, that's** the lot!; **¿nada —? anything** else?; **ocurrió nada — iniciado el partido** it happened when the game had scarcely begun; **aparecen nada — terminado el invierno** they come when the winter is hardly over; **ni — ni menos** neither more nor less; just; **es un genio ni — ni menos** he's nothing more nor less than a genius, he's a real genius; **no — no more; habían llegado no — they** had just arrived; **vengo no — a verlo** I've come just to see it; **ayer.no — (SAm)** only yesterday; **¡espera no —! (SAm)** just you wait!; **no trabaja — he no** longer works, he doesn't work any more; **por — que se esfuerce** however much (or hard) he tries, no matter how (hard) he tries; **por — que quisiera ayudar** much as I should like to help; **¿qué —? what** else?; what next?; **sin — (ni —)** without more ado; **todo lo — at** most, at the most; see **allá, bien, cuento, nunca** etc.
2 conj and, plus; 2 — **3 son 5** 2 and 3 are 5, 2 plus 3 are 5; **con éstos — los que había antes** with these and (or together with) what there were before; **España — Portugal** Spain together with Portugal.
3 nm (a) (Math) plus, plus sign.
(b) **tiene sus — y sus menos** it has its good and bad points, there are things to be said on both sides.

mas conj (lit) but.

masa¹ nf (a) (Cook) dough. (b) (RPl) small bun, tea-

cake; (Chi, Ec) puff pastry. (c) (Archit) mortar, plaster.

masa² nf (a) (Phys etc) mass; (fig) mass; bulk; volume, quantity; **las —s** the masses; — **coral** choir; **en — en** masse; in a body, all together; (Arg, Chi, Per) as a whole, altogether; **reunir(se) en — to** mass; **llevar algo en la — de la sangre** to have something in one's blood, have a natural inclination towards something.
(b) (Elec) earth, ground (US); **conectar un aparato con — to** earth a piece of apparatus, ground a piece of apparatus (US).

masacrar [1a] vt to massacre.

masacre nf massacre.

masada nf farm.

masadero nm farmer.

masaje nm massage; **dar — a** to massage; **hacerse dar —s** to have oneself massaged.

masajista 1 nm masseur. 2 nf masseuse.

masato nm (SAm) drink made from fermented maize, bananas, yucca etc.

mascada nf (a) (SAm) plug of chewing tobacco. (b) (CAm, Ec) buried treasure; store of money, nest egg; (Col, Ec) money; (RPl) illicit gains; rake-off (fam), cut. (c) (CAm) rebuke. (d) (Guat, Mex) silk handkerchief.

mascadura nf chewing.

mascar [1g] 1 vt (a) food to chew.
(b) (fam) words to mumble, mutter.
(c) (fam) — **un asunto, dar mascado un asunto** to explain something in very simple terms.
2 vi to chew; (SAm, esp) to chew tobacco.

máscara 1 nf (a) mask; — **antigás** gasmask; — **para esgrima** fencing mask; — **de oxígeno** oxygen mask.
(b) —s masque, masquerade.
(c) (fig) mask; disguise; **quitar la — a uno** to unmask someone; **quitarse la — to** reveal oneself.
2 nmf masked person.

mascarada nf (a) masque, masquerade. (b) (fig) masquerade; farce, charade.

mascarilla nf mask (also Med); plaster cast (of the face); — **mortuoria** death mask.

mascarón nm large mask; — **de proa** figurehead.

mascota nf mascot.

masculinidad nf masculinity, manliness.

masculino 1 adj masculine, manly; (Bio) male; (Gram) masculine; **ropa masculina** men's clothing. 2 nm (Gram) masculine.

mascullar [1a] vt to mumble, mutter.

masera nf kneading trough.

masía nf (Aragon) farm.

masilla nf putty.

masillo nm (Cu) plaster.

masita nf (Bol, RPl, SD) small bun, teacake, pastry.

masitero nm (Bol, RPl, SD) pastrycook, confectioner.

masivo adj attack, dose etc massive; evacuation etc en masse, general; execution mass (attr), wholesale.

masocotudo adj (Chi, Per) heavy, ponderous; thick.

masón nm (free)mason.

masonería nf (free)masonry.

masónico adj masonic.

masoquismo nm masochism.

masoquista 1 adj masochistic. 2 nmf masochist.

mastate nm (CAm, Mex) loincloth; short skirt.

mastelero nm topmast.

masticación nf mastication.

masticar [1g] vt to masticate, chew.

mástil nm (a) pole, post, support; flagpole; (Naut) mast; (Archit) upright; — **de tienda** tent pole. (b) (Mus) neck. (c) (of feather) shaft.

mastín nm mastiff; — **danés** Great Dane.

mastique nm plaster; cement; putty.

mastitis nf mastitis.

masto nm (Agr, Hort) stock (for grafting).

mastodonte nm mastodon.

mastodóntico adj (fig) elephantine.

mastoides 1 adj mastoid. 2 nf mastoid.

mastuerzo nm (a) (Bot) cress; — **de agua** watercress. (b) (fam) dolt.

masturbación nf masturbation.

masturbarse [1a] vr to masturbate.

mata nf (a) bush, shrub; (esp SAm: any) plant; — **de coco** (Ant) coconut palm; — **de plátano** (Ant) banana tree; — **rubia** kermes oak.
(b) sprig; tuft, blade; clump, root; bunch.
(c) —s thicket, bushes; scrub.
(d) (Agr) field, plot, patch; — **de olivos** field of olive trees, olive grove.
(e) (SAm) clump, group (of trees), grove; (Col) orchard; (Mex, Ven) forest, jungle; — **de bananos** clump of banana trees, banana plantation.
(f) — **de pelo** head of hair; mop of hair.

mataburro nm (CAm, Col, Ec) liquor, rum.

mataburros *nm, pl* **mataburros** (*Cu, RPl: hum*) dictionary.

matacán *nm* (**a**) (*Ec, Ven*) fawn, young deer. (**b**) (*Hond*) calf.

matachín *nm* bully.

matadero *nm* (**a**) slaughterhouse, abattoir. (**b**) (*fig*) drudgery. (**c**) (*fig: Mil*) exposed position, dangerous place. (**d**) (*Mex, RPl*) brothel.

matador 1 *adj* (**a**) killing.
(**b**) (*fam*) ridiculous; absurd; **el vestido le está** — the dress looks absurd on her.
2 *nm*, **matadora** *nf* killer.
3 *nm* (*Taur*) matador, bullfighter.

matadura *nf* (*Vet*) sore.

matafuego *nm* fire extinguisher.

mátalas callando *nm* (*fam*) smooth type, sly sort.

matalobos *nm, pl* **matalobos** aconite, wolf's-bane.

matalón 1 *adj* horse old, broken-down. **2** *nm* broken-down old horse.

matamoros *nm, pl* **matamoros** swashbuckler, braggart.

matamoscas *nm, pl* **matamoscas** fly swat; flypaper.

matanza *nf* (**a**) slaughter, killing; (*Agr*) slaughtering, (*esp*) pig-killing; slaughtering season; (*fig*) slaughter, massacre, butchery.
(**b**) (*Ven*) slaughterhouse; (*Col*) butcher's (shop); (*CAm*) meat market.

mataperrear [1a] *vi* (*Arg, Ec, Per*) to behave like a hooligan.

mataperros *nm, pl* **mataperros** *nm* (*fam*) urchin, hooligan.

matar [1a] **1** *vt* (**a**) to kill; to slay, slaughter; **— a uno a disgustos** to wear someone out with burdens, heap troubles on someone; **así me maten . . .** for the life of me . . .; **que me maten si . . .** I'll eat my hat if . . .; believe me, I never . . .; **—las callando** to do oneself a lot of good on the quiet, go about things slyly.
(**b**) (*fig*) *time* to kill; *hunger* to stay; *dust* to lay; *lime* to slake; *corner, edge etc* to file down, smooth, round off; *colour* to tone down; *violence etc* to diminish, reduce.
2 *vi* (**a**) to kill; **no mataréis** thou shalt not kill; **estar a — con uno** to be at daggers drawn with someone.
(**b**) (*Chess*) to mate.
3 matarse *vr* (**a**) to kill oneself, commit suicide; (*in accident*) to be killed, get killed.
(**b**) (*fig*) to wear oneself out, kill oneself; **— a trabajar** to kill oneself with work, overwork; **— por** + *infin* to struggle to + *infin*, make a great effort to + *infin*.

matarife *nm* butcher, slaughterman; **— de caballos** knacker.

matarratas *nm* rat poison; (*fig*) hooch, bad liquor.

matasanos *nm, pl* **matasanos** (*fam*) quack (doctor).

matasellado *nm* cancellation, postmark.

matasellos *nm, pl* **matasellos** cancellation, postmark.

matasiete *nm* braggart, bully.

matasuegras *nm, pl* **matasuegras** streamer, blower (*toy*).

matazón *nm* (*CAm, Col, Cu, Ven*)=**matanza**.

match [maʃ] *nm, pl* **matchs** [maʃ] (*Sport: angl*) match.

mate¹ *adj* dull, matt, unpolished.

mate² *nm* (*Chess*) mate, checkmate; **dar — a** to mate, checkmate.

mate³ *nm* (*SAm*) (**a**) maté, Paraguayan tea (*herb and drink similar to tea*).
(**b**) gourd, drinking vessel; maté pot; **pegar — (CAm)** to go crazy; **tener mucho — (CAm)** to be sly, be sharp.
(**c**) (*Chi, RPl: fam*) head, nut (*sl*).

matear¹ [1a] **1** *vt* (*Agr*) to plant at regular intervals, sow in groups. **2** *vi* (**a**) (*Bot*) to sprout. (**b**) (*Hunting: of dog*) to hunt among the bushes.

matear² [1a] *vi* (*SAm*) to drink maté.

matear³ [1a] *vt* (*Chi*) to checkmate.

matemáticamente *adv* mathematically.

matemáticas *nfpl* mathematics; **— aplicadas** applied mathematics; **— puras** pure mathematics.

matemático 1 *adj* mathematical. **2** *nm* mathematician.

Mateo *m* Matthew.

materia *nf* (**a**) matter (*also Med, Phys*); material; stuff; **— colorante** dyestuff; **— prima** raw material.
(**b**) (*Lit etc*) matter, subject matter; (*School etc*) subject; **índice de —s** table of contents; **en — de** in the matter of, on the subject of; as regards; **entrar en —** to begin on one's subject (after a preamble); **será — de muchas discusiones** it will be

the subject of a lot of argument, it will give rise to a lot of argument.

material 1 *adj* (**a**) material.
(**b**) physical; **la presencia — de uno** someone's physical (*or* bodily) presence; **dolor —** physical pain; **daños —es** physical damage; damage to property.
(**c**) real, true; literal; **el autor — del hecho** the real instigator of the deed, the person really responsible for the affair.
2 *nm* (**a**) (*in general*) material; **hecho de mal —** made of bad material(s); **— bélico, — de guerra** war material; **— de construcción** building material; **—es de derribo** rubble; **—es plásticos** plastics, plastic materials.
(**b**) (*Tech*) equipment, plant; materials; **— escolar** teaching materials, school equipment; **— fijo** permanent way; **— de limpieza** cleaning materials; **— móvil, — rodante** rolling stock; **el nuevo — de la fábrica** the new factory plant.
(**c**) (*Typ*) copy.
(**d**) (*of footwear*) leather.
(**e**) (*SAm*) **de —** made of adobe; made of bricks, brick-built.

materialidad *nf* material nature; outward appearance; literalness; substance; **percibe solamente la — del asunto** he sees only the basic aspects of the question; **no hablo de la — del insulto** I'm not talking about the substance of the insult, I'm not talking about what the insult actually consisted of.

materialismo *nm* materialism.

materialista 1 *adj* materialist(ic). **2** *nmf* materialist. **3** *nm* (*Mex*) lorry driver, truckdriver (*US*).

materializar [1f] **1** *vt* to materialize. **2 materializarse** *vr* to materialize.

materialmente *adv* (**a**) materially; physically, in the physical sense.
(**b**) absolutely; literally; **nos es — imposible** it is quite (*or* absolutely) impossible for us; **estaba — mojado** he was literally soaked.

maternal *adj* motherly; maternal.

maternidad *nf* (**a**) motherhood, maternity. (**b**) (*also* **casa de —**) maternity hospital.

materno *adj* (**a**) *language etc* mother (*attr*); *home etc* mother's. (**b**) **abuelo —** maternal grandfather, grandfather on the mother's side.

matero *adj* (*Chi, RPl*) (**a**) of maté, relating to maté. (**b**) fond of drinking maté.

matete *nm* (*Arg, Urug*) (**a**) confused mess, mixture, hash. (**b**) (*fig*) quarrel, brawl. (**c**) (*fig*) confusion.

Matilde *f* Mat(h)ilda.

matinal *adj* morning (*attr*).

matiz *nm* (**a**) shade, hue, tint. (**b**) (*of meaning*) shade, nuance; (*of irony etc*) touch.

matizado *adj*: **— de, — en** tinged with, touched with (*also fig*).

matizar [1f] *vt* (**a**) (*Art*) to blend.
(**b**) to tinge, tint (*de* with; *also fig*); **— un discurso de ironía** to introduce ironical notes into a speech, give a speech an ironical slant.
(**c**) *tone etc* to vary, introduce some variety into.

matojal *nm* (*Cu, PR*), **matojo** *nm* (*Ant, Col, Mex*) = **matorral**.

matón *nm* bully, lout, thug.

matonismo *nm* bullying, loutishness.

matorral *nm* thicket; brushwood, scrub.

matorro *nm* (*Col*) = **matorral**.

matra *nf* (*RPl*) horseblanket.

matraca 1 *nf* (**a**) rattle.
(**b**) (*fam*) nuisance, bore; chaff, banter; **dar — a uno** to pester someone, keep bothering someone; to banter someone.
2 *nmf* (*fam: person*) nuisance, bore.

matraquear [1a] *vt* (**a**) to rattle. (**b**) (*fam*) = **dar matraca a**.

matraz *nm* (*Chem*) flask.

matreraje *nm* (*RPl*) banditry, brigandage.

matrero 1 *adj* (**a**) cunning, sly, knowing. (**b**) (*SAm*) suspicious, distrustful. **2** *nm* (*SAm*) bandit, brigand; trickster.

matriarca *nf* matriarch.

matriarcado *nm* matriarchy.

matriarcal *adj* matriarchal.

matricida *nmf* matricide (*person*).

matricidio *nm* matricide (*act*).

matrícula *nf* (**a**) register, list, roll; (*Naut*) register.
(**b**) (*act: Naut*) registration; (*Univ*) registration, matriculation; **un buque de — extranjera** a foreign ship, a ship with foreign registration; **un barco con — de Bilbao** a boat registered in Bilbao; **en los exámenes le dieron una — de honor** as a result of the examinations his fees for the following year were remitted.

(c) licence; (*Aut*) registration number; licence plate.

matriculación *nf* registration; enrolment; licensing.

matricular [1a] **1** *vt* to register; to enrol; to license. **2 matricularse** *vr* to register; to enrol, sign on; — **en el curso de . . .** to sign on for the course in . . .

matrimonial *adj* matrimonial; **enlace** — link by marriage; **capitulaciones** —es marriage settlement; **vida** — married life, conjugal life.

matrimonio *nm* (a) (*in general*) marriage, matrimony; married state; (*act*) marriage; — **civil** civil marriage; — **clandestino** secret marriage; — **de conveniencia**, — **de interés** marriage of convenience; — **por la iglesia** church marriage; **contraer** — (**con**) to marry.
(b) (*persons*) couple, married couple; **el** — **García** the Garcías, Mr and Mrs García; **de** — **bed** etc double.

matritense = **madrileño**.

matriz **1** *nf* (a) (*Anat*) womb, uterus.
(b) (*Tech*) mould, die; (*Typ*) matrix.
(c) (*Math*) matrix.
(d) (*of cheque book etc*) stub.
(e) (*Law*) original, master copy.
2 *attr*: **casa** — (*Comm* etc) head office; parent company; **convento** — (*Eccl*) parent house.

matrona *nf* (a) matron. (b) (*Med*) midwife.

matronal *adj* matronly.

matungo (*Ant, RPl*) **1** *adj* old, worn-out. **2** *nm* old horse, nag; thin person, weakling.

maturrango **1** *adj* (*Arg, Chi, Urug*) clumsy, awkward; (*Arg, Per, Urug*) *rider* poor, incompetent. **2** *nm* (*Per, RPl*) poor rider, incompetent horseman.

matute *nm* (a) smuggling, contraband; **de** — (*Comm*) smuggled, contraband; (*as adv*) secretly, stealthily; **introducir una idea de** — to bring in a (dangerous) notion from outside.
(b) smuggled goods, contraband.
(c) gambling den.

matutero *nm* smuggler.

matutino *adj* morning (*attr*).

maula **1** *adj* (*SAm*) *animal* useless, vicious, lazy; (*Arg, Mex*) *person* good-for-nothing, unreliable; (*Arg*) cowardly.
2 *nf* (a) (*Sew*) remnant.
(b) piece of junk, useless object; white elephant.
(c) (*person*) useless individual, dead loss.
(d) dirty trick, fraud.
3 *nmf* (a) idler, slacker.
(b) cheat, trickster; tricky individual; (*Fin*) bad payer.

maulería *nf* cunning, trickiness.

maulero *nm* (a) cheat, trickster; smooth and deceitful type. (b) (*Ec*) conjurer.

maullar [1a] *vi* to mew, miaow.

maullido *nm* mew, miaow.

Mauricio[1] *m* Maurice.

Mauricio[2] *m* (*Geog*) Mauritius.

mausoleo *nm* mausoleum.

maxifalda *nf* maxiskirt.

maxilar **1** *adj* maxillary. **2** *nm* jaw, jawbone.

máxima *nf* maxim.

máxime *adv* especially; principally; all the more so.

máximo **1** *adj* maximum; top; highest, greatest; **el** — **premio** the highest award, the top prize; **su** — **esfuerzo** their greatest effort; **llegar al punto** — to reach the highest point; **es lo** — **en la moda juvenil** (*sl*) it's the most in young people's fashions (*sl*).
2 *nm* maximum; **como** — at most, at the outside; **al** — to the maximum, to the utmost.

máximum *nm* maximum.

maya[1] *nf* (a) (*Bot*) daisy. (b) May Queen, Queen of the May.

maya[2] (*Hist*) **1** *adj* Mayan. **2** *nmf* Maya, Mayan.

mayal *nm* flail.

mayo *nm* (a) May. (b) maypole.

mayonesa *nf* mayonnaise.

mayor **1** *adj* (a) *part* etc main, major, larger; **y otros animales** —es and other larger animals.
(b) *altar, mass, street* etc high; *square* main, principal; *mast* main; *see* **colegio, libro** etc.
(c) (*Mus*) major.
(d) *person* grown up, adult; of age; elderly; **ser** — **de edad** to be of age, be adult; **hacerse** — to grow up.
(e) (*of rank* etc) head, chief; **montero** — head huntsman.
2 *adj comp* (a) (*in size*) bigger, larger, greater (*que* than).
(b) (*in age*) older (*que* than), elder; (*in rank*) senior (*que* to).
3 *adj superl* (a) (*in size*) biggest, largest, greatest

(*also fig*); **su** — **cuidado** his biggest worry; **su** — **enemigo** his greatest enemy; **viven en la** — **miseria** they live in the greatest poverty.
(b) (*in age*) oldest, eldest; (*in rank*) most senior.
4 *nmf* (a) (*of rank*) chief, boss, superior; (*in office*) chief clerk.
(b) — **de edad** adult, person legally of age; —**es** grown-ups, adults; elders (and betters); **eso es sólo para** —**es** that's only for grown-ups; **¡más respeto con los** —**es!** be more respectful to your elders (and betters)!
(c) —**es** ancestors, forefathers.
(d) **llegar a** — **es** (*of situation*) to get out of hand, get out of control.
5 *nm*: **al por** — wholesale (*also fig*); **vender al por** — to sell wholesale; **repartir golpes al por** — to deal out punches wholesale, throw punches left and right.

mayoral *nm* (*Tech* etc) foreman, overseer, gaffer; (*Agr*) head shepherd; steward; farm manager; (*Arg*) tram conductor; (*Hist*) coachman.

mayorazgo *nm* (a) primogeniture. (b) entailed estate.
(c) eldest son, first-born.

mayordomo *nm* steward, butler; (*Naut*) steward; (*of estate*) steward; (*Chi*) foreman; (*Per*) servant.

mayoreo *nm* (*Chi, Mex*) wholesale (trade).

mayoría *nf* (a) majority, greater part, larger part; **la** — **de los españoles** the majority of Spaniards, most Spaniards; **en la** — **de los casos** in most cases; **en su** — in the main; **la abrumadora** —, **la inmensa** — the overwhelming majority, the vast majority; **por una** — **arrolladora** by an overwhelming majority.
(b) (*Pol* etc) majority; **una** — **de las cuatro quintas partes** a four-fifths majority; **gobierno de la** — majority rule, majority government.
(c) — **de edad** majority, adult age; **cumplir** (*or* **llegar a**) **la** — **de edad** to come of age.

mayorista *nmf* wholesaler.

mayoritario *adj* majority (*attr*); **gobierno** — majority government.

mayormente *adv* chiefly, mainly; especially; all the more so.

mayúscula *nf* capital (letter).

mayúsculo *adj* (a) *letter* capital. (b) (*fig*) big, tremendous; **un susto** — a big scare; **un error** — a tremendous mistake.

maza *nf* (a) (*Hist*) mace; war club; (*Sport*) bat; (*in polo*) stick, mallet; (*Mus*) drumstick; (*of billiard cue* etc) thick end; (*Tech*) flail; — **de fraga** drop hammer; — **de gimnasia** Indian club.
(b) (*fam*) pest, bore.
(c) (*SAm*) hub.
(d) (*Col, Cu, PR*) drum (*of a sugar mill*).

mazacote *nm* (a) hard mass; (*Cook*) dry doughy food; (*Archit*) concrete; **el arroz se ha hecho un** — the rice has gone lumpy, the rice has set like concrete.
(b) (*Art, Lit* etc) crude piece of work; mess, hotchpotch.
(c) (*fam*) bore.

mazacotudo *adj* = **amazacotado**.

mazada *nf* (a) bash (*fam*), blow (with a club); **dar** — **a** (*fig*) to hurt, injure. (b) (*fig*) blow; **fue una** — **para él** it came as a blow to him.

mazamorra *nf* (a) (*SAm*) maize mush, maize pudding, porridge. (b) (*CAm, Col, Cu, PR*) blister (on a horse's hoof); sore, soreness (on the foot).

mazapán *nm* marzipan.

mazmorra *nf* dungeon.

mazo *nm* (a) club; mallet; pestle; (*Sport*) club, bat, (*for croquet*) mallet; (*Agr*) flail; (*Aragon: of bell*) clapper.
(b) bunch, handful; bundle, packet; — **de papeles** sheaf of papers, bundle of papers; — **de naipes** stack of cards; — **de billetes** wad of notes (*or* bills: US).
(c) (*fam*) bore.

mazorca *nf* (a) (*Bot*) spike; (*of maize*) cob, ear; — **de maíz** corncob; **maíz en la** — corn on the cob.
(b) (*Tech*) spindle.
(c) (*Chi, RPl*) despotic government; political gang, terrorist band.

mazorquero *nm* (*Chi, RPl*) member of a despotic government; member of a political gang.

me *personal pron* (a) (*acc*) me.
(b) (*dative*) (to) me; **¡dámelo!** give it to me!; **me lo compró** he bought it from me; he bought it for me; **me rompí el brazo** I broke my arm.
(c) (*reflexive*) (to) myself; **me lavé** I washed, I washed myself; **me retiro** I withdraw.

meada *nf* (a) (*tabu*) piss (*tabu*). (b) mark (*or* stain etc) of urine.

meadero *nm* (*tabu*) bog (*sl*), jakes (*fam*).

meados nmpl (tabu) piss (tabu).
meaja nf crumb.
meandro nm meander.
mear [1a] (tabu) **1** vt to piss on (tabu).
  2 vi to piss (tabu), have a piss (tabu).
  3 mearse vr to wet oneself; — **de risa** to laugh so much that one has an accident.
Meca: La — Mecca.
meca nf (Ec, Per) prostitute.
mecachis interj (euph for ¡me cago!) see **cagar**.
mecánica nf **(a)** mechanics. **(b)** mechanism, works.
mecánicamente adv mechanically.
mecánico 1 adj **(a)** mechanical; power-driven, power-operated; machine (attr).
  (b) trade etc manual.
  2 nm mechanic; machinist; fitter, repair man; (Aut) driver, chauffeur; (Aer) rigger, fitter.
mecanismo nm **(a)** mechanism; works, machinery; gear; — **de dirección** steering gear.
  (b) action, movement.
  (c) (fig) mechanism; machinery, structure; process.
mecanización nf mechanization.
mecanizar [1f] vt to mechanize.
mecanografía nf typing, typewriting; — **al tacto** touch-typing.
mecanografiado 1 adj typewritten, typescript. **2** nm typescript.
mecanografiar [1c] vt to type.
mecanógrafo nm, **mecanógrafa** nf typist.
mecapalero nm (CAm, Mex) porter.
mecatazo nm (CAm) **(a)** lash, slash. **(b)** swig of liquor (fam).
mecate nm (CAm, Col, Mex, Ven) **(a)** strip of pita fibre; string, cord; twine. **(b)** coarse individual.
mecateada nf (CAm, Mex) lashing, beating.
mecatear[1] [1a] **1** vt **(a)** (CAm, Mex) to tie up; to lash, whip.
  (b) (Ven) to fawn on, flatter.
  2 mecatearse vr (Mex): **—las** to run away, beat it (fam).
mecatear[2] [1a] vi (Col) to eat cakes.
mecato nm (Col) cakes, pastries.
mecedor 1 adj rocking; swinging. **2** nm **(a)** swing. **(b)** (Cu, Mex, Pan) rocking chair. **(c)** (Cu) stirrer, spoon.
mecedora nf rocking chair.
Mecenas m Maecenas; **m—** (fig) patron.
mecenazgo nm patronage.
mecer [2b] **1** vt **(a)** to swing; cradle etc to rock; child to rock (to and fro), dandle; branch etc to sway, move to and fro.
  (b) container, liquid to stir, shake (up), agitate.
  2 mecerse vr to swing; to rock (to and fro); to sway, move to and fro.
meción nm (CAm, PR) jerk, jolt.
meco adj (Mex) Indian uncivilized; rebellious, treacherous; (CAm, Mex) coarse, rough, vile.
mecha nf **(a)** wick; (Mil etc) fuse; — **tardía** time fuse; **aguantar (la)** — (fig) to take one's punishment; to put up with everything.
  (b) (Cook) slice of bacon.
  (c) =**mechón**.
  (d) (Arg, Chi, Per) bit (of brace).
  (e) (Col, Ec, Ven) joke.
  (f) (Mex) fear.
mechar [1a] vt (Cook) to lard; to stuff.
mechera nf shoplifter.
mechero nm **(a)** cigarette lighter; (of stove) burner; jet; (Arg, Col) oil lamp; — **Bunsen** Bunsen burner; — **encendedor** pilot light; — **de gas** gas burner, gas jet.
  (b) (Guat, Mex) mop of hair.
  (c) (Ven) joker.
mechificar [1g] vt (Ec, Per, Ven) to trick, deceive; to mock.
mecho nm (Guat, Col) candle; candle end; candlestick.
mechón nm tuft, wisp; (of threads) bundle; (of hair) lock.
mechudo adj (SAm) tousled, unkempt.
medalla nf medal.
medallón nm **(a)** medallion. **(b)** locket. **(c)** (Typ) inset.
médano nm, **medaño** nm sand dune; sandbank.
media nf **(a)** stocking; (SAm: man's) sock; — **de malla** net stocking; — **de nylon** nylon stocking.
  (b) de — knitting (attr); knitting plain; **hacer —** to knit.
  (c) (Sport) half-back line.
  (d) (Math) mean.
mediación nf **(a)** mediation; intercession. **(b)** instrumentality.

mediado adj **(a)** half full; halfway through, half completed; **el local estaba —** the place was half full; **mediada la tarde** halfway through the afternoon; **llevo — el trabajo** I am halfway through the job, I have completed half the work.
  (b) a —s de marzo in the middle of March, halfway through March; **hacia —s del siglo pasado** about the middle of last century.
mediador nm, **mediadora** nf mediator.
medial adj medial.
medialuna nf croissant, breakfast roll.
medianamente adv moderately, fairly; moderately well; **un trabajo — bueno** a moderately good piece of work; **quedó — en los exámenes** he did moderately well in the exams.
medianera nf (RPl) party wall, dividing wall.
medianería nf **(a)** party wall. **(b)** (Mex, Ven) partnership.
medianero 1 adj **(a)** wall party (attr), dividing; fence boundary (attr).
  (b) adjacent, next.
  2 nm **(a)** owner of the adjoining house (or property etc).
  (b) (Ven) partner.
medianía nf **(a)** average; halfway point; middling position; (Econ) moderate means, modest circumstances; undistinguished social position.
  (b) (person) ordinary sort, mediocrity; **no pasa de ser una —** he's no better than average, he's rather a mediocrity.
mediano adj middling, medium, average; indifferent, undistinguished; (euph) mediocre (euph), rather poor; **de tamaño —** medium-sized; **es — de talento** he has average talent; **es mediana de guapa** she has average looks, she's not outstandingly pretty.
medianoche nf midnight.
mediante prep by means of, through, by.
mediar [1b] vi **(a)** to be in the middle; to get to the middle, get halfway; **entre A y B median 30 kms** there are 30 kms between A and B; **entre estas 2 casas median otras 3** there are 3 other houses between those 2; **media un abismo entre los dos gobiernos** there is a wide gap between the two governments; **entre los dos sucesos mediaron varios años** several years elapsed between the two events, there were some years between the two events; **mediaba el otoño** autumn was half over; **mediaba el mes de julio** it was halfway through July.
  (b) to come up, happen; to intervene; to exist; **pero medió la muerte de su madre** but his mother's death intervened; **media el hecho de que . . .** there is the fact that . . . to be considered; there is an obstacle in the fact that . . .; **median relaciones cordiales entre los dos** cordial relations exist between the two.
  (c) to mediate (en in, entre between), intervene; — **con uno** to intercede with someone.
médica nf woman doctor.
medicación nf medication, treatment.
médicamente adv medically.
medicamento nm medicine, drug; — **de patente** patent medicine.
medicastro nm (pej) quack (doctor).
medicina nf medicine; — **forense,** — **legal** forensic medicine; — **preventiva** preventive medicine; **estudiante de —** medical student.
medicinal adj medicinal.
medicinar [1a] **1** vt to treat, prescribe for. **2 medicinarse** vr to dose oneself.
medición nf measurement, measuring; **hacer —es** to take measurements.
médico 1 adj medical.
  2 nm doctor; medical practitioner, physician; — **de cabecera** family doctor; — **dentista** dental surgeon; — **forense** forensic surgeon, expert in forensic medicine; — **general** general practitioner; — **partero** obstetrician; — **puericultor** paediatrician; — **residente** house physician, resident, intern (US).
medida nf **(a)** (Math) measurement; (act) measuring, measurement; **a la —** in proportion; suitable; **el precio es a la —** the price goes according to the size; **una caja a la —** a specially made box, a box made for the purpose; **un traje a la —,** un traje hecho a la — a made-to-measure suit; **tiene una novia a la —** he has a girl who is just right for him; **es una solución a la —** the solution is exactly the right one; **a la — de mi deseo** just as I would have wished, exactly as I wanted (it); **a — de** in proportion to, in keeping with; **a — que . . . as . . .,** according as . . ., in keeping with the rate at which . . .; **a — que vaya bajando el agua** as the water goes

down; **en cierta** — up to a point, in a way; **en gran** — to a great extent; **—s vitales** vital statistics; **tomar las —s a uno** to measure someone, take someone's measurements; (fig) to size someone up; **tomar sus —s** to size a situation up.

(**b**) (system, container etc) measure; **pesos y —s** weights and measures; **— agraria** land measure; **— para áridos** dry measure; **— para líquidos** liquid measure; **esto colma la —** (fig) this is the last straw; **con esto se colmó la — de la paciencia de su padre** this finally exhausted her father's patience.

(**c**) (of shirt, shoe etc) size, fitting.

(**d**) (Lit) (correct) scansion.

(**e**) (fig) measure, step, move; **— preventiva** preventive measure; **— represiva** deterrent, check (contra to); **tomar —s** to take steps (para que to ensure that).

(**f**) (fig) moderation, prudence; restraint; **sin —** immoderately, in an unrestrained fashion.

medidor nm (SAm) meter; gauge; **— de lluvia** rain gauge.

mediería nf hosiery.

medieval adj medieval.

medievalismo nm medievalism.

medievalista nmf medievalist.

medio 1 adj (**a**) half (a).

(**b**) **media naranja** half an orange, a half orange; **media hora** half an hour; **nos queda media botella** we've half a bottle left; **media luna** half-moon, (fig) crescent; **medio luto** half-mourning; **media luz** half-light; **acudió media provincia** half the province turned up.

(**c**) point etc mid, midway, middle; **clase —** middle class(es); **dedo —** middle finger; **a media tarde** halfway through the afternoon; **café de media mañana** (mid-)morning coffee.

(**d**) (Math) mean, average; (fig) average; **el hombre —** the average man, the ordinary man, the man in the street; see **término** etc.

(**e**) (SAm) big, huge.

(**f**) **a medias** half; by halves; **está escrito a medias** it's half-written; **lo dejó hecho a medias** he left it half-done; **estoy satisfecho sólo a medias** I am only partly satisfied; **ir a medias** to go fifty-fifty (con with), divide the costs (etc) equally; **lo pagamos a medias** we share the cost.

2 adv half; **— dormido** half asleep; **estar — borracho** to be half drunk; **está — escrito, está a — escribir** it is half-written; **eso no está ni — bien** that isn't at all right.

3 nm (**a**) middle, centre; halfway point (etc); (Math) mean; **— aritmético** arithmetical mean; **justo —** happy medium, golden mean; fair compromise; **equivocarse de — a —** to be completely wrong; **en — in** the middle; **in between; en — de la plaza** in the middle of the square; **en — de tanta confusión** in the midst of such confusion; **la casa de en —** the middle house; the house in between; **quitar algo de en —** to remove something; to get rid of something, get something out of the way; **quitarse de en —** to get out of the way; to duck, dodge; to remove oneself; **pasar por — de** to go through (the middle of); **tomar algo por el —** to grasp something round the middle; **de por — in** between; **hay dificultades de por —** there are snags in the way; **meterse de por —** to intervene; **día (de) por —** (SAm) every other day.

(**b**) (Sport) half-back; **— centro** centre-half.

(**c**) (Spiritualism) medium.

(**d**) means, way, method; medium; measure, expedient; **—s de transporte** means of transport; **por — de** by means of, by, through; **por todos los —s** by all possible means, in every possible way; **no hay — de conseguirlo** there is no way of getting it; **poner todos los —s para + infin, no regatear — para + infin** to spare no effort to + infin.

(**e**) **—s** (Econ, Fin) means, resources.

(**f**) atmosphere; milieu, ambience; environment; circle; (Bio: also **— ambiente**) environment; **— de cultivo** culture medium; **en los —s financieros** in financial circles; **encontrarse en su —** to be in one's element.

mediocre adj middling, average; (pej) mediocre, rather poor.

mediocridad nf middling quality; (pej) mediocrity; **es una —** he's a nonentity, he's a dead loss.

mediodía nm (**a**) midday, noon; **a — at** noon. (**b**) (Geog) south.

Medio Oriente m Middle East.

mediquillo nm (pej) quack (doctor).

medir [3l] **1** vt (**a**) to measure; to survey, plot; **— a**

millas, **— por millas** to measure in miles; **— a uno** (con la vista: fig) to size someone up.

(**b**) plan, possibility etc to weigh up.

(**c**) (Lit) verse to scan (properly).

2 vi (**a**) to measure, be; **la tela mide 90 cms** the cloth measures 90 cms; **el papel mide 20 cms de ancho** the paper is 20 cms wide; **ella mide 1,50 m** she is 1.50 m tall; **mide 88 cms de pecho** she is 88 cms round the chest, her bust measurement is 88 cms.

(**b**) (Lit) to scan (properly).

3 medirse vr (**a**) **— con uno** to measure up to someone; to test oneself against someone.

(**b**) (fig) to be moderate, act with restraint.

(**c**) (SAm: Sport) to play each other, meet; to quarrel, come to blows.

meditabundo adj pensive, thoughtful.

meditación nf meditation; pondering; **—es** meditations (sobre on).

meditar [1a] **1** vt to ponder, think over, meditate (on); plan etc to think out, work out, plan. **2** vi to ponder, think, meditate; to muse.

Mediterráneo m Mediterranean.

mediterráneo adj Mediterranean.

médium nm, pl **médiums** medium.

medo nm: **los —s y los persas** the Medes and the Persians.

medra nf increase, growth; improvement; (Econ etc) prosperity.

medrar [1a] vi to increase, grow; to improve, do well, do better; (Econ etc) to prosper, thrive, do well; (animal, plant) to grow, thrive; **¡medrados estamos!** (iro) a fine thing you've done!

medro nm = **medra**.

medroso adj fearful, timid, fainthearted.

médula nf, **medula** nf (**a**) (Anat) marrow; medulla; **— espinal** spinal cord; **hasta la —** (fig) to the core; through and through; **estoy convencido hasta la —** I am profoundly convinced.

(**b**) (Bot) pith.

(**c**) (fig) essence; substance; pith.

medusa nf jellyfish.

Mefistófeles m Mephistopheles.

megaciclo nm megacycle.

megáfono nm megaphone.

megalítico adj megalithic.

megalito nm megalith.

megalomanía nf megalomania.

megalómano nm, **megalómana** nf megalomaniac.

megatón nm megaton.

megavatio nm megawatt.

megavoltio nm megavolt.

mejicanismo nm mexicanism, word (or phrase etc) peculiar to Mexico.

mejicano 1 adj Mexican. **2** nm, **mejicana** nf Mexican.

Méjico m Mexico.

mejido adj egg beaten.

mejilla nf cheek.

mejillón nm mussel.

mejor 1 adj (**a**) (comp) better (que than).

(**b**) (superl) best; bidder highest; **es el — de todos** he's the best of all; **lo — the** best thing, the best part (etc); **lo — de la novela** the best part of the novel, the best thing about the novel; **lo — de la vida** the prime of life; **hice lo — que pude** I did the best I could, I did my best; **llevar lo — to** get the best of it; **a lo — probably**, maybe; with any luck; suddenly, when least expected; **"¿crees que lo hará?" ... "a lo —"** "do you think he'll do it?" ... "he may do" (or "maybe").

2 adv (**a**) (comp) better; **A canta — que B** A sings better than B; **— quisiera + infin** I would rather + infin; **¡—!** good!, that's fine!; **— que** — better and better, all the better; **tanto — all** the better, so much the better (para for); **está mucho —** he's much better; **"nunca habéis estado —"** (slogan) "you never had it so good".

(**b**) (superl) best.

mejora nf (**a**) improvement; **—s** (to property) improvements; alterations, repairs. (**b**) (at auction) higher bid. (**c**) (Mex: Agr) weeding, cleaning.

mejorable adj improvable; **esto es fácilmente —** this can easily be improved.

mejoramiento nm improvement.

mejorana nf marjoram.

mejorar [1a] **1** vt (**a**) to improve, make better, ameliorate; to enhance; bid to raise; offer to improve, increase; record to break.

(**b**) **— a** to be better than, be superior to.

2 vi and **mejorarse** vr (**a**) to improve, get better; (Med) to get better; (Meteorol) to improve, clear up;

(Fin etc) to do well, prosper; **los negocios mejoran** business is improving, business is picking up; **¡que se mejore!** get well soon!

(b) *(at auction)* to raise one's bid.

mejoría *nf* improvement; recovery; **¡que siga la —!** I hope the improvement continues.

mejunje *nm* **(a)** brew, mixture, concoction. **(b)** *(fam)* fraud. **(c)** *(Arg, Mex, PR)* mess, tangle, mix-up.

melado 1 *adj* honey-coloured. **2** *nm* treacle, syrup; *(SAm)* cane syrup.

meladura *nf (Cu, Mex)* cane syrup.

melancolía *nf* melancholy, gloom(iness), sadness; *(Med)* melancholia.

melancólicamente *adv* gloomily, sadly, in a melancholy way; wistfully.

melancólico *adj* melancholy, gloomy, sad; dreamy, wistful.

melanismo *nm* melanism.

melarchía *nf (CAm)* = **melancolía**.

melaza *nf (also —s)* molasses; treacle.

melcocha *nf* molasses; treacle; candy, molasses toffee.

melcochado *adj fruit etc* candied; *(in colour)* golden, honey-coloured.

melcocharse [1a] *vr* to thicken *(in boiling)*.

mêlée [me'le] *nf (Rugby)* scrum.

melena *nf* long hair; loose hair, flowing hair; *(pej)* mop of hair, bushy hair; *(as style)* ponytail; *(Zool)* mane; **andar a la —** to pull one another's hair, *(fig)* to quarrel; **estar en —** to have one's hair down; **soltar la —** *(fig)* to break out, shatter the conventions; to lose all restraint.

melenudo *adj* long-haired.

melga *nf (Arg, Mex)* plot of land prepared for sowing; *(Chi)* furrow.

melifluo *adj* mellifluous, sweet.

melindre *nm* **(a)** sweet cake, iced bun; honey fritter. **(b)** **—s** daintiness, dainty ways; *(pej)* affectation, affected ways; squeamishness; prudery, prudishness; **gastar —s** = **melindrear**.

melindrear [1a] *vi* to be affected, indulge in affectation; to be squeamish; to be prudish; to be excessively finicky, be terribly fussy.

melindroso *adj* affected; squeamish; prudish; finicky, fussy.

melisca *nf (Arg)* gleaning.

melocotón *nm* peach.

melocotonero *nm* peach tree.

melodía *nf* **(a)** *(una —)* melody; tune, air. **(b)** *(quality)* melodiousness.

melódico *adj* melodic.

melodiosamente *adv* melodiously, tunefully.

melodioso *adj* melodious, tuneful.

melodrama *nm* melodrama.

melodramáticamente *adv* melodramatically.

melodramático *adj* melodramatic.

melón[1] *nm* **(a)** *(Bot)* melon. **(b)** *(fam)* head, nut *(sl)*. **(c)** *(fam)* idiot.

melón[2] *nm (Zool)* = **meloncillo**.

melonada *nf (fam)* silly thing, idiotic remark *(etc)*.

meloncillo *nm (Zool)* ichneumon, (kind of) mongoose.

melosidad *nf* **(a)** sweetness; *(pej)* sickliness. **(b)** *(fig)* sweetness; gentleness; *(pej)* smoothness.

meloso *adj* **(a)** honeyed, sweet; *(pej)* sickly, cloying. **(b)** *(fig)* voice etc sweet, musical; gentle; *(pej)* smooth, soapy.

mella *nf* **(a)** nick, dent, notch; *(in teeth etc)* gap; **hacer —** *(fig)* to make an impression, sink in, strike home; **hacer — en** *(or* **a)** to make an impression on, tell on. **(b)** *(fig)* harm, damage; **hacer — en** to do damage to, harm.

mellado *adj edge* jagged, nicked, ragged; *person* gap-toothed.

mellar [1a] *vt* **(a)** to nick, dent, notch; to take a chip out of. **(b)** *(fig)* to damage, harm.

mellizo 1 *adj* twin. **2** *nm*, **melliza** *nf* twin.

membrana *nf* **(a)** membrane; *(Orn)* membrane, web; **— mucosa** mucous membrane; **— virginal** hymen. **(b)** *(Chi)* diphtheria.

membranoso *adj* membranous.

membrete *nm* letterhead, heading.

membrillero *nm* quince tree.

membrillo *nm* quince; *(carne de)* **— quince jelly.**

membrudo *adj* burly, brawny, tough.

memela *nf (CAm, Mex)* thick pancake of maize flour.

memez *nf* silly thing; farce, absurdity.

memo 1 *adj* silly, stupid. **2** *nm* idiot.

memorable *adj* memorable.

memorablemente *adv* memorably.

memorando *nm (Acad)*, **memorándum** *nm*, *pl* **memorándums** **(a)** notebook. **(b)** *(Pol etc)* memorandum.

memoria *nf* **(a)** *(in general)* memory; **de buena —**, **de feliz —** of happy memory; **digno de —** memorable; **falta de —** forgetfulness; **flaco de —** forgetful; **aprender algo de —** to learn something by heart; to memorize something, commit something to memory; **hablar de —** to speak from memory; **se le fue de la —** he forgot it, it slipped his mind; **en — de** in memory of; **la peor tormenta de que hay —** the worst storm in living memory; the worst storm on record; **hacer — de algo** to recall something, bring something to mind; **no queda — de eso** there is no memory *(or* record) of that; **tener mala —** to have a bad memory; **si tengo buena —** if my memory serves me; **traer algo a la —** to recall something.

(b) note, report, statement; record; aide-mémoire, memorandum; petition; *(learned)* paper; **— anual** annual report; **—s** *(of person)* memoirs, *(of society)* transactions.

(c) **—s** *(to person)* regards, remembrances.

memorial *nm* memorial, petition; *(Law)* brief.

memorialista *nm* amanuensis.

memorión *nm (fam)* good memory, amazing memory.

memorioso *adj (SAm)* having a retentive memory, that remembers everything.

memorista *adj (SAm)* having a retentive memory; **es —** *(pej)* he just memorizes things.

memorización *nf (SAm)* memorizing.

memorizar [1f] *vt (SAm)* to memorize.

mena *nf* ore.

menaje *nm* **(a)** family, household; **vida de —** *(SAm)* family life, domestic life.

(b) housekeeping; housework, upkeep of the house.

(c) *(Comm etc)* household equipment, furnishings; **sección de —** *(in store)* hardware and kitchen department.

mención *nf* mention; **— honorífica** honourable mention; **hacer — de** to mention.

mencionado *adj* aforementioned.

mencionar [1a] *vt* to mention, refer to; to name; **sin —** . . . let alone . . .; **dejar de —** to fail to mention, leave unmentioned.

mendacidad *nf* **(a)** mendacity, untruthfulness. **(b)** *(una —)* untruth, gross lie.

mendaz *adj* mendacious; lying, untruthful.

mendeliano *adj* Mendelian.

mendelismo *nm* Mendelism, Mendelianism.

mendicante 1 *adj* mendicant. **2** *nmf* mendicant.

mendicidad *nf* begging; mendicity.

mendigar [1h] **1** *vt* to beg (for). **2** *vi* to beg (for alms).

mendigo *nm*, **mendiga** *nf* beggar.

mendrugo *nm* **(a)** (hard) crust. **(b)** *(fam)* dolt, blockhead.

mene *nm (Col, Ven)* pitch, asphalt.

menear [1a] **1** *vt* **(a)** to move, shift; *head etc* to shake, toss; *tail* to wag; *hips* to sway, swing, waggle; **sin — el dedo** without lifting a finger; **peor es meneallo** it's best to leave that alone; don't go stirring all that up.

(b) **— cálamo** to wield a pen.

(c) *affair* to get on with, get moving; *business etc* to handle, conduct.

2 menearse *vr* **(a)** to move; to shake; to wag; to sway, swing, waggle.

(b) to hustle, bestir oneself, get a move on; **¡—!** get going!, jump to it!

Menelao *m* Menelaus.

meneo *nm* **(a)** movement; shake, toss; wag; sway(ing), swing(ing); waggle; jerk, jolt; **dar un — a** to jerk, jolt, move suddenly. **(b)** *(fam)* hiding.

menequear [1a] *vt*, **menequetear** [1a] *vt (Arg, Mex)* to shake, wag.

menequе(te)o *nm (Arg, Mex)* shaking, wagging.

menester *nm* **(a)** **ser —** to be necessary; **cuando sea —** when it is necessary; **es — + infin** it is necessary to + infin, we *(etc)* must + infin; **todo es —** everything is welcome.

(b) job, piece of business; errand; **—es** duties, jobs, business; occupation; function; **salir para un —** to go out on an errand; **hacer sus —es** *(euph)* to do one's business *(euph)*.

(c) **—es** *(Tech)* gear, tackle, tools.

menesteroso *adj* needy.

menestra *nf* **(a)** vegetable soup, stew. **(b)** **—s** dried vegetables.

menestral *nm* workman, artisan.

mengano *nm*, **mengana** *nf* Mr *(etc)* So-and-so; *see* **fulano.**

mengua *nf* **(a)** decrease, diminishment; dwindling;

decay, decline; **ir en — de** to contribute to the lessening of, assist the decrease (*or* restriction *etc*) of; **sin —** complete, whole; untouched.
(b) lack, want; loss.
(c) poverty.
(d) (*of person*) spinelessness, weakness of character.
(e) discredit; **ir en — de uno** to be to someone's discredit.
menguadamente *adv* (a) (*fig*) wretchedly; weakly, spinelessly. (b) meanly. (c) foolishly.
menguado 1 *adj* (a) decreased, diminished.
(b) (*fig*) wretched, miserable; weak, spineless, weak in character; cowardly.
(c) unlucky; **en hora menguada** at an unlucky moment.
(d) mean.
(e) foolish.
2 *nm* (*knitting*) decrease.
menguante 1 *adj* decreasing, diminishing; dwindling; decaying; *moon* waning; *tide* ebb (*attr*).
2 *nf* (a) (*Naut*) ebb tide, low water.
(b) (*of moon*) waning.
(c) (*fig*) decay, decline; **estar en —** to be in decline.
menguar [1i] **1** *vt* (a) to lessen, diminish, reduce; (*knitting*) to decrease (by).
(b) (*fig*) to discredit.
2 *vi* (a) to diminish, get less, dwindle, decrease; (*of number, tide etc*) to go down; (*of moon*) to wane.
(b) (*fig*) to wane, decay, decline.
mengue *nm* (*fam*) the devil; **¡malos —s te lleven!** go to hell!
meningitis *nf* meningitis.
menjunje *nm*, **menjurje** *nm* see **mejunje**.
menopausia *nf* menopause.
menor 1 *adj* (*Eccl*) order minor; (*Mus*) minor.
2 *adj comp* (a) (*in size*) smaller (*que* than); less, lesser; **en — número** in smaller numbers; **celidonia — lesser** celandine.
(b) (*in age*) younger (*que* than); junior (*que* to); **el hermano —** the younger brother; **Juanito es — que Pepe** Johnnie is younger than Joe; see **edad**.
3 *adj superl* (a) (*in size*) smallest; least; **éste es el — de todos** this is the smallest of the lot; **no le concedo la — importancia** I don't attach the least (*or* slightest) importance to it.
(b) (*in age*) youngest; most junior; **ella es la — de todas** she is the youngest of all.
4 *nmf* young person, juvenile, (*Law*) minor; **un — de 14** an under-14; **los —es de edad** those who are under age, the juveniles; **apto para —es** (*Cine*) for all ages, "Universal" (U); **no apto para —es** (*Cine*) not suitable for juveniles.
5 *nm* (a) **al por —** (*Comm*) retail; **vender un género al por —** to sell goods retail.
(b) **contar algo por —** to recount something in detail.
Menorca *f* Minorca.
menoría *nf* (a) (*Law*) minority. (b) inferiority; subordination.
menorista (*Chi, Mex*) **1** *adj* retail (*attr*). **2** *nmf* retailer.
menorquín 1 *adj* Minorcan. **2** *nm*, **menorquina** *nf* Minorcan.
menos 1 *adj* (a) (*Math*) sign minus.
(b) (*comp*) less; fewer; **con — ruido** with less noise; **con — hombres** with fewer men; **A tiene — ventajas que B** A has fewer advantages than B; **A tiene — años que B** A is younger than B; **éste es — coche que el anterior** (*fam*) this is not such a good car as the old one.
(c) (*superl*) least; fewest; **es el que — culpa tiene** least blame attaches to him, he is least to blame.
2 *adv* (a) (*comp*) less, (*superl*) least; **hoy se va —** people don't go so much nowadays, nowadays people go less; **es el — inteligente de los 4** he is the least intelligent of the 4; **no quiero alquilarlo ni — comprarlo** I don't want to rent it and still less to buy it; **¿qué —?** (*fam*) what else did you expect?; **— de, — de lo que, — que** less than; **— de lo que piensas** less than you think; **fue nada — que un rey** he was nothing less than a king, he was a king no less; **hay 7 de —** we're 7 short, there are 7 missing; **me dieron un paquete con medio kilo de —** they gave me a packet which was half a kilo short (*or* under weight); **me han pagado 2 libras de —** they have underpaid me by £2.
(b) (*phrases with* lo) **lo — 10** 10 at least; **lo — posible** as little as possible; **eso es lo de —** that's the least of it; **es lo — que se puede esperar** it's the

least one can expect; **al —, a lo —, por lo —** at least.
(c) (*idioms*) **a — de** without; **tener a — + infin** to consider it beneath oneself to + *infin*; **ir a —, venir a —** to come down in the world; to decline, decay; to run to seed; **darse de —** to underestimate oneself, hide one's light under a bushel; **echar a uno de —** to miss someone; **hacer a uno de —** to despise someone; to belittle someone; **no se quedó en —** he was not to be outdone; see **cuando, mucho, poder.**
3 *prep* (a) except; **todos — él** everybody except him; **¡todo — eso!** anything but that!
(b) (*Math*) minus, less; **7 — 2 son 5** 2 from 7 leaves 5, 7 take away 2 leaves 5; **las 7 — 20** (*time*) 20 to 7.
4 *conj*: **a — que . . . unless . . .**
5 *nm* (a) (*Math*) minus sign (-).
(b) see **más.**
menoscabar [1a] *vt* (a) to lessen, reduce, diminish; to damage, harm, impair. (b) to discredit.
menoscabo *nm* lessening, reduction; damage, harm; loss; **con — de, en — de** to the detriment of; **sin —** unimpaired; **sufrir —** to suffer damage, suffer loss.
menospreciable *adj* contemptible.
menospreciador *adj* scornful.
menospreciar [1b] *vt* (a) to scorn, despise. (b) to slight. (c) to underrate, undervalue.
menospreciativo *adj* scornful, contemptuous; slighting.
menosprecio *nm* (a) scorn, contempt.
(b) underrating, undervaluation.
(c) disrespect; **con — del sexo de la víctima** without regard for the sex of the victim.
mensaje *nm* message; **— de buenos augurios** goodwill message; **— de la corona** (*Parl*) speech from the throne.
mensajero *nm*, **mensajera** *nf* messenger.
menso *adj* (*Mex*) silly, stupid.
menstruación *nf* menstruation.
menstrual *adj* menstrual.
menstruar [1e] *vi* to menstruate.
menstruo *nm* (a) menstruation. (b) menses.
mensual *adj* monthly; **50 dólares —es** 50 dollars a month.
mensualidad *nf* monthly payment (*or* salary, instalment *etc*).
mensualmente *adv* monthly.
mensuario *nm* (*SAm*) monthly journal.
ménsula *nf* bracket; (*Archit*) corbel.
mensura *nf* (*SAm*) measurement.
mensurable *adj* measurable.
mensuración *nf* mensuration.
menta *nf* mint; **— romana, — verde** spearmint.
mentado *adj* (a) aforementioned. (b) well-known, famous.
mental *adj* mental; *capacity, work etc* intellectual.
mentalidad *nf* mentality, mind.
mentalmente *adv* mentally.
mentar [1k] *vt* to mention, name.
mentas *nfpl* (*Arg, Bol, Urug*) (a) reputation. (b) rumours, gossip.
mente *nf* mind; intelligence, understanding; **— consciente** conscious mind; **— subconsciente** subconscious mind; **cambiar de —** to change one's mind; **no está en mi — + infin, no tengo en — + infin** it is not in my mind to + *infin*, it is not my intention to + *infin*; **se le fue completamente de la —** it completely slipped his mind.
mentecatería *nf*, **mentecatez** *nf* stupidity, foolishness.
mentecato 1 *adj* silly, stupid. **2** *nm*, **mentecata** *nf* idiot, fool.
mentidero *nm* place where people gossip.
mentir [3i] **1** *vt* (*lit*) to feign, pretend; to suggest (falsely) to; **la sed me mintió un arroyo cercano** my thirst led me to suppose there was a stream nearby.
2 *vi* to lie, tell a lie, tell lies; to be deceptive; **¡miento!** sorry, I'm wrong!, my mistake!; **¡esta carta no me dejará —!** this letter will bear me out!, this letter will confirm what I say!
mentira *nf* (a) (*una —*) lie, falsehood; (*in general*) lying, untruthfulness, deceitfulness; (*Lit*) fiction, invention; (*in text*) error, misprint; **¡—!** it's a lie!; **una mentira como una casa** a whopping great lie (*sl*); **— oficiosa, — piadosa** white lie; **¡parece —!** well (I never)!; you don't say so!; **aunque parezca —** however incredible it seems; **parece — que . . . it** seems impossible that . . .; **parece — que no te acuerdas** I'm surprised you don't remember it; **no**

hay — **que no salga** truth will out; **coger a uno en una** — to catch someone in a lie.
(**b**) white mark (*on fingernail*).
(**c**) (*Arg, Chi, CAm*) cracking of knuckles; **sacar —s** to crack one's knuckles.
mentirijillas: es de —, **va de** — it's only a joke; (*to child*) just pretend, it's just make-believe; **jugar de** — to play for fun (*ie not for money*).
mentirilla *nf* fib; white lie.
mentirosillo *nm*, **mentirosilla** *nf* fibber.
mentiroso 1 *adj* (**a**) lying, deceitful, untruthful; deceptive, false. (**b**) *text* full of errors, full of misprints. **2** *nm*, **mentirosa** *nf* liar; deceiver.
mentís *nm*, *pl* **mentís** denial; **dar el** — **a** to refute, deny, give the lie to.
mentol *nm* menthol.
mentolado *adj* mentholated.
mentón *nm* chin.
mentor *nm* mentor.
menú *nm* menu.
menudear [1a] **1** *vt* (**a**) to repeat frequently, do repeatedly; *story etc* to tell in great detail.
(**b**) (*Col*) to sell retail.
2 *vi* (**a**) to be frequent, happen frequently; (*of missiles etc*) to rain, come thick and fast; to come in abundance.
(**b**) to go into great detail.
(**c**) (*Arg, Mex*) to abound; to increase, grow in number.
menudencia *nf* (**a**) trifle, small thing; —s little things, odds and ends. (**b**) minuteness; exactness; meticulousness. (**c**) —s pork products; offal.
menudeo *nm* (*Comm*) retail trade; **vender al** — to sell retail.
menudillos *nmpl* giblets.
menudo 1 *adj* (**a**) small, tiny, minute; (*fig*) slight, petty, insignificant; **moneda menuda** small change, coins of low denomination.
(**b**) *person* exact, meticulous.
(**c**) (*iro*) fine, some; **¡— negocio!**[1] some deal!; **¡menuda plancha!** what a bloomer! (*fam*); **¡menuda vidorra nos vamos a dar!** we won't half live it up! (*fam*); **¡menuda me la han hecho!** they've done it on me!
(**d**) (*with prep*) **a** — frequently, often; **a la menuda, por la menuda** (*Comm*) retail; **contar algo por** — to tell something in detail.
2 *nm* (**a**) small change.
(**b**) —s offal; giblets.
meñique 1 *adj* tiny, very small; **dedo** — = **2** *nm* little finger.
meollo *nm* (**a**) (*Anat*) marrow, brains.
(**b**) (*of bread*) soft part, inside, crumb.
(**c**) (*fig: of person*) brains.
(**d**) (*fig: of matter etc*) gist, essence, core; solid substance, solid part, meat.
meón 1 *adj* child that constantly wets itself. **2** *nm*, **meona** *nf* baby (boy, girl).
meque *nm* (*Cu*) slap, punch.
mequetrefe *nm* good-for-nothing, whippersnapper.
meramente *adv* merely, only, solely.
merca *nf* (*Mex*) shopping, purchases.
mercachifle *nm* (**a**) small-time trader, dealer; hawker, huckster. (**b**) (*fig*) money grubber.
mercadear [1a] *vi* to deal, trade.
mercadeo *nm* marketing.
mercader *nm* (*esp Hist*) merchant.
mercadería *nf* commodity; —s goods, merchandise.
mercado *nm* market; **M— Común** Common Market; — **de dinero** money market; — **exterior** overseas market; — **interior**, — **nacional** home market; — **libre** free market (*de* in); — **mundial** world market; — **negro** black market; — **de valores** stock market; — **de viejo** rag fair; — **de signo favorable al comprador** buyer's market; — **de signo favorable al vendedor** seller's market; **inundar el** — **de** to flood the market with.
mercadotecnia *nf* marketing; **estudios de** — market research.
mercancía 1 *nf* commodity; —s goods, merchandise.
2 —s *nm* goods train, freight train (*US*).
mercante 1 *adj* merchant (*attr*), trading, commercial; **buque** — = **2** *nm* merchantman, merchant ship.
mercantil *adj* mercantile, trading, commercial; *law* commercial.
mercantilismo *nm* mercantilism.
mercar [1g] *vt* to buy.
merced *nf* (**a**) (*arch*) favour; benefit, reward; pleasure, will; **hacer la** — **de** + *infin* to do someone the favour of + *ger*; **tenga la** — **de** + *infin* please be so good as to + *infin*.
(**b**) — **a** thanks to.

(**c**) (*arch*) **vuestra** — your honour, your worship, sir.
(**d**) **estar a la** — **de** to be at the mercy of.
mercenario 1 *adj* mercenary. **2** *nm* (*Mil*) mercenary; (*Agr*) day labourer; (*fig*) hack, hireling.
mercería *nf* (**a**) haberdashery, notions (*US*).
(**b**) haberdasher's (shop), notions store (*US*); (*Mex, Per, PR*) draper's (shop), dry-goods store (*US*); (*Chi*) hardware store.
mercero *nm* haberdasher; (*Mex, Per, PR*) draper.
mercurial *adj* mercurial.
Mercurio m Mercury.
mercurio *nm* mercury.
merdoso *adj* (*tabu*) filthy; sluttish.
merecedor *adj* deserving, worthy (*de* of); — **de crédito** solvent; — **de confianza** trustworthy; **ser** — **de** to deserve, be deserving of.
merecer [2d] **1** *vt* (**a**) to deserve, be worthy of, merit; — + *infin* to deserve to + *infin*; **merece que se le dé el premio** he deserves (to receive) the prize.
(**b**) (*Col, Ec*) to catch; to snatch, pinch (*fam*); to find.
2 *vi* to be deserving, be worthy; — **mucho** to be very deserving; — **bien de la patria** to deserve well of one's country, deserve one's country's gratitude.
3 merecerse *vr*: — **algo** to earn something.
merecidamente *adv* deservedly.
merecido 1 *adj* well deserved, fully deserved; **bien** — **lo tiene** it serves him right. **2** *nm* (just) deserts; **llevar su** — to get one's deserts.
merecimiento *nm* (**a**) deserts. (**b**) merit, worthiness.
merendar [1k] **1** *vt* (**a**) to have for tea.
(**b**) — **lo que escribe otro** to look at what someone else is writing; — **las cartas de otro** to peep at someone else's cards, take a sly look at an opponent's cards.
2 *vi* to have tea; (*in country*) to picnic, take tea out.
3 merendarse *vr* (*fam*) (**a**) — **algo** to wangle something (*fam*), get something by a fiddle (*fam*).
(**b**) — **una fortuna** to squander a fortune.
(**c**) — **a uno** (*Col*) to beat someone; (*Col, Chi, Mex*) to kill someone.
merendero *nm* tearoom; picnic spot.
merengue *nm* (**a**) (*Cook*) meringue. (**b**) (*Ant, Col, Chi, Per*) sickly person, invalid. (**c**) (*Arg*) row, fuss.
meretriz *nf* prostitute.
mergo *nm* cormorant.
meridiana *nf* (**a**) divan, couch; chaise longue. (**b**) **a la** — at noon.
meridiano *nm* meridian.
meridional 1 *adj* southern. **2** *nmf* southerner.
merienda *nf* tea; afternoon snack; (*on journey*) packed meal; (*in country*) picnic, picnic tea (*also* — **campestre**); — **de negros** (*fam*) bedlam; (*fam*) crooked deal, dishonest share-out; **ir de** — to go for a picnic; **juntar** —s (*fig*) to join forces, pool one's resources.
merienda-cena *nf* high tea.
merino 1 *adj* merino. **2** *nm* merino (sheep); merino wool.
mérito *nm* merit; worth, value; excellence; **de** — worthy, of merit; —s **de guerra** *equivalent to* mention in dispatches; **hacer** — **de** to mention; **hacer** —s **to** strive to be deserving; **restar** — **de** to detract from; **alega los siguientes** —s he quotes the following facts in support (*or* in his favour).
meritocracia *nf* meritocracy.
meritorio 1 *adj* meritorious, worthy, deserving; praiseworthy. **2** *nm* unpaid employee, apprentice, (*esp*) office boy.
merla *nf* = **mirlo**.
Merlín m Merlin; **saber más que** — to know the lot.
merlo[1] *nm* (*Fish*) black wrasse.
merlo[2] *nm* (*SAm*) idiot.
merluza *nf* (**a**) (*Fish*) hake. (**b**) (*sl*) **coger una** — to get sozzled (*sl*); **estar** —; **estar con la** — to get boozed up.
merma *nf* decrease; shrinkage; wastage, loss.
mermar [1a] **1** *vt* to reduce, lessen; to deplete; *pay, rations etc* to cut down.
2 *vi and* **mermarse** *vr* to decrease, dwindle; to be depleted; (*liquid*) to go down; (*fig*) to waste away.
mermelada *nf* jam; — **de albaricoques** apricot jam; — **de manzanas** apple sauce; — **de naranjas amargas** marmalade.
mero[1] **1** *adj* (**a**) mere; pure, simple.
(**b**) (*Mex*) exact, real.
2 *adv* (**a**) (*Col, Ven*) only.
(**b**) (*Guat, Mex, Salv*) soon.
(**c**) (*Guat*) really, truly.
(**d**) (*Mex*) just; right, exactly; **aquí** — right here; **él va** — **adelante** he's just ahead.
mero[2] *nm* (*Fish*) grouper.

merodeador 1 *adj* marauding; prowling. **2** *nm* (*Mil etc*) marauder; raider; (*at night*) prowler.
merodear [1a] *vi* (a) (*Mil etc*) to maraud; (*at night*) to prowl (about), rove about. (b) (*Mex*) to make money by illicit means.
merodeo *nm* marauding; prowling, roving.
merolico *nm* (*Mex*) quack, seller of quack remedies.
merovingio 1 *adj* Merovingian. **2** *nm*, **merovingia** *nf* Merovingian.
mes *nm* (a) month; **50 dólares al** — 50 dollars a month; — **lunar** lunar month; **el** — **corriente** the current month, this month; **el** — **que viene, el** — **próximo** next month.
(b) (*Fin*) month's pay; monthly payment.
(c) (*Med*) menses.
mesa *nf* (a) table; (*also* — **de trabajo**) desk; (*Comm*) counter; — **de alas abatibles** gate-leg(ged) table, table with flaps; — **de billar** billiard table; — **de café** coffee table; café table; — **de despacho** office desk; — **de noche** bedside table; — **de operaciones**, — **operatoria** operating table; — **redonda** (*restaurant*) table d'hôte; (*Hist*) Round Table; (*Pol*) round table; — **de tijera** folding table; **alzar la** —, **levantar la** —, **quitar la** — (*SAm*) to clear away; **bendecir la** — to say grace; **poner la** — to lay the table; **sentarse a la** — to sit down to table; **servir a la** — to wait at table; **vino de** — table wine.
(b) board; — **y cama** bed and board; **tratar a uno a** — **y mantel** to entertain someone royally.
(c) (*Geog*) meseta, tableland, plateau.
(d) (*Archit*) landing.
(e) (*of tool, blade*) side, flat.
(f) (*persons*) presiding committee, board.
mesana *nf* mizzen.
mesarse [1a] *vr* (a) (*of 2 persons*) to pull each other's hair. (b) — **el pelo** (*or* **los cabellos**) to tear one's hair.
mescalina *nf* mescaline.
mescolanza *nf* =**mezcolanza**.
mesenterio *nm* mesentery.
mesera *nf* (*Mex*) waitress.
mesero *nm* (*Mex*) waiter.
meseta *nf* (a) (*Geog*) meseta, tableland, plateau. (b) (*Archit*) landing.
mesiánico *adj* messianic.
Mesías *m* Messiah.
mesilla *nf* (a) small table, side table, occasional table; — **de chimenea** mantelpiece; — **de noche** bedside table; — **plegable** folding table; — **de ruedas** trolley.
(b) (*Cu*) market stall.
mesmeriano *adj* mesmeric.
mesmerismo *nm* mesmerism.
mesón[1] *nm* (*Phys*) meson.
mesón[2] *nm* (a) (*arch*) inn; (*modern*) hotel with period décor, olde-worlde pub. (b) (*Chi*) counter; bar.
mesonero *nm*, **mesonera** *nf* (*arch*) innkeeper; landlord, landlady.
mesteño (*Mex*) **1** *adj* horse wild, untamed. **2** *nm* mustang.
mestizaje *nm* (a) crossbreeding; miscegenation. (b) half-castes (*collectively*).
mestizar [1f] *vt* to crossbreed; *race* to adulterate by crossbreeding.
mestizo 1 *adj* half-caste, half-breed, racially mixed; (*Zool*) crossbred; hybrid; mongrel.
2 *nm*, **mestiza** *nf* half-caste, half-breed; (*Zool*) crossbred animal; hybrid; mongrel.
mesura *nf* (a) gravity, dignity, calm. (b) moderation, restraint. (c) courtesy.
mesurado *adj* (a) grave, dignified, calm. (b) moderate, restrained. (c) courteous.
mesurar [1a] **1** *vt* (a) to restrain, temper. (b) (*SAm*) to measure. **2 mesurarse** *vr* to restrain oneself, act with restraint.
meta 1 *nf* (a) (*Sport*) goal; (*in race*) winning post, finishing line. (b) (*fig*) goal, aim, objective. **2** *nm* goalkeeper.
metabólico *adj* metabolic.
metabolismo *nm* metabolism.
metacarpiano *nm* metacarpal.
metafísica *nf* metaphysics.
metafísico 1 *adj* metaphysical. **2** *nm* metaphysician.
metáfora *nf* metaphor.
metafórico *adj* metaphoric(al).
metal *nm* (a) metal; (*Mus*) brass; (*Mex*) ore; — **en láminas**, — **laminado** sheet metal; **el vil** — filthy lucre. (b) (*of voice*) timbre; (*fig*) quality.
metalero *adj* (*Bol, Chi, Per*) metal (*attr*).
metálico 1 *adj* metallic; metal (*attr*). **2** *nm* (a) specie, bullion, coin; cash; **pagar en** — to pay (in) cash; **premio en** — cash prize. (b) metalworker.
metalista *nm* metalworker.

metalistería *nf* metalwork.
metalizado *adj* mercenary, dedicated to making money; who sees everything in terms of money.
metalizarse [1f] *vr* (*fig*) to become mercenary.
metalurgia *nf* metallurgy.
metalúrgico 1 *adj* metallurgic(al). **2** *nm* metallurgist.
metamórfico *adj* metamorphic.
metamorfosear [1a] **1** *vt* to metamorphose, transform, change (*en* into). **2 metamorfosearse** *vr* to be metamorphosed, be transformed, change.
metamorfosis *nf*, *pl* **metamorfosis** metamorphosis, transformation, change.
metano *nm* methane.
metatarsiano *nm* metatarsal.
metate *nm* (*CAm, Mex*) flat stone for grinding.
metátesis *nf*, *pl* **metátesis** metathesis.
metedor *nm* smuggler.
metedura *nf* (a) putting, placing; insertion. (b) — **de pata** (*fam*) blunder, bloomer (*fam*), clanger (*sl*).
meteduría *nf* smuggling.
metejón *nm* (a) (*Arg*) violent love; passion, fanatical enthusiasm. (b) (*Col*) fuss.
metelón *adj* (*Mex*) meddling.
meteórico *adj* meteoric (*also fig*).
meteorito *nm* meteor, meteorite.
meteoro *nm* (*esp fig*) meteor.
meteoroide *nm* meteoroid.
meteorología *nf* meteorology.
meteorológico *adj* meteorological, weather (*attr*).
meteorologista *nmf* meteorologist.
meter [2a] **1** *vt* (a) (*general sense*) to put, place; to insert, introduce (*en* in, into); to fit in; to squeeze in; (*Cook*) *ingredient* to add (*en* to), put (*en* in); *tool* to use, ply; **le están poniendo inyecciones a todo** — they're pumping injections into him as fast as they can.
(b) (*Sport*) *goal* to score (*a* against).
(c) (*Comm*) *goods* to smuggle (in; *also* — **de contrabando**).
(d) to make, cause; — **ruido** to cause a stir (*and see* **ruido**); — **un lío** to make a fuss, stir up trouble; — **miedo a uno** to scare someone, frighten someone, fill someone with fear; — **un susto a uno** to put the wind up someone; — **prisa a uno** to make someone get a move on.
(e) *money* to stake, wager (*en* on); (*Fin*) to invest (*en* in).
(f) **no hay quien le meta aquello** nobody seems able to make him understand that, nobody is able to get that idea into his head.
(g) *person* to involve (*en* in); **tú me metiste en este lío** you got me into this mess; **A le metió a B en muchos disgustos** A let B in for a lot of trouble; **¿quién le mete en esto?** who told you to interfere?
(h) — **a uno a trabajar** to put someone to work; — **a uno a un oficio** to put someone to a trade; — **a un chico de panadero** to apprentice a lad to a baker, put a lad to the baking trade.
(i) (*Sew*) *dress* to take in, take up, gather.
(j) (*fam*) *blow* to give, deal.
(k) (*fam*) — **algo a uno** to palm something off on someone; to force someone to accept something; **nos metió un largo discurso** he gave us a terribly long speech; **le metieron 5 años de cárcel** they did him for 5 years (*fam*); **nos van a** — **más trabajo** they're going to lumber us with more work; **no me meta esas peras** don't try to foist those pears off on me.
(l) (*Col*) — **las** to beat it (*fam*).
2 meterse *vr* (a) — **en** to go into, get into, enter; — **en un agujero** to get into a hole, squeeze into a hole; **se metió en la tienda** he went into the shop; — **en un negocio turbio** to take part in a shady deal, get involved in a shady deal; — **en peligro** to get into danger; — **en sí mismo** to withdraw into one's shell; **¿dónde se habrá metido el lápiz?** where can the pencil have got to?
(b) (*Geog*) to extend, project; **el cabo se mete en el mar** the cape extends (*or* goes out) into the sea; **el río se mete en el mar** the river flows into the sea.
(c) — **en** (*fig*) to interfere in, meddle in; **¡no se meta en lo que no le importa!, ¡no se meta donde no le llaman!** mind your own business!
(d) — **con uno** to provoke someone, pick a quarrel with someone; to accost someone, molest someone.
(e) — **con una herramienta** to misuse a tool, use a tool in ways for which it was not designed.
(f) — **monja** to become a nun; — **a escritor** to

become a writer, (*pej*) set oneself up as a writer; — **de aprendiz en un oficio** to go into a trade as an apprentice.

(**g**) — **a** + *infin* to start (without due preparation) to + *infin*; to take it upon oneself to + *infin*.
meterete *nm*, **metereta** *nf* (*RPl*), **metete** *nm* (*CAm, Chi, Per*), **meticón** *nm* (*fam*) busybody, meddler.
meticulosamente *adv* meticulously, scrupulously, thoroughly.
meticulosidad *nf* meticulousness, scrupulousness, thoroughness.
meticuloso *adj* meticulous, scrupulous, thorough; (*esp SAm: pej*) fussy, petty, small-minded.
metiche *adj* (*Mex*) meddling, meddlesome.
metido 1 *adj* (**a**) — **en sí,** — **para adentro** introspective.

(**b**) **estar muy** — **en un asunto** to be deeply involved in a matter.

(**c**) — **en años** elderly, advanced in years; **está algo metidita en años** she must be getting on a bit now; — **en carnes** plump.

(**d**) **estar muy** — **con uno** to be well in with someone.

(**e**) (*SAm*) meddling, meddlesome.

(**f**) (*PR, SD, Urug*) half tight.
2 *nm* (*fam*) (**a**) ticking-off; **dar** (*or* **pegar**) **un** — **a uno** to give someone a dressing-down.

(**b**) touch (*sl*); **pegar un** — **a uno** to touch someone for money (*sl*).

(**c**) **pegar un buen** — **a una tarta** to make a cake look silly (*fam*), dispose of a good chunk out of a cake.
metijón *nm* (*fam*) busybody, meddler.
metilado *adj*: **alcohol** — methylated spirit.
metilo *nm* methyl.
metimiento *nm* (**a**) insertion. (**b**) (*fig*) influence, pull.
metódicamente *adv* methodically.
metódico *adj* methodical.
metodismo *nm* Methodism.
metodista 1 *adj* Methodist. **2** *nmf* Methodist.
método *nm* method.
metodología *nf* methodology.
metomentodo *nm* meddler, busybody.
metraje *nm* (*Cine*) length; **cinta de largo** — full-length film; *see* **cortometraje.**
metralla *nf* shrapnel.
metralleta *nf* submachine gun, tommy gun.
métrica *nf* metrics.
métrico *adj* metric(al).
metro[1] *nm* (**a**) (*Math*) metre, meter (*US*); — **cuadrado** square metre; — **cúbico** cubic metre.

(**b**) (*Math*) rule, ruler (*also* — **plegable**); — **de cinta** tape measure.
metro[2] *nm* (*Rail*) underground, tube, subway (*US*); — **aéreo** overhead railway, elevated railway.
metrónomo *nm* metronome.
metrópoli *nf* metropolis; (*of empire*) mother country.
metropolitano 1 *adj* metropolitan. **2** *nm* (**a**) (*Eccl*) metropolitan. (**b**) (*Rail*) = **metro**[2].
mexicano (*SAm*) = **mejicano.**
México *m* (*SAm*) Mexico.
mezcla *nf* (**a**) (*act*) mixing.

(**b**) (*substance*) mixture; (*fig*) blend, combination; medley; (*Sew*) mixture; tweed; **sin** — pure, un-adulterated; *drink* neat; — **explosiva** explosive mixture; (*fam*) unholy mixture.

(**c**) (*Archit*) mortar.
mezclador *nm* mixing bowl.
mezcladora *nf* (*Cook*) mixer; — **de hormigón** concrete mixer.
mezclar [1a] **1** *vt* (**a**) to mix, mix up (together); to blend; to merge, combine; *cards* to shuffle.

(**b**) (*fig*) — **a A con B** to involve A with B, get A into trouble with B; — **a la Iglesia en el debate** to drag the Church into the debate.
2 mezclarse *vr* (**a**) to mix, mingle (*con* with); to blend (*con* with).

(**b**) — **con cierta gente** to mix with certain people; **hizo mal en** — **con esa familia** she did wrong to marry (beneath herself) into that family.

(**c**) — **en** to get mixed up in, get involved in; to meddle in.
mezcolanza *nf* hotchpotch, jumble.
mezquinar [1a] **1** *vt* (**a**) (*SAm*) to be stingy with, give sparingly.

(**b**) (*Arg*) — **el cuerpo** to dodge, duck; — **el saludo** to refuse to greet someone.

(**c**) (*Col*) — **a uno** to defend someone; — **a un niño** to let a child off a punishment.
2 *vi* (*SAm*) to be mean, be stingy.
mezquindad *nf* (**a**) (*quality*) meanness, stinginess;

poor spirit; pettiness; ignoble nature; paltriness, wretchedness. (**b**) (*act*) mean action, petty deed.
mezquino 1 *adj* (**a**) mean, stingy.

(**b**) poor-spirited; small-minded, petty; ignoble, materialistic, lacking the finer sentiments.

(**c**) *quality etc* miserable, paltry, tiny; *pay etc* wretched, wretchedly small.
2 *nm* (**a**) mean person, miser; petty individual, wretch.

(**b**) (*CAm, Col, Mex*) wart, callosity.
mezquita *nf* mosque.
mezzo-soprano ['metso-] *nf* mezzo-soprano.
mi *poss adj* my.
mí *pron* (*used after prep*) me; myself; **¡a** —! help!; **¡a con ésas!** come off it!, tell me another!; **¿y a** — **qué?** so what?, what has that got to do with me?; **para** — **no hay duda** so far as I'm concerned there's no doubt, I don't believe there can be any doubt; **por** —, **puede ir** so far as I'm concerned she can go; **por** — **mismo** by myself; on my own account.
miaja *nf* (**a**) crumb.

(**b**) (*fig*) bit, tiny portion; **ni** (**una**) — **de** not the least little bit of.

(**c**) (*as adv*) a bit; **me quiere una** — she likes me a bit.
miasma *nm* miasma.
miau *nm* mew, miaow.
mica[1] *nf* (*Min*) mica.
mica[2] *nf* (*Col*) chamberpot.
mica[3] *nf* (*CAm*) drunkenness; **ponerse una** — to get drunk.
micada *nf* (*CAm, Mex*) affected expression, simper.
mico *nm*, **mica** *nf* (**a**) (*Zool*) monkey, (*esp*) long-tailed monkey.

(**b**) (*fam*) ugly devil; conceited person, swank (*fam*); flirt; randy man, old goat; **¡**—**!** (*to child*) you little monkey!

(**c**) **dar** —, **hacer** — to miss a date, fail to turn up for an appointment (*a* with); **dar el** — to cheat; to disappoint, behave differently from what had been hoped; **volverse** — **para hacer algo** to be at one's wit's end to know how to do something.
micología *nf* mycology.
micro ... **micro** ...; **mini** ...
micro[1] *nm* (*Radio*) mike (*sl*), microphone.
micro[2] *nm* (*Chi, Per*) bus.
microbiano *adj* microbial.
microbio *nm* microbe.
microbiología *nf* microbiology.
microbiólogo *nm* microbiologist.
microbús *nm* minibus.
microcosmo(s) *nm* microcosm.
microfilm *nm*, *pl* **microfilms**, **microfilme** *nm* (*Acad*) microfilm.
micrófono *nm* microphone; (*Tel*) mouthpiece.
microfundio *nm* smallholding, small farm.
microlentillas *nfpl* contact lenses.
micrómetro *nm* micrometer.
microorganismo *nm* microorganism.
microscopia *nf* microscopy.
microscópico *adj* microscopic.
microscopio *nm* microscope.
microsurco *nm* microgroove; **disco** (**de**) — long-playing record (*L.P.*).
microtaxi *nm* minicab.
microteléfono *nm* (*Tel*) handset; mouthpiece.
miche *nm* (**a**) (*Mex*) cat. (**b**) (*Ven*) liquor, rum. (**c**) (*Ven*) native hut. (**d**) (*Chi*) game of marbles. (**e**) (*CR*) fight, brawl.
micho *nm*, **micha** *nf* (*fam*) puss, pussy cat.
Midas *m* Midas.
mieditis *nf* (*fam*) permanent fear, funkiness (*fam*).
miedo *nm* (**a**) fear, dread (*a, de* of); apprehension, nervousness; — **cerval**, — **espantoso** great fear; — **al público** (*Theat*) stage fright; **por** — **a**, **por** — **de** for fear of; **por** — **de que** ... for fear that ...; **dar** — **a**, **infundir** — **a**, **meter** — **a** to scare, frighten, fill with fear; **me da** — he scares me, he makes me nervous; **le daba** — **hacerlo** he was nervous about doing it; **en este punto siempre me entra un** — **terrible** I always get terribly nervous at this point; **tener** — to be afraid (*a* of); **tener** — **de** + *infin* to be afraid to + *infin*, be afraid (*or* nervous) of + *ger*.

(**b**) (*fam*) **¡qué** —**!** how awful! (*fam*); **de** — (*adj*) wonderful, smashing (*sl*), marvellous; (*pej*) awful, ghastly (*fam*); (*adv*) wonderfully, marvellously; (*pej*) awfully; **es un coche de** — it's a smashing car (*sl*); **eso fue de** — it was tremendous (*fam*), (*pej*) it was ghastly (*fam*); **hace un frío de** — it's terribly cold (*fam*).

miedoso *adj* fearful, fainthearted; timid, nervous, shy.
miel *nf* (a) honey.
    (b) (*esp* SAm) molasses (*also* — de caña, — negra *etc*).
    (c) (*idioms*) es — sobre hojuelas it's marvellous, it's even better than I (*etc*) expected; no hay — sin hiel nothing is ever entirely perfect; dejar a uno con la — en los labios to snatch something away from someone, spoil someone's fun; hacerse de — to be excessively kind, be almost too sweet; hazte de — y te comerán las moscas if you are too nice people will take advantage of you.
mielga *nf* alfalfa.
miembro 1 *nm* (a) (*Anat*) limb, member; — viril male member, penis.
    (b) (*Gram, Math etc*) member.
    (c) (*person*) member; fellow, associate; no — non-member; hacerse — de to become a member of.
    2 *as adj* member; los países —s the member countries.
mientes: ¡ni por —! never!, not on your life!; parar — en to reflect on, consider carefully; traer a las — to recall; se le vino a las — it occurred to him, it came to his mind.
mientras 1 *conj* (a) while; as long as; — duraba la guerra while the war lasted, as long as the war lasted; — él estaba fuera while he was abroad; — no venga until he comes.
    (b) — (que) whereas; — más tienen más quieren the more they have the more they want.
    2 *adv* meanwhile, meantime (*also* y —, — tanto); all the while.
miércoles *nm, pl* miércoles Wednesday; — de ceniza Ash Wednesday.
mierda *nf* (*tabu*) (a) shit (*tabu*); (*fig*) filth, dirt.
    (b) (*fig*) es una — he's a shit (*tabu*); es un don M— he's a nobody; coger (*or* pillar) una — to get sozzled (*sl*); ¡vaya Vd a la —! go to hell!
mies *nf* (a) (ripe) corn, wheat, grain. (b) harvest time.
    (c) —es cornfields.
miga *nf* (a) crumb; (*fig*) bit; —s (*Cook*) fried bread-crumbs.
    (b) (*fig*) core, substance, essence; esto tiene su — there's something in this; there's more in this than meets the eye.
    (c) hacer algo —s to break something up, smash something into little pieces; hacer —s a uno to leave someone in a sorry state; tener los pies hechos —s to be footsore; hacer buenas —s to get on well, hit it off (*con* with).
migajas *nfpl* crumbs; bits; (*fig*) leavings.
migar [1h] *vt* to crumble, break up.
migración *nf* migration.
migraña *nf* migraine.
migratorio *adj* migratory.
Miguel *m* Michael; — Ángel Michaelangelo.
miguelear [1a] *vt* (CAm) to court.
miguelero *nm* (CAm) wolf (*fam*).
mijo *nm* millet.
mil *adj and nm* thousand; tres — coches three thousand cars; — doscientos dólares one thousand two hundred dollars; lo ha hecho — veces he's done it hundreds of times; —es y —es thousands and thousands; a las — at some ungodly hour, terribly late.
miladi *nf* (*angl*) milady.
milagro *nm* miracle; (*fig*) miracle, wonder, marvel; ¡ni de —! not a bit of it!; es un — que ... it is a miracle (*or* wonder) that ...; — (sería) que ... it would be a miracle if ...; salvarse de — to escape miraculously, have a miraculous escape; vivir de — to have a hard time of it, keep going somehow; to manage to stay alive; hacer —s (*fig*) to work wonders.
milagrosamente *adv* miraculously.
milagroso *adj* miraculous.
Milán Milan.
milano *nm* (*Orn*) kite.
mildeu (*also* mildiu, mildiú) *nm* mildew.
mildo *adj* (Chi) timid, shy.
milenario 1 *adj* millennial; (*fig*) very ancient, age-old. **2** *nm* millennium.
milenio *nm* millennium.
milenrama *nf* yarrow.
milésima *nf* thousandth.
milésimo 1 *adj* thousandth. **2** *nm* thousandth.
mili *nf* (*fam*) military service; estar en la — to be in the army; hacer la — to do one's military service.
miliar *adj*: piedra — milestone.
milicia *nf* (a) militia; military, soldiery.
    (b) art of war; science of warfare; soldiering, military profession.
    (c) (period of) military service.

    (d) M—s universitarias *equivalent to* cadet corps, O.T.C.
miliciano *nm*, **milico** *nm* (Bol, Chi, RPl) militiaman, conscript.
miligramo *nm* milligramme, milligram (US).
mililitro *nm* millilitre, milliliter (US).
milímetro *nm* millimetre, millimeter (US).
militante 1 *adj* militant. **2** *nmf* militant.
militar 1 *adj* military; spirit *etc* warlike; ciencia — art of war.
    2 *nm* soldier, military man; serviceman.
    3 [1a] *vi* (a) (Mil) to serve (in the army); to soldier.
    (b) (*fig*) — en un partido to belong to a party, be a member of a party.
    (c) (*fig*) — contra to militate against; — en defensa de, — en favor de to speak for, argue in favour of, lend weight to.
militarada *nf* military rising, putsch.
militarismo *nm* militarism.
militarista 1 *adj* militaristic. **2** *nmf* militarist.
militarizar [1f] *vt* to militarize.
militarote *nm* (SAm: *pej*) rough soldier; blustering soldier; sergeant-major type.
milonga *nf* (a) (Arg, Bol, Chi) kind of dance; cabaret; party. (b) (Bol, RPl) gossip.
milord [mi'lor] *nm* (*angl*) milord.
milpa *nf* (CAm, Mex) maize field, cornfield (US).
milpear [1a] **1** *vt* (CAm, Mex) to prepare for the sowing of maize. **2** *vi* (a) (CAm, Mex) to make a maize field. (b) (Mex: *of maize*) to sprout.
milpero *nm* (CAm, Mex) maize grower.
milla *nf* mile; — marina nautical mile.
millar *nm* thousand; a —es in thousands, by the thousand; los había a —es they were there in thousands.
millarada *nf* (about a) thousand.
millas-pasajero *nfpl* passenger miles.
millo *nm* (CAm, Mex) (*variety of*) millet.
millón *nm* million; un — de sellos a million stamps; 3 —es de niños 3 million children; ¡un — de gracias! a thousand thanks!
millonada *nf* (*fam*) million.
millonario *nm*, **millonaria** *nf* millionaire.
millonésimo 1 *adj* millionth. **2** *nm* millionth.
mimado *adj* spoiled.
mimar [1a] *vt* child *etc* to spoil, pamper, indulge; powerful person to humour, flatter.
mimbre *nm or f* (a) (Bot) osier, willow. (b) (*material*) wicker; de — wicker, wickerwork.
mimbrearse [1a] *vr* to sway.
mimbrera *nf* osier, willow.
mimbreral *nm* osier bed.
mimeografiar [1c] *vt* to mimeograph.
mimeógrafo *nm* mimeograph.
mimetismo *nm* mimicry.
mimetizarse [1f] *vr* (SAm: *Zool*) to change colour, camouflage oneself.
mímica *nf* (a) sign language; gesticulation. (b) mimicry; (una —) mime.
mímico *adj* mimic; imitative; lenguaje — sign language.
mimo *nm* (a) (Theat: Hist) mime; hacer — de to mime, mimic.
    (b) affectionate caress; nice remark (*etc*); (*in general*) pampering, indulgence; dar —s a un niño to spoil a child; hacer —s a uno to make a great fuss of someone, fuss over someone; hacer —s a los poderosos to humour the powerful, flatter the great.
mimosa *nf* mimosa.
mimoso *adj* (a) spoilt, pampered; soft; fussy, finicky. (b) (*to opposite sex*) arch, coy, provocative; kittenish.
mina *nf* (a) (Min) mine; — de carbón, — hullera coalmine.
    (b) underground passage; gallery; shaft.
    (c) (Mil, Naut) mine.
    (d) (*of pencil*) lead; refill.
    (e) (*fig*) mine, storehouse; gold mine; — de información mine of information.
minador *nm* (a) (Mil) sapper; (Min) mining engineer. (b) (Naut: *also* buque —) minelayer.
minar [1a] *vt* (a) (Min) to mine. (b) (Mil, Naut) to mine. (c) (*fig*) to undermine, sap, wear away.
minarete *nm* minaret.
mineral 1 *adj* mineral. **2** *nm* (Geol) mineral; (Min) ore; — - de hierro iron ore.
mineralogía *nf* mineralogy.
mineralogista *nmf* mineralogist.
minería *nf* mining.
minero 1 *adj* mining. **2** *nm* miner; — de carbón coalminer.
minga[1] *nf* (*tabu*) prick (*tabu*).

minga² *nf* (*SAm*) (a) voluntary communal labour, cooperative work. (b) crew, team, gang (of cooperative workers).

mingaco *nm* (*Chi*, *Per*) = **minga²** (a).

mingar [1h] *vt* (a) (*Arg*, *Chi*, *Ec*) to work communally on, contribute cooperatively to.
(b) (*Arg*, *Chi*, *Ec*) *workers* to call together for a communal task.
(c) (*Col*) to set on, attack.

mini . . . mini . . .; (*as hum prefix*) **minibikini** microscopic bikini; **mininovillo** (*Taur*) baby bull, tiny bull.

miniatura 1 *adj* miniature; *dog etc* toy; **golf** — miniature golf (course); **relojes** — miniature watches. **2** *nf* miniature; **en** — in miniature.

minicoche *nm* minicar.

minifalda *nf* miniskirt.

minifaldero *adj* short-skirted, miniskirted.

minifundio *nm* smallholding, small farm.

minimizar [1f] *vt* to minimize.

mínimo 1 *adj* minimum; minimal; smallest, slightest, least; **cifra mínima** minimum number, smallest figure; **sin el más** — **esfuerzo** without the slightest effort; **no contribuye en lo más** — it doesn't help at all, it doesn't help in the least; **no me importa en lo más** — it doesn't matter to me in the least.
2 *nm* minimum; **como** — as a minimum, at the very least; — **de presión** (*Meteorol*) low-pressure area, trough.

mínimum *nm* minimum.

minina *nf* (*fam*) prick (*tabu*); (*child's*) John Thomas.

minino *nm*, **minina** *nf* (*fam*) puss, pussy cat.

minio *nm* red lead, minium.

ministerial *adj* ministerial; governmental.

ministerio *nm* ministry; *see* **asunto, gobernación** *etc*.

ministro *nmf* minister; **primer** — prime minister; — **sin cartera** minister without portfolio.

minoración *nf* reduction, diminution.

minorar [1a] *vt* to reduce, diminish.

minoría *nf* minority; — **de edad** minority.

minoridad *nf* minority (*of age*).

minorista *nm* (*Ant*, *Chi*, *RPl*) retailer, retail trader.

minoritario *adj* minority (*attr*); **gobierno** — minority government.

minorizar [1f] *vt* to minimize.

Minotauro *m* Minotaur.

minucia *nf* trifle, insignificant detail; mere nothing; morsel, tiny bit; —s petty details, minutiae.

minuciosamente *adv* thoroughly, meticulously; in a very detailed way, minutely.

minuciosidad *nf* thoroughness, meticulousness; detailed nature; minuteness.

minucioso *adj* thorough, meticulous; very detailed; minute.

minué *nm* minuet.

minúscula *nf* small letter.

minúsculo *adj* tiny, minute, minuscule; (*Typ*) small.

minuta *nf* (a) rough draft, first draft; carbon copy.
(b) note, memorandum.
(c) list, roll.
(d) (*Cook*) menu; **a la** —, (*Ant*, *RPl*) rolled in breadcrumbs.
(e) (*Chi*) junk, trash; secondhand goods; junk shop.

minutar [1a] *vt* to draft.

minutario *nm* minute book.

minutero *nm* minute hand.

minutisa *nf* sweet william.

minuto *nm* minute.

miñango *nm* (*Bol*, *RPl*) bit, small piece; **hecho** —s smashed to pieces.

miñoco *nm* (*Col*) wry face; grimace.

miñón *adj* (*SAm*: *gall*) sweet, cute.

mío *adj and pron* mine, of mine; **es** —, **es el** — it is mine; **lo** — (what is) mine, what belongs to me; **no es amigo** — he's no friend of mine; **¡hijo** —! my dear boy!; **los** —s (*freq*) my people, my relations, my family.

miope 1 *adj* short-sighted, myopic. **2** *nmf* short-sighted person.

miopía *nf* short-sightedness, myopia.

mira *nf* (a) **estar a la** — to be on the look-out, keep watch (*de* for).
(b) (*Mil*, *Tech etc*) sight(s); — **de bombardeo** bombsight; — **telescópica** telescopic sight; **con la** — **puesta en** (*fig*) with one's sights set on.
(c) (*Mil*) watchtower, look-out post.
(d) (*fig*) aim, intention; **con la** — **de** + *infin* with the aim of + *ger*; **con** —s **a** with a view to; **llevar una** — **interesada** to have a selfish end in view; **poner la** — **en** to aim at, aspire to; **tener** —s **sobre** to have designs on.
(e) (*fig*) **de amplias** —s broad in outlook; tolerant,

broad-minded; **de** —s **estrechas** narrow-minded; insular, parochial.

mirada *nf* (a) look, glance; gaze; — **fija** stare; hard look; — **de soslayo** sidelong glance; — **perdida**, — **vaga** vague look, distant look; **apartar la** — to look away (*de* from); **apuñalar a uno con la** — to look daggers at someone; **echar una** — **a** to glance at; to keep an eye on; **lanzar una** — **a** to glance at, cast a glance at; **levantar la** — to raise one's eyes; **no levanta la** — **del libro** he never takes his eyes off the book; **resistir la** — **de uno** to stare back at someone, stare someone out.
(b) (*of face*) look, expression; **con una** — **triste** with a sad look.

miradero *nm* (a) look-out, vantage point. (b) cynosure (of every eye), person (*etc*) that attracts every eye.

mirado *adj* (a) **bien** — well thought of, well liked, highly regarded; **no está bien** — **que . . .** it is not thought proper that . . .; **mal** — disliked (*see also* **malmirado**).
(b) sensible; well-behaved; considerate, thoughtful; **ser** — **en los gastos** to be sensible about what one spends, be a careful spender.
(c) (*pej*) finicky, fussy.
(d) **bien** — (*as adv*) by rights, in justice, if everything is weighed up.

mirador *nm* (a) (*Archit*) bay window; (enclosed) balcony; — **de popa** (*Naut*) stern gallery. (b) viewpoint, vantage point.

miramiento *nm* (a) considerateness; courtesy; **sin** — without consideration, discourteously.
(b) caution, circumspection, care; (*pej*) timidity, excessive caution.
(c) —s courtesies, attentions; **sin** —s unceremoniously; high-handed(ly); **sin** —s **de** regardless of; **tratar sin** —s **a uno** to treat someone without consideration, ride roughshod over someone.

mirar [1a] **1** *vt* (a) to look at; to gaze at; to watch; **miraba la foto** she was looking at the photo; **miraba los barcos** she was watching the boats; **la miré subir la escalera** I watched her go (*or* going) upstairs; **le miraron la cartera** they looked at his wallet; — **fijamente a uno** to stare at someone, look hard at someone; — **algo por encima** to glance over something, glance cursorily at something.
(b) (*fig*) to consider, think over, think carefully about; **lo hago mirando el porvenir** I do it bearing the future in mind; **no mira las dificultades** he doesn't take account of the difficulties; **mirándolo bien** all in all; by rights; on second thoughts; **¡mira lo que haces!** just think what you're doing!; **¡mira con quien hablas!** just remember who you're talking to!
(c) (*fig*) — **a uno como** to look on someone as, consider someone to be.
(d) (*fig*) to watch, keep an eye on, be careful about; **conviene** — **el bolso** it's best to keep an eye on your handbag.
(e) (*fig*) to value, think highly of (*also* — **bien**); — **mal** to dislike, have a poor opinion of.
(f) (*SAm*) to see.
2 *vi* (a) to look; to glance; **no habla pero mira mucho** he never speaks but he keeps on looking; **¡mira!, ¡mire!** look!; (*as protest*) look here!; **¡pero mire!** now look here!; **¡mira que no tenemos dinero!** remember that we haven't any money!; **¡mira que tenemos que aguantar!** look at what we have to put up with!; **¡mira que si es mentira!** just suppose it isn't true!, what if it's not true?; **mira si ha venido el taxi** look and see if the taxi has come; — **alrededor** to look around; — **atrás** to look back (*fig*), think about the past; — **hacia otro lado** to look the other way; — **por la ventana** to look out of the window; — **por un agujero** to look through a hole; — **de través** to squint (*see also* **través** 2).
(b) (*Archit*) to face; to look on to, open on to; **la casa mira al sur** the house faces south.
(c) (*fig*) — **a** to aim at, have in mind.
(d) **por lo que mira a** as for, as regards.
(e) (*fig*) — **por** to look after, take care of; — **por sí** to look out for oneself, consider one's own safety.
3 mirarse *vr* (a) to look at oneself; — **al espejo** to look at oneself in the mirror.
(b) (2 *persons*) to look at one another; **nos miramos asombrados** we looked at each other in amazement; — **a los ojos** to look into each other's eyes.
(c) — **muy bien de hacer algo** to be very careful about doing something; to think carefully before doing something; — **en ello** to watch one's step.

mirasol nm sunflower.
miríada nf myriad; —(s) **de moscas** a myriad flies.
mirilla nf peephole, spyhole; (Phot) viewer.
miriñaque nm (a) (Hist) crinoline, hoop skirt. (b) (Arg: Rail) cowcatcher. (c) (Cu) thin cotton cloth.
miriópodo nm millipede.
mirlarse [1a] vr to put on airs, act important.
mirlo nm (a) (Orn) blackbird.
  (b) — **blanco** (fig) exceptional thing, highly unusual thing; one in a million; impossible dream.
  (c) (fig) self-important air, pompousness.
mirobrigense 1 adj of Ciudad Rodrigo. **2** nmf native (or inhabitant) of Ciudad Rodrigo; **los** —s the people of Ciudad Rodrigo.
mirón 1 adj inquisitive, curious.
  2 nm, **mirona** nf onlooker, watcher, observer; (pej) nosey-parker; (Cards) kibitzer; **los** —**s son de piedra** those watching the game are not allowed to speak; **estar de** — to look on (without doing anything), to stand by (doing nothing); **ir de** — to go along just to see.
mirra nf myrrh.
mirtilo nm bilberry, whortleberry.
mirto nm myrtle.
misa nf mass; — **del gallo** midnight mass (on Christmas Eve); — **mayor** high mass; — **de prima** early mass; — **rezada** low mass; **como en** — in dead silence; **celebrar** — to celebrate mass; **ir a** — to go to mass, go to church; **oír** — to go to mass, attend mass; **ser como** — **de pobre** to last all too short a time; **no saber de la** — **la media** to be woefully ill-informed; **to know only a part of the story**; **estos datos van a** — (fig) these facts are utterly trustworthy.
misal nm missal.
misantropía nf misanthropy.
misantrópico adj misanthropic.
misántropo nm misanthrope, misanthropist.
misario nm acolyte, altar boy.
miscelánea nf (a) miscellany. (b) (Mex) small shop, (esp) hardware store.
misceláneo adj miscellaneous.
miserable 1 adj (a) person mean, stingy; miserly; sum etc miserable, paltry, pitifully small.
  (b) (morally) rotten (fam), vile, contemptible, despicable; **¡—!** you rotter!, you wretch!
  (c) place, room etc squalid, sordid.
  2 nmf wretch; rotter, cad; **¡eres un —!** you're a rotter!
miserando adj (esp SAm) pitiful.
miseria nf (a) poverty, destitution; want; **caer en la** — to fall into abject poverty; **vivir en la** — to live in poverty.
  (b) squalor, squalid conditions.
  (c) fleas, lice; **estar lleno de** — to be covered with vermin.
  (d) (Fin) **una** — a tiny sum, a mere pittance; a tiny amount.
  (e) meanness, stinginess.
misericordia nf (a) pity, compassion. (b) forgiveness; mercy.
misericordioso adj (a) compassionate. (b) forgiving; merciful.
misero adj (fam) churchy (fam), fond of going to church.
mísero adj (a) wretched. (b) =**miserable**.
mísil nm (angl) missile; — **antimísil** antimissile missile; — **autodirigido** guided missile.
misión nf mission; —**es** (Eccl) overseas missions, missionary work; — **de buena voluntad** goodwill mission.
misional adj missionary.
misionero nm, **misionera** nf missionary.
Misisipí m Mississippi.
misiva nf missive.
mismamente adv (fam) only, just; literally; **ayer** — **vino** it was only yesterday he came.
mismísimo adj superl selfsame, very same; **por mis** —**s ojos** with my very own eyes; **es Vd el** — **diablo** you're the very devil in person; **estuvo el** — **obispo** the bishop himself was there; **es el** — **que yo perdí** it's the very (same) one I lost.
mismo 1 adj (a) same (que as, that); **el** — **coche** the same car; **viven en la misma calle** they live in the same street; **es el** — **que vi ayer** it's the (same) one as I saw yesterday; **el policía y el ladrón son el** — the policeman and the thief are one and the same; **quedar en las mismas** to be no further forward, show no progress.
  (b) (with lo) **lo** — the same, the same thing; **es lo** — it's the same thing, it comes to the same thing; **no es lo** — it's not the same (at all); **él diría lo** —

he would say the same; **por lo** — for the same reason; **lo** — **A que B** both A and B; **o lo que es lo** — or what amounts to the same thing; **lo** — **si viene que si no viene** whether he comes or not; see **dar**.
  (c) (with personal pron) -self; **yo** — I myself; **yo** — **lo vi** I saw it myself; **lo hizo por sí** — he did it by himself; **perjudicarse a sí** — to harm one's own interests.
  (d) (emphatic) very; selfsame; **en ese** — **momento** at that very moment; **en Argentina misma, en la misma Argentina** in Argentina itself; **estuvo el** — **ministro** the (very) minister himself was there; **ella es la misma caridad** she is charity itself; **eso** — **digo yo** that's just what I say.
  2 adv right; **aquí** — right here, on this very spot; **ayer** — only yesterday; **delante** — **de la casa** right in front of the house.
  3 as conj: **lo** — **que** just like, just as (if); **lo** — **que Vd es médico yo soy ingeniero** just as you are a doctor I am an engineer; **nos divertimos lo** — **que si hubiéramos ido al baile** we had just as good a time as if we had gone to the dance; **lo** — **que me levanto a las 6 me levantaría a las 5** just as I get up at 6 so I would gladly get up at 5.
misogamia nf misogamy.
misógamo nm, **misógama** nf misogamist.
misoginia nf misogyny.
misógino nm misogynist.
miss [mis] nf (angl) beauty queen; **M— España 1978** Miss Spain 1978.
misterio nm (a) mystery; **no hay** — there's no mystery about it.
  (b) secrecy; **obrar con** — to go about something secretly, go to work in secrecy.
  (c) (Theat: Hist) mystery play.
misteriosamente adv mysteriously; puzzlingly.
misterioso adj mysterious; mystifying, puzzling.
mística nf, **misticismo** nm mysticism.
místico 1 adj mystic(al). **2** nm, **mística** nf mystic.
mistificación nf hoax, practical joke; hocus-pocus.
mistificar [1g] vt (a) to hoax, play a practical joke on.
  (b) to mix up, make a mess of.
Misurí m Missouri.
mitad nf (a) half; — **y** — half-and-half; (fig) so-so, yes and no; **es** — **blanco y** — **rojo** it's half white and half red; **mi otra** —, **mi cara** — my better half; **me queda la** — I have half left; **a** — **de precio** half-price, at half the cost; **reducir en una** — to cut by half, halve.
  (b) middle; **a** — **de, en** — **de** halfway along (or through etc); **a** — **de la distancia entre A y Z** halfway between A and Z; **estar a** — **de camino** to be halfway there; **hacia la** — **de la película** halfway through the film; **cortar por la** — to cut down the middle; **partir a uno por la** — (fig) to upset someone's plans, queer someone's pitch; see **dividir**.
mítico adj mythical.
mitigación nf mitigation; relief; quenching; appeasement; tempering; reduction.
mitigar [1h] vt to mitigate, allay; pain to relieve; thirst to quench; anger to appease, mollify; harshness etc to temper, mitigate; worry to allay; heat to reduce; solitude to alleviate, relieve.
mitin nm (esp Pol: angl) meeting; — **popular** mass meeting.
mito nm myth.
mitología nf mythology.
mitológico adj mythological.
mitón nm mitten.
mitote nm (Mex) a kind of dance; brawl; uproar; —**s** rowdyism; merrymaking.
Mitra m Mithras.
mitra nf mitre.
mitrado nm bishop, prelate.
mitraico adj Mithraic.
mitraísmo nm Mithraism.
mítulo nm mussel.
mixomatosis nf myxomatosis.
mixtión nf mixture.
mixto 1 adj (all senses) mixed. **2** nm (a) match; (Mil) explosive compound. (b) (Rail) passenger and goods train.
mixtolobo nm Alsatian (dog).
mixtura nf mixture (also Pharm).
mixturar [1a] vt to mix.
mnemotécnica nf mnemonics.
mnemotécnico adj mnemonic.
moaré nm moiré.
mobiliario nm furniture; household goods; suite (of furniture).
moblaje nm =**mobiliario**.
moca[1] nf mocha.

moca² *nf* (*Ec*) quagmire, muddy place.

moca³ *nf* (*Mex*) coffee-flavoured cake (*or* biscuit).

mocasín *nm* moccasin.

mocear [1a] *vi* to play around, live a bit wildly, sow one's wild oats.

mocedad *nf* (a) youth; **en mis —es** in my young days. (b) **—es** youthful pranks; wild living; **pasar las —es** to sow one's wild oats.

moceril *adj* youthful; typical of youth.

mocerío *nm* young people, lads and lasses (*collectively*).

mocero *adj* rakish, loose-living; fond of the girls.

mocetón *nm* strapping youth.

mocetona *nf* big girl, hefty wench.

moción *nf* (a) motion, movement.
(b) (*Parl etc*) motion; **— de censura** motion of censure, censure motion; **hacer** (*or* **presentar**) **una —** to propose a motion.

mocionante *nmf* (*SAm*) proposer (of a motion).

mocionar [1a] *vti* (*SAm*) to move, propose.

mocito 1 *adj* very young. **2** *nm*, **mocita** *nf* youngster.

moco *nm* (a) mucus; snot (*fam*); **limpiarse los —s** to blow one's nose; **llorar a — y baba, llorar a — tendido** to sob one's heart out, cry uncontrollably; **soltar el —** to burst into tears.
(b) (*Orn*) crest; **no es — de pavo** it's not just a small thing; you can't laugh this one off.
(c) (*of candle*) snuff, burnt wick; candle grease; **a — de candil** by candlelight.
(d) (*Tech*) slag.

mocoso 1 *adj* snivelling; (*fig*) ill-bred, rude. **2** *nm* (*fam*) brat.

mochales *adj* (*fam*): **estar —** to be round the bend (*sl*).

mochar [1a] *vt* (a) **= desmochar.**
(b) (*Per, PR*) to chop off, hack off (clumsily); (*Col, PR*) to amputate.
(c) (*Arg*) to pinch (*fam*).
(d) (*Col*) to fire (*fam*), sack (*fam*).

mochila *nf* rucksack, knapsack; (*Mil*) pack.

mocho 1 *adj* (a) cut off, short, truncated; stubby; *tool etc* blunt, short; *tree* lopped, pollarded; *cow* hornless, polled; *tower* flat-topped; *person* (*fam*) close-cropped, shorn.
(b) (*Col*) big, huge.
(c) (*Guat, Mex*) reactionary.
2 *nm* (a) butt; blunt end, thick end.
(b) (*fam*) burden, chore, bind (*sl*); blame; **cargar el —** to get landed with it; to carry the can (*sl*); **le echaron el —** they gave him the job; they made him carry the can (*sl*).
(c) (*Cu*) **— de tabaco** cigar butt.
(d) (*Col, PR, Ven*) nag.

mochuelo *nm* (a) (*Orn: also* **— común**) little owl; **cada — a su sitio** everything in its place. (b) (*fam*) **=mocho** (b).

moda *nf* fashion; style; **a la —** (*adj*) in fashion, fashionable; (*adv*) fashionably; **un sombrero a la —** a fashionable hat; **a la — de** after the fashion of; **estar a la —** to be in fashion, be fashionable; **ponerse a la —** to smarten up, get some new clothes; (*fam*) to get with it (*fam*); **de —** in fashion, fashionable; **fuera de —** out of fashion; **pasado de —** old-fashioned, out-dated; **pasarse de —** to go out of fashion; **ponerse de —** to become fashionable; **estar muy de —** to be highly fashionable; **ha entrado la — de las medias amarillas** the fashion for yellow stockings has begun, yellow stockings are in.

modal 1 *adj* modal. **2 —es** *nmpl* manners.

modalidad *nf* form, kind, variety; fashion; modality; **una nueva — teatral** a new dramatic form; a new fashion in the theatre; **hay varias —es del juego** there are various forms of the game, there are several ways of playing the game.

modelado *nm* modelling.

modelador *nm*, **modeladora** *nf* modeller.

modelar [1a] **1** *vt* (a) to model (*sobre, según* on). (b) to fashion, shape, form. **2 modelarse** *vr*: **— sobre** to model oneself on.

modelo 1 *nm* model; pattern; standard; **presentar algo como un —** to hold something up as a model; **servir de —** to serve as a model; **tomar por —** to take as a model; **— de maridos** model husband.
2 *nmf* (*Art, Phot, Fashion etc*) model; **servir de — a un pintor** to sit for a painter, pose for a painter.
3 *as adj* model; **cárcel —** model prison; **empresa —** model company; pilot plant.

moderación *nf* moderation; **con —** in moderation.

moderadamente *adv* moderately.

moderado *adj* (*all senses*) moderate.

moderar [1a] **1** *vt* to moderate; *violence etc* to restrain, control; *speed* to reduce.
2 moderarse *vr* (*fig*) to restrain oneself, control oneself; to calm down.

modernamente *adv* nowadays, in modern times; recently.

modernidad *nf* modernity.

modernismo *nm* modernism.

modernista 1 *adj* modernist(ic). **2** *nmf* modernist.

modernización *nf* modernization.

modernizar [1f] **1** *vt* to modernize. **2 modernizarse** *vr* to modernize (oneself); to catch up, get up to date.

moderno *adj* modern; present-day; up-to-date; **a la moderna** in the modern way; modern.

modestamente *adv* modestly.

modestia *nf* modesty.

modesto *adj* modest.

modicidad *nf* reasonableness, fairness, moderateness.

módico *adj* reasonable, fair, moderate.

modificación *nf* modification.

modificar [1g] *vt* to modify.

modismo *nm* idiom.

modista *nf* dressmaker, modiste; **— de sombreros** milliner.

modistilla *nf* dressmaker, seamstress.

modisto *nm* fashion designer, couturier.

modo *nm* (a) way, manner; fashion; mode, method; **"— de empleo"** (*on label*) "instructions for use"; **— de gobierno** form of government; **— de pensar** way of thinking; **según mi — de pensar** according to my way of thinking; **— de ser =manera de ser; a mi — de ver** in my view; as I see it.
(b) (*phrases with prep*) **a mi —** in my (own) way; **lo interpretan a su —** they interpret it each in his own way; **a — de** like; **uno a — de saco** a sort of bag, some kind of bag; **al — inglés** in the English way (*or* style); **de este —** (in) this way, like this; **de ese —** (*fig*) at that rate; **del mismo — (que), de igual — (que)** in the same way (as), just (as); **de igual —, . . .** in the same way, . . .; **de diversos —s** in various ways; **declaraba su edad de diversos —s** she gave her age variously; **de un — o de otro** (in) one way or another; by some means or other; *for numerous other phrases, see* **manera** (a) *and* (b).
(c) **—s** (*of person*) manners; **buenos —s** good manners; **contestar con buenos —s** to answer courteously.
(d) (*Mus*) mode.
(e) (*Gram*) mood; **— imperativo** imperative mood; **— indicativo** indicative mood; **— subjuntivo** subjunctive mood.
(f) (*fig*) moderation; **beber con —** to drink in moderation.

modorra *nf* (a) drowsiness, heaviness. (b) (*Vet*) staggers.

modorro *adj* (a) drowsy, heavy. (b) *fruit* soft, sleepy. (c) (*fam*) dull, stupid.

modoso *adj* quiet, well-mannered, nicely-behaved; *girl* demure.

modulación *nf* modulation; **— de frecuencia** (*Radio*) frequency modulation.

modulado *adj* modulated.

modular [1a] *vt* to modulate.

moer *nm* mohair.

mofa *nf* (a) (*in general*) mockery, ridicule, derision; **exponer a uno a la — pública** to hold someone up to public ridicule; **hacer — de** to scoff at, jeer at.
(b) (*una —*) jibe, taunt, sneer.

mofador 1 *adj* mocking, scoffing, sneering. **2** *nm* mocker, scoffer.

mofar [1a] **1** *vi* to mock, scoff, sneer. **2 mofarse** *vr*: **— de** to mock, scoff at, sneer at.

mofeta *nf* (a) (*Zool*) skunk. (b) (*Min*) firedamp. (c) (*fam*) fart (*tabu*).

moflete *nm* (a) fat cheek. (b) **—s** (*fig*) chubbiness.

mofletudo *adj* fat-cheeked, chubby.

mogol 1 *adj* Mongol, Mongolian. **2** *nm*, **mogola** *nf* Mongol, Mongolian; **el Gran M—** the Great Mogul. **3** *nm* (*language*) Mongol.

Mogolia *f*: **la —** Mongolia.

mogolismo *nm* mongolism.

mogollón *nm* (*fam*) sponger (*fam*), hanger-on; spiv (*sl*); **colarse de — en un sitio** to get into a place without paying; **comer de —** to scrounge a meal (*fam*); **lograr un puesto de —** to get a job without effort, get a job the easy way.

mogote *nm* flat-topped hillock; heap, pile; (*of sheaves etc*) stack, rick.

mohín *nm* (wry) face, grimace; pout; **hacer un —** to make a face; **con un leve — de chanza** with a faintly humorous expression.

mohina nf (a) annoyance, displeasure; resentment. (b) (una —) grudge. (c) the sulks, sulkiness; **ser fácil a las —s** to be easily depressed.

mohino adj gloomy, depressed; sulky, sullen, resentful; peevish.

moho nm (a) (on metal) rust. (b) (Bot) mould, mildew; **cubierto de —** mouldy, mildewed. (c) lazy feeling; workshyness; **no cría —** he's not exactly idle, he's always on the go; **no dejar criar — a uno** to keep someone on the go.

mohoso adj (a) rusty. (b) mouldy, mildewed; musty. (c) (fig) joke etc stale.

Moisés m Moses.

moisés nm Moses basket, cradle; carrycot.

mojada nf (a) wetting, soaking. (b) stab (wound).

mojado adj wet; damp, moist; drenched, soaked; **llover sobre —** to be quite unnecessary, be entirely superfluous; **luego llovió sobre —** then on top of all that something else happened; **llueve sobre —** it never rains but it pours.

mojadura nf wetting, soaking.

mojama nf salted tuna.

mojar [1a] **1** vt (a) to wet; to damp(en), moisten; to drench, soak; **la lluvia mojó a todos** the rain soaked everybody; **moje ligeramente el sello** moisten the stamp a little; **— la ropa en un líquido** to soak (or steep) clothes in a liquid.
(b) **— la pluma en la tinta** to dip one's pen into the ink; **— el pan en el café** to dip one's bread into one's coffee.
(c) (Ling) to palatalize.
(d) to stab.
(e) (PR, SD) to tip; (PR) to bribe.
2 vi: **— en** (fig) to dabble in; to meddle in, get involved in.
3 mojarse vr to get wet; to get drenched, get soaked.

mojarra nf (SAm) short broad knife.

mojicón nm (a) (Cook) sponge cake; bun. (b) (fam) punch in the face, biff (fam), slap.

mojiganga nf (a) (Hist) masquerade, mummery; farce, piece of clowning. (b) (fam) pretentious thing.

mojigatería nf hypocrisy; sanctimoniousness, affected piety; prudery, prudishness.

mojigato 1 adj hypocritical; sanctimonious, affectedly pious; prudish, strait-laced. **2** nm, **mojigata** nf hypocrite; sanctimonious person; prude.

mojinete nm (a) (of roof) ridge; (of wall) tiling, coping. (b) (Arg, Chi) gable.

mojón nm landmark, boundary stone; (also **— kilométrico**) milestone; signpost; heap, pile.

mola nf rounded mountain.

molar nm molar.

molde nm (a) (Tech) mould; (Cook) mould, shape; (of plaster etc) cast.
(b) (Sew) pattern; knitting needle.
(c) (fig) model.
(d) **de —** very suitably; **el vestido le está de —** the dress suits her perfectly, the dress is just right for (or on) her; **venir de —** to come just right; see **letra.**

moldear [1a] vt (a) to mould, shape; (in plaster etc) to cast. (b) (fig) to mould, shape, form.

moldura nf moulding.

mole nf mass, bulk; (of building) pile; **se sentó con toda su —** he sat down with his full weight; **la enorme — del buque** the vast mass of the ship; **esa mujer es una —** that woman is a lump.

molécula nf molecule.

molecular adj molecular.

moledor 1 adj (a) grinding, crushing. (b) (fam) boring. **2** nm (a) (Tech) grinder, crusher; roller. (b) (fam) bore.

moledora nf (Tech) grinder, crusher; mill.

moler [2h] vt (a) to grind, crush; to pound; to mill; (fam) to chew (up); **— a uno a palos** to give someone a beating.
(b) (fig) to tire out, weary, exhaust.
(c) (fig) to annoy; to bore.

molestar [1a] **1** vt to annoy; to bother, inconvenience, put out; to upset; (of pain) to trouble, bother, hurt; **me molesta ese ruido** that noise upsets me, that noise gets on my nerves; **¿le molesta el ruido?** do you mind (or object to) the noise?, does the noise bother you?; **los niños me molestan para estudiar** the kids disturb my work, the kids stop me working; **me molesta tener que repetirlo** I hate having to repeat it; **¿le molesta que abra la ventana?** do you mind if I open the window?; **¿le molesta que fume?** will it bother you if I smoke?

2 vi to be a nuisance; to get in the way, be awkward; **no quiero —** I don't want to intrude, I don't want to be in the way, I don't wish to cause any trouble.

3 molestarse vr (a) to bother (con about); to go to trouble, put oneself out; **— en + infin** to bother to + infin; **¡no se moleste!** don't bother!, don't trouble yourself!
(b) to get cross; to take offence, get upset.

molestia nf bother, trouble, nuisance; inconvenience; (Med) discomfort; **es una —** it's a nuisance; **no es —** it's no trouble; **ahorrarse —s** to save oneself trouble, spare oneself effort; **darse la — de + infin, tomarse la — de + infin** to take the trouble to + infin, go out of one's way to + infin.

molesto adj (a) troublesome, annoying; trying, tiresome; arrangement inconvenient; task irksome; smell, taste nasty; **es muy — para mí** it's very inconvenient for me; **si no cs — para Vd** if it's no trouble to you; **es una persona muy molesta** she's a very trying person.
(b) discontented; restless; ill-at-ease; uncomfortable; upset, offended; embarrassed; **estar —** (Med) to be in some discomfort; **estar — con uno** to be cross with someone; **me sentí —** I felt uncomfortable; I felt embarrassed.

molestoso adj (Cu, Chi, Ec, PR) annoying.

moletón nm flannelette.

molibdeno nm molybdenum.

molicie nf (a) softness. (b) (fig) soft living, luxurious living; effeminacy.

molido adj (a) ground, crushed; powdered. (b) **estar —** (fig) to be exhausted, be dead beat.

molienda nf (a) (act) grinding; milling. (b) quantity of corn (etc) to be ground. (c) mill. (d) (fam) weariness. (e) (fam) nuisance.

molinero nm miller.

molinete nm (toy) windmill.

molinillo nm (a) hand mill; **— de café** coffee mill, coffee grinder; **— de carne** mincer.
(b) (toy) windmill.

molino nm (a) mill; grinder; **— de agua** water mill; **— de viento** windmill. (b) (fam) restless person; bore, tedious individual.

molo nm (Chi, Ven) breakwater, sea wall.

molote nm (a) (Mex) ball of wool (etc). (b) (Mex) fried maize pancake. (c) (Col, Mex) dirty trick. (d) (CAm, Cu, SD) riot, commotion.

molusco nm mollusc.

mollar adj (a) fruit soft, tender; easily shelled; (pej) mushy, rotten. (b) meat lean. (c) (fam) gullible.

molledo nm (a) (Anat) fleshy part (of a limb). (b) (of bread) crumb.

molleja nf gizzard; **—s** sweetbreads.

mollejón nm fat listless man.

mollera nf (Anat) crown of the head; (fam) brains, sense; **cerrado de —, duro de —** dense, dim; pigheaded; **secar la — a uno** to drive someone crazy; **tener buena —** to have brains, be brainy.

mollete nm (a) (Cook) muffin. (b) (Anat) fleshy part of the arm; fat cheek.

momentáneamente adv momentarily.

momentáneo adj momentary.

momento nm (a) moment; instant; time; **—s después** a few moments later; **al —** at once; **a cada —** every instant, all the time; **de —** at the moment, for the moment; **no los vi de —** I didn't see them at first; **de un — a otro** at any moment; **en el — actual** at the present time; **en el — bueno** at the right moment, at the proper time; **en este — at** this moment; right now; **hace un —** not a moment ago; **por el —** for the moment; **está cambiando por —s** it is changing all the time; **atravesamos un — difícil** we are going through a difficult time; **ha llegado el — de + infin** the time has come to + infin.
(b) (Mech) momentum; moment.
(c) (fig) consequence, importance; **de poco —** unimportant.

momería nf mummery, clowning.

momia nf mummy.

momificación nf mummification.

momificar [1g] **1** vt to mummify. **2 momificarse** vr to mummify, become mummified.

momio 1 adj meat lean. **2** nm bargain; extra; cushy job (sl); profitable deal; **de —** free, gratis.

momo nm (a) funny face. (b) clowning, buffoonery.

mona nf (a) (Zool) female monkey; (species) Barbary ape; **estar hecho una —** to be embarrassed, be quite

put out; **mandar a uno a freír —s** (*fam*) to tell someone to go to blazes.
   (**b**) (*fam*: *person*) ape, copycat (*fam*).
   (**c**) (*fam*) drunk (*fam*); hangover; **coger** (*or* **pillar**) **una —** to get tight; **dormir la —** to sleep off a hangover.
   (**d**) (*Col*) blonde.
monacal *adj* monastic.
monacato *nm* monasticism; monastic life, monk's way of life.
monacillo *nm* acolyte, altar boy.
monada *nf* (**a**) (*act*) monkey face; monkeyish way (*or* movement *etc*); silly habit; silly thing (to say *etc*).
   (**b**) (*child's*) charming habit, sweet little way.
   (**c**) (*quality*) silliness, childishness.
   (**d**) (*fam*) lovely thing; beauty, cute little thing; (*person*) pretty girl; **la casa es una —** the house is lovely, the house is a gem; **¡qué —!** isn't it cute?, isn't it lovely?; **¡hola, —!** hullo, beautiful!
   (**e**) (*fam*) **—s** flattery.
mónada *nf* monad.
monago *nm*, **monaguillo** *nm* acolyte, altar boy.
monarca *nm* monarch, ruler.
monarquía *nf* monarchy.
monárquico **1** *adj* monarchic(al); (*Pol*) royalist, monarchist. **2** *nm* royalist, monarchist.
monarquismo *nm* monarchism.
monasterio *nm* monastery.
monástico *adj* monastic.
monda[1] *nf* (**a**) (*act*) pruning, lopping, trimming; peeling. (**b**) pruning season. (**c**) peel, peelings, skin. (**d**) (*Col, Cu, Mex, PR*) beating.
monda[2] *nf* (*fam*): **¡es la —!** (**a**) it's great! (*fam*); (*pej*) it's the limit, it's the end; it's sheer hell (*fam*); **este nuevo baile es la —** this new dance is the greatest (*fam*), (*pej*) this new dance is awful (*fam*).
   (**b**) (*of person*) he's the most (*sl*), he's a knockout (*sl*); (*pej*) he's a shocker, he's a terror.
mondadientes *nm*, *pl* **mondadientes** toothpick.
mondadura *nf* (**a**) = **monda**[1] (**a**); cleaning, cleansing.
   (**b**) **—s** = **monda**[1] (**c**).
mondar [1a] **1** *vt* (**a**) *tree* to prune, lop, trim.
   (**b**) *fruit* to peel, skin; *potato* to peel; *nut, peas* to shell; *stick* to peel, pare, remove the bark from; **— a uno** to cut someone's hair.
   (**c**) to clean, cleanse; *canal etc* to clean out.
   (**d**) (*fam*) to fleece, strip bare, clean out (*sl*).
   (**e**) (*fam*) **¡que te monden!** get away!, rubbish!
   (**f**) (*Col, Cu, PR*) to beat, thrash; (*Cu: Sport etc*) to wipe the floor with (*fam*).
   2 mondarse *vr*: **— los dientes** to pick one's teeth.
mondo *adj* (**a**) clean; pure; plain; neat; *head* completely shorn.
   (**b**) (*fig*) bare, plain, without addition; **el asunto — es esto** the plain fact of the matter is; **tiene su sueldo — y nada más** he has his bare salary and nothing more; **me he quedado —** I'm cleaned out (*sl*), I haven't a cent; **— y lirondo** (*fam*) *fact, truth etc* plain, pure and simple.
mondongo *nm* guts, insides.
mondongudo *adj* (*esp RPl*) fat, potbellied.
monear [1a] *vi* (**a**) to act like a monkey; to make monkey faces. (**b**) (*Chi, Mex, Urug*) to boast, swank (*fam*).
moneda *nf* (**a**) (*in general*) currency, money, coinage; **— blanda, — débil** soft currency; **— dura, — fuerte** hard currency; **— menuda, — suelta** small change, coins of low denomination; **en — española** in Spanish money; **pagar a uno con** (*or* **en**) **la misma —** to pay someone back in his own coin.
   (**b**) (*una —*) coin, piece; **— falsa** false coin, dud coin; **una — de 5 dólares** a 5-dollar piece; **es tan probable como que ahora lluevan —s de 5 duros** it's about as likely as my becoming pope.
moned(e)ar [1a] *vt* = **amonedar**.
monedero *nm* (**a**) **— falso** counterfeiter. (**b**) purse.
monería *nf* (**a**) funny face, monkey face; mimicry. (**b**) antic, prank, playful trick. (**c**) (*pej*) trifle, triviality.
monetario *adj* monetary, financial.
Mongolia *f* = **Mogolia**.
moni *nf* (*SAm: angl*) money.
monigote *nm* (**a**) rag doll; puppet; grotesque figure; **— de nieve** snowman.
   (**b**) (*fig*) colourless individual, weak character, little man; **¡—!** (*to child*) you chump! (*fam*).
   (**c**) (*Art*) humorous sketch, cartoon; (*pej*) bad painting (*or* statue), daub; doodle.
monises *nmpl* (*fam: angl*) brass (*sl*), dough (*sl*).
monitor *nm* monitor.
monitorio *adj* admonitory.
monja *nf* nun; sister.

monje *nm* monk.
monjil **1** *adj* nun's, of (*or* like) a nun; (*fig*) excessively demure. **2** *nm* nun's habit.
mono[1] *nm* (**a**) (*Zool*) monkey, ape; **¡—!** (*to child*) you little monkey!
   (**b**) (*fig*) ape, mimic; **— de imitación** (*child etc*) copycat (*fam*).
   (**c**) (*fam*) brash youth; affected youth.
   (**d**) (*Art*) = **monigote** (**c**).
   (**e**) (*Cards*) joker.
   (**f**) (*fam*) ugly devil, ugly monkey.
   (**g**) (*fam*) sign (*between lovers etc*); **hacerse —s** to make eyes at each other, make little signs to each other.
   (**h**) (*idioms*) **no lo aguantaría ni que fuera yo un —** I wouldn't put up with it at any price; **no me mirarían más ni que tuviera —s en la cara** they couldn't have stared at me more if I had come from the moon; **estar de —s** to be at daggers drawn; **meter los —s a uno** (*Col, Cu, PR*) to put the wind up someone.
mono[2] *adj* pretty, lovely, attractive; nice, charming, cute; **una chica muy mona** a very attractive girl, a very nice girl; **¡qué sombrero más —!** what a cute little hat!
mono[3] *nm* overalls; boiler suit; (*child's*) rompers.
mono[4] **1** *adj* (*Col*) yellow; blond, reddish blond; yellow with age. **2** *nm* (*Chi*) pile (*of fruit etc*); slice of melon; bunch of cherries.
mono . . . mono . . .
monocarril *nm* monorail.
monocromo **1** *adj* monochrome. **2** *nm* monochrome.
monóculo *nm* monocle.
monocultivo *nm* monoculture, single crop; one-crop farming; **el — es un peligro para muchos países** in many countries dependence upon a single crop is dangerous.
monogamia *nf* monogamy.
monógamo *adj* monogamous.
monografía *nf* monograph.
monográfico *adj*: **estudio —** monograph.
monograma *nm* monogram.
monohombre *adj* one-man (*attr*).
monolingüe *adj* monolingual.
monolítico *adj* monolithic.
monolito *nm* monolith.
monologar [1h] *vi* to soliloquize.
monólogo *nm* monologue.
monomanía *nf* monomania; mania, obsession; **— de grandezas** megalomania.
monomio *nm* monomial.
monomotor *adj* single-engined.
monoplano *nm* monoplane.
monoplaza *nm* single-seater.
monopolio *nm* monopoly.
monopolizar [1f] *vt* to monopolize.
monorail *nm* monorail.
monorrimo *adj* *stanza etc* having the same rhyme throughout.
monosabio *nm* (**a**) (*Zool*) trained monkey. (**b**) (*Taur*) *picador's assistant*; *employee who leads the horse team dragging the dead bull*.
monosilábico *adj* monosyllabic.
monosílabo **1** *adj* monosyllabic. **2** *nm* monosyllable.
monoteísmo *nm* monotheism.
monoteísta **1** *adj* monotheistic. **2** *nmf* monotheist.
monotipia *nf* Monotype (*Protected Trade Name*).
monotonía *nf* (*sound*) monotone; (*fig*) monotony; sameness, dreariness.
monótono *adj* on one note; (*fig*) monotonous; humdrum, dreary.
monóxido *nm* monoxide; **— de carbono** carbon monoxide.
monseñor *nm* monsignor.
monserga *nf* (**a**) gibberish, jargon. (**b**) drivel, tedious talk; **dar la —** to get on someone's nerves, be a bore.
monstruo **1** *nm* monster (*also fig*); (*Bio*) freak, sport, monster.
   2 *as adj* (*invar*) (*fam*) fantastic, fabulous (*fam*); **idea —** fantastic idea; **es un plan —** it's a fabulous scheme.
monstruosidad *nf* monstrosity; (*Bio*) freak.
monstruoso *adj* monstrous, huge, monster (*attr*); (*Bio*) freakish, freak (*attr*); (*fig*) monstrous, hideous; **es — que . . .** it is monstrous that . . .
monta *nf* (**a**) (*act*) mounting.
   (**b**) (*Math*) total, sum.
   (**c**) (*fig*) value; **de poca —** of small account, unimportant.
   (**d**) (*Agr*) stud; mating season (*of horses*).
montacargas *nm*, *pl* **montacargas** service lift, hoist, freight elevator (*US*).

montado *adj* (a) mounted; **artillería montada** horse artillery; **guardias montadas** horse guards. (b) (*Tech*) built-in.
montador *nm* (a) mounting block. (b) (*person*) fitter; — **de escena** (*Cine*) design craftsman.
montadura *nf* (a) mounting. (b) = **montura.**
montaje *nm* (a) (*Mech etc*) assembly; fitting-up; (*Archit*) erection.
(b) (*Radio*) hookup.
(c) (*Art, Cine, Phot*) montage; (*Theat*) stage designing, décor.
montante *nm* (a) (*Hist*) broadsword.
(b) (*Tech*) upright, post; stanchion; (*Archit*) transom; (*of window*) mullion.
(c) (*Archit*) small window over a door.
(d) (*SAm*) total, amount.
montaña *nf* (a) mountain; mountains, mountainous area; — **rusa** switchback, scenic railway. (b) (*Per, PR*) forest.
montañero 1 *adj* mountain (*attr*). 2 *nm*, **montañera** *nf* mountaineer, climber.
montañés 1 *adj* (a) mountain (*attr*); hill (*attr*); highland (*attr*).
(b) of (*or from*) the Santander region.
2 *nm*, **montañesa** *nf* (a) highlander.
(b) native of the Santander region.
montañismo *nm* mountaineering, climbing.
montañoso *adj* mountainous.
montaplatos *nm*, *pl* **montaplatos** service lift, dumbwaiter (*US*).
montar [1a] 1 *vt* (a) *horse etc* to mount, get on; to ride; **hoy ella monta mi caballo** she's riding my horse today.
(b) — **a uno sobre un tronco** to lift someone on to a log; **montó al niño en el burro** he lifted the child on to the donkey, he put the child up on the donkey, he sat the child on the donkey.
(c) (*Bio*) to cover, mate with.
(d) to overlap; — **un color sobre otro** to overlap one colour with another, to cover one colour partially with another.
(e) (*Mech*) to assemble, fit (up), put together, set up; (*Archit*) to erect, put up; *jewel* to set, mount; *gun* to cock; *clock, spring* to wind (up); *stitches* to cast on; *guard* to mount.
(f) — **una casa** to set up house; — **una tienda** to open a shop; — **un negocio** to start a business, found a business.
(g) (*Cook*) *egg* to beat, whip.
2 *vi* (a) to mount (*a un caballo, en un caballo* a horse), get up (*a, en* on); to get on; to ride; — **a caballo** to ride; — **en bicicleta** to ride a bicycle, cycle; **me ayudó a** — he helped me up; he helped me to mount; **montó en la bicicleta y desapareció** he got on his bicycle and disappeared; **mi hermana monta a diario** my sister rides every day; — **para una cuadra de carreras** to ride for a racing stable.
(b) to overlap; **el mapa monta sobre el texto** the map overlaps the text, the map covers part of the text.
(c) — **en cólera,** — **en indignación** to get angry.
(d) (*Fin*) — **a** to amount to, come to, add up to.
(e) **tanto monta** it makes no odds; it's all the same, it doesn't matter either way; **tanto monta que vengas o no** it's all the same whether you come or not.
3 **montarse** *vr* = 2 (a) (b) *and* (c).
montaraz 1 *adj* (a) mountain (*attr*), highland (*attr*). (b) wild, untamed; (*pej*) rough, coarse, uncivilized; unsociable. 2 *nm* gamekeeper, game warden.
montarrón *nm* (*Col*) forest.
monte *nm* (a) mountain; M—s Apalaches Appalachians; M—s Cárpatos Carpathians; M—de la Mesa Table Mountain; los M—s Pirineos the Pyrenees; **echarse al** — to take to the hills.
(b) woodland; wilds, wild country; — **alto** forest; — **bajo** scrub; **batir el** — to beat for game, go hunting.
(c) — **de piedad** (state-owned) pawnshop.
(d) (*Cu, Pan, PR, Urug, Ven*) outskirts, surrounding country.
(e) (*Mex*) grass, pasture.
(f) (*Cards*) pile; bank; *a card game.*
(g) (*fam*) obstacle, snag; **todo se le hace un** — he sees difficulties everywhere, he makes a mountain out of every molehill.
montear [1a] *vt* to hunt.
montecillo *nm* mound, hummock, hump.
montepío *nm* (a) charitable fund for dependents, friendly society. (b) (*SAm*) pawnshop.
montera *nf* cloth cap; bullfighter's hat.
montería *nf* (a) (art of) hunting; hunt, chase. (b)

(*Art*) hunting scene. (c) hunting party. (d) (*SAm*) animals, game; hunting ground. (e) (*Bol, Ec*) canoe.
montero *nm* huntsman, hunter; beater.
montés *adj* *cat etc* wild.
montevideano 1 *adj* Montevidean. 2 *nm*, **montevideana** *nf* Montevidean.
montículo *nm* = **montecillo.**
monto *nm* total, amount.
montón *nm* (a) heap, pile; (*of snow*) drift.
(b) (*fig*) **del** — ordinary, average, commonplace; **un hombre del** — an ordinary chap; **salirse del** — to be exceptional, stand out from the crowd.
(c) (*fam*) stack (*fam*), heap, lot; (*of people*) crowd, mass; **un** — **de gente** a crowd, a mass of people, masses of people; **tengo un** — **de cosas que decirte** I have lots (*or* heaps, stacks) of things to tell you; **tenemos** —**s** we have heaps (*or* tons, loads: *fam*); **a** — together, all lumped together; **a** —**es** in great abundance, by the score (*etc*), galore.
montonera *nf* (a) (*SAm*) band of guerrilla fighters.
(b) (*PR*) pile, heap; (*Col*) haystack, strawstack.
montonero 1 *adj* (*Mex etc*) *person* overbearing, that chucks his weight about. 2 *nm* (*SAm*) guerrilla fighter.
montuno *adj* (a) mountain (*attr*); forest (*attr*). (b) (*SAm*) wild, untamed; rustic.
montuosidad *nf* hilliness, mountainous nature.
montuoso *adj* hilly, mountainous.
montura *nf* (a) mount.
(b) saddle; harness, trappings; **cabalgar sin** — to ride bareback.
(c) (*of jewel etc*) mount, mounting, setting; (*of spectacles etc*) frame.
monumental *adj* monumental; (*fam*) tremendous (*fam*), terrific (*fam*).
monumento 1 *nm* (a) monument (*also fig*); memorial; —**s prehistóricos** prehistoric remains; **visitar los** —**s de una ciudad** to see the sights of a town, visit the places of interest in a city.
(b) (*historical*) —**s** documents, source material.
2 *as adj* (*fam*) **un éxito** — a tremendous success (*fam*), a huge success.
monzón *nm or f* monsoon.
monzónico *adj* monsoon (*attr*); **lluvias monzónicas** monsoon rains.
moña *nf* (a) hair ribbon, bow; bullfighter's ribbon; sash, prize ribbon. (b) (*fam*) doll. (c) (*fam*) **estar con la** — to be tight.
moño *nm* (a) bun, chignon; topknot; (*Chi*) man's hair; (*Chi*) horse's forelock; **agarrarse del** — to tear each other's hair; **estar hasta el** — (*fam*) to be fed up to the back teeth; **ponerse** —**s** (*fam*) to give oneself airs, put it on.
(b) (*Orn*) crest.
(c) = **moña** (a).
(d) —**s** (*fig*) frippery, buttons and bows.
(e) (*SAm*) pride, haughtiness; **bajar el** — **a uno** to take someone down a peg.
moquero *nm* handkerchief.
moqueta *nf* moquette.
moquete *nm* punch on the nose.
moquillo *nm* (*Vet*) distemper; pip.
mora[1] *nf* (a) (*Bot*) mulberry; blackberry. (b) (*Bol*) bullet.
mora[2] *nf* (*Law*) delay; **ponerse en** — to default, get into arrears.
mora[3] *nf* (*Chi*) blood sausage, black pudding.
morada *nf* (a) dwelling, abode, home; **la eterna** — the great beyond; **última** — (last) resting place; **no tener** — **fija** to be of no fixed abode.
(b) stay, period of residence.
morado 1 *adj* purple, violet; **pasarlas moradas** to have a tough time of it. 2 *nm* bruise.
morador *nm*, **moradora** *nf* inhabitant.
moradura *nf* bruise.
moral[1] *nm* (*Bot*) mulberry tree.
moral[2] 1 *adj* moral. 2 *nf* (a) morals, morality; (*as study*) ethics. (b) (*of army etc*) morale.
moraleja *nf* moral.
moralidad *nf* (a) morals, morality, ethics. (b) (*of story etc*) moral.
moralista *nmf* moralist.
moralizador 1 *adj* moralizing. 2 *nm*, **moralizadora** *nf* moralist.
moralizar [1f] *vt* to moralize.
moralmente *adv* morally.
morapio *nm* (*fam*) red wine.
morar [1a] *vi* to live, dwell; to stay.
moratoria *nf* moratorium.
morbidez *nf* (*Art etc*) softness, delicacy.
mórbido *adj* (a) morbid; diseased. (b) (*Art etc*) soft, delicate.

morbosidad *nf* (a) morbidity, morbidness; unhealthiness. (b) (*of nation*) state of health; medical statistics.

morboso *adj* (a) morbid; unhealthy, likely to cause disease(s). (b) (*fig*) diseased, morbid.

morcilla *nf* (a) (*Cook*) blood sausage, black pudding. (b) (*Theat*) gag, unscripted lines, improvised part.

morcillo *adj* horse black with reddish hairs.

morcón *nm* (a) (*Cook*) big blood sausage. (b) (*fam*) stocky person. (c) (*fam*) sloppy individual, shabby sort.

mordacidad *nf* sharpness, pungency; bite.

mordaga *nf* (*fam*), **mordaguera** *nf* (*fam*) drunkenness; **coger** (*or* **pillar**) **una** — to get boozed.

mordaz *adj* wit etc biting, scathing, pungent.

mordaza *nf* (a) gag. (b) (*Tech*) clamp, jaw.

mordazmente *adv* bitingly, scathingly.

mordedura *nf* bite.

mordelón 1 *adj* (a) (*CAm, Mex*) given to taking bribes. (b) (*Col, Ven*) dog snappy. 2 *nm* (*Mex: fam*) traffic cop (*sl*).

morder [2h] 1 *vt* (a) to bite; to nip; to nibble (at).
(b) (*Chem*) to corrode, eat away, eat into; *resources etc* to eat into.
(c) (*Mech*) to catch; to clutch, seize.
(d) (*fam*) to gossip about, run down.
(e) (*Ant, Mex, Ven*) to cheat; (*CAm, Mex*) to exact a bribe from.
2 *vi* to bite (*also fig*); **estoy que muerdo** I'm simply furious; **está que muerde** he's hopping mad.

mordicar [1g] *vi* to smart, sting.

mordida *nf* (a) (*SAm*) bite. (b) (*CAm, Mex*) bribe; money obtained by graft, illegal payment.

mordiscar [1g] 1 *vt* to nibble at, gnaw at; to nip; (*of horse*) to champ. 2 *vi* to nibble; to champ.

mordisco *nm* (a) bite, nip; nibble; **deshacer algo a** **—s** to bite something to pieces. (b) bite, piece bitten off.

mordisquear [1a] = **mordiscar**.

morena[1] *nf* (*Geol*) moraine.

morena[2] *nf* (*Fish*) moray.

morena[3] *nf* dark girl, brunette.

moreno *adj* (dark) brown; *person* dark; swarthy; dark-haired; *hair* dark, black; (*euph*) coloured (*euph*), Negro; (*Cu, Ec, PR*) mulatto.

morera *nf* mulberry tree.

morería *nf* (*Hist*) Moorish lands, Moorish territory; (*in town*) Moorish quarter.

morfema *nm* morpheme.

morfina *nf* morphia, morphine.

morfinómano 1 *adj* addicted to drugs. 2 *nm*, **morfinómana** *nf* drug addict.

morfología *nf* morphology.

morfológico *adj* morphological.

morganático *adj* morganatic.

morgue *nf* (*CAm*) morgue.

moribundo 1 *adj* dying; (*esp fig*) moribund. 2 *nm*, **moribunda** *nf* dying person.

moricho *nm* (*Ven*) hammock.

morigerado *adj* well-behaved, law-abiding.

morigerar [1a] *vt* to restrain, moderate.

morillo *nm* firedog.

morir [3k; *ptp* **muerto**] 1 *vt* (*only in ptp and perfect tense*) to kill; **le han muerto** they have killed him; **fue muerto en un accidente** he was killed in an accident; **fue muerto a tiros** he was shot (dead).
2 *vi* (a) to die (*also fig*); — **de difteria** to die of diphtheria; — **joven** to die young; — **de vejez** to die of old age; — **ahogado** to drown; — **ahorcado** to be hanged, die by hanging; — **de frío** to die of cold, freeze to death; — **fusilado** to be shot; — **de hambre** to die of (*or* from) starvation, starve to death; — **sin decir Jesús** to die very suddenly; **¡muera!** kill him!; **¡muera el tirano!** down with the tyrant!; **¡así se muera!** (*fam*) God rot him!
(b) (*of fire*) to die down, burn low; to go out; (*of light*) to get dim, go out; **moría el día** the day was almost over, night was falling.
(c) (*Rail etc: of line*) to end (*en* at); (*of street*) to come out (*en* at).
3 **morirse** *vr* (a) to die; **se le murió el tío** an uncle of his died; **se nos va a** — **el burro** the donkey is going to die on us; — **de hambre** = **morir de hambre; ¡me muero de hambre!** (*fig*) I'm starving!; **no es cosa de** — it's not as bad as all that.
(b) (*fig*) to be dying; **me moría de vergüenza** I nearly died of shame; **me moría de miedo** I was half-dead with fright; **se van a** — **de risa** they'll die of laughing.
(c) — **por algo** to be dying for something; — **por uno** to be crazy about someone; **se muere por el**

fútbol he's mad keen on football; — **por** + *infin* to be dying to + *infin*.
(d) — to go to sleep, go numb.

morisco 1 *adj* Moorish; (*Archit*) Mauresque, in the Moorish style.
2 *nm*, **morisca** *nf* (a) (*Hist*) Moslem convert to Christianity, subject Moslem (*of 15th and 16th centuries*).
(b) (*Mex*) quadroon.

morisqueta *nf* fraud, dirty trick.

mormón *nm*, **mormona** *nf* Mormon.

mormónico *adj* Mormon.

mormonismo *nm* Mormonism.

moro 1 *adj* (a) Moorish.
(b) horse dappled, piebald.
2 *nm*, **mora** *nf* (a) Moor; — **de paz** peaceful person; **¡hay —s en la costa!** watch out!; **dar a** — **muerto gran lanzada** to kick a man when he's down.
(b) (*SAm*) piebald horse.

morocha *nf* (*Ven*) double-barrelled gun.

morocho 1 *adj* (a) (*SAm*) dark, swarthy; brunette.
(b) (*Col, Chi, Ec, PR*) strong, tough; well-preserved.
(c) (*Ven*) twin.
2 *nm* (a) (*SAm*) hard maize, corn (*US*).
(b) (*Col, Chi, Ec, PR*) tough person.
(c) (*Ven*) twin.

morondaga *nf* hotchpotch.

morondo *adj* (a) bald; leafless, bare. (b) (*fig*) bare, plain.

moronga *nf* (*CAm, Mex*) blood sausage, black pudding.

morosidad *nf* slowness, sluggishness; dilatoriness; apathy.

moroso 1 *adj* (a) slow, sluggish; dilatory; (*Comm, Fin*) slow to pay up; **deudor** — slow payer, defaulter; **una película de acción morosa** a film with slow action, a slow-moving film.
(b) **delectación morosa** lingering enjoyment, (*pej*) morbid enjoyment, unhealthy enjoyment.
2 *nm* (*Comm, Fin*) slow payer, bad debtor, defaulter.

morra *nf* top of the head; **andar a la** — to exchange blows.

morrada *nf* butt; bang on the head; bash (*fam*), punch.

morral *nm* (a) haversack, knapsack; (*Hunting*) pouch, gamebag; (*horse's*) nosebag. (b) (*fam*) lout, rough type.

morrillo *nm* (*Zool*) fleshy part of the neck; (*fam*) neck, back of the neck.

morriña *nf* depression, depressed state, blues; — **de** **la tierra** homesickness.

morrión *nm* (*Mil*) helmet, bearskin.

morro *nm* (a) (*Zool*) snout, nose; (*fam*) lip, thick lip; **andar de** — **con uno** to be at odds with someone; **estar de —s** to be in a bad mood; **estar de** — **(s) con** **uno** to be cross with someone; **¡cierra los —s!** shut your trap! (*sl*); **poner** —, **torcer el** — to look cross.
(b) (*Aer, Aut etc*) nose; **caer de** — to nose-dive (into the ground).
(c) (*Geog*) headland, promontory.
(d) pebble.
(e) small rounded hill, rounded rock.

morrocotudo *adj* (*fam*) (a) smashing (*sl*), terrific (*fam*), splendid; *row, blow etc* tremendous.
(b) heavy; heavy.
(c) *affair* sticky, awkward; important, weighty.
(d) (*Arg, Mex, Urug*) big.
(e) (*Col*) rich.
(f) (*Chi*) dull, monotonous.

morrocoyo *nm* (*Ant*) (a) turtle. (b) (*fam*) fat person; deformed person.

morrongo *nm*, **morronga** *nf* cat.

morronguero *adj* (*Cu*) mean; cowardly.

morroñoso *adj* (a) (*CAm*) rough. (b) (*Per*) small, feeble; mean.

morrudo *adj* (a) thick-lipped. (b) (*Arg*) tough, brawny.

morsa *nf* walrus.

mortaja *nf* (a) shroud. (b) (*Tech*) mortise. (c) (*SAm*) cigarette paper.

mortal 1 *adj* (a) mortal.
(b) *wound etc* mortal, fatal; *blow* deadly.
(c) (*fam*) *distance, wait etc* deadly, unending.
(d) (*fam*) **quedarse** — to be utterly taken aback.
2 *nmf* mortal.

mortalidad *nf* (a) mortality. (b) mortality; loss of life, toll, number of victims; death rate; — **infantil** (rate of) infantile mortality.

mortalmente *adv* (a) mortally. (b) fatally.

mortandad *nf* toll, loss of life, number of victims; (*Mil*) slaughter, carnage.
mortecino *adj* (a) weak, failing; **hacerse la mortecina** to pretend to be dead. (b) *light* dim, fading, failing; *colour* dull, faded.
mortero *nm* (*all senses*) mortar.
mortífero *adj* deadly, lethal.
mortificación *nf* mortification; humiliation.
mortificar [1g] **1** *vt* (a) (*Med*) to damage, affect seriously.
　(b) *flesh* to mortify; (*of insect, shoe*) to torment, plague; **me han mortificado toda la noche los mosquitos** the mosquitos tormented me all night; **estos zapatos me mortifican** these shoes are killing me.
　(c) (*fig*) to mortify, humiliate; to spite.
　2 mortificarse *vr* (*Mex*) to feel ashamed; to be embarrassed, feel bashful.
mortuorio *adj* mortuary, death (*attr*); **casa mortuoria** house of mourning, home of the deceased.
morucco *nm* (*Zool*) ram.
Mosa *m* Meuse.
mosaico[1] *adj* Mosaic, of Moses.
mosaico[2] *nm* mosaic; tessellated pavement; **— de madera** marquetry.
mosca *nf* (a) (*Ent*) fly; **— de burro** horsefly; **— de la carne** meat fly; **— doméstica** housefly; **— de España** Spanish fly, cantharides; **— muerta** (*fig*) hypocrite, slyboots (*fam*); **— tsetsé** tsetse fly; **por si las —s** just in case; **estar —** to smell a rat, be distrustful; **estar —** to be utterly fed up; **estar — con uno** to be cross with someone; **mandar a uno a capar —s** to tell someone to go to blazes; **papar —s** to gape, gawp (*fam*); **pescar a —** to fish with a fly; **le picó la —** (*fig*) he suddenly got worried; **tener la — en** (*or* **detrás de**) **la oreja** to be wary, be suspicious.
　(b) (*sl*) dough (*sl*); **aflojar la —, soltar la —** to fork out (*fam*), stump up.
　(c) (*fam: person*) pest, bore.
　(d) tuft of hair, small growth of hair; small goatee beard.
　(e) **—s** sparks; **—s volantes** spots before the eyes.
　(f) (*Mex*) sponger (*fam*).
moscarda *nf* blowfly, bluebottle.
moscardón *nm* (a) (*Ent*) botfly, blowfly; hornet.
　(b) (*fam*) pest, bore, nuisance.
moscatel[1] **1** *adj grape* muscatel. **2** *nm* muscatel.
moscatel[2] *nm* (a) bore, pest. (b) big lad, overgrown lad.
moscón *nm* (a) (*Ent*) = **moscarda**. (b) (*Bot*) maple.
　(c) (*fam*) pest, nuisance.
Moscú Moscow.
Mosela *m* Moselle.
mosqueado *adj* spotted.
mosqueador *nm* fly-whisk; (*fam*) tail (*of horse etc*).
mosquearse [1a] *vr* (*fig*) to get cross, take offence.
mosquete *nm* musket.
mosquetero *nm* (*Hist: Mil*) musketeer; (*Theat*) groundling.
mosquita *nf*: **— muerta** (*fig*) hypocrite, slyboots (*fam*); **hacerse la — muerta** to look as if butter would not melt in one's mouth.
mosquitero *nm* mosquito net.
mosquito *nm* mosquito; gnat.
mostacera *nf*, **mostacero** *nm* mustard pot.
mostacho *nm* moustache.
mostachón *nm* macaroon.
mostaza *nf* mustard.
mostela *nf* sheaf.
mosto *nm* must, unfermented grape juice.
mostrador *nm* (a) counter; (*of café, pub etc*) bar. (b) (*of clock*) face, dial.
mostrar [1m] **1** *vt* to show; to display, exhibit; to point out; to explain; to demonstrate.
　2 mostrarse *vr* (a) to show oneself; to appear.
　(b) (*with adj*) to appear, show oneself to be; **se mostró muy amable** he was very kind, he proved to be very kind; **'se mostró ofendido** he appeared (to be) cross; **no se muestra muy imaginativa** she does not seem to be very imaginative.
mostrenco *adj* (a) ownerless, unclaimed; *title* in abeyance; *animal* stray; *person* (*fam*) homeless, rootless.
　(b) (*fam*) *person* dense, slow; fat.
　(c) (*fam*) *object* crude, roughly made.
mota *nf* (a) speck, tiny piece; piece of fluff; **— de carbonilla** smut, speck of coaldust; **— de polvo** speck of dust; **ver la — en el ojo ajeno** to see the mote in someone else's eye.
　(b) (*in pattern*) dot; **diseño a —s** design with (*or* of) dots.

　(c) (*in cloth*) burl, kink; (*fig*) fault, blemish, defect.
　(d) **no . . . —** nothing, no, *eg* **no hace — de aire** there isn't a breath of air.
　(e) (*Geog*) hillock.
　(f) (*Agr*) ridge, boundary mark.
　(g) (*Agr*) turf, clod (*used to block off irrigation channel*).
　(h) (*SAm*) lock of kinky hair.
　(i) (*Cu, Mex, PR*) powder puff.
　(j) (*Mex*) marijuana plant.
mote[1] *nm* (a) (*Hist*) motto, device. (b) nickname, by-name.
mote[2] *nm* (*SAm*) boiled maize, boiled corn (*US*).
moteado *adj skin* speckled, mottled, dappled (*de* with); *fabric etc* dotted, with a design of dots.
motear [1a] *vt* to speck (*de* with); to speckle, dapple.
motejar [1a] *vt* to nickname; **— a uno de** to brand someone as, accuse someone of being.
motel *nm* (*angl*) motel.
motete *nm* motet.
motín *nm* revolt, rising; riot, disturbance.
motivación *nf* motivation.
motivar [1a] *vt* (a) to cause, motivate, give rise to. (b) to explain, justify (*con, en* by, by reference to).
motivo 1 *adj* motive.
　2 *nm* (a) motive, reason (*de* for), cause (*de* of); **—s de divorcio** grounds for divorce; **— oculto** ulterior motive; **con — de** because of, owing to; on the occasion of; **fue allí con — de la boda de su hija** he went there for his daughter's wedding; **con este —** for this reason, because of this; **por cuyo —** for which reason, on account of which; **sin —** for no reason at all, without good reason; **un crimen sin —** a crime without a motive, a pointless crime; **tengo mis —s** I have my reasons.
　(b) (*Art, Mus*) motif; **— conductor** leitmotif; **— principal** (*of musical etc*) theme song.
moto[1] *nf* (*fam*) motorbike (*fam*); scooter.
moto[2] *adj* (a) (*CAm*) orphaned, abandoned. (b) (*Bol*) tailless.
motobomba *nf* fire engine.
motocarro *nm* three-wheeler, light delivery van.
motocicleta *nf* motorcycle; **— con sidecar** motorcycle combination.
motociclista *nmf* motorcyclist; **— de escolta** outrider.
moto-cross *nm* (*angl*) moto-cross.
motón *nm* (*Naut*) pulley.
motonave *nf* motor ship, motor vessel.
motoniveladora *nf* bulldozer.
motor 1 *adj* (a) (*Tech*) motive; **potencia motora** motive power.
　(b) (*Anat*) motor.
　2 *nm* motor, engine; **con 6 —es** 6-engined; **— de arranque, — de puesta en marcha** starter, starting motor; **— de aviación** aircraft engine; **— de combustión interna, — de explosión** internal combustion engine; **— a chorro** jet engine; **— delantero** front-mounted engine; **— Diesel** Diesel engine; **— de fuera de borda** outboard motor; **— de pistón** piston engine; **— radial** radial engine; **— de reacción** jet engine; **— refrigerado por aire** air-cooled engine; **— trasero** rear-mounted engine.
motora *nf*, **motorbote** *nm* motorboat, speedboat.
motorismo *nm* motorcycling.
motorista *nm* (a) motorcyclist. (b) (*SAm*) motorman.
motorización *nf* motorization.
motorizado *adj* motorized.
motorizar [1f] *vt* to motorize.
motosierra *nf* mechanical saw.
motosilla *nf* scooter, light motorcycle.
motoso *adj* (*Arg, Col, Ec, Per*) hair kinky.
motriz *adj* motive, driving; *see* **fuerza**.
motudo *adj* (*Chi*) hair kinky.
movedizo *adj* (a) easily moved, movable; loose, unsteady, shaky; *sands* shifting. (b) *person* fickle; *situation etc* shifting, unsettled, changeable; troubled.
mover [2h] **1** *vt* (a) *object etc* to move; to shift; to move about, move along; *head* to shake; to nod; *tail* to wag; (*Chess etc*) to move.
　(b) (*Mech*) to drive, power, work; to pull; **el agua mueve la rueda** the water turns (*or* drives) the wheel; **la máquina mueve 14 coches** the engine pulls 14 coaches; **el vapor mueve el émbolo** the steam drives (*or* works) the piston.
　(c) (*fig*) to cause, provoke, induce; *trouble etc* to stir up; **— un jaleo** to cause a row, make a fuss; **— guerra a uno** to wage war on someone; **— pleito a uno** to take proceedings against someone; **— a uno a piedad** to move someone to pity, arouse compassion in someone; **— a uno a risa** to make someone

laugh; — **a uno a hacer algo** to move (or prompt, lead) someone to do something.

2 vi (a) (Bot) to bud, sprout.

(b) (fam) to start to leave, get ready to go, make a move.

3 moverse vr (a) to move; to stir (de from); **no se ha movido de su asiento** he has not stirred from his place.

(b) (sea) to get rough; (wind) to rise.

(c) (fig) to move oneself, get a move on; to be on the move; **hay que** — we must get a move on; **si no te mueves lo perderás** if you don't hustle (or unless you do something) it will be lost; **la moda masculina se mueve** men's fashions are changing, men's fashions are on the move.

movible adj (a) movable; mobile. (b) (fig) changeable; fickle.

movida nf (Chess etc) move.

movido adj (a) (Phot) blurred (by camera shake etc).
(b) person active; restless, always on the go; meeting etc lively; turbulent.
(c) (Col, CR, Chi) egg soft-shelled.
(d) (CAm, Col, Chi) weak, feeble; stiff; paralytic; (CAm, Mex) slow, sluggish; irresolute.

móvil 1 adj =**movible a)** and (b); see **material** etc.
2 nm motive (de for); incentive.

movilidad nf mobility.

movilización nf mobilization.

movilizar [1f] vt (a) to mobilize. (b) (Arg) to unblock, free.

movimiento nm (a) (in general) movement; (Mech, Phys) motion; (statistical etc) movement; (of head) shake; nod; — **ascensional de los precios** upward trend (or movement) of prices; — **ascendente de las líneas** (Archit etc) upward sweep of the lines; — **continuo, — perpetuo** perpetual motion; — **de mercancías** (Comm) turnover, volume of business; — **de pinza** (Mil) pincer movement; — **de los precios** changes in prices; — **sísmico** earth tremor; **estar en** — to be in motion, be moving; to be on the move; **mantener algo en** — to keep something moving; **mantener en** — **la circulación** to keep the traffic on the move; **poner algo en** — to set something in motion, start something, get something going.

(b) (of street etc) movement; activity; bustle, stir; (Aut) traffic; **una tienda de mucho** — a busy shop, a much-frequented shop; — **máximo** (Aut) peak traffic; **había mucho** — **en el tribunal** there was great activity in the court.

(c) (Lit, Theat etc) action; **el libro no tiene bastante** — the book does not have enough action, not enough happens in the book.

(d) (Mus) tempo.

(e) (of emotions) change, alteration; — **de ánimo** perturbation; **en un** — **de celos** in a rush of jealousy; **obró en un** — **de pasión** he acted in a surge of passion.

(f) (Art, Lit, Pol etc) movement; **el** — **revolucionario** the revolutionary movement; **el** — **iniciado por Picasso** the movement started by Picasso; **el M**— (Spain, 1936 etc) the Falangist Movement.

moviolas nfpl magic-lantern (show); (Cine) hand viewer for film editing.

moza nf girl; servant; (pej) wench; **buena** —, **real** — handsome girl, good-looking girl; — **de partido** prostitute; — **de servicio** maid of all work; — **de taberna** barmaid.

mozalbete nm lad.

mozárabe 1 adj Mozarabic. **2** nmf Mozarab. **3** nm (dialect) Mozarabic.

mozo 1 adj (a) young.
(b) single, unmarried.

2 nm youth, young fellow, lad; servant; (in café) waiter; (Rail etc) porter; **buen** — handsome lad; well set-up young man; — **de caballos** groom; — **de café** waiter; — **de cámara** cabin boy; — **de cuerda, — de estación, — de equipajes** porter; — **de hotel** page, buttons, bellhop (US); — **de laboratorio** laboratory assistant; — **de panadería** baker's boy.

mozuela nf girl; (pej) wench.

mozuelo nm (young) lad.

muaré nm moiré.

mucama nf (SAm) maid, servant.

mucamo nm (RPl) servant, houseboy.

muceta nf (Univ) hood.

mucilaginoso adj mucilaginous.

mucílago nm mucilage.

mucosa nf mucous membrane; mucus.

mucosidad nf mucus.

mucoso adj mucous.

muchá nmf (SAm) =**muchacho, muchacha**.

muchacha nf (a) girl. (b) maid, servant (also — **de servicio**).

muchachada nf childish prank.

muchacha-guía nf, pl **muchachas-guías** girl guide, girl scout (US).

muchachería nf (a) childish prank. (b) boys and girls, kids (collectively) (fam); crowd of kids (fam).

muchachil adj boyish, girlish.

muchacho nm (a) boy, lad. (b) (SAm) clamp, holdfast; (RPl) reel; (Chi) shoehorn; (Per) miner's lamp; (Per) prop.

muchedumbre nf crowd, mass, throng; (pej) mob, herd; **una** — **de** a great crowd of, a great number of.

muchísimo adj, adv superl of **mucho**; very much, a very great deal (etc).

mucho 1 adj (a) (sing) a lot of; much, great; — **tiempo** a long time (and see **tiempo**); — **dinero** a lot of money; **con** — **valor** with much courage, with great courage; **hace** — **calor** it's very hot.

(b) (sing, collective) **había** — **borracho** there were a lot of drunks (fam); **aquí hay** — **maricón** there are lots of queers here (fam).

(c) (sing: fam) **es** — **jugador** he's a great player; **es mucha mujer** what a woman she is!, there's a woman for you!; **ésta es mucha casa para nosotros** this house is far too big for us.

(d) (pl) — **s** many, lots of; many a; **hay** — **s conejos** there are lots of rabbits; — **s de los ausentes** many of those absent; **somos** — **s** there are a lot of us; **son** — **s los que no quieren** there are many who don't want to.

2 pron: **tengo** — **que hacer** I have a lot to do; — **s dicen que** . . . a lot of people say that . . .

3 adv (a) a lot, a great deal, much; — **más** much more, a lot more; — **menos** much less; — **peor** much worse; **toca** — she plays a lot, she plays a great deal; **me alegro** — I'm very glad; **correr** — to run fast; **trabajar** — to work hard; **viene** — he comes a lot, he comes often; **es** — it's a lot, it's too much; **si no es** — **pedir** if that's not asking too much; **se guardará muy** — **de hacerlo** (fam) he'll jolly well be careful not to do it (fam); see **antes** etc.

(b) (of time) long; **¿te vas a quedar** —? are you staying long?

(c) (used alone, in answers) very; **¿estás cansado?** . . . ¡—! are you tired? . . . very (or I certainly am, yes indeed).

(d) (idioms) ¡— **que sí!** I should jolly well think so! (fam), of course!; **con** — by far, far and away, easily; **con** — **el mejor** far and away the best; **ni con** — not nearly, nothing like; not by a long chalk; **ni** — **menos** far from it; **no es** — **que** . . . it is no wonder that . . .; **no es para** — it's not up to much; **tener a uno en** — to think highly of someone, have a high opinion of someone.

muda nf (a) change of clothing. (b) (Orn, Zool) moult; (of snake) slough. (c) moulting season. (d) **está de** — (boy) his voice is breaking.

mudable adj changeable, variable; shifting; character etc fickle.

mudanza nf (a) change; **sufrir** — to undergo a change.

(b) (of house) move, removal; **camión de** — **s** removal van; **estar de** — to be moving.

(c) (Dancing) figure.

(d) — **s** (fig) fickleness; moodiness, uncertainty of mood.

mudar [1a] **1** vt (a) to change, alter; — **en** to change into, transform into; **me van a** — **la pluma** they're going to change the pen for me; **le han mudado a otra oficina** they've moved (or switched) him to another office; **esto mudó la tristeza en alegría** this changed (or turned, transformed) the sadness into joy; **le mudan las sábanas todos los días** they change his sheets every day.

(b) (Orn, Zool) to shed, moult; skin to slough.

2 vi to change; — **de ropa** to change one's clothes; — **de color** to change colour; **he mudado de parecer** I've changed my mind.

3 mudarse vr (a) = vi.

(b) to move, move house (also — **de casa**).

(c) (of voice) to break.

mudéjar 1 adj Mudejar. **2** nmf (Hist) Mudejar (Moslem permitted to live under Christian rule).

mudenco adj (CAm) stuttering; silly.

mudengo adj (Per) silly.

mudez nf dumbness.

mudo adj (a) dumb, silent, mute; **quedarse** — **de** (fig) to be dumb with; **quedarse** — **de asombro** to be dumbfounded, be speechless; **se quedó** — **durante 3 horas** he remained silent for 3 hours, he did not speak for 3 hours.

(b) (Ling) letter mute, silent.

(c) film silent; **papel** — (Theat) walking-on part.

mueblaje *nm* = mobiliario.

mueble 1 *adj* movable.

2 *nm* piece of furniture; —s furniture; (*of shop etc*) fittings; con —s furnished; sin —s unfurnished; — combinado, — de elementos adicionales piece of unit furniture; —s y enseres furniture and fittings.

mueble-bar *nm* cocktail cabinet.

mueblería *nf* furniture factory; furniture shop.

mueca *nf* (wry) face, grimace; hacer —s a to make faces at.

muela *nf* (a) (*Anat*) tooth, (*strictly*) molar, back tooth; — del juicio wisdom tooth; dolor de —s toothache; está que echa las —s he's hopping mad.

(b) (*Tech*) millstone; grindstone.

(c) (*Geog*) mound, hillock.

(d) (*Col*) gluttony.

(e) (*Ant*) trickery.

muellaje *nm* wharfage.

muelle¹ 1 *adj* (a) soft; delicate; springy, bouncy.

(b) (*fig*) life soft, easy, luxurious.

2 *nm* spring; — real mainspring; colchón de —s spring mattress, interior sprung mattress.

muelle² *nm* (a) (*Naut*) wharf, quay; pier. (b) (*Rail*) unloading bay.

muérdago *nm* mistletoe.

muérgano *nm* (a) (*Col, Ven*) useless object, piece of junk. (b) (*Col*) shabby person; (*Ec*) ill-bred person, lout. (c) (*Col*) vicious horse.

muerte *nf* (a) death (*also fig*); murder; — civil loss of civil rights; — a mano airada, — violenta violent death; — natural natural death; — repentina sudden death; dar — a to kill; causar la — a, producir la — a to kill (*in an accident*), cause the death of, bring about the death of, encontrar la — to meet one's death; estar a la — to be at death's door.

(b) (*fig phrases*) guerra a — war to the knife, war to the bitter end; luchar a — to fight to the death; un susto de — a terrible fright; odiar a uno de — to hate someone implacably; aburrirse de — to be bored to death; un empleo de mala — an awful job (*fam*), a lousy job (*fam*).

muerto 1 *adj* (a) dead; lifeless; — nacido — stillborn; más — que vivo half-dead, more dead than alive; más — que mi abuela, más — que una piedra as dead as a doornail, stone-dead; dar por — a uno to give someone up for dead; no tener donde caerse — to be utterly destitute, not have a thing; resultó — en el acto he died instantly.

(b) (*fig*) estar — de cansancio to be dead tired, be dog-tired; estar — de hambre to be dying of hunger; estar — de miedo to be half-dead with fear, be panic-stricken.

(c) *colour* dull.

(d) *language* dead; see marea, naturaleza *etc*.

(e) *lime* slaked.

2 *nm*, **muerta** *nf* dead man, dead woman; deceased; corpse; los —s the dead; callarse como un — to keep absolutely quiet; cargar con el — (*fam*) to carry the can (*sl*); doblar a —, tocar a — to toll (for a death); echar el — a uno to put the blame on someone else; no hablan los —s dead men tell no tales; hacer el — (*of swimmer*) to float; hacerse el — to pretend to be dead.

3 *nm* (*Cards*) dummy.

muesca *nf* notch, nick; groove, slot.

muestra *nf* (a) indication, sign; example; demonstration; proof; token; es — de cariño it is a token of affection; el no hacerlo es — de desprecio not doing it is an indication of contempt; quieren hacer una — de su poder they want to give a demonstration of their power; da —s de deterioro it's showing signs of wear.

(b) (*Comm etc*) sample; specimen; — gratuita free sample.

(c) (*statistical*) sample.

(d) model, pattern, guide; (*Sew*) pattern; es — de cómo debe hacerse it is a model of how it should be done.

(e) (*of watch*) face.

(f) (*of shop etc*) sign, signboard.

muestrario *nm* collection of samples (*or specimens*); pattern book.

muestreo *nm* (*statistical*) sampling.

mugido *nm* moo, lowing; bellow; roar, howl.

mugir [3c] *vi* (*cow*) to moo, low; (*bull*) to bellow; (*with pain*) to roar, howl; (*of sea etc*) to roar.

mugre *nf* dirt, filth; grease, grime.

mugriento *adj* dirty, filthy; greasy, grimy.

mugrón *nm* (*of vine*) sucker, layer; shoot, sprout.

muguete *nm* lily of the valley.

mujer *nf* (a) woman; — alegre, — de vida alegre, —

de (mala) vida, — pública prostitute; — de la limpieza charwoman, cleaner; ser muy — de su casa to be a good housewife; to be very houseproud; — fatal femme fatale; — policía policewoman.

(b) wife; mi — my wife; tomar — to take a wife, marry.

(c) ¡—!: in direct address, not translated.

mujeraza *nf* shrew, bitch, horrid woman.

mujerengo *adj* (*CAm, RPl*) (a) effeminate. (b) fond of women.

mujerero *adj* (*SAm*) fond of women.

mujeriego 1 *adj* (a) fond of women, given to chasing the girls, wolfish (*fam*).

(b) cabalgar a mujeriegas to ride sidesaddle.

2 *nm* man who is fond of the women, wolf (*fam*).

mujeril *adj* womanly.

mujerzuela *nf* whore.

mújol *nm* grey mullet.

mula *nf* (a) mule. (b) (*Mex*) trash, junk, unsaleable goods. (c) (*Guat, Hond*) shame. (d) (*Col*) pipe. (e) (*Col*) idiot. (f) (*Mex*) tough guy (*US jam*).

mulada *nf* drove of mules.

muladar *nm* dungheap, dunghill, midden.

mulato 1 *adj* mulatto. 2 *nm*, **mulata** *nf* mulatto.

mulero *nm* muleteer.

muleta *nf* (a) crutch. (b) (*Taur*) matador's stick with red cloth attached. (c) (*fig*) prop, support.

muletilla *nf* (a) cross-handled cane; (*Tech*) wooden toggle; large wooden button; (*Taur*) = muleta (b). (b) (*fig*) pet word, tag, cliché.

mulo *nm* mule.

mulón *adj* (*Chi, Per*) stammering; slow in learning to talk, backward.

multa *nf* fine; (*Sport etc*) penalty; echar una — a, imponer una — a to impose a fine (*or penalty*) on.

multar [1a] *vt* to fine; (*Sport etc*) to penalize; — a uno en 100 dólares to fine someone 100 dollars.

multi . . . multi . . .

multicanal *adj* (*TV*) multichannel.

multicolor *adj* multicoloured, many-coloured; motley, variegated.

multicopista *nm* duplicator.

multiforme *adj* manifold, multifarious; multiform; having different forms.

multilaminar *nm* plywood.

multilateral *adj*, **multilátero** *adj* mutilateral, many-sided.

multimillonario *nm*, **multimillonaria** *nf* multi-millionaire.

múltiple *adj* (a) (*Math*) multiple; (*fig*) many-sided.

(b) —s (*fig*) many, numerous; manifold, multifarious; tiene —s actividades he has multifarious activities, he has very numerous activities.

multiplicación *nf* multiplication.

multiplicado *nm* multiplicand.

multiplicar [1g] **1** *vt* (*Math and fig*) to multiply (por by); *possibilities etc* to increase; (*Mech*) to gear up. 2 **multiplicarse** *vr* (a) (*Math, Bio etc*) to multiply; to increase.

(b) (*fig*) to be everywhere at once; to attend to a lot of things all at once.

multiplicidad *nf* multiplicity.

múltiplo 1 *adj* multiple. 2 *nm* multiple; mínimo común — lowest common multiple.

multirracial *adj* multiracial.

multisecular *adj* age-old, centuries-old, very ancient.

multitud *nf* multitude; (*of people*) crowd; la — (*pej*) the multitude, the masses; — de (*fam*) lots of, heaps of; tengo — de cosas que hacer I have lots of things to do.

multitudinario *adj* multitudinarious; of the multitude, mass (*attr*).

mullido 1 *adj* (a) *bed etc* soft, sprung; fluffy; *grass etc* soft, springy.

(b) (*fam*) dejar a uno — to leave someone all in (*fam*), wear someone out.

2 *nm* stuffing, filling.

mullir [3a] *vt* (a) *wool etc* to make fluffy, fluff up; to soften; *bed* to shake up; *earth* to hoe, loosen.

(b) *plants* to hoe round, loosen the earth round.

mullo *nm* (red) mullet.

mundanal *adj* (*lit*) worldly, of the world.

mundanalidad *nf* (*lit*) worldliness.

mundanería *nf* worldliness.

mundano 1 *adj* (a) worldly, of the world.

(b) society (*attr*); fashionable; social; son gente muy mundana they're great society people; una reunión mundana a fashionable gathering, a gathering of society people.

2 *nm*, **mundana** *nf* society person, socialite.

mundial *adj* world-wide, universal; *record, war, distribution etc* world (*attr*); las comunicaciones —es world communications; **un invento de aplicación —** an invention of world-wide application; **otra guerra —** another world war.

mundialmente *adv* throughout the world; universally; **— famoso** world-famous; **hacer algo — popular** to make something universally popular.

mundillo *nm* (a) world, circle; **en el — teatral** in the theatre world, in theatrical circles. (b) (*Bot*) viburnum.

mundo *nm* (*in most senses*) world, people; society; (*Eccl*) world, secular life; **— antiguo** ancient world; **Nuevo M—** New World; **el — hispánico** the Hispanic world; **el gran —** high life, high society; **el — del espectáculo** show business; **este pícaro —** this wicked world; **en el — de las ideas** in the world of ideas, in the realm of ideas; **estaba medio —** there were hordes of people; **el otro —** the other world, the next world; **no es nada del otro —** it's nothing extraordinary; **hacer algo del otro —** to do something quite extraordinary; **todo el —** everybody; **en todo el —** everywhere; throughout the world; **es lo que más desea en el —** it's what she wants most in the world; **por esos —s (de Dios)** there; all over, in all parts; **el — es un pañuelo** it's a small world; **desde que el — es —** since time began; **echar al —** to bring into the world; **echarse al —** to take to prostitution; **aunque se hunda el —** come what may; **no por eso se hundirá el —** it won't be too much of a disaster; **así va el —** that's the way it is; **ponerse el — por montera** to care nothing for public opinion; **tener (mucho) —** to be experienced, be sophisticated, know one's way around; **tener poco —** to be inexperienced; **ver —** to see life, see the world; **ha visto mucho —** he's knocked around a lot.

mundología *nf* (*iro*) worldly-wisdom, experience of the world.

mundonuevo *nm* peep show.

munición *nf* (a) (*also* **—es**) ammunition; munitions; stores, supplies; **—es de boca** provisions.
(b) **de —** army (*attr*), service (*attr*); **botas de —** army boots.
(c) (*CAm*) uniform.

municionera *nf* (*Ven*) ball bearing.

municipal 1 *adj* municipal; town (*attr*). 2 *nm* policeman.

municipalidad *nf* municipality.

municipio *nm* (a) municipality; town, township. (b) corporation; town council.

munificiencia *nf* munificence.

munífico *adj* munificent.

muñeca *nf* (a) (*Anat*) wrist. (b) (*child's*) doll; (*tailor's*) dummy, manikin; **— de trapo** rag doll. (c) bunch of rags, cleaning (*or* polishing) rag.

muñeco *nm* (a) figure; (boy) doll; guy, scarecrow; puppet, marionette; (*tailor's*) dummy; **— de nieve** snowman.
(b) (*fig*) puppet, pawn.
(c) (*fam*) pretty little boy, little angel; (*pej*) sissy.

muñequera *nf* wristband; wrist watch.

muñir [3h] *vt* (a) to summon, convoke, call. (b) (*pej*) to rig, fix, arrange in a fraudulent fashion.

muñón *nm* (a) (*Anat*) stump. (b) (*Mech*) trunnion; pivot, journal.

mural *adj* 1 *adj* mural, wall (*attr*); **mapa —** wall map. 2 *nm* mural.

muralla *nf* (city) wall, walls; rampart; (*SAm*) (*any*) wall.

murar [1a] *vt* to wall.

murciano 1 *adj* Murcian. 2 *nm*, **murciana** *nf* Murcian.

murciélago *nm* bat.

murga *nf* (a) band of street musicians. (b) (*fam*) bore, nuisance, bind (*sl*).

murguista *nm* (a) street musician; (*fam*) bad musician, poor player. (b) (*fam*) bore.

murmullo *nm* (a) murmur(ing); whisper(ing); mutter(ing). (b) murmur, rippling; rustle, rustling; hum(ming).

murmuración *nf* gossip; slanderous talk, backbiting; constant complaining.

murmurador 1 *adj* gossip; backbiting; critical; complaining, grumbling. 2 *nm*, **murmuradora** *nf* gossip; backbiter; critic; complainer, grumbler.

murmurar [1a] *vi* (a) (*person*) to murmur, whisper; to mutter.
(b) (*of water*) to murmur, ripple; (*of leaves, wind etc*) to rustle; (*of bees, crowd etc*) to hum.
(c) (*fig*) to gossip (*de* about); to criticize (*de uno* someone), grumble (*de* about), mutter (*de* about);

siempre están murmurando del jefe they're always grumbling about the boss, they're always criticizing the boss.

muro *nm* wall; **— de contención** containing wall.

murria *nf* depression, blues; sulks; **tener —** to feel blue, be down in the dumps (*fam*); to feel sulky.

murrio *adj* depressed, dejected; sulky, sullen.

mus[1] *nm* a card game.

mus[2] *see* **chus**; **sin decir ni —** without saying a word.

musa *nf* Muse; **las M—s** the Muses.

musaraña *nf* (a) (*Zool*) shrew; (*any*) small creature, bug, creepy-crawly (*fam*).
(b) speck floating in the eye; **mirar a las —s** to stare vacantly; **pensar en las —s** to go woolgathering.

muscovita 1 *adj* Muscovite. 2 *nmf* Muscovite.

muscular *adj* muscular.

musculatura *nf* muscles, musculature; **preparar su —** to flex one's muscles (*also fig*).

músculo *nm* muscle.

musculoso *adj* muscular; tough, brawny.

muselina *nf* muslin.

museo *nm* museum; gallery; **— de arte, — de pintura** art gallery; **— de cera** waxworks.

musgaño *nm* shrew.

musgo *nm* moss.

musgoso *adj* mossy, moss-covered.

música *nf* (a) music; **— de cámara** chamber music; **— celestial** (*fam*) bunk (*sl*), drivel; **— coreada** choral music; **— de fondo** background music; **— mundana, — de las esferas, — de los planetas** music of the spheres; **— sagrada** sacred music; **poner — a** to set to music; **irse con la — a otra parte** to take one's troubles elsewhere; to go away, go somewhere else; **¡con la — a otra parte!** off with you!, get out!
(b) (*persons*) band.
(c) **—s** (*fam*) drivel; **no estoy para —s** I'm not in the mood to listen to such drivel.

musical *adj* musical.

musicalidad *nf* musicality, musical quality.

músico 1 *adj* musical. 2 *nm* musician, player; **— mayor** bandmaster.

musicología *nf* musicology.

musicólogo *nm* musicologist.

musitar [1a] *vti* to mumble, mutter.

muslo *nm* thigh.

mustango *nm* (*SAm*) mustang.

mustela *nf* weasel.

mustio *adj* (a) (*Bot*) withered, faded. (b) soft, slack. (c) depressed, gloomy. (d) (*Mex*) hypocritical.

musulmán 1 *adj* Moslem. 2 *nm*, **musulmana** *nf* Moslem.

mutabilidad *nf* mutability; changeableness.

mutación *nf* (a) (sudden) change. (b) (*Bio*) mutation. (c) (*Ling*) mutation. (d) (*Theat*) change of scene.

mutante *nm* mutant.

mutil *nm* (*Hist*) Carlist soldier.

mutilación *nf* mutilation.

mutilado *nm*, **mutilada** *nf* cripple, disabled person; **— de guerra** war cripple.

mutilar [1a] *vt* (a) to mutilate; to cripple, maim, disable. (b) (*fig*) text etc to mutilate, hack about, spoil; tale to garble; object to deface.

mutis *nm*, *pl* **mutis** (*Theat*) exit; **¡—!** sh!; **hacer —** (*Theat*) to exit, go off; (*fig*) to say nothing, keep quiet.

mutismo *nm* dumbness; (*fig*) silence, uncommunicativeness.

mutualidad *nf* (a) mutuality, mutual character. (b) mutual aid, reciprocal aid. (c) (*Fin*) friendly society, mutual benefit society.

mutuamente *adv* mutually, reciprocally.

mutuo *adj* mutual, reciprocal; joint.

muy *adv* very; greatly, highly; too; **— bueno** very good; **— lentamente** very slowly; **— buscado** very much sought-after, highly prized; **— de noche** very late at night; **tener — en cuenta** to bear very much in mind; **venir — tarde** to come too late; **es — de sentir** it is much to be regretted; **eso es — español** that's very Spanish, that's typically Spanish; **eso es — de él** that's just like him; **una enfermera — de minifalda** a nurse in a very short skirt, a nurse in what one could undoubtedly describe as a miniskirt; **es — hombre** he's a real man, he's pretty tough; **es — mujer** she's very feminine; as a woman she's terribly attractive; **el — bestia de Pedro** that great idiot of a Peter; **¡el — bandido!** the rotter!

N

naba nf (Bot) rape.
nabab nm nabob.
nabina nf rapeseed.
nabo nm **(a)** (Bot) turnip; (any) root vegetable, thick root; — **gallego** rape; — **sueco** swede.
  (b) (Anat) root of the tail.
  (c) (Archit) newel, stair post.
  (d) (Naut) mast.
  (e) (Anat: tabu) prick (tabu).
Nabucodonosor m Nebuchadnezzar.
nácar nm mother-of-pearl, nacre.
nacarado adj, **nacarino** adj mother-of-pearl (attr), pearly, nacreous.
nacatete nm (Mex), **nacatón** nm, **nacatona** nf (CAm, Mex) unfledged chick.
nacedera nf (CAm: also **cerca** —) hedge.
nacencia nf (SAm) =**nacimiento**.
nacer [2d] **1** vi **(a)** to be born; (from egg) to hatch; **nací en Cuba** I was born in Cuba; **cuando nazca el niño** when the baby is born; — **al amor** to awaken to love; **con esa exposición nació a la vida artística** that exhibition saw the beginning of his artistic career; **no nació para sufrir** she was not born to suffer; **nació para poeta** he was born to be a poet; **nadie nace enseñado** we all have to learn.
  (b) (Bot) to sprout, bud; to come up; (of star etc) to rise; (of river) to rise; (of water) to spring up, appear, begin to flow; (of roads) to begin, start (de from, en in); **le nacieron alas** it grew wings; **le nació mucho pelo** it sprouted a lot of hair.
  (c) (fig: of idea etc) to be born; to begin, originate, have its origin (en in); **nació una sospecha en su mente** a suspicion formed in her mind; **el error nace del hecho de que . . .** the error springs (or stems) from the fact that . . .; **entre ellos ha nacido una fuerte simpatía** a strong friendship has sprung up between them; **¿de dónde nace la idea?** whence comes the idea?
  2 nacerse vr **(a)** (Bot) to bud, sprout.
  (b) (seam) to split.
nacido 1 adj born; — **a la libertad** born to be free; — **para el amor** born to love; — **de padres ricos** born of wealthy parents; **bien** — of noble birth; **well-bred; mal** — mean, base, wicked; ill-bred; **recién** — newborn.
  2 nm **(a)** human being; **todos los** —s everybody, all mankind; **ningún** — nobody.
  (b) (Med) tumour, growth; boil.
  (c) (Sew) split.
naciente 1 adj nascent; new, recent; growing; sun rising; **el** — **interés por . . .** the new-found interest in . . ., the growing interest in . . .
  2 nm **(a)** east.
  (b) (Arg, Par: also —s) spring, source.
nacimiento nm **(a)** birth; (Orn etc) hatching; **ciego de** — blind from birth; **tonto de** — born fool; **este defecto lo tiene de** — he has had this defect since birth, he was born with this defect.
  (b) (fig) descent, family; **de** — **noble** of noble birth, of noble family.
  (c) (of water) spring; (of river) source.
  (d) (fig) birth; origin, beginning, start; **dar** — **a** to give rise to; **el partido tuvo su** — **en . . .** the party had its origins in . . .
  (e) (Art, Eccl) nativity (scene).
nación 1 nf nation; people; **N**—s **Unidas** United Nations; **de** — **ruritana** Ruritanian by birth, of Ruritanian nationality. **2** nmf (Arg) foreigner.
nacional 1 adj national; industry, product etc home.
  2 nmf national; **los** —es (Spain, 1936 etc) the Franco forces.
nacionalidad nf nationality.
nacionalismo nm nationalism.
nacionalista 1 adj nationalist(ic). **2** nmf nationalist.

nacionalización nf **(a)** naturalization. **(b)** nationalization.
nacionalizar [1f] **1** vt **(a)** person to naturalize. **(b)** industry to nationalize. **2 nacionalizarse** vr to become naturalized.
naco 1 adj (Mex) stupid.
  2 nm **(a)** (CAm) coward; milksop.
  (b) (Bol, RPl) chewing tobacco.
  (c) (Col) maize kernels cooked with salt; mashed potatoes.
  (d) (Arg) fright, scare.
  (e) —s (Arg) roll of banknotes.
nada 1 pron nothing; **no dijo** — she said nothing, she didn't say anything; **¡**—**, —!** not a bit of it!; — **de eso** nothing of the kind, far from it; **¡**— **de eso!** not a bit of it!; **¡**— **de excusas!** no excuses!; — **de marcharse!** forget about leaving!; **no tiene** — **de particular** there's nothing special about it; — **entre dos platos** a lot of fuss, much ado about nothing; **see más; a cada de** — (SAm) every moment, at every step; **antes de** — very soon, right away; **antes de** — **tengo que . . .** before I do anything else I must . . .; **casi** — next to nothing; **como si** — as if it didn't matter, as if it were only a small thing; **¡de** —**!** not at all!, don't mention it!; **estuvo en** — **que lo perdiesen** they very nearly lost it; **quedar(se) en** — to come to nothing; **no reparar en** — to stop at nothing; **en** — **de tiempo** in no time at all; **hace** — just a moment ago; **¡ni curas ni** —**!** blow the priests!; I don't want to hear about the priests!; **no los mencionó para** — he never mentioned them at all; **no servir para** — to be no use at all, be utterly useless; **llorar por** — to cry for no reason at all; **por** — **del mundo** not for anything in the world; **por menos de** — for two pins; **no lo hago por** — **ni por nadie** I won't do it and that's flat; **¡pues** —**!** not to worry!; **no ha sido** — it's nothing; **y** — and that was that, so there it was.
  2 adv not at all, by no means; **no es** — **fácil** it's not at all easy, it's far from easy.
  3 nf nothingness; **la** — the void; **el avión parecía salir de la** — the aircraft seemed to come from nowhere.
nadaderas nfpl water wings.
nadador nm, **nadadora** nf swimmer.
nadar [1a] vi **(a)** to swim; (of cork etc) to float; (Col) to take a bath.
  (b) (Sew) **en estos pantalones va nadando** he rattles about inside these trousers, these trousers are much too big for him.
  (c) — **en** (fig) to wallow in, be rolling in.
nadería nf small thing, mere trifle.
nadie pron **(a)** nobody, no-one; — **lo tiene, no lo tiene** — nobody has it; **no he visto a** — I haven't seen anybody; **apenas** — hardly anybody.
  (b) **no es** — he's nobody (that matters); **es un don** — he's a nobody.
nadir nm nadir.
nadita (SAm) =**nada**.
nado: cruzar (or **pasar**) **a** — to swim, swim across.
nafta nf naphtha; (Arg) petrol, gasoline (US).
naftaleno nm, **naftalina** nf naphthaline.
nagual nm **(a)** (CAm, Mex) sorcerer, wizard. **(b)** (Guat, Hond) inseparable companion. **(c)** (Mex) lie.
nagualear [1a] vi (Mex) **(a)** to lie. **(b)** to go thieving at night; to spend the night in revelry.
naguas nfpl petticoat.
nagüeta nf (CAm) overskirt.
nailon nm (angl) nylon.
naipe nm playing card; — **de figura** court card, picture; —s cards.
naipeador adj (Arg) fond of cards.
naipear [1a] vi (Arg) to play cards.
naja: salir de — (fam) to get out, beat it (fam).

najarse [1a] *vr* (*fam*) to beat it (*fam*).
najencia *interj* (*fam*) scram! (*sl*).
nalga *nf* buttock; —s buttocks, backside, rump; **dar de** —s to fall on one's bottom.
nalgada *nf* (a) (*Cook*) ham, shoulder. (b) smack on the bottom; —s spanking.
nalguiento *adj* (*Per*), **nalgón** *adj* (*SAm*), **nalgudo** *adj* big-bottomed, broad in the beam (*fam*).
nana¹ *nf* (a) grandma (*fam*), granny (*fam*); *see* año. (b) (*Mus*) lullaby, cradlesong. (c) baby's sleeping bag. (d) (*CAm, Mex*) wet-nurse; nurserymaid.
nana² *nf* (*Chi, RPl*) minor ailment of children.
nanai *interj* (*sl*) no!
napias *nfpl* (*sl*) nose, snitch (*sl*).
Napoleón *m* Napoleon.
napoleónico *adj* Napoleonic.
Nápoles Naples.
napolitano 1 *adj* Neapolitan. **2** *nm*, **napolitana** *nf* Neapolitan.
naranja *nf* (a) orange; — **cajel** Seville orange; — **sanguina** blood orange.
(b) (*fam*) ¡—s!, ¡—s chinas!, ¡—s de la China! nonsense!, rubbish!
(c) **la media** — one's better half; **esperar la media** — to wait for Mr Right; **encontrar su media** — to find one's life partner.
(d) (*PR*) bitter orange.
naranjada *nf* orangeade, orange squash.
naranjado *adj* orange, orange-coloured.
naranjal *nm* orange grove.
naranjo *nm* orange tree.
Narbona Narbonne.
narcisismo *nm* narcissism.
narcisista *adj* narcissistic.
narciso *nm* (a) narcissus; — **atrompetado,** — **trompón** daffodil. (b) (*fig*) dandy, fop.
narcosis *nf* narcosis.
narcótico 1 *adj* narcotic. **2** *nm* narcotic; sleeping pill; —s (*loosely*) drugs, dope.
narcotismo *nm* narcosis.
narcotizar [1f] *vt* to narcotize; (*loosely*) to drug, dope.
nardo *nm* nard; spikenard.
narguile *nm* hookah.
naricear [1a] *vt* (*Per*) to smell (out).
narigón 1 *adj* big-nosed. **2** *nm* (*Cu, Mex, SD*) ring (*in animal's nose*).
narigudo *adj* big-nosed.
narigueta *adj* (*Arg, Chi*) big-nosed.
nariz *nf* (a) nose; nostril.
(b) **narices** *pl* nostrils; (*fam*) nose; ¡**narices!** (*fam*) rubbish!, nonsense!; **cerrar la puerta en las narices de uno** to shut the door in someone's face; **dar de narices** to fall flat on one's face; **dar de narices contra la puerta** to bang one's face on the door; **estar hasta las narices** to be completely fed up; **hablar por las narices** to talk through one's nose, speak with a nasal twang; **hacer algo por narices** to do something under compulsion; **se le hincharon las narices** he got very cross; **meter las narices en algo** to poke one's nose into something.
(c) sense of smell.
(d) (*of wine*) bouquet.
narizota *nf* big nose; ¡—s! (*fam*) you villain!; you idiot!
narizudo *adj* (*CAm, Mex, PR*) big-nosed.
narración *nf* narration, account.
narrador *nm*, **narradora** *nf* narrator.
narrar [1a] *vt* to tell, narrate, recount.
narrativa *nf* (a) narrative, story. (b) narrative skill, skill in storytelling.
narrativo *adj* narrative.
narval *nm* narwhal.
nasa *nf* bread bin, flour bin; (*Fish*) basket, creel; (*Fish*) fish trap.
nasal 1 *adj* nasal. **2** *nf* nasal.
nasalidad *nf* nasality.
nasalizar [1f] *vt* to nasalize.
nasalmente *adv* nasally.
nata *nf* (a) cream; (*on custard etc*) skin; — **batida** whipped cream. (b) (*fig*) cream, choicest part, best part; *see* flor.
natación *nf* (a) swimming.
(b) style (of swimming), stroke; — **a braza,** — **de pecho** breast-stroke; — **de costado,** — **en cuchillo** sidestroke; — **de espalda** backstroke; — **submarina** underwater swimming; skin diving.
natal *adj* natal; *soil etc* native; *town etc* home (*attr*).
natalicio 1 *adj* birthday (*attr*). **2** *nm* birthday.
natalidad *nf* birth rate.
natillas *nfpl* custard.
natividad *nf* nativity.
nativo 1 *adj* (a) native; *country etc* native, home

(*attr*); **lengua nativa** native language, mother tongue.
(b) natural, innate.
(c) (*Min*) native.
2 *nm*, **nativa** *nf* native; **los** —s **son gente pacífica** the natives are friendly.
nato *adj* born; **un actor** — a born actor; **un criminal** — a hardened criminal, an incorrigible criminal; **es un pintor** — he's a natural painter.
natural 1 *adj* (a) (*in most senses*) natural; **es — que . . .** it is natural that . . .
(b) *fruit* fresh, raw.
(c) (*Mus*) natural.
2 *nmf* native, inhabitant; **fue — de Sigüenza** he was a native of Sigüenza; **trató sin miramientos a los —es** he treated the inhabitants unceremoniously.
3 *nm* (a) nature, disposition, temperament; **buen** — good nature.
(b) **fruta al** — fruit in its own juice; **ginebra al** — neat gin, gin with nothing added; **una descripción al** — a true-to-life description, a realistic description; **vivir al** — to live according to nature; **está muy guapa al** — she is very pretty just as she is (without make-up *etc*); **pintar del** — to paint from life, paint from nature.
(c) (*Taur*) a kind of pass with the cape.
naturaleza *nf* (a) (*in most senses*) nature.
(b) — **muerta** (*Art*) still life.
(c) (*Pol*) nationality; **una mujer de** — **suiza** a woman of Swiss nationality.
(d) (*Pol*) citizenship (*granted to a foreigner*); **carta de** — naturalization papers.
naturalidad *nf* naturalness; **con la mayor** — (**del mundo**) as if nothing had happened; as if it were the most natural thing in the world; **lo dijo con la mayor** — he said it in a perfectly ordinary tone; **allí le pegan un tiro con la mayor** — they'll shoot you there and think nothing of it.
naturalismo *nm* naturalism; realism.
naturalista 1 *adj* naturalistic; realistic. **2** *nmf* naturalist.
naturalización *nf* naturalization.
naturalizar [1f] **1** *vt* to naturalize. **2 naturalizarse** *vr* to become naturalized.
naturalmente *adv* (a) naturally; in a natural way.
(b) ¡—! naturally!, of course!; you bet!
naturismo *nm* naturism.
naturista *nmf* naturist.
naufragar [1h] *vi* (a) (*ship*) to be wrecked, sink; (*person*) to be shipwrecked. (b) (*fig*) to fail, miscarry, suffer a disaster.
naufragio *nm* (a) shipwreck. (b) (*fig*) failure, disaster, ruin.
náufrago 1 *adj* shipwrecked. **2** *nm* shipwrecked sailor, shipwrecked person; castaway.
náusea *nf*, **náuseas** *nfpl* nausea, sick feeling; (*fig*) disgust, repulsion; **dar —s a** to nauseate, sicken, disgust; **tener —s** to feel nauseated, feel sick, (*fig*) to be nauseated, be sickened.
nauseabundo *adj* nauseating, sickening.
náutica *nf* navigation, seamanship.
náutico *adj* nautical.
nautilo *nm* nautilus.
navaja *nf* (a) clasp knife, jack-knife; penknife; — (**de afeitar**) razor.
(b) (*Zool: of boar*) tusk; (*mollusc*) razor shell; (*Ent*) sting.
(c) (*fig*) sharp tongue, evil tongue.
navajada *nf*, **navajazo** *nm* slash, gash, razor wound.
naval *adj* naval; ship (*attr*), sea (*attr*).
Navarra *f* Navarre.
navarro 1 *adj* Navarrese. **2** *nm*, **navarra** *nf* Navarrese. **3** *nm* (*dialect*) Navarrese.
nave *nf* (a) (*Naut*) ship, vessel; **quemar las —s** to burn one's boats; **la N— de San Pedro** (*Eccl*) the Roman Catholic Church.
(b) (*Aer*) — **espacial** spaceship, spacecraft.
(c) (*Archit*) nave; — **lateral** aisle.
(d) (*Tech*) large building, large shed; factory, mill, plant; — **de laminación** rolling mill.
navegable *adj* navigable.
navegación *nf* (a) navigation.
(b) sea voyage; — **costanera** coasting, coastal traffic; — **fluvial** sailing by inland waterways, river navigation.
(c) ships, shipping; **cerrado a la** — closed to shipping.
navegador *nm*, **navegante** *nm* navigator.
navegar [1h] **1** *vt* to sail; to navigate; — **los mares** to sail the seas.
2 *vi* to sail; — **a 15 nudos** to sail at 15 knots, go at 15 knots; — **a la vela** to sail, go sailing.

Navidad nf Christmas; (**día de**) — Christmas Day; —es Christmas time; **por** —es at Christmas time; ¡**feliz** —! happy Christmas!
naviero 1 adj shipping (attr). **2** nm shipowner.
navío nm ship; — **de alto bordo**, — **de línea** (Hist) ship of the line.
náyade nf naiad.
nazarenas nfpl (Bol, Chi, RPl) large gaucho spurs.
nazareno 1 adj Nazarene. **2** nm, **nazarena** nf Nazarene.
Nazaret Nazareth.
nazi 1 adj Nazi. **2** nmf Nazi.
nazismo nm Nazism.
nazista adj Nazi.
neblina nf mist; mistiness; (fig) fog.
nebulosa nf nebula.
nebulosidad nf (a) nebulosity; cloudiness; mistiness; gloominess. (b) (fig) vagueness; obscurity.
nebuloso adj (a) (Astron) nebular, nebulous; sky cloudy; air misty, foggy; dark, gloomy. (b) (fig) nebulous, vague; obscure.
necedad nf (a) foolishness, silliness. (b) (**una** —) silly thing; —es nonsense.
necesariamente adv necessarily.
necesario adj necessary; **es** — **que lo hagas** it is necessary that you should do it, it is necessary for you to do it; **todo es** — it all helps, every little helps.
neceser nm toilet case, dressing case; holdall; — **de belleza** vanity case; — **de costura** workbox; — **de fin de semana** weekend bag, weekend case.
necesidad nf (a) necessity; need (**de** for); — **imperiosa**, — **primordial** absolute necessity, pressing need; **de** —, **por** — of necessity; **esto es de primera** — this is absolutely essential; **no hay** — **de** + infin there is no need to + infin; **satisfacer las** —**es de uno** to satisfy someone's needs.
(b) necessity; tight spot, awkward situation; **en caso de** — in case of need; **encontrarse en una** — to be in a difficult situation.
(c) need, necessity, want; poverty; **están en la mayor** — they are in great need.
(d) —es hardships; **pasar** —es to suffer hardships.
(e) (euph) business (euph); **hacer sus** —**es** to do one's business, relieve oneself; **sentir una gran** — to be dying to relieve oneself.
necesitado adj (a) — **de** in need of; **estamos** —**s de mano de obra** we need workers, we are in need of labour.
(b) needy, necessitous; **los** —**s** the needy, those in need.
necesitar [1a] **1** vt to need, want; to necessitate, require; **necesitamos 2 más** we need 2 more; **necesita un poco de cuidado** it needs (or requires, takes) a little care; — + infin to need to + infin, must + infin; **no necesitas hacerlo** you don't need to do it, you don't have to do it.
2 vi: — **de** to need.
3 necesitarse vr to be needed, be wanted; "**necesítase coche**" (advert) "car wanted".
neciamente adv foolishly, stupidly.
necio adj (a) silly, stupid.
(b) (Col etc) peevish.
(c) (Arg, Col, PR) touchy, hypersensitive.
(d) (Guat etc) illness stubborn, long-lasting.
necrófago nm ghoul.
necrología nf obituary (notice), necrology.
necrológico adj necrological, obituary (attr).
necromancia nf, **necromancía** nf necromancy.
necrópolis nf, pl **necrópolis** necropolis.
néctar nm nectar (also fig); **el** — **de la amabilidad humana** the milk of human kindness.
nectarina nf nectarine.
neerlandés 1 adj Dutch, Netherlands (attr). **2** nm, **neerlandesa** nf Dutchman, Dutchwoman, Netherlander. **3** nm (language) Dutch.
nefando adj unspeakable, abominable.
nefario adj nefarious.
nefasto adj unlucky, ill-fated, inauspicious.
nefato adj (Ven) stupid, dim.
nefritis nf nephritis.
negación nf (a) negation; refusal, denial. (b) (Gram) negation; negative.
negado adj (a) dull, stupid. (b) — **para** inept at, unfitted for.
negar [1h and 1k] **1** vt (a) fact, truth etc to deny; charge to deny, reject, refute; — **que algo sea así** to deny that something is so.
(b) permission etc to deny, refuse (a to); to withhold (a from); — **la mano a uno** to refuse to shake hands with someone; — **el saludo a uno** to cut someone; **le negaron el paso por la frontera** they refused to let him cross the frontier; **pasé por la casa**

pero me la negaron I called at the house but they refused to let me see her.
(c) relationship, responsibility etc to disclaim, disown.
2 negarse vr (a) — **a** + infin to refuse to + infin.
(b) — **a una visita** to refuse to see a visitor, be not at home to a caller.
negativa nf (a) negative; denial, refusal; — **rotunda** flat refusal; **la** — **a comer es peligrosa** the refusal to eat is dangerous.
(b) (Phot) negative.
negativamente adv negatively; **contestar** — to answer in the negative.
negativo 1 adj (a) negative. (b) (Math) minus. (c) (Phot) negative. **2** nm (Phot) negative.
negligencia nf negligence; neglect, slackness, carelessness; nonchalance.
negligente adj negligent; neglectful, slack, careless; posture etc careless, nonchalant.
negligentemente adv negligently; slackly, carelessly; nonchalantly.
negociable adj negotiable.
negociación nf negotiation; deal, transaction; (of cheque) clearance; **entrar en** —**es con** to enter into negotiations with.
negociado nm (a) department, section. (b) (Chi) shop, store. (c) (Arg, Chi, Ec, Per) illegal transaction, shady deal.
negociador nm, **negociadora** nf negotiator.
negociante nm businessman; merchant, dealer.
negociar [1b] **1** vt to negotiate. **2** vi (a) (Pol etc) to negotiate. (b) (Comm) — **en** to deal in, trade in.
negocio nm (a) affair; **mal** — bad business; ¡**mal** —**!** it looks bad!; **eso es** — **tuyo** that's your affair.
(b) (Comm, Fin) business; **el** — **del libro** the book trade, the book business; **el** — **del espectáculo** show business; **montar un** — **de frutas** to start a fruit business; **traspasar un** — to transfer a business, sell a business.
(c) (Comm, Fin) deal, transaction, piece of business; (iro) bargain; **buen** — profitable deal, (good) bargain; — **sucio**, — **turbio** shady deal; **hacer un buen** — to pull off a profitable deal; ¡**hiciste un buen** —**!** (iro) that was a fine deal you did!; **hacer su propio** — to look after one's own interests.
(d) —**s** (Comm, Fin: in general) business; trade; **hombre de** —**s** businessman; **el mundo de los** —**s** the business world; "**los** —**s, como de costumbre**" "business as usual"; **a malos** —**s sombrero de copa** one must accept losses with dignity, one must make the best of a bad job; **estar de** —**s** to be (away) on business; **retirarse de los** —**s** to retire from business.
(e) (Arg, Chi, Per, Urug) firm, business house; place of business.
(f) (Per, PR, Ven) **el** — the fact, the truth; **pero el** — **es que** . . . but the fact is that . . .
(g) (Col) tale, piece of gossip.
negocioso adj industrious; businesslike.
negra nf (a) Negress, black woman.
(b) (Mus) crotchet.
(c) (Chess) black piece.
(d) (CAm: fig) black mark.
(e) bad luck; **tener la** — to be out of luck, have a run of bad luck; **le tocó la** — he had bad luck; **ése me trae la** — he brings me bad luck; he mucks things up for me.
negrada nf (SAm) (a) group of Negroes; Negroes (collectively). (b) remark (or act etc) typical of a Negro.
negrear [1a] vi to turn black; to look black, appear black.
negrería nf (SAm), **negrerío** nm (SAm) = **negrada** (a).
negrero nm slave trader; (RPl) exploiter of labour, cruel boss.
negrilla nf (a) (Typ) = **negrita** (a). (b) (Bot) elm.
negrita nf (a) (Typ) bold face; **en** — in bold type, in heavy type. (b) (CAm: fig) black mark.
negrito nm golliwog.
negro 1 adj (a) black; dark; person Negro; dark, swarthy; — **como boca de lobo**, — **como un pozo** as black as pitch, pitch-dark; as black as your hat; **más** — **que el azabache** (etc) as black as ink, coal-black.
(b) (fig) mood, state etc sad; black, gloomy; luck awful (fam), atrocious; **pasarlas negras** to have a tough time of it; **la cosa se pone negra** it's not going well, it looks bad; **ve muy** — **el porvenir** he's very gloomy about the future; **lo ve todo** — he's terribly pessimistic about everything; **verse** — to be in a jam;

verse — **para** + *infin* to have one's work cut out to + *infin*; **nos veíamos** —s **para salir del apuro** we had a tough time getting out of it.

(c) (*fam*) cross, peeved (*fam*); **estoy** — **con esto** I'm getting desperate about it; **poner** — **a uno** (*fam*) to make someone cross, upset someone; **ponerse** — (*fam*) to get cross, cut up rough.

2 *nm* (a) (*colour*) black; **en** — (*Phot*) in black and white; — **de humo** lampblack.

(b) (*person*) Negro, black; **¡no somos** —s! we won't stand for it!, you can't do that to us!; **sacar lo que el** — **del sermón** to understand nothing of what has been said.

(c) (*SAm: in direct address*) dear, honey (*US*).

negroide *adj* negroid.
negrura *nf* blackness.
negruzco *adj* blackish.
neme *nm* (*Col*) asphalt.
nemorosa *nf* wood anemone.
nene *nm*, **nena** *nf* baby, small child; **¡sí, nena!** (*to woman*) yes dear!, yes darling!
nenúfar *nm* water lily.
neo *nm* neon.
neo . . . neo . . .
neoclasicismo *nm* neoclassicism.
neoclásico *adj* neoclassical.
neofascismo *nm* neofascism.
neofascista 1 *adj* neofascist. 2 *nmf* neofascist.
neófito *nm*, **neófita** *nf* neophyte.
neolatino *adj*: **lenguas neolatinas** Romance languages.
neolítico *adj* neolithic.
neologismo *nm* neologism.
neón *nm* neon.
neonazi 1 *adj* neonazi. 2 *nmf* neonazi.
neonazista *adj* neonazi.
neoperonista *adj* (*Arg*) neoperonist.
neoplatónico *adj* neoplatonic.
neoplatonismo *nm* neoplatonism.
neoplatonista *nmf* neoplatonist.
neoyorquino 1 *adj* New York (*attr*), of New York. 2 *nm*, **neoyorquina** *nf* New Yorker.
neozelandés 1 *adj* New Zealand (*attr*), of New Zealand. 2 *nm*, **neozelandesa** *nf* New Zealander.
Nepal *m* Nepal.
nepalés 1 *adj* Nepalese. 2 *nm*, **nepalesa** *nf* Nepalese.
nepotismo *nm* nepotism.
Neptuno *m* Neptune.
nereida *nf* nereid.
Nerón *m* Nero.
nervadura *nf* (*Archit, Bot*) ribs; (*Ent*) veins (*of wing*).
nervio *nm* (a) (*Anat*) nerve; **crispar los** —s **a uno, poner los** —s **en punta a uno** to get on someone's nerves; to jar on someone, grate on someone; **tener los** —s **en punta** to be all keyed up, have one's nerves on edge.

(b) (*Anat*) tendon, sinew; (*in meat*) sinew, tough part.

(c) (*Archit, Bot*) rib; (*Ent*) vein; (*of book*) rib, fillet; (*Mus*) string.

(d) (*fig*) vigour, strength; fibre; stamina, toughness; moral fibre, moral strength; **un hombre sin** — a weak man, a spineless man; **tener** — to have character.

(e) (*fig: person*) soul, leading light, guiding spirit; **él es el** — **de la sociedad** he is the guiding spirit of the club.

(f) (*fig: of question*) core, crux.

nerviosamente *adv* nervously.
nerviosidad *nf*, **nerviosismo** *nm* nervousness; nervous anticipation, nerves; agitation, restlessness, impatience.
nervioso *adj* (a) (*Anat*) nerve (*attr*), nervous; **centro** — nerve centre; **crisis nerviosa** nervous breakdown; **sistema** — nervous system.

(b) (*Anat*) hand *etc* sinewy, wiry.

(c) *person* (*by temperament*) nervy, highly-strung, excitable; (*temporarily*) nervous, nervy; restless, impatient; overwrought; upset, agitated; **poner** — **a uno** to make someone nervous, get on someone's nerves; to get someone worked up; to make someone cross; **ponerse** — to get nervous; to get worked up; to get upset, get cross; to get rattled; **¡no te pongas** —! take it easy!, keep calm!

(d) *style etc* vigorous, forceful.

nervoso *adj* (a) *person* = **nervioso** (c). (b) *meat* sinewy, tough.
nervudo *adj* (a) tough, strong. (b) *hand etc* sinewy, wiry.
nesga *nf* (*Sew*) flare, gore.
nesgado *adj* *skirt etc* flared.
nesgar [1h] *vt* (*Sew*) to flare, gore.

netamente *adv* clearly; purely; genuinely; **una construcción** — **española** a purely Spanish construction, a genuinely Spanish construction.
neto *adj* (a) clear; clean, pure; neat; *truth etc* pure, simple; **tiene su sueldo** — he has (just) his bare salary.

(b) (*Comm, Fin*) net; **peso** — net weight; **sueldo** — net salary, salary after deductions.

neumático 1 *adj* pneumatic; air (*attr*). 2 *nm* tyre; — **de recambio**, — **de repuesto** spare tyre.
neural *adj* neural.
neuralgia *nf* neuralgia.
neurastenia *nf* (a) neurasthenia; nervous exhaustion.

(b) excitability, highly-strung nature, nerviness.

neurasténico *adj* (a) neurasthenic. (b) excitable, highly-strung, nervy, neurotic.
neuritis *nf* neuritis.
neurología *nf* neurology.
neurólogo *nm* neurologist.
neurona *nf* neuron, nerve cell.
neurópata *nmf* neuropath.
neurosis *nf*, *pl* **neurosis** neurosis; — **de guerra** shellshock.
neurótico 1 *adj* neurotic. 2 *nm*, **neurótica** *nf* neurotic.
neutral 1 *adj* neutral. 2 *nmf* neutral.
neutralidad *nf* neutrality.
neutralismo *nm* neutralism.
neutralista 1 *adj* neutralist. 2 *nmf* neutralist.
neutralización *nf* neutralization.
neutralizar [1f] *vt* to neutralize; *tendency etc* to counteract.
neutro *adj* (a) (*in most senses*) neutral.

(b) (*Bio*) neuter, sexless, without sex; **abeja neutra** worker bee.

(c) (*Gram*) neuter; **género** — neuter; **verbo** — intransitive verb.

neutrón *nm* neutron.
nevada *nf* snowstorm; snowfall; **una copiosa** — a heavy snowfall.
nevado 1 *adj* (a) snow-covered; *mountain* snow-capped; (*Arg*) permanently snow-covered.

(b) (*fig*) snowy, snow-white.

2 *nm* (*Chi, Ec*) snow-capped mountain.

nevar [1k] 1 *vt* to cover with snow; (*fig*) to whiten. 2 *vi* to snow.
nevasca *nf* snowstorm.
nevazón *nf* (*Arg, Chi, Ec*) snowstorm.
nevera *nf* refrigerator, icebox; (*fig*) icebox.
nevero *nm* snowfield, icefield, place of perpetual snow.
nevisca *nf* light snowfall, flurry of snow; sleet.
neviscar [1g] *vi* to snow lightly; to sleet.
nevoso *adj* snowy.
nexo *nm* link, connection; nexus.
ni *conj* (a) nor, neither; **no bebe** — **fuma** he neither smokes nor drinks; — **el uno** — **el otro** neither one nor the other; — **vino** — **llamó por teléfono** he neither came nor rang up; **no quiere** — **sal** — **mostaza** he doesn't want either salt or mustard; **sin temor** — **favor** without fear or favour; **sin padre** — **madre** without father or mother; — **yo** nor me; *see* **siquiera**.

(b) not . . . even; **no lo sabrán** — **por fuerza** they won't find it out even by force; — **a ti te lo dirá** he won't tell even you.

(c) — **que** . . . not even if . . .; — **que fueses su mujer** not even if you were his wife; — **que fuera de plomo pesaría tanto** it wouldn't weigh so much even if it were lead.

Niágara *m* Niagara.
niara *nf* (*Agr*) stack, rick.
nica *nmf* (*CAm: fam*) Nicaraguan.
Nicaragua *f* Nicaragua.
nicaragüense 1 *adj* Nicaraguan. 2 *nmf* Nicaraguan.
nicaragüismo *nm* word (*or phrase etc*) peculiar to Nicaragua.
Nicolás *m* Nicholas.
nicotina *nf* nicotine.
nicho *nm* niche; recess; hollow.
nidada *nf* (*of eggs*) sitting, clutch; (*of chicks*) brood.
nidal *nm* (a) *nest*; nesting box. (b) nest egg. (c) (*fam*) haunt, hangout (*fam*); hiding place. (d) (*of birdwatcher*) hide.
nido *nm* (a) nest; — **de amor** love nest; **caer del** — (*fig*) to come down to earth with a bump; **se ha caído de un** — he's dreadfully innocent, he's terribly naïve (*fam*); **manchar el propio** — to foul one's own nest.

(b) (*fig*) nest, haunt, abode, den; — **de ladrones** nest of thieves, den of thieves.

(c) (*fig*) hiding place; secret store.

(d) (*fig*) centre, hotbed; **el reparto de premios fue**

un — de polémicas the prize giving was a centre of controversy, the prize giving gave rise to heated arguments.

niebla nf (a) fog, mist; — artificial smoke screen; un día de — a foggy day; hay — it is foggy. (b) (fig) fog, confusion. (c) (Bot) mildew.

nieta nf granddaughter.

nieto nm (a) grandson; —s grandchildren. (b) (fig) descendant.

nieve nf (a) snow; las primeras —s the first snows, the first snowfall; — abundante, copiosa — heavy snow. (b) (SAm) sherbet, ice cream.

Nigeria f Nigeria.

nigeriano 1 adj Nigerian. **2** nm, **nigeriana** nf Nigerian.

nigromancia nf, **nigromancía** nf necromancy, black magic.

nigromante nm necromancer.

nihilismo nm nihilism.

nihilista 1 adj nihilistic. **2** nmf nihilist.

Nilo m Nile.

nilón nm (Acad) nylon.

nimbo nm (Art, Astron, Eccl) halo; (Meteorol) nimbus.

nimiamente adv (a) trivially; with a host of petty details. (b) fussily; small-mindedly; long-windedly. (c) excessively.

nimiedad nf (a) (quality) triviality; fussiness; small-mindedness; long-windedness; excess; tratar un asunto con — to discuss a subject in great detail, treat a theme exhaustively; (pej) to discuss a subject in excessive detail. (b) (una —) very small thing, tiny detail; riñeron por una — they quarrelled over some triviality.

nimio adj (a) insignificant, trivial, tiny; un sinfín de detalles —s a host of petty details. (b) person fussy (about details), too meticulous; small-minded; long-winded. (c) excessive (en in).

ninfa nf nymph.

ninfilla nf, **ninfita** nf nymphet.

ninfómana nf nymphomaniac.

ninfomanía nf nymphomania.

ninfómano adj nymphomaniac.

ningún see ninguno.

ningunear [1a] vt (Mex) to deny; to refuse; — a uno to look down one's nose at someone; to pretend that someone is not there, pay no attention to someone; to make someone feel small; to treat someone badly.

ninguno 1 adj (ningún before m sing noun) no; ningún hombre no man; ninguna belleza no beauty; no hay ningún libro que valga más there is no book that is worth more; en ninguna fiesta me he divertido tanto I haven't enjoyed myself so much at any other party; sin ningún sentimiento without any regret, without regret of any kind; no es ningún tonto he's no fool, he's no sort of fool. **2** pron nobody, no-one; none; neither; no lo sabe — nobody knows; — de ellos none of them; — de los dos neither of them; ¿cuál prefieres? . . . — which do you prefer? . . . neither (of them).

niña nf (a) girl, little girl, child; — exploradora girl guide, girl scout (US). (b) (fam) tart (sl), whore. (c) (SAm: in direct address) miss, mistress; la — the mistress of the house. (d) (Anat) pupil; ser las —s de los ojos de uno to be the apple of someone's eye.

niñada nf = niñería.

niñear [1a] vi to act childishly.

niñera nf nursemaid, nanny.

niñería nf (a) (quality) childishness. (b) (act) childish thing; silly thing, triviality; llora por cualquier — she cries about any triviality.

niñero adj fond of children.

niñez nf childhood; infancy (also fig); segunda — second childhood.

niño 1 adj (a) young; immature, inexperienced; (pej) childish; es muy — todavía he's still very young (or small). (b) (Col) fruit green, unripe. **2** nm (a) boy, little boy, child; (in general) child; (unborn, newborn) baby; (in direct address) my boy, my lad; ¡—! (look) look out!, be careful!; los —s the children; el N— the Child, Jesus; el N— Jesús the Christ-child, (less formally) Baby Jesus; — azul blue baby; — bien, — bonito, — gótico playboy, elegant layabout; — de coro choirboy; — explorador boy scout; — expósito foundling; — de pecho small baby, babe-in-arms; — prodigio child prodigy; de

— as a child; when a child; desde — since childhood, since I (etc) was a child; ¡no seas — baby!; ser el — mimado de uno to be someone's pet, be someone's white-haired boy (fam); hacer un — a una to get a girl in the family way; va a tener un — she's going to have a baby; cuando nazca el — when the baby (or child) is born. (b) (SAm: in direct address) master, sir; el — the (young) master. (c) (Chi) unsavoury individual.

nipón 1 adj Japanese. **2** nm, **nipona** nf Japanese.

níquel nm (a) nickel; (Tech) nickel-plating, chromium-plating. (b) (SAm) small coin, nickel (US); —es (esp Arg, Mex) money, wealth.

niquelado adj nickel-plated, chromium-plated.

niquelar [1a] vt to nickel-plate; to chromium-plate.

niquelera nf (Col) purse.

níspero nm, **níspola** nf medlar.

nítidamente adv brightly, cleanly; spotlessly; clearly, sharply.

nitidez nf (a) brightness; spotlessness; clarity, sharpness. (b) (fig) unblemished nature.

nítido adj (a) bright, clean; spotless; outline (also Phot) clear, sharp. (b) (fig) pure, unblemished.

nitral nm nitrate deposit.

nitrato nm nitrate.

nitrera nf (Chi) nitrate deposit.

nítrico adj nitric.

nitro nm nitre, saltpetre.

nitrogenado adj nitrogenous.

nitrógeno nm nitrogen.

nitroglicerina nf nitroglycerin(e).

nitroso adj nitrous.

nivel nm (a) (Geog etc) level, height; — de(l) aceite (Aut etc) oil level; — del agua water level; — del mar sea level; a los 900 m sobre el — del mar at 900 m above sea level, at a height of 900 m; la nieve alcanzó un — de 1,5 m the snow reached a depth of 1½ m; a — level; true; flush; horizontal; al — de on the same level as, on a level with, at the same height as. (b) (fig) level, standard; el — cultural del país the cultural standard of the country; — de vida standard of living; alto — de trabajo high level of employment; conferencia al más alto —, conferencia de alto — high-level conference, top-level conference; estar al — de to be on a level with, be equal to; no está al — de los demás he is not up to the standard of the others; estar al — de las circunstancias to rise to the occasion. (c) (Tech) — de aire, — de burbuja spirit level.

nivelación nf levelling.

nivelado adj level, flat; flush.

niveladora nf bulldozer.

nivelar [1a] vt (a) to level (out); (Rail etc) to grade. (b) (fig) to level (up), even (out, up), make even; (Fin etc) to balance (con against), adjust (con to).

níveo adj (lit) snowy, snow-white.

Niza f Nice.

no adv (a) (used alone) no; not; (qualifying verb) not; ¡no! no!; ¡yo no! not I!; ¡rey no! we don't want a king!; ¡Paco no, Pepe sí! Paco out, no sé I do not know, I don't know; me rogó no hacerlo he asked me not to do it; ¿vives aquí, no? see ¿no es verdad? (in verdad); decir que no to say no; creo que no I don't think so; ¡que no! I tell you it isn't! (or doesn't etc); ¡a que no! I bet you can't!, I bet you it isn't! (etc); ¡no?; ¿a que no? oh no?; do you dare me to?, do you think I can't?; ¡a que no lo sabes! I bet you don't know!; está de no he is in a mood to refuse, I guess he'll say no; no sea que . . . lest . . .; si no if not, otherwise; unless you (etc) do; todavía no not yet; see más, sino etc. (b) (in double negatives) no tengo nada I have nothing, I don't have anything; see nada, nunca etc. (c) (in compounds) eg el no conformismo nonconformism; pacto de no agresión non-aggression pact; la política de no intervención the policy of non-intervention, the non-intervention policy; cosa no esencial non-essential thing, inessential; la no necesidad del latín en partes de la misa the fact that Latin is not to be insisted upon in parts of the mass; for other cases, see the noun or adj.

nobiliario adj (a) title etc noble. (b) book etc genealogical.

noble 1 adj noble; honest, upright. **2** nm noble, nobleman; los —s the nobles, the nobility.

noblemente adv nobly; honestly, uprightly.

nobleza nf (a) (quality) nobility; honesty, uprightness. (b) (persons) nobility, aristocracy.

nocaut nm (SAm: angl) knockout.

noción *nf* (a) notion, idea; **no tener la menor —
de algo** to have not the faintest idea about something.
(b) **—es** elements, rudiments; smattering; **tiene
algunas —es de árabe** he has a smattering of Arabic.
nocional *adj* notional.
nocivo *adj* harmful, injurious (*para* to).
noctambulismo *nm* sleepwalking.
noctámbulo *nm*, **noctámbula** *nf* sleepwalker.
noctiluca *nf* (*Ent*) glow-worm.
nocturno 1 *adj* night (*attr*); evening (*attr*); (*Zool etc*)
nocturnal; **clase nocturna** evening class; **vida
nocturna** night life. **2** *nm* (*Mus*) nocturne.
noche *nf* night; night-time; (late) evening; dark,
darkness (*fig*); **ayer —** last night; **esta —**
¡**buenas —s!** good evening!, (*on parting or going to
bed*) good night!; **— de estreno** (*Theat*) first night; **—
toledana** sleepless night; **— vieja** New Year's Eve;
a primera — shortly after dark; **a la —** at nightfall;
de — (*adv*) at night, by night, in the night-time; **de
—** (*adj*) late-night (*attr*), evening (*attr*), eg **función
de —** late-night show, evening performance, **traje
de —** evening dress; **de la — a la mañana** overnight
(*also fig*); **en toda la —** all night; **hasta muy entrada
la —** until late at night; on into the small hours;
por la — at night, during the night; **se ha cerrado
la —** the darkness has come down, night has closed
in; **hacer — en un sitio** to spend the night in a place;
se hace de — it's getting dark, night is falling;
pasar la — en blanco, pasar la — de claro en claro
to have a sleepless night.
Nochebuena *nf* Christmas Eve.
nochecita *nf* (*SAm*) dusk, nightfall.
nocherniego 1 *adj* nocturnal, that goes out (*etc*) at
night, given to wandering about at night. **2** *nm*
night-bird (*fig*).
nochero 1 *adj* (*SAm*) = **nocherniego. 2** *nm* (a) (*Col,
Chi*) night watchman; (*Guat*) night worker. **(b)**
(*Guat*) bedside table.
nodo *nm* node.
nodriza *nf* wet-nurse.
nodular *adj* nodular.
nódulo *nm* nodule.
Noé *m* Noah.
nogal *nm* walnut (*wood*); walnut tree.
nogalina *nf* imitation walnut (*wood*).
noguera *nf* walnut tree.
nómada 1 *adj* nomadic. **2** *nmf* nomad.
nomadismo *nm* nomadism.
nomás *adv* (*SAm*) just; only.
nombradía *nf* fame, renown.
nombrado *adj* (a) aforementioned. (b) (*fig*) famous,
renowned.
nombramiento *nm* (a) naming; designation. (b)
mention. (c) nomination; appointment; commission.
nombrar [1a] *vt* (a) to name; to designate.
(b) to mention.
(c) to nominate; to appoint; (*Mil*) to commission;
— a uno embajador to nominate someone as ambassador, appoint someone ambassador.
nombre *nm* (a) name; **mal —** nickname; **A, por mal
— B A**, nicknamed B; **A**, wrongly named B; **A**,
improperly called B; **— y apellidos** name in full,
full name; **— artístico** nom de plume, pen name;
— comercial trade name; **— gentilicio** family
name; *see* **hipocorístico**; **— de lugar** place name;
— de pila first name, Christian name; **— propio**
proper name; **— de religión** name in religion; **bajo
el — de** under the name of; **de — by** name, *eg* **de —
García** García by name; **conocer a uno de — to**
know someone by name; **era rey tan sólo de —,
de rey no tenía más que el —** he was king in name
only; **no existe sino de —** it exists in name only; **en
— de** in the name of, on behalf of; **en — de la
libertad** in the name of liberty; ¡**abran en — de la
ley!** open up, in the name of the law!; **por — de by**
the name of, called; **sin — nameless; poner — a to**
call, name; ¿**qué — le van a poner?** what are they
going to call him, what name are they giving him?;
le pusieron el — de su abuelo they named him after
his grandfather; **su conducta no tiene —** his conduct
is utterly despicable.
(b) (*Gram*) noun.
(c) (*fig*) name, reputation; **un médico de — a**
famous doctor; **tiene — en el mundo entero** it has a
world-wide reputation.
nomenclatura *nf* nomenclature.
nomeolvides *nf*, *pl* **nomeolvides** forget-me-not.
nómina *nf* list, roll; (*Comm, Fin*) payroll; **tiene una
— de 500 personas** he has 500 on his payroll.
nominación *nf* (*esp SAm*) nomination.

nominal *adj* (a) *head, king etc* nominal, titular, in
name only. (b) *value* face (*attr*), nominal; *salary etc*
nominal. (c) (*Gram*) noun (*attr*), substantival.
nominalismo *nm* nominalism.
nominalmente *adv* nominally, in name; **al menos —**
at least in name.
nominativo 1 *adj* (a) (*Gram*) nominative.
(b) (*Comm, Fin*) bearing a person's name, made
out to an individual; **el cheque será — a favor de X**
the cheque should be made out to X.
2 *nm* (*Gram*) nominative.
non 1 *adj number* odd, uneven.
2 *nm* odd number; **pares y —es** odds and evens;
los —es the odd ones; **un zapato de —** an odd shoe;
queda uno de — there's an odd one, there's one left
over; **estar de — (***person*) to be odd man out, (*fig*) be
useless; **andar de —es** to have nothing to do.
nonada *nf* trifle, mere nothing.
nonagenario 1 *adj* nonagenarian, ninety-year old.
2 *nm*, **nonagenaria** *nf* nonagenarian, person in his
(*or* her) nineties.
nonagésimo *adj* ninetieth.
nonato *adj* unborn.
noneco *adj*, **nonejo** *adj* (*CAm, Pan*) dolt.
nones *adv* (*fam*) no; **decir que —** to say no.
nono *adj* ninth.
nopal *nm* prickly pear.
nopalera *nf* patch of prickly pears, area where
prickly pears grow.
noqueada *nf* (*esp SAm: angl*) knockout; knockout
blow.
noquear [1a] *vt* (*esp SAm: angl*) to knock out.
noray *nm* bollard.
norcoreano 1 *adj* North Korean. **2** *nm*, **norcoreana**
nf North Korean.
nordeste 1 *adj part* north-east, north-eastern;
direction north-easterly; *wind* north-east, north-
easterly.
2 *nm* (a) north-east.
(b) north-east wind.
nórdico 1 *adj* (a) northern, northerly; **es la ciudad
más nórdica de Europa** it is the most northerly city
in Europe.
(b) (*Hist*) Nordic, Norse.
2 *nm*, **nórdica** *nf* (a) northerner.
(b) (*Hist*) Northman.
3 *nm* (*language*) Norse.
noreste *see* **nordeste**.
noria *nf* (a) (*Agr*) waterwheel, chain pump. (b) (*at
fair*) big wheel.
norma *nf* (a) standard, norm, rule; pattern; method;
— de comprobación (*Phys etc*) control; **—s de
conducta** (*of newspaper*) policy; **— de vida** standard
of living; **está sujeto a ciertas —s** it is subject to
certain rules.
(b) (*Archit, Tech*) square.
normal *adj* normal; regular, usual, natural; *gauge etc*
standard; **es perfectamente —** it's perfectly normal,
it's completely usual.
normalidad *nf* normality, normalcy; (*Pol*) calm,
normal conditions; **la situación ha vuelto a la —**
the situation has returned to normal; **la vuelta a la
— es completa en la provincia** calm has been completely restored in the province.
normalizar [1f] **1** *vt* to normalize, restore to normal;
(*Tech*) to standardize.
2 normalizarse *vr* to return to normal, settle
down.
normalmente *adv* normally; usually.
Normandía *f* Normandy.
normando 1 *adj* Norman; **— francés** Norman-
French; **Islas Normandas** Channel Isles.
2 *nm*, **normanda** *nf* Norman; Northman, Norseman.
3 *nm* (*language*) **— francés** Norman-French.
normánico *adj* (*Archit*) Norman.
normar [1a] *vt* (*SAm*) to lay down rules for, establish
norms for.
normativo *adj*: **es — en todos los coches nuevos** it is
standard in all new cars, it is the norm in all new
cars.
noroeste 1 *adj part* north-west, north-western;
direction north-westerly; *wind* north-west, north-
westerly.
2 *nm* (a) north-west.
(b) north-west wind.
norsa *nf* (*SAm: angl*) nurse; governess; nursemaid.
nortada *nf* (steady) northerly wind.
norte 1 *adj part* north, northern; *direction* northerly;
wind north, northerly.
2 *nm* (a) north; **en la parte del —** in the northern
part; **al — de Segovia** to the north of Segovia, on the

north side of Segovia; **eso cae más hacia el —** that lies further (to the) north.
(**b**) north wind.
(**c**) (*fig*) guide; aim, objective; lodestar.
(**d**) (*Cu*) *used loosely to refer to the* United States.
(**e**) (*Cu, PR*) drizzle.
Norteamérica *f* North America.
norteamericano 1 *adj* North American, (*esp*) American. **2** *nm*, **norteamericana** *nf* North American, (*esp*) American.
nortear *vi* (*CAm, Per, PR*): **nortea** the north wind is blowing.
norteño 1 *adj* northern. **2** *nm*, **norteña** *nf* northerner.
nortino =**norteño.**
Noruega *f* Norway.
noruego 1 *adj* Norwegian. **2** *nm*, **noruega** *nf* Norwegian. **3** *nm* (*language*) Norwegian.
norvietnamita 1 *adj* North Vietnamese. **2** *nmf* North Vietnamese.
nos *personal pron pl* (**a**) (*acc*) us.
(**b**) (*dative*) (to) us; **— lo dará** he will give it to us; **— lo compró** he bought it from us; he bought it for us; **— cortamos el pelo** we had our hair cut.
(**c**) (*reflexive*) (to) ourselves; (*reciprocal*) (to) each other; **— lavamos** we washed; **no — hablamos** we don't speak to each other; **— levantamos a las 7** we get up at 7.
nosotros, nosotras *personal pron pl* (**a**) (*subject*) we.
(**b**) (*after prep*) us; ourselves; **no irán sin —** they won't go without us; **no pedimos nada para —** we ask nothing for ourselves.
nostalgia *nf* nostalgia, homesickness; longing.
nostálgico *adj* nostalgic, homesick; longing.
nostalgioso *adj* (*Chi*) =**nostálgico.**
nota *nf* (**a**) note; memorandum; (*Lit*) footnote, marginal note; (*Comm*) account; (*in newspaper*) note; (*SAm*) IOU, promissory note; **— de gastos** expense account; **— de inhabilitación** (*Aut*) endorsement (*in licence*); **— de la redacción** editor's note; **— de sociedad** gossip column, column of society news; **texto con —s de . . .** text edited with notes by . . ., text annotated by . . .; **tomar —s** to take notes.
(**b**) (*school etc*) grade, mark, class; (*terminal*) report; **obtener buenas —s** to get good marks.
(**c**) (*Mus and fig*) note; **— de adorno** grace note; **una — de buen gusto** a tasteful note; **como — de color** as a colourful note; as a bit of local colour; **— dominante** dominant feature; **entonar la —** to pitch a note, give the note (*for singers to start*).
(**d**) (*fig*) reputation; **de —** of note, famous; **de mala —** notorious; of ill fame; **tiene — de tacaño** he has a reputation for meanness.
(**e**) **digno de —** notable, worthy of note; **tomar —** to take note.
notabilidad *nf* (**a**) noteworthiness, notability. (**b**) (*person*) notable, worthy.
notable 1 *adj* noteworthy, notable; remarkable; outstanding. **2** *nmf* notable, worthy.
notablemente *adv* notably; remarkably, outstandingly.
notación *nf* notation.
notar [1a] **1** *vt* (**a**) to note, notice; to feel, perceive; to see; **no noto frío alguno** I don't feel cold at all; **no lo había notado** I hadn't noticed it; **hacer — que . . .** to note that . . ., observe that . . .; **hacerse —** to stand out, catch the eye, draw attention to oneself.
(**b**) to note down.
(**c**) to mark, indicate.
(**d**) to criticize; to discredit; **— a uno de oscuro** to brand someone as obscure, criticize someone for being obscure.
2 notarse *vr* to show, be apparent, be obvious; **se nota que . . .** one observes that . . ., one notes that . . .; **la combinación no se le nota** your slip doesn't show; **su origen extranjero no se nota en absoluto** his foreign origin is not in the least obvious, you can't tell at all that he is foreign.
notaría *nf* (**a**) profession of notary. (**b**) notary's office.
notarial *adj* notarial; *style etc* legal, lawyer's.
notario *nm* notary, notary public; (*in some functions, equivalent to*) solicitor.
noticia *nf* (**a**) piece of news; (*in newspaper etc*) news item; **—s** news; information; **necrológica** notice of a death, obituary notice; **según nuestras —s** according to our information; **estar atrasado de —s** to be behind the times, lack up-to-date information; **tener —s de uno** to have news of someone, hear from someone; **hace tiempo que no tenemos —s suyas** we haven't heard from her for a long time.
(**b**) knowledge; notion; **no tener la menor — de algo** to know nothing at all about a matter, be completely ignorant of something.

noticiar [1b] *vt* to notify.
noticiario *nm* (*Radio*) news bulletin; (*Cine*) newsreel.
noticiero 1 *adj* (**a**) news-bearing, news-giving. (**b**) fond of receiving news. **2** *nm* (**a**) newspaper, gazette. (**b**) (*Cu*) newsreel.
noticioso *adj* (**a**) *source etc* well-informed.
(**b**) **— de que Vd quería verme . . .** hearing that (*or* on being informed that) you wished to see me . . .
notificación *nf* notification.
notificar [1g] *vt* to notify, inform.
notoriamente *adv* obviously; glaringly, blatantly, flagrantly; **una sentencia — injusta** a glaringly injust sentence.
notoriedad *nf* fame, renown; wide knowledge.
notorio *adj* (**a**) well-known, publicly known; **un hecho —** a well-known fact; **es — que . . .** it is well-known that . . .
(**b**) obvious; glaring, blatant, flagrant.
novador 1 *adj* innovating, revolutionary. **2** *nm* innovator.
noval *adj* ground newly-broken.
novatada *nf* (**a**) rag, ragging, hazing (US) (*of new member etc*). (**b**) beginner's mistake, elementary blunder.
novato 1 *adj* raw, green, new. **2** *nm* beginner, tyro.
novecientos *adj* nine hundred.
novedad *nf* (**a**) (*quality*) newness, novelty; strangeness.
(**b**) (*object etc*) novelty; surprise; **—es** (*newspaper*) latest news; **—es, últimas —es** (*Comm*) novelties, latest fashions, latest models.
(**c**) new feature, new development, change; **sin — en el frente** all quiet on the front; **llegar sin —** to arrive without mishap, arrive safely; **la jornada ha sido sin —** it has been a quiet (*or* normal) day, it has been a day without incident; **el enfermo sigue sin —** the patient's condition is unchanged.
novedoso *adj* (**a**) novel; full of novelties. (**b**) (*Arg, Chi, Mex*) =**novelesco.**
novel 1 *adj* new; inexperienced; **una escritora — a** new writer. **2** *nm* beginner.
novela *nf* novel; **— de amores** love story, romance; **—s científicas** science fiction; **— por entregas** serial; **— histórica** historical novel; **— policíaca** detective story, whodunit (*sl*); **— radiofónica** radio serial; **la — española en el siglo XX** the 20th century Spanish novel.
novelar [1a] **1** *vt* to make a novel out of; to tell in novel form. **2** *vi* to write novels.
novelero 1 *adj* (**a**) *person* highly imaginative; dreamy, romantic.
(**b**) *person* fond of novelty.
(**c**) *person* fond of novels.
(**d**) *story etc* romantic, novelettish.
(**e**) *person* (*pej*) gossipy, fond of gossiping. **2** *nm*, **novelera** *nf* novel reader.
novelesco *adj* (**a**) (*Lit*) fictional; **el género —** fiction, the novel. (**b**) romantic, fantastic, novelettish.
novelista *nmf* novelist.
novelística *nf*: **la —** fiction, the novel.
novelón *nm* big novel, three-decker novel.
novelucha *nf* (*pej*) cheap novel, yellowback, shocker.
noveno *adj* ninth.
noventa *adj* ninety; ninetieth.
noventón 1 *adj* ninety-year old, ninetyish. **2** *nm*, **noventona** *nf* person of about ninety.
novia *nf* girlfriend, sweetheart; fiancée; bride; newly-married girl; **echarse una —** to get oneself a girlfriend; **Juan y su —** John and his girlfriend, John and his fiancée; **traje de —** bridal gown, wedding dress.
noviar [1b] *vi* (*RPl*): **— con** to court, keep company with.
noviazgo *nm* engagement.
noviciado *nm* apprenticeship, training; (*Eccl*) novitiate.
novicio *nm*, **novicia** *nf* beginner, novice; apprentice; (*Eccl*) novice.
noviembre *nm* November.
noviero *adj* (*CAm, Mex*) =**enamoradizo.**
novilunio *nm* new moon.
novilla *nf* heifer.
novillada *nf* (*Taur*) bullfight with young bulls (*and novice bullfighters*).
novillero *nm* (**a**) (*Taur*) novice, young bullfighter. (**b**) (*fam*) truant.
novillo *nm* (**a**) young bull, bullock, steer; **—s =novillada.**
(**b**) (*fam*) cuckold.
(**c**) **hacer —s** to stay away, not turn up, (*School*) play truant.

novio *nm* boyfriend, sweetheart; fiancé; bridegroom; newly-married man; **los —s** the engaged couple; the bride and groom; the newly-weds; **ser —s formales** to be formally engaged; **Maruja y su —** Mary and her boyfriend, Mary and her fiancée; **viaje de —s** honeymoon.

novísimo *adj* newest, latest, most recent; brand-new.
nubada *nf*, **nubarrada** *nf* (a) downpour, sudden shower. (b) (*fig*) shower; abundance; mass.
nubarrón *nm* storm cloud.
nube *nf* (a) cloud; **— de lluvia** raincloud; **— de tormenta** storm cloud.
(b) (*fig*: *of insects, smoke etc*) cloud; crowd, mass, multitude; **una — de pordioseros** a crowd of beggars; **una — de críticas** a storm of criticism.
(c) (*Med*: *in eye*) cloud, film.
(d) **los precios están por las —s** prices are terribly high; **poner a uno en** (*or* **por, sobre**) **las —s** to praise someone to the skies; **ponerse por las —s** (*person*) to go up the wall (*fam*); (*price*) to rocket, soar; **andar por las —s, estar en las —s** to be up in the clouds, be daydreaming, be remote from it all.
núbil *adj* marriageable, nubile.
nublado **1** *adj* cloudy, overcast.
2 *nm* (a) storm cloud, black cloud; **todo — tiene su claridad** every cloud has a silver lining.
(b) (*fig*) threat; impending danger.
(c) (*fig*) swarm, crowd, multitude; **un — de a** swarm of, a host of.
(d) (*fig*) anger, black mood.
nublar [1a] **1** *vt* (a) to darken, obscure. (b) (*fig*) sight to cloud, disturb; reason to affect; happiness etc to cloud, destroy. **2 nublarse** *vr* to become cloudy, cloud over.
nublazón *nm* (*SAm*) =**nublado**.
nublo *adj* (*SAm*) cloudy.
nubloso *adj* (a) cloudy. (b) (*fig*) unlucky, unfortunate; gloomy.
nubosidad *nf* cloudiness.
nuboso *adj* cloudy.
nuclear *adj* nuclear.
nuclearizado *adj*: **países —s** countries possessing nuclear weapons.
núcleo *nm* nucleus; (*Elec*) core; (*Bot*) kernel, stone; (*fig*) core, essence; **— rural** (new) village, village settlement.
nudillo *nm* knuckle.
nudismo *nm* (*angl*) nudism.
nudista *nmf* (*angl*) nudist.
nudo *nm* (a) knot; **— corredizo** slipknot; **— llano, — de rizos** reef knot.
(b) (*Naut*) knot.
(c) (*Bot*) knot; node.
(d) thick part, thickening, lump; **con un — en la garganta** with a lump in one's throat; **se me hizo un — en la garganta** I got a lump in my throat.
(e) (*of communications etc*) centre; (*of road system*) cloverleaf, system of flyovers.
(f) (*fig*) bond, tie, link.
(g) (*fig*: *of problem*) knotty point; core, crux; (*of play etc*) crisis, point of greatest complexity.
nudoso *adj* wood etc knotty, full of knots; trunk gnarled; stick knobbly.
nuégado *nm* nougat.
nuera *nf* daughter-in-law.
nuestro **1** *poss adj* our; (*after n*) of ours, eg **un barco — a** boat of ours, one of our boats; **no es amigo —** he's no friend of ours; **lo —** (what is) ours, what belongs to us. **2** *poss pron* ours, of ours; **es el —** it is ours; **los —s** (*freq*) our people, our relations, our family; our men, our side.
nueva *nf* piece of news; **—s** news; **me cogió de —s** it was news to me, it took me by surprise; **hacerse de —s** to pretend that one had not heard a piece of news before.
Nueva Escocia *f* Nova Scotia.
Nueva Gales *f* **del Sur** New South Wales.
Nueva Guinea *f* New Guinea.
Nueva Inglaterra *f* New England.
nuevamente *adv* again; anew.
Nueva Orléans New Orleans.
Nueva York New York.
Nueva Zelanda *f* New Zealand.
nueve **1** *adj* nine; (*date*) ninth; **las — nine** o'clock. **2** *nm* nine.
nuevo *adj* (*in most senses*) new; fresh; novel; further, additional; stamp mint, unused; **es — en la ciudad** he's new to the town; **es — en el oficio** he's new to the trade; **somos —s aquí** we're new here; **no hay nada —** there's nothing fresh; **no hay nada — bajo las estrellas** there's nothing new under the sun; **es más — que yo** he is junior to me; **con —s argumentos** with new arguments, with further arguments; **la**

casa es nueva the house is new; **la casa está nueva** the house is as good as new; **¿qué hay de —?** (*fam*) what's new? (*fam*), what's the news?
nuevomejicano **1** *adj* New Mexican. **2** *nm*, **nuevomejicana** *nf* New Mexican.
Nuevo Méjico *m* New Mexico.
nuez *nf* nut, (*esp*) walnut; **— moscada** nutmeg; **— de la garganta** Adam's apple.
nulidad *nf* (a) (*Law*) nullity. (b) incompetence, incapacity. (c) (*person*) nonentity; **es una —** he's a dead loss, he's useless.
nulo **1** *adj* (a) (*Law*) void, null and void; invalid, without force.
(b) person useless; **es — para la música** he's useless at music, he's no good at music, he's a dead loss as a musician.
(c) (*Sport*) game drawn, tied.
2 —s *nmpl* (*Cards*) misère; **bridge con —s** bridge with the misère variation.
numen *nm* inspiration; talent, inventiveness; **— poético** poetic inspiration; **de propio —** out of one's head.
numeración *nf* (a) numeration. (b) numbers, numerals; **— arábiga** Arabic numerals; **— romana** Roman numerals.
numerador *nm* numerator.
numeral **1** *adj* numeral, number (*attr*). **2 nm** numeral.
numerar [1a] **1** *vt* to number; **páginas sin —** unnumbered pages. **2 numerarse** *vr* (*Mil etc*) to number off.
numerario *nm* hard cash.
numéricamente *adv* numerically.
numérico *adj* numerical.
número *nm* (a) number (*also Gram, Tel*); numeral; **— arábigo** Arabic numeral; **— cardinal** cardinal number; **— entero** whole number; **— impar** odd number; **— de matrícula** (*Aut etc*) registration number; **— ordinal** ordinal number; **— par** even number; **— primo** prime number; **— quebrado** fraction; **— redondo** round number; **en —s redondos** in round numbers, in round figures; **— de referencia** reference number; **— romano** Roman numeral; **— de serie** serial number; **el jugador — uno de su país** the number one player of his country; **en — de** to the number of; **miembro de — full** member; **sin — (fig)** numberless, unnumbered; countless.
(b) (*of shoe etc*) size.
(c) (*of journal etc*) number, issue; **— atrasado** back number; **— extraordinario** special edition, special issue.
(d) (*in programme*) item, number; (*Theat etc*) turn, act, number; sketch.
(e) (*Arg*) **de —** best, first.
(f) **¡vaya —!** (*fam*) what a character!
numeroso *adj* numerous; **familia numerosa** large family.
numismática *nf* numismatics.
numismático **1** *adj* numismatic. **2 nm** numismatist.
nunca *adv* never; ever; **no viene —, — viene** he never comes, he doesn't ever come; **¡—! never!; casi —** almost never, hardly ever; **¡hasta —!** I don't care if I never see you again!; **más que —** more than ever; **— jamás, — más** never again, nevermore; **¿has visto — cosa igual?** have you ever seen anything like this?
nunciatura *nf* nunciature.
nuncio *nm* (a) (*Eccl*) nuncio; **— apostólico** papal nuncio; **¡cuéntaselo al —!** tell that to the marines!; **¡que lo haga el —!** let someone else to do it!
(b) messenger; (*fig*) herald, harbinger; **— de la primavera** harbinger of spring.
nunquita *adv* (*SAm*) =**nunca**.
nupcial *adj* wedding (*attr*), nuptial.
nupcias *nfpl* wedding, nuptials; **casarse en segundas — to** marry again, get married a second time; **A, que se casó en segundas — con B** A, who made a second marriage to B.
nurse ['nurse] *nf* (*angl*) nurse; governess; nursemaid.
nutria *nf* otter.
nutrición *nf* nutrition.
nutrido *adj* (a) **bien — well-nourished; mal — undernourished.**
(b) (*fig*) large, considerable; numerous; abundant; **— de full** of, abounding in; **una nutrida concurrencia** a large attendance; **—s aplausos** deafening applause; **fuego — (Mil)** heavy fire.
nutrimento *nm* nutriment, nourishment.
nutrir [3a] *vt* (a) to feed, nourish. (b) (*fig*) to feed, strengthen; to support, foment, encourage.
nutritivo *adj* nourishing, nutritious; **valor — nutritional** value, food value.
nylon [ni'lon, 'nailon] *nm* (*angl*) nylon.

Ñ

ña *nf* (*SAm: fam*) = **doña, señora.**
ñácara *nf* (*CAm*) ulcer, sore.
ñame *nm* yam.
ñandú *nm* (*RPl*) rhea, American ostrich.
ñanga *nf* (**a**) (*CAm*) marsh, swampy estuary. (**b**) (*Ec*) bit, small portion.
ñangada *nf* (*CAm*) (**a**) nip, bite. (**b**) harmful and foolish act.
ñangado *adj* (*Cu*) knock-kneed; bow-legged.
ñango *adj* (**a**) (*Arg, Urug*) awkward, clumsy. (**b**) (*Chi*) short-legged, waddling. (**c**) (*Mex*) weak, feeble. (**d**) (*PR*) = **ñangado.**
ñangotarse [1a] *vr* (**a**) (*Col, PR*) to squat, crouch down. (**b**) (*PR*) to get scared.
ñaña *nf* (**a**) (*Arg, Chi*) elder sister; (*Chi, PR*) nursemaid, wet-nurse. (**b**) (*CAm*) excrement.
ñaño **1** *adj* (**a**) (*Col, Chi, Ec, Pan*) friend close; (*Col, Pan*) spoiled, pampered.
   (**b**) (*Chi*) silly.
   2 *nm* (*Col, Chi, Ec, Pan*) close friend, chum; (*Arg, Ec*) elder brother; (*Col, Per*) baby, child; **estar — s** to be on very close terms.
ñapa *nf* (*SAm*) extra, bonus; tip; **de —** (*Col, PR*) as an extra, in addition.
ñapango *nm* (*Col*) mulatto, mestizo, half-breed.
ñaque *nm* junk, worthless stuff; odds and ends.
ñata *nf* (**a**) (*SAm*) nose. (**b**) (*Per*) death.
ñato *adj* (**a**) (*SAm*) flat-nosed, snub-nosed. (**b**) (*Col*) nasal, twangy. (**c**) (*Arg*) ugly; bent, deformed; wicked. (**d**) (*Pan*) effeminate.
ñeque **1** *adj* (*CAm, Chi, Ec, Ven*) strong; vigorous; clever, capable; (*CAm, Cu*) brave. **2** *nm* (**a**) (*CAm, Col, Chi, Ec, Per, Ven*) strength; energy, vigour; courage. (**b**) (*CAm, Mex*) blow, punch. (**c**) **—s** (*Ec*) fists.

ñique *nm* (*CAm, Chi*) butt, thrust; (*CAm*) punch.
ñiquiñaque *nm* (**a**) trash, junk, rubbish. (**b**) worthless individual.
ñisca *nf* (**a**) (*CAm, Chi, Ec, Per*) bit, small piece. (**b**) (*CAm, Col*) excrement.
ñoca *nf* (*Col*) crack, fissure.
ñoco **1** *adj* (*Col, PR, SD, Ven*) lacking a finger; one-handed. **2** *nm* (*Chi*) straight punch.
ñola *nf* (**a**) (*Col, Guat*) excrement. (**b**) (*Guat, Hond*) ulcer, sore.
ñongarse [1h] *vr* (*Col*) (**a**) to squat, crouch down. (**b**) **— el pie** to twist one's foot.
ñongo *adj* (**a**) (*Cu, Chi*) stupid; (*Chi*) slow, lazy; good-for-nothing; excessively humble.
   (**b**) (*Col, Ven*) crippled; damaged, defective.
   (**c**) (*Ven*) tricky, deceitful; unsightly; of ill omen; touchy.
ñoñería *nf*, **ñoñez** *nf* (**a**) insipidness; spinelessness; shyness, bashfulness, fussiness.
   (**b**) (*Arg, Chi*) senility; dotage.
   (**c**) (*Cu*) inanity, stupid thing.
   (**d**) (*PR, SD*) endearment; caress.
ñoño **1** *adj* (**a**) characterless, insipid; unsubstantial; *person* spineless.
   (**b**) shy, bashful.
   (**c**) fussy, finicky.
   (**d**) (*SAm*) senile, decrepit.
   (**e**) (*Per, PR, SD*) vain, that likes to be flattered.
   2 *nm*, **ñoña** *nf* spineless person, drip (*sl*).
ñorbo *nm* (*CAm, Ec, Per*) passionflower.
ñudoso *adj* = **nudoso.**
ñufla *nf* (*Chi*) worthless object.
ñusca *nf* (*Col, Ec*) excrement.
ñutir [3a] *vi* (*Col*) to grunt.

O

o *conj* or; — . . .— either . . . or.

oasis *nm, pl* **oasis** oasis.

obcecación *nf* blindness, blind obstinacy; mental blockage, disturbance; **en un momento de** — when the balance of his (*etc*) mind was disturbed.

obcecadamente *adv* blindly; stubbornly, obdurately; in a disturbed state.

obcecado *adj* blind, mentally blinded; stubborn, obdurate; disturbed.

obcecar [1g] *vt* to blind (mentally), disturb the mind of; **el amor le ha obcecado** love has blinded him (to all else).

obedecer [2d] *vti* **(a)** to obey.
(b) — **a** (*of disease etc*) to yield to, respond to (treatment by).
(c) — **a,** — **al hecho de que** . . . to be due to . . ., arise from . . .; **su viaje obedece a dos motivos** his journey has two reasons.

obediencia *nf* obedience.

obediente *adj* obedient.

obelisco *nm* obelisk; (*Typ*) dagger.

obenques *nmpl* (*Naut*) shrouds.

obertura *nf* overture.

obesidad *nf* obesity.

obeso *adj* obese.

óbice *nm* obstacle, impediment; **eso no es** — **para que lo haga** that is not an obstacle to my doing it.

obispado *nm* bishopric.

obispo *nm* bishop.

óbito *nm* (*lit*) decease, demise (*lit*).

obituario *nm* (*SAm*) **(a)** decease, demise. **(b)** (*angl*) obituary; obituary section (*of a newspaper*).

objeción *nf* objection; **hacer** —**es** to raise objections; **no hacen ninguna** — they make (*or* raise) no objection.

.objetable *adj* objectionable, open to objection.

objetante *nmf* objector; (*in meeting*) heckler, protester.

objetar [1a] *vti* to object; *objection* to make, offer, raise; *argument* to present, put forward; **le objeté que no había dinero para ello** I pointed out to him (*or* I protested to him) that there was no money for it.

objetivamente *adv* objectively.

objetividad *nf* objectivity.

objetivo 1 *adj* objective. **2** *nm* **(a)** objective, aim, end. **(b)** (*Mil*) objective, target. **(c)** (*Phot*) lens; object lens.

objeto *nm* **(a)** object, thing; —**s de escritorio** writing materials; —**s de tocador** toilet articles.
(b) object, aim, end, purpose; **al** — **de** + *infin* with the object of + *ger*, with the aim of + *ger*; **esta carta tiene por** — + *infin* this letter has the aim of + *ger*, this letter aims to + *infin*.
(c) (*of speech etc*) theme, subject matter.
(d) (*Gram*) object.

objetor *nm* objector; — **de conciencia** conscientious objector.

oblación *nf* oblation, offering.

oblar [1a] *vt* (*Arg*) *debt* to pay in cash.

oblata *nf* oblation, offering.

oblea *nf* **(a)** (*Eccl and fig*) wafer; very thin slice; **quedar como una** — to be as thin as a lath. **(b)** (*Chi: Post*) stamp.

oblicuamente *adv* obliquely.

oblicuar [1d] **1** *vt* to slant, place obliquely, cant, tilt. **2** *vi* to deviate from the perpendicular.

oblicuidad *nf* obliquity, oblique angle (*or* position *etc*).

oblicuo *adj* oblique; slanting; *glance* sidelong.

obligación *nf* **(a)** obligation; duty; responsibility; —**es** (*esp*) family responsibilities; **cumplir con una** — to fulfil a duty; **faltar a sus** —**es** to fail in one's duty, fail to carry out one's obligations; **tener**
— **de** + *infin* to have a duty to + *infin*, be under an obligation to + *infin*; **primero es la** — **que la devoción** business before pleasure.
(b) (*Comm, Fin*) bond; —**es** bonds, securities; — **de banco** bank bill.

obligacionista *nmf* bondholder.

obligar [1h] **1** *vt* **(a)** to force, compel, oblige; — **a uno a hacer algo** to force (*or* compel) someone to do something; **verse obligado a** + *infin* to be obliged to + *infin*, find oneself compelled to + *infin*; **estar** (*or* **quedar**) **obligado a uno** to be obliged to someone, be in someone's debt.
(b) *shoes etc* to force, stretch; **el libro sólo entra allí obligándolo** the book goes in there but only with a hard push (*or* but only by forcing it).
2 obligarse *vr* to put oneself under an obligation; — **a** + *infin* to bind oneself to + *infin*.

obligatoriedad *nf* obligatory nature.

obligatorio *adj* obligatory, compulsory; binding; **es** — + *infin* it is obligatory to + *infin*; **escolaridad obligatoria** compulsory schooling, compulsory attendance at school.

obliteración *nf* (*Med*) obliteration.

obliterar [1a] *vt* **(a)** (*Med*) to obliterate. **(b)** (*SAm: angl*) to obliterate, efface, destroy.

oblongo *adj* oblong.

oboe *nm* **(a)** oboe. **(b)** oboist, oboe player.

óbolo *nm* (*fig*) mite, small contribution.

obra *nf* **(a)** (*in general*) work; piece of work; — **de arte** work of art; — **benéfica,** — **de misericordia,** — **piadosa** charity; **buenas** —**s,** —**s de caridad** good works; — **maestra** masterpiece; — **pía** religious foundation; —**s públicas** public works; **Ministerio de O**—**s Públicas** Ministry of Works; **es** — **de benedictinos** (*or* **romanos**) it's a huge task, it's a long job; **¡manos a la** —**!** to work!, let's get on with it!; **por** — **de** thanks to, thanks to the efforts of; **poner algo por** — to carry something out, put something into effect; —**s son amores y no buenas razones** actions speak louder than words.
(b) (*Lit*) work, book; — **de consulta** reference book, work of reference; — **literaria** literary work; — **de vulgarización** popular work; —**s completas** complete works, collected works; **las** —**s de Cervantes** the works of Cervantes.
(c) (*Theat: also* — **dramática,** — **de teatro**) play.
(d) (*Mus*) work, opus, composition.
(e) (*Archit: also* —**s**) work; construction, building; (*Arg*) building under construction; — **de hierro** ironwork; —**s** (*freq*) repairs, alterations; **"cerrado por** —**s"** "closed for repairs (*or* alterations)"; **estamos en** —**s** there are building repairs going on; we have the workmen in; **se han comenzado las** —**s del nuevo embalse** work has been begun on the new dam.
(f) workmanship, craftsmanship; handiwork; **la** — **es buena pero con malos materiales** the workmanship is good but the materials were bad.
(g) (*Chi*) brickworks.
(h) — **de** about; **en** — **de 8 semanas** in about 8 weeks, in a matter of 8 weeks.

obradera *nf* (*Col, Guat, Pan*) diarrhoea.

obrador *nm* working table, bench; workroom, workshop.

obraje *nm* **(a)** (*Bol, RPl*) sawmill, timberyard. **(b)** (*Mex*) pork butcher's (shop).

obrajero *nm* **(a)** foreman, overseer. **(b)** (*RPl*) lumberman. **(c)** (*Bol*) craftsman, skilled worker. **(d)** (*Mex*) pork butcher.

obrar [1a] **1** *vt* **(a)** *wood etc* to work.
(b) (*of medicine*) to work on, have an effect on.
(c) (*Arg*) to build.
(d) *miracle etc* to work, bring about.
2 *vi* **(a)** to act, behave; to proceed; — **de acuerdo**

con to proceed in accordance with; — **con precaución** to act cautiously, proceed warily.
(**b**) (of medicine) to work, have an effect.
(**c**) (formal phrases) **su carta obra en mi poder** I have received your letter, your letter is to hand; **el acusado obra en manos del juez** the accused man is in the judge's hands.
(**d**) (fam) to relieve nature.
obrerismo nm working-class movement.
obrero 1 adj class working; action, union etc labour (attr); **el movimiento** — the working-class movement; **condiciones obreras** working conditions.
2 nm worker (also Pol), workman; man, hand; labourer; — **escenógrafo** stagehand; — **portuario** dock worker.
3 obrera nf worker, woman worker.
obscenamente adv obscenely.
obscenidad nf obscenity.
obsceno adj obscene.
obscu . . . see **oscu** . . .
obseder [2a] vt (SAm) to obsess.
obsequiar [1b] vt (**a**) to lavish attentions on, make a fuss of; **le obsequiaron con un reloj** they presented him with a clock, they gave him a clock; **le van a — con un banquete** they are going to hold a dinner for him, they are going to honour him with a dinner.
(**b**) (SAm) **le obsequiaron un reloj** they presented him with a clock.
obsequio nm (**a**) present, gift; (on retirement etc) presentation; **ejemplar de** — complimentary copy, presentation copy.
(**b**) attention, kindness, courtesy; **en — de** in honour of; **hágame el — de** + infin please + infin.
obsequiosamente adv obligingly, helpfully.
obsequioso adj (**a**) obliging, helpful, attentive. (**b**) (Mex) fond of giving presents.
observable adj observable.
observación nf (**a**) observation; (of law) observance.
(**b**) observation, remark, comment; objection; **hacer una** — to make a remark, comment, observe; **hacer una — a** (freq) to raise an objection to.
observador 1 adj observant. **2** nm, **observadora** nf observer; — **extranjero** foreign observer.
observancia nf observance.
observar [1a] vt (**a**) to observe, watch; to see, notice, spot; (Astron) to observe; — **que** . . . to observe that . . ., notice that . . .
(**b**) law to observe, respect; to keep; rule to abide by, adhere to; — **buena conducta** (Per) to behave oneself.
(**c**) (SAm) — **algo a uno** to point out something to someone, draw someone's attention to something.
observatorio nm observatory; — **del tiempo** weather station.
obsesión nf obsession.
obsesionante adj haunting; obsessive.
obsesionar [1a] vt to obsess, haunt; **estar obsesionado con** (or **por**) **algo** to be obsessed by something; to have something on the brain.
obsesivo adj obsessive.
obseso adj obsessed, haunted.
obsidiana nf obsidian.
obsoleto adj (SAm: angl) obsolete.
obstaculizar [1f] vt to hinder, hamper, hold up; to prevent, stand in the way of.
obstáculo nm obstacle; hindrance; handicap, drawback; (Mil, Sport etc) obstacle; **no es — para que yo** + subj it is no obstacle to my + ger.
obstante: no — 1 adv nevertheless, however; all the same. **2** prep in spite of.
obstar [1a] vi: — **a**, — **para** to hinder; to prevent; **eso no obsta para que lo haga** that is no obstacle to his doing it, that does not prevent him from doing it.
obstetricia nf obstetrics.
obstétrico 1 adj obstetric(al). **2** nm obstetrician.
obstinación nf obstinacy, stubbornness.
obstinadamente adv obstinately, stubbornly.
obstinado adj obstinate, stubborn.
obstinarse [1a] vr to be obstinate; to dig one's heels in; — **en** + infin to persist in + ger, continue obstinately to + infin.
obstrucción nf obstruction (also Parl).
obstruccionar [1a] vt (SAm) to obstruct.
obstruccionismo nm obstructionism.
obstruccionista 1 adj obstructionist, obstructive. **2** nmf obstructionist.
obstructivo adj, **obstructor** adj obstructive.
obstruir [3g] vt to obstruct; to block; to hinder, impede; to interfere with.
obtención nf obtaining, securing.

obtener [2l] vt to get, obtain, secure; — **un subproducto del carbón** to obtain a by-product from coal.
obtenible adj obtainable.
obturación nf plugging, stopping; sealing off; filling.
obturador nm plug, stopper; (Aut) choke; (Phot) shutter.
obturar [1a] vt to plug, stop (up); to seal off; tooth to fill.
obtuso adj (**a**) edge etc blunt, dull. (**b**) (Math and fig) obtuse.
obús nm (**a**) (Mil) howitzer; shell. (**b**) (Aut) tyre valve.
obvención nf bonus, perquisite.
obvencional adj bonus, extra; incidental.
obviar [1c] **1** vt to obviate, remove. **2** vi to stand in the way.
obvio adj obvious.
oca nf goose.
ocasión nf (**a**) occasion, time; **con — de** on the occasion of; **en algunas —es** sometimes; **en aquella** — on that occasion; **venir en una mala** — to come at a bad moment.
(**b**) chance, opportunity, occasion; **aprovechar la** — to take one's chance, seize one's opportunity; **dar a uno la — de** + infin to give someone a chance (or opportunity) to + infin.
(**c**) cause, motive; **no hay — para quejarse** there is no cause to complain.
(**d**) **de** — (Comm) secondhand; old, used; **librería de** — secondhand bookshop.
(**e**) (SAm) bargain; **precio de** — bargain price, reduced price.
ocasional adj (**a**) chance, accidental; incidental. (**b**) composition etc occasional.
ocasionalmente adv by chance, accidentally; incidentally.
ocasionar [1a] vt to cause, produce, occasion.
ocaso nm (**a**) (Astron) sunset; (of star) setting. (**b**) (Geog) west. (**c**) (fig) decline, end, fall.
occidental 1 adj western. **2** nmf westerner.
occidentalizar [1f] vt to westernize.
occidente nm west.
occipucio nm occiput.
occiso nm, **occisa** nf: **el** — the deceased, (of crime) the victim.
Oceanía f Oceania.
oceánico adj oceanic.
océano nm ocean; **O— Atlántico** Atlantic Ocean; **O— Glacial Ártico** Arctic Ocean; **O— Índico** Indian Ocean; **O— Pacífico** Pacific Ocean.
oceanografía nf oceanography.
ocelote nm ocelot.
ocio nm (**a**) leisure, idleness; (pej) idleness; —**s**, **ratos de** — leisure, spare time, free time; **entretener los —s de uno** to help someone to enjoy his leisure, occupy someone's spare time.
(**b**) —**s** pastime, diversion.
ociosamente adv idly.
ociosear [1a] vi (Arg, Bol, Chi, Ec) to be at leisure; (pej) to idle, loaf about.
ociosidad nf idleness; **la — es madre de todos los vicios** the devil finds work for idle hands.
ocioso adj (**a**) idle; at leisure; inactive; **estar —** to be idle.
(**b**) act, words etc useless, pointless, idle; **dinero —** money lying idle; **es — especular** it is idle to speculate.
oclusión nf (**a**) (Ling etc) occlusion. (**b**) (Meteorol) occluded front.
oclusiva nf (Ling) occlusive, plosive.
oclusivo adj (Ling) occlusive, plosive.
ocote nm (CAm, Mex) torch; a species of pine.
ocre nm ochre; — **amarillo** yellow ochre; — **rojo** red ochre.
octaedro nm octahedron.
octagonal adj octagonal.
octágono nm octagon.
octanaje nm octane number; **de alto —** high-octane (attr).
octano nm octane.
octava nf (Mus, Poet) octave.
octavilla nf pamphlet, leaflet.
octavín nm piccolo.
Octavio m Octavian.
octavo 1 adj eighth. **2** nm (**a**) eighth. (**b**) (Typ) **libro en —** octavo book. (**c**) —**s de final** (Sport) quarter finals.
octeto nm octet(te).
octogenario 1 adj octogenarian, eighty-year-old. **2** nm, **octogenaria** f octogenarian, person in his (or her) eighties.
octogésimo adj eightieth.

octosílabo 1 *adj* octosyllabic. **2** *nm* octosyllable.
octubre *nm* October.
ocular 1 *adj* ocular; eye (*attr*); **testigo** — eyewitness. **2** *nm* eyepiece.
oculista *nmf* oculist.
ocultamente *adv* secretly; mysteriously; stealthily.
ocultar [1a] **1** *vt* to hide, conceal (*a, de* from); to screen, mask.
 2 ocultarse *vr* to hide (oneself); **— a la vista** to keep out of sight; **— con, — tras** to hide behind; **se me oculta la razón** I do not know the reason, the reason is a mystery to me.
ocultismo *nm* occultism.
ocultista *nmf* occultist.
oculto *adj* **(a)** hidden, concealed; **permanecer** — to stay hidden, remain in hiding.
 (b) (*fig*) secret; mysterious; *science* occult; *thought* secret, inner; *motive* ulterior.
ocupación *nf* (*all senses*) occupation.
ocupado *adj* **(a)** *place etc* occupied, taken; **¿está ocupada la silla?** is that seat taken?
 (b) la línea esta ocupada (*Tel*) the line is engaged, the line is busy (*US*); **señal de** — engaged tone, busy signal (*US*).
 (c) *person* busy; **estoy muy** — I'm very busy (*en* with).
 (d) estar ocupada (*woman*) to be pregnant.
ocupante *nmf* occupant.
ocupar [1a] **1** *vt* **(a)** *seat, space etc* to occupy, fill, take up; *room* to occupy, live in, inhabit; *atmosphere* to fill, pervade; *country, town* (*Mil*) to occupy; to take over, take control of.
 (b) *post* to occupy, fill.
 (c) *person* to occupy, engage; to keep busy; *workers* to employ, provide work for; **las obras ocupan más de 1000 hombres** the work keeps more than 1000 men busy, the work employs more than 1000 men.
 (d) *time* to occupy, fill up, take up; **ocupa sus ratos libres pintando** he uses his spare time to paint, he paints in his spare time.
 (e) *object* to seize, confiscate; **la policía le ocupó la navaja con que hirió a su mujer** the police took from him (*or* found on him) the razor with which he wounded his wife; **les ocuparon todo el contrabando** they seized all the contraband from them.
 (f) (*Mex*) to use.
 2 ocuparse *vr*: **— con, — de, — en** to concern oneself with; to pay attention to; to busy oneself with; to take care of, look after; **los críticos no se ocuparon del libro** the critics paid no attention to the book, the critics did not take note of the book; **me ocuparé de ello mañana** I will deal with it tomorrow; I will look into it tomorrow; **en esta sección el autor se ocupa de los peces** in this section the author deals with fish; **conviene — de lo suyo** it's best to mind one's own business.
ocurrencia *nf* **(a)** occurrence; incident, event.
 (b) idea, bright idea; **me dio la — de + infin** it occurred to me to + *infin*, I had the idea of + *ger*; **¡qué —!** what a bright idea!
 (c) witty remark, witticism.
ocurrente *adj* witty; bright, clever.
ocurrido *adj* **(a) lo** — what has happened. **(b)** (*Ec, Per*) witty.
ocurrir [3a] **1** *vi* to happen, occur; **¿qué ocurre?** what's going on?; **por lo que pudiera** — because of what might happen.
 2 ocurrirse *vr*: **se le ocurre + infin** it occurs to him to + *infin*; **si se le ocurre huir** if he takes it into his head to escape; **se me ocurre que . . .** it occurs to me that . . .; **nunca se me había ocurrido** it had never crossed my mind.
ochar [1a] **1** *vt* **(a)** (*Arg, Chi*) *dog* to urge on, provoke to attack. **(b)** (*Chi*) to spy on. **2** *vi* (*Arg*) to bark.
ochavado *adj* eight-sided, octagonal.
ochavero *nm* miser, skinflint.
ochenta *adj* eighty; eightieth.
ochentón 1 *adj* eighty-year-old, eightyish. **2** *nm*, **ochentona** *nf* person of about eighty.
ocho 1 *adj* eight; (*date*) eighth; **las** — eight o'clock. **2** *nm* eight.
ochocientos *adj* eight hundred.
oda *nf* ode.
odalisca *nf* odalisque.
odiar [1b] *vt* **(a)** to hate. **(b)** (*Chi*) to irk, annoy.
odio *nm* **(a)** hatred; ill will; dislike; **— de clases** class hatred; **— de sangre** feud, vendetta; **almacenar** — to store up hatred; **tener — a** to hate.
 (b) (*Chi*) annoyance, bother.
odiosear [1a] *vt* (*Chi, Per*) to weary, annoy.

odiosidad *nf* **(a)** odiousness, hatefulness; nastiness.
 (b) (*Arg, Chi, Per, SD*) irksomeness, annoyance.
odioso *adj* **(a)** odious, hateful, detestable; nasty, unpleasant; **hacerse — a uno** to incur someone's dislike.
 (b) (*Arg, Chi, Per*) irksome, annoying.
Odisea *f* Odyssey; **o—** odyssey.
Odiseo *m* Odysseus.
odómetro *nm* odometer.
odontología *nf* dentistry, dental surgery, odontology.
odontólogo *nm* dentist, dental surgeon, odontologist.
odorífero *adj* sweet-smelling, odoriferous.
odorífico *adj* (*pej*) smelly.
odre *nm* **(a)** wineskin. **(b)** (*fam*) toper, old soak (*fam*).
oeste 1 *adj part* west, western; *direction* westerly; *wind* west, westerly.
 2 *nm* **(a)** west; **en la parte del** — in the western part; **al — de Bilbao** to the west of Bilbao, on the west of Bilbao; **eso cae más hacia el** — that lies further (to the) west.
 (b) west wind.
Ofelia *f* Ophelia.
ofender [2a] **1** *vt* **(a)** to offend, slight, insult; **to wrong; por temor a —le** for fear of offending him.
 (b) *sense* to offend, be offensive to; **— a la vista** to offend one's sight.
 2 ofenderse *vr* to take offence (*de, por* at).
ofendido *adj* offended; **darse por** — to take offence.
ofensa *nf* offence; slight; wrong.
ofensiva *nf* offensive; **— de paz** peace offensive; **tomar la** — to take the offensive.
ofensivo *adj* **(a)** (*Mil*) offensive. **(b)** offensive; rude, insulting; nasty, disgusting.
ofensor 1 *adj* offending. **2** *nm*, **ofensora** *nf* offender.
oferta *nf* **(a)** offer; proposal, proposition.
 (b) (*Comm*) offer; tender; bid; **— y demanda** supply and demand; **la — es superior a la demanda** the supply exceeds the demand; **estar en** — to be on offer.
 (c) gift, present.
ofertar [1a] *vt* **(a)** (*Chi, Guat, Mex, RPl*) to offer. **(b)** (*Comm*) to tender.
ofertorio *nm* offertory.
off [of] *nm*: **voz en** — (*Cine etc: angl, gall*) voice off; **hay una discusión en** — there is an argument offstage, there is an argument spoken by unseen actors.
office ['ofis] *nm* (*gall*) pantry; scullery.
offset [of'set] *nm* (*Typ: angl*) offset.
offside [or'sai] *interj* (*Sport: angl*) offside!
oficial 1 *adj* official.
 2 *nm* official, officer; (*Mil*) officer; (*Tech*) skilled workman; craftsman; journeyman; (*in office*) clerk; **primer** — (*Naut*) mate; **— del día** orderly officer; **— de enlace** liaison officer; **— de guardia** (*Naut*) officer of the watch; **— mayor** chief clerk; **— médico** medical officer; **— pagador** paymaster.
oficiala *nf* skilled woman worker; clerk.
oficialada *nf* (*Mex, RPl*) = **oficialidad**.
oficialidad *nf* (*Mil*) officers (*collectively*).
oficializar [1f] *vt* (*CAm*) to make official, give official status to.
oficialmente *adv* officially.
oficiante *nm* (*Eccl*) officiant.
oficiar [1b] **1** *vt* to inform officially. **2** *vi* **(a)** (*Eccl*) to officiate. **(b)** **— de** to officiate as, act as.
oficina *nf* office; (*Mil*) orderly room; (*Pharm*) laboratory; (*Tech*) workshop; (*Chi*) nitrate works; **horas de** — business hours, office hours; **— de colocación** labour exchange, employment agency; **— de información** information bureau; **— meteorológica** weather bureau; **— de objetos perdidos** lost-property office, lost-and-found department (*US*).
oficinesco *adj* office (*attr*); clerical, white-collar (*attr*); (*pej*) bureaucratic.
oficinista *nmf* office worker, clerk; white-collar worker.
oficio *nm* **(a)** job, profession, occupation; (*Tech*) craft, trade; **es del** — he's an old hand; **sabe su** — he knows his job; **aprender un** — to learn a trade; **mi — es enseñar** my job is to teach; my profession is teaching.
 (b) job, role, post; office; (*Mech etc*) function; **los deberes del** — the duties of the post; **el — de esta pieza es de . . .** the function (*or* job) of this part is to . . .
 (c) buenos —s good offices; **ofrecer sus buenos —s** to offer one's good offices.
 (d) Santo O— (*Hist*) Holy Office, Inquisition.
 (e) official letter.
 (f) (*Eccl*) service; mass; **— de difuntos** office for

the dead, funeral service; — **divino** divine service; canonical hours.
(**g**) (*Archit*) scullery.
(**h**) de —: **miembro de** — ex officio member; **4 matones de** — 4 professional thugs, 4 hired toughs (*fam*); **fue enterrado de** — he was buried at the State's expense; **le informaremos de** — we will inform you officially.

oficiosamente *adv* (**a**) semiofficially; informally. (**b**) helpfully. (**c**) (*pej*) officiously.

oficiosidad *nf* (**a**) helpfulness. (**b**) (*pej*) officiousness, meddlesomeness.

oficioso *adj* (**a**) semiofficial; unofficial, informal; **de fuente oficiosa** from a semiofficial source.
(**b**) kind, helpful, obliging.
(**c**) (*pej*) officious, meddlesome, interfering.
(**d**) *see* **mentira**.

ofrecer [2d] **1** *vt* (*in most senses, also Comm*) to offer; to present; *thanks* to give, offer; *respects* to pay; *welcome* to extend; — **a uno hacer algo** to offer to do something for someone; **me ha ofrecido no fumar más** she has promised me that she won't smoke any more.
2 ofrecerse *vr* (**a**) to offer oneself, volunteer; — **a** + *infin* to offer to + *infin*, volunteer to + *infin*; **me ofrezco de guía** I offer myself as a guide.
(**b**) (*of object, view etc*) to offer itself, present itself.
(**c**) to occur; **¿qué se ofrece?** what's going on?, what's happening?; **se me ofrece una duda** a doubt occurs to me.
(**d**) **¿se le ofrece algo?** do you want anything?; is there anything I can get you?; **no se me ofrece nada por ahora** I don't want anything for the moment.

ofrecimiento *nm* offer, offering; — **de paz** peace offer.

ofrenda *nf* offering, gift; (*Eccl*) offering; (*fig*) tribute.

ofrendar [1a] *vt* to give, contribute.

oftalmía *nf* ophthalmia.

oftálmico *adj* ophthalmic.

oftalmología *nf* ophthalmology.

oftalmólogo *nm* ophthalmologist.

ofuscación *nf*, **ofuscamiento** *nm* (*fig*) dazzled state; blindness; bewilderment, confusion, mystification.

ofuscar [1g] *vt* (**a**) to dazzle.
(**b**) (*fig*) to dazzle; to bewilder, confuse, mystify.
(**c**) (*fig*) to blind; **estar ofuscado por la cólera** to be blinded by anger.

ogro *nm* ogre.

oh *interj* oh!

ohmio *nm* ohm.

oíble *adj* audible.

oída *nf* hearing; **de —s** by hearsay.

oído *nm* (**a**) (sense of) hearing; **duro de** — hard of hearing.
(**b**) (*Anat*) ear; — **interno** inner ear; — **a la caja!**, ¡— **al parche!** pay attention!; **aguzar los —s** to prick up one's ears; **dar —s a** to listen to, give ear to; **apenas pude dar crédito a mis —s** I could scarcely believe my ears; **decir algo al** — **de uno** to whisper something to someone, whisper something in someone's ear; **entra por un** — **y sale por otro** it goes in one ear and out (of) the other; **hacer —s sordos a** to turn a deaf ear to; **es una canción que se pega al** — it's a catchy song; **prestar** —(s) **a** to give ear to; **ser todo —s** to be all ears; **le estarán zumbando los —s** his ears must be burning.
(**c**) (*Mus*) ear; **de** — by ear; **duro de** — tone-deaf; **tener (buen)** — to have a good ear.

oidor *nm* (*Hist*) judge.

oigo *etc see* **oír**.

oír [3q] *vti* (**a**) to hear; to listen (to); *confession* to hear; *mass* to go to, attend, hear; *advice* to hear, pay attention to, heed; — **decir que** . . . to hear about . . ., hear of . . .; — **hablar de** to hear about, hear of; — **de** (*SAm: angl*) to hear from; **le oí abrir la puerta** I heard him open (*or* opening) the door; **como lo oyes, lo que oyes** it really is so, just like I'm telling you; **lo oyó como quien oye llover** she paid no attention, she turned a deaf ear to it.
(**b**) (*as interj etc*) ¡**oye!**, ¡**oiga!** listen!, listen to this!; (*calling attention*) hi!, hey!; I say!; (*objecting*) now look here!; (*surprise*) I say!, say! (*US*) ¡**oiga!** (*Tel*) hullo!
(**c**) *entreaty* to hear, heed, answer; **Dios oyó mi ruego** God answered my prayer.
(**d**) (*Law*) case to hear.

ojada *nf* (*Col*) skylight.

ojal *nm* buttonhole.

ojalá 1 *interj* (*used alone*) if only it were so!, if only it would! (*etc*); no such luck!, some hope!; "**mañana**

puede que haga sol" . . . "**¡—!**" "it may be fine tomorrow" . . . "I hope it will be!" (*or pessimistically*, "some hope!").
2 *conj* (*also* — **que**) (**a**) I wish . . .!, if only . . .!, (*rhetorically*) would that . . .!; ¡— **venga pronto!** I hope he comes soon!, I wish he'd come!; ¡— **pudiera!** I wish I could!, if only I could!
(**b**) (*SAm*) even though; **no lo haré**, — **me maten** I won't do it even if they kill me.

ojazos *nmpl* big eyes, wide eyes; **echar los** — **a uno** to make eyes at someone.

ojeada *nf* glance; **echar una** — **a** to glance at, take a quick look at.

ojeador *nm* (*Hunting*) beater.

ojear[1] [1a] *vt* to stare at; **voy a** — **cómo va el trabajo** I'm going to see how the work is getting on.

ojear[2] [1a] *vt* (**a**) to drive away, drive off, shoo. (**b**) (*Hunting*) game to beat, put up, drive.

ojeo *nm* (*Hunting*) beating.

ojera *nf* (**a**) ring under the eye; **tener —s** to have rings (*or* circles) under the eyes. (**b**) eyebath.

ojeriza *nf* spite, ill will; **tener** — **a** to have a grudge against, have it in for.

ojeroso *adj* with rings under the eyes; tired, haggard; seedy.

ojete *nm* (**a**) (*Sew*) eyelet. (**b**) (*SAm: tabu*) arse (*tabu*).

ojillos *nmpl* bright eyes; lovely eyes; roguish eyes; ¡**tiene unos —!** you should see what eyes she's got!

ojinegro *adj* black-eyed.

ojituerto *adj* cross-eyed.

ojiva *nf* ogive, pointed arch.

ojival *adj* ogival, pointed.

ojo *nm* (**a**) eye; **—s de almendra** almond eyes; — **de cristal** glass eye; — **a la funerala**, — **amoratado** black eye; **—s saltones** bulging eyes, goggle eyes; **—s que hablan** expressive eyes; **a los —s de** in the eyes of; **a** — (**de buen cubero**) by guesswork; roughly, at a rough guess; **a —s cerrados** blindly; on trust; **dependiente a —s cerrados** en blindly dependent on; **a** — **vistas** publicly, openly; *grow etc* before one's (very) eyes; *happen etc* right under one's nose; **con buenos —s** kindly, favourably; **delante de mis propios —s** before my very eyes; **estar hasta los —s de trabajo** to be up to one's eyes in work; — **por** — an eye for an eye; tit for tat; **abrir el** — to keep one's eyes open; **abrir los —s a uno** to open someone's eyes to something; **en un abrir y cerrar de —s** in the twinkling of an eye; **avivar el** — to be on the alert; **cerrar los —s a algo** (*fig*) to shut one's eyes to something; **clavar los —s en** to fix one's eyes on, stare at; **costar un** — **de la cara** to cost a small fortune; **dar en los —s** to be conspicuous; to be self-evident; **echar el** — **a** to have one's eye on, covet; **guiñar el** — to wink (*a at*); to turn a blind eye (*a on*); **hacer del** — to wink; **se le fueron los —s tras la chica** he couldn't keep his eyes off the girl; **pasar los —s por algo** to look something over; **no pegué los —s en toda la noche** I didn't get a wink of sleep all night; **en mi vida le puse los —s encima** I never set eyes on him in my life; **recrear los —s en** to feast one's eyes on; **ser todo —s** to be all eyes; ¡**no es nada lo del —!** there's a lot more to it than that!; **tener a uno entre —s** to loathe someone; **tener los —s puestos en** (*fig*) to have set one's heart on; **torcer los —s** to squint; **—s que no ven, corazón que no siente** out of sight, out of mind; *see* **alerta, avizor, besugo, blanco** *etc*.
(**b**) (*of needle etc*) eye; (*in cheese etc*) hole; — **de la llave** keyhole.
(**c**) (*of bridge*) span; space underneath the span; **un puente de 4** — a bridge with 4 arches (*or* spans).
(**d**) (*SAm*) — **de agua** spring.
(**e**) — **del culo** (*tabu*) arse (*tabu*).
(**f**) (*Archit*) skylight; — **de buey** (*Naut*) porthole; (*Mex*) round church window.
(**g**) — **de gallo**, — **de pollo** (*SAm*) corn, callus; — **de pescado** (*Ant*) callus (on the hand).
(**h**) (*fig*) perspicacity; judgement; sharpness; **tener** — **para conocer algo** to have the perspicacity to recognize something.
(**i**) (*fig*) care, caution; ¡—! careful!, look out!; (*as marginal sign*) N.B.; **hay que tener mucho** — **con los carteristas** one must be very careful of pickpockets, one must beware of pickpockets.

ojón *adj* (*SAm*) big-eyed, having big eyes.

ojota *nf* (**a**) (*SAm*) sandal. (**b**) (*Arg, Bol, Chi*) tanned llama leather.

ojotes *nmpl* (*CAm, Col*) bulging eyes, goggle eyes.

ojuelos *nmpl* = **ojillos**.

ola *nf* wave (*also fig*); — **de calor** heat wave; — **de frío** cold wave; — **de marea**, — **sísmica** tidal wave; **la nueva** — the latest fashion, the current trend, the most modern style; (*persons*) the new generation; (*Cine*) the new wave; **batir las —s** (*fig*) to ply the seas.

olé *interj* bravo!; well done!, jolly good! (*fam*).

oleada *nf* (a) (*Naut*) big wave; surge, swell.
(b) (*fig*) wave; surge; **una gran — de gente** a great surge of people; **la primera — del ataque** the first wave of the attack; **esta última — de huelgas** this latest wave of strikes.
(c) (*Mex*) run of luck.

oleaginoso *adj* oily, oleaginous.

oleaje *nm* swell, surge; surf.

oleo . . . oleo . . .

óleo *nm* (a) (*Eccl*) oil; (*Art*) oil; **santo —** holy oil.
(b) (*Art*) oil painting; **pintar al —** to paint in oils.
(c) (*SAm*) baptism.

oleoducto *nm* (oil) pipeline.

oleoso *adj* oily.

oler [2i] **1** *vt* (a) to smell.
(b) (*fig*) to pry into, poke one's nose into.
(c) (*fig*) to smell out, sniff out, uncover.
2 *vi* to smell (*a* of, like; *also* fig); **huele mal it** smells bad.

oletear [1a] *vt* (*Per*) to pry into.

oletón *adj* (*Per*) prying.

olfa *nmf* (*RPl*) creep (*sl*), bootlicker (*fam*).

olfatear [1a] *vt* (a) to smell, sniff (*also* fig); (*of dog*) to smell out, scent out, nose out (*also* fig).
(b) (*fig*) to pry into, poke one's nose into.

olfativo *adj* olfactory.

olfato *nm* (a) (sense of) smell. (b) (*fig*) good nose; instinct, intuition.

olfatorio *adj* olfactory.

oligarquía *nf* oligarchy.

oligárquico *adj* oligarchic(al).

olimpíada *nf* Olympiad; **las O—s** the Olympics.

olímpico *adj* Olympian; *games* Olympic.

Olimpo *m* Olympus.

oliscar [1g] **1** *vt* (a) to smell, sniff (gently). (b) (*fig*) to investigate, look into. **2** *vi* to smell (bad).

olisco *adj* (*Arg, Chi, Mex*), **oliscón** *adj* (*Per*), **oliscoso** *adj* (*Cu, Ec*) smelly.

olisquear [1a] =**oliscar**.

oliva *nf* (a) olive; olive tree. (b) (*Orn*) =**lechuza**.

oliváceo *adj* olive, olive-green.

olivar *nm* olive grove.

Oliverio *m* Oliver.

olivo *nm* olive tree; **tomar el —** (*fam*) to beat it (*fam*).

olmeda *nf*, **olmedo** *nm* elm grove.

olmo *nm* elm, elm tree.

ológrafo 1 *adj* holograph. **2** *nm* holograph.

olor *nm* (a) smell; odour, scent; **buen —** nice smell, pleasant smell; **mal —** bad smell, nasty smell, stink; **tiene mal —** it smells bad; **— de santidad** odour of sanctity.
(b) (*fig*) smell; suspicion; **acudir al — del dinero** to come to where the money is, get wind of the money.
(c) (*Chi, Mex*) spice.

oloroso *adj* sweet-smelling, scented, fragrant.

olote *nm* (*CAm, Mex*) (a) corncob. (b) (*fig*) **un — a** nobody, a nonentity.

olotear [1a] *vi* (*CAm, Mex*) to gather maize, gather corn (*US*).

olotera *nf* (*CAm, Mex*) (a) head of corncobs. (b) maize thresher.

olvidadizo *adj* forgetful; absent-minded.

olvidado *adj* (a) forgotten.
(b) *person* forgetful; **— de** forgetful of, oblivious to.
(c) (*fig*) ungrateful.
(d) (*Arg, Col, Par*) =**olvidadizo**.

olvidar [1a] **1** *vt* to forget; to leave behind; to leave out, omit; **— hacer algo** to forget to do something.
2 olvidarse *vr* (a) **se me olvidó** I forgot; **se me olvidó el paraguas** I forgot my umbrella; **se me olvida la fecha** I forget the date, the date escapes me, I can't think of the date; **— de hacer algo** to forget to do something, neglect to do something.
(b) (*fig*) to forget oneself.

olvido *nm* (a) (*state*) oblivion; **caer en el —** to fall into oblivion; **echar al —** to forget; **enterrar** (*or* **hundir**) **en el —** to forget (deliberately), cast into oblivion.
(b) (*state*) forgetfulness; (*act*) omission, oversight; slip; **ha sido por —** it was an oversight.

olvidón *adj* (*Ec*) forgetful.

olla *nf* (a) (*vessel*) pot, pan; kettle; **— eléctrica** electric kettle; **— exprés . — de** (*or* **a**) **presión** pressure cooker.
(b) (*Cook*) stew; **— podrida** Spanish stew, (*fig*) hotchpotch.
(c) (*of river*) pool; eddy, whirlpool.
(d) (*Mountaineering*) chimney.

ollero *nm* maker of (*or* dealer in) pots and pans.

ombligo *nm* navel; **encogérsele el — a uno** to get the wind up, get cold feet; **meter a uno el — para dentro** to put the wind up someone.

ombliguera *nf* (*Per*) striptease artiste.

omega *nf* omega.

ominoso *adj* (a) awful, dreadful. (b) ominous.

omisión *nf* (a) omission; oversight; **su — de +** *infin* his failure to + *infin*, the fact that he omits to + *infin*. (b) (*quality*) neglect.

omiso *adj* see **caso**.

omitir [3a] *vt* (a) to leave out, miss out, omit. (b) — **hacer algo** to omit to do something, fail to do something.

ómnibus 1 *adj* see **tren**. **2** *nm* (*Hist*) omnibus.

omnímodo *adj* all-embracing.

omnipotencia *nf* omnipotence.

omnipotente *adv* omnipotent, all-powerful.

omnipresencia *nf* omnipresence.

omnipresente *adj* omnipresent.

omnisapiente *adj* omniscient, all-knowing.

omnisciencia *nf* omniscience.

omnisciente *adj*, **omniscio** *adj* omniscient, all-knowing.

omnívoro *adj* omnivorous.

omóplato *nm* shoulder blade.

—ón, —ona *n and adj suffix* (a) (*augmentative*) **librón** big book, massive tome; **fortunón** vast fortune, pile (*fam*); **barrigón** fat, potbellied; see **gritón, llorón** etc.
(b) (*pej*) **hombrón** hulking great brute; **caserón** large (ramshackle) house, barracks (of a place); see **solterona, valentón** etc.
(c) (*of age*) see **sesentón** etc.
(d) (*of blow*) see **empujón**.
(e) (*of habit*) see **mirón, tragón** etc.

onanismo *nm* onanism.

once 1 *adj* eleven; (*date*) eleventh; **las —** eleven o'clock; **las —** (*fam*) elevenses (*fam*), mid-morning snack, (*Col, Chi, Ven*) tea, afternoon snack.
2 *nm* eleven.

oncear [1a] *vi* (*Col, Ven*) to have an afternoon snack.

onceno *adj* eleventh.

onda *nf* (in most senses) wave; (*Sew*) scallop; **— corta** short wave; **de — corta** shortwave (*attr*); **— de choque, — sísmica** shock wave; **— extracorta** ultra-short wave; **— larga** long wave; **— luminosa** light wave; **— media** medium wave; **— sonora** sound wave; **tratamiento de — ultravioleta** ultra-violet treatment.

ondeante *adj* =**ondulante**.

ondear [1a] **1** *vt* *flag* to wave; *hair* to wave; (*Sew*) to pink, scallop.
2 *vi* to wave (up and down), undulate; to be wavy; to fluctuate; (*of water*) to ripple; (*of flag etc*) to fly, flutter, wave; (*of hair*) to flow, fall, (*in wind*) to stream; **la bandera ondea en lo alto del edificio** the flag flies (*or* flutters) from the top of the building; **la bandera ondea a media asta** the flag is flying at half mast.
3 ondearse *vr* to swing, sway.

ondímetro *nm* wavemeter.

ondulación *nf* undulation; wavy motion; (*in water*) wave, ripple; (*in hair*) wave; **—es** (*of surface*) undulations, ups and downs; unevenness; **— permanente** permanent wave.

ondulado 1 *adj* *hair etc* wavy; *surface* undulating, uneven; *road* uneven, rough; *country* undulating, rolling; *iron, paper etc* corrugated.
2 *nm* (*in hair*) wave.

ondulante *adj* (a) *movement* undulating; from side to side, (gently) swaying; *sound* rising and falling.
(b) =**ondulado**.

ondular [1a] **1** *vt* *hair* to wave; **hacerse — el pelo** to have one's hair waved. **2** *vi and* **ondularse** *vr* to undulate; to sway; to wriggle.

ondulatorio *adj* undulatory, wavy.

oneroso *adj* onerous, burdensome.

ónice *nm* onyx.

onomástica *nf* personal names, proper names; study of personal names.

onomástico 1 *adj* onomastic, name (*attr*), of names; **lista onomástica** list of names; **fiesta onomástica =**
2 *nm* one's saint's day, one's name day (*celebrated in Spain etc as equivalent to one's birthday*).

onomatopeya *nf* onomatopoeia.

onomatopéyico *adj* onomatopoeic.

ontología *nf* ontology.

ontológico *adj* ontological.

onubense 1 *adj* of Huelva. **2** *nmf* native (*or* inhabitant*) of Huelva; **los —s** the people of Huelva.

onza *nf* ounce.

oolítico *adj* oolitic.

oolito *nm* oolite.

opa[1] *adj* (*Bol, Per, RPl*) (a) deaf and dumb. (b) (*fig*) stupid.

opa[2] *interj* (*SAm*)=hola; (*Arg*) stop it!

opacar [1g] **1** *vt* (*SAm*) to make opaque; to darken; to mist up; to dull, tarnish.
  2 opacarse *vr* (a) (*SAm*) to become opaque; to darken; to mist up; to lose its shine, become tarnished.
  (b) (*Col, Guat*) to cloud over.

opacidad *nf* (a) opacity, opaqueness. (b) (*fig*) dullness, lifelessness. (c) gloominess.

opaco *adj* (a) opaque; dark; **una pantalla opaca a los rayos X** a screen which does not let X-rays through, a screen resistant to X-rays.
  (b) (*fig*) dull, lustreless, lifeless.
  (c) (*fig*) gloomy, sad.

opalescencia *nf* opalescence.

opalescente *adj* opalescent.

ópalo *nm* opal.

opción *nf* (a) option, choice; **no hay** — there is no choice, you (*etc*) do not have the option.
  (b) right; **tiene** — **a viajar gratis** he has the right to travel free.
  (c) (*Comm*) option (*a* on); **con** — **a 8 más, con** — **para 8 más** with an option on 8 more; **este dispositivo es de** — this gadget is optional; **suscribir una** — **para la compra de** to take out an option on.

opcional *adj* optional.

opear [1a] *vi* (*Bol, Per, RPl*) to act the fool.

ópera *nf* opera; — **bufa** comic opera; — **semiseria** light opera; — **seria** grand opera.

operación *nf* (a) (*Med*) operation; — **cesárea** Caesarean operation; — **quirúrgica** surgical operation; — **de estómago** stomach operation, operation on the stomach.
  (b) (*Mil etc*) operation; — **de ablandamiento** softening-up operation; —**es conjuntas** joint operations; — **de limpieza** mopping-up operation; —**es de rescate**, —**es de salvamento** rescue operations.
  (c) (*Comm*) transaction, deal; operation; — **es de bolsa** stock-exchange transaction; — **mercantil** business deal.
  (d) (*Math*) operation.
  (e) (*SAm: Min*) operation; working, exploitation; (*Comm*) management.

operacional *adj* operational.

operador *nm* operator; (*Med*) surgeon; (*Cine*) cameraman, film cameraman; (*in cinema*) projectionist, operator; — **del telégrafo** (*SAm*) telegraph operator.

operante *adj* (a) operating. (b) powerful, influential; active; **los medios más** —**s del país** the most influential circles in the country.

operar [1a] **1** *vt* **a** *cure, change etc* to produce, bring about, effect; *miracle* to work.
  (b) (*Med*) to operate on; — **a uno de apendicitis** to operate on someone for appendicitis.
  (c) (*SAm*) *machine* to use, operate; *business* to manage; (*Min*) to work, exploit.
  2 *vi* (a) to operate (*also Math*).
  (b) (*Comm*) to operate; to deal, do business; **hoy no se ha operado en la bolsa** there has been no dealing on the stock exchange today.
  3 operarse *vr* (a) to occur, come about; **se han operado grandes cambios** great changes have come about, there have been great changes.
  (b) (*Med*) to have an operation (*de* for).

operario *nm*, **operaria** *nf* operative; worker, hand; — **de máquina** machinist.

operativo *adj* operative.

opereta *nf* operetta, light opera.

opería *nf* (*Bol, Per, RPl*) stupidity.

operista *nmf* opera singer.

operístico *adj* operatic, opera (*attr*).

opiata *nf* opiate.

opimo *adj* plentiful, abundant, rich.

opinable *adj* debatable, open to a variety of opinions.

opinar [1a] *vi* (a) to think; — **que . . .** to think that . . ., be of the opinion that . . .
  (b) — **bien de** to think well of, have a good opinion of.
  (c) to give one's opinion; **fueron opinando uno tras otro** they gave their opinions in turn; **hubo un 7 por 100 que no quisieron** —, **no opinaron el 7 por 100** (*in poll*) there were 7% "don't knows".

opinión *nf* opinion, view; — **pública** public opinion; **en mi** — in my opinion; **abundar en la** — **de uno** to share someone's opinion (*or* view) wholeheartedly; **cambiar** (*or* **mudar**) **de** — to change one's mind;

formarse una — to form an opinion; **ser de** — **que . . .** to be of the opinion that . . ., take the view that . . .

opio *nm* opium; **dar el** — **a uno** (*fam*) to fill someone with wonder, leave someone open-mouthed; **ella le dio el** — she knocked him all of a heap (*fam*).

opíparo *adj* *meal* sumptuous.

oponente *nmf* (*angl*) opponent; opposite number; **tener de** — **a uno** to have someone as one's opposite number, (*Theat*) play opposite someone.

oponer [2r] **1** *vt* (a) — **A a B** to pit A against B, set up A in opposition to B; to play off A against B; — **dos opiniones** to contrast two views.
  (b) *objection* to raise (*a* to); *resistance* to put up, offer (*a* to); *weapon* to use (*a* against); — **la razón a la pasión** to use reason against passion, rely on reason and not passion; — **un dique al mar** to set up defences against the sea.
  2 oponerse *vr* to be opposed; (*of 2 persons*) to oppose each other, be in opposition; **yo no me opongo** I don't oppose it, I don't object; — **a** to oppose, be opposed to, be against; to object to; to defy, resist; **se opone a hacerlo** he resists the idea of doing it, he is unwilling to do it, he objects to doing it; **se opone rotundamente a ello** he is flatly opposed to it.

oportunamente *adv* opportunely, in a timely way; appropriately, suitably; conveniently; expediently.

oportunidad *nf* (a) (*quality*) opportuneness; timeliness; appropriateness; expediency.
  (b) (*una* —) opportunity, chance; **igualdad de** —**es** equality of opportunity; **en la primera** — at the first opportunity; **tener la** — **de** + *infin* to have the chance of + *ger*, have a chance to + *infin*.

oportunismo *nm* opportunism.

oportunista 1 *adj* opportunist. **2** *nmf* opportunist.

oportuno *adj* (a) opportune, timely; appropriate, suitable; convenient; expedient; **una respuesta oportuna** a suitable reply; **en el momento** — at the right moment; at a convenient time; **las medidas que se estimen oportunas** the measures which may be considered appropriate; **sería** — **hacerlo en seguida** it would be best to do it at once.
  (b) *person* witty.

oposición *nf* (a) opposition.
  (b) —**es** public competition (for a post), public entrance (*or* promotion) examination; **hacer** —**es a**, **presentarse a unas** —**es a** to be a candidate for, go in for; **hacer** —**es para una cátedra** (*etc*) to try to win a chair (*etc*) by public competitive examination; **ganar unas** —**es** to be successful in a public competition.

opositar [1a] *vi* to go in for a public competition (for a post), sit for a public entrance (*or* promotion) examination; — **a una cátedra** (*etc*) to try to win a chair (*etc*) by public competitive examination.

opositor *nm*, **opositora** *nf* competitor, candidate (*a* for).

opresión *nf* (a) oppression; oppressiveness. (b) (*Med*) difficulty in breathing, tightness of the chest; **sentir** — to find it difficult to breathe.

opresivo *adj* oppressive.

opresor *nm*, **opresora** *nf* oppressor.

oprimir [3a] *vt* (a) to squeeze, press, exert pressure on; *handle etc* to grasp, clutch; *button etc* to press; *gas* to compress; (*of clothing*) to be too tight for, constrict; to strangle.
  (b) (*fig*) to oppress; to burden, weigh down, bear down on; to crush.

oprobio *nm* shame, ignominy, opprobrium.

oprobioso *adj* shameful, ignominious, opprobrious.

optar [1a] *vi* (a) to choose, decide; — **entre** to choose between; — **por** to choose, decide on, opt for; — **por** + *infin* to choose to + *infin*.
  (b) **poder** — **a** to (have the right to) apply for, go in for; **ésos no pueden** — **a las becas** those do not have the right to apply for scholarships.

optativo 1 *adj* (a) optional. (b) (*Gram*) optative. **2** *nm* (*Gram*) optative.

óptica *nf* optics.

óptico 1 *adj* optic(al). **2** *nm* optician.

optimismo *nm* optimism.

optimista 1 *adj* optimistic, hopeful. **2** *nmf* optimist.

óptimo *adj* very good, very best; *conditions etc* optimum.

optometrista *nm* optometrist.

opuesto *adj* (a) *angle, side etc* opposite; **en dirección opuesta** in the opposite direction. (b) *opinion etc* contrary, opposing, opposite.

opugnar [1a] *vt* to attack.

opulencia *nf* opulence; luxury; affluence; **vivir en la** — to live in luxury, live in affluence.

opulento *adj* opulent, rich; luxurious; affluent.
opúsculo *nm* booklet; short work, tract, brief treatise.
oquedad *nf* hollow, cavity; (*fig*) void; hollowness, emptiness.
oquedal *nm* wood of grown timber, plantation.
ora *adv* (*lit*): — A, — B now A, now B; sometimes A, at other times B.
oración *nf* (a) oration, speech; — **fúnebre** funeral oration; **pronunciar una** — to make a speech.
   (b) (*Eccl*) prayer; —**es por la paz** prayers for peace; **estar en** — to be at prayer.
   (c) (*SAm, freq*) pagan invocation, magic charm.
   (d) (*Gram*) sentence; clause; — **compuesta** complex sentence; — **subordinada** subordinate clause; **partes de la** — parts of speech.
oráculo *nm* oracle.
orador *nm*, **oradora** *nf* speaker, orator.
oral *adj* oral.
orangután *nm* orang-outang.
orante 1 *adj*: **actitud** — kneeling position, posture of prayer. **2** *nmf* worshipper.
orar [1a] *vi* (a) (*Eccl*) to pray (*a* to, *por* for). (b) to speak, make a speech.
orate *nmf* lunatic.
orático *adj* (*CAm*) crazy, lunatic.
oratoria *nf* oratory.
oratorio 1 *adj* oratorical. **2** *nm* (*Mus*) oratorio; (*Eccl*) oratory, chapel.
orbe *nm* (a) orb, sphere. (b) (*fig*) world; **en todo el** — throughout the world.
órbita *nf* orbit (*also fig*); **estar en** — to be in orbit; **entrar en** — **alrededor de la luna** to go into orbit round the moon.
orbital *adj* orbital.
orbitar [1a] *vt* to orbit.
orca *nf* grampus, killer whale.
Órcadas *fpl* Orkneys, Orkney Islands.
órdago: de — *adj* (*fam*) first-class, jolly good (*fam*), swell (*US*).
ordalías *nfpl* (*Hist*) ordeal, trial by ordeal.
orden 1 *nm* (a) order; arrangement; — **del día** agenda; **de primer** — first-rate, of the first order; **en** — in order; **en** — **a** with regard to; **en** — **de batalla** in battle order; **en** — **de marchar** in marching order; **fuera de** — out of order; out of turn; **por** (**su**) — in order; **por** — **de antigüedad** in order of seniority; **por** — **cronológico** in chronological order; **poner en** — to put in order, arrange (properly); to tidy up.
   (b) (*Law etc*) order; — **público** public order, law and order; **las fuerzas del** — the forces of law and order; **llamar al** — to call to order; **mantener el** — to keep order.
   (c) **una cifra del** — **de 600** a figure of the order of 600.
   (d) (*Archit*) order; — **dórico** Doric order.
   2 *nf* (a) order; (*Law*) order, warrant, writ; — **del día** (*Mil*) order of the day; **eso ahora está a la** — **del día** that is now the order of the day; **O**— **Real** Order in Council; **a la** — (*Comm*) to order; **a la** — **de Vd, a sus** —**es** at your service; **¡a las** —**es!** (*Mil*) yes sir?; **hasta nueva** — till further orders; **por** — **de** on the orders of, by order of; **¡es una** —**!** that's an order!; **dar una** — to give an order; **dar la** — **de** + *infin* to give the order to + *infin*.
   (b) (*Eccl*) order; —**es menores** minor orders; — **monástica** monastic order; — **religiosa** religious order; —**es sagradas** holy orders; **O**— **de San Benito** Benedictine Order.
   (c) (*Hist, Mil*) — **de caballería** order of knighthood; — **militar** military order; **O**— **del Imperio Británico** Order of the British Empire.
   (d) (*SAm: Comm: angl*) order.
ordenación *nf* (a) order; arrangement; (*act*) ordering, arranging. (b) (*Eccl*) ordination.
ordenada *nf* ordinate.
ordenadamente *adv* in an orderly way; tidily; methodically.
ordenado *adj* (a) orderly; tidy; well arranged. (b) *person* methodical; tidy. (c) (*Eccl*) in holy orders.
ordenador *nm* computer.
ordenancista *nm* disciplinarian, martinet.
ordenando *nm* (*Eccl*) ordinand.
ordenanza 1 *nf* ordinance, decree; —**s municipales** by-laws; **ser de** — to be the rule.
   2 *nm* (*Comm etc*) office boy, messenger; errand boy; (*Mil*) orderly, batman.
ordenar [1a] **1** *vt* (a) to arrange, put in order; to marshal; to draw up; — **sus asuntos** to put one's affairs in order; — **su vida** to arrange one's life.
   (b) to order; — **a uno hacer algo** to order someone to do something.
   (c) (*Eccl*) to ordain.
   2 ordenarse *vr* (*Eccl*) to take holy orders, be ordained (*de* as).
ordeña *nf* (*Chi, Mex*) milking.
ordeñadero *nm* milking pail.
ordeñadora *nf* milking machine.
ordeñar [1a] *vt* to milk.
ordeñe *nm* (*Cu*), **ordeño** *nm* milking.
ordinal 1 *adj* ordinal. **2** *nm* ordinal.
ordinariamente *adv* ordinarily, usually.
ordinariez *nf* (a) (*quality*) commonness, coarseness, vulgarity. (b) (*una* —) coarse remark (*or* joke *etc*), piece of vulgarity.
ordinario 1 *adj* (a) ordinary; usual; current; *expenses* daily; **de** — usually, ordinarily.
   (b) common, coarse, vulgar; *joke* coarse, crude; **son gente muy ordinaria** they're very common people.
   2 *nm* (a) daily household expenses.
   (b) carrier, delivery man.
orear 1 *vt* to air. **2 orearse** *vr* (a) to air. (b) (*person*) to get some fresh air, take a breather.
orégano *nm* marjoram.
oreja *nf* (a) (*Anat*) ear; **con las** —**s gachas** (*fig*) ashamed; embarrassed; **aguzar las** —**s** to prick up one's ears; **asomar** (*or* **descubrir, enseñar**) **la** — to give oneself away, reveal one's true nature; **calentar las** — **a uno** to box someone's ears; **estar hasta las** —**s** to be utterly fed up; **hacer** —**s de mercader** to turn a deaf ear.
   (b) (*of shoe etc*) tab; tag; (*of vessel*) lug, handle; (*Mech*) lug, flange; (*of chair*) wing; (*of book jacket*) flap.
   (c) (*SAm*) curiosity; eavesdropping; caution.
   (d) (*SAm*) secret police.
orejano 1 *adj* (a) (*SAm*) *animal* unbranded, ownerless.
   (b) (*SAm*) shy, easily scared; unsociable.
   (c) (*Ven*) cautious.
   2 *nm* (*Pan, SD*) peasant, countryman.
orejear [1a] *vi* (a) (*CAm, Chi, Mex, Per, PR*) to eavesdrop.
   (b) (*Ant, Bol, Chi*) to suspect, be distrustful.
   (c) (*RPl*) to uncover one's cards one by one.
orejera *nf* earflap.
orejero 1 *adj* (a) (*SAm*) suspicious; cautious. (b) (*Arg*) telltale. (c) (*Col*) malicious. **2** *nm* (*Arg*) boss's right-hand man.
orejeta *nf* (*Tech*) lug.
orejón 1 *adj* (a) (*SAm*) =**orejudo**.
   (b) (*CAm, Col, Mex*) rough, coarse.
   2 *nm* (a) pull on the ear, tug at one's ear.
   (b) strip of dried peach (*or* apricot).
   (c) (*Col*) goitre.
   (d) (*Col*) herdsman, plainsman.
   (e) (*Mex*) complaisant husband.
   (f) (*Per*) Inca nobleman.
orejonas *nfpl* (*Col, Ven*) big spurs.
orejudo *adj* big-eared, with big ears.
orensano 1 *adj* of Orense. **2** *nmf* native (*or* inhabitant) of Orense; **los** —**s** the people of Orense.
orfanato *nm*, **orfanatorio** *nm* (*SAm*) orphanage.
orfandad *nf* (a) orphanhood. (b) (*fig*) helplessness, destitution.
orfebre *nm* goldsmith, silversmith.
orfebrería *nf* gold work, silver work, craftsmanship in precious metals.
orfelinato *nm* (*gall*) orphanage.
Orfeo *m* Orpheus.
orfeón *nm* glee club, choral society.
organdí *nm* organdie.
orgánicamente *adv* organically.
orgánico *adj* organic.
organillero *nm* organ-grinder.
organillo *nm* barrel organ, hurdy-gurdy.
organismo *nm* (a) (*Bio*) organism.
   (b) (*Pol etc*) organization; body, institution; —**s de gobierno** organs of government, state bodies; — **de sondaje** public-opinion poll, institute of public opinion.
organista *nmf* organist.
organito *nm* (*RPl*) =**organillo**.
organización *nf* organization; **O**— **de Estados Americanos** Organization of American States; **O**— **de las Naciones Unidas** United Nations Organization.
organizador *nm*, **organizadora** *nf* organizer.
organizar [1f] *vt* to organize.
órgano *nm* (a) (*Anat, Mech etc*) organ. (b) (*Mus*) organ. (c) (*fig*) organ, means, medium.
orgasmo *nm* orgasm.
orgía *nf* orgy.

orgiástico adj orgiastic.

orgullo nm pride; (pej) pride, haughtiness.

orgullosamente adv proudly; haughtily.

orgulloso adj proud; haughty; **estar — de algo** to be proud of something; **estar — de + infin** to be proud to + infin.

orientación nf (a) orientation, position(ing); direction, course; (Archit) aspect, prospect; **la — actual del partido** the party's present course (or position); **una casa con — sur** a house with a southerly aspect, a house facing south.
    (b) (of person) guidance; training; **me ayudó en la — bibliográfica** he helped me with bibliographical information; **importa mucho en la — de los maestros** it is very important in the training of teachers; **lo hizo para mi —** he did it for my guidance.

oriental 1 adj oriental; eastern. 2 nmf oriental.

orientar [1a] 1 vt (a) to orientate, position; to point (hacia towards); to give a direction to, direct; (Naut) sail to trim; **la casa está orientada hacia el suroeste** the house faces (or looks) south-west; **hay que — las investigaciones en otro sentido** you will have to change the direction of your inquiries, you will have to pursue your researches in another direction.
    (b) person to guide, direct; to train; **me ha orientado en la materia** he has guided me through the subject, he has given me guidance about the subject.
    2 **orientarse** vr (a) (object etc) to point, face (hacia towards).
    (b) (person) to get one's bearings, orient oneself, get orientated; (fig) to get one's bearings; to establish oneself; to decide on a course of conduct (etc); **es difícil — en este terreno** it's hard to get one's bearings (or find one's way about) in this country.

oriente nm (a) east.
    (b) **el O—** the Orient, the East; **Cercano O—, Próximo O—** Near East; **Extremo O—, Lejano O—** Far East; **O— Medio** Middle East.
    (c) east wind.
    (d) masonic lodge.

orificación nf gold filling.

orificar [1g] vt tooth to fill with gold.

orificio nm orifice, hole; vent.

origen nm origin; source; **los —es de la guerra** the origins of the war, the causes of the war; **país de —** country of origin; **de — argentino** of Argentinian origin; **dar — a** to cause, give rise to.

original 1 adj (a) original.
    (b) (fig) original; novel; odd, eccentric, strange.
    (c) = originario (b).
    2 nm (a) original; **el — es mejor que la copia** the original is better than the copy.
    (b) (Typ) manuscript, original; copy; **tenemos exceso de —** we have too much copy.
    (c) (person) character, eccentric, original type.

originalidad nf (a) originality. (b) eccentricity, oddness.

originar [1a] 1 vt to originate; to start, cause, give rise to. 2 **originarse** vr to originate (de from, en in); to be started, be caused.

originariamente adv originally.

originario adj (a) original; **en su forma originaria** in its original form.
    (b) **ser — de** to originate from, be a native of; **una familia originaria de Sicilia** a family originating from Sicily.
    (c) país — country of origin, native country.
    (d) **una decisión originaria de disgustos** a decision which gave rise to trouble, a decision which was a source of trouble.

orilla nf (a) edge, border; (of river) bank; (of lake) side, shore; (of sea) shore; (of table etc) edge; (of cup, vessel) rim, lip; **del mar** seashore; **a —s de** on the banks of; **vive — de mi casa** (fam) he lives next door to me.
    (b) (Sew) edge, border, trimming; hem.
    (c) (Ant) de — trivial, of no account; worthless.

orillar [1a] vt (a) (Sew) to edge, trim (de with).
    (b) lake, wood etc to skirt, go round; to pass along the edge of.
    (c) subject to touch briefly on.
    (d) affairs to put in order, tidy up; to wind up.
    (e) obstacle to overcome; difficulty to avoid, get round.

orillero adj (SAm) = **arrabalero**.

orillo nm selvage.

orín nm rust; **tomarse de —** to get rusty.

orina nf urine.

orinacamas nm, pl **orinacamas** dandelion.

orinal nm chamberpot; **— de cama** bedpan.

orinar [1a] 1 vti to urinate. 2 **orinarse** vr to urinate (involuntarily); to wet oneself; **— en la cama** to wet one's bed.

orines nmpl urine.

oriundo 1 adj: **— de** native to; **ser — de** to be a native of, come from, hail from. 2 nm, **oriunda** nf native, inhabitant.

orla nf, **orladura** nf border, fringe, trimming.

orlar [1a] vt to border, edge, trim (de with).

ornamentación nf ornamentation, adornment.

ornamental adj ornamental.

ornamentar [1a] vt to adorn (de with).

ornamento nm (a) ornament, adornment; **—s** (Eccl) ornaments, vestments. (b) **—s** (fig) good qualities, moral qualities.

ornar [1a] vt to adorn (de with).

ornato nm adornment, decoration.

ornitología nf ornithology.

ornitológico adj ornithological.

ornitólogo nm ornithologist.

ornitorrinco nm platypus.

oro nm (a) gold; **— en barras** gold bars, bullion; **— batido** gold leaf; **— laminado** rolled gold; **— molido** ormulu; **— en polvo** gold dust; **de —** gold, golden; **como un —** like new; spick and span; **no es — todo lo que reluce** all that glitters is not gold; **es de —** (fig) he's a treasure; he's a marvel; he has a heart of gold; **tiene una voz de —** she has a marvellous voice; **apalear —** to be rolling in money; **guardar algo como — en paño** to treasure something; **tratar algo como — en paño** to treat something as if it were terribly fragile; **hacerse de —** to make a fortune; **poner a uno de — y azul** to lay into someone (verbally) (fam), heap insults on someone; **prometer el — y el moro** to promise the moon.
    (b) (Cards) **—s** hearts.

orondo adj (a) pot etc big, big-bellied, rounded; person fat, potbellied.
    (b) person smug, self-satisfied; pompous.
    (c) (SAm) calm, serene.

oropel nm tinsel; **de —** flashy, bright but tawdry; unsubstantial; **gastar mucho —** to put on a bold front; **tener mucho —** to be all show, (esp) make a pretence of being wealthy.

oropéndola nf golden oriole.

oroya nf (Bol, Per) basket of a rope bridge (for conveying people across ravines).

orozuz nm liquorice.

orquesta nf orchestra; **— de baile** dance band; **— de jazz** jazz band; **— sinfónica** symphony orchestra.

orquestación nf orchestration.

orquestal adj orchestral.

orquestar [1a] vt to orchestrate.

orquídea nf orchid, orchis.

ortiga nf nettle, stinging nettle.

ortodoncia nf orthodontics.

ortodoxia nf orthodoxy.

ortodoxo adj orthodox.

ortografía nf spelling; orthography.

ortográfico adj spelling (attr); orthographic(al); **reforma ortográfica** spelling reform.

ortopedia nf orthopaedics.

ortopédico adj orthopaedic.

ortopedista nmf orthopaedist.

oruga nf (a) (Ent, Tech) caterpillar; **tractor de —** caterpillar tractor. (b) (Bot) rocket.

orujo nm refuse of grapes (or olives) after pressing.

orza nf (Naut) luff, luffing.

orzar [1f] vi (Naut) to luff.

orzuelo nm stye.

os personal pron pl (a) (acc) you.
    (b) (dative) (to) you; **lo di** I gave it to you; **lo compré** I bought it from you; I bought it for you; **quitáis el abrigo** you take off your coats.
    (c) (reflexive) (to) yourselves; (reciprocal) (to) each other; **vosotros — laváis** you wash yourselves; **cuando — marchéis** when you leave.

osa nf she-bear; **O— Mayor** Ursa Major, Great Bear; **O— Menor** Ursa Minor, Little Bear; **¡anda la —!** what a carry-on! (fam).

osadamente adv daringly, boldly.

osadía nf daring, boldness.

osado adj daring, bold.

osamenta nf bones; skeleton.

osar [1a] vi to dare; **— hacer algo** to dare to do something.

osario nm ossuary, charnel house.

oscense 1 adj of Huesca. 2 nmf native (or inhabitant) of Huesca; **los —s** the people of Huesca.

oscilación nf (a) oscillation; swing, sway, to and fro movement; rocking; winking, blinking. (b) fluctuation. (c) hesitation, wavering.

oscilador 1 *adj* oscillating. **2** *nm* oscillator.

oscilante *adj* oscillating.

oscilar [1a] *vi* (**a**) to oscillate; to swing, sway, move to and fro; to rock; (*of light*) to wink, blink.

(**b**) (*fig*) to fluctuate (*entre* between); to range (*entre* between); **la distancia oscila entre los 100 y 500 m** the distance ranges between 100 and 500 m; **los precios oscilan mucho** prices are fluctuating a lot.

(**c**) (*person*) to hesitate; to waver (*entre* between); **oscila entre la alegría y el pesimismo** he passes from cheerfulness to pessimism.

oscilatorio *adj* oscillatory.

oscular [1a] *vt* (*lit*) to osculate, kiss.

ósculo *nm* (*lit*) osculation, kiss; — **de paz** kiss of peace.

oscuramente *adv* obscurely; in an obscure way.

oscurana *nf* (*Hond*) cloud of volcanic dust; (*Mex, Per*) darkness.

oscurantismo *nm* obscurantism.

oscurantista 1 *adj* obscurantist. **2** *nmf* obscurantist.

oscurear [1a] (*Mex*) = **oscurecer**.

oscurecer [2d] **1** *vt* (**a**) to obscure, darken; to dim; to black out.

(**b**) (*fig*) *issue* to confuse, cloud, fog; *rival* to overshadow, put in the shade; *fame* to dim, tarnish.

(**c**) (*Art*) to shade.

2 *vi* to grow dark, get dark.

oscuridad *nf* (**a**) darkness, obscurity; gloom, gloominess. (**b**) (*fig*) obscurity.

oscuro *adj* (**a**) dark; dim, gloomy, obscure; *outline* confused, indistinct; **a oscuras** in the dark (*also fig*), in darkness.

(**b**) *colour* dark, deep; **un hermoso azul** — a beautiful dark blue.

(**c**) (*Meteorol*) overcast, cloudy.

(**d**) (*fig*) obscure; confused; *future etc* uncertain; **de origen** — of obscure origin(s).

óseo *adj* bony, osseous.

osezno *nm* bear cub.

osificación *nf* ossification.

osificar [1g] **1** *vt* to ossify. **2 osificarse** *vr* to ossify, become ossified.

osito *nm*: — **de felpa** teddy bear.

osmosis *nf*, **ósmosis** *nf* osmosis.

osmótico *adj* osmotic.

oso *nm* (**a**) bear; — **blanco** polar bear; — **gris** grizzly bear; — **hormiguero** anteater; — **pardo** brown bear; — **de peluche** teddy bear; **ser un** — to be a prickly sort; **hacer el** — to play the fool; to play the sentimental lover.

(**b**) (*Cu*) braggart; bully.

Ostende Ostend.

ostensible *adj* obvious, evident; **hacer algo** — to reveal something, make something clear; **procurar no hacerse** — to keep out of the way, lie low.

ostensiblemente *adv* obviously, evidently; openly; perceptibly, visibly; **se mostró — conmovido** he was visibly affected.

ostenta *nf* (*Chi, Ec*) = **ostentación**.

ostentación *nf* (**a**) ostentation, display; pomp. (**b**) (*act*) show, display; **hacer — de** to show off, display, parade.

ostentar [1a] *vt* (**a**) to show; (*pej*) to show off, display, make a parade of, flaunt.

(**b**) to have, carry, show; **ostenta todavía las cicatrices** he still has (*or* carries) the scars.

(**c**) *legal powers etc* to have, possess; *title, honour* to have, hold; — **el título mundial en el deporte** to hold the world title in the sport, be the world record holder.

ostentativo *adj* ostentatious.

ostentosamente *adv* ostentatiously.

ostentoso *adj* ostentatious.

osteoartritis *nf* osteoarthritis.

osteópata *nm* osteopath.

osteopatía *nf* osteopathy.

ostión *nm* large oyster.

ostra *nf* (**a**) (*Zool*) oyster; — **perlera** pearl oyster.

(**b**) (*fig*) dull person; retiring individual; **las —s del café** the café regulars, the café habitués; **es una** — he's a fixture here.

ostracismo *nm* ostracism.

ostral *nm* oyster bed.

ostrero *nm* (**a**) oyster bed. (**b**) (*Orn*) oystercatcher.

osuno *adj* bear-like.

otario *adj* (*Arg, Urug*) simple, gullible.

otate *nm* (*Mex*) bamboo; cane, stick.

—ote, —ota *n and adj suffix* (**a**) (*augmentative*) **un toro grandote** a whacking great bull (*fam*), a whopping bull (*sl*).

(**b**) (*pej*) **barbarote** terribly rough (*fam*), awfully

uncouth (*fam*); **presumidote** awfully vain (*fam*); **papelote** useless bit of paper, worthless document; (*Lit*) trashy piece of writing; *see* **machote, palabrota** etc.

(**c**) (*diminutive*) **islote** small island, rocky isle.

otear [1a] *vt* (**a**) to descry, make out, glimpse; to look down on, look over; to watch (from above), spy on. (**b**) (*fig*) to examine, look into.

Otelo *m* Othello.

otero *nm* low hill, hillock, knoll.

otitis *nf* earache.

otomana *nf* ottoman.

otomano 1 *adj* Ottoman. **2** *nm*, **otomana** *nf* Ottoman.

otomía *nf* (*Mex*) = **atomía**.

Otón *m* Otto.

otoñada *nf* autumn, fall (*US*).

otoñal *adj* autumnal, autumn (*attr*), fall (*attr*: *US*).

otoño *nm* autumn, fall (*US*).

otorgamiento *nm* (**a**) (*act*) granting, conferring; consent; (*Law*) execution. (**b**) (*Law*) legal document, deed.

otorgar [1h] *vt* (**a**) to grant, give (*a* to); to confer (*a* on); *prize etc* to award (*a* to); *privilege etc* to grant; (*Law*) *deed etc* to execute; *will* to make.

(**b**) to consent, agree to.

otramente *adv* in a different way.

otro 1 *adj* (*sing*) another, (*pl*) other; **otra taza de café** another cup of coffee; **con —s trajes** with other dresses; with different dresses; **con otras 8 personas** with another 8 people, with 8 other people; **¡otra!** (*Theat*) encore!; **otra cosa** something else; **tropezamos con otra nueva dificultad** we run up against yet another (*or* a further) difficulty; **va a ser — Manolete** he's going to be another (*or* a second) Manolete; — **que** other than; different from; **fue no — que el obispo** it was none other than the bishop, it was no lesser person than the bishop; **ser muy** — to be quite changed; **los tiempos son —s** times have changed.

2 *pron* (*sing*) another one, (*pl*) others; **el** — the other one; **los —s** the others; the rest; **¿—? another one?;** **lo — es más triste** the rest of it is sadder; **lo — no importa** the rest isn't important; **tomar el sombrero de** — to take somebody else's hat; **conformarse con las costumbres de los —s** to adapt oneself to other people's habits; **algún** — somebody else; **que lo haga** — let somebody else do it; — **dijo que . . .** somebody else said . . .; **como dijo el** — as someone said; **¡— que tal!** here we go again!, we've heard all that before!; *see* **alguno, parte, tanto** *etc*.

otrora *adv* (*arch, lit*) formerly, in older times; **el — señor del país** the one-time ruler of the country.

ovación *nf* ovation.

ovacionar [1a] *vt* to cheer, applaud, give an ovation to.

oval *adj*, **ovalado** *adj* oval.

óvalo *nm* oval.

ovario *nm* ovary.

oveja *nf* (**a**) sheep, ewe; — **negra** (*fig*) black sheep (of the family); **cada** — **con su pareja** it's best to stick to people like oneself; birds of a feather flock together; **apartar las —s de los cabritos** (*fig*) to separate the sheep from the goats; **cargar con la — muerta** to be left holding the baby.

(**b**) (*Arg*) whore.

ovejera *nf* (*Mex*) sheepfold.

ovejería *nf* (*Chi*) sheep farm; sheep farming.

ovejo *nm*, **ovejón** *nm* (*SAm*) ram.

ovejuno *adj* sheep (*attr*).

overear [1a] *vt* (*Bol, RPl*) to cook to a golden colour, brown.

overol *nm* (*SAm*: *angl*) overalls.

ovetense 1 *adj* of Oviedo. **2** *nmf* native (*or* inhabitant) of Oviedo; **los —s** the people of Oviedo.

Ovidio *m* Ovid.

oviducto *nm* oviduct.

oviforme *adj* egg-shaped, oviform.

ovillar [1a] **1** *vt* *wool etc* to wind, wind into a ball. **2 ovillarse** *vr* to curl up into a ball.

ovillo *nm* (*of wool etc*) ball; (*fig*) tangle; **hacerse un** — to curl up into a ball; (*in fear*) to crouch, cower; (*in speech etc*) to get tied up in knots.

ovino *adj* sheep (*attr*), ovine; **ganado** — sheep.

ovíparo *adj* oviparous.

ovoide 1 *adj* ovoid. **2** *nm* ovoid.

ovulación *nf* ovulation.

óvulo *nm* ovule, ovum.

oxálico *adj* oxalic.

oxear [1a] *vt* to shoo (away).

oxiacanta *nf* hawthorn.

oxiacetilénico *adj* oxyacetylene (*attr*).
oxidación *nf* rusting; (*Chem*) oxidation.
oxidado *adj* rusty; (*Chem*) oxidized.
oxidar [1a] **1** *vt* to rust; (*Chem*) to oxidize. **2 oxidarse** *vr* to rust, go rusty, get rusty; (*Chem*) to oxidize.
óxido *nm* oxide.
oxigenación *nf* oxygenation.
oxigenado 1 *adj* **(a)** (*Chem*) oxygenated.
    (b) *hair* peroxided, bleached; **una rubia oxigenada** a peroxide blonde.
    2 *nm* peroxide (*for hair*).

oxigenar [1a] **1** *vt* to oxygenate. **2 oxigenarse** *vr* **(a)** to become oxygenated. **(b)** (*fig*) to get some fresh air.
oxígeno *nm* oxygen.
oxte *interj* shoo!; get out!, hop it! (*fam*); **sin decir — ni moxte** without a word.
oye, oyendo *etc see* **oír**.
oyente *nmf* **(a)** listener, hearer; **"queridos —s . . ."** (*Radio*) "dear listeners . . .".
    (b) (*Univ*) unregistered student, occasional student.
ozono *nm* ozone.

P

pabellón *nm* (a) bell tent.

(b) (*of bed*) canopy, hangings.

(c) (*Archit*) pavilion; (*in garden*) summerhouse, hut; (*of hospital etc*) block, section; **— de caza** shooting box; **— de conciertos,** **— de música** bandstand; **— de hidroterapia** pumproom.

(d) (*of trumpet etc*) mouth; **— de la oreja** outer ear.

(e) (*Mil*) stack.

(f) flag; **— de conveniencia** flag of convenience; **— nacional** national flag; **un buque de — panameño** a ship of Panamanian registration, a ship flying the Panamanian flag.

pabilo *nm,* **pábilo** *nm* wick; snuff.

Pablo *m* Paul.

pábulo *nm* (a) food.

(b) (*fig*) food, fuel; encouragement; **dar — a** to feed, encourage; **dar — a las llamas** to add fuel to the flames; **dar — a los rumores** to encourage rumours.

Paca *f pet name for* **Francisca.**

paca[1] *nf* bale.

paca[2] *nf* (*SAm: Zool*) paca, spotted cavy.

pacatería *nf* (a) timidity. (b) excessive modesty, prudishness.

pacato *adj* (a) timid. (b) excessively modest, prudish, shockable.

pacense 1 *adj* of Badajoz. 2 *nmf* native (*or* inhabitant) of Badajoz; **los —s** the people of Badajoz.

paceño 1 *adj* of La Paz. 2 *nm,* **paceña** *nf* native (*or* inhabitant) of La Paz; **los —s** the people of La Paz.

pacer [2d] 1 *vt* (a) *grass etc* to eat, graze. (b) *flocks* to graze, pasture. 2 *vi* to graze.

paciencia *nf* patience; forbearance; **¡—!** be patient!; **¡— y barajar!** keep trying!, don't give up!; **se me acaba** (*or* **agota**) **la —, no tengo más —** my patience is exhausted; **armarse** (*or* **cargarse, revestirse**) **de —** to arm oneself with patience, resolve to be patient; **perder la —** to lose one's temper.

paciencioso *adj* (*Chi, Ec*) patient.

paciente 1 *adj* patient. 2 *nmf* patient.

pacientemente *adv* patiently.

pacienzudo *adj* very patient, long-suffering.

pacificación *nf* pacification.

pacificador 1 *adj:* **operación pacificadora** peace-keeping operation. 2 *nm,* **pacificadora** *nf* peace-maker.

pacíficamente *adv* pacifically, peaceably.

pacificar [1g] 1 *vt* to pacify; to calm; to appease. 2 **pacificarse** *vr* to calm down.

Pacífico *nm* (*also* **Océano —**) Pacific (Ocean).

pacífico *adj* pacific, peaceable; peace-loving.

pacifismo *nm* pacifism.

pacifista 1 *adj* pacifist. 2 *nmf* pacifist.

Paco *m pet name for* **Francisco; ya vendrá el tío — con la rebaja** the day of reckoning will come.

paco[1] *nm* (*Mil*) sniper, sharpshooter.

paco[2] *nm* (*Col, Chi, Ec, Pan, Per*) policeman.

paco[3] 1 *adj* (*Chi, Per, RPl*) reddish. 2 *nm* (*Chi, Per*) alpaca.

pacota *nf* (*Mex*) = **pacotilla.**

pacotilla *nf* (a) trash, junk, inferior stuff; **de —** trashy, shoddy; **hacer su —** to be doing nicely, make a nice profit.

(b) (*Chi, Ec, Guat*) rabble, crowd, mob.

pacotillero 1 *adj* (*Ec*) rustic, uncouth. 2 *nm* (*Chi, Ec, Ven*) pedlar, peddler (*US*), hawker.

pactar [1a] 1 *vt* to agree to, agree on; to stipulate, contract for. 2 *vi* to come to an agreement; to compromise.

pacto *nm* pact; agreement, covenant; **— de no agresión** non-aggression pact.

pachá *nm* pasha.

pachaco *adj* (*CAm*) weak, feeble; useless.

pachacho *adj* (*Chi*) chubby, squat.

pachamama *nf* (*Arg, Bol, Ec, Per*) the good earth, Earth (*as a deity*).

pachamanca *nf* (*Per*) barbecue; (*fig*) disorder, confusion.

pacho *adj* (a) (*CAm, Chi*) chubby, squat; (*CAm*) *object* flat, flattened. (b) (*Cu*) slow, phlegmatic.

pachocha *nf* (*SAm*) = **pachorra.**

pachol *nm* (*Mex*) mat of hair.

pachón 1 *adj* (a) (*Chi, Hond*) shaggy, hairy; (*Guat, Mex*) woolly.

(b) (*Per*) plump.

(c) (*Per*) dim, dense.

2 *nm* (a) dull person, slow sort.

(b) (*also* **perro —**) pointer.

pachorra *nf* slowness, sluggishness; phlegm, phlegmatic nature; **Juan, con su santa — ...** John, as slow as ever ...

pachorrada *nf* (*Ant, Par*) = **patochada.**

pachorrear [1a] *vi* (*CAm*) to be slow, be sluggish.

pachorriento *adj* (*Per, RPl*), **pachorro** *adj* (*Col, Per, PR*), **pachorrudo** *adj* slow, sluggish; phlegmatic.

pachotada *nf* (*Mex, Per*) = **patochada.**

pachuco *adj* (*Mex*) flashy, flashily dressed; coarse, common.

pachucho *adj fruit* overripe; soft, sleepy; *person* droopy, off-colour, poorly.

padecer [2d] *vti* to suffer; to endure, put up with; *error etc* to labour under, be a victim of; **— de** to suffer from; **padece del corazón** he suffers w :h his heart, he has heart trouble; **padece en su amor propio** his self-respect suffers; **ella padec: por todos** she suffers on everybody's account; **eso hace — el metal de los goznes** that puts a strain on the metal of the hinges; **se embala bien para que no padezca en el viaje** it is well packed so that it should not get damaged on the journey.

padecimiento *nm* suffering.

padrastro *nm* (a) stepfather; (*fig*) harsh father, cruel parent. (b) (*fig*) obstacle, difficulty. (c) (*Anat*) hangnail.

padrazo *nm* indulgent father.

padre 1 *nm* (a) father; (*Zool*) father, sire; **—s** father and mother, parents; ancestors; **García —** García senior, the elder García; **— de familia** father of a family, man with family responsibilities, (*in census etc*) head of a household; **— de pila** godfather; **— político** father-in-law; **su señor —** your father; **es el — de estos estudios** he is the father of this discipline.

(b) (*Eccl*) father; **el P— Las Casas** Father Las Casas; **— espiritual** confessor; **P— Nuestro** Lord's Prayer, Our Father; **P— Santo** Holy Father, Pope.

(c) (*fam*) **una paliza de — y muy señor mío** a terrific bashing (*fam*), a beating and a half, the father and mother of a thrashing.

2 *adj* (*fam*) huge, tremendous (*fam*); **un éxito —** a terrific success (*fam*); **un lío —** an almighty row (*fam*); **un susto —** an awful fright (*fam*).

padrejón *nm* (*Arg*) stallion.

padrenuestro *nm* Lord's Prayer, paternoster; **en menos que se reza un —** in no time at all.

padrillo *nm* (*Per, RPl*) stallion.

padrinazgo *nm* godfathership; (*fig*) sponsorship, patronage.

padrino *nm* (*Eccl*) godfather; (*also* **— de boda**) best man; (*in duel*) second; (*fig*) sponsor, patron; **—s** godparents.

padrón *nm* (a) list of inhabitants, roll, census; (*of members etc*) register.

(b) (*Tech*) pattern.

(c) (*Archit*) inscribed column, commemorative column.

(d) (*fig*) stain, blot (*also* **— de ignominia**); **el**

trabajo es un — para su autor the work is a disgrace to its author; **será un — para todos nosotros** it will be a stain on all of us. **(e)** (*fam*) indulgent father. **(f)** (*SAm*) stallion; (*Col*) breeding bull.

padrote *nm* **(a)** (*SAm*) stallion; breeding bull. **(b)** (*Mex*) brothel keeper; pimp.

paella *nf* (*originally Valencian*) *dish of rice with meat, shellfish etc.*

paf *interj* bang!; plop!, splash!

paga *nf* **(a)** payment; **entrega contra —** cash on delivery. **(b)** pay, wages; fee. **(c)** (*fam*) **mala —** bad payer.

pagadero *adj* payable, due; **— a la entrega** payable on delivery; **— a plazos** payable in instalments.

pagado *adj* (*fig*) pleased; **— de sí mismo** self-satisfied, smug.

pagador *nm* **(a)** payer; **mal —** bad payer. **(b)** (*in bank*) teller, cashier; (*Mil: also* **oficial —**) paymaster.

pagaduría *nf* paymaster's office.

paganismo *nm* paganism, heathenism.

pagano[1] **1** *adj* pagan, heathen. **2** *nm*, **pagana** *nf* pagan, heathen.

pagano[2] *nm*, **pagana** *nf* person who pays for others; scapegoat, dupe.

pagar [1h] **1** *vti* **(a)** to pay; *debt* to pay, pay off, repay; *purchase* to pay for; *insurance policy* to pay out on; **su tío le paga los estudios** his uncle is paying for his education; **no lo podemos —** we can't afford it; **paga 20 dólares de habitación** he pays 20 dollars for his room; **a —** (*Post*) postage due; **cuenta a —, cuenta por —** unpaid bill, outstanding account; **— por adelantado** to pay in advance; **— al contado** to pay (in) cash.
(b) (*fig*) *favour* to repay; *love* to return, requite; *visit* to return; *crime, offence* to pay for, atone for; **lo pagó con la vida** he paid for it with his life; **¡me las pagarás!** I'll pay you out for this!, I'll get you for this!; **¡las vas a —!** you'll catch it! (*fam*), you've got it coming to you!
2 *vi* **(a)** (*SAm*) to pay; **el negocio no paga** the business doesn't pay.
(b) (*Arg, Chi*) to take bets, make a book.
3 pagarse *vr* **(a)** **— con algo** to be content with something.
(b) **— de algo** to be pleased with something; to take a liking to something; (*pej*) to boast of something; **— de sí mismo** to be conceited, be smug; **se paga mucho de su pelo** she's terribly vain about her hair.

pagaré *nm* promissory note, IOU.

página *nf* page.

paginación *nf* pagination.

paginar [1a] *vt* to paginate, number the pages of; **con 6 hojas sin —** with 6 unnumbered pages.

pago[1] **1** *nm* **(a)** payment; repayment; **— anticipado** advance payment; **— al contado** cash payment; **— a cuenta** payment on account; **— a la entrega, — contra recepción** cash on delivery; **— en especie** payment in kind; **— inicial** first payment, down payment, deposit; **— a plazos** payment by instalments, deferred payment; **"nada de —"** (*at customs*) "nothing to declare"; **atrasarse en los —s** to be in arrears; **efectuar un —** to make a payment; **faltar en los —s** to default on one's payments; **suspender los —s** to stop payments.
(b) (*fig*) return, reward; **en — de** in return for; as a reward for.
2 *adj* paid; **estar —** to be paid; (*fig*) to be even, be quits.

pago[2] *nm* district; estate, property (*esp* planted with vines or olives); (*Arg, Urug*) region, area; home area, native part.

pagoda *nf* pagoda.

pagote *nm* (*fam*) scapegoat.

pagua *nf* (*Chi*) hernia; large swelling.

paguacha *nf* (*Chi*) **(a)** = **pagua**. **(b)** gourd, vessel; (*any*) large round fruit; moneybox; (*Anat*) hump; (*fam*) head.

paguala *nf* (*PR*) swordfish.

pai *nm* (*SAm: angl*) pie.

paila *nf* large pan; (*SAm*) frying pan.

pailero *nm* **(a)** (*Col, Mex*) immigrant Italian. **(b)** (*Cu, Mex, Nic*) coppersmith; tinker.

pailón *nm* **(a)** (*Col, Cu*) pot, pan. **(b)** (*Bol, Ec, Hond: Geog*) bowl, round flat area. **(c)** (*Ven*) whirlpool.

paiño *nm* petrel.

país *nm* **(a)** country; land, region, area; landscape; **— natal** native land; **— satélite** satellite country; **los —es miembros, los —es participantes** the member countries; **vivir sobre el —** to live off the country.

(b) **P—es Bajos** Low Countries; **P— de los Lagos** Lake District; **P— Vasco** Basque Country.

paisa *nmf* (*SAm: fam*) = **paisano**.

paisaje *nm* landscape, countryside, scenery.

paisajista *nmf* landscape painter.

paisajístico *adj* landscape (*attr*), scenic.

paisanada *nf* (*RPl*) group of peasants, peasants (*collectively*).

paisanaje *nm* **(a)** civil population. **(b)** (*RPl*) = **paisanada**.

paisano **1** *adj* of the same country.
2 *nm*, **paisana** *nf* **(a)** (*Mil*) civilian; **vestir de —** (*soldier*) to be in mufti, be in civvies (*fam*), (*policeman*) be in plain clothes.
(b) compatriot, fellow countryman, fellow countrywoman; **es — mío** he's a fellow countryman (of mine).
(c) (*Arg*) countryman, peasant; (*Ec, Per*) (Indian) highlander; (*Mex*) Spaniard; (*Chi, Per*) Chinese.

paja *nf* **(a)** straw; (*SAm*) dried brushwood; **hombre de —** (*fam*) stooge (*sl*); **techo de —** thatched roof; **hacerse una —** (*fam*) to masturbate; **riñeron por un quítame allá esas —s** they fell out over some tiny thing, they quarrelled over some trifle; **ver la — en el ojo ajeno y no la viga en el propio** to see the mote in someone else's eye and not the beam in one's own.
(b) (*fig*) trash, rubbish; (*Lit*) padding, waffle (*fam*); **hinchar un libro con mucha —** to pad a book out.
(c) (*CAm, Col*) **— de agua** tap, faucet (*US*); canal.

pajar *nm* straw loft; straw rick.

pájara *nf* **(a)** (*Orn*) hen, hen bird; (*esp*) hen partridge.
(b) kite; paper bird.
(c) loose woman; thieving woman.
(d) **— pinta** (game of) forfeits.
(e) (*Col, CR*) **dar — a uno** to swindle someone.

pajarada *nf* (*Ec*) flock of birds.

pajarear [1a] **1** *vt* **(a)** (*SAm*) *birds* to scare, keep off.
(b) (*Col*) to watch intently.
(c) (*Col*) to murder.
2 *vi* **(a)** to loaf; to loiter.
(b) (*SAm: of horse*) to shy.
(c) (*Chi*) to pay no attention, be absent-minded.
(d) (*Mex*) to take notice, listen carefully.

pajarera *nf* aviary.

pajarero **1** *adj* **(a)** (*Orn*) bird (*attr*).
(b) *person* merry, fun-loving.
(c) *dress etc* gaudy, flashy, loud.
(d) (*SAm*) *horse* nervous; (*Mex, Per, PR*) *horse* spirited.
(e) (*Ven*) meddlesome.
2 *nm* bird catcher; bird fancier, breeder of birds; (*Col, Guat*) bird-scarer.

pajarilla *nf* paper kite; **se le alegraron las —s** he laughed himself silly.

pajarita *nf* **(a)** **— de las nieves** white wagtail. **(b)** paper kite; paper bird. **(c)** bow tie.

pajarito *nm* **(a)** baby bird, fledgling; (*hum*) birdie; (*fig*) very small person; **quedarse como un —** to die peacefully, fade away.
(b) (*PR*) bug, insect.

pájaro **1** *nm* **(a)** bird; **— de mal agüero** bird of ill omen; **P— del Alba** Early Bird (*satellite*); **— azul** bluebird; **— bobo** penguin; **— cantor, — cantarín** songbird; **— carpintero** woodpecker; **— mosca** hummingbird; **matar dos —s de un tiro** to kill two birds with one stone; **más vale — en mano que ciento volando** a bird in the hand is worth two in the bush; **tener la cabeza a —s** (*or* **llena de —s**) to be featherbrained.
(b) (*fam: person*) bird (*sl*), chap (*fam*), guy (*US fam*); (*pej*) clever fellow, sharp sort; **— de cuenta** big shot (*fam*).
2 *adj* **(a)** (*Arg*) scatty, featherbrained; shady, dubious; loud, flashy.
(b) (*Cu*) effeminate; queer (*fam*).
(c) (*Chi*) vague, distracted.
(d) (*SD*) (*any*) animal.

pajarón (*Arg*) **1** *adj* vague, ineffectual, stupid.
2 *nm*, **pajarona** *nf* **(a)** untrustworthy sort, unbusinesslike person.
(b) flashily dressed person.

pajarota *nf* (*fam*) hoax.

pajarraco *nm* **(a)** big bird; mysterious bird. **(b)** (*fam*) slyboots (*fam*).

paje *nm* page; (*Naut*) cabin boy.

pajera *nf* straw loft.

pajilla *nf* (*Cu, Mex, Pan*) straw hat.

pajita *nf* (drinking) straw.

pajizo *adj* (**a**) straw, made of straw; *roof* thatched. (**b**) straw-coloured.

pajolero *adj* (*fam*) blessed, wretched, annoying.

pajón *adj* (*Mex*) hair straight, lank.

pajonal *nm* (*SAm*) weedy place, scrubland.

pajoso *adj* (**a**) *grain* full of chaff. (**b**) straw-coloured; like straw.

pajuela *nf* spill; (*Bol*) match; (*Bol, Col, Chi*) toothpick; (*Ven: Mus*) plectrum.

Pakistán *m* Pakistan.

pakistaní 1 *adj* Pakistani. **2** *nmf* Pakistani.

pala *nf* (**a**) shovel, spade; scoop; **— mecánica** power shovel; **— de patatas** potato fork; **— topadora** (*Arg*) bulldozer.
 (**b**) (*Cook*) slice; **— para el pescado** fish slice.
 (**c**) (*Sport*) bat; racquet.
 (**d**) (*of oar, propeller*) blade.
 (**e**) **— matamoscas** fly swat.
 (**f**) (*of shoe*) uppers.
 (**g**) (*fig*) cunning, wiliness.

palabra *nf* (**a**) word; **—s cruzadas** crossword; **—s gruesas, —s mayores** strong words, abuse; **dos —s, cuatro —s** a couple of words; **¡ni una — más!** not another word!; **a media —** at the least hint; **de —** by word of mouth; **en una —** in a word; **— por word for word; verbatim; **a —s necias, oídos sordos** it's best not to listen to such nonsense; **ser la última —** en lujo to be the last word in luxury; **cambiar unas —s con uno** to have a few words with someone; **coger a uno la —** to take someone at his word; **sin chistar —** without a word; **dejar a uno con la — en la boca** to interrupt someone; **no encuentro —s para expresarme** words fail me; **no entiendo —** it's Greek to me; **gastar —s** to waste words, waste one's breath; **negar la — de Dios a uno** to concede absolutely nothing to someone; **quedarse con la — en la boca** to stop short; **tuvo —s de elogio para el ministro** he praised the minister; **trabarse de —s** to get involved in an argument; to wrangle, squabble.
 (**b**) speech, power of speech, faculty of speech; **de — fácil** fluent; **perder la —** to lose one's power of speech.
 (**c**) (*Parl*) right to speak; **conceder la — a uno** to invite someone to speak; **dirigir la — a uno** to address someone; **hacer uso de la —, tomar la —** to speak; **pedir la —** to ask to be allowed to speak; **tener la —** to have the floor; **Vd tiene la —** the floor is yours; **yo no tengo la —** it's not for me to say.
 (**d**) word, promise; **— de casamiento, — de matrimonio** promise to marry; **— de honor** word of honour; **bajo —** (*Mil*) on parole; **es hombre de —** he is a man of his word; **dar su —, empeñar su —** to give one's word, give a pledge; **faltar a su —** to go back on one's word.

palabrear [1a] *vt* (**a**) (*Col, Chi, Ec*) to agree verbally to; **— a una** to promise to marry someone. (**b**) (*Chi*) to abuse.

palabreja *nf* strange word; nasty-sounding word.

palabrería *nf*, **palabrerío** *nm* (*Guat, RPl*) wordiness; verbiage, hot air.

palabrero 1 *adj* wordy, windy. **2** *nm*, **palabrera** *nf* windbag.

palabrota *nf* rude word, swearword.

palabrudo *adj* (*Chi*) foulmouthed.

palacete *nm* small palace; outlying building of a palace; court, manor.

palacial *adj* (*SAm: angl*) palatial.

palaciego 1 *adj* palace (*attr*), court (*attr*). **2** *nm* courtier.

palacio *nm* palace; mansion, large house; **— episcopal** bishop's palace; **— de justicia** courthouse; **— municipal** city hall; **— real** royal palace; **el — de los Marqueses de Tal** the house of the Marquis of Tal; **ir a —** to go to court; **tener un puesto en —** to have a post at court.

palada *nf* (**a**) shovelful, spadeful. (**b**) (*of oar*) stroke.

paladar *nm* (hard) palate, roof of the mouth; (*fig*) palate, taste; **tener un — delicado** to have a delicate palate.

paladear [1a] *vt* to taste; to relish, savour; **beber algo paladeándolo** to sip a drink (to see what it tastes like).

paladeo *nm* tasting; relishing, savouring; sipping.

paladín *nm* (*Hist*) paladin; (*fig*) champion.

paladinamente *adv* openly, publicly.

paladino *adj* open, public.

palafrén *nm* palfrey.

palafrenero *nm* groom.

palana *nf* (*Per*) = **pala.**

palanca *nf* (**a**) lever; crowbar; (*Mech*) lever; **— de cambio** gear-lever, gearshift (*US*); **— de freno** brake lever; **— de mando** control lever.
 (**b**) (*fig*) lever; pull, influence; **mover —s** to pull strings.
 (**c**) (*Col, Mex, Ven*) punting pole.

palangana 1 *nf* (**a**) washbasin.
 (**b**) (*CAm, Col*) platter, wooden bowl.
 2 *nmf* (*also* **—s**; *Chi*) intruder; (*SAm*) shallow person; charlatan; braggart.

palanganear [1a] *vi* (*SAm*) to brag; to show off.

palanganero *nm* washstand.

palanquear [1a] **1** *vt* (*Ec, Guat*) to lever (along), move with a lever; (*Col, Mex, Ven*) boat to punt, pole along.
 2 *vi* (*Cu, Per, RPl*: *fig*) to pull strings.

palanquera *nf* stockade.

palanquero *nm* (*Bol, Chi: Rail*) brakeman; (*Col*) lumberman; (*Chi*) burglar, housebreaker.

palanqueta *nf* small lever; (*burglar's*) jemmy; (*Chi, Mex*) metal bar, weight (in weight lifting).

palatal 1 *adj* palatal. **2** *nf* palatal.

palatalizar [1f] **1** *vt* to palatalize. **2 palatalizarse** *vr* to palatalize.

palatinado *nm* palatinate.

palatino *adj* (**a**) (*Pol*) palace (*attr*), court (*attr*), palatine. (**b**) (*Anat*) palatal.

palatosquisis *nf* cleft palate.

palco *nm* (*Theat etc*) box; **— de la presidencia** (*Taur*) president's box; **— de proscenio** stage box.

palde *nm* (*Chi*) pointed digging tool; dagger.

palear [1a] *vt* (**a**) (*SAm*) boat to punt, pole. (**b**) (*SAm*) earth to shovel; trench to dig. (**c**) (*Arg*) to thresh.

palenque *nm* (**a**) fence, stockade, palisade.
 (**b**) arena, ring, enclosure; (*for cockfighting*) pit.
 (**c**) (*Bol, RPl*) tethering post, rail.
 (**d**) (*Chi*) noisy place.

palenquear [1a] *vt* (*RPl*) to hitch, tether.

paleo . . . pal(a)eo . . .

paleografía *nf* paleography.

paleógrafo *nm* paleographer.

paleolítico *adj* paleolithic.

paleontología *nf* paleontology.

Palestina *f* Palestine.

palestino 1 *adj* Palestinian. **2** *nm*, **palestina** *nf* Palestinian.

palestra *nf* arena; (*fig*) lists; **salir a la —** (*fig*) to take the field, take the floor.

paleta *nf* (**a**) small shovel, small spade; scoop; fire shovel; (*Archit*) trowel.
 (**b**) (*Art*) palette.
 (**c**) (*Tech*: *of turbine etc*) blade; vane; (*of wheel*) paddle; bucket.
 (**d**) (*Anat*) shoulder blade.
 (**e**) (*SAm*) wooden paddle for beating clothes.
 (**f**) (*SAm*) lollipop.

paletear [1a] **1** *vt* (*Arg*) horse to pat; (*fig*) to flatter. **2** *vi* (*Chi*) to lose one's job.

paletero *nm* (*Ec*) tuberculosis.

paletilla *nf* shoulder blade.

paleto *nm* (**a**) (*Zool*) fallow deer. (**b**) (*fam*) yokel, country bumpkin.

palia *nf* altar cloth, pallium.

paliar [1b] *vt* (**a**) to palliate, mitigate, alleviate; pain to relieve; effect to lessen, cushion; importance to diminish.
 (**b**) defect to conceal, gloss over.
 (**c**) offence etc to mitigate, excuse.

paliativo 1 *adj* palliative; mitigating; concealing. **2** *nm* palliative.

palidecer [2d] *vi* to pale, turn pale.

palidez *nf* paleness, pallor; wanness; sickliness.

pálido *adj* pale, pallid (*also fig*); wan; sickly.

palidoso *adj* (*Per*) = **pálido.**

palillo *nm* (**a**) small stick; toothpick; (*Mus*) drumstick; (*CAm, Mex*) penholder; **—s** (*Mus*) castanets; **—s chinos** chopsticks; **unas piernas como —s de dientes** legs like matchsticks.
 (**b**) (*hum*) very thin person; **estar hecho un —** to be as thin as a rake.

palimpsesto *nm* palimpsest.

palindromo *nm* palindrome.

palinodia *nf* recantation; **cantar la —** to recant.

palio *nm* cloak; canopy; (*Eccl*) pallium.

palique *nm* (*fam*) chat; small talk, chitchat; **estar de —** to be chatting, have a chat.

palitroque *nm* (*Chi*) skittles, bowling (*US*); skittle alley, bowling alley (*US*).

paliza *nf* (**a**) beating, thrashing; beating-up; **dar una**

— **a uno** to give someone a beating, beat someone up.

(**b**) (*fig: Sport etc*) beating, drubbing; **¡qué — aquélla!** what a beating that was!; **el viaje fue una** — the journey was ghastly (*fam*); **le espera una — en la oficina** he'll get a dressing-down at the office, he's got it coming to him at the office; **los críticos le dieron una — a la novela** the critics panned the novel (*sl*), the novel took a beating from the critics.

palizada *nf* (**a**) fence, stockade, palisade. (**b**) fenced enclosure.

palma *nf* (**a**) (*Anat*) palm; **batir —s, dar —s** to clap hands, applaud; (*Mus*) to clap hands; **como la — de la mano** as flat as the palm of one's hand; very easy, straightforward.

(**b**) **—s** (*fig*) clapping, applause.

(**c**) (*Bot*) palm, palm tree; palm leaf; **ganar la —, llevarse la —** to carry off the palm, triumph, win.

palmada *nf* (**a**) slap, pat (*on the shoulder etc*); **darse una — en la frente** to clap one's hand to one's brow.

(**b**) **—s** clapping, applause; **dar —s** to clap, applaud.

palmadita *nf* pat, light tap.

palmar[1] *nm* (*Bot*) palm grove, cluster of palms.

palmar[2] [1a] *vi* (*fam*) to die, peg out (*sl*).

palmar[3] *adj*, **palmario** *adj* clear, obvious, self-evident.

palmarote *nm* (*Ven*) rustic, peasant.

palmatoria *nf* (**a**) candlestick. (**b**) (*for punishment*) cane.

palmeado *adj* foot webbed.

palmear [1a] *vi* to clap.

palmera *nf*, **palmero** *nm* (*Arg, Ec, Mex*) palm, palm tree.

palmeta *nf* cane; caning, swish with a cane; **— matamoscas** fly swat.

palmetazo *nm* caning, swish with a cane; (*fig*) blow, slap in the face.

palmillas *nfpl*: **llevar a uno en —** to treat someone with great consideration.

palmípedo *adj* web-footed.

palmista *nmf* (*Cu, Mex, PR: angl*) palmist.

palmito *nm* (*SAm*) top of the palm tree (*an edible delicacy*).

palmo *nm* span; (*fig*) few inches, small amount; **— a —** inch by inch; **avanzar — a —** to go forward inch by inch; **conocer el terreno — a —** (*or a —s*), **tener medido el terreno a —s** to know every inch of the ground; **crecer a —s** to shoot up; **dejar a uno con un — de narices** to disappoint someone greatly, leave someone very crestfallen; **no hay un — de A a B** there's hardly any distance (*or* difference) between A and B.

palmotear [1a] *vi* to clap, applaud.

palmoteo *nm* clapping, applause.

palo *nm* (**a**) stick; post, pole; club; (*of tool etc*) handle, haft, shaft; (*Sport*) club; bat; **— ensebado** greasy pole; **— de escoba** broomstick; **— de golf** golf club; **— de tienda** tent pole; **de tal — tal astilla** like father like son; **estar hecho un —** to be as thin as a rake; **meter —s en las ruedas** (*fig*) to put a spanner in the works.

(**b**) (*Naut*) mast; spar; **— mayor** mainmast; **— de mesana** mizzenmast; **— de trinquete** foremast.

(**c**) (*Bot*) stalk (*of grape etc*).

(**d**) wood; **cuchara de —** wooden spoon.

(**e**) (*esp SAm*) tree; **— dulce** liquorice root; **— de hule** (*Guat etc*) rubber tree; **— de mango** mango tree; **— santo** lignum vitae.

(**f**) (*Typ: of letter*) upright, straight part.

(**g**) blow, hit (with a stick); **andar a —s** to be always squabbling; **dar un — a uno** (*fig*) to criticize someone severely, take someone to task; **los críticos le dieron un — a la obra** the critics lashed (*or* panned: *sl*) the play; **dar de —s a uno, doblar** (*or* **moler**) **a uno a —s** to give someone a beating; **dar —s de ciego** to lash out wildly.

(**h**) (*Cards*) suit; **seguir el —, servir del —** to follow suit.

(**i**) (*SAm*) swig (*fam*), draught of liquor; **a medio —** half-drunk; **darse al —** to take to drink; **pegarse unos —s** to have a few drinks.

(**j**) **a — seco** bare; by itself, pure, with nothing else; **vermut a — seco** straight vermouth; **beber a — seco** to drink without having anything to eat; **tiene el sueldo a — seco** he has just his salary, he has his bare salary and nothing else.

(**k**) (*SAm*) **un — de casa** a splendid house, a marvellous house; **es un — de hombre** he's a great guy (*US fam*); **cayó un — de agua** there was a tremendous lot of rain (*fam*).

(**l**) (*Chi*) **— grueso** (*fig*) big shot (*fam*).

paloma *nf* (**a**) (*Orn*) dove, pigeon; **— mensajera** carrier pigeon, homing pigeon; **— torcaz** wood-pigeon, ringdove.

(**b**) (*fig*) meek and mild person.

(**c**) (*Sport*) handstand.

(**d**) (*Cu, Hond*) kite.

(**e**) (*Naut*) **—s** white caps (*of waves*), white horses.

palomar *nm* dovecot(e), pigeon loft.

palomear [1a] *vt* (**a**) (*Cu*) to swindle. (**b**) (*Ec, Per*) enemies to hunt down one by one; to shoot to kill, shoot dead.

palomilla *nf* (**a**) (*Ent*) moth; moth which is a pest on stored grain; (*stage*) nymph, chrysalis.

(**b**) (*Tech*) wing nut.

(**c**) (*Tech*) wall bracket, angle iron.

(**d**) (*of horse*) back, backbone.

(**e**) (*Chi, Per*) urchin, ragamuffin; (*Chi, Hond, Mex*) mob of kids (*fam*); crowd of layabouts, band of hooligans.

palomino 1 *adj* (*Arg, Mex, Per*) horse white. 2 *nm* (**a**) young pigeon. (**b**) (*Arg, Mex, Per*) white horse, palomino horse.

palomitas *nfpl* popcorn.

palomo 1 *adj* (*Arg, Col, Mex*) = **palomino**. 2 *nm* (cock) pigeon; **— de arcilla** clay pigeon.

palotada *nf*: **no dar —** not to do a stroke of work; to do nothing; to get nothing right.

palote *nm* (**a**) (*Mus*) drumstick. (**b**) (*in writing*) downstroke; pothook. (**c**) (*Arg, Cu*) rolling pin; (*Chi*) tall thin person.

palotear [1a] *vi* to bicker, wrangle.

paloteo *nm* bickering, wrangling.

palpable *adj* palpable; (*fig*) tangible, palpable; concrete.

palpar [1a] **1** *vt* (**a**) to touch, feel; (*amorously*) to feel, caress, fondle; *wall etc* to feel one's way along, grope one's way past.

(**b**) **— a uno** (*of police etc*) to frisk someone, search someone for weapons.

(**c**) (*fig*) to feel; to appreciate, understand; **ahora palpa las consecuencias** now he's really feeling the consequences; **ya palparás lo que es esto** one day you'll really understand all this.

2 palparse *vr* (*fig*) to be felt; **se palpaba el descontento** you could feel the restlessness; **es una enemistad que se palpa** it's a hostility which one can feel.

palpitación *nf* palpitation, throb(bing), beat(ing); quiver(ing); stutter(ing).

palpitante *adj* (**a**) palpitating, throbbing. (**b**) (*fig*) interest, question burning.

palpitar [1a] *vi* (**a**) to palpitate; to throb, beat; to quiver; to flutter.

(**b**) (*fig*) to throb; **en la poesía palpita la emoción** the poem throbs with emotion.

(**c**) (*RPl*) **me palpita** I have a hunch; **ya me palpitaba ese fracaso** I had a hunch about that disaster, I had a presentiment of that disaster.

palpite *nm*, **pálpito** *nm* (*Chi, Per, RPl*) hunch, presentiment; **tener un —** to have a hunch.

palta *nf* (*SAm*) avocado pear.

paltó *nm* (*Col, CR, Ven: gall*) jacket.

palúdico *adj* marshy; (*Med*) malarial.

paludismo *nm* malaria.

palurdo 1 *adj* rustic; coarse, uncouth. 2 *nm* rustic, yokel, hick (*US*); (*pej*) lout.

palustre[1] *nm* (*Tech*) trowel.

palustre[2] *adj* marsh (*attr*); marshy.

palla *nf* (*Chi, Per*) mistress, kept woman.

pallador *nm* (*SAm*) *etc* see **payador** *etc*.

pallar *nm* (*Arg, Chi, Per*) Lima bean.

pallasa *nf* (*Chi, Per: gall*) mattress.

pamela *nf* (*woman's*) broad straw hat.

pamema *nf* (**a**) silly thing, stupid remark (*etc*); **—s** nonsense, humbug; **¡déjate de —s!** stop your nonsense!

(**b**) triviality, trifle.

(**c**) **—s** flattery; coaxing, wheedling.

(**d**) **—s** fuss; **¡déjate de —s!** stop your fussing!, that's enough of that!

pampa[1] *nf* (**a**) (*SAm*) pampa(s), prairie; **la P—** the Pampas.

(**b**) (*Chi*) region of nitrate deposits; open area on the outskirts of a town.

(**c**) **a la —** (*SAm*) in the open, out of doors; **en —** (*Chi, Guat*) in the open; naked; disappointed, frustrated.

pampa[2] **1** *adj* (**a**) (*Arg, Bol, Urug*) deal shady, dishonest.

(**b**) (*Bol*) weak, feeble.

2 *nmf* (*Arg*) pampean Indian.

3 *nm* language of the pampean Indians.

pámpana *nf* (a) vine leaf. (b) (*fam*) **zurrar la — a uno** to give someone a hiding.

pámpano *nm* vine shoot, vine tendril.

pampeano *adj* (*SAm*) of (*or* from) the pampas.

pampear[1] [1a] *vi* (*Arg*) to travel over a plain.

pampear[2] [1a] *vt* (*Col*) (a) to tap, pat (on the shoulder). (b) *pastry* to roll out.

pampero (*SAm*) 1 *adj* of (*or* from) the pampas. 2 *nm* (a) inhabitant of the pampas, plainsman. (b) strong wind (*blowing over the pampas from the Andes*).

pampino 1 *adj* (*SAm*) of (*or* from) the pampas. 2 *nm*, **pampina** *nf* (*Chi*) inhabitant of the Chilean pampas.

pamplina *nf* (a) (*Bot*) chickweed. (b) (*fam*) silly remark; **—s** nonsense; fuss; ¡**—s!** rubbish!; **esas son —s** that's a load of rubbish; **no me venga Vd con —s** don't come to me with such nonsense.

pamplinero *adj* (a) silly, nonsensical. (b) fussy, emotional, given to making a great fuss. (c) vain.

pamplonada *nf* (*SAm*) triviality; silly thing, piece of nonsense.

pamplonés *adj and nm*, **pamplonesa** *nf* = **pamplonica**.

pamplonica 1 *adj* of Pamplona. 2 *nmf* native (*or* inhabitant) of Pamplona; **los —s** the people of Pamplona.

pamporcino *nm* cyclamen.

pan[1] *nm* (a) (*in general*) bread; (*un —*) loaf; (*fig*) bread, daily bread; **— candeal, — de flor** white bread; **— de centeno** rye bread; **— integral** wholemeal bread; **el — nuestro de cada día** our daily bread; **estar a — y agua** to be on (*or* condemned to a diet of) bread and water; **ganarse el —** to earn one's living. (b) (*Bot*) wheat; **—es** (*fig*) crops, harvest; **año de mucho —** good year for wheat, year of a heavy wheat crop; **tierras de — llevar** arable land, corn-growing land. (c) **— de azúcar** sugar loaf; **— de higos** block of dried figs; **— de jabón** bar of soap, cake of soap. (d) (*Tech*) gold leaf, silver leaf. (e) **— de cuco** stonecrop. (f) (*idioms*) **eso es — comido** it's a cinch (*sl*); **contigo — y cebolla** (with you I'd gladly have) love in a cottage; **con su — se lo coma** that's his look-out, let him get on with it; **echar —es** (*Arg, Bol*) to boast, brag; **llamar al — — y al vino vino** to call a spade a spade; **venderse como — bendito** to sell like hot cakes.

pan[2] ... **pan** ..., *eg* **panasiático** pan-Asiatic.

pana[1] *nf* velveteen, corduroy.

pana[2] *nf* (*SAm: Aut: gall*) breakdown.

pana[3] *nf* (*Chi*) liver; (*fig*) guts, courage.

panacea *nf* panacea, cure-all.

panadería *nf* bakery, bakehouse; baker's (shop).

panadero *nm* baker.

panadizo *nm* (*Med*) whitlow.

panal *nm* honeycomb.

Panamá *m* Panama.

panamá *nm* (*SAm*) panama hat.

panameñismo *nm* word (*or* phrase *etc*) peculiar to Panama.

panameño 1 *adj* Panamanian. 2 *nm*, **panameña** *nf* Panamanian.

panamericanismo *nm* Pan-Americanism.

panamericano *adj* Pan-American.

panamitos *nmpl*, **panamos** *nmpl* (*Per*) beans; (*fig*) food, daily bread.

panca *nf* (*Bol, Per*) green leaf of maize.

pancarta *nf* placard, banner.

pancista *adj* unprincipled; always ready to compromise, concerned only to keep on good terms with those in power.

páncreas *nm* pancreas.

pancreático *adj* pancreatic.

pancromático *adj* panchromatic.

pancha *nf* (*fam*) = **panza**.

pancho[1] *adj* (a) (*Chi*) brown, tan. (b) (*Col, Ven*) broad and flat; squat.

pancho[2] *adj* calm, unruffled; **estar tan — to remain** perfectly calm.

panda[1] *nf* (*Zool*) panda.

panda[2] *nf* (*Cu*) = **pandeo**.

panda[3] *nf* (*fam*) = **pandilla**.

pandear [1a] *vi and* **pandearse** *vr* to bend, warp; to sag; to bulge.

pandeo *nm* bend; sag(ging); bulge, bulging.

pandereta *nf* tambourine; **zumbar la — a uno** (*fam*) to tan someone's hide (*fam*).

panderetear [1a] *vi* to play the tambourine.

pandero *nm* (a) (*Mus*) tambourine. (b) kite. (c) (*fam*) idiot.

pandilla *nf* set, group; (*pej*) clique, coterie; (*criminal etc*) gang; (*Comm*) ring.

pandillero *nm* member of a clique (*etc*); (*SAm*) gangster.

pando *adj* (a) *beam etc* sagging, warped. (b) *dish* shallow; flat. (c) *river, person* slow.

Pandora *f*: **la caja de —** Pandora's box.

pandorga *nf* (a) fat woman. (b) kite. (c) (*Col*) bother, nuisance. (d) (*Mex*) practical joke, hoax; student rag.

pandorgo *adj* (a) (*Mex*) dim, stupid. (b) (*PR*) fat and slow-moving.

panecillo *nm* roll.

panegírico *nm* panegyric.

panel *nm* panel; plywood; (*Archit*) panelling.

panela *nf* (a) (*SAm*) brown sugar, coarse sugar; sugar loaf. (b) (*Mex*) straw hat. (c) (*Col, Mex, Ven*) bore, tedious person; flatterer, smooth type.

pánfilo *adj* (a) simple, gullible; stupid. (b) (*Col*) pale, discoloured.

panfletario *adj* (*SAm*) *style* violent, highly-coloured.

panfletista *nm* (*SAm: angl*) pamphleteer; satirist, lampoonist.

panfleto *nm* (*angl*) pamphlet; (*SAm*) satire, lampoon, scandal sheet.

panga *nf* (*Mex, Nic, Pan*) barge, lighter.

paniaguado *nm* (*Hist*) henchman; protégé.

paniaguarse [1i] *vr* (*Mex*) to become friends, pal up (*fam*).

pánico 1 *adj* panic. 2 *nm* (a) panic, fear; **yo le tengo un — tremendo** (*fam*) I'm scared stiff of him. (b) **de — = de miedo.**

panizo *nm* (a) millet; maize. (b) (*Chi*) mineral deposit; (*fig*) treasure, gem, valuable object; (*Comm*) profitable deal, gold mine.

panocha *nf*, **panoja** *nf* (a) corncob, ear of maize; ear of wheat (*etc*). (b) (*Mex*) brown sugar; brown sugar candy. (c) (*Col, CR, Chi*) large pancake of maize and cheese.

panolis *nmf, pl* **panolis** (*fam*) chump (*fam*), idiot.

panoplia *nf* panoply.

panorama *nm* panorama (*also fig*); vista, view, scene; (*Art, Phot*) view.

panoramicar [1g] *vti* (*Cine*) to pan.

panorámico *adj* panoramic; **punto — viewpoint,** vantage point.

panqué *nm* (*Cu, Guat: angl*), **panqueque** *nm* (*SAm: angl*) pancake.

pantaleta *nf* (*SAm*) bloomers, drawers.

pantalón *nm*, **pantalones** *nmpl* (a) (*man's*) trousers, pants (*US*); (*woman's: outer*) slacks, trousers, (*inner*) knickers; **—es cortos** shorts; **—es de esquí** ski pants; **—es (de) pirata, —es tejanos, —es vaqueros** jeans. (b) (*Ec, Per*) man, male. (c) (*Ant*) guts, courage.

pantalla *nf* (a) screen; shade, lampshade. (b) (*Cine etc*) screen; **— de radar** radar screen; **— de televisión** television screen; **los personajes de la —** screen personalities; **llevar una historia a la —** to film a story. (c) (*SAm*) fan. (d) (*fig*) blind, pretext; decoy; **servir de — a** to be a blind for. (e) (*SAm*) henchman, bodyguard. (f) (*Guat*) large mirror.

pantanal *nm* marshland.

pantano *nm* (a) (*natural*) marsh, swamp, bog; (*artificial*) reservoir, artificial lake; **los nuevos —s del Tajo** the new artificial lakes along the Tagus. (b) (*fig*) jam, fix (*fam*), difficulty; **salir de un — to** get out of a jam.

pantanoso *adj* marshy, swampy, boggy.

panteísmo *nm* pantheism.

panteísta 1 *adj* pantheistic. 2 *nmf* pantheist.

panteón *nm* (a) pantheon; **— familiar** family vault; **el — de los reyes** the burial place of the royal family, the pantheon of the kings. (b) (*Andalusia, SAm*) cemetery. (c) (*Chi*) ore, mineral.

panteonero *nm* (*SAm*) gravedigger.

pantera *nf* (a) panther; (*Ven*) jaguar, ocelot. (b) (*Cu, PR*) trickster; (*Mex*) bully; bold person.

pantógrafo *nm* pantograph.

pantomima *nf* pantomime, dumb show.

pantoque *nm* (*Naut*) bilge; **agua de —** bilge water.

pantorrilla *nf* (a) calf (of the leg). (b) (*Ec, Per*) brazenness, nerve.

pantorrilludo *adj* (a) fat in the leg, thick-calved. (b) (*Ec, Per*) brazen, cheeky.

pantufla *nf*, **pantuflo** *nm* slipper.

panul *nm* (*Chi*) celery.

panza *nf* belly, paunch; — **de burro** (*Mountaineering*) overhang; — **mojada** (*Mex*) wetback (*US*).

panzada *nf* (a) bellyful; **darse una** —, **darse las grandes** —s to have a blow-out (*sl*).
(b) blow in the belly.
(c) (*fig*) **una** — **de** a lot of, a bellyful of.

panzazo *nm* (a) (*Arg, Par, Per*) blow in the belly.
(b) (*Mex*) = **panzada** (a).

panzón *adj*, **panzudo** *adj* paunchy, fat, potbellied.

pañal *nm* (a) nappy, diaper (*US*); shirttail.
(b) —es baby clothes, swaddling clothes; (*fig*) early stages, infancy; **de humildes** —es of humble origins; **criarse en buenos** —es to be born with a silver spoon in one's mouth; **estar todavía en** —es to be very innocent still.

pañería *nf* drapery; draper's (shop), dry-goods store (*US*), clothier's (shop).

pañero *nm* draper, dry-goods dealer (*US*), clothier.

pañete *nm* (a) light cloth. (b) —s shorts, trunks. (c) (*Col*) coat of fine plaster. (d) (*Chi*) horse blanket.

pañi *nm* (*Chi*) sun trap, sunny place.

pañito *nm* table runner; traycloth.

paño *nm* (a) (*in general*) cloth; stuff, material; **el buen** — **en el arca se vende** good wine needs no bush; **le conozco el** — I know his sort, I know all about him, I recognize the type.
(b) (*un* —) (piece of) cloth; duster, rag, cleaning cloth; (*Eccl*) altar cloth; —s **calientes** (*fig*) half-measures, ineffective remedies; **no andarse con** —s **calientes** to pull no punches, not go in for half-measures; — **de cocina** dishcloth; — **higiénico** sanitary towel, sanitary napkin (*US*); — **de lágrimas** (*fig*) standby, consolation; — **de manos** towel; — **mortuorio** pall; — **de los platos**, — **de secar** tea towel; **jugar a dos** —s to play a double game.
(c) (*Sew*) piece of cloth, width; panel.
(d) —s clothes; (*Art*) drapes; —s **menores** underclothes, undies (*fam*).
(e) **al** — (*Theat*) offstage.
(f) (*Archit*) stretch, length (*of wall*).
(g) (*on glass etc*) mist, cloud, cloudiness.
(h) (*Cu*) fishing net.
(i) (*Cu, Mex*) plot of land made ready for cultivation.

pañol *nm* (*Naut*) store, storeroom; — **del agua** water store; — **del carbón** coal bunker.

pañoleta *nf* fichu.

pañolón *nm* shawl.

pañuelo *nm* handkerchief; scarf, headscarf, shawl.

papa[1] *nm* (*Eccl*) pope.

papa[2] *nf* (a) (*esp SAm*) potato. (b) *see* **entender** *etc*. (c) (*Arg*) bash (*fam*), blow. (d) (*Cu*) soft job, plum. (e) (*Mex*) lie, fib; hoax.

papa[3] *adj* (*Arg, Chi*) jolly good (*fam*), first-rate.

papá *nm* (a) (*fam*) dad, daddy, papa, pop (*US*).
(b) (*CAm, Mex etc*) father; —s mother and father, parents; **felicitamos a los** —s **de la damita** we congratulate the young lady's parents.

papacote *nm* (*CAm*) kite.

papachar [1a] *vt* (*Mex*) to pat, caress.

papada *nf* double chin; dewlap.

papadilla *nf* dewlap.

papado *nm* papacy.

papagayo *nm* (a) (*Orn*) parrot.
(b) (*fig*) parrot; chatterbox; person who repeats parrot fashion.
(c) (*Cu, Mex*) large kite.
(d) (*Per*) chamberpot.

papal[1] *adj* (*Eccl*) papal.

papal[2] *nm* (*SAm*) potato field.

papalina *nf* (a) cap with earflaps; bonnet; mobcap.
(b) (*fam*) binge (*sl*); **coger una** — to get tight.

papalón *nm* (*Mex*) cad, rotter.

papalote *nm* (*Ant, Guat, Mex*) kite.

papalotear [1a] *vi* (*Guat, Mex*) to roam, wander.

papamoscas *nm*, *pl* **papamoscas** (a) (*Orn*) flycatcher. (b) = **papanatas**.

papanatas *nm*, *pl* **papanatas** simpleton, sucker (*sl*).

papanatería *nf*, **papanatismo** *nm* gullibility, simple-mindedness.

papandujo *adj* soft, overripe.

papapa *nf* (*CAm*) stupidity.

papar [1a] 1 *vt* to swallow, gulp (down).
2 **paparse** *vr*: — **algo** (*fam*) to eat up, scoff (*fam*); **se lo papó todo** he scoffed the lot; **¡pápate ésa!** put that in your pipe and smoke it! (*fam*).

paparrucha *nf* (a) piece of nonsense, silly thing.
(b) botch, worthless object. (c) hoax.

paparruta *nmf* (*Chi*) humbug.

papas *nfpl* pap, mushy food; (*fam*) grub (*sl*).

papaya *nf* (a) (*Bot: SAm*) papaya. (b) (*Cu, PR, Ven: tabu*) cunt (*tabu*).

papayo *nm* (*SAm*) papaya tree.

papel *nm* (a) (*in general*) paper; — **atrapamoscas** flypaper; — **de calcar** tracing paper; — **biblia**, — **de China** India paper; — **carbón** carbon paper, carbon; — **de cartas** notepaper, stationery; — **cuadriculado** squared paper; — **de embalar**, — **de envolver** brown paper, wrapping paper; — **de empapelar** wallpaper; — **encerado** wax(ed) paper; — **de estaño** tinfoil; — **engomado** gummed paper; — **de estraza** brown paper, wrapping paper; **es como el** — **de estraza** it's worthless, it's not worth the paper it's written on; — **de excusado** toilet paper; — **de filtro** filter paper; — **de fumar** cigarette paper; **entre A y B no cabía un** — **de fumar** you couldn't have got a razor's edge between them; — **de lija** sandpaper; — **para máquinas de escribir** typing paper; — **mojado** (*fig*) scrap of paper, worthless bit of paper; — **de oficio** (*SAm*) official foolscap paper; — **ondulado** corrugated paper; — **de paja de arroz** rice paper; — **de paredes**, — **pintado** wallpaper; — **de plata** silver paper; — **prensa** newsprint; — **sanitario** (*CAm*) toilet paper; — **secante** blotting paper; blotter; — **sellado** stamped paper; — **de tina** handmade paper; — **de tornasol** litmus paper; — **transparente** tracing paper; — **vitela** vellum paper; **sobre el** — (*fig*) on paper, in theory.
(b) (*un* —) piece of paper, sheet (of paper); —es papers; —es **usados**, —es **viejos** waste paper.
(c) (*official*) —es papers, documents; identification papers; **los** —es, **por favor** your papers, please; **tiene los** —es **en regla** his papers are in order.
(d) (*Fin*) — **moneda** paper money, banknotes; **mil dólares en** — a thousand dollars in notes.
(e) (*Fin*) stocks and shares; — **del Estado** government bonds.
(f) (*Col*) one-peso note.
(g) (*Cine, Theat etc*) part, role; **desempeñar un** — (*fig*), **hacer un** — to play a part; **el** — **del gobierno en este asunto** the government's role in this matter; **hizo el** — **de Cleopatra** she played the part of Cleopatra; **el equipo hizo un buen** — **en el torneo** the team did well in the tournament, the team put up a good show in the tournament; **tuvo que desempeñar un** — **secundario** he had to play second fiddle, he had to take a minor role.

papelada *nf* (*CAm*) farce, pretence, charade.

papelear [1a] *vi* (a) to rummage through papers.
(b) to make a splash, draw attention to oneself.

papeleo *nm* (*fig*) red tape.

papelera *nf* (a) litter bin; wastepaper basket. (b) desk.

papelería *nf* (a) stationery. (b) stationer's (shop).
(c) mass of papers, heap of papers; sheaf of papers.

papelerío *nm* (*SAm*) = **papelería** (c).

papelero 1 *adj* (*SAm*) paper (*attr*). 2 *nm* (a) stationer; paper manufacturer. (b) (*Mex*) paper-boy. (c) (*RPl*) ridiculous person.

papeleta *nf* slip of paper, bit of paper; card, index card, file card; (*Pol*) voting paper, ballot paper; (*School*) report; (*Guat*) visiting card, calling card (*US*); — **de empeño** pawn ticket; **¡vaya** —! this is a tough one.

papelillo *nm* cigarette.

papelista *nmf* (*Arg, Cu, PR*) = **picapleitos**.

papelito *nm* slip of paper, bit of paper.

papelón *nm* (a) (piece of) wastepaper; pasteboard.
(b) impostor; bluffer, show-off (*fam*).
(c) ridiculous act, ridiculous state; **hacer un** — to do something ridiculous, make oneself a laughing stock.
(d) (*Col, Ven*) sugar loaf.

papelonero *adj* (*RPl*) ridiculous.

papelote *nm*, **papelucho** *nm* useless bit of paper; worthless document; (*Lit*) trashy piece of writing.

papera *nf* goitre; (*also* —s) mumps.

papero 1 *adj* (a) (*SAm*) potato (*attr*). (b) (*Mex*) lying, deceitful. 2 *nm* potato grower; potato dealer.

papilla *nf* (a) pap, mush. (b) (*fig*) guile, deceit.
(c) **estar hecho** — to be smashed to pieces (*or* to pulp); to be dog-tired.

papiro *nm* papyrus.

pápiro *nm* (*fam*) thousand-peseta note; —s (*fig*) dough (*sl*), brass (*sl*); **tener afán de** —s to be greedy for money.

papirotazo *nm*, **papirote** *nm* flick.

papismo *nm* papistry, popery.

papista 1 *adj* papist, popish. **2** *nmf* papist.
papo *nm* **(a)** (*Orn*) crop; (*Zool*) dewlap; (*of person*) jowl, double chin. **(b)** (*Med*) goitre.
papudo *adj* with a heavy jowl, double-chinned.
papujado *adj* swollen, puffed up.
papujo *adj* **(a)** (*Mex*) swollen, puffed up; (*Col*) fat-cheeked. **(b)** (*Mex*) wan, sickly, anaemic.
paquebote *nm* packet boat, packet.
paquete 1 *nm* **(a)** packet, parcel (*also Post*), package; —s postales (*as service*) parcel post; — de cigarrillos packet (pack *US*) of cigarettes; — de flores bunch of flowers.
　(b) (*Naut*) packet boat, packet.
　(c) (*fam*) toff (*fam*), dandy; **estar hecho un —** to be all dressed up, be dressed in style.
　(d) (*Mil: fam*) **meter un — a uno** to put someone on a charge.
　(e) (*SAm*) nuisance, bore; ¡menudo —!, ¡vaya —! what a bore!
　(f) (*Guat, Mex*) **darse —** to give oneself airs. **2** *adj* (*SAm*) chic, elegant, spruce.
paquetear [1a] *vi* (*SAm*) to be very smart.
paquetería *nf* (*RPl*) **(a)** adornments, accessories. **(b)** excess of adornment, overdressed state.
paquetudo *adj* (*SAm*) = **paquete 2**.
paquidermo *nm* pachyderm.
paquistaní (*Acad*) = **pakistaní**.
Paquita *f pet name for* **Francisca**.
Paquito *m pet name for* **Francisco**.
par 1 *adj* like, equal; *number* even.
　2 *nm* **(a)** pair; couple; **un — de guantes** a pair of gloves; **por un — de dólares** for a couple of dollars; **solamente un — de veces** only a couple of times; **a —es** in pairs, in twos.
　(b) equal; **al —** equally; together, jointly; **es útil a — que** (*or* **y al —**) **divertido** it is both useful and amusing, it is useful and amusing at the same time; **está al — de los mejores** it is on a level with the best, it's up to the standard of the best; **caminar al — de** to walk abreast of; **sin —** matchless, peerless; unparalleled; **no tener —** to have no parallel, be unique.
　(c) (*Math*) even number; **—es o nones** odds or evens.
　(d) (*Golf*) par; **lo hizo con 4 por debajo del —** he did it in 4 under par.
　(e) (*Mech*) **— de fuerzas** couple; **— de torsión** torque.
　(f) **estar abierto de — en —** to be wide open.
　(g) (*person*) peer; **los doce —es** the twelve peers.
　3 *nf* (*esp Comm, Fin*) par; **a la —** at par; (*fig*) = **al par**; **estar a la —** to be at par; **estar por encima de la —** to be above (*or* over) par; **estar por debajo de la —** to be under (*or* below) par.
para *prep* **(a)** (*destination, aim, use etc*) for; intended for; **un regalo — ti** a present for you; **lo traje — ti** I brought it for you; **un hotel — turistas** a hotel (intended) for tourists, a tourist hotel; **una taza — café** a coffee cup, a cup for coffee; **no es — comer** it's not for eating, it's not to be eaten; **nació — poeta** he was born to be a poet; **ir — casa** to go home, head for home; **salir — Panamá** to leave for Panama; **decir — sí** to say to oneself; **léelo — ti** read it to yourself; **— esto, podíamos habernos quedado en casa** if this is all it is we might as well have stayed at home.
　(b) **¿— qué?** why?, for what purpose?, what's the use?; **¿— qué lo quieres?** why do you want it?
　(c) **— + infin** (*purpose*) to + *infin*, in order to + *infin*; **lo hizo — salvarse** he did it (in order) to save himself; **— comprarlo necesitas 5 dólares más** to buy it you need another 5 dollars.
　(d) (*bastante, demasiado, muy*) **— + infin**: **tengo bastante — vivir** I have enough to live on; **es demasiado cara — nuestros recursos** it's too dear for our means; **tiene demasiada inteligencia — pensar así** he's too intelligent to think that.
　(e) **— que** in order that, so that; **lo traje — que lo veas** I brought it so that you could see it, I brought it for you to see; **— que eso fuera posible habría que trabajar mucho** you would have to work hard for that to be possible (*or* to bring that about).
　(f) **— + infin** (*result*) only to + *infin*; **se casaron — separarse en seguida** they married only to separate at once.
　(g) (*expressions of time*) **— mañana** for tomorrow; by tomorrow; **lo dejamos — mañana** we left it till tomorrow; **lo tendré listo — fin de mes** I'll have it ready by (*or* for) the end of the month; **— las 2 estaba lloviendo** by 2 o'clock it was raining; **ahora — la feria de agosto hará un año** it'll be a

year ago this (*or* come the) August holiday; *see* **ir** *etc*.
　(h) (*relationships: also —* **con**) to, towards; **tan amable — todos** so kind to everybody; **no hay hombre grande — su ayuda de cámara** no man is a hero to (*or* in the eyes of) his valet.
　(i) (*contrasts*) — **profesor habla muy mal** he talks very badly for a professor; — **niño lo hace muy bien** he does it very well for a child; **es mucho — lo que suele dar** this is a lot in comparison with what he usually gives; **¿quién es Vd — gritar así?** who are you to shout like that?
　(j) *see* **estar 1 (r)** *and* **(s)**; *see* **ir 1 (b)** *etc*.
parabién *nm* congratulations; **dar el — a uno** to congratulate someone (*por* on).
parábola *nf* **(a)** (*Math*) parabola. **(b)** (*Lit*) parable.
parabólico *adj* parabolic.
parabrisas *nm, pl* **parabrisas** windscreen, windshield (*US*).
paracaídas *nm, pl* **paracaídas** parachute; **lanzar algo en —** to send something down by parachute; **lanzarse en —** to parachute (down), (*in emergency*) bale out.
paracaidista *nm* parachutist; (*Mil*) paratrooper; **los —s** (*Mil*) the paratroops.
parachoques *nm, pl* **parachoques** (*Aut*) bumper, fender (*US*); (*Rail*) buffer(s); (*Mech etc*) shock absorber.
parada *nf* **(a)** stop; stopping; stopping place; (*of industry etc*) shutdown, stoppage; standstill; (*of payments*) suspension; — **de autobús** bus stop; — **discrecional** request stop; — **en seco** sudden stop; — **de taxis** taxi stand, cab rank.
　(b) (*of horses*) relay, team.
　(c) bet, stake.
　(d) dam.
　(e) (*Fencing*) parry.
　(f) (*of horses*) stud, breeding establishment.
　(g) (*Mil etc*) parade; (*CAm, Mex, Per, PR*) civic procession; **formar en —** to parade.
　(h) (*CAm, Mex*) clip of cartridges.
　(i) (*SAm*) vanity, pride, presumption; boastfulness; **meter —** to boast, be proud.
　(j) (*Col*) crafty trick.
　(k) (*Per*) farmer's market (*US*), open market.
paradear [1a] *vi* (*RPl*) to brag; to swank, show off; **— con algo** to brag about something, show something off.
paradero *nm* **(a)** whereabouts; **no sabemos su —** we do not know where it is; **averiguar el — de** to ascertain the whereabouts of, locate.
　(b) stopping place; lodging; (*SAm: Rail*) wayside halt; (*Col*) bus stop.
　(c) end; **seguramente tendrá mal —** he'll surely come to a bad end.
paradigma *nm* paradigm.
paradisíaco *adj* heavenly.
parado 1 *adj* **(a)** **estar —** (*person*) to be motionless, be standing still; (*factory*) to be closed, be at a standstill; (*car*) to be stopped, be standing; **salida parada** (*Sport*) standing start.
　(b) **estar —** (*worker*) to be unemployed, be idle; **los —s** the unemployed.
　(c) **estar —** (*SAm*) to be standing (up); **estuve — durante 2 horas** I was standing for 2 hours, I stood for 2 hours.
　(d) **dejar a uno —** (*fig*) to amaze someone; to bewilder someone, leave someone confused; to leave someone in doubt; **¡me deja Vd —!** you amaze me!; **me quedé —** I was completely confused.
　(e) **salir bien —** to come off well, come out of it well; **salió mejor — de lo que cabía esperar** he came out of it better than could be expected; **estar bien —** (*SAm*) to be well placed; to have influence; (*Ec, Per, PR*) to be lucky; **estar mal —** (*Ec, Per, PR*) to be unlucky; **caer — (como los gatos)** to land on one's feet, be lucky.
　(f) **ser —** (*person*) to be slow, be dull, be inactive; to lack character, be weak.
　(g) (*SAm*) hair stiff, straight; *post etc* upright.
　(h) (*Chi, PR*) proud, haughty; vain.
　2 *nm* (*Mex*) air, look, resemblance.
paradoja *nf* paradox.
paradójicamente *adv* paradoxically.
paradójico *adj* paradoxical.
parador *nm* **(a)** (*Hist*) inn; (*modern*) tourist hotel. **(b)** (*heavy*) gambler.
paraestatal *adj body* semi-official, public.
parafina *nf* paraffin wax.
parafrasear [1a] *vt* to paraphrase.
paráfrasis *nf, pl* **paráfrasis** paraphrase.

paragolpes *nm*, *pl* **paragolpes** (*RPl*) = **parachoques**.

paraguas *nm*, *pl* **paraguas** (a) umbrella. (b) (*Col, Cu, Mex*) fungus.

Paraguay: el — Paraguay.

paraguayismo *nm* word (*or* phrase *etc*) peculiar to Paraguay.

paraguayo 1 *adj* Paraguayan. **2** *nm*, **paraguaya** *nf* Paraguayan. **3** *nm* (a) (*Bol*) whip. (b) (*Cu*) long straight knife.

paragüero *nm* umbrella stand.

paraíso *nm* (a) paradise, heaven. (b) (*Theat*) upper gallery, gods.

paraje *nm* place, spot.

paral *nm* (*Mex*) shore, prop; post.

paralela *nf* parallel (line); —s parallel bars.

paralelamente *adv* parallel; (*fig*) in a parallel way, comparably.

paralelismo *nm* parallelism.

paralelo 1 *adj* parallel (*also fig: a* to). **2** *nm* (*all senses*) parallel; **en** — (*Elec*) in parallel.

paralelogramo *nm* parallelogram.

parálisis *nf* paralysis; — **cerebral** cerebral palsy; — **infantil** infantile paralysis; — **progresiva** creeping paralysis.

paralítico 1 *adj* paralytic. **2** *nm*, **paralítica** *nf* paralytic.

paralización *nf* paralysation.

paralizar [1f] **1** *vt* to paralyse (*also fig*); **estar paralizado de un brazo** to be paralysed in one arm; **estar paralizado de miedo** to be paralysed with fright.
2 paralizarse *vr* to become paralysed; (*fig*) to be paralysed, come to a standstill; to stagnate.

paramar *nm* (*Col, Ec, Ven*) season of wind and snow.

param(e)ar [1a] *vi* (*Col, Ec, Ven*) to drizzle.

paramento *nm* (a) ornament, ornamental cover; hangings; (*of horse*) trappings; —s **sacerdotales** liturgical vestments. (b) (*of stone, wall*) face.

paramera *nf* (a) high moorland. (b) (*Ven*) mountain sickness.

paramero 1 *adj* (*Col, Ven*) upland, highland. **2** *nm*, **paramera** *nf* highlander.

paramilitar *adj* paramilitary.

páramo *nm* (a) bleak plateau, high moor. (b) waste land. (c) (*Bol, Col, Ec*) drizzle; storm of wind and snow. (d) (*Ven*) mountain heights.

paramoso *adj* (*Col*) drizzly.

paramuno *adj* (*Col*) upland, highland.

paranera *nf* (*SAm*) grassland.

parangón *nm* comparison; **sin** — incomparable, matchless.

parangonable *adj* comparable (con to).

parangonar [1a] *vt* to compare (con to).

paraninfo *nm* (*Univ*) central hall.

paranoia *nf* paranoia.

paranoico *nm* paranoic.

paranza *nf* (*Hunting*) hide.

parapetarse [1a] *vr* (a) to protect oneself, shelter (*tras* behind). (b) (*fig*) — **tras una razón** to take refuge in a reason (for not doing something).

parapeto *nm* parapet, breastwork; defence, barricade.

paraplejía *nf* paraplegia.

parapléjico 1 *adj* paraplegic. **2** *nm*, **parapléjica** *nf* paraplegic.

parar [1a] **1** *vt* (a) to stop; *breathing, car, engine etc* to stop; *progress* to stop, check, halt.
(b) *blow, threat* to ward off; (*Fencing*) to parry; *pass* (*Sport*) to intercept, cut off; *shot* to stop, save.
(c) *attention* to fix (en on).
(d) (*fig*) to lead; **ahí le paró esa manera de vida** that's where that way of life led him.
(e) (*Cards etc*) to bet, lay, stake.
(f) to prepare, arrange; (*esp SAm*) to stand upright.
2 *vi* (a) to stop; to come to rest; to come to an end; **¡pare!** stop!; **el coche ha parado** the car has stopped; **el autobús para enfrente** the bus stops opposite; **sin** — without stopping; without a break; — **en seco** to stop dead, stop suddenly; **no parará hasta conseguirlo** he won't give up until he gets it; **¡y no para!** (*of speaker*) he just goes on and on!, there's no stopping him!; **vino a** — **a mis pies** it came to rest at my feet.
(b) — **de** + *infin* to stop + *ger*; **ha parado de llover** it has stopped raining; **no para de quejarse** he never stops complaining, he complains all the time; **... y pare Vd de contar** ... and that's the lot, ... and that was it.
(c) — **en** (*of plan etc*) to end up as, result in;

come down to; (*of person*) to end up at; **no sabemos en qué va a** — **todo esto** we don't know where all this is going to end; **el edificio paró en hotel** the building ended up as a hotel; **fueron a** — **en la comisaría** they finished (*or* ended) up at the police station; **irá a** — (**en**) **mal** he'll come to a bad end.
(d) to stay, put up, lodge (en at); **siempre paro en este hotel** I always stay at this hotel.
(e) (*Hunting: of dog*) to point.
3 pararse *vr* (a) (*person etc*) to stop; (*car etc*) to stop, pull up, draw up; (*process*) to come to a halt; (*work etc*) to stop, come to a standstill, cease; — **a** + *infin* to stop to + *infin*, pause to + *infin*.
(b) — **en algo** to pay attention to something, notice something.
(c) (*SAm*) to stand up, get up; to straighten up, sit (*etc*) erect; (*from bed*) to get up; (*hair*) to stand on end.
(d) (*Arg, Cu, Ec, Guat*) to prosper, become wealthy.

pararrayos *nm*, *pl* **pararrayos** lightning conductor.

parasitario *adj*, **parasítico** *adj* parasitic(al).

parasitismo *nm* parasitism.

parásito 1 *adj* parasitic (de on). **2** *nm* (a) parasite (*also fig*). (b) (*Radio*) —s atmospherics, statics.

parasitología *nf* parasitology.

parasol *nm* parasol, sunshade.

paratifoidea *nf* paratyphoid.

paratopes *nm*, *pl* **paratopes** (*Rail*) buffer(s).

Parcas: las — the Parcae.

parcela *nf* plot, piece of ground; smallholding.

parcelar [1a] *vt* to divide into plots; *estate* to break up, parcel out.

parcial *adj* (a) partial; part-. (b) partial, prejudiced, biassed; partisan.

parcialidad *nf* (a) partiality, prejudice, bias; partisanship. (b) party, faction, group, (*esp*) rebel group.

parcidad *nf* = **parquedad**.

parcamente *adv* frugally, sparingly; parsimoniously; moderately.

parco *adj* frugal, sparing; parsimonious; moderate, temperate; **muy** — **en comer** very frugal in one's eating habits; — **en elogios** sparing in one's praises.

parcómetro *nm* parking meter.

parchar [1a] *vt* (*SAm*) to patch, put a patch on, mend.

parche *nm* (a) (*Med*) sticking plaster; (*Aut etc*) patch; (*fig*) patch, mend, botch.
(b) (*Mus*) drumhead; drum.
(c) **pegar un** — (*fam*) to get money by a trick.

parcho (*Ant, Ven*) = **parche**.

pardal *nm* (a) (*Orn*) sparrow; linnet. (b) (*Bot*) aconite. (c) (*fam*) sly fellow, rogue; **¡—!** (*to child*) you rascal!

pardear [1a] *vi* to look brown(ish).

pardiez *interj* good heavens!

pardillo *nm* (a) brown cloth; **gente del** — country folk. (b) (*person*) yokel, rustic. (c) (*Orn*) linnet (*also* — **común**).

pardo 1 *adj* brown; dun; drab, dark grey; *cloud, beer* black, dark; *sky* overcast. **2** *nm* (*Ant, Arg*) mulatto, half-breed; (*Mex*) low-class person.

pardusco *adj* = **pardo**.

parear [1a] **1** *vt* (a) to match, put together; to form pairs of. (b) (*Bio*) to mate, pair. **2 parearse** *vr* to pair off.

parecer 1 *nm* (a) opinion, view; **a mi** — in my opinion; **al** — apparently, seemingly; **por el bien** (*or* **buen**) — for form's sake, as a matter of courtesy; in order not to seem rude; **soy de** — **que ...** I am of the opinion that ... , I take the view that ...; **mudar de** — to change one's mind.
(b) looks; **de buen** — good-looking, nice-looking, handsome; **de mal** — plain, ugly.
2 [2d] *vi* (a) to seem; to look; **parece muy difícil** it seems very difficult, it looks very difficult; **parecía volar** it seemed to fly; **así parece** so it seems; **a lo que parece, según parece** evidently, apparently; **aunque no lo parezca** surprising though it may seem, incredible though it is; **parece como si quisieras ...** it looks as if you wanted to ...; **parece que va a llover** it looks as though it's going to rain, it seems that it's going to rain.
(b) (*hum* comparisons) **parece un alfeñique** he's terribly thin (*fam*); **parece una ballena** (*fam*) she's as fat as a cow (*fam*); **parece un juez** he looks terribly serious (*fam*).
(c) (*with personal pron*) **me parece que ...** I think (that) ... , it seems to me that ...; **como te parece, si a Vd le parece** as you wish; if you think so, if you want to; **¿qué te parece?** what do you

think (of it)?; **vamos a la piscina, ¿te parece?** do you fancy the swimming pool?, what about going to the swimming pool?; **me parece bien que vayas** I think you should go, it seems to be proper you should go; **si a Vd le parece mal** if you don't like it; **le parece mal que no vayas** she takes a poor view of your not going, she doesn't like the idea of your not going; **¡me parece muy mal!** I think it's shocking!

(d) to look like, seem like, resemble; **una casa que parece un palacio** a house that looks like a palace; **¡pareces una reina!** you look like a queen!

(e) to appear, show; (*person*) to turn up, show up, appear; (*lost object*) to turn up, reappear; **pareció el sol entre las nubes** the sun showed (*or* shone) through the clouds; **cuando la luna parezca** when the moon comes up; **ya parecieron los guantes** the gloves turned up; **¡ya pareció aquello!** so that was it!

3 parecerse *vr* (a) (*2 objects etc*) to look alike, resemble each other; **se parecen mucho** they look very much alike, they resemble each other closely; **ni cosa que se parezca** nor anything of the sort; far from it.

(b) — a to look like, resemble; **se parece al abuelo** he takes after his grandfather, he has his grandfather's looks; **el retrato no se le parece** the picture isn't a bit like him.

parecido 1 *adj* (a) similar (*de, en* in, in respect of); — a like, similar to; **son muy —s** they are very similar, they are very much alike.

(b) **bien** — good-looking, nice-looking, handsome; **no es mal parecida** she's not bad-looking.

2 *nm* similarity, likeness, resemblance (*a* to, *entre* between); **tienen mucho** — they are very alike.

parecimiento *nm* (a) (*Arg, Mex, Par*) = **parecido 2**. (b) (*Chi*) appearance.

pared *nf* wall; — **medianera** party wall; — **por medio** next door; **ni que hablara uno a la** — I might as well talk to a brick wall; **ponerse como la** — to go as white as a sheet; **subirse por las —es** (*fam*) to go up the wall (*fam*); **me hace subirme por las —es** it drives me up the wall (*fam*).

paredaño *adj* adjoining, next-door (*con* to).

paredón *nm* (a) thick wall; standing wall (*of ruined house etc*).

(b) wall of rock, rock face.

(c) **llevar a uno al** — to put someone up against a wall, shoot someone; **¡al —!** shoot him!

pareja *nf* (a) pair, couple; pair of Civil Guards; (*Cards*) pair.

(b) other one (of a pair); — **de baile** dancing partner; **no encuentro la** — **de este guante** I can't find the glove that goes with this one, I can't find the other half of my pair of gloves; **correr —s** to be on a par, go together, keep pace (*con* with).

(c) (*SAm*) pair of horses; team of draught animals; yoke of oxen.

parejería *nf* (*Ant, Ven*) vanity, conceit.

parejero 1 *adj* (a) (*Cu, PR, SD*) bold, brazen; presumptuous.

(b) (*Ven*) vain, conceited; given to social climbing.

2 *nm* (a) (*SAm*) racehorse.

(b) (*Ven*) friend, companion.

parejo 1 *adj* (a) equal; **6 todos —s** 6 all the same; **por** — on a par; **ir —s** to be neck and neck; **ir con** to be on a par with, be paralleled by.

(b) *joint etc* smooth, even, flush; (*SAm*) flat, level.

2 *adv* (a) (*SAm*) at the same time, together.

(b) (*Ven*) often.

3 *nm* (*Ant, CAm*) dancing partner, escort.

parentela *nf* relations.

parentesco *nm* relationship, kinship.

paréntesis *nm, pl* **paréntesis** (a) (*Ling*) parenthesis; digression; aside.

(b) (*Typ*) parenthesis, bracket; — **rectos** square brackets; **entre** — (*adj*) parenthetical, incidental; (*adv*) parenthetically, incidentally; **y, entre** — ... and, by the way ..., and, I may add in passing ...

(c) (*fig*) interruption, interval, break.

paria *nmf* pariah.

parián *nm* (*SAm*) market.

parida *nf* woman who has recently given birth.

paridad *nf* (a) parity, equality; similarity. (b) comparison.

parienta *nf* (a) relative, relation. (b) (*fam*) **la** — the wife (*fam*), the missus (*fam*).

pariente *nm* (a) relative, relation; — **político** relative by marriage; **los —s políticos** the in-laws.

(b) (*fam*) **el** — the old man, my (*etc*) hubby (*fam*).

parietal *adj* parietal.

parihuela *nf* stretcher.

parir [3a] **1** *vt* to give birth to, bear.

2 *vi* (*woman*) to give birth, have a baby; to be delivered; (*cow*) to calve (*and similar words for many other species*); **ha parido 4 veces** she has had 4 children, she has given birth 4 times.

París Paris.

parisién *adj*, **parisiense** *adj*, **parisino** *adj* Parisian.

parisiense *nmf* Parisian.

parla *nf* chatter, gossip.

parlador *adj* talkative; **ojos —es** eyes that speak, expressive eyes.

parlamentar [1a] *vi* to converse, talk; (*of enemies*) to parley.

parlamentario 1 *adj* parliamentary. **2** *nm*, **parlamentaria** *nf* parliamentarian; member of parliament.

parlamento *nm* (a) (*Pol*) parliament. (b) (*between enemies*) parley. (c) (*Law, Theat*) speech.

parlanchín 1 *adj* loose-tongued, indiscreet. **2** *nm*, **parlanchina** *nf* (a) chatterbox, great talker. (b) indiscreet person.

parlante *adj machine etc* talking.

parlar [1a] *vi* to chatter (away), talk (a lot), gossip; (*of parrot*) to talk.

parlero *adj* (a) talkative, garrulous; gossipy. (b) *bird* talking; singing, song (*attr*); *stream* musical; *eyes* expressive.

parleta *nf* chat, small talk.

parlotear [1a] *vi* to chatter, prattle.

parloteo *nm* chatter, prattle.

Parnaso *m* Parnassus.

parné *nm* (*sl*) dough (*sl*), brass (*sl*).

paro[1] *nm* (*Orn*) tit.

paro[2] *nm* (a) stoppage (of work); standstill; **hay — en la industria** work in the industry is at a standstill.

(b) (*also* — **forzoso,** — **obrero**) unemployment; — **estacional** seasonal unemployment; **subsidio de** — unemployment benefit, unemployment compensation (US).

(c) (*Col, SD, Ven*) throw (*at dice*).

(d) (*Col*) **en** — all at once, in one go.

parodia *nf* parody, travesty, takeoff; (*fig*) travesty.

parodiar [1b] *vt* to parody, travesty, take off.

parodista *nmf* parodist, writer of parodies.

parola *nf* (a) fluency; verbosity; gift of the gab (*fam*).

(b) chitchat; wearisome talk; —**s** (*Arg*) empty talk, hot air.

parón *nm* sudden halt, complete stop.

paroxismo *nm* paroxysm; — **histérico** hysterics; — **de risa** convulsions of laughter; **en un** — **de celos** in a fit of jealousy, in a paroxysm of jealousy.

parpadear [1a] *vi* (*eye*) to blink, wink; (*light*) to blink, flicker; (*star*) to twinkle.

parpadeo *nm* blinking, winking; flickering; twinkling.

párpado *nm* eyelid; **restregarse los —s** to rub one's eyes.

parque *nm* (a) park; — **de automóviles,** — **de estacionamiento** carpark, parking lot (US); — **de atracciones** fun fair, fairground; — **nacional** national park; — **zoológico** zoo.

(b) (*Mil etc*) depot; — **de artillería** artillery depot, artillery stores; — **de bomberos** fire station; **el** — **nacional de automóviles** the total number of cars in the country; **el** — **provincial de tractores** the number of tractors in use in the province.

(c) — **de jugar** playpen.

(d) (*SAm: Mil*) equipment; ammunition.

parqué *nm* (*Acad*) parquet.

parqueadero *nm* (*Col*) carpark, parking lot (US); parking place.

parquear [1a] *vti* (*SAm: angl*) to park.

parquedad *nf* frugality, sparingness; parsimony; moderation.

parqueo *nm* (*SAm: angl*) parking; carpark, parking lot (US); parking place.

parquet [par'ke] *nm* (*gall*) parquet.

parquímetro *nm* parking meter.

parra *nf* grapevine; climbing vine, trained vine; **subirse a la** — (*fam*) to blow one's top (*fam*).

párrafo *nm* paragraph; **echar un** — (*fam*) to have a chat (*con* with).

parral *nm* vine arbour.

parranda *nf* (a) spree (*fam*), party (*fam*); **andar** (*or* **ir** *etc*) **de** — to go on a binge (*sl*), have a party. (b) (*Col, Chi, Mex*) lot, group, heap; **una** — **de** a lot of.

parricida *nmf* parricide (*person*).

parricidio *nm* parricide (*act*).

parrilla *nf* (a) grating, gridiron, grille; (*Cook*) grill; **carne a la** — grilled meat. (b) grillroom, steak restaurant.

parrillada nf grill; barbecue.
párroco nm parish priest.
parroquia nf (a) (Eccl) parish; parish church.
 (b) (Comm) clientèle, customers; **hoy hay poca —** there are few customers today; **una tienda con mucha —** a shop with a large clientèle, a well-patronized shop.
parroquial adj parochial, parish (attr).
parroquiano nm, **parroquiana** nf (a) (Eccl) parishioner.
 (b) (Comm) client, customer, patron; **ser — de** to be a regular client of, shop regularly at, patronize.
parsi nmf Parsee.
parsimonia nf (a) carefulness (about money etc); sparingness.
 (b) deliberateness, calmness; phlegmatic nature; **con —** deliberately, calmly, unhurriedly.
parsimonioso adj (a) sensible, careful (about money etc); economical; sparing. (b) slow, deliberate, calm, unhurried; phlegmatic.
parte[1] nm (Tel) message; report; (Mil) dispatch, communiqué; **— meteorológico** weather report, weather forecast; **dar — a uno** to report to someone, inform someone.
parte[2] nf (a) (in general) part; portion, section; **cuarta —** quarter, fourth part; **tercera —** third; **reducir algo en una tercera —** to reduce something by a third; **la mayor — de** most of; the greater part of, the great majority of; **la mayor — de los argentinos** most Argentinians, most of the Argentinians; **— del mundo** part of the world; **en las cinco —s del mundo** in the four corners of the earth; **— de la oración** part of speech; **ser — esencial** (or **integrante**) **de** to be an essential part of; **de algún tiempo a esta —** for some time past; **como — del pago** in part payment; in part exchange; **de una — a otra** back and forth, to and fro; **de — a —** through and through, right through; **de — de** from, on behalf of; in the name of; **de parte de todos nosotros** on behalf of us all; **salúdale de mi —** give him regards from me, give him my regards; **en — en parte**, partly; **en gran —** to a large extent, in large measure; **por — de** on the part of; **con concesiones por ambas —s** with concessions on both sides; **por —s** bit by bit; stage by stage, systematically; **por otra — (or)** again, on the other hand; **por una — ... por otra (—)** on the one hand, ... on the other; **yo por mi —** I for my part; **por la mayor —** mostly, for the most part; **echar algo a mala —** to look on something with disapproval, be offended about something; **echar una palabra a mala —** to use a word incorrectly; **(entrar a) formar — de** to form a part of, be a part of; (person) to be a member of; **no formaba — del equipo** he was not in the team; **tomar algo en buena —** to take something in good part.
 (b) share; **la — del león** the lion's share; **a —s iguales** in equal shares; **ir a la —** to go shares; **llevar la mejor —** to have the advantage, be on the way to winning; **llevarse la mejor —** to come off best, get the best of it; **tener — en** to share in; **tomar —** to take part (en in).
 (c) (of place, Geog etc) part; **en alguna —** somewhere; **en alguna — de Europa** somewhere in Europe; **en cualquier —** anywhere; **por ahí no se va a ninguna —** that leads nowhere, (fig) this is getting us nowhere; **en ninguna — del país** in no part of the country, nowhere in the country; **de ninguna — esperes ayuda** don't expect help from any quarter; **ir a otra —** to go somewhere else; **mirar a otra —** to look the other way, look in another direction; **ha de estar en otra —** it must be somewhere else; **¿en qué — del país?** in which part of the country? **¿en qué — lo dejaste?** whereabouts did you leave it?; **en todas —s** everywhere; **en todas —s de España** in all parts of Spain, everywhere in Spain, all over Spain; **por todas —s se va a Roma** all roads lead to Rome.
 (d) (of object) side; **por cualquier — que lo mires** from whichever side you look at it.
 (e) (Mus, Theat) part.
 (f) (of relationship) side; **por — de madre** on the mother's side.
 (g) (person) contender; (Law) party, side; **— actora** prosecution; plaintiff; **las —s contratantes** the contracting parties; **— contraria** opposing party, other side; **tercera —** third party; **ponerse de — de** to take the side of, side with.
 (h) **—s** (of person) parts, qualities, talents; **buenas —s** good parts.
 (i) (Anat) **—s** parts; **—s pudendas** pudenda, private parts; **la — donde la espalda pierde su**

honesto nombre (hum, euph) one's anatomy; **le dio en salva sea la —** (euph) it hit her on a part of her anatomy.
 (j) (Mex: Mech) = **pieza**.
parteaguas nm, pl **parteaguas** divide, ridge; **— continental** continental divide.
partear [1a] vt woman to deliver.
partenogénesis nf parthenogenesis.
partenueces nm, pl **partenueces** nutcracker.
partera nf midwife.
partición nf division, sharing-out; (Pol etc) partition.
participación nf (a) (act) participation, taking part.
 (b) share; (Fin) share, stock (US), investment; **— en los beneficios** profit-sharing; **su — en estos asuntos** his share (or part) in these matters.
 (c) (Sport) entry; **hubo una nutrida —** there was a big entry, there were numerous entrants.
 (d) (part of a) lottery ticket.
 (e) notice, notification; **— de boda** notice of a forthcoming wedding; **dar — a uno de algo** to inform someone of something.
participante nmf participant; (Sport) entrant, entry.
participar [1a] **1** vt to notify, inform; **— algo a uno** to notify someone of something; **le participo que ...** I have to tell you that ...; I warn you that ...
 2 vi (a) to take part, participate (en in); **— en una carrera** to enter for a race, run in a race, take part in a race.
 (b) **— de** (or **en**) **una herencia** to share in an estate; **— en una empresa** (Fin) to invest in an enterprise.
 (c) **— de una cualidad** to share a quality, partake of a quality, have a quality in common.
partícipe nmf participant; **hacer — a uno de algo** to share something with someone, inform someone of something.
participial adj participial.
participio nm participle; **— de pasado** past participle; **— de presente** present participle.
partícula nf particle.
particular **1** adj (a) particular, special; peculiar (a to); **nada de —** nothing special; **lo que tiene de — es que ...** what's remarkable about it is that ...; **en —** in particular; **en este caso —** in this particular case; **tiene un sabor —** it has a special flavour, it has a flavour of its own.
 (b) private, personal; **tiene coche —** he has a car of his own, he has a car to himself; **secretario —** private secretary; **en —** in private.
 2 nm (a) particular, point, matter; **no dijo mucho sobre el —** he didn't say much about the matter.
 (b) individual, private individual; **no comerciamos con —es** we don't do business with individuals.
particularidad nf (a) particularity, peculiarity; **tiene la — de que ...** one of its special features is ..., it has the characteristic that ...
 (b) friendship, intimacy.
particularizar [1f] **1** vt (a) to distinguish, characterize, mark out.
 (b) to particularize, specify.
 (c) to show special friendship to.
 (d) to give details about.
 2 particularizarse vr (a) to distinguish itself, stand out, mark itself out; (person) to make one's mark, do something outstanding.
 (b) **— con uno** to single someone out (for special treatment etc).
partida nf (a) departure.
 (b) register; certificate; entry (in a register etc); **— de bautismos** register of baptisms; **— de bautismo** certificate of baptism; **— de defunción** death certificate; **— de matrimonio** marriage certificate, marriage lines; **— de nacimiento** birth certificate.
 (c) (Comm, Fin: of account) entry, item; (in budget etc) item, section, heading; **— doble** double entry; **— simple** single entry.
 (d) (Comm: of goods) consignment.
 (e) (Cards) game, hand; (Chess etc) game; **— de dobles** doubles match; **— de individuales**, **— de simples** singles match; **echar una —** to have a game.
 (f) stake, wager, bet.
 (g) (persons) party; (Mil etc) band, group; faction; **— de caza** hunting party; **— de campo** picnic (party); **— de excursión** group of trippers.
 (h) (mala) **—**, **— serrana** dirty trick.

partidario 1 *adj* partisan. **2** *nm,* **partidaria** *nf* (a) supporter, follower (*de* of); partisan. (b) (*Cu, Ec*) sharecropper.

partidismo *nm* partisanship, bias; partisan spirit; (*Pol, pej: also* —**s**) party feeling, party politics.

partidista 1 *adj* partisan. **2** *nmf* partisan.

partido *nm* (a) (*Pol etc*) party; — **político** political party; — **de la reforma** reforming party; — **republicano** republican party; **sistema de** — **único** one-party system, single-party system.

(b) (*Sport etc*) game, match; fixture; — **amistoso** friendly game; — **de fútbol** football match; — **internacional** international match.

(c) (*Sport etc: persons*) team, side.

(d) (*also* — **judicial**) district, administrative area.

(e) **darse a** —, **venir(se) a** — to give way; **tomar** — to decide, make up one's mind; to take sides.

(f) advantage, profit; **sacar** — **de** to profit from, benefit from; to put to use.

(g) support; **tiene** — **en todas las clases** he has support among all classes.

(h) **de** — *bachelor* eligible; **Lola es un** — (*sl*) Lola's a girl with money; Lola's hot stuff (*sl*).

(i) (*Chi: Cards*) hand.

(j) (*Mex*) smallholding; portion of a crop given to the landlord.

(k) (*Bol, Cu*) **a** —, **al** — equal shares.

partija *nf* (a) partition, division. (b) (*pej*) = **parte²**.

partir [3a] **1** *vt* (a) to split (up, into two *etc*), divide (up); *nut etc* to crack; to break open, split open; — **la cabeza a uno** to split (*or* crack) someone's head open.

(b) *slice etc* to cut off.

(c) to share (out), distribute, divide (up); — **algo con otros** to share something with others.

(d) *cards* to cut.

2 *vi* (a) to start, set off, set out, depart (*de* from, *para* for, *con rumbo a* for, in the direction of).

(b) to start (*de* from); **a** — **del lunes** from Monday, starting on (*or* from) Monday; **es el tercero a** — **de la esquina** it's the third one counting from the corner; **a** — **de estos datos** starting from these data; **hemos partido de un supuesto falso** we have started from a false assumption.

3 partirse *vr* to crack, split, break (in two *etc*).

partisano 1 *adj* partisan. **2** *nm* (*Mil*) partisan.

partitivo *adj* partitive.

partitura *nf* (*Mus*) score.

parto *nm* (a) birth, childbirth; delivery; labour; **asistir un** — to deliver a baby; **estar de** — to be in labour; **tener un** — **difícil** to have a difficult labour.

(b) (*fig*) product, creation; — **del ingenio** brainchild; **el ensayo ha sido un** — **difícil** I sweated blood over the essay.

parturición *nf* parturition.

parturienta *nf* woman in labour; woman who has just given birth.

party *nm or f* (*angl*) party.

parva *nf* (heap of) unthreshed corn; (*fig*) heap, pile.

parvada *nf* (*SAm*) flock.

parvedad *nf* littleness, smallness; fewness; **una** — a very small amount, a tiny bit.

parvulario *nm* nursery school, kindergarten.

párvulo *nm,* **párvula** *nf* child, infant; (*School*) infant.

pasa *nf* raisin; — **de Corinto** currant; — **de Esmirna** sultana.

pasable *adj* (a) passable, tolerable. (b) (*SAm*) *stream etc* fordable, that can be forded. (c) (*Arg*) saleable.

pasablemente *adv* passably, tolerably (well).

pasada *nf* (a) (*act*) passing, passage; (*with cloth etc*) rub, clean, polish; — **de pintura** coat of paint; **dar dos** —**s de jabón a la ropa** to soap the clothes twice.

(b) **de** — in passing, incidentally.

(c) (*Sew*) row of stitches; tacking stitch; —**s** patch, mend, botch.

(d) **mala** — dirty trick.

(e) (*fam*) **una** — **de** a lot of, a whole heap of.

(f) (*CAm, Arg*) telling-off.

(g) (*Col*) shame, embarrassment.

pasadera *nf* stepping stone.

pasadero *adj* passable, tolerable.

pasadizo *nm* passage, corridor; passageway, alley, (*with shops*) arcade; gangway; catwalk.

pasado 1 *adj* (a) past; **lo** — the past; **lo** —, — let bygones be bygones; **el mes** (**próximo**) — last month; — **mañana** the day after tomorrow; —**s dos días** after two days.

(b) *food* stale, bad; *fruit* overripe; *cooked dish* overdone; *news, story* stale; *idea* antiquated, out of date; *clothing etc* old, worn, threadbare; *beauty* faded; **la carne está pasada** the meat is off (*or* bad); **ella está un poco pasada** she's a little past her best.

2 *nm* (a) past.

(b) (*Gram*) past (tense).

(c) —**s** ancestors.

pasador *nm* (a) (*of window etc*) bolt, fastener; (*for hair, tie etc*) pin; (*Tech*) bolt; split pin.

(b) (*Cook*) colander; (*Tech*) filter.

(c) —**es** cufflinks; (*Per*) shoelaces.

(d) (*person*) smuggler.

pasaje *nm* (a) (*act*) passage, passing; (*Naut*) voyage, crossing.

(b) fare; **cobrar el** — to collect fares.

(c) passengers (*collectively*).

(d) passageway, alleyway; (*with shops*) arcade; (*Arg, Cu, Mex*) cul-de-sac.

(e) (*Lit, Mus*) passage.

(f) (*Col, Ven*) story, anecdote.

(g) (*Col*) tenement building.

pasajeramente *adv* fleetingly.

pasajero 1 *adj* (a) passing, fleeting, transient.

(b) *pájaro* — bird of passage, migratory bird.

(c) *street etc* busy.

2 *nm,* **pasajera** *nf* passenger; traveller.

3 *nm* (*Mex*) ferryman.

pasamano(s) *nm* (a) rail, handrail; bannister(s). (b) (*Arg, Chi*) strap (*for standing passenger*). (c) (*Chi*) tip.

pasamontaña(s) *nm* Balaclava (helmet).

pasante *nm* assistant; assistant teacher.

pasapasa *nm* sleight of hand.

pasaporte *nm* passport; **dar el** — **a uno** (*sl*) to bump someone off (*sl*).

pasapurés *nm, pl* **pasapurés** grinder, mincer.

pasar [1a] **1** *vt* (a) (*general sense*) to pass; *object* to hand, give, pass (*a* to); *message, news* to give, pass on; *bill* to send; *property* to transfer; *person* to take, lead, conduct (*a* to, into); **¿me pasas la sal, por favor?** would you please pass the salt?; **nos pasaron a otra habitación** they led us into another room; **nos pasaron a ver al director** they took us to see the director; *see* **lista**, **revista** etc.

(b) *illness* to give, infect with; **me has pasado tu tos** you've given me that cough.

(c) *visit etc* to make, carry out; **el médico pasará visita** the doctor will call.

(d) *river, street etc* to cross, go over.

(e) *armour etc* to pierce, penetrate, go through; *barrier* to pass through (*or* across, over), go through; *boundary etc* to cross, go beyond; **el túnel pasa la montaña** the tunnel goes right through the mountain; **esto pasa los límites de lo razonable** this goes beyond anything that is reasonable.

(f) *pin etc* to insert, put in; to put through; — **el café por el colador** to put the coffee through a filter, strain the coffee.

(g) *drink, pill etc* to swallow; (*SAm*) to bear, stand, put up with; **no puedo** — **este vino** I can't get this wine down; **no puedo** — **a ese hombre** (*SAm*) I can't bear that chap.

(h) *exam etc* to pass.

(i) *fault etc* to overlook, tolerate; *person* to forgive, indulge, be soft on; **no te voy a** — **más** I'm not going to indulge you any more.

(j) *false coin* to pass (off); *goods* to smuggle (in, out); **a ése se le puede** — **cualquier cosa** you can get anything past him.

(k) to surpass, excel; *competitor* to do better than, beat, outdistance; (*Aut*) to pass, overtake; **él me pasa ya 3 cms** he's already 3 cms taller than I am.

(l) *event, date etc* to pass, go past; *illness* to get over; **hemos pasado el aniversario** we are past the anniversary, the anniversary is behind us.

(m) to omit, leave out, pass over; to skip; to overlook; *see* **alto 3** (f).

(n) *time* to spend, pass; — **las vacaciones** to spend one's holidays; **fuimos a** — **el día en la playa** we went to the seaside for a day; **lo bien** to have a good time; **¡que lo pases bien!** have a good time!, enjoy yourself!; **lo pasaremos tan ricamente** we'll have such a good time; **lo mal** to have a bad time (of it); —**las moradas** (*etc*) to have a tough time of it.

(o) *hardships* to suffer, endure, go through.

(p) — **la mano por algo** to pass (*or* run) one's hand over something; to stroke something; — **el rosario** to tell one's beads; — **el cepillo por el pelo** to run a brush through (*or* over) one's hair.

2 *vi* (**a**) (*general sense*) to pass, go; **pasó de mis manos a las suyas** it passed from my hands into his; **la cuerda pasa de un lado a otro de la calle** the rope goes from one side of the street to the other; **el hilo pasa por el agujero** the thread goes through the hole; **el río pasa por la ciudad** the river flows (*or* goes, runs) through the city; **el autobús pasa por nuestra casa** the bus goes past our house.

(**b**) (*general sense: of person*) to pass, go; to move; to come in, go in; **¡pase Vd!** come in!; after you!; **— a un cuarto contiguo** to go into an adjoining room, move into an adjoining room; **no se puede —** you can't go in; you can't go through; **pasamos directamente a ver al jefe** we went straight in to see the chief; **nos hicieron —** they showed us in (*a* to), they ushered us in; **— a decir algo** to go on to say something; **y luego pasaron a otra cosa** and then they went on to something else; **los moros pasaron a España** the Moors crossed into (*or* over to) Spain; **— adelante** to go on, continue, proceed; **— de Inglaterra al Canadá** to move (*or* go, migrate) from England to Canada; **— de teniente a general** to go from lieutenant to general; **— por una crisis** to go through a crisis; **pasaré por tu casa** I'll call on you (at home), I'll drop in.

(**c**) (*of proposal*) to pass, get through, be approved; (*of excuse*) to be accepted; **puede —** it's passable, it's O.K. (*fam*); **esta moneda no pasa** this coin is a dud, this coin is no good.

(**d**) **— de** to go beyond; to exceed; **— de los límites** to exceed the limits; **pasa ya de los 70** he's over 70; **esto pasa de ser una broma** this goes beyond a joke; **no pasa de ser una mediocridad** he's no more than a mediocrity; **no pasan de 60 los que lo tienen** those who have it do not number more than 60; **de ésta no pasa** this is the very last time; **de hoy no pasa que le escriba** I'll write to him this very day; **yo de ahí no paso** that's as far as I can go; I draw the line at that; there I stick.

(**e**) (*Cards*) to pass; **paso** I pass, no bid.

(**f**) **Juan pasa por francés** John could be taken for a Frenchman; **pasa por buen pintor** he is considered to be a good painter; **pasa por sabio** he has a reputation for learning; **se hace — por médico** he passes himself off as a doctor, he poses as a doctor.

(**g**) **ir pasando** (*fig*) to get by, manage (somehow); **— con poco** to get along with very little; **tendrá que — sin coche** he'll have to get along without a car; **pasa por todo con tal que no le hagan trabajar** he'll put up with anything as long as they don't make him work.

(**h**) (*of time*) to pass, go by, elapse; **han pasado 4 años ya** 4 years have gone by; **¡cómo pasa el tiempo!** how time passes!

(**i**) (*of event, state etc*) to be over; to pass away; (*of effect*) to pass off, wear off; **ha pasado la crisis** the crisis is over; **ya pasó aquello** that's all over (and done with) now.

(**j**) to happen; **aquí pasa algo misterioso** something odd is going on here; **¿qué pasa?** what's happening?, what's going on?, what's up?; **¿qué le pasa a ése?** what's the matter with him?; **algo le pasa al motor** something's the matter with the engine; **lo que pasa es que . . .** , **pasa una cosa y es que . . .** what's happening is that . . . , it's like this . . . ; **como si no hubiese pasado nada** as if nothing (unusual) had happened, come what may; **no me ha pasado otra (igual) en la vida** nothing like it has ever happened to me before.

3 pasarse *vr* (**a**) (*state, effects etc*) to pass, pass off; **ya se te pasará** you'll get over it.

(**b**) **se me pasó el turno** I missed my turn; **no se te pase la oportunidad** don't miss the chance this time.

(**c**) (*movement etc*) = **1** (**a**); **— al enemigo** to go over to the enemy.

(**d**) (*flower, beauty etc*) to fade; (*fruit*) to go soft, get overripe; (*food*) to go bad, go off, get stale; (*tea*) to stew; (*cloth*) to wear, show signs of wear, get threadbare; (*woman*) to lose her charms; **no se pasará si se tapa la botella** it will keep if you put the cap on the bottle.

(**e**) to go too far, go over the line (*etc*); (*fig*) to overdo it; to say too much, go too far; **se pasa en mostrar agradecimiento** he overdoes the gratitude.

(**f**) (*time*) = **1** (**n**); **se ha pasado todo el día leyendo** he has spent the whole day reading.

(**g**) **— con**, **— sin**; *see* **2** (**g**).

(**h**) **no se le pasa nada** nothing escapes him, nothing gets past him, he misses nothing; **se me pasó + *infin*** I forgot to + *infin*.

(**i**) **— de + *adj*** to be too + *adj*, be excessively + *adj*; **se pasa de generoso** he's too generous; *see* **listo**.

4 *nm*: **un modesto —** modest means, modest income; **tener un buen —** to be well off.

pasarela *nf* footbridge; catwalk; (*Naut*) gangway, gangplank.

pasarrato *nm* (*Mex, PR*) = **pasatiempo**.

pasatiempo *nm* pastime, (leisure) pursuit; hobby; amusement.

pascana *nf* (**a**) (*Arg, Bol, Per*) wayside inn. (**b**) (*Arg, Bol, Per*) stage, part (of a journey); (*Col, Ec*) part of a journey done without stopping.

Pascua *nf*, **pascua** *nf* (**a**) **— florida**, **— de Resurrección** Easter; **— de Navidad** Christmas; **— de Pentecostés** Whitsun, Whitsuntide; **—s** Christmas holiday, Christmas time (*strictly*, Christmas Day to Twelfth Night); **¡felices —s!** merry Christmas!

(**b**) **— de los hebreos**, **— de los judíos** Passover.

(**c**) (*idioms*) . . . **y santas —s** . . . and that's that, . . . and that's the lot; . . . and there's nothing one can do about it; **de —s a Ramos** once in a blue moon; **estar como unas —s** to be as happy as a sandboy; **hacer la — a uno** (*fam*) to do the dirty on someone.

pascual *adj* paschal.

pase *nm* (*all senses*) pass.

paseandero *adj* (*Arg, Chi, Par*) fond of strolling.

paseante *nmf* (**a**) walker, stroller; passer-by; (*pej*) loafer, idler. (**b**) (*of woman*) suitor.

pasear [1a] **1** *vt* (**a**) *child, dog etc* to take for a walk, walk; *child* (*fig*) to keep amused, entertain.

(**b**) *banner etc* to parade, show off, exhibit; to walk about (the streets) with.

(**c**) **— la calle a una muchacha** to prowl up and down the street where a girl lives.

(**d**) (*CAm*) *money* to squander.

2 *vi* and **pasearse** *vr* (**a**) to walk, go for a walk, stroll; to walk about, walk up and down; **— en bicicleta** to go for a ride, go cycling; **— en coche** to go for a drive, go driving, go for a run; **— a caballo** to ride, go riding; **— en bote** (*etc*) to go sailing, go on a trip.

(**b**) **pasearse** (*fig*) to idle, loaf about.

(**c**) **pasearse por un tema** to deal superficially with a subject.

(**d**) **pasear** (*Mex*) to take a day off.

paseíllo *nm* (*Taur*) inaugural procession (*or* ceremonial entry) of bullfighters.

paseo *nm* (**a**) (*act*) stroll, walk; outing; **— en bicicleta**, **— a caballo** ride; **— en coche** drive, run, ride, outing; **— de vigilancia** round, tour of inspection; **dar un —** to go for a walk, take a walk (*or* stroll); to go for a ride (*etc*); **dar el — a uno** (*sl*) to bump someone off (*sl*); **estar de —** to be out for a walk; **enviar** (*or* **mandar**) **a uno a —** to tell someone to go to blazes; to chuck someone out, send someone packing; **¡vete a —!** get lost! (*fam*); **llevar** (*or* **sacar**) **a un niño de —** to take a child out for a walk.

(**b**) parade, avenue; **— marítimo** promenade, esplanade.

(**c**) (*distance*) short walk; **entre las dos casas no hay más que un —** it's only a short walk between the two houses.

(**d**) (*SAm*) **— cívico** civic procession.

pasero *nm* (*Col*) ferryman.

pasillo *nm* (**a**) passage, corridor; (*Parl: fig*) lobby; (*Naut*) gangway. (**b**) (*Theat*) short piece, sketch.

pasión *nf* (**a**) (*in most senses*) passion; **tener — por** to be passionately fond of, have a passion for. (**b**) (*pej*) bias, prejudice, partiality.

pasional *adj* (**a**) *person etc* passionate; **crimen —** crime of passion. (**b**) temperamental.

pasionaria *nf* passionflower.

pasito *adv* gently, softly.

pasivamente *adv* passively.

pasividad *nf* passiveness, passivity.

pasivo 1 *adj* (**a**) passive; inactive. (**b**) (*Gram*) passive. **2** *nm* (**a**) (*Comm, Fin*) liabilities, debts; (*of account*) debit side. (**b**) (*Gram*) passive (voice).

pasmado *adj* (**a**) **dejar — a uno** to amaze someone; **estar** (*or* **quedar**) **— de** to be amazed at, be astonished at.

(**b**) (*fam*) **estar** (*or* **quedar**) **—** to stand gaping, be bewildered, look silly; **se quedó ahí —** he just stood there gaping; **¡oye, —!** hey, you idiot!

(**c**) (*SAm*) *wound* infected, unhealthy; *person* unhealthy-looking, ill-looking, seedy.

(**d**) (*CAm, Mex*) dull, stupid; clumsy.

(**e**) (*CAm, PR*) sluggish, phlegmatic.

pasmar [1a] **1** vt **(a)** to amaze, astonish, astound; to stun, dumbfound.
(b) to chill (to the bone); *plants* to nip, cut.
2 pasmarse vr **(a)** to be amazed (*etc*; *de* at); to be dumbfounded; to marvel, wonder (*de* at).
(b) to be chilled to the bone; to catch a chill.
(c) (*SAm*) to become infected; to fall ill, look seedy; to catch a fever.
(d) (*Mex, PR: fruit*) to dry up, wither.
pasmarota nf, **pasmarotada** nf display of shocked surprise, exaggerated reaction.
pasmazón nm (*CAm, Mex, PR*) = **pasmo.**
pasmo nm **(a)** amazement, astonishment; awe; (*fig*) wonder, marvel, prodigy; **es el — de cuantos lo ven** it is a marvel (*or* a source of wonder) to all who see it.
(b) (*Med*) lockjaw, tetanus.
(c) (*Med*) chill.
(d) (*SAm*) fever; inflammation.
pasmosamente adv amazingly; awesomely; wonderfully.
pasmoso adj amazing, astonishing; awesome, breathtaking; wonderful.
paso[1] adj *fruit* dried.
paso[2] **1** nm **(a)** (*act*) passing, passage; crossing; (*Aut*) overtaking, passing; (*Orn, Zool*) migration, passage; (*fig*) transition; progress; **el — del tiempo** the passage of time; **lo recogeré al —** I'll pick it up when I'm passing; **salir al — a** (*or* **de**) to waylay; to confront; (*fig*) to nip in the bud; to strangle at birth; **de —** in passing; by the way, incidentally; **estar de —** to be passing through; **entrar de —** to drop in, call in (for a moment).
(b) way through, passage; (*Archit*) passage; **¡—!** make way!, gangway!; **— elevado, — a distinto nivel** (*Aut*) flyover; **— franco, — libre** free passage, free access; clear way through; **— inferior** underpass; **— a nivel** level crossing, grade crossing (*US*); **— de** (*or* **para**) **peatones** pedestrian crossing; **— subterráneo** subway, underpass (*US*); **"prohibido el —"** "no thoroughfare" (*Aut*), "no entry"; **abrir — para** to make way for; **abrirse —** to make one's way (*entre, por* through), force a way through; **abrirse — luchando** to fight one's way through; **abrirse — a tiros** to shoot one's way through; **ceder el —** to make way; (*Aut*) to give way, yield (*US*); **"ceda el —"** (*Aut*) "give way"; **ceder el — a** (*fig*), **dar — a** to give way to, give place to; **cerrar el —** to block the way.
(c) (*Geog*) pass; (*Naut*) strait.
(d) (*of foot*) step, pace; (*mark*) footprint; (*sound*) footstep, footfall; (*distance*) pace; **— atrás** step backwards, (*fig*) backward step; **— a —** step by step; **a cada —** at every step, at every turn; **a grandes —s, a —s agigantados** (*fig*) by leaps and bounds; **a dos —s de aquí** two steps from here, very near here; **estar a un — mínimo de** to border on, verge closely on; **por sus —s contados** step by step, systematically; **coger el —** to fall into step (*con* with; *also fig*); **dar un —** to take a step; **dar un — en falso** to step on something that is not there, trip; (*fig*) to take a false step; **no da un — sin hacer alguna barbaridad** he can't take a step without doing something awful; **llevar el —** to keep in step, keep time; **marcar el —** (*SAm*) to keep time, (*fig*) to mark time; **seguir los —s a uno** to tail someone, shadow someone; **seguir los —s de uno** to follow in someone's footsteps; **volver sobre los —s** to retrace one's steps.
(e) walk, gait; speed, pace, rate; (*of horse*) gait; **— de andadura** amble; **buen —** quick step, good pace; **a buen —** quickly; (*fig*) at a good rate; **a — lento** at a slow pace, slowly; **a — ligero** (*Mil*), **a — redoblado** (*SAm*) at the double; **a — de tortuga** at a snail's pace; **a ese —** (*fig*) at that rate; **al — slowly; al — que vamos** at the rate we're going; **al — que . . .** (*as conj*) at the same time as . . . ; while . . . , whereas . . . ; **acelerar** (*or* **apretar, avivar** *etc*) **el —** to go faster, quicken one's pace; **aflojar el —** to slow down, slacken one's pace; **establecer el —** to make the pace, set the pace; **romper el —** to break step.
(f) (*of dance*) step; **— a dos** pas de deux; **— de vals** waltz step.
(g) (*fig*) step, move; measure; **es un — hacia nuestro objetivo** it's a step towards our objective; **andar en malos —s** to be mixed up in shady affairs; **dar un mal —** to take a false step, make a false move; to get in the family way; **dar los primeros —s** to make the first moves; *see also fig senses in* **(d).**
(h) episode, incident, event.

(i) (*Theat: Hist*) sketch, interlude; (*Eccl*) float (*or series of sculptures etc*) representing part of the Easter story, carried in procession.
(j) (*Elec, Tech*) pitch.
(k) **— de armas** (*Mil: Hist*) passage of arms.
(l) difficulty, awkward situation, crisis; **salir del —** to get out of a jam, get out of trouble.
(m) (*SAm*) ford.
2 adv softly, gently; **¡—!** not so fast!, easy there!
pasoso adj **(a)** (*Col, Chi, Guat, Per, Ven*) porous, permeable; absorbent. **(b)** (*Chi*) perspiring, sweaty. **(c)** (*Ec*) contagious.
paspa nf (*Bol, Ec, Per*), **paspadura** nf (*RPl*) chapped skin, cracked skin.
pasparse [1a] vr (*SAm: skin*) to chap, crack.
paspartú nm passe-partout.
pasquín nm skit, satire, lampoon.
pasta nf **(a)** (*in general*) paste; **— de carne** meat paste; **— de dientes, — dentífrica** toothpaste; **— de madera** wood pulp.
(b) (*of tooth*) filling; (*of pencil*) lead.
(c) cardboard; papier mâché; (*Typ*) boards; **— española** marbled leather binding; **media —** half-binding; **libro en —** book in boards.
(d) (*Cook*) dough; pastry (*mixture*); **—s** pastries, cakes; noodles, spaghetti.
(e) (*sl*) money, dough (*sl*).
(f) de buena — equable; kindly, good-natured.
pastaje nm (*Arg, Col, Guat, Urug*) pasture.
pastal nm (*SAm*) pasture, grazing land.
pastar [1a] vti to graze.
pastear [1a] vt to graze.
pastejón nm solid mass, lump.
pastel nm **(a)** (*Cook: of fruit etc*) cake; (*of meat etc*) pie; **—es** pastry, confectionery.
(b) (*Art*) pastel; pastel drawing (*also* **pintura al —**).
(c) (*Cards*) sharp practice; (*fig*) plot; undercover agreement, cynical compromise, deal; **se le descubrió el —** his little game was found out.
(d) (*fam*) botch, mess.
pastelear [1a] vi **(a)** to indulge in sharp practice; to make an undercover agreement. **(b)** to stall, spin it out to gain time.
pastelería nf **(a)** (*art of*) confectionery, pastrymaking. **(b)** pastry, pastries (*collectively*). **(c)** confectioner's, pastry shop, cake shop.
pastelero 1 adj (*Arg*) meddlesome, intriguing. **2** nm, **pastelera** nf pastrycook; confectioner.
pastelillo nm small cake; **— de mantequilla** pat of butter; **— de hígado de ganso** pâté de foie gras.
pastelón nm (*Chi*) large paving stone.
pasteurización nf pasteurization.
pasteurizado adj pasteurized.
pasteurizar [1f] vt to pasteurize.
pastilla nf tablet, pastille; (*of soap etc*) cake, bar; (*of chocolate*) bar, piece; **— para la tos** cough drop, throat lozenge.
pastinaca nf parsnip.
pastizal nm pasture.
pasto nm **(a)** grass, herbage, fodder; grazing; **un sitio abundante en —s** a place with rich grazing.
(b) (*any*) food, feed (*for cattle*).
(c) pasture, field; (*SAm*) grass, lawn; **echar el ganado al —** to put animals out to pasture.
(d) (*fig*) food, nourishment; fuel; **fue — del fuego** it was fuel to the flames, the flames devoured it; **es — de la murmuración** it is a subject for gossip, gossip thrives on it; **— espiritual** spiritual nourishment.
(e) a — abundantly; **había fruta a —** there was fruit in unlimited quantities; **beber a todo —** to drink for all one is worth, drink to excess; **cita refranes a todo —** he quotes vast quantities of proverbs, he greatly overdoes the proverbs.
(f) vino de — ordinary wine.
pastor nm **(a)** (*Agr*) shepherd; herdsman, goatherd, cowman (*etc*). **(b)** (*Eccl*) (*protestant*) minister, clergyman, pastor. **(c) el Buen P—** the Good Shepherd.
pastora nf shepherdess.
pastoral 1 adj pastoral. **2** nf pastoral, idyll.
pastorear [1a] vt **(a)** *flock* to pasture, shepherd; to look after; (*Eccl*) to guide, lead.
(b) (*CAm, Arg, Urug*) to lie in wait for.
(c) (*CAm*) to spoil, pamper.
(d) (*Arg, Urug*) to court.
pastorela nf (*Lit*) pastourelle.
pastoril adj (*Lit*) pastoral.
pastoso adj **(a)** *material* doughy; soft; pasty. **(b)** *voice* rich, mellow, pleasant. **(c)** (*Arg, Chi*) grassy. **(d)** (*Col*) lazy.

pastura nf (a) pasture. (b) food, fodder, ration of feed.

pasudo adj (Mex) hair kinky.

pata nf (a) (Zool) foot, leg; paw; (Orn) foot; (of person, hum) foot; (of furniture etc) leg; — de cabra (Tech) crowbar; — de gallina (Ant, Col, Ven) crow's-feet (wrinkles); — de gallo crow's-feet; (fam) silly remark, piece of nonsense; bloomer (fam); — hendida cloven hoof; la — coja, la — sola (Col) hopscotch; eso lo sé hacer a la — coja I can do that blindfold; —s arriba on one's back, upside down; (fig) upside down, topsy-turvy; a — on foot; a cuatro —s on all fours; a la — la llana plainly, simply, directly; bluntly; andar a —s (child) to crawl, go on all fours; andar a — renca (SAm) to limp; enseñar la —, sacar la — to give oneself away; estirar la — (sl) to peg out (sl); meter la — to put one's foot in it, make a blunder; to blot one's copybook; to butt in; ser —(s) to be even, tie; es un diccionario con dos —s he's a walking dictionary; es la virtud con dos —s she is virtue personified; tener buena — to be lucky; tener mala — to be unlucky; to be clumsy; ser de mala — to be unlucky, bring bad luck.
(b) (Zool) (female) duck.
(c) P—s the devil; —s cortas shorty, little man.

patacón nm (a) (Col) slice of fried banana. (b) (Chi) bruise, welt.

patache nm (a) (Arg) flat-bottomed boat. (b) (Ec, Per) soup; food (in general).

patacho nm (a) (Arg, Par) flat-bottomed boat. (b) (CAm, Mex) train of mules.

patada nf kick; stamp; a —s in abundance, in great quantity; (treat etc) roughly, inconsiderately; dar —s to kick; to stamp; dar —s para conseguir algo to take steps to obtain something; dar la — a uno (fam) to give someone the boot (fam); dar a uno una — en el culo (fam) to kick someone up the backside (fam); me da cien —s it gets on my nerves; he gives me a pain in the neck, I can't stand him; echar a uno a —s to kick someone out.

patagón 1 adj Patagonian. 2 nm, **patagona** nf Patagonian.

patagónico adj Patagonian.

patalear [1a] vi (a) to stamp (angrily).
(b) por mí, que patalee so far as I'm concerned he can make all the fuss he likes.
(c) (child etc) to kick out, kick about.

pataleo nm stamping; kicking.

patán nm rustic, yokel; (pej) lout.

pataplún (SAm) = cataplum.

patarata nf (a) gush, affectation, emotional fuss; excessive show of feeling. (b) silly thing; triviality; —s nonsense, tomfoolery.

pataratero adj (a) gushing, affected. (b) silly.

pataruco adj (Ven) (a) coarse, rough. (b) cowardly.

patata nf (a) potato; — de siembra seed potato; — temprana early potato; —s enteras potatoes in their jackets; —s a la española, —s fritas chips, French fries (US); —s inglesas crisps, potato chips (US); —s mojadas, puré de —s mashed potatoes.
(b) no se me da una —, (no) me importa una — I don't care two hoots (de about); no entendió una — he didn't understand a word of it.

patatal nm, **patatar** nm potato field, potato patch.

patato adj (Cu), **patatuco** adj (Cu) chubby, plump.

patatús nm dizzy spell, queer turn.

pateada nf (Arg) long tiring walk; = pateadura.

pateadura nf, **pateamiento** nm (a) stamping, kicking. (b) (in argument) flat denial; violent interjection; (Theat) noisy protest.

patear [1a] 1 vt (a) to stamp on, trample (on); to kick, boot.
(b) (fig) to trample on, treat roughly, treat inconsiderately.
(c) (Ven) to abuse.
2 vi (a) to stamp (with rage), stamp one's foot; (Theat etc) to stamp.
(b) (SAm: of animal, gun) to kick.
(c) (Chi, RPl: of food etc) to cause an upset, be harmful.
(d) (Chi, RPl) to go long distances on foot.
(e) (fam) to be always on the go, bustle about.

patena nf paten.

patentado adj patent; proprietary.

patentar [1a] vt to patent.

patente 1 adj (a) patent, obvious, evident; hacer — to show clearly, establish.
(b) (Comm etc) patent.
2 nf (a) grant; warrant; (Comm) patent; — de invención patent; — de navegación ship's certificate of registration; — de privilegio letters patent; — de sanidad bill of health; de — patent; (Chi) first-rate.
(b) (Arg, Par: Aut) licence plate.
2 nm (Cu) patent medicine.

patentizar [1f] vt to show, reveal, make evident.

pateo nm stamping; (Theat) stamping, noisy protest, the bird (sl).

páter nm (fam): el — the pater (fam).

paternal adj fatherly, paternal.

paternalmente adv paternally, in a fatherly fashion.

paternidad nf (a) (in general) fatherhood, parenthood. (b) (of child) paternity; — literaria authorship.

paterno adj paternal; abuelo — paternal grandfather, grandfather on the father's side.

patero adj (a) (Chi) fawning. (b) (Per) tricky, untrustworthy.

patéticamente adv pathetically, movingly, poignantly.

patético adj (a) pathetic, moving, poignant. (b) (Chi) clear, evident.

patetismo nm pathos, poignancy.

patiabierto adj bow-legged.

patibulario adj (a) horrifying, harrowing. (b) person of criminal appearance.

patíbulo nm scaffold; gallows, gibbet.

patidifuso adj (fam) aghast, shattered; openmouthed; nonplussed; dejar a uno — to shatter someone; to nonplus someone.

patiestevado adj bandy-legged.

patihendido adj cloven-hoofed.

patilla 1 nf (a) (Arg) bench.
(b) (Col, Ven) watermelon.
(c) (Chi: Bot) layer.
(d) —s whiskers, sideburns.
2 —s nm: P—s Old Nick; ser un —s to be a weak character, be a poor fish.

patín nm skate; (of sledge) runner; (Aer) skid; — de cola (Aer) tailskid; — de cuchilla, — de hielo iceskate; — de ruedas roller skate.

pátina nf patina.

patinadero nm skating rink.

patinador nm, **patinadora** nf skater.

patinadura nf (Ven) skid, skidding.

patinaje nm skating; — artístico, — de figuras figure skating.

patinar [1a] vi (a) (person) to skate. (b) (Aut etc) to skid, slip. (c) (fam) to boob (sl), make a blunder. (d) (Arg) to fail.

patinazo nm (a) skid. (b) (fam) boob (sl), blunder; dar un — to make a boob, blunder.

patinete nm (child's) scooter.

patio nm court, courtyard, patio; (Theat) pit; (Mex) shunting yard; — de recreo playground.

patiquín nm (Ven) fop, dandy.

patita nf: see calle (a).

patitieso adj (a) paralysed with cold (or fright etc). (b) (fig) = patidifuso. (c) (fig) vain, conceited.

patito nm duckling.

patituerto adj with crooked legs.

patizambo adj knock-kneed.

pato nm (a) duck; — (macho) drake; — real, — silvestre mallard, wild duck; pagar el — (fam) to foot the bill; to take the blame, carry the can (sl); ser el — de la boda (or fiesta) (SAm) to be the one who pays; to be an object of ridicule, be a laughing stock; salga — o gallareta (SAm) whatever the results.
(b) (fam) bore, dull person; estar hecho un — to be terribly dull.
(c) (fam) boredom; boring time; boring party (etc).
(d) (Col) stowaway; sponger (fam); gatecrasher.
(e) (Ec) victim (of a swindle).
(f) (Arg) ser un —, estar — to be broke (fam).
(g) (SAm: Med) bedpan.

patochada nf blunder, bloomer (fam).

patojo 1 adj (SAm) having deformed legs (or feet); waddling; lame. 2 nm, **patoja** nf (CAm, Col) child; sweetheart; (pej) street urchin, ragamuffin.

patología nf pathology.

patológico adj pathological.

patólogo nm pathologist.

patomachera nf (Ven) loud argument.

patoso 1 adj boring, tedious; would-be clever. 2 nm bore; smart-aleck (fam).

patota nf (RPl) street gang, mob of young thugs.

patotero nm (RPl) rowdy, young thug.

patraña nf story, fib; hoax; long involved story.

patraquear [1a] vt (Chi) object to steal; person to hold up, attack.

patraquero nm (Chi) thief; holdup man.

patria *nf* native land, mother country; fatherland; — **adoptiva** country of adoption; — **chica** home town, home area; **madre** — mother country; **luchar por la** — to fight for one's country; *see* **merecer**.
patriada *nf* (RPl) rising, revolt.
patriarca *nm* patriarch.
patriarcado *nm* patriarchy.
patriarcal *adj* patriarchal.
Patricia *f* Patricia.
Patricio *m* Patrick.
patricio 1 *adj* patrician. 2 *nm*, **patricia** *nf* patrician.
patrimonial *adj* hereditary.
patrimonio *nm* (a) inheritance.
 (b) *(fig)* heritage; birthright; **el — artístico de la nación** our national art heritage, the national art treasures; **nuestro — forestal** our national stock of trees, the forestry resources we have inherited.
patrio *adj* (a) native, home *(attr)*; **el suelo** — one's native land, one's native soil. (b) *(Law)* power *etc* paternal.
patriota 1 *nmf* patriot. 2 *nm* (CAm) banana.
patriotería *nf* ostentatious patriotism, flag-wagging; chauvinism; jingoism.
patriotero 1 *adj* ostentatiously patriotic; chauvinistic; jingoistic. 2 *nm*, **patriotera** *nf* flag-wagger; chauvinist; jingoist.
patrióticamente *adv* patriotically.
patriótico *adj* patriotic.
patriotismo *nm* patriotism.
patrocinador *nm*, **patrocinadora** *nf* sponsor, patron(ess).
patrocinar [1a] *vt* to sponsor, act as patron to; to back, support; **un movimiento patrocinado por . . .** a movement under the auspices of . . . (*or* under the patronage of).
patrocinio *nm* sponsorship, patronage; backing, support.
patrón *nm* (a) patron; *(Eccl: also* **santo** —) patron saint; *(of slave)* master; *(fig)* master, boss, chief; *(Naut)* skipper; *(of boarding house etc)* landlord.
 (b) *(Sew, Tech)* pattern; *(for measurement etc)* standard; — **oro** gold standard; — **picado** stencil.
 (c) *(Agr)* prop, shore.
 (d) *(Agr)* stock *(for grafting)*.
patrona *nf* patron(ess); *(Eccl)* patron saint; employer, owner; *(of boarding house etc)* landlady.
patronal *adj* (a) **organización** — employers' organization, owners' organization; **la clase** — management, the managerial class; **cerrado por acto** — closed by the employers, closed by the owners *(or* management).
 (b) *(Eccl)* of a patron saint.
patronato *nm* (a) *(act)* patronage; sponsorship; **bajo el** — **de** under the auspices of, under the patronage of.
 (b) *(Comm, Fin)* employers' association, owners' organization; *(Pol)* the owners *(as a class)*, management; **el** — **francés** *(loosely)* French industrialists, French capitalism.
 (c) board of trustees, board of management; **el** — **de turismo** the tourist board, the tourist organization.
patronímico 1 *adj* patronymic. 2 *nm* patronymic.
patronizar [1a] *vt* (SAm: angl) to patronize.
patrono *nm* patron; sponsor; protector, supporter; *(Eccl)* patron saint; *(Comm, Fin)* owner, employer.
patrulla *nf* patrol.
patrullar [1a] 1 *vt* to patrol, police. 2 *vi* to patrol.
patrullero *nm* patrol boat.
patucho *adj* (Ec) short, squat.
patudo *nm* (Per): **el** — the devil.
patueco *adj* (CAm) = **patojo**.
patulea *nf* (fam) mob, rabble.
patuleco *adj* (SAm), **patulejo** *adj* (Chi), **patuleque** *adj* (Cu) = **patojo, patituerto**.
patullar [1a] *vi* (a) to trample about, stamp around. (b) to bustle about, keep very busy, be always on the go. (c) to chat.
paturro *adj* (Col, Chi) chubby, plump; squat.
paulatinamente *adv* gradually, slowly.
paulatino *adj* gradual, slow.
paulina *nf* (fam) (a) telling-off. (b) poison-pen letter.
Paulo *m* Paul.
pauperismo *nm* pauperism.
paupérrimo *adj* very poor, terribly poor.
pausa *nf* (a) pause; break, respite; interruption; *(Mus)* rest. (b) **con** — slowly, deliberately.
pausadamente *adv* slowly, deliberately.
pausado *adj* slow, deliberate.
pausar [1a] 1 *vt* to slow down; to interrupt. 2 *vi* to go slow.

pauta *nf* (a) line, guide line.
 (b) ruler.
 (c) *(fig)* guide, guide lines, model; standard, norm; outline, plan, key; **dar** *(or* **marcar)** **la** — to set a standard, lay down a norm; **servir de** — **a** to act as a model for.
pautado *adj*: **papel** — ruled paper.
pautar [1a] *vt* (a) *paper* to rule. (b) *(fig: esp CAm)* to establish a norm for, lay down a pattern for, give directions for.
pava *nf* (a) *(Orn)* turkey (hen); — **real** peahen; **pelar la** — *(fam: of lovers)* to talk, whisper sweet nothings, canoodle *(sl)*.
 (b) *(Arg, Bol, Per, Urug)* kettle; teapot; pot for making maté.
 (c) *(Col, Ec, PR, Ven)* broad-brimmed straw hat.
 (d) *(Col, CR)* fringe.
 (e) *(Chi, Mex)* chamber pot.
 (f) *(Bol, Chi, Per)* coarse banter; tasteless joke; **hacer la** — **a** to play a joke on.
 (g) *(Ec, Pan)* fag end.
 (h) *(fam)* **es una** — she's a dull person.
pavada *nf* (RPl) (a) silly thing; silliness, stupidity.
 (b) triviality; very small amount.
pavear [1a] 1 *vt* (a) *(Col)* to kill treacherously.
 (b) *(Chi, Per)* to play a joke on.
 2 *vi* (a) *(Chi, RPl)* to act the fool, do silly things.
 (b) *(Arg, Chi)* = **pelar la pava**.
 (c) *(Ec, Pan)* to play truant; *(PR)* to malinger, slack.
pavería *nf* (Chi, RPl) silliness, stupidity.
pavero *nm*, **pavera** *nf* (Chi, Per) practical joker.
pavimentar [1a] *vt* to pave; to floor.
pavimento *nm* pavement, paving; *(inside house)* flooring.
pavisoso *adj* (fam), **pavitonto** *adj* (fam) nice but a bit dull.
pavo *nm* (a) *(Orn)* turkey (cock); — **real** peacock.
 (b) **comer** — *(fam)* to be a wallflower *(at a dance)*; *(SAm)* to be disappointed; to get embarrassed.
 (c) *(fam)* silly thing, idiot; **¡no seas** —**!** don't be silly!
 (d) *(sl)* 5 pesetas, one *duro*.
 (e) **ponerse hecho un** —, **subirse a uno el** — to blush like a lobster; **tener mucho** — to blush a lot.
 (f) *(Col)* large kite.
 (g) *(Col)* big shot *(fam)*; evil-looking person.
 (h) *(SAm)* **ir de** — *(on bus etc)* to travel free, travel without paying one's fare.
 (i) *(Ant)* telling-off.
pavón *nm* (a) *(Orn)* peacock. (b) *(Tech)* bluing, bronzing.
pavonearse [1a] *vr* to swagger, strut (about); to swank, show off.
pavoneo *nm* swagger(ing), strutting; swanking *(fam)*, showing-off.
pavor *nm* dread, terror.
pavorosamente *adv* frighteningly, terrifyingly.
pavoroso *adj* dreadful, frightening, terrifying.
pavoso *adj* (Ven) unlucky; that brings bad luck.
payacate *nm* (Mex) handkerchief.
payada *nf* (Chi, RPl) extemporized song (of *gaucho* minstrel); — **de contrapunto** contest between two *payadores*.
payador *nm* (Chi, RPl) *gaucho* minstrel, popular musician *(poet and guitarist)*.
payar [1a] *vi* (Chi, RPl) to improvise songs to a guitar accompaniment.
payasada *nf* clownish trick, stunt; *(pej)* ridiculous thing (to do); —**s** clowning, tomfoolery; *(Theat etc)* slapstick, knockabout humour.
payasear [1a] *vi* (SAm) to clown, do clownish things.
payaso *nm* clown *(also fig)*.
payés *nm* (Catalonia, Balearics) peasant farmer.
payo 1 *adj* (a) *(Arg)* albino. (b) *(Mex)* rustic, simple. (c) *(Mex)* dress *etc* loud, flashy, tasteless. 2 *nm* (in *gipsy speech*) non-gipsy.
payuelas *nfpl* chickenpox.
paz *nf* (a) peace; peacefulness, tranquility; **¡a la** — **de Dios!** God be with you!; **en** — **y en guerra** in peace and war, in peacetime and wartime; **no dar** — **a** to give no rest *(or* respite to); **no dar** — **a la lengua** to keep on and on; **dejar a uno en** — to leave someone alone, leave someone in peace; **¡déjame en** —**!** leave me alone!; **descansar en** — to rest in peace; **su madre, que en** — **descanse, lo decía** her mother (God rest her soul) used to say so; **estar en** — to be at peace; *(fig)* to be quits, be all square *(con* with); **¡haya** —**!** stop it!, that's enough!; **mantener la** — to keep the peace; **¡aquí** — **y después gloria!** and that's that!, Bob's your uncle! *(fam)*.

(b) peace, peace treaty; **la — de los Pirineos** the Peace of the Pyrenees (1659); **hacer las paces** to make peace, (*fig*) to make it up.

pazguato *adj* (a) simple, stupid. (b) prudish.

pe: de — a pa from A to Z, from beginning to end.

peaje *nm* toll.

peal *nm* (*SAm*) lasso.

pealar [1a] *vt* (*SAm*) to lasso.

peana *nf* stand, pedestal, base.

peatón *nm* pedestrian, person on foot; walker.

pebete 1 *nm* (a) joss stick. (b) (*Mil*) fuse. (c) (*fam*) small object. **2** *nm*, **pebeta** *nf* (*RPl*) kid (*fam*), child; short person.

peca *nf* freckle.

pecado *nm* sin; **— capital, — grave, — mortal** mortal sin; **— de comisión** sin of commission; **— nefando** sodomy; **— original** original sin; **— venial** venial sin; **por mis —s** for my sins; **sería un — no aprovecharlo** it would be a crime (*or* sin, pity) not to make use of it.

pecador 1 *adj* sinful, sinning. **2** *nm*, **pecadora** *nf* sinner.

pecaminoso *adj* sinful.

pecar [1g] *vi* (a) (*Eccl*) to sin; (*fig*) to err, go astray; **si he pecado en esto, ha sido por . . .** if I have been at fault in this, it has been because . . .; **si me lo pones delante, acabaré pecando** if you put temptation in front of me, I shall fall.
   (b) (*fig*) **— de + adj** to be too + *adj*; **peca de generoso** he is too generous, he is excessively generous; **nunca se peca por demasiado cuidado** one can't be too careful; **peca por exceso de confianza** he is too confident, he errs on the side of over-confidence.

pececillos *nmpl* (*Fish*) fry.

pecera *nf* fishbowl, fishtank.

pecios *nmpl* flotsam, wreckage.

pécora *nf* (*esp* **mala —**) bitch; loose woman, whore.

pecoso *adj* freckled.

pecotra *nf* (*Chi: Anat*) bump, swelling; (*on wood*) knot.

pectina *nf* pectin.

pectoral 1 *adj* pectoral. **2** *nm* (*Eccl*) pectoral cross.

pecuaca *nf* (*Col, Ec, Ven*) = **pecueca**.

pecuario *adj* cattle (*attr*).

pecueca *nf* (*Col, Ec, Ven*) hoof; (*hum*) smell of feet.

peculado *nm* peculation.

peculiar *adj* special, peculiar; typical, characteristic.

peculiaridad *nf* peculiarity; special feature, characteristic.

peculio *nm* one's own money; modest savings.

pecunia *nf* (*fam*) brass (*sl*), cash.

pecuniario *adj* pecuniary, money (*attr*).

pecha *nf* (*Arg, Chi*), **pechada** *nf* (*SAm*) push, shove.

pechar[1] [1a] *vti* to pay (as a tax).

pechar[2] [1a] *vt* (a) (*SAm*) to push, shove. (b) (*SAm*) **— a uno** to touch someone for a loan (*sl*). (c) (*Chi*) to collar (*fam*), grab.

pechazo *nm* (*SAm*) push, shove; (*fig*) bold act, unprincipled deed; (*fam*) touch (for a loan: *sl*).

pechblenda *nf* pitchblende.

peche (*CAm*) **1** *adj* skinny, weak. **2** *nm* child.

pechera *nf* (a) shirt front; (*of dress*) front, bosom; (*Mil etc*) chest protector; **— postiza** dicky. (b) (*Anat: hum*) (big) bosom. (c) (*Chi: Tech*) apron.

pechero[1] *nm* (*Hist*) commoner, plebeian.

pechero[2] *nm* (*Sew*) front (*of dress*); bib.

pechicato *adj* (*Cu*) = **pichicato**.

pecho[1] *nm* (a) (*Anat*) chest; **de — plano** flat-chested; **a — descubierto** unarmed, defenceless; (*fig*) openly, frankly; **dar el —** to face things squarely; **estar de —s sobre una barandilla** to be leaning on a railing; **gritar a todo —** (*Col, PR*) to shout at the top of one's voice; **quedarse con algo entre — y espalda** to keep something back; to have something on one's mind; **sacar el —** to thrust one's chest out, draw oneself up.
   (b) (*woman's*) breast; **los —s** the breasts, the bosom, the bust; **dar el —** to feed, suckle, nurse.
   (c) (*fig*) heart, breast; **abrir** (*or* **descubrir**) **su — a uno** to unbosom oneself to someone; **no le cabía en el —** he just had to talk about it; he was bursting with happiness; **tomar algo a —** to take something to heart.
   (d) (*fig*) courage, spirit; **¡— al agua!** courage!
   (e) (*Geog*) slope, gradient.

pecho[2] *nm* (*Hist*) tax, tribute.

pechoño *adj* (*Bol, Chi*) sanctimonious.

pechuga *nf* (a) (*of chicken etc*) breast; (*hum: woman's*) bosom; cleavage.
   (b) (*Geog*) slope, hill.

(c) (*SAm*) sangfroid; (*pej*) nerve, insolence.
   (d) (*Ec, Pan, Per*) abuse of trust.
   (e) (*Guat, Hond, Nic, Pan*) trouble, annoyance.

pechugón 1 *adj* (a) (*Arg, Mex, PR*) big-bosomed.
   (b) (*SAm*) shameless, brazen, insolent; sponging (*fam*), parasitical; on the make (*fam*).
   (c) (*Chi*) bold, single-minded.
   2 *nm* (*SAm*) shameless individual, impudent person; sponger (*fam*), parasite; go-getter.

pechuguera *nf* (*Bol, Col, Mex*) hoarseness; chest trouble, bronchitis.

pedagogía *nf* pedagogy.

pedagógico *adj* pedagogic(al).

pedagogo *nm* teacher; educator; (*pej*) pedagogue.

pedal *nm* pedal; **— de acelerador** accelerator (pedal); **— de embrague** clutch (pedal); **— de freno** footbrake, brake (pedal); **— dulce, — piano, — suave** (*Mus*) soft pedal; **— fuerte** (*Mus*) loud pedal.

pedalear [1a] *vi* to pedal; **— en agua** to tread water.

pedante 1 *adj* pedantic. **2** *nm* pedant.

pedantería *nf* pedantry.

pedantescamente *adv* pedantically.

pedantesco *adj* pedantic.

pedazo *nm* (a) piece, bit; scrap; morsel; **un — de papel** a piece of paper; **un — de pan** a bit of bread, a scrap of bread; **es un — de pan** (*fig*) he's a terribly nice person; **trabaja por un — de pan** he works for a mere pittance; **hacer algo a —s** to do something in pieces, do something piecemeal; **hacer —s** to break to pieces, tear (*or* pull) to pieces; to shatter, smash; **se hizo —s** it fell to pieces, it came apart; it broke up; it shattered, it smashed (itself); **estoy hecho —s** I'm worn out.
   (b) (*fig*) **— del alma, — de las entrañas, — del corazón** one's darling, the apple of one's eye; (*in direct address*) my darling; **— de animal** blockhead; **¡— de animal!, ¡— de bruto!** you idiot!; you beast!

pederasta *nm* pederast.

pederastia *nf* pederasty.

pedernal *nm* flint; **como un —** (*fig*) of flint, flinty.

pederse [2a] *vr* (*tabu*) to fart (*tabu*).

pedestal *nm* pedestal, stand, base.

pedestre *adj* (a) traveller *etc* on foot; walking. (b) (*fig*) pedestrian.

pedestrismo *nm* walking (*as a sport*).

pediatra *nmf* paediatrician.

pediatría *nf* paediatrics.

pedicura *nf* chiropody.

pedicuro *nm* chiropodist.

pedidera *nf* (*CAm, Col, Ec, Ven*) = **petición**.

pedido *nm* (*Comm*) order; **— de ensayo** trial order; **— de repetición** repeat order; **a — on** request; **a — de** at the request of.

pedigüeño *adj* insistent, importunate; demanding.

pedilón 1 *adj* (*SAm*) = **pedigüeño**. **2** *nm* (*SAm*) pest, nuisance.

pedimento *nm* petition; (*Law*) claim, bill.

pedir [3l] **1** *vt* (a) to ask for, request; **meal to** order; (*Comm*) to order (*a* from); **— algo a uno** to ask someone for something; **— la paz** to sue for peace; **— que . . .** to ask that . . .; **me pidió que cerrara la puerta** he asked me to shut the door; **pidió que se volviera a estudiar la cuestión** he asked that the matter should be studied afresh; **el pescado es tal que no hay más que —** the fish is as good as it could possibly be.
   (b) (*Comm*) *price* to ask; **¿cuánto piden por él?** how much are they asking for it?
   (c) **— a una joven** to ask for a girl's hand in marriage; **fue anoche a —la a su padre** he went last night to ask for permission to marry the girl.
   (d) (*Law*) to file a claim against.
   (e) (*fig*) to need, demand, require; to cry out for; **la casa está pidiendo una mano de pintura** the house is crying out for a dab of paint; **ese color pide una cortina azul** that colour needs a blue curtain to go with it; **el triunfo pide que bebamos algo** the victory demands to be celebrated with a drink.
   2 *vi* (a) to ask.
   (b) (*also* **— por Dios**) to beg.
   (c) see **boca** (a).

pedo *nm* (*tabu*), **pedorrera** *nf* (*tabu*) fart (*tabu*).

pedorrero *adj* (*tabu*) given to farting (*tabu*), windy.

pedrada *nf* (a) throw of a stone; hit (*or* blow) from a stone; **matar a uno a —s** to stone someone to death; **pegar una — a uno** to throw a stone at someone.
   (b) (*fig*) wounding remark, snide remark, dig.
   (c) **la cosa le sentó como una —** he took it very ill, the affair went down very badly with him; **me sienta como una — tener que irme** I don't in the

least want to go; **venir como — en ojo de boticario** to come just right, be just what the doctor ordered.

pedrea nf (a) stone-throwing, fight with stones. (b) (*Meteorol*) hailstorm. (c) small prizes in the lottery.

pedregal nm stony place, rocky ground.

pedregón nm (*SAm*) big stone, rock, boulder.

pedregoso adj stony, rocky.

pedregullo nm (*RPl, Ven*) crushed stone, grit; small loose stones.

pedrejón nm big stone, rock, boulder.

pedrera nf stone quarry.

pedrería nf precious stones, jewels.

pedrero nm (a) quarryman, stone cutter. (b) (*CAm, Col, Chi*) = **pedregal**.

pedrisco nm (a) shower of stones; (*Meteorol*) hailstorm. (b) heap of stones.

Pedro m Peter; **entrar como — por su casa** to come in as if one owned the place.

pedrusco nm (a) rough stone; piece of stone, lump of stone. (b) (*Meteorol*) hailstorm; hailstones. (c) (*SAm*) = **pedregal**.

pedúnculo nm stem, stalk.

peerse [2a] vr = **pederse**.

pega nf (a) (*act*) sticking.
(b) beating; beating-up.
(c) practical joke; hoax, trick.
(d) snag, difficulty; **todo son —s** there's nothing but problems; **poner —s** to raise objections; to make trouble.
(e) searching question; catch question, trick question.
(f) **de —** false, dud; fake, sham, bogus; **un billete de —** a dud banknote.
(g) (*Cu, Chi*) job.
(h) (*Cu*) birdlime.
(i) (*Chi: of disease*) infectious period.
(j) (*Chi*) **estar en la —** to be at one's best.

pegada nf (a) (*Arg*) (a) fib, lie. (b) piece of luck.

pegadillo nm (*Ec*) lace.

pegadizo 1 adj (a) sticky.
(b) (*Med*) infectious, catching.
(c) (*Mus*) tune catchy.
(d) sham, imitation.
(e) person parasitic, sponging (*fam*).
2 nm sponger (*fam*), hanger-on.

pegado 1 adj (*fig*) **dejar a uno —** to leave someone nonplussed; **estar —** to have no idea, not have a clue; **quedarse —** to be bewildered, be nonplussed.
2 nm patch, sticking plaster.

pegadura nf (*Col, Ec*) practical joke.

pegajoso adj (a) sticky, adhesive; viscous.
(b) (*Med*) infectious, catching; (*fig*) contagious; tempting.
(c) person over-sweet; sloppy, cloying; too free with one's hands.

pegamento nm gum, sticky stuff; **— de caucho** (*Aut etc*) rubber solution.

pegar [1h] 1 vt (a) to stick (on, together, up); to glue, gum, paste; poster to post, stick up; (*Sew*) to sew (on), fasten (on); parts to join, fix together; **— un sello** to stick a stamp on; **— una estantería a una pared** to put a set of shelves against a wall; **— una silla a una pared** to move a chair up against a wall.
(b) (*Med*) disease to give, infect with; idea etc to give, communicate (a to).
(c) blow to give, hit, deal; ball to hit; person to hit, strike; to smack, slap; **dicen que pega a su mujer** they say he knocks his wife about; **es un crimen — a los niños** it's a crime to hit (*or* smack) children; **"pegad fuerte a Eslobodia"** (*slogan*) "hit Slobodia hard"; **hazlo o te pego** do it or I'll bash you (*fam*).
(d) (*fam*) **— un grito** to let out a yell; **— un puntapié a uno** to give someone a kick; **— un salto** to jump (with fright etc); see susto, fuego etc.
(e) (*SAm*) **—la** to be lucky; to manage it, get what one wants; to make a hit (con with).
(f) (*Mex*) to tie, fasten (down); horse etc to hitch up.
(g) (*Ven*) work to start.
2 vi (a) to stick, adhere; see cola.
(b) **— en** to touch; **el piano pega en la pared** the piano is touching the wall.
(c) (*Bot*) to take root; (of remedy) to take; (of fire) to catch.
(d) **— con uno** to run into someone.
(e) (of colours etc) to match, go together; **— con** to match, go with; **ese sombrero no pega con el abrigo** that hat doesn't go with the coat.
(f) to hit; to beat; **— en** to hit, strike (against); **la flecha pegó en el blanco** the arrow hit the target;

pegaba con un palo en la puerta he was hitting (*or* pounding on) the door with a stick; **las ramas pegan en los cristales** the branches beat against the windows.
(g) (of sun) to strike hot; **a estas horas el sol pega fuerte** the sun strikes very hot at this time; **el sol pega en esta ventana** the sun comes (*or* shines) in through this window.
3 **pegarse** vr (a) to stick.
(b) (2 persons) to hit each other, fight.
(c) **— a uno** to stick to someone, attach oneself to someone; **— a una reunión** to intrude on a meeting, go to a meeting uninvited.
(d) (*Med*) to be catching.
(e) (*Cook*) to catch, burn.
(f) (*fam*) **ella se la pega a su marido** she's deceiving her husband, she's unfaithful to her husband.
(g) **— un tiro** to shoot oneself; **se pega una vida de millonario** (*fam*) he lives the life of Riley, he has a whale of a time (see also vida).

Pegaso m Pegasus.

pegativo adj (*Chi, Hond*) sticky.

pegoste nm (*CAm, Col, Mex, Ven*) sticking plaster.

pegote nm (a) sticking plaster; (*fig*) patch, ugly mend, botch.
(b) (*Cook: fam*) sticky mess, sticky lump.
(c) (*fam*) botch, clumsy job.
(d) (*fam*) sponger (*fam*), hanger-on.

pegotear [1a] vi (*fam*) to sponge (*fam*), cadge.

peina nf ornamental comb.

peinada nf combing; **darse una —** to comb one's hair, have a brush up.

peinado 1 adj (a) **bien —** well combed; neat, well-groomed.
(b) (*fig*) foppish, over elegant, overdressed; affected, overdone.
2 nm hairdo; coiffure, hair style.

peinador nm (a) hairdresser. (b) peignoir, dressing gown. (c) (*SAm*) dressing table.

peinadora nf hairdresser.

peinadura nf (a) combing. (b) **—s** combings.

peinar [1a] 1 vt (a) hair to comb; to do, arrange, style; horse, skin to dress.
(b) (*SAm*) rock to cut.
(c) (*Arg*) to flatter.
2 **peinarse** vr to comb one's hair, do one's hair; **— a la griega** to do one's hair in the Greek style.

peine nm comb; **¡ya pareció el —!** so that was it!

peinecillo nm fine comb.

peineta nf ornamental comb.

peinilla nf (*Col, Ven*) machete.

peje 1 adj (*Mex*) stupid. 2 nm (a) fish. (b) (*fam*) sly fellow, twister (*fam*).

pejiguera nf (*fam*) bother, nuisance.

Pekín Pekin(g).

pela nf (a) peeling. (b) (*sl*) one peseta. (c) (*SAm*) beating. (d) (*Mex*) slog, hard work.

pelada nf (a) (*SAm*) haircut.
(b) (*Chi, RPl*) bald head; head of close-cropped hair.
(c) (*Col, Ec, Guat, Pan, Ven*) blunder.
(d) (*Cu, Chi, Ec*) **la —** death.
(e) (*Mex*) **la —** the plain truth.

peladar nm (*Arg, Mex*) bare land, wasteland.

peladera nf (*CAm, Mex*) (a) gossip, backbiting. (b) = **peladar**.

peladero nm (*CAm, Col, Chi, Mex*) = **pelador**.

peladez nf (a) (*Col*) poverty. (b) (*Mex*) rudeness.

pelado 1 adj (a) head etc shorn; hairless; trunk etc bare, smooth; bone clean; apple peeled; field etc treeless, bare; countryside bleak.
(b) (*fig*) bare; **cobra el sueldo —** he gets just the bare salary; **el cinco mil —** exactly five thousand; five thousand as a round number.
(c) (*SAm*) poor; broke (*fam*), penniless.
(d) (*Mex*) coarse, rude.
(e) (*CAm, PR*) impudent; barefaced.
2 nm (a) bare patch.
(b) poor man, member of the lowest class; (*fig*) poor devil, wretch.
(c) (*Mex*) fellow, chap (*fam*).
(d) (*Bol, Col, Pan*) child, baby.

peladura nf (a) (*act*) peeling. (b) bare patch. (c) **—s** peel, peelings.

pelafustán nm, **pelafustana** nf layabout, good-for-nothing.

pelagallos nm, pl **pelagallos** = **pelagatos**.

pelagatos nm, pl **pelagatos** poor man, member of the lowest class; poor devil, wretch.

pelágico adj pelagic.

pelaje nm (a) (Zool) fur, coat. (b) = **pelambre** (a).
(c) (fig) appearance; quality; **y otros de ese —** and others like him, and others of that ilk.

pelambre nm (a) thick hair, long hair, mop of hair; unkempt hair. (b) fur, fleece (cut from animal). (c) bare patch. (d) (Chi) gossip, slander.

pelambrera nf = **pelambre** (a).

pelanas nm, pl **pelanas** = **pelado** 2 (b).

pelar [1a] **1** vt (a) to cut the hair of, shear; dead animal to flay, skin; fowl to pluck; fruit to peel, skin, take the skin off; potatoes etc to peel; peas etc to shell.
(b) (fam) to blacken, slander, speak ill of; to criticize.
(c) (fam: Cards etc) to fleece, clean out (sl).
(d) (SAm) to beat.
2 vi: hace un frío que pela it's bitterly cold.
3 pelarse vr (a) to peel off.
(b) (person) to lose one's hair; **voy a pelarme** I'm going to get my hair cut.
(c) **—las por algo** (fam) to crave (for) something; **—las por +** infin (fam) to crave to + infin, long to + infin.
(d) (fam) **corre que se las pela** he runs like nobody's business (fam).

pelazón nf (CAm, Mex) (a) gossip, backbiting. (b) chronic poverty.

peldaño nm step, stair; (of ladder) rung.

pelea nf (a) fight, tussle, scuffle; quarrel, row; **armar una —** to kick up a row, start a fight. (b) **— de gallos** cockfight; **gallo de —** gamecock, fighting cock.

peleador adj brawling; combative, quarrelsome.

pelear [1a] **1** vi to fight; to scuffle, brawl; (fig) to fight, struggle (por for); to vie.
2 pelearse vr (a) to fight; to scuffle, brawl; to come to blows; **— con uno** to fight someone (por for).
(b) (fig) to fall out, quarrel (con with; por about, over); **estamos peleados** (SAm) we're at daggers drawn.

pelechar [1a] vi (a) to moult, shed its hair; to get new hair.
(b) (fig) to regain one's strength, be on the mend; (RPl, Ven) to improve one's position, prosper.

pelecho nm (Mex, RPl) (a) moulted fur; sloughed skin. (b) old clothing.

pelele nm (a) guy, dummy, figure of straw; (fig) tool, cat's-paw, puppet. (b) (child's) rompers.

peleón adj pugnacious, aggressive; quarrelsome; argumentative.

peleona nf row, set-to (fam); brawl.

peleonero adj (SAm) = **peleón**.

pelero nm (a) (CAm, Chi) horse blanket. (b) (Ven) = **pelambre**.

pelete nm = **pelado** 2 (b); **en —** stark naked.

peletería nf furrier's, fur shop; (Cu) shoe shop.

peletero nm furrier.

peliagudo adj subject tricky, ticklish.

pelicano adj grey-haired.

pelícano nm pelican.

pelicorto adj short-haired.

película nf (a) film; thin covering.
(b) (Cine) film, movie (US), motion picture (US); **— en colores** colour film; **— de dibujos (animados)** cartoon film; **— estereofónica** stereophonic film; **— muda** silent film; **— sonora** talkie.
(c) (Phot) film; roll of film, reel of film.
(d) (Ant) silly remark; row, rumpus (fam).

peliculero 1 adj film (attr), cine (attr), movie (US attr). **2** nm film maker; scenario writer; film actor.

peligrar [1a] vi to be in danger; **— de +** infin to be in danger of + ger.

peligro nm danger, peril; risk; menace, threat; **"— de muerte"** (notice) "danger"; **con — de la vida** at the risk of one's life; **estar en —** to be in danger; to be at stake; **estar fuera de —** to be out of danger; **correr —** to be in danger; to run a risk; **correr — de +** infin to run the risk of + ger; **poner algo en —** to endanger something; **estar enfermo de —** to be seriously ill, be dangerously ill.

peligrosamente adv dangerously; riskily.

peligrosidad nf danger; riskiness.

peligroso adj dangerous; risky; wound etc ugly, nasty.

pelillo nm slight annoyance; triviality; **echar —s a la mar** to make it up, bury the hatchet; **no se para en —s** he doesn't stick at trifles, he won't let a little thing like that deter him.

pelinegro adj black-haired.

pelirrojo adj red-haired, red-headed; **la pequeña pelirroja** the little redhead.

pelirubio adj fair-haired.

pelma 1 nmf (fam) bore; **¡no seas —!** don't be such a bore!, don't go on about it! **2** nm lump, solid mass.

pelmazo nm = **pelma** 1 and 2.

pelo nm (a) hair; (of beard, moustache) whisker; (of animal) hair, fur, coat; (of corn) beard; (of bird, fruit) down; (of carpet, cloth) nap, pile; (Tech) fibre, filament, strand; (in jewel) flaw; (of watch) hairspring; **un — rubio** a blonde hair; **tiene — rubio** she has blonde hair; **— de camello** camel-hair, camel's hair (US); **dos caballos del mismo —** two horses of the same colour; **cortarse el —** to have one's hair cut; **hacer el — a una** to do someone's hair.
(b) (idioms etc) **a —** bareheaded, hatless; **a medios —s** (fam) half-seas over; **al —** just right; **venir al —** to come just right, be exactly what one needs; **con (sus) —s y señales** with full details, with chapter and verse; **de medio —** person of no social standing, socially unimportant; thing mediocre; **hombre de — en pecho** brave man; real man, he-man (fam), tough guy; (pej) hard-hearted man; **en —** bareback; (fam) naked; **por los —s** by the skin of one's teeth; **escaparse por un —** to have a narrow escape, have a close shave; **pasó el examen por los —s** he scraped through the exam; **agarrarse (or asirse) a un —** to clutch at any opportunity; **cortar un — en el aire** (fig) to be pretty smart; **dar a uno para el —** to knock someone silly; (in argument) to flatten someone; to dress someone down; **estuvo en un — que lo perdiéramos** we very nearly lost it; **no se mueve un — de aire** (or viento) there isn't a breath of air stirring; **se me pusieron los —s de punta** my hair stood on end; **soltarse el —** to burst out, drop all restraint; **tener el — de la dehesa** to betray one's rustic (or humble) origins; **no tiene — de tonto** he's no fool; **no tener —s en la lengua** to be outspoken, not mince words; to talk nineteen to the dozen; **no tocar un — de la ropa a uno** not to lay a finger on someone; **tomar el — a uno** to pull someone's leg; to rag someone.
(c) (Tech) hairline, fine crack.
(d) (Tech) fine saw.

pelón 1 adj (a) hairless, bald; close-cropped.
(b) (fam) poor; broke (fam), penniless.
(c) (Ec) hairy, long-haired.
2 nm (a) (fam) = **pelado** 2 (b).
(b) (SAm) child, baby.
(c) (Arg) smooth-skinned peach.
(d) (Guat, Mex) **el —** death.
(e) (Ven) blunder.

pelona nf (a) baldness. (b) (fam) **la —** death.

peloso adj hairy.

pelota 1 nf (a) ball; (sl) nut (sl), head; **— base** baseball; **— vasca** pelota; **devolver la — a uno** (fig) to turn the tables on someone; **la — sigue en el tejado** (fig) the situation is still unresolved.
(b) **en —** stark naked; **dejar a uno en —** to strip someone of all that he has; **estar en —s** (fam) to be broke (fam).
(c) (SAm) ferryboat.
(d) (Cu, Mex, Nic, Ven) passion; **tener — por** to have a passion for; to be madly in love with.
(e) (Cu, Mex, Nic, Ven) girlfriend, mistress.
2 nm (fam) = **pelotillero**.

pelotari nm pelota player.

pelotear [1a] **1** vt account to audit.
2 vi (a) to knock (or kick) a ball about; (Tennis) to knock up (before a game).
(b) to bicker, argue.
(c) (SAm) to cross by ferry.

peloteo nm (Tennis) knock-up (before a game); rally, long exchange of shots.

pelotera nf row, scrap (fam), set-to (fam).

pelotero nm (SAm) ball player, sportsman, (esp) footballer, baseball player.

pelotilla nf: **hacer la — a** (fam) to suck up to (fam), ingratiate oneself with.

pelotillero (fam) **1** adj creeping (sl), soapy. **2** nm toady, creep (sl); yes man (sl), stooge (sl).

pelotón nm (a) big ball.
(b) (of threads etc) mass, tangle, mat.
(c) (of people) knot, crowd.
(d) (Mil) squad, party, detachment; **— de ejecución** firing squad.

pelotudo adj (RPl) good-for-nothing, useless; slack, negligent.

peltre nm pewter.

peluca nf (a) wig. (b) (fam) dressing-down.

peluco nm (sl) watch.

pelucón 1 adj (Per) long-haired. **2** nm (Chi) conservative; (Ec) bigwig, big shot (fam).

peluche nm felt; see **oso**.

peludo 1 *adj* hairy, shaggy; *animal* long-haired, shaggy; furry; *beard etc* bushy. **2** *nm* **(a)** round felt mat.
  (b) (*Arg, Urug*) (species of) armadillo.
  (c) (*Arg, Urug*) **agarrarse un —** to get drunk.
peluquearse [1a] *vr* (*SAm*) to have a haircut.
peluquería *nf* hairdresser's, barber's (shop), barbershop (*US*).
peluquero *nm* **(a)** hairdresser, barber. **(b)** wigmaker.
pelusa *nf* **(a)** (*Bot*) down; (*on face*) down, fuzz; (*of cloth*) fluff; (*under furniture etc*) fluff, dust. **(b)** (*fam*) envy, jealousy.
pelusiento *adj* (*Per, PR*) hairy, shaggy.
pélvico *adj* pelvic.
pelvis *nf* pelvis.
pella *nf* **(a)** ball, pellet, round mass; roll; dollop; (*Cook*) lump of raw lard. **(b)** (*Bot*) head. **(c)** (*fam*) sum of money.
pelleja *nf* **(a)** skin, hide. **(b)** (*fam*) whore. **(c)** (*fam*) thin person.
pellejería *nf* **(a)** skins, hides. **(b)** tannery. **(c)** (*Arg, Chi*) difficulty, jam; setback; **—s** hard work to no avail.
pellejo *nm* **(a)** (*of animal*) skin, hide, pelt; (*of person: esp SAm*) skin; (*Bot*) skin, peel, rind.
  (b) wineskin; (*fam*) drunk (*fam*), toper.
  (c) (*fam*) whore.
  (d) (*fig*) skin, hide; **perder el —** to lose one's life; **no quisiera estar en su —** I wouldn't like to be in his shoes; **quitar el — a uno** to flay someone, criticize someone harshly; **salvar el —** to save one's skin; **no tener más que el —** to be all skin and bones.
pellingajo *nm* (*Col, Chi*) **(a)** floor cloth.
  (b) (*fig*) shabby individual; worthless object.
pellizcar [1g] *vt* to pinch, nip; *food etc* to take a small bit of.
pellizco *nm* **(a)** pinch, nip. **(b)** small bit; **un — de sal** a pinch of salt. **(c)** (*in hat*) pinch, dent.
pellón *nm* (*SAm*) sheepskin (*used as a saddle cushion*).
pena *nf* **(a)** grief, sadness, sorrow; distress; anxiety; regret; **¡allá —s!** I don't care!, that's not my worry!; **es una —** it's a shame, it's a pity (*que* that); **me dan — they** grieve me; **da — verlos así** it grieves me to see them like that; **da — que no vengan más** it's a pity they don't come more often; **¡qué —!** what a shame!; **merecer·la —, valer la —** to be worthwhile; **no merece la —** it's not worth the trouble; **merece la — (de)** ir it's worth taking the trouble to go and see it, it's worth seeing; **morir de —** to die of a broken heart.
  (b) (*fam*) pain; **tener una —** to have a pain.
  (c) trouble; **—s** hardships; toil; **alma en —** soul in torment; **a duras —s** with great difficulty; (*fig*) hardly, scarcely; **ahorrarse la —** to save oneself trouble; **pasar las —s del purgatorio** (*fig*) to go through purgatory; **con muchas —s llegamos a la cumbre** after much toil we reached the top.
  (d) (*Law*) punishment, penalty; (*Comm*) penalty; **— capital** capital punishment; **— de muerte** death penalty; **— pecuniaria** fine; **bajo — de, so — de** on pain of, on penalty of.
  (e) (*SAm*) bashfulness; shyness, timidity.
  (f) (*Per*) ghost.
penable *adj* punishable.
penacho *nm* **(a)** (*Orn*) tuft, crest; (*on helmet*) plume. **(b)** (*of smoke etc*) plume; wreath; pall. **(c)** (*fig*) pride, arrogance.
penado 1 *adj* = **penoso. 2** *nm* convict.
penal 1 *adj* penal; criminal. **2** *nm* **(a)** prison. **(b)** (*SAm: Sport*) foul (in the penalty area); penalty (kick).
penalidad *nf* **(a)** trouble, hardship. **(b)** (*Law*) penalty, punishment.
penalista *nm* penologist, expert in criminal law.
penalización *nf* penalty; penalization.
penalizar [1f] *vt* (*SAm: angl*) to penalize.
penálty *nm, pl* **penálty(e)s, penalties** (*etc*) (*angl*) penalty (kick).
penar [1a] **1** *vt* to penalize; to punish.
  2 *vi* **(a)** to suffer; (*of soul*) to be in torment; **— de amores** to be unhappy in love, go through the pains of love; **ella pena por todos** she takes everybody's sufferings upon herself.
  (b) **— por** to pine for, long for.
  3 penarse *vr* to grieve, mourn.
penca *nf* **(a)** fleshy leaf; main rib of a leaf; (*SAm*) palm leaf; (*Cu*) fan; (*Mex: of knife*) blade.
  (b) **hacerse de —s** to have to be coaxed into doing something.
  (c) (*Col*) **— de hombre** a fine man; **— de casa** a great big house.
  (d) (*SAm*) **agarrar una —** to get drunk.

penco 1 *adj* (*CAm*) rustic; stupid. **2** *nm* **(a)** (*Mex, Nic*) horse. **(b)** (*Col*) **un — de hombre** a fine man.
pendango *adj* (*Cu*) effeminate; (*PR*) cowardly.
pendejada *nf* (*SAm*) **(a)** foolish act; cowardly act. **(b)** foolishness, stupidity; cowardliness.
pendejear [1a] *vi* (*Col, Mex*) to act the fool; to act irresponsibly.
pendejeta *nmf* (*Col*) idiot.
pendejo 1 *adj* **(a)** (*CAm, Mex, Ven*) silly, stupid; irresponsible; contemptible; cowardly.
  (b) (*Col, Per*) alert; cunning.
  2 *nm* (*RPl*) lad, youth; (*pej*) pretentious adolescent.
pendencia *nf* quarrel; fight, brawl; **armar — to** fight, brawl; to stir up trouble.
pendenciero 1 *adj* quarrelsome, argumentative; brawling, given to fighting. **2** *nm* rowdy, lout, tough (*fam*).
pender [2a] *vi* **(a)** to hang (*de, en* from; *sobre* over); to hang down, dangle; to droop.
  (b) (*Law*) to be pending.
  (c) (*fig: of threat etc*) **— sobre** to hang over.
pendiente 1 *adj* **(a)** hanging; **estar — to** be hanging; to hang, dangle.
  (b) (*fig*) *matter* pending, unsettled; *account* outstanding, unpaid.
  (c) (*fig*) **estar — de un cabello** to hang by a thread; **estar — de los labios de uno** to hang on someone's lips (*or* words); **estamos —s de lo que él decida** we are dependent on what he may decide, everything hangs for us on his decision.
  2 *nm* earring; pendant.
  3 *nf* (*Geog*) slope, incline; (*Aut etc*) hill, slope; (*Archit*) pitch.
pendil *nm* (woman's) cloak; **tomar el — (fam)** to pack up, clear out.
péndola *nf* **(a)** pen, quill. **(b)** (*of bridge etc*) suspension cable.
pendolear [1a] *vi* **(a)** (*SAm*) to write a lot; (*Arg*) to write neatly. **(b)** (*Mex*) to be good in difficult situations, know how to manage people sensibly.
pendolista *nm* penman, calligrapher.
pendón *nm* **(a)** banner, standard; pennant. **(b)** (*fam*) tall shabby person. **(c)** (*fam*) lazy woman; worthless woman, slut; whore.
pendona *nf* (*fam*) whore.
pendonear [1a] *vi* (*fam*) to loaf around the streets.
pene *nm* penis.
peneque *adj* (*sl*): **estar — to** be pickled (*sl*).
penetrable *adj* penetrable.
penetración *nf* **(a)** (*act*) penetration. **(b)** (*quality*) penetration, sharpness, acuteness; insight.
penetrador *adj* = **penetrante (c).**
penetrante *adj* **(a)** *wound* deep.
  (b) *weapon* sharp; *cold, wind* biting; *sound* penetrating, piercing; *look* searching; sharp, penetrating; *sight* acute; *irony etc* biting.
  (c) *person, mind* sharp, acute, keen.
penetrar [1a] **1** *vt* **(a)** to penetrate, pierce; to permeate.
  (b) *mystery etc* to fathom, grasp, see the explanation of; *secret* to lay bare, understand; *intention* to see through, grasp; *meaning* to grasp.
  2 *vi* **(a)** to penetrate; to go in; (*of liquid etc*) to sink in, soak in; **— en, — entre, — por** to penetrate; **el cuchillo penetró en la carne** the knife went into (*or* entered, penetrated) the flesh; **penetramos poco en el mar** we did not go far out to sea; **el frío penetra en los huesos** the cold gets right into one's bones.
  (b) (*of person*) to enter, go in; **— en un cuarto** to go into a room.
  (c) (*of emotion etc*) to pierce; **la ingratitud penetró hondamente en su corazón** the ingratitude pierced him to the heart (*or* wounded him deeply).
  3 penetrarse *vr*: **— de (a)** to become imbued with.
  (b) to understand fully, become fully aware of (the significance of).
penga *nf* (*Bol*) bunch of bananas.
penicilina *nf* penicillin.
península *nf* peninsula; **P— Ibérica** Iberian Peninsula.
peninsular *adj* peninsular.
penique *nm* penny.
penitencia *nf* **(a)** (*condition*) penitence.
  (b) (*act, punishment*) penance; **en — as** a penance; **imponer una — a uno** to give someone a penance; **hacer — (Eccl)** to do penance (*por* for); to do something unpleasant; (*fam*) to take potluck.
penitenciado *nm* (*SAm*) convict.
penitencial *adj* penitential.

penitenciar [1b] *vt* to impose a penance on.
penitenciaría *nf* prison, penitentiary (*esp US*).
penitenciario 1 *adj* penitentiary, prison (*attr*). **2** *nm* (*Eccl*) confessor.
penitente 1 *adj* (**a**) (*Eccl*) penitent. (**b**) (*Ec*) silly. **2** *nmf* (*Eccl*) penitent. **3** *nm* (*Arg*, *Chi*) rock pinnacle, isolated cone of rock; snowman.
penol *nm* yardarm.
penosamente *adv* (**a**) painfully, distressingly. (**b**) laboriously, with difficulty.
penoso *adj* (**a**) painful, distressing. (**b**) arduous, laborious, difficult. (**c**) (*Col*, *Mex*, *Ven*) bashful; timid, shy.
pensado *adj* (**a**) **un proyecto poco** — a badly thought-out scheme; **lo tengo bien** — I have thought it over (*or* out) carefully; **tengo** — **hacerlo mañana** I have formed the intention of doing it tomorrow.
(**b**) **bien** — well-intentioned; **mal** — *see* **malpensado**.
(**c**) **en el momento menos** — when least expected; much sooner than one thinks.
pensador *nm* thinker.
pensamiento *nm* (**a**) (*faculty*) thought; **como el** — (*fig*) in a flash.
(**b**) mind; **acudir** (*or* **venir**) **al** — to come to someone's mind; **no le pasó por el** — it never occurred to him.
(**c**) (**un** —) thought; **mal** — nasty thought, wicked thought; **el** — **de Quevedo** Quevedo's thought; **nuestro** — **sobre este tema** our thinking on this subject; **adivinar los** —**s de uno** to read someone's thoughts.
(**d**) idea, intention; **mi** — **es** + *infin* my idea is to + *infin*.
(**e**) (*Bot*) pansy.
pensante *adj* thinking.
pensar [1k] **1** *vt* (**a**) *thought etc* to think; — **que . . .** to think that . . .; **cuando menos lo pensamos** when we least expect it; **¿qué piensas de ella?** what do you think of her?, what is your opinion of her?; **dar que** — **a uno** to give someone food for thought; to give someone pause; **dar que** — **a la gente** to arouse suspicions, set people thinking; **¡ni** —**lo!** not a bit of it!
(**b**) *problem etc* to think over, think out; **lo pensaré** I'll think about it; **esto es para** —**lo** this needs thinking about; **pensándolo bien** on reflection, after mature consideration.
(**c**) — **que . . .** to decide that . . ., come to the conclusion that . . .
(**d**) — + *infin* to intend to + *infin*, plan to + *infin*, propose to + *infin*.
(**e**) *scheme etc* to think up, invent; **¿quién pensó este plan?** who thought this one up?
2 *vi* (**a**) to think; — **en** to think of, think about; **¿en qué piensas?** what are you thinking about?; — **entre sí,** — **para sí** to think to oneself; — **sobre** to think about, think over; **sin** — without thinking, rashly; involuntarily; unexpectedly.
(**b**) — **en** to aim at, aspire to; **piensa en una cátedra** he's aiming at a chair.
pensativamente *adv* thoughtfully, pensively.
pensativo *adj* thoughtful, pensive.
penseque *nm* (*fam*) excuse.
Pensilvania *f* Pennsylvania.
pensión *nf* (**a**) (*Fin*) pension; allowance; — **de retiro** retirement pension; — **vitalicia** annuity.
(**b**) (*Univ etc*) scholarship, fellowship; travel grant. (**c**) boarding house, guest-house, lodging house; (*for students etc*) lodgings.
(**d**) board and lodging; — **completa** full board, room and all meals.
(**e**) (*fig*) nuisance; burden.
(**f**) (*Col*, *Chi*, *Mex*) worry, anxiety; regret.
pensionado 1 *nm* boarding school. **2** *nm*, **pensionada** *nf* pensioner.
pensionar [1a] *vt* (**a**) to pension, give a pension to; *student* to give a grant to. (**b**) (*Chi*, *Ec*, *Per*) to cause trouble to, make work for; to worry.
pensionista *nmf* (**a**) pensioner, old-age pensioner. (**b**) lodger, paying guest. (**c**) boarder; boarding-school pupil.
pentagonal *adj* pentagonal.
pentágono *nm* pentagon; **el P**— (*Washington*) the Pentagon.
pentagrama *nm* (*Mus*) stave, staff.
pentámetro *nm* pentameter.
Pentateuco *nm* Pentateuch.
pentatlon *nm* pentathlon.
pentatónico *adj* pentatonic; **escala pentatónica** pentatonic scale.

Pentecostés *nm* (*sometimes f*) (**a**) Whitsun, Whitsuntide; **domingo de** — Whit Sunday. (**b**) (*Jewish*) Pentecost.
penúltima *nf* (*Gram*) penult.
penúltimo *adj* penultimate, last but one, next to last.
penumbra *nf* penumbra; half-light, semi-darkness; shadows; **sentado en la** — seated in the shadows.
penuria *nf* shortage, dearth.
peña *nf* (**a**) cliff, crag; — **viva** bare rock, living rock.
(**b**) group, circle; (*pej*) coterie, clique; — **deportiva** (*Sport*) supporters' club; **forma parte de la** — he's a member of the circle; **hay** — **en el café los domingos** the group meets in the café on Sundays.
(**c**) (*Ec*, *Guat*, *PR*) deaf person.
(**d**) (*Chi*) pawnshop; moneylender's.
peñascal *nm* rocky place; rocky hill.
peñasco *nm* (**a**) large rock, boulder. (**b**) rock, crag; pinnacle of rock.
peñascoso *adj* rocky, craggy.
peñón *nm* mass of rock; wall of rock, crag; **el P**— the Rock (of Gibraltar).
peños *nmpl* (*sl*) ivories (*sl*), teeth.
peñusco *nm* (*Arg*, *PR*) crowd, squash.
peón *nm* (**a**) (*Tech*) unskilled workman; (*Agr*, *esp SAm*) labourer, farmhand; (*Mex*) apprentice; — **de albañil** building labourer, bricklayer's mate; — **caminero** navvy, roadman, roadmender.
(**b**) (*Mil: Hist*) infantryman, foot-soldier.
(**c**) (*Chess*) pawn.
(**d**) spinning top.
(**e**) (*Mech*) spindle, shaft, axle.
peonada *nf* (**a**) (*Agr*) day's stint. (**b**) gang of workmen, gang of labourers.
peonaje *nm* labourers (*collectively*), group of labourers.
peonar [1a] *vi* (*Arg*) to work as a labourer.
peonía *nf* peony.
peonza *nf* (**a**) spinning top, whipping top. (**b**) (*fam*) busy little person. (**c**) (*fam*) **ir a** — to go on foot, walk it.
peor *adj and adv* (*comp*) worse; (*superl*) worst; — **que** — worse and worse; **A es** — **que B** A is worse than B; **Z es el** — **de todos** Z is the worst of all; **lo** — **es que . . .** the worst of it is that . . .; **llevar lo** — to get the worst of it; **o si no, será** — **para Vd** or if you don't, it will be the worse for you; *see* **mal, tanto** *etc*.
peoría *nf* worsening, deterioration.
Pepa *f pet name for* **Josefa**; **¡viva la** —**!** as if he (*etc*) cared!, and to blazes with everybody else!; jolly good! (*fam*).
pepa *nf* (**a**) (*SAm*) seed, pip, stone. (**b**) (*SAm*) marble. (**c**) (*Col*) lie; fraud, hoax. (**d**) (*Ec*) rogue.
pepazo *nm* (**a**) (*SAm*) shot, hit, throw; accurate shot. (**b**) (*Col*) = **pepa** (**c**).
Pepe *m pet name for* **José**.
pepe *nm* (**a**) (*Bol*, *Ven*) fop, toff (*fam*). (**b**) (*Guat*, *Hond*) feeding bottle.
pepenado *nm*, **pepenada** *nf* (*CAm*, *Mex*) orphan; foundling.
pepenar [1a] *vt* (**a**) (*CAm*, *Col*, *Mex*) to pick up; to search out; to choose; to get, obtain.
(**b**) (*Mex*) to grab hold of; to go through the pockets of; to steal; *orphan* to take in, bring up.
pepinillo *nm* gherkin.
pepino *nm* cucumber; **no se me da un** —, **(no) me importa un** — I don't care two hoots (*de* about).
Pepita *f pet name for* **Josefa**.
pepita *nf* (**a**) (*Vet*) pip; **no tener** — **en la lengua** to be outspoken, not mince words; to talk nineteen to the dozen.
(**b**) (*Bot*) pip.
(**c**) (*Min*) nugget.
Pepito *m pet name for* **José**.
pepito *nm* (*Col*, *Pan*, *Ven*) fop, toff (*fam*).
pepitoria *nf* (*fig*) hotchpotch, mixture.
pepsina *nf* pepsin.
péptico *adj* peptic.
peptona *nf* peptone.
peque *nmf* (*fam*) kid (*fam*), child.
pequeñez *nf* (**a**) smallness, littleness, small size; shortness; (*of child*) infancy.
(**b**) (*pej*) pettiness, small-mindedness.
(**c**) trifle, triviality; **preocuparse por pequeñeces** to worry about trifles.
pequeño *adj* small, little; *number*, *figure* small, low; (*in stature*) short; **los** —**s** the children, the kids (*fam*), the little ones; **un castillo en** — a miniature castle; **un negocio en** — a small-scale business.
pequero *nm* (*RPl*) cardsharper.
pequinés *nm* (*dog*) Pekinese.
pera[1] *nf* (**a**) (*Bot*) pear; (*sl*) nut (*sl*), head; **partir** —**s con uno** to fall out with someone; **eso es pedir** —**s**

al olmo that's asking the impossible; **poner a uno las —s a cuarto** to tell someone a few home truths. (b) goatee; (Chi) chin.
(c) (of spray, horn etc) bulb.
(d) (Elec) bulb; switch.
(e) (sl) **hacerse una** — to masturbate.

pera[2] adj invar (sl) elegant; classy (fam), posh (fam); **niño** — spoiled upper-class child; **es un pollo** — he's a real toff (fam); **fuimos a un restaurante muy** — we went to a really swish restaurant (sl).

peral nm pear tree.

perca f (Fish) perch.

percal nm, **percala** nf (Mex, Per) percale.

percán nm (Chi) mould.

percance nm (a) misfortune, mishap; (in plan etc) setback, hitch; **sufrir un —, tener un —** to have a mishap. (b) (Fin) perquisite.

percanque nm (Chi) mould.

percatarse [1a] vr: — **de** to notice, take note of; to heed; to guard against.

percebe nm (a) (Zool) barnacle. (b) (fam) idiot.

percepción nf (a) perception; — **extrasensoria** extrasensory perception. (b) notion, idea. (c) (Comm, Fin) collection; receipt.

perceptible adj (a) perceptible, noticeable, detectable. (b) (Comm, Fin) payable, receivable.

perceptiblemente adv perceptibly, noticeably.

perceptivo adj perceptive.

perceptor nm, **perceptora** nf recipient; (of taxes etc) receiver.

percibir [3a] vt (a) to perceive, notice, detect; to see, observe; danger etc to sense, scent; — **que ...** to perceive that ..., observe that ...
(b) (Comm, Fin) salary to earn, receive, get.

percollar [1a] vt (Arg) to acquire illegally; (Bol, Per) to monopolize.

percuchante nm (Ec, Per) fool.

percudir [3a] vt to tarnish, dull; clothing etc to dirty, mess up; complexion to spoil.

percusión nf percussion; **instrumento de** — percussion instrument.

percusor nm, **percutor** nm (Tech) striker, hammer.

percutir [3a] vt to strike, tap.

percha nf (a) pole, support; rack; coat stand, hallstand; coat hanger; (Orn) perch; — **de herramientas** toolrack.
(b) (Col, Ec) elegance, luxury; showiness; **tener** — (Arg) to be smart.
(c) (Col) new clothes, smart clothing; (Cu) jacket; (SD) suit, dress.
(d) (Chi) pile.
(e) (Mex) bunch, crowd (of people).

perchero nm clothes rack, hallstand.

perchudo adj (Col), smart, elegant.

perdedor 1 adj (a) team, trick etc losing. (b) forgetful, given to losing things.
2 nm, **perdedora** nf loser; **buen** — good loser, good sport.

perder [2g] **1** vt (a) (general sense) to lose; **¿dónde lo perdió?** where did you lose it?; **he perdido 5 kilos** I've lost 5 kilos; **he perdido la costumbre** I have got out of the habit (and see **costumbre**).
(b) effort, time, words etc to waste; chance to miss, lose, waste; train etc to miss; (Law) to lose, forfeit, give up; **no pierde nada** he doesn't miss a thing; **sin** — **un momento** without wasting a moment.
(c) to ruin, spoil; **ese vicio le perderá** that vice will be his ruin, that vice will destroy him; **ese error le perdió** that mistake was his undoing.
(d) (Univ) course to fail.

2 vi (a) to lose; **el equipo perdió por 2-5** the team lost 2-5; **salir perdiendo** to lose, be the loser; to lose on a deal; **tener buen** — to be a good loser.
(b) to decline, deteriorate, go down(hill); to lose influence; **ha perdido mucho en mi estimación** he has gone down a lot in my estimation; **era guapísima, pero ha perdido bastante** she used to be very pretty, but she's deteriorated a bit.
(c) (of cloth) to fade, discolour.
(d) **echar a** — food etc to spoil, ruin; chance to waste; **echarse a** — to be spoiled, be ruined; to go downhill.

3 perderse vr (a) to get lost (also fig), lose oneself; to stray; to lose one's way; **se perdieron en el bosque** they got lost in the wood; **se perdió en un mar de contradicciones** he got lost in a mass of contradictions.
(b) to disappear, be lost (to view); **el tren se perdió en la niebla** the train disappeared into the fog, the train was lost to sight in the fog; **el arroyo**

se pierde en la roca the stream disappears into the rock.
(c) to be wasted; to go (or run) to waste.
(d) to be ruined, get spoiled; **con la lluvia se ha perdido la mitad de la cosecha** with so much rain half the crop has been ruined (or lost).
(e) (Naut) to sink, be wrecked.
(f) (person) to be ruined; **se perdió por el juego** he was ruined through gambling.
(g) — **por** to be mad about, long for; — **por** + infin to be mad keen to + infin, long to + infin.
(h) (SAm) to become a prostitute.

perdición nf perdition (also Rel), undoing, ruin; **fue su** — it was his undoing; **será mi** — it will be the ruin of me.

pérdida nf loss; (of time etc) waste; (Law) forfeiture, loss; —**s** (Fin, Mil etc) losses; (of liquid etc) wastage; **¡no tiene** —! you can't miss!, you can't go wrong!; **vender algo con** — to sell something at a loss.

perdidamente adv: — **enamorado** passionately in love, hopelessly in love.

perdidizo adj: **hacer algo** — to hide something away, deliberately lose something; **hacerse el** — to lose deliberately (in a game); to make oneself scarce, hide oneself away.

perdido 1 adj (a) lost; bullet stray; moments idle; spare; **dar algo por** — to give something up for lost; **darse por** — to give oneself up for lost.
(b) vicious; incorrigible; drinker etc inveterate, hardened.
(c) **estar** — **por** to be mad about, be crazy about.
(d) (SAm) idle; down and out.
2 nm rake, libertine, profligate.

perdidoso adj (a) team etc losing. (b) easily lost, easily mislaid.

perdigar [1h] vt to half-cook, brown.

perdigón nm (a) young partridge. (b) pellet; — **zorrero** buckshot; —**es** shot, pellets.

perdiz nf partridge; — **blanca,** — **nival** ptarmigan.

perdón nm pardon (also Law), forgiveness; mercy; (of sin etc) remission; **¡—!** sorry!, I beg your pardon!; **¡le pido —!** I am so sorry!, do forgive me!; **pedir** — **a uno** to ask someone's forgiveness, apologize to someone; **con** — if I may, if you don't mind, by your leave; excuse me; **con** — **de los presentes** present company excepted; **hablando con** — if I may say so, if you'll pardon the expression; **no cabe** — it's inexcusable.

perdonable adj pardonable, excusable.

perdonador adj forgiving.

perdonar [1a] vti (a) offence etc, person to pardon (also Law), forgive, excuse; **¡perdone (Vd)!** sorry!, I beg your pardon!; **perdone, pero me parece que ...** excuse me, but I think ...; **perdónanos nuestras deudas** forgive us our trespasses; **Dios le haya perdonado** may God have mercy on him.
(b) — **la vida a uno** to spare someone's life.
(c) (from duty etc) to exempt, excuse; **les he perdonado las clases** I have excused them from classes.
(d) **no** — **esfuerzo** to spare no effort; **no** — **ocasión** to miss no chance (de + infin to + infin); **no** — **medio para** + infin to use all possible means to + infin; **sin** — **detalle** without omitting a single detail.

perdonavidas nm, pl **perdonavidas** bully, tough (fam), thug.

perdulario 1 adj (a) forgetful, given to losing things. (b) careless, sloppy, inefficient. (c) (pej) vicious, dissolute. **2** nm rake.

perdurable adj lasting, abiding; everlasting.

perdurar [1a] vi to last, endure, survive; to stand, still exist.

perecedero adj perishable; life etc transitory, which must come to an end; person mortal.

perecer [2d] **1** vi to perish, die; (hum) to expire; (of object) to shatter; — **ahogado** to drown; to suffocate.
2 perecerse (a) — **de risa** to die (of) laughing; — **de envidia** to be dying of jealousy.
(b) — **por algo** to long for, be dying for, crave; — **por una mujer** to be crazy about a woman; **se perece por los calamares** he's passionately fond of squid; — **por** + infin to long to + infin, be dying to + infin.

peregrinación nf (a) long tour, travels; (hum) peregrination.
(b) (Eccl) pilgrimage; **ir en** — to go on a pilgrimage, make a pilgrimage (a to).

peregrinar [1a] vi (a) to go to and fro; to travel extensively (abroad). (b) (Eccl) to go on a pilgrimage (a to).

peregrino 1 adj (a) *person* wandering; travelling; *bird* migratory.
(b) *custom, plant etc* alien, newly introduced; adventitious.
(c) *(fig)* odd, strange, surprising.
(d) *(fig) beauty etc* fine, extraordinary, rare; exotic.
2 nm, **peregrina** nf pilgrim.
perejil nm (a) *(Bot)* parsley.
(b) *(fam)* —**es** buttons and bows, trimmings, fripperies.
(c) —**es** *(fam)* extra titles, handles (to one's name) *(fam)*.
perendengue nm trinket, cheap ornament; silly adornment.
perenne adj everlasting, constant, perennial; *(Bot)* perennial; **de hoja** — evergreen.
perennemente adv everlastingly, constantly, perennially.
perentoriamente adv urgently, peremptorily.
perentorio adj (a) urgent, peremptory. (b) *term* set, fixed.
pereza nf (a) sloth, laziness; slowness; idleness. (b) *(Ven)* deck chair. (c) *(Col)* nuisance.
perezosa nf *(Arg, Per)* deck chair.
perezosamente adv lazily; slowly; sluggishly.
perezoso 1 adj slothful, lazy; slow, sluggish, idle. **2** nm (a) *(Zool)* sloth. (b) *(Cu, Mex)* safety pin. (c) headrest.
perfección nf (a) perfection; **a la** — to perfection. (b) *(act)* completion.
perfeccionamiento nm perfection; improvement.
perfeccionar [1a] vt (a) to perfect; to improve. (b) *process etc* to complete, finish.
perfeccionista nmf perfectionist.
perfectamente adv perfectly; ¡—! precisely!, just so!; of course!
perfectibilidad nf perfectibility.
perfectible adj perfectible.
perfecto 1 adj (a) perfect. (b) complete, finished; perfected. **2** nm *(Gram)* perfect (tense).
pérfidamente adv perfidiously, treacherously.
perfidia nf perfidy, treachery.
pérfido adj perfidious, treacherous.
perfil nm (a) profile; silhouette, outline; *(Archit, Geol etc)* section, cross section, sectional view; *(Phot)* side view; — **aerodinámico** streamlining; **en** — in profile, from the side.
(b) —**es** *(fig)* features, characteristics.
(c) —**es** *(fig)* social courtesies; finishing touches.
perfilado adj well-shaped, well-finished; *face* long; *nose* well-formed, shapely; *(Aer)* streamlined.
perfilar [1a] **1** vt (a) to outline; *(fig)* to shape, give character to; **son los lectores los que perfilan los periódicos** it is the readers who shape their newspapers.
(b) *(Aer etc)* to streamline.
(c) *(fig)* to put the finishing touches to; to round off, perfect.
2 perfilarse vr (a) *(person)* to show one's profile, give a side view; *(Taur)* to draw oneself up (and prepare for the kill); *(building etc)* to show in outline, appear in silhouette.
(b) *(fig)* to take shape; to become more definite; **el proyecto se va perfilando** the plan is taking shape.
(c) *(SAm)* to slim, get slim.
(d) *(Arg: Sport)* to dribble and shoot.
perforación nf (a) perforation; piercing; drilling; boring; punching. (b) *(for oil)* drilling; drill, bore.
perforadora nf punch; drill; — **neumática** pneumatic drill.
perforar [1a] **1** vt to perforate; to pierce; to puncture; *hole* to make, drill, bore; *well* to sink; *card etc* to punch, punch a hole in.
2 vi *(for oil etc)* to drill, bore.
performance [per'formans] nm or f *(Aut, Mech, Sport etc: angl)* performance.
perfumado adj scented; sweet-smelling.
perfumar [1a] vt to scent, perfume.
perfume nm scent, perfume.
perfumería nf perfume shop; perfumery.
pergamino nm parchment; **una familia de muchos** —**s** a very blue-blooded family, a very ancient family.
pergenio nm (a) *(SAm)* small unpleasant person; ragamuffin. (b) *(Arg)* bright boy, clever youngster.
pergeñar [1a] vt (a) to sketch; to do roughly, do in rough; *text etc* to do a draft of, prepare. (b) *(fam)* to fix up, arrange.
pergeño nm (a) aspect, appearance. (b) sketch; rough draft. (c) *(fam)* arrangement.
pérgola nf pergola.

perica nf (a) *(Col, Pan)* razor, knife; machete; short sword. (b) *(Col, Ec, Pan)* **agarrar una** — to get drunk.
pericia nf skill, skilfulness; expertness, expertise.
pericial adj: **testigo** — expert witness.
Perico m Pete; — **el de los palotes** anybody, somebody; so-and-so; any Tom, Dick or Harry; **ser p— entre ellas** to be a ladies' man.
perico nm (a) *(Orn)* parakeet.
(b) wig, toupé.
(c) *(fam)* chamberpot.
(d) *(Col)* coffee with milk.
(e) —**s** *(Col, Ven)* scrambled eggs with fried onions.
pericote nm (a) *(Arg, Bol, Ec, Per)* mouse. (b) *(Arg, Per)* child.
periferia nf periphery; *(of town)* outskirts.
periférico adj peripheral.
perifollo nm (a) *(Bot)* chervil. (b) —**s** *(fig)* buttons and bows, trimmings, fripperies.
perifrasis nf, pl **perifrasis** periphrasis.
perifrástico adj periphrastic.
perilla nf pear-shaped ornament, drop; switch; doorknob; goatee; — **de la oreja** lobe of the ear; — **del timbre** bell-push; **venir de** —**s** to come just right, be very welcome, be perfect.
perillán nm *(fam)* rogue, rascal; ¡—! *(to child)* you rascal!
perímetro nm perimeter.
perinola nf teetotum.
periódicamente adv periodically.
periodicidad nf periodicity; regular recurrence, regular nature.
periódico 1 adj periodic(al); *(Math)* recurrent. **2** nm newspaper; periodical; — **del domingo** Sunday newspaper; — **de la tarde** evening newspaper.
periodicucho nm *(fam: pej)* rag *(fam)*.
periodismo nm journalism.
periodista nmf journalist; *(m)* pressman, newsman, newspaperman.
periodístico adj (a) journalistic; newspaper *(attr)*; **estilo** — journalistic style, journalese. (b) *report etc* newsworthy.
período nm (a) period *(also Med)*. (b) *(Gram)* sentence, period.
peripatética nf *(hum)* whore.
peripatético adj peripatetic.
peripecia nf vicissitude; sudden change, unforeseen change; —**s** vicissitudes, ups and downs; adventures, incidents.
periplo nm journey, tour; wanderings; *(hum)* peregrination.
peripuesto adj *(fam)* dressed up, smart; overdressed, dressy; **tan** — all dressed up (to the nines).
periquete nm *(fam)*: **en un** — in a tick.
periquito nm parakeet.
periscopio nm periscope.
peristilo nm peristyle.
peritaje nm (a) expert work; report of an expert; specialist's report. (b) expert's fee. (c) professional training.
perito 1 adj skilled, skilful; expert; experienced, seasoned; — **en** skilled in, expert at.
2 nm expert; skilled man, qualified man; technician; — **electricista** qualified electrician; — **forense** legal expert; — **en metales** metal expert, specialist in metals.
peritoneo nm peritoneum.
peritonitis nf peritonitis.
perjudicar [1g] vt (a) to damage, harm, impair; *chances etc* to damage, prejudice; **me perjudica que digan eso** for them to say that lowers me in the eyes of others.
(b) to be unbecoming to; **ese sombrero le perjudica** that hat does not become her, she doesn't look well in that hat.
perjudicial adj harmful, injurious, damaging *(a, para* to*)*; detrimental, prejudicial *(a, para* to*)*.
perjuicio nm damage, harm; *(Fin)* financial loss; **en** — **de** to the detriment of; **redundar en** — **de** to be detrimental to, harm; **sin** — **de** without prejudice to; **sufrir grandes** —**s** to suffer great damage.
perjurar [1a] **1** vi (a) to perjure oneself, commit perjury. (b) to swear a lot. **2 perjurarse** vr to perjure oneself.
perjurio nm perjury.
perjuro 1 adj perjured. **2** nm perjurer.
perla nf (a) pearl; — **cultivada** cultivated pearl, cultured pearl; —**s de imitación** imitation pearls.
(b) *(fig)* pearl *(de of, among)*; gem; **me está de** —**s, me viene de** —**s** it comes just right; it suits me perfectly; **me parece de** —**s** it all seems splendid to me.

perlático adj paralytic, palsied.
perlesía nf paralysis, palsy.
perlífero adj pearl-bearing; **ostra perlífera** pearl oyster.
perlino adj pearly.
permanecer [2d] vi (a) to stay, remain; ¿cuánto tiempo vas a —? how long are you staying?
(b) — + adj to go on being + adj, remain + adj; — indeciso to remain undecided; — dormido to go on sleeping.
permanencia nf (a) permanence. (b) stay.
permanente 1 adj permanent; constant; colour fast; committee, army etc standing.
2 nf permanent wave, perm (fam); **hacerse una** — to have one's hair permed.
permanentemente adv permanently; constantly.
permanganato nm permanganate.
permeabilidad nf permeability, pervious nature.
permeable adj permeable, pervious (a to).
permisible adj allowable, permissible.
permisionario nm (SAm) official agent, official agency, concessionaire.
permisivo adj permissive.
permiso nm (a) (in general) permission; **con** — if I may; excuse me; **con** — de Vds me voy excuse me but I must go, if you don't mind I must go; **dar su** — to give one's permission; **tener** — **para** + infin to have permission to + infin.
(b) (document) permit, licence; — de conducción, — de conducir, — de conductor driving licence; — de entrada entry permit; — de exportación export permit; — de importación import permit; — de salida exit permit.
(c) (Mil etc) leave; — de convalecencia sick leave; **estar de** — to be on leave.
permitir [3a] **1** vt to permit, allow; to allow of; — **a uno hacer algo** to allow someone to do something; **¿me permite?** may I?, do you mind?; **permítame que le diga que . . .** permit me to tell you that . . .; **si lo permite el tiempo** weather permitting; **la fábrica permitirá una producción anual de . . .** the factory will provide an annual production of . . ., the factory will make possible an annual production of . . .
2 **permitirse** vr (a) to be permitted, be allowed; **eso no se permite** that is not allowed; **si se me permite la expresión** if you'll pardon the expression; so to speak; **no se permite fumar** no smoking, you can't smoke here; **¿se permite fumar?** may I smoke?
(b) — **algo** to permit oneself something; to (be able to) afford something.
permuta nf barter, exchange; interchange.
permutación nf (a) (Math etc) permutation. (b) = permuta.
permutar [1a] **1** vt (a) (Math etc) to permute.
(b) to exchange (con with, por for); to interchange (con with); — **algo con uno** to exchange something with someone; — **destinos con uno** to exchange jobs with someone.
2 vi: — **con uno** to exchange (jobs) with someone, swap with someone.
pernear [1a] vi (a) to shake one's legs; to kick one's legs. (b) to stamp one's foot (with rage). (c) (fam) to hustle, get cracking (fam).
pernera nf trouser leg.
perneta nf: **en** —s bare-legged, with bare legs.
perniabierto adj bow-legged.
pernicioso adj pernicious (also Med); person wicked, evil; insect etc injurious (para to).
pernicorto adj short-legged.
pernil nm (a) (Zool) upper leg, haunch; (Cook) leg.
(b) trouser leg.
pernio nm hinge.
perno nm bolt.
pernoctar [1a] vi to spend the night, stay for the night.
pero[1] **1** conj (a) but; yet.
(b) (fam) **una chica guapa,** — **muy guapa** what you really call a pretty girl, a pretty girl and no mistake; **hizo muy mal,** — **muy mal** he was wrong, a thousand times wrong; I should jolly well say he was wrong (fam); — **vamos a ver** well let's see; ¡— **que muy bien!** jolly good! (fam); ¡— **si no tiene coche!** I tell you he hasn't got a car!
2 nm (a) flaw, defect; snag; **el plan no tiene** — there's nothing wrong with the plan, the plan hasn't any snags; **he encontrado un** — I've found a snag.
(b) objection; **poner** —s a to raise objections to, find fault with; **el programa tiene dos** —s the programme is open to two objections; ¡**no hay que valga!** there are no buts about it!
pero[2] nm (Arg, Bol) pear tree.

perogrullada nf platitude, truism.
Pero Grullo: verdad de — platitude, truism.
perol nm pan; (Cu) saucepan; (Chi, Mex) metal pot, pot with legs and handles; (Ven) kitchen utensil; (Ven: fig) piece of junk, worthless object.
perolero nm (Ven) tinsmith; plumber.
peroné nm fibula.
peronista (Arg etc) **1** adj Peronist. **2** nmf Peronist, supporter of Perón.
peroración nf (a) peroration, speech. (b) conclusion of a speech.
perorar [1a] vi to make a speech; (hum) to orate (hum), spout.
perorata nf long-winded speech; violent speech, harangue.
peróxido nm peroxide; — de hidrógeno hydrogen peroxide.
perpendicular 1 adj (a) perpendicular (a to).
(b) at right angles (a to); **el camino es** — **al río** the road is at right angles to the river.
2 nf perpendicular; vertical; **salir de la** — to be out of the perpendicular (or vertical).
perpendicularmente adv perpendicularly; vertically.
perpetración nf perpetration.
perpetrador nm, **perpetradora** nf perpetrator.
perpetrar [1a] vt to perpetrate.
perpetuación nf perpetuation.
perpetuamente adv perpetually; everlastingly, ceaselessly.
perpetuar [1e] vt to perpetuate.
perpetuidad nf perpetuity; **a** — in perpetuity, for ever; **condena a** — life sentence, sentence of life imprisonment; **le condenaron a prisión a** — he was sentenced to life imprisonment.
perpetuo adj perpetual; everlasting; ceaseless; exile, sentence etc life (attr); (Bot) everlasting.
Perpiñán Perpignan.
perplejamente adv perplexedly; in a puzzled way; in perplexity.
perplejidad nf (a) perplexity; bewilderment; puzzlement; hesitation. (b) perplexing situation; dilemma.
perplejo adj perplexed; bewildered; puzzled; **me miró** — he looked at me in perplexity, he looked at me in a puzzled way; **dejar a uno** — to perplex someone, puzzle someone; **se quedó** — **un momento** he looked perplexed for a moment, he hesitated a moment.
perra nf (a) (Zool) bitch; female dog, lady dog (euph).
(b) (Fin: fam) — **chica** 5-céntimo coin; — **gorda** 10-céntimo coin; —s small change; **costó unas** —s it cost a few coppers.
(c) (fam) tantrum (fam), pet; **el niño cogió una** — the child had a tantrum, the child began to cry violently.
(d) (fam) mania, crazy idea; **está con la** — **de un abrigo de pieles** she's got the crazy idea that she must have a fur coat; **le cogió la** — **de ir a Eslobodia** he got an obsession about going to Slobodia.
(e) (Chi) old hat; leather water bottle.
perrada nf (a) pack of dogs. (b) (fam) dirty trick.
perraje nm (Col, Ven) pack of dogs.
perramus nm (Bol, RPl) raincoat.
perrera nf (a) kennel; kennels.
(b) cart in which stray dogs are picked up.
(c) badly-paid job; drudgery.
(d) (fam) = **perra** (c).
(e) (Cu, Ven) row, shindy.
perrería nf (a) pack of dogs; (fig) gang of villains.
(b) harsh word, angry word; **decir** —s de uno to say harsh things about someone.
(c) (fam) dirty trick.
perrillo nm (a) puppy; small (breed of) dog; miniature dog; (sentimentally) doggie. (b) (Mil) trigger.
perrito nm, **perrita** nf puppy.
perro 1 nm (a) (Zool) dog; "— **peligroso**" "beware of the dog"; — **afgano** Afghan hound; — **de aguas** spaniel; — **callejero** mongrel; — **cobrador** retriever; — **danés** Great Dane; — **dogo** (angl) bulldog; — **esquimal** husky; — **faldero** lapdog; — **guardián** watchdog; — **del hortelano** dog in the manger; — **de lanas** poodle; — **lebrel** whippet; — **lobo** alsatian; — **marino** dogfish; — **de muestra** pointer, setter; — **pastor** sheepdog; — **pequinés** Pekinese; — **policía** police dog; — **de presa** bulldog; — **raposero** foxhound; — **rastreador**, — **rastrero** tracker dog; — (**de**) **San Bernardo** St Bernard; — **tejonero** dachshund; — **de Terranova** Newfoundland dog.
(b) (idioms) **ser** — **viejo** to be an old hand; to be an old fox; **tiempo de** —s dirty weather, awful weather (fam); ¡**a otro** — **con ese hueso!** tell that to the marines!; **darse a** —s to get wild; **echar a uno los**

—s encima to persecute someone, keep after someone; echar una hora a —s to waste a whole hour, get absolutely nothing done in an hour; hacer — muerto (Bol, Per) to avoid paying; heder a — muerto to stink to high heaven; se llevan como —s y gatos they're always squabbling; meter los —s en danza to set the cat among the pigeons; — que ladra no muerde, — ladrador, poco mordedor his bark is worse than his bite.

(c) (pej) dog, swine, hound.

(d) (Col) drowsiness.

2 adj (fam) awful (fam), wretched; esta perra vida this wretched life; he pasado una temporada perra I've had a ghastly time (fam).

perrucho nm (pej) hound, cur.

perruna nf dog biscuit.

perruno adj canine, dog (attr); devotion etc doglike.

persa 1 adj Persian. 2 nmf Persian. 3 nm (language) Persian.

persecución nf (a) pursuit, hunt, chase; estar en plena — to be in full cry. (b) (Eccl, Pol etc) persecution.

persecutorio adj: manía persecutoria persecution mania; trato — cruel treatment.

perseguidor nm, **perseguidora** nf (a) pursuer. (b) (Eccl, Pol etc) persecutor.

perseguimiento nm pursuit, hunt, chase; en — de in pursuit of.

perseguir [3d and 3l] vt (a) fugitive, prey to pursue, hunt, chase; to hunt out, hunt down.

(b) (fig) post, girl etc to chase after, go after; aim to pursue; la persiguió durante 2 años he was after her for 2 years, he pursued her for 2 years.

(c) (Eccl, Pol etc) to persecute; (fig) to persecute, harass; to pester, annoy; me persiguieron hasta que dije que sí they pestered me until I said yes; le persiguen los remordimientos he is gnawed by remorse, his conscience pricks him constantly; le persigue la mala suerte he is dogged by ill luck.

perseverancia nf perseverance, persistence.

perseverante adj persevering, persistent.

perseverantemente adv perseveringly.

perseverar [1a] vi to persevere, keep on, persist; — en to persevere in, persist with.

Persia f Persia.

persiana nf (Venetian) blind; slatted shutter (also — enrollable).

persignarse [1a] vr to cross oneself.

persistencia nf persistence.

persistente adj persistent.

persistentemente adv persistently.

persistir [3a] vi to persist (en in; en + infin in + ger).

persoga nf (CAm, Mex) halter (of plaited vegetable fibre.)

persona nf person; 20 —s 20 people; aquellas —s que lo deseen those who wish; es para animales y no para — s it's for animals not people; es buena — he's a good sort, he's a decent chap (fam); tercera — third party; (Gram) third person; un pronombre de primera — a first person pronoun; — no grata persona non grata; — de historia person with a past, dubious individual; — jurídica legal entity; —s reales royalty, king and queen; en — in person; in the flesh; en la — de in the person of; 3 caramelos por — 3 sweets per person, 3 sweets each; pagaron 2 dólares por — they paid 2 dollars a head (or each).

personaje nm (a) personage, important person; celebrity; ser un — to be somebody, be important. (b) (Lit, Theat etc) character.

personal 1 adj (a) personal.

(b) room, seat etc single, for one person.

2 nm (a) personnel, staff; (as total) establishment; (esp Mil) force; (Naut) crew, complement; — de tierra (Aer) ground crew, ground staff; estar falto de — to be short-handed.

(b) (fam) people; había exceso de — en el cine there were too many people in the cinema.

personalidad nf (a) personality; — desdoblada split personality. (b) (Law) legal entity.

personalísimo adj intensely personal, highly individualistic.

personalismo nm (a) personal reference, personal nature (of attack etc); tenemos que proceder sin —s we must proceed without indulging in personalities (or personal attacks).

(b) selfishness, egoism.

(c) personal preference, partiality; obrar sin —s to act with partiality towards none, act fairly with regard to the persons involved.

personalizar [1f] 1 vt to personalize; virtue etc to embody, personify. 2 vi to make a personal reference. 3 personalizarse vr to become personal.

personalmente adv personally.

personarse [1a] vr to appear in person; — en to present oneself at; to report to; — en forma (Law) to be officially represented; el juez se personó en el lugar del accidente the judge made an official visit to the scene of the accident.

personería nf (RPl) personality; aptitude, talent.

personificación nf personification; embodiment.

personificar [1g] vt (a) to personify; to embody, be the embodiment of.

(b) en esta mujer el autor personifica la maldad the author makes this woman a symbol of wickedness.

(c) (in speech etc) to single out for special mention.

perspectiva nf (a) (Art and fig) perspective; en — in perspective; le falta — he lacks a sense of perspective.

(b) view, scene, panorama.

(c) outlook, prospect; future development; "buenas —s de mejora" (job advert) "good prospects"; las —s de la cosecha son favorables the harvest outlook is good; es una — nada halagüeña it's a most unwelcome prospect; se alegró con la — de pasar un día en el campo he cheered up with the prospect of spending a day in the country; encontrarse ante la — de + infin to be faced with the prospect of + ger; tener algo en — to have something in view, have a prospect of something; hay ocupaciones en — there's a busy time ahead.

perspicacia nf (a) keen-sightedness. (b) (fig) perspicacity, shrewdness, discernment.

perspicaz adj (a) sight keen; person keen-sighted. (b) (fig) perspicacious, shrewd, discerning.

perspicuidad nf perspicuity, clarity.

perspicuo adj clear, intelligible.

persuadir [3a] 1 vt to persuade; to convince, prevail upon; — a uno a hacer algo to persuade someone to do something; dejarse — to allow oneself to be persuaded.

2 persuadirse vr to be persuaded, become convinced.

persuasión nf (a) (act) persuasion. (b) (state) conviction; tener la — de que . . . to have the conviction that . . ., be convinced that . . .

persuasiva nf persuasiveness.

persuasivo adj persuasive; convincing.

pertenecer [2d] vi (a) to belong (a to). (b) (fig) — a to concern; to apply to, pertain to; le pertenece a él hacerlo it's his job to do it.

perteneciente adj (a) los países —s the member countries, the countries which belong. (b) — a pertaining to, relevant to.

pertenencia nf (a) ownership; las cosas de su — the things which belong to him, his possessions, his property.

(b) —s possessions, property; estate.

(c) (of estate etc) —s appurtenances, accessories.

pértica nf land measure = 2.571m, approx = rod.

pértiga nf pole; — de trole trolley pole.

pertinacia nf (a) persistence; prolonged nature. (b) pertinacity, obstinacy.

pertinaz adj (a) cough etc persistent; drought persistent, long-lasting, prolonged. (b) person pertinacious, obstinate.

pertinencia nf relevance, pertinence; appropriateness.

pertinente adj (a) relevant, pertinent; appropriate; no es — hacerlo ahora this is not the appropriate time to do it.

(b) — a concerning, relevant to; en lo — a libros as regards books, as far as books are concerned.

pertinentemente adv relevantly, pertinently; appropriately.

pertrechar [1a] 1 vt to supply (con, de with); to equip (con, de with); (Mil) to supply with ammunition and stores.

2 pertrecharse vr: — de algo to provide oneself with something.

pertrechos nmpl implements, equipment; gear; (Mil) supplies and stores, provisions; (Mil) ammunition.

perturbación nf (a) (Meteorol, Pol etc) disturbance; — del orden público breach of the peace.

(b) (Med) upset, disturbance; (mental) perturbation, (serious) mental disorder, alienation.

perturbado 1 adj mentally unbalanced. 2 nm, **perturbada** nf mentally unbalanced person.

perturbador 1 adj (a) perturbing, disturbing.

(b) unruly, disorderly; subversive.

2 nm disturber (of the peace); (Pol) disorderly element, unruly person; subversive.

perturbar [1a] *vt* (a) *order etc* to disturb; *calm* to disturb, ruffle, upset.
(b) (*Med*) to upset, disturb; (*mentally*) to perturb; to cause mental disorder in.
Perú: el — Peru.
peruanismo *nm* word (*or* phrase *etc*) peculiar to Peru.
peruano 1 *adj* Peruvian. **2** *nm*, **peruana** *nf* Peruvian.
peruétano 1 *adj* (Col, Cu, Mex) boring, tedious; stupid. **2** *nm* (Col, Cu, Mex) bore; dolt; (Chi) meddlesome youngster; (Mex) rascal.
perulero *nm* (SAm: *hum*) Peruvian.
perversamente *adv* perversely; wickedly.
perversidad *nf* (a) perversity; depravity; wickedness.
(b) (*una* —) evil deed, wrongdoing.
perversión *nf* (a) perversion; — **sexual** sexual perversion. (b) wickedness.
perverso *adj* perverse; depraved; wicked.
pervertido 1 *adj* perverted. **2** *nm*, **pervertida** *nf* pervert.
pervertimiento *nm* perversion, corruption.
pervertir [3i] **1** *vt* to pervert, corrupt; *text etc* to distort, corrupt; *taste* to corrupt. **2 pervertirse** *vr* to become perverted.
pervinca *nf* periwinkle.
pesa *nf* (a) weight; (*Sport*) weight, shot; dumbbell. (b) (CAm, Col, Ven) butcher's shop.
pesadamente *adv* (a) heavily; **caer** — to fall heavily. (b) slowly, ponderously; sluggishly; stiffly. (c) boringly, tediously.
pesadez *nf* (a) heaviness; weight.
(b) slowness, ponderousness; sluggishness.
(c) drowsiness; dull feeling, heavy feeling.
(d) tediousness, boring nature; annoyance; **es una — tener que . . .** it's a bore having to . . .
pesadilla *nf* (a) nightmare, bad dream.
(b) (*fig*) worry, obsession, nightmare; bogey; (*person*) pet aversion; bogeyman; **ese equipo es nuestra —** that is our bogey team; **ha sido la — de todos** it has been a nightmare for everybody.
pesado 1 *adj* (a) heavy (*also fig*), weighty.
(b) *person etc* slow, slow-moving, ponderous; sluggish; *work etc* slow; *mechanism* stiff.
(c) (*Meteorol*) heavy, sultry.
(d) *sleep* deep, heavy.
(e) **tengo la cabeza pesada** my head feels heavy, I can hardly keep my head up, my head feels like lead; **tener el estómago —** to feel blown out.
(f) *task etc* tough, hard; tedious; boring; *reading etc* boring, stodgy; *person* tedious, boring; annoying; **esto se hace —** this is becoming tedious; **la lectura del libro resultó pesada** the book was heavy going, I got bored with the book; **es una persona de lo más —** he's a terribly dull sort, he's a person of the most boring kind; **es — tener que . . .** it's such a bore having to . . ., it's tough having to . . .; **¡no seas —!** come off it!; don't be so difficult!
(g) (Col) very good, excellent.
2 *nm*, **pesada** *nf* boring person, bore; **es un —** he's such a bore.
pesador *nm* (CAm, Col, Ven) butcher.
pesadumbre *nf* grief, sorrow, affliction.
pésame *nm* expression of condolence, message of sympathy; **dar el —** to express one's condolences, send one's sympathy (*por* for, on).
pesantez *nf* weight, heaviness; (*Phys*) gravity.
pesar [1a] **1** *vt* (a) to weigh.
(b) to weigh down, be heavy for; **me pesa el abrigo** the coat weighs me down.
(c) (*fig*) to weigh heavily on; **le pesa tanta responsabilidad** so much responsibility bears heavily on him (*or* is a burden to him).
(d) (*fig*) to weigh; to appraise, value; to reckon up; **— las posibilidades** to weigh up one's chances; **— las palabras** to weigh one's words.
(e) (*fig*) to grieve, afflict, distress; **me pesa mucho** it grieves me, I am very sorry about it (*or* to hear it *etc*); **no me pesa haberlo hecho** I'm not sorry I did it; **le pesa que no le hayan nombrado** it grieves him that they should not have nominated him; **¡ya le pesará!** you'll be sorry!; **pese a las dificultades** in spite of the difficulties; **pese a quien pese** regardless of the consequences; in spite of everything; *see* **mal**.
2 *vi* (a) to weigh; (*Phys*) to have weight; **pesa 5 kilos** it weighs 5 kilos.
(b) to weigh a lot, be heavy; (*of time*) to drag, hang heavy; **ese paquete no pesa** that parcel isn't heavy, that parcel hardly weighs anything; **¿pesa mucho?** is it heavy?
(c) (*fig*) to weigh heavily; **sobre ella pesan muchas obligaciones** many obligations bear

heavily on her; **la hipoteca que pesa sobre la finca** the mortgage with which the estate is burdened.
(d) (*fig: of opinion etc*) to carry weight, count for a lot; **esa consideración no ha pesado conmigo** that consideration has not weighed with me (*or* influenced me).
(e) (CAm, Col, Ven) to sell meat.
3 *nm* (a) regret; grief, sorrow; **a mi —** to my regret; **con gran — mío** much to my sorrow; **causar — a uno** to grieve someone, cause grief to someone; **tener — por no haber . . .** to regret not having . . .
(b) **a — de** in spite of, despite; **a — de eso** in spite of that, notwithstanding that; **a — de que no tiene dinero** in spite of the fact that he has no money.
pesario *nm* pessary.
pesaroso *adj* sorrowful, regretful, sad.
pesca *nf* (a) fishing; **— de altura** deep-sea fishing; **— en bajura** shallow water fishing, coastal fishing; **— de la ballena** whaling; **— de perlas** pearl fishing; **— submarina** underwater fishing; skin diving; **allí la — es muy buena** the fishing is very good there; **ir de —** to go fishing; **andar a la — de** (*fig*) to fish for, angle for.
(b) catch, quantity (of fish) caught; **la — ha sido mala** it's been a poor catch.
pescada *nf* hake.
pescadera *nf* fishmonger; (*esp pej*) fishwife.
pescadería *nf* fish market; fish shop.
pescadero *nm* fishmonger.
pescadilla *nf* whiting; small hake.
pescado *nm* (a) fish. (b) (Ec, RPl: *hum*) secret police.
pescador *nm* fisherman; **— de caña** angler, fisherman; **— a mosca** fly fisherman.
pescaduría *nf* fishery; **— de perlas** pearl fishery.
pescante *nm* (a) coachman's seat, driver's seat. (b) (*Theat*) wire. (c) (*Tech*) jib; (*Naut*) davit.
pescar [1g] **1** *vt* (a) to catch; to land.
(b) to fish for, try to catch; **¿qué pescáis aquí?** what are you fishing for here?, what fish are you after here?
(c) (*fam*) to catch, get hold of, land; *job etc* to land, manage to get; *meaning* to grasp; *facts etc* to dredge up; **viene a — un marido** she's come to get a husband; **logró — unos cuantos datos** he managed to bring up a few facts, he was able to find a few facts.
(d) (*fam*) *person* to catch (out), catch in a lie; to catch unawares; **¡ya te pesqué!** now I've found you out!
2 *vi* (a) to fish; to go fishing; **— a mosca** to fish with a fly; **— al arrastre, — a la rastra** to trawl.
(b) (*fam*) **la chica viene a ver si pesca** the girl is coming to see if she can get hitched (*sl*).
(c) (Col, RPl) to nod, doze.
3 pescarse *vr*: **no sabe lo que se pesca** (*fam*) he hasn't a clue, he has no idea.
pescocear [1a] *vt* (SAm) to punch.
pescozudo *adj* thick-necked, fat in the neck.
pescuezo *nm* (a) neck; scruff of the neck; **retorcer el — a una gallina** to wring a chicken's neck; **¡calla, o te retuerzo el —!** shut up, or I'll wring your neck!
(b) (*fig*) vanity; haughtiness.
pescuezón *adj* (SAm) (a) = **pescozudo**. (b) long-necked.
pese: — a (*as prep*) *see* **pesar 1** (e).
pesebre *nm* (a) manger; stall. (b) (SAm) Nativity scene, crib.
pesebrera *nf* (Chi, Mex) = **pesebre** (b).
pesero *nm* (a) (CAm, Col, Ven) butcher; slaughterman. (b) (Mex) small bus.
peseta *nf* peseta; **cambiar la —** (*fam*) to be sick.
pesetada *nf* (SAm) joke, trick.
pesetera *nf* (*fam*) prostitute.
pesetero *adj* (a) money-grubbing, mercenary. (b) (Mex) *dealer* small-time. (c) (Cu) mean. (d) (Ant, Guat, Per, Ven) sponging (*fam*), parasitic.
pésimamente *adv* abominably, wretchedly.
pesimismo *nm* pessimism.
pesimista 1 *adj* pessimistic. **2** *nmf* pessimist.
pésimo *adj* abominable, wretched, vile.
peso *nm* (a) (*in general*) weight; weightiness, heaviness; (*Phys*) gravity; **—s y medidas** weights and measures; **— atómico** atomic weight; **— bruto** gross weight; **— específico** specific gravity; **— muerto** dead weight; **— neto** net weight; **— en vivo** live weight; **comprar algo a — de oro** to buy something at a very high price; **vender a —** to sell by weight; **de poco —** light, lightweight; **de mucho —** (very) heavy; **eso cae de su —** that goes without saying, that's obvious; **coger algo en —** to catch something in the

air; **echar a uno en — por una ventana** to throw someone bodily through a window; **sostener algo en —** to support the full weight of something; **lleva toda la dirección en —** he carries all the burden of the management; **llevar el — de un ataque** to bear the brunt of an attack.

(b) (*object*) weight, weighty object; burden, load; (*Sport*) weight; shot; **lanzar el —** to put the shot; **levantamiento de —s** weight lifting.

(c) (*Boxing*) weight; **— completo** (*CAm, Mex*), **— fuerte** heavyweight; **— gallo** bantam-weight; **— ligero** lightweight; **— medio** middle-weight; **— medio fuerte** light heavyweight, cruiser weight; **— mosca** flyweight; **— pesada** heavyweight; **— pluma** featherweight.

(d) heavy feeling, dull feeling (*in head etc*).

(e) (*fig*) weight; **el — de los años** the weight of the years, the burden of age; **argumento de —** weighty argument.

(f) scales, balance, weighing machine; **— de baño** bathroom scales; **— de muelle** spring balance.

(g) (*Fin*) standard monetary unit of certain SAm countries.

pesor nm (*Ant, CAm*) weight, heaviness.
pespunt(e)ar [1a] vti to backstitch.
pespunte nm backstitch(ing).
pesquera nf **(a)** fishing ground, fishery. **(b)** (*on river*) weir.
pesquería nf fishing ground, fishery.
pesquero 1 adj fishing (*attr*). **2** nm fishing boat.
pesquisa nf **(a)** investigation, inquiry; search. **(b)** (*Ec, RPl: euph*) secret police.
pesquisador nm (*Ec, RPl: euph*) member of the secret police, detective.
pesquisar [1a] vt to investigate, inquire into.
pesquisidor nm investigator, inquirer.
pestaña nf **(a)** (*Anat, Bot etc*) fringe (*of hairs*); **no pegué —** (*fam*) I didn't get a wink of sleep. **(b)** (*Tech*) flange; (*of tyre*) rim.
pestañar [1a] vi (*SAm*), **pestañear** [1a] vi to blink, wink; **sin —** without batting an eyelid.
pestañeo nm blink(ing), wink(ing).
peste nf **(a)** (*Med*) plague, epidemic; (*Per, PR*) bubonic plague; (*Chi*) smallpox; (*Col, Per*) cold; (*RPl*) (*any*) infectious disease; **— aviar** fowl pest; **— bubónica** bubonic plague; **— negra** Black Death.

(b) (*fig*) plague; evil menace; nuisance; **una — de ratones** a plague of mice; **los chiquillos son una —** the kids are a pest, the kids are a nuisance (*fam*).

(c) stink, stench, foul smell; **¡qué — hay aquí!** what a stink!

(d) **echar —s de** to swear about, fume at, utter bitter words about.
pesticida nm pesticide.
pestífero adj pestiferous; *smell* foul; *influence etc* noxious, harmful.
pestilencia nf **(a)** pestilence, plague. **(b)** stink, stench.
pestilencial adj pestilential.
pestilente adj **(a)** pestilent. **(b)** smelly, foul.
pestillo nm bolt, latch; catch, fastener.
petaca 1 nf **(a)** cigarette case, cigar case; tobacco pouch.

(b) wicker basket; hamper; (*SAm*) leather-covered chest; (*Mex*) suitcase, grip; piece of luggage.

(c) (*CAm: Anat*) hump; **—s** (*Ant, Mex*) buttocks; big breasts.

2 nmf (*SAm*) **(a)** short squat person.

(b) lazy person.

3 adj invar **(a)** (*SAm*) idle, lazy; (*Chi*) slow, ponderous, sluggish.

(b) (*PR*) coarse.
petacón adj **(a)** (*Mex, Per, RPl*) plump; squat, short. **(b)** (*Col*) lazy. **(c)** (*Col*) potbellied, fat; (*Mex*) broad in the beam (*fam*). **(d)** (*CAm*) bent.
petacudo adj **(a)** (*Bol*) stout, fat; (*Guat*) hunchbacked; (*Mex*) broad in the beam (*fam*). **(b)** slow, ponderous, sluggish.
pétalo nm petal.
petardear [1a] **1** vt to cheat, swindle. **2** vi (*Aut*) backfire.
petardista nm cheat, swindler; (*in strike*) blackleg; (*Mex*) crooked politician.
petardo nm **(a)** firework, firecracker; (*Mil*) petard. **(b)** (*fam*) fraud, swindle; **pegar un —** to practise a fraud, pull a fast one (*a on*).
petate nm **(a)** grass mat; (*SAm*) mat of palm leaves, sleeping mat.

(b) roll of bedding; baggage; **liar el —** (*fam*) to pack up; to pack up and go, clear out; to peg out (*sl*).

(c) (*fam*) cheat, trickster.

(d) (*fam*) poor fish, worthless individual.

petatearse [1a] vr (*Mex*) to peg out (*sl*), die.
peteneras nfpl: **salir por —** to butt in with some silly remark, say (*or* do) something quite inappropriate.
peteretes nmpl sweets.
petición nf request, plea; petition; (*Law*) plea; claim; **a —** by request; **a — de** at the request of; **programa a —** de radioyentes listeners' request programme; **— de aumento de salarios** demand for higher wages, wage demand, wage claim; **— de divorcio** petition for divorce; **cometer — de principio** to beg the question.
peticionar [1a] vt (*SAm*) to petition.
peticionario nm, **peticionaria** nf petitioner.
petimetre nm fop, dandy.
petirrojo nm robin.
petizo (*Bol, Chi, RPl*) **1** adj small, short; stocky, chubby. **2** nm small horse; small person.
petizón adj (*Bol, Chi, RPl*) = **petizo 1**.
peto nm bodice; bib; (*Mil*) breastplate; (*Taur*) protective covering of picador's horse.
petral nm breast-strap (*of harness*).
Petrarca m Petrarch.
petrarquismo nm Petrarchism.
petrarquista adj Petrarchan.
petrel nm petrel.
pétreo adj stony; rocky.
petrificación nf petrifaction.
petrificado adj petrified.
petrificar [1g] **1** vt to petrify (*also fig*), turn to stone. **2 petrificarse** vr to petrify, become petrified (*also fig*), turn to stone.
petróleo nm (*Min*) oil, petroleum; **— de alumbrado** paraffin (oil); **— combustible** fuel oil; **— crudo** crude oil.
petrolero 1 adj oil (*attr*), petroleum (*attr*). **2** nm **(a)** (*Comm*) oil man. **(b)** (*fam*) extremist, revolutionary. **(c)** (*Naut*) tanker.
petrolífero adj petroliferous, oil-bearing.
petrología nf petrology.
petulancia nf vanity, self-satisfaction, opinionated nature.
petulante adj vain, self-satisfied, opinionated.
petunia nf petunia.
peuquino adj (*Chi*) greyish.
peyorativo adj pejorative.
pez[1] nm **(a)** fish; **— de color(es)** goldfish; **— espada** swordfish; **— mujer** manatee; **— sierra** sawfish; **— volador, — volante** flying fish; **estar como el — en el agua** to feel completely at home.

(b) (*fam*) **— gordo** big shot (*fam*), big pot (*fam*).

(c) (*fam*) **buen —** rogue, rascal.

(d) **estar — de** (*or* **en**) **algo** to be completely ignorant of something, know nothing at all about something.
pez[2] nf pitch, tar.
pezón nm **(a)** (*Anat*) teat, nipple. **(b)** (*Bot*) stalk. **(c)** (*Mech*) **— de engrase** nipple, lubrication point.
pezonera nf (*Arg*) feeding bottle.
pezuña nf **(a)** hoof. **(b)** (*Mex, Per*) dirt hardened on the feet.
piache nm (*Ven*) medicine man; quack doctor.
piada nf **(a)** (*Orn*) cheep, cheeping. **(b)** (*fig*) catch phrase.
piadosamente adv **(a)** piously, devoutly. **(b)** kindly, mercifully.
piadoso adj **(a)** (*Rel*) pious, devout. **(b)** kind, merciful (*para con* to); see **mentira**.
piafar [1a] vi (*horse*) to paw the ground, stamp.
pial nm (*etc*) see **peal** (*etc*).
Piamonte m Piedmont.
piamontés 1 adj Piedmontese. **2** nm, **piamontesa** nf Piedmontese.
pianista nmf pianist.
piano nm piano; **— de cola** grand piano; **— de media cola** baby grand; **— mecánico** pianola; **— recto, — vertical** upright piano; **tocar el —** to play the piano, (*fam*) do the washing up; **tocar —** (*SAm*) to rob, steal.
piar [1c] vi **(a)** (*Orn*) to cheep. **(b)** (*fam*) **— por** to cry for, be dying for.
piara nf herd; drove.
piastra nf piastre.
pibe nm, **piba** nf (*Bol, Chi, RPl*) kid (*fam*), child.
pica[1] nf (*Orn*) magpie.
pica[2] nf (*Mil*) pike; (*Taur*) goad; **poner una — en Flandes** to bring off something difficult, achieve a signal success.
pica[3] nf (*Col, Ec, Per*) tapping (of rubber trees).
pica[4] nf (*Col*) pique, resentment; (*Chi*) annoyance, impatience.
pica[5] nf (*Col, Ec, Guat, Ven*) forest trail, narrow path.

picacera *nf* (*Chi*, *Per*) pique, resentment.

picacho *nm* peak, summit.

picada[1] *nf* (a) prick; sting; bite; peck. (b) (*Chi*) bad temper, anger.

picada[2] *nf* (*SAm*) forest trail, narrow path; (*Bol*) ford.

picadero *nm* (a) riding school. (b) (*Col*) slaughterhouse.

picadillo *nm* mince, minced meat.

picado 1 *adj* (a) *material* pricked, perforated; with a row of holes; *surface* pitted; — **de viruelas** pockmarked.

(b) *meat etc* minced; *tobacco* cut; *sea* choppy.
(c) **estar** — to be offended, be cross.
(d) **estar** — **por algo** (*SAm*) to go for something in a big way.
2 *nm* (a) (*Aer*, *Orn*) dive.
(b) (*Mus*) pizzicato.

picador *nm* (a) horse-trainer, horse-breaker. (b) (*Taur*) picador, bullfighter's assistant (*mounted, with a pike*). (c) (*Min*) faceworker.

picadora *nf*: — **de carne** mincer, mincing machine.

picadura *nf* (a) prick; puncture; sting; bite. (b) cut tobacco.

picaflor *nm* (*SAm*) (a) hummingbird. (b) (*fam*) wolf (*fam*), flirt; lover, boyfriend.

picafuego *nm* poker.

picajón *adj* (*fam*), **picajoso** *adj* (*fam*) touchy.

picamaderos *nm*, *pl* **picamaderos** woodpecker.

picana *nf* (*SAm*) spur, goad.

picanear [1a] *vt* (*SAm*) to spur on, goad on.

picante 1 *adj* (a) *food, flavour* hot; peppery; highly seasoned.
(b) (*fig*) *remark* sharp, stinging, cutting; *joke etc* racy, spicy; *situation, contrast* piquant.
2 *nm* (a) hot taste.
(b) (*fig*) sharpness, pungency; raciness, spiciness; piquancy.
(c) (*Bol*, *Chi*, *Per*) highly seasoned sauce (*or* dish).

picantería *nf* (*Bol*, *Chi*, *Per*) restaurant specializing in seasoned dishes.

picapedrero *nm* stonecutter, quarryman.

picapica: **polvos** *nmpl* **de** — itching powder.

picapleitos *nm*, *pl* **picapleitos** (*pej*) lawyer; litigious person.

picaporte *nm* door-handle; latch; doorknocker; latchkey.

picar [1g] **1** *vt* (a) to prick, puncture; *paper etc* to prick (a line of) holes in, pierce with holes, perforate; *surface* to pit, pock; (*Art*) to stipple; (*Sew*) to pink; *ticket* to punch, clip.
(b) (*of insect*) to sting; to bite; (*of snake*) to bite; (*of thorn*) to prick.
(c) (*of bird*) to peck; to peck at; (*of person*) *food* to nibble (at), pick at; (*of fish*) to bite.
(d) *horse* to put spurs to, spur on; *bull* to stick, prick (with the goad); (*fig*) to incite, goad, stimulate; (*fig*) to wound; to pique; to annoy, bother; **le pican los celos** jealousy is pricking him, he is feeling pangs of jealousy.
(e) (*Mus*) to play pizzicato.
(f) *stone* to chip, chip pieces off; *millstone* to sharpen; *stone* to grind (up); (*Cook*) to mince, chop (up); *tobacco* to cut.
(g) *tongue* to burn, sting.
(h) (*Mil*) to harass.
2 *vi* (a) (*of thorn*) to prick; (*of insect*) to sting, bite; **no es de los que pican** it's not the kind that stings.
(b) (*of bird*) — **en** to peck at; (*of person etc*) to nibble at, pick at; (*fig*) to dabble in, study superficially; **ha picado en todos los géneros literarios** he's dabbled in (*or* had a go at) all the literary genres.
(c) (*of fish*) to bite, take the bait; (*fig*) to rise to the bait; **por fin picó** he swallowed the bait eventually; **ha picado mucha gente** lots of people have fallen for it, it has caught on with lots of people.
(d) — **en** (*fig*) to border on, be akin to; **eso pica en frescura** that borders (*or* verges) on cheek.
(e) (*Med*) to itch, sting; **me pican los ojos** my eyes hurt; **me pica la lengua** my tongue is smarting (*or* stinging); **me pica el brazo** my arm itches.
(f) (*of sun*) to burn, scorch; **hoy sí pica el sol** the sun is really burning today.
(g) (*Aer*, *Orn*) to dive.
(h) — **muy alto** to aim too high, be over-ambitious.
(i) (*Aut*) — **por autoencendido** to pink.
3 picarse *vr* (a) (*clothing*) to get moth-eaten; (*substance*) to get holes in it; (*tooth*) to decay.

(b) (*wine etc*) to turn sour, go off; (*fruit etc*) to spoil, go rotten.
(c) (*sea*) to get choppy.
(d) (*person*) to take offence, get piqued; to get cross; to bridle (*por at*).
(e) — **con algo** to get a longing for, get an obsession about; to take a strong liking to.
(f) — **de puntual** to take a pride in being punctual, make a strong point of punctuality; — **de caballero** to boast of being a gentleman.
(g) (*Ant*) — **de pecho** to become consumptive.

picarazado *adj* (*Cu*, *PR*) pockmarked.

picardear [1a] **1** *vt*: — **a uno** to get someone into bad habits, lead someone into evil ways.
2 *vi* to play about; to play up, be mischievous.
3 picardearse *vr* to get into evil ways, go to the bad.

Picardía *f* Picardy.

picardía *nf* (a) (*quality*) crookedness; villainy, knavery; slyness, craftiness; naughtiness.
(b) (**una** —) dirty trick; naughty thing (to do), mischievous act.
(c) rude thing (to say), naughty word; insult; **le gusta decir** —**s a las chicas** he likes saying naughty things to the girls.

picaresco *adj* (a) roguish, rascally. (b) (*Lit*) *novel* picaresque, of roguery.

pícaro 1 *adj* (a) crooked; villainous, knavish; sly, crafty; *child* naughty, mischievous.
(b) *child etc* precocious, knowing, (*esp*) sexually aware before the proper age.
(c) (*hum*) naughty, wicked; **¡este** — **siglo!** what naughty times we live in!; **tiene inclinación a los** —**s celos** she gives way to that wicked jealousy.
2 *nm* (a) crook; villain, knave, scoundrel, rogue, rascal; sly sort; (*child*) rascal, scamp; **¡**—**!** you rascal!
(b) (*Lit*) rogue, pícaro.

picarón *nm* (a) rogue. (b) (*Chi*, *Mex*, *Per*) fritter.

picaruelo *adj* *look etc* roguish, naughty, sly; **me miró picaruela** she gave me a roguish look.

picatoste *nm* fried bread.

picaza *nf* magpie.

picazo *nm* peck; jab, poke.

picazón *nf* (a) itch; sting, stinging feeling; smart, smarting. (b) (*fig*) annoyance, pique; uneasy feeling, pang of conscience.

piccolo *nm* piccolo.

pícea *nf* spruce.

pick-up [pi'kap *or* pi'ku] *nm* (*angl*) pickup.

pico *nm* (a) (*Orn*) beak, bill; (*Ent etc*) beak; (*hum*) mouth, lips; **callar** (*or* **cerrar**) **el** — (*fam*) to shut one's trap (*sl*), keep one's trap shut (*sl*); **hincar el** — (*fam*) to peg out (*sl*); to give up, give in.
(b) corner, peak, sharp point; (*of page*) corner; **sombrero de tres** —**s** cocked hat, three-cornered hat; **andar** (*or* **irse**) **de** —**s pardos** to go on the spree (*fam*); to go whoring.
(c) (*of jug etc*) lip, spout.
(d) (*Tech*) pick, pickaxe.
(e) (*Geog*) peak, summit; pinnacle of rock.
(f) **y** — and a bit; **son las 3 y** — it's just after 3; **tiene 50 libros y** — he has 50-odd books; **quédese con el** — keep the change, keep the odd amount; **me costó un** — it cost me quite a bit.
(g) (*Orn*: *species*) woodpecker.
(h) (*fam*) talkativeness; **ser un** — **de oro**, **tener buen** — (*or* **mucho**) — to have the gift of the gab (*fam*), be a great talker; **irse del** — to talk too much; **perderse por el** — to harm oneself by saying too much.
(i) (*Cards*) —**s** spades.
(j) (*Col*, *Guat*, *Mex*) kiss.
(k) (*Chi*: *tabu*) prick (*tabu*).

picolargo *adj* (*Arg*) pert, saucy; backbiting; intriguing, scheming.

picón 1 *adj* (a) (*Col*, *PR*) pert, saucy. (b) (*Per*, *PR*) touchy. (c) (*PR*) mocking. **2** *nm* (*Col*) gossip, talebearer.

picor *nm* = **picazón** (a).

picoreto *adj* (*CAm*, *Col*, *PR*, *Ven*) talkative, indiscreet.

picoso *adj* pockmarked.

picota *nf* (a) pillory; **poner a uno en la** — (*fig*) to ridicule someone, show someone up (for what he is).
(b) (*Archit*) point, top; (*Geog*) peak.

picotada *nf*, **picotazo** *nm* peck; sting, bite.

picotear [1a] **1** *vt* to peck. **2** *vi* to nibble, pick.
(b) (*fam*) to chatter, gas (*fam*), gab (*fam*). **3 picotearse** *vr* to squabble.

picotero (*fam*) **1** *adj* chattering, gossipy, talkative.
2 *nm*, **picotera** *nf* gossip, chatterer, gasbag (*fam*).

picotón nm (Arg, Chi, Ec) peck.
picto 1 adj Pictish. **2** nm, **picta** nf Pict. **3** nm (language) Pict.
pictóricamente adv pictorially.
pictórico adj (a) pictorial.
  (b) scene etc worth painting.
  (c) gift, skill etc artistic; **tiene dotes pictóricas** she has artistic gifts, she has talent for painting.
picúa nf (Cu, PR) (a) small kite. (b) sharp business-man. (c) prostitute.
picuda nf (a) (Orn) woodcock. (b) (Cu, PR: Fish) barracuda.
picudo adj (a) pointed, with a point; jar with a spout; person long-nosed, sharp-nosed.
  (b) (fam) = picotero 1.
  (c) (Cu) = cursi.
  (d) (Mex) crafty, clever.
picure nm (a) (Col) fugitive; slacker. (b) (Ven) highly seasoned sauce.
picurearse [1a] vr (Col, Ven) to flee.
picha[1] nf (Mex) blanket; (hum) mistress.
picha[2] nf (tabu) prick (tabu).
pichado adj (RPl) easily embarrassed.
pichana nf (Arg, Chi, Per) bass broom.
pichanga nf (Col) bass broom.
pichango nm (Chi) dog.
piche nm (a) (CAm) miser, skinflint.
  (b) (Arg, Bol, Chi) (kind of) armadillo.
  (c) (Arg, Cu) fear, cowardice.
  (d) (Col) shove.
  (e) (Col) whey.
  (f) (Col) red.
pichel nm tankard, mug.
pichicata nf (Per) cocaine powder.
pichicatero nm, **pichicatera** nf (Per) dope addict.
pichicato adj (SAm) mean, miserly.
pichicote adj (Bol, Ec) mean, miserly.
pichilingo nm (Mex) lad, kid.
pichincha nf (Bol, RPl) bargain; low price, reduced price; advantageous deal, lucky break.
pichingo nm (CAm) jar, vessel; piece of junk.
pichirre adj (Per, Ven) mean, stingy.
picholear [1a] vi (a) (Chi, Hond) to make merry.
  (b) (Guat) to win by cheating. (c) (Hond, Mex) to lay small bets.
pichón 1 nm (a) young pigeon; (SAm) chick, young bird; — **de barro** clay pigeon.
  (b) (SAm) novice, greenhorn; tyro; young player, inexperienced player.
  (c) (Arg) **un — de hombre** a well-bred man.
  2 nm, **pichona** nf darling, dearest.
pichonear [1a] **1** vt (a) (Arg, Mex) to swindle.
  (b) (Col, Pan) to catch out; to kill, murder.
  (c) (Chi) = pinchar.
  (d) (Ec, Pan etc) to borrow, use temporarily; to occupy temporarily.
  2 vi (Arg, Col, Mex) to beat an inexperienced player.
pichuleador nm (RPl) money grubber.
pichulear [1a] vi (a) (CAm, RPl) to be in a small-time business; to be mercenary, be greedy for money. (b) (CR, Mex) to lay small bets; to spend very little.
pichuleo nm (a) (RPl) meanness. (b) (Mex, Nic) small business, retail business; small-time gambling.
pídola nf leapfrog.
pie nm (a) (Anat etc) foot; — **de atleta** athlete's foot; — **de cabra** crowbar; — **marino** sea legs; — **s planos** flat feet; **ligero de —s** light-footed, quick; **a — on foot; ir a —** to go on foot, walk; **a cuatro —s** on all fours; **a — enjuto** dry-shod, (fig) without danger, without any risk; **a — firme** steadfastly; **a — juntillo, a —s juntillos** with both feet together, (fig) believe firmly, absolutely; **al — close, handy; con el — bien sentado** calmly, thoughtfully; **with due care; con —s de plomo** warily, gingerly; **andar con —s de plomo** to go very carefully; **con un — en el hoyo** with one foot in the grave; **entrar con buen —** (or **con — derecho**) to get off to a good start; **hacer algo con los —s** to bungle something, make a mess of something; **estar de —** to be standing (up); **ponerse de** (or **en**) — to stand up, get up, rise; **caer de —** (fig) to fall on one's feet; **nacer de —** to be born with a silver spoon in one's mouth, be born lucky; **cojear del mismo —** to have the same faults as someone else; **saber de qué — cojea uno** to know someone's weak spots (or weaknesses); **de —s a cabeza** from head to foot, from top to toe; **soldado de a —** (Hist) foot-soldier; **en — standing; upright; mantenerse en —** to remain upright; **la duda sigue en —** the doubt remains; **saltar en —** to leap to one's feet; **irse** (or **salir**) **por —s** to make off;

argumento sin —s ni cabeza pointless argument, absurd argument; **asentar el —** to make a cautious start; **buscar tres —s al gato** to split hairs, quibble; to look for trouble; **no dar — con bola** to do every-thing wrong, be no good at anything; **se le fueron los —s** he slipped, he stumbled; **parar los —s a uno** to curb someone, clip someone's wings; to stop some-one going too far; to take someone down a peg; **poner el —** to tread, put one's foot; **poner los —s en** (fig) to set foot in; **sacar los —s del plato** to abandon all restraint; to kick over the traces; **tomar —** (Aer) to land, come down; **volverse —s atrás** to retrace one's steps.
  (b) (Math) foot; — **cuadrado** square foot; — **cúbico** cubic foot; **tiene 6 —s de largo** it is 6 feet long.
  (c) trunk, stem; (of rose etc) root, stock, stand; (of glass) stem; (of statue) foot, base; (of bed, hill, page, slope, stairs etc) foot, bottom; (of document, letter) ending; (of picture, photo) caption; — **de imprenta** imprint; **al — del monte** at the foot (or bottom) of the mountain; **a los —s de la cama** at the foot of the bed; **al — de la fábrica** cost price, ex works; **al — de la letra** quote etc literally, verbatim; copy exactly, word for word; **morir al — del cañón** to die in harness.
  (d) (Theat) cue.
  (e) (of wine etc) sediment.
  (f) (fig) motive, basis; pretext; **dar — a** to give cause for; **dar — para que uno haga algo** to give someone a motive for doing something; **tomar — para hacer algo** to use something as a basis for action.
  (g) (fig) foothold; **perder el —** to lose one's foot-hold, slip.
  (h) (fig) standing, footing; **en — de guerra** on a war footing; **estar sobre un (mismo) — de igualdad** to be on an equal footing, be on equal terms (con with).
  (i) (Lit) foot; measure, verse form.
piedad nf (a) (Rel) piety, devotion, devoutness; respect; — **filial** filial respect.
  (b) pity; mercy; **¡por —!** for pity's sake!; **mover a uno a —** to move someone to pity, arouse com-passion in someone; **tener — de** to take pity on; **¡ten un poco de —!** show some sympathy!; **no tuvieron — de ellos** they showed them no mercy.
piedra nf (a) stone; rock; (of lighter etc) flint; (Med) stone; (Meteorol) hailstone; hail; **un puente de —** a stone bridge; **tener el corazón de —** to be hard-hearted; **primera — foundation stone;** — **de afilar** hone; — **de amolar** grindstone; — **angular** corner-stone (also fig); — **arenisca** sandstone; — **de cal,** — **caliza** limestone; — **de escándalo** source of scandal; **bone of contention;** — **filosofal** philosopher's stone; — **fundamental** (fig) basis, cornerstone; — **imán** lodestone; — **miliar** milestone; — **de molino** mill-stone; — **pómez** pumice (stone); — **preciosa** precious stone; — **de toque** touchstone; **a tiro de —** within a stone's throw; **no dejar — sobre —** to raze to the ground; **no dejar — por mover** to leave no stone unturned; **¿quién se atreve a lanzar la primera —?** which of you shall cast the first stone?; **pasar a uno por la —** to put someone through the mill; **quedarse de —** to be thunderstruck.
  (b) (Cu, PR) bore.
piel 1 nf (a) (Anat) skin.
  (b) (Zool) skin, hide, pelt; fur; leather; — **de ante** buckskin, buff, suède; — **de becerro,** — **de ternera** calf, calfskin; — **de cabra** goatskin; — **de cerdo** pigskin; — **de Suecia** suède; **abrigo de —es** fur coat; **artículos de —** leather goods; **una maleta de —** a leather suitcase.
  (c) (Bot) skin, peel, rind.
  2 nmf: — **roja** redskin; **los —es rojas** the redskins.
piélago nm (lit) (a) ocean, deep. (b) (fig) **un — de dificultades** a sea of difficulties.
pienso[1] nm (Agr) feed, fodder; —s feeding stuffs.
pienso[2]: **¡ni por —!** never!, the very idea!
pierna nf (a) leg; — **artificial** artificial leg; **en —s** bare-legged; **estirar las —s** (fig) to stretch one's legs; see **dormir**.
  (b) (of letter) stroke; (with pen) downstroke.
  (c) (Arg) player; partner.
piernicorto adj short-legged.
pierrot [pie'ro] nm pierrot.
pieza 1 nf (a) piece; (of cloth) piece, roll; — **de museo** museum exhibit, (fig) object fit only for a museum; — **de ropa** piece of clothing, article of clothing; **de una —** in one piece; solid; (SAm) person straight, honest; **formar — única con** to be all of a piece

with, (Mech) be integral with; **traje de dos —s** two-piece costume; **dejar a uno de una** — to strike someone all of a heap; **quedarse de una** — to be dumbfounded; **vender algo por —s** to sell something by the piece.

(b) (Mech) part; — **de recambio**, — **de repuesto** (SAm) spare, spare part, extra (US).

(c) (Fin) coin, piece; — **de oro** gold coin, gold piece.

(d) (Chess etc) piece, man.

(e) (Hunting) example; **cobró dos bellas —s** he obtained (or shot etc) two fine specimens (or examples.)

(f) (Archit) room; — **amueblada** furnished room; — **de recibo** reception room.

(g) (Mus) piece, composition; (Theat) piece, work, play; — **corta** sketch; — **oratoria** speech.

(h) — **de artillería** piece, gun.

(i) — **de convicción** (Law) exhibit, document, piece of evidence; (fig) convincing argument; — **de examen** thing worth examining; point to bear in mind.

(j) **buena** — (iro) rogue, villain.

2 nm: **un dos —s** a two-piece (costume etc).
pífano nm fife.
pifia nf (a) (Billiards) bad shot.

(b) (fig) blunder, bloomer (fam).

(c) (Arg, Chi, Per) joke; mockery; **hacer — de** to joke about, mock.

(d) (Ec, Per) hiss.
pifiador adj (Chi, Per) joking, mocking.
pifiar [1b] **1** vt (Arg, Chi, Per) to joke about, mock; to hoax; to play a practical joke on.

2 vi (a) (RPl) to fail, come a cropper (fam); to mess up one's game.

(b) (Col, CR, Ec) to be disappointed, suffer a setback.

(c) to blunder, make a bloomer (fam).
pigmentación nf pigmentation.
pigmentado 1 adj pigmented; person (euph) coloured. **2** nm, **pigmentada** nf (euph) coloured person.
pigmento nm pigment.
pigmeo 1 adj pigmy. **2** nm, **pigmea** nf pigmy.
pignorar [1a] vt to pawn.
pigricia nf (a) laziness; sluggishness. (b) (Chi, Ec, Per) trifle, bagatelle; small bit, pinch.
pija nf (SAm: tabu) prick (tabu).
pijama nm pyjamas.
pije nm (Chi) toff (fam), fop.
pijotada nf (Mex) (a) nuisance, annoying thing. (b) insignificant sum.
pijotear [1a] vi (Col, Mex, RPl) to haggle over trifles; to behave meanly.
pijotería nf (a) (fam) nuisance, small annoyance; trifling request.

(b) (SAm) insignificant sum, tiny amount; trifle, small thing.

(c) (SAm) meanness.
pijotero 1 adj (a) (fam) tedious, annoying; wretched.

(b) (SAm) mean, given to haggling over small amounts.

(c) (Arg) untrustworthy.

2 nm (fam) wretch, rogue; ¡no seas —! don't be a beast!
pila[1] nf (a) heap, pile; stack.

(b) (fam) heap; **tengo una — de cosas que hacer** I have heaps (or stacks) of things to do (fam).

(c) (SAm) **una — de** a heap of, a lot of; **una — de años** very many years; **una — de ladrones** a whole lot of thieves.
pila[2] nf (a) sink; trough; drinking trough; (of fountain) basin; (SAm) fountain; — **de cocina** kitchen sink.

(b) (Eccl: also — **bautismal**) font; — **de agua bendita** holy-water stoup; **sacar de — a uno** to act as godparent to someone.

(c) (Elec) battery; cell; — **atómica** atomic pile; — **seca** dry cell.

(d) (Cu) tap, faucet (US).
pilado adj (Col) sure (to succeed); easy, simple.
pilar[1] nm (a) post, pillar; milestone.

(b) (Post) pillar box.

(c) (Archit) pillar; column, pier.

(d) (fig) prop, (chief) support, mainstay; **un — de la monarquía** a mainstay of the monarchy.
pilar[2] nm (of fountain) basin, bowl.
pilastra nf pilaster; (Chi: of door etc) frame.
Pilatos m Pilate.
pilatuna nf (SAm) dirty trick; vile deed.
pilatuno adj (Col) manifestly unjust.
pilcate nm (Mex) grubby child; child.
pilcha nf (a) (Chi, RPl) garment, article of clothing;

— **s** old clothes; fine clothes. (b) (Arg) mistress, one's beloved.
pilche nm (Bol, Col, Ec) gourd, calabash.
píldora nf pill; — **anticonceptiva** contraceptive pill; — **antifatiga** anti-fatigue pill, pep pill (fam); **dorar la** — to gild the pill.
pileta nf (a) basin, bowl; sink; — **de cocina** kitchen sink. (b) (Arg) — **de natación** swimming pool.
pilgua nf (Chi) wicker basket.
piligüe 1 adj (CAm) fruit shrivelled, empty. **2** nmf (CAm, Mex) poor fish, weak person.
pililo nm (Chi) tramp; ragged person.
pilintruca nf (Chi) slut.
pilmama nf (Mex) wet-nurse; nursemaid.
pilón[1] nm (a) pillar, post; (Elec etc) pylon; — **de azúcar** sugar loaf. (b) (of steelyard) weight. (c) (Cu: Agr) dump, store.
pilón[2] nm (a) drinking trough; (of fountain) basin; (Mex) drinking fountain. (b) mortar. (c) (Chi) pannier. (d) (Mex, Ven) tip, gratuity.
pilongo adj thin, lean.
pilotar [1a] vt plane to pilot; car to drive; ship to steer, navigate; (fig) to guide, direct.
pilote nm (Archit) pile.
pilotear [1a] vt (a) =**pilotar**. (b) (SAm) person to guide, direct; business to run, manage. (c) (Chi) person to exploit.
piloto 1 nm (a) (Aer) pilot; — **automático** automatic pilot; — **de caza** fighter pilot; — **de prueba** test pilot.

(b) (Naut) first mate; navigator, navigation officer; — **de puerto** harbour pilot.

(c) (Aut) driver.

(d) (fig) guide; (in exploration) pathfinder.

(e) (Elec) rear light, tail light.

2 attr: **planta** — pilot plant; see **luz**.
pilpinto nm (Arg, Bol) butterfly.
pilsen nf (Chi) (any) beer.
piltrafa nf (a) useless bit of meat, skinny meat; — **s** offal, scraps.

(b) (fig) useless lump, worthless object; (person) poor specimen, poor fish, weakling.

(c) (Chi, Per) bargain; piece of luck; profit.

(d) (SAm) —**s** rags, old clothes.
piltrafiento adj (a) (Chi, Mex) ragged. (b) (Chi) withered.
piltrafoso adj (Per) ragged.
piltrafudo adj (Per) weak, languid.
piltre adj (a) (Col, Cu, Ven) foppish. (b) (Chi) over-ripe; shrivelled, dried up; person wizened.
pilucho adj (Chi) naked (from the waist down).
pillada nf (a) dirty trick. (b) (RPl) surprise revelation; surprise encounter.
pillaje nm pillage, plunder.
pillar [1a] vt (a) to pillage, plunder, sack.

(b) (fam) to grasp, seize, lay hold of; (of dog) to catch, worry; **la pillará el dedo** the door trapped his finger, he got his finger caught in the door; **el perro le pilló el pantalón** the dog seized his trouser leg (in its teeth).

(c) (fam) culprit etc to catch; (fig) to catch, catch out, catch in the act; **por fin le pilló la policía** the police nabbed him eventually; ¡te he pillado! got you!

(d) (fam) bargain, job etc to get, land, lay hold of.

(e) (fam) meaning to grasp, catch on to.

(f) (of horse, coach etc: fam) to knock down.

(g) (fam) — **una enfermedad** to catch a disease; — **una borrachera** to get drunk.
pillastre nm (fam) scoundrel.
pillería nf (a) dirty trick. (b) gang of scoundrels.
pillete nm, **pillín** nm rascal, scamp.
pillo 1 adj villainous, knavish; blackguardly; sly, crafty; child naughty. **2** nm rascal, rogue, scoundrel; rotter; (child) rascal, scamp.
pilluelo nm =**pillo**; urchin.
pimentero nm (a) pepperpot. (b) (Bot) pepper plant.
pimentón nm cayenne pepper, red pepper; paprika.
pimienta nf pepper; — **inglesa** allspice.
pimiento nm (a) pepper, pimiento; **no se me de un —**, **(no) me importa un —** I don't care two hoots (de about). (b) (Bot) pepper plant.
pimpante adj (fam) (a) charming, attractive; chic. (b) (pej: esp tan —) smug, self-satisfied.
Pimpinela m: **el — escarlata** the Scarlet Pimpernel.
pimpinela nf pimpernel.
pimpollo nm (a) (Bot) sucker, shoot; sapling; rosebud. (b) (fam) bonny 'child; attractive woman; **estar hecho un —** to look very smart; to look very young (still).
pinabete nm fir, fir tree.
pinacoteca nf art gallery.

pináculo *nm* pinnacle.
pinar *nm* pinewood, pine grove.
pinaza *nf* pinnace.
pincel *nm* (a) paintbrush, artist's brush; estar hecho un — to be very smartly dressed. (b) (*fig*) painter.
pincelada *nf* brush-stroke; última — (*fig*) finishing touch.
pinciano 1 *adj* of Valladolid. 2 *nm*, pinciana *nf* native (*or* inhabitant) of Valladolid; los —s the people of Valladolid.
pinchar [1a] 1 *vt* (a) to prick, pierce, puncture; tyre to puncture; no — ni cortar (*fam*) to cut no ice; tener un neumático pinchado to have a puncture, have a flat tyre; — a uno (*Med: fam*) to give someone a jab (*or* injection).
　(b) (*fig*) to prod; hay que —le he needs prodding; le pinchan para que se case they keep prodding him to get married.
　(c) (*fig*) to wound, mortify; to provoke, stir up. 2 pincharse *vr* (a) to prick oneself.
　(b) (*tyre*) to get punctured, go flat, burst.
pinchazo *nm* (a) prick; puncture (*also Aut*), flat (*US Aut*). (b) (*fig*) prod.
pinche *nm* (a) kitchen boy, scullion. (b) (*Arg*) minor office clerk. (c) (*Mex, PR*) rascal. (d) (*Col*) bad horse, nag. (e) (*Arg*) hatpin.
pinchitos *nmpl* hors d'oeuvres, snacks (*served on bar counter*).
pincho *nm* (a) point; pointed stick, spike; (*RPl*) spike, prickle. (b) —s (*Cook*) =pinchitos.
pindárico *adj* Pindaric.
Píndaro *m* Pindar.
pindonga *nf* (*fam*) gadabout.
pinga *nf* (*Col, Cu, Mex, PR: tabu*) prick (*tabu*).
pingajo *nm* rag, shred; tag.
pinganilla *nm* (a) (*SAm*) poor man with pretensions to elegance; (*Arg*) toff (*fam*), masher (*fam*).
　(b) en —s (*Col, Mex*) on tiptoe; (*Mex*) squatting, in an unsteady position.
pinganillo *adj* (a) (*Bol, Ec*) smart, elegant. (b) (*Col*) chubby.
pinganitos: estar en — to be well up, be well-placed socially; poner a uno en —s to give someone a leg up (socially).
pingo *nm* (a) rag, shred; tag; old garment, shabby dress; —s (*fam*) clothes; odds and ends; no tengo ni un — que ponerme (*fam*) I haven't a single thing I can wear; andar (*or* ir) de — to gad about; poner a uno como un — to abuse someone.
　(b) (*fam*) slut; prostitute.
　(c) (*RPl*) horse; good horse; (*Chi, Per*) worthless horse, nag.
　(d) (*Mex*) naughty child; el — the devil.
　(e) (*Chi*) lively child.
pingonear [1a] *vi* (*fam*) to gad about.
pingorotear [1a] *vi* (*SAm*), pingotear [1a] *vi* (*SAm*) to skip about, jump.
ping-pong ['pinpon] *nm* (*angl*) ping-pong.
pingucho (*Chi*) 1 *adj* poor, wretched. 2 *nm* urchin, ragamuffin.
pingüe *adj* (a) greasy, fat. (b) (*fig*) abundant, copious; profits rich, fat; crop heavy, bumper, rich; business lucrative.
pingüino *nm* penguin.
pininos *nmpl* (*SAm*), pinitos *nmpl*: hacer — (*child*) to toddle, walk alone, take one's first steps; (*convalescent*) to start to get about again; (*novice*) to take one's first steps, try for the first time.
pino[1] *nm* (*Bot*) pine, pine tree; — albar Scots pine; — bravo, — marítimo, — rodeno cluster pine; — de tea pitch pine; vivir en el quinto — to live at the back of beyond; eso está en el quinto — that's terribly far away.
pino[2] *nm* (a) en — upright, vertical; standing. (b) —s = pinitos.
pinocha *nf* pine needle.
pinsapo *nm* Spanish fir.
pinta[1] *nf* (a) spot, dot; (*Zool etc*) spot, mark, marking; una tela a —s azules a cloth with blue spots.
　(b) (*Cards*) spot (*indicating value*); ¿a qué —? what's trumps?, what suit are we in?
　(c) (*of water etc*) drop, spot; drop of rain; (*fam*) drink, drop to drink; una — de grasa a grease spot.
　(d) (*fig*) appearance, look(s); tener buena — to look good, look well; tener — de listo to look clever, have a bright look about one; tiene — de criminal he has a criminal look.
　(e) (*fam*) worthless creature.
　(f) (*Arg, Per, PR: Zool etc*) colouring, coloration; (*Arg, Col, Ec, Mex, PR*) family characteristic, distinguishing mark.
　(g) (*Bol, Chi, Per*) draughts.

　(h) (*Chi*) high-grade ore.
　(i) hacer la — (*Mex*), irse de — (*CAm*) to play truant.
　(j) (*SD*) ser de la — to be a Negro, be of the Negro race.
pinta[2] *nf* (*British measure*) pint.
pintado *adj* (a) spotted; mottled, dappled; (*fig*) many-coloured, colourful.
　(b) (*fam*) podría pasarle al más — it could happen to anybody; lo hace como el más — he does it with (*or* as well as) the best.
　(c) (*fam*) me sienta que ni —, viene que ni — it comes just right; it suits me a treat.
　(d) (*SAm*) like, identical; el niño salió — al padre the boy looked exactly like his father.
pintar [1a] 1 *vt* (a) to paint; letter, sign etc to draw, make; — algo de azul to paint something blue.
　(b) (*fig*) to paint, depict, describe; lo pinta todo con colores muy negros he paints it all very black.
　(c) (*fam*) —la to put it on, show off.
　(d) (*fam*) no pinta nada he cuts no ice, he doesn't count; he has no say.
　(e) (*SAm*) to flatter.
　2 *vi* (a) to paint; "ojo, que pinta" (*notice*) "wet paint"; — como querer to daydream, indulge in wishful thinking.
　(b) (*Bot*) to ripen, turn red.
　(c) (*fam*) to show; to turn out (as), give signs of (being).
　3 pintarse *vr* (a) to use make-up; to put on make-up, (*pej*) paint oneself.
　(b) —las solo para algo to manage to do something by oneself.
pintarraj(e)ar [1a] *vti* (*fam*) to daub.
pintarrajo *nm* (*fam*) daub.
pintear [1a] *vi* to drizzle, spot with rain.
pintiparado *adj* (a) identical (*a* to). (b) me viene (que ni) — it comes just right, it's just what the doctor ordered.
pintiparar [1a] *vt* to compare.
pinto *adj* (a) (*SAm*) spotted; mottled, dappled; marked (*esp* with black and white); motley, colourful; complexion blotchy.
　(b) (*Cu*) clever; (*pej*) sharp, shrewd.
Pinto: estar entre — y Valdemoro (*fam*) to be unable to decide between two alternatives.
pintor *nm*, pintora *nf* painter; — de brocha gorda house painter, (*fig*) bad painter, dauber; — decorador house painter, decorator.
pintoresco *adj* picturesque.
pintura *nf* (a) (*in general*) painting; (*fig*) painting, depiction, description.
　(b) (*una* —) painting; — a la acuarela, — a la aguada watercolour; — al óleo oil painting; — al pastel pastel drawing; — rupestre cave painting.
　(c) (*material*) paint; — a la cola, — al temple distemper, (*Art*) tempera.
pinturero (*fam*) 1 *adj* conceited, swanky (*fam*). 2 *nm*, pinturera *nf* show-off (*fam*), swank (*fam*).
pinza *nf* (*also* —s) clothes peg, clothespin (*US*); tweezers, forceps; tongs; (*Tech*) pincers; (*Zool*) claw; —s de azúcar sugar tongs; no se lo sacan ni con —s wild horses won't drag it out of him.
pinzón *nm* finch; — vulgar chaffinch; — real bullfinch.
piña *nf* (a) pine cone.
　(b) (*also* — de América, — de las Indias) pineapple.
　(c) (*fig*) group; cluster, knot; (*pej*) clique, closed circle.
　(d) (*Ant, Mex*) hub.
　(e) (*Mex, RPl*) punch, bash (*fam*); darse —s to fight, exchange blows.
　(f) (*Mex: of revolver*) chamber.
piñal *nm* (*SAm*) pineapple plantation.
piñata *nf* (*Chi*) brawl, scrap (*fam*).
piñatería *nf* (*Chi*) armed holdup.
piño *nm* (*Chi*) lot, crowd.
piñón[1] *nm* (*Bot*) pine kernel; estar a partir un — to be bosom pals (*fam*).
piñón[2] *nm* (*Orn, Tech*) pinion.
piñonate *nm* candied pine kernel.
piñonear [1a] *vi* to click.
piñoneo *nm* click.
Pío *m* Pius.
pío[1] *adj* horse piebald, dappled.
pío[2] *adj* (a) (*Rel*) pious, devout; (*pej*) sanctimonious; excessively pious. (b) merciful.
pío[3] *nm* (a) (*Orn*) cheep, chirp; no decir ni — not to breathe a word; ¡de esto no digas ni —! you keep your mouth shut about this!
　(b) (*fam*) tener el — de algo to long for something.

piocha *nf* (a) jewel (worn on the head). (b) (*SAm: gall*) pickaxe. (c) (*Mex*) goatee.

piojería *nf* (a) lousy place, verminous place. (b) poverty. (c) (*fam*) tiny amount, very small portion.

piojo *nm* (a) louse; — **resucitado** (*fam*) jumped-up fellow, vulgar parvenu; **estar como** —**s en costura** to be packed in like sardines. (b) (*Col*) gambling den.

piojoso *adj* (a) lousy, verminous; (*fig*) dirty, ragged. (b) (*fig*) mean.

piojuelo *nm* louse.

piola *nf* (a) (*SAm*) rope, tether. (b) (*Per, Ven*) cord, string, twine.

piolet [pio'le] *nm, pl* **piolets** [pio'les] (*gall*) ice axe.

piolín *nm* (*SAm*) cord, twine.

pionco *adj* (a) (*Chi*) naked from the waist down. (b) (*Mex*) squatting. (c) (*Mex*) horse short-tailed.

pionero (*angl*) 1 *adj* pioneering. 2 *nm* pioneer.

piorrea *nf* pyorrhoea.

pipa *nf* (a) pipe; **fumar una** —, **fumar en** — to smoke a pipe.
    (b) (*of wine*) cask, barrel; (*as measure*) pipe.
    (c) (*Bot*) pip, seed, edible sunflower seed.
    (d) (*Mus*) reed.
    (e) (*SAm*) belly.
    (f) (*CR, Ec, Pan*) green coconut.

pipeta *nf* pipette.

pipí *nm* (*fam*) weewee (*fam*); **hacer** — to go weewee (*fam*).

pipiar [1c] *vi* to cheap, chirp.

pipiciego *adj* (*Col*) short-sighted.

pipil *nm* (*CAm: hum*) Mexican.

pipiolero *nm* (*Mex*) crowd of kids (*fam*).

pipiolo *nm* (a) youngster; (*SAm*) little boy; (*fig*) novice, greenhorn, tyro. (b) (*Ec*) short person. (c) (*Arg, Ven*) fool. (d) —**s** (*CAm*) money.

pipiripao *nm* (a) (*fam*) slap-up do (*fam*), spread (*fam*). (b) (*SAm*) **de** — worthless.

pipo 1 *adj* (*Ant, Ec*) potbellied; **estar** — (*PR*) to be blown out.
    2 *nm* (a) (*Ant, Ec*) child.
    (b) (*Ant, Ec*) crooked employee.
    (c) (*Col*) punch, bash (*fam*).
    (d) (*Col*) contraband liquor.

pipón *adj* (*Ant, Ec, RPl*) potbellied; full, blown out (*after a meal*).

pipote *nm* keg, cask.

pique[1] *nm* (a) pique, resentment; ill will; grudge; rivalry, competition; self-respect; **estar de** — to have a grudge, be at loggerheads; **tener un** — **con uno** to have a grudge against someone.
    (b) **estar a** — **de** + *infin* to be on the point of + *ger*; to be in danger of + *ger*; **estuvo a** — **de hacerlo** he very nearly did it.
    (c) **echar a** — *ship* to sink; (*fig*) to wreck, ruin; **irse a** — to sink, founder; (*hope, family etc*) to be ruined.
    (d) (*SAm*) bounce, rebound.
    (e) (*Chi, Hond*) mine shaft; (*Mex*) drill, well.
    (f) (*Arg, Guat*) trail, narrow path.

pique[2] *nm* (*Cards: gall*) spades.

piquera *nf* (a) hole, vent. (b) (*CAm, Mex*) night-club hostess.

piquero *nm* (a) (*Hist*) pikeman. (b) (*Chi, Ec*) miner.

piqueta *nf* pick, pickaxe.

piquetazo *nm* (*SAm*) =**picotazo**; (*Col*) =**tijeretazo**.

piquete *nm* (a) prick, jab, slight wound.
    (b) small hole (*in clothing*).
    (c) (*Mil*) squad, party; (*of strikers*) picket.
    (d) (*Arg*) yard, small corral.
    (e) (*Col*) picnic.
    (f) (*Cu*) small band; poor-quality band.

piquiña *nf* (a) (*Ant, Col, Ven*) =**picazón**. (b) (*PR*) envy; grudge.

pira *nf* pyre.

piragua *nf* canoe; (*Sport*) shell.

piragüismo *nm* canoeing.

piragüista *nmf* canoeist; oarsman.

piramidal *adj* (a) pyramidal. (b) (*Col*) terrific (*fam*), tremendous (*fam*).

pirámide *nf* pyramid.

piraña *nf* (*SAm*) piranha.

pirarse [1a] *vr* (*fam; also* —**las**) (a) to beat it (*fam*). (b) (*Univ*) to cut class.

pirata *nm* (a) pirate. (b) (*fig*) hard-hearted person. (c) (*fam*) plagiarist, borrower of other people's ideas (*etc*).

piratear [1a] *vi* to buccaneer, practise piracy; (*fig*) to steal.

piratería *nf* piracy; (*fig*) theft, stealing; —**s** depredations.

pirático *adj* piratical.

piraya *nf* (*SAm*) piranha.

pirca *nf* (*SAm*) dry-stone wall.

pirenaico *adj* Pyrenean.

pirético *adj* pyretic.

piretro *nm* pyrethrum.

pirgua *nf* (*Arg, Bol, Chi*) shed, outhouse, small barn.

pirineo *adj* Pyrenean.

Pirineo *m*, **Pirineos** *mpl* Pyrenees; **el** — **catalán** the Catalan (part of the) Pyrenees.

pirinola *nf* (*Mex*) kid (*fam*), child.

piripez *nf* (*fam*): **coger una** — to get sozzled (*sl*).

piripi *adj* (*fam*): **estar** — to be sozzled (*sl*).

piritas *nfpl* pyrites.

pirlán *nm* (*Col*) doorstep.

piro . . . pyro . . .

pirófago *nm* fire-eater.

piropear [1a] *vt* to pay an amorous compliment to, make a flirtatious remark to.

piropo *nm* (a) amorous compliment, flirtatious remark; nice (and witty) thing to say; **echar** —**s a** = **piropear**.
    (b) garnet; ruby.
    (c) (*Col*) ticking-off.

pirotecnia *nf* pyrotechnics; firework display (*also fig*).

pirotécnico *adj* pyrotechnic, firework (*attr*).

pirrarse [1a] *vr* (*fam*): — **por** to rave about, be crazy about.

pírrico *adj*: **victoria** *f* **pírrica** Pyrrhic victory.

pirueta *nf* (a) pirouette; caper. (b) (*fig*) remark which helps someone out of an awkward situation. (c) —**s** (*fig*) balancing act (*between two policies etc*).

piruetear [1a] *vi* to pirouette; to caper.

pirulí *nm* toffee apple; (*Ant, CAm, Mex, RPl*) lollipop.

pirulo *nm*, **pirula** *nf* (*Chi, RPl*) slim child.

pisa *nf* (a) treading (*of grapes etc*). (b) (*fam*) beating.

pisada *nf* footstep, footfall, tread; footprint.

pisadera *nf* (*Per*) carpet.

pisadero *nm* (*Mex*) brothel.

pisapapeles *nm, pl* **pisapapeles** paperweight.

pisar [1a] 1 *vt* (a) to tread (on), walk on; (*accidentally*) to step on; (*destructively*) to flatten, crush, trample (on, underfoot); *grapes etc* to tread; *earth* to tread down; — **el acelerador** to step on the accelerator, press the accelerator; **no volvimos a** — **ese sitio** we never went to that place again.
    (b) (*Mus*) *key* to play, strike, press; *string* to pluck.
    (c) to lie on, cover (part of).
    (d) (*fig*) to trample on, walk all over; to disregard; to abuse; **no se deja** — **por nadie** he doesn't let anybody trample over him.
    (e) (*fam*) to pinch (*fam*), steal; **A le pisó la novia a B** A pinched B's girl; — **una baza a uno** to trump someone's trick; **otro le pisó el puesto** someone got in first and collared the job (*fam*); **el periódico le pisó la noticia** the newspaper got in first with the news.
    2 *vi* (a) to tread, step, walk; **hay que** — **con cuidado** you have to tread carefully.
    (b) (*fig*) — **fuerte** to act determinedly; to make a strong showing, make a real impression; **entrar pisando fuerte** to get off to a good start.
    3 **pisarse** *vr* (*Arg*) to be mistaken.

pisaverde *nm* fop, toff (*fam*).

pisca *nf* (*Mex*) maize harvest, corn harvest (*US*).

piscador *nm* (*Mex*) harvester.

piscar [1g] *vi* (*Mex*) to harvest maize (*or* corn: *US*).

piscina *nf* (a) swimming pool. (b) fishpond, fishtank.

pisco[1] *nm* (*Col*) (a) turkey. (b) (*fig*) fellow, guy (*US fam*).

pisco[2] *nm* (*SAm*) brandy, liquor.

piscoiro *nm*, **piscoira** *nf* (*Chi*) kid (*fam*), child.

piscolabis *nm, pl* **piscolabis** (*fam*) snack.

pisicorre *nm* (*Ant*) small bus.

piso *nm* (a) floor; flooring.
    (b) (*Archit*) storey, floor; (*of bus*) deck; (*of rocket*) stage; — **alto** top floor; — **bajo** ground floor, first floor (*US*); — **primer** — first floor, second floor (*US*); **un edificio de 8** —**s** an 8-storey building; **viven en el quinto** — they live on the fifth floor; **autobús de dos** —**s** double-decker bus; **ir en el** — **de arriba** to travel on the top deck, travel upstairs.
    (c) flat, apartment (*US*); **poner un** — **a una** to make a girl one's mistress.
    (d) (*Aut: of tyre*) tread.
    (e) (*of shoe*) sole; **poner** — **a un zapato** to sole a shoe.
    (f) (*Min*) set of workings; (*Geol*) layer, stratum.
    (g) (*Chi*) stool; bench.
    (h) (*Chi, Mex*) table runner; (*Chi, Per*) long narrow rug.

pisón nm (a) ram, rammer. (b) (SAm)=**pisotón**. (c) (RPl) mortar.

pisotear [1a] vt (a) to tread down, trample (on, underfoot); to stamp on. (b) (fig) to trample on; law etc to abuse, disregard.

pisotón nm (a) stamp on the foot. (b) (fam) newspaper scoop, reporting scoop.

pispar [1a] vi (Chi, RPl) to keep watch, spy.

pisporra nf (CAm) wart.

pista nf (a) (Zool and fig) track, trail; (fig) clue; — **falsa** false trail, false clue; (in argument etc) red herring; **estar sobre la** — to be on the scent; **estar sobre la** — **de uno** to be on someone's trail, be after someone; **seguir la** — **de uno** to be on someone's track, trail someone; **la policía tiene una** — **ya** the police already have a lead (or clue).
  (b) (Sport etc) track, course; court; (Aut) motorway; — **de aterrizaje** runway; landing strip; — **de baile** dance floor; — **de bolos** bowling alley; — **de carreras** racetrack; — **de ceniza** dirt track; — **de esquí** ski run; — **de hielo** ice rink; — **de patinaje** skating rink; — **de tenis** tennis court; **atletismo en** — track events.

pistacho nm pistachio.

pistero adj (CAm) mercenary, fond of money.

pistilo nm pistil.

pisto nm (a) (Med) chicken broth. (b) (Cook) fried vegetable hash. (c) (fig) mixture, hotchpotch. (d) a —s little by little; sparingly. (e) **darse** — (fam) to show off, swank (fam). (f) (CAm, Per) money. (g) (Col) barrel (of gun). (h) (Mex) shot of liquor.

pistola nf pistol; (Tech) spray, sprayer; — **ametralladora** submachine gun, tommy gun; — **engrasadora**, — **de engrase** grease gun; — **de juguete** toy pistol; — **rociadora de pintura** paint spray.

pistolera nf holster.

pistolero nm gunman, gangster.

pistoleta nf (Arg, Col, Chi) pistol.

pistoletazo nm pistol shot.

pistolete nm pocket pistol.

pistón nm (a) (Mech) piston. (b) (Mus) key; (SAm) bugle, cornet. (c) (fam) **de** —=**pistonudo**.

pistonudo adj (fam) smashing (sl), terrific (fam).

pistudo adj (CAm) rich.

pita nf (SAm) agave; pita fibre, pita thread.

pitada nf (a) whistle; hiss. (b) (SAm) puff (at cigarette etc). (c) (fam) silly remark.

pitador nm, **pitadora** nf (SAm) smoker.

Pitágoras m Pythagoras.

pitandero nm (Chi) smoker.

pitanza nf (a) dole, daily ration; (fam) grub (sl). (b) (fam) price. (c) (Chi) bargain; profit.

pitar [1a] 1 vt (a) whistle to blow. (b) referee etc to whistle at, boo; actor, play to hiss, give the bird to (sl). (c) (SAm) to smoke.
  2 vi (a) to whistle, blow a whistle; to hiss, boo; (Aut) to sound one's horn. (b) (SAm) to smoke. (c) (fam) **esto no pita** this is no good, this doesn't work; — **bien** to give a good account of oneself; **salir pitando** to beat it (fam).

pitay nm (Arg, Bol) rash.

pitazo nm (Mex, Per) whistle, hoot.

pitear [1a] vi (SAm)=**pitar** 2 (a).

pitido nm whistle.

pitillera nf cigarette case.

pitillo nm (a) cigarette; **echarse un** — to have a smoke. (b) (Ec, Ven) drinking straw.

pitiyanqui nmf, **pitiyanki** nmf (PR) slavish imitator of Yankee mannerisms.

pito nm (a) whistle; (Aut) horn, hooter; (Rail etc) whistle, hooter; **tener voz de** — to have a squeaky voice. (b) (Orn) — **real** green woodpecker. (c) (SAm: Zool) tick. (d) cigarette; (SAm) pipe. (e) (SAm: tabu) prick (tabu). (f) (idioms) —s **flautos** (fam) tomfoolery, absurdities; **cuando** —s, **flautas** it's always the same, one way or another it always happens; **no se me da un** —, (no) **me importa un** — I don't care two hoots (de about); **en este asunto no toca** — he's got nothing to do with this matter; **me tomaron por el** — **del sereno** they thought I was something the cat had brought in; **no vale un** — it's not worth tuppence.

pitón[1] nm (Zool) python.

pitón[2] nm bump, lump, protuberance; (Zool) budding

horn; (Bot) sprig, young shoot; (of jar etc) spout; (SAm: of hose) nozzle; — **de roca** sharp point of rock.

pitongo[1] adj (Chi) drunk.

pitongo[2] adj (sl): **niño** — spoiled upper-class child.

pitonisa nf fortuneteller; witch, sorceress.

pitorrearse [1a] vr: — **de** (fam) to scoff at, make fun of.

pitorro nm spout.

pitra nf (Chi) rash.

pitre adj (Col, Cu, PR, Ven) foppish.

pituitario adj pituitary; **glándula pituitaria** pituitary (gland).

pituco nm (RPl) fop, toff (fam).

piuco adj (Chi) timid, scared.

piular [1a] vi to cheep, chirp.

pivote nm pivot.

píxide nf pyx.

piyama nm (SAm) pyjamas.

pizarra nf (a) slate; shale. (b) (School etc) blackboard.

pizarral nm slate quarry; shale bed.

pizarrín nm slate pencil.

pizarrón nm (SAm: School) blackboard; (Sport) scoreboard.

pizarroso adj slaty.

pizca nf (a) pinch, spot; crumb; **una** — **de sal** a pinch of salt. (b) (fig) spot, speck, trace, jot; **ni** — not a bit, not a scrap; **no tiene ni** — **de verdad** there's not a jot of truth in it.

pizcar [1g] vt to pinch, nip.

pizco nm pinch, nip.

pizpireta nf (fam) bright girl, lively (little) girl; smart little piece (sl).

placa nf (a) plate; thin piece of material, (thin) sheet; tab; plaque, tablet; dental plate, denture; — **conmemorativa** commemorative plaque; — **giratoria** turntable; — **de matrícula** number plate, registration plate; — **del nombre** nameplate. (b) (Phot: also — **fotográfica**) plate; — **esmerilada** focusing screen. (c) (Mus) gramophone record, phonograph record (US). (d) badge, insignia. (e) (SAm) blotch, skin blemish.

placaminero nm persimmon.

pláceme nm congratulations, message of congratulations; **dar el** — **a uno** to congratulate someone.

placenta nf placenta.

placentero adj pleasant, agreeable.

placentino 1 adj of Plasencia. 2 nm, **placentina** nf native (or inhabitant) of Plasencia; **los** —s the people of Plasencia.

placer[1] 1 nm (a) pleasure; enjoyment, delight; **a** — at one's pleasure; as much as one wants; **es un** — + infin it is a pleasure to + infin; **con mucho** —, **con sumo** — with great pleasure; **tengo** — **en** + infin it is my pleasure to + infin, I have pleasure in + ger.
  (b) pleasure; **los** —**es del ocio** the pleasures of idleness; **darse a los** —**es** to give oneself over to pleasures.
  2 [2x] vt to please; **me place poder** + infin I am glad to be able to + infin.

placer[2] nm (a) (Geol, Min) placer. (b) (Naut) sandbank. (c) (Col) ground prepared for sowing; plot, patch; (Cu) field.

placero nm, **placera** nf (a) stallholder, market trader. (b) (fig) loafer, gossip.

placeta nf (Chi) piece of level ground.

plácidamente adv placidly.

placidez nf placidity.

plácido adj placid.

plaga nf (a) (Agr: Zool) pest, (Bot) blight; — **del jardín** garden pest; — **de la vid** pest of vines, pest on the vine; —s **forestales** pests on timber, forest pests. (b) (Med, of locusts etc) plague; (fig) scourge; calamity, disaster; blight; **aquí la sequía es una** — drought is a menace here; **una** — **de gitanos** a plague of gipsies. (c) (fig) glut, abundance; **ha habido una** — **de lechugas** there has been a glut of lettuces. (d) (fig) hardship.

plagar [1h] 1 vt (a) to infest, plague; to fill; **han plagado la ciudad de carteles** they have covered (or plastered) the town with posters; **un texto plagado de errores** a text full of errors, a text riddled with errors. (b) — **de minas** to sow with mines.
  2 **plagarse** vr to become infested with.

plagiar [1b] vt (a) to plagiarize. (b) (SAm) to kidnap.

plagiario nm, **plagiaria** nf (a) plagiarist. (b) (SAm) kidnapper.

plagio nm (a) plagiarism. (b) (SAm) kidnapping.

plan nm (a) plan; scheme; idea, intention; — **de desarrollo** development plan; — **del ensanche de la capital** plan for the expansion of the capital; — **quinquenal** five-year plan; **mi** — **era comprar otro nuevo** my idea was to buy a new one; **realizar su** — to put one's plan into effect.

(b) (fam) (idea for an) activity, amusement; **ha sido un** — **muy pesado** it turned out to be a very tedious kind of amusement; **tengo un** — **estupendo para mañana** I've got a splendid idea about what to do tomorrow.

(c) (fam: between sexes) date; (pej) affair; **¿tienes** — **para esta noche?** are you booked for tonight?, have you a date for tonight?; **tiene un** — **con la mujer del alcalde** he's having an affair with the mayor's wife.

(d) programme; — **de estudios** curriculum, syllabus.

(e) (Med) régime; course of treatment; **estar a** — to be on a course of treatment.

(f) (Surveying) level; height.

(g) (fam) **a todo** — with great ceremony; in a very posh way (fam).

(h) (fam) **no me hace** — + infin it doesn't suit me to + infin.

(i) (fam) set-up, system, arrangement; basis, footing; attitude; **en** — **económico** in an economical way, on the cheap; **en ese** — in that way; at that rate; **como sigas en ese** — if you go on like that; **si te pones en ese** — if that's your attitude; **no puedo con este** — **de esperar** I can't stand this business of waiting; **está en un** — **imposible** it's on an impossible basis, it's an impossible set-up; **en** — **de** as; on a basis of; **vamos en** — **de turismo** we're going as tourists; **estaban en** — **de viaje** they were making preparations for the trip; **unos jóvenes en** — **de divertirse** some youngsters out for a good time; **está en** — **de rehusar** he's in a mood to refuse, he's likely to refuse at the moment.

(j) (Mex, RPl) flat bottom (of boat etc).

(k) (Chi, Guat, Mex, Ven) level ground; plain; (Arg, Chi) flat area at the foot of a hill.

(l) (Cu, Ec, Guat, Ven) flat (of a sword etc).

plana nf (a) sheet (of paper), page; (School) writing exercise, copy writing; (Typ) page; — **de anuncios** advertisement page; **en primera** — on the front page; **noticias de primera** — front-page news; **corregir** (or **enmendar) la** — **a uno** to put someone right, (pej) find fault with someone; to improve upon someone's efforts.

(b) (Mil) — **mayor** staff; (fig) persons in charge.

(c) (Tech) trowel; cooper's plane.

planazo nm (a) (SAm) blow with the flat of a sword (etc). (b) (Cu) shot of liquor.

plancha nf (a) plate, sheet; slab; (Typ) plate; (Naut) gangway; (Med) dental plate; **hacer la** — (bather) to float.

(b) iron; (act) ironing; pressing; ironed clothes; clothes to be ironed, ironing; — **eléctrica** electric iron.

(c) (fam) bloomer (fam); **hacer una** —, **tirarse una** — to make a bloomer, drop a clanger (sl).

planchada nf (SAm) (a) landing stage. (b) (fam) = **plancha** (c).

planchado 1 adj (a) clothes ironed; pressed.

(b) (Arg, Guat, Salv) very smart, dolled up.

(c) (Cu, Chi, Per) broke (fam).

(d) (Mex) clever; brave.

2 nm ironing; pressing; **dar un** — **a** to iron; to press; **prenda que no necesita** — non-iron garment.

planchar [1a] **1** vt (a) clothes to iron; suit, trousers to press; **prenda de no** — non-iron garment.

(b) (SAm) to flatter, suck up to (fam).

2 vi (a) to iron, do the ironing.

(b) (SAm) to sit out (a dance), be a wallflower.

(c) (Chi, RPl) to make a bloomer (fam), drop a clanger (sl); to make oneself look ridiculous.

planchear [1a] vt to plate.

plancheta nf (a) (Surveying) plane table. (b) (fam) **echárselas de** — to show off, swank (fam).

planchón nm (SAm) snowcap; ice field.

planeador nm glider.

planeadora nf leveller, bulldozer.

planear [1a] **1** vt to plan. **2** vi (Aer) to glide.

planeta nm planet.

planetario 1 adj planetary. **2** nm planetarium.

planicie nf plain; flat area, level ground; flat surface.

planificación nf planning; — **de familia**, — **familiar** family planning.

planificador 1 adj planning (attr). **2** nm planner.

planificar [1g] vt to plan.

planilla nf (a) (SAm) list; table, tabulation; payroll.

(b) (SAm: Rail etc) ticket.

(c) (Ec, Per, RPl) form, application form, blank; (Fin) account; expense account.

(d) (CAm, Ec, Mex) voting paper; (Pol) ticket.

planimetría nf surveying, planimetry.

plankton nm plankton.

plano 1 adj (a) flat, level, even; plane (also Math, Mech); smooth; **caer de** — to fall flat.

(b) **de** — (fig): **le daba el sol de** — the sun shone directly on it; the sun was directly over it; **confesar de** — to make a full confession; **rechazar algo de** — to turn something down flat, reject something outright; see **cortar**.

2 nm (a) (Math, Mech) plane; — **focal** focal plane; — **inclinado** inclined plane.

(b) (fig) plane; position, level; **de distinto** — **social** of a different social level; **están en un** — **distinto** they're on a different plane.

(c) (Cine, Phot) shot; **primer** — foreground; close-up; **un primer** — **de la famosa actriz** a close-up of the famous actress.

(d) (Aer) plane; — **de cola** tailplane.

(e) (Archit, Mech etc) plan; (Geog) map; (of city) map, street plan; — **acotado** contour map; **levantar el** — **de** country to survey, map, make a map of; building etc to draw up the designs for.

(f) (of sword) flat.

planta nf (a) (Anat) sole of the foot, foot; **asentar sus** —**s en** to establish oneself in.

(b) (Archit) ground plan; **construir un edificio de** (**nueva**) — to build a completely new building, rebuild from the foundations up.

(c) (Archit) floor, storey; — **baja** ground floor, first floor (US); **una ventana de la** — **baja** a downstairs window, a ground-floor window.

(d) (Dancing, Fencing) position (of the feet).

(e) **de buena** — well-built; shapely; **tener buena** — to have a fine physique; to be good-looking.

(f) (Tech) plant; — **de ensamblaje** assembly plant; — **piloto** pilot plant.

(g) plan, programme, scheme.

(h) (Bot) plant.

(i) (fam) **echar** —**s** to swagger; to brag.

plantación nf (a) (Agr) planting. (b) plantation; — **de tabaco** tobacco plantation.

plantado adj (a) (fam) **dejar a uno** — to leave someone suddenly, leave someone in mid-sentence; to leave someone in the lurch, leave someone high and dry; **dejar** — **al novio** to jilt one's boyfriend, walk out on one's boyfriend; (on a date) to stand one's boyfriend up (fam).

(b) **bien** — well-built; shapely; good-looking.

plantador nm (a) (Agr) dibber. (b) (person) planter.

plantaje nm (Col, Ec, PR) looks.

plantar [1a] **1** vt (a) (Bot) to plant.

(b) post etc to put in; monument etc to erect, set up; tent to pitch; belief, reform etc to implant; institution to set up.

(c) blow to plant (en on).

(d) remark to make.

(e) — **a uno en la calle** to pitch someone into the street, chuck someone out; — **a un obrero en la calle** to sack a workman (fam).

(f) (fam) — **a uno** to curb someone, check someone; **le planté para que no dijera más** I stopped him before he could say any more.

(g) (fam) = **dejar plantado** (see **plantado** (a)).

2 plantarse vr (a) to stand firm, stay resolutely where one is; to plant oneself; (fig) to stand firm, dig one's heels in, refuse to compromise.

(b) (horse) to balk, refuse.

(c) — **en** to reach, get to; **en 3 horas se plantó en Sevilla** he got to Seville in 3 hours.

(d) (Cards) to stick.

(e) (CAm, Col, Mex) to doll oneself up.

plante nm stand, agreed basis for resistance, common programme of demands.

plantear [1a] vt (a) belief, reform etc to implant; change to get under way; institution to set up, establish.

(b) to plan.

(c) problem to create, pose; difficulty, question to raise; discussion, lawsuit etc to start; **nos ha planteado muchos problemas** it has created a lot of problems for us; **se lo plantearé** I'll put it to him; I'll have it out with him.

plantel nm (a) (Hort) nursery.

(b) training establishment, nursery.

(c) (RPl) stud animals; best animals on a farm; (fig) group, set, establishment.

(d) (Mex) school.

plantificarse [1g] *vr* (a) (*Cu, Mex, RPl*) to plant oneself. (b) (*CAm, Mex*) to doll up.

plantilla *nf* (a) (*of shoe*) inner sole, insole; (*of stocking etc*) sole.
(b) (*Tech*) pattern, template; stencil.
(c) (*persons*) establishment, personnel; list, roster; — **de personal** staff; **ser de** — to be established, be on the establishment.

plantío *nm* (a) (*act*) planting. (b) plot, вea, patch.

plantista *nm* braggart.

plantón *nm* (a) (*Bot*) seedling; cutting.
(b) (*Mil etc*) guard, sentry.
(c) (*fam*) long wait, tedious wait; **dar (un)** — a uno to stand someone up (on a date; *fam*); **estar de** — to be stuck, have to wait around; **tener a uno de** — to keep someone waiting around.

plañidera *nf* (paid) mourner.

plañidero *adj* mournful, plaintive.

plañir [3h] *vt* to mourn, grieve over.

plasma *nm* plasma.

plasmar [1a] **1** *vt* to mould, shape, form; to create; to represent, give visible (*or* concrete) form to. **2** *vi*: — **en** to take the form of, emerge as.

plasta *nf* (a) soft mass, lump; flattened mass.
(b) (*fam*) botch, mess; **es una** — **de edificio** it's a mess of a building; **el plan es una** — the plan is one big mess, the plan is a complete botch.

plástica *nf* (art of) sculpture, modelling.

plasticidad *nf* (a) plasticity. (b) (*fig*) expressiveness, descriptiveness; richness, evocative character.

plasticina *nf* plasticine.

plástico 1 *adj* (a) (*in most senses*) plastic; **artes plásticas** plastic arts.
(b) (*fig*) image etc expressive, descriptive; description rich, poetic, evocative.
2 *nm* plastic.

plastificado *adj* treated with plastic.

plastrón *nm* (*SAm*) floppy tie, cravate.

plata *nf* (a) silver; silverware; (*Fin*) silver, silver coin(s); **como una** — shining bright, like a new pin.
(b) (*esp SAm*) money; wealth; **apalear** — to be rolling in money.
(c) **hablar en** — to speak bluntly, speak frankly.

platada *nf* (*SAm*) dish, plateful.

plataforma *nf* (a) platform; stage; (*Rail*) turntable; — **de lanzamiento** launching pad; — **de perforación** submarine drilling rig.
(b) (*SAm: Pol: angl*) platform.

platal *nm* (*SAm*) fortune; wealth.

platanal *nm*, **platanar** *nm*, **platanera** *nf* (*Col, Mex, PR*) banana plantation.

platanero 1 *adj* banana (*attr*). **2** *nm* (*CAm, Mex*) banana grower; dealer in bananas.

plátano *nm* (a) plane; plane tree. (b) banana; banana tree.

platea *nf* (*Theat*) pit, orchestra (*US*).

plateado 1 *adj* (a) silver; silvery; (*Tech*) silver-plated. (b) (*Mex*) wealthy. **2** *nm* silver-plating.

platear [1a] *vt* (a) to silver; to silver-plate. (b) (*Mex, Nic*) to sell, turn into money.

platense *adj* (*SAm*) = **rioplatense**.

platería *nf* (a) silversmith's craft. (b) silversmith's; jeweller's.

platero *nm* silversmith; jeweller.

plática *nf* talk, chat; (*Eccl*) sermon; **estar de** — to be chatting, have a talk.

platicar [1g] *vi* (a) to talk, chat. (b) (*Mex*) to say, tell.

platija *nf* plaice.

platillo *nm* (a) saucer; small plate; collecting bowl; — **de balance** scale, pan (*of scales*); — **volador**, — **volante** flying saucer; **pasar el** — to pass the hat round, make a collection.
(b) —**s** (*Mus*) cymbals.
(c) (*CAm, Mex*) dish; course; **el tercer** — **de la comida** the third course of the meal.

platina *nf* miscroscope slide.

platino 1 *nm* platinum; —**s** (*Aut*) contact points. **2** as *adj*: **rubia** — platinum blonde.

plato *nm* (a) plate, dish; (*Tech*) plate; (*of balance*) scale, pan; — **frutero** fruit dish; — **hondo**, — **sopero** soup dish; **del** — **a la boca se pierde la sopa** there's many a slip 'twixt cup and lip; **fregar** (*or* **lavar**) **los** —**s** to wash the dishes, wash up; **pagar los** —**s rotos** to pay for the damage, (*fig*) to carry the can (*sl*); *see* **nada**.
(b) plateful, dish; **un** — **de arroz** a dish of rice; **vender algo por un** — **de lentejas** to sell something for a mess of pottage.
(c) dish; course; — **dulce** sweet course; — **fuerte** main course; heavy dish, meal in itself; **sopa y 4** —**s** soup and 4 courses; **es un** — **típico español** it's a

typical Spanish dish; **es mi** — **favorito** it's my favourite dish (*or* meal); **ser** — **de segunda mesa** (*fam*) to be second-best; to feel neglected, be left out in the cold.

plató *nm* (*Cine*) set.

Platón m Plato.

platón *nm* (*SAm*) (a) large dish; serving dish. (b) washbasin.

platónicamente *adv* Platonically.

platónico *adj* Platonic.

platonismo *nm* Platonism.

platonista *nmf* Platonist.

platudo *adj* (*SAm*) rich, well heeled (*sl*).

plausible *adj* (a) commendable, laudable, praiseworthy. (b) reason etc acceptable, admissible.

plausiblemente *adv* commendably, laudably.

playa *nf* (a) shore, beach; **una** — **de arenas doradas** a beach of golden sands; **pasar el día en la** — to spend the day on the beach; **pescar desde la** — to fish from the beach.
(b) (*fig*) seaside; seaside resort; **ir a veranear a una** — to spend the summer at the seaside, go to the seaside for one's summer holidays.
(c) (*Arg, Bol, Ven*) flat open space; (*Rail*) yard; — **de estacionamiento** carpark, parking place, parking lot (*US*); — **de juegos** playground.

playeras *nfpl* sandals, sandshoes; tennis shoes.

playero *adj* beach (*attr*).

playo *adj* (*Mex, RPl*) shallow.

plaza *nf* (a) square; public square, open space; market (place); — **de armas** parade ground; — **mayor** main square; — **de toros** bullring; **hacer la** — to do the daily shopping.
(b) (*Comm*) town, city, centre; **en esa** — there, in your town.
(c) room, space; place; (*on vehicle etc*) seat, place; ¡—! make way!; **abrir** — to make way; **el avión tiene 90** —**s** the plane has 90 seats, the plane carries 90 passengers; **de dos** —**s** (*Aut etc*) two-seater; **reservar una** — to reserve a seat.
(d) post, job; vacancy; **cubrir una** — to fill a job, appoint to a post; **sentar** — (*Mil*) to enlist, sign on (*de as*).
(e) (*Mil*) fortress, fortified town (*also* — **fuerte**).

plazo *nm* (a) time, period, term; time limit; date, expiry date; (*Comm, Fin*) date; **en un** — **de 6 meses** in the space of 6 months, in a period of 6 months; **within a term of 6 months, before 6 months are up; nos dan un** — **de 8 días** they allow us a week, they give us a week's grace; ¿**cuándo vence el** —? when is the payment due?, what is the time limit?; **se ha cumplido el** — the time is up; **a** — (*Comm*) on credit; **a corto** — loan short-dated, (*fig*) short-term; **a largo** — loan long-dated, (*fig*) long-term; **es una tarea a largo** — it's a long-term job.
(b) instalment, payment; **pagar el** — **de marzo** to pay the March instalment; **comprar a** —**s** to buy on hire purchase, pay for in instalments.

plazoleta *nf*, **plazuela** *nf* small square.

pleamar *nf* high tide.

plebe *nf*: **la** — the common people, the masses, the mass of the population; (*pej*) the plebs; the mob, the rabble.

plebeyez *nf* plebeian nature; (*fig*) coarseness, commonness.

plebeyo 1 *adj* plebeian; (*pej*) coarse, common. **2** *nm*, **plebeya** *nf* plebeian, commoner; (*pej*) plebeian.

plebiscito *nm* plebiscite.

plectro *nm* plectrum.

plegable 1 *adj* pliable, that bends; chair etc folding, that folds up, collapsible. **2** *nm* playpen.

plegadera *nf* paper knife.

plegadizo *adj* = **plegable 1**.

plegado *nm*, **plegadura** *nf* (a) (*act*) folding; bending; creasing. (b) fold; crease.

plegar [1h *and* 1k] **1** *vt* to fold; to bend; to crease; (*Sew*) to pleat. **2 plegarse** *vr* (a) to bend; to crease. (b) (*fig*) to yield, submit (*a* to).

plegaria *nf* prayer.

pleitear [1a] *vi* (a) to plead, conduct a lawsuit; to go to law (*con, contra* with; *sobre* over), indulge in litigation. (b) (*esp SAm*) to argue.

pleitesía *nf*: **rendir** — **a** to show respect for, treat respectfully, show courtesy to; (*SAm*) to pay tribute to.

pleitista 1 *adj* litigious; (*fig*) quarrelsome, argumentative. **2** *nmf* litigious person; quarrelsome individual.

pleitisto *adj* (*SAm*) quarrelsome, argumentative.

pleito *nm* (a) (*Law*) lawsuit, case; —**s** litigation; — **de acreedores** bankruptcy proceedings; — **civil** civil action; **andar a** —**s** to be engaged in lawsuits;

entablar — to bring an action, bring a lawsuit; **ganar el** — to win one's case; **poner** — to sue, bring an action; **poner** — **a uno** to bring an action against someone, take someone to court.
  (b) (*fig*) dispute, feud; controversy; (*SAm*) quarrel, argument; **estar a** — **con uno** to be at odds with someone.
  (c) — **homenaje** homage.

plenamente *adj* fully; completely.

plenario *adj* plenary, full.

plenilunio *nm* full moon.

plenipotenciario *nm* plenipotentiary.

plenitud *nf* plenitude, fullness; abundance; **en la** — **de** in the fullness of; at the height of.

pleno 1 *adj* full; complete; (*powers*) full; *session* plenary, full; **en** — **día** in broad daylight; **en** — **verano** at the height of summer; **tiene frío en** — **mes de julio** he's cold even though it's July; **en plena rebeldía** in open revolt; **en plena vista** in full view; **le dio en plena cara** it hit him full in the face.
  2 *nm* (a) plenum.
  (b) **en** — as a whole, collectively; unanimously.

pleonasmo *nm* pleonasm.

pleonástico *adj* pleonastic.

plepa *nf* sickly person.

plétora *nf* plethora, abundance; flood; excess, surplus.

pletórico *adj* abundant; — **de** abounding in, full of, brimming with.

pleuresía *nf* pleurisy.

plexiglás *nm* perspex (*Protected Trade Name*).

plexo *nm*: — **solar** solar plexus.

plica *nf* sealed envelope, sealed document; (*in competition*) sealed entry.

pliego *nm* (a) sheet; folder; (*Typ*) gathering.
  (b) sealed letter, sealed document; — **cerrado** (*Naut*) sealed orders; — **de condiciones** details, specifications (*of a tender etc*); — **de cargos** list of accusations; *see* **descargo**.

pliegue *nm* (a) fold, crease; (*Sew*) pleat, crease; tuck. (b) (*Geol etc*) fold.

Plinio *m* Pliny; — **el Joven** Pliny the Younger; — **el Viejo** Pliny the Elder.

plinto *nm* plinth.

plisado *nm* pleating.

plisar [1a] *vt* to pleat.

plomada *nf* (*Archit etc*) plumb; (*Naut*) lead; (*on fishing net*) weights, sinkers.

plomar [1a] *vt* to seal with lead.

plomazo *nm* (*CAm, Mex*) shot; bullet wound.

plombagina *nf* plumbago.

plomería *nf* (a) (*Archit*) leading, lead roofing. (b) (*SAm*) plumbing; plumber's workshop, plumber's shop.

plomero *nm* (*SAm*) plumber.

plomizo *adj* (a) leaden, lead-coloured. (b) (*fig*) leaden.

plomo 1 *nm* (a) lead; — **derretido** molten lead; **soldado de** — tin soldier.
  (b) =**plomada**; (*Fishing*) weight, sinker; **a** — plumb, true, vertical(ly); (*fig*) just right, exactly right; **caer a** — to fall heavily, fall flat.
  (c) (*Elec*) fuse; **se ha fundido el** — it's fused.
  (d) (*esp SAm*) bullet, shot.
  (e) (*fam*) bore, dull affair, dull person.
  (f) (*Mex*) gunfight.
  2 *adj* (*SAm*) leaden, lead-coloured.

plomoso *adj* (*CAm*) boring.

plugo, pluguiere *etc see* **placer**[1].

pluma *nf* (a) (*Orn*) feather; quill; (*adornment*) plume, feather; **colchón de** —**s** feather bed; **hacer algo a** — **y a pelo** to waste nothing, do something using every scrap.
  (b) pen (*also fig*); — **esferográfica** (*SAm*) ball-point pen; — **estilográfica** fountain pen; **y otras obras de su** — and other works from his pen; **dejar correr la** — to write spontaneously; **escribir a vuela** — to write quickly, write without much thought.
  (c) (*fig*) penmanship, writing.
  (d) (*CAm*) fib, tale; hoax.
  (e) (*Arg, Mex*) prostitute.
  (f) (*Col, PR, Urug*) tap, faucet (*US*).
  (g) (*Chi*) crane, derrick.

plumada *nf* stroke of the pen; flourish.

plumado *adj* feathered, with feathers; *chick* fledged.

plumafuente *nf* (*SAm*) fountain pen.

plumaje *nm* (a) (*Orn*) plumage, feathers. (b) (*adornment*) plume, crest; bunch of feathers.

plumario *nm*, **plumaria** *nf* (*CAm, Mex*) hack journalist.

plumazo *nm* (a) stroke of the pen (*also fig*); **de un** — with one stroke of the pen.
  (b) piece of rapid writing (*or sketching*).
  (c) feather mattress; feather pillow.

plúmbeo *adj* leaden.

plúmbico *adj* plumbic.

plumear [1a] **1** *vt* (*CAm, Mex*) to write. **2** *vi* (*Mex*) to be (*or become*) a prostitute.

plumero *nm* (a) feather duster.
  (b) (*adornment*) plume; bunch of feathers; **se le ve el** — (*fam*) you can see what he's really thinking.
  (c) penholder.
  (d) (*Col, Ec*) plumber.
  (e) (*Chi*) powder puff.

plumífero *nm* (*hum*) poor writer, hack; hack journalist.

plumilla *nf*, **plumín** *nm* nib, pen nib.

plumista *nm* clerk, scrivener.

plumón *nm* (a) (*Orn*) down. (b) feather bed.

plumoso *adj* feathery, downy.

plural 1 *adj* (a) plural. (b) (*fig: esp SAm*) many, manifold, numerous. **2** *nm* plural; **en** — in the plural.

pluralidad *nf* (a) plurality.
  (b) — **de votos** majority of votes.
  (c) **una** — **de** a number of; numerous, diverse; **el asunto tiene** — **de aspectos** there are a number of sides to this question; **existe una** — **de textos para esta asignatura** there is a duplication of textbooks for this course.

plurilingüe *adj* multilingual.

plurivalencia *nf* many-sided value; diversity of uses (*etc*); wide applicability.

plurivalente *adj* having numerous values; having diverse uses (*etc*); widely applicable.

plus *nm* extra pay, bonus; — **de carestía de vida** cost-of-living bonus; **con 5 dólares de** — with a bonus of 5 dollars.

pluscafé *nm* (*SAm*) liqueur.

pluscuamperfecto *nm* pluperfect.

plusmarca *nf* record; **batir la** — to break the record.

plusmarquista *nmf* record holder; record breaker; top scorer.

plusvalía *nf* appreciation, added value.

Plutarco *m* Plutarch.

plutocracia *nf* plutocracy.

plutócrata *nmf* plutocrat.

plutocrático *adj* plutocratic.

Plutón *m* Pluto.

plutonio *nm* plutonium.

pluvial *adj* rain (*attr*).

pluviómetro *nm* rain gauge, pluviometer.

pluvioso *adj* rainy.

población *nf* (a) population; — **activa** working population. (b) town, city; village; (*Arg*) small hamlet; (*on ranch*) main building and outbuildings.

poblacho *nm* down-at-heel town, miserable village.

poblachón *nm* dump (*fam*), one-horse town.

poblada *nf* (a) (*Bol, Col, Chi, Ec, Per, Ven*) riot; revolt, armed rising. (b) (*Chi, Ec, Per, Ven*) crowd.

poblado 1 *adj* (a) inhabited.
  (b) **poco** — underpopulated, with a sparse population; **densamente** — thickly populated; **la ciudad más poblada del país** the most populous city in the country.
  (c) — **de** peopled with, populated with; (*fig*) full of, filled with; covered with.
  (d) *beard* big, thick; *eyebrows* bushy.
  2 *nm* village; town; inhabited place; (*Aut etc*) built-up area; — **de absorción** new town, satellite town.

poblador *nm*, **pobladora** *nf* settler, colonist; founder.

poblano 1 *adj* (*SAm*) village (*attr*), town (*attr*); (*Mex*) of Puebla. **2** *nm*, **poblana** *nf* (*SAm*) villager; (*Mex*) native of Puebla.

poblar [1m] **1** *vt* (a) *place* to settle, people, colonize; *hive, river etc* to stock (*de* with); *ground* to plant (*de* with).
  (b) to people, inhabit; **los peces que pueblan las profundidades** the fish that inhabit the depths; **las estrellas que pueblan el espacio** the stars that dwell in (*or* fill) space.
  2 poblarse *vr* (a) to fill (*de* with); to fill up, become stocked (*de* with); to become covered (*de* with).
  (b) (*Bot*) to come into leaf.

pobo *nm* white poplar.

pobre 1 *adj* (*all senses*) poor (*de, en* in); ¡— **de mí!** poor old me!; ¡— **de él!** poor fellow!; ¡— **de ti si te pillo!** it'll be tough on you if I catch you!
  2 *nmf* (a) poor person; beggar, pauper; **un** — **a** poor man; **los** —**s** the poor, poor people.

(b) (*fig*) poor wretch, poor devil; **la — estaba mojada** the poor girl was wet through; **el — está fatal de los ojos** (*fam*) he's terribly short-sighted, poor chap (*fam*).

pobremente *adv* poorly.

pobrería *nf*, **pobrerío** *nm* (*SAm*) poor people (*collectively*).

pobrete 1 *adj* poor, wretched. **2** *nm*, **pobreta** *nf* poor thing, poor wretch.

pobretería *nf* **(a)** poor people (*collectively*); gathering of poor people. **(b)** poverty. **(c)** miserliness, meanness.

pobretón 1 *adj* terribly poor. **2** *nm* poor man.

pobreza *nf* poverty; work, penury; **— de espíritu** poorness of spirit, small-mindedness; **— no es vileza** poverty is not a crime.

poca *nm* (*SAm*), **pócar** *nm* (*Mex*) poker.

pocero *nm* well-digger.

pocerón *nm* (*CAm, Mex*) pool.

pocilga *nf* piggery, pigsty; (*fig*) pigsty.

pocillo *nm* (*SAm*) cup; (*Mex*) tankard.

pócima *nf*, **poción** *nf* (*Pharm*) potion, draught; (*Vet*) drench; (*fig*) brew, concoction, nasty drink.

poco 1 *adj* **(a)** (*sing*) little; small; slight, scanty; **con — respeto** with little respect, with scant respect; **de — interés** of small interest; **de poca extensión** of small extent, not extensive; **hay — queso** there isn't much cheese; **nos queda — tiempo** we haven't much time; **el provecho es —** the gain is small; **con lo — que me quedaba** with what little I had left; **ya sabes lo — que me interesa** you know how little it interests me.

(b) (*pl*) **—s** few; **unos —s** a few, some; **—s de entre ellos** few of them; **—s niños saben que . . .** few (*or* not many) children know that . . .; **—s son los que . . .** there are few who . . .; **me quedan pocas probabilidades** I don't have much chance; **un canalla como hay —s** a real rotter, an absolute rotter.

2 *adv* **(a)** little, not much; only slightly; **cuesta —** it doesn't cost much; **ahora trabaja —** he only works a little now; **los estiman —** they hardly value it at all; **¡a — a little by little; ¡— a —!** gently!, easy there!; **— más o menos** more or less; **ser para —** to be weak, be characterless, be very negative; **tener a uno en —** to think little of someone, have no use for someone; **tiene la vida en —** he holds his life cheap.

(b) (*with adj: often translated by prefixes* dis-, un-) **— dispuesto a ayudar** disinclined to help; **— amable** unkind; **— inteligente** unintelligent.

(c) **por —** almost, nearly; **por — me ahogo** I very nearly drowned; **en — estuvo que el coche le atropellara** the car almost knocked him down.

(d) (*time expressions*) **a —** shortly (after), presently; **a — de haberlo firmado** shortly after he had signed it; **dentro de —** shortly; soon after; **hace — a short while back, a short time ago.**

(e) (*SAm*) **¿a —?** not really!, you don't say!

3 *nm*: **un —** a little, a bit; **estoy un — triste** I am a little sad; **le conocía un —** I knew him slightly; **un — de dinero** a little money, some money.

pocha *nf* (*Chi*) lie; trick.

pochismo *nm* (*Mex etc*) gross *anglicism introduced into Spanish*.

pocho 1 *adj* **(a)** faded, discoloured; *person* pale; *fruit* soft, overripe; withered.

(b) (*fig*) depressed, gloomy.

(c) (*Chi*) chubby; squat.

2 *nm*, **pocha** *nf* (*Mex etc*) United States national *of Mexican origin; Mexican influenced in language etc by North America*.

pochola *nf* (*fam*) nice girl, attractive girl; (*in direct address*) dear, darling.

pocholez *nf* (*fam*) gem, treasure; **el vestido es una —** it's a dear little dress.

poda *nf* **(a)** (*act*) pruning. **(b)** pruning season.

podadera *nf* pruning knife, billhook; pruning shears, secateurs.

podar [1a] *vt* **(a)** to prune; to lop, trim (off). **(b)** (*fig*) to prune, cut out.

podenco *nm* hound.

poder 1 [2t] *vi* **(a)** (+ *infin*) can, to be able to; **puede venir** he can come, he is able to come; **no puede venir** he cannot come; **puede ser** maybe, it may be so; **puede ser que . . .** it may be that . . .; **puede que esté en la biblioteca** he may be in the library, perhaps he's in the library; **este vino no se puede beber** this wine is not fit to drink.

(b) (+ *infin*) may; **puede no venir** he may not come, it is possible that he won't come; **por lo que pudiera pasar** because of what might happen;

¡**podías habérmelo dicho**! you might have told me!; **bien puedes pasar la noche aquí** you might as well spend the night here.

(c) (*absolutely*) can; **lo haré si puedo** I'll do it if I can; **no puedo I can't**; **¡puede!** who knows!, maybe!; **¿se puede?** may I?, may I come in?; do you mind?; **los que pueden** those who can, those who are able (to); **el dinero puede mucho** money can do anything, money talks; **él puede mucho en el partido** he has great influence in the party; **causas respecto a las cuales nada puede el fabricante** causes over which the manufacturer has no control; **¿tú puedes con eso?** can you manage that?; **no puedo con él** I can't stand him; **no puedo con la maleta** I can't manage the case; **no puedo más** I've had enough; I can't go on any longer; I'm exhausted; **a más no —** to the utmost; as hard as possible, for all one is worth; **es terco a más no —** he's utterly obstinate, he's as obstinate as they come; **comió a más no —** he ate to excess; **me gusta al cine a más no —** I'm passionately fond of the cinema; **no — menos de** + *infin* not to be able to help + *ger*; to have no alternative but to + *infin*.

(d) **puede que vaya** I may go, I might go; **puede que tenga uno ya** he may have one already; **puede que sí** it may be, maybe.

(e) (*fam*) **A le puede a B** A can beat B; A is tougher than B; A is more than a match for B.

(f) (*CAm, Mex*) to affect, upset; **me pudo esa broma** that joke upset me.

2 *nm* **(a)** power; authority; possession; **— adquisitivo, — de compra** purchasing power; **— de repercusión** resilience, recuperative power; **a — de** by dint of; **bajo el — de** in the hands of; under the power of; **estar en — de** to be in the hands of, be in the possession of; **pasar a — de** to pass to, pass into the possession of; **el dinero es —** money is power; **tiene — para arruinarnos** he has the power to ruin us; **esa droga no tiene — contra la enfermedad** that drug has no power (*or* is not effective) against the disease.

(b) (*Mech*) power; strength; capacity; **el — del motor** the power of the engine; **tiene — para levantar X kilos** it has the power to lift X kilos.

(c) (*Pol etc*) power; authority; **— absoluto** absolute power; **— ejecutivo** executive power; **— legislativo** legislative power; **división de poderes** separation of powers; **estar en el —**, **ocupar el —** to be in power.

(d) (*Law*) power of attorney, proxy; **plenos poderes** full power, full authority (to act); **por poder(es)** by proxy.

poderhabiente *nmf* (*Law*) proxy.

poderío *nm* **(a)** power; might; authority, jurisdiction. **(b)** (*Fin*) wealth.

poderosamente *adv* powerfully.

poderoso *adj* (*all senses*) powerful.

podiatría *nf* podiatry.

podio *nm* podium; (*Mex*) rostrum; **estar en el — de la actualidad** to be in the limelight, be the centre of current interest.

podómetro *nm* pedometer.

podón *nm* billhook.

podre *nf* pus.

podredumbre *nf* **(a)** (*matter*) pus; rotten part, rot. **(b)** (*quality*) rottenness, putrefaction; (*fig*) rottenness, decay, corruption. **(c)** (*fig*) gnawing doubt, secret uneasiness.

podrido *adj* **(a)** rotten, bad; putrid. **(b)** (*fig*) rotten, corrupt; "**algo está — en Dinamarca**" "something is rotten in the state of Denmark"; **está — por dentro** he's rotten inside; **están —s de dinero** they're rotten with money (*fam*).

podrir [3a] = **pudrir**.

poema *nm* **(a)** poem, (*esp*) long poem. **(b)** (*fig*) **fue todo un —** it was just like a fairy tale; it was all terribly romantic (*fam*); (*hum*) it was a proper farce.

poemario *nm* book of poems.

poemático *adj* poetic.

poesía *nf* **(a)** (*in general*) poetry; **la — del Siglo de Oro** Golden Age poetry. **(b)** (*una —*) poem, (*esp*) short poem, lyric.

poeta *nm* **(a)** poet. **(b)** (*SAm*) writer, author, literary man.

poetastro *nm* poetaster.

poética *nf* poetics, art of poetry, theory of poetry.

poéticamente *adv* poetically.

poético *adj* poetic(al).

poetisa *nf* poetess.

poetizar [1f] **1** *vt* to poeticize; to idealize; to turn into poetry, make poetry out of. **2** *vi* to write poetry.

pogrom(o) nm pogrom.
póker nm (Cards: angl) poker.
polaco 1 adj Polish. **2** nm, **polaca** nf Pole. **3** nm (language) Polish.
polaina nf (a) gaiter, legging. (b) (Arg, Bol, Hond) annoyance; setback.
polar adj polar.
polaridad nf polarity.
polarización nf polarization.
polarizar [1f] **1** vt to polarize. **2 polarizarse** vr to polarize (en torno a around).
polca nf (a) (Mus) polka. (b) (Ec, Per) blouse; (Chi, Per) long jacket.
polea nf pulley; (Naut) tackle, tackle block.
polémica nf (a) (in general) polemics. (b) (una —) polemic, controversy.
polémico adj polemic(al).
polemista nmf polemicist; debater, controversialist.
polemizar [1f] vi to indulge in a polemic, argue (en torno a about); **no quiero** — I have no wish to get involved in an argument; — **con uno en la prensa** to have a debate with someone in the press.
polen nm pollen.
poli 1 nm (fam) bobby (sl), copper (sl), cop (sl). **2** nf (fam): **la** — the cops (sl).
poli . . ., **poly** . . ., **many** . . .
poliandria nf polyandry.
poliándrico adj polyandrous.
policía 1 nm policeman; — **femenino** policewoman.
　　2 nf (a) police; police force; — **fluvial** river police; — **militar** military police; — **montada** mounted police; — **secreta** secret police; — **de tráfico** traffic police.
　　(b) administration, (good) government; public order.
　　(c) courtesy, politeness.
　　(d) cleanliness.
policíaco adj police (attr); see **novela**.
policial 1 adj police (attr). **2** nm (CAm) policeman.
policromo adj, **polícromo** adj polychromatic; many-coloured, colourful.
Polichinela m Punch.
polietileno nm polythene, polyethylene (US).
polifacético adj person, talent etc many-sided, versatile.
Polifemo m Polyphemus.
polifonía nf polyphony.
polifónico adj polyphonic.
poligamia nf polygamy.
polígamo 1 adj polygamous. **2** nm polygamist.
poligloto nm, **poliglota** nf (also **polígloto** nm, **políglota** nmf) polyglot.
poligonal adj polygonal.
polígono nm (a) (Math) polygon.
　　(b) site (for development), building lot; area; housing estate; — **industrial** industrial estate; — **de descongestión** industrial overspill area.
polígrafo nm writer on a wide variety of subjects.
polilla nf moth, (esp) clothes moth; grub, destructive larva; bookworm.
polimerización nf polymerization.
polímero nm polymer.
polimorfismo nm polymorphism.
polimorfo adj polymorphic.
Polinesia f Polynesia.
polinesio 1 adj Polynesian. **2** nm, **polinesia** nf Polynesian.
polinización nf pollination; — **cruzada** cross-pollination.
polio nf polio.
poliomielitis nf poliomyelitis.
pólipo nm polyp, polypus.
polisílabo 1 adj polysyllabic. **2** nm polysyllable.
polisón nm bustle.
polista nm polo player.
politeísmo nm polytheism.
politeísta adj polytheistic.
politene nm, **politeno** nm polythene, polyethylene (US).
política nf (a) (Pol) politics; **la** — **ruritana en la posguerra** postwar Ruritanian politics; **mezclarse en la** — to go in for politics, get mixed up in politics.
　　(b) policy; — **agraria** farming policy, agricultural policy; — **económica** economic policy; — **exterior** foreign policy; — **de ingresos y precios**, — **de jornales y precios** prices and incomes policy; — **de mano dura** strong-arm policy, tough policy.
　　(c) tact, skill; politeness; good manners.
políticamente adv politically.
politicastro nm (pej) politician.

político 1 adj (a) (Pol) political.
　　(b) politic; tactful, skilful; polite, well-mannered, courteous.
　　(c) stiff, reserved, stand-offish.
　　(d) (of family relationships) in-law, eg **padre** — father-in-law; **es tío** — **mío** he's an uncle of mine by marriage; see **familia** etc.
　　2 nm politician.
politicón adj (fam) (a) strongly political, keenly interested in politics. (b) very ceremonious, obsequious.
politiquear [1a] vi to play at politics, dabble in politics; to talk politics.
politiqueo nm, **politiquería** nf party politics, the political game; political gossip.
politiquero nm (pej) politician, party politician; political intriguer.
póliza nf (a) certificate, voucher; (Fin) draft; (Fin) insurance certificate; insurance policy; — **dotal** endowment policy; — **de seguro(s)** insurance policy; **pagar una** — to pay out on an insurance.
　　(b) tax stamp, fiscal stamp.
polizón nm (a) tramp, vagrant, bum (US). (b) (Aer, Naut, etc) stowaway; **viajar de** — to stow away (en on).
polizonte nm (sl) bobby (sl), copper (sl), cop (sl).
polo[1] nm (a) (Geog) pole; **P— Norte** North Pole; **P— Sur** South Pole; — **magnético** magnetic pole, magnetic north; **de** — **a** — from pole to pole.
　　(b) (Elec) pole; terminal; pin, point; — **negativo** negative pole; — **positivo** positive pole; **una clavija de 4** —**s a** a 4-pin plug.
　　(c) (fig) pole; focus, centre; — **de atracción** focus of interest, centre of attraction; **los dos generales son** —**s opuestos** the two generals are at opposite extremes; **esto es el** — **opuesto de lo que dijo antes** this is the exact opposite of what he said before.
　　(d) (fig: Comm etc) — **de desarrollo**, — **de promoción** growth point; development area.
　　(e) — **helado** iced lolly.
polo[2] nm (Sport) polo; — **acuático** water polo.
polo[3] nm polo-necked sweater.
polola nf (Chi, Ec) flirtatious girl; steady girlfriend.
pololear [1a] (Bol, Chi, Ec, Per) **1** vt to court; to flirt with. **2** vi to flirt (con with); to be going steady (fam).
pololo nm (Chi) (a) (species of) buzzing insect. (b) bore, tedious person; flirt; steady boyfriend, (persistent) suitor. (c) pimp.
polonesa nf polonaise.
Polonia f Poland.
poltrón adj idle, lazy.
poltrona nf reclining chair, easy chair.
poltronear [1a] vi (Arg, Chi, Mex) to idle, loaf.
polución nf pollution; — **de la atmósfera** air pollution.
polvareda nf (a) dust cloud, cloud of dust. (b) (fig) storm, fuss, rumpus (fam); **levantar una** — to create a storm, cause a rumpus.
polvera nf (a) powder compact, vanity case. (b) (Mex) =**polvareda**.
polvero nm (a) (Col, CR, Mex, Ven) =**polvareda**. (b) (CAm) handkerchief.
polvillo nm (a) (Arg, Col) blight. (b) (Chi, Per) tobacco refuse. (c) (CAm) leather for shoemaking. (d) (Ec, Per) rice bran.
polvo nm (a) dust; **lleno de** — dusty; **dust-covered**; **limpiar un mueble de** —, **quitar el** — **de** (or **a**) **un mueble** to dust a piece of furniture; **hacer algo** — to smash something, ruin something; **hacer** — **a uno** to shatter someone; to wear someone out; to depress someone; (in argument) to flatten someone, crush someone; **estoy hecho** — I'm worn out; **hacer morder el** — **a uno** to make someone bite the dust; **matar el** — to lay the dust; **sacudir el** — **a uno** to thrash someone; to beat someone up.
　　(b) (Chem, Cook, Med etc) powder (freq —**s**); —**s** (esp) face powder; —**(s) de arroz** rice powder; —**s de blanqueo** bleaching powder; —**(s) de hornear**, —**(s) de levadura** baking powder; — **dentífrico**, —**s para dientes** tooth powder; —**s de talco** talcum powder; **en** —, **powdered**, in powdered form; **ponerse** —**s** to powder one's face.
　　(c) pinch; **un** — **de rapé** a pinch of snuff.
　　(d) (sl: tabu) screw (tabu); **echar un** — to have a screw (tabu).
pólvora nf (a) gunpowder; — **de algodón** guncotton; **no ha descubierto** (or **inventado**) **la** — he'll never set the Thames (or world) on fire; **gastar la** — **en salvas** to waste time and energy, fuss around uselessly; **propagarse como la** — to spread like wildfire.
　　(b) fireworks.
　　(c) (fig) bad temper, crossness.
　　(d) (fig) life, liveliness.

polvorear [1a] *vt* to powder, dust, sprinkle (*de* with).
polvoriento *adj* (a) *surface etc* dusty. (b) *substance* powdery.
polvorilla *nmf* (*fam*) (a) live wire, lively spark (*fam*). (b) touchy person, bad-tempered person.
polvorín *nm* (a) fine powder; —**es atómicos** atomic dust, atomic fallout.
 (b) (*Mil*) powder magazine; (*fig*) powder keg.
 (c) (*Arg*) =**jején**.
 (d) (*Chi, Mex*) =**polvorilla** (b).
 (e) (*Col, PR*) cloud of dust.
polvorosa: poner pies en — (*fam*) to beat it (*fam*).
polvoroso *adj* (*SAm*) dusty.
polvoso *adj* = **polvoriento**.
polla *nf* (a) (*Orn*) pullet; chick; — **de agua** moorhen.
 (b) (*Cards*) pool, kitty; (*Arg, Chi, Guat, Per*) stakes, pool.
 (c) (*fam*) girl, chick (*fam*), bird (*sl*).
 (d) (*Anat: tabu*) prick (*tabu*).
pollada *nf* (*Orn*) brood.
pollastre *nm* (*fam*) =**pollo** (b).
pollastro *nm*, **pollastrón** *nm* (*fam*) sly fellow.
pollera *nf* (a) hencoop; chicken run; basket for chickens. (b) (*Bol, Chi, RPl*) skirt, overskirt; (*Chi: Eccl*) soutane.
pollería *nf* poulterer's (shop).
pollero *nm* (a) chicken farmer; poulterer. (b) (*SAm*) gambler.
polludo *adj* (*RPl*) (a) cowardly; backbiting, gossipy. (b) *priest* (*pej*) holy, sanctimonious.
pollino *nm*, **pollina** *nf* (a) donkey. (b) (*fam*) ass, idiot.
pollita *nf* young pullet.
pollito *nm* (a) (*Orn*) chick. (b) (*fam*) =**pollo** (b).
pollo *nm* (a) (*Orn*) chicken; chick, young bird; (*Cook*) chicken; — **asado** roast chicken.
 (b) (*fam*) young man; elegant youth, playboy; **¿quién es ese** —? who is that chap? (*fam*); **es un** — **nada más** he's only a youngster.
 (c) (*fam*) spittle, sputum.
polluelo *nm* chick.
poma *nf* (a) (*fig*) apple. (b) (*Chi*) small flask; scent bottle; (*Ec*) carafe. (c) (*Mex*) pumice (stone).
pomada *nf* pomade.
pomar *nm* apple orchard.
pomelo *nm* grapefruit.
pómez: piedra *f* — pumice (stone).
pomo *nm* (a) (*Bot*) pome, fruit with pips. (b) scent bottle. (c) (*of sword*) pommel; (*of door*) round knob, handle. (d) (*Col*) powder puff.
pompa *nf* (a) bubble; — **de jabón** soap bubble. (b) (*Naut*) pump. (c) pomp, splendour; show, display; procession; pageant, pageantry; —**s fúnebres** funeral.
Pompeya Pompeii.
Pompeyo *m* Pompey.
pompo *adj* (*Col*) blunt.
pomposamente *adv* splendidly, magnificently; majestically; (*pej*) pompously.
pomposidad *nf* splendour, magnificence; majesty; (*pej*) pomposity.
pomposo *adj* splendid, magnificent; majestic; (*pej*) pompous.
pómulo *nm* cheekbone; (*fig*) cheek.
Poncio Pilatos *m* Pontius Pilate.
ponchada[1] *nf* bowlful of punch.
ponchada[2] *nf* (*Chi, RPl*) large quantity, large amount; **costó una** — it cost a lot.
ponchar [1a] *vt* (*Ant, Mex: angl*) (a) *ticket* to punch. (b) *tyre* to puncture.
ponche *nm* punch.
ponchera *nf* (a) punch bowl. (b) (*Col, Mex, Ven*) washbasin; (*Col*) bath.
poncho[1] *adj* (a) lazy, indolent; quiet, peaceable. (b) (*Col*) chubby.
poncho[2] *nm* (*SAm*) poncho, blanket, cape.
ponderación *nf* (a) weighing, consideration; deliberation. (b) high praise. (c) weighting. (d) calmness, steadiness, balance.
ponderado *adj* calm, steady, balanced.
ponderar [1a] *vt* (a) to weigh up, consider.
 (b) to praise highly, speak in praise of; — **algo a uno** to speak warmly of something to someone, tell someone how good something is; **le ponderan de inteligente** they speak highly of his intelligence.
 (c) (*Statistics*) to weight.
ponedero *nm* nest, nesting box.
ponedora *adj*: **gallina** — laying hen, hen in lay; **ser buena** — to be a good layer.
ponencia *nf* (learned) paper, communication; report.
poner [2r] **1** *vt* (a) (*general sense*) to put; to place, set; *clothes, hat* to put on; *care* to take, exercise (*en* in);

objection to raise; *table* to lay, set; *window* (*Comm*) to dress, arrange; *emphasis* to place (*en* on); — **algo a secar al sol** to put something (out) to dry in the sun; — **la experiencia al servicio de** to put one's experience at the disposal of; — **algo como ejemplo** to give (*or* quote) something as an example, use something as an illustration; — **a uno por testigo** to cite someone as a witness; — **algo en duda** to cast doubt on something, call something in question; — **algo aparte** to put something aside, put something on one side.
 (b) *egg* to lay.
 (c) *watch etc* to adjust, set (right); **pone el reloj por esa campana** he sets his watch by that bell.
 (d) *radio etc* to switch on, turn on, put on; **ponlo más fuerte** turn it up.
 (e) *letter, telegram* to send (*a* to).
 (f) *problem* to set; *fine, tax* to impose (*a* on); *task* to give, assign (*a* to); **nos pone mucho trabajo** he gives us a lot of work.
 (g) *shop* to open, set up, establish; *house* to fit up, equip; **han puesto la casa con todo lujo** they have fitted the house up most luxuriously.
 (h) *money* to contribute, subscribe, give; (*in gambling*) to stake; (*Fin*) to put, invest; (*fig*) to contribute; *time* to put, give; **yo pongo el dinero pero ella escoge** I put up the money but she chooses; **he puesto 5 minutos en firmarlo** it took me 5 minutes to sign it; **esto no pone nada para la solución del problema** this does not contribute at all towards solving the problem.
 (i) *name* to give; **al niño le pusieron Luis** they called the child Luis; **¿qué nombre le van a** —? what are they going to call him?, what name are they giving him?
 (j) — **a uno de cochino** to call someone a swine.
 (k) to add; **pongo 3 más para llegar a 100** I'll add 3 more to make it 100.
 (l) (*Theat*) *play* to put on, do, perform; *film* to show, put on; to screen; **¿qué ponen en el cine?** what's on at the cinema?
 (m) *emotion, fear etc* to cause; **me pone miedo** it frightens me, it scares me.
 (n) *words, language etc* to translate, put (*en* into); **puso el discurso en alemán** he translated the speech into German.
 (o) to suppose; **pongamos 120** let's say 120, let's put it at 120; **pongamos que** . . . let us suppose that . . .; **poniendo que** . . . supposing that . . ., assuming that . . .
 (p) (*Tel*) — **a X con Y** to connect X to Y, give X a line to Y; **póngame con el conserje** get me the porter, put me through to the porter; **le pongo en seguida** I'm trying to connect you.
 (q) **poner a P bien con Q** to reconcile P and Q, make things up between P and Q; **poner a Z mal con A** to cause a rift between Z and A, make Z fall out with A.
 (r) (+ *adj*) to make, turn; **si añades eso lo pones azul** if you add that you turn it blue; **la medicina le puso bueno** the medicine made him better; **la has puesto colorada** now you've made her blush; **para no** —**le de mal humor** so as not to make him cross.
 (s) — **a uno a** + *infin* to set someone to + *infin*; to start someone + *ger*.
 (t) **puso a su hija de sirvienta** she got her daughter a job as a servant; **puso a sus hijos a trabajar** she sent her children out to work; *see* **aprendiz**; *for many other uses and idioms, see noun entries.*
2 *vi* (a) (*Orn*) to lay, lay eggs.
 (b) **no pongo a la lotería** I don't go in for the lottery, I don't invest in the lottery.
 (c) **eso pone mucho** that's asking a lot.
3 ponerse *vr* (a) to put oneself, place oneself; **se ponía debajo de la ventana** he used to stand under the window; *see* **cómodo** *etc.*
 (b) — **un traje** to put a suit on; *see* **largo** *etc.*
 (c) — **de barro** to get covered in mud.
 (d) — **de conserje** to take a job as a porter.
 (e) — **a** (*place*), — **en** to reach, get to, arrive at; **en 2 horas se puso a su lado** in 2 hours he reached her side, in 2 hours he was at her side.
 (f) (*sun etc*) to set.
 (g) — **delante** to get in the way; to intercede, intervene; (*difficulty*) to arise, come up; **destruye al que se le pone delante** he destroys anyone who gets in his way.
 (h) — **a bien con uno** to get on good terms with someone, (*pej*) get in with someone; — **a mal con uno** to get on the wrong side of someone.
 (i) — **con uno** to quarrel with someone; to

oppose someone; to compete with someone, play (against) someone.

(j) (+ *adj*) to turn, get, become; **se puso serio** he became serious; **en el agua se pone verde** it turns green in the water; **¡no te pongas así!** don't be like that!; *see* **furioso** *etc*.

(k) — **a** + *infin* to begin to + *infin*, set about + *ger*; to proceed to + *infin*; **se pusieron a gritar** they started to shout.

poney ['poni] *nm*, *pl* **poneys** ['ponis] (*angl*) pony.

ponga, pongo[1] *etc see* **poner**.

pongaje *nm* (*Bol, Chi, Ec, Per*) domestic service which Indian tenants are obliged to give free.

pongo[2] *nm* orang-outang.

pongo[3] *nm* (*Bol, Chi, Ec, Per*) Indian servant, Indian tenant.

poniente *nm* (a) west. (b) west wind.

pontaje *nm* (*SAm*), **pontazgo** *nm* toll.

pontevedrés 1 *adj* of Pontevedra. **2** *nm*, **pontevedresa** *nf* native (*or* inhabitant) of Pontevedra; **los —es** the people of Pontevedra.

pontificado *nm* papacy, pontificate.

pontifical *adj* papal, pontifical.

pontificar [1g] *vi* to pontificate (*also fig*).

pontífice *nm* pope, pontiff; **el Sumo P—** His Holiness the Pope.

pontificio *adj* papal, pontifical.

pontón *nm* (a) pontoon; (*Aer: of seaplane*) float. (b) pontoon bridge (*also* — **flotante**); bridge of planks. (c) (*Naut*) hulk.

pony ['poni] *nm*, *pl* **ponys** ['ponis] (*angl*) pony.

ponzoña *nf* poison, venom; (*fig*) poison.

ponzoñoso *adj* poisonous, venomous; (*fig*) *attack etc* venomous; *propaganda* poisonous; *custom, idea etc* harmful.

popa *nf* stern; **a —** astern, abaft; **de — a proa** fore and aft, from stem to stern.

popar [1a] *vt* (a) *child etc* to spoil; (*fig*) to make a fuss of, flatter. (b) to scorn, jeer at.

popelín *nm*, **popelina** *nf* (*Acad*), **poplín** *nm* (*SAm*) poplin.

poporo *nm* (a) (*Col, Ven*) bump, swelling. (b) (*Ven*) stick.

popote *nm* (*Mex*) long thin stem; tough grass used for making brooms; drinking straw.

populachería *nf* cheap popularity, playing to the gallery.

populachero *adj* common, vulgar; cheap; *speech, policy* rabble-rousing; *politician* demagogic, who appeals to the lower orders, who plays to the gallery.

populacho *nm* populace, plebs, mob.

popular *adj* (in most senses) popular; *word etc* colloquial; *culture etc* of the people; folk (*attr*).

popularidad *nf* popularity.

popularismo *nm* colloquial word (*or* phrase *etc*).

popularización *nf* popularization.

popularizar [1f] **1** *vt* to popularize. **2 popularizarse** *vr* to become popular.

populoso *adj* populous.

poquedad *nf* (a) scantiness, paucity; smallness; fewness. (b) (**una —**) small thing, trifle; small quantity. (c) (*fig*) timidity.

póquer *nm* poker.

poquísimo *adj* (a) (*sing*) very little; hardly any, almost no. (b) (*pl*) **—s** very few, terribly few (*fam*).

poquito *nm* (a) **un —** a little bit (*de* of); (*as adv*) a little, a bit. (b) **a —s** bit by bit; in dribs and drabs; **¡— a poco!** gently!, easy there!

por *prep* (a) (+ *infin*) in order to; **— no llegar tarde** in order not to be late, so as not to arrive late; **lo hizo — complacerle** he did it to please her; **hablar — hablar** to talk just for talking's sake; **moverse — no estar quieto** to move about simply so as to have a change from sitting still; *see also* (c).

(b) (*objective*) for; **luchar — la patria** to fight for one's country; **trabajar — dinero** to work for money; **su amor — la pintura** his love for painting; **hazlo — mí** do it for me, do it for my sake.

(c) (*cause*) out of, because of, from; **fue — necesidad** it was from (*or* out of, because of) necessity; **— temor** from fear; **— temor a** for fear of; **lo hago — gusto** I do it because I like to; **no se realizó — escasez de fondos** it was not put into effect because of lack of money; **— venir tarde perdió la mitad** through coming late he missed half of it; **se hundió — mal construido** it collapsed because it was badly built; **le expulsaron — revoltoso** they expelled him as a troublemaker; **lo dejó — imposible** he gave it up as (being) impossible.

(d) (*evidence*) **— lo que dicen** from what they say, judging by what they say; **— las señas no piensa**

hacerlo judging by the signs he's not intending to do it.

(e) (*person affected*) — **mí, que se vaya** so far as I'm concerned (*or* for myself, for my part) he can go.

(f) (*agent*) by; — **su propia mano** by his own hand; — **correo** by post, through the post; — **mar** by sea, by boat; — **sí mismo** by oneself; **hablar — señas** to talk by signs, communicate by means of signs; **lo obtuve — un amigo** I got it through a friend, I got it with the help of a friend.

(g) (*Math*) 7 — 2 **son** 14 7 times 2 are 14.

(h) (*manner*) in; by; according to; — **centenares** by the hundred, by hundreds; — **orden** in order; **están dispuestos — tamaños** they are arranged according to size (*or* by sizes, in sizes); **punto — punto** point by point; **día — día** day by day.

(i) (*of place*) by, by way of; through; along; **ir a Bilbao — Santander** to go to Bilbao via Santander; — **el lado izquierdo** on (*or* along) the left side; **cruzar la frontera — Canfranc** to cross the frontier at Canfranc; — **la calle** along the street; — **la caña** through the pipe, along the pipe; — **todo el país** over the whole country, throughout the country; **llevar periódicos — las casas** to deliver papers round the houses; **pasar — Madrid** to pass through Madrid; to go via Madrid; **pasearse — el parque** to walk round the park, stroll through the park.

(j) (*of time*) — **la mañana** in the morning; during the morning; **no sale — la noche** he doesn't go out at night.

(k) (*of present and future time*) for; **se quedarán — 15 días** they will stay for a fortnight; **será — poco tiempo** it won't be for long.

(l) for, in exchange for; **te doy éste — aquél** I'll swap you this one for that one; **le dieron uno nuevo — el viejo** they gave him a new one (in exchange) for the old one; **se vendió — 15 dólares** it was sold for 15 dollars; **me dieron 13 francos — una libra** they gave me 13 francs for a pound; **ha puesto B — V** he has put B as being equivalent to V.

(m) **vino — su jefe** he came instead of (*or* in place of) his boss; **interceder — uno** to intercede for someone, intercede on someone's behalf; **hablo — todos** I speak on behalf of (*or* in the name of) everybody.

(n) **contar a uno — amigo** to count someone as a friend; **no se admite — válido** it is not accepted as valid; *see* **tener, tomar** *etc*.

(o) (*rate*) **tres dólares — hora** three dollars an hour; **revoluciones — minuto** revolutions per minute; *see* **persona** *etc*.

(p) (*approximation*) **eso está allá — el norte** that's somewhere up in the north; — **la feria** about carnival time, round about the carnival; *see* **fecha, Navidad** *etc*.

(q) — **difícil que sea** however hard it is, however hard it may be; **por mucho que lo quisieran** however much they would like to; *see* **más**.

(r) (*fam*) **ir a — uno** to go for someone, go and fetch someone; *see* **ir —, venir —** *etc*.

(s) — **qué** why; **¿— qué?** why?

porcachón *adj* (*fam*) filthy, dirty.

porcada *nf* (*fam*) = **porquería**.

porcallón *adj* (*fam*) filthy, dirty.

porcelana *nf* porcelain; china, chinaware; **tienda de —** china shop.

porcentaje *nm* percentage; proportion, ratio; rate; **un elevado — de** a high percentage of, a high proportion of; **el — de defunciones** the death rate.

porcentual *adj* percentage (*attr*).

Porcia *f* Portia.

porcino 1 *adj* porcine; pig (*attr*); **ganado —** pigs. **2** *nm* (a) young pig. (b) (*Med*) bump, swelling.

porción *nf* (a) portion; part, share; (*in recipes etc*) quantity, amount, part; (*of chocolate bar*) piece, segment.

(b) **una —** **de** (*fig*) a number of; **tengo una — de cosas que hacer** I have a number of things to do; **tuvimos una — de problemas** we had quite a few problems.

porcuno *adj* pig (*attr*).

porche *nm* (a) arcade (*of shops, round village square etc*). (b) (*of house*) porch.

pordiosear [1a] *vi* to beg (*also fig*).

pordiosero *nm*, **pordiosera** *nf* beggar.

porende *adv* (*arch or lit*) hence, therefore.

porfía *nf* (a) persistence; obstinacy, stubbornness. (b) dispute; continuous struggle, continuous competition. (c) **a — in** competition.

porfiadamente *adv* persistently; obstinately, stubbornly.

porfiado 1 *adj* persistent; obstinate, stubborn. **2** *nm* (*SAm*) doll; manikin, dummy.

porfiar [1c] *vi* to persist, insist; to argue stubbornly, doggedly maintain one's point of view; — **con uno** to argue with someone; — **en algo** to persist in something; **porfía en que es así** he insists that it is so, he will have it that it is so; — **por** + *infin* to struggle obstinately to + *infin*.

pórfido *nm* porphyry.

pormenor *nm* detail, particular.

pormenorizar [1f] **1** *vt* to detail, set out in detail; to particularize; to describe in detail. **2** *vi* to go into detail, particularize.

pornografía *nf* pornography.

pornográfico *adj* pornographic.

poro[1] *nm* (*Anat*) pore.

poro[2] *nm* (*Mex*) leek.

porongo *nm* (*SAm*) gourd, calabash.

pororó *nm* (*RPl*) popcorn.

porosidad *nf* porousness, porosity.

poroso *adj* porous.

porotal *nm* (*SAm*) (a) beanfield, bean patch. (b) (*fig*) **un** — **de** a lot of, a whole heap of.

poroto *nm* (a) (*Arg, Chi, Per*) bean; (*fig*) food (*in general*). (b) (*Arg: Sport etc*) point. (c) (*Chi, RPl*) weak person, feeble individual. (d) (*Chi*) child.

porque *conj* (a) (+ *indic*) because; since, for. (b) (+ *subj*) so that, in order that.

porqué *nm* (a) reason (*de* for), cause (*de* of); the whys and wherefores; **el** — **de la revolución** the factors that underlie the revolution; "**El** — **de los dichos**" "Origins of our Sayings". (b) (*fam: Fin*) wherewithal; **no tenemos el** — we haven't the wherewithal.

porquería *nf* (a) (*substance*) filth, muck, dirt; **me lo devolvieron cubierto de** — they gave it back to me filthy all over; **estar hecho una** — to be covered in muck, be dirty all over. (b) (*quality*) nastiness; indecency. (c) (*objects*) small thing, trifle; —**s** old things, junk, lumber; **le regalaron alguna** — they gave her some worthless present; **lo vendieron por una** — they sold it for next to nothing. (d) (*act*) dirty trick, mean action; indecent act; **me han hecho una** — they've played a dirty trick on me. (e) (*Cook*) nasty food, awful meal (*fam*); attractive but unwholesome dish. (f) (*fig*) rubbish; **la novela es una** — the novel is just rubbish; **escribió 3 o 4** —**s** he wrote 3 or 4 rubbishy books.

porqueriza *nf* pigsty.

porquerizo *nm*, **porquero** *nm* pigman, swineherd (*arch*).

porra *nf* (a) stick, club, cudgel; truncheon; (*Mus*) drumstick; (*Tech*) large hammer; (*Anat: tabu*) prick (*tabu*). (b) (*fam*) bore. (c) (*fam*) swank (*fam*), conceit; **gasta mucha** — he's got loads of swank. (d) (*fam*) ¡ —**s**! bother!, dash it!; (*to another person*) rubbish! (e) (*fam*) **mandar a uno a la** — to chuck someone out, send someone packing; **¡vete a la** —! go to blazes! (f) (*Bol, RPl*) curl, forelock. (g) (*CAm, Mex*) political gang; terrorist band; (*Theat*) claque.

porracear [1a] *vt* (*Mex, Ven*) to hit, beat.

porrada *nf* (a) thwack, thump, blow. (b) (*fam*) pile, heap; lot; **una** — **de** a whole heap of, a lot of.

porrazo *nm* (a) thwack, thump, blow; (*in falling*) bump. (b) (*SAm*) **de** — in one go, at one blow.

porrear [1a] *vi* to go on and on, harp on a theme.

porrería *nf* (*fam*) (a) annoying request, footling demand. (b) stupidity.

porreta *nf* (a) (*Bot*) green leaf. (b) (*fam*) **en** — stark naked.

porretada *nf* = **porrada** (b).

porrillo: a — *adv* in abundance, by the ton.

porro (*fam*) **1** *adj* stupid, oafish. **2** *nm* idiot, oaf.

porrón[1] *adj* slow, stupid; dull; sluggish.

porrón[2] *nm* *glass wine jar with a long spout*.

porrudo *adj* (a) big, bulging. (b) (*Arg, Urug*) long-haired; tousle-headed. (c) (*Arg, Urug*) big-headed.

porsiacaso *nm* (*Arg, Ven*) knapsack.

porta *nf* (*Naut*) port.

porta(a)viones *nm*, *pl* **porta(a)viones** aircraft carrier.

portacargas *nm*, *pl* **portacargas** crate; (*of bicycle*) carrier.

portación *nf* (*SAm*): — **de armas** carrying (of) a weapon.

portacubiertos *nm*, *pl* **portacubiertos** knife box, cutlery box.

portada *nf* (a) (*Archit*) main front; façade; porch, doorway. (b) (*Typ*) frontispiece, title page; (*of magazine*) cover.

portado *adj*: **bien** — well-dressed; well-behaved; respectable.

portador *nm*, **portadora** *nf* carrier, bearer; (*Comm, Fin*) bearer; payee; — **de gérmenes** germ carrier; **el** — **de esta carta** the bearer of this letter.

portaequipajes *nm*, *pl* **portaequipajes** (*Aut etc*) boot, trunk (*US*); luggage rack, grid; (*on bicycle*) carrier.

portaestandarte *nm* standard bearer.

portafolio *nm* (*Ven*) briefcase.

portafusil *nm* rifle sling.

portahachón *nm* torchbearer.

portal *nm* (a) vestibule, hall. (b) porch, doorway; street door, main door; (*of city*) gate; —**es** arcade. (c) (*Sport*) goal. (d) (*Eccl*) — **de Belén** Nativity scene, crèche.

portalada *nf* large doorway; imposing entrance; gate.

portalámpara(s) *nm*, *pl* **portalámparas** lamp-holder, socket.

portaligas *nm*, *pl* **portaligas** suspender belt, garter belt (*US*).

portalón *nm* (a) (*Archit*) = **portalada**. (b) (*Naut*) gangway.

portamaletas *nm*, *pl* **portamaletas** (*Aut*) luggage rack, grid.

portamantas *nm*, **portamantas** valise.

portamanteo *nm* travelling bag.

portaminas *nm*, *pl* **portaminas** propelling pencil.

portamonedas *nm*, *pl* **portamonedas** pocketbook, purse.

portañuela *nf* fly (*of trousers*).

portaobjeto(s) *nm*, *pl* **portaobjetos** slide; stage (*of microscope*).

portapapeles *nm*, *pl* **portapapeles** briefcase.

portaplacas *nm*, *pl* **portaplacas** (*Phot*) plateholder.

portaplumas *nm*, *pl* **portaplumas** penholder.

portar [1a] **1** *vt* (*lit*) to carry, bear. **2 portarse** *vr* (a) to behave, conduct oneself; — **mal** to misbehave, behave badly; **se ha portado como un cochino** he has behaved like a swine; **se portó muy bien conmigo** he was very decent to me, he treated me very well. (b) (*fam*) to show up well, come through creditably. (c) (*SAm*) to behave well; to behave nobly (*or* bravely).

portarretratos *nm*, *pl* **portarretratos** picture frame, photograph frame.

portátil *adj* portable.

portatostadas *nm*, *pl* **portatostadas** toast rack.

portaviandas *nm*, *pl* **portaviandas** lunch tin, dinner pail (*US*).

portavoz *nm* (a) megaphone, loudhailer. (b) (*person*) spokesman; (*pej*) mouthpiece.

portazgo *nm* toll.

portazo *nm* bang (*of a door*), slam; **dar un** — to slam the door.

porte *nm* (a) (*Comm*) carriage, transport; (costs of) carriage, transport charges; (*Post*) postage; — **pagado** (*Comm*) carriage paid, (*Post*) post-paid; **franco de** — (*Comm*) carriage free, (*Post*) post-free. (b) (*esp Naut*) capacity. (c) conduct, behaviour. (d) bearing, demeanour; air, appearance; **de** — **distinguido** with a distinguished air.

porteador *nm* carrier; (*Mountaineering etc*) porter; (*Hunting etc*) bearer.

portear[1] [1a] *vt* (*Comm*) to carry, convey, transport.

portear[2] [1a] *vi* (*of door*) to slam, bang. (b) (*Arg*) to get out in a hurry.

portento *nm* marvel, wonder, prodigy; **es un** — **de belleza** she is extraordinarily beautiful.

portentosamente *adv* marvellously, extraordinarily; extraordinarily well.

portentoso *adj* marvellous, extraordinary.

porteño 1 *adj* of Buenos Aires. **2** *nm*, **porteña** *nf* native (*or* inhabitant) of Buenos Aires; **los** —**s** the people of Buenos Aires.

porteo *nm* carriage, transport, conveyance.

portera *nf* portress.

portería *nf* (a) porter's lodge, porter's office. (b) (*Sport*) goal.

portero *nm* (a) porter, janitor; doorman; caretaker. (b) (*Sport*) goalkeeper.

portezuela *nf* (a) little door; (*of vehicle*) door. (b) (*Sew*) pocket flap.

portezuelo *nm* (Arg, Chi: *Geog*) pass.

pórtico *nm* (a) portico, porch; (*fig*) gateway (*de* to). (b) arcade.

portilla *nf* porthole.

portillo *nm* (a) gap, opening; breach; wicket, wicket gate; side entrance, private door.
(b) (*Geog*) narrow pass.
(c) (*of vessel etc*) dent; chip.
(d) (*fig*) weak spot, vulnerable point; opening (*affording solution to a problem*).

pórtland *nm* or *f* (*esp* SAm) cement.

portón *nm* large door, main door; (SAm) gate; (Chi) back door.

portorriqueño 1 *adj* Puerto Rican. 2 *nm*, **portorriqueña** *nf* Puerto Rican.

portuario *adj* port (*attr*), harbour (*attr*); dock (*attr*); **trabajador** — docker.

Portugal *m* Portugal.

portugués 1 *adj* Portuguese. 2 *nm*, **portuguesa** *nf* Portuguese. 3 *nm* (*language*) Portuguese.

portuguesimo *nm* portuguesism, word (or phrase *etc*) borrowed from Portuguese.

porvenir *nm* future; **en el** —, **en lo** — in the future; **un hombre sin** — a man with no future, a man with no prospects; **le espera un brillante** — a brilliant future awaits him.

pos: en — **de** *prep* after, in pursuit of; **ir en** — **de** to chase (after), pursue; **ella va en** — **de un marido** she's after a husband.

posada *nf* (a) shelter, lodging; **dar** — **a** to give shelter to, take in. (b) inn; lodging house. (c) house, dwelling, abode.

posaderas *nfpl* backside, buttocks.

posadero *nm* innkeeper.

posar [1a] 1 *vt* load to lay down, put down; *hand etc* to place, put gently; — **los ojos en** to look vaguely at, glance briefly at.
2 *vi* (Art, Cine, Phot) to sit, pose.
3 **posarse** *vr* (a) (*bird, insect*) to alight, settle, rest; (*bird*) to perch, sit; (*aircraft*) to land, come down; **el avión se encontraba posado** the aircraft was on the ground.
(b) (*liquid*) to settle, form sediment; (*dust*) to settle.

posas *nfpl* backside, buttocks.

posdata *nf* postscript.

pose [pouz or 'pose] *nf* (angl, gall) (a) (Art, Cine, Phot) pose; (Phot) time exposure.
(b) (*fig*) attitude.
(c) (*fig*) composure; poise.
(d) (*fig*) pose; affectedness; affected posture.

poseedor *nm*, **poseedora** *nf* owner, possessor; (*of post, record*) holder.

poseer [2e] *vt* to have, possess, own; *advantage* to have, enjoy; *language, subject* to know perfectly, have a complete mastery of; *post, record* to hold.

poseído 1 *adj* (a) possessed (*por* by); (*fig*) maddened, crazed.
(b) **estar muy** — **de** to be very vain about, have an excessively high opinion of.
2 *nm*, **poseída** *nf*: **gritar como un** — to shout like one possessed.

posesión *nf* (a) (*in general*) possession; (*of office*) tenure, occupation; (*of language, subject*) complete knowledge, perfect mastery; **dar** — **a** to hand over to, make formal transfer to; **él está en** — **de las cartas** he is in possession of the letters; **las cartas están en** — **de su padre** the letters are in the possession of his father; **está en** — **del récord** he holds the record; **tomar** — to take over, enter upon office (*etc*); **tomar** — **de** to take possession of, take over; **tomar** — **de un oficio** to take up a post.
(b) (*una* —) possession (*also* Pol); property; piece of property, estate.
(c) (Chi) country house and lands; (Ven) ranch, estate.

posesionar [1a] 1 *vt*: — **a uno de algo** to hand something over to someone. 2 **posesionarse** *vr*: — **de** to take possession of, take over.

posesivo 1 *adj* possessive. 2 *nm* possessive.

poseso = **poseído**.

posfechar [1a] *vt* to postdate.

posibilidad *nf* possibility; chance; **no existe** — **alguna de que venga** there is no possibility of his coming; **tiene pocas** —**es** he hasn't much chance.

posibilitar [1a] *vt* to make possible, facilitate, permit; to make feasible.

posible 1 *adj* possible; feasible; **una** — **tragedia** a possible tragedy; **todas las concesiones** —**s** all possible concessions; **a serme** — if I possibly can; **de**

ser — if possible; **en lo** — as far as possible; **lo antes** — as soon as possible; as quickly as possible; **lo más frecuentemente** — as often as possible; **hacer lo** — to do all that one can (*para* or *por* + *infin* to + *infin*); **es** — **que** + *subj* it is possible that . . .; perhaps . . .; **¿es** —? surely not?; can it really be true?; **¿será** — **que haya venido?** can he really have come (after all)?; **¿será** — **que no haya venido?** surely he has come, hasn't he?; **si es** — if possible; **si me es** — if I possibly can; *see* **dentro, pronto** *etc*.
2 —**s** *nmpl* means; funds, assets; **vivir dentro de sus** —**s** to live within one's means.

posiblemente *adv* possibly.

posición *nf* (a) (*in most senses*) position; status, standing, social position.
(b) (Sport) position; (*in table etc*) place, position; **terminar en primera** — to finish first; **ganó A con B en segunda** — A won with B in second place.
(c) (SAm: *angl*) position, post, job.

positiva *nf* (Phot) positive, print.

positivamente *adv* positively.

positivismo *nm* positivism.

positivista 1 *adj* positivist. 2 *nmf* positivist.

positivo 1 *adj* (*in most senses*) positive; (Math) positive, plus; *idea* useful, practical, constructive. 2 *nm* (a) (Ling) positive. (b) (Phot) positive, print.

pósito *nm* (a) (public) granary. (b) cooperative, association.

positrón *nm* positron.

posma *nmf* (*fam*) bore, dull person.

poso *nm* sediment, deposit; dregs.

posponer [2r] *vt* (a) — **A a B** to put A behind (or below) B; — **el amor propio al interés general** to subordinate one's self-respect to the general interest; — **a uno** to assign an unduly low position (*etc*) to someone.
(b) (*esp* SAm: *angl*) to postpone.

posposición *nf* (a) postposition; relegation; subordination. (b) postponement.

posta 1 *nf* (a) (*of horses*) relay, team; stage; staging post; **a** — on purpose, deliberately; **por la** — posthaste, as quickly as possible.
(b) (Cards) stake.
(c) slice (*of meat etc*).
(d) (Hunting) slug, pellet.
2 *nm* courier.

postal 1 *adj* postal. 2 *nf* postcard; — **ilustrada** picture postcard.

poste *nm* post, pole; pillar; stake; (Sport) post, upright; —**s** (Sport) goalposts, goal; — **de cerca** fencing post; — **indicador** signpost; — **de llegada** winning post; — **de portería** goalpost; — **de salida** starting post; — **telegráfico** telegraph pole; **dar** — **a uno** (*fam*) to keep someone hanging about; **oler el** — to scent danger, see trouble ahead; to smell a rat.

postema *nf* (a) (Med) abscess, tumour; (Mex) pus; (Mex) boil. (b) (*fam*) bore, dull person.

postemilla *nf* (SAm) gumboil.

postergación *nf* (a) passing over, ignoring. (b) delaying; deferment, postponement.

postergar [1h] *vt* (a) *person* to pass over, disregard; to ignore the seniority (or better claim) of. (b) (*esp* SAm) to delay; to defer, postpone.

posteridad *nf* posterity.

posterior *adj* (a) (*place*) back, rear; posterior; *engine* rear-mounted.
(b) (*in order*) later, following.
(c) (*time*) later, subsequent; **ser** — **a** to be later than.

posterioridad *nf* later nature; **con** — later, subsequently; **con** — **a** subsequent to, later than.

posteriormente *adv* later, subsequently, afterwards.

postglacial *adj* postglacial.

postgraduado 1 *adj* postgraduate. 2 *nm*, **postgraduada** *nf* postgraduate.

pos(t)guerra *nf* postwar period; **los años de la** — the postwar years; **en la** — in the postwar period, after the war.

postigo *nm* (a) wicket, wicket gate; postern; small door, side door. (b) shutter.

postillón *nm* postillion.

postimpresionismo *nm* post-impressionism.

postimpresionista 1 *adj* post-impressionist. 2 *nmf* post-impressionist.

postín *nm* (*fam*) (a) elegance, luxury, poshness (*fam*), tone (*fam*); **de** — posh (*fam*), swanky (*fam*), smart.
(b) side (*fam*), swank (*fam*); **darse** — to show off, swank (*fam*); **se da mucho** — **de que su padre es ministro** he swanks about his father being a minister.

postinear [1a] *vi* (*fam*) to show off, swank (*fam*).

postinero adj (fam) (a) person, vain, conceited (de about); swanky (fam). (b) dress etc posh (fam), swish (sl).

postizas nfpl castanets.

postizo 1 adj false, artificial; teeth false; collar detachable; front etc dummy; smile etc false, phoney (fam), sham. **2** nm switch, false hair, hairpiece.

postludio nm postlude.

postmeridiano adj postmeridian.

postnatal adj postnatal.

postor nm bidder; **mejor** — highest bidder.

postración nf prostration; — **nerviosa** nervous exhaustion.

postrado adj prostrate (also fig); — **por el dolor** prostrate with grief.

postrar [1a] **1** vt (a) to cast down, overthrow; to humble. (b) (Med) to weaken, exhaust, prostrate. **2 postrarse** vr to prostrate oneself.

postre 1 nm (also — s) sweet, sweet course; dessert; **¿qué hay de** —? what is there for dessert?; **para** — (fam) to crown it all, on top of all that; **llegar a los** —**s** (fig) to come too late, come after everything is over.

2 nf: **a la** — at last, in the end; when all is said and done.

postremo adj, **postrero** adj (**postrer** before m sing noun) last; rear, hindermost.

postrimerías nfpl (a) dying moments; final stages, closing stages; **en las** — **del siglo** in the last few years of the century, right at the end of the century. (b) (Eccl) four last things.

postulación nf (a) postulation. (b) collection.

postulado nm postulate, proposition; assumption, hypothesis.

postulante nmf petitioner; (Eccl) postulant, candidate.

postular [1a] vt (a) to postulate.
(b) to seek, demand; to petition for; to claim; **en el artículo postula la reforma de . . .** in the article he sets out demands for the reform of . . .
(c) to collect (for charity).
(d) (CAm, Mex) candidate to nominate.

póstumo adj posthumous.

postura nf (a) (of body) posture, position; stance; pose. (b) (fig) attitude, position; stand; **adoptar una poco razonable** to take an unreasonable attitude; **la** — **del gobierno en este asunto** the government's position in this matter. (c) (in auction) bid; (Gambling) bet, stake; **hacer una** — to lay a bet; to make a bid. (d) (Orn) egg-laying; eggs (laid).

post-venta adj after-sales (attr); **servicio** (or **asistencia**) **de** — after-sales service.

potable adj drinkable; **agua** — drinking water.

potaje nm (a) (Cook) stew; —**s** mixed vegetables; (dish of) dried vegetables. (b) (fig) mixture; jumble.

potasa nf potash.

potasio nm potassium.

pote nm (a) pot; jar; jug; (Pharm) jar; (Mex) tin, can; (Mex) tankard; (Hort) flowerpot, pot; (Ec, PR) flask; **a** — in plenty; see **beber**.
(b) (Prov) stew.
(c) (fam) pout.
(d) (fam) **darse** — to show off, swank (fam).

potencia nf (a) (in general) power; potency; — **electoral** voting power, power in terms of votes; — **hidráulica** hydraulic power; — **muscular** muscular power, muscular strength.
(b) (Mech) power; capacity; — (**en caballos**) horsepower; — **al freno** brake horsepower; — **real** effective power.
(c) (Pol) power; **las** —**s** the Powers; **las grandes** —**s** the great powers; — **colonial** colonial power; — **mundial** world power; **éramos una** — **naval** we used to be a naval power.
(d) (Math) power.
(e) (Rel: also — **del alma**) faculty.
(f) **en** — potential, in the making; **es una guerra civil en** — it is a civil war in the making.

potencial 1 adj potential. **2** nm (a) potential. (b) (Gram) conditional.

potencialidad nf potentiality.

potencialmente adv potentially.

potentado nm potentate; (fig) tycoon; baron, magnate; big shot (fam).

potente adj (a) powerful. (b) (fam) big, mighty, strong; **un grito** — a great yell.

potestad nf power, authority, jurisdiction; — **marital** husband's authority; **patria** — paternal authority.

potestativo adj optional, not mandatory; permissive.

potingue nm (fam) concoction, brew.

poto nm (a) (Arg, Bol, Chi, Per) backside, bottom; lower end. (b) (Chi, Ec, Per) calabash; earthenware vessel.

potoco adj (Bol, Chi) squat.

potón (Chi) **1** adj coarse. **2** nm rustic, peasant.

potosí nm fortune; **cuesta un** — it costs the earth; **vale un** — it's worth a fortune; **ella vale un** — she's a treasure; **en ese negocio tienen un** — they've got a gold mine in that business.

potra nf (a) (Zool) filly. (b) (Med) rupture, hernia. (c) (fam) **tener** — to be lucky.

potranca nf filly, young mare.

potranco nm (Col, CR, Mex, PR) colt, young horse.

potrear [1a] **1** vt (a) (Guat, Per) to beat. (b) (Mex, PR) to break, tame. **2** vi (Arg, Hond, Urug) to gambol, caper about, chase around.

potrero nm (a) pasture; paddock. (b) (SAm) cattle ranch. (c) (Arg) playground.

potrillo nm (a) (Chi, RPl) colt. (b) (Chi) tall glass. (c) (Col, Ec) small canoe.

potro nm (a) (Zool) colt; — **de madera** vaulting horse. (b) rack (for torture); stocks; shoeing frame. (c) (SAm) hernia, tumour.

poyo nm stone bench.

poza nf puddle, pool; (Mex) pool, backwater (of river).

pozanco nm puddle, pool.

pozo nm (a) well; — **artesiano** artesian well; — **negro** cesspool; — **de petróleo** oil well; — **séptico** septic tank; **caer en el** — (fig) to fall into oblivion.
(b) (Geog) deep pool, deep part (of river).
(c) (Min) shaft; pit; — **de aire** air shaft; — **de registro**, — **de visita** manhole; inspection hatch; — **de ventilación** ventilation shaft.
(d) (fig) **ser un** — **de ciencia** to be immensely learned; **es un** — **de maldad** he is utterly wicked.

práctica nf (in most senses) practice; method; skill; **en la** — in practice; —**s restrictivas** (**de la competencia**) restrictive practices; —**s profesionales** professional training, practical training for a profession; **la** — **hace maestro** practice makes perfect; **aprender con la** — to learn by practice; **hacer** —**s de piano** to practise (on) the piano; **hacer** — **de clínica** to do one's hospital training, walk the wards (fam); **poner algo en** — to put something into practice.

practicable adj (a) practicable; workable, feasible. (b) road etc passable, usable. (c) door that opens, that is meant to open.

prácticamente adv practically.

practicante 1 adj (Eccl) practising. **2** nmf practitioner; (Med) medical assistant, doctor's assistant; male nurse.

practicar [1g] **1** vt (a) skill, virtue etc to practise, exercise.
(b) activity etc to practise; sport to go in for, play; profession to practise; — **el francés con su profesor** to practise one's French with one's teacher.
(c) to perform, carry out; arrest to make.
(d) hole to cut, make; to bore, drill.
2 practicarse vr: — **en la enseñanza** to do teaching practice, do one's school practice.

práctico 1 adj (a) practical; tool etc handy; house etc convenient; clothing sensible, practical; **no resultó ser muy** — it turned out to be not very practical; **resulta** — **vivir tan cerca de la fábrica** it's convenient (or handy) to live so close to the factory.
(b) study, training etc practical.
(c) person skilled, expert (en at); **ser muy** — **en** to be very skilled at, be very adept at.
2 nm (Med) practitioner; (Naut) pilot.

pradera nf meadow, meadowland; (Canada etc) prairie; **unas extensas** —**s** extensive grasslands.

pradería nf meadowlands, grasslands.

prado nm meadow, field; pasture; green grassy area; — **de juego** playground, play area.

Praga Prague.

pragmático adj pragmatic.

pragmatismo nm pragmatism.

pragmatista nmf pragmatist.

preámbulo nm (a) preamble, introduction.
(b) (pej) evasive talk, annoying digression; **gastar** —**s** to talk evasively, beat about the bush; **decir algo sin** —**s** to say something without beating about the bush.

prebélico adj prewar.

prebenda nf (a) (Eccl) prebend. (b) (fam) sinecure, soft job.

prebendado nm prebendary.

preboste nm provost.

precalentar [1k] vt to preheat.

precariamente adv precariously.

precario *adj* precarious; **estar de —** to be in a precarious position.

precaución *nf* **(a)** *(act)* precaution; preventive measure; **tomar —es** to take precautions.

(b) *(quality)* foresight; caution, wariness; **ir con —** to go cautiously, proceed warily; **lo hicimos por —** we did it to be on the safe side.

precautorio *adj* *(SAm)* precautionary.

precaver [2a] **1** *vt* to guard against, try to prevent; to forestall; to stave off.

2 precaverse *vr* to be on one's guard, take precautions, be forewarned; **— contra** to guard against; **— de** to be on one's guard against, beware of.

precavidamente *adv* cautiously, warily.

precavido *adj* cautious, wary.

precendencia *nf* precedence; priority; greater importance, superiority.

precedente **1** *adj* preceding, foregoing; former; **cada uno mejor que el —** each one better than the one before.

2 *nm* precedent; **de acuerdo con el —** according to precedent; **contra todos los —s** against all the precedents; **sin —(s)** unprecedented; unparalleled; **establecer un —, sentar un —** to establish (*or* set up) a precedent.

preceder [2a] **1** *vt:* **— a (a)** to precede, go before; **le precedía un coche** he was preceded by a car; **el título precede al nombre** the title goes before the name.

(b) *(fig)* to have priority over; to take precedence over.

2 *vi* to precede; **todo lo que precede** all the preceding (part), all that which comes before.

preceptista *nmf* theorist.

precepto *nm* precept; order, rule; **de —** *(Eccl)* obligatory.

preceptor *nm* teacher; (private) tutor.

preceptorado *nm* tutorship.

preceptoral *adj* tutorial.

preces *nfpl* prayers, supplications.

preciado *adj* **(a)** esteemed, valuable. **(b)** presumptuous.

preciarse [1b] *vr* to boast; **— de algo** to pride oneself on something, boast of being something; **— de inteligente** to think oneself clever, pride oneself on one's intelligence; **— de + infin** to boast of + *ger*.

precintado *adj* sealed, presealed; *(Comm)* prepackaged.

precinto *nm* seal.

precio *nm* **(a)** price; cost; value, worth; *(of journey)* fare; *(in hotel etc)* rate, charge; **— de compra** purchase price; **— al contado** cash price; **— de coste** cost price; **a —, de coste, a — de costo** at cost price; **— en fábrica** price ex-factory; **— irrisorio, — de oportunidad, — de situación** *(SAm)* bargain price; **— de lista** list price; **— de mercado** market price; **— neto** net price; **— obsequio** giveaway price; **— de pensión** school fees; **— tope** top price, ceiling price; **último —** closing price; **— de venta** sale price; **— del viaje** fare (for the journey); **al — de** *(fig)* at the cost of; **lo hará a cualquier —** he'll do it whatever the cost; **evítelo a cualquier —** avoid it at all costs; **"no importa —"** "cost no object"; **poner** *(or* **señalar) — a la cabeza de uno** to put a price on someone's head; **no tener —** *(fig)* to be priceless.

(b) *(fig)* value, worth; **hombre de gran —** a man of great worth.

preciosamente *adv* *(fam)* beautifully; charmingly.

preciosidad *nf* **(a)** preciousness; value, worth.

(b) *(pej)* preciosity.

(c) *(fam)* beautiful thing; precious object; **es una —** it's lovely, it's really beautiful; **¡oye, —!** hey, beautiful!

preciosismo *nm* *(Lit etc)* preciosity.

preciosista *(Lit etc)* **1** *adj* precious, affected. **2** *nmf* precious writer, affected writer *(etc)*.

precioso *adj* **(a)** precious; valuable.

(b) *(fam)* pretty, lovely, beautiful; charming; **una edición preciosa** a beautiful edition; **tienen un niño —** they have a lovely child; **¿verdad que es —?** isn't it lovely?

preciosura *nf* *(SAm)* = **preciosidad (c)**.

precipicio *nm* **(a)** cliff, precipice.

(b) *(fig)* chasm, abyss; **tiene el — abierto a sus pies** the chasm yawns before him, he stands on the brink of disaster.

(c) *(fig)* ruin.

precipitación *nf* **(a)** haste; rashness; **con —** hastily; rashly, precipitately. **(b)** *(Meteorol)* precipitation, rainfall. **(c)** *(Chem)* precipitation.

precipitadamente *adv* headlong; hastily, suddenly; rashly, precipitately.

precipitado **1** *adj* *flight etc* headlong; *departure etc* hasty, sudden; *act* hasty, rash, precipitate. **2** *nm* *(Chem)* precipitate.

precipitar [1a] **1** *vt* **(a)** to hurl down, cast down, throw *(desde* from).

(b) to hasten; to speed up, accelerate; to precipitate; **aquello precipitó su salida** that affair hastened his departure; **la dimisión precipitó la crisis** the resignation precipitated *(or* brought on, sparked off) the crisis.

(c) *(Chem)* to precipitate.

2 precipitarse *vr* **(a)** to throw oneself, hurl oneself *(desde* from); to launch oneself.

(b) to rush, dash; to dart; **— a hacer algo** to rush to do something, hasten to do something; **— sobre** *(bird etc)* to swoop on, pounce on; **— sobre uno** to rush at someone, hurl oneself on someone; **— hacia un sitio** to rush towards a place.

(c) to act rashly; **se ha precipitado rehusándolo** he acted rashly in rejecting it, it was rash of him to refuse it.

precipitoso *adj* **(a)** *place* precipitous, steep, sheer. **(b)** *act etc* = **precipitado 1**.

precisado *adj* *(Arg, CAm, Mex):* **verse — a + infin** to be obliged to + *infin*.

precisamente *adv* **(a)** precisely, in a precise way.

(b) precisely, exactly; just; **¡—!** exactly!, precisely!; **just so!; — por eso** for that very reason, precisely because of that; **— fue él quien lo dijo** it so happens it was he who said it, as a matter of fact he said it; **— estábamos hablando de eso** we were just talking about that; **llegó — cuando nos íbamos** he arrived just as we were leaving; **yo no soy un experto —** I'm not exactly an expert; **no es eso —** it's not quite that, it's not really that.

precisar [1a] **1** *vt* **(a)** to need, require; **no precisa lavado** it needs no washing; **"vendedores precisa agencia internacional"** *(advert)* "salesmen wanted by international agency"; **precisa que vengas** you must come; **no precisamos que el candidato tenga experiencia** we do not insist *(or* demand) that the candidate should be experienced.

(b) to determine exactly, fix; to pinpoint, put one's finger on; *details etc* to specify, state precisely; **hay alguna rareza que no puedo —** there is some oddity which I cannot pin down *(or* put my finger on).

2 *vi* to be necessary; to be urgent; **— de algo** to need something; **precisamos de más tiempo** we need more time.

precisión *nf* **(a)** precision; preciseness, accuracy, exactness; **instrumento de —** precision instrument.

(b) need, necessity; **tener — de algo** to need something, have need of something.

(c) *(Mex)* urgency.

preciso *adj* **(a)** precise; exact, accurate; **una descripción precisa** a precise description.

(b) **en aquel — momento** at that precise moment, at that very moment, just at that moment.

(c) necessary, essential; **las cualidades precisas** the essential qualities, the requisite qualities; **tener el tiempo — para + infin** to have (just) enough time to + *infin*; **cuando sea —** when it becomes necessary; **es — que lo hagas** it is essential that you should do it, you must do it; **es — tener coche** it is essential to have a car.

precitado *adj* above-mentioned.

preclaro *adj* *(lit)* illustrious.

precocidad *nf* precociousness, precocity; *(Bot etc)* earliness.

precognición *nf* precognition.

precolombino *adj* pre-Columbian; **la América precolombina** America before Columbus.

preconcebido *adj* preconceived; **idea preconcebida** preconception.

preconcepción *nf* preconception.

preconizable *adj* foreseeable, that can be envisaged.

preconización *nf* **(a)** recommendation; favouring. **(b)** visualizing, envisaging.

preconizar [1f] **1** *vt* **(a)** to advise, recommend; *policy* to favour.

(b) to foresee, visualize, envisage *(que* that).

2 preconizarse *vr:* **se preconiza que . . .** it is envisaged that . . ., it is thought that . . .

precordillera *nf* *(Arg)* Andean foothills.

precoz *adj* precocious; forward; *baldness etc* premature; *(Bot etc)* early.

precursor *nm*, **precursora** *nf* predecessor, forerunner.

predador *nm*, **predator** *nm* predator.

predecesor *nm*, **predecesora** *nf* predecessor.

predecir [3p] *vt* to predict, foretell, forecast.

predestinación *nf* predestination.
predestinado *adj* predestined; **ser — a** + *infin* to be predestined to + *infin*.
predestinar [1a] *vt* to predestine.
predeterminación *nf* predetermination.
predeterminar [1a] *vt* to predetermine.
prédica *nf* sermon; harangue; **—s** preaching (*also fig*).
predicación *nf* (a) preaching. (b) (*una —*) = **prédica**.
predicado *nm* predicate.
predicador *nm* preacher.
predicamento *nm* (a) standing, prestige; **no goza ahora de tanto —** it has less prestige now, it is not so well thought of now. (b) (*SAm: angl*) predicament.
predicar [1g] *vti* to preach.
predicativo *adj* predicative.
predicción *nf* prediction; forecast; **— del tiempo** weather forecast(ing).
predicho *adj* aforementioned.
predilección *nf* predilection; **tener — por** to have a predilection for; **—es y aversiones** likes and dislikes.
predilecto *adj* favourite.
predio *nm* property, estate; **— rústico** country estate; **— urbano** town property.
predisponer [2r] *vt* to predispose; (*pej*) to prejudice, bias (*contra* against).
predisposición *nf* predisposition, inclination; (*pej*) prejudice, bias (*contra* against); (*Med*) tendency, predisposition (*a* to).
predispuesto *adj* predisposed; **ser — a los catarros** to have a tendency to get colds; **ser — al abatimiento** to be inclined to depression; **estar — contra uno** to be prejudiced against someone.
predominante *adj* predominant; major; prevailing; (*Comm*) *interest* controlling.
predominantemente *adv* predominantly.
predominar [1a] **1** *vt* to dominate, predominate over. **2** *vi* (a) to predominate; to prevail.
　(b) **esta casa predomina a áquella** this house is higher than that one.
predominio *nm* predominance; prevalence; sway, ascendancy, influence; superiority.
preeminencia *nf* pre-eminence, superiority.
preeminente *adj* pre-eminent; superior.
preeminentemente *adv* pre-eminently.
preempción *nf* pre-emption.
preenfriar [1c] *vt* to precool.
pre(e)scoger [2c] *vt* *players* to seed.
preestreno *nm* preview, press view, private showing.
preexistencia *nf* pre-existence.
preexistente *adj* pre-existent, pre-existing.
preexistir [3a] *vti* to pre-exist, exist before.
prefabricado *adj* prefabricated.
prefabricar [1g] *vt* to prefabricate.
prefacio *nm* preface, foreword.
prefecto *nm* prefect.
prefectura *nf* prefecture.
preferencia *nf* preference; **de —** for preference, preferably; **localidad de —** reserved seat; **tratamiento de —** preferential treatment; **mostrar — por** to show preference to, be biassed in favour of.
preferente *adj* (a) preferred; preferable. (b) (*Fin*) *share* preference (*attr*); *duty, treatment etc* preferential; *right* prior.
preferentemente *adv* preferably.
preferible *adj* preferable (*a* to).
preferiblemente *adv* preferably.
preferir [3i] *vt* to prefer; **— té a café** to prefer tea to coffee; **¿cuál prefieres?** which do you prefer?; **prefiero ir a pie** I prefer to walk, I'd rather go on foot.
prefiguración *nf* foreshadowing, prefiguration.
prefigurar [1a] *vt* to foreshadow, prefigure.
prefijar [1a] *vt* (a) to fix beforehand, arrange in advance, prearrange. (b) (*Gram*) to prefix (*a* to).
prefijo *nm* prefix.
pregón *nm* proclamation, announcement; (*Comm*) street cry, vendor's cry; **— literario de un acto** speech (*etc*) about a forthcoming public ceremony.
pregonar [1a] *vt* to proclaim, announce; *secret* to disclose, reveal; *wares* to cry, hawk, advertise verbally; *merits etc* to praise publicly, proclaim (for all to hear).
pregonero *nm* town crier.
preguerra *nf* prewar period; **el nivel de la —** the prewar level; **en la —** in the prewar period, before the war.
pregunta *nf* question; **— capciosa** catch question, loaded question; **— retórica** rhetorical question; **andar (*or* estar) a la cuarta —** (*fam*) to be broke (*fam*); **contestar a una —** to answer a question; **hacer una —** to ask (*or* put) a question; **estrechar a uno a —s** to press someone closely with questions.

preguntar [1a] **1** *vt* to ask; to question, interrogate; **— algo a uno** to ask someone something; **— si** to ask if, ask whether; **le fue preguntada su edad** he was asked his age; *see* **caber**.
　2 *vi* to ask, inquire; **— por uno** to ask for someone, inquire for someone; **— por la salud de uno** to ask after someone's health, ask about someone's health.
　3 preguntarse *vr* to wonder; **me pregunto si vale la pena** I wonder if it's worth while.
preguntón *adj* inquisitive.
prehistoria *nf* prehistory.
prehistórico *adj* prehistoric.
preignición *nf* preignition.
prejuiciado *adj* (*SAm: angl*) prejudiced (*contra* against).
prejuicio *nm* (a) prejudgement. (b) (*pej*) prejudice, bias (*contra* against); preconception.
prejuzgar [1h] *vt* to prejudge.
prelación *nf* priority.
prelado *nm* prelate.
preliminar 1 *adj* preliminary. **2** *nm* preliminary.
preludio *nm* (a) (*Mus and fig*) prelude (*de* to). (b) (*Mus*) tuning up, practice notes, scales.
preludir [1b] **1** *vt* to announce, herald; to introduce; to start off. **2** *vi* (*Mus*) to tune up, play a few scales.
premarital *adj* premarital.
prematuramente *adv* prematurely.
prematuro *adj* premature.
premeditación *nf* premeditation; **con —** with premeditation, deliberately.
premeditadamente *adv* with premeditation, deliberately.
premeditado *adj* premeditated, deliberate; wilful; *insult etc* studied.
premeditar [1a] *vt* to premeditate; to plan, think out (in advance).
premiado 1 *adj* *novel etc* prize (*attr*), prize-winning. **2** *nm*, **premiada** *nf* prizewinner.
premiar [1b] *vt* to reward (*con* with); to give a prize to, make an award to; **salir premiado** to win a prize.
premio *nm* (a) reward, recompense; **como — a sus servicios** as a reward for his services.
　(b) (*in competition*) prize; award; **— de consolación** consolation prize; **— extraordinario** award (*of a degree etc*) with special distinction; **— gordo** first prize, big prize.
　(c) (*Comm, Fin*) premium; **a —** at a premium.
premioso *adj* (a) *dress etc* tight.
　(b) *order etc* strict.
　(c) *person* tongue-tied, slow of speech; slow in writing; slow in movement, heavy, awkward.
　(d) (*fig*) troublesome.
premisa *nf* premise.
premonición *nf* premonition.
premonitorio *adj* indicative, warning.
premunirse [3a] *vr* (*SAm*) = **precaverse**.
premura *nf* (a) pressure; **con — de tiempo** under (time) pressure, with very little time; **debido a — de espacio** because of pressure on space.
　(b) haste, urgency.
prenatal *adj* antenatal, prenatal.
prenda *nf* (a) pledge; (*fig*) pledge, token; **dejar algo en —** to pawn something; to leave something as security; **en — de** as a pledge of, as a token of; **no doler —s** to make a promise without conditions; to spare no effort (*or* expense *etc*); **a mí no me duelen —s** I don't mind saying nice things about others, it doesn't worry me that I'm not as good as others; **no soltar —** to give nothing away, avoid committing oneself; to give someone no chance (*or* opening).
　(b) (*also — de vestir*) garment, article of clothing; **— interior** undergarment, piece of underclothing; **—s de cama** bedclothes; **—s de mesa** table linen.
　(c) **—s** (*fig*) talents, gifts; (*also* **buenas —s**) good qualities.
　(d) **—s** (*game*) forfeits.
　(e) (*esp SAm*) jewel.
　(f) (*in direct address*) darling!, my treasure!
　(g) (*RPl*) **la —** one's sweetheart, one's lover.
prendar [1a] **1** *vt* to captivate, enchant; to win over; **volvió prendado con (*or* de) la ciudad** he came back enchanted with the town.
　2 prendarse *vr*: **— de** to be captivated by, be enchanted with; to take a fancy to; **— de uno** to fall in love with someone.
prendedera *nf* (*Col*) waitress.
prendedero *nm*, **prendedor** *nm* clasp, brooch.
prender [2a] **1** *vt* (a) *person* to catch, capture; to arrest.
　(b) (*Sew etc*) to fasten; to pin, attach (*en* to); to

tie, do up; — **el pelo con horquillas** to fix one's hair with grips, put grips in one's hair.

(c) (*esp SAm*) *fire, oven etc* to light; *match* to strike; *light* to switch on; *cigarette, candle* to light; *room* to light up.

2 *vi* (a) to catch, stick; to grip; **el ancla prendió en el fondo** the anchor buried itself in the seabed, the anchor gripped firmly.

(b) (*of fire*) to catch; (*of injection*) to take; (*of plant*) to take, take root; **el mal prendió más en la juventud** the evil spread most among young people, the evil infected youth most strongly.

3 prenderse *vr* (a) to catch fire (*en* on).

(b) (*woman*) to dress up.

prendería *nf* secondhand (clothes) shop; pawnbroker's (shop).

prendero *nm* secondhand (clothes) dealer, junk dealer; pawnbroker.

prendido 1 *adj*: **quedar** — to be caught (fast), be stuck; (*fig*) to be captivated. **2** *nm* clip, brooch.

prendimiento *nm* (a) capture, seizure; arrest. (b) (*Chi*) constipation.

prensa *nf* (a) (*Mech*) press; (*Mech*) gland, stuffing box; (*Typ*) press, printing press; (*of racquet*) press, frame; — **de copiar** printing frame; — **hidráulica** hydraulic press; — **de ropa** linen press, clothes press; — **rotativa** rotary press.

(b) (*fig*) **la P—** the press; **aprobar un libro para la** — to pass a book for (the) press; **dar algo a la** — to publish something; **entrar en** — to go to press; **estar en** — to be in press; **tener mala** — to have (or get) a bad press; **"libros en —"** (*advert*) "books in press", "forthcoming publications".

prensado *nm* sheen, shine, gloss.

prensador *nm* press, pressing machine; — **de paja** (*Agr*) straw baler.

prensaestopas *nm*, *pl* **prensaestopas** (*Mech*) packing gland.

prensalimones *nm*, *pl* **prensalimones** lemon squeezer.

prensar [1a] *vt* to press.

prensil *adj* prehensile.

preñada *adj* pregnant; (*Zool*) pregnant, with young.

preñado 1 *adj* (*fig*) (a) *wall* bulging, sagging.

(b) — **de** pregnant with, full of; **una situación preñada de peligros** a situation full of danger, a situation fraught with dangers; **ojos** —**s de lágrimas** eyes filled with tears, eyes brimming with tears.

2 *nm* pregnancy.

preñar [1a] *vt* (*fam*) to get pregnant; (*Zool*) to impregnate, fertilize.

preñez *nf* pregnancy.

preocupación *nf* (a) worry, anxiety, concern, preoccupation.

(b) prejudice.

(c) preconception; unfounded fear, silly fear; notion, silly idea; **tiene la** — **de que su mujer le es infiel** he has the silly idea that his wife is unfaithful to him.

(d) (*SAm*) special consideration, priority, preference.

preocupado *adj* worried, anxious, concerned, preoccupied.

preocupar [1a] **1** *vt* (a) to worry, preoccupy; to bother, exercise; **esto me preocupa muchísimo** this worries me greatly; **me preocupa cómo decírselo** it bothers me to know how to tell him; **no le preocupa el qué dirán** public opinion doesn't bother him.

(b) to prejudice, influence.

2 preocuparse *vr* (a) to worry, care (*de, por* about); to concern oneself (*de* about); **¡no se preocupe!** don't worry!, don't bother!; **no te preocupes por eso** don't worry about that; **no se preocupa en lo más mínimo** he doesn't care in the least.

(b) **yo me preocuparé de que esté listo** I'll see to it that everything is ready; **tú preocúpate de que todo esté listo** you ensure that (*or* see to it that) everything is ready.

(c) (*SAm*) — **de algo** to give special attention to something, give something priority.

preparación *nf* (a) (*act*) preparation; **estar en** — to be in preparation.

(b) (*state*) preparedness, readiness; — **militar** military preparedness.

(c) training (*also Sport*); **le falta** — **matemática** he lacks mathematical training, he is not trained in maths.

(d) (*Bio, Pharm*) preparation.

preparado 1 *adj* prepared (*para* for); (*Cook*) ready to serve, ready cooked; **¡**—**s, listos, ya!** ready, steady, go!

2 *nm* (*Pharm*) preparation.

preparador *nm* (*Sport*) trainer, coach; (*of horse*) trainer.

preparar [1a] **1** *vt* (a) to prepare, get ready; (*Tech*) to prepare, process, treat.

(b) to teach, train; (*Sport*) to train, coach; **X le prepara a Y de física** X is coaching Y in physics.

2 prepararse *vr* (a) to prepare, prepare oneself, get ready; — **a** + *infin*, — **para** + *infin* to prepare to + *infin*, get ready to + *infin*.

(b) (*storm, trouble etc*) to be brewing.

preparativo 1 *adj* preparatory, preliminary.

2 —**s** *nmpl* preparations; preliminaries; **hacer sus** —**s** to make one's preparations (*para* + *infin* to + *infin*).

preparatorio *adj* preparatory.

preponderancia *nf* preponderance; superiority.

preponderante *adj* preponderant; superior.

preponderar [1a] *vi* to preponderate; to dominate, prevail.

preposición *nf* preposition.

preposicional *adj* prepositional.

prepucio *nm* foreskin, prepuce.

prerrogativa *nf* prerogative, right, privilege.

presa *nf* (a) (*act*) capture, seizure; **hacer** — to seize.

(b) clutch, hold; — **de pie** foothold; **hacer** — **en** to clutch (on to), seize; to get a hold on; **el fuego hizo** — **en la cortina** the fire set light to (*or* caught, began to burn) the curtain.

(c) (*object*) capture, catch, prize; (*Mil*) spoils, booty; loot; (*Naut*) prize; (*Orn*) prey; (*Zool*) prey, catch; **ave de** — bird of prey; **ser** — **de** (*fig*) to be a prey to, be a victim of.

(d) (*Orn*) claw; (*Zool*) tusk, fang.

(e) (*in river etc*) dam; weir, barrage.

(f) (*Agr*) ditch, channel.

(g) (*esp SAm*) piece of food, piece of meat (*esp* chicken).

presagiar [1b] *vt* to betoken, forebode, presage.

presagio *nm* omen, portent.

presbicia *nf* long-sightedness.

presbiopía *nf* presbyopia.

présbita *adj*, **présbite** *adj* long-sighted.

presbiteriano 1 *adj* Presbyterian. **2** *nm*, **presbiteriana** *nf* Presbyterian.

presbiterio *nm* presbytery, chancel.

presbítero *nm* priest.

presciencia *nf* prescience, foreknowledge.

presciente *adj* prescient.

prescindencia *nf* (*SAm*) doing without, going without; non-participation (in a dispute).

prescindente *adj* (*SAm*) non-participating.

prescindible *adj* dispensable; expendable; **y cosas fácilmente** —**s** and things we can easily do without.

prescindir [3a] *vi*: — **de** to do without, go without; to dispense with, get rid of; to disregard; to omit, overlook; **han prescindido del coche** they've given up their car, they've got rid of their car; **no podemos** — **de él** we can't manage without him; **prescindamos de todo aquello** let's forget about all that, let's leave all that aside.

prescribir [3a; *ptp* **prescrito**] *vt* to prescribe.

prescripción *nf* prescription; — **facultativa** medical prescription.

prescrito *adj* prescribed.

presea *nf* jewel; treasure, precious thing.

preselección *nf* (*Sport*) seeding.

preseleccionar [1a] *vt* (*Sport*) to seed.

presencia *nf* (*all senses*) presence; — **de ánimo** presence of mind; **en** — **de** in the presence of; **tener** (**buena**) — to have a good presence, be impressive, have an impressive bearing.

presencial *adj*: **testigo** — eyewitness.

presenciar [1b] *vt* to be present at; to attend; to see, witness, watch.

presentable *adj* presentable.

presentación *nf* (a) presentation; introduction; — **en** (**la**) **sociedad** coming-out, début. (b) (*SAm*) petition.

presentador *nm* (*TV etc*) compère.

presentar [1a] **1** *vt* (a) (*general sense*) to present; to offer; to show, display; *arms, excuse, petition, proof etc* to present; *resignation* to tender; *motion* to propose, put forward; **presenta señales de deterioro** it shows signs of wear; **el coche presenta ciertas modificaciones** the car has certain modifications.

(b) *play* to perform, put on; *film* to show; *star* to present, feature.

(c) *person* to introduce; **le presento a Vd a mi hermana** may I introduce my sister to you?; **ser presentada en** (**la**) **sociedad** to come out, make one's début.

2 presentarse *vr* (a) to present oneself; to appear

(unexpectedly), turn up; — **a la policía** to report to the police, (*criminal*) give oneself up to the police; **hay que — el lunes a las 9** you should report at 9 on Monday; **se presentó en un estado lamentable** he turned up in a dreadful state.

(b) to introduce oneself (*a* to); — **en (la) sociedad** to come out, make one's début.

(c) (*as candidate*) to run, stand; — **a** *post* to put in for, apply for; — **para** *exam* to sit (for), enter for.

(d) to present itself; to show, appear; **el día se presenta muy hermoso** it looks like being a lovely day, there are prospects of a fine day; **se presentó un caso singular** a strange case came up.

presente 1 *adj* (a) *person* present; **¡—!** present!, here!; **los —s** those present; **los señores aquí —s** the gentlemen here present; **estar — en** to be present at; **mejorando lo —, salvando a los —s** present company excepted.

(b) **la — carta, la —** this letter.

(c) *time, tense* present; **hacer —** to state, declare; **tener — to** remember, bear in mind; **ten —s a nosotros** don't forget us; **ten muy — que . . .** be sure to remember that . . .; understand clearly that . . .

2 *nm* (a) present; **al —** at present; **hasta el —** up to the present.

(b) (*Gram*) present (tense).

presentimiento *nm* premonition, presentiment; foreboding.

presentir [3i] *vt* to have a premonition of; **— que . . .** to have a premonition that . . .

preservación *nf* protection, preservation.

preservar [1a] *vt* (a) to protect, preserve (*contra* against, *de* from). (b) (*SAm*: *angl*) to keep, preserve.

presidencia *nf* presidency; chairmanship; **ocupar la —** to preside, be in (*or* take) the chair.

presidencial *adj* presidential.

presidente *nm* (*Pol, of association, Taur etc*) president; (*of committee, meeting*) chairman; (*Parl*) speaker; (*Law*) presiding magistrate (*etc*).

presidiario *nm* convict.

presidio *nm* (a) prison, penitentiary; **echar a uno a —** to put someone in prison.

(b) hard labour, penal servitude.

(c) (*Pol*) praesidium.

(d) (*Mil*) garrison; fortress.

presidir [3a] **1** *vt* (a) to preside at, preside over; to take the chair at.

(b) (*fig*) to dominate, rule, be the dominant element in.

2 *vi* to preside; to take the chair.

presilla *nf* (a) fastener, clip. (b) loop. (c) (*SAm*) shoulder badge, flash; (*Mex*) epaulette.

presión *nf* (a) pressure; (*with hand etc*) press, squeeze; (*Meteorol, Phys, Tech*) pressure; (*of explosion*) blast; **— arterial, — sanguínea** blood pressure; **— atmosférica** atmospheric pressure, air pressure; **a — under** pressure; **de —** (*Tech*) pressure (*attr*); **hacer —** to press (*sobre* on).

(b) (*fig*) pressure; **ejercer** (*or* **hacer**) **— para que se haga algo** to press for something to be done; **hay —es dentro del partido** there are pressures within the party.

presionar [1a] **1** *vt* (a) *button etc* to press.

(b) (*fig*) to press, put pressure on; **el ministro, presionado por los fabricantes, accedió** the minister, under pressure from the manufacturers, agreed.

2 *vi* to press; **— para, — por** to press for; **— para que sea permitido algo** to press for something to be granted.

preso 1 *ptp of* **prender**; **llevar — a uno** to take someone away under arrest; **estar — de un terror pánico** to be panic-stricken.

2 *nm*, **presa** *nf* convict, prisoner.

prestación *nf* (a) lending, loan; **— de ayuda** giving of help; **— personal** obligatory service (*of individual on communal work*).

(b) **— de juramento** oath-taking, swearing.

prestado *adj*: **dar algo —** to lend something; **eso está —** that is on loan; **pedir — algo, tomar — algo** to borrow something; **vivir de —** to live at someone else's expense, live on what one can borrow.

prestador *nm*, **prestadora** *nf* lender.

prestamista *nm* moneylender; pawnbroker.

préstamo *nm* (a) (*act*) loan, lending, borrowing. (b) loan. (c) (*Ling*) loanword.

prestancia *nf* distinction, excellence; elegance, dignity.

prestar [1a] **1** *vt* (a) *money etc* to lend, loan.

(b) (*fig*) to lend, give; *help, support* to give; *attention* to pay (*a* to); *service* to do, render; *enchantment etc* to lend.

(c) *oath* to take, swear.

(d) (*SAm*) to borrow (*a* from).

(e) (*Arg, Ven*) to do good to, be good for; to suit; **no le prestó el viaje** the trip was not good for him.

2 *vi* (a) to give, stretch.

(b) **— para** to be big enough for.

3 prestarse *vr* (a) **no se presta a esas maniobras** he does not lend himself to manoeuvres of that kind; **la situación se presta a muchas interpretaciones** the situation lends itself to many interpretations.

(b) **— a + infin** to offer to **+ infin**, volunteer to **+ infin**.

prestatario *nm*, **prestataria** *nf* borrower.

presteza *nf* speed, promptness; alacrity; **con —** promptly, with alacrity.

prestidigitación *nf* conjuring, juggling; sleight of hand.

prestidigitador *nm* conjurer, juggler.

prestigiado *adj* (*SAm*) worthy, estimable, prestigious.

prestigiar [1b] *vt* to give prestige to; to make famous; to honour (*con* with).

prestigio *nm* (a) prestige; face; good name. (b) (*magic*) spell. (c) trick.

prestigioso *adj* worthy, estimable, prestigious; reputable; famous.

prestímano *nm* conjurer, juggler.

presto 1 *adj* (a) quick, prompt. (b) ready (*para* for). (c) (*Mus*) presto. **2** *adv* quickly; at once, right away.

presumible *adj* presumable; probable; **es — it** is to be presumed.

presumido *adj* conceited.

presumir [3a] **1** *vt* (a) to presume, conjecture, surmise; **— que . . .** to presume that . . ., guess that . . .

(b) (*Arg, Bol*) to court; to flirt with.

2 *vi* (a) **según cabe —** as may be presumed, presumably.

(b) to be conceited; to give oneself airs, swank (*fam*), show off; **para — ante las amistades** in order to show off before one's friends; **no presumas tanto** don't be so conceited; **— de listo** to think oneself very smart, boast of being clever; **— de experto** to pride oneself on being an expert; **— demasiado de las fuerzas** to overestimate one's strength.

presunción *nf* (a) supposition, presumption; (*pej*) suspicion. (b) (*quality*) conceit, presumption; pretentiousness.

presunto *adj* supposed, presumed; so-called; *heir* presumptive; **el — asesino** the alleged murderer; **estos —s expertos** these so-called experts.

presuntuosamente *adv* conceitedly, presumptuously; pretentiously.

presuntuoso *adj* conceited, presumptuous; pretentious.

presuponer [2r] *vt* to presuppose.

presuposición *nf* presupposition.

presupuestal *adj* (*Mex etc*) budgetary, budget (*attr*).

presupuestar [1a] *vt* to budget for; to reckon up, estimate for.

presupuestario *adj* budgetary, budget (*attr*).

presupuestívoro *nm* (*SAm*: *hum, pej*) public employee.

presupuesto *nm* (*Fin*) budget; (*for job, plan etc*) estimate.

presurosamente *adv* quickly, promptly; hastily.

presuroso *adj* quick, prompt, speedy; hasty; *step etc* light, quick.

pretal *nm* (*esp SAm*) strap, girth.

pretencioso *adj* (a) pretentious, presumptuous; showy. (b) (*SAm*) vain, boastful.

pretender [2a] *vt* (a) **— + infin** to try to **+ infin**, seek to **+ infin**, endeavour to **+ infin**; **pretendió convencerme** he sought to convince me; **han pretendido robarme** they have attempted to rob me; **¿qué pretende Vd decir con eso?** what do you mean by that?; **no pretendo ser feliz** it's not happiness I'm after.

(b) to claim; **— ser rico** to claim to be rich, profess to be rich; **— haber hecho algo** to claim to have done something; **el libro pretende ser importante** the book tries to look (*or* make out that it is) important; **esto pretende poder curarlo todo** this purports to cure everything; **pretende que el coche le atropelló** he alleges that the car knocked him down.

(c) to seek, try for; *post* to apply for; *honour* to aspire to; *objective* to aim at, try to achieve; **¿qué pretende Vd?** what are you after?; what do you hope to achieve?

(d) **— que + subj** to expect that . . ., suggest that . . ., intend that . . .; **él pretende que yo le**

escriba he suggests that I should write to him, he wants me to write to him; ¿**cómo pretende Vd que lo compre yo?** how do you expect me to buy it?

(e) *woman* to woo, court; to seek the hand of.

pretendido *adj* supposed, pretended; alleged.

pretendiente 1 *nm* suitor. **2** *nm,* **pretendienta** *nf* claimant; (*for post*) candidate, applicant (*a* for); (*royal*) pretender (*a* to).

pretensado *adj* prestressed.

pretensión *nf* (a) claim.

(b) aim, object; aspiration.

(c) (*pej*) pretension; exaggerated claim, false claim; **tener —es de** to have pretensions to, lay claim to; **tener pocas —es** to be undemanding, be content with very little; **tiene la — de que le acompañe yo** he expects me to go with him, he says unreasonably that I ought to go with him.

(d) (*SAm*) vanity; presumption.

pretensioso *adj* (*SAm*) = **pretencioso** (b).

pretérito 1 *adj* (a) (*Gram*) past. (b) past, former; **las glorias pretéritas del país** the country's former glories. **2** *nm* preterite, past historic.

preternatural *adj* preternatural.

pretextar [1a] *vt* to plead, use as an excuse; **— que . . .** to plead that . . ., allege that . . .

pretexto *nm* pretext; excuse, plea; **a — de** on the pretext of; **so — de** under pretext of.

pretil *nm* (a) parapet; handrail, guardrail, railing.

(b) (*Ec*) forecourt; (*Mex, Ven*) bench; (*Mex*) kerb.

pretina *nf* girdle, belt, waistband; (*Arg, Col, Urug*) leather strap; (*Cu*) trouser fly.

preuniversitario 1 *adj* pre-university; **curso — course** taken between the end of one's school career and beginning of university studies.

2 *nm,* **preuniversitaria** *nf* student on a pre-university course.

prevalecer [2d] *vi* (a) to prevail (*sobre* against, over); to triumph, win through; to come to dominate.

(b) (*Bot*) to take root and grow.

prevaleciente *adj* prevailing, prevalent; dominant.

prevalerse [2q] *vr:* **— de** to avail oneself of; (*pej*) to take advantage of.

prevención *nf* (a) preparation; (*state*) preparedness, readiness; **las —es para la ceremonia** the preparations for the ceremony.

(b) prevention.

(c) (*quality*) foresight, forethought; **obrar con —** to act with foresight.

(d) precaution; precautionary measure, safety measure; **de —** spare, reserve, emergency (*attr*); **hemos tomado ciertas —es** we have taken certain precautions.

(e) prejudice; **tener — contra uno** to have a prejudice against someone, be prejudiced against someone.

(f) police station; (*Mil*) guardroom, guardhouse.

prevenido *adj* (a) **ser —** to be cautious; to be far-sighted.

(b) **estar —** to be prepared, be ready; to be forewarned, be on one's guard (*contra* against); **hombre — vale por dos** forewarned is forearmed.

prevenir [3s] **1** *vt* (a) to prepare, get ready, make ready (*para* for).

(b) **— a uno de algo** to provide someone with something.

(c) to prevent; to alert; to forestall; **hay accidentes que no se pueden —** some accidents cannot be prevented.

(d) **— a uno** to warn someone, forewarn someone, put someone on his guard (*contra* against, *de* about); **pudieron —le a tiempo** they were able to warn him in time.

(e) to foresee, anticipate; to provide for.

(f) to prejudice, bias (*a favor de* in favour of, *en contra de* against).

2 prevenirse *vr* (a) to get ready, prepare; **— para un viaje** to get ready for a trip; **— de ropa adecuada** to provide oneself with suitable clothing.

(b) **— contra** to take precautions against, prepare for.

(c) **— en contra de uno** to take up a hostile attitude to someone.

preventivo *adj* preventive, precautionary; (*Med*) preventive.

prever [2v] *vt* (a) to foresee.

(b) to anticipate, envisage, visualize; **— que . . .** to anticipate that . . ., envisage that . . ., expect that . . .; **ya lo preveía** I expected as much.

previamente *adv* previously.

previo 1 *adj* previous, prior, earlier; *exam* preliminary.

2 *as prep* after, following; **— acuerdo de los otros**

subject to the agreement of the others; **— pago de los derechos** on payment of the fees.

3 *nm* (*Cine*) playback.

previsible *adj* foreseeable.

previsión *nf* (a) (*quality*) foresight, far-sightedness; caution.

(b) (*act*) precaution, precautionary measure; **en — de** as a precaution against.

(c) **— social** social security.

(d) forecast; **— del tiempo** weather forecast(ing); **las —es del plan quinquenal** the forecasts of the five-year plan.

previsivo *adj* (*Mex*) = **previsor**.

previsor *adj* far-sighted; thoughtful.

prez *nf* honour, glory.

prieto *adj* (a) blackish, dark; (*SAm*) dark, swarthy; *woman* brunette.

(b) *person* mean.

(c) tight, compressed, tightly packed; **un siglo — de historia** a century packed full of history, a century rich in history.

prietuzco *adj* (*Ant, CAm, Mex*) blackish.

prima *nf* (a) (*female*) cousin.

(b) (*on wages etc*) bonus, extra payment; (*insurance*) premium; (*on exports etc*) subsidy; **— de incentivo** incentive bonus; **— por rendimiento** output bonus; **— por trabajos peligrosos** danger money.

(c) (*Eccl*) prime.

(d) (*RPl*) **bajar la —** to moderate one's language; **subir la —** to use strong language.

primacía *nf* (a) primacy, first place; priority; supremacy; **— de paso** (*Aut*) priority, right of way; **tener la — entre** to be supreme among.

(b) (*Eccl*) primacy.

primada *nf* (*fam*) (a) piece of stupidity; silly mistake.

(b) trick, hoax.

primado *nm* (*Eccl*) primate.

primadon(n)a *nf* prima donna.

primal 1 *adj* yearling. **2** *nm,* **primala** *nf* yearling.

primar [1a] *vi* to occupy first place, be supreme; **— sobre** to have priority over, take precedence over; to outweigh.

primariamente *adv* primarily.

primario *adj* primary.

primate *nm* (a) (*Zool*) primate. (b) important person, outstanding figure.

primavera 1 *nf* (a) spring; springtime (*also fig*). (b) (*Orn*) blue tit. (c) (*Bot*) primrose. **2** *nm* (*fam*): **ser un —** to be a simple soul.

primaveral *adj* spring (*attr*); springlike.

primer *adj see* **primero**.

primera *nf* (a) (*Aut etc*) first gear, bottom gear.

(b) (*Rail*) first class; **viajar en —** to travel first.

(c) (*fam*) **de —** first-class, first-rate; **comer de —** to eat really well, have a first-class meal; **estar de —** to feel fine.

(d) (*Comm*) **— de cambio** first of exchange; *see* **cambio** (c).

primeramente *adv* first, firstly; chiefly.

primerear [1a] *vi* (*RPl*) to land the first blow, get in first.

primerizo 1 *adj* green, inexperienced. **2** *nm,* **primeriza** *nf* novice, beginner.

primero 1 *adj* (**primer** *before m sing noun*) (a) first; former; *page* first, front; **en los —s años del siglo** in the early years of the century; **en los —s años treinta** in the early thirties; **a —s de siglo** at the start of the century, early in the century; **llegar el —** to arrive first; **ser el — en + *infin*** to be the first to + *infin*.

(b) (*fig*) first; prime; basic, fundamental; urgent; *material* raw; **lo — es que . . .** the fundamental thing is that . . .; **es nuestro primer deber** it is our first duty; **es el primer país en estos estudios** it is the foremost country in these studies.

2 *adv* (a) first.

(b) rather, sooner; **— se quedará en casa que pedir permiso para salir** she'd rather stay at home than have to ask for permission to go out; **¡— morir!** we'd rather die!

primicias *nfpl* (a) first fruits. (b) (*fig*) first fruits, first effort, first attempt.

primitivamente *adv* (a) at first; originally. (b) primitively, in a primitive way.

primitivo *adj* (a) early; first, original; **el texto —** the original text; **quedan 200 de los — 850** there remain 200 from the original 850; **es una obra primitiva** it is an early work; **devolver algo a su estado —** to restore something to its original state.

(b) *colour* primary.

(c) (*Fin*) *share* ordinary.

(d) (*Hist etc*) primitive; uncivilized; **en condiciones primitivas** in primitive conditions.

primo 1 adj (a) (Math) prime.
(b) material raw.
2 nm (a) cousin; — **carnal**, — **hermano** first cousin; **ser** —**s carnales** (fig) to be extraordinarily alike, be very closely related.
(b) (fam) fool; dupe, sucker (sl); **hacer el** — to be easily taken in, be taken for a sucker (sl); to carry the can (sl).
primogénito adj first-born.
primogenitura nf primogeniture; birthright.
primor nm (a) exquisiteness, beauty; elegance; delicacy.
(b) care, skill; **hecho con** — done most skilfully, delicately made.
(c) fine thing, lovely thing; **hace** —**es con la aguja** she makes lovely things with her needlework; **cose que es un** — she sews beautifully, she sews in a way that is a delight to see; **hijos que son un** — delightful children, charming children.
primordial adj basic, fundamental, essential; **es de interés** — it is of fundamental concern; **es** — **saberlo** it is essential to know it.
primordialmente adv basically, fundamentally.
primorosamente adv exquisitely, delicately, elegantly; neatly, skilfully.
primoroso adj exquisite, fine, delicate, elegant; neat, skilful.
princesa nf princess.
principado nm principality.
principal 1 adj (a) principal, chief, main; foremost; floor first, second (US); **lo** — **es** . . . the main thing is to . . .
(b) person illustrious.
2 nm (a) (person) head, chief, principal.
(b) (Fin) principal, capital.
(c) (Theat) dress circle.
principalmente adv principally, chiefly, mainly.
príncipe nm (a) prince; — **consorte** prince consort; — **encantador** Prince Charming; — **heredero** crown prince. (b) see **edición**.
principesco adj princely.
principiante 1 adj who is beginning; novice; inexperienced, green. **2** nm, **principianta** nf beginner; learner; novice.
principiar [1b] vti to begin; — **a** + infin to begin to + infin, begin + ger; — **con** to begin with.
principio nm (a) beginning, start; origin; early stage; **al** — at first, in the beginning; **a** —**s de** at the beginning of; **a** —**s del verano** at the beginning of the summer, early in the summer; **desde el** — from the first; **desde el** — **hasta el fin** from start to finish, from beginning to end; **en un** — at first; **dar** — **a** to start off; **tener** (or **tomar**) — **en** to start from, be based on.
(b) —**s** (of subject) rudiments, first notions; "**P**—**s de física**" "Introduction to Physics", "Outline of Physics".
(c) (moral) principle; **persona de** —**s** man of principles; **en** — in principle; **por** — on principle; **es inmoral por** — it is immoral in principle; **sin** —**s** unprincipled.
(d) (Philos) principle; (Chem) element, constituent.
(e) (Cook) entrée.
principote nm (fam) swank (fam), show-off (fam); parvenu, social climber.
pringar [1h] **1** vt (a) (Cook) to dip in fat (etc); roast to baste; — **el pan en la sopa** to dip one's bread in the soup.
(b) to dirty, soil (with grease); to splash grease (or fat) on; (esp SAm) to splash.
(c) (fam) — **a uno** to wound someone, make someone bleed.
(d) (fam) to blacken, run down.
(e) (fam) — **a uno en un asunto** to involve someone in a matter.
(f) (Chi) disease to give.
(g) (Chi) woman to put in the family way.
(h) (sl) —**las** to peg out (sl).
2 vi (a) (fam) to take a beating, lose badly; to come a cropper (fam); **hemos pringado** we're done for.
(b) (Mil etc) to sweat one's guts out (fam).
(c) (fam) — **en** to dabble in; to take a hand in, get mixed up in.
(d) (CAm, Mex, Ven) to drizzle.
3 pringarse vr (a) to get splashed, get soiled (con, de with).
(b) (fam) = **2** (c).
(c) (fam) to make money on the side; to get a rake-off (fam); to make a packet (fam).
pringo nm (SAm) drop (of liquid); **con un** — **de leche** with a drop of milk.

pringón 1 adj dirty, greasy. **2** nm (a) grease stain, grease spot. (b) (fam) rake-off (fam); packet (fam).
pringoso adj greasy.
pringue nm (sometimes f) (a) grease, fat, dripping.
(b) grease stain, grease spot; (any) dirty object, sticky thing.
(c) (fam) nuisance; cause of trouble; **es un** — **tener que** . . . it's a bind having to . . . (sl).
(d) (CAm, Mex) drop (of liquid); (Mex, Nic) splash (of mud etc); (Ec) burn.
prior nm prior.
priora nf, **prioresa** nf prioress.
priorato nm priory.
prioridad nf priority; seniority, greater age; **tener** — to have priority (sobre over).
prioritario adj prior, priority (attr); **un proyecto de carácter** — a plan with top priority, a plan in the priority class.
prisa nf hurry, haste; speed; (sense of) urgency; **temporada de más** —(s) rush period, busy period; **a** —, **de** — quickly, hurriedly; **a toda** — as quickly as possible; **estar de** — to be in a hurry; **voy con mucha** — I'm in a great hurry; **correr** — to be urgent; **¿te corre** —? are you in a hurry?; **¿corren** — **estas cartas?** are these letters urgent?, is there any hurry for these letters?; **dar** — **a uno, meter** — **a uno** to make someone get a move on; **darse** — to hurry (up); **¡date** —! hurry (up)!, come along!; **tener** — to be in a hurry.
prisco nm (esp SAm) apricot.
prisión nf (a) prison. (b) imprisonment; **cinco años de** — five years' imprisonment, prison sentence of five years. (c) —**es** shackles, fetters.
prisionero nm prisoner (of war); **hacer** — **a uno** to take someone prisoner.
prisma nm prism.
prismático 1 adj prismatic. **2** —**s** nmpl binoculars, field glasses.
prístino adj pristine, original.
privación nf (a) (act) deprivation, deprival; **sufrir** — **de libertad** to suffer loss of liberty. (b) (state) deprivation; want, privation; —**es** hardships, privations.
privadamente adv privately.
privado 1 adj (a) private; personal; " — **y confidencial**" "private and confidential".
(b) (SAm) mad, senseless; (Ven) weak, faint.
2 nm (a) (Pol) favourite, protégé; (Hist) royal favourite, chief minister.
(b) **en** — privately, in private.
privanza nf favour; **durante la** — **de Lerma** when Lerma was royal favourite, when Lerma was chief minister.
privar [1a] **1** vt (a) — **a uno de algo** to deprive someone of something, take something away from someone; — **a uno del conocimiento** to render someone unconscious; **le privaron del carnet de conducir** they suspended his driving licence, they took away his driving licence; **nos vemos privados de** . . . we find ourselves without . . ., we find ourselves bereft of . . .
(b) — **a uno de** + infin to forbid someone to + infin, prevent someone from + ger; **lo cual me privó de verlos** which prevented me from seeing them; **no me prives de verte** don't forbid me to come to see you, don't tell me not to come again.
(c) to delight, overwhelm.
2 vi (a) (Pol) to be in favour (at court).
(b) to obtain, be present; to prevail; (fam) to be in fashion, be the thing; **la cualidad que más priva entre ellos** the quality which is most strongly present in them; **en ese período privaba la minifalda** at that time miniskirts were in (fam).
3 privarse vr: — **de** to deprive oneself of; to give up, go without, forgo; **no se privan de nada** they lack nothing, they have everything they want.
privativo adj exclusive; — **de** exclusive to; **esa función es privativa del presidente** that function is the president's alone; **la planta es privativa del Brasil** the plant is peculiar to Brazil, the plant is restricted to Brazil.
privilegiado 1 adj privileged; memory etc exceptionally good. **2** nm, **privilegiada** nf privileged person; **los** —**s** the privileged.
privilegiar [1b] vt to grant a privilege to; to favour.
privilegio nm privilege; concession; immunity, exemption; (Law) sole right; (Lit) copyright; — **fiscal** tax concession; — **de invención** patent.
pro 1 nm and f profit, advantage; **hombre de** — worthy man, honest man; **los** —**s y los contras** the pros and the cons, for and against; **buena** — **le haga** and much good may it do him; **en** — **de** for, on behalf of; for the benefit of.

2 *prep* for, on behalf of; **campaña — paz** peace campaign; **asociación — ciegos** association for (aid to) the blind.

pro . . . pro- . . ., *eg* **prosoviético** pro-Soviet.

proa *nf* (*Naut*) bow, bows; prow; (*Aer*) nose; **de —** bow (*attr*), fore; **en la —** in the bows; **poner la — a** (*Naut*) to head for, set a course for; (*fig*) to aim at; **poner — a la tempestad** to ride out the storm (*also fig*); **poner la — a uno** to take a stand against someone.

probabilidad *nf* (**a**) probability, likelihood; **según toda —** in all probability.
   (**b**) chance, prospect; **—es** chances; **—es de vida** expectation of life; **hay pocas —es de que venga** there is little prospect of his coming; **apenas tiene —es** he hasn't much chance.

probable *adj* probable, likely; **es — que + *subj*** it is probable (or likely) that . . .; **es — que no venga** he probably won't come.

probablemente *adv* probably.

probado *adj remedy etc* proven.

probador *nm* (**a**) (*person*) taster (*of wine etc*). (**b**) fitting room. (**c**) (*SAm*) tailor's dummy.

probanza *nf* proof, evidence.

probar [1m] **1** *vt* (**a**) *fact, case etc* to prove; to show, demonstrate; to establish; **— que . . .** to prove that . . .
   (**b**) *apparatus, weapon etc* to test, try (out); *garment* to try on.
   (**c**) *food etc* to try, taste, sample; **prueba un poco de esto** try a bit of this; **no han probado nunca un jerez fino** they have never tasted fine sherry; **no lo pruebo nunca** I never touch it.
   2 *vi* (**a**) to try; **¿probamos?** shall we try?, shall we have a go?; **— a + *infin*** to try to + *infin*.
   (**b**) **— de = 1** (**c**).
   (**c**) to suit; **no me prueba (bien) el café** coffee doesn't agree with me; **le probó mal ese oficio** that trade did not suit him.
   3 probarse *vr*: **— un traje** to try a suit on.

probatorio *adj* (**a**) evidential; **documentos —s del crimen** documents in proof of the crime, documents which prove the crime. (**b**) convincing.

probeta *nf* test tube; graduated cylinder.

probidad *nf* integrity, honesty, rectitude.

problema *nm* problem; puzzle.

problemático *adj* problematic.

probo *adj* honest, upright.

probóscide *nf* proboscis.

procacidad *nf* (**a**) insolence, impudence; brazenness. (**b**) indecency.

procaz *adj* (**a**) insolent, impudent; brazen. (**b**) indecent.

procedencia *nf* (**a**) source, origin; point of departure; (*Naut*) port of origin. (**b**) properness; (*Law*) propriety.

procedente *adj* (**a**) **— de** coming from, proceeding from, originating in. (**b**) reasonable; proper, fitting; (*Law*) proper; duly established.

proceder [2a] **1** *vi* (**a**) to proceed; **— a una elección** to proceed to an election; **— contra uno** (*Law*) to take proceedings against someone.
   (**b**) **— de** to come from, originate in; to flow from, spring from; **todo esto procede de su negativa** all this springs from his refusal; **estas patatas proceden de Israel** these potatoes come from Israel; **de donde procede que . . .** (from) whence it happens that . . .
   (**c**) to act; to proceed, behave; **ha procedido precipitadamente** he has acted hastily; **conviene — con cuidado** it is best to go carefully.
   (**d**) to be right (and proper), be fitting; **si el caso procede** if the case warrants it; **no procede obrar así** it is not right to act like that; **luego, si procede, . . .** then, if appropriate, . . .
   2 *nm* course of action; behaviour, conduct.

procedimiento *nm* procedure; process; means, method; (*Law*) proceedings; **un — para abaratar el producto** a method of making the product cheaper; **por un — deductivo** by a deductive process.

proceloso *adj* (*lit*) stormy, tempestuous.

prócer *nm* worthy, notable; important person; (*Pol*) great man, leader.

procesado *nm*, **procesada** *nf* accused (person).

procesal *adj* (**a**) (*Parl etc*) procedural. (**b**) (*Law*) *costs etc* legal.

procesar [1a] *vt* to try, put on trial; to prosecute; to sue, bring an action against.

procesión *nf* procession; **la — va por dentro** still waters run deep; there is more in this than meets the eye; **la — le va por dentro** he's a quiet one; he keeps his troubles to himself.

procesional *adj* processional.

proceso *nm* (**a**) process (*also Anat, Chem etc*); **— mental** mental process; **— de datos** data processing; **— de una enfermedad** course (or progress) of a disease.
   (**b**) lapse of time; **en el — de un mes** in the course of a month.
   (**c**) (*Law*) trial; prosecution; action, lawsuit, proceedings; **— verbal** record; **abrir** (*or* **entablar, formar**) **—** to bring a suit (*a* against).

proclama *nf* (**a**) proclamation. (**b**) poster; **— electoral** election poster. (**c**) **—s** (*Eccl*) banns.

proclamación *nf* proclamation.

proclamar [1a] **1** *vt* to proclaim. **2 proclamarse** *vr*: **— rey** to proclaim oneself king.

procreación *nf* procreation, breeding.

procrear [1a] *vti* to procreate, breed.

procura *nf* (*SAm*) obtaining, getting; **andar en — de algo** to be trying to get something.

procuración *nf* (*Law*) power of attorney; proxy.

procurador *nm* (**a**) (*Law*) attorney, (*approx*) solicitor. (**b**) (*Law*) proxy. (**c**) (*Pol*) **— en Cortes, — a Cortes** (*Hist*) deputy, member of (the Spanish) parliament.

procurar [1a] **1** *vt* (**a**) **— + *infin*** to try to + *infin*, endeavour to + *infin*; **procura conservar la calma** do try to keep calm; **procura que no te vean** take care not to let them see you, don't let them see you.
   (**b**) to get, obtain; to secure; to yield, produce; **— un puesto a uno** to get someone a job, find a job for someone; **esto nos procurará grandes beneficios** this will bring us great benefits, this will secure great benefits for us.
   (**c**) **— + *infin*** to manage to + *infin*, succeed in **+ *ger***; **por fin procuró dominarse** eventually he managed to control himself.
   2 procurarse *vr*: **— algo** to secure something for oneself.

Procustes *m*, **Procusto** *m* Procrustes; **lecho de —** Procrustes' bed.

prodigalidad *nf* (**a**) bounty; richness. (**b**) lavishness, generosity. (**c**) (*pej*) prodigality; extravagance, wastefulness.

pródigamente *adv* (**a**) bountifully; richly. (**b**) lavishly. (**c**) (*pej*) prodigally; wastefully.

prodigar [1h] **1** *vt* to lavish, give lavishly; (*pej*) to squander; **prodiga las alabanzas** he is lavish in his praise (*a* of); **nos prodigó sus atenciones** he was very generous in his kindnesses to us.
   2 prodigarse *vr* to be generous with what one has, lay oneself out to please.

prodigio *nm* prodigy; wonder, marvel; **niño — child** prodigy; **es un — de talento** he is wonderfully talented.

prodigiosamente *adv* prodigiously, marvellously.

prodigioso *adj* prodigious, marvellous.

pródigo 1 *adj* (**a**) bountiful; rich; productive; **— en** rich in, generous with; **la pródiga naturaleza** bountiful nature.
   (**b**) lavish, generous (*de* with); **ser — de sus talentos** to be generous in offering one's talents.
   (**c**) (*pej*) prodigal; extravagant, wasteful; **hijo — prodigal son**.
   2 *nm*, **pródiga** *nf* spendthrift, prodigal.

producción *nf* (**a**) production; output; yield; **— en serie** mass production. (**b**) (*object*) product; (*Cine*) production.

producido *nm* (*Arg, Mex*) profit, yield.

producir [3o] **1** *vt* (*in most senses*) to produce; to make; to give, yield; to cause, generate; *change etc* to bring about; *impression* to give, cause; *interest* (*Fin*) to bear; **le produjo gran tristeza** it caused her much sadness; **¿qué impresión le produce?** how does it impress you?, what impression do you get from it?; **Ruritania no produce cohetes** Ruritania does not make rockets; **estos factores produjeron la revolución** these factors caused the revolution; **— en serie** to mass-produce.
   2 producirse *vr* (**a**) to be produced, be made (*etc*).
   (**b**) (*change etc*) to come about; (*difficulty, crisis*) to arise; (*accident*) to happen, take place; (*riot etc*) to break out; **así se produjo la nueva creencia de que . . .** in this way there arose the new belief that . . .; **en ese momento se produjo una explosión** at that moment there was an explosion; **a no ser que se produzca un cambio** unless a change takes place, unless there is a change.

productividad *nf* productivity.

productivo *adj* productive; *business* profitable; **— de interés** *bond etc* that bears interest.

producto *nm* product (*also Math*); production; (*Comm, Fin*) yield, profit; proceeds, revenue; **—s** products, (*Agr*) produce; **—s agrícolas** agricultural produce, farm produce; — **alimenticio** foodstuff; — **bruto** gross (national) product; — **de desecho** waste product; —**s estancados** goods sold by state monopoly; —**s de marca** branded goods; — **secundario** by-product; — **terminado** finished product.

productor 1 *adj* productive, producing; **clase productora** producing class, class of producers; **nación productora** producer nation.

2 *nm*, **productora** *nf* producer (*also Cine*).

produje, produzco *etc see* **producir**.

proemio *nm* preface, introduction.

proeza *nf* (a) exploit, feat, heroic deed. (b) (*Col, Mex*) boast.

profanación *nf* desecration.

profanar [1a] *vt* to desecrate, profane; to defile; — **la memoria de uno** to blacken the memory of someone, slander someone who is dead.

profano 1 *adj* (a) profane, secular.
(b) irreverent.
(c) lay; ignorant.
(d) indecent, immodest.
2 *nm* layman; **soy — en música** I'm ignorant of music, I'm a layman in matters of music.

profecía *nf* prophecy.

proferir [3i] *vt word, sound* to utter; *hint* to drop, throw out; *sigh* to fetch; *insult* to hurl, let fly (*contra* at); *curse* to utter.

profesar [1a] **1** *vt* (a) *admiration, belief etc* to profess; to declare.
(b) *subject* to teach; to hold a chair in.
(c) *profession* to practise.
2 *vi* (*Eccl*) to take vows.

profesión *nf* (a) (*of faith etc*) profession, declaration; avowal; (*Eccl*) taking of vows.
(b) profession; calling, vocation; **abogado de —, de — abogado** a lawyer by profession; — **liberal** liberal profession.

profesional 1 *adj* professional; **no — ** non-professional. **2** *nmf* professional.

profesionalismo *nm* professionalism.

profesionalmente *adv* professionally.

profeso *adj* (*Eccl*) professed.

profesor *nm*, **profesora** *nf* (a) (*in general*) teacher; instructor; — **de esgrima** fencing master; — **de gimnasia** gym instructor; — **de natación** swimming instructor; — **de piano** piano teacher; — **robot** teaching machine.
(b) (*School: in general*) teacher; — (**de instituto**) schoolmaster, schoolmistress; — **de biología** biology teacher (*or* master, mistress).
(c) (*Univ*) professor; lecturer; — **adjunto** (*kind of*) assistant lecturer, associate professor (*US*); — **agregado** assistant professor (*US*); — **numerario**, — **titular** full professor; **es — de griego** he is professor of Greek, he is a lecturer in Greek; **nuestros —es de universidad** our university teachers; **se reunieron los —es** the staff met, the faculty met (*US*).

profesorado *nm* (a) teaching profession; teaching, lecturing. (b) teaching staff, faculty (*US*). (c) professorship.

profesoral *adj* professorial.

profeta *nm* prophet.

proféticamente *adv* prophetically.

profético *adj* prophetic.

profetisa *nf* prophetess.

profetizar [1f] *vti* to prophesy.

profiláctico 1 *adj* prophylactic. **2** *nm* prophylactic.

profilaxis *nf* prophylaxis.

prófugo *nm* fugitive; (*Mil*) deserter; — **de la justicia** fugitive from justice.

profundamente *adv* deeply, profoundly; *sleep* deeply, soundly.

profundidad *nf* (a) depth; (*Math*) depth, height; **la poca — del río** the shallowness of the river; **tener una — de 30 cm** to be 30 cm deep (*or* in depth).
(b) **las —es del océano** the depths of the ocean.
(c) (*fig*) depth, profundity.

profundizar [1f] **1** *vt* (a) to deepen, make deeper.
(b) (*fig*) *subject* to study in depth, make a profound study of, go deeply into; *mystery* to fathom, get to the bottom of.
2 *vi* (a) — **en** to penetrate into, enter.
(b) — **en** (*fig*) = **1** (b).

profundo *adj* (a) deep; **poco —** shallow; **tener 20 cm de —** to be 20 cm deep (*or* in depth); **¿cuánto tiene de —?** how deep is it?
(b) (*fig*) *bow* low; *breath, sigh, voice* deep; *note* low, deep; *sleep* deep, sound; *darkness* deep; *effect, impression etc* deep; *mystery, thinker* profound; **conocedor — del arte** a very knowledgeable expert in the art; **en lo — del alma** in the depths of one's soul.

profusamente *adv* profusely; lavishly, extravagantly.

profusión *nf* profusion; wealth, extravagance.

profuso *adj* profuse; lavish, extravagant.

progenie *nf* (a) progeny, offspring; (*pej*) brood. (b) family, lineage.

progenitor *nm* ancestor; —**es** (*hum*) parents.

progenitura *nf* offspring.

programa *nm* programme; plan; — **continuo** (*Cine*) continuous showing; — **de estudios** curriculum, syllabus.

programación *nf* programming; programme planning.

programado *adj* programmed; *visit etc* planned.

programador *nm*, **programadora** *nf* programmer.

programar [1a] *vt* (a) (*for computer etc*) to program. (b) (*Arg, Ec, Mex*) to plan; to draw up a programme for.

progresar [1a] *vi* to progress, make progress.

progresión *nf* progression; — **aritmética** arithmetic progression; — **geométrica** geometric progression.

progresista (*Pol*) **1** *adj* progressive. **2** *nmf* progressive.

progresivamente *adv* progressively; gradually, little by little.

progresivo *adj* progressive; gradual; continuous; (*Gram*) continuous.

progreso *nm* progress; advance; —**s** progress; **hacer —s** to progress, make progress, advance.

prohibición *nf* prohibition (**de** of); ban (**de** on); embargo (**de** on); **levantar la — de** to remove the ban on, lift the embargo on.

prohibicionismo *nm* prohibitionism.

prohibicionista 1 *adj* prohibitionist. **2** *nmf* prohibitionist.

prohibir [3a] **1** *vt* to prohibit, forbid, stop, ban; — **una droga** to prohibit a drug, ban a drug; — **algo a uno** to forbid someone something; — **a uno + infin** to forbid someone to + *infin*; to stop someone + *ger*, ban someone from + *ger*; **"prohibido fumar"** "no smoking"; **está prohibido fumar aquí** smoking is not allowed here, you can't smoke in here; **queda terminantemente prohibido + infin** it is strictly forbidden to + *infin*.
2 prohibirse *vr*: **"se prohíbe fumar"** "no smoking".

prohibitivo *adj* prohibitive.

prohibitorio *adj* prohibitory.

prohijar [1a] *vt* to adopt (*also fig*).

prohombre *nm* outstanding man, great man; leader.

prójima *nf* woman of dubious character, loose woman.

projimidad *nf* (*Arg, Per, PR*) fellow feeling, compassion (for one's fellows).

prójimo *nm* fellow man, fellow creature, neighbour; **nuestros —s los animales** our fellow animals.

prolapso *nm* prolapse.

prole *nf* offspring; (*pej*) brood, spawn; **padre de numerosa —** father of a large family.

proletariado *nm* proletariat.

proletariar [1b] *vt* to proletarianize.

proletario 1 *adj* proletarian. **2** *nm*, **proletaria** *nf* proletarian.

proletarismo *nm* proletarianism.

proliferación *nf* proliferation; — **de armas nucleares** proliferation of atomic weapons, spread of nuclear arms.

proliferar [1a] *vi* to proliferate.

prolífico *adj* prolific (**en** of).

prolijamente *adv* long-windedly; tediously; with an excess of detail.

prolijidad *nf* prolixity, long-windedness; tediousness; excess of detail.

prolijo *adj* (a) prolix, long-winded; tedious; excessively detailed; excessively meticulous. (b) (*RPl*) untiring.

prologar [1h] *vt* to preface, write an introduction to; **un libro prologado por Ortega** a book with a preface by Ortega.

prólogo *nm* (a) prologue (**de** to); preface, introduction; **un texto con — y notas de X** a text edited by X. (b) (*fig*) prelude (**de** to).

prolongación *nf* (a) (*act*) prolongation, extension.
(b) extension; **por la — de la Castellana** along the new part of the Castellana, along the extension of the Castellana.

prolongado *adj* *envelope, room etc* long; *meeting, stay* lengthy.

prolongar [1h] **1** *vt* to prolong, extend; *line* (*Math*) to produce; *tube etc* to make longer, extend; *meeting* to prolong.
2 prolongarse *vr* to extend; to go on; **la carretera**

se prolonga más allá del bosque the road goes on (or extends, stretches) beyond the wood; **el paisaje se prolonga hasta lo infinito** the countryside stretches away to infinity; **la sesión se prolongó bastante** the meeting went on long enough, it was a pretty long meeting.

promediar [1b] **1** *vt* **(a)** *object etc* to divide into two halves, divide equally.

(b) (*Math etc*) to work out the average of, average (out).

2 *vi* **(a)** to mediate (*entre* between).

(b) promediaba el mes it was halfway through the month; **antes de — el mes** before the month is halfway through.

promedio *nm* **(a)** average; **el — de asistencia diaria** the average daily attendance; **el — es de 35 por 100** the average is 35%.

(b) (*of distance etc*) middle, mid-point.

promesa *nf* **1** promise; pledge; **— de matrimonio** promise of marriage; **absolver a uno de su —** to release someone from his promise; **faltar a una —** to break a promise, go back on one's word.

2 *attr*: **jugador —** promising player, bright hope among players.

promesante *nmf* (Arg), **promesero** *nm*, **promesera** *nf* (Arg, Col, Per) pilgrim.

prometedor *adj* promising.

Prometeo *m* Prometheus.

prometer [2a] **1** *vt* to promise; to pledge; **— hacer algo** to promise to do something, (*Eccl*) to take a vow to do something; **esto promete ser interesante** this promises to be interesting; **esto no nos promete nada bueno** this does not look at all hopeful for us, this promises to be pretty bad for us.

2 *vi* to have promise, show promise; **es un jugador que promete** he's a promising player, he's a player with promise.

3 prometerse *vr* **(a)** to expect, promise oneself; **— algo bueno** to promise oneself a treat; **nos habíamos prometido algo mejor** we had expected something better; **se prometía que todo iba a ser fácil** he anticipated that everything was going to be easy.

(b) (*2 persons*) to get engaged; **se prometió con él en abril** she got engaged to him in April.

prometida *nf* fiancée.

prometido **1** *adj* **(a)** promised. **(b)** engaged; **estar — con** to be engaged to. **2** *nm* **(a)** fiancé. **(b)** promise.

prominencia *nf* **(a)** protuberance; swelling, bump; (*in ground*) rise. **(b)** (*fig: esp S Am*) prominence.

prominente *adj* **(a)** prominent, protuberant; that sticks out. **(b)** (*fig*) prominent.

promiscuidad *nf* **(a)** mixture, jumble, confusion; confused nature. **(b)** ambiguity.

promiscuo *adj* **(a)** mixed (up), in disorder; *crowd*, *gathering* motley. **(b)** *sense* ambiguous.

promisión *nf*: **tierra de —** land of promise, promised land.

promoción *nf* **(a)** promotion, advancement, furtherance; (*in table*, *Sport etc*) promotion; **— de ventas** sales promotion.

(b) (*professional*) promotion; class, year; **la — de 1975** the 1975 class; **fue de mi —** he belonged to the same class as I did, he graduated (*or* got his commission *etc*) at the same time as I did.

promocionar [1a] *vt* (*Comm*) to promote.

promontorio *nm* promontory, headland.

promotor *nm* promoter; pioneer; instigator, prime mover; **— de ventas** sales promoter; **el — de los disturbios** the instigator of the rioting.

promovedor *nm* promotor; instigator.

promover [2h] *vt* **(a)** *process etc* to promote, advance, further; *interests* to promote; *plan etc* to pioneer; *action* to begin, set on foot, get moving; *lawsuit* to bring.

(b) *scandal etc* to cause; *riot*, *trouble* to instigate, stir up.

(c) *person*, *team* to promote (*a* to).

promulgación *nf* promulgation; (*fig*) announcement, publication.

promulgar [1h] *vt* to promulgate; (*fig*) to proclaim, announce publicly.

pronombre *nm* pronoun; **— personal** personal pronoun; **— posesivo** possessive pronoun; **— reflexivo** reflexive pronoun.

pronominal *adj* pronominal.

pronosticación *nf* prediction, prognostication, forecasting.

pronosticador *nm* forecaster; (*Racing*) tipster.

pronosticar [1g] *vt* to predict, foretell, forecast, prognosticate.

pronóstico *nm* **(a)** prediction, forecast; omen; **— del tiempo** weather forecast; **—s para el año nuevo** predictions for the new year, prognostications for the new year.

(b) (*Med*) prognosis; **de — leve** slight, not serious; **de — reservado** of uncertain gravity, of unknown extent, possibly serious.

prontitud *nf* **(a)** speed, quickness, promptness. **(b)** (*of mind*) quickness, sharpness.

pronto **1** *adj* **(a)** ready; **la comida está pronta** lunch is ready; **estar — para + infin** to be ready to + *infin*.

(b) *reply etc* prompt, quick, (*esp Comm*) early; *cure* speedy; *service* quick, rapid, prompt.

(c) *person* quick, sharp; **de inteligencia pronta** of keen (*or* sharp) intelligence; **es — en las decisiones** he is quick about taking decisions; **estuvo muy — para resolverse** he was quick to make up his mind, he decided on the spot.

2 *adv* **(a)** quickly, promptly, speedily; at once, right away; soon; **lo más — posible** as soon as possible, as quickly as possible; **tan — como** as soon as; **tan — como me lo traigan** as soon as they bring it to me; **¡—!** hurry!, get on with it!; **al —** at first; **de —** suddenly; unexpectedly, without warning; **¡hasta —!** see you soon!; **por de —, por lo —** meanwhile, for the present; at least, anyway.

(b) early; **levantarse —** to get up early; **todavía es — para hacerlo** it's too early yet to do it, it's too soon to be doing it yet; **todavía es — para decidir si . . .** it's early days to decide whether to . . .; **iremos a comer un poco —** we'll go and lunch a bit early.

3 *nm* urge, strong impulse; sudden feeling; **tener —s de enojo** to be quick-tempered.

prontuario *nm* handbook, manual, compendium.

prónuba *nf* bridesmaid.

pronuncia *nf* (*Mex*) = **pronunciamiento**.

pronunciación *nf* pronunciation; **— figurada** phonetic transcription.

pronunciado *adj* pronounced, strong; *bend etc* sharp; *feature etc* marked, noticeable.

pronunciamiento *nm* revolt, insurrection, military rising.

pronunciar [1b] **1** *vt* **(a)** (*Ling*) to pronounce; to make, utter.

(b) (*fig*) *speech* to make, deliver; *toast* to propose; **— palabras de elogio para . . .** to say a few words of tribute to . . .

(c) (*Law*) *sentence* to pass, pronounce.

2 pronunciarse *vr* **(a)** to be pronounced; **ese sonido se pronuncia más abierto** that sound is pronounced more openly.

(b) to declare oneself, state one's opinion; to make a pronouncement; **— a favor de** to pronounce in favour of, declare oneself in favour of; **— sobre** to pronounce on, make a pronouncement about.

(c) (*Pol*) to revolt, rise, rebel.

(d) (*fig*) to become (more) pronounced.

pronuncio *nm* (*Col*) = **pronunciamiento**.

propagación *nf* propagation; (*fig*) propagation, spread(ing), dissemination.

propaganda *nf* **(a)** propaganda. **(b)** (*Comm*) advertising; **hacer — de un producto** to advertise a product.

propagandista *nmf* propagandist.

propagandístico *adj* propaganda (*attr*); (*Comm*) advertising (*attr*).

propagar [1h] **1** *vt* (*Bio*) to propagate; (*fig*) to propagate, spread, disseminate. **2 propagarse** *vr* (*Bio*) to propagate; (*fig*) to spread, be disseminated.

propalar [1a] *vt* to divulge, disclose; to publish an account of.

propasarse [1a] *vr* to go too far, overstep the bounds; (*sexually*) to take liberties, overstep the bounds of propriety.

propela *nf* (*Cu*, *Mex*: *angl*) propeller; outboard motor.

propender [2a] *vi*: **— a** to tend towards, incline to; **— a + infin** to tend to + *infin*, have a tendency to + *infin*.

propensión *nf* inclination, propensity, tendency (*a* to).

propenso *adj*: **— a** inclined to; prone to, subject to; **ser — a + infin** to be inclined to + *infin*, have a tendency to + *infin*.

propi *nf* (*fam*) = **propina**.

propiamente *adv* properly; really, exactly; *see* **dicho**.

propiciación *nf* propitiation.

propiciar [1b] *vt* **(a)** to propitiate, to win over. **(b)** to favour; to cause, give rise to; **tal secreto**

propicia muchas conjeturas such secrecy causes a lot of speculation.

propiciatorio adj propitiatory.

propicio adj propitious, auspicious; *moment etc* favourable; *person* kind, well-disposed, helpful.

propiedad nf (a) possession, ownership; **ser de la —** de to be the property of, belong to; **una finca de la — del marqués** an estate belonging to the marquis; **ceder algo a uno en —** to transfer something completely to someone, transfer to someone the full rights over something.

(b) (*object etc*) property; **— particular** private property; **una —** a property, a piece of property; **es — del municipio** it is the property of the town.

(c) (*Chem etc*) property; (*fig*) property, attribute.

(d) (*quality*) propriety, properness; suitability, appositeness; **discutir la — de una palabra** to discuss the appropriateness of a word.

(e) (*quality*) accuracy, faithfulness; naturalness; **lo reproduce con toda —** he reproduces it faithfully.

(f) (*Comm etc*) right(s); **— industrial** patent rights; **— intelectual, — literaria** copyright; **"es —" "copyright".**

propietaria nf owner, proprietress.

propietario 1 adj proprietary. 2 nm owner, proprietor; (*Agr etc*) landowner.

propina nf tip, gratuity; **dar algo de —** to give something extra, give something as a bonus; **con dos más de —** (*fig*) with two more into the bargain.

propinar [1a] 1 vt (a) to tip, give a tip to.

(b) **— a uno** to treat someone to a drink, buy someone a drink.

(c) (*fam*) *blow* to deal, hit; *beating* to give; **le propinó una serie de consejos** he gave him a lot of advice, he made him listen to several bits of advice.

2 **propinarse** vr: **— algo** to treat oneself to something.

propincuidad nf propinquity, nearness, proximity.

propincuo adj near.

propio 1 adj (a) own, of one's own; **con su propia mano** with his own hand; **lo vi con mis —s ojos** I saw it with my own eyes; **los rizos son —s** her curls are natural, her curls are her own; **lo hizo en beneficio —** he did it for his own good; he did it in his own interest; **tienen casa propia** they have a house of their own; **ahora tiene una bicicleta suya propia** now she has a bicycle of her very own.

(b) peculiar (*de* to); special; characteristic, typical (*de* of); of one's own; **una bebida propia del país** a typical drink of the country; **hace un sol — de país mediterráneo** this sunshine is more typical of a Mediterranean country; **fruta propia del tiempo** fruit in season; **eso es muy — de él** that's very characteristic of him; **tiene un olor muy —** it has a very special smell, it has a smell of its own.

(c) proper; correct, suitable, fitting (*para* for); **con los honores que le son —s** with the honours which are proper (*or* due) to him; **ese bikini no es — para esta playa** that bikini is not suitable for this beach.

(d) selfsame, very; **sus propias palabras** his very words; **me lo dijo el — ministro** the minister himself told me so; **yo haría lo — que tú** I'd do the same as you, I'd do exactly what you're doing.

(e) *sense* proper, true; basic.

(f) **de —** especially, deliberately, expressly.

2 nm (*fam*) messenger.

proponente nmf proposer.

proponer [2r] 1 vt *scheme etc* to propose, put forward; *theory* to propound; *problem* to pose; to outline, put up (for discussion); *motion* to propose; *candidate* to propose, nominate, put forward; **— a uno para una beca** to propose someone for a scholarship; **le propuse que fuéramos juntos** I proposed to him that we should go together.

2 **proponerse** vr (a) **— hacer algo** to propose to do something, plan to do something, intend to do something.

(b) (*pej*) **te has propuesto hacerme perder el tren** you set out deliberately to make me miss the train.

proporción nf (a) proportion; (*Math etc*) ratio; relationship; rate; **—es** proportions, (*fig*) dimensions; size, scope; **la — entre azules y verdes** the proportion of blues to greens; **en — con** in proportion to; **en una —** de 5 a 1 in a ratio of 5 to 1; at a rate of 5 to 1; **guarda bien las —es** it remains in proportion; **esto no guarda — con lo otro** this is out of proportion to the rest; **una máquina de gigantescas —es** a machine of huge proportions (*or* size); **se descono-**

cen las **—es del desastre** the size (*or* extent, scope) of the disaster is unknown.

(b) chance, opportunity, right moment.

(c) (*SAm*) **de —es** huge, vast; considerable; (*Mex*) wealthy.

proporcionadamente adv proportionately, in proportion.

proporcionado adj (a) proportionate (*a* to).

(b) medium, middling, just right; **de tamaño —** of the right size.

(c) **bien —** well proportioned; shapely, of pleasing shape.

proporcional adj proportional.

proporcionalmente adv proportionally.

proporcionar [1a] vt (a) to give, supply, provide, furnish; (*fig*) to lend; **— dinero a uno** to give someone money, supply someone with money; **esto le proporciona una renta anual de . . .** this brings him in a yearly income of . . .; **esto proporciona gran encanto a la narración** this lends (*or* gives) great charm to the story.

(b) to adjust, adapt (*a* to).

proposición nf proposition; proposal.

propósito nm purpose; aim, intention, objective; **buenos —s** good intentions; good resolutions; **¿cuál es su —?** what is his aim?; **nuestro — es de + infin** our aim is to + infin; **hacer(se) el — de + infin** to form an intention to + infin, set oneself the aim of + ger; **a —** (*as adj*) appropriate, suitable, fitting (*para* for); *remark etc* relevant, apt; **a —** (*as adv*) by the way, incidentally; **a — de** about, with regard to; **y a — de los toros . . .** and talking of bulls . . ., and while we're on the subject of bulls . . .; **eso no viene a —** that's not relevant, that's nothing to do with it; **de —** on purpose, purposely, deliberately; **fuera de —** irrelevant(ly), off the point, out of place; **sin — fijo** aimless(ly), pointless(ly).

propuesta nf proposal.

propulsado adj: **— a cohete** rocket-driven; **— a chorro** jet-propelled.

propulsar [1a] vt (a) (*Mech*) to drive, propel. (b) (*fig*) to promote, encourage.

propulsión nf propulsion; **— a cohete** rocket propulsion; **— a chorro, — por reacción** jet propulsion; **con — a chorro** jet-propelled.

propulsor nm propellent, fuel.

prorrata nf share, quota; prorate (*US*); **a —** pro rata, proportionately.

prorratear [1a] vt to share out, apportion, distribute proportionately; to prorate (*US*); **prorratearemos el dinero** we will share out the money pro rata.

prorrateo nm sharing (in proportion), apportionment; **a —** pro rata, proportionately.

prórroga nf prorogation; (*Comm*) extension; (*Mil*) deferment; (*Law*) stay (of execution), respite; (*Sport*) extra time.

prorrogable adj which can be extended.

prorrogación nf prorogation.

prorrogar [1h] vt *sitting etc* to prorogue, adjourn; *period* to extend; (*Mil*) to defer; (*Law*) to grant a stay of execution to; *decision etc* to defer, postpone; **prorrogamos una semana las vacaciones** we extended our holiday by a week.

prorrumpir [3a] vi to burst forth, break out; **— en gritos** to start shouting; **— en lágrimas** to burst into tears.

prosa nf (a) (*Lit*) prose.

(b) (*fig*) prosaic nature, tedium; **la — de la vida** the tedium of life, the dreariness of life.

(c) (*fam*) chatter, idle talk.

(d) (*Chi*) vanity, haughtiness.

(e) (*Ec, Guat, Per*) pomposity, affectation.

prosador nm, **prosadora** nf (a) (*Lit*) prose writer.

(b) (*fam*) chatterbox, great talker, gossip.

prosaicamente adv (a) prosaically. (b) (*fig*) prosaically; tediously, monotonously.

prosaico adj (a) (*Lit*) prosaic, prose (*attr*). (b) (*fig*) prosaic, prosy; tedious, monotonous; ordinary.

prosaísmo nm (*fig*) prosaic nature; tediousness, monotony; ordinariness.

prosapia nf lineage, ancestry.

proscenio nm proscenium.

proscribir [3a; *ptp* **proscrito**] vt to prohibit, ban; *party etc* to proscribe; *criminal* to outlaw; to banish; *subject etc* to ban; **— un tema de su conversación** to banish a topic from one's conversation.

proscripción nf prohibition (*de* of), ban (*de* on); proscription; outlawing; banishment.

proscrito 1 *ptp* of **proscribir**. 2 adj banned; outlawed; proscribed; **un libro —** a banned book. 3 nm exile; outlaw.

prosecución nf continuation; pressing; pursuit.

proseguir [3d *and* 3l] **1** *vt* to continue, carry on, go on with, proceed with; *demand* to go on with, push, press; *investigation, study* to pursue.
2 *vi* (a) — **en** (*or* **con**) **una actitud** to continue in one's attitude, maintain one's attitude.
(b) (*of state etc*) to continue, go on; **prosiguió con el cuento** he went on with the story; **¡prosigue! continue!; prosigue el mal tiempo** the bad weather continues.
proselitismo *nm* proselytism.
proselitista *adj* proselytizing.
prosélito *nm,* **prosélita** *nf* proselyte.
prosificación *nf* prose version; rewriting as prose, turning into prose.
prosificar [1g] *vt* to rewrite as prose, write a prose version of.
prosista *nmf* prose writer.
prosodia *nf* (set of) rules for pronunciation and accentuation.
prosopopeya *nf* (a) (*Lit*) personification. (b) (*fig*) pomposity, affectation.
prospección *nf* exploration; (*Mil*) prospecting (*de* for); — **del petróleo** prospecting for oil, drilling for oil.
prospectivo *adj* (*SAm: angl*) prospective.
prospecto *nm* prospectus; (*Comm etc*) leaflet, sheet of instructions.
prospector *nm* prospector.
prósperamente *adv* prosperously; successfully.
prosperar [1a] *vi* to prosper, thrive, flourish; (*of idea etc*) to prosper.
prosperidad *nf* prosperity; success; **en época de** — in a period of prosperity, in good times; **desear a uno muchas** —**s** to wish someone success.
próspero *adj* (a) prosperous, thriving, flourishing; successful. (b) **con próspera fortuna** with good luck, favoured by fortune.
próstata *nf* prostate.
prosternarse [1a] *vr* to prostrate oneself; to bow low, bow humbly.
prostético *adj* (*Gram, Med*) prosthetic.
prostíbulo *nm* brothel.
prostitución *nf* prostitution (*also fig*).
prostituir [3g] **1** *vt* to prostitute (*also fig*). **2 prostituirse** *vr* to prostitute oneself, take up prostitution, become a prostitute.
prostituta *nf* prostitute; — **callejera** streetwalker.
prosudo *adj* (*Chi, Ec, Per*) affectedly solemn, pompous.
protagonista *nmf* protagonist; (*Lit etc, freq*) main character; hero, heroine.
protagonizar [1f] *vt* to take the chief role in, play the main part in.
protección *nf* protection.
proteccionismo *nm* protectionism.
proteccionista 1 *adj policy* protectionist; *duty etc* protective. **2** *nmf* protectionist.
protector 1 *adj* (a) protective, protecting. (b) *tone etc* patronizing. **2** *nm,* **protectora** *nf* protector; (*Lit etc*) patron; (*of tradition etc*) guardian.
protectorado *nm* protectorate.
protectoramente *adv* (a) protectively. (b) patronizingly.
proteger [2c] *vt* to protect (*contra* against, *de* from); to shield; to defend; to act as patron to.
protegida *nf* protégée.
protegido *nm* protégé.
proteico *adj* protean.
proteína *nf* protein.
protervidad *nf* wickedness, perversity.
protervo *adj* wicked, perverse.
protesta *nf* (a) protest; **bajo** — under protest. (b) (*of innocence etc*) protestation; **hacer** —**s de lealtad** to protest one's loyalty.
protestación *nf* protestation; — **de lealtad** protestation of loyalty, declaration of loyalty; — **de fe** profession of faith.
protestante 1 *adj* Protestant. **2** *nmf* Protestant.
protestantismo *nm* Protestantism.
protestar [1a] **1** *vt* (a) *innocence etc* to protest, declare, avow; *faith* to profess.
(b) (*Fin*) **cheque protestado por falta de fondos** cheque referred to drawer (*R/D*).
2 *vi* (a) to protest (*contra, de* about, against; *de que* that); to object, remonstrate; — **contra una demora** to protest about a delay; **¡protesto contra esa observación!** I resent that!, I object to that remark!
(b) — **de** *innocence etc* to protest.
proto . . . proto . . .
protocolario *adj* (a) established by protocol, required by protocol. (b) (*fig*) formal.

protocolo *nm* (a) (*Pol*) protocol. (b) (*fig*) protocol, social etiquette, convention. (c) (*fig*) **sin** —**s** informal(ly); without formalities, without a lot of fuss.
protón *nm* proton.
protoplasma *nm* protoplasm.
prototipo *nm* prototype.
protuberancia *nf* protuberance.
protuberante *adj* protuberant.
provecto *adj:* **de edad provecta** elderly.
provecho *nm* advantage, benefit, profit; (*Fin*) profit; **de** — *deal* profitable; *activity* useful; *person* worthy, honest; **¡buen** —**!** *phrase used to those at table, hoping they will enjoy their meal*; **¡buen** — **le haga!** and much good may it do him!; **en** — **de** to the benefit of; **en** — **propio** to one's own advantage, for one's own profit; **ese alimento no le hace** — **a uno** that food-(stuff) doesn't do one any good; **sacar** — **de algo** to benefit from something, profit by (*or* from) something.
provechosamente *adv* advantageously, beneficially, profitably.
provechoso *adj* advantageous, beneficial, profitable; useful; (*Fin*) profitable.
proveedor *nm,* **proveedora** *nf* supplier, purveyor; dealer; — **casero** roundsman, deliveryman (*US*); "—**es de la Real Casa**" "by appointment to His (*or* Her) Majesty"; **consulte a su** — **habitual** consult your usual dealer.
proveer [2a; *ptp* **provisto** *and* **proveído**] **1** *vt* (a) to provide, supply, furnish (*de* with).
(b) to provide, get ready; — **todo lo necesario** to provide all that is necessary (*para* for).
(c) *vacancy* to fill.
(d) *business* to transact, dispatch.
(e) (*Law*) to decree.
2 *vi:* — **a** to provide for; — **a las necesidades de uno** to provide for someone's wants; — **a un vicio de uno** to pander to someone's vice.
3 proveerse *vr:* — **de** to provide oneself with.
provenir [3s] *vi:* — **de** to come from, arise from, stem from; **esto proviene de no haberlo curado antes** this comes from (*or* is due to) not having treated it earlier.
Provenza *f* Provence.
provenzal 1 *adj* Provençal. **2** *nm* Provençal. **3** *nm* (*language*) Provençal.
proverbial *adj* proverbial.
proverbialmente *adv* proverbially.
proverbio *nm* proverb.
próvidamente *adv* providently.
providencia *nf* (a) (*quality*) foresight; forethought, providence; (**Divina**) **P—** (Divine) Providence.
(b) —**s** measures, steps; **dictar** (*or* **tomar**) —**s para** + *infin* to take steps to + *infin*.
(c) (*Law*) ruling, decision.
providencial *adj* providential.
providencialmente *adv* providentially.
providente *adj,* **próvido** *adj* provident.
provincia *nf* province; **las P—s Vascongadas** the Basque Provinces, the Basque Country; **un pueblo de** —**(s)** a provincial town, a country town; **la vida en** — provincial life.
provincial 1 *adj* provincial. **2** *nm,* **provinciala** *nf* (*Eccl*) provincial.
provincialismo *nm* (*Ling*) provincialism, dialect(al) word (*or* phrase etc).
provincianismo *nm* provincialism; — **de cortas luces,** — **de vía estrecha** narrow provincialism, deadening provincialism.
provinciano 1 *adj* (a) provincial (*also pej*); country (*attr*).
(b) Basque, of the Basque Provinces.
2 *nm,* **provinciana** *nf* (a) provincial (*also pej*); country dweller.
(b) Basque.
provisión *nf* (a) (*act*) provision.
(b) provision, supply; —**es** provisions, supplies, stores.
(c) (*Fin*) — **de fondos** financial cover; **cheque sin** — bad cheque.
(d) (*precautionary*) measure, step.
provisional *adj* provisional.
provisionalidad *nf* provisional nature, temporary character.
provisionalmente *adv* provisionally.
provisorio *adj* (*SAm*) provisional.
provista *nf* (*RPl*) provisions, supplies.
provisto 1 *ptp* of **proveer. 2** *adv:* — **de** provided with, supplied with; having, possessing.
provocación *nf* provocation.
provocador *adj* provocative, provoking.

provocar [1g] **1** *vt* (a) *person* to provoke; to rouse, stir up (to anger *etc*); to tempt, invite; **— a uno a cólera** (*or* **indignación**) to rouse someone to fury; **— a uno a lástima** to move someone to pity; **— a uno a risa** to make someone laugh; **el mar provoca a bañarse** the sea tempts one to bathe, the sea invites one to go for a swim.

(b) *change etc* to bring about, lead to; *process to* promote; *explosion, protest, war etc* to cause, spark off.

(c) (*of woman*) to rouse, stir, stimulate (sexually). **2** *vi* (*fam*) to be sick.

provocativo *adj* (a) provocative, provoking.

(b) *woman* provocative, sexually stimulating; (*pej*) openly sexy; *dress* daring, immodest; *laugh, gesture etc* inviting.

proxeneta *nmf* go-between; pimp, procurer.
próximamente *adv* shortly, soon.
proximidad *nf* nearness, closeness, proximity.
próximo *adj* (a) near, close; neighbouring; *relative* close; **en fecha próxima** soon, at an early date; **estar — a** to be close to, be near; **estar — a + *infin*** to be on the point of + *ger*, be about to + *infin*.

(b) next; **el mes —** next month; **el mes — pasado** last month; **el — 5 de junio** on 5th June next; **se bajarán en la próxima parada** they will get off at the next stop.

proyección *nf* (a) (*act etc, part*) projection.

(b) (*Cine etc*) showing; **el tiempo de — es de 35 minutos** the showing lasts 35 minutes, the film runs for 35 minutes.

(c) (*Cine, Phot*) slide, projection; transparency.

(d) (*fig*) hold, sway, influence; **la — de los periódicos sobre la sociedad** the hold of newspapers over society, the influence which newspapers have on society.

proyectable *adj*: **asiento —** (*Aer*) ejector seat.
proyectar [1a] *vt* (a) *object* to hurl, throw; *light* to cast, shed, project; *jet, liquid etc* to send out, give out; to direct (*hacia* at); *shadow* to cast.

(b) (*Cine, Phot*) to project; to screen, show.

(c) (*Math etc*) to project.

(d) (*Archit etc*) to plan; (*Mech*) to design; **está proyectado para + *infin*** it is designed to +*infin*.

(e) **— + *infin*** to plan to + *infin*.

proyectil *nm* projectile, missile; (*Mil*: *of gun*) shell, (*with rocket*) missile; **— de aire a aire** air-to-air missile; **— balístico intercontinental** intercontinental ballistic missile; **— (tele)dirigido** guided missile; **— de iluminación** flare, rocket.

proyectista *nm* planner; (*Aer, Aut, Tech etc*) designer; draughtsman.

proyecto *nm* (a) (*Tech*) plan, design; project.

(b) (*fig*) plan; scheme, project; **cambiar de —** to change one's plans; **tener —s para** to have plans for; **tener algo en —** to be planning something; **tener sus —s sobre algo** to have designs on something.

(c) (*Fin*) detailed estimate.

(d) (*Parl*) **— de ley** bill.

proyector *nm* (a) (*Cine*) projector. (b) (*Mil etc*) searchlight; (*Theat*) spotlight.

prudencia *nf* wisdom, prudence; care; soundness, sound judgement.

prudencial *adj* (a) prudential; sensible.

(b) *amount, distance etc* roughly correct, more or less correctly guessed.

prudenciarse [1b] *vr* (*CAm, Col, Mex*) to be sensible; to remain calm, control oneself.

prudente *adj* sensible, wise, prudent; *driver etc* careful; *choice etc* sensible, judicious, sound.

prudentemente *adv* sensibly, wisely, prudently; carefully; judiciously, soundly.

prueba *nf* (a) proof (*also Math*); (*Law*) proof, evidence; **—s** (*Law*) documents; **— documental** documentary evidence; **— indiciaria** circumstantial proof; **a la — me remito** the proof of the pudding is in the eating, the event will show; **en — de** in proof of; /**en — de lo cual** in proof whereof; **en — de que no es así te lo ofrezco gratis** to prove that it isn't so I offer it to you free; **¿tiene Vd — de ello?** can you prove it?; do you have proof?

(b) (*fig*) proof, sign, token; **es buena —** it's a good sign; **sin dar la menor — de ello** without giving the faintest sign of it.

(c) (*Tech etc*) test, trial; (*Chem etc*) experiment; **—s** (*Aer, Aut, Naut*) trials; **— por carretera** road trials; **— de fuego** (*fig*) acid test; **— de inteligencia** intelligence test; **— nuclear** nuclear test; **por un procedimiento de — y desacierto** by a process of trial and error; **a —** (*Tech*) on trial; (*Comm*) on approval, on trial; **ingresar con un nombramiento a —** to take up a post for a probationary period; to

come in with a probationary appointment; **a — de** proof against; **a — de agua** waterproof; **a — de bala** bulletproof; **a — de bombas** bombproof, shellproof; **a — de choques** shockproof; **a — de grasa** greaseproof; **a — de herrumbre** rustproof, rust-resistant; **a — de impericia** foolproof; **a — de ladrones** burglarproof; **a — de lluvia** rainproof; **a — de ruidos** soundproof; **a — de viento** windproof; **poner a —,** **someter a —** to test, put to the test, try out; **poner a — los nervios de uno** to test someone's nerves; **poner a — la paciencia de uno** to try someone's patience; **hacer — de** to tesr, put to the test.

(d) (*of food etc*: *act*) testing, sampling; (*quantity*) taste, sample.

(e) (*Sew*) fitting, trying on; **sala de —s** fitting room.

(f) (*Typ*) **—s** proofs; **primeras —s** first proofs, galleys; **—s de planas** page proofs.

(g) (*Phot*) proof, print; **— negativa** negative; **— positiva** positive, print.

(h) (*Sport*) event; **—s** trials; **— clasificatoria, — eliminatoria** heat; **— de vallas** hurdles, hurdles race.

(i) (*SAm*) circus act; acrobatic act, piece' of juggling (*or* contortionism *etc*), display of acrobatic (*etc*) skill; (*Ec, Per*) circus show, performance.

pruebista *nmf* (a) (*SAm*) acrobat, tightrope walker; conjurer, juggler; contortionist. (b) (*Arg*) proofreader.

prurito *nm* (a) (*Med*) itch.

(b) (*fig*) itch; urge (to perfectionism); **tener el — de + *infin*** to have the urge to + *infin*; **por un — de exactitud** out of an excessive desire for accuracy, because of his urge to get everything just right.

Prusia *f* Prussia.
prusiano 1 *adj* Prussian. **2** *nm*, **prusiana** *nf* Prussian.
pse . . ., psi . . .: *the Academy recommends the spellings* **se . . ., si . . .**; *all forms are pronounced* [se—, si—].
psefología *nf* psephology.
psefólogo *nm* psephologist.
psic . . ., psiqu . . .: psych . . .
psicoanálisis *nm* psychoanalysis.
psicoanalista *nmf* psychoanalyst.
psicoanalizar [1f] *vt* to psychoanalyse.
psicología *nf* psychology.
psicológicamente *adv* psychologically.
psicológico *adj* psychological.
psicólogo *nm* psychologist.
psiconeurosis *nf*, *pl* **psiconeurosis** psychoneurosis.
psicopatología *nf* psychopathology.
psicópata *nmf* psychopath.
psicopático *adj* psychopathic.
psicosis *nf*, *pl* **psicosis** psychosis.
psicosomático *adj* psychosomatic.
psicoterapia *nf* psychotherapy.
psicótico 1 *adj* psychotic. **2** *nm*, **psicótica** *nf* psychotic.
Psique *f* Psyche.
psique *nf* (a) psyche. (b) cheval glass.
psiquedélico *adj* psychedelic.
psiquiatra *nmf* psychiatrist.
psiquiatría *nf* psychiatry.
psiquiátrico *adj* psychiatric.
psíquico *adj* psychic(al).
psitacosis *nf* psittacosis.
pterodáctilo [te—] *nm* pterodactyl.
ptomaína [to—] *nf* ptomaine.
ptomaínico [to—] *adj*: **envenenamiento m —** ptomaine poisoning.
púa *nf* sharp point; (*Bot, Zool*) prickle, spike, spine; (*of hedgehog*) quill; (*of comb*) tooth; (*of fork*) prong, tine; (*of hook, wire*) barb; (*SAm*: *of fighting cock*) spur; (*Mus*) plectrum; (*Mus*) gramophone needle, phonograph needle (*US*); (*Bot*) graft, cutting.
puazo *nm* (*SAm*) slash (*with cock's spur*).
púber 1 *adj* adolescent. **2** *nmf* adolescent child, child approaching puberty.
pubertad *nf* puberty.
pubescencia *nf* pubescence.
pubescente *adj* pubescent.
púbico *adj* pubic.
pubis *nm* pubis.
publicación *nf* publication.
públicamente *adv* publicly.
publicar [1g] *vt* (*in most senses*) to publish; to publicize; *secret etc* to make public, disclose, divulge.
publicidad *nf* (a) publicity; **dar — a** to publicize, give publicity to.

(b) (*Comm*) advertising; **— de lanzamiento** advance publicity, advertising campaign to launch a product; **hacer — por** to advertise; **se ha prohibido la — de cigarrillos** cigarette advertising has been banned.

publicista nmf publicist.
publicitario adj advertising (attr); publicity (attr).
público 1 adj public; **hacer** — to publish, make public; to disclose.
  2 nm public; (Mus, Theat etc) audience; (Sport) spectators, crowd; (of restaurant etc) clients, clientèle, patrons; (of newspaper) readers, readership; **hay poco** — there aren't many people; **el** — **que se paseaba por la calle** the people who were strolling in the street; **hubo un** — **de 800** there was a crowd (or gathering, audience etc) of 800; **el gran** — the general public; **en** — in public.
puco nm (SAm) earthenware bowl.
pucha[1] nf (a) (Cu, PR) bouquet. (b) (Mex) ring-shaped loaf.
pucha[2] nf (SAm: euph)=**puta**; **¡(la)** —**!** well I'm damned!
puchera nf stew.
pucherazo nm (fam) electoral fiddle (fam); **dar** — to rig an election, fiddle the votes (fam).
puchero nm (a) (Cook) cooking pot. (b) (Cook) stew; (fig) daily bread, ordinary sustenance; **apenas gana para el** — he hardly earns enough to live on. (c) (fam) pout; **hacer** —**s** to pout, make a face, screw up one's face.
puches nmpl porridge, gruel.
puchito nm, **puchita** nf (Chi, Ec) youngest child.
pucho nm (a) fag end, cigar stub.
  (b) (SAm) scrap, left-over(s); dregs; (Sew) remnant; (Fin) coppers, small change; (fig) trifle, mere nothing; **a** —**s** in dribs and drabs.
  (c) (Chi, Ec) youngest child.
pude etc see **poder**.
pudendo 1 adj: **partes pudendas** pudenda, private parts. 2 nm penis.
pudibundez nf false modesty, affected modesty; excess of modesty.
pudibundo adj affectedly modest; over-shy (about sexual matters), excessively modest; prudish.
pudicicia nf modesty; chastity.
púdico adj modest; chaste.
pudiendo see **poder**.
pudiente adj wealthy, well-to-do; powerful, influential; **las gentes menos** —**s** the less well-off.
pudín nm (angl) pudding.
pudinga nf pudding stone.
pudor nm (a) modesty; shyness; (sense of) shame, (sense of) decency; **con** — modestly; discreetly. (b) chastity, virtue; **atentado al** — indecent assault.
pudorosamente adv (a) modestly; shyly. (b) chastely, virtuously.
pudoroso adj (a) modest; shy. (b) chaste, virtuous.
pudrición nf (a) rotting. (b) rot, rottenness; — **seca** dry rot.
pudridero nm rubbish heap, midden.
pudrimiento nm (a) rotting. (b) rot, rottenness.
pudrir [3a] 1 vt (a) to rot.
  (b) (fam) to upset, vex, annoy.
  2 vi (fig) to rot, be dead and buried.
  3 **pudrirse** vr (a) to rot, decay; to rot away.
  (b) (fig) to rot, languish; **mientras se pudría en la cárcel** while he was languishing in jail; **te vas a** — **de aburrimiento** you'll die of boredom; **¡que se pudra!** let him rot!
pueblada nf (SAm) riot; revolt, uprising; (Arg) mob, gathering of workers.
pueblerino 1 adj countrified, small-town (attr); person rustic, provincial. 2 nm, **pueblerina** nf rustic, country person, provincial.
pueblero (SAm) 1 adj town (attr), city (attr). 2 nm townsman, city dweller; (pej) city slicker (US); (pej) toff (fam), fop.
pueblo nm (a) (Pol etc) people, nation; — **elegido** chosen people; **el** — **español** the Spanish people; **la voluntad del** — the nation's will; **hacer un llamamiento al** — to call on the people, call on the nation.
  (b) (pej) common people, lower orders; — **de mala muerte** dregs of the populace.
  (c) village; small town, country town.
puedo etc see **poder**.
puente nm (a) bridge (also fig); — **aéreo** airlift; — **de barcas**, — **de pontones** pontoon bridge; — **colgante** suspension bridge; — **giratorio** swing bridge; — **levadizo** drawbridge; — **para peatones** footbridge; **tender un** — (fig) to offer a compromise, go part-way to meet someone's wishes.
  (b) (fig: of glasses, Mus etc) bridge.
  (c) (Naut) bridge (also — **de mando**); deck; — **del timón** wheelhouse.
  (d) (fig) gap; hiatus; **habrá que salvar el** — **de una cosecha a otra** something will have to be done to fill the gap between one harvest and the next.

  (e) (fam) **hacer (el)** — to take a long weekend, take extra days off work between two public holidays.
  (f) (Col) collarbone.
puerca nf (a) sow. (b) (fam) slut. (c) woodlouse.
puercada nf (CAm, Per, PR) dirty trick, mean act; obscene remark.
puercamente adv (a) dirtily. (b) nastily, disgustingly; coarsely. (c) vilely, meanly.
puerco 1 nm (a) pig, hog (US); wild boar; — **espín** porcupine; — **jabalí**, — **montés**, — **salvaje** wild boar, wild pig; — **de mar** porpoise; — **marino** dolphin; see **Martín**.
  (b) (fam) pig; swine, rotter.
  2 adj (a) dirty, filthy.
  (b) nasty, disgusting; coarse.
  (c) vile, rotten (fam), mean.
puericia nf boyhood.
puericultor nm (also **médico** —) paediatrician.
puericultura nf paediatrics.
pueril adj (a) childish, child (attr); **edad** — childhood. (b) (pej) puerile, childish.
puerilidad nf puerility, childishness.
puerperal adj puerperal.
puerqueza nf (Arg, Par) (a) dirty thing, filthy object. (b) dirty trick. (c) (Zool) bug, creepy-crawly (fam).
puerro nm leek.
puerta nf door; gate; doorway; (esp fig) gateway (de to); — **accesoria** side door; — **de artistas** stage door; — **de corredera** sliding door; — **de cristales** glass door; — **excusada** private door, side door; — **chica** side door, private door; **entrar por la** — **chica** (fam) to get in by the back door (fig); — **giratoria** swing door, revolving door; — **principal** front door; main entrance; — **de servicio** tradesmen's entrance; — **trasera** back door; — **ventana** French window; — **vidriera** glass door; **a** — **cerrada** behind closed doors; **a las** —**s de la muerte** at death's door; **tenemos la guerra a las** —**s** war is upon us, the threat of war is imminent; **coche de 2** —**s** 2-door car; **coche de 4** —**s** 4-door car; **política de** —**s adentro** home policy; **lo que pasa de** —**s afuera** what happens abroad, foreign affairs; **de** — **en** — from door to door; **abrir la** — **a** (fig) to open the door to; **coger la** — (fam) to leave in a huff; **coger a uno detrás de la** — to catch someone at a disadvantage; **enseñar la** — **a uno** to show someone the door; **franquear las** —**s a uno** to welcome someone in; **querer poner** —**s al campo** to try to stem the tide; **salir por la** — **de los carros** to fail, be a disaster; **tomar la** — (fam) to leave, get out.
puertaventana nf shutter.
puertear [1a] vi (SAm) to stand about in the doorway.
puerto nm (a) port, harbour; seaport; — **comercial** trading port; — **de escala** port of call; — **de entrada** port of entry; — **franco** free port; — **de origen** home port; — **naval** naval port, naval harbour; — **pesquero** fishing port; **entrar a** —, **tomar** — to enter port, come into port.
  (b) (fig) haven, refuge; **llegar a** — to solve a problem, get over a difficulty, come through safely.
  (c) (Geog) pass.
Puerto m Rico Puerto Rico.
puertorriqueñismo nm word (or phrase etc) peculiar to Puerto Rico.
puertorriqueño 1 adj Puerto Rican. 2 nm, **puertorriqueña** nf Puerto Rican.
pues 1 adv (a) then; well, well then; so; — **no voy** well I'm not going, in that case I'm not going; **¿no vas con ella,** —**?** aren't you going with her after all?; so you're not going with her?; **llegó,** —, **con 2 horas de retraso** so he arrived 2 hours late; — **sí** well yes, why yes; certainly; — **no** well no; not at all; **¡**— **qué!** come now!; what else did you expect!; **¿**—**?** so?, well?; what next?
  (b) (hesitant) — **. . . no sé** well . . . I don't know.
  (c) (affirmation) **¡**—**!** yes!, certainly!; see **ahora**, **bien** etc.
  2 conj since, for; **cómpralo,** — **lo necesitas** buy it, since you need it; **nos marchamos,** — **no había más remedio** we went, since there was no alternative.
puesta nf (a) — **en marcha** starting; — **en escena** staging.
  (b) (Astron) setting; — **del sol** sunset.
  (c) (Orn) egg-laying; **una** — **anual de 300 huevos** an annual lay (or output) of 300 eggs.
  (d) (Cards etc) stake, bet.
  (e) (RPl) **¡**—**!** it's a tie!, it's a draw!; (Racing) it's a dead heat!
puestero nm (a) (SAm) stallholder, market vendor. (b) (Chi, RPl) farm overseer; small farmer, tenant farmer.

puesto 1 *ptp of* **poner.**
   2 *adj* (a) **con el sombrero** — with one's hat on, wearing a hat; **una mesa puesta para 9** a table laid for 9.
   (b) **bien** — well dressed, smartly turned out.
   3 *nm* (a) place; position; **el** — **de la especie en la clasificación** the place of the species in the classification; **ocupa el tercer** — **en la liga** it is in third place in the league; **ceder el** — **a uno** to give up one's place to someone; **quedar** (*or* **mantener**) **su** — to know one's place; to keep the proper distance.
   (b) post, position, job; **tiene un** — **de conserje** he has a post as a porter; **se creerán 200** —**s de trabajo** 200 new jobs will be created.
   (c) (*Mil etc*) post; — **de escucha** listening post; — **de policía** police post, police station; — **de socorro** first-aid post.
   (d) (*Hunting*) stand, place.
   (e) (*Comm*) stall; stand, booth; kiosk; pitch; — **de mercado** market stall.
   (f) (*RPl*) small farm.
   3 — **que** *conj* since, as.
puf *interj* ugh!
púgil *nm* boxer.
pugilato *nm* boxing.
pugilista *nm* (*SAm*) boxer.
pugio *nm* (*Arg, Per*) spring.
pugna *nf* battle, struggle, conflict; **entrar en** — **con** to clash with, come into conflict with; **estar en** — **con** to clash with, conflict with.
pugnacidad *nf* pugnacity, aggressiveness.
pugnar [1a] *vi* (a) to fight; — **en defensa de** to fight in defence of; — **por** to fight for.
   (b) to struggle, fight, strive (**por** + *infin* to + *infin*); — **por no reírse** to struggle not to laugh.
   (c) — **con** (*of opinion etc*) to clash with, conflict with.
pugnaz *adj* pugnacious, aggressive.
puja *nf* (a) attempt, effort. (b) (*at auction*) bid. (c) **sacar de la** — **a uno** to get ahead of someone; to get someone out of a jam. (d) (*Col*) ticking-off.
pujante *adj* strong, vigorous; powerful; pushful, forceful.
pujanza *nf* strength, vigour; power; pushfulness, forcefulness, drive.
pujar [1a] **1** *vt price* to raise, push up.
   2 *vi* (a) (*at auction*) to bid, bid up; (*Cards*) to bid.
   (b) to struggle, strain; — **para hacer algo** o **para adentro** (*SAm*) to grin and bear it.
   (c) to falter, dither, hesitate.
   (d) to struggle for words, be at a loss for words.
   (e) to be on the verge of tears.
puje *nm* (*Per*) ticking-off.
pujo *nm* (a) (*Med*) difficulty in relieving oneself.
   (b) (*fig*) longing, strong urge; **sentir** — **de llorar** to be on the verge of tears; **sentir** — **de reírse** to have an uncontrollable urge to laugh.
   (c) (*fig*) attempt, try, shot; —**s** pretensions; **tiene** —**s de caballero** he has pretensions to being a gentleman.
pulcramente *adv* neatly, tidily, smartly; exquisitely; delicately.
pulcritud *nf* neatness, tidiness, smartness; exquisiteness, delicacy.
pulcro *adj* neat, tidy, smart; smartly dressed, smartly turned out; *style etc* exquisite; dainty, delicate.
pulga *nf* (a) flea.
   (b) (*idioms*) **un tío de malas** —**s** a bad-tempered chap, a peppery individual; **tener malas** — to be bad-tempered, be violent, be unpredictable; **no aguantar** —**s** (*fam*) to stand no nonsense; **buscar las** —**s a uno** to tease someone, needle someone (*fam*); **hacer de una** — **un elefante** to make a mountain out of a molehill.
pulgada *nf* inch.
pulgar *nm* thumb.
pulgarada *nf* (a) flick, flip. (b) (*of snuff etc*) pinch.
Pulgarcito *m* Tom Thumb.
pulgón *nm* plant louse; bug.
pulgoso *adj,* **pulguiento** *adj* (*SAm*) full of fleas, verminous.
pulidamente *adv* (a) neatly, tidily; carefully; in a polished way; (*pej*) affectedly. (b) courteously.
pulido *adj* neat, tidy, clean; careful, polished; refined; (*pej*) over-nice, affected, finicky.
pulidor *nm,* **pulidora** *nf* polisher.
pulimentar [1a] *vt* to polish; to put a gloss on, put a shine on; to smooth.
pulimiento *nm* (a) polish, shine; gloss. (b) (*substance*) polish.

pulir [3a] **1** *vt* (a) to polish; to put a gloss on, put a shine on.
   (b) to smooth; to finish (off).
   (c) (*fig*) to polish up, touch up, rub up; *person* to polish up.
   (d) (*fam*) to pinch (*fam*); to sell, flog (*fam*).
   2 pulirse *vr* (*fig*) to acquire polish; to spruce oneself up.
pulmón *nm* lung; — **de acero** iron lung; **a pleno** — **breathe** deeply; *shout* at the top of one's voice.
pulmonar *adj* pulmonary, lung (*attr*).
pulmonía *nf* pneumonia; — **doble** double pneumonia.
pulóver *nm* (*angl*) pullover.
pulpa *nf* pulp; soft mass; (*of fruit, plant*) flesh, soft part; (*Anat*) soft flesh; (*RPl*) boneless meat, fillet; — **de madera** wood pulp.
pulpejo *nm* fleshy part, soft part.
pulpería *nf* (*SAm*) general store, food store; bar, tavern.
pulpero *nm* (*SAm*) storekeeper, grocer; tavern-keeper.
púlpito *nm* pulpit.
pulpo *nm* octopus.
pulposo *adj* pulpy; soft, fleshy.
pulque *nm* (*Ec, Mex*) fermented drink made from maguey juice.
pulquear [1a] (*Mex*) **1** *vi* to drink *pulque*. **2 pulquearse** *vr* to get drunk on *pulque*.
pulquería *nf* (*Mex*) bar, tavern.
pulquérrimo *adj superl of* **pulcro.**
pulsación *nf* (a) beat, pulsation; (*Anat*) throb(bing), beat(ing). (b) (*on typewriter etc*) tap; (*of pianist, typist*) touch.
pulsador *nm* button, push-button; (*Elec*) switch.
pulsar [1a] **1** *vt* (a) *key etc* to strike, touch, tap; *button, switch* to press; (*Mus*) to play.
   (b) (*Med*) — **a uno** to take someone's pulse, feel someone's pulse.
   (c) (*fig*) *opinion etc* to sound out, take, explore.
   2 *vi* to pulsate; to throb, beat.
pulsear [1a] *vi* (*RPl*) to aim at a target.
pulsera *nf* wristlet, bracelet; — **para reloj** watch strap; **reloj de** — wristwatch.
pulso *nm* (a) (*Anat*) pulse; **tomar el** — **a uno** to take someone's pulse, feel someone's pulse; **tomar el** — **a la opinión** to sound out opinion.
   (b) (*Anat*) wrist; (*fig*) strength of wrist; **a** — by sheer strength; with arm upraised, with arm up in the air; (*fig*) by sheer hard work; (*fig*) unaided, all alone; the hard way; **a** — **sudando** by the sweat of one's brow; **dibujo** (**hecho**) **a** — freehand drawing; **tomar un mueble a** — to lift a piece of furniture clean off the ground.
   (c) (*fig*) steadiness, steady hand, firmness of touch; **tener** — (*RPl*) to have a good aim.
   (d) (*fig*) tact, good sense; **con mucho** — very sensibly; with great tact.
   (e) (*Col*) =**pulsera.**
pulular [1a] **1** *vt* (*SAm*) to infest, swarm in, overrun.
   2 *vi* to swarm, abound.
pulverización *nf* (a) pulverization. (b) spray; spraying.
pulverizador *nm* spray, sprayer, spray gun.
pulverizar [1f] *vt* (a) *substance* to pulverize; to powder, convert into powder. (b) *liquid* to spray. (c) (*fig*) *enemy, city* to pound, pulverize, smash.
pulverulento *adj* (a) powdered, powdery. (b) *surface* dusty.
pulla *nf* (a) cutting remark, wounding remark; taunt; dig. (b) obscene remark, rude word.
pum *interj* bang!; thud!; pop!
puma *nf* puma.
puna *nf* (*SAm*) (a) high Andean plateau, bleak upland. (b) (*Med*) mountain sickness.
punción *nf* (*Med*) puncture.
punch *nm* (*SAm: angl*) (a) punch. (b) (*fig*) vigour, strength, punch; agility.
punchar [1a] *vt* (*SAm: angl*) to punch.
punching ['punʃin] *nm* (*angl*) punchball.
pundonor *nm* self-respect, amour propre; honour; face.
pundonoroso *adj* honourable; punctilious, scrupulous.
punga 1 *nf* (*Arg*) thieving. **2** *nmf* (*Chi*) pickpocket, thief.
punguista *nm* (*Arg, Urug*) pickpocket, thief.
pungir [3c] *vt* (a) to prick, puncture; to sting. (b) to cause suffering to.
punible *adj* punishable.
punición *nf* punishment.
púnico 1 *adj* Punic. **2** *nm* (*language*) Punic.
punitivo *adj* punitive.

punta 1 nf **(a)** end; tip, point, sharp end; (of timber etc) thin end; (Geog) point; headland; (Sew etc) corner; — **de lanza** spearhead (also fig); **con la — de la lengua** with the tip of one's tongue; **tener algo en la — de la lengua** to have something on the tip of one's tongue; — **del pie** toe; **de** — on end; endways; **de — a** — fròm one end to the other; **ir de — en blanco** to be all dressed up to the nines; **hacer** — to be first, go first; **sacar** — **a** to sharpen, point, put a point on; **sacar** — **a una observación** to read too much into a remark, force the sense of a remark; **sacar** — **a una máquina** to get the most out of a machine; to use a machine in ways which were never intended; **se le pusieron los pelos de** — her hair stood on end; **estoy hasta la** — **de los pelos con él** I'm utterly fed up with him.

(b) (fig) touch, trace; tinge; **tiene** — **de loco** he has a streak of madness, he's a bit mad; **tiene sus** —**s de filósofo** there's a little of the philosopher about him.

(c) (fig: idioms) **andar** (or **estar**) **de** — to be at odds (con with); **estar de** — to be edgy; to be in a bad mood; **ponerse de** — **con uno** to fall out with someone; to adopt a hostile attitude to someone; **tener de** — **a uno** to be at daggers drawn with someone.

(d) (Tech) small nail.

(e) (of cigar) stub, butt.

(f) (Zool: of bull) horn; (of antler) point, tine.

(g) (Agr) group of cows.

(h) (Cu, PR) leaf of best tobacco.

(i) (Mex) sharp weapon.

(j) (Ven) taunt, snide remark.

(k) (SAm) group, gathering; lot; **una** — **de a lot of**, a bunch of.

(l) (CAm) **en** — wholesale.

2 attr: **horas** — peak hours, rush hours; **velocidad** — maximum speed, top speed.

puntada nf **(a)** (Sew) stitch; — **cruzada** cross-stitch; — **invisible** invisible mending; **dar unas** —**s en** to put a few stitches in, stitch up; **no ha dado** — (fig) he hasn't done a stroke; he's done nothing at all about it.

(b) (fam) hint; **pegar** (or **soltar**) **una** — to drop a hint.

(c) (SAm: Med) stitch; sharp pain.

(d) (Mex) witty remark.

puntal nm **(a)** (Archit) prop, shore, support; (Agr) prop; (Tech) strut, crosspiece; stanchion. **(b)** (fig) prop, support; chief supporter. **(c)** (SAm) snack.

puntapié nm kick; **echar a uno a** —**s** to kick someone out; **pegar un** — **a uno** to give someone a kick.

puntazo nm (Taur) jab (with a horn); (SAm) jab, poke; stab; stab wound, knife wound.

punteado 1 adj dotted, covered with dots; stippled; flecked (de with); design of dots.

2 nm **(a)** series of dots; stippling; flecking.

(b) (Mus) twang; twanging; plucking.

puntear [1a] **1** vt **(a)** to dot, cover (or mark) with dots; to stipple; to fleck.

(b) items to tick, put a mark against; (SAm) list to check off.

(c) (Sew) to stitch (up).

(d) (Mus) to pluck; to twang.

(e) (Chi, RPl) ground to fork over.

(f) (Chi, RPl) march etc to head, lead.

2 vi (Naut) to tack.

punteo nm plucking, twanging.

puntera nf **(a)** toecap. **(b)** pencil top. **(c)** (fam) kick.

puntería nf **(a)** aim, aiming; **enmendar** (or **rectificar**) **la** — to correct one's aim; **hacer la** — **de un cañón** to aim a gun, sight a gun.

(b) (fig) marksmanship; **tener buena** — to be a good shot; **tener mala** — to be a bad shot.

puntero nm **(a)** pointer.

(b) stonecutter's chisel.

(c) outstanding individual; leader, top man.

(d) (SAm) leading team, team which is ahead; leading animal (of a flock or team); leader (of a procession).

(e) (SAm: of watch) hand.

puntiagudo adj sharp, sharp-pointed.

puntilla nf **(a)** (Tech) tack, brad.

(b) (of pen) point, nib.

(c) (Sew) lace edging.

(d) (Taur) short dagger for giving the coup de grâce; **dar la** — to give the coup de grâce, finish off the bull.

(e) de —**s** on tiptoe; **andar de** —**s** to walk on tiptoe.

puntillismo nm pointillisme.

puntillo nm punctilio; exaggerated sense of honour, excessive amour propre.

puntilloso adj punctilious; touchy, sensitive.

punto nm **(a)** (in design etc) dot, spot; fleck; (on plumage etc) spot, speckle; (on card, domino) spot, pip; **diseño a** —**s** design of dots, pattern of dots.

(b) (Typ) point; (also — **final**) full stop; **dos** —**s** colon; — **y coma** semicolon; — **de admiración**, — **de exclamación** exclamation mark; — **de interrogación** question mark, query; —**s suspensivos** dots, suspension points (. . .); — **acápite** full stop, new paragraph; **" — y aparte"** (in dictating) "new paragraph"; **sin faltar** — **ni coma** accurately, faithfully; minutely; **poner los** —**s sobre las íes** to dot the i's and cross the t's.

(c) (in scoring) point; (in exam) mark; **con 8** —**s a favor y 3 en contra** with 8 points for and 3 against; **vencer por** —**s** to win on points.

(d) (in argument, discussion) point; item, matter, question; **contestar** — **por** — to answer point by point; — **capital** crucial point, basic point; crux; —**s de consulta** terms of reference; —**s a tratar** matters to be discussed, agenda.

(e) — **de taxis** taxi stand, cabrank.

(f) (Mus) pitch.

(g) (Sew) stitch; (of fabric) mesh; (in stocking) ladder, run; (Med) stitch; — **de media** plain knitting; **hacer** — to knit; **¡** — **en boca!** mum's the word!, keep it under your hat!; **chaqueta de** — knitted jacket.

(h) (Med) — **de costado** stitch, pain in the side.

(i) (in strap, belt etc) hole; **darse dos** —**s en el cinturón** to let out one's belt, (fig) overeat; **calzar muchos** —**s** to know a lot; **calzar pocos** —**s** to know very little, be pretty dim.

(j) (of place etc) spot, place, point; (Geog) point; (Math) point; (of process) point, stage; (in time) point, moment; — **de apoyo** fulcrum; — **de arranque** starting point; — **cardinal** cardinal point; — **céntrico** central point; — **ciego** (Anat) blind spot; — **clave de las defensas** key point in the defences; — **de congelación** freezing point; — **de contacto** point of contact; — **crítico** critical point, critical moment; — **culminante** culminating moment; topmost point, limit; — **débil**, — **flaco** weak spot, weak point; — **de ebullición** boiling point; — **de fuga** vanishing point; — **de fusión** melting point; — **de inflamación** flash point; — **muerto** (Mech) dead centre; (Aut etc) neutral (gear); (fig) deadlock, stalemate; **las negociaciones están en un** — **muerto** the negotiations are deadlocked, there is stalemate in the talks; **hemos llegado a un** — **muerto** we have reached deadlock; — **neutro** (Mech) dead centre; (Aut etc) neutral (gear); — **panorámico** viewpoint, vantage point; — **de partida** starting point; — **de referencia** point of reference; — **de veraneo** summer resort, holiday resort; — **de vista** point of view, viewpoint; criterion; **él lo mira desde otro** — **de vista** he looks at it from another point of view.

(k) (idioms etc with prep) **a** — ready; **con sus máquinas a** — **para disparar** with their cameras ready to shoot; **llegar a** — to come just at the right moment; **al llegar a este** — at this moment, at this stage; **saber algo a** — **fijo** to know something for sure; **al** — at once, instantly; **está a** — it's ready; **estar a** — **de** + infin to be on the point of + ger, be about to + infin; **poner un motor a** — to tune an engine; **de todo** — completely, absolutely; **bajar de** — to decline, fall off, fall away; **subir de** — to grow, increase; to get worse; **a las 7 en** — at 7 sharp, at 7 on the dot, punctually at 7; **en** — **a** with regard to; **estar en su** — (Cook) to be done to a turn; **una medida muy puesta en su** — a very timely (or proper) measure; **para dejar las cosas en su** — to be absolutely precise; **pongamos las cosas en su** — let's be absolutely clear about this; **poner algo en su** — to bring something to perfection; **hasta el** — **de** + infin to the extent of + ger; **hasta cierto** — up to a point, to some extent; **hasta tal** — **que** . . . to such an extent that . . .

(l) (fam) **¡vaya un** —**!**, **¡está hecho un** — **filipino!** he's a right rogue! (fam).

puntuable adj: **una prueba** — **para el campeonato** a race which counts towards (or scores in) the championship.

puntuación nf **(a)** (Gram, Typ) punctuation.

(b) (act: School etc) marking; (Sport) scoring; **sistema de** — system of scoring.

(c) (School etc) mark(s); class, grade; (Sport) score.

puntual adj **(a)** person reliable, conscientious; prompt, (in timing) punctual.

(b) arrival etc punctual.

(c) report etc reliable; precise; calculation exact, accurate.

puntualidad nf (a) reliability, conscientiousness; promptness; punctuality. (b) precision; exactness, accuracy.

puntualizar [1f] vt (a) to fix, specify, state in detail; to settle, determine. (b) to fix in one's mind (or memory).

puntualmente adv (a) reliably, conscientiously; promptly; punctually. (b) precisely, exactly, accurately.

puntuar [1c] 1 vt (a) (Gram, Typ) to punctuate. (b) exam to mark. 2 vi (Sport etc) to score, count; **eso no puntúa** that doesn't count.

puntudo adj (SAm) sharp.

puntura nf puncture, prick.

punzada nf (a) puncture, prick; jab. (b) (Med) stitch; twinge (of pain), shooting pain; spasm. (c) (fig) pang, twinge (of regret etc). (d) (Cu) silliness.

punzante adj (a) pain shooting, sharp. (b) tool etc sharp. (c) (fig) remark etc biting, caustic.

punzar [1f] 1 vt (a) to puncture, prick, pierce; (Tech) to punch; to perforate. (b) (fig) to hurt, grieve; **le punzan remordimientos** he feels pangs of regret, his conscience pricks him. 2 vi (of pain) to shoot, stab; to sting.

punzó adj (SAm) bright red.

punzón nm (Tech) punch; graver, burin; bodkin.

puñada nf punch, clout; **dar de —s en** to punch, pound, beat on.

puñado nm handful (also fig); **a —s** by handfuls; in plenty, galore.

puñal nm dagger; **poner el — al pecho a uno** (fig) to put someone on the spot.

puñalada nf (a) stab, thrust; **— de misericordia** coup de grâce; see **coser**. (b) (fig) stab, grievous blow; **— encubierta** stab in the back, treacherous thrust.

puñeta nf (a) **¡—!, ¡qué —(s)!** hell!, damnation! (b) **hacer —s** (tabu) to masturbate; **mandar a uno a hacer —s** to tell somebody to go to hell.

puñetazo nm punch; **a —s** with (blows of) one's fists; **dar a uno de —s** to punch someone.

puñetero adj (fam) bloody.

puño nm (a) (Anat) fist; **— cerrado** with one's clenched fist; **apretar los —s** (fig) to struggle hard; **comerse los —s** to be starving; **como un — house** etc tiny, very small; truth etc obvious; tangible, visible; (see also **verdad**); **mentiras como —s** whopping great lies (sl); **de propio —** in one's own handwriting **de — y letra del poeta** in the poet's own handwriting; **meter a uno en un —** to intimidate someone, cow someone; to bring someone under control; **su mujer le tiene en un —** his wife's got him completely under her thumb. (b) (quantity) handful, fistful. (c) (Sew) cuff. (d) (of sword) hilt; (of tool) handle, haft, grip; (of vessel) handle. (e) (fig) **—s** strength; brute force; **es hombre de —s** he's strong, he's tough; **ganar algo con los —s** to get something by sheer hard work; **hacer algo a —s** to do something by hand. (f) (fig) **un — de casa** a tiny house, a very small house.

pupa nf (a) (Med) pimple, blister; lip sore, ulcer. (b) (Ent) pupa.

pupila nf (a) (Anat) pupil. (b) (Law) ward. (c) (Chi, RPl) prostitute.

pupilo nm (a) (of institution) inmate; boarder. (b) (Law) ward.

pupitre nm desk.

pupo nm (Arg, Chi, Ec, Per) navel.

pupón adj (Arg, Mex) (a) replete, full (of food). (b) pot-bellied, fat.

puque nm (Mex) rotten, bad; weak, sickly; sterile.

puquío nm (SAm) spring, fountain.

puramente adv purely, simply.

pura-sangre nmf, pl **pura-sangres** thoroughbred.

puré nm purée, (thick) soup; **— de patatas** mashed potatoes; **— de guisantes** (fig) pea souper, thick fog.

purear [1a] vi (Ec) to drink one's liquor neat.

pureza nf purity (also fig).

purga nf (a) (Med) purge, cathartic, purgative. (b) (Pol) purge. (c) (Mech) venting, draining, airing; **válvula de —** vent.

purgación nf (a) purging, purgative. (b) menstruation. (c) **tener —es** (fam) to have the clap (fam).

purgante nm purgative.

purgar [1h] 1 vt (a) to purge, cleanse (de of); (Mech) to vent, drain, air; (Pol) to purge, liquidate. (b) to purify, refine. (c) (Med) to purge, administer a purgative to. (d) (fig) sin to purge, expiate; passions to purge. 2 **purgarse** vr (a) (Med) to take a purge. (b) (fig) **— de** to purge oneself of.

purgativo adj purgative.

purgatorio nm purgatory (also fig); **¡fue un —!** it was purgatory!

puridad nf (lit) secrecy; **en —** plainly, directly; in secret.

purificación nf purification.

purificar [1g] vt to purify; to cleanse; (Tech) to purify, refine.

Purísima adj superl: **la — the** Virgin.

purismo nm purism.

purista nmf purist.

puritanismo nm puritanism.

puritano 1 adj attitude etc puritanical; church, tradition etc puritan. 2 nm, **puritana** nf puritan.

puro 1 adj (a) substance, colour, language etc pure; unadulterated; gold solid; sky clear. (b) (fig) pure, simple; sheer; truth plain, simple; **de — aburrimiento** out of sheer boredom; **por pura casualidad** by sheer chance. (c) (morally) pure, virtuous, chaste. (d) (SAm) only, just; **me queda una pura porción** I have just one ration left, I have only one ration left. (e) (Mex, Ven) identical; **el hijo es — el padre** the son is exactly like his father. 2 as adv: **de —** out of sheer stupidity; **de — cansado** out of sheer tiredness; **no se le ve el color de — sucio** it's so dirty you can't tell what colour it is. 3 nm (a) cigar. (b) **a — de** by dint of, thanks only to.

púrpura nf purple.

purpurado nm (Eccl) cardinal.

purpurar [1a] vt to dye purple.

purpúreo adj, **purpurino** adj purple.

purpurina nf (Ec, Per) metallic paint (gold, silver etc).

purrela nf (a) bad wine, cheap wine. (b) (fig) **una — a** mere trifle, chicken feed.

purrete nm (RPl) kid (fam), child.

purulento adj purulent.

pus nm pus, matter.

puse etc see **poner**.

pusilánime adj fainthearted, pusillanimous.

pusilanimidad nf faintheartedness, pusillanimity.

pústula nf pustule, sore, pimple.

puta nf (a) whore, prostitute; **— callejera** streetwalker; **casa de —s** brothel; **ir de —s** to go whoring. (b) (SAm: Cards) jack.

putañear [1a] vi to go whoring, consort with prostitutes.

putañero adj that consorts with prostitutes; (fig) randy, oversexed, wolfish (fam).

putativo adj putative, supposed.

puteada nf (Mex, RPl) shower of gross insults.

putear [1a] vi =**putañear**.

putería nf (a) prostitution, whoring. (b) gathering of prostitutes; brothel. (c) (fam) womanly wile(s).

putrefacción nf (a) (act) rotting, putrefaction; decay. (b) rot, rottenness; **— fungoide** dry rot; **sujeto a — food** etc perishable.

putrefacto adj rotten, putrid; decayed.

putrescente adj rotting, putrefying, putrescent.

pútrido adj putrid, rotten.

puya nf goad, pointed stick; point; (Taur) point of the picador's lance.

puyar [1a] 1 vt (a) (SAm) to jab, wound, prick. (b) (Ant, CAm) to upset, needle (fam). 2 vi (Ven: of plant) to shoot, sprout.

puyo nm (Arg) coarse woollen poncho.

puyón nm (a) (Arg, Bol) cock's spur; (Mex) sharp point; (Mex: Bot) prickle, spine, thorn; (CAm, Col, Mex) shoot, bud. (b) (Col, Guat, PR) jab, prick.

Q

que[1] **1** *rel pron* **(a)** (*of person: subject*) who, that; (*acc*) whom, that; (*but relative often omitted, eg*) **la joven — invité** the girl I invited.

(b) (*of thing*) that, which; (*but relative often omitted, eg*) **el coche — compré** the car I bought; **la cama en — pasé la noche** the bed in which I spent the night, the bed I spent the night in; **el día — ella nació** the day (that) she was born, the day when she was born; **la reunión a — yo asistí** the meeting I attended, the meeting at which I was present; **los disgustos — tiene que aguantar** the unpleasantness he has to put up with.

2 *rel pron* (*with article*) see **el**[3], **lo**.

que[2] *conj* **(a)** (*following verb*) that; (*but often omitted, eg*) **creo — va a venir** I think (that) he will come; **no sabía — tuviera coche** I didn't know he had a car; **decir — sí** to say yes; **la idea de — haya oro en Ruritania** the idea that there is gold in Ruritania; **estoy seguro de — lloverá** I am sure (that) it will rain; **¿— no estabas allí?** (are you telling me) you weren't there?; *see* **claro, decir** *etc*.

(b) (*introducing subj verb*) that; **esperar — uno haga algo** to hope that somebody will do something; **querer — uno haga algo** to want someone to do something; **alegrarse de — uno haya llegado** to be glad (that) someone has arrived; **no digo — sea traidor** I'm not saying (that) he's a traitor; **¡— lo haga él!** let him do it!, get him to do it!; **¡— entre!** let him come in!, send him in!; **¡— venga pronto!** let's hope he comes soon!

(c) (*elliptical*) **¡a — no!** *etc: see* **no** (a).

(d) **el que** + *subj* the fact that . . .; **el — tenga dos hermanas guapas no me interesa** the fact that he has two pretty sisters doesn't concern me; **el — quiera estar con su madre es natural** it is natural (that) he should want to be with his mother.

(e) (*result*) that; **soplaba tan fuerte — no podíamos salir** it was blowing so hard (that) we couldn't go out; **huele — es un asco** it smells so much that it's disgusting; *see* **bendición, primor** *etc*.

(f) (*idiom*) **siguió toca — toca** he just kept on playing, he played and played; **estuvieron habla — habla toda la noche** they talked and talked all night.

(g) for, since, because; **vine un poco pronto — está lloviendo** I came a bit early because it's raining; **¡vamos, — cierro!** off with you, (because) I'm closing!; **¡cuidado, — nos vamos!** hold tight, we're off!; **¡suélteme, — voy a gritar!** let go or I'll scream!

(h) (*comparisons*) than; *see* **más** *etc*.

(i) (*idiom*) **yo — tú** if I were you, if I were in your place.

qué 1 *interrog pron*: **¿—?** what?; **¿— dijiste?** what did you say?; **no sé — quiere decir** I don't know what it means; **¿a —?** why?; **¿y a mí —?** so what?, what has that got to do with me?; **¿y —?** so what?, well?; **¿con — lo vas a pagar?** what are you going to pay with?; **how are you going to pay it?; ¿de — le conoces?** how do you recognize him?; **¿en — lo notas?** in what way do you see that?; **sin — ni para —** without rhyme or reason; *see* **más, para** *etc*.

2 *adj* **(a)** (*interrog*) **¿— libro?** what book?; which book?; **¿— edad tiene?** what age is he?, how old is he?; **¿— traje te vas a poner?** which dress are you wearing?; **¿a — velocidad?** at what speed?, how fast?; **¿de — tamaño es?** what size is it?, how big is it?; **dime — libro buscas** tell me which book you are looking for.

(b) (*excl*) **¡— día más espléndido!** what a glorious day!; **¡— bonito!** isn't it pretty!, how pretty it is!; very nice too! (*also iro*); **¡— asco!** how awful!, how revolting!; **¡— susto!** what a scare!; **¡— de cosas te diría!** what a lot I'd have to say to you!; **¡— de gente había!** what a lot of people there were!

quebrada *nf* **(a)** gorge, ravine; gap, pass. **(b)** (*SAm*) brook, stream.

quebradero *nm*: **— de cabeza** headache, worry.

quebradizo *adj* **(a)** fragile, brittle, delicate; *pastry* short; *biscuit etc* crumbly.
(b) (*Med*) sickly, frail.
(c) emotionally fragile, sensitive, readily upset.
(d) (*morally*) frail, easily tempted.

quebrado 1 *adj* **(a)** *ground* broken, rough, uneven, *line* irregular, zigzag.
(b) *face* pale; *complexion* pallid.
(c) (*Med*) ruptured.
(d) (*Fin*) bankrupt.
2 *nm* **(a)** (*Math*) fraction.
(b) (*Fin*) bankrupt.

quebradura *nf* **(a)** fissure, slit, crack. **(b)** (*Geog*) =**quebrada** (a). **(c)** (*Med*) rupture.

quebraja *nf* fissure, slit, crack.

quebrantadura *nf*, **quebrantamiento** *nm* **(a)** (*act*) breaking; cracking; weakening; forcing; violation.
(b) (*state*) exhaustion, exhausted state; broken health.

quebrantar [1a] **1** *vt* **(a)** to break; to crack; to shatter.
(b) *foundations, fury, morale etc* to weaken; *resistance* to break, weaken; *health, position* to undermine, shatter, destroy; *person* to shatter, break.
(c) *lock* to force; *safe, seal* to break open; *prison* to break out of; *sanctuary* to break into, violate; *forbidden ground etc* to trespass on.
(d) *law, promise* to break.
(e) *colour* to tone down.
(f) (*SAm*) *horse* to break in.
2 quebrantarse *vr* (*person*) to be shattered, be broken (in health etc).

quebranto *nm* **(a)** damage, harm; severe loss. **(b)** exhaustion, weakness; broken health; depression, shattered state. **(c)** sorrow, affliction.

quebrar [1k] **1** *vt* **(a)** to break, smash.
(b) *body* to bend (at the waist); to twist.
(c) *career, training, process etc* to interrupt; to alter the course of, interfere seriously with.
(d) *colour* to tone down.
(e) =**quebrantar** (*various senses*).
2 *vi* **(a)** (*Fin*) to fail, go bankrupt.
(b) to weaken.
(c) **— con uno** to break with someone.
3 quebrarse *vr* **(a)** to break, smash, get broken.
(b) (*Med*) to be ruptured; to have a rupture.

quebraza *nf* crack; (*Med*) crack (on the skin), chap.

quebrazón *nf* (*SAm*) smash-up, general shattering, multiple breakage.

quebroso *adj* (*Per*) brittle, fragile.

queco *nm* (*Arg*) brothel.

queche *nm* smack, ketch.

queda *nf* curfew.

quedada *nf* (*Mex, Nic, SD*) spinster, old maid.

quedado *adj* (*Chi, Mex*) feeble, slow, lazy.

quedar [1a] **1** *vi* **(a)** to stay, remain; **quedamos una semana** we stayed a week; **— atrás** to remain behind; to fall behind.
(b) (*in state*) to remain, be; **— asombrado** to be amazed; **— inmóvil** to remain (*or* be, stand *etc*) motionless; (*vehicle etc*) to remain stationary; **— de pie** to remain standing; **— ciego** to go blind; **— cojo** to go lame; **después de eso ha quedado en ridículo** as a result of that he was ridiculed; **A pretendía que B quedara en ridículo** A was trying to make B look ridiculous; **ha quedado sin hacer** it remained undone, nothing was done about it; **el proyecto quedó sin realizar** the plan was never carried out; **ir quedando lejos** to fall behind; **con las reformas el edificio queda feo** as a result of the

alterations the building is ugly; **la cosa queda así** there the matter rests, that's how the affair stands; **¿cuánto te quedo a deber?** how much do I owe you?; **quedó heredero del título** he became heir to the title, that made him heir to the title.

(c) (— **bien** etc) — **bien** to come off well; to do oneself justice; — **bien con uno** to be on good terms with someone, stand well with someone; **por** — **bien** in order to do the right thing; — **mal** to do badly, come off badly; — **mal con uno** to be at odds with someone; **por no** — **mal** in order to do the right thing, so as not to cause any offence; **ha quedado como un canalla** he showed himself to be a rotter, he was shown up as the rotter he is.

(d) (place) to be; **eso queda muy lejos** that's a long way (away); **queda un poco más al oeste** it is (or lies) a little further west; **esa cuestión queda fuera de nuestros límites** that matter lies (or falls, is) outside the bounds of our inquiry.

(e) to remain, be left; **quedan 6** there are 6 left; **me quedan 6** I have 6 left; **nos queda poco dinero** we haven't much money left; **no quedan más que escombros** there is nothing left but rubble; **ya no queda motivo para ello** there is no longer any reason for it; **no me queda otro remedio** I have no alternative (left).

(f) to be . . . still; **quedan pocos días para la fiesta** only a few days remain till the party, there are only a few days to go to the party; **nos quedan 12 kms para llegar al pueblo** there are still 12 kms to go to the village.

(g) — **en** to turn out to be, result in, end up as; **todo ese trabajo quedó en nada** all that work came to nothing; **las discusiones quedaron en un informe más** the discussions merely resulted in one more report.

(h) — **en** + infin to agree to + infin, arrange to + infin; — **en que** . . . to agree that . . .; **¿en qué quedamos?** what do we decide to do then?

(i) — **por** + infin to be still to be + ptp, remain to be + ptp; **las cartas quedan aún por escribir** the letters are still to be written; **eso queda todavía por estudiar** that remains to be studied.

(j) — + ger to be + ger, go on + ger; **él quedaba trabajando en casa** he went on working at home.

2 **quedarse** vr (a) in basic sense, = 1 (a) and (b), eg — **atrás** to remain behind; to fall behind; (additional senses) to stay on, stay behind, linger (on); — **en una pensión** to stay at a boarding house, put up at a boarding house; — **con unos amigos** to stay with some friends; **se me queda pequeña esta camisa** this shirt has got too small for me, I've outgrown this shirt; — **sin** to find oneself out of, run out of; **nos hemos quedado sin café** we've run out of coffee.

(b) (sea, wind) to fall calm.

(c) — **con** to keep, hold on to, retain; to acquire, get hold of; (fig) to take, prefer; **se quedó con mi pluma** he kept my pen, he walked off with my pen; **quédese con la vuelta** keep the change; **entre A y B, me quedo con B** if I have to choose between A and B, I'll take B; **así que me quedé con la más fea de las tres** so I got left with the plainest of the three.

(d) — **con uno** (fam) to swindle someone, cheat someone.

(e) (idioms) **no se queda con la cólera dentro** he can't control his anger, he can't keep his anger bottled up; — **en nada** to come to nothing; **no se quedó en menos** he was not to be outdone.

(f) (Chi: limb) to become paralysed; (person) to die.

(g) — + ger to be + ger, go on + ger; **se nos quedó mirando asombrado** he stood (etc) looking at us in amazement.

quedito adv very softly, very gently.

quedo 1 adj (a) still. (b) voice quiet, soft, gentle; step etc soft. **2** adv softly, gently; **¡—!** gently now!

quehacer nm job, task; —**es** (domésticos) household jobs, chores; **agobiado de** — overburdened with work; **tener mucho** — to have a lot to do.

queja nf (a) complaint; protest; grumble, grouse (fam); grudge, resentment; (Law) protest; **una** — **infundada** an unjustified complaint; **formar** — **de uno** to make a complaint about someone; **tener** — **de uno** to have a complaint to make about someone; **tengo** — **de ti** I've a bone to pick with you.

(b) moan, groan; — **de dolor** groan of pain.

quejadera nf (Col, Mex), **quejambre** nf (Col, Mex) moan.

quejarse [1a] vr (a) to complain (de about, of), grumble (de about, at); to protest (de about, at);

— **de que** . . . to complain (about the fact) that . . .; — **a un oficial** to complain to an official.

(b) to moan, groan; to whine.

quejica nmf (fam), **quejicoso** nm, **quejicosa** nf (fam) = **quejón**.

quejido nm moan, groan; whine; **dar** —**s** to moan, groan; to whine.

quejón (fam) **1** adj grumbling, complaining. **2** nm, **quejona** nf grumbler, constant complainer.

quejoso adj person complaining; tone querulous, whining; plaintive.

quejumbre nf moan, groan.

quejumbroso adj = **quejoso**.

quelite nm (CAm, Mex) greens, vegetables; shoot, tip, green part.

quelonia nf (Ven) turtle.

quelpo nm kelp.

quema nf (a) fire; burning, combustion. (b) (Arg) rubbish dump. (c) (Mex) burning-off (of scrub). (d) (Mex: fig) danger.

quemado adj (a) burned, burnt; **aquí huele a** — I smell something burning in here; **esto sabe a** — this has a burnt taste. (b) (Arg, Mex) very dark.

quemador nm burner; — **de gas** gas burner.

quemadura nf (a) burn; scald; sunburn; (of fuse) blowing, blow-out. (b) (Bot: by frost) cutting; withering. (c) (Bot: disease) smut.

quemar [1a] **1** vt (a) to burn (also Cook; of acid, sun); to burn up; to set on fire, kindle; to scorch; (with liquid) to scald; fuse to blow, burn out.

(b) plants (of frost) to cut, wither, burn.

(c) (fig) fortune etc to burn up, squander; sum to spend quickly, get through in no time; prices to slash, cut.

(d) (fig) to annoy, upset; **estar muy quemado** to have suffered an unpleasant experience.

(e) (CAm, Mex) to denounce, inform on.

(f) (Cu, Mex, PR) to swindle.

(g) (Ven) to shoot.

2 vi (a) to be burning hot; **esto está que quema, está quemando** it's burning hot; **es una especia que quema en la lengua** it's a spice that tastes really hot, it's a spice that burns the tongue.

(b) (of skin) to get tanned.

3 quemarse vr (a) to burn up, burn away; to burn down; to scorch, get scorched; to get sunburnt; — **con la sopa** to burn one's mouth on the soup; **¡que me quemo!** (fig) I'm scorching!, I'm terribly hot!

(b) (in search) to get warm; **¡que te quemas!** you are getting warm!

(c) (fig) to fret.

(d) (Arg, Cu) to get depressed.

quemarropa: a — adv point-blank (also fig).

quemazón nf (a) burn; burning, combustion; (Ant, CAm, Mex) fire.

(b) intense heat.

(c) burning sensation; (fig) itch; smarting, sting.

(d) (fig) cutting remark, wounding thing (to say).

(e) (fig) pique, resentment, annoyance.

(f) (Comm: fam) bargain sale, cut-price sale.

(g) (Bol, Chi) mirage (on the pampas).

quena nf (Arg, Bol, Per) rustic flute.

quepo etc see **caber**.

queque nm (SAm) pancake; (CAm, Mex) bun, cake.

querella nf (a) complaint. (b) (Law) charge, accusation. (c) dispute, controversy.

querellante 1 adj actionable; giving grounds for complaint. **2** nmf (Law) plaintiff.

querellar [1a] **1** vt to scold, reprimand.

2 querellarse vr (a) to complain.

(b) (Law) to file a complaint, bring an action (ante before; contra, de against).

querencia nf (a) (Zool) lair, haunt; (fig) favourite spot, home ground, haunt; **buscar la** — to home, head for home.

(b) (Zool) homing instinct; (fig) longing for home, homesickness.

querendón (SAm) **1** adj affectionate, loving, of an affectionate nature; susceptible to women. **2** nm favourite, pet; spoiled child.

querer [2u] **1** vti (a) to want, wish (for); **¿cuál quieres?** which one do you want?; **no quiero más** I don't want any more; **¿qué más quieres?** what more do you want?; **¿cuánto quieren por el coche?** how much do they want for the car?, what are they asking for the car?; **como Vd quiera** as you wish, as you please; **ven cuando quieras** come when you like; **quiera o no, quiera que no** willy-nilly, whether he (etc) likes it or not; **lo hizo queriendo** (fam) he did it deliberately; **lo hizo sin** — he didn't mean to do it, he did it inadvertently, he did it by mistake; — **es poder** where there's a will there's a way.

(b) (*with verb construction*) — **hacer algo** to want to do something, wish to do something; — **que uno haga algo** to want someone to do something; **no quiso pagar** he didn't want to pay; he refused to pay; **ha querido quedarse en casa** he preferred to stay at home, he decided to stay at home; **¿quiere abrir la ventana?** would you mind opening the window?, please open the window; **más quiero +** *infin* I would rather + *infin*, I would prefer to + *infin*; **mejor quisiera +** *infin* I would rather + *infin*; **la ley quiere que seamos buenos** the law wants us to be good; **este crítico quiere que Góngora haya sido loco** this critic tries to make out that Góngora was mad, this critic would have us believe that Góngora was mad; **la tradición quiere que . . .** tradition has it that . . .; **éste quiere que le rompan la cabeza** (*fam*) this fellow is asking for a crack on the head.

(c) (*absolute*) **¡no quiero!** I won't!, I refuse!; **sí quiero** (*marriage*) I will; **lo hago porque quiero** I do it because I want to; **pero no quiso** but he refused; but he was unwilling; **¿quiere?** do you want some?, would you like some?

(d) to need, demand; **tal traje quiere un sombrero ancho** that dress needs a big hat to go with it; **¡esto quiere unas copas!** we must have a drink on that!, that deserves a drink to celebrate it!

(e) (*impersonal use*) **quería amanecer** dawn was about to break; **parece que quiere llover** it looks like rain, it seems that it's trying to rain.

(f) *person* to love; to like; — **bien a uno** to be fond of someone; **¡te quiero, bobo!** I love you, you idiot!; **en la oficina le quieren mucho** he is well liked at the office; **¿no me quieres siquiera un poquito?** don't you like me just a little bit?; **hace tiempo que te quiero** I've been in love with you for a long time; **hacerse — por uno** to endear oneself to someone; **¡por lo que más quieras!** by all that's sacred!; **me quiere . . . no me quiere** (*picking off petals etc*) she loves me . . . she loves me not.

(g) **como quiera** etc: see **comoquiera, cuandoquiera, dondequiera.**

2 *nm* love, affection; **tener — a** to be fond of.

querida *nf* **(a)** darling, beloved; **¡sí, —!** yes, darling! **(b)** (*pej*) mistress.

querido 1 *adj* dear, darling, beloved; (*in letters*) dear; **nuestra querida patria** our beloved country.

2 *nm* darling, beloved; **¡sí, —!** yes, darling!; **el — de las musas** the darling of the muses.

querindongo *nm*, **querindonga** *nf* (*SAm*) lover.

querosén *nm*, **queroseno** *nm* (*Acad*), **querosín** *nm* (*SAm*) kerosene, paraffin.

querúbico *adj* cherubic.

querubín *nm* cherub.

quesera *nf* **(a)** dairymaid; cheesemaker. **(b)** cheese-dish.

quesería *nf* dairy; cheese factory.

quesero *nm* dairyman; cheesemaker.

queso *nm* cheese; — **de bola** Dutch cheese; — **crema** cream cheese; — **helado** ice-cream brick; — **rallado** grated cheese; **darla a uno con —** (*fam*) to swindle someone, pull a fast one on someone.

quetzal *nm standard monetary unit of Guatemala.*

quiá *interj* never!, not on your life!; surely not!

quicio *nm* hinge; **estar fuera de —** (*fig*) to be out of joint; **sacar a uno de —** (*fig*) to irritate someone, get on someone's nerves; to get someone worked up; **estas cosas me sacan de —** these things make me see red.

Quico: ponerse como el — (*fam*) to stuff oneself; to get as fat as a pig.

quichuista *nm* **(a)** (*SAm*) Quichua specialist. **(b)** (*Arg, Bol, Per*) Quichua speaker.

quid *nm* gist, core, root, crux; **dar en el —** to hit the nail on the head.

quídam *nm* **(a)** somebody, somebody or other. **(b)** (*pej*) nobody, nonentity.

quiebra *nf* **(a)** crack, fissure; slit.

(b) (*Fin*) bankruptcy; failure; (*Econ*) slump, crash, collapse; (*fig*) failure; risk of failure; **es una cosa que no tiene —** it just can't go wrong, it's a venture that carries no risk.

quiebro *nm* **(a)** (*Taur etc*) dodge, swerve; avoiding action; **dar el — a uno** (*fig*) to dodge someone. **(b)** (*Mus*) grace note(s), trill.

quien *rel pron* **(a)** (*subject*) who, (*acc*) whom; **la señorita con — hablaba** the young lady to whom I was talking, the young lady I was talking to; **las personas con —es estabas** the people you were with; **esta señora es a — tienes que dar el recado** this is the lady to whom you are to give the message.

(b) (*indefinite*) — **dice eso es tonto** whoever says

that is a fool; — **lo sepa, que lo diga** or **que lo diga — lo sepa** let whoever knows it speak up about it; — **habla más trabaja menos** he who talks most works least; **contestó como — no quería** he answered as if he was reluctant to.

(c) — **más, — menos tiene sus problemas** everybody has problems.

quién *interrog pron* (*subject*) who, (*acc*) whom; **¿— es?** who is it?; who's there?; (*Tel*) who's calling?; **"¿Q— es Q—?"** "Who's Who?"; **¿a — lo diste?** to whom did you give it?, who did you give it to?; **¿a quién le toca jugar?** whose turn is it to play?, whose go is it?; **¿con — estabas anoche?** who were you with last night?; **¿de — es la bufanda esa?** whose scarf is that?, who does that scarf belong to?; **¿— de ustedes lo reconoce?** which of you recognizes it?; **no sé — lo dijo primero** I don't know who said it first.

quienquiera *indef pron*, *pl* **quienesquiera** whoever; **le cazaremos — que sea** we'll catch him whoever he is.

quietismo *nm* quietism.

quietista *nmf* quietist.

quieto *adj* **(a)** still; motionless; **¡—!** (*to dog*) down boy!; **¡estáte —!** keep still!, stop fidgeting!; behave yourself!; **dejar — a uno** to leave someone alone; **estar — como un poste** (*or* **una estatua**) to stand stock-still.

(b) *character* calm, staid, placid.

quietud *nf* stillness; quietude; calm.

quijada *nf* jaw, jawbone.

quijotada *nf* quixotic act.

quijote *nm* quixotic person; hopelessly unrealistic person, do-gooder (*fam*); well-meaning busybody; **Don Q—** Don Quixote.

quijotería *nf* **(a)** = quijotismo. **(b)** = quijotada.

quijotescamente *adv* quixotically.

quijotesco *adj* quixotic.

quijotismo *nm* quixotism.

quilatar [1a] *vt* = aquilatar.

quilate *nm* carat.

quilco *nm* (*Chi*) large basket.

quiligua *nf* (*Mex*) large basket.

quilo[1] *nm* (*Anat*) chyle; **sudar el —** (*fam*) to have a tough time; to slave, work like a nigger.

quilo[2] *nm* kilo, kilogramme.

quilo . . . *alternative spelling of* **kilo** . . .

quilombear [1a] *vi* (*RPl*) to patronize brothels.

quilombera *nf* (*RPl*) prostitute.

quilombo *nm* **(a)** (*Bol, Chi, Per, RPl*) brothel. **(b)** (*Bol, Chi, Per, RPl*) row, set-to (*fam*). **(c)** (*Col, Ec, Ven*) out-of-the-way spot; rustic hut, shack.

quiltrear [1a] *vt* (*Chi*) to annoy.

quiltro *nm* (*Chi*) **(a)** small dog, yapping dog. **(b)** nobody, nonentity.

quilla *nf* (*all senses*) keel; **colocar la — de un buque** to lay down a ship; **dar de — to keel over.**

quillango *nm* (*Bol, Chi, RPl*) fur blanket.

quimba *nf* **(a)** (*Col, Ec, Ven*) sandal. **(b)** (*Ec*) grimace. **(c)** (*Col*) — **s** difficulties; debts.

quimbo *nm* (*Ant*) knife, machete.

quimera *nf* **(a)** (*Myth*) chimera.

(b) hallucination; fancy, fantastic idea; impossible notion, pipe dream.

(c) unfounded suspicion; **tener la — de que . . .** to suspect quite wrongly that . . .

(d) quarrel.

quimérico *adj* fantastic, fanciful; *hope, plan etc* impossible.

quimerista 1 *adj* quarrelsome; rowdy. **2** *nmf* quarrelsome person; rowdy, brawler.

quimerizar [1f] *vi* to indulge in fantasy, indulge in pipe dreams.

química *nf* chemistry.

químico 1 *adj* chemical. **2** *nm* chemist.

quimono *nm* kimono.

quina *nf* quinine, Peruvian bark.

quincalla *nf* hardware, ironmongery.

quincallería *nf* ironmonger's (shop), hardware store (*US*).

quincallero *nm* ironmonger, hardware dealer (*US*).

quince 1 *adj* fifteen; fifteenth; — **días** (*freq*) fortnight; **dar — y raya a uno** to be able to beat someone hollow (**en** at), be more than a match for someone (**en** at).

2 *nm* fifteen.

quinceañero 1 *adj* fifteen-year old, (*loosely*) teenage. **2** *nm*, **quinceañera** *nf* fifteen-year old, (*loosely*) teenager.

quincena *nf* **(a)** fortnight. **(b)** fortnight's imprisonment. **(c)** fortnightly pay.

quincenal *adj* fortnightly.

quinceno *adj* fifteenth.
Quincuagésima *f* Quincuagesima.
quincuagésimo *adj* fiftieth.
quincha *nf* (SAm) wall (or roof etc) made of rushes and mud.
quinchar [1a] *vt* (SAm) to build walls (etc) of quincha.
quincho *nm* (Arg, Urug) mud hut; (Bol, Chi) mud fence.
quindécimo *adj* fifteenth.
quinfa *nf* (Col) sandal.
quingentésimo *adj* five-hundredth.
quingo *nm* (Col, Per) twist, turn; zigzag.
quinguear [1a] *vi* (Ec, Col) to twist, turn; to zigzag.
quiniela *nf* pools coupon; —s football pool(s).
quinielista *nmf* punter, participant in a football pool.
quinientos *adj* five hundred.
quinina *nf* quinine.
quinqué *nm* (a) oil lamp. (b) (fam) know-how, shrewdness; **tener mucho** — to know what's going on, know what the score is.
quinquenal *adj* quinquennial; **plan** — five-year plan.
quinquenio *nm* quinquennium, five-year period.
quinqui *nm* (fam) bandit, gangster.
quinta *nf* (a) villa, country house; (SAm) estate on the outskirts of a town.
  (b) (Mil) draft, call-up; **la** — **de 1978** the 1978 call-up, the class called up in 1978; **ser de la** — **de uno** to be the same age as someone; **entrar en** —**s** to reach the call-up age; to be called up.
  (c) (Mus) fifth.
quintacolumnista *nmf* fifth columnist.
quintada *nf* (fam) rag, trick.
quintaescencia *nf* quintessence.
quintal *nm* (Castile) measure of weight, = 46 kg; — métrico = 100 kg.
quintar [1a] *vt* (Mil) to call up, conscript, draft (US).
quintería *nf* farmhouse.
quintero *nm* farmer; farmhand, labourer.
quinteto *nm* quintet(te).
quintilla *nf* (Lit: Hist) a five-line stanza.
quintillizos *nmpl*, **quintillizas** *nfpl* quintuplets.
quinto 1 *adj* fifth. 2 *nm* (a) (Math) fifth. (b) (Mil) conscript, recruit, national serviceman. (c) (fam) bingo.
quintuplicar [1g] 1 *vt* to quintuple. 2 **quintuplicarse** *vr* to quintuple.
quintuplo 1 *adj* quintuple, fivefold. 2 *nm* quintuple; **X es el** — **de Y** X is five times the size of Y.
quinzavo *adj* fifteenth.
quiñazo *nm* (SAm) smash, collision.
quiosco *nm* (in street) kiosk, stand, stall; (in garden) summerhouse, pavilion; (in park: also — **de música**) bandstand; — **de necesidad** public lavatory; — **de periódicos** news stand.
quipe *nm* (Bol, Ec) knapsack, bag; (Per) bundle, roll.
quiquiriquí *nm* cock-a-doodle-doo.
quirico *nm* (Ven) servant; messenger; petty thief.
quirófano *nm* operating theatre.
quiromancia *nf* palmistry.
quiromántico *nm*, **quiromántica** *nf* palmist.
quiropedia *nf* chiropody.
quiropodista *nmf* chiropodist.
quirúrgico *adj* surgical.
quise *etc* see **querer**.
quisicosa *nf* (fam) puzzle, conundrum.
quisling ['kizlin] *nm*, *pl* **quislings** ['kizlin] quisling.
quisquilla *nf* (a) trifle, triviality.
  (b) slight snag, minor difficulty.
  (c) —s quibbles, quibbling, hair-splitting; **¡déjate de** —**s!** stop fussing!; don't quibble! **pararse en** —**s** to bicker; to quibble.
  (d) (Zool) shrimp.
quisquilloso *adj* (a) touchy, oversensitive; irritable; pernickety (fam), choosy (fam). (b) quibbling, hair-splitting.
quiste *nm* cyst.
quisto *adj*: **bien** —, **mal** — see **bienquisto**, **malquisto**.
quita *nf* (a) release (from a debt); (SAm) rebate.
  (b) **de** — **y pon** see **quitapón**.

quitaesmalte *nm* nail-polish remover.
quitagusto *nm* (Ec, Per) intruder, gatecrasher.
quitalodos *nm*, *pl* **quitalodos** boot-scraper.
quitamanchas *nm*, *pl* **quitamanchas** (a) cleaning material, stain remover. (b) (person) dry cleaner; dry-cleaner's (shop).
quitamiedos *nm*, *pl* **quitamiedos** handrail.
quitamotas *nm*, *pl* **quitamotas** (fam) bootlicker (fam).
quitanieves *nm*, *pl* **quitanieves** snowplough.
quitapelillos *nm*, *pl* **quitapelillos** (fam) bootlicker (fam).
quitapenas *nm*, *pl* **quitapenas** (fam) pistol, rod (US sl).
quitapesares *nm*, *pl* **quitapesares** comfort; distraction.
quitapiedras *nm*, *pl* **quitapiedras** (Rail) cowcatcher.
quitapón: **pieza** *f* **de** — detachable part, removable part.
quitar [1a] 1 *vt* (a) to take away, remove; clothing etc to take off; stain to remove, get rid of, get out; pain etc to relieve, stop, kill; happiness to destroy; life to take; part (Mech etc) to remove, take out, take off; table to clear; abuse, difficulty, obstacle to remove, do away with, put an end to; time to take (up); trouble, worry to save, prevent; (Math) to take away, subtract; value etc to reduce; (pej) to remove, steal; — **extensión a un campo** to reduce the size of a field; — **importancia a un acontecimiento** to diminish the importance of an event; **no quita nada de su valor** it does not detract at all from its value; **me quita mucho tiempo** it takes up a lot of my time; **le van a** — **ese privilegio** they are going to take that privilege away from him; **le quitaron la cartera en el tren** he had his wallet stolen on the train; **me quitó las ganas de comer** it took away my appetite; **el café me quita el sueño** coffee stops me sleeping; **quitando 3 o 4, van a ir todos** except for 3 or 4 everybody is going; see **medio** etc.
  (b) blow to avert, ward off; (Fencing) to parry.
  (c) — **a uno de hacer algo** to stop someone doing something, prevent someone (from) doing something; **eso no quita para que me ayudes** that doesn't stop you helping me, that is no bar to your helping me.
  2 *vi* (a) **¡quita!, ¡quita de ahí!** get away!
  (b) **ni quito ni pongo** I'm not saying one thing or the other; I'm strictly neutral.
  3 **quitarse** *vr* (a) to remove oneself; to withdraw (de from); — **de la vista de uno** to remove oneself from someone's sight; **esa mancha de vino no se quita** that wine stain won't come off (or come out); **¡quítate de ahí!** come (or get) out of there!, off with you!; see **medio** etc.
  (b) — **algo de encima** to get rid of something; to cast something off, shake something off; — **la ropa** to take off one's clothing; — **una jaqueca andando** to walk off a headache.
  (c) — **de un vicio** to give up a vice, wean oneself away from a vice; — **del tabaco** to give up smoking; **se me ha quitado el gusto de fumar** I've lost my taste for smoking; **quitémonos de tonterías** let's stop being silly.
quitasol *nm* sunshade, parasol.
quite *nm* (a) removal.
  (b) (Fencing) parry.
  (c) dodge, sidestep, swerve; (Taur) manoeuvre whereby bullfighters draw the bull away from an injured colleague; **estar al** — to be ready to go to someone's aid; **esto no tiene** — there's no help for it.
  (d) (SAm: Sport) tackle.
quiteño 1 *adj* of Quito. 2 *nm*, **quiteña** *nf* native (or inhabitant) of Quito; **los** —**s** the people of Quito.
quitrín *nm* (Ant, Chi, Guat) open two-wheeled carriage.
quizá(s) [ki'θa] *adv* perhaps, maybe.
quórum ['korum] *nm*, *pl* **quórums** ['korum] quorum; **constituir** — to constitute (or make up) a quorum.

R

rabada nf hindquarter, rump.

rabadán nm head shepherd.

rabadilla nf (Anat) coccyx.

rábano nm radish; — **picante** horseradish; **¡un —!** (fam) get away!; **no se me da un —**, **(no) me importa un —** I don't care two hoots (de about); **tomar el — por las hojas** to get hold of the wrong end of the stick, bark up the wrong tree.

rabear [1a] vi (dog) to wag its tail.

rebelasiano adj Rabelaisian.

rabí nm (before name) rabbi.

rabia nf (a) (Med) rabies.
(b) (fig) fury, rage, anger; bad feeling; **¡qué —!** isn't it infuriating!; **me da —** it maddens me, it infuriates me; **tener — a uno** to have a grudge against someone, have it in for someone; **el maestro le tiene —** the teacher has it in for him, the teacher doesn't like him; **tomar — a** to take a dislike to.
(c) **con —** (SAm) extremely, terribly (fam); **es fea con —** she's terribly ugly.

rabiadero nm (Col) annoyance.

rabiar [1b] vi (a) (Med) to have rabies.
(b) (fig) to suffer terribly, be in great pain; **estaba rabiando de dolor de muelas** she had raging toothache.
(c) (fig) **esto quema** (or **pica**) **que rabia** this is hot enough to burn your mouth; **este cóctel está que rabia** this cocktail has got a real kick to it.
(d) (fig) to rage, rave, be furious; — **contra** to storm at, rave about; **hacer — a uno** to rouse someone to a fury; **las cosas así le hacen** — things like that make him see red; **está que rabia** he's hopping mad, he's furious; **¡para que rabies!** so there!; just to turn you green with envy!
(e) (fig) — **por algo** to long for, be dying for; — **por — + infin** to be dying to + infin.
(f) **me gusta a —** I'm terribly fond of it (fam).

rabiasca nf (Cu, PR) fit of temper.

rabieta nf (fam) fit of temper; paddy (fam), pet, tantrum (fam); **tomarse una —** to get cross, fly into a rage.

rabietas nmf, pl **rabietas** (fam) touchy sort, bad-tempered person.

rabillo nm (a) (Anat) small tail.
(b) (Bot) leaf stalk.
(c) tip; corner; thin part; thin strip of material; **mirar con el — del ojo** to look out of the corner of one's eye.

rabimocho adj (Col, Mex, Per, PR) cut-tailed.

rabina nf rapeseed.

rabínico adj rabbinical.

rabino nm rabbi; **gran —** chief rabbi.

rabión nm (also **—es**) rapids.

rabiosamente adv (fig) furiously; terribly, violently; rabidly.

rabioso adj (a) (Med) rabid, suffering from rabies; **perro —** (fig) mad dog.
(b) (fig) furious; pain terrible, raging, violent; supporter etc rabid; taste hot; **poner — a uno** to enrage someone.

rabo nm (a) (Anat) tail; **con el — entre las piernas** crestfallen, dejected; **queda el — por desollar** we've still got the most difficult part to do.
(b) (fig) tail, train, hanging part; **=rabillo (b)** and (c).

rabón adj (a) short-tailed; bobtailed; tailless.
(b) (SAm) short, small.
(c) (Chi) stark naked; half-naked.
(d) (Arg, Ven) knife damaged.
(e) (Mex) wretched.

rabona nf (a) **hacer —** to play truant. (b) (SAm) camp follower.

rabonear [1a] vi (SAm) to play truant.

rabosear [1a] vt to mess up, rumple, crumple.

rabotada nf rude remark; coarse expression.

rabudo adj long-tailed.

racanear [1a] vi (fam) to slack; to swing the lead (fam).

racaneo nm (fam) slackness, idleness.

rácano nm (fam) (a) slacker, idler; **hacer el —** to slack; to swing the lead (fam). (b) (Aut) grid, old car.

racial adj racial, race (attr); **odio —** race hatred.

racimo nm bunch, cluster; (Bot) raceme.

raciocinación nf ratiocination.

raciocinar [1a] vi to reason.

raciocinio nm (a) (faculty) reason. (b) (act) reasoning.

ración nf (a) ratio; portion, helping; **—es** (Mil) rations; — **de hambre** starvation ration; — **de reserva** emergency ration; iron ration.
(b) (Eccl) prebend.

racional adj (a) (Math, Philos etc) rational. (b) rational, reasonable, sensible.

racionalidad nf rationality.

racionalismo nm rationalism.

racionalista 1 adj rationalist. 2 nmf rationalist.

racionalización nf rationalization.

racionalizar [1f] vt to rationalize.

racionalmente adv rationally, reasonably, sensibly.

racionamiento nm rationing.

racionar [1a] vt (a) to ration; **estar racionado** to be rationed, be on the ration. (b) to ration out, share out.

racionero nm (Eccl) prebendary.

racionista nmf (a) person living on an allowance. (b) (Theat) player of bit parts; ham (sl), third-rate actor (or actress).

racismo nm racialism, racism.

racista 1 adj racial, racialist. 2 nmf racialist.

racha nf (a) (Meteorol) gust of wind; squall.
(b) (fig) string, series; **buena —** piece of luck, stroke of luck, lucky break; **mala —** piece of bad luck; unlucky spell, spell when everything goes wrong; **a —s** by fits and starts.

racheado adj wind gusty, squally.

rada nf (Naut) roads, roadstead; natural bay.

radar nm radar.

radiación nf (a) radiation. (b) broadcasting.

radiactividad nf radioactivity.

radiactivo adj radioactive.

radiado adj (a) (Bot etc) radiate. (b) radio (attr), broadcast; **en una interviú radiada** in a radio interview.

radiador nm radiator.

radial adj (a) (Mech etc) radial. (b) (SAm) radio (attr), broadcasting (attr).

radiante adj (Phys and fig) radiant; **estaba —** she was radiant (de with).

radiar[1] [1b] vt (a) (Phys etc) to radiate; to irradiate. (b) to broadcast. (c) (Med) to treat with X-rays.

radiar[2] [1b] vt (SAm) to delete, cross off (a list); to expel; to remove.

radical 1 adj radical. 2 nm (a) (Gram, Math) root; square-root sign. (b) (Pol) radical.

radicalismo nm radicalism.

radicalmente adv radically.

radicar [1g] 1 vi (a) (Bot and fig) to take root.
(b) to be, be situated, lie.
(c) (of difficulty etc) — **en** to lie in.
2 **radicarse** vr to establish oneself, put down one's roots (en in).

radicula nf (Bot) radicle.

radio[1] nm (a) (Math) radius; — **de acción** sphere of jurisdiction, extent of one's authority; (Aer) range; **un avión de largo — de acción** a long-range aircraft; **en un — de 10 km alrededor de la ciudad** within a radius of 10 km round the city.
(b) (of wheel) spoke.
(c) (Anat) radius.

(d) (*Chem*) radium.

(e) (*fam*) wireless message.

(f) (*SAm*) =radio².

radio² *nf* (a) (*in general*) radio, wireless; broadcasting; R— Eslobodia Radio Slobodia; **por** — by radio, on the radio, over the radio; **hablar por** — to talk on the radio.

(b) radio (set), wireless (set).

radio . . . **radio** . . .

radioactivo *adj* =radiactivo.

radioastronomía *nf* radio astronomy.

radiobiología *nf* radiobiology.

radiocaptar [1a] *vt station* to monitor.

radiodifusión *nf* broadcasting.

radiodifusora *nf* (*SAm*) radio station, transmitter.

radiodifusorio *adj* broadcasting (*attr*).

radioemisora *nf* radio station, transmitter.

radioescucha *nmf* listener.

radioexperimentador *nm* radio fan, ham (*sl*).

radiofaro *nm* radio beacon, wireless beam.

radiofonía *nf* radio, wireless.

radiofónico *adj* radio (*attr*).

radiofonógrafo *nm* (*SAm*) radiogram.

radiogoniómetro *nm* direction finder.

radiografía *nf* (a) (*in general*) radiography, X-ray photography. (b) (*una* —) radiograph, X-ray photograph (*or* picture).

radiografiar [1c] *vt* (a) (*Med*) to X-ray. (b) to radio, send by radio.

radiográfico *adj* X-ray (*attr*).

radiograma *nm* wireless message.

radiogramola *nf* radiogram; — **tragamonedas**, — **tragaperras** jukebox.

radioisótopo *nm* radioisotope.

radiología *nf* radiology.

radiólogo *nm* radiologist.

radiooperador *nm* (*SAm*) radio operator, wireless operator.

radiorreceptor *nm* radio (set), wireless (set), receiver; — **de contrastación** monitor set.

radioscopia *nf* radioscopy.

radiotelefonía *nf* radiotelephony.

radioteléfono *nm* radiotelephone.

radiotelegrafía *nf* radiotelegraphy, wireless (telegraphy).

radiotelegrafista *nm* radio operator, wireless operator.

radiotelescopio *nm* radiotelescope.

radioterapia *nf* radiotherapy.

radioyente *nmf* listener.

raedera *nf* scraper.

raedura *nf* (a) scrape, scraping; (*Med*) abrasion, graze. (b) —s scrapings, filings.

raer [2z] **1** *vt* (a) to scrape; to scrape off; to erase; (*Med*) to abrade, graze; to chafe; *cloth etc* to fray.

(b) *contents of vessel* to level off, level with the brim.

2 raerse *vr* to chafe; (*cloth*) to fray.

Rafael m Raphael.

ráfaga *nf* (a) (*Meteorol*) gust, squall; sudden blast.

(b) (*of shots*) burst.

(c) (*of light, intuition*) flash.

(d) (*Arg, Per*) run of luck; **estar de** (*or* **en**) — to have a spell of bad luck.

rafañoso *adj* (*Arg*) dirty; coarse, common.

rafia *nf* raffia.

raglán *nm* raglan.

raicear [1a] *vi* (*CAm, Ven*) to take root.

raicero *nm* (*SAm*) mass of roots, root system.

raid [raid] *nm, pl* **raids** [raid] (*angl, gall*) (a) (*Mil*) raid, attack; expedition.

(b) police raid; criminal raid.

(c) attempt, endeavour; enterprise; heroic undertaking.

(d) endurance test; (*Aer*) long-distance flight; (*Aut*) rally drive; transcontinental expedition by car.

(e) (*Mex: Aut*) lift.

raído *adj* (a) *cloth* frayed, threadbare; *garment, person* shabby. (b) (*fig*) shameless.

raigambre *nf* (*often* m) (a) (*Bot*) mass of roots; root system.

(b) (*fig*) tradition; antecedents, history; **una familia de fuerte** — local a family with deep roots in the area; **tienen** — **liberal** they have a liberal tradition.

raigón *nm* (*Bot*) thick root, stump; (*Anat*) root, stump.

rail, raíl *nm* (*angl*) rail.

Raimundo m Raymond.

raíz *nf* (a) (*Bot etc*) root; **arrancar algo de** — to root something out completely, destroy something root

and branch; **cortar un peligro de** — to nip a danger in the bud; **echar raíces** to take root (*algo fig*).

(b) (*Math*) root; — **cuadrada** square root; — **cúbica** cube root.

(c) root.

(d) (*fig*) root, origin; **a** — **de** immediately after, immediately following; as a result of.

raja *nf* (a) slit, split; crack; gash, chink.

(b) sliver, splinter, thin piece; (*of lemon etc*) slice.

(c) (*fam*) **sacar** — to get a rake-off (*fam*), get a share.

(d) (*PR*) **tener** — to have Negro blood.

rajá *nm* rajah.

rajada *nf* (a) (*Arg*) flight, hasty exit. (b) (*Mex*) cowardly act; backing down, going back on one's word.

rajador *adj* (*Arg*) fast.

rajadura *nf* =raja (a) *and* (b).

rajamacana *nm* (*Ven*) (a) hard work, drudgery; tough job. (b) tough character; stubborn person. (c) expert. (d) **a** — =a rajatabla.

rajante *adj* (*Arg*) peremptory, sharp.

rajar [1a] **1** *vt* (a) to split, crack; to cleave; to slit; *fruit etc* to slice; *log etc* to chop (up), split.

(b) (*SAm*) to slander, run down.

(c) (*SAm: Univ*) to plough (*sl*).

(d) (*Col, Per, PR*) to crush, defeat; to ruin; to annoy.

(e) (*Arg*) *worker* to fire (*fam*).

2 *vi* (a) (*fam*) to chatter, talk a lot; to brag.

(b) (*SAm*) to rush out, rush out.

3 rajarse *vr* (a) to split, crack.

(b) (*esp SAm*) to back out (*de* of), quit; to get cold feet; to go back on one's word; ¡me rajé! that's enough for me!, I'm quitting!

(c) (*Ant, Bol, Arg*) to run away; to rush off; **salir rajando** to go off at top speed.

(d) (*Arg, Col*) to be mistaken.

(e) (*PR*) to get drunk.

(f) (*CAm, Chi, Per, PR*) — **con** to give generously, dish out lavishly; to make a splurge with (*fam*).

rajatabla: a — *adv* strictly, rigorously; exactly; without fear or favour; at all costs; regardless (of the consequences); **cumplir las órdenes a** — to carry out one's orders to the letter; **pagar** (*etc*) **a** — (*SAm*) to pay (*etc*) on the dot, pay (*etc*) promptly.

rajatablas *nm, pl* **rajatablas** (*Col, Ven*) ticking-off.

raje *nm* (*Arg*) firing (*fam*), sacking (*fam*); **dar el** — **a uno** to fire someone (*fam*); **tomar(se) el** — to flee; to rush off.

rajo *nm* (*SAm*) tear, rip.

rajón 1 *adj* (a) (*Andalusia, Ant, CAm, Chi, Per*) generous, lavish, free-spending.

(b) (*Andalusia, CAm, Mex*) easily scared, cowardly; readily disheartened; (*Mex*) unreliable.

2 *nm* (a) (*Ant, Col, Guat, Urug*) tear, rip.

(b) (*Andalusia, CAm, Mex*) quitter.

(c) (*CAm, Mex*) bully; braggart.

rajonada *nf* (*CAm*) (a) boast, brag; bragging. (b) ostentation.

rajuñar [1a] *vt* (*Arg*) =rasguñar.

rala *nf* (*Col*) birdlime.

rale *nm* (*Chi*) wooden bowl, wooden trough.

ralea *nf* (*pej*) kind, sort, breed; **de esa** — of that ilk; **de baja** — evil, wicked; wretched.

ralear [1a] *vi* to become thin, become sparse; to thin out; to become less dense.

ralenti *nm* (*gall*) (a) (*Cine*) slow motion; **al** — in slow motion. (b) (*Aut*) neutral; **estar al** — to be ticking over.

ralo *adj* *hair etc* thin, sparse; *cloth* loosely woven; *woodland* open; (*Phys*) rare; (*Arg*) unsubstantial, lacking body.

rallado *adj* *cheese etc* grated.

rallador *nm* grater.

rallar [1a] *vt* (a) (*Cook*) to grate. (b) (*fam*) to grate on; to annoy, needle (*fam*). (c) (*Cu*) to goad.

rallo *nm* (*Cook*) grater; (*Tech*) file, rasp.

rallye ['rali] *nm* (*angl, gall: Aut*) rally.

rallye-paper *nm* (*angl, gall*) paper chase.

rama *nf* (*all senses*) branch; **en** — cotton, silk raw; *book* unbound; **de olivo** olive branch; **andarse por las** —**s** to beat about the bush; to get bogged down in details; **poner algo en la última** — to leave something till last; to consider something unimportant.

ramada *nf* (a) branches, foliage. (b) (*SAm*) shed, hut; shelter (*or* covering *etc*) made of branches.

ramadán *nm* Ramadan.

ramaje *nm* branches, foliage.

ramal *nm* (a) strand (of a rope); halter. (b) (*fig*) offshoot; (*Aut*) branch, branch road; (*Rail*) branch line.

ramalazo nm (a) lash; weal, bruise, mark left by a lash.
(b) (fig) stab of pain, sharp pain; fit of depression, sudden grief; blow; fit of madness.
(c) (fig) gust of wind; lash of rain.
(d) (fig: Pol etc) backlash, reaction; outbreak of violence.

ramazón nf (Arg, CAm, Mex) antler, horns.

rambla nf (a) watercourse; stream, torrent. (b) avenue.

ramera nf whore.

ramificación nf ramification.

ramificarse [1g] vr to ramify, divide, branch (out).

ramillete nm (a) bouquet, bunch of flowers, posy; (worn on dress) corsage; (Bot) cluster. (b) (fig) collection; choice bunch, select group.

ramita nf twig, spring; (of flowers) spray.

ramo nm (a) (of tree) branch (also fig).
(b) (fig) branch; (Comm) section, department; (of goods) line.
(c) (Med; also —s) touch; **tiene —s de loco** he has a streak of madness.

ramojo nm brushwood.

Ramón m Raymond.

ramonear [1a] vt (a) trees to lop, lop the twigs of. (b) (of sheep) to browse on, nibble.

rampa nf ramp, incline; **— de lanzamiento** launching ramp.

ramplón adj common, coarse, uncouth.

ramplonería nf commonness, coarseness, uncouthness.

rana nf frog; **— toro** bullfrog; **no es —** (fig) he's no fool, he knows his stuff; **pero salió —** (fam) but he turned out badly, but he was a big disappointment; **cuando las —s críen pelo** when pigs learn to fly; **¡hasta que las —s críen pelo!** if I never see you again it'll be too soon!

rancidez nf, **ranciedad** nf (a) age, mellowness; (pej) rankness, rancidness; mustiness. (b) (fig) great age, antiquity; (pej) antiquatedness.

rancio 1 adj (a) wine old, mellow; food (pej) rank, rancid, stale; musty.
(b) (fig) lineage ancient; tradition etc very ancient, time-honoured; (pej) antiquated, old-fashioned.
2 nm =**rancidez**.

rancotán adv (Col, Pan, PR, Ven) in cash.

ranchada nf (a) (CAm) canoe. (b) (Arg, Par) shed, improvised hut.

ranchar [1a] vi (a) (Arg, Mex) to wander from farm to farm. (b) (Col, Mex, Ven) to spend the night, make a camp; to settle.

ranchear [1a] **1** vt (Cu, Mex, PR) to loot, pillage; to rob. **2** vi (SAm) (a) to build a camp, make a settlement. (b) (Arg, Per) to have a meal.

ranchería nf (a) (RPl) =**rancherío**. (b) (Per) labourers' quarters (on an estate). (c) (Ven) poor country inn.

rancherío nm (SAm) settlement.

ranchero nm **1** adj (Mex) uncouth. **2** (a) (SAm) rancher, farmer. (b) mess cook.

rancho nm (a) hut, thatched hut; (Col, Per) shed; (Per) country house, villa.
(b) (Naut) crew's quarters.
(c) (SAm) ranch, large farm; (Mex) small farm.
(d) (of gipsies etc) camp, settlement; (Mex) village.
(e) (Mil etc) mess, communal meal; (pej) bad food, grub; **asentar el —** to prepare a meal; (fig) to get things organized, settle in; **hacer —** to make room; **hacer el —** to have a meal; **hacer — aparte** to set up on one's own, go one's own way.
(f) (RPl) straw hat.

randa nm (fam) pickpocket, petty thief; suspicious character, prowler.

randevú nm (RPl: gall) rendez-vous.

randevuses nmpl (RPl: gall) courtesies.

ranfaña nm (Chi, Per) shabby person.

ranfañoso nm (Arg) shabby person; mean individual; (Comm) crook.

ranfla nf (Col, Mex) ramp, incline.

ranga nf (Col, Ec) nag, old horse.

rango¹ nm (a) rank; standing, status, class; **de —** of high standing, of some status. (b) (SAm) luxury; pomp, splendour.

rango² nm (Col) =**ranga**.

rangosidad nf (Chi) generosity.

rangoso adj (CAm, Cu, Chi) generous.

Rangún Rangoon.

rantifuso adj (Arg) dirty, grubby; common; suspicious.

ranúnculo nm ranunculus, (esp) buttercup.

ranura nf groove; slot.

rapacidad nf rapacity, greed.

rapadura nf (a) shave, shaving; close haircut. (b) (SAm) brown sugar; home-made sweet.

rapapolvo nm ticking-off; **echar un — a uno** to give someone a ticking-off, tick someone off.

rapar [1a] vt (a) to shave; to crop, cut very close. (b) (fam) to pinch (fam).

rapaz¹ 1 adj rapacious, greedy; thieving; (Zool) predatory; (Orn) raptorial, of prey. **2** nf (Zool) predatory animal; (Orn) bird of prey.

rapaz² nm lad, youngster; kid; **sí, —** yes, my lad.

rapaza nf lass, girl, youngster.

rape nm (a) quick shave, rough haircut; **al — cut** close. (b) (fam) ticking-off.

rapé nm snuff.

rápida nf (Mex) chute.

rápidamente adv rapidly, fast, quickly, swiftly.

rapidez nf rapidity, speed; speediness, swiftness.

rápido 1 adj (a) rapid, fast, quick, swift; train fast, express.
(b) (Col, Chi, Ven) field open; country flat, monotonous.
(c) (Ven) weather clear.
2 adv (fam) quickly; **¡y —, eh?** and make it snappy!
3 nm (a) (Rail) express.
(b) (Col, Chi, Ven) open field, bare field.
(c) **—s** rapids.

rapiña nf robbery (with violence); see **ave**.

rapiñar [1a] vt to steal.

raposa nf fox (also fig), vixen.

raposera nf foxhole.

raposero adj: **perro —** foxhound.

raposo nm (a) fox, dog fox. (b) (Ec, PR) urchin.

rapsodia nf rhapsody.

rapsódico adj rhapsodic.

raptar [1a] vt to kidnap, abduct; to carry off.

rapto nm (a) kidnapping, abduction; carrying-off.
(b) (fig) sudden impulse; **en un — de celos** in a sudden fit of jealousy. (c) (fig) ecstasy, rapture.

raptor nm kidnapper.

raque¹ nm beachcombing.

raque² nm (Cu) bargain.

raquear¹ [1a] vi to go beachcombing.

raquear² [1a] vt (Cu) to rob, hold up.

Raquel f Rachel.

raquero nm beachcomber.

raqueta nf racquet; **— de nieve** snowshoe.

raquetazo nm (SAm) shot, hit, stroke.

raquítico adj (a) (Med) rachitic; tree etc weak, stunted. (b) (fig) small, inadequate, miserly.

raquitis nf, **raquitismo** nm rickets.

raramente adv rarely, seldom.

rarefacción nf rarefaction.

rareza nf (a) (quality) rarity, rareness, scarcity.
(b) (object) rarity.
(c) (fig) oddity, peculiarity; eccentricity; **tiene alguna —** there's something odd about him; **tiene sus —s** he has his peculiarities, he has his little ways.

raridad nf rarity.

rarificar [1g] vt to rarefy.

rarífico adj (Chi) =**raro (b)**.

raro adj (a) rare, scarce, uncommon; **son —s los que saben hacerlo** very few people know how to do it; **con alguna rara excepción** with rare exceptions.
(b) odd, peculiar, strange; eccentric; notable, remarkable; **de rara perfección** of rare perfection, of remarkable perfection; **es — que . . .** it is odd that . . ., it is strange that . . .; **¡qué —!** how (very) odd!; **¡qué cosa más rara!** how strange!, most odd!; **es un hombre muy —** he's a very odd man.
(c) (Phys) rare, rarefied.

ras¹ nm levelness, evenness; **— con —** level, on a level; flush; **a — de** level with; flush with; **volar a — de tierra** to fly (almost) at ground level.

ras² interj snap!

rasar [1a] **1** vt (a) contents to level (with the rim).
(b) to skim, graze; **la bala pasó rasando su sombrero** the bullet grazed his hat.
(c) =**arrasar**.
2 rasarse vr (sky) to clear.

rascacielos nm, pl **rascacielos** skyscraper.

rascadera nf scraper.

rascado adj (a) (SAm) drunk. (b) (CAm) featherbrained.

rascador nm (a) scraper; file, rasp. (b) hairpin.

rascaespalda nf backscratcher.

rascamoño nm (a) hairpin. (b) (Bot) zinnia.

rascar [1g] **1** vt (a) to scrape, rasp; to scrape off; to scratch.
(b) (Mus: hum) to scrape, scratch away.
2 vi (Chi) to itch.

3 rascarse *vr* (a) to scratch, scratch oneself.
(b) (*SAm*) to get drunk.
(c) — **juntos** (*Arg*, *Guat*) to band together (for a criminal purpose); — **la barriga**, — **la panza** (*Mex*, *RPl*) to take it easy; **no** — **con uno** (*Col*) not to hit it off with someone.

rascatripas *nm, pl* **rascatripas** (*fam*) fiddler, third-rate violinist.

rascón[1] *adj* (a) sharp, sour. (b) (*Mex*) quarrelsome.

rascón[2] *nm* (*Orn*) water rail.

rascuache *adj* (*Guat*, *Mex*) poor, penniless; (*Mex*) wretched; ridiculous, in bad taste; worthless; coarse, vulgar.

rasete *nm* satinet(te).

rasgado *adj* (a) *window* wide; *eyes* wide, large; almond-shaped; *mouth* wide, big. (b) (*SAm*) outspoken. (c) (*Col*) generous.

rasgadura *nf* tear, rip, slash.

rasgar [1h] *vt* (a) to tear, rip, slash; *paper* to tear up, tear to pieces. (b) =**rasguear**.

rasgo *nm* (a) (*with pen*) stroke, flourish; adornment; dash; —s characteristics (*of one's handwriting*); **a grandes** —**s** (*fig*) with broad strokes, in outline.
(b) —**s** (*Anat*) features; **de** —**s enérgicos** of energetic appearance, with an energetic look.
(c) (*fig*) characteristic, feature, trait; —**s características** typical features; —**s distintivos** distinctive features.
(d) generous deed; noble gesture; — **de ingenio** flash of wit; stroke of genius.
(e) (*Chi*) irrigation channel.
(f) (*Chi*) plot (of land); piece, portion.

rasgón *nm* tear, rent.

rasguear [1a] *vt* (a) (*Mus*) to strum. (b) to write with a flourish; (*fig*) to write.

rasguñadura *nf* (*SAm*) scratch.

rasguñar [1a] *vt* (a) to scratch. (b) (*Art*) to sketch, draw in outline.

rasguño *nm* (a) scratch; **salir sin un** — to come out of it without a scratch. (b) sketch, outline drawing.

rasmillar [1a] *vt* (*Chi*) to scratch.

rasmillón *nm* (*Chi*) scratch.

raso 1 *adj* (a) flat, level; clear, bare, open; smooth; *seat* backless.
(b) *sky* clear; **está** — the sky is clear, the weather is clear.
(c) level (with the brim); **una cucharada rasa** a level teaspoonful.
(d) *ball, flight etc* very low, almost at ground level.
(e) **soldado** — private.
2 *adv:* **tirar** — (*Sport*) to shoot low.
3 *nm* (a) (*Sew*) satin.
(b) flat country; open country; **al** — in the open.

raspa *nf* (a) (*Bot: of corn*) beard; (*of grape*) stalk.
(b) (*Fish*) fishbone, (*esp*) backbone.
(c) (*fam*) sharp-tongued woman.
(d) (*SAm*) scolding; dressing-down.
(e) (*Ant*, *Mex*) brown sugar.
(f) (*RPl*) rasp.

raspada *nf* (*Mex*, *PR*) scolding; dressing-down.

raspado *adj* (*CR*, *Ven*) shameless.

raspador *nm* scraper, rasp.

raspadura *nf* (a) scrape, scraping, rasping. (b) —**s** scrapings; filings. (c) scratch, mark; erasure. (d) (*SAm*) brown sugar.

raspante *adj* *wine* sharp, rough.

raspar [1a] **1** *vt* (a) to scrape; to rasp, file; to smooth (down); *paint etc* to scrape off, remove by scraping; *surface* to scratch; *skin* to chafe; to graze; *word* to erase, scratch out.
(b) (*fig*) to skim, graze; to scrape past.
(c) **este vino raspa la boca** this wine is rough on the mouth, this wine takes the skin off your mouth.
(d) (*fam*) to pinch (*fam*).
(e) (*Ven*) to kill.
(f) (*Mex*, *PR*) to scold; to dress down.
(g) (*Mex*) to say unkind things to, make wounding remarks to.
2 *vi* (a) (*of hands*) to be rough.
(b) (*of wine*) to be sharp, have a rough taste.
(c) (*Ven*) to leave, go off; to die.

raspear [1a] **1** *vt* (*Chi*, *Ec*) to tick off. **2** *vi* (*of pen*) to scratch.

raspón *nm* (a) scratch, graze; (*SAm*) abrasion; bruise.
(b) (*Col*, *Chi*, *Hond*, *Mex*) scolding; ticking-off.
(c) (*Mex*) cutting remark.
(d) (*Col*) straw hat.

rasponear [1a] *vt* (*Col*) to scold; to tick off.

rasposo *adj* (a) sharp-tasting, rough. (b) (*Mex*) joking, teasing. (c) (*Arg*) stingy.

rasqueta *nf* (*SAm*) scraper, rasp; currycomb.

rasquetear [1a] *vt* (*SAm*) *horse* to brush down; (*Arg*) to scrape.

rasquiña *nf* (*SAm*) itch.

rastacuerismo *nm* (*SAm*) social climbing; rich living; ostentation, display; public lavishness.

rastacuero *nm* (*SAm*) upstart, parvenu, wealthy social climber.

rastra *nf* (a) (*Agr*) rake; harrow.
(b) =**rastro**; =**ristra**.
(c) sledge (*for moving heavy objects*); weighty object, thing being pulled along.
(d) (*Fish*) trawl; dredge; **pescar a la** — to trawl.
(e) (*Arg*, *Urug*) thick leather belt, gaucho's belt.
(f) (*Mex*) prostitute.
(g) (*fig*) unpleasant consequence, disagreeable result; punishment; deserts.
(h) **a** —**s** by dragging, by pulling; (*fig*) unwillingly; **avanzar a** —**s** to crawl (along), drag oneself along; **llevar un piano a** —**s** to pull a piano along; **andar a** —**s** (*fig*) to have a difficult time of it, suffer hardships.

rastreador *nm* (a) tracker. (b) (*Naut: also* **barco** —) trawler; — **de minas** minesweeper.

rastrear [1a] **1** *vt* (a) to track, trail, follow the trail of; *satellite* to track; to track down, trace, run to ground.
(b) to dredge (up), drag (up); to trawl; *mines* to sweep.
2 *vi* (a) (*Agr*) to rake, harrow.
(b) (*Fish*) to trawl.
(c) (*Aer*) to skim the ground; to fly low, hedgehop.

rastreo *nm* (a) dredging, dragging; trawling. (b) (*of satellite*) tracking.

rastrerismo *nm* (*SAm*) toadyism, bootlicking (*fam*).

rastrero *adj* (a) (*Zool*) creeping, crawling; (*Bot*) creeping.
(b) *dress etc* trailing, hanging close to the ground; (*Aer*) *flight* very low.
(c) (*fig*) *conduct* mean, despicable; *method* low; *apology* abject, humble; *person* cringing; soapy, bootlicking (*fam*), fawning.

rastrillada *nf* (*RPl*) track, trail.

rastrillar [1a] **1** *vt* (a) (*Agr*) to rake; to rake up, rake together; to rake smooth.
(b) *flax etc* to dress.
(c) (*SAm*) *weapon* to fire; *match* to strike.
(d) (*CR*, *Mex*) *feet* to drag.
2 *vi* (a) (*Col*, *Cu*, *RPl*) to miss (with a shot).
(b) (*Chi*) to shoplift, steal from shops.

rastrillazo *nm* (*CAm*) light sleep; light meal, snack.

rastrillero *nm*, **rastrillera** *nf* (*Chi*) shoplifter.

rastrillo *nm* (a) (*Agr etc*) rake.
(b) (*Tech*) hackle, flax comb.
(c) (*of key*) ward.
(d) (*Mil*) portcullis; (*Archit etc*) spiked gate.
(e) (*Rail*) — **delantero** cowcatcher.
(f) (*Col*) barter; deal.

rastro *nm* (a) (*Agr etc*) rake; harrow.
(b) track, trail; mark on the ground; scent; (*of rocket etc*) track, course; (*of storm*) path; **perder el** — to lose the scent; **seguir el** — **de uno** to follow someone's trail.
(c) (*fig*) trace, sign; **desaparecer sin dejar** — to vanish without trace; **no quedaba ni** — **de ello** not a trace of it was to be seen.
(d) slaughterhouse; **el R**— *secondhand market in Madrid*.

rastrojear [1a] *vi* (*Col*, *Chi*, *Guat*, *Mex*) to glean; (*of animals*) to feed in the stubble.

rastrojera *nf* stubble field.

rastrojero *nm* (a) (*Chi*, *Mex*) stubble field. (b) (*Arg*) jeep. (c) (*Mex*) maize plant, corn plant (*US*) (*used as fodder*).

rastrojo *nm* (a) stubble. (b) —**s** (*SAm*) waste, remains, left-overs.

rasura *nf* (a) flatness, levelness; smoothness. (b) shave, shaving; scrape, scraping. (c) —**s** scrapings; filings.

rasurado *nm* shave.

rasurador *nm*, **rasuradora** *nf* (electric) shaver, electric razor.

rasurar [1a] **1** *vt* (a) to shave. (b) (*Tech*) to scrape. **2 rasurarse** *vr* to shave.

rata 1 *nf* rat. **2** *nm* (*fam*) sneak thief.

rataplán *nm* drumbeat, rub-a-dub.

ratear[1] [1a] **1** *vt* to steal, pilfer; to filch. **2** *vi* to crawl, creep (along).

ratear[2] [1a] *vt* (a) to share out. (b) to reduce proportionately.

ratera *nf* (*Mex*) rattrap.

ratería nf (a) petty larceny, small-time thieving, pilfering. (b) (una —) theft. (c) (quality) crookedness, dishonesty.

raterismo nm (SAm) art of thieving; tendency to thievishness.

ratero 1 adj thievish, light-fingered. **2** nm pickpocket, sneak thief, small-time thief.

raticida nm (SAm) rat poison.

ratificación nf ratification.

ratificar [1g] vt to ratify.

Ratisbona Regensburg, Ratisbon.

rato nm (short) time, while; spell, period; **un** — (as adv) a while, a time; **un buen** —, **largo** — a long time, a good while; **—s libres**, **—s de ocio** leisure, spare time, free time; **a —s** at times, from time to time; **a —s perdidos** at (or in) odd moments; **al poco** — shortly after; ¡hasta cada —! (SAm), ¡hasta otro —! so long!; **matar el** —, **pasar el** — to kill time, pass the time, while away the time; **pasar un buen** — to have a good time; **pasar un mal** — to have a bad time of it, have a rough time; **dar malos —s a uno** to give someone a hard time of it; to cause someone a lot of worry; **hay para** — there's still a long way to go; **tenemos para** — we've still a lot to do, we're still far from finished.

ratón nm (a) mouse; — **de archivo**, — **de biblioteca** bookworm; — **almizclero** muskrat; **mandar a uno a capar —es** (fam) to tell someone to go to blazes. (b) (Ven) squib, cracker. (c) (Ven) hangover. (d) (fam) ball of fluff.

ratonar [1a] vt to gnaw, nibble.

ratonera nf (a) mousetrap. (b) mousehole. (c) (Arg, Chi, Per) hovel, slum; (PR, Ven) poky little shop.

ratonero nm buzzard.

raudal nm (a) torrent, flood. (b) (fig) plenty, abundance; great quantity; **a —es** in abundance, in great numbers; **entrar a —es** to pour in, come flooding in.

raudo adj swift; rushing, impetuous.

raya[1] nf (a) line; streak; (on stone etc) scratch, mark; (on hand) line; (on cloth, pattern) stripe, pinstripe; — **de puntos** dotted line; — **en negro** black line; **a —s** striped.
(b) (in hair) parting; (in trousers) crease; **hacerse la** — to part one's hair.
(c) line, boundary, limit; (Sport) line, mark; **hacer** — to mark off (also fig); **pasar de la** — to overstep the mark, go too far; **poner a** — to check, hold back; **tener a** — to keep off, keep at bay, keep in check, control.
(d) (Typ) line, dash; (Tel) dash.
(e) (Mex) pay, wages.

raya[2] nf (Fish) ray, skate.

rayado 1 adj paper ruled; cheque crossed; cloth, pattern striped. **2** nm ruling, ruled lines; crossing; stripes, striped pattern; (Tech) rifling.

rayador nm (a) (Mex) paymaster, accountant. (b) (Chi) umpire. (c) (RPl) =**rallador**.

rayano adj (a) adjacent, contiguous; borderline. (b) — **en** bordering on.

rayar [1a] **1** vt (a) paper to line, rule lines on; cheque to cross; stone etc to scratch, score, mark; text to underline, underscore; mistake to cross out; (as pattern) to stripe, streak; (Tech) to rifle.
(b) (Mex) to pay (his wages to).
(c) (RPl) =**rallar**.
(d) (SAm) horse to spur on.
2 vi (a) — **con** to border on, be next to, be adjacent to.
(b) — **en** (fig) to border on, verge on; **esto raya en lo increíble** this verges on the incredible, this is well-nigh incredible.
(c) to scratch, make scratches; **este producto no raya al fregar** this product scrubs without scratching.
(d) **al** — **el alba** at break of day, at first light.
(e) (Mex) to draw one's wages; to earn.
3 rayarse vr (a) to get scratched.
(b) (Col, Mex) to get all one wants; to get rich.

rayero nm (RPl) umpire, judge.

rayo[1] nm (a) ray, beam; shaft (of light); — **de luna** moonbeam; — **de sol**, — **solar** sunbeam, ray of sunlight; **—s catódicos** cathode rays; **—s cósmicos** cosmic rays; **—s gamma** gamma rays; **—s infrarrojos** infrared rays; **—s luminosos** light rays; **—s ultravioleta** ultraviolet rays; **—s X** X-rays.
(b) (Tech) spoke.
(c) (Meteorol) lightning, flash of lightning; thunderbolt; **cayó un** — **en la torre** the tower was struck by lightning; **como un** — like lightning, like a shot; **la noticia cayó como un** — the news was a bombshell; **entrar como un** — to dash in; **salir como un** —

— to dash out; **pasar como un** — to rush past, flash past; **echar —s y centellas** to rage, fume; ¡que le **parta un** —!, ¡mal — le **parta**! God's curse on him!
(d) (fig) blow, misfortune.
(e) (fig: person) fast worker, speedy and efficient person; **es un** — he's like lightning.

rayo[2] etc see **raer**.

rayón nm rayon.

raza[1] nf race; breed, strain; stock; (Bio) race; — **blanca** white race; — **humana** human race; — **negra** black race; **de** —, **de pura** — horse thoroughbred; dog etc pedigree.

raza[2] nf (a) crack, slit, fissure; (in cloth) run. (b) ray of light.

razano adj (Col, Ec) thoroughbred.

razón nf (a) (faculty) reason; **hacer que uno entre en** —, **meter** (or **poner**) **a uno en** — to make someone see sense; **meterse en** — to see sense, listen to reason; **perder la** — to lose one's reason, go out of one's mind; **muy puesto en** — very reasonable; ¡eso es **ponerse en** —! that's better!, now you're talking!
(b) right, rightness; justice; **con** — **o sin ella** rightly or wrongly; **le asiste la** — he has right on his side; **cargarse de** — to justify oneself completely; **dar la** — **a uno** to agree that someone is right; **tener** — to be right; **no tener** — to be wrong; **tener plenamente** — **en** + infin to be fully justified in + ger; **tratar de quitar a uno la** — to try to put someone in the wrong.
(c) reason, motive, cause; "—: **Princesa 4**" "inquiries to 4 Princesa Street"; "for further details, apply to 4 Princesa Street"; ¿**cuál es la** —? what is the reason?; **la** — **por qué** the reason why; **la** — **por la que lo hizo** the reason why he did it, the reason for his doing it; — **de estado** reasons of state; — **de más** all the more reason (para + infin to + infin); — **de ser** raison d'être; **con** — with good reason; ¡**con** —! naturally!; **en** — **de** with regard to; **no atiende a —es** he'll not listen to reason, he's not open to argument; **dar** — **de** to give an account of, report on; to give information about; **nadie me daba** — **de ella** nobody could tell me anything about her; **dar** — **de sí** to give an account of oneself; **tener** — **para** + infin to have cause to + infin.
(d) (Comm) — **social** trade name, firm's name.
(e) (fam) message; **mandar a uno** — **de que haga algo** to send someone a message telling him to do something.
(f) (Math) ratio, proportion; rate; **a** — **de 5 a 7** in the ratio of 5 to 7; **a** — **de 8 por persona** at the rate of 8 per head; **abandonan el país a** — **de 800 cada año** they are leaving the country at the rate of 800 a year; **en** — **directa con** in direct ratio to.

razonable adj reasonable.

razonablemente adv reasonably.

razonado adj reasoned; account etc itemized, detailed.

razonamiento nm reasoning.

razonar [1a] **1** vt (a) to reason, argue. (b) problem etc to reason out. (c) account to itemize. **2** vi (a) to reason, argue. (b) to talk (together).

re . . . (a) (prefix) re . . .
(b) (intensifying prefix) very, awfully (fam), terribly (fam), eg **rebueno** very good, jolly good (fam); **reguapa** awfully pretty; **resalada** terribly attractive; ¡**rebomba**! how utterly amazing!; ¡**rediez**! well I'm damned!

reabastecer [2d] **1** vt (also — **de combustible**, — **de gasolina**) to refuel. **2 reabastecerse** vr to refuel.

reabastecimiento nm refuelling.

reabrir [3a; ptp **reabierto**] **1** vt to reopen. **2 reabrirse** vr to reopen.

reacción nf (a) reaction (a, ante to; also Med); response (a to); — **en cadena** chain reaction; **la** — **blanca** the white backlash.
(b) (Pol) reaction.
(c) (Tech) **avión a** (or **de**) — jet plane; **propulsión por** — jet propulsion.

reaccionar [1a] vi to react (a, ante to; contra against; sobre on); to respond (a to); ¿**cómo reaccionó**? how did she react?

reaccionario 1 adj reactionary. **2** nm, **reaccionaria** nf reactionary.

reacio adj stubborn; **ser** — **a**, **estar** — **a** to be opposed to, resist (the idea of), be unwilling to accept (the need for); **estar** — **a** + infin to be unwilling to + infin.

reacondicionar [1a] vt to recondition.

reactivo nm reagent.

reactor nm (a) (Phys) reactor; — **nuclear** nuclear reactor; — **generador**, — **reproductor** breeder reactor. (b) (Aer) jet engine; jet plane.

readaptación *nf:* — **profesional** industrial re-training.

readmisión *nf* readmission.

readmitir [3a] *vt* to readmit.

readquirir [3a] *vt power etc* to recover.

reafirmación *nf* reaffirmation; reassertion.

reafirmar [1a] *vt* to reaffirm; to reassert.

reagrupación *nf* regrouping.

reagrupar [1a] **1** *vt* to regroup. **2 reagruparse** *vr* to regroup.

reagudizarse [1f] *vr* (*Med*) to become acute again, get worse again.

reajustar [1a] **1** *vt* to readjust. **2 reajustarse** *vr* to readjust.

reajuste *nm* readjustment; (*fig*) readjustment, re-appraisal; — **agonizante**, — **doloroso** agonizing reappraisal.

real[1] *adj* real.

real[2] **1** *adj* (**a**) royal.

(**b**) (*fig*) royal; grand, splendid; *see* **moza** *etc.*

2 *nm* (**a**) (*Hist*) army camp; fairground.

(**b**) (*Fin*) coin of 25 céntimos, *one quarter of a peseta;* **costó 6 reales** it cost 1½ pesetas; **está sin un** —, **no tiene un** — (*fam*) he hasn't a bean (*fam*).

realada *nf* (*Mex*) roundup, rodeo.

realar [1a] *vt* (*Mex*) *cattle* to round up.

realce *nm* (**a**) (*Tech*) raised work, embossing.

(**b**) (*Art*) highlight.

(**c**) (*fig*) lustre, splendour; importance, significance; enhancement; **dar** — **a** to add lustre to, enhance the splendour of; **un asunto sin** — a matter of no importance.

realengo *adj* (**a**) (*SAm*) *animal* stray, lost, ownerless.

(**b**) (*Mex, Ven*) idle; out of work; carefree.

realeza *nf* royalty.

realidad *nf* reality; truth; **la** — **de la política** the realities of politics; **atengámonos a la** — let's stick to realities; **en** — in fact, really, actually; **la** — **es que . . .** the fact of the matter is that . . .

realismo *nm* realism.

realista 1 *adj* realistic. **2** *nmf* realist.

realizable *adj* (**a**) *assets etc* realizable. (**b**) *aim* attainable; *plan* practical, feasible.

realización *nf* (**a**) (*Fin*) realization; sale, selling-up; — **de plusvalías** profit-taking. (**b**) realization; fulfilment, carrying out; achievement.

realizador *nm* (*TV etc*) producer.

realizar [1f] **1** *vt* (**a**) (*Fin*) *assets* to realize; *stock* to sell off, sell up; *profit* to take.

(**b**) *aim etc* to attain, achieve, realize; *promise* to fulfil, carry out; *plan* to carry out, put into effect.

(**c**) *journey etc* to make; *visit* to carry out; *expedition, flight etc* to undertake, make; *purchase* to make.

(**d**) — **que** (*SAm: angl*) to realize that . . .

2 realizarse *vr* (*dream etc*) to come true; to materialize; (*plan*) to be carried out.

realmente[1] *adv* really; in fact, actually.

realmente[2] *adv* (*fig*) royally.

realquilar [1a] *vt* to sublet, sublease; to relet.

realzar [1f] *vt* (**a**) (*Tech*) to emboss, raise. (**b**) (*Art*) to highlight. (**c**) (*fig*) to enhance, heighten, add to.

reanimar [1a] **1** *vt* (**a**) to revive. (**b**) (*fig*) to revive, encourage, stimulate; to give new life to. **2 reanimarse** *vr* to revive; to acquire new life.

reanudación *nf* renewal; resumption.

reanudar [1a] *vt* to renew; *story, journey etc* to resume.

reaparecer [2d] *vi* to reappear; to return; to recur.

reaparición *nf* reappearance; return; recurrence.

reapertura *nf* reopening.

reaprovisionamiento *nm* replenishment, restocking.

reaprovisionar [1a] *vt* to replenish, restock.

rearmar [1a] **1** *vt* to rearm. **2 rearmarse** *vr* to rearm.

rearme *nm* rearmament.

reasegurar [1a] *vt* to reinsure; to underwrite.

reaseguro *nm* to reinsure.

reasumir [3a] *vt* to resume, reassume.

reata *nf* (**a**) rope (*joining string of pack animals*); (*SAm*) rope, lasso; strap; (*Ec*) strip of cotton cloth.

(**b**) string (of horses *etc*), pack train; **de** — in single file, one after the other; (*fig*) submissively.

(**c**) (*Ant, Col, Mex*) flowerbed, border.

rebaja *nf* lowering, lessening, reduction; (*Comm*) discount, rebate; (*in sale*) reduction; "**grandes —s**" "big reductions".

rebajamiento *nm* (**a**) =**rebaja**. (**b**) — **de sí mismo** self-abasement.

rebajar [1a] **1** *vt* (**a**) *ground etc* to lower, lower the level of.

(**b**) *price* to reduce, lower, cut (down); *value* to detract from, reduce; — **el precio a uno en un 5 por**

100 to give someone a discount of 5%, knock 5% off the price for someone.

(**c**) *intensity etc* to lessen, diminish; *colour* to tone down; *sound* to turn down, reduce; *heat* to lessen.

(**d**) *person etc* to humble; to bring down a peg or two, deflate; *advantages etc* to decry, disparage; **llamarlo así es** —**lo de categoría** calling it by that name reduces its (real) importance, calling it that makes it less important than it is.

2 rebajarse *vr:* — **ante uno** to bow before some-one; — **a** + *infin* to humble oneself sufficiently to + *infin*; to stoop to + *ger*, descend to + *ger*, condescend to + *infin*.

rebajo *nm* recess; (*Tech*) rabbet.

rebalsa *nf* pool, puddle.

rebalsar [1a] **1** *vt* (**a**) *water* to dam, dam up. (**b**) (*SAm*) *banks etc* to burst, overflow. **2 rebalsarse** *vr* to form a pool (or lake); to become dammed up.

rebanada *nf* (**a**) slice. (**b**) (*Mex*) latch.

rebanar [1a] *vt food* to slice, cut in slices; *tree etc* to slice through, slice down; *limb etc* to slice off.

rebañar [1a] *vt* (**a**) to scrape up, scrape together; to sweep up, sweep into a pile; **logró** — **ciertos fondos** he managed to scrape some money together; — **el plato del arroz** to scrape a dish clean of rice.

(**b**) (*fig*) — **una tienda de joyas** to clear a shop of jewellery, clean out all the jewellery from a shop.

rebaño *nm* flock, herd; (*fig*) flock.

rebasar [1a] *vt* (*also vi:* — **de**) (*in quality, number*) to exceed, surpass; (*in range, progress*) to overtake, leave behind; (*Aut*) to overtake, pass; *point* to pass, go beyond; (*Naut*) to sail past; *time limit* to exceed; (*of water*) to overflow, rise higher than; **han rebasado ya los límites razonables** they have already gone beyond all reasonable limits; **la cifra no rebasa de mil** the number does not exceed a thousand.

rebatible *adj* (**a**) *argument* easily refuted. (**b**) *seat* tip-up.

rebatinga *nf* (*Mex*) =**rebatiña**.

rebatiña *nf* (*CAm, Mex*) scramble, rush; **les echó caramelos a la** — he threw sweets so that they could scramble for them; **andar a la** — **de algo** to scramble for something, fight over something; (*fig*) to argue fiercely over something.

rebatir [3a] *vt* (**a**) *attack* to repel; *thrust* to parry, ward off.

(**b**) *arguments etc* to reject, rebut, refute; *tempta-tion* to resist; *suggestion* to reject.

(**c**) *sum* to reduce; *discount* to deduct, knock off.

rebato *nm* (*Mil*) alarm, warning of attack, call to arms; surprise attack; **llamar** (*or* **tocar**) **a** — to sound the alarm (*also fig*).

rebautizar [1f] *vt* to rechristen.

Rebeca *f* Rebecca.

rebeca *nf* cardigan.

rebeco *nm* chamois, ibex.

rebelarse [1a] *vr* to revolt, rebel, rise; — **contra** (*fig*) to rebel against.

rebelde 1 *adj* (**a**) rebellious; mutinous; **el gobierno** — the rebel government; **ser** — **a** (*fig*) to be in revolt against, rebel against; to resist.

(**b**) *child etc* unruly; unmanageable, uncontroll-able; stubborn; *problem etc* difficult; *cough etc* per-sistent, hard to cure; *substance* difficult to work, awkward to treat.

2 *nmf* (**a**) (*Mil, Pol*) rebel.

(**b**) (*Law*) defaulter; person in contempt of court.

rebeldía *nf* (**a**) rebelliousness; defiance, disobedience; **estar en plena** — to be in open revolt.

(**b**) (*Law*) default; contempt of court; **caer en** — to be in default; to be in contempt of court; **fue juzgado en** — he was sentenced by default.

rebelión *nf* revolt, rebellion, rising.

rebelón *adj horse* restive.

rebencudo *adj* (*Cu*) stubborn.

rebenque *nm* (*SAm*) whip.

rebenquear [1a] *vt* (*SAm*) to whip.

reblandecer [2d] *vt* to soften.

reblandecimiento *nm* softening; — **cerebral** soften-ing of the brain.

rebolludo *adj* thickset, chunky (*fam*).

reborde *nm* ledge; (*Tech*) flange, rim; border.

rebosadero *nm* overflow.

rebosante *adj:* — **de** brimming with, overflowing with (*also fig*).

rebosar [1a] *vi* (**a**) (*of container, liquid*) to overflow, run over; **el café rebosa de la taza** the coffee cup is running over, the coffee is running over the cup.

(**b**) to abound, be plentiful; **allí rebosa el mineral** the mineral abounds there, a lot of the mineral is

found there; **le rebosa la alegría** merriment bubbles out of him.
(c) — **de**, — **en** to overflow with, be brimming with; — **de salud** to be busting with health, be brimming with health; **ellos rebosan en dinero** they have pots of money.

reboso nm (Arg, PR) driftwood.

rebotar [1a] **1** vt (a) ball to bounce; attack to repel; rays etc to send back, turn back, cause to bounce off.
(b) nail to clinch.
(c) person to annoy; to put out, upset.
(d) (Col, Mex) water to muddy, stir up.
2 vi (of ball etc) to bounce; to rebound (de off); (of bullet) to ricochet (de off), glance (de off).

rebote nm bounce, rebound; **de** — on the rebound; (fig) indirectly, as an indirect consequence.

rebozado adj (Cook) fried in batter (or breadcrumbs etc).

rebozar [1f] **1** vt (a) to muffle up, wrap up. (b) (Cook) to roll in batter (or breadcrumbs etc), fry in batter.
2 rebozarse vr to muffle (oneself) up.

rebozo nm (a) muffler, wrap; (SAm) shawl. (b) (fig) disguise; dissimulation; **de** — secretly; **sin** — (adv) openly, frankly, (adj) plain, straight; aboveboard.

rebufar [1a] vi to recoil.

rebufo nm recoil.

rebujo nm mass, knot, tangle, ball; badly-wrapped parcel.

rebultado adj bulky.

rebullicio nm hubbub, uproar; agitation.

rebullir [3a] **1** vt (Mex) to stir up. **2** vi and **rebullirse** vr to stir, begin to move; to show signs of life.

rebumbio nm (Mex) shouting, row, hubbub.

rebusca nf (a) search.
(b) (Agr) gleaning.
(c) leavings, left-overs, remains.
(d) (Arg, Ec) small business; undercover business, illicit trading; (Col) profit made on the side.

rebuscado adj recherché; out-of-the-way; studied, elaborate; (SAm) affected.

rebuscar [1g] **1** vt (a) object etc to search carefully for, search out; (Agr) to glean.
(b) place to search carefully; pile etc to search through, rummage in.
2 vi to search carefully; (Agr) to glean.
3 rebuscarse vr (Col, RPl) to look for work.

rebuznar [1a] vi to bray.

rebuzno nm bray; braying.

recabar [1a] vt (a) to obtain by entreaty, manage to get (de from).
(b) to claim as of right, assert one's claim to.
(c) (SAm) to ask for, apply for; to ask insistently for.

recadero nm messenger; errand boy, deliveryman; carrier.

recado nm (a) message; errand; gift, small present; **coger** (or **tomar**) **un** — (Tel etc) to take a message; **dejar** — to leave a message; **enviar a uno a un** — to send someone on an errand; **mandar** — to send word.
(b) provisions, daily shopping.
(c) equipment, materials; — **de escribir** writing case, set of writing materials.
(d) —**s** regards, remembrances.
(e) (SAm) saddle and trappings, horseman's equipment.

recaer [2o] vi (a) (Med) to suffer a relapse.
(b) (of criminal etc) to fall back, relapse (en into); to backslide.
(c) — **en** (of choice etc) to fall on, fall to; (of bequest) to pass to; (of duty) to devolve upon; (of prize) to go to; **las sospechas recayeron sobre el conserje** the suspicions fell on the porter; **este peso recaerá más sobre los pobres** this burden will bear most heavily on the poor; **la acusación recayó sobre él mismo** the charge recoiled upon him.
(d) (Archit) — **a** to look out on, look over.

recaída nf relapse (en into); backsliding.

recalar [1a] **1** vt to saturate, soak. **2** vi (a) to sight land, reach port. (b) (SAm) to end up (en at). (c) (SAm) — **a uno** to go to someone for help.

recalcar [1g] **1** vt (a) contents to press down, press in, squeeze in; container to cram, stuff (de with).
(b) (fig) to stress, emphasize; to make great play with; — **algo a uno** to insist on something to someone; — **a uno que** . . . to tell someone emphatically that . . .
2 vi (Naut) to list, heel.
3 recalcarse vr (SAm): — **un hueso** to dislocate a bone.

recalcitrante adj recalcitrant.

recalcitrar [1a] vi (a) to take a step back (the better to resist). (b) to resist, be stubborn, refuse to take heed.

recalentado adj warmed-up (also fig).

recalentar [1k] **1** vt (a) to overheat. (b) food etc to warm up, reheat. **2 recalentarse** vr to become overheated, get too hot.

recalmón nm lull.

recamado nm embroidery.

recamar [1a] vt to embroider.

recámara nf (a) side room; dressing room; (CAm, Col, Mex) bedroom.
(b) (of gun) breech, chamber.
(c) (fig) caution, wariness; reserve; **tener mucha** — to be on the careful side, be wary by nature.

recamarera nf (Mex) chambermaid.

recamarero nm (Mex) houseboy, hotel servant.

recambiar [1b] vt part to change over.

recambio nm spare; refill; —**s** spares, spare parts, extras (US); **neumático de** — spare tyre.

recapacitar [1a] **1** vt to think over, reflect on. **2** vi to think things over, reflect.

recapitulación nf recapitulation, summing-up, summary.

recapitular [1a] vti to recapitulate, sum up, summarize.

recargado adj (a) overloaded. (b) adornment, style etc overelaborate.

recargar [1h] vt (a) to overload; to overload on one side, unbalance.
(b) (Fin) to put an additional charge on, increase (the price of, the tax on etc).
(c) (Law) sentence to increase.
(d) (Tech) to reload, recharge; battery to recharge.
(e) (fig) to overload (de with); — **a uno de deberes** to overload someone with duties; — **el café de azúcar** to put too much sugar in the coffee, make the coffee too sweet; — **un diseño de adornos** to overload a pattern with decoration.

recargo nm (a) new burden; extra load, additional load.
(b) (Fin) extra charge, surcharge; increase.
(c) (Law) new charge, further charge; increase of sentence.
(d) (Med) rise in temperature.

recatado adj (a) woman modest, shy, demure. (b) cautious, circumspect.

recatar [1a] **1** vt to hide.
2 recatarse vr (a) to hide oneself away (de from).
(b) to act discreetly; **sin** — openly.
(c) to be cautious; to hesitate; — **de algo** to fight shy of something.

recato nm (a) modesty, shyness, demureness. (b) caution, circumspection; reserve, restraint; **sin** — openly, unreservedly.

recatón nm (Col) miner's pick.

recauchutado nm (a) retread. (b) (process) retreading, remoulding.

recauchutar [1a] vt tyre to retread, remould.

recaudación nf (a) (act) collection; recovery. (b) (sum) takings, sum taken, income; (Sport) gate, gate money. (c) tax office.

recaudador nm: — **de contribuciones** tax collector.

recaudar [1a] vt taxes to collect; sum to collect, take (in), receive; debt to recover.

recaudo nm (a) (Fin) collection.
(b) (Law) surety, security.
(c) care, protection; precaution; **estar a buen** — to be in safekeeping; **poner algo a buen** — to put something in a safe place.
(d) (Chi, Guat, Mex) spices, condiments.
(e) (Chi, Guat, Mex) daily supply of vegetables.

rececar [1a] vt game to stalk.

recelar [1a] **1** vt: — **que** . . . to suspect that . . ., fear that . . .
2 vi and **recelarse** vr: — **de** to suspect, fear, distrust; **recelarse** + infin to be afraid of + ger.

receloso adj suspicious, distrustful; apprehensive.

recensión nf recension.

recepción nf (a) (act) reception, receiving; (Radio) reception; (to academy etc) admission.
(b) (ceremony) reception.
(c) drawing room; (at hotel) reception, reception desk.

recepcionar [1a] vt (SAm) to receive.

recepcionista nf (hotel) receptionist.

receptáculo nm receptacle; holder.

receptividad nf receptivity.

receptivo adj receptive.

receptor nm (all senses) receiver; — **de control** (TV) monitor; — **de televisión** television receiver, television set; **descolgar el** — (Tel) to pick up the receiver.

recesión nf (Comm, Fin) recession; slump.

recesivo adj (Bio) recessive.

receso nm (SAm: Parl) recess.
receta nf (Cook) recipe (de for); (Med) prescription.
recetar [1a] vt (a) (Med) to prescribe. (b) (Guat, Mex) blow to deal, hit.
recial nm rapids.
reciamente adv strongly; severely; intensely; loudly.
recibí nm "received with thanks", receipt; **poner el —** en to sign one's receipt on.
recibida nf (Arg) reception, welcome.
recibidero adj receivable.
recibidor nm, **recibidora** nf receiver, recipient.
recibimiento nm (a) (act) reception, welcome; **dispensar a uno un — apoteósico** to give someone an enthusiastic welcome.
(b) anteroom, vestibule, lobby; hall; reception room.
recibir [3a] 1 vt (a) (general sense) to receive.
(b) person to welcome, receive, greet; to go and meet; proposal etc to receive; to welcome, greet; — **a uno con los brazos abiertos** to welcome someone with open arms; **el torero recibe al toro** the bullfighter awaits the bull's charge; **le recibió el ministro** the minister received him, the minister granted him an interview; **la oferta fue mal recibida** the offer was badly received.
(c) degree etc to receive, take.
2 vi to receive; to entertain; **reciben mucho en casa** they entertain at home a good deal; **la baronesa recibe los lunes** the baroness receives visitors on Mondays, the baroness's "at home" day is Monday.
3 **recibirse** vr: — de to qualify as; see **abogado**; — **de doctor** to take one's doctorate, receive one's doctor's degree.
recibo nm (a) = **recibimiento** (a) and (b); **acusar —** to acknowledge receipt (de of); **estar de —** (dress etc) to be ready for collection; (person) to be at home (to callers).
(b) (Comm) receipt.
recidiva nf (Med) relapse.
reciedumbre nf strength, toughness; solidity; severity, harshness; loudness.
recién adv (a) newly, recently (+ ptp).
(b) (SAm) just, just now; — **llegó** he has just arrived, he arrived recently; — **se acordó** he only just then remembered it; — **ahora** right now, this very moment; — **aquí** right here, just here.
recién casado adj newly-wed; **los —s** the newly-weds.
recién hecho adj newly-made.
recién llegado 1 adj newly arrived. 2 nm, **recién llegada** nf newcomer, new person; (at party etc) latecomer.
recién nacido 1 adj newborn. 2 nm, **recién nacida** nf newborn child.
recién puesto adj egg new-laid.
reciente adj recent; bread etc new, fresh, newly-made.
recientemente adv recently.
recinto nm enclosure; precincts; area, spot, place; — **amurallado** walled enclosure; — **fortificado** fortified place; strongpoint; **dentro del — universitario** within the university precincts.
recio 1 adj (a) rope etc thick, strong; person strong, tough, robust; ground solid; test etc tough, demanding, severe.
(b) voice loud.
(c) weather harsh, severe.
(d) swift, fast, quick.
(e) **en lo más — del combate** in the thick of the fight; **en lo más — del invierno** in the depths of winter.
2 adv hit hard; blow hard, strongly; pass etc swiftly; shout, sing loud, loudly.
recipiente nm (a) (person) recipient. (b) recipient, receptacle, container.
recíproca nf (Math) reciprocal.
recíprocación nf reciprocation.
recíprocamente adv reciprocally, mutually.
reciprocar [1g] vt to reciprocate.
reciprocidad nf reciprocity; mutual character; **usar de —** to reciprocate.
recíproco adj (a) reciprocal, mutual. (b) inverse. (c) **a la recíproca** vice versa; **estar a la recíproca** to be ready to respond.
recitación nf recitation.
recitado nm recitation; (Mus) recitative.
recital nm (Mus) recital; (Lit) reading; — **de poesías** poetry reading.
recitar [1a] vt to recite.
recitativo nm recitative.
reclamable adj reclaimable.
reclamación nf (a) reclamation. (b) claim, demand; — **salarial** wage claim. (c) objection; complaint, protest; **formular una —** to make (or lodge) a complaint.

reclamar [1a] 1 vt (a) to claim, demand (de from); — **algo para sí** to claim something for oneself; — **su porción de la herencia** to claim one's share of the estate; **esto reclama toda nuestra atención** this demands our full attention.
(b) — **a uno ante los tribunales** to take someone to court, file a suit against someone.
2 vi: — **contra** to protest against, complain about; — **contra una sentencia** (Law) to appeal against a sentence.
reclame nm and f (SAm) advertisement; **mercadería de —** loss leader.
reclamo nm (a) (Orn) call, bird call; (Hunting) decoy, lure.
(b) (to person) call; **acudir al —** to answer the call.
(c) (Typ) catchword.
(d) (fig) inducement, lure, attraction; (Comm) advertisement; advertising slogan; publisher's blurb.
(e) (Law) claim.
reclinar [1a] 1 vt to lean, recline (contra against, sobre on). 2 **reclinarse** vr to lean; to recline, lean back.
recluir [3g] 1 vt to shut away; to confine; (Law) to imprison. 2 **recluirse** vr to shut oneself away.
reclusión nf (a) seclusion; (Law) imprisonment, confinement; — **perpetua** life imprisonment. (b) place of imprisonment, prison.
recluso 1 adj imprisoned; **población reclusa** prison population. 2 nm, **reclusa** nf (a) recluse. (b) (Law) inmate (of a prison), prisoner.
recluta 1 nf recruitment. 2 nm recruit.
reclutamiento nm recruitment.
reclutar [1a] vt (a) (Mil) to recruit. (b) (Arg) cattle to round up; (RPl) workmen to sign up, engage; members etc to recruit.
recobrar [1a] 1 vt to recover, get back, retrieve; fugitive, city etc to recapture; friendship etc to win back; time to make up (for).
2 **recobrarse** vr (a) (Med) to recover, convalesce; to come to, regain consciousness.
(b) (fig) to collect oneself.
recobro nm recovery, retrieval; recapture.
recocer [2b and 2h] 1 vt (a) (Cook) to cook again, warm up; to overcook.
(b) (Metal) to anneal.
(c) (Urug) to cook.
2 **recocerse** vr (fam) to be eaten up inside, suffer a lot.
recocina nf scullery.
recodar [1a] vi to twist, turn; to form a bend.
recodo nm turn, bend; elbow; loop.
recogedor nm (a) (person) picker, harvester; gleaner.
(b) (tool) rake, scraper; (container) pan.
recoger [2c] 1 vt (a) fallen object to pick up; scattered objects to gather (up), gather together; ball (Sport) to gather, stop, field; detail, information etc to pick up, come across; to collect; **este romance fue recogido en Esmirna** this ballad was picked up in Smyrna.
(b) money etc to collect, get together; stamps etc to collect.
(c) newspaper etc to take up, ban; **las autoridades recogieron todos los ejemplares** the authorities took up all the copies; **van a — las monedas antiguas** they are going to call in the old coins.
(d) (Agr) crop to harvest, get in; fruit to pick; (fig) to harvest, reap; to get as one's reward; **no recogió más que censuras** all he got was criticisms; **de todo esto van a — muy poco** they won't get much back out of all this.
(e) water etc to absorb, take up; dust to gather; (in receptacle) to collect.
(f) rope, sails to take in; wings to fold; horns etc to draw in; skirt to roll up, lift, gather up; sleeves to roll up; (Sew) to take in, reduce, shorten.
(g) washing to take in, get in; apparatus, materials, crockery etc to put away.
(h) person to pick up; to get, fetch, come for; **te vendremos a — a las 8** we'll come for you at 8 o'clock; **me recogieron en la estación** they picked me up at the station.
(i) needy person to take in, shelter.
2 **recogerse** vr (a) to withdraw, retire; to go home; to go to bed; to take shelter; to go off alone (to meditate etc).
(b) (Fin) to retrench.
recogida nf (a) withdrawal, retirement.
(b) (Agr) harvest; (of post, rubbish etc) collection; **hay 6 —s diarias** there are 6 collections daily.
(c) (Arg, Mex: Agr) roundup; (Arg: by police) sweep, raid.

recogido 1 *adj* **(a)** *life* quiet; *place, setting* secluded; *character* modest, retiring, (*pej*) shy, inhibited; **ella vive muy recogida** she lives very quietly.
(b) small; bunched up, tight.
2 *nm* tuck, gathering.

recogimiento *nm* **(a)** (*act*) harvesting, picking; collection; gathering.
(b) (*act*) withdrawal, retirement; (*Fin*) retrenchment.
(c) (*state*) absorption, concentration; seclusion; quietness.
(d) (*Eccl*) retreat, withdrawal.

recolección *nf* **(a)** (*act*) harvesting, picking; collection; gathering.
(b) (*time*) harvest time, picking season.
(c) (*Lit*) compilation; summary.
(d) (*Eccl*) retreat.

recolecta *nf* (*Mex*) collection.

recolectar [1a] *vt* = **recoger** (d).

recomendable *adj* recommendable; laudable; advisable; **poco —** inadvisable.

recomendación *nf* **(a)** recommendation; suggestion.
(b) praise.
(c) (*written*) reference, testimonial; **carta de —** letter of introduction (*para* to); **tiene muchas —es** he is strongly recommended to us, (*fig*) there's a lot to be said for him.
(d) (*Eccl*) **— del alma** prayers for the dying.

recomendar [1k] *vt* **(a)** to recommend; to suggest, advise; **— a uno que haga algo** to recommend someone to do something, advise someone to do something; **se lo recomiendo** I recommend it to you.
(b) to entrust, confide (*a* to).
(c) to praise, command.

recomendatorio *adj* recommendatory.

recomenzar [1f *and* 1k] *vti* to begin again, recommence.

recomerse [2a] *vr* to bear a secret grudge, harbour resentment.

recompensa *nf* recompense, reward; compensation (*de una pérdida* for a loss); **en — de** in return for, as a reward for.

recompensar [1a] *vt* to reward, recompense (*por* for); to compensate (*algo* for something).

recomponer [2r] **1** *vt* **(a)** (*Tech*) to mend, repair; (*Typ*) to reset. **(b)** (*fam*) *person* to dress up, doll up. **2 recomponerse** *vr* (*fam*) to dress up, doll up.

reconcentrar [1a] **1** *vt* **(a)** *attention etc* to concentrate (*en* on), devote (*en* to).
(b) *persons etc* to bring together.
(c) *solution* to make more concentrated; to reduce the volume of, compress, increase the density of.
(d) *emotion* to hide.
2 reconcentrarse *vr* **(a)** to concentrate hard, become totally absorbed.
(b) *emotion* to harbour, conceal in one's heart.

reconciliable *adj* reconcilable.

reconciliación *nf* reconciliation.

reconciliar [1b] **1** *vt* to reconcile. **2 reconciliarse** *vr* to become (*or* be) reconciled.

reconcomerse [2a] *vr* to bear a secret grudge, harbour resentment.

reconcomio *nm* **(a)** grudge, resentment. **(b)** urge, longing, itch. **(c)** suspicion.

recóndito *adj* recondite; **en lo más — de** in the depths of; **en lo más — del corazón** in one's heart of hearts.

reconfortante 1 *adj* comforting; cheering. **2** *nm* (*SAm*) tonic; strengthening food (*or* drink), pick-me-up.

reconfortar [1a] **1** *vt* to comfort; to cheer, encourage; (*Med*) to strengthen. **2 reconfortarse** *vr*: **— con** to fortify oneself with.

reconocer [2d] *vt* **(a)** to recognize (*por* by); to identify, know, tell, distinguish (*por* by); **se le reconoce por el pelo** you can recognize him by his hair.
(b) to recognize (*por* as); *child, government, signature etc* to recognize; **no le reconocieron por jefe** they did not recognize (*or* accept) him as their leader; **le reconocen por inteligente** they agree that he is intelligent; **reconoció al nino por suyo** he recognized that the child was his, he recognized the child as his.
(c) *merit, obligation, quality, right etc* to recognize, admit, acknowledge; **— los hechos** to face the facts; **— que . . .** to admit that . . .; to realize that . . .; **reconozco que no existen pruebas de ello** I realize that there is no proof of it; **hay que — que no es normal** one must admit that it isn't normal; **por fin reconocieron abiertamente que era falso** eventually they openly admitted that it was untrue.
(d) *gift, service etc* to be grateful for.

(e) *person* to search; *luggage etc* to search, inspect, examine; *terrain* to survey; (*Mil*) to reconnoitre, spy out; (*Med*) to examine.

reconocible *adj* recognizable.

reconocido *adj* **(a)** *leader etc* recognized, accepted. **(b) estar —** to be grateful.

reconocimiento *nm* **(a)** recognition; identification.
(b) recognition, admission, acknowledgement.
(c) gratitude; **en — de** in gratitude for.
(d) search(ing); inspection, examination; survey; (*Mil*) reconnaissance; (*Med*) examination, checkup; **vuelo de —** reconnaissance flight.

reconquista *nf* reconquest; recapture; **la R—** the Reconquest (of Spain).

reconquistar [1a] *vt* **(a)** (*Mil*) *territory* to reconquer; *position, town* to recapture (*a* from). **(b)** (*fig*) *esteem etc* to recover, win back.

reconsideración *nf* reconsideration.

reconsiderar [1a] *vt* to reconsider.

reconstitución *nf* reconstitution, reforming; reconstruction.

reconstituir [3g] *vt* to reconstitute, reform; *crime, scene* to reconstruct.

reconstituyente *nm* tonic, restorative, pick-me-up.

reconstrucción *nf* reconstruction; reshuffle.

reconstruir [3g] *vt* (*in most senses*) to reconstruct; *cabinet* to reshuffle.

recontar [1m] *vt* **(a)** *quantity* to recount, count again; to count up carefully. **(b)** *story* to retell, tell again.

recontra **(a)** (*SAm: intensifying prefix*) extremely, terribly; *eg* **recontracaro** terribly dear, **recontrabueno** jolly good. **(b) ¡—! interj** (*euph*) well I'm . . .!

reconvención *nf* **(a)** reprimand; expostulation, remonstrance. **(b)** (*Law*) countercharge.

reconvenir [3s] *vt* **(a)** to reprimand; to expostulate with, remonstrate with. **(b)** (*Law*) to countercharge.

reconversión *nf* reconversion; **— profesional** industrial retraining.

reconvertir [3i] *vt* to reconvert (*en* to); **— profesionalmente** to retrain for industry, give industrial retraining to.

recopilación *nf* summary; compilation; (*Law*) code; **la R—** Spanish law code of 1567; **la Nueva R—** Spanish law code of 1775.

recopilador *nm* compiler.

recopilar [1a] *vt* **(a)** to compile, gather, collect (together); to summarize. **(b)** *laws* to codify.

record, récord [re'kor, 'rekor] (*angl*) **1** *adj invar* record; **cifras —** record quantities; **en un tiempo —** in a record time.
2 *nm, pl* **records, récords** [re'kor, 'rekor] record; **batir el —** to break the record.

recordable *adj* memorable.

recordación *nf* recollection; remembrance; **de feliz —** of happy memory; **de infeliz** (*or* **triste**) **—** of unhappy memory; **digno de —** memorable.

recordar¹ [1m] **1** *vt* **(a)** to remember; to recollect, recall; **no lo recuerdo** I don't remember it; **recuerda haberlo dicho** he remembers having said it.
(b) to recall; to call up, evoke (memories of); bring to mind; **esto recuerda aquella escena de la película** this recalls that scene in the film; **la frase recuerda a Garcilaso** the phrase is reminiscent of Garcilaso, the phrase has echoes of Garcilaso.
(c) to remind; **— algo a uno** to remind someone of something; **— a uno que haga algo** to remind someone to do something; **recuérdale que me debe 5 dólares** remind him that he owes me 5 dollars.
(d) (*Arg, Mex*) to rouse, awaken.
2 *vi* to remember; **no recuerdo** I don't remember; **que yo recuerde** as far as I can remember; **creo —, si mal no recuerdo** if my memory serves me right; *see* **desde**.
3 recordarse *vr* **(a) — que . . .** to remind oneself that . . .
(b) (*Arg, Mex*) to wake up.

recordar² [1m] *vt* (*CAm, Mex, PR: angl*) *voice etc* to record.

recordativo *adj* reminiscent; **carta recordativa** follow-up letter, reminder.

recordatorio *nm* **(a)** reminder; memento. **(b)** notice of death.

recordman *nm, pl* **recordmans** (*angl, gall*) record holder; champion; outstanding player (*etc*).

recorrer [2a] *vt* **(a)** *area, place* to go over, go across, go through, traverse; *country* to cross, tour, travel; (*of searchers*) to cover, range, scour; *distance* to travel, cover, do; (*Mech*) to travel (along); **— una provincia a pie** to go over a province on foot, have a walking tour through a province; **— un escrito** to run one's eye over a document, look through a

document; **en 14 días los Jones han recorrido media Europa** the Jones have done half Europe in a fortnight.
 (**b**) to look over, go over, survey; to check; to search.
 (**c**) (*Mech etc*) to repair, mend; to overhaul.
 (**d**) *chairs etc* to move along, put closer together; (*Typ*) *letters* to take over.
recorrido *nm* (**a**) run, journey; route, course, path; distance covered, distance travelled; (*of roundsman, golf, show jumping etc*) round; (*of piston etc*) stroke; **el — del primer día fue de 450 km** the first day's run was 450 kms; **un — en 5 bajo par** a round in 5 under par; **un — sin penalizaciones** a clear round; **— de aterrizaje** (*Aer*) landing run.
 (**b**) (*Mech etc*) repair; overhaul.
 (**c**) (*fam*) detailed reprimand.
recortable *nm* cutout.
recortadito *adj* (*fam*) fussy, very particular, strict.
recortado 1 *adj* (**a**) *edge* jagged; uneven, irregular. (**b**) (*Cu, Mex*) squat. (**c**) (*Nic, Ven*) needy. **2** *nm* (*Arg, Per, Ven*) sawn-off rifle, pistol.
recortar [1a] **1** *vt* (**a**) *excess* to cut away, cut off, cut back, trim; *hair* to trim; *cutting, figure, picture etc* to cut out.
 (**b**) (*Art*) to draw in outline.
 (**c**) (*fig*) to cut out, remove, suppress; *rations etc* to cut down.
 2 recortarse *vr* to stand out, be outlined, be silhouetted (*en, sobre* against).
recorte *nm* (**a**) (*act*) cutting, trimming; (*of hair*) trim.
 (**b**) (*child's*) cutout.
 (**c**) **—s** trimmings, clippings; **—s de periódico** newspaper cuttings, press clippings; **álbum de —s** scrapbook; **el libro está hecho de —s** (*pej*) the book is a scissors-and-paste job.
 (**d**) (*CAm, Mex*) nasty remark, piece of gossip.
recoser [2a] *vt* to patch up, darn.
recosido *nm* patch, darn.
recostado *adj* reclining, recumbent; **estar —** to be lying down.
recostar [1m] **1** *vt* to lean (*en* on). **2 recostarse** *vr* (**a**) to recline, lie back; to lie down. (**b**) (*fig*) to have a short rest.
recotín *adj* (*Chi, Mex*) nervous, restless.
recova *nf* (**a**) poultry business, dealing in poultry; poultry market.
 (**b**) (*Bol, Chi, Ec, Per, Urug*) food market; (*Arg*) butcher's (shop).
 (**c**) (*RPl*) arcade, covered corridor (*along the front of a house*); porch.
recoveco *nm* (**a**) (*in street etc*) turn, bend.
 (**b**) (*in house*) nook, odd corner; cubbyhole.
 (**c**) **—s** (*fig*) ins and outs; **el asunto tiene muchos —s** it's a very complicated matter, the affair has lots of pitfalls.
 (**d**) **—s** (*fig: of person*) subterfuges, devious ways; **sin —s** plainly, frankly.
recreación *nf* (**a**) recreation. (**b**) =**recreo.**
recrear [1a] **1** *vt* (**a**) to recreate.
 (**b**) to amuse, divert, entertain.
 2 recrearse *vr* to enjoy oneself; to amuse oneself, entertain oneself (*con* with); **— viendo algo** (*pej*) to enjoy watching something, take a fiendish delight in seeing something.
recreativo *adj* recreative; recreational.
recrecer [2d] **1** *vt* to increase. **2** *vi* (**a**) to increase, grow. (**b**) to happen again. **3 recrecerse** *vr* to cheer up, recover one's spirits.
recreo *nm* (**a**) recreation, relaxation; amusement. (**b**) (*School*) break, playtime, recreation.
recriminación *nf* recrimination; **— mutua** mutual recrimination.
recriminar [1a] **1** *vt* to reproach. **2** *vi* to recriminate. **3 recriminarse** *vr* to reproach each other, indulge in mutual recrimination.
recrudecer [2d] **1** *vt* to cause to break out again; to worsen, exacerbate. **2** *vi and* **recrudecerse** *vr* to recrudesce, break out again; to worsen.
recrudecimiento *nm*, **recrudescencia** *nf* recrudescence, new outbreak, upsurge.
recrudescente *adj* recrudescent.
recta *nf* straight line; **la —** (*Sport*) the straight; **— de llegada** home straight.
rectal *adj* rectal.
rectangular *adj* =**rectángulo 1.**
rectángulo 1 *adj* rectangular, oblong; *triangle etc* right-angled. **2** *nm* rectangle, oblong.
rectificable *adj* rectifiable; **fácilmente —** easily rectified, easy to put right.
rectificación *nf* rectification; correction; **publicar una —** to publish a correction.
rectificador *nm*, **rectificadora** *nf* (*Mech*) rectifier.

rectificar [1g] **1** *vt* (**a**) *road etc* to straighten (out).
 (**b**) (*Mech etc*) to rectify; to balance; *cylinder* to rectify, rebore.
 (**c**) *calculation etc* to rectify, correct; *conduct* to change, reform.
 2 *vi* to correct oneself; **"No, eran 4", rectificó** "No", he said, correcting himself, "there were 4".
rectilíneo *adj* rectilinear.
rectitud *nf* (**a**) straightness. (**b**) (*fig*) rectitude, honesty, uprightness.
recto 1 *adj* (**a**) *line etc* straight; *angle* right; *part etc* upright; *course* straight, direct, unswerving; **la flecha fue recta al blanco** the arrow went straight to the target.
 (**b**) (*fig*) *person* honest, upright; *judge etc* fair, just, impartial; *judgement* sound; *intention* lawful, proper.
 (**c**) (*fig*) *sense* literal, proper, basic; **en el sentido — de la palabra** in the proper sense of the word.
 (**d**) (*Gram*) *case* nominative.
 2 *nm* (*Anat*) rectum.
rector 1 *adj* *person* leading; governing, managing; *idea, principle* guiding, governing; **los deberes —es del régimen** the régime's duty to govern; **una figura rectora** an outstanding figure, a leading figure.
 2 *nm* (**a**) head, chief, leader; principal.
 (**b**) (*Univ*) rector, president (*US*), (*approx*) vice-chancellor.
rectorado *nm* (*Univ*) (**a**) rectorship, presidency (*US*), (*approx*) vice-chancellorship. (**b**) rector's office.
rectorar [1a] *vt* (*CAm*) to rule, govern, direct.
rectoría *nf* (**a**) =**rectorado** (**a**) *and* (**b**). (**b**) (*Eccl*) rectory.
recua *nf* mule train, train of pack animals.
recubrir [3a; *ptp* **recubierto**] *vt* to cover (*con, de* with); to coat (*con, de* with).
recuento *nm* count, recount; inventory, survey; **hacer el — de** to make a survey of, draw up an inventory of; to count up, reckon up.
recuerdo 1 *adj* (*Ven*) awake.
 2 *nm* (**a**) memory; recollection; reminiscence; **"R—s de la vida de hace 80 años"** "Reminiscences of life 80 years ago"; **contar los —s** to reminisce; **guardar un feliz — de uno** to have happy memories of someone.
 (**b**) souvenir, memento, keepsake; **"R— de Mallorca"** "A present from Majorca"; **toma esto como —** take this as a keepsake.
 (**c**) **—s** regards, best wishes; **¡dale —s míos!** give him my regards!, remember me to him!; **os manda muchos —s para todos** he sends you all his warmest regards.
recuero *nm* muleteer.
recuesto *nm* slope.
reculada *nf* (**a**) backward movement; (*of gun*) recoil.
 (**b**) (*fig*) retreat; backing down, weakening.
recular [1a] *vi* (**a**) (*of animal, vehicle*) to go back, back; (*of gun*) to recoil; (*of army etc*) to fall back, retreat.
 (**b**) (*fig*) to back down, weaken (in one's resolve).
reculativa *nf* (*Mex*) =**reculada** (**b**).
reculón *nm* (**a**) (*SAm*) =**reculada**. (**b**) **andar a —es** to go backwards.
recuperable *adj* recoverable, retrievable.
recuperación *nf* recovery, recuperation; retrieval.
recuperar [1a] **1** *vt* (**a**) to recover, recuperate, retrieve; *loss* to recoup; *lost time* to make up.
 (**b**) (*Tech*) *waste etc* to reclaim, process for re-use.
 2 recuperarse *vr* (*Med etc*) to recover, recuperate.
recuperativo *adj* recuperative.
recurrente *adj* recurrent.
recurrir [3a] *vi* **— a** *a means etc* to resort to, have recourse to; to fall back on; *person* to turn to, appeal to. (**b**) (*Law*) to appeal (*a* to; *contra, de* against).
recurso *nm* (**a**) recourse, resort; means; expedient; **como último —** as a last resort.
 (**b**) **—s** (*Fin etc*) resources; means; **—s económicos** economic resources; **—s naturales** natural resources; **la familia está sin —s** the family has nothing to fall back on.
 (**c**) (*Law*) appeal.
recusante 1 *adj* recusant. **2** *nmf* recusant.
recusar [1a] *vt* (**a**) to reject, refuse. (**b**) (*Law*) to challenge (the authority of).
rechazamiento *nm* (**a**) repelling, beating off; driving back; reflection. (**b**) rejection; refusal; resistance.
rechazar [1f] *vt* (**a**) *person* to push back, push away; *attack* to repel, beat off; *enemy* to throw back, drive back; *light etc* to reflect, turn back; *water etc* to throw off.
 (**b**) *accusation, idea, motion* to reject; *offer* to reject, refuse, turn down; *temptation* to resist.

rechazo nm (of ball) bounce, rebound; (of gun) recoil; (fig) repulse, rebuff; **de —** on the rebound; (of bullet) as it glanced off, as it richocheted; (fig) in consequence, as a result.

rechifla nf (a) whistle, whistling. (b) hissing, hooting, booing; (Theat) catcall. (c) (fig) mockery, derision.

rechiflar [1a] **1** vt to whistle at, hiss, hoot, boo. **2** vi to whistle, hiss. **3 rechiflarse** vr (a) to take things as a joke. (b) (Arg) to get cross.

rechín nm (Col) piece of burnt food; **oler a —** to smell burnt.

rechinamiento nm creaking, grating; squeaking; clanking, clattering; humming, whirring; grinding, gnashing (of teeth).

rechinar [1a] **1** vi (a) to creak, grate; to squeak; (of wood, door etc) to creak; (of machine) to clank, clatter; (of unoiled parts) to grate; (of engine) to hum, whirr; (of teeth) to grate, grind, gnash; **hacer — los dientes** to grind one's teeth, gnash one's teeth.
(b) (fig) to do (or accept etc) something with an ill grace.
(c) (Arg, Col, Mex, Per) to rage; (Ven) to grumble; (Ven) to answer rudely.
2 rechinarse vr (a) (CAm, Mex) to burn, over-cook.
(b) (Arg) to get furious.

rechinido nm, **rechino** nm =**rechinamiento**.

rechoncho adj thickset, stocky, squat; plump.

rechupete: de — (fam) **1** adj splendid, jolly good (fam); meal delicious, scrumptious (fam).
2 adv splendidly, jolly well (fam); **me ha salido de —** it turned out marvellously for me; **pasarlo de —** to have a fine time.

red nf (a) (Fish etc) net; hairnet; mesh, meshes; (Rail) rack; fence; grille; **— de alambre** wire mesh, wire netting; **— barredera** trawl.
(b) (fig) network, system; (Elec, of water etc) mains, supply system; (of shops etc) chain; **— de emisoras** radio network; **— de espionaje** spy network; spy ring; **— ferroviaria** railway network, railway system; **— rastreadora, — de rastreo** tracking network; **con agua de la —** with mains water, with water from the mains; **estar conectado con la —** to be connected to the mains.
(c) (fig) snare, trap; **aprisionar a uno en sus —es** to have someone firmly caught in one's toils, have someone well and truly snared; **caer en la —** to fall into the trap; **tender una — para uno** to set a trap for someone.

redacción nf (a) (act) writing, redaction; editing. (b) wording. (c) newspaper office. (d) (persons) editorial staff.

redactar [1a] vt (a) to write; to draft, draw up; to word, express; **una carta mal redactada** a badly-worded letter. (b) newspaper etc to edit.

redactor nm (a) writer, drafter. (b) editor; sub-editor.

redada nf (a) (act) cast, casting, throw. (b) (by police) sweep, raid. (c) catch, haul (also fig).

redaje nm (Ec) net; mass, tangle.

redaño nm (a) (Anat) mesentery; caul. (b) **—s** (fam) guts, pluck.

redargüir [3g] **1** vt (Law) to impugn, hold to be invalid. **2** vi to turn an argument against its proposer; **— que . . .** to argue on the other hand that . . .

redecilla nf hairnet.

rededor: al — see **alrededor**.

redención nf redemption.

redentor 1 adj redeeming. **2** nm redeemer; **R—** Redeemer, Saviour; **meterse a —** to intervene (with the best intentions).

redescubrir [3a; ptp **redescubierto**] vt to rediscover.

redespachar [1a] vt (Arg) to send on, forward (directly).

redicho adj (fam) affected, overrefined, stilted.

redil nm sheepfold.

redimible adj redeemable.

redimir [3a] vt to redeem (also Fin, fig); captive to ransom; slave to purchase the freedom of.

rédito nm interest, yield, return.

redituar [1e] vt to yield, produce, bear.

redoblado adj (a) (Mech) part reinforced, extra strong; person stocky, thickset. (b) zeal etc redoubled. (c) pace double-quick.

redoblante nm drum.

redoblar [1a] **1** vt (a) paper etc to bend back, bend over, bend down; nail to clinch.
(b) watchfulness, zeal etc to redouble.
(c) (Bridge) to redouble.
2 vi (Mus) to play a roll on the drum; (of thunder) to roll, rumble.

redoble nm (Mus) drumroll, drumbeat; (of thunder) roll, rumble.

redoma nf (a) flask, phial. (b) (Chi) fishbowl. (c) (Ven) large lamp.

redomado adj (a) sly, artful. (b) rogue etc complete, utter, out-and-out.

redomón adj (SAm) horse half-tamed, half-trained; (Chi, Mex) person untrained; (Mex) rustic.

redonda nf (a) (Mus) semibreve.
(b) (Typ) roman, rounded characters, ordinary letters.
(c) **en muchas millas a la —** for many miles round about; **se olía a un kilómetro a la —** you could smell it a mile off.

redondear [1a] **1** vt (a) to round, round off. (b) (fig) to round off. **2 redondearse** vr (a) to acquire money, become wealthy. (b) to get clear of debts.

redondel nm (a) bullring, arena. (b) (fam) ring, circle. (c) (Aut) roundabout, traffic circle (US).

redondez nf roundness; **en toda la — de la tierra** in the whole wide world.

redondilla nf (Lit: Hist) quatrain.

redondo adj (a) round; rounded; **3 m en —** 3 metres round; **¿cuánto tiene de —?** how far is it round?; **caer —** to fall in a heap; **girar en —** to turn right round; **rehusar en —** to give a flat refusal, refuse flatly.
(b) number, quantity round; **en números —s** in round numbers, in round figures.
(c) trip round.
(d) refusal etc straight, flat, square; oath etc frank.
(e) deal etc complete, finished; successful; **todo le ha salido —** it all went well for him.
(f) (Mex) person dim, dense; weak, unresisting.

redopelo nm (a) (fam) row, shindy. (b) **a — = a contrapelo; traer al — a uno** to treat someone very badly, ride roughshod over someone.

redro adv (fam) behind; backwards.

redrojo nm (a) (Bot) late fruit, withered fruit.
(b) puny child, runt; (Mex) worthless individual, poor fish; poor wretch.
(c) (Arg) surplus, remainder.
(d) (Mex) rag.

reducción nf (a) reduction; diminution, lessening, cut. (b) (Med) setting. (c) (SAm: Hist) settlement of converted Indians.

reducible adj reducible.

reducido adj (a) reduced; limited; number etc small; income, resources limited, small; space confined, limited; price low. (b) **quedar — a** to be reduced to.

reducir [3o] **1** vt (a) number, quantity etc to reduce; to diminish, lessen, cut (down); speech etc to cut down, abridge; size to reduce, cut down; activity, intervention etc to limit (a to).
(b) (Math etc) to reduce (a to), convert (a into); **— las millas a kilómetros** to convert miles into kilometres; **— los dólares en pesetas** to change dollars into pesetas; to express dollars as pesetas; **— una casa a escombros** to reduce a house to rubble; **todo lo reduce a cosas materiales** he reduces everything to material terms.
(c) country etc to subdue; rebels to overcome, bring under control; fortress to reduce; **— a uno al silencio** to silence someone, reduce someone to silence; **— a uno a la obediencia** to bring someone to heel.
(d) (Med) bone to set.
2 reducirse vr (a) to diminish, lessen, fall, be reduced (a to).
(b) (Fin) to economize.
(c) **— a** to come down to, amount to no more than; **el escándalo se redujo a un simple chisme** the scandal amounted to nothing more than a piece of gossip; **— a + infin** to come down to + ger, find oneself reduced to + ger.

reductible adj (Arg, Mex) reducible.

reducto nm (Mil and fig) redoubt; **el último — de** the last redoubt of.

reduje etc see **reducir**.

redundancia nf redundancy, superfluity.

redundante adj redundant, superfluous.

redundar [1a] vi: **— en** to redound to; **— en beneficio de** to be to the advantage of.

reduplicación nf reduplication; redoubling.

reduplicar [1g] vt to reduplicate; effort etc to redouble.

reedición nf reissue, reprint(ing).

reedificación nf rebuilding.

reedificar [1g] vt to rebuild.

reeditar [1a] vt to reissue, republish, reprint.

reeducación nf re-education; **— profesional** industrial retraining.

reeducar [1g] *vt* to re-educate; **— profesionalmente** to give industrial retraining to.

reelección *nf* re-election.

reelegible *adj* re-elegible.

reelegir [3c *and* 3l] *vt* to re-elect.

reembalar [1a] *vt* to repack.

reembolsable *adj* repayable; returnable; **no —** (*Fin*) stock irredeemable; *deposit* non-returnable.

reembolsar [1a] **1** *vt person* to reimburse; to repay; *money* to repay, pay back; *deposit* to refund, return. **2 reembolsarse** *vr* to reimburse oneself; **— una cantidad** to recover a sum.

reembolso *nm* reimbursement; repayment, refund; **enviar algo contra —** to send something cash on delivery (*abbr:* C.O.D.).

reemplazable *adj* replaceable.

reemplazante *nmf* (*Mex*) replacement, substitute.

reemplazar [1f] *vt* (*all senses*) to replace (*con* with, *por* by).

reemplazo *nm* (a) replacement. (b) (*Mil*) reserve; annual draft of recruits; **de —** reserve (*attr*), from the reserve.

reencarnación *nf* reincarnation.

reencarnar [1a] **1** *vt* to reincarnate. **2** *vi* to be reincarnated.

reencender [1k] *vt* to light again, rekindle.

reencuadernar [1a] *vt* to rebind.

reengancharse [1a] *vr* to re-enlist.

reentrada *nf* re-entry.

reenvasar [1a] *vt* to repack, rewrap.

reenviar [1c] *vt* to forward, send on; to send back.

reestatificación *nf* renationalization.

reestatificar [1g] *vt* to renationalize.

reestrenar [1a] *vt* (*Theat*) to revive, put on again; (*Cine*) to reissue.

reestreno *nm* (*Theat*) revival; (*Cine*) reissue.

reexaminación *nf* re-examination.

reexaminar [1a] *vt* to re-examine.

reexpedir [3l] *vt* to forward; to redirect.

reexportar [1a] *vt* to re-export.

refacción *nf* (a) light refreshment, refection. (b) (*SAm: Archit, Mech*) repair(s). (c) (*Cu, Mex, Per, PR*) upkeep costs. (d) (*Mex, PR*) short-term loan, financial aid. (e) (*Mex: Mech*) spare part.

refaccionar [1a] *vt* (a) (*SAm*) to repair. (b) (*Cu, Mex, Per, PR*) to give financial aid to, subsidize.

refajo *nm* flannel underskirt; short extra skirt; slip.

refalar [1a] **1** *vt* (a) (*Chi, RPl*) **— algo a uno** to take something from (*or* off) someone. (b) (*Arg, Bol*) to steal. **2 refalarse** *vr* (*RPl*) (a) **— los zapatos** to take one's shoes off. (b) to leave, make off; to beat it (*fam*); to slip.

refaloso *adj* (*Arg*) (a) slippery. (b) shy, timid.

refectorio *nm* refectory.

referencia *nf* (a) (*in most senses*) reference; **con — a** with reference to; **hacer — a** to refer to, allude to. (b) account, report; **una — completa del suceso** a complete account of what took place.

referente *adj:* **— a** relating to, about, concerning.

referéndum *nm, pl* **referéndums** referendum.

referí *nm* (*SAm: angl*) referee, umpire.

referible *adj:* **— a** referable to.

referir [3i] **1** *vt* (a) to recount, report; to tell; **— que . . .** to say that . . ., tell how . . ., relate how . . . (b) **— al lector a un apéndice** to refer the reader to an appendix. (c) to refer, apply, relate; **todo lo refiere a su teoría favorita** he refers (*or* relates) everything to his favourite theory; **han referido el cuadro al siglo XVII** they have referred the picture to the 17th century, they have placed the picture in the 17th century. (d) **— a** (*Fin*) to convert into, express in terms of. (e) (*CAm*) to abuse, insult. (f) (*Mex*) **— algo a uno** to reproach someone with something. **2 referirse** *vr:* **— a** to refer to; **me refiero a lo de anoche** I refer to what happened last night; **por lo que se refiere a eso** as for that, as regards that.

**refilón: de — ** *adv* obliquely, slantingly, aslant; **el sol da de — ** the sun strikes obliquely, the sun comes slanting in; **mirar a uno de — ** to take a sideways glance at; to take a quick look at.

refinación *nf* refining.

refinado *adj* refined.

refinador *nm* refiner.

refinadura *nf* refining.

refinamiento *nm* refinement; **con todos los —s modernos** with all the modern refinements.

refinar [1a] *vt* (a) (*Tech*) to refine. (b) (*fig*) *system etc* to refine, perfect; *style etc* to polish.

refinería *nf* refinery.

refino 1 *adj* extra fine, pure, refined. **2** *nm* refining.

refirmar [1a] *vt* (*SAm*) to reaffirm.

refistolería *nf* (a) (*CAm, Ven*) scheming nature; scheming, troublemaking. (b) (*Ant, Ec, Mex*) conceit; affectation; pedantry. (c) (*Cu, SD*) oiliness, soapiness.

refistolero *adj* (a) (*CAm, Ven*) intriguing, scheming; mischievous. (b) (*Ant, Ec, Mex*) vain, stuck-up (*fam*), affected; pedantic. (c) (*Cu, SD*) oily, soapy.

reflector *nm* (a) reflector; **— posterior** (*Aut*) rear reflector. (b) (*Elec*) spotlight; (*Aer, Mil*) searchlight.

reflejar [1a] **1** *vt* (a) to reflect. (b) (*fig*) to reflect, mirror, show, reveal. **2 reflejarse** *vr* to be reflected (*also fig*).

reflejo 1 *adj* (a) *light* reflected. (b) *action* reflex. (c) (*Gram*) *verb* reflexive. **2** *nm* (a) reflection; **mirar su — en el agua** to look at one's reflection in the water. (b) (*fig*) reflection. (c) (*Anat etc*) reflex; reflex action. (d) **—s** gleam, glint; **tiene —s metálicos** it has a metallic glint. (e) (*for hair*) rinse; **darse un — azul** to give one's hair a blue rinse.

reflexión *nf* (a) (*Phys*) reflection. (b) (*fig*) reflection; thought; meditation; **mis —es sobre el problema** my reflections on the problem.

reflexionar [1a] **1** *vt* to reflect on, think about, think over. **2** *vi* to reflect (*en, sobre* on); (*before acting*) to think, pause, reflect; **¡reflexione!** you think it over!, think for a moment!

reflexivamente *adv* (a) (*Gram*) reflexively. (b) thoughtfully, reflectively.

reflexivo *adj* (a) (*Gram*) *verb* reflexive. (b) *person etc* thoughtful, reflective. (c) *act* considered.

refluir [3g] *vi* to flow back.

reflujo *nm* ebb, ebb tide.

refocilación *nf* huge enjoyment, great pleasure; unhealthy pleasure, cruel pleasure; coarse merriment.

refocilar [1a] **1** *vt* to give great pleasure to; to amuse hugely, amuse in a coarse way; to cheer up. **2** *vi* (*RPl: of lightning*) to flash. **3 refocilarse** *vr* (a) to enjoy oneself hugely; to enjoy oneself in a coarse way; **— con algo** to enjoy something hugely, have a fine time with something; **— viendo lo que sufre otro** to take a cruel pleasure in watching someone else's sufferings. (b) to cheer up no end.

refocilo *nm* (a) = **refocilación**. (b) (*RPl*) lightning, flash of lightning.

reforma *nf* (a) reform; reformation; improvement; **R—** (*Eccl*) Reformation; **— agraria** land reform. (b) (*Archit etc*) **—s** alterations, repairs, improvements; **"cerrado por —s"** "closed for repairs".

reformación *nf* reform, reformation.

reformado *adj* reformed.

reformador *nm*, **reformadora** *nf* reformer.

reformar [1a] **1** *vt* (a) to reform; to change, alter, improve; to reorganize; *abuse etc* to correct, put right; *text* to revise. (b) to re-form. (c) (*Archit etc*) to alter, repair; to improve; (*Mech*) to mend, repair; (*Sew*) to alter. **2 reformarse** *vr* to reform, mend one's ways.

reformatorio *nm* reformatory; **— de menores** remand home.

reformista *nmf* reformist, reformer.

reforzador *nm* (*Elec*) booster; (*Phot*) intensifier.

reforzamiento *nm* reinforcement, strengthening.

reforzar [1f *and* 1m] *vt* (a) (*Archit etc*) to reinforce, strengthen; (*Mil*) to reinforce; (*Elec etc*) to boost, raise, step up; *dose* to increase. (b) (*fig*) *resistance etc* to strengthen, buttress, bolster up; *person* to encourage.

refracción *nf* refraction.

refractar [1a] *vt* to refract.

refractario *adj* (a) (*Tech*) fireproof, heat-resistant; (*Cook*) ovenproof. (b) (*fig*) refractory, recalcitrant; stubborn; **ser — a una reforma** to resist a reform, be opposed to a reform; **ser — a las lenguas** to have a total blank where languages are concerned.

refractivo *adj* refractive.

refractor *nm* refractor.

refrán *nm* proverb, saying; **como dice el —** as the saying goes.

refranero *nm* collection of proverbs.

refraniento *adj* (*Chi*) much given to quoting proverbs.

refregar [1h *and* 1k] *vt* (a) to rub (hard), brush (repeatedly); to scrub.
(b) (*fig*) — algo a uno to rub something in so that someone remembers it, drive something home; to harp on something to someone; to reproach someone with something.

refregón *nm* (a) rub(bing), brush(ing); scrub(bing).
(b) mark left by rubbing (*etc*).

refrenar [1a] *vt* (a) horse to rein back, rein in; to hold back. (b) (*fig*) to curb, restrain, hold in check.

refrendar [1a] *vt* (a) to endorse, countersign; to authenticate; to give one's approval to; *passport* to stamp. (b) (*fam*) to do again, repeat; *food* to order more of, have a second helping of. (c) (*Mex*) to redeem (from pawn).

refrescante *adj* refreshing, cooling.

refrescar [1g] 1 *vt* (a) to refresh, to cool (down).
(b) *memory* to refresh; *knowledge, subject* to brush up, polish up.
(c) *action* to repeat; *enmity etc* to renew.
2 *vi* (a) (*Meteorol*) to get cooler, cool down.
(b) (*person*) to refresh oneself; to take the air, go out for a walk.
(c) (*person*) to take some refreshment, have a drink.
(d) (*Mex: Med*) to get better.
3 **refrescarse** *vr* = *vi* (*esp* b).

refresco *nm* cool drink, soft drink; —s refreshments; "R—s" "Refreshments".

refresquería *nf* (*SAm*) refreshment stall.

refriega *nf* scuffle, set-to (*fam*); affray, brawl.

refrigeración *nf* refrigeration; (*Mech*) cooling; air conditioning; — por agua water-cooling; — por aire air-cooling.

refrigerado *adj* cooled; *cinema, room etc* air-conditioned; — por agua water-cooled; — por aire air-cooled.

refrigerador *nm* refrigerator; cooling unit, cooling system.

refrigeradora *nf* (*SAm*) refrigerator.

refrigerante 1 *adj* cooling, refrigerating. 2 *nm* (*Chem*) refrigerant.

refrigerar [1a] *vt* to cool, refresh; (*Tech*) to refrigerate; (*Mech*) to cool; *room* to air-condition.

refrigerio *nm* (a) snack; cooling drink. (b) (*fig*) relief.

refucilar [1a] *vi* (*Arg, Ec*) = **refocilar** 2.

refucilo *nm* (*Arg*) = **refocilo** (b).

refuerzo *nm* (a) (*act*) strengthening; reinforcement (also *Mil*). (b) (*Tech*) brace, support. (c) —s (*Mil*) reinforcements. (d) (*fig*) aid.

refugiado 1 *adj* refugee. 2 *nm*, **refugiada** *nf* refugee.

refugiarse [1b] *vr* to take refuge; to shelter (*en* in); to go into hiding; — en un país vecino to flee to a neighbouring country, seek asylum in a neighbouring country.

refugio *nm* (a) (*in general*) refuge, shelter; asylum; (*Eccl*) sanctuary; (*fig*) refuge, haven; acogerse a un — to take refuge, shelter (*en* in); to seek sanctuary.
(b) refuge, shelter; (*Aut*) street island; — alpino, — de montaña mountain hut; — antiaéreo air-raid shelter; — subterráneo (*Mil*) underground shelter, dugout.

refulgencia *nf* brilliance, refulgence.

refulgente *adj* brilliant, refulgent.

refulgir [3c] *vi* to shine (brightly).

refundición *nf* (a) (*act*) revision, recasting. (b) new version, adaptation, rehash; revision.

refundidor *nm*, **refundidora** *nf* reviser, adapter.

refundir [3a] 1 *vt* (a) (*Tech*) to recast.
(b) (*Lit etc*) to adapt, rehash; to revise, rewrite; to remodel.
(c) (*CAm, Col, Mex*) to lose, mislay.
(d) (*Arg*) to ruin, crush; *candidate* to plough (*sl*).
(e) (*Guat, Mex*) to keep carefully.
2 **refundirse** *vr* (*CAm, Col, Mex*) to get lost, be mislaid.

refunfuñar [1a] *vi* to growl, grunt; to grumble.

refunfuño *nm* growl, grunt; grumble.

refunfuñón (*fam*) 1 *adj* growling, grunting; grumbling, grouchy (*fam*). 2 *nm* grumbler, groucher (*fam*).

refutable *adj* refutable; fácilmente — easily refuted.

refutación *nf* refutation.

refutar [1a] *vt* to refute.

regadera *nf* (a) sprinkler; (*Hort*) watering can. (b) (*Mex*) shower bath. (c) (*fam*) estar como una —, ser una — to have a memory like a sieve; to be crazy.

regadío 1 *adj* irrigable. 2 *nm* irrigated land, irrigable

land (*also* tierra de —); cultivo de — crop that grows on irrigated land, crop that needs irrigation.

regadizo *adj* irrigable.

regador *nm* (*Chi*) watering can.

regadura *nf* sprinkling, watering; (*Agr*) irrigation.

regala *nf* gunwale.

regaladamente *adv* live in luxury.

regalado *adj* (a) *life etc* of luxury; comfortable, pleasant; (*pej*) soft.
(b) dainty, delicate.
(c) (*Comm, Fin*) free, given away; me lo dio medio — he gave it to me for a song; no lo quiero ni — I won't have it at any price, I don't want it even as a present.

regalar [1a] 1 *vt* (a) to give, present; to give away; — algo a uno to give someone something, make someone a present of something; en su jubilación le regalaron este reloj they gave him this clock on his retirement, they presented him with this clock on his retirement; están regalando plumas they're giving pens away, they're issuing pens free.
(b) *person* to treat royally, make a great fuss of; (*pej*) to indulge, pamper; — a uno con un banquete to entertain someone to a dinner, (*less formally*) treat someone to a dinner; le regalaron con toda clase de atenciones they regaled him with all manner of hospitality, they lavished attentions on him.
2 **regalarse** *vr* (a) to indulge oneself, pamper oneself; to do oneself well.
(b) — con to regale oneself with.

regalía *nf* (a) —s (*Hist*) royal prerogatives.
(b) (*fig*) privilege, prerogative; (*Fin*) perquisite, bonus.
(c) (*Ant, CAm, Col*) gift, present.
(d) (*Arg, Cu, Mex*) royalty; advance payment.
(e) (*Ven*) excellence, goodness; beauty.

regaliz *nm*, **regaliza** *nf* liquorice, licorice.

regalo *nm* (a) gift, present; — de boda wedding present; entrada de — complimentary ticket.
(b) (*fig*) pleasure; (*food*) treat, delicacy, dainty; es un — del oído it's a treat to listen to.
(c) (*fig*) luxury, comfort.

regalón *adj* (a) *child* spoiled, pampered; *person* comfort-loving, (*pej*) soft, lapped in luxury.
(b) *life* of luxury, comfortable; (*pej*) soft.
(c) (*Arg*) éste es el — de su padre this is the son that his father spoils most, this is daddy's pet.

regalonear [1a] 1 *vt* (*Arg, Chi*) to spoil, pamper.
2 *vi* (*Chi*) to allow oneself to be pampered.

regaña *nf* (*CAm, Mex, Per*) = **regaño**.

regañadientes: a — *adv* unwillingly, reluctantly.

regañado *adj*: estar — con uno to be at odds with someone.

regañar [1a] 1 *vt* to scold; to tell off, reprimand; to nag (at).
2 *vi* (a) (*of dog*) to snarl, growl.
(b) (*of person*) to grumble, grouse (*fam*); to nag.
(c) (*of two persons*) to fall out, quarrel.

regaño *nm* (a) snarl, growl; scowl; grumble, grouse (*fam*). (b) scolding; telling-off; merecerse un — to get a telling off.

regañón *adj* grumbling, grouchy (*fam*); irritable; *woman* nagging, shrewish.

regar [1h *and* 1k] 1 *vt* (a) *plant* to water; *land* to water, irrigate; *street* to water, hose (down), wash; *wound etc* to wash, bathe (*con, de* with); (*with insecticide etc*) to spray (*con, de* with); — la garganta to spray one's throat; — un papel de lágrimas to let tears fall on a sheet of paper, cover a sheet of paper with teardrops.
(b) (*Geog: of river*) to water; (*of sea*) to wash, lap against; una costa regada por un mar tranquilo a coast washed by a calm sea.
(c) (*fig*) to sprinkle, strew (in all directions), scatter; iba regando monedas he was dropping money all over the place.
(d) (*Col, CR*) to spill; to knock over.
(e) (*PR*) to hit.
2 *vi* (a) (*PR*) to joke; to fib.
(b) (*Ven*) to act rashly.
3 **regarse** *vr* (a) (*CAm, Mex, Ven*) to scatter (in all directions).
(b) (*SD*) to get cross.

regata[1] *nf* (*Agr*) irrigation channel.

regata[2] *nf* (*Naut*) race, boat race; regatta.

regate *nm* (a) swerve, dodge; (*Sport*) dribble. (b) (*fig*) dodge, ruse.

regatear[1] [1a] *vi* (*Naut*) to race.

regatear[2] [1a] 1 *vt* (a) (*Comm*) *deal, object* to haggle over, bargain over; *price* to try to beat down.
(b) *supply etc* to be mean with, economize on; to give (*or* issue *etc*) sparingly; su padre no le regatea

dinero her father does not keep her short of money; **aquí regatean el vino** they are mean with their wine here; **no hemos regateado esfuerzo para** + *infin* we have spared no effort to + *infin*.

(c) (*fig*) to deny, refuse to allow; **no le regateo buenas cualidades** I don't deny his good qualities.

2 *vi* (a) (*Comm*) to haggle, bargain; (*fig*) to bicker. (b) to swerve, dodge; to duck; (*Sport*) to dribble.

regateo *nm* (a) haggling, bargaining. (b) (*Sport*) dribbling.

regatón[1] *nm* (*of stick*) tip, ferrule.

regatón[2] **1** *adj* (*Comm*) haggling; (*fig*) bickering, niggling, argumentative. **2** *nm* (a) (*Ven*) dregs. (b) (*Mex*) retailer, small-time dealer.

regazo *nm* lap (*also fig*).

regencia *nf* regency.

regeneración *nf* (a) regeneration. (b) (*Tech*) reclaiming.

regenerado *adj* regenerate.

regenerador *adj* regenerative.

regenerar [1a] *vt* (a) to regenerate. (b) (*Tech*) to reclaim, process for re-use.

regentar [1a] *vt* (a) *chair etc* to occupy, hold; *post to* hold temporarily; (*fig*) *destinies etc* to guide, preside over. (b) (*fam*) to domineer, boss.

regente 1 *adj* (a) *prince etc* regent. (b) *director etc* managing.

2 *nm* (*also f, and* **regenta** *nf*) (a) (*Pol*) regent. (b) (*of estate, factory*) manager; (*Pharm*) chief pharmacist; (*Typ*) foreman.

regiamente *adv* regally.

regicida *nmf* regicide (*person*).

regicidio *nm* regicide (*act*).

regidor *nm* (*Hist*) alderman.

regiego = **rejego**.

régimen *nm* (a) (*Pol*) régime; rule; **antiguo —** ancien régime; — **marioneta** puppet régime; **bajo el — del dictador** under the dictator's régime (*or* rule).

(b) (*Med*) diet (*also* — **alimenticio**); — **lácteo** milk diet; **estar a —** to be on a diet; **poner a uno a —** to put someone on a diet.

(c) rules, set of rules, régime, system; way of life; **he cambiado de —** I have changed my whole way of life, I have made myself a new set of rules.

(d) (*Gram*) government.

regimentación *nf* regimentation.

regimiento *nm* (a) administration, government, organization. (b) (*Mil*) regiment. (c) (*SAm*) regiment, mass, crowd.

Reginaldo *m* Reginald.

regio *adj* (a) royal, regal; kingly. (b) (*fig*) royal, splendid, majestic.

región *nf* (a) region; district, area, part; (*Pol*) region. (b) (*Anat*) region, tract.

regional *adj* regional.

regionalismo *nm* regionalism.

regionalista 1 *adj* regionalist. **2** *nmf* regionalist.

regir [3c *and* 3l] **1** *vt* (a) *country etc* to rule, govern; *college etc* to run, be in charge of, be at the head of; *business* to manage, run, control.

(b) (*Law, Gram etc*) to govern; **según el reglamento que rige estos casos** according to the statute which governs these cases; **ese verbo rige el dativo** that verb takes the dative; **los factores que rigen los cambios del mercado** the factors which govern (*or* determine, control) changes in the market.

2 *vi* (a) (*Law*) to be in operation, be in force, apply; (*of price*) to be in force; (*of condition etc*) to prevail, obtain; **esa ley ya no rige** that law no longer applies; **el mes que rige** the present month, the current month; **cuando estas condiciones ya no rijan** when these conditions no longer obtain.

(b) (*Mech*) to work, go; **el timbre no rige** the bell doesn't work.

(c) (*fam*) **no —** to have a screw loose (*fam*), be not all there (*fam*).

3 regirse *vr*: — **por** to be ruled by, be guided by, go by.

registrado *adj* registered.

registrador *nm* recorder, registrar.

registrar [1a] **1** *vt* (a) *fact etc* to register, record; to enter; to file.

(b) (*Mus etc*) to record; — **la voz en una cinta** to record one's voice on tape.

(c) *luggage, person, place* to search; *archive, document* to survey, inspect; to look through; lo **hemos registrado todo de arriba abajo** we have searched the whole place from top to bottom.

2 registrarse *vr* (a) (*person*) to register. (b) (*fact etc*) to be recorded; (*event, accident*) to happen; **se han registrado algunos casos de tifus**

a few cases of typhus have been reported; **no se ha registrado nunca nada parecido** nothing of the kind has ever been recorded before; **el cambio que se ha registrado en su actitud** the change which has occurred in his attitude.

registro *nm* (a) (*act*) registration, recording.

(b) register; visitor's book; — **de casamientos** register of marriages; — **de defunciones** register of deaths; — **electoral** voting register, electoral roll; — **de hotel** hotel register; — **de nacimientos** register of births; — **parroquial** parish register; **firmar el —** to sign the register.

(c) list, roll, record; note; — **de erratas** list of errata.

(d) entry (in a register).

(e) registry, record office; — **civil** register office; — **de patentes y marcas** patents office; — **de la propiedad** land registry (office).

(f) search; survey, inspection; — **domiciliario** search of a house; — **policíaco** police search; **practicar un —** to make a search (*en* of).

(g) (*Mus etc*) recording; **es un buen — de la sinfonía** it is a good recording of the symphony.

(h) (*Mus*) register; (*of organ*) stop; (*of piano*) pedal; **salir por** (*or* **adoptar**) **un — muy raro** (*fig*) to adopt a very odd tone, adopt a most inappropriate tone; **tocar todos los —s** (*fig*) to pull out all the stops.

(i) (*Tech*) manhole, manhole cover; (*of fire*) damper; inspection plate, inspection hatch.

(j) bookmark.

(k) (*of watch*) regulator.

(l) (*Typ*) register; **estar en —** to be in register.

(m) (*Bol, RPl*) wholesale textiles store.

regla *nf* (a) ruler, rule; — **de cálculo** slide rule; — **de un pie** foot rule; — **T**, — **en T** T-square.

(b) rule; regulation; (*Sport etc*) rule; (*scientific*) law, principle; norm; —**s del juego** rules of the game, laws of the game; —**s de la circulación** traffic regulations; —**s para utilizar una máquina** instructions for the use of a machine, points to be observed in using a machine; **no hay — sin excepción** every rule has its exception; **en —** in order; **todo está en —** everything is in order; all is as it should be; **poner algo en —** to put something straight; **no tenía los papeles en —** his papers were not in order; **por — general** generally, usually, as a rule; on the average; **hacerse una — de** + *infin* to make it a rule to + *infin*; **ser de —** to be the rule, be usual, be the norm; **salir de —** to overstep the mark; to be abnormal, have abnormal features.

(c) (*Math*) rule; law; — **de 3** rule of 3.

(d) (*Eccl*) rule, order; **viven según la — benedictina** they live according to the Benedictine rule.

(e) (*Med*) —**s** period.

(f) (*fig*) moderation, restraint; **comer con —** to eat in moderation.

reglaje *nm* (a) (*Mech*) checking, overhaul; adjustment. (b) (*Mil*) correction (*of aim*).

reglamentación *nf* (a) (*act*) regulation. (b) rules, regulations (*collectively*).

reglamentar [1a] *vt* to regulate; to make rules for, establish regulations for.

reglamentariamente *adv* in due form, according to the rules; properly.

reglamentario *adj* regulation (*attr*), set; statutory; proper, due; **en el traje —** in the regulation dress; **en la forma reglamentaria** in due form, in the properly established way; **es — + infin** the law requires that . . ., the regulation makes it obligatory to + *infin*.

reglamento *nm* rules, regulations (*collectively*); (*of meeting, society*) standing order(s); (*municipal etc*) by-law; (*of profession*) code of conduct; — **de aduana** customs regulations; — **del tráfico** rule of the road, highway code.

reglar [1a] **1** *vt* (a) *line etc* to rule. (b) (*Mech*) to check, overhaul; to adjust; (*Mil*) *aim* to correct.

(c) (*fig*) to regulate, make regulations for.

2 reglarse *vr*: — **a** to abide by, conform to; — **por** to be guided by.

regleta *nf* (*Typ*) space.

regletear [1a] *vt* (*Typ*) to space out.

regocijadamente *adv* merrily; joyously, joyfully; exultantly.

regocijado *adj* (a) *character* jolly, cheerful, merry. (b) *state* merry; joyous, joyful; exultant.

regocijar [1a] **1** *vt* to gladden, delight, cheer (up); **un chiste que regocijó a todos** a joke which made everyone laugh; **crear un personaje para — a los niños** to create a character to amuse children; **la**

noticia **regocijó a la familia** the news delighted the family, the news filled the family with joy.

2 regocijarse *vr* (a) to rejoice, be glad, express one's happiness (*de, por* about, at).

(b) to laugh; — **con un chiste** to laugh at a joke.

(c) to make merry, have a merry time, celebrate.

(d) (*pej*) to exult; — **por un desastre ajeno** to exult in someone else's misfortune, take a cruel pleasure in a disaster which has befallen someone else.

regocijo *nm* (a) joy, happiness; rejoicing; elation; gaiety, merriment.

(b) (*pej*) exultation; unhealthy pleasure, cruel delight (*por* in).

(c) —**s** festivities, rejoicings, celebrations; —**s navideños** Christmas festivities; —**s públicos** public rejoicings.

regodearse [1a] *vr* (a) to crack jokes (*fam*); to indulge in coarse humour.

(b) to be glad, be delighted; — **haciendo algo** to enjoy oneself hugely doing something; (*pej*) — **con,** — **en** to take a cruel delight in; — **porque otro está sufriendo** to be perversely glad that somebody else is suffering.

(c) (*Col, Chi, Ven*) to be fussy, be hard to please.

regodeo *nm* (a) joking; coarse humour. (b) delight; huge enjoyment; (*pej*) cruel delight, perverse pleasure.

regodeón *adj* (*Col, Chi*) fussy, hard to please.

regodiente *adj* (*Col, Ven*) fussy, hard to please.

regoldar [1m] *vi* to belch.

regordete *adj person* chubby, plump; *hands etc* fat.

regosto *nm* longing, craving (*de* for).

regresar [1a] **1** *vt* (*SAm*) to give back, return. **2** *vi* to come back, go back, return. **3 regresarse** *vr* (*SAm*)=**2.**

regresión *nf* regression; (*fig*) retreat; backward step; fall, decrease.

regresivo *adj movement* backward; (*fig*) regressive, retrogressive, backward; downward.

regreso *nm* return; **viaje de** — return trip, homeward journey; **emprender el** — **a** to return to, come back to; **estar de** — to be back, be home.

regüeldo *nm* belch, belching.

reguera *nf* (a) (*Agr*) irrigation channel. (b) (*Naut*) cable, mooring rope, anchor chain.

reguero *nm* (a) (*Agr*) irrigation ditch; (*SAm*) furrow.

(b) track; streak, line, mark; (*of blood etc*) trickle; (*of gunpowder etc*) train; (*of smoke, vapour*) trail; **propagarse como un** — **de pólvora** to spread like wildfire.

reguío *nm* (*Col, Ec, SD*)=**riego.**

regulable *adj* adjustable.

regulación *nf* regulation; adjustment; control; — **de la natalidad** birth control; — **del tráfico** traffic control; — **del volumen sonoro** (*Radio*) volume control.

regulador *nm* (*Mech*) regulator, throttle, governor; (*Radio etc*) control, knob, button; — **del volumen sonoro** volume control.

regular 1 *adj* (a) (*in most senses, also Eccl, Math, Mil*) regular; normal, usual, customary; ordinary; *life etc* regular, orderly, well-organized; **a intervalos** —**es** at regular intervals; **tiene un latido** — it has a regular beat.

(b) (*fig*) regular; middling, medium, average; fair; (*pej*) fair, so-so, not too bad; (*fam: euph*) tremendous (*fam*), whopping (*sl*); **es una novela** — it's an average sort of novel, it's a fair novel; **de tamaño** — medium-sized, fair-sized; "**¿cómo es la chica?**" . . . "**—**" "what's the girl like?" . . . "an ordinary sort of girl" (or "not too bad", "nothing outstanding").

(c) **por lo** — as a rule, generally.

2 *adv* (*fam*) **estar** — to be all right, be so-so; "**¿qué tal estás?**" . . . "**—**" "how are you?" "so-so" (or "all right", "can't complain").

3 [1a] *vt* (a) to regulate, control; (*of law etc*) to govern; *traffic* to control, direct; *price etc* to control.

(b) (*Mech etc*) to adjust, regulate; *watch* to put right; *alarm clock* to set.

(c) (*Mex*) to calculate.

regularcillo *adj* (*fam*)=**regular 1**(b).

regularidad *nf* regularity; **con** — regularly.

regularizar [1f] *vt* to regularize; to standardize, bring into line.

regularmente *adv* regularly.

regurgitación *nf* regurgitation.

regurgitar [1a] *vt* to regurgitate.

regustado *adj* (*Cu, PR*) satisfied.

regustar [1a] *vt* (*Cu, Mex*) to taste, relish, savour.

regusto *nm* (a) aftertaste (*also fig*). (b) additional pleasure; unhealthy pleasure.

rehabilitación *nf* (a) rehabilitation; reinstatement. (b) restoration; overhaul.

rehabilitar [1a] *vt* (a) *person* to rehabilitate; (*in office*) to reinstate. (b) (*Archit etc*) to restore, renovate; (*Mech*) to overhaul.

rehacer [2s] **1** *vt* (a) to redo, do again; to repeat.

(b) to remake; to mend, repair; to refurbish, renew, do up.

2 rehacerse *vr* (a) (*Med*) to recover; to regain one's strength; (*fig*) to recover one's calm (or self esteem etc).

(b) (*Mil*) to re-form; to rally.

rehecho *adj* thickset, chunky (*fam*).

rehén *nm* hostage.

rehenchir [3l] *vt* to fill, stuff, pack (*de* with).

rehilar [1a] *vi* (a) to quiver, shake. (b) (*of arrow etc*) to whizz.

rehilete *nm* (a) dart (*also Taur*). (b) shuttlecock; badminton. (c) (*fig*) dig, cutting remark, taunt.

rehuir [3g] *vt* to shun, avoid; to shrink from; — + *infin* to avoid + *ger*, shrink from + *ger*.

rehusar [1a] **1** *vt* to refuse, decline; — **hacer algo** to refuse to do something. **2** *vi* to refuse (*also of horse*).

reidero *adj* (*fam*) amusing, funny.

reidor *adj* merry, laughing.

reilón *adj* (*Ec, Ven*) given to laughing a lot, giggly; merry.

reimponer [2r] *vt* to reimpose.

reimpresión *nf* reprint(ing).

reimprimir [3a] *vt* to reprint.

reina *nf* queen (*also Chess, Ent etc*); — **de belleza** beauty queen; — **de la fiesta** carnival queen; — **madre** queen mother; — **viuda** dowager queen.

reinado *nm* reign; **bajo el** — **de** in the reign of.

Reinaldos *m* Reginald.

reinante *adj* (a) reigning. (b) (*fig*) prevailing.

reinar [1a] *vi* (a) (*Pol*) to reign, rule.

(b) (*fig*) to reign; to prevail, be general; **reinan las bajas temperaturas** there are low temperatures everywhere; **reina una confusión total** total confusion reigns; **entre la población reinaba el descontento** unrest was rife in the population; there was widespread discontent in the population.

reincidencia *nf* relapse (*en* into).

reincidente *nmf* recidivist; hardened offender; backslider.

reincidir [3a] *vi* to relapse (*en* into); to repeat an offence; to backslide.

reincorporarse [1a] *vr*: — **a** to rejoin.

reingresar [1a] *vi*: — **a** to re-enter.

reingreso *nm* re-entry (*en* into).

reino *nm* (*all senses*) kingdom.

reinoso *nm* (a) (*Col*) inlander, inhabitant of the interior (*esp of the cold eastern upland*). (b) (*Ven*) Colombian.

reinstalar [1a] *vt* to reinstall; *person* to reinstate.

reintegrable *adj deposit* returnable, repayable.

reintegración *nf* (a) reinstatement (*a* in). (b) (*Fin*) refund, repayment, reimbursement. (c) return (*a* to).

reintegrar [1a] **1** *vt* (a) to make whole again, reintegrate.

(b) *person* to reinstate (*a* in).

(c) (*Fin*) — **a uno una cantidad** to refund (or repay, pay back) a sum to someone, reimburse someone for a sum; **ha sido reintegrado de todos sus gastos** he has been reimbursed in full for all his expenses.

(d) *sum* to pay back.

(e) *document* to attach a fiscal stamp to.

2 reintegrarse *vr* (a) — **a** to return to.

(b) — **de una cantidad** to recover a sum, recoup a sum, secure repayment of a sum; — **de los gastos** to reimburse oneself for one's expenses.

reintegro *nm* (a) refund, repayment, reimbursement; (*from bank account*) withdrawal. (b) (*in lottery*) return of one's stake. (c) (*cost of a*) fiscal stamp.

reinversión *nf* reinvestment.

reinvertir [3i] *vt* to reinvest.

reír [3m] **1** *vt* to laugh at; **todos le ríen los chistes** everybody laughs at his jokes.

2 *vi* (a) to laugh; **sólo para hacer** — just to make people laugh, just for a laugh; **el último que ríe, ríe más fuerte** he who laughs last laughs longest.

(b) (*fig: of eyes etc*) to laugh, sparkle, be merry; (*of morning, nature, countryside*) to smile, be bright.

3 reírse *vr* (a) to laugh (*con, de* about, at, over); — **con uno** to laugh at someone's jokes; — **de uno** to laugh at someone, make fun of someone; **¿se ríe Vd de mí?** are you laughing at me?; **¡déjeme que me ría!** that's a good one!; **fue para** — it was utterly absurd; *see echar etc.*

(b) (*fam*) to tear, come apart; **la chaqueta se me**

rie por los codos my jacket is out at the elbows, my jacket is coming apart at the elbows.
reiteración nf reiteration, reaffirmation; repetition.
reiteradamente adv repeatedly.
reiterado adj repeated.
reiterar [1a] vt to reiterate, reaffirm; to repeat.
reiterativo adj reiterative; (pej) repetitive, repetitious.
reivindicable adj recoverable (at law).
reivindicación nf (a) claim (de to). (b) vindication; restoration. (c) (Law) recovery.
reivindicar [1g] **1** vt (a) to claim (the right to), claim as of right; to assert one's claim to.
(b) (reputation etc) to vindicate; to restore; to win back.
(c) (Law) right to recover.
2 reivindicarse vr (SAm) to vindicate oneself; to restore one's reputation.
reja nf (a) grating, grid, gridiron; (of window) bars, grille; **estar entre —s** to be behind bars.
(b) (Agr) — **del arado** ploughshare.
(c) (SAm) prison.
(d) (Mex) darning.
(e) (Chi) cattle truck.
rejado nm grille, grating.
rejeada nf (CAm, Col) thrashing.
rejear [1a] vt (CAm) to jail, put in jail.
rejego 1 adj (a) (CAm, Mex) wild, untamed; troublesome, unruly. (b) (Mex) slow, sluggish. **2** nm (CAm) stud bull.
rejiego adj (Cu, Mex) = **rejego.**
rejilla nf (a) grating, grille; lattice; screen; (Radio) grille; (Rail) luggage rack; (of furniture) wickerwork; **silla de —** wicker chair.
(b) small stove, footwarmer.
(c) (Chi) meat safe.
rejo nm (a) spike, sharp point.
(b) (Ent) sting.
(c) (Bot) radicle.
(d) (fig) strength, vigour, toughness.
(e) (SAm) whip; (Col, Ven) strip of raw leather.
(f) (Ven) stick, club.
(g) (Ec) milking; herd of cows.
rejón nm pointed iron bar; (Taur) lance.
rejoneador nm (Taur) mounted bullfighter who uses the lance.
rejonear [1a] (Taur) **1** vt to wound the bull with the lance. **2** vi to fight the bull on horseback with the lance.
rejudo adj (Col, Ven) sticky, viscous.
rejugado adj (CAm, Col, Cu) shy.
rejunta nf (Arg, Mex) roundup, rodeo.
rejuntar [1a] vt (Mex, RPl) to collect, gather in; cattle to round up; sum to add up.
rejuvenecer [2d] **1** vt to rejuvenate. **2 rejuvenecerse** vr to be rejuvenated, become young again.
relación nf (a) relation, relationship (con to, with); **—es** relations, relationship; **la — entre X y Z** the relationship between X and Z; **sus —es con el jefe** his relations with the boss; **buenas —es** good relations; **—es amistosas** friendly relations; **—es carnales** sexual relations; **—es comerciales** business connections, trade relations; **—es humanas** human relations, (as department, profession) personnel management; **—es públicas** public relations; **estar en buenas —es con** to be on good terms with; **mantener —es con** to keep in touch with; **romper las —es con** to break off relations with; **con — a, en — a** in relation to; **un aumento de 3 por cien con — al año anterior** an increase of 3% over the previous year.
(b) (Math) ratio; proportion; **en una — de 7 a 2** in a ratio of 7 to 2; **— real de intercambio** terms of trade; **guardar cierta — con** to bear a certain relation to; **no guardar — alguna con** to be out of all proportion to, bear no relation whatsoever to.
(c) **—es** (amorosas) courting, courtship; **—es formales** engagement; **—es ilícitas** illicit sexual relations; **llevan varios meses de —es** they've been going out (or courting) for some months; **A está en (or tiene) —es con B** A and B are going out together, A and B are courting.
(d) **—es** (persons) acquaintances; (esp) influential friends, contacts, connections; **para eso conviene tener —es** for that it helps to have contacts; **tener buenas —es** to be well connected, have powerful friends.
(e) account, report; story; (of difficulties etc) tale, recital; **hizo una larga — de su viaje** he gave a lengthy account of his trip.
(f) list; record, (official) return.

(g) (Theat) long speech.
(h) (Mex) buried treasure.
relacionado adj (a) related; **un tema — con Lorca** a subject that has to do with Lorca, a subject that concerns Lorca; **A está íntimamente — con B** A is closely connected with B; A is much bound up with B.
(b) **una persona relacionada** (SAm), **una persona bien relacionada** a well-connected person.
relacionar [1a] **1** vt to relate (con to), connect (con with).
2 relacionarse vr (a) **es hombre que se relaciona** he's a man with (powerful) connections.
(b) (two things etc) to be connected, be related.
(c) **— con uno** to get to know someone; to get into touch with someone.
(d) **en lo que se relaciona con** as for, with regard to.
relai(s) [re'le] nm (Elec) relay.
relajación nf (a) relaxation; slackening, loosening; weakening. (b) (fig) relaxation, amusement. (c) (fig: moral) laxity, looseness. (d) (Med) hernia, rupture.
relajado adj (a) life etc dissolute, loose. (b) (Med) ruptured.
relajadura nf (Mex) hernia, rupture.
relajante 1 adj (a) (Med) laxative. (b) (Arg, Chi) food cloying, excessively sweet; repellent. **2** nm laxative.
relajar [1a] **1** vt (a) to relax; to slacken, loosen; to weaken.
(b) (fig: morally) to weaken, corrupt, make lax.
(c) (SAm: of food) to cloy, sicken, disgust.
(d) (Ant) to mock; to abuse, be disrespectful to.
2 relajarse vr (a) to relax; to slacken, loosen; to weaken.
(b) (fig) to relax; **tiene mucha facilidad para —** he has a great capacity for relaxing.
(c) (fig: morally) to become dissolute, go to the bad; (morality etc) to become lax.
(d) (Med) **— un tobillo** to lose the use of an ankle, lose the feeling in an ankle; **— un órgano** to rupture an organ.
relajo nm (SAm) (a) laxity, dissipation, depravity; lewdness.
(b) immoral act; indecent act.
(c) boisterous gathering; lewd party; commotion, disorder.
(d) rude joke; practical joke; derision; **cuento de — blue joke; echar algo a —** to make fun of something.
relajón adj (Ant) (a) mocking; coarsely humorous.
(b) depraved, lewd.
relamer [2a] **1** vt to lick repeatedly.
2 relamerse vr (a) (animal) to lick its chops; (person) to lick one's lips (also **— los labios**).
(b) (fig) **— con algo** to relish something in advance, relish the prospect of something; to smack one's lips over (the idea of) something; (pej) to gloat over the prospect of something.
(c) (fig) to brag.
(d) (fig) to paint one's face.
relamido adj (a) prim and proper; affected; overdressed. (b) (CAm, Cu, Mex) shameless, brazen.
relámpago 1 nm lightning, flash of lightning; (fig) flash; **— difuso** sheet lightning; **como un —** as quick as lightning, in a flash.
2 as adj lightning; **guerra —** blitzkrieg; **visita —** rushed visit, rapid visit; **viaje —** lightning trip.
relampaguear [1a] vi (Cu, Mex) to twinkle; to flicker; to gleam.
relampagueo nm (Cu, Mex) twinkle; flicker, gleam.
relampagueante adj flashing.
relampaguear [1a] vi (a) to lighten; to flash; **relampagueó toda la noche** the lightning was flashing all night, there was lightning all night.
relampagueo nm flashing.
relampuso nm (Cu) shameless, brazen.
relance nm (Chi) = **piropo.**
relanzar [1f] vt to repel, repulse.
relatar [1a] vt to relate, tell; to report.
relativamente adv relatively.
relativismo nm relativism.
relativista 1 adj relativistic. **2** nmf relativist.
relativo 1 adj relative (also Gram); **— a** a relative to; regarding, relating to. **2** nm (Gram) relative.
relato nm story, tale; account, report.
relator nm teller, narrator; (Law) court reporter.
relauchar [1a] vi (Chi) to knock off work for a rest.
relé nm (Elec: Acad) relay.
releer [2e] vt to reread.
relegación nf (a) relegation. (b) (Hist) exile, banishment.

relegar [1h] *vt* (**a**) to relegate; **— algo al olvido** to banish something from one's mind; to consign something to oblivion. (**b**) (*Hist*) to exile, banish.

releso *adj* (*Chi*) stupid.

relevación *nf* (**a**) relief (*also Mil*); replacement. (**b**) (*Law*) exoneration; release (*de* from).

relevante *adj* outstanding.

relevar [1a] *vt* (**a**) (*Tech*) to emboss; to carve (*or* paint *etc*) in relief.
(**b**) (*Mil*) *guard* to relieve.
(**c**) **— a uno de una obligación** to relieve someone of a duty, free someone from an obligation; **— a uno de la culpa** to exonerate someone, free someone from blame; **relevar a uno de** + *infin* to free someone from the obligation to + *infin*.
(**d**) **— a uno de un cargo** to relieve someone of his post, replace someone in his post; **ser relevado de su mando** to be relieved of one's command.

relevo *nm* (*Mil*: *act*) relief, change; (*persons*) relief; **— de los tiros** change of horses. (**b**) (*Sport*) **—s** relay (race); **100 metros —s** 100 metres relay.

relicario *nm* (**a**) (*Eccl*) shrine; reliquary. (**b**) locket.

relieve *nm* (**a**) (*Art, Tech*) relief; raised work, embossing; raised part; **alto —** high relief; **bajo —** bas-relief; **en —** raised pattern, embossed pattern, pattern in relief; **película en —** stereoscopic film, three-dimensional (*abbr*: 3-D) film; **estampar en —** to emboss.
(**b**) importance, prominence; social standing; **un personaje de —** an important man, a man of some importance; **dar — a** to enhance; to give prominence to, bring out; **poner algo de —** to emphasize (the importance of), point out the interest of, stress the qualities of.
(**c**) **—s** left-overs.

religión *nf* (**a**) religion.
(**b**) (*fig*) religion, cult; **tiene la — de la promesa** he believes utterly in keeping his word.
(**c**) religiousness; religious sense, piety.
(**d**) (*Eccl*) the religious life, religion; **entrar en —** to take vows, enter a religious order.

religiosa *nf* nun.

religiosamente *adv* religiously.

religiosidad *nf* religiosity, religiousness; (*fig*) religiousness.

religioso **1** *adj* religious (*also fig*). **2** *nm* religious, member of a religious order, monk.

relimpio *adj* absolutely clean; spick and span.

relinchada *nf* (*Mex*) = **relincho**.

relinchar [1a] *vi* to neigh, whinny, snort.

relincho *nm* neigh(ing), whinny, snort(ing).

reliquia *nf* (**a**) (*Eccl*) relic; (*Mex*) votive offering.
(**b**) **—s** relics, remains; traces, vestiges; **— de familia** heirloom, family treasure.
(**c**) (*Med*) **—s** after-effects, lingering effects, resultant weakness.

reloj [re'lo] *nm* clock; watch; (*Tech*) clock, meter; **— de arena** sandglass, hourglass; **— automático** timer, timing mechanism; **— de bolsillo** pocket watch; **— de caja** grandfather clock; **— de carillón** chiming clock; **— despertador** alarm clock; **— eléctrico** electric clock; **— de estacionamiento** parking meter; **— de la muerte** (*Ent*) deathwatch beetle; **— de pie** grandfather clock; **— de pulsera** wristwatch; **— registrador** time clock; **— de sol** sundial; **como un —** like clockwork; **estar como un —** (*fam*) to feel on top of the world, be on top form; to be as fit as a fiddle; **contra (el) —** against the clock.

relojear [1a] *vt* (*Arg*) (**a**) *race* to time. (**b**) (*fig*) to watch, spy on; to check.

relojería *nf* (**a**) watchmaking, clockmaking. (**b**) watchmaker's (shop). (**c**) (*also* **aparato de —**) clockwork; **bomba de —** time bomb.

relojero *nm* watchmaker, clockmaker.

reluciente *adj* (**a**) shining, brilliant; glittering, gleaming, sparkling; bright. (**b**) *person* sleek; well-fed; healthy-looking.

relucir [3f] *vi* (**a**) to shine; to glitter, gleam, sparkle; to be bright. (**b**) **sacar algo a —** to bring something out, show something off.

relujar [1a] *vt* (*Guat, Mex*) *shoes* to shine.

relumbrante *adj* brilliant, dazzling; glaring.

relumbrar [1a] *vi* to shine brilliantly, be bright; to dazzle; to glare.

relumbrón *nm* (**a**) flash; sudden glare. (**b**) (*fig*) flashiness, ostentation; **joyas de —** flashy jewellery; **vestirse de —** to dress flashily, dress ostentatiously.

rellano *nm* (*Archit*) landing.

rellena *nf* (*Col, Mex*) black pudding.

rellenado *nm* refill; replenishment; (*Aer etc*) refuelling.

rellenar [1a] **1** *vt* (**a**) to refill, replenish; (*Aer etc*) to refuel.
(**b**) to fill up; to pack, stuff, cram (*de* with); (*Cook*) to stuff; (*Sew etc*) to pad; *spaces etc* to fill in; *form* to fill in, fill up.
2 rellenarse *vr* to stuff oneself (*de* with).

relleno **1** *adj* packed, stuffed, crammed (*de* with); very full, full right up (*de* of); (*Cook*) stuffed. **2** *nm* filling; (*Archit*) plaster filling; (*Cook*) stuffing; (*Sew*) padding; wadding; (*Mech*) packing.

remachado *adj* (*Col*) quiet, reserved.

remachador *nm* rivetter.

remachar [1a] **1** *vt* (**a**) (*Tech*) *nail etc* to clinch; *metals* to rivet.
(**b**) (*fig*) *point* to hammer home, drive home; to stress; **para —lo todavía** to clinch matters; to make it entirely certain.
2 remacharse *vr* (*Col*) to remain stubbornly silent.

remache *nm* (**a**) (*Tech*) rivet. (**b**) (*act*) clinching; rivetting. (**c**) (*Col*) stubbornness.

remada *nf* stroke.

remador *nm* rower, oarsman.

remadura *adj* (*SAm*) overripe.

remandingo *nm* (*Cu*) row, uproar.

remanente **1** *adj* remaining; (*Phys*) remanent; (*Comm etc*) surplus. **2** *nm* remainder; (*Comm, Fin*) balance; (*of production*) surplus.

remansarse [1a] *vr* to form a pool; to become stagnant.

remanso *nm* (**a**) pool; backwater. (**b**) (*fig*) quiet place, peaceful area; **un — de paz** an oasis of peace, a haven of peace.

remar [1a] *vi* (**a**) to row. (**b**) (*fig*) to toil, struggle; to suffer hardships.

remarcable *adj* (*SAm*: *angl*) remarkable.

remarcar [1g] *vt* (*SAm*: *angl*) (**a**) to notice, observe, remark on. (**b**) to distinguish.

rematadamente *adv* terribly, hopelessly; **— mal** terribly bad; **es — tonto** he's utterly stupid.

rematado *adj* (**a**) hopeless, complete, out-and-out; **es un loco —** he's a raving lunatic; **es un tonto —** he's an utter fool. (**b**) *child* very naughty.

rematador *nm* (*Bol, RPl*) auctioneer.

rematante *nm* highest bidder.

rematar [1a] **1** *vt* (**a**) *person* to finish off; to kill off; *animal* to shoot dead, kill instantly.
(**b**) (*fig*) *work etc* to finish off, bring to a conclusion; *process* to finish, round off; *abuse* to put an end to; *drink etc* to finish up, drink (*etc*) the last of.
(**c**) (*Archit etc*) to top, be at the very top of, crown.
(**d**) (*Comm*) to sell off cheap (to clear).
(**e**) (*Comm*) **— algo a uno** to knock something down to someone (*en* for).
(**f**) (*SAm*) to buy at an auction; to sell at auction; (*CAm, Mex*) to sell.
(**g**) (*Chi*) *horse* to rein in suddenly.
2 *vi* (**a**) to end, finish off; **rematό con un par de chistes** he finished with a couple of jokes.
(**b**) **— en** to end in, come to; **es del tipo que remata en punta** it's the sort which comes to a point; **fue una broma que rematό en tragedia** it was a joke which ended in tragedy.
(**c**) (*Sport*) to shoot, score; **— de cabeza** to head a goal.

remate *nm* (**a**) (*act*) finishing (off); killing off.
(**b**) (*of object*) end; tip, point; (*Archit*) top, crest; (*of sideboard etc*) ornamental top.
(**c**) (*fig*) conclusion; finishing touch; **de — =** **rematado** (a); **para —** to crown it all, on top of all that; **por —** finally, as a finishing touch; **poner — a** to cap; to put the finishing touch to, round off.
(**d**) (*Comm*) highest bid.
(**e**) (*Comm*) sale (by auction); (*Bridge*) bidding, auction; (*SAm*) auction.

rematista *nm* (*Per, PR*) auctioneer.

remecer [2d] **1** *vt* to rock, swing (to and fro); (*Mex*) to shake; to wave. **2 remecerse** *vr* to rock, swing (to and fro).

remedar [1a] *vt* to imitate, copy; (*pej*) to ape; (*jokingly*) to ape, mimic.

remediable *adj* remediable, that can be remedied; **fácilmente —** easy to remedy, easily remedied.

remediar [1b] *vt* (**a**) to remedy; *damage, loss* to make good, repair; to make up for; *abuse* to correct, put right, put a stop to; **llorando no remedias nada** you won't do any good by crying.
(**b**) *needs etc* to meet, help with; *needy person* to help (out); *endangered person* to help, save.
(**c**) to avoid, prevent; **sin poder —lo** without being able to prevent it; **a ver si lo remediamos** let's

see if we can do anything about it; **no poder** — **el echarse a reír** not to be able to help laughing.

remedio *nm* (a) remedy (*also Med*; *contra* against); help; — **casero** ordinary remedy, simple domestic remedy; — **heroico** extreme remedy; (*fig*) extreme measure; **como último** — as a last resort; **sin** — inevitable; irremediable; **es un tonto sin** — he's a hopeless idiot, he's so stupid he's past redemption; **no se podía encontrar ni para un** — it couldn't be had for love nor money; **¡ni por un** —**!** not on your life!; **no hay más** — there's no help for it, there's nothing one can do, there's no other way; **no hay más** — **que** + *infin* the only thing is to + *infin*; **no hay** — **para él** it's all up with him; **esto no tiene** — it is unavoidable; there's nothing one can do about it; it's beyond repair; **él no tiene** — he's hopeless, he's past redemption; **¿qué** — **tengo?** what else can I do?; **no tener más** — **que** + *infin* to have no alternative but to + *infin*; **poner** — **a un abuso** to correct an abuse, put a stop to an abuse.

(b) relief, help; **buscar** — **en su aflicción** to look for some relief in one's distress.

(c) (*Law*) remedy, recourse.

remedo *nm* imitation, copy; (*pej*) poor imitation, travesty, parody.

rememorar [1a] *vt* (*lit*) to remember, recall.

remendar [1k] *vt* (a) to mend, repair; to patch, darn. (b) (*fig*) to correct.

remendón *nm* cobbler.

remero *nm* oarsman.

remesa *nf* remittance; shipment, consignment.

remesar [1a] *vt money* to remit, send; *goods* to send, ship, consign.

remeter [2a] *vr* to put back; *bedclothes, shirt etc* to tuck in.

remezón *nm* (*SAm*) earth tremor, slight earthquake.

remiendo *nm* (a) (*act*) mending; patching. (b) mend; patch, darn; **a** —**s** piecemeal; **echar un** — **a** to patch, put a patch on. (c) (*fig*) correction. (d) (*Zool*) spot, patch.

remilgado *adj* prudish, prim; affected; finicky, fussy, particular, overnice; squeamish, oversensitive.

remilgarse [1h] *vr* to react prudishly; to show one's affectation; to be fussy; to be squeamish.

remilgo *nm* (a) prudery, primness; affectation; fussiness; squeamishness, excess of sensitivity.

(b) prim look; simper; simply; **hacer** —**s a** to react in a prudish (*etc*) way to; **él no hace** —**s a ninguna clase de trabajo** he won't turn up his nose at any kind of work.

(c) **don R**—**s** (*hum*) Lord Muck.

remilgoso *adj* (*SAm*) = **remilgado**.

reminiscencia *nf* reminiscence.

remirado *adj* (a) cautious, circumspect, careful; (*pej*) overcautious. (b) (*pej*) prudish; affected, overnice; fussy, pernickety (*fam*).

remirar [1a] **1** *vt* to look at again; to look hard at. **2 remirarse** *vr* to be extra careful (*en* about), take great pains (*en* over).

remise *nm or f* (*Arg: gall*) hired car, taxi.

remisión *nf* (a) sending; (*SAm*) shipment, consignment. (b) reference (*a* to). (c) postponement; adjournment. (d) remission (*also Med*); slackening. (e) (*Eccl*) forgiveness, remission.

remiso *adj* (a) slack, slow (to obey), remiss. (b) *movement* slow, sluggish.

remisor *nm* (*SAm: Comm*) sender.

remitente *nmf* sender.

remitido *nm* (a) (*in newspaper*) paid insertion; note (*or* article) reprinted from another newspaper. (b) (*Mex*) shipment, consignment.

remitir [3a] **1** *vt* (a) (*Post*) to send; *money* to remit; (*Comm*) to send, ship, consign. (b) *reader, user* to refer (*a* to). (c) *event etc* to postpone; *session* to adjourn. (d) — **una decisión a uno** to leave a decision to someone, refer a matter to someone for a decision. (e) *sins* to forgive, pardon.

2 *vi* (a) to slacken, diminish, let up. (b) "**remite: X . . .**" (*on envelope*) "sender: X . . ."

remo *nm* (a) oar; **a** — **y vela** (*fig*) speedily; **andar al** — (*fig*) to be hard at it; **cruzar un río a** — to row across a river; **pasaron los cañones a** — they rowed the guns across. (b) (*as sport*) rowing; **practicar el** — to row, go in for rowing. (c) (*Anat*) arm, leg; (*Orn*) wing. (d) (*fig*) toils, hardships.

remoción *nf* (a) removal. (b) (*Mex*) sacking (*fam*), dismissal.

remodelar [1a] *vt* to remodel.

remojar [1a] *vt* (a) to steep, soak (*en* in); to dip (*en* in, into); (*accidentally*) to soak, drench (*con* with); *biscuit etc* to dip, dunk (*en* in). (b) (*fam*) *event* to celebrate with a drink.

remojo *nm* (a) steeping, soaking; drenching; dip, dipping; **dejar la ropa en** — to leave clothes to soak; **poner los garbanzos a** — to put chickpeas in to soak. (b) (*SAm*) gift made to mark an occasion; tip.

remojón *nm* (a) soaking, drenching. (b) (*Cook*) piece of bread soaked in milk (*etc*).

remolacha *nf* beet, beetroot; — **azucarera** sugar beet.

remolcador *nm* (*Naut*) tug; (*Aut*) tow car, breakdown lorry.

remolcar [1g] *vt* to tow, tow along; to take in tow.

remoledor *adj* (*Chi, Per*) roistering, merry.

remoler [2h] **1** *vt* (a) to grind up small. (b) (*Guat, Per*) to annoy. **2** *vi* (*Chi, Per*) to live it up (*fam*).

remolienda *nf* (*Chi, Per*) carousal, revelry.

remolinar(se) [1a], **remolinear(se)** [1a] = **arremolinarse**.

remolino *nm* (a) (*of water*) swirl, eddy; whirlpool; (*of air*) whirl; disturbance; whirlwind; (*of dust, smoke*) whirl, cloud. (b) (*of hair*) tuft. (c) (*of people*) crowd, throng, crush, moving mass. (d) (*fig*) commotion.

remolón 1 *adj* (a) stubborn; awkward, cantankerous. (b) slack, lazy. **2** *nm*, **remolona** *nf* stubborn individual; slacker, shirker; **hacerce el** — = **remolonear**.

remolonear [1a] *vi* (a) to be stubborn, refuse to budge; to hold out on someone. (b) to slack, shirk.

remolque *nm* (a) (*act*) towing; **a** — on tow, being towed; **ir a** — to be on tow; **llevar un coche a** — to tow a car; **lo hizo a** — (*fig*) he did it reluctantly; they had to push him to do it, he did it because somebody made him; **dar** — **a** to tow, take in tow. (b) (*Naut*) towrope; cable, hawser; (*Aut etc*) towrope. (c) (*vehicle etc: Aut*) tow; car being towed; trailer, caravan; (*Naut*) ship on tow.

remonda *nf* (*sl*): **¡es la** —**!** this is the end!; it's sheer hell!

remonta *nf* (a) mending, repair. (b) (*Mil*) remount, supply of cavalry horses; cavalry horses; cavalry depot.

remontar [1a] **1** *vt* (a) *stocking* to mend (a ladder in); *shoes* to mend, repair, resole. (b) — **el vuelo** to soar (up). (c) *river etc* to go up. (d) *obstacle* to negotiate, get over, surmount. (e) (*Mil*) *cavalry* to remount. (f) *watch* to wind. (g) (*Hunting*) *game* to frighten away.

2 remontarse *vr* (a) (*Aer, Orn etc*) to rise, soar; (*building*) to soar, tower; (*fig*) to soar; — **en alas de la imaginación** to take flight on the wings of fantasy. (b) (*Fin*) — **a** to amount to. (c) (*in time*) — **a** to go back to; **sus recuerdos se remontan al siglo pasado** her memories go back to the last century; **este texto se remonta al siglo XI** this text dates from (*or* back to) the 11th century; **tenemos que remontarnos a los mismos orígenes** we must get back to the very origins.

remoquete *nm* (a) punch. (b) (*fig*) cutting remark, dig. (c) nickname; **poner** — **a uno** to give someone a nickname. (d) (*fam*) flirting, spooning (*fam*); suitor.

rémora *nf* (*fig*) drawback; hindrance.

remorder [2h] **1** *vt person* to grieve, distress; to cause remorse to; *conscience* to prick; *mind* to afflict, prey upon.

2 remorderse *vr* to suffer (*or* show) remorse; to suffer inwardly, harbour a grudge (*or* jealousy *etc*).

remordimiento *nm* remorse, regret (*also* —**s**); **tener** —**s** to feel remorse, suffer pangs of conscience.

remotamente *adv* (a) resemble, *remember* vaguely, slightly; **no se le parece ni** — he doesn't look even remotely like him. (b) *think etc* vaguely, tentatively.

remotidad *nf* (*CAm*) (a) remoteness. (b) remote spot, distant place.

remoto *adj* (*all senses*) remote; **¡ni por lo más** —**!** not on your life!

remover [2h] *vt* (a) *earth etc* to turn over, dig up; *objects* to move round, change over, shift about; *cocktail etc* to shake; *porridge etc* to stir (round); *feelings* to disturb, upset; — **un asunto** to turn a matter over, go into a matter again; — **el pasado** to stir up the past; to rake up the past; — **un proyecto** to revive a scheme.

(b) *obstacle etc* to remove; (*Med*) to excise, cut out; *person* to discharge, remove (from office).

removimiento *nm* removal.
remozamiento *nm* rejuvenation.
remozar [1f] **1** *vt person etc* to rejuvenate; *appearance etc* to brighten up, polish up.
2 remozarse *vr* to be rejuvenated; to look much younger; **la encuentro muy remozada** I find her looking much younger.
rempujar [1a] *vt* (*fam*) to shove, jostle.
rempujón *nm* (*fam*) shove, push.
remuda *nf* change, alteration; replacement; — **de caballos** change of horses; — (**de ropa**) change of clothes, spare clothes.
remudar [1a] *vt* to remove; to change, alter; to replace.
remuneración *nf* remuneration.
remunerado *adj*: **trabajo mal** — badly-paid job.
remunerador *adj* remunerative; rewarding, worthwhile; **poco** — unremunerative.
remunerar [1a] *vt* to remunerate; to pay; to reward.
renacentista *adj* Renaissance (*attr*).
renacer [2d] *vi* (**a**) to be reborn; (*Bot*) to appear again, come up again.
(**b**) (*fig*) to revive; to acquire new vigour (*or* life); **hacer** — to revive; **hoy me siento** — today I feel renewed, I feel I am coming to life again today; **sentían** — **la esperanza** they felt new hope.
renaciente *adj* renascent.
renacimiento *nm* rebirth, revival; **R**— Renaissance.
renacuajo *nm* (**a**) (*Zool*) tadpole. (**b**) (*fam*) shrimp; (*pej*) runt, little squirt (*fam*); **¡ven, —!** (*to child*) come along, pet!
renal *adj* renal, kidney (*attr*).
Renania *f* Rhineland.
renano *adj* Rhenish, Rhine (*attr*).
rencilla *nf* (**a**) quarrel; feud; **—s** dissension; arguments, bickering. (**b**) bad blood; ill will; grudge; **me tiene** — he's got it in for me, he bears me a grudge.
rencilloso *adj* quarrelsome.
renco *adj* lame.
rencor *nm* rancour, bitterness; ill feeling, resentment; spitefulness; **guardar** — to bear malice, have a grudge (*a* against); **no le guardo** — I bear him no malice.
rencorosamente *adv* (**a**) spitefully, maliciously. (**b**) resentfully; bitterly.
rencoroso *adj* (**a**) (*ser*) spiteful, nasty, malicious. (**b**) (*estar*) resentful; bitter, embittered.
rendición *nf* (**a**) (*Mil etc*) surrender; — **incondicional** unconditional surrender. (**b**) (*Fin*) yield, profit(s), return. (**c**) (*Arg*) trading balance.
rendidamente *adv* submissively; obsequiously; humbly, devotedly.
rendido *adj* (**a**) submissive; obsequious; *admirer* humble, devoted. (**b**) **estar** — (**de cansancio**) to be exhausted, be all in.
rendidor *adj* (*SAm*) highly productive; (*Fin*) highly profitable.
rendija *nf* (**a**) crack, cleft, crevice; chink; aperture. (**b**) (*fig*) rift, split. (**c**) (*Law*) loophole.
rendimiento *nm* (**a**) usable part, proportion of usable material.
(**b**) (*Mech*) efficiency, performance; capacity; output; **el** — **del motor** the performance of the engine; **aumentar el** — **de una máquina** to increase the output of a machine.
(**c**) (*Fin*) yield, profit(s), return; **ley del** — **decreciente** law of diminishing returns.
(**d**) (*quality*) submissiveness; obsequiousness; devotion; **su** — **total a la voluntad de ella** his complete submissiveness to her will.
(**e**) exhaustion.
rendir [3l] **1** *vt* (**a**) to produce, yield, bear; *product, total etc* to produce; *profit etc* to yield; *interest* to bear.
(**b**) *enemy* to defeat, conquer, overcome; *country* to conquer, subdue; *fortress* to take, capture, reduce.
(**c**) *person* to exhaust, tire out; **le rindió el sueño** sleep overcame him.
(**d**) *will* to subject to one's own will, dominate, assume control of; **logró** — **el albedrío de la joven** he came to dominate the young woman's will completely; **había que** — **su entereza** he had to overcome his honest doubts, he had to fight down his moral objections.
(**e**) to give back, return; to hand over; (*Mil*) to surrender; (*Mil*) *guard* to hand over; (*fam*) to vomit, bring up.
(**f**) (*Comm*) *account* to send.
(**g**) (*Mil*) *flag* to dip; *arms* to lower, reverse.
(**h**) *tribute* to pay; *homage* to do, pay; *thanks* to give; — **culto a** to worship; (*fig*) to pay homage to, pay tribute to.

(**i**) (*RPl*) — **examen** to sit an exam, take an exam.
2 *vi* (**a**) to yield, produce; **el negocio no rinde** the business doesn't pay; **este año ha rendido poco** it has done poorly this year; **la finca rinde para mantener a 8 familias** the estate produces enough to keep 8 families.
(**b**) (*SAm*) to last longer than usual.
(**c**) (*SAm*) to swell up (in the cooking *etc*).
3 rendirse *vr* (**a**) to yield (*a* to); (*Mil*) to surrender; to give oneself up; — **a la evidencia** to bow before the evidence; — **a la fuerza** to yield to violence; — **a la razón** to yield to reason.
(**b**) to wear oneself out, exhaust oneself.
renegado 1 *adj* (**a**) renegade.
(**b**) (*fam*) gruff; cantankerous, bad-tempered.
2 *nm*, **renegada** *nf* (**a**) renegade; turncoat.
(**b**) (*fam*) bad lot, nasty piece of work (*fam*).
renegar [1h *and* 1k] **1** *vt* (**a**) to deny vigorously, deny repeatedly.
(**b**) to abhor, detest.
2 *vi* (**a**) to turn renegade, turn one's coat, be a traitor; (*Eccl*) to apostatize.
(**b**) — **de** to forsake, disown; to renounce, give up; — **de su familia** to disown one's family; — **de la amistad de uno** to break completely with someone; **reniego de ti** I want nothing more to do with you.
(**c**) — **de** to abhor, detest.
(**d**) to curse, swear; (*Rel*) to blaspheme.
(**e**) to grumble; to protest, complain.
(**f**) (*Mex, Per, RPl*) to get angry, be upset.
renegón *adj* (*fam*) grumbling, cantankerous, grouchy (*fam*).
renegrido *adj* (*SAm*) very black, very dark; blackened.
renglón *nm* (**a**) line (of writing); **a** — **seguido** in the very next line, (*fig*) straight after, without a break; **escribir un** — **a, poner unos** — **es a** to drop a line to; **leer entre** — **es** to read between the lines; **estos pobres** — **es** these humble jottings.
(**b**) (*Comm etc*) item (of expenditure).
(**c**) (*SAm: Comm*) line of goods.
renguear [1a] *vi* (**a**) (*SAm*) to limp, hobble. (**b**) (*Arg*) to be courting.
renguera *nf* (*SAm*) limp, limping; lameness.
reniego *nm* (**a**) curse, oath; (*Rel*) blasphemy, blasphemous remark. (**b**) grumble; complaint.
reno *nm* reindeer.
renombrado *adj* renowned, famous.
renombre *nm* (**a**) renown, fame; **de** — renowned, famous. (**b**) surname.
renovable *adj* renewable.
renovación *nf* (**a**) renewal; renovation; — **espiritual** spiritual renewal; — **de la suscripción** renewal of one's subscription.
(**b**) (*Archit etc*) renovation; restoration; redecoration.
(**c**) (*Pol etc*) reorganization, remodelling, transformation.
renovado *adj* renewed, redoubled; **con renovada energía** with renewed energy.
renoval *nm* (*Arg, Chi, Mex*) area of young trees.
renovar [1m] *vt* (**a**) (*general sense*) to renew; *warning etc* to renew, repeat; *subscription* to renew.
(**b**) (*Archit etc*) to renovate; to restore; *room* to redecorate.
(**c**) (*Pol etc*) to reorganize, remodel, transform.
renquear [1a] *vi* (**a**) to limp, hobble. (**b**) (*fam*) to get along, manage with difficulty.
renta *nf* (**a**) income; (*from stock etc*) interest, return, yield; **política de** — **s** incomes policy; — **gravable, — imponible** taxable income; — **nacional** national income; — **bruta nacional** gross national income; — **s públicas** revenue; — **del trabajo** earned income; — **vitalicia** annuity; **tiene** — **s particulares** she has a private income; **vivir de sus** — **s** to live on one's income.
(**b**) public debt, national debt.
(**c**) (*for a property etc*) rent.
rentabilidad *nf* profitability.
rentable *adj* profitable; **no** — unprofitable; uneconomical; **el avión no es** — the aircraft is not an economic proposition; **la línea ya no es** — the line is no longer economic (to run).
rentado *adj* (*Arg, Chi*) work paid.
rentar [1a] *vt* (**a**) to produce, yield. (**b**) (*Mex*) to let, rent out; "**rento casa**" "house to let".
rentero *nm* tenant farmer.
rentista *nmf* (**a**) stockholder, person who lives on income from shares, (*as member of class*) rentier; person of independent means. (**b**) financial expert.

rentístico *adj* financial.
renuencia *nf* **(a)** unwillingness, reluctance. **(b)** awkwardness.
renuente *adj* **(a)** *person* unwilling, reluctant. **(b)** *material* awkward, difficult.
renuevo *nm* **(a)** *(act)* renewal. **(b)** *(Bot)* shoot, sprout.
renuncia *nf* renunciation; resignation; relinquishment; abdication.
renunciar [1b] **1** *vt (also vi: —* **a)** *right etc* to renounce *(en* in favour of), surrender, relinquish; *plan, habit etc* to give up; *claim* to drop, waive; *post, responsibility* to resign; *throne* to abdicate *(en* in favour of); **— a hacer algo** to give up doing something, stop doing something.
2 *vi (Cards)* to revoke.
renuncio *nm* **(a)** *(Cards)* revoke. **(b) coger a uno en un —** to catch someone in a fib, catch someone out.
reñidamente *adv fight etc* bitterly, hard, stubbornly.
reñidero *nm:* **— de gallos** cockpit.
reñido *adj* **(a)** battle, contest bitter; **un partido —** a hard-fought game; a bitter struggle; **en lo más — de la batalla** in the thick of the fight.
(b) estar — con uno to be at odds with someone, be on bad terms with someone; **está — con su familia** he has fallen out with his family.
(c) estar — con *(of principle etc)* to be at variance with, be divorced from, be in opposition to.
reñidor *adj* quarrelsome.
reñir [3h *and* 3l] **1** *vt* **(a)** to scold; to tell off, reprimand *(por* for).
(b) *battle* to fight, wage.
2 *vi* to quarrel, fall out *(con* with); to fight, scrap, come to blows; **ha reñido con su novio** she's fallen out with her boyfriend; **she's broken it off with her fiancé; se pasan la vida riñendo** they spend their whole time quarrelling; **riñeron por cuestión de dinero** they quarrelled about *(or* over) money.
reo *nmf* **(a)** culprit, offender; criminal; *(Law)* accused, defendant; **— de estado** person accused of a crime against the state; **— de muerte** person under sentence of death.
(b) *(Arg)* shabby individual, tramp.
reojo: mirar a uno de — to look at someone out of the corner of one's eye; *(fig)* to look askance at someone, look dubiously at someone.
reorganización *nf* reorganization.
reorganizar [1f] **1** *vt* to reorganize. **2 reorganizarse** *vr* to reorganize.
reorientar [1a] *vt* to reorientate; to give a new direction to; to readjust.
reóstato *nm* rheostat.
repanchigarse [1h] *vr*, **repantigarse** [1h] *vr* to lounge, sprawl, loll (back); **estar repanchigado en un sillón** to loll back in a chair.
reparable *adj* repairable.
reparación *nf* **(a)** *(act)* repairing, mending.
(b) *(Tech)* repair; **"—es en el acto", "—es instantáneas"** "repairs while you wait"; **efectuar —es en** to carry out repairs to.
(c) *(fig)* amends, reparation, redress.
reparador 1 *adj* **(a)** *person* critical, faultfinding.
(b) *food* fortifying, strengthening, restorative.
2 *nm* *(Tech)* repairer.
3 *nm,* **reparadora** *nf* carping critic, faultfinder.
reparar [1a] **1** *vt* **(a)** *(Tech)* to repair, mend.
(b) *energies etc* to repair, restore; *fortunes* to retrieve.
(c) *offence etc* to make amends for; *damage, loss* to make good; *bad effect* to undo.
(d) *blow* to parry.
(e) to observe, notice.
(f) *(RPl)* to mimic, imitate.
2 *vi* **(a) — en** to observe, notice, note, see; **no reparó en la diferencia** he didn't notice the difference; **sin — en que ya no funcionaba** without noticing that it was no longer working.
(b) — en to pay attention to, take heed of; to consider; **no — en las dificultades** to take no heed of the difficulties, refuse to consider the difficulties; **repara en lo que vas a hacer** reflect on what you are going to do; **sin — en los gastos** heedless of expense, regardless of the cost; **no — en nada** to stop at nothing.
(c) *(Guat, Mex: of horse)* to rear, buck.
3 repararse *vr* to check oneself, restrain oneself.
reparista *adj (CAm, Col, PR),* **reparisto** *adj (CAm, Ven)* **=reparón 1.**
reparo *nm* **(a)** *(Tech)* repair; *(Archit etc)* restoration.
(b) *(Fencing)* parry; *(fig)* defence, protection.
(c) *(Med)* remedy; restorative.
(d) objection; criticism; doubt; **poner —s** to raise

objections *(a* to); to criticize, express one's doubts; *(pej)* to find fault *(a* with).
(e) hesitation; scruple, doubt; **no tuvo — en +** *infin* he did not hesitate to **+** *infin*; he did not scruple to **+** *infin*.
(f) *(CAm, Mex)* buck, rearing; **tirar un —** to rear, buck.
reparón 1 *adj* carping, critical, faultfinding. **2** *nm,* **reparona** *nf* critic, faultfinder.
repartición *nf* **(a)** distribution; sharing out, division. **(b)** *(Chi, RPl)* government department, administrative section.
repartida *nf (Arg, Guat)* **=repartición (a).**
repartido *nm (Post)* delivery; *(of milkman etc)* round.
repartidor *nm* distributor; *(Comm)* roundsman, deliveryman; **— de leche** milkman; **— de periódicos** paperboy.
repartija *nf (RPl: pej)* share-out, carve-up *(fam).*
repartimiento *nm* distribution; division; *(of tax)* assessment.
repartir [3a] **1** *vt* to distribute; to divide (up), share (out); to parcel out; *task* to allot, assign; *land* to parcel up, divide, split up; *country* to partition; *pamphlets etc* to give out, hand out; *food* to serve out; *drinks, glasses* to hand round; *dividend* to declare, pay out; *bread, milk, papers, post etc* to deliver; *cards* to deal; *parts (Theat)* to cast; *punishments* to issue, impose, mete out; **las cartas están repartidas en 4 palos** the cards are distributed among 4 suits; **las guarniciones están repartidas por toda la costa** the garrisons are distributed all round the coast, there are garrisons dotted about all along the coast.
2 repartirse *vr* to be distributed, be shared out *(etc);* **"se reparte a domicilio"** "home delivery service".
reparto *nm* **(a)** *(act)* **=repartición (a).**
(b) distribution *(also Bridge);* **un — poco uniforme** a very uneven distribution.
(c) *(Comm, Post)* delivery.
(d) *(Theat)* cast(ing); cast list; **dar — francés a uno** to put someone at the top of the bill.
(e) *(Cu, Mex)* building site, building lot *(US);* *(Mex)* suburb, real-estate development.
repasador *nm (Arg)* dishcloth.
repasar [1a] *vt* **(a)** *place* to pass (by) again; *street* to go along again; **pasar y — una calle** to go up and down a street repeatedly.
(b) — la plancha por una prenda to put the iron again over a garment.
(c) *(Sew)* to sew, sew up, darn; to mend.
(d) *(Mech)* to check, overhaul.
(e) *accounts etc* to check; *text* to revise, re-examine; *notes* to go over again; to read through rapidly, flick through; *lesson* to revise; *publication etc* to put the finishing touches to, polish up.
(f) *(Arg)* *plates etc* to dust, rub the cloth over; *furniture* to polish; *clothes* to brush down.
repasata *nf (fam)* ticking-off.
repaso *nm* review, revision; check; *(Sew)* mending; *(Mech)* checkup, overhaul; rapid reading, quick re-reading; **— general** general overhaul; **curso de —** revision course, refresher course; **ropa de —** mending, darning; **dar un — a una lección** to revise a lesson; **los técnicos daban el último — al cohete** the technicians were giving the rocket a final check.
repatriación *nf* repatriation.
repatriado 1 *adj* repatriated. **2** *nm,* **repatriada** *nf* repatriate, repatriated person.
repatriar [1b] **1** *vt* to repatriate; *criminal etc* to deport; to send home, send back to one's country of origin; **van a — el famoso mármol** they are going to send the famous marble back to its original country.
2 repatriarse *vr* to return home, go back to one's own country.
repecho *nm* **(a)** sharp gradient, steep slope; **a — uphill. (b)** *(Mex)* parapet; shelter, refuge, hut.
repela *nf (CAm, Col, Ec)* gleaning *(of coffee crop).*
repelar [1a] **1** *vt* **(a)** to leave completely bare, shear; *grass* to nibble, crop; *nails* to clip.
(b) — a uno to pull someone's hair.
(c) *(Mex)* to raise objections to.
(d) *(Mex)* to reprimand.
2 repelarse *vr (Chi)* to feel uneasy; to feel unwell; to feel regret.
repelencia *nf (Per, PR, Ven)* revulsion, disgust.
repelente *adj* **(a)** repellent, repulsive, disgusting. **(b)** *(SAm)* tedious, annoying.
repeler [2a] **1** *vt* **(a)** *enemy etc* to repel, repulse, drive back; *person* to push away.
(b) este material repele el agua this material resists water, this material makes water roll off it;

la pared **repele** la pelota the wall sends the ball back, the ball bounces off the wall.
  (c) *idea, offer* to reject.
  (d) *(fig)* to repel, disgust, fill with repulsion.
  2 **repelerse** *vr*: los dos se **repelen** the two are (mutually) incompatible.
repelo *nm* (a) hair out of place, hair *(etc)* that sticks up; *(in wood)* snag, knot; *(Anat)* hangnail.
  (b) *(fam)* tiff, slight argument.
  (c) *(fig)* aversion.
  (d) *(Ec, Mex)* old dress; worn-out object; piece of junk; *(Mex)* rag, tatter.
repelón 1 *adj (Mex)* grumbling, complaining, grouchy *(fam)*.
  2 *nm* (a) tug (at one's hair).
  (b) *(Sew)* ruck, snag.
  (c) small bit, tag, pinch.
  (d) *(of horse)* dash, short run.
  (e) *(Mex)* sharp reprimand.
repelús *nm (fam)* inexplicable fear; me da — it gives me the willies *(sl)*, it gives me the shivers.
repeluzno *nm (fam)* nervous shiver, slight start of fear.
repellar [1a] *vt* to plaster, stucco; *(SAm)* to white-wash.
repello *nm* (a) *(SAm)* whitewash(ing). (b) *(Cu etc)* lewd movement, lewd gesture *(in a dance)*.
repensar [1k] *vt* to rethink, reconsider, think out again.
repente *nm* (a) sudden movement, start, jerk; *(fig)* sudden impulse; — de ira fit of anger.
  (b) **de** — suddenly; unexpectedly; all at once.
  (c) *(Mex)* fit, fainting fit.
repentinamente *adv* suddenly; unexpectedly; **torcer** — to turn sharply, make a sharp turn.
repentino *adj* (a) sudden; unexpected; *change* sudden, swift; *turn* sharp. (b) **tener repentina compasión** to be quick to pity.
repentizar [1f] *vi (Mus)* to sight-read, improvise.
repentón *nm (fam)* violent start.
repercusión *nf* (a) repercussion; reverberation; re-echo.
  (b) *(fig)* repercussion; las —es de esta decisión the repercussions of this decision; de amplia —, de ancha — far-reaching, of profound effects; tener —(es) en to have repercussions on.
repercutir [3a] 1 *vt (Col)* to contradict.
  2 *vi* (a) *(object)* to rebound, bounce off; *(sound)* to re-echo; to reverberate, go on sounding *(or beating etc)*.
  (b) *(fig)* — en to have repercussions on, have effects on.
  (c) *(Mex)* to smell bad.
  3 **repercutirse** *vr* to reverberate.
reperiquete *nm (Mex)* (a) cheap adornment. (b) brag, boast.
repertorio *nm* (a) list, index, compendium. (b) *(Theat)* repertoire, repertory.
repeso *nm (Col)* bonus, extra.
repetición *nf* (a) repetition; recurrence. (b) *(Theat etc)* encore; pedir la — de una canción to encore a song. (c) fusil de — repeater rifle.
repetidamente *adv* repeatedly.
repetido *adj* (a) repeated; numerous; el tan — aviso the oft-repeated warning; repetidas veces repeatedly, over and over again. (b) aforementioned.
repetidor *nm (Radio, TV)* booster, booster station.
repetir [3l] 1 *vt* to repeat; to say again, do again; *(Theat)* to give as an encore, sing *(etc)* again; *lesson* to recite, rehearse, go over; *sound* to echo; *recording* to repeat, play back; le repito que es imposible I repeat that it is impossible, I tell you again it is impossible; los niños repiten lo que hacen las personas mayores children imitate adults, children ape their seniors.
  2 *vi* (a) to repeat; el pepino repite mucho cucumber keeps coming back, cucumber gives one bad hiccups.
  (b) — de un plato to have a second helping of a dish.
  3 **repetirse** *vr* (a) to repeat oneself; *(artist etc)* to copy oneself, use an earlier theme *(etc)* again.
  (b) *(event)* to recur.
repicar [1g] 1 *vt* (a) *meat etc* to chop up small.
  (b) to prick (again).
  (c) *bells* to ring, peal (merrily).
  (d) *(fam)* — gordo un acontecimiento to celebrate an event in style.
  2 **repicarse** *vr* to boast *(de* about, of).
repintar [1a] 1 *vt* to repaint; to paint hastily, paint roughly. 2 **repintarse** *vr* to pile the make-up on.
repipi *adj (fam)* posh *(fam)*; la-di-dah *(fam)*, affected;

arty *(fam)*; precocious, knowing for one's years; stuck-up *(fam)*; es una niña — she's a little madam, she's an insufferably affected child.
repique *nm* (a) *(Mus)* peal(ing), ringing; chime. (b) *(fam)* tiff, squabble.
repiquete *nm* (a) *(Mus)* merry peal(ing). (b) *(Mil)* clash. (c) *(Chi: Orn)* trill, song. (d) *(Col)* pique, resentment.
repiquetear [1a] 1 *vt* (a) *bells* to peal joyfully, ring merrily.
  (b) *drum, table etc* to tap, beat rapidly, drum lightly on.
  2 *vi* (a) *(Mus)* to peal out, ring.
  (b) *(of machine)* to clatter.
  3 **repiquetearse** *vr (fam)* to squabble.
repiqueteo *nm* (a) *(Mus)* joyful peal(ing), merry ringing. (b) tapping, drumming; clatter.
repisa *nf* ledge, shelf; *(wall)* bracket; — de chimenea mantelpiece; — de ventana windowsill.
replana *nf (Per)* underworld slang.
replantar [1a] *vt* to replant.
replantear [1a] *vt question* to raise again, reopen.
replantigarse [1h] *vr (SAm)* =repanchigarse.
repleción *nf* repletion.
replegable *adj* folding, that folds (up); *(Aer)* under-carriage retractable.
replegar [1h and 1k] 1 *vt* to fold over; to fold again, refold; *undercarriage* to retract, draw up.
  2 **replegarse** *vr (Mil)* to withdraw, fall back (in good order; *sobre* on).
repletar [1a] 1 *vt* to fill completely, stuff full, pack tight. 2 **repletarse** *vr* to eat to repletion.
repleto *adj* (a) replete, full up; — de filled with, absolutely full of, crammed with; la plaza estaba repleta de gente the square was solid with people; una colección repleta de rarezas a collection containing innumerable rarities.
  (b) estar — to be full up *(with food)*, be replete.
  (c) *appearance* sleek, well-fed.
réplica *nf* (a) answer; retort, rejoinder; rebuttal; *(Law)* answer to a charge; —s backchat. (b) *(Art)* replica, copy.
replicar [1g] *vi* to answer, retort, rejoin; *(pej)* to argue, answer back; ¡no repliques! don't answer back!, I don't want any backchat!
replicón *adj (fam)* argumentative; cheeky, saucy.
repliegue *nm* (a) fold, crease. (b) *(Mil)* withdrawal, retirement.
repoblación *nf* repopulation, repeopling; restocking; — forestal (re)afforestation.
repoblar [1m] *vt area, country* to repopulate; repeople; *river etc* to restock; *(Bot)* to (re)afforest, plant trees on.
repollo *nm* cabbage.
repolludo *adj* tubby, chunky *(fam)*.
reponer [2r] 1 *vt* (a) to replace, put back; *person* to reinstate; *fuel, stock etc* to replenish; *(Fin)* to plough back, reinvest; *damaged article etc* to replace, pay for (the replacement of).
  (b) *(Theat)* to revive, put on again.
  (c) to reply *(que* that).
  2 **reponerse** *vr (Med etc)* to recover; — de to recover from, get over.
reportaje *nm* report, article, news item; — gráfico illustrated report, story in pictures.
reportar [1a] 1 *vt* (a) to bring, fetch, carry.
  (b) *benefit etc* to obtain.
  (c) to give, bring; esto le habrá reportado algún beneficio this will have brought him some benefit; la cosa no le reportó sino disgustos the affair brought him nothing but trouble.
  (d) *(fig)* to check, restrain.
  (e) *(SAm: angl)* to report; to denounce, accuse; to notify.
  2 **reportarse** *vr* to control oneself; to calm down; ¡repórtate! control yourself!
reporte *nm (CAm, Cu, Mex: angl)* report.
reportear [1a] *vt (SAm)* to interview (for the purpose of writing an article); to photograph (for the press).
repórter *nm*, **reportero** *nm (angl)* reporter.
reposacabezas *nm*, *pl* **reposacabezas** headrest.
reposadamente *adv* quietly; gently, restfully; un-hurriedly, calmly.
reposado *adj* quiet; gentle, restful; unhurried, calm.
reposaplatos *nm*, *pl* **reposaplatos** tablemat.
reposar [1a] 1 *vt*: — la comida to let one's meal go down, settle one's stomach.
  2 *vi* to rest, repose; to sleep; *(of dead)* to lie, rest.
  3 **reposarse** *vr (liquid)* to settle.
reposición *nf* (a) replacement. (b) *(Fin)* ploughing back, reinvestment. (c) *(Theat)* revival. (d) *(Med and fig)* recovery.

repositorio nm repository.
reposo nm rest, repose; — **absoluto** (Med) complete rest.
repostada nf (CAm) rude reply, sharp answer.
repostar [1a] **1** vt stock etc to replenish, renew; — **combustible**, — **gasolina** (Aer) to refuel, (Aut) to fill up (with petrol).
　2 vi to refuel.
　3 **repostarse** vr to replenish stocks, take on supplies; — **de combustible** to refuel.
repostería nf (a) confectioner's (shop), cake shop. (b) confectionery; (art of) pastrymaking. (c) larder, pantry.
repostero nm, **repostera** nf confectioner, pastrycook.
repostón adj (CAm, Mex) rude, surly.
repregunta nf (Law) cross-examination, cross-questioning.
repreguntar [1a] vt (Law) to cross-examine, cross-question.
reprender [2a] vt to reprimand, tell off, take to task; child to scold; — **algo a uno** to reprimand someone for something; to criticize someone about something, reproach someone for something.
reprensible adj reprehensible.
reprensión nf reprimand, rebuke; scolding; criticism, reproach.
represa nf (a) recapture. (b) repression; check, stoppage. (c) (on river) dam; weir; pool, lake; — **de molino** millpond.
represalia nf reprisal; **como** — **por** as a reprisal for; **tomar** —**s** to take reprisals, retaliate (contra against).
represar [1a] vt (a) (Naut) to recapture. (b) to repress; to check, put a stop to; to restrain. (c) water to dam (up); (fig) to stem.
representable adj (Theat): **la obra no es** — the play cannot actually be staged, it is not a play for the stage.
representación nf (a) (in most senses) representation; — **proporcional** proportional representation; **en** — **de** representing, as a representative of; **por** — by proxy; **hacer** —**es a** to make representations to. (b) (Theat) performance; production; (of actor) playing, acting; **una serie de 350** —**es** a run of 350 performances. (c) (fig) importance, standing; **hombre de** — man of some standing.
representante nmf (a) (Comm, Pol etc) representative. (b) (Theat) performer, actor, actress.
representar [1a] **1** vt (a) (general sense) to represent; to act for; to stand for, symbolize; to express. (b) (Theat) play to perform, put on, do; to produce; part to act, play, take. (c) age etc to look; **representa unos 55 años** he looks about 55, from his appearance he's about 55; **ella no representa los años que tiene** she doesn't look her age; **el conserje no representaba ser muy listo** the porter didn't seem to be any too intelligent; **ese traje no representa lo que has gastado en él** that suit does not look as though it's worth what you paid for it. (d) details, facts etc to state, explain; to enumerate; to express; — **una dificultad a uno** to represent a difficulty to someone, explain a snag to someone. (e) to mean; **tal acto representaría la guerra** such an act would mean war.
　2 **representarse** vr: — **una escena** to imagine a scene, picture a scene to oneself; — **una solución** to envisage a solution; **se me representa la cara que pondrá** I can just imagine what a face he'll pull.
representativo adj representative.
represión nf repression; suppression.
represivo adj repressive.
reprimenda nf reprimand, rebuke.
reprimido adj repressed.
reprimir [3a] **1** vt to repress, suppress; to curb, check; giggle, yawn etc to suppress, hold in, smother; revolt etc to suppress.
　2 **reprimirse** vr: — **de** + ger to stop oneself from + ger.
reprisar [1a] vt (Arg, Chi, Mex, Nic: gall) play to revive, put on again.
reprise nf (SAm: Theat: gall) revival.
reprobable adj blameworthy, to be condemned, reprehensible.
reprobación nf reproval, reprobation; blame; condemnation; **escrito en** — **de** ... written in condemnation of ...
reprobador adj look etc reproving, disapproving.
reprobar [1m] vt (a) to reprove, condemn; to blame; to damn. (b) candidate to fail.
reprobatorio adj = **reprobador**.

réprobo adj (Eccl) damned.
reprochar [1a] **1** vt to reproach; to condemn, censure; — **algo a uno** to reproach someone for something; **le reprochan (por) su descuido** they reproach him for his negligence.
　2 **reprocharse** vr to reproach oneself; **no tienes nada que reprocharte** you have nothing to reproach yourself for (or about).
reproche nm reproach (a for); reflection (a on); **es un** — **a su honradez** it is a reflection on his honesty; **nos miró con** — he looked at us reproachfully.
reproducción nf reproduction.
reproducir [3c] **1** vt to reproduce; (Bio) to reproduce, breed.
　2 **reproducirse** vr (a) to reproduce; to breed. (b) (conditions etc) to be reproduced; (event) to happen again, recur; **se le ha reproducido la enfermedad** the complaint has made a reappearance; **si se reproducen los desórdenes** if the disorders happen again.
reproductor adj reproductive.
reps nm (fabric) rep.
reptar [1a] vi to creep, crawl; to snake along.
reptil 1 adj reptilian. **2** nm reptile.
república nf republic; **R— Dominicana** Dominican Republic; **R— Árabe Unida** United Arab Republic; **Segunda R— Española** Second Spanish Republic.
republicanismo nm republicanism.
republicano 1 adj republican. **2** nm, **republicana** nf republican.
repudiación nf repudiation.
repudiar [1b] vt wife, violence etc to repudiate; to disown, disavow; inheritance to renounce.
repudio nm repudiation.
repudrir [3a] **1** vt (a) to rot. (b) (fig) to gnaw at, eat up, devour.
　2 **repudrirse** vr to suffer inwardly, suffer gnawing doubts (etc); to eat one's heart out, pine away.
repuesto nm (a) stock, store; supply. (b) replacement; refill. (c) (Aut, Mech) spare, spare part, extra (US); **rueda de** — spare wheel; **y llevamos otro de** — and we have another as a spare (or in reserve). (d) (Cook) sideboard, buffet.
repugnancia nf (a) disgust, loathing, repugnance; aversion (hacia, por to). (b) (moral) repugnance. (c) reluctance; **lo hizo con** — he did it reluctantly. (d) (Philos) opposition.
repugnante adj disgusting, loathsome, revolting.
repugnar [1a] **1** vt (a) to disgust, revolt, nauseate; to fill with loathing; **ese olor me repugna** that smell revolts me, I loathe that smell; **me repugna tener que mirarlo** I hate having to watch it, I loathe having to watch it. (b) to hate, loathe; **siempre repugnaba el engaño** he always hated deceit.
　2 vi (a) to be disgusting, be revolting. (b) = **3 repugnarse** vr to conflict, be in opposition; to contradict each other; **las dos teorías se repugnan** the two theories are not compatible; the two theories contradict each other.
repujar [1a] vt to emboss, work in relief.
repulgado adj affected.
repulgar [1h] vt (a) (Sew) to hem, edge. (b) (Cook) to edge, put an edging on.
repulgo nm (a) (Sew) hem; hemstitch. (b) (Cook) fancy edging, decorated border; — **de empanada** (fig) mere trifle.
repulido adj (a) polished, repolished. (b) (fig) dressed up, dolled up; spick and span, very smart.
repulir [3a] **1** vt (a) to polish up; to repolish. (b) (fig) to try to make absolutely perfect, seek the greatest perfection in. (c) (fig) to dress up; to spruce up.
　2 **repulirse** vr (fig) to dress up, doll up; to smarten up.
repulsa nf (a) (Mil) check. (b) (fig) rejection, refusal; rebuff; **sufrir una** — to meet with a rebuff. (c) (fig) strong condemnation; severe reprimand.
repulsar [1a] vt (a) (Mil) to repulse; to check. (b) (fig) request to reject, refuse; offer, person to rebuff. (c) (fig) to condemn in strong terms.
repulsión nf (a) = **repulsa**. (b) (feeling) repulsion, disgust, aversion. (c) (Phys) repulsion.
repulsivo adj disgusting, revolting, loathsome.
repunta nf (a) (Geog) point, headland. (b) sign, indication, hint. (c) pique. (d) slight upset, tiff. (e) (SAm: Agr) roundup. (f) (Col, Per) sudden rise (of a river).

repuntar [1a] **1** vt (*Chi, Mex, RPl*) *cattle* to round up. **2** vi (a) (*of tide*) to turn.
(b) (*SAm*) to begin to show, give the first signs; (*of person*) to turn up unexpectedly.
(c) (*SAm: of river*) to rise suddenly.
(d) (*RPl*) to recover lost ground.
3 repuntarse vr (a) (*wine*) to begin to sour, turn.
(b) (*person*) to get cross.
(c) (*two persons*) to fall out, have a tiff.
repunte nm (a) (*Naut*) turn of the tide. (b) (*SAm: Agr*) roundup. (c) (*RPl: Fin*) rise in share prices.
reputación nf reputation; standing.
reputado adj (*also bien* —) highly reputed, reputable.
reputar [1a] vt to repute; to esteem; to deem, consider; **— a uno de** (*or por*) **inteligente** to consider someone intelligent; **le reputan no apto para el cargo** they think him unsuitable for the post; **una colección reputada en mucho** a highly esteemed collection.
requebrar [1k] vt to say nice things to, flatter, compliment; **— a una de amores** to court someone.
requemado adj scorched; parched; *skin* tanned, bronzed; *food* overdone.
requemar [1a] **1** vt (a) (*of fire etc*) to scorch; *plant* to parch, scorch, dry up; *skin* to tan; *food* to overdo, burn; *tongue* to burn, sting.
(b) (*fig*) *blood* to inflame, set afire.
2 requemarse vr (a) to scorch; to parch, get parched, dry up; to tan; to burn.
(b) (*fig*) to harbour resentment, smoulder with indignation (*etc*).
requenete adj (*Ven*), **requeneto** adj (*Col, Ven*) = **rechoncho**.
requerimiento nm (a) request; demand; summons (*also Law*). (b) notification.
requerir [3i] vt (a) to need, require; **esto requiere cierto cuidado** this requires some care.
(b) to request, ask, invite; **— a uno para que haga algo** to ask someone to do something.
(c) to send for, call for; *person* to send for, summon; **el ministro requirió sus gafas** the minister sent for his spectacles; **el ministro le requirió para que lo explicara** the minister summoned him to explain it.
(d) *woman* (*also — de amores*) *see* **requebrar**.
requesón nm cottage cheese; curd(s).
requeté nm *soldier of the Carlist forces* (*esp 19th century*).
requete... *intensifying prefix* (*fam*), eg **requeteguapa** quite extraordinarily pretty; **me parece requetebién** it seems absolutely splendid to me; **una joven requetemonísima** a fabulously attractive girl; **una requetesuperminifalda** an ultrashort miniskirt.
requiebro nm amorous compliment, flirtatious remark.
réquiem nm, pl **réquiems** requiem.
requilorios nmpl (a) tedious formalities, annoying bits of red tape; petty conditions.
(b) silly adornments, unnecessary frills.
(c) time-wasting preliminaries; roundabout way of saying something.
(d) bits and pieces.
requintar [1a] **1** vt (a) (*SAm*) *rope* to tighten, tauten.
(b) (*Col, Mex*) **— a uno** to impose one's will on someone, exact obedience from someone.
(c) (*Per*) to insult, abuse.
2 vi (*PR*) to resemble each other.
requisa nf (a) survey, inspection. (b) (*Mil*) requisition. (c) (*Arg*) seizure, confiscation.
requisar [1a] vt (a) (*Mil*) to requisition. (b) (*Arg*) to seize, confiscate. (c) (*Arg*) to search.
requisición nf (a) (*Mil*) requisition. (b) (*Arg, Chi, Mex*) seizure, confiscation. (c) (*Arg, Chi, Mex*) search.
requisito nm requirement, requisite; qualification; **— previo** prerequisite; **llenar los —s** to fulfil the requirements; **tener los —s para un cargo** to have the essential qualifications for a post.
requisitoria nf (*SAm: Law*) examination, interrogation.
res nf (a) beast, animal; **— lanar** sheep; **— vacuna** cow, bull, ox; **100 —es** 100 animals, 100 head of cattle. (b) (*SAm: Cook*) steak. (c) (*RPl*) body.
resabiado adj knowing, crafty; that has learned his lesson; *horse* vicious.
resabiarse [1b] vr to acquire a bad habit, get into evil ways.
resabido adj (a) thoroughly well known; **lo tengo sabido y —** of course I know all that perfectly well.
(b) (*fam*) pretentious, pedantic, would-be knowledgeable.

resabio nm (a) nasty taste (in the mouth), unpleasant aftertaste; **tener —s de** (*fig*) to smack of. (b) bad habit, unpleasant way; (*of horse*) vicious nature.
resabioso adj (*Cu, Mex, Per*) = **resabiado**.
resaca nf (a) (*Naut*) undertow, undercurrent; backward movement (*of the waves*).
(b) (*fam*) hangover.
(c) (*fig*) reaction, backlash; **la — blanca** the white backlash.
(d) (*CAm, Col, Mex*) high-quality liquor; bad liquor.
(e) (*Arg, Chi, Urug*) line of driftwood and rubbish (*left by the tide*).
(f) (*Arg, Chi, Urug*) worthless individual; very poor person.
(g) (*Cu, PR*) beating.
(h) (*Mex*) the best thing (*etc*) of its kind; (*iro*) hardened criminal.
resacado 1 adj (*Mex*) mean; weak; stupid. **2** nm (*Col, Ec*) (contraband) liquor.
resacar [1g] vt (*Col, Ec, Mex*) to distil (a second time).
resalado adj lively, vivacious, attractive; *see* **re ...**
resaltante adj (*SAm*) outstanding.
resaltar [1a] vi (a) to jut out, stick out, stick up, project.
(b) (*fig*) to stand out; to be outstanding; **hacer — algo** to throw something into relief, set something off (*contra* against a background of); (*fig*) to emphasize something.
resalte nm, **resalto** nm projection.
resanar [1a] vt to restore, repair, make good.
resaque nm (*Ven*) = **resaca** (d).
resaquero adj (*CAm*) = **remolón**.
resarcimiento nm repayment; indemnification, compensation.
resarcir [3b] **1** vt to repay; to indemnify, compensate; **— a uno de una cantidad** to repay someone a sum; **— a uno de una pérdida** to compensate someone for a loss.
2 resarcirse vr: **— de** to make up for, compensate oneself for; to retrieve.
resbalada nf (*SAm*) slip.
resbaladero nm slippery place; slide.
resbaladizo adj slippery.
resbalar [1a] **1** vi (a) to slip, slip up (*en, sobre* on); to slide, slither (*por* along, down); (*Aut etc*) to skid; **el embrague resbala** the clutch is slipping; **le resbalaban las lágrimas por las mejillas** tears were trickling down her cheeks.
(b) (*fig*) to slip up, make a slip.
2 resbalarse vr = **1**.
resbalón nm (a) slip; slide, slither; skid. (b) (*fig*) slip, error; **dar un —** to slip up.
resbaloso adj (*SAm*) slippery.
rescatar [1a] **1** vt (a) *captive* to ransom; *town etc* to recapture, recover; *pledge* to redeem.
(b) *person in danger etc* to save, rescue.
(c) *object, money etc* to get back, recover, regain possession of.
(d) *lost time* to make up; *misdeeds* to atone for, redeem, expiate.
(e) *land* to reclaim.
(f) (*Mex*) to resell.
2 vi (*Col*) to peddle goods from village to village.
rescate nm (a) ransom; recapture, recovery; redemption.
(b) rescue; **operaciones de —** rescue operations; **acudir al — de** to go to the rescue of.
(c) recovery.
(d) atonement, expiation.
(e) reclamation; **— de terrenos** land reclamation.
rescindir [3a] vt to rescind, cancel; to withdraw.
rescisión nf cancellation; withdrawal.
rescoldo nm (a) embers, hot ashes. (b) (*fig*) lingering doubt, scruple; **avivar el —** (*fig*) to stir up the dying embers.
rescontrar [1m] vt (*Comm, Fin*) to offset, balance.
resecar[1] [1g] **1** vt to dry off, dry thoroughly; to parch, scorch, burn. **2 resecarse** vr to dry up, get too dry.
resecar[2] [1g] vt (*Med*) to cut out, remove; to amputate.
resección nf resection.
reseco adj (a) very dry, too dry; parched. (b) (*fig*) skinny, lean.
reseda nf, **resedá** nf (*SAm*) mignonette.
resellarse [1a] vr (*fam*) to switch parties, change one's views.
resembrar [1k] vt to resow, reseed.
resentido adj resentful; bitter; sullen; **es un —** he's bitter, he's got a chip on his shoulder, he feels hard done by.
resentimiento nm resentment; bitterness.

resentirse [3i] *vr* (a) — **con algo,** — **por algo** to resent something, be offended about something, feel bitter about something.

(b) to remain weak, be weakened, suffer; **con los años se resintió su salud** his health suffered (*or* was affected) over the years; **los cimientos se resintieron con el terremoto** the foundations were weakened by the earthquake.

(c) — **de** *defect* to suffer from, labour under; *consequences etc* to feel the effects of; **me resiento todavía del golpe** I can still feel the effects of the injury.

reseña *nf* (a) outline, account, summary; (*Lit*) review; (*Sport etc*) report (*de* on), account (*de* of).

(b) brief description (*for identification purposes*).

(c) (*Mil*) review.

reseñar [1a] *vt* (a) to describe (*for identification purposes*); to write up, write a brief account of; (*Lit*) to review; *match* to report on.

(b) (*fam*) *offender* to book (*fam*); **la policía le reseñó por alguna infracción** the police booked him for some offence.

resero *nm* (*Arg, Bol, Guat*) cowboy, herdsman; cattle dealer.

reserva *nf* (a) (*act*) reservation; **la** — **de asientos no se paga** there is no charge for seat reservation (*or* for reserving seats).

(b) reserve (*also Comm*); stock, holding; — **en metálico** cash reserves; — **de oro** gold reserve; **las** —**s mundiales de petróleo** world reserves of oil; **de** — spare, reserve (*attr*), emergency (*attr*); **tener algo de** — to have something in reserve, keep something for an emergency.

(c) (*Geog etc*) reserve, reservation; — **de indios** Indian reservation; — **natural** nature reserve.

(d) (*Mil*) reserve.

(e) (*quality*) reserve; discretion, reticence; (*pej*) coldness, distance.

(f) privacy; **con** — in confidence; **escribir con la mayor** — to write in the strictest confidence; "**absoluta** —" (*adverts*) "strictest confidence".

(g) reserve, reservation; — **mental** mental reservation; **con ciertas** —**s** with certain reservations; **hay que tomar esa noticia con** — that news should be taken with reservations; **sin** —(**s**) unreservedly.

(h) **a** — **de** except for; **a** — **de que ... unless ...,** unless it should turn out that ...

reservación *nf* reservation.

reservadamente *adv* confidentially, privately.

reservado 1 *adj* (a) *seat etc* reserved.

(b) *person, manner* reserved; discreet, reticent; (*pej*) cold, distant.

(c) *matter etc* confidential, private.

2 *nm* (*in restaurant etc*) private room; (*Rail*) reserved compartment.

reservar [1a] **1** *vt* (a) to reserve; to keep, keep in reserve, set aside; *seats etc* to reserve, book; **lo reserva para el final** he's keeping it till last; **ha reservado lo mejor para sí** he has kept the best part for himself.

(b) to conceal; to keep to oneself, refuse to tell; *opinion etc* to reserve; **prefiero** — **los detalles** I prefer to keep the details to myself.

2 reservarse *vr* to save oneself (*para* for); to keep up one's strength; to bide one's time; **no bebo porque me reservo para más tarde** I'm not drinking because I have to be fit for later on.

reservista *nm* reservist.

reservón *adj* (*fam*) excessively reserved.

resfriado 1 *adj* (*Arg*) indiscreet. **2** *nm* cold; chill; **coger un** — to catch a cold.

resfriar [1c] **1** *vt* (a) to cool, chill.

(b) (*fig*) *ardour* to cool.

(c) (*Med*) — **a uno** to give someone a cold. **2** *vi* (*Meteorol*) to turn cold.

3 resfriarse *vr* (a) (*Med*) to catch (a) cold.

(b) (*fig: relations*) to cool off.

resguardar [1a] **1** *vt* to protect, shield (*de* from); to safeguard.

2 resguardarse *vr* (a) to defend oneself, protect oneself; to safeguard oneself.

(b) to go warily, proceed with caution.

resguardo *nm* (a) defence, protection; safeguard; **servir de** — **a uno** to be a protection to someone; — **de consigna** cloakroom check.

(b) (*Comm etc*) voucher, certificate; guarantee; slip, check, cover note; receipt.

(c) (*Naut*) sea room; safe distance.

residencia *nf* residence; (*Univ*) hall of residence, hostel; — **para ancianos,** — **para jubilados** rest home, old people's home.

residencial *adj* residential.

residenciar [1b] **1** *vt* (*Law*) to conduct a judicial inquiry into, investigate. **2 residenciarse** *vr* to take up residence, establish oneself, settle.

residente 1 *adj* resident; **no** — non-resident. **2** *nmf* resident; **no** — non-resident.

residir [3a] *vi* (a) to reside, live, dwell.

(b) (*fig*) — **en** to reside in, lie in; to consist in; **la autoridad reside en el gobernador** authority rests with the governor; **la dificultad reside en que ...** the difficulty lies in the fact that ...

residual *adj* residual, residuary; **aguas** —**es** sewage.

residuo *nm* residue; (*Math*) remainder; (*Chem etc*) residuum; —**s** remains; refuse, waste; rubbish; leftovers; —**s atmosféricos,** —**s radiactivos** fallout.

resignación *nf* resignation.

resignadamente *adv* resignedly, with resignation.

resignado *adj* resigned.

resignar [1a] **1** *vt* to resign, give up, renounce; *command* to hand over (*en* to); *post* to resign.

2 resignarse *vr* to resign oneself (*a, con* to); — **a** + *infin* to resign oneself to + *ger*.

resina *nf* resin.

resinoso *adj* resinous.

resistencia *nf* (a) (*in most senses*) resistance; stand; **la R**— (*Pol*) the Resistance; — **a la enfermedad** resistance to disease; — **pasiva** passive resistance; **oponer** — **a** to resist, oppose, stand out against.

(b) (*of body etc*) endurance, stamina; strength; staying power; toughness; (*of material*) strength, toughness; **carrera de** — endurance race, long-distance race; **la** — **que necesitan tener los montañistas** the toughness (*or* stamina) which mountaineers need.

(c) opposition; **luchar con la** — **de sus colegas** to fight against the opposition of one's colleagues, try to overcome the hostility of one's colleagues.

resistente *adj* resistant (*a* to); *material* strong, tough; hard-wearing; (*Bot*) hardy; — **al calor** resistant to heat, heat-resistant; **hacerse** — (*Med*) to build up a resistance (*a* to).

resistible *adj* resistible.

resistir [3a] **1** *vt* (a) *weight* to bear, support; *pressure etc* to bear, withstand.

(b) *enemy* to resist; *attack* to resist, withstand; to stand up to; *proposal* to resist, oppose, make a stand against; *temptation* to resist.

(c) *disappointment, tiredness etc* to put up with, endure, withstand; **no puedo** — **este frío** I can't bear (*or* stand) this cold; **no lo resisto un momento más** I'm not putting up with this a moment longer.

(d) — **la mirada de uno** to stare back at someone; to stare someone out.

2 *vi* (a) to resist; to struggle; to put up a fight, fight back; to hold out.

(b) to last, still go on, endure; **el coche resiste todavía** the car is still going; **el equipo no puede** — **mucho tiempo más** the team can't last out much longer; **no podíamos** — **de cansados** we were so tired we couldn't go on any longer.

3 resistirse *vr* (a) = **2** (a).

(b) — **a** + *infin* to refuse to + *infin*, find it hard to + *infin*, resist + *ger*; **no me resisto a citar algunos versos** I can't resist quoting a few lines; **me resisto a creerlo** I refuse to believe it; **se me resiste pasar sin saludarle** I cannot possibly pass by without calling on him.

(c) **se le resiste la química** she can't get on with chemistry, chemistry comes very hard to her.

resma *nf* ream.

resobado *adj* (*fig*) hackneyed, trite, well-worn.

resobar [1a] *vt* (a) to finger, paw; to muck about. (b) (*fig*) *subject* to work to death.

resobrino *nm*, **resobrina** *nf* second cousin.

resol *nm* glare of the sun; reflected sunlight.

resolana *nf* (*SAm*) sunlight; warmth of the sun; = **resol**; = **resolano**.

resolano *nm* suntrap, sunny place.

resoltarse [1m] *vr* (*Col*) to overstep the mark.

resolución *nf* (a) decision; — **fatal** decision to take one's own life; **tomar una** — to take a decision.

(b) (*of problem*) solving; solution; **un problema de** — **nada fácil** a problem which it is not easy to (re)solve.

(c) (*Parl etc*) resolution; motion; — **judicial** legal ruling.

(d) (*quality*) resolution, resolve, determination; decisiveness; **obrar con** — to act with determination, act boldly.

(e) **en** — in a word, in short, to sum up.

resoluto *adj* = **resuelto**.

resolver [2h; *ptp* **resuelto**] **1** *vt* (**a**) *problem* to solve, resolve; *doubt* to settle; *matter* to decide, settle; *course of action* to decide on.
(**b**) (*Chem*) to dissolve.
(**c**) *body of material etc* to analyse, divide up, resolve (*en into*).
2 *vi* (**a**) to resolve, decide; — **a favor de uno** to resolve in someone's favour.
(**b**) — **hacer algo** to resolve to do something.
3 resolverse *vr* (**a**) (*problem etc*) to resolve itself, work out.
(**b**) — **en** to resolve itself into; to be transformed into; **todo se resolvió en una riña más** in the end it came down to one more quarrel.
(**c**) to decide, make up one's mind; — **a** + *infin* to resolve to + *infin*; — **por algo** to decide on something; **hay que** — **por el uno o el otro** you'll have to make up your mind one way or the other.
resollar [1m] *vi* (**a**) to breathe heavily, breathe noisily; to puff and blow; to wheeze.
(**b**) (*fig*) **escuchar sin** — to listen without saying a word in reply, listen scarcely daring to breathe; **hace tiempo que no resuella** he has given no sign of life for some time, it's a long time since we heard from him.
resonador *nm* resonator.
resonancia *nf* (**a**) resonance; echo. (**b**) (*fig*) wide importance, widespread effect; **tener** — to have repercussions, cause a stir, have a considerable effect.
resonante *adj* (**a**) resonant; ringing, echoing, re-sounding. (**b**) (*fig*) *success etc* tremendous, resounding.
resonar [1m] *vi* to resound, ring, echo (*de with*).
resoplar [1a] *vt* = **resollar**; (*with anger etc*) to snort.
resoplido *nm* (**a**) heavy breathing, noisy breathing; puff, puffing; wheeze; snort; **dar** —**s** to breathe heavily, puff; (*of engine*) to chug, puff; to labour.
(**b**) (*fig*) sharp answer.
resopón *nm* nightcap.
resorber [2a] *vt* to reabsorb.
resorción *nf* resorption, reabsorption.
resorte *nm* (**a**) spring.
(**b**) (*quality*) elasticity; springiness, resilience.
(**c**) (*fig*) means, expedient; contact; influence; **tocar** —**s** to pull strings; **tocar todos los** —**s** to mobilize all one's influential friends, bring influence to bear from all sides.
(**d**) (*SAm*) elastic band.
(**e**) (*SAm*) responsibility; concern; (*Law*) authority; jurisdiction; **no es de mi** — it's not my concern.
respaldar [1a] **1** *vt* (**a**) *document* to endorse.
(**b**) (*fig*) to back, support.
(**c**) (*SAm*) to ensure; to guarantee, safeguard.
2 respaldarse *vr* (**a**) to lean back, sprawl, loll (*contra against, en on*).
(**b**) (*fig*) — **con**, — **en** to take one's stand on, base oneself on.
respaldo *nm* (**a**) (*of chair etc*) back.
(**b**) (*Hort*) wall.
(**c**) (*of documents*) back; endorsement; **firmar al** —, **firmar en el** — to sign on the back.
(**d**) (*fig*) support, backing; (*esp SAm*) help; guarantee.
respectar [1a] *vt* to concern, relate to; **por lo que respecta a** as for, with regard to.
respectivamente *adv* respectively.
respectivo 1 *adj* respective. **2 en lo** — **a** *as prep* as regards, with regard to.
respecto *nm*: **al** — in the matter, with regard to the subject under discussion; **a ese** — on that score; **bajo ese** — in that respect; (**con**) — **a**, — **de** with regard to, in relation to.
respetabilidad *nf* respectability.
respetable *adj* (*all senses*) respectable.
respetablemente *adv* respectably.
respetar [1a] *vt* to respect; **hacerse** — to win respect; to establish oneself, win a proper position; to impose one's will.
respeto *nm* (**a**) respect, regard, consideration; — **a la opinión ajena** respect for somebody else's opinion; — **de sí mismo** self-respect; — **a la conveniencia**, —**s humanos** respect for the conventions, consideration for the susceptibilities of others; **por** — **a** out of consideration for; **campar por sus** —**s** to act independently, strike out on one's own; (*pej*) (**a**) to show no consideration for others, be entirely self-centred; **faltar al** —, **perder el** — to be disrespectful (*a to*).
(**b**) —**s** respects; **presentar sus** —**s a** to pay one's respects to.
(**c**) **de** — spare, reserve (*attr*); special; **cuarto de** — spare room; **estar de** — to be all dressed up.

respetuosamente *adv* respectfully.
respetuosidad *nf* respectfulness.
respetuoso *adj* respectful.
réspice *nm* (**a**) sharp answer, curt reply. (**b**) severe reprimand.
respingado *adj* nose snub, turned-up.
respingar [1h] **1** *vi* (**a**) (*of horse*) to shy, balk; to start.
(**b**) (*fig*) to kick, show oneself unwilling, dig one's heels in.
(**c**) = **2 respingarse** *vr* (*dress*) to ride up, curl up.
respingo *nm* (**a**) shy; start, sudden movement (of alarm etc); wince (of pain); jump (of surprise); **dar un** — to start, jump.
(**b**) (*fig*) gesture of disgust; flounce.
(**c**) (*Sew*) part that is too short, part that rides up; **la chaqueta me hace un** — **aquí** the jacket rides up here.
(**d**) (*fig*) = **réspice** (**a**) *and* (**b**).
respingón *adj* nose snub, turned-up.
respiración *nf* (**a**) breathing, respiration; breath; **contener la** — to hold one's breath; **quedarse sin** — to be knocked all of a heap (*fam*); **llegar sin** — to arrive exhausted.
(**b**) (*of room etc*) ventilation.
respiradero *nm* (**a**) (*Tech*) vent, valve. (**b**) (*fig*) respite, breathing space.
respirador *nm* breathing tube, snorkel.
respirar [1a] **1** *vt* to breathe; *gas etc* to breathe in, inhale.
2 *vi* (**a**) to breathe; to draw breath; — **con dificultad** to breathe with difficulty, gasp for breath; **sin** — without a break, without respite; **paramos durante 5 minutos para** — we stopped for 5 minutes to get our breath back.
(**b**) (*fig*) (*after shock, effort etc*) to breathe again; **¡respiro!** that's a relief!; **no dejar** — **a uno** to keep on at someone, badger someone, make someone's life a misery; **no poder** — to be all in; to be up to one's eyes (*with work etc*).
(**c**) **no** — (*fig*) to say absolutely nothing; **estuvo escuchándole sin** — he listened to him in complete silence; **los niños le miraban sin** — the children watched him with bated breath.
(**d**) (*of room*) to be ventilated.
(**e**) (*fig*) **respira confianza** he oozes confidence, he breathes out confidence through every pore.
respiratorio *adj* respiratory; breathing (*attr*).
respiro *nm* (**a**) breathing. (**b**) (*fig*) respite, breathing space; rest; (*Comm etc*) extension of time, period of grace; (*Law*) suspension; reprieve.
respis *nm see* **réspice**.
resplandecer [2d] *vi* (**a**) to shine; to gleam, glitter, glow; to blaze. (**b**) (*fig*) to shine; — **de felicidad** to shine with happiness, be radiant with happiness.
resplandeciente *adj* (**a**) shining; gleaming, glittering, glowing; blazing. (**b**) (*fig*) radiant (*de with*).
resplandor *nm* (**a**) brilliance, brightness, radiance; gleam, glitter, glow; blaze. (**b**) (*Arg, Mex*) = **resolana**.
responder [2a] **1** *vt* to answer; to reply to; **pero él responde con injurias** but he answers with insults.
2 *vi* (**a**) to answer, reply; (*of echo*) to answer; — **a una pregunta** to answer a question.
(**b**) (*fig*) to reply, respond; — **con grosería a una cortesía** to return rudeness for courtesy, answer a courteous request rudely.
(**c**) (*fig: after order etc*) to answer back.
(**d**) — **a** *need* to answer, obey; *controls etc* to obey; *situation, treatment etc* to respond to; **la cápsula no responde a los mandos** the capsule is not obeying the controls; **pero no respondió a tal tratamiento** but he did not respond to such treatment.
(**e**) (*of material*) to be workable, be easily worked.
(**f**) (*of results etc*) to correspond (*a to*); — **a una descripción** to fit a description, agree with a description; **la obra no responde al título** the book is not what the title implies.
(**g**) — **de** to be responsible for; to answer for; **yo no respondo de lo que hagan mis colegas** I am not responsible for what my colleagues may do; **yo no respondo de él** I cannot answer for him; **en estas circunstancias, ¿quién responde?** who is responsible in these circumstances?
(**h**) — **por uno** to vouch for someone, guarantee someone.
(**i**) — **al nombre de** to be called, go by the name of.
respondón *adj* cheeky, saucy.
responsabilidad *nf* responsibility; liability; **solidaria** joint responsibility; **de** — **limitada** limited liability (*attr*); **bajo mi** — on my responsibility.

responsabilizar [1f] **1** *vt* (*SAm*): — **a uno** to make someone responsible; to put someone in charge.

2 responsabilizarse *vr* to make oneself responsible; to acknowledge one's responsibility; to take charge.

responsable *adj* (a) responsible (*de* for); **la persona** — the person in charge; **la policía busca a los —s** the police are hunting for those responsible; **hacer a uno** — to hold someone responsible (*de* for); **hacerse** — **de algo** to assume responsibility for something; to acknowledge one's responsibility for something; **no me hago** — **de lo que pueda pasar** I take no responsibility for what may happen.

(b) accountable, answerable; **ser** — **ante uno de algo** to be answerable to someone for something.

responsorio *nm* (*Eccl*) response.

respuesta *nf* answer, reply; response.

resquebra(ja)dura *nf* crack, split, cleft.

resquebrajar [1a] **1** *vt* to crack, split. **2 resquebrajarse** *vr* to crack, split.

resquebrar [1k] *vi* to begin to crack.

resquemar [1a] *vt* (a) to burn slightly; (*Cook*) to burn; *tongue* to burn, sting; *plant* to parch, dry up. (b) (*fig*) to cause bitterness to, upset.

resquemor *nm* (a) burn, sting, stinging feeling; (*Cook*) burnt taste. (b) (*fig*) resentment, bitterness; concealed anger; secret suspicion.

resquicio *nm* (a) chink, crack.

(b) (*fig*) chance, possibility; opening, opportunity.

(c) (*Col, Per, PR, Ven*) sign, vestige, trace.

(d) (*Cu, PR, Ven*) bit, small piece.

resta *nf* (*Math*) (a) subtraction. (b) remainder.

restablecer [2d] **1** *vt* to re-establish; to restore. **2 restablecerse** *vr* (*Med*) to recover.

restablecimiento *nm* re-establishment; restoration; (*Med*) recovery.

restallar [1a] *vi* to crack; to click one's tongue; to crackle.

restallido *nm* crack; click; crackle.

restante *adj* remaining; **lo** — the rest, the remainder; **los —s** the remaining ones, the rest, those that are left (over).

restañar [1a] *vt* to stanch, stop (the flow of).

restañasangre *nm* bloodstone.

restar [1a] **1** *vt* (a) to take away, reduce; to deduct; (*Math*) to take away, subtract (*de* from); — **autoridad a uno** to take away authority from someone, reduce someone's authority.

(b) (*Sport*) *ball* to return.

2 *vi* to remain, be left; **restan 3 días para terminarse el plazo** there are 3 days left before the period expires.

restauración *nf* restoration.

restaurador **1** *nm*, **restauradora** *nf* restorer. **2** *nm*: — **del cabello** hair restorer.

restaurán *nm*, **restaurante** [resto'ran] *nm* restaurant.

restaurar [1a] *vt* (*all senses*) to restore.

restinga *nf* sandbar, shoal, mudbank.

restitución *nf* return; restoration.

restituir [3g] **1** *vt* (a) to return, give back, restore (*a* to). (b) (*Archit etc*) to restore. **2 restituirse** *vr*: — **a** to return to, go back to, rejoin.

resto *nm* (a) rest, remainder; (*Math*) remainder; **—s** remains; (*Cook*) left-overs, scraps; (*Naut etc*) wreckage; debris, rubble; **—s de edición** remainders; **—s humanos** human remains; **—s mortales** mortal remains.

(b) (*Sport*) return (of a ball); (*person*) receiver.

(c) stake; **a** — **abierto** with no limit on stakes; (*fig*) without limit; **echar el** — (*fam*) to stake all one's money; (*fig*) to go all out, go the whole hog; **echar el** — **por** + *infin* to do one's utmost to + *infin*.

restorán *nm* restaurant.

restregar [1h *and* 1k] *vt* (a) to scrub; to rub (hard).

(b) (*of furniture etc*) to rub on, rub against.

restricción *nf* restriction; limitation; restraint; — **mental** mental reservations; **—es eléctricas** electricity cuts; **sin** — **de** without restrictions as to, with no limitation upon; **hablar sin —es** to talk freely.

restrictivo *adj* restrictive.

restrillar [1a] **1** *vt* (*Per, PR*) *whip* to crack. **2** *vi* (*Per, PR: of wood*) to crack, creak.

restringido *adj* restricted, limited.

restringir [3c] *vt* to restrict, limit (*a* to).

resucitación *nf* resuscitation.

resucitar [1a] **1** *vt* (a) to resuscitate, revive.

(b) (*fig*) to revive; to resurrect, give a new existence to.

2 *vi* (a) to revive, return to life.

(b) (*fig*) to be resuscitated, be resurrected; to revive.

resudar [1a] *vti* to sweat a little; (*of bottle etc*) to leak slightly.

resueltamente *adv* resolutely, with determination; boldly; steadfastly.

resuelto **1** *ptp of* **resolver**.

2 *adj* resolute, resolved, determined; bold; steadfast; **estar** — **a algo** to be set on something; **estar** — **a** + *infin* to be determined to + *infin*.

resuello *nm* (a) breath; breathing; **corto de** — short of breath, short-winded.

(b) puff; heavy breathing; wheeze.

(c) **meter a uno el** — **en el cuerpo** to put the wind up someone, give someone a nasty fright; to puncture someone's vanity.

(d) (*SAm*) breathing space; rest; **tomar un** — to take a breather.

resulta *nf* result; **de —s de** as a result of.

resultado *nm* result; outcome, sequel; effect; **dar** — to produce results.

resultante *adj* resultant, consequential.

resultar [1a] *vi* (a) to be; to prove (to be), turn out (to be); **si resulta (ser) verdadero** if it proves (to be) true; **el conductor resultó muerto** the driver was killed; **resultó (ser) el padre de mi cocinera** he turned out to be my cook's father, it emerged that he was my cook's father; **la casa nos resulta muy pequeña** we find the house very small; **resulta difícil decidir si . . .** it is difficult to decide whether . . .; **resulta que . . .** it follows that . . .; it seems that . . ., it emerges that . . .; **ahora resulta que no vamos** now it turns out that we're not going; **resulta de todo esto que no lo podemos pagar** it follows from all this that we can't afford it.

(b) — **de** to result from; to stem from; to be evident from; — **en** to result in, produce; **de ese negocio resultaron 4 más** from that deal there resulted 4 others, that deal produced 4 more; **me resultan 8 menos que a ti** that leaves me with 8 less than you.

(c) (*in absolute use*) to ensure; **con lo que después resultó** with what ensued, with what happened in consequence; **no resultó** it didn't work; **no me resultó muy bien aquello** that didn't work out very well for me; **este tema no me resulta** I can't get along with this subject.

(d) (*Fin*) to cost, work out at, amount to; **la serie completa nos resultó en 50 dólares** the complete set cost us 50 dollars; **resultan con unos y otros a 80 pesetas** all together they amount to 80 pesetas.

(e) (*fam*) — + *infin* to be best to + *infin*, be wise to + *infin*; **no resulta dejar el coche fuera** it's best not to leave the car outside.

(f) (*fam*) to look well, have a pleasing effect; **esa corbata no resulta con ese traje** that tie doesn't go with the suit.

resumen *nm* summary, résumé; abstract; **en** — to sum up; in short.

resumidero *nm* (*SAm*) = **sumidero**.

resumir [3a] **1** *vt* to sum up; summarize; to abridge, shorten, cut down.

2 resumirse *vr* (a) **la situación se resume en pocas palabras** the situation can be summed up in a few words.

(b) — **en** to be reduced to, come down to; **todo se resumió en algunos porrazos** the affair amounted to no more than a few bashes (*fam*).

resurgimiento *nm* resurgence; revival.

resurgir [3c] *vi* (a) to reappear, revive; to be resurrected. (b) to acquire a new spirit, pick up again; (*Med*) to recover.

resurrección *nf* resurrection.

retablo *nm* reredos, altarpiece.

retacarse [1g] *vr* (*Chi*) to refuse to budge; to go back on a promise (*etc*).

retacear [1a] *vt* (*RPl*) *grant etc* to give grudgingly, give in small amounts.

retacón *adj* (*Per, RPl*) short, squat.

retachar [1a] *vti* (*SAm*) to bounce.

retador **1** *adj* challenging; defiant. **2** *nm* (*SAm: Sport*) challenger.

retaguardia *nf* rearguard; **a** — in the rear; **3 millas a** — 3 miles to the rear, 3 miles further back.

retahíla *nf* string, series; (*of abuse etc*) volley, stream.

retajado *adj* (*Arg*) castrated, gelded.

retajar [1a] *vt* (a) to cut out, cut round. (b) (*SAm*) to castrate, geld.

retal *nm* remnant, piece left over.

retaliación *nf* (*SAm: angl*) retaliation.

retama *nf* (*Bot*), **retamo** *nm* (*SAm: Bot*) broom.

retar [1a] *vt* (a) to challenge; to defy. (b) to reprimand, tell off; to scold. (c) (*Chi, RPl*) to insult, abuse.

retardación *nf* retardation, slowing down; delaying; (*Mech*) deceleration.

retardar [1a] *vt* to slow down, slow up, retard; *progress etc* to hold up, retard; *train etc* to delay, make late; *clock* to put back.

retardatriz *adj* (*f*) *action etc* delaying.

retardo *nm* delay; time lag.

retazar [1f] *vt* to cut up, snip into pieces; to divide up; *firewood* to chop.

retazo *nm* remnant; snippet; bit, piece, fragment; —s (*Lit etc*) snippets, bits and pieces; disjointed fragments.

rete . . . *intensifying prefix* (*fam*) very . . . eg, **retebién** very well, jolly well (*fam*); **una persona retefina a** terribly refined person (*fam*).

retemblar [1k] *vi* to shudder, shake (*de* at, with).

retemplar [1a] *vt* (*Arg, Chi, Guat, Per*) to cheer up, revive, raise the spirits of.

retén *nm* (a) (*Tech*) stop, catch; lock. (b) reserve, store. (c) police post; post of armed men kept in reserve for an emergency.

retención *nf* (a) retention (*also Med*). (b) (*Fin*) deduction, part (of pay *etc*) withheld.

retener [2l] *vt* to retain; to keep (back), hold back; (*Fin*) to deduct; to withhold (part of); *attention* to hold; *memory* to retain; *borrowed article* to keep, hold on to; *treasures, rationed goods* to hoard; — **a uno preso** to keep someone in detention.

retenida *nf* guy-rope.

retentivo *adj* retentive.

reteñir [3h and 3l] *vt* to redye.

reticencia *nf* (a) insinuation, (malevolent) suggestion; implication; irony, sarcasm. (b) half-truth, misleading statement. (c) (*angl*) reticence, reserve.

reticente *adj* (a) insinuating; ironical, sarcastic; full of (unpleasant) implications. (b) deceptive, misleading. (c) (*angl*) reticent, reserved.

retícula *nf* (*Opt*) reticle; (*Phot*) screen.

reticular *adj* reticulated.

retículo *nm* reticle; net, network; (*in measuring etc*) grid.

retina *nf* retina.

retintín *nm* (a) tinkle, tinkling; jingle, jangle; (*in the ears*) ringing. (b) (*fig*) sarcastic tone; **decir algo con** — to say something sarcastically.

retinto *adj* (*SAm*) *complexion* very dark.

retiñir [3a] *vi* to tinkle; to jingle, jangle; to go on ringing (in one's ears).

retirada *nf* (a) (*Mil*) retreat, withdrawal; **batirse en** —, **emprender la** — to retreat. (b) (*of money, ambassador etc*) withdrawal. (c) retreat, safe place, place of refuge.

retiradamente *adj* live quietly, in seclusion.

retirado *adj* (a) *life* quiet; *place* remote, secluded, quiet. (b) *officer etc* retired.

retirar [1a] 1 *vt* (a) *chair etc* to move away, move back; to put away, take away, remove; *horn, tentacle etc* to draw in; *cover, hand etc* to draw back; *lid* to take off; *part* (*Mech*) to take out, remove; (*Mil*) *forces* to withdraw.
(b) (*Fin*) to withdraw (*de* from), take out; *ambassador* to recall, withdraw; *horse, runner* to scratch.
(c) *coins, stamps etc* to withdraw (from circulation); *permission* to withdraw, cancel; *driving licence* to suspend, confiscate, take away.
(d) *person* to retire, pension off.
(e) *accusation, words* to withdraw.
2 **retirarse** *vr* (a) to move back, move away (*de* from); (*Mil*) to retreat, withdraw; — **ante un peligro** to shrink back from a danger.
(b) (*Sport*) to retire; to scratch.
(c) to go into seclusion, go off into retreat, withdraw from active life; (*with pension*) to retire (*de* from); **se retiró a vivir a Mallorca** he went off to live in Majorca, he retired to Majorca; **cuando me retire de los negocios** when I retire from business.
(d) to retire (to one's room *or* to bed), go off to bed.

retiro *nm* (a) (*act*) retirement; withdrawal; (*Sport*) retirement; scratching; (*of money etc*) withdrawal.
(b) (*state*) retirement; **un oficial en** — an officer in retirement, a retired officer.
(c) (*Fin*) retirement pay, pension.
(d) quiet place, secluded spot; seclusion; retreat; **vivir en el** — to live in seclusion; live quietly.
(e) (*Eccl*) retreat.

reto *nm* (a) (*act*) challenge; threat, defiant statement (*etc*). (b) (*Chi, RPl*) reprimand; scolding. (c) (*Chi*) insult.

retobado *adj* (a) (*SAm*) *animal* wild, untamed; *person* wild, unruly, rebellious; obstinate; sullen; unpredictable, capricious.
(b) (*CAm, Ec, Mex*) grumbling; saucy, cheeky.
(c) (*Col, Chi, Per, RPl*) sly, crafty.

retobar [1a] 1 *vt* (a) (*SAm*) to line (*or* cover) with leather; (*Chi, Per*) *crate etc* to line (*or* cover) with leather (*or* sacking *or* oilcloth).
(b) (*Col*) *hides* to tan.
2 *vi* and **retobarse** *vr* (*SAm*) to be stubborn, dig one's heels in; to rebel; to grumble, protest.

retobo *nm* (a) (*SAm*) lining, covering; (*Chi*) sacking, oilcloth, wrapping material.
(b) (*SAm*) stubbornness; rebelliousness; grumble, protest; whim.
(c) (*Col, Hond: Agr*) old stock, useless animals; (*fig*) useless person, worthless object; junk, rubbish.

retobón *adj* (*Arg*) =**retobado** (a).

retocar [1g] *vt* (a) to retouch, touch up. (b) *recording* to play back.

retoñar [1a] *vi* (a) (*Bot*) to sprout, shoot. (b) (*fig*) to reappear, recur.

retoño *nm* (*Bot*) sprout, shoot, new growth.

retoque *nm* (a) retouching, touching-up; finishing touch. (b) (*Med*) symptom, sign, indication.

retorcer [2b and 2h] 1 *vt* (a) *arm etc* to twist; *hands, neck, washing* to wring; *strands* to twine (together).
(b) (*fig*) *argument* to turn, twist; *sense* to twist, force.
2 **retorcerse** *vr* (a) (*string etc*) to get into knots, twist up, curl up.
(b) — **el bigote** to twirl one's moustache.
(c) (*person*) to writhe; to squirm; — **de dolor** to writhe in pain, squirm with pain; — **de risa** to double up with laughter.

retorcido *adj* (a) *style* involved. (b) *person, manner* crafty, devious.

retorcijón *nm* (*SAm*) =**retortijón**.

retorcimiento *nm* (a) twisting; wringing; entwining; writhing. (b) (*fig*) involved nature. (c) (*fig*) craftiness, deviousness.

retórica *nf* (a) rhetoric; (*pej*) affectedness, windiness, grandiloquence. (b) —s (*fam*) hot air, mere words; quibbles.

retóricamente *adv* rhetorically.

retórico 1 *adj* rhetorical; (*pej*) affected, windy; grandiloquent. 2 *nm* rhetorician.

retornar [1a] 1 *vt* (a) to return, give back. (b) to replace, return to its place. (c) to move back. 2 *vi* to return, come back, go back.

retorno *nm* (a) return. (b) reward; repayment; exchange, barter; (*of present, service etc*) return. (c) (*Elec*) — **terrestre** earth wire, ground wire (US).

retorsión *nf* =**retorcimiento** (a).

retorta *nf* (*Chem*) retort.

retortero: andar al — to bustle about, have heaps of things to do; **andar al** — **por algo** to crave for something; **andar al** — **por uno** to be madly in love with someone; **llevar** (*or* **traer**) **a uno al** — to have someone under one's thumb; to keep someone constantly on the go; (*fig*) to push someone around.

retortijón *nm* rapid twist; —'**de tripas** gripe, stomach cramp.

retostar [1m] *vt* to burn, overcook.

retozar [1f] *vt* to romp, frolic, frisk about; to gambol.

retozo *nm* (a) romp, frolic; gambol; —s romping, frolics; gambolling. (b) — **de la risa** giggle, titter, suppressed laugh.

retozón *adj* (a) playful, frolicsome, frisky. (b) *laughter* bubbling.

retracción *nf* retraction, retractation.

retractable *adj* retractable.

retractación *nf* retraction, recantation.

retractar [1a] 1 *vt* to retract, withdraw. 2 **retractarse** *vr* to retract, recant; **me retracto** I take that back.

retráctil *adj* (*Aer etc*) retractable.

retraer [2p] 1 *vt* (a) *horns etc* to draw in, retract.
(b) to bring back, bring again.
(c) (*fig*) to dissuade.
2 **retraerse** *vr* to withdraw, retire, retreat (*de* from); — **a** to take refuge in; — **de** (*fig*) to withdraw from; to give up, avoid, shun.

retraído *adj* retiring, shy, reserved; aloof, unsociable.

retraimiento *nm* (a) (*act*) withdrawal, retirement; (*state*) seclusion. (b) (*quality*) retiring nature, shyness, reserve; aloofness. (c) (*place*) refuge, retreat.

retranca *nf* (*SAm*) brake.

retrancar [1g] 1 *vt* (*SAm*) to brake. 2 **retrancarse** *vr* (a) (*SAm*) to brake, apply the brakes. (b) (*Mex*) to be held up, reach deadlock.

retransmisión *nf* repeat broadcast, rebroadcast.

retransmitir [3a] *vt* *message* to relay, pass on; (*Radio, TV*) to repeat, rebroadcast, retransmit; to broadcast live (*direct from a theatre etc*), do an outside broadcast of.

retrasado *adj* **(a)** **estar** — (*of person, industry etc*) to be behind, be behindhand, lag behind; **está — en química** he is behind in chemistry, he has a lot to make up in chemistry; **vamos —s en la producción** we lag behind in production, our production is lagging; **estar — en los pagos** to be behind in one's payments, be in arrears.
(b) **estar** — (*of watch*) to be slow; **tengo el reloj 8 minutos** — my watch is 8 minutes slow.
(c) *country* backward, underdeveloped; *way of life* antiquated, old-fashioned.
(d) *food etc* unused, left over; **tengo trabajo —** I have work piling up, I am behindhand in my work.
(e) (*Med*) *child* subnormal, mentally retarded.
retrasar [1a] **1** *vt* **(a)** *departure, event etc* to delay, put off, postpone; *development, progress* to retard, slow down; to hold up.
(b) *watch* to put back.
2 *vi and* **retrasarse** *vr* (*watch*) to be slow; (*person, train etc*) to be late, be behind time; (*in production, studies etc*) to lag behind; (*production etc*) to decline, fall away.
retraso *nm* **(a)** delay; time lag; slowness, lateness; **llegar con —** to be late, arrive late; **llegar con 25 minutos de —** to be 25 minutes late; **llevo un — de 6 semanas** I'm 6 weeks behind (with my work *etc*).
(b) (*of country*) backwardness, backward state.
(c) (*Med*) — **mental** subnormality, mental deficiency.
(d) —**s** (*Comm, Fin*) arrears; deficit, debts.
retratar [1a] **1** *vt* **(a)** to portray; (*Art*) to paint a picture of, paint the portrait of; (*Phot*) to photograph, take a picture of; **hacerse —** to have one's portrait painted.
(b) (*fig*) to portray, depict, describe.
2 **retratarse** *vr* **(a)** to have one's picture painted; (*Phot*) to have one's photograph taken.
(b) (*sl*) to pay (up), fork out (*fam*).
retratería *nf* (*SAm*) photographer's (studio).
retratista *nmf* (*Art*) portrait painter; (*Phot*) photographer.
retrato *nm* **(a)** (*Art*) portrait; (*Phot*) photograph, portrait.
(b) (*fig*) portrayal, depiction, description.
(c) (*fig*) likeness; **ser el vivo — de** to be the very image of.
retrato-robot *nm* identikit picture.
retrechería *nf* **(a)** (*fam: act*) dodge, wheeze (*fam*), crafty trick; (*hum*) rascally trick.
(b) (*fam*) —**s** winning ways, charming ways.
(c) (*fam: quality*) charm, attractiveness.
(d) (*SAm*) meanness; deceitfulness; suspicious nature.
retrechero *adj* **(a)** (*fam*) full of dodges; wily, crafty; (*hum*) rascally.
(b) (*fam*) *child, woman* winning, charming, attractive.
(c) (*SAm*) mean; unreliable, deceitful; suspicious.
retreparse [1a] *vr* to lean back; to sprawl, loll, lounge.
retreta *nf* **(a)** (*Mil*) retreat; tattoo, display. **(b)** (*SAm*) open-air band concert. **(c)** (*SAm*) series, string.
retrete *nm* lavatory.
retribución *nf* **(a)** pay, payment; reward; compensation. **(b)** (*Tech*) compensation.
retribuido *adj* *work* paid; *post* salaried, that carries a salary; **un puesto mal —** an ill-paid post.
retribuir [3g] *vt* **(a)** to pay; to reward, compensate. **(b)** (*SAm*) *favour etc* to repay, return.
retro . . . retro . . .
retroactivo *adj* retroactive, retrospective; **dar efecto — a un pago** to backdate a payment.
retrocarga: de — breechloading; **arma de —** breechloader.
retroceder [2a] *vi* **(a)** (*of person*) to move back; to draw back, stand back; to go backwards; (*on journey*) to turn back; (*Mil*) to fall back, retreat; (*of gun*) to recoil; (*of water level etc*) to fall, go down; **retrocedió unos pasos** he went back a few steps; **la policía hizo — a la multitud** the police forced the crowd back, the police pushed the crowd back.
(b) (*fig*) to back down; to give up; to flinch (*ante un peligro* from a danger); **no —** to stand firm.
retroceso *nm* **(a)** backward movement; drawing back; (*Mil*) withdrawal, retreat; (*of gun*) recoil.
(b) (*fig*) backing down.
(c) (*Comm, Fin*) recession (of trade), slump, depression.
(d) (*Med*) renewed attack, new outbreak.
retrocohete *nm* retrorocket.
retrogradación *nf* retrogression.

retrógrado *adj* retrograde, retrogressive; (*Pol etc*) reactionary.
retrogresión *nf* retrogression.
retronar [1m] *vi* =**retumbar**.
retropropulsión *nf* retropropulsion; (*Aer*) jet propulsion.
retrospección *nf* retrospection.
retrospectivamente *adv* retrospectively; in retrospect.
retrospectivo *adj* retrospective; **escena retrospectiva** flashback; **mirada retrospectiva** backward glance, look back (*a* at).
retrotraer [2p] *vt* to carry back (in time), take back; **retrotrajo su relato a los tiempos del abuelo** he carried his tale back into his grandfather's day; **ahora podemos — su origen al siglo XI** now we can take its origin further back to the 11th century; **piensa — el problema a su origen** he hopes to trace the problem back to its origin.
retrovisor **1** *adj*: **espejo —** = **2** *nm* driving mirror, rear-view mirror.
retrucar [1g] *vt* **(a)** *argument* to turn against its user. **(b)** (*Prov, SAm*) to retort; **le retruqué diciendo que . . .** I retorted to him that . . .
retruécano *nm* pun, play on words.
retruque *nm* **(a)** (*Per, RPl*) sharp retort, brusque reply. **(b)** (*Chi, Mex*) **de —** on the rebound; as a consequence.
retumbante *adj* **(a)** booming, rumbling; resounding.
(b) (*fig*) bombastic.
retumbar [1a] *vi* (*of guns, thunder etc*) to boom, roll, thunder, rumble; (*of voice, steps*) to echo, resound; to reverberate; **la cascada retumbaba a lo lejos** the waterfall boomed (*or* roared) in the distance; **la caverna retumbaba con nuestros pasos** the cave echoed with our steps; **sus palabras retumban en mi cabeza** his words are still reverberating in my mind.
retumbo *nm* boom, roll, thunder, rumble; echo; reverberation.
reuma, reúma *nm* rheumatism.
reumático *adj* rheumatic.
reumatismo *nm* rheumatism.
reumatoideo *adj* rheumatoid.
reunificación *nf* reunification.
reunificar [1g] *vt* to reunify.
reunión *nf* **(a)** reunion, gathering; social gathering, party; (*Pol*) meeting; rally; (*Sport*) meeting; **— en la cumbre** summit meeting; **— plenaria** plenary session.
(b) reunion.
reunir [3a] **1** *vt* **(a)** *parts etc* to reunite, join (together); **— dos cuartos** to knock two rooms together, make one room out of two.
(b) *scattered objects etc* to gather (together), get together, put together; *data etc* to assemble, collect, gather; *resources* to pool; *collection* to make; *money* to collect; *funds* to raise; **los 4 reunidos no valen lo que él** the 4 of them together are not as good as he is; **la producción de los demás países reunidos no alcanzará al nuestro** the production of the other countries put together will not come up to ours.
(c) *persons* to assemble, bring together, invite together; **reunió a sus amigos para discutirlo** he assembled his friends to talk it over.
(d) *qualities* to combine; **la casa reúne la comodidad con la economía** the house combines comfort with economy.
2 **reunirse** *vr* **(a)** to unite, join together; to reunite.
(b) (*persons*) to meet, gather, assemble; to get together; **— para + infin** to get together to + *infin*; **— con uno para una excursión** to join someone for an outing.
(c) (*circumstances*) to conspire (*para + infin* to + *infin*).
revalida *nf* (*School etc*) final examination.
revalidar [1a] *vt* **(a)** to confirm, ratify. **(b)** (*School etc*) to sit a final examination for, take a final examination in.
revalor(iz)ación *nf* revaluation; reassessment.
revalorar [1a] *vt*, **revalorizar** [1f] *vt* to revalue; to reassess.
revaluación *nf* (*SAm*) revaluation.
revancha *nf* **(a)** revenge; **tomar su —** to get one's revenge, get one's own back. **(b)** (*Sport*) return match; (*Boxing*) return fight.
revejido *adj* (*Col*) weak, feeble.
revelación *nf* revelation; disclosure; **fue una — para mí** it was a revelation to me.
revelado *nm* (*Phot*) developing.
revelador **1** *adj* revealing; telltale. **2** *nm* (*Phot*) developer.

revelar [1a] *vt* (a) to reveal; to disclose; to betray, show; to give away. (b) (*Phot*) to develop.

revendedor *nm* retailer; (*pej*) speculator; vendor, hawker, seller; (*Sport, Theat etc*) ticket tout.

revender [2a] *vt* to resell; to retail; (*pej*) to speculate in; to hawk; *tickets* to tout.

revendón *nm* (*Ec, Per*) middleman.

revenirse [3s] *vr* (a) to shrink.
(b) (*food*) to go bad, go off; (*wine etc*) to sour, turn.
(c) (*plaster etc*) to dry out; to give off moisture.
(d) (*Cook*) to get tough; get leathery.
(e) (*fig*) to give way (at last).

reventa *nf* resale; speculation; hawking; touting.

reventadero *nm* (a) rough ground; steep terrain. (b) (*fig*) tough job, heavy work, grind. (c) (*Col, Mex*) bubbling spring. (d) (*Chi*)=**rompiente**.

reventar [1k] 1 *vt* (a) *balloon etc* to burst, explode, pop; *pipe, tyre etc* to burst; *barrier etc* to break, smash; **tengo una cubierta reventada** I have a puncture, I have a burst tyre, I have a flat (US).
(b) *horse* to flog, ride hard, ride to death; *person* to work to death, overwork, exhaust.
(c) (*fam*) *plan etc* to sink, ruin; *play* to hiss off the stage.
(d) (*fam*) *person* to do down, do serious harm to.
(e) (*fam*) to annoy, rile (*fam*); **me revienta tener que ponérmelo** it riles me to have to wear it; **me revienta de aburrimiento** it bores me to tears.
2 *vi* (a) (*of balloon etc*) to burst, pop, go off pop; to explode; (*of shell, pipe, tyre etc*) to burst; (*of contents*) to burst forth, burst out.
(b) (*of wave*) to break.
(c) (*sl*) to peg out (*sl*).
(d) — **de** (*fig*) to be bursting with; — **de indignación** to be bursting with indignation; **casi reventaba de ira** he almost exploded with anger; — **de risa** to burst out laughing, split one's sides; — **de ganas de decirlo todo** to be bursting to tell all about it; — **por algo** to crave something; — **por** + *infin* to be bursting to + *infin*, be dying to + *infin*.
3 **reventarse** *vr* =2 (a).
(b) (*horse*) to die of overwork, die of exhaustion; (*in race*) to blow up.
(c) (*sl*) to peg out (*sl*); **se revienta trabajando** he's killing himself with work, he's working his guts out.

reventazón *nf* (a) (*Arg*) low ridge. (b) (*Mex*) flatulence. (c) (*Mex*) bubbling spring.

reventón *nm* (a) burst, bursting; explosion; (*Aut*) puncture, blow-out, flat (*US*); **dar un** — to burst, explode.
(b) (*fam*) death (from overeating); **dar un** — to peg out (*sl*).
(c) steep slope; tough climb.
(d) (*fam*) killing effort; toil, slog; **le dio un** — **al caballo** he flogged his horse, he half-killed his horse; **darse un** —, **pegarse un** — to slog, flog oneself (*fam*), sweat one's guts out (*para* + *infin* to + *infin*).
(e) jam, difficulty.
(f) (*Arg, Chi*) outcrop of ore.
(g) (*Chi*) violent outburst; (*Med*) relapse.
(h) (*CR*) shove.

rever [2v] *vt* (a) to see again, look again at. (b) (*Law*) *sentence* to review; *case* to retry.

reverberación *nf* reverberation.

reverberador *nm* reverberator.

reverberar [1a] *vi* (a) (*of light*) to play, be reflected; (*of surface*) to shimmer, shine; (*of snow etc*) to glare; **la luz reverberaba en el agua** the light played (or danced) on the water; **la luz del farol reverberaba en la calle** the lamplight lay in a pool on the street, the lamplight was reflected on the street.
(b) (*of sound*) to reverberate.

reverbero *nm* (a) play, reflection; shimmer, shine; glare; **el** — **de la nieve** the glare of the snow, the dazzle of the snow.
(b) reverberation.
(c) reflector; adornment of glass (*or* steel).
(d) (*CAm, Col, Mex*) small spirit stove.
(e) (*Mex*) brazier.

reverdecer [2d] *vi* (a) (*Bot*) to grow green again.
(b) (*fig*) to come to life again, revive, acquire new vigour.

reverencia *nf* (a) reverence. (b) bow, curtsy; **hacer una** — to bow, curtsy. (c) (*as title*) **R**— (*also* **Su R**—, **Vuestra** —) Your Reverence.

reverencial *adj* reverential.

reverenciar [1b] *vt* to revere, venerate.

reverendísimo *adj* right reverend.

reverendo *adj* (a) respected, revered.
(b) (*Eccl*) reverend; **el** — **padre X** Reverend Father X.
(c) (*fam*) solemn.
(d) (*SAm*) big, tremendous (*fam*), awful (*fam*); **un** — **imbécil** an awful idiot.

reverente *adj* reverent.

reverentemente *adv* reverently.

reversa *nf* (*Col, Cu, Mex, PR: Aut*) reverse.

reversible *adj* reversible.

reversión *nf* reversion.

reversionario *adj* reversionary.

reverso *nm* back, other side; wrong side; (*of coin*) reverse; **el** — **de la medalla** (*fig*) the other side of the coin; the exact opposite.

revertir [3i] *vi* (a) (*of possession*) to revert (*a* to).
(b) — **a su estado primitivo** to revert to its original state.
(c) — **en** to end up as, come to be.
(d) — **en beneficio de** to be to the advantage of; — **en perjuicio de** to be to the detriment of.

revés *nm* (a) back; other side, wrong side; underside.
(b) backhand (*blow or shot etc*); slap, swipe; (*Sport*) backhand.
(c) (*fig*) reverse (*also fig*), setback; **sufrir un** — to suffer a setback; **los** —**es de la fortuna** the blows of fate.
(d) **al** — the wrong (*or* other) way round; upside down; *dress etc* inside out; **y al** — and vice versa; **entender algo al** — to get hold of the wrong end of the stick; to have quite a different idea; **todo nos salió al** — it all turned out wrong for us; **al** — **de lo que se cree** contrary to what is believed; **al** — **de lo corriente** against the usual practice, contrary to what normally happens; **llevar algo del** — to wear something the wrong way round (*or* inside out); **volver algo del** — to turn something round (the other way); to turn something inside out.

revesado *adj* (a) *matter* complicated, involved. (b) *child etc* unruly, uncontrollable.

revesero *adj* (*Col*) treacherous.

revestimiento *nm* (*Tech*) coating, facing, covering; lining; (*Mil*) revetment.

revestir [3l] 1 *vt* (a) *dress* to put on, don; to wear.
(b) (*Tech*) to coat, face, cover (*de* with); to line (*de* with); to sheathe (*de* in); (*fig*) *floor etc* to carpet (*de* with).
(c) (*fig*) to cloak, disguise (*de* in); *person* to invest (*con, de* with); *tale etc* to adorn (*de* with); **revistió su acto de generosidad** he gave his action an appearance of generosity.
(d) *importance, quality* to have, possess; **el acto revestía gran solemnidad** the ceremony had great dignity, the ceremony was a very solemn one.
2 **revestirse** *vr* (a) (*Eccl*) to put on one's vestments.
(b) (*fig*) to deck oneself in, put on; **los árboles se revisten de hojas** the trees put on their leaves again.
(c) (*fig*) — **con**, — **de** *authority etc* to be invested with, have; *quality etc* to arm oneself with; **se revistió de valor y fue a hablarle** he screwed up his courage and went to speak to her; *see also* **paciencia**.
(d) (*fig*) to get carried away; to be vain, be haughty.

reviejo *adj* very old.

revirado *adj* (*RPl*) (a) bad-tempered; unruly, uncontrollable. (b) crazy.

revirar [1a] 1 *vt* to turn (round), twist (round); to turn over. 2 **revirarse** *vr* (a) (*Cu, Chi, RPl*) to disobey, rebel. (b) (*Arg*) to go crazy.

revirón 1 *adj* (*Cu*) disobedient, rebellious, unruly. 2 *nm* (*Ant, CAm, Mex*) disobedience, revolt.

revisación *nf* (*RPl*), **revisada** *nf* (*SAm*)=**revisión**.

revisar [1a] *vt* (a) *notes, text etc* to revise, look over, go through; *edition* to revise; *account* to check; to audit; (*Law*) to review; *case, theory etc* to re-examine.
(b) (*Mil*) *troops* to review.
(c) (*Mech*) to check, overhaul.

revisión *nf* (a) revision; check, checking; re-examination, review; — **aduanera** customs inspection; — **de cuentas** audit. (b) (*Mech*) check, overhaul.

revisionismo *nm* revisionism.

revisionista 1 *adj* revisionist. 2 *nmf* revisionist.

revisor *nm* reviser; inspector; (*Rail*) ticket collector, inspector, conductor (*US*); — **de cuentas** auditor.

revista *nf* (a) review, revision; inspection; (*Law*) retrial; *pasar* — **a** to review, revise, re-examine.
(b) (*Mil*) review, inspection; (*Naut*) review; *pasar* — **a** to review, inspect.

(c) review, journal, magazine; — **comercial** trade paper; — **cómica** comic; — **gráfica** illustrated paper; — **juvenil** teenage magazine; — **literaria** literary review; — **de modas** fashion paper; — **para mujeres** women's magazine; — **semanal** weekly review.

(d) (*Lit*) section, page; — **de libros** book review section, literary page; — **de toros** bullfighting page, section of bullfight reports.

(e) (*Theat*) revue; variety show, vaudeville show (*US*).

revistar [1a] *vt* (*Mil*) to review, inspect; (*Naut*) to review.

revistero *nm* (a) reviewer, critic; contributor; — **deportivo** sporting journalist; — **literario** literary critic, book reviewer. (b) magazine rack.

revitalizar [1f] *vt* (*SAm*: *angl*) to revitalize.

revivificar [1g] *vt* to revitalize.

revivir [3a] 1 *vt event etc* to revive memories of; to relive, live again; *suspicions* to revive. 2 *vi* to revive, be revived; to come to life again; **hacer** — =1.

revocación *nf* revocation, repeal; reversal.

revocar [1g] *vt* (a) *decision* to revoke, repeal; to cancel; to reverse.

(b) *smoke etc* to send in a different direction, blow back, blow the wrong way.

(c) *person* to dissuade (**de** from).

(d) (*Archit*) to plaster, stucco; to whitewash.

revocatoria *nf* (*SAm*) revocation, repeal; reversal.

revoco *nm* (a) = **revocación**. (b) = **revoque**.

revolar [1m] *vi* to take to flight again; to flutter about, fly around.

revolcadero *nm* (*Zool*) mudhole, mudbath.

revolcar [1g *and* 1m] 1 *vt* (a) *person* to knock down, knock over, send flying; (*Taur*) to knock down and trample on.

(b) (*fam*) *opponent* to floor, crush; to wipe the floor with (*fam*).

(c) *proud person* to deflate, puncture.

(d) (*Univ*: *sl*) to plough (*sl*).

2 **revolcarse** *vr* (a) to roll about, flounder about; to turn over and over; (*animal*) to wallow; — **en la tumba** to turn over in one's grave; — **en los vicios** to wallow in vice.

(b) (*fig*) to dig one's heels in.

revolcón *nm* (*fam*) fall, tumble; (*Fin*) slump; **dar un** — **a uno** (*fig*) to floor someone, crush someone; to wipe the floor with someone (*fam*); to deflate someone.

revolear [1a] 1 *vt* (*Mex*, *RPl*) *lasso* to whirl, twirl. 2 *vi* to fly round.

revolotear [1a] *vi* to flutter, fly about; to flit; to wheel, circle; to hover.

revoloteo *nm* fluttering; flitting; wheeling, circling; hovering.

revoltijo *nm*, **revoltillo** *nm* (a) jumble, confusion; mess, litter; (*fig*) mess; — **de huevos** scrambled eggs. (b) (*Arg*, *Guat*, *Mex*) badly-tied bundle.

revoltoso 1 *adj* rebellious, unruly, turbulent; *child* naughty, uncontrollable. 2 *nm* rebel; (*Pol*) trouble-maker, agitator; rioter.

revoltura *nf* (a) (*Ant*, *Col*, *Chi*, *Mex*) confusion, jumble. (b) (*Mex*) mixture; (*Cook*) mixed egg and vegetable dish; (*Archit*) plaster; concrete.

revolución *nf* (*all senses*) revolution; —**es por minuto** revolutions per minute.

revolucionar [1a] *vt* (a) *fashion etc* to revolutionize, cause a revolution in.

(b) *person* to arouse intense excitement in, rouse to a pitch of excitement.

(c) (*Pol*) to stir up, sow discontent among; to rouse to revolt.

revolucionario 1 *adj* revolutionary. 2 *nm*, **revolucionaria** *nf* revolutionary.

revoluta *nf* (*CAm*) revolution.

revolvedora *nf* (*Arg*, *Mex*) concrete mixer.

revolver [2h; *ptp* **revuelto**] 1 *vt* (a) *objects* to move about; *object* to turn round, turn over, turn upside-down; (*Cook*) to turn over; *earth* to turn over, turn up, dig over; *container* to shake; *liquid etc* to stir; *papers etc* to look through; to rummage through, rummage among.

(b) *order, ordered things* to disturb, disarrange, mix up, mess up; **han revuelto toda la casa** they've messed up the whole house, they've turned the whole house upside-down.

(c) *affair* to go into, inquire into, investigate; — **algo en la cabeza** to turn something over in one's mind.

(d) (*Pol etc*) to stir up, rouse, cause unrest

among; *person* to provoke, rouse to anger; — **a Eslobodia con Ruritania** to stir up trouble between Slobodia and Ruritania; — **al secretario con el jefe** to get the secretary into trouble with his boss.

(e) *eyes, head, horse* to turn.

(f) *parcel* to wrap up.

(g) (*Col*) to weed.

2 *vi*: — **en una maleta** to rummage (about) in a case, hunt through the contents of a case; — **en los bolsillos** to feel in one's pockets, fumble in one's pockets.

3 **revolverse** *vr* (a) to turn (right) round; to turn over; (*in bed*) to toss and turn; (*with pain*) to writhe, squirm; (*Astron*) to revolve; — **al enemigo** to turn to face the enemy; **hay tantos muebles que resulta imposible** — there is so much furniture you can't turn round; **se revolvía en su silla** he was fidgeting about on his chair; he was squirming uncomfortably on his chair.

(b) (*fig*) — **contra uno** to turn on someone, turn against someone, attack someone.

(c) (*sediment*) to be stirred up, be disturbed; (*liquid*) to become cloudy.

(d) (*Meteorol*) to break, turn stormy.

(e) (*Col*) to have a piece of luck, begin to do well; (*pej*) to look after number one.

revólver *nm* revolver.

revoque *nm* (a) (*act*) plastering; whitewashing. (b) (*material*) plaster, stucco; whitewash.

revuelco *nm* fall, tumble.

revuelo *nm* (a) second flight; wheeling flight.

(b) mass flight.

(c) flutter(ing).

(d) (*fig*) stir, commotion, disturbance; row, rumpus; **de** — incidentally, in passing; **armar** (*or* **levantar** *etc*) **un gran** — to cause a great stir.

revuelta *nf* (a) turn; **dar vueltas y** —**s a algo** to go on turning something over and over.

(b) (*in road etc*) bend, turn.

(c) (*fig*) commotion, disturbance; fuss; quarrel, row; (*Pol*) disturbance, riot; revolt.

(d) (*Col*, *Ven*) weeding.

revuelto 1 *ptp of* **revolver**.

2 *adj* (a) *objects* mixed up, in disorder, confused; *eggs* scrambled; *water* cloudy, muddy; *sea* rough; *weather* unsettled, changeable; stormy; **todo estaba** — everything was in disorder, everything was upside-down; **los tiempos están** —**s** the times are out of joint, these are disturbed times; **viven** —**s los animales y las personas** people and animals live on top of each other.

(b) *character* unruly; restless, discontented; *child etc* mischievous, naughty; *populace* rebellious, mutinous; **la gente está revuelta por tales abusos** people feel mutinous about such scandals, people are properly on the boil about such abuses.

(c) *matter* complicated, involved.

3 *nm* (a) (*Arg*) mixed egg and vegetable dish.

(b) (*Col*) must, grape juice.

revulsar [1a] *vt* (*Mex*) to vomit, bring up.

revulsivo *nm* (a) enema, revulsive. (b) (*fig*) nasty but salutary shock.

rey *nm* king (*also Cards, Chess and fig*); **los** —**es** (*freq*) the king and queen; royalty; **los Reyes Católicos** the Catholic Monarchs (*Ferdinand and Isabella of Castile and Aragon*); **los Reyes Magos** *see* **Mago**; — **de armas** king of arms; — **de la evasión** escapologist; **ni** — **ni roque** no-one at all, not a single living soul; **lo mismo me da** — **que roque** it's all the same to me.

reyerta *nf* quarrel; fight, brawl, affray.

reyezuelo *nm*: — **sencillo** goldcrest.

rezaga *nf* (*SAm*) =**zaga**.

rezagado 1 *adj* (a) **quedar** — to be left behind; to be late, be behindhand; (*in payment, progress etc*) to fall behind, be backward.

(b) (*Mex*, *Per*) **carta rezagada** unclaimed letter.

2 *nm* latecomer, loiterer, dawdler; (*Mil*) straggler.

rezagar [1h] 1 *vt* (a) to leave behind; to outpace, outdistance.

(b) *event etc* to postpone.

2 **rezagarse** *vr* to stay behind, fall behind, get left behind; to lag (behind); to loiter, dawdle; to struggle; **nos rezagamos en la producción** we are falling behind in production.

rezago *nm* (a) left-over goods (*etc*); unused material which is left over; (*Arg*) unsold goods, articles being remaindered.

(b) group of straggling cattle.

(c) (*Mex*, *Per*) unclaimed letters.

rezar [1f] **1** *vt* (a) *prayer* to say.
(b) to call for, plead for; **el periódico reza agua** the paper says we need rain.
2 *vi* (a) (*Rel*) to pray (*a* to); to say one's prayers; to be at prayer.
(b) (*of text*) to read, say, run, go; **el anuncio reza así** the notice reads as follows.
(c) (*fam*) to grumble.
(d) (*fam*) — **con** to concern, have to do with; **eso no reza conmigo** that has nothing to do with me; that doesn't apply to me.
rezo *nm* (a) prayer(s); devotions; daily service; **estar en el** — to be at prayer. **(b)** (*act, in general*) praying.
rezongador *adj* =**rezongón**.
rezongar [1h] **1** *vt* (*Arg, CAm*) to reprimand; to scold. **2** *vi* to grumble; to mutter; to growl.
rezongo *nm* (a) grumble, moan. **(b)** (*CAm*) reprimand; scolding.
rezongón *adj* grumbling, grouchy (*fam*), cantankerous.
rezumar [1a] **1** *vt* to ooze, exude; to leak.
2 *vi* (a) (*of contents*) to ooze (out), seep, leak out; (*of container*) to ooze, leak.
(b) (*fig*) to ooze; **le rezuma el orgullo** he oozes pride; **le rezuma el entusiasmo** he is bursting with enthusiasm, he overflows with enthusiasm.
3 rezumarse *vr* (a) = **2** (a).
(b) (*fig*) to leak out, become known.
ría[1] *etc see* **reír**.
ría[2] *nf* estuary.
riachuelo *nm* brook, stream.
riada *nf* flood (*also fig*).
ribazo *nm* steep slope, steep bank.
ribera *nf* (a) (*of river, lake*) bank; (*of sea*) beach, shore; (*as area*) riverside.
(b) (*Agr*) irrigated plain.
(c) (*Mex, RPl*) group of riverside houses; shantytown, slum quarter.
riberano *adj* (*SAm*) =**ribereño**.
ribereño **1** *adj* riverside (*attr*); (*Law*) riparian. **2** *nm*, **ribereña** *nf* person who lives near a river.
ribete *nm* (a) (*Sew*) edging, border, trimming.
(b) (*fig*) addition, adornment; —**s** (*of story*) embellishments, trimmings, personal touches.
(c) (*fig*) —**s** touch, quality; **tiene sus** —**s de pintor** he has some pretensions to being a painter, he is not without some of the painter's talents.
ribetear [1a] *vt* to edge, border, trim (*de* with).
ribo *nm* (*Col*) bank; shore.
ricacho *nm*, **ricachón** *nm* (*fam*) fabulously rich man (*fam*); nouveau riche; (*Pol: as abuse*) well-heeled bourgeois (*fam*), dirty capitalist (*fam*).
ricamente *adv* (a) richly.
(b) (*fig*) **muy** —, **tan** — very well, jolly well (*fam*); **comeremos tan** — we'll have a really good meal; **he dormido tan** — I've slept splendidly; **viven muy** — **sin él** they manage perfectly well without him.
Ricardo *m* Richard.
ricino *nm* castor-oil plant; **aceite de** — castor oil.
rico **1** *adj* (a) (*Fin*) rich, wealthy.
(b) (*fig*) *soil, vein etc* rich; —**de**, — **en** rich in.
(c) *gem etc* valuable, precious; *furnishings etc* luxurious, sumptuous, valuable; *cloth* fine-quality, rich.
(d) *food* delicious, tasty; *fruit* luscious; **estos pasteles son riquísimos** these cakes are exceptionally tasty, these cakes are really lovely.
(e) *child* bonny; cute, lovely; (*in direct address*) ¡—! darling!; ¡**oye, rica!** hey, beautiful! (*fam*); hullo, gorgeous! (*fam*); ¡**qué** — **está el pequeño!** isn't he a lovely baby!; ¡**qué** —! (*iro*) isn't that just splendid?
2 *nm*, **rica** *nf* rich person; wealthy man, wealthy woman; **nuevo** — nouveau riche.
rictus *nm* (*involuntary*) curl of the lip; sneer; grin; — **de dolor** wince of pain; — **de amargura** bitter smile.
ricura *nf* (*fam*) (a) (*of food*) tastiness, delicious quality.
(b) smashing girl (*sl*); ¡**oye,** —! hey, beautiful! (*fam*); hullo, gorgeous (*fam*)!
(c) ¡**qué** — **de pastel!** aren't these cakes lovely?, what smashing cakes! (*sl*); ¡**qué** — **de criatura!** what a lovely baby!
ridículamente *adv* ridiculously, absurdly.
ridiculez *nf* absurdity.
ridiculizar [1f] *vt* to ridicule, to deride; to mock, guy, parody; — **a sus adversarios** (*Sport etc*) to make one's opponents look silly.
ridículo **1** *adj* ridiculous, absurd, ludicrous.
2 *nm* (a) **hacer el** — to make oneself ridiculous.
(b) ridicule; **exponerse al** — to lay oneself open to ridicule; **poner a uno en** — to ridicule someone, make a fool of someone; **ponerse en** — to make oneself ridiculous, make a fool of oneself.

riego *nm* watering; irrigation; (*fig*) sprinkling; — **por aspersión** watering by spray, watering by sprinklers; **la política del** — **en esta provincia** irrigation policy in this province; **con el** — **se triplica la producción** productivity is increased threefold by irrigation.
riel *nm* (a) (*Rail*) rail; —**es** rails, track, permanent way. **(b)** (*Tech*) ingot.
rielar [1a] *vi* (*poet*) to shimmer; to glitter, gleam.
rielero *nm* (*Mex*) railwayman.
rienda *nf* rein; (*fig*) restraint, moderating influence; **a** — **suelta** at top speed; (*fig*) without the least restraint; violently; **aflojar las** —**s** to let up; **dar** — **suelta a** to give free rein to; **dar** — **suelta al llanto** to weep uncontrollably; **dar** — **suelta a los deseos** to indulge one's desires freely; **dar** — **suelta a uno** to give someone a free hand; **empuñar las** —**s** to take charge; **llevar las** —**s** to be in charge, be in control; **soltar las** —**s** to relinquish control; to take off the brakes; to kick over the traces.
riente *adj* (a) laughing, merry. **(b)** (*fig*) *countryside etc* bright, pleasant.
riesgo *nm* risk, danger; **con** — **de** at the risk of; **seguro a** (*or* **contra**) **todo** — comprehensive insurance; **correr** — **de** + *infin* to run the risk of + *ger*, be in danger of + *ger*.
riesgoso *adj* (*SAm*) risky, dangerous.
rifa *nf* (a) raffle. **(b)** quarrel, dispute, fight.
rifar [1a] **1** *vt* to raffle; — **algo para fines benéficos** to raffle something for charity.
2 *vi* to quarrel, fight.
3 rifarse *vr* (*fam*): — **algo** to quarrel over something, fight for something; — **el amor de una** to vie for someone's love.
rifeño **1** *adj* Riffian, of the Riff. **2** *nm*, **rifeña** *nf* Riffian.
rifle *nm* rifle; sporting rifle; hunting gun.
riflero **1** *adj* (*Arg, Chi, Mex*) marksman expert, crack. **2** *nm* (a) (*Mil*) rifleman. **(b)** (*Arg, Chi, Mex*) marksman, crack shot.
rígidamente *adv* (a) rigidly, stiffly. **(b)** (*fig*) rigidly. **(c)** (*fig*) strictly, sternly, harshly. **(d)** *stare etc* woodenly.
rigidez *nf* (a) rigidity, stiffness; — **cadavérica** rigor mortis. **(b)** (*fig*) rigidity; inflexibility. **(c)** (*fig*) strictness, sternness, harshness. **(d)** woodenness.
rígido *adj* (a) rigid, stiff; **quedarse** — to go rigid; to get stiff (with cold).
(b) (*fig: in attitude*) rigid, inflexible, unadaptable.
(c) (*fig: morally*) strict, stern (*con, para* towards), harsh, unbending.
(d) *face* wooden, expressionless.
rigor *nm* (a) severity, harshness; strictness; toughness, stringency.
(b) (*Meteorol*) harshness, severity; **el** — **del verano** the worst of the summer, the hottest part of the summer; **los** —**es del clima** the rigours of the climate.
(c) rigour; exacting nature; accuracy, meticulousness; **con todo** — **científico** with complete scientific rigour; **una edición hecha con el mayor** — **crítico** an edition produced with absolute meticulousness.
(d) **ser de** — to be de rigueur, be absolutely essential; **después de los saludos de** — after the inevitable greetings; **me dio los consejos de** — he gave the expected advice, he gave me the advice which he felt he had to; **en** — strictly speaking.
(e) (*Col*) **un** — **de cosas** a whole lot of things.
(f) (*RPl*) **dar un** — **a uno** to give someone a thrashing.
rigorismo *nm* strictness, severity; austerity.
rigorista *nmf* strict disciplinarian; strict observer (*de* of), stickler (*de* for).
rigurosamente *adv* (a) severely, harshly; strictly; stringently.
(b) rigorously; accurately, meticulously.
(c) **un estudio** — **científico** an absolutely scientific study; **eso no es** — **exacto** that is not strictly accurate, that is not wholly true.
rigurosidad *nf* rigour, harshness, severity.
riguroso *adj* (a) *attitude, discipline etc* severe, harsh; *application etc* strict; *measure* severe, tough, stringent; **su tratamiento** — **de los empleados** his harsh treatment of the employees.
(b) (*Meteorol*) harsh, severe, hard; extreme.
(c) *method, study etc* rigorous; exacting; accurate; meticulous.
(d) (*lit*) cruel; **los hados** —**s** the cruel fates.
rija *nf* quarrel, dispute, fight.
rijio *nm* (a) (*Guat*) =**rijo**. **(b)** (*Mex, Nic*) spirit, spirited temperament (*of a horse*).
rijioso *adj* (*CAm, Mex*) =**rijoso**.
rijo *nm* lustfulness.

rijosidad nf (a) sensitivity, susceptible nature; quarrelsomeness. (b) lustfulness, sensuality; randiness.

rijoso adj (a) sensitive, susceptible; quarrelsome. (b) lustful, sensual; randy.

rikisha nf rickshaw.

rila nf (a) (Col, Mex) gristle. (b) (Col) bird droppings.

rima nf (a) rhyme; — imperfecta assonance, half-rhyme; octava — ottava rima; tercia — terza rima. (b) —s poems, verse, poetry.

rimador nm, **rimadora** nf rhymester.

rimar [1a] vti to rhyme (con with).

rimbombancia nf (a) resonance, echo. (b) (fig) pomposity, bombast. (c) (fig) showiness, flashiness.

rimbombante adj (a) resounding, echoing. (b) (fig) pompous, bombastic. (c) (fig) showy, flashy.

rimbombar [1a] vi to resound, echo, boom.

rimel nm (esp SAm) mascara; eyeshadow.

rimero nm stack, pile, heap.

Rin m Rhine.

rincón nm (a) (inside) corner. (b) (fig) corner, nook; retreat; niche. (c) (Agr: esp SAm) patch of ground.

rinconada nf corner.

rinconera nf (a) corner piece (of furniture); corner cupboard, dresser. (b) (Archit) wall between corner and window.

rinche[1] adj (Col) full to the brim.

rinche[2] nm (fam) secret place, hiding place.

rinde nm (Arg: also —s) yield, revenue.

ringla nf, **ringle** nm, **ringlera** nf row, line; (Agr) swath.

ringorrango nm (a) (in writing) flourish. (b) —s frills, buttons and bows, useless adornments.

ringuelete nm (a) (Arg, Col, Chi) restless person; busybody, gadabout. (b) (Col) dart; toy windmill.

ringueletear [1a] vi (Col, Chi) = callejear.

rinoceronte nm rhinoceros.

riña nf quarrel, argument; fight, brawl, scuffle; — de gallos cockfight.

riñón nm (a) (Anat) kidney; (loosely) lower part of the back; tener el — bien cubierto (fam) to be well heeled (sl); me costó un — (fam) it cost the earth. (b) (fig) heart, core; innermost part; aquí en el — de Castilla here in the very heart of Castile.

río[1] nm river; (fig) stream, torrent; — abajo downstream; — arriba upstream; un — de gente a stream of people, a flood of people; es un — de oro it's a gold mine; a — revuelto, ganancia de pescadores there are bound to be pickings for some, it's an ill wind that blows nobody any good; cuando el — suena, agua lleva there's no smoke without fire.

río[2], **rió** etc see **reír**.

riojano 1 adj Riojan, of La Rioja. 2 nm, **riojana** nf Riojan. 3 nm (wine) Riojan.

riolada nf (fam) flood, stream.

rioplatense 1 adj of the River Plate region. 2 nmf native (or inhabitant) of the River Plate region; los —s the people of the River Plate region.

riostra nf brace, strut.

ripiado adj (a) (Col) ragged. (b) (Cu) very poor.

ripiar [1b] vt (a) (Archit) to fill with rubble. (b) (Ant, Col) to cut up, cut into shreds; to crumble. (c) (Col, Cu) to squander. (d) (Col) person to leave badly off; two persons to mix up. (e) (Mex) to glean. (f) (Ant) to hit.

ripiería nf mob, populace.

ripio nm (a) refuse, waste; (Archit) rubble; debris. (b) (Lit) padding, word (or phrase) put in to fill up the line; (fig) padding, verbiage, empty words; no perder — not to miss a trick, to miss nothing of what is going on.

ripioso adj (Col, SD) ragged.

riquerío nm (Chi) rich people (collectively).

riqueza nf (a) wealth, riches; — imponible part of one's property qualifying for the wealth tax; vivir en la — to live in luxury. (b) (fig: quality) richness.

riquiña nf (Ven) wicker basket.

risa nf (una —) laugh; (in general, also —s) laughter; hubo —s there was laughter; no es cosa de — it's no laughing matter; ¡qué —! how very funny!, what a joke!; el libro es una verdadera — the book is a laugh from start to finish; — retozona suppressed giggle, titter; caerse (or descoserse, desternillarse, mondarse, morirse) de — to split one's sides with laughing, die of laughing; causar a uno, mover (or provocar) a uno a — to make someone laugh; soltar la — to burst out laughing; tomar algo a — to take something as a joke, laugh something off.

risco nm (a) cliff, crag; steep rock. (b) —s rough parts, difficult pieces (of a terrain).

riscoso adj steep, craggy.

risible adj ludicrous, laughable.

risotada nf guffaw, loud laugh.

rispiar [1b] vi (CAm) to rush off.

rispidez nf (Ec, Mex) roughness, coarseness.

risquería nf (Chi) craggy place.

ristra nf string (also fig).

ristre nm: en — at the ready, all set; see **lanza**.

risueño adj (a) face smiling; muy — smiling all over, with a big smile, wreathed in smiles. (b) disposition etc cheerful, sunny, gay; countryside etc smiling, pleasant. (c) outlook bright.

rítmico adj rhythmic(al).

ritmo nm (a) (Mus etc) rhythm. (b) (fig) rhythm; rate, pace; speed; — de crecimiento, — de expansión rate of growth; el trabajo se mantiene a un — intenso the work is going on at a good rate (or pace); trabajar a — lento (of workers) to go slow; de acuerdo con el — de las estaciones in keeping with the rhythm of the seasons.

rito nm rite, ceremony.

ritual 1 adj ritual. 2 nm ritual; de — ritual, customary.

ritualismo nm ritualism.

ritualista 1 adj ritualistic. 2 nmf ritualist.

rival 1 adj rival, competing. 2 nmf rival, competitor; contender.

rivalidad nf rivalry, competition; enmity.

rivalizar [1f] vi to vie, compete, contend; — con to rival, compete with; los dos rivalizan en habilidad they rival each other in skill.

rizado adj hair curly; surface ridged, crinkly; undulating.

rizador nm curling iron, hair-curler.

rizar [1f] 1 vt hair to curl; to ruffle; surface to ridge, crinkle; water to ripple, ruffle; see **rizo** (b). 2 **rizarse** vr (water) to ripple.

rizo[1] 1 adj curly. 2 nm (a) curl, ringlet; (of surface) ridge; (on water) ripple. (b) (Aer) loop; hacer el —, rizar el — to loop the loop.

rizo[2] nm (Naut) reef; tomar —s to reef in (the sails).

rizoma nm rhizome.

roano 1 adj roan. 2 nm roan (horse).

robar [1a] vt (a) possessor to rob; object to steal (a from); house etc to break into, burgle; safe to break open, break into, rifle (the contents of); — algo a uno to steal something from someone, rob someone of something; en ese negocio me han robado I was cheated in that deal. (b) person to steal away, kidnap, abduct. (c) (fig) attention etc to steal, capture; interest to command; patience to exhaust; peace of mind to destroy; life to take; — el corazón a uno to steal someone's heart; tuve que — 3 horas al sueño I had to use up 3 hours when I should have been sleeping. (d) (of river) to carry away. (e) (Cards) to draw, take (from the pile).

Roberto nm Robert.

roblar [1a] vt to rivet, clinch.

roble nm oak, oak tree; de — oak (attr), oaken; de — macizo of solid oak.

robledal nm, **robledo** nm oakwood.

roblón nm rivet.

roblonar [1a] vt to rivet.

robo nm (a) (un —) theft; (in general) robbery, theft, thieving; — con escalamiento housebreaking, burglary; — relámpago smash-and-grab raid; — en la vía pública highway robbery; ¡esto es un —! this is sheer robbery! (b) stolen article, stolen goods.

robot [ro'βo] nm, pl **robots** [ro'βo] (a) robot. (b) (fig) puppet, tool.

robustecer [2d] 1 vt to strengthen. 2 **robustecerse** vr to grow stronger.

robustez nf strength, toughness, robustness.

robusto adj strong, tough, robust.

roca nf rock; en — viva in(to) the living rock.

rocalla nf small stones, pebbles; stone chippings.

rocalloso adj pebbly, stony.

roce nm (a) (act) rub, rubbing; (Tech) friction. (b) rub, mark of rubbing; (on skin) graze, chafing mark. (c) (fam) close contact; familiarity; tener — con to be in close contact with, have a lot to do with.

rociada nf (a) shower, spray, sprinkling; (in drink etc) dash, splash; (Agr) spray. (b) (fig: of stones) shower; (of bullets) hail; (of shot) scatter; (of abuse etc) hail, stream, torrent.

rociadera nf watering can.

rociador nm spray, sprinkler.
rociar [1c] **1** vt to sprinkle, spray (de with); (with mud etc) to spatter, bespatter (de with); (with bullets) to spray (de with).
2 vi: **empieza a —** the dew is beginning to fall; **rocía esta mañana** there is a dew this morning.
rocín nm (a) hack, nag, poor horse; (Arg) riding horse; (Bol) draught ox. (b) (fam) lout, ignorant fellow.
rocinante nm broken-down old horse.
rocío nm (a) (Meteorol) dew; light drizzle. (b) (fig) sprinkling; dew; drops of condensation (etc).
rococó 1 adj rococo. **2** nm rococo.
rocosidades nfpl rocky places.
rocoso adj rocky.
rocote nm, **rocoto** nm (SAm) large pepper, large chili.
Rochela: La — La Rochelle.
rochela nf (Col, Mex, PR, Ven) noisy gathering, rowdy party.
rochelear [1a] vi (Col, PR, Ven) to play about, live it up (fam).
rochelero adj (PR, Ven) unruly, rowdy; mischievous; quarrelsome.
roda nf (Naut) stem.
rodaballo nm turbot; **— menor** brill.
rodada nf (a) rut, wheel track. (b) (Mex, RPl) fall (from a horse).
rodadero nm (Ec) cliff, precipice.
rodado 1 adj (a) traffic wheeled, on wheels.
(b) stone etc rounded; **esto vino —** this just happened (without my having to do anything); by luck the chance came up.
(c) horse dappled.
(d) style well-rounded, fluent.
2 nm (Arg, Chi) wheeled vehicle.
rodadura nf (a) roll, rolling. (b) rut. (c) (of tyre) tread.
rodaja nf (a) small wheel; small disc; (of furniture) castor. (b) (of bread, fruit etc) slice; **limón en —s** sliced lemon.
rodaje nm (a) (Tech) wheels, set of wheels. (b) (Cine) shooting, filming. (c) (Aut) running-in; "**en —**" "running in". (d) (Per) vehicle tax.
rodamiento nm (a) **— a bolas, — de bolas** ball bearing. (b) (Aut: on tyre) tread.
Ródano m Rhône.
rodante adj rolling; **material —** rolling stock.
rodapié nm skirting board, baseboard (US).
rodar [1m] **1** vt (a) vehicle to wheel (along); object to roll, drag (along).
(b) staircase to roll down, go tumbling down.
(c) area to travel, go over; **ha rodado medio mundo** he's been over half the world.
(d) car, make of car to race, drive; new car to run in.
(e) (Cine) to shoot, film.
(f) (Ven) to seize; to imprison.
(g) (SAm) **— (a patadas)** to knock down, knock over.
2 vi (a) to roll (por along, down, over etc); (on wheels) to go, run, travel; **— de suelo** (Aer) to taxi; **se oía el — de los carros** one could hear the rumbling of the tanks; **echarlo todo a —** (fig) to mess it all up, spoil everything; to throw one's hand in.
(b) (on axle etc) to go round, turn, rotate.
(c) **andar** (or **ir**) **rodando** (of person) to move about (from place to place); to roll around, drift; **no hace más que ir rodando** he just drifts about; **me han hecho ir rodando de acá para allá** they kept shunting me about from place to place.
(d) (fig) to be still going, exist still; **no sabía que ese modelo rodaba todavía por esos mundos** I didn't know that model was still about.
(e) **— por uno** to be at someone's beck and call, dance attendance on someone.
(f) (Cine) to shoot, film; **llevamos 2 meses de — en Méjico** we've spent 2 months filming in Mexico.
(g) (Arg, Mex: of horse) to stumble, fall forwards.
Rodas f Rhodes.
rodear [1a] **1** vt (a) to surround (de by, with); to ring, encircle, enclose, shut in; (of arms, dress etc) to encircle, enclose; **los soldados rodearon el edificio** the soldiers surrounded the building; **le rodeó el cuello con los brazos** she threw her arms round his neck.
(b) (SAm) cattle to round up.
2 vi (a) to go round, go by an indirect route; to make a detour.
(b) (fig) to beat about the bush.
3 rodearse vr (a) **— de** to surround oneself with.
(b) to turn round; to turn over (and over), toss and turn.

rodela nf (a) (Hist) buckler, round shield. (b) (Chi) padded ring (for carrying loads on one's head).
rodeo nm (a) long way round, roundabout way; detour.
(b) (in pursuit) dodge; (fig) dodge, stratagem, subterfuge.
(c) (in speech) circumlocution; evasion; **andarse con —s, ir por —s** to beat about the bush; **no andarse con —s, dejarse de —s** to talk straight, stop beating about the bush; **hablar sin —s** to speak out plainly.
(d) (SAm) roundup, rodeo.
rodera nf rut, wheel track.
Rodesia f Rhodesia.
rodesiano 1 adj Rhodesian. **2** nm, **rodesiana** nf Rhodesian.
rodete nm (a) (of hair) coil, bun; (of fat) roll; (of support weight) pad. (b) (of lock) ward. (c) (Tech) articulator.
rodilla nf (a) (Anat) knee; **de —s** kneeling; **caer de —s** to fall on one's knees; **doblar** (or **hincar**) **la —** to kneel down; (fig) to bow, humble oneself, bend the knee (ante to); **estar de —s** to kneel, be kneeling (down); **hincarse de —s, ponerse de —s** to kneel (down); **poner de —s a un país** to bring a country to its knees.
(b) (to support weight) pad.
(c) floorcloth, mop.
rodillazo nm push with the knee; **dar un — a** to knee.
rodillera nf (a) knee guard; kneepad, patch on the knee. (b) baggy part (in knee of trousers). (c) (to support weight) pad.
rodillo nm roller; (Cook) rolling pin; (Typ) ink roller; (of typewriter) cylinder, roller; (for washing) mangle; (Agr) roller; **— pintor** paint roller; **— de vapor** steamroller.
rodillón nm (Col) old man, feeble individual.
rodillona nf (Ven) old maid.
rododendro nm rhododendron.
Rodrigo m 'Roderick; **— el último godo** Roderick, the last of the Goths.
rodrigón nm (Agr) stake, prop, support.
roedor 1 adj (a) (Zool) gnawing. (b) (fig) regret etc gnawing, ever-present, nagging. **2** nm rodent.
roer [2z] vt (a) food to gnaw; to nibble at; bone to gnaw, pick.
(b) metal to corrode, eat away, eat into.
(c) (fig) capital etc to eat into bit by bit.
(d) (fig) (of remorse etc) to gnaw, nag, torment.
rogación nf (a) (Eccl) rogations.
rogar [1h and 1m] **1** vt (a) person to beg; to plead with; thing to ask for, beg for, plead for; **— a uno + infin** to ask someone to + infin, beg someone to + infin; **— que + subj** to ask that . . .; **ruegue a este señor que nos deje en paz** please ask this gentleman to leave us alone.
(b) (Rel) to pray.
2 vi (a) to beg, plead; **hacerse —** to have to be coaxed, be unwilling to agree; **no se hace de —** he doesn't have to be asked twice.
(b) (Rel) to pray.
3 rogarse vr: "**se ruega la mayor puntualidad**" "please be punctual"; "**se ruega no fumar**" "please do not smoke".
rogativas nfpl (Eccl) rogations.
rogatoria nf (SAm) request; pleading.
rojear [1a] vi (a) to redden, turn red; to show red.
(b) to tend towards red.
rojete nm rouge.
rojez nf redness.
rojiblanco adj red-and-white.
rojillo adj (Pol) pink; suspicious, subversive.
rojizo adj reddish; ruddy.
rojo 1 adj (a) red; ruddy; **— cereza** cherry red; **poner — a uno** to make someone blush; **ponerse —** to turn red, blush.
(b) hair red; sandy.
(c) (Pol) red; (in Nationalist parlance in Spain, 1936 and subsequently) Republican.
2 nm (a) red, red colour; **calentar al —** to make red-hot; **la atmósfera está al — vivo** the atmosphere is electric; **la emoción está al — vivo** excitement is at fever pitch.
(b) **— de labios** rouge, lipstick.
(c) (Pol) red; Republican (see **1 c**).
rojura nf redness.
rol nm (a) list, roll; catalogue; (Naut) muster. (b) SAm: Theat and fig) role, part.
rola 1 nf (Ven) police station. **2** nmf (Chi) lout; dimwit (fam).
Rolando m Roland.

rolar [1a] **1** *vt* **(a)** (Arg, Bol, Chi, Per) to touch on (in conversation).
(b) (Arg, Chi, Per) to associate with, be in contact with.
(c) (Mex) to pass from hand to hand.
2 *vi* **(a)** (Naut: *of wind*) to veer round.
(b) (Arg) to be a social climber.
(c) (Bol, Chi) to talk, converse (con with).
Roldán m Roland.
rollista *nmf* (fam) bore.
rollizo *adj* **(a)** *object* round, cylindrical. **(b)** *person* plump; stocky; *child* chubby; *woman* plump, buxom.
rollo 1 *adj* (fam) boring, tedious.
2 *nm* **(a)** (*of cloth, film, paper etc*) roll; (*of rope*) coil; (Hist) scroll; **en —** rolled, rolled up; *log* whole, uncut.
(b) (Cook) rolling pin.
(c) round log, uncut log.
(d) (Cook) roll.
(e) (Anat: fam) roll of fat.
(f) (fam) bore; boring speech; tedious explanation, lengthy justification; sermon; **la conferencia fue un —** the lecture was an awful bore (fam); **¡menudo — nos colocó!** some sermon he gave us!; **iba a soltarnos un —** he was about to start off on a lengthy explanation.
(g) (Bol, RPl) **largar el —** to be sick.
Roma Rome; **— no se construyó en un día** Rome was not built in a day; **por todas partes se va a —** all roads lead to Rome; **revolver — con Santiago** to leave no stone unturned.
romadizo *nm* head cold; catarrh; (PR) rheumatism.
romana *nf* steelyard; **cargar la —** (RPl) to heap the blame on somebody.
romance 1 *adj language* Romance.
2 *nm* **(a)** (Ling) Romance language; Spanish, Spanish language; **hablar en —** (fig) to speak plainly.
(b) (Lit) ballad.
(c) (angl) romance, love affair.
romancear [1a] **1** *vt* to translate into Spanish. **2** *vi* (Chi) **(a)** to waste time chatting. **(b)** to flirt.
romancero *nm* collection of ballads; **el R—** the Spanish ballads (collectively).
románico *adj* **(a)** (Ling) Romance. **(b)** (Archit) Romanesque, Romanic; (*in England*) Norman.
romanizar [1f] **1** *vt* to romanize. **2 romanizarse** *vr* to become romanized.
romano 1 *adj* Roman. **2** *nm*, **romana** *nf* Roman.
románticamente *adv* romantically.
romanticismo *nm* romanticism.
romántico 1 *adj* romantic. **2** *nm* romantic.
romaza *nf* dock, sorrel.
rombal *adj* rhombic.
rombo *nm* rhomb, rhombus.
romboidal *adj* rhomboid.
romboide *nm* rhomboid.
romereante *nmf* (Ec, PR) pilgrim.
romería *nf* **(a)** (Eccl) pilgrimage; gathering at a local shrine; **ir en —** to go on a pilgrimage. **(b)** (fig) trip, excursion; fair, open-air dance; festivities.
romero[1] *nm*, **romera** *nf* pilgrim.
romero[2] *nm* (Bot) rosemary.
romo[1] *adj* **(a)** blunt; *person* snub-nosed. **(b)** (fig) dull, lifeless.
romo[2] *nm* (Ant, Ven) rum.
rompecabezas *nm*, *pl* **rompecabezas (a)** puzzle; riddle; jigsaw (puzzle). **(b)** (fig) puzzle; problem, teaser, headache.
rompedero 1 *adj* breakable, delicate, fragile. **2** *nm* (Arg) **— de cabeza** puzzle, problem.
rompedora-cargadora *nf* (Min) power loader.
rompehielos *nm*, *pl* **rompehielos** icebreaker.
rompehuelgas *nm*, *pl* **rompehuelgas** strikebreaker, blackleg.
rompeolas *nm*, *pl* **rompeolas** breakwater.
rompenueces *nm*, *pl* **rompenueces** nutcrackers.
romper [2a; *ptp* **roto**] **1** *vt* **(a)** *plate, toy etc* to break, smash, shatter; *barrier, fence etc* to break down, break through; to breach; *rope etc* to snap, break; *paper, cloth* to tear (up), rip (up); *mist, clouds* to break through.
(b) *clothing, shoes* to wear out, wear a hole in.
(c) *waves (of breakwater)* to break the force of; (*of ship*) to cleave.
(d) *land* to break (up), plough.
(e) (Mil) *line etc* to break (through); see **fila**.
(f) *continuity, fast, silence, succession etc* to break.
(g) *contract, pact* to break; *friendship, relations* to break off.
(h) — el fuego to open fire; **— las hostilidades** to start hostilities.

2 *vi* **(a)** (*of waves*) to break.
(b) (*of bud*) to open, burst.
(c) (*of war*) to break out.
(d) — la naturaleza to reach puberty; to begin to menstruate.
(e) (*of tooth*) to break through; (*of sun*) to break through, appear, begin to shine; (*of dawn, day*) to break; **— entre** to burst one's way through; **— por** to break through.
(f) — a + *infin* to start (suddenly) to + *infin*; **— a proferir insultos** to begin to pour forth abuse; **— a llorar** to burst into tears; **luego rompió a hacer calor** then it suddenly began to get hot.
(g) — en llanto to burst into tears.
(h) — con uno to fall out with someone, break with someone; **ha roto con su novio** she has broken it off with her fiancé.
(i) de rompe y rasga brash, tearaway, impetuous; full of self-confidence; utterly inconsiderate; **rompe por todo** he presses on regardless (fam).
3 romperse *vr* to break, smash; to snap; to tear, rip; to wear out.
rompiente *nm* **(a)** reef, shoal. **(b) —s** breakers, surf.
rompimiento *nm* **(a)** (*act*) breaking, smashing, shattering; breaching; snapping; tearing.
(b) opening, breach; crack.
(c) (*act: fig*) break (con with); **— de relaciones** breaking-off of relations.
(d) — de hostilidades outbreak of hostilities.
romplón: de — adv (CAm, Mex) suddenly, unexpectedly.
rompopo *nm* (CAm, Mex) eggnog.
Rómulo m Romulus.
ron *nm* rum; **— de laurel, — de malagueta** bay-rum.
ronca *nf* **(a)** (Zool) roar (*of rutting stag*); rutting season. **(b)** (fig) threat; **echar —s** to bully, threaten.
roncadoras *nfpl* (SAm) large spurs.
roncar [1g] *vi* **(a)** to snore. **(b)** (*of stag, sea, wind*) to roar. **(c)** to threaten, bully; (Arg) to be bossy, domineer; to be jealous of one's authority.
roncear [1a] **1** *vt* **(a)** to cajole, pester, keep on at. **(b)** (SAm)=**ronzar**[1]. **(c)** (SAm) to keep watch on, spy on. **2** *vi* to work (etc) unwillingly; to slack, kill time.
roncería *nf* **(a)** unwillingness. **(b)** cajolery.
roncero *adj* **(a)** (Naut) slow, slow-moving, sluggish.
(b) *person* unwilling; slack, slow; **estar —** to find reasons for shirking work (etc).
(c) *person* grumpy, grouchy (fam).
(d) *person* smooth, smarmy (fam).
(e) (CAm, Col) sly.
ronco *adj person* hoarse; *voice* throaty, husky; *sound* harsh, raucous.
roncón *adj* (Col, Ven) boastful.
roncha *nf* bruise, weal, welt; (*of sting*) swelling.
ronda *nf* **(a)** (*esp* Hist) night patrol, night watch; (*of policeman*) beat; (*persons*) watch, patrol, guard; **ir de —** to go the rounds, do one's round.
(b) (Mus) group of serenaders.
(c) (*of drinks etc, negotiations*) round; **pagar una —** to pay for a round.
(d) (Cards) hand, round, game; (*in competition*) round.
(e) (Mil) sentry walk (*on wall*).
(f) outer road, ring road.
(g) (Arg, Chi) ring-a-ring-a-roses.
(h) (Arg) **en —** in a ring, in a circle.
rondalla *nf* **(a)** band of street musicians. **(b)** fiction, invention.
rondana *nf* (SAm) pulley; winch.
rondar [1a] **1** *vt* **(a)** (Mil etc) to patrol; to inspect, go the rounds of; (fig) to haunt, frequent, hang about; **— la calle a una joven** to patrol up and down (*or* hang about) the street where a girl lives.
(b) *person* to hang round; to harass, pester; *girl* to court.
(c) *light (of moth)* to flutter round, fly about.
(d) (fig) **me está rodando un catarro** I've got a cold hanging about.
2 *vi* (*of police*) to patrol, go on patrol, go the rounds; (fig) to prowl round, go up and down, hang about; to roam the streets after dark; (Mus) to go serenading.
rondín[1] *nm* (Bol, Chi) policeman; night watchman.
rondín[2] *nm* (Bol, Ec, Per) harmonica.
rondó *nm* (Lit) rondeau; (Mus) rondo.
rondón: de — adv unexpectedly; unannounced, without warning; **entrar de —** to rush in.
ronquear [1a] *vi* to be hoarse, talk hoarsely.
ronquedad *nf*, **ronquera** *nf* hoarseness; huskiness.
ronquido *nm* snore; snoring; (fig) roar(ing); snort.
ronronear [1a] *vi* to purr.
ronroneo *nm* purr.

ronzal nm halter.
ronzar[1] [1f] vt (Naut) to move with levers, lever along.
ronzar[2] [1f] **1** vt to munch, crunch, eat noisily. **2** vi to crunch.
roña 1 nf **(a)** (Vet: on sheep) scab, (on dog) mange; (Bot) rust.
 (b) crust of dirt, filth, grime; (on metal) rust.
 (c) (Bot) pine bark.
 (d) (fig) moral danger, contagion.
 (e) (fig) meanness, stinginess.
 (f) stratagem.
 (g) (Cu, PR) envy; rancour; (Mex) grudge, ill will.
 (h) (Col) feigned illness.
 (i) jugar a la — to play for fun, play without money stakes.
 2 nmf (fam) mean person.
 3 adj (Arg, CR) mean, stingy.
roñería nf meanness, stinginess.
roñoso adj **(a)** (Vet) scabby, mangy.
 (b) dirty, filthy, grimy; rusty; (fig) wretched, broken down, useless.
 (c) (fig) mean, stingy.
 (d) (Col, Ec) rough, unpolished, coarse.
 (e) (Ec) tricky.
 (f) (Mex, PR) bitter, hostile.
ropa nf clothes, clothing; dress; **— blanca** linen; **— blanca de mujer** lingerie; **— de cama** bed linen, bedclothes; **— hecha** ready-made clothes; **— interior** underwear, underclothes; **— lavada, — por lavar** washing; **— de mesa** table linen; **— planchada** ironing; **— sucia** dirty clothes, washing; **— usada** used clothing, secondhand clothes; **a quema —** point-blank; **hay — tendida** be careful what you say, walls have ears; **guardar la —** to speak cautiously; **nadar y guardar la —** to be able to do two things well at the same time; **tentarse la —** to think long and hard (before doing anything); **no tocar la — a uno** not to touch a hair of someone's head, keep one's hands off someone; see **ligero** etc.
ropaje nm **(a)** gown, robes, ceremonial garb; **—s** (Eccl) vestments.
 (b) (fig) drapes, drapery.
 (c) (pej) odd garb; heavy clothing, excessive amount of clothes.
 (d) (Lit) trappings, rhetorical adornments.
ropavejero nm old-clothes dealer.
ropería nf **(a)** clothier's, clothes shop. **(b)** clothing trade.
ropero 1 adj for clothes, clothes (attr); **armario —** wardrobe, clothes cupboard.
 2 nm **(a)** clothier, dealer in ready-made clothing.
 (b) wardrobe, clothes cupboard.
ropón nm **(a)** long robe; loose coat, housecoat. **(b)** (Col, Chi, Ven) woman's riding habit.
roque nm (Chess) rook, castle.
roquedal nm rocky place.
roqueño adj **(a)** rocky. **(b)** hard as rock, rock-like, flinty.
rorro nm **(a)** (fam) baby, kid (fam). **(b)** (Mex) fair blue-eyed person.
Rosa f Rose.
rosa 1 nf **(a)** (Bot) rose; **— almizcleña** musk rose; **no hay — sin espinas** there's no rose without a thorn; **un cutis como una —** a skin as soft as silk; **estar como una —** to be fresh and clean; to feel as fresh as a daisy; **estar como las propias —s** to feel entirely at ease.
 (b) — de —, color de — pink, rose, rose-coloured; **vestidos color de —** pink dresses; see also **color**.
 (c) (Anat) red spot, red mark, birth mark.
 (d) (Archit) rose window.
 (e) — náutica, — de los vientos compass (card), compass rose.
 (f) —s popcorn.
 2 adj pink, rose, rose-coloured.
rosáceo adj =**rosado** 1.
rosado 1 adj pink, rosy, roseate. **2** nm rosé.
rosal nm **(a)** rosebush, rosetree; **— silvestre** wild rose, dog rose; **— de China, — japonés** japonica. **(b)** (Chi, PR, RPl) rosebed, rosegarden.
rosaleda nf rosebed, rosegarden.
rosario nm **(a)** rosary; chaplet, beads; **rezar el —** to say one's rosary, tell one's beads.
 (b) (Agr) chain of buckets (of a waterwheel).
 (c) (fam) backbone.
 (d) (fig) string, series; **un — de maldiciones** a string of curses.
 (e) (Archit) beading.
rosbif nm roast beef.
rosca nf **(a)** coil, spiral, ring; (Cook) ring, ring-shaped

roll; **estaba hecho una —** he was all curled up in a ball.
 (b) (of screw) thread; (of spiral) turn; **hacer la — a uno** (fam) to suck up to someone (fam); **pasarse de — (screw)** to have a crossed thread; (fig) to go too far, overdo it.
 (c) (Anat etc) swelling; (Anat) roll of fat.
 (d) (Chi) pad (for carrying loads on the head).
 (e) (Chi) circle (of card players).
 (f) (Arg, Chi) noisy argument, general set-to (fam); uproar, commotion.
 (g) (Univ sl) **tirarse una —** to plough (sl).
rosedal nm (Arg) =**rosaleda**.
Rosellón m Roussillon.
róseo adj rosy, roseate.
roseta nf **(a)** (Bot) small rose.
 (b) (Sport etc) rosette.
 (c) (of watering can) rose, nozzle.
 (d) (Anat) red spot (on the cheek).
 (e) (Arg, Mex) prickly fruit, prickly seed, burr.
 (f) (Per, RPl) rowel (of a spur).
 (g) —s (Cook) popcorn.
rosetón nm **(a)** (Archit) rose; rose window. **(b)** (Sport etc) rosette. **(c)** (Aut) cloverleaf (junction).
rosicler nm dawn pink, rosy tint of dawn.
rosita nf **(a)** (Bot) small rose. **(b)** (Chi) earring. **(c) de — (Bol, Mex)** free, gratis; **andar de — (Arg, Mex)** to be out of work. **(d) —s** (Cook) popcorn.
rosquero adj (Chi) quarrelsome.
rosquete nm **(a)** (CAm, Per) bun. **(b)** (Per) queer (fam), homosexual.
rosquilla nf **(a)** (of smoke) ring. **(b)** (Ent) grub, small caterpillar.
rosticería nf (Mex) =**rotisería**.
rostro nm **(a)** (Anat) countenance, face (for idioms and phrases, compare **cara**). **(b)** (Naut) beak. **(c)** (Zool, Hist etc) rostrum.
rotación nf rotation; turn, revolution; (Tech: of production etc) turnover; **— de cultivos** rotation of crops; **— de la tierra** rotation of the earth.
rotariano adj and nm (SAm) =**rotario**.
rotario 1 adj Rotarian. **2** nm Rotarian.
rotativo 1 adj rotary, revolving; press rotary. **2** nm newspaper.
rotería nf (Chi) **(a)** common people, plebs. **(b)** dirty trick; coarse remark, coarse action.
rotisería nf (Arg, Mex: gall) grillroom, steak restaurant.
roto 1 ptp of **romper**.
 2 adj **(a)** broken, smashed; dress etc torn; ragged; life shattered, destroyed; wasted.
 (b) (fig) debauched, dissipated.
 3 nm **(a)** (in dress) hole, torn piece, worn part; **nunca falta un — para un descosido** you can always find someone else just as contemptible as he (etc) is.
 (b) (Chi) very poor person, down-and-out; (iro) fop, toff (fam).
 (c) (Arg, Per) nickname given to a Chilean.
 (d) (Ec) half-breed.
rotograbado nm rotogravure.
rotonda nf (Archit) rotunda; circular gallery; (Rail) engine shed, roundhouse.
rotor nm rotor.
rotoso adj **(a)** (SAm) ragged, shabby. **(b)** (Chi) low-class, common.
rótula nf **(a)** (Anat) kneecap. **(b)** (Mech) ball-and-socket joint.
rotulación nf **(a)** labelling; lettering. **(b)** (as profession) sign painting.
rotular [1a] vt object to label, put a label (or ticket etc) on; map etc to letter, inscribe; letter, document to head, entitle.
rotulata nf **(a)** labels, inscriptions etc (collectively).
 (b) (fam) =**rótulo**.
rotulista nm sign painter.
rótulo nm (on goods) label, ticket, tag; (on specimen etc) label; (on document) heading, title; (on map etc) lettering; inscription; (Comm) sign; placard, poster.
rotundamente adv deny flatly, roundly; agree etc emphatically.
rotundidad nf **(a)** rotundity. **(b)** forthrightness. **(c)** well-rounded character, expressiveness.
rotundo adj **(a)** round. **(b)** denial etc flat, round, forthright; **me dio un "sí" —** he gave me an emphatic "yes". **(c)** style well-rounded, expressive.
rotura nf **(a)** (act) breaking etc (see **rompimiento** (a)). **(b)** opening, breach; crack; (in cloth) tear, rip, hole. **(c)** (act: fig) break (con with); **— de relaciones** breaking-off of relations.
roturación nf breaking-up, ploughing.
roturar [1a] vt to break up, plough.
roya nf (Bot) rust, blight.

roza *nf* (a) (*Archit*) groove, hollow (*in a wall*). (b) (*Prov, Chi, Mex*) weeds, brushwood. (c) (*Col*) planting in newly-broken ground.

rozado *adj* worn, grazed.

rozador *nm* (*Ven*) machete.

rozadura *nf* mark of rubbing, chafing mark; (*Med*) abrasion, graze, sore place.

rozagante *adj* (a) *dress etc* showy, gorgeous; striking. (b) (*fig*) proud.

rozamiento *nm* (a) rubbing, chafing; (*Mech*) friction; wear. (b) (*fam*) **tener un — con uno** to have a slight disagreement with someone.

rozar [1f] **1** *vt* (a) to rub (on), rub against; to scrape (on); to chafe; (*Mech*) to grate on, cause friction with; (*Med*) to chafe, graze; (*of vehicle etc*) to graze, shave, touch lightly; *surface etc* (*of bird*) to skim; **— a uno al pasar** to brush past someone.
(b) *dress* to rumple, crumple; to dirty.
(c) (*fig*) to touch on, border on; **es cuestión que roza la política** it's a question which partly concerns politics.
(d) (*Archit*) to make a groove (*or* hollow) in.
(e) (*Agr*) *grass* to graze, crop, nibble.
(f) (*Agr*) *land* to clear.
2 *vi* (a) **— en = 1** (a).
(b) **= con** (*fig*) **= 1** (c).
3 rozarse *vr* (a) **— el cuello** to rub (*or* wear, chafe) one's collar; **— los puños** to graze one's knuckles.
(b) to get worn, get rubbed (*etc*).
(c) (*fam*) to trip over one's own feet.
(d) (*fam*) **— con** to hobnob with, rub shoulders with, mix with.
(e) **— en un sonido** to stutter over a sound, have trouble pronouncing a sound.

roznar[1] [1a] *vti* =**ronzar**.

roznar[2] [1a] *vi* to bray.

roznido *nm* bray(ing).

Ruán Rouen.

ruana *nf* (*Col, Ven*) peasant poncho.

ruanetas *nmf, pl* **ruanetas** (*Col*) peasant.

ruano *adj and nm* = **roano**.

rubéola *nf* German measles.

rubí *nm* ruby; (*of watch*) jewel.

rubia *nf* (a) blonde; **— de bote, — de frasco** peroxide blonde; **— platino** platinum blonde. (b) (*Aut*) shooting brake, station wagon. (c) (*sl*) one-peseta coin.

rubiales *nmf, pl* **rubiales** (*fam*) blond(e), fair-headed person.

Rubicón *m* Rubicon; **pasar el — to** cross the Rubicon.

rubicundo *adj* (a) ruddy, rubicund. (b) reddish.

rubio *adj* (a) *hair, person* fair, fair-haired, blond(e); *animal, fur etc* light-coloured, golden. (b) **tabaco — Virginian tobacco.

rublo *nm* rouble.

rubor *nm* (a) bright red. (b) (*on face*) blush, flush; **causar — a una** to make someone blush (*also fig*). (c) (*fig*) bashfulness.

ruborizado *adj* blushing; flushed.

ruborizar [1f] **1** *vt* to cause to blush, make blush (*also fig*). **2 ruborizarse** *vr* to blush, flush, redden (*de at*).

ruboroso *adj* (a) **ser —** to have a tendency to blush, blush easily. (b) **estar —** to blush, be blushing, have a flush; (*fig*) to feel bashful.

rúbrica *nf* (a) red mark. (b) flourish (*added to a signature*). (c) title, heading, rubric; **bajo la — de** under the heading of. **de — = de rigor**.

rubricar [1g] *vt* to sign with a flourish; (*loosely*) to sign and seal.

rubro *nm* (a) (*SAm*) heading, title; (*Typ*) headline; section heading.
(b) (*Chi, RPl*) book-keeping entry.
(c) (*Chi, RPl*) section, department (*of a business*).
(d) (*Arg*) **— social** trading name, firm's name.

ruca *nf* (a) (*Arg, Chi*) hut, cabin. (b) (*Mex*) old maid.

rucio **1** *adj* *horse* grey, silver-grey; *person* grey-haired; (*Chi*) fair, blond(e). **2** *nm* grey (*horse*).

ruco *adj* (*CAm*) worn-out, useless.

rucho *adj* (*Col*) (a) rough. (b) *fruit* overripe.

ruda *nf* rue.

rudamente *adv* simply, plainly; (*pej*) roughly, coarsely.

rudeza *nf* (a) simplicity; plainness; (*pej*) roughness, coarseness, commonness. (b) stupidity (*also* **— de entendimiento**).

rudimental *adj*, **rudimentario** *adj* rudimentary.

rudimento *nm* (a) (*Anat etc*) rudiment. (b) **—s** rudiments.

rudo *adj* (a) *wood etc* rough; unpolished, unworked. (b) (*Mech*) part stiff.

(c) *person* simple, uncultured; plain; (*pej*) rough, coarse, common.
(d) *blow* hard.
(e) (*in intelligence*) simple, stupid.

rueca *nf* distaff.

rueda *nf* (a) (*Mech etc*) wheel; (*of furniture*) roller, castor; **— de agua, — hidráulica** waterwheel; **— de alfarero** potter's wheel; **—s de aterrizaje** (*Aer*) landing wheels; **— de atrás** rear wheel, back wheel; **— de cadena** sprocket wheel; **— dentada** cog, cog wheel; gear wheel; **— de la fortuna** wheel of fortune; **— libre** freewheel; **— de molino** millwheel; **— de paletas** paddle wheel; **— de recambio** spare wheel; **— de trinquete** ratchet wheel; **ir sobre —s** (*fam*) to go smoothly; to go with a swing.
(b) (*of objects, persons*) circle, ring; **en — in** a ring; **— de prensa** press conference.
(c) (*Cook*) slice, round.
(d) (*of tournament*) round.
(e) (*Hist*) rack.
(f) (*Fish*) sunfish.
(g) (*Orn: of peacock*) spread tail; **hacer la — to** spread its tail; **hacer la — a una** to court someone; **hacer la — a uno** (*fig*) to play up to someone, ingratiate oneself with someone.

ruedecilla *nf* small wheel; roller, castor.

ruedero *nm* wheelwright.

ruedo *nm* (a) turn, rotation. (b) edge, circumference; border; (*of skirt*) hem, bottom. (c) (*Taur*) bullring, arena. (d) (round) mat.

ruego *nm* request, entreaty; **a — de** at the request of; **accediendo a los —s de** . . . in response to the requests of . . .; **"—s y preguntas"** (*on agenda*) "any other business".

rufián *nm* (a) pimp, pander. (b) lout, hooligan; scoundrel.

rufiancete *nm* villain, rogue.

rufianesca *nf* criminal underworld.

rufianesco *adj* (a) pimping, pandering. (b) loutish; villainous.

rufo *adj* (a) sandy-haired, red-haired; curly-haired. (b) (*fam*) smug, self satisfied; cocky (*fam*), boastful.

rugbista *nm* rugby player.

rugby ['rugbi] *nm* rugby.

rugido *nm* roar; bellow; howl; **— de dolor** howl of pain; **— de tripas** intestinal rumblings, collywobbles (*fam*).

rugir [3c] *vi* (*of lion etc*) to roar; (*of bull*) to bellow; (*of sea*) to roar; (*of storm, wind*) to roar, howl, rage; (*of person*) to roar; (*of stomach*) to rumble; **— de dolor** to roar with pain, howl with pain.

rugoso *adj* wrinkled, creased; ridged; rough.

ruibarbo *nm* rhubarb.

ruido *nm* (a) noise, sound; din, row; noisiness; **— de fondo** background noise; **sin —** quietly, soundlessly, without making a noise; **no hagas —** don't make a sound; **no hagas tanto —** don't make such a noise; **mucho — y pocas nueces** much ado about nothing; **es más el — que las nueces** there's a lot of talk but nothing much gets done.
(b) (*fig*) commotion, stir; fuss; row, rumpus (*fam*); outcry; **hacer —, meter — to** cause a stir, be a sensation; to have repercussions; to cause an outcry; **quitarse de —s** to keep out of trouble.

ruidosamente *adv* (a) noisily, loudly. (b) (*fig*) sensationally.

ruidoso *adj* (a) noisy, loud. (b) (*fig*) sensational; much talked-of.

ruin **1** *adj* (a) *person* mean, despicable, low, contemptible; *treatment etc* mean, shabby; heartless, callous.
(b) mean, stingy.
(c) (*in size*) small, weak.
(d) *animal* vicious.
2 *nm* mean person (*etc*); **en nombrando al — de Roma, luego asoma** talk of the devil!; well, look who's here!

ruina *nf* (a) (*Archit etc*) ruin; **—s** ruins, remains; **estar hecho una —** to be a wreck; to be a shadow of one's former self.
(b) (*Archit: act*) collapse; **amenazar — to** threaten to collapse, be about to fall down.
(c) (*fig*) ruin, destruction; (*of empire*) fall, decline; (*of person*) ruin, downfall; (*of hopes*) destruction; **será mi —** it will be the ruin of me; **la empresa le llevó a la —** the venture ruined him (financially).

ruindad *nf* (a) (*quality*) meanness, lowness; shabbiness; callousness. (b) (*act*) mean act, low trick, piece of villainy.

ruinoso *adj* (a) (*Archit*) ruinous; tumbledown. (b) (*Fin etc*) ruinous, disastrous.

ruiseñor *nm* nightingale.

rula *nf* (a) roulette. (b) (*Col, Pan*) hunting knife.

rulemán *nm* (*Arg*) ball bearing, roller bearing.
rulenco, rulengo *adj* (*Chi*) weak, underdeveloped.
ruleta *nf* roulette.
ruletero *nm* (*Mex*) taxi driver.
rulo[1] *nm* (a) ball, round mass. (b) roller; (*Cook*) rolling pin. (c) hair-curler. (d) (*Arg*) (natural) curl.
rulo[2] *nm* (*Chi*) well-watered ground.
rulota *nf* (*gall*) caravan, trailer (*US*).
ruma *nf* (*SAm*) heap, pile.
Rumania *f* Rumania.
rumano 1 *adj* Rumanian. **2** *nm*, **rumana** *nf* Rumanian. **3** *nm* (*language*) Rumanian.
rumba[1] *nf* (a) (*Mus*) rumba. (b) (*Ant*) party, celebration, spree (*fam*).
rumba[2] *nf* (*Chi*) =**ruma**.
rumbar [1a] **1** *vt* (*Col*, *Hond*) to throw. **2** *vi* (a) (*Col*) to buzz. (b) (*Col*, *Chi*) to follow a direction; to get one's bearings. **3 rumbarse** *vr* (*Col*) to go off.
rumbeador *nm* (*Bol*, *RPl*) pathfinder, tracker, man with expert knowledge of the countryside.
rumbear [1a] *vi* (a) (*SAm*: *Mus*) to dance the rumba.
  (b) (*SAm*) to follow a direction; to find one's way, get one's bearings.
  (c) (*Ant*, *Guat*, *Mex*, *Per*) to have a party, carouse, go on the spree (*fam*).
  (d) (*Mex*) to open up a forest path.
rumbero 1 *adj* (a) (*Col*) knowledgeable about the countryside, expert in pathfinding.
  (b) (*Ant*) merry, fond of carousing.
  2 *nm* (*Col*) pathfinder, guide; (*Per*) river guide.
rumbo[1] *nm* (a) route, direction; (*Naut*) course; bearing; **con — a** in the direction of; **ir con — a** to be heading for, be going in the direction of, be bound for; (*Naut*) to be bound for; **corregir el —** to correct one's course; **hacer — a** (*or* **hacia**) to head for; **poner — a** (*Naut*) to set a course for; **ir al —** find one's way by guesswork.
  (b) (*fig*) course of events; line of conduct; **— nuevo** new departure; **los nuevos —s de la estrategia occidental** the new lines of western strategy; **tomar — nuevo** to set off on a different tack, change one's approach; **los acontecimientos vienen tomando un — sensacional** events are taking a sensational turn.
  (c) (*fig*) generosity, lavishness; lavish display; showiness, pomp; **de mucho —** =**rumboso**; **viajar con —** to travel in style, travel in state.
  (d) (*CAm*) party, binge (*sl*).
  (e) (*Arg*) cut on the head.
rumbo[2] *nm* (*Col*) hummingbird.
rumbón *adj* (*fam*) =**rumboso**.
rumboso *adj* (a) *person* generous, lavish; free-spending. (b) *present* lavish; *wedding etc* big, splendid, slap-up (*fam*).
rumia *nf*, **rumiación** *nf* rumination.
rumiante 1 *adj* ruminant. **2** *nm* ruminant.

ruminar [1b] **1** *vt* (a) to chew.
  (b) (*fig*) *matter* to chew over; to brood over, ponder (over).
  2 *vi* (a) to chew the cud.
  (b) (*fig*) to ruminate, brood, ponder; (*pej*) to take too long to make up one's mind.
rumor *nm* (a) murmur, mutter; confused noise, low sound; (*of voices*) buzz; (*of water*) murmur. (b) (*fig*) rumour.
rumorearse [1a] *vr*: **se rumorea que . . . it is rumoured that . . .**
rumoreo *nm* murmur(ing).
rumoroso *adj* full of sounds; *stream etc* murmuring, musical.
runa *nf* rune.
runcho *adj* (a) (*Col*) stupid. (b) (*Pan*) mean.
rundir [3a] (*Mex*) **1** *vt* to keep; to hide, put away. **2** *vi* to become drowsy. **3 rundirse** *vr* to fall fast asleep.
rundún *nm* (*Arg*) hummingbird.
runfla *nm* (*SAm*) mass, lot, heap; crowd; gang.
rúnico *adj* runic.
runrún *nm* (a) sound of voices, buzz of conversation, murmur. (b) (*fig*) rumour, buzz (*fam*). (c) (*of machine etc*) whirr.
runrunearse [1a] *vr*: **se runrunea que . . . it is rumoured that . . .**
runruneo *nm* =**runrún** (a).
ruñir [3h] *vti* (*Col*, *Mex*, *PR*, *Ven*) =**roer**.
rupestre *adj* rock (*attr*); **pintura —** cave painting; **planta —** rock plant.
rupia *nf* rupee.
ruptura *nf* (*fig*) rupture; split; (*of contract*) breaking; (*of relations*) breaking-off.
rural *adj* rural, country (*attr*).
Rusia *f* Russia; **— Soviética** Soviet Russia.
ruso 1 *adj* Russian. **2** *nm*, **rusa** *nf* Russian. **3** *nm* (*language*) Russian.
rústica *nf*: **libro en —** paperback (book).
rusticidad *nf* (a) rusticity, rural character. (b) coarseness, uncouthness; crudity; unmannerliness.
rústico 1 *adj* (a) rustic, rural, country (*attr*). (b) (*pej*) coarse, uncouth; crude; unmannerly. **2** *nm* rustic, peasant, yokel.
ruta *nf* route; (*fig*) course, course of action; **— aérea** air route, airway.
rutilante *adj* (*lit*) shining, sparkling, glowing.
rutilar [1a] *vi* (*lit*) to shine, sparkle, glow.
rutina *nf* routine; **— diaria** daily routine, daily round; **por —** as a matter of course, as a matter of routine; (*fig*) from force of habit.
rutinariamente *adv* in a routine way; unimaginatively.
rutinario *adj* (a) routine; ordinary, everyday. (b) *person* ordinary; unimaginative.
rutinero 1 *adj* who sticks to routine; ordinary; unimaginative. **2** *nm* person who sticks to routine; ordinary sort, unimaginative person.

S

sábado *nm* Saturday; (*Jewish*) Sabbath; **S— de Gloria, S— Santo** Easter Saturday; **hacer — to** have a good cleanup, do the weekly clean.

sábalo *nm* (*Fish*) shad.

sabana *nf* (*SAm*) savannah.

sábana *nf* (a) sheet; (*Eccl*) altar cloth; **— de agua** (*fig*) sheet of rain; **estirarse más de lo que dan de sí las —s** to bite off more than one can chew, over-reach oneself; **se le pegan las —s** he gets up late.

(b) (*sl*) 1000-*peseta* note.

sabandija *nf* (a) bug, insect, creepy-crawly (*fam*), creature; **—s** bugs, vermin. (b) (*fig*) wretch, louse.

sabanear [1a] **1** *vt* (a) (*CAm*) to catch.

(b) (*CAm*) to flatter.

(c) (*Guat, Ven*) to pursue.

2 *vi* (*SAm*) to travel over a plain; to round up cattle on the savannah, scour the plain for cattle.

sabanero 1 *adj* (*SAm*) plain (*attr*), savannah (*attr*); of (*or* from) the plains. **2** *nm* (a) (*SAm*) plainsman.

(b) (*CAm*) bully, thug.

sabanilla *nf* small sheet, piece of cloth; (*Eccl*) altar cloth; (*Chi*) bedspread.

sabañón *nm* chilblain.

sabara *nf* (*Ven*) light mist, haze.

sabatario 1 *adj* sabbatarian. **2** *nm*, **sabataria** *nf* sabbatarian.

sabateño *nm* (*Ven*) boundary stone.

sabático *adj* (*Rel*) sabbatical.

sabedor *adj*: **ser — de** to know about; to be aware of.

sabelotodo *nm* (*fam*) know-all.

saber [2n] **1** *vti* (a) (*general sense*) to know; **— de** to know about, be aware of; to know; **desde hace 6 meses no sabemos nada de él** we haven't heard from him for 6 months, it's 6 months since we had news of him; **lo sé** I know; **sin —lo yo** without my knowledge; **hacer — algo a uno** to inform someone of something, let someone know about something.

(b) (*in past tenses, freq*) to find out, learn; to hear, get to know; **cuando lo supe** when I heard about it; **lograron — el secreto** they managed to learn the secret.

(c) (*phrases and idioms*) **a —** namely; **a — dónde lo tiene guardado** I wonder if he really has got it hidden away; **a — si realmente lo compró** I wonder whether he really did buy it; **es a —** namely, that is to say; **¡haberlo sabido!** if only I'd known!; **¡yo qué sé!, ¡qué sé yo!** how should I know!, search me! (*fam*); **demasiado sé que . . .** I know only too well that . . .; **que yo sepa** as far as I know; **que sepamos** as far as we know; **ya lo sabía yo** I thought as much; **un no sé qué** a certain something; **un no sé qué de afectado** a certain (element of) affectation; **nos sirvió no sé qué vino** he gave us some wine or other; **¿tú qué sabes?** what do you know about it?; **vete a —** your guess is as good as mine; **¡vete a — de dónde ha venido!** goodness only knows where he came from!; **cualquiera sabe** si . . . it's anybody's guess whether . . .; **¿sabe?** (*fam*) you know?, you know what I mean?; **costó muy caro, ¿sabe Vd?** it was very dear, you know; **¿quién sabe?** who knows?, who can tell?; **who's to say?; sepa Vd, para que lo sepa** let me tell you, just for your information; *see* **cuánto, más, convenir, Briján** *etc.*

(d) **— + *infin*** to know how to + *infin*, can + *infin*; **sé conducir** I can drive, I know how to drive; **¿sabes nadar?** can you swim?; **tiene que — contenerse** he must know how to control himself, he must be able to control himself.

(e) **— + *infin*** (*verbs of motion*): **— ir a un sitio** to know one's way to a place; **no sabe todavía andar por la ciudad** he still doesn't know his way about the town.

(f) (*SAm*) **— + *infin*** to be in the habit of + *ger*; **no sabe venir por aquí** he doesn't usually come

this way, he's not in the habit of coming along here.

2 *vi*: **— a** to taste of, taste like; (*fig*) to smack of; **esto sabe a queso** this tastes of cheese; **esto sabe mal, sabe a demonio(s)** this tastes awful (*fam*); **le sabe mal que otro la saque a bailar** it upsets him that anybody else should ask her to dance, he doesn't like other people dancing with her.

3 saberse *vr* (a) **se sabe que . . .** it is known that . . ., we know that . . .; **no se sabe** nobody knows; **¿se puede — si . . .?** may one inquire whether . . .?; **¿quién es Vd, si puedo —?** who are you, may I ask?; **tiene que perder sépase cuánto tiempo para recuperarlo** he has to waste goodness knows how much time getting it back.

(b) **se supo que . . .** it was learnt that . . ., it was discovered that . . .; **por fin se supo el secreto** finally the secret was revealed.

4 *nm* knowledge, learning; **según mi leal — y entender** to the best of my knowledge, as far as I can honestly tell.

sabiamente *adv* (a) learnedly; expertly. (b) wisely, sensibly.

sabichoso *adj* (*Ant*) = **sabihondo**.

sabidillo *nm*, **sabidilla** *nf* (*fam*) know-all.

sabido 1 *ptp* of **saber; es — que . . .** it is well known that . . .; **como es —** as we know, as is well known.

2 *adj* (a) = **consabido**.

(b) (*iro*) highly knowledgeable, learned.

(c) **de —** for sure, certainly.

(d) (*Col*) lively.

sabiduría *nf* wisdom; learning, knowledge; **— popular** popular knowledge; folklore.

sabiendas: a — *adv* knowingly; consciously, deliberately; **a — de que . . .** knowing full well that . . ., in the full knowledge that . . .

sabihondo 1 *adj* know-all. **2** *nm*, **sabihonda** *nf* know-all, self-proclaimed expert; smart-aleck.

sabio 1 *adj* (a) *person* (*in a subject*) learned; expert; (*iro*) know-all.

(b) *person* (*in acting*) wise, sensible, judicious.

(c) *act, decision etc* wise, sensible.

(d) *animal* trained.

2 *nm*, **sabia** *nf* learned man, learned woman; wise person; scholar, expert, savant; (*Hist*) sage; **¡hay que escuchar al —!** (*iro*) just listen to the professor!

sablazo *nm* (a) sword wound; slash with a sword.

(b) (*fam*) sponging (*fam*); **dar un —, pegar un —** to make a touch (*sl; de* for); **dar un — a uno** to touch someone for a loan (*sl*); **vivir de —s** to live by sponging (*fam*).

sable[1] *nm* sabre, cutlass.

sable[2] *nm* (*Her*) sable.

sablear [1a] *vi* (*fam*) to live by sponging (*fam*); to ask for a loan.

sablista *nmf* (*fam*) sponger (*fam*), cadger.

sabor *nm* taste, flavour; savour, savouriness; (*fig*) flavour; **con — a queso** with a cheese flavour(ing), cheese-flavoured; **con ligero — arcaico** with a slightly archaic flavour (to it); **sin —** tasteless; **le deja a uno mal — de boca** (*fig*) it leaves a nasty taste in the mouth.

saborcillo *nm* slight taste.

saborear [1a] **1** *vt* (a) to savour, relish (the savour of); to taste; to enjoy.

(b) to flavour, add a flavour to.

(c) (*fig*) to relish, enjoy; **— el triunfo** to enjoy one's triumph, relish one's victory (to the full).

2 saborearse *vr* (a) to smack one's lips (in anticipation).

(b) **— algo** (*fig*) to relish the thought of something.

saborete *nm* slight taste.

sabotaje *nm* sabotage.

saboteador nm saboteur.
sabotear [1a] vt to sabotage (also fig).
Saboya f Savoy.
sabré etc see **saber**.
sabrosera nf (CAm) tasty thing, delicacy.
sabroso adj (a) food tasty, delicious; nice, rich.
   (b) (Cook) too salty.
   (c) (fig) lecture etc solid, meaty.
   (d) (fig) story etc salty, racy, daring.
   (e) (Col, Ven) lovely, nice, pleasant.
   (f) (Mex, Per, PR, SD) talkative.
sabrosón adj (a) (SAm)=**sabroso** (a). (b) (Cu, Per, PR, Ven) talkative.
sabrosura nf (SAm) (a) tastiness. (b) pleasantness, delightfulness, sweetness; delight, enjoyment.
sabueso nm (a) (Zool) bloodhound. (b) (fig) sleuth.
saburra nf coat, fur (on tongue etc).
saca[1] nf (a) big sack; — de correo(s) mailbag. (b) (SAm) herd of cattle.
saca[2] nf taking out; withdrawal; (Comm) export; estar de — (Comm) to be on sale; (fig) to be at the right age to marry.
sacabocados nm, pl **sacabocados** (Tech) punch.
sacabotas nm, pl **sacabotas** bootjack.
sacabuche nm sackbut.
sacaclavos nm, pl **sacaclavos** nail-puller, pincers.
sacacorchos nm, pl **sacacorchos** corkscrew.
sacacuartos nm, pl **sacacuartos**=**sacadineros**.
sacada nf (Arg, Col, Per)=**sacadura**.
sacadera nf (Fish) landing net.
sacadineros nm, pl **sacadineros** (a) cheap trinket. (b) money-wasting spectacle, worthless sideshow (etc), small-time racket. (c) (person) cheat.
sacador nm (Tennis) server.
sacadura nf (Col, Chi, Per) extraction, removal.
sacafaltas nmf, pl **sacafaltas** faultfinder.
sacamanchas nm, pl **sacamanchas** cleaning material.
sacamuelas nm, pl **sacamuelas** (hum) dentist.
sacapuntas nm, pl **sacapuntas** pencil sharpener.
sacar [1g] vt (a) (general sense) to take out, get out; to pull out, draw out, extract; (Chem) to extract; coal etc to mine, bring up; (from pocket etc) to get out; weapon to draw; money (from bank) to draw out, withdraw; (from list etc) to remove, exclude; to except.
   (b) (general and fig sense) to get (out); — una información a uno to get information out of someone; los datos están sacados de 2 libros the data is taken from 2 books; — un secreto a uno to get (or worm) a secret out of someone; ¿de dónde has sacado esa idea? where did you get that idea?; no conseguirán —le nada they'll get nothing out of him; lo que se saca de todo esto es que ... what I gather from all this is that . . .
   (c) stain etc to remove, get out, get off.
   (d) (Tennis) to serve; (Football) to throw in.
   (e) part of body to stick out, put out, thrust out; — la barbilla to stick one's chin out; — la lengua to put one's tongue out; — la mano (Aut etc) to put one's hand out.
   (f) garment (Sew) to let out.
   (g) clothing etc (esp SAm) to take off; — la funda a un fusil to take the cover off a rifle.
   (h) tickets etc to get; reservations to make, book.
   (i) answer, solution to reach, obtain, get; conclusion to draw.
   (j) piece of work to produce, make; product to make; novel etc to bring out, publish; new model to bring out; fashion to create; song etc to compose, make up; aquí sacan 200 coches diarios they make 200 cars a day here; he sacado 20 páginas de notas I've made 20 pages of notes; a este propósito han sacado unos versos they've made up some verses about this.
   (k) (Phot) to take; copy to make, have made; saca buen retrato he takes well; nos quiso — una foto he wanted to take a photo of us; no tenía la intención de — ese coche I didn't mean to include that car in the photograph.
   (l) prize, benefit, legacy, post etc to get; to receive; profit to make; (fig) to derive (de from); sacó el premio gordo he got (or won) the big prize; así no vas a — nada you won't get anything that way; sacó un buen número para la lotería he drew a good number for the lottery; la sociedad saca una ganancia de . . . the company makes a profit of . . .
   (m) (Parl etc) to elect; han sacado 35 diputados they have got 35 members elected; por fin sacaron presidente a X they finally elected X (as) president.
   (n) quality etc to show; en esto sacó por fin su habilidad in this he finally showed (or demonstrated,

proved) his skill; — faltas a uno to point out someone's defects.
   (o) polish etc to put on, bring up, bring out; — los colores a la cara de uno to bring the colour to someone's cheeks, put some colour into someone's cheeks.
   (p) (in newspaper etc) to mention, put; no me vayas a — en tu discurso don't mention me in your speech; le han sacado en el periódico they've put him in the paper.
   (q) (fam) le saca 10 cm a su hermano he is 10 cm taller than his brother, he has an advantage in height of 10 cm over his brother; al terminar la carrera le sacaba 10 metros al adversario at the end of the race he was 10 metres ahead of his rival.
   (r) — adelante child to bring up; graduate, trainee etc to turn out; business to carry on, go on with; — a una adelante (fam) to get a girl in the family way.
   (s) — a uno de sí to infuriate someone.
   (t) (CAm, Ec) to flatter, fawn on.
   (u) (Ec, Mex) — algo a uno to reproach someone for something.
sacarina nf saccharin(e).
sacarino adj saccharine.
sacatín nm (Col) still.
sacerdocio nm priesthood.
sacerdotal adj priestly.
sacerdote nm priest; — obrero worker priest; sumo — high priest.
sacerdotisa nf priestess.
saciado adj: — de (fig) steeped in, saturated in, full of.
saciar [1b] 1 vt (a) to satisfy, satiate.
   (b) (fig) desires etc to appease; curiosity, longing etc to satisfy; ambition to fulfil, more than satisfy.
   2 **saciarse** vr to satiate oneself; to be satiated (con, de with).
saciedad nf satiation, satiety; demostrar algo hasta la — to prove something up to the hilt; repetir algo hasta la — to repeat something over and over again.
saco[1] nm (a) bag; sack; (Mil) kitbag; (as measure) bagful; sackful; — de arena (Mil) sandbag, (Sport) punchball; — de dormir, — manta sleeping bag; — de mano, — de noche, — de viaje travelling bag; — terrero sandbag; a —s (fig) by the ton; no echar algo en — roto to be careful not to forget something; no es (or no parece) — de paja he can't be written off as unimportant.
   (b) (Anat) sac.
   (c) (fam) ser un — de gracia to be very witty; es un — de picardías he's full of tricks; ser un — de huesos (SAm) to be a bag of bones.
   (d) long coat, loose-fitting jacket; (Arg) woman's outdoor coat.
   (e) (sl) 1000 pesetas.
saco[2] nm (Mil) sack; entrar a — en to sack, loot, plunder.
sacón 1 adj (CAm) (a) talebearing, sneaking. (b) flattering, soapy.
   2 nm, **sacona** nf (CAm) flatterer, soapy individual.
   3 nm (Arg) woman's outdoor coat.
saconear [1a] vt (CAm) to flatter, soap up (fam).
saconería nf (CAm) flattery, soft soap (sl).
sacramental adj (a) (Eccl) sacramental. (b) (fig) ritual, ritualistic; time-honoured; pronunció las palabras —es he spoke the time-honoured words.
sacramentar [1a] vt to administer the last sacraments to.
sacramento nm sacrament; el Santísimo S— the Blessed Sacrament; recibir los —s to receive the last sacraments.
sacrificar [1g] 1 vt (a) to sacrifice (also fig; a to).
   (b) animal (for meat) to slaughter; pet to put to sleep, destroy painlessly.
   2 **sacrificarse** vr to sacrifice oneself; to make a sacrifice.
sacrificio nm (a) sacrifice (also fig); el — de la misa the sacrifice of the mass. (b) slaughter(ing); painless destruction.
sacrilegio nm sacrilege.
sacrílego adj sacrilegious.
sacristán nm verger, sacrist(an); sexton.
sacristía nf vestry, sacristy.
sacro[1] adj sacred, holy.
sacro[2] nm (Anat) sacrum.
sacrosanto adj most holy; (fig) sacrosanct.
sacudida nf (a) shake, shaking; jerk; jolt, jar, bump; (of earthquake) shock; (of explosion) blast; (with head) jerk, toss; — eléctrica electric shock; dar una — a una alfombra to beat a carpet; el coche avanzaba dando —s the car moved forward

in a series of jolts, the car went jerkily forwards; **la — de la bomba llegó hasta aquí** the blast of the bomb was felt as far away as this.

    (b) (*fig*) violent change; sudden jolt; (*Pol etc*) upheaval; **hay que darle una** — he needs a jolt.

sacudido *adj* (a) ill-disposed, unpleasant; intractable. (b) determined.

sacudidura *nf*, **sacudimiento** *nm* =sacudida.

sacudir [3a] **1** *vt* (a) *building, ground, limb, person, tree etc* to shake; *person (as punishment)* to beat, thrash; *wing etc* to flap, move up and down; *carpet* to beat; *mattress* to shake (the dust out of); *rope etc* to jerk, tug; *passenger, vehicle etc* to shake, jolt, jar, bump; to rock (to and fro); *head* to jerk, toss.

    (b) *flies etc* to chase away, brush off; *burden* to shake off.

    (c) (*of emotion etc*) to shake; **una tremenda emoción sacudió a la multitud** a great wave of excitement ran through the crowd; **— a uno de su depresión** to shake someone out of his depression; **— los nervios a uno** to shatter someone's nerves.

    (d) (*fam*) **— a uno** to belt someone (*fam*); to beat someone up; to shoot someone.

    2 sacudirse *vr*: **— (de) un peso** to shake off a burden, get rid of a burden; **por fin se le han sacudido** they've finally got rid of him; **el caballo se sacudía las moscas con la cola** the horse brushed off the flies with his tail.

sacudón *nm* (*SAm*) violent shake, severe jolt; (*fig*) big shake-up, almighty upheaval (*fam*).

sacha *adj invar* (*SAm*) (a) false, sham; **— médico** quack. (b) bungling, unskilled; **— carpintero** clumsy carpenter.

sádico *adj* sadistic.

sadismo *nm* sadism.

sadista *nmf* sadist.

saeta *nf* (a) (*Mil*) arrow, dart.

    (b) (*Mech*) hand; magnetic needle.

    (c) (*Mus*) *sacred song in flamenco style sung during Holy Week processions.*

    (d) (*Rel*) short prayer.

saetera *nf* (*Mil*) loophole.

saetín *nm* (a) millrace. (b) (*Tech*) tack, brad.

safado *adj* (*SAm*) impudent, shameless.

safagina *nf* (*Col*) uproar, commotion.

safari *nm* safari; **estar de —** to be on safari.

saga *nf* saga.

sagacidad *nf* shrewdness, cleverness, sagacity; astuteness.

sagaz *adj* (a) shrewd, clever, sagacious; astute. (b) *dog* keen-scented.

sagazmente *adv* shrewdly, cleverly, sagaciously; astutely.

sagrado 1 *adj* sacred, holy (*also fig*); *orders, scripture etc* holy. **2** *nm* sanctuary, asylum; **acogerse a —** to seek sanctuary.

sagú *nm* sago.

Sahara *m*, **Sáhara** *m* Sahara.

sahumar [1a] *vt* to perfume (with incense); to smoke, fumigate.

saibó *nm* (*SAm*: *angl*), **saibor** *nm* (*Col, Ven*: *angl*) sideboard.

saín *nm* (a) animal fat, grease; fish oil (*used for lighting*). (b) (*on clothing*) dirt, grease.

sainete *nm* (a) (*Cook*) seasoning, sauce; (*fig*) titbit, delicacy, pleasant adornment, nice extra.

    (b) (*fig*) spice, relish, tastiness.

    (c) (*Theat*) one-act farce (*or* comedy); comic sketch, skit.

sajar [1a] *vt* (*Med*) to cut open, lance.

sajín *nm* (*CAm*), **sajino** *nm* (*CAm*) underarm odour.

sajón 1 *adj* Saxon. **2** *nm*, **sajona** *nf* Saxon.

Sajonia *f* Saxony.

sajornar [1a] *vt* (*Cu*) to bother, upset.

sal[1] *nf* (a) salt; **— amoníaca** sal ammoniac; **—es (aromáticas)** smelling salts; **—es de baño** bath salts; **— de cocina, — gorda** kitchen salt, cooking salt; **— de fruta(s)** fruit salts; **— gema** rock salt; **— de la Higuera** Epsom salts; **— de mesa** table salt; **— volátil** sal volatile.

    (b) (*fig*) salt; wit, wittiness; charm, liveliness; **— de la tierra** salt of the earth; **esto es la — de la vida** this is the spice of life; **tiene mucha —** he's a great wit, he's very amusing, he's good company; **ella tiene mucha —** she's delightful, she's absolutely charming.

    (c) (*fig*: *CAm, SD*) misfortune, bad luck.

sal[2] see **salir**.

sala *nf* (a) (*in house: also* **— de estar**) drawing room; (large) room; hall; (*Theat*) house, auditorium; (*Law*) court; (*Med*) hospital ward, section; **— de alum-**

---

bramiento delivery ward; **— capitular** chapter house, meeting room; **— de lo civil** civil court; **— de conferencias** lecture room, lecture hall; **— de lo criminal** criminal court; **— de espectáculos** concert room, hall; **— de espera** waiting room; **— de fiestas** dance hall; **— de juntas** (*Comm*) boardroom; **— de justicia** law court; **— de lectura** reading room; **— de máquinas** (*Naut*) engine room; **— de muestras** showroom; **— de operaciones** operating theatre; **— de pruebas** fitting room; **— de recibo** parlour; **— de subastas** saleroom, auction room; **— del trono** throne room; **deporte en —** indoor sport, indoor game.

    (b) suite of drawing-room (*etc*) furniture.

salacidad *nf* salaciousness, prurience.

saladar *nm* salt marsh, saltings.

salado *adj* (a) (*Cook*) salt, salty; *water* salt; **muy —** strongly salted, over-salted.

    (b) (*fig*) witty, amusing; lively; charming, attractive, cute; *language* rich, racy; **es un tipo muy —** he's a very amusing chap, he's a very lively sort; **¡qué —!** how amusing!, (*iro*) very droll!, wasn't that clever of you?

    (c) (*SAm*) unlucky, unfortunate; wretched.

    (d) (*Chi, RPl*) *article* expensive; *price* very high.

salamanca *nf* (*Chi, RPl*) (a) cave, grotto; dark place. (b) witchcraft, sorcery.

salamandra *nf* salamander.

salamanquesa *nf* lizard.

salame *nm* (*Arg*) idiot.

salami *nm* salami.

salar 1 *nm* (*Arg, Bol, Chi*) salt mine; salt pan. **2** [1a] *vt* (a) (*Cook*) to put salt in, add salt to.

    (b) (*Cook*) to salt, cure.

    (c) (*Col, Ec*) *cattle* to feed salt to.

    (d) (*Ant, CAm, Ec, Mex, Per*) to ruin, spoil; to bring bad luck to.

    (e) (*Cu, Hond*) to dishonour.

salarial *adj* wage (*attr*); **reclamación —** wage claim.

salario *nm* wages, pay; (*SAm*: *angl*) salary.

salaz *adj* salacious, prurient.

salazón *nf* (*Ant, Guat, Par*) bad luck.

salceda *nf*, **salcedo** *nm* willow plantation.

salcochar [1a] *vt* to boil in salt water.

salchicha *nf* pork sausage.

salchichería *nf* pork butcher's (shop).

salchichón *nm* (salami-type) sausage.

saldar [1a] *vt* (a) *bill* to pay; *debt* to pay off. (b) (*fig*) *differences* to settle, resolve; see **cuenta**. (c) *stocks* to sell off, sell up; *books* to remainder.

saldo *nm* (a) (*act*) settlement; payment.

    (b) balance (*also fig*); **— acreedor, — a favor** credit balance; **— deudor, — en contra** debit balance, adverse balance; **el — es a su favor** (*fig*) the balance is in his favour, on balance he comes off best.

    (c) (*Comm*) clearance sale.

    (d) remnant(s), remainder, left-over(s).

saledizo 1 *adj* projecting. **2** *nm* projection; overhang; **en —** projecting, overhanging.

salera *nf* (*Chi*) =**salina**.

salero *nm* (a) (*Cook*) saltcellar. (b) salt store. (c) (*Agr*) salt lick. (d) (*fig*) wit, wittiness; charm; sex appeal, allure, glamour. (e) (*Chi*) =**salina**.

saleroso *adj* (*fam*) =**salado** (b).

salida *nf* (a) (*act*) leaving, going out, exit; emergence; (*Aer, Rail etc*) departure; (*Astron*) rising; (*of gas etc*) leak, escape; (*Sport*) start; (*Theat*) appearance, entry, coming-on; (*Theat*) curtain call; **"S—s"** (*Rail*) "Departures"; **— lanzada** running start, flying start; **— parada** standing start; **— del sol** sunrise; **la — fue triste** leaving was sad, our departure was sad; **a la — del trabajo** on leaving work; **a la — del teatro** as we (*etc*) came out of the theatre; **para García, dos orejas y — en hombros** (*Taur*) García won two ears and was carried out shoulder-high.

    (b) (*Mil*) sally, sortie; (*Aer*) sortie.

    (c) (*Cards*) lead; **si la — es a trébol** if the lead is in clubs.

    (d) (*Tech*) output, production; (*Fin*) outlay.

    (e) (*place etc*) exit, way out; (*Mech*) outlet, vent, valve; (*Geog*) outlet; **"S—"** "Exit", "Way Out"; **— de artistas** (*Theat*) stage door; **— de urgencia** emergency exit; **dar — a su indignación** to vent one's anger; **tener — a** (*Archit*) to lead to, open on to, (*Geog*) have an outlet to.

    (f) (*fig*) way out; pretext, loophole; dodge; **es una — cómoda** it's a simple solution; **no hay —** there's no way out of it; **no tenemos otra — que firmarlo** there's nothing we can do but sign it, there is no solution open to us except to sign it;

dio con una — **ingeniosa** he hit upon a clever way out.

(g) (*fig*) issue, result, outcome.

(h) (*fig*) argument, counterargument.

(i) (*Comm*) sale, sales outlet, opening; **dar — a** to sell, place, find an outlet for; **tener —** to sell well; **el bikini no tiene — en Groenlandia** bikinis don't sell in Greenland; **tener una —** difícil to be a hard sell; **tener una — fácil** to have a ready market, be a soft sell.

(j) (*on surface*) projection, protuberance.

(k) — de baño bathrobe; **— de teatro** evening wrap.

(l) (*Comm: in account*) item.

(m) (*fig*) crack (*fam*), joke, witty remark; **tener —s** to be amusing, be full of wisecracks; to have amusing ideas.

(n) (*fig*) **— de pie de banco, — de tono** inept remark, ill-judged remark, unfortunate intervention.

salido *adj* **(a)** projecting, sticking out; bulging. **(b) estar salida** (*Zool*) to be on heat.

salidor *adj* (*Chi, RPl, Ven*) restless, roving; fond of going out a lot.

saliente 1 *adj* **(a)** (*Archit etc*) projecting, protuberant; raised, overhanging; *feature* prominent.

(b) (*fig*) salient; outstanding.

(c) *sun* rising.

(d) *member etc* outgoing, retiring.

2 *nm* projection; (*of road etc*) shoulder; (*Mil*) salient.

salina *nf* salt mine; salt pan; **—s** saltworks.

salinera *nf* (*Per, PR*) = **salina**.

salinidad *nf* salinity; saltness, saltiness.

salino *adj* saline; salty.

salir [3t] **1** *vi* **(a)** (*general sense: of person*) to come out, go out (*de* of); to leave; to appear, emerge (*de* from); to get out (*de* of), escape (*de* from); **salimos a la calle** we went out into the street; **— a ver algo** to go out to see something; **— de la calle; al — del cine** on leaving the cinema, when we (*etc*) came out of the cinema; **lo buscaremos al — de aquí** we'll look for it on the way out of here; **¿de dónde ha salido Vd?** where did you spring from?; **— del coma** to emerge from a coma; **— del enojo** to get over one's anger; **— de un apuro** to get out of a jam; **— de un puesto** to leave one's post, give up one's post; **este año sale de presidente** this year he ceases to be chairman, he gives up the chairmanship this year; **por fin salió de pobre** he finally left poverty behind him; **— para** to leave for.

(b) (*general sense: other subjects*) to come out; to emerge, appear; (*Astron*) to rise, come up; (*Bot*) to appear, come up, show; (*of journal etc*) to come out, appear, be published; (*of fashion etc*) to come in; (*of stain, dirt*) to come off, come out; **el agua sale aquí** the water comes out here; **le salió un diente** he cut a tooth; **esta calle sale a la plaza** this street comes out in the square, this street leads to the square; **el vino sale de la uva** wine comes from grapes; **el anillo no le sale del dedo** the ring won't come off her finger, she can't get the ring off her finger; **le salió la satisfacción a la cara** satisfaction showed in his face; **la noticia salió en el periódico de ayer** the news came out in yesterday's paper; **por fin salió la causa de todo ello** eventually the reason for the whole thing came to light; **¡ya salió aquello!** so that was it!, so now we know!; **cuando salga la ocasión** when the opportunity comes up (*or* arises, presents itself); **si sale un puesto a propósito** if the right job comes up; **no le sale novio** she doesn't seem to get a boyfriend; **— adelante** to do well, make progress, get on.

(c) (*of result etc*) to turn out; to prove, be, turn out to be; **salga lo que salga** (*or* **saliere**) come what may; regardless of the consequences; whatever turns up; **si sale verdad** if it proves (to be) true; **nos salió la criada muy trabajadora** the girl turned out to be very hard-working; **el conserje salió un sinvergüenza** the porter turned out to be a rogue; **si sale cara** (*tossing coin*) if it comes down heads; **este crucigrama no me sale** this crossword won't work out, I can't do this crossword; **le salen los problemas sin dificultad** he works problems out with no trouble at all; **— a** (*of price*) to come to, amount to, work out at; **el traje le salió muy caro** the suit worked out very expensive for him; **esto nos va a — carísimo** this is going to cost us a fortune; **me sale a menor precio que a ti** it's working out cheaper for me than it is for you; **— ganando** to gain, be the gainer; to come out on top; to emerge as the winner; to gain on a deal; **— perdiendo** to lose, be the loser; to lose on a deal; **— bien** (*person*)

to succeed, make good; to do well; (*in exam*) to pass; (*event*) to go off well; **— mal** (*person*) to fail, do badly, come unstuck; (*in exam*) to fail; (*event*) to be a failure; **les salió mal el proyecto** the scheme miscarried, the plan went badly for them.

(d) (*Theat: also* **— a escena**) to enter, come on; **sale vestido de policía** he comes on dressed as a policeman; **"sale el rey"** (*stage direction*) "enter the king".

(e) (*of bus, train etc*) to leave, depart; (*Naut*) to sail; **sale a las 8** it departs at 8; **— para** to leave for.

(f) — con (*of boyfriend etc*) to go out with, date (*US*); **salen juntos desde hace 2 años** they've been going around together for two years.

(g) (*of chick, egg*) to hatch.

(h) (*Archit etc*) to project, jut out; to stick out; to overhang; **sale un poco más cada día** it comes out a little further each day; **el balcón sale unos 2 metros** the balcony projects about 2 metres.

(i) (*of lottery number etc*) to come up, win (a prize); (*Pol: also* **— elegido**) to be elected, win; **salió alcalde por 3 votos** he was elected mayor by 3 votes.

(j) (*Cards*) to lead; (*Chess*) to have first move; (*Sport*) to start; **— con un as** to lead an ace.

(k) — con una observación to come out with a remark, come up with some (inept) remark.

(l) — por uno to come out in defence of someone.

(m) — con un propósito to carry out a plan; **— con una pretensión** to succeed in a claim; **ella sale con todo el trabajo** she manages to keep up with all the work; she is fully up to all the work.

(n) — a to take after; **salió a su padre** he took after his father, he was exactly like his father.

(o) (*Fin*) **— a los gastos de uno** to meet (or pay, defray) someone's expenses; **— por uno** to back someone financially; to stand security for someone.

2 salirse *vr* **(a)** (*in most senses*) = **1**; **— del tema** to wander from the point; to make a digression, go outside one's subject; **se salió del partido** he left the party.

(b) (*animal, bird etc*) to escape (*de* from), get out (*de* of); (*air, liquid etc*) to leak out; to overflow; to boil over; (*container*) to leak; to overflow; to boil over; **el barril se sale** the barrel is leaking.

(c) (*Mech*) to become disconnected; **— de la vía** (*Rail*) to leave the rails, jump the track.

(d) — de costumbre to break with custom, depart from tradition; **— de lo normal** to go beyond what is normal; **— de los límites** to go beyond the limits.

(e) — de un compromiso to get out of an obligation.

salitre *nm* saltpetre, nitre.

salitrera *nf* nitre works; nitrate fields.

saliva *nf* saliva, spit; **gastar —** (*fig*) to waste one's breath (*en* on); **tragar —** to swallow one's feelings; to swallow hard.

salivación *nf* salivation.

salivadera *nf* (*Andalusia, Chi, RPl*) spittoon, cuspidor (*US*).

salival *adj* salivary.

salivar [1a] *vi* to salivate.

salivazo *nm* spittle, gobbet, spit; **arrojar un —** to spit.

salivera *nf* (*RPl*) spittoon, cuspidor (*US*).

salmantino 1 *adj* of Salamanca. **2** *nm*, **salmantina** *nf* native (*or* inhabitant) of Salamanca; **los —s** the people of Salamanca.

salmear [1a] *vi* to sing psalms.

salmo *nm* psalm.

salmodia *nf* **(a)** (*Eccl*) psalmody. **(b)** (*fam*) monotonous singing; drone, singsong.

salmodiar [1b] *vi* **(a)** to sing psalms. **(b)** (*fig*) to drone, sing monotonously; to chant.

salmón *nm* salmon.

salmonete *nm* red mullet.

salmuera *nf* pickle, brine.

salobre *adj* salt, salty; *water* salt, brackish.

saloma *nf* sea shanty, sea song; working song.

Salomón *m* Solomon.

salón *nm* **(a)** drawing room, lounge; (*Art and Hist*) salon; hall, assembly room; (*Naut*) saloon; (*of college etc*) common room; **— del automóvil** motor show; **— de baile** ballroom, dance hall; **— de belleza** beauty parlour; **— de demostraciones** showroom; **— de fiestas** dance hall; **— de fumar** smoking room; **— de pintura** art exhibition, art gallery; **— de sesiones** assembly hall; (*Pol*) chamber; **— de té** tearoom; **juego de —** parlour game.

(b) suite of drawing-room furniture.

(c) (*Mex, Pan: angl*) saloon (*US*).

saloncillo nm (*Theat etc*) private room; rest room.
salpicado adj (a) — de splashed with, spattered with; sprinkled with; **un diseño — de puntos rojos** a pattern with red dotted about in it; **una llanura salpicada de granjas** a plain with farms dotted about on it, a plain dotted with farms.
(b) **un discurso — de citas latinas** a speech sprinkled with Latin quotations, a speech full of Latin quotations.
(c) (*Arg, Mex*) animal spotted, dappled, mottled.
salpicadura nf (a) (*act*) splashing, spattering; sprinkling; flecking. (b) splash, spatter; sprinkle; dot, fleck. (c) (*fig*) spatter, peppering; sprinkling.
salpicar [1g] vt (a) (*with mud, paint etc*) to splash, spatter (*de* with); (*with water etc*) to sprinkle (*de* with); *flowers etc* to scatter, strew (about); *cloth, design* to dot, fleck (*de* with); — **un coche de barro** to splash a car with mud, splash mud over a car; **agua sobre el suelo** to sprinkle water on the floor; **la multitud de islas que salpican el océano** the host of islands dotted about the ocean.
(b) (*fig*) conversation, speech etc to sprinkle, interlard (*de* with); to pepper (*de* with).
salpicón nm (a) =**salpicadura**. (b) (*Cook*) salmagundi. (c) (*Ec*) drink of cold fruit juice.
salpimentar [1a] vt (a) (*Cook*) to season, add salt and pepper to. (b) (*fig*) to season, improve, sweeten (*de* with).
salpiquear [1a] vt (*Col, PR*) =**salpicar**.
salpresar [1a] vt to salt (down).
salpreso adj (*Cook*) salted, salt.
salpullido nm (a) (*Med*) rash, skin disease. (b) flea-bite, swelling (from a bite).
salsa nf (a) sauce; (*with roast*) gravy; (*with sweet*) sauce; (*with salad*) dressing; — **de ají** chili sauce; — **mayonesa** mayonnaise; — **de tomate** tomato sauce, ketchup; — **tártara** tartar sauce.
(b) (*fig*) seasoning, spice; appetizer; **es la — de la vida** it's the spice of life.
salsera nf sauce boat; gravy boat.
salsifí nm salsify.
saltabanco nm (a) (*Hist*) quack, mountebank. (b) rogue. (c) =**saltimbanqui**.
saltado adj (a) estar — to be chipped, be damaged; **la corona tiene varias piedras saltadas** the crown has several stones missing. (b) *eyes* bulging.
saltador nm (a) (*Sport*) jumper. (b) skipping rope.
saltadura nf chip.
saltamontes nm, pl **saltamontes** grasshopper.
saltante adj (*Chi, Per*) outstanding.
saltaperico nm (a) (*Cu*) squib, firecracker. (b) (*Ven*) row, uproar.
saltar [1a] 1 vt (a) to jump (over), leap (over), vault.
(b) to remove; **le saltó 3 dientes** he knocked out 3 of his teeth; **me has saltado un botón** you've torn off one of my buttons.
(c) (*fig*) meal, name, passage etc to skip, miss out, leave out; **saltó un párrafo entero** he skipped a whole paragraph; **me ha saltado dos renglones** I've left out a couple of lines.
2 vi (a) (*of persons etc*) to jump, leap, spring (*a* on to, into; *por, por encima de* over); to vault; to bound; (*of child*) to hop, skip; to gambol; — **a la silla** to leap into the saddle; — **al agua** to jump (*or* dive, plunge) into the water; — **de la cama** to leap out of bed; — **de alegría** to jump with joy, jump for joy; — **en una silla** to jump up on (to) a chair; — **en tierra** to leap ashore; — **en paracaídas** to jump, come down by parachute; — **por una ventana** to jump out of a window, leap from a window; — **sobre uno** to pounce on someone; **hacer — un caballo** to jump a horse, make a horse jump.
(b) (*fig: in speech etc*) to skip about, skip from one subject to another.
(c) (*of ball*) to bounce, fly up; (*of spring*) to unroll suddenly; (*of liquid*) to spurt up, shoot up; (*of tears*) to well up; (*of figure*) to leap (up); — **a la mente** to leap to one's mind; **estar a lo que salta** to watch out for an opportunity, look for an opening; to live for the day; **la mayoría ha saltado a 900 votos** the majority has shot up (*or* leaped up) to 900 votes.
(d) (*of part*) to come off, fly off; (*of cork*) to blow out, pop out; (*of chip etc*) to fly off; (*of button*) to come off; (*of wood etc*) to crack, snap, break; (*of spring*) to break; (*of vessel*) to crack; (*of explosive*) to explode, burst; **hacer — un edificio** to blow a building up; **hacer — una trampa** to spring a trap.
(e) (*fig: with anger*) to explode, blow up (*fam*).

(f) (*fig*) — **con una observación** to come out with a remark, make a ridiculous remark.
(g) (*fig*) — **de un puesto** to leave a post, give up a job; **hacer — a uno de un puesto** to boot someone out of a job.
(h) (*Bio*) — **atrás** to revert (to type).
3 **saltarse** vr (a) — **un párrafo** to skip a paragraph; see 1 (c).
(b) — **todas las reglas** to break all the rules.
(c) (*of part*) to come off, fly off; see 2 (d).
saltarín 1 adj restless; full of movement, always on the go; (*pej*) unstable. 2 nm, **saltarina** nf dancer.
salteado adj (*Cook*) sauté.
salteador nm (*also* — **de caminos**) holdup man; (*Hist*) highwayman, footpad.
salteamiento nm robbery, holdup.
saltear [1a] 1 vt (a) to hold up; to rob, assault, attack; to take by surprise.
(b) (*fig: of doubt etc*) to assail, overcome suddenly.
(c) (*Cook*) to sauté.
2 vi to work (*etc*) fitfully, do something by fits and starts; **lo leyó salteando** he read bits of it here and there.
salterio nm (a) (*Eccl*) psalter; (*Bib*) Book of Psalms. (b) (*Mus*) psaltery.
saltimbanqui nm juggler; acrobat; tightrope walker, mountebank; (*fig*) playboy.
salto nm (a) jump, leap; bound, spring; vault; hop, skip; (*into water*) jump, dive, plunge; (*on to prey*) pounce; — **a ciegas** leap in the dark; **el gran —** (*hacia*) **adelante** the great leap forward; **a —s** by jumping, in a series of jumps; (*fig*) by fits and starts; **avanzar a —s** to jump along, go hopping along; **de un —** at one bound, with one jump; **subió de un —** he jumped up; **bajó de un —** he jumped down; **en un —** (*fig*) in a jiffy; **en dos —s estoy de vuelta** I'll be back in a moment; **dar un —, pegar un —** to jump (with fright etc); **me daba —s el corazón** my heart was pounding; **vivir a — de mata** to live from hand to mouth, keep one's head just above water; to keep one jump ahead of justice; **escapar a — de mata** to flee headlong; **hacer algo a — de mata** to do something thoughtlessly, do something unmethodically.
(b) (*Sport etc*) jump; (*into water*) dive; — **de altura** high jump; high dive; — **de cabeza** header; — **de carpa** jack-knife dive; — **a la** (*or* **con**) **garrocha**, — **con** (*or* **de**) **pértiga** pole vault; — **de longitud** long jump; — **mortal** somersault; — **ornamental** fancy dive; **triple —** hop, step and jump; — **de trampolín** springboard dive.
(c) (*Bio*) — **atrás** throwback, reversion to type.
(d) (*Geol*) fault; chasm, rift.
(e) (*fig*) gap; jump; passage skipped, part missed; **aquí hay un — de 50 versos** there is a gap here of 50 lines; **de él al otro hermano hay un — de 9 años** there is a gap of 9 years between him and the other brother, there are 9 years between him and the other brother.
(f) (*Sport*) jump; fence; hurdle, obstacle; — **de agua** water jump.
(g) — **de agua** (*Geog*) waterfall, cascade; (*Tech*) chute.
(h) — **de cama** négligé, peignoir.
(i) (*Cu*) **a —** in cash.
saltón 1 adj (a) *eyes* bulging, popping; *teeth* prominent, protruding.
(b) (*Col, Chi, Ven*) undercooked, half raw.
2 nm grasshopper; (*Mex*) immature locust.
saltona nf (*RPl*) immature locust.
salubre adj healthy, salubrious.
salubridad nf (a) healthiness, salubrity, salubriousness. (b) health statistics.
salud nf (a) (*Med*) health; state of health; **estar bien de —** to be in good health; **estar mal de —** to be in bad health; **¿cómo vamos de —?** how are we today?; **mejorar de —** to improve in health, get better; **devolver la — a uno** to give someone back his health, restore someone to health.
(b) (*fig*) health; welfare, wellbeing; **la — moral de la nación** the country's moral welfare.
(c) **¡—!, ¡a su —!, — y pesetas!** good health!, here's to you!, here's luck!; **beber a la — de** to drink to the health of.
(d) (*Rel*) salvation; state of grace.
saludable adj (a) (*Med*) healthy. (b) (*fig*) salutary, good, beneficial; **un aviso —** a salutary warning.
saludar [1a] vt (a) to greet; to bow to, take off one's hat to; **ir a — a uno** to go and say hullo to someone, drop in to see someone; **salude de mi parte a X** give

my regards to X; **no — a uno** to cut someone, refuse to acknowledge someone.

(b) (*formula in letter*) **le saluda atentamente** yours faithfully.

(c) (*Mil*) to salute.

(d) (*fig*) to salute, hail, welcome.

saludo *nm* (a) greeting; bow.

(b) (*formula in letter*) **—s** best wishes, greetings, regards; **un — afectuoso, un — cordial** yours sincerely; **os envía muchos —s** he sends you warmest regards.

(c) (*Mil*) salute.

Salustio *m* Sallust.

salutación *nf* greeting, salutation.

salva *nf* (a) (*Mil etc*) salute, salvo; (*fig: of applause*) storm, volley. (b) greeting. (c) oath, solemn promise.

salvabarros *nm, pl* **salvabarros** mudguard.

salvación *nf* (a) rescue, delivery (de from), salvation.

(b) (*Rel*) salvation; **— eterna** eternal salvation.

salvada *nf* (*SAm*) = **salvación** (a).

salvado *nm* bran.

salvador *nm* rescuer, saviour; **el S—** the Saviour.

salvadoreñismo *nm* word (*or* phrase *etc*) peculiar to Salvador.

salvadoreño **1** *adj* Salvadoran. **2** *nm,* **salvadoreña** *nf* Salvadoran.

salvaguardar [1a] *vt* to safeguard.

salvaguardia *nf* safe-conduct; (*fig*) safeguard.

salvajada *nf* savage deed, piece of savagery; barbarity, atrocity; brutal act.

salvaje **1** *adj* (a) (*Bot, Zool etc*) wild; *land* wild, uncultivated. (b) *people, tribe etc* savage. **2** *nmf* savage (*also fig*).

salvajería *nf* = **salvajada**.

salvajez *nf* = **salvajismo**.

salvajino *adj* (a) wild, savage. (b) **carne salvajina** meat from a wild animal.

salvajismo *nm* savagery.

salvamanteles *nm, pl* **salvamanteles** tablemat.

salvamento *nm* (a) rescue; delivery; salvage; (*fig*) salvation; **de — life-saving** (*attr*); rescue (*attr*); **bote de — lifeboat; operaciones de — rescue** operations.

(b) place of safety, refuge; haven.

salvaplatos *nm, pl* **salvaplatos** tablemat.

salvar [1a] **1** *vt* (a) *person etc* to save, rescue (de from); *ship* to salvage; *appearances* to save, keep up; **me salvó la vida** he saved my life; **apenas salvaron nada del incendio** they hardly rescued anything from the fire; **— a uno de tener que** + *infin* to save someone from having to + *infin*.

(b) (*Rel*) to save.

(c) *barrier, line, mountains, river etc* to cross; *rapids* to shoot; *ditch, stream* to jump across, jump over, clear; *difficulty* to overcome, resolve; *obstacle* to get round, negotiate.

(d) *distance* to cover, do, travel; **el tren salva la distancia en 2 horas** the train covers the distance in 2 hours.

(e) to except, exclude.

(f) (*of building, tree etc*) to rise above.

(g) (*of water level etc*) to reach, rise as high as; **el agua salvaba el peldaño más alto** the water came up to the topmost step.

2 salvarse *vr* (a) to save oneself, escape (de from); **¡sálvese el que pueda!** every man for himself!

(b) (*Rel*) to save one's soul, be saved.

salvavidas *nm, pl* **salvavidas** (a) lifebelt. (b) (*as adj*) life-saving (*attr*); **bote — lifeboat; cinturón — lifebelt**.

salvedad *nf* reservation, qualification, proviso; **con la — de que . . .** with the proviso that . . .; **hacer una — to** make a qualification.

salvia *nf* (*Bot*) sage.

salvilla *nf* salver, tray; (*Chi*) cruet.

salvo **1** *adj* safe; see **sano**.

2 *adv and prep* (a) except (for), save; barring; **aquellos que ya contamos** except for those we have already counted; **de todos los países — de Ruritania** from all countries except Ruritania.

(b) **a — safely**; out of danger; **a — de** safe from; **en — out of danger, in a safe place; dejar algo a — to** make an exception of something, leave something out of it; **para dejar a — su reputación** in order to keep his reputation safe; **poner algo a — to** put something in a safe place, put something out of harm's way; **ponerse a — to** escape, reach safety; **nada ha quedado a — de sus ataques** nothing has been safe from his attacks.

3 — que, — si *conj* unless . . .; except that . . .; **iré — que me avises al contrario** I'll go unless you tell me not to.

salvoconducto *nm* safe-conduct.

salvohonor *nm* (*hum*) backside.

samaritano **1** *adj* Samaritan. **2** *nm,* **samaritana** *nf* Samaritan; **buen — good** Samaritan.

samaruco *nm* (*Chi*) hunter's pouch, gamebag.

samba *nf* (*SAm*) samba.

sambenito *nm* (*fig*) dishonour, disgrace, infamy; **echar el — a otro** to pin the blame on someone else; **quedó con el — toda la vida** he was disgraced for life.

sambumbia *nf* (a) (*Col, Mex, PR*) badly-made drink, watery drink; badly-made object.

(b) (*Cu*) drink of sugar-cane syrup, water and peppers; (*Mex*) pineapple drink; (*Mex*) barley-water drink.

(c) (*Col*) old thing, battered object; **volver algo — to** smash something to pieces.

sambutir [3a] *vt* (*Mex*) = **embutir**.

samotana *nf* (*CAm*) row, uproar.

samovar *nm* samovar.

sampablera *nf* (*Ven*) noisy argument; fuss, row.

sampán *nm* sampan.

Samuel *m* Samuel.

samurar [1a] *vi* (*Ven*) to walk with bowed head.

San *nm* (*apocopated form of* **santo**) saint; **San Juan** Saint John, (*mostly written*) St John; **cerca de San Martín** near St Martin's (church); **se casarán por San Juan** they'll get married sometime in midsummer (*strictly*, round about St John's Day); *see also* **santo**.

sanable *adj* curable, susceptible to treatment.

sanaco *adj* (*Ant*) silly.

sanalotodo *nm* cure-all, universal remedy.

sanamente *adv* healthily; wholesomely.

sananería *nf* (*Ant*) silly thing, stupid remark.

sanar [1a] **1** *vt* to heal; to cure (de of). **2** *vi* (*of person*) to recover, get well; (*of wound*) to heal.

sanativo *adj* healing, curative.

sanatorio *nm* sanatorium; (*private*) nursing home.

sanción *nf* sanction; imponer **—es** to impose sanctions; levantar **—es a uno** to lift sanctions against someone.

sancionable *adj* punishable.

sancionado *nm* guilty person; **los —s** (*Pol*) those who have been punished for a political offence, those guilty of political crimes.

sancionar [1a] *vt* (*all senses*) to sanction.

sancochado *nm* (*Per*) = **sancocho**.

sancochar [1a] *vt* to parboil.

sancocho *nm* (a) undercooked food, parboiled meat. (b) (*SAm*) stew (of meat, yucca *etc*). (c) (*CAm, Mex, PR, Ven*) fuss; confusion; row. (d) (*Cu*) pigswill.

San Cristóbal *m* (a) (*Eccl*) St Christopher. (b) (*Geog*) St Kitts.

sancho *nm* (a) (*Prov*) pig. (b) (*Mex*) ram, lamb; billy-goat; (*any*) domestic animal.

sandalia *nf* sandal.

sándalo *nm* sandal, sandalwood.

sandez *nf* (a) (*quality*) foolishness. (b) (*act*) stupid thing, piece of stupidity; **decir sandeces** to talk nonsense; **fue una — obrar así** it was silly to do that.

sandía *nf* watermelon.

sandío *adj* foolish, silly, stupid.

sandunga *nf* (a) (*fam*) charm; wit. (b) (*Chi, Mex, Per, PR*) carousal, celebration.

sandunguero *adj* (*fam*) charming; witty, amusing.

sandwich [saŋ'gwitʃ, sam'bitʃ] *nm, pl* **sandwichs** *or* **sandwiches** (*angl*) sandwich.

saneamiento *nm* (a) draining; drainage (system), sanitation; sewerage.

(b) (*fig*) remedy; ending; cleaning-up.

(c) guarantee; insurance.

(d) compensation, indemnification.

sanear [1a] *vt* (a) *land* to drain; *house* to remove the dampness from; (*Tech*) to instal drainage (*or* sewerage) in, lay sewers in.

(b) (*fig*) *damage* to remedy, repair; *abuse* to end; *centre of vice* to clean up.

(c) *goods* to guarantee; to insure.

(d) (*Law*) *purchaser* to compensate, indemnify.

**sanfasón: a la — — *adv* (*SAm: gall*) unceremoniously, informally; (*pej*) carelessly.

sanforizar [1f] *vt* to sanforize (*Protected Trade Name*).

sangradera *nf* (a) (*Med*) lancet. (b) (*Agr*) irrigation channel; sluice, outflow.

sangradura *nf* (a) (*Anat*) inner angle of the elbow.

(b) (*Med*) cut made into a vein; bleeding, blood-letting. (c) (*Agr*) outlet, drainage channel.

sangrante *adj* (a) *person, wound* bleeding. (b) (*fig*) *injustice etc* crying, flagrant.

sangrar [1a] **1** *vt* (a) (*Med*) to bleed.

(b) (*Agr etc*) to drain, drain the water from;

water to drain off, let out, allow to drain away; *tree* to tap; *furnace* to tap.
   (c) (*Typ*) to indent.
   (d) (*fam*) to filch, filch from.
  2 *vi* (a) to bleed (*also fig*).
   (b) (*fig*) **estar sangrando** to be still fresh, be very new still; to be obvious; **aún sangra la humillación** the humiliation still rankles.

sangre *nf* blood (*also fig*); — **azul** blue blood; — **fría** sangfroid, coolness; (*pej*) callousness; **a — fría in** cold blood, callously; **mala** — bad blood; **pura** — (*nmf*) thoroughbred; — **vital** lifeblood; **a** — by animal power, by horsepower; **a** — **caliente** in the heat of the moment; **a** — **y fuego** by fire and sword; **es de** — **de reyes** he has royal blood, he is of the blood royal; **fue de** — **de conquistadores** he came of a line of conquerors; **le bulle la** — **(en las venas)** he is full of youthful vigour, he is bursting with energy; **esto chorrea** — this cries out to heaven; **chupar la** — **a uno** (*fig*) to exploit someone, suck out someone's lifeblood; to bleed someone white; **dar su** — to give one's blood; **echar** — to bleed (*de* from); **echar** — **por los ojos** to be furious; **encender** (*or* **quemar, revolver**) **la** — **a uno** to infuriate someone, make someone's blood boil; **freír la** — **a uno** (*fam*) to rile someone (*fam*), needle someone (*fam*); **se me heló la** — my blood froze, my blood ran cold; **llegar a la** — to come to blows; **sin que la** — **llegue al río** without disastrous results, without going to extremes; **no creo que llegue la** — **al río** I don't think it will be too disastrous; **sudar** — to undergo hardships; to slog, toil; **tener la** — **gorda** (*or* **de horchata**), **no tener** — **en las venas** to be excessively phlegmatic, be unemotional, be stone cold; to be dull, be boring.

sangregorda *nmf* (*fam*) bore.

sangría *nf* (a) (*Med*) bleeding, bloodletting; — **suelta** excessive flow of blood; (*fig*) outflow, drain, continuous loss.
   (b) (*Anat*) inner angle of the elbow.
   (c) (*Agr*) irrigation channel; outlet, outflow; ditch; drainage.
   (d) (*Tech*) tapping (*of a furnace*); stream of molten metal.
   (e) (*Cook*) *sweetened and chilled drink of red wine with fruit*, (*approx*) fruit cup.
   (f) (*Typ*) indentation.

sangrientamente *adv* bloodily.

sangriento *adj* (a) *wound* bleeding.
   (b) *dress, weapon etc* bloody, bloodstained, gory.
   (c) *battle, clash* bloody.
   (d) (*lit*) blood-red.
   (e) (*fig*) *injustice etc* crying, flagrant; *insult* deadly; *joke* cruel.

sangrigordo *adj* (*Ant*) tedious; annoying.

sangriligero *adj* (*SAm*), **sangriliviano** *adj* (*SAm*) pleasant, nice, congenial.

sangripesado *adj* (*SAm*), **sangrón** *adj* (*Cu, Mex*), **sangruno** *adj* (*PR*) rude; unpleasant, nasty, uncongenial.

sanguarañas *nfpl* (*Arg, Ec, Per*) circumlocutions.

sanguijuela *nf* leech (*also fig*).

sanguinario *adj* bloodthirsty, cruel, callous.

sanguíneo *adj* (a) (*Anat*) blood (*attr*); **vaso** — blood vessel. (b) (*fig*) blood-red.

sanguinolento *adj* (a) bleeding; bloody, bloodstained; streaked (*or* tinged) with blood; *eyes* bloodshot.
   (b) (*Cook*) underdone, rare.
   (c) (*fig*) blood-red.

sanidad *nf* (a) health, healthiness; (*fig*) salubrity.
   (b) public health; sanitation; **Ministerio de S—** Ministry of Health; — **pública** public health (department); **inspector de —, oficial de —** sanitary inspector.

sanitario *adj* sanitary; health (*attr*); sanitation (*attr*).

sano *adj* (a) (*Med etc*) healthy; fit; *organ, wood etc* sound; *fruit* good; **cortar por lo** — to take extreme measures, go right to the root of the trouble; to cut one's losses.
   (b) *climate etc* healthy; *food* good, wholesome.
   (c) *object* whole, intact, undamaged; — **y salvo** safe and sound; **esa silla no es muy sana** that chair is not too strong; **no ha quedado plato** — **en toda la casa** there wasn't a plate left whole (*or* unbroken) in the house.
   (d) (*fig*) (morally) healthy, wholesome; *doctrine, teaching* sound; *desire* earnest, sincere; *objective etc* worthy.

sánscrito 1 *adj* Sanskrit. **2** *nm* Sanskrit.

sanseacabó (*fam*): **y** — and that's the end of it, and there's no more to be said.

Sansón *m* Samson; **es un** — he's tremendously strong.

santa *nf* saint; *see* **santo**.

santabárbara *nf* (*Naut*) magazine.

santamente *adv*: **vivir** — to live a saintly (*or* holy) life.

santanderino 1 *adj* of Santander. **2** *nm*, **santanderina** *nf* native (*or* inhabitant) of Santander; **los** —**s** the people of Santander.

santateresa *nf* (*Ent*) praying mantis.

santería *nf* (a) (*SAm*) *shop selling religious images, prints etc.* (b) (*fam*) = **santidad**.

santero 1 *nm* (*SAm*) *maker* (*or* *seller*) *of religious images, prints etc.* **2** *nm*, **santera** *nf* person excessively devoted to the saints.

Santiago *m* St James; — **de Compostela** St James of Compostela.

santiamén *nm*: **en un** — in an instant.

santidad *nf* holiness, sanctity; saintliness; **su S—** His Holiness.

santificación *nf* sanctification.

santificar [1g] *vt* (a) to sanctify, make holy, hallow; to consecrate; *festivity* to keep; **santificado sea Tu Nombre** hallowed be thy name. (b) (*fam*) to forgive.

santiguar [1i] **1** *vt* (a) to make the sign of the cross over; to bless.
   (b) (*SAm*) to heal (by blessing).
   (c) (*fam*) to slap, hit.
  2 santiguarse *vr* (a) to cross oneself, make the sign of the cross.
   (b) (*fam*) to make a great fuss, react in an exaggerated way, overdo the emotion.

santísimo *adj superl* (most) holy.

santo 1 *adj* (a) holy; sacred; *ground* holy, consecrated; *person* saintly; *martyr* blessed.
   (b) (*fig*) *remedy etc* wonderful, miraculous.
   (c) (*fam*) utter, complete; blessed; — **y bueno** well and good; **todo el** — **día** the whole livelong day; the whole blessed day; **y él con su santa calma** he utterly unmoved, and he so completely calm; *see* **voluntad** etc.
  2 *nm* (a) (*Eccl*) saint; — **patrón**, — **titular** patron saint; **S— Domingo** (*Eccl*) St Dominic; (*Geog*) Santo Domingo, Dominican Republic; **S— Tomás** St Thomas; *see* **sano**.
   (b) (*idioms*) ¿**a qué** —? what on earth for?; ¿**a** — **de qué . . .**? why on earth . . .?; **¡por todos los** —**s!** for pity's sake!; **no es** — **de mi devoción** I'm not very keen on him; **alzarse con el** — **y la limosna** to clear off with the whole lot; **comerse los** —**s** to be terribly devout; **desnudar a un** — **para vestir otro** to rob Peter to pay Paul; **se le fue el** — **al cielo** he forgot what he was about to say; **llegar y besar el** — to pull it off at the first attempt; **nacer con el** — **de espaldas** to be born unlucky; **poner a uno como un** — to give someone a telling-off; **quedar para vestir** —**s** to be on the shelf; **tener el** — **de cara** to have tremendous luck.
   (c) (*fig*) saint; **es un** — he's a saint; **estaba hecho un** — he was terribly sweet (*fam*).
   (d) saint's day; — **y seña** (*Mil*) password; (*fig*) watchword, slogan; **mañana es mi** — tomorrow is my saint's day, tomorrow is my name day (*celebrated in Spain etc as equivalent to a birthday*).
   (e) (*Chi: Sew*) patch, darn.

santuario *nm* (a) sanctuary, shrine. (b) (*Col, Ven*) native idol; buried treasure.

santulario *adj* (*RPl*) = **santurrón**.

santurrón 1 *adj* sanctimonious; hypocritical. **2** *nm*, **santurrona** *nf* sanctimonious person; hypocrite.

saña *nf* anger, rage, fury; cruelty; (*fig*) fury, viciousness.

sañoso *adj* = **sañudo**.

sañudamente *adv* angrily, furiously; cruelly; viciously.

sañudo *adj* furious, enraged; cruel; *blow etc* vicious, cruel.

sapaneco *adj* (*CAm*) plump, chubby.

sáparo *nm* (*Col*) wicker basket.

sapo[1] *nm* (a) (*Zool*) toad; (*fig*) small/ animal, bug, creature; **echar** —**s y culebras** to produce a stream of abuse, swear black and blue.
   (b) (*prov, SAm*) *game of throwing coins into the mouth of an iron toad.*

sapo[2] *adj* (*Chi, Par, Per*) sly, cunning; hypocritical; (*Pan*) telltale.

saporro *adj* (*CAm, Col*) chubby.

sapotear [1a] *vt* (*Col*) to finger, handle.

saque *nm* (a) (*act: Tennis*) service, serve; (*Football*) throw-in, (*Rugby*; *also* — **de banda**) line-out; — **de castigo** penalty kick; — **de esquina** corner kick; —

inicial kick-off; — **libre** free kick; — **de portería**, — **de puerta** goal-kick.

  (b) (*Tennis: person*) server.

  (c) **tener buen** — to eat heartily, be a good trencherman.

  (d) (*Chi*) distilling; distillery.

saqueador *nm* looter.

saquear [1a] *vt* (*Mil*) to sack; to loot, plunder, pillage; (*fig*) to rifle, ransack; to turn upside down.

saqueo *nm* sacking; looting, plundering; (*fig*) rifling, ransacking.

saquito *nm* small bag; sachet; — **de papel** paper bag.

saracutear [1a] *vi* (*RPl*) to move about restlessly, be always on the go.

sarampión *nm* measles.

sarao *nm* soirée, evening party.

sarape *nm* (*Guat, Mex*) blanket.

saraviado *adj* (*Col*) spotted, mottled; *person* freckled.

sarazo (*SAm*) = **zarazo**.

sarazón *adj* (*Mex*) = **zarazo**.

sarcasmo *nm* sarcasm.

sarcásticamente *adv* sarcastically.

sarcástico *adj* sarcastic.

sarcófago *nm* sarcophagus.

sardina *nf* sardine; — **arenque** pilchard; — **noruega** brisling; **como** —**s en banasta** packed like sardines.

sardinero *adj* sardine (*attr*).

sardo 1 *adj* Sardinian. 2 *nm*, **sarda** *nf* Sardinian.

sardónico *adj* (*esp SAm*) sardonic; ironical, sarcastic.

sargentear [1a] 1 *vt* (*Mil*) to command; (*fam*) to boss about. 2 *vi* (*fam*) to be bossy, boss people about.

sargento *nm* sergeant; **ser** — **de caballería** (*of woman*) to be very tough and mannish.

sargentona *nf* (*fam*) tough mannish woman.

sargo *nm* bream.

sari *nm* sari.

sarita *nf* (*Per*) straw hat.

sarmentoso *adj* (a) *plant* twining, climbing. (b) *finger etc* long and thin; gnarled.

sarmiento *nm* vine shoot.

sarna *nf* itch, scabies; (*Vet*) mange.

sarniento *adj* (*CAm, Mex*), **sarnoso** *adj* (a) itchy, infected with the itch; (*Vet*) mangy. (b) (*fig*) weak, feeble. (c) (*Arg, Bol*) contemptible, lousy (*fam*).

sarpullido *nm* = **salpullido**.

sarraceno 1 *adj* Saracen. 2 *nm*, **sarracena** *nf* Saracen.

sarracina *nf* (a) quarrel; brawl, free fight.

  (b) mass slaughter; (*fig*) wholesale destruction.

  (c) (*Univ: fam*) **han hecho una** — they've ploughed almost everybody (*sl*).

Sarre *m* Saar.

sarro *nm* (a) incrustation, deposit; (*on teeth*) tartar; (*on kettle, tongue*) fur. (b) (*Bot*) rust.

sarroso *adj* incrusted; covered with tartar; furred, furry.

sarta *nf*, **sartal** *nm*, **sartalada** *nf* (*Chi*) string; line, row, series; (*fig*) string; **una** — **de mentiras** a string of lies.

sartén *nf* frying pan; **coger la** — **por donde quema** to act rashly; **saltar de la** — **y dar en la brasa** to jump out of the frying pan into the fire; **tener la** — **por el mango** to be the master, rule the roost.

sarteneja *nf* (*Ec, Mex*) dried-out pool; (*Mex*) deep bog.

sasafrás *nm* sassafras.

sastre *nm* tailor; — **de teatro** costumier; **hecho por** — tailor-made.

sastrería *nf* (a) tailoring, tailor's trade. (b) tailor's (shop).

Satanás *m* Satan.

satánico *adj* satanic; devilish, fiendish.

satélite 1 *nm* (a) (*Astron*) satellite; — **artificial** artificial satellite.

  (b) (*person*) satellite; minion; henchman; boon companion, crony.

  2 *as adj* satellite; **ciudad** — satellite town; **país** — satellite country.

satén *nm* sateen.

satín *nm* (*SAm*) sateen, satin.

satinado 1 *adj* glossy, shiny. 2 *nm* gloss, shine.

satinar [1a] *vt* to gloss, make glossy.

sátira *nf* satire.

satíricamente *adv* satirically.

satírico *adj* satiric(al).

satirizar [1f] *vt* to satirize.

sátiro *nm* satyr.

satisfacción *nf* (a) (*in most senses*) satisfaction; **a** — **de** to the satisfaction of; **a su entera** — to his complete satisfaction; **con** — **de todos** to the general satisfaction.

  (b) (*for an offence*) satisfaction, redress; apology;

pedir una — **a uno** to demand an apology from someone, demand satisfaction from someone.

  (c) — **de sí mismo** self-satisfaction, smugness.

satisfacer [2s] 1 *vt* (a) (*in most senses*) to satisfy; (*of achievement etc*) to gratify, please; *need, request* to meet, satisfy; *debt, wages etc* to pay; *draft* (*Comm*) to honour; *expenses* to meet.

  (b) *guilt* to expiate; *loss* to make good.

  (c) — **a uno de** (*or* **por**) **una ofensa** to give someone satisfaction for an offence.

  2 **satisfacerse** *vr* (a) to satisfy oneself, be satisfied; — **con muy poco** to be content with very little.

  (b) to obtain redress, obtain satisfaction; to take revenge.

satisfactoriamente *adv* satisfactorily.

satisfactorio *adj* satisfactory.

satisfecho *adj* (a) satisfied; content(ed); **darse por** — **con algo** to declare oneself satisfied (*or* content) with something; **dejar** —**s a todos** to satisfy everybody.

  (b) (*also* — **consigo mismo**, — **de sí mismo**) self-satisfied, smug; conceited; **nos miró** — he looked at us smugly.

saturación *nf* saturation; permeation.

saturar [1a] *vt* to saturate; to permeate.

saturnales *nfpl* Saturnalia.

saturnino *adj* saturnine.

Saturno *m* Saturn.

sauce *nm* willow; — **de Babilonia**, — **llorón** weeping willow.

saucedal *nm* willow plantation.

saúco *nm* (*Bot*) elder.

Saúl *m* Saul.

sauna *nf* sauna.

saurio *nm* saurian.

savia *nf* sap.

saxífraga *nf* saxifrage.

saxofón *nm*, **saxófono** *nm* saxophone.

saya *nf* (a) skirt; petticoat; dress. (b) (*Col*) woman.

sayal *nm* coarse woollen cloth.

sayo *nm* smock, tunic; loose garment, long loose gown.

sayón *nm* (a) (*Law*) executioner. (b) (*fig*) cruel henchman; (*fam*) fierce-looking chap (*fam*), ugly customer (*fam*).

sayuela *nf* (*Cu*) serge skirt.

sazo *nm* (*sl*) hankie (*fam*).

sazón 1 *nf* (a) (*Agr*) good heart; proper condition (*of land*) for planting.

  (b) (*of fruit*) ripeness, maturity; **en** — ripe, ready (to eat); (*fig*) opportunely; **fuera de** — at the wrong moment, inopportunely.

  (c) (*lit*) time, moment, season; **a la** — then, at that time.

  (d) (*Cook*) flavour.

  2 *adj* (*CAm, Mex, Per*) ripe.

sazonado *adj* (a) *fruit etc* ripe; mellow; *dish* tasty. (b) — **de** (*Cook*) seasoned with, flavoured with. (c) (*fig*) witty.

sazonar [1a] 1 *vt* (a) *fruit* to ripen, bring to maturity. (b) (*Cook*) to season, flavour (*de* with). (c) *PR* to sweeten. 2 *vi* to ripen.

se[1] *reflexive pron* (a) (*sing: m*) himself, (*f*) herself, (*of thing*) itself, (*relating to* **Vd**) yourself; (*pl*) themselves, (*relating to* **Vds**) yourselves; **se está lavando**, **está lavándose** he's washing, he's washing himself; **se retira** he withdraws; **se tiró al suelo** she threw herself to the ground; **¡siéntese!** sit down!

  (b) (*reciprocal*) each other, one another; **se ayudan** they help each other; **se miraron el uno al otro** they looked at one another; **no se hablan** they are not on speaking terms, they don't speak; **procuran no verse** they try not to run into each other.

  (c) (*in general*) oneself; **conviene lavarse de vez en cuando** it is advisable to wash oneself occasionally.

  (d) (*dative use*) **se ha comprado un sombrero** he has bought himself a hat, he has bought a hat for himself; **se rompió la pierna** he broke his leg; **han jurado no cortarse la barba** they have sworn not to cut their beards.

  (e) (*impersonal use: often translated by English passive, by one, by some or people*) **se compró hace 3 años** it was bought 3 years ago; **se comprende que . . .** it can be understood that . . ., it is understandable that . . .; **no se sabe por qué** it is not known why; **en esa parte se habla galés** in that area Welsh is spoken, in that area people speak Welsh; **en ese hotel se come realmente bien** the food is really good in that hotel, you eat (*or* one eats) really well in that hotel; **se hace cuando se puede** one does it when one can; **se avisa a los interesados que . . .** those concerned are informed that . . .; "**véndese: solar . . .**" (*advert*) "for sale: plot . . ."; "**véndese coche**" (*advert*) "car for sale".

se² *personal pron* (*corresponding to* **le, les**)**: se lo arrancó** he snatched it from her; **voy a dárselo** I'll give it to him; **se lo buscaré** I'll look for it for you; **no se lo agradecerán** they won't thank you for it.

sé *see* **saber, ser.**

sebear [1a] *vi* (*Ven*) to make love.

sebo *nm* (a) grease, fat; (*for candles*) tallow; (*Cook*) suet.
(b) (*fam: on person*) fat; (*on object*) grease, filth, grime.
(c) **helarse a uno el —** (*Arg, Bol*) to fail; to peg out (*sl*); **hacer un —** (*RPl*) to idle, loaf; **dar — a** (*Col, Ven*) to pester; **hacer** (*or* **volver**) **— a** (*Cu*) to finish off, ruin.

sebón *adj* (*Arg, Guat*) idle, lazy.

seboso *adj* (a) greasy, fatty; tallowy; suety. (b) (*fam*) greasy, filthy, grimy.

seca *nf* (a) (*Agr*) drought; (*Meteorol*) dry season. (b) (*Naut*) sandbank.

secadero *nm* (a) place where fruit (*etc*) is laid to dry. (b) (*Col*) dry land.

secador *nm* (a) place where clothes are hung to dry. (b) **— de cabello, — para el pelo** hair-drier; **— centrífugo** spin-drier.

secadora *nf* wringer; **— centrífuga** spin-drier.

secamente *adv* brusquely, sharply, curtly; drily.

secano *nm* (a) (*Agr: also* **tierra de —**) dry land, dry region; unirrigated land; **cultivo de —** crop of dry regions, crop not requiring irrigation; crop suitable for a region of low rainfall.
(b) (*Naut*) sandbank; small sandy island.
(c) (*fig*) very dry thing.

secante¹ **1** *adj* (a) *wind etc* drying; **papel — =2.** (b) (*RPl*) annoying. **2** *nm* blotting paper, blotter.

secante² *nf* (*Math*) secant.

secar [1g] **1** *vt* (a) to dry, dry up, dry off; *dish, surface* to wipe dry; *tears* to dry; *brow* to wipe, mop; *spilt liquid* to mop up; *ink* to blot; *plant* to dry up, wither.
(b) (*fig*) to annoy, vex; to bore.
2 secarse *vr* (a) (*washing etc*) to dry, dry off; (*river*) to dry up, run dry; (*plant*) to dry up, wither, wilt; (*person*) to dry oneself, get dry (*con una toalla* on a towel, with a towel).
(b) (*wound*) to close up, heal up.
(c) (*fam: person*) to get thin.
(d) (*fam: also* **— de sed**) to have a raging thirst.

secarropa *nm* clothes horse.

sección *nf* (a) (*Archit, Math etc*) section; (*also* **— transversal**) cross-section; **— cónica** conic section; **— longitudinal** longitudinal section; **— vertical** vertical section.
(b) (*fig*) section; division, department, branch.
(c) (*Mil*) section, platoon.

seccional *adj* sectional.

seccionar [1a] *vt* to divide up, divide into sections.

secesión *nf* secession.

secesionista **1** *adj* secessionist. **2** *nmf* secessionist.

seco *adj* (a) (*general sense*) dry; *fruit etc* dried; *plant* dried up, withered, dead; *battery, climate, lake, season etc* dry; **— al tacto** touch-dry; **estar en —** (*Naut and fig*) to be high and dry.
(b) *person* thin, skinny.
(c) *character* cold; disagreeable; blunt; *manner, reply etc* brusque, sharp, curt; *style* plain, bare, flat, inexpressive; *explanation* plain, unvarnished; *subject, study* dry.
(d) *blow, sound, thud etc* dull; *cough* dry.
(e) bare; *brandy* pure, unadulterated; **vivir a pan — to** live on bread alone, eat only bread; **tiene el sueldo —** he has just his salary.
(f) **dejar a uno —** to kill someone stone-dead; (*fig*) to dumbfound someone; **quedarse —** to be dumbfounded.
(g) **a secas: habrá pan a secas** there will be just bread; **decir algo a secas** to say something curtly, say something abruptly; **se llama Rodríguez a secas** he is called plain Rodríguez, he is just called Rodríguez.
(h) **callarse en —** to stop talking suddenly; to stop talking at once; **frenar en —** to brake sharply, pull up sharply; **parar en —** to stop dead, stop suddenly.

secoya *nf* redwood, sequoia.

secreción *nf* secretion.

secretamente *adv* secretly.

secretar [1a] *vt* to secrete.

secretaría *nf* (a) secretariat. (b) secretary's office. (c) secretaryship.

secretariado *nm* (a) secretariat. (b) secretaryship. (c) (*SAm*) secretarial course. (d) (*SAm*) career as a secretary, profession of secretary.

secretario *nm*, **secretaria** *nf* secretary; **— general** general secretary, (*Pol*) secretary general; **— municipal** town clerk; **— particular** private secretary.

secretear [1a] *vi* (a) to talk confidentially, exchange secrets. (b) to whisper unnecessarily; to whisper ostentatiously.

secreter *nm* (*gall*) writing desk.

secreto **1** *adj* (a) secret; hidden; *information* secret, confidential, (*Mil*) classified; **todo es de lo más —** it's all highly secret.
(b) *person* secretive.
2 *nm* (a) (*un —*) secret; **— de confesión** confessional secret; **— de estado** state secret; **— de fabricación** industrial secret; **— a voces** open secret; **estar en el —** to be in on the secret; **guardar un —** to keep a secret; **hacer — de algo** to be secretive about something.
(b) (*quality*) secrecy; **— de correspondencia** sanctity of the mails; **en —** in secret, secretly, in secrecy; **lo han hecho con mucho —** they have done it in great secrecy.
(c) (*of desk*) secret drawer.
(d) (*of lock*) combination.

secta *nf* sect; denomination.

sectario **1** *adj* sectarian; denominational; **no — non**-sectarian, non-denominational.
2 *nm*, **sectaria** *nf* follower, devotee; member; (*Eccl*) sectarian, member of a sect (*or* denomination).

sectarismo *nm* sectarianism.

sector *nm* sector; (*of opinion etc*) section; **— privado** (*Comm*) private sector; **— público** (*Comm*) public sector.

secuaz *nm* follower, supporter; (*pej*) underling, hireling.

secuela *nf* consequence.

secuencia *nf* (*Cine, Gram etc*) sequence.

secuestración *nf* sequestration; **= secuestro.**

secuestrador *nm*, **secuestradora** *nf* kidnapper.

secuestrar [1a] *vt* (a) *child* to kidnap; *person* to kidnap, abduct. (b) (*Law*) *goods* to seize, confiscate.

secuestro *nm* (a) kidnapping, abduction. (b) (*Law*) seizure, confiscation.

secular *adj* (a) (*Eccl*) secular; lay. (b) century-old; (*fig*) centuries-old, age-old, ancient; **según una tradición —** according to an age-old tradition.

secularización *nf* secularization.

secularizar [1f] *vt* to secularize.

secundar [1a] *vt* to second, help, support.

secundario *adj* secondary; minor, of lesser importance; *question* (*Parl*) supplementary.

secundinas *nfpl* afterbirth.

secuoia *nf* (*SAm*) = **secoya.**

sed *nf* thirst; thirstiness; (*Agr*) thirst, drought, dryness; (*fig*) thirst, lust, longing (*de* for); **— inextinguible, — insaciable** unquenchable thirst; **apagar la —** to quench one's thirst; **tener —** to be thirsty; **tener mucha —** to be very thirsty; **tener — de** (*fig*) to thirst for, long for.

seda *nf* (a) silk; **— artificial** artificial silk; **— de coser** sewing silk; **— floja** floss silk; **— hilada** spun silk; **— en rama** raw silk; **como una —** (*adj*) as smooth as silk, beautifully smooth; *person* very meek, very sweet-tempered; (*adv*) smoothly; **de — silk** (*attr*); silken, silky.
(b) (*Zool*) bristle.

sedal *nm* fishing line.

sedalina *nf* artificial silk.

sedán *nm* (*Aut*) sedan (*US*).

sedante **1** *adj* sedative; (*fig*) soothing, calming. **2** *nm* sedative.

sedativo *adj* sedative.

sede *nf* (a) (*of government*) seat; (*of company, society*) headquarters, central office; **— social** head office, central office. (b) (*Eccl*) see; **Santa S—** Holy See.

sedentario *adj* sedentary.

sedeño *adj* (a) silken, silky. (b) (*Zool*) bristly.

sedería *nf* (a) silk raising, silk manufacture; sericulture; silk trade. (b) silks, silk goods. (c) silk shop.

sedero **1** *adj* silk (*attr*); **industria sedera** silk industry. **2** *nm* silk dealer; draper, haberdasher.

sedicente *adj* self-styled; so-called, would-be.

sedición *nf* sedition.

sedicioso **1** *adj* seditious; mutinous, rebellious. **2** *nm*, **sediciosa** *nf* subversive element, disloyal individual; rebel; troublemaker.

sediento *adj* (a) thirsty (*also Agr*). (b) (*fig*) thirsty, eager (*de* for).

sedimentación *nf* sedimentation.

sedimentar [1a] **1** vt (a) to deposit. (b) (fig) to calm, quieten. **2 sedimentarse** vr (a) to settle. (b) (fig) to calm down, quieten down.
sedimentario adj sedimentary.
sedimento nm sediment, deposit.
sedosidad nf silkiness.
sedoso adj silky, silken.
seducción nf (a) (act) seduction. (b) (quality) seductiveness; charm, allure; lure, fascination.
seducir [3o] **1** vt (a) woman to seduce.
　(b) (fig) to lead on, seduce from one's duty; to bribe.
　(c) (fig) to charm, attract, captivate, fascinate; **seduce a todos con su simpatía** she captivates everyone with her charm; **la teoría ha seducido a muchos** the theory has attracted many people.
　2 vi to be charming, be fascinating; **es una película que seduce** it's a captivating film.
seductivo adj = **seductor 1**.
seductor 1 adj (a) seductive. (b) (fig) charming, captivating, fascinating; tempting. **2** nm seducer.
sefardí 1 adj Sephardic. **2** nmf Sephardi, Sephardic Jew(ess); **sefardíes** Sephardim (descendants of the Jews expelled from Spain in 1492).
segable adj corn ready to cut.
segadera nf sickle.
segador nm harvester, reaper.
segadora nf (a) (person) harvester, reaper. (b) (Mech) mower, reaper, mowing machine; **— de césped** lawnmower.
segadora-atadora nf binder.
segadora-trilladora nf combine harvester.
segar [1h and 1k] vt (a) (Agr) corn etc to reap, cut, harvest; grass, hay to mow, cut; other object to cut off.
　(b) (fig) to mow down.
　(c) (fig) hopes etc to ruin, destroy; **— la juventud de uno** to cut someone off in his prime.
seglar 1 adj secular, lay. **2** nm layman.
segmento nm segment; **— de émbolo** piston ring.
segoviano 1 adj of Segovia. **2** nm, **segoviana** nf native (or inhabitant) of Segovia; **los —s** the people of Segovia.
segregación nf (a) segregation; **— racial** racial segregation, apartheid. (b) (Anat) secretion.
segregacionista nmf segregationist, supporter of racial segregation.
segregar [1h] vt (a) to segregate, separate. (b) (Anat) to secrete.
seguida nf (a) normal way (of doing something); proper rhythm, habitual speed; **coger la —** to get into the swing of it, get into the proper way (of doing something).
　(b) **a —** = **seguidamente**; **de —** uninterruptedly, straight off; at once; **en —** at once, right way; **en — termino** I've very nearly finished, I shan't be long now; **en — tomó el avión para Madrid** he immediately caught the plane to Madrid.
seguidamente adv (a) uninterruptedly, straight off, without a break; continuously. (b) immediately after, next; **dijo — que . . .** he went on at once to say that . . .
seguido 1 adj (a) row etc continuous, unbroken.
　(b) road, route etc straight.
　(c) **—s** consecutive, successive; **5 días —s** 5 days running; **5 blancos —s** 5 bull's-eyes in a row, 5 consecutive bull's-eyes.
　(d) long-lasting; **una enfermedad muy seguida** a very lengthy illness, a long drawn-out illness.
　2 adv (a) straight; **vaya Vd todo —** just keep straight on; **por aquí —** straight on past here.
　(b) after; **ese coche iba primero y — el mío** that car was in front and mine was immediately behind it.
seguidor nm, **seguidora** nf follower; (Sport) fan (fam), follower, supporter.
seguimiento nm chase, pursuit; continuation; **estación de —** tracking station; **ir en — de** to go in pursuit of, chase (after).
seguir [3d and 3l] **1** vt (a) (general sense) to follow; to follow on, come next to, come after.
　(b) quarry to chase, pursue; to hound; track to follow; satellite to track; steps to dog; clue to follow up; woman to court.
　(c) authority, leader, instruction, inclination, text etc to follow; advice to follow, adopt, take.
　(d) career, course to follow, pursue.
　(e) **— su camino** to continue on one's way.
　2 vi (a) (general sense) to follow; to follow on, come next, come after; **y los que siguen** and the next ones, and those that come next; **como sigue** as follows.
　(b) to continue, to carry on, go on; **¡siga!** go on!; (Col) come in!; **siga a la derecha** keep to the right; **— con una idea** to go on with an idea; **sigue en su sitio** it is still in its place; **sigue en Caracas** he is still in Caracas; **seguía en su error** he continued in his error; **— adelante** to go on, carry on; to go straight on; (Aut) to drive on, go straight ahead; **siga Vd adelante hasta Toboso** go straight ahead as far as Toboso; **— por un camino** to carry on along a path; **hacer — una carta** to forward a letter; **¿cómo sigue?** how is he?; **sigue bien, que siga Vd bien** I hope you keep well, look after yourself.
　(c) (with adj or n etc) to be still, go on being; **sigue enfermo** he's still ill; **si el tiempo sigue bueno** if the weather continues fine; **sigue tan misterioso como antes** it's still as mysterious as ever; **sigue soltera** she's still single; **sigue sin poderlo comprar** he is still unable to buy it; **sigo sin comprender** I still don't understand.
　(d) **— + ger** to go on + ger, keep (on) + ger; **sigue lloviendo** it's still raining; **sigue siendo lo mismo** it's still the same, it remains unchanged; **siguió mirándola** he went on looking at her; **siguió sentado** he stayed sitting down, he remained seated.
　3 seguirse vr (a) to follow; **una cosa se sigue a otra** one thing follows another.
　(b) to follow, ensue, happen in consequence; **de esto se sigue que . . ., síguese que . . .** it follows that . . .
según 1 adv (fam) according to circumstances; **— y como, — y conforme** it all depends; "**¿lo vas a comprar?**" . . . "**—**" "are you going to buy it?" . . . "it all depends".
　2 prep (a) according to; in accordance with, in line with; **— el jefe** according to the boss; **— este mapa** according to this map; **obrar — las instrucciones** to act in accordance with one's instructions; **— lo que dice** from what he says, according to what he says; **iremos o no, — el tiempo** we'll go or not, depending on the weather; **eso es — el dinero de que se disponga** that depends on what money is available.
　(b) **está — lo dejaste** it is just as you left it.
　3 conj as; **— me consta** as far as I know; **— esté el tiempo** depending on the weather; **— que vengan 3 or 4** depending on whether 3 or 4 come.
segunda nf (a) (Mus) second. (b) second meaning, veiled meaning; **decir algo con —(s)** to say something with an implied second meaning.
segundante nm (Boxing) second.
segundar [1a] **1** vt (a) to do again. (b) (RPl) blow to return. (c) (Mex) to earth up. **2** vi to come second, be in second place.
segundero nm second hand (of a watch).
segundo 1 adj second.
　2 nm (a) second; second one; second in authority; (Naut) mate; **ser el — de a bordo** (fig) to be second in command; **sin —** unrivalled.
　(b) (of time) second.
　(c) (Mex) **—s** upstairs seats (in a theatre etc).
segundón nm second son, younger son.
segur nf sickle; axe.
seguramente adv (a) know etc for sure, with certainty.
　(b) surely; **— tendrán otro** surely they'll have another, they must have another; "**¿lo va a comprar?**" . . . "**—**" "is he going to buy it?" . . . "I should think so".
　(c) (SAm) probably, possibly.
seguridad nf (a) safety; security; safeness; (Mil, Pol) security; **— en la carretera** road safety; **— colectiva** collective security; **— contra incendios** fire precautions; **— social** social security; **de —** safety (attr), eg **cinturón de —** safety belt; **con la mayor —** with (or in) complete safety; **para mayor —** to be on the safe side, for safety's sake; **estar en —** to be in a safe place.
　(b) certainty; **en la — de su victoria** in the certainty of winning, being sure of winning; **con toda —** with complete certainty; **no lo sabemos con —** we don't know for sure; **tener la — de que . . .** to have the certainty that . . ., be sure that . . .; **tengan Vds la — de que . . .** rest assured that . . .
　(c) (also **— en sí mismo**) confidence, self-confidence.
　(d) trustworthiness; reliability.
　(e) firmness; stability, steadiness.
　(f) (Law) security, surety.
seguro 1 adj (a) safe; secure; **un puerto —** a safe harbour; **está más — en el banco** it's safer in the

bank; **lo más — es** + *infin* the safest thing is to + *infin*, the best thing is to + *infin*; **conviene atenerse a lo —** it's best to be on the safe side.
(b) *method, result etc* sure, certain; bound to come, certain to happen; **ir a una muerte segura** to go to certain death; **es — que ... it** is certain that ...; **en estas investigaciones no hay nada —** nothing is certain in these researches.
(c) *(of person)* sure, certain; **¿estás —?** are you sure?; **estar — de** to be sure of; **estar — de que ...** to be sure that ...
(d) estar — de sí mismo to be confident, be self-confident, be sure of oneself.
(e) *friend etc* firm, sure, trustworthy; *source* reliable, dependable, trustworthy.
(f) *object* firm; firmly fastened, securely tied *(etc)*; stable, steady; *date etc* firm, definite.
(g) *(SAm)* honest, straight.
2 *adv* **(a)** for sure; **todavía no lo ha dicho —** he still hasn't said for sure.
(b) ¡—! sure!, I'm sure it is! *(etc)*.
3 *nm* **(a)** safety device; *(of lock)* tumbler; *(Mil)* safety catch; *(Tech)* catch, pawl, lock, stop.
(b) *(fig)* safety, certainty, assurance; **a buen —, de —** surely; truly; **en —** in a safe place; **sobre —** safely, without risk; **ir sobre —** to be on safe ground.
(c) *(Comm, Fin)* insurance; **S— de Enfermedad** *equivalent to* National Health Insurance; **— de incendios** fire insurance; **— social** social insurance, social security; **— contra terceros** third-party insurance; **— a** *(or* **contra)** **todo riesgo** comprehensive insurance; **— de vida, — sobre la vida** life insurance.
seibó *nm (Col, PR, SD, Ven: angl)* sideboard.
seis 1 *adj* six; *(date)* sixth; **las — six** o'clock. **2** *nm* six.
seiscientos *adj* six hundred.
seísmo *nm* tremor, shock, earthquake.
selección *nf* selection; **—es** *(Lit, Mus)* selections; **— biológica, — natural** natural selection.
seleccionador *nm (Sport)* selector.
seleccionar [1a] *vt* to pick, choose, select.
selectividad *nf* selectivity.
selectivo *adj* selective.
selecto *adj* **(a)** *(in quality)* select, choice, fine; *club etc* select, exclusive. **(b)** *(Lit)* works selected.
seltz [selθ,sel]: **agua (de) —** seltzer (water).
selva *nf* forest, woods; jungle.
selvático *adj* **(a)** woodland *(attr)*, sylvan; *(fig)* rustic. **(b)** *(Bot etc)* wild.
selvoso *adj* wooded, well-wooded.
sellado 1 *adj* sealed; stamped, franked. **2** *nm* **(a)** sealing; stamping. **(b)** *(Arg)* postage, value in stamps.
selladura *nf* **(a)** seal. **(b)** *(act)* sealing; stamping.
sello *nm* **(a)** seal; *(official etc)* stamp; signet; **— de caucho, — de goma** rubber stamp.
(b) impression, mark; stamp; *(Comm)* brand, seal; **— fiscal** revenue stamp; **lleva el — de esta oficina** it carries the stamp of this office.
(c) *(Post)* stamp; **— aéreo** airmail stamp; **— conmemorativo** commemorative stamp; **— de correo** postage stamp; **— de urgencia** express-delivery stamp.
(d) *(Med)* capsule, pill.
(e) *(fig)* hallmark, stamp *(also —* **distintivo)**; **lleva el — de su genialidad** it carries the hallmark of his genius.
semáforo *nm (Naut etc)* semaphore; *(Rail)* signal; *(Aut)* traffic lights.
semana *nf* week; **— inglesa** working week of 5½ days; **— laboral** working week; **S— Santa** Holy Week; **entre —** during the week; **vuelo de entre —** mid-week flight.
semanal *adj* weekly.
semanalmente *adv* weekly, each week.
semanario 1 *adj* weekly. **2** *nm* weekly.
semanero *nm*, **semanera** *nf (SAm)* weekly-paid worker; worker specially engaged for a week's work.
semántica *nf* semantics.
semántico *adj* semantic.
semblante *nm (lit)* face, visage; *(fig)* face, appearance; outlook; aspect; **alterar** *(or* **demudar)** **el — a uno** to make someone look alarmed, upset someone; **componer el —** to regain one's composure; **mudar de —** to change colour.
semblantear [1a] *vt* **(a)** *(Chi, Guat, Mex, RPI)* *person* to look straight in the face, scrutinize the face of. **(b)** *(Mex)* to study, examine, look at.
semblanza *nf* biographical sketch.
sembradera *nf* seed drill.
sembrado *nm* sown field.

sembrador 1 *nm*, **sembradora** *nf* sower. **2 sembradora** *nf (Mech)* seed drill.
sembradura *nf* sowing.
sembrar [1k] *vt* **(a)** *(Agr)* *field, seed* to sow; **— de** to sow with.
(b) *(Naut)* **— minas en un estrecho, — un estrecho de minas** to mine a strait, lay mines in a strait.
(c) *(fig)* *objects* to sprinkle, scatter about, spread around; *surface* to sprinkle, strew *(de* with); *discord* to sow; *news* to spread; **el que siembra recoge** one reaps what one has sown.
(d) *(Mex)* *rider* to throw; to knock down.
sembrío *nm (SAm)* sown field.
semejante 1 *adj* **(a)** similar; **—s** alike, similar, the same; **— a** like; **es — a ella en el carácter** she is like her in character; **son muy —s** they are very much alike.
(b) *(Math)* similar.
(c) such; **nunca hizo cosa —** he never did such a thing, he never did anything of the kind; **¿se ha visto frescura —?** did you ever see such cheek?
(d) *(Arg, Mex)* huge.
2 *nm* **(a)** fellow man, fellow creature; **nuestros —s** our fellow men.
(b) no tiene — it has no equal, there is nothing to equal it.
semejanza *nf* similarity, resemblance; **a — de** like, as; **— de familia** family likeness; **tener — con** to look like, resemble, bear a resemblance to.
semejar [1a] **1** *vi* to seem like, resemble, seem to be. **2 semejarse** *vr* to look alike, be similar, resemble each other; **— a** to look alike, resemble.
semen *nm* semen.
semental 1 *adj* stud, breeding *(attr)*. **2** *nm* sire, stud animal.
sementera *nf* **(a)** sowing. **(b)** seedtime, sowing season. **(c)** sown land, sown field. **(d)** *(fig)* hotbed *(de* of), breeding ground *(de* for).
semestral *adj* half-yearly, biannual.
semestralmente *adv* half-yearly, biannually.
semestre *nm* **(a)** period of six months; *(US: Univ etc)* semester. **(b)** *(Fin)* half-yearly payment.
semi- prefix semi..., half-...
semibola *nf (Bridge)* small slam.
semibreve *nf* semibreve.
semicircular *adj* semicircular.
semicírculo *nm* semicircle.
semiconsciente *adj* semiconscious, half-conscious.
semiconsonante *nf* semiconsonant.
semicorchea *nf* semiquaver.
semicualificado *adj* semiskilled.
semicultismo *nm* half-learned word.
semiculto *adj* half-learned.
semicupio *nm (Cu, Guat)* hip-bath.
semidesierto *adj* half-empty.
semidesnudo *adj* half-naked.
semidiós *nm* demigod.
semidormido *adj* half-asleep.
semiexperto *adj* semiskilled.
semifallo *nm (Bridge)* singleton *(a* in).
semifinal *nf* semifinal.
semifinalista *nmf* semifinalist.
semilla *nf* **(a)** *(Bot)* seed; **— de césped** grass seed. **(b)** *(Arg, Par)* brad, tack. **(c)** *(Chi)* baby, child; kids *(collectively; fam)*.
semillero *nm* **(a)** seedbed; nursery.
(b) *(fig)* hotbed *(de* of), breeding ground *(ae* for); **un — de delincuencia** a hotbed of crime; **la decisión fue un — de disgustos** the decision caused a host of troubles, the decision became a battleground of controversy.
semimedio *nm (Boxing)* welterweight.
seminal *adj* seminal.
seminario *nm* **(a)** *(Agr)* seedbed; nursery. **(b)** *(Eccl)* seminary. **(c)** *(Univ etc)* seminar.
seminarista *nm* seminarist.
semioficial *adj* semi-official.
semiprecioso *adj* semiprecious.
semiseparado *adj* semidetached.
semisótano *nm* semibasement.
semita 1 *adj* Semitic. **2** *nmf* Semite.
semítico *adj* Semitic.
semitono *nm* semitone.
semiverdad *nf* half-truth.
semivocal *nf* semivowel.
sémola *nf* semolina.
sempiterna *nf* evergreen.
sempiterno *adj* everlasting.
sen *nm*, **sena** *nf (Bot, Med)* senna.
Sena *m* Seine.
senado *nm* senate; *(fig)* assembly, gathering.

senador *nm* senator.
senatorial *adj* senatorial.
sencillamente *adv* simply; **es — imposible** it's simply impossible.
sencillez *nf* (a) simplicity, plainness. (b) simplicity, straightforwardness. (c) naturalness, unaffectedness, lack of sophistication; (*pej*) simplicity.
sencillo 1 *adj* (a) (*general sense*) simple, plain, unadorned; *custom, dress, style etc* simple.
　(b) *matter, problem* simple, easy, straightforward; **es muy —** it's very simple.
　(c) *person* natural, unaffected, unsophisticated; (*pej*) simple.
　(d) *flower, thread, ticket etc* single.
　2 *nm* (*SAm*) small change, loose change.
senda *nf* path, track; (*fig*) path; (*Aut*) lane.
sendero *nm* path, track.
sendos *adj pl*: **les dio — golpes** he hit both of them, he gave each of them a blow; **llevaban — sombreros** they both wore hats, each of them wore a hat; **con sendas peculiaridades** with individual peculiarities.
Séneca *m* Seneca.
senectud *nf* old age.
Senegal: El — Senegal.
senegalés 1 *adj* Senegalese. **2** *nm*, **senegalesa** *nf* Senegalese.
senil *adj* senile.
senilidad *nf* senility.
seno[1] *nm* (a) (*Anat*) bosom, bust; **—s** breasts; **— frontal** sinus; **— materno** womb; (*fig*) bosom; **en el — de Abrahán** on Abraham's bosom; **morir en el — de la familia** to die in the bosom of one's family; **lo escondió en su —** she hid it in her bosom, she put it down the front of her dress.
　(b) hollow, cavity; (*Naut*) trough (*between waves*).
　(c) (*Geog*) small bay, inlet; gulf.
　(d) (*fig*) refuge, haven.
　(e) (*of club etc*) headquarters.
seno[2] *nm* (*Math*) sine.
sensación *nf* (a) sensation, feeling; sense; feel; **una — de placer** a feeling of pleasure; **tengo una — de inutilidad** I have a feeling of being useless.
　(b) (*fig*) sensation; **causar —, hacer —** to cause a sensation.
sensacional *adj* sensational.
sensacionalismo *nm* sensationalism.
sensacionalista *adj* sensationalist.
sensatamente *adv* sensibly.
sensatez *nf* good sense, sensibleness.
sensato *adj* sensible.
sensibilidad *nf* sensitivity (*a* to), sensitiveness; sensibility; **— artística** artistic feeling, sensitivity to art.
sensibilizado *adj* sensitized; (*Phot*) sensitive.
sensibilizar [1f] *vt* to sensitize.
sensible *adj* (a) *creature* feeling, sentient; sensitive (*a* to); (*Med*) *spot* sensitive, tender, sore; (*Phot*) sensitive; **un aparato muy —** a very sensitive (*or* delicate) piece of apparatus; **una placa — a la luz** a plate sensitive to light; **es muy — a los cambios de temperatura** it is very sensitive to changes in temperature.
　(b) *person* sensitive (*a* to); responsive (*a* to); impressionable, emotional.
　(c) *change etc* perceptible, appreciable, noticeable; *difference etc* tangible, palpable; *blow* heavy; *loss* heavy, considerable; **una — mejoría** a noticeable improvement, a marked improvement.
　(d) **— de** capable of; **— de mejora** capable of improvement, having a capacity for improvement.
　(e) **soy — del honor que se me hace** I am conscious of the honour being done me.
　(f) regrettable, lamentable; **es muy —** it is highly regrettable; **es — que . . .** it is regrettable that . . .
sensiblemente *adv* perceptibly, appreciably, noticeably; markedly.
sensiblería *nf* sentimentality; mushiness, sloppiness; squeamishness.
sensiblero *adj* sentimental; mushy, sloppy; squeamish.
sensitiva *nf* (a) (*Bot*) mimosa. (b) (*fam*) highly sensitive person, delicate flower.
sensitivo *adj* (a) *organ etc* sense (*attr*). (b) *being etc* sentient; sensitive.
sensorio *adj* sensory.
sensual *adj* (a) sensual; sensuous. (b) (*esp SAm*) attractive, alluring, sexy.
sensualidad *nf* sensuality; sensuousness.
sensualismo *nm* sensualism.
sensualista *nmf* sensualist.

sentada *nf* (a) sitting; **de una —, en una —** at one sitting. (b) (*Pol etc*) sit-down (protest); sit-in.
sentadera *nf* (*SAm*) seat (*of a chair etc*).
sentadero *nm* seat.
sentado *adj* (a) **estar —** to sit, be sitting (down), be seated; **permanecer —** to remain seated.
　(b) (*fig*) settled, established; firm; **dar algo por —** to take something for granted, assume something; **dejar algo —** to establish something firmly; **dejar — que . . .** to lay down that . . ., have it clearly understood that . . .
　(c) (*fig*) *character* solid, sensible, steady; sedate.
sentador *adj* (*Chi, RPl*) *dress* becoming, smart.
sentadura *nf* mark (*on skin, fruit etc*).
sentar [1k] **1** *vt* (a) *person* to sit, seat.
　(b) *object* to place (firmly), settle (in its place); **— el último ladrillo** to tap the last brick into place; **— las costuras** to press the seams.
　(c) (*Comm*) **— una suma en la cuenta de uno** to put a sum down to someone's account.
　(d) *basis, foundations* (*fig*) to lay, establish, create; *principle* to set up, establish; *precedent* to lay down, set up.
　(e) (*Col, PR*) *person* to crush, squash.
　(f) (*Col*) *horse* to rein in sharply.
　2 *vti* (a) (*of dress etc*) to suit; to fit; to look well on, be becoming to; **ese peinado le sienta horriblemente** that hair style doesn't suit her one little bit, she looks awful with that hairdo (*fam*).
　(b) (*of food*) **— bien a** to agree with; **— mal a** to disagree with; **no me sientan las gambas** prawns disagree with me.
　(c) (*fig*) **— bien** to go down well; **— mal** to go down badly, produce a bad impression; **le ha sentado mal que lo hayas hecho tú** he took it badly that you should do it, he didn't like your doing it.
　3 sentarse *vr* (a) (*person*) to sit, sit down; to seat oneself; to settle oneself; **¡siéntese!** (do) sit down, take a seat; **sentémonos aquí** let's sit (down) here; **se sentó a comer** he sat down to eat.
　(b) (*sediment etc*) to settle.
　(c) (*weather etc*) to settle (down); to become steady, stabilize.
　(d) (*Archit*) to settle.
　(e) (*shoes etc*) to leave a mark, rub.
sentencia *nf* (a) (*Law*) sentence; (*fig*) decision, ruling; opinion; **— de muerte** death sentence; **dictar —, pronunciar —** to pronounce sentence. (b) (*Lit*) maxim, saying; dictum.
sentenciar [1b] **1** *vt* (a) (*Law*) to sentence (*a* to). (b) (*SAm*) **— a uno** to swear vengeance against someone. **2** *vi* to pronounce, give one's opinion.
sentenciosamente *adv* (a) pithily. (b) sententiously; dogmatically.
sentenciosidad *nf* (a) pithiness; oracular nature. (b) sententiousness; dogmatism.
sentencioso *adj* (a) *saying* pithy; oracular. (b) *person* sententious; dogmatic.
sentidamente *adv* (a) regretfully. (b) sincerely, with great feeling.
sentido 1 *adj* (a) regrettable; deeply felt; **una pérdida muy sentida** a deeply felt loss, a most regrettable loss.
　(b) *sympathy etc* sincere, deeply felt, keen; **le doy mi más — pésame** I send my deepest sympathy.
　(c) *character* sensitive, tender, easily wounded.
　(d) (*Arg, Mex*) having sharp hearing.
　2 *nm* (a) (*bodily*) sense; **los cinco —s** the five senses; **— del olfato** sense of smell; **— del color** sense of colour; **— del humor** sense of humour; **— de la medida, — de las proporciones** sense of proportion; **— de orientación** sense of direction; **no tiene — del ritmo** he has no sense of rhythm; **sin —** senseless, unconscious; **aguzar el —** to prick up one's ears; **costar un — (fam)** to cost the earth; **embargar los —s a uno** to enrapture someone; **perder el —** to lose consciousness; **poner los cinco —s en algo** to give one's whole attention to something; **recobrar el —** to regain consciousness.
　(b) (*fig*) sense; discernment, judgement; **buen —** good sense; **— común** common sense; **tener — para distinguir algo** to have enough sense to distinguish something.
　(c) (*Ling*) sense, meaning; **doble —** double meaning; **— figurado** figurative sense; **en el buen — de la palabra** in the best sense of the word; **en el — amplio** in the broad sense; **en el — estricto** in the strict sense; **en cierto —** in a sense; **en tal — to this effect; sin —** meaningless; **cobrar —** to begin to make sense; **no le encuentro ningún —** I can't

make any sense of it; **tener** — to make sense; **no tiene** — **que lo haga él** it doesn't make any sense for him to do it.

(d) (in reading, for music etc) feeling; **leer con** — to read with feeling; **tener** — **de la música** to have a feeling for music.

(e) (Geog) direction; way; "**— único**" "one way (street)"; **en** — **contrario, en** — **opuesto** in the opposite direction, the other way; **algo en este** — (fig) something along these lines; **iban en** — **inverso al nuestro** they were travelling in the opposite direction to us.

(f) (Mex) ear.

sentimental adj (a) sentimental; **look** soulful. (b) **affair, life** etc love (attr); **aventura** — love affair, affair of the heart.

sentimentalismo nm sentimentality.

sentimentero adj (Mex, PR) = **sensiblero.**

sentimiento nm (a) feeling, emotion, sentiment; **un** — **de insatisfacción** a feeling of dissatisfaction; **buenos** —**s** fellow-feeling, sympathy; **herir los** —**s de uno** to hurt (or wound) someone's feelings.

(b) sense; — **del deber** sense of duty; — **de la responsabilidad** sense of responsibility.

(c) regret, grief, sorrow; **con profundo** — with profound regret; see **acompañar.**

sentina nf (a) (Naut) bilge; (in town) sewer, drain. (b) (fig) sink, sewer.

sentir [3i] **1** vt (a) (general sense) to feel; to perceive, sense; to hear (esp SAm); to smell; **emotion** to feel; **dignity, responsibility** etc to feel, be aware of, realize; **music, painting** etc to feel, have a feeling for; — **un dolor** to feel a pain; — **el ruido de un coche** to hear the noise of a car; **sin** — **el frío** without feeling the cold; — **ganas de** + infin to feel an urge to + infin; **lo siento ajeno a mí** I feel it is foreign to me, I feel detached from it; **siente la profesión como un sacerdocio** he feels the profession like a sacred calling; **dejarse** —, **hacerse** — to let itself be felt.

(b) **illness** etc to feel the effects of, suffer from the aftermath of.

(c) to regret, be sorry for; **lo siento** I'm sorry; ¡**lo siento muchísimo!, ¡cuánto lo siento!** I'm very sorry!, I'm so sorry!; **sintió profundamente esa pérdida** he felt (or regretted, mourned etc) that loss deeply; — **que . . .** to regret that . . ., be sorry that . . .; **sentiré que me obligue Vd a venderlo** I shall be sorry if you force me to sell it; **siento no haberlo hecho antes** I am sorry not to have done it before; **siento molestarle** I'm sorry to bother you.

2 vi (a) to feel; **estaba que ni oía ni sentía** he was in such a state that he could neither hear nor feel anything; **sin** — without noticing, quite inadvertently; imperceptibly, so quickly (or smoothly etc) that one does not notice.

(b) to feel sorry; **dar que** — to give cause for regret.

3 sentirse vr (a) to feel; — **pesimista** to feel pessimistic; — **herido** (fig) to feel hurt; — **mal(o)** to feel ill, feel bad; — **como en su casa** to feel at home; — **en ridículo** to feel ridiculous; — **actor** to feel oneself to be an actor.

(b) (Med) — **del costado** to have a pain in one's side; — **del paludismo** to suffer from malaria.

(c) to be offended, feel resentful (de about, at); — **de una observación** to take offence at a remark.

(d) (SAm) to get cross, get angry; — **con uno** to fall out with someone.

(e) (container, vessel) to crack.

4 nm opinion, judgement; **a mi** —, **en mi** — in my opinion; **compartir el** — **de** to share the view of, echo the opinion of.

sentón nm (a) (CAm, Mex) bump on one's bottom, heavy fall. (b) (CAm, Ec) **dar un** — to rein in suddenly.

seña nf (a) mark, distinguishing mark; —**s descripción**; —**s personales** personal description; **las** —**s son mortales** (fam) we know all about that already; **dar las** —**s de uno** to give a personal description of someone.

(b) sign; (fig) sign, token; secret sign; (Mil) password; **por las** —**s** so it seems; **por más** —**s** just to prove it, to clinch matters; into the bargain, moreover; **dar** —**s de** to show signs of; **hablar por** —**s** to talk by signs, communicate by means of signs; **hacer una** — **a uno** to make a sign to someone; **hacer una** — **a uno para que** + subj to signal to someone to + infin.

(c) (Post) —**s** address.

señal nf (a) sign; symptom; token, indication; **en** —

de as a token of, as a sign of, in sign of; **es buena** — it's a good sign; **dar** —**es de** to show signs of; **hacer la** — **de la cruz** to make the sign of the Cross.

(b) (Comm, Fin) token payment; deposit; pledge; **dejar una suma en** — to leave a sum as a deposit.

(c) (with hand) sign, signal; **dar la** — **de** (or para) to give the signal for; **hacer una** — **a uno** to make a sign to someone; **hacer una** — **grosera** to make a rude sign; **al hacerse una** — **predeterminada** at a prearranged signal.

(d) mark; trace, vestige; sign; (Med) scar, mark; (on animal) mark, marking; brand; (Geog) landmark; (Lit) bookmark; **sin la menor** — **de** without the least trace of, without the slightest sign of; **no quedaba ni** — there wasn't the slightest trace of it; **lo hicieron sin dejar** — they did it without leaving a trace.

(e) (Aut, Rail etc) signal; — **de alto** stop sign; — **de auxilio** distress signal; — **de carretera** road sign; —**es luminosas,** —**es de tráfico** traffic lights, traffic signals; — **óptica** (Aut) trafficator; — **de peligro** danger signal.

(f) (Radio) signal; — **horario** time signal.

(g) (Tel) signal, tone; buzz; — **de llamada** calling signal; — **para marcar** dialling tone; — **de ocupado** (or **comunicando**) engaged tone, busy signal (US).

(h) (SAm) earmark.

señala nf (Chi) earmark.

señaladamente adv (a) especially. (b) clearly, plainly.

señalado adj (a) **estar** — **como** to be marked down as, be known to be.

(b) **dejar** — **a uno** to scar someone permanently.

(c) distinct, clear, plain.

(d) **day, favour** etc special; **person** distinguished, notable, (pej) notorious.

señalar [1a] **1** vt (a) to mark; to denote, betoken; **señalan la llegada de la primavera** they announce the arrival of spring; **eso señaló el principio del descenso** that marked the start of the decline.

(b) **paper** etc to mark; to stamp; **person** to mark (for life), scar (permanently); (Med) to leave a scar on; (SAm) **livestock** to brand.

(c) **road** etc to put up signs on; **route** to signpost.

(d) (with finger) to point to, point out, indicate; (fig) to show, indicate; (of clock hand etc) to show, point to, say; **iba señalando los edificios notables** he went round pointing out the interesting buildings; **tuve que** —**le varios errores** I had to point out several mistakes to him.

(e) (in conversation) to allude to; (pej) to criticize.

(f) **date, price** etc to fix, settle; **task** to set; **person** to appoint; **¿qué precio ha señalado al cuadro?** what price has he put on the picture?; **se negó a** —**me hora** he refused to offer me an appointment.

2 señalarse vr to make one's mark (como as); to distinguish oneself (por by, by reason of), achieve distinction.

señalero nm (Chi) signalman.

señalización nf signposting; system of signs (or signals), signal code.

señalizar [1f] vt **road** etc to put up signs on; **route** to signpost.

señor 1 nm (a) man; gentleman; **le espera un** — there's a gentleman waiting to see you; **es todo un** — he's a real gentleman; **hacer el** — to lord it; **quiere parecer un** — he tries to look like a gentleman.

(b) (of property) owner, master; (of servants) master; (fig) master; **el** — **de la casa** the master of the household; **¿está el** —? is the master in?; **no es** — **de sus pasiones** he cannot control his passions.

(c) (before proper name) Mister (always written Mr); **es para el Sr Meléndez** it's for Mr Meléndez; **los** —**es Poblet** the Poblets, Mr and Mrs Poblet; **Señor Don Jacinto Benavente** (on envelope) Mr J. Benavente, J. Benavente Esq.

(d) (before professional title: not translated) **el** — **alcalde** the mayor; **el** — **cura** the priest; **el** — **presidente** the president (but see (e)).

(e) (in direct address) sir (but often not translated); (to noble) my lord; —**es** (in speech) gentlemen; ¡**mire Vd,** —! look here!; ¡**oiga Vd,** —! I say!; — **alcalde** Mr Mayor; — **director . . .** (to editor) Dear Sir . . .; — **juez** my lord; — **presidente** Mr Chairman, Mr President; ¡**no** —! (fig) not a bit of it!, never!, absolutely not!; ¡**sí** —! (fig) yes indeed!,

I should jolly well think it is! (*fam*), it certainly does! (*etc*); **pues sí** — well that's how it is.

(**f**) (*Comm etc*) **muy — mío** Dear Sir; **muy —es nuestros** Gentlemen.

(**g**) (*Hist*) noble, lord; **— feudal** feudal lord; lord of the manor; **— de horca y cuchillo** (*fig*) despot.

(**h**) (*Rel*) **El S—** The Lord; **Nuestro S—** Our Lord; **S— de los Ejércitos** Lord of Hosts; **recibir al S—** to take communion.

2 *adj* (*fam*) (**a**) lordly; **un coche muy —** a really lordly car.

(**b**) real, really big; **una casa para un — —** a house for a gentleman who really is a gentleman; **eso es un — melón** now that really is a melon, that's some melon; **fue una señora herida** it was a real big wound.

señora *nf* (**a**) lady; **— de compañía** chaperon; companion; **le espera una —** there's a lady waiting to see you.

(**b**) (*of property*) owner, mistress; **¿está la —?** is the mistress in?

(**c**) wife; **mi —** my wife; **el jefe y su —** the boss and his wife; **la — de Smith** Mrs Smith.

(**d**) (*in direct address*) madam (*but often not translated*); (*to noble*) my lady; **¡—s y señores!** ladies and gentlemen!; **sí, —** yes, madam; **¡oiga Vd, —!** I say!

(**e**) (*Comm etc*) **muy — mía** Dear Madam.

(**f**) (*Rel*) **Nuestra S—** (*to Catholics*) Our Lady, (*to Protestants*) the Virgin (Mary).

señorear [1a] **1** *vt* (**a**) (*as ruler*) to rule, control; to domineer, lord it over.

(**b**) (*of building*) to dominate, soar above, tower over.

(**c**) *passions* to master, control.

2 señorearse *vr* (**a**) to control oneself.

(**b**) to adopt a lordly manner.

(**c**) **— de** to seize, seize control of.

señoria *nf* (**a**) rule, sway. (**b**) (*titles*) **su S—** (*also* **vuestra S—**) your lordship, his lordship, your ladyship, her ladyship; my lord, my lady.

señorial *adj*, **señoril** *adj* lordly; aristocratic; noble, majestic, stately.

señorío *nm* (**a**) (*Hist*) manor, feudal estate; domain.

(**b**) (*fig*) rule, sway, dominion (*sobre* over).

(**c**) (*quality*) lordliness; majesty, stateliness.

(**d**) (*fam*) distinguished people; (*pej*) toffs (*fam*), nobs (*sl*).

señorita *nf* (**a**) young lady.

(**b**) (*before proper name*) Miss.

(**c**) (*in direct address, not translated*) **¿qué busca Vd, —?** what are you looking for?

(**d**) (*SAm*) schoolteacher.

señorito *nm* (**a**) young gentleman; (*in servants' parlance*) master, young master. (**b**) (*pej*) playboy, toff (*fam*), young swell (*fam*).

señorón *nm* (*fam*) big shot (*fam*).

señuelo *nm* (**a**) decoy. (**b**) (*fig*) bait, lure. (**c**) (*Arg, Bol*) leading ox.

separable *adj* separable; (*Mech etc*) detachable, removable.

separación *nf* (**a**) (*act etc*) separation; division; (*Mech*) removal; (*from post*) removal, dismissal (*de* from); **— del matrimonio** legal separation; **— racial** racial segregation.

(**b**) gap, distance.

separadamente *adv* separately.

separado *adj* separated; separate; (*Mech*) detached; **vive — de su mujer** he is separated from his wife, he doesn't live with his wife; **por —** separately; individually, one by one; (*Post*) under separate cover; **firmar una paz por —** to sign a separate peace.

separador *nm* separator.

separar [1a] **1** *vt* (**a**) *object* to separate (*de* from); *chair etc* to move away (*de* from), take away, remove; **— un trozo de pan** to put aside a piece of bread.

(**b**) *fighters etc* to separate, pull apart, keep apart; *syllables, words* to divide; *connection* to sever, cut; *letters etc* to sort (out); **saber — las buenas de las malas** to know how to separate (*or* tell, distinguish) the good ones from the bad; **los negocios le separan de su familia** business keeps him away from his family.

(**c**) (*Mech*) *part* to detach, remove (*de* from).

(**d**) *person* (*from post*) to remove, dismiss (*de* from).

2 separarse *vr* (**a**) (*part*) to come away, detach itself (*de* from); (*parts*) to come apart; (*Pol*) to secede.

(**b**) (*person*) to leave, go away, withdraw; **— de un grupo** to leave a group; to part company with a group; **se ha separado de todos sus amigos** he has cut himself off from all his friends; **me separé de ella a las 11** I left her at 11; **se ha separado de su mujer** he has left his wife.

(**c**) (*Law*) to withdraw (*de* from).

separata *nf* offprint.

separatismo *nm* separatism, separatist tendency.

separatista 1 *adj* separatist. **2** *nmf* separatist.

separo *nm* (*Mex*) cell.

sepia *nf* (**a**) (*Fish*) cuttlefish. (**b**) (*Art etc*) sepia.

sepsis *nf* sepsis.

septentrión *nm* north.

septentrional *adj* north, northern.

septicemia *nf* septicaemia.

séptico *adj* septic.

se(p)tiembre *nm* September.

séptimo 1 *adj* seventh. **2** *nm* seventh.

septuagenario 1 *adj* septuagenarian, seventy-year-old. **2** *nm*, **septuagenaria** *nf* septuagenarian, person in his (*or* her) seventies.

septuagésimo *adj* seventieth.

séptuplo *adj* sevenfold.

sepulcral *adj* sepulchral; (*fig*) sepulchral, gloomy, dismal.

sepulcro *nm* tomb, grave; (*esp Bib*) sepulchre; **— blanco, — blanqueado** whited sepulchre.

sepultación *nf* (*Chi*) burial.

sepultar [1a] *vt* (**a**) to bury; (*fig: in mine etc*) to bury, entomb; **quedaban sepultados en la caverna** they were trapped in the cave, they were cut off in the cave.

(**b**) (*fig*) to hide away, bury, conceal.

sepultura *nf* (**a**) (*act*) burial; **dar — a** to bury; **dar cristiana — a uno** to give someone a Christian burial; **recibir —** to be buried.

(**b**) grave, tomb.

sepulturero *nm* gravedigger, sexton.

sequedad *nf* (**a**) dryness. (**b**) (*fig*) bluntness; brusqueness, curtness; plainness, bareness (*see* seco).

sequía *nf* (**a**) drought; dry season. (**b**) (*Prov, Col*) thirst.

sequiar [1c] *vi* (*Arg: of smoker*) to inhale.

séquito *nm* (**a**) retinue, suite, entourage.

(**b**) (*Pol etc*) group of supporters, adherents, devotees.

(**c**) (*of events*) train; aftermath; **con todo un — de calamidades** with a whole train of disasters.

ser [2w] **1** *vi* (**a**) (*general sense: absolute, of character, identity etc*) to be; **— o no —** to be or not to be; **es difícil** it's difficult; **él es pesimista** he's a pessimist, he's a pessimistic sort; **soy ingeniero** I'm an engineer; **soy yo** it's me, it is I (*lit*); **¡soy Pedro!** (*Tel*) this is Peter, Peter here, Peter speaking; **¿quién es?** who is it?; who's there?; (*Tel*) who's calling?; **es él quien debiera hacerlo** it is he who should do it, he's the one who ought to do it; **¿qué ha sido?** what happened?, what goes on?

(**b**) (*origin*) **— de** to be from, come from; **ella es de Calatayud** she's from Calatayud; **estas naranjas son de España** these oranges come from Spain; **¿de dónde es Vd?** where are you from?

(**c**) (*material*) **— de** to be (made) of; **es de piedra** — it is of stone, it is made of stone, it's a stone one.

(**d**) (*possession*) **— de** to belong to; **éste es suyo** this is his; **el parque es del municipio** the park belongs to the town; **esta tapa es de otra caja** this top belongs to another box; **¿de quién es este lápiz?** whose is this pencil?, who does this pencil belong to?

(**e**) (*destination*) **¿qué será de mí?** what will become of me?; **¿qué ha sido de él?** what has become of him?, what happened to him?

(**f**) (*appropriateness*) **esas finuras no son para mí** those niceties are not for me; **ese coche no es para correr mucho** that car isn't made to go very fast; **esa manera de hablar no es de una dama** that talk does not come well from a lady, one does not expect to hear a lady say such things.

(**g**) (*time of day*) **es la una** it is one o'clock; **son las 7** it is 7 o'clock; **serán las 8** it would be about 8 o'clock; **serían las 9 cuando llegó** it would have been about 9 when he arrived; *see* **hora** *etc*.

(**h**) (*special use of imperfect: in games*) **yo era la reina** pretend I was the queen, let's pretend I'm the queen.

(**i**) (*special use of preterite: of offices*) **presidente que fue de Ruritania** ex-president of Ruritania, former(ly) president of Ruritania.

(**j**) (*as equivalent to estar*) **soy en todo con Vd**

I entirely agree with you, I'm with you all the way; **en un momento soy con Vd** I'll be with you in a moment.

(**k**) (**— de** + *infin*) **es de creer que . . .** it may be assumed that . . .; **es de desear que . . .** it is to be wished that . . .; **es de esperar que . . .** it is to be hoped that . . .; **era de ver** it was worth seeing, you ought to have seen it.

(**l**) (*idioms with indicative*) **siendo así que . . .** since . . .; **¡o somos o no somos!** (*fam*) let's get on with it!, make your minds up!; **érase que se era** once upon a time; **a no — por** but for; were it not for, had it not been for; **a no — que . . .** unless . . .; **¡ahí fue ella!** what a row there was!, you should have heard the fuss!; **¿cómo es que . . .?** how is it that . . .?, how does it happen that . . .? **¡cómo ha de ser!** what else do you expect!; **hizo como quien es** he acted as one might expect, he did what one could expect of him; **con — ella su madre** even though she is his mother, despite the fact that she's his mother; **de no — esto así** if it were not so, were it not so.

(**m**) (*idioms with subjunctive*) **¡sea!** agreed!, all right!; **o sea . . .** that is to say . . ., or rather . . .; **sea . . . sea . . .** either . . . or, whether . . . or whether; **sea lo que sea** (*or* **fuere**) be that as it may; **no sea que . . .** lest . . ., for fear that . . .; **hable con algún abogado que no sea Pérez** speak to some lawyer other than Pérez, consult any lawyer you like except Pérez.

2 *v aux* used to form passive: **fue construido** it was built; **ha sido asaltada una joyería** there has been a raid on a jeweller's; **será fusilado** he will be shot; **está siendo estudiado** it is being examined.

3 *nm* being; life; essence; **— humano** human being; **— imaginario** imaginary being; **S— Supremo** Supreme Being; **— vivo** living creature, living organism; **la que le dio su —** she who gave him life, she who brought him into the world; **en lo más íntimo de su —** in his inmost being, deep within himself.

sera *nf* pannier, basket.

seráficamente *adv* angelically, like an angel.

seráfico *adj* (**a**) angelic, seraphic. (**b**) (*fam*) poor, humble.

serafín *nm* (**a**) seraph; (*fig*) angel; cherub. (**b**) (*Ven*) fastener.

serbal *nm*, **serbo** *nm* service tree.

serenamente *adv* (**a**) calmly, serenely. (**b**) peacefully, quietly.

serenar [1a] **1** *vt* (**a**) to calm; to quieten, pacify.
(**b**) *liquid* to clarify.
2 *vi* (*Col*) to drizzle.
3 serenarse *vr* (**a**) (*person etc*) to calm down, grow calm; to compose oneself.
(**b**) (*sea*) to grow calm; (*weather*) to clear up.
(**c**) (*liquid*) to clear, settle.

serenata *nf* serenade.

serenera *nf* (*CAm, Col, Ven*) cape, wrap.

serenero *nm* headscarf.

serenidad *nf* (**a**) calmness, serenity, (**b**) peacefulness, quietness.

sereno **1** *adj* (**a**) *person* calm, serene, unruffled.
(**b**) *weather* settled, fine; *sky* cloudless, clear.
(**c**) *atmosphere* calm, peaceful, quiet.
(**d**) (*fam*) **estar —** to be sober.
2 *nm* (**a**) night dew, night dampness; **dormir al —** to sleep out in the open; **le perjudica el —** the night air is harmful to her.
(**b**) night watchman.

serial *nm* serial; **— radiofónico** radio serial.

seriamente *adv* seriously.

sericultura *nf* silk raising, sericulture.

serie *nf* series (*also Bio, Elec, Math*); set, sequence, succession; (*Lit, Radio etc*) series, serial; **una — inacabable de** an endless series of; **arrollado en —** (*Elec*) series-wound; **fabricación en —** mass production; **fabricar en —** to mass-produce; **casas construidas en —** mass-produced houses, prefabricated houses; **matanzas en —** mass murders; **fuera de —** out of order, not in the proper sequence; (*fig*) special; **artículos fuera de —** (*Comm*) goods left over, remainders, remnants.

seriedad *nf* (**a**) seriousness; gravity, solemnity; staidness; **hablar con —** to speak seriously, speak in earnest.
(**b**) dignity; properness; seriousness, (sense of) responsibility; **falta de —** frivolity; irresponsibility.
(**c**) (*in business etc*) reliability, dependability, trustworthiness; straightness, honesty; fair-mindedness.
(**d**) (*of crisis etc*) gravity, seriousness.

serio *adj* (**a**) *person, attitude, expression etc* serious; grave, solemn; staid; **ponerse —** to look serious, adopt a solemn expression (*etc*); **se quedó mirándome muy —** he looked at me very seriously, he stared gravely at me; **pareces muy —** you're looking very serious.
(**b**) *person, attitude etc* dignified; proper; serious, responsible; **el negro es el único color — para esto** black is the only proper colour for this; **un traje —** a formal suit; **poco —** undignified; frivolous, not to be taken seriously; **es una persona poco seria** he's an irresponsible sort, he's rather a silly individual.
(**c**) (*in business etc*) *person* reliable, dependable, trustworthy; responsible; fair-minded; *deal, dealing* straight, honest; **poco —** unreliable; irresponsible; **es una casa seria** it's a reliable firm.
(**d**) *book, study etc* serious.
(**e**) *crisis, illness, loss etc* grave, serious; **esto se pone —** this is getting serious.
(**f**) **en —** seriously; **hablo perfectamente en —** I'm perfectly serious, I'm in dead earnest; **tomar un asunto en —** to take a matter seriously.

sermón *nm* sermon (*also fam*); **el S— de la Montaña** the Sermon on the Mount.

sermonear [1a] (*fam*) **1** *vt* to lecture, read a lecture to. **2** *vi* to sermonize.

sermoneo *nm* (*fam*) lecture, sermon.

sernambí *nm* (*Bol, Col, Ven*) inferior rubber.

serón *nm* pannier, large basket.

seroso *adj* serous.

serpa *nf* (*Bot*) runner.

serpenteante *adj* (*fig*) winding, twisting; meandering.

serpear [1a] *vi*, **serpentear** [1a] *vi* (**a**) (*Zool*) to wriggle; to creep. (**b**) (*fig: of road*) to wind, snake, twist and turn; (*of river*) to wind, meander.

serpenteo *nm* (**a**) wriggling; creeping. (**b**) (*fig*) winding, twisting; meandering.

serpentín *nm* coil.

serpentina *nf* (**a**) (*Min*) serpentine. (**b**) (*of paper*) streamer.

serpentino *adj* snaky, sinuous; winding, meandering; serpentine.

serpiente *nf* snake; serpent; **— boa** boa constrictor; **— de cascabel** rattlesnake; **— de mar** sea serpent; **— pitón** python; **— de vidrio** slow worm.

serpol *nm* thyme.

serpollo *nm* sucker, shoot.

serrado *adj* serrated; toothed; jagged, uneven, rough.

serraduras *nfpl* sawdust.

serrallo *nm* seraglio, harem.

serranía *nf* mountainous area, hilly country; range of mountains.

serraniego *adj* = **serrano**.

serrano **1** *adj* (**a**) (*Geog*) highland (*attr*), hill (*attr*), mountain (*attr*).
(**b**) (*fig*) coarse, rustic.
(**c**) **partida serrana** dirty trick.
2 *nm* highlander.

serrar [1k] *vt* to saw (off, up).

serrería *nf* sawmill.

serrín *nm* sawdust.

serrote *nm* (*Mex*) = **serrucho**.

serruchar [1a] *vt* (*SAm*) to saw (off, up).

serrucho *nm* (**a**) saw, handsaw.
(**b**) (*Cu*) whore.
(**c**) (*Col, Cu*) **al —** by halves; fifty-fifty.
(**d**) (*Ant, Col*) **hacer un —** to split the cost.

Servia *f* Serbia.

servible *adj* serviceable, usable.

servicial **1** *adj* helpful, obliging. **2** *nm* (*Bol, Col*) servant.

servicio *nm* (**a**) (*general sense*) service; **a su —** at your service; **al — de** in the service of; **estar al — de** to be in the service of; **estar al — del gobierno** to be on government service; **estar de —** to be serviceable, be in service; **entrar en —** to come into service; **tiene 8 camiones en —** he has 8 lorries in service; **hacer un —** to do someone a service; **hacer un flaco —** a uno to do someone an ill turn, play a dirty trick on someone.
(**b**) (*Mil etc*) service; **— activo** active service; **— militar** military service; **apto para el —** fit for military service; **en condiciones de —** operational; **estar de —** to be on duty; **beber estando de —** to drink while on duty; **prestar —** to serve, see service (*de* as).
(**c**) (*individual —s*) **— aduanero, — de aduana** customs service; **— de asistencia, — de atención, — post-venta** after-sales service; **— de contra-espionaje** secret service; **— doméstico** domestic service; domestic help; (*persons*) servants; **— a**

domicilio delivery service; "— a domicilio" "we deliver"; — de incendios fire service; — de información (Mil) intelligence service; — médico medical service; —s postales postal services; —s públicos public services; — secreto secret service; —s sociales social services; welfare work; — de transportes transport service.

(d) (Cook etc) service, set; — de café coffee set; — de mesa set of dishes; — de tocador toilet set.

(e) (euph: esp SAm) lavatory; chamberpot.

(f) —s (of house) services; (euph) sanitation; "todos —s" "all main services".

(g) (Eccl) service; — divino divine service.

(h) (in hotel etc) service, service charge.

(i) (Tennis) serve, service.

servidor nm, **servidora** nf (a) servant; un — (referring to speaker or writer) my humble self; your humble servant; aquí tiene un — para lo que se le ofrezca I am always at your service, please count on me for whatever it may be; ¡— de Vd! at your service!

(b) (in class etc) ¡—! present!

(c) (formulae in letters) su seguro —, atento y s.s. (= seguro servidor) yours faithfully.

servidumbre nf (a) servitude; — de la gleba serfdom.

(b) (fig) compulsion.

(c) (Law) obligation; — de paso right of way.

(d) (persons) servants, staff.

servil adj (a) slave (attr), serf's; work etc menial. (b) attitude etc servile; obsequious, grovelling; imitation etc slavish.

servilismo nm servility; obsequiousness; slavishness.

servilla nf slipper, pump.

servilleta nf serviette, napkin.

servilletero nm serviette ring.

servio 1 adj Serbian. **2** nm, **servia** nf Serb. **3** nm (language) Serbo-Croat.

servir [3l] **1** vt (a) (general sense) to serve; to do a favour to, oblige; — a Dios to serve God; — a la patria to serve one's country; dígame en qué puedo —le tell me in what way I can be of service, tell me how I can help you; para —le at your service; ser servido de + infin to be pleased to + infin.

(b) diners to wait on, serve.

(c) (Comm) customer to serve; order to attend to, fill; ¿ya le sirven, señora? are you being attended to, madam?

(d) (Cook) food to serve (out or up); — patatas a uno to serve someone with potatoes, help someone to potatoes; la cena está servida dinner is served; — vino a uno to pour out wine for someone.

(e) post to hold, fill; duties to carry out.

(f) gun to man; machine to tend, mind, man.

(g) (Tennis etc) to serve.

2 vi (a) (general sense) to serve; (of servant) to be in service; sirvió 10 años he served 10 years, he did 10 years; está sirviendo (Mil) he's doing his military service; para — a Vd at your service.

(b) (at table) to serve, wait (a at, on).

(c) to serve (de as, for); to be of use, be useful; eso no sirve that's no good, that won't do; — en lugar de to do duty for; — de guía to act as guide, serve as a guide; no sirve de nada que vaya él it's no use his going; — para to be good for, be used for; no sirve para nada it's no use at all, it's utterly useless; él no sirve para nada he's a dead loss; yo no serviría para futbolista I shouldn't be any good as a footballer.

(d) (Cards) — del palo to follow suit.

3 servirse vr (a) (at table) to serve oneself, help oneself; se sirvió patatas · he helped himself to potatoes; se sirvió café he poured himself some coffee; ¡sírvete más! have some more!; ¿no se sirve más guisantes? wouldn't you like more peas?

(b) — de algo to make use of something, use something; to put something to use.

(c) — + infin to be kind enough to + infin; to deign to + infin, condescend to + infin; sírvase sentarse please sit down; si la señora se sirve pasar por aquí if madam would care to come this way.

servocroata 1 adj Serbo-Croatian. **2** nmf Serbo-Croatian. **3** nm (language) Serbo-Croat.

sésamo nm sesame; ¡— ábrete! open sesame!

sesear [1a] vt to pronounce c (before e, i) and z [θ] as [s] (a feature of Andalusian and much SAm pronunciation).

sesenta adj sixty; sixtieth.

sesentón 1 adj sixty-year old, sixtyish. **2** nm, **sesentona** nf person of about sixty.

seseo nm pronunciation of c (before e, i) and z [θ] as [s].

sesera nf (Anat) brainpan; (fam) brains, intelligence.

sesgado adj slanted, slanting, oblique; leaning; awry, askew.

sesgar [1h] vt (a) to slant, slope, place obliquely; to put askew, twist to one side.

(b) (Sew) to cut on the slant, cut on the bias; (Tech) to bevel.

(c) (Aut) to cut across, cut in on.

sesgo nm (a) slant, slope; warp, twist, twisted position; (Sew) bias; (Tech) bevel; estar al — to be aslant, be awry; cortar algo al — to cut something on the bias.

(b) (fig) direction; twist, turn; ha tomado otro — it has taken a new turn.

(c) (fam) dodge.

sésil adj sessile.

sesión nf (a) (Parl etc) session, sitting, meeting; — secreta secret session; abrir la — to open the meeting; levantar la — to close the meeting, adjourn.

(b) (Theat) show, performance; — de espiritismo séance; — de prestidigitación conjuring show, exhibition of conjuring; — de lectura de poesías poetry reading.

(c) (Cine) showing; — continua continuous showing; iremos a la segunda — we'll go to the second house; hay 3 —es diarias there are 3 showings a day.

sesionar [1a] vi to sit; to be in session; to hold a meeting.

seso nm (a) (Anat) brain; —s (Cook) brains.

(b) (fig) brains, sense, intelligence; calentarse los —s, devanarse los —s to rack one's brains; perder el — to go off one's head (por over); eso le tiene sorbido el — he's crazy about it.

sesquipedal adj sesquipedalian.

sestear [1a] vi to take a siesta, have a nap.

sesteo nm (SAm) siesta, nap.

sesudamente adv sensibly, wisely.

sesudo adj (a) sensible, wise. (b) brainy. (c) (Chi) stubborn.

set nm, pl set or sets (Tennis) set.

seta nf (a) mushroom. (b) (tabu) vagina.

setecientos adj seven hundred.

setenta adj seventy; seventieth.

setentón 1 adj seventy-year old, seventyish. **2** nm, **setentona** nf person of about seventy.

setiembre nm September.

seto nm (a) fence; — vivo hedge. (b) (PR, SD) wall, partition.

seudo ... pseudo ...

seudónimo 1 adj pseudonymous. **2** nm pseudonym; pen name, nom de plume.

severamente adv (a) severely, harshly; strictly. (b) severely; grimly, sternly.

severidad nf (a) severity, harshness; strictness; stringency. (b) severity; grimness, sternness.

severo adj (a) character etc severe, harsh; discipline strict; critic, punishment harsh; parent etc strict, harsh; conditions harsh, stringent; ser — con uno to be hard on someone, treat someone harshly.

(b) winter etc severe, harsh, hard; cold bitter.

(c) expression severe; grim, stern; dress, style etc severe.

seviche nm = cebiche.

Sevilla Seville.

sevillano 1 adj Sevillian. **2** nm, **sevillana** nf Sevillian.

sexagenario 1 adj sexagenarian, sixty-year old. **2** nm, **sexagenaria** nf sexagenarian, person in his (or her) sixties.

sexagésimo adj sixtieth.

sexar [1a] vt chicks to sex.

sexo nm sex; el bello — the fair sex; el — débil the gentle sex; el — femenino the female sex; el — masculino the male sex; de ambos —s of both sexes; sin — sexless.

sexología nf sexology.

sexólogo nm sexologist.

sextante nm sextant.

sexteto nm sextet(te).

sexto 1 adj sixth. **2** nm sixth.

séxtuplo adj sixfold.

sexual adj sexual; sex (attr); vida — sex life.

sexualidad nf (a) sexuality. (b) sex; determinar la — de to determine the sex of.

sexualmente adv sexually.

sexy nm (false angl) sex appeal.

shock [ʃok] nm, pl **shock** or **shocks** [ʃok] (angl) shock.

si *conj* (a) if; — **lo quieres te lo doy** if you want it I'll give it to you; — **me lo pedía se lo daba** if he asked me for it I gave it to him; — **me lo hubiese pedido se lo hubiera dado** if he had asked me for it I would have given it to him; — **lo sé te lo digo** *(fam)* if I had known about it I would have told you.

(b) if, whether; **me pregunto — vale la pena** I wonder whether *(or* if*)* it's worth the trouble; **no sé — hacerlo o no** I don't know whether to do it or not; **hablaban de — hacerlo o no** they were talking about whether to do it or not; **que — lavar los platos, que — limpiar el suelo, que —** ... what with washing up and sweeping the floor and ...

(c) *(idioms etc)* — **no** if not; otherwise, or else; **¿— vendrá?** I wonder if he'll come?; **¿— será verdad?** what if it's true?; **¿— nos lo roban?** what if someone steals it?, suppose it gets stolen?; **lleva un revólver por — resulta útil** he carries a gun in case it should come in handy; **¡— fuera verdad!** if only it were true!; **¡— viniese pronto!** I wish he'd come!; **¡— no sabía que estabas allí!** but I didn't know you were there!; **¡— es el cartero!** why, it's the postman!

sí[1] **1** *adv* (a) yes; indeed, certainly; **él no quiere pero yo —** he doesn't want to but I do; **ellos no van pero nosotros —** they aren't going but we are; **—, pero menos** *(iro)* that's a bit much, that's pushing things a bit; **creo que —** I think so; **¡que —, hombre!** I tell you it is! *(etc)*; **está de que —** *(fam)* he seems likely to agree; **¡(pues) — que estoy yo para bromas!** *(iro)* I should say I'm in the mood for jokes!; **por — o por no** in any case, just in case; **porque —** because that's the way it is; **because I say so; lo hizo porque —** he did it because he just felt like doing it; he did it because he thought it had to be done; *(pej)* he did it out of sheer cussedness; **una semana — y otra no** in alternate weeks, every other week.

(b) *(emphatic)* **ella — vendrá** she will certainly come, she is sure to come; **ellos — tienen uno** they certainly have one; **¡— que lo es!** I'll say it is!, you're dead right there!; **¡eso — que no!** never!, not on your life!

2 *nm* consent, agreement; **dar el —** to agree, consent; *(of woman)* to accept a proposal; **todavía no tengo el —** I have not yet received his consent, he still hasn't said yes.

sí[2] *reflexive pron (used after preps)* (a) *(sing: m)* himself, *(f)* herself, *(of thing)* itself, *(relating to Vd)* yourself, *(used generally)* oneself; *(pl)* themselves, *(relating to Vds)* yourselves; — **mismo** himself *etc*; **lo quieren todo para —** they want the whole lot for themselves; **no lo podrá hacer por — solo** he won't be able to do it by himself; **conviene guardarlo para —** it's best to keep it to oneself; **se ríe de — misma** she laughs at herself.

(b) *(reciprocal)* each other; **cambiaron una mirada entre —** they exchanged a look, they gave each other a look.

(c) *(idioms)* **de —** in itself; spontaneously; **el problema es bastante difícil de —** the problem is difficult enough in itself; **de por —** in itself; per se; separately, individually; **estar en —** to be in one's right mind; **pensar entre —, pensar para —** to think to oneself; **estar fuera de —** to be beside oneself; **estar sobre —** to be on one's guard; to be puffed up with conceit; *see* **decir, volver** *etc*.

Siam *m* Siam.
siamés 1 *adj* Siamese. **2** *nm*, **siamesa** *nf* Siamese.
sibarita 1 *adj* sybaritic, luxury-loving; epicurean. **2** *nmf* sybarite, lover of luxury; epicure, bon vivant.
sibarítico *adj* sybaritic, luxury-loving; epicurean.
sibaritismo *nm* sybaritism, love of luxury; epicureanism.
Siberia *f* Siberia.
siberiano 1 *adj* Siberian. **2** *nm*, **siberiana** *nf* Siberian.
sibil *nm* cave; vault, underground store; corn-storage pit.
Sibila *f* Sibyl.
sibila *nf* sibyl.
sibilante 1 *adj* sibilant. **2** *nf* sibilant.
sibilino *adj* sibylline.
sic ... = **psic** ..., *eg for* **sicología** *see* **psicología**.
sicalipsis *nf* eroticism, suggestiveness; pornography.
sicalíptico *adj* erotic, suggestive; pornographic.
Sicilia *f* Sicily.
siciliano 1 *adj* Sicilian. **2** *nm*, **siciliana** *nf* Sicilian. **3** *nm* *(dialect)* Sicilian.
sicofante *nm* sycophant.
sicomoro *nm*, **sicómoro** *nm* sycamore.

sicote *nm* (Ant, CR), **sicotera** *nf* (Ant) smell of dirty feet.
sidecar ['saikar] *nm* *(angl)* sidecar.
sideral *adj*, **sidéreo** *adj* astral, sidereal; space *(attr)*.
siderurgia *nf* iron and steel industry.
siderúrgico *adj* iron and steel *(attr)*; **la siderúrgica** iron and steel works.
sidra *nf* cider.
siega *nf* (a) reaping, harvesting; mowing. (b) harvest *(time)*.
siembra *nf* (a) sowing; **patata de —** seed potato. (b) sowing time.
siembre *nm* (Ven) sowing.
siempre 1 *adv* (a) always; all the time; ever; **como —** as usual, as always; **la hora de —** the usual time; **somos amigos de —** we're old friends; **es lo de —** it's the same thing as it always is, it's the same old story; **lo vienen haciendo así desde —** they've always done it this way; **para —, por —** for ever; for good (and all); **por — jamás** for ever and ever.

(b) *(SAm)* certainly, for sure; *(Mex)* — **no** certainly not; — **sí** indeed yes, of course.

2 *conj*: — **que** ... (a) (+ *indic*) whenever; each time that ..., as often as ...

(b) (+ *subj*) provided that ...

sien *nf* (Anat) temple.
siena *nf* sienna.
sierpe *nf* snake, serpent.
sierra *nf* (a) *(Tech)* saw; — **de arco para metales** hacksaw; — **de calados** fretsaw; — **circular** circular saw; — **de espigar** tenon saw; — **mecánica** power saw; — **de vaivén** jigsaw.

(b) *(Geog)* mountain range, sierra; **van a la — a pasar el fin de semana** they're off to the mountains for the weekend.
Sierra *f* **Leona** Sierra Leone.
siervo *nm*, **sierva** *nf* slave; — **de la gleba** serf.
siesta *nf* (a) hottest part of the day, afternoon heat.

(b) siesta, nap; **dormir la —, echarse una —, tomar una —** to have one's afternoon nap, have a doze.
siete[1] **1** *adj* seven; *(date)* seventh; **las —** seven o'clock; **hablar más que —** to talk nineteen to the dozen. **2** *nm* seven.
siete[2] *nm* (SAm: *euph*) arse *(tabu)*.
sietecueros *nm*, *pl* **sietecueros** (SAm) gumboil, whitlow.
sífilis *nf* syphilis.
sifilítico 1 *adj* syphilitic. **2** *nm*, **sifilítica** *nf* syphilitic.
sifón *nm* (a) *(Tech)* trap, U-bend; siphon. (b) siphon (of soda water); **whisky con —** whisky and soda.
siga *nf* (Chi) pursuit, chase; **ir a la — de** to chase after.
sigilo *nm* secrecy; discretion; *(pej)* stealth; slyness; — **sacramental** secrecy of the confessional; **con mucho —** with great secrecy.
sigilosamente *adv* secretly; discreetly; *(pej)* stealthily, slyly.
sigiloso *adj* secret; discreet; *(pej)* stealthy, sly.
sigla *nf* symbol; abbreviation; acronym, *set of initials pronounced as a word* (eg NATO, CAMPSA).
siglo *nm* (a) century; **S— de las Luces** Age of Enlightenment (18th century); — **de oro, — dorado** (Myth) golden age; **S— de Oro** Golden Age (Spain: about 1492-1650); **los —s medios** the Middle Ages.

(b) *(fig)* age, time, times.

(c) *(fig)* age(s); **hace un — que no le veo** I haven't seen him for ages.

(d) *(Rel)* **por los —s de los —s** world without end.

(e) *(Eccl)* **el —** the world; worldly affairs; **retirarse del —** to withdraw from the world, become a monk.
signar [1a] **1** *vt* (a) to seal; to put one's mark on.

(b) to sign.

(c) *(Rel)* to make the sign of the cross over. **2 signarse** *vr* to cross oneself.
signatario 1 *adj* signatory. **2** *nm* signatory.
signatura *nf* (a) *(Mus, Typ)* signature. (b) *(of library)* catalogue number, press mark.
significación *nf* significance.
significado 1 *adj* well-known; outstanding.

2 *nm* significance; *(of word etc)* meaning; **su — principal es** ... its chief meaning is ...; **una palabra de — dudoso** a word of uncertain meaning.
significante *adj* (*esp* SAm) significant.
significar [1g] **1** *vt* (a) to mean; to signify *(also fig)*; **¿qué significa "nabo?"** what does "nabo" mean?; **5 dólares significan muy poco para él** 5 dollars doesn't mean much to him; **significará la ruina de la sociedad** it will mean the ruin of the company; **él no significa gran cosa en estos asuntos** he doesn't count for much in these matters.

(b) to make known, express *(a* to*)*; **le significó**

la condolencia de la familia **real** he expressed (*or* conveyed) the royal family's sympathy.

2 significarse *vr* (**a**) to become known, make a name, become famous (*or* notorious); — **como** to become known as, be recognized as.

(**b**) **no** — to refuse to take sides.

significativamente *adv* significantly; meaningly.

significativo *adj* significant; *glance etc* meaning, expressive; **es** — **que** . . . it is significant that . . .

signo *nm* (**a**) (*in most senses*) sign; (*Math*) sign, symbol; (*of illiterate*) mark; — **de admiración** exclamation mark; — **de la cruz** sign of the Cross; — **igual** equals sign; — **de interrogación** question mark; — (**de**) **más**, — **de sumar** plus sign; — (**de**) **menos** minus sign; — **positivo** positive sign; —**s de puntuación** punctuation marks; — **del zodíaco** sign of the zodiac. '

(**b**) (*fig*) quantity; tendency; **una situación de** — **alentador** an encouraging situation; *see* **mercado**.

sigo *etc see* **seguir**.

siguetear [1a] *vti* (*Per*) = **seguir**.

siguiente *adj* following; next; **dijo lo** — he said the following; **¡que pase el** —**!** next please!; **el día** — the following day, next day.

sílaba *nf* syllable.

silabario *nm* spelling book.

silabear [1a] *vt* to syllabicate, divide into syllables; to pronounce syllable by syllable.

silabeo *nm* syllabication, division into syllables.

silábico *adj* syllabic.

silba *nf* hissing, catcalls; **armar una** —, **dar una** — (**a**) to hiss.

silbar [1a] **1** *vt* (**a**) *tune* to whistle; *whistle etc* to blow.

(**b**) *speaker, play etc* to hiss.

2 *vi* (**a**) (*Mus*) to whistle; (*Anat*) to wheeze; (*of wind*) to whistle; (*of bullet*) to whistle, whine; (*of arrow etc*) to whizz, swish, hum.

(**b**) (*Theat etc*) to hiss, catcall, boo.

silbatina *nf* (*Chi, Per, RPl*) hissing.

silbato *nm* whistle.

silbido *nm*, **silbo** *nm* whistle, whistling; hiss; wheeze; whine, whizz, swish, hum; — **de oídos** ringing in the ears.

silenciador *nm* silencer.

silenciar [1b] *vt* (**a**) *event etc* to hush up; *fact etc* to keep silent about, pass over in silence. (**b**) *person etc* to silence. (**c**) (*Tech*) to silence.

silencio 1 *nm* (**a**) silence; quiet, hush; **¡**—**!** silence!, quiet!; — **administrativo** policy of doing nothing about a matter; **en** — in silence; **en el** — **más absoluto** in dead silence; **entregar algo al** — to cast something into oblivion; **guardar** — to keep silent, say nothing (**sobre** about); **había un** — **sepulcral** it was as quiet as the grave; **imponer** — **a uno** to make someone be quiet; to force someone to remain silent; **mantener el** — **radiofónico** to keep radio silence; **pasar algo en** — to pass over something in silence; **reducir al** — *person* to silence, reduce to silence; *guns* to silence.

(**b**) (*Mus*) rest.

2 *adj* (*CAm, Ec, Mex*) silent, quiet; still.

silenciosamente *adv* silently, quietly; soundlessly; noiselessly.

silencioso 1 *adj* silent, quiet; soundless; *machine* silent, noiseless. **2** *nm* silencer, muffler.

silense *adj* of Silos, of Santo Domingo de Silos (*Riojan monastery*).

sílex *nm* silex, flint.

sílfide *nf* sylph (*also fig*).

silfo *nm* sylph.

silicato *nm* silicate.

sílice *nf* silica.

silíceo *adj* siliceous.

silicio *nm* silicon.

silicosis *nf* silicosis.

silo *nm* (*Agr*) silo; underground store; storage pit.

silogismo *nm* syllogism.

silogístico *adj* syllogistic.

silueta *nf* silhouette; (*of building*) outline; (*of city*) skyline; (*of person*) figure; (*Art*) silhouette, outline drawing.

silvático *adj* = **selvático**.

silvestre *adj* (*Bot*) wild; (*fig*) rustic, rural.

silvicultor *nm* forestry expert.

silvicultura *nf* forestry.

silla *nf* (**a**) seat; chair; — **alta** high chair; — **de balanza**, — **de hamaca** (*SAm*) rocking chair; — **eléctrica** electric chair; — **de manos** sedan chair; — **plegadiza**, — **de tijera** folding chair, folding stool, camp stool; — **de ruedas** wheelchair; **calentar la** — to stay too long, overstay one's welcome.

(**b**) (*also* — **de montar**) saddle.

sillar *nm* block of stone, ashlar.

sillería *nf* (**a**) chairs, set of chairs; seating; (*Eccl*) choir stalls. (**b**) chairmaker's workshop. (**c**) (*Archit*) masonry.

sillero *nm* (**a**) chairmaker. (**b**) (*Arg*) horse, mule.

silleta *nf* (**a**) small chair; (*SAm*) seat, chair; (*SAm*) low stool. (**b**) (*Med*) bedpan.

sillico *nm* chamberpot; commode.

sillín *nm* saddle.

sillita *nf* small chair; — **de ruedas** pushchair.

sillón 1 *adj* (*Chi, RPl, SD*) saddle-backed.

2 *nm* (**a**) armchair; easy chair; (*SAm*) rocking chair; — **de lona** deckchair; — **de orejas** wing chair; — **de ruedas** wheelchair.

(**b**) woman's saddle, sidesaddle.

sima *nf* abyss, chasm; pit; deep fissure, pothole.

Simbad *m* Sinbad; — **el marinero** Sinbad the sailor.

simbar [1a] *vt* (*Arg*) to plait.

simbiosis *nf* symbiosis.

simbólicamente *adv* symbolically.

simbólico *adj* symbolic(al); token.

simbolismo *nm* symbolism.

simbolista 1 *adj* symbolist. **2** *nmf* symbolist.

simbolizar [1f] *vt* to symbolize; to represent, stand for, be a token of; to typify.

símbolo *nm* symbol; — **de los apóstoles**, — **de la fe** Creed; — **de prestigio** status symbol.

simetría *nf* symmetry; (*fig*) harmony.

simétricamente *adv* symmetrically; (*fig*) harmoniously.

simétrico *adj* symmetrical; (*fig*) harmonious.

símico *adj* = **simiesco**.

simiente *nf* seed.

simiesco *adj* simian, apish.

símil 1 *adj* similar. **2** *nm* comparison; (*Lit*) simile.

similar *adj* similar.

similitud *nf* similarity, resemblance, similitude.

similor *nm* pinchbeck; **de** — (*fig*) showy but valueless; fake, sham.

similñaca *nf* (*Cu*) tangle, complicated affair.

Simón *m* Simon.

simonía *nf* simony.

simpatía *nf* (**a**) liking; affection; — **hacia**, — **por** liking for; —**s y antipatías** likes and dislikes; **coger** — **a uno** to take to someone, take a liking to someone; **ganarse la** — **de todos** to win everybody's affection, come to be well liked by everybody; **tener** — **a** to like; **no le tenemos** — **en absoluto** we don't like him at all; **no tiene** —**s en el colegio** nobody at school likes him, he has no friends at school.

(**b**) (*of atmosphere etc*) friendliness, warmth, congeniality; (*of person, place etc*) charm, attractiveness, likeableness; **la famosa** — **andaluza** that well-known Andalusian charm.

(**c**) fellow feeling; mutual support, solidarity, sympathy; **mostrar su** — **por** to show one's support for, show one's solidarity with.

(**d**) (*angl*) sympathy, compassion.

simpático *adj person* nice, likeable, genial, pleasant; kind; charming, attractive; *atmosphere etc* congenial, agreeable; **¡qué policía más** —**!** what a nice policeman!; **no le hemos caído muy** —**s** she didn't much take to us; **siempre procura hacerse** — he's always trying to ingratiate himself; **me es** — **ese muchacho** I like that lad.

simpatizante *nmf* sympathizer (**de** with).

simpatizar [1f] *vi* (**a**) (*of 2 persons*) to get on (well together); **pronto simpatizaron** they hit it off at once, they soon became friends.

(**b**) — **con** to get on well with, take to, hit it off with; to be congenial to.

simplada *nf* (*CAm, Col*) simplicity, stupidity; stupid thing (*to do etc*).

simple 1 *adj* (**a**) simple; uncomplicated, unadorned, bare; (*Chem, Gram etc*) simple; (*Bot*) single; *method etc* simple, easy, straightforward.

(**b**) (*preceding n*) mere; pure; sheer; alone; **por** — **descuido** through sheer (*or* pure) carelessness; **es cosa de una** — **plumada** it's a matter of a mere stroke of the pen; **me basta con tu** — **palabra** your word alone is good enough for me.

(**c**) (*preceding n*) ordinary; **un** — **soldado** an ordinary soldier.

(**d**) *person* simple, simple-minded, innocent; gullible; (*pej*) foolish, silly.

2 *nm* (**a**) (*person*) simpleton.

(**b**) (*Col*) liquor.

(**c**) —**s** (*Bot*) simples.

(**d**) —**s** (*Tennis*) singles.

simplemente *adv* (**a**) simply. (**b**) simply, merely; purely.

simpleza nf (a) (quality) simpleness, simple-mindedness; gullibility; (pej) foolishness.
   (b) (una —) silly thing (to do etc); —s nonsense.
   (c) (fig) trifle, small thing; **se contenta con cualquier** — she's happy with any little thing.
simplicidad nf (all senses) simplicity, simpleness.
simplificable adj simplifiable.
simplificación nf simplification.
simplificar [1g] vt to simplify.
simplón 1 adj simple, gullible. **2** nm, **simplona** nf simple soul, gullible person.
simplote = **simplón**.
simposio nm symposium.
simulación nf simulation; make-believe; (pej) pretence.
simulacro nm (a) simulacrum; image, idol. (b) semblance; sham, pretence; **un — de ataque a** mock attack; **un — de combate** a sham fight.
simulado adj simulated; feigned; mock, sham.
simular [1a] vt to simulate; to feign, sham.
simultáneamente adv simultaneously.
simultanear [1a] vt: — **dos cosas** to do two things simultaneously; — **A con B** to contrive to do A at the same time as B, fit in A and B at the same time, synchronize A and B; **jugar con 16 tableros simultaneados** (Chess) to play 16 boards simultaneously.
simultaneidad nf simultaneity.
simultáneo adj simultaneous.
simún nm sandstorm.
sin 1 prep (a) without; with no . . .; apart from, not counting, not including; — **nosotros** without us; **costó 5 dólares — los gastos de envío** it cost 5 dollars not counting postage and packing; **salió — sombrero** he went out without a hat (or hatless); **me he quedado — cerillas** I've run out of matches; — **protección contra el sol** with no protection against the sun.
   (b) — + infin without + ger, eg — **verlo** without seeing it; — **verlo yo** without my seeing it; (often translated by un prefix + ptp, eg) — **lavar** unwashed, — **pagar** unpaid.
   2 — **que** conj without + ger; — **que lo sepa él** without his knowing; **entraron — que nadie les observara** they came in without anyone seeing them.
sinagoga nf synagogue.
sinalefa nf elision.
sinalefar [1a] vt to elide.
sinapismo nm (a) (Med) mustard plaster; **hay que ponerle un —** (fam) he needs shaking up, you'll have to give him a jolt.
   (b) (fam) bore; nuisance, pest.
sinceramente adv sincerely.
sincerarse [1a] vr to vindicate oneself; — **a**, — **con** to open one's heart to; to square oneself with, give a full explanation to; — **ante el juez** to justify one's conduct to the judge; — **de su conducta** to explain one's conduct, justify one's conduct.
sinceridad nf sincerity; **con toda —** in all sincerity.
sincero adj sincere.
síncopa nf (a) (Ling) syncope. (b) (Mus) syncope, syncopation.
sincopar [1a] vt to syncopate.
síncope nm (a) (Ling) syncope. (b) (Med) syncope; fainting fit, queer turn.
sincronía nf synchronous character; simultaneity.
sincrónico adj synchronous; (Tech) synchronized; events etc simultaneous, coincidental; (Ling) synchronic.
sincronismo nm synchronism; simultaneity; (of dates etc) coincidence.
sincronización nf synchronization.
sincronizar [1f] vt to synchronize (con with).
síncrono adj synchronous.
sindical adj union (attr), trade-union (attr); (Pol) syndical.
sindicalismo nm trade(s) unionism; (Pol) syndicalism.
sindicalista 1 adj union (attr), trade-union (attr); (Pol) syndicalist. **2** nmf trade(s) unionist; (Pol) syndicalist.
sindicar [1g] **1** vt workers to unionize, form into a trade(s) union.
   2 sindicarse vr (worker) to join a union; (workers) to form themselves into a union.
sindicato nm (a) syndicate. (b) trade(s) union, labor union (US).
síndico nm trustee; (Law) official receiver.
síndrome nm syndrome.
sinécdoque nf synecdoche.
sinecura nf sinecure.
sinfín nm = **sinnúmero**.

sinfonía nf (a) symphony. (b) (Ven) harmonica.
sinfónico adj symphonic; **orquesta sinfónica** symphony orchestra.
Singapur Singapore.
singar [1h] vt (Cu) to bother, annoy.
singladura nf (Naut) day's run; nautical day (from noon to noon).
singuisarra nf (Col, Ven) row, shindy.
singular 1 adj (a) (Gram) singular.
   (b) **combate** — single combat.
   (c) (fig) outstanding, exceptional; (pej) singular, peculiar, odd.
   2 nm (Gram) singular; **en —** in the singular; (fig) **en —** in particular; **se refiere a él en —** it refers to him in particular; **que hable él en —** let him speak solely for himself.
singularidad nf singularity, peculiarity, oddity.
singularizar [1f] **1** vt to single out; to refer specifically to.
   2 singularizarse vr to distinguish oneself, stand out, excel; to be conspicuous; — **con uno** to single someone out for special treatment.
singularmente adv (a) singularly, peculiarly, oddly. (b) especially.
sinhueso nf (fam) tongue; **soltar la —** to shoot one's mouth off (fam).
siniestrado nm, **siniestrada** nf victim (of an accident etc), person who has suffered a loss (or damage).
siniestro 1 adj (a) (lit) left.
   (b) (fig) sinister; ominous; evil, malign.
   (c) (fig) fateful, disastrous.
   2 nm natural disaster, catastrophe, calamity; accident; — **marítimo** shipwreck, disaster at sea.
siniquitate nm (PR, Ven) fool.
sinnúmero nm: **un — de** a great many, no end of, a huge number of.
sino[1] nm fate, destiny.
sino[2] conj (a) but; **no son 8 — 9** there are not 8 but 9; **no cabe otra solución — que vaya él** there is no other solution but that he should go; **no lo hace sólo para sí — para todos** he's not doing it only for himself but for everybody.
   (b) except, save; only; **todos aplaudieron — él** everybody except him applauded; **no te pido — una cosa** I ask only (or but) one thing of you; **no deseo — verte** my sole wish is to see you; **no lo habría dicho — en broma** he could only have said it jokingly, he wouldn't have said it except as a joke.
sino . . . Chinese . . ., Sino . . .
sínodo nm synod.
sinonimia nf synonymy.
sinónimo 1 adj synonymous (con with). **2** nm synonym.
sinopsis nf, pl **sinopsis** synopsis.
sinóptico adj synoptic(al).
sinrazón nf wrong, injustice, outrage.
sinsabor nm (a) trouble, unpleasantness. (b) (of mind) sorrow; uneasiness, worry.
sinsilico adj (Mex) stupid.
sinsombrerismo nm hatlessness, custom of going hatless.
sinsonte nm mockingbird.
sinsustancia nmf (fam) idiot.
sintáctico adj syntactic(al).
sintaxis nf syntax.
síntesis nf, pl **síntesis** synthesis.
sintéticamente adv synthetically.
sintético adj synthetic(al).
sintetizar [1f] vt to synthesize.
síntoma nm symptom; sign, indication.
sintomático adj symptomatic.
sintonía nf (a) (Elec) syntomy; (Radio) tuning. (b) (Mus, Radio) signature tune.
sintonización nf (Radio) tuning.
sintonizar [1f] vt (Elec) to syntonize; (Radio) station to tune (in) to, pick up.
sinuosidad nf (a) sinuosity; waviness. (b) bend, curve, wave; **las —es del camino** the windings of the road, the bends in the road.
sinuoso adj (a) road etc winding, sinuous; line wavy; course devious. (b) person, means etc devious.
sinusitis nf sinusitis.
sinvergonzón nm (fam) rotter, bounder (fam).
sinvergüencería nf (a) (quality) villainy; rottenness, caddishness; shamelessness. (b) (act) = **sinvergüenzada**.
sinvergüenza nmf (a) scoundrel, villain, rascal; rotter, cad; ¡—! (hum) you villain! (b) shameless person.
sinvergüenzada nf (SAm) villainous trick, rotten thing (to do) (fam).

sinvergüenzura *nf* (SAm) shamelessness.
Sión *m* Zion.
sionismo *nm* Zionism.
sionista 1 *adj* Zionist. **2** *nmf* Zionist.
sipo *adj* (Ec) pockmarked.
sipotazo *nm* (CAm) slap, punch.
siqu ... = **psiqu ...**, *eg for* **siquiatría** *see* **psiquiatría.**
siquiera 1 *adv* (a) at least; **una vez** — once at least, just once; **dame un abrazo** — at least give me a hug; **deja — trabajar a los demás** at least let the others work.
　(b) **ni —, ni . . .** — not even, not so much as; **ni él — vino** not even he came; **ella ni me miró** — she didn't even look at me.
　2 *conj* (a) even if, even though; **ven — sea por pocos días** do come even if only for a few days.
　(b) **— venga, — no venga** whether he comes or not.
Siracusa Syracuse.
sirena *nf* (a) siren; mermaid; **— de la playa** bathing beauty. (b) (Tech) siren, hooter; **— de buque** ship's siren; **— de niebla** foghorn.
sirga *nf* towrope.
sirgar [1h] *vt* to tow.
Siria *f* Syria.
sirimba *nf* (Cu) faint, fainting fit.
sirimbo *adj* (Cu) silly.
sirimbombo *adj* (Cu) weak; cowardly, timid.
Sirio *m* Sirius.
sirio 1 *adj* Syrian. **2** *nm*, **siria** *nf* Syrian.
siró *nm* (PR), **sirope** *nm* (SAm: *angl*) syrup.
sirsaca *nf* seersucker.
sirte *nf* shoal, sandbank.
sirvienta *nf* servant, maid.
sirviente *nm* servant; waiter.
sisa *nf* (a) petty theft; dishonest profit (*made by a servant*); **—s** pilfering, petty thieving. (b) (Sew) dart; armhole.
sisal *nm* sisal; sisal plant.
sisar [1a] *vt* (a) to thieve, pilfer, filch; *person* to cheat; *account* to cheat on. (b) (Sew) to put darts in, take in.
sisear [1a] *vti* to hiss.
siseo *nm* hiss(ing).
Sísifo *m* Sisyphus.
sísmico *adj* seismic.
sismo *nm* = **seísmo.**
sismografía *nf* seismography.
sismógrafo *nm* seismograph.
sismología *nf* seismology.
sisón[1] **1** *adj* thieving, light-fingered. **2** *nm*, **sisona** *nf* petty thief.
sisón[2] *nm* (Orn) little bustard.
sistema *nm* system; method; **— de calefacción** heating (system); **— impositivo, — tributario** taxation, tax system; **— nervioso** nervous system; **— pedagógico** educational system; teaching method; **— rastreador** (*in space research*) tracking system; **trabajar con —** to work systematically, work methodically; **yo por — lo hago así** I make it a rule to do it this way.
sistemáticamente *adv* systematically.
sistemático *adj* systematic.
sistematización *nf* systematization.
sistematizar [1f] *vt* to systematize.
sitiador *nm* besieger.
sitial *nm* seat of honour; ceremonial chair.
sitiar [1b] *vt* to besiege, lay siege to; (*fig*) to surround, hem in.
sitio *nm* (a) place; spot; part; site, location; **— real** royal residence; **en cualquier —** anywhere; **en todos los —s** everywhere, all over; **en el mejor — de la ciudad** in the best part of the city; **cambiar de —** to shift, move; **cambiar de — con uno** to change places with someone; **dejar a uno en el —** to kill someone (on the spot); **poner a uno en su —, volver a uno a su —** (*fig*) to put someone firmly in his place; **quedarse en el —** to die instantly, die on the spot.
　(b) room, space; **¿hay —?** is there any room?; **hay — de sobra** there's plenty of room; **hacer —** to make room (*a uno* for someone).
　(c) (Mil) siege; **en estado de —** in a state of siege; under martial law; **levantar el —** to raise the siege; **poner — a** to besiege.
　(d) (Arg, Chi, Guat) building site, vacant lot.
　(e) (Cu, Mex) small farm.
　(f) (SAm) taxi rank.
sito *adj* situated, located (*en* at, in).
situación *nf* situation, position; (*social*) position, standing; **— económica** financial position; **crearse una —** to attain a position of financial security,

make good; **estar en — de + infin** to be in a position to + infin.
situado *adj* (a) situated, placed. (b) (Fin) **estar —** to be financially secure, be well placed.
situar [1e] *vt* (a) to place, put, set; *building etc* to locate, situate, site; (Mil) to post, station; **sitúan esta etapa en el siglo XIII** they place this stage in the 13th century; **esto le sitúa entre los mejores** this places him among the best.
　(b) (Fin) *money* to place, invest; to bank; *grant etc* to set aside; to assign, earmark; **— una pensión para uno** to settle an income on someone; **ha venido situando fondos en el extranjero** he has been placing money in accounts abroad.
siútico *adj* (Chi) = **cursi.**
siutiquería *nf* (Chi) = **cursilería.**
slam [ez'lam] *nm* (Bridge: *angl*) slam; **gran —** grand slam; **pequeño —** little slam.
slip [ez'lip] *nm*, *pl* **slips** [ez'lip] (*angl*) briefs, pants; (SAm) bathing trunks.
slogan [ez'loɣan] *nm*, *pl* **slogans** [ez'loɣan] (*angl*) slogan.
smoking [ez'mokin] *nm*, *pl* **smokings** [ez'mokin] (*false angl*) dinner jacket, tuxedo (US).
snack [ez'nak] *nm*, *pl* **snacks** [ez'nak] (*angl*) snack; snack bar.
snob [ez'noβ] *etc see* **esnob** *etc.*
so[1] *prep* under; *see* **capa** *etc.*
so[2] *interj* (a) whoa! (b) (SAm) quiet!, shut up! (c) (PR) shoo!
so[3] *as interj* (*contraction of* señor): **¡— indecente!** you swine!; **¡— burro!** you idiot!, you great oaf!
soba *nf* (a) kneading. (b) (*fam*) slap, punch; hiding; **dar — a uno** to wallop someone. (c) (*fam*) telling-off.
sobacal *adj* underarm (*attr*).
sobaco *nm* (Anat) armpit; (Sew) armhole.
sobado *adj* (a) worn, shabby; rumpled, crumpled, messed up; *book* well-thumbed, dog-eared.
　(b) (*fig*) *subject* well-worn.
　(c) (Cook) *pastry* short.
　(d) (Chi) big, huge.
sobador *nm* (a) (Col, Mex) bonesetter; quack. (b) (Ec, Mex, Per, PR) flatterer.
sobajar [1a] *vt* (a) to crush, rumple, mess up. (b) (Ec, Mex, Ven) to humiliate.
sobajear [1a] *vt* (SAm) to handle; to squeeze, press; to mess up.
sobandero *nm* (Col, Ven) bonesetter; quack.
sobaquera *nf* (a) (Sew) armhole. (b) shoulder holster. (c) (CAm, Mex, PR) underarm odour.
sobaquina *nf* underarm odour.
sobar [1a] **1** *vt* (a) *material* to handle, finger, dirty (with one's fingers); *dress etc* to crush, rumple, crumple, mess up; *dough* to knead; *putty etc* to squeeze (in the hands), soften; *muscle* to massage, rub.
　(b) *person* to fondle, feel (amorously); (*pej*) to finger, paw, lay hands on.
　(c) (SAm) *bones* to set.
　(d) (Col) to skin, flay.
　(e) (*fam*) to wallop.
　(f) to pester; to annoy.
　(g) (Ec, Mex, Per, PR) to flatter.
　(h) (Guat *etc*) to tell off.
　2 sobarse *vr* (*lovers*) to pet, fondle, cuddle.
sobasquera *nf* (CAm, Mex, PR) = **sobaquina.**
soberanamente *adv* (*fig*) supremely.
soberanía *nf* sovereignty.
soberano 1 *adj* (a) (Pol *etc*) sovereign.
　(b) (*fig*) supreme.
　(c) (*fam*) real, really big; **una soberana paliza** a real walloping.
　2 *nm*, **soberana** *nf* sovereign; **los —s** the king and queen, the royal couple.
soberbia *nf* (a) pride; haughtiness, arrogance. (b) (*fig*) magnificence, grandeur, pomp. (c) anger; irritable nature.
soberbio *adj* (a) proud; haughty, arrogant. (b) (*fig*) magnificent, grand, superb; **¡—!** splendid! (c) angry; irritable. (d) (*fam*) = **soberano** (c).
sobijo *nm* (a) (CAm, Col, Pan) = **soba.** (b) (Col) skinning, flaying.
sobijón *nm* (CAm) = **sobijo.**
sobón *adj* (a) too free with one's hands, given to pawing; (*fig*) fresh, too familiar by half; *lovers* mushy, spoony (*fam*).
　(b) lazy, workshy.
　(c) (Per) soapy.
sobornable *adj* bribable, venal.
sobornar [1a] *vt* to bribe, suborn; to buy off; (*hum*) to get round.

soborno *nm* (a) (*un* —) bribe; (*el* —) bribery, graft. (b) (*Arg, Bol, Chi*) extra load; extra, bonus.

sobra *nf* (a) excess, surplus; —s leavings, left-overs, scraps; (*Sew*) remnants.

(b) **de** — spare, surplus, extra; **aquí tengo de** — I've more than enough here, I've got plenty (and to spare) here; **tuvo motivos de** — he had plenty of justification, he was more than justified; **lo sé de** — I know it only too well; **aquí estoy de** — I'm not needed here; I'm in the way here.

sobradamente *adv* too; amply; over . . .; *know* only too well; **con eso queda** — **satisfecho** he is only too happy with that, with that he is more than fully satisfied.

sobradero *nm* overflow pipe.

sobradillo *nm* penthouse.

sobrado 1 *adj* (a) more than enough; superfluous, excessive; superabundant; **hay tiempo** — there's plenty of time; **tuvo razón sobrada** he was amply justified; **sobradas veces** repeatedly.

(b) **estar** — **de algo** to have more than enough of something, be well provided with something.

(c) wealthy; **no anda muy** — he's not very well off.

(d) bold, forward.

(e) (*Chi*) colossal.

2 *adv* too, exceedingly.

3 *nm* (a) attic, garret.

(b) (*Arg*) kitchen shelf.

(c) (*Andalusia, Chi*) —s left-overs.

sobrancero *adj* unemployed.

sobrante 1 *adj* spare, remaining, extra, surplus; *worker* redundant.

2 *nm* (a) surplus, remainder; (*Comm, Fin*) surplus; balance in hand.

(b) —s odds and ends.

3 *nmf* redundant worker, person made redundant.

sobrar [1a] **1** *vt* to exceed, surpass.

2 *vi* to remain, be left (over), be to spare; to be more than enough; to be superfluous; **por este lado sobra** there's too much on this side; **no es que sobre talento** it's not that there's a surplus of talent; **todo lo que has dicho sobra** all that you've said is quite unnecessary; **nos sobra tiempo** we have plenty (*or* lots, heaps) of time; **al terminar me sobraba medio metro** I had half a metre left over when I finished; **veo que aquí sobro** I see that I'm not needed here; I see that I'm in the way.

sobre[1] *nm* envelope; — **de primer día (de circulación)** first-day cover; — **de paga** pay packet; — **de sellos** packet of stamps; — **de té** tea bag.

sobre[2] *prep* (a) (*of place*) on, upon; on top of; over, above; **está** — **la mesa** it's on the table; **volamos** — **Cádiz** we're flying over Cadiz; **prestar juramento** — **la Biblia** to swear on the Bible.

(b) (*of quantity etc*) over, over and above; more than; (*of addition*) in addition to, on top of, besides; **un aumento** — **el año anterior** an increase over last year; **10 dólares** — **lo estipulado** 10 dollars over and above what was agreed; — **todas mis obligaciones hay una nueva** on top of all my duties here comes another; **crimen** — **crimen** crime upon crime; — **ser traidor es asesino** in addition to being a traitor he is a murderer.

(c) **estar** — **uno** (*fig*) to keep on at someone; to keep constant watch over someone.

(d) (*of loan etc*) on; **un préstamo** — **una propiedad** a loan on a property; **un tributo** — **las medias a** tax on stockings.

(e) (*of numbers*) about; — **las 6** at about 6 o'clock; **ocupa** — **20 páginas** it fills about 20 pages, it fills about 20 pages, it occupies roughly 20 pages.

(f) (*of proportions*) in, out of; **3** — **100** 3 in a 100, 3 out of every 100.

(g) (*of subject*) about, on; **un libro** — **Tirso** a book about Tirso.

sobre . . . *super* . . ., *over* . . .

sobreabundancia *nf* superabundance, overabundance.

sobreabundante *adj* superabundant, overabundant.

sobreabundar [1a] *vi* to superabound (*en* in, with), be very abundant.

sobrealimentado *adj* (*Mech*) supercharged.

sobrealimentador *nm* supercharger.

sobrealimentar [1a] *vt* (a) *person etc* to overfeed. (b) (*Mech*) to supercharge.

sobreañadir [3a] *vt* to give in addition, add (as a bonus); to superinduce.

sobrecalentar [1k] *vt* to overheat.

sobrecama *nm* bedspread.

sobrecarga *nf* (a) extra load; excess weight; (*fig*) new burden.

(b) (*Comm*) surcharge; (*Post*) surcharge, overprint(ing); — **de importación** import surcharge.

(c) rope.

sobrecargar [1h] *vt* (a) *lorry etc* to overload; (*Elec*) to overcharge; *person* to weigh down, overburden; — **el mercado** (*Arg*) to glut the market.

(b) (*Comm*) to surcharge; (*Post*) to surcharge, overprint (*de* with).

sobrecargo *nm* (*Naut*) supercargo, purser.

sobrecejo *nm* (a) frown. (b) (*Archit*) lintel.

sobreceño *nm* frown.

sobrecoger [2c] **1** *vt* to startle, take by surprise; to scare, frighten.

2 sobrecogerse *vr* (a) to be startled, start (*a* at, *de* with); to get scared, be frightened.

(b) to be overawed (*de* by); — **de emoción** to be overcome with emotion.

sobrecubierta *nf* outer cover; (*of book*) jacket.

sobredicho *adj* aforementioned.

sobredorar [1a] *vt* to gild; (*fig*) to gloss over.

sobre(e)ntender [2g] **1** *vt* to understand; to guess, deduce, infer.

2 sobre(e)ntenderse *vr*: **aquí se sobre(e)ntienden dos palabras** here two words are understood; **se sobre(e)ntiende que** . . . it is implied that . . ., one infers that . . .

sobre(e)stimación *nf* overestimate.

sobre(e)stimar [1a] *vt* to overestimate.

sobre(e)xcitación *nf* overexcitement.

sobre(e)xcitado *adj* overexcited.

sobre(e)xcitar [1a] **1** *vt* to overexcite. **2 sobre(e)xcitarse** *vr* to get overexcited.

sobre(e)xponer [2r] *vt* to overexpose.

sobre(e)xposición *nf* (*Phot*) overexposure.

sobrefunda *nf* (*CAm*) pillowslip.

sobregirar [1a] *vti* to overdraw.

sobregiro *nm* overdraft.

sobrehumano *adj* superhuman.

sobreimpresión *nf* (*Post*) overprint(ing).

sobreimprimir [3a] *vt* (*Post*) to overprint.

sobrellevar [1a] *vt burden* to carry, help to carry, help with; *another's burden* to ease; *illness, disaster, troubles etc* to bear, endure; *another's faults* to be tolerant towards.

sobremanera *adv* exceedingly.

sobremarca *nf* (*Bridge*) overbid; raise (in a suit).

sobremarcha *nf* (*Aut*) overdrive.

sobremesa *nf* (a) table cover.

(b) dessert.

(c) sitting on after a meal; **charla de** — after-dinner speech; **conversación de** — table talk; **un cigarro de** — an after-dinner cigar, a postprandial cigar; **hablaremos de eso de** — we'll talk about that after dinner.

sobrenadar [1a] *vi* to float.

sobrenatural *adj* supernatural; weird, unearthly; **lo** — the supernatural; **ciencias** —**es** occult sciences; **vida** — life after death.

sobrenombre *nm* by-name, extra name; nickname.

sobrentender *etc see* **sobre(e)ntender** *etc*.

sobrepaga *nf* extra pay, bonus; rise, raise (*US*).

sobreparto *nm* confinement; **dolores de** — afterpains; **morir de** — to die in childbirth.

sobrepasar [1a] *vt* to exceed, surpass, outdo; *limit* to exceed; *hope etc* to surpass; *competitor, record* to beat; *runway* (*Aer*) to overshoot.

sobrepelo *nm* (*RPl*) saddlecloth.

sobrepelliz *nf* surplice.

sobrepeso *nm* extra load; excess weight.

sobrepoblación *nf* overcrowding.

sobreponer [2r] **1** *vt* (a) to put on top (*en* of), superimpose (*en* on), add (*en* to).

(b) — **A a B** to give A preference over B, give more weight to A than to B.

2 sobreponerse *vr* (a) to master oneself, pull oneself together; to win through, pull through, overcome adversity (*etc*).

(b) — **a una enfermedad** to pull through an illness; — **a un rival** to triumph over a rival; — **a un enemigo** to overcome an enemy; — **a un susto** to get over a fright, recover from a fright.

sobreprecio *nm* surcharge; increase in price.

sobreproducción *nf* overproduction.

sobrepuesto *adj* added, superimposed.

sobrepujar [1a] *vt* to outdo, excel, surpass; **sobrepuja a todos en talento** he excels all the rest in talent.

sobrero *adj* extra, spare.

sobresaliente 1 *adj* (a) projecting; overhanging.

(b) (*fig*) outstanding, excellent; (*Univ etc*) *mark* first class.

2 *nmf* substitute; (*Theat*) understudy.

3 *nm* (*Univ etc*) first class (mark), distinction.

sobresalir [3r] *vi* **(a)** to project, jut out; to overhang; to stick out, protrude; to stick up, stand up.
(b) (*fig*) to stand out, be outstanding, excel.
sobresaltar [1a] **1** *vt* to startle, scare, frighten. **2 sobresaltarse** *vr* to start, be startled (*con, de* at).
sobresalto *nm* start; scare; sudden shock; **de —** suddenly.
sobresanar [1a] *vi* (*Med*) to heal superficially; (*fig*) to conceal itself, hide its true nature.
sobrescrito *nm* address; superscription.
sobreseer [2e] **1** *vt:* **— una causa** (*Law*) to stop a case, rule that a case should not continue. **2** *vi:* **— de** to desist from, give up.
sobresello *nm* double seal.
sobrestante *nm* foreman, overseer; site manager.
sobresueldo *nm* = **sobrepaga.**
sobretasa *nf* surcharge.
sobretiro *nm* (*Mex*) offprint.
sobretodo *nm* overcoat.
sobrevalorar [1a] *vt* to overvalue.
sobrevenir [3s] *vi* to happen (unexpectedly), come up, supervene; to follow, ensue.
sobreviviente = **superviviente.**
sobrevivir [3a] *vi* to survive; **— a** *disaster etc* to survive; *person* to survive, outlive; to outlast.
sobrevolar [1m] *vt* to fly over, overfly.
sobriedad *nf* soberness; moderation; restraint; quietness; plainness.
sobrina *nf* niece.
sobrino *nm* nephew.
sobrio *adj* sober; moderate, temperate, restrained; *colour* quiet; *style etc* plain, sober; **ser — en la bebida** to be temperate in one's drinking habits; **ser — de palabras** to speak with restraint.
sobros *nmpl* (*CAm*) leavings, scraps.
soca[1] *nf* **(a)** (*Bol*) young shoots of rice; (*Ec*) top leaf of tobacco plant, high-quality tobacco. **(b)** (*CAm*) drunkenness.
soca[2] *nm* (*fam*): **hacerse el —** to act dumb (*fam*).
socaire *nm* (*Naut*) lee; **al —** to leeward; **al — de** (*fig*) enjoying the protection of; **using . . . as an excuse; estar** (*or* **ponerse**) **al —** (*fig*) to shirk.
socaliña 1 *nf* craft, cunning; clever persistence. **2** *nmf* (*fam*) twister (*fam*), swindler.
socaliñar [1a] *vt* to get by a swindle.
socaliñero *adj* crafty, cunning; cleverly persistent.
socapa *nf* (*fam*) dodge, subterfuge; **a —** surreptitiously.
socapar [1a] *vt* (*Bol, Ec, Mex*): **— a uno** to cover up for someone.
socar [1g] **1** *vt* (*CAm*) **(a)** to press down, squeeze, compress.
(b) (*fig*) to annoy, upset.
2 socarse *vr* (*CAm*) **(a)** to get drunk.
(b) — con uno to fall out with someone, get into a fight with someone.
socarrar [1a] *vt* to scorch, singe.
socarrón *adj* **(a)** sarcastic, ironical; *humour* sly. **(b)** crafty, cunning.
socarronería *nf* **(a)** sarcasm, irony; sly humour. **(b)** craftiness, cunning.
socava *nf*, **socavación** *nf* undermining.
socavar [1a] *vt* **(a)** to undermine; to dig under, dig away; (*of water*) to hollow out. **(b)** (*fig*) to sap, undermine.
socavón *nm* **(a)** (*Min*) gallery, tunnel; hollow; cavern; (*in street*) hole. **(b)** (*Archit etc*) subsidence, sudden collapse.
sociabilidad *nf* sociability, friendliness; gregariousness; conviviality.
sociable *adj* *person* sociable, friendly; *animal* social, gregarious; *gathering etc* convivial.
sociablemente *adv* sociably; gregariously; convivially.
social *adj* **(a)** social. **(b)** (*Comm, Fin*) company (*attr*), company's.
socialdemócrata *nmf* social democrat.
socialdemocrático *adj* social-democratic.
socialismo *nm* socialism.
socialista 1 *adj* socialist(ic). **2** *nmf* socialist.
socialización *nf* socialization; nationalization.
socializar [1f] *vt* to socialize; to nationalize.
socialmente *adv* socially.
sociedad *nf* **(a)** (*in general*) society; **los males de la — actual** the ills of contemporary society; **la — benéfica** the welfare state; **la — opulenta** the affluent society; **hacer —** to join forces.
(b) society, association; body; **— científica, — docta** learned society; **— inmobiliaria** building society; **S— de Jesús** Society of Jesus; **S— de las Naciones** League of Nations; **— secreta** secret society; **— de socorro mutuo** friendly society, provident society.

(c) (*Comm, Fin*) company; partnership; **— anónima** limited liability company, corporation; **Góngora y Quevedo S— Anónima** (*abbr* SA) Góngora and Quevedo Limited (Incorporated US); **— de cartera, — de control** holding company; **— mercantil** company, trading company.
(d) society; **alta —, buena —** (high) society; **notas de —** gossip column, column of society news; **entrar en —, presentarse en (la) —** to come out, make one's début.
socio *nm*, **socia** *nf* **(a)** associate; (*of club*) member; (*of learned society etc*) fellow; **se ruega a los señores —s . . .** members are asked to . . .; **— honorario, — de honor** honorary member; **— de número** full member.
(b) (*Comm, Fin*) partner; **— comanditario, — pasivo** sleeping partner, silent partner (*US*).
socioeconómico *adj* socioeconomic.
sociología *nf* sociology.
sociológico *adj* sociological.
sociólogo *nm* sociologist.
soco 1 *adj* **(a)** (*CAm*) drunk.
(b) *see* **zoco 1.**
2 *nm* **(a)** (*Col: Anat, Bot*) stump.
(b) (*Col*) short blunt machete.
(c) *see* **zoco 2.**
socola *nf* (*CAm, Col*) clearing of land.
socolar [1a] *vt* **(a)** (*CAm, Col, Ec, Pan*) *land* to clear, clear of scrub.
(b) (*Col*) to bungle, do clumsily.
socollón *nm* (*CAm, Cu*) violent shake.
socollonear [1a] *vt* (*CAm*) to shake violently.
soconusco *nm* **(a)** snack, bite to eat, refreshment.
(b) (*Cu*) chocolate; (*Guat, Mex*) high-quality chocolate. **(c)** (*Cu*: *fig*) shady deal.
socorrer [2a] *vt person* to help; *needs* to relieve, meet, help with; *city* to relieve; *expedition etc* to bring aid to.
socorrido *adj* **(a)** *place* well-stocked. **(b)** *object etc* handy; useful. **(c)** *person* helpful, obliging, co-operative. **(d)** (*fig*) hackneyed, trite, well-worn.
socorrismo *nm* life-saving.
socorro *nm* **(a)** help, aid, assistance; relief (*also Mil*); **¡—!** help!; **—s mutuos** mutual aid; **trabajos de —** relief work, rescue work.
(b) (*Chi*) advance payment.
socoyote *nm* (*Mex*) youngest son.
socucha *nf*, **socucho** *nm* (*Mex, RPl*) small room, den; small house; ruinous house, slum.
soche *nm* (*Col*) tanned sheepskin (*or* goatskin).
Sócrates *m* Socrates.
socrático *adj* Socratic.
soda *nf* **(a)** soda. **(b)** soda water.
sodio *nm* sodium.
sodomía *nf* sodomy.
sodomita *nm* sodomite.
soez *adj* dirty, rude, obscene.
sofá *nm* sofa, settee.
sofá-cama *nm* studio couch, sofa bed.
sofero *adj* (*Per*) huge, tremendous.
Sofía *f* Sophia.
sofión *nm* sharp rebuke; sharp retort.
sofisma *nm* sophism.
sofista *nm* sophist; (*fig*) quibbler.
sofistería *nf* sophistry.
sofisticación *nf* sophistication; (*pej*) affectation.
sofisticado *adj* sophisticated; (*pej*) affected.
sofístico *adj* sophistic(al); false, fallacious.
soflama *nf* **(a)** dull glow, flicker. **(b)** (*of face*) blush. **(c)** (*fig*) fiery speech, harangue. **(d)** (*fig*) deceit. **(e)** (*Mex*) unimportant piece of news.
soflamar [1a] *vt* **(a)** to scorch; (*Cook*) to singe. **(b)** *person* to shame, make blush. **(c)** (*fam*) to deceive, swindle, blarney.
sofocación *nf* **(a)** suffocation. **(b)** (*fig*) = **sofoco (b).**
sofocado *adj*: **estar —** (*fig*) to be out of breath; to feel stifled; to be hot and bothered.
sofocante *adj* stifling, suffocating.
sofocar [1g] **1** *vt* **(a)** *person* to suffocate, stifle; to get out of breath.
(b) *fire* to smother, put out; *revolt etc* to crush, put down; *epidemic* to stop.
(c) (*fig*) **— a uno** to make someone blush; to put someone to shame; to embarrass someone; to anger someone, get someone worked up, provoke someone, upset someone.
2 sofocarse *vr* **(a)** to suffocate, stifle; to get out of breath, (begin to) pant; to choke.
(b) (*fig*) to blush; to feel embarrassed; to get angry, get worked up, get upset, upset oneself; **no vale la pena de que te sofoques** it's not worth upsetting yourself about it.

Sófocles m Sophocles.
sofoco nm (a) suffocation; stifling sensation.
(b) (fig) embarrassment; anger, rage, feeling of indignation.
(c) **pasar un** — to have an embarrassing time.
sofocón nm (fam) nasty blow; **se le dio un** — he really blew up (fam), he got really worked up.
sofoquina nf (fam) (a) stifling heat; **hace una** — it's stifling hot. (b) = **sofocón**.
sofreír [3m; ptp **sofrito**] vt to fry lightly.
sofrenada nf (a) sudden check, sudden jerk on the reins. (b) (fam) ticking-off.
sofrenar [1a] vt (a) horse to rein back sharply. (b) (fig) to restrain, control. (c) (fam) to tick off.
soga nf rope, cord; halter; hangman's rope; **dar** — **a uno** to make fun of someone; **echar la** — **tras el caldero** to chuck it all up, throw in one's hand; **estar con la** — **al cuello** to be in imminent danger, be in a real fix; **hablar de la** — **en casa del ahorcado** to say something singularly inappropriate; **hacer** — to lag behind.
soguear [1a] vt (a) to measure with a rope; (Arg, CAm, Ec) to tie with a rope; (Cu) to lasso. (b) (Cu) to tame. (c) (Col) to make fun of.
soguero adj (Cu) tame.
sois see **ser**.
soja nf soya; **semilla de** — soya bean.
sojuzgar [1h] vt to conquer; to subdue; to rule despotically.
sol nm (a) sun; sunshine, sunlight; — **naciente** rising sun; — **poniente** setting sun; **como un** — as bright as a new pin; **día de** — sunny day; **de** — **a** — from sunrise to sunset; **dejar algo al** — to leave something in the sun; **tostarse al** — to sit in the sun, acquire a sun tan; **arrimarse al** — **que más calienta** to know which side one's bread is buttered; **no dejar a uno a** — **ni a sombra** to chase someone all over, pester someone continually; **hay** —, **hace** — it is sunny, the sun is shining; **salga el** — **por donde quiera** come what may; press on regardless (fam); **tomar el** — to sun oneself, sunbathe, bask.
(b) standard monetary unit of Peru.
solada nf sediment.
solado nm tiling, tiled floor.
solamente adv only; solely; just.
solana nf sunny spot, suntrap; sun lounge, solarium.
solanera nf scorching sunshine; (Med) sunburn; sunstroke.
solano nm east wind.
solapa nf (a) (of jacket) lapel; (of envelope, book, pocket) flap. (b) (fig) pretext.
solapadamente adv slyly, in an underhand way, by underhand means.
solapado adj sly, underhand, sneaky.
solapar [1a] **1** vt (a) to overlap.
(b) (fig) to cover up, cloak, keep dark.
2 vi to overlap.
3 solaparse vr: **se ha solapado** it has got covered up, it has got hidden underneath.
solapo nm (a) (Sew) lapel; overlap. (b) **a** — (fam) = **solapadamente**.
solar[1] nm (a) (Archit) lot, piece of ground, site; — **para edificaciones** building site.
(b) ancestral home, family seat; (fig) family, lineage, line.
(c) (CAm, Ven) backyard.
(d) (Cu, Per) tenement house.
solar[2] [1m] vt floor to floor, tile; shoes to sole.
solar[3] adj solar, sun (attr).
solariego adj (a) casa **solariega** family seat, ancestral home. (b) (Hist) family ancient and noble; rights etc manorial; **tierras solariegas** demesne.
solaz nm recreation, relaxation; solace, spiritual relief.
solazar [1f] **1** vt to amuse, provide relaxation for; to console; to comfort, cheer. **2 solazarse** vr to enjoy oneself, amuse oneself, relax.
solazo nm (fam) = **solanera**.
soldada nf pay.
soldadesca nf (a) military profession. (b) (pej) soldiery, brutal and licentious soldiery.
soldadesco adj soldierly.
soldadito nm: — **de plomo** tin soldier.
soldado[1] nm soldier; — **de infantería** infantryman; — **de marina** marine; — **de plomo** tin soldier; — **de primera** lance-corporal; — **raso** private; **la tumba del S— Desconocido** the tomb of the Unknown Warrior.
soldado[2] adj seam etc welded; **totalmente** — welded throughout.
soldador nm (a) (Tech) soldering iron. (b) (person) welder.

soldadura nf (a) (material) solder. (b) (act) soldering, welding; — **autógena** welding. (c) soldered joint, welded seam.
soldar [1m] **1** vt (a) (Tech) to solder, weld.
(b) to join, unite; to cement; diverse parts to weld together; quarrel to patch up.
2 soldarse vr (bones) to knit (together).
soleado adj sunny.
solear [1a] vt to put in the sun; to bleach.
solecismo nm solecism.
soledad nf (a) solitude; loneliness. (b) grieving, mourning. (c) lonely place; —**es** wilderness.
solemne adj (a) solemn; dignified, impressive. (b) (fam) lie downright; nonsense utter; mistake complete, terrible.
solemnemente adv solemnly; impressively.
solemnidad nf (a) solemnity; impressiveness; formality, gravity, dignity.
(b) (act) solemnity, solemn ceremony; —**es** solemnities.
(c) —**es** (bureaucratic) formalities.
(d) (fam) **pobre de** — miserably poor; **rico de** — stinking rich (fam).
solemnización nf solemnization, celebration.
solemnizar [1f] vt to solemnize, celebrate.
solenoide nm solenoid.
soler [2h; defective] vi (a) — + infin to be in the habit of + ger, be accustomed to + infin, be wont to + infin; **suele pasar por aquí** he usually comes this way; **solíamos ir todos los años** we used to go every year; **como se suele** as is normal, as is customary; ¿**beber? pues no suele** drink? well he doesn't usually.
(b) (Chi) to occur rarely, happen only occasionally.
solera nf (a) prop, support; plinth.
(b) (of ditch etc) bottom.
(c) lower millstone.
(d) (Mex) floor tile, paving stone.
(e) (Chi) kerb.
(f) inherited character, collective character; traditional nature; **éste es país de** — **celta** this is a country of basically Celtic character; **es de** — **de médicos** he comes from a line of doctors; **vino de** — vintage wine; **es un barrio con** — it is a typically Spanish (etc) quarter, it is a quarter with a strong flavour to it.
soleta nf (a) (Sew) patch, darn.
(b) (fam) shameless woman.
(c) (fam) **dar** — **a uno** to chuck someone out; **tomar** — to beat it (fam).
(d) (Mex) wafer, ladyfinger.
solevantamiento nm (a) pushing up, raising. (b) (Pol) rising; upheaval.
solevantar [1a] vt (a) to push up, raise, heave up. (b) (Pol etc) to rouse, stir up.
solfa nf (a) (Mus) solfa; musical notation; (fig) music.
(b) (fam) tanning (fam).
(c) (fam) **poner a uno en** — to make someone look ridiculous, hold someone up to mockery.
solfear [1a] vt (a) (Mus) to solfa. (b) (fam) to tan (fam). (c) (fam) to tick off.
solfeo nm (a) (Mus) solfa. (b) (fam) tanning (fam); ticking-off.
solicitación nf request; solicitation; canvassing.
solicitante nmf applicant; petitioner.
solicitar [1a] vt (a) permission etc to ask for, request, seek; approval to seek; post to apply for; support to solicit, canvass for; votes to canvass; — **algo a uno** to ask someone for something, request something of someone.
(b) attention, interest, (also Phys) to attract.
(c) person to pursue, chase after, try to attract; woman to court; **le solicitan en todas partes** he is in great demand all over, he is much sought after.
solícito adj diligent, careful; solicitous, concerned (por about, for); affectionate.
solicitud nf (a) (quality) diligence, care; solicitude, concern; affection.
(b) (act) request (de for); petition; application (de un puesto for a post); **a** — on request; **presentar una** — to put in an application, make an application; **denegar** (or **desestimar** etc) **una** — to refuse a request, reject an application.
sólidamente adv solidly.
solidariamente adv jointly, mutually.
solidaridad nf solidarity; **por** — **con** (Pol etc) out of sympathy with, out of solidarity with.
solidario adj (a) obligation etc mutually binding, jointly shared, shared in common; participación etc joint, common; person jointly liable.

(b) hacerse — de to sympathize with, declare one's solidarity with; **hacerse — de una opinión** to echo an opinion.

solidarizarse [1f] *vr*: **— con** to declare one's solidarity with, affirm one's support for, line up with.

solidez *nf* solidity; hardness.

solidificación *nf* solidification; hardening.

solidificar [1g] **1** *vt* to solidify, harden. **2 solidificarse** *vr* to solidify, harden.

sólido[1] **1** *adj* **(a)** solid (*also Math, Phys*); hard.
(b) (*Tech etc*) solidly made; well built; *shoes etc* stout, strong; *colour* fast.
(c) (*fig*) solid, sound; firm, stable, secure; *basis, principle, morality etc* sound. **2** *nm* solid.

sólido[2] *adj* (*Andalusia, Per*) lonely.

soliloquiar [1b] *vi* to soliloquize, talk to oneself; to meditate aloud.

soliloquio *nm* soliloquy, monologue.

solimán *nm* corrosive sublimate; (*fig*) poison.

solio *nm* throne.

solipsismo *nm* solipsism.

solista *nmf* soloist.

solitaria *nf* tapeworm.

solitario 1 *adj* **(a)** *person, life* lonely, solitary; **vivir — to** live alone.
(b) *place* lonely, desolate; bleak; **a tal hora la calle está solitaria** at such a time the street is deserted (*or* empty).
2 *nm*, **solitaria** *nf* recluse; hermit; solitary person. **3** *nm* (*game, diamond*) solitaire.

sólito *adj* usual, customary.

soliviantar [1a] *vt* **(a)** to stir up, rouse (to revolt).
(b) to anger; to irritate, exasperate.
(c) to worry, cause anxiety to; **le tienen soliviantado los celos** he is eaten up with jealousy.
(d) to fill with longing; to buoy up with false hopes; to make vain, fill with conceit; **anda soliviantado con el proyecto** he has tremendous hopes for the scheme.

soliviar [1b] **1** *vt* **(a)** to lift, push up. **(b)** (*Arg*) to steal. **2 soliviarse** *vr* to half rise, partly get up; to get up on one elbow.

solo 1 *adj* **(a)** single, sole; only one; unique; **hay una sola dificultad** there is just one difficulty; **con esta sola condición** with this single condition; **su sola preocupación es ganar dinero** his one concern is to make money; **no hubo ni una sola objeción** there was not a single objection; **es — en su género** it is unique of its kind.
(b) alone; lonely; by oneself; **venir — to** come alone; **pasa los días — en su cuarto** he spends the days alone in his room; **iré —** I'll go alone; **estos días me siento muy —** I feel very lonely nowadays; **dejar — a uno** to leave someone all alone; **tendremos que comer pan —** we shall have to eat plain bread, we shall have to eat bread and nothing with it; **se quedó — a los 7 años** he was left an orphan (*or* alone in the world) at 7; **se queda — en esta especialidad** there's nobody to touch him in this particular field.
(c) a solas alone, by oneself; **lo hizo a solas** he did it (all) by himself; **volar a solas** to fly solo; **vuelo a solas** solo flight.
(d) (*Mus*) solo; **cantar — to** sing solo.
2 *nm* **(a)** (*Mus*) solo; **un — para tenor** a tenor solo.
(b) (*Cards*) solitaire, patience.
(c) (*Arg*) tedious conversation.

sólo *adv* only, solely, merely, just; **— quería verlo** I only (*or* just) wanted to see it; **es — un teniente** he's only a lieutenant, he's merely a lieutenant; **no — A sino también B** not only A but also B; **— que . . .** except that . . .; but for the fact that . . .; **ven aunque — sea para media hora** come even if it's just for half an hour; **con — que sepas tocar algunas notas** even if you only know how to play a few notes; **con — que estudies dos horas diarias** by studying for as little as two hours a day; **tan —** only, just.

solomillo *nm* sirloin.

solomo *nm* sirloin; loin of pork.

solón *nm* (*Ven*) scorching heat.

solsticio *nm* solstice; **— de estío** summer solstice; **—** de invierno winter solstice.

soltar [1m] **1** *vt* **(a)** (*from hand etc*) to let go of; to drop; to release; *knot* to undo, untie; *mooring* to cast off; *buckle etc* to undo, unfasten, loosen; *clutch* (*Aut*) to release, disengage; *brake* to release, take off; *rope etc* to loosen, slacken; to pay out; *tangled rope etc* to free; *water* to let out, run off; *captive* to release, let go, set free; *animals* to let out,

turn out, turn loose; to set free; *prey* to let go of; *money* (*fam*) to cough up (*fam*); *post, privilege etc* (*fam*) to give up; **¡suéltame, querido!** let go of me, dear!; **¡suélteme, señor!** unhand me, sir! (*lit*); **no quiere — el puesto por nada del mundo** he won't give up the job for anything.
(b) *exclamation, laugh, sneeze etc* to let out; *sigh* to fetch, heave; *oath etc* to utter, come out with, let fly; *hint* to drop; *truth* to let out, let slip; **soltó un par de palabrotas** he came out with a couple of rude words, he let fly a couple of obscenities; **les volvió a — el mismo sermón** he read them the same lecture all over again.
(c) *blow* to deal, strike, let fly.
(d) *skin* (*of snake*) to cast, slough.
(e) *difficulty* to solve; *doubt* to resolve; *objection etc* to satisfy, deal with.
(f) (*Col*) to cede, give, hand over.
2 soltarse *vr* **(a)** (*knot, laces etc*) to come undone, come untied; (*seam etc*) to come unstitched; (*animal etc*) to get loose, break loose, free itself; to escape; (*Mech: part*) to work loose; to come off, fly off, fall off; **— de las manos de uno** to escape from someone's clutches; **se le soltó un grito** a cry escaped him, he let out a yell; **no se vaya a — el perro** don't let the dog get out (*or* get loose etc); **— del estómago** to have diarrhoea.
(b) (*fig*) to achieve one's independence, win freedom.
(c) (*fig*) to lose control (of oneself); **— a su gusto** to let fly, let oneself go.
(d) (*fig: in a skill etc*) to become expert, acquire real proficiency; (*in a language*) to become fluent.
(e) — a + infin to begin to + *infin*.
(f) — con una idea absurda to come up with a silly idea; **— con una contribución de 50 dólares** to come up with a 50-dollar contribution; **por fin se soltó con algunos peniques** he eventually parted with a few coppers.

soltera *nf* single woman, unmarried woman, spinster; **apellido de —** maiden name.

solterear [1a] *vi* (*Arg*) to stay single.

soltería *nf* single state, unmarried state; bachelorhood, spinsterhood.

soltero 1 *adj* single, unmarried. **2** *nm* bachelor, unmarried man.

solterón *nm* confirmed bachelor, old bachelor.

solterona *nf* spinster, maiden lady; (*pej*) old maid; **tía —** maiden aunt.

soltura *nf* **(a)** (*of rope etc*) looseness, slackness; (*Mech*) looseness; (*of limbs*) agility, nimbleness, ease of movement, freedom of action.
(b) (*Med, also — de vientre*) looseness of the bowels, diarrhoea.
(c) (*in speaking etc*) fluency, ease; **habla árabe con —** he speaks Arabic fluently.
(d) (*pej*) shamelessness; licentiousness; dissipation.

solubilidad *nf* solubility.

soluble *adj* **(a)** (*Chem*) soluble; **en agua soluble in** water. **(b)** *problem* solvable, that can be solved.

solución *nf* **(a)** (*Chem*) solution.
(b) (*of problem etc*) solution; answer (*de* to); **esto no tiene —** there's no answer to this, there's no solution to this one.
(c) (*Theat*) climax, dénouement.
(d) — de continuidad break in continuity, interruption.

solucionar [1a] *vt* to solve; to resolve, settle.

solucionista *nmf* solver.

solvencia *nf* **(a)** (*Fin*) solvency.
(b) (*Fin: act*) settlement, payment.
(c) (*fig*) **— moral** character; **de toda — moral** of excellent character, completely trustworthy.

solventar [1a] *vt* **(a)** *account, debt* to settle, pay. **(b)** *difficulty* to resolve; *matter* to settle.

solvente 1 *adj* solvent, free of debt. **2** *nm* (*Chem*) solvent.

sollamar [1a] *vt* to scorch, singe.

sollastre *nm* rogue, villain.

sollo *nm* sturgeon.

sollozar [1f] *vi* to sob.

sollozo *nm* sob; **decir algo entre —s** to sob something.

somalí 1 *adj* Somali. **2** *nm* Somali.

Somalia *nf* Somaliland.

somanta *nf* beating.

somatada *nf* (*CAm, Pan*) blow, bang; punch.

somatar [1a] **1** *vt* **(a)** (*CAm*) to beat, thrash; to punch.
(b) (*Hond*) to sell off cheap.
2 somatarse *vr* (*CAm, Pan*) to fall heavily, knock oneself about badly.

somatón *nm* (*CAm*) = **somatada**.

sombra nf (a) (cast by object) shadow; (as protection etc) shade; (Art) shaded part, shaded area, dark part; —s shadows, darkness; **luz y** — light and shade; **lugar de** — shady spot; **a la** — **de** in the shade of; (fig) under the protection of; thanks to the support of; (pej) under the cloak of; **estar a la** — to be in the shade; (sl) to be in clink (sl); **dar** —, **hacer** — (of tree etc) to give shade; to cast a shadow; **dar** — a to shade; **hacer** — a uno (fig) to put someone in the shade; **no quiere que otros le hagan** — he doesn't want to be overshadowed by anybody else, he refuses to tolerate any rivals; **se ha constituido en** — **de sí mismo** he is a shadow of his former self.

(b) (fig) —s darkness, obscurity; ignorance; sombreness, pessimism.

(c) (Rel) shade, ghost.

(d) (on mirror etc) dark patch, stain; (fig) stain, blot; **es una** — **en su carácter** it is a stain on his character.

(e) (fig) shadow; sign, trace, bit; **sin** — **de avaricia** without a trace of greed; **sin** — **de duda** without a shadow of doubt; **no tiene ni** — **de talento** he hasn't the least bit of talent; **tiene una** — **de parecido con su tío** he has a faint resemblance to his uncle; **ni por** — by no means; not in the least bit.

(f) luck; **tener buena** — to be lucky; **ser de mala** — to be unlucky.

(g) charm; wit; talent, aptitude; **tiene mucha** — **para contar chistes** he's got a great talent for telling jokes; **tener buena** — to be likeable, have lots of charm; **tener mala** — to be a nasty piece of work; to have an unfortunate effect (on people etc); **el cuento tiene (buena)** — it's a good story.

(h) (CAm, Chi) parasol, sunshade; (CAm) awning; porch.

(i) (CAm, Chi) guide lines (in writing).

sombraje nm, **sombrajo** nm shelter from the sun; **hacer** —s to get in the light.

sombreado 1 adj shady. 2 nm (Art etc) shading; hatching.

sombreador nm: — **de ojos** eyeshadow.

sombrear [1a] vt to shade; (Art etc) to shade; to hatch.

sombrerera nf (a) milliner. (b) hatbox. (c) (Ec, Per, PR) hatstand.

sombrerería nf (a) hats, millinery. (b) hat shop; hat factory.

sombrerero nm (a) hatter, hatmaker. (b) (Arg, Col) hatstand.

sombrerete nm (a) little hat. (b) (of mushroom) cap. (c) (Tech) bonnet; (of hub etc) cap; (of chimney) cowl.

sombrero nm (a) hat; headgear; — **apuntado**, — **de candil**, — **de tres picos** cocked hat, three-cornered hat; — **de bola** (Mex), — **hongo** bowler (hat); — **de copa**, — **de pelo** (SAm) top hat; — **flexible** soft hat, trilby; — **gacho** slouch hat; — **de jipijapa** Panama hat; — **de paja** straw hat; **quitarse el** — (**y hacer reverencia) a** (fig) to take off one's hat to. (b) (Bot) cap.

sombríamente adv sombrely; dismally; gloomily.

sombrilla nf parasol, sunshade.

sombrío 1 adj (a) place shaded, (too much) in the shade, dark.

(b) (fig) place sombre, sad, dismal; person gloomy; outlook etc sombre.

2 nm (Mex) shady place.

someramente adv superficially.

somero adj superficial; shallow.

someter [2a] 1 vt (a) country to conquer; person to subject to one's will, force to yield.

(b) — **una decisión a lo que se resuelva en una reunión** to make one's decision depend on what is resolved in a meeting; — **su opinión a la de otros** to subordinate one's opinion to that of others.

(c) report etc to present, submit (a to); to send in; — **algo a la aprobación de uno** to submit something for someone's approval; — **un trabajo a la censura** to send a work to the censor.

(d) — **un asunto a una autoridad** to refer a matter to an authority for decision.

(e) — **a test** etc to put to, subject to; — **una sustancia a la acción de un ácido** to subject a substance to the action of an acid; see **prueba** etc.

2 **someterse** vr (a) to give in, yield, submit; — **a la mayoría** to give way to the majority.

(b) — **a una operación** to undergo an operation; — **a un tratamiento con drogas** to have treatment with drugs.

sometico adj (Col), **sometido** adj (CR, Ec) = **entrometido**.

sometimiento nm (a) (state) submission, subjection.

(b) (act) presentation, submission; reference.

somier nm, pl **somiers** (gall) spring mattress.

somnambulismo nm sleepwalking, somnambulism.

somnámbulo nm, **somnámbula** nf sleepwalker, somnambulist.

somnífero 1 adj sleep-inducing. 2 nm sleeping pill.

somnílocuo 1 adj given to talking in one's sleep. 2 nm, **somnílocua** nf person who talks in his (or her) sleep.

somnolencia nf sleepiness, drowsiness, somnolence.

somnolento adj = **soñoliento**.

somorgujar [1a] 1 vt to duck; to plunge, dip, submerge. 2 **somorgujarse** vr to dive, plunge (en into).

somormujo nm grebe; — **menor** dabchick.

somos see **ser**.

son[1] nm (a) sound; pleasant sound, sweet sound; **a** — **de** to the sound of; **a los** —**es de la marcha nupcial** to the sounds (or strains) of the wedding march.

(b) (fig) rumour; **corre el** — **de que** ... there is a rumour that ...

(c) (fig) manner, style; **¿a qué** —...?, **¿a** — **de qué** ...? why ...?; **en** — **de** as, like, in the manner of; by the way of; **en** — **de broma** as a joke; **en** — **de guerra** in a warlike fashion; **lo dijo en** — **de riña** he said it as though he was trying to pick a quarrel; **no vienen en** — **de protesta** they're not coming in a protesting mood; **por este** — in this way; **sin** — for no reason at all; see **bailar**.

son[2] see **ser**.

sonado adj (a) talked-of; famous; sensational; scandalous; **un crimen muy** — a particularly ghastly crime, a most notorious crime; **un suceso muy** — a much talked-of event, an event which made a great stir.

(b) **hacer una (que sea) sonada** to do something really frightful; to cause a major scandal.

sonaja nf little bell.

sonajera nf (Arg, Chi), **sonajero** nm rattle.

sonante adj audible; resounding; tinkling, jingling; see **contante**.

sonar [1m] 1 vt (a) bell, coin to ring; trumpet etc to play, blow; hooter to blow.

(b) (las narices) **a un niño** to blow a child's nose.

2 vi (a) to sound, make a noise; to sound out, make itself heard; to be heard; (Mus) to play; (of bell) to ring; (of clock) to chime, strike; **han sonado las 10** it has struck 10; **le estaban sonando las tripas** his stomach was rumbling; — **a cascado** to sound cracked; — **a hueco** to sound hollow.

(b) (Ling) to be sounded, be pronounced; **la h de "hombre"** no suena the h in "hombre" is not pronounced (or is silent); **en esa región "fue" suena casi como "juez"** in that area "fue" sounds (or is pronounced) almost like "juez".

(c) (fig) to sound; **esas palabras suenan extrañas** those words sound strange; **no me suena bien** it sounds all wrong to me; **no le ha sonado muy bien aquello** that did not make a good impression on him, he wasn't very well impressed with that; **me suena a camelo** it sounds like a hoax to me; **se llama Anastasio, así como suena** he's called Anastasius, just like I'm telling you.

(d) (fig) to be talked of; **es un nombre que suena** it's a name that's in the news, it's a name that people are talking about; **no quiere que suene su nombre** he doesn't want his name mentioned; **el asunto no ha sonado para nada en la reunión** the matter did not come up at all at the meeting.

(e) (fig) to sound familiar, seem familiar; **no me suena el nombre** the name doesn't ring a bell with me; **me suena ese coche** that car looks familiar.

(f) (Arg) to have a setback, suffer a disappointment.

(g) (Arg, Chi) **hacer** — **a uno** to punish someone severely.

3 **sonarse** vr (a) (also — **las narices**) to blow one's nose.

(b) **se suena que** ... it is rumoured that ...

sonata nf sonata.

sonda nf (a) (act) sounding. (b) (Naut) lead; (Tech) bore, drill; (Med) probe; — **acústica** echo-sounder.

sondaje nm (Naut) sounding; (Tech) boring, drilling; **conversaciones de** — exploratory talks; **organismo de** — public-opinion poll, institute of public opinion.

sond(e)ar [1a] vt (Naut) to sound, take soundings of; (Med) to probe, sound; (Tech) to bore, bore into, drill; (fig) ground etc to explore; mystery to plumb, delve into, inquire into; person, intentions etc to sound out.

sondeo *nm* sounding; (*Tech*) boring, drilling; (*fig*) poll, inquiry, investigation; (*Pol etc*) feeler, overture, approach.

sonería *nf* (*of clock*) chimes.

soneto *nm* sonnet.

songa *nf* (**a**) (*Cu, PR*) sarcasm, irony. (**b**) (*Mex*) coarseness, vulgarity. (**c**) (*CAm, Chi, Ec*) **a la songasonga** slyly.

songo 1 *adj* (**a**) (*Col, Mex*) stupid. (**b**) (*Col, Mex*) sly, crafty. **2** *nm* (*Col*) buzz, hum.

sónico *adj* sonic, sound (*attr*).

sonido *nm* sound.

sonoridad *nf* sonority, sonorousness.

sonorizar [1f] (*Ling*) **1** *vt* to voice. **2 sonorizarse** *vr* to voice, become voiced.

sonoro *adj* (**a**) sonorous; loud, resonant, resounding; *verse etc* sonorous; *cave etc* echoing.
(**b**) (*Ling*) voiced.
(**c**) **banda sonora** sound track; **efectos —s** sound effects.

sonreír [3m] **1** *vi* (**a**) to smile; **— a uno** to smile at someone, beam at someone; **— de un chiste** to smile at a joke; **— forzadamente** to force a smile.
(**b**) (*fig*) **le sonríe la fortuna** fortune smiles upon him; **el porvenir le sonríe** he has a bright future. **2 sonreírse** *vr* to smile.

sonriente *adj* smiling.

sonrisa *nf* smile; **— amarga** bitter smile, wry smile; **— forzada** forced smile.

sonrojar [1a] **1** *vt*: **— a uno** to make someone blush. **2 sonrojarse** *vr* to blush, flush (*de at*).

sonrojo *nm* (**a**) blush. (**b**) offensive word, naughty remark (that brings a blush).

sonrosado *adj* rosy, pink.

sonrosarse [1a] *vr* to turn pink.

sonsacar [1g] *vt* to get by cunning; to remove surreptitiously; *servant etc* to entice away; **— a uno** to pump someone for information; **— un secreto a uno** to worm a secret out of someone.

sonsear [1a] *vi* (*Chi, RPl*) see **zoncear.**

sonsera *nf*, **sonsería** *nf* (*SAm*) see **zoncera** *etc.*

sonso *adj* (*SAm*) see **zonzo.**

sonsonete *nm* (**a**) tap, tapping; rattle; jangling; monotonous din.
(**b**) monotonous delivery, singsong (voice), chant.
(**c**) jingle, rhyming phrase.
(**d**) mocking undertone.

sonsoniche *nm* (*Cu*) = **sonsonete.**

sonza *nf* (**a**) (*Cu*) slyness, deceit. (**b**) (*Mex*) sarcasm, mockery.

soñación: ¡**ni por —**! not on your life!

soñado *adj* (**a**) dreamed-of, that one has dreamed of; **el hombre —** one's ideal man, one's dream man; Mr Right.
(**b**) (*fam*) **hemos encontrado un sitio que ni —** we've found an absolutely perfect spot; **me va que ni —** it suits me a treat (*fam*).

soñador 1 *adj* dreamy. **2** *nm*, **soñadora** *nf* dreamer.

soñar [1m] *vti* to dream (*also fig*); **— con algo** to dream of something; **soñé contigo anoche** I dreamed about you last night; **soñaba con una lavadora** she dreamed of one day having a washing machine; **— con + infin, — en + infin** to dream of + *ger*; **— que ...** to dream that ...; **— despierto** to daydream; **— en voz alta** to talk in one's sleep; ¡**ni —lo!** (*fam*) not on your life!

soñarra *nf*, **soñarrera** *nf*, **soñera** *nf* (**a**) drowsiness, deep desire to sleep. (**b**) deep sleep.

soñolencia *nf* = **somnolencia.**

soñolientamente *adv* sleepily, drowsily.

soñoliento *adj* sleepy, drowsy, somnolent.

sopa *nf* (**a**) soup; **— de cebolla** onion soup; **— del hortelano** vegetable soup; **— de pastas** noodle soup; **comer** (*or* **andar a, vivir a**) **la — boba** to scrounge one's meals (*fam*), live on other people; **poner a uno como — de Pascua** to give someone a ticking-off.
(**b**) (*in milk etc*) sop; **—s de leche** bread and milk; **dar —s con honda a uno** to be streets ahead of someone; **estar hecho una —** to be sopping wet.
(**c**) (*Mex: also* **seca**) dish.
(**d**) (*fam*) hangover; **quitar la — a uno** to sober someone up; **quitarse la —** to sober up.

sopapear [1a] *vt* to punch, bash (*fam*); to shake violently.

sopapié *nm* (*Col*) kick.

sopapina *nf* series of punches, bashing (*fam*).

sopapo *nm* punch (on the jaw), bash (*fam*).

sopar [1a] (*Arg*) **1** *vt* bread etc to dip, dunk. **2** *vi* to meddle.

sopera *nf* soup tureen.

sopero 1 *adj*: **plato —** = **2** *nm* soup plate.

sopesar [1a] *vt* to try the weight of, try to lift.

sopetón *nm* (**a**) punch.
(**b**) **de —** — suddenly, unexpectedly; **entrar de —** to pop in, drop in; **entrar de — en un cuarto** to burst into a room, appear unexpectedly in a room.

sopimpa *nf* (*Cu*) series of punches; beating, bashing (*fam*).

soplado *adj* (**a**) clean; extra smart, overdressed; affected; stuck-up (*fam*). (**b**) (*fam*) **estar —** to be tight.

soplador *nm* (**a**) glass blower. (**b**) fan, ventilator. (**c**) (*fig*) troublemaker. (**d**) (*Ec, Guat: Theat*) prompter.

soplamocos *nm*, *pl* **soplamocos** (**a**) punch, slap. (**b**) (*Mex*) rude remark.

soplar [1a] **1** *vt* (**a**) *dust etc* to blow away, blow off; *surface* to blow on; *candle* to blow out; *balloon* to blow up, inflate; *glass* to blow; *fire, ashes* to blow on.
(**b**) (*fig: of muse etc*) to inspire.
(**c**) **— a uno** to whisper to someone; to prompt someone, help someone along; (*CAm: Theat*) to prompt; **— a X algo referente a Y** to tell X something to Y's discredit.
(**d**) (*fam*) to split on (*fam*).
(**e**) (*fam*) to pinch (*fam*).
(**f**) (*fam*) to charge, rush (*sl*), sting (*fam*); ¿**cuánto te soplaron?** what did they rush you?; **me han soplado 8 dólares** they stung me for 8 dollars.
(**g**) (*fam*) *blow* to deal, fetch.
2 *vi* (**a**) (*of person, wind*) to blow; to puff; ¡**sopla!** well I'm blowed!
(**b**) (*fam*) to split (*fam*), squeal (*sl*).
(**c**) (*fam*) to drink, booze.
3 soplarse *vr* (**a**) (*fam*) **— un pastel** to wolf a cake.
(**b**) (*fam*) to get conceited.
(**c**) (*fam*) **— de uno** to split on someone (*fam*), sneak on someone.

soplete *nm* (**a**) blowlamp, torch; **— oxiacetilénico** oxyacetylene burner; **— soldador** welding torch. (**b**) (*Chi, RPl*) = **soplón**; (*Theat*) prompter.

soplido *nm* strong puff, blast.

soplo *nm* (**a**) (*from mouth*) blow, puff; (*of wind*) puff, gust; (*Tech*) blast; **la semana pasó como** (*or* **en**) **un —** the week sped by, the week seemed no more than an instant.
(**b**) (*fam*) tip, tip-off, secret warning; denunciation, informing; **dar el —** to tell tales; to split (*fam*), squeal (*sl*); to inform; **ir con el — al director** to take one's tales to the headmaster, go and split to the head.
(**c**) (*fam*) telltale, talebearer, sneak (*fam*); (*of police etc*) informer.

soplón *nm*, **soplona** *nf* (**a**) (*fam*) = **soplo** (**c**). (**b**) (*Mex*) policeman; (*Per*) member of the secret police. (**c**) (*CAm: Theat*) prompter.

soponcio *nm* queer turn, dizzy spell.

sopor *nm* (*Med*) drowsiness; (*fig*) torpor, lethargy.

soporífero 1 *adj* sleep-inducing; (*fig*) soporific. **2** *nm* nightcap; (*Med*) sleeping pill, sleeping draught.

soportable *adj* bearable.

soportal *nm* (**a**) porch; portico. (**b**) **—es** arcade; colonnade.

soportar [1a] *vt* (**a**) (*Archit etc*) to bear, carry, support, hold up; *pressure etc* to resist, withstand.
(**b**) (*fig*) to stand, bear, endure, put up with.

soporte *nm* (**a**) support; base, stand, mounting; holder, bracket. (**b**) (*Her*) supporter. (**c**) (*fig*) pillar, support.

soprano *nf* soprano.

sor *nf* (*before names*) Sister; **S— María** Sister Mary.

sorber [2a] *vt* (**a**) (*with lips*) to sip; to suck up; **— por una paja** to drink through a straw; **— por las narices** to sniff (in, up); (*Med*) to inhale.
(**b**) (*of sponge*) to soak up, absorb, suck up; (*of blotter*) to dry up; (*with cloth*) to mop up.
(**c**) (*fig: of sea*) to suck down, swallow up.
(**d**) (*fig*) *words* to drink in.

sorbete *nm* (**a**) sherbet; iced fruit drink, water ice. (**b**) (*PR, Urug*) drinking straw. (**c**) (*Mex*) top hat.

sorbetera *nf* (**a**) ice-cream freezer. (**b**) (*fam*) top hat.

sorbetón *nm* gulp, mouthful.

sorbito *nm* sip.

sorbo *nm* sip; gulp, swallow; sniff; **un — de té** a sip of tea; **beber a —s** to sip.

sordamente *adv* dully, in a muffled way.

sordera *nf* deafness.

sordidez *nf* (**a**) dirt, dirtiness, squalor. (**b**) (*fig*) meanness.

sórdido *adj* (**a**) dirty, squalid. (**b**) *word etc* nasty, dirty. (**c**) (*fig*) mean.

sordina *nf* (a) (*Mus*) mute, muffle, damper. (b) **a la** — on the quiet, surreptitiously, by stealth.

sordo 1 *adj* (a) *person* deaf; — **como una tapia** as deaf as a post, stone-deaf; **quedarse** — to go deaf; **a la sorda, a sordas** on the quiet, surreptitiously, by stealth; **mostrarse** — **a, permanecer** — **a** (*fig*) to remain deaf to.

(b) *machine etc* quiet, noiseless; *noise* dull, muffled; *pain* dull; (*Ling*) voiceless; *anger, emotion* suppressed, inward.

2 *nm*, **sorda** *nf* deaf person; **hacerse el** — to pretend not to hear, turn a deaf ear.

sordomudez *nf* condition of being deaf and dumb.

sordomudo 1 *adj* deaf and dumb. **2** *nm*, **sordomuda** *nf* deaf-mute.

sorgo *nm* sorghum.

soriano 1 *adj* of Soria. **2** *nm*, **soriana** *nf* native (or inhabitant) of Soria; **los** —**s** the people of Soria.

Sorlinga, Sorlingen: **Islas** *fpl* — Scilly Isles.

sorna *nf* (a) slyness; sarcasm, sarcastic tone; **con** — slyly, mockingly, sarcastically. (b) slowness; (humorous) deliberation.

sorocharse [1a] *vr* (a) (*Bol, Chi, Ec, Per*) = **asorocharse**. (b) (*Chi*) to blush.

soroche *nm* (a) (*SAm*) mountain sickness, sickness caused by great altitudes. (b) (*Chi*) blush(ing). (c) (*Bol, Chi*) galena, silver-bearing ore.

sorprendente *adj* surprising; amazing; startling; **no es** — **que...** it is hardly surprising that..., it is small wonder that...

sorprender [2a] **1** *vt* (a) to surprise; to amaze; to startle.

(b) (*Mil etc*) to surprise; to catch unawares, take by surprise; *conversation* to overhear; *secret* to find out, discover; *hiding place* to come across; — **a uno en el hecho** to catch someone in the act.

2 sorprenderse *vr* to be surprised (*de* at), be amazed (*de* at); **no me sorprendería de que fuera así** I shouldn't be surprised if it were like that; **se sorprendió mucho** he was very surprised.

sorpresa 1 *nf* (a) (*emotion*) surprise; amazement; **causar** — **a, producir** — **a** to surprise; **con gran** —**mía, para mi** — much to my surprise, to my great surprise.

(b) (*act*) surprise; ¡**qué** —!, ¡**vaya** —! what a surprise!; **coger a uno de** — to take someone by surprise, come as a surprise to someone.

(c) (*fig*) surprise package.

(d) (*Mil*) surprise attack; **coger por** — to surprise.

2 *as adj* surprise (*attr*); **resultado** — surprise result.

sorpresivo *adj* (*SAm*) surprising; sudden, unexpected.

sorrajar [1a] *vt* (*Mex*) to hit; to wound.

sorrasear [1a] *vt* (*Mex*) to roast partially, grill.

sorrongar [1h] *vi* (*Col*) to grumble.

sorrostrigar [1h] *vt* (*Col*) to pester, annoy.

sortario *adj* (*Ven*) lucky.

sortear [1a] **1** *vt* (a) to draw lots for, decide by lot; to draw out of a hat; *object etc* to raffle (for charity); (*Sport*) *ends* to toss up for.

(b) *obstacle* to dodge, avoid; to get round; to manage to miss, swerve past; **el torero sorteó al toro** the bullfighter eluded the bull; **el esquiador sorteó muy bien las banderas** the skier swerved round the flags skilfully.

(c) (*fig*) *difficulty* to avoid; to get round, overcome; *question* to handle, deal with (skilfully).

2 *vi* to draw lots; to toss, toss up.

sorteo *nm* (a) draw, drawing lots; raffle; (*Sport*) toss; **ganar el** — to win the toss. (b) dodging, avoidance; swerving.

sortija *nf* (a) ring; — **de sello** signet ring. (b) curl, ringlet.

sortilegio *nm* (a) sorcery; fortunetelling; magical prediction. (b) (*un* —) spell, charm. (c) (*fig*) charm, magical attraction; unnatural influence.

sosa *nf* soda; — **cáustica** caustic soda.

sosco *nm* (*Col*) bit, piece.

sosegadamente *adv* quietly, calmly, peacefully; gently.

sosegado *adj* (a) quiet, calm, peaceful; gentle. (b) *person* calm, sedate, steady.

sosegar [1h *and* 1k] **1** *vt* to calm, quieten; to lull; *mind etc* to reassure; *doubts, fears* to allay.

2 *vi* to rest.

3 sosegarse *vr* to calm down, become calm; to quieten down.

sosería *nf* (a) insipidity. (b) (*fig*) dullness; flatness, colourlessness. (c) **es una** — it's boring, it's terribly dull.

sosiego *nm* (a) calm(ness), quiet(ness); peacefulness.

(b) calmness, sedateness, steadiness, composure; **hacer algo con** — to do something calmly.

soslayar [1a] *vt* (a) to put across, put sideways, place obliquely. (b) (*fig*) *difficulty* to get round; *question* to dodge, sidestep; *meeting* to avoid.

soslayo: al —, **de** — *adv* obliquely, sideways, aslant; **mirada de** — sidelong glance; **mirar de** — to look out of the corner of one's eye (at); (*fig*) to look askance (at), look down one's nose (at).

soso *adj* (a) (*Cook*) tasteless, insipid; unsalted; unsweetened. (b) (*fig*) dull, uninteresting, flat, colourless.

sospecha *nf* (*all senses*) suspicion.

sospechar [1a] **1** *vt* to suspect. **2** *vi*: — **de** to suspect, be suspicious of, have one's suspicions about.

sospechosamente *adv* suspiciously.

sospechoso 1 *adj* suspicious; suspect; **todos son** —**s** everybody is under suspicion; **es** — **de desafecto al régimen** he is suspected of being hostile to the régime, it is suspected that he is hostile to the régime; **tiene amistades sospechosas** some of his acquaintances are suspect.

2 *nm*, **sospechosa** *nf* suspect.

sosquín *nm* (*Cu*) (a) wide corner, obtuse angle. (b) treacherous blow.

sosquinar [1a] *vt* (*Cu*) to hit (or wound *etc*) treacherously.

sostén *nm* (a) (*Archit etc*) support, prop; stand; pillar, post.

(b) (*woman's*) brassière, bra (*fam*).

(c) sustenance, food, nourishment.

(d) (*fig*) support, pillar, mainstay; **el principal** — **del gobierno** the mainstay of the government; **el único** — **de su familia** the sole support of his family.

sostener [2l] **1** *vt* (a) (*Archit etc*) to hold up, support; to prop up; *load* to carry; *weight* to bear; (*of person*) to hold up, hold on to; ¡**sostén!** hold this!; **los dos sosteníamos la cuerda** we were both holding the rope; **la cinta le sostiene el pelo** the ribbon keeps her hair in place.

(b) (*fig*) *person* to support, back; to help; to defend; **su partido le sostiene en el poder** his party keeps him in power; **esta manifestación de apoyo sirve para** — **me** this demonstration of support strengthens my resolve; **le sostienen los nervios** his nerves keep him going.

(c) (*with food*) to sustain, keep going.

(d) (*Mus*) *note* to hold.

(e) (*fig*) *charge etc* to maintain; *opinion* to stand by, stick to, uphold; *promise* to stand by; *proposition, theory* to maintain; *pressure* to keep up, sustain; *resistance* to strengthen, boost, bolster up; — **que ...** to maintain that..., hold that...

(f) (*fig*) *position, speed, struggle etc* to keep up, maintain.

(g) (*Fin*) to maintain, pay for; *costs* to meet, defray.

(h) — **la mirada de uno** to stare someone out, look someone in the eye without flinching.

2 sostenerse *vr* (a) to hold oneself up, support oneself; to stand up; **apenas podía** — **de puro cansado** he was so utterly tired he could hardly stand.

(b) (*fig*) to support oneself; to keep (oneself) going; to last out; — **en el poder** to stay in power; — **vendiendo corbatas** to support oneself by selling ties.

(c) (*fig*) to continue, remain; **el mercado se sostiene firme** the market remains firm, the market continues steady; **se sostiene el régimen lluvioso** rainy conditions prevail.

sostenidamente *adv* steadily, continuously.

sostenido 1 *adj* (a) steady, continuous, sustained; prolonged. (b) (*Mus*) sharp. **2** *nm* (*Mus*) sharp.

sostenimiento *nm* (a) support; holding up; maintenance; upholding; strengthening; bolstering. (b) (*Fin*) maintenance; (*of body*) sustenance.

sota[1] *nf* (a) (*Cards*) jack, knave. (b) (*fam*) hussy, brazen woman; whore.

sota[2] *nm* (*Chi*) overseer, foreman.

sotabanco *nm* (a) attic, garret. (b) (*Arg*) poky little room, dirty room.

sotabarba *nf* double chin, jowl.

sotacura *nm* (*Arg, Col, Chi*) curate.

sotana *nf* (a) (*Eccl*) cassock, soutane. (b) (*fam*) hiding.

sotanear [1a] *vt* (*fam*) to tick off.

sótano *nm* basement; cellar; (*of bank etc*) vault.

Sotavento: Islas *fpl* **de** — Leeward Isles.

sotavento *nm* lee, leeward; **a** — to leeward; **de** — leeward (*attr*).

sotechado *nm* shed.

soterrar [1k] *vt* to bury; (*fig*) to bury, hide away.

soto *nm* (a) thicket; grove, copse. (b) (*Ec*) rough patch, bump (*on the skin*); knot, tangle.

sotobosque *nm* undergrowth.

sotreta *nf* (*Bol, RPl*) (a) vicious horse; useless horse, old horse. (b) (*person*) useless individual; idler; unreliable person.

soturno *adj* taciturn, silent; unsociable.

soviet [so'βie] *nm, pl* **soviets** [so'βie] soviet.

soviético 1 *adj* Soviet (*attr*). 2 *nm*: **los —s** the Soviets, the Russians.

soy *see* **ser**.

spleen [es'plin] *nm* (*angl*) *see* **esplín**.

sport [es'por] *nm* (*angl*) sport; **chaqueta (de) —** sports coat; **un hombre vestido de —** a man wearing sports clothes.

sprint [es'prin] *nm* (*angl*) *etc see* **esprint** *etc*.

stand [es'tan] *nm, pl* **stands** [es'tan] (*angl*) stand.

stándard [es'tandar] *adj and nm etc* (*angl*) *see* **estándar** *etc*.

stárter [es'tarter] *nm* (a) (*Aut: angl*) self-starter, starting motor. (b) (*SAm, Sport: angl*) starter; starting gate.

statu quo *nm* status quo.

status *nm, pl* **status** status.

stock [es'tok] *nm, pl* **stocks** [es'tok] (*Comm: angl*) stock, supply.

stop [es'top] *nm* (*angl*) (a) (*Tel*) stop. (b) (*Aut*) stop sign, halt sign.

store [es'tor] *nm* (*gall*) sunblind, awning.

su *poss adj* (a) (*one possessor*) his, hers, its; one's; (*relating to* **Vd**) your. (b) (*plural possessors*) their; (*relating to* **Vds**) your.

suampo *nm* (*CAm: angl*) swamp.

suato *adj* (*Mex*) silly.

suave *adj* (a) *surface* smooth, even; *skin* smooth; *mixture, paste etc* smooth.
(b) *colour, curve, slope, movement, touch, rebuke, wind etc* gentle; *air* soft, mild, sweet; *climate* mild; *work* easy; *working of machine* smooth, easy; *music, voice* soft, sweet, mellow; *noise* soft, gentle, quiet; *smell* sweet; *flavour* smooth, mild.
(c) *person, character* gentle; meek, docile; **estuvo muy — conmigo** he was very sweet to me, he was very helpful to me, he behaved very nicely to me.
(d) (*Chi, Mex*) big, huge; outstanding.
(e) (*Mex*) charming, attractive; splendid; **¡—!** yes of course!

suavemente *adv* smoothly; gently; softly, sweetly.

suavidad *nf* smoothness, evenness; gentleness; softness, mildness; sweetness.

suavizador *nm* razor strop.

suavizar [1f] *vt* (a) to smooth (out, down); to soften; *paste etc* to make smoother; *razor* to strop; *slope etc* to ease, make more gentle; *colour* to tone down; *tone* to soften.
(b) *person* to mollify, soften, make gentler; *character* to mellow; *harshness* to soften, temper.

sub ... **sub ...**, **under ...**, *eg* **subempleo** underemployment, **subprivilegiado** underprivileged, **subvalorar** to undervalue.

suba *nf* (*CAm*) rise (in prices).

subalimentación *nf* underfeeding, undernourishment.

subalimentado *adj* underfed, undernourished.

subalpino *adj* subalpine.

subalterno 1 *adj importance etc* secondary; *personnel etc* minor, auxiliary. 2 *nm* subordinate.

subametralladora *nf* submachine gun.

subarrendador *nm*, **subarrendadora** *nf* subtenant.

subarrendar [1k] *vt* to sublet, sublease.

subarrendatario *nm*, **subarrendataria** *nf* subtenant.

subarriendo *nm* subtenancy, sublease.

subártico *adj* subarctic.

subasta *nf* (a) auction, sale by auction; (*for work etc*) tender(ing); **poner en** (*or* **sacar a**) **pública —** to put up for auction, sell at auction.
(b) (*Cards*) auction.

subastador *nm* auctioneer.

subastar [1a] *vt* to auction, auction off, sell at auction.

subcampeón *nm* runner-up.

subcomisión *nf* subcommittee.

subconsciencia *nf* subconcious.

subconsciente 1 *adj* subconscious. 2 *nm*: **el — the** subconscious; **en el — in the** subconscious.

subcontinente *nm* subcontinent.

subcontratista *nmf* subcontractor.

subcontrato *nm* subcontract.

subcutáneo *adj* subcutaneous.

subdesarrollado *adj* underdeveloped.

subdesarrollo *nm* underdevelopment.

subdirector *nm*, **subdirectora** *nf* subdirector; **— de biblioteca** sub-librarian.

súbdito 1 *adj* subject. 2 *nm*, **súbdita** *nf* (*Pol*) subject.

subdividir [3a] 1 *vt* to subdivide. 2 **subdividirse** *vr* to subdivide.

subdivisión *nf* subdivision.

subespecie *nf* subspecies.

subestación *nf* substation.

subestimación *nf* underestimation; undervaluation; understatement.

subestimar [1a] *vt capacity, enemy etc* to underestimate, underrate; *object, property* to undervalue; *case* to understate.

subexpuesto *adj* (*Phot*) underexposed.

subida *nf* (a) climb, climbing; ascent; **una — en globo** a balloon ascent; **en la — había muchas flores** there were a lot of flowers on the way up; **es una — difícil** it's a tough climb.
(b) (*in price, quantity etc*) rise, increase (*de* in); (*in rank*) promotion (*a* to); **esto va de —** this is increasing, this is on the increase; **el calor va de —** it's getting hotter.
(c) slope, hill; (*as street name*) rise, hill.

subido *adj* (a) *price etc* high. (b) *colour* bright, strong, intense; *smell* strong; *see* **color**. (c) *person* vain, proud.

subienda *nf* (*Col: Fish*) shoal.

subilón *adj* (*Per*) *liquor* strong, heady.

subilla *nf* awl.

subinquilino *nm*, **subinquilina** *nf* subtenant.

subir [3a] 1 *vt* (a) *object* to raise, lift up; to put up; to take up, get up; *head etc* to raise; **que me suban los equipajes** please see that my luggage is brought up (*or* taken up); **lo subieron a la reja** they put it up on the rack.
(b) *slope, street etc* to go up; *stairs* to climb, mount, ascend.
(c) *person* to promote (*a* to).
(d) (*Archit*) to build, raise, put up; **— una pared** to build a wall.
(e) *price, salary etc* to raise, put up, increase; *article* to put up the price of.
(f) (*Mus*) to raise the pitch of.
2 *vi* (a) to go up, come up; to move up; to climb; (*on horse etc*) to get on, mount; (*into vehicle*) to get in, get on; **le subieron los colores a la cara** she blushed; **el vino me sube a la cabeza** wine goes to my head; **— a caballo** to mount, get on one's horse; **— al tren** to get into the train, get on to the train; **seguíamos subiendo** we went on climbing; **bajar es peor que —** coming down is worse than going up.
(b) (*of mercury, river, tide etc*) to rise.
(c) (*Fin*) **— a** to amount to.
(d) (*of person: fig*) to be promoted (*a* to), rise, move up.
(e) (*of price, value etc*) to rise, increase, go up; (*of epidemic etc*) to spread; (*of fever etc*) to get worse; **sigue subiendo la bolsa** the market is still rising; **— de tono** to get louder, increase in volume.
3 **subirse** *vr* (a) to get up, climb (*a* on to); to go up, rise; **— al tren** to get on the train; **el niño se subió a las rodillas** the child climbed on to her knees; **se me sube el vino a la cabeza** wine goes to my head; *see* **tono** *etc*.
(b) (*fig*) to get conceited; to become bolder; to forget one's manners.
(c) (*Bot*) to grow very tall, shoot up.

súbitamente *adv* suddenly; unexpectedly.

súbito 1 *adj* (a) sudden; unexpected. (b) (*fam*) hasty, rash. (c) (*fam*) irritable. 2 *adv* (*also* **de —**) suddenly; unexpectedly.

subjetivamente *adv* subjectively.

subjetividad *nf* subjectivity.

subjetivismo *nm* subjectivism.

subjetivo *adj* subjective.

subjuntivo 1 *adj* subjunctive. 2 *nm* subjunctive (mood).

sublevación *nf* revolt, rising.

sublevar [1a] 1 *vt* (a) to rouse to revolt, stir up a revolt among.
(b) (*fig*) to upset, put out, irritate; to rouse to fury.
2 **sublevarse** *vr* to revolt, rise, rebel.

sublimación *nf* sublimation.

sublimado *nm* (*Chem*) sublimate.

sublimar [1a] *vt* (a) *person* to exalt, praise. (b) *desires etc* to sublimate. (c) (*Chem*) to sublimate.

sublime *adj* (a) sublime; noble, lofty, grand; **lo — the** sublime. (b) (*lit*) high, tall, lofty.

sublimemente *adv* sublimely.

sublimidad *nf* sublimity.

subliminal *adj* subliminal.
submarinista *nmf* underwater fisherman, underwater diver (*or* explorer *etc*).
submarino 1 *adj* underwater, submarine. **2** *nm* submarine.
suboficial *nm* non-commissioned officer; sergeant-major.
subordinación *nf* subordination.
subordinado 1 *adj* subordinate; **X queda — a Y** X is subordinate to Y. **2** *nm*, **subordinada** *nf* subordinate.
subrayable *adj* worth emphasizing; **el punto más —** the point which is particularly to be noted, the most important point.
subrayado 1 *adj* underlined; italicized, in italics. **2** *nm* underlining; italics; **el — es mío** my italics, the italics are mine.
subrayar [1a] *vt* (a) to underline; to italicize, put in italics. (b) (*fig*) to underline, emphasize.
subrepticiamente *adv* surreptitiously.
subrepticio *adj* surreptitious.
subsanable *adj* excusable; repairable; **un error fácilmente —** an error which is easily rectified; **un obstáculo difícilmente —** an obstacle which is hard to overcome.
subsanar [1a] *vt fault* to overlook, excuse; *damage*, *defect* to repair, make good; *error* to rectify, put right; *shortcoming* to make up for; *difficulty*, *obstacle* to get round, overcome.
subscr . . . *see* **suscr . . .**
subsecretaría *nf* undersecretaryship.
subsecretario *nm*, **subsecretaria** *nf* undersecretary.
subsector *nm* subsection.
subsecuente *adj* subsequent.
subsidiario *adj* subsidiary.
subsidio *nm* (a) subsidy, grant; aid, financial help; benefit; **— de enfermedad** sick benefit, sick pay; **— de exportación** export subsidy; **— familiar** family allowance; **— de huelga** strike pay; **— de natalidad** maternity benefit; **— de paro** unemployment benefit, unemployment compensation (US); **— de vejez** old-age pension.
(b) (*Col, Ec*) anxiety, worry.
subsiguiente *adj* subsequent.
subsistencia *nf* subsistence; sustenance.
subsistente *adj* lasting, enduring; surviving; **una costumbre aún —** a still surviving custom.
subsistir [3a] *vi* (a) to subsist, live (*con, de* on); to survive, last out, endure; **todavía subsiste el edificio** the building still stands; **es una creencia que subsiste** it is a belief which still exists; **sin ayuda económica no podrá — el colegio** the college will not be able to survive without financial aid.
(b) (*Per*) to live together.
subsónico *adj* subsonic.
subst . . . *see* **sust . . .**
subsuelo *nm* subsoil.
subteniente *nm* sub-lieutenant, second lieutenant.
subterfugio *nm* subterfuge.
subterráneo 1 *adj* underground, subterranean.
2 *nm* (a) underground passage; underground store (*or* cellar *etc*).
(b) (*SAm*) underground railway, subway (US).
subtitular [1a] *vt* to subtitle.
subtítulo *nm* subtitle, subheading.
subtropical *adj* subtropical.
suburbano 1 *adj* suburban. **2** *nm* suburban train.
suburbio *nm* (a) suburb, outlying area. (b) slum quarter; shantytown, collection of shacks.
subvención *nf* subsidy, subvention, grant; **— estatal** state subsidy; **—es agrícolas** agricultural subsidies.
subvencionar [1a] *vt* to subsidize, aid.
subvenir [3s] *vi*: **— a** *costs* to meet, defray; *needs etc* to provide for; **con eso subviene a sus vicios** with that he pays for his vices; **así subviene a la escasez de su sueldo** in that way he makes up for his low salary.
subversión *nf* (a) (*in general*) subversion.
(b) (*una —*) revolution; **la — del orden establecido** the overthrow of the established order.
subversivo *adj* subversive.
subvertir [3i] *vt* to subvert; to overthrow, undermine; to disturb.
subyacente *adj* underlying.
subyugación *nf* subjugation.
subyugador *adj* (*fig*) captivating, enchanting.
subyugar [1h] *vt* (a) *country etc* to subjugate, subdue; *enemy* to overpower; *will etc* to dominate, gain control over.
(b) (*fig*) to captivate, charm.
succión *nf* suction.
succionar [1a] *vt* to suck; to apply suction to;

(*Tech*) to absorb, soak up, suck up; **— su pipa** to suck (at) one's pipe, puff (at) one's pipe.
sucedáneo *nm* substitute (food).
suceder [2a] **1** *vti* (a) to happen; **pues sucede que no vamos** well it happens we're not going; **no le había sucedido eso nunca** that had never happened to him before; **suceda lo que suceda** come what may, whatever happens; **¿qué sucede?** what's going on?, whatever's all this?; **lo que sucede es que . . .** the fact is that . . ., the trouble is that . . .; **lo más que puede — es que . . .** the worst that can happen is that . . .; **llevar algo por lo que pueda —** to take something just in case.
(b) to succeed, follow; to inherit; **— a uno en un puesto** to succeed someone in a post; **— al trono** to succeed to the throne; **— a una fortuna** to inherit a fortune; **al otoño sucede el invierno** winter follows autumn; **a este cuarto sucede otro mayor** a larger room leads off this one, a large room lies beyond this one.
2 sucederse *vr* to follow one another.
sucesión *nf* (a) succession (*a* to); sequence, series; **una — de acontecimientos** a succession of events, a series of happenings; **en rápida —** in quick succession; **la princesa ocupa el quinto puesto en la línea de — al trono** the princess is fifth in the line of succession to the throne.
(b) inheritance; estate.
(c) issue, offspring; **morir sin —** to die without issue.
sucesivamente *adv* successively, in succession; **y así — and so on.**
sucesivo *adj* successive, following; consecutive; **3 días —s** 3 days running; 3 successive days; **en lo —** henceforth, in future; (*in past*) thereafter, thenceforth.
suceso *nm* (a) event, happening; incident; **capítulo de —s** (*newspaper*) section of accident and crime reports.
(b) issue, outcome; **buen —** happy outcome.
sucesor *nm*, **sucesora** *nf* successor; heir.
suciamente *adv* (a) dirtily, filthily. (b) (*fig*) vilely, meanly; obscenely, unfairly.
suciedad *nf* (a) dirt, filth, grime; dirtiness; filthiness.
(b) (*fig*) vileness, meanness; obscenity; unfairness.
(c) (*una —*) dirty act; filthy remark; obscenity.
sucintamente *adv* succinctly, concisely, briefly.
sucinto *adj* (a) succinct, concise, brief. (b) *garment* short, brief, scanty.
sucio 1 *adj* (a) (*general sense*) dirty; filthy, grimy, grubby, soiled; *colour* dirty; blurred, smudged; *sketch etc* rough, messy; *tongue* coated, furred.
(b) (*fig*) *conduct* vile, mean, despicable; *act*, *word etc* dirty, filthy, obscene; *play* foul, dirty; *tactics* unfair.
(c) *conscience* bad.
2 *adv*: **jugar —** to play unfairly, indulge in dirty play.
3 *nm* (*Col*) smut, bit of dirt.
suco[1] *adj* (*Bol, Ven*) muddy, swampy.
suco[2] *adj* (*Ec*) bright reddish; blond, fair; (*Per*) orange.
sucre *nm standard monetary unit of Ecuador.*
sucrosa *nf* sucrose.
suculencia *nf* tastiness, richness; succulence, lusciousness, juiciness.
suculento *adj* tasty, rich; succulent, luscious, juicy.
sucumbir [3a] *vi* to succumb (*a* to).
sucursal *nf* branch, branch office; subsidiary.
sucusumuco: a lo — *adv* (*Col, Cu, PR*) in a mock-foolish way, as if one were stupid.
suche 1 *adj* (*Ven*) sharp, bitter.
2 *nm* (a) (*Arg*) pimple.
(b) (*Chi*) subordinate.
(c) (*Chi*) pimp.
súchil *nm* (*Mex*) bouquet of sweet-smelling flowers.
sucho *adj* (*Arg, Ec*) maimed, paralytic.
sud *nm* south.
sudafricano 1 *adj* South African. **2** *nm*, **sudafricana** *nf* South African.
Sudamérica *f* South America.
sudamericano 1 *adj* South American. **2** *nm*, **sudamericana** *nf* South American.
Sudán *m* Sudan.
sudanés 1 *adj* Sudanese. **2** *nm*, **sudanesa** *nf* Sudanese.
sudar [1a] **1** *vt* (a) to sweat; *see* **sangre** *etc*.
(b) (*Bot etc*) to ooze, give out, give off; (*of container*) to ooze; (*of wall etc*) to sweat, give off moisture.
(c) *garment etc* to make sweaty, make damp with sweat.
(d) (*fam*) **— un aumento de sueldo** to sweat for

a rise in pay, work hard for some extra money; **ha sudado el premio** he really sweated to get the prize.

(e) *(sl)* money to cough up *(sl)*, part with.

2 *vi* to sweat; **hacer — a uno** *(fig)* to make someone sweat.

sudario *nm* shroud.

sudeste 1 *adj part* south-east, south-eastern; *direction* south-easterly; *wind* south-east, south-easterly.

2 *nm* (a) south-east.

(b) south-east wind.

sudoeste *adj and nm see* **suroeste**.

sudón *adj* (SAm) sweaty.

sudor *nm* sweat; *(fig: also* **—es**) sweat, toil, labour; **con el — de su frente** by the sweat of one's brow.

sudoriento *adj*, **sudoroso** *adj*, **sudoso** *adj* sweaty, sweating; covered with sweat; **trabajo sudoroso** thirsty work, work that makes one sweat a lot.

Suecia *f* Sweden.

suecia *nf* suède.

sueco 1 *adj* Swedish.

2 *nm*, **sueca** *nf* Swede; **hacerse el — (***fam***)** to pretend not to hear *(or* understand); to act dumb *(fam)*, not let on.

3 *nm (language)* Swedish.

suegra *nf* mother-in-law.

suegro *nm* father-in-law.

suela *nf* (a) *(of shoe)* sole; piece of strong leather; *(Tech)* tap washer; **media —** half sole; *(fig)* patch, botch; *(fig)* temporary remedy; temporary relief; **A no le llega a la — del zapato a B** A can't hold a candle to B.

(b) **—s** *(Eccl)* sandals; **de siete —s** utter, downright.

(c) *(Fish)* sole.

suelazo *nm* (SAm) heavy fall, nasty bump.

sueldo *nm* salary, pay; **estar a —** to be on a salary, earn a salary; **estar a — de una potencia extranjera** to be in the pay of a foreign power.

suelear [1a] *vt* (Arg) to throw, hurl.

suelo *nm* (a) ground; surface; **— natal, — patrio** native land, native soil; **arrastrar** *(or* **poner,** *tirar)* **por los —s** to blacken, run down, speak ill of; **caer al —** to fall to the ground; **caerse al —** *(fig)* to fail, collapse; **echar al —** *building* to demolish; *hopes* to dash; *plan* to ruin; **echarse al —** to hurl oneself to the ground; to fall on one's knees; **los precios están por el —** prices are at rock-bottom; **esos géneros están por los —s** those goods are dirt cheap; **medir el —** to measure one's length (on the ground), fall full-length; **venirse al —** *(fig)* to fail, collapse, be ruined.

(b) *(of house etc)* floor; flooring.

(c) (Arg) ground, soil, land; **— vegetal** topsoil.

(d) *(of vessel etc)* bottom.

sueltista *nmf* (SAm) freelance journalist.

suelto 1 *adj* (a) free; untied, undone; detached, unattached, separate; loose; unhampered; *dress etc* loose, loose-fitting; **— de lengua** talkative; cheeky, given to answering back; not to be trusted with secrets; foulmouthed; **— de vientre** loose; **el libro tiene dos hojas sueltas** the book has two pages loose; **llevas —s los cordones** your shoelaces are undone; **el perro anda —** the dog is loose; **lo ató con el cabo —** he tied it up with the free *(or* loose) end; **lo dejamos —** we leave it untied, we leave it free.

(b) *fragment, passage etc* detached, isolated; *individual; number, volume* single; **es un trozo — de la novela** it's a separate piece from the novel, it's an isolated passage from the novel; **son 3 poesías sueltas** these are 3 separate poems; **los tomos no se venden —s** the volumes are not sold singly *(or* separately); **hay un calcetín —** there is one odd sock; **una mesa con números —s de revistas** a table with odd copies of magazines.

(c) *(in movement)* free; light; quick, agile, unhampered; *style* fluent, free, flowing.

(d) *(morally)* free and easy; daring; licentious, lax.

(e) *(Lit) verse* blank.

2 *nm* (a) *(Fin)* change, loose change, small change.

(b) *(Typ)* paragraph; *(in paper)* item, note, short article.

sueñera *nf* (SAm) drowsiness, sleepiness.

sueño *nm* (a) sleep; **— eterno** *(euph)* eternal rest; **— invernal** *(Zool)* winter sleep; **— pesado,** **— profundo** deep sleep, heavy sleep; **coger el —,** **conciliar el —** to get to sleep; **descabezar un —** to have a nap; **pasar una noche sin —** to have a sleepless night; **perder el — por algo**

to lose sleep over something; **tener el — ligero** to be a light sleeper; **tener el — pesado** *(or* **profundo)** to be a heavy sleeper.

(b) sleepiness, drowsiness; **caerse de —** to be so sleepy one can hardly stand; **espantar el —** to struggle to keep awake; **tener —** to be sleepy.

(c) dream *(also fig)*; **¡ni en —s!, ¡ni por —!** not on your life!; **es su — dorado** it's the dream of his life, it's his great dream; **ver algo en *(or* entre) —s** to see something in a dream; **vive en un mundo de —s** she lives in a dream world; **tiene una casa que es un —** she has a real dream of a house.

suero *nm* (a) *(Med)* serum. (b) whey; **— de manteca** buttermilk.

suerte *nf* (a) fate, destiny; chance, fortune; **por —** by chance, as it happened; **confiar algo a la —** to leave something to chance; **dejar a uno a su —** to abandon someone to his fate; **la — que les espera** the fate which awaits them; **quiso la — que . . .** as fate would have it . . ., as luck would have it . . .; **seguir la — a uno** to keep track of someone; **tentar a la —** to tempt fate; **unirse a la — de uno** to throw in one's lot with someone, make common cause with someone.

(b) lot; **caber en — a uno, caer en — a uno** to fall to someone, fall to someone's lot; **no me cupo tal —** I had no such luck; **echaron —s entre los 4** the 4 of them drew lots, the 4 of them tossed up; **lo echaron a —s** they drew lots for it, they tossed up for it; **la — está echada** the die is cast.

(c) luck; **buena —** luck, good luck; **¡buena —!** good luck!; **mala —** bad luck, hard luck; **hombre de —** lucky man; **un número de mala —** an unlucky number; **por —** luckily, fortunately; **dar —, traer —** to bring luck; **trae mala — escupir allí** it's unlucky to spit there; **estar de —** to be in luck; **probar —** to try one's luck; **tener —** to be lucky; to have a piece of luck; **¡que tengas —!** good luck!, I wish you luck!, and the best of luck!; **tuvo una — loca** he was fantastically lucky; **tuvo la — de que hacía buen tiempo** he was lucky that it was fine.

(d) lot; state, condition; **mejorar de —** to improve one's lot.

(e) lottery ticket.

(f) sort, kind; **es una — de** it is a kind of; **no podemos seguir de esta —** we cannot go on in this way; **de otra —** otherwise, if not; **de — que . . .** in such a way that . . ., so that . . ; **¿de — que no hay más dragones?** so there are no more dragons?

(g) *(Taur)* stage, part *(of the bullfight)*; **— de varas** opening section *(of play with the capes)*.

(h) (Arg) lot, piece of ground.

suertero 1 *adj* (SAm) lucky. 2 *nm* (CAm, Per) seller of lottery tickets.

suertoso *adj* (Ec) lucky.

suertudo *adj* (SAm) lucky.

sueste *nm* (a) *(Naut etc)* sou'wester. (b) (SAm) south-east wind.

suéter *nm (angl)* sweater.

Suetonio *m* Suetonius.

Suez Suez; **Canal de —** Suez Canal.

suficiencia *nf* (a) sufficiency; adequacy; **una — de . . .** enough . . .; **con —** sufficiently, adequately.

(b) competence; suitability; fitness; adequacy; capacity; **demostrar su —** to prove one's competence, show one's capabilities.

(c) *(pej)* self-importance; superiority; condescension; smugness, self-satisfaction, complacency; *see* **aire**.

suficiente *adj* (a) enough, sufficient *(para* for); adequate.

(b) *person* competent; suitable, fit; adequate; capable.

(c) *(pej)* self-important; superior; condescending; smug, self-satisfied, complacent.

suficientemente *adv* sufficiently, adequately.

sufijo *nm* suffix.

suflé *nm* soufflé.

sufragáneo *adj* suffragan.

sufragar [1h] 1 *vt* (a) to aid, help, support.

(b) *costs* to meet, defray, cover; *project etc* to pay for, defray the costs of.

2 *vi* (SAm) to vote *(por* for).

sufragio *nm* (a) vote; **los —s emitidos a favor de X** the votes cast for X.

(b) suffrage; franchise; **— universal** universal suffrage.

(c) help, aid.

(d) *(Eccl)* intercession for souls in purgatory.

sufragista *nf* suffragette.

sufrible *adj* bearable.

sufrido 1 *adj* (a) *person* tough; long-suffering, patient.
(b) *cloth etc* hard-wearing, long-lasting, tough; *colour* that does not show the dirt, that wears well.
(c) *husband* complaisant.
2 *nm* complaisant husband.

sufridor 1 *adj* suffering. **2** *nm* (a) sufferer. (b) (*Col, Ven*) saddlecloth.

sufrimiento *nm* (a) (*state*) suffering; misery, wretchedness.
(b) (*quality*) toughness; patience; tolerance; **tener — en las dificultades** to be patient in hard times, bear troubles patiently.

sufrir [3a] **1** *vt* (a) (*general sense*) to suffer; *accident, attack* to have, suffer; *consequences, disaster, disappointment etc* to suffer; *change* to undergo, *experience*; *loss* to suffer, sustain; *operation* to have, undergo.
(b) to bear, stand, put up with; **no sufre la menor descortesía** he won't tolerate the slightest rudeness; **A no le sufre a B** A can't stand B.
(c) *object* to hold up, support.
(d) *exam, test* to take, undergo.
2 *vi* to suffer; **— de** to suffer from, suffer with; **sufre de reumatismo** she suffers from (*or* with) rheumatism; **sufre mucho de los pies** she suffers a lot with her feet; **aprender a — silenciosamente** to learn to suffer in silence.

sugerencia *nf* suggestion.

sugerente *adj* full of suggestions, rich in ideas, thought-provoking.

sugerible *adj* = **sugestionable**.

sugerir [3i] *vt* to suggest; to hint, hint at; *thought etc* to prompt; **— que . . .** to suggest that . . .

sugestión *nf* (a) suggestion; hint; prompting, stimulus; **las —es del corazón** the promptings of the heart; **un sitio de muchas —es** a place rich in associations.
(b) autosuggestion, self-hypnotism.
(c) fascination (for others), hypnotic power, power to influence others; **emanaba de él una fuerte —** a strong hypnotic power flowed from him.

sugestionable *adj* impressionable, suggestible; open to influence, readily influenced.

sugestionar [1a] **1** *vt* to influence, dominate the will of, hypnotize; to exercise a powerful fascination over; **— a uno para que haga algo** to influence someone to do something.
2 **sugestionarse** *vr* to indulge in autosuggestion; **es probable que se haya dejado — por . . .** he may have allowed himself to be influenced by . . .; **te lo has sugestionado** you've talked yourself into it.

sugestivo *adj* (a) stimulating, thought-provoking.
(b) attractive; fascinating.

suicida 1 *adj* suicidal.
2 *nmf* suicidal case, person with a tendency to suicide; person who has committed suicide; **es un — conduciendo** he drives in a suicidal way.

suicidarse [1a] *vr* to commit suicide, kill oneself.

suicidio *nm* suicide.

Suiza *f* Switzerland.

suiza[1] *nf* (a) (*CAm, Cu*) skipping, skipping game.
(b) (*CAm, Ec, Ven*) beating.

suizo[1] **1** *adj* Swiss. **2** *nm*, **suiza**[2] *nf* Swiss.

suizo[2] *nm* sugared bun.

sujeción *nf* (a) (*state*) subjection. (b) (*act*) fastening; seizure; (*fig*) subjection (*a* to); **con — a** a subject to.

sujetador *nm* fastener; (*for hair*) clip, pin, grip; (*for papers*) clip; (*of pen*) clip; (*garment*) brassière, bra (*fam*); **— de libros** book end.

sujetapapeles *nm*, *pl* **sujetapapeles** paper clip.

sujetar [1a] **1** *vt* (a) *nation, people* to subdue, conquer; to hold down, keep down, keep under; to exercise control over; **— a A a B** to put A under B's authority, subordinate A to B.
(b) *object* to seize, clutch, lay hold of; to hold tight; *person* to hold down, keep hold of; (*Tech*) to fasten; to nail down, stick down, screw down (*etc*); *hair etc* to keep in place, hold in place; *papers etc* to fasten together.
2 **sujetarse** *vr*: **— a** to subject oneself to; *rule* to abide by; *circumstance, pay etc* to act in accordance with, recognize the limitations of; *authority* to submit to; **— a + infin** to agree to + *infin*, give way before the necessity of + *ger*.

sujeto 1 *adj* (a) fastened, secure; firm; tight; **la cuerda está bien sujeta** the rope is securely fastened.
(b) **— a** a subject to; liable to; **— a la aprobación de** subject to the approval of; **— a derechos** subject to duty, dutiable; **ser — a cambios inesperados** to be liable to sudden changes.
2 *nm* (a) (*Gram*) subject.

(b) individual; (*Med etc*) subject, case; (*fam*) fellow, character (*fam*), chap (*fam*); **un — sospechoso** a suspicious character; **buen —** good chap.

sulfa *nf*: **fármacos —** sulpha drugs.

sulfato *nm* sulphate; **— de cobre** copper sulphate.

sulfonamida *nf* sulphonamide.

sulfurar [1a] **1** *vt* (a) (*Chem*) to sulphurate.
(b) (*fam*) to annoy, rile (*fam*).
2 **sulfurarse** *vr* (*fam*) to get riled (*fam*), see red, blow up (*fam*).

sulfúreo *adj* sulphurous.

sulfúrico *adj* sulphuric.

sulfuro *nm* sulphide.

sulfuroso *adj* sulphurous.

sultán *nm* sultan.

sultana *nf* sultana.

sultanato *nm* sultanate.

suma *nf* (a) (*Math*: *act*) adding (up), addition; (*quantity*) total, sum; (*of money*) sum: "**— y sigue**" (*in account*) "carried forward"; (*fam*) and it's still going on; **— global** lump sum; **en —** in short.
(b) (*fig*) summary; essence; **una — de perfecciones** perfection itself; **es la — y compendio de todas las virtudes** she is the personification of all the virtues.

sumadora *nf* adding machine.

sumamente *adv* extremely, exceedingly, highly.

sumar [1a] **1** *vt* (a) (*Math*) to add (up), total; (*fig*) *argument etc* to summarize, sum up.
(b) to collect, gather.
(c) **la cuenta suma 6 dólares** the bill adds up to (*or* comes to, amounts to, works out at) 6 dollars.
2 *vi* to add up.
3 **sumarse** *vr*: **— a un partido** to join a party; **— a una protesta** to associate oneself with a protest, join in a protest.

sumariamente *adv* summarily.

sumario 1 *adj* brief, concise; (*Law*) summary.
2 *nm* (a) summary. (b) (*Law*) indictment.

sumergible *adj* submersible; that can go under water.

sumergido *adj* submerged, sunken.

sumergimiento *nm* submersion, submergence.

sumergir [3c] **1** *vt* (a) to submerge; to sink; to immerse, dip, plunge (*en* in).
(b) (*fig*) to plunge (*en* into).
2 **sumergirse** *vr* (a) to submerge, sink beneath the surface; to dive.
(b) (*fig*) **— en** to immerse oneself in, become absorbed in.

sumersión *nf* (a) submersion, submergence; immersion. (b) (*fig*) absorption (*en* in).

sumidero *nm* (a) drain, sewer; sink; (*Tech*) sump; (*Per, PR*) cesspool.
(b) (*PR*) quagmire.
(c) (*fig*) drain; **es el gran — de las reservas** it is the chief drain on our reserves.

suministrador *nm*, **suministradora** *nf* supplier.

suministrar [1a] *vt* *goods, information etc* to supply, furnish, provide; *person* to supply; **me ha suministrado muchos datos** he has given me a lot of data, he has supplied me with a lot of information.

suministro *nm* supply; (*act*) supplying, furnishing, provision; **—s** (*Mil*) supplies; **—s de combustible** fuel supply.

sumir [3a] **1** *vt* (a) to sink, plunge, submerge; (*of sea*) to swallow up, suck down.
(b) (*fig*) to plunge (*en* into); **el desastre le sumió en la tristeza** the disaster plunged him into sadness.
(c) (*SAm*) **— el resuello a uno** to kill someone.
(d) (*Mex*) to dent.
2 **sumirse** *vr* (a) (*object*) to sink; (*water etc*) to run away, disappear.
(b) (*mouth, chest etc*) to sink, be sunken, become hollow.
(c) **— en el estudio** to become absorbed in one's work; **— en la tristeza** to plunge into grief, give oneself over entirely to one's grief.
(d) (*SAm*) to cower, cringe; to lose heart; to fall silent from fear.
(e) (*SAm*) **— el sombrero** to pull one's hat right down.

sumisamente *adv* submissively, obediently; unresistingly; uncomplainingly.

sumisión *nf* (a) (*act*) submission. (b) (*quality*) submissiveness, docility.

sumiso *adj* submissive, docile, obedient; unresisting; uncomplaining.

sumo *adj* (a) great, extreme, supreme; **con suma dificultad** with the greatest difficulty; **con suma indiferencia** with supreme indifference.
(b) (*in rank*) high, highest; **— sacerdote** high

priest; *see* **pontífice; la suma autoridad** the highest authority, the supreme authority.

(c) **a lo** — at most.

sunco *adj* (*Col*) = **manco.**

sungo *adj* (*Col*) Negro; with a shiny skin, tanned.

suntuario *adj* sumptuary.

suntuosamente *adj* sumptuously, magnificently; lavishly, richly.

suntuosidad *nf* sumptuousness, magnificence; lavishness.

suntuoso *adj* sumptuous, magnificent; lavish, rich.

supeditar [1a] **1** *vt* (a) to subordinate (*a* to); **tendrá que ser supeditado a lo que decidan ellos** it will have to depend on what they decide.

(b) to subdue; to oppress, crush.

2 supeditarse *vr*: — **a** to make oneself subordinate to, come to depend on; to give way to, allow oneself to be overridden by; **no voy a supeditarme a su capricho** I am not going to depend on her whims.

super . . . super . . ., over . . .; *eg* (a) **superambicioso** overambitious; **superdesarrollo** overdevelopment; **superpetrolero** supertanker.

(b) *as prefix to adj, often equivalent to superlative*: **superfamoso** extremely famous; **superreservado** excessively shy; **un texto supercomentado** a text which has so often been commented on.

superable *adj* difficulty surmountable, that can be overcome; *task etc* that can be performed; **un obstáculo difícilmente** — an obstacle not easily surmounted.

superabundancia *nf* superabundance.

superabundante *adj* superabundant.

superación *nf* (a) overcoming, surmounting; transcending; excelling. (b) improvement, doing better; *see* **afán.**

superar [1a] **1** *vt* (a) *rival* to surpass, excel (*in* en), beat, do better than; *opponent* to overcome; *expectations* to exceed; *limit, point* to go beyond, transcend; *record* to break; **las escenas superan a toda imaginación** the scenes are more extraordinary than anyone could imagine, the scenes defeat one's imagination; — **a uno en brillantez** to outshine someone; **superó 2 veces la marca de los 200 metros** he twice broke the 200-metre record.

(b) *difficulty* to overcome, surmount; *task* to perform, carry out.

(c) *period* to get past, leave behind, emerge from; **ya hemos superado lo peor** we're over the worst now.

2 superarse *vr* to do extremely well, excel oneself.

superávit *nm*, *pl* **superávits** surplus.

supercarburante *nm* high-grade fuel.

supercarretera *nf* superhighway.

superconsumo *nm* overconsumption.

supercotizado *adj* much sought-after, in very great demand.

superchería *nf* fraud, trick, swindle.

superchero *adj* fraudulent; sham, bogus.

superdirecta *nf* (*Aut*) overdrive.

superempleo *nm* overemployment.

superentender [2g] *vt* to supervise, superintend.

supererogación *nf* supererogation.

superestructura *nf* superstructure.

superferolítico *adj* (*fam*) (a) affected; excessively refined. (b) overnice, finicky, choosy (*fam*).

superficial *adj* (a) *measurement etc* surface (*attr*), of the surface; *wound etc* superficial, skin (*attr*). (b) (*fig*) *interest, glance etc* superficial; brief, perfunctory; *character* superficial, shallow; facile.

superficialidad *nf* superficiality; shallowness.

superficialmente *adv* superficially.

superficie *nf* (a) surface; face; outside; (*of sea etc*) surface; — **inferior** lower surface, underside; — **de rodadura** (*Aut*) tread; **el ave rozó la** — the bird skimmed the surface; **el submarino salió a la** — the submarine surfaced, the submarine came to the surface; **ruta de** — surface route, land (*or* sea) route.

(b) (*in measurements etc*) area; **se regará una** — **de 200 hectáreas** an area of 200 hectares will be irrigated; **todo quedó destruido en una extensa** — everything was destroyed over a wide area.

(c) (*fig*) surface, outward appearance.

superfino *adj* superfine.

superfluamente *adv* superfluously.

superfluidad *nf* superfluity.

superfluo *adj* superfluous.

superfosfato *nm* superphosphate.

superhombre *nm* superman.

superintendencia *nf* supervision, superintendence.

superintendente *nm* supervisor, superintendent; overseer; — **de división** sectional head; (*Comm*) floorwalker.

superior 1 *adj* (a) (*in position etc*) upper; uppermost, top; higher; *class* upper; *study* advanced, higher; **labio** — upper lip; **vive en el piso** — he lives on the upper (*or* top) floor; **viven en el piso** — **al mío** they live on the floor above mine; **un estudio de nivel** — **a los existentes** a study on a higher plane than the present ones.

(b) (*in quality etc*) superior, better; **ser** — **a** to be superior to, be better than; **de calidad** — of superior quality.

(c) (*in number*) higher, greater, larger; **cualquier número** — **a 12** any number above (*or* higher than) 12.

2 *nm* superior; **mis** —**es** my superiors, those above me (*in rank*); (*fig*) my betters.

superiora *nf* mother superior.

superioridad *nf* superiority.

superlativo 1 *adj* superlative. **2** *nm* superlative.

superlujo *nm*: **hotel de** — super-luxury hotel; **tiene categoría de** — it is in the extra luxurious class.

supermercado *nm* supermarket.

superministro *nm* minister with an overall responsibility, senior minister, overlord.

supernumerario 1 *adj* supernumerary. **2** *nm* supernumerary.

superpetrolero *nm* supertanker.

superpoblación *nf* overpopulation, excess of population; overcrowding, congestion.

superpoblado *adj* country, region overpopulated; *quarter etc* overcrowded, congested.

superponer [2r] *vt* to superimpose, superpose, put on top.

superposición *nf* superposition.

superpotencia *nf* superpower, great power.

superproducción *nf* overproduction.

superrealismo *nm* (*Art, Lit*) surrealism.

supersecreto *adj* top secret.

supersimplificación *nf* oversimplification.

supersónico *adj* supersonic.

superstición *nf* superstition.

supersticiosamente *adv* superstitiously.

supersticioso *adj* superstitious.

supertalla *nf* (*Sew*) outsize.

supervalorar [1a] *vt* to overvalue, overstate.

supervigilancia *nf* (*SAm*) supervision.

supervisar [1a] *vt* to supervise.

supervisión *nf* supervision.

supervisor *nm* supervisor.

supervivencia *nf* survival; — **de los más aptos,** — **de los mejor dotados** survival of the fittest.

superviviente 1 *adj* surviving. **2** *nmf* survivor.

supino 1 *adj* supine. **2** *nm* supine.

súpito *adj* (a) = **súbito.** (b) (*Col*) dumbfounded.

suplantación *nf* (a) supplanting; impersonation. (b) (*Col*) fraudulent alteration, forgery.

suplantar [1a] *vt* (a) to supplant; to take the place of (fraudulently), impersonate. (b) (*Col*) to alter fraudulently, forge.

suplefaltas *nmf*, *pl* **suplefaltas** (a) scapegoat. (b) substitute, stopgap, fill-in.

suplemental *adj* supplementary.

suplementario *adj* supplementary; extra, additional; **empleo** —, **negocio** — sideline; **tren** — extra train, relief train.

suplementero *nm* (*Chi*) newsboy.

suplemento *nm* supplement; (*Rail etc*) excess fare.

suplencia *nf* (*SAm*) substitution, replacement; period during which one deputizes (*etc*).

suplente 1 *adj* substitute, deputy; reserve; **maestro** — supply teacher.

2 *nmf* substitute, deputy; replacement; (*Sport*) reserve; (*Theat*) understudy.

supletorio *adj* supplementary; extra, reserve, additional; stopgap (*attr*); **con la ventaja supletoria de que** . . . with the additional advantage that . . .; **llevar una lámpara supletoria** to take a spare bulb.

súplica *nf* request; entreaty, supplication; (*Law*) petition; —**s** entreaties, pleading; **acceder a las** —**s de uno** to grant someone's request; **se publica a** —**(s) de** . . . it is published at the request of . . .

suplicante 1 *adj* tone etc imploring, pleading. **2** *nmf* applicant; (*Law*) petitioner, supplicant.

suplicar [1g] **1** *vt* (a) *thing* to beg (for), plead for, implore.

(b) *person* to beg, plead with, implore; — **a uno**

no hacer algo to implore someone not to do something.

(c) (*Law*) to appeal to, petition (*de* against).

2 **suplicarse** *vr*: "se suplica cerrar la puerta" (*sign*) "please shut the door".

suplicio *nm* torture; (*Hist*) punishment, execution; (*fig*) torment, torture; (*mental*) anguish; ordeal; — **de Tántalo** torments of Tantalus; **es un — tener que escucharle** it's torture having to listen to him.

suplir [3a] 1 *vt* (a) *need, omission* to supply; *lack* to make good, make up for; *missing word etc* to supply; to understand.

(b) — **A con B** to replace A by B, substitute B for A; **suplen el aceite con grasa animal** they replace olive oil by animal fat.

2 *vi*: — **a, — por** to replace, take the place of, substitute for, do duty for; **suple en el equipo al portero lesionado** he's replacing the injured goalkeeper in the team.

suponer [2r] 1 *vt* (a) to suppose, assume; **supongamos que . . .** let us suppose (*or* assume) that . . .; **supongo que sí** I suppose so; **era de — que . . .** it was to be expected that . . .; **con las dificultades que son de —** with all the difficulties that one might expect.

(b) to think, imagine; to guess; **ya puedes — lo que ella sufría** you can just imagine how she was suffering; **Vd puede — lo que pasó** you can guess what happened; **no puedes — lo bruto que es** you can't begin to imagine what a lout he is; **es un —** I was only thinking aloud, of course that's just guesswork.

(c) to attribute; to credit (with); **le supongo unos 60 años** I give him an age of about 60; **se le supone una gran antigüedad** it is thought to be very ancient, it is credited with great antiquity, great antiquity is attributed to it; **hubo poco público y se ve que el equipo no tenía tanta "fuerza" como se le suponía** there were few spectators and it is clear that the team did not have the "pull" it was credited with.

(d) to mean, imply, involve, entail; **el traslado le supone grandes gastos** the move involves a lot of expense for him; **tal distancia no supone nada yendo en coche** that distance doesn't amount to anything in a car; **esa cantidad supone mucho para ellos** that amount means a lot to them.

2 *vi* to have authority, count (for a lot); **casi no supone en la organización** he hardly counts for anything in the organization.

suposición *nf* (a) supposition, assumption, surmise.

(b) authority; distinction. (c) slander; imposture.

supositorio *nm* suppository.

supra . . . supra . . .

supradicho *adj* aforementioned.

supranacional *adj* supranational.

supremacía *nf* supremacy.

supremo *adj* supreme.

supresión *nf* suppression; abolition; removal, elimination; cancellation, lifting; deletion, omission; banning.

supresivo *adj* suppressive.

supresor *nm* (*Elec*) suppressor.

suprimido *adj book etc* suppressed, banned.

suprimir [3a] *vt revolt, criticism etc* to suppress; *custom, right, institution etc* to abolish; *difficulty, obstacle, waste* to remove, eliminate; *restrictions* to cancel, lift; *detail, passage etc* to delete, cut out, omit; *book etc* to suppress, ban.

supuestamente *adv* (*SAm*) supposedly.

supuesto 1 *ptp of* **suponer**.

2 *adj* (a) supposed, ostensible; self-styled; **el — jefe del movimiento** the self-styled leader of the movement; **bajo un nombre —** under an assumed name, under a false name.

(b) **dar por — algo** to take something for granted; **demos por — que . . .** let us take it for granted that . . .

3 **— que** *conj* since; granted that; inasmuch as.

4 *nm* (a) assumption, hypothesis; **— previo** prior assumption; **en el — de que . . .** on the assumption that . . .

(b) **¡por —!** of course!, naturally!

supuración *nf* suppuration.

supurar [1a] *vi* to suppurate, discharge, fester.

sur 1 *adj part* south, southern; *direction* southerly; *wind* south, southerly.

2 *nm* (a) south; **en la parte del —** in the southern part; **al — de León** to the south of Leon, on the

south side of Leon; **eso cae más hacia el —** that lies further (to the) south.

(b) south wind.

sura *nm* sura.

surazo *nm* (*Arg, Bol*) strong southerly wind.

surafricano = **sudafricano**.

surcar [1g] *vt* (a) *earth* to plough (through), furrow; *surface* to cut, score, groove; to make lines across; **una superficie surcada de . . .** a surface lined with . . ., a surface criss-crossed with . . .

(b) (*fig*) *water* to cut through, cleave; **los barcos que surcan los mares** (*lit*) the ships which ply the seas; **las aves que surcan los aires** (*lit*) the birds which ride the winds.

surco *nm* (*Agr etc*) furrow; (*of wheel*) rut, track; (*on metal etc*) groove, score, line; (*on record*) groove; (*Anat*) wrinkle; (*on water*) track, wake; **echarse al —** to sit down on the job; to knock off, think one has done enough.

surcoreano 1 *adj* South Korean. 2 *nm*, **surcoreana** *nf* South Korean.

sureño *nm*, **sureña** *nf* (*Chi, SD*) southerner.

surero *nm* (*Bol*) cold southerly wind.

surestada *nf* (*RPl*) persistent wet south-easterly wind.

sureste *adj and nm see* **sudeste**.

surgir [3c] *vi* (a) to arise, emerge, spring up, appear; (*of liquid*) to spout (out), spurt (up), gush (forth); (*in fog etc*) to loom up; (*of person*) to appear unexpectedly; (*of difficulty*) to arise, come up, crop up; **la torre surge en medio del bosque** the tower rises (*or* soars up) in the middle of the woods; **han surgido varios problemas** several problems have arisen.

(b) (*Naut*) to anchor.

suriano *adj* (*Mex*) southern.

suroeste 1 *adj part* south-west, south-western; *direction* south-westerly; *wind* south-west, south-westerly.

2 *nm* (a) south-west.

(b) south-west wind.

surrealismo *nm* surrealism.

surrealista 1 *adj* surrealist(ic). 2 *nmf* surrealist.

surtido 1 *adj* (a) mixed, assorted, varied.

(b) **estar bien — de** to be well supplied with, have good stocks of; **estar mal — de** to be badly off for.

2 *nm* selection, assortment, range; supply, stock; **gran —** large assortment, wide range; **artículo de —** article from stock.

surtidor *nm* (a) jet, spout; fountain. (b) **— de gasolina** petrol pump.

surtir [3a] 1 *vt* (a) to supply, furnish, provide; **— a uno de combustible** to supply someone with fuel; **— el mercado** to supply the market; **— un pedido** to fill an order.

(b) *effect* to have, produce; *see* **efecto** (a).

2 *vi* to spout, spurt (up), rise.

3 **surtirse** *vr*: **— de** to provide oneself with.

suruco *nm* (*Chi*) excrement.

surumbático *adj* (*SAm*) = **zurumbático**.

surumbiar [1b] *vt* (*Arg*) to beat, whip.

surumbo *adj* (*CAm*) = **zurumbo**.

surumpe *nm* (*Bol, Per*) inflammation of the eyes (*caused by snow glare*).

surupa *nf* (*Ven*) cockroach.

survietnamita 1 *adj* South Vietnamese. 2 *nmf* South Vietnamese.

susceptibilidad *nf* (a) susceptibility (*a* to); sensitivity; touchiness; impressionable nature.

(b) **—es** susceptibilities; **ofender las —es de uno** to offend someone's susceptibilities.

susceptible *adj* (a) **— de** capable of; **— de mejora(r)** capable of improvement, open to improvement; **— de sufrir daño** liable to suffer damage.

(b) *person* susceptible; sensitive; touchy; impressionable.

suscitar [1a] *vt revolt etc* to stir up; *trouble, scandal, stir etc* to make, cause, provoke; *discussion* to start; *doubt, problem* to raise; *interest, hostility, suspicion* to arouse.

suscribir [3a; *ptp* **suscrito**] 1 *vt* (a) *contract, petition etc* to sign; *promise* to make, agree to, ratify.

(b) *opinion* to subscribe to, endorse.

(c) *shares etc* to take out an option on.

(d) **— a uno a una revista** to enter someone as a subscriber to a journal, put someone on the subscription list of a journal; **A le suscribió a B por 100 dólares** A put B down for a 100-dollar contribution.

2 **suscribirse** *vr* to subscribe (*a* to, for); **¿te vas a suscribir?** are you going to subscribe?

suscripción *nf* subscription; **abrir una —** to take out a subscription; **cerrar su —** to cancel one's subscription.

suscriptor *nm*, **suscriptora** *nf* subscriber.

susodicho *adj* above-mentioned.

suspender [2a] *vt* (**a**) *object* to hang, hang up, suspend (*de* from, on).
(**b**) (*fig*) *payment, work etc* to stop, suspend; *meeting, session* to adjourn; *process etc* to interrupt; **— hasta más tarde** to put off till later, postpone for a time.
(**c**) (*Univ etc*) *candidate, subject* to fail.
(**d**) (*fig*) to astound, astonish; to fill with wonder, cause to marvel.

suspense *nm* (*Lit, Theat etc*: *angl*) suspense.

suspensión *nf* (**a**) (*act*) hanging (up), suspension.
(**b**) (*Aut, Mech*) suspension.
(**c**) (*fig*) stoppage, suspension; adjournment; interruption; postponement; (*Law*) stay; **— de fuego, — de hostilidades** ceasefire, cessation of hostilities; **— de pagos** suspension of payments.
(**d**) astonishment; wonderment; (*Lit, Theat etc*) suspense.

suspensivo *adj*: **puntos —s** dots, suspension points (. . .).

suspenso 1 *adj* (**a**) hanging, suspended; hung (*de* from).
(**b**) (*Univ etc*) *candidate* failed.
(**c**) (*fig*) **estar —, quedarse —** to be astonished, be amazed; to be filled with wonder; to be bewildered, be baffled.
2 *nm* (**a**) (*Univ etc*) fail, failure.
(**b**) **estar en —, quedar en —** to be in suspense, be pending; (*Law*) to be suspended, be in abeyance; (*case*) to stand over, be postponed.

suspensores *nmpl* (*SAm*) braces, suspenders (*US*).

suspensorio 1 *adj* suspensory. 2 *nm* jockstrap; (*Med*) suspensory (bandage).

suspicacia *nf* suspicion, mistrust.

suspicaz *adj* suspicious, distrustful.

suspirado *adj* longed-for, yearned-for.

suspirar [1a] *vi* to sigh (*also fig*; *por* for).

suspiro *nm* sigh; (*fig*) sigh, breath, rustle, whisper; **deshacerse en —s** to sigh deeply, fetch a great sigh; **exhalar el último —** to breathe one's last.

sustancia *nf* substance; essence; matter; **— gris** (*Anat*) grey matter; **en —** in substance, in essence; **sin —** lacking in substance; shallow, superficial.

sustancial *adj* (**a**) substantial; essential, vital, fundamental. (**b**) = **sustancioso**.

sustancialmente *adv* substantially; essentially, vitally, fundamentally.

sustancioso *adj* *speech etc* solid; meaty; *food* solid, substantial, nourishing.

sustantivar [1a] *vt* to use as a noun.

sustantivo 1 *adj* substantive; (*Gram*) substantival, noun (*attr*). 2 *nm* noun, substantive.

sustentación *nf* sustenance; support; (*Aer*) lift.

sustentar [1a] 1 *vt* (**a**) *object* to hold up, support, bear (the weight of).
(**b**) (*of food*) to sustain, nourish, feed, keep going.
(**c**) (*fig*: *of hope etc*) to sustain, keep going, buoy up.
(**d**) *idea, theory* to maintain, uphold, defend.
2 **sustentarse** *vr*: **— con** to sustain oneself with, subsist on; **— de esperanzas** to sustain oneself with hopes, buoy oneself up with hopes; **— del aire** to live on air.

sustento *nm* support; sustenance, food; maintenance; (*fig*) livelihood; **ganarse el —** to earn one's living, earn a livelihood; **es el — principal de la institución** it is the lifeblood of the institution.

sustitución *nf* substitution (*por* for), replacement (*por* by).

sustituible *adj* replaceable; expendable.

sustituir [3g] 1 *vt* to substitute, replace; **— A por B** to substitute B for A, replace A by B, replace A with B, put A in place of B; **tendremos que — el neumático pinchado** we shall have to change (*or* replace) the flat tyre; **le quieren —** they want to remove him, they want him replaced.

2 *vi* to substitute; to deputize; **— a** to replace; to substitute for, deputize for; **los sellos azules sustituyen a los verdes** the blue stamps are replacing the green ones.

sustitutivo 1 *adj* substitute. 2 *nm* substitute (*de* for); **es un — del café** it is a coffee substitute.

sustituto *nm*, **sustituta** *nf* substitute, replacement; deputy.

susto *nm* (**a**) fright, scare; **¡qué —!** what a scare!; **dar un — a uno** to give someone a fright (*or* scare); **darse un —, pegarse un —** (*fam*) to have a fright, give oneself a fright; **meter un — a uno** to put the wind up someone.
(**b**) (*Per*) nervous breakdown; tuberculosis.

sustracción *nf* (**a**) removal; (*Math*) subtraction, taking away; deduction; extraction. (**b**) theft.

sustraer [2p] 1 *vt* to remove, take away; (*Math*) to subtract, take away; to deduct; *water etc* to extract.
2 **sustraerse** *vr*: **— a** to avoid; to withdraw from, contract out of; **— a + infin** to avoid + *ger*, get out of + *ger*; **no pude sustraerme a la tentación** I could not resist the temptation; **me era imposible sustraerme a un terrible dolor de cabeza** I couldn't shake off (*or* get rid of) an awful headache.

sustrato *nm* substratum.

susurrante *adj* whispering, murmuring; rustling.

susurrar [1a] 1 *vi* (**a**) (*of person*) to whisper; **— al oído de uno** to whisper to someone, whisper in someone's ear.
(**b**) (*fig*: *of wind*) to whisper; (*of insects*) to hum; (*of stream*) to murmur; (*of leaves*) to rustle.
2 **susurrarse** *vr*: **se susurra que . . .** it is being whispered that . . ., it is rumoured that . . .

susurro *nm* (**a**) whisper. (**b**) (*fig*) whisper; hum, humming; murmur; rustle.

sutil *adj* (**a**) *strand etc* fine, delicate, tenuous; *slice* thin; *material* thin, light; very soft; *air* thin; *scent* delicate; subtle; *breeze etc* gentle.
(**b**) *difference* fine, subtle, nice.
(**c**) *mind, person* sharp, keen, observant; subtle; *observation* subtle.

sutileza *nf* (**a**) fineness, delicacy; thinness; subtlety, subtleness; sharpness, keenness. (**b**) (*una —*) subtlety; (*pej*) artifice, artful deceit.

sutilizar [1f] 1 *vt* (**a**) *object etc* to thin down, fine down; (*fig*) to polish, perfect; (*fig*) to refine (upon).
(**b**) *concept etc* (*pej*) to quibble about, split hairs about.
2 *vi* (*pej*) to quibble, split hairs.

sutura *nf* suture.

suturar [1a] *vt* to suture; to stitch.

suyo *poss adj and pron* 1 (*following verb* ser *or with article*) (**a**) (*one possessor*) his, hers, its, one's; (*relating to* **Vd**) yours; **es —, es el —** it is his (*etc*); **¿es — esto?** is this yours?; **lo —** (what is) his, what belongs to him; **los —s** (*freq*) his people, his relations, his family.
(**b**) (*plural possessors*) theirs; (*relating to* **Vds**) yours.
2 (*after n*) (**a**) (*one possessor*) of his, of hers; of its own, of one's own; (*relating to* **Vd**) of yours; **no es amigo —** he is no friend of hers.
(**b**) (*plural possessors*) of theirs; (*relating to* **Vds**) of yours.
3 *adj and pron* (*idioms*): **de —** in itself, per se; intrinsically; on its own; **eso es muy —** that's just like him, that's typical of him; **aguantar lo —** to shoulder one's burden; to put up with a lot; **eso cae de —** that's obvious, that goes without saying; **estar en lo mejor —** (*fam*) to be on top form, be in one's best form; **hizo suyas mis palabras** he echoed my words, he supported what I had said; **hacer de las suyas** to get up to one's old tricks; **ir a la suya, ir a lo —** to go one's own way; (*pej*) to act selfishly, think only of oneself; **salirse con la suya** to get one's way; (*in argument*) to carry one's point; **valorar lo —** to be worth one's keep; **cada cual a lo —** it's best to mind one's own business.

svástica *nf* swastika.

T

taba *nf* (*Anat*) ankle bone; (*game*) knucklebones, jackstones (*US*); **menear las —s** (*fam*) to hustle about; to get cracking (*fam*), get moving; **tomar la — (*fam*)** to start speaking; to show who is boss.
tabacal *nm* (*SAm*) tobacco field; tobacco plantation.
Tabacalera *nf Spanish state tobacco monopoly.*
tabacalero 1 *adj* tobacco (*attr*). **2** *nm* tobacconist; tobacco grower, tobacco merchant.
tabaco 1 *nm* (a) tobacco; cigarettes, cigar (*esp SAm*); (*Bot*) tobacco plant; **— de hebra** loose tobacco; **— de pipa** pipe tobacco; **— en polvo** snuff; **— en rama** leaf tobacco; **— rubio** Virginian tobacco; **— turco** Turkish tobacco; **¿tienes —?** have you any cigarettes?; **se me acabó el —** I ran out of cigarettes, I had nothing left to smoke; **se le acabó el — (*Arg, Chi: fig*)** he ran out of money; **estar de mal — (*CAm*)** to be in a bad mood; **estaba hecho — (*fam*)** he was all in; it was all torn to pieces.
(b) (*Cu*) punch, blow.
2 *adj* (*SAm*) dusty brown.
tabacón *nm* (*Mex*) marijuana.
tabacoso *adj* tobacco-stained.
tabalada *nf* punch; knock, bump, blow (from a fall).
tabalear [1a] **1** *vt* to rock; to shake. **2** *vi* to drum (with one's fingers), tap.
tabaleo *nm* rocking; shaking; drumming, tapping.
tabanco *nm* (*CAm*) attic.
tábano *nm* horsefly.
tabaqueada *nf* (*Mex*) beating-up; fist fight.
tabaquear [1a] *vi* (*Col*) to smoke.
tabaquera *nf* tobacco jar; snuffbox; (*of pipe*) bowl; (*SAm*) tobacco pouch, cigar case, cigarette case.
tabaquería *nf* tobacconist's (shop), cigar store (*US*).
tabaquero 1 *adj* (*SAm*) tobacco (*attr*). **2** *nm* tobacconist; (*SAm*) tobacco grower, tobacco merchant.
tabaquito *nm* (*SAm*) small cigar.
tabarra *nf* (*fam*) nuisance, bore; **dar la —** to be a nuisance, be a bore; **dar la — a uno** to get on someone's nerves, annoy someone.
tabear [1a] *vi* (*RPl*) to chat, gossip; to gossip about someone not present.
taberna *nf* bar, pub; (*Hist*) tavern; (*Arg*) gambling joint; (*Cu*) = **pulpería**.
tabernáculo *nm* tabernacle.
tabernario *adj* rude, dirty.
tabernero *nm* publican, landlord; barman, bartender.
tabicar [1g] **1** *vt* to wall up; to partition off. **2 tabicarse** *vr* to get stopped up.
tabique *nm* thin wall, partition (wall).
tabla *nf* (a) (*of wood*) plank, board; shelf; (*of stone etc*) slab; (*Art*) panel; (*Cu*) shop counter; **— de dibujo** drawing board; **— de lavar** washboard; **— de picar** chopping board; **— de planchar** ironing board; **— de salvación** (*fig*) last resort, sole hope; thing that saves one's life; **— del suelo** floorboard; **escaparse** (*or* **salvarse**) **en una —** to have a narrow escape, have a close shave; **hacer — rasa** to make a clean sweep; to clear away all obstacles; **hacer — rasa de** (*pej*) to disregard utterly, ride roughshod over.
(b) **—s** (*Taur*) boards, fence.
(c) **—s** (*Theat*) boards, stage; **pisar las —s** to walk the stage; **salir a las —s** to go on the stage, become an actor; **tener muchas —s** to be an old hand, be an expert.
(d) **—s** (*Chess*) draw; tie; (*fig*) stalemate, deadlock; **—s por ahogado** stalemate; **hacer —s, quedar (en) —s** to draw, reach a drawn position; (*fig*) to reach stalemate, be deadlocked; **el partido quedó —s** the game was a draw, the game was drawn.
(e) (*Anat*) flat area, wide part.
(f) (*Agr*) plot, patch, bed.
(g) (*Sew*) broad pleat.
(h) (*Comm*) meat stall.

(i) (*fig*) table, list, chart; (*Math*) table; (*Typ*) table, index; **— de materias** table of contents; **— de multiplicar** multiplication table.
(j) (*Arg, Col*) tablet, pastille.
tablada *nf* (*Bol, RPl*) stockyard, cattlepen; (*Par*) slaughterhouse.
tablado *nm* plank floor, boards; stand, stage, platform; (*Hist*) scaffold; (*Theat*) stage.
tablaje *nm*, **tablazón** *nf* planks, planking, boards.
tablear [1a] *vt* (a) *wood* to cut into boards (*or* planks).
(b) *land* to divide up into plots.
(c) *ground* to level off; *dough* (*Chi*) to roll out.
(d) (*Sew*) to pleat.
tablero *nm* (a) (*of wood*) board(s), plank(s); panel; (*of marble etc*) slab; (*School etc*) blackboard; (*Comm*) counter; (*for games*) board; (*RPl*) notice board, bulletin board (*US*); (*Elec*) switchboard; **— de ajedrez** chessboard; **— de dibujo** drawing board; **— de instrumentos** instrument panel, (*Aut*) dashboard; **— posterior** tail board.
(b) (*Agr*) bed(s), plot(s).
(c) gambling den.
tableta *nf* (a) small board. (b) writing pad, tablet. (c) (*Med*) tablet; (*of chocolate*) bar, stick.
tabletear [1a] *vi* to rattle, clatter; (*of machine gun*) to rattle.
tableteo *nm* rattle, clatter.
tablilla *nf* (a) small board; (*Med*) splint. (b) (*Mex*) bar (of chocolate).
tablón *nm* (a) plank, beam; **— de anuncios** notice board, bulletin board (*US*).
(b) (*fam*) coger un —, **pillar un —** to get tight.
(c) (*SAm: Agr*) plot, bed.
tablonazo *nm* (*Cu*) trick, swindle.
tabú *nm* taboo.
tabuco *nm* slum, shack; tiny room, poky little room.
tabular 1 [1a] *vt* to tabulate. **2** *adj* tabular.
taburete *nm* stool.
tacana *nf* (a) (*Arg, Bol*) cultivated hillside terrace.
(b) (*Arg, Mex*) pestle.
tacanear [1a] *vt* (*Arg*) to tread down; to pound, crush.
tacañería *nf* (a) meanness, stinginess. (b) craftiness.
tacaño *adj* (a) mean, stingy. (b) crafty.
tacar [1g] *vt* (*Col*) (a) to shoot at. (b) to fill, pack tightly (*de* with).
tacita *nf* small cup; **la T— de Plata** (*affectionate name for*) Cadiz; **como una — de plata** as bright as a new pin.
tácitamente *adv* tacitly.
Tácito *m* Tacitus.
tácito *adj* tacit; *comment etc* unspoken; *law* unwritten; (*Ling*) unexpressed, understood.
taciturnidad *nf* taciturnity, silent nature; moodiness, sullenness; glumness.
taciturno *adj* taciturn, silent; moody, sullen, sulky; glum.
tacizo *nm* (a) (*Col, Ven*) narrow-bladed axe. (b) (*Col*) small prison cell.
taco[1] *nm* (a) wad, wadding; wooden peg; stopper, plug, bung.
(b) (*in boot*) stud; (*SAm*) heel.
(c) pad; calendar; book of travel tickets (*or* coupons *etc*); stub; **— de papel** writing pad, pad of notepaper.
(d) (*Billiards*) cue.
(e) (*Mil: Hist*) ramrod.
(f) popgun.
(g) snack, bite; swig of wine (*fam*).
(h) (*fam*) rude word, swearword; **dice muchos —** he swears a lot; **soltar un —** to swear.
(i) (*fam*) tangle, mess; **armarse un —, hacerse un —** to get into a mess, get all tied up; **dejar a uno hecho un —** to flatten someone (in an argument).
(j) (*Chi, Mex*) obstruction, blockage.

(**k**) (*Mex*) rolled pancake.

(**l**) (*Arg, Chi*) short stocky person.

(**m**) (*CAm, PR*) worry, anxiety; fear.

taco[2] **1** *adj* (*Cu, PR*) (**a**) foppish. (**b**) bold, enterprising. **2** *nm* (**a**) (*Ant, CAm, Mex*) fop, dandy, toff (*fam*); **darse** — to put on airs. (**b**) (*Col*) big shot (*fam*).

tacómetro *nm* tachometer.

tacón *nm* heel; — (**de**) **aguja** stiletto heel; —**es altos** high heels; **de** — **alto** high-heeled.

taconazo *nm* heel tap; kick with one's heel, blow with the heel; —**s** (*Mil etc*) heel-clicking; **entró y dio un** — he came in and clicked his heels.

taconear [1a] **1** *vt* (*Chi*) to pack tight, fill right up. **2** *vi* (**a**) to tap (*or* stamp) with one's heels; (*Mil etc*) to click one's heels; to walk noisily on one's heels.

(**b**) (*fam*) to bustle about.

taconeo *nm* tapping (*or* stamping) with one's heels; heel-clicking; noisy walking on one's heels.

tacote *nm* (*Mex*) marijuana.

táctica *nf* tactics; (*una* —) tactic, move, method; gambit; — **de cerrojo** stonewalling, negative play.

tácticamente *adv* tactically.

táctico 1 *adj* tactical. **2** *nm* tactician.

táctil *adj* tactile.

tacto *nm* (**a**) (*bodily*) touch, sense of touch; (*of typist etc*) touch.

(**b**) (*act*) touch, touching; feel; **ser áspero al** — to feel rough, be rough to the touch.

(**c**) (*quality*) feel; **tiene un** — **viscoso** it has a sticky feel (to it).

(**d**) (*fig*) tact.

tacuaco *adj* (*Chi*) chubby.

tacuache *nm* (*Cu*) fib, lie.

tacuche *nm* (*Mex*) bundle of rags; (*Univ: fam*) dress; (*fig*) worthless object, useless person, dead loss.

tacha[1] *nf* (**a**) (*Tech*) large tack, brad, stud. (**b**) (*SAm*) = **tacho**.

tacha[2] *nf* flaw, blemish, defect; **sin** — perfect, flawless; **poner** — **a** to find fault with.

tachadura *nf* erasure, correction.

tachar [1a] *vt* (**a**) to cross out, erase; to correct.

(**b**) to criticize, attack, find fault with; **witness** (*Law*) to challenge; — **a uno de incapaz** to accuse someone of being incompetent.

tachero *nm* (*Arg, Chi*) tinsmith.

tachines *nmpl* (*sl*) feet.

tacho *nm* (*SAm*) boiler, large boiling pan; sugar pan, sugar evaporator; bin, container; (*RPl*) washbasin; — **para la basura** dustbin, garbage can (*US*); — **para lavar la ropa** clothes boiler; **irse al** — to be ruined, fail.

tachón[1] *nm* (**a**) (*Tech*) large stud, ornamental stud, boss. (**b**) (*Sew*) trimming.

tachón[2] *nm* erasure, stroke, crossing-out.

tachonado *adj*: — **de estrellas** star-studded, star-spangled.

tachonar [1a] *vt* to stud, adorn with studs; to trim; (*fig*) to stud (*de* with).

tachoso *adj* defective, faulty.

tachuela *nf* (**a**) tack, tintack; (*Cu*) long pin.

(**b**) (*Col, Cu, Ven*) metal pan, boiler, bowl; (*Mex, Ven*) metal cup, dipper.

(**c**) (*Arg, Chi, Guat, Mex*) short stocky person, runt.

tafetán *nm* (**a**) taffeta; — **adhesivo**, — **inglés** sticking plaster. (**b**) —**es** (*fig*) flags; (*fam*) frills, buttons and bows.

tafia *nf* (*SAm*) rum.

tafilete *nm* morocco leather.

tagarnia *nf* (*CAm, Col*) surfeit, blow-out (*sl*); drunkenness.

tagarnina *nf* (**a**) (*Mex*) leather tobacco pouch. (**b**) (*Col, Guat, Mex*) drunkenness.

tagarote *nm* (**a**) (*Zool*) sparrowhawk. (**b**) (*fam*) tall shabby person. (**c**) (*fam*) lawyer's clerk, penpusher. (**d**) (*CR, Per*) big shot (*fam*).

tagua *nf* (*Ec*) ivory palm.

tahalí *nm* swordbelt.

Tahití *m* Tahiti.

tahona *nf* bakery, bakehouse; flourmill.

tahonero *nm* baker; miller.

tahur *nm* gambler; (*pej*) cardsharper, cheat.

taifa *nf* (*fam*) gang, crew; gang of thieves.

Tailandia *f* Thailand.

tailandés 1 *adj* Thai. **2** *nm*, **tailandesa** *nf* Thai. **3** *nm* (*language*) Thai.

taima *nf* (**a**) slyness, craftiness, slickness. (**b**) (*Chi*) obstinacy, sullenness.

taimado *adj* (**a**) sly, crafty, slick. (**b**) sullen. (**c**) (*Arg, Ec*) lazy.

taimarse [1a] *vr* (**a**) to get sly, adopt crafty tactics. (**b**) to be stubborn, be sullen, sulk.

taita *nm* (**a**) (*fam*) dad, daddy; uncle.

(**b**) (*Arg, Chi, Par etc*) in direct address, term of respect used before a name.

(**c**) (*Arg*) tough (*fam*), bully; quarrelsome person.

(**d**) pimp.

taja *nf* (**a**) cut. (**b**) division (of taxes).

tajada *nf* (**a**) (*Cook*) slice; slab, chunk.

(**b**) (*fam*) rake-off (*fam*); **sacar** — to get one's share, get something out of it; to get a rake-off, take one's cut; (*fig*) to look after number one.

(**c**) (*Med*) hoarseness.

(**d**) (*fam*) **coger una** —, **pillar una** — to get tight.

(**e**) cut, slash; **¡te haré** —**s!** I'll cut you up!

tajadera *nf* (**a**) chopper; cold chisel. (**b**) chopping block.

tajadero *nm* chopping block.

tajado *adj* rock sheer.

tajalán *adj* (*Cu*) lazy.

tajaleo *nm* (*Cu*) (**a**) food, grub (*sl*). (**b**) row, brawl.

tajamar *nm* (**a**) (*Naut*) stem; (*of bridge*) cutwater. (**b**) (*CAm, Chi*) mole; (*Per, RPl*) dam, dike.

tajante *adj* (**a**) sharp, cutting.

(**b**) (*fig*) incisive, sharp, emphatic; *distinction etc* sharp; **contestó con un "no"** — he answered with an emphatic "no"; **una crítica** — **del gobierno** some sharp criticism of the government; **es una persona** — he's an incisive person.

tajantemente *adv* (*fig*) incisively, sharply, emphatically.

tajar [1a] *vt* to cut, slice, chop.

tajarrazo *nm* (*CAm, Mex*) slash, wound; (*fig*) damage, harm.

tajeadura *nf* (*Chi, RPl*) long scar.

tajear [1a] *vt* (*SAm: fam*) to cut up, chop; to slash.

Tajo *m* Tagus.

tajo *nm* (**a**) cut, slash; **darse un** — **en el brazo** to cut one's arm; **tirar** —**s a uno** to slash at someone.

(**b**) (*Geog*) cut, cleft; steep cliff, sheer drop.

(**c**) working area; (*fam*) work, job; **largarse al** — to get off to work, go back on the job; **¡vamos al** —**!** let's get on with it!

(**d**) cutting edge.

(**e**) (*Cook*) chopping block; (*Hist*) block (*for executions*).

(**f**) (*Sew: Hist*) slash.

(**g**) small three-legged stool.

tajón *nm* (*Mex*) slaughterhouse.

tal 1 *adj* such; — **cosa** such a thing; —**es cosas** such things; **no hay** — **cosa** there's no such thing; **con** — **atrevimiento** with such boldness; **coi un resultado** — with such a result; **el** — **paí no existió nunca** such a country never existed; **necesitas tanto dinero para** — **cosa** you need so much money for such-and-such a thing; **un** — **García** a man called García, one García; **el** — **cura** this priest, the aforementioned priest, this priest we were talking about; (*pej*) this priest person.

2 *pron* such a one, someone; such a thing, something; **el** — this man (*etc*) I mentioned, this man we're talking about; such a person; **una** — (*euph*) a prostitute; **no haré** — I won't do anything of the sort; **¡no hay** —**!** nothing of the sort!; **en la calle de** — in such-and-such a street; — **como es, todavía vale algo** such as it is, it is still worth something; **y como** —, **tiene que pagar los derechos** and such, he has to pay the fees; **se para aquí** — **cual autocar** an odd coach stops here, a coach stops here occasionally; **vive en** — **o cual hotel** he lives in such-and-such a hotel; **son** — **para cual** they're two of a kind; **sí** — yes indeed, yes of course; — **hay que lo piensa** there are some who think so; **hablábamos de que si** — **que si cual** we were talking about this that and the other; **había ruritanos y eslobodos y** — there were Ruritanians and Slobodians and such (*or* such like, others of that kind); **fuimos al cine y** — we went to the pictures and that kind of thing.

3 *adv* so; in such a way; — **como** just as; **estaba** — **como lo dejé** it was just as I had left it; — **cual** (*adv*) just as it is; **es** — **cual siempre deseaba** it is just what he had always wanted; **ella sigue** — **cual** she's so-so, she's middling fair; — **la madre, cual la hija** like mother, like daughter; **tomaremos algo ligero** — **que una tortilla** (*fam*) we'll have something light such as an omelette; **¿qué** —**?** how goes it?, how's things?; **¿qué** — **el partido?** what was the game like?, how did the game go?;

¿qué — tu tío? how's your uncle?; ¿qué — del profesor? what's the news of the professor?; ¿qué — te gusta? what do you think of it?, how do you like it?; *see also* cual *for other comparative phrases.*

4 *conj*: con — (de) que . . . provided (that) . . ., on condition that . . .; con — de no volver nunca on condition that he (*etc*) never comes back; no importa el frío con — de ir bien abrigado the cold doesn't matter if you're well wrapped up.

tala *nf* (a) tree felling, wood cutting; (*fig*) havoc, destruction. (b) (*Ven*) axe. (c) (*PR*) vegetable garden. (d) (*Chi*) grazing.

talabarte *nm* swordbelt.

talabartería *nf* saddlery, harness-maker's shop.

talabartero *nm* saddler, harness maker.

talacha *nf*, **talache** *nm* (*Mex*) mattock.

taladradora *nf* drill; — de fuerza power drill; — neumática pneumatic drill.

taladrar [1a] *vt* (a) to bore, drill, punch, pierce; *ticket* to punch; *lobe of ear* to pierce.
(b) (*fig: of pain, sound*) to pierce; un ruido que taladra los oídos an ear-splitting noise; es un ruido que taladra it's a shattering noise.

taladro *nm* (a) drill; auger, gimlet; borer; — neumático pneumatic drill. (b) drill hole.

talaje *nm* (a) (*Arg, Chi*) pasture. (b) (*Chi, Mex*) grazing, pasturage.

tálamo *nm* marriage bed.

talamoco *adj* (*Ec*) albino.

talante *nm* (a) mood, disposition, frame of mind; will, willingness; estar de buen — to be in a good mood, be in the right frame of mind; hacer algo de buen — to do something willingly; recibir a uno de buen — to give someone a warm welcome; estar de mal — to be in a bad mood; responder de mal — to answer with an ill grace, answer bad-temperedly.
(b) mien, look, appearance.

talar [1a] *vt* (a) *tree* to fell, cut down. (b) (*fig*) to lay waste, devastate. (c) (*Prov, SAm*) to prune.

talco *nm* talcum powder; (*Min*) talc.

talcualillo *adj* (*fam*) so-so, middling, fair (*also Med*).

talega *nf* (a) sack, bag. (b) baby's nappy, diaper (*US*). (c) —s (*fam*) money.

talegada *nf*, **talegazo** *nm* heavy fall, severe bump.

talego *nm* (a) big sack, long sack, poke. (b) (*fam*: *person*) fat person, lump. (c) (*fam*) tener — to have money stashed away (*fam*), have brass (*sl*).

taleguilla *nf* bullfighter's breeches.

talento *nm* (a) talent; ability, gift; —s talents; accomplishments. (b) (*Bib*) talent.

talentoso *adj* talented, gifted.

talero *nm* (*Chi, RPl*) whip.

talidomida *nm* thalidomide.

talismán *nm* talisman.

talmente *adv* so, in such a way; to such an extent; exactly, literally; la casa es — una pocilga the house is such a pigsty, the house is literally a pigsty.

Talmud *m* Talmud.

talmúdico *adj* Talmudic.

talón *nm* (a) (*Anat*) heel; (*of shoe etc*) heel; — de Aquiles Achilles' heel; pisar los —es a uno to be on someone's heels, follow close behind someone; (*fig*) to run someone very close.
(b) (*Aut*) flange, rim (*of tyre*).
(c) (*Comm etc*) stub, counterfoil; (*Rail*) luggage receipt.

talonar [1a] *vt* to heel.

talonario 1 *adj*: libro — = 2 *nm* receipt book; book of tickets, book of counterfoils; — de cheques cheque book.

talonear [1a] 1 *vt* (*SAm*) to dig one's heels into, spur along. 2 *vi* to walk briskly, hurry along.

talonera *nf* (*Col*) heel.

talquina *nf* (*Chi*) deceit, treachery.

talud *nm* slope, bank; (*Geol*) talus.

talla[1] *nf* (a) (*Art*) carving; sculpture; engraving (*also* obra de —).
(b) (*of person*) height, stature; (*fig*) stature; (*of garment*) size, fitting; camisas de todas las —s shirts in all sizes; tener poca — to be short, be on the short side; ha crecido de — (*fig*) he has grown in stature.
(c) measuring rod.
(d) (*Med*) gallstones operation.
(e) (*Cards*) hand.
(f) (*Law*) reward (*for capture of a criminal*); poner a uno a — to offer a reward for the capture of someone.

talla[2] *nf* (a) (*CAm*) fib, lie. (b) (*Chi, RPl*) gossip, chitchat. (c) (*Col*) beating.

tallado 1 *adj* (a) carved; sculpted; engraved.
(b) bien — shapely, well-formed; mal — misshapen.
2 *nm* carving; sculpting; engraving; — en madera wood carving.

tallador *nm* (a) carver; sculptor; engraver. (b) (*SAm: Cards*) dealer, banker.

tallar[1] [1a] 1 *vt* (a) to carve, shape, work; to sculpt; to engrave; *gem* to cut.
(b) *person* to measure (the height of).
(c) (*Cards*) to deal.
2 *vi* (*Cards*) to deal, be banker.

tallar[2] [1a] 1 *vt* (a) (*Col*) to bother, annoy.
(b) (*Col*) to beat.
2 *vi* (*Chi, RPl*) to chat, gossip; to gossip maliciously; (*Chi*) to exchange sweet nothings.

tallarín *nm* (*Cook*) noodle.

talle *nm* (a) (*Anat, Sew*) waist; — de avispa wasp waist.
(b) (*Sew etc*) waist and chest measurements; size, fitting.
(c) (*Anat: woman's*) figure; (*man's*) build, physique; de — esbelto with a slim figure; tiene buen — she has a good figure.
(d) (*fig*) look, appearance; outline.
(e) (*Chi, Guat*) bodice.

taller *nm* (*Tech*) workshop; mill, factory; (*Art*) studio; (*Sew*) workroom; (*industrial and trade-union parlance*) shop; — agremiado union shop, closed shop; —es gráficos printing works; — de máquinas machine shop; — de montaje assembly shop; — de reparaciones repair shop; (*Aut*) service station.

tallero *nm* (*SAm*) vegetable merchant, greengrocer.

tallista *nm* = tallador (a), (*esp*) wood carver.

tallo *nm* (a) stem, stalk; (*of grass*) blade, sprig; shoot.
(b) (*Col*) cabbage.
(c) (*SAm*) —s vegetables, greens.
(d) (*Cook*) candied peel; crystallized fruit.

talludo *adj* (a) (*Bot*) tall; *person* big, tall, lanky; (*fig*) grown-up; ya eres una talluda you're a big girl now, you're too big for that at your age; es una talluda ya (*pej*) she's not exactly a youngster, she's no chicken.
(b) (*CAm, Mex*) tough, leathery; hard to peel.
(c) (*CAm, Mex*) *person* old but still active; *object* old but still useful.

tamal *nm* (a) (*SAm: Cook*) tamale.
(b) (*Chi*) bundle of clothing; (*Mex*) shapeless mass, rough bundle.
(c) (*SAm: fig*) fraud, trick, hoax; intrigue; hacer un — to prepare a trick, set a trap.

tamalero (*SAm*) 1 *adj* (a) fond of tamales. (b) intriguing, fond of intrigue. 2 *nm* tamale maker, tamale seller.

tamango *nm* (*Chi, RPl*) (a) clog, sandal, rough shoe; old shoe. (b) baby boy.

tamañito *adj*: dejar a uno — to make someone feel very small; to crush someone, flatten someone (in an argument); me quedé — I felt about so high; I felt utterly bewildered.

tamaño 1 *adj* so big, such a big; so small, such a small; parece absurdo que cometiera — error it seems absurd that he should make so grave an error (*or* such a great error); una piedra tamaña como una naranja a stone as big as an orange.
2 *nm* size; — de bolsillo pocket-size; de — extra, de — extraordinario outsize, extra large; de — natural full-size, life-size; ser del mismo —, tener el mismo — to be the same size; ¿de qué — es? what size is it?, how big is it?

tamarindo *nm* (a) tamarind. (b) (*Mex: fam*) policeman, cop (*sl*).

tamarisco *nm*, **tamariz** *nm* tamarisk.

tambache *nm* (*Mex*) bundle of clothes.

tambaleante *adj* staggering, tottering; *gait* unsteady; *vehicle* swaying.

tambalearse [1a] *vr* (*person*) to stagger, totter, reel; to zigzag; to wobble (from side to side); (*vehicle*) to lurch, sway; ir tambaleándose to stagger along; to lurch along, sway about (as one walks *etc*).

tambar [1a] *vt* (*Ec*) to swallow.

tambarria *nf* (*CAm, Col, Ec*) party, carousal.

tambero *nm* (*Chi, RPl*) innkeeper; dairy farmer.

también *adv* also, as well, too; besides; ¿Vd —? you too?; y bebe — and he drinks as well, he also drinks; no sólo A sino — B not only A but also B; "¿y es guapa?" . . . "—" "and is she pretty?" . . . "she's that as well".

tambo *nm* (*Bol, Col, Ec, Per*) country inn, roadside inn; (*RPl*) milking yard; (*Chi*) brothel.

tambor *nm* **(a)** (*Mus, Tech*) drum; (*Archit, Sew*) tambour; (*Anat*) eardrum; — **de tostar café** coffee roaster; — **del freno** brake drum; **venir a — batiente** to come out with flying colours, emerge in triumph.
(b) (*Mus*) drummer; — **mayor** drum major.
(c) (*Cu, Mex*) burlap, sackcloth.
tambora *nf* **(a)** (*Mus*) bass drum. **(b)** (*Cu*) lie, fib.
tamboril *nm* small drum.
tamborilada *nf*, **tamborilazo** *nm* bump on one's bottom, severe jolt; slap on the shoulder.
tamborilear [1a] **1** *vt* (*fam*) to praise up, boost. **2** *vi* (*Mus*) to drum, play the drum; to drum with one's fingers; (*of rain*) to patter, drum.
tamborileo *nm* drumming; patter(ing).
tamborilero *nm* drummer.
tambre *nm* (*Col*) dam.
tamegua *nf* (*CAm, Mex*) weeding, cleaning.
tameguar [1d] *vt* (*CAm, Mex*) to weed, clean.
Tamerlán *m* Tamberlane.
Támesis *m* Thames.
tamiz *nm* sieve.
tamizar [1f] *vt* to sieve, sift.
tamo *nm* fluff, down, dust; (*Agr*) dust; chaff.
tampa *nf* (*Arg*) matted hair.
tampoco *adv* neither, not . . . either; nor; **ni A ni B** — neither A nor B, not A nor B either; **yo — lo compré, yo no lo compré** — I didn't buy one either; **ni yo** — nor I; "**¿lo sabes tú?**" . . . "**—**" do you know?" . . . "No, I don't either"; "**pero ¿vendrás a la fiesta?**" . . . "**—**" "but you'll be coming to the party?" . . . "No, I shan't come to that either".
tampón *nm* plug (*also Med*); (*Med*) tampon; — **de entintar** inking pad.
tamuga *nf* (*CAm, Pan*) bundle, pack; knapsack.
tan *adv* so; — **rápido** so fast; — **rápidamente** so fast; **no es buena idea comprar un coche — grande** it's not a good idea to buy such a big car; **¡qué idea — rara!** what an odd notion!; **A es — feo como B** A is as ugly as B; **es — caro que nadie puede comprarlo** it's so expensive that nobody can afford it; **no te esperaba — pronto** I wasn't expecting you so soon; **de — rico resulta incomible** it's so rich that one can't eat it; — **es así que . . .** so much so that . . .
tanaca *nf* (*Bol*) slut.
tanaceto *nm* tansy.
tanate *nm* (*CAm, Mex*) **(a)** basket, pannier. **(b)** —**s** (*fig*) odds and ends, bits and pieces, gear (*fam*).
tanda *nf* **(a)** series, set; batch; (*of eggs etc*) layer; (*of injections*) course, series; (*of bricks*) course; (*of blows*) series.
(b) (*at work*) shift, turn, spell; job; task, piece of work; (*in irrigation*) turn (to use water); (*persons*) shift, relay; gang; — **de noche** nightshift, spell of night work; **ahora estás de** — now it's your turn.
(c) (*Billiards etc*) game; (*Baseball*) innings.
(d) (*SAm: Theat*) show, performance; (*Chi*) light comedy, farce, musical; **primera** — first show, early performance.
tándem *nm* tandem; **en** — (*Elec*) tandem.
tanganear [1a] *vt* (*Col, Ec, Ven*) to beat.
tanganillas: en — *adv* unsteadily; (*fig*) uncertainly, dubiously; unsafely.
tanganillo *nm* prop, wedge, temporary support.
tangencial *adj* tangential; (*fig*) oblique.
tangencialmente *adv* tangentially; (*fig*) obliquely.
tangente *nf* tangent; **salirse por la** — (*fig*) to go off at a tangent; to dodge the issue, give an evasive answer.
Tánger Tangier(s).
tangerino 1 *adj* of Tangier(s). **2** *nm*, **tangerina** *nf* native (*or* inhabitant) of Tangier(s); **los** —**s** the people of Tangier(s).
tangibilidad *nf* tangibility.
tangible *adj* tangible; (*fig*) tangible, concrete.
tango *nm* tango.
tanguear [1a] *vi* **(a)** (*SAm*) to tango; to dance. **(b)** (*Ec*) to reel drunkenly.
tánico *adj* tannic; **ácido** — tannic acid.
tanino *nm* tannin.
tano *nm* (*Arg, Urug: pej*) Neapolitan, Italian.
tanque *nm* (*in most senses*) tank; water store, reservoir; (*Mil*) tank; (*Aut*) tanker, tanker lorry.
tanquero *nm* (*Ven etc*) tanker.
tanquista *nm* (*Mil*) member of a tank-crew.
tanta *nf* (*Bol, Per*) maize bread.
tantán *nm* gong; tomtom.
tantarán *nm*, **tantarantán** *nm* **(a)** drumbeat, rub-a-dub. **(b)** (*fam*) hefty punch; violent shaking.
tanteada *nf* **(a)** (*SAm*) = **tanteo. (b)** (*Mex*) dirty trick; hoax, swindle.

tanteador *nm* **(a)** scoreboard. **(b)** scorer.
tantear [1a] **1** *vt* **(a)** *number, value etc* to reckon (up), work out roughly, try to calculate, guess; *cloth, quantity etc* to size up, take the measure of; *weight* to feel, get the feel of, try the weight of; (*fig*) to weigh up, consider carefully.
(b) to test, try out; to probe; *intentions, person* to sound out; — **si la superficie está bien segura** to test the surface to see if it is safe, see if the surface is safe.
(c) (*Art*) to sketch in, draw the outline of.
(d) (*Sport*) to keep the score of.
(e) (*Hond, Mex*) to lie in wait for.
(f) (*Mex*) to swindle; to make a fool of, take for a ride (*fam*).
2 *vi* **(a)** (*Sport*) to score, keep (the) score.
(b) (*SAm*) to grope, feel one's way; **¡tantee Vd!** fancy that!
tanteo *nm* **(a)** reckoning, rough calculation, guesswork; weighing up, careful consideration; **a** —, **por** — by guesswork.
(b) test(ing), trial; trial and error; **al** — by trial and error; **conversaciones de** — exploratory conversations.
(c) (*Sport*) scoring.
tantico: un — *adv* (*fam*) a bit, quite a bit; **es un** — **difícil** it's a wee bit awkward (*fam*).
tantísimo *adj superl* so much; —**s** so many; **había tantísima gente** there was such a crowd, there were so many people; **te lo he dicho tantísimas veces** I've told you lots of times.
tanto 1 *adj* so much, as much; so many, as many; **tiene — dinero como yo** he has as much money as I have; **tiene — dinero que no sabe qué hacer con él** he has so much money he doesn't know what to do with it; **hay — s sellos verdes como azules** there are as many green stamps as (there are) blue ones; **hubo tanta manzana** there were so many apples; **es uno de —s** it's one of many, it's one of a number; **hay otros —s candidatos** there are as many other candidates; **quedan por ver otros —s candidatos** there are as many candidates again still to be seen; **se dividen el trabajo en otras tantas porciones** they divide up the work into a like number of parts; **20 y —s** 20-odd; **hay ciento y —s concursantes** there are 100-odd competitors; **a —s de marzo** on such-and-such a day in March; **a —s de —s** on such-and-such a day in this or that month; **volver a casa a las tantas** to come home terribly late; **estar fuera hasta las tantas** to stay out until all hours.
2 *adv* so much, as much; **permanecer — to** stay so long; **trabajar — to** work so hard; **venir — to** come so often; **él gasta — como yo** he spends as much as I do; **gastó — que se quedó sin dinero** he spent so much that he ran out of money; — **A como B** both A and B; — **como eso . . .** I don't think it's as bad as all that, I think you're exaggerating; **es — más difícil** it is all the more difficult; **es — más loable cuanto que . . .** it is all the more praiseworthy because . . .; — **mejor** all the better, so much the better (*para* for); — **peor** so much the worse; **¡y —!** and how!, I'll say it is! (*etc*); — **es así que . . .** so much so that . . .; — **si viene como si no viene** whether he comes or whether he doesn't; **en —, entre** — meanwhile, meantime; **no es para** — it's not as bad as all that; there's no need to make such a fuss; **por —, por lo** — so, therefore; **¡ni — así!** not a scrap!; **no le tengo ni — así de lástima** I haven't a scrap of pity for him.
3 *conj*: **con — que . . .** provided (that) . . .; **en — que . . . while . . .; until . . .; hasta — que . . .** until (such time as) . . .
4 *nm* **(a)** (*Comm, Fin etc*) certain amount, so much; — **alzado** agreed price; overall estimate; **por un — alzado** for a lump sum; — **por palabra** rate per word, so much a word; — **por ciento** percentage; rate; **un — por cada semana de trabajo** so much for each week's work; **al** — at the same price.
(b) (*Sport*) point; goal; (*Gambling*) counter, chip; — **en contra** point against; — **a favor** point for; **apuntar los —s** to keep score; **apuntarse un** — to score a point; (*fig*) to stay one up.
(c) estar al — to be fully informed; to know the score (*fig*); **estar al — de los acontecimientos** to be fully abreast of events, be in touch with events; **poner a uno al** — to give someone the news (*de* about), put someone in the picture (*de* about).
(d) al — de because of; **al — de que . . .** because of the fact that . . .; with the excuse that . . ., on the pretext that . . .

(e) algún —, un — (*as adv*) rather, somewhat; **estoy un — cansado** I'm rather tired; **es un — difícil** it's a bit awkward.

Tanzanía *f* Tanzania.

tañer [2f] **1** *vt* (*Mus*) to play; *bell* to ring; **2** *vi* to drum with one's fingers.

tañido *nm* (*Mus*) sound; strains, notes; (*of bell*) ringing, pealing.

tapa *nf* **(a)** lid; cover, top, cap; (*of book*) cover; (*of cylinder*) head; **— de registro** manhole cover, inspection cover; **— de los sesos** brainbox, skull; **levantarse la — de los sesos** to blow one's brains out.
(b) (*of shoe*) heelplate.
(c) (*of canal*) sluice gate.
(d) (*Cook*) dish of hors d'oeuvres; snack, delicacy (*taken at the bar counter with drinks*).

tapa(a)gujeros *nm*, *pl* **tapa(a)gujeros** (*fam*) **(a)** jerry-builder. **(b)** (*fig*) stopgap, temporary measure.

tapabalazo *nm* (*Col, Hond, Mex*) trouser fly.

tapabarro *nm* (*Chi, Per*) mudguard.

tapaboca *nf*, **tapabocas** *nm*, *pl* **tapabocas** **(a)** slap. **(b)** muffler.

tapacubos *nm*, *pl* **tapacubos** hub cap.

tapadera *nf* lid, cover; cap.

tapadero *nm* stopper.

**tapadillo: de — ** *adv* secretly, stealthily.

tapado 1 *adj* **(a)** (*Chi, RPl*) *animal* all one colour.
(b) (*Col, Per*) lazy, slack; ignorant.
2 *nm* **(a)** (*Arg, Bol, Per*) buried treasure.
(b) (*Chi, RPl, Salv*) woman's coat; child's coat; (*SAm*) headscarf, shawl.
(c) (*Col, Guat, Hond*) dish of plantain and meat.

tapalcate *nm* (*CAm, Mex*) piece of junk, useless object; useless person.

tapalodo *nm* (*Per, PR*) mudguard.

tapanca *nf* (*Col, Chi, Ec, Per*) horse trappings.
(b) (*Chi*) backside.

tapaojo *nm* (*SAm*) blindfold, bandage (over the eyes); patch.

tapar [1a] **1** *vt* **(a)** (*general sense*) to cover, cover up (*de* with); *container, pot* to put the lid on; *bottle* to put the cap on, put the stopper in, stopper, cork; *face* to cover up, hide; to muffle up; (*in bed*) to wrap up; *pipe etc* to stop (up), block (up), obstruct; *hole* to plug; (*Archit*) to fill up, wall up, wall in; (*SAm*) *tooth* to fill; *object* to hide; *view* to obstruct, block; **el árbol tapa el sol a la ventana** the tree keeps the sunlight off the window, the tree prevents the sun from reaching the window; **el muro nos tapaba el viento** the wall protected us from the wind.
(b) (*fig*) *defeat etc* to cover up, conceal; *fugitive* to hide, conceal; *criminal* to cover up for.
(c) (*Col*) to crush, flatten; to rumple.
(d) (*Col: fig*) to abuse, insult.
2 taparse *vr* to wrap (oneself) up, (*esp*) to wrap up warmly (in bed).

tapara *nf* (*Arg, Ven*) calabash, gourd.

táparo *nm* (*Col*) **(a)** tinderbox. **(b)** one-eyed person; (*fig*) dolt.

tapayagua *nf* (*CAm, Mex*), **tapayagüe** *nm* (*Mex*) stormcloud; drizzle.

tapeque *nm* (*Bol*) equipment for a journey.

tapera *nf* (*SAm*) ruined farm, tumbledown house; abandoned village.

taperujarse [1a] *vr* (*fam*) to cover up one's face.

tapesco *nm* (*CAm, Mex*) hurdle (used as a bed), rough bed.

tapete *nm* table runner, table cover; **— verde** card table; **estar sobre el —** (*fig*) to be under discussion.

tapetusa *nf* (*Col*) contraband goods, contraband liquor.

tapia *nf* garden wall; mud wall, adobe wall.

tapial *nm* = **tapia.**

tapialera *nf* (*Ec*) = **tapia.**

tapiar [1b] *vt* to wall in; (*fig*) to block, stop up.

tapicería *nf* **(a)** (*art*) tapestry making; upholstery.
(b) tapestry; (*collectively*) tapestries, hangings; (*of furniture, car etc*) upholstery.

tapioca *nf* tapioca.

tapir *nm* tapir.

tapisca *nf* (*CAm, Mex*) maize harvest, corn harvest (*US*).

tapiscar [1g] *vt* (*CAm, Mex*) *maize* to harvest.

tapiz *nm* tapestry; carpet.

tapizado *nm* tapestries; carpeting; upholstery.

tapizar [1f] *vt* **(a)** *wall* to hang with tapestries; *furniture* to upholster, cover; *car* to upholster; *floor* to carpet, cover.
(b) (*fig*) to carpet (*con, de* with).

tapón 1 *adj* (*Pan, Par, Urug*) tailless.
2 *nm* **(a)** (*of bottle*) stopper, cap, top; cork; (*Tech*)

plug, bung, wad; (*Med*) tampon; **al primer —, zurrapa** (*fam*) well, the first shot was a failure.
(b) (*fam*) chubby person.
(c) (*Aut: fam*) slowcoach, slow driver.
(d) (*PR: Aut*) traffic jam.

taponar [1a] *vt* *bottle* to stopper, cork, put the cap on; *pipe* to plug, stop up, block; (*Med*) to tampon; **— los oídos** to stop up one's ears.

taponazo *nm* pop (*of a cork*).

tapujarse [1a] *vr* (*fam*) to muffle oneself up.

tapujo *nm* **(a)** muffler.
(b) (*fam*) deceit, humbug; subterfuge, dodge; **sin —s** honestly, openly, aboveboard; without beating about the bush; **andar con —s** to behave deceitfully, be involved in some shady business; **llevan no sé qué — entre manos** they're up to some dodge or other.

taquear [1a] **1** *vt* **(a)** (*SAm*) to shoot at.
(b) (*SAm*) to fill right up, pack tight (*de* with).
2 *vi* **(a)** (*Arg, Mex, Per*) to play billiards.
(b) (*Cu*) to dress in style.
(c) (*Mex*) to have a snack.
3 taquearse *vr* (*Col*) to get rich.

taquería *nf* (*Cu*) brazenness.

taquigrafía *nf* shorthand, stenography.

taquigráficamente *adv*: **coger un discurso —** to take a speech down in shorthand.

taquigráfico *adj* shorthand (*attr*).

taquígrafo *nm*, **taquígrafa** *nf* shorthand writer, stenographer.

taquilla *nf* **(a)** (*Rail*) booking office, ticket office; ticket window; (*Theat*) box office.
(b) (*Theat: Fin*) takings; (*Sport etc*) gate money, proceeds.
(c) file; filing cabinet; (*for tools etc*) locker.
(d) (*CAm*) bar, liquor store.
(e) (*CR, Chi, Ec, Per*) tack, brad.

taquillero 1 *adj*: **ser —** to be good (for the) box office, be a draw, be popular; **función taquillera** box-office success, big draw; **el actor más — del año** the actor who has been the biggest box-office draw of the year.
2 *nm*, **taquillera** *nf* clerk, ticket clerk.

taquimeca *nf* (*fam*), **taquimecanógrafa** *nf* shorthand typist.

taquímetro *nm* speedometer; (*Surveying*) tachymeter.

tara¹ *nf* **(a)** (*Comm*) tare. **(b)** (*fig*) defect, blemish.
(c) (*Arg*) **—s** physical defects.

tara² *nf* tally stick.

tarabilla 1 *nf* **(a)** (*Orn*) stonechat. **(b)** (*fam*) chatter.
2 *nmf* chatterbox; featherbrained person; useless individual, dead loss.

tarabita *nf* **(a)** tongue (*of belt, buckle*). **(b)** (*Col, Ec, Per*) cable of a rope bridge (*with hanging basket for carrying passengers across ravines*).

taracea *nf* inlay, marquetry.

taracear [1a] *vt* to inlay.

tarado *adj* **(a)** (*Comm etc*) damaged, defective, imperfect; *animal etc* maimed, weak. **(b)** (*RPl*) *person* physically impaired, crippled; odd, eccentric.

tarambana(s) *nmf* (*fam*) **(a)** harum-scarum, fly-by-night; crackpot; unreliable person. **(b)** chatterbox.

taranta *nf* **(a)** (*Arg, Ec*) tarantula. **(b)** (*CR, Ec*) mental disturbance, madness; (*Hond*) bewilderment.
(c) (*Mex*) drunkenness.

tarantear [1a] *vi* (*Arg*) to do something unexpected; to chop and change a lot; to behave strangely, be eccentric.

tarantela *nf* tarantella.

tarantín *nm* **(a)** (*CAm, Cu*) kitchen utensil. **(b)** (*Cu*) scaffold. **(c)** (*Ven*) mean little shop. **(d)** (*CAm, Mex*) **—es** things, gear (*fam*), odds and ends.

taranto *adj* (*Col*) dazed, bewildered.

tarántula *nf* tarantula.

tarar [1a] *vt* (*Comm*) to tare.

tararear [1a] *vti* to hum.

tarasca *nf* **(a)** carnival dragon, monster.
(b) (*fig*) glutton; person who is a drain on one's resources.
(c) (*fam*) old hag, old bag (*sl*).
(d) (*CR, Chi, Per*) big mouth; deformed mouth.

tarascada *nf* **(a)** bite; snap. **(b)** (*fam*) tart reply, snappy answer.

tarascar [1g] *vt* to bite, snap at.

tarasco *nm* (*Ec*) bite; snap.

tarascón *nm* (*SAm*) bite; snap.

tarasquear [1a] *vt* (*Arg, Mex, Nic*) to bite, snap at; to bite off.

tardanza *nf* **(a)** slowness. **(b)** delay.

tardar [1a] *vi* **(a)** to take a long time, be long; to be late; to delay, linger (on); **a más —, a todo —** at the latest; **aquí tardan mucho** they are very slow here, they take a long time here; **he tardado un poco debido a la lluvia** I'm a bit late because of the rain, I took longer (to get here) because of the rain; **tardamos 3 horas de A a B** we took 3 hours (to get) from A to B; **escribiré sin** — I'll write without delay.

(b) — **a** + *infin* to delay + *ger*, be slow to + *infin*; **no tardes a hacerlo** don't put off doing it.

(c) — **en** + *infin* to be slow to + *infin*, take a long time to + *infin*, be long in + *ger*; to be late in + *ger*; **tardó mucho en repararlo** he took a long time to repair it; **tardó 3 horas en encontrarlo** it took him 3 hours to find it, he spent 3 hours looking for it; **no tarde Vd en informarme** tell me at once, inform me without delay; **¿cuánto tardaremos en terminarlo?** how long shall we take to finish it?; **el público no tardó en reaccionar** the spectators were not slow to react.

2 *nf* afternoon; evening, early evening; **¡buenas —s!** good afternoon!; good evening!; **a la** — in the evening; by evening; **por la** — in the afternoon, in the evening; **función de la** — matinée; **de la** — **a la mañana** overnight, during the night; (*fig*) in no time at all.

tardecer [2d] *vi* = **atardecer**.
tardecica *nf*, **tardecita** *nf* nightfall, dusk.
tardecito *adv* (*Arg*, *Guat*, *PR*) rather late.
tardíamente *adv* late, belatedly; too late.
tardío *adj* late; overdue, belated, slow to arrive (*etc*); *fruit*, *vegetable* late.
tardo *adj* (a) slow, sluggish; dilatory. (b) slow (of understanding), dull, dense; — **de oído** hard of hearing.
tardón *adj* (*fam*) (a) slow; dilatory. (b) dim.
tarea *nf* job, task; chore; set piece of work, stint, amount of work set; — **de ocasión** chore; — **suelta** odd job; **todavía me queda mucha** — I've still got a lot left to do; **es una** — **poco grata** it's not a very satisfying job; **¡— le mando!** (*fam*) you've got a job on there!; you'll have your work cut out!
tareco *nm* (*Cu*, *Ec*, *Ven*) old thing, piece of junk; **—s** (*fig*) things, gear (*fam*), odds and ends.
tarifa *nf* tariff; rate; price list, list of charges; (*on vehicle*) fare; — **de agua** water rate, water charges; — **de suscripción** subscription rate; — **turística** tourist class, tourist rates.
tarifar [1a] **1** *vt* to price. **2** *vi* to fall out, quarrel.
tarima *nf* platform; low dais; stand; low bench, stool; bunk.
tarimaco *nm* (*Cu*) = **tareco**.
tarja[1] *nf* tally, tally stick.
tarja[2] *nf* (*fam*) swipe, bash (*fam*).
tarjar [1a] *vt* (a) to keep a tally of, notch up. (b) (*Chi*, *Per*) to cross out.
tarjeta *nf* card; — **de crédito** credit card; — **de identidad** identity card; — **de Navidad**, — **navideña** Christmas card; — **postal** postcard; — **de visita** visiting card, calling card (*US*); **dejar** — to leave one's card; **pasar** — to send in one's card.
tarpón *nm* tarpon.
tarquín *nm* mud, slime, ooze.
tarraconense 1 *adj* of Tarragona. **2** *nmf* native (*or* inhabitant) of Tarragona; **los —s** the people of Tarragona.
tarrajazo *nm* (a) (*Ec*, *PR*) unpleasant happening. (b) (*Guat*) blow; wound.
tarramenta *nf* (*Cu*, *Mex*) horns.
tarrayazo *nm* (a) (*Ant*, *Col*, *Mex*, *Ven*) cast (of a net). (b) (*PR*, *Ven*) violent blow.
tarrear [1a] *vt* (*Cu*) to cuckold.
tarro *nm* (a) pot, jar.
(b) (*Chi*, *Per*, *RPl*) tin, can; drum.
(c) (*Cu*, *Mex*, *PR*, *Urug*) horn.
(d) (*Bol*, *Col*, *Ec*, *Per*) top hat.
(e) (*Arg*) stroke of luck, fluke.
(f) (*Cu*) cuckolding.
(g) (*Cu*) difficult matter, complicated affair.
tarsana *nf* (*SAm*) soapbark.
tarso *nm* tarsus.
tarta *nf* cake; tart; sponge; — **de cumpleaños** birthday cake; — **de Reyes** Christmas cake.
tártago *nm* (a) (*Bot*) spurge.
(b) (*fam*) mishap, misfortune.
(c) (*fam*) practical joke.
(d) **darse un** — (*fam*) to slave, slog; to bustle about.
tartajear [1a] *vi* to stammer.
tartajeo *nm* stammer(ing).
tartajoso *adj* stammering, tongue-tied.

tartalear [1a] *vi* (a) to walk in a daze; to stagger, reel. (b) to stammer, be stuck for words.
tartamudear [1a] *vi* to stutter, stammer.
tartamudeo *nm* stutter(ing), stammer(ing).
tartamudez *nf* stutter, stammer, speech defect.
tartamudo 1 *adj* stuttering, stammering. **2** *nm*, **tartamuda** *nf* stutterer, stammerer.
tartán *nm* tartan.
tartancho *adj* (*Arg*, *Bol*) = **tartamudo**.
Tartaria *f* Tartary.
tartárico *adj* tartaric; **ácido** — tartaric acid.
tártaro[1] *nm* (*Chem etc*) tartar.
tártaro[2] **1** *adj* Tartar. **2** *nm*, **tártara** *nf* Tartar.
tarugo 1 *adj* (a) (*Guat*, *Mex*, *RPl*) stupid.
(b) (*SD*) fawning.
2 *nm* (a) lump, chunk (of wood *etc*); wooden peg; plug, stopper; chunk of stale bread; wooden paving block.
(b) (*Cu*) fright, scare.
(c) (*Guat*, *Mex*, *RPl*) chump (*fam*), blockhead.
tarumba *adj* (*fam*): **volver** — **a uno** to get someone all mixed up; to daze someone, fog someone; **volverse** — to get all mixed up, get completely bewildered; **esa chica me tiene** — I'm crazy about that girl.
tasa *nf* (a) (*act*) valuation; estimate, appraisal.
(b) measure, standard, norm.
(c) fixed price, official price, standard rate; — **de interés** rate of interest; **sin** — (*fig*) boundless, limitless; unstinted.
tasable *adj* ratable.
tasación *nf* valuation, assessment; (*fig*) appraisal; — **de un artículo** fixing of a price for an article.
tasadamente *adv* sparingly.
tasador *nm* valuer.
tasajear [1a] *vt* (*SAm*) = **atasajar**.
tasajo *nm* (a) dried beef, jerked beef; (*any*) piece of meat. (b) (*Col*) tall thin person.
tasajudo *adj* (*SAm*) tall and thin.
tasar [1a] *vt* (a) *article* to fix a price for, price (*en* at); to regulate; *work etc* to rate (*en* at).
(b) (*fig*) to value, appraise, assess (*en* at).
(c) to limit, put a limit on, restrict; to be sparing with, (*pej*) be mean with, stint; **les tasa a los niños hasta la leche** she even stints her children for milk.
tasca *nf* (*fam*) pub (*fam*), bar; dive (*fam*), joint (*sl*); **ir de** —**s** to go on a pub crawl (*fam*).
tascar [1g] *vt* (a) *flax etc* to swingle, beat. (b) *grass* to munch, champ; *bit* to champ; (*Ec*) to chew, crunch.
Tasmania *f* Tasmania.
tata 1 *nm* (a) (*Murcia*, *SAm*: *fam*) dad, daddy. (b) (*SAm*) = **taita** (b). 2 *nf* (a) (*fam*) nanny, nursemaid; maid. (b) (*SAm*) younger sister.
tatarabuelo *nm* great-great-grandfather; **los** —**s** one's great-great-grandparents.
tataranieto *nm* great-great-grandson.
tatas: andar a — to toddle; to crawl, get down on all fours.
tate *interj* (*surprise*) good heavens!, well well!; (*admiration*) bravo!; (*anger*) come now!; watch your step!; (*understanding*) so that's it!; oh I see!; (*warning*) look out!
tato *nm* (*prov*, *SAm*: *fam*) younger brother.
tatuaje *nm* (a) tattoo. (b) (*act*) tattooing.
tatuar [1d] *vt* to tattoo.
taumaturgo *nm* miracle-worker; (*fig*) wonder-worker.
taurino *adj* bullfighting (*attr*); **el negocio** — the bullfighting business; **leía una revista taurina** he was reading a bullfighting magazine.
taurómaco 1 *adj* bullfighting (*attr*). **2** *nm* bull-fighting expert.
tauromaquia *nf* (art of) bullfighting, tauromachy.
tauromáquico *adj* bullfighting (*attr*).
tautología *nf* tautology.
tautológico *adj* tautological.
taxativamente *adv* in a restricted sense, specifically.
taxativo *adj* limited, restricted; *sense* particular, concrete; specific.
taxi *nm* taxi, cab, taxicab.
taxidermia *nf* taxidermy.
taxidermista *nmf* taxidermist.
taxímetro *nm* taximeter, clock (*fam*).
taxista *nm* taxidriver, taximan, cabby (*fam*).
taxonomía *nf* taxonomy.
taxonomista *nmf* taxonomist.
taza *nf* (a) cup; cupful; — **de café** cup of coffee; — **para café** coffee cup, cup for coffee.
(b) (*of fountain*) basin, bowl; (*of lavatory*) bowl.
(c) (*Chi*) washbasin.
(d) (*Arg*) — **de noche** chamberpot.

tazado adj dress frayed, worn; person shabby.

tazar [1f] **1** vt (a) to cut; to cut up, divide. (b) to fray. **2 tazarse** vr to fray.

tazón nm large cup; bowl, basin; (Prov) washbasin.

te personal pron (a) (acc) you; (arch, to God) thee.
  (b) (dative) (to) you; (arch, to God) (to) thee; **te he traído esto** I've brought you this, I've brought this for you; **¿te duele mucho el brazo?** does your arm hurt much?
  (c) (reflexive) (to) yourself; (arch, to God) (to) thyself; **te vas a caer** you'll fall; **te equivocas** you're wrong; **¡cálmate!** calm yourself!

té nm (a) tea; tea party; **dar un —** to give a tea party. (b) (fam) **dar el — a uno** to bore someone to tears.

tea nf (a) torch; firelighter. (b) (fam) **coger una —**, **pillar una —** to get tight.

teatral adj (a) theatre (attr); dramatic; **obra —** dramatic work; **temporada —** theatre season.
  (b) (fig) theatrical, dramatic; (pej) histrionic, stagey.

teatralidad nf drama; sense of the theatre, stage sense; (pej) showmanship; histrionics, staginess.

teatralmente adv (a) dramatically. (b) (fig) theatrically, dramatically; (pej) histrionically.

teatro nm (a) (in general) theatre; **el — (as profession)** the theatre, the stage, acting; **— de aficionados** amateur theatre, amateur theatricals; **— de la ópera** opera house; **— de variedades** variety theatre, music hall, vaudeville theater (US); **escribir para el —** to write for the stage; **en el — es una persona muy distinta** she's a very different person on the stage; **hacer que se venga abajo el —** to bring the house down.
  (b) (Lit) drama, plays; **el — de Cervantes** Cervantes' plays, Cervantes' dramatic works; **selecciones del — del siglo XVIII** selections from 18th century drama.
  (c) (of event) scene; (Mil) theatre; **— de guerra** theatre of war, front.
  (d) (fig) **hacer —** to exaggerate, act affectedly; **ella tiene mucho —** she's terribly dramatic, she's given to histrionics.

Tebas Thebes.

tebeo nm children's comic.

teca nf teak.

tecla nf (Mus, of typewriter etc) key; **— de cambio** shift key; **dar en la —** (fam) to get it right; to get the hang of something; **dar en la — de + infin** (fam) to fall into the habit of + ger; **hay que tocar muchas —s a la vez** (fam) there are too many things to think about all together; **no le queda ninguna — por tocar** there's nothing else left for him to try.

teclado nm (Mus, of typewriter) keyboard, keys; (of organ) manual.

tecle adj (Chi) weak, sickly.

teclear [1a] **1** vt (a) (SAm) instrument to play clumsily, mess about on; typewriter to use clumsily.
  (b) (fam) problem to approach from various angles.
  2 vi (a) (Mus) to strum, thrum, play a few chords.
  (b) (fam) to drum, tap (with one's fingers).
  (c) (Arg, Chi) to be weak, be ill.
  (d) (Chi) to be very poor.
  (e) (Col, Chi, RPl: of business) to be going very badly.

tecleo nm (a) (Mus) fingering, playing; touch; strumming, thrumming. (b) (fam) drumming, tapping.

técnica nf technique; method; craft, skill **— electrónica** electronics.

técnicamente adv technically.

tecnicidad nf technicality.

tecnicismo nm (a) technical nature. (b) (Ling) technical term, technicality.

técnico **1** adj technical. **2** nm technician; expert, specialist; **es un — en la materia** he's an expert on the subject.

tecnicolor nm Technicolor (Protected Trade Name); **en —** in Technicolor.

tecnología nf technology.

tecnológico adj technological.

tecnólogo nm technologist.

teco adj (CAm, Mex) drunk.

tecolote **1** adj (a) (CR) reddish-brown. (b) (CAm, Mex) drunk. **2** nm (a) (CAm, Mex) eagle owl. (b) (Mex) policeman, cop (sl).

tecomate nm (CAm, Mex) gourd, calabash; earthenware cup, pan.

tecorral nm (Mex) dry-stone wall.

tecuán **1** adj (CAm, Mex) greedy, voracious. **2** nm monster.

techado nm roof, covering; **bajo —** under cover, indoors.

techar [1a] vt to roof (in, over).

techo nm (a) roof; ceiling; **bajo —** under cover, indoors; **tenis bajo —** indoor tennis. (b) (Aer) ceiling.

techumbre nf roof.

tedio nm (a) boredom, tedium. (b) lack of interest; depression; sense of emptiness; **a mí no me produce sino —** it just depresses me.

tedioso adj boring, tedious; wearisome; depressing.

tefe nm (a) (Col, Ec) strip of leather, strip of cloth. (b) (Ec) scar on the face; bruise.

tegumento nm tegument.

teísmo nm theism.

teísta **1** adj theistic. **2** nmf theist.

teja[1] nf tile; **pagar a toca —** to pay cash; to pay on the nail; **de —s abajo** in this world, in the natural way of things; **de —s arriba** in the next world; up aloft; with God's help.

teja[2] nf lime (tree).

tejadillo nm top, cover.

tejado nm roof, tiled roof; (fig) housetop; **tiene el — de vidrio** he himself is open to the same charge, he lives in a glass house and should not throw stones.

tejamaní nm, **tejamanil** nm (SAm) roofing board, shingle.

tejano **1** adj Texan. **2** nm, **tejana** nf Texan. **3 —s** nmpl jeans.

tejar [1a] vt to tile, roof with tiles.

Tejas m Texas.

tejaván nm (SAm) shed; corridor, gallery; eaves; rustic dwelling.

tejavana nf shed; shed roof, plain tile roof.

tejedor nm, **tejedora** nf (a) weaver. (b) (Chi, Per) intriguer, meddler.

tejedura nf (a) weaving. (b) weave, texture.

tejeduría nf (a) (art of) weaving. (b) textile mill.

tejemaneje nm (fam) (a) bustle; fuss, to-do (fam); **se trae un tremendo — con sus papeles** he's making a tremendous to-do with his papers, he's getting all worked up with his papers.
  (b) intrigue, shady business.

tejer [2a] **1** vt (a) to weave; to make; cobweb to make, spin; cocoon to spin; (esp SAm) to knit; to sew; to crochet.
  (b) (fig) to weave; to bring about little by little; lie, scandal etc to fabricate.
  2 vi: **— y destejer** to chop and change, blow hot and cold.

tejido nm (a) weave, woven material; web; fabric; **—s** textiles; **— de punto** knitting; knitted fabric. (b) weave, texture. (c) (Anat) tissue.

tejo[1] nm (a) ring, quoit. (b) hopscotch.

tejo[2] nm (Bot) yew (tree).

tejoleta nf bit of tile, sherd; brickbat.

tejón nm badger.

tela nf (a) cloth, fabric, material; **—s del corazón** (fig) heartstrings; **— cruzada** twill; **— metálica** wire netting; **— de saco** sackcloth; **en —** (Typ) clothbound.
  (b) (SAm: Art) canvas, painting.
  (c) (Ent etc) web; **— de araña** spider's web, cobweb.
  (d) (on liquid) skin, film.
  (e) (Bot) skin.
  (f) (sl) dough (sl).
  (g) (fig) subject, matter; **hay — que cortar, hay — para rato** there's plenty of material, there's lots to talk about; it's a long job; it's a tricky business.
  (h) **poner algo en — de juicio** to question, call in question, cast doubt on.
  (i) (Col) thin maize pancake.

telabrejos nmpl (SAm) things, gear (fam), odds and ends.

telar nm (a) loom; **—es** (fig) textile mill. (b) (Theat) gridiron.

telaraña nf spider's web, cobweb.

tele nf (fam) telly (fam).

tele ... tele ...

telebrejos nmpl (Mex) = **telabrejos**.

telecomando nm remote control.

telecomunicación nf telecommunication.

telecontrol nm remote control.

telediario nm television news bulletin.

teledifusión nf telecast.

teledirigido adj remote-controlled, radio-controlled.

teleférico nm ski lift; cable railway, cableway.

telefilm nm, **telefilme** nm (Acad) telefilm.

telefonazo *nm* telephone call; **te daré un — I'll give you a ring**, I'll call you up.
telefonear [1a] *vti* to telephone.
telefonema *nm* telephone message.
telefonía *nf* telephony.
telefónico *adj* telephonic; telephone (*attr*).
telefonista *nmf* (telephone) operator, telephonist.
teléfono *nm* telephone, phone; **el — rojo** (*Pol*) the hot line; **está hablando por —** he's on the phone; **llamar a uno al** (*or* **por**) **—** to telephone someone, phone someone, ring someone up, call someone (up); **le llaman al —** you're wanted on the phone.
telefoto(grafía) *nf* telephoto.
telefotográfico *adj* telephoto (*attr*).
telegrafía *nf* telegraphy.
telegrafiar [1c] *vti* to telegraph.
telegráfico *adj* telegraphic; telegraph (*attr*).
telegrafista *nmf* telegraphist.
telégrafo *nm* (a) telegraph. (b) **—s** (*fam*) telegram boy.
telegrama *nm* telegram; **poner un — a uno** to send someone a telegram.
teleimpresor *nm* teleprinter.
telémetro *nm* rangefinder.
telengues *nmpl* (*CAm*) things, gear (*fam*), odds and ends.
telenque *adj* (*Chi*) weak, feeble.
teleobjetivo *nm* telephoto lens.
teleología *nf* teleology.
telépata *nmf* telepathist.
telepático *adj* telepathic.
telescopar [1a] **1** *vt* to telescope. **2 telescoparse** *vr* to telescope.
telescópico *adj* telescopic.
telescopio *nm* telescope.
telesilla *nm* skilift, chairlift.
telespectador *nm*, **telespectadora** *nf* viewer, televiewer.
telesquí *nm* ski lift.
teletipista *nmf* teletypist, teleprinter operator.
teletipo *nm* teletype, teleprinter; **el — rojo** (*Pol*) the hot line.
teletubo *nm* cathode-ray tube, television tube.
televidente *nmf* viewer, televiewer.
televisar [1a] *vt* to televise.
televisión *nf* television; **— en colores** colour television; **— pagada** pay-television; **mirar la —** to watch television; **hacer —** to be doing television, be working in television, be engaged in television work.
televisivo *adj* television (*attr*); **serie televisiva** television serial (*or* series).
televisor *nm* television set.
telón *nm* (a) (*Theat*) curtain; **— de boca** front curtain; **— de fondo, — de foro** backcloth, backdrop; **— metálico** fire curtain; **— de seguridad** safety curtain. (b) (*Pol*) **— de acero** iron curtain.
telúrico *adj* of the earth, telluric; (*fig*) earthy.
tema[1] *nm* (a) theme; subject, topic; (*Mus*) theme, motif; (*Art*) subject; **— de actualidad** current issue; **—s de actualidad** current affairs; **el — de su discurso** the theme (*or* subject) of his speech; **es un tema muy manoseado** it's a subject which has often been discussed; **las autoridades tienen — de meditación** the authorities have food for thought, the authorities have something to think about. (b) (*Gram*) stem.
tema[2] *nf* (a) fixed idea, mania, obsession; **tener —** to be stubborn. (b) ill will, unreasoning hostility; **tener — a uno** to have a grudge against someone.
temar [1a] *vi* (*Arg, Par*) (a) to have a mania, be obsessed. (b) to bear ill will; **— con uno** to have a grudge against someone.
temario *nm* set of themes, collection of subjects; (*of meeting*) agenda, subjects for discussion.
temascal *nm* (*CAm, Mex*) bathroom; (*fig*) hot place, oven.
temático *adj* (a) thematic. (b) (*Gram*) stem (*attr*). (c) (*Col*) injudicious, tasteless.
tembladera *nf* (a) (*fam*) violent shaking. (b) (*SAm*) = **tembladeral**.
tembladeral *nm* (*Arg, Mex, Urug*) quaking bog, quagmire.
temblar [1k] *vi* (a) (*of person: with fear*) to tremble, shake; (*with cold*) to shiver; (*of building etc*) to shake, quiver, shudder; **— de frío** to shiver with cold; **— de miedo** to tremble with fright; **— ante una escena** to shudder at a sight; **— como un azogado** to shake like a leaf, tremble all over; **dejar una botella temblando** (*fam*) to use most of a bottle, make a bottle look pretty silly (*fam*).
(b) (*fig*) to tremble; **tiemblo de pensar en lo que pueda ocurrir** I tremble (*or* shudder) to think what may happen; **— por su vida** to fear for one's life.

tembleque *nm* (a) (*fam*) violent shaking; **le entró un —** he began to shake violently. (b) (*SAm*) sickly person, weakling.
temblequear [1a] *vi* (*fam*) to shake violently, be all of a quiver.
temblequera *nf* (*Per, PR*) fear; cowardice.
temblón **1** *adj* trembling, shaking; tremulous; **álamo — = 2** *nm* aspen.
temblor *nm* trembling, shaking; shiver, shivering, shudder, shuddering; (*SAm*) **— de tierra** earthquake; **le entró un — violento** he began to shake violently.
tembloroso *adj* trembling, tremulous; quivering; shivering; **con voz temblorosa** in a shaky voice, in a tremulous tone.
tembo *adj* (*Col*) featherbrained, stupid.
temer [2a] **1** *vt* (a) to fear, be afraid of; to dread; to go in awe of; **— + infin** to fear to + *infin*; **— a Dios** to fear God.
(b) (*fig*) **temo que lo ha perdido** I'm afraid he has lost it, I fear he has lost it; **teme que no vaya a volver** she's afraid (lest) he won't come back.
2 *vi* to be afraid; **no temas** don't be afraid, (*fig*) don't worry; **— por la seguridad de uno** to fear for someone's safety.
3 temerse *vr* = **1** (b).
temerariamente *adv* rashly, recklessly; boldly; hastily.
temerario *adj* act, person rash, reckless; bold; judgement etc hasty, rash.
temeridad *nf* (a) rashness, recklessness; boldness; hastiness. (b) rash act, folly.
temerón **1** *adj* bullying, ranting, loud-mouthed. **2** *nm* bully, ranter.
temerosamente *adv* timidly, fearfully.
temeroso *adj* (a) timid; fearful, frightened. (b) **— de Dios** full of the fear of God. (c) dread, frightful.
temible *adj* fearsome, dread, frightful; *opponent etc* redoubtable.
temor *nm* fear, dread; suspicion, mistrust; **— a fear of; — de Dios** fear of God; **por — from fear; por — a** for fear of; **sin — a** fearless of; regardless of; **sin — ni favor** without fear or favour.
témpano *nm* (a) (*also* **— de hielo**) ice floe; **quedarse como un —** (*fam*) to be chilled to the marrow. (b) (*Mus*) small drum, kettledrum. (c) (*Mus*) drumhead. (d) (*Archit*) tympan. (e) (*Cook*) **— de tocino** flitch of bacon.
temperadero *nm* (*SAm*) summer resort.
temperado *adj* (*Col*) = **templado**.
temperamental *adj* (a) temperamental. (b) (*angl*) temperamental.
temperamento *nm* (a) temperament, nature, disposition. (b) constitution. (c) (*angl*) temperament; **tener — to have a temperament**, be temperamental. (d) (*Pol etc*) compromise. (e) (*SAm*) climate, weather; summer.
temperancia *nf* temperance, moderation.
temperante (*SAm*) **1** *adj* teetotal. **2** *nmf* teetotaller, abstainer.
temperar [1a] **1** *vt* to temper, moderate; to calm; to relieve. **2** *vi* (*SAm*) to spend the summer, summer; to go to a warmer climate; to have a change of air.
temperatura *nf* temperature.
temperie *nf* state of the weather.
tempestad *nf* storm (*also fig*); **— en un vaso de agua** storm in a teacup; **levantar una — de protestas** to cause a storm of protests.
tempestuoso *adj* stormy (*also fig*).
templado *adj* (a) moderate, restrained; (*in eating*) frugal; (*in drinking*) of sober habits, abstemious. (b) *water* lukewarm; *climate* mild, temperate; *zone* (*Geog*) temperate. (c) (*Mus*) in tune, well-tuned. (d) (*fam*) bold, forthright; courageous. (e) (*fam*) *child* bright, lively; (*CAm, Mex*) clever; competent. (f) (*Col*) severe. (g) (*SAm*) half drunk. (h) (*Bol, Col, Chi*) **estar — to be in love.**
templanza *nf* (a) moderation, restraint; frugality; abstemiousness. (b) (*Meteorol*) mildness.
templar [1a] **1** *vt* (a) (*general sense*) to temper; to moderate, soften; *anger* to restrain, control; *climate* to make mild; *heat* to reduce; *solution* to dilute. (b) *room, water* to warm up (slightly). (c) (*Mus*) to tune (up). (d) (*Mech*) to adjust; *screw etc* to tighten up; *spring etc* to set properly.

(e) *steel* to temper.
(f) (*Art*) *colours* to blend.
(g) (*Col, Ec*) to knock down; (*CR*) to hit; to beat; (*Ec, Per*) to kill.
2 *vi* (a) (*of cold etc*) to moderate.
(b) (*Cu*) to flee.
3 templarse *vr* (a) (*person*) to be moderate, be restrained, act with restraint; **— en la comida** to eat frugally.
(b) (*water*) to warm up, get warm.
(c) (*Ec, Guat, Hond*) to die.
(d) (*Arg, Cu*) to flee; **—las** (*Cu, Mex*) to flee.
(e) (*Col, Per, PR*) to get drunk.
(f) (*Chi*) to fall in love.
(g) (*Chi*) to go too far, overstep the mark.
(h) (*Col*) **—las** to stand firm.
templario *nm* Templar.
temple *nm* (a) (*Tech*) temper; tempering.
(b) (*Mus*) tuning.
(c) (*Meteorol*) state of the weather, temperature.
(d) (*of person*) mood; **estar de mal —** to be in a bad mood.
(e) (*of person*) spirit, temper, mettle; (*SAm*) courage, boldness, resoluteness.
(f) distemper; (*Art*) tempera; **pintar al —** to distemper; (*Art*) to paint in tempera.
templete *nm* bandstand; pavilion.
templo *nm* (*pagan, masonic, fig*) temple; (*Eccl*) church, chapel; **— metodista** Methodist chapel; **— protestante** Protestant church; **como un —** (*esp SAm*) huge, tremendous; first-rate, excellent.
temporada *nf* time, period, spell; (*Meteorol*) spell; (*of year, social, sporting etc*) season; **— de fútbol** football season; **— de ópera** opera season; **— de exámenes** examination period; **— de lluvias** rainy spell; rainy season; **en plena —** at the height of the season; **estar fuera de —** to be out of season.
temporal 1 *adj* (a) temporary.
(b) (*Eccl etc*) temporal; **poder —** temporal power.
2 *nm* (a) storm; rainy weather, spell of rough weather; **capear el —** to weather the storm, ride out the storm (*also fig*).
(b) (*Cu*) shady character.
temporalmente *adv* temporarily.
temporáneo *adj* temporary.
témporas *nfpl* ember days.
temporero *adj worker* temporary, casual.
temporizar [1f] *vi* to temporize.
tempozonte *adj* (*Mex*) hunchbacked.
tempranal *adj land, plant etc* early.
tempranear [1a] *vi* (a) (*SAm*) to get up early. (b) (*Arg*) to sow early.
tempranero *adj* (a) (*Bot*) early. (b) *person* early, early-rising.
temprano 1 *adj* (a) *fruit etc* early.
(b) *years* youthful; *period, work etc* early.
2 *adv* early; too early, too soon; **lo más — posible** as soon as possible.
tenacidad *nf* (a) toughness. (b) tenacity. (c) ingrained nature; persistence; stubbornness.
tenacillas *nfpl* sugar tongs; curling tongs; (*Med etc*) tweezers, forceps; (*for candle*) snuffers.
tenamaste 1 *adj* (*CAm, Mex*) stubborn. **2** *nm* (a) (*CAm, Mex*) cooking stone. (b) (*Guat*) = **cachivache**.
tenaz *adj* (a) *material* tough, durable, resistant.
(b) *person* tenacious.
(c) *stain etc* hard to remove, that sticks fast; *ingrained*; *pain* persistent; *belief, resistance etc* stubborn.
tenaza *nf* (a) (*Bridge*) squeeze (a in). (b) **—s** (*Tech*) pliers, pincers; tongs; forceps; **unas —s** a pair of pliers (*etc*).
tenazmente *adv* tenaciously; stubbornly.
**tenazón: a —, de — ** *adv* suddenly; *shoot* without taking aim.
tenca¹ *nf* (*Fish*) tench.
tenca² *nf* (*Chi*) lie, swindle.
tencal *nm* wicker box, wicker poultry cage.
tendajo *nm* = **tendejón**.
tendal *nm* (a) awning.
(b) sheet spread to catch olives (*when shaken from the tree*).
(c) (*SAm*) heap, lot, abundance; lot of scattered objects (*or bodies etc*); confusion, disorder; **un — de** a lot of, a whole heap of.
(d) (*RPl*) shearing shed; (*Col, PR*) brickworks, tileworks; (*Cu, Nic*) sunny place for drying coffee; (*Chi*) small travelling shop.
(e) (*Bol*) flat field.
tendalada *nf* (*SAm*) = **tendal** (c).
tendalera *nf* mess, litter (of scattered objects).

tendear [1a] *vi* (*Mex*) to go window shopping.
tendedera *nf* (a) (*Cu, Guat, Mex*) clothesline. (b) (*Col*) = **tendal** (c).
tendedero *nm* drying place; clothesline, frame for drying clothes.
tendejón *nm* small shop; stall, booth.
tendencia *nf* tendency; trend; inclination; **— imperante** dominant trend, prevailing tendency; **— del mercado** (*Fin*) run of the market, price movement; **la — hacia el sinsombrerismo** the tendency (*or* trend) towards hatlessness; **una palabra con — a quedarse arcaica** a word tending to become archaic; **tener — a + infin** to have a tendency to + infin, tend to + infin, be inclined to + infin; **tener —s de zurdo** to have a tendency towards left-handedness.
tendenciosidad *nf* tendentiousness.
tendencioso *adj* tendentious.
ténder *nm* (*Rail*) tender.
tender [2g] **1** *vt* (a) to stretch; to spread, spread out, extend, lay out; *paint etc* to put on, apply; *tablecloth* to lay, spread; **tendieron el cadáver sobre el suelo** they stretched the corpse out on the floor.
(b) *washing* to hang out; *rope etc* to stretch (a to, de from), hang (de from); *hand* to stretch out, reach out; *bridge, railway* to build; *cable, track* to lay.
(c) *bow* to draw; *trap* to set (a for).
(d) (*SAm*) **— la cama** to make the bed; **— la mesa** to lay the table.
2 *vi*: **— a** to tend to, tend towards, have a tendency towards; **— a + infin** to tend to + infin; **las plantas tienden a la luz** plants grow (*or* turn) towards the light; **el color tiende a verde** the colour tends towards green; **ella tiende al pesimismo** she has a tendency to be pessimistic.
3 tenderse *vr* (a) to lie down, stretch (oneself) out.
(b) (*fig*) to let oneself go; to give up, let things go, stop bothering.
(c) (*horse*) to run at full gallop.
(d) (*Cards*) to lay down.
tenderete *nm* (a) = **tendedero**. (b) stall, barrow, market booth. (c) display of goods for sale (*etc*); (*fig*) litter (of objects), mess.
tendero *nm*, **tendera** *nf* shopkeeper, (*esp*) grocer.
tendida *nf* (*Arg*) shy, start (*of horse*).
tendido 1 *adj* (a) lying down; flat.
(b) *gallop* fast, flat out.
2 *nm* (a) (*Archit*) coat of plaster.
(b) (*also* **—s**) washing, clothes (hung out to dry).
(c) (*Taur*) front rows of seats.
(d) (*of cable, track*) laying.
(e) (*Cook*) batch of loaves.
(f) (*Col, Ec, Mex*) bedclothes.
(g) (*Cu, Pan*) long tether, rope.
(h) (*Mex*) stall, booth.
tendinoso *adj* sinewy.
tendón *nm* tendon, sinew.
tendré *etc see* **tener**.
tenducho *nm* poky little shop.
tenebrosidad *nf* (a) darkness; gloom(iness). (b) (*fig*) gloominess, dimness, blackness. (c) (*fig*) sinister nature, shadiness. (d) (*fig*) obscurity.
tenebroso *adj* (a) dark; gloomy, dismal. (b) (*fig*) *outlook etc* gloomy, dim, black. (c) (*pej*) *plot etc* sinister, dark, shady. (d) (*fig*) *style etc* obscure.
tenedor *nm* (a) (*Cook*) fork.
(b) (*Comm, Fin etc*) holder, bearer; **— de acciones** shareholder; **— de libros** book-keeper; **— de obligaciones** bondholder; **— de póliza** policyholder.
teneduría *nf*: **— de libros** book-keeping.
tenencia *nf* (a) tenancy, occupancy; (*of office*) tenure; (*of property*) possession; **— ilícita de armas** illegal possession of weapons.
(b) mayorship, period of office as mayor.
(c) (*Mil*) lieutenancy.
tener [2l] **1** *vt* (a) (*general sense*) to have; to have got; to possess; **— ojos azules** to have blue eyes; **hemos tenido muchas dificultades** we have had a lot of difficulties; **hoy no tenemos clase** we have no class today, we are not having a class today; **¿tienes una pluma?** have you got a pen?; **¿tiene Vd permiso para esto?** do you have permission for this?, have you (got) permission for this?; **va a — un niño** she's going to have a baby; **tiene un tío en Venezuela** he has an uncle in Venezuela; **tiene muchas preocupaciones encima** he has a lot of worries, he is burdened with anxieties; **el cargo tiene una buena retribución** the post carries a good salary; **de bueno no tiene nada** there's nothing good about it; *see* **particular, suerte** *etc*.
(b) (*idiomatic uses with certain nouns*) **— 7 años**

to be 7, be 7 years old; — **hambre** to be hungry; — **mucha sed** to be very thirsty; — **calor** to be hot; — **mucho frío** to be very cold; *for a full exposition see the noun in question, also* **celos, cuidado, ganas, miedo** *etc.*

(c) *(measurements)* — **5 cm de ancho** to be 5 cm wide; *see* **ancho, largo** *etc.*

(d) *object* to hold; to hold on to, hold up, grasp; to carry, bear; **ten esto** take this, hold on to this; **¡ten!, ¡tenga!** here you are!; catch!; **lo tenía en la mano** he was holding it in his hand; he was carrying it in his hand; **los dos que tenían la bandera** the two who were carrying the flag.

(e) *(of container)* to hold, contain; **una caja para** — **el dinero** a box to hold the money, a box to keep (*or* put) the money in.

(f) *promise* to keep.

(g) *(of feelings etc)* to have, profess *(a* for); — **gran admiración a uno** to have (a) great admiration for someone; **le tengo mucho cariño** I'm very fond of him; *see* **cariño** *etc.*

(h) to think, consider, deem; — **a bien** + *infin* to see fit to + *infin*, deign to + *infin*; to think it proper to + *infin*; — **a menos** + *infin* to consider it beneath oneself to + *infin*; — **a uno en más** to think all the more of someone; **te tendrán en más estima** they will hold you in higher esteem; — **para sí que** . . . to think that . . .; — **a uno por** + *adj* to think someone + *adj*, consider someone to be + *adj*, deem someone to be + *adj*; **no quiero que me tengan por informal** I don't want them to think me unreliable; **le tengo por poco honrado** I consider him to be rather dishonest; **lo tienen por cosa cierta** they believe it to be true; **ten por seguro que** . . . rest assured that . . .; *see* **más, mucho** *etc*; *see* **gala, honra** *etc.*

(i) (+ *adj)* **procura** — **contentos a todos** he tries to keep everybody happy; **me tiene perplejo la falta de noticias** the lack of news perplexes me, I am bewildered by the absence of news; *see* **cuidado, frito** *etc.*

(j) (+ *infin)* **no tengo nada que deciros** I have nothing to tell you; **tengo trabajo que hacer** I have work to do.

(k) — **que** + *infin* to have to + *infin*, must + *infin*; **tengo que comprarlo** I have to buy it; **tenemos que marcharnos** we have to leave, we must go; **así tiene que ser** it has to be this way; **¡tú tenías que ser!** it would be you!, it had to be you!

(l) (+ *ptp)* **tenemos alquilado un piso** we have rented a flat; **tenía el sombrero puesto** he had his hat on; **te lo tengo dicho muchas veces** I've told you hundreds of times; **nos tenían preparada una sorpresa** they had prepared a surprise for us; **teníamos andados unos 10 kilómetros** we had walked (*or* covered) some 10 kilometres.

(m) *(idioms)* **¿qué tienes?** what's the matter with you?; **¿ésas tenemos?** what's all this?; what on earth . . .? **no** —**las todas consigo** to be worried, feel uneasy; **no las tengo todas conmigo de que lo haga** I'm none too sure that he'll do it; **ten con ten** *(as n)* good sense, tact; ability to find a middle way.

(n) *(SAm)* **tienen 3 meses de no cobrar** they haven't been paid for 3 months; **este cadáver tiene un mes de muerto** this corpse has been dead for a month.

2 tenerse *vr* (a) to stand, stand up; **la muñeca se tiene de pie** the doll stands up; — **firme** to stand upright; *(fig)* to stand firm; **no poder** — to be all in, be tired out; to be incapable (with drink).

(b) — **sobre algo** to lean on something, support oneself on something.

(c) *(fig)* to control oneself; to stop in time.

(d) — **por** to consider oneself to be, think oneself; **se tiene por muy listo** he thinks himself very clever; — **en mucho** to have a high opinion of oneself; *(fig)* to be dignified; to be incapable of a mean action.

teneraje *nm (SAm)* calves.
tenería *nf* tannery.
tenga, tengo *etc see* **tener**.
tenguerengue *nm (Cu)* shack.
tenia *nf* tapeworm.
tenida *nf* (a) *(SAm)* meeting, session; meeting of a masonic lodge. (b) *(Arg, Chi)* suit, dress; uniform; — **de gala** *evéning* dress; — **de luto** mourning.
teniente *nm* lieutenant; — **coronel** lieutenant-colonel.
tenis *nm* tennis; — **de mesa** table tennis.
tenista *nmf* tennis player.
tenístico *adj* tennis *(attr)*.
tenor[1] *nm (Mus)* tenor.

tenor[2] *nm* tenor; meaning, sense, purport; **el** — **de esta declaración** the sense of this statement, the tenor of this declaration; **a este** — like this, in this fashion; **a** — **de** on the lines of, like; *(Comm)* in accordance with.
tenorio *nm* ladykiller, wolf *(fam)*, Don Juan.
tensamente *adv* tensely.
tensar [1a] *vt* to tauten; *bow* to draw.
tensión *nf* (a) *(in physical sense)* tension, tautness; *(Mech)* stress, strain; rigidity; — **superficial** surface tension.

(b) *(Phys: of gas etc)* pressure.

(c) *(Elec)* voltage; tension; **alta** — high tension; **cable de alta** — high-tension cable.

(d) *(Anat)* — **arterial** blood pressure; **tener** — to have blood pressure; **tener la** — **alta** to have high blood pressure.

(e) *(Med)* tension; strain, stress; — **excesiva** (over)strain; — **nerviosa** nervous strain.

(f) *(fig)* tension, tenseness; — **racial** racial tension; **la** — **de la situación política** the tenseness of the political situation.
tenso *adj* (a) tense, taut.

(b) *(fig)* tense; strained; **es una situación muy tensa** it is a very tense situation; **las relaciones entre los dos están muy tensas** relations between the two are very strained.
tensor 1 *adj* tensile. **2** *nm (Tech)* guy, strut; *(Anat)* tensor; *(of collar)* stiffener.
tentación *nf* (a) temptation; **resistir (a) la** — to resist temptation; **no puedo resistir (a) la** — **de** + *infin* I can't resist the temptation of + *ger*; **vencer la** — to overcome temptation.

(b) *(fam)* tempting thing; **las gambas son mi** — I can't resist prawns; **¡eres mi** —**!** you'll be the ruin of me!
tentáculo *nm* tentacle; feeler.
tentador 1 *adj* tempting. **2** *nm* tempter.
tentadora *nf* temptress.
tentar [1k] *vt* (a) to touch, feel; *(Med)* to probe; **ir tentando el camino** to feel one's way, grope one's way along.

(b) to try, test, try out; to undertake, venture on; — **(a) hacer algo** to try to do something, attempt to do something.

(c) to tempt *(also Rel)*; to attract, lure, entice; **me tentó con una copita de anís** she tempted me with a glass of anise; **no me tienta nada la idea** the idea doesn't attract me at all; — **a uno a hacer algo** to tempt someone to do something; **ella podría estar tentada también a probarlo** she might be tempted to try it too.
tentativa *nf* attempt; effort; *(Law)* criminal attempt; — **de asesinato** attempted murder.
tentativo *adj* tentative.
tentempié *nm (fam)* snack, bite.
tenue *adj* (a) *stick etc* thin, slim, slender; *wire* fine.

(b) *(fig)* tenuous; insubstantial, slight; *air, scent* thin; *mist* light; *line* faint; *sound* faint, weak; *connection etc* slight, tenuous; *style* simple.
tenuidad *nf* (a) thinness, slimness, slenderness; fineness.

(b) tenuousness; slightness; thinness; lightness; faintness; simplicity.

(c) *(una* —) triviality.
teñir [3h *and* 3l] *vt* (a) to dye; to tinge, colour; to stain; — **una prenda de azul** to dye a garment blue; **el jersé ha teñido los pañuelos** the jersey has come out on the handkerchiefs.

(b) *(Art) colour* to darken.

(c) *(fig)* to tinge *(de* with); **una poesía teñida de añoranza** a poem tinged with longing.
teocali *nm (Mex)* Aztec temple.
teocracia *nf* theocracy.
teocrático *adj* theocratic.
teodolito *nm* theodolite.
teología *nf* theology.
teológico *adj* theological.
teólogo *nm* theologian, theologist.
teorema *nm* theorem.
teorético *adj (SAm: angl)* theoretic(al).
teoría *nf* theory; — **atómica** atomic theory; — **cuántica,** — **de los cuanta** quantum theory; **en** — in theory, theoretically.
teóricamente *adv* theoretically, in theory.
teórico 1 *adj* theoretic(al). **2** *nm* theoretician.
teorizante *nm* theoretician, theorist; *(pej)* theorizer.
teorizar [1f] *vi* to theorize.
teosofía *nf* theosophy.
teosófico *adj* theosophical.
teósofo *nm* theosophist.

tepalcate nm (*Guat, Mex*) (**a**) earthenware jar; old pot, broken vessel; fragment of pottery, sherd. (**b**) = tapalcate.

tepalcatero nm (*Mex*) potter.

tepe nm sod, turf, clod.

tepetate nm (**a**) (*Hond, Mex*) mining waste, refuse. (**b**) (*Mex, Nic*) building stone; stone block, building block.

tepocate nm (*Guat, Mex*) (**a**) stone, pebble. (**b**) small boy.

tequila nf (*Mex*) liquor, brandy, tequila.

tequío nm (*CAm, Mex*) trouble; burden; harm, damage.

tequioso adj (*CAm, Mex*) burdensome; harmful; annoying, bothersome.

terapeuta nmf therapist.

terapéutica nf therapeutics; therapy.

terapéutico adj therapeutic(al).

ↄ **terapia** nf therapy; — **laboral** occupational therapy.

tercamente adv obstinately, stubbornly.

tercena nf (**a**) (*Mex*) government warehouse. (**b**) (*Ec*) butcher's (shop).

tercenista nm (**a**) (*Mex*) government warehouseman. (**b**) (*Ec*) butcher.

tercer see tercero.

tercera nf (**a**) (*Mus*) third. (**b**) (*pej*) go-between, procuress.

tercería nf mediation, arbitration; good offices; (*pej*) pimping, procuring.

tercero 1 adj (**tercer** before m sing noun) third; **a la tercera va la vencida** third time lucky.

2 nm (**a**) mediator, arbitrator; (*Law*) third person, third party.

(**b**) (*pej*) pimp, pander, procurer.

tercerola nf (*Ven*) shotgun.

terceto nm (**a**) (*Mus*) trio. (**b**) (*Lit*) tercet, triplet.

terciado adj (**a**) **azúcar terciada** brown sugar.

(**b**) **llevar algo** — to wear something diagonally (or across one's chest etc); **con el sombrero** — with his hat on the slant, with his hat at a rakish angle.

(**c**) **está terciado ya** a third of it has gone (or been used etc) already.

terciana nf (tertian) fever.

terciar [1b] 1 vt (**a**) (*Math*) to divide into three.

(**b**) (*Agr*) to plough a third time.

(**c**) to slant, slope; sash etc to wear (diagonally) across one's chest; hat etc to tilt, wear on the slant, put on at a rakish angle.

(**d**) (*Arg, Col, Mex*) to hoist on to (or carry on) one's shoulder.

(**e**) (*SAm*) wine etc to water down; (*Mex*) to mix, blend.

2 vi (**a**) to fill in, stand in, make up the number.

(**b**) — **en** to take part in, join in; — **con uno** to intervene on behalf of someone; — **entre dos rivales** to mediate between two rivals.

3 **terciarse** vr (**a**) **si se tercia una buena oportunidad** if a good chance presents itself (or comes up); **si se tercia, él también sabe hacerlo** on occasion he knows how to do it too, in the right circumstances he can manage it too.

(**b**) **si se tercia alguna vez que yo pase por allí** if I should happen sometime to go that way.

terciario adj tertiary.

tercio nm (**a**) third; **dos** —**s** two thirds.

(**b**) (*Mil: Hist*) regiment, corps; — **extranjero** foreign legion; — **de la guardia civil** division of the civil guard.

(**c**) (*Taur*) stage, part (of the bullfight).

(**d**) **hacer buen** — **a uno** to do a service for someone; to serve someone well, be useful to someone; **hacer mal** — **a uno** to do someone a bad turn; **estar mejorado en** — **y quinto** to come out of it very well.

(**e**) (*SAm*) pack, package, bale.

(**f**) (*Ven*) fellow, chap (fam).

terciopelo nm velvet.

terco adj (**a**) obstinate, stubborn. (**b**) material hard, tough, hard to work. (**c**) (*Ec*) harsh, unfeeling, indifferent.

tere adj (*Col*) (**a**) weepy, tearful. (**b**) weak, sickly.

terebrante adj pain sharp, piercing.

tereco nm (*Ec*) = tereque.

Terencio m Terence.

tereque nm (*Ant, Col, Ven*) (**a**) = **cachivache**. (**b**) —**s** things, gear (fam), odds and ends.

Teresa f Theresa.

tergiversación nf (**a**) distortion, misrepresentation. (**b**) prevarication.

tergiversar [1a] 1 vt to distort, twist (the sense of), misrepresent. 2 vi to prevaricate; to chop and change, blow hot and cold.

terliz nm ticking.

termal adj thermal.

termas nfpl hot springs, hot baths.

termes nm, pl **termes** (*Acad*) termite.

térmico adj thermic, heat (attr).

terminación nf (**a**) (act) ending, termination. (**b**) (part) ending, conclusion. (**c**) (*Gram*) ending, termination.

terminacho nm ugly word; incorrect word, malapropism, linguistic monstrosity; nasty word, rude word.

terminado nm (*Tech*) finish, finishing.

terminajo nm = terminacho.

terminal 1 adj terminal. 2 nm (*Elec*) terminal. 3 nf (*Naut, Rail* etc) terminal; (*SAm: Rail* etc) terminus.

terminante adj final, decisive, definitive; decision final; reply categorical, conclusive; refusal flat, forthright; prohibition strict.

terminantemente adv finally, decisively, definitively; categorically, conclusively; flatly; strictly; **queda** — **prohibido** + infin it is strictly forbidden to + infin.

terminar [1a] 1 vt to end; to conclude; to finish, complete.

2 vi (**a**) (of object etc) to end, finish; **termina en punta** it ends in a point, it comes to a point; **esto va a** — **en tragedia** this will end in tragedy.

(**b**) to end (up), finish; to stop; **al** — **el acto se fueron todos** at the end of the ceremony everyone went off; **¡hemos terminado!** that's an end of the matter!; — **de hacer algo** to finish doing something; to stop doing something; **cuando termine de hablar** when he finishes speaking; **terminaba de salir del baño** she had just got out of the bath; **terminó de llenar el vaso con helado** he topped (or filled) the glass up with ice cream; — **por hacer algo** to end (up) by doing something; **terminó marchándose enfadado** he ended up by going off in a huff, he finally went off very cross; **terminó diciendo que . . .** he ended by saying that . . . , he said in conclusion that . . .

3 **terminarse** vr to end, come to an end, draw to a close, stop.

terminista nm (*Chi*) pedant, affected speaker.

término nm (**a**) end, finish, conclusion; **dar** — **a** to finish off, conclude; **llevar a feliz** — to carry through to a happy conclusion; **poner** — **a** to put an end to, put a stop to.

(**b**) (of land etc) boundary, limit; boundary stone.

(**c**) (*Rail* etc) terminus.

(**d**) (*Pol*) area, district; (*Law*) jurisdiction; — **municipal** township.

(**e**) (*Art, Theat*) **primer** — foreground; **segundo** — middle distance; **último** — background.

(**f**) (*Math, Philos*) term; **medio** middle term; average; (fig) compromise, middle way; **de** — **medio** average; **por** — **medio** on the average; **tendrán que buscar un** — **medio** they will have to look for a compromise (or middle way); **en último** — in the last analysis; as a last resort, if there is no other way out.

(**g**) (of contract etc) term, time, period; **en el** — **de 10 días** within a period of 10 days.

(**h**) (in argument etc) point; **invertir los** —**s** to stand an argument on its head; (fig) to switch things round completely, turn a situation upside down.

(**i**) (*Ling*) term; **según los** —**s del contrato** according to the terms of the contract; **en** —**s sencillos** in simple terms; **en otros** —**s** in other words; **en** —**s de la productividad** in terms of productivity; **se expresó en** —**s conciliatorios** he expressed himself in conciliatory terms.

(**j**) **estar en buenos** —**s con uno** to be on good terms with someone.

terminología nf terminology.

terminológico adj terminological.

termita nf, **termite** nm termite.

termo[1] nm thermos (bottle, flask).

termo[2] . . . thermo . . .

termodinámica nf thermodynamics.

termodinámico adj thermodynamic.

termoeléctrico adj thermoelectric.

termoiónico adj thermionic.

termómetro nm thermometer.

termonuclear adj thermonuclear.

termopar nm thermocouple.

termopila nf thermopile.

Termópilas: Las — Thermopylae.

termos nm, pl **termos** = **termo**[1].

termostático adj thermostatic.

termostato nm thermostat.

ternario *adj* ternary.
terne 1 *adj* (a) tough, strong, husky; (*pej*) bullying. (b) stubborn; — **que** — out of sheer stubbornness. **2** *nm* bully, tough (*fam*).
ternejo *adj* (*Ec*, *Per*) active, vigorous.
ternera *nf* (a) (*Agr*) calf, heifer calf. (b) (*Cook*) veal.
ternero *nm* calf, bull calf.
ternerón *adj* (a) (*fam*) soft-hearted. (b) (*Chi*, *Mex*) lad overgrown, big.
terneza *nf* (a) tenderness. (b) —s nice things, endearments, tender words.
ternilla *nf* gristle, cartilage; (*Cu*, *Mex*, *Nic*) cartilage of the nose.
ternilloso *adj* gristly, cartilaginous.
terno *nm* (a) set of three, group of three; trio; three-piece suit; (*Cu*, *PR*) set of three jewels.
(b) (*fam*) curse, swearword; **echar** (*or* **soltar**) —s to curse, swear.
ternura *nf* (a) tenderness; fondness, affection. (b) endearment, tender word.
Terpsícore *f* Terpsichore.
terquedad *nf* (a) obstinacy, stubbornness. (b) hardness, toughness. (c) (*Ec*) harshness, lack of feeling; indifference.
terracota *nf* terracotta.
terrado *nm* terrace; flat roof.
terraja *nf* diestock.
terral *nm* cloud of dust.
Terranova *f* Newfoundland.
terranova *nm* Newfoundland dog.
terraplén *nm* (a) (*Rail etc*) embankment; (*Agr*) terrace; (*Mil*) rampart, bank, earthwork; mound. (b) slope, gradient.
terraplenar [1a] *vt* to level (off); (*Agr*) to terrace; **hole** to fill in; to bank up, raise.
terrateniente *nmf* landowner.
terraza *nf* (a) (*Archit*) flat roof; balcony; terrace. (b) (*Agr*) terrace. (c) (*Hort*) flowerbed, border, plot. (d) (*Cook*) two-handled glazed jar.
terregal *nm* (*SAm*) clod, hard lump of earth; (*Mex*) loose earth, dusty soil.
terremoto *nm* earthquake.
terrenal *adj* earthly, worldly.
terreno 1 *adj* terrestrial; earthly, worldly.
2 *nm* (a) (*in general*, *Geol etc*) terrain; soil, earth, ground, land; (*Agr*) soil, land; **los accidentes del** — the characteristics of the terrain, the features of the landscape; — **abonado para el vicio** hotbed of vice, breeding ground of vice; **en todos los** —s in any place you care to name; **un coche para todo** — a car for every type of surface, a car for all conditions; **sobre el** — on the spot; **hay que fiarse del hombre sobre el** — you have to trust the man on the spot; **resolveremos el problema sobre el** — we will solve the problem as we go along; **ceder** —, **perder** — to give ground, lose ground (*a*, *ante* to); **ganar** — to gain ground; **llegar al** — to arrive on the scene, get to the spot; **medir el** — (*fig*) to see how the land lies; **mirar** (*or* **socavar**) **el** — **a uno** to undermine someone's position; **preparar el** — (*fig*) to pave the way (*a* for).
(b) (**un** —) piece of land, piece of ground; (*for building*) plot, lot, site; (*Agr*) plot, field, patch; (*Sport*) field, pitch, ground; — **beneficial** (*Eccl*) glebe, glebe land; — **de camping** camping site; — **de fútbol** football ground, football pitch; — **de pasto** pasture; **un** — **plantado de patatas** a field planted with potatoes; **vender unos** —s to sell some land; **repartir** — **a los campesinos** to distribute land to the peasants.
(c) (*fig*) field, sphere; **en el** — **de la química** in the field of chemistry; **eso no es mi** — that's not (in) my field.
térreo *adj* earthen; earthy.
terrero 1 *adj* (a) earthy; of earth. (b) *flight* low, skimming. (c) (*fig*) humble. **2** *nm* pile, heap; (*Min*) dump.
terrestre *adj* terrestrial; earthly; ground (*attr*), land (*attr*); *route* land (*attr*), overland (*attr*); *forces* (*Mil*) ground (*attr*).
terrible *adj* terrible, dreadful, awful (*also fam*).
terriblemente *adv* terribly, dreadfully, awfully (*also fam*).
terrier *nm* terrier.
terrífico *adj* terrifying.
territorial *adj* territorial.
territorialidad *nf* territoriality.
territorio *nm* territory; — **bajo mandato** mandated territory.
terrón *nm* (a) (*Geol*) clod, lump, sod. (b) (*of flour*, *sugar etc*) lump; **azúcar en** — lump sugar. (c) (*Agr*) field, patch; —es (*fig*) land.

terronera *nf* (*Col*) terror, fright.
terror *nm* terror; — **pánico** panic.
terrorífico *adj* terrifying, frightening.
terrorismo *nm* terrorism.
terrorista 1 *adj* terrorist. **2** *nm* terrorist.
terroso *adj* earthy.
terruño *nm* (a) lump, clod. (b) plot, piece of ground; (*fig*) native soil, home (ground); **apego al** — attachment to one's native soil.
terso *adj* (a) smooth; glossy, polished, shining; **piel tersa** smooth skin, soft skin. (b) *style* smooth, polished, flowing.
tersura *nf* (a) smoothness; glossiness, polish, shine. (b) smoothness, flow.
tertulia *nf* (a) social gathering, regular informal gathering; (*in café etc*) group, circle, set; — **literaria** literary circle, literary gathering; **estar de** —, **hacer** — to get together, meet informally and talk; **hoy no hay** — there's no meeting today, the group is not meeting today.
(b) clubroom, games room.
(c) (*Arg*, *Cu*) upper gallery.
Tertuliano *m* Tertullian.
tertuliano *nm*, **tertuliana** *nf* member of a social gathering (*etc*).
tertuliar [1b] *vi* (*SAm*) to attend a social gathering; to get together, meet informally and talk.
terylene *nm* Terylene (*Protected Trade Name*).
Tesalia *f* Thessaly.
tesar [1k] *vt* to tauten, tighten up.
tescal *nm* (*Mex*) stony ground, rocky area.
Teseo *m* Theseus.
tesina *nf* minor thesis, dissertation (*for first degree*).
tesis *nf*, *pl* **tesis** thesis.
teso *adj* taut, tight; tense.
tesón *nm* insistence; tenacity, persistence; firmness; **resistir con** — to resist firmly, resist staunchly.
tesonero *adj* (*SAm*) tenacious, persistent; firm.
tesorería *nf* treasurership, office of treasurer.
tesorero *nm*, **tesorera** *nf* treasurer.
tesoro *nm* (a) treasure; hoard; — **escondido** buried treasure; secret hoard; **valer un** — to be worth a fortune; (*person*) to be a real treasure.
(b) (*Fin*, *Pol etc*) treasury; **T— público** Exchequer, Treasury.
(c) (*Lit*) thesaurus.
(d) (*fig*) treasure; **¡sí, —!** yes, my treasure!; **el libro es un** — **de datos** the book is a mine of information; **es un** — **de recuerdos** it is a treasure-house of memories; **tenemos una cocinera que es todo un** — we have a real gem of a cook, we have a cook who is a real treasure.
Tespis *m* Thespis.
test [tes] *nm*, *pl* **tests** [tes] (*angl*) test; aptitude test, psychological test.
testa *nf* (a) head; — **coronada** crowned head. (b) (*fam*) brains; gumption (*fam*).
testador *nm* testator.
testadora *nf* testatrix.
testaduro *adj* (*Ant*) =**testarudo**.
testaferro *nm* (a) figurehead; front man. (b) (*Comm*) dummy.
testamentaria *nf* executrix.
testamentaría *nf* (a) execution of a will. (b) estate.
testamentario 1 *adj* testamentary. **2** *nm* executor.
testamento *nm* (a) will, testament; **hacer** —, **otorgar** — to make one's will.
(b) **Antiguo T** — Old Testament; **Nuevo T** — New Testament.
(c) (*fam*) screed.
testar[1] [1a] *vi* to make a will.
testar[2] [1a] *vt* (*Ec*) to underline.
testarada *nf*, **testarazo** *nm* (*fam*) bump on the head; **darse una testarada** to bump one's head, give oneself a bang on the head.
testarudez *nf* stubbornness, pigheadedness.
testarudo *adj* stubborn, pigheaded.
testear [1a] (*SAm*: *angl*) **1** *vt* to test. **2** *vi* to do a test, undergo a test.
testera *nf* front, face; (*Zool*) forehead.
testero *nm* (a) =**testera**. (b) bedhead. (c) (*Archit*) wall.
testes *nmpl* testes.
testículo *nm* testicle.
testificación *nf* (a) testification. (b) =**testimonio**.
testificar [1g] **1** *vt* (a) to attest; to testify to, give evidence of. (b) (*fig*) to attest, testify to. **2** *vi* to testify, give evidence; — **de** = **1** (a).
testigo *nmf* (a) (*Law etc*) witness;' — **de cargo** witness for the prosecution; — **de descargo** witness for the defence; — **del novio** (*approx*) best man; — **ocular**, — **presencial**, — **de vista** eyewitness; —

pericial expert witness; **poner a uno por —** to cite someone as a witness.
(b) (in experiment) control.
(c) (in relay race) baton.
testimoniar [1b] vt to testify to, bear witness to; (fig) to show, demonstrate.
testimonio nm testimony, evidence; affidavit; **falso —** perjured evidence; **dar —** to testify (de to), give evidence (de of); **en — de mi afecto** as a token (or mark) of my affection.
teta nf teat; nipple; (fam) breast; **dar (la) — a** to suckle, breast-feed; **quitar la — a** to wean; **niño de — baby** still at the breast.
tétanos nm tetanus.
tetelque adj (CAm, Mex) sharp, bitter.
tetera[1] nf teapot; tea urn.
tetera[2] nf (Cu, Mex, PR) rubber teat; (PR) feeding bottle; (Mex) vessel with a spout.
tetero nm (Col, PR, Ven) feeding bottle.
tetilla nf (a) (Anat) (man's) nipple. (b) rubber teat.
Tetis f Thetis.
tetón[1] nm bubble, swelling (on a tyre etc).
tetón[2] adj (Chi) stupid.
tetraedro nm tetrahedron.
tetrágono nm tetragon.
tetrámetro nm tetrameter.
tetramotor adj four-engined.
tétrico adj gloomy, dismal; mood gloomy, pessimistic; sullen; light dim, wan.
tetuda adj (fam) big-breasted, bosomy (fam).
tetunte nm (CAm) large shapeless mass; rough bundle.
teutón nm, **teutona** nf Teuton.
teutónico adj Teutonic.
teveo nm=**tebeo**.
textil 1 adj textile. 2 **—es** nmpl textiles.
texto nm text; **grabado fuera de —** full-page illustration.
textual adj (a) textual. (b) (fig) exact; literal; **son sus palabras —es** those are his exact words.
textualmente adv (a) textually. (b) (fig) exactly; literally.
textura nf texture (also fig).
tez nf complexion, skin; colouring.
ti pron (used after prep) you; yourself; (arch, to God) thee, thyself; **es para —** it's for you; **¿lo has comprado para —?** did you buy it for yourself?; **esto no se refiere a —** this doesn't refer to you.
tía nf (a) aunt; **— abuela** great-aunt; **¡no hay tu —!** nothing doing!; **¡cuéntaselo a tu —!** tell that to the marines!
(b) before name as title of respect, not translated: **unos dulces para la — Dulcinea** some sweets for Dulcinea.
(c) (sl) bird (sl), dame (sl), girl; (pej) coarse woman, old bag (sl); whore.
tiamina nf thiamine.
tiangue nm (CAm) small market; booth, stall; (Ec) cattle market.
tibante adj (Col) haughty.
tibe nm (Col, Cu) whetstone.
Tíber m Tiber.
Tiberio m Tiberius.
tiberio 1 adj (Guat, Mex) drunk. 2 nm (a) (fam) uproar, row; set-to (fam). (b) (Guat, Mex) drinking spree (fam).
Tibet: **El —** Tibet.
tibetano 1 adj Tibetan. 2 nm, **tibetana** nf Tibetan. 3 nm (language) Tibetan.
tibia nf tibia.
tibiarse [1b] vr (CAm, Col, Per, Ven) to get cross.
tibieza nf (a) lukewarmness, tepidness. (b) (fig) lukewarmness; coolness, lack of enthusiasm.
tibio adj (a) water etc lukewarm, tepid.
(b) (fig) person, belief etc lukewarm; cool, unenthusiastic; **estar — con uno** to be cool to someone, behave distantly towards someone.
(c) **poner — a uno** to hurl abuse at someone, give someone a verbal battering; to say dreadful things about someone.
(d) (CAm, Col, Per, Ven) cross, angry.
tiburón nm (a) shark. (b) (fig) go-getter, unscrupulous person; (Arg) wolf (fam), Don Juan.
tic, nm, pl **tics** [tik] (a) tap; click; (of clock) tick, tick tock. (b) (Med) tic (also **— nervioso**).
Ticiano m Titian.
tico (CAm) 1 adj Costa Rican. 2 nm, **tica** nf Costa Rican.
tictac nm (of clock) tick, tick tock; (of heart) beat; (of typewriter) tapping, tip-tap; **hacer —** to tick; to beat, go pit-a-pat; to tip-tap.
tiempecito nm (SAm) (spell of) very bad weather.
tiempla nf (Chi) drunkenness.

tiemple nm (Chi) (a) love-making, courting. (b) lover.
tiempo nm (a) (in general) time; **— libre** spare time, free time, leisure; **a —** in time, in good time, early; at the right time; **a un —, al mismo —** at the same time; **a su debido —** in due course; **al poco —** very soon, soon after; **a — que . . . a** at the time that . . ., while . . .; **al mismo — que . . .** at the same time as . . .; **cada cierto —** every so often; **con — in** time, in good time, early; **con el —** eventually, in time; **¿cuánto — se va a quedar?** how long is he staying?; **de — en —** from time to time; **de algún — a esta parte** for some time past; **una costumbre de mucho —** a long-standing custom; **fuera de —** at the wrong time; **necesito más —** I need longer, I need more time; **no puede quedarse más —** he can't stay any longer; **mucho —** a long time, a long while; **todo el — all** the time; **el — es de oro** time is money; time is precious; **el — lo es todo** time is everything, time is of the essence; **es — perdido hablar con él** it's a waste of time talking to him; **andando el —** in due course, in time; in the fullness of time; **el — apremia** time presses; **dar — al —** to consider all the possibilities; to let matters take their course; **darse buen —** to have a good time; **el — dirá** time will tell; **apenas dispongo de mi —** I can scarcely call my time my own; **engañar el —, matar el —** to kill time; **hacer —** to while away the time; to mark time; **hace mucho —** a long time ago; **hace bastante — que lo compré** I bought it a good while ago; **desde hace mucho —** for a long time; **hace mucho — que no voy** I haven't been for a long time; **perder el —** to waste time; to fool around; **sin perder —** without delay; **tener — para** to have time for.
(b) (limited, specific) time, period, age; **—s modernos** modern times; **en — de los griegos** in the time of the Greeks; **en estos —s nuestros** in this day and age; **en los —s que corremos** in these dreadful times; **en mis —s** in my day; **en los buenos —s** in the good old days; **en mis buenos —s** when I was in my prime; **en otro —** formerly; once upon a time; **en — de Maricastaña, en — del rey que rabió** way back, long ago; in the good old days; **estar en el — de las vacas flacas** to have fallen on hard times; **los —s están revueltos** the times are out of joint, these are disturbed times; **hay que ir con los —s** one must keep abreast of the times.
(c) (of person) age; **A y B son del mismo —** A and B are the same age; **¿cuánto — tiene el pequeño?** how old is the child?
(d) (Sport) half; **primer —** first half.
(e) (Mus) tempo, time.
(f) (Mus: of symphony etc) movement.
(g) (Gram) tense; **— compuesto** compound tense; **en — presente** in the present tense.
(h) (Meteorol) weather; **si dura el mal —** if the bad weather continues; **hace buen —** it's fine, the weather is good, the weather is fine; **¿qué — hará mañana?** what will the weather be like tomorrow?; **a mal —, buena cara** one must make the best of a bad job.
(i) (Naut) stormy weather, rough weather.
(j) (Mech) cycle; **motor de 2 —s** two-stroke engine.
tienda nf (a) (Comm) shop, store; (esp) grocer's; (Cu, Chi, RPl, Ven) draper's, clothier's; **— de coloniales, — de comestibles, — de ultramarinos** grocer's (shop), grocery (US); **ir de —s** to go shopping; **poner —** to set up shop.
(b) (Naut etc) awning; **— de campaña** tent; **— de oxígeno** oxygen tent.
tienta nf (a) (Med) probe.
(b) cleverness; wisdom, good sense.
(c) **a —s** gropingly, blindly; **andar a —s** to grope one's way along, feel one's way; (fig) to feel one's way; **decir algo a —s** to throw out a remark at random, say something to see what effect it has.
tiento nm (a) feel, feeling, touch; (fam) touch (sl), tickle; (fam) pass; **a — by** touch; gropingly; (fig) uncertainly; **echar un — a una chica** to make a pass at a girl, try it on with a girl; **a 40 dólares nadie le echó un —** at 40 dollars nobody was biting, at 40 dollars he didn't get a tickle; **perder el —** to lose one's touch.
(b) (fig) tact; care; wariness, circumspection; **ir con —** to go carefully, go cautiously.
(c) (Art etc) steadiness of hand, steady hand.
(d) (Zool) feeler, tentacle; (Circus) balancing pole; blind man's stick.
(e) (Mus) preliminary flourish, scale, notes played in tuning up.
(f) (fam) blow, punch; **dar —s a uno** to hit someone.

(g) (*fam*) swig (*fam*); **dar un —** to take a swig (*a from*).

(h) (*SAm*) thong of raw leather, rawhide strap.

(i) (*Arg, PR*) snack.

tiernamente *adv* tenderly.

tierno *adj* (*in most senses*) tender; soft; *bread etc* new, fresh.

tierra *nf* **(a)** (*Astron*) earth, world.

(b) (*as surface, not sea*) land; **— firme** mainland; dry land; **— de nadie** no-man's land; **— quemada** scorched earth; **— adentro** inland; (*SAm*) interior, remote area; **por —** by land, overland; **besar la —** to fall flat; **caer a —** to fall down; **caer por —** to fall to the ground (*also fig*); **dar con algo en —** to drop something; to knock something over; (*fig*) to overthrow something; **echar a —** to demolish, pull down; to raze to the ground; **echar** (*or* **tirar**) **algo por —** to ruin something, upset something; **perder —** to lose one's footing; to get out of one's depth; **poner un avión en —** to land a plane; **poner — por medio** to get out quick, get as far away as possible; **saltar en** (*or* **a**) **—** (*from boat*) to leap ashore; **tocar —** (*Aer*) to touch down; **tomar —** (*Aer*) to land, come down; (*Naut*) to reach harbour.

(c) (*Geol etc*) land, soil, earth, ground; **— de batán** fuller's earth; **— de brezo** peat; **— vegetal** topsoil; **echar — a un asunto** to hush an affair up; to forget about a matter; **echar — a uno** (*Mex, RPl*) to speak damagingly of someone.

(d) (*Agr*) land; **—s** lands, estate(s); **— baldía** wasteland; **— de labor** agricultural land; **— de pan llevar** arable land, corn-growing land; **en cualquier — de garbanzos** all over; **heredó unas —s en la provincia** he inherited some land in the province.

(e) (*Pol etc*) country; **su —** one's own country, one's native land; one's own region, one's home area; **— natal** native land; **— prometida,** *or* **— de promisión** land of promise, promised land; **ver —s** to see the world; **vamos a nuestra — a pasar las Navidades** we go home for Christmas; **no es de estas —s** he's not from these parts; **¿tienen tractores en tu —?** do they have tractors where you come from?, do they have tractors in your part of the world?

(f) (*Elec*) earth, ground (*US*); **conectar un aparato a —** to earth a piece of apparatus, ground a piece of apparatus (*US*).

(g) (*SAm*) dust.

tierrafría *nmf* (*Col*) highlander.

tierral *nm* (*SAm*) cloud of dust.

Tierra *f* **Santa** Holy Land.

tierrero *nm* (*SAm*) cloud of dust.

tieso 1 *adj* **(a)** stiff, rigid; erect; taut; **con las orejas tiesas** with its ears erect; **quedarse —** (*fig*) to be frozen stiff.

(b) (*fig*) fit; sprightly; chirpy; **le encontré muy — a pesar de su enfermedad** I found him very fit in spite of his illness.

(c) (*fig*) stiff (in manner); rigid (in attitude); **— como un ajo** as stiff as a poker; **me recibió muy —** he received me very stiffly.

(d) (*fam*) proud; conceited, stuck-up (*fam*); smug; **— de cogote** haughty; **iba tan — con la novia al brazo** he was walking so proudly with his girl on his arm; *see* **ajo**.

(e) stubborn; firm, confident; **— que —** as stubborn as they come; **ponerse — con uno** to stand one's ground, insist on one's rights; (*pej*) to be stubborn; **tenerlas tiesas con uno** to put up a firm resistance to someone, stand up for oneself.

2 *adv* strongly, energetically, hard.

tiesto *nm* **(a)** (*Hort*) flowerpot. **(b)** sherd, piece of pottery. **(c)** (*Chi, Urug*) pot, vessel; (*Chi*) chamberpot.

tiesura *nf* **(a)** stiffness, rigidity; erectness; tautness. **(b)** (*fig*) stiffness; rigidity. **(c)** (*fam*) conceit. **(d)** stubbornness; firmness, confidence.

tifiar [1b] *vt* (*Cu*) to steal.

tifitifi *nm* (*Cu, PR*) theft.

tifo *nm* typhus; **— de América** yellow fever; **— asiático** cholera; **— de Oriente** bubonic plague.

tifoidea *nf* (*also* **fiebre —**) typhoid.

tifón *nm* **(a)** typhoon. **(b)** waterspout. **(c)** (*Mex*) outcrop of ore.

tifus *nm* **(a)** (*Med*) typhus; **— exantemático** spotted fever; **— icteroides** yellow fever.

(b) (*Theat: fam*) persons having complimentary tickets (*or* free seats); claque; **entrar de —** to get in free.

tigra *nf* (*SAm*) female tiger; female jaguar; (*Arg, Col*) **ponerse como una — parida** to fly into a violent rage.

tigre *nm* **(a)** tiger; (*SAm*) jaguar. **(b)** (*Col*) black coffee with a dash of milk; (*Col, Ec*) cocktail.

tigrero 1 *adj* (*Arg*) brave. **2** *nm* (*SAm*) jaguar hunter.

tigresa *nf* tigress.

tigridia *nf* tiger lily.

tigrillo *nm* (*SAm*) member of the cat tribe, eg ocelot, lynx.

Tigris *m* Tigris.

tigrón *nm* (*Ven*) bully, braggart.

tigüila *nf* (*Mex*) trick, swindle.

tijera *nf* **(a)** (*SAm*) scissors.

(b) (*SAm: Zool*) claw, pincer.

(c) (*person*) gossip; **ser una buena —, tener buena —** to be a great gossip; to have a sharp tongue; to indulge constantly in backbiting, be a scandalmonger.

(d) **de —** folding; **escalera de —** steps, step-ladder; **silla de —** folding chair, folding stool, camp stool.

(e) **es un trabajo de —** it's a piece of paste-and-scissors work, he's put it together by copying from other people.

tijeras *nfpl* scissors; (*Hort etc*) shears, clippers; **— para las uñas** nail scissors; **unas —** a pair of scissors (*etc*), some scissors (*etc*).

tijereta *nf* **(a)** (*Ent*) earwig. **(b)** (*Bot*) vine tendril.

tijeretada *nf*, **tijeretazo** *nm* snip, snick, small cut.

tijeretear [1a] **1** *vt* to snip, snick, cut. **2** *vi* **(a)** to meddle. **(b)** (*Arg, Mex, Nic*) to gossip, backbite.

tijereteo *nm* **(a)** snipping, snicking, cutting. **(b)** meddling. **(c)** (*Arg, Mex, Nic*) gossiping, backbiting.

tila *nf* **(a)** (*Bot*) lime tree. **(b)** (*Cook*) *tila*, infusion of lime flowers.

tildar [1a] *vt* **(a)** (*Typ*) to put a tilde over. **(b)** (*fig*) **— a uno de** + *adj* to brand someone as (being) + *adj*, stigmatize someone as (being) + *adj*.

tilde *gen nf* **(a)** (*Typ*) tilde (~). **(b)** (*fig*) blemish, defect, flaw. **(c)** (*fig*) triviality; jot, bit; **en una —** (*fam*) in a jiffy (*fam*).

tilichera *nf* (*CAm, Mex*) hawker's box, glass-covered box.

tilichero *nm* (*CAm, Mex*) hawker, pedlar, peddler (*US*).

tiliches *nmpl* (*CAm, Mex*) fancy articles, trinkets, hawker's wares.

tilín *nm* **(a)** tinkle, ting-a-ling.

(b) (*fig*) **hacer —** to be well liked; **tener —** to be nice, be attractive, have a way with people.

(c) (*fig*) **a mí no me hace —** it doesn't ring a bell with me.

(d) (*Col, Chi, Ven*) **en un —** in an instant.

tilinches *nmpl* (*Mex*) rags.

tilingada *nf* (*RPl*) silly thing (to do *etc*).

tilingo (*Mex, Per, RPl*) **1** *adj* silly, stupid. **2** *nm* fool.

tilinguear [1a] *vi* (*RPl*) to act the fool, do (*etc*) silly things.

tilinguería *nf* (*Mex, RPl*) **(a)** silliness, stupidity. **(b)** **—s** nonsense.

tilintar [1a] *vt* (*CAm*) to stretch, tauten.

tilinte *adj* **(a)** (*CAm*) tight, taut. **(b)** (*Guat*) elegant. **(c)** (*Hond*) replete.

tilma *nf* (*SAm*) blanket, poncho.

tilo *nm* **(a)** (*Bot*) lime tree. **(b)** (*Chi, RPl*) = **tila (b)**.

tiloso *adj* (*CAm*) dirty, filthy.

timador *nm* swindler, trickster.

timar [1a] **1** *vt* **(a)** *property* to steal; to swindle someone out of.

(b) *person* to swindle, play a confidence trick on.

2 timarse *vr* (*fam*) to make eyes at each other; **— con uno** to make eyes at someone, ogle someone.

timba *nf* **(a)** game of chance. **(b)** gambling den. **(c)** (*CAm, Mex, SD, Ven*) belly. **(d)** (*Cu, Mex, PR*) **tener —** to be a tough proposition; to be very odd.

timbal *nm* **(a)** (*Mus*) small drum, kettledrum. **(b)** (*Cook*) meat pie.

timbembe *adj* (*Chi*) weak, trembling.

timbiriche *nm* (*Cu, Mex, Ven*) small shop.

timbrar [1a] *vt* **(a)** to stamp; to seal. **(b)** (*Post*) to postmark.

timbrazo *nm* ring; **dar un —** to ring the bell.

timbre *nm* **(a)** (*Comm, Fin*) fiscal stamp, revenue stamp; seal; (*Fin*) stamp duty.

(b) (*SAm*) postage stamp.

(c) (*SAm*) personal description; description of goods (*etc*).

(d) (*fig*) **— de gloria** mark of honour; action (*etc*) which is to one's credit.

(e) (*Elec etc*) bell; **— de alarma** alarm bell; **tocar el —** to ring the bell.

(f) (*Mus etc*) timbre; **— nasal** (*Ling*) nasal timbre, twang.

timbusca *nf* (*Col, Ec*) thick soup; (*any*) low-class dish with a strong flavour; (*Per*) stew.

tímidamente *adv* timidly, shyly, nervously; bashfully.

timidez *nf* timidity, shyness, nervousness; bashfulness.

tímido *adj* timid, shy, nervous; bashful.

timo *nm* swindle, confidence trick, confidence game (*US*); gag, hoax; **dar un — a uno** to swindle someone; to hoax someone.

timón *nm* **(a)** (*Aer, Naut*) rudder; helm; **— de dirección** (*Aer*) rudder; **— de profundidad** (*Aer*) elevator; **poner el — a babor** to turn to port, port the helm.
   (b) (*of carriage*) pole; (*of plough*) beam.
   (c) (*also fig*) helm; **coger el —, empuñar el —** to take the helm, take charge.

timonear [1a] **1** *vt* (*Col, Guat, Mex, SD*) to direct, manage; to guide. **2** *vi* to steer.

timonel *nm* (*Naut*) steersman, helmsman; (*of racing boat*) cox.

timonera *nf* wheelhouse.

timonero *nm* = **timonel**.

timorato *adj* God-fearing; (*pej*) excessively pious; sanctimonious.

Timoteo *m* Timothy.

tímpano *nm* **(a)** (*Anat*) tympanum, eardrum. **(b)** (*Archit*) tympanum. **(c)** (*Mus*) small drum, kettle-drum; **—s** (*in orchestra*) tympani.

tina *nf* vat, tub; bathtub; **— de lavar** washtub.

tinaco *nm* (*Ec, Mex*) tall earthenware vessel; (*Mex*) water tank.

tinaja *nf* large earthen jar.

tinca *nf* **(a)** (*Arg, Chi*) flip, flick. **(b)** (*Per*) bowls. **(c)** (*Chi*) presentiment, hunch.

tincanque *nm* (*Chi*) = **tinca (a)**.

tincar [1g] *vt* **(a)** (*Arg, Chi*) to flip, flick. **(b)** (*Chi*) to have a presentiment of. **(c)** (*Chi* to like, fancy; **no me tinca** I don't like the idea, I don't fancy it.

tincazo *nm* (*Arg, Chi*) = **tinca (a)**.

tinctura *nf* tincture.

tinerfeño 1 *adj* of Tenerife. **2** *nm*, **tinerfeña** *nf* native (*or* inhabitant) of Tenerife; **los —s** the people of Tenerife.

tinga *nf* (*Mex*) row, confusion, uproar.

tingar [1h] *vt* (*Ec*) to flip, flick.

tinglado *nm* **(a)** platform; shed, covering.
   (b) (*fig*) trick; plot, intrigue; **armar un —** to lay a plot; **conocer el —** to see through it, see someone's little game.

tingo *nm*, **tingue** *nm* (*Ec*) = **tinca (a)**.

tinieblas *nfpl* **(a)** darkness, dark; shadows; gloom.
   (b) (*fig*) confusion, fog; black ignorance; **estamos en — sobre sus proyectos** we are in the dark about his plans, we are entirely ignorant of what he plans to do.

tino *nm* **(a)** skill, knack; feel; (sureness of) touch; (good) guesswork, (good) reckoning, (*Mil*) (accurate) aim, (good) marksmanship; **a —** gropingly; **a buen —** by guesswork; **coger el —** to get the feel of it, get the hang of it.
   (b) (*fig*) tact; good judgement; insight, acumen; **sin —** foolishly; aimlessly; **obrar con mucho —** to act wisely, act with great good sense; **perder el —** to act foolishly, go off the rails; **sacar de — a uno** to bewilder someone; to exasperate someone, infuriate someone.
   (c) (*fig*) moderation; **sin —** immoderately; **comer sin —** to eat to excess; **gastar sin —** to spend recklessly.

tinoso *adj* (*Col, Ven*) skilful, clever; sensible; moderate; tactful.

tinque *nm* (*Arg, Chi*) = **tinca (a)**.

tinta *nf* **(a)** (*Typ etc*) ink; **— china** Indian ink; **— de imprenta** printer's ink, printing ink; **— indeleble, — de marcar** marking ink; **— simpática** invisible ink; **con —** in ink; **sudar —** (*fam*) to slog, slave; **saber algo de buena —** to know something on good authority.
   (b) (*Tech*) dye.
   (c) (*Fish*) dye, ink.
   (d) (*Art*) colour; **—s** (*fig*) tints, shades, hues; **media —** half-tone, tint; **medias —s** (*fig*) half measures; half-baked ideas; inadequate answers; **presentar una situación bajo —s muy negras** to paint a situation very black; **recargar las —s** to exaggerate.

tinte *nm* **(a)** (*act*) dyeing.
   (b) (*Chem*) dye, dyestuff; stain.
   (c) (*Comm*) dyer's (shop); dry-cleaning establishment, dry cleaner's.
   (d) (*fig*) tinge, colouring; **sin el menor — político** without the slightest political colouring, devoid of all political character.

(e) (*fig*) veneer, gloss, light covering; **tiene cierto — de hombre de mundo** he has a slight touch of the man of the world about him.

tinterillo *nm* **(a)** penpusher, small-time clerk. **(b)** (*SAm*) shyster lawyer.

tintero *nm* **(a)** inkpot, inkwell, inkstand; **lo dejó en el —, se le quedó en el —** he clean forgot about it. **(b)** (*SAm*) writing materials, desk set.

tintillo *nm* (*Arg*) red wine.

tintín *nm* (*of bell*) tinkle, tinkling; ting-a-ling; (*of chain etc*) jingle, chink; (*of cups etc*) clink, chink.

tintinear [1a] *vi* to tinkle; to go ting-a-ling; to jingle; to clink, chink.

tintineo *nm* = **tintín**.

tinto 1 *adj* **(a)** dyed; stained; tinged; **— en sangre** stained with blood, bloodstained. **(b)** wine red. **2** *nm* **(a)** red wine. **(b)** (*Col*) black coffee.

tintorera *nf* shark; (*Guat, Mex, Per*) female shark.

tintorería *nf* **(a)** (*art*) dyeing. **(b)** (*Comm*) dyeworks; dyer's (shop); dry-cleaning establishment, dry cleaner's.

tintorero *nm* dyer; dry cleaner.

tintura *nf* **(a)** (*act*) dyeing.
   (b) (*Chem*) dye, dyestuff; (*Tech*) stain; (*Pharm*) tincture; **— de tornasol** litmus; **— de yodo** iodine.
   (c) (*fig*) smattering; thin veneer.

tinturar [1a] *vt* **(a)** to dye; to tinge. **(b)** (*fig*) **— a uno** to give someone a rudimentary knowledge, teach someone superficially.

tiña *nf* **(a)** (*Med*) ringworm. **(b)** (*fig*) poverty. **(c)** (*fig*) meanness.

tiñoso *adj* **(a)** (*Med*) scabby, mangy. **(b)** (*fig*) poor, wretched. **(c)** (*fig*) mean.

tío *nm* **(a)** uncle; **— abuelo** great-uncle; **— carnal** real uncle; **mi — Eduardo** my uncle Edward; **T— Sam** Uncle Sam; **mis —s** (*freq*) my uncle and aunt.
   (b) before name as title of respect, not translated; **ha muerto el — Francisco** Francis has died.
   (c) (*fam*) old fellow; fellow, chap (*fam*), guy (*US fam*); **¿quién es ese —?** who's that chap?; **ese — del sombrero alto** that chap with the tall hat; **¡qué —!** what a fellow!; (*pej*) isn't he a so-and-so?; **es un — grande, es un — con toda la barba** he's a great guy.

tiovivo *nm* roundabout, merry-go-round.

tipa[1] *nf* (*Arg, Bol, Per*) wicker basket.

tipa[2] *nf* (*SAm*) bitch, awful woman.

tipear [1a] *vti* (*SAm*) to type.

tiperrita *nf* (*Cu*) typist.

tipiadora *nf* (*fam*) **(a)** typewriter. **(b)** typist.

típicamente *adv* typically; characteristically.

típico *adj* **(a)** typical; characteristic.
   (b) custom etc typical; quaint, picturesque; full of local colour; rich in folklore, full of folkloric interest; traditional; of interest to tourists; **es la taberna más típica de la ciudad** it's the most picturesque pub in town; **unas jóvenes con su — peinado** some girls with their hair done in the traditional (and local) fashion; **no hay que perderse tan típica fiesta** you shouldn't miss a festivity so rich in local colour and tradition.

tipificar [1g] *vt* to typify.

tipismo *nm* quaintness, picturesqueness; local colour; folkloric interest; traditionalism; **estoy harto de tanto — bobo** I'm fed up with all this nonsensical local colour and traditionalism.

tiple 1 *nm* **(a)** treble, boy soprano. **(b)** soprano (voice). **2** *nf* soprano.

tipo *nm* **(a)** type; norm, standard; pattern, model.
   (b) type, sort, kind; **un nuevo — de bicicleta** a new kind of bicycle; **de otro — pero del mismo precio** of a different type but at the same price.
   (c) (*Lit etc*) type, character.
   (d) (*fam*) fellow, chap (*fam*), guy (*US fam*); **dos —s sospechosos** two suspicious characters; **un — que yo conozco** a fellow I know; **¿quién es ese —?** who's that chap?
   (e) (*Comm, Fin*) rate; **— bancario, — de descuento** bank rate; **— de cambio** exchange rate, rate of exchange; **— de interés** interest rate; **— (de) oro** gold standard.
   (f) (*Anat: man's*) build, physique; (*woman's*) figure; **él tiene buen —** he's well built; **ella tiene buen —** she has a good figure; **tener mal —** to be misshapen.
   (g) (*Typ: also* **—s**) type; **— gótico** Gothic type, black letter; **— menudo** small print.
   (h) (*fam*) **aguantar el —** to put up with a lot; **jugarse el —** to risk one's neck.

tipografía *nf* **(a)** typography; printing. **(b)** printing works; printing press.

tipográfico *adj* typographical; printing (*attr*).

tipógrafo nm typographer; printer.
tiposo adj (Per) ridiculous, eccentric.
típula nf cranefly, daddy-long-legs.
tiquear [1a] vt (Chi) ticket to punch.
tíquet ['tike] nm, pl **tíquets** ['tike] (SAm: angl) ticket.
tiquete nm (CAm, Col, Cu, Mex: angl) ticket; (Col) label.
tiquismiquis 1 nm, pl **tiquismiquis** fussy person.
  2 nmpl (a) silly scruples.
    (b) affected courtesies, bowing and scraping.
    (c) bickering, squabbles.
    (d) minor irritations, pinpricks.
tira¹ 1 nf strip; long strip, narrow strip; band; slip of paper; — **de películas** film strip; — **cómica** comic strip.
  2 nm: — **y afloja** (a) prudence, caution; tact.
    (b) tug-of-war (fig); give and take, mutual concessions.
tira² nm (Arg, Col, Chi) detective.
tirabuzón nm (a) corkscrew; **sacar algo a uno con** — (fig) to worm something out of someone. (b) curl, ringlet.
tirada nf (a) (act) cast, throw.
    (b) distance; stretch; (Sew) length; (fig) series, number; time; (Lit) stanza; sequence; epic laisse; **de una** — at one go, in a stretch; **lo recitó todo de una** — he recited the whole lot straight off, he reeled the lot off; **estuvo con nosotros una** — **de días** he spent a number of days with us; **de B a C hay una** — **de 18 kms** from B to C there is a distance of 18 kms.
    (c) (Typ) printing, edition; — **aparte** offprint, reprint.
    (d) (SAm) boring speech, tedious discourse.
    (e) (Arg) hint.
    (f) (PR) dirty trick.
tiradera nf (a) (CAm, Cu, Chi) sash, belt, strap; (Cu) harness strap, trace. (b) (Col, Pan) taunt.
tirado adj (a) (Naut) rakish; writing cursive.
    (b) **estar** — (Comm) to be dirt-cheap; to be a glut on the market; (task etc) to be very simple; **esa asignatura está tirada** (fam) that subject is dead easy, that subject is a cinch (sl).
tirador nm (a) (person) marksman, shot; shooter; (Mex, Nic) hunter; — **apostado**, — **certero** sniper.
    (b) handle, knob, button; doorknob; (Elec) flex, cord; — **de campanilla** bellrope, bellpull.
    (c) catapult.
    (d) (Art, Tech) drawing pen.
    (e) (Bol, RPl) wide gaucho belt.
    (f) (Bol, RPl) —**es** braces, suspenders (US).
tiraje nm (Arg, Chi, Mex, Nic) chimney flue.
tiralevitas nm, pl **tiralevitas** (fam) bootlicker (fam); creep (sl).
tiralíneas nm, pl **tiralíneas** drawing pen, ruling pen.
tiranía nf tyranny.
tiránicamente adv tyrannically.
tiranicida nmf tyrannicide (person).
tiranicidio nm tyrannicide (act).
tiránico adj tyrannical; despotic; love possessive, domineering; attraction irresistible, all-powerful.
tiranizar [1f] vt to tyrannize, rule despotically; to domineer.
tirano 1 adj tyrannical, despotic; domineering. **2** nm, **tirana** nf tyrant, despot.
tirantas nfpl (Col, Mex) braces, suspenders (US).
tirante 1 adj (a) rope etc tight, taut; tensed; drawn tight.
    (b) relations, situation etc tense, strained; **estamos algo** —**s** things are rather strained between us.
    (c) (Fin) tight.
  2 nm (a) (Archit) tie, brace, crosspiece; (Mech) brace, stay, strut.
    (b) (of harness) trace; (of dress) shoulder strap; —**s** braces, suspenders (US).
tirantear [1a] vt (Chi, Guat) to stretch.
tirantez nf (a) tightness, tautness; tension.
    (b) (fig) tension, strain; **la** — **de las relaciones con Eslobodia** the strained relations with Slobodia, the tense state of relations with Slobodia; **ha disminuido la** — the tension has lessened.
    (c) (Fin) tightness; stringency.
tirar [1a] **1** vt (a) to throw; to hurl, fling, cast, sling; (accidentally) to drop; to knock over, knock down; building to pull down; shot to fire, shoot; rocket to fire, launch; bomb to drop; **el aparato tira el proyectil a 2000 metros** the machine throws the projectile 2000 metres; **estaban tirando la fruta con palos largos** they were knocking the fruit down with long poles; **el viento ha tirado la valla** the

wind has knocked the fence down; **me tiró un beso** she blew me a kiss.
    (b) rubbish etc to throw away; to chuck out; fortune to waste, squander; **estos calcetines están para** —**los** these socks are ready to be thrown away; **hay que** — **los podridos** the rotten ones ought to be thrown out; **has tirado el dinero comprando eso** you've thrown your money away buying that.
    (c) wire to draw out.
    (d) line to draw, trace, rule.
    (e) (Typ) to print, run off.
    (f) blow etc to give, deal, fetch; — **una coz a uno** to give someone a kick; — **un mordisco a uno** to give someone a bite; — **tajos a uno** to slash at someone.
    (g) (Col) to use; to work with; — **azada** to hoe, work with the hoe; — **brazo** to swim; — **canoa** to sail a canoe.
    (h) (Col, Cu, Chi) to cart, haul, transport.
    (i) —**la de** to fancy oneself as, pose as.
  2 vi (a) (Mil etc) to shoot (a at), fire (a at, on); — **a matar** to shoot to kill; — **con bala** to use live ammunition; **¡no tires!** don't shoot!
    (b) — **de** to pull, tug; to draw (along), haul; rope etc to pull (on), tug (at); handkerchief, wallet etc to pull out, take out (suddenly), yank out; sword to draw; — **de la manga de uno** to tug at someone's sleeve; **tire de ese cabo** pull that end; **tiraron de cuchillos** they drew their knives; "—", "**tirad**" (on doors etc) "pull".
    (c) (of magnet etc) to draw, attract; (fig) to draw, pull, have a pull; to appeal; **no le tira el estudio** study does not attract him; **la patria tira siempre** one's native land always exerts a powerful pull.
    (d) (of chimney etc) to draw.
    (e) (fam) **ir tirando** to get along, manage; **vamos tirando** we manage, we keep going; **esos zapatos tirarán todavía otro invierno** those shoes will last out another winter.
    (f) (fam) to go; **tire Vd adelante** go straight on; **¡tira (adelante)!** get on with it!; — **a la derecha** to turn right; to keep right; — **por una calle** to turn down a street, go off along a street.
    (g) — **a** to tend to, tend towards; — **a rojo** to have some red in it, have a touch of red about it; — **a viejo** to be getting old, be elderly; — **a su padre** to take after one's father, resemble one's father; **él tira más bien a cuidadoso** he's on the careful side; **tira a hacerse servir** he tends to make others wait on him; — **para médico** to have inclinations towards a medical career, feel like becoming a doctor, be attracted towards a career in medicine.
    (h) — **a** to aim at being, work to become; (pej) to intrigue to become; — **a** + infin to aim to + infin; (pej) to intrigue in order to + infin, go surreptitiously to work to + infin.
    (i) (Sport) to shoot; to go, play, have one's turn; **tira tú ahora** it's your go now; **tiró fuera de la portería** he shot wide of the goal; **¡tira!** shoot!
    (j) — **a todo** — at the most; **nos queda gasolina para 20 kms a todo** — we have only enough petrol for 20 kms at the outside (or at the most); **llegará el martes a todo** — he'll arrive on Tuesday at the latest.
  3 tirarse vr (a) to throw oneself, hurl oneself; — **al agua** to dive (or plunge) into the water; — **al suelo** to throw oneself to the ground; — **por una ventana** to throw oneself out of a window; to jump from a window; — **por un risco** to throw oneself over a cliff; — **en paracaídas** to parachute (down), (in emergency) bale out; — **en la cama** to lie down on one's bed; — **a uno** to rush at someone, spring on someone.
    (b) (fig) to cheapen oneself, demean oneself; to waste oneself in an unworthy job.
    (c) — **a una** (tabu) to screw someone (tabu).
tirilla nf (a) band, strip; (Sew) neckband. (b) (Chi) shabby dress, ragged garment.
tirillas nmf (fam) (a) unimportant person, nobody; **¡vete,** —**!** get along, little man! (b) undersized individual, runt.
tirillento adj (SAm) ragged, shabby.
tiritaña nf (fam) mere trifle.
tiritar [1a] vi (a) to shiver (de with).
    (b) (fam) **dejaron el pastel tiritando** they almost finished the cake off, they made the cake look pretty silly (fam); **este plato ha quedado tiritando** there isn't much left of this dish.
tiritón nm shiver.
tiritona nf shivering (fit).
Tiro Tyre.
tiro nm (a) throw.
    (b) (Mil etc) shot; sound of a shot, report; impact of a shot, hit; bullet mark; (in general) shooting,

firing; — **con arco** archery; — **de pichón** clay-pigeon shooting; — **al blanco** target practice, shooting practice; — **de escopeta,** — **de fusil** gunshot; **cañón de** — **rápido** quick-firing gun; **descargar un** — to fire a shot; **errar el** — to miss, miss with one's shot; **se oyó un** — a shot was heard; **se pegó un** — he shot himself; **le pegó un** — **a su novio** she shot her boyfriend; **le salió el** — **por la culata** the scheme (etc) backfired; **hacer** — **a** (fig) to have designs on, aim at; **no lo haría ni a** —**s** I wouldn't do it for love nor money; **matar a uno a** —**s** to shoot someone (dead); **tendrán que decidirlo a** —**s** they'll have to shoot it out.

(c) (Sport) shot; drive; — **a gol** shot at goal; — **de revés** backhand drive; **parar un** — to stop a shot.

(d) (Mil etc) range; **a** — **de fusil** within gunshot; **a** — **de piedra** within a stone's throw; **estar a** — to be within range; (fig) to be accessible; **si se pone a** — **se lo diré** if he comes my way I'll tell him.

(e) rifle range; shooting gallery.

(f) team of horses (etc); **caballo de** — cart-horse, draught horse.

(g) (Sew) length (of cloth etc); **andar de** —**s largos** to be all dressed up, be very smartly turned out.

(h) rope; cord, chain; bellpull; (of harness) trace, strap; —**s** (Mil) swordbelt; —**s** (Arg) braces, suspenders (US).

(i) (Archit) flight of stairs.

(j) (of chimney etc) draught; (Min) shaft; — **de mina** mineshaft.

(k) (fig) blow; setback.

(l) (fig) veiled attack; damaging allusion.

(m) (fig) trick, hoax; practical joke.

(n) (fig) petty theft; petty deceit.

(o) (Chi, Mex, Per) marble.

(p) (Arg, Chi: Racing) distance, course.

(q) (Mex) issue, edition.

(r) (Chi) hint.

(s) (Ven) craftiness, cunning.

(t) (SAm: idioms) **al** — at once, right away; **a** — **de** + infin about to + infin, on the point of + ger; **de a** — completely; **del** — consequently.

tiroideo adj thyroid.

tiroides nf (also **glándula** —) thyroid (gland).

Tirol: El — the Tyrol.

tirolés 1 adj Tyrolese. 2 nm, **tirolesa** nf Tyrolese.

tirón[1] nm (a) pull, tug, sudden jerk; hitch; **dar un** — **a** to pull at, tug at; to jerk suddenly; **me lo arrancó de un** — she suddenly jerked it away from me; **el coche se movía a** —**es** the car moved along in a series of jerks, the car went jerkily forward.

(b) **de un** — all at once; in one go, straight off, without a break; **leyó la novela de un** — he read the novel straight through; **se lo bebió de un** — he drank it down in one go; **trabajan 10 horas de un** — they work 10 hours at a stretch.

(c) (RPl) **ganar el** — to get ahead, jump the gun successfully.

tirón[2] nm tyro, novice.

tirona nf (fam) whore.

tironear [1a] vt (SAm) =**tirar** 2 (b).

tirotear [1a] 1 vt to shoot at, fire on; to blaze away at; to snipe at. 2 **tirotearse** vr to exchange shots; to blaze away at each other.

tiroteo nm firing, shooting, exchange of shots; skirmish.

tirria nf dislike; ill will; **tener** — **a** to dislike, have a grudge against.

tisana nf tisane, infusion.

tísico 1 adj consumptive, tubercular. 2 nm, **tísica** nf consumptive.

tisiqu(i)ento adj (RPl) consumptive; pale and thin.

tisis nf consumption, tuberculosis.

tisú nm tissue.

tita nf (fam) auntie, aunty (fam).

titán nm Titan.

titánico adj titanic.

titanio nm titanium.

titeador adj (Bol, RPl) mocking, given to scoffing.

titear [1a] vt (Bol, RPl) to mock, scoff at; to make fun of.

titeo nm (Bol, RPl) mockery, scoffing; **tomar a uno para el** — to scoff at someone; to make fun of someone.

títere nm (a) puppet, marionette; —**s** puppets; puppet show; puppetry; **no dejar** — **con cabeza** to turn everything upside down; to leave nothing intact, break up everything in sight.

(b) (fig) puppet; cat's-paw; weak person, colourless individual; untrustworthy person; odd-looking person.

titi nm (SAm) small monkey.

titilar [1a] vi (of eyelid etc) to flutter, tremble; (of light, star) to twinkle.

titiritaña nf (Mex) (a) puppet show. (b) (fig) triviality.

titiritero nm puppeteer; acrobat, juggler, circus artist.

tito nm (fam) uncle.

titubeante adj (a) tottery, unstable, shaky. (b) stammering; halting. (c) hesitant.

titubear [1a] vi (a) to totter; to stagger; to be unstable, be shaky, be unsteady; to reel.

(b) (Ling) to stammer; to falter.

(c) to hesitate, vacillate; **no** — **en** + infin not to hesitate to + infin.

titubeo nm (a) tottering; staggering; instability, shakiness, unsteadiness.

(b) (Ling) stammering; faltering.

(c) hesitation, vacillation; **proceder sin** —**s** to act resolutely, act without hesitation.

titulado adj (a) entitled; **escribió una obra titulada "Sotileza"** he wrote a book entitled "Sotileza".

(b) person titled.

(c) person (Univ etc) qualified; (Tech etc) trained, skilled.

titular 1 adj titular, official.

2 nm (Typ) headline.

3 nmf (of office) holder, occupant; (Eccl) incumbent; (of passport, record etc) holder.

4 vt [1a] to title, entitle, call.

5 **titularse** vr to be entitled, be called; to call oneself, style oneself.

titulillo nm (Typ) running title, page heading; **andar en** —**s** (fam) to watch out for every little thing.

título nm (a) (general sense) title; (Law etc) section heading; article; (of budget) item; (Typ) title; (of newspaper) headline; **a** — **de** by way of; in the capacity of; **a** — **de curiosidad** as a matter of interest; **el dinero fue a** — **de préstamo** the money was given as a loan, the money was by way of being a loan; **nos lo dijo a** — **de noticia alentadora** he told us it as being a cheering piece of news.

(b) (of person) title; — **de nobleza,** — **nobiliario** title of nobility.

(c) (fig) titled person; **casarse con un** — to marry a titled person, marry into the nobility.

(d) professional qualification; diploma, certificate; (Univ) degree; (fig) qualification; —**s** qualifications, credentials; — **universitario** university degree; **maestro sin** — unqualified teacher; **obtener un** — to obtain a qualification; to take a degree; **tener los** —**s para un puesto** to have the qualifications for a job.

(e) (of character etc) quality; **no es precisamente un** — **de gloria para él** it is not exactly a quality on which he can pride himself; **tiene varios** —**s honrosos** he has several noble qualities, he has a number of worthy attributes.

(f) (Law) title; — **de propiedad** title deed.

(g) (Fin) bond; — **al portador** bearer bond.

(h) (fig) right; **con justo** — rightly; **tener** — **de** + infin to be entitled to + infin, have the right to + infin; **le sobran** —**s para hacerlo** he has every right to do it.

tiza nf (a) chalk; whitening; **una** — a piece of chalk.

(b) (Col) exaggeration.

tizar [1f] vt (Chi) to plan; to design, model; (Per) suit to mark out for cutting.

tizate nm (CAm, Mex) chalk.

tizna nf black, grime; (Art) crayon.

tiznado nm (pej) nigger, blackie.

tiznajo nm (fam) black mark, dirty smear.

tiznar [1a] 1 vt to blacken, black; to smudge, soil, stain, spot; to smear (de with).

(b) (fig) to stain, tarnish; to defame, blacken.

2 **tiznarse** vr (a) — **la cara con un corcho quemado** to blacken one's face with burnt cork.

(b) to get smudged, get soiled (etc).

(c) (Chi, Guat, Mex) to get drunk.

tizne nm (a) soot; black smear, blackening; grime; smut. (b) (fig) stain.

tiznón nm smut, speck of soot; smudge.

tizo nm burning piece of wood, brand.

tizón nm (a) burning piece of wood, brand; half-burned piece of wood. (b) (Bot) smut. (c) (fig) stain.

tizonazos nmpl (fig) pains of hell.

tizonear [1a] vt fire to poke, stir.

tizos nmpl (sl) fingers.

tlacanear [1a] vt (Mex) to touch, feel, handle.

tlacote nm (Mex) growth, tumour.

tlacual nm (Mex) (a) food; meal. (b) cooking pot.

tlachique nm (Mex) unfermented *pulque*.

tlapalería nf (Mex) paint shop.

tlapiloya nf (Mex) jail.

tlapisquera nf (Mex) shed, barn, granary.

tlecuil nm (Mex) hearth, fire; stove.

toa nf (SAm) hawser, rope, towrope.

toalla nf towel; — **de baño** bath towel; — **de rodillo** roller towel.

toallero nm towel rail.

tobar [1a] vt (Col) to tow.

tobera nf nozzle.

tobillera nf (a) ankle sock. (b) (fam) teenager, bobbysoxer (US fam).

tobillo nm ankle.

tobo nm (Ven) bucket.

tobogán nm (a) toboggan. (b) (at fair) switchback. (c) (into pool) chute, slide.

toca[1] nf headdress; bonnet; toque; —s **de viuda** widow's weeds.

toca[2] nmf (SAm) = tocayo.

tocadiscos nm, pl tocadiscos record player, phonograph (US); — **automático** auto-change record player; — **tragamonedas**, — **tragaperras** jukebox.

tocado[1] adj (a) fruit bad, rotten; meat etc tainted, bad; **estar** — **de la cabeza** to be weak in the head.

(b) **una creencia tocada de heterodoxia** a belief tinged with heterodoxy.

(c) **estar** — **de piedad** to be full of pious feelings.

tocado[2] 1 adj: — **con un sombrero de paja** wearing a straw hat, with a straw hat on his head.

2 nm (a) headdress, headgear, hat.

(b) coiffure, hair-do.

(c) toilet.

tocador[1] nm (a) dressing table; **jabón de** — toilet soap; **juego de** — toilet set.

(b) toilet case.

(c) boudoir, dressing room; — **de señoras** ladies' room.

tocador[2] nm, **tocadora** nf (Mus) player.

tocante 1 — a prep with regard to, about; **en lo** — a so far as concerns, as for. 2 adj (RPl) moving, touching.

tocar[1] [1g] 1 vt (a) to touch; to feel; to handle; — **las cosas de cerca** to experience things for oneself, learn about things at first hand; **sin** — **un pelo de su ropa** without laying a finger on her; **¡no me toques!** don't touch me!; **que nadie toque mis papeles** don't let anyone touch my papers, don't interfere with my papers.

(b) (of objects) to touch, be touching; **la mesa toca la pared** the table touches the wall, the table is up against the wall.

(c) (Mus) to play; bell to ring; to toll, peal; drum to play, beat; trumpet to play, blow, sound; siren etc to sound; record to play; hour of day to chime, strike; — **la generala** (Mil) to sound the call to arms; — **la retirada** to sound the retreat; **¡a pagar tocan!** it's time to pay up!

(d) (Art) to touch up.

(e) (fig) to touch; — **el corazón de uno** to touch someone's heart.

(f) obstacle etc to hit, strike, collide with, run into; (Naut) to go aground on, run on to; (Hunting) to hit, wing; target etc to hit.

(g) subject to touch on, refer to, allude to; **no tocó para nada esa cuestión** he didn't refer to that matter at all.

(h) consequences to suffer, undergo, come in for; **él tocará las consecuencias de todo esto** he will suffer the consequences of all this.

(i) (fam) to be related to; **X no le toca para nada a Y** X is not related at all to Y, X is no relation to Y.

2 vi (a) — **a una puerta** to knock on (or at) a door.

(b) **tocan a misa** they are ringing the bell for mass; **ese timbre toca a fuego** that bell sounds the fire alarm; see **muerto** etc.

(c) — **le a uno** to fall to someone, fall to someone's lot; to fall to someone's share; **les tocó un dólar a cada uno** each one got a dollar as his share; **¿les tocará algo de herencia?** will they get anything under the will?; **le ha tocado otro premio** he has won another prize; **te toca jugar** it's your turn (to play), it's your go; **¿a quién le toca?** whose turn is it?; **¿a quién le toca pagar esta vez?** whose turn is it to pay this time?; **le toca a Vd reprenderle** it is up to you to reprimand him.

(d) (impersonal) **no toca hacerlo hasta el mes que viene** it's not due to be done until next month; **ahora toca torcer a la derecha** now you have to turn right, now there's a right turn coming up.

(e) to concern, affect; **esto no te toca a ti** this doesn't concern you; **ello me toca de cerca** it con-

cerns me intimately; **por lo que a mí me toca** so far as I am concerned.

(f) (Naut) — **en** to call at, touch at; **el barco no toca en Barcelona** the ship does not call at Barcelona.

(g) (fig) — **en** to border on, verge on; **esto toca en locura** this verges on madness.

3 **tocarse** vr (a) to touch each other, be in contact.

(b) (fam) —las to beat it (fam).

tocar[2] [1g] 1 vt hair to do, arrange, set. 2 **tocarse** vr to cover one's head, put on one's hat.

tocateja: a — adv on the nail.

tocayo nm, **tocaya** nf (a) namesake. (b) (Per) friend.

tocino nm bacon (also — **de panceta**); salt pork.

toco[1] nm (CAm) = tocayo.

toco[2] nm (Ven) = tocón.

tocolotear [1a] vi (Cu) to shuffle (the cards).

tocón 1 adj (Col) tailless; (PR, Ven) hornless. 2 nm (Anat, Bot) stump.

tocuyo nm (Bol, Per, RPl) coarse cotton cloth.

tochimbo nm (Per) smelting furnace.

todavía adv (a) still, yet; — **no** not yet; — **en 1970** as late as 1970, right up to 1970; — **no lo ha encontrado** he still has not found it, he has not found it yet; **está nevando** — it is still snowing; **es más inteligente que su hermano** he is still (or yet) more intelligent than his brother.

(b) (SAm) not yet.

todo 1 adj (a) all; whole, entire; every; — **el bosque** all the wood, the whole wood, the entire wood; **el universo** — the whole universe; **lo sabe** — **Madrid** all Madrid knows it, the whole of Madrid knows it; **lo golpeó con toda su fuerza** he hit him with his full strength, he hit him with all his might; **a toda velocidad** at full speed, at top speed; **con toda prisa** in all haste, with all speed; **en toda España** all over Spain, throughout Spain; **en toda España no hay más que 5** there are only 5 in the whole of Spain; — **lo demás** all the rest, all else; — **s vosotros** all of you; — **s los libros** all the books; **todas las semanas** every week; **viene todos los martes** he comes every Tuesday; — **el que quiera** . . . everyone who wants to . . .; whoever wants to . . .; — **s los que quieran** . . . all those who want to . . .; — **lo que Vd ve aquí** all that you see here; — **lo que Vd necesite** whatever you need; **con toda su inteligencia** with all his intelligence; **in spite of all his intelligence; de todas todas** (fam) the whole lot, all of them without exception; **¡te digo que sí de todas todas!** I tell you it jolly well is! (fam); **es verdad de todas todas** it's absolutely true; see **cuanto** etc.

(b) (neg sense) **en** — **el día** not once all day; **en toda la noche he dormido** I haven't slept all night; **en toda España lo encuentra Vd** you won't find it anywhere in Spain.

(c) (idiomatic use) **es** — **un hombre** he's every inch a man; **es** — **un palacio** it's a real palace; **es** — **un héroe** he's a real hero; **la hija es toda su madre** the daughter is exactly like her mother; **tiene toda la nariz de su abuela** her nose is exactly like her grandmother's; **el niño estaba** — **ojos** the child was all eyes; **ese hombre es** — **ambición** that man is all ambition (and nothing else).

2 adv (a) all, entirely, completely; **estaba** — **rendido** he was completely worn out; **para las 8 estará** — **hecho** it will be completely finished by 8 o'clock; **lleva un vestido** — **roto** she's wearing a dress that's all torn.

(b) **puede ser** — **lo sencillo que Vd quiera** it can be as simple as you wish; see **más** etc.

3 **con** — **y** conj (SAm) in spite of; **el equipo, con** — **y estar integrado por buenos jugadores** . . . the team, in spite of being (or for all that it is) made up of good players . . .

4 nm and pron (a) all, everything; —s everybody; every one of them; **el** — the whole; **en un** — together, as a whole; —**s y cada uno** all and sundry; **lo comió** — he ate it all; **lo han vendido** — they've sold it all, they've sold the lot; — **lo sabemos** we know everything; — **o nada** all or nothing; — **es** (or **son**) **reveses** it's all setbacks, there's nothing but troubles; **y luego** — **son sonrisas** and then it's all smiles; — **cabe en él** he is capable of anything; **ser el** — to be the most important thing; (of person: fam) to be the mainstay; to run the show, dominate everything; **y** — and so on, and what not; **tienen un coche nuevo y** — they have a new car and everything; **los zapatos, viejos y** —, **durarán otro año** these shoes, old though they are, will last another year; **andando rápidamente y** —, **no llegaron a tiempo** even though they walked quickly they still didn't get there in time; see **jugarse** etc.

(b) (*phrases with prep*) **ante** — first of all, in the first place; primarily; **a pesar de** — even so, in spite of everything; all the same; **con** — still, however; in spite of everything; **de** — **como en botica** everything under the sun; **de** — **hay en este mundo de Dios, de** — **hay en la viña del Señor** it takes all sorts to make a world; **del** — wholly, completely; **no es del** — **verdad** it is not entirely true, it is not quite true; **no es del** — **malo** it is not wholly bad; **después de** — after all; **para** — all-purpose; **por** — all in all; **sobre** — especially; above all, most of all.

todopoderoso *adj* almighty, all-powerful; **el T** — the Almighty.

tofo *nm* (*Arg, Chi*) white clay; fireclay.

toga *nf* (*Hist*) toga; (*Law etc*) gown, robe; (*Univ*) gown; **tomar la** — (*approx*) to take silk.

Togolandia *f* Togoland.

tojo[1] *nm* gorse, furze.

tojo[2] *adj* (*Bol*) twin.

tol *nm* (*CAm*) gourd; large vessel; bowl.

tolda *nf* **(a)** (*Col, Ec, PR*) coarse material, canvas. **(b)** (*Col*) tent, improvised hut; shelter; (*of boat*) awning. **(c)** (*PR*) large sack. **(d)** (*Ven*) overcast sky.

toldería *nf* (*Bol, Chi, RPl*) Indian village, camp of Indian huts.

toldillo *nm* (*Ant, Col, Ven*) mosquito net.

toldo *nm* **(a)** sunshade, awning; marquee; cover, cloth, tarpaulin. **(b)** (*Bol, Chi, RPl*) Indian hut. **(c)** (*Col, Per, PR*) mosquito net. **(d)** (*Mex: Aut*) hood, top (*US*). **(e)** (*fig*) pride, haughtiness.

tole[1] *nm* (*fam*) **(a)** hubbub, commotion, uproar; outcry; **levantar el** — to kick up a fuss. **(b)** (*also* **tole tole**) gossip, rumour; slander campaign. **(c)** **coger el** —, **tomar el** — to get out, pack up and go.

tole[2] *nm* (*Col*) track, trail.

toledano 1 *adj* Toledan. **2** *nm*, **toledana** *nf* Toledan.

tolempo *nm* (*Col*) = **lempo**.

tolerable *adj* tolerable.

tolerancia *nf* **(a)** tolerance; toleration. **(b)** (*Mech*) tolerance.

tolerante *adj* tolerant.

tolerantismo *nm* religious toleration.

tolerar [1a] *vt* to tolerate; to bear, endure, put up with; to allow; **no se puede** — **esto** this cannot be tolerated; **no tolera que digan eso** he won't allow them to say that, he won't put up with their saying that; **su madre le tolera demasiado** his mother spoils him, his mother lets him get away with too much; **su estómago no tolera los huevos** eggs don't agree with him; **el cosmonauta toleró muy bien esta situación difícil** the cosmonaut stood up very well to this awkward situation; **el puente no tolera el peso de los tanques** the bridge will not support the weight of the tanks.

tolete *nm* **(a)** (*Naut*) tholepin. **(b)** (*SAm*) short club, stick, cudgel. **(c)** (*Col, Cu*) piece, bit. **(d)** (*Col*) raft.

toletero *nm* (*Ven*) rowdy, tough (*fam*).

toletole *nm* **(a)** (*Arg*) row. **(b)** (*Col*) obstinacy, persistence. **(c)** (*Ven*) gay life, roving life; *see also* **tole**[1] **(b)**.

Tolomeo *m* Ptolemy.

Tolón Toulon.

toloncho *nm* (*Col*) piece of wood.

tolondro 1 *adj* scatterbrained. **2** *nm* (*Med*) bump, lump, swelling.

tolondrón *adj and nm* = **tolondro**.

Tolosa (de Francia) Toulouse.

tolva *nf* **(a)** hopper; chute. **(b)** (*Chi, Mex: Rail*) hopper wagon, hopper car (*US*). **(c)** (*Mex*) shed for storing ore.

tolvanera *nf* dustcloud.

tolla *nf* **(a)** marsh, quagmire. **(b)** (*Cu, Mex*) drinking trough.

tollina *nf* (*fam*) hiding; bashing (*fam*).

toma *nf* **(a)** (*general sense*) taking; — **de declaración** taking of evidence; — **de hábito** (*Eccl*) taking of vows; — **de posesión** taking over; (*by president*) taking up of office, inauguration; — **de tierra** (*Aer*) landing, touchdown. **(b)** (*Mil*) capture, taking; seizure. **(c)** amount, portion; (*Med*) dose; — **de rapé** pinch of snuff. **(d)** (*Mech etc*) inlet, intake; outlet; (*of water etc*) tap, outlet; (*Elec*) plug, socket; lead; terminal; — **de antena** (*Radio*) aerial socket; — **de corriente** power

point, plug; — **directa** (*Aut*) top gear; — **de fuerza** power takeoff; — **de tierra** earth wire, ground wire (*US*). **(e)** (*Cine, TV*) take, shot; — **directa** live shot; live broadcast. **(f)** (*SAm*) channel; irrigation ditch; (*Guat*) brook.

tomacorriente *nm* (*Elec*) plug.

tomada *nf* (*SAm: Elec*) plug.

tomadero *nm* **(a)** handle. **(b)** inlet, intake; tap.

tomado *adj* **(a)** (*also* — **de orín**) rusty. **(b)** *voice* hoarse. **(c)** **estar** — (*SAm*) to be drunk.

tomador 1 *adj* (*SAm*) drunken, boozy. **2** *nm* **(a)** (*Comm*) drawee. **(b)** (*fam*) thief. **(c)** (*SAm*) drunkard, boozer.

tomadura *nf* = **toma (a)** *and* **(b)**; — **de pelo** hoax, deception; mockery; abuse.

tomaína *nf* ptomaine.

tomar [1a] **1** *vt* **(a)** (*general sense*) to take; to accept; to get, acquire; *air, bath, bend, decision, measure, opportunity, route, step, sun, temperature etc* to take; *arms, pen etc* to take up; *attitude* to adopt, take up; to strike; *appearance, aspect, shape etc* to take on; *ball* to catch, stop; *cold* to take, get, catch; *habit* to get into, fall into, acquire; *business* to take over; *lesson* to have; *name* to take, adopt; *servant* to take on. engage; *strength* to get, gain, acquire; *ticket* to take, get, buy; **¡toma!** here you are!, here!, catch!; **¡tómate ésa!** take that!; — **y dejar pasajeros** to take up and set down passengers; — **a uno por policía** to take someone for a policeman, think that someone is a policeman; — **a uno por loco** to think someone mad; **¿por quién me toma Vd?** what do you take me for?, who do you think I am?; — **algo sobre sí** to take something upon oneself; *see* **mal, serio** *etc*. **(b)** (*Mil*) to take, capture; to seize. **(c)** (*Cook*) to eat, drink, have; — **el pecho** to suck, feed at the breast; **tomamos unas cervezas** we had a few beers; **¿qué quieres** —? what will you have?, what would you like? **(d)** *bus, train etc* to take. **(e)** (*Cine, Phot, TV*) to take; (*Cine*) to shoot; — **una foto de** to take a photo of. **(f)** *notes* to take; *speech etc* to take down; — **por escrito** to write down; — **en taquigrafía** to take down in shorthand; — **en cinta** to record on tape. **(g)** *affection, loathing etc* to acquire, take (*a* to); *see* **cariño** *etc*. **(h)** (*of feeling*) to overcome; **le tomaron ganas de reír** she was overcome by an urge to laugh. **(i)** — **la con uno** to pick a quarrel with someone; **tenerla tomada con uno** to have a down on someone (*fam*), adopt a consistently hostile attitude to someone. **(j)** (*Col*) to upset, annoy.

2 *vi* **(a)** (*Bot*) to take, take root; (*of graft*) to take. **(b)** — **a la derecha** to go off to the right, turn right; — **por una calle** to go off along a street, turn down a street. **(c)** (*SAm*) to drink; **estaba tomando en varios bares** he was drinking in a number of bars. **(d)** (*fam*) **tomó y lo rompió** he went and broke it; **tomó y se fue** off he went, he upped and went (*fam*). **(e)** **toma y daca** (*as n*) give and take; (*pej*) mutual concessions (for selfish reasons), log rolling; **más vale un** — **que dos te daré** a bird in the hand is worth two in the bush. **(f)** **¡toma!** well!; there!, fancy that!; I told you so!; (*to dog*) here boy!

3 tomarse *vr* **(a)** to take; — **la venganza por su mano** to take vengeance with one's own hands; **no te lo tomes así** don't take it that way; **se lo sabe tomar bien** he knows how to take it, he can take it in his stride; **se tomó unas vacaciones larguísimas** he took tremendously long holidays; **se tomó un tremendo disgusto** he received a very severe blow; **se tomó 13 cervezas seguidas** he drank down 13 beers one after the other. **(b)** — **por** to think oneself, consider oneself to be; **¿por quién se toma aquel ministro?** who does that minister think he is? **(c)** — (**de orín**) to get rusty.

Tomás *m* Thomas; — **Moro** Thomas More.

tomatal *nm* **(a)** tomato bed, tomato field. **(b)** (*SAm*) tomato plant.

tomate *nm* tomato; **ponerse como un** — to turn as red as a beetroot.

tomatera *nf* **(a)** tomato plant. **(b)** (*Chi*) drunken spree (*fam*); rowdy party.

tomatero *nm* tomato grower; tomato dealer.

tomavistas *nm*, *pl* **tomavistas** film camera, cine-camera.

tómbola *nf* tombola.

tomillo *nm* thyme; — **salsero** savory.

tominero *adj* (*Mex*) mean.

tomismo *nm* Thomism.

tomista 1 *adj* Thomist. **2** *nmf* Thomist.

tomo[1] *nm* volume; **en 3** —**s** in 3 volumes.

tomo[2] *nm* bulk, size; (*fig*) importance; **de** — **y lomo** utter, out-and-out; **un canalla de** — **y lomo** a real rotter.

tomón *adj* (*Col*) teasing, jokey.

tompiate *nm* (*Mex*) basket made of palm leaves; bag, pouch, knapsack.

ton: sin — **ni son** for no particular reason; without rhyme or reason.

tonada *nf* (**a**) tune, song, air. (**b**) (*SAm*) accent, local peculiarity, typical intonation. (**c**) (*Cu*) fib, hoax.

tonadilla *nf* little tune; merry tune, light-hearted song.

tonal *adj* tonal.

tonalidad *nf* (**a**) (*Mus*) key; tonality; (*Radio*) tone; — **mayor** major key; — **menor** minor key; **control de** — tone control.
(**b**) (*Art*) shade; colour scheme; **una bella** — **de verde** a beautiful shade of green; **cambiar la** — **de un cuarto** to change the colour scheme of a room.

tonel *nm* barrel, cask, keg.

tonelada *nf* ton; — **métrica** metric ton; — **de registro** register ton; **un buque de 30.000** —**s de registro bruto** a ship of 30,000 gross register tons.

tonelaje *nm* tonnage.

tonelería *nf* cooperage, barrel making.

tonelero *nm* cooper.

tonelete *nm* (**a**) cask, keg. (**b**) short skirt; (*man's*) kilt.

tonga *nf* (**a**) layer, stratum; (*of bricks*) course. (**b**) (*Cu, Mex*) pile. (**c**) (*Aragón, Arg, Col*) job, task; spell of work. (**d**) (*Col*) nap.

tongada *nf* layer, coat, covering.

tongo[1] *nm* (*Sport*) fixing, throwing of a game (*or* fight *etc*); **¡hay** —! it's been fixed!, it's been rigged!; **hubo** — **en las elecciones** the elections were rigged.

tongo[2] *nm* (*Chi*) (**a**) bowler hat. (**b**) rum punch.

tongonearse [1a] *vr* (*SAm*) = **contonearse**.

tongoneo *nm* (*SAm*) = **contoneo**.

tongorí *nm* (*Arg, Bol*) liver (of cow *etc*); offal; lights.

tongoy *nm* (*SAm*) bowler hat.

tónica *nf* (*Mus*) tonic; keynote (*also fig*); **es una de las** —**s del estilo moderno** it is one of the keynotes of the modern style.

tonicidad *nf* tonicity.

tónico 1 *adj* (**a**) (*Mus*) tonic; (*Ling*) syllable tonic, stressed, accented. (**b**) (*Med*) tonic, invigorating, stimulating (*also fig*). **2** *nm* tonic (*also fig*).

tonificador *adj*, **tonificante** *adj* invigorating, stimulating.

tonificar [1g] *vt* to tone up; to invigorate, fortify.

tonillo *nm* (**a**) singsong, monotone, monotonous voice. (**b**) sarcastic tone, mocking undertone.

tono *nm* (**a**) (*Mus*) tone; pitch; key; — **mayor** major key; — **menor** minor key; **estar a** — to be in key; **estar a** — **con** (*fig*) to be in tune with.
(**b**) (*of voice etc, also fig*) tone; — **de marcar** (*Tel*) dialling tone; — **de voz** tone of voice; **a este** — **in** the same fashion, in the same vein; **en** — **bajo** in low tones; **en** — **de enojo** in an angry tone; **bajar el** — to lower one's voice; (*fig*) to change one's tune, quieten down; **cambiar el** (*or* **de**) — to change one's tune; **la expresión tiene un** — **despectivo** the expression has a pejorative tone; **la discusión tomó un** — **áspero** the discussion took on a harsh tone.
(**c**) (*social etc*) tone; **buen** — tone, good tone; **una familia de** — a good family, a family of some social standing; **de buen** — elegant, fashionable; (*hum*) genteel, refined; **de mal** — common, coarse; **eso no es de** — that's not done, that's not nice; **fuera de** — inappropriate; **dar el** — to set the tone; **darse** — to put on airs; **subirse de** — to get more haughty (*or* angry), take a more arrogant (*or* indignant) line; **no venir a** — to be inappropriate, be out of place.
(**d**) (*Mus*) tuning fork.
(**e**) (*Mus: of wind instrument*) slide.
(**f**) (*Anat, Med*) tone.
(**g**) (*of colour*) shade, hue; — **pastel** pastel shade.

tonsura *nf* tonsure.

tonsurado *adj* tonsured.

tonsurar [1a] *vt* to clip, shear; (*Eccl*) to tonsure.

tontada *nf* = **tontería**.

tontaina *nmf* (*fam*) idiot, dimwit (*fam*).

tontamente *adv* foolishly, stupidly.

tontear [1a] *vi* (*fam*) (**a**) to fool about, act the fool; to talk nonsense. (**b**) (*of lovers*) to exchange witty talk, flirt humorously.

tontería *nf* (**a**) (*quality*) silliness, foolishness, stupidity.
(**b**) (*una* —) silly thing; foolish act, stupid remark; —**s** nonsense, rubbish; **¡déjate de** —**s**! stop that nonsense!, quit fooling!; **dejémonos de** —**s** let's be serious; **hacer una** — to do a silly thing, do something silly; **no es ninguna** — it's not such a bad idea; it's not just a small thing, it's more serious than you think.
(**c**) (*fig*) triviality; **lo vendió por una** — he sold it for a song; **estima cualquier** — **de ese autor** he values any little thing by that writer.
(**d**) (*fig*) silly scruple; —**s** display of delicacy (*or* squeamishness *etc*).

tonto 1 *adj* (**a**) silly, foolish, stupid; (*Med*) imbecile; **¡qué** — **soy!** how silly of me!; **¡no seas** —! don't be silly!; **es lo bastante** — **como para** + *infin* he's fool enough to + *infin*; **dejar a uno** — to dumbfound someone.
(**b**) *lover* silly, soft, mushy.
(**c**) **a tontas y a locas** anyhow, unsystematically, haphazardly; **lo hace a tontas y a locas** he does it just anyhow; **repartir golpes a tontas y a locas** to hit out wildly, hit out blindly.
2 *nm*, **tonta** *nf* (**a**) fool, idiot; (*Med*) imbecile; —! you idiot!; **soy un** — I'm an idiot, I must be crazy; — **del bote**, — **de capirote** prize idiot, utter fool; **hacer(se) el** — to act the fool, play the fool.
(**b**) (*Circus, Theat*) clown, funny man.
(**c**) (*Col, CR, Chi*) jemmy.

tontón[1] *nm*, **tontona** *nf* (*fam*) = **tonto 2**.

tontón[2] *nm* (*fam*) smock, maternity dress.

tontura *nf* = **tontería (a)**.

tontureco *adj* (*CAm*) = **tonto 1**.

tonudo *adj* (*Arg*) classy (*fam*).

tony ['toni] *nm* (*SAm: angl*) clown.

topacio *nm* topaz.

topar [1a] **1** *vt* (**a**) (*Zool*) to butt, horn.
(**b**) *person* to run into, come across, bump into; *object* to find, come across; **le topé por casualidad en el museo** I happened to bump into him in the museum.
(**c**) (*Chi, Mex, Per*) to wager, stake.
2 *vi* (**a**) — **contra**, — **en** to run into, hit, bump into, knock against.
(**b**) — **con** = **1** (**b**); — **con un obstáculo** to run up against an obstacle, encounter an obstacle.
(**c**) **la dificultad topa en eso** that's where the trouble lies, there's the rub.
(**d**) (*Mex*) to quarrel.
3 toparse *vr* = **2** (**b**).

tope[1] **1** *adj* top, maximum; **edad** — **para un puesto** maximum (*or* minimum) age for a job; **fecha** — closing date, last date; **precio** — top price, ceiling price; **sueldo** — top salary, maximum salary.
2 *nm* (**a**) end; top, maximum, limit; ceiling; (*Naut*) top, masthead; **al** — **end to end; hasta el** — to the brim, to the limit; **estar hasta los** —**s** (*Naut*) to be overloaded, be loaded to the gunwales; (*fig*) to be full to bursting; **estoy hasta los** —**s** I'm utterly fed up.
(**b**) (*Naut: person*) lookout.
(**c**) (*Arg, Col*) peak, summit.

tope[2] *nm* (**a**) bump, knock, bang; (*with head*) butt; collision.
(**b**) (*fig*) quarrel; scuffle.
(**c**) (*Mech etc*) catch, stop, check; (*Rail*) buffer; (*Aut*) bumper; (*of gun*) catch.
(**d**) (*fig*) snag, difficulty; **ahí está el** — that's just the trouble.

topera *nf* molehill.

toperol *nm* (*Chi, Mex*) brass tack.

topetada *nf* butt, bump, bang, collision.

topetar [1a] *vt* (**a**) to butt, bump. (**b**) (*fig*) to bump into.

topetazo *nm* = **topetada**.

topetear [1a] *vt* (*Col*) = **topetar**.

topetón *nm* = **topetada**.

tópico 1 *adj* (*Med*) local; for external application.
2 *nm* (**a**) commonplace, platitude; cliché; catchphrase.
(**b**) (*SAm: angl*) topic, subject.

topillo *nm* (*Mex*) trick, swindle.

topo[1] *nm* (**a**) (*Zool*) mole. (**b**) (*fig*) clumsy person, blunderer.

topo[2] *nm* (*SAm*) large pin.

topocho *adj* (*Ven*) (**a**) plump, chubby. (**b**) full up.

topografía *nf* topography.

topográfico *adj* topographic(al).

topógrafo *nm* topographer; surveyor.

topolino 1 _nf_ teenager, bobbysoxer (_US fam_). **2** —s _nmpl_ wedge-heeled shoes.
topón _nm_ (_SAm_) = **topetada**.
toponimia _nf_ (**a**) toponymy, place-names; **la** — visigótica de España the Visigothic place-names of Spain. (**b**) study of place-names.
topónimo _nm_ place-name.
toposo _adj_ (_Ven_) (**a**) meddlesome. (**b**) pedantic.
toque _nm_ (**a**) (_act_) touch; **dar los primeros** —s a to make a start on; **dar el último** — a to put the finishing touch to; **faltan algunos** —s **para completarlo** it needs a few touches to finish it off.
　(**b**) (_Art_) touch; dab (of colour); — **de luz** light.
　(**c**) (_Chem_) test; assay; **dar un** — a to test; _person_ to sound out.
　(**d**) (_Mus_) (_of bell_) peal, chime; stroke; ring; (_of drum_) beat; (_of siren_) hoot, blast; (_Mil_) bugle call; — **de atención** (_fig_) warning note; — **de diana** reveille; — **de difuntos** passing bell, knell; — **de queda** curfew; — **de retreta** tattoo; **al — de las doce** on the stroke of twelve.
　(**e**) (_fig_) crux; essence, heart of the matter; **ahí está el** — that's the crux of the matter.
　(**f**) (_Bol_) turn.
toquetear [1a] _vt_ (**a**) to touch repeatedly, handle, keep fingering. (**b**) (_Mus_) to mess about on, play idly. (**c**) (_SAm_) to fondle, feel, caress.
toqueteo _nm_ (_SAm_) fondling, feeling, caressing.
toquido _nm_ (_Guat, Mex_) = **toque**.
toquilla _nf_ headscarf; knitted shawl, woollen bonnet; (_Par, Per etc_) straw hat.
torácico _adj_ thoracic.
torada _nf_ herd of bulls.
tórax _nm_ thorax.
torbellino _nm_ (**a**) whirlwind; dust cloud. (**b**) (_fig_) whirl. (**c**) (_fig_) restless and unsound individual, energetic but disorganized person.
torcaz _adj_: see **paloma**.
torcecuello _nm_ (_Orn_) wryneck.
torcedor _nm_ (**a**) (_Tech_) spindle. (**b**) (_fig_) torture, torment.
torcedura _nf_ (**a**) twist(ing); (_Med_) sprain, strain, wrench. (**b**) weak wine.
torcer [2b _and_ 2h] **1** _vt_ (**a**) (_general sense_) to twist; to bend; _wood etc_ to warp; _limb_ to twist, wrench, put out; _muscle_ to strain; _ankle_ to sprain, twist; _eyes_ to turn; _ball_ to spin, cut; — **el gesto**, — **el hocico** (_sl_) to make a (wry) face; to scowl, look cross.
　(**b**) _clothes, hands, neck_ to wring; _strands, rope_ to plait.
　(**c**) (_fig_) _decision, course of events_ to influence, affect; _will_ to bend; _thoughts_ to turn (_de_ from); _person_ to dissuade, turn (_de_ from).
　(**d**) (_fig_) _justice_ to pervert; _person_ to corrupt, bribe.
　(**e**) (_fig_) _sense_ to twist, pervert, distort.
　2 _vi_ (**a**) (_of road, vehicle, traveller_) to turn; **el coche torció a la izquierda** the car turned left; **al llegar allí tuerza Vd a la derecha** when you reach there turn right.
　(**b**) (_of ball_) to spin; to swerve.
　3 torcerse _vr_ (**a**) to twist; to bend; to warp.
　(**b**) — **un pie** to twist one's foot, sprain one's foot.
　(**c**) (_fig_) to go astray, be perverted; (_Med etc_) to suffer in one's development; (_events_) to take a strange turn; (_hope, plan etc_) to go all wrong, go awry.
　(**d**) (_milk, wine_) to turn sour.
torcida _nf_ wick.
torcidamente _adv_ (**a**) in a twisted way, crookedly. (**b**) (_fig_) deviously, in a crooked way.
torcido 1 _adj_ (**a**) twisted; bent; _road etc_ crooked, twisty, full of turns; **el cuadro está** — the picture is askew, the picture is not straight; **llevaba el sombrero algo** — he had his hat on not quite straight.
　(**b**) (_fig_) devious, crooked.
　(**c**) (_CAm, Col, S D, Ven_) unlucky.
　2 _nm_ curl; (_of silk etc_) twist.
torcijón _nm_ (**a**) sudden twist. (**b**) = **retortijón**.
torcimiento _nm_ = **torcedura**.
tordillo _adj_ dappled, dapple-grey.
tordo 1 _adj_ dappled, dapple-grey. **2** _nm_ (_Orn_) thrush.
torear [1a] **1** _vt_ (**a**) _bull_ to fight, play.
　(**b**) (_fig_) to dodge, avoid.
　(**c**) (_fig_) to keep at bay; to tease, draw on; to put off, keep guessing.
　(**d**) (_fig_) to plague, confuse.
　(**e**) (_Arg, CAm_) _animal_ to provoke, enrage; (_Arg, Mex_) _person_ to infuriate.
　(**f**) (_Bol, RPl: of dog_) to bark furiously at.
　2 _vi_ (**a**) (_Taur_) to fight, fight bulls; to be a bull-

fighter; **toreó bien Suárez** Suárez fought well; **no volverá a** — he will never fight again; **el muchacho quiere** — the boy wants to be a bullfighter.
　(**b**) (_Bol, RPl_) to bark furiously.
toreo _nm_ (**a**) (art of) bullfighting. (**b**) (_Mex_) illicit still.
torera _nf_ (**a**) short tight jacket. (**b**) **saltarse algo a la** — to pay no attention to something.
torería _nf_ (**a**) (class of) bullfighters; bullfighting world. (**b**) (_Cu, Guat_) mischief, prank.
torero _nm_ bullfighter.
torete _nm_ (**a**) small bull, young bull. (**b**) (_fig_) strong boy, robust child; (_pej_) rough child; bad-tempered boy.
toril _nm_ bullpen.
torio _nm_ thorium.
tormenta _nf_ (**a**) storm.
　(**b**) (_fig_) storm; turmoil, upheaval; — **en un vaso de agua** storm in a teacup; **sufrió una** — **de celos** she suffered a great pang of jealousy; **desencadenó una** — **de pasiones** it unleashed a storm of passions.
　(**c**) (_fig_) misfortune; reverse, setback.
tormento _nm_ torture; (_fig_) torture, torment; anguish, agony; **dar** — a to torture; (_fig_) to torment, plague; **darse** — to torment oneself; **estos zapatos son un** — these shoes are agony; **sus dos hijos son un** — **perpetuo** her two sons are a perpetual torment to her.
tormentoso _adj_ stormy (_also fig_).
tormo _nm_ lump, mass.
torna _nf_ (**a**) return.
　(**b**) **volver las** —s **a uno** to make everything come out all wrong for someone; **se han vuelto las** —s now it's all changed, now the boot's on the other foot.
tornada _nf_ return.
tornadera _nf_ pitchfork, winnowing fork.
tornadizo 1 _adj_ changeable; fickle. **2** _nm_, **tornadiza** _nf_ (_Hist_) renegade.
tornado _nm_ tornado.
tornar [1a] **1** _vt_ (**a**) to give back, return.
　(**b**) to change, alter, transform (_en_ into).
　2 _vi_ (**a**) to go back, come back, return.
　(**b**) — **a hacer algo** to do something again; **tornó a llover** it began to rain again; **tornó a estudiar el problema** he returned to the study of the problem.
　(**c**) — **en sí** to regain consciousness, come to.
　3 tornarse _vr_ (**a**) to return.
　(**b**) to turn, become.
tornasol _nm_ (**a**) (_Bot_) sunflower. (**b**) (_Chem_) litmus; **papel de** — litmus paper. (**c**) (_fig_) sheen, iridescence.
tornasolado _adj_ iridescent, sheeny; full of different lights; _fabric_ shot.
tornasolar [1a] **1** _vt_ to make iridescent, put a sheen on. **2 tornasolarse** _vr_ to be (_or become_) iridescent, show different lights.
tornavía _nf_ (_Rail_) turntable.
tornavoz _nf_ baffle; sounding board; (_of pulpit_) canopy; **hacer** — to cup one's hands to one's mouth.
torneado _adj_ (**a**) (_Tech_) turned (on a lathe). (**b**) _arm etc_ shapely, delicately curved; pleasingly rounded.
tornear [1a] _vt_ to turn (on a lathe).
torneo _nm_ tournament, competition; (_Hist_) tourney, joust; — **de tenis** tennis tournament; — **por equipos** team tournament.
tornero _nm_ machinist, turner, lathe operator.
tornillo _nm_ (**a**) screw; bolt; — **de banco** vice, vise (_US_), clamp; — **sin fin** worm gear; **apretar los** —s **a uno** to apply pressure on someone, put the screws on someone; **le falta un** — (_fam_) he has a screw loose (_fam_).
　(**b**) (_Mil_) **hacer** — to desert.
torniquete _nm_ (**a**) turnstile. (**b**) (_Med_) tourniquet.
torniscón _nm_ (**a**) pinch, squeeze. (**b**) slap on the face; smack on the head, cuff.
torno _nm_ (**a**) (_Tech_) winch, windlass; drum; winding machine.
　(**b**) (_Tech_) lathe; — **de banco** vice, vise (_US_), clamp; — **de tornero** turning lathe; **labrar a** — to turn on the lathe.
　(**c**) (_Tech_) — **de alfarero** potter's wheel; — **de asador** spit; — **de hilar** spinning wheel.
　(**d**) revolving door.
　(**e**) (_of cart etc_) brake.
　(**f**) (_of river_) bend; race, rapids.
　(**g**) **en** — a round, about; **se reunieron en** — **suyo** they gathered round him; **todo estaba inundado en muchos kilómetros en** — for many miles all round everything was flooded; **en** — **a este tema** on this theme, about this subject; **polemizar en** — **a un texto** to argue about a text.

toro nm (a) (*Zool*) bull; — **bravo,** — **de lidia** fighting bull; **coger el** — **por los cuernos, irse a la cabeza del** — to take the bull by the hórns; **echar** (*or* **soltar**) **el** — **a uno** to give someone a severe dressing-down. (b) (*fig*) strong man, he-man (*fam*); solidly-built man; tough guy (*fam*); **ser** — **corrido** to be an old hand at it, be an old fox. (c) **los** —**s** bullfight; (art of) bullfighting; **los** —**s cuestan más cada año** the bullfighting business grows more expensive each year; **este año no habrá** —**s** there will be no bullfight this year; **ir a los** —**s, ir de** —**s** to go to the bullfight; **no me gustan los** —**s** I don't like bullfighting; **ciertos son los** —**s** it turns out that it's true; **ver los** —**s desde la barrera** to be able to take an independent view, remain uncommitted; to sit on the fence. (d) **hacer** —**s** (*fam*) to play truant, cut class.

torombolo adj (*Cu*) plump, potbellied.
toronja nf grapefruit.
toronjil nm balm.
toronjo nm grapefruit tree.
torpe adj (a) *person* clumsy, awkward; slow, ungainly; *movement* slow, sluggish, heavy. (b) *handle, key etc* stiff. (c) *person (mentally)* dense, dim, slow-witted. (d) (*fig*) morally vile; dishonest, dishonourable. (e) (*fig*) crude, obscene.
torpear [1a] vi (*Chi*) to be dishonest, behave dishonourably.
torpedear [1a] vt to torpedo (*also fig*).
torpedero nm torpedo boat.
torpedo nm torpedo.
torpemente adv (a) clumsily, awkwardly; slowly, sluggishly, heavily. (b) stiffly. (c) slow-wittedly. (d) (*fig*) vilely, dishonestly. (e) (*fig*) crudely, obscenely.
torpeza nf (a) clumsiness, awkwardness; slowness, ungainliness; sluggishness, heaviness. (b) stiffness. (c) denseness, dimness, slowness of wit. (d) (*fig*) moral vileness; dishonesty. (e) (*fig*) crudeness, obscenity. (f) (*una* —) mistake, error of taste, lack of tact; **fue una** — **más** it was yet another instance of tastelessness.
torpón adj (*Chi*) =**torpe.**
torrados nmpl toasted chickpeas.
torrar [1a] vt to toast, roast.
torre nf (a) (*Archit etc*) tower; (*Radio, TV etc*) mast, tower, (*of oil well*) derrick; **T—** **de Babel** Tower of Babel; — **de conducción eléctrica** electricity pylon; — **de control** (*Aer*) control tower; — **del homenaje** keep; — **de marfil** ivory tower; — **de refrigeración** cooling tower; — **de vigía** (*Naut*) crow's-nest. (b) (*Chess*) rook, castle. (c) (*Aer, Mil, Naut*) turret; (*Mil*) watchtower; — **de mando** conning tower. (d) (*Ant, Mex*) factory chimney.
torrefacción nf toasting, roasting.
torrefacto adj toasted, roasted.
torreja nf (*SAm*) (fried) slices of fruit and vegetables; (*Chi*) slice of fruit.
torrencial adj torrential.
torrente nm (a) rushing stream, mountain stream, torrent; **llover a** —**s** to rain cats and dogs, rain in torrents. (b) (*Anat:* also — **de sangre**) bloodstream. (c) (*fig*) stream, torrent, rush, flood; onrush; — **de palabras** torrent of words, rush of words; — **de voz** loud strong voice.
torrentera nf gully, watercourse.
torrentoso adj (*SAm*) torrential, rushing.
torreón nm tower; (*Archit*) turret.
torrero nm lighthouse keeper.
torreta nf (a) (*Aer, Mil, Naut*) turret; (*of submarine*) conning tower. (b) (*Elec*) pylon, mast.
torrezno nm rasher, slice of bacon.
tórrido adj torrid.
torrificar [1g] vt (*Mex*) to toast, roast.
torrija nf slice of fried bread.
torsión nf twist(ing); warp(ing); (*Mech*) torsion, torque.
torsional adj torsional.
torso nm (*Anat*) torso; (*Art*) head and shoulder; (*Sculpture*) bust.
torta nf (a) cake; tart, flan; (*fig*) cake, flat mass, round lump; **la** — **costó un pan** it worked out dearer than expected, (*fig*) it was more trouble than it was worth; **eso es** —**s y pan pintado** it's child's play, it's

a cinch (*sl*); **no entendió ni** — he didn't understand a word of it. (b) (*CAm, Mex;* also — **de huevos**) omelet(te). (c) (*Typ*) fount. (d) (*fam*) slap, punch, sock (*fam*).
tortazo nm (*fam*) slap, punch, sock (*fam*).
tortear [1a] **1** vt (*Chi*) *dough* to flatten, roll; (*CAm, Mex*) *pancake* to shape (with the palms of one's hands). **2** vi (*Mex*) to clap, applaud.
tortero adj (*Bol, Par*) round and flat, disc-shaped.
tortícolis nm, **torticolis** nm crick in the neck, stiff neck.
tortilla nf (a) omelet(te); — **a la española,** — **de patatas** Spanish potato omelette; **cambiar** (*or* **volver**) **la** — **a uno** to turn the tables on someone; **se le volvió la** — it came out all wrong for him, his luck let him down; **se ha vuelto la** — now the boot is on the other foot; **hacer algo una** — to smash something up; **hacer a uno una** — to beat someone up; **van a hacer el negocio una** — they're sure to mess the deal up. (b) (*CAm, Mex*) flat maize pancake, *tortilla*. (c) (*tabu*) lesbian intercourse.
tortillera nf (a) (*CAm, Mex*) nf woman who sells maize pancakes. (b) (*tabu*) lesbian.
tortita nf pancake.
tórtola nf turtledove.
tortoleo nm (*Mex*) billing and cooing (*fig*).
tórtolo nm (male) turtledove; (*fam*) lovebird, loverboy (*fam*); —**s** (*fam*) pair of lovers, lovebirds.
tortuga nf tortoise; — **marina** turtle.
tortuoso adj (a) winding, tortuous, full of bends. (b) (*fig*) devious.
tortura nf torture (*also fig*).
torturar [1a] vt to torture.
toruno nm (a) (*CAm*) stud bull; (*RPl*) old bull; (*Chi, Ven*) ox. (b) (*Arg, Chi, Par*) elderly but still robust man.
torvisca nf, **torvisco** nm spurge flax.
torvo adj grim, stern, fierce.
torzal nm cord, twist (of silk); (*Chi, RPl*) plaited rope.
tos nf cough; coughing; — **ferina** whooping cough.
toscamente adv coarsely, roughly, crudely.
Toscana: La — Tuscany.
toscano 1 adj Tuscan. **2** nm, **toscana** nf Tuscan. **3** nm (*dialect*) Tuscan; (*Hist*) Italian.
tosco adj coarse, rough, crude (*also fig*).
tosedera nf (*CAm, Col, Ec*) persistent cough.
toser [2a] **1** vt (*fig*) **a no le tose nadie, no hay quien le tosa** nobody can compete with him, he's in a class by himself. (b) **a mí no me tose nadie** I'll not stand for that, I'm not taking that from anybody. **2** vi to cough.
tosido nm (*Chi, Guat, Mex*) cough.
tósigo nm poison.
tosquedad nf coarseness, roughness, crudeness (*also fig*).
tostada nf (a) toast, piece of toast. (b) (*fam*) **dar una** — **a uno, pegar una** — **a uno** to have someone on, cheat someone. (c) (*Arg*) long boring conversation; interminable visit.
tostado 1 adj (a) (*Cook*) toasted. (b) *colour* dark brown, ochre, burnt; *person, skin* (also — **por el sol**) brown, tanned, sunburnt. **2** nm tan.
tostador nm toaster; roaster; — **eléctrico,** — **de pan** electric toaster.
tostadora nf toaster.
tostar [1m] **1** vt (a) *bread etc* to toast; *coffee* to roast; (*Cook*) to brown. (b) *person, skin* to tan. (c) (*Chi, PR*) to tan, beat. (d) to continue vigorously what one has begun. (e) (*Mex*) to offend; to harm, hurt; to kill. **2 tostarse** vr (also — **al sol**) to tan, brown, get brown.
tostón nm (a) (*Cook*) small cube of toast, crouton; toast dipped in oil; toasted chickpea. (b) (*Cook*) roast sucking-pig. (c) (*Cook*) piece of bread (*etc*) toasted too much. (d) (*fam*) bore, boring thing; long boring speech, tedious tale; **dar el** — to be a bore, get on everybody's nerves. (e) (*fam*) bad play (*or* film *etc*), dreadful piece of work. (f) (*Ant, Ven*) slice of fried green banana. (g) (*Mex*) 50-cent piece.
tostonear [1a] vti (*Mex*) to sell at bargain prices.
total 1 adj total; whole, complete, utter, sheer; *anaesthetic* general; **una revisión** — **de su teoría a**

complete revision of his theory; **ha sido una calamidad** — it was an utter disaster.
2 *adv* in short, all in all; and so; when all is said and done; — **que . . .** to cut a long story short . . ., the upshot of it all was that . . .; —, **usted manda** well, you're the boss, after all; — **que no fuimos** so we didn't go after all.
3 *nm* (a) (*Math*) total, sum; whole; **el** — **de la población** the whole (of the) population; **en** — in all. **(b) en** — (*fig*) = **2**.

totalidad *nf* whole; totality; **en su** — as a whole, in its entirety; **la** — **de los obreros** all the workers; **la** — **de la población** the whole (of the) population; **pero el hombre en su** — **se nos escapa** but the whole man eludes us.

totalista *adj* complete, thoroughgoing.

totalitario *adj* totalitarian.

totalitarismo *nm* totalitarianism.

totalizador *nm* totalizator.

totalizar [1f] **1** *vt* to totalize, add up. **2** *vt* to add up to; to come to, amount to.

totalmente *adv* totally, wholly, completely.

totazo *nm* (a) (*Col*) bursting, explosion. (b) (*Col, Cu*) bang on the head; (*Ven*) blow.

totear [1a] **1** *vi* (*Col, Ven*) to burst, explode. **2 totearse** *vr* (*Col, Ven*) to burst; to crack, split.

tótem *nm*, *pl* **tótems** totem.

totémico *adj* totemic.

totemismo *nm* worship of totems.

totora *nf* (*SAm*) reed.

totoreco *adj* (*CAm*) stupid.

totovía *nf* woodlark.

totuma *nf* (a) (*Col, SD, Ven*) gourd, calabash. (b) (*Chi*) bump, bruise; abscess; bump on the back. (c) (*Per, Ven*) head.

totumo *nm* (a) (*Col, Ec, Per, Ven*) calabash tree. (b) (*Chi*) bump on the head; bump on the back.

tóxico 1 *adj* toxic, poisonous. **2** *nm* poison.

toxicología *nf* toxicology.

toxicológico *adj* toxicological.

toxicólogo *nm* toxicologist.

toxicomanía *nf* drug addiction.

toxicómano 1 *adj* addicted to drugs. **2** *nm*, **toxicómana** *nf* drug addict.

toxina *nf* toxin.

tozudez *nf* obstinacy.

tozudo *adj* obstinate.

traba *nf* (a) (*general sense*) bond, tie; (*of table etc*) crosspiece; (*Mech*) lock; (*on horse*) hobble; (*on prisoner*) fetter, shackle.
(b) (*fig*) bond, link, tie; (*pej*) hindrance, obstacle; —s trammels, shackles; **desembarazado de** —s free, unrestrained; **poner** —**s a** to shackle; to restrain, check; **ponerse** —**s** to place restrictions on oneself, limit one's own freedom to act.
(c) (*Cu, Mex*) cockfight; cockpit.

trabacuenta *nf* mistake; **andar con** —**s** to be engaged in endless controversies.

trabado *adj* (a) joined; linked; *speech etc* coherent, well constructed. (b) (*fig*) strong, tough. (c) (*Col*) cross-eyed. (d) (*Mex*) stammering.

trabajado *adj* (a) *person* worn out, weary from over-work. (b) carefully worked, elaborately fashioned; (*pej*) forced, strained, artificial.

trabajador 1 *adj* hard-working, industrious. **2** *nm* worker, workman; labourer; (*Pol*) worker; — **eventual** casual worker; — **portuario** docker.

trabajar [1a] **1** *vt* (a) *land* to work, till; *material, wood etc* to work; *dough* to knead; *ingredients* to mix, stir, work in.
(b) *subject, study* to work at, work on; *aspect, detail* to give special attention to, work to bring out; *deal, project etc* to work at, carry forward, pursue, follow up; (*Comm*) *goods* to run a line in, deal particularly with, handle; **estoy trabajando el latín** I am working away at Latin; **es mi colega quien trabaja esos géneros** it is my colleague who handles that line; **el pintor ha trabajado muy bien los árboles** the painter has taken special care over the trees.
(c) *horse* to train.
(d) *person* to work, drive, push.
(e) *person* (*fig*) to work on, get to work on, persuade; **trabaja a su tía para sacarle los ahorros** he's working on his aunt in order to get hold of her savings.
(f) *mind etc* to trouble, bother.
2 *vi* (a) to work (*de* as; *en* in, at); — **mucho** to work hard; — **más** to work harder; — **como un buey** (*etc*) to work like a Trojan; — **por horas** to be paid by the hour; to work part-time; — **a ritmo lento** (*of workers*) to go slow; — **por** + *infin* to

strive to + *infin*; **hacer** — *money etc* to put to good use, make work; *water power, resources etc* to harness.
(b) (*fig*) — **con uno para que** + *subj* to work on someone to + *infin*, persuade someone to + *infin*.
(c) (*fig*: *of process, time etc*) to work, operate; **el tiempo trabaja a nuestro favor** time is working for us.
(d) (*fig*: *of soil, tree etc*) to bear, produce, yield.

trabajo *nm* (a) (*in general*) work; (*Mech*) work; (*un* —) job, task; (*Art, Lit etc*) work, piece of work; — **de campo**, — **en el propio campo** fieldwork; — **a destajo** piecework; — **en equipo** teamwork; — **excesivo**, — **intenso** overwork; —**s forzados** hard labour; — **intelectual** brainwork; — **manual** manual labour; —**s manuales** (*School etc*) handicraft; — **nocturno** night work; — **por turno** shift work; **ropa de** — working clothes; **los sin** — the unemployed; **estar sin** — to be out of a job, be unemployed; **hacer** — **lento** to go slow; **ir al** — to go to work.
(b) (*Pol*) labour; the workers, the working class.
(c) (*fig*) effort, labour; trouble; —**s** troubles, difficulties, hardships; **ahorrarse el** — to save oneself the trouble; **tomarse el** — **de** + *infin* to take the trouble to + *infin*; **lo hizo con mucho** — he did it after a lot of trouble, it took him a lot of effort to do it; **le cuesta** — + *infin* he finds it hard to + *infin*, it is difficult for him to + *infin*; **dar** — to cause trouble; — **te doy**, — **te mando** it's no easy task, it's a tough job; **tener** — **de sobra para poder** + *infin* to have one's work cut out to + *infin*.

trabajosamente *adv* laboriously; painfully.

trabajoso *adj* (a) hard, laborious; painful.
(b) (*Med*) pale, sickly.
(c) (*Arg, Mex*) exacting, demanding; wily.
(d) (*Col*) unhelpful; bad-tempered.
(e) (*Chi*) annoying.

trabalenguas *nm*, *pl* **trabalenguas** tongue twister.

trabar [1a] **1** *vt* (a) to join, unite, link.
(b) to seize; to lay hold of, catch, grasp; to tie down; to shackle, fetter; (*Mech*) to lock, fasten; to jam; *horse* to hobble.
(c) (*Cook etc*) to thicken.
(d) *saw* to set.
(e) (*fig*) *conversation, discussion etc* to start (up); *battle* to join, engage in; *friendship* to strike up.
(f) (*fig*) to impede, hinder, obstruct.
(g) (*Cu, Guat*) to deceive.
2 *vi* (*of plant*) to take, strike; (*of anchor etc*) to grip, hold.
3 trabarse *vr* (a) (*in rope etc*) to get entangled, get tangled up; (*of mechanism*) to lock, jam; to seize up; **se le traba la lengua** he gets tongue-tied, he stammers.
(b) (*SAm*) to get tongue-tied, stammer.
(c) (*also* — **de palabras**) to get involved in an argument; to wrangle, squabble.
(d) (*Cu*) to ramble, lose the thread.

trabazón *nf* (a) (*Tech*) joining, assembly; (*fig*) link, bond, (close) connection. (b) (*of liquid*) consistency; (*fig*) coherence.

trabilla *nf* small strap; clasp, belt loop; dropped stitch.

trabucar [1g] **1** *vt* to confuse, to jumble up, mix up, mess up; *sounds, words* to switch over, misplace, interchange. **2 trabucarse** *vr* to get all mixed up.

trabuco *nm* (*Hist*) catapult; (*also* — **naranjero**) blunderbuss; (*prov*) popgun.

traca *nf* string of fireworks.

trácala *nf* (a) (*Ec*) crowd, mob. (b) (*Mex, PR*) trick, ruse. (c) (*Mex*) trickster.

tracalada *nf* (a) (*SAm*) crowd; lot, mass; **una** — **de** a lot of. (b) (*Mex*) trick, ruse.

tracalero (*Mex, PR, Ven*) **1** *adj* tricky; sly, deceitful. **2** *nm* cheat, trickster.

tracamundana *nf* (*fam*) (a) row, rumpus (*fam*). (b) swap, exchange.

tracción *nf* traction; haulage; (*Mech*) drive, traction; — **delantera** front-wheel drive; — **trasera** rear-wheel drive; — **a las cuatro ruedas** four-wheel drive.

tracería *nf* tracery.

tracoma *nm* trachoma.

tractivo *adj* tractive.

tractor *nm* tractor; — **agrícola** agricultural tractor, farm tractor; — **de oruga** caterpillar tractor.

tractorista *nmf* tractor driver.

tradición *nf* tradition.

tradicional *adj* traditional.

tradicionalismo *nm* traditionalism.

tradicionalista 1 *adj* traditionalist. **2** *nmf* traditionalist.

tradicionalmente *adv* traditionally.

traducción *nf* translation (*a* into, *de* from); (*fig*) rendering, interpretation.

traducible *adj* translatable.

traducir [3f] **1** *vt* to translate (*a* into, *de* from); (*fig*) to render, interpret; to express. **2 traducirse** *vr*: — **en** (*fig*) to mean in practice; to entail, result in.

traductor *nm*, **traductora** *nf* translator.

traer [2p] **1** *vt* **(a)** to bring, get, fetch; to carry; to take; **¡trae!, ¡traiga!** hand it over!, give it here!; **el muchacho que trae los periódicos** the lad who brings the papers; **¿has traído el dinero?** have you brought the money?

(b) *clothing etc* to wear; *object* to wear, carry, have about one.

(c) (*of magnet etc*) to draw, attract, pull.

(d) (*fig*) to bring (about), cause; to involve; *consequences* to bring, have; — **consigo** to involve, entail; **nos trajo grandes perjuicios** it did us great harm, it caused a lot of trouble for us.

(e) (*of newspaper etc*) to carry, have, print; **este periódico no trae nada sobre el particular** this newspaper doesn't carry anything about the affair.

(f) *authority, reason etc* to adduce, bring forward; *see* **colación, cuento.**

(g) — + *adj etc* to have + *adj*, keep + *adj*; — **de cabeza a uno** to upset someone, bother someone; **el juego le trae perdido** gambling is his ruin; **la ausencia de noticias me trae muy inquieto** the lack of news is making me very anxious; *see* **frito, loco** *etc.*

(h) (*idioms*) — **a mal** — **a uno** to abuse someone, maltreat someone; to upset someone; to exasperate someone; to keep someone chasing about all over the place; = — **a mal** —. — **y llevar a uno** to gossip about someone; = — **a mal** —.

2 traerse *vr* **(a)** — **algo** to have something (improper) on hand; to be planning something (disreputable); **los dos se traen algún manejo sucio** the two of them are up to something shady.

(b) — **bien** to dress well; to behave properly; — **mal** to dress shabbily; to behave badly.

(c) — **las** to be annoying; to be difficult, be awkward; to be excessive; **es un problema que se las trae** it's a difficult problem; **ese punto realmente se las trae** that point really is a sticky one; **hace un calor que se las trae** this heat is too much of a good thing; **tiene un padre que se las trae** she has an excessively severe father.

trafagar [1h] *vi* to bustle about; to be on the move, keep on the go.

tráfago *nm* **(a)** (*Comm*) traffic, trade. **(b)** drudgery, toil; routine job. **(c)** bustle, hustle, intense activity.

trafaguear [1a] *vi* (*Mex*) to bustle about, keep on the go.

traficante *nm* trader, dealer (*en* in).

traficar [1g] *vi* **(a)** to trade, deal (*con* with, *en* in); to buy and sell; (*pej*) to traffic (*en* in).

(b) (*pej*) — **con** to deal illegally in, do illegal business in.

(c) to be on the move, keep on the go; to travel a lot.

tráfico *nm* **(a)** (*Comm*) trade, business; (*esp pej*) traffic (*en* in); — **en narcóticos** drug traffic.

(b) (*Aut, Rail etc*) traffic; — **de carga** (*SAm*), — **de mercancías** goods traffic; — **por ferrocarril** rail traffic.

(c) (*SAm*) transit, passage.

tragabalas *nm, pl* **tragabalas** (*Mex*) bully, braggart.

tragaderas *nfpl* **(a)** throat, gullet.

(b) (*fig*) gullibility; tolerance, broad-mindedness; **tener buenas** — to be gullible, be prepared to swallow anything; to be very easy-going, be prepared to put up with a lot, be excessively tolerant.

tragadero *nm* throat, gullet.

tragador *nm* glutton; — **de leguas** (*fam*) great walker.

trágala *nm* (*fam*) **(a)** glutton, greedy sort. **(b)** **cantar el** — **a uno** to mock someone's authority by doing precisely what he has forbidden.

tragaldabas *nmf, pl* **tragaldabas** (*fam*) glutton, greedy sort.

tragaleguas *nmf, pl* **tragaleguas** (*fam*) quick walker, great walker.

tragaluz *nm* skylight.

tragallón *adj* (*Chi*) greedy.

tragamonedas *nm, pl* **tragamonedas** = **tragaperras.**

tragantada *nf* swig, mouthful.

tragantón *adj* (*fam*) greedy, gluttonous.

tragantona *nf* (*fam*) **(a)** blow-out (*sl*), slap-up meal (*fam*). **(b)** (act of) swallowing hard.

tragaperras *nm, pl* **tragaperras** slot machine; *see* **máquina, tocadiscos** *etc.*

tragar [1h] **1** *vt* **(a)** (*general sense*) to swallow; to swallow down, drink up; (*pej*) to bolt, devour, swallow whole (*or* quickly *etc*); to gulp down, get down.

(b) (*of land etc*) to absorb, soak up, drink in; *see also* **3.**

(c) *abuse, reprimand* to have to listen to; *trick etc* to swallow, fall for, be taken in by; **hacer** — **algo a uno** to force someone to listen to something; to force someone to swallow something, make someone believe something.

(d) **no le puedo** — I can't stand him, I can't stomach him.

2 *vi* (*sl*) to screw (*tabu*); to sleep around.

3 tragarse *vr* **(a)** to swallow; to eat, get down; **se lo tragó entero** he swallowed it whole; **el perro se ha tragado un hueso** the dog has swallowed a bone; **eso me lo trago en dos minutos** I could eat that up in a couple of minutes.

(b) (*of land etc*) to absorb, soak up; (*of chasm, sea*) to swallow up, engulf; to suck down; *material, savings etc* to swallow up, use up, absorb.

(c) (*fig*) *unpleasant fact, tale etc* to swallow; **se tragará todo lo que se le diga** he'll swallow whatever he's told; **ya se lo tenía tragado** he had already learned to live with the idea, he had already prepared himself for that happening.

(d) = **1 (d).**

tragasables *nm, pl* **tragasables** sword-swallower.

tragasantos *nmf, pl* **tragasantos** excessively pious person.

tragavenado *nm* (*Col, Ven*) boa constrictor.

tragedia *nf* tragedy.

trágicamente *adv* tragically.

trágico 1 *adj* tragic(al); **lo** — **es que** ... the tragedy of it is that ..., the tragic thing about it is that ... **2** *nm* tragedian.

tragicomedia *nf* tragicomedy.

tragicómico *adj* tragicomic.

trago *nm* **(a)** drink, draught; swallow, mouthful, swig (*fam*); sip; **beber algo de un** — to drink something at a gulp; **brindar el** — **a uno** (*SAm*) to stand someone a drink; **echarse un** — to have a drink, have a swig; **no vendría mal un** — **de vino** a drop of wine would not come amiss.

(b) drink, drinking; (*SAm*) hard liquor; **ser demasiado aficionado al** — to be too fond of the drink.

(c) (*fig*) **mal** —, — **amargo** hard time, rough time; nasty blow; misfortune, calamity; **fue un** — **amargo** it was a cruel blow; **nos quedaba todavía el** — **más amargo** the worst of it was still to come.

(d) **hacer algo a** —**s** to do something bit by bit.

tragón *adj* greedy, gluttonous.

traguear [1a] **1** *vti* (*CR*) to drink; (*Ven*) to get drunk. **2 traguearse** *vr* (*CAm, Col, Mex*) to get drunk.

traición *nf* treachery; (*Law etc*) treason; (*una* —) betrayal, act of treason, treacherous act; **alta** — high treason; **matar a uno a** — to kill someone treacherously; **hacer** — **a uno** to betray someone.

traicionar [1a] *vt* to betray (*also fig*).

traicionero *adj* treacherous.

traída *nf* carrying, bringing; — **de aguas** water supply.

traído 1 *adj* **(a)** worn, old, threadbare. **(b)** (*fig*) — **y llevado** well-worn, trite, hackneyed. **2** —**s** *nmpl* (*Col*) presents.

traidor 1 *adj person* treacherous; *act* treasonable. **2** *nm* traitor; betrayer; (*Theat*) villain, bad character.

traidora *nf* traitress; betrayer.

traidoramente *adv* treacherously, traitorously.

traiga *etc see* **traer.**

tráiler *nm, pl* **tráilers** (*Cine: angl*) trailer.

traílla *nf* **(a)** (*Tech*) scraper, leveller; (*Agr*) harrow. **(b)** (*of dog*) lead, leash; lash. **(c)** team of dogs.

traillar [1a] *vt* to scrape; to level; (*Agr*) to harrow.

trainera *nf* small fishing boat.

Trajano *m* Trajan.

traje¹ *etc see* **traer.**

traje² *nm* (*in general*) dress, costume; (*man's*) suit; (*esp Chi, Pan, Per*) woman's dress; (*fig*) garb, guise; — **de baño** bathing costume, swimming costume, swimsuit; — **de calle** lounge suit; **un policía en** — **de calle** a policeman in plain clothes; — **de campaña** battledress; — **de ceremonia**, — **de etiqueta** full dress; dress suit, evening dress (*man's*); — **de cuartel** (*Mil*) undress; — **espacial** spacesuit; — **hecho** ready-made suit; — **(hecho) a la medida** made-to-measure suit; — **de luces** bullfighter's costume; — **de malla** tights; — **de**

montar riding habit; — **de noche** evening dress (*woman's*); — **de novia** wedding dress, bridal gown; — **de paisano** civilian clothes; — **pantalón** trouser suit; — **de playa** sunsuit; — **regional** regional costume, regional dress; **cortar un — a uno** (*fig*) to gossip about someone.

trajeado *adj*: **ir bien** — to be well dressed, be well turned out; **estar** — **de** to be dressed in; (*hum*) to be got up in, be rigged out in; **estar bien** — **para la temporada** to be well equipped with clothes for the season.

trajear [1a] **1** *vt* to clothe, dress (*de* in); (*hum*) to get up, rig out (*de* in). **2 trajearse** *vr* to dress up; to provide oneself with clothes.

trajín *nm* (a) haulage, carriage, transport.
(b) (*fam*) coming and going, movement; hustle, bustle, commotion; fuss.
(c) —**es** (*fam*) affairs, (suspicious) doings, goings-on.

trajinante *nm* (a) carrier, carter; haulage contractor.
(b) (*fam*) person who indulges in a lot of useless activity.

trajinar [1a] **1** *vt* (a) to carry, cart; to transport.
(b) (*Arg, Chi*) to swindle, deceive.
(c) (*Chi*) to search.
2 *vi* to bustle about; to travel around a lot; to be on the go, keep on the move.

trajinería *nf* carriage; haulage.

trajinista *nmf* (*Arg, Chi, PR*) busybody, snooper.

tralla *nf* whipcord, whiplash; lash.

trallazo *nm* (a) crack of a whip; lash. (b) (*fig*) telling-off.

trama *nf* (a) (*Tech*) weft, woof. (b) (*fig*) connection, link; correlation. (c) (*fig*) plot, scheme, intrigue; (*Lit*) plot.

tramar [1a] **1** *vt* (a) (*Tech*) to weave.
(b) (*fig*) to plan, plot; to scheme for, intrigue for; *plot* to lay, hatch; **están tramando algo** they're up to something; **¿qué estarán tramando?** I wonder what they're up to?
2 tramarse *vr* (*fig*): **algo se está tramando** there's something afoot, there's something going on.

trambucar [1g] *vi* (a) (*Col, Ven*) to be shipwrecked.
(b) (*Ven*) to go out of one's mind.

trambuque *nm* (*Col*) shipwreck.

trámil *adj* (*Chi*) awkward, clumsy.

tramitación *nf* transaction; negotiation; steps, procedure; handling.

tramitar [1a] *vt* to transact; to negotiate; to proceed with, carry forward; to handle.

trámite *nm* step, stage; transaction; —**s** procedure; (*Law*) proceedings; —**s de costumbre** usual channels; —**s oficiales** official channels; **los** —**s para la obtención de un visado** the procedure for obtaining a visa; **para acortar los** —**s de costumbre lo hacemos así** in order to get it quickly through the usual procedure we do it this way.

tramo *nm* (a) section, stretch; (*of road etc*) section, length; (*of bridge*) span; (*of stairs*) flight. (b) (*Agr*) plot.

tramontana *nf* (a) north wind; north. (b) (*fig*) conceit, pride; luxury. (c) (*fam*) **perder la** — to lose one's head.

tramontar [1a] **1** *vi* (*of sun*) to go behind the mountains. **2 tramontarse** *vr* to escape over the mountains.

tramoya *nf* (a) (*Theat*) piece of stage machinery. (b) trick, scheme, swindle; concealed part, secret part (of a deal). (c) (*fam*) **armar una** — to kick up a fuss.

tramoyar [1a] *vt* (*Per, Ven*) to swindle.

tramoyero *adj* (*Guat, PR*) tricky, sharp.

tramoyista *nm* (a) (*Theat*) scene shifter, stagehand.
(b) (*fig*) swindler, trickster; humbug; impostor; schemer.

trampa *nf* (a) trapdoor; hatch.
(b) (*Hunting etc*) trap; snare; (*Golf*) bunker; (*fig*) snare; catch, pitfall; — **explosiva** (*Mil*) booby trap; — **para ratas** rat-trap; **caer en la** — to fall for it, fall into the trap; **hay** — there's a catch in it; there's something fishy here; **esto es s¹ᵉ** — **ni cartón** this is the real thing; **este juego no tiene** — **ni cartón** there are no catches in this game.
(c) conjuring trick; **hacer** —**s** to juggle, conjure.
(d) (*fig*) trick, swindle, fraud; wangle (*fam*), fiddle (*fam*); hoax; (*Fin etc*) racket; **hacer** —**s** to cheat; to be on the fiddle; **hicieron una** — **con los votos** they fiddled the voting, they juggled with the votes; **hecha la ley, hecha la** — as soon as a new law is brought in someone finds a way to beat it.
(e) (*Comm*) bad debt.
(f) (*of trousers*) fly.

trampantojo *nm* (*fam*) sleight of hand, trick; (*fig*) fiddle (*fam*), cheat; underhand method.

trampear [1a] **1** *vt* to cheat, swindle. **2** *vi* (a) to cheat; to get money by false pretences. (b) **ir trampeando** to manage, get by; (*of dress, shoes etc*) to last out.

trampería *nf* = **tramposería**.

trampero 1 *adj* (*Guat, Mex, Par*) = **tramposo**. **2** *nm* (a) trapper. (b) (*Arg, Chi*) trap for birds.

trampilla *nf* (a) peephole. (b) trap, hatchway; (*of trousers*) fly.

trampista *nm* = **tramposo 2**.

trampolín *nm* springboard, diving board; trampoline.

tramposería *nf* crookedness; guile, deceit.

tramposo 1 *adj* crooked, tricky, swindling. **2** *nm* crook, twister (*fam*), swindler; cardsharper; (*Fin*) bad payer.

tranca *nf* (a) stick, cudgel, club. (b) beam, pole; (*of door, window*) bar. (c) = **tranquera** (b). (d) (*fam*) drunken spree (*fam*), binge (*sl*); **tener una** — (*SAm*) to be drunk. (e) (*Arg, Par*) safety catch. (f) (*PR, SD*) dollar, peso. (g) **a** —**s y barrancas** with great difficulty, against many obstacles; through fire and water.

trancada *nf* stride; **en dos** —**s** in a couple of strides; (*fig*) in a couple of ticks.

trancar [1g] **1** *vt door, window* to bar. **2** *vi* to stride along. **3 trancarse** *vr* (a) (*Cu, Ven*) to get drunk. (b) (*Chi, Mex, RPI*) to be constipated.

trancazo *nm* (a) blow, bang (with a stick). (b) (*Med: fam*) flu (*fam*).

trance *nm* (a) (difficult) moment, (awkward) juncture, (tough) situation; critical juncture, moment of peril; — **mortal, último** —, **postrer** — last moments, dying moments; **a todo** — at all costs; **estar en** — **de muerte** to be at the point of death, be at death's door; **estar en** — **de** + *infin* to be on the point of + *ger*, be in process of + *ger*; **puesto en tal** — placed in such a situation.
(b) hypnotic state; drugged condition; (spiritualistic) trance.

tranco *nm* (a) stride, big step; **a** —**s** (*fam*) pell-mell, hastily, in a rush; **andar a** —**s** to walk with long strides, take big steps; **en dos** —**s** in a couple of strides; (*fig*) in a couple of ticks.
(b) (*Archit*) threshold.

tranquera *nf* (a) palisade, fence. (b) (*SAm*) large gate in a fence (*for cattle*).

tranquero *nm* (*Col, Chi, Ven*) = **tranquera** (b).

tranquilamente *adv* calmly; peacefully; quietly.

tranquilidad *nf* stillness, calmness, tranquillity; peacefulness; quietness; freedom from anxiety; unruffled state; **dijo con toda** — he said calmly; **perder la** — to lose patience; to get worked up.

tranquilino *nm* (*SAm*) drunkard.

tranquilizador *adj music etc* soothing; lulling; *fact etc* reassuring.

tranquilizante 1 *adj* = **tranquilizador**. **2** *nm* (*Med*) tranquillizer.

tranquilizar [1f] **1** *vt* to calm, quieten, still; *mind* to reassure, relieve, set at ease; *person* to calm down; to reassure.
2 tranquilizarse *vr* to calm down; to stop worrying; **¡tranquilícese!** calm yourself!; don't worry!, never fear!

tranquilo *adj* (a) still, calm, tranquil; peaceful; quiet; *sea etc* calm; *mind* calm, free of worry, untroubled; *character, state* calm, unruffled; **dejar a uno** — to leave someone alone; **ir con la conciencia tranquila** to go with a clear conscience; **¡estad tranquilos!** don't worry!; keep calm!; **tú estáte** — **hasta que yo vuelva** you stay put till I come back, you just sit tight till I get back.
(b) (*pej*) thoughtless, unreliable, inconsiderate; **es un tío de lo más** — he's an utterly inconsiderate chap.

tranquilla *nf* (a) latch; pin. (b) (*in conversation*) trap; catch.

tranquillo *nm* (*fam*) knack; **coger el** — **a un problema** to get the hang of a problem, find the knack of solving a problem.

tranquiza *nf* (*Mex*) beating.

trans . . . **trans** . . . ; *for alternative spellings, see also* **tras** . . .

transacción *nf* (a) (*Comm etc*) transaction; deal, bargain; — **comercial** business deal. (b) compromise, compromise settlement; **llegar a una** — to reach a compromise.

transalpino 1 *adj* transalpine; from the other side of the Alps, (*esp*) Italian. **2** *nm*, **transalpina** *nf* person from the other side of the Alps, (*esp*) Italian.

transandino *adj* trans-Andean.

transar [1a] *vi* (*SAm*) = **transigir**.
transatlántico 1 *adj* *cable etc* transatlantic; *crossing* Atlantic; **los países** **—s** the countries on the other side of the Atlantic. **2** *nm* (*Naut*) liner.
transbordador *nm* (**a**) ferry; **— para coches** car ferry. (**b**) **puente —** transporter bridge.
transbordar [1a] **1** *vt* to transfer, move across, switch; (*Naut*) to tranship; (*across river*) to ferry across. **2** *vi* and **transbordarse** *vr* (*Rail etc*) to change.
transbordo *nm* (**a**) transfer; move, switch; (*Naut*) transhipment; ferrying. (**b**) (*Rail etc*) change; **hacer —, realizar —** to change (*en* at).
transcribir [3a; *ptp* **transcrito**] *vt* to transcribe; (*from different alphabet*) to transliterate.
transcripción *nf* transcription; transliteration.
transcurrir [3a] *vi* (**a**) to pass, go by, elapse; **han transcurrido 7 años** 7 years have passed.
   (**b**) (*of event etc*) to be, turn out; **la tarde transcurrió aburrida** the evening was boring; **las fiestas transcurren con gran alegría** the festivities are being held in a very happy atmosphere, the celebrations are turning out to be very merry.
transcurso *nm*: **— del tiempo** course of time, passing of time, lapse of time; **en el — de 8 días** in the course of a week, in the space of a week; **en el — de los años** in the course of the years.
transepto *nm* transept.
transeúnte 1 *adj* transient, transitory; *member etc* temporary. **2** *nmf* passer-by; temporary member (*or* inhabitant *etc*), non-resident.
transferencia *nf* transference; (*Law, Sport*) transfer; **— bancaria** banker's order; **— de crédito** credit transfer.
transferible *adj* transferable.
transferir [3i] *vt* (**a**) to transfer. (**b**) to postpone.
transfiguración *nf* transfiguration.
transfigurar [1a] *vt* to transfigure (*en* into).
transformable *adj* transformable; (*Aut*) convertible.
transformación *nf* transformation (*en* into); change, conversion (*en* into); changeover; (*Rugby*) conversion.
transformador *nm* (*Elec*) transformer.
transformar [1a] *vt* to transform (*en* into); to change, convert (*en* into).
transformismo *nm* (*Bio*) evolution, transmutation.
transformista *nmf* (*Theat*) quick-change artist(e).
tránsfuga *nm* (*Mil*) deserter; (*Pol*) turncoat.
transfundir [3a] *vt* (**a**) to transfuse. (**b**) *news etc* to tell, spread, disseminate.
transfusión *nf* transfusion; **— de sangre** blood transfusion; **hacer una — de sangre a uno** to give someone a blood transfusion.
transgredir [3a] *vti* to transgress.
transgresión *nf* transgression.
transgresor *nm*, **transgresora** *nf* transgressor.
transiberiano *adj* trans-Siberian.
transición *nf* transition (*a* to, *de* from); **período de —** transitional period.
transicional *adj* transitional.
transido *adj*: **— de angustia** beset with anxiety; **— de dolor** racked with pain; **— de frío** frozen to the marrow; **— de hambre** overcome with hunger.
transigencia *nf* (**a**) compromise; yielding. (**b**) accommodating attitude, spirit of compromise.
transigente *adj* accommodating, compromising; tolerant.
transigir [3c] *vi* to compromise (*con* with; *en cuanto a* on, about); to give way, yield, make concessions; **— en + infin** to agree to + *infin*; **yo no transijo con tales abusos** I cannot tolerate such abuses, I cannot compromise with such abuses; **hemos transigido con la demanda popular** we have bowed to the people's demand.
transistor *nm* transistor.
transistorizado *adj* transistorized.
transitable *adj* passable.
transitar [1a] *vi* to go, go from place to place, travel; **— por** to go along, pass along.
transitivamente *adv* transitively.
transitivo *adj* transitive.
tránsito *nm* (**a**) (*act*) transit, passage, movement; **"se prohíbe el —"** "no thoroughfare"; **estar de —** to be in transit, be passing through; **el — de este camino presenta dificultades** this road has its problems, the going on this road is not easy.
   (**b**) (*Aut etc*) movement, traffic; **— rodado** wheeled traffic, vehicular traffic; **calle de mucho —** busy street; **horas de máximo —** rush hours, peak traffic hours.
   (**c**) (*to job*) move, transfer.
   (**d**) (*Rel*) passing, death.

(**e**) (*on route*) stop; stopping place; **hacer —** to make a stop.
   (**f**) passageway.
transitoriedad *nf* transience.
transitorio *adj* transitory; fleeting; temporary; *period etc* transitional.
translucidez *nf* translucence.
translúcido *adj* translucent.
transmarino *adj* overseas.
transmigración *nf* migration, transmigration.
transmigrar [1a] *vi* to migrate, transmigrate.
transmisible *adj* transmissible.
transmisión *nf* (**a**) (*act*) transmission; (*Law etc*) transfer; **— de dominio** (*Law*) transfer of ownership.
   (**b**) (*Mech*) transmission.
   (**c**) (*Elec*) transmission; (*Radio, TV*) transmission, broadcast(ing); **— en circuito** hookup; **— exterior** outside broadcast.
   (**d**) **—es** (*Mil*) signals (corps).
transmisor 1 *adj* transmitting; **aparato —** transmitter; **estación transmisora** transmitter. **2** *nm* transmitter.
transmisora *nf* transmitter; radio relay station.
transmitir [3a] *vti* to transmit (*a* to); (*Radio, TV*) to transmit, broadcast; *possessions* to pass on, hand down; (*Law*) to transfer (*a* to); (*Med*) *disease* to give, infect with; *germs* to carry.
transmutable *adj* transmutable.
transmutación *nf* transmutation.
transmutar [1a] *vt* to transmute (*en* into).
transparencia *nf* transparency; clarity, clearness.
transparentar [1a] **1** *vt* to reveal, allow to be seen; *emotion etc* to show, reveal, betray.
   2 *vi* to be transparent; to allow the contents (*etc*) to show through.
   3 transparentarse *vr* (**a**) (*glass etc*) to be transparent, be clear; (*object etc*) to show through, be able to be seen.
   (**b**) (*fig*) to show clearly, become perceptible; **se transparentaba su verdadera intención** his real intention became plain, his true intention was betrayed.
   (**c**) (*fam: clothing*) to become threadbare, show what is underneath.
   (**d**) (*fam: person*) to be dreadfully thin.
transparente 1 *adj* transparent; *air* clear; *garment* diaphanous, filmy; (*fig*) transparent, clear, plain. **2** *nm* curtain, blind, shade.
transpiración *nf* perspiration; (*Bot*) transpiration.
transpirar [1a] *vi* (**a**) to perspire; (*Bot*) to transpire; (*of liquid*) to seep through, ooze out. (**b**) (*fig*) to transpire, become known.
transpirenaico *adj* *route etc* trans-Pyrenean; *traffic* passing through (*or* over) the Pyrenees; **los países —s** the countries on the other side of the Pyrenees.
transponer [2r] **1** *vt* (**a**) to transpose; to switch over, move about, change the places of.
   (**b**) to transplant.
   (**c**) **— la esquina** to disappear round the corner.
   2 *vi* to disappear from view; to go beyond, get past; (*of sun*) to go down, go behind the mountain (*etc*).
   3 transponerse *vr* (**a**) to change places.
   (**b**) to hide, hide behind something; (*sun*) to go down, go behind the mountain (*etc*).
   (**c**) (*person*) to get sleepy.
transportable *adj* transportable; **fácilmente —** easily carried, easily transported.
transportación *nf* transportation.
transportador *nm* (**a**) (*Mech*) conveyor, transporter; **— de banda, — de correa** belt conveyor. (**b**) (*Math*) protractor.
transportar [1a] **1** *vt* (**a**) to transport; to haul, carry, take; (*Naut*) to ship; (*of cable etc*) to carry, transmit; **el avión podrá — 100 pasajeros** the plane will be able to carry 100 passengers.
   (**b**) *design etc* to transfer (*a* to).
   (**c**) (*Mus*) to transpose.
   2 transportarse *vr* (*fig*) to get carried away, be enraptured.
transporte *nm* (**a**) (*act*) transport; haulage, carriage; **—s** transport, transportation; (*as business*) haulage business, transport company; removals company; **Ministerio de T—s** Ministry of Transport.
   (**b**) (*of design etc*) transfer.
   (**c**) (*Naut*) transport, troopship.
   (**d**) (*fig*) transport, rapture, ecstasy.
transposición *nf* transposition (*also Mus*).
transustanciación *nf* transubstantiation.
transustanciar [1b] *vt* to transubstantiate.
transvasar [1a] *vt* to decant.

transversal 1 *adj* transverse, cross; oblique; **calle — cross street; otra calle — de la calle mayor** another street which crosses the high street. **2** *nf* cross street.

transversalmente *adv* transversely, across; obliquely.

transverso *adj* = **transversal 1**.

transvestido 1 *adj* transvestite. **2** *nm*, **transvestida** *nf* transvestite.

transvestismo *nm* transvestism.

tranvía *nm* tram, tramcar, streetcar (*US*); (*system*) tramway.

trapacear [1a] *vi* to cheat, be on the fiddle (*fam*); to run a racket; to make mischief.

trapacería *nf* racket, fiddle (*fam*), swindle; piece of gossip, malicious tale.

trapacero 1 *adj* dishonest, swindling. **2** *nm* cheat, swindler; racketeer; gossip, mischief-maker.

trapacista *nm* = **trapacero 2**.

trapajoso *adj* (a) *dress* shabby, ragged. (b) *pronunciation* defective; incorrect; *person* who talks incorrectly; who has a speech defect.

trápala 1 *nf* (a) clatter, noise of hooves, clip-clop, hoofbeat. (b) (*fam*) row, uproar, shindy. (c) (*fam*) swindle. (d) (*fam*) talkativeness, garrulity. **3** *nmf* (*fam*) (a) chatterbox. (b) cheat, trickster, swindler.

trapalear [1a] *vi* (a) (*of horse*) to clatter, beat its hooves, clip-clop; (*of person*) to clatter, go clattering along. (b) (*fam*) to chatter, jabber. (c) to fib, lie; to be on the fiddle (*fam*).

trapalero *adj* (*Cu*) = **trapalón**.

trapalón *adj* (*fam*) lying; dishonest, swindling.

trapalonear [1a] *vi* (*Arg*, *Chi*) = **trapalear** (c).

trapatiesta *nf* (*fam*) commotion, 'shindy; roughhouse (*fam*).

trapaza *nf* = **trapacería**.

trapeador *nm* (*Chi*, *Guat*, *Mex*) floor mop.

trapear [1a] *vt* (a) (*SAm*) *floor* to mop. (b) (*CAm*) to beat, tan (*fam*); (*fig*) to insult; (*fig*) to dress down.

trapecio *nm* trapeze; (*Math*) trapezium.

trapecista *nmf* trapeze artist(e).

trapería *nf* (a) rags; old clothes. (b) old-clothes shop; junk shop.

trapero *nm* ragman.

trapezoide *nm* trapezoid.

trapicar [1g] *vi* (*Chi*) to taste very hot; to sting, smart.

trapichar [1a] *vt* (*Col*, *Mex*) to smuggle (in); (*Cu*, *PR*) to deal in.

trapiche *nm* olive-oil press; sugar mill; (*Arg*, *Chi*, *Per*) orecrusher.

trapichear [1a] *vi* (a) to be on the fiddle (*fam*); to be mixed up in something shady; to plot, scheme. (b) (*Arg*, *Mex*) to manage to live on small-time buying and selling.

trapicheos *nmpl* (a) fiddles (*fam*), shady dealing; plots, schemes, tricks. (b) (*Arg*) small-time business. (c) (*Mex*) clandestine affair.

trapichero *nm* (a) (*SAm*) sugar-mill worker. (b) (*Col*, *PR*) busybody. (c) (*Arg*) shady businessman, dishonest dealer.

trapiento *adj* ragged, tattered.

trapillo: **estar de —**, **ir de —** to be dressed in ordinary clothes, be informally dressed; to be all dressed up to the nines.

trapío *nm* (a) elegant carriage, attractive way of moving; **tener buen —** to have a fine presence, carry oneself elegantly, move beautifully; (*fig*) to have real class. (b) (*of bull*) fine appearance.

trapisonda *nf* (a) row, commotion; shindy; brawl, scuffle. (b) swindle; monkey business, shady affair, fiddle (*fam*); intrigue; fib.

trapisondear [1a] *vi* to scheme, plot, intrigue; to fiddle (*fam*), wangle (*fam*).

trapisondista *nm* schemer, intriguer; fiddler (*fam*), wangler (*fam*).

trapito *nm* rag; **—s** (*fam*) clothes; **—s de cristianar** (*fam*) Sunday best, glad rags (*fam*).

trapo *nm* (a) rag; **dejar a uno hecho un —**, **poner a uno como un —** to give someone a dressing-down; **to haul someone over the coals;** (*in argument*) to flatten someone, give someone a battering; to shower abuse on someone.
(b) (*also* **— del polvo**) duster; rag, cleaning cloth.
(c) (*Taur: fam*) cape.
(d) (*fam*) **—s** (*woman's*) clothes, dresses; **gasta una barbaridad en —s** she spends an awful lot on clothes; **lavar los —s sucios ante el mundo entero** to wash one's dirty linen in public; **sacar los —s a relucir** to let fly, tell someone a lot of home truths.
(e) (*Naut*) canvas, sails; **a todo — with all sails**

set, under full sail; (*fig*) quickly; **llorar** (*etc*) **a todo — to cry** (*etc*) uncontrollably.
(f) **soltar el — (a llorar)** to burst into tears; **soltar el — (a reír)** to burst out laughing, collapse in helpless laughter.

traposiento *adj* (*Per*) ragged.

traposo *adj* (a) (*Chi*, *Per*, *PR*) ragged. (b) (*Chi*) = **trapajoso** (b). (c) (*Chi*) *food* tough, stringy.

traque *nm* (a) crack, bang. (b) (*tabu*) noisy fart (*tabu*).

tráquea *nf* trachea, windpipe.

traquear [1a] **1** *vti* = **traquetear**.
2 *vt* (a) (*Arg*, *CR*, *Mex*) to make deep tracks on. (b) (*PR*) *person* to take about from place to place; (*Arg*) *cattle* to switch from place to place. (c) (*PR*, *SD*) to test, try out; to train.
3 *vi* (a) (*Arg*) to pass frequently, frequent a place. (b) (*PR*) to drink.
4 traquearse *vr* (*Ven*) to go out of one's mind.

traqueo *nm* = **traqueteo**.

traquetear [1a] **1** *vt* (a) *container* to shake; *chairs etc* to rattle, bang about, make a lot of noise with. (b) (*fam*) to mess up, muck about with.
2 *vi* (a) (*of rocket etc*) to crackle, bang; (*of vehicle etc*) to rattle, jolt; (*of machine gun*) to rattle, clatter. (b) (*Arg*, *Mex*) to bustle about, go to and fro a lot; (*Arg*) to tire oneself out at work.

traqueteo *nm* (a) crack, crackle, bang; rattle, rattling, jolting; clatter. (b) (*Col*, *Mex*, *PR*) row, din; noisy movement.

traquidazo *nm* (*Mex*) = **traquido**.

traquido *nm* (*of whip*) crack; (*of shot*) crack, bang, report.

traquinar [1a] *vi* (*PR*) = **trajinar**.

tras[1] 1 *prep* (a) (*place*) behind; after; **día — día** day after day; **uno — otro** one after the other; **andar — algo, estar — algo** to be looking for something, be on the track of something; **andamos — un coche que han anunciado** we're after a car which has been advertised; **correr — uno, ir — uno** to chase (after) someone.
(b) (*time*) after.
(c) **— de** + *infin* besides + *ger*, in addition to + *ger*.
2 *nm* (*fam*) bottom, backside.

tras[2] *interj* **¡—, —!** bang, bang! (*sound of knocking on door*).

tras . . . trans . . . ; *for alternative spellings, see also* **trans . . .**

trasalcoba *nf* dressing room.

trasaltar *nm* space behind the altar.

trasbocar [1g] *vti* (*Arg*, *Col*, *Chi*) to vomit.

trasbucar [1g] *vt* (*Chi*, *PR*) to upset, overturn.

trasbuscar [1g] *vt* (*Chi*) to search carefully.

trascendencia *nf* (a) importance, significance, momentousness; far-reaching nature; implications, consequences; **encuentro sin — casual meeting; discusión sin — discussion of no particular significance.**
(b) (*Philos*) transcendence.

trascendental *adj* (a) important, significant, momentous; vital; far-reaching. (b) (*Philos*) transcendental.

trascendente *adj* = **trascendental**.

trascender [2g] *vi* (a) to smell (*a* of); to reek (*a* of); **el olor de la cocina trascendía hasta nosotros** the smell of the kitchen floated across to us, the kitchen smell reached as far as us; **la carne trasciende a pasada** the meat smells bad.
(b) **— a** (*fig*) to reek of, smack of, be suggestive of; to evoke, suggest; **en esta novela todo trasciende a romanticismo** everything in this novel smacks of romanticism; **de su gesto trasciende cierta serenidad** his expression suggests a certain calmness, a certain serenity shines through his expression.
(c) (*of news*) to come out, leak out; **— a to become** known to, spread to; **por fin ha trascendido la triste noticia** the sad news has come out at last; **no queremos que ello trascienda a los demás** we do not want this to be known to the others.
(d) (*of event, feeling etc*) to spread, have a wide effect; **— a to reach, get across to, have an effect on; su influencia trasciende a los países más remotos** his influence extends to the most remote countries; **— de to go beyond, go outside of, go beyond the limits of.**

trascocina *nf* scullery.

trascolar [1m] *vt* to strain.

trasconejarse [1a] *vr* (*fam*) to get lost, be misplaced.

trascordarse [1m] *vr*: **— algo** to forget something, lose all memory of something; **estar trascordado** to be completely forgotten.

trascoro nm retrochoir.
trascorral nm (a) backyard. (b) (fam) bottom.
trascuarto nm back room.
trasegar [1h and 1k] **1** vt (a) to move about, switch round; posts to reshuffle; wine etc to decant; to pour into another container (or bottle).
　(b) to mix up; to upset, turn upside down.
　2 vi (fam) to drink, booze.
trasera nf back, rear.
trasero 1 adj back, rear; hind; **motor** — rear-mounted engine; **rueda trasera** back wheel, rear wheel. **2** nm (a) (Anat) bottom, buttocks; (Zool) hindquarters, rump. (b) **—s** ancestors.
trasfondo nm background; (of criticism etc) undertone, undercurrent.
trasgo nm (a) goblin, imp. (b) (child) imp.
trashojar [1a] vt book to leaf through, glance through.
trashumación nf seasonal migration, move to new pastures.
trashumante adj flock migrating, on the move to new pastures; person, tribe nomadic.
trashumar [1a] vi to make the seasonal migration, move to new pastures.
trasiego nm (a) move, switch; reshuffle; decanting. (b) mixing; upset.
trasigar [1h] vt (Ec, Per) to upset, turn upside down.
trasijado adj skinny.
traslación nf (a) (Astron) movement, passage; removal. (b) copy; copying. (c) (Lit) metaphor; figurative use.
trasladar [1a] **1** vt (a) to move; to remove; person to move, change, transfer (a to).
　(b) event etc to postpone (a until), move (a to); meeting to adjourn (a to).
　(c) document to copy, transcribe.
　(d) feelings, thoughts etc to translate; to express, interpret; to convey in a different form; — **su pensamiento al papel** to put one's thoughts on paper; — **una novela a la pantalla** to transfer a novel to the screen, interpret a novel as a film.
　(e) language to translate (a into).
　2 trasladarse vr to go, move (a to); to betake oneself (a to); — **a otro puesto** to move to a new job, change to a new post; **los que se trasladan a la oficina en coche** those who go to their offices by car; **después nos trasladamos al bar** later we moved to the bar.
traslado nm (a) move; removal; change, transfer. (b) copy; (Law) notification; **dar — a uno de una orden** to give someone a copy of an order.
traslapar [1a] **1** vt to overlap. **2 traslaparse** vr to overlap.
traslapo nm overlap, overlay.
traslaticiamente adv figuratively.
traslaticio adj figurative.
traslucir [3f] **1** vt to show, reveal, betray; **dejar — algo** to hint at something, suggest something.
　2 traslucirse vr (a) to be translucent, be transparent.
　(b) to show through, be perceptible.
　(c) (fig) to reveal itself, be revealed; to be plain to see; **en su cara se traslucía cierto pesimismo** a certain pessimism was revealed in his expression, a certain pessimism was written on his face.
　(d) (fig: news) to leak out, come to light.
　(e) (fig: person) to reveal one's inmost thoughts, betray one's hidden feelings.
traslumbrar [1a] **1** vt to dazzle.
　2 traslumbrarse vr (a) to be dazzled.
　(b) to appear and disappear suddenly, come and go unexpectedly.
trasluz nm (a) diffused light; reflected light, glint, gleam.
　(b) **mirar algo al —** to look at something against the light; **estudió el cuadro al —** he held the picture up to the light.
　(c) (PR, SD) resemblance.
trasmano (a) a — adv out of reach; (fig) out of the way, remote.
　(b) (SAm) **por —** adv secretly, stealthily; in an underhand way.
trasminante adj (Chi) cold bitter, piercing.
trasminarse [1a] vr to filter through, pass through.
trasnochada nf (a) vigil, watch; sleepless night.
　(b) (Mil) night attack.
　(c) last night, previous night, night before.
trasnochado adj (a) food etc stale, old; (fig) stale, obsolete, ancient; plan etc that has been too long in the preparation, that has been overtaken by events.
　(b) person wan, haggard, run-down, hollow-eyed.

trasnochador 1 adj given to staying up late; **son muy —es** they turn in very late, they keep very late hours. **2** nm night-bird (fig).
trasnochar [1a] **1** vt problem to sleep on.
　2 vi (a) to stay up late, go to bed late; (fig) to have a sleepless night; (fig) to have a night out, have a night on the tiles.
　(b) **— en un sitio** to spend the night in a place.
　3 trasnocharse vr (SAm) = **2**.
trasnocheo nm staying up late; (fig) night-time revelry, living it up in the small hours (fam).
trasoír [3q] vti to mishear.
trasojado adj haggard, hollow-eyed.
traspaís nm interior, hinterland.
traspalar [1a] vt to shovel about, move with a shovel.
traspapelar [1a] **1** vt to lose, mislay, misplace.
　2 traspapelarse vr to get mislaid.
traspasar [1a] **1** vt (a) (of bullet, sword etc) to pierce, penetrate, go through; to transfix; (of liquid) to go through, come through, soak through; **la bala le traspasó el pulmón** the bullet pierced his lung; **— a uno con una espada** to run someone through with a sword.
　(b) (fig) to pierce; to pain, grieve mortally; **un ruido que traspasa el oído** a noise which pierces your ear, a noise which drills into your ear; **ese grito me traspasó** that yell transfixed me; **la escena me traspasó el corazón** the scene pierced me to the core.
　(c) river, street etc to cross over.
　(d) bounds, limit to go beyond, overstep; to transcend; **esto traspasa los límites de lo tolerable** this goes beyond the limits of what is tolerable.
　(e) law to break, infringe, transgress.
　(f) player, property etc to transfer; to sell, make over; (Law) to convey; **"traspaso negocio"** (advert) "business for sale".
　2 traspasarse vr to go too far, overstep the mark.
traspaso nm (a) transfer, sale; (Law) conveyance.
　(b) property transferred, goods (etc) sold; (Law) property being conveyed.
　(c) (Fin) sale price.
　(d) (fig) anguish, pain; grief.
　(e) (of law) infringement, transgression.
traspatio nm (SAm) backyard.
traspié nm (a) slip, stumble; **dar un —** to slip, trip, stumble. (b) trip. (c) (fig) slip, blunder.
traspintarse [1a] vr (a) (on paper) to come through, show through. (b) (fam) to backfire, turn out all wrong.
trasplantar [1a] **1** vt (Bot, Med) to transplant.
　2 trasplantarse vr to emigrate, uproot oneself.
trasplante nm (a) (Bot) transplanting. (b) (Med) transplant, transplantation.
traspontín nm (fam) bottom, backside.
trasportín nm (a) extra seat, pillion seat. (b) (fam) = **traspontín**.
traspuesta nf (a) transposition; switching, changing over; removal.
　(b) (Geog) rise.
　(c) flight, escape; hiding.
　(d) backyard.
traspunte nm (Theat) callboy; prompter.
traspuntín nm (a) = **trasportín**. (b) = **traspontín**.
trasque conj (SAm) in addition to the fact that . . ., besides being . . .
trasquiladura nf shearing, clipping.
trasquilar [1a] vt (a) sheep to shear, clip; hair, person to crop. (b) (fam) to cut down, curtail, chop off.
trastada nf (fam) (a) stupid act, senseless act; mischief, prank; practical joke; piece of bad behaviour.
　(b) dirty trick; **hacer una — a uno** to play a dirty trick on someone.
trastajo nm piece of junk.
trastazo nm bump, bang, thump.
traste[1] nm (a) (Mus) fret.
　(b) **dar al — con algo** to ruin something, spoil something, mess something up; **dar al — con una fortuna** to squander a fortune; **dar al — con los planes** to ruin one's plans; **esto ha dado al — con mi paciencia** this has exhausted my patience; **ir al —** to fail, fall through, be ruined.
traste[2] nm (a) (SAm) = **trasto**. (b) (Chi, RPl) bottom, backside.
trastear [1a] **1** vt (a) (Mus) to play (well).
　(b) objects to move around; to mess up, disarrange.
　(c) (Taur) to play with the cape.
　(d) (fig) person to direct cleverly the way one wants, lead by the nose.

(e) (fig) *person* to keep waiting, keep at bay, keep dangling.
(f) (Mex) to feel, fondle.
2 *vi* **(a)** to move things around; **— con, — en** to rummage among; to mess up, disarrange.
(b) (CAm, Col) to move house.
(c) to make bright conversation.

trastera nf **(a)** lumber room. **(b)** (Mex) cupboard. **(c)** (PR) heap of junk.

trastería nf **(a)** lumber, junk. **(b)** junkshop. **(c)** = **trastada.**

trastero nm lumber room.

trastienda nf **(a)** back room (of a shop); **obtener algo por la —** to get something under the counter; (fig) to get something by underhand means.
(b) (fam) **tiene mucha —** he's a sharp one; he's a deep one, he hides a lot inside himself.
(c) (Chi, Mex) bottom, backside.

trasto nm **(a)** piece of furniture; household utensil; (pej) piece of lumber, piece of junk; old crock, old pot; **—s viejos** lumber, junk, rubbish; **tirarse los —s a la cabeza** to have a blazing row; to be at daggers drawn.
(b) (Theat) **—s** scenery; stage furniture, properties.
(c) (fam) **—s** gear, tackle; **—s de matar** weapons; **—s de pescar** fishing tackle; **coger los —s, liar los —s** to pack up and go.
(d) (fam) useless individual, good-for-nothing; dead loss; nuisance; unreliable person; odd type (fam).

trastornado adj person mad, crazy; mind unhinged.

trastornar [1a] **1** vt **(a)** to overturn, upset; to turn upside down; objects to mix up, jumble up, turn upside down; order to confuse, disturb.
(b) (fig) ideas etc to upset, confuse; plans to upset; life to disturb, disorganize; senses to daze, confuse; nerves to shatter; public order etc to disturb; person to upset, trouble, disturb; to make dizzy.
(c) (fig) mind, person to unhinge; to drive crazy, disturb mentally; **esa chica le ha trastornado** that girl has bowled him over, that girl is driving him crazy.
(d) (fam) to delight; **la trastornan las joyas** she's crazy about jewels, she just lives for jewels.
2 trastornarse vr **(a)** (plan etc) to fall through, be ruined.
(b) (person) to go crazy, go out of one's mind.

trastorno nm **(a)** (act) overturning, upsetting; mixing up, jumbling up.
(b) (fig) confusion, disturbance; (Pol) disturbance, upheaval; **los —s políticos de Eslobodia** the Slobodian political disturbances.
(c) (Med) upset, disorder; **— estomacal** stomach upset.
(d) **— mental** mental disorder, breakdown.

trastrocar [1g and 1m] vt **(a)** to switch over, change round; order to reverse, invert. **(b)** to change, transform.

trastrueco nm, **trastrueque** nm **(a)** switch, change-over; reversal. **(b)** change, transformation.

trastumbar [1a] vt (Mex) = **transponer.**

trasudar [1a] vi to sweat a little.

trasudor nm slight sweat.

trasuntar [1a] vt **(a)** to copy, transcribe. **(b)** to summarize.

trasunto nm **(a)** copy, transcription.
(b) (fig) image, likeness; second edition; **fiel —** exact likeness; faithful representation; **esto es un — en menor escala de lo que ocurrió ayer** this is a repetition on a smaller scale of what happened yesterday.

trasvasar [1a] vt to pour into another container, decant.

trasvase nm pouring, decanting.

trasvasijar [1a] vt (Chi) = **trasvasar.**

trasvolar [1m] vt to fly over, cross in an aeroplane.

trata nf (also **— de esclavos, — de negros**) slave trade; **— de blancas** white slave trade.

tratable adj **(a)** friendly, sociable, easy to get on with. **(b)** (Chi) passable.

tratadista nmf writer (of a treatise); essayist.

tratado nm **(a)** (Comm etc) agreement; (Pol) treaty, pact; **— de paz** peace treaty.
(b) (Lit) treatise, tract; essay; **un — de física** a treatise on physics.

tratamiento nm **(a)** (Chem, Med, Tech etc) treatment; (Tech) processing; (of person, problem) treatment, handling; management; **— médico** medical treatment; **— con rayos X** X-ray treatment.
(b) title, style (of address); **— de tú** familiar address (in 2nd person singular of verb); **apear el —**

a uno to drop someone's title, address someone without formality; **dar — a uno** to give someone his full title.

tratante nm dealer, trader (en in).

tratar [1a] **1** vt **(a)** (general sense) to treat, handle; **la tratan muy bien en esa pensión** they treat her well in that boarding house; **hay que — los libros con cuidado** books should be handled carefully; **trata a todos con poca ceremonia** he treats everyone very unceremoniously.
(b) (Chem, Med, Tech) to treat (con, por with); to process; **— a uno con un nuevo fármaco** to treat someone with a new drug.
(c) **— a uno** to have dealings with someone, have to do with someone, know someone; **le trato desde hace 6 meses** I have known him for 6 months.
(d) **— a uno de tú** to address someone as "tú" (familiar 2nd person singular pronoun); **¿cómo le hemos de —?** how should we address him?, what ought we to call him?; **— a uno de vago** to call someone idle.
2 vi **(a)** **— de** (of book) to deal with, be about, discuss; (of meeting, persons) to talk about, discuss; **este libro trata de las leyendas épicas** this book is about the epic legends; **ahora van a — del programa** they're going to talk about the programme now.
(b) (Comm) **— con** to deal in, trade in, handle.
(c) **— con** subject etc to have to do with, deal with; person to know, have dealings with, have contacts with; enemy to negotiate with, treat with; **el geólogo trata con rocas** the geologist deals with rocks; **no tratamos con traidores** we do not treat with traitors, there can be no negotiations with traitors; **no había tratado con personas de esa clase** I had not had dealings with people of that class.
(d) **— de + infin** to try to + infin, endeavour to + infin.
3 tratarse vr **(a)** (1 person) **— bien** to do oneself well, live well; **ahora se trata con mucho cuidado** he looks after himself very carefully now.
(b) (2 persons) to treat each other, behave towards each other.
(c) (2 persons) **se tratan de usted** they address each other as "usted" (polite form of verb); **¿aquí nos tratamos de tú o de usted?** are we on "tú" or "usted" terms here?; **¿cómo nos hemos de —?** how should we address each other?
(d) **— con uno** to have to do with someone, have dealings with someone.
(e) **se trata de la nueva piscina** it's about the new pool, it's a question of the new pool; **se trata de aplazarlo un mes** it's a question of putting it off for a month; **¿de qué se trata?** what's it about?; what's up?, what's the trouble?; **ahora, tratándose de Vd . . .** now, in your case . . .; **si no se trata más que de eso** if there's no more to it than that, if that's all it is.

trato nm **(a)** (between persons) intercourse, dealings; relationship; **— carnal, — sexual** sexual intercourse; **— doble** double-dealing, dishonesty; **entrar en —s con uno** to enter into relations (or negotiations) with someone; **no querer —s con uno** to want no dealings with someone; **romper el — con uno** to break off relations with someone.
(b) (of person; also **—s**) treatment; **malos —s** ill treatment, rough treatment, ill usage.
(c) manner; behaviour; **de fácil —** easy to get on with; **de — agradable** pleasant, affable; **— de gentes = don de gentes; tener buen —** to be easy to get on with, have a pleasant manner, be affable.
(d) (Comm, Law) agreement, contract; deal, bargain; (fig) deal; **—s** dealings; **— colectivo** collective bargaining; **— comercial** business deal; **— equitativo** fair deal, square deal; **— preferente** preferential treatment; **¡— hecho!** it's a deal!; **cerrar un —** to do a deal, strike a bargain; **hacer buenos —s a uno** to offer someone advantageous terms.
(e) (Ling) title, style of address; **dar a uno el — debido** to give someone his proper title.
(f) (Mex) market stall.
(g) (Mex) small business.

trauma nm trauma.

traumático adj traumatic.

traumatismo nm traumatism.

travelín nm (Cine) travelling.

través 1 nm **(a)** (Archit) crossbeam.
(b) (Mil) traverse; protective wall.
(c) bend, turn; slant; bias; warp.
(d) (fig) reverse, misfortune; upset.

2 al — *adv* across, crossways; **de —** across, crossways; obliquely; sideways; **con el sombrero puesto de —** with his hat on askew; **hubo que introducirlo de —** it had to be squeezed in sideways; **ir de —** (*Naut*) to drift off course, be blown (*etc*) to the side; **mirar de —** to squint; **mirar a uno de —** to look at someone out of the corner of one's eye, (*fig*) look askance at.

3 a — de, al — de *prep* across; over; through; **un árbol caído a — de los carriles** a tree fallen across the lines; **lo sé a — de un amigo** I know about it through a friend.

travesaño *nm* (a) (*Archit*) crosspiece, crossbeam; (*Sport*) crossbar.
(b) (*of bed*) bolster.
(c) (*Cu, Mex: Rail*) sleeper.

travesear [1a] *vi* (a) to play around; to play up, be mischievous, be naughty; (*pej*) to live a dissipated life.
(b) (*fig*) to talk wittily, sparkle. (c) (*Mex*) to show off one's horsemanship.

traveseo *nm* (*Mex*) display of horsemanship.

travesero 1 *adj* cross (*attr*); slanting, oblique. **2** *nm* bolster.

travesía *nf* (a) cross-street, short street which joins two others; road that passes through a village.
(b) (*Naut*) crossing, voyage; (*Aer*) crossing; distance travelled, distance to be crossed.
(c) (*Naut*) crosswind; (*Chi*) west wind.
(d) (*in gambling*) amount won, amount lost.
(e) (*Arg, Bol*) arid plain, desert region.

travestido *adj* disguised, in disguise.

travesura *nf* (a) prank, lark, piece of mischief; escapade; **son —s de niños** they're just childish pranks; **las —s de su juventud** the wild doings of his youth, the waywardness of his young days.
(b) sly trick.
(c) wit, sparkle.

traviesa *nf* (a) (*Archit*) tie, crossbeam, rafter.
(b) (*Rail*) sleeper.
(c) (*Min*) cross gallery.
(d) = **travesía** (b).

travieso *adj* (a) *child* naughty, mischievous; *adult* restless; lively, unpredictable; (*pej*) dissolute.
(b) bright, clever, shrewd; witty.
(c) **a campo travieso** (*adj*, *adv*) across country, cross-country.

trayecto *nm* (a) road, route, way; stretch, section; **destrozó un — de varios kilómetros** it destroyed a stretch several kilometres long; **final del —** end of the line, terminus; **recorrer un —** to cover a distance.
(b) (*by person*) journey; (*of vehicle*) run, journey; (*of bullet etc*) flight, trajectory; **comeremos durante el —** we'll eat on the journey, we'll lunch on the way.

trayectoria *nf* (a) trajectory, path.
(b) (*fig*) course of development, evolution, path; **la — poética de Garcilaso** Garcilaso's poetic development; **la — actual del partido** the party's present line (*or* course, path).

traza *nf* (a) (*Archit, Tech*) plan, design; layout.
(b) (*of person etc*) looks, general appearance, air; **por las —s, según las —s** from all the signs, to judge by appearances; **llevar buena —** to look well, seem impressive; (*of plan etc*) to seem promising; **llevar (or tener) —s de + infin** to look like + *ger*; **esto tiene —s de nunca acabar** this looks as though it will never end.
(c) means; (*pej*) trick, device, expedient; **darse — to find a way**, get along, manage; **darse — para hacer algo, discurrir —s para hacer algo** to contrive (schemes) to do something, look for a way of achieving something.
(d) skill, ability; **tener (buena) — para hacer algo** to be skilful at doing something; **para pianista tiene poca —** she's not much of a pianist.
(e) (*Chi*) trace, vestige; trail.

trazado 1 *adj*: **bien —** shapely, well-formed; good-looking; **mal —** ill-favoured, unattractive.
2 *nm* (a) (*Archit, Tech*) plan, design; layout; outline, sketch; (*of road etc*) line, route.
(b) (*fig*) lines, outline, shape, appearance.
(c) (*Bol*) machete.

trazador 1 *adj* (a) (*Mil, Phys*) tracer (*attr*); **bala trazadora** tracer bullet; **elemento —** tracer element.
2 *nm* (a) (*person*) planner, designer.
(b) (*Phys*) tracer.

trazadora *nf* tracer, tracer bullet.

trazar [1f] *vt* (a) (*Archit, Tech*) to plan, design; to lay out; *line etc* to draw, trace; (*Art*) to sketch, outline; *boundaries* to mark out; *course, path* to trace, plot, follow.

(b) (*fig*) *line of development etc* to lay down, mark out.
(c) (*fig: in speech etc*) to trace, describe, explain, outline.
(d) *means etc* to contrive, devise.

trazo *nm* (a) line, stroke; **— de lápiz** pencil stroke, pencil mark.
(b) sketch, outline; **—s** (*of face*) lines, features, cast; **de —s enérgicos** vigorous-looking; **de —s indecisos** with an indecisive look about him (*etc*).
(c) (*Art*) fold (*in drapery*).

trébede(s) *nf*, *pl* **trébedes** trivet.

trebejos *nmpl* (a) equipment, gear, things; **— de cocina** kitchen utensils, kitchen things.
(b) chessmen.
(c) (*fig*) old-fashioned things.

trébol *nm* (a) (*Bot*) clover, trefoil. (b) (*Archit*) trefoil. (c) (*Cards*) **—es** clubs.

trece *adj* thirteen; (*date*) thirteenth; **estar** (*or* **mantenerse, seguir** *etc*) **en sus —** to stand firm, stick to one's guns.

trecho *nm* (a) stretch; length, distance; (*of time*) while; **andar un buen —** to walk a good way, go on a good distance; **a —s** in parts, here and there; intermittently; by fits and starts; **de — en —** at intervals, every so often; **muy de — en —** very occasionally, only once in a while.
(b) (*Agr*) plot, patch.
(c) (*fam*) bit, piece, part; **he terminado ese — de punto** I've finished that bit of knitting; **queda un buen — que hacer** there's still quite a bit to do.

trefilar [1a] *vt wire* to draw (out).

trefinar [1a] *vt* to trephine.

tregua *nf* (a) (*Mil*) truce. (b) (*fig*) lull, respite, let-up; **sin —** without respite; **dar —s** (*of pain etc*) to come and go, let up from time to time; (*of matter*) not to be urgent; **no dar —** to give no respite.

treinta *adj* thirty; (*date*) thirtieth.

treintena *nf* thirty, about thirty.

trematodo *nm* (*Zool*) fluke.

tremebundo *adj* terrible, frightening; *words etc* fierce, threatening, savage.

tremedal *nm* quaking bog.

tremendamente *adv* (*fam*) tremendously (*fam*); awfully (*fam*), terrifically (*fam*).

tremendismo *nm* crudeness, coarse realism; use of realism to shock.

tremendista 1 *adj* crude, coarsely realistic. **2** *nmf* coarsely realistic writer, writer who shocks by his realism.

tremendo *adj* (a) terrible, dreadful, frightful.
(b) imposing, awesome.
(c) (*fam*) tremendous (*fam*); awful (*fam*), terrific (*fam*); **una roca tremenda de alta** a terrifically high rock; **le dio una tremenda paliza** he gave him a tremendous beating.
(d) (*fam*) *person* inventive, witty, entertaining; **es —, ¿eh?** isn't he a scream?, isn't he great? (*fam*).
(e) **echar la tremenda** to speak angrily; **dar** (*or* **tomar**) **algo por la tremenda** to make a great fuss about something.

trementina *nf* turpentine.

tremolar [1a] **1** *vt flag* to wave. (b) (*fig*) to show off, flaunt. **2** *vi* to wave, flutter.

tremolina *nf* (*fam*) row, fuss, commotion; shindy; **armar una —** to start a row, make a fuss.

tremotiles *nmpl* (*Col, PR*) tools, tackle.

trémulamente *adv* tremulously; quaveringly; timidly.

trémulo *adj* quivering, tremulous; *voice* quavering; timid, small; *light etc* flickering.

tren *nm* (a) (*Rail*) train; **— ascendente** up train; **— botijo, — de excursión, — de recreo** excursion train; **— de cercanías** suburban train; **— correo** slow train; (*Post*) mail train; **— descendente** down train; **— directo** through train; **— expreso** fast train; **— (de) mercancías** goods train, freight train (*US*); **— mixto** passenger and goods train; **— ómnibus** stopping train, local train, accommodation train (*US*); **— de pasajeros** passenger train; **— postal** mail train; **— rápido** express (train); **— suplementario** extra train, relief train; **cambiar de —** to change trains; **coger un —, tomar un —** to catch a train; **ir en —** to go by train.
(b) baggage; outfit, equipment; **— de viaje** equipment for a journey.
(c) (*Mech*) set; set of gears (*or* wheels *etc*); **— de aterrizaje** (*Aer*) undercarriage, landing gear; **— de laminación** rolling mill.
(d) (*Mil*) convoy.
(e) **— de vida** (flamboyant *etc*) way of life, (luxurious *etc*) style of living; **vivir a todo —** to

live in style, live expensively; **no pudo sostener ese — de vida** he could not keep up that style of living.
(f) speed; **a fuerte** — at a rapid pace, fast; **ir a buen** — to go at a good speed.
(g) (*RPl*) **en** — in process of, in the course of; **estamos en — de realizarlo** we are carrying it out; **estar en — de recuperación** to be on one's way to recovery.
(h) (*Cu*) workshop; firm, company; **— de mudanzas** removal company; **— de lavado** laundry.
(i) (*Guat, Mex*) = **trajín.**
(j) (*Mex, Urug*) tram, streetcar (*US*).
(k) (*Cu*) stupid act, foolish remark.
trena *nf* (*sl*) clink (*sl*).
trencilla *nf*, **trencillo** *nm* braid.
trenista *nm* (a) (*Cu*) owner of a workshop; company manager. (b) (*Mex*) railwayman.
Trento *m* Trent; **Concilio de —** Council of Trent.
trenza *nf* (a) (*of hair*) plait; pigtail; ponytail; tress; (*Sew*) braid; (*of straw etc*) plait; (*of thread*) twist; **— postiza** switch, hairpiece; **encontrar a una en —** to find someone with her hair down.
(b) (*SAm: of onions etc*) string.
(c) (*Ven*) —**s** shoelaces.
(d) (*Arg*) hand-to-hand fight.
trenzado 1 *adj* plaited; braided; twisted together, intertwined. 2 *nm* plaits.
trenzar [1f] 1 *vt hair* to plait, braid; *straw etc* to plait; *threads etc* to twist (together), intertwine, weave.
2 *vi* (*dancers*) to weave in and out; (*horse*) to caper.
3 **trenzarse** *vr* (a) (*SAm*) **— en una discusión** to get involved in an argument.
(b) (*Chi, Per, RPl*) to come to blows; to fight hand to hand.
trepa¹ 1 *nf* (a) climb, climbing.
(b) somersault.
(c) (*Hunting*) hide.
(d) trick, ruse, deception.
(e) (*fam*) tanning (*fam*).
2 *nmf* (*fam*) creep (*sl*); social climber.
trepa² *nf* (a) (*Tech*) drilling, boring. (b) (*Sew*) trimming. (c) (*in wood*) grain.
trepadera *nf* (*Cu, Mex*) climbing irons.
trepado *nm* (a) (*Tech*) drilling, boring. (b) (*of stamp etc*) perforation.
trepador 1 *adj plant* climbing, rambling.
2 *nm* (a) (*Bot*) climber, rambler.
(b) (*Orn*) nuthatch.
(c) —**es** climbing irons.
trepadora *nf* (*Bot*) climber, rambler.
trepanar [1a] *vt* to trepan.
trepar¹ [1a] *vti* to climb (*a* up), clamber up; to scale; (*Bot*) to climb (*por* up); **— a un avión** to climb into an aircraft; **— a un árbol** to climb (up) a tree.
trepar² [1a] *vt* (a) (*Tech*) to drill, bore. (b) (*Sew*) to trim.
trepe *nm* (*fam*) telling-off; **echar un — a uno** to tell someone off.
trepetera *nf* (*Ven*) jargon, jibberish.
trepidación *nf* shaking, vibration.
trepidar [1a] *vi* (a) to shake, vibrate. (b) (*Chi, Per, RPl*) to hesitate, waver; **— en +** *infin* to hesitate to + *infin*.
treque *adj* (*Ven*) witty, funny.
tres 1 *adj* three; (*date*) third; **las — three o'clock; como — y 2 son 5** as sure as sure can be, without a shadow of doubt; **de — al cuarto** cheap, poorquality; **ni a la de —** on no account, not by a long shot; **not by any manner of means.**
2 *nm* three.
trescientos *adj* three hundred.
tresillo *nm* (a) three-piece suite. (b) (*Mus*) triplet.
tresnal *nm* shock, stack.
treso *adj* (*Mex*) dirty.
treta *nf* (a) (*Fencing*) feint. (b) (*fig*) trick; ruse, stratagem; (*Comm etc*) stunt, gimmick; **— publicitaria** advertising gimmick.
tri . . . tri . . .; three-
tríada *nf* triad.
triangulación *nf* triangulation.
triangular 1 *adj* triangular; three-cornered. 2 [1a] *vt* to triangulate.
triángulo *nm* triangle (*also Mus*).
tribal *adj* tribal.
tribu *nf* tribe.
tribual *adj* tribal.
tribulación *nf* tribulation.

tribuna *nf* (a) (*orator's*) platform, rostrum, dais; (*at meeting*) platform.
(b) (*Sport etc*) stand, grandstand; **— de la prensa** press box.
(c) (*Eccl*) gallery; **— del órgano** organ loft.
(d) (*Law*) **— del acusado** dock; **— del jurado** jury box.
(e) (*fig*) political oratory, public speechmaking.
tribunal *nm* (a) (*Law*) court; (*persons*) court, bench; **— juvenil, — (tutelar) de menores** juvenile court; **T— Supremo** High Court, Supreme Court (*US*); **en pleno —** in open court; **llevar a uno ante los —es** to take someone to court.
(b) (*Pol, of inquiry etc*) tribunal.
(c) (*Univ*) board of examiners; appointments committee.
(d) (*fig*) tribunal; forum; **— de la conciencia** one's own conscience; **el — de la opinión pública** the forum of public opinion.
tribuno *nm* tribune.
tributación *nf* (a) payment. (b) taxation.
tributar [1a] *vt* (a) (*Fin*) to pay. (b) (*fig*) homage, respect etc to pay; thanks to give; affection etc to have, show (*a* for).
tributario 1 *adj* (a) (*Geog, Pol*) tributary.
(b) (*Fin*) tax (*attr*), taxation (*attr*); **privilegio —** tax concession; **sistema —** taxation, tax system.
2 *nm* tributary.
tributo *nm* (a) (*Hist*) tribute (*also fig*). (b) (*Fin*) tax.
tricentenario *nm* tercentenary.
triciclo *nm* tricycle.
tricófero *nm* (*Arg, Chi, Mex*) hair-restorer.
tricola *nf* (*RPl*) knitted waistcoat.
tricolor 1 *adj* tricolour, three-coloured; **bandera —** = 2 *nm* tricolour.
tricornio *nm* three-cornered hat.
tricotosa *nf* (*gall*) knitting machine.
trichina *nf* (*SAm*) trichina.
tridente *nm* trident.
tridentino *adj* of Trent; **Concilio T—** Council of Trent.
tridimensional *adj* three-dimensional.
trienal *adj* triennial.
trienalmente *adv* triennially.
trienio *nm* period of three years.
trifásico *adj* (*Elec*) three-phase, triphase.
triforio *nm* triforium.
trifulca *nf* (*fam*) row, shindy.
trifurcarse [1g] *vr* to divide into three.
trigal *nm* wheat field.
trigésimo *adj* thirtieth.
trigo *nm* (a) (*Bot*) wheat; **— candeal** bread wheat; **— sarraceno** buckwheat; **de — entero** wholemeal; **no es — limpio** (*fig*) he's dishonest.
(b) —**s** wheat, wheat field(s); **meterse en —s ajenos** to meddle in someone else's affairs; to trespass on someone else's subject (*etc*).
(c) (*sl*) dough (*sl*), brass (*sl*).
trigonometría *nf* trigonometry.
trigonométrico *adj* trigonometric(al).
trigueño *adj* hair corn-coloured, dark blonde; skin olive, darkish; person olive-skinned, (*SAm*) dark, swarthy, (*euph*) Negro.
triguero 1 *adj* wheat (*attr*). 2 *nm* (a) corn merchant. (b) corn sieve.
trilátero *adj* trilateral, three-sided.
trilingüe *adj* trilingual.
trilogía *nf* trilogy.
trilla *nf* (a) (*Agr*) threshing. (b) (*Chi, PR*) thrashing, beating. (c) (*Mex*) track.
trillado 1 *adj* (a) (*Agr*) threshed.
(b) (*fig*) path beaten, well-trodden.
(c) (*fig*) subject trite, hackneyed, well-worn; well-known; straightforward.
2 *nm* (*Cu, PR*) path, track.
trillador *nm* thresher.
trilladora *nf* threshing machine.
trilladura *nf* threshing.
trillar [1a] *vt* (a) (*Agr*) to thresh. (b) (*fig*) to frequent; to use a lot, wear out by frequent use.
trillizos *nmpl*, **trillizas** *nfpl* triplets.
trillo *nm* (a) threshing machine. (b) (*Ant, CAm*) path, track.
trillón *nm* trillion (*Brit*), quintillion (*US*).
trimestral *adj* quarterly, three-monthly; (*Univ*) termly.
trimestralmente *adv* quarterly, every three months.
trimestre *nm* (a) quarter, period of three months; (*Univ*) term. (b) (*Fin*) quarterly payment; quarter's rent (*etc*).

trinado nm (Orn) song, warble; (Mus) trill.

trinar [1a] vi (a) (Mus) to trill; (Orn) to sing, warble. (b) (fam) to fume, be angry; (Arg) to shout; **está que trina** he's hopping mad.

trinca nf (a) group of three, set of three, threesome. (b) (Arg, Ec) band, gang; faction; meeting of plotters. (c) (Cu, PR, Mex) drunkenness. (d) (Chi) marbles.

trincar[1] [1g] **1** vt (a) to tie up, tie firmly; (Naut) to lash. (b) to pinion, hold by the arms; (fam) to arrest, catch. (c) (Arg, CAm, Mex) to squeeze, press. **2 trincarse** vr (CAm, Mex): — **a** + infin to start to + infin, set about + ger.

trincar[2] [1g] vt to break up; to chop up; to tear up.

trincar[3] [1g] **1** vti to drink. **2 trincarse** vr (Cu, Mex) to get drunk.

trinco nm (Mex, PR) drunkard.

trinchador nm carving knife.

trinchante nm (a) carving knife; carving fork. (b) side table; (RPl) sideboard.

trinchar [1a] vt (a) to carve, slice, cut up. (b) (sl) to do in (sl).

trinche nm (a) (SAm) fork. (b) (Chi, Ec, Mex) side table. (c) (Mex) pitchfork.

trinchera nf (a) trench, entrenchment; (Mil) trench; (Rail) cutting; **guerra de —s** trench warfare. (b) trench coat. (c) (SAm) fence, stockade. (d) (Mex) curved knife.

trinchete nm shoemaker's knife; (Col) table knife.

trincho nm (Col) parapet; trench, ditch.

trineo nm sledge, sleigh; — **de balancín** bobsleigh; — **de perros** dog sleigh.

Trinidad nf (a) (Rel) Trinity; **t—** (fig) trio, set of three. (b) (Geog) Trinidad.

trinitaria nf pansy; (wild) heart's-ease.

trinitrotolueno nm trinitrotoluene.

trino nm (Orn) warble; trill; (Mus) trill.

trinomio 1 adj trinomial. **2** nm trinomial.

trinque nm (Per) liquor.

trinquetada nf (Cu) period of danger; (Mex, Per) period of hardship (or bad luck).

trinquete[1] nm (Mech) pawl, trip, catch; ratchet.

trinquete[2] nm (a) (Naut) foremast; foresail. (b) pelota court.

trinquete[3] nm (Mex) (a) bribe; shady deal, corrupt affair. (b) **es un — de hombre** he really is a tough guy (US fam), he's mighty strong (fam).

trinquis nm, pl **trinquis** (fam) drink, swig (fam).

trío nm trio.

tripa nf (a) (Anat) intestine, gut; **—s** (Anat) guts, insides, innards (fam); (Cook) tripe; **me duelen las —s** I have a stomach ache; **echar las —s** to retch, vomit violently; **le gruñían las —s** his tummy was rumbling (fam); **hacer de —s corazón** to pluck up courage, screw up one's courage; **llenar la — (fam)** to eat well at someone else's expense; **quitar las —s a un pez** to gut a fish; **revolver las —s a uno** (fig) to turn someone's stomach; **¡te sacaré las —s!** I'll tear your guts out!; **tener malas —s** to be cruel. (b) (fig, fam) belly, tummy (fam); (of pregnancy) bulge; **echar —** to start to get a paunch; **tener mucha —** to be fat, be paunchy. (c) (of fruit) core, seeds. (d) (Mech: fam) **—s** innards (fam), works; parts; **sacar las —s de un reloj** to take out the works of a watch. (e) (of vessel) belly, bulge. (f) (Comm, Law etc) file, dossier. (g) (Ven) inner tube, tyre.

tripartito adj tripartite.

triperío nm (Col, Mex) guts, entrails.

tripicallos nmpl (Cook) tripe.

triple 1 adj triple; threefold; of three layers (or thicknesses etc). **2** nm triple; **es el — de lo que era** it is three times what (or as big as) it was; **su casa es el — de grande que la nuestra** their house is three times bigger than ours. **3** adv (fam): **esta cuerda es — gruesa que ésa** this string is three times thicker than that bit.

triplicado adj triplicate; **por —** in triplicate.

triplicar [1g] **1** vt to treble, triple. **2 triplicarse** vr to treble, triple.

trípode nm tripod.

tripón 1 adj fat, potbellied. **2** nm, **tripona** nf (Mex) little boy, little girl.

tríptico nm (a) (Art) triptych. (b) form in three parts, three-part document.

triptongo nm triphthong.

tripudo adj fat, potbellied.

tripulación nf crew.

tripulado adj: **vuelo —** manned flight; **— por** manned by.

tripulante nm crew member, crewman; **—s** crew, men.

tripular [1a] vt (a) ship etc to man. (b) (Aut etc) to drive. (c) (Chi) to mix (up).

tripulina nf (Chi) row, brawl.

trique nm (a) crack, sharp noise, swish. (b) **a cada —** at every moment; repeatedly. (c) (Col, Mex) trick, dodge. (d) (Mex) **—s** things, gear (fam), odds and ends.

triquina nf trichina.

triquinosis nf trichinosis.

triquiñuela nf trick, dodge; **—s** dodges, funny business; **es un tío —s** (fam) he's an artful old cuss (fam); **saber las —s del oficio** to know the tricks of the trade, know all the dodges.

triquis nmpl (Mex) see **trique** (d).

trirreme nm trireme.

tris nm (a) crack; tearing noise; pop; swish; tinkle. (b) **está en un —** it's touch and go; **estaba en un — que lo perdiera** he very nearly lost it, he was within an inch of losing it; **los dos coches evitaron el choque por un —** the two cars avoided a collision by a hair's breadth.

trisar [1a] vt (Chi) to crack; to chip.

trisca nf (a) crunch, crushing noise. (b) uproar, rumpus (fam), row. (c) (Cu) mockery; private joke.

triscar [1g] **1** vt (a) to mix, mingle; to mix up. (b) saw to set. (c) (Col, Cu) to mock, joke about; to tease. **2** vi (a) to stamp one's feet about. (b) (of lambs etc) to gambol, frisk about; (of persons) to romp, play about.

trisecar [1g] vt to trisect.

trisemanal adj triweekly.

trisemanalmente adv triweekly, thrice weekly.

trisilábico adj trisyllabic, three-syllabled.

trisílabo 1 adj trisyllabic, three-syllabled. **2** nm trisyllable.

trismo nm lockjaw.

Tristán m Tristram.

triste 1 adj (a) (of person) state sad; miserable; gloomy; sorrowful; character gloomy, melancholy; appearance, face sad-looking; **poner — a uno** to make someone sad, make someone unhappy, make someone miserable; **ponerse —** to become sad; to look sad. (b) news, story etc sad; song sad, mournful; countryside dismal, desolate, dreary; room etc gloomy, dismal. (c) (fig) sorry, sad; **hizo un — papel** he cut a sorry figure; **la — verdad es que . . .** the sorry truth is that . . .; **es — verle así** it is sad to see him like that, it grieves one to see him like that; **es — no poder ir, es — que no podamos ir** it's a pity we can't go. (d) (fam) flower etc old, withered. (e) (fam) miserable, wretched; single; **no queda sino un — penique** there's just one miserable penny left, there's just one poor little penny left; **su padre es un — vigilante** his father is just a poor old watchman; **le mató algún — campesino** some wretched peasant killed him. (f) (SAm) poor, valueless, wretched. (g) (Bol, Mex) shy, timid. **2** nm (Bol, Ec, Per, RPl) sad love song.

tristemente adv sadly; miserably; gloomily; sorrowfully; mournfully; **el — famoso lugar** the place which is well known for such unhappy reasons, the place which enjoys a sorry fame.

tristeza nf (a) sadness; misery; gloom; sorrow; gloominess, melancholy. (b) dismalness, desolation, dreariness. (c) **—s** (fam) sad news, unhappy events.

tristón adj rather sad; given to melancholy; pessimistic, gloomy.

tristura nf (SAm) sadness.

Tritón m Triton.

tritón nm (Zool) newt.

trituración nf trituration; grinding, crushing.

trituradora nf grinder, crushing machine.

triturar [1a] vt to triturate; to grind, crush, pulverize.

triunfador 1 adj triumphant; winning. **2** nm victor, winner.

triunfal adj (a) arch etc triumphal. (b) cry, smile etc triumphant.

triunfalmente adv triumphantly.

triunfante *adj* (a) triumphant; winning; **salir — to come out the winner, emerge victorious. (b)** jubilant, exultant.

triunfar [1a] *vi* (a) to triumph (*de, sobre* over); to win; to emerge victorious; **— de los enemigos** to triumph over one's enemies; **— en la vida** to succeed in life, make a success of one's life; **— en un concurso** to win a competition.
    (b) *(pej)* to exult (*de, sobre* over).
    (c) *(Cards)* to trump (in), play a trump.
    (d) *(Cards)* to be trumps; **triunfan corazones** hearts are trumps.

triunfo *nm* (a) triumph; win, victory; success; **ha sido un verdadero —** it has been a real triumph; **fue el sexto — consecutivo del equipo** it was the team's sixth consecutive win.
    (b) *(Mus etc)* hit, success; **lista de —s, lista del — hit** parade, top ten (*or* twenty *etc*).
    (c) *(Cards)* trump; **6 sin —s** 6 no-trumps; **palo del —** trump suit, trumps; **tener todos los —s en la mano** *(fig)* to hold all the cards.

triunvirato *nm* triumvirate.

trivial *adj* trivial, trite, commonplace.

trivialidad *nf* (a) *(quality)* triviality, triteness.
    (b) *(una —)* trivial matter; trite remark (*etc*); **—es** trivia, trivialities; **decir —es** to talk trivially, talk in platitudes.

trivializar [1f] *vt* to minimize (the importance of), play down.

trivialmente *adv* trivially, tritely.

triza *nf* bit, fragment; shred; **hacer algo —s** to smash something to bits; to tear something to shreds; **hacer —s a uno** to wear someone out; to flatten someone, crush someone; **los críticos dejaron la obra hecha —s** the critics pulled the play to pieces, the critics tore the play to shreds.

trizar [1f] *vt* to smash to bits; to tear to shreds.

trocaico *adj* trochaic.

trocar [1g *and* 1m] **1** *vt* (a) *(Comm)* to exchange, barter (*por* for).
    (b) *money* to change (*en* into).
    (c) to change (*con, por* for); to interchange, switch round, move about; *words* to exchange (*con* with); **— la alegría en tristeza** to change gaiety into sadness.
    (d) to mix up, confuse.
    (e) *food* to vomit.
    (f) *(Chi)* to sell; *(Per)* to buy.
    2 trocarse *vr* to change (*en* into); to get switched round; to get mixed up.

trocha *nf* (a) by-path, narrow path; short cut. **(b)** *(SAm: Rail)* gauge; **— normal** standard gauge. **(c)** *(Col, Ven)* trot. **(d)** *(Col, Ven)* portion, helping (of meat).

trochar [1a] *vi* *(Col, Ven)* to trot.

troche: a — y moche, a trochemoche *adv run etc* helter-skelter, pell-mell; *scatter etc* all over the place; *distribute, use etc* haphazardly, unsystematically, regardless of distinctions.

trofeo *nm* (a) trophy. **(b)** *(fig)* victory, success, triumph.

troglodita *nm* (a) *(Hist)* caveman, cave dweller, troglodyte. **(b)** *(fig)* brute, coarse person; unsociable individual, recluse. **(c)** *(fam)* glutton.

troica *nf* troika.

troja *nf* *(SAm)* = **troj(e)**.

troj(e) *nf* granary, barn.

trola[1] *nf* *(fam)* fib, lie.

trola[2] *nf* *(Col)* slice of ham; piece of raw hide; piece of loose bark.

trole *nm* (a) *(Elec)* trolley, trolley pole. **(b)** *(Arg)* trolley bus.

trolebús *nm* trolley bus.

trolero *nm* *(fam)* fibber, liar.

tromba *nf* whirlwind; **— marina** waterspout; **— terrestre** whirlwind, tornado; **— de agua** violent downpour; **— de polvo** column of dust; **pasar como una —** to go by like a whirlwind.

trombón *nm* (a) trombone. **(b)** trombonist.

trombosis *nf* thrombosis.

trompa 1 *nf* (a) *(Mus)* horn; **— de caza** hunting horn; **sonar la — marcial** to sound a warlike note, blow a martial trumpet.
    (b) humming-top; whipping top.
    (c) *(Ent)* proboscis; *(Zool)* trunk; *(Anat: hum)* snout, *(fam)* hooter *(fam)*; *(SAm)* thick lips, blubber lips.
    (d) *(Anat)* tube, duct.
    (e) *(Meteorol)* = **tromba**.
    (f) *(fam)* drunkenness; **cogerse una —** to get tight.
    (g) *(Mex: Rail)* cow catcher.
    2 *nm* horn player.

trompada *nf*, **trompazo** *nm* (a) bump, bang; head-on collision. **(b)** punch, swipe.

trompeadura *nf* *(SAm)* (a) bumping, banging. **(b)** series of punches; beating-up.

trompear [1a] *(SAm)* **1** *vt* to bump, bang into; to collide head-on with. **2** *vi* (a) to spin a top. **(b)** = **3 trompearse** *vr* to exchange blows, fight.

trompeta 1 *nf* (a) *(Mus)* trumpet; bugle; *(fig)* clarion. **(b)** *(Mex)* drunkenness. **2** *nm* (a) *Mus)* trumpeter; bugler. **(b)** *(fam)* worthless individual, silly little man.

trompetazo *nm* *(Mus)* trumpet blast; *(fig)* blast, blare.

trompetear [1a] *vi* to play the trumpet.

trompetero *nm* *(orchestral)* trumpet player; *(Mil etc)* trumpeter; bugler.

trompetilla *nf* (a) *(also — acústica)* ear trumpet. **(b)** *(Cu, PR)* hiss, unpleasant whistle.

trompetista *nm* *(Mex etc)* trumpet player.

trompeto *adj* *(Mex)* drunk.

trompezar [1f] *vi* *(SAm)* = **tropezar**.

trompezón *nm* *(SAm)* = **tropezón**.

trompicar [1g] **1** *vt* (a) to trip up.
    (b) **— a uno** to fiddle someone's promotion *(fam)*, promote someone improperly.
    2 *vi* (a) to trip up a lot, stumble repeatedly.
    (b) to turn a somersault.

trompicón *nm* stumble, trip; **a —es** in fits and starts; with difficulty.

trompis *nm*, *pl* **trompis** *(fam)* punch, bash *(fam)*.

trompiza *nf* *(Ec, Mex)* punch-up *(fam)*.

trompo *nm* (a) spinning top; **— de música** humming-top; **ponerse como un —** *(fam)* to eat to bursting point. **(b)** *(SAm)* clumsy person; rotten dancer *(fam)*.

trompón *nm* (a) bump, bang; hefty punch, vicious swipe. **(b)** = **trompo** (b). **(c)** *(Bot: also* **narciso —**) daffodil.

trompudo *adj* *(SAm)* thick-lipped, blubber-lipped.

tronada *nf*, **tronadera** *nf* *(Mex)* thunderstorm.

tronado *adj* (a) old, broken-down, useless. **(b)** *(fam)* **estar —** to be broke *(fam)*; to be ruined.

tronamenta *nf* *(Col, Mex)* thunderstorm.

tronar [1m] **1** *vt* *(CAm, Mex)* to shoot, execute.
    2 *vi* (a) to thunder; *(of guns etc)* to thunder, rumble, boom; **por lo que pueda —** just in case, to be on the safe side.
    (b) *(fam)* to go broke *(fam)*; to fail, be ruined.
    (c) *(fam)* **con uno** to fall out with someone.
    (d) *(fig)* to rave, rage; **— contra** to fulminate against, thunder against; to storm at.

tronazón *nf* *(CAm, Mex)* thunderstorm.

troncal *adj*: **línea —** main line, trunk line.

troncar [1g] *vt* = **truncar**.

tronco *nm* (a) *(Bot: of tree)* trunk; *(of plant)* stem, stalk; log; *(SAm)* tree stump; **estar hecho un —** to be sound asleep; to be completely deprived of movement.
    (b) *(Anat)* trunk.
    (c) *(Rail)* main line, trunk line.
    (d) *(of family)* stock.

troncha *nf* (a) *(SAm)* slice; chunk, piece. **(b)** *(SAm)* sinecure, soft job. **(c)** *(Mex)* soldier's rations; meagre meal.

tronchado *nm* *(Mex: Fin)* gold mine, prosperous business.

tronchar [1a] **1** *vt* (a) *tree* to bring down; to chop down, lop off; to cut up, cut off; to split, rend, smash.
    (b) *(fig)* *life* to cut off, cut short; *hopes etc* to shatter.
    (c) *(fam)* *person* to tire out.
    2 troncharse *vr* (a) *(tree)* to fall down, split.
    (b) *(fam)* to tire oneself out.
    (c) **— de risa** to split one's sides with laughing.

troncho 1 *adj* *(Arg)* maimed, crippled. **2** *nm* (a) *(Bot)* stem, stalk (of cabbage *etc*). **(b)** *(Arg)* piece, chunk. **(c)** *(Col)* knot, tangle.

tronera 1 *nf* (a) *(Mil)* loophole, embrasure; *(Archit)* small window.
    (b) *(Billiards)* pocket.
    (c) *(Mex)* chimney, flue.
    2 *nmf* *(fam)* crazy person, harum-scarum.
    3 *nm* *(fam)* rake, libertine.

tronido *nm* thunderclap; loud report, bang, detonation; boom; **—s** thunder, booming.

tronío *nm* lavish expenditure, extravagance.

trono *nm* throne; *(fig: freq)* crown; **heredar el —** to inherit the crown; **subir al —** to ascend the throne, come to the throne; **nuestra lealtad al —** our loyalty to the crown.

tronzar [1f] *vt* (a) to cut up; to split, rend, smash. **(b)** *(Sew)* to pleat. **(c)** *(fam)* *person* to tire out.

tropa nf (a) troop, body, crowd; (pej) troop, mob.
(b) (Mil) army, military; —s troops; —s de asalto storm troops; ser de — (fam) to be in the army, be a soldier.
(c) (Mil) men, rank and file, ordinary soldiers.
(d) (SAm: Agr) flock, herd.
(e) (RPl) convoy of carts; stream of vehicles; line of cars.
(f) (CAm, Cu, Mex) ill-bred person; rake, libertine.

tropel nm (a) mob, crowd, throng. (b) jumble, mess, litter. (c) rush, haste; **acudir** (etc) **en** — to come in a mad rush, all rush together, come thronging in confusion.

tropelía nf (a) = **tropel** (c). (b) outrage, abuse of authority, violent act; **cometer una** — to commit an outrage.

tropero nm (a) (RPl) cowboy; carter. (b) (Mex) ill-bred person.

tropezar [1f and 1k] **1** vt = vi (b).
2 vi (a) to trip, stumble (con, contra, en on, over); — **con** to run into, run up against.
(b) (fig) — **con uno** to run into someone, bump into someone; — **con algo** to run across something.
(c) (fig) — **con una dificultad** to run into a difficulty, run up against a difficulty.
(d) (fig) — **con uno** to have an argument with someone; to fall out with someone.
(e) (fig) to slip up, blunder; (morally) to slip, fall.
3 tropezarse vr to run into each other.

tropezón nm (a) trip, stumble; **dar un** — to trip, stumble; **proceder a** —es to proceed by fits and starts; **hablar a** —es to talk jerkily, talk falteringly.
(b) (fig) slip, blunder; (moral) slip, lapse.
(c) (Cook: fam) small piece of meat (added to soup etc).

tropical adj (a) tropical. (b) (Arg) rhetorical, melodramatic, highly-coloured.

tropicalismo nm (Arg) rhetoric, melodramatic style, excessive colourfulness.

trópico nm (a) tropic; —s tropics; — **de Cáncer** Tropic of Cancer; — **de Capricornio** Tropic of Capricorn.
(b) (Col, Cu, PR) —s hardships, difficulties; **pasar los** —s to suffer hardships.

tropiezo nm (a) slip, blunder; moral lapse. (b) misfortune, mishap, setback; disappointment in love. (c) obstacle, snag; stumbling block. (d) quarrel, tiff, argument.

tropilla nf (RPl) drove, flock, herd.

tropo nm trope, figure of speech.

troquel nm (Tech) die.

troqueo nm trochee.

trotamundos nm, pl **trotamundos** globetrotter.

trotar [1a] vi (a) to trot. (b) (fam) to travel about, chase around here and there; to hustle.

trote nm (a) trot; — **cochinero**, — **de perro** jog-trot; **ir al** — to trot, go at a trot; **irse al** — to go off in a great rush.
(b) (fam) travelling, chasing around; bustle; **yo ya no estoy para esos** —s I can't go chasing around like that any more; **tomar el** — to dash off.
(c) **de mucho** — garment tough, hard-wearing; **chaqueta para todo** — a jacket for everyday use, a jacket for ordinary wear.
(d) (fam) —s shady affair, dark doings; **meterse en malos** —s to get mixed up in something improper.
(e) (fam) —s hardships; **andar en malos** —s to have a rough time of it, suffer hardships.

trovador nm troubadour.

Troya Troy; **aquí fue** — and now this is all you see, now there's nothing but ruins; **¡aquí fue** —! (fam) you should have heard the fuss!; **¡arda** —! press on regardless! (fam), never mind the consequences!

troyano 1 adj Trojan. **2** nm, **troyana** nf Trojan.

troza nf log.

trozo nm (a) bit, piece; chunk; fragment; **a** —s in bits, piecemeal. (b) (Lit, Mus) passage; section; —s **escogidos** selections, selected passages.

trucaje nm (Cine) trick photography.

truco nm (a) trick, device, dodge; knack; (Cine) trick effect, piece of trick photography; **arte de los** —s conjuring; — **de naipes** card trick; — **publicitario** advertising stunt, publicity gimmick; **el tío tiene muchos** —s the fellow is up to all the dodges; **coger el** — to get the knack, get the hang of it, catch on; **coger el** — **a uno** to see how someone works a trick; (fig) to catch on to someone's little game.
(b) —s billiards, pool.
(c) (Bol, Chi) punch, bash (fam).

truculento adj cruel; horrifying, terrifying; full of extravagant effects.

trucha¹ nf (a) (Fish) trout; — **arco iris** rainbow trout; — **marina** sea trout. (b) (Tech) crane, derrick.

trucha² nf (CAm) stall, portable stand.

trucha³ nmf (fam) tricky individual, wily bird (sl); cheat.

truche nm (Col) toff (fam), dude (US).

truchero nm (CAm) hawker, vendor.

trucho adj (Col) sharp, rascally.

trueco nm = **trueque**.

trueno nm (a) (in general) thunder; (un —) clap of thunder, thunderclap; (of gun etc) bang, boom, report.
(b) (fam) wild youth, madcap; rake.
(c) (fam) — **gordo** finale (of firework display); (fig) big row, major scandal.
(d) (Ven) carousal, binge (sl), noisy party.
(e) (Ven) —s stout shoes.

trueque nm (a) exchange; switch; (Comm) barter; **a** — **de** in exchange for; in place of; **aun a** — **de perderlo** even at the cost of losing it. (b) (Col) —s change.

trufa nf (a) (Bot) truffle. (b) (fam) fib, story.

trufado adj stuffed with truffles.

trufar [1a] **1** vt (a) (Cook) to stuff with truffles. (b) (fam) to take in, swindle. **2** vi (fam) to fib, tell stories.

truhán nm (a) (Hist) jester, buffoon, funny man. (b) rogue, crook, swindler; mountebank.

truhanería nf (a) (Hist) buffoonery. (b) roguery, crookedness, swindling.

truhanesco adj (a) buffoonish. (b) crooked, dishonest.

truísmo nm truism.

trujal nm winepress; olive-oil press.

trulla nf (a) bustle, commotion, noise. (b) crowd, throng. (c) (Col) joke, tease.

trullada nf (Cu, PR) crowd, throng.

truncado adj truncated, shortened; incomplete.

truncamiento nm (a) truncation, shortening; curtailing; cutting; mutilation. (b) truncated state.

truncar [1g] vt (a) to truncate, shorten; text etc to cut off; to cut short, curtail; speech to cut, slash; quotation to mutilate; sense to affect, upset, destroy.
(b) (fig) career, life to cut short; hopes, plans to ruin; development to stunt, check, seriously affect.

trunco adj truncated, shortened; incomplete.

truquero (SAm) **1** adj tricky. **2** nm, **truquera** nf trickster.

trusa nf (Ant) bathing trunks.

trust [trus] nm, pl **trusts** [trus] (Fin: angl) trust, cartel.

tu poss adj your; (arch, to God) thy.

tú pers pron you; (arch, to God) thou.

tualé (SAm: gall) **1** nm toilet, lavatory. **2** nf (feminine) toilet.

tubercular adj tubercular.

tubérculo nm (a) (Bot) tuber; potato. (b) (Anat, Med etc) tubercle.

tuberculosis nf tuberculosis.

tuberculoso adj tuberculous, tubercular.

tubería nf pipes, piping; tubes, tubing; pipeline.

tubo nm tube (also Anat, TV etc); pipe; (SAm: Tel) handset, earpiece; — **acústico** speaking tube; — **capilar** capillary; — **de chimenea** chimney pot; — **de desagüe** drainpipe, waste pipe; — **digestivo** alimentary canal; — **de ensayo** test tube; — **de escape** exhaust (pipe); — **de humo** chimney, flue; — **de imagen** television picture tube; — **intestinal** intestine; — **de lámpara** lamp glass; — **lanzatorpedos** torpedo tube; — **de órgano** organ pipe; — **de radio** wireless valve, tube (US); — **de rayos católicos** cathode-ray tube; — **de respiración** breathing-tube.

tubular 1 adj tubular. **2** nm (garment) roll-on.

tucán nm, **tucano** nm (Arg, Ven) toucan.

tuco¹ 1 adj (SAm) maimed, limbless; lacking a finger (or hand). **2** nm (SAm) (a) (Anat) stump. (b) cripple.

tuco² nm (Arg, Bol) glow worm.

tuco³ nm, **tuca** nf (CAm) namesake.

tucucho nm (Bol) bladder; balloon.

tucura nf (Arg, Urug) locust larva; (Bol) dragonfly; praying mantis; (fig) immoral priest.

tucuso nm (Ven) hummingbird.

tudesco 1 adj German. **2** nm, **tudesca** nf German.

tuerca nf nut; — **mariposa** wingnut.

tuerce nm (CAm) misfortune, setback.

tuerto 1 adj (a) twisted, bent, crooked.
(b) one-eyed, blind in one eye.
(c) **a tuertas** upside-down; back to front; **a**

tuertas o a derechas rightly or wrongly; by hook or by crook; thoughtlessly, hastily.
2 *nm*, **tuerta** *nf* one-eyed person, person blind in one eye.
3 *nm* wrong, injustice.

tuesta *nf* (*PR, SD*) binge (*sl*); beating.

tuétano *nm* (a) (*Anat*) marrow; (*Bot*) pith; **hasta los —s** through and through, utterly, to the core; **enamorado hasta los —s** head over heels in love.
(b) (*fig*) core, essence.

tufarada *nf* bad smell; gust of foul smell, cloud of evil-smelling gas (*etc*).

tufillas *nmf*, *pl* **tufillas** (*fam*) bad-tempered person.

tufo[1] *nm* (a) vapour, gas, exhalation.
(b) (*pej*) bad smell, stink; body odour; bad breath; (*of room etc*) fug; **se le subió el — a las narices** (*fig*) he got very cross.
(c) **—s** (*fam*) swank (*fam*), conceit; **tener —s** to be swanky (*fam*), be conceited.

tufo[2] *nm* curl, ringlet.

tugurio *nm* (*Agr*) shepherd's hut; hovel, slum, shack; poky little room; den, joint (*sl*).

tuja *nf* (*Bol*) hide-and-seek.

tul *nm* tulle, net.

tulenco *adj* (*CAm*) splay-footed.

tulipa *nf* lampshade.

tulipán *nm* tulip.

tulipanero *nm*, **tulipero** *nm* tulip tree.

tulis *nm*, *pl* **tulis** (*Mex*) thief, brigand.

tullida *nf* (*Cu*) dirty trick.

tullido 1 *adj* crippled; paralysed, paralytic. 2 *nm*, **tullida** *nf* cripple.

tullir [3h] *vt* (a) to cripple, maim; to paralyse. (b) (*fig*) to wear out, exhaust. (c) (*fig*) to abuse, maltreat.

tumba[1] *nf* tomb, grave; **ser (como) una —** to keep one's mouth shut; **llevar a uno a la —** (*euph*) to carry someone off, take someone.

tumba[2] *nf* (a) shake, jolt; lurch.
(b) somersault.
(c) (*SAm*) felling of timber, clearing of ground; ground cleared for sowing; forest clearing.
(d) (*Arg, Chi*) boiled meat of poor quality.

tumba[3] *nf* (*Cu, RPl*) African drum.

tumbacuartillos *nm*, *pl* **tumbacuartillos** (*fam*) old soak (*fam*).

tumbacuatro *nm* (*Cu*) braggart.

tumbadero *nm* (a) (*Ant, Mex*) ground cleared for sowing. (b) (*Cu, Mex*) brothel.

tumbar [1a] 1 *vt* (a) to knock down, knock over, knock to the ground; (*of wine: fam*) to lay out.
(b) (*tabu*) to lay, screw (*tabu*).
(c) (*Univ: sl*) to plough (*sl*).
(d) (*fam: of smell etc*) to lay out, knock back (*fam*); (*of impression etc*) to amaze, stun; **su presunción tumbó a todos** his conceit amazed everybody, his conceit knocked everybody sideways (*fam*).
(e) (*SAm*) trees to fell; land to clear.
2 *vi* (a) to fall down.
(b) (*Naut*) to capsize.
(c) (*fam*) **un olor que tumba** a smell which knocks you back (*fam*); **tiene una desfachatez que tumba de espaldas** his brazenness is enough to stun you.
3 **tumbarse** *vr* (a) to lie down; to stretch out; to sprawl, loll; **estar tumbado, quedar tumbado** to lie, be lying down.
(b) (*corn etc*) to go flat.
(c) (*fig*) to give up, decide to take it easy; to let oneself go (*after achieving a success etc*).

tumbo *nm* (a) fall, tumble; (*of vehicle*) shake, jolt; lurch; **dar un —** to tumble; to jolt; to lurch; **dando —s** (*fig*) with all sorts of difficulties, despite the upsets, after a lot of setbacks.
(b) critical moment.

tumbón *adj* (*fam*) slack, lazy, bone-idle.

tumbona *nf* easy chair; deckchair.

tumefacción *nf* swelling, tumefaction.

tumescente *adj* tumescent.

tumido *adj* swollen, tumid.

tumor *nm* tumour, growth; **— maligno** malignant growth, cancer.

túmulo *nm* tumulus, barrow, burial mound; (*Geog*) mound.

tumulto *nm* turmoil, commotion, uproar, tumult; (*Pol etc*) riot, disturbance; **— popular** popular rising.

tumultuario *adj* = **tumultuoso**.

tumultuosamente *adv* tumultuously; (*pej*) riotously; rebelliously.

tumultuoso *adj* tumultuous; (*pej*) riotous, disorderly; rebellious.

tuna[1] *nf* (*Bot*) prickly pear.

tuna[2] *nf* (a) (*Mus*) student music group (*guitarists and singers*).
(b) (*fam*) loose woman, amateur prostitute.
(c) rogue's life, vagabond life; (*fig*) merry life; **correr la —** to have a good time, live it up (*fam*).
(d) (*Guat, Mex*) drunkenness.

tunantada *nf* dirty trick, villainous act.

tunante *nm* rogue, villain, crook; **¡—!** you villain!, (*to child*) you young scamp!

tunantear [1a] *vi* to live a rogue's life, be a crook.

tunantería *nf* (a) (*quality*) villainy, crookedness. (b) (*una —*) villainy, dirty trick.

tunar [1a] *vi* to loaf, idle, bum around (*US*).

tunco (*CAm, Mex*) 1 *adj* maimed, crippled. 2 *nm* (a) cripple. (b) (*Zool*) pig.

tunda[1] *nf* shearing.

tunda[2] *nf* (a) beating, thrashing. (b) **darse una —** to wear oneself out.

tundir[1] [3a] *vt* cloth to shear; grass etc to mow, cut.

tundir[2] [3a] *vt* (a) to beat, thrash. (b) (*fig*) to exhaust, tire out.

tundra *nf* tundra.

tunear [1a] *vi* (a) to live a rogue's life. (b) to loaf, idle; to have a good time.

tunecino 1 *adj* Tunisian. 2 *nm*, **tunecina** *nf* Tunisian.

túnel *nm* tunnel; **— aerodinámico, — de pruebas aerodinámicas** wind-tunnel.

tunes *nmpl* (*CAm, Col*) first steps (*of a child*); **hacer —** to start to walk, take one's first steps.

Túnez *m* (*city*) Tunis; (*country*) Tunisia.

tungo 1 *adj* (*Col*) short, shortened; blunt. 2 *nm* (a) (*Col*) bit, chunk. (b) (*Chi*) neck; jowl.

tungsteno *nm* tungsten.

túnica *nf* (a) tunic; robe, gown, long dress. (b) (*Anat, Bot*) tunic.

túnico *nm* (*SAm*) shift, long undergarment.

tuno *nm* (a) (*hum*) rogue, villain; scamp; **el muy —** the old rogue. (b) (*Mus*) member of a student tuna (see **tuna**[2]).

tunoso *adj* (*Col*) prickly.

tuntún: al (buen) — *adv* thoughtlessly, without due calculation; trusting to luck; **juzgar al buen —** to judge hastily, jump to conclusions.

tuntuneco *adj* (*CAm, PR*) stupid and ugly.

tuñeco *adj* (*Ven*) maimed, crippled.

tupé *nm* (a) toupée. (b) (*fam*) nerve, cheek.

tupi *nm* (*SAm*) Brazilian Indian.

tupia *nf* (*Col*) dam.

tupiar [1b] *vt* (*Col*) to dam up.

tupición *nf* (a) (*SAm*) blockage, stoppage, obstruction; (*Med*) catarrh.
(b) (*SAm*) dense crowd, throng.
(c) (*Bol, Mex*) dense part of a forest.
(d) (*Chi*) **una — de cosas** a lot of things.
(e) (*SAm: fig*) bewilderment, confusion; embarrassment.

tupido 1 *adj* (a) thick, dense; impenetrable; cloth close-woven.
(b) (*SAm*) blocked, stopped up, obstructed.
(c) (*fig*) dense, dim.
(d) (*Mex*) common, frequent.
2 *adv* (*Mex*) perseveringly, steadily; keenly.

tupir [3a] 1 *vt* (a) to pack tight, press down, compact.
(b) (*SAm*) to block, stop up, obstruct.
2 **tupirse** *vr* (a) (*fam*) to stuff oneself.
(b) (*SAm*) to feel silly, get embarrassed.

turba[1] *nf* (*Geog*) peat, turf.

turba[2] *nf* crowd, throng; swarm; (*pej*) mob; rabble.

turbación *nf* (a) disturbance. (b) perturbation, worry, alarm; embarrassment; bewilderment, confusion; trepidation.

turbado *adj* disturbed, worried, upset; embarrassed; bewildered.

turbador *adj* disturbing, alarming; embarrassing.

turbal *nm* peat bog.

turbamulta *nf* mob, rabble.

turbante *nm* (a) turban. (b) (*Mex*) gourd, calabash.

turbar [1a] 1 *vt* (a) order, peace, reason etc to disturb.
(b) person to disturb, worry, alarm; to disconcert; to upset; to embarrass; to bewilder.
(c) water etc to stir up.
2 **turbarse** *vr* to be disturbed, get worried, become alarmed; to be embarrassed; to be bewildered, get confused, get all mixed up.

turbera *nf* peat bog.

turbiedad *nf* (a) cloudiness, thickness.
(b) dimness, mistiness; disturbance; lack of clarity, confusion.
(c) turbulence.
(d) (*pej*) shadiness; dubious character.

turbina *nf* turbine; **— de gas** gas turbine; **— a** (*or* **de**) **vapor** steam engine.

turbio 1 *adj* (**a**) *water etc* cloudy, thick, turbid, muddy. (**b**) *vision* dim, misty, blurred; disturbed; *language, matter* unclear, confused. (**c**) (*fig*) *period etc* restless, unsettled, turbulent. (**d**) (*pej*) *deal* shady; *means* dubious. **2** *adv*: **ver** — to have disturbed vision, not see clearly. **3** —s *nmpl* sediment; sludge.

turbión *nm* (**a**) (*Meteorol*) heavy shower, downpour; squall. (**b**) (*fig*) shower, torrent; swarm; (*of bullets*) hail.

turbohélice 1 *adj* turboprop. **2** *nm* turboprop (aeroplane).

turbonada *nf* (*Arg*) sudden storm, squall.

turbopropulsor, turborreactor 1 *adj* turbojet. **2** *nm* turbojet (aeroplane).

turbulencia *nf* (**a**) turbulence; troubled nature, unsettled character; storminess. (**b**) restlessness; unruliness, rebelliousness; disorderly state, mutinous state.

turbulento *adj* (**a**) *elements, river etc* turbulent; *period* troubled, unsettled, turbulent; *meeting* stormy. (**b**) *character* restless; unruly, rebellious; *child* noisy, troublesome, unruly; *army etc* disorderly, mutinous.

turca *nf* (*fam*) booze-up (*fam*), binge (*sl*); **coger** (*or* **pillar** *etc*) **una** — to get sozzled (*fam*).

turco 1 *adj* Turkish. **2** *nm*, **turca** *nf* (**a**) Turk. (**b**) (*SAm*) Arab, Syrian, Middle Easterner; pedlar, peddler (*US*), hawker. **3** *nm* (*language*) Turkish.

túrdiga *nf* thong, strip of leather.

Turena *f* Touraine.

turf *nm* (*angl*) (**a**) the turf, horse-racing. (**b**) (*SAm*) racetrack.

turfista (*SAm*: *angl*) **1** *adj* horsy, fond of horse-racing. **2** *nm* racing man.

turgencia *nf* turgidity.

turgente *adj*, **túrgido** *adj* turgid, swollen.

turismo *nm* (**a**) tourism; touring, sightseeing; tourist trade; **hacer** — to go touring (abroad), go travelling as tourists; **ahora se hace más** — **que nunca** numbers of tourists are greater now than ever; **se desarrolla mucho el** — **en Eslobodia** facilities for tourists are being much developed in Slobodia; **el** — **constituye su mayor industria** the tourist trade is their biggest industry. (**b**) (*Aut*) saloon car, sedan (*US*); tourer.

turista *nmf* tourist; sightseer, visitor, holidaymaker, vacacionist (*US*).

turístico *adj* tourist (*attr*).

turma *nf* (**a**) (*Anat*) testicle. (**b**) (*Bot*) truffle; (*Col*) potato.

turnar [1a] *vi and* **turnarse** *vr* to take (it in) turns; **ellos se turnan para usarlo** they take it in turns to use it.

turné *nm* (*gall*) tour, trip.

turno *nm* (**a**) rota, order (of priority). (**b**) turn; (*at work*) spell, period of duty; shift; (*at games*) turn, go; (*in meeting etc*) opportunity to speak; — **de día** day shift; — **de noche** night shift; **por** — in rotation, in turn; **por** —s by turns; **trabajar por** —s to work shifts; **es su** —, **es el primero en** —, **le toca el** — it's his turn (next); **esperar su** — to wait one's turn, take one's turn; **cuando le llegue el** — when her turn comes; **estar de** — to be on duty.

turolense 1 *adj* of Teruel. **2** *nmf* native (*or* inhabitant) of Teruel; **los** —s people of Teruel.

turón *nm* polecat.

turquesa *nf* turquoise.

turquesco *adj* Turkish.

turquí *adj*: **color** — indigo, deep blue.

Turquía *nf* Turkey.

turra *nf* (*Arg*) loose woman, prostitute.

turrón *nm* (**a**) (*Cook*) a kind of nougat, made of almond, honey etc. (**b**) (*sl*) cushy government job (*sl*); sinecure, political plum.

turulato *adj* (*fam*) dazed, stunned, flabbergasted; **quedó** — **con la noticia** he was stunned by the news.

tus[1] *interj* good dog!, here boy!

tus[2]: **sin decir** — **ni mus** without saying a word; **no decir** — **ni mus** to remain silent, say nothing.

tusa *nf* (**a**) (*Ant, CAm, Col*) cob of maize, corncob; maize husk; (*Cu*) cigar rolled in a maize leaf; (*Chi*) cornsilk. (**b**) (*Chi, RPl*) horse's mane. (**c**) (*Chi, RPl*) clipping, shearing. (**d**) (*Col*) pockmark. (**e**) (*Ec*) fright; anxiety. (**f**) (*CAm, Cu, PR*) whore. (**g**) (*CAm, PR*) **no vale ni una** — it's worthless. (**h**) (*Mex*) *nm* field mouse.

tusar [1a] *vt* (*SAm*) to cut, clip, shear; to cut roughly, cut badly.

tuse *nm* (*Chi, RPl*) = **tusa**.

tuso *adj* (**a**) (*Col, PR*) cropped, shorn. (**b**) (*PR*) docked, tailless. (**c**) (*Col, Ven*) pockmarked.

tútano *nm* (*SAm*) = **tuétano**.

tute *nm* a card game similar to bezique; **darse un** — to work extra hard, make a special effort.

tutear [1a] **1** *vt*: — **a uno** to address someone as "tú" (*familiar 2nd person singular*). **2 tutearse** *vr*: **se tutean desde siempre** they have always addressed each other as "tú", they have always been on familiar terms.

tutela *nf* (*Law*) guardianship; (*fig*) protection, tutelage; (*fig*) guidance; **bajo** — in ward; **estar bajo la** — **de** (*fig*) to be under the protection of; to be under the auspices of.

tutelaje *nm* (*SAm*) = **tutela**.

tutelar 1 *adj* tutelary; **ángel** — guardian angel. **2** [1a] *vt* to protect, guard; to advise, guide.

tuteo *nm* addressing a person as "tú", familiar usage; **se ha extendido mucho el** — the use of "tú" has greatly increased.

tutilimundi *nm* (*SAm*) everybody.

tutiplé(n): a — *adv give etc* freely; haphazardly, without discernment; *eat etc* hugely, to excess.

tutor *nm* (**a**) (*Law*) guardian; (*Univ*) tutor; — **de curso** (*School*) form master. (**b**) (*Agr*) prop, stake.

tutora *nf* (*Law*) guardian; — **de curso** (*School*) form mistress.

tutoría *nf* guardianship.

tutú *nm* tutu.

tutuma *nf* (*Chi, Per*) head; bump, welt; hump (on one's back).

tutumito *nm* (*CAm, Col*) idiot.

tuturuto 1 *adj* (**a**) (*CAm, Mex, Ven*) drunk. (**b**) (*CAm, Col, Ec, Ven*) stupid; dumbfounded, stunned. **2** *nm* (*Chi*) pimp.

tuve *etc see* **tener**.

tuyo *adj and pron* yours, of yours; (*arch, to God*) thy, of thine; **es** —, **es el** — it is yours; **lo** — (what is) yours, what belongs to you; **cualquier amigo** — any friend of yours; **los** —s (*freq*) your people, your relations, your family.

tweed [twi] *nm* (*angl*) tweed.

U

u *conj* (*used instead of* **o** *before* **o—**, **ho—**) or; **siete u ocho** seven or eight.

ualabi *nm* wallaby.

ubérrimo *adj* exceptionally fertile, marvellously productive, very rich; (*SAm*) abundant.

ubicación *nf* placing; siting; (*esp SAm*) place, position, location, situation.

ubicado *adj*: **una tienda ubicada en la calle X** a shop situated in X street.

ubicar [1g] **1** *vt* (*SAm*) (**a**) to place, put, locate, situate; to site.
(**b**) (*fig*) person to instal in a place (*or* post *etc*).
(**c**) (*fig*) to classify, place, judge.
2 *vi* to be, be situated, be located; to lie, stand.
3 ubicarse *vr* (**a**) (*SAm*) = **2**.
(**b**) (*Arg*) to get a job, find a position; to get into a good position to see.

ubicuidad *nf* ubiquity.

ubicuo *adj* ubiquitous.

ubre *nf* udder; teat.

ubrera *nf* (*Med*) thrush.

—uco *n suffix* (**a**) (*diminutive, mock-scornful*), *eg* **mujeruca** odd little woman; **ventanuco** useless little window.
(**b**) (*prov: diminutive*) *eg* **niñuco** very small boy.

Ucrania *f* Ukraine.

ucraniano, ucranio 1 *adj* Ukrainian. **2** *nm*, **ucrania** *nf*, **ucraniana** *nf* Ukrainian.

—ucho *n* and *adj suffix* (**a**) (*strongly pej*) **medicucho** rotten doctor (*fam*), bungling doctor; **delgaducho** terribly thin (*fam*); *see* **casucha, periodicucho** *etc*.
(**b**) (*softening*) *eg* **delicaducho** rather delicate; **maluchо** (*Med: fam*) poorly, under the weather.

uchuvito *adj* (*Col*) drunk.

—udo *adj suffix* (*denoting a lot or excess of*), *eg* **bigotudo** with a big moustache, **nalgudo** big-bottomed, broad in the beam (*fam*); *see* **peludo, tripudo** *etc*.

—uelo *n* and *adj suffix* (*diminutive*), *eg* **muchachuelo** little boy; **pequeñuelo** very small, tiny; *see* **arroyuelo, ojuelos** *etc*.

uf *interj* (*tiredness, lack of air etc*) phew!; (*repugnance*) ugh!

ufanamente *adv* proudly; cheerfully; exultantly; (*pej*) conceitedly; boastfully; smugly.

ufanarse [1a] *vr* to boast; to be vain, be conceited; **— con, — de** to boast of, pride oneself on, be vain about; to glory in.

ufanía *nf* (**a**) pride; (*pej*) vanity, conceit; boastfulness.
(**b**) (*Bot*) = **lozanía**.

ufano *adj* (**a**) proud; gay, cheerful; exultant; (*pej*) vain, conceited; boastful; overweening; smug; **iba muy — en el nuevo coche** he was going along so proudly in his new car; **está muy — porque le han dado el premio** he is very proud that they have awarded him the prize.
(**b**) (*Bot*) = **lozano**.

ujier *nm* usher; doorkeeper, attendant.

—ujo *n* and *adj suffix* (**a**) (*diminutive*) **pequeñujo** tiny, miserably small. (**b**) (*pej*) **papelujo** wretched bit of paper.

úlcera *nf* ulcer, sore; **— de decúbito** bedsore.

ulceración *nf* ulceration.

ulcerar [1a] **1** *vt* to make sore, make a sore on, ulcerate. **2 ulcerarse** *vr* to ulcerate; to fester.

ulceroso *adj* ulcerous; full of sores, covered with sores.

ulecear [1a] *vt* (*Chi*) dough to roll out.

ulero *nm* (*Chi*) rolling pin.

Ulises *m* Ulysses.

ulpo *nm* (*Chi, Per*) maize gruel.

ulterior *adj* (**a**) *place* farther, further. (**b**) *occasion etc* later, subsequent.

ulteriormente *adv* later, subsequently.

ultimación *nf* completion, conclusion.

últimamente *adv* (**a**) lastly, finally. (**b**) as a last resort. (**c**) recently, lately. (**d**) (*SAm*) ¡—! well I'm damned!, that's the absolute end!

ultimar [1a] *vt* (**a**) to finish, complete, conclude; *details, preparations* to finalize; *agreement* to conclude.
(**b**) (*SAm*) to finish off, give the coup de grâce to.

ultimátum *nm*, *pl* **ultimátums** ultimatum.

último *adj* (**a**) (*in order, time*) last; latest, most recent; (*of two*) latter; **éste —, éstos —s** the latter; **el — día del mes** the last day of the month; **a —s del mes** in the latter part of the month, towards the end of the month; **las últimas noticias** the latest news; **en estos —s años** in recent years, in the last few years; **llegó el —** he arrived last, he came last, he was last; (*in race*) he came (in) last; **ser el — en + infin** to be the last to + *infin*; **estar a lo — de** to be nearly at the end of, have nearly finished; **estar en las últimas** (*fam*) to be about to peg out (*sl*); to be down and out, be on one's last legs, to be down to one's last little bit (of a stock *etc*); **por —** lastly, finally; **por última vez** for the last time.
(**b**) (*in place*) furthest, most remote; back; top; topmost; lowest, bottom; **en el — rincón del país** in the furthest corner of the country; **un asiento de última fila** a seat in the back row; **el equipo en última posición** the team in the lowest position, the bottom team; **viven en el — piso** they live on the top floor.
(**c**) (*fig*) final, extreme, last; utmost; **la última solución** the final solution; **el — remedio** the ultimate remedy; **en — caso** as a last resort, in the last resort.
(**d**) (*Comm*) *price* lowest, bottom; **dígame lo —, dígame el — precio** tell me what your lowest price is.
(**e**) (*fig*) *quality* finest, best, superior.
(**f**) (*fam*) **vestido a la última** dressed in the latest style; **tienen un coche que es lo —** they have the very latest thing in cars; **¡es lo —!** it's the greatest! (*fam*), it's tremendous! (*fam*); (*pej*) this is the end!; **viven en un pueblucho que es lo —** they live in a dump which is unbelievably awful (*fam*); **pedirme eso encima ya es lo —** for him to ask that of me as well really is the limit.

**ultra ... ** *ultra* . . ., *extra* . . .

ultracorto *adj* ultra-short.

ultraísmo *nm* revolutionary poetic movement of the 1920's (*imagist, surrealist etc*).

ultrajador *adj*, **ultrajante** *adj* outrageous; offensive; insulting.

ultrajar [1a] *vt* (**a**) to outrage; to offend; to insult, revile, abuse. (**b**) (*lit*) to spoil, to crumple, disarrange.

ultraje *nm* outrage; insult.

ultrajoso *adj* outrageous; offensive; insulting.

ultramar *nm* countries beyond the seas, foreign parts; **de —, en —** overseas; **los países de —** the overseas countries; **productos venidos de —** products from overseas, goods from abroad; **pasó 8 años en —** he spent 8 years overseas.

ultramarino 1 *adj* overseas; foreign. **2 —s** *nmpl* (**a**) groceries, foodstuffs; **tienda de —s** = (**b**) (*fam*) **un —s** a grocer's (shop), a grocery (*US*).

ultramoderno *adj* ultramodern.

ultramontanismo *nm* ultramontanism.

ultramontano 1 *adj* ultramontane. **2** *nm* ultramontane.

ultranza: a — ** *adv* (a**) **luchar a —** to fight to the death; **lo quiere hacer a —** he wants to do it at all costs (*or* come what may, regardless of the difficulties); **paz a —** peace at any price.
(**b**) **revolucionario a —** out-and-out revolutionary, utterly uncompromising revolutionary.

ultrapotente *adj* extra powerful.
ultrarrápido *adj* extra fast.
ultrarrojo *adj* = **infrarrojo.**
ultrasónico *adj* ultrasonic.
ultratumba *nf* what lies beyond the grave; **la vida de** — life beyond the grave, life in the next world; **una voz de** — a voice from beyond the grave.
ultravioleta *adj* ultraviolet; **rayos** — ultraviolet rays.
ulular [1a] *vi* (*of animal, wind*) to howl, shriek; (*of owl*) to hoot, screech.
ululato *nm* howl, shriek; hoot, screech.
ulluco *nm* (*Ec, Per*) *a potato-like tuber.*
umbilical *adj* umbilical.
umbral *nm* (a) threshold; **pasar** (*or* **traspasar**) **el** — **de uno** to set foot in someone's house.
  (b) (*fig*) threshold; first step, beginning; **estar en los** —**es de** to be on the threshold of, be on the verge of, be on the point of; **eso está en los** —**es de lo imposible** that borders (*or* verges) on the impossible.
umbralada *nf* (*Col, Chi*), **umbralado** *nm* (*Col, Chi*), **umbraladura** *nf* (*Ec*) threshold.
umbrío *adj,* **umbroso** *adj* shady.
un, una 1 *indefinite article* a, (*before a vowel and silent* h) an.
  2 *adj* one; **la una** one o'clock; **¡a la una, a las dos, a las tres!** (*at auction*) going, going, gone!; (*in racing*) ready, steady, go!
  3 *nm* one.
unánime *adj* unanimous.
unánimemente *adv* unanimously.
unanimidad *nf* unanimity; **por** — unanimously.
uncial 1 *adj* uncial. 2 *nf* uncial.
unción *nf* (a) (*Med*) anointing. (b) (*Eccl and fig*) unction.
uncir [3b] *vt* to yoke.
undécimo *adj* eleventh.
undoso *etc see* **ondoso.**
ungido *adj* anointed; **el U—** **del Señor** the Lord's Anointed.
ungir [3c] *vt* (a) (*Med*) to anoint, put ointment on, rub with ointment. (b) (*Eccl*) to anoint.
ungüento *nm* ointment, unguent; (*fig*) salve, balm.
ungulado 1 *adj* ungulate, hoofed. 2 *nm* ungulate, hoofed animal.
uni . . . uni . . ., one- . . .
únicamente *adv* only; solely.
unicameral *adj* (*Pol*) single-chamber.
unicelular *adj* unicellular, single-cell.
unicidad *nf* uniqueness.
único *adj* (a) only; sole, single, solitary; unique; **hijo** — only child; **sistema de partido** — one-party system, single-party system; **la única dificultad es que . . .** the only difficulty is that . . .; **es el** — **ejemplar que existe** it is the only copy in existence; **este ejemplar es** — this specimen is unique.
  (b) (*fig*) unique; unusual, extraordinary.
unicolor *adj* one-colour, all one colour.
unicornio *nm* unicorn.
unidad *nf* (a) (*quality*) unity; oneness; togetherness; — **de acción** (*Lit*) unity of action; — **de lugar** (*Lit*) unity of place.
  (b) (*Math, Mil, Tech etc*) unit; — **de cola** (*Aer*) tail unit; — **móvil** (*TV*) mobile unit; — **vecinal de absorción de Toboso** overspill town for Toboso.
unido *adj* (a) joined (*por* by), linked (*por* by).
  (b) (*fig*) united; **una familia muy unida** a very united family; **mantenerse** —**s** to remain united, maintain their (*etc*) unity, keep together.
unificación *nf* unification.
unificar [1g] *vt* to unite, unify.
uniformado 1 *adj* uniformed. 2 *nm* man in uniform, (*esp*) policeman.
uniformar [1a] *vt* (a) to make uniform; to level up, make the same. (b) *person* to put into uniform, provide a uniform for.
uniforme 1 *adj* uniform; *surface etc* level, even, smooth; *speed, rate etc* uniform, steady; regular. 2 *nm* uniform.
uniformemente *adv* uniformly.
uniformidad *nf* uniformity; levelness, evenness, smoothness; steadiness; regularity.
unigénito *adj* (*Rel*) only-begotten; **el U—** the Only Begotten Son.
unilateral *adj* unilateral, one-sided.
unilateralmente *adv* unilaterally.
unión *nf* (a) (*act*) union, uniting, joining.
  (b) (*quality*) unity; closeness, togetherness.
  (c) (*Comm, Pol etc*) union; (*Law*) union, marriage;

en — **con** with, together with, accompanied by; — **aduanera** customs union; **U—** **Panamericana** Pan-American Union; **U—** **Soviética** Soviet Union; **U—** **Sudafricana** Union of South Africa; **vivir en** — **libre con** to live with.
  (d) (*Mech*) joint, union; (*also* **punto de** —) junction (*entre* between).
unipersonal *adj* for one (person); single, individual.
unir [3a] 1 *vt* (a) *objects, parts* to join, unite; to tie (*or* fasten, bolt *etc*) together; *persons* to unite; *families* to unite (by marriage); *companies, interests etc* to merge, join; to pool; *qualities* to combine (a with); **les une una fuerte simpatía** they are bound by a strong affection, there are bonds of affection between them.
  (b) *liquids etc* to mix; *dough, sauce etc* to mix thoroughly, make smooth; to beat (up).
  2 *vi* (*of ingredients*) to mix well, make a smooth mixture.
  3 **unirse** *vr* (a) (2 *persons etc*) to join together, unite; (*companies*) to merge, combine; — **en matrimonio** to marry, be united in marriage.
  (b) — **a** to join; — **con** to unite with, merge with; **se unen las ramas por encima** the branches meet overhead.
  (c) (*of ingredients*) to mix well, cohere.
unísono *adj* unisonous, on the same tone; *voices etc* in harmony; **al** — on the same tone; (*fig*) in unison, with one voice, in harmony, harmoniously; **al** — **con** (*fig*) in tune with, in harmony with.
unitario 1 *adj* unitary; (*Eccl*) Unitarian. 2 *nm,* **unitaria** *nf* Unitarian.
unitarismo *nm* Unitarianism.
univalente *adj* univalent.
univalvo *adj* univalve.
universal *adj* universal; world (*attr*), world-wide; **historia** — world history; **de fama** — known all over the world, internationally famous; **una especie de distribución** — a species with a world-wide distribution.
universalidad *nf* universality.
universalizar [1f] *vt* to universalize, make universal; to extend widely, bring into general use.
universalmente *adv* universally; all over the world.
universidad *nf* university; — **laboral** technical college.
universitario 1 *adj* university (*attr*); academic. 2 *nm* university teacher; university student, university man.
universo *nm* universe; world.
uno 1 *adj* (a) one; one and the same, identical; **es todo** —, **es** — **y lo mismo** it's all one, it's all the same; **Dios es** — God is one; **la verdad es una** truth is one and indivisible.
  (b) —**s** some, a few (*also* —**s cuantos**); about, *eg* —**s 80 dólares** about 80 dollars.
  2 *pron* (a) one; somebody; — **mismo** oneself; **ha venido** — **que dice que te conoce** somebody who says he knows you came; —**s que estaban allí protestaron** some (people) who were there protested; **los** —**s dicen que sí y los otros que no** some say yes and some say no; **es mejor hacerlo** — **mismo** it's better to do it oneself.
  (b) **cada** — each one, every one; **cada** — **a lo suyo** everyone should mind his own business; **había 3 manzanas para cada** — there were 3 apples each.
  (c) (*indef subject*) one, you; — **nunca sabe qué hacer** one never knows what to do; — **necesita descansar** a man has to rest, you have to rest.
  (d) **uno(s) a otro(s)** each other, one another; **se detestan** —**s a otros** they hate each other; **se miraban fijamente el** — **al otro** they stared at each other.
  (e) (*idioms*) — **a** —, — **por** —, **de** — **en** — one by one; **a una** all together; **juntarlo todo en** — to put it all together; **estar en** — to be at one; **no gustará a más de** — there are quite a few who will not like this; **una de dos** either one thing or the other; — **con otro salen a 3 dólares** on an average they work out at 3 dollars each; — **y otro están locos** they're both mad; **para mí es** — **de tantos** so far as I'm concerned he's just one of many; in my view he's a very ordinary sort; **lo** — **por lo otro** it comes to the same thing, what you lose on the swings you gain on the roundabouts.
untadura *nf* (a) (*act*) smearing, dabbing, rubbing; greasing; spreading. (b) (*Med*) ointment; (*Mech etc*) grease, oil. (c) mark, smear, dab.
untar [1a] 1 *vt* (a) to smear, dab, rub (*con, de* with); (*Med*) to anoint, rub (*con, de* with); (*Mech etc*) to

grease, oil; — **su pan en la salsa** to dip one's bread in the gravy, soak one's bread in the gravy; — **los dedos de tinta** to smear one's fingers with ink; — **el pan con manteca** to spread butter on one's bread, put butter on one's bread.
   (b) (*fam*) to bribe, grease the palm of.
   2 **untarse** *vr* (a) — **con**, — **de** to smear oneself with.
   (b) (*fam*) to indulge in immorality, get involved in wrongdoing; (*Fin*) to take a rake-off (*fam*), get a cut in the profits; to find that somebody else's money (*etc*) has stuck to one.
unto *nm* (a) soft substance; (*Med*) ointment, unguent; (*Zool*) grease, animal fat. (b) (*Chi*) shoe polish.
untuosidad *nf* greasiness, oiliness; stickiness.
untuoso *adj* greasy, oily, sticky.
untura *nf* = **untadura**.
uña *nf* (a) (*Anat*) nail, fingernail; toenail; (*Zool etc*) claw; **ser** — **y carne** to be inseparable, be as thick as thieves; **largo de** —**s** light-fingered, thieving; **estar de** —**s con uno** to be at daggers drawn with someone; **caer en las** —**s de uno** to fall into someone's clutches; **comerse las** —**s** to bite one's nails; (*fig*) to get very impatient, get furious; (*SAm*) to be terribly poor; **se dejó las uñas en ese trabajo** he wore his fingers to the bone at that job; **enseñar** (*or* **mostrar, sacar**) **las** —**s** to show one's claws (*also fig*).
   (b) (*of horse etc*) hoof; — **de caballo** (*Bot*) coltsfoot; **escapar a** — **de caballo** to ride off at full speed; — **de vaca** (*Cook*) cow heel.
   (c) (*of scorpion*) sting.
   (d) (*Tech*) claw; nailpuller.
   (e) (*of anchor*) fluke.
uñada *nf* nail mark; scratch.
uñalarga *nmf* (*SAm*) thief.
uñarada *nf* = **uñada**.
uñatear [1a] *vt* (*Arg, Bol*) to steal.
uñero *nm* (a) whitlow. (b) ingrowing nail.
uñetas *nmf, pl* **uñetas** (*CAm, Col*) thief.
uñetear [1a] *vt* (*Chi*) to steal.
uñilargo *nm* (*Col, Per*), **uñón** *nm* (*Col, Per*) thief.
upa¹ *nm* (*Ec, Per*) idiot.
upa² *interj* up, up!
upar [1a] *vt* (*fam*) to lift up, lift in one's arms; (*SAm*) = **aupar**.
Urales *mpl* (*also* **Montes** —) Urals.
uranio *nm* uranium.
Urano *m* Uranus.
urbanidad *nf* courtesy, politeness, urbanity.
urbanismo *nm* (a) town planning; urban development. (b) (*Ven*) real-estate development.
urbanista *nm* town planner.
urbanístico *adj* town-planning (*attr*); urban, city (*attr*).
urbanización *nf* urbanization; urban development.
urbanizado *adj* built-up.
urbanizar [1f] *vt* (a) *land* to develop, build on, urbanize; to lay out and prepare for city development. (b) *person* to civilize.
urbano *adj* (a) urban, town (*attr*), city (*attr*). (b) courteous, polite, urbane.
urbe *nf* large city, metropolis; capital city; **La U**— (*in Spain*) Madrid, the Capital.
urbícola *nmf* city dweller.
urco *nm* (*Bol, Chi*) ram; male alpaca.
urdimbre *nf* (a) warp. (b) (*fig*) scheme, intrigue.
urdir [3a] *vt* (a) to warp. (b) (*fig*) to plot, scheme for, contrive.
urdu *nm* Urdu.
urea *nf* urea.
urente *adj* (*Med etc*) burning, stinging.
uréter *nm* ureter.
uretra *nf* urethra.
urgencia *nf* (a) urgency; pressure; haste, rush; **con toda** — with the utmost urgency, posthaste; **de** — urgent, pressing; (*Post*) express; **pedir algo con** — to press for something.
   (b) emergency; **medida de** — emergency measure; **salida de** — emergency exit.
   (c) pressing need; **en caso de** — in case of necessity, if the need arises; **acudió a mí en una** — **de dinero** he came to me with a pressing need for money.
urgente *adj* urgent; pressing; *demand etc* pressing, imperative, insistent; **carta** — special-delivery letter; **pedido** — rush order.
urgentemente *adv* urgently; imperatively, insistently.
urgir [3c] *vi* to be urgent, be pressing; **urge el dinero** the money is urgently needed; **me urge la respuesta** the reply is required with the utmost urgency; **el tiempo urge** time presses, time is short; **me urge terminarlo** I must finish it as soon as I can, I

must finish it with the utmost speed; **me urge partir** I have to leave at once; "**Úrgeme vender: dos gatos . . .**" (*advert*) "Must be sold: two cats."
úrico *adj* uric.
urinario 1 *adj* urinary. 2 *nm* urinal, public lavatory, comfort station (*US*).
urna *nf* urn; glass case; (*Pol etc: also* — **electoral**) ballot box; **acudir a las** —**s** (*fig*) to vote, go and vote, go to the polls.
uro *nm* aurochs.
urogallo *nm* capercaillie.
urogenital *adj* urogenital.
urología *nf* urology.
urólogo *nm* urologist.
urpo *nm* (*Arg, Chi*) = **ulpo**.
urraca *nf* magpie.
urticaria *nf* urticaria, nettlerash.
Uruguay: **El** — Uruguay.
uruguayismo *nm* word (*or* phrase *etc*) peculiar to Uruguay.
uruguayo 1 *adj* Uruguayan. 2 *nm*, **uruguaya** *nf* Uruguayan.
usado *adj* *stamp etc* used; *clothing* worn; secondhand; **muy** — worn out, old, shabby.
usagre *nm* (*Med*) impetigo; (*Vet*) mange.
usanza *nf* usage, custom; **a** — **india, a** — **de los indios** according to the custom of the Indians, in the Indian fashion.
usar [1a] 1 *vt* (a) to use, make use of; *clothing* to wear; **sin** — unused.
   (b) — + *infin* to be accustomed to + *infin*, to be in the habit of + *ger*.
   2 *vi*: — **de** to use, make use of.
   3 **usarse** *vr* to be used, be in use; (*clothing*) to be worn; to be in fashion; to be the custom; **la chistera ya no se usa** top hats are not worn nowadays, top hats are no longer in fashion.
usina *nf* (*SAm*: *gall*) factory, plant; (*RPl*) power plant; gasworks; tram depot.
uslero *nm* (*Chi*) rolling pin.
uso *nm* (a) use; **objeto de** — **personal** article for personal use; **de** — **externo** (*Med*) for external application; **estar fuera de** — to be out of use, be obsolete; **estar en** — to be in use; **estar en buen** — to be in good condition; **estar en el** — **de la palabra** to be speaking, have the floor; **hacer** — **de** to make use of; **hacer** — **de la palabra** to speak; **retirar algo del** — to withdraw something from service.
   (b) (*Mech etc*) wear, wear and tear; — **y desgaste** wear and tear; **deteriorado por el** — worn.
   (c) custom, usage; fashion, style; **es un** — **muy antiguo** it is a very ancient custom; **al** — as is customary, in keeping with custom; **con bigotes al** — with the usual sort of moustache, with the sort of moustache which was then fashionable; **un hombre al** — an ordinary man; **al** — **de** in the style of, in the fashion of; **un libro hecho al** — **de los principiantes** a book written for beginners.
usted, *pl* **ustedes** *personal pronoun* (*normally abbr* **Vd, Vds**) you (*polite or formal address*); **el coche de** — your car; **mi coche y el de** — my car and yours; **para** — for you; **sin** — without you; **¡a** —**!** (*reciprocating thanks*) thank you!
usual *adj* usual, customary; ordinary; regular.
usualmente *adv* usually; ordinarily, regularly.
usuario *nm*, **usuaria** *nf* user; — **de la vía pública** road user.
usufructo *nm* usufruct, use; — **vitalicio** life interest (*de in*).
usufructuario *nm*, **usufructuaria** *nf* usufructuary.
usura *nf* usury; (*fig*) profiteering, racketeering.
usurario *adj* usurious.
usurear [1a] *vi* to lend money at an exorbitant rate of interest; (*fig*) to profiteer, run a racket.
usurero *nm* usurer; (*fig*) profiteer, racketeer.
usurpación *nf* usurpation; seizure, illegal taking; (*fig*) encroachment (*de* upon), inroads (*de* into).
usurpador *nm* usurper.
usurpar [1a] *vt* *crown, rights etc* to usurp; *land etc* to seize, take illegally; (*fig*) to encroach upon, make inroads into.
usuta *nf* (*Arg, Bol, Per*) = **ojota**.
utensilio *nm* tool, implement; (*Cook*) utensil; —**s de cirujano** surgeon's instruments; —**s para escribir** writing materials; —**s para pescar** fishing tackle; —**s de pintor** painter's materials; **con los** —**s de su oficio** with the tools of his craft, with the equipment of his trade.
uterino *adj* uterine; **hermanos** —**s** children born of the same mother.
útero *nm* womb, uterus.
útil 1 *adj* (a) useful; usable, serviceable; handy; **las**

plantas —es para el hombre the plants which are useful to man; **el coche es viejo pero todavía está — **the car is old but but it is still serviceable; **es muy — tenerlo aquí cerca** it's very handy having it here close by; **¿en qué puedo serle —?** can I do anything for you?, can I be of any help?
(b) **día —** working day, weekday.
(c) (*Mil*) **— para el servicio** *person* fit for military service, *vehicle etc* operational.
2 **—es** *nmpl* tools, implements; tackle, equipment; **—es de chimenea** fire irons; **—es de labranza** agricultural implements.

utilería *nf* (*Arg, Mex: Theat*) properties, props (*fam*).
utilidad *nf* (a) usefulness, utility; benefit. (b) (*Comm, Fin etc*) profit, benefit; **—es** profits, earnings; **—es líquidas** net profits.
utilitario *adj* (a) utilitarian. (b) *car, clothing etc* utility (*attr*).
utilitarismo *nm* utilitarianism.
utilitarista *nmf* utilitarian.
utilizable *adj* usable; serviceable; fit for use, ready to use; (*Tech*) *waste* reclaimable.

utilización *nf* use, utilization; (*Tech*) reclamation.
utilizar [1f] *vt* to use, make use of, utilize; *power, resources etc* to harness; (*Tech*) *waste* to reclaim.
útilmente *adv* usefully.
utillaje *nm* (set of) tools; tackle, equipment.
utopía *nf*, **utopia** *nf* Utopia.
utópico *adj* Utopian.
utopista 1 *adj* Utopian. 2 *nmf* Utopian.
utrículo *nm* utricle.
uva *nf* (a) grape; **— blanca** green grape; **— de Corinto** currant; **— crespa, — espina** gooseberry; **— moscatel** muscatel grape; **— pasa** raisin; **—s verdes** (*fig*) sour grapes; **de —s a peras** very occasionally, once in a blue moon; **estar hecho una —** to be drunk as a lord. (b) (*Chi*) kiss.
uve *nf name of the letter* V; **de forma de —** V-shaped; **escote en —** V-neck.
úvula *nf* uvula.
uvular *adj* uvular.
uxoricidio *nm* wife-murder.
—uzo *n and adj suffix* (*pej*), *eg* **carnuza** bad meat, awful meat (*fam*); *see* **gentuza** etc.

V

va *etc see* **ir.**

vaca *nf* (a) cow; **— de leche, — lechera** dairy cow, milking cow; (*SAm: fig*) good business, profitable deal; **— marina** manatee, sea cow; **— de San Antón** ladybird, ladybug (*US*); **—s gordas** (*fig*) period of prosperity, boom; **pasar las —s gordas** (*fig*) to have a grand time of it.
(b) (*Cook*) beef; cowhide.
(c) (*SAm*) enterprise with profits on a pro rata basis.
(d) (*Per*) **hacerse la —** to play hooky.

vacación *nf* vacation; **—es** holiday(s), vacation; **—es escolares** school holidays; **—es pagadas, —es retribuidas** holidays with pay; **estar de —es** to be (away) on holiday; **hacer —es** to take a day off; **marcharse de —es** to go off on holiday.

vacacionista *nmf* holidaymaker, vacationist (*US*).

vacada *nf* herd of cows.

vacaje *nm* (*Chi, RPl*) cows, cattle; herd of cows; (*Mex*) herd of beef cows.

vacante 1 *adj* vacant, empty, unoccupied; *post* vacant. **2** *nf* vacancy, place, (unfilled) post; **proveer una —** to fill a post.

vacar [1g] *vi* (a) to fall vacant, become vacant; to remain unfilled.
(b) (*of person*) to cease work; to be idle.
(c) **— a, — en** to attend to, engage in, devote oneself to.
(d) **— de** to lack, be without.

vacarí *adj* cowhide (*attr*).

vaccinio *nm* bilberry; blueberry (*US*).

vaciadero *nm* (a) sink, drain; sump. (b) rubbish tip, dumping ground.

vaciado 1 *adj statue etc* cast in a mould; *tool* hollow-ground. **2** *nm* (a) cast, mould(ing); **— de yeso** plaster cast. (b) hollowing out; excavation. (c) (*Aer*) **— rápido** jettisoning.

vaciar [1c] **1** *vt* (a) *container* to empty (out); *glass etc* to drain; *contents* to empty out; *liquid* to pour, pour away; to run off; to drink up; (*Aer etc*) to jettison; **vació los bolsillos en la mesa** he emptied out his pockets on the table; **vació la leche en un vaso** he poured (*or* emptied) the milk into a glass; **lo vació todo sobre su cabeza** he poured the lot over his head.
(b) *wood, stone etc* to hollow out; *statue etc* to cast.
(c) *knife etc* to grind, sharpen.
(d) *subject, theory* to expound at length.
(e) *writing, text* to copy out.
2 *vi* (*of river*) to flow, empty, run (*en* into).
3 vaciarse *vr* (a) to empty.
(b) (*also* **— por la lengua**; *sl*) to blab, spill the beans (*sl*).

vaciedad *nf* (a) emptiness. (b) (*fig*) silliness; piece of nonsense; **—es** nonsense, rubbish.

vacilación *nf* hesitancy, hesitation, vacillation; **sin —es** unhesitatingly.

vacilada *nf* (*Mex*) (a) spree (*fam*), binge (*sl*). (b) joke.

vacilante *adj* (a) unsteady; wobbly, tottery; *speech* faltering, halting; *memory* uncertain. (b) light flickering. (c) (*fig*) hesitant, uncertain, vacillating; indecisive, dithery.

vacilar [1a] *vi* (a) (*of furniture etc*) to be unsteady; to wobble, rock, move, shake; (*of person*) to totter; to reel, stagger; to stumble; (*fig: of morality etc*) to be indecisive, be collapsing; (*in speech*) to falter; (*of memory*) to fail.
(b) (*of light*) to flicker.
(c) (*fig*) to hesitate, waver, vacillate; to hang back; **sin —** unhesitatingly; **— en + infin** to hesitate to + *infin*; **— entre dos posibilidades** to hesitate between two possibilities; **es un hombre que vacila mucho** he is a very indecisive man, he is

a man who dithers a lot; **no vaciles en decírmelo** don't hesitate to tell me about it.
(d) (*fig*) **— entre** to vary between; **un sabor que vacila entre agradable y desagradable** a taste which varies between nice and nasty, a taste which ranges from nice to nasty.
(e) (*CAm, Mex, PR*) to get tight; to go on a spree (*fam*); to revel, carouse.

vacilón *nm* (*Mex*) reveller, merrymaker.

vacío 1 *adj* (a) empty; *post etc* vacant, unoccupied; unfilled; *flat* unfurnished; *paper* blank; **— de todo contenido serio** empty of any serious contents, devoid of any serious purpose; **el teatro estaba medio —** the theatre was half empty.
(b) (*fig*) insubstantial; superficial; *talk etc* light, idle, frivolous; *effort* vain, useless.
(c) (*fig*) vain; proud.
(d) (*fig*) idle, unemployed.
(e) (*Col, CR, SD*) **pan —** bread alone, just bread, bread by itself.
2 *nm* (*in general*) emptiness; void; (*Phys*) vacuum; (*un —*) empty space, gap; vacant place; hollow; (*Anat*) side, flank, ribs; **han dejado un — para el nombre** they have left a space for the name; **se nota ahora un gran — en la familia** one is conscious now of a big gap in the family; **el libro llenará un bien sentido —** the book will fill a long-felt want; **el camión volvió de —** the lorry came back empty; **lo pedí pero tuve que marcharme de —** I asked for it but had to go away empty-handed; **caer en el —** to fall flat; to fail, be ineffective, produce no result; **dar un golpe en —** to miss, fail to connect; **esta viga parece que está en el —** this beam seems to be unsupported, this beam seems to rest on nothing at all; **marchar en —** (*Mech*) to tick over; **hacer el — a uno** to send someone to Coventry, pretend that someone does not exist.

vacuidad *nf* (a) emptiness. (b) (*fig*) vacuity; superficiality, frivolity; empty-headedness.

vacuna *nf* (a) vaccine. (b) (*SAm*) vaccination.

vacunación *nf* (a) vaccination. (b) (*fig*) preparation; inuring; forearming.

vacunar [1a] *vt* (a) to vaccinate. (b) (*fig*) to prepare; to inure; to forearm.

vacuno *adj* bovine; cow (*attr*); **ganado —** cattle.

vacuo *adj* (a) empty; vacant. (b) (*fig*) vacuous; superficial, frivolous, empty-headed.

vade *nm* (*School etc*) satchel, case.

vadeable *adj* (a) fordable, which can be forded. (b) (*fig*) not impossible, not insuperable.

vadear [1a] **1** *vt* (a) *river* to ford; *water* to wade through, wade across.
(b) (*fig*) *difficulty* to surmount, get round, overcome.
(c) (*fig*) *person* to sound out.
2 *vi* to wade; **cruzar un río vadeando** to wade across a river; **llegar a tierra vadeando** to wade ashore.

vademécum *nm, pl* **vademécums** (a) vademecum. (b) (*School etc*) satchel, case.

vadera *nf* wide ford.

vado *nm* (a) ford. (b) (*fig*) way out, solution, expedient; **no hallar —** to see no way out, find no solution; **tentar el —** to look into possible solutions. (c) (*fig*) respite.

vagabundear [1a] *vi* to wander, roam, rove; to loaf, idle, bum (*US*).

vagabundeo *nm* wandering, roving; tramp's life; loafing, idling, bumming (*US*).

vagabundo 1 *adj* wandering, roving; (*pej*) vagrant; vagabond. **2** *nm*, **vagabunda** *nf* wanderer, rover; (*pej*) vagrant; vagabond, tramp, bum (*US*).

vagación *nf* (*Mech*) free play.

vagamente *adv* vaguely.
vagamundería *nf* (*SAm*) idleness, laziness.
vagamundo *adj* (*SAm*) idle, lazy.
vagancia *nf* vagrancy; idleness, laziness.
vagante *adj* (a) wandering, vagrant. (b) (*Mech*) *etc* free, loose.
vagar 1 [1h] *vi* (a) to wander (about), roam, rove; to prowl about; to saunter up and down, wander about the streets; to loiter; to idle, loaf, laze about.
 (b) (*Mech*) to be free, be loose, move about.
 2 *nm* leisure, free time; idleness; lack of anxiety, freedom from worry; **andar de —** to be at leisure; to feel at ease.
vagido *nm* (baby's) wail, cry.
vagina *nf* vagina.
vaginal *adj* vaginal.
vago 1 *adj* (a) vague; ill-defined, indistinct; indeterminate; (*Art*) blurred.
 (b) roving, wandering.
 (c) *person* lazy, slack; unreliable; idle, unemployed; *object* idle, unused; *space etc* empty.
 (d) **en — stand** *etc* unsteadily; unsupported; *strive* in vain; aimlessly, pointlessly; **dar golpes en —** to flail about, beat the air.
 2 *nm* (a) tramp, vagrant; down-and-out.
 (b) lazy sort, slacker; unreliable person; useless individual, dead loss.
vagón *nm* (*Rail*: for passengers) coach, carriage, car; (for goods) truck, wagon; car, van; **— cisterna, — tanque** tanker, tank wagon; **— directo** through carriage; **— de ganado, — de hacienda** (*Arg*), **— de reja** (*Chi*) cattle truck; **— de mercancías** goods van, freight car (*US*); **— de primera** first-class carriage; **— de segunda** second-class carriage; **— restaurante** dining car; **— tolva** hopper.
vagonada *nf* truckload, wagonload.
vagoneta *nf* light truck.
vaguada *nf* watercourse, stream bed.
vaguear [1a] *vi* =**vagar 1**.
vaguedad *nf* (a) vagueness; indistinctness; indeterminacy. (b) (*una —*) vague remark; woolly idea; **hablar sin —es** to talk in a down-to-earth way, speak with precision.
vaguería *nf* laziness, slackness; unreliability.
vaharada *nf* puff, gust of breath; whiff, reek; smell.
vahear [1a] *vi* to steam; to fume, give off fumes, smoke; to whiff, reek, smell.
vahído *nm* dizzy spell, queer turn, vertigo.
vaho *nm* (a) vapour, steam, fumes; breath; whiff, reek, smell. (b) **—s** (*Med*) inhalation.
vaina 1 *nf* (a) (*Mil etc*) sheath, scabbard; (of tool) sheath, case.
 (b) (*Bot*) pod; husk, shell.
 (c) (*SAm*) nuisance, troublesome thing.
 (d) (*Col*) flute, piece of luck.
 (e) (*Chi*) swindle.
 (f) (*Cu*: *tabu*) screw (*tabu*).
 2 *adj* (*SAm*) annoying.
vainetilla *nf* (*Per*) annoyance, vexation.
vainica *nf* (*Sew*) hemstitch.
vainilla *nf* vanilla.
vainillina *nf* vanillin.
vainita *nf* (*SD, Ven*) string bean.
vaivén *nm* (a) to-and-fro movement, oscillation; rocking, backward and forward movement; swing(ing), sway(ing); lurch(ing).
 (b) (of vehicles etc) coming and going, constant movement.
 (c) (fig) change of fortune; **—es** ups and downs, vicissitudes.
 (d) (fig: *Pol etc*) swing, seesaw, violent change of opinion.
vaivenear [1a] *vt* to oscillate; to rock, move backwards and forwards; to swing, sway.
vajear [1a] *vt* (*CAm, Cu, Mex*) (of snake) to fascinate, hypnotize; (fig) to use black magic on; (fig) to win over by flattery.
vajilla *nf* (in *general*) crockery, china; dishes; (*una —*) service, set of dishes; **— de oro** gold plate; **— de porcelana** chinaware; **lavar la —** to wash up.
valdré *etc* see **valer**.
vale[1] *nm* promissory note, IOU; receipt; voucher, warrant; **— de correo, —** postal money order; **dar el —** (fig) to pass as suitable; to give the go-ahead.
vale[2] *nm* (*SAm*: abbr of **valedor**) pal (fam), chum, buddy (US); **— corrido** (*Ven*) old crony; **ser — con** (*Col*) to be pals with.
valedero *adj* valid; **— para 6 meses** valid for 6 months; **— hasta el día 16** valid until the 16th.
valedor *nm* (a) protector. (b) (*SAm*) =**vale**[2].

valedura *nf* (a) (*Mex*) help; protection; favour. (b) (*Col, Cu*) gift made by a gambler out of his winnings.
Valencia Valencia.
valencia *nf* (*Chem*) valency.
valencianismo *nm* word (or phrase etc) peculiar to Valencia.
valenciano 1 *adj* Valencian. **2** *nm*, **valenciana** *nf* Valencian. **3** *nm* (dialect of Catalan) Valencian.
valentía *nf* (a) bravery, courage; boldness; resoluteness.
 (b) (pej) boastfulness.
 (c) (*una —*) brave deed, heroic exploit; bold act.
 (d) (*una —*: pej) brag, boast.
valentón 1 *adj* boastful; blustering, bullying; arrogant. **2** *nm* braggart; bluster, bully.
valentonada *nf* boast, brag; piece of bluster; arrogant act.
valer [2q] **1** *vt* (a) to aid, protect; to serve; to help, avail; **¡válgame (Dios)!** see **Dios**; **no le vale ser hijo del ministro** it's of no help to him being the minister's son, it doesn't help his case that he's the minister's son; **su situación privilegiada no le valió** his privileged position did not save him; **no le valdrán excusas** excuses won't help him, excuses will avail him nothing.
 (b) (*Math etc*) to equal, be equal to; to amount to, come to; **la suma vale 99** the total comes to 99; **el ángulo B vale 38°** angle B is 38°; **en ese caso X vale 9** in that case X equals 9.
 (c) to cause; to earn; to win; to lose, cost; **el asunto le valió muchos disgustos** the affair caused him lots of trouble; **esa tontería le valió un rapapolvo** that piece of stupidity got (or earned) him a dressing-down; **son las cualidades que le valieron el premio** these are the qualities which won him the prize; **su ausencia le valió la pérdida del contrato** his absence lost (or cost) him the contract.
 2 *vti* (a) (*Comm, Fin*) to be worth; to cost, be priced at, be valued at; (in *absolute sense*) to be valuable; (fig) to be equivalent to, represent; **este libro vale 5 dólares** this book costs (or is worth) 5 dollars; **ésas valen 20 pesetas el kilo** those are 20 pesetas a kilo; **esta tela vale a 60 pesetas** this cloth costs 60 pesetas; **¿cuánto vale?** how much is it?; **¿vale mucho?** is it valuable?; **4 fichas azules valen por una negra** 4 blue counters are worth one black one; **cada cupón vale por un paquete** each coupon represents (or counts for) a packet.
 (b) (fig) to be worth; **no vale nada** it's worthless, it's rubbish; **no vale un higo** (*etc*) it's not worth a brass farthing; **vale lo que pesa** it's worth its weight in gold; **esa mirada suya me valió un sinfín de cartas** that look of hers told me more (or was worth more to me) than a hundred letters; **más vale así** it's better this way; **A vale más que B** A is better than B; **más vale tarde que nunca** better late than never; **más vale no hacerlo** it's better not to do it; **más vale que vayas tú** it would be better for you to go; **más vale que me vaya** I had better go; see **pena**.
 (c) (fig: of person) to be worthy; to have one's merits (or qualities); **es un hombre que vale** he's a worthy man, he's a man of some quality, he has his points; **no vale para nada** he's useless, he's a dead loss.
 3 *vi* (a) to be of use, be useful; **es viejo pero todavía vale** it's old but it still serves; **este sombrero me vale aún** this hat is still useful to me; **hay que tirar todo lo que no vale** we must throw out everything that is no use; **este trozo no me vale para hacer la cortina** this piece is not big enough to make the curtain.
 (b) to be valid; to be applicable, apply; (in games) to count, score; to be permitted; **¿vale?** is that all right?, will that do?; how about that?; **¡vale!** that's right!, O.K.! (fam); that'll do!, that's enough!; **es una teoría que no vale ya** it is a theory which no longer holds; **esa sección no vale ahora** that section is not now applicable; **¡eso no vale!** that doesn't count!; that's not allowed!, you can't do that!; **ese tanto no vale** that point doesn't score; **no vale golpearlo segunda vez** you aren't allowed to have a second shot at it; **¡no hay "querido" que valga!** it's no good saying "darling" to me!
 (c) **hacer — su derecho** to assert one's right; **hacer — sus argumentos** to make one's arguments felt, establish the validity of one's arguments.
 (d) **está un poco chiflado, valga la expresión** he's a bit cracked, so to speak; he's a bit cracked, for want of a better way of putting it.

4 valerse *vr* **(a)** — **de** to make use of, avail oneself of; to take advantage of; *right* to exercise. **(b)** — **por sí mismo** to help oneself, shift for oneself, manage by oneself; **poder** — to be able to manage; **no poder** — to be helpless.
5 *nm* worth, value.

valeriana *nf* valerian.

valerosamente *adv* bravely, valiantly.

valeroso *adj* brave, valiant.

valet [ba'le] *nm*, *pl* **valets** [ba'le] (*Cards*: *gall*) jack, knave.

valetudinario 1 *adj* valetudinarian. **2** *nm*, **valetudinaria** *nf* valetudinarian.

valga *etc see* **valer.**

Valhala *m* Valhalla.

valía *nf* **(a)** worth, value; **de gran** — of great worth, very valuable; *person* worthy, estimable. **(b)** (*fig*) influence.

validación *nf* validation; ratification.

validar [1a] *vt* to validate, give effect to; to ratify.

validez *nf* validity; **dar** — **a** to validate, give effect to; to ratify.

válido *adj* **(a)** valid (*hasta* until, *para* for). **(b)** (*Med*) strong, robust; fit.

valido *nm* (*Hist*) (royal) favourite.

valiente 1 *adj* **(a)** brave, valiant; bold. **(b)** (*pej*) boastful, blustering. **(c)** (*fig*) fine, excellent; noble; strong; (*iro*) fine, wonderful; ¡— **amigo!** a fine friend you are!; ¡— **gobierno!** some government!, do you call this a government?
2 *nm* **(a)** brave man, gallant man; hero. **(b)** (*pej*) braggart.

valientemente *adv* **(a)** bravely, valiantly; boldly. **(b)** (*pej*) boastfully. **(c)** (*fig*) excellently; nobly; (*iro*) wonderfully.

valija *nf* **(a)** case. **(b)** valise; satchel; (*Post*) mailbag; (*fig*) mail, post; — **diplomática** diplomatic bag.

valijería *nf* (*Chi*, *RPl*) travel-goods shop.

valimiento *nm* **(a)** value; benefit. **(b)** (*Pol etc*) favour, protection; position of royal favourite, status of the royal favourite; — **con uno,** — **cerca de uno** influence with someone.

valioso *adj* **(a)** valuable; useful, beneficial; estimable. **(b)** wealthy; powerful.

valisoletano = **valisoletano.**

valona *nf* **(a)** (*Col, Ec, Ven*) artistically trimmed mane; **hacer la** — (*Cu*) to shave. **(b)** (*Mex*) = **valedura (a).**

valonar [1a] *vt* (*Col, Ec, Ven*) to trim, cut; to shear.

valonearse [1a] *vr* (*CAm*) to lean from the saddle.

valor *nm* **(a)** (*general sense*) value, worth; price; (*of coin, stamp*) value, denomination; (*Math, Mus etc*) value; (*of words etc*) value, importance; meaning; **objetos de** — valuables; **sin** — worthless, valueless; — **adquisitivo** purchasing power; — **alimenticio** food value, nutritional value; — **facial,** — **nominal** face value, nominal value; (*of shares*) par value; — **sentimental** sentimental value; **conceder** — **a, dar** — **a** to attach importance to; to value, esteem; **quitar** — **a** to minimize the importance of; **esas cosas ya no tienen** — **para mí** such things no longer have any importance for me, I no longer value such things.
(b) (*fig*) great name, great figure; **Cervantes, máximo** — **nacional** Cervantes, one of our country's greatest figures; Cervantes, part of our great national heritage.
(c) —**es** (*Comm, Fin*) securities, bonds; stock; (*Arg, Col*) assets; —**es en cartera,** —**es habidos** investments, holdings, share portfolio; —**es fiduciarios** fiduciary issue, banknotes.
(d) bravery, courage, valour; — **cívico** (sense of) civic duty; **armarse de** — to gather up one's courage.
(e) (*fam*) nerve, cheek; ¡**qué** —! of all the cheek!; **tuvo el** — **de pedírmelo** he had the nerve to ask me for it.

valoración *nf* **(a)** valuation; (*fig*) assessment, appraisal. **(b)** (*Chem*) titration.

valorar [1a] *vt* **(a)** to value (*en* at); to price; (*esp fig*) to assess, appraise; to rate; — **mucho** to value highly, esteem; — **poco** to attach little value to. **(b)** (*Chem*) to titrate.

valorizar [1f] *vt* **(a)** = **valorar.** **(b)** (*Col, RPl*) to put up the price of.

Valquiria *nf* Valkyrie.

vals *nm*, *pl* **vals** waltz.

valsar [1a] *vi* to waltz.

valse *nm* (*SAm*) waltz.

valsear [1a] *vi* (*SAm*) to waltz.

valsón *nm* (*fam*) burst of activity; **dar** —**es** to rush around, display great energy.

valuable *adj* (*SAm*) **(a)** (*angl*) valuable. **(b)** calculable.

valuación *nf* = **valoración (a).**

valuador *nm* (*SAm*) valuer.

valuar [1e] *vt* = **valorar (a).**

valumen *nm* **(a)** (*Chi*: *Bot*) luxuriance, rankness. **(b)** (*Mex*) bundle; mass, bulk.

valumoso *adj* **(a)** (*CAm, Chi*) luxuriant, rank. **(b)** (*CAm, Ec, Mex*) bulky. **(c)** (*Ven*) vain, conceited.

valva *nf* (*Bot, Zool*) valve.

válvula *nf* (*Mech etc*) valve; — **de admisión** inlet valve; — **de escape** exhaust valve; — **de purga** vent; — **de seguridad** safety valve.

valla *nf* **(a)** fence; (*Mil*) barricade; palisade, stockade; (*Sport*) hurdle; — **paranieves** snow fence. **(b)** (*fig*) barrier; limit; obstacle, hindrance; **romper las** —**s, saltar(se) la** — to disregard the social conventions, do away with social niceties; to burst through the barriers of convention. **(c)** (*Cu, Col, Mex, PR*) cockpit. **(d)** (*Col*) ditch.

valladar *nm* **(a)** = **valla (a).** **(b)** (*fig*) defence, barrier.

vallado *nm* **(a)** = **valla (a).** **(b)** defensive wall, rampart. **(c)** (*Mex*) deep ditch.

vallar [1a] *vt* to fence in, put up a fence round, enclose.

valle *nm* valley; vale, dale; — **de lágrimas** vale of tears.

vallero (*Mex*) **1** *adj* valley (*attr*). **2** *nm*, **vallera** *nf* valley dweller.

vallino *adj* (*Per*) valley (*attr*).

vallisoletano 1 *adj* of Valladolid. **2** *nm*, **vallisoletana** *nf* native (*or* inhabitant) of Valladolid; **los** —**s** the people of Valladolid.

vallisto *adj* (*Arg, Mex*) valley (*attr*).

vallunco *adj* (*CAm*) rustic, peasant (*attr*).

vamos *etc see* **ir.**

vampi *nf* (*fam*) = **vampiresa.**

vampiresa *nf* vamp.

vampiro *nm* **(a)** (*Zool*) vampire. **(b)** (*fig*) vampire; exploiter, bloodsucker.

vanagloria *nf* vainglory.

vanagloriarse [1b] *vr* to boast; to be vain, be arrogant; — **de** to boast of; — **de** + *infin* to boast of + *ger*, boast of being able to + *infin*.

vanaglorioso *adj* vainglorious; vain, boastful, arrogant.

vanamente *adv* uselessly, vainly.

vanarse [1a] *vr* (*Col, Chi, Ven*) to shrivel up; (*fig*) to fall through, come to nothing, produce no results.

vandálico *adj* Vandal(ic); (*fig*) loutish, destructive.

vandalismo *nm* vandalism.

vándalo 1 *adj* Vandal(ic). **2** *nm*, **vándala** *nf* (*Hist*) Vandal; (*fig*) vandal.

vanguardia *nf* vanguard, van (*also fig*); **estar en la** — **del progreso** to be in the van of progress; **ir a** —, **ir en** — to be in the vanguard; to be foremost, be ahead, be in front; **un pintor de** — an ultramodern painter, a painter with a revolutionary style; a far-out painter.

vanguardismo *nm* (*Art, Lit etc*) ultramodern manner, revolutionary style; new tendency, far-out tendencies.

vanidad *nf* **(a)** unreality; groundlessness; uselessness, futility; shallowness; inanity, pointlessness. **(b)** vanity; **por pura** — out of sheer vanity; **halagar la** — **de uno** to play up to someone's vanity. **(c)** —**es** vanities.

vanidoso *adj* vain, conceited; smug.

vano 1 *adj* **(a)** unreal, imaginary, vain; *fear etc* idle; *suspicion* groundless; *superstition* foolish, unreasonable. **(b)** *attempt* vain, useless; *pastime* idle; **en** — in vain. **(c)** *person* shallow, superficial; frivolous; *pleasure etc* empty, inane, pointless; *adornment* silly. **(d)** *shell* empty, hollow.
2 *nm* (*Archit*) space, gap.

vapor *nm* **(a)** vapour; (*Tech*) steam; fumes; (*Meteorol*) mist, haze; — **de agua** water vapour; **al** — by steam, (*fig*) very fast; **cocer un plato al** — to steam a dish; **de** — steam (*attr*); **acumular** — to get steam up; **echar** — to give off steam, steam. **(b)** (*Naut*) steamer, steamship; — **correo** mailboat; — **de ruedas** paddle steamer; — **volandero** tramp steamer. **(c)** (*Med*) giddiness, faintness; dizzy spell; —**es** vapours, hysteria.

vapora *nf* **(a)** steam launch. **(b)** (*PR*) steam engine.

vapor(e)ar [1a] **1** *vt* to evaporate. **2** *vi* to give off vapour. **3 vapor(e)arse** *vr* to evaporate.

vaporización *nf* vaporization.

vaporizador *nm* vaporizer; spray.

vaporizar [1f] **1** *vt* to vaporize, convert into vapour; *scent etc* to spray. **2 vaporizarse** *vr* to vaporize, turn into vapour.

vaporizo *nm* (*Mex, PR*) (a) strong heat, steamy heat. (b) (*Med*) inhalation.

vaporoso *adj* (a) vaporous; steamy, misty; steaming. (b) *cloth* light, airy, diaphanous.

vapulear [1a] *vt* (a) *carpet etc* to beat; *person* to beat; to thrash, flog; to beat up. (b) (*fig*) to give a tongue-lashing to.

vapuleo *nm* (a) beating; thrashing, flogging; beating-up. (b) (*fig*) tongue-lashing.

vaquerear [1a] *vi* (*Per*) to play truant.

vaquería *nf* (a) dairy. (b) (*SAm*) cattle management, cattle tending; craft of the cowboy. (c) (*Cu, Per, PR*) milking pail; milking parlour. (d) (*Cu, PR*) herd of dairy cows. (e) (*Ven*) hunting with a lasso. (f) (*Mex*) country dance in cowboy dress.

vaqueriza *nf* cowshed; cattle yard.

vaquerizo 1 *adj* cattle (*attr*). **2** *nm* cowman; herdsman.

vaquero 1 *adj* cattle (*attr*). **2** *nm* (a) cowman; herdsman, cattle tender; (*in US, SAm*) cowboy. (b) (*SAm*) milkman. (c) (*Per*) truant. (d) (*Ven*) rawhide whip.

vaqueta 1 *nf* (a) cowhide, leather. (b) (*PR*) razor strop. **2** *nm* (*Cu*) shifty sort.

vaquetón *adj* (a) (*Cu*) unreliable, shifty. (b) (*Mex*) dim-witted; phlegmatic, slow. (c) (*Mex*) barefaced, brazen.

vaquetudo *adj* (*Cu, Mex*) = **vaquetón, baquetudo.**

vaquilla *nf* (*SAm*) (a) heifer. (b) **—s** amateur bullfight with young bulls.

vaquillona *nf* (*SAm*) heifer.

vara *nf* (a) stick, pole; rod, bar; (*Mech*) rod; (of *carriage*) shaft; (*Bot*) branch, twig (stripped of its leaves), wand, switch; (*Bot*) central stem, main stalk; **— mágica, — de las virtudes** magic wand; **— de medir** yardstick, measuring rod; **— de oro, — de San José** goldenrod; **— de pescar** fishing rod. (b) (*Pol etc*) wand (of office); sign of authority; **— alta** authority, power; influence; dominance; **doblar la — de la justicia** to pervert justice; **empuñar la —** to take over, take up office (as *mayor etc*). (c) (*Math: prov, SAm*) *approx* yard (=.836 m, =2.8 feet). (d) (*Taur*) lance, pike; wound with the lance; **poner —s al toro** to wound the bull with the lance.

varada *nf* (a) launching. (b) stranding, running aground.

varadero *nm* shipyard.

varado 1 *adj* (a) (*Naut*) stranded; **estar —** to be aground; to be beached. (b) **estar —** (*Chi*) to be without regular work; (*Arg, CAm, Mex*) to be helpless for lack of money. **2** *nm* (*Chi*) drifter, man without a regular job.

varadura *nf* stranding, running aground.

varal *nm* (a) long pole, stout stick; framework of poles; strut, support. (b) (*fam*) thin person, lamp-post.

varapalo *nm* (a) long pole. (b) blow with a stick; beating. (c) (*fig*) dressing-down. (d) (*fig*) setback, disappointment, blow.

varar [1a] **1** *vt* (a) to launch. (b) to beach, run up on the beach. **2** *vi and* **vararse** *vr* (a) (*Naut*) to be stranded, run aground. (b) (*fig*) to get stuck, get bogged down; to come to a standstill.

varayoc *nm* (*Per*) Indian Chief.

varazo *nm* blow with a stick.

varazón *nf* (a) (*Col, Cu, Mex*) sticks, bunch of sticks. (b) (*Chi*) shoal.

vardasca *nf* green twig; switch, swishy stick.

varear [1a] *vt* (a) *person* to beat, hit; *fruit* to knock down (with poles); *carpet etc* to beat; *bull* to prick with the lance, goad, stir up. (b) (*Comm*) *cloth* to sell by the yard. (c) (*RPl*) to exercise, train.

varec *nm* seaweed, wrack.

varejón *nm* (*SAm*) = **vardasca**; stick, straight branch (stripped of leaves).

vareta *nf* (a) twig, small stick; lime twig for catching birds. (b) (*Sew*) stripe. (c) insinuation; taunt; **echar —s** to make insinuations.

(d) (*Med: fam*) **estar de —, irse de —** to have diarrhoea.

varetazo *nm* (*Taur*) sideways thrust with the horn.

variabilidad *nf* variability.

variable 1 *adj* variable, changeable; (*Math*) variable. **2** *nf* (*Math*) variable.

variación *nf* variation (*also Mus*); **sin —** without varying, unchanged.

variado *adj* varied; mixed; assorted; *surface, colours* variegated.

variante 1 *adj* variant. **2** *nm* (*Col*) path; short cut. **3** *nf* variant.

variar [1c] **1** *vt* to vary, change, alter; to modify; *menu etc* to vary, introduce some variety into; *positions* to change round, switch about. **2** *vi* to vary; to change; **— de opinión** to change one's mind; **varía de 3 a 8** it ranges from 3 to 8, it goes from 3 to 8; **este producto varía mucho de precio** this article varies a lot in price; **esto varía de lo que dijo antes** this differs from what he said earlier.

varicela *nf* chickenpox.

várices *nfpl* varicose veins.

varicoso *adj* (a) varicose. (b) suffering from varicose veins.

variedad *nf* (a) variety; variation; (*Bio*) variety. (b) (*Theat*) **—es** variety show; **teatro de —es** variety theatre, music hall, vaudeville theater (*US*).

varietés *nmpl* (*Theat: gall*) = **variedades.**

varilla *nf* (a) (thin) stick; (*Bot*) twig, wand, switch; (*Mech*) rod, bar; link; (of *wheel*) spoke; (of *corset*) rib, stay; (of *fan, umbrella*) rib; (*Anat*) jawbone; **— mágica, — de virtudes** magic wand; **— de zahorí** divining rod. (b) (*Mex*) small wares, trinkets. (c) (*Ven*) = **vaina** (c).

varillaje *nm* (*Mech*) rods, links, linkage; (of *fan, umbrella*) ribs, ribbing.

varillar [1a] *vt* (*Ven*) *racehorse* to try out, train.

varillero *nm* (*Mex*) hawker, pedlar, peddler (*US*).

vario *adj* (a) varied; (*in colour*) variegated, motley. (b) varying, variable, changeable; fickle. (c) **—s** several, some; a number of; **hay varias posibilidades** there are several (*or various*) possibilities; **en —s libros que he visto** in a number of books which I have seen; **los inconvenientes son —s** there are several drawbacks.

varioloso *adj* pockmarked.

variopinto *adj* many-coloured, colourful; of diverse colours.

varita *nf* wand; **— mágica, — de las virtudes** magic wand.

varón 1 *adj* male; **hijo —** male child, boy, son. **2** *nm* (a) man, male; adult male; (*fig*) worthy man, great man; **— de Dios** saintly man; **santo —** nice old chap (*fam*); extraordinarily kind man; **tuvo 4 hijos, todos —es** she had 4 children, all boys. (b) (*Col*) husband. (c) (*Chi, Mex*) beam, timber.

varona *nf*, **varonesa** *nf* mannish woman.

varonil *adj* (a) manly, virile; vigorous. (b) (*Bio*) male. (c) **una mujer de aspecto —** a woman of mannish appearance.

Varsovia Warsaw.

vasallaje *nm* (*Hist*) vassalage; (*fig*) subjection, serfdom.

vasallo *nm* vassal.

vasar *nm* kitchen shelf, rack.

vasco 1 *adj* Basque. **2** *nm*, **vasca** *nf* Basque. **3** *nm* (*language*) Basque.

vascófilo *nm* expert in Basque studies.

Vascongadas: las — the Basque Provinces.

vascongado = **vasco.**

vascuence *nm* (*Ling*) Basque.

vascular *adj* vascular.

vase (= **se va**) *see* **ir.**

vaselina *nf* Vaseline (*Protected Trade Name*), petroleum jelly.

vasera *nf* kitchen shelf, rack.

vasija *nf* vessel; container, recipient.

vaso *nm* (a) (*Cook*) glass, tumbler; vessel; container; (*lit*) vase, urn; (*Col*) small cup; **— de agua** glass of water; **— para vino** wineglass; **— de engrase** (*Mech*) grease cup; **— de noche** chamberpot; **— litúrgico, — sagrado** holy vessel, chalice; **ahogarse en un — de agua** to get worked up about nothing at all. (b) (*quantity*) glassful, glass. (c) (*Anat*) vessel; tube, duct; **— capilar** capillary; **— sanguíneo** blood vessel. (d) (*Zool*) hoof. (e) (*Naut*) hull; boat, ship, vessel.

vástago *nm* (a) (*Bot*) shoot, sprout, bud.
   (b) (*Mech*) rod; stem; — **de émbolo** piston rod.
   (c) (*fig*) scion, offspring.
   (d) (*Col, CR, Ven*) trunk of the banana tree.
vastedad *nf* vastness, immensity.
vasto *adj* vast, huge, immense.
vate *nm* (a) (*Hist*) seer, prophet. (b) (*Lit*) poet, bard.
vatiaje *nm* wattage.
Vaticano *m* Vatican.
vaticano *adj* Vatican; papal.
vaticinador *nm* seer, prophet.
vaticinar [1a] *vt* to prophesy, predict.
vaticinio *nm* prophecy, prediction.
vatio *nm* watt.
vaya *etc see* **ir.**
vecinal *adj* (a) road *etc* local; *tax* local, municipal; **padrón** — list of residents. (b) (*SAm*) neighbouring, adjacent.
vecindad *nf* (a) neighbourhood, vicinity.
   (b) (*persons*) neighbours, neighbourhood; local community; residents (of a block of flats).
   (c) (*Law etc*) residence, abode; **declarar su** — to state where one lives, give one's place of abode.
vecindario *nm* neighbourhood; local community, residents; (*as total etc*) population, inhabitants.
vecino 1 *adj* (a) neighbouring, adjacent, adjoining; near, nearby, close; *house etc* next; **el garaje** — **del mío** the garage next to mine; **no aquí sino en el pueblo** — not here but in the next village; **las dos fincas son vecinas** the two estates adjoin.
   (b) (*fig*) alike, similar; — **a** like, similar to.
   2 *nm*, **vecina** *nf* (a) neighbour.
   (b) resident, inhabitant, citizen; **un pueblo de 800** — **s** a village of 800 inhabitants; **una vecina de la calle X** a resident in X street.
vector *nm* vector.
Veda *m* Veda.
veda *nf* (a) (*act*) prohibition; imposition of a close season. (b) close season.
vedado *nm* preserve; — **de caza** game preserve; **cazar** (*or* **pescar**) **en** — to poach, hunt (*or* fish) illegally.
vedar [1a] *vt* to prohibit, forbid, ban; to stop, prevent; *idea, plan etc* to veto; — **a uno hacer algo** to forbid someone to do something; to stop someone doing something, prevent someone from doing something.
vedette [be'ðet] *nf* (*gall*) star; starlet; (*fig*) star turn, main attraction.
védico *adj* Vedic.
vedija *nf* (a) tuft of wool. (b) mat of hair, matted hair.
vega *nf* (a) fertile plain, rich lowland area; water meadow(s); (*Ec*) stretch of alluvial soil. (b) (*Ant*) tobacco plantation.
vegetación *nf* (a) vegetation. (b) growth, growing.
   (c) (*Med*) — **es adenoideas** adenoids.
vegetal 1 *adj* vegetable, plant (*attr*); **patología** — plant pathology. **2** *nm* plant, vegetable; — **es** (*CAm, Mex: angl*) vegetables.
vegetar [1a] *vi* (a) (*Bot*) to grow. (b) (*fig*) to vegetate, live like a vegetable, stagnate.
vegetarianismo *nm* vegetarianism.
vegetariano 1 *adj* vegetarian. **2** *nm*, **vegetariana** *nf* vegetarian.
vegetativo *adj* vegetative.
vegoso *adj* (*Chi*) land moist, damp.
veguero 1 *adj* lowland (*attr*), of the plain. **2** *nm* (a) lowland farmer. (b) (*Ant*) tobacco planter. (c) coarse cigar; (*Arg*) good-quality Cuban tobacco, good cigar.
vehemencia *nf* vehemence; passion, impetuosity; fervour; eagerness, violence.
vehemente *adj* (a) vehement; passionate, impetuous; *supporter etc* fervent, passionate; *desire* strong, eager, violent; *speaker* passionate, forceful.
   (b) *sign, suspicion etc* strong.
vehículo *nm* (a) (*Aut etc*) vehicle; — **carretero** road vehicle; — **astral**, — **cósmico** spacecraft.
   (b) (*fig*) vehicle (*de* for); (*Med*) carrier, transmitter (*de* of).
veinte *adj* twenty; (*date*) twentieth.
veintena *nf* twenty, about twenty, a score.
veintiuna *nf* (*Cards*) pontoon.
vejación *nf* vexation, annoyance; **sufrir** — **es** to suffer vexations.
vejamen *nm* (a) = **vejación**. (b) satire, satirical composition; shaft, taunt.
vejaminoso *adj* (*Per, PR*) vexatious, annoying.
vejancón, vejarrón (*fam*) **1** *adj* ancient, doddery. **2** *nm* old chap (*fam*), old dodderer.

vejar [1a] *vt* to vex, annoy; to make feel small, humiliate; to harass.
vejarano *adj* (*SAm*) ancient, doddery, decrepit.
vejatorio *adj* vexatious, annoying; humiliating, degrading; **es** — **para él tener que pedirlo** it is humiliating for him to have to beg for it.
vejestorio *nm*, **vejete** *nm* old chap (*fam*), old boy (*fam*).
vejez *nf* (a) old age; **los males de la** — the ills of old age; **lo escribió en su** — he wrote it in old age.
   (b) (*fig*) peevishness; grouchiness (*fam*), grumpiness.
   (c) (*fig*) old story; piece of stale news.
vejiga *nf* (a) (*Anat*) bladder; — **de la bilis** gallbladder; — **natatoria** air bladder. (b) (*Med, on paint etc*) blister.
vela¹ *nf* (a) wakefulness, state of being awake; sleeplessness; **estar en** — to be unable to get to sleep, be still awake; **pasar la noche en** — to have a sleepless night, not sleep all night.
   (b) vigil; evening work, night work; (*Mil*) (period of) sentry duty.
   (c) candle; — **de sebo** tallow candle; **no se le dará** — **en este entierro** he will not be given any say in this matter.
   (d) (*Taur: fam*) horn.
   (e) (*fam*) — **s** mucus, snot (*fam*).
   (f) (*CAm, SD*) funeral wake.
   (g) (*Arg*) nuisance, bother; **¡qué** — **!** what a nuisance!; **aguantar la** — to put up with it for someone else's sake.
   (h) (*Cu, Mex*) telling-off; **aguantar la** — to face the music.
vela² *nf* (*Naut*) sail; — **mayor** mainsail; **a toda** —, **a** — **s desplegadas** under full sail, (*fig*) vigorously, energetically, straining every nerve; **barco de** — sailing ship; **estar a dos** — **s** (*fam*) to be broke (*fam*); **estar entre dos** — **s** (*fam*) to be half-seas over; **darse a la** —, **hacerse a la** —, **largar las** — **s** to set sail, get under way; **arriar** — **s**, **recoger** — **s** (*fig*) to back down; to give up, chuck it up.
velada *nf* (evening) party, social gathering, soirée; — **musical** musical evening; **pasar una buena** — to have a pleasant evening.
velado *adj* veiled (*also fig*); (*Phot*) fogged, blurred; *sound* muffled.
velador *nm* (a) watchman, caretaker; (*Hist*) sentinel.
   (b) candlestick.
   (c) pedestal table; (*SAm*) night table.
   (d) (*RPl*) night light.
   (e) (*Mex*) lampshade.
veladora *nf* (a) (*Mex*) table lamp, bedside lamp. (b) (*Mex: Eccl*) paraffin lamp.
velamen *nm* sails, canvas.
velar¹ [1a] **1** *vt* (a) to watch, keep watch over; *sick person* to sit up with, stay by the bedside of.
   (b) (*SAm*) to look covetously at.
   2 *vi* (a) to stay awake; to go without sleep; to stay up, sit up at night; to work late, do night duty; to keep watch, (*Eccl*) keep vigil.
   (b) to be solicitous; — **por** to watch over, look after; to guard, protect; — **por que se haga algo** to see to it (*or* ensure) that something is done; **no hay quien vele por sus intereses** there is nobody to watch over his interests.
   (c) (*Naut: of reef*) to appear.
velar² [1a] **1** *vt* (a) to veil. (b) (*fig*) to shroud, hide, veil. (c) (*Phot*) to fog, blur. **2 velarse** *vr* (a) to hide itself. (b) (*Phot*) to fog, blur.
velar³ *adj* (*Ling*) velar.
velarte *nm* (*Hist*) broadcloth.
velatorio *nm* funeral wake.
Velázquez *m* Velasquez.
veleidad *nf* (a) (*quality*) fickleness, capriciousness, flightiness. (b) (*una* —) whim, caprice; unpredictable mood; strange fancy.
veleidoso *adj* fickle, capricious, flighty.
velero 1 *adj* ship fast. **2** *nm* (a) (*Naut*) sailing ship. (b) (*Aer*) glider. (c) (*Naut*) sailmaker.
veleta 1 *nf* (a) weather vane, weather cock. (b) (*Fish*) float. **2** *nmf* person who chops and changes, fickle person.
veletería *nf* (*Chi*) chopping and changing, fickleness.
velís *nm*, **veliz** *nm* (*Mex*) valise; bag, grip; **velices**, **velises** cases, luggage.
velo *nm* (a) veil; **tomar el** — to take the veil, become a nun.
   (b) (*fig*) veil, light covering; shroud; film; (*Phot*) fog, veiling.
   (c) (*fig*) pretext, cloak.
   (d) (*fig*) mental fog, confusion, lack of clarity.
   (e) (*Anat*) — **del paladar** soft palate, velum.

velocidad *nf* (a) speed; rate, pace, velocity; speediness, swiftness; **de alta** — high-speed; — **de crucero**, — **económica** cruising speed; — **limitada** speed limit; — **máxima**, — **punta** maximum speed, top speed; — **máxima permitida** speed limit; **a gran** — at high speed; **a máxima** —, **a toda** — at full speed, at top speed; **¿a qué** —? at what speed?, how fast?; **¿a qué** — **ibas**? what speed were you doing?; **cobrar** — to pick up speed, gather speed; **disminuir** —, **moderar la** — to slow down; **exceder la** — **permitida** to speed, exceed the speed limit.

(b) (*Mech*) gear, speed; **primera** — low gear, bottom gear, first gear; **segunda** — second gear; —**es de avance** forward gears; **4** —**es hacia adelante** 4 forward gears.

velocímetro *nm* speedometer.
velocípedo *nm* velocipede.
velódromo *nm* cycle track.
velomotor *nm* autocycle.
velón *nm* (a) oil lamp. (b) (*Chi, Mex, Per*) thick tallow candle. (c) (*CAm*) sponger (*fam*), parasite. (d) (*Col, Ec, SD*) person who casts covetous glances.
velorio[1] *nm* (a) party, celebration; (*Ant, Arg, Ec*) dull party, flat affair.
(b) (*esp SAm*) funeral wake, vigil for the dead; — **del angelito** wake for a dead child.
velorio[2] *nm* (*Eccl*) taking the veil.
veloz *adj* fast, quick, swift; — **como un relámpago** as quick as lightning.
velozmente *adv* fast, quickly, swiftly.
vello *nm* (*Anat*) down, fuzz, hair; (*Bot*) down; (*on fruit*) bloom; (*on antlers*) velvet.
vellocino *nm* fleece; V— **de Oro** Golden Fleece.
vellón[1] *nm* (a) fleece; sheepskin. (b) tuft of wool.
vellón[2] *nm* (a) (*Tech*) copper and silver alloy. (b) (*PR, Pan*) five-cent coin.
vellonera *nf* (*PR, SD*) musical box; jukebox.
vellosidad *nf* downiness, fuzziness, hairiness; fluffiness.
velloso *adj* downy, fuzzy, hairy; fluffy.
velludo 1 *adj* hairy, shaggy. **2** *nm* plush, velvet.
vena *nf* (a) (*Anat*) vein; — **yugular** jugular vein.
(b) (*Min*) vein, seam, lode.
(c) (*in stone, wood*) grain.
(d) (*Bot*) vein, rib.
(e) (*Geog*) underground stream.
(f) (*fig*) vein; mood, disposition; — **de loco** streak of madness; oddity, mania; **coger a uno de** (*or* **en**) — to catch someone in the right mood; **le daba la** — **por ello** he took a fancy to it, the mood took him that way; **estar de** (*or* **en**) — to be in the vein, be in the mood (*para* for); to be in good form.
(g) (*fig*) talent, promise; **tiene** — **de pintor** he has the makings of a painter, he shows a talent for painting.
venablo *nm* javelin, dart; **echar** —**s** (*fig*) to burst out angrily.
venado *nm* (a) deer, stag.
(b) (*Cook*) venison.
(c) (*Cu*) deerskin.
(d) (*Cu*) whore.
(e) (*Ec*) contraband.
(f) (*Guat, Mex*) **correr el** —, **pintar el** — to play truant.
venal[1] *adj* (*Anat*) venous.
venal[2] *adj* (a) (*Comm*) commercial, that can be bought (*or* sold). (b) (*pej*) venal, corrupt.
venalidad *nf* venality, corruptness.
venático *adj* rather crazy, a bit mad.
venatorio *adj* hunting (*attr*).
vencedor 1 *adj player, team* winning, victorious; *general etc* victorious, successful; *nation* conquering, victorious.
2 *nm*, **vencedora** *nf* winner, victor; conqueror.
vencejo[1] *nm* (*Orn*) swift.
vencejo[2] *nm* (*Agr*) straw plait, string (*used in binding sheaves*).
vencer [2b] **1** *vt* (a) *enemy* to defeat, beat; to conquer, vanquish, overcome; (*Sport*) to beat; *rival* to outdo, surpass; *passion etc* to master, control, fight down; *temptation* to overcome; (*of sleep etc*) to overcome; **vence a todos en elegancia** he outdoes them all in elegance, he beats them all for elegance; **por fin le venció el sueño** finally sleep overcame him; **dejarse** — to yield, give in; **no te dejes** — don't give in, don't let yourself be beaten (by it).
(b) *difficulty, obstacle* to overcome, surmount, get round.
(c) *branch, support etc* to break down, snap, prove too heavy for; **el peso de los libros ha vencido el estante** the weight of the book has broken the shelf.

(d) *mountain, slope* to get to the top of, reach the summit of.
2 *vi* (a) to win; to win through, succeed, triumph; **¡venceremos!** we shall win!; we shall overcome!
(b) (*Comm etc: of term*) to expire, end; (*of payment etc*) to fall due; (*of bond*) to mature, become due for redemption; (*of policy etc*) to become invalid, cease to apply.
3 vencerse *vr* (a) to control oneself.
(b) (*support etc*) to break, snap, collapse (under the weight); (*Chi, RPI*) to break down, get worn out.
vencido 1 *adj* (a) beaten, defeated; *team etc* losing; **¡ay de los** —**s!** woe to the conquered!; **darse por** — to give up, acknowledge defeat; **ir de** — to be all in, be on one's last legs; **la enfermedad va de vencida** the illness is past its worst; **la tormenta va de vencida** the worst of the storm is over.
(b) (*Comm etc*) mature; due, payable; **con los intereses** —**s** with the interest which is due; **pagar por meses** —**s** to pay by the month in arrears.
2 *adv*: **pagar** — to pay in arrears, pay for the month (*etc*) which is past.
vencimiento *nm* (a) (*under weight*) breaking, snapping; collapse. (b) (*Comm etc*) expiration; maturity; **al** —, **a su** — when it matures, when it falls due.
venda *nf* bandage.
vendaje[1] *nm* (*Med*) dressing, bandaging; —**provisional** first-aid bandage.
vendaje[2] *nm* (a) commission. (b) (*SAm*) bonus, small extra.
vendar [1a] *vt* (a) *wound* to bandage, dress; *eyes etc* to cover, put a bandage over, tie a cloth (*etc*) round. (b) (*fig*) to blind; to hoodwink.
vendaval *nm* gale, strong wind, hurricane; (*fig*) storm.
vendedor *nm* seller, vendor; retailer; (*in shop*) salesman; — **ambulante** hawker, pedlar, peddler (*US*).
vendedora *nf* seller; (*in shop*) salesgirl, saleswoman.
vendeja *nf* (a) public sale. (b) collection of goods offered for sale.
vender [2a] **1** *vt* (a) to sell; to market; (*pej*) to sell (improperly); — **por las casas** to peddle round the houses; — **al contado** to sell for cash; — **al por mayor** to sell wholesale; — **al por menor** to sell retail; **estar sin** — to remain unsold; **¡a mí que las vendo!** you can't catch an old bird with chaff!, I'm not falling for that one!
(b) (*fig*) to sell, betray.
2 venderse *vr* (a) to sell; to be sold; — **a**, — **por** to sell at, sell for; to fetch, bring in; **este artículo se vende muy bien** this article is selling very well; **"se vende"** (*advert*) "for sale"; **"véndese coche"** (*advert*) "car for sale"; **no se vende** not for sale.
(b) (*fig*) — **caro** to play hard to get, be terribly choosy about one's friends (*fam*).
(c) (*fig*) to betray oneself, give oneself away.
vendí *nm* certificate of sale.
vendible *adj* saleable; marketable.
vendimia *nf* (a) grape harvest, wine harvest; (*with reference to quality, year*) year; **la** — **de 1973** the 1973 vintage. (b) (*fig*) big profit, killing.
vendimiador *nm*, **vendimiadora** *nf* vintager.
vendimiar [1b] *vt* (a) *grapes* to harvest, pick, gather. (b) (*fig*) to take a profit from, squeeze a profit out of, make a killing with. (c) (*sl*) to bump off (*sl*).
vendré *etc see* **venir**.
venduta *nf* (a) (*Col, Cu, Guat, Mex, Ven*) auction, public sale.
(b) (*Cu, SD*) greengrocer's (shop), fruiterer's (shop); small grocery store.
(c) (*PR*) betrayal.
vendutero *nm* (a) (*Col, Cu, Guat, Mex, Ven*) auctioneer. (b) (*Cu, SD*) greengrocer, fruiterer.
Venecia Venice.
veneciano 1 *adj* Venetian. **2** *nm*, **veneciana** *nf* Venetian.
veneno *nm* poison, venom.
venenoso *adj* poisonous, venomous.
venera *nf* scallop; scallop shell.
venerable *adj* venerable.
veneración *nf* veneration; worship.
venerando *adj* venerable.
venerar [1a] *vt* to venerate, revere; to worship.
venéreo *adj* venereal; **enfermedad venérea** venereal disease.
venero *nm* (a) (*Min*) lode, seam. (b) spring. (c) (*fig*) source, origin; — **de datos** mine of information.
venezolanismo *nm* word (*or* phrase *etc*) peculiar to Venezuela.

venezolano 1 adj Venezuelan. **2** nm, **venezolana** nf Venezuelan.

Venezuela f Venezuela.

vengador 1 adj avenging. **2** nm, **vengadora** nf avenger.

venganza nf vengeance, revenge; retaliation; **tomar — en uno** to take vengeance on someone.

vengar [1h] **1** vt to avenge. **2 vengarse** vr to take revenge (de una ofensa for an offence; de uno, en uno on someone), avenge oneself; to retaliate (en against, on).

vengativo adj person, spirit vindictive; step retaliatory.

vengo etc see **venir**.

venia nf **(a)** pardon, forgiveness.
(b) permission, consent; **con su —** by your leave, with your permission; **casarse sin la — de sus padres** to marry without the consent of one's parents.
(c) (SAm: Mil) salute.

venial adj venial.

venialidad nf veniality.

venida nf **(a)** coming; arrival; return. **(b)** (fig) impetuosity, rashness.

venidero adj coming, future; **los —s** future generations, posterity, our (etc) descendants; **en lo —** in (the) future.

venir [3s] **1** vi **(a)** (general sense) to come (a to, de from); to arrive; **¡ven!, ¡venga!** come along!; **¡ven acá!** come (over) here!; **vino a vernos** she came to see us; **— por** to come for; **no me vengas con historias** don't come telling tales to me; **hacer — a uno** to summon someone; to call someone, have someone fetched; **le hicieron — desde Londres** they fetched him (all the way) from London.
(b) (of event) to come, happen; **le vino una desgracia** she had a mishap, something untoward happened to her; **venga lo que viniere** come what may; **con todo lo que vino después** with everything that happened afterwards, with all that ensued; **(estar a) ver —** to wait and see what happens; to sit on the fence; **se puede ver — la noche** one can face the evening ahead; **vinieron sobre él muchos desastres** a host of disasters fell upon him.
(c) (of time) ... **que viene** next ..., eg **el mes que viene** next month.
(d) (fig) to come; **— de** to come from, proceed from, stem from; to originate in; **la finca le viene de su hermano** the estate is come to him from his brother; **de ahí vienen muchos males** many evils spring from that; **de ahí viene que ...** hence it is that ..., and so it is that ...; thus it follows that ...
(e) (fig: of feeling etc) to come; **le vino la idea de + infin** there came to him the idea of + ger; **sentía —me sueño** I felt sleep coming over me; **me vinieron ganas de llorar** I felt like crying, I had an urge to cry.
(f) **— a + infin** to come to + infin, serve to + infin; **el desastre vino a turbar nuestra tranquilidad** the disaster served to destroy our peace; **viene a llenar un gran vacío** it serves to fill a large gap; **viene a cumplir lo que habíamos empezado** it helps to finish off what we had begun; **venimos a conocerle en Bolivia** we got to know him in Bolivia; **vino a dar en la cárcel** he ended up in jail; see **caso, menos** etc.
(g) **— a ser: viene a ser lo mismo** it comes to (about) the same thing; **viene a ser 84 en total** it amounts to 84 in all, it comes to 84 all together; **viene a ser más difícil que nunca** it's turning out to be more difficult than ever.
(h) **— bien** to come just right; to be suitable, be convenient; to fit; (Bot) to do well, grow nicely; **eso vendrá bien para el invierno** that will come in handy for the winter; **no me viene muy bien aquello** that doesn't suit me all that well; **— bien a** (of dress) to suit, look well on, fit, be right for; **el tapón viene justo a la botella** the stopper fits the bottle exactly; **el abrigo te viene algo pequeño** the coat is rather small on you; **te viene estrecho por las espaldas** it's too tight round your shoulders; **— mal** to come awkwardly, be inconvenient (a for); **— mal a** (of dress) to look wrong on, not fit.
(i) (idioms) **¿a qué viene afligirte?** why get so worked up?, what's the point of distressing yourself?; **¡venga!** (fam) let's have it!, hand it over!; **¡venga la pluma esa!** let's have (a look at) that pen!; **¡venga una canción!** let's have a song!
(j) (in continuous tenses) **venían andando desde mediodía** they had been walking since midday; **viene gastando mucho** she has been spend-

ing a lot; **eso vengo diciendo** that's what I've been saying all along.
(k) (+ ptp) **vengo cansado** I'm tired; **venía hecho polvo** he was worn out.

2 venirse vr **(a)** (of wine) to ferment; (of dough) to work.
(b) **— abajo, — al suelo, — a (la) tierra** to fall down, collapse, tumble down; (fig) to fail, collapse, be ruined.
(c) **se nos vino encima la guerra** the war came upon us; **parece que todo se nos viene encima a la vez** everything seems to be happening to us all at once; **cualquier cosita se le viene encima** any little thing gets him down.
(d) see **mano** etc.

venoso adj **(a)** blood venous. **(b)** leaf etc veined, ribbed.

venta nf **(a)** (Comm) sale; selling; marketing; **— por balance, — postbalance** stocktaking sale; **— al contado** cash sale; **— de liquidación** sale, clearance sale; **— a plazos** hire purchase; **— al (por) mayor** wholesale; **— al (por) menor, — al detalle** retail; **— pública** public sale, auction; **precio de —** sale price; **poner algo a la —** to put something on sale, put something up for sale; to market a product; **estar de (or en) —** to be (up) for sale, be on the market.
(b) country inn.
(c) (Mex, SD) small shop, stall; (Chi) stall, booth (at fair etc).

ventada nf gust of wind.

ventaja nf **(a)** advantage; (in a race) start, advantage; (Tennis) vantage; (in betting) odds; **es un plan que tiene muchas —s** it is a plan that has many advantages; **me dio una — de 4 metros, me dio 4 metros de —** he gave me 4 metres start; **me dio una — de 20 puntos** he gave me an advantage of 20 points, he handicapped himself by 20 points; **llevar (la) — a** to have the advantage over; to be ahead of; to be one up on; **la — que A le lleva a B es grande** A has a big advantage over B; **sacar — de** to derive profit from, (pej) use to one's own advantage.
(b) (Fin: esp SAm) profit, gain; **dejar buena —** to bring in a good profit.
(c) **—s** (in a job) extras, perks (fam).

ventajear [1a] vt (Col, Guat, RPl) **(a)** = **aventajar**.
(b) (pej) **— a uno** to beat someone to it, get an improper advantage over someone.

ventajero adj (SAm) = **ventajista**.

ventajista adj unscrupulous; self-seeking, grasping; sly, treacherous.

ventajosamente adv advantageously; (Fin) profitably; **estar — colocado** to be well placed.

ventajoso adj **(a)** advantageous; (Fin) profitable.
(b) (SAm) = **ventajista**.

ventana nf **(a)** window; **— de guillotina** sash window; **— de la nariz** nostril; **— salediza** bay window; **tirar algo por la —** to throw something out of the window; (fig) to throw something away, fail to make any use of something.
(b) (Col, Ven) forest clearing, glade.

ventanaje nm windows.

ventanal nm large window.

ventanear [1a] vi to be always at the window, be forever peeping out.

ventanilla nf **(a)** small window; window (of booking office etc); (Aut) window. **(b)** (Anat: also — de la nariz) nostril.

ventanillo nm small window; peephole.

ventarrón nm (fam) gale, violent wind, blast.

ventear [1a] **1** vt **(a)** (of dog etc) air to sniff.
(b) clothes etc to air, put out to dry, expose to the wind.
(c) (CAm, Mex) animal to brand.
(d) (Arg, Par) competitor to get far ahead of, leave far behind.
(e) (Col, PR) to fan, winnow.
2 vi to snoop, pry, come poking about; to inquire, investigate.
3 ventearse vr **(a)** to split, crack; to blister; to get too dry, spoil.
(b) (Anat) to break wind.
(c) (Arg, Chi, Per, PR) to be outdoors a great deal; to spend a long time away from home.
(d) (Col, Ec, Per, PR) to get conceited.

ventero nm, **ventera** nf innkeeper.

ventilación nf **(a)** ventilation; **sin —** unventilated. **(b)** draught, air. **(c)** ventilator, opening for ventilation. **(d)** (fig) airing, discussion.

ventilado adj draughty, breezy.

ventilador nm ventilator; fan.

ventilar [1a] **1** *vt* (a) *room etc* to ventilate.
　(b) *clothing etc* to air, put out to air, dry in the air.
　(c) *(fig) matter* to air, discuss, talk over.
　(d) *(fig) private matter* to make public, reveal.
　2 ventilarse *vr* (a) to ventilate, air.
　(b) *(person)* to get some air, take a breather.
ventisca *nf* blizzard, snowstorm.
ventiscar [1g] *vi*, **ventisquear** [1a] *vi* to blow a blizzard, snow with a strong wind; *(of snow)* to drift.
ventisquero *nm* (a) blizzard, snowstorm. (b) glacier; snowdrift; gully *(etc)* where the snow lies.
ventolera *nf* (a) gust of wind, blast.
　(b) *(toy)* windmill.
　(c) *(fig)* vanity, conceit; smugness; arrogance; boastfulness.
　(d) *(fig)* whim, wild idea; **le dio la — de** + *infin* he had a sudden notion to + *infin*.
　(e) *(Mex)* wind, flatulence.
ventolina *nf* (a) *(Naut)* light wind. (b) *(Arg, Chi, Mex)* sudden gust of wind. (c) *(Chi)* wind, flatulence.
ventorrillo *nm* (a) small inn, roadhouse. (b) *(SAm)* small shop.
ventosa *nf* (a) vent, airhole. (b) *(Zool)* sucker; *(Tech)* peg *(etc)* that adheres by suction. (c) *(Med)* cupping glass.
ventosear [1a] *vi* to break wind.
ventosidad *nf* wind; flatulence, windiness.
ventoso *adj* (a) windy. (b) *(Anat)* windy, flatulent.
ventral *adj* ventral.
ventregada *nf* brood, litter.
ventrículo *nm* ventricle.
ventrílocuo *nm*, **ventrílocua** *nf* ventriloquist.
ventriloquia *nf* ventriloquism.
ventrudo *adj* fat, potbellied.
ventura *nf* (a) happiness.
　(b) luck, (good) fortune; chance; **mala —** ill luck; **por su mala —** as ill luck would have it; **a la — at** random; **ir a la —** to go haphazardly, go without a fixed plan; **vivir a la —** to live in a disorganized way; **todo lo hace a la —** he does it all in a hit-or-miss fashion; **por —** fortunately; perhaps, by chance, *eg* **¿piensas ir, por —?** are you by any chance thinking of going?; **echar la buena — a uno** to tell someone's fortune; **probar la —** to try one's luck; **— te dé Dios** I wish you luck; **viene la — a quien la procura** fortune favours the brave.
venturero *adj (Mex) crop* out of season; *(fig)* temporary; casual; irregular.
venturoso *adj* happy; lucky, fortunate.
Venus *nf* **1** Venus. **2** *nm (Astron)* Venus.
venus *nf (fig)* venery, love-making, sexual delights.
venusiano **1** *adj* Venusian. **2** *nm,* **venusiana** *nf* Venusian.
ver [2v] **1** *vti* (a) *(general sense)* to see; *(esp SAm)* to look at, watch; **la vi bajar la escalera** I saw her come downstairs; **lo he visto hacer muchas veces** I have often seen it done; **no lo veo** I can't see it; **desde aquí lo verás** you can see it from here; **¡lo que ves!** can't you see?, it's there for you to see!; **no veo nada en contra de eso** I see nothing against it; **— es creer** seeing is believing; **— y callar** it's best to keep one's mouth shut about this; **ir a — a uno** to go to see someone, go and see someone; **voy a —** I'll go and see; **¡a —!** let's see!, let's have a look!, show me!; *(fig)* **¡ya sí!, hey!; ¿a —?** what's all this?; **a — qué nos dices** let's see what you've got to say; **¡a — qué pasa!** *(fam)* just you dare!; **a — si . . .** I wonder if . . .; **a — si acabas pronto** I hope you can finish this off quickly; **es de —** it's worth seeing, you really should see it; **eso está por —** that remains to be seen.
　(b) *(fig)* to see, understand; **¿ves?** do you see?, (do you) get it?; **lo veo I see!; ¡verás!** you'll see!; **veremos** we'll see (about that); **¿no ves que . . .?** don't you see that . . .?; **como vimos ayer en la conferencia** as we saw in the lecture yesterday; **como veremos más adelante** as we shall see later; **según voy viendo** as I am now beginning to see; **no veo claro por qué lo quiere** I don't really see why he wants it; **a mi modo de ver** in my view; as I see it.
　(c) *(fig)* to look into, examine, inquire into; **lo veremos** we'll look into it.
　(d) *(Law) case, appeal* to try, hear.
　(e) **— de** + *infin* to see about + *ger.*
　(f) *(idioms)* **¡para que veas!** so there!; **si te vi no me acuerdo** they *(etc)* just don't want to know; **me lo estoy viendo de almirante** I can just imagine him as an admiral; **lo estaba viendo** it's just what I expected, one could see this coming; **dejarse —**

(effect etc) to show, become apparent; to begin to tell; *(person)* to show up, show one's face; **no dejarse —** to keep away; to lie low, stay hidden; **la preocupación se dejaba —** en su cara the worry showed in his face; **echar de —** algo to notice something; **¡hay que —!** it just goes to show!; **hacer — que . . .** to point out that . . ., prove that . . .; **no le puedo —** I hate the sight of him, I can't stand him; **tener que — con** to concern, have to do with; **A no tiene nada que — con B** A has nothing to do with B; **vamos a — let's see . . .,** let me see . . .; **¿por qué no lo compraste, vamos a —?** why didn't you buy it, I'd like to know?; *see also* **visto.**
　(g) *(SAm idioms)* **¡nos estamos viendo!** *(Mex)* au revoir!; **eso está en veremos** *(SAm)* that's still a long way off, that's very much in the future; **lo dijo por —** *(Ant),* **lo dijo por de —** *(Chi)* he said it just as a joke.
　2 verse *vr* (a) *(two persons)* to see each other; to meet; **— con uno** to see someone, have a talk *(or* interview) with someone; **ahora apenas nos vemos** we hardly see (anything of) each other nowadays.
　(b) *(one person: etc)* to see oneself; to be seen; **véase la página 9** see page 9; **se le veía mucho en el parque** he used to be seen a lot in the park; **desde aquí no se ve** you can't see it from here; **ya se ve** naturally, plainly; **ya se ve que . . .** it is obvious that . . .; **¿cuándo se vio nada igual?** when did you hear of anything like this?; **no se ha visto un lío parecido** you never saw such a mess, it was the biggest mess ever; **¡habráse visto!** did you ever! *(fam);* of all the cheek!; **¡que se vean los forzudos!** let's see how tough you are!; come on, you tough guys! *(US fam).*
　(c) to find oneself, be; **— en un apuro** to be in a jam; **se veía en la cumbre de la fama** he was at the height of his fame.
　3 *nm* (a) looks, appearance; **de buen —** good-looking, of agreeable appearance; **tener buen —** to be good-looking; **no tiene mal —** she's not bad-looking.
　(b) **a mi —** in my view, as I see it.
　(c) **a más —, hasta más —** au revoir.
vera *nf* edge, verge, border; *(of river)* bank; **a la — de** near, beside, next to; **se sentó a mi —** he sat down beside me.
veracidad *nf* truthfulness, veracity.
veragua *nf (CAm)* mildew *(on cloth).*
veranda *nf* veranda(h).
veraneante *nmf* holidaymaker, (summer) vacationist *(US).*
veranear [1a] *vi* to spend the summer (holiday); **veranean en Jaca** they go to Jaca for the summer, they holiday in Jaca; **es un buen sitio para —** it's a nice place for a summer holiday.
veraneo *nm* summer holiday; **lugar de —, punto de — summer** resort, holiday resort; **estar de —** to be away on one's summer holiday; **ir de — a la montaña** to go off to spend one's summer holidays in the mountains.
veraniego *adj* (a) summer *(attr).* (b) *(fig)* slight, trivial.
veranillo *nm* (a) **— de San Martín** Indian summer. (b) *(CAm)* dry spell in the rainy season; **— de San Juan** *(RPl)* warm spell in June.
verano *nm* (a) summer. (b) *(Ec, Mex)* dry season.
veranoso *adj (SAm)* dry.
veras *nfpl* (a) truth, reality; serious things; hard facts; **burlas y —** light-hearted and serious things.
　(b) **de —** really, truly; sincerely; in earnest; **¿de —?** really?, indeed?, is that so?; **lo siento de —** I am truly sorry; **ahora me duele de —** now it really does hurt me; **esto va de —** this is serious; I'm in earnest; **ahora va de —** que lo hago now I really am going to do it; **esta vez va de —** this time it's the real thing.
veraz *adj* truthful, veracious.
verbal *adj* verbal; oral.
verbalmente *adv* verbally; orally.
verbena *nf* (a) *(Bot)* verbena. (b) fair; open-air celebration on the eve of a saint's day; open-air dance.
verbenero *adj* of *(or* relating to) a *verbena (see* **verbena** (b)); **alegría verbenera** fun of the fair; **música verbenera** fairground music.
verbigracia *adv* for example, eg.
verbo *nm* (a) *(Gram)* verb; **— activo** transitive verb; **— auxiliar** auxiliary verb; **— defectivo** defective verb; **— deponente** deponent verb; **— finito** finite verb; **— intransitivo, — neutro** intransitive verb; **— reflexivo** reflexive verb; **— transitivo** transitive verb.

(b) curse, oath; **echar —s** to swear, curse.
(c) (*Lit*) language, diction, style; **de — elegante** elegant in style.
(d) el V— (*Rel*) the Word.
verborragia *nf*, **verborrea** *nf* verbosity, verbal diarrhoea (*fam*); verbiage.
verbosidad *nf* verbosity, wordiness; verbiage.
verboso *adj* verbose, wordy.
verdad *nf* **(a)** truth; truthfulness; reliability, trustworthiness; **la — de su relato** the truthfulness of his tale, the reliability of his account; **la — lisa y llana** the plain truth; **la pura — es que . . .** the plain truth is that . . . ; **a la —** really, in truth; **de —** (*adj*) real, proper, *eg* **un héroe de —** a real hero; (*adv*) really, properly, *eg* **entonces la pegó de —** then he really did hit her; **¿de —?** really?; **en —** really, truly; **pues, la — no sé** well, the truth is I don't know; **well, truth to tell, I don't know; decir la — to** tell the truth; **decir la — al lucero del alba** to be very outspoken; to be utterly truthful; **faltar a la —** to lie, be untruthful; **hablar con —** to speak truthfully; **hay una parte de — en esto** there is some truth in this.
(b) **es —** it is true, it is so; (*as confession*) yes; I'm afraid so; **eso no es —** that is not true; **es — que . . .** it is true that . . . ; **bien es — que . . .** it is of course true that . . . , it is certainly true that . . . ; **si bien es — que . . .** even though . . . , despite the fact that . . . ; **¿—?**, **¿no es —?** isn't it?, aren't you?, don't you? (*etc*), isn't that so?
(c) — de clavo pasado, — de Pero Grullo platitude, truism; **—es del barquero** plain truths; **es una — como un puño** it's as plain as a pikestaff; **decir cuatro —es a uno** to tell someone a few home truths, give someone a piece of one's mind.
verdaderamente *adv* really, indeed; truly; **—, no sé** I really don't know; **un hombre — bueno** a truly good man; **es — triste** it's really sad.
verdadero *adj* **(a)** *account, description etc* true, truthful; reliable, trustworthy.
(b) *person* truthful.
(c) (*fig*) true, real, veritable; **es un — héroe** he's a real hero; **fue un — desastre** it was a real disaster, it was a veritable disaster; **es un — amigo** he's a true friend.
verde 1 *adj* **(a)** green.
(b) *fruit etc* green, unripe; *plant* green; *vegetables* green, fresh; *wood* unseasoned; (*fig*) *plan etc* premature; **¡están —s!** sour grapes!; **segar la hierba en —** to cut the grass while it is still green.
(c) (*fig*) *person* unduly amorous, sexy (despite one's advanced years); **viejo —** randy old man, dirty old man; **viuda —** merry widow (*euph*).
(d) (*fig*) *joke, song etc* blue, smutty, scabrous, dirty.
(e) (*idioms*) **estar — de envidia** to be green with envy; **¡si piensan eso, están —s!** if that's what they think, they've got another think coming!; **pasar las —s y las maduras** to have a rough time of it; **poner — a uno** (*fam*) to give someone a dressing-down; to abuse someone violently; to run someone down.
2 *nm* **(a)** green, green colour.
(b) (*Bot*) green, green grass; foliage; (*Agr*) green fodder; **sentarse en el —** to sit on the grass.
(c) darse un — to eat a lot, eat one's fill (*de* of); **darse un — de conciertos** to have a surfeit of concerts, have one's fill of concerts.
(d) (*RPl*) grass, pasture; maté; salad.
(e) (*Col, Ec*) green banana.
(f) (*PR, Mex*) country, countryside.
(g) (*Cu*) policeman.
verdear [1a] *vi* **(a)** to look green; to incline to green, be greenish.
(b) to turn green, grow green.
(c) (*RPl*) to drink maté.
(d) (*RPl: Agr*) to graze.
verdecer [2d] *vi* to turn green, grow green; (*of person*) to go green.
verdegay 1 *adj* light green. **2** *nm* light green.
verdemar 1 *adj* sea-green. **2** *nm* sea green.
verde-oliva *adj invar* olive-green.
verderón *nm* (*Orn*) greenfinch.
verdete *nm* verdigris.
verdiblanco *adj* green and white.
verdín *nm* **(a)** bright green, fresh green. **(b)** (*Bot*) scum; moss; verdigris. **(c)** (*on clothing etc*) green stain.
verdinegro *adj* dark green.
verdino *adj* bright green.
verdirrojo *adj* green and red.

verdón 1 *adj* (*Arg*) **(a)** bright green. **(b)** *fruit* slow to ripen. **2** *nm* **(a)** (*Orn*)=**verderón**. **(b)** (*Arg*) bruise, welt.
verdor *nm* **(a)** greenness; (*Bot*) verdure, lushness. **(b)** (*fig: also* **—es**) youthful vigour, lustiness.
verdoso *adj* greenish.
verdugo *nm* **(a)** (*Hist*) executioner; hangman.
(b) (*fig*) cruel master, slave driver; tyrant; tormentor.
(c) (*fig*) torment.
(d) lash.
(e) weal, welt.
(f) (*Bot*) twig, shoot, sprout.
(g) slender rapier.
verdugón *nm* **(a)** weal, welt. **(b)** (*Bot*) twig, shoot, sprout. **(c)** (*Bol*) rent, rip.
verdulera *nf* **(a)** greengrocer. **(b)** (*pej*) coarse woman, fishwife.
verdulería *nf* greengrocer's (shop).
verdulero *nm* greengrocer.
verdura *nf* **(a)** greenness; (*Bot*) greenery, verdure. **(b)** **—s** (*Cook*) greens, green vegetables, (*esp*) cabbage. **(c)** (*fig*) smuttiness, scabrous nature.
verdusco *adj* dark green, dirty green.
verecundia *nf* bashfulness, sensitivity.
verecundo *adj* bashful, sensitive.
vereda *nf* **(a)** path, lane; **ir por la —** (*fig*) to do the right thing; to keep to the straight and narrow.
(b) (*SAm*) pavement, sidewalk (*US*).
(c) (*Col*) village, settlement; section of a village.
(d) (*Mex*) parting (*in the hair*).
veredicto *nm* verdict; **— de culpabilidad** verdict of guilty.
veredón *nm* (*Arg*) broad pavement, broad sidewalk (*US*).
verga *nf* **(a)** rod, stick; (*Naut*) yard, spar. **(b)** (*Anat: Zool*) penis.
vergajo *nm* **(a)** pizzle; lash, whip. **(b)** (*Col*) rotter, cad.
vergonzante *adj* **(a)** shamefaced, full of shame; **pobre —** poor but too ashamed to beg. **(b)** shameful, shaming.
vergonzosamente *adv* **(a)** bashfully, shyly; modestly. **(b)** shamefully, disgracefully.
vergonzoso *adj* **(a)** *person* bashful, shy, timid; modest. **(b)** *act, matter etc* shameful, disgraceful, shocking; **es — que . . .** it is disgraceful that . . .
(c) (*Anat*) **partes vergonzosas** private parts.
vergüenza *nf* **(a)** shame; sense of shame, feelings of shame; **perder la —** to lose all sense of shame, cast aside all restraints; **sacar a uno a la —** to hold someone up to shame; **tener —** to be ashamed; **tener — de** + *infin* to be ashamed to + *infin*; **si tuviera — no lo haría** if he had any shame he wouldn't do it.
(b) bashfulness, shyness, timidity; embarrassment; (*sexual*) shame, modesty; **me da — decírselo** I feel too shy to say it to him, it embarrasses me to say it to him, it upsets me to say it to him.
(c) disgrace; **¡qué —!** what a disgrace!, what a scandal!; shame (on you)!; **el hijo es la — de su familia** the son is a disgrace to his family; **es una — que esté tan sucio** it's a disgrace that it should be so dirty.
(d) **—s** (*Anat*) private parts.
vericueto *nm* rough part, rough track, piece of difficult terrain.
verídico *adj* true, truthful.
verificable *adj* verifiable.
verificación *nf* **(a)** check, checkup, inspection; testing; verification; proving. **(b)** carrying out; performance; holding. **(c)** realization.
verificar [1a] **1** *vt* **(a)** *machine, meter etc* to check, inspect; to test; *results* to check (up on); *facts* to verify, establish, substantiate; *will* to prove.
(b) *test etc* to carry out; *marriage, ceremony* to perform; *election* to hold.
2 verificarse (a) (*event etc*) to occur, happen; (*meeting etc*) to be held, take place.
(b) (*prediction etc*) to come true, prove true, be realized.
verija *nf* **(a)** (*Anat*) groin, genital region. **(b)** (*SAm*) flank (*of a horse*).
verijón *adj* (*Mex*) slow, sluggish.
veringo *adj* (*Col*) nude, naked.
veringuearse *vr* (*Col*) to undress.
verismo *nm* realism, truthfulness; factual nature.
verista *adj* realistic, true to life; factual.
verja *nf* grating, grille; railing(s); iron gate.
vermicida *nm* vermicide.
vermífugo *nm* vermifuge.
verminoso *adj* infected, wormy.

vermut [ber'mu] *nm, pl* **vermuts** [ber'mu] (*gall*) (a) vermouth. (b) (*Chi, RPl: Theat*) early performance.

vernáculo *adj* vernacular; **lengua vernácula** vernacular.

vernal *adj* spring (*attr*), vernal.

Verónica *f* Veronica.

verónica *nf* (a) (*Bot*) veronica, speedwell. (b) (*Taur*) *a kind of pass with the cape*.

verosímil *adj* likely, probable; *story* credible.

verosimilitud *nf* likeliness, probability; credibility; (*Lit*) verisimilitude.

verosímilmente *adv* in a likely way; credibly.

verraco *nm* boar, male pig; (*Col*) ram; (*Cu*) wild boar.

verraquear [1a] *vi* (a) to grunt. (b) (*of child*) to wail, howl with rage.

verraquera *nf* (a) crying spell, fit of rage, tantrum (*fam*). (b) (*Cu*) drunken spell.

verruga *nf* (a) (*Anat, Bot*) wart. (b) (*fam*) bore, pest, nuisance. (c) (*fam*) defect; stain (on one's character).

verrugoso *adj* warty, covered in warts.

versación *nf* (*Arg, Chi, Mex*) expertise, expertness.

versada *nf* (*SAm*) long tedious poem.

versado *adj:* — **en** versed in, conversant with; expert in, skilled in.

versal (*Typ*) **1** *adj* capital. **2** *nf* capital (letter).

versalitas *nfpl* (*Typ*) small capitals.

Versalles Versailles.

versar [1a] *vi* (a) to go round, turn.

  (b) — **sobre** to deal with, discuss, be about; to turn on.

  (c) (*Cu, PR*) to versify, improvise verses.

  (d) (*Cu*) to chat, talk.

  (e) to tease, crack jokes.

versátil *adj* (a) (*Anat etc*) mobile, loose, easily turned. (b) (*fig*) versatile. (c) (*fig: pej*) fickle, changeable.

versatilidad *nf* (a) mobility, looseness, ease of movement. (b) (*fig*) versatility. (c) (*fig: pej*) fickleness, changeableness.

versículo *nm* (*Bible*) verse.

versificación *nf* versification.

versificador *nm*, **versificadora** *nf* versifier.

versificar [1g] **1** *vt* to versify, put into verse. **2** *vi* to write verses, versify.

versión *nf* version; translation.

verso *nm* (a) (*in general*) verse; — **libre** free verse; — **suelto** blank verse; **teatro en** — verse drama. (b) (*un* —) line; **en el segundo** — **del poema** in the second line of the poem. (c) (*Mex, Ven*) **echar** — to gab (*fam*), talk just for talking's sake; to talk nonsense.

vértebra *nf* vertebra.

vertebrado 1 *adj* vertebrate. **2** *nm* vertebrate.

vertebral *adj* vertebral.

vertedero *nm* (a) rubbish dump, tip. (b) =**vertedor** (a). (c) (*Arg*) slope, hillside, cliff.

vertedor *nm* (a) runway, overflow; drain, outlet; spillway. (b) (*Naut*) scoop, bailer. (c) (*in shop etc*) scoop, small shovel.

verter [2g] **1** *vt* (a) *contents, liquid etc* to pour (out); to empty (out); (*by accident*) to pour, spill; *light, blood* to shed; *rubbish* to dump, tip, shoot; — **los granos del saco en el camión** to pour grain from a sack into a lorry; — **el café sobre el mantel** to spill (*or* upset) one's coffee on the tablecloth. (b) *container* to empty (out); to tip up; (*accidentally*) to upset. (c) (*Ling*) to translate (*a* into).

  2 *vi* (*of river*) to flow, run (*a* into); (*of slope etc*) to fall (*a* towards).

vertical 1 *adj* vertical; upright. **2** *nf* vertical.

verticalidad *nf* vertical position; vertical direction.

verticalmente *adv* vertically.

vértice *nm* (a) vertex, apex; top; — **geodésico** bench mark, survey point. (b) (*Anat*) crown of the head.

verticilo *nm* whorl.

vertiente *nf* (a) slope. (b) (*Col, Chi, Mex, RPl*) spring, fountain.

vertiginosamente *adv* (a) giddily, dizzily. (b) (*fig*) excessively; very rapidly; **los precios suben** — prices are rising rapidly, prices are spiralling up.

vertiginoso *adj* (a) giddy, dizzy, vertiginous. (b) (*fig*) *speed* dizzy, excessive; *rise etc* very rapid.

vértigo *nm* (a) (*Med*) giddiness, dizziness, vertigo; dizzy spell; **puede provocar** —**s** it may cause giddiness; **bajar así me produce** — going down like that makes me dizzy. (b) (*fig*) sudden frenzy; fit of madness, aberration. (c) (*fig*) intense activity; whirl, maelstrom; frenzy; **el** — **de los negocios** the frenzied rush of

business; **el** — **de los placeres** the whirl of pleasures. (d) **de** — (*fam*): **con una velocidad de** — at a giddy speed; **fue un jaleo de** — it was an almighty row (*fam*); **tiene un talento de** — he has a fantastic talent; **es de** — **cómo crece la ciudad** the city grows at a frenzied speed, the town spreads at a tremendous rate (*fam*).

vesania *nf* rage, fury.

vesánico *adj* raging, furious.

vesícula *nf* vesicle; blister; — **biliar** gall-bladder.

vespasiana *nf* (*Arg, Chi: gall*) public lavatory, urinal.

vespertino *adj* evening (*attr*).

vestal 1 *adj* vestal. **2** *nf* vestal.

vestíbulo *nm* vestibule, lobby, hall; (*Theat*) foyer.

vestido *nm* (a) (*in general*) dress, costume, clothing; **historia del** — history of costume. (b) (*un* —: *woman's*) dress, frock; costume, suit; (*Chi, Pan, Per: man's*) suit; — **de debajo** undergarment; — **de encima** outer garment.

vestidor *nm* dressing room.

vestidura *nf* (a) (*lit*) clothing, apparel. (b) (*Eccl*) —**s** vestments; —**s sacerdotales** priestly vestments; **rasgarse las** —**s** (*fig*) to make a great show of being shocked.

vestigial *adj* vestigial.

vestigio *nm* vestige, trace; sign; —**s** remains, relics; **no quedaba el menor** — **de ello** there was not the slightest trace of it.

vestimenta *nf* (a) clothing; (*pej*) gear (*fam*), stuff (*fam*), things. (b) (*Eccl*) —**s** vestments.

vestir [3l] **1** *vt* (a) *body, person* to dress (*de* in), clothe (*de* in, with); *statue, surface etc* to clothe, cover, drape (*de* in, with); *wall* to hang (*de* with); to dress up, adorn, deck, embellish (*de* with); **estar vestido de** to be dressed in, be clad in; (*as disguise*) to be dressed as.

  (b) *garment* to don, put on; to wear; **vestía traje azul con sombrero** he was wearing a blue suit and a hat; **lo viste siempre** she always wears it.

  (c) (*of parent etc*) to clothe, pay for the clothing of.

  (d) (*of tailor*) to dress, make clothes for; **le viste un buen sastre** he has his clothes made at a good tailor's.

  (e) *idea etc* to express (*de* in); *defect etc* to conceal, cover up, disguise; — **el rostro de gravedad** to put on a serious expression.

  2 *vi* (a) to dress; — **bien** to dress well; — **con elegancia** to dress smartly; — **de negro** to dress in black, wear black; — **de uniforme** to wear a uniform; **el mismo que viste y calza** the selfsame, the very same.

  (b) (*of dress*) to look well, be right (for an occasion); **traje de** (**mucho**) — formal suit, (*pej*) suit that is too dressy; **el vestido negro viste más que el azul** the black dress is more formal (*or* suitable) than the blue one.

  3 vestirse *vr* (a) to dress oneself, get dressed, put on one's clothes; (*fig*) to cover itself, become covered (*de* in); — **de azul** to wear blue, dress in blue; **el árbol se está vistiendo de verde** the tree is coming out in leaf, the tree is turning green; **su querida se viste en París** his mistress buys her clothes in Paris; **apenas gana para** — she hardly earns enough to keep her in clothes.

  (b) (*fig: Med*) to get up again (after an illness). (c) (*fig*) — **de cierta actitud** to adopt a certain attitude; — **de severidad** to adopt a severe tone (*etc*).

vestón *nm* (*Chi: gall*) jacket.

vestuario *nm* (a) clothes, wardrobe; (*Theat*) wardrobe, costumes; (*Mil*) uniform. (b) (*Theat*) dressing room, (*loosely*) backstage area; (*in public building etc*) cloakroom; (*Sport*) changing room; pavilion.

Vesubio *m* Vesuvius.

veta *nf* (*Min*) seam, vein, lode; (*in wood*) grain; (*in stone, meat etc*) streak, stripe.

vetar [1a] *vt* to veto.

vetazo *nm* (*Ec*) lash.

veteada *nf* (*Ec*) flogging, beating.

veteado 1 *adj* veined; grained; streaked, striped (*de* with). **2** *nm* veining; graining; streaks, markings.

vetear [1a] *vt* (a) to grain; to streak. (b) (*Ec*) to flog, beat.

veteranía *nf* status (*or* dignity *etc*) of being a veteran; long service; seniority.

veterano 1 *adj* veteran. **2** *nm* veteran; (*fig*) old hand, old stager.

veterinaria *nf* veterinary science.

veterinario *nm* veterinary surgeon, vet (*fam*), veterinarian (*US*).

veto *nm* veto; **poner (su) — a** to veto; **tener — to have a veto.**

vetulio *nm* (*Ec*) old man.

vetustez *nf* (*lit*) great age, antiquity; (*iro*) venerable nature; hoariness.

vetusto *adj* (*lit*) very old, ancient, venerable; (*iro*) venerable, ancient; hoary.

vez *nf* (a) time, occasion; instance; **aquella — en Tánger** that time in Tangiers; **a veces** at times; **a la — at a time, at the same time; a la — que . . .** at the same time as . . . ; **alguna —, algunas veces** sometimes; **¿lo viste alguna —?** did you ever see it?; **alguna que otra —** occasionally, now and again; **cada — every time; cada — que . . .** (*as conj*) each time that . . . , whenever . . . ; **cada — más** increasingly, more and more; **iba cada — más lento** it went slower and slower; **le encuentro cada — más inaguantable** he gets more and more unbearable; **contadas veces** seldom, rarely; **¿cuántas veces?** how often?, how many times?; **de — en cuando** now and again, from time to time, occasionally; **en veces** by fits and starts; with interruptions; **las más veces** most of the times, mostly, in most cases; **muchas veces** often; **otra — again; pocas veces** seldom, rarely; **por esta — this time, this once; rara — seldom, rarely; repetidas veces** repeatedly, over and over again; **tal — perhaps; toda — que . . .** (*as conj*) since . . . ; in view of the fact that . . . ; **varias veces** several times; repeatedly.

(b) (*with numeral*) **una — once; una — que** (*as conj*) once . . . ; **una — dice que sí y otra que no** first he says yes and then he says no; **érase una — once upon a time (there was); había una — una princesa** there was once a princess; **de una — in one go, all at once; outright; without a break, straight off; ¡acabemos de una —!** let's get it over!, let's have done with it!; **de una — para siempre** once and for all, for good; **dos veces** twice; **dos veces tanto** twice as much; **con una velocidad dos veces superior a la del sonido** at a speed twice that of sound; **tres veces** three times; **cien veces** (*fig*) hundreds of times, lots of times; **la primera — que le vi** the first time I saw him; **por primera — for the first time; por última — for the last time; por enésima — for the umpteenth time** (*fam*); **no se permite golpearlo segunda —** you can't hit it again, you aren't allowed a second shot at it.

(c) (*Math*) **7 veces 9** 7 times 9.

(d) turn; **a su — in his turn; en — de instead of, in place of; ceder la — to give up one's turn, (in queue etc)** give up one's place; **cuando le llegue la — when his turn comes; hacer las veces de** to take the place of, act for, stand in for; to serve as, do duty as.

veza *nf* vetch.

vía 1 *nf* (a) road; route; track; (*fig*) way; (*Rel etc*) way; **— aérea** airway; (*Post*) airmail; **por — aérea** by air, (*Post*) (by) airmail; **— de agua** leak; **abrirse una — de agua** to spring a leak; **— de circunvalación** bypass, ring road; **— de comunicación** communication route; **— férrea** railway; **— fluvial** waterway; **V— Láctea** Milky Way; **¡— libre!** make way!, clear the way!; **— marítima** sea route, seaway; **por — marítima** by sea; **— pública** public thoroughfare; **— romana** Roman road; **— terrestre** overland route, (*Post*) surface route; **por — terrestre** overland, by land, (*Post*) by surface mail; **por — de** via, by way of; through; (*fig*) by way of, as, as a kind of; **dejar la — libre al desafuero** to leave the way open for abuse.

(b) (*Rail*) track; line; (*in width*) gauge; **— ancha** broad gauge; **— doble** double track; **de — estrecha** narrow-gauge (*attr*); **— muerta** siding; **— normal** standard gauge; **de — única** single-track (*attr*); **el tren está en la — 8** the train is at platform 8; **la estación tiene 18 —s** the station has 18 platforms.

(c) (*Anat*) passage, tube; tract; **—s digestivas** digestive tract; **por — bucal** through the mouth, by mouth; **por — interna** (*Med*) internally.

(d) (*fig*) system; way, means; channel; **— judicial** process of law, legal means; **recurrir a la — judicial** to go to law, have recourse to the law; **por — oficial** through official channels; by official means; **— sumarísima** (*Law*) summary proceedings.

(e) (*fig*) **en —s de** in process of; **un país en —s de desarrollo** a developing country; **el asunto está en —s de una solución** the matter is on its way to a

solution, the question is in process of being solved.

2 *prep* (*Rail etc*) via, by way of; through.

viabilidad *nf* viability; feasibility.

viable *adj* viable; **plan etc** feasible.

viada *nf* (*Per*) speed.

viaducto *nm* viaduct.

viajante 1 *adj* travelling. 2 *nm* (*also — de comercio*) commercial traveller, salesman; **— en jabones** traveller in soap.

viajar [1a] *vi* to travel (*also Comm*); to journey; **ha viajado mucho** he has travelled a lot; **— en coche** to go in a car, ride (in a car); **— por Ruritania** to travel through (*or* across) Ruritania; to tour Ruritania.

viajazo *nm* (a) (*Mex*) push, shove. (b) (*Ven*) lash. (c) (*CR*) telling-off.

viaje[1] *nm* (a) journey; trip; tour; (*Naut*) voyage; **el —, los —s** (*in general*) travel; **— en coche** ride, trip by car; **— en barco** boat trip, sail; **— de buena voluntad** goodwill trip, goodwill mission; **— de ensayo** trial run; **— de ida** outward journey, trip out; **— de ida y vuelta, — redondo** (*SAm*) round trip, journey there and back; **— de novios** honeymoon; **— de recreo** pleasure trip; **¡buen —!, ¡feliz —!** bon voyage!, have a good trip!; **estar de — to** be travelling, be on a trip.

(b) (*Comm etc*) load; cartload, cartful (*etc*); **un — de leña** a load of wood.

(c) (*PR, Ven*) time; **lo repitió varios —s** he repeated it several times; **de un — (*SAm*)** all in one go, at one blow; all at once.

(d) (*CAm*) **echar un — a uno** to give someone a telling-off.

viaje[2] *nm* (*fam*) slash (with a razor); **tirar un — a uno** to take a slash at someone.

viajero 1 *adj* travelling; (*Zool*) migratory. 2 *nm*, **viajera** *nf* traveller; (*in vehicle, Rail etc*) passenger; **¡señores —s, al tren!** will passengers kindly board the train?

vial *adj* (*esp SAm*) road (*attr*); traffic (*attr*); **reglamento — traffic control; rule of the road, highway code; fluidez — free movement of traffic.

vianda *nf* (a) (*also —s*) food. (b) (*Ant*) vegetables. (c) (*Chi, RPl*) lunch tin, dinner pail (*US*).

viandante *nmf* traveller, wayfarer; (*in town*) passerby; pedestrian.

viaraza *nf* (*Col, Guat, RPl*) fit of anger; spell of bad temper; **estar con la —** to be in a bad mood.

viático *nm* (a) (*Hist*) food for a journey. (b) (*Fin*) travel allowance. (c) (*Eccl*) viaticum.

víbora *nf* (a) viper (*also fig*). (b) (*Mex*) money belt.

viborear [1a] *vi* (a) (*RPl*) to twist, snake along. (b) (*Cu*) to cheat by marking the cards.

vibración *nf* (a) vibration; shaking; throbbing, pulsating. (b) (*Ling*) roll, trill.

vibrador *nm* vibrator.

vibrante 1 *adj* (a) vibrant, vibrating.
(b) (*Ling*) rolled, trilled.
(c) (*fig*) *voice, slogan etc* ringing; **— de ringing with, vibrant with.
2 *nf* (*Ling*) vibrant.

vibrar [1a] 1 *vt* (a) to vibrate; to shake, rattle. (b) (*Ling*) to roll, trill. 2 *vi* to vibrate; to shake, rattle; to throb, beat, pulsate.

vibratorio *adj* vibratory.

viburno *nm* viburnum.

vicario *nm* (*Eccl*) curate; deputy; **— general** vicar-general; **V— de Cristo** Vicar of Christ (*the Pope*).

vice . . . vice . . .

vicealmirante *nm* vice-admiral.

vicecónsul *nm* vice-consul.

vicegerente *nm* assistant manager.

Vicente *m* Vincent.

vicepresidencia *nf* vice-presidency; vice-chairmanship.

vicepresidente *nm* (*Pol*) vice-president; (*of committee etc*) vice-chairman.

vicetiple *nf* chorus girl.

viceversa *adv* vice versa.

viciado *adj* (a) *air* foul, thick, stale. (b) *text* corrupt.

viciar [1b] 1 *vt* (a) *customs etc* to corrupt, pervert, subvert.
(b) (*Law*) to nullify, invalidate.
(c) *text* to corrupt, vitiate, falsify; to interpret erroneously.
(d) *substance* to adulterate; *air* to make foul; *food etc* to spoil, taint, contaminate.
(e) *object* to bend, twist, put out of shape; to warp.
2 **viciarse** *vr* (a) to take to vice, get depraved, become corrupted; *see also* **enviciarse**.
(b) (*object*) to warp, lose its shape.

vicio nm (a) vice; viciousness, depravity.

(b) bad habit, vice; — **inveterado**, — **de origen** ingrained bad habit; **tiene el** — **de no contestar las cartas** he has the bad habit of not answering letters; **no le podemos quitar el** — we can't get him out of the habit; **de** —, **por** — out of sheer habit; for no reason at all; **hablar de** — to chatter away; **quejarse de** — to complain for no reason at all.

(c) defect, blemish; (*Law etc*) error; (*Ling*) mistake, incorrect form; solecism; **adolece de ciertos** —s it has a number of defects, there are certain things wrong with it.

(d) (*of surface etc*) warp; twist, bend.

(e) (*towards child*) excessive indulgence.

(f) (*Bot*) rankness, luxuriance, lushness.

(g) (*SAm*) **estar de** — to be idle.

viciosamente adv (a) viciously; dissolutely. (b) (*Bot*) rankly, luxuriantly.

viciosidad nf viciousness.

vicioso 1 adj (a) vicious; depraved, dissolute; *child* spoiled.

(b) (*Mech etc*) faulty, defective.

(c) (*Bot*) rank, luxuriant, lush.

2 nm, **viciosa** nf (a) vicious person, depraved person.

(b) addict, fiend.

vicisitud nf accident, upset, mishap; sudden change; —es vicissitudes.

víctima nf (a) victim; (*fig*, *also of bird etc*) prey; **fue** — **de una estafa** she was the victim of a swindle; **es** — **de alguna neurosis** he is a prey to some neurosis; **no hay que lamentar** —s **del accidente** there were no casualties in the accident.

(b) (*Hist*) sacrifice.

victimar [1a] vt (*SAm*) to wound; to kill.

victimario nm (a) person responsible for someone's suffering (*or accident etc*).

(b) (*SAm*) person responsible for wounding (*or killing*).

Victoria f Victoria.

victoria nf victory; triumph; — **moral** moral victory; — **pírrica** Pyrrhic victory.

victoriano 1 adj Victorian. 2 nm, **victoriana** nf Victorian.

victoriosamente adv victoriously.

victorioso adj victorious.

victrola nf (*SAm*) gramophone, phonograph (*US*).

vicuña nf vicuna.

vichadero nm (*RPl*) see **bichadero**.

vich(e)ar [1a] vt (*RPl*) see **bichear**.

vid nf vine.

vida nf (a) (*in most senses*) life; way of life; lifetime; livelihood; **tuvo una** — **ejemplar** he lived an exemplary life; **la** — **de estos edificios es breve** the life of these buildings is short; **así es la** — such is life, that's life; **¿qué es de tu** —? what's the news?; **este sol es la** — this sunshine is a real tonic; **¡esto es** —! this is living!; **está escribiendo la** — **de Quevedo** he is writing the life (*or* a biography) of Quevedo.

(b) (*phrases with prep*) **¡hermana de mi** —! my dear sister!; **de por** — for life, for the rest of one's life; **un amigo de toda la** — a lifelong friend; **en** — during his (*etc*) lifetime, while still alive; **en la** —, **en mi** — (*negative sense*) never, never in my life; **entre** — **y muerte** at death's door; **¡por de . . .** ! upon my soul!; **¡por** — **del chápiro verde!** by the toe of the Prophet!

(c) (*phrases with adj etc*) — **airada** criminal life; underworld; **de** — **airada** criminal; loose-living, immoral; — **arrastrada** wretched life; — **eterna** everlasting life; — **íntima** private life; **de** — **libre** loose-living, immoral; **mala** — dissolute life; prostitution; **mujer de** — **alegre**, **mujer de mala** — prostitute; — **y milagros de uno** (*fam*) full details about someone; **la otra** — the next life; the life to come; — **perra**, — **de perros** dog's life, wretched life; — **privada** private life; — **sentimental** love life.

(d) (*phrases with verb*) **estar con** — to be still alive; **amargar la** — **a uno** to make someone's life a misery; **complicarse la** — to make life difficult for oneself; **cortar la** — **de uno** to cut someone off (in his prime); **darse buena** —, **darse** — **de canónigo** to live well, live in style, do oneself proud (*fam*); **dar la** — to sacrifice one's life; **dar mala** — **a uno** to ill-treat someone, give someone a wretched time of it; **enterrarse en** — to go into seclusion; **escapar con** — to escape alive; **ganarse la** — to make a living; **hacer** — **marital** to live together (as man and wife); **hacer por la** — (*fam*)

to eat; **no le va la** — **en esto** it's not as though his life depends on it; **meterse en** —s **ajenas** to pry, snoop; to meddle; **pasar a mejor** — (*euph*) to pass away; **pasar la** — **a tragos** (*fam*) to have a miserable life; **pegarse la gran** —, **pegarse la** — **padre** (*fam*) to live it up (*fam*), live the life of Riley; **perder la** — to lose one's life; **quitar la** — **a uno** to take someone's life; **quitarse la** — to kill oneself, do away with oneself; **vender cara la** — to sell one's life dearly.

(e) (*of look*, *eyes etc*) liveliness, brightness.

(f) (*in direct address*) **¡**—**!**, **¡**— **mía!** my love!

(g) (*euph*) prostitution; **una mujer de la** — a prostitute, a woman on the game; **echarse a la** — to take up prostitution.

vidente nmf seer, prophet; clairvoyant(e).

video nm video; **de** — video (*attr*).

vidorra nf (*fam*) gay life, easy life.

vidorria nf (a) (*Arg*) gay life, easy life. (b) (*Col, Ven*) miserable life.

vidriado 1 adj glazed. 2 nm (a) glaze, glazing. (b) glazed earthenware.

vidriar [1b] 1 vt to glaze. 2 **vidriarse** vr to become glazed.

vidriera nf (a) (*Eccl*; *also* — **de colores**) stained-glass window; (*also* **puerta** —) glass door; glass partition.

(b) (*SAm*) shop window; showcase.

(c) (*Cu*) tobacco stall, tobacco kiosk.

vidriería nf (a) glassworks. (b) glassware.

vidriero nm glazier.

vidrio nm (a) glass; — **cilindrado** plate glass; — **de color(es)**, — **pintado** stained glass; — **deslustrado** frosted glass, ground glass; — **inastillable** laminated glass, splinter-proof glass; — **tallado** cut glass; **bajo** — under glass; **pagar los** —s **rotos** (*fam*) to carry the can (*sl*).

(b) (*Arg*) bottle of liquor.

vidrioso adj (a) glassy; glass-like; brittle, fragile, delicate.

(b) *eye* glassy; fishy; *expression*, *look* glazed; *surface* slippery as glass, glassy.

(c) *person* touchy, sensitive.

(d) *matter* delicate.

vidurria nf (*Arg, Col, Ven*) = **vidorria**.

vieira nf (*Galicia*) scallop.

vieja nf (a) old woman.

(b) (*RPl*: *fam*) **la** — my old woman (*fam*).

(c) (*Chi*) cracker, squib.

(d) (*Mex*) cigar stub.

viejada nf (*Arg*) group of old people.

viejales nm, pl **viejales** (*fam*) old chap (*fam*).

viejera nf (a) (*PR, Ven*) old age. (b) (*PR*) old useless thing.

viejo 1 adj (a) (*all senses*) old; **se cae de** — he's so old he can hardly walk; **hacerse** — to grow old, get old; **no parece más** — **de un día** he doesn't look a day older.

(b) **zapatero de** — cobbler.

(c) **Plinio el V**— Pliny the Elder.

2 nm (a) old man; *see* **verde**.

(b) (*SAm*) **mi** — (*fam*) my old man (*fam*); **los** —s the old folks.

viejón adj (*Col, Mex, RPl*) elderly.

Viena Vienna.

vienés 1 adj Viennese. 2 nm, **vienesa** nf Viennese.

viento nm (a) wind, breeze; **corre** —, **hay** —, **hace** — it is windy, there is a wind; **hace mucho** — it is very windy; **cuando sopla el** — when the wind blows; — **s alisios** trade winds; — **ascendente** (*Aer*) up-current; — **de cola**, — **de espalda**, — **trasero** tailwind; — **colado** draught; — **de costado** crosswind, sidewind; — **contrario**, — **de proa** headwind; — **de la hélice** slipstream; — **huracanado** hurricane wind, violent wind; — **en popa** following wind; **ir** — **en popa** to go splendidly; to do extremely well; (*of business*) to prosper, boom; — **terral** (*Naut*) land breeze; **estar lleno de** — to be empty, have nothing inside; **beber los** —s **por uno** to be crazy about someone; **echar a uno con** — **fresco** to chuck someone out; **¡vete con** — **fresco!** go to blazes!, and good riddance!; **publicar algo a los cuatro** —s to tell all and sundry about something, shout something from the rooftops; **soplan** —s **de fronda** there's trouble brewing; **como el** — like the wind; **contra** — **y marea** regardless of all the difficulties, at all costs, come what may.

(b) (*Anat*) wind, flatulence.

(c) (*Mus*) wind; wind instruments, wind section.

(d) (*Hunting*) scent.

(e) (*of dog*) keen scent, sense of smell.

(f) (fig) conceit, vanity; **estar lleno de —** to be puffed up (with conceit).
(g) (of tent, post) guy, guy-rope.
(h) (Col) strings of a kite.
(i) (Pan, PR) rheumatism.
vientre nm **(a)** (Anat) belly; womb; **bajo —** lower abdomen; **llevar un hijo en su —** to carry a child in one's womb.
(b) bowels; **— flojo** looseness of the bowels; **descargar el —, exonerar el —, hacer de —** to have a movement of the bowels.
(c) (of slaughtered animal) guts, entrails, offal.
(d) (Zool) foetus, unborn young.
(e) (of vessel) belly, wide part.
viernes nm, pl **viernes** Friday; **V— Santo** Good Friday.
Vietnam m Vietnam; **— del Norte** North Vietnam; **— del Sur** South Vietnam.
vietnamita 1 adj Vietnamese. **2** nmf Vietnamese. **3** nm (language) Vietnamese.
viga nf balk, timber; (Archit) beam, rafter; girder; **— maestra** main beam; **— transversal** crossbeam; **estar contando las —s** (fig) to gaze vacantly at the ceiling.
vigencia nf **(a)** operation; validity, applicability; **estar en —** to be in force; to be valid, apply; **entrar en —** to take effect, come into operation; **tener —** to be valid, apply; to prevail.
(b) social convention, norm of society.
vigente adj valid, applicable, in force; prevailing.
vigésimo 1 adj twentieth. **2** nm twentieth.
vigía 1 nm look-out, watchman; **los —s** (Naut) the watch. **2** nf **(a)** (Mil etc) watchtower. **(b)** (Geog) reef, rock.
vigilancia nf vigilance, watchfulness; **burlar la — de uno** to escape someone's vigilance.
vigilante 1 adj vigilant, watchful; alert.
2 nm **(a)** watchman, caretaker; (of prison) warder; (in shop) shopwalker, store detective; **— de noche, — nocturno** night watchman.
(b) (Arg) policeman.
vigilantemente adv vigilantly, watchfully.
vigilar [1a] **1** vt to watch, watch over; to look after, keep on eye on; installations, prisoners etc to guard; machine to tend; frontier etc to guard, police, patrol; work etc to supervise, superintend; **— a los niños para que no se hagan daño** to see that the children come to no harm; **— la leche para que no se salga** to keep an eye on the milk so that it does not boil over.
2 vi to be vigilant, be watchful, stay alert; to keep watch; **— por, — sobre** to watch over.
vigilia nf **(a)** wakefulness, being awake; watchfulness; **pasar la noche de —** to spend a night without sleep, stay awake all night.
(b) night work, late work; time spent working late; night-time study, lucubrations.
(c) (Eccl) fast; **día de —** day of abstinence; **comer de —** to fast, abstain from meat.
(d) (Eccl) vigil.
(e) (Eccl) eve (of a religious festivity).
vigor nm **(a)** vigour; vitality; toughness, stamina, hardiness; drive; **con —** vigorously.
(b) =**vigencia; en —** in force; valid, applicable, operative; **entrar en —** to take effect, come into force; **poner en —** to put into effect, put into operation, enforce; see **mantenerse**.
vigorizador adj, **vigorizante** adj invigorating; bracing; revitalizing; medicine tonic.
vigorizar [1f] vt to invigorate; to strengthen, encourage, stimulate; to revitalize.
vigorosamente adv vigorously; strongly, forcefully; strenuously.
vigoroso adj vigorous; strong, tough, forceful; effort strenuous; protest etc vigorous, forceful; child sturdy, strong.
viguería nf beams, rafters; girders, metal framework.
vigués 1 adj of Vigo. **2** nm, **viguesa** nf native (or inhabitant) of Vigo; **los —es** the people of Vigo.
vigueta nf joint, small beam.
vihuela nf (Hist) an early form of the guitar.
vihuelista nmf (Hist) vihuela player.
vijúa nf (Col) rock salt.
vikingo nm Viking.
vil adj person low, villainous, blackguardly; act vile, foul, rotten; treatment unjust, shabby, mean.
vileza nf **(a)** (quality) low character, villainy; vileness, foulness; injustice, shabbiness, meanness.
(b) (una —) vile act, base deed, villainy.
vilipendiar [1a] vt **(a)** to vilify, revile, abuse. **(b)** to despise, scorn.
vilipendio nm **(a)** vilification, abuse. **(b)** contempt, scorn; humiliation.

vilipendioso adj contemptible; humiliating.
vilmente adv villainously; vilely, foully; unjustly, shabbily, meanly.
vilo: en — adv **(a) en —** (up) in the air; suspended, unsupported; **sostener algo en —** to hold something up.
(b) (fig) **estar en —, quedar en —** to be left in the air, be left in suspense.
vilote nm (Arg) coward.
villa nf **(a)** (Hist etc) villa. **(b)** small town; (Pol) borough, municipality; **la V—** (esp) Madrid.
Villadiego: tomar las de — (fam) to beat it quick (fam).
villalata nf shack, tin hut.
villanaje nm **(a)** humble status, peasant condition. **(b)** peasantry, villagers.
villancico nm (Christmas) carol.
villanesco adj peasant (attr); village (attr), rustic.
villanía nf **(a)** (Hist) humble birth, lowly status.
(b) (quality) villainy, baseness.
(c) (una —) =**vileza (b)**.
(d) obscene expression, filthy remark.
villano 1 adj **(a)** (Hist) peasant (attr); rustic.
(b) (fig) coarse.
(c) (fig) villainous, base.
2 nm, **villana** nf **(a)** (Hist) villein, serf; (esp fig) peasant, rustic.
(b) (fig) low individual, rotter, cad.
(c) (SAm: angl) villain.
villoría nf country house.
villorrio nm one-horse town, dump (fam).
vinagre nm vinegar.
vinagrera nf **(a)** vinegar bottle; **—s** cruet stand. **(b)** (SAm) heartburn, acidity of the stomach.
vinagroso adj **(a)** vinegary, tart. **(b)** (fig) bad-tempered, sour.
vinatería nf **(a)** wine shop. **(b)** wine trade.
vinatero nm wine merchant, vintner.
vinaza nf nasty wine, wine from the dregs.
vinazo nm strong wine.
vinculación nf **(a)** linking, binding; (fig) bond, connexion. **(b)** (Law) entail.
vincular [1a] **1** vt **(a)** to link, bind, tie (a to); hopes etc to base, found (en on); **— su suerte a la de otro** to make one's fate depend on someone else's; **están estrechamente vinculados entre sí** they are closely bound together.
(b) (Law) to entail.
2 **vincularse** vr to link oneself (a to).
vínculo nm **(a)** link, bond, tie; **— de parentesco** family ties, ties of blood; **hay un fuerte — histórico** there is a strong historical link.
(b) (Law) entail.
vincha nf (Per, RPl) = **bincha**.
vindicación nf vindication.
vindicar [1g] **1** vt **(a)** to avenge.
(b) to vindicate.
(c) (Law) =**reivindicar**.
2 **vindicarse** vr **(a)** to avenge oneself.
(b) to vindicate oneself.
vine etc see **venir**.
vinería nf (Bol, Chi, Per, RPl) wineshop.
vínico adj (Chem) wine (attr).
vinícola adj wine (attr); wine-growing (attr); wine-making (attr).
vinicultor nm wine grower.
vinicultura nf wine growing, wine production.
vinificación nf fermentation.
vinilo nm vinyl.
vinillo nm thin wine, weak wine.
vino nm wine; **— añejo** mellow wine, mature wine; **— blanco** white wine; **— espumoso** sparkling wine; **— generoso** strong wine, full-bodied wine; **— de Jerez** sherry; **— de Málaga** Malaga (wine); **— de mesa** table wine; **— de Oporto** port (wine); **— de pasto** ordinary wine; **— peleón** coarse wine, pub wine; **— de postre** dessert wine; **— seco** dry wine; **— de solera** vintage wine; **— tinto** red wine; **aguar** (or **bautizar, cristianar**) **el —** to water the wine; **dormir el —** to sleep off a hangover; **echar agua al —** (fig) to water down a statement; **tener buen —** to know how to carry one's liquor; **tener mal —** to get wild after a few drinks.
vinolento adj boozy, fond of the bottle.
vinoso adj like wine, vinous; wine-coloured.
vinotería nf (CAm, Mex) wineshop.
viña nf **(a)** vineyard. **(b)** (Mex) rubbish dump.
viñador nm vine grower; wine grower.
viñal nm (Arg) vineyard.
viñatero nm (Chi, Per, RPl) vine grower; wine grower.
viñedo nm vineyard.

viñeta *nf* vignette; emblem, badge, device.

viola *nf* (a) (*Bot*) viola. (b) (*Mus*) viola; (*Hist*) viol.

violáceo *adj* violet.

violación *nf* (a) violation. (b) rape. (c) offence, infringement.

violado 1 *adj* violet. 2 *nm* violet (colour).

violador 1 *nm* rapist. 2 *nm*, **violadora** *nf* violator; offender (*de* against).

violar [1a] *vt* (a) *sanctuary, territory etc* to violate.
(b) *woman* to rape.
(c) *law etc* to break, offend against, infringe; *agreement, principle etc* to violate, break.

violencia *nf* (a) violence; force; (*Law*) violence, assault; (*Pol*) rule by force; **no** — non-violence; **usar** — **para abrir una caja** to use force to open a box; **no se consigue nada con él usando la** — you will not achieve anything with him by using force; **amenazar** — to threaten violence, (*of crowd etc*) to turn ugly; **apelar a la** — to resort to violence, use force; **hacer** — **a** = **violentar**.
(b) (*una* —) unjust act, damaging act; outrage.
(c) embarrassment; embarrassing situation; **si eso te cuesta** — if that embarrasses you; **estar con** — to be (*or* feel) embarrassed.

violentamente *adv* (a) violently; furiously, wildly.
(b) awkwardly, unnaturally.
(c) embarrassingly, awkwardly.
(d) distortedly.
(e) (*SAm*) quickly.

violentar [1a] 1 *vt* (a) *door etc* to force; *branch etc* to bend, twist (out of shape); *house* to break into, enter forcibly.
(b) *person* to force, use force on, persuade forcibly; to subject to violence; (*Law*) to assault.
(c) (*fig*) *principle* to violate, outrage.
(d) (*fig*) *sense* to distort, twist, force.
2 **violentarse** *vr* to force oneself.

violento *adj* (a) violent; furious, wild; *means, person, speech, temperament etc* violent; *sport* tough, physically demanding, (*pej*) rough; **mostrarse** — to turn violent, offer violence.
(b) *position of body etc* awkward, unnatural; cramped; *act* unnatural, forced; **me es muy** — **consentir en ello** it goes against the grain with me to agree with it.
(c) *situation etc* embarrassing, awkward; **para mí todo esto es un poco** — this is all a bit awkward for me.
(d) *person's state* embarrassed, awkward; **estar** (*or* **sentirse**) — to be (*or* feel) embarrassed; **me encuentro** — **estando con ellos** I feel awkward when I'm with them; **la discusión entre los dos me hacía estar** — the argument between them made me feel embarrassed.
(e) (*fig*) *interpretation* forced, distorted.

violeta 1 *nf* violet; — **de genciana** gentian violet. 2 *adj invar* violet.

violín *nm* (a) violin.
(b) violinist; **primer** — first violin.
(c) — **de Ingrés** (*gall*) spare-time occupation (*or* art, hobby *etc*) at which one shines.
(d) (*Ven*) bad breath.
(e) (*Mex*) **de** — gratis, free.
(f) (*Arg, Ven*) **embolsar el** — to be embarrassed.

violinista *nmf* violinist.

violón *nm* double bass; **tocar el** — (*fam*) to come out with something silly, reveal one's ignorance and stupidity.

violoncelista *nmf* cellist.

violoncelo *nm* cello.

viperino *adj* viperish.

vira[1] *nf* (*Mil etc*) dart.

vira[2] *nf* (*of shoe*) welt.

viracho *adj* (*Chi*) cross-eyed.

virada *nf* (*Naut*) tack, tacking.

virago *nf* mannish woman.

viraje *nm* (a) (*Naut*) tack; turn, going about; (*of vehicle*) turn; swerve; (*in road etc*) bend, curve; — **en horquilla** hairpin bend.
(b) (*fig*) change of direction; (*in policy*) abrupt switch, volte-face; (*in voting*) swing.
(c) (*Phot*) toning.

virar [1a] 1 *vt* (a) (*Naut*) to put about, turn.
(b) (*Phot*) to tone.
(c) (*Arg, Cu*) to turn round; to turn over, turn upside down.
(d) (*Cu*) to whip.
2 *vi* (a) to change direction; (*Naut*) to tack; to turn, go about, put about; (*of driver, vehicle*) to turn; to swerve; — **a estribor** to turn to starboard; — **hacia el sur** to turn towards the south; — **en redondo** to turn completely round; **tuve que** —

a la izquierda para no atropellarle I had to swerve left to avoid hitting him.
(b) (*fig*) to change one's views, switch round; to veer (*a, hacia* a, towards); (*Pol: of voting*) to swing; — **en redondo** to switch round completely, veer round, make a complete volte-face; **el país ha virado a la derecha** the country has swung (to the) right.
(c) (*Arg, Cu etc*) to turn.

virgen 1 *adj* virgin.
2 *nf* virgin; **la V** — the Virgin; **la Santísima V** — the Blessed Virgin; **¡Santísima V** —! by all that's holy!; **es un viva la V** — (*fam*) he doesn't give a damn, he doesn't care one little bit.

Vírgenes: Islas *fpl* — Virgin Isles.

virgiliano *adj* Virgilian.

Virgilio *m* Virgil.

virginal *adj* (a) maidenly, virginal. (b) (*Eccl*) of (*or* relating to) the Virgin.

virginidad *nf* virginity.

virgo *nm* virginity.

Virgo *f* Virgo.

virguería *nf* silly adornment, frill.

viril *adj* virile; manly; *see* **edad** *etc*.

virilidad *nf* (a) virility; manliness. (b) manhood.

viringo *adj* (*Col, Ec*) (a) bare, naked. (b) skinned, skinless.

viroca *nf* (*Chi*) serious mistake.

virola *nf* (a) metal tip, ferrule; (*on lance, tool etc*) collar. (b) (*Mex, RPl*) silver ring; metal disc (*fixed to harness etc as an adornment*).

virolento *adj* pockmarked.

virología *nf* virology.

virólogo *nm* virologist.

virote *nm* (a) arrow.
(b) (*Mex*) bread roll.
(c) (*fam*) young man about town, idle youth; solemn person, stiff person.
(d) (*Col, Mex, Ven*) simpleton.

virreinato *nm* viceroyalty.

virrey *nm* viceroy.

virriondo *adj* (*Mex*) = **cachondo**.

virtual *adj* (a) virtual. (b) *strength, wealth etc* potential; future, possible. (c) (*Phys*) apparent.

virtualidad *nf* potentiality; **tiene ciertas** — **es** it has certain potentialities.

virtualmente *adv* virtually.

virtud *nf* (a) virtue; — **cardinal** cardinal virtue.
(b) virtue, power, efficacy; **en** — **de** by virtue of, by reason of; **tener la** — **de** + *infin* to have the virtue of + *ger*, have the power to + *infin*; **una planta que tiene** — **contra varias enfermedades** a plant which is effective against certain diseases.
(c) (*Cu*) penis.

virtuosamente *adv* virtuously.

virtuosismo *nm* virtuosity.

virtuoso 1 *adj* virtuous. 2 *nm* virtuoso.

viruela *nf* (a) smallpox. (b) —**s** pockmarks; **picado de** —**s** pockmarked.

virulé: a la — (*gall*) *adj* (a) old; damaged; bent, twisted; shabby. (b) *person* cracked, potty (*fam*).

virulencia *nf* virulence.

virulento *adj* virulent.

virus *nm*, *pl* **virus** virus; **enfermedad por** — virus disease.

viruta *nf* shaving.

vis *nf*: — **cómica** comic sense, sense of comedy; **tener** — **cómica** to be witty, sparkle.

visa *nf* (*SAm*: *angl*) visa.

visado *nm* visa; permit; — **de permanencia** residence permit; — **de tránsito** transit visa.

visaje *nm* (wry) face, grimace; **hacer** —**s** to pull faces, grimace, smirk.

visar [1a] *vt* (a) *passport* to visa. (b) *document* to pass, approve, endorse.

vísceras *nfpl* viscera, entrails; (*fig*) guts, bowels.

visco *nm* birdlime.

viscosa *nf* viscose.

viscosidad *nf* (a) (*quality*) viscosity, stickiness; thickness. (b) (*Bot, Zool*) slime; sticky secretion.

viscoso *adj* viscous, sticky; *liquid* thick, stiff; *secretion* slimy.

visera *nf* (a) (*Mil*) visor; (*of cap*) peak; eyeshade.
(b) (*Cu, PR*) (horse's) blinkers.

visibilidad *nf* visibility; **la** — **es de 200 m** there is a visibility of 200 m; **la** — **queda reducida a cero** visibility is down to nil; **una curva de escasa** — (*Aut*) a corner that leaves a driver with a poor view.

visible *adj* (a) visible.
(b) (*fig*) clear, plain; evident, obvious.
(c) *person* free (to receive a visit); **¿está** — **el profesor?** is the professor free?, could the professor see me?

visiblemente *adv* (a) visibly.

(b) (*fig*) clearly; evidently; **parecía crecer** — it seemed to grow as one watched it, it seemed to get bigger before one's eyes.

visigodo 1 *adj* Visigothic. 2 *nm*, **visigoda** *nf* Visigoth.

visigótico *adj* Visigothic.

visillo *nm* (a) small curtain, lace curtain. (b) antimacassar.

visión *nf* (a) (*Anat*) vision, (eye)sight; **perder la** — **de un ojo** to lose the sight in one eye.

(b) vision (*also Rel*); fantasy; illusion; **se le apareció en** — it came to him in a vision; **ver** —**es** to be seeing things, suffer delusions.

(c) view; — **de conjunto** complete picture, overall view; **su** — **del problema** his view of the problem.

(d) (*pej*) scarecrow, fright; **ella iba hecha una** — she looked a real fright; **han comprado una** — **de cuadro** they've bought a frightful picture, they've bought an absolutely ghastly picture (*fam*).

visionario 1 *adj* (a) visionary.

(b) (*pej*) deluded, subject to hallucinations.

2 *nm*, **visionaria** *nf* (a) visionary.

(b) (*pej*) deluded person, crazy individual.

visir *nm* vizier; **gran** — grand vizier.

visita *nf* (a) visit; call; **derecho de** — right of search; — **de cortesía**, — **de cumplido** formal visit, courtesy call; — **de despedida** farewell visit; — **de médico** (*fam*) very short call; — **de pésame** call to express one's condolences; **estar de** — **en** to be on a visit to; **hacer una** —, **rendir una** — to visit, pay a visit; **devolver una** —, **pagar una** — to return a visit.

(b) (*person*) visitor, caller; **hoy tenemos** — we have visitors today.

(c) (*Per*, *PR*) enema.

visitación *nf* (*Eccl*) visitation.

visitador *nm*, **visitadora** *nf* (a) frequent visitor, person much given to calling.

(b) inspector.

(c) **visitadora** *nf* (*SAm*) syringe; enema.

visitante 1 *adj* visiting. 2 *nmf* visitor.

visitar [1a] 1 *vt* to visit; to call on, go and see; *museum*, *city etc* to visit; (*officially*) to visit; inspect.

2 **visitarse** *vr* (a) (*two persons*) to visit each other.

(b) (*Med*) to ask the doctor to call.

visiteo *nm* frequent visiting, constant calling.

visitero 1 *adj* fond of visiting, much given to calling.

2 *nm*, **visitera** *nf* frequent visitor, constant caller.

visitón *nm* (*fam*) long and boring visit; visitation.

vislumbrar [1a] *vt* (a) to glimpse, catch a glimpse of, see briefly.

(b) (*fig*) to glimpse, see some slight possibility of; *solution etc* to begin to see; *future* to get a slight idea of, make a conjecture about; *unknown fact etc* to surmise.

vislumbre *nf* (a) glimpse, brief view.

(b) gleam, glimmer.

(c) (*fig*) glimmer; slight possibility; vague idea; conjecture; **tener** —**s de** to get an inkling of, get a vague idea of.

viso *nm* (a) (*of metal*) gleam, glint.

(b) (*of cloth*) —**s** sheen, gloss; shot-silk appearance; **negro con** —**s azules** black with a bluish sheen, black with bluish lights in it; **a dos** —**s**, **de dos** —**s** (*fig*) with a double purpose, two-edged; **hacer** —**s** to shimmer.

(c) (*fig*) appearance; **hay un** — **de verdad en esto** this has the appearance of truth, there is an element of truth in this; **tiene** —**s de ser puro cuento** it looks like being just a tale; **tenía** — **de nunca acabar** it seemed that it was never going to finish.

(d) (*Sew*) coloured undergarment (*worn under a filmy outer garment*).

(e) (*Geog*) viewpoint, vantage point.

(f) **ser persona de** — to be a somebody, have some standing.

visón *nm* mink.

visor *nm* (a) (*Aer*) bombsight. (b) (*Phot*: *also* — **de imagen**) viewfinder.

víspera *nf* eve, day before, evening before; — **de Navidad** Christmas Eve; **la** — **de**, **en** —**s de** on the eve of (*also fig*); **estar en** —**s de** + *infin* to be on the point of + *ger*, be on the verge of + *ger*.

vista 1 *nf* (a) (*Anat*) sight, eyesight, vision; (*act*) look, gaze, glance; — **de águila**, — **de lince** very keen sight, eagle eye; — **corta** short sight; — **doble** double vision; second sight; ¡— **a la derecha!** (*Mil*) eyes right!

(b) (*general sense*: *phrases with prep*) **a primera** — at first sight; on the face of it; **traducción hecha a primera** — unseen translation; **a simple** — with

the naked eye; at a glance; **lo teníamos a la** — we could see it, we had it before our eyes; **la parte que quedaba a la** — the part that was visible (*or* uncovered); **no tenemos ningún cambio a la** — we do not have any change in view; **está a la** — **que** ... it is obvious that ...; **estar a la** — **de** to be within sight of; **a la** — **de muchas personas** in the presence of many people; **a la** — **de todo el mundo** openly, publicly, for all to see; **a la** — **de tal espectáculo** at the sight of such a scene, on beholding such a scene; **a la** — **de sus informes** in the light of his reports; **estaré a la** — **de lo que pase** I will keep an eye on developments; **yo me quedo a la** — **del fuego** I'll keep an eye on the fire; **con la** — **puesta en** with one's eyes (*fig*: thoughts) fixed on; **conocer a uno de** — to know somebody by sight; **en plena** — in full view; **en** — **de** (*fig*) in view of; **en** — **de que** ... in view of the fact that ...; **¡hasta la** —! au revoir!; so long!; **hasta donde alcanza la** — as far as the eye can see; **no muy agradable para la** — not a pretty sight, not nice to look at.

(c) (*general sense*: *phrases with verb*) **aguzar la** — to look sharp, look more carefully; **alzar la** — to look up; (*fig*) to raise one's eyes to; **alzar la** — **a uno** (*fig*) to turn to someone for help; **apartar la** — to look away, glance away; (*fig*) to turn a blind eye (*de* to); **bajar la** — to look down; to cast one's eyes down; **clavar la** — **en** to stare at, fix one's eyes on; to clap eyes on; **comer** (*or* **devorar**) **con la** — to look angrily at; to look curiously at; to look lovingly (*pej*: lustfully) at; **dirigir la** — **a** to look at, look towards; to turn one's gaze on; **echar una** — **a** to take a look at; **fijar la** — **en** to stare at, fix one's eyes on; **hacer la** — **gorda** to pretend not to notice, turn a blind eye; **hacer la** — **gorda a** to wink at, close one's eyes to; **luz que hiere la** — light that dazzles, light that hurts one's eyes; **medir a uno con la** — to size someone up; **se me nubló la** — my eyes became dazed; **pasar la** — **por** to look over, glance quickly at; **perder algo de** — to lose sight of something (*also fig*); **se pierde de** — (*fig*) he's very sharp, he's terribly clever; **no perder a uno de** — to keep someone in sight; **poner algo a la** — to put something on view; **recorrer algo con la** — to run one's eye over something; **salta a la** — it hits you in the eye; **torcer la** — to squint; **volver la** — to look back (*also fig*); to look away; **nunca volvió la** — **atrás** he never looked back, he never had regrets about the past.

(d) (*Comm*) **a la** — at sight, on sight; **a 30 días** — thirty days after sight.

(e) (*of object*) appearance, looks; **un coche con una** — **estupenda** a splendid-looking car; **de** — **poco agradable** of unattractive appearance, unprepossessing; **a la** —, **no son pobres** from what one can see, they're not poor.

(f) (*fig*) foresight, perception; **ha tenido mucha** — he was very far-sighted.

(g) (*fig*) intention; **con** —**s a una solución del problema** with a view to solving the problem.

(h) (*of scene etc*) view, scene, vista, panorama; —**s** (*from house etc*) outlook; (*fig*) outlook, prospect; **la** — **desde el castillo** the view from the castle; — **anterior**, — **frontal** front view; **con** —**s a la montaña** with views across to the mountains; **con** —**s al mar** overlooking the sea; **con** —**s al oeste** facing west, with westerly aspect.

(i) (*Art*, *Phot etc*) view; — **fija** still; — **de pájaro** bird's-eye view; **una tarjeta con una** — **de Venecia** a card with a view of Venice.

(j) (*Law*) hearing; trial; — **de una causa** hearing of a case.

(k) (*Hist*) —**s** meeting, conference.

2 *nm* customs inspector.

vistazo *nm* look, glance; **de un** — at a glance; **dar un** — (*fam*) to pop in, drop in; **dar un** — **a**, **echar un** — **a** to glance at, take a look at, have a quick look at.

vistillas *nfpl* viewpoint, height, high place.

visto 1 *ptp of* **ver**.

2 *ptp and adj* (a) — **todo esto** in view of all this; **por lo** — evidently, apparently; by the look of it; **ni** — **ni oído** like lightning; **cosa no vista**, **cosa nunca vista** an unheard-of thing.

(b) — **bueno** approved, passed, O.K. (*fam*).

(c) **está muy** — it is very commonly worn (*or* used), one sees it about a lot; (*pej*) it's old, it's right out of fashion.

(d) **está** — **que** ... it is clear that ...; **estaba** — **que** it had to be, it was expected all along.

(e) **lo que está bien** — what is socially acceptable, what is done; **eso está muy mal** — that's not done, that is thought highly improper; **está muy**

mal — que una joven vaya sola it is thought most improper for a girl to go alone.
3 — que . . . *conj* seeing that . . .; since . . ., inasmuch as . . .
4 — bueno *nm* approval, O.K. (*fam*), authorization.
vistosamente *adv* showily, colourfully; attractively; (*pej*) gaudily.
vistosidad *nf* showiness, colourfulness; attractiveness; (*pej*) gaudiness.
vistoso *adj* showy, colourful; gay, attractive; (*pej*) gaudy.
visual 1 *adj* visual. **2** *nf* (a) line of sight. (b) (*fam*) look, glance; **echar una —** to take a look (*a* at).
visualizar [1f] *vt* (*SAm*: *angl*) (a) to see, make out, descry. (b) (*fig*) to visualize.
visualmente *adv* visually.
vital *adj* life (*attr*), living (*attr*); **espacio —** living space, (*Pol*) lebensraum.
  (b) (*fig*) vital, essential, fundamental; **de importancia —** of vital importance.
  (c) (*fig*) person vital, full of vitality.
vitalicio 1 *adj* life (*attr*); for life; **cargo —** post held for life; **interés —** life interest. **2** *nm* life annuity.
vitalidad *nf* vitality.
vitalizar [1f] *vt* (*esp SAm*: *angl*) to vitalize; to revitalize.
vitamina *nf* vitamin.
vitaminado *adj* vitaminized.
vitaminar [1a] *vt* to vitaminize, add vitamins to.
vitamínico *adj* vitamin (*attr*).
vitela *nf* vellum.
vitícola *adj* vine (*attr*), vine-growing (*attr*).
viticultor *nm* vine grower; proprietor of a vineyard.
viticultura *nf* vine growing, viticulture.
vitoco *adj* (*Ven*) vain, swanky (*fam*).
vitola *nf* (a) cigar band. (b) looks, appearance, general air.
vitoquear [1a] *vi* (*Ven*) to be conceited, swank (*fam*).
vítor 1 *interj* hurrah! **2** *nm* cheer; **entre los —es de la multitud** among the cheers of the crowd.
vitorear [1a] *vt* to cheer, acclaim.
vítreo *adj* glassy, vitreous; glass-like.
vitrificación *nf* vitrification.
vitrificar [1g] **1** *vt* to vitrify. **2 vitrificarse** *vr* to vitrify.
vitrina *nf* (a) glass case, showcase; display cabinet. (b) (*SAm*) shop window.
vitriolo *nm* vitriol.
vitrola *nf* (*SAm*) gramophone, phonograph (*US*).
vitualla *nf*, **vituallas** *nfpl* provisions, victuals.
vituperable *adj* to be condemned, worthy of censure.
vituperación *nf* condemnation, censure.
vituperar [1a] *vt* to condemn, censure, inveigh against.
vituperio *nm* (a) condemnation; reproach, censure; insult; **—s** abuse, insults; vituperation. (b) stigma, dishonour.
vituperioso *adj* abusive; vituperative.
viuda *nf* (a) widow; **— verde** merry widow (*euph*). (b) (*Arg, Ec, Per*) ghost. (c) (*Col*) fish stew. (d) (*Cu*) large kite.
viudedad *nf* (a) (*esp SAm*) widowhood. (b) (*Fin*) widow's pension.
viudez *nf* widowhood.
viudo 1 *adj* widowed; **estar viuda** (*fam*) to be temporarily widowed, have one's husband away. **2** *nm* widower.
viva *nm* cheer; **dar un —** to give a cheer; **prorrumpir en —s** to start to cheer, burst out cheering.
vivac *nm*, *pl* **vivacs** bivouac.
vivacidad *nf* (a) vigour. (b) liveliness, vivacity; keenness, sharpness; brightness.
vivales *nm*, *pl* **vivales** (*fam*) person who is quick to look after his own interests, clever person on the make (*fam*).
vivamente *adv* in lively fashion; *describe, remember etc* vividly; *protest* sharply, strongly; *feel* acutely, intensely; **lo siento —** I am deeply sorry, I sincerely regret it; **se lo deseo —** I sincerely hope he gets it.
vivaque *nm* bivouac.
vivaquear [1a] *vi* to bivouac.
vivar[1] *nm* (a) (*Zool*) warren. (b) (*Fish*) fishpond; fish nursery.
vivar[2] [1a] *vt* (*SAm*) to cheer.
vivaracho *adj* person jaunty, lively, sprightly; *girl* vivacious; superficially attractive; bouncy; *eyes* bright, lively, twinkling.
vivaz *adj* (a) long-lived; enduring, lasting; (*Bot*) perennial. (b) vigorous. (c) lively; keen, sharp, quick-witted.
víveres *nmpl* provisions; (*esp Mil*) stores, supplies.
vivero *nm* (a) (*Hort etc*) nursery; seedbed; tree nursery.

(b) (*Fish*) fishpond; fish nursery; (*Zool*) vivarium; **— de ostras** oyster bed.
  (c) (*fig*) hotbed; **es un — de discordias** it's a hotbed of discord.
viveza *nf* liveliness, vividness; brightness; sharpness; strength, depth, intensity; acuteness; **la — de su inteligencia** the sharpness of his mind; **la — de sus sentimientos** the strength of his feelings; the sincerity of his regret; **contestar con —** to answer sharply, answer with spirit.
vividero *adj* habitable, inhabitable, that can be lived in.
vivido *adj* personally experienced; **un episodio — por el autor** an episode which the author himself lived (through).
vívido *adj* vivid, graphic.
vividor 1 *adj* (*pej*) sharp, clever; unscrupulous. **2** *nm* wide boy (*fam*).
vivienda *nf* (a) (*in general*) housing, accommodation; **escasez de —s** housing shortage; **el problema de la —** the housing problem.
  (b) (*una —*) dwelling, accommodation unit; flat, apartment (*US*), tenement; **— campestre** small house in the country, cottage; **bloque de —s** block of flats, block of tenements; **—s para obreros** workers' flats.
viviente *adj* living; **los —s** the living.
vivificador *adj*, **vivificante** *adj* life-giving; (*fig*) revitalizing.
vivificar [1g] *vt* (a) to give life to, vivify. (b) (*fig*) to revitalize, bring to life, bring new life to; to enliven.
vivillo *adj* and *nm* (*RPl*) = **vividor**.
vivíparo *adj* viviparous.
vivir [3a] **1** *vt* to live through; to experience, go through; **los que hemos vivido la guerra** those of us who lived through the war; **ha vivido momentos de verdadera angustia** she went through moments of real agony.
  2 *vi* (a) to live (*en* at, in); **— bien** to live well, be prosperous; to live an honest life; (*of 2 people*) to live happily together, live in harmony; **— para ver** to live and learn; **¡viva!** hurray!; **¡viva el rey!** long live the king!; hurray for the king!; **¿quién vive?** (*Mil*) who goes there?; **dar el quién vive a uno** to challenge someone; **saber —** to know how to get the best out of life; **no dejar — a uno** to bother someone, harass someone; **no le dejan —** los celos she is eaten up with jealousy; **no vivo de intranquilidad** I'm worried to death; **ya no vivo de vergüenza** the shame of it is killing me.
  (b) (*Fin*) to live (*de* by, off, on); **— muy justo** to be hard up, have only just enough to live on; **— dentro de los medios** to live within one's means; **— por encima de sus posibilidades** to live beyond one's means; **— de la pluma** to live by one's pen; **— de las rentas** to live on one's income (from property *etc*); **no tienen con qué —** they haven't enough to live on; **ganar lo justo para —** to earn a bare living.
  (c) (*fig*) to last (out); **el abrigo no vivirá mucho** the coat won't last much longer.
  (d) (*fig* of memory) to live, remain.
  3 *nm* life, way of life; living; **de mal —** dissolute, loose-living; criminal, delinquent.
vivisección *nf* vivisection.
vivo 1 *adj* (a) (*general sense*) living; live, alive; *flesh* living, raw; *language* living; **los —s y los muertos** the living and the dead; **los venden en —** they sell them alive; **transmitir algo en —** to broadcast something live; **le ha llegado al —** it touched him on the raw, it really came home to him; **me dio** (*or* **hirió**) **en lo más —** it got me on the raw, it cut me to the quick.
  (b) (*fig*) *description* lively, vivid, graphic; *memory, scene* vivid; *flash etc* bright, sudden; *eyes, look, rhythm* lively; *movement, pace* quick, lively; *colour* bright; rich, vivid; *edge* sharp; *protest etc* sharp, strong; *feeling* strong, deep, intense; *pain* sharp, acute; *temper* sharp, quick; *intelligence* sharp, keen, acute; *wit* ready; *imagination* lively; **¡—!** hurry up!; **describir algo al —** (*or a lo —*) to describe something to the life, describe something very realistically; **lo explica al —** (*or a lo —*) he explains it very expressively.
  (c) (*fig*) person sharp, clever; lively; (*pej*) sharp; (*esp SAm*) sly, crafty; unscrupulous.
  (d) (*Chi*) naughty.
  2 *nm* (*Sew*) trimming, edging, border.
vizcaíno 1 *adj* Biscayan. **2** *nm*, **vizcaína** *nf* Biscayan.
Vizcaya *f* Biscay (*Spanish province*).
vizcondado *nm* viscounty.
vizconde *nm* viscount.
vizcondesa *nf* viscountess.

vocablo nm word; term; **jugar del —** to make a pun, play on words.

vocabulario nm vocabulary.

vocación nf vocation, calling; **errar la —** to miss one's vocation; **tener — por** to have a vocation for.

vocacional adj vocational.

vocal 1 adj vocal. 2 nm member (of a committee etc); director, member of the board of directors. 3 nf (Ling) vowel.

vocálico adj vocalic, vowel (attr).

vocalismo nm vowel system.

vocalista nmf vocalist, singer.

vocalizar [1f] 1 vt to vocalize. 2 vi (Mus) to hum; to sing scales, practise. 3 **vocalizarse** vr to vocalize.

vocalmente adv vocally.

vocativo nm vocative.

voceador 1 adj loud, loud-mouthed, vociferous. 2 nm (a) town crier. (b) (Col, Ec, Mex) newsboy, paperboy.

vocear [1a] 1 vt (a) wares to cry.
  (b) person to call loudly to, shout to, shout the name of.
  (c) person to cheer, acclaim.
  (d) secret etc to shout to all and sundry, proclaim from the rooftops; (fig) to proclaim; **su cara voceaba su culpabilidad** his face proclaimed his guilt.
  (e) (fam) to boast publicly about, lay public claim to.
  2 vi to shout, yell, bawl.

vocejón nm loud voice, big voice.

voceo nm shouting, yelling, bawling.

vocería nf, **vocerío** nm shouting, yelling; clamour, uproar, hullabaloo (fam).

vocero nm spokesman.

vociferación nf vociferation.

vociferador adj loud, loud-mouthed.

vociferar [1a] 1 vt (a) to shout, scream, vociferate. (b) to proclaim boastfully. 2 vi to shout, yell, clamour.

vocinglería nf (a) clamour, uproar. (b) (quality) loudness, noisiness; garrulity.

vocinglero adj (a) vociferous, loud, loud-mouthed. (b) loquacious, garrulous. (c) (fig) blatant.

vodevil nm (gall) vaudeville (US), music hall, variety show (or theatre).

vodka nf vodka.

vodú nm (SAm) voodoo.

voduísmo nm (SAm) voodooism.

volada nf (a) short flight, single flight. (b) (SAm: various senses) = **bolada**.

voladizo adj (Archit) projecting.

volado 1 adj (a) (Typ) superior, raised.
  (b) **estar — to** be worried, feel anxious (con about); to be ill-at-ease.
  (c) (Arg, Mex) projecting; protuberant, big.
  (d) (Arg, Mex) **— de genio** quick-tempered.
  (e) (Cu, Guat, Mex) **estar —** to be in love; to be full of hope.
  2 nm (a) (CAm) = **bolado** (c).
  (b) (RPl, Ven) flounce, ruffle.
  (c) (Mex) game of heads or tails.
  (d) (Mex) adventure; incident, happening.
  3 adv (Col, Guat, Mex) hastily.

volador 1 adj (a) flying.
  (b) (fig) swift; fleeting.
  2 nm (a) (Fish) flying fish; (Zool) (species of) squid.
  (b) rocket.
  (c) (CAm, Col) toy windmill; (Ven) kite.

voladura nf blowing up, demolition; blast.

volandas: en — adv (a) in the air, through the air. (b) (fig) swiftly, as if on wings; **¡voy en —!** (hum) I fly!

volandera nf (a) millstone, grindstone. (b) (on wheel) washer. (c) (fam) fib.

volandero adj (a) part loose, movable, not fixed; leaf, rope etc loose; pain that moves about.
  (b) random, casual; unexpected.
  (c) (Orn) fledged, ready to fly; (fig) person restless.

volanta nf (a) (Col, PR) flywheel; large wheel. (b) (Cu, Mex, PR) cart with big wheels; (Mex) small car.

volante 1 adj (a) flying; **ciervo —** stag beetle; **escuadrón —** flying squad; **hoja —** leaflet, handbill, pamphlet.
  (b) (fig) unsettled.
  2 nm (a) (Tech) flywheel; (of watch) balance.
  (b) (Aut) steering wheel; **ir al —** to be at the wheel, be driving.
  (c) note.
  (d) (Sport) shuttlecock; (**juego del**) — badminton.

  (e) (Sport: person) winger.
  (f) (Sew) flounce, ruffle.
  (g) (SAm) driver; racing driver.

volantín 1 adj loose, unattached. 2 nm (a) fishing line. (b) (SAm) kite. (c) (Bol) rocket. (d) (SAm) somersault.

volantista nm driver; racing driver.

volantón 1 adj fledged, ready to fly. 2 nm fledgling.

volantusa nf (SAm) prostitute.

volantuzo nm (Per) toff (fam), dandy.

volapié nm (Taur) wounding thrust; **a —** (of bird) half walking and half flying; **de —** (fam) in a split second.

volar [1m] 1 vt (a) building, bridge etc to blow up, demolish (with explosive); mine to explode; rock to blast.
  (b) (Hunting) to put up, put to flight, rouse.
  (c) (fam) to irritate, upset, exasperate.
  (d) (SAm) to put to flight.
  (e) (CAm) **— lengua** to talk, speak; **— diente** to eat; **— pata** to walk; **— máquina** to type.
  (f) (Mex) to pinch (fam).
  (g) (Mex) to swindle.
  (h) (Mex) to flirt with.
  2 vi (a) (general sense) to fly; to fly away, fly off; to get blown away; **una alfombra que vuela** a carpet that flies, a flying carpet; **— a solas** to fly solo; **echar a — una noticia** to spread a piece of news; **echarse a —** (fig) to leave the parental nest.
  (b) (fig: of time) to fly, pass swiftly; (of news) to spread rapidly.
  (c) (fig) to fly; to rush, hurry; (of car etc) to scorch, hurtle (along, past etc), go like the wind; **¡volando!** get a move on!; **voy volando** I'll go as quickly as I can; **prepárame volando la cena** get my supper double-quick, please; **— a + infin** to fly to + infin, rush to + infin.
  (d) (fam) to fly, disappear, vanish, walk (fam); **han volado mis pitillos** my fags have walked.
  (e) (SAm: Cards) to bluff.
  3 **volarse** vr (a) to fly away.
  (b) (SAm) to get angry, lose one's temper.
  (c) (Mex) **— algo** to spirit something away.

volate nm (a) (Col) confusion, mess. (b) (Col) lot of odd things. (c) (Ven) great show of despair (or impatience etc).

volatería nf (a) (Hunting) hawking, falconry; fowling.
  (b) (Orn) birds; fowls; flock of birds.
  (c) (fig) random thoughts, formless collection of ideas.
  (d) (Ec) fireworks.

volatero nm (Ec) rocket.

volátil adj (a) volatile. (b) (fig) changeable, inconstant.

volatilidad nf (a) volatility, volatile nature. (b) (fig) changeableness, inconstancy.

volatilizar [1f] 1 vt (a) to volatilize, vaporize.
  (b) (fig) to spirit away, cause to vanish.
  2 **volatilizarse** vr (a) to volatilize, vaporize.
  (b) (fig) to vanish into thin air.

volatín nm (a) acrobatics, tightrope walking. (b) = **volatinero**.

volatinero nm, **volatinera** nf acrobat, tightrope walker.

volcán nm (a) volcano.
  (b) (Arg, Bol, Col) summer torrent, avalanche.
  (c) (CAm, PR) pile, heap; **un — de cosas** a lot of things, a whole heap of things.
  (d) (PR) deafening noise; confusion, hubbub.
  (e) (Col) breakdown; collapse, fall.

volcanada nf (Chi) puff of air; whiff (of smell).

volcanarse [1a] vr (Col) to break down; to collapse, fall down.

volcánico adj volcanic.

volcar [1g and 1m] 1 vt (a) container to upset, overturn, tip over, knock over; (deliberately) to empty out; contents to upset; to empty out; lorry etc to tip; contents to dump, shoot; car etc to overturn; boat to overturn, capsize, upset.
  (b) (fig) **— a uno** to make someone dizzy, make someone's head swim.
  (c) (fig) **— a uno** to force someone to change his mind.
  (d) (fig) to irritate, exasperate; to upset; to tease.
  2 vi (of car etc) to overturn.
  3 **volcarse** vr (a) (container) to be upset, get overturned; to tip over; (car etc) to overturn; (boat) to capsize.
  (b) (fig) to go out of one's way, be excessively kind; **— para (or por) conseguir algo** to do one's

utmost to get something; — **por complacer a uno** to lean over backwards to satisfy someone.
volea *nf* volley; **media** — half-volley.
volear [1a] *vti* to volley.
voleibol *nm* (*SAm*) volleyball.
voleo *nm* (**a**) volley; **de un** —, **del primer** — quickly; brusquely, suddenly; at one blow; **sembrar a** (*or* **al**) — to broadcast the seed, sow the seed by the handful; **repartir algo a** (*or* **al**) — to distribute something haphazardly.
   (**b**) (*fam*) punch.
volframio *nm* wolfram.
volibol *nm* volleyball.
volición *nf* volition.
volido *nm* (*SAm*) flight; **de un** — quickly, at once.
volquete *nm* tipcart; dumping lorry, dumper, dump truck (*US*).
voltaico *adj* voltaic.
voltaje *nm* voltage.
voltario *adj* (*Chi*) (**a**) fickle, changeable. (**b**) wilful, headstrong. (**c**) spruce, dapper.
volteada *nf* (**a**) (*RPl*) roundup. (**b**) (*CAm, Chi, Mex*) defection.
volteado *nm* (*Col*) deserter; switch of political allegiance.
volteador *nm*, **volteadora** *nf* acrobat.
voltear [1a] **1** *vt* (**a**) to turn over, roll over; to turn upside down; to turn round; *container* to upset, overturn; (*SAm*) *back etc* to turn; (*Chi, Mex, RPl*) to knock down; to knock over, spill.
   (**b**) *bells* to peal.
   (**c**) to throw into the air; (*of bull*) to toss.
   (**d**) (*esp SAm*) *lasso etc* to whirl, twirl.
   (**e**) (*Col, Chi, PR*) — **a uno** to force someone to change his mind.
   (**f**) (*Arg, PR*) to search all over.
   2 *vi* to roll over, go rolling over and over; to somersault.
   3 voltearse *vr* (*SAm*) to change one's allegiance, go over to the other side; to change one's ideas.
voltereta *nf* somersault; roll, tumble; — **sobre las manos** handspring.
voltímetro *nm* voltmeter.
voltio *nm* volt.
volubilidad *nf* fickleness, changeableness; unpredictability; instability.
voluble *adj* (**a**) (*Bot*) twining, clinging; climbing. (**b**) *person* fickle, changeable; erratic, unpredictable; unstable.
volumen *nm* (**a**) volume; bulk, bulkiness; mass; — **sonoro** volume (of sound); — **de negocios**, — **de ventas** amount of business done, volume of business, turnover; — **de capital invertido** amount of capital invested; **una operación de mucho** — a sizeable operation; **poner la radio a todo** — to turn the radio up full (*or* as loud as possible).
   (**b**) (*Typ*) volume.
volumétrico *adj* volumetric.
voluminoso *adj* voluminous; sizeable, bulky, massive.
voluntad *nf* (**a**) will; willpower; volition; wish, desire; intention; **buena** — goodwill; good intention, honest intention; **mala** — ill will, malice; evil intent; **última** — last wish, (*Law*) last will and testament; — **débil** weak will, lack of willpower; — **divina** divine will; — **férrea**, — **de hierro** will of iron; **a** — at will; at one's discretion; *quantity* as much as one likes; **se abre a** — it opens whenever you want it to; **a** — **de uno** as one wishes; **por causas ajenas a mi** — for reasons beyond my control; **por** — **propia** of one's own volition, of one's own free will; **su** — **es** + *infin* his wish is to + *infin*; **no lo dije con** — **de** + *infin* I did not say so with any wish to + *infin*, I did not say it with any intention of + *ger*; **hacer su santa** — to do exactly as one pleases, have one's own way at all costs; **hace falta** — **para escucharlo hasta el final** you need a strong will to sit right through it; **ganar(se) la** — **de uno** to win someone over; to dominate someone's will; **no tener** — **propia** to have no will of one's own; **no tiene** — **para dejar de beber** he hasn't the willpower to give up drinking; **reiterar su** — **de** + *infin* to reaffirm one's intention to + *infin*; **le viene** — **de** + *infin* he feels a need to + *infin*, he feels like + *ger*.
   (**b**) (*fam*) fondness, affection; **tener** — **a** to be fond of, feel affection for.
voluntariamente *adv* voluntarily.
voluntariedad *nf* wilfulness, unreasonableness.
voluntario 1 *adj* (**a**) voluntary. (**b**) (*Mil*) voluntary; *force etc* voluntary. **2** *nm* volunteer.
voluntariosamente *adv* wilfully, unreasonably. (**b**) dedicatedly, in a well-intentioned way.

voluntarioso *adj* (**a**) (*pej*) headstrong, wilful, unreasonable. (**b**) dedicated, full of honest endeavour, well-intentioned.
voluptuosamente *adv* voluptuously; (*pej*) sensually.
voluptuosidad *nf* voluptuousness; (*pej*) sensuality.
voluptuoso 1 *adj* voluptuous; (*pej*) sensual. **2** *nm*, **voluptuosa** *nf* voluptuary; sensualist.
voluta *nf* (**a**) (*Archit*) scroll, volute. (**b**) (*of smoke*) spiral, column; (*from cigarette etc*) curl, ring.
volvedor 1 *adj* (*Col, Guat, RPl*) *horse etc* that knows its way home; that tends to make for its home area.
   2 *nm* (**a**) wrench; screwdriver.
   (**b**) (*Col*) bonus, extra.
volver [2h; *ptp* **vuelto**] **1** *vt* (**a**) *object* to turn, turn round, turn over, turn upside down; to turn back to front; *back, head* to turn; (*Cook*) to turn (over); (*Sew*) to turn inside out; *soil* to turn over; *eyes* to turn (*a* on, towards), cast (*a* on); *weapon* to aim (*a* at), turn (*a* on); — **un calcetín** to turn a sock inside out; **tener a uno vuelto como un calcetín** (*or* **media**) to have got someone where one wants him; — **el pensamiento a Dios** to turn one's thoughts to God; **me volvió la espalda** he turned his back on me (*see also* **espalda**); — **la proa al viento** to turn the bow into the wind; — **la vista atrás** to look back.
   (**b**) *page* to turn (over); *door, window* to push open, swing open; to close, pull to, swing to.
   (**c**) *sleeves etc* to roll up.
   (**d**) *object thrown etc* to turn back, send back, return; *food* to bring up; *image* to reflect.
   (**e**) (*fam*) to return, give back, send back; *change* to give; *visit* to repay, return; — **algo a su lugar** to return something to its place, put something back (in its place); — **bien por mal** to return good for evil.
   (**f**) to change, turn, transform; (+ *adj*) to turn, make, render; — **la casa a su estado original** to restore a house to its original state; **vuelve fieras a los hombres** it turns men into wild beasts; **esto le vuelve furioso** this makes him mad; **todo lo volvió muy triste** it made it all very sad; **el ácido lo vuelve azul** the acid turns it blue; *see* **loco**.
   (**g**) (*Ling*) to translate (*a* into).
   2 *vi* (**a**) (*of road, traveller etc*) to turn (*a* to).
   (**b**) to return (*a* to, *de* from), come back, go back, get back; — **atrás** to go back, turn back; — **victorioso** to come back victorious, return in triumph; **volvió muy cansado** he got back tired out; — **a una costumbre** to revert to a habit; **volviendo ahora a mi tema . . .** returning (*or* reverting) now to my theme . . .
   (**c**) — **a hacer algo** to do something again; **han vuelto a pintar la casa** they have painted the house again; **he vuelto a salir con ella** I've started going out with her again.
   (**d**) — **en sí** to come to, come round, regain consciousness; — **sobre sí** to give up an idea, change one's mind; — **por** to come out in defence (*or* support) of, stand up for.
   3 volverse *vr* (**a**) to turn round, turn over, turn upside down, turn inside out; **se le volvió el paraguas** his umbrella turned inside out; **se volvió riendo a mí** she turned laughingly to me; **se volvió para mirarlo** he turned (round) to look at it; — **atrás** (*fig*) to look back; (*fig*) to back down, go back on one's word; — **contra uno** to turn on someone.
   (**b**) = **2** (**b**); **vuélvete a buscarlo** go back and look for it.
   (**c**) (+ *adj*) to turn, become, go, get; **se ha vuelto imposible** he has become quite impossible; **en el ácido se vuelve más oscuro** it turns darker in the acid; **todo se le vuelve dificultades** troubles come thick and fast for him; *see* **loco** *etc*.
   (**d**) (*wine etc*) to go off, turn sour.
vomitado *adj person* sickly, seedy.
vomitar [1a] **1** *vt* (**a**) to vomit, bring up, throw up; — **sangre** to spit blood.
   (**b**) (*fig*) *flames, smoke etc* to belch, belch forth; *lava* to spew, throw up, hurl out; *insults* to hurl (*contra* at).
   (**c**) (*fig*) *secret* to tell reluctantly, finally come out with; *profits etc* to disgorge, shed.
   2 *vi* (**a**) to vomit, be sick.
   (**b**) (*fig*) **eso me da ganas de** — that makes me sick, that turns my stomach.
vomitera *nf* (*Cu, PR*), **vomitina** *nf* vomiting, retching.
vomitivo 1 *adj* emetic. **2** *nm* (**a**) (*Med*) emetic. (**b**) (*Chi*) nuisance, bore.
vómito *nm* (**a**) (*act*) vomiting, being sick; — **de sangre** spitting of blood. (**b**) vomit.
vomitona *nf* (*fam*) bad sick turn.

voquible nm (hum) word.
voracear [1a] vt (Arg) to challenge in a loud voice.
voracidad nf voracity, voraciousness.
vorágine nf whirlpool, vortex, maelstrom; (fig) maelstrom; whirl.
voraz adj (a) voracious, ravenous; greedy. (b) (fig) fire all-devouring, fierce. (c) (Mex) bold.
vorazmente adv voraciously, ravenously; greedily.
vórtice nm (a) whirlpool, vortex; whirlwind. (b) (Meteorol) cyclone, hurricane.
vos personal pronoun pl (arch) you, ye; (in certain SAm countries) you (in singular sense).
vosear [1a] vt (SAm) to address as "vos" (ie, treat familiarly).
voseo nm (SAm) addressing a person as "vos", familiar usage.
Vosgos nmpl Vosges.
vosotros, vosotras personal pronoun pl (a) (subject) you.
(b) (after prep) you; yourselves; **entre —** among yourselves; **irán sin —** they'll go without you; ¿no **pedís nada para —?** are you not asking anything for yourselves?
votación nf voting; vote; **— por manos levantadas** show of hands; **por — popular** by popular vote; **por — secreta** by secret vote, by secret ballot; **la — ha sido nutrida** voting has been heavy; **someter algo a —** to put something to the vote, take a vote on something.
votante 1 adj voting. **2** nmf voter.
votar [1a] **1** vt (a) (Pol) candidate, party to vote for; bill, motion to pass, approve (by vote).
(b) (Eccl) to vow, promise (a to).
2 vi (a) (Pol etc) to vote (por for).
(b) (Eccl) to vow, take a vow.
votivo adj votive.
voto nm (a) (Pol etc) vote; **— de calidad, — decisivo** casting vote; **— de censura** vote of censure; **— de confianza** vote of confidence; **— de desconfianza** vote of no confidence; **— de gracias** vote of thanks; **— secreto** secret vote, secret ballot; **dar su — to** cast one's vote (a for), give one's vote (a to); **emitir su —** to cast one's vote, give one's opinion; **ganar por 7 —s** to win by 7 votes; **hubo 13 —s a favor y 11 en contra** there were 13 votes for and 11 against; **tener —** to have a vote.
(b) (Eccl) vow; **— de castidad** vow of chastity; **— de pobreza** vow of poverty; **—s monásticos** monastic vows; **hacer — de + infin** to take a vow to + infin.
(c) (Eccl) ex voto.
(d) oath, curse; swearword.
(e) **—s** wishes; good wishes; **mis mejores —s por su éxito** my best wishes for its success; **hacer —s por el restablecimiento de uno** to wish someone a quick recovery, hope that someone will get well; **hago —s para que se remedie pronto** I pray that it may be speedily put right, I earnestly hope that something will soon be done about it.
voy etc see **ir**.
voz nf (a) voice; **— argentina** silvery voice; **— empañada, — opaca** thin voice, voice weak with emotion; **la — de la conciencia** the voice of conscience, the promptings of conscience; **la — del pueblo** the voice of the people; **a una —** with one voice, unanimously; **a media —** in a low voice; **a — en cuello, a — en grito** at the top of one's voice; **de viva —** viva voce; by word of mouth, verbally; **en alta —** loud(ly), in a loud voice; see **bajo**; **estar en —** to be in good voice; (fam) to be fit, be ready for anything; **aclarar la —** to clear one's throat; **alzar la —,** **levantar la —** to raise one's voice; **ahuecar la —** to adopt a serious tone, try to make oneself sound impressive; **se me anudó la — (en la garganta)** I got a lump in my throat; **desanudar la —** to manage to speak again, find one's voice; **tener la — tomada** to be hoarse.
(b) (Mus etc) sound, note; (of thunder etc) noise; **la — del órgano** the sound of the organ, the strains of the organ.
(c) (Mus) voice, part; **canción a cuatro voces** song for four voices, four-part song; **cantar a dos voces** to sing a duet; **— cantante** leading part; **llevar la — cantante** (fig) to be the boss, have the chief say.
(d) shout; yell; **voces** shouts, shouting, yelling; **— de mando** (Mil) command; **dar (or pegar) voces** to shout, call out, yell; **dale una —** give him a shout; **dar la — de alarma** to sound the alarm; **dar cuatro voces** to make a great fuss; **discutir a voces** to argue noisily; **llamar a uno a voces** to shout to someone; **está pidiendo a voces que se remedie** it's crying out (to heaven) to be put right.
(e) (Cards) call.

(f) (fig) rumour; **— común** hearsay, gossip, rumour; **corre la — de que . . .** there is a rumour going round that . . .
(g) (fig: in meeting etc) voice, say; vote, support; **asistir con — y voto** to be present as a full member; **tener — y voto** to have a say; to have the right to speak; **no tener — en capítulo** to have no say in a matter; to have no influence, not count.
(h) (Ling) word; **una — de origen árabe** a word of Arabic origin.
(i) (Gram) voice; **— activa** active voice; **— pasiva** passive voice.
vozarrón nm loud voice, big voice.
vudú nm voodoo.
vuduísmo nm voodooism.
vuelco nm (a) upset, overturning, spill; **dar un —** to overturn.
(b) **mi corazón dio un —** my heart missed a beat; I had a presentiment.
(c) (fig) collapse; catastrophe, ruin; **este negocio va a dar un —** this business is heading for a catastrophe.
vuelillo nm lace, frill.
vuelo nm (a) flight; **— a ciegas** blind flying, flying on instruments; **— de ensayo** test flight; **— espacial** space flight; **— sin etapas** non-stop flight; **— sin motor, — a vela** gliding; **— de órbita** orbital flight; **— en picado** dive; **— a solas** solo flight; **alzar el —** to take flight, take off; (fig) to dash off; (fig) to leave the parental nest, spread one's wings; **se oía el — de una mosca** you could hear a pin drop; **remontar el —** to soar (up); **tocar las campanas a —** to peal the bells; **tomar —** to grow, develop; to assume great importance; **de —, en un —** (fig) rapidly.
(b) **al —:** **cazar (or coger) algo al —** to catch something in flight; (fig) to overhear something in passing; **tirar al —** to shoot at a bird on the wing; **cogerlas (or pescarlas, pillarlas etc) al —** (fig) to catch on immediately, get it at once; to be pretty smart.
(c) (Orn: also **—s**) flight feathers; wing, wings; **de altos —s** (fig) grandiose, far-reaching; **cortar los —s a uno** to clip someone's wings.
(d) (Sew: on cuff) lace, frill.
(e) (Sew: of skirt etc) loose part; **el — de la falda** the spread of the skirt, the swirl of the skirt; **falda de mucho —** full skirt, wide skirt.
(f) (Archit) projection, projecting part.
(g) (Bot) timber, trees, woodland.
vuelta nf (a) turn; (Astron, Mech etc) revolution; **una — de la tierra** one revolution of the earth; **— al mundo** trip round the world; **— atrás** backward step (also fig); **¡media —!** (Mil) about turn!; **— en redondo** complete turn; **a — de** by dint of; **andar a —s con** to be engaged in, be immersed in; **dar la — a una página** to turn a page; **dar la — al mundo** to go round the world; **el coche dio la —** the car turned over; **dar una — de campana** to overturn, turn completely over, somersault; **dar media —** (Mil) to face about; to turn half round; (fam) to beat it (fam); **al llegar allí hay que dar media —** when you get there make a half turn; **dar — a una llave** to turn a key; **dar — a un coche** to reverse a car, turn a car round; **el libro dio la — por muchas oficinas** the book went round a lot of offices, the book went the rounds in many offices; **dar —s** to turn, revolve, go round; (of head) to spin, swim, be in a whirl; **dar —s alrededor de un eje** to spin round an axle; **dar —s alrededor de un planeta** to revolve round a planet, go round a planet; **dar —s a una manivela** to turn (or wind, crank) a handle; **dar —s a un botón** to turn a knob; **dar —s a un asunto** to think a matter over, turn a matter over in one's mind; **le estás dando demasiadas —s** you're worrying too much about it; **dar —s a un palo entre los dedos** to twirl a stick in one's fingers; **no hay que darle —s** that's the way it is, there's no mistake about it; **poner a uno de — y media** to heap abuse on someone; to give someone a good telling-off.
(b) (fig) turn, change; volte-face, reversal; **— de la marea** turn of the tide; **las —s de la vida** the ups and downs of life; **dar la —, dar una —** to change right round, alter radically.
(c) (of river, road) bend, curve, turn; **— cerrada** sharp turn, tight bend; **en una — del río** at a bend in the river; **dar —s** to twist and turn.
(d) (of rope) loop; coil; **— de cabo** (Naut) hitch.
(e) (of election, talks, tournament etc) round; (in racing) lap, circuit; **— ciclista** long-distance cycle race; **V— de Francia** Tour de France (cycle race); **— de honor** lap of honour; **— al ruedo** (Taur) circuit of the ring made by a triumphant bullfighter;

dio 3 —s al ruedo he went round the ring 3 times; segunda — (*Univ*) repeat examinations, resits.

(**f**) (*of sausage etc*) round, slice.

(**g**) (*Sew*) row of stitches.

(**h**) (*Sew*) strip; facing; cuff; (*of trousers*) turn-up, cuff (*US*).

(**i**) (*of paper, cloth etc*) back, reverse, other side; a la — on the next page, overleaf; a la — de la esquina round the corner; a la — de varios años after some years; lo escribió a la — del sobre he wrote it on the back of the envelope; buscar las —s a uno to try to catch someone out; no tiene — de hoja there's no alternative; there are no two ways about it; there's no gainsaying it, it's unanswerable.

(**j**) (*act*) return; (*Rail etc*) return journey, homeward journey; a — de correo by return (of post); a la — on one's return; lo haré a la — I'll do it when I get back; de —, iremos a verlos we'll go and see them on the way back; estar de — to be back, be home (again); (*fam*) to have no illusions, know from experience; (*fam*) to be pretty clever; ¡hasta la —! au revoir!, good-bye for now!

(**k**) (*act*) = devolución.

(**l**) (*Fin: also* —s) change; quédese con la — keep the change.

(**m**) stroll, walk; dar una — to take a stroll, go for a walk.

(**n**) (*fam*) beating, tanning (*fam*).

vueltero adj (*Arg*) person difficult.

vuelto 1 ptp of **volver**. **2** nm (*SAm*) = **vuelta (1)**.

vuestro 1 poss adj your; (*after n*) of yours, eg una idea vuestra an idea of yours, one of your ideas; lo — (what is) yours, what belongs to you.

2 poss pron yours, of yours; es el — it is yours; los —s (*freq*) your people, your relations, your family; your men, your side.

vulcanita nf vulcanite.

vulcanización nf vulcanization.

vulcanizar [1f] vt to vulcanize.

Vulcano m Vulcan.

vulgar adj (**a**) *tongue* vulgar; *term* common, ordinary; (*pej*) vulgar; latín — Vulgar Latin.

(**b**) *person* ordinary, common; *features, manners etc* coarse; el hombre — the ordinary man, the common man.

(**c**) *event, life etc* ordinary, everyday; humdrum; *remark etc* banal, trivial, commonplace; inane.

vulgaridad nf (**a**) (*quality*) ordinariness, commonness; coarseness; banality; triviality; inanity.

(**b**) (*act*) vulgarity, coarse thing; coarse expression.

(**c**) —es banalities, trivialities, platitudes; inanities.

vulgarismo nm popular form (of a word); (*pej*) slang word, vulgarism, popular expression.

vulgarización nf (**a**) popularization; obra de — popular work. (**b**) (*Ling*) translation into the vernacular.

vulgarizar [1f] vt (**a**) to popularize; to spread a knowledge of. (**b**) (*Ling*) to translate into the vernacular.

vulgarmente adv commonly, ordinarily; vulgarly; A, llamado — B A, popularly (*or* commonly) known as B.

Vulgata nf Vulgate.

vulgo 1 nm common people; (*pej*) lower orders, common herd; mob.

2 adv: el mingitorio, — "meadero" the urinal, commonly (*or* popularly) known as the "bog".

vulnerabilidad nf vulnerability.

vulnerable adj vulnerable (*de* to).

vulnerar [1a] vt (**a**) to damage, harm; *custom, right etc* to interfere with, affect seriously. (**b**) *law* to break.

vulpeja nf fox; vixen.

vulpino adj vulpine; (*fig*) foxy.

vulva nf vulva.

W

[in initial position pronounced like Spanish b, v, but sometimes like English w]

wáter ['bater] *nm* (*angl*) lavatory, water closet.
wélter ['belter] *nm* (*angl*) welterweight.
whisk(e)y ['wiski, 'gwiski] *nm* (*angl*) whisk(e)y.

wolfram ['bolfram] *nm*, **wolframio** [b—] *nm* (*angl*) wolfram.

X

[in initial position pronounced like Spanish s]

xeno *nm* xenon.
xenofobia *nf* xenophobia.
xenófobo *nm* xenophobe.
xenón *nm* xenon.

xilófono *nm* xylophone.
xilografía *nf* (a) xylography. (b) (*una* —) xylograph, wood engraving.
xilográfico *adj* xylographic.

Y

y ...: *for some words so spelled in* S Am, *see also* **ll** ...
y *conj* and.
ya 1 *adv* (a) (*basic sense: past*) already; **lo hemos visto** — we've seen it already; **han dado las 8** — it's past 8 already; — **en el siglo X** as long ago as the 10th century, as early as the 10th century; — **no viene** he no longer comes, he doesn't come any more.
(b) (*present, future*) now; at once, right away; soon, presently; in due course; — **es hora de irnos** it's time for us to go now; — **viene el autobús** the bus is coming now, here's the bus; — **se lo traerán** they'll bring it for you right away; — **no lo volverás a ver** you won't see it any more; — **arreglarán todo eso** they'll soon put all that right.
(c) (*as interj*) ¡—! of course!, that's it!, now I remember!; at last!, so you've managed it at last!; ¡—, —! yes, yes!; all right!; O.K.! (*fam*).
(d) (*emphatic: often not translated*) ¡— voy! coming!; — **lo sé** I know; — **se acabó** it's all over; ¿— **estás aquí otra vez?** are you here again?; — **te llegará el turno a ti**, — your turn will come (don't you worry).
2 *conj* (a) — **por una cosa**, — **por otra** now for one thing, now for another; — **dice que sí**, — **dice que no** first he says yes, then he says no; — **te vas**, — **te quedas, me es igual** whether you go or stay is all the same to me.

(b) **no** — **not only**; **no** — **aquí, sino en todas partes** not only here, but everywhere.
(c) — **que** as, since; now that, seeing that.
yac *nm*, *pl* **yacs** [jak] yak.
yacaré *nm* (S Am) alligator.
yacente *adj statue* reclining, recumbent.
yacer [2y] *vi* (*mostly arch*) to lie; **aquí yace X** here lies X; — **con** to sleep with.
yacija *nf* (a) bed; rough bed; **ser de mala** — to sleep badly, have a restless night; (*fig*) to be a vagrant, be a ne'er-do-well. (b) grave, tomb.
yacimiento *nm* bed, deposit; — **petrolífero** oilfield.
yagua *nf* (Ant, Col, Mex, Per, Ven) royal palm; fibrous tissue from the wood of the royal palm.
yagual *nm* (CAm, Mex) padded ring (*for carrying loads on the head*).
yaguareté *nm* (Bol, RPl) jaguar.
yaguré *nm* (S Am) skunk.
yaíta *adv* (S Am)=**ya**.
yak *nm*, *pl* **yaks** [jak] yak.
Yakarta Jakarta.
yámbico *adj* iambic.
yana *adj* (Ec) black.
yanacón *nm*, **yanacona** *nf* (Arg, Bol, Chi, Per) Indian tenant farmer, Indian sharecropper; unpaid Indian servant.
yancófilo *adj* (S Am) pro-American, pro-United States.

yanqui (*fam*) **1** *adj* Yankee. **2** *nmf* Yank (*fam*), Yankee (*fam*).
Yanquilandia *f* (*SAm: hum*) United States.
yapa *nf* (a) (*SAm*) extra, extra bit, bonus; **dar algo de** — to add a bit, give something as a bonus; (*fig*) to add something for good measure. (b) (*Mex*) tip. (c) (*Chi, RPl*) attachment, end piece.
yapada *nf* (*SAm*) extra, extra bit, bonus.
yapar [1a] (*SAm*) **1** *vt* (a) to give as a bonus, add as an extra. (b) *rope etc* to stretch; to add a bit to, lengthen. **2** *vi* to add an extra, give an extra bit.
yarará *nm or f* (*Bol, RPl*) rattlesnake.
yarda *nf* (*angl*) yard.
yate *nm* yacht.
yaya *nm* (a) (*CAm, Col*) wound; (*Col, Cu, Chi, Per*) slight wound; scar; small pain. (b) (*Cu*) stick, walking stick.
yaz *nm* (*Acad*) jazz.
ye . . .: *for some words, see* **hie . . .,** *eg for* **yerra** *see* **hierra.**
yedra *nf* ivy.
yegua 1 *nf* (a) mare. (b) (*Chi, Per, RPl*) woman; coarse woman, slattern. (c) (*Bol, CAm*) cigar stub. **2** *adj* (a) (*CAm, PR*) stupid; rough, coarse. (b) (*Chi*) big, huge.
yeguada *nf* (a) stud; (*RPl*) group of breeding mares. (b) (*CAm, PR*) piece of stupidity, foolish act (*etc*).
yeguarizo *nm* (*RPl*) (a) stud, group of breeding mares. (b) horses (*in general*).
yegüerío *nm* (*CAm, PR*) =**yeguarizo** (a).
yelmo *nm* helmet.
yema *nf* (a) (*of egg*) yoke; (*SAm*) egg: **— mejida** egg flip. (b) (*Bot*) leaf bud, eye; young shoot. (c) (*Anat*) **— del dedo** fingertip. (d) (*fig*) best part. (e) (*fig*) snag; **dar en la —** to put one's finger on the spot, hit the nail on the head. (f) (*fig*) **en la — del invierno** in the dead of winter.
yendo *see* **ir.**
yerba *nf* (a) =**hierba.** (b) (*SAm*) green. (c) (*Bol, Chi, RPl: also* **— mate, — de mate**) maté. (d) (*Mex*) marijuana. (e) (*RPl*) **—s** herb, medicinal plant.
yerbal *nm* (*RPl*), **yerbatal** *nm* (*Ec*) maté plantation.
yerbatero *nm* (a) (*SAm*) herbalist; quack doctor. (b) (*RPl*) dealer in maté.
yerbear [1a] *vi* (*RPl*) to drink maté.
yerbera *nf* (*RPl*) maté container.
yermar [1a] *vt* to lay waste.
yermo 1 *adj* uninhabited; waste, uncultivated. **2** *nm* waste land; waste, wilderness.
yerna *nf* (*Col, PR, SD*) daughter-in-law.
yerno *nm* son-in-law.
yeros *nmpl* lentils.
yerro *nm* error, mistake.
yersey *nm* (*Acad*), **yersi** *nm* (*Acad*) jersey.
yerto *adj* stiff, rigid; **— de frío** stiff with cold.
yesca *nf* (a) tinder; (*Arg*) flint; **—s** tinderbox; **arder como si fuera —** to burn like tinder. (b) (*fig*) fuel; inflammable situation, group (*etc*) which is easily inflamed. (c) (*fig*) food (*etc*) which makes one thirsty (for wine). (d) (*Ec*) debt.

yesería *nf* plastering, plasterwork.
yesero *nm* plasterer.
yeso *nm* (a) (*Geol*) gypsum. (b) (*Archit etc*) plaster; **— mate** plaster of Paris; **dar de — a una pared** to plaster a wall. (c) (*Art etc*) plaster cast. (d) (*School*) chalk.
yesquero *nm* (*Ec, Ven*) cigarette lighter.
yeta *nf* (*Mex, RPl*) bad luck, misfortune.
yetar [1a] *vt* (*RPl*) to bring bad luck to.
yeti *nm* yeti.
ye-yé (*fam*) **1** *adj* ultramodern; mod (*fam*); cool (*fam*), groovy (*sl*); trendy (*sl*); **cantante —** pop singer; **música —** pop music, beat music; **es una chica —** she's an ultramodern girl, she's really with it (*fam*). **2** *nmf* ultramodern person, member of the modern generation, mod (*fam*); person who is with it (*fam*); **ser un —** to be ultramodern, be with it, be a mod.
yeyeísmo *nm* (*fam*) ultramodern fashions (*or tendencies etc*); trendiness (*sl*); devotion to (*or cult of*) pop music *etc*.
yeyería *nf* (*fam*) (a) modern generation, mods (*fam*), people who are with it (*fam*). (b) =**yeyeísmo.**
yip *nm* (*SAm*) jeep.
yo *pers pron* (a) I; **soy —** it's me, it is I (*lit*). (b) **el —** the self, the ego.
yod *nf* yod.
yodo *nm* iodine.
yodoformo *nm* iodoform.
yoga[1] *nf* yoga.
yoga[2] *nf* (*Mex*) dagger.
yogui *nm* yogi.
yogur *nm* yogourt.
yol *nm* yawl.
yola *nf* gig, yawl; sailing boat, shell.
yóquey *nm* (*Acad*) jockey.
yuca *nf* (a) yucca; (*SAm*) manioc root, cassava. (b) (*Ant*) poverty. (c) (*Col*) food (*in general*). (d) (*Col*) leg. (e) (*CAm, Bol*) lie.
yugo *nm* yoke (*also fig*); **— del matrimonio** marriage tie; **sacudir el —** (*fig*) to throw off the yoke.
Yugo(e)slavia *f* Yugoslavia, Jugoslavia.
yugo(e)slavo 1 *adj* Yugoslavian, Jugoslavian. **2** *nm*, **yugo(e)slava** *nf* Yugoslav, Jugoslav.
yuguero *nm* ploughman.
yugular *adj* jugular.
yungas *nfpl* (*Bol, Chi, Ec, Per*) hot valleys.
yungla *nf* jungle.
yunque *nm* (a) anvil. (b) (*fig*) stoical person; tireless worker; **hacer de —, servir de —** to have to put up with hardships (*or abuse etc*).
yunta *nf* (a) yoke, team (of oxen). (b) (*esp SAm*) **—s** couple, pair; cufflinks.
yuntero *nm* ploughman.
yuta *nf* (a) (*Chi*) slug. (b) (*Arg, Bol*) **hacer la —** to play truant.
yute *nm* jute.
yuxtaponer [2r] *vt* to juxtapose.
yuxtaposición *nf* juxtaposition.
yuyal *nm* (*Chi, RPl*) weedy ground.
yuyerío *nm* (*Bol, Chi, RPl*) weeds; wild plants.
yuyero *nm* (*Arg*) herbalist.
yuyo *nm* (a) (*Bol, Chi, RPl*) weed; wild plant, useless plant; (*RPl*) medicinal plant, herb; (*Ec*) herb flavouring; (*Per*) cooking herb; **estar como un —** (*Arg, Chi*) to be weak, be lifeless. (b) (*Col*) herbal poultice. (c) (*CAm*) **—s** blisters on the feet.

Z

zabordar [1a] *vi* to run aground.
zabullir [3h] *vi etc* = **zambullir** *etc*.
zacapel(l)a *nf* rumpus (*fam*), row.
zacatal *nm* (*CAm*, *Mex*) pasture.
zacate *nm* (*CAm*, *Mex*) grass; hay, fodder.
zacatear [1a] (*CAm*, *Mex*) **1** *vt* to beat. **2** *vi* to graze.
zacatera *nf* (*CAm*, *Mex*) pasture; haystack.
zafacoca *nf* (a) (*SAm*) row, quarrel; brawl. (b) (*Mex*) beating. (c) (*Cu*) riot.
zafado *adj* (a) (*prov*, *SAm*) brazen, shameless; insolent. (b) (*RPl*) alert, sharp, wide awake. (c) (*Col*, *Mex*) crazy.
zafadura *nf* (*SAm*) dislocation, sprain.
zafaduría *nf* (*SAm*) (a) effrontery, brazenness; insolence. (b) (*una* —) shameless remark (*or act etc*).
zafante *prep* (*Ant*) except (for).
zafar [1a] **1** *vt* (a) to loosen, untie.
  (b) *ship* to lighten; *surface etc* to clear, free.
  (c) (*Col*, *Cu*, *Mex*, *Nic*) to exclude.
  2 zafarse *vr* (a) to escape, run away; to slip away; to break loose; to hide oneself away.
  (b) (*Mech*) to slip off, come off.
  (c) — **de** *person* to get away from; to dodge, shake off; *duty*, *work* to get out of, dodge; *agreement* to get out of, wriggle out of; *difficulty* to get round.
  (d) (*fam*) — **con algo** to pinch something (*fam*).
  (e) (*SAm*) — **un brazo** to dislocate one's arm, wrench one's arm.
  (f) (*Arg*, *CAm*) to dodge (a blow).
  (g) (*Col*) to go a bit crazy.
zafarrancho *nm* (a) (*Naut*) clearing for action; — **de combate** call to action stations.
  (b) (*fig*) havoc, destruction; mess; **hacer un** — to cause havoc; to break everything up; to make a dreadful mess.
  (c) (*fam*) quarrel, row.
zafio *adj* coarse, uncouth.
zafiro *nm* sapphire.
zafo 1 *adj* (a) (*Naut*) clear; unobstructed. (b) unharmed; undamaged, intact; **salir** — **de** to come unscathed out of. (c) (*SAm*) free. **2** *prep* (*Arg*, *CAm*) except (for).
zafón *nm* (*Col*) slip, error.
zafra[1] *nf* oil jar, oil container.
zafra[2] *nf* (*esp SAm*) sugar harvest; sugar making.
zaga *nf* rear; **a la** —, **en** — behind, in the rear; **dejar en** — to leave behind, outstrip; **A no le va a la** (*or* **en**) — **a B** A is every bit as good as B, A is in no way inferior to B; **no le va a la** — **a nadie** he is second to none.
zagal *nm* boy, lad, youth; (*Agr*) shepherd boy.
zagala *nf* girl, lass; (*Agr*) shepherdess.
zagalejo *nm* lad; shepherd boy.
zagalón *nm* big boy, strapping lad.
zagalona *nf* big girl, hefty wench.
zagual *nm* paddle.
zaguán *nm* vestibule, hallway, entry.
zaguero *adj* (a) rear, back; *cart* too heavily laden at the back; **equipo** — bottom team, team that is trailing. (b) (*fig*) slow, laggard.
zahareño *adj* wild; shy, unsociable.
zaherimiento *nm* criticism; mortification; reprimand; reproach.
zaherir [3i] *vt* to criticize sharply (*or* sarcastically), attack, lash; to wound, mortify; to upbraid; — **a uno con algo** to reproach someone for something, cast something in someone's teeth.
zahones *nmpl* riding breeches.
zahorí *nm* seer, clairvoyant; water diviner; (*fig*) highly perceptive person.
zahurda *nf* (a) (*Agr*) pigsty. (b) (*fam*) hovel, shack.
zahurra *nf* (*Col*) din, hullabaloo (*fam*).
zaino[1] *adj* *horse* chestnut; *cow* black.

zaino[2] *adj* treacherous; *animal* unreliable, vicious; **mirar a lo** (*or* **de**) — to look sideways, look shiftily.
zainoso *adj* (*Chi*) treacherous.
zalagarda *nf* (a) (*Mil*) ambush, trap; ruse; (*Hunting*) trap. (b) row, din; noisy quarrel; shindy, hullabaloo (*fam*).
zalamerear [1a] *vi* (*Arg*, *Mex*) to flatter, cajole, wheedle.
zalamería *nf* (a) (*also* —**s**) flattery; cajolery, wheedling. (b) (*quality*) suaveness; oiliness, soapiness.
zalamero 1 *adj* flattering; cajoling, wheedling; suave; oily, soapy. **2** *nm* flatterer; wheedler; suave person; oily sort, soapy individual.
zalea *nf* sheepskin.
zalema *nf* salaam, deep bow; —**s** (*fig*) bowing and scraping, flattering courtesies.
zalenquear [1a] *vi* (*Col*) to limp.
zamarra *nf* sheepskin; sheepskin jacket, fur jacket.
zamarrazo *nm* (*fig*) blow; setback; nasty jolt.
zamarrear [1a] *vt* (a) (*of dog*) to shake, worry.
  (b) (*fam*) to shake up, knock around; to shove around.
  (c) (*fam: in argument etc*) to stamp on, humiliate, squash.
zamarro *nm* (a) sheepskin; sheepskin jacket. (b) (*Col*, *Ec*, *Ven*) —**s** riding breeches. (c) (*fam*) boor, yokel; sly person.
zamba *nf* (*esp SAm*) samba.
zambada *nf* (*Per*) group of half-breeds.
zambardo *nm* (a) (*Chi*) clumsy person. (b) (*Arg*, *Chi*) clumsiness; damage, breakage. (c) (*Arg*) fluke.
zambeque 1 *adj* (*Cu*) silly. **2** *nm* (a) (*Cu*) idiot. (b) (*Cu*, *Ven*) uproar, hullabaloo (*fam*).
zambequería *nf* (*Cu*) silliness.
zamberío *nm* (*Col*, *Ec*, *Per*) half-breeds (*collectively*).
Zambeze *m* Zambesi.
Zambia *f* Zambia.
zambo 1 *adj* knock-kneed. **2** *nm*, **zamba** *nf* (a) (*SAm*) half-breed (*of Negro and Indian parentage*). (b) (*Bol*, *Col*, *Chi*) mulatto.
zambomba *nf* (a) *a kind of rustic drum*. (b) (*fam*) ¡—! phew!
zambombazo *nm* (a) bang, explosion. (b) blow, punch.
zambombo *nm* boor, yokel.
zambra *nf* (a) gipsy dance. (b) (*fam*) uproar, shindy; commotion.
zambrate *nm* (*CAm*), **zambrera** *nf* (*Ven*) row, commotion.
zambucar [1g] *vt* (a) to hide, tuck away, cover up. (b) to mix up, jumble up.
zambuir [3g] *vi* (*Col*, *Ec*, *PR*) = **zambullir**.
zambullida *nf* dive, plunge; dip; ducking.
zambullir [3h] **1** *vt* to dip, plunge (**en** into); to duck (**en** under).
  2 zambullirse *vr* (a) to dive, plunge (**en** into); to duck (**en** under).
  (b) to hide, cover oneself up.
zambullón *nm* (*Col*, *Ec*, *RPl*) = **zambullida**.
zambutir [3a] *vt* (*CAm*, *Mex*) to stuff, pack hastily (**en** into).
zamorano 1 *adj* of Zamora. **2** *nm*, **zamorana** *nf* native (*or* inhabitant) of Zamora; **los** —**s** the people of Zamora.
zampa *nf* (*Archit*) pile.
zampabollos *nmf*, *pl* **zampabollos** (*fam*) (a) greedy pig, glutton. (b) coarse individual.
zampar [1a] **1** *vt* (a) *object* to put away hurriedly (**en** in), whip smartly (**en** into); to dip, plunge (**en** into).
  (b) to hurl, dash (**en** against, to); **lo zampó en el suelo** he dashed it to the floor.
  (c) *food* to gobble, wolf.
  (d) (*SAm*) *blow* to fetch, deal.
  2 *vi* to gobble, eat voraciously.
  3 zamparse *vr* (a) to bump, crash, hurtle; **se**

zampó en medio del corro he thrust himself roughly into the circle.
(b) (*fig*) to gatecrash, go along uninvited.
(c) — **en** to dart into, whip into, shoot into; **pero se zampó en el cine** but he shot into the cinema.
(d) — **algo** to wolf something, tuck something away (*fam*); **se zampó 4 porciones enteras** he wolfed 4 whole helpings.
zampatortas *nmf, pl* **zampatortas** (*fam*)=**zampabollos**.
zampón *adj* (*fam*) greedy.
zampoña *nf* shepherd's pipes, rustic flute.
zampullín *nm* grebe.
zampuzar [1f] *vt*=**zambullir**; =**zampar**.
zanahoria 1 *nf* carrot. **2** *nm* (*RPl*) (a) errand boy. (b) idiot, nitwit (*sl*); clumsy person; poor wretch.
zanca *nf* (*Orn, also fam*) shank.
zancada *nf* stride; **alejarse a grandes** —s to go off with big strides, stride away; **en dos** —s (*fig*) in a couple of ticks; very easily.
zancadilla *nf* (a) trip; (*fig*) stratagem, trick (*to get someone out of a job*); **echar la** — **a uno** to trip someone up; (*fig*) to put the skids under someone (*fam*), scheme to get someone out.
(b) booby trap.
zancajear [1a] *vi* to rush around.
zancajo *nm* (a) (*Anat, Sew*) heel; **A no le llega a los** —s **a B** A can't hold a candle to B, A is much inferior to B. (b) (*fam*) dwarf, runt.
zancajón *adj* (*Mex*) (a) tall, lanky. (b) clumsy, misshapen.
zancarrón *nm* (a) leg bone; big bone. (b) (*fam*) old bag of bones. (c) (*fam*) poor teacher.
zanco *nm* stilt; **estar en** —s (*fig*) to be well up, be in a good position.
zancón *adj* (a) long-legged. (b) (*CAm*) lanky; clumsy-looking. (c) (*SAm*) *dress* too short.
zancudero *nm* (*Ant, CR, Mex, Ven*) swarm of mosquitoes.
zancudo 1 *adj* long-legged; **ave zancuda** wader, wading bird. **2** *nm* (*SAm*) mosquito.
zangamanga *nf* (*fam*) trick; funny business.
zanganada *nf* stupid remark, silly thing (to say).
zanganear [1a] *vi* (a) to idle, loaf; to fool around, waste one's time. (b) to make stupid remarks.
zángano *nm* (a) (*Ent*) drone. (b) (*fig*) drone; idler, slacker. (c) idiot, fool. (d) bore. (e) (*CAm, Mex*) rogue.
zangarri(an)a *nf* (a) (*Med*) headache, migraine; minor upset. (b) (*fig*) blues, depression.
zangolotear [1a] **1** *vt* to keep playing with, fiddle with; to shake, jiggle.
2 *vi* and **zangolotearse** *vr* (a) (*of window etc*) to rattle, shake.
(b) (*of person*) to fidget; to jiggle; to fiddle about, fuss around.
zangoloteo *nm* fiddling; shaking, jiggling; fidgeting; rattling.
zangolotino *adj*: **niño** — older boy with childish habits (*or* clothes *etc*); weedy youth, overgrown baby.
zangón *nm* big lazy lad.
zanguanga *nf* fictitious illness; **hacer la** — to swing the lead (*fam*), malinger.
zanguango 1 *adj* idle, slack. **2** *nm* slacker, shirker; malingerer.
zanja *nf* (a) ditch; drainage channel; trench; pit; grave; **abrir las** —s (*Archit*) to lay the foundations (*de* for).
(b) (*SAm*) gully, watercourse.
(c) (*Ec*) fence, low wall.
zanjar [1a] *vt* (a) to ditch, trench; to dig trenches in. (b) (*fig*) difficulty to get around, surmount; *disagreement* to resolve, clear up.
zanjón *nm* (a) deep ditch. (b) (*Cu, Chi, RPl*) cliff; gully, ravine.
zanquear [1a] **1** *vt* (*CAm, Mex, SD*) to hunt for. **2** *vi* (a) to walk awkwardly. (b) to stride along. (c) (*fig*) to rush about, bustle about.
zanquilargo *adj* long-legged, leggy.
zanquivano *adj* spindly-legged.
Zanzíbar *m* Zanzibar.
zapa[1] *nf* sharkskin.
zapa[2] *nf* (a) spade. (b) (*Mil*) sap, trench.
zapador *nm* sapper.
zapallada *nf* (a) (*Chi, RPl*) fluke; lucky break; lucky guess (*etc*). (b) (*Col*) silly remark.
zapallo *nm* (a) (*SAm*) gourd, pumpkin. (b) (*Chi, RPl*) =**zapallada** (a). (c) (*Ec*) fat person. (d) (*CAm, Col*) dull individual.
zapallón *adj* (*Chi, Ec, Per*) chubby, fat.
zapapico *nm* pick, pickaxe; mattock.

zapar [1a] *vti* to sap, mine.
zaparrazo *nm* claw, scratch.
zapata *nf* (a) half-boot. (b) (*Mech, Naut*) shoe; — **de freno** brake shoe.
zapatazo *nm* (a) blow with a shoe; (*fam*) thud; bump; bang; **tratar a uno a** —s (*fam*) to treat someone very rudely. (b) (*Naut*) violent flapping of a sail.
zapateado *nm* tap-dance.
zapatear [1a] **1** *vt* (a) to tap with one's foot.
(b) to kick, prod with one's foot.
(c) (*fam*) to ill-treat, treat roughly.
2 *vi* (a) to tap with one's feet; to tap-dance; (*of rabbit*) to thump.
(b) (*Naut: of sail*) to flap violently.
zapatería *nf* (a) shoemaking. (b) shoeshop; shoe factory, footwear factory.
zapatero 1 *adj* *potatoes etc* hard, undercooked; poor-quality.
2 *nm* shoemaker; — **remendón**, — **de viejo** cobbler; —, **a tus zapatos** the cobbler should stick to his last.
zapatilla *nf* (a) slipper; pump. (b) (*Mech*) washer, gasket.
zapato *nm* shoe; —s **de color** brown shoes; —s **de goma** (*SAm*), —s **de hule** (*Mex*) rubber shoes, gym shoes; —s **de tenis** tennis shoes; **estaban como tres en un** — they were packed in like sardines; **meter a uno en un** — to bring someone to heel; **saber dónde aprieta el** — to be alive to all the difficulties, have the right feeling about a situation; to know which side one's bread is buttered; to know where someone's weakness lies.
zapatón *nm* (*SAm*) overshoe, galosh.
zape *interj* (a) shoo!, scat! (b) good gracious!
zapear [1a] *vt* (a) *cat* to shoo, scare away; *person* to shoo away, get rid of. (b) (*Pan, Per*) to spy on, watch.
zaporro *nm* (*Col, Ven*) dwarf, runt.
zaque *nm* (a) wineskin. (b) (*fam*) boozer, old soak (*fam*).
zaquizamí *nm* (a) attic, garret. (b) (*fig*) poky little room, hole; hovel.
zar *nm* tzar, czar.
zarabanda *nf* (a) (*Hist*) sarabande. (b) (*fig*) confused movement, rush, whirl. (c) (*Mex*) beating.
zaragata *nf* (a) (*fam*) bustle, turmoil; hullabaloo (*fam*); row, set-to (*fam*). (b) (*Cu, PR*) —s cajolery, wheedling.
zaragate *nm* (a) (*SAm*) rogue, rascal; busybody. (b) (*Cu*) flatterer, creep (*sl*).
zaragatero (*fam*) **1** *adj* rowdy, noisy; quarrelsome. **2** *nm* rowdy, hooligan.
Zaragoza Saragossa.
zaragozano 1 *adj* of Saragossa. **2** *nm*, **zaragozana** *nf* native (*or* inhabitant) of Saragossa; **los** —s the people of Saragossa.
zaramullo 1 *adj* (a) (*Col, Cu, Hond*) affected; conceited; finicky.
(b) (*Ec, SD*) amusing, witty.
2 *nm* (a) (*Bol*) silly thing.
(b) (*Per, Ven*) busybody; fool.
zaranda *nf* (a) sieve. (b) (*Mex*) cruet. (c) (*Ven*) spinning top; (*Mus*) horn.
zarandajas *nfpl* (*fam*) trifles, odds and ends, little things.
zarandear [1a] **1** *vt* (a) to sieve, sift.
(b) (*fam*) to shake vigorously to and fro, shake up, toss about.
(c) (*fam*) *person* to keep on the go, keep bustling about.
(d) (*SAm*) to swing, push to and fro; (*fig*) to abuse publicly.
2 zarandearse *vr* (a) (*prov, SAm*) to strut about.
(b) to keep on the go, bustle about.
zarandillo *nm* active person, bustler; (*pej*) restless individual; (*child*) fidget; **llevar a uno como un** — to keep someone on the go.
zarapito *nm* (*also* — **real**) curlew.
zaraza *nf* printed cotton cloth, chintz.
zarazas *nfpl* rat poison.
zarazo *adj* (*SAm*) (a) *fruit* half-ripe. (b) rather drunk, tight.
zarcillo *nm* (a) earring. (b) (*Bot*) tendril. (c) (*Arg, Mex, Ven: Agr*) earmark.
zarco *adj* light blue.
zarigüeya *nf* opossum.
zarina *nf* tsarina.
zaroche *nm* (*SAm*)=**soroche**.
zarpa *nf* (a) claw, paw; **echar la** — **a** to claw at, paw; (*fam*) to grab, lay hold of. (b) splash of mud, smear of mud.

zarpada *nf* clawing; blow with the paw; **dar una — a** to claw, scratch; to hit with its paw.

zarpar [1a] *vi* to weigh anchor, set sail, get under way.

zarpazo *nm* (a)=zarpada. (b) (*fig*) thud; bang, bump. (c) (*fam*) **dar un —** to beat it quick (*fam*).

zarpear [1a] *vt* (*CAm*, *Mex*) to splash with mud, bespatter.

zarrapastrón *adj* (*fam*), **zarrapastroso** *adj* shabby, dirty, rough-looking.

zarria *nf* (a) splash of mud, spattering of mud, smear of mud. (b) rag, tatter.

zarza *nf* bramble, blackberry (bush).

zarzal *nm* bramble patch, clump of brambles.

zarzamora *nf* blackberry.

zarzaparrilla *nf* sarsaparilla.

zarzo *nm* (a) (*Agr etc*) hurdle; (*in building*) wattle. (b) (*Col*) attic.

zarzuela *nf* operetta, light opera, (Spanish-style) musical comedy.

zarzuelista *nmf* composer of light opera, musical-comedy writer.

zas *interj* bang!, slap!; crash!; **le pegó un porrazo . . .,** ¡—! . . . que . . . he gave him a swipe . . . bang! . . . which . . .; **apenas habíamos puesto la radio y . . .** ¡—! . . . **se cortó la corriente** we had only just switched on the radio when . . . click! . . . and off went the current.

zascandil *nm* (a) featherbrained person; unreliable person; frivolous individual. (b) busybody.

zascandilear [1a] *vi* (a) to buzz about uselessly, fuss a lot; to behave frivolously, do featherbrained things. (b) to pry, meddle.

Zenón *m* Zeno.

zepelín *nm* zeppelin.

Zetlandia: Islas *fpl* **de —** Shetland Isles.

zigzag 1 *adj* zigzag. 2 *nm* zigzag (line *etc*); **relámpago en —** forked lightning, chain lightning (US).

zigzagueante *adj* (*SAm*) zigzag.

zigzaguear [1a] *vi* to zigzag.

zinc *nm* zinc.

zipizape *nm* (*fam*) set-to (*fam*), rumpus (*fam*); brawl, disturbance; **armar un —** to start a rumpus; **los dos están de —** the two of them are always squabbling.

zócalo *nm* (a) (*Archit*) socle; plinth, base. (b) skirting board, baseboard (US); panelling. (c) (*Mex*) parade ground; public square; walk, boulevard; park.

zocato 1 *adj* (a) *fruit*, *vegetable* hard, rubbery; damaged. (b) *person* left-handed. 2 *nm* (a) (*Col*) stale bread. (b) (*Mex*) sickly child.

zoclo *nm*=zueco.

zoco 1 *adj* (a) left-handed. (b) (*Col*) one-armed; (*Col*, *Chi*, *PR*) maimed, limbless. 2 *nm* (a) left-handed person. (b) (*Ven*) fool. (c) (*Chi*, *Par*) hefty punch.

zocotroco *nm* (*Arg*, *Bol*, *Col*) chunk, big lump; **— de hombre** hefty man.

zodíaco *nm* zodiac.

zollenco *adj* (*Mex*) big and tough.

zollipar [1a] *vi* to sob.

zona *nf* zone; belt, area; **— de desastre** disaster area; **— edificada** built-up area; **— de ensanche** zone of future urban development; **— fronteriza** border area, border land; **— de pruebas** testing ground; **— de tiendas** shopping centre; **— tórrida** torrid zone.

zonal *adj* zonal.

zoncear [1a] *vi* (*Chi*, *Guat*, *RPl*) to behave stupidly.

zoncera *nf* (a) (*SAm*)=zoncería. (b) (*Chi*, *RPl*) mere trifle; small amount; **costar una —** to cost next to nothing; **comer una —** to have a bite to eat.

zoncería *nf* silliness, stupidity; dullness; boredom, boring nature.

zonchiche *nm* (*CAm*, *Mex*) buzzard.

zonda *nf* (*Arg*, *Bol*) hot northerly wind.

zonzo 1 *adj* (*esp SAm*) silly, stupid; boring, inane; (*Mex*) dazed, weary. 2 *nm* (*SAm*) idiot; bore, tedious person.

zonzoneco *adj* (*CAm*), **zonzoreco** *adj* (*CAm*), **zonzoreno** *adj* (*CAm*) stupid.

zoo *nm* zoo.

zoo . . . zoo . . .

zoología *nf* zoology.

zoológico 1 *adj* zoological. 2 *nm* zoo.

zoólogo *nm* zoologist.

zoomórfico *adj* zoomorphic.

zopenco (*fam*) 1 *adj* dull, stupid. 2 *nm* clot (*sl*), nitwit (*sl*).

zopilote *nm* (*SAm*) buzzard; (*fam*) thief.

zopilotear [1a] *vt* (*Mex*) to eat greedily, wolf; (*fig*) to steal.

zopo *adj* crippled, maimed.

zoquetada *nf* (*SAm*) stupidity.

zoquetazo *nm* (*Mex*, *RPl*) swipe, punch.

zoquete *nm* (a) block, piece, chunk (of wood). (b) crust of old bread. (c) (*fam*) squat person. (d) (*fam*) duffer, blockhead; lout, oaf. (e) (*SAm*) body dirt, human dirt. (f) (*Cu*, *Mex*) punch.

zoquetillo *nm* shuttlecock.

zorenco *adj* (*CAm*) stupid.

Zoroastro *m* Zoroaster.

zorra *nf* (a) fox; vixen. (b) (*fam*) whore, tart (*sl*).

zorral *adj* (a) (*CAm*, *Col*) annoying. (b) (*Ec*) obstinate.

zorrera *nf* (a) foxhole; (*fig*) smoky room, room with a fug. (b) dismay; worry, anxiety. (c) (*fig*) drowsiness, lethargy.

zorrería *nf* (a) (*quality*) foxiness, craftiness. (b) (*una —*) sly trick.

zorrero *adj* foxy, crafty.

zorrillo *nm* (*Arg*), **zorrino** *nm* (*Arg*) skunk.

zorro 1 *adj* foxy, crafty. 2 *nm* (a) (*Zool*) fox, dog fox. (b) fox fur, foxskin. (c) (*fig*) old fox, crafty person, rascal; (*at work*) slacker, shirker; **hacerse el —** to act dumb; **estar hecho un —** to be very drowsy; **estar hecho unos —s** (*fam*) to be all in, be done up (*fam*).

zorruno *adj* foxy, fox-like.

zorzal *nm* (a) (*Orn*) thrush. (b) (*fig*) shrewd person; sly fellow. (c) (*Arg*, *Chi*) simpleton; dupe, innocent person.

zorzalear [1a] *vi* (*Chi*) to sponge (*fam*).

zorzalero *adj* (*Chi*) sponging (*fam*), parasitical.

zorzalino *adj* (*Chi*) *life* rich, luxurious, easy.

zosco *nm* (*Ven*) idiot.

zote (*fam*) 1 *adj* dense, dim, stupid. 2 *nm* dimwit (*fam*).

zozobra *nf* (a) (*Naut*) capsizing, overturning; sinking. (b) (*fig*) worry, anxiety; jumpiness, nervous state.

zozobrar [1a] *vi* (a) (*Naut*) to be in danger (of foundering); to capsize, overturn; to founder, sink. (b) (*fig*: *of plan*, *intention*) to fail, come to naught, collapse; (*of business*) to be ruined. (c) (*fig*: *of person*) to be anxious, worry, fret.

zueco *nm* clog, wooden shoe.

—zuelo, —zuela *n suffix* (a) (*diminutive*) *eg* **pernezuela** little leg. (b) (*pej*) *eg* **autorzuelo** scribbler, hack, penpusher; **mujerzuela** whore.

zulú 1 *adj* Zulu. 2 *nmf* Zulu.

Zululandia *nf* Zululand.

zulla *nf* (*tabu*) shit (*tabu*).

zullarse [1a] *vr* to dirty oneself; to fart (*tabu*).

zullón *nm* (*tabu*) fart (*tabu*).

zumaque *nm* sumac(h).

zumba *nf* (a) banter, chaff, teasing; humour; satirical intention; **dar — a**, **hacer — a** to rag, tease. (b) (*SAm*) beating. (c) (*Mex*) drunkenness.

zumbador *nm* (a) (*Elec*) buzzer. (b) (*Ant*, *Mex*) hummingbird.

zumbar [1a] 1 *vt* (a) *person* to rag, tease. (b) (*Univ*: *sl*) to plough (*sl*). (c) *blow* to fetch, hit. (d) (*SAm*) to throw, chuck, toss; to chuck out. 2 *vi* (a) (*of insect*) to buzz, hum, drone; (*of machine*) to hum, whirr; (*of buzzer*) to buzz; (*of ears*) to hum, sing, buzz; **me zumban los oídos** I have a buzzing in my ears (*see also* **oído**). (b) (*fam*) to be very close; **no está en peligro ahora, pero le zumba** he's not actually in danger now, but it's not far away. 3 **zumbarse** *vr* (a) **— de** to rag, tease; to poke fun at. (b) (*Ant*, *Col*) to clear off. (c) (*Cu*) to overstep the mark.

zumbido *nm* (a) buzz(ing), hum(ming), drone; whirr(ing); **— de oídos** buzzing in the ears, ringing in the ears. (b) (*fam*) punch, biff (*fam*).

zumbo[1] *nm* (*CAm*, *Col*) gourd, calabash.

zumbo[2] *nm*=zumbido (a).

zumbón 1 *adj* waggish, funny; *tone etc* teasing, bantering; sarcastic. 2 *nm* wag, joker, funny man; tease.

zumiento *adj* juicy.

zumo *nm* (a) juice; (*as drink*) juice, squash; **— de naranja** orange squash. (b) (*fig*) (solid) profit, (real) gain.

zumoso *adj* juicy.

zuncho *nm* band, hoop, ring.

zupia *nf* (a) dregs; muddy wine; nasty drink, evil-tasting liquid. (b) (*fig*) dregs; human trash, worthless people. (c) (*Bol*, *Ven*) coarse liquor.

zurcido *nm* (a) darning, mending. (b) darn, mend, patch.

zurcidura *nf* = zurcido.
zurcir [3b] *vt* (a) to darn, mend, sew up.
  (b) (*fig*) to join, combine, put together; *lie* to concoct, think up; *tale* to spin.
  (c) (*fam*) **¡que las zurzan!** to blazes with them!
zurdazo *nm* (*SAm*) left-handed punch.
zurdear [1a] *vt* (*SAm*) to do with the left hand.
zurdo 1 *adj hand* left; *person* left-handed; **a zurdas** with the left hand, (*fig*) the wrong way, clumsily; **no es** — (*fig*) he's no fool.
  2 *nm*, **zurda** *nf* left-handed person.
zurra *nf* (a) (*Tech*) dressing, tanning. (b) (*fam*) tanning (*fam*), hiding. (c) (*fam*) hard grind (*fam*), drudgery. (d) (*fam*) roughhouse (*fam*).
zurrador *nm* tanner.
zurrapa *nf* (a) soft lump, dollop, spot; thread, stream (of dirt *etc*); —s dregs. (b) (*fig*) trash, muck, rubbish.
zurraposo *adj* full of dregs, thick, muddy.
zurrar [1a] *vt* (a) (*Tech*) to dress, tan.
  (b) (*fam*) to tan, wallop, lay into (*fam*).
  (c) (*fam: in argument*) to sit heavily on, flatten.
  (d) (*fam*) to lash into, criticize ferociously.

zurria *nf* (a) (*CAm, Col*) tanning (*fam*), hiding. (b) (*Col*) lot, crowd, mass.
zurriaga *nf* whip, lash.
zurriagar [1h] *vt* to whip, lash.
zurriagazo *nm* (a) lash, stroke, cut. (b) (*fig*) severe blow, bad knock; stroke of bad luck. (c) (*fig*) piece of unjust (*or* harsh) treatment.
zurriago *nm* whip, lash.
zurribanda *nf* (*fam*) = zurra (b) *and* (d).
zurriburri *nm* (*fam*) (a) turmoil, bustle, confusion; mess, mix-up; hubbub. (b) worthless individual.
zurrón *nm* pouch, bag.
zurullo *nm*, **zurullón** *nm* (a) lump, hard bit (in liquid *etc*). (b) (*tabu*) turd (*tabu*). (c) lout, hooligan.
zurumato *adj* (*Mex*) stunned, dazed; stupid.
zurumbanco *adj* (*CR, Mex*) (a) = zurumato. (b) half-drunk.
zurumbático *adj*: **estar** — to be stunned, be dazed.
zurumbo *adj* (*CAm*) (a) = zurumato. (b) fuddled, stupid with drink.
zutano *nm*, **zutana** *nf* (*Mr etc*) So-and-so; **si se casa fulano con zutana** if Mr X marries Miss Y; *see* **fulano.**

A

a [ei, ə], **an** [æn, ən, n] (*before words starting with a vowel sound*), *indef art* (a) un, una.
  (b) (*omitted*) **half an hour** media hora; **a fine excuse!** ¡bonita disculpa!; **have you a passport?** ¿tiene Vd pasaporte?; (*omitted in negative uses*) **I haven't got a car** no tengo coche; **you don't stand a chance** no tienes posibilidad alguna; **without a doubt** sin duda; **without saying a word** sin decir palabra; (*omitted in apposition*) **the Duero, a Spanish river** el Duero, río de España.
  (c) (*a certain*) **a Mr Smith called to see you** vino a verle un tal Sr Smith.
  (d) (*distributive*) **2 apples a head** 2 manzanas por persona.
  (e) (*rate*) **30 miles an hour** 30 millas por hora; **£10 a week** 10 libras por semana; **3 times a month** 3 veces al mes; **he reads 3 books a week** lee 3 libros cada semana; **3 pence a dozen** 3 peniques la docena.
A 1 ['ei'wʌn] *adj* de primera clase, de primera categoría; excelente; **to be — at Lloyds** ser de máxima garantía; **to feel —** estar como un reloj.
Aachen ['ɑːxən] Aquisgrán.
aback [ə'bæk] *adv*: **to take —** desconcertar, coger de improviso; **to be taken —** quedar desconcertado; **I was quite taken — by the news** la noticia me causó gran sorpresa, la noticia me cogió de improviso.
abacus ['æbəkəs] *n*, *pl* **abaci** ['æbəsai] ábaco *m*.
abaft [ə'bɑːft] 1 *adv* a popa, en popa. 2 *prep* detrás de.
abandon [ə'bændən] 1 *vt* (a) (*leave*) abandonar, desamparar; **fog made the motorists — their cars** la niebla hizo que los conductores abandonasen sus coches; **to — someone to his fate** abandonar a uno a su suerte.
  (b) (*give up*) renunciar a; **the attempt had to be —ed** tuvieron que renunciar a la empresa; **the game was —ed after 20 minutes' play** después de 20 minutos de juego se dio por nulo el partido.
  2 *vr*: **to — oneself to** abandonarse a, entregarse a.
  3 *n* abandono *m*; libertad *f*, desenfado *m*, desenfreno *m*; **to dance with wild —** abandonarse al éxtasis del baile, bailar desenfrenadamente.
abandoned [ə'bændənd] *adj* **house** etc abandonado, desierto; **child** desamparado; (*vicious*) vicioso, entregado a los vicios; **— woman** mujer perdida; **in an — fashion** con abandono, desenfrenadamente.
abandonment [ə'bændənmənt] *n* (*state*) desamparo *m*, abandono *m*; (*act*) acto *m* de desamparar, el abandonar (etc); (*moral*) = abandon 3.
abase [ə'beis] 1 *vt* humillar, rebajar, degradar; envilecer. 2 *vr*: **to — oneself** humillarse, envilecerse.
abasement [ə'beismənt] *n* humillación *f*, rebajamiento *m*, degradación *f*; envilecimiento *m*.
abash [ə'bæʃ] *vt* avergonzar; **—ed** avergonzado, confuso, corrido; **to be —ed** quedar confuso; **to be —ed at** avergonzarse de; **not a bit —ed** sin inmutarse, como si tal cosa; **he was not a bit —ed at this** no dio la menor señal de vergüenza, siguió como si tal cosa.
abate [ə'beit] 1 *vt* disminuir, reducir; (*Law*) suprimir; **price** rebajar; **violence** mitigar, suavizar; **energy** debilitar; **enthusiasm** moderar; **pride** abatir.
  2 *vi* disminuir, reducirse; ceder, menguar; (*violence, enthusiasm*) moderarse; (*wind*) calmarse, amainar; (*pain*) ceder; (*courage*) desfallecer; (*flood, price*) bajar.
abatement [ə'beitmənt] *n* disminución *f*; moderación *f*; amaine *m*; (*of pain*) alivio *m*; (*Law*) supresión *f*.
abattoir ['æbətwɑː*] *n* matadero *m*.
abbess ['æbis] *n* abadesa *f*.
abbey ['æbi] *n* abadía *f*; monasterio *m*, convento *m*.
abbot ['æbət] *n* abad *m*.
abbreviate [ə'briːvieit] *vt* abreviar.

abbreviation [ə,briːvi'eiʃən] *n* (*short form*) abreviatura *f*; (*act*) abreviación *f*.
ABC ['eibiː'siː] *n* abecé *m*; abecedario *m*; (*fig*) abecé *m*; **— of politics** nociones *fpl* de política, introducción *f* a la política.
abdicate ['æbdikeit] 1 *vt* **throne** abdicar; **responsibility, rights** renunciar a; **principles** abdicar de. 2 *vi* abdicar (*in favour of* en, en favor de).
abdication [,æbdi'keiʃən] *n* abdicación *f*; renuncia *f*.
abdomen ['æbdəmen, *Med* æb'dəumen] *n* abdomen *m*.
abdominal [æb'dɔminl] *adj* abdominal.
abduct [æb'dʌkt] *vt* raptar, secuestrar.
abduction [æb'dʌkʃən] *n* rapto *m*, secuestro *m*.
abductor [æb'dʌktə*] *n* raptor *m*, secuestrador *m*; (*Anat*) abductor *m*.
abed [ə'bed] *adv* en cama, acostado; **we are always — by 12** nos acostamos siempre antes de las 12.
aberrant [ə'berənt] *adj* (*Bio*) aberrante, anormal; (*Anat*) anómalo.
aberration [,æbe'reiʃən] *n* (*all senses*) aberración *f*; **in a moment of mental —** en un momento de aberración.
abet [ə'bet] *vt* **criminal** incitar; ayudar; **crime** instigar; **to — someone in a crime** ser cómplice de uno en un crimen; **X, aided and —ted by Y** X, persuadido y ayudado por Y; **accused of aiding and —ting** acusado de ser cómplice en un crimen.
abetter, abettor [ə'betə*] *n* instigador *m*, ora *f*, promovedor *m*, ora *f*; cómplice *mf*, fautor *m*.
abeyance [ə'beiəns] *n*: **to be in —** estar en suspenso; **to fall into —** caer en desuso.
abhor [əb'hɔː*] *vt* aborrecer, abominar (de), detestar.
abhorrence [əb'hɔrəns] *n* aborrecimiento *m*, detestación *f*; **violence fills me with —** aborrezco la violencia; **to hold in —** detestar.
abhorrent [əb'hɔrənt] *adj* aborrecible, detestable, repugnante; **war is — to me** aborrezco la guerra.
abide [ə'baid] (*irr: pret and ptp* **abode** *or* **abided**) 1 *vt* aguantar, soportar; **I can't — him** no le puedo ver; **I can't — a coward** aborrezco los cobardes; **I can't — tea** me da asco el té.
  2 (*arch: dwell*) morar; (*stay*) permanecer, continuar; **to — by** atenerse a, obrar de acuerdo con, guiarse por; **rules of competition** ajustarse a, aceptar; **promise** cumplir.
abiding [ə'baidiŋ] *adj* permanente, perdurable.
ability [ə'biliti] *n* habilidad *f*, capacidad *f*; talento *m*, aptitud *f*; **— to pay** (*Comm*) solvencia *f*, recursos *mpl*, medios *mpl*; **he has great —** tiene un gran talento (*for* para); **his — in French** su aptitud para el francés; **to the best of my —** lo mejor que yo pueda (*or* sepa); **my — to come depends on el que yo asista depende de; **abilities** talento *m*, dotes *fpl*.
abject ['æbdʒekt] *adj* abyecto, vil; abatido; **apology** rastrero; **to live in — poverty** vivir en la mayor miseria.
abjure [əb'dʒuə*] *vt* renunciar (a), abjurar.
ablative ['æblətiv] *n* ablativo *m*; **— absolute** ablativo *m* absoluto.
ablaze [ə'bleiz] *adv* en llamas, ardiendo; **the house was — in 5 minutes** en 5 minutos la casa estuvo envuelta en llamas; **the house was — with light** brillaban todas las luces de la casa; **the garden was — with colour** resplandecía el jardín con sus flores multicolores; **— with excitement** emocionadísimo, fervoroso.
able ['eibl] 1 *adj* (*talented*) hábil, capaz, talentoso; **seaman of primera; **he's a very — man** es un hombre de mucho talento; **it's an — piece of work** es un trabajo sólido, es un trabajo que vale; **— to pay** (*Comm*) solvente.
  2 **to be — to** + *infin* poder + *infin*; (*of acquired skills*) saber + *infin*, eg **you can go when you are —**

to swim te permitiré ir cuando sepas nadar; **I was eventually — to escape** por fin pude escaparme, por fin logré escaparme; **come as soon as you are —** venga en cuanto pue as.

able-bodied ['eibl'bɔdid] *adj* sano, robusto; **— seaman** marinero *m* de primera.

ablution [ə'bluːʃən] *n* ablución *f*; **—s** (*fam*) lavabo *m*.

ably ['eibli] *adv* hábilmente, con mucha habilidad.

abnegation [ˌæbni'geiʃən] *n* abnegación *f*.

abnormal [æb'nɔːməl] *adj* anormal; irregular; deforme, mal formado.

abnormality [ˌæbnɔː'mæliti] *n* anormalidad *f*; irregularidad *f*; deformidad *f*.

abnormally [æb'nɔːməli] *adv* anormalmente, de modo anormal.

aboard [ə'bɔːd] **1** *adv* a bordo; **to go —** embarcarse, ir a bordo; **to take —** tomar a bordo, embarcar, cargar; **he was not — when we sailed** no estaba a bordo cuando salimos; **all —!** (*Rail etc*) ¡señores viajeros, al tren! (*etc*).
2 *prep:* **— the ship** a bordo del barco; **— the train** en el tren.
3 *as adj:* **life — is pleasant** es agradable la vida de a bordo.

abode [ə'baud] **1** *pret and ptp* of **abide.**
2 *n* domicilio *m*, morada *f*; **place of —** domicilio *m*; **of no fixed —** sin domicilio fijo; **to take up one's —** avecindarse, establecerse.

abolish [ə'bɔliʃ] *vt* suprimir, abolir; anular, revocar.

abolishment [ə'bɔliʃmənt] *n*, **abolition** [ˌæbəu'liʃən] *n* supresión *f*, abolición *f*; anulación *f*.

abolitionist [ˌæbəu'liʃənist] *n* abolicionista *mf*.

A-bomb ['eibɔm] *n* bomba *f* A.

abominable [ə'bɔminəbl] *adj* abominable; *taste etɑ* detestable, pésimo.

abominably [ə'bɔminəbli] *adv* abominablemente; **to behave —** comportarse de una manera detestable; **to be — rude to** estar terriblemente grosero con; **he writes —** escribe pésimamente.

abominate [ə'bɔmineit] *vt* abominar (de), detestar.

abomination [əˌbɔmi'neiʃən] *n* abominación *f*.

aboriginal [ˌæbə'ridʒənl] **1** *adj* aborigen, indígena.
2 *n* aborigen *mf*, indígena *mf*.

aborigines [ˌæbə'ridʒiniːz] *npl* aborígenes *mpl*.

abort [ə'bɔːt] **1** *vt* abortar. **2** *vi* abortar, malparir.

abortion [ə'bɔːʃən] *n* (*Med*) aborto *m* (provocado); (*Vet*) abortón *m*; (*creature*) engendro *m*; (*fig*) malogro *m*, fracaso *m*; **illegal —** aborto *m* ilegal; **to have an —** hacerse abortar; **to procure an —** hacer abortar a una mujer.

abortionist [ə'bɔːʃənist] *n* abortista *mf*.

abortive [ə'bɔːtiv] *adj* abortivo; *attempt, plan* ineficaz, fracasado; **to prove —** fracasar, no dar resultado.

abound [ə'baund] *vi* abundar (*in, with* en).

about [ə'baut] **1** *adv* (a) (*approximately*) casi, alrededor de, más o menos; **— 20** unos 20, 20 más o menos; **— 7 years ago** hace unos 7 años; **— 2 o'clock** a eso de las 2; **— a month** un mes poco más o menos, cosa de un mes; **he must be — 40** tendrá alrededor de 40 años; **— half** alrededor de la mitad; **it's just — finished** está terminado casi; **he's — the same** sigue más o menos lo mismo; **that's — it, that's — right** eso es.
(b) (*place*) **all —** por todas partes; **to run —** correr, correr por todas partes; **to walk —** pasearse de aquí para allá; *see* **play, turn** *etc.*
(c) (*with verb* to be) **to be — again** (*after illness*) estar levantado; **we were — early** nos levantamos temprano; **is Mr Brown —?** ¿está por aquí el Sr Brown?; **he must be — somewhere** debe de andar por aquí; **there's a thief —** anda por aquí un ladrón; **there's a lot of measles —** hay mucho sarampión; **to be — to** + *infin* estar a punto de + *infin*, estar para + *infin*.
2 *prep* (a) (*place*) alrededor de; **the fields — the house** los campos alrededor de la casa; **all — the house** por todas partes alrededor de la casa, (*inside*) por todas partes de la casa; **the fire junto a la lumbre**; **to walk — the house** andar por la casa; **to wander — the town** pasearse sin propósito fijo por la ciudad; **you're — the house all day** pasas todo el día en casa; **to do jobs — the house** hacer los quehaceres domésticos; **he looked — him** miró alrededor de sí, miró a su alrededor; **he took her — the waist** la cogió por la cintura; **I have no money — me** no llevo dinero encima.
(b) (*place: fig*) **he had a mysterious air — him** había algo misterioso en él; **there's something — him (that I like)** tiene un no sé qué que me gusta; **there's something — a soldier** los soldados tienen un no sé qué de atractivo; **while you're — it**

mientras lo estés haciendo; **you've been a long time — it** has tardado bastante en hacerlo.
(c) (*relating to*) de, acerca de, sobre, con respecto a; **a book — travel** un libro sobre los viajes; **I can tell you nothing — him** no le puedo decir nada acerca de él; **they fell out — money** riñeron por cuestión de dinero; **how — me?** ¿y yo?; **how — that book?** ¿y el libro ese?; **how — that?** ¿qué te parece?; **what — that book?** ¿y el libro ese?; **what — it?** (*what do you say*) ¿quieres?; (*what of it*) ¿y qué?; **what — a song?** ¿queréis que os cante algo?; **— what no nos cantas algo?; what's that book —?** ¿de qué trata ese libro?; **what's it all —?** ¿de qué se trata?, ¿qué pasa?; **what are you —?** ¿qué haces ahí?, ¿qué pretendes con eso?; **what did he talk —?** ¿de qué te habló?

about-face [ə'baut'feis] **1** *n* media vuelta *f*; cambio *m* de postura. **2** *vi* dar media vuelta, cambiar de postura.

above [ə'bʌv] **1** *adv* encima, por encima, arriba; (*in text*) arriba; **as — según** lo dicho antes; **as set out — según** lo arriba expuesto; **as I said — según** dije ya; **from — desde** encima, desde arriba; de lo alto; del cielo; **orders from — órdenes** de fuente superior; **the flat — el** piso de arriba; **the air — el** aire por encima; **those — los** de categoría superior; los que están en el cielo.
2 *prep* (a) (*place*) encima de; **— my head** encima de mi cabeza; **— ground** sobre la tierra; **the Tagus — Toledo** el Tajo más arriba de Toledo; (*more northerly than*) al norte de; **2000 metres — sea level** 2000 metros sobre el nivel del mar.
(b) (*place: fig*) **he is — me in rank** tiene categoría superior a la mía; **I couldn't hear — the din** no podía oír con tanto ruido; **we are — that sort of thing** nosotros quedamos por encima de aquello; **it is — criticism** queda por encima de toda crítica; **it's — me** no lo entiendo; **he is not — a bit of blackmail** es capaz de hacer un poco de chantaje.
(c) (*number*) más de; superior a; **— 100** más de 100; **there were not — 40 people** no había más de 40 personas; **any number — 12** cualquier número superior a 12; **she can't count — 10** no sabe contar más allá de 10.
3 *adj* susodicho, citado, arriba escrito.

aboveboard [ə'bʌv'bɔːd] **1** *adv* sin rebozo, abiertamente. **2** *adj* legítimo.

above-mentioned [ə'bʌv'menʃənd] *adj* sobredicho, susodicho.

abracadabra [ˌæbrəkə'dæbrə] *n* abracadabra *f*.

abrade [ə'breid] *vt* raer, raspar.

Abraham ['eibrəhæm] *m* Abrahán, Abraham.

abrasion [ə'breiʒən] *n* raedura *f*, raspadura *f*; (*Med*) abrasión *f*.

abrasive [ə'breiziv] **1** *adj* abrasivo. **2** *n* abrasivo *m*.

abreast [ə'brest] *adv* de frente, de fondo; **to march 4 — marchar** 4 de frente; **he was walking — of the last two** caminaba a par de los dos últimos; **to come — of** llegar a la altura de; **to be — of** (*fig*) estar al corriente de; **to keep — of** mantenerse al corriente de; **to keep — of the times** mantenerse al día.

abridge [ə'bridʒ] *vt book* compendiar, resumir; (*cut short*) abreviar, acortar; (*deprive*) privar (*of* de).

abridgement [ə'bridʒmənt] *n* compendio *m*, resumen *m*; abreviación *f*; privación *f*.

abroad [ə'brɔːd] *adv* (a) (*in foreign parts*): **to be — estar** en el extranjero; **to go — ir** al extranjero; **he had to go — (*fleeing*)** tuvo que salir del país; **troops brought in from — tropas** traídas de fuera.
(b) (*outside*) fuera; fuera de casa; **there were not many — at that hour** había poca gente por las calles a tal hora; **there is a rumour — that** corre un rumor de que; **it has got — that** se tiene noticia de que, (*falsely*) se ha divulgado la especie de que; **how did the news get —?** ¿cómo se divulgó la noticia?

abrogate ['æbrəugeit] *vt* abrogar.

abrogation [ˌæbrəu'geiʃən] *n* abrogación *f*.

abrupt [ə'brʌpt] *adj* (*sudden*) repentino, brusco; precipitado; *terrain* escarpado; *style* cortado, lacónico; *manner of person* áspero; **he was very — with me** me trató sin miramientos.

abruptly [ə'brʌptli] *adv* repentinamente, bruscamente; precipitadamente; **a cliff rose — before them** delante de ellos se alzaba un risco cortado a pico; **to leave — salir** repentinamente; **everything changed — de** pronto cambió todo.

abruptness [ə'brʌptnis] *n* brusquedad *f*; precipitación *f*; lo escarpado; lo cortado.

abscess ['æbsis] *n* absceso *m*.

abscond [əb'skɔnd] *vi* fugarse, huir de la justicia; **to — with the funds** huir (*or* largarse, alzarse) con el dinero.

absence ['æbsəns] n (of person) ausencia f; (of thing) falta f; in the — of person en ausencia de, thing a falta de; sentenced in one's — condenado en ausencia; to be conspicuous by one's — brillar por su ausencia; — of mind distracción f, despiste m.

absent ['æbsənt] adj ausente (from de); (fig) distraído; where liberty is — donde falta la libertad; why were you — from class? ¿por qué faltó Vd a la clase?

absent [æb'sent] vr: to — oneself ausentarse (from de).

absentee [,æbsən'ti:] n ausente mf; — landlord absentista m.

absenteeism [,æbsən'ti:izəm] n absentismo m.

absently ['æbsəntli] adv distraídamente.

absent-minded ['æbsənt'maindid] adj distraído, despistado.

absent-mindedly ['æbsənt'maindidli] adv distraídamente, por distracción.

absent-mindedness ['æbsənt'maindidnis] n distracción f, despiste m.

absinth(e) ['æbsinθ] n (Bot) ajenjo m; (drink) absenta f.

absolute ['æbsəlu:t] adj (Math, Gram, power, monarch, alcohol etc) absoluto; certainty, confidence etc completo; support incondicional; prohibition terminante, total; denial rotundo, categórico; liar redomado; the — (Philos) lo absoluto; the man's an — idiot es un puro imbécil; it's — rubbish! ¡es puro disparate!; it's an — scandal es simplemente escandaloso.

absolutely ['æbsəlu:tli] adv rule etc absolutamente; (wholly) completamente, totalmente; —! ¡perfectamente!, ¡eso es!; that is — untrue eso es completamente falso; it is — forbidden to + infin queda terminantemente prohibido + infin; I deny it — lo niego rotundamente.

absolution [,æbsə'lu:ʃən] n absolución f.

absolutism ['æbsəlu:tizəm] n absolutismo m.

absolve [əb'zɔlv] vt absolver (from de).

absorb [əb'zɔ:b] vt absorber; shock etc amortiguar; (Comm) absorber; the business —s a lot of my time el negocio me lleva mucho tiempo, el negocio me trae ocupadísimo; she —s chemistry readily le entra con facilidad la química; the country —ed 1000 refugees el país dio entrada a 1000 refugiados; to be —ed in (fig) estar absorto en; to get —ed in (fig) engolfarse en, empaparse de, dedicarse de lleno al estudio de.

absorbency [əb'zɔ:bənsi] n absorbencia f.

absorbent [əb'zɔ:bənt] adj absorbente; cotton etc hidrófilo.

absorbing [əb'zɔ:biŋ] adj study etc absorbente, interesantísimo; I find history very — la historia tiene para mí un fuerte atractivo, me apasiona la historia.

absorption [əb'zɔ:pʃən] n absorción f (also fig).

abstain [əb'stein] vi abstenerse (from de); (not drink) abstenerse de las bebidas alcohólicas; to — from comment no ofrecer comentario alguno.

abstainer [əb'steinə*] n (also total —; approx) abstemio m, abstinente m, persona f que no bebe alcohol.

abstemious [əb'sti:miəs] adj sobrio, abstemio, templado.

abstemiousness [əb'sti:miəsnis] n sobriedad f, moderación f.

abstention [əb'stenʃən] n abstención f; (Parl) abstención f de votar; there were 20 —s hubo 20 que no votaron.

abstinence ['æbstinəns] n abstinencia f (from de); day of — día m de ayuno.

abstinent ['æbstinənt] adj abstinente.

abstract ['æbstrækt] 1 adj abstracto (also Art, Gram); in the — en abstracto. 2 n resumen m, sumario m.

abstract [æb'strækt] 1 vt (remove) extractar, quitar, separar; (steal) robar; (Chem) extraer; book resumir, compendiar.
2 vr: to — oneself abstraerse, ensimismarse.

abstracted [æb'stræktid] adj distraído, ensimismado.

abstraction [æb'strækʃən] n abstracción f; distraimiento m, ensimismamiento m.

abstruse [æb'stru:s] adj profundo, recóndito, abstruso.

absurd [əb'sə:d] adj absurdo, ridículo, disparatado; it is — that es absurdo que; how —! ¡qué ridículo!; don't be —! ¡no digas tonterías!; you look — in that hat con ese sombrero pareces ridículo; theatre of the — teatro m de lo absurdo.

absurdity [əb'sə:diti] n absurdo m, disparate m; locura f; (of situation etc) lo absurdo.

absurdly [əb'sə:dli] adv absurdamente, ridiculamente.

abundance [ə'bʌndəns] n abundancia f; (of heart) plenitud f; in — en abundancia, abundantemente, a granel; we had an — of rain llovió copiosamente; we have a great — of books tenemos gran copia de libros.

abundant [ə'bʌndənt] adj abundante (in en); copioso.

abundantly [ə'bʌndəntli] adv abundantemente; copiosamente; to make it — clear that hacer constar con toda claridad que.

abuse [ə'bju:s] n (a) (insults) improperios mpl, injurias fpl; to heap — on somone llenar a uno de injurias.
(b) (misuse) abuso m; — of confidence, — of trust abuso m de confianza; — of one's authority abuso m de su autoridad.

abuse [ə'bju:z] vt (a) (revile) maltratar (de palabra), injuriar, llenar de injurias; he roundly —d the government dijo mil improperios contra el gobierno.
(b) (misuse) abusar de.

abusive [ə'bju:siv] adj practice etc abusivo; (insulting) ofensivo, injurioso, insultante; to be — to decir cosas injuriosas a; to become — empezar a soltar injurias (to contra).

abut [ə'bʌt] vi confinar, estar contiguo; to — against, to — on confinar con, lindar con; (penthouse etc) apoyarse en; (end in) terminar en.

abutment [ə'bʌtmənt] n (Archit) estribo m, contrafuerte m, botarel m; (Carpentry) empotramiento m.

abutting [ə'bʌtiŋ] adj colindante, contiguo.

abysmal [ə'bizməl] adj abismal; (fig) profundo; the most — ignorance la ignorancia más profunda; to live in — poverty vivir en la mayor miseria; an — result un malísimo resultado; an — performance una pésima actuación; the play was — la obra fue una catástrofe.

abysmally [ə'bizməli] adv (fig) malísimamente, terriblemente; — bad terriblemente malo.

abyss [ə'bis] n abismo m, sima f.

Abyssinia [,æbi'siniə] Abisinia f.

Abyssinian [,æbi'siniən] 1 adj abisinio. 2 n abisinio m, a f.

acacia [ə'keiʃə] n acacia f.

academic [,ækə'demik] 1 adj académico; (Univ) universitario; argument bizantino, poco provechoso, estéril; question puramente teórico, sin trascendencia práctica; — dress vestidura f universitaria; — freedom libertad f de cátedra; — interests intereses mpl eruditos; — year (Univ) año m universitario, (School) año m escolar.
2 n universitario m, catedrático m (de universidad).

academicals [,ækə'demikəlz] npl vestidura f universitaria.

academician [ə,kædə'miʃən] n académico m.

academy [ə'kædəmi] n academia f; (Scot) instituto m, colegio m; military — escuela f militar; — for young ladies colegio m para señoritas; secretarial — escuela f para secretarias; Royal A— (of Arts) Real Academia f (de Bellas Artes); the Spanish A— la Real Academia Española.

acanthus [ə'kænθəs] n acanto m.

accede [æk'si:d] vi: to — to request consentir en, acceder a; office, post tomar posesión de, entrar en; party adherirse a; throne subir a; treaty firmar.

accelerate [æk'seləreit] 1 vt acelerar; apresurar. 2 vi acelerarse; darse prisa.

acceleration [æk,selə'reiʃən] n aceleración f.

accelerator [æk'seləreitə*] n acelerador m.

accent ['æksənt] n acento m; acute — acento m agudo; grave — acento m grave; in a broken — con marcado acento extranjero; with a strong provincial — con fuerte acento de provincia; in —s of some surprise en cierto tono de asombro; the minister put the — on exports el ministro subrayó la importancia de la exportación; this year the — is on bright colours este año están de moda los colores brillantes.

accent [æk'sent] vt acentuar.

accentuate [æk'sentjueit] vt acentuar; (fig) recalcar, subrayar, dar énfasis a.

accentuation [æk,sentju'eiʃən] n acentuación f.

accept [ək'sept] vt aceptar (also Comm); aprobar; admitir; recibir, acoger, dar acogida a; the Academy —s the word la Academia aprueba la palabra; the Academy —ed the word in 1936 la Academia admitió la palabra en 1936; to — orders (Comm) admitir pedidos; I do not — that way of doing it no apruebo ese modo de hacerlo; it is —ed that se reconoce que; we — that it is so reconocemos que es así; he was —ed as one of us pasaba por ser uno de nosotros.

acceptable [ək'septəbl] *adj* acceptable; admisible; grato; **tea is always** — el té siempre agrada; **that would be most** — eso me gustaría muchísimo; **that would not be** — **to the government** eso no le sería grato al gobierno; **that policy is not** — esa política no es admisible; **it is not easy to find an** — **gift** no es fácil encontrar un regalo adecuado.

acceptance [ək'septəns] *n* aceptación *f* (*also Comm*); aprobación *f*; (buena) acogida *f*; **to win** — lograr la aprobación; **to meet with general** — ser bien recibido.

acceptation [,æksep'teiʃən] *n* acepción *f*.

accepted [ək'septid] *adj* acepto; **it's the** — **thing** es cosa corriente; **he's an** — **expert** es un experto reconocido como tal.

acceptor [ək'septə*] *n* aceptador *m*, ora *f*; (*Comm*) aceptante *mf*.

access ['ækses] *n* (**a**) acceso *m*, entrada *f*; **easy of** — asequible, de fácil acceso; **person** abordable, tratable; **to give** — **to a room** comunicar con una habitación; **this gives** — **to the garden** por aquí se sale al jardín; **to have** — **to the minister** poder libremente hablar con el ministro, tener libre acceso al ministro; **he had** — **to the family papers** pudo leer los papeles de la familia, se le facilitaron los papeles de la familia.
(**b**) (*Med*) acceso *m*, ataque *m*; **in an** — **of rage** en un arranque de cólera.

accessibility [æk,sesi'biliti] *n* accesibilidad *f*.

accessible [æk'sesəbl] *adj* accesible, asequible (*to* a); **person** tratable; **the duke is not** — **to visitors** el duque no recibe visitas.

accession [æk'seʃən] *n* acceso *m*, entrada *f*; (*increase*) aumento *m*; (*to treaty*) accesión *f*; (*new library book*) libro *m* recién adquirido; (*Law*) entrada *f* en posesión (*to an estate* de una propiedad); (*of king*) subida *f*, ascenso *m* (*to the throne* al trono); — **to power** ascenso *m* al poder; **a sudden** — **of strength** un aumento inesperado de fuerzas.

accessory [æk'sesəri] **1** *adj* accesorio.
2 *n* (**a**) accesorio *m*; **accessories** accesorios *mpl*; (*Aut etc*) complementos *mpl*; **toilet accessories** artículos *mpl* de tocador.
(**b**) (*Law*) cómplice *mf*; — **after the fact** cómplice *m* encubridor, ora *f*; — **before the fact** cómplice *m* instigador, ora *f*.

accidence ['æksidəns] *n* (*Gram*) accidentes *mpl*.

accident ['æksidənt] *n* accidente *m*; — **insurance** seguro *m* contra accidentes; **road** — accidente *m* de carretera; **traffic** — accidente *m* de circulación; **by** — (*by chance*) por casualidad, (*unintentionally*) accidentalmente, sin querer, por descuido; **by some** — **I found myself there** me encontré no sé cómo allí; —**s will happen** hay accidentes que no se pueden prever; **to have an** —, **to meet with an** — sufrir un accidente; **I'm sorry, it was an** — lo siento, lo hice sin querer.

accidental [,æksi'dentl] *adj* accidental, fortuito; — **death** muerte *f* por accidente.

accidentally [,æksi'dentəli] *adv* (*by chance*) por casualidad; (*unintentionally*) sin querer, por inadvertencia, por descuido; **we met quite** — nos encontramos por pura casualidad.

accident-prone ['æksidənt,prəun] *adj* con tendencia a sufrir (*or* causar) accidentes.

acclaim [ə'kleim] **1** *vt* aclamar; vitorear, ovacionar; **he was** —**ed king** le aclamaron rey; **he was** —**ed** (**as**) **the winner** le aclamaron por vencedor; **the play was** —**ed** la obra fue muy aplaudida, la obra recibió muchos aplausos. **2** *n* aclamación *f*, aplausos *mpl*.

acclamation [,æklə'meiʃən] *n* aclamación *f*, aplausos *mpl*; **amid the** —**s of the crowd** entre los vítores de la multitud; **by** — por aclamación.

acclimate [ə'klaimət] *vt* (*US*) aclimatar.

acclimatization [ə,klaimətai'zeiʃən] *n* aclimatación *f*.

acclimatize [ə'klaimətaiz] **1** *vt* aclimatar. **2** *vi*, *vr*: **to** — **oneself** aclimatarse (*to* a); **to become** —**d** aclimatarse.

acclivity [ə'kliviti] *n* subida *f*, cuesta *f*.

accolade ['ækəuleid] *n* (*Hist*) acolada *f*, espaldarazo *m*; (*fig*) premio *m*; (*Mus*) acolada *f*.

accommodate [ə'kɔmədeit] **1** *vt* (**a**) (*lodge, have room for*) **person** alojar, hospedar; **thing** tener espacio para, tener cabida para, contener; **can you** — **4 people in July?** ¿tiene Vd habitaciones para 4 personas en julio?; **can you** — **2 more in your car?** ¿caben 2 más en su coche?
(**b**) (*reconcile*) **differences** acomodar, concertar; **quarrel** componer; **quarrellers** reconciliar.
(**c**) (*adapt*) acomodar, adaptar (*to* a).

(**d**) (*supply*) proveer (*with* de); **to** — **someone with a loan** ayudar a uno prestándole dinero.
(**e**) (*oblige*) complacer; **we will do our best to** — **you** haremos todo lo que podamos por complacerle.
2 *vi* (*eye*) adaptarse (*to* a).

accommodating [ə'kɔmədeitiŋ] *adj* servicial, complaciente, atento; (*pej*) acomodadizo, que a todo se aviene fácilmente.

accommodation [ə,kɔmə'deiʃən] *n* (**a**) (*lodging*) alojamiento *m*; (*rooms*) habitaciones *fpl*; — **to let** se alquila habitación; **have you any** — **available?** ¿tiene Vd habitación disponible?; — **bureau** oficina *f* de hospedaje; — **train** (*US*) tren *m* de pasajeros.
(**b**) (*space*) espacio *m*, sitio *m*; cabida *f*; **seating** — plazas *fpl*, asientos *mpl*; **there is** — **for 20 passengers** hay sitio para 20 pasajeros; **the plane has limited** — el avión tiene un número fijo de plazas.
(**c**) (*agreement*) acuerdo *m*, convenio *m*.
(**d**) (*adaptation*) acomodación *f*, adaptación *f*.
(**e**) (*loan*) crédito *m*, préstamo *m*; — **bill,** — **note** (*Comm*) pagaré *m* de favor.

accompaniment [ə'kʌmpənimənt] *n* acompañamiento *m* (*also Mus*).

accompanist [ə'kʌmpənist] *n* acompañante *m*, a *f*.

accompany [ə'kʌmpəni] **1** *vt* acompañar (*by, with* de; *also Mus, on* con); **he accompanied this with a grimace** al decir esto hizo un visaje.
2 *vr*: **to** — **oneself on the piano** acompañarse del piano.

accomplice [ə'kʌmplis] *n* cómplice *mf*.

accomplish [ə'kʌmpliʃ] *vt* (*finish*) acabar, concluir; (*carry out*) llevar a cabo, hacer; (*bring about*) efectuar, lograr; **one's design** realizar; **prophecy** cumplir.

accomplished [ə'kʌmpliʃt] *adj* **person** experto, consumado, hábil; **fact** consumado.

accomplishment [ə'kʌmpliʃmənt] *n* (*finishing*) conclusión *f*; (*bringing about*) efectuación *f*, logro *m*, realización *f*; **a great** — una hazaña; **it's quite an** — **to** + **infin** exige mucho talento + *infin*; **difficult of** — de difícil consecución; —**s** talentos *mpl*, prendas *fpl*, dotes *fpl*.

accord [ə'kɔ:d] **1** *n* (*treaty*) acuerdo *m*, convenio *m*; (*harmony*) armonía *f*; **of one's own** — espontáneamente, de su propio acuerdo, por impulso propio; **with one** — de común acuerdo; **to be in** — estar de acuerdo (*with* con).
2 *vt* conceder, otorgar; *welcome* dar.
3 *vi* concordar (*with* con); **how does this** — **with your plan?** ¿cómo se aviene esto con su proyecto?

accordance [ə'kɔ:dəns] *n*: **in** — **with** conforme a, con arreglo a, de acuerdo con.

according [ə'kɔ:diŋ]: — **as** según que, a medida que; — **to** según; (*in accordance with*) con arreglo a, conforme a.

accordingly [ə'kɔ:diŋli] *adv* en conformidad, de acuerdo con esto; (**and**) — así pues, por consiguiente.

accordion [ə'kɔ:diən] *n* acordeón *m*.

accordionist [ə'kɔ:diənist] *n* acordeonista *mf*.

accost [ə'kɔst] *vt* abordar, dirigirse a, entablar conversación con; (*prostitute*) abordar con fines deshonestos; **he** —**ed me in the street** se dirigió a mí en la calle; **he** —**ed me for a light** se acercó a mí para pedir fuego.

account [ə'kaunt] **1** *n* (**a**) (*Fin etc*) cuenta *f*; (*invoice*) factura *f*; (*statement of* —) estado *m* de cuenta; —**s department** sección *f* de teneduría de libros; **blocked** — cuenta *f* bloqueada; **current** — cuenta *f* corriente; **deposit** — cuenta *f* a plazo fijo; **joint** — cuenta *f* indistinta; **profit and loss** — cuenta *f* de ganancias y pérdidas; — **payable** cuenta *f* a pagar; — **rendered** cuenta *f* pasada; **on** — a cuenta; **payment on** — pago *m* a cuenta; **could I have £50 on** —? ¿puede Vd darme 50 libras anticipadas?; **on his** — por él, por causa de él; **on his own** — por cuenta propia; **on** — **of** por, a causa de, por motivo de; **on that** — por eso; **on no** —, **not on any** — de ninguna manera, bajo ningún concepto; **to bring someone to** —, **to call someone to** — pedir cuentas a uno; **to charge something to someone's** — cargar algo en cuenta a uno; **to close an** — liquidar una cuenta; **to go to one's** — morir; **to keep the** —**s** llevar las cuentas; **to open an** — abrir una cuenta; **to render an** —, **to send an** — pasar factura; **to settle an** — liquidar una cuenta; **to settle** —**s with** (*fig*) ajustar cuentas con; **to turn to** — aprovechar, sacar provecho de.
(**b**) (*estimation*) importancia *f*; **of no** —, **of little** —, **of small** — de poca importancia; **of some** — de cierta importancia, de alguna consideración.

(c) (*report*) relato *m*, relación *f* (*of* de), informe *m* (*of* sobre); **by all** —s a decir de todos, por lo que dicen todos; **to give an** — of dar cuenta de, informar sobre; **to give an** — of oneself justificar su conducta; **to give a good** — of oneself dar buena cuenta de sí; **to leave something out** of — no tomar algo en consideración; **to take something into** —, **to take** — of something tener algo en cuenta, tener algo presente.

2 *vt* considerar; **I** — him a fool considero que es tonto; **I** — myself lucky creo que tengo suerte; **he is** —ed an expert se le considera como un experto; **I should** — it a favour if agradecería que.

3 *vi*: **to** — for (*answer for*) responder de; (*explain*) dar cuenta de, dar razón de, justificar; (*kill*) acabar con; **that** —s for it ésa es la razón, ha sido por eso; **I can't** — for it no me lo explico; **how do you** — for it? ¿cómo lo explica Vd?; **everything is now** —ed for todo está completo ya; **there is no** —ing for tastes sobre gustos no hay disputa.

accountable [ə'kauntəbl] *adj* responsable (*for* de, *to* ante); **he is** — only to himself no reconoce más responsabilidad que ante sí mismo; **not** — for one's actions no responsable de sus propios actos.

accountancy [ə'kauntənsi] *n* contabilidad *f*.

accountant [ə'kauntənt] *n* contable *m*, contador *m*; —'s office contaduría *f*; **chartered** — contable *m* diplomado.

account book [ə'kauntbuk] *n* libro *m* de cuentas.

account day [ə'kauntdei] *n* día *m* de ajuste de cuentas.

accounting [ə'kauntiŋ] *n* contabilidad *f*.

accounting machine [ə'kauntiŋmə,ʃi:n] *n* máquina *f* de contabilidad, calculadora *f*.

accoutred [ə'ku:təd] *ptp and adj* equipado.

accoutrements [ə'ku:trəmənts] *npl* equipo *m*, avíos *mpl*, arreos *mpl*.

accredit [ə'kredit] *vt* acreditar (*someone to someone* a uno cerca de uno); **to** — something to someone, **to** — someone with something atribuir algo a uno.

accredited [ə'kreditid] *adj* autorizado.

accretion [ə'kri:ʃən] *n* aumento *m*, acrecentamiento *m*; (*Min*) acreción *f*; (*Law*) acrecencia *f*.

accrue [ə'kru:] *vi* (*grow*) aumentarse, acumularse; **to** — from proceder de; **to** — to corresponder a; **some benefit will** — to you from this de esto resultará algo a beneficio de Vd; —d income renta *f* acumulada; —d interest interés *m* acumulado.

accumulate [ə'kju:mjuleit] 1 *vt* acumular, amontonar; acopiar. 2 *vi* acumularse, amontonarse.

accumulation [ə,kju:mju'leiʃən] *n* (*amassing*) acumulación *f*, amontonamiento *m*; (*mass*) montón *m*, acopio *m*.

accumulative [ə'kju:mjulətiv] *adj* acumulativo; acumulador.

accumulator [ə'kju:mjuleitə*] *n* acumulador *m*.

accuracy ['ækjurəsi] *n* exactitud *f*, precisión *f*.

accurate ['ækjurit] *adj* number, observation etc exacto, preciso, correcto; copy fiel; answer correcto, acertado; shot certero; instrument de precisión; **to be strictly** — para decirlo con toda exactitud.

accurately ['ækjuritli] *adv* exactamente, correctamente; fielmente; acertadamente; certeramente.

accursed, accurst [ə'kə:st] *adj* (*lit*) maldito; (*ill-fated*) infausto, desventurado; — be he who . . .! ¡maldito sea quien . . .!, ¡mal haya quien . . .!

accusation [,ækju'zeiʃən] *n* acusación *f*, cargo *m*; denuncia *f*, delación *f*.

accusative [ə'kju:zətiv] *n* acusativo *m*.

accuse [ə'kju:z] *vt* acusar (*of* de); denunciar, delatar; echar la culpa a.

accused [ə'kju:zd] *n* acusado *m*, a *f*.

accuser [ə'kju:zə*] *n* acusador *m*, ora *f*.

accusing [ə'kju:ziŋ] *adj* acusatorio, lleno de reproches.

accusingly [ə'kju:ziŋli] *adv*: **he looked at me** — me lanzó una mirada acusatoria.

accustom [ə'kʌstəm] 1 *vt* acostumbrar, habituar (*to* a); **to be** —ed to + infin acostumbrar + infin, soler + infin; **I'm not really** —ed to + ger en realidad no tengo la costumbre de + infin, no estoy realmente acostumbrado a + infin; **to get** —ed to something acostumbrarse a algo, habituarse a algo; **to get** —ed to + ger acostumbrarse a + infin.

2 *vr*: **to** — oneself to acostumbrarse a; **to** — oneself to + ger acostumbrarse a + infin.

accustomed [ə'kʌstəmd] *adj* acostumbrado, usual.

ace [eis] *n* (*all senses*) as *m*; **to be within an** — of estar a dos dedos de, estar a pique de.

acerbity [ə'sə:biti] *n* aspereza *f*.

acetate ['æsiteit] *n* acetato *m*.

acetic [ə'si:tik] *adj* acético; — acid ácido *m* acético.

acetone ['æsitəun] *n* acetona *f*.

acetylene [ə'setili:n] 1 *adj* acetilénico; — lamp, — torch soplete *m* oxiacetilénico; — welding soldadura *f* oxiacetilénica. 2 *n* acetileno *m*.

ache [eik] 1 *n* dolor *m*; **I have an** — in my side me duele el costado; **full of** —s and pains lleno de goteras; **with an** — in one's heart con dolor del corazón.

2 *vi* doler; **my head** —s me duele la cabeza; **it makes my head** — me da un dolor de cabeza; **I** — all over tengo dolores por todas partes; **it was enough to make your heart** — era para romper el alma; **my heart** —s for you lo siento en el alma; **I am aching for you** suspiro por ti; **I** —d to help him quería con todo mi ser acudir en su auxilio.

achieve [ə'tʃi:v] *vt* lograr, conseguir, alcanzar, realizar; llevar a cabo; acabar; **he will never** — anything él no hará nunca nada.

achievement [ə'tʃi:vmənt] *n* (*act*) realización *f*, consecución *f*; (*thing achieved*) éxito *m*, hazaña *f*; **that's quite an** — eso representa un éxito nada despreciable; **it's an** — to do that hacer aquello ya es algo.

Achilles [ə'kili:z] *m* Aquiles; —' heel talón *m* de Aquiles; —' tendon tendón *m* de Aquiles.

aching ['eikiŋ] 1 *adj* dolorido; heart etc afligido. 2 *n* dolor *m*.

acid ['æsid] 1 *adj* (*Chem*) ácido; (*sour*) agrio; comment etc mordaz, punzante. 2 *n* ácido *m*.

acidify [ə'sidifai] 1 *vt* acidificar. 2 *vi* acidificarse.

acidity [ə'siditi] *n* acidez *f*; (*of stomach*) acedía *f*.

acid-proof ['æsidpru:f] *adj*, **acid-resisting** ['æsidri'zistiŋ] *adj* a prueba de ácidos.

acidulous [ə'sidjuləs] *adj* acídulo.

ack-ack ['æk'æk] *n* (*fam*) fuego *m* antiaéreo; (*guns*) artillería *f* antiaérea; — gun cañón *m* antiaéreo.

acknowledge [ək'nɔlidʒ] 1 *vt* reconocer; truth etc confesar; claim admitir; crime confesarse culpable de; favour agradecer; letter acusar recibo de; present dar las gracias por; greeting contestar a; **to** — defeat darse por vencido; **to** — receipt acusar recibo de; **I** — that reconozco que; **to** — someone as leader reconocer a uno por jefe; **to** — someone to be superior reconocer que uno es mejor.

2 *vr*: **to** — oneself beaten darse por vencido; **I** — myself the loser reconozco que he perdido.

acknowledged [ək'nɔlidʒd] *adj*: **an** — expert un experto reconocido como tal.

acknowledgement [ək'nɔlidʒmənt] *n* reconocimiento *m*; confesión *f*; agradecimiento *m*; contestación *f* (*of a greeting* a un saludo); (*Comm*) acuse *m* de recibo; (*reward*) recompensa *f*; **to make** —s expresar su agradecimiento; **I wish to make public** — of the help quiero agradecer públicamente la ayuda; **to quote without** — citar sin mencionar la fuente.

acme ['ækmi] *n* colmo *m*, cima *f*; — of perfection suma perfección *f*; **he is the** — of good taste es el buen gusto en persona.

acne ['ækni] *n* acné *m*.

acolyte ['ækəulait] *n* acólito *m*.

aconite ['ækənait] *n* acónito *m*.

acorn ['eikɔ:n] *n* bellota *f*.

acoustic [ə'ku:stik] *adj* acústico.

acoustics [ə'ku:stiks] *npl* acústica *f*.

acquaint [ə'kweint] 1 *vt* (a) **to** — someone with avisar a uno de, informar a uno sobre; poner a uno al corriente de.

(b) **to be** —ed conocerse; **to become** —ed (llegar a) conocerse.

(c) **to be** —ed with person conocer, fact saber, situation estar enterado de, estar al corriente de; **to become** —ed with person (llegar a) conocer, fact saber, situation ponerse al tanto de.

2 *vr*: **to** — oneself with informarse sobre; **I intend to make myself** —ed with the facts me propongo averiguar los hechos.

acquaintance [ə'kweintəns] *n* (a) conocimiento *m* (*with* de); familiaridad *f* (*with* con); **I have not the honour of his** — no tengo el honor de conocerle; **to have a nodding** — with conocer ligeramente; **it improves on** — parece mejor después de conocido; **to make someone's** — conocer a uno; **I am very glad to make your** — tengo mucho gusto en conocerle; **to scrape** — with hacerse conocer por.

(b) (*person*) conocido *m*; **we're just** —s nos conocemos ligeramente nada más; **an** — of mine una persona que yo conozco; **to have a wide circle of** —s conocer a muchísimas personas.

acquaintanceship [ə'kweintənsʃip] *n* (a) conocimiento *m* (*with* de), familiaridad *f* (*with* con). (b) (*between two persons*) relaciones *fpl*.

acquiesce [,ækwi'es] *vi* consentir (*in* en), asentir (*in* a), conformarse (*in* con); (*unwillingly*) someterse.

acquiescence [,ækwi'esns] n consentimiento m (in en), conformidad f (in con).

acquiescent [,ækwi'esnt] adj condescendiente, conforme; **he was perfectly** — consintió de buena gana.

acquire [ə'kwaiə*] vt adquirir; obtener; conseguir; proporcionarse; language etc aprender; territory tomar (from a), tomar posesión de; **he** —**d a fine tan** se dio un espléndido bronceado; **where did you** — **that?** ¿dónde conseguiste eso?; **she** —**d many followers** se le pegaron muchos pretendientes; **to** — **a name for honesty** crearse una reputación de honrado; **to** — **a taste for** tomar gusto a, cobrar afición a; —**d character** (Bio) carácter m adquirido; —**d taste** gusto m adquirido.

acquirement [ə'kwaiəmənt] n adquisición f; —**s** conocimientos mpl.

acquisition [,ækwi'ziʃən] n adquisición f.

acquisitive [ə'kwizitiv] adj codicioso; — **instincts** instintos mpl acaparadores.

acquisitiveness [ə'kwizitivnis] n codicia f.

acquit [ə'kwit] **1** vt absolver, exculpar (of de); debt pagar.

2 vr: **to** — **oneself** portarse; **how did he** — **himself?** ¿cómo se portó?, ¿cómo desempeñó el cometido?; **to** — **oneself well** tener éxito, hacerlo bien, salir airoso; **to** — **oneself of** duty desempeñar.

acquittal [ə'kwitl] n absolución f, exculpación f; (of debt) descargo m.

acre ['eikə*] n (= 40,47 áreas) acre m; **God's** — camposanto m; **the family's broad** —**s** los extensos terrenos de la familia.

acreage ['eikəridʒ] n superficie f (or extensión f) medida en acres; **the 1970 wheat** — el área sembrada de trigo en 1970; **what** — **have you here?** ¿cuánto miden estos terrenos?; **they farm a large** — cultivan unos terrenos muy extensos.

acrid ['ækrid] adj acre, punzante; (fig) áspero, desapacible.

acrimonious [,ækri'məuniəs] adj áspero; remark mordaz; argument amargo, reñido.

acrimony ['ækriməni] n aspereza f, acrimonia f.

acrobat ['ækrəbæt] n acróbata mf.

acrobatic [,ækrəu'bætik] adj acrobático.

acrobatics [,ækrəu'bætiks] npl acrobacia f; (Aer) vuelo m acrobático.

acronym ['ækrənim] n sigla f (eg ONU = Organización de las Naciones Unidas).

Acropolis [ə'krɔpəlis] Acrópolis f.

across [ə'krɔs] **1** adv (a) a través, al través, de través; **don't go round, go** — no des la vuelta, ve al través; **shall I go** — **first?** ¿paso yo el primero?

(b) (from one side to the other) de una parte a otra, de un lado a otro; **we shall have to cut it** — tendremos que cortarlo por medio; **he helped an old lady** — ayudó a una vieja a cruzar la calle.

(c) **the plank is 4 inches** — la tabla tiene 4 pulgadas de ancho; **it's not very far** — es corta la travesía.

(d) (crossways) en cruz, transversalmente.

2 prep (a) a través de, al través de; **to go** — **a bridge** pasar a través de un puente.

(b) al otro lado de, del otro lado de; **from** — **the sea** desde más allá del mar; — **the street from our house** en el otro lado de la calle enfrente de nuestra casa; **he'll be** — **the water by now** ya estará al otro lado del mar.

(c) **it is 12 miles** — **the strait** el estrecho tiene 12 millas de ancho.

acrostic [ə'krɔstik] n acróstico m.

act [ækt] **1** vt play representar; part hacer; **to** — **the part of** hacer el papel de; **I have** —**ed Othello** he hecho el papel de Otelo; **to** — **the fool** hacer el tonto.

2 vi (a) (Theat) actuar, trabajar, representar; **I** —**ed in my youth** en mi juventud fui actor; **to** — **in a film** tener un papel en una película; **have you ever** —**ed?** ¿ha hecho Vd algún papel?; **who's** —**ing in it?** ¿quiénes hacen los papeles?; (fig: pretend) fingir; **he's only** —**ing** lo está fingiendo nada más; **to** — **ill** fingirse enfermo; **to** — **up** travesear.

(b) (function: machine) funcionar, marchar; (person) actuar; **the brakes did not** — no funcionaron los frenos; —**ing in my capacity as chairman** de acuerdo con las funciones atribuidas a mi cargo de presidente; **he declined to** — se negó a servir; **to** — **as** actuar de, hacer de, servir de; **it** —**s as a safety valve** funciona como una válvula de seguridad; **he was** —**ing as ambassador** estaba de embajador; **to** — **for someone** representar a uno.

(c) (behave) actuar, obrar, comportarse; **he is** —**ing strangely** se está comportando de una manera rara; **he always** —**s sensibly** obra siempre con juicio; **to** — **with caution** obrar con precaución;

she —**ed as if she was crying** hizo como si llorase; **to** — **up to a principle** obrar con arreglo a un principio.

(d) (take action) obrar, tomar medidas; **he** —**ed to stop it** tomó medidas para impedirlo; **now is the time to** — es hora ya de ponerse en acción; **he** —**ed for the best** hizo lo que mejor le parecía; **to** — **on a suggestion** seguir una indicación; **to** — **on the evidence** obrar de acuerdo con los hechos.

(e) (affect): **to** — **upon** afectar, obrar sobre; **the drug** —**s upon the brain** la droga afecta el cerebro; **acids** — **upon metals** los ácidos atacan los metales.

3 n (a) acto m, acción f; obra f; **A**—**s of the Apostles** Hechos mpl de los Apóstoles; — **of faith** acto m de fe; — **of God** fuerza f mayor; **an** — **of folly** una locura; **an** — **of treason** una traición; **we need** —**s not words** queremos ver hechos no palabras; **I was in the** — **of writing to him** precisamente le estaba escribiendo a él; **to catch someone in the** — coger a uno en flagrante, coger a uno con las manos en la masa.

(b) (Parl) decreto m, ley f.

(c) (Theat: division) acto m.

(d) (Theat: turn) número m; **to get into the** — introducirse en el asunto.

actable ['æktəbl] adj representable.

acting ['æktiŋ] **1** adj interino, suplente.

2 n (a) (Theat: of play) representación f; (by actor) desempeño m, actuación f; **what was his** — **like?** ¿qué tal hizo el papel?

(b) (as profession) profesión f de actor; — **is not in my line** yo no soy actor; **to go in for** — hacerse actor.

actinic [æk'tinik] adj actínico.

action ['ækʃən] n (a) acción f, acto m, hecho m; **man of** — hombre m de acción; **to bring into** —, **to put into** — poner en movimiento; **to go into** — entrar en acción; **to put out of** — inutilizar, destrozar, parar; **to suit the** — **to the word** unir la acción a la palabra; **to take** — tomar medidas.

(b) (Mil) acción f, batalla f; **killed in** — muerto en batalla; **to go into** — entrar en batalla.

(c) (Mech etc) mecanismo m, accionado m; funcionamiento m, movimiento m; (of horse) marcha f.

(d) (Law) demanda f, proceso m; **civil** — demanda f civil; **to bring an** — entablar demanda (against contra).

actionable ['ækʃnəbl] adj justiciable, procesable; querellante.

activate ['æktiveit] vt activar.

active ['æktiv] adj activo (also Gram, Comm); personality etc enérgico, vigoroso; **to take an** — **interest in** interesarse vivamente por; **to play an** — **part in** colaborar activamente a.

actively ['æktivli] adv activamente; enérgicamente, vigorosamente.

activist ['æktivist] n activista mf.

activity [æk'tiviti] n actividad f; (of personality) energía f, vigor m; (of busy scene) movimiento m, bullicio m; **in full** — en pleno vigor; **activities** actividades fpl; **his activities were wide** tuvo una ancha esfera de actividad; **social activities** vida f social.

actor ['æktə*] n actor m.

actress ['æktris] n actriz f.

actual ['æktjuəl] adj verdadero, real, efectivo; (of the present time) actual; **in** — **fact** en realidad; **let's take an** — **case** tomemos un caso concreto; **what were his** — **words?** ¿qué es lo que dijo, concretamente?; **is this the** — **book?** ¿es éste el mismo libro?; **what was the** — **price?** ¿cuál fue el precio real?; **there is no** — **contract** no hay contrato propiamente dicho.

actuality [,æktju'æliti] n realidad f; realismo m.

actualize ['æktjuəlaiz] vt realizar.

actually ['æktjuəli] adv (a) (really) realmente, en realidad, en efecto, efectivamente; — **I am her husband** en realidad soy su marido; **I wasn't** — **there** en realidad yo no estuve allí; **did you** — **see him?** ¿le vieron Vds realmente?; **what did he** — **say?** ¿qué es lo que dijo, concretamente?

(b) (even) **he** — **hit her** incluso llegó a pegarla; **we** — **caught a fish** con gran sorpresa nuestra cogimos un pez.

(c) **that's not true,** — eso no es verdad, que digamos; **as for** — **working, he didn't** pues trabajar, como trabajar, no lo hizo.

actuary ['æktjuəri] n actuario m de seguros.

actuate ['æktjueit] vt mover, animar; (Mech) impulsar, accionar; **he was** —**d by envy** la envidia le movió a ello.

acuity [ə'kjuːiti] n acuidad f, agudeza f.
acumen ['ækjumen] n perspicacia f.
acupuncture ['ækjupʌŋktʃə*] n acupuntura f.
acute [ə'kjuːt] adj (in most senses) agudo; **the situation is** — la situación es sumamente peligrosa; — **anxiety exists** existe una honda preocupación; **that was very** — **of you** te has mostrado muy perspicaz.
acutely [ə'kjuːtli] adv agudamente; **I am** — **aware that** me doy perfectamente cuenta de que; **I feel my position** — no se me oculta que es muy difícil mi situación.
acuteness [ə'kjuːtnis] n agudeza f.
ad [æd] n (fam) = **advertisement**.
adage ['ædidʒ] n adagio m, refrán m.
Adam ['ædəm] m Adán; —**'s apple** nuez f de la garganta; **the old** — la inclinación al pecado; **I don't know him from** — no le conozco en absoluto.
adamant ['ædəmənt] adj (fig) firme, inexorable; **he was** — **se mostró inexorable; he was** — **in his refusal** reiteró inexorablemente su denegación.
adapt [ə'dæpt] **1** vt (a) adaptar (to a); acomodar, ajustar (to a); **it is perfectly** —**ed to its environment** se ajusta perfectamente a su ambiente.
   (b) text arreglar, refundir; **a novel** —**ed by X** una novela en versión de X; **a novel** —**ed as a play** una novela en versión dramática; —**ed from the Spanish** inspirado en una obra española.
   2 vr: **to** — **oneself to** adaptarse a, ajustarse a.
adaptability [ə,dæptə'biliti] n adaptabilidad f; capacidad f para acomodarse.
adaptable [ə'dæptəbl] adj adaptable; person capaz para acomodarse; **he's very** — se acomoda en seguida a las circunstancias.
adaptation [,ædæp'teiʃən] n adaptación f; (of text) arreglo m, versión f, refundición f.
adapter [ə'dæptə*] n (Elec, Radio) adaptador m.
add [æd] **1** vt (a) añadir, agregar (to a); (to drink etc) añadir, echar, sumar (to a); (Math) sumar; **he that** añadió que, agregó que; **we gave £100 and he** —**ed the rest** nosotros dimos 100 libras y él contribuyó con lo demás; **to** — **in** añadir, incluir; **to** — **together, to** — **up** sumar.
   2 vi: **to** — **to** aumentar, acrecentar; realzar; **to** — **to our troubles** para colmo de desgracias; **to** — **up to** sumar, ascender a; (fig) venir a ser, equivaler a; querer decir; **it all** —**s up** es lógico, hace sentido; **it doesn't** — **up** no tiene sentido, no tiene pies ni cabeza; **it's beginning to** — **up** la cosa nos deja ya entrever una solución; **it doesn't** — **up to much** es poca cosa, no tiene gran importancia.
addendum [ə'dendəm] n, pl **addenda** [ə'dendə] adenda f, adición f, artículo m suplementario.
adder ['ædə*] n víbora f.
addict ['ædikt] n partidario m, a f (of de), entusiasta mf; drug — toxicómano m, a f; **I'm a guitar** — me apasiona la guitarra; **I'm a detective-story** — yo soy un apasionado de la novela policíaca.
addicted [ə'diktid] adj: **to be** — **to something** ser adicto a algo, ser aficionado a algo, (viciously) estar enviciado con algo; **to be** — **to drugs** ser toxicómano; **to be** — **to** + ger ser aficionado a + infin, acostumbrar + infin, (viciously) tener la manía de + infin; **to become** — **to something** enviciarse con algo, entregarse a algo.
addiction [ə'dikʃən] n afición f (to a); (vicious) hábito m morboso; (to drugs) toxicomanía f.
adding machine ['ædiŋmə,ʃiːn] n sumadora f, calculadora f.
Addis Ababa ['ædis'æbəbə] Addis Abeba.
addition [ə'diʃən] n (act) el añadir; (Math) adición f, suma f; (thing added) adición f, añadidura f; — **sign** signo m de sumar; **if my** — **is correct** si he hecho bien el cálculo; **we made** —**s to our stocks** aumentamos nuestras existencias; **this is a welcome** — **to** books on X; **in** — además; **in** — **to** además de.
additional [ə'diʃənl] adj adicional; supletorio; **we need** — **men** necesitamos más hombres; **an** — **reason for** razón de más para; **this gave him** — **confidence** esto aumentó su confianza.
additionally [ə'diʃənli] adv adicionalmente; **and** — y además; **this makes it** — **difficult for me** esto aumenta mis dificultades.
additive ['æditiv] n aditivo m.
addled ['ædld] adj huero, podrido.
address [ə'dres] **1** n (a) (of house etc) señas fpl, dirección f.
   (b) (on envelope) sobrescrito m.
   (c) (Comm) consignación f.
   (d) (style) tratamiento m, título m; **what form of** — **should I use?** ¿qué tratamiento debo darle?

   (e) (speech) discurso m; (lecture) conferencia f; **election** —, **electoral** — carta f de propaganda electoral; **public** — **system** sistema m amplificador de discursos públicos.
   (f) (Parl etc) petición f, memorial m.
   (g) (skill) destreza f, habilidad f.
   (h) (behaviour) modales mpl; conducta f, comportamiento m.
   (i) **to pay one's** —**es to** hacer la corte a, pretender.
   2 vt (a) person dirigirse a, dirigir la palabra a; meeting pronunciar un discurso ante; **he** —**ed us on politics** nos habló de política.
   (b) **to** — **someone as** dar a uno el tratamiento de; **to** — **someone by his proper title** dar el debido tratamiento a uno; **to** — **someone as "tú"** tutear a uno, tratar a uno de tú.
   (c) letter, protest dirigir (to a); **I** —**ed it to your home** lo mandé a su casa; **this letter is wrongly** —**ed** en esta carta se han puesto incorrectamente las señas.
   (d) (Comm) consignar.
   3 vr: **to** — **oneself to** person dirigirse a; problem aplicarse a.
addressee [,ædre'siː] n destinatario m, a f; (Comm) consignatario m.
Addressograph [ə'dresəugraːf] n (Protected Trade Name) máquina f de direcciones.
adduce [ə'djuːs] vt alegar, aducir, presentar.
Aden ['eidn] Adén m.
adenoidal ['ædinɔidl] adj adenoideo; **the child is** — (fam) el niño padece inflamación adenoidea.
adenoids ['ædinɔidz] npl vegetaciones fpl adenoideas; (fam) inflamación f adenoidea.
adept ['ædept] **1** adj experto, hábil, ducho (at, in en). **2** n experto m, perito m; **to be an** — at ser maestro en; **he's an** — **at thieving** es un ladrón consumado.
adequacy ['ædikwəsi] n suficiencia f.
adequate ['ædikwit] adj suficiente; **to feel** — **to a task** sentirse con fuerzas para una tarea.
adequately ['ædikwitli] adv suficientemente.
adhere [əd'hiə*] vi pegarse (to a); (fig) **to** — **to party, policy** adherirse a; promise cumplir; rule observar.
adherence [əd'hiərəns] n adherencia f, adhesión f (to a); observancia f (to a rule de una regla).
adherent [əd'hiərənt] **1** adj adhesivo. **2** n partidario m, a f.
adhesion [əd'hiːʒən] n see **adherence**.
adhesive [əd'hiːziv] adj adhesivo, pegajoso.
adieu [ə'djuː] **1** interj ¡adiós! **2** n adiós m; **to bid** — **to** person despedirse de; thing renunciar a, separarse de; **to make one's** — despedirse.
ad infinitum [,ædinfi'naitəm] adv a lo infinito; **it carries on** — es inacabable, es cosa de nunca acabar; **it varies** — tiene un sinfín de variaciones.
ad interim ['æd'intərim] **1** adv en el interín, interinamente. **2** adj interino.
adipose ['ædipəus] adj adiposo.
adiposity [,ædi'pɔsiti] n adiposidad f.
adjacent [ə'dʒeisənt] adj contiguo, inmediato (to a); angle adyacente.
adjectival [,ædʒek'taivəl] adj adjetivo, adjetival.
adjective ['ædʒektiv] n adjetivo m.
adjoin [ə'dʒɔin] **1** vt estar contiguo a, lindar con. **2** vi estar contiguo, colindar.
adjoining [ə'dʒɔiniŋ] adj contiguo, vecino, colindante; **the** — **house** la casa de al lado; **in an** — **room** en un cuarto inmediato.
adjourn [ə'dʒəːn] **1** vt (postpone) aplazar; session suspender, levantar; **the meeting was** —**ed** se suspendió la sesión.
   2 vi (meeting) suspenderse; **the house then** —**ed** luego se suspendió la sesión; **to stand** —**ed** estar en suspenso; **to** — **to** trasladarse a.
adjournment [ə'dʒəːnmənt] n suspensión f, clausura f.
adjudge [ə'dʒʌdʒ] vt matter juzgar, decidir; **to** — **that** estimar que, considerar que; **he was** —**d the winner** se le decretó el premio; **to** — **someone guilty** declarar culpable a uno.
adjudicate [ə'dʒuːdikeit] **1** vt claim decidir, juzgar. **2** vi ser juez, sentenciar.
adjudication [ə,dʒuːdi'keiʃən] n juicio m, sentencia f, decisión f.
adjudicator [ə'dʒuːdikeitə*] n juez m, árbitro m.
adjunct ['ædʒʌŋkt] n adjunto m, accessorio m.
adjure [ə'dʒuə*] vt ordenar solemnemente (to do hacer); suplicar, implorar.
adjust [ə'dʒʌst] **1** vt (change) modificar, cambiar; (arrange) arreglar; machine ajustar, regular; differences concertar, componer; insurance claim liquidar.
   2 vr: **to** — **oneself to** adaptarse a.

adjustable [ə'dʒʌstəbl] *adj* ajustable, graduable, regulable.

adjustment [ə'dʒʌstmənt] *n* modificación *f*, cambio *m*; arreglo *m*; (*Mech*) ajuste *m*, regulación *f*; composición *f*; **to make a small — to one's plans** modificar ligeramente sus proyectos.

adjutant ['ædʒətənt] *n* ayudante *m*.

ad lib [æd'lib] (*fam*) **1** *adv* a voluntad, a discreción. **2 ad-lib** *vi* improvisar.

adman ['ædmæn] *n*, *pl* **admen** ['ædmen] hombre *m* que trabaja en una agencia de publicidad, profesional *m* de la publicidad comercial.

admass ['ædmæs] *n parte de la población que está considerada como fácilmente influida por los actuales medios de la publicidad o propaganda comercial, conjunto de consumidores que tiene poco sentido crítico.*

administer [əd'ministə*] *vt* administrar; *shock etc* proporcionar; **to — an oath** to tomar juramento a.

administration [əd,minis'treiʃən] *n* (*act*) administración *f*; (*system*) gobierno *m*, dirección *f*; (*ministry*) gobierno *m*.

administrative [əd'ministrətiv] *adj* administrativo.

administrator [əd'ministreitə*] *n* administrador *m*.

admirable ['ædmərəbl] *adj* admirable, digno de admiración, excelente; **—! ¡muy bien!**

admiral ['ædmərəl] *n* almirante *m*.

Admiralty ['ædmərəlti] *n* Ministerio *m* de Marina, Almirantazgo *m*; **First Lord of the —** Ministro *m* de Marina.

admiration [,ædmə'reiʃən] *n* admiración *f*.

admire [əd'maiə*] *vt* admirar; (*express admiration for*) manifestar su admiración por, elogiar; **she was admiring herself in the mirror** se estaba mirando satisfecha al espejo.

admirer [əd'maiərə*] *n* admirador *m*, ora *f*; (*suitor*) enamorado *m*, pretendiente *m*.

admiring [əd'maiəriŋ] *adj look* de admiración.

admiringly [əd'maiəriŋli] *adv*: **he looked at her —** le lanzó una mirada llena de admiración; **to speak — of** hablar en términos elogiosos de.

admissibility [əd,misə'biliti] *n* admisibilidad *f*.

admissible [əd'misəbl] *adj* admisible.

admission [əd'miʃən] *n* (a) (*entry*) entrada *f* (*to* a); (*to academy etc*) ingreso *m* (*to* a); "**— free**" "entrada gratis"; "**no —**" "se prohibe la entrada"; **we gained — by a window** logramos entrar por una ventana. **(b)** (*acknowledgement*) confesión *f* (*of* de); **it would be an — of defeat** sería reconocer nuestra derrota.

admit [əd'mit] **1** *vt* (a) (*allow to enter*) dejar entrar, dar entrada a; (*fig*) admitir; **children not —ted** se prohibe entrar a los menores de edad; **ticket which —s two** entrada *f* para dos personas; **to be —ed to** *academy etc* ingresar en. **(b)** (*accept*) aceptar. **(c)** (*acknowledge*) reconocer, confesar; **it must be —ted that** hay que reconocer que; **it is hard, I —** es difícil, lo reconozco; **he —ted himself beaten** reconoció que había sido vencido. **2** *vi*: **to — of** admitir, dar lugar a, permitir; **it —s of no delay** no admite dilación; **to — to** *crime* confesarse culpable de.

admittance [əd'mitəns] *n* entrada *f*; **he was refused —** se le negó la entrada; "**no —**" "se prohibe la entrada".

admittedly [əd'mitidli] *adv* se reconoce que, es verdad que, de acuerdo que.

admixture [əd'mikstʃə*] *n* mezcla *f*, adición *f*; (*fig*) dosis *f*.

admonish [əd'mɔniʃ] *vt* (*reprimand*) reprender, amonestar; (*warn*) amonestar, prevenir; (*advise*) aconsejar (*to do* hacer).

admonition [,ædmɔu'niʃən] *n* (*reproof*) reprensión *f*; (*warning*) amonestación *f*, advertencia *f*; (*advice*) consejo *m*.

ad nauseam [,æd'nɔ:siæm] *adv*: **he repeated it —** lo repitió incansablemente; **you've told me that —** ya me lo has dicho mil veces.

ado [ə'du:] *n*: **much — about nothing** mucho ruido y pocas nueces, nada entre dos platos; **without more —** sin más.

adobe [ə'dəubi] *n* adobe *m*.

adolescence [,ædəu'lesns] *n* adolescencia *f*.

adolescent [,ædəu'lesnt] **1** *adj* adolescente. **2** *n* adolescente *mf*; joven *mf*.

Adolf ['ædɔlf], **Adolphus** [ə'dɔlfəs] *m* Adolfo.

Adonis [ə'dəunis] *m* Adonis.

adopt [ə'dɔpt] *vt* adoptar; *report, motion* aprobar; *suggestion* seguir, aceptar.

adopted [ə'dɔptid] *adj child* adoptivo.

adoption [ə'dɔpʃən] *n* adopción *f*; **country of —** patria *f* adoptiva.

adoptive [ə'dɔptiv] *adj* adoptivo.

adorable [ə'dɔ:rəbl] *adj* adorable; (*fam*) encantador, mono; **the child is —** el niño es un encanto.

adoration [,ædɔ:'reiʃən] *n* adoración *f*.

adore [ə'dɔ:rə*] *vt* adorar.

adoring [ə'dɔ:riŋ] *adj look* lleno de adoración.

adoringly [ə'dɔ:riŋli] *adv*: **she looked at him — le** miró con adoración.

adorn [ə'dɔ:n] *vt* adornar, embellecer.

adornment [ə'dɔ:nmənt] *n* adorno *m*.

adrenal [ə'dri:nl] *adj* suprarrenal; **— gland** glándula *f* suprarrenal.

adrenalin [ə'drenəlin] *n* adrenalina *f*.

Adriatic (Sea) [,eidri'ætik (si:)] (*Mar m*) Adriático *m*.

adrift [ə'drift] *adv* al garete, a la deriva; **to be all —** (*fig*) ir a la deriva; **to break —** perder las anclas; **to come —** (*fig*) soltarse, desprenderse; **to cut a boat —** cortar las amarras de una barca; **to turn someone —** abandonar a uno a su suerte.

adroit [ə'drɔit] *adj* diestro, hábil.

adroitly [ə'drɔitli] *adv* hábilmente.

adroitness [ə'drɔitnis] *n* destreza *f*, habilidad *f*.

adulate ['ædjuleit] *vt* adular.

adulation [,ædju'leiʃən] *n* adulación *f*.

adult ['ædʌlt] **1** *adj* adulto; mayor. **2** *n* adulto *m*, a *f*; persona *f* mayor; "**—s only**" (*Cine*) "mayores".

adulterate [ə'dʌltəreit] *vt* adulterar.

adulteration [ə,dʌltə'reiʃən] *n* adulteración *f*.

adulterer [ə'dʌltərə*] *n* adúltero *m*.

adulteress [ə'dʌltəris] *n* adúltera *f*.

adulterous [ə'dʌltərəs] *adj* adúltero.

adultery [ə'dʌltəri] *n* adulterio *m*.

adumbrate ['ædʌmbreit] *vt* bosquejar; (*foreshadow*) presagiar, anunciar.

advance [əd'vɑ:ns] **1** *n* (a) (*Mil*) avance *m*; (*progress*) avance *m*, progreso *m*, adelanto *m*.
    (b) (*loan*) anticipo *m*; préstamo *m*; (*in share price*) alza *f*, aumento *m*.
    (c) **—s** insinuaciones *fpl*; (*amorous*) requerimiento *m* amoroso; **to accept someone's —s** aceptar las intenciones de uno; **to make —s** to requerir de amores a; **to make the first —s** dar los primeros pasos.
    (d) (*phrases with* in) **in —** por adelantado, de antemano; **to arrive in — of someone** llegar antes que uno; **to be in — of** adelantarse a; **to book in —** reservar con anticipación; **to let someone know a week in —** avisar a uno con ocho días de anticipación; **to pay in —** pagar por adelantado; **to thank in —** anticipar las gracias a; **thanking you in —** dándole anticipadas gracias.
    2 *adj* anticipado, adelantado; **— booking office** despacho *m* de venta por adelantado; **— copy** anticipo *m* editorial; **— guard** avanzada *f*; **— party** (*Mil*) brigada *f* móvil; **— payment** anticipo *m*.
    3 *vt* (a) (*move forward*) avanzar, adelantar; *person* (*in rank*) ascender (*to* a).
    (b) (*encourage*) promover, fomentar.
    (c) (*put forward*) *idea* proponer para la discusión; *suggestion* hacer; *claim* presentar.
    (d) *money* anticipar; *loan* prestar.
    4 *vi* (a) (*move forward*) avanzar, adelantarse; **to — on someone** acercarse (de modo amenazador) a uno; **to — on a town** avanzar hacia una ciudad.
    (b) (*fig*) avanzar, adelantarse; **the work is advancing quickly** el trabajo se está adelantando rápidamente.
    (c) (*in rank*) ascender.
    (d) (*price*) subir.

advanced [əd'vɑ:nst] *adj gen, ideas etc* avanzado; *student* adelantado; *study* superior, alto; **— in years** entrado en años; **the corn is well —d** el trigo está muy avanzado; **the season is well —d** la estación está avanzada.

advancement [əd'vɑ:nsmənt] *n* adelantamiento *m*, progreso *m*; (*in rank*) ascenso *m*.

advantage [əd'vɑ:ntidʒ] *n* ventaja *f* (*also Tennis*); **to be to someone's —** ser ventajoso para uno; **to have the — of someone** llevar ventaja a uno; **I'm sorry, you have the — of me** lo siento, pero no recuerdo su nombre; **to have the — in numbers** llevar ventaja en cuanto al número; **to show to —** lucir; **to take — of** aprovechar(se) de; sacar partido de; *kindness etc* abusar de; (*euph*) seducir.

advantageous [,ædvən'teidʒəs] *adj* ventajoso, provechoso.

advent ['ædvənt] *n* advenimiento *m*, venida *f*; **A—** (*Eccl*) Adviento *m*.

adventitious [,ædven'tiʃəs] *adj* adventicio.

adventure [əd'ventʃə*] *n* aventura *f*.

adventurer [əd'ventʃərə*] n aventurero m.
adventuress [əd'ventʃəris] n aventurera f.
adventurous [əd'ventʃərəs] adj aventurero, emprendedor.
adverb ['ædvə:b] n adverbio m.
adverbial [əd'və:biəl] adj adverbial.
adversary ['ædvəsəri] n adversario m, a f, contrario m, a f.
adverse ['ædvə:s] adj adverso, contrario (to a); desfavorable (to para); balance negativo.
adversity [əd'və:siti] n infortunio m; companion in — compañero m de desgracias.
advert [əd'və:t] vi: to — to referirse a.
advert ['ædvə:t] n = advertisement.
advertise ['ædvətaiz] 1 vt (Comm etc) anunciar; publicar; weakness etc revelar públicamente.
   2 vi hacer publicidad, hacer propaganda; poner un anuncio (in a paper en un periódico; for solicitando); to — for buscar por medio de anuncios; it pays to — compensa hacer publicidad.
advertisement [əd'və:tismənt, US ædvər'taizmənt] n anuncio m.
advertiser ['ædvətaizə*] n anunciante mf.
advertising ['ædvətaiziŋ] 1 n publicidad f, propaganda f; (advertisements collectively) anuncios mpl; my brother's in — mi hermano trabaja en una agencia de publicidad.
   2 attr: — agency agencia f de publicidad; — campaign campaña f publicitaria; — rates tarifa f para anuncios.
advice [əd'vais] n consejo m; (report) informe m, noticia f; a piece of — un consejo; my — to you is + infin te aconsejo + infin; to ask for —, to seek — pedir consejos; to take someone's — seguir los consejos de uno; to take legal — consultar a un abogado; to take medical — consultar a un médico.
advisability [əd,vaizə'biliti] n conveniencia f, prudencia f.
advisable [əd'vaizəbl] adj aconsejable, conveniente, prudente; it would be — to + infin sería aconsejable + infin; if you think it — si le parece bien.
advise [əd'vaiz] 1 vt (a) (counsel) aconsejar (to do hacer); (as paid adviser) asesorar; what do you — me to do? ¿qué me aconsejas (que haga)?; the doctor —s complete rest el médico recomienda un descanso total.
   (b) (inform) avisar, informar; to keep someone —d of something tener a uno al corriente de algo.
   2 vi: he —s against the plan aconseja que no aceptemos el proyecto; to — on ser asesor en.
advised [əd'vaizd] adj: well— prudente; you would be well — to + infin sería aconsejable + infin.
advisedly [əd'vaizidli] adv deliberadamente; I say so — lo digo después de pensarlo bien.
adviser [əd'vaizə*] n consejero m; (eg business —) asesor m; legal — abogado m; spiritual — confesor m.
advisory [əd'vaizəri] adj consultivo; in an — capacity como asesor; — board junta f consultiva.
advocacy ['ædvəkəsi] n defensa f.
advocate ['ædvəkit] n (Law) abogado m; (of cause) defensor m, partidario m.
advocate ['ædvəkeit] vt abogar por, ser partidario de, recomendar; what do you —? ¿qué nos aconseja Vd?
adze [ædz] n azuela f.
Aegean Sea [i:'dʒi:ən si:] Mar m Egeo.
aegis ['i:dʒis] n égida f; under the — of (protection) bajo la tutela de, (patronage) patrocinado por.
Aeneas [i:'ni:æs] m Eneas.
Aeneid ['i:niid] Eneida f.
aeon ['i:ən] n eón m; (loosely) eternidad f.
aerate ['eəreit] vt airear.
aerated ['eəreitid] adj: — water gaseosa f.
aerial ['eəriəl] 1 adj aéreo; — cableway funicular m aéreo; — photograph aerofoto f.
   2 n antena f; directional — antena f dirigida; indoor — antena f de interior; — (mast) torre f de antena.
aero . . . ['eərəu] aero . . .
aerobatics [,eərəu'bætiks] npl acrobacia f aérea.
aerodrome ['eərədrəum] n aeródromo m.
aerodynamic ['eərəudai'næmik] adj aerodinámico.
aerodynamics ['eərəudai'næmiks] npl aerodinámica f.
aero-engine ['eərəu,endʒin] n motor m de aviación.
aerogram ['eərəugræm] n aerograma m, radiograma m.
aerolite ['eərəlait] n aerolito m.
aeromodelling ['eərəu'mɔdliŋ] n aeromodelismo m.
aeronaut ['eərənɔ:t] n aeronauta mf.
aeronautic(al) [,eərə'nɔ:tik(əl)] adj aeronáutico.
aeronautics [,eərə'nɔ:tiks] npl aeronáutica f.

aeroplane ['eərəplein] n avión m; model — aeromodelo m.
aerosol ['eərəsɔl] n aerosol m.
Aeschylus ['i:skiləs] m Esquilo.
Aesop ['i:sɔp] m Esopo.
aesthete ['i:sθi:t] n esteta mf.
aesthetic(al) [i:s'θetik(əl)] adj estético.
aesthetically [i:s'θetikəli] adv estéticamente.
aestheticism [i:s'θetisizəm] n esteticismo m.
aesthetics [i:s'θetiks] npl estética f.
afar [ə'fɑ:*] adv: — off lejos, en lontananza; from — desde lejos.
affability [,æfə'biliti] n afabilidad f.
affable ['æfəbl] adj afable.
affably ['æfəbli] adv afablemente.
affair [ə'feə*] n asunto m; episodio m; (event) acontecimiento m; (love —) aventura f amorosa; —s pl (business) negocios mpl; man of — s hombre m de negocios; the Cuba — el asunto de Cuba; current —s actualidades fpl; foreign —s asuntos mpl exteriores; — of honour lance m de honor; —s of state asuntos mpl de estado; — of the heart aventura f sentimental; how are —s with you? ¿qué tal van tus cosas?; it was an odd — fue una cosa rara; it will be a big — será un acontecimiento importante; that's my — eso me toca únicamente a mí, ésa es cosa mía; that's his — allá él, con su pan se lo coma; to have an — with andar en relaciones con, tener un plan con; to put one's —s in order arreglar sus asuntos personales.
affect [ə'fekt] vt (a) (concern) afectar, tener que ver con, influir en; (Med) interesar, afectar; (harm) perjudicar; it did not — my decision no influyó en mi decisión; it —s me considerably para mí tiene gran importancia.
   (b) (move) conmover, enternecer; he seemed much —ed estuvo muy emocionado, se conmovió mucho.
   (c) he —s the rebel se las echa de rebelde; to — indifference afectar indiferencia; she —ed to cry fingió llorar.
affectation [,æfek'teiʃən] n afectación f.
affected [ə'fektid] adj afectado.
affectedly [ə'fektidli] adv de manera afectada, con afectación.
affecting [ə'fektiŋ] adj conmovedor, enternecedor.
affection [ə'fekʃən] n afecto m, cariño m; to have an — for tener cariño a.
affectionate [ə'fekʃənit] adj cariñoso, afectuoso.
affectionately [ə'fekʃənitli] adv cariñosamente, afectuosamente; yours — un abrazo cariñoso.
affective [ə'fektiv] adj afectivo.
affidavit [,æfi'deivit] n declaración f jurada, afidávit m.
affiliate [ə'filieit] vi: to — to, to — with afiliarse a.
affiliated [ə'filieitid] adj company filial, subsidiario; member, society afiliado.
affiliation [ə,fili'eiʃən] n afiliación f; political —s relaciones fpl políticas; its —s are rather with this school está relacionado más bien con esta escuela.
affinity [ə'finiti] n afinidad f; A has certain affinities with B entre A y B existe cierta afinidad; I feel no — whatsoever with him no nos une ningún lazo de simpatía.
affirm [ə'fə:m] vt afirmar.
affirmation [,æfə'meiʃən] n afirmación f.
affirmative [ə'fə:mətiv] adj afirmativo; to answer in the — dar una respuesta afirmativa, contestar afirmativamente.
affix ['æfiks] n (Gram) afijo m.
affix [ə'fiks] vt signature etc poner, añadir; stamp poner, pegar; seal imprimir.
afflict [ə'flikt] vt afligir; the —ed los afligidos; to be —ed with sufrir de.
affliction [ə'flikʃən] n aflicción f, congoja f; infortunio m, desgracia f; (bodily) mal m; the —s of old age los males de la vejez.
affluence ['æfluəns] n riqueza f, opulencia f.
affluent ['æfluənt] 1 adj acaudalado, opulento; the — society la sociedad opulenta. 2 n afluente m.
afflux ['æflʌks] n afluencia f; (Med) aflujo m.
afford [ə'fɔ:d] vt (a) (provide) dar, proporcionar; this —s me a chance to speak esto me da la oportunidad de hablar; that —ed me some relief eso me proporcionó cierto alivio; it —s shade da sombra.
   (b) (pay for) we can — it tenemos con que comprarlo, podemos permitírnoslo; can we — it? ¿tenemos bastante dinero?
   (c) (spare, risk) I can't — the time to go no tengo bastante tiempo para ir; we can — to wait bien podemos esperar; an opportunity you cannot — to miss una ocasión que no es para desperdiciar;

I can't — to be idle no puedo permitirme el lujo de no hacer nada; can we — the risk? ¿podemos arriesgarnos?

afforest [æ'fɒrist] vt repoblar (de árboles).

afforestation [æ,fɔris'teiʃən] n repoblación f forestal.

affray [ə'frei] n refriega f, reyerta f.

affright [ə'frait] vt asustar, espantar.

affront [ə'frʌnt] 1 n afrenta f, ofensa f; to offer an — to afrentar. 2 vt afrentar; he was much —ed se ofendió mucho.

Afghan ['æfgæn] 1 adj afgano. 2 n afgano m, a f; (dog) perro m afgano.

Afghanistan [æf'gænistæn] Afganistán m.

afield [ə'fiːld] adv: far — muy lejos; you'll have to go further — for that para eso hará falta buscar más lejos.

afire [ə'faiə*] adv: to be — arder, estar en llamas; to be — with a desire to + infin anhelar ardiente-mente + infin.

aflame [ə'fleim] adv en llamas.

afloat [ə'fləut] adv a flote; en el mar; by a miracle we were still — por maravilla quedamos a flote; to keep — mantener(se) a flote; to set — poner a flote; the largest navy — la mayor marina del mundo; to spend one's life — pasar toda la vida a bordo.

afoot [ə'fut] adv: there is something — algo se está tramando; what is —? ¿qué estarán tramando?; there is a plan — to + infin existe un proyecto para + infin; to set — poner en movimiento.

aforementioned [ə,fɔː'menʃənd] adj, **aforesaid** [ə'fɔːsed] adj susodicho, mencionado.

aforethought [ə'fɔːθɔːt] adj: with malice — con premeditación.

afraid [ə'freid] adj (a) to be — tener miedo; all were very — todos se espantaron mucho; don't be — no tengas miedo, no temas; to make someone — infundir miedo a uno; to be — for temer por; to be — of person tener miedo a, thing tener miedo de; to be — to + infin tener miedo de + infin, temer + infin; I'm — he won't come me temo que no venga.

(b) I'm — he's out lo siento, pero no está; I'm — I have to go now siento tener que irme ahora; I'm — so! lo siento, pero es así.

afresh [ə'freʃ] adv de nuevo, otra vez; to do some-thing — volver a hacer algo.

Africa ['æfrikə] África f.

African ['æfrikən] 1 adj africano. 2 n africano m, a f.

Afrikaans [,æfri'kɑːns] n africaans m.

Afrikander [,æfri'kændə*] n africander m.

Afro-Asian ['æfrəu'eiʃən] adj afroasiático.

aft [ɑːft] adv (be) en popa; (go) a popa.

after ['ɑːftə*] 1 adv (time, order) después; long — mucho tiempo después; soon — poco después.

(b) (place) detrás.

2 prep (a) (time, order) después de; soon — eating it poco después de comerlo; do you put Lope — Calderón? ¿crees que Lope le es inferior a Calderón?

(b) (place, order) detrás de; tras; day — day día tras día; one — the other uno tras otro; he ran — me with my umbrella corrió tras de mí con mi paraguas; — you! ¡pase Vd!; — you with the salt ¿me das la sal, por favor?

(c) this is — Goya esto se pintó según el estilo de Goya; — the English fashion a la manera inglesa.

(d) (on account of) he is named — Churchill se le llamó así por Churchill.

(e) (idioms with to be): the police are — him la policía le está buscando; I have been — that for years eso lo busco desde hace años; what are you —? ¿qué pretendes con eso?; she's — a husband ella va en pos de un marido.

3 conj después (de) que.

4 adj part posterior, trasero; (Naut) de popa; in — years en los años siguientes, años después.

afterbirth ['ɑːftəbəːθ] n secundinas fpl.

aftercare ['ɑːftəkeə*] n asistencia f postoperatoria.

afterdeck ['ɑːftədek] n cubierta f de popa.

after-dinner ['ɑːftə'dinə*] adj de sobremesa.

after-effect ['ɑːftərifekt] n consecuencia f.

afterglow ['ɑːftəgləu] n (in sky) resplandor m crepuscular; (bodily) sensación f de bienestar.

afterlife ['ɑːftəlaif] n vida f futura; (on earth) resto m de la vida.

aftermath ['ɑːftəmæθ] n consecuencias fpl, resultados mpl, efectos mpl.

afternoon ['ɑːftə'nuːn] n tarde f; good —! ¡buenas tardes!

after-sales service ['ɑːftəseilz'səːvis] n servicio m de asistencia post-venta.

after-shave lotion ['ɑːftəʃeiv'ləuʃən] n loción f para después del afeitado.

aftertaste ['ɑːfteist] n dejo m, resabio m.

afterthought ['ɑːftəθɔːt] n ocurrencia f tardía, idea f adicional.

after-treatment ['ɑːftətriːtmənt] n tratamiento m postoperatorio.

afterwards ['ɑːftəwədz] adv después, más tarde; shortly —, soon — poco después; long — mucho tiempo después.

again [ə'gen] adv otra vez, nuevamente, de nuevo; often translated by volver a + infin, eg he climbed up — volvió a subir; —, it may not be true por otra parte, puede no ser verdad; these are different — también estos son distintos; never — nunca más; as much — otro tanto; as many — otros tantos.

against [ə'genst] prep (a) (next to) contra; (close to) al lado de, junto a, cerca de; over — the church enfrente de la iglesia.

(b) — that, as — that en contraste con eso.

(c) (for) — his arrival para su llegada.

(d) (fig) contra; en contra de; he was — it estaba en contra, se opuso a ello; I see nothing — it no veo nada en contra de eso; I spoke — the plan hablé en contra del proyecto; I know nothing — him yo no sé nada que le sea desfavorable; what have you got — me? ¿por qué me tiene Vd inquina?; it's — the rules no lo permiten las reglas; is there a law — it? ¿es que hay ley que lo prohiba?; luck was — him la suerte le era contraria; to be up — it estar en un aprieto.

agape [ə'geip] adj and adv boquiabierto.

agate ['ægət] n ágata f.

agave [ə'geivi] n agave f, pita f.

age [eidʒ] 1 n (a) (in general) edad f; (old —) vejez f, senectud f; mental — edad f mental; middle — mediana edad f; he is 20 years of — tiene 20 años; when I was your — cuando yo tenía los años de Vd; what — are you? ¿qué edad tiene Vd?; she doesn't look her — no representa la edad que tiene; — is beginning to tell on him los años empiezan a pesar sobre él; at the — of a la edad de; at my — a la edad que yo tengo; of — mayor de edad; to be of an — to ser de edad para; to come of — llegar a la mayoría de edad; over — demasiado viejo; under — menor de edad.

(b) (period) época f, era f, siglo m; the — we live in el siglo en que vivimos; atomic — era f atómica; in the — of Queen Elizabeth en la época (or en tiempos) de la reina Isabel; golden — (Myth) edad f dorada, edad f de oro; Golden A— (of Spain) Siglo m de Oro; Bronze A— Edad f de Bronce; Iron A— Edad f de Hierro; Stone A— Edad f de Piedra; Dark A—s Edades fpl Bárbaras; Middle A—s Edad f Media; A— of Enlighten-ment Siglo m de las Luces.

(c) (long time) siglo m, eternidad f, muchísimo tiempo m; we waited an —, we waited (for) —s esperamos una eternidad; it's —s since I saw him hace muchísimo tiempo que no le veo.

2 vt envejecer.

3 vi envejecer(se).

aged adj (a) ['eidʒid] viejo, anciano. (b) [eidʒd]: — 15 de 15 años, que tiene 15 años.

age group ['eidʒgruːp] n grupo m de personas de la misma edad; the 40 to 50 — el grupo que comprende los de 40 a 50 años; children of the same — niños mpl de la misma edad; to arrange people by —s clasificar las personas según su edad.

ageless ['eidʒlis] adj eternamente joven; perenne, inmemorial.

age limit ['eidʒlimit] n edad f mínima or edad f máxima; (retirement) edad f de jubilación.

agency ['eidʒənsi] n (a) (office) agencia f; advertising — agencia f de publicidad; news — agencia f de información; tourist —, travel — agencia f de viajes.

(b) (instrumentality): through the — of por medio de, por la mediación de.

agenda [ə'dʒendə] n orden m del día, asuntos mpl a tratar.

agent ['eidʒənt] n (a) (representative) representante m, delegado m; (Law) apoderado m; (Comm, Police etc) agente m; (US) jefe m de estación; foreign — agente m extranjero; special — agente m especial; he is not a free — no puede actuar libremente; land — (on estate) administrador m; literary — agente m literario; publicity — agente m de publicidad; shipping — agente m marítimo; sole — agente m único; to be sole — for tener la representación exclusiva de.

(b) (*Chem*) bleaching — decolorante *m*; **chemical —** agente *m* químico.

agent provocateur ['æʒɑ̃:prɔvɔkə'tə:*] *n* agente *m* provocador.

age-old ['eidʒəuld] *adj* secular, antiquísimo.

agglomeration [ə,glɔmə'reiʃən] *n* aglomeración *f*.

agglutinate [ə'glu:tineit] **1** *vt* aglutinar. **2** *vi* aglutinarse.

agglutination [ə,glu:ti'neiʃən] *n* aglutinación *f*.

agglutinative [ə'glu:tinətiv] *adj* aglutinante.

aggrandizement [ə'grændizmənt] *n* engrandecimiento *m*, agrandamiento *m*.

aggravate ['ægrəveit] *vt* agravar; (*fam*) irritar, sacar de quicio.

aggravating ['ægrəveitiŋ] *adj* (*fam*) irritante, molesto; **it's very —** es para volverse loco; **he's an — child** es un niño molesto.

aggravation [,ægrə'veiʃən] *n* agravación *f*; circunstancia *f* agravante; (*angering*) irritación *f*.

aggregate ['ægrigit] **1** *adj* total, global. **2** *n* agregado *m*, conjunto *m*; **in the —** en conjunto, en total.

aggregate ['ægrigeit] **1** *vt* agregar, juntar, reunir. **2** *vi* ascender a.

aggression [ə'greʃən] *n* agresión *f*.

aggressive [ə'gresiv] *adj* (*pej*) agresivo; (*zealous etc*) dinámico, enérgico.

aggressively [ə'gresivli] *adv* de manera agresiva; con dinamismo, enérgicamente, con empuje.

aggressiveness [ə'gresivnis] *n* agresividad *f*, acometividad *f*; dinamismo *m*, energía *f*, empuje *m*.

aggressor [ə'gresə*] *n* agresor *m*, ora *f*.

aggrieved [ə'gri:vd] *adj*: **he was much —** se ofendió mucho; **in an — tone** en un tono de queja.

aghast [ə'gɑːst] *adj* horrorizado; **to be — pasmarse** (*at* de).

agile ['ædʒail] *adj* ágil.

agility [ə'dʒiliti] *n* agilidad *f*.

aging ['eidʒiŋ] **1** *adj* ya bastante viejo. **2** *n* envejecimiento *m*.

agitate ['ædʒiteit] **1** *vt* (*shake*) agitar; (*perturb*) inquietar, perturbar; **to be very —d** estar muy inquieto (*about* por), estar en ascuas.

2 *vi*: **to — for** hacer propaganda por, hacer una campaña en pro de.

agitation [,ædʒi'teiʃən] *n* (*Pol etc*) agitación *f*; propaganda *f*, campaña *f*; (*mental*) inquietud *f*, perturbación *f*; nerviosismo *m*.

agitator ['ædʒiteitə*] *n* agitador *m*, ora *f*, alborotador *m*, ora *f*, elemento *m* revoltoso; (*Chem*) agitador *m*.

aglow [ə'gləu] *adj*: **to be — with** brillar de; **to be — with happiness** irradiar felicidad.

Agnes ['ægnis] *f* Inés.

agnostic [æg'nɔstik] **1** *adj* agnóstico. **2** *n* agnóstico *m*, a *f*.

agnosticism [æg'nɔstisizəm] *n* agnosticismo *m*.

ago [ə'gəu] *adv*: **a week —** hace una semana; **just a moment —** hace un momento nada más; **a little while —** hace poco; **long —** hace mucho tiempo, tiempo ha; **how long — was it?** ¿hace cuánto tiempo?; **as long —** as 1965 ya en 1965.

agog [ə'gɔg] *adj*: **to be —** estar ansioso, sentir gran curiosidad; **the country was —** el país estaba emocionadísimo, el país estaba pendiente de lo que pudiera pasar; **he was — to hear the news** tenía enorme curiosidad por saber las noticias; **to set — emocionar**, infundir curiosidad a.

agonized ['ægənaizd] *adj cry etc* angustiado, de angustia.

agonizing ['ægənaiziŋ] *adj pain* atroz, agudo; *indecision, suspense* angustioso; *moment* de angustia; *reappraisal* agonizante, doloroso.

agony ['ægəni] *n* (*pain*) dolor *m* agudo, dolor *m* punzante; (*mental anguish*) angustia *f*, aflicción *f*; **— of death, mortal —** agonía *f*; **I was in —** sufría unos dolores horrorosos; **to suffer agonies of doubt** ser atormentado por las dudas; **the play was sheer —** la obra era una birria; **— column** sección *f* de anuncios relativos a asuntos personales.

agrarian [ə'greəriən] *adj* agrario.

agree [ə'gri:] *vi* **(a)** (*be in harmony: things*) concordar (*with* con; *also Gram*), corresponder (*with* a).

(b) (*be in agreement: persons*) estar de acuerdo (*with* con, *that* en que); **to — with** *plan, policy* aprobar; **I — estoy** conforme; **I quite —** estoy completamente de acuerdo; **I — that it was foolish** reconozco que era tonto; **he's an idiot, don't you —?** es un imbécil, ¿no es así?

(c) (*come to an agreement*) ponerse de acuerdo (*with* con); **eventually he —d** por fin consintió; **"it's impossible", he —d** "es imposible", asintió; **you'll never get him to —** no lograrás nunca su

consentimiento; **to — on** convenir en; **it was —d that** se resolvió que, (*Parl*) se acordó que; **it is —d that** (*in legal contract*) se acuerda que; **to — to plan** convenir en, aprobar; **he'll — to anything** se aviene a todo; **to — to** + *infin* consentir en + *infin*, quedar en + *infin*; **it was —d to** + *infin* (*Parl etc*) se acordó + *infin*.

(d) (*get on well*) **we simply don't —, that's all** es que no existe simpatía entre nosotros, no congeniamos.

(e) (*of food*) **garlic does not — with me** el ajo no me sienta bien.

agreeable [ə'gri:əbl] *adj* (*pleasing*) agradable, *person* simpático; (*in agreement*) **if you are —** si estás de acuerdo; **is that — to everybody?** ¿estamos de acuerdo todos?; **he was — to that** estaba conforme con eso, lo aprobó; **he is — to help** está dispuesto a ayudar.

agreeably [ə'gri:əbli] *adv* agradablemente.

agreed [ə'gri:d] *adj plan etc* convenido; **—!** ¡conformes!

agreement [ə'gri:mənt] *n* **(a)** (*treaty etc*) acuerdo *m*, pacto *m*, convenio *m*; (*Comm*) contrato *m*; **gentlemen's —** acuerdo *m* verbal; **to differ** desacuerdo *m* amistoso; **by mutual —** por acuerdo mutuo; **to come to** (*or* **reach**) **an —** ponerse de acuerdo, llegar a un acuerdo; **to enter into an —** firmar un contrato (*to* + *infin* para + *infin*).

(b) (*harmony*) concordancia *f* (*also Gram*); (*between persons*) conformidad *f*, armonía *f*; **in — with** de acuerdo con; **to be in — with** estar de acuerdo con.

agricultural [,ægri'kʌltʃərəl] *adj* agrícola; **— college** escuela-granja *f* agrícola; **— expert** agrónomo *m*.

agriculture ['ægrikʌltʃə*] *n* agricultura *f*.

agricultur(al)ist [,ægri'kʌltʃər(əl)ist] *n* agricultor *m*, ora *f*.

agronomist [ə'grɔnəmist] *n* agrónomo *m*.

agronomy [ə'grɔnəmi] *n* agronomía *f*.

aground [ə'graund] *adv*: **to be —** estar encallado; **to run —** encallar, embarrancar; **to run a ship —** hacer que encalle un barco.

ah [ɑ:] *excl* ¡ah!

aha [ɑː'hɑː] *excl* ¡ajá!

ahead [ə'hed] **1** *adv*: **to be —** estar delante; **can you see who is —?** ¿ves quién va al frente?; **there's trouble —** habrá un lío, han de sobrevenir disgustos; **there's a busy time —** hay ocupaciones en perspectiva; **straight —** todo seguido; **full speed —!** ¡avante a toda máquina!; **to go —** ir adelante; continuar, avanzar; **to go — with one's plans** seguir adelante con sus proyectos; **go —!** ¡adelante!; **to look —** tener en cuenta el futuro; **to send someone — enviar** a uno por delante.

2 — of *prep* delante de; **to be — of** (*in progress*) llevar la ventaja a; **to be — of one's time** anticiparse a su época; **to get — of someone** adelantarse a uno; **you'll get there — of us** llegarás antes de nosotros.

ahoy [ə'hɔi] *excl*: **ship —!** ¡ah del barco!

aid [eid] **1** *n* ayuda *f*, auxilio *m*, socorro *m*; **audiovisual —s** ayudas *fpl* audiovisuales; **economic —** ayuda *f* económica; **mutual —** socorros *mpl* mutuos; **navigational —s, —s to navigation** ayudas *fpl* a la navegación; **by** (*or* **with**) **the — of** con la ayuda de; **in — of** a beneficio de, pro; **what's all this in — of?** ¿qué motivo tiene esto?, ¿para qué sirve esto?, ¿qué pasa aquí?; **to come to the — of** acudir en ayuda de, (*in argument*) acudir en defensa de.

2 *vt* ayudar, auxiliar, socorrer; **—ed by darkness** al amparo de la noche; *see* **abet**.

aide [eid] *n*, **aide-de-camp** ['eiddə'kɑ̃:ŋ] *n* edecán *m*.

aide-mémoire [eid'meimwɑ:] *n* memorándum *m*.

ail [eil] **1** *vt* afligir; **what —s you?** ¿qué tienes?, ¿qué te pasa? **2** *vi* sufrir, estar enfermo.

aileron ['eilərɔn] *n* alerón *m*.

ailing ['eiliŋ] *adj* enfermo, achacoso.

ailment ['eilmənt] *n* enfermedad *f*, achaque *m*.

aim [eim] **1** *n* (*of weapon*) puntería *f*; (*fig*) propósito *m*, intención *f*, meta *f*, blanco *m*; **his one — is to** + *infin* su único propósito es de + *infin*; **to have no — in life** no saber qué hacer con su vida; **with the — of** + *ger* con miras a + *infin*, con la intención de + *infin*; **to take —** apuntar (*at* a).

2 *vt gun* apuntar (*at* a); *missile, remark* dirigir (*at* a); *blow* asestar (*at* a).

3 *vi* apuntar (*at* a); **to — at** *objective* aspirar a, pretender, ambicionar; **what are you —ing at?** ¿qué intentas?; **to — high** (*fig*) picar muy alto; **to — to** + *infin* aspirar a + *infin*, pretender + *infin*, tener la intención de + *infin*.

aimless ['eimlis] *adj* sin propósito fijo, sin objeto.

aimlessly ['eimlisli] *adv* a la ventura.

ain't [eint] (*fam*) = **is not, are not; has not, have not.**

air [ɛə*] **1** *n* (a) aire *m*; **foul** — aire *m* viciado; **fresh** — aire *m* fresco; **he's a breath of fresh** — es una persona con ideas nuevas; **to get some fresh** — (salir a) tomar el fresco; **hot** — palabrería *f*; **by** — en avión, (*Post*) por avión, por vía aérea; **to be in the** — (*fig*) estar en el aire, estar en proyecto; **it's still very much in the** — está todavía en el aire, queda todavía sin resolver; **there's something in the** — se está tramando algo; **spring is in the** — se presiente ya la llegada de la primavera; **to go up in the** — (*fig*) ponerse negro, subirse por las paredes; **in mid** — entre cielo y tierra; **in the open** — al aire libre; **war in the** — guerra *f* aérea; **to vanish into thin** — desaparecer por completo; **to be on the** — (*Radio*) estar en el aire, hablar por radio; **we are on the** — **from 6 to 7** emitimos de 6 a 7; **one can't live on** — no se vive de aire solo; **to walk on** — estar bañado en agua de rosas; **to clear the** —, **to let in fresh** — airear la atmósfera, (*fig*) aclarar las cosas; **to fly through the** — volar por los aires; **to give someone the** — (*sl*) despedir a uno, dar calabazas a uno; **to take the** — tomar el fresco.

(b) (*Mus*) aire *m*, tonada *f*.

(c) (*appearance*) aire *m*, aspecto *m*; (*mien*) porte *m*, ademán *m*; **—s and graces** afectación *f*, melindres *mpl*; **with an** — con toda confianza, con aplomo, con garbo; **he has a distinguished** —, **he has an** — **about him** se ve que es un hombre distinguido; **to give oneself** —**s, to put on** —**s** presumir, darse tono.

2 *attr* aéreo; aeronáutico.

3 *vt* airear, ventilar; *idea, grievance* airear; **to** — **one's knowledge** lucir sus conocimientos, hacer alarde de sus conocimientos.

air base ['ɛəbeis] *n* base *f* aérea.

airborne ['ɛəbɔ:n] *adj* (*Mil*) aerotransportado; *germ* transmitido por el aire; *seed* llevado por el aire; **suddenly we were** — de pronto nos vimos en el aire.

air brake ['ɛəbreik] *n* freno *m* neumático.

air bubble ['ɛə‚bʌbl] *n* burbuja *f* de aire.

air chamber ['ɛə‚tʃeimbə*] *n* cámara *f* de aire.

air-conditioned ['ɛəkən‚diʃənd] *adj* con aire acondicionado, refrigerado.

air conditioner ['ɛəkən‚diʃənə*] *n* acondicionador *m* de aire.

air conditioning ['ɛəkən‚diʃəniŋ] *n* acondicionamiento *m* de aire.

air-cooled ['ɛəku:ld] *adj* refrigerado por aire.

aircraft ['ɛəkra:ft] *n* avión *m*.

aircraft carrier ['ɛəkra:ft‚kæriə*] *n* porta(a)viones *m*.

aircrew ['ɛəkru:] *n* tripulación *f* de avión.

air cushion ['ɛəkuʃən] *n* cojín *m* de aire, almohada *f* neumática; (*Aer*) colchón *m* de aire.

airdrome ['ɛə‚drəum] *n* (*US*) *see* **aerodrome.**

air duct ['ɛədʌkt] *n* tubo *m* de aire.

airfield ['ɛəfi:ld] *n* campo *m* de aviación.

air force ['ɛəfɔ:s] *n* aviación *f*, fuerzas *fpl* aéreas.

airgun ['ɛəgʌn] *n* escopeta *f* de aire comprimido.

airhole ['ɛəhəul] *n* respiradero *m*.

air hostess ['ɛə‚həustis] *n* azafata *f*.

airily ['ɛərili] *adv* *say etc* muy a la ligera, sin dar importancia a la cosa; confiado, satisfecho.

air intake ['ɛər‚inteik] *n* toma *f* de aire.

airless ['ɛəlis] *adj* *room* mal ventilado; *day* sin viento.

air letter ['ɛəletə*] *n* carta *f* por correo aéreo.

airlift ['ɛəlift] *n* puente *m* aéreo.

airline ['ɛəlain] *n* línea *f* aérea.

airliner ['ɛəlainə*] *n* avión *m* de pasajeros.

airlock ['ɛəlɔk] *n* esclusa *f* de aire.

airmail ['ɛəmeil] *n* correo *m* aéreo; **by** — por avión.

airman ['ɛəmən] *n, pl* —**men** [mən] aviador *m*, piloto *m*.

air marshal ['ɛə‚ma:ʃəl] *n* (*Brit*) mariscal *m* de aire.

airplane ['ɛəplein] *n* (*US*) avión *m*.

air pocket ['ɛə‚pɔkit] *n* bache *m* aéreo.

airport ['ɛəpɔ:t] *n* aeropuerto *m*.

air pressure ['ɛə‚preʃə*] *n* presión *f* atmosférica.

air pump ['ɛəpʌmp] *n* bomba *f* de aire.

air raid ['ɛəreid] *n* ataque *m* aéreo; **air-raid shelter** refugio *m* antiaéreo; — **warden** vigilante *m* contra ataques aéreos; — **warning** alarma *f* antiaérea.

airscrew ['ɛəskru:] *n* hélice *f* de avión.

air-sea base ['ɛə'si:beis] *n* base *f* aeronaval.

airship ['ɛəʃip] *n* aeronave *f*.

airsick ['ɛəsik] *adj:* **to be** —, **to get** — marearse (en un avión).

airspeed indicator ['ɛəspi:d'indikeitə*] *n* velocímetro *m* aéreo, tacómetro *m*.

airstrip ['ɛəstrip] *n* pista *f* de aterrizaje.

airtight ['ɛətait] *adj* hermético.

airway ['ɛəwei] *n* línea *f* aérea.

airwoman ['ɛə‚wumən] *n, pl* —**women** [‚wimin] aviadora *f*.

airworthy ['ɛəwə:ði] *adj* en condiciones de vuelo.

airy ['ɛəri] *adj* *place* de mucho viento; *room* bien ventilado; espacioso; *cloth etc* ligero, diáfano; (*unsubstantial*) etéreo; *step* ligero; *remark etc* dicho a la ligera.

aisle [ail] *n* nave *f* lateral; (*Theat*) pasillo *m*; **it had them rolling in the** — los hizo desternillarse de risa.

aitch [eitʃ] *n* *nombre de la h inglesa*; **to drop one's** —**es** no pronunciar las haches.

Aix-la-Chapelle ['eikslæʃə'pel] Aquisgrán.

ajar [ə'dʒa:*] *adv* entreabierto, entornado; **to leave the door** — no cerrar completamente la puerta.

Ajax ['eidʒæks] *m* Áyax.

akimbo [ə'kimbəu] *adv:* **with arms** — en jarras.

akin [ə'kin] *adj* relacionado (*to* con), análogo (*to* a), semejante (*to* a).

alabaster ['æləba:stə*] **1** *n* alabastro *m*. **2** *adj* alabastrino.

à la carte [ælæ'ka:t] *adv* a la carta.

alacrity [ə'lækriti] *n:* **with** — con presteza, con la mayor prontitud.

Aladdin [ə'lædin] *m* Aladino.

alarm [ə'la:m] **1** *n* alarma *f*; (*fear etc*) inquietud *f*, temor *m*; — **and despondency** confusionismo *m* y desconcierto *m*; —**s and excursions** sobresaltos *mpl*; **false** — falsa alarma *f*; **there was some** — **at this** esto produjo cierta inquietud, esto sobresaltó a la gente; **to give** (*or* **sound, raise**) **the** — dar la alarma; **to take** — alarmarse, sobresaltarse.

2 *vt* alarmar; inquietar, asustar; **to be** —**ed at** alarmarse de; **don't be** —**ed** no te vayas a asustar.

alarm bell [ə'la:mbel] *n* timbre *m* de alarma.

alarm clock [ə'la:mklɔk] *n* despertador *m*.

alarming [ə'la:miŋ] *adj* alarmante.

alarmingly [ə'la:miŋli] *adv* de modo alarmante, alarmantemente.

alarmist [ə'la:mist] *n* alarmista *mf*.

alarm signal [ə'la:m‚signəl] *n* señal *f* de alarma.

alas [ə'læs] *excl* ¡ay!, ¡ay de mí!; — **for the country!** ¡ay del país!

Albania [æl'beiniə] Albania *f*.

Albanian [æl'beiniən] **1** *adj* albanés. **2** *n* albanés *m*, esa *f*. **3** *n* (*language*) albanés *m*.

albatross ['ælbatrɔs] *n* albatros *m*.

albeit [ɔ:l'bi:it] *conj* (*lit*) aunque, no obstante.

Albert ['ælbət] *m* Alberto.

albinism ['ælbinizəm] *n* albinismo *m*.

albino [æl'bi:nəu] **1** *adj* albino. **2** *n* albino *m*, a *f*.

Albion ['ælbiən] Albión *f*.

album ['ælbəm] *n* álbum *m*.

albumen ['ælbjumin] *n* (*Bot*) albumen *m*; (*Chem*) albúmina *f*.

albumin ['ælbjumin] *n* (*Chem*) albúmina *f*.

albuminous [æl'bju:minəs] *adj* albuminoso.

alchemist ['ælkimist] *n* alquimista *m*.

alchemy ['ælkimi] *n* alquimia *f*.

alcohol ['ælkəhɔl] *n* alcohol *m*.

alcoholic [‚ælkə'hɔlik] **1** *adj* alcohólico. **2** *n* alcohólico *m*, a *f*, alcoholizado *m*, a *f*.

alcoholism ['ælkəhɔlizəm] *n* alcoholismo *m*; **to die of** — morir alcoholizado.

alcove ['ælkəuv] *n* hueco *m*.

alder ['ɔ:ldə*] *n* aliso *m*.

alderman ['ɔ:ldəmən] *n, pl* —**men** [mən] concejal *m* (de cierta antigüedad).

ale [eil] *n* cerveza *f*.

Alec ['ælik] *nombre cariñoso de* **Alexander**; (*fam*) **smart** — sabelotodo *m*.

alert [ə'lə:t] **1** *adj* alerta (*invariable:* eg estaban alerta); vigilante; *character* listo; (*wide-awake*) despierto, despabilado; *expression* vivo.

2 *n* alarma *f*, alerta *f*; **to be on the** — estar alerta, estar sobre aviso.

3 *vt* alertar, poner sobre aviso, avisar.

Alexander [‚ælig'za:ndə*] *m* Alejandro; — **the Great** Alejandro Magno.

Alexandria [‚ælig'za:ndriə] Alejandría.

alexandrine [‚ælig'zændrain] *n* alejandrino *m*.

alfalfa [æl'fælfə] *n* alfalfa *f*.

Alfred ['ælfrid] *m* Alfredo.

alfresco [æl'freskəu] **1** *adv* al aire libre. **2** *adj* de aire libre, al aire libre.

alga ['ælgə] *n, pl* **algae** ['ældʒi:] alga *f*.

algebra ['ældʒibrə] *n* álgebra *f*.

algebraic [‚ældʒi'breiik] *adj* algebraico, algébrico.

Algeria [æl'dʒiəriə] Argelia *f*.

Algerian [æl'dʒiəriən] **1** *adj* argelino. **2** *n* argelino *m*, a *f*.

Algiers [æl'dʒiəz] Argel m.
alias ['eiliæs] **1** adv alias, por otro nombre. **2** n alias m.
alibi ['ælibai] n coartada f; (excuse) excusa f, pretexto m.
Alice ['ælis] f Alicia; — **in Wonderland** Alicia en el país de las maravillas; — **through the Looking-glass** Alicia en el país del espejo.
alien ['eiliən] **1** adj ajeno, extraño (to a); (of foreign country) extranjero. **2** n extranjero m, a f.
alienate ['eiliəneit] vt property enajenar, traspasar; friend indisponerse con, alejar, ofender; other people ganarse la antipatía de; sympathies perder, enajenar.
alienation [ˌeiliə'neifən] n (of property) enajenación f, traspaso m; (of friend) alejamiento m; (Med) enajenación f mental.
alienist ['eiliənist] n alienista mf.
alight¹ [ə'lait] adj: **to be** — (fire) estar ardiendo, estar quemando; (light) estar encendido; **to set** — pegar fuego a, incendiar.
alight² [ə'lait] vi bajar, apearse (from de); (from air) posarse (on sobre); (Aer) aterrizar.
align [ə'lain] **1** vt alinear. **2** vr: **to** — **oneself with** ponerse al lado de.
alignment [ə'lainmənt] n alineación f; **in** — alineados, en línea recta; **out of** — fuera de alineación.
alike [ə'laik] **1** adj semejantes, parecidos, iguales; **you're all** —! ¡todos sois iguales!; **to look** — parecerse; **they all look** — **to me** yo no veo diferencia entre ellos, para mí todos son iguales.
2 adv del mismo modo, igualmente; **winter and summer** — tanto en invierno como en verano, lo mismo en invierno que en verano.
alimentary [ˌæli'mentəri] adj alimenticio; canal digestivo.
alimony ['æliməni] n alimentos mpl.
alive [ə'laiv] adj (a) **to be** — estar vivo, vivir; **to be still** — vivir todavía, estar todavía con vida; — **and kicking** vivito y coleando; **dead or** — vivo o muerto; **man** —! ¡hombre!; **he's the best footballer** — es el mejor futbolista de los que hay ahora viven; **it's good to be** —! ¡qué bueno es vivir!; **to be buried** — ser enterrado vivo; **to keep someone** — conservar con vida a uno; **to keep a tradition** — conservar una tradición; **to keep a memory** — guardar fresco un recuerdo.
(b) — **with** lleno de, hormigueante en, rebosante de.
(c) (fig) activo, enérgico; **look** —! ¡menearse!
(d) (fig) — **to** sensible a, consciente de; **I am** — **to the danger** estoy consciente del peligro, me doy cuenta del peligro; **I am** — **to the fact that** no ignoro que; **I am fully** — **to the honour you do me** soy consciente del honor que se me hace.
alkali ['ælkəlai] n álcali m.
alkaline ['ælkəlain] adj alcalino.
alkaloid ['ælkəbid] n alcaloide m.
all [ɔːl] **1** adj todo, todos; — **day** todo el día; — **men** todos los hombres; — **Spain** toda España; (with it: subject) **it's** — **done** todo está hecho, (object) **he ate it all** se lo comió todo; **and** — that y cosas así, y otras cosas por el estilo; **it's not as bad as** — **that** no es para tanto; **for** — **that** con todo, así y todo.
2 n (a) (sing) todo m, (pl) todos mpl, todas fpl; **my** — todo lo que tengo; — (**that**) **I can tell you is** lo único que puedo decirle es; — **is lost, it's** — **up** se acabó; **it's** — **up with him** no hay remedio para él; **that's** — nada más, eso es todo; **is that** —? ¿eso es todo?, ¿nada más?; **it cost him** — **of £50** le costó 50 libras largas; — **of us** todos nosotros, nosotros todos; **what with the rain and** — con la lluvia y todo.
(b) above — sobre todo; **after** — con todo, después de todo; **did you speak at** —? ¿dijiste algo?; **if I go at** — si es que voy; **if it's at** — **possible** si existe la menor posibilidad de ello; **not at** — de ninguna manera, nada de eso, (answer to thanks) de nada, no hay de qué; **not at** — **nice** nada agradable; **I'm not at** — **tired** no estoy cansado en lo más mínimo; **you mean he didn't sing at** —? ¿quieres decir que ni cantó siquiera?; **I don't know him at** — no le conozco en absoluto; **for** — **I know** que yo sepa, quizá; **for** — **his boasting** a pesar de toda su jactancia; **50 men in** — 50 hombres en total; — **in** — con todo, en resumen; **most of** — más que nada, sobre todo.
3 adv completamente, enteramente, del todo; **dressed** — **in black** vestido enteramente de negro; **it's** — **dirty** está todo sucio; — **but casi**; **he** — **but died** casi murió, por poco se nos murió; **it's** — **but impossible** es punto menos que imposible; — **but 7**

todos menos 7; **to draw 2** — empatar a 2; see **in, over, right** etc.
Allah ['ælə] Alá.
allay [ə'lei] vt pain aliviar; fears aquietar.
all clear (**signal**) ['ɔːl'kliə(ˌsignəl)] n cese m de alarma.
allegation [ˌæle'geifən] n aseveración f, alegación f.
allege [ə'ledʒ] vt declarar, afirmar, pretender (that que); (with n) alegar, pretextar; **he is** —**d to be wealthy** se pretende que es rico; **he is** —**d to be the leader** se dice que él es el jefe.
alleged [ə'ledʒd] adj supuesto, pretendido.
allegedly [ə'ledʒidli] adv según se afirma.
allegiance [ə'liːdʒəns] n lealtad f; **to owe** — **to** deber lealtad a; **to swear** — **to** rendir homenaje a.
allegoric(al) [ˌæli'gɔrik(əl)] adj alegórico.
allegorically [ˌæli'gɔrikəli] adv alegóricamente.
allegorize ['æligəraiz] vt alegorizar.
allegory ['æligəri] n alegoría f.
alleluia [ˌæli'luːjə] n aleluya f.
all-embracing ['ɔːlim'breisiŋ] adj que lo abarca todo, de vasto alcance, universal.
allergic [ə'lɜːdʒik] adj alérgico (to a).
allergy ['ælədʒi] n alergia f.
alleviate [ə'liːvieit] vt aliviar, mitigar.
alleviation [əˌliːvi'eifən] n alivio m, mitigación f.
alley ['æli] n callejuela f, callejón m; (in park) paseo m; **blind** — callejón m sin salida (also fig).
alleyway ['æliwei] n see alley.
All Fools' Day ['ɔːl'fuːlzdei] n día m de inocentes (en Inglaterra el 1 abril, en España el 28 diciembre).
All Hallows' (Day) ['ɔːl'hæləuz(dei)] n Día m de Todos los Santos (1 noviembre).
alliance [ə'laiəns] n alianza f.
allied ['ælaid] adj conexo, parecido; — **to** (fig) relacionado con.
alligator ['æligeitə*] n caimán m.
all-important ['ɔːlim'pɔːtənt] adj sumamente importante, importantísimo.
all-in ['ɔːlin] adj sum global; charge todo incluido; wrestling libre.
alliteration [əˌlitə'reifən] n aliteración f.
alliterative [ə'litərətiv] adj aliterado.
all-metal ['ɔːl'metl] adj enteramente metálico.
all-night ['ɔːl'nait] adj café abierto toda la noche; vigil, party, journey que dura toda la noche.
allocate ['æləukeit] vt asignar, señalar (to a); repartir, distribuir.
allocation [ˌæləu'keifən] n (act) asignación f; reparto m; (share, amount) ración f, cupo m, cuota f.
allot [ə'lɔt] vt asignar, adjudicar (to a).
allotment [ə'lɔtmənt] n (act) asignación f; (share) ración f, porción f; (land) parcela f.
all-out ['ɔːl'aut] **1** adj supporter acérrimo, incondicional; effort máximo; **to make an** — **attack on poverty** desplegar todas sus fuerzas para acabar con la pobreza.
2 adv all out con todas sus fuerzas; a fondo; (of speed) a máxima velocidad; **to go** — (Sport) emplearse a fondo; **to go** — **for something** volcarse por conseguir algo.
allover ['ɔːl'əuvə*] (US) **1** adj que tiene un diseño repetido sobre toda la superficie.
2 n tela f con diseño repetido sobre toda la superficie; diseño m repetido sobre toda la superficie.
allow [ə'lau] **1** vt (a) (with n) permitir; (grant) dar, conceder; request, claim admitir, aceptar; discount dar; allowance pagar, dar; **it** —**s very little time** deja muy poco tiempo; **how much should I** — **for expenses?** ¿cuánto debo poner para los gastos?; — **me!** permita que le ayude (etc).
(b) to — **to** + infin permitir + infin, dejar + infin, permitir que + subj; **it is not** —**ed to speak** no se permite hablar; **smoking not** —**ed** prohibido fumar.
(c) to — **that** reconocer que, confesar que; **he is** —**ed to be strong** se reconoce que es fuerte.
2 vi: **to** — **for** tener en cuenta, tomar en consideración; **after** —**ing for** después de considerar; **to** — **of** permitir; **it** —**s of no excuse** no admite disculpa.
allowable [ə'lauəbl] adj permisible; admisible; lícito; expense deducible.
allowance [ə'lauəns] n concesión f; (amount) ración f; (payment) subsidio m, subvención f, pago m, pensión f; (discount) descuento m, rebaja f; (Mech) tolerancia f; family — subsidio m familiar; subsistence — dietas fpl; **one must make** —**s** hay que ser comprensivo, hay que ser indulgente; **to make** —(**s**) **for someone** ser indulgente con uno, disculpar a uno; **to make** —(**s**) **for something** tener algo en cuenta.

alloy ['ælɔɪ] n aleación f, liga f; (fig) mezcla f.
alloy [ə'lɔɪ] vt alear, ligar.
all-powerful ['ɔːl'pauəful] adj omnipotente.
all-purpose ['ɔːl'pəːpəs] adj universal, para todo uso.
all-round ['ɔːl'raund] adj success etc completo; view amplio, global; person que hace de todo, hábil para todo.
all-rounder ['ɔːl'raundə*] n persona f (esp jugador m) que hace de todo.
All Saints' Day ['ɔːl'seintsdei] n Día m de Todos los Santos (1 noviembre).
All Souls' Day ['ɔːl'səulzdei] n Día m de Difuntos (2 noviembre).
allspice ['ɔːlspais] n pimienta f inglesa.
all-star ['ɔːl'stɑː] adj compuesto de primeras figuras.
all-time ['ɔːl'taim] adj: an — record un récord mundial de todos los tiempos; exports have reached an — high las exportaciones han alcanzado cifras nunca conocidas antes; to reach an — low llegar al punto más bajo.
allude [ə'luːd] vi: to — to referirse a, aludir a.
allure [ə'ljuə*] 1 n atractivo m, encanto m, fascinación f; aliciente m. 2 vt atraer, captarse la voluntad de, tentar.
alluring [ə'ljuəriŋ] adj atractivo, seductor, tentador.
allusion [ə'luːʒən] n alusión f, referencia f (to a); he said in — to dijo refiriéndose a.
allusive [ə'luːsiv] adj alusivo, referente (to a); style lleno de alusiones.
alluvial [ə'luːviəl] adj aluvial.
alluvium [ə'luːviəm] n aluvión m, depósito m aluvial.
all-weather ['ɔːl'weðə*] adj para todo tiempo.
ally ['ælai] n aliado m; the Allies los Aliados.
ally [ə'lai] vr: to — oneself to (or with) aliarse con; (by marriage) emparentar con.
ally ['æli] n bolita f, canica f.
alma mater ['ælmə'meitə*] n alma mater f, universidad f donde uno se ha graduado.
almanac ['ɔːlmənæk] n almanaque m.
almighty [ɔːl'maiti] 1 adj omnipotente, todopoderoso; (fam) imponente, enorme de grande; the A— el Todopoderoso.
  2 adv (fam) terriblemente, la mar de.
almond ['ɑːmənd] n (fruit) almendra f; (tree) almendro m; burnt —s almendras fpl dulces tostadas; sugar —s almendras fpl garapiñadas.
almond-eyed ['ɑːmənd'aid] adj de ojos almendrados.
almond oil ['ɑːmənd,ɔil] n aceite m de almendra.
almond tree ['ɑːməndtriː] n almendro m.
almoner ['ɑːmənə*] n (Hist) limosnero m; (Med) oficial mf de asistencia social (de un hospital).
almost ['ɔːlməust] adv casi; he — died en poco estuvo que muriese, por poco se nos murió.
alms [ɑːmz] n sing and pl limosna f.
alms box ['ɑːmzbɔks] n cepillo m para los pobres.
alms house ['ɑːmzhaus] n, pl — houses [,hauziz] hospicio m, asilo m de pobres.
aloe ['æləu] n áloe m; —s (juice) acíbar m.
aloft [ə'lɔft] adv arriba, en alto; (Naut) en la arboladura.
alone [ə'ləun] 1 adj (a) solo; to be — estar solo, estar a solas; to be all — estar completamente solo; am I — in thinking so? ¿soy yo el único en pensar así?
  (b) to leave someone — dejar a uno solo; to leave (or let) someone — (fig) no molestar a uno, dejar de molestar a uno; leave me —! ¡déjame en paz!; to leave (or let) something — no tocar algo; leave it —! ¡déjalo!; I advise you to let that severely — le aconsejo no meterse de ninguna manera en eso.
  (c) let — (as prep etc) sin mencionar, sin tomar en cuenta; he can't read, let — write nada de escribir, no sabe leer siquiera.
  2 adv solamente, sólo, únicamente; it is mine — es todo mío; you — can do it sólo Vd puede hacerlo.
along [ə'lɔŋ] 1 adv: all — desde el principio, todo el tiempo; — with junto con; I'll be — in a moment ahora voy.
  2 prep (a) a lo largo de; — the river a lo largo del río; all — the street todo lo largo de la calle.
  (b) por; to go — the tunnel ir por el túnel; it's — here es por aquí.
  (c) sign — this line firme Vd en este renglón.
alongside [ə'lɔŋ'said] 1 adv (Naut) al costado, costado con costado; to bring — acostar; to come — atracarse al costado.
  2 prep junto a, al lado de; (Naut) al costado de; to come — a ship atracarse al costado de un navío.
aloof [ə'luːf] 1 adj character reservado, frío; he was very — with me conmigo se mostró muy reservado.
  2 adv: to keep (or stand) — mantenerse a distancia, mantenerse apartado (from de).

aloofness [ə'luːfnis] n reserva f, frialdad f.
alopecia [,æləu'piːʃə] n alopecia f.
aloud [ə'laud] adv en voz alta, alto.
alpaca [æl'pækə] n alpaca f.
alpenstock ['ælpinstɔk] n alpenstock m, bastón m montañero.
alpha ['ælfə] n alfa f.
alphabet ['ælfəbet] n alfabeto m.
alphabetic(al) [,ælfə'betik(əl)] adj alfabético.
alphabetically [,ælfə'betikəli] adv alfabéticamente, en orden alfabético.
Alphonso [æl'fɔnsəu] m Alfonso.
alpine ['ælpain] adj alpino, alpestre.
alpinist ['ælpinist] n alpinista mf.
Alps [ælps] pl Alpes mpl.
already [ɔːl'redi] adv ya.
Alsace ['ælsæs] Alsacia f.
Alsace-Lorraine ['ælsæslə'rein] Alsacia-Lorena f.
Alsatian [æl'seiʃən] 1 adj alsaciano. 2 n alsaciano m, a f; (dog) perro m lobo.
also ['ɔːlsəu] adv también, además.
altar ['ɔːltə*] n altar m; high — altar m mayor; on the —s of (fig) en aras de.
altar boy ['ɔːltəbɔi] n acólito m, monaguillo m.
altar cloth ['ɔːltəklɔθ] n sabanilla f, paño m de altar.
altarpiece ['ɔːltəpiːs] n retablo m.
alter ['ɔːltə*] 1 vt cambiar, modificar, (esp for the worse) alterar; (Archit) reformar; opinion, course etc cambiar de; that —s things la cosa cambia; circumstances — cases el caso depende de las circunstancias.
  2 vi cambiar(se), mudarse; I find him much —ed le veo muy cambiado.
alteration [,ɔːltə'reiʃən] n cambio m, modificación f, (esp for the worse) alteración f (in, to de); —s (Archit) reformas fpl.
altercation [,ɔːltə'keiʃən] n altercado m.
alter ego ['æltər'iːgəu] n álter ego m.
alternate [ɔl'təːnit] adj alterno, alternativo; on — days un día sí y otro no, cada dos días.
alternate ['ɔːltəːneit] vti alternar.
alternately [ɔl'təːnitli] adv alternativamente; por turno.
alternating ['ɔːltəːneitiŋ] adj alterno.
alternation [,ɔːltəː'neiʃən] n alternación f; in — alternativamente.
alternative [ɔl'təːnətiv] 1 adj alternativo.
  2 n alternativa f; I have no — no tengo más remedio, no puedo hacer otra cosa; you have no — but to go Vd no tiene más remedio que ir.
alternatively [ɔl'təːnətivli] adv por otra parte.
alternator ['ɔːltəːneitə*] n alternador m.
although [ɔːl'ðəu] conj aunque; si bien.
altimeter ['æltimiːtə*] n altímetro m.
altitude ['æltitjuːd] n altitud f, altura f.
alto ['æltəu] 1 adj alto; — saxophone saxofón m alto. 2 n contralto f.
altogether [,ɔːltə'geðə*] adv (a) en conjunto, en total; how many are there —? ¿cuántos hay en total?; in the — (fam) en cueros.
  (b) enteramente; del todo; we haven't — finished no hemos terminado del todo; I'm not — sure no estoy del todo seguro; this is — too hard esto es demasiado difícil con mucho; you're — wrong Vd está completamente equivocado.
altruism ['æltruizəm] n altruismo m.
altruist ['æltruist] n altruista mf.
altruistic [,æltru'istik] adj altruista.
alum ['æləm] n alumbre m.
aluminium [,ælju'miniəm] n, aluminum [ə'luːminəm] n (US) aluminio m.
alumnus [ə'lʌmnəs] nm, pl alumni [ə'lʌmnai] graduado m, a f.
alumna [ə'lʌmnə] nf, pl alumnae [ə'lʌmniː] (US) graduada f.
alveolar [æl'viələ*] adj alveolar.
always ['ɔːlweiz] adv siempre; as — como siempre.
am [æm] see be.
amalgam [ə'mælgəm] n amalgama f.
amalgamate [ə'mælgəmeit] 1 vt amalgamar; companies etc unir. 2 vi amalgamarse; unirse.
amalgamation [ə,mælgə'meiʃən] n amalgamación f; unión f.
amanuensis [ə,mænju'ensis] n, pl amanuenses [ə,mænju'ensiːz] amanuense m.
Amaryllis [,æmə'rilis] f Amarilis.
amass [ə'mæs] vt amontonar, acumular.
amateur ['æmətə*] 1 n amateur mf, aficionado m, a f; (pej) principiante mf, chapucero m.
  2 adj see amateurish; — tennis tenis m para aficionados (or amateur); I have an — interest in pottery me interesa como aficionado la cerámica.

amateurish ['æmətəriʃ] *adj* superficial, inexperto, torpe, chapucero.

amateurism ['æmətərizəm] *n* amateurismo *m*, estado *m* de aficionado; **there must be room for — in sport** en los deportes debe haber sitio para los aficionados.

amatory ['æmətəri] *adj* amatorio, erótico.

amaze [ə'meiz] *vt* asombrar, pasmar; **to be —d** quedar estupefacto; **to be —d at** asombrarse de; **you — me!** ¡me admiras!

amazement [ə'meizmənt] *n* asombro *m*, sorpresa *f*, estupefacción *f*; **they looked on in —** miraron asombrados; **the news caused general —** se asombraron todos al saber la noticia.

amazing [ə'meiziŋ] *adj* asombroso, pasmoso; **he's an — man** es un hombre extraordinario.

amazingly [ə'meiziŋli] *adv* milagrosamente, por maravilla; **— enough** aunque parece mentira; **—, nobody was killed** por milagro, no hubo víctimas; **he did —** well tuvo un éxito formidable; **he is — fit for his age** su estado físico es extraordinario para un hombre de su edad.

Amazon[1] ['æməzən] *n* (*Myth*) amazona *f*; (*fig*) marimacho *m*.

Amazon[2] ['æməzən] (*Geog*) Amazonas *m*.

ambassador [æm'bæsədə*] *n* embajador *m*.

ambassadorial [æm,bæsə'dɔ:riəl] *adj* embajatorio.

ambassadorship [æm'bæsədəʃip] *n* embajada *f*.

amber ['æmbə*] **1** *n* ámbar *m*. **2** *adj* ambarino, color de ámbar; *traffic light* amarillo.

ambergris ['æmbəgri:s] *n* ámbar *m* gris.

ambidextrous [,æmbi'dekstrəs] *adj* ambidextro.

ambient ['æmbiənt] *adj* ambiente.

ambiguity [,æmbi'gjuiti] *n* (*quality*) ambigüedad *f*; (*of meaning*) doble sentido *m*.

ambiguous [æm'bigjuəs] *adj* ambiguo; (*in bad sense*) doble, equívoco.

ambit ['æmbit] *n* ámbito *m*.

ambition [æm'biʃən] *n* ambición *f*; **to have an — for** ambicionar; **to have an — to be** ambicionar ser.

ambitious [æm'biʃəs] *adj* ambicioso; *idea, plan* grandioso; **to be — of** ambicionar.

ambitiously [æm'biʃəsli] *adv* ambiciosamente; grandiosamente.

ambivalence [æm'bivələns] ambivalencia *f*; (*pej*) lo equívoco, lo doble.

ambivalent [æm'bivələnt] *adj* ambivalente; (*pej*) equívoco, doble.

amble ['æmbl] **1** *n* (*horse*) paso *m* de andadura; **to walk at an —** (*person*) andar muy despacio.
2 *vi* (*horse*) amblar; (*person*) andar muy despacio; **he —d up to me** se acercó despacio a mí.

Ambrose ['æmbrəuz] *m* Ambrosio.

ambrosia [æm'brəuziə] *n* ambrosía *f*.

ambulance ['æmbjuləns] *n* ambulancia *f*; **— man** ambulanciero *m*.

ambush ['æmbuʃ] **1** *n* emboscada *f*; **to fall into an —** caer en una emboscada; **to lay an —** tender una emboscada (*for* a); **to lie in —** estar emboscado (*for* para coger).
2 *vt* tender una emboscada a, coger por sorpresa; **to be —ed** caer en una emboscada.

ameba [ə'mi:bə] *n* = **amoeba**.

ameliorate [ə'mi:liəreit] **1** *vt* mejorar. **2** *vi* mejorar(se).

amelioration [ə,mi:liə'reiʃən] *n* mejora *f*, mejoramiento *m*.

amen ['ɑ:men] *interj* amén.

amenable [ə'mi:nəbl] *adj* sumiso, dócil, tratable; (*Law*) responsable; **— to argument** que se deja convencer; **— to reason** que se deja convencer por la lógica; **— to treatment** (*Med*) susceptible de ser curado, curable.

amend [ə'mend] *vt* enmendar; rectificar, corregir.

amendment [ə'mendmənt] *n* enmienda *f*; rectificación *f*, corrección *f*.

amends [ə'mendz] *n sing*: **to make —** dar cumplida satisfacción, enmendarlo; **to make — for** dar satisfacción por, enmendar, expiar.

amenity [ə'mi:niti] *n* (*pleasantness*) amenidad *f*; (*pleasant thing*) atractivo *m*, cosa *f* agradable; **amenities** atractivos *mpl*, conveniencias *fpl*, comodidades *fpl*; **the amenities of life** las cosas agradables de la vida; **a house with all amenities** una casa con todo confort.

America [ə'merikə] América *f*; (*USA*) Estados *mpl* Unidos.

American [ə'merikən] **1** *adj* americano; (*of USA*) norteamericano, estadounidense.
2 *n* americano *m*, a *f*; (*of USA*) norteamericano *m*, a *f*, estadounidense *mf*.

americanism [ə'merikənizəm] *n* americanismo *m*.

americanize [ə'merikənaiz] *vt* americanizar; **to become —d** americanizarse.

amethyst ['æmiθist] *n* amatista *f*.

amiability [,eimiə'biliti] *n* afabilidad *f*, amabilidad *f*.

amiable ['eimiəbl] *adj* afable, amable, simpático; bonachón.

amiably ['eimiəbli] *adv* afablemente, amablemente.

amicable ['æmikəbl] *adj* amistoso, amigable.

amicably ['æmikəbli] *adv* amistosamente, amigablemente.

amid [ə'mid] *prep* en medio de, entre.

amidships [ə'midʃips] *adv* en medio del navío.

amidst [ə'midst] *prep* = **amid**.

amiss [ə'mis] *adv*: **there's something —** pasa algo malo, no va todo bien; (*with machine etc*) esto no marcha bien; **what's —?** ¿qué pasa?; **what's — with him?** ¿qué le pasa?; **it would not be — for him to + infin** no le estaría mal + *infin*; **a cup of tea would not come —** me gustaría mucho una taza de té; **a little politeness would not come —** no le vendría mal un poco de cortesía; **to take something —** llevar algo a mal; **don't take it —, will you?** ¿no te vas a ofender, eh?

amity ['æmiti] *n* concordia *f*, amistad *f*.

ammeter ['æmitə*] *n* amperímetro *m*.

ammo ['æməu] *n* (*Mil sl*) = **ammunition**.

ammonia [ə'məuniə] *n* amoníaco *m*; **liquid —** amoníaco *m* líquido.

ammunition [,æmju'niʃən] *n* municiones *fpl*; (*fig*) argumentos *mpl*, artillería *f*.

ammunition dump [,æmju'niʃən'dʌmp] *n* depósito *m* de municiones.

amnesia [æm'ni:ziə] *n* amnesia *f*.

amnesty ['æmnisti] **1** *n* amnistía *f*, indulto *m* general; **to grant an — to** amnistiar. **2** *vt* amnistiar, indultar.

amoeba [ə'mi:bə] *n* amiba *f*.

amok [ə'mɔk] *adv see* **amuck**.

among(st) [ə'mʌŋ(st)] *prep* entre, en medio de; **from —** de entre; **he is — those who** es de los que; **it is not — the names I have** no figura entre los nombres que tengo.

amoral [æ'mɔrəl] *adj* amoral.

amorous ['æmərəs] *adj* amoroso; enamorado, enamoradizo; **an — old man** un viejo mujeriego.

amorously ['æmərəsli] *adv* amorosamente.

amorphous [ə'mɔ:fəs] *adj* amorfo, sin forma fija.

amortize [ə'mɔ:taiz] *vt* amortizar.

amount [ə'maunt] **1** *n* cantidad *f*, (*of bill etc*) suma *f*, importe *m*; **in small —s** en pequeñas cantidades; **to the — of** hasta un total de; por la suma de, por el valor de; **we used to drink any — of that** bebíamos grandes cantidades de eso; **we have had any — of trouble** hemos tenido la mar de dificultades.
2 *vi*: **to —** to: ascender a, sumar, subir a; (*fig*) equivaler a, significar; **it —s to the same thing es** igual, viene a ser lo mismo; **this —s to a refusal** esto equivale a una negativa; **he'll never — to** **much** siempre será una nulidad, es un pobre hombre.

amour [ə'muə*] *n* amorío *m*, intriga *f* amorosa.

amour-propre [ə'muə'prɔpr] *n* amor *m* propio.

amp [æmp] *n*, **ampère** ['æmpɛə*] *n* amperio *m*.

ampersand ['æmpəsænd] *n* el signo & (*que significa* and, et).

amphibia [æm'fibiə] *npl* anfibios *mpl*.

amphibian [æm'fibiən] **1** *adj* anfibio. **2** *n* anfibio *m*.

amphibious [æm'fibiəs] *adj* anfibio.

amphitheatre ['æmfi,θiətə*] *n* anfiteatro *m*.

Amphitryon [æm'fitriən] *m* Anfitrión.

amphora ['æmfərə] *n* ánfora *f*.

ample ['æmpl] *adj* (*spacious*) amplio, ancho, extenso; (*abundant*) liberal, abundante; (*enough*) bastante, suficiente.

amplification [,æmplifi'keiʃən] *n* amplificación *f*; explicación *f*.

amplifier ['æmplifaiə*] *n* amplificador *m*.

amplify ['æmplifai] *vt* amplificar (*also Radio*), aumentar; *statement etc* explicar, añadir comentarios a.

amplitude ['æmplitju:d] *n* amplitud *f*.

amply ['æmpli] *adv* bastante, suficientemente; abundantemente; **you were — justified** Vd tuvo plenamente razón; **we are — supplied with food** tenemos abundancia de comida.

ampoule ['æmpu:l] *n* ampolla *f*.

amputate ['æmpjuteit] *vt* amputar.

amputation [,æmpju'teiʃən] *n* amputación *f*.

amuck [ə'mʌk] *adv*: **to run —** enloquecer, desbocarse; (*fig*) conducirse como un loco, hacer locuras, mostrarse violento, atacar a ciegas.

amulet ['æmjulit] *n* amuleto *m*.

amuse [ə'mjuːz] **1** *vt* divertir, entretener, distraer; **to be —d at** (*or* **by**) divertirse con, reírse con; **we are not —d** no nos cae en gracia.
2 *vr*: **to — oneself** distraerse (*doing* haciendo); **run along and — yourselves** idos a jugar; **you'll have to — yourselves for a time** tendréis que buscaros algo en que ocuparos durante un rato.
amusement [ə'mjuːzmənt] *n* (**a**) (*amusing thing*) diversión *f*, entretenimiento *m*; **— park** parque *m* de atracciones; **place of —** sitio *m* de recreo.
(**b**) (*pastime*) pasatiempo *m*, recreo *m*; **they do it for —** only lo hacen sólo para divertirse, es un pasatiempo nada más.
(**c**) (*laughter*) risa *f*; **there was general — at this** al oír esto se rieron todos; **much to my —** con gran regocijo mío.
amusing [ə'mjuːziŋ] *adj* divertido, gracioso.
amusingly [ə'mjuːziŋli] *adv* de modo divertido, graciosamente.
an [æn, ən, n] *indef art see* **a**.
anachronism [ə'nækrənizəm] *n* anacronismo *m*.
anachronistic [ə,nækrə'nistik] *adj* anacrónico.
anaconda [,ænə'kɔndə] *n* anaconda *f*.
Anacreon [ə'nækriən] *m* Anacreonte.
anaemia [ə'niːmiə] *n* anemia *f*.
anaemic [ə'niːmik] *adj* anémico; (*fig*) soso, insípido, débil.
anaesthesia [,ænis'θiːziə] *n* anestesia *f*.
anaesthetic [,ænis'θetik] **1** *adj* anestésico. **2** *n* anestésico *m*.
anaesthetist [æ'niːsθitist] *n* anestesista *mf*.
anaesthetize [æ'niːsθitaiz] *vt* anestesiar.
anagram ['ænəgræm] *n* anagrama *m*.
anal ['einəl] *adj* anal.
analgesia [,ænæl'dʒiːziə] *n* analgesia *f*.
analgesic [,ænæl'dʒiːsik] **1** *adj* analgésico. **2** *n* analgésico *m*.
analogical [,ænə'lɔdʒikəl] *adj* analógico.
analogous [ə'næləgəs] *adj* análogo (*to* a); afín, semejante.
analogue ['ænəlɔg] *n* análogo *m*.
analogy [ə'nælədʒi] *n* analogía *f*; afinidad *f*, semejanza *f*; **on the — of** por analogía con; **to draw an — between** hacer ver la semejanza que existe entre.
analyse, (*US*) **analyze** ['ænəlaiz] *vt* analizar.
analysis [ə'næləsis] *n*, *pl* **analyses** [ə'næləsiːz] análisis *m*; **in the last —** en último término, en fin de cuentas.
analyst ['ænəlist] *n* analizador *m*; **public —** jefe *m* del laboratorio municipal.
analytic(al) [,ænə'litik(əl)] *adj* analítico.
anapaest ['ænəpiːst] *n* anapesto *m*.
anarchic(al) [æ'nɑːkik(əl)] *adj* anárquico.
anarchism ['ænəkizəm] *n* anarquismo *m*.
anarchist ['ænəkist] *n* anarquista *mf*.
anarchy ['ænəki] *n* anarquía *f*, desorden *m*.
anathema [ə'næθimə] *n* anatema *m*.
anathematize [ə'næθimətaiz] *vt* anatematizar.
anatomical [,ænə'tɔmikəl] *adj* anatómico.
anatomize [ə'nætəmaiz] *vt* anatomizar; (*fig*) analizar minuciosamente.
anatomy [ə'nætəmi] *n* anatomía *f*; (*fig*) cuerpo *m*, carnes *fpl*.
ancestor ['ænsistə*] *n* antepasado *m*; **—s** *pl* abuelos *mpl*.
ancestral [æn'sestrəl] *adj* ancestral, hereditario; **— home** casa *f* solariega, solar *m*.
ancestry ['ænsistri] *n* ascendencia *f*, abolengo *m*, linaje *m*.
anchor ['æŋkə*] **1** *n* ancla *f*, áncora *f*; **to be** (*or* **lie**, **ride**) **at —** estar al ancla, estar anclado; **to cast** (*or* **drop**) **—** echar anclas; **to weigh —** levar anclas.
2 *vt* poner sobre el ancla; (*fig*) sujetar, asegurar.
3 *vi* anclar, fondear.
anchorage ['æŋkəridʒ] *n* ancladero *m*, fondeadero *m*.
anchorite ['æŋkərait] *n* anacoreta *mf*.
anchovy ['æntʃəvi] *n* anchoa *f*.
ancient ['einʃənt] *adj* antiguo; **the —s** los antiguos; **he's getting pretty —** (*fam*) va para viejo.
ancillary [æn'siləri] *adj* subordinado (*to* a), auxiliar, secundario.
and [ænd, ənd, nd, ən] *conj* (**a**) y, (*before* i-, hi-) e; **— ?** ¿y después?, ¿y qué más?; **better — better** cada vez mejor; **more — more** cada vez más.
(**b**) (*negative sense*) ni: **you can't buy — sell here** aquí no se permite comprar ni vender.
(**c**) **he talked — talked, but . . .** habló incansablemente, pero . . . , por mucho que hablase, no . . .
(**d**) (*before infins*) **try — do it** trata de hacerlo, hazlo si puedes; **come — see me** ven a verme.
Andalusia [,ændə'luːziə] Andalucía *f*.

Andalusian [,ændə'luːziən] **1** *adj* andaluz. **2** *n* andaluz *m*, uza *f*.
Andean ['ændiən] *adj* andino.
Andes ['ændiːz] *pl* Andes *mpl*.
andiron ['ændaiən] *n* morillo *m*.
Andrew ['ændruː] *m* Andrés.
anecdote ['ænikdəut] *n* anécdota *f*.
anemia [ə'niːmiə] *n etc* = **anaemia** *etc*.
anemone [ə'neməni] *n* (*Bot*) anemone *f*; (*Zool*) anémona *f* (de mar).
aneroid ['ænərɔid] *adj* aneroide; **— barometer** barómetro *m* aneroide.
anesthesia [,ænis'θiːziə] *n etc* = **anaesthesia** *etc*.
anew [ə'njuː] *adv* de nuevo, otra vez.
angel ['eindʒəl] *n* ángel *m*; **yes, (my) —** ! ¡sí, querida!; **guardian —** ángel *m* custodio, ángel *m* de la guarda; **talk of —s** ! hablando del ruin de Roma, por la puerta asoma.
angelic(al) [æn'dʒelik(əl)] *adj* angélico.
angelica [æn'dʒelikə] *n* angélica *f*.
angelus ['ændʒiləs] *n* ángelus *m*.
anger ['æŋgə*] **1** *n* cólera *f*, ira *f*; **to rouse someone to —** provocar a uno a cólera, encolerizar a uno; **to speak in —** hablar indignado, hablar coléricamente. **2** *vt* enojar, provocar, encolerizar.
angina pectoris [æn'dʒainə'pektəris] *n* angina *f* del pecho.
angle¹ ['æŋgl] *n* (**a**) ángulo *m*; **acute —** ángulo *m* agudo; **alternate —** ángulo *m* alterno; **obtuse —** ángulo *m* obtuso; **right —** ángulo *m* recto; **— iron** hierro *m* angular; **— of climb** (*Aer*) ángulo *m* de subida; **it is leaning at an — of 80°** esta ladeado en un ángulo de 80°; **to be at an —** to formar ángulo con; **to look at a building from a different —** contemplar un edificio desde otro sitio, tener de un edificio una nueva perspectiva.
(**b**) (*fig*) punto *m* de vista; opinión *f*; **look at it from my —** considere la cosa desde mi punto de vista; **he has a different —** tiene otro modo de enfocar la cuestión; **that's a new — to the problem** ése es otro aspecto nuevo del problema.
angle² ['æŋgl] *vi* pescar con caña (*for a fish* un pez); **to — for** (*fig*) ir a la caza de, intrigar por conseguir.
angler ['æŋglə*] *n* pescador *m* (de caña).
Angles ['æŋglz] *npl* anglos *mpl*.
Anglican ['æŋglikən] **1** *adj* anglicano. **2** *n* anglicano *m*, a *f*.
Anglicanism ['æŋglikənizəm] *n* anglicanismo *m*.
anglicism ['æŋglisizəm] *n* anglicismo *m*, inglesismo *m*.
anglicist ['æŋglisist] *n* anglicista *mf*.
anglicize ['æŋglisaiz] *vt* inglesar.
angling ['æŋgliŋ] *n* pesca *f* con caña.
Anglo . . . ['æŋgləu] anglo . . .
Anglo-Catholic ['æŋgləu'kæθlik] **1** *adj* anglo-católico. **2** *n* anglocatólico *m*, a *f*.
Anglo-Catholicism ['æŋgləukə'θɔlisizəm] *n* anglo-catolicismo *m*.
Anglo-Indian ['æŋgləu'indiən] **1** *adj* angloindio. **2** *n* angloindio *m*, a *f*.
anglophile ['æŋgləufail] *n* anglófilo *m*, a *f*.
anglophobe ['æŋgləufəub] *n* anglófobo *m*, a *f*.
Anglo-Saxon ['æŋgləu'sæksən] **1** *adj* anglosajón. **2** *n* anglosajón *m*, ona *f*. **3** *n* (*language*) anglosajón *m*.
angora [æŋ'gɔːrə] *n* angora *m* f.
Angoulême [ũːŋgu'lɛm] Angulema.
angrily ['æŋgrili] *adv* coléricamente, airadamente.
angry ['æŋgri] **1** *adj* colérico, enojado, enfadado, airado; (*Med*) inflamado; *sky* tormentoso, que amenaza tormenta; **in an — voice** en tono colérico; **— young man** joven *m* airado; **to be — at** estar enfadado (*about* por; *at, with* con); **you won't be —** if I tell you? no te vayas a ofender si te lo digo; **to get —** enfadarse, ponerse furioso, indignarse; **to make someone —** irritar a uno, provocar a uno; **this sort of thing makes me —** estas cosas me sacan de quicio.
2 *n*: **the angries** los airados *mpl*.
anguish ['æŋgwiʃ] *n* (*bodily*) dolor *m* agudo, tormentos *mpl*; (*mental*) angustia *f*.
anguished ['æŋgwiʃt] *adj* acongojado, afligido, angustiado.
angular ['æŋgjulə*] *adj* angular; *face etc* anguloso.
aniline ['æniliːn] *n* anilina *f*; **— dyes** colores *mpl* de anilina.
animal ['æniməl] **1** *adj* animal. **2** *n* animal *m*; (*horse etc*) bestia *f*; (*insect etc*) bicho *m*.
animate ['ænimit] *adj* vivo, que tiene vida.
animate ['ænimeit] *vt* animar, infundir vida a; vivificar, estimular; alentar.
animated ['ænimeitid] *adj* vivo, vivaz, vigoroso; *discussion* vivo; **— cartoon** película *f* de dibujos.
animatedly ['ænimeitidli] *adv* *talk etc* animadamente.

animation [,æni'meiʃən] *n* vivacidad *f*, viveza *f*, animación *f*; **suspended** — muerte *f* aparente.

animosity [,æni'mɔsiti] *n* animosidad *f*, rencor *m*, hostilidad *f*.

animus ['ænimǝs] *n* odio *m*, rencor *m*.

anise ['ænis] *n* anís *m*.

aniseed ['ænisiːd] *n* anís *m*; (*strictly*) grano *m* de anís.

anisette [,æni'zet] *n* anisete *m*, anís *m*.

Anjou [ɑ̃:n'ʒu:] Anjeo *m*.

ankle ['æŋkl] *n* tobillo *m*.

anklebone ['æŋklbǝun] *n* hueso *m* del tobillo.

ankle-deep ['æŋkl'diːp] *adv*: **to be** — **in something** estar metido hasta los tobillos en algo; **the water is only** — el agua llega a los tobillos nada más.

anklet ['æŋklit] *n* brazalete *m* para el tobillo, ajorca *f* para el pie.

ankle sock ['æŋklsɔk] *n* escarpín *m*.

Ann [æn] *f* Ana; — **Boleyn** Ana Bolena.

annalist ['ænǝlist] *n* analista *mf*, cronista *mf*.

annals ['ænǝlz] *npl* anales *mpl*, crónica *f*; **never in the** — **of human endeavour** nunca en la historia de los esfuerzos humanos.

Anne [æn] *f* Ana; **Queen** —**'s dead!** eso lo tenemos archisabido.

anneal [ǝ'niːl] *vt* recocer; templar.

annex [ǝ'neks] *vt territory* anexar; *document* adjuntar, añadir (*to* a).

annexation [,ænek'seiʃǝn] *n* anexión *f*.

annexe ['æneks] *n* pabellón *m* separado, dependencia *f*, edificio *m* anexo.

annihilate [ǝ'naiǝleit] *vt* aniquilar.

annihilation [ǝ,naiǝ'leiʃǝn] *n* aniquilación *f*, aniquilamiento *m*.

anniversary [,æni'vǝːsǝri] *n* aniversario *m*; — **dinner** banquete *m* para festejar el aniversario de . . .

Anno Domini ['ænǝu'dɔminai] (*gen abbr* A.D.) **(a) 250** — el año 250 después de Jesucristo; **the second century** — el siglo segundo de Cristo.

(b) (*fam*) vejez *f*, edad *f*.

annotate ['ænǝuteit] *vt* anotar, comentar.

annotation [,ænǝu'teiʃǝn] *n* anotación *f*, apunte *m*; **a book with** —**s by X** un libro con notas de X.

announce [ǝ'nauns] *vt* anunciar; proclamar; declarar; hacer saber, comunicar; **then he** —**d "I won't"** luego declaró "No quiero"; **it is** —**d from London that** se comunica desde Londres que; **we regret to** — **the death of** lamentamos tener que participar la muerte de.

announcement [ǝ'naunsmǝnt] *n* anuncio *m*; proclama *f*; declaración *f*; aviso *m*; — **of birth** natalicio *m*; — **of death** necrológica *f*.

announcer [ǝ'naunsǝ*] *n* (*Radio*) locutor *m*, ora *f*.

annoy [ǝ'nɔi] *vt* molestar, fastidiar, irritar; **to be** —**ed** estar enfadado (*about* por; *at, with* con); **to get** —**ed** enfadarse, molestarse, incomodarse.

annoyance [ǝ'nɔiǝns] *n* (*state*) enojo *m*, irritación *f*; (*thing*) molestia *f*.

annoying [ǝ'nɔiiŋ] *adj* molesto, fastidioso, engorroso; *person* pesado, importuno; **it's** — **to have to** + *infin* me molesta tener que + *infin*.

annoyingly [ǝ'nɔiiŋli] *adv* de modo fastidioso; pesadamente, importunamente; **and then,** — **enough . . .** y luego, para fastidiarnos . . .; **the radio was** — **loud** la radio nos molestó con su ruido.

annual ['ænjuǝl] **1** *adj* anual. **2** *n* (*book*) anuario *m*; (*Bot*) planta *f* anual, anual *m*.

annually ['ænjuǝli] *adv* anualmente, cada año; **£500** — 500 libras al año.

annuity [ǝ'njuːiti] *n* (*also* **life** —) renta *f* vitalicia, pensión *f* vitalicia; **deferred** — cuota *f* de pensión; **to settle an** — **on** señalar una renta a.

annul [ǝ'nʌl] *vt* anular, invalidar; cancelar; *law* revocar.

annulment [ǝ'nʌlmǝnt] *n* anulación *f*; cancelación *f*; revocación *f*.

Annunciation [ǝ,nʌnsi'eiʃǝn] *n* Anunciación *f*.

anode ['ænǝud] *n* ánodo *m*.

anodyne ['ænǝudain] **1** *adj* anodino. **2** *n* anodino *m*.

anoint [ǝ'nɔint] *vt* untar; (*Eccl*) ungir.

anomalous [ǝ'nɔmǝlǝs] *adj* anómalo.

anomaly [ǝ'nɔmǝli] *n* anomalía *f*.

anon[1] [ǝ'nɔn] *adv* (*arch*) luego, dentro de poco; **ever and** — a menudo, de vez en cuando.

anon[2] [ǝ'nɔn] *abbr* = **anonymous.**

anonymity [,ænǝ'nimiti] *n* (*in general*) anonimato *m*; (*special case*) anónimo *m*; **to preserve one's** — conservar el anónimo.

anonymous [ǝ'nɔnimǝs] *adj* anónimo; **he wishes to remain** — no quiere que se publique su nombre.

anonymously [ǝ'nɔnimǝsli] *adv* anónimamente; **the book came out** — salió el libro sin nombre de autor; **he gave £100** — dio 100 libras sin revelar su nombre.

anorak ['ænǝræk] *n* anorak *m*.

another [ǝ'nʌðǝ*] **1** *adj* otro (*no art needed, eg* — **man** otro hombre); — **glass?** ¿otra copita?; **in** — **10 years** en otros 10 años; **we need** — **2 men** necesitamos 2 hombres más; **there are** — **2 months to go** faltan todavía 2 meses; **that is** — **matter altogether** eso es un asunto totalmente distinto; **without** — **word** sin decir palabra.

2 *pron* otro *m*, otra *f*; **just such** — otro tal; — **would have done it this way** cualquier otro lo hubiera hecho de este modo.

3 *reflexive pron*: **they love one** — (*2 persons*) se quieren (uno a otro), (*more than 2 persons*) se quieren unos a otros; **they don't speak to one** — no se hablan.

answer ['ɑːnsǝ*] **1** *n* **(a)** (*to question etc*) contestación *f*, respuesta *f* (*to* a); (*Law*) contestación *f* a la demanda, réplica *f*; **in** — **to** contestando a; **he smiled in** — contestó con una sonrisa; **his only** — **was to smile** por toda respuesta, se sonrió; **to know all the** —**s** saberlo todo, ser una hacha; **he's not exactly the** — **to a maiden's prayer** no es precisamente el hombre soñado.

(b) (*to problem*) solución *f* (*to* de); **what do you make the** —**?** ¿qué solución tienes?; **my** — **is to do nothing** yo lo resuelvo no haciendo nada; **there is no easy** — esto no se resuelve fácilmente.

(c) (*defence, reason*) **there must be an** — debe de haber una razón, debe de haber una explicación; **he's got an** — **to everything** lo justifica todo; **he has a complete** — **to the charges** puede probar su inocencia; **there is no** — **to the H-bomb** contra la bomba H no hay defensa posible.

2 *vt* **(a)** contestar a, responder a; *letter* contestar (a); **that should** — **your question** eso debe resolver (*or* satisfacer) sus dudas; **God will** — **our prayers** Dios escuchará nuestras oraciones; **our prayers have been** —**ed** nuestras súplicas han sido oídas; **to** — **the bell, to** — **the door** acudir a la puerta; **to** — **the telephone** contestar el teléfono; **to** — **one's name** contestar a su nombre; **to** — **a call for help** acudir a una llamada de socorro; **to** — **the helm** obedecer al timón.

(b) *description* corresponder a, cuadrar con; *expectations* corresponder a; *purpose* convenir para.

3 *vi* **(a)** contestar, responder; **to** — **back** replicar, ser respondón; **don't** — **back!** ¡no repliques!; **to** — **for** *thing* responder de, ser responsable de, *person* responder por; **I'll not** — **for the consequences** yo no me considero responsable de las consecuencias; **he's got a lot to** — **for** tiene la culpa de muchas cosas; **to** — **to the name of** (*dog*) atender por.

(b) (*suffice*) servir, convenir.

(c) **to** — **to** *description* corresponder a, cuadrar con.

answerable ['ɑːnsǝrǝbl] *adj* **(a) to be** — **to someone for something** ser responsable ante uno de algo; **he's not** — **to anyone** no tiene que dar cuentas a nadie.

(b) the question is not — el problema no tiene solución.

ant [ænt] *n* hormiga *f*.

antacid ['ænt'æsid] **1** *adj* antiácido. **2** *n* antiácido *m*.

antagonism [æn'tægǝnizǝm] *n* antagonismo *m*; oposición *f*, hostilidad *f* (*to* a); rivalidad *f* (*between* entre).

antagonist [æn'tægǝnist] *n* antagonista *mf*, adversario *m*, a *f*.

antagonistic [æn,tægǝ'nistik] *adj* antagónico; contrario, opuesto (*to* a).

antagonize [æn'tægǝnaiz] *vt* enemistarse con, provocar la enemistad de; **he managed to** — **everybody** logró ponerse a malas con todo el mundo.

Antarctic [ænt'ɑːktik] **1** *adj* antártico. **2** *n*: **the** — el Antártico.

Antarctica [ǝ,nʌnsi'eiʃǝn] Antártida *f*.

Antarctic Circle [ænt'ɑːktik'sǝːkl] *n* Círculo *m* Polar Antártico.

ante ['ænti] (*US*) **1** *n* apuesta *f*, tanto *m*. **2** *vt* apostar. **3** *vi* poner su apuesta; (*fig, also* **to** — **up**) contribuir, pagar su cuota.

anteater ['ænt,iːtǝ*] *n* oso *m* hormiguero.

antecedent [,ænti'siːdǝnt] **1** *adj* antecedente. **2** *n* antecedente *m*; —**s** antecedentes *mpl*.

antechamber ['ænti,tʃeimbǝ*] *n* antecámara *f*.

antedate ['ænti'deit] *vt* **(a) this building** —**s the** Norman conquest este edificio se construyó antes de la conquista normanda; **this text** —**s that by 50 years** este texto es anterior a ése en 50 años.

(b) *cheque etc* antedatar.

antediluvian ['æntidi'luːviǝn] *adj* antediluviano.

antelope ['æntilǝup] *n* antílope *m*.

antenatal ['ænti'neitl] *adj* antenatal.
antenna [æn'tenə] *n*, *pl* **antennae** [æn'teni:] antena *f*.
antepenultimate ['æntipi'nʌltimit] *adj* antepenúltimo.
anterior [æn'tiəriə*] *adj* anterior (*to* a).
anteroom ['æntirum] *n* antecámara *f*.
anthem ['ænθəm] *n* (*Eccl*) antífona *f*, motete *m*; **national** — himno *m* nacional.
anther ['ænθə*] *n* antera *f*.
ant-hill ['ænthil] *n* hormiguero *m*.
anthology [æn'θɔlədʒi] *n* antología *f*.
Anthony ['æntəni] *m* Antonio.
anthracite ['ænθrəsait] *n* antracita *f*.
anthrax ['ænθræks] *n* ántrax *m*.
anthropoid ['ænθrəupɔid] **1** *adj* antropoide. **2** *n* antropoideo *m*.
anthropological [,ænθrəpə'lɔdʒikəl] *adj* antropológico.
anthropologist [,ænθrə'pɔlədʒist] *n* antropólogo *m*.
anthropology [,ænθrə'pɔlədʒi] *n* antropología *f*.
anthropomorphism [,ænθrəupə'mɔːfizəm] *n* antropomorfismo *m*.
anthropophagi [,ænθrəu'pɔfəgai] *npl* antropófagos *mpl*.
anti ... ['ænti] *in compounds*: anti ...; **he's rather —** (*fam*) está más bien opuesto a ello.
anti-aircraft ['ænti'ɛəkrɑːft] *adj* antiaéreo; **— gun** cañón *m* antiaéreo.
antibiotic ['æntibai'ɔtik] **1** *adj* antibiótico. **2** *n* antibiótico *m*.
antibody ['ænti,bɔdi] *n* anticuerpo *m*.
Antichrist ['æntikraist] *n* Anticristo *m*.
anticipate [æn'tisipeit] *vt* (**a**) (*forestall*) *person* anticiparse a, adelantarse a; *event* anticiparse a, prevenir; *pleasure* disfrutar de antemano.
　(**b**) (*foresee*) prever; **you have —d my wishes** Vd se ha anticipado (*or* adelantado) a mis deseos; **you have —d my orders** Vd se ha anticipado a mis órdenes, (*wrongly*) Vd ha obrado sin esperar mis órdenes.
　(**c**) (*expect*) esperar; contar con; **this is more than I —d** esto es más de lo que esperaba; **the police —d trouble** la policía contaba con algunos disturbios; **to — that** prever que, calcular que; **do you — that this will be easy?** ¿crees que esto va a resultar fácil?
　(**d**) (*look forward to*) prometerse.
anticipation [æn,tisi'peiʃən] *n* (**a**) (*forestalling*) anticipación *f*, prevención *f*.
　(**b**) (*foresight*) previsión *f*, prevención *f*; **in —** de antemano.
　(**c**) (*foretaste*) anticipación *f*.
　(**d**) (*expectation*) esperanza *f*, esperanzas *fpl*; **in — of a fine week** esperando una semana de buen tiempo; **it did not come up to our —s** no correspondió con nuestras esperanzas.
　(**e**) (*advance excitement*) expectación *f*, ilusión *f*; **we waited with growing —** esperábamos con creciente ilusión; **we waited in great —** esperábamos muy ilusionados.
anticlerical ['ænti'klerikl] *adj* anticlerical.
anticlericalism ['ænti'kleriklizəm] *n* anticlericalismo *m*.
anticlimax ['ænti'klaimæks] *n* acontecimiento *m* (*etc*) que marca un descenso de la emoción, decepción *f*; **the book ends in —** la emoción desfallece hacia el fin de la novela, la novela termina de modo decepcionante; **the game came as an —** el partido no correspondió con las esperanzas.
anticlockwise ['ænti'klɔkwaiz] *adv* en dirección contraria a la de las agujas del reloj.
anticoagulant ['æntikəu'ægjulənt] **1** *adj* anticoagulante. **2** *n* anticoagulante *f*.
anticorrosive ['æntikə'rɔuziv] *adj* anticorrosivo.
antics ['æntiks] *npl* bufonadas *fpl*, payasadas *fpl*; (*of child, animal etc*) gracias *fpl*, travesuras *fpl*; **he's up to his — again** ha vuelto a hacer de las suyas.
anticyclone ['ænti'saiklɔun] *n* anticiclón *m*.
anti-dazzle ['ænti'dæzl] *adj* antideslumbrante.
antidote ['æntidɔut] *n* antídoto *m* (*for, against, to* contra).
antifreeze ['ænti'friːz] **1** *adj* anticongelante. **2** *n* solución *f* anticongelante.
anti-friction ['ænti'frikʃən] *adj* antifriccional.
anti-glare ['ænti'glɛə*] *adj* antideslumbrante.
Antigone [æn'tigəni] *f* Antígona.
antihistamine [,ænti'histəmin] **1** *adj* antihistamínico. **2** *n* antihistamínico *m*.
anti-knock ['ænti'nɔk] *adj* antidetonante.

Antilles [æn'tiliːz] *pl* Antillas *fpl*.
antilogarithm [,ænti'lɔgəriθəm] *n* antilogaritmo *m*.
antimacassar ['æntimə'kæsə*] *n* antimacasar *m*.
antimissile ['ænti'misail] *adj*, *attr* antimísil, antiproyectil.
antimony ['æntiməni] *n* antimonio *m*.
Antioch ['æntiɔk] Antioquía *f*.
antipathetic [,æntipə'θetik] *adj* antipático (*to* a).
antipathy [æn'tipəθi] *n* antipatía *f* (*between* entre; *to* por, hacia); (*thing disliked*) aversión *f*, cosa *f* aborrecida.
antiphony [æn'tifəni] *n* antífona *f*.
antipodes [æn'tipədi:z] *npl* antípodas *fpl*.
antiquarian [,ænti'kwɛəriən] **1** *adj* anticuario. **2** *n* anticuario *m*.
antiquary ['æntik,wəri] *n* anticuario *m*.
antiquated ['æntikweitid] *adj* anticuado.
antique [æn'ti:k] **1** *adj* antiguo, viejo; anticuado; *furniture etc* clásico, de época.
　2 *n* antigüedad *f*, antigualla *f*; **— dealer** anticuario *m*, comerciante *m* en antigüedades; **— shop** tienda *f* de antigüedades.
antiquity [æn'tikwiti] *n* antigüedad *f*; **high —** remota antigüedad *f*; **in —** en la antigüedad.
anti-roll device ['ænti'rəuldi'vais] *n* dispositivo *m* para contrarrestar el balanceo.
antirrhinum [,ænti'rainəm] *n* antirrino *m*.
anti-rust ['ænti'rʌst] *adj* antioxidante.
anti-semite ['ænti'si:mait] *n* antisemita *mf*.
anti-semitic ['æntisi'mitik] *adj* antisemítico.
anti-semitism ['ænti'semitizəm] *n* antisemitismo *m*.
antiseptic [,ænti'septik] **1** *adj* antiséptico. **2** *n* antiséptico *m*.
anti-skid ['ænti'skid] *adj* antideslizante, antiderrapante.
antisocial ['ænti'səuʃəl] *adj* antisocial.
anti-tank ['ænti'tæŋk] *adj* antitanque.
antithesis [æn'tiθisis] *n*, *pl* **antitheses** [æn'tiθisi:z] antítesis *f*.
antithetic(al) [,ænti'θetik(əl)] *adj* antitético.
anti-trust law ['ænti'trʌstlɔ:] *n* ley *f* antimonopolios.
antivivisectionist ['ænti,vivi'sekʃənist] *n* antivivisecciónista *mf*.
antler ['æntlə*] *n* cuerna *f*; **—s** cuernas *fpl*, cornamenta *f*.
Antony ['æntəni] *m* Antonio.
antonym ['æntənim] *n* antónimo *m*.
Antwerp ['æntwə:p] Amberes *f*.
anus ['einəs] *n* ano *m*.
anvil ['ænvil] *n* yunque *m*.
anxiety [æŋ'zaiəti] *n* (**a**) (*worry*) inquietud *f*, preocupación *f*; **some — is felt about it** existe cierta inquietud sobre esto; **it is a great — to me** me preocupa muchísimo.
　(**b**) (*eagerness*) ansia *f*, anhelo *m* (*for* de; *to do* de hacer, por hacer); **in his — to be gone he forgot his maleta** tanto ansiaba partir que olvidó su maleta.
　(**c**) (*Med*) ansiedad *f*; **— neurosis** neurosis *f* de ansiedad.
anxious ['æŋkʃəs] *adj* (**a**) (*worried*) inquieto, preocupado, angustiado; **to be — about, to be — for** inquietarse por; **I'm very — about you** me tienes muy preocupado; **in an — voice** en un tono angustiado; **with an — glance** con una mirada llena de inquietud.
　(**b**) (*causing worry*) **it is an — time** es un período de gran ansiedad; **you gave me some — moments** en ciertas ocasiones me causaste gran inquietud; **it was an — moment** fue un momento de ansiedad.
　(**c**) (*eager*) deseoso (*for*; *to do* de hacer); **he is — for success** ansía el triunfo, ambiciona el triunfo; **to be — to do** desear hacer, tener ganas de hacer, tener empeño en hacer; **I am very — that he should go** quiero a toda costa que vaya; **I'm not very — to go** tengo pocas ganas de ir.
anxiously ['æŋkʃəsli] *adv* con inquietud, de manera angustiada; **we waited —** esperábamos con ansiedad.
anxiousness ['æŋkʃəsnis] *n* inquietud *f*.
any ['eni] **1** *adj* (**a**) algún, alguna; **— day now** algún día de éstos; **if there are — tickets left** si le queda alguna entrada.
　(**b**) (*partitive: gen not translated*) **have you — money?** ¿tienes dinero?; **have you — bananas?** ¿hay plátanos?; **is there — man who ...?** ¿hay hombre que ...?
　(**c**) (*any ... you like*) cualquier; **— farmer will tell you** te lo dirá cualquier agricultor; **wear — hat (you like)** ponte el sombrero que quieras, ponte un sombrero no importa cuál.
　(**d**) (*negative sense*) ningún, ninguna; **I don't see — cows** no veo ninguna vaca, no veo vaca alguna.

2 *pron* (a) alguno, alguna; **if there are — who ...** si hay algunos que ...; **few, if — pocos**, si es que los hay.

(b) (*any ... you like*) cualquiera; **take — you like** tome cualquiera.

(c) (*negative sense*) ninguno, ninguna; **I haven't — of them** no tengo ninguno de ellos.

3 *adv* (a) (*gen not translated*) — **more** más; **don't wait — longer** no esperes más tiempo; **are there — others?** ¿hay otros?; **is he — better?** ¿está algo mejor?

(b) (*fam, esp US*) **it doesn't help us —** eso no nos ayuda en lo más mínimo.

anybody ['enibɔdi] *pron* (a) alguien, álguno; **did you see —?** ¿vio a alguien?; **— but you** todos menos Vd; **— would have said he was mad** se hubiera dicho que estaba loco.

(b) (**— ... you like**) cualquiera; **— will tell you the same** cualquiera te dirá lo mismo; **— else would have laughed** cualquier otro se hubiera reído; **it's not available to just —** no se hace asequible a todos sin distinción; **I'm not going to marry just —** yo no me caso con un cualquiera.

(c) (*negative sense*) nadie, ninguno; **I can't see —** no veo a nadie.

(d) (*person of importance*) **is he —?** ¿es una persona de importancia?

anyhow ['enihau] *adv* (a) (*at any rate*) de todas formas, de todos modos, con todo.

(b) (*in spite of everything*) **I shall go —** voy a pesar de todo, sin embargo voy.

(c) (*haphazard*) **he leaves things just —** deja sus cosas en la mayor confusión; **she makes the beds just —** hace las camas de cualquier modo.

anyone ['eniwʌn] *pron* = **anybody**.

anything ['eniθiŋ] *pron* (a) algo, alguna cosa; **is there — inside?** ¿hay algo dentro?; **are you doing — tonight?** ¿tienes compromiso para esta noche?; **— else?** (*in shop etc*) ¿algo más?, ¿alguna cosita más?; **is there — in this idea?** ¿tiene algún valor esta idea?

(b) (**— you like**) cualquier cosa; **he will give you — you ask for** te dará todo lo que pidas; **sing — you like** canta lo que quieras; **— but that** todo menos eso; **— else is ruled out** todo lo demás está excluido; **I'll read — else** leeré otra cosa cualquiera; **I'm not buying just —** yo no compro una cosa cualquiera.

(c) (*negative sense*) nada; **I can't see —** no veo nada; **can't — be done?** ¿no se puede hacer nada?; **we can't do — else** no podemos hacer otra cosa; **not for — in the world** por nada del mundo.

(d) (*fam*) **like —** hasta más no poder.

anytime ['enitaim] *adv see* **time**.

anyway ['eniwei] *adv* = **anyhow**.

anywhere ['eniwɛə*] *adv* (a) en todas partes, en (*or* a) cualquier parte, dondequiera; **— in the world** en todas partes del mundo; **go — you like** vaya adonde quiera; **— you go you'll see the same** dondequiera que vaya Vd verá lo mismo; **— else** en cualquier otra parte; **I'm not going to live just —** yo no voy a vivir en un sitio cualquiera; **do you see him —?** ¿le ves en alguna parte?

(b) (*negative sense*) en (*or* a) ninguna parte; **I'm not going —** yo no voy a ninguna parte; **he was first and the rest didn't come —** él se clasificó primero y los demás quedaron muy por debajo.

aorta [ei'ɔːtə] *n* aorta *f*.

apace [ə'peis] *adv* aprisa, rápidamente.

apache [ə'pætʃi] *n* apache *m*.

apart [ə'pɑːt] *adv* (a) aparte, separadamente; **this is something quite —** esto es una cosa totalmente distinta; **to come —** romperse, deshacerse; **but joking —** pero en serio; **to keep —** separar; mantener aislado; **they live — now** ahora están separados; **to set —** guardar, reservar (*for* para), poner aparte; **the house stands somewhat —** la casa está algo aislada; **to take —** desmontar; **to tear — tear —** despedazar, romper; **to tell —** distinguir entre.

(b) **— from** aparte de; **but quite — from that** pero además de eso; **he lives — from his wife** vive separado de su mujer.

apartheid [ə'pɑːteit] *n* separación *f* racial.

apartment [ə'pɑːtmənt] *n* (*flat*) piso *m*, apartamento *m*; (*room*) aposento *m*; **— house** (*US*) casa *f* de pisos.

apathetic [.æpə'θetik] *adj* apático, indiferente; **to be — towards** ser indiferente a, no mostrar interés alguno en.

apathy ['æpəθi] *n* apatía *f*, indiferencia *f* (*towards* a), falta *f* de interés (*towards* en).

ape [eip] **1** *n* mono *m* (*esp* los antropomorfos), antropoideo *m*; (*fig*) mono de imitación *m*, imitador *m*, ora *f*. **2** *vt* imitar, remedar.

aperient [ə'piəriənt] **1** *adj* laxante. **2** *n* laxante *m*.

apéritif [ə'peritiv] *n* aperitivo *m*.

aperture ['æpətʃjuə*] *n* abertura *f*, rendija *f*, resquicio *m*.

apex ['eipeks] *n*, *pl* **apices** ['eipisiːz] ápice *m*; (*fig*) cumbre *f*.

aphasia [æ'feiziə] *n* afasia *f*.

aphis ['eifis] *n*, *pl* **aphides** ['eifidiːz] áfido *m*.

aphorism ['æfərizəm] *n* aforismo *m*.

aphrodisiac [.æfrəu'diziæk] **1** *adj* afrodisíaco. **2** *n* afrodisíaco *m*.

Aphrodite [.æfrəu'daiti] *f* Afrodita.

apiarist ['eipiərist] *n* apicultor *m*.

apiary ['eipiəri] *n* colmenar *m*.

apiculture ['eipikʌltʃə*] *n* apicultura *f*.

apiece [ə'piːs] *adv* cada uno, **eg they had a gun —** tenía cada uno un revólver; **he gave them an apple —** dio una manzana a cada uno; por persona, por cabeza, **eg the rule is a shilling —** la regla es un chelín por persona.

aplomb [ə'plɔm] *n* aplomo *m*, confianza *f*, sangre *f* fría, serenidad *f*; **with the greatest —** con la mayor serenidad.

Apocalypse [ə'pɔkəlips] *n* Apocalipsis *m*.

apocalyptic [ə.pɔkə'liptik] *adj* apocalíptico.

apocopate [ə'pɔkəpeit] *vt* apocopar.

Apocrypha [ə'pɔkrifə] *npl* libros *mpl* apócrifos de la Biblia.

apocryphal [ə'pɔkrifəl] *adj* apócrifo.

apogee ['æpəudʒiː] *n* apogeo *m*.

Apollo [ə'pɔləu] *m* Apolo.

apologetic [ə.pɔlə'dʒetik] *adj* lleno de disculpas; **with an — air** como si viniera a pedir perdón; **he was very — about it** dijo que lo sentía profundamente.

apologetically [ə.pɔlə'dʒetikəli] *adv* con aire del que pide perdón, con muchas excusas, excusándose.

apologize [ə'pɔlədʒaiz] *vi* disculparse (*for* de; *to* con), pedir perdón (*to* a); (*for absence etc*) presentar sus excusas.

apology [ə'pɔlədʒi] *n* (a) disculpa *f*, excusa *f*; **I demand an —** reclamo la satisfacción, insisto en que Vd pida perdón; **to make** (*or* **offer**) **an —** disculparse, presentar sus excusas.

(b) (*Lit etc*) apología *f*, defensa *f*.

(c) **an — for a house** una birria de casa; **this — for a letter** ésta que apenas se puede llamar carta.

apoplectic [.æpə'plektik] *adj* apopléctico; **to get —** (*fig*) enfurecerse.

apoplexy ['æpəpleksi] *n* apoplejía *f*.

apostasy [ə'pɔstəsi] *n* apostasía *f*.

apostate [ə'pɔstit] *n* apóstata *mf*.

apostatize [ə'pɔstətaiz] *vi* apostatar (*from* de).

apostle [ə'pɔsl] *n* apóstol *m*.

apostolic [.æpəs'tɔlik] *adj* apostólico.

apostrophe [ə'pɔstrəfi] *n* (*written sign*) apóstrofo *m*; (*address*) apóstrofe *gen m*.

apostrophize [ə'pɔstrəfaiz] *vt* apostrofar.

apothecary [ə'pɔθikəri] *n* (*Hist*) boticario *m*.

apotheosis [ə.pɔθi'əusis] *n* apoteosis *f*.

appal [ə'pɔːl] *vt* horrorizar, aterrar; **everyone was —led** se horrorizaron todos, todos quedaron aterrados; **I was —led by the news** me horrorizó la noticia.

Appalachians [.æpə'leiʃənz] *pl* Montes *mpl* Apalaches.

appalling [ə'pɔːliŋ] *adj* espantoso, horroroso; *taste etc* detestable, pésimo.

appallingly [ə'pɔːliŋli] *adv* espantosamente, horrorosamente; detestablemente; **it was quite — bad** fue del todo horrible; **he's — self-centred** es terriblemente egocéntrico.

apparatus [.æpə'reitəs] *n* aparato *m*.

apparel [ə'pærəl] (*arch or hum*) **1** *n* ropa *f*, vestidos *mpl*; (*hum*) atavío *m*. **2** *vt* vestir; (*hum*) trajear, ataviar (*in* de).

apparent [ə'pærənt] *adj* (*seeming*) aparente; (*clear*) claro, evidente, manifiesto; *heir* forzoso; **more — than real** más aparente que real; **it is — that** está claro que; **to become —** manifestarse, hacerse patente; **it is becoming — that** ya se está viendo que.

apparently [ə'pærəntli] *adv* por lo visto, según parece, al parecer.

apparition [.æpə'riʃən] *n* (*act*) aparición *f*; (*ghost*) fantasma *m*, aparecido *m*.

appeal [ə'piːl] **1** *n* (a) (*call*) llamamiento *m*; **a national — for funds** un llamamiento a todo el país para que contribuya dinero; **he made an — for calm**

hizo un llamamiento a todos para que mantuvieran la calma; **a charity** — una cuestación para obras benéficas.

(b) (*petition*) súplica *f*, ruego *m*, petición *f*; **an** — **for help** una petición de socorro.

(c) (*Law*) apelación *f*, recurso *m* de casación; **without** — inapelable; **there is no** — **from his decision** su fallo es inapelable; **to give notice of** — entablar apelación; **to lodge an** — apelar (*against* de).

(d) (*attraction*) atractivo *m*, encanto *m*, interés *m*; **the** — **of children** el encanto de los niños; **a book of general** — un libro de interés para todos.

2 *vi* (a) (*call, beg*) **to** — **for** suplicar, reclamar; **I** — **for its return** ruego que se me devuelva; **he** —**ed for silence** rogó que se callasen todos; **to** — **to someone for something** suplicar algo a uno; **I** — **to you!** ¡se lo ruego!; **it's no good** —**ing to me** de nada sirve acudir a mí; **to** — **to the country** celebrar elecciones generales; **to** — **to arms** recurrir a las armas; **to** — **to someone's finer feelings** apelar a los sentimientos nobles de uno.

(b) (*Law*) apelar (*against* de; **to** a).

(c) (*attract*) atraer, tener atractivo para, interesar; **jazz does not** — **to me** el jazz no tiene atractivo para mí; **it** —**s to the imagination** estimula la imaginación.

appealing [ə'piːliŋ] *adj* (*begging*) suplicante; (*attractive*) atrayente, atractivo, encantador.

appealingly [ə'piːliŋli] *adv* de modo suplicante.

appear [ə'piə*] *vi* (a) (*present oneself*) aparecer; mostrarse, presentarse; **he** —**ed from nowhere** apareció como cosa llovida del cielo; **he** —**ed from behind a tree** salió de detrás de un árbol; **he** —**ed without a tie** se presentó sin corbata; **as will** — **in due course** según se verá luego; **to** — **to someone** (*as vision*) aparecerse a uno.

(b) (*book etc*) salir a luz, publicarse; **the magazine** —**s weekly** la revista sale cada semana.

(c) (*Law*) comparecer (*before* ante); **to** — **for someone** representar a uno.

(d) (*seem*) parecer; **he** —**s tired** parece cansado; **how does it** — **to you?** ¿qué le parece esto?; **it** —**s that** resulta que, parece que; **so it** —**s, so it would** — según parece; **in daylight it** —**s red** a la luz del sol se muestra rojo.

appearance [ə'piərəns] *n* (a) (*act of appearing*) aparición *f*; **to make an** — aparecer, presentarse, dejarse ver; **to make one's first** — aparecer por primera vez; **to put in an** — hacer acto de presencia; **to put in an** — hacer acto de presencia.

(b) (*Law*) comparecencia *f*; **to make an** — **in court** comparecer ante el tribunal.

(c) (*aspect*) apariencia *f*, aspecto *m*; **to have a good** — tener buen aspecto.

(d) —**s** (*seeming*) apariencias *fpl*; —**s are deceptive** las apariencias engañan; **to all** —**s** al parecer, según todos los indicios.

(e) (*face*) apariencias *fpl*; **for the sake of** —**s** para salvar las apariencias; **to keep up** (*or* **save**) —**s** salvar las apariencias.

appease [ə'piːz] *vt* apaciguar; *hunger* satisfacer, saciar; *passion* mitigar; *person* satisfacer, dar contento a; *angry person* desenojar.

appeasement [ə'piːzmənt] *n* apaciguamiento *m*, pacificación *f*.

appellant [ə'pelənt] *n* apelante *mf*.

appellation [ˌæpe'leiʃən] *n* nombre *m*, título *m*.

append [ə'pend] *vt* (*add*) añadir; (*enclose*) adjuntar, enviar adjunto; *signature* poner.

appendage [ə'pendidʒ] *n* añadidura *f*, apéndice *m*; (*fig*) pegote *m*.

appendectomy [ˌæpen'dektəmi] *n* apendectomía *f*.

appendicitis [əˌpendi'saitis] *n* apendicitis *f*.

appendix [ə'pendiks] *n*, *pl* **appendices** [ə'pendisiːz] apéndice *m*.

Appenines [ˈæpənainz] *pl* Apeninos *mpl*.

appertain [ˌæpə'tein] *vi*: **to** — **to** relacionarse con, tener que ver con.

appetite [ˈæpitait] *n* (a) apetito *m*; **to eat with an** — comer con buen apetito; **to whet one's** — abrir el apetito.

(b) (*fig*) deseo *m*, anhelo *m* (*for* de); **they had no** — **for further fighting** ya no les apetecía seguir luchando; **to spoil one's** — **for** quitar a uno las ganas de.

appetizer [ˈæpitaizə*] *n* apetite *m*, aperitivo *m*.

appetizing [ˈæpitaiziŋ] *adj* apetitoso.

applaud [ə'plɔːd] **1** *vt* aplaudir; (*fig*) aplaudir, celebrar, alabar. **2** *vi* aplaudir, palmotear.

applause [ə'plɔːz] *n* aplausos *mpl*; (*fig*) aplausos *mpl*, aprobación *f*; **there was loud** — sonaron fuertes aplausos; **to win the** — **of** ganarse la aprobación de.

apple ['æpl] *n* (*fruit*) manzana *f*; (*tree*) manzano *m*; **stewed** —**s** compota *f* de manzanas; — **of discord** manzana *f* de la discordia; **the** — **of one's eye** la niña de los ojos.

applecart ['æplkɑːt] *n*: **to upset the** — echarlo todo a rodar; **to upset someone's** — dar al traste con los planes de uno.

apple core ['æplkɔː*] *n* corazón *m* de manzana.

applejack ['æpldʒæk] *n* (*US*) aguardiente *m* de manzana.

apple orchard ['æplˌɔːtʃəd] *n* manzanar *m*, pomar *m*.

apple pie ['æpl'pai] *n* tarta *f* de manzanas; **in apple-pie order** en perfecto orden; **apple-pie bed** cama *f* en petaca.

apple-sauce ['æpl'sɔːs] *n* compota *f* de manzanas; (*US sl*) coba *f*.

appliance [ə'plaiəns] *n* aparato *m*, instrumento *m*, dispositivo *m*.

applicability [ˌæplikə'biliti] *n* aplicabilidad *f*.

applicable [ə'plikəbl] *adj* aplicable (*to* a); **a rule** — **to all** una regla que se extiende a todos; **this is not** — **to you** esto no se refiere a Vd; **delete what is not** — táchese lo que no interese.

applicant ['æplikənt] *n* aspirante *mf*, candidato *m* (*for a post* a un puesto); suplicante *mf*, solicitante *mf*.

application [ˌæpli'keiʃən] *n* (a) (*in most senses*) aplicación *f*; **for external** — **only** (*Med*) para uso externo.

(b) (*request*) solicitud *f*, petición *f* (*for* de, por); —**s in triplicate** las solicitudes por triplicado; **are you going to put in an** —? ¿te vas a presentar?; **to make an** — **for** solicitar; **to make an** — **to** dirigirse a; **details may be had on** — **to X** para los detalles dirigirse a X.

applied [ə'plaid] *adj* *science etc* aplicado.

appliqué [æ'pliːkei] *n* (*also* — **lace,** — **work**) encaje *m* de aplicación.

apply [ə'plai] **1** *vt* aplicar (*to* a); *rule* emplear, recurrir a; *law* poner en vigor; **how can we best** — **this money?** ¿cómo podemos utilizar mejor este dinero?; **to** — **one's mind to a problem** dedicarse a resolver un problema.

2 *vi* (a) (*refer to*) ser aplicable, interesar; **cross out what does not** — táchese lo que no interese; **to** — **to** tener que ver con, ser aplicable a, referirse a; **the law applies to everybody** la ley a todos comprende.

(b) (*request*) presentarse, ser candidato; **are you** —**ing?** ¿te vas a presentar?; **to** — **for** solicitar, pedir, *post* solicitar, presentarse a; **patent applied for** se ha solicitado patente; **to** — **to** dirigirse a, acudir a; **to** — **to someone for something** dirigirse a uno pidiendo algo.

3 *vr*: **to** — **oneself to** aplicarse a, dedicarse a.

appoint [ə'pɔint] *vt* (a) *time, date etc* fijar, señalar (*for* para); **at the** — **ed time** a la hora señalada.

(b) (*nominate*) nombrar (*to* a); **they** —**ed him chairman** le nombraron presidente; **they** —**ed him to do it** le nombraron para que lo hiciese.

(c) **well** —**ed** bien amueblado, bien equipado.

appointment [ə'pɔintmənt] *n* (a) (*act*) nombramiento *m* (*to* a); **by** — **to . . .** (*with royal arms*) proveedores de . . .

(b) (*engagement*) cita *f*, compromiso *m*; **I have an** — **at 10** tengo una cita a las 10; **have you an** — **tonight?** ¿tienes compromiso para esta noche?; **have you an** —? (*to caller*) ¿tiene Vd hora?; **to keep an** — acudir a una cita; **to make an** — (*2 persons*) darse una cita; **to make an** — **with** citarse con; **to make an** — **for 3 o'clock** citarse para las 3.

(c) (*post*) puesto *m*, empleo *m*; —**s bureau** bolsa *f* de trabajo.

(d) —**s** mobiliario *m*, moblaje *m*, equipo *m*.

apportion [ə'pɔːʃən] *vt* prorratear; repartir, distribuir; **the blame is to be** —**ed equally** todos tienen la culpa por partes iguales.

apposite ['æpəzit] *adj* apropiado (*to* a); a propósito, oportuno.

apposition [ˌæpə'ziʃən] *n* aposición *f*; **in** — en aposición.

appraisal [ə'preizəl] *n* tasación *f*, valoración *f*; (*fig*) estimación *f*, apreciación *f*.

appraise [ə'preiz] *vt* tasar, valorar; (*fig*) apreciar.

appreciable [ə'priːʃəbl] *adj* sensible, perceptible; **an** — **sum** una cantidad importante; **an** — **loss** una pérdida sensible.

appreciably [ə'priːʃəbli] *adv* sensiblemente, perceptiblemente.

appreciate [ə'priːʃieit] **1** *vt* (a) (*estimate worth of*) apreciar, valorar.

(b) (*estimate correctly*) apreciar, saber valorar en su justo precio.

(c) (*esteem*) apreciar, tener en mucho, tener un alto concepto de; **he does not — music** no sabe apreciar la música, no entiende de música; **I am not —d here** aquí no me estiman; **we much — your work** tenemos un alto concepto de su trabajo.

(d) (*understand*) comprender; **I — your wishes in the matter** comprendo sus deseos en este asunto; **yes, I — that** sí, lo comprendo; **to — that comprender que**; **we fully — that** comprendemos perfectamente que.

(e) (*be grateful for*) agradecer; **I — the gesture** agradezco el detalle.

(f) (*be sensitive to*) percibir; **the smallest change can be —d on this machine** en esta máquina se percibe el más pequeño cambio.

2 *vi* aumentar(se) en valor, subir.

appreciation [ə‚priːʃiˈeiʃən] *n* **(a)** (*estimation*) aprecio *m*, apreciación *f*, estimación *f*; (*obituary*) necrológica *f*; (*praise*) elogio *m*; **literary —** crítica *f* literaria.

(b) (*esteem*) aprecio *m*; **you have no — of art** Vd no sabe apreciar el arte, Vd no entiende de arte.

(c) (*gratitude*) reconocimiento *m*, agradecimiento *m*; **as a token of my —** en señal de reconocimiento.

(d) (*rise in value*) aumento *m* en valor, subida *f*.

appreciative [əˈpriːʃiətiv] *adj* agradecido; *audience* atento; **an — look** una mirada llena de agradecimiento; **he was very — of what I had done** agradeció mucho lo que yo había hecho; **he spoke in — terms of my work** habló de mi trabajo en términos elogiosos.

apprehend [‚æpriˈhend] *vt* **(a)** (*arrest*) prender. **(b)** (*perceive*) percibir; comprender. **(c)** (*fear*) recelar, sospechar; **to — that** sospechar que.

apprehension [‚æpriˈhenʃən] *n* **(a)** (*arrest*) prendimiento *m*.

(b) (*perception*) percepción *f*; comprensión *f*.

(c) (*fear*) recelo *m*, aprensión *f*; **my chief — is that** sobre todo me temo que + *subj.*

apprehensive [‚æpriˈhensiv] *adj* aprensivo; **to be — for** temer por, inquietarse por; **to be — that** recelar que, temer que + *subj*; **to grow —** inquietarse.

apprehensively [‚æpriˈhensivli] *adv* con aprensión.

apprentice [əˈprentis] **1** *n* aprendiz *m*, iza *f*; (*fig*) novicio *m*, a *f*. **2** *vt* poner de aprendiz (*to* con); **to be —d to** estar de aprendiz con.

apprenticeship [əˈprentiʃip] *n* aprendizaje *m*; **to serve one's —** hacer su aprendizaje.

apprise [əˈpraiz] *vt* informar, avisar (*of* de); **I will — him of it** se lo diré; **to be —d of** estar enterado de; **I was never —d of your decision** no se me comunicó nunca su decisión.

appro [ˈæprəu] (*fam*) = **approval**; **on — a prueba.**

approach [əˈprəutʃ] **1** *vt* **(a)** acercarse a; aproximarse a.

(b) (*fig*) **we must — the subject with care** tenemos que considerar el asunto con mucho cuidado; **it all depends on how we — it** depende de cómo enfocamos la cuestión; **I — it with an open mind** empiezo a estudiarlo sin prejuicios.

(c) *person* abordar, dirigirse a; **a man —ed me in the street** un hombre me abordó en la calle; **you should — the boss about that** Vd debiera dirigirse al jefe sobre aquello; **have you —ed him yet?** ¿has hablado ya con él?

(d) (*approximate to*) aproximarse a, parecerse a, ser semejante a; **here the colour —es blue** aquí el color tira a azul.

2 *vi* acercarse.

3 *n* **(a)** (*act*) acercamiento *m*; **— light** (*Aer*) luz *f* de acercamiento; **we watched his —** le vimos acercarse; **at the — of the enemy** al acercarse el enemigo; **at the — of night** al entrar la noche.

(b) (*fig*) aproximación *f* (*to* a).

(c) (*to problem*) aproximación *f* (*to* a), modo *m* de enfocar una cuestión, método *m* de abordar un problema; **an — to Spanish history** una aproximación a la historia de España; **I don't like your — to this matter** no me gusta su modo de enfocar esta cuestión; **we must think of a new —** tenemos que inventar otro método.

(d) (*access*) acceso *m* (*to* a), vía *f* de entrada; **— road** camino *m* de acceso; **—es** accesos *mpl*, (*Mil*) aproches *mpl*; **the northern —es of Madrid** las rutas de acceso a Madrid por la parte norte; **easy of —** asequible, de fácil acceso.

(e) (*advance*) propuesta *f*, proposición *f*; oferta *f*; **to make —es to** dirigirse a, tratar de hablar con.

approachable [əˈprəutʃəbl] *adj* *person* abordable, afable; *place* accesible.

approaching [əˈprəutʃiŋ] *adj* *event* próximo, venidero; *car etc* que se acerca; *traffic* que viene en dirección opuesta.

approbation [‚æprəˈbeiʃən] *n* aprobación *f*; consentimiento *m*.

appropriate [əˈprəupriit] *adj* apropiado, conveniente, a propósito; *moment etc* oportuno; *authority etc* competente; **— for, — to** apropiado para; **whichever seems more —** el que le parezca más apropiado; **would it be — for me to wear it?** ¿convendría que yo me lo pusiera?; **and where —** . . . y en su caso . . .

appropriate [əˈprəupriit] *vt* *thing* apropiarse; *funds etc* asignar, destinar (*for* a).

appropriately [əˈprəupriitli] *adv* apropiadamente, convenientemente; **he was very — named Moor** tuvo el nombre tan apropiado de Moro; **in an — designed house** en una casa convenientemente distribuida.

appropriateness [əˈprəupriitnis] *n* propiedad *f*, conveniencia *f*.

appropriation [ə‚prəupriˈeiʃən] *n* apropiación *f*; asignación *f*.

approval [əˈpruːvəl] *n* aprobación *f*; consentimiento *m*; (*formal OK*) visto bueno *m*; **on — a prueba**; **has this your —?** ¿Vd ha aprobado esto?; **to meet with someone's —** obtener la aprobación de uno; **he nodded his —** asintió con la cabeza.

approve [əˈpruːv] **1** *vt* aprobar; **read and —d** visto bueno.

2 *vi*: **to — of** aprobar, dar por bueno; **they don't — of my fiancé** no les cae en gracia mi novio; **I cannot — of your going** no puedo consentir en que vayas.

approved [əˈpruːvd] *adj* aprobado, acreditado; **in the — fashion** del modo acostumbrado; **— school** correccional *m*.

approving [əˈpruːviŋ] *adj* de aprobación.

approvingly [əˈpruːviŋli] *adv* con aprobación.

approximate [əˈprɔksimit] *adj* aproximado.

approximate [əˈprɔksimeit] *vi* aproximarse (*to* a).

approximately [əˈprɔksimətli] *adv* aproximadamente, poco más o menos.

approximation [ə‚prɔksiˈmeiʃən] *n* aproximación *f*.

appurtenance [əˈpəːtinəns] *n* (*appendage*) dependencia *f*; (*accessory*) accesorio *m*.

apricot [ˈeiprikɔt] *n* (*fruit*) albaricoque *m*; (*tree*) albaricoquero *m*.

April [ˈeiprəl] *n* abril *m*.

April Fools' Day [ˈeiprəlˈfuːlzˈdei] *n see* **All Fools' Day.**

apron [ˈeiprən] *n* delantal *m*; (*workman's, mason's etc*) mandil *m*; (*Theat*) visera *f*; (*Aer*) pista *f*.

apron strings [ˈeiprənˈstriŋz] *npl*: **tied to the — of** cosido a las faldas de.

apropos [‚æprəˈpəu] **1** *adv* a propósito. **2** *prep*: **— of** a propósito de. **3** *adj* oportuno.

apse [æps] *n* ábside *m*.

apt [æpt] *adj* **(a)** (*suitable*) apropiado, conveniente; *remark* acertado, oportuno; *description* exacto, atinado.

(b) (*tending*) **to be — to** + *infin* tener tendencia a + *infin*, ser propenso a + *infin*; **to be rather — to** + *infin* tener cierta tendencia a + *infin*; **I am — to be out on Mondays** por regla general no estoy los lunes; **we are — to forget that** . . . es fácil que olvidemos que . . .; **it is — to cause trouble** suele motivar disgustos.

(c) (*sharp*) listo (*at* en); **to be an — pupil** ser un alumno aprovechado.

aptitude [ˈæptitjuːd] *n* aptitud *f* (*for*, *in* para), capacidad *f*, habilidad *f*; **— test** prueba *f* de aptitud.

aptly [ˈæptli] *adv* oportunamente, acertadamente.

aptness [ˈæptnis] *n* lo apropiado, lo acertado.

Apuleius [‚æpjəˈliəs] *m* Apuleyo.

aqualung [ˈækwəlʌŋ] *n* aparato *m* de aire comprimido (que suministra aire al buzo).

aquamarine [‚ækwəməˈriːn] **1** *adj* (de color) verde mar. **2** *n* aguamarina *f*.

aquatint [ˈækwətint] *n* acuatinta *f*.

aquarium [əˈkwɛəriəm] *n* acuario *m*.

aquatic [əˈkwætik] **1** *adj* acuático. **2** *n* (*Bot*) planta *f* acuática; **—s** deportes *mpl* acuáticos.

aqueduct [ˈækwidʌkt] *n* acueducto *m*.

aqueous [ˈeikwiəs] *adj* ácueo, acuoso.

aquiline [ˈækwilain] *adj* aguileño.

Aquinas [əˈkwainəs] *m* Aquino.

Arab [ˈærəb] **1** *adj* árabe. **2** *n* árabe *mf*; **street —** golfillo *m*.

arabesque [‚ærəˈbesk] *n* arabesco *m*.

Arabia [əˈreibiə] Arabia *f*.

Arabian [ə'reibiən] **1** adj árabe, arábigo; — **Desert** Desierto m Arábigo; — **Sea** Mar m de Omán; **the — Nights** Las Mil y Una Noches. **2** n árabe mf.
Arabic ['ærəbik] **1** adj árabe, arábigo; — **numeral** número m arábigo. **2** n árabe m.
arable ['ærəbl] **1** adj cultivable; — **land** = **2** n tierra f de labrantío, labranza f.
arachnid [ə'ræknid] n arácnido m.
Aragon ['ærəgən] Aragón m.
Aragonese [ˌærəgə'ni:z] **1** adj aragonés. **2** n aragonés m, esa f. **3** n (dialect) aragonés m.
arbiter ['ɑ:bitə*] n árbitro m.
arbitrarily ['ɑ:bitrərili] adv arbitrariamente.
arbitrary ['ɑ:bitrəri] adj arbitrario.
arbitrate ['ɑ:bitreit] vi arbitrar (in en, between entre).
arbitration [ˌɑ:bi'treiʃən] n arbitraje m; **industrial** — arbitraje m industrial; **the question was referred to** — se confió el asunto a un juez árbitro.
arbitrator ['ɑ:bitreitə*] n juez árbitro m.
arboreal [ɑ:'bɔ:riəl] adj arbóreo.
arbour ['ɑ:bə*] n cenador m, pérgola f.
arc [ɑ:k] n arco m.
arcade [ɑ:'keid] n (Archit) arcada f; (round public square) soportales mpl; (with shops) galería f, pasaje m, pasadizo m.
Arcadian [ɑ:'keidiən] **1** adj árcade; (fig) arcádico. **2** n árcade mf.
Arcady ['ɑ:kədi] Arcadia f.
arch[1] [ɑ:tʃ] **1** n (a) (Archit) arco m; (vault) bóveda f; — **of heaven** bóveda f celeste; **horseshoe** — arco m de herradura; **pointed** — arco m ojival; **round** — arco m redondo; **triumphal** — arco m triunfal.
　(b) (Anat) empeine m; (dental) arcada f, arco m; **fallen** —es pies mpl planos.
　2 vt (a) back, body etc arquear; eyebrows enarcar.
　(b) (Archit) **to** — **over** abovedar.
　3 vi arquearse, formar un arco.
arch[2] [ɑ:tʃ] adj (cunning) astuto; (roguish) zumbón, picaruelo; look, remark etc malicioso, lleno de malicia; woman coqueta.
arch[3] [ɑ:tʃ] (gen in compounds, see below) principal; consumado; **the** — **criminal** el mayor de los criminales; in compounds: archi . . .
archaeological [ˌɑ:kiə'lɔdʒikəl] adj arqueológico.
archaeologist [ˌɑ:ki'ɔlədʒist] n arqueólogo m.
archaeology [ˌɑ:ki'ɔlədʒi] n arqueología f.
archaic [ɑ:'keiik] adj arcaico.
archaism ['ɑ:keiizəm] n arcaísmo m.
archangel ['ɑ:kˌeindʒəl] n arcángel m.
archbishop ['ɑ:tʃ'biʃəp] n arzobispo m.
archbishopric [ɑ:tʃ'biʃəprik] n arzobispado m.
archdeacon ['ɑ:tʃ'di:kən] n arcediano m.
archdiocese ['ɑ:tʃ'daiəsis] n archidiócesis f.
archduchess ['ɑ:tʃ'dʌtʃis] n archiduquesa f.
archduchy ['ɑ:tʃ'dʌtʃi] n archiducado m.
archduke ['ɑ:tʃ'dju:k] n archiduque m.
arched [ɑ:tʃt] adj en forma de arco(s); abovedado.
arch-enemy ['ɑ:tʃ'enimi] n archienemigo m; (devil) el enemigo malo, Satanás.
archer ['ɑ:tʃə*] n arquero m.
archery ['ɑ:tʃəri] n tiro m con arco.
archetype ['ɑ:kitaip] n arquetipo m.
Archimedes [ˌɑ:ki'mi:di:z] m Arquímedes.
archipelago [ˌɑ:ki'peligəu] n archipiélago m.
architect ['ɑ:kitekt] n (a) arquitecto m; **naval** — constructor m naval. (b) (fig) artífice m; **the** — **of victory** el artífice de la victoria.
architectural [ˌɑ:ki'tektʃərəl] adj arquitectónico.
architecture ['ɑ:kitektʃə*] n arquitectura f.
archive ['ɑ:kaiv] n archivo m.
archivist ['ɑ:kivist] n archivero m.
archness ['ɑ:tʃnis] n astucia f; socarronería f; malicia f, coquetería f.
archway ['ɑ:tʃwei] n arco m, arcada f.
arc lamp [ɑ:'klæmp] n lámpara f de arco; (in welding) arco m voltaico.
arctic ['ɑ:ktik] **1** adj ártico; (fig) glacial. **2** n: **the A—** el Ártico.
Arctic Circle ['ɑ:ktik'sə:kl] n Círculo m Polar Ártico.
Arctic Ocean ['ɑ:ktik'əuʃən] Océano m Glacial Ártico.
Ardennes [ɑ:'denz] pl Ardenas fpl.
ardent ['ɑ:dənt] adj ardiente, vehemente, apasionado; supporter fervoroso, entusiasmado; desire vivo; lover apasionado.
ardently ['ɑ:dəntli] adv ardientemente, con vehemencia, apasionadamente; fervorosamente, con entusiasmo.
ardour ['ɑ:də*] n ardor m; fervor m, entusiasmo m; vehemencia f; pasión f; **to dampen someone's** — enfriar la pasión de uno.

arduous ['ɑ:djuəs] adj arduo, fuerte, riguroso; climb, journey penoso; task difícil.
arduousness ['ɑ:djuəsnis] n lo riguroso; lo penoso; dificultad f.
are [ɑ:*] see **be**.
area ['ɛəriə] n (a) (Math, surface extent) área f, superficie f; extensión f.
　(b) (Geog, space) región f, zona f; (Sport, eg goal —) área f; **the London** — la región londinense; **postal** — distrito m postal; **depressed** — zona f deprimida, región f de elevado paro obrero; **prohibited** — zona f prohibida.
　(c) (Archit) corral m, patio m.
arena [ə'ri:nə] n arena f, redondel m; (Taur) plaza f, ruedo m; (Circus) pista f.
aren't [ɑ:nt] = **are not**.
Argentina [ˌɑ:dʒən'ti:nə] la Argentina.
Argentine ['ɑ:dʒəntain] **1** adj argentino. **2** n: **the** — la Argentina.
Argentinian [ˌɑ:dʒən'tiniən] **1** adj argentino. **2** n argentino m, a f.
argon ['ɑ:gɔn] n argo m, argón m.
Argonaut ['ɑ:gənɔ:t] n Argonauta m.
arguable ['ɑ:gjuəbl] adj discutible; **it is** — **whether** . . . es dudoso si . . .
argue ['ɑ:gju:] **1** vt (a) case sostener; matter razonar acerca de; point discutir; **a well—d case** un argumento razonado; **how will you** — **the case?** ¿cómo va Vd a presentar el pleito?; **to** — **one's way out of a jam** salir de un apuro a fuerza de argumentos.
　(b) (point to) argüir, indicar; **it —s his untrustworthiness** le arguye de poco confiable; **it —s him to be untrustworthy** ello hace creer que es poco confiable; **to** — **that** sostener que; **I have heard it —d that** he oído sostener que.
　(c) **to** — **someone into** + ger persuadir a uno a + infin; **to** — **someone out of** + ger disuadir a uno de + infin; **to** — **someone out of something** persuadir a uno a abandonar algo.
　2 vi (a) (two persons) discutir, disputar (about acerca de, with con); **we —d all night** pasamos toda la noche discutiendo; **don't** —! ¡no discutas!, ¡no repliques!
　(b) (reason) razonar, argüir, discurrir; **I** — **this way** yo pienso de este modo, yo razono así; **he —s well** razona bien, presenta de modo convincente sus argumentos; **this —s in his favour** esto habla en su favor; **to** — **against** person hablar en contra de, thing alegar razones contra, combatir por argumentos; **to** — **for** abogar por.
argument ['ɑ:gjumənt] n (a) (reason) argumento m. (against en contra de, for en pro de); **his** — **is that** él sostiene que; **I don't follow your** — no comprendo su razonamiento; **to be open to** — estar dispuesto a dejarse convencer.
　(b) (debate) discusión f, disputa f, debate m; **there was a heated** — hubo una discusión acalorada; **for the sake of** — pongamos por caso, como hipótesis; **to have the better of the** — salir airoso de un debate; **let's not have any —s** no discutamos; **you've heard only one side of the** — le han contado solamente una parte de la discusión.
　(c) (Law) alegato m.
argumentation [ˌɑ:gjumən'teiʃən] n argumentación f, argumentos mpl.
argumentative [ˌɑ:gju'mentətiv] adj discutidor, argumentador.
Argus ['ɑ:gəs] m Argos.
aria ['ɑ:riə] n aria f.
Arian ['ɛəriən] **1** adj arriano. **2** n arriano m, a f.
Arianism ['ɛəriənizəm] n arrianismo m.
arid ['ærid] adj árido (also fig).
aridity [ə'riditi] n aridez f.
aright [ə'rait] adv correctamente, acertadamente; **if I heard you** — si le oí bien; **if I understand you** — si le entiendo correctamente; **to set** — rectificar.
arise [ə'raiz] (irr: pret **arose**, ptp **arisen**) vi (a) (lit) levantarse, alzarse; —! (slogan) ¡arriba!
　(b) (fig) surgir; presentarse, producirse; **difficulties have —n** han surgido dificultades; **should the occasion** — si se presenta la ocasión; **should the occasion** — si nos vemos en el caso; **a storm arose** hubo un temporal; **a great clamour arose** se produjo un tremendo clamor; **the question does not** — no hay tal, no existe ese problema; **the question —s whether** . . . se plantea el problema de si . . .
　(c) **to** — **from** provenir de, resultar de; **arising from this, can you say . . .?** partiendo de esta base, ¿puede Vd decir . . .?
arisen [ə'rizn] ptp of **arise**.
aristocracy [ˌæris'tɔkrəsi] n aristocracia f.
aristocrat ['æristəkræt] n aristócrata mf.

aristocratic [ˌærɪstəˈkrætik] *adj* aristocrático.
Aristophanes [ˌærɪsˈtɔfəniːz] *m* Aristófanes.
Aristotelian [ˌærɪstəˈtiːliən] *adj* aristotélico.
Aristotle [ˈærɪstɔtl] *m* Aristóteles.
arithmetic [əˈriθmətik] *n* aritmética *f*; **mental —** cálculo *m* mental.
arithmetical [ˌæriθˈmetikəl] *adj* aritmético.
arithmetician [əˌriθməˈtiʃən] *n* aritmético *m*.
ark [ɑːk] *n* arca *f*; **A— of the Covenant** Arca *f* de la Alianza; **Noah's A—** Arca *f* de Noé.
Arles [ɑːl] Arlés.
arm[1] [ɑːm] *n* (*Anat and fig*) brazo *m*; **— in —** cogidos del brazo, de bracete; **baby in —s** niño *m* de pecho; **with open —s** con los brazos abiertos; **within —'s reach** al alcance del brazo; **to chance one's —** arriesgarse, aventurarse; **to give someone one's —** ofrecer el brazo a uno; **to keep someone at —'s length** mantener a uno a distancia; **to put one's — round someone** rodear a uno del brazo; **to take someone in one's —s** abrazar a uno.
arm[2] [ɑːm] (*Mil*) **1** *n* arma *f*; **—s** (*Her*) escudo *m*, blasón *m*; **—s race** carrera *f* de armamentos; **under —s** sobre las armas; **to be up in —s** poner el grito en el cielo; **to lay down one's —s** rendir las armas; **to rise up in —s** alzarse en armas; **to take up —s** tomar las armas; **present —s!** ¡presenten armas!; **shoulder —s!, slope —s!** ¡armas al hombro!
  2 *vt* armar.
  3 *vr*: **to — oneself** armarse; **to — oneself with arguments** pertrecharse de argumentos.
Armada [ɑːˈmɑːdə] *n*: **the —** la (Armada) Invencible.
armadillo [ˌɑːməˈdiləu] *n* armadillo *m*.
Armageddon [ˌɑːməˈgedn] Armagedón *m*, lucha *f* suprema.
armament [ˈɑːməmənt] *n* armamento *m*.
armature [ˈɑːmətjuə*] *n* (*Elec, Zool, Bot*) armadura *f*; (*of dynamo*) inducido *m*.
armband [ˈɑːmbænd] *n* brazal *m*, brazalete *m*.
armchair [ˈɑːmtʃɛə*] **1** *n* sillón *m*, butaca *f*. **2** *attr*: **— politician** político *m* de café.
armed [ɑːmd] **1** *pret and ptp of* **arm**[2]. **2** *adj* armado, provisto de armas; **— to the teeth** armado hasta los dientes; **— robbery** robo *m* a mano armada.
-armed [ɑːmd] *adj* de brazos . . . , *eg* **strong-armed** de brazos fuertes; **one-armed** manco.
Armenia [ɑːˈmiːniə] Armenia *f*.
Armenian [ɑːˈmiːniən] **1** *adj* armenio. **2** *n* armenio *m*, a *f*.
armful [ˈɑːmful] *n* brazado *m*, brazada *f*.
armhole [ˈɑːmhəul] *n* sobaquera *f*.
armistice [ˈɑːmistis] *n* armisticio *m*.
armlet [ˈɑːmlit] *n* brazal *m*.
armorial [ɑːˈmɔːriəl] *adj* heráldico; **— bearings** escudo *m* de armas.
armour, (US) armor [ˈɑːmə*] **1** *n* (*Mil, Zool, fig*) armadura *f*; (*steel plates*) blindaje *m*; (*tanks*) tanques *mpl*, fuerzas *fpl* blindadas. **2** *vt* blindar, acorazar.
armour-clad, (US) armor— [ˈɑːməklæd] *adj*, **armoured, (US) armored** [ˈɑːməd] *adj* blindado, acorazado.
armourer, (US) armorer [ˈɑːmərə*] *n* armero *m*.
armour-plated, (US) armor— [ˈɑːməˈpleitid] *adj* blindado, acorazado.
armoury, (US) armory [ˈɑːməri] *n* armería *f*; arsenal *m*.
armpit [ˈɑːmpit] *n* sobaco *m*, axila *f*.
armrest [ˈɑːmrest] *n* apoyo *m* para el brazo, apoyabrazos *m*.
army [ˈɑːmi] *n* ejército *m*; (*fig*) ejército *m*, multitud *f*; **standing —** ejército *m* permanente; **— corps** cuerpo *m* de ejército; **— life** vida *f* militar; **— list** lista *f* de oficiales del ejército; **— doctor** médico *m* militar; **to join the —** hacerse soldado, engancharse, alistarse.
aroma [əˈrəumə] *n* aroma *m* (*of* a), fragancia *f*.
aromatic [ˌærəuˈmætik] *adj* aromático, fragante.
arose [əˈrəuz] *pret of* **arise.**
around [əˈraund] **1** *adv* alrededor; a la redonda, *eg* **for 5 miles —** en 5 millas a la redonda; **all —** por todas partes, por todos lados; **is he —?** ¿está por aquí? **he must be somewhere —** debe de andar por aquí.
  2 *prep* alrededor de, en torno de; **— 50** unos 50, 50 más o menos; **all — me** por todas partes alrededor de mí; **it's just — the corner** está precisamente a la vuelta de la esquina; **to go — the world** dar la vuelta al mundo; *see also* **about, round.**
arouse [əˈrauz] *vt* despertar; (*fig*) mover, incitar, estimular; **it —d great interest** despertó mucho interés; **it should — you to greater efforts** esto deberá incitarle a esforzarse más todavía.
arrack [ˈærək] *n* aguardiente *m* de palma.
arraign [əˈrein] *vt* procesar, acusar (*before* ante).

arrange [əˈreindʒ] **1** *vt* (a) (*put into order*) arreglar, ordenar, organizar; **to — one's affairs** poner en orden sus asuntos; **how did we — matters last time?** ¿cómo lo organizamos la última vez?
  (b) (*draw up*) disponer; **how is the room —d?** ¿qué disposición tienen los muebles?
  ·(c) (*Mus*) adaptar, refundir.
  (d) (*fix upon*) fijar, señalar; **to — a time for** fijar una hora para.
  (e) (*agree*) **it was —d that** se decidió que; **what did you — with him?** ¿qué decidieron Vds?; **a marriage has been —d between . . .** se ha concertado la boda de . . .
  2 *vi*: **to — for** prevenir, disponer; **I have —d for you to go** he hecho los arreglos para que vaya Vd; **can you — for my luggage to be sent up?** por favor, que me suban el equipaje; **I —d to meet him at the café** me cité con él en el café; **I have —d to see him tonight** nos hemos dado una cita para esta noche; **to — with someone to +** *infin* ponerse de acuerdo con uno para que **+** *subj*; **to — with someone that** convenir con uno en que **+** *subj*.
arrangement [əˈreindʒmənt] *n* (a) (*order*) arreglo *m*, orden *m*, disposición *f*.
  (b) (*act of ordering*) arreglo *m*, ordenación *f*.
  (c) (*Mus*) adaptación *f*.
  (d) (*agreement*) acuerdo *m*, convenio *m*; **to come to an —** llegar a un acomodo; **we have an — with them** existe un acuerdo con ellos; **larger orders by —** los pedidos de mayor cantidad, por acuerdo mutuo; **by — with Covent Garden** con permiso de Covent Garden; **salary by —** sueldo a convenir.
  (e) (*plan, line of action*) plan *m*, medida *f*; **—s** (*preparations*) preparativos *mpl*; (*order of events*) programa *m*; **what are the —s for your holiday?** ¿qué plan tiene Vd para sus vacaciones?; **we must make —s to help them** tenemos que tomar medidas para ayudarles; **to make one's own —s** obrar por cuenta propia; **all the —s are made** todo está arreglado; **if this — doesn't suit you** si esto no le conviene; **all the —s were made by X** todos los preparativos los hizo X.
arrant [ˈærənt] *adj* **knave** *etc* consumado, de siete suelas; **— nonsense** puro disparate *m*.
array [əˈrei] **1** *n* (a) (*Mil*) orden *m* de batalla; **in battle —** en orden de batalla; **in close —** en filas apretadas.
  (b) (*fig*) serie *f* impresionante, colección *f* imponente; **a fine — of flowers** un bello conjunto de flores; **a great — of hats** una magnífica colección de sombreros.
  (c) (*dress*) adorno *m*, atavío *m*.
  2 *vt* ataviar, engalanar (*in* de).
arrears [əˈriəz] *npl* atrasos *mpl* (**— of rent** atrasos *mpl* de alquiler; **in —** atrasado en pagos; **to get into —** atrasarse en los pagos.
arrest [əˈrest] **1** *n* detención *f*; (*of goods*) secuestro *m*; **to be under —** estar detenido; **you're under —** queda Vd detenido.
  2 *vt* **criminal** detener, arrestar, prender; **progress, decay** *etc* detener, parar; **attention** llamar; **judgement** prorrogar.
arresting [əˈrestiŋ] *adj* llamativo, impresionante.
arrival [əˈraivəl] *n* llegada *f*; (*fig*) advenimiento *m*; **new —** recién llegado *m*, a *f*, persona *f* que acaba de llegar; (*fam*) recién nacido *m*, a *f*; **— platform** andén *m* de vacío; **on —** al llegar.
arrive [əˈraiv] *vi* llegar (*at, in* a); (*fam*) llegar a ser un auténtico personaje, triunfar, hacerse famoso.
arriviste [ˌæriˈviːst] *n* arribista *mf*.
arrogance [ˈærəgəns] *n* arrogancia *f*.
arrogant [ˈærəgənt] *adj* arrogante.
arrogate [ˈærəugeit] *vt*: **to — something to oneself** arrogarse algo; **quality** atribuirse, apropiarse.
arrow [ˈærəu] *n* flecha *f*.
arrowhead [ˈærəuhed] *n* punta *f* de flecha.
arrowroot [ˈærəuruːt] *n* arruruz *m*.
arse [ɑːs] *n* (*tabu*) culo *m*.
arsenal [ˈɑːsinl] *n* arsenal *m*.
arsenic [ˈɑːsnik] *n* arsénico *m*.
arson [ˈɑːsn] *n* delito *m* de incendiar.
art[1] [ɑːt] *n* (a) arte gen *m* in *sing*, *f* in *pl*; (*skill*) habilidad *f*, destreza *f*; (*technique*) técnica *f*; **—s and crafts** artes *fpl* y oficios; **— exhibition** exposición *f* de arte; **— gallery** museo *m* de bellas artes; **— school** escuela *f* de arte; **work of —** obra *f* de arte; **black —s** magia *f* negra; **commercial —** arte *m* comercial; **fine —s** bellas artes *fpl*; **graphic —s** artes *fpl* gráficas; **liberal —s** artes *fpl* liberales; **the noble —** el boxeo.
  (b) **—s** (*Univ*) Artes *fpl* (*arch*), Filosofía y Letras *f*; **Faculty of A—s** Facultad *f* de Filosofía y Letras;

Bachelor of A—s (*abbr* B.A.) Licenciado *m*, a *f*, en Filosofía y Letras; **Master of A—s** (*abbr* M.A.) Maestro *m*, a *f* en Artes.

art² [ɑːt] *see* be.

artefact ['ɑːtifækt] *n* artefacto *m*.

arterial [ɑːˈtiəriəl] *adj* arterial; *road* principal.

arteriosclerosis [ɑːˈtiəriəuskliəˈrəusis] *n* arteriosclerosis *f*.

artery ['ɑːtəri] *n* arteria *f*; (*fig*) arteria *f*, vía *f* principal; (*road*) camino *m* troncal.

artesian well [ɑːˈtiːzionˈwel] *n* pozo *m* artesiano.

artful ['ɑːtful] *adj* mañoso, artero, astuto; (*skilful*) ingenioso.

artfully ['ɑːtfəli] *adv* astutamente, con mucha maña, ingeniosamente.

artfulness ['ɑːtfulnis] *n* maña *f*, astucia *f*; ingenio *m*.

arthritic [ɑːˈθritik] *adj* artrítico.

arthritis [ɑːˈθraitis] *n* artritis *f*.

arthropoda [ɑːˈθrɔpədə] *npl* artrópodos *mpl*.

Arthur ['ɑːθə*] *m* Arturo; **King —** el rey Artús, el Rey Arturo.

Arthurian [ɑːˈθjuəriən] *adj* arturiano, artúrico.

artichoke ['ɑːtitʃəuk] *n* alcachofa *f*; **Jerusalem —** aguaturma *f*.

article ['ɑːtikl] **1** *n* artículo *m*; objeto *m*, cosa *f*; **—s of apprenticeship** contrato *m* de aprendizaje; **—s of association** estatutos *mpl* de asociación (de una sociedad anónima); **— of clothing** prenda *f* de vestir; **— of faith** artículo *m* de fe; **—s of value** objetos *mpl* de valor; **definite —** artículo *m* definido; **indefinite —** artículo *m* indefinido; **leading —** artículo *m* de fondo; **toilet —s** artículos *mpl* de tocador.

2 *vt text* articular; *items* poner en lista, poner en forma detallada; *apprentice* pactar, comprometer por contrato; **to be —d to** estar de aprendiz con, servir bajo contrato a.

articulate [ɑːˈtikjulit] *adj* (*jointed*) articulado; *speech* claro, distinto; **at 2 a child is hardly —** a los 2 años el niño es apenas capaz de hablar claramente; **he's not very —** no se expresa bien, no habla con confianza.

articulate [ɑːˈtikjuleit] *vt* articular.

articulation [ɑːˌtikjuˈleiʃən] *n* articulación *f*.

artifice ['ɑːtifis] *n* artificio *m*; ardid *m*, estratagema *f*.

artificial [ˌɑːtiˈfiʃəl] *adj* artificial; *hair, teeth etc* postizo; *person* afectado; *manure* químico.

artificiality [ˌɑːtifiʃiˈæliti] *n* lo artificial; afectación *f*.

artificially [ˌɑːtiˈfiʃəli] *adv* artificialmente; afectadamente, con afectación.

artillery [ɑːˈtiləri] *n* artillería *f*; **heavy —** artillería *f* pesada.

artilleryman [ɑːˈtilərimən], *pl* **—men** [mən] *n* artillero *m*.

artisan ['ɑːtizæn] *n* artesano *m*.

artist ['ɑːtist] *n* artista *mf*.

artist(e) [ɑːˈtiːst] *n* (*Theat*) artista *mf* de teatro; (*Mus*) intérprete *mf*; **variety —** artista *mf* de variedades.

artistic [ɑːˈtistik] *adj* artístico.

artistically [ɑːˈtistikəli] *adv* artísticamente; **to be — gifted** tener talento artístico.

artistry ['ɑːtistri] *n* arte *m*, habilidad *f* artística.

artless ['ɑːtlis] *adj* natural, sencillo; ingenuo; (*clumsy*) desmañado.

arty ['ɑːti] *adj* (*fam*) ostentosamente artístico; *person* de gusto muy afectado, que se las echa de muy artista, repipi.

arty-crafty ['ɑːtiˈkrɑːfti] *adj* (*fam*), **artsy-craftsy** ['ɑːtsiˈkrɑːftsi] *adj* (*US fam*) ostentosamente artístico, afectadamente artístico.

Aryan ['ɛəriən] **1** *adj* ario. **2** *n* ario *m*, a *f*.

as [æz, əz] *adv, conj and prep* **(a)** (*comparisons*) como: **he does — I** do hace como yo; **— . . . —** tan . . . como; **— tall —** tan alto como; **— quickly —** tan rápidamente como; **is it — big —** all that? ¿tan grande es en efecto?; **the same —** (or la, lo) mismo que; **such countries — France** los países tales como Francia; **large books (such) —** dictionaries los libros grandes tales como los diccionarios; **he is not so silly — to** do that no es bastante tonto para hacer eso, no es tan tonto como para hacer eso.

(b) (*comparisons: intensifying similes*) (**—**) **pale — death** pálido como la muerte; **— dead — a doornail** más muerto que mi abuela.

(c) (*comparisons:* as if *etc*) **—, if, — though** como si + *subj*: **— if (he were) drunk** como si estuviera borracho; **— if to +** *infin* como para + *infin*.

(d) (*concessive*) **interesting — the book is** por interesante que sea el libro; **stupid — he is** aunque es estúpido; **be that — it may** sea como fuere eso.

(e) (*in the quality or capacity of*) como: **— a husband and father** como marido y padre; **Vivien Leigh — Cleopatra** Vivien Leigh en el papel de Cleopatra; **I don't think much of him — an actor** no le estimo como (*or* en cuanto, en tanto que) actor; **he was often ill — a child** estuvo a menudo enfermo de niño; **we're going — tourists** vamos en plan de turismo; (*after certain verbs*) de: **to act —** actuar de, estar de; **to be dressed —** estar vestido de.

(f) (*concerning*) **— for that, — to that, — regards that** en cuanto a eso, por lo que se refiere a eso.

(g) (*manner*) **— often happens** como (*or* según) ocurre a menudo; **do — you wish** haga lo que quiera, haga como quiera; **to leave things — they are** dejar las cosas tal como están; **just — you are an engineer, (so) I am a doctor** lo mismo que Vd es ingeniero, yo soy médico; **her door is the first —** you go up the stairs su puerta es la primera según se sube la escalera; **you've got plenty — it is** Vd tiene bastante ya; **— it is we can do nothing** así las cosas, no podemos hacer nada.

(h) (*time*) **he came in — I was leaving** entró como yo salía; **— I was sitting there he came up** mientras yo estaba sentado allí se acercó; **— he learned more a medida** que iba aprendiendo más; **— I was passing the house al pasar** yo delante de la casa; **— from tomorrow** a partir de mañana.

(i) (*result*) **he did it in such a way — to please everyone** lo hizo de tal modo que logró contentar a todos.

(j) (*because*) **— I don't talk Arabic** como yo no hablo árabe; **I can't come — I have an appointment** no puedo venir, pues (*or* ya que, porque) tengo un compromiso.

asbestos [æzˈbestəs] *n* asbesto *m*, amianto *m*.

ascend [əˈsend] **1** *vt stairs, river* subir; *mountain, throne* subir a. **2** *vi* subir; (*soar*) elevarse, encaramarse.

ascendancy [əˈsendənsi] *n* ascendiente *m*, dominio *m* (*over* sobre).

ascendant [əˈsendənt] *n*: **to be in the —** predominar, tener una influencia cada vez mayor.

ascension [əˈsenʃən] *n* ascensión *f*; **A— Day** Día *m* de la Ascensión.

ascent [əˈsent] *n* (*act*) subida *f*, ascensión *f*; (*promotion*) ascenso *m*; (*slope*) cuesta *f*, pendiente *f*.

ascertain [ˌæsəˈtein] *vt* averiguar, determinar, descubrir.

ascertainable [ˌæsəˈteinəbl] *adj* averiguable.

ascertainment [ˌæsəˈteinmənt] *n* averiguación *f*.

ascetic [əˈsetik] **1** *adj* ascético. **2** *n* asceta *mf*.

asceticism [əˈsetisizəm] *n* ascetismo *m*.

ascribable [əsˈkraibəbl] *adj* atribuible.

ascribe [əsˈkraib] *vt* atribuir (*to* a).

ascription [əsˈkripʃən] *n* atribución *f*.

aseptic [eiˈseptik] *adj* aséptico.

asexual [eiˈseksjuəl] *adj* asexual.

ash¹ [æʃ] *n* (*Bot*) fresno *m*.

ash² [æʃ] *n* ceniza *f*; **—es** cenizas *fpl* (*also of dead*); **A— Wednesday** Miércoles *m* de Ceniza.

ashamed [əˈʃeimd] *adj*: **to be** (*or* feel) **—** avergonzarse, estar avergonzado (*at, of* de; *for* por; *of being* de ser); **I am — of you** me das vergüenza; **I was — to ask for money** me daba vergüenza pedir dinero; **your generosity makes me feel —** su generosidad me produce vergüenza; **to be — of oneself** tener vergüenza de sí; **you ought to be — of yourself!** ¿no te da vergüenza esto?

ash-bin ['æʃbin] *n* cubo *m* de la basura.

ashcan ['æʃkæn] *n* (*US*) cubo *m* de la basura.

ash-coloured ['æʃkʌləd] *adj*, **ashen** ['æʃn] *adj* ceniciento; *face* pálido.

ashlar ['æʃlə*] *n* sillar *m*.

ashore [əˈʃɔː*] *adv*: **to be —** estar en tierra; **to come —, to go —** desembarcar; **to put someone —** desembarcar a uno.

ash pan ['æʃpæn] *n* guardacenizas *m*.

ashtray ['æʃtrei] *n* cenicero *m*.

ashy ['æʃi] *adj* cenizoso.

Asia ['eiʃə] Asia *f*; **— Minor** Asia *f* Menor.

Asiatic [ˌeisiˈætik] **1** *adj* asiático. **2** *n* asiático *m*, a *f*.

aside [əˈsaid] **1** *adv* aparte, a un lado. **2** *prep*: **— from** aparte de. **3** *n* (*Theat*) aparte *m*; **to say in an —** decir aparte.

asinine ['æsinain] *adj* asnal; (*fig*) estúpido.

ask [ɑːsk] **1** *vt* **(a)** (*inquire, inquire of*) preguntar; **to — someone something** preguntar algo a uno; **to — someone a question** hacer una pregunta a uno; **they —ed me about my passport** me hicieron preguntas acerca de mi pasaporte; **they —ed me about the new missile** me interrogaron sobre el nuevo proyectil; **don't — me!** ¡yo qué sé!

(b) (*request, demand*) pedir; **to — someone a favour** pedir un favor a uno; **how much are they —ing for it?** ¿cuánto piden por él?; **I don't — much from you** no soy muy exigente con Vds; **that's —ing the impossible** eso es pedir lo imposible; **to write —ing for help** escribir en demanda de ayuda; **that's —ing a lot** eso pone mucho; **to — something from** (*or* **of**) **someone** pedir algo a uno; **to — someone for something** pedir algo a uno; **to — that** pedir que + *subj,* rogar que + *subj;* **to — someone to do something** pedir que uno haga algo.

(c) (*invite*) invitar; **have they —ed you?** ¿te han invitado a ti?; **to — someone back** invitar a uno a que pague la visita; **to — someone in** rogar a uno que pase; **to — someone out** invitar a uno a que salga, rogar a uno que le dé una cita; **to — someone to dinner** invitar a uno a cenar.

2 *vi* preguntar; (*request, demand*) pedir; **I was only —ing** era una simple pregunta; **for the —ing** sin más que pedirlo, con solo pedir; **this is the third time of —ing** ésta es la tercera vez que te lo pido; **to — about, to — after, to — for** (*inquire*) preguntar por; **to — for** (*request*) pedir, reclamar; **to — for something back** pedir que se devuelva algo; **he —ed for it** (*fam*) se la buscó, bien merecido lo tiene; **it's just —ing for trouble** eso es buscar tres pies al gato.

askance [ə'skɑːns] *adv:* **to look — at** mirar con recelo, mirar con desdén.

askew [ə'skjuː] *adv* sesgado, ladeado, oblicuamente; **the picture is —** el cuadro está torcido.

aslant [ə'slɑːnt] **1** *adv* a través, oblicuamente. **2** *prep* a través de.

asleep [ə'sliːp] *adj:* **to be —** estar dormido; **to be fast** (*or* **sound**) **—** estar profundamente dormido; **to drop —, to fall —** dormirse, quedar dormido.

asp [æsp] *n* áspid *m.*

asparagus [əs'pærəgəs] *n* (*plant*) espárrago *m;* (*as food*) espárragos *mpl.*

aspect ['æspekt] *n* aspecto *m;* apariencia *f;* **to study all —s of a question** estudiar una cuestión bajo todos los aspectos; **a house with a southern —** una casa orientada hacia el sur.

aspen ['æspən] *n* álamo *m* temblón.

asperity [æs'periti] *n* aspereza *f.*

aspersion [əs'pəːʃən] *n* calumnia *f;* **to cast —s on** difamar, calumniar.

asphalt ['æsfælt] **1** *n* asfalto *m;* (*place*) pista *f* asfaltada, recinto *m* asfaltado. **2** *vt* asfaltar.

asphyxia [æs'fiksiə] *n* asfixia *f.*

asphyxiate [æs'fiksieit] **1** *vt* asfixiar. **2** *vi* morir asfixiado.

asphyxiation [æs.fiksi'eiʃən] *n* asfixia *f.*

aspic ['æspik] *n* manjar a base de gelatina, que contiene huevos, carne etc.

aspidistra [.æspi'distrə] *n* aspidistra *f.*

aspirant ['æspirənt] *n* aspirante *mf,* candidato *m* (*after, for,* to a).

aspirate ['æspərit] **1** *adj* aspirado. **2** *n* aspirada *f.*

aspirate ['æspəreit] *vt* aspirar.

aspiration [.æspə'reiʃən] *n* (*Med, Gram*) aspiración *f;* (*fig*) anhelo *m,* deseo *m,* ambición *f.*

aspire [əs'paiə*] *vi:* **to — to** aspirar a, ambicionar; **we can't — to** that nuestras pretensiones son más modestas; **he —s to a new car** anhela tener un nuevo coche; **to — to** + *infin* aspirar a + *infin,* anhelar + *infin,* tener vivo deseo de + *infin,* ambicionar + *infin.*

aspirin ['æsprin] *n* aspirina *f.*

aspiring [əs'paiəriŋ] *adj* ambicioso, deseoso de tener éxito.

ass[1] [æs] *n* asno *m,* burro *m;* (*fig*) burro *m,* imbécil *m;* **the man's an —** es un imbécil; **what an — I am!** ¡soy un imbécil!; **to make an — of oneself** ponerse en ridículo.

ass[2] [æs] *n* (*US tabu*) culo *m.*

assail [ə'seil] *vt* acometer, atacar; *task* acometer, emprender; *doubts began to —* him empezaron a asaltarle algunas dudas; **he was —ed by critics on all sides** por todos lados le atacaron los críticos; **a sound —ed my ear** un ruido penetró en mis oídos.

assailant [ə'seilənt] *n* asaltador *m,* ora *f;* agresor *m,* ora *f;* **there were 4 —s** los que le atacaron eran 4; **he disarmed his —** le quitó las armas al agresor.

assassin [ə'sæsin] *n* asesino *m.*

assassinate [ə'sæsineit] *vt* asesinar.

assassination [ə.sæsi'neiʃən] *n* asesinato *m.*

assault [ə'sɔːlt] **1** *n* asalto *m* (*on* sobre), ataque *m* (*on* a, contra); (*Law*) violencia *f;* **— and battery** violencias *fpl* físicas; **indecent —, sexual —** atentado *m* contra el pudor.

2 *vt* asaltar, atacar; (*Law*) agredir; *woman* violar, tratar de violar.

assay [ə'sei] **1** *n* ensaye *m.* **2** *vt* *metals* ensayar; (*fig*) intentar, probar; **to — to** + *infin* intentar + *infin.*

assemblage [ə'semblidʒ] *n* reunión *f;* colección *f;* (*Mech*) montaje *m.*

assemble [ə'sembl] **1** *vt* reunir, juntar; (*Mech*) montar. **2** *vi* reunirse, juntarse.

assembly [ə'sembli] *n* reunión *f;* (*Pol etc*) asamblea *f;* (*people present*) concurrencia *f,* asistentes *mpl;* (*Mech*) montaje *m;* **unlawful —** reunión *f* ilegal.

assembly line [ə'semblilain] *n* línea *f* de montaje.

assembly room [ə'semblirum] *n* sala *f* de fiestas.

assembly shop [ə'sembliʃɔp] *n* taller *m* de montaje.

assent [ə'sent] **1** *n* asentimiento *m,* consentimiento *m,* aprobación *f;* **royal —** aprobación *f* real. **2** *vi* consentir (*to* en), asentir (*to* a).

assert [ə'səːt] **1** *vt* afirmar, declarar; *rights* hacer valer. **2** *vr:* **to — oneself** imponerse, hacer valer sus derechos.

assertion [ə'səːʃən] *n* afirmación *f,* declaración *f.*

assertive [ə'səːtiv] *adj* enérgico.

assess [ə'ses] *vt* valorar, apreciar, tasar, calcular (*at* en); enjuiciar, juzgar; *property* gravar (con impuestos); *tax, damages* fijar (*at* en); **how did you — this candidate?** ¿qué juicio formó Vd sobre este candidato?; **how do you — the situation now?** ¿cómo ve Vd la situación actual?

assessment [ə'sesmənt] *n* (*act*) valoración *f,* tasación *f;* (*tax*) gravamen *m,* imposición *f;* (*fig*) aprecio *m,* juicio *m.*

assessor [ə'sesə*] *n* asesor *m;* (*of taxes etc*) tasador *m.*

asset ['æset] *n* **(a)** posesión *f;* (*book-keeping item*) partida *f* del activo; (*useful quality*) ventaja *f.*

(b) **—s** (*Comm*) activo *m,* haber *m,* capital *m,* fondos *mpl;* (*fig*) valores *mpl* positivos, ventajas *fpl;* **—s in hand** bienes *mpl* disponibles; **liquid —s** activo *m* líquido; **personal —s** bienes *mpl* muebles.

asseverate [ə'sevəreit] *vt* aseverar.

asseveration [ə.sevə'reiʃən] *n* aseveración *f.*

assiduous [ə'sidjuəs] *adj* asiduo.

assiduously [ə'sidjuəsli] *adv* asiduamente.

assign [ə'sain] **1** *vt* asignar; *reason etc* señalar, indicar; *share, task* señalar; *property* traspasar, ceder; *literary work etc* atribuir; **they —ed him to the Paris embassy** le nombraron para la embajada de París; **which is the room —ed to me?** ¿qué habitación es la que me destinan a mí?; **the event is to be —ed to the year 1600** hemos de referir este suceso al año 1600.

2 *n* (*Law*) cesionario *m.*

assignation [.æsig'neiʃən] *n* asignación *f;* traspaso *m;* nombramiento *m;* (*meeting*) cita *f* (*esp* amorosa).

assignment [ə'sainmənt] *n* (*act*) asignación *f* etc; (*task*) cometido *m,* tarea *f;* misión *f.*

assimilate [ə'simileit] **1** *vt* asimilar. **2** *vi* asimilarse.

assimilation [ə.simi'leiʃən] *n* asimilación *f.*

assist [ə'sist] **1** *vt* ayudar; *development, progress etc* favorecer, estimular, fomentar; **we —ed him to his car** le ayudamos para que llegara a su coche.

2 *vi* (*help*) ayudar; **to — at** asistir a; **to — in** tomar parte en, participar en; **to — in** + *ger* ayudar a + *infin,* contribuir a + *infin.*

assistance [ə'sistəns] *n* **(a)** ayuda *f,* auxilio *m;* **to be of —** to ayudar a, prestar ayuda a; **can I be of —?** ¿puedo ayudarle?; **to come to someone's —** acudir en auxilio de uno, socorrer a uno.

(b) (*also national* **—**) subsidio *m* al necesitado.

assistant [ə'sistənt] **1** *adj* auxiliar; **— manager** subdirector *m;* **— secretary** subsecretario *m;* **— professor** (*US*) profesor *m* auxiliar.

2 *n* ayudante *mf;* **laboratory —** ayudante *mf* de laboratorio; **shop —** vendedor *m,* ora *f,* dependiente *m,* a *f.*

assizes [ə'saiziz] *npl* sesión *f* de un tribunal.

associate [ə'səuʃiit] **1** *adj* asociado; *member* correspondiente; *professor* adjunto.

2 *n* asociado *m,* colega *m;* compañero *m;* (*in crime*) cómplice *m;* (*member*) miembro *m* correspondiente; (*Comm*) socio *m,* consocio *m.*

associate [ə'səuʃieit] **1** *vt* asociar; relacionar; juntar, unir; **I don't wish to be —d with it** no quiero tener nada que ver con ello; **was he —d with that scandal?** ¿estuvo mezclado con ese escándalo?

2 *vi* asociarse (*with* a, con); juntarse, unirse; **to — in** mancomunarse en, participar juntamente en; **to — with** *person* ir con, tratar con, frecuentar la compañía de.

3 *vr:* **to — oneself with someone in a venture** participar con uno en una empresa; **I should like to — myself with that** quiero hacerme eco de esa opinión.

associated [ə'səuʃieitid] *adj* asociado; conexo; company afiliado.

association [ə,səusi'eiʃən] *n* (**a**) asociación *f*; (*Comm*) sociedad *f*; (*producers'* —) cooperativa *f*; (*connection*) conexión *f*, relación *f*; **by** — **of ideas** por asociación de ideas.

  (**b**) —**s** (*memories*) recuerdos *mpl*, sugestiones *fpl*; **the town has historic** —**s** la ciudad tiene importancia en la historia; **the word has nasty** —**s** la palabra hace pensar en cosas feas.

assonance ['æsənəns] *n* (*in general*) asonancia *f*; (*word*) asonante *f*; **words in** — palabras *fpl* asonantadas.

assort [ə'sɔːt] *vi* concordar (*with* con), convenir (*with* a); **it** —**s ill with his character** no cuadra con su carácter; **this does not** — **with what you said** esto no corresponde con lo que dijo Vd.

assorted [ə'sɔːtid] *adj* surtido, variado; (*hum*) **he dined with** — **ministers** cenó con este y con el otro ministro.

assortment [ə'sɔːtmənt] *n* (*Comm*) surtido *m*; variedad *f*, colección *f* variada; **there was a strange** — **of guests** los invitados pertenecían a tipos muy diversos; **quite an** —! ¡aquí hay de todo!

assuage [ə'sweidʒ] *vt feelings* calmar; *pain* aliviar; *passion* mitigar, suavizar; *desire* satisfacer; *appetite* saciar; *person* apaciguar, contentar; **he was not easily** —**d** no era fácil darle satisfacción, no era fácil desalterarle.

assume [ə'sjuːm] *vt* (**a**) *aspect, name, possession, importance, large proportions* tomar; *air* darse; *attitude* adoptar; *authority* (*unjustly*) apropiarse, arrogarse; *control, responsibility* asumir; *power* ocupar; *burden* asumir, tomar sobre sí.

  (**b**) (*suppose*) suponer, dar por sentado; **to** — **that** suponer que, imaginar que; **let us** — **that** pongamos por caso que; **you resigned, I** — imagino que Vd dimitió; **assuming (that)** dado que.

assumed [ə'sjuːmd] *adj* falso, fingido.

assumption [ə'sʌmpʃən] *n* (**a**) (*act*) asunción *f*; **el** tomar, adopción *f*; **A**— (*Rel*) Asunción *f*.

  (**b**) (*supposition*) suposición *f*, presunción *f*; **that is a dangerous** — es peligroso dar aquello por sentado; **on the** — **that** suponiendo que; **to start from a false** — partir de una base falsa.

  (**c**) (*arrogance*) presunción *f*.

assurance [ə'ʃuərəns] *n* (**a**) (*guarantee*) garantía *f*, promesa *f*; **you have my** — **that** les aseguro que; **I can give you no** — **about that** no les puedo hacer ninguna promesa sobre ello.

  (**b**) (*confidence*) confianza *f*; aplomo *m*, serenidad *f*.

  (**c**) (*certainty*) certeza *f*, seguridad *f*; **to make** — **doubly sure** para mayor seguridad.

  (**d**) (*insurance*) seguro *m*.

assure [ə'ʃuə*] *vt* (**a**) (*make certain*) asegurar, garantizar.

  (**b**) (*insure*) asegurar; **his life is** —**d for £5000** su vida está asegurada en 5000 libras.

  (**c**) *person* asegurar; **I** —**ed him of my support** le aseguré de mi apoyo; **you may rest** —**d that** Vd puede estar completamente seguro de que; **let me** — **you that** permita que le asegure que; **it is so, I** — **you** es así, se lo aseguro.

assured [ə'ʃuəd] **1** *adj* confiado, sereno; **you have an** — **future** Vd tiene un porvenir de éxito seguro. **2** *n* (*Comm*) asegurado *m*, a *f*.

assuredly [ə'ʃuəridli] *adv* seguramente, sin duda.

Assyria [ə'siriə] Asiria *f*.

Assyrian [ə'siriən] **1** *adj* asirio. **2** *n* asirio *m*, a *f*.

aster ['æstə*] *n* aster *f*.

asterisk ['æstərisk] **1** *n* asterisco *m*. **2** *vt* señalar con un asterisco, poner asterisco a.

astern [ə'stəːn] **1** *adv* a popa, por la popa; **to fall** — quedarse atrás; **to go** — ciar, ir hacia atrás; **to make a boat fast** — amarrar un barco por la popa. **2** *prep*: — **of** detrás de.

asteroid ['æstərɔid] *n* asteroide *m*.

asthma ['æsmə] *n* asma *f*.

asthmatic [æs'mætik] **1** *adj* asmático. **2** *n* asmático *m*, a *f*.

astigmatic [,æstig'mætik] *adj* astigmático.

astigmatism [æs'tigmətizəm] *n* astigmatismo *m*.

astir [ə'stəː*] *adv* activo, en movimiento; (*up and about*) levantado; **we were** — **early** nos levantamos temprano ; **at that hour nobody was** — a tal hora todos estaban todavía en cama.

astonish [ə'stɔniʃ] *vt* asombrar, pasmar; **you** — **me**! ¡esto es asombroso!; **to be** —**ed** asombrarse (*at* de), maravillarse (*at* de, con), quedarse asombrado (*at* de).

astonishing [ə'stɔniʃiŋ] *adj* asombroso, pasmoso; **I find it** — **that** se me hace muy cuesta arriba creer que, para mí es increíble que.

astonishingly [ə'stɔniʃiŋli] *adv*: **it was** — **easy** era increíblemente fácil; **it was an** — **lovely scene** la escena era de una belleza totalmente inesperada; — **enough** por milagro, por maravilla.

astonishment [ə'stɔniʃmənt] *n* asombro *m*, sorpresa *f*, estupefacción *f*; **there was general** — todos quedaron estupefactos; **to my** — con gran sorpresa mía.

astound [ə'staund] *vt*, **astounding** [ə'staundiŋ] *adj etc see* **astonish, astonishing** *etc.*

astrakhan [,æstrə'kæn] *n* astracán *m*.

astral ['æstrəl] *adj* astral.

astray [ə'strei] *adv*: **to go** — extraviarse; (*fig*: *make a mistake*) equivocarse, (*morally*) ir por mal camino; **to lead** — llevar por mal camino; **I was led** — **by his voice** su voz hizo que me equivocara.

astride [ə'straid] **1** *adv* a horcajadas. **2** *prep* a caballo sobre, a horcajadas sobre.

astringent [əs'trindʒənt] *adj* (*Med*) astringente; (*fig*) adusto, austero.

astrologer [əs'trɔlədʒə*] *n* astrólogo *m*.

astrological [,æstrə'lɔdʒikəl] *adj* astrológico.

astrology [əs'trɔlədʒi] *n* astrología *f*.

astronaut ['æstrənɔːt] *n* astronauta *mf*.

astronautics [,æstrəu'nɔːtiks] *n* astronáutica *f*.

astronomer [əs'trɔnəmə*] *n* astrónomo *m*.

astronomical [,æstrə'nɔmikəl] *adj* astronómico; (*fig*) tremendo, inmenso, increíble.

astronomy [əs'trɔnəmi] *n* astronomía *f*.

astrophysics ['æstrəu'fiziks] *n* astrofísica *f*.

astute [əs'tjuːt] *adj* astuto.

astutely [əs'tjuːtli] *adv* astutamente.

astuteness [əs'tjuːtnis] *n* astucia *f*.

asunder [ə'sʌndə*] *adv*: **to tear** — hacer pedazos, romper en dos; **to put** — separar.

asylum [ə'sailəm] *n* asilo *m*; (*lunatic* —, *mental* —) manicomio *m*; **to afford** — **to** (*place*) servir de asilo a, (*person*) dar asilo a; **to ask for political** — pedir asilo político.

asymmetric(al) [,eisi'metrik(əl)] *adj* asimétrico.

at [æt] *prep* (**a**) (*position*) en; — **the edge** en el borde; — **the top** en la cumbre; — **Toledo** en Toledo; — **school** en la escuela; — **sea** en el mar; — **peace** en paz; — **John's** en casa de Juan; — **the hairdresser's** en la peluquería; — **table** a la mesa; **to stand** — **the door** estar a la puerta; **to be** — **the window** mirar por la ventana; **he came in** — **the window** entró por la ventana.

  (**b**) (*time*) — **4 o'clock** a las cuatro; — **midday** a mediodía; — **night** de noche, por la noche; — **this season** en esta época del año; — **Christmas** por Navidades; — **a time like this** en un momento como el actual; **two** — **a time** de dos en dos.

  (**c**) (*price*) — **a shilling a pound** a chelín la libra; — **4% interest** al 4 por 100 de interés; — **a high price** a un precio elevado.

  (**d**) — **my request** a petición mía; **to awaken** — **the least sound** despertarse al menor ruido; — **his suggestion** siguiendo su sugerencia, de acuerdo con su sugerencia; — **one stroke** de un golpe; **he's good** — **games** tiene talento para los juegos; **I'm no good** — **that** yo soy inútil para eso.

  (**e**) (*with verb* to be) **to be** — **work** estar en el trabajo; **to be hard** — **it** estar trabajando con ahinco; **I've been** — **it for 3 hours** estoy ocupado en esto desde hace 3 horas; **what are you** — ? ¿qué haces ahí?; **while we are** — **it** mientras lo estemos haciendo; **you've been** — **me all day** ha estado persiguiéndome todo el día; **she's** — **it again** ella está siempre con la misma canción.

atavism ['ætəvizəm] *n* atavismo *m*.

atavistic [,ætə'vistik] *adj* atávico.

ate [eit] *pret of* **eat**.

atheism ['eiθiizəm] *n* ateísmo *m*.

atheist ['eiθiist] *n* ateo *m*, a *f*.

atheistic [,eiθi'istik] *adj* ateo, ateísta.

Athenian [ə'θiːniən] **1** *adj* ateniense. **2** *n* ateniense *mf*.

Athens ['æθinz] Atenas *f*.

athirst [ə'θəːst] *adj* (*fig*): **to be** — **for** tener sed de.

athlete ['æθliːt] *n* atleta *mf*.

athlete's foot ['æθliːts'fut] *n* (*Med*) pie *m* de atleta.

athletic [æθ'letik] *adj* atlético.

athletics [æθ'letiks] *n sing* atletismo *m*.

at-home [ət'həum] *n* recepción *f* (en casa particular).

athwart [ə'θwɔːt] **1** *adv* de través, al través. **2** *prep* a través de.

Atlantic (Ocean) [ət'læntik('əuʃən)] (Océano) Atlántico *m*.

Atlantis [ət'læntis] Atlántida *f*.

atlas ['ætləs] *n* atlas *m*; **A**— Atlante *m*.

atmosphere ['ætməsfiə*] n atmósfera f; (fig) ambiente m.
atmospheric [,ætməs'ferik] adj atmosférico.
atmospherics [,ætməs'feriks] npl (Radio) mala atmósfera f, parásitos mpl.
atoll ['ætɔl] n atolón m.
atom ['ætəm] n átomo m; **if you had an — of sense** si Vd tuviera la más mínima parte de inteligencia; **to smash to —s** hacer añicos.
atomic [ə'tɔmik] adj atómico.
atomic-powered [ə'tɔmik'pauəd] adj impulsado por energía atómica.
atomize ['ætəmaiz] vt reducir a átomos; **liquid** atomizar.
atomizer ['ætəmaizə*] n atomizador m.
atom smasher ['ætəm,smæʃə*] n rompeátomos m.
atonal [æ'təunl] adj atonal.
atone [ə'təun] vi: **to — for** expiar.
atonement [ə'təunmənt] n expiación f; **Day of A—** Día m dc la Expiación.
atonic [æ'tɔnik] adj átono.
atop [ə'tɔp] **1** adv encima. **2** prep encima de; sobre, en la cumbre de.
atrocious [ə'trəuʃəs] adj atroz; (fig) horrible, infame.
atrocity [ə'trɔsiti] n atrocidad f.
atrophy ['ætrəfi] **1** n atrofia f. **2** vt atrofiar. **3** vi atrofiarse.
attach [ə'tætʃ] **1** vt (a) (fasten) sujetar; (stick) pegar; (tie) atar, liar; (with pin etc) prender; (join) unir; seal poner; trailer etc acoplar, enganchar.
   (b) (in letter) adjuntar; **the document is —ed** enviamos adjunto el documento; **the —ed letter** la carta adjunta.
   (c) (fig) importance, value dar, conceder (to a); **the salary —ed to the post is £2000** el sueldo que corresponde al puesto es de 2000 libras; **to be —ed to an embassy** estar agregado a una embajada; **there are no strings —ed to this** esto es sin compromiso alguno, esto es libre de condiciones.
   (d) (Law) property incautar, embargar.
   (e) **to be —ed to** person etc tener cariño a.
   2 vi: **to — to** corresponder a, pertenecer a; **no blame —es to you** Vd no tiene culpa alguna.
   3 vr: **to — oneself to** group agregarse a, entrar a formar parte de; (in bad sense) pegarse a.
attaché [ə'tæʃei] n agregado m; **commercial —** agregado m comercial; **cultural —** agregado m cultural; **military —** agregado m militar; **naval —** agregado m naval.
attaché case [ə'tæʃeikeis] n maletín m.
attachment [ə'tætʃmənt] n (a) (act) atadura f, unión f etc.
   (b) (device) accesorio m, dispositivo m; (coupling) acoplamiento m.
   (c) (affection) cariño m, apego m (to a); (loyalty) adhesión f.
   (d) (Law) incautación f, embargo m.
attack [ə'tæk] **1** n (a) (Mil etc) ataque m (on a, contra, sobre), asalto m; (criminal — on person) agresión f; **air —** ataque m aéreo; **flank —** ataque m de flanco; **frontal —** ataque m de frente; **surprise —** ataque m por sorpresa; **— on someone's life** atentado m contra la vida de uno; **— on the security of the state** atentado m contra la seguridad del estado; **to be under —** ser atacado; **— is the best form of defence** la mejor defensa está siempre en el ataque; **to launch an —** lanzar un ataque; **to leave oneself open to —** dejarse expuesto al ataque; **to return to the —** volver al ataque.
   (b) (Med) ataque m, acceso m; **an — of pneumonia** una pulmonía; **an — of nerves** una crisis nerviosa.
   2 vt (Mil etc) atacar (also Med, Chem); acometer; (criminally) agredir, asaltar; (bull etc) embestir; (gratuitously) emprenderla con; problem acometer, tratar de resolver; opinion, theory impugnar; **we must — poverty** debemos acabar con la pobreza; **he was —ed by doubts** le asaltaron dudas.
attackable [ə'tækəbl] adj atacable.
attacker [ə'tækə*] n agresor m, ora f, asaltante mf.
attain [ə'tein] **1** vt alcanzar, lograr, conseguir. **2** vi: **to — to** llegar a.
attainable [ə'teinəbl] adj alcanzable, realizable.
attainment [ə'teinmənt] n (act) logro m, consecución f, obtención f; **—s** dotes fpl, talento m (in para), conocimientos mpl (in de); **difficult of —** de difícil consecución.
attempt [ə'tempt] **1** n (a) tentativa f, intento m, conato m; **to make an — to** + infin hacer una tentativa de + infin, intentar + infin; **he made two —s at it** trató dos veces de lograrlo; **to make an — on the record** tratar de batir la marca; **it was**

a good — fue un esfuerzo loable; **this is my first —** es la primera vez que lo intento; **we had to give up the —** tuvimos que renunciar a la empresa.
   (b) atentado m (on someone's life contra la vida de uno).
   2 vt (a) probar, ensayar, intentar; tratar de efectuar (or conseguir etc); (undertake) emprender.
   (b) **to — to** + infin intentar + infin, tratar de + infin; **to accuse someone of —ed murder** acusar a uno de tentativa de asesinato.
attend [ə'tend] **1** vt (wait on) servir; (escort) acompañar; (Med) atender, asistir; (be present at) asistir a; **a well—ed meeting** una reunión muy concurrida; **the policy was —ed by many difficulties** la política tropezó con muchas dificultades.
   2 vi (be present) asistir; (pay attention) prestar atención; **to — to** words, work prestar atención a; task ocuparse de; order (Comm) ejecutar; **can you — to this customer?** ¿está Vd libre para atender a este cliente?; **I'll — to you in a moment** un momentino y estoy con Vd.
attendance [ə'tendəns] n (a) (act) asistencia f (at a), presencia f (at en); **is my — necessary?** ¿es preciso que asista yo?
   (b) (those present) concurrencia f, asistentes mpl; **what was the — at the meeting?** ¿cuántos asistieron a la reunión?; **we need an — of 1000** hace falta atraer a un público de 1000.
   (c) (Med) asistencia f.
   (d) **to be in —** asistir; estar de servicio; **to dance — on** estar pendiente de los menores detalles de.
attendant [ə'tendənt] **1** adj: **the — crowd** la multitud que asistió a ello; **the — difficulties** las dificultades con que ello tropezó; **the — circumstances** las circunstancias concomitantes.
   2 n acompañante m; (servant) sirviente m, a f; mozo m; (Theat) acomodador m, ora f; (in carpark, museum) celador m.
attention [ə'tenʃən] n (a) atención f; **it requires daily —** hay que atenderlo a diario; **it shall have my earliest —** lo atenderé lo más pronto posible; **to attract** (or catch) **someone's —** llamar la atención de uno; **to call** (or draw) **someone's — to** llamar la atención de uno sobre; **to come to someone's —** hacérsele presente a uno; **to give** (or pay) **—** prestar atención (to a); **he paid no —** no hizo caso (to that de eso); **to pay special — to** fijarse de modo especial en; **to turn one's — to** pasar a considerar, pasar a estudiar.
   (b) (Mil) **—!** ¡firme(s)!; **to come to —** ponerse firme(s), cuadrarse; **to stand at —** estar firme(s).
   (c) **—s** atenciones fpl, cortesías fpl.
attentive [ə'tentiv] adj (heedful) atento; (polite) cortés, obsequioso (to con).
attentively [ə'tentivli] adv atentamente; cortésmente.
attentiveness [ə'tentivnis] n atención f; cortesía f.
attenuate [ə'tenjueit] vt atenuar.
attenuating [ə'tenjueitiŋ] adj atenuante.
attest [ə'test] **1** vt atestiguar (that que); dar fe de; signature confirmar, autenticar. **2** vi: **to — to** dar fe de.
attic ['ætik] n desván m, ático m.
Attila ['ætilə] m Atila.
attire [ə'taiə*] **1** n traje m, vestido m; (hum) atavío m. **2** vt vestir (in de); (hum) ataviar (in de).
attitude ['ætitju:d] n actitud f; (posture in painting etc) ademán m; postura f; **— of mind** actitud f, disposición f de ánimo; **to strike** (or adopt, take up) **an —** tomar una postura, adoptar una actitud; **if that's your —** si te pones en ese plan; **what is your — to this?** ¿cuál es su posición con respecto a esto?
attitudinize [,æti'tju:dinaiz] vi tomar posturas afectadas.
attorney [ə'tə:ni] n (lawyer) abogado m; (representative) apoderado m, a f; **district —** (US) fiscal m; **A— General** fiscal m de la corona, (US) procurador m general; **power of —** poder m, procuración f.
attract [ə'trækt] vt atraer; attention llamar.
attraction [ə'trækʃən] n atracción f; (attractive feature) atractivo m; (inducement) aliciente m; **the film has the special — of featuring X** la película tiene el aliciente especial de presentar a X; **the main — at the party was Y** el interés de la fiesta se cifraba en Y; **one of the —s of the quiet life** uno de los encantos de la vida retirada; **spring —s in Madrid** las diversiones de la primavera madrileña.
attractive [ə'træktiv] adj atractivo; (interesting) atrayente; idea, plan sugestivo; child, girl mono, guapo, atractivo; offer interesante; prospect halagüeño.
attractively [ə'træktivli] adv atractivamente; de modo atrayente; de modo sugestivo; de modo

halagüeño; **an — designed garden** un jardín de trazado atractivo.
attributable [ə'tribjutəbl] *adj*: **— to** atribuible a.
attribute ['ætribjuːt] *n* atributo *m*.
attribute [ə'tribjuːt] *vt* atribuir; achacar; **to what would you — this?** ¿cómo explica Vd esto?
attribution [,ætri'bjuːʃən] *n* atribución *f*.
attributive [ə'tribjutiv] *adj* atributivo.
attrition [ə'triʃən] *n*: **war of —** guerra *f* de agotamiento.
attune [ə'tjuːn] *vt* (*fig*): **to — to** armonizar con; **to be —d to** estar en armonía con.
atypical [,ei'tipikəl] *adj* atípico.
aubergine ['əubəʒiːn] *n* berenjena *f*.
auburn ['ɔːbən] *adj* castaño rojizo.
auction ['ɔːkʃən] **1** *n* subasta *f*, almoneda *f*, licitación *f* (*SAm*); (*at bridge*) subasta *f*; **— sale, sale by —** subasta *f*; **Dutch —** *subasta en la que el precio se reduce poco a poco hasta encontrar comprador*; **to put up for —**, **to sell at —** subastar, poner en pública subasta.
2 *vt* subastar (*also* **— off**), licitar (*SAm*).
auctioneer [,ɔːkʃə'niə*] *n* subastador *m*, licitador *m* (*SAm*).
auction room ['ɔːkʃənrum] *n* sala *f* de subastas.
audacious [ɔː'deiʃəs] *adj* audaz, atrevido; (*in bad sense*) descarado.
audacity [ɔː'dæsiti] *n* audacia *f*, atrevimiento *m*; (*in bad sense*) descaro *m*; **and you have the — to say that!** ¡y Vd me lo dice tan fresco!, ¡y usted se atreve a decirlo!
audibility [,ɔːdi'biliti] *n* audibilidad *f*.
audible ['ɔːdibl] *adj* audible, que se puede oír; **the speech was barely —** apenas se podía oír nada del discurso.
audibly ['ɔːdibli] *adv* de modo que se puede oír; **he said quite —** lo dijo de modo que se podía oír claramente.
audience ['ɔːdiəns] *n* (a) (*gathering*) auditorio *m*, público *m*; **there was a big —** asistió un público numeroso; **those in the —** los que formaban parte del auditorio.
(b) (*interview*) audiencia *f* (*of*, *with* con); **to grant someone an —**, **to receive someone in —** recibir a uno en audiencia; **to have an — of** (*or* **with**) ser recibido en audiencia por.
audio-visual [,ɔːdiəu'vizjuəl] *adj* audiovisual.
audit ['ɔːdit] **1** *n* revisión *f* de cuentas, intervención *f*. **2** *vt* revisar, intervenir.
audition [ɔː'diʃən] **1** *n* audición *f*. **2** *vt* dar audición a; **he was —ed for the part** le hicieron una audición para el papel.
auditor ['ɔːditə*] *n* censor *m* de cuentas, interventor *m*.
auditorium [,ɔːdi'tɔːriəm] *m* auditorio *m*, sala *f*.
auditory ['ɔːditəri] *adj* auditivo.
Augean Stables [ɔː'dʒiːən'steiblz] *pl* establos *mpl* de Augias.
aught [ɔːt] *n* algo, alguna cosa *f*; (*with negation*) nada; **if there is —** I can do si puedo ayudarles en alguna manera; **for —** I care igual me da; **for —** I know que yo sepa.
augment [ɔːg'ment] **1** *vt* aumentar. **2** *vi* aumentar(se).
augmentation [,ɔːgmen'teiʃən] *n* aumento *m*.
augmentative [ɔːg'mentətiv] *adj* aumentativo.
augur ['ɔːgə*] **1** *vt* **thing** augurar, pronosticar; **it —s no good** esto no nos promete nada bueno.
2 *vi*: **it —s ill** es de mal agüero; **to — well** ser de buen agüero (*for* para).
augury ['ɔːgjuri] *n* augurio *m*; **to take the auguries** consultar los augurios.
August ['ɔːgəst] *n* agosto *m*.
august [ɔː'gʌst] *adj* augusto.
Augustan [ɔː'gʌstən] *adj* augustal; **the — age** (*Latin*) el siglo de Augusto, (*English*) la época neoclásica (del siglo XVIII).
Augustine [ɔː'gʌstin] *m* Agustín.
Augustus [ɔː'gʌstəs] *m* Augusto.
auk [ɔːk] *n* alca *f*; **little —** mérgulo *m* marino.
aunt [ɑːnt] *n* tía *f*; **my — and uncle** mis tíos.
auntie, aunty ['ɑːnti] *n* (*fam*) tía *f*.
au pair ['əu'pɛə] *adv* au pair.
aura ['ɔːrə] *n* emanación *f*; (*atmosphere*) ambiente *m*.
aural ['ɔːrəl] *adj* aural.
au revoir [əurə'vwɑː*] *adv* hasta la vista.
auricle ['ɔːrikl] *n* (*Anat*) aurícula *f*.
aurochs ['ɔːrɔks] *n* uro *m*.
aurora borealis [ɔː'rɔːrəbɔːri'eilis] *n* aurora *f* boreal(is).
auspices ['ɔːspisiz] *npl*: **under the — of** bajo los auspicios de.

auspicious [ɔːs'piʃəs] *adj* propicio, favorable, de buen augurio; **to make an — start** comenzar felizmente.
auspiciously [ɔːs'piʃəsli] *adv* propiciamente, favorablemente; **to start —** comenzar felizmente.
Aussie ['ɔzi] (*fam*) **= Australian**.
austere [ɔs'tiə*] *adj* austero; *style* adusto.
austerely [ɔs'tiəli] *adv* austeramente; adustamente.
austerity [ɔs'teriti] *n* austeridad *f*; adustez *f*.
Australia [ɔs'treiliə] Australia *f*.
Australian [ɔs'treiliən] **1** *adj* australiano. **2** *n* australiano *m*, a *f*.
Austria ['ɔstriə] Austria *f*.
Austrian ['ɔstriən] **1** *adj* austríaco. **2** *n* austríaco *m*, a *f*.
authentic [ɔː'θentik] *adj* auténtico.
authenticate [ɔː'θentikeit] *vt* autenticar; autentificar.
authenticity [,ɔːθen'tisiti] *n* autenticidad *f*.
author ['ɔːθə*] *n* autor *m*, ora *f*.
authoress ['ɔːθəris] *n* autora *f*.
authoritarian [,ɔːθɔri'tɛəriən] **1** *adj* autoritario. **2** *n* autoritario *m*, a *f*.
authoritarianism [,ɔːθɔri'tɛəriənizəm] *n* autoritarismo *m*.
authoritative [ɔː'θɔritətiv] *adj* *version* autorizado; *manner etc* autoritario.
authority [ɔː'θɔriti] *n* autoridad *f*; **the authorities** las autoridades; **he is the greatest living —** es la máxima autoridad actual; **he is an — on the subject** es muy perito en la materia; **to apply to the proper —** dirigirse a la autoridad competente; **I have no — to + infin** yo no estoy autorizado para + *infin*; **to give someone — to + infin** autorizar a uno para que + *subj*; **to do something without —** hacer algo sin tener autorización para ello; **those in —** los que tienen la autoridad; **in — over** al mando de; **who is in — here?** ¿quién manda aquí?; **on the — of Plato** con la autoridad de Platón; **I have it on good — that** sé de buena tinta que.
authorization [,ɔːθərai'zeiʃən] *n* autorización *f*.
authorize ['ɔːθəraiz] *vt* autorizar; **to — someone to + infin** autorizar a uno para + *infin*; **the A—d Version** la Versión Autorizada (de la Biblia).
authorized ['ɔːθəraizd] *adj* autorizado.
authorship ['ɔːθəʃip] *n* (a) profesión *f* de autor. **(b)** (*of book*) autoría *f*, paternidad *f* literaria.
autism ['ɔːtizəm] *n* autismo *m*.
autistic [ɔː'tistik] *adj* autístico.
auto¹ . . . ['ɔːtəu] *in compounds*: auto . . .
auto² ['ɔːtəu] *n* (*US*) coche *m*, automóvil *m*.
autobiographic(al) ['ɔːtəu,baiəu'græfik(əl)] *adj* autobiográfico.
autobiography [,ɔːtəubai'ɔgrəfi] *n* autobiografía *f*.
autocade ['ɔːtəukeid] *n* (*US*) caravana *f* de automóviles.
autocracy [ɔː'tɔkrəsi] *n* autocracia *f*.
autocrat ['ɔːtəukræt] *n* autócrata *mf*.
autocratic [,ɔːtəu'krætik] *adj* autocrático.
autocycle ['ɔːtəusaikl] *n* velomotor *m*, ciclomotor *m*.
auto-da-fé ['ɔːtəudɑː'fei] *n* auto *m* de fe.
autogiro ['ɔːtəu'dʒaiərou] *n* autogiro *m*.
autograph ['ɔːtəgrɑːf] **1** *adj* autógrafo *m*; **— album** álbum *m* de autógrafos.
2 *n* (*MS*) autógrafo *m*; (*signature*) firma *f*.
3 *vt* (*sign*) firmar; *book*, *photo* dedicar, poner su nombre en.
automate ['ɔːtəmeit] *vt* automatizar.
automatic [,ɔːtə'mætik] **1** *adj* automático. **2** *n* pistola *f* automática.
automatically [,ɔːtə'mætikəli] *adv* automáticamente.
automation [,ɔːtə'meiʃən] *n* automatización *f*.
automaton [ɔː'tɔmətən] *n*, *pl* **automata** [ɔː'tɔmətə] autómata *m*.
automobile ['ɔːtəməbiːl] *n* (*US*) coche *m*, automóvil *m*.
automotive [ɔːtə'məutiv] *adj* automotor.
autonomous [ɔː'tɔnəməs] *adj* autónomo.
autonomy [ɔː'tɔnəmi] *n* autonomía *f*.
autopsy ['ɔːtɔpsi] *n* autopsia *f*.
autosuggestion ['ɔːtəusə'dʒestʃən] *n* (auto)sugestión *f*.
autumn ['ɔːtəm] *n* otoño *m*.
autumnal [ɔː'tʌmnəl] *adj* otoñal.
Auvergne [əu'vɛən] Auvernia *f*.
auxiliary [ɔːg'ziliəri] **1** *adj* auxiliar. **2 auxiliaries** *npl* tropas *fpl* auxiliares.
avail [ə'veil] **1** *n*: **it is of no —** es inútil; **of what — is it to + infin?** ¿de qué sirve + *infin*?; **to be of little —** ser de poco provecho; **to no — en** vano, sin resultado.
2 *vt* aprovechar, valer.
3 *vi*: **it —s nothing to + infin** de nada sirve + *infin*.
4 *vt*: **to — oneself of** aprovechar(se de), valerse de.

availability [ə‚veilə'biliti] n disponibilidad f.
available [ə'veiləbl] adj disponible; asequible, aprovechable; **to make something — to someone** poner algo a la disposición de uno; **is the manager —?** ¿está libre el gerente?, ¿puedo pasar a ver al gerente?; **are you — next Thursday?** ¿tienes compromiso para el jueves que viene?; **I am not — to visitors** no estoy para las visitas; **that ticket is no longer —** ese billete ya no vale.
avalanche ['ævəlɑːnʃ] n alud m, avalancha f; (fig) torrente m, avalancha f.
avant-garde ['ævːɑ̃ŋ'gɑːd] adj ultramoderno, de vanguardia, nueva ola.
avarice ['ævəris] n avaricia f.
avaricious [‚ævə'riʃəs] adj avaro, avariento.
avenge [ə'vendʒ] **1** vt vengar. **2** vr: **to — oneself** vengarse (on en).
avenger [ə'vendʒə*] n vengador m, ora f.
avenging [ə'vendʒiŋ] adj vengador.
avenue ['ævənjuː] n avenida f; (fig) vía f, camino m; **to explore every —** tentar todas las vías.
aver [ə'vəː*] vt afirmar, declarar.
average ['ævəridʒ] **1** adj medio, de término medio; regular, corriente; (pej) mediano, ordinario; **the — man** el hombre medio; **of — height** de regular estatura; **of — ability** de capacidad regular; **the — height of players** el promedio de talla por jugador.
  2 n (a) promedio m, término m medio; **on (an or the) —** por término medio; por regla general.
  (b) (Comm) avería f.
  3 vt (also **to — out**) calcular el término medio de; prorratear.
  4 vi (also **to — out at**) ser por término medio, resultar por término medio; ser por regla general; **we — 8 hours a day** trabajamos (etc) por regla general 8 horas diarias; **he —d 50 all the way** sacó un promedio de 50 millas por hora por todo el recorrido.
averse [ə'vəːs] adj: **I am — to** siento repugnancia por, tengo antipatía a; **I am not — to an occasional drink** no me repugna tomar algo de vez en cuando; **I am — to getting up early** tengo pocas ganas de levantarme temprano.
aversion [ə'vəːʃən] n (a) aversión f (for, from, to hacia), repugnancia f (for, from, to por); **to feel an — for** sentir repugnancia por; **I have an — to him** me resulta antipático; **I took an — to it** empezó a repugnarme.
  (b) (hated thing) cosa f aborrecida; **pet —** bestia f negra, pesadilla f; (person) hincha mf.
avert [ə'vəːt] vt eyes, thoughts apartar (from de); suspicion desviar (from de); possibility quitar; blow impedir, desviar; accident, illness, rebellion prevenir.
aviary ['eiviəri] n pajarera f, avería f.
aviation [‚eivi'eiʃən] n aviación f; **— spirit** gasolina f de aviación.
aviator ['eivieitə*] n aviador m, ora f.
avid ['ævid] adj ávido, ansioso (for, of de).
avidity [ə'viditi] n avidez f, ansia f.
avidly ['ævidli] adv ávidamente, ansiosamente; **to read —** leer con avidez.
Avignon ['ævinjɔ̃] Aviñón.
avocado [ævə'kɑːdəu] n aguacate m.
avocation [‚ævəu'keiʃən] n diversión f, distracción f, ocupación f accesoria; (loosely) vocación f.
avoid [ə'vɔid] vt evitar; guardarse de; duty etc eludir; danger salvarse de; **to — + ger** evitar + infin; **he managed to — the tree** evitó chocar con el árbol; **are you trying to — me?** ¿se está esforzando Vd por no hablar conmigo?; **I try to — him** procuro no tener nada que ver con él; **he —s all his friends** huye de todos sus amigos; **it's to be —ed like the plague** esto hay que evitarlo como la peste; **this way we — London** por esta ruta evitamos entrar en Londres.
avoidable [ə'vɔidəbl] adj evitable, eludible.
avoidance [ə'vɔidəns] n el evitar (etc), evitación f.
avoirdupois [ævədə'pɔiz] n sistema de pesos británico y estadounidense (1 libra = 16 onzas = 453,50 gramos); (fam) peso m, gordura f.
avow [ə'vau] **1** vt reconocer, confesar. **2** vr: **he —ed himself beaten** reconoció que había perdido.
avowal [ə'vauəl] n confesión f; declaración f.
avowed [ə'vaud] adj declarado.
avowedly [ə'vauidli] adv declaradamente, abiertamente.
avuncular [ə'vʌŋkjulə*] adj como de tío.
await [ə'weit] vt esperar, aguardar; **the fate that —s him** la suerte que le espera; **we — your reply with interest** nos interesa mucho saber su contestación;

a long **—ed event** un acontecimiento que se viene esperando desde hace mucho tiempo.
awake [ə'weik] **1** adj despierto; **to lie —** quedar despierto, estar sin poder dormir; **to stay — all night** pasar toda la noche en vela; **the noise kept me —** el ruido me impidió dormir; **coffee keeps me —** el café me desvela; **to be — to** ser consciente de.
  2 (irr: pret **awoke**, ptp **awaked**) vt despertar.
  3 vi despertar(se).
awaken [ə'weikən] **1** vt despertar (also fig); **to — someone to something** hacer que uno se dé cuenta de algo.
  2 vi despertar(se) (also fig); **to — to** darse cuenta de.
awakening [ə'weikniŋ] n despertamiento m, el despertar; **a rude —** una sorpresa desagradable.
award [ə'wɔːd] **1** n (act of —ing) adjudicación f; concesión f; (prize) premio m; (Law) sentencia f, fallo m; (Mil etc) condecoración f.
  2 vt conceder, otorgar; prize, damages etc adjudicar, decretar; medal dar; **the prize is not being —ed this year** este año el premio se declaró desierto.
aware [ə'wɛə*] adj (a) (alert) enterado; despierto.
  (b) **to be — of** saber, estar enterado de, ser consciente de; **not that I am — of** que yo sepa; **our employees are — of this advert** los empleados de la empresa ya conocen este anuncio; **so far as I am —** según mi leal saber y entender; **to be — that** saber que; **I am fully — that** yo sé perfectamente que; **to become — of** darse cuenta de, enterarse de.
awareness [ə'wɛənis] n conciencia f, conocimiento m.
awash [ə'wɔʃ] adv: **the deck is —** la cubierta está a flor de agua; **the house was —** la casa estaba inundada.
away [ə'wei] **1** adv: (a) **3 miles —** a 3 millas (de aquí); **— in the distance** allá a lo lejos; **— from the noise** lejos del ruido; **— with you!** ¡vete!, ¡fuera de aquí!; **— with him!** ¡que le lleven de aquí!; **— with taxes!** ¡abajo los impuestos!
  (b) (with verb to be) **to be — (from home)** estar fuera, estar ausente; **he's — for a week** pasa una semana fuera; **it's 10 miles —** dista de aquí 10 millas, está a 10 millas de aquí; **we are 20 miles — from London** estamos a 20 millas de Londres.
  (c) (other verbs) **I must —** tengo que marcharme; **to play —** jugar fuera.
  2 adj: **the — team** el equipo de fuera.
awe [ɔː] **1** n temor m reverencial, pavor m y respeto; **to go in — of, to hold in —, to stand in — of** tener temor reverencial a. **2** vt imponer respeto a.
awe-inspiring ['ɔːin‚spaiəriŋ] adj, **awesome** ['ɔːsəm] adj imponente, pasmoso.
awe-struck ['ɔːstrʌk] adj pasmado.
awful ['ɔːfəl] adj (a) tremendo, imponente, terrible, pasmoso.
  (b) (fam) horrible, malísimo, fatal; **it was simply —** fue francamente horrible; **how —!** ¡qué horror!; **what — weather!** ¡qué tiempo más feo!; **his English is —** tiene un inglés fatal; **he's an — fool** es un puro tonto; **there were an — lot of people** había la mar de gente.
awfully ['ɔːfli] adv (fam) terriblemente; **it's — hard** es terriblemente difícil; **it's — funny** es divertidísimo; **I'm — sorry** lo siento muchísimo; **thanks —!** ¡muchísimas gracias!; **he's — nice** es simpatiquísimo.
awfulness ['ɔːfulnis] n horror m.
awhile [ə'wail] adv un rato, algún tiempo; **not yet —** todavía no.
awkward ['ɔːkwəd] adj problem, question difícil; situation violento, difícil; time inoportuno; task delicado, desagradable; shape incómodo; corner peligroso; phrasing poco elegante; (clumsy) desmañado, desgarbado, torpe; **it's — for me** es difícil para mí; **it's all a bit —** todo esto es un poco violento; **he's being — about it** está poniendo peros; **to feel —** sentirse molesto; **to be at the — age** estar en la edad del pavo; **the — squad** la sección de los bisoños.
awkwardness ['ɔːkwədnis] n dificultad f; violencia f; incomodidad f; molestia f; desmaña f, torpeza f.
awl [ɔːl] n lezna f, subilla f.
awning ['ɔːniŋ] n toldo m; (of cart) entalamadura f; (Naut) toldilla f; (over window) marquesina f.
awoke [ə'wəuk] pret and ptp of **awake**.
awry [ə'rai] adv: **to be —** estar de través, estar al sesgo, estar puesto mal; **to go —** salir mal, fracasar.
ax (US), **axe** [æks] **1** n hacha f; **when the — fell** (fig) cuando se descargó el golpe; **to have an — to grind** actuar de una manera interesada.
  2 vt (fig) reducir, cercenar; person despedir.

axial ['æksiəl] *adj* axial.
axiom ['æksiəm] *n* axioma *m*.
axiomatic [,æksiəu'mætik] *adj* axiomático.
axis ['æksis] *n*, *pl* **axes** ['æksiːz] eje *m*; (*Anat*) axis *m*; **the A—** (*Pol*) el Eje; **the A— powers** las potencias del Eje.
axle ['æksl] *n* eje *m*, árbol *m*; **rear —** eje *m* trasero.
axle-box ['ækslbɔks] *n* caja *f* de eje.
ay(e) [ai] **1** *adv* sí; **— — sir**! sí, mi capitán (*etc*).

2 *n* sí *m*; **the —s have it** se ha aprobado la moción; **there were 50 —s and 3 noes** votaron 50 a favor y 3 en contra.
aye [ei] *adv*: **for ever and —** para siempre jamás.
azalea [ə'zeiliə] *n* azalea *f*.
Azores [ə'zɔːz] *pl* Azores *fpl*.
Aztec ['æztek] **1** *adj* azteca. **2** *n* azteca *mf*.
azure ['eiʒə*] **1** *adj* azul celeste. **2** *n* azul *m* celeste; (*Her*) azur *m*.

B

baa [bɑ:] **1** n balido m. **2** interj ¡bee! **3** vi balar.

baa-lamb ['bɑ:læm] n (fam) corderito m, borreguito m.

babble ['bæbl] **1** n barboteo m; (of stream) murmullo m; **a — of voices arose** se oyó un ruido confuso de voces.

    2 vt decir balbuceando.

    3 vi barbullar, barbotear; (talk to excess) parlotear; (tell secrets) hablar indiscretamente; (stream) murmurar.

babe [beib] n (lit or hum) criatura f; (US sl) chica f, (in direct address) ricura f, nena f.

Babel ['beibəl] Babel m or f; **Tower of —** Torre f de Babel.

baboon [bə'bu:n] n mandril m.

baby ['beibi] **1** n niño m, a f; (more sentimental) bebé mf, crío m, a f, rorro m, a f, nene m, a f; (US sl) chica f, (in direct address) ricura f, nena f; **she's having a — in May** va a tener un niño en mayo; **she's having the — in hospital** va a dar a luz en el hospital; **— of the family** benjamín m; **don't be such a —!** ¡no seas niño!

    2 attr and adj: **— boy** nene m; **— girl** nena f; **— clothes,** — linen ropa f de niño; **— face** cara f de niño; **— car** coche m pequeño.

baby carriage ['beibi,kærid3] n (US) cochecito m de niño.

baby grand ['beibi'grænd] n piano m de media cola.

babyhood ['beibihud] n infancia f.

babyish ['beibiiʃ] adj infantil.

Babylon ['bæbilən], **Babylonia** [,bæbi'ləuniə] Babilonia f.

Babylonian [,bæbi'ləuniən] **1** adj babilonio, babilónico. **2** n babilonio m, a f.

baby-sit ['beibisit] vi hacer de niñero, vigilar (a los niños dormidos, en ausencia de sus padres).

baby-sitter ['beibi,sitə*] n guardián m, ana f de niños.

baby talk ['beibitɔ:k] n habla f infantil.

baccarat ['bækərɑ:] n bacará m, bacarrá m (Acad).

bacchanalia [,bækə'neiliə] npl bacanales fpl; (fig) bacanal f.

bacchanalian [,bækə'neiliən] adj bacanal, báquico.

Bacchic ['bækik] adj báquico.

Bacchus ['bækəs] n Baco.

baccy ['bæki] n (fam) tabaco m.

bachelor ['bætʃələ*] n **(a)** soltero m; **confirmed —, old —** solterón m; **— flat** piso m para soltero; **— girl** soltera f (que se dedica a una carrera); **— party** guateque m para hombres solos.

    (b) (Univ) licenciado m, a f (of en).

bachelorhood ['bætʃələhud] n soltería f, estado m de soltero.

bacillary [bə'siləri] adj bacilar.

bacillus [bə'siləs] n, pl **bacilli** [bə'silai] bacilo m.

back [bæk] **1** n trasero, de atrás, posterior; view desde atrás; issue, number atrasado; pay retrasado.

    2 adv **(a)** atrás, hacia atrás; **— and forth** de acá para allá, de una parte a otra; **a house standing — from the road** una casa situada no demasiado cerca de la carretera; **to make one's way —** regresar; **to fly to Madrid and — ir** en avión a Madrid y volver del mismo modo.

    (b) (time) **— in the 12th century** allá en el siglo XII; **as far — as 1900** ya en 1900; **some months —** hace unos meses.

    (c) (with verb to be) **to be —** estar de vuelta; **when will he be —?** ¿cuándo volverá?

    3 prep: **— of** (US) = behind.

    4 n (Anat) espalda f; (of animal, knife) lomo m; (of chair) respaldo m; (of coin) reverso m; (of cheque, document, hand) dorso m; (end of book) final m; (spine of book) lomo m; (of stage, cave etc) fondo m; (Sport) defensa m; **— to —** espalda con espalda; **to front** al revés; **at the — of** tras, detrás de; al fondo de; **what's at the — of it?** ¿qué motivo oculto tendrá esto?; **who's at the — of it?** ¿quién lo está dirigiendo (entre bastidores)?; **behind one's — a** espaldas de uno, por detrás de uno (also fig); **she wears her hair down her —** el pelo le cae por la espalda; **with one's — to** de espaldas a; **to be on one's — (**Med) estar postrado (en la cama); **to carry something on one's —** llevar algo a cuestas; **he lay on his —** estaba tumbado boca arriba; **to sign on the —** firmar al dorso; **his — is broad** bien es capaz de soportarlo; **to break one's —** deslomarse; **the ship broke its —** el buque se rompió por medio; **to break the — of the work** haber terminado lo más difícil del trabajo; **to get (or put) someone's — up** enojar a uno, incordiar a uno; **to have one's — to the wall** estar entre la espada y la pared; **to put one's — into it** esforzarse al máximo, hacer todo lo que puede uno; **put your —s into it!** ¡dale!; **to scratch someone's —** (fig) hacer un favor a uno; **to see the — of someone** librarse de uno; **we were glad to see the — of him** nos alegramos de que se fuera; **to turn one's —** volver las espaldas (on a).

    5 vt (support) apoyar, respaldar; defender; favorecer; (bet on) apostar a; vehicle dar marcha atrás a; horse recular; **to — up** apoyar, secundar, defender.

    6 vi moverse hacia atrás, retroceder; (vehicle) dar marcha atrás; **the car —ed into the garage** el coche entró en el garaje marcha atrás; **the house —s on to the park** la parte trasera de la casa da al parque; **to — down** volverse atrás, echarse atrás, desdecirse, rajarse (fam); **to — out** retirarse (of de); **to — up** retroceder.

backache ['bækeik] n dolor m de riñones.

backbencher ['bæk'bentʃə*] n diputado m que no es ministro.

backbite ['bækbait] vi murmurar.

backbiting ['bækbaitiŋ] n murmuración f.

backbone ['bækbəun] n espinazo m; (fig) (guts) firmeza f, agallas fpl, (chief support) espina f dorsal, piedra f angular; **to the —** hasta los tuétanos.

back-breaking ['bækbreikiŋ] adj deslomador, matador.

backchat ['bæktʃæt] n réplicas fpl.

back-cloth ['bækkləθ] n telón m de foro.

backdate ['bæk'deit] vt poner fecha atrasada a; dar efecto retroactivo a; **a salary award —d to January** un aumento de sueldo con efecto retroactivo desde enero.

backdrop ['bækdrɔp] n telón m de foro.

backer ['bækə*] n (Pol) partidario m, a f; (Comm) promotor m, impulsor m, caballo m blanco; (better) apostador m.

backfire ['bæk'faiə*] **1** n (Aut) petardeo m. **2** vi (Aut) petardear; (fig) salir el tiro por la culata; **the idea —d** la idea perjudicó a sus propios inventores.

background ['bækgraund] **1** n **(a)** fondo m; (Art) fondo m, último término m; **in the —** al fondo, en el fondo, en último término; **against a dim —** sobre un fondo oscuro; **to stay in the —** preferir no destacar, no buscar la luz de la publicidad.

    (b) (of person etc) antecedentes mpl, historial m, educación f; **the — to the crisis** los antecedentes de la crisis.

    2 attr: **— music** música f de fondo; **— studies** estudios mpl del ambiente histórico (etc) (en que vivió un autor etc).

backhand(ed) ['bæk'hænd(id)] adj dado con la vuelta de la mano; (fig) irónico, equívoco; **— shot, — stroke** revés m.

backhander ['bæk'hændə*] n revés m.

backing ['bækiŋ] n apoyo m; garantía f; (Comm) respaldo m; (funds) reserva f.

backlash ['bæklæʃ] n reacción f, contragolpe m; **the white —** (US Pol) la resaca blanca.

backlog ['bæklɔg] *n* atrasos *mpl*; reserva *f* de pedidos pendientes.

back number ['bæk'nʌmbə*] *n* número *m* atrasado; *(fig)* cero *m* a la izquierda.

back pay ['bækpei] *n* paga *f* con efecto retroactivo.

back-pedal ['bæk'pedl] *vi* contrapedalear.

back room ['bæk'rum] *n* cuarto *m* interior, cuarto *m* en la parte trasera (de una casa); **back-room boy** investigador *m*, inventor *m* (que hace el trabajo preliminar sin reclamar ningún reconocimiento público).

back seat ['bæk'si:t] *n* asiento *m* de atrás; **to take a —** ceder su puesto, dejar de tener influencia.

backseat ['bæksi:t] *attr:* **— driver** *(Aut)* pasajero *m* que molesta al conductor dándole consejos *etc.*

backside ['bæk'said] *n* trasero *m*, culo *m*.

backslapping ['bæk,slæpiŋ] *n* espaldarazos *mpl*; **mutual —** bombo *m* mutuo.

backslide ['bæk'slaid] *(irr: see* **slide***) vi* reincidir, volver a las andadas.

backslider ['bæk'slaidə*] *n* reincidente *mf*.

backsliding ['bæk'slaidiŋ] *n* reincidencia *f*.

backstage ['bæk'steidʒ] **1** *n* espacio *m* entre bastidores. **2** *adv:* **to be —** estar entre bastidores.

backstairs ['bæk'stɛəz] **1** *npl* escalera *f* de servicio; **by the —** *(fig)* por enchufe. **2** *attr* clandestino.

backstitch ['bækstitʃ] **1** *n* pespunte *m*. **2** *vt* pespuntar.

backstroke ['bækstrəuk] *n* braza *f* de espaldas.

backtrack ['bæktræk] *vi* volver pies atrás.

backward ['bækwəd] *adj motion etc* hacia atrás; *pupil, country* atrasado; *(shy)* tímido; **he's not — in coming forward** no peca de tímido.

backward(s) ['bækwəd(z)]. *adv* atrás, hacia atrás; *(back to front)* al revés; **to walk —** andar de espaldas; **to read something —** leer algo para atrás; **to go — and forward** ir de acá para allá.

backwardness ['bækwədnis] *n* atraso *m*, estado *m* atrasado; timidez *f*.

backwash ['bækwɔʃ] *n* agua *f* de rechazo; *(fig)* reacción *f*, consecuencias *fpl*.

backwater ['bækwɔːtə*] *n* brazo *m* de río estancado, remanso *m*; *(fig)* lugar *m* atrasado, lugar *m* de agradable tranquilidad.

backwoods ['bækwudz] *npl* región *f* apartada *(freq* = Las Batuecas *in Spain).*

backwoodsman ['bækwudzmən] *n, pl* **—men** [mən] patán *m*, rústico *m*; *(Pol)* miembro de la Cámara de los Lores que rara vez asiste al Parlamento.

backyard ['bæk'jɑːd] *n* patio *m* trasero, traspatio *m*.

bacon ['beikən] *n* tocino *m* (entreverado, de panceta); **to bring home the —** *(fam)* sacarse el gordo; **to save one's —** *(fam)* salvar el pellejo.

bacterial [bæk'tiəriəl] *adj* bacteriano, bactérico.

bacteriological [bæk,tiəriə'lɔdʒikəl] *adj* bacteriológico.

bacteriologist [bæk,tiəri'ɔlədʒist] *n* bacteriólogo *m*.

bacteriology [bæk,tiəri'ɔlədʒi] *n* bacteriología *f*.

bacterium [bæk'tiəriəm] *n, pl* **bacteria** [bæk'tiəriə] bacteria *f*.

bad [bæd] **1** *adj* malo; *(ill)* malo, enfermo; *(rotten)* podrido, dañado, pasado; *(harmful)* nocivo, dañoso; *accident, mistake* grave; *air* viciado; *cheque* no cubierto, descubierto; *coin* falso; *debt* incobrable; *joke* de mal gusto, nada divertido; *law, treatment* injusto; *shot* descuidado, errado; *tooth* cariado; *voting paper* inválido; **he's a — man** es un hombre malo; **he's a — one** es un mal sujeto; **he's a very — poet** es un poeta malísimo; **my — leg** mi pierna lisiada; **to have a — cold** estar fuertemente acatarrado; **to talk — Spanish** hablar mal el español; **to be — at French** ser malo en francés; **I'm — about getting up** levantarme exige un gran esfuerzo, me repuga la idea de levantarme; **not —** bastante bueno, nada malo, *(less enthusiastic)* regular; **that's too — es** una pena; **it's really too — of you** te has comportado de una manera vergonzosa; **it would be — for you to** + *infin* sería poco aconsejable que Vd + *subj*; **it's — for you** te hace daño; **what's — about it?** ¿qué hay de malo en ello?; **he looks —** tiene mal aspecto; **this is beginning to look —** esto se está poniendo feo; **he's not as — as he looks** es mejor persona de lo que parece; **to go from — to worse** ir de mal en peor; **to be taken — (fam)** caer enfermo; **to go —** *(food)* echarse a perder, pasarse, alterarse.

2 *n* lo malo; **I'm £5 to the —** he perdido 5 libras; **to be in — with someone** estar a malas con uno; **to go to the —** echarse a perder, arruinarse; **to take the — with the good** aceptar lo malo con lo bueno.

baddie ['bædi] *n (US sl)* mal sujeto *m*, tipo *m* nada confiable; criminal *m*; *(Theat etc)* malo *m*.

baddish ['bædiʃ] *adj* bastante malo, más bien malo.

bade [bæd] *pret of* **bid**.

badge [bædʒ] *n* divisa *f*, insignia *f*; *(worn on coat)* distintivo *m*; *(metal disc)* chapa *f*, placa *f*; *(fig)* señal *f*, indicio *m*.

badger ['bædʒə*] **1** *n* tejón *m*. **2** *vt* acosar, atormentar *(for* para obtener*)*; **stop —ing me!** ¡no me fastidies!

badinage ['bædinɑːʒ] *n* chanzas *fpl*, bromas *fpl*.

badlands ['bædlændz] *npl (US)* tierras *fpl* malas (región yerma, *esp* en los estados de Nebraska y Dakota del Sur).

badly ['bædli] *adv* mal; **to be — mistaken** equivocarse gravemente; **we were — beaten** sufrimos una grave derrota; **we came off — in the deal** el negocio resultó ser desfavorable para nosotros; **I want it —** lo deseo muchísimo; **we — need another assistant** nos hace gran falta otro ayudante; **to be — off** andar mal de dinero; **how did he take it? ...—** ¿qué impresión le produjo la noticia? ... malísima.

bad-mannered ['bæd'mænəd] *adj* sin educación, grosero.

badminton ['bædmintən] *n* volante *m*.

badness ['bædnis] *n* lo malo, mala calidad *f*; *(wickedness)* maldad *f*.

bad-tempered ['bæd'tempəd] *adj (permanently)* de mal genio; *(temporarily)* de mal humor; *argument* fuerte; *tone etc* áspero, malhumorado.

baffle ['bæfl] **1** *n (also — **plate***)* deflector *m*; *(Radio)* pantalla *f* acústica.

2 *vt progress* impedir, estorbar; *mind etc* desconcertar; *searchers* confundir; **at times you — me a** veces no te comprendo; **the problem —s me al** problema no le veo solución alguna; **the police are —d** la policía no tiene pista alguna; **the crime —d the police for months** durante meses el crimen dejó perpleja a la policía; **it —s description** es imposible describirlo.

baffling ['bæfliŋ] *adj crime* de solución nada fácil, misterioso; *action* incomprensible; *problem* dificilísimo.

bag [bæg] **1** *n* **(a)** saco *m*; talega *f*; *(large sack)* costal *m*; *(handbag)* bolso *m*; *(suitcase)* maleta *f*; *(carried over shoulder)* zurrón *m*, mochila *f*; *(in dress)* bolsa *f*; *(in trousers)* rodillera *f*; *(sl)* puta *f*, mujeraza *f*; **diplomatic — valija** *f* diplomática; **the whole — of tricks** todo el negocio; **it's in the — (fam)** es cosa segura, está en la talega; **to pack — and baggage** liar el petate.

(b) *(Hunting)* cacería *f*, caza *f*, número *m* de piezas cazadas.

(c) —s *(fam)*: *(baggage)* equipaje *m*; *(trousers)* pantalones *mpl*; **—s under the eyes** bolsas *fpl* de los ojos; **there's —s of** hay un montón de, hay la mar de; **we've —s of time** tenemos tiempo de sobra.

2 *vt* ensacar; *(Hunting)* cazar, coger, capturar; *(shoot down)* derribar; *(sl)* birlar.

3 *vi* hacer bolsa.

bagatelle [,bægə'tel] *n* bagatela *f*.

bagful ['bægful] *n* saco *m* (lleno).

baggage ['bægidʒ] *n* equipaje *m*; *(Mil)* bagaje *m*; *(fam)* mujercilla *f*.

baggage car ['bægidʒkɑː*] *n (US)* furgón *m* de equipajes.

baggy ['bægi] *adj* muy holgado; que hace bolsa; *trousers* con rodilleras.

bagpiper ['bægpaipə*] *n* gaitero *m*.

bagpipes ['bægpaips] *npl* gaita *f*.

bag-snatcher ['bæg'snætʃə*] *n* ladrón *m* de bolsos.

Bahamas [bə'hɑːməz] *pl* Islas *fpl* Bahama, las Bahamas.

bail[1] [beil] *(Law)* **1** *n* caución *f*, fianza *f*; **on — bajo** fianza; **to be (or go, stand) — for** salir fiador por; **to jump one's — (fam)** fugarse estando bajo fianza; **to be released on — ser** puesto en libertad bajo fianza. **2** *vt* afianzar; **to — someone out** obtener la libertad de uno bajo fianza, *(fig)* echar un cable a uno.

bail[2] [beil] *vt (Naut)* achicar.

bailiff ['beilif] *n (Law)* alguacil *m*, corchete *m*; *(steward)* administrador *m*.

bairn [bɛən] *n (Scot)* niño *m*, a *f*.

bait [beit] **1** *n* cebo *m*, *(live)* carnada *f*; *(fig)* aliciente *m*, añagaza *f*; **he wouldn't rise to the — no** quería picar; **to swallow the — tragar** el anzuelo.

2 *vt hook, trap* cebar, poner cebo en; *(fig)* acosar, atormentar.

baize [beiz] *n* bayeta *f*; **green — tapete** *m* verde.

bake [beik] *vt* cocer al horno; *bricks etc* cocer; *(harden)* endurecer; **it's baking hot** hace un calor terrible.

bakehouse ['beikhaus] *n, pl* **—houses** [hauziz] tahona *f*, panadería *f*.

Bakelite ['beikəlait] *n (Protected Trade Name)* baquelita *f*.

baker ['beikə*] *n* panadero *m*; **—'s (shop)** panadería *f*.

bakery ['beikəri] n tahona f, panadería f.
baking ['beikiŋ] n cocción f; (batch) hornada f.
baking powder ['beikiŋ,paudə*] n polvos mpl de levadura.
baksheesh ['bækʃiːʃ] n propina f.
Balaclava [,bælə'klɑːvə] n (also — helmet) pasamontañas m.
balance ['bæləns] 1 n (a) (state) equilibrio m; — of power equilibrio m político; when the — of his mind was disturbed en un momento de obcecación; to lose one's — perder el equilibrio; to throw someone off — hacer que uno pierda el equilibrio, (fig) desconcertar a uno.
  (b) (scales) balanza f.
  (c) (Comm) balance m; (remainder) resto m; (still to be paid over) remanente m; (eg credit —) saldo m; adverse — saldo m negativo; credit — saldo m positivo; — in hand alcance m, sobrante m; — of payments balance m de pagos; — of trade balance m de comercio; on — pensándolo bien; to be (or hang) in the — estar pendiente de un hilo; to hold the — tener una influencia decisiva.
  2 vt (a) equilibrar; (make up for) contrapesar (with con); this has to be —d against that hay que pesar esto contra aquello; the match is nicely —d el partido lo podrá ganar tanto un equipo como el otro; —d diet régimen m bien equilibrado; —d personality personalidad f estable; —d view opinión f juiciosa.
  (b) account saldar; budget nivelar; to — the books hacer balance, cerrar los libros.
  3 vi (a) equilibrarse.
  (b) (Comm) now the account —s ahora está bien, el balance de esta cuenta; to — up finiquitar.
  4 vr: to — oneself equilibrarse (on en).
balance sheet ['bælənsfiːt] n balance m, avanzo m.
balcony ['bælkəni] n balcón m; (covered) mirador m; (of block of flats) galería f, terraza f; (Theat) paraíso m.
bald [bɔːld] adj calvo; style escueto, desnudo; as — as a coot completamente calvo; to go — quedarse calvo.
balderdash ['bɔːldədæʃ] n tonterías fpl.
bald-headed ['bɔːld'hedid] adj calvo; to go — into (fam) meterse de ligero en.
baldly ['bɔːldli] adv escuetamente, desnudamente.
baldness ['bɔːldnis] n (a) calvicie f; premature — calvicie f precoz. (b) (fig) lo escueto, desnudez f.
bale[1] [beil] 1 n bala f; (Agr) paca f, fardo m. 2 vt (also to — up) embalar; (Agr) empacar.
bale[2] [beil] vi: to — out (Aer) lanzarse en paracaídas.
Bâle [bɑːl] Basilea.
Balearic [,bæli'ærik] 1 adj balear. 2: the —s, — Islands pl Baleares fpl, Islas fpl Baleares.
baleful ['beilful] adj influence funesto, siniestro; look triste.
baler ['beilə*] n (Agr) empacadora f, enfardadora f.
balk [bɔːk] 1 n (Agr) lomo m; (of timber) viga f. 2 vt (thwart) burlar, impedir; (miss) perder, no aprovechar.
  3 vi (stop) detenerse bruscamente; (horse) plantarse, repropiarse (at al ver); he —ed at this se resistió a considerarlo, lo rechazó.
Balkan ['bɔːlkən] 1 adj balcánico. 2: the —s pl los Balcanes.
ball[1] [bɔːl] n (in general) bola f; globo m, esfera f; (eg tennis ball) pelota f; (eg football) balón m; (M il) bala f; (of wool) ovillo m; crystal — bola f de cristal; to be on the — ser un hacha; estar al tanto; you have to be on the — for this para esto hay que fijarse mucho; to keep one's eye on the — (fig) no perder de vista lo principal del asunto; to play — jugar a la pelota, (fig) cooperar (with con), ser acomodaticio; to roll up into a — hacerse una pelota, arrollarse; to start the — rolling empezar, hablar (etc) primero.
ball[2] [bɔːl] n (dance) baile m (gen de etiqueta).
ballad ['bæləd] n balada f, (Spanish) romance m.
ballade [bæ'lɑːd] n (Mus) balada f.
ballast ['bæləst] 1 n (Naut and fig) lastre m; (Rail) balasto m; in — en lastre. 2 vt (Naut) lastrar; (Rail) balastar.
ball bearing ['bɔːl'beəriŋ] n cojinete m a (or de) bolas, rodamiento m a bolas.
ballboy ['bɔːlbɔi] n recogedor m de pelotas.
ballcock ['bɔːlkɔk] n (Tech) llave f de bola, llave f de flotador.
ballerina [,bælə'riːnə] f bailarina f (de ballet).
ballet ['bælei] n ballet m, baile m.
ballet dancer ['bælei,dɑːnsə*] n bailarín m, ina f (de ballet).
ballistic [bə'listik] adj balístico.
ballistics [bə'listiks] n sing balística f.

balloon [bə'luːn] 1 n globo m. 2 vi subir en un globo; (sail etc) hincharse como un globo (also to — out).
balloon barrage [bə'luːn,bærɑː3] n (M il) barrera f de globos.
balloonist [bə'luːnist] n ascensionista mf.
ballot ['bælət] 1 n (voting) votación f; (paper) balota f, papeleta f (para votar); to take a — on something someter algo a votación; there will be a — for the remaining places se sortearán las plazas restantes. ╦ 2 vt members etc invitar a votar.
  3 vi votar; to — for elegir (or determinar etc) por votación; to — for tickets rifar, sortear.
ballot box ['bælətbɔks] n urna f electoral.
ballot paper ['bælətpeipə*] n papeleta f (para votar).
ball-point pen ['bɔːlpɔint'pen] n bolígrafo m.
ballroom ['bɔːlrum] n salón m de baile; — dance baile m de salón.
ballyhoo [,bæli'huː] n (fam) propaganda f sensacional.
balm [bɑːm] m bálsamo m (also fig).
balmy ['bɑːmi] adj balsámico; breeze etc suave, fragante.
baloney [bə'ləuni] n (sl) tonterías fpl.
balsa ['bɔːlsə] n balsa f.
balsam ['bɔːlsəm] n bálsamo m.
Baltic Sea ['bɔːltik'siː] Mar m Báltico.
balustrade [,bæləs'treid] n balaustrada f, barandilla f.
bamboo [bæm'buː] n bambú m.
bamboozle [bæm'buːzl] vt (fam) embaucar, capear.
ban [bæn] 1 n prohibición f (on de); to be under a — estar prohibido; to put a — on prohibir (el uso de), proscribir; to raise the — on levantar el entredicho a.
  2 vt prohibir, proscribir; person excluir (from de); he was —ned from driving for life le prohibieron conducir de por vida; the bullfighter was —ned for 3 months el torero fue inhabilitado para ejercer la profesión durante 3 meses.
banal [bə'nɑːl] adj banal, vulgar.
banality [bə'næliti] n banalidad f, vulgaridad f.
banana [bə'nɑːnə] n plátano m, banana f (esp SAm).
banana tree [bə'nɑːnə,triː] n plátano m, banano m.
band [bænd] 1 n (a) (strip of material) banda f, tira f, faja f; (ribbon) cinta f; (edging) cenefa f, franja f; (armband) brazalete m; (hatband) cintillo m; (of harness) correa f; (stripe) lista f, raya f; (of territory) faja f; zona f; metal — fleje m, precinto m; rubber — goma f, gomita f.
  (b) (Radio) banda f.
  (c) (Mus) orquesta f; (M il Mus) banda f, música f; (brass —) charanga f, banda f; jazz — orquesta f de jazz; to beat the — (fam) hasta más no poder.
  (d) (group) grupo m; cuadrilla f; (pej) gavilla f; (gang) pandilla f.
  2 vt (stripe) rayar.
  3 vi: to — together juntarse, asociarse; (pej) apandillarse.
bandage ['bændidʒ] 1 n venda f, vendaje m. 2 vt vendar.
bandbox ['bændbɔks] n sombrerera f.
bandit ['bændit] n bandido m; one-armed — máquina f tragaperras.
banditry ['bænditri] n bandolerismo m, bandidaje m.
bandmaster ['bændmɑːstə*] n director m de banda.
bandsman ['bændzmən] n, pl —men [mən] músico m de banda.
bandstand ['bændstænd] n quiosco m de música.
bandwagon ['bænd,wægən] n: to climb on the — adherirse al partido ganador; seguir la moda.
bandy[1] ['bændi] vt words, stories cambiar; don't — words with me ! ¡no replique Vd!; to — someone's name about mencionar el nombre de uno en rumores.
bandy[2] ['bændi] adj, **bandy-legged** ['bændi'legd] adj estevado.
bane [bein] n: it's the — of my life será mi ruina.
baneful ['beinful] adj nocivo; funesto, fatal.
bang [bæŋ] 1 interj ¡pum!; (of a blow) ¡zas!; to go (off) — hacer explosión, estallar.
  2 adv precisamente, exactamente; it hit him — on the ear le dio en la oreja precisamente; it was — on the target dio en el mismo centro del blanco.
  3 n (a) (explosion) estallido m, detonación f; (of door) portazo m; (any loud noise) golpe m, estrépito m; supersonic — estampido m supersónico; it started off with a — empezó con muchísimo ímpetu; it all went with a — todo fue a las mil maravillas.
  (b) (blow) golpe m.
  (c) (US) flequillo m.
  4 vt (explode) volar, hacer estallar; door cerrar de golpe; table etc dar golpes en; (strike) golpear; he —ed it down on the table lo arrojó violentamente sobre la mesa; I —ed his head on the table di con su

cabeza en la mesa; **I'll — your heads together!** ¡voy a dar un coscorrón a los dos!

5 *vt* hacer explosión, estallar; hacer estrépito; **the balloons were —ing** estallaban los globos; **the guns were —ing away** disparaban estrepitosamente los cañones; **she was —ing away on the piano** aporreaba el piano; **downstairs a door —ed** abajo se cerró de golpe una puerta.

6 *vr*: **he —ed himself against the wall** dio consigo contra la pared.

banger ['bæŋə*] *n* (*sl*) = **sausage.**

bangle ['bæŋgl] *n* ajorca *f*.

banish ['bænɪʃ] *vt* desterrar (*also fig*); **to — a topic from one's conversation** proscribir un tema de su conversación.

banishment ['bænɪʃmənt] *n* destierro *m*.

banisters ['bænɪstəz] *npl* barandilla *f*, pasamanos *m*.

banjo ['bændʒəu] *n* banjo *m*.

bank [bæŋk] **1** *n* (**a**) (*of river etc*) ribera *f*, orilla *f*; (*small hill*) loma *f*; (*of earth*) terraplén *m*; (*sandbank*) banco *m*; (*of snow, clouds*) montón *m*; (*rise in road*) cuesta *f*; (*escarpment*) escarpa *f*; (*of oars*) hilera *f*. (**b**) (*Comm*) banco *m*; (*in games*) banca *f*; **to break the —** hacer que se quiebre la banca.

2 *vt* (*also freq* **to — up**) (*pile*) amontonar; *fire* cubrir; (*Aer*) ladear; (*Comm*) depositar, ingresar.

3 *vi* (*Aer*) ladearse; **to — on** contar con; **to — up** (*clouds etc*) amontonarse; **we — with Smith** tenemos la cuenta en el Banco Smith, (*of company*) llevamos relaciones bancarias con Smith.

bank account ['bæŋkə,kaunt] *n* cuenta *f* de banco.

bank-book ['bæŋkbuk] *n* libreta *f* (de depósitos); (*in savings bank*) cartilla *f*.

bank clerk ['bæŋkklɑːk] *n* empleado *m* de banco.

banker ['bæŋkə*] *n* banquero *m*; **to be —** (*at games*) tener la banca.

bank holiday ['bæŋk'hɔlədi] *n* día *m* festivo (*en que están cerrados los bancos y el comercio en general*).

banking ['bæŋkɪŋ] **1** *adj* bancario. **2** *n* (*of earth etc*) terraplén *m*, rampas *fpl*; (*Comm*) banca *f*.

banking house ['bæŋkɪŋhaus] *n*, *pl* **— houses** [,hauziz] casa *f* de banca.

banknote ['bæŋknəut] *n* billete *m* de banco.

bank rate ['bæŋkreit] *n* tipo *m* de interés bancario.

bankrupt ['bæŋkrʌpt] **1** *adj* quebrado, insolvente; **to be —** estar en quiebra; **to be — of ideas** estar totalmente falto de ideas; **to go —** quebrar, (*esp fraudulently*) hacer bancarrota.

2 *n* quebrado *m*; **—'s estate** activo *m* de la quiebra.

3 *vt* hacer quebrar, arruinar.

4 *vr*: **to — oneself buying pictures** arruinarse comprando cuadros.

bankruptcy ['bæŋkrʌptsi] *n* quiebra *f*, insolvencia *f*, (*esp fraudulent*) bancarrota *f*; (*fig*) falta *f* (*of de*); **— proceedings** juicio *m* de insolvencia; **moral —** insolvencia *f* moral.

banner ['bænə*] *n* bandera *f*, estandarte *m*; (*carried in demonstration*) pancarta *f*; **— headlines** titulares *mpl* sensacionales.

banns [bænz] *npl* amonestaciones *fpl*; **to call** (*or put up*) **the —** correr las amonestaciones.

banquet ['bæŋkwit] **1** *n* banquete *m*. **2** *vt* festejar, banquetear. **3** *vi* banquetear.

banqueting hall ['bæŋkwitɪŋ,hɔːl] *n* comedor *m* de gala.

banshee ['bænʃiː] *n* (*Scot, Ir*) hada que anuncia una muerte en la familia.

bantam ['bæntəm] *n* gallinilla *f* de Bantam.

bantam-weight ['bæntəmweit] *n* peso *m* gallo.

banter ['bæntə*] **1** *n* burlas *fpl*, zumba *f*. **2** *vt* chancearse con, tomar el pelo a.

baptise [bæp'taiz] *vt* bautizar (*also fig*); **he was —d John** le bautizaron con el nombre de Juan.

baptism ['bæptizəm] *n* (*in general*) bautismo *m*; (*act*) bautizo *m*.

baptismal [bæp'tizməl] *adj* bautismal.

Baptist ['bæptist] *n* bautista *mf*; **the — Church** la Iglesia Baptista; **St John the —** San Juan Bautista.

bar [bɑː*] **1** *n* (*in general, of metal, in harbour, Her*) barra *f*; (*on door*) tranca *f*; (*lever*) palanca *f*; (*of soap*) pastilla *f*; (*of chocolate*) tableta *f*; (*tavern*) bar *m*; (*counter*) mostrador *m*; (*of public opinion*) tribunal *m*; (*Mus*) compás *m*; (*hindrance*) obstáculo *m*, impedimento *m* (*to para*); (*Law*) **the B—** (*persons*) el cuerpo de abogados, (*profession*) la abogacía; **parallel —s** paralelas *fpl*; **prisoner at the —** acusado *m*, a *f*; **to be called to the B—** recibirse de abogado; **to be behind —s** estar en la cárcel; **to put someone behind —s** encarcelar a uno.

2 *vt door* atrancar; *road* obstruir; *progress* impedir; (*ban*) prohibir; (*exclude*) excluir (*from de*); **to —**

someone from doing something prohibir a uno hacer algo; **to be —red from a club** ser excluido de un club.

3 *prep*: **all — 2** todos con excepción de 2; **— none** sin excluir a ninguno, sin excepción.

barb [bɑːb] *n* lengüeta *f*; (*Zool*) púa *f*.

Barbados [bɑː'beidɔs] Barbados *m*.

barbarian [bɑː'bɛəriən] **1** *adj* bárbaro. **2** *n* bárbaro *m*, a *f*.

barbaric [bɑː'bærik] *adj* bárbaro, barbárico; de ruda magnificencia.

barbarism ['bɑːbərizəm] *n* barbarie *f*; (*Gram*) barbarismo *m*.

barbarity [bɑː'bæriti] *n* barbaridad *f*.

barbarous ['bɑːbərəs] *adj* bárbaro.

barbarously ['bɑːbərəsli] *adv* bárbaramente.

Barbary ['bɑːbəri] Berbería *f*.

barbecue ['bɑːbikjuː] *n* barbacoa *f*.

barbed [bɑːbd] *adj arrow etc* armado de lengüetas; *criticism* incisivo, mordaz.

barbed wire ['bɑːbd'waiə*] *n* alambre *m* de espino, (*Mil*) alambre *m* de púas; **barbed-wire entanglement** alambrada *f*.

barbel ['bɑːbəl] *n* (*Anat*) barbilla *f*, cococha *f*; (*Fish*) barbo *m*.

barber ['bɑːbə*] *n* peluquero *m*, barbero *m*; **—'s** (*shop*) peluquería *f*.

barbican ['bɑːbikən] *n* barbacana *f*.

barbiturate [bɑː'bitjurit] *n* barbiturato *m*.

barcarol(l)e [,bɑːkə'rəul] *n* barcarola *f*.

bard [bɑːd] *n* bardo *m*; **the B— of Avon** el Cisne del Avon.

bare [bɛə*] **1** *adj* desnudo; *head* descubierto; *landscape* pelado; *ground* raso; *room* (*casi*) desprovisto de muebles; *style* escueto, desnudo; **with one's — hands** con las manos desnudas; **— of** desprovisto de; **the trees are —** los árboles están sin hojas; **the pantry is —** la despensa está vacía; **to earn a — living** ganar lo justo para vivir; **by a — majority** por una mayoría escasa; **the — thought frightens me** me horroriza sólo pensar en ello; **to lay —** poner al descubierto, poner al desnudo.

2 *vt* desnudar; descubrir; **to — one's head** descubrirse.

bareback ['bɛəbæk] *adv* en pelo, sin montura.

barefaced ['bɛəfeist] *adj* descarado, fresco; **a — lie** una mentira descarada.

barefoot(ed) ['bɛə'fut(id)] *adj* descalzo, con los pies desnudos.

bareheaded ['bɛə'hedid] *adj* con la cabeza descubierta, sin sombrero.

barelegged ['bɛə'legid] *adj* en pernetas.

barely ['bɛəli] *adv* apenas.

bareness ['bɛənis] *n* desnudez *f*.

bargain ['bɑːgin] **1** *n* (*agreement*) pacto *m*; (*business deal*) negocio *m*, contrato *m*; (*cheap thing*) ganga *f*; (*advantageous deal*) negocio *m* ventajoso; **— counter** baratillo *m*; **— price** precio *m* de ganga; **— sale** saldo *m*; **into the —** por añadidura, además; **it's a real —** es una verdadera ganga; **to drive a good —** hacer un buen trato; **you drive a hard —** Vd es un hombre terrible para sacar la última peseta; **to get the better of the —** salir ganando del negocio; **to make** (*or strike*) **a —** cerrar un trato; **I'll make a — with you** hagamos un pacto.

2 *vt*: **to — away** regatear.

3 *vi* negociar (*about sobre, for* para obtener, *with* con); (*haggle*) regatear; **I wasn't —ing for that** yo no contaba con eso; **he got more than he —ed for** le resultó peor de lo que esperaba.

bargaining ['bɑːginiŋ] *n* negociación *f*; (*haggling*) regateo *m*; **collective —** trato *m* colectivo.

barge [bɑːdʒ] **1** *n* barcaza *f*; (*towed*) lancha *f* a remolque, gabarra *f*; (*ceremonial*) falúa *f*.

2 *vt* (*fam*) empujar; (*Sport*) atajar.

3 *vi* (*fam*): **to — about** moverse pesadamente, dar tumbos; **to — in** entrar sin pedir permiso, irrumpir; (*fig*) entrometerse; **to — into** chocar contra, dar contra.

bargee [bɑː'dʒiː] *n* gabarrero *m*.

barge pole ['bɑːdʒpəul] *n*: **I wouldn't touch it with a —** no lo quiero ver ni de lejos.

baritone ['bæritəun] *n* barítono *m*.

barium ['bɛəriəm] *n* bario *m*.

bark[1] [bɑːk] (*Bot*) **1** *n* corteza *f*; **Peruvian —** quina *f*.

2 *vt tree* descortezar; *skin* raer, raspar.

bark[2] [bɑːk] **1** *n* ladrido *m*; (*fam*) tos *f*; **his — is worse than his bite** perro que ladra no muerde.

2 *vt*: **to — (out)** *order* escupir, dar en un tono muy brusco.

3 *vi* ladrar (*at a*).

barker ['bɑːkə*] *n* pregonero *m*.

barley ['bɑːli] n cebada f.
barley field ['bɑːlifiːld] n cebadal m.
barley sugar ['bɑːliˌʃugə*] n azúcar m cande.
barley water ['bɑːliˌwɔːtə*] n hordiate m.
barmaid ['bɑːmeid] n camarera f.
barman ['bɑːmən] n, pl —men [mən] barman m.
barmy ['bɑːmi] adj (sl) lelo, gili.
barn [bɑːn] n granero m, troje f; (US) establo m, cuadra f.
barnacle ['bɑːnəkl] n percebe m.
barndoor ['bɑːnˈdɔː*] n puerta f de granero; — fowls aves fpl de corral.
barnstorm ['bɑːnstɔːm] vi (US) hacer una campaña electoral por el campo.
barnyard ['bɑːnjɑːd] n corral m; — fowls aves fpl de corral.
barometer [bəˈrɔmitə*] n barómetro m.
barometric [ˌbærəuˈmetrik] adj barométrico.
baron ['bærən] n barón m; (fig) magnate m, potentado m.
baroness ['bærənis] n baronesa f.
baronet ['bærənit] n baronet m.
baronial [bəˈrəuniəl] adj baronial.
baroque [bəˈrɔk] 1 adj barroco; (fig) complicado; grotesco. 2 n barroco m.
barque [bɑːk] n (Hist, poet) barca f.
barrack ['bærək] vt befar, mofarse de; lanzar improperios a; aplaudir irónicamente.
barracking ['bærəkiŋ] n befas fpl; improperios mpl; aplausos mpl irónicos.
barrack-room ['bærəkˌrum] adj cuartelero; — ballad canción f cuartelera.
barracks ['bærəks] npl (a) cuartel m; to be confined to — estar bajo arresto en el cuartel.
(b) (house) caserón m; a great — of a place una casa enorme de grande.
barrack square ['bærəkˈskweə*] n plaza f de armas.
barrage ['bærɑːʒ] n presa f; (Mil) cortina f de fuego; (of balloons etc) barrera f; creeping — cortina f de fuego móvil; a — of noise un estrépito; a — of questions una descarga cerrada de preguntas; there was a — of protests estallaron ruidosamente las protestas.
barrage balloon ['bærɑːʒbəˌluːn] n globo m de barrera.
barrel ['bærəl] n tonel m, barril m; (of gun, pen) cañón m; (Tech) cilindro m, tambor m; to scrape the bottom of the — rebañar las últimas migas.
barrel organ ['bærəlˌɔːgən] n organillo m.
barren ['bærən] adj estéril, árido; woman estéril; — of falto de, desprovisto de.
barrenness ['bærənnis] n esterilidad f, aridez f.
barricade [ˌbæriˈkeid] 1 n barricada f. 2 vt barrear, cerrar con barricadas. 3 vr: to — oneself in a house hacerse fuerte en una casa.
barrier ['bæriə*] n barrera f (also fig: to para).
barring ['bɑːriŋ] prep excepto, salvo; we shall be there, — accidents iremos, si Dios quiere.
barrister ['bæristə*] n abogado m (que tiene derecho a alegar en los tribunales superiores).
barrow[1] ['bærəu] n (Hist) túmulo m.
barrow[2] ['bærəu] n carretilla f, carretón m de mano.
barrow-boy ['bærəubɔi] n carretonero m (que vende frutas etc en la calle).
bartender ['bɑːtendə*] n barman m.
barter ['bɑːtə*] 1 n permuta f, trueque m. 2 vt permutar, trocar (for por, con); to — away malvender.
Bartholomew [bɑːˈθɔləmjuː] m Bartolomé.
basalt ['bæsɔːlt] n basalto m.
base[1] [beis] 1 n base f; (Archit) basa f; naval — base f naval.
2 vt basar, fundar (on en); to be —d on (fig) estar basado en, fundarse en; (Mil) we were —d on Malta tuvimos nuestra base en Malta.
3 vr: I — myself on the following facts yo me fundo en los hechos siguientes.
base[2] [beis] adj bajo, infame, vil; metal bajo de ley.
baseball ['beisbɔːl] n béisbol m.
Basel ['bɑːzəl] Basilea.
baseless ['beislis] adj infundado.
base line ['beislain] n (Surveying) línea f de base; (Tennis) línea f de saque.
basement ['beismənt] n sótano m.
baseness ['beisnis] n bajeza f, vileza f.
bash [bæʃ] (fam) 1 n golpe m; to have a — at probar, intentar, echar un tiento a. 2 vt golpear; person aporrear, vapulear.
bashful ['bæʃful] adj tímido, vergonzoso.
bashfully ['bæʃfuli] adv timidamente.
bashfulness ['bæʃfulnis] n timidez f, vergüenza f.
bashing ['bæʃiŋ] n (fam) tunda f, vapuleo m.

basic ['beisik] adj básico (also Chem), fundamental.
basically ['beisikli] adv fundamentalmente, en el fondo, esencialmente.
basil ['bæzl] n albahaca f.
basilica [bəˈzilikə] n basílica f.
basilisk ['bæzilisk] n basilisco m.
basin ['beisn] n (in kitchen) escudilla f, tazón m, cuenco m; (washbasin) jofaina f, palangana f; (large fixed washbasin) lavabo m; (of fountain) taza f; (Geog) cuenca f; (of port) dársena f.
basis ['beisis] n, pl bases ['beisiːz] base f; on the — of a base de; partiendo de una base de.
bask [bɑːsk] vi tostarse; to — in the sun tomar el sol.
basket ['bɑːskit] n cesta f; (big) cesto m; (two-handled) canasta f; (hamper) excusabaraja f.
basketball ['bɑːskitbɔːl] n baloncesto m.
basketwork ['bɑːskitwəːk] n cestería f.
basking shark ['bɑːskiŋˈʃɑːk] n cetorrino m.
Basle [bɑːl] Basilea.
Basque [bæsk] 1 adj vasco. 2 n vasco m, a f. 3 n (language) vasco m, vascuence m, éuscaro m.
Basque Country ['bæskˈkʌntri] País m Vasco.
Basque Provinces ['bæskˈprɔvinsiz] pl las Vascongadas.
bas-relief ['bæsriˌliːf] n bajorrelieve m.
bass[1] [beis] (Mus) 1 adj bajo. 2 n (voice, note) bajo m; (instrument) contrabajo m.
bass[2] [bæs] n (Fish) róbalo m.
basset ['bæsit] n perro m basset.
bassoon [bəˈsuːn] n bajón m.
basso profundo [ˌbæsəuprəˈfundəu] n bajo m profundo.
bastard ['bɑːstəd] 1 adj bastardo. 2 n bastardo m, a f.
bastardy ['bɑːstədi] n bastardía f.
baste [beist] vt (Cook) pringar.
bastion ['bæstiən] n baluarte m (also fig).
Basutoland [bəˈsuːtəulænd] Basutolandia f.
bat[1] [bæt] n (Zool) murciélago m; to be —s, to have —s in the belfry estar chiflado.
bat[2] [bæt] 1 n (eg cricket —) maza f, palo m; (Baseball) bate m; (fam) golpe m; off one's own — sin ayuda de nadie; right off the — de repente, sin deliberación.
2 vt (fam) golpear.
3 vi (Baseball) batear.
bat[3] [bæt] vt: without —ting an eyelid sin pestañear.
batch [bætʃ] n colección f, serie f, grupo m, cantidad f, lote m, montoncito m; (of papers) lío m; (Cook) hornada f.
bated ['beitid] adj: with — breath sin respiración.
bath [bɑːθ] 1 n, pl baths [bɑːðz] baño m, bañera f; (swimming pool) piscina f; Turkish — baño m turco; to have (or take) a — tomar un baño.
2 vt bañar, dar un baño a.
3 vi tomar un baño.
bathchair ['bɑːθtʃeə*] n silla f de ruedas.
bathe [beið] 1 n baño m (en el mar etc); to go for a —, to have a —, to go bathing ir a bañarse.
2 vt bañar; —d in tears bañado en lágrimas.
3 vi bañarse.
bather ['beiðə*] n bañista mf.
bathing ['beiðiŋ] n baño m (de mar etc), el bañarse; no — prohibido bañarse.
bathing beauty ['beiðiŋ,bjuːti] n sirena f de la playa.
bathing cap ['beiðiŋ,kæp] n gorro m de baño.
bathing costume ['beiðiŋ,kɔstjuːm] n traje m de baño.
bathing hut ['beiðiŋ,hʌt] n caseta f.
bathing suit ['beiðiŋ,suːt] n traje m de baño.
bathing trunks ['beiðiŋ,trʌŋks] n taparrabo m, calzón m.
bathing wrap ['beiðiŋ,ræp] n albornoz m.
bathmat ['bɑːθmæt] n estera f de baño.
bathos ['beiθɔs] n paso m de lo sublime a lo trivial.
bathrobe ['bɑːθrəub] n albornoz m.
bathroom ['bɑːθrum] n cuarto m de baño; — fittings aparatos mpl sanitarios; — scales peso m de baño.
bath salts ['bɑːθsɔlts] npl sales fpl de baño.
bath towel ['bɑːθtauəl] n toalla f de baño.
bathtub ['bɑːθtʌb] n bañadera f.
bathwater ['bɑːθwɔːtə*] n agua f de baño.
bathysphere ['bæθisfiə*] n batisfera f.
batiste [bæˈtiːst] n batista f.
batman ['bætmən] n, pl —men [mən] ordenanza m.
baton ['bætən] n (Mil) bastón m; (Mus) batuta f; (in race) testigo m.
batrachian [bəˈtreikiən] n batracio m.
battalion [bəˈtæliən] n batallón m.
batten ['bætn] 1 n alfarjía f, lata f, listón m. 2 vt: to — down the hatches asegurar las escotillas con listones.

batten² ['bætn] *vi*: to — on vivir (*etc*) a costa de, cebarse en.

batter ['bætə*] 1 *n* batido *m* (para rebozar).

2 *vt person* apalear; (*of boxer*) magullar; (*of the elements*) embravecerse contra; (*Mil*) cañonear, bombardear; (*verbally etc*) criticar ásperamente, poner como un trapo; to — down, to — in derribar a palos.

3 *vi*: to — at, to — away at dar grandes golpes en.

battered ['bætəd] *adj* (*bruised*) magullado; (*damaged*) estropeado; maltrecho, malparado; *hat etc* ajado.

battering ['bætəriŋ] *n* (*blows*) paliza *f*; (*Mil*) bombardeo *m*; the — of the waves el golpear de las olas; he got a — from the critics los críticos le pusieron como un trapo.

battering ram ['bætəriŋræm] *n* ariete *m*.

battery ['bætəri] *n* (*Mil, for hens, of lights*) batería *f*; (*Elec*) pila *f*, batería *f*, acumulador *m*; (*Law*) violencia *f*; (*of questions*) serie *f*; **dry** — pila *f* seca.

battery charger ['bætəri,tʃɑːdʒə*] *n* cargador *m* de baterías.

battle ['bætl] 1 *n* (a) batalla *f*; **pitched** — batalla *f* campal; **in** — order en orden de batalla; **to do** — librar batalla (*with* con); **to do** — for luchar por; **to fight a** — luchar; **the** — was fought in 1346 se libró la batalla en 1346; **to join** — trabar batalla.

(**b**) (*fig*) lucha *f* (*for control of* por el control de, *to control* por controlar); — royal pelotera *f*; — of wits duelo *m* de inteligencias; **confidence is half the** — tener confianza es vencer una buena parte de las dificultades; **to fight a losing** — ir perdiendo poco a poco, ir de vencida.

2 *vi* luchar (*against* contra, *for* por, *to do* por hacer); the two armies —d all day los dos ejércitos se batieron todo el día; **to** — against the wind luchar contra el viento.

battle-axe ['bætlæks] *n* hacha *f* de combate; **old** — (*fam*) arpía *f*.

battle cruiser ['bætl,kruːzə*] *n* crucero *m* de batalla.

battle cry ['bætlkrai] *n* grito *m* de combate.

battle dress ['bætldres] *n* traje *m* de campaña.

battlefield ['bætlfiːld] *n*, **battleground** ['bætlgraund] *n* campo *m* de batalla.

battlements ['bætlmənts] *npl* almenas *fpl*.

battleship ['bætlʃip] *n* acorazado *m*.

batty ['bæti] *adj* (*fam*) lelo.

bauble ['bɔːbl] *n* chuchería *f*.

baulk [bɔːlk] *see* **balk**.

bauxite ['bɔːksait] *n* bauxita *f*.

Bavaria [bə'veəriə] Baviera *f*.

Bavarian [bə'veəriən] 1 *adj* bávaro. 2 *n* bávaro *m*, a *f*.

bawd [bɔːd] *n* alcahueta *f*.

bawdy ['bɔːdi] *adj* obsceno, indecente; *joke, song* verde.

bawdyhouse ['bɔːdihaus] *n*, *pl* —houses [hauziz] lupanar *m*.

bawl [bɔːl] 1 *vt*: to — out *song etc* cantar (*etc*) en voz muy fuerte; to — someone out echarle un rapapolvo a uno.

2 *vi* gritar, vocear, desgañitarse; hablar (*or* cantar *etc*) muy fuerte; to — at reñir en voz alta.

bay¹ [bei] *n* (*Bot*) laurel *m*.

bay² [bei] *n* (*Geog*) bahía *f*; (*small*) abra *f*; (*very large*) golfo *m*; **B**— of Biscay Golfo *m* de Vizcaya.

bay³ [bei] *n* (*Archit*) intercolumnio *m*; crujía *f*; (*Rail*) nave *f*; (*of window*) parte *f* saldiza.

bay⁴ [bei] 1 *n* (*bark*) ladrido *m*, aullido *m*; at — acorralado; **to bring to** — acorralar; **to keep at** — mantener a raya. 2 *vi* ladrar, aullar.

bay⁵ [bei] 1 *adj horse* bayo. 2 *n* caballo *m* bayo.

bay leaf ['beiliːf] *n* hoja *f* de laurel.

bayonet ['beiənit] 1 *n* bayoneta *f*; **with fixed** —s con las bayonetas caladas. 2 *vt* herir (*or* matar) con la bayoneta.

bayonet charge ['beiənit,tʃɑːdʒ] *n* carga *f* a la bayoneta.

Bayonne [bai'jɔn] Bayona.

bay rum ['bei'rʌm] *n* ron *m* de laurel, ron *m* de malagueta.

bay window ['bei'windəu] *n* ventana *f* saldiza.

bazaar [bə'zɑː*] *n* bazar *m*.

bazooka [bə'zuːkə] *n* bazuca *f*.

be [biː] (*irr*: *pres* **am, is,** are; *pret* **was, were;** *ptp* **been**) 1 (*absolute*) to — or not to — ser o no ser; as things are tal como están las cosas; you're busy enough as it is estás bastante ocupado ya; some are and some aren't algunos lo son y otros no; let it —! ¡déjalo!; let me —! ¡déjame en paz!

2 (*with noun, pronoun, numeral or verb complement* [*but see also* 7, 8, 9, 10 *below*]) ser; **I am a man** soy hombre; **he's a pianist** es pianista; **he was a com-** munist era comunista; **he will be pope** será papa; **I was a bullfighter for 2 days** durante 2 días fui torero; **it's a fact** es un hecho; **it is I, it's me** soy yo; **it's 8 o'clock** son las 8; **it's the 3rd of May** es el 3 de mayo; **seeing is believing** ver es creer.

3 (*with adj complement*) (a) (*when a permanent or essential quality is expressed*) ser; **I'm English** soy inglés; **she's tall** es alta; **it was very bad** fue malísimo; **I used to be poor but now I'm rich** antes era pobre pero ahora soy rico; **when I was young** cuando era joven; **when I'm old** cuando sea viejo.

(**b**) (*when a temporary or reversible state is indicated, also fig*) estar; **it's dirty** está sucio; **he's ill** está enfermo; **they're tired** están cansados; **the glass is empty** el vaso está vacío; **the pond is always full** el estanque siempre está lleno; **the symphony is full of tunes** la sinfonía está llena de melodías.

(**c**) (*of persons*, ser + *adj indicates a permanent quality of character*, estar + *adj indicates a more temporary mood or state*): **he's a cheerful sort** es alegre, **he's very cheerful** (*about something*) está alegre; **he's always very smart** siempre es muy elegante, **you're very smart** (*today, for once*) ¡qué guapo estás!; **they're very happy together** son muy felices, **are you happy in your work?** ¿estás contento con tu trabajo?

(**d**) (to be + *adj, impersonal*) ser: **it is possible that . . . es** posible que . . .; **is it certain that . . .?** ¿es cierto que . . .?

4 (*expressions of authorship, origin, possession, construction*) ser: **it's a Picasso** es de Picasso; **I'm from the south** soy del Sur; **it's mine** es mío; **it's of gold, it's a gold one** es de oro.

5 (*place, geographical location, temporary circumstances*) estar: **he's here** está aquí; **it's on the table** está en la mesa; **Burgos is in Spain** Burgos está en España; **the issue was in doubt** el resultado estaba en duda; **I'm in a jam** estoy en un aprieto; **to — on a journey** estar de viaje; **to — in a hurry** estar de prisa; **to — in mourning** estar de luto.

6 (*health*) **how are you?** ¿cómo estás?; **how are you now?** ¿qué tal te encuentras ahora?; **I'm very well, thanks** estoy muy bien, gracias.

7 (*age*) **I'm 8** tengo 8 años; **how old are you?** ¿cuántos años tienes?

8 (*weather, temperatures, certain adjs*) **it is hot** (*weather*) hace calor; **I'm hot** tengo calor; **the water is hot** el agua está caliente; **it's sunny** hay sol; **it's foggy** hay niebla; **it's windy** hace viento; **to — hungry** tener hambre; **to — afraid** tener miedo.

9 (*certain expressions of time*) **we've been here a year** hace un año que estamos aquí, llevamos un año aquí; **it's a long time since I saw him** hace mucho tiempo que no le veo.

10 **there is, there are** hay; **there was, there were** había, hubo; **there may not** — any puede no haber ninguno.

11 (*idioms*) **so** — it así sea; — **that as it may** sea como fuere; **what is it to you?** ¿a ti qué te importa?; **mother to** — futura madre *f*; **my wife to** — mi futura esposa; **what's it to** —? (*in bar etc*) ¿qué vas a tomar?

12 *v aux* (a) (*conditional sentences*) **if I were to say so** si dijera eso; **if I were you** yo en tu lugar, yo que tú.

(**b**) (*obligation*) **I am to do it** he de hacerlo; **he was to have come** había de venir; **what am I to say?** ¿qué he de decir?

(**c**) (*continuous tenses*) to be + *ger* estar + *ger*, eg **I was singing** estaba cantando, **were you waiting for me?** ¿me estabas esperando?; (*but a simple tense is used in such cases as*) **he is coming tomorrow** viene (*or* vendrá) mañana, **what are you doing?** ¿qué haces?, **I shall** — **seeing him** voy a verle, **will you** — **wanting more?** ¿vas a necesitar más?

(**d**) (to be + *ptp, passive*) ser + *ptp*: **the window was opened by the servant** la ventana fue abierta por el criado; **it is being studied** está siendo estudiado; (*but the passive is often replaced by a reflexive or active construction*) **the window was opened by the servant** la ventana la abrió el criado; **it is being studied** se está estudiando; **it is said that** se dice que, dicen que; **he was nowhere to** — **seen** no se le veía en ninguna parte; **what's to** — **done?** ¿qué hay que hacer?; **it is to be regretted that** es de lamentar que; **it is to** — **hoped that** es de esperar que; **it's a film not to** — **missed** es una película que no hay que perder.

(**e**) (to be + *ptp, state*) estar + *ptp*: **the window was open** la ventana estaba abierta; **it's made of wood** está hecho de madera; **the book is bereft of ideas** el libro está desprovisto de ideas.

beach [biːtʃ] **1** n playa f. **2** vt varar.
beachcomber ['biːtʃˌkəumə*] n raquero m.
beachhead ['biːtʃhed] n cabeza f de playa.
beachwear ['biːtʃweə*] n trajes mpl de playa.
beacon ['biːkən] n almenara f; (in port) faro m, fanal m; (on aerodrome) baliza f, aerofaro m; (Radio) radiofaro m; (hill) hacho m.
bead [biːd] n cuenta f; (of glass) abalorio m; (of dew, sweat) gota f; (of gun) mira f globular; —s sarta f de cuentas, (Eccl) rosario m; to draw a — on apuntar a; to tell one's —s rezar el rosario.
beading ['biːdiŋ] n (Archit) astrágalo m, contero m.
beadle ['biːdl] n bedel m; (Eccl) pertiguero m.
beady ['biːdi] adj eyes parecidos a dos gotas brillantes.
beagle ['biːgl] n sabueso m.
beak [biːk] n pico m; (nose) nariz f (corva); (Naut) rostro m; (sl) magistrado m; — of land promontorio m.
beaked [biːkt] adj picudo.
beaker ['biːkə*] n taza f alta; (Chem) vaso m de precipitación.
be-all ['biːˈɔːl] n (also — and end-all) único objeto m, única cosa f que importa; he is the — of her life él es lo único que le importa en la vida; money is not the — el dinero no es lo único que vale, hay cosas que valen tanto como el dinero.
beam [biːm] **1** n (a) (Archit) viga f; travesaño m; (of plough) timón m; (of balance) astil m; (Mech) balancín m.
(b) (Naut) (timber) bao m; (width) manga f; broad in the — (fam) ancho de caderas, nalgudo; on her — ends a punto de volcar; on one's — ends (fam) sin un cuarto; on the port — a babor.
(c) (of light) rayo m; (from beacon, lamp) haz m de luz; (from radio beacon) haz m de radiofaro; (smile) sonrisa f, mirada f agradecida; with a — of pleasure con una sonrisa de placer; to be on the — (fam) seguir el buen camino; to be off the — (fam) estar despistado, estar equivocado.
2 vt light, signal emitir; she —ed her thanks me lanzó una mirada agradecida.
3 vi (shine) brillar; (smile) sonreírse alegremente (at a).
beam-ends ['biːm'endz] npl (Naut) cabezas fpl de los baos (de un buque); she was on her — (Naut) el buque escoraba peligrosamente; they are on their — (fig) están en un grave aprieto, no tienen donde caerse muertos.
beaming ['biːmiŋ] adj sonriente, radiante.
bean [biːn] n (a) (plant) runner — judía f, habichuela f; scarlet runner — judía f escarlata; dwarf —, French —, kidney — judía f enana f, fríjol m; broad — haba f gruesa.
(b) (served as food) —s judías fpl; (broad, haricot) habas fpl; (of coffee) granos mpl.
(c) I haven't a — (fam) no tengo un céntimo; to be full of —s (fam) rebosar de vitalidad; to spill the —s (sl) tirar de la manta.
beanfeast ['biːnfiːst] n, **beano** ['biːnəu] n (fam) fiesta f, juerga f; (meal) comilona f.
bear[1] [beə*] n oso m; (Comm) bajista m; — market mercado m bajista; Great B— (Astron) Osa f Mayor; Little B— Osa f Menor.
bear[2] [beə*] (irr: pret bore, ptp borne) **1** vt (a) (carry) llevar; arms, date, inscription etc llevar; character, name, relation, responsibility tener; weight sostener; fruit dar, producir; interest devengar; child parir, tener; cost pagar, correr con; love etc sentir, tener (for para); grudge, ill will guardar, tener (against a); it is borne in upon me that ya voy comprendiendo que.
(b) (stand up to) inspection etc sufrir, resistir a; it doesn't — close examination no resiste a la inspección de cerca; it doesn't — thinking about da horror sólo pensar en ello; the film will — a second viewing la película vale la pena de verse por segunda vez.
(c) (endure) soportar, aguantar, resistir; I can't — delays yo no aguanto los retrasos; I can't — him no le puedo ver; I can't — spiders odio las arañas; I can't — to look! ¡no puedo mirar!; can you — me to look at it? ¿quieres dejarme verlo?; I could — it no longer ya no resistía más.
(d) to — away, to — off llevarse; to — out llevar; (confirm) confirmar, corroborar.
2 vi (a) a tree that —s well un árbol que rinde bien; the ship —s north el barco lleva dirección norte; to — left torcer a la izquierda.
(b) to — down on (ship etc) correr sobre, (person) avanzar hacia, acercarse majestuosamente (or de manera amenazadora etc) a; to — on person interesar, subject tener que ver con, referirse a;

it —s hard on the old esto pesa bastante sobre los viejos; to — up animarse; — up! ¡ánimo!; to — with tener paciencia con, ser indulgente con.
(c) to bring a gun to — on apuntar a; to bring pressure to — on ejercer presión sobre.
3 vr: to — oneself comportarse, portarse.
bearable ['beərəbl] adj soportable, llevadero.
beard [biəd] **1** n barba f; (Bot) arista f; to have (or wear) a — llevar barba. **2** vt desafiar.
bearded ['biədid] adj barbado, (pej) barbudo.
beardless ['biədlis] adj lampiño; youth imberbe.
bearer ['beərə*] n (servant) mozo m; (Comm) portador m, ora f; (of office) poseedor m, ora f.
bear garden ['beəˌgɑːdn] n guirigay m.
bearing ['beəriŋ] n (a) (of person) porte m, comportamiento m; soldierly — porte m militar.
(b) (relationship) relación f (on con); this has no — on the matter esto no tiene que ver con el asunto.
(c) (Mech) cojinete m.
(d) (Naut) marcación f; to get one's —s orientarse; to lose one's —s desorientarse; to take a — marcarse; to take one's —s orientarse.
(e) (Her) blasón m.
(f) beyond all — que ya no se puede sufrir más.
bearskin ['beəskin] n piel f de oso; (Mil) morrión m.
beast [biːst] n bestia f; (fig: person) bruto m, salvaje m; (thing) cosa f muy difícil; — of burden bestia f de carga; wild — fiera f; the king of —s el rey de los animales; you —! ¡animal!; that — of a policeman aquel bruto de policía; what a — he is! ¡qué bruto!; it's a — esto es horrible; it's a — of a day es un día horrible.
beastliness ['biːstlinis] n bestialidad f.
beastly ['biːstli] **1** adj bestial; (fam) detestable, horrible; condenado, maldito; that was a — thing to do aquello sí que fue cruel; you were — to me fuiste cruel conmigo; where's that — book? ¿dónde está el maldito libro ese?
2 adv (fam): it's — awkward es terriblemente difícil.
beat [biːt] **1** n (blow) golpe m; (of drum) redoble m; (of heart) latido m; (Mus) compás m, ritmo m; (of policeman) ronda f; it's off my — está fuera de mi competencia; I like music with a — me gusta la música de ritmo fuerte.
2 (irr: pret beat, ptp beaten) vt (a) (strike) golpear; table, door dar golpes en; metal etc batir, martillar; person pegar, (as punishment) dar una paliza a; carpet sacudir, (Cook) batir; drum tocar; time (Mus) marcar, llevar; path abrir; he — him on the head le dio un golpe en la cabeza; he — him about the head le dio una serie de golpes por la cabeza; to — someone to death apalear a uno hasta dejarlo muerto; the bird — its wings el pájaro batió las alas; to — it (fam) poner pies en polvorosa; — it! ¡lárgate!
(b) (Hunting) ojear.
(c) (defeat) vencer, derrotar; record batir, superar, mejorar; to — someone to it ganar por la mano a uno, llegar antes que uno.
(d) (be better than) sobrepasar; that —s everything! ¡eso es el colmo!
(e) (mystify) confundir; the police confess themselves —en la policía confiesa no tener pista alguna; the problem has me —en el problema me deja totalmente perplejo.
(f) to — back rechazar; to — down abatir, derribar a golpes; corn acamar; resistance, opponent vencer; price conseguir rebajar (regateando), seller persuadir a que venda a precio más bajo; to — off rechazar; to — out metal martillar, formar a martillazos; tune tocar (con fuerte ritmo); to — up (Cook) batir, person aporrear, vapulear.
3 vi (heart) latir, pulsar; the rain was —ing down caía la lluvia con violencia; the drums were —ing redoblaban los tambores; to — on a door dar golpes en una puerta; the waves — on the shore las olas azotaban la playa; to — about (Naut) barloventear.
4 ptp (fam) = beaten.
beaten ['biːtn] **1** ptp of beat. **2** adj (a) metal etc batido, martillado; track trillado. (b) team etc derrotado, vencido.
beater ['biːtə*] n (Hunting) ojeador m, batidor m.
beatific [ˌbiːə'tifik] adj beatífico; with a — smile con una sonrisa de puro contento.
beatification [biːˌætifi'keiʃən] n beatificación f.
beatify [biːˈætifai] vt beatificar.
beating ['biːtiŋ] n (a) (blows) golpes mpl, golpeo m; (of waves) el batir, el azotar; (of heart) latido m,

pulsación *f*; (*punishment*) paliza *f*; **to get a —** recibir una paliza.
(b) (*Hunting*) ojeo *m*, batida *f*.
(c) (*defeat*) derrota *f*; **to take a —** salir derrotado, ser cascado (*from por, at the hands of* a manos de).
beatitude [bi'ætitjuːd] *n* beatitud *f*; **the B—s** las Bienaventuranzas.
beatnik ['biːtnik] *n* beatnik *m*.
Beatrice ['biətris] *f* Beatriz.
beau [bəu] **1** *adj:* **— ideal** lo bello ideal. **2** *n* (*fop*) petimetre *m*, dandy *m*; (*ladies' man*) galán *m*; (*suitor*) pretendiente *m*; (*sweetheart*) novio *m*.
beauteous ['bjuːtiəs] *adj* (*poet*) bello.
beautician [bjuː'tiʃən] *n* especialista *mf* en belleza, maquillador *m*, ora *f*.
beautiful ['bjuːtiful] *adj* hermoso, bello; precioso.
beautifully ['bjuːtifli] *adv* maravillosamente.
beautify ['bjuːtifai] *vt* embellecer.
beauty ['bjuːti] *n* **(a)** (*in general*) belleza *f*, hermosura *f*; (*concrete*) belleza *f*, eg **the beauties of Majorca** las bellezas de Mallorca.
(b) (*fig*) **the — of it** is that lo bueno es que.
(c) **B— and the Beast** la Bella y la Bestia.
(d) (*person*) belleza *f*, beldad *f*; (*thing, specimen*) ejemplar *m* hermoso; **it's a —** es maravilloso; **that was a —!** (*stroke etc*) ¡qué golpe más fino!; **isn't he a little —?** (*child*) ¡mira qué rico está el niño!
beauty contest ['bjuːti,kɔntest] *n* concurso *m* de belleza.
beauty cream ['bjuːtikriːm] *n* crema *f* de belleza.
beauty parlour ['bjuːti,pɑːlə*] *n* salón *m* de belleza.
beauty queen ['bjuːtikwiːn] *n* reina *f* de la belleza.
beauty sleep ['bjuːtisliːp] *n* primer sueño *m*; **to lose one's —** (*hum*) perder el tiempo en que uno debiera estar dormido.
beauty spot ['bjuːtispɔt] *n* (*on face*) lunar *m* postizo; (*in country*) sitio *m* pintoresco, lugar *m* de excepcional belleza natural.
beaver ['biːvə*] *n* castor *m*.
becalm [bi'kɑːm] *vt:* **to be —ed** estar encalmado.
became [bi'keim] *pret of* **become**.
because [bi'kɔz] **1** *conj* porque; **— he has two cars he thinks he's somebody** como tiene dos coches se cree un personaje.
2 *prep:* **— of** a causa de, debido a, por motivo de.
beck[1] [bek] *n:* **to be at the — and call of** estar a disposición de, estar sometido a la voluntad de.
beck[2] [bek] *n* (*prov*) arroyo *m*, riachuelo m.
beckon ['bekən] **1** *vt* llamar con señas; (*fig*) llamar, atraer. **2** *vi:* **to —** to hacer señas a.
become [bi'kʌm] (*irr: see* **come**) **1** *vt* (*of clothes etc*) sentar a, favorecer; (*action etc*) convenir a; **that thought does not — you** ese pensamiento es indigno de ti.
2 *vi* **(a)** (*absolute*) **what has become of him?** ¿qué es de él?; **what will — of me?** ¿qué será de mí?; **what can have become of that book?** ¿adónde diablos se habrá metido aquel libro?
(b) (*followed by n: entering profession etc*) hacerse, (*by promotion etc*) llegar a ser, (*of material things*) transformarse en, convertirse en; **to — a soldier** hacerse soldado; **to — professor** llegar a ser catedrático; **he became king in 1911** subió al trono en 1911; **to — a father** ser padre; **the gas —s liquid** el gas se convierte en líquido; **the building has become a cinema** el edificio se ha transformado en cine.
(c) (*followed by adj*) ponerse, volverse, (*by effort*) hacerse; **this is becoming difficult** esto se está poniendo difícil; **to — rich** hacerse rico; **to — mad** volverse loco; (*freq* **to become** + *adj is translated by a reflexive verb*) **to — red** ponerse rojo, enrojecerse; **to — ill** ponerse enfermo, enfermar; **to — angry** enfadarse; **he became quite blind** quedó totalmente ciego; **to — accustomed to** acostumbrarse a; **it became known that** se supo que, llegó a saberse que; **we became very worried** empezamos a inquietarnos muchísimo.
(d) (*of age*) **when he —s 21** cuando llegue a tener 21 años, cuando cumpla los 21 años.
becoming [bi'kʌmiŋ] *adj clothes* favorecedor, que sienta bien, que le va bien a uno; *action* decoroso, conveniente.
bed [bed] **1** *n* cama *f*, (*of animal*) lecho *m*; (*of river*) cauce *m*, lecho *m*; (*of flowers*) arriate *m*, cuadro *m*, macizo *m*; (*Geol*) capa *f*, estrato *m*, yacimiento *m*; (*Archit etc*) base *f*; **— and board** comida *f* y casa; **single —** cama *f* individual; **double —** cama *f* de matrimonio; **— of roses** caminito *m* de rosas; **to be brought to —** of dar a luz, parir; **to get out of — on the wrong side** levantarse por los pies de la cama; **to get into —** meterse en la cama; **to go to —**

acostarse (*with* con); **to give someone a — for the night** hospedar a uno una noche; **to make the —** hacer la cama; **you've made your —** and you must lie on it quien mala cama hace en ella se yace; **to put a child to —** acostar a un niño; **to put a paper to —** terminar la redacción de un número; **to stay in —** (*ill*) guardar cama, (*lazy*) seguir en la cama; **to take to one's —** encamarse.
2 *vt* (*Archit etc*) fijar, engastar (*also* **to — down**); **to — down** (*for the night*) hacer un lecho para; **to — out** plantar en un macizo.
bedaub [bi'dɔːb] *vt* embadurnar.
bedbug ['bedbʌg] *n* chinche gen *f*.
bedclothes ['bedkləuðz] *npl* ropa *f* de cama.
bedcover ['bedkʌvə*] *n* colcha *f*, cubierta *f* de cama; **—s** ropa *f* de cama.
bedding ['bediŋ] *n* ropa *f* de cama; (*for animal*) lecho *m*.
Bede [biːd] *m* Beda; **the Venerable —** el venerable Beda.
bedeck [bi'dek] *vt* adornar, engalanar.
bedevil [bi'devəl] *vt* endiablar; **the problem is —led by several factors** hay diversos factores que complican el problema; **the team has been —led by injuries** el equipo ha sufrido mucho de lesiones.
bedfellow ['bedfeləu] *n* compañero *m*, a *f* de cama.
bedhead ['bedhed] *n* testero *m*, cabecera *f*.
bed jacket ['bedʒækit] *n* mañanita *f*.
bedlam ['bedləm] *n:* **it was sheer —** la confusión era total; **— broke out** estallaron ruidosamente los gritos.
bed linen ['bedlinin] *n* ropa *f* de cama, sábanas *fpl*.
Bedouin ['beduin] **1** *adj* beduino. **2** *n* beduino *m*, a *f*.
bedpan ['bedpæn] *n* bacinilla *f* de cama.
bedraggled [bi'drægld] *adj* ensuciado, mojado.
bedridden ['bedridn] *adj* postrado en cama.
bedrock ['bedrɔk] *n* lecho *m* de roca, roca *f* sólida; **to get down to —** ir a lo fundamental.
bedroom ['bedrum] *n* dormitorio *m*, alcoba *f*.
bedside ['bedsaid] **1** *n:* **to wait at the — of** esperar a la cabecera de.
2 *attr:* **— lamp** lámpara *f* para leer en la cama; **— table** mesita *f* de noche; **to have a good — manner** tener mucho tacto con los enfermos.
bed-sitter ['bed'sitə*] *n*, **bed-sitting room** ['bed-'sitiŋrum] *n* salón *m* con cama.
bedsocks ['bedsɔks] *npl* calcetines *mpl* de cama.
bedsore ['bedsɔː*] *n* úlcera *f* de decúbito.
bedspread ['bedspred] *n* sobrecama *m*, colcha *f*, cobertor *m*.
bedstead ['bedsted] *n* cuja *f*, armazón *m* de cama.
bedstraw ['bedstrɔː] *n* cuajaleche *m*, amor *m* de hortelano.
bedtime ['bedtaim] *n* hora *f* de acostarse.
bedwetting ['bedwetiŋ] *n* enuresis *f*.
bee [biː] *n* abeja *f*; **to have a — in one's bonnet** tener una idea fija.
beech [biːtʃ] *n* haya *f*.
beechmast ['biːtʃmɑːst] *n* hayucos *mpl*.
beechnut ['biːtʃnʌt] *n* hayuco *m*.
beech tree ['biːtʃtriː] *n* haya *f*.
beechwood ['biːtʃwud] *n* hayedo *m*.
beef [biːf] **1** *n* carne *f* de vaca; (*fam*) fuerza *f* muscular, corpulencia *f*; **corned —** carne *f* de vaca acecinada; **roast —** rosbif *m*; **salt —** carne *f* de vaca salada.
2 *vi* (*sl*) quejarse.
beef cattle ['biːf'kætl] *n* ganado *m* vacuno de engorde.
beefeater ['biːf,iːtə*] *n* alabardero *m* de la Torre de Londres.
beefsteak ['biːf'steik] *n* biftec *m*, bistec *m*.
beef tea ['biːf'tiː] *n* caldo *m* concentrado de carne.
beefy ['biːfi] *adj* (*fam*) fornido, corpulento.
beehive ['biːhaiv] *n* colmena *f*.
beekeeper ['biːkiːpə*] *n* apicultor *m*, colmenero *m*.
beeline ['biːlain] *n:* **to make a — for** ir en línea recta hacia, ir derecho a.
Beelzebub [biː'elzibʌb] *m* Belcebú.
been [biːn] *ptp of* **be**.
beer [biə*] *n* cerveza *f*; **bottled —** cerveza *f* de botella; **dark —** cerveza *f* negra; **draught —** cerveza *f* al grifo (*or* de barril); **light —** cerveza *f* clara; **small —** (*fig*) cosa *f* sin importancia, bagatela *f*; **life isn't all — and skittles** la vida no es toda diversiones.
beery ['biəri] *adj smell* a cerveza; *person* muy aficionado a la cerveza; *party* donde se bebe mucha cerveza; **it was a — affair** allí se bebió una barbaridad.
beeswax ['biːzwæks] *n* cera *f* (de abejas).
beet [biːt] *n* remolacha *f*.

beetle ['biːtl] **1** *n* escarabajo *m*. **2** *vi*: **to — off** (*sl*) marcharse.

beetroot ['biːtruːt] *n* (raíz *f* de) remolacha *f*.

beet sugar ['biːt‚ʃugə*] *n* azúcar *m* de remolacha.

befall [bi'fɔːl] (*irr*: *see* **fall**) **1** *vt* acontecer a. **2** *vi* acontecer.

befallen [bi'fɔːlən] *ptp of* **befall**.

befell [bi'fel] *pret of* **befall**.

befit [bi'fit] *vt* convenir a, venir bien a, corresponder a.

befitting [bi'fitiŋ] *adj* conveniente, decoroso.

befog [bi'fɔg] *vt* (*fig*) entenebrecer; *person* ofuscar, confundir.

before [bi'fɔː*] **1** *adv* **(a)** (*place*) delante, adelante; **— and behind** por delante y por detrás.

(b) (*time*) antes; anteriormente; **a moment —** un momento antes; **the day —** el día anterior; **on this occasion and the one —** en esta ocasión y la anterior.

2 *prep* **(a)** (*place*) delante de; (*in the presence of, faced with*) ante, en presencia de; **we still have 2 hours — us** tenemos todavía 2 horas por delante.

(b) (*time*) antes de; *see* **long, now** *etc*.

(c) (*rather than*) **I should choose this one — that** yo escogería éste antes que aquél.

(d) (*with verb*) **— going out** antes de salir.

3 *conj* antes (de) que.

beforehand [bi'fɔːhænd] *adv* de antemano, con anticipación; **to prepare something well —** preparar algo con mucha antelación.

befoul [bi'faul] *vt* ensuciar.

befriend [bi'frend] *vt* ofrecer amistad a; amparar, favorecer.

befuddled [bi'fʌdld] *adj* aturdido; (*drunk*) borracho.

beg [beg] **1** *vt* **(a)** pedir, suplicar, rogar (*from, of* a); **to — someone for something** pedir algo a uno; **he —ged my help** suplicó mi ayuda; **he —ged me to help him** me suplicó que le ayudara; **he —ged the book from me** rogó que le diese el libro; **I — you! ¡**se lo suplico!

(b) (*as beggar*) mendigar; pedir; **he —ged a shilling** pidió un chelín.

2 *vi* **(a)** pedir, rogar; **to — for** pedir, solicitar; **I — to inform you that** tengo el gusto de informarle que.

(b) (*as beggar*) mendigar, pedir por Dios, pedir limosna; **it's going —ging** no se ha presentado nadie que lo quiera aceptar (*or* comprar *etc*).

began [bi'gæn] *pret of* **begin**.

beget [bi'get] (*irr*: *pret* **begot**, (*arch*) **begat**, *ptp* **begotten**) *vt* engendrar (*also fig*).

beggar ['begə*] **1** *n* mendigo, a *f*; (*fam*) tío *m*, sujeto *m*; **lucky —! ¡**qué chorra tiene el tío!; **poor —! ¡**pobre diablo!; **—s can't be choosers** los pobres no escogen.

2 *vt* empobrecer, arruinar, reducir a la miseria; (*fig*) excederse a; **it —s description** es imposible describirlo.

beggarly ['begəli] *adj* indigente, (*fig*) miserable, mezquino.

beggary ['begəri] *n* mendicidad *f*; miseria *f*; **to reduce to —** reducir a la miseria.

begin [bi'gin] (*irr*: *pret* **began**, *ptp* **begun**) **1** *vt* comenzar, empezar; iniciar; (*undertake*) emprender; **the work will be begun tomorrow** mañana se iniciará el trabajo, mañana se dará principio al trabajo; **I was foolish ever to — it** hice mal en emprenderlo.

2 *vi* comenzar, empezar; **to — to +** *infin* comenzar (*or* empezar) a **+** *infin*; **to — talking** empezar a hablar; **it doesn't — to be possible** dista mucho de ser posible; **to — by saying** comenzar diciendo; **to — on** emprender; **to — with something** comenzar por (*or* con) algo; **to — with** (*as phrase*) en primer lugar, para empezar; **—ning from Monday** a partir del lunes.

beginner [bi'ginə*] *n* principiante *mf*.

beginning [bi'giniŋ] *n* **(a)** principio *m*, comienzo *m*; **at the — of** al principio de; **at the — of the century** a principios del siglo; **from the —** desde el principio; **from — to end** desde el principio hasta el final, de cabo a rabo; **in the —** al principio; **the — of the end** el comienzo del fin; **to make a —** empezar.

(b) origen *m*; **from small —s** de orígenes modestos, de antecedentes humildes; **he had the —s of a beard** tenía lo que iba a ser su barba.

begone [bi'gɔn] *interj* ¡fuera de aquí!

begonia [bi'gəunia] *n* begonia *f*.

begot [bi'gɔt] *pret of* **beget**.

begotten [bi'gɔtn] *ptp of* **beget**; **the only B— Son** el Unigénito.

begrime [bi'graim] *vt* tiznar, ensuciar.

begrudge [bi'grʌdʒ] *vt* (*give*) dar de mala gana; (*envy*) tener envidia a; **I don't — him his success** no le tengo envidia a causa de su éxito.

beguile [bi'gail] *vt* (*delude*) engañar; (*charm away*) seducir; *time etc* entretener; **to — someone into doing something** persuadir a uno por engaños a hacer algo.

beguiling [bi'gailiŋ] *adj* seductor, persuasivo.

begun [bi'gʌn] *pret of* **begin**.

behalf [bi'hɑːf]: **on —of** *prep*: **on — of everybody** en nombre de todos; **a collection on — of orphans** una colecta en beneficio de los huérfanos, una colecta por huérfanos; **I interceded on his —** intercedí por él; **don't worry on my —** no os inquietéis por mí.

behave [bi'heiv] **1** *vi* (*person*) portarse (*to, towards* con), comportarse, conducirse; (*Mech etc*) comportarse, funcionar.

2 *vr*: **to — oneself** portarse (bien); **— yourself! ¡**estáte formal!; **if you — yourself (properly)** si te conduces debidamente.

behaviour, (US) behavior [bi'heivjə*] *n* conducta *f*, comportamiento *m*; (*Mech etc*) comportamiento *m*, funcionamiento *m*; **good —** buena conducta *f*; **to be on one's best —** estar todo lo formal que sepa uno.

behavioural, (US) behavioral [bi'heivjərəl] *adj* comportamentista, behaviorístico.

behaviourism, (US) behaviorism [bi'heivjərizəm] *n* behaviorismo *m*.

behead [bi'hed] *vt* decapitar, descabezar.

beheld [bi'held] *pret and ptp of* **behold**.

behest [bi'hest] *n*: **at the — of** por orden de.

behind [bi'haind] **1** *adv* **(a)** detrás, por detrás; atrás; **to come from —** venir desde atrás; **to follow close —** seguir muy de cerca; **to attack someone from —** atacar a uno por la espalda.

(b) (*with verb to be*) **to be a bit —** estar un poco atrasadillo; **to be — with one's work** estar atrasado en su trabajo, tener atrasos de trabajo.

2 *prep* detrás de; **what's — all this? ¿**qué motivo oculto tendrá esto?; **he has all of us — him** (*fig*) tiene el apoyo de todos nosotros; **we are much — them in technology** les somos muy inferiores en tecnología; **it's all — us now** todo eso ha quedado ya a la espalda.

3 *n* (*fam*) trasero *m*, culo *m*.

behindhand [bi'haindhænd] *adv* atrasado, con retraso; **to be — with the rent** tener atrasos de alquiler.

behold [bi'həuld] (*irr*: *see* **hold**) *vt* contemplar; **—! ¡**fíjese bien!; **— the results! ¡**he aquí los resultados!; *see* **lo**.

beholden [bi'həuldən] *adj*: **to be — to** estar bajo una obligación a; **I don't want to be — to anybody** yo no quiero tener obligaciones con nadie.

beholder [bi'həuldə*] *n* espectador *m*, ora *f*, observador *m*, ora *f*.

behove [bi'həuv] *vt*: **it —s him to +** *infin* le incumbe **+** *infin*.

beige [beiʒ] **1** *adj* (color de) beige. **2** *n* beige *m*.

being ['biːiŋ] *n* ser *m*; **human —** ser *m* humano; **Supreme B—** Ser *m* Supremo; **in —** existente; **to come into —** nacer, empezar a existir.

bejewelled [bi'dʒuːəld] *adj* enjoyado.

belabour [bi'leibə*] *vt* apalear; (*fig*) criticar, dar un palo a.

belated [bi'leitid] *adj* atrasado, tardío.

belay [bi'lei] *vt* (*Naut*) amarrar (dando vueltas en una cabilla).

belch [beltʃ] **1** *n* eructo *m*. **2** *vt* (*fig*) vomitar, arrojar. **3** *vi* eructar.

beleaguered [bi'liːgəd] *adj* sitiado, asediado.

belfry ['belfri] *n* campanario *m*.

Belgian ['beldʒən] **1** *adj* belga. **2** *n* belga *mf*.

Belgium ['beldʒəm] *n* Bélgica *f*.

Belgrade [bel'greid] *n* Belgrado.

belie [bi'lai] *vt* desmentir, contradecir; *hopes etc* defraudar.

belief [bi'liːf] *n* **(a)** creencia *f* (*that* de que); opinión *f*; **a man of strong —s** un hombre de opiniones firmes; **to the best of my —** según mi leal saber y entender; **it is my firm — that** creo firmemente que; **it passes —, it is beyond —** es increíble (*that* que).

(b) (*Rel etc*) fe *f*; **his — in God** su fe en Dios; **to have lost one's —** haber perdido su fe.

believable [bi'liːvəbl] *adj* creíble.

believe [bi'liːv] **1** *vt* creer; *ears, story* dar crédito a; **don't you — it! ¡**no lo creas!; **he is —d to be abroad** se cree que está en el extranjero.

2 *vi* creer; **to — in God** creer en Dios; **we don't — in drugs** no aprobamos (el uso de) las drogas; **I — so** creo que sí; **I — not** creo que no.

believer [bi'li:və*] n (Rel) creyente mf, fiel mf; (Pol etc) partidario m, a f; **I am a — in letting things take their course** yo soy partidario de dejar que las cosas se desarrollen por símismas.

belittle [bi'litl] vt despreciar, minimizar, conceder poca importancia a.

bell [bel] n (church —) campana f; (hand —) campanilla f; (animal's) cencerro m; (on toy, dress etc) cascabel m; (electric) timbre m; (of trumpet) pabellón m; (Bot) campanilla f; **that rings a —** eso me suena; **it doesn't ring a — with me** no me suena.

bell-bottomed ['bel'bɔtəmd] adj acampanado, abocinado.

bellboy ['belbɔi] n botones m.

belle [bel] n belleza f, beldad f; **the — of the ball** la reina del baile.

belles-lettres ['bel'letr] npl bellas letras fpl.

bell glass ['belglɑ:s] n campana f de cristal.

bellhop ['belhɔp] n (US) botones m.

bellicose ['belikəus] adj belicoso.

bellicosity [,beli'kɔsiti] n belicosidad f.

belligerency [bi'lidʒərənsi] n beligerancia f.

belligerent [bi'lidʒərənt] 1 adj beligerante; person, tone agresivo. 2 n beligerante m.

bellow ['beləu] 1 n bramido m; (of person) rugido m. 2 vt gritar, vociferar. 3 vi bramar; (person) rugir.

bellows ['beləuz] npl fuelle m; **a pair of —** un fuelle.

bell ringer ['bel,riŋə*] n campanero m.

bell rope ['belrəup] n cuerda f de campana.

bell-shaped ['belʃeipt] adj acampanado.

bell tent ['beltent] n pabellón m.

belly ['beli] 1 n vientre m; (with offensive connotations) barriga f, panza f; (of vessel) barriga f. 2 vi (sail) hacer bolso, llenarse de viento (also to — out).

bellyache ['belieik] 1 n dolor m de barriga. 2 vi (sl) quejarse (about de).

bellyful ['beliful] n panzada f; **I've had a —** estoy harto ya (of de).

belly-landing ['beli,lændiŋ] n (Aer) aterrizaje m de barriga.

belong [bi'lɔŋ] vi (a) (be the possession of) pertenecer (to a); **who does this — to?** ¿a quién pertenece esto?, **¿de quién es esto?; the countryside —s to everyone** el campo es de todos.

(b) (be incumbent on): **that duty —s to me** ese deber me corresponde.

(c) (of membership etc) **to — to a club** ser socio de un club; **to — to a party** ser miembro de un partido; **why don't you —?** ¿por qué no te haces socio?

(d) (have rightful place) **this —s with that** éste va con aquél; **that card —s under K** esa ficha debiera estar en la K; **where does this —?** ¿esto dónde lo pongo?; **it —s on the shelf** tiene un puesto en el estante.

(e) (be resident, be at ease) **I — here** yo soy de aquí; **I feel I — here** aquí me siento cómodo; **that feeling of not —ing** esa sensación de estar fuera de su ambiente natural.

belongings [bi'lɔŋiŋz] npl pertenencias fpl, bártulos mpl, cosas fpl.

beloved [bi'lʌvid] 1 adj querido (by, of de). 2 n querido m, amada f.

below [bi'ləu] 1 adv abajo, (por) debajo; **that flat —** ese piso de abajo; **the passage quoted —** el pasaje abajo citado; **here —** aquí abajo; **it was 5 —** la temperatura era de 5 grados bajo cero.

2 prep bajo, debajo de; (fig) inferior a, eg **temperatures — normal** temperaturas inferiores a las normales.

Belshazzar [bel'ʃæzə*] m Baltasar; **—'s Feast** la Cena de Baltasar.

belt [belt] 1 n cinturón m; (Med) faja f; (Mech) correa f, cinta f; (Geog and fig) zona f, faja f; **endless — correa** f sin fin; **industrial — zona** f industrial; **green — zona** f verde; **a blow below the —** un golpe bajo; **to tighten one's — (fig)** apretarse el cinturón, ceñirse.

2 vt (fam) golpear (con una correa).

3 vi (fam): **to — along** ir como una bala; **to — past** pasar como un rayo; **to — out** salir disparado.

bemoan [bi'məun] vt lamentar.

bemuse [bi'mju:z] vt aturdir, confundir.

Ben [ben] m nombre abreviado de **Benjamin**.

ben [ben] n (Scot) montaña f; cuarto m interior.

bench [bentʃ] n banco m; (court) tribunal m; (persons) judicatura f; **to be on the — (Law)** ser juez, ser magistrado; **he's on the — today** hoy forma parte del tribunal.

bench mark ['bentʃmɑ:k] n cota f, punto m topográfico.

bend [bend] 1 n curva f; recodo m, vuelta f; ángulo m; (Her) banda f; (Naut) gaza f; **hairpin — viraje**

m en horquilla; sharp — curva f cerrada; **to be round the — (sl)** estar chiflado; **to go round the — (sl)** volverse loco.

2 (irr: pret and ptp **bent**) vt encorvar; (buckle) doblar, torcer; (cause to sag) combar; body, head inclinar; knee doblar; sail envergar; efforts, steps etc dirigir (to a); **to — someone to one's will** someter a uno a su voluntad; **to — back** doblar hacia atrás; **to — down** doblar hacia abajo, head inclinar.

3 vi encorvarse; (buckle) doblarse, torcerse; (sag) combarse; (road) torcer(se) (to the left a la izquierda); (person) encorvarse, inclinarse (also **to — down, to — over**).

bender ['bendə*] n (sl): **to go on a —** ir de juerga.

beneath [bi'ni:θ] adv and prep = **below**; (fig) **it is — him** es indigno de él; **it is — him to do such a thing** él es incapaz de hacer tal bajeza; **she married — her** se casó con hombre de clase inferior.

Benedict ['benidikt] m Benito; (pope) Benedicto.

Benedictine [,beni'diktin] 1 adj benedictino. 2 n benedictino m.

benediction [,beni'dikʃən] n bendición f.

benefaction [,beni'fækʃən] n (gift) beneficio m.

benefactor ['benifæktə*] n bienhechor m.

benefactress ['benifæktris] n bienhechora f.

benefice ['benifis] n beneficio m.

beneficence [bi'nefisəns] n beneficencia f.

beneficent [bi'nefisənt] adj benéfico.

beneficial [,beni'fiʃəl] adj provechoso, beneficioso.

beneficiary [,beni'fiʃəri] n beneficiario m, a f; (Eccl) beneficiado m.

benefit ['benifit] 1 n beneficio m; provecho m, utilidad f; (payment) subsidio m; (Theat, Sport) beneficio m; **maternity — subsidio** m de natalidad; **unemployment — subsidio** m de paro; **match —** partido homenaje m; **— performance** función f benéfica; **— society** sociedad f de socorro mutuo; **for the — of a** beneficio de; **to be to the — of** ser provechoso a; **to give someone the — of the doubt** dar a uno el beneficio de la duda; **to have the — of** tener la ventaja de; **to reap the — of** sacar el fruto de.

2 vt beneficiar, aprovechar.

3 vi aprovecharse; **to — by, to — from** sacar provecho de.

benevolence [bi'nevələns] n benevolencia f.

benevolent [bi'nevələnt] adj benévolo; **society** de socorro mutuo.

Bengal [beŋ'gɔ:l] Bengala f.

benighted [bi'naitid] adj (fig) ignorante.

benign [bi'nain] adj benigno (also Med).

benignant [bi'nignənt] adj benigno; (healthy) saludable.

Benjamin ['bendʒəmin] m Benjamín.

bent [bent] 1 adj, pret and ptp of **bend**; encorvado; doblado, torcido; (fam) sospechoso, de tendencias criminales; **on pleasure — intentando** divertirse; **to be — on + ger** estar resuelto a + infin, estar empeñado en + infin; **to be — on a quarrel** estar resuelto a provocar una riña.

2 n inclinación f (to, towards, for a); **to follow one's — seguir** su inclinación; **to have a — towards** estar inclinado a.

benumb [bi'nʌm] vt entumecer; (fig) entorpecer; mind etc paralizar.

Benzedrine ['benzidri:n] n (Protected Trade Name) bencedrina f.

benzene ['benzi:n] n benceno m.

benzine ['benzi:n] n bencina f.

bequeath [bi'kwi:ð] vt legar.

bequest [bi'kwest] n legado m.

berate [bi'reit] vt censurar; reñir, regañar.

Berber ['bə:bə*] 1 adj bereber. 2 n bereber mf.

bereaved [bi'ri:vd] adj afligido; **the — los** afligidos.

bereavement [bi'ri:vmənt] n aflicción f (por la muerte de un pariente).

bereft [bi'reft] ptp: **to be — of** (act) ser privado de, (state) estar desprovisto de.

beret ['berei] n boina f.

Berlin [bə:'lin] Berlín m; (attr) berlinés.

Berliner [bə:'linə*] n berlinés m, esa f.

Bermuda [bə:'mju:də] Islas fpl Bermuda, las Bermudas.

Bernard ['bə:nəd] m Bernardo.

Berne [bə:n] Berna f.

berry ['beri] n baya f.

berserk [bə'sə:k] adj: **to go — perder** los estribos.

Bert [bə:t] m nombre abreviado de **Albert, Herbert** etc.

berth [bə:θ] 1 n (place at wharf) amarradero m; (cabin) camarote m; (bunk) litera f; (fam) puesto m, lugar m; **to give someone a wide — evitar** el encuentro de uno, huir el trato de uno. 2 vti atracar.

beryl ['beril] n berilo m.

beseech [bi'si:tʃ] (irr: pret and ptp **besought**) vt suplicar (for something algo, to do hacer).

beseeching [bi'si:tʃiŋ] adj suplicante.

beseechingly [bi'si:tʃiŋli] adv en tono (etc) de súplica.

beset [bi'set] (irr: see **set**) vt person acosar, perseguir; road obstruir, dificultar; **a policy — with dangers** una política llena de peligros; **a way — with difficulties** un camino erizado de dificultades.

besetting [bi'setiŋ] adj obsesionante; sin dominante.

beside [bi'said] prep (a) cerca de, junto a, al lado de; **to be — oneself** (with anger) estar fuera de sí, (with anxiety) volverse loco de inquietud.

(b) (fig) **whom can we set — him?** ¿con quién podemos compararle?; **what is that — victory?** y eso ¿qué importa en comparación con la victoria?

besides [bi'saidz] **1** adv además. **2** prep además de; (with negation) excepto, fuera de.

besiege [bi'si:dʒ] vt asediar, sitiar; **we are —d with calls** nos están llamando incesantemente; **we were —d with inquiries** hubo un torrente de preguntas.

besieger [bi'si:dʒə*] n sitiador m.

besmear [bi'smiə*] vt embarrar, embadurnar.

besmirch [bi'smə:tʃ] vt (fig) manchar, mancillar.

besotted [bi'sɔtid] adj entontecido; **— with alcohol** embrutecido por el alcohol; **he is — with her** anda loco por ella.

besought [bi'sɔ:t] pret and ptp of **beseech**.

bespatter [bi'spætə*] vt salpicar (with de).

bespeak [bi'spi:k] (irr: see **speak**) vt (engage) apalabrar; goods etc encargar, reservar; (be evidence of) indicar.

bespectacled [bi'spektikld] adj con gafas, que lleva gafas.

bespoke [bi'spəuk] **1** pret and ptp of **bespeak**. **2** adj **— clothing** ropa f hecha a la medida; **— tailor** sastre m que confecciona a medida.

bespoken [bi'spəukən] ptp of **bespeak**.

besprinkle [bi'spriŋkl] vt salpicar, rociar (with de); espolvorear (with de).

Bess [bes], **Bessie** or **Bessy** ['besi] f Isabelita.

best [best] **1** adj superl (el, la) mejor; **to know what is — for someone** saber lo que más conviene a uno. **2** adv superl (lo) mejor; **as — I could** lo mejor que pude; **I had — go** más vale que yo vaya; **I had — see him at once** sería aconsejable verle en seguida; **you know —** Vd sabe mejor que yo; **Mummy knows —** estas cosas las decide mamá, mamá sabe lo que más conviene; **when it comes to hotels I know —** yo soy el más experto en asunto de hoteles; **to come off —** salir ganando.

3 n (a) lo mejor; **Sunday —** trapos mpl de cristianar; **to dress up in one's Sunday —** endomingarse; **the — of it is that** lo mejor del caso es que; **is that the — you can do?** y eso ¿es todo lo que Vd puede hacer?; **we have had the — of the day** el buen tiempo se acabó por hoy.

(b) (phrases with prep) **at —, at the —** a lo más, en el mejor de los casos; **the garden is at its — in June** en junio el jardín está en todo su esplendor; **he wasn't at his —** no estuvo en forma; **it's all for the —** todo conduce al bien a la larga; **I acted for the —** obré con la mejor intención; **we drank of the —** bebimos el mejor vino (etc); **I can sing with the — (of them)** yo canto como el que más.

(c) (phrases with verb) **to do one's —** hacer como mejor puede uno; **to get the — of it** salir ganando, imponerse; **in order to get the — out of the car** para obtener el máximo rendimiento del coche; **to look one's —** mostrarse en todo su esplendor; **she's not looking her —** está algo desmejorada; **to make the — of it** (or of a bad job) salir de un mal negocio lo mejor posible.

4 vt vencer.

bestial ['bestiəl] adj bestial.

bestiality [,besti'æliti] n bestialidad f.

bestir [bi'stə:*] vr: **to — oneself** menearse.

bestow [bi'stəu] vt (grant) otorgar (on a); (give) dar (on a); affections ofrecer (on a); compliment hacer (on a).

bestowal [bi'stəuəl] n otorgamiento m; donación f; ofrecimiento m.

bestraddle [bi'strædl] vt montar a horcajadas, estar a horcajadas sobre; (fig) estar a caballo sobre.

bestrew [bi'stru:] (irr: see **strew**) vt things desparramar, esparcir; surface sembrar, cubrir (with de).

bestridden [bi'stridn] ptp of **bestride**.

bestride [bi'straid] (irr: see **stride**) vt horse montar a horcajadas; stream etc cruzar de un tranco; (fig) dominar.

bestrode [bi'strəud] pret of **bestride**.

bestseller ['best'selə*] n éxito m de librería.

bet [bet] **1** n apuesta f; (sum) postura f; **to lay** (or **make, put**) **a —** on apostar a.

2 (irr: pret and ptp **bet** or **betted**) vt apostar (on a); **I — you a shilling that** te apuesto un chelín a que; **I'll — you anything you like!** ¡apuesto lo que quieras!; **you — (your life)!** ¡ya lo creo!

3 vi apostar, jugar; **I — you can't!** ¡a que no puedes!; **I — it isn't!** ¡a que no!; **I don't —** yo no juego.

betake [bi'teik] (irr: see **take**) vr: **to — oneself to** dirigirse a, trasladarse a, acudir a.

betaken [bi'teikən] ptp of **betake**.

betel ['bi:təl] n betel m.

bête noire ['beit'nwɑ:*] n bestia f negra, pesadilla f; (person) hincha mf.

bethink [bi'θiŋk] (irr: see **think**) vr: **to — oneself of** acordarse de.

Bethlehem ['beθlihem] Belén.

bethought [bi'θɔ:t] pret and ptp of **bethink**.

betide [bi'taid] vti acontecer; see **woe**.

betimes [bi'taimz] adv temprano; con tiempo.

betoken [bi'təukən] vt presagiar, anunciar.

betook [bi'tuk] pret of **betake**.

betray [bi'trei] vt (a) person, country traicionar; **to — someone to the enemy** vender a uno al enemigo; **his accent —s him** su acento le traiciona; **his accent —s him as a foreigner** su acento le acusa de extranjero.

(b) (reveal) plot etc revelar, delatar; **ignorance etc** hacer patente.

(c) (show signs of) dejar ver, dar muestras de, descubrir; **his face —ed a certain surprise** su cara acusó cierto asombro.

betrayal [bi'treiəl] n (a) traición f; **— of trust** abuso m de confianza. (b) revelación f. (c) descubrimiento m.

betroth [bi'trəuð] vt prometer en matrimonio (to a); **to be —d** (act) desposarse, (state) estar desposado.

betrothal [bi'trəuðəl] n desposorios mpl, esponsales mpl.

better[1] ['betə*] **1** adj comp mejor; **— and —** cada vez mejor; **that's —** eso va mejor; más vale así; **that's —!** ¡bien!; **he's much —** (Med) está mucho mejor; **it couldn't be —** no podría ser mejor; **it is — to + infin** más vale + infin; **it would be — to + infin** más valdría + infin, sería aconsejable + infin; **she's no — than she ought to be** es una mujer que tiene historia; **to get —** mejorar(se), (Med) reponerse; **to go one —** hacer mejor todavía (than que).

2 adv comp mejor; **all the —, so much the —** tanto mejor (for para); **to be all the — for** haber mejorado mucho a consecuencia de; **it would be all the — for a drop of paint** no le vendría mal una mano de pintura; **they are — off than we are** son más acomodados que nosotros; **I had — go** más vale que yo vaya; **but he knew —** pero él tuvo otra idea; **he thinks he knows —** él cree que se lo sabe todo; **he knows — than the experts** él sabe más que los expertos; **to think —** of it mudar de parecer.

3 n (a) **my —s** mis superiores.

(b) **it's a change for the —** es un cambio beneficioso; **for — or worse** en la fortuna como en la adversidad; **to get the — of** vencer, quedar por encima de.

4 vt mejorar; record, score superar.

5 vr: **to — oneself** mejorar su posición.

better[2] ['betə*] n apostador m, ora f.

betterment ['betəmənt] n mejoramiento m.

betting ['betiŋ] **1** adj aficionado al juego; **I'm not a — man** yo no juego, el apostar.

betting shop ['betiŋ,ʃɔp] n oficina f de un corredor de apuestas (esp sobre las carreras de caballos).

betting slip ['betiŋslip] n boleto m de apuestas.

Betty ['beti] f Isabelita.

between [bi'twi:n] **1** adv en medio (also **in —**).

2 prep entre; **— ourselves** entre nosotros; **we bought it — 4 of us** lo compramos entre los 4; **they shared it — them** se lo repartieron; **— now and May** de ahora a mayo; **the shops are shut — 2 and 4** las tiendas están cerradas de 2 a 4.

betwixt [bi'twikst] **1** adv en medio; **— and between** entre lo uno y lo otro. **2** prep entre; en medio de.

bevel ['bevəl] **1** adj biselado. **2** n (tool) cartabón m, escuadra f falsa; (surface) bisel m. **3** vt biselar.

beverage ['bevəridʒ] n bebida f.

bevy ['bevi] n (birds) bandada f; (women etc) grupo m.

bewail [bi'weil] vt lamentar.

beware [bi'weə*] vi (a) **to — of** precaverse de, tener cuidado con, guardarse de.

(b) **—!** ¡cuidado!, ¡atención!, ¡ojo!; **— of the dog!** ¡ojo con el perro!, (as notice) "perro peligroso"; **— of pickpockets!** ¡ojo con los carteristas!; **— of imitations** desconfíe de las imitaciones.

bewilder [bi'wildə*] *vt* aturdir, dejar perplejo, desconcertar.
bewildering [bi'wildəriŋ] *adj* desconcertante.
bewilderingly [bi'wildəriŋli] *adv* de modo desconcertante; **a — complicated matter** un asunto tan complicado que desconcierta a uno.
bewilderment [bi'wildəmənt] *n* aturdimiento *m*, perplejidad *f*.
bewitch [bi'witʃ] *vt* hechizar (*also fig*).
bewitching [bi'witʃiŋ] *adj* hechicero, encantador.
beyond [bi'jɔnd] **1** *adv* más allá, más lejos.
 2 *prep* (a) más allá de; **— the seas** allende los mares. (b) (*over and above*) además de, fuera de. (c) (*fig*) **the task is — him** la tarea es superior a sus fuerzas; **it's — me** está fuera de mi alcance, no lo entiendo; **it's — me to see how** no alcanzo a ver cómo; **this is getting — me** se me está haciendo imposible esto; **it's — a doubt** está fuera de toda duda; **it's — praise** queda por encima de todo elogio; **to go — one's authority** exceder a su autoridad.
 3 *n*: **the great —** el más allá; **at the back of —** en el quinto infierno.
bi . . . [bai] **bi . . .**
biannual [bai'ænjuəl] *adj* semestral.
bias ['baiəs] **1** *n* (a) sesgo *m*, diagonal *f*; **to cut something on the —** cortar algo al sesgo. (b) (*inclination*) propensión *f*, predisposición *f* (*to, towards* a); **to have a — towards** tener propensión a, estar inclinado a. (c) (*prejudice*) pasión *f*, prejuicio *m*.
 2 *vt* (*fig*) influir en, torcer; **to — someone against something** predisponer a uno en contra de algo; **to be —sed** tener prejuicio (*against* contra), ser partidista (*in favour of* de).
bib [bib] *n* babero *m*, babador *m*; **in one's best — and tucker** llevando el mejor traje que tiene uno.
Bible ['baibl] *n* Biblia *f*; **the Holy —** la Santa Biblia.
Biblical ['biblikəl] *adj* bíblico.
bibliographer [ˌbibli'ɔɡrəfə*] *n* bibliógrafo *m*.
bibliographic(al) [ˌbibliəu'ɡræfik(əl)] *adj* bibliográfico.
bibliography [ˌbibli'ɔɡrəfi] *n* bibliografía *f*.
bibliomania [ˌbibliəu'meiniə] *n* bibliomanía *f*.
bibliophile ['bibliəufail] *n* bibliófilo *m*.
bibulous ['bibjuləs] *adj* bebedor, borrachín.
bicameral [bai'kæmərəl] *adj* bicameral.
bicarbonate of soda [bai'kɑ:bənitəv'səudə] *n* bicarbonato *m* sódico.
bicentenary [ˌbaisen'ti:nəri] *n* bicentenario *m*.
biceps ['baiseps] *n* bíceps *m*.
bicker ['bikə*] *vi* reñir, altercar; (*stream*) murmurar.
bickering ['bikəriŋ] *n* riñas *fpl*, altercados *mpl*.
bicuspid [bai'kʌspid] *adj* bicúspide.
bicycle ['baisikl] **1** *n* bicicleta *f*. **2** *vi* ir en bicicleta; **to — to Dover** ir en bicicleta a Dover.
bid [bid] **1** *n* (a) (*at auction*) oferta *f*, postura *f*; **highest —** mejor postura *f*. (b) (*Cards*) marca *f*; **no —** paso. (c) (*fig*) tentativa *f*, conato *m*; **to make a — for** tratar de asegurar el control de; **to make a — to +** *infin* hacer una tentativa de + *infin*.
 2 (*irr: pret* **bade, bid,** *ptp* **bidden, bid**) *vt* (a) (*order*) ordenar, mandar; **to — someone to do something** mandar a uno hacer algo. (b) (*at auction*) licitar, ofrecer; **to — £10 for** ofrecer 10 libras por; **to — someone up to £12** hacer que uno siga haciendo posturas hasta 12 libras. (c) (*Cards*) marcar, pujar, declarar. (d) **to — someone good-day** dar a uno los buenos días; **to — defiance to** desafiar a; *see* **adieu.**
 3 *vi* (a) **to — for** pujar por, hacer una oferta por; **to — up** pujar. (b) **to — fair to +** *infin* prometer + *infin*, dar esperanzas de + *infin*.
biddable ['bidəbl] *adj* mandable.
bidden ['bidn] *ptp of* **bid.**
bidder ['bidə*] *n* (a) postor *m*; **highest —** mejor postor *m*. (b) (*Cards*) declarante *mf*.
bidding ['bidiŋ] *n* (a) (*order*) orden *f*, mandato *m*; **to do someone's —** cumplir el mandato de uno. (b) (*at auction*) licitación *f*, ofertas *fpl*; **the — opened at £5** la primera oferta fue de 5 libras; **there was keen — for the picture** hubo una rápida serie de ofertas por el cuadro. (c) (*Cards*) remate *m*, declaración *f*; **to open the —** abrir la declaración.
bide [baid] *vt*: **to — one's time** esperar la hora propicia.
bidet ['bi:dei] *n* bidet *m*, bidé *m* (*Acad*).
biennial [bai'eniəl] **1** *adj* bienal; (*Bot*) bianual. **2** *n* planta *f* bienal, bianual *m*.

bier [biə*] *n* féretro *m*.
biff [bif] (*fam*) **1** *n* bofetada *f*. **2** *vt* dar una bofetada a.
bifocal ['bai'fəukəl] **1** *adj* bifocal. **2** *n* lente *m* bifocal; **—s** gafas *fpl* bifocales.
bifurcate ['baifəkeit] *vi* bifurcarse.
big [big] **1** *adj* grande; abultado, voluminoso; importante; (*fam*) generoso; **my — brother** mi hermano mayor; **the B— Four** las cuatro Grandes (Potencias); **it's a — shame** es una terrible lástima; **to be — with child** estar encinta; **that's very — of you** (*fam*) es Vd muy amable.
 2 *adv* (*sl*): **to talk —** darse mucha importancia, darse bombo; **to think —** hacer proyectos de gran envergadura.
bigamist ['bigəmist] *n* bígamo *m*, a *f*.
bigamous ['bigəməs] *adj* bígamo.
bigamy ['bigəmi] *n* bigamia *f*.
bighead ['bighed] *n* (*sl*) orgulloso *m*, a *f*, listillo *m*, a *f*.
bigheaded ['big'hedid] *adj* (*sl*) engreído.
big-hearted ['big'hɑ:tid] *adj* generoso.
bight [bait] *n* (a) (*Geog*) ensenada *f*, cala *f*; (*bend*) recodo *m*. (b) (*of rope*) gaza *f*.
bigmouth ['bigmauθ] *n* (*sl*) hablador *m*, ora *f*, charlador *m*, ora *f*; chismoso *m*, a *f*; soplón *m*.
big-mouthed ['big'mauθt] *adj* (a) de boca grande, de boca ancha, bocudo. (b) (*sl*) hablador, charlador; chismoso; soplón.
bigot ['bigət] *n* fanático *m*, a *f*, intolerante *mf*.
bigoted ['bigətid] *adj* fanático, intolerante.
bigotry ['bigətri] *n* fanatismo *m*, intolerancia *f*.
big-time ['big'taim] *adj* (*fam*) de postín, de rumbo.
bigwig ['bigwig] *n* pez *m* gordo, señorón *m*, espadón *m*.
bike [baik] (*fam*) **1** *n* bici *f*. **2** *vi* ir en bicicleta.
bikini [bi'ki:ni] *n* bikini *m*.
bilateral [bai'lætərəl] *adj* bilateral.
bilberry ['bilbəri] *n* arándano *m*.
bile [bail] *n* bilis *f*; (*fig*) mal genio *m*, displicencia *f*.
bilge [bildʒ] *n* (*Naut*) pantoque *m*; (*water*) agua *f* de pantoque; (*sl*) tonterías *fpl*.
bilge water ['bildʒwɔ:tə*] *n* agua *f* de pantoque.
bilingual [bai'liŋgwəl] *adj* bilingüe.
bilingualism [bai'liŋgwəlizəm] *n* bilingüismo *m*.
bilious ['biliəs] *adj* bilioso (*also fig*); **— attack** trastorno *m* biliar.
biliousness ['biliəsnis] *n* tendencia *f* a sufrir trastornos biliares.
bilk [bilk] *vt* estafar, defraudar.
bill[1] [bil] **1** *n* (*bird's*) pico *m*; (*of anchor*) uña *f*; (*Agr*) podadera *f*, podón *m*; (*Geog*) promontorio *m*. **2** *vi*: **to — and coo** besuquearse, acariciarse.
bill[2] [bil] **1** *n* (a) (*account*) cuenta *f*; (*invoice*) factura *f*; **wages —** (*in industry*) coste *m* de salarios; **to foot the —** pagar la cuenta; correr con los gastos; (*fig*) pagar el pato. (b) (*Parl*) proyecto *m* de ley; **— of rights** declaración *f* de derechos, ley *f* fundamental; **to fill the —** llenar los requisitos. (c) (*banknote*) billete *m*; **— of exchange** letra *f* de cambio. (d) (*notice*) cartel *m*; **stick no —s** prohibido fijar carteles. (e) **— of fare** lista *f* (de platos), menú *m*; **— of health** (*Naut*) patente *f* de sanidad; **— of lading** conocimiento *m* de embarque; **— of sale** escritura *f* de venta.
 2 *vt* (*Theat*) anunciar; **he is —ed to appear next week** figura en el programa de la semana que viene.
Bill [bil] *m nombre abreviado de* **William.**
billboard ['bilbɔ:d] *n* (*US*) cartelera *f*.
billet ['bilit] **1** *n* alojamiento *m*. **2** *vt* alojar (*on* en casa de).
billet-doux ['bilei'du:] *n* carta *f* amorosa.
billfold ['bilfauld] *n* (*US*) billetero *m*, cartera *f*.
billhook ['bilhuk] *n* podadera *f*, podón *m*.
billiard ball ['biliəd.bɔ:l] *n* bola *f* de billar.
billiard cue ['biliəd.kju:] *n* taco *m*.
billiards ['biliədz] *n sing* billar *m*.
billiard table ['biliəd.teibl] *n* mesa *f* de billar.
billion ['biliən] *n* billón *m*, (*US*) mil millones *mpl*.
billow ['biləu] **1** *n* oleada *f*; **—s** las olas, el mar. **2** *vi* ondular, ondear; **to — out** hincharse (de viento *etc*).
billowy ['biləui] *adj* ondoso; hinchado.
billposter ['bil.pəustə*] *n*, **billsticker** ['bil.stikə*] *n* cartelero *m*.
Billy ['bili] *m nombre abreviado de* **William.**
billy goat ['biligəut] *n* macho *m* cabrío.
billy-ho ['bilihəu] *adv* (*fam*): **like —** hasta más no poder.
bimonthly ['bai'mʌnθli] **1** *adj* (*every* 2 *months*) bimestral; (*twice monthly*) bimensual, quincenal.

2 *adv* bimestralmente; bimensualmente, quincenalmente.

3 *n* revista *f* bimestral; revista *f* bimensual, revista *f* quincenal.

bin [bin] *n* hucha *f*, arcón *m*; (*for bread*) nasa *f*; (*for rubbish*) cubo *m*; (*for litter*) papelera *f*.

binary ['bainəri] *adj* binario.

bind [baind] (*irr: pret and ptp* **bound**) 1 *vt* (a) (*tie*) atar, liar (*to* a); *hands* atar; *wound* vendar (*also to* — **up**); *corn* agavillar; *book* encuadernar; (*Med*) estreñir; (*encircle*) rodear (*with* de), ceñir (*with* con, de); (*fig*) liar (*to* a), unir (*to* con).

(b) (*force*) obligar; **to** — **someone to do something** obligar a uno a hacer algo; **to** — **someone to a promise** obligar a uno a cumplir su promesa; **to** — **someone apprentice to** poner a uno de aprendiz con; **to** — **someone over** obligar a uno a comparecer ante el magistrado; **to** — **someone over to** + *infin* imponer a uno el deber legal de + *infin*; *see also* **bound**[1].

2 *vi* (*cement etc*) endurecerse; cuajarse; adherirse; (*parts of machine*) trabarse.

3 *n* (*sl*): **it's a** — es una lata; **what a** —! ¡qué lata!

binder ['baində*] *n* (*Agr*) agavilladora *f*; (*file*) cartera *f*, (*of book*) encuadernador *m*.

binding ['baindiŋ] 1 *adj* obligatorio (*on* a, para); *promise* que hay que cumplir; (*Med*) que estriñe. 2 *n* (*of book*) encuadernación *f*; (*Sew*) ribete *m*.

bindweed ['baindwi:d] *n* convólvulo *m*, enredadera *f*.

binge [bindʒ] *n* (*sl*) borrachera *f*; **to go on a** — ir de juerga.

bingo ['biŋgəu] *n* lotería *f* casera, quinto *m*.

binoculars [bi'nɔkjuləz] *npl* gemelos *mpl*, prismáticos *mpl*, (*Mil*) anteojo *m* de campaña.

binomial [bai'nəumiəl] 1 *adj* de dos términos. 2 *n* binomio *m*.

biochemical ['baiəu'kemikəl] *adj* bioquímico.

biochemist ['baiəu'kemist] *n* bioquímico *m*.

biochemistry ['baiəu'kemistri] *n* bioquímica *f*.

biographer [bai'ɔgrəfə*] *n* biógrafo *m*.

biographic(al) [‚baiəu'græfik(əl)] *adj* biográfico.

biography [bai'ɔgrəfi] *n* biografía *f*.

biological [‚baiə'lɔdʒikəl] *adj* biológico.

biologist [bai'ɔlədʒist] *n* biólogo *m*.

biology [bai'ɔlədʒi] *n* biología *f*.

biophysics [‚baiəu'fiziks] *n sing* biofísica *f*.

biopsy ['baiɔpsi] *n* biopsia *f*.

bipartisan [‚bai'pɑ:tizæn] *adj* *policy etc* que tienen en común los dos partidos.

bipartite [bai'pɑ:tait] *adj* bipartido.

biped ['baiped] *n* bípedo *m*.

biplane ['baiplein] *n* biplano *m*.

birch [bə:tʃ] 1 *n* abedul *m*; (*for punishment*) vara *f*, férula *f*. 2 *vt* castigar con la vara.

birch tree ['bə:tʃtri:] *n* abedul *m*.

birchwood ['bə:tʃwud] *n* bosque *m* de abedules.

bird [bə:d] *n* (a) ave *f*, (*gen small*) pájaro *m*; (*sl*) (*man*) tío *m*, tipo *m*, (*girl*) chica *f*, (*girlfriend*) novia *f*; — **of ill omen** pájaro *m* de mal agüero; — **of passage** ave *f* de paso (*also fig*); — **of prey** ave *f* de rapiña; **early** — madrugador *m*, ora *f*.

(b) (*Theat sl*) **to get the** — ganarse un abucheo, ser pateado; **to give someone the** — abuchear a uno, patear a uno.

(c) (*proverbs*) **the early** — **catches the worm** al que madruga Dios le ayuda; **a** — **in the hand is worth two in the bush** más vale pájaro en mano que ciento volando; —**s of a feather flock together** Dios los cría y ellos se juntan; **they're** —**s of a feather** son lobos de una camada; **to kill two** — **with one stone** matar dos pájaros de un tiro.

bird brain ['bə:dbrein] *n* (*sl*) casquivano *m*, a *f*.

birdcage ['bə:dkeidʒ] *n* jaula *f* de pájaro; (*large, outdoor*) pajarera *f*.

bird call ['bə:dkɔ:l] *n* reclamo *m*.

bird fancier ['bə:d‚fænsiə*] *n* pajarero *m*.

birdlime ['bə:dlaim] *n* liga *f*.

birdseed ['bə:dsi:d] *n* alpiste *m*.

bird's-eye view ['bə:dzai'vju:] *n* vista *f* de pájaro.

bird's nest ['bə:dznest] 1 *n* nido *m* de pájaro. 2 *vi* (*esp* **to go** —**ing**) buscar nidos.

bird watcher ['bə:dwɔtʃə*] *n* ornitólogo *m*.

birth [bə:θ] *n* nacimiento *m*; (*Med*) parto *m*; (*fig*) nacimiento *m*, origen *m*, comienzo *m*; **the** — **of an idea** el origen de una idea; **by** — de nacimiento; **of humble** — de nacimiento humilde; **to give** — **to** dar a luz, parir, (*fig*) dar lugar a, ser el origen de; **to be in at the** — **of** (*fig*) asistir al nacimiento de.

birth certificate ['bə:θsə'tifikit] *n* partida *f* de nacimiento.

birth control ['bə:θkən'trəul] *n* control *m* de natalidad; **method of** — método *m* anticonceptivo, método *m* anticoncepcional.

birthday ['bə:θdei] *n* cumpleaños *m*; (*of event etc*) aniversario *m*; (*the Spaniard more commonly celebrates each year his*) día *m* del santo de uno, fiesta *f* onomástica; **on my 21st** — cuando cumplí los 21 años; **in one's** — **suit** en cueros.

birthday present ['bə:θdei'preznt] *n* regalo *m* de cumpleaños.

birthmark ['bə:θmɑ:k] *n* rosa *f*, marca *f* de nacimiento.

birthplace ['bə:θpleis] *n* lugar *m* de nacimiento.

birth rate ['bə:θreit] *n* natalidad *f*.

birthright ['bə:θrait] *n* derechos *mpl* de nacimiento; primogenitura *f*; (*fig*) patrimonio *m*, herencia *f*; **it is the** — **of every Englishman** pertenece por derecho natural a todo inglés.

birthstone ['bə:θstəun] *n* *piedra preciosa que simboliza las influencias astrológicas de la fecha en que uno nació.*

Biscay ['biskei] Vizcaya *f*.

biscuit ['biskit] *n* galleta *f*; **that takes the** —! (*fam*) ¡eso es el colmo!

biscuit barrel ['biskit‚bærəl] *n* galletero *m*.

bisect [bai'sekt] *vt* bisecar.

bisexual ['bai'seksjuəl] *adj* bisexual.

bishop ['biʃəp] *n* obispo *m*; (*Chess*) alfil *m*.

bishopric ['biʃəprik] *n* obispado *m*.

bismuth ['bizməθ] *n* bismuto *m*.

bison ['baisən] *n* bisonte *m*.

bit[1] [bit] *n* (*horse's*) freno *m*, bocado *m*; (*tool*) barrena *f*; **to get the** — **between one's teeth** desbocarse, rebelarse.

bit[2] [bit] *n* (a) trozo *m*, pedacito *m*, porción *f*.

(b) (*noun phrases*) **a** — **of advice** un consejo; **a** — **of news** una noticia; **I had a** — **to eat** tomé un bocado; **I'll have a** — **of cake** tomo un poco de tarta; **they have a** — **of money** tienen dinerillos; **to blow something to** —**s** hacer algo añicos; **to come to** —**s** hacerse pedazos, romperse, desmontarse; **to do one's** — contribuir, hacer la debida contribución, servir como se debe (a la patria *etc*).

(c) (*adjectival uses*) **he's a** — **of a liar** es algo mentiroso; **I'm a** — **of a musician** yo sé algo de música; **I'm a** — **of a socialist** yo soy socialista hasta cierto punto; **it was a** — **of a shock** fue un golpe bastante duro; **I've a** — **of a cold** estoy ligeramente acatarrado; **not a** — **of it!** ¡ni hablar!, ¡nada, nada!; **it's not a** — **of use** no sirve para nada en absoluto; **every** — **as good as** de ningún modo inferior a; **every** — **a** **man** todo un hombre.

(d) (*adverbial uses*) — **by** — poco a poco; **it's a** — **awkward** es un poco difícil; **a** — **later** poco después, un poco más tarde; **wait a** —! ¡espere un momento!, ¡un momento, por favor!; **so I waited a** — así que esperé un ratito; **it's a good** — **further than we thought** queda bastante más lejos de lo que creíamos; **a good** — **bigger** bastante más grande; **are you tired?** ... **not a** —! ¿estás cansado? ... ¡en absoluto!

bit[3] [bit] *pret of* **bite**.

bitch [bitʃ] 1 *n* (a) perra *f*; (*woman*) lagarta *f*, mujer *f* de mal genio; **you** —! ¡lagarta!; ¡perra salida! (b) (*sl*) queja *f*. 2 *vi* (*sl*) quejarse.

bitchy ['bitʃi] *adj* (*fam*) maldiciente, malicioso; de mal genio; rencoroso; *remark etc* malintencionado, horrible.

bite [bait] 1 *n* (a) mordedura *f*; (*toothmark*) dentellada *f*; (*of bird, insect*) picadura *f*.

(b) (*food*) bocado *m*; (*snack*) bocadillo *m*; **1 not had a** — **to eat** no he comido un solo bocado; **will you have a** — **to eat?** ¿le traigo algo de comer?; **I'll get a** — **on the train** tomaré un bocadillo en el tren.

(c) (*Fishing*) **are you getting any** —**s?** ¿están picando?

(d) (*fig*) mordacidad *f*, penetración *f*; **a novel with** — una novela penetrante; **a speech with** — un discurso tajante; **without any** — sin garra.

2 (*irr: pret* **bit**, *ptp* **bitten**) *vt* morder; (*bird, fish, insect*) picar; (*acid*) corroer; (*Mech*) asir, trabar; **what's biting you?** (*fam*) ¿qué mosca te ha picado?; **to** — **off** arrancar con los dientes; **to** — **off more than one can chew** abarcar más de lo que se puede apretar; **once bitten twice shy** el gato escaldado del agua fría huye; **to be bitten, to get bitten** (*fig*) ser engañado; **to be bitten with** (*fam*) estar contagiado con.

3 *vi* morder; picar; (*fish*) picar; (*fig*) tragar el anzuelo; **to** — **at** tratar de morder; **to** — **into** *earth etc* devorar, tragar.

biter ['baitə*] n: **the — bit** el cazado cazador.
biting ['baitiŋ] adj cold, wind penetrante, cortante; criticism etc mordaz.
bitten ['bitn] ptp of **bite**.
bitter ['bitə*] **1** adj amargo; cold penetrante, cortante; battle encarnizado; enemy, hatred implacable; disappointment agudo; protest amargo; person resentido; **to feel — about something** resentirse por algo, tener rencor por motivo de algo.
2 n cerveza f clara.
bitterly ['bitəli] adv amargamente; **it's — cold** hace un frío cortante; **he protested —** se quejó amargamente; **I was — disappointed** sufrí una terrible decepción; **she spoke — of her experiences** habló con mucho rencor de sus experiencias.
bittern ['bitə:n] n avetoro m común.
bitterness ['bitənis] n amargura f; encarnizamiento m; implacabilidad f; agudeza f; **there is great — between them** entre ellos existe un odio implacable; **I accepted it without —** lo acepté sin rencor; **I have no — towards you** no le guardo rencor.
bitters ['bitəz] npl bítter m.
bittersweet ['bitəswi:t] adj agridulce.
bitumen ['bitjumin] n betún m.
bituminous [bi'tjuminəs] adj bituminoso.
bivalve ['baivælv] **1** adj bivalvo. **2** n molusco m bivalvo.
bivouac ['bivuæk] **1** n vivaque m, vivac m. **2** vt vivaquear.
bi-weekly ['bai'wi:kli] **1** adj (every 2 weeks) quincenal; (twice weekly) bisemanal.
2 adv quincenalmente; bisemanalmente.
3 n revista f quincenal; revista f bisemanal.
bizarre [bi'za:*] adj event extraño, raro; appearance etc estrafalario.
blab [blæb] **1** vt divulgar, soltar. **2** vi chismear; (to police etc) soplar.
black [blæk] **1** adj **(a)** negro; (in darkness) oscuro, tenebroso; (with smoke) negro, ennegrecido; (with dirt) sucio; event, day negro, funesto, aciago; look ceñudo, de desaprobación; **things look pretty —** la situación es desconsoladora; **a — forecast** una predicción pesimista; **a — day on the roads** una jornada trágica en las carreteras; **as — as pitch** (or night or your hat) negro como boca de lobo; **— man** negro m; **— woman** negra f.
(b) (trade-union parlance) **— goods** géneros mpl boicoteados; **to declare something —** boicotear algo.
(c) his face was — and blue tuvo la cara amoratada; **— and blue** echar sapos y culebras; **— and white photo** foto f en blanco y negro; **I should like it in — and white** quisiera tenerlo por escrito; **there it is in — and white!** ¡ahí lo tiene en letra de molde!
2 n (colour) negro m, color m negro; (person) negro m, a f; (mourning) luto m; **to be in —, to wear —** estar de luto; **to put up a —** (sl) meter la pata.
3 vt ennegrecer; shoes limpiar, lustrar; **to — someone's eye** dar a uno una bofetada en el ojo; **to — out a house** hacer que no sean visibles por fuera las luces de una casa; **the storm —ed out the town** la tormenta causó un apagón en la ciudad.
4 vi: **to — out** (Med) padecer una amnesia temporal, desmayarse.
blackball ['blækbɔ:l] vt dar bola negra a.
blackberry ['blækbəri] n (fruit) zarzamora f; (plant) zarza f.
blackbird ['blækbə:d] n mirlo m.
blackboard ['blækbɔ:d] n pizarra f, encerado m.
black box ['blæk'bɔks] n (Aer) registrador m de vuelo.
black-coated ['blæk'kəutid] adj: **— worker** oficinista mf.
blackcock ['blækkɔk] n grigallo m.
blackcurrant ['blæk'kʌrənt] n grosella f negra.
blacken ['blækən] vt ennegrecer; (by fire) calcinar; face tiznar de negro; (fig) denigrar, desacreditar.
blackguard ['blæga:d] **1** n pillo m, canalla m. **2** vt vilipendiar.
blackguardly ['blæga:dli] adj vil, canallesco.
blackhead ['blækhed] n comedón m, espinilla f.
black-hearted ['blæk'ha:tid] adj malvado, perverso.
blacking ['blækiŋ] n betún m.
blackish ['blækiʃ] adj negruzco.
blackjack ['blækdʒæk] n cachiporra f (con puño flexible).
black lead ['blæk'led] n grafito m.
blackleg ['blækleg] **1** n esquirol m. **2** vi ser esquirol, trabajar durante una huelga.
blacklist ['blæklist] **1** n lista f negra. **2** vt poner en la lista negra.
blackmail ['blækmeil] **1** n chantaje m. **2** vt chantajear, sacar dinero por chantaje a.

blackmailer ['blækmeilə*] n chantajista mf.
Black Maria ['blækmə'raiə] n coche m celular.
blackness ['blæknis] n negrura f; (darkness) oscuridad f.
blackout ['blækaut] n apagón m; (Med) amnesia f temporal, desmayo m.
Black Sea ['blæk'si:] Mar m Negro.
blackshirt ['blækʃə:t] n fascista mf.
blacksmith ['blæksmiθ] n herrero m; **—'s (forge)** herrería f.
blackthorn ['blækθɔ:n] n endrino m.
bladder ['blædə*] n vejiga f.
blade [bleid] n (of weapon etc) hoja f; (cutting edge) filo m; (sword) espada f; (of propeller) paleta f, aleta f; (of oar, hoe) pala f; (Elec) cuchilla f; **a — of grass** una brizna de hierba.
blame [bleim] **1** n culpa f; **to bear the —** tener la culpa; **to lay** (or put) **the — for something on someone** echar a uno la culpa de algo.
2 vt culpar, echar la culpa a; **to — someone for something** echar a uno la culpa de algo; **to be to — for** tener la culpa de; **I am not to —** yo no tengo la culpa; **who's to —?** ¿quién tiene la culpa?; **you have only yourself to —** tú eres el único culpable; **and I don't — him** y lo comprendo perfectamente.
blameless ['bleimlis] adj person inocente (of de); action intachable.
blameworthy ['bleimwə:ði] adj censurable.
blanch [bla:ntʃ] vi palidecer.
blancmange [blə'mɔnʒ] n (approx) crema f (de vainilla etc).
bland [blænd] adj suave.
blandish ['blændiʃ] vt engatusar, halagar.
blandishments ['blændiʃmənts] npl halagos mpl, lisonjas fpl.
blandly ['blændli] adv suavemente.
blank [blæŋk] **1** adj paper, space, cheque etc en blanco; verse suelto, blanco; cartridge sin bala, shell de fogueo; **a — look** una mirada sin expresión, una mirada de incomprensión; **a — stare** una mirada vaga; **when I asked him he looked —** cuando se lo pregunté puso la mirada en el vacío; **a look of — amazement** una mirada de profundo asombro; **in a state of — despair** en un estado de desesperación total; **my mind went —** no pude recordar nada.
2 n (space) blanco m, espacio m en blanco; (form) formulario m, hoja f; (coin) cospel m; (Mil) cartucho m sin bala, granada f de fogueo; **to fire —** usar municiones de fogueo; **my mind was a complete —** no pude recordar nada; **to draw a —** no encontrar nada, no tener éxito alguno.
blanket ['blæŋkit] **1** n manta f; (fig) manto m, capa f; **a — of snow** una manta de nieve; **electric —** manta f eléctrica; **wet —** aguafiestas mf.
2 adj comprensivo, general.
3 vt (fig) cubrir (in, with de), envolver (by, in, with en).
blankly ['blæŋkli] adv: **he looked at me —** me miró sin comprender.
blare [blɛə*] **1** n estrépito m, sonido m fuerte; (of trumpet) trompetazo m. **2** vt: **to — out** vociferar.
3 vi resonar, sonar muy fuerte.
blarney ['bla:ni] **1** n coba f; labia f. **2** vt dar coba a.
blasé ['bla:zei] adj hastiado; **he's very — about it** habla de ello en términos de hastío, habla con indiferencia de ello.
blaspheme [blæs'fi:m] vi blasfemar.
blasphemer [blæs'fi:mə*] n blasfemador m, ora f.
blasphemous ['blæsfiməs] adj blasfemo.
blasphemy ['blæsfimi] n blasfemia f.
blast [bla:st] **1** n **(a)** (of wind) ráfaga f; (of air) soplo m; (of sand, water) chorro m.
(b) (sound) trompetazo m; (of whistle etc) toque m.
(c) (explosive) carga f explosiva; (force of explosion) sacudida f, choque m, presión f.
(d) (of criticism etc) tempestad f, oleada f.
2 vt (with explosive) volar; (by lightning) derribar, destruir; (Mil) bombardear; (Bot) marchitar, (with blight) añublar; (fig) arruinar; criticar duramente; **to — open** abrir con carga explosiva; **— (it)!** ¡maldición!
blasted ['bla:stid] adj condenado.
blast furnace ['bla:st'fə:nis] n alto horno m.
blast-off ['bla:stɔf] n lanzamiento m, disparo m inicial.
blatant ['bleitənt] adj (shameless) descarado; agresivo; (noisy) estrepitoso, vociglero; colour etc chillón.
blatantly ['bleitəntli] adv descaradamente.
blather ['blæðə*] **1** n disparates mpl. **2** vi charlatanear.
blaze[1] [bleiz] **1** n (with flames) llamarada f, (steady

glow) resplandor *m*; *(fire)* incendio *m*; *(bonfire)* hoguera *f*; **the garden is a — of colour** el jardín está radiante de color; **in a — en llamas; in a — of anger** en un arranque de cólera; **in a — of publicity** bajo los focos de la publicidad; **like —s** *(fam)* hasta más no poder, con todas sus fuerzas; **what the —s . . .?** ¿qué diablos . . .?; **go to —s!** ¡vete al diablo!

2 *vi* arder en llamas; *(fig)* brillar, resplandecer; **all the lights were blazing** brillaban todas las luces; **to — with anger** estar encendido de ira; **to — away** seguir tirando rápidamente; **the sun was blazing down** brillaba implacable el sol, picaba muy fuerte el sol; **to — up** (volver a) encenderse vivamente, *(fig)* estallar.

blaze² [bleiz] **1** *n* *(on animal)* mancha *f*, estrella *f*; *(on tree)* señal *f* (hecha para servir de guía). **2** *vt*: **to — a trail** abrir un camino *(also fig)*.

blazer ['bleizə*] *n* chaqueta *f* ligera (de deporte *etc*).

blazing ['bleiziŋ] *adj* *sun* abrasador; *light* brillante; *anger* irreprimible; *row* violento.

blazon ['bleizn] **1** *n* blasón *m*. **2** *vt* *(fig)* proclamar.

bleach [bliːtʃ] **1** *n* lejía *f*. **2** *vt* blanquear. **3** *vi* blanquearse.

bleachers ['bliːtʃəz] *npl* *(US)* gradas *fpl* al sol.

bleaching powder ['bliːtʃiŋ,paudə*] *n* polvos *mpl* de blanqueo.

bleak [bliːk] *adj* *landscape* desierto, *(treeless)* pelado; *weather* crudo; *smile* poco afable; *welcome* inhospitalario; *prospect* nada prometedor.

bleary ['bliəri] *adj* *eye* legañoso.

bleary-eyed ['bliəriaid] *adj* de ojos legañosos.

bleat [bliːt] **1** *n* balido *m*. **2** *vi* balar; *(fig)* quejarse *(about* de).

bled [bled] *pret and ptp of* **bleed**.

bleed [bliːd] *(irr: pret and ptp* **bled**) **1** *vt (Med)* sangrar; *(fig)* desangrar; **to — someone white** desangrar a uno, arrancar hasta el último céntimo a uno; **to — a country white** explotar despiadadamente un país.

2 *vi* sangrar; *(tree)* exudar; **to be —ing at the nose** echar sangre por las narices; **to — to death** morir de desangramiento; **to — for** sangrar de dolor por; **those who have bled for England** los que han vertido su sangre por Inglaterra.

bleeder ['bliːdə*] *n (Med)* hemofílico *m*.

bleeding ['bliːdiŋ] *adj (sl)* puñetero.

bleep [bliːp] **1** *n* sonido *m* agudo; *(Radio)* señal *f* (aguda, continua). **2** *vi (Radio)* emitir una señal (aguda, continua).

blemish ['blemiʃ] *n* tacha *f*, mancha *f*.

blench [blentʃ] *vi* cejar, recular; palidecer.

blend [blend] **1** *n* mezcla *f*, combinación *f*.

2 *vt* mezclar, combinar, armonizar; *colours* casar.

3 *vi* combinarse, armonizarse; **to — in with** armonizarse con, formar un conjunto armonioso con; **to — into** transformarse poco a poco en.

blender ['blendə*] *n* catador *m*; **tea —** catador *m* de té.

bless [bles] *vt* bendecir; **God — you!** ¡Dios te bendiga!; **well I'm —ed!, God — my soul!** ¡caramba!; **I'm —ed if I know** que me maten si lo sé; **they were —ed with children** Dios les dio la bendición de los hijos; **she is —ed with every virtue** le adornan mil virtudes; **I — the day I bought it** bendigo el día que lo compré.

blessed ['blesid] *adj* **(a)** bendito, bienaventurado; **the B— Virgin** la Santísima Virgen; **— be Thy Name** bendito sea tu Nombre; **a day of — calm** un día de bendita tranquilidad.

(b) *(fig)* santo; **the whole — day** todo el santo día; **where's that — book?** ¿dónde diablos estará el libro ese?; **we didn't find a — thing** no encontramos nada en absoluto.

blessing ['blesiŋ] *n* **(a)** bendición *f*.

(b) *(advantage)* beneficio *m*, ventaja *f*; **the —s of electricity** los beneficios de la electricidad; **the —s of science** los adelantos que nos proporciona la ciencia; **to count one's —s** pensar en los muchos beneficios que tiene uno; **it's a — in disguise** no hay mal que por bien no venga; **it's a mixed —** está muy bien pero trae algunas desventajas, no es ganancia limpia en todos los aspectos.

blest [blest] *adj and ptp (poet)* of **bless**.

blether ['bleðə*] *see* **blather**.

blew [bluː] *pret of* **blow**.

blight [blait] **1** *n (Bot)* añublo *m*, tizón *m*, roya *f*; *(fig)* plaga *f*, infortunio *m*; desperfecto *m*, mancha *f*; **to cast a — on** *(or over)* arruinar.

2 *vt (Bot)* añublar, atizonar; arruinar *(also fig)*.

blighter ['blaitə*] *n (sl)* tío *m*, sujeto *m*; **you —!** *(hum)* ¡cacho cabrón!; **what a lucky —!** ¡es un chorrón!

Blighty ['blaiti] *(Mil sl)* Inglaterra *f*.

blimey ['blaimi] *interj (sl)* ¡caray!

blimp [blimp] *n* globo *m*; *(person)* reaccionario *m*, militarista *m*, patriotero *m*.

blind [blaind] **1** *adj* ciego *(also fig, Archit; to* a, para; *with* de); *alley* sin salida; *corner* sin visibilidad; **— in one eye** tuerto; **as — as a bat** más ciego que un topo; **a — man** un ciego; **the — los ciegos; it's a case of the — leading the —** tan ciego el uno como el otro; **to be — to** no ver, *(deliberately)* hacer la vista gorda a; **he is — to all dangers** no comprende en absoluto los peligros; **he is — to her true character** se le oculta su verdadero carácter; **to fly —** volar a ciegas; **to go —** quedar ciego.

2 *n* **(a)** *(also* **Venetian —)** persiana *f*; *(outside window)* toldo *m*.

(b) pretexto *m*, subterfugio *m*; **it's all a —** no es más que un pretexto.

3 *vt* cegar; *(dazzle)* deslumbrar; **to be —ed in an accident** quedar ciego después de un accidente; **to be —ed by anger** estar cegado por la ira, estar ciego de ira.

blindfold ['blaindfəuld] **1** *adj* con los ojos vendados *(also fig); game of chess* a la ciega. **2** *n* venda *f*. **3** *vt* vendar los ojos a.

blinding ['blaindiŋ] *adj* *light* intenso, que ciega, cegador.

blindly ['blaindli] *adv* a ciegas *(also fig)*.

blind man's buff ['blaindmænz'bʌf] *n* gallina *f* ciega.

blindness ['blaindnis] *n* ceguera *f*, ceguedad *f*.

blindworm ['blaindwə:m] *n* lución *m*.

blink [bliŋk] **1** *n* parpadeo *m*; *(gleam)* destello *m*.

2 *vt* guiñar, cerrar momentáneamente; **to — one's eyes** parpadear; **there is no —ing the fact that** es imposible soslayar el hecho de que.

3 *vi* parpadear, pestañear; *(light)* oscilar.

blinkers ['bliŋkəz] *npl* anteojeras *fpl*.

blinking ['bliŋkiŋ] *adj (fam)* maldito.

bliss [blis] *(Rel)* bienaventuranza *f*; *(fig)* éxtasis *m*, arrobamiento *m*; **the concert was —!** ¡el concierto fue una gloria! **what —!** ¡qué bien!; **isn't he —?** ¡qué hombre más estupendo!

blissful ['blisful] *adj* bienaventurado; *(happy)* feliz; *(fig)* deleitoso; *(fam)* maravilloso, estupendo.

blissfully ['blisfuli] *adv* felizmente; deleitosamente; maravillosamente, estupendamente.

blister ['blistə*] **1** *n* ampolla *f*. **2** *vt* ampollar, causar ampollas en. **3** *vi* ampollarse.

blistering ['blistəriŋ] *adj* *heat* abrasador; *criticism* feroz, devastador.

blithe [blaið] *adj* alegre.

blithely ['blaiðli] *adv* alegremente.

blithering ['bliðəriŋ] *adj*: **— idiot** imbécil *mf*.

blitz [blits] **1** *n* guerra *f* relámpago; *(Aer)* bombardeo *m* aéreo; *(fig)* campaña *f (on* contra); **the B— el bombardeo alemán de Inglaterra en 1940–42**. **2** *vt* bombardear.

blizzard ['blizəd] *n* ventisca *f*.

bloated ['bləutid] *adj* hinchado *(also fig; with* de), abotagado.

bloater ['bləutə*] *n* arenque *m* ahumado.

blob [blɔb] *n (drop)* gota *f*; *(lump)* burujo *m*; *(blot)* borrón *m*; *(stain)* mancha *f*.

bloc [blɔk] *n* bloque *m*; **en —** en bloque.

block [blɔk] **1** *n (of stone, stamps, cylinder, Pol etc)* bloque *m*; *(for paving)* adoquín *m*; *(of wood)* zoquete *m*; *(butcher's, executioner's)* tajo *m*; *(children's toys)* tarugos *mpl*; *(of houses)* manzana *f*, cuadra *f* *(S Am)*; *(fig)* obstáculo *m*, estorbo *m*; **— and tackle** aparejo *m* de poleas; **— of flats** bloque *m* de pisos; **to knock someone's — off** *(sl)* romper la crisma a uno.

2 *adj*: **— letter** mayúscula *f*; **please write in — letters** escribir por favor en caracteres de imprenta.

3 *vt* obstruir, cerrar; *traffic, progress* estorbar, impedir; *(Parl) bill* bloquear; *(Comm) account* bloquear; *road* **—ed** cerrado (por obras); **the line is —ed in 4 places** la vía está cortada en 4 lugares; **to — in, to — out** esbozar; **to — up** tapar, cegar.

4 *vi* obstruirse, cerrarse.

blockade [blɔ'keid] **1** *n* bloqueo *m*; **to run the —** forzar *(or* burlar) el bloqueo. **2** *vt* bloquear.

blockage ['blɔkidʒ] *n* obstrucción *f*; obstáculo *m*, estorbo *m*.

blockbuster ['blɔk,bʌstə*] *n (Mil: fam)* bomba *f* revientamanzanas.

blockhead ['blɔkhed] *n* zopenco *m*, a *f*; **you —!** ¡imbécil!

blockhouse ['blɔkhaus] *n* blocao *m*.

bloke [bləuk] *n (sl)* tío *m*, sujeto *m*.

blond(e) [blɔnd] **1** *adj* rubio. **2** *n* rubia *f*; **platinum — rubia** *f* platino.

blood [blʌd] n sangre f; (family) sangre f, linaje m; parentesco m; (person) galán m; **bad** — mala f leche, mala f uva; **blue** — sangre f azul; — **royal** estirpe f regia; **in cold** — a sangre fría; **that man of** — aquel monstruo; — **is thicker than water** son muy fuertes los lazos de parentesco; **it's in the** — lo lleva en la sangre; **they're out for** — están dispuestos a verter sangre; **he's after my** — me tiene un odio mortal, (hum) quiere darme una paliza; **when my** — **is up** cuando me encolerizo; **to draw** — hacer que sangre uno, herir, (fig) herir en lo vivo; **he has X's** — **on his hands** tiene las manos manchadas con la sangre de X; **it makes my** — **boil** me saca de quicio; **we need new** — **in the company** hace falta gente nueva en la compañia; **my** — **ran cold** se me heló la sangre; **to shed one's** — verter su sangre; **to shed (or spill) the** — **of** derramar la sangre de; **without shedding** — sin efusión de sangre; **it's like trying to get** — **out of a stone** es como sacar agua de las piedras.

blood-and-thunder ['blʌdən'θʌndə*] **1** adj aparatosamente violento, intencionadamente cruel; melodramático.

2 n violencia f aparatosa, crueldad f intencionada; melodrama m.

blood bank ['blʌdbæŋk] n banco m de sangre.

blood bath ['blʌdbɑ:θ] n carnicería f, baño m de sangre.

blood count ['blʌdkaunt] n recuento m sanguíneo.

bloodcurdling ['blʌd,kə:dliŋ] adj espeluznante, horripilante.

blood donor ['blʌd,dəunə*] n donador m de sangre.

blood feud ['blʌdfju:d] n odio m de sangre.

blood group ['blʌdgru:p] n grupo m sanguíneo.

blood heat ['blʌdhi:t] n temperatura f de la sangre.

bloodhound ['blʌdhaund] n.sabueso m.

bloodless ['blʌdlis] adj exangüe, (lacking spirit) soso; revolt etc incruento, sin efusión de sangre.

blood money ['blʌd,mʌni] n dinero m manchado de sangre.

blood orange ['blʌd,ɔrindʒ] n naranja f sanguina.

blood poisoning ['blʌd,pɔizniŋ] n envenenamiento m de la sangre.

blood pressure ['blʌd,preʃə*] n presión f sanguínea, tensión f arterial; (ie high —) hipertensión f.

blood-red ['blʌd'red] adj sanguíneo, sanguinolento.

blood relation ['blʌdri'leiʃən] n pariente m consanguíneo, parienta f consanguínea.

bloodshed ['blʌdʃed] n efusión f de sangre; mortandad f.

bloodshot ['blʌdʃɔt] adj inyectado en sangre.

blood sports ['blʌdspɔ:ts] npl caza f.

bloodstained ['blʌdsteind] adj manchado de sangre.

bloodstock ['blʌdstɔk] n caballos mpl de raza.

bloodstone ['blʌdstəun] n restañasangre m; hematites f.

bloodstream ['blʌdstri:m] n corriente f sanguínea.

bloodsucker ['blʌdsʌkə*] n (fig) sanguijuela f.

blood test ['blʌdtest] n análisis m de sangre.

bloodthirsty ['blʌdθə:sti] adj sanguinario.

blood transfusion ['blʌdtrænz'fju:ʒən] n transfusión f de sangre.

blood vessel ['blʌd,vesl] n vaso m sanguíneo.

bloody ['blʌdi] **1** adj battle sangriento, cruento; steak sanguinolento; hands, dress ensangrentado, manchado de sangre; (fig) puñetero.

2 adv (fig, fam) muy, terriblemente, condenadamente.

bloody-minded ['blʌdi'maindid] adj (sl) malintencionado; de mal genio, de malas pulgas; **to be** — **about a matter** mostrarse poco dispuesto a ayudar en un asunto, crear dificultades para la solución de un problema; **don't be so** — ! ¡no seas malintencionado!, ¡qué mala idea!

bloody-mindedness ['blʌdi'maindidnis] n (sl) mala intención f; mal genio m; mala disposición f (para ayudar etc).

bloom [blu:m] **1** n flor f; floración f, (fig) perfección f; lozanía f; (on fruit) vello m; **in** — en flor; **in full** — en plena floración; **in the full** — **of youth** en la flor de su edad; **to come into** — florecer.

2 vi florecer, (fig) prosperar, lozanear, hacer eclosión.

bloomer ['blu:mə*] n (fam) plancha f.

bloomers ['blu:məz] npl pantalones mpl (de señora).

blooming ['blu:miŋ] adj floreciente; (euph, fam) condenado.

blossom ['blɔsəm] **1** n flor f; **in** — en flor.

2 vi florecer; **to** — **into** transformarse en, convertirse (algo inesperadamente) en; **to** — **out** desarrollarse, mostrar las muchas posibilidades que tiene uno, hacer eclosión.

blot [blɔt] **1** n borrón m (also fig); **a** — **on the family escutcheon** una mancha en el honor de la familia; **a** — **on the landscape** una cosa que afea el paisaje.

2 vt (with ink) manchar, emborronar; (with blotter) secar; reputation desacreditar; **to** — **out** oscurecer, hacer desaparecer; (fig) aniquilar, arrasar; **to** — **up** ink secar; mist beber, absorber.

3 vi (pen) echar borrones.

blotch [blɔtʃ] n mancha f; (on skin) erupción f.

blotchy ['blɔtʃi] adj manchado, lleno de manchas; skin lleno de erupciones.

blotter ['blɔtə*] n secante m tipo rodillo, secafirmas m; (sheet) hoja f de papel secante.

blotting paper ['blɔtiŋ,peipə*] n papel m secante.

blotto ['blɔtəu] adj (sl): **to be** — estar mamao.

blouse [blauz] n blusa f.

blow¹ [bləu] n (a) golpe m; bofetada f; (a — with may often be translated by the suffix -azo, eg) **a** — **with a hammer** un martillazo, **a** — **with the fist** un puñetazo; **at one** — de un solo golpe; **to deal (or strike) someone a** — dar (or asestar) un golpe a uno; **to strike a** — **for freedom** dar un golpe por la libertad; **without striking a** — sin efusión de sangre, sin violencia; **to come to** —s venir a las manos.

(b) (fig) golpe m; **that's a** — ! ¡qué lástima!; **it is a cruel** — **for everybody** es un golpe cruel para todos; **the news came as a great** — la noticia me causó un gran disgusto; **the affair was a** — **to his pride** la cosa le hirió en el amor propio; **it was a final** — **to our hopes** esto terminó de arruinar nuestras esperanzas; **on Monday the** — **fell** el lunes se descargó el golpe.

blow² [bləu] **1** n soplo m, soplido m; **to go for a** — (fam) dar una vuelta.

2 (irr: pret **blew**, ptp **blown**) vt **(a)** (of wind) llevar; **the wind blew the ship towards the coast** el viento llevó el barco hacia la costa; **the wind has blown dust all over it** el viento lo ha cubierto todo de polvo.

(b) glass soplar; organ dar viento a; trumpet etc tocar, sonar; nose sonarse; bubble hacer; kiss tirar, echar; at one — de un solo golpe; fuse quemar; money (fam) gastar, despilfarrar.

(c) — **me!, well I'm** —**ed!** ¡caramba!; **I'll be** —**ed if que me cuelguen si;** — **the expense!** ¡no hagamos caso del precio!

(d) **to** — **about** leaves etc llevar de acá para allá; **to** — **away** llevarse; arrancar; **to** — **down** derribar; **to** — **off** quitar, arrebatar; **to** — **the dust off a table** quitar el polvo de una mesa soplando; **to** — **open** door abrir de golpe, safe abrir con explosivos; **to** — **out** candle apagar, flames henchir; **to** — **over** derribar, volcar; **to** — **up** tyre etc inflar; photo ampliar; (with explosive) volar; (with publicity) dar bombo a; **to** — **someone up into a great novelist** hacer creer que alguien es gran novelista.

3 vi (wind, whale) soplar; (puff and —) jadear, resoplar; (siren etc) sonar; (fuse) quemarse; (sl) irse; **it's** —**ing a gale** hace muchísimo viento; **to** — **in** (sl) entrar de sopetón, llegar inesperadamente; **to** — **on one's fingers** soplarse los dedos; **to** — **on one's soup** enfriar la sopa soplando; **to** — **open** abrirse de golpe; **to** — **out** apagarse; **to** — **over** pasar, quedar olvidado, no tener consecuencias de importancia; **to** — **up** (explosive) estallar, hacer explosión; (container) reventar; (fam) reventar (de ira); **now something else has blown up** ahora ha surgido otra cosa; **it's** —**ing up for rain** con este viento tendremos lluvia.

blower ['bləuə*] n (sl) teléfono m.

blowfly ['bləuflai] n moscarda f, mosca f azul.

blowlamp ['bləulæmp] n soplete m, lámpara f de soldar.

blown [bləun] **1** ptp of **blow²**. **2** adj **(a)** flower marchito. **(b)** bridge etc volado, destruido.

blow-out ['bləuaut] n (Aut) pinchazo m; (Elec) quemadura f; (sl) banquetazo m, atracón m.

blowpipe ['bləupaip] n cerbatana f.

blow-up ['bləuʌp] n (a) (Phot) ampliación f. (b) (fam) explosión f de ira; riña f, pelea f (between entre).

blowy ['bləui] adj ventoso; de mucho viento; **on a** — **day in March** un día de marzo de mucho viento; **it's** — **here** aquí hay mucho viento.

blowzy ['blauzi] adj desaliñado; de aspecto muy ordinario; (red in face) colorado.

blubber¹ ['blʌbə*] n grasa f de ballena.

blubber² ['blʌbə*] **1** vt decir lloriqueando. **2** vi lloriquear, llorar a lágrima viva.

bludgeon ['blʌdʒən] **1** n cachiporra f. **2** vt aporrear; **to** — **someone into doing something** obligar a uno a porrazos a hacer algo.

blue [blu:] **1** adj azul; body, bruise amoratado; (Pol) conservador; blood azul, noble; joke, song verde; (sad) deprimido, triste, melancólico; **to feel —** estar melancólico; **to look —** tener aspecto triste.

2 n (a) azul m; (Chem) añil m; **the —** (sky) el cielo, (sea) el mar; **electric —** azul m eléctrico; **navy —** azul m de mar; **Prussian —** azul m de Prusia; **to come out of the —** venir como cosa llovida del cielo, bajar del cielo, (bad news) caer como una bomba.

(b) (Pol) conservador m, ora f; **a true —** un conservador de los más leales.

(c) **—s** melancolía f, murrias fpl, morriña f.

3 vt azular; washing añilar, dar azulete a; (fam) despilfarrar.

bluebell ['blu:bel] n campánula f azul.
blueberry ['blu:beri] n (US) vaccinio m.
bluebird ['blu:bə:d] n pájaro m azul, azulejo m de América.
blue-blooded ['blu:'blʌdid] adj de sangre noble, linajudo.
bluebottle ['blu:,bɔtl] n moscarda f, mosca f azul.
blue-eyed ['blu:,aid] adj de ojos azules.
bluejacket ['blu:,dʒækit] n marinero m (de buque de guerra).
blueness ['blu:nis] n azul m, lo azul.
blue-pencil ['blu:'pensl] vt tachar, suprimir (en la censura).
blueprint ['blu:print] n cianotipo m, ferroprusiato m; (fig) anteproyecto m (for de).
bluestocking ['blu:,stɔkiŋ] n literata f, marisabidilla f.
blue tit ['blu:tit] n primavera f.
bluff [blʌf] **1** adj escarpado; person brusco, francote.
2 n (a) (Geog) risco m, peñasco m.

(b) bluff m, farol m; **to call someone's —** coger a uno en un abrenuncio.

3 vt hacer un bluff a, engañar, intimidar con amenazas que no se pueden cumplir.

4 vi hacer un bluff, farolear, tirarse un farol.
bluish ['blu:iʃ] adj azulado, azulino.
blunder ['blʌndə*] **1** n patochada f, patinazo m; error m garrafal.

2 vt: **to — out** descolgarse con.

3 vi hacer una patochada, tirarse una plancha; **to — about** andar a ciegas, andar a tontas y a locas; **to — into** chocar con; **to — upon** tropezar con.
blunderbuss ['blʌndəbʌs] n trabuco m.
blunt [blʌnt] **1** adj edge embotado, desafilado; point despuntado; manner directo, franco, abrupto; statement terminante, franco; person francote; **with a — instrument** con un instrumento contundente.

2 vt embotar (also fig), desafilar, despuntar.
bluntly ['blʌntli] adv francamente, de modo terminante.
bluntness ['blʌntnis] n embotadura f; (fig) franqueza f, brusquedad f.
blur [blə:*] **1** n contorno m borroso, impresión f imprecisa; **my mind was a —** me veía imposibilitado de recordar con precisión nada, todo se había vuelto borroso en mi mente.

2 vt hacer borroso, oscurecer, empañar, desdibujar; **a —red photo** una foto desenfocada; **a —red image** una imagen borrosa; **my eyes were —red with tears** las lágrimas enturbiaban mi vista.

3 vi desdibujarse, hacerse borroso.
blurb [blə:b] n anuncio m efusivo (de un libro).
blurt [blə:t] vt: **to — out** descolgarse con, decir a bulto; secret revelar.
blush [blʌʃ] **1** n rubor m, sonrojo m; (glow) color m de rosa; **the first — of dawn** la primera luz del alba; **in the first — of youth** en la inocencia de la edad juvenil; **at first —** a primera vista; **it should not bring a — to the face of a bishop** no haría sonrojar a una hermana de la caridad; **to spare someone's —es** dejar de contar algo para no ofender a uno.

2 vi ruborizarse, sonrojarse, ponerse colorado (at por, with de); **to — like a lobster** (or **tomato**) ponerse colorado como un pavo; **I — for you me das vergüenza; **I — to + infin** me avergüenzo de + infin; **to make someone —** sofocar a uno, hacer que uno se ruborice.
blushing ['blʌʃiŋ] adj ruboroso; bride candoroso.
bluster ['blʌstə*] **1** n jactancia f; fanfarronadas fpl, bravatas fpl.

2 vt: **to — it out** defenderse echando bravatas.

3 vi fanfarronear, echar bravatas.
blustery ['blʌstəri] adj wind tempestuoso.
boa ['bəuə] n boa f.
boar [bɔ:*] n verraco m, cerdo m padre; **wild —** jabalí m.
board [bɔ:d] **1** n (a) (of wood) tabla f, tablero m, tablón m; (notice-) tablón m; (table) mesa f; (in bookbinding) cartón m; (for chess etc) tablero m; **the —s** (Theat) las tablas; **in —s** (book) en cartoné; **to**

sweep the — ganar todas las bazas, (in election) copar todos los escaños.

(b) pensión f; **full —** pensión f completa; **— and lodging** comida f y casa.

(c) (Naut) **on —** a bordo; en el tren, en el autobús etc; **on — (the) ship** a bordo del barco; **to go on —** ir a bordo; **to go by the —** ser abandonado, ser olvidado.

(d) (persons) junta f, consejo m de administración; **— of directors** junta f directiva; **B— of Trade** Ministerio m de Comercio; **medical —** tribunal m médico; **planning —** comisión f planificadora; **— meeting** reunión f de la junta directiva.

2 vt (with boards) entablar, enmaderar (also **to — up**); ship ir a bordo de, embarcarse en; enemy ship abordar; bus, train subir a; person hospedar, dar pensión (completa) a.

3 vi: **to — with** hospedarse en casa de.
boarder ['bɔ:də*] n huésped m, eda f; (School) interno m, a f.
boarding ['bɔ:diŋ] n entablado m.
boarding house ['bɔ:diŋhaus] n, pl **— houses** [,hauziz] pensión f, casa f de huéspedes.
boarding school ['bɔ:diŋsku:l] n internado m.
board room ['bɔ:drum] n sala f de juntas.
boardwalk ['bɔ:dwɔ:k] n (US) paseo m entablado (a la orilla del mar).
boast [bəust] **1** n baladronada f; **it is his — that se jacta de que.

2 vt enorgullecerse de poseer, ostentar.

3 vi jactarse; **to — about**, **to — of** jactarse de, hacer alarde de; **that's nothing to — about** eso no es motivo para vanagloriarse.
boasted ['bəustid] adj alardeado, cacareado.
boaster ['bəustə*] n jactancioso m, a f, fanfarrón m.
boastful ['bəustful] adj jactancioso, fanfarrón.
boastfully ['bəustfuli] adv jactanciosamente.
boastfulness ['bəustfulnis] n jactancia f.
boasting ['bəustiŋ] n jactancia f, baladronadas fpl.
boat [bəut] n (in general) barco m; (large ship) buque m, navío m; (small) barca f, embarcación f; (racing eight, ship's —) bote m; **we're all in the same —** todos estamos embarcados en la misma nave; **to burn one's —s** quemar las naves; **to go by —** ir en barco; **to launch** (or **lower**) **the —s** botar los botes al agua; **to miss the —** (fig) perder la ocasión, llegar tarde; **to push the — out** (sl) ir de parranda; **to rock the —** (fig) perturbar el equilibrio.
boatbuilder ['bəut,bildə*] n constructor m de barcos.
boat deck ['bəut,dek] n cubierta f de botes.
boater ['bəutə*] n sombrero m de paja.
boat hook ['bəuthuk] n bichero m.
boathouse ['bəuthaus] n cobertizo m para botes.
boating ['bəutiŋ] n canotaje m.
boatload ['bəutləud] n barcada f.
boatman ['bəutmən] n, pl **—men** [mən] barquero m.
boat race ['bəutreis] n regata f.
boatswain ['bəusn] n contramaestre m.
boat train ['bəuttrein] n tren m que enlaza con un barco.
Bob [bɔb] m nombre abreviado de **Robert**.
bob[1] [bɔb] **1** n (of hair) pelo m a lo garçon. **2** vt hair cortar a lo garçon.
bob[2] [bɔb] n (sl) chelín m.
bob[3] [bɔb] **1** n (jerk) sacudida f, meneo m, movimiento m brusco; (curtsy) reverencia f.

2 vi menearse, agitarse; **to — about** (in wind etc) bailar, (on water) fluctuar; **to — down** sentarse; agacharse; esconderse; **to — to someone** hacer una reverencia a uno; **to — up** levantarse, aparecer; (fig) surgir, presentarse inesperadamente; **to — up and down** subir y bajar, (person) levantarse y sentarse repetidas veces.
bobbin ['bɔbin] n carrete m, bobina f (also Elec); (Sew) canilla f.
Bobby ['bɔbi] m nombre abreviado de **Robert**.
bobby ['bɔbi] n (sl) guili m, poli m.
bobbysocks ['bɔbisɔks] npl (US) escarpines mpl.
bobbysoxer ['bɔbisɔksə*] n (US fam) tobillera f.
bobsled ['bɔbsled] n, **bobsleigh** ['bɔbslei] n bob m, trineo m de balancín.
bobtail ['bɔbteil] n cola f corta; animal m de cola corta, animal m rabón.
Boccaccio [bɔ'kætʃiəu] m Bocacio.
Boche [bɔʃ] **1** adj alemán, tudesco. **2** n alemán m; **the —** los alemanes.
bod [bɔd] n (sl) tío m, individuo m.
bode [bəud] **1** vt presagiar; **it —s no good** esto no nos promete nada bueno. **2** vi: **this —s ill for** esto es mala señal para.
bodice ['bɔdis] n corpiño m, almilla f.

-bodied ['bɔdid] *adj* de cuerpo . . ., *eg* **small-bodied** de cuerpo pequeño; **full-bodied** cry fuerte, *wine* generoso.

bodily ['bɔdili] **1** *adj* corpóreo, corporal; — **needs** necesidades *fpl* corporales. **2** *adv* (*in person*) en persona; (*as a whole*) en conjunto; **to lift someone** — levantar a uno en peso.

bodkin ['bɔdkin] *n* (*Sew*) aguja *f* de jareta; (*Typ*) punzón *m*; (*for hair*) espadilla *f*.

body ['bɔdi] *n* (**a**) cuerpo *m*; (*corpse*) cadáver *m*; (*fam*) persona *f*; (*frame*) armazón *f*, bastidor *m*; (*Aut*) caja *f*, carrocería *f*; — **and soul** (*as adv*) de todo corazón, con el alma; **the** — **politic** el estado; **heavenly** — astro *m*, cuerpo *m* celeste; **over my dead** —! ¡bajo ningún concepto!; **to keep** — **and soul together** vivir justo, seguir viviendo.

(**b**) (*corporation etc*) corporación *f*; **learned** — academia *f*; **legislative** — cuerpo *m* legislativo; **public** — corporación *f* estatal.

(**c**) (*group*) grupo *m*, conjunto *m*; **a considerable** — **of evidence** una colección importante de datos; **there is a** — **of opinion that** hay quien opina que; **a large** — **of people** un nutrido grupo de personas; **main** — grueso *m*; **the main** — **of his speech** la parte principal de su discurso; **in a** — todos juntos, en bloque.

bodyguard ['bɔdigɑːd] *n* (*man*) guardaespaldas *m*; (*men*) guardia *f* personal.

bodywork ['bɔdiwəːk] *n* (*Aut*) carrocería *f*.

Boer ['bəuə*] **1** *adj* bóer. **2** *n* bóer *mf*.

Boer War ['bəuə,wɔː*] *n* Guerra *f* Bóer, Guerra *f* del Transvaal.

boffin ['bɔfin] *n* científico *m*, inventor *m*.

bog [bɔg] **1** *n* pantano *m*, ciénaga *f*; (*sl*) wáter *m*.

2 *vt*: **to get** —**ged down** quedar atascado en el lodo, hundirse en el lodo; (*fig*) empantanarse, atrancarse (*in* en).

bogey ['bəugi] *n* (*goblin*) duende *m*, trasgo *m*; (*bugbear*) pesadilla *f*; (*policeman*: *sl*) guindilla *m*; **that is our** — **team** ese equipo es nuestra pesadilla.

boggle ['bɔgl] *vi* sobresaltarse, pasmarse; **don't just stand and** — no sirve para nada estar ahí boquiabierto; **the imagination** —**s** la imaginación es incapaz de representárselo; **to** — **at** vacilar ante, titubear ante.

boggy ['bɔgi] *adj* pantanoso.

bogie ['bəugi] *n* (*Rail*) bogie *m*, boga *f*.

bogus ['bəugəs] *adj* falso, fraudulento; *person* fingido; (*of person's character*) artificial, afectado.

bogy ['bəugi] *n see* **bogey, bogie.**

Bohemia [bəu'hiːmiə] *n* Bohemia *f*.

Bohemian [bəu'hiːmiən] **1** *adj* bohemo; (*fig*) bohemio. **2** *n* bohemo *m*, a *f*; (*fig*) bohemio *m*, a *f*.

boil[1] [bɔil] *n* (*Med*) divieso *m*.

boil[2] [bɔil] **1** *n*: **to be on the** — estar hirviendo; (*fig*) (*situation*) estar a punto de estallar, (*person*) estar furioso; **to bring to the** — calentar hasta que hierva; **to come to the** — comenzar a hervir, (*fig*) entrar en ebullición; **to go off the** — dejar de hervir.

2 *vt* hervir, hacer hervir, calentar hasta que hierva; (*Cook*) *liquid* hervir; *vegetables* herventar, cocer; *meat* salcochar; *egg* pasar por agua; **to** — **down** reducir por cocción; (*fig*) reducir a forma más sencilla.

3 *vi* hervir; **to** — **over** irse, rebosar; **it makes me** — me hace rabiar; **to** — **with rage** estar furioso; **to** — **with indignation** estar indignado; **it all** —**s down to this** la cosa se reduce a lo siguiente.

boiler ['bɔilə*] *n* caldera *f*.

boiler house ['bɔiləhaus] *n* edificio *m* de la caldera.

boiler room ['bɔilərum] *n* sala *f* de calderas.

boiler suit ['bɔiləsuːt] *n* mono *m*.

boiling ['bɔiliŋ] *adj* hirviendo (*invariable*), en ebullición; **it's** — **hot** (*weather*) hace un calor terrible; **on a** — **hot day** un día de mucho calor.

boiling point ['bɔiliŋpɔint] *n* punto *m* de ebullición.

boisterous ['bɔistərəs] *adj* *wind* borrascoso; *behaviour* ruidoso, turbulento; *child* bullicioso; (*in high spirits*) muy alegre, de excelente humor; *meeting* nada tranquilo, alborotado; *welcome* tumultuoso.

bold [bəuld] *adj* (*courageous*) valiente, audaz; (*excessively* —) atrevido, osado, temerario; (*shameless*) descarado; *move, stroke* enérgico; *relief, contrast* fuerte; *headland* escarpado; *line* claro, vigoroso; — **face**, — **type** negrita *f*; **he came up as** — **as brass** se acercó tan fresco; **if I may make so** — si Vd me lo permite; **if I may make so** — **as to** + *infin* si se me permite + *infin*.

boldly ['bəuldli] *adv* audazmente; atrevidamente, con temeridad; descaradamente; enérgicamente; vigorosamente.

boldness ['bəuldnis] *n* audacia *f*, osadía *f*; temeridad *f*; descaro *m*; energía *f*; fuerza *f*, lo marcado.

bole [bəul] *n* tronco *m*.

bolero [bə'lɛərəu] *n* bolero *m*.

Bolivia [bə'liviə] Bolivia *f*.

Bolivian [bə'liviən] **1** *adj* boliviano. **2** *n* boliviano *m*, a *f*.

boll [bəul] *n* cápsula *f*.

bollard ['bɔləd] *n* bolardo *m*, noray *m*.

Bologna [bə'ləunjə] Bolonia.

boloney [bə'ləuni] *n* (*sl*) *see* **baloney.**

Bolshevik ['bɔlʃəvik] **1** *adj* bolchevique. **2** *n* bolchevique *mf*.

Bolshevism ['bɔlʃəvizəm] *n* bolchevismo *m*.

Bolshevist ['bɔlʃəvist] **1** *adj* bolchevista. **2** *n* bolchevista *mf*.

Bolshie ['bɔlʃi] *adj* (*fam*) turbulento, rebelde.

bolster ['bəulstə*] **1** *n* travesero *m*, cabezal *m*; (*Tech*) plancha *f* de garnitura, cojín *m*. **2** *vt* (*also to* — **up**) reforzar; (*fig*) alentar, dar aliento a.

bolt [bəult] **1** *n* (**a**) (*of door, rifle*) cerrojo *m*; (*arrow*) cuadrillo *m*; (*of cloth*) rollo *m*; (*Tech*) perno *m*, tornillo *m*; (*of thunder*) rayo *m*; — **from the blue** suceso *m* inesperado, sorpresa *f* desagradable; **he has shot his** — ha hecho todo cuanto en él cabe.

(**b**) fuga *f* precipitada, salida *f* repentina; **to make a** — **for it** evadirse corriendo, escapar repentinamente; **he made a** — **for the door** se precipitó hacia la puerta.

2 *as adv*: — **upright** rígido, erguido.

3 *vt* *door* echar el cerrojo a; (*Tech*) sujetar con tornillos, empernar; *food* engullir, comer rapidísimamente; **to** — **two things together** unir dos cosas con pernos; **to** — **someone out** dejar fuera a uno echando el cerrojo a la puerta.

4 *vi* (*escape*) fugarse; (*horse*) desbocarse, dispararse; (*rush*) precipitarse; (*US Pol*) separarse del partido; **to** — **out** salir de golpe; **to** — **past** pasar como un rayo.

bolt-hole ['bəulthəul] *n* refugio *m*.

bomb [bɔm] **1** *n* bomba *f*; **atomic** — bomba *f* atómica; **hydrogen** — bomba *f* de hidrógeno; **incendiary** — bomba *f* incendiaria.

2 *vt* bombardear; **to be** —**ed out** ser desalojado por el bombardeo.

bombard [bɔm'bɑːd] *vt* bombardear; (*fig*) asediar, llenar (*with* de); **I was** —**ed with questions** me hicieron muchísimas preguntas.

bombardment [bɔm'bɑːdmənt] *n* bombardeo *m*.

bombast ['bɔmbæst] *n* ampulosidad *f*, rimbombancia *f*; (*words*) palabras *fpl* altisonantes; (*boasts*) bravatas *fpl*.

bombastic [bɔm'bæstik] *adj* altisonante, ampuloso, rimbombante; *person* jactancioso, farolero.

bomb crater ['bɔm,kreitə*] *n* cráter *m* de bomba.

bomber ['bɔmə*] *n* bombardero *m*.

bombing ['bɔmiŋ] *n* bombardeo *m*.

bombproof ['bɔmpruːf] *adj* a prueba de bombas.

bombshell ['bɔmʃel] *n*: **it fell like a** — cayó como una bomba.

bomb shelter ['bɔm,ʃeltə*] *n* refugio *m* antiaéreo.

bombsight ['bɔmsait] *n* mira *f* de bombardeo.

bomb site ['bɔmsait] *n* lugar *m* donde ha estallado una bomba; solar *m* arrasado por una bomba.

bona fide ['bəunə'faidi] *adj* genuino, auténtico.

bona fides ['bəunə'faidiz] *n* buena fe *f*; autenticidad *f*.

bonanza [bə'nænzə] *n* (*US*) bonanza *f* (*also fig*).

bonbon ['bɔnbɔn] *n* (*arch*) bombón *m*.

bond [bɔnd] *n* lazo *m*, vínculo *m*; (*Comm*) obligación *f*, bono *m*; (*bail, customs*) fianza *f*; —**s** (*fetters etc*) cuerdas *fpl*, cadenas *fpl*; **in** — en depósito bajo fianza.

bondage ['bɔndidʒ] *n* esclavitud *f*, cautiverio *m*.

bonded warehouse ['bɔndid'wɛəhaus] *n*, *pl* — **houses** [,hauziz] almacén *m* de depósito.

bondholder ['bɔnd,həuldə*] *n* obligacionista *mf*.

bond paper ['bɔnd,peipə*] *n* papel *m* blanco de calidad extra (para cartas).

bondsman ['bɔndzmən] *n*, *pl* —**men** [mən] (*Hist*) fiador *m*.

bone [bəun] **1** *n* hueso *m*; (*of fish*) espina *f*; —**s** (*of dead*) huesos *mpl*, (*more respectfully*) restos *mpl* mortales; — **of contention** manzana *f* de la discordia; **to feel something in one's** —**s** estar seguro de algo pero sin saber cómo, tener un presentimiento de algo; **to have a** — **to pick with someone** tener que arreglar cuentas con uno; **to make no** —**s about** + *ger* no vacilar en + *infin*; **to make no** —**s about something** no andarse con rodeos en (el asunto de) algo; **he won't make old** —**s** no llega a pájaros nuevos.

2 *vt meat* deshuesar, *fish* quitar las espinas a; (*sl*) birlar.

3 *vi* (*US*): **to — up** quemarse las cejas (*on* estudiando), empollar (*on* sobre).

bone china ['bəun'tʃainə] *n* porcelana *f* fina.

bone-dry ['bəun'drai] *adj* enteramente seco.

boneheaded ['bəun'hedid] *adj* estúpido.

bone-idle ['bəun'aidl] *adj* muy gandul.

bone meal ['bəunmi:l] *n* harina *f* de huesos.

boner ['bəunə*] *n* (*US*) plancha *f*, patochada *f*.

bonesetter ['bəun,setə*] *n* ensalmador *m*.

bone-shaker ['bəun,ʃeikə*] *n* (*Aut etc*) armatoste *m*, rácano *m*.

bonfire ['bɔnfaiə*] *n* hoguera *f*, fogata *f*.

bongo drum ['bɔŋgəudrʌm] *n* bongó *m*.

bonhomie ['bɔnɔmi:] *n* afabilidad *f*.

bon mot ['bɔn'məu] *n* aforismo *m*, chiste *m*, agudeza *f*.

bonnet ['bɔnit] *n* (*woman's*) gorra *f*, cofia *f*; (*large, showy*) papalina *f*, toca *f*; (*baby's*) capillo *m*; (*Scot's*) gorra *f* escocesa; (*Aut*) capó *m*.

bonny ['bɔni] *adj* (*esp Scot*) bonito, robusto, rollizo.

bonus ['bəunəs] **1** *n* plus *m*; (*on wages*) sobrepaga *f*, prima *f*, suplemento *m*; (*insurance etc*) prima *f*; **cost-of-living —** plus *m* de carestía de vida; **incentive —** prima *f* de incentivo; **output —** prima *f* por rendimiento.

2 *adj* adicional, extra.

bony ['bəuni] *adj* huesudo; (*like bone*) óseo, huesoso; (*thin*) descarnado, flaco.

boo[1] [bu:] (*equivalents in Spain etc*) **1** *n* silbido *m*, rechifla *f*, pateo *m*.

2 *vt* abuchear, silbar, rechiflar, patear; **to — an** actor patear a un actor; **he was —ed off the stage** tuvo que abandonar la escena a fuerza de pateo.

boo[2] [bu:] *n*: **not to say —** (**to a goose**) no decir chus ni mus.

boob [bu:b] (*sl*) **1** *n* (*person*) bobo *m*, a *f*; (*mistake*) patochada *f*. **2** *vt* tirar una plancha.

booby prize ['bu:bipraiz] *n* pequeño premio *m* de consolación.

booby trap ['bu:bitræp] *n* trampa *f* explosiva.

boogie-woogie ['bu:gi,wu:gi] *n* bugui-bugui *m*.

booing ['bu:iŋ] *n* abucheo *m*, silbos *mpl*, rechifla *f*.

book [buk] **1** *n* libro *m*; (*notebook*) libreta *f*, librito *m*; (*exercise book*) cuaderno *m*; (*of cheques, tickets*) libro *m* talonario; **reference —** libro *m* de consulta; **the —** (*Comm*) las cuentas, el balance; **the good —** la Biblia; **to be in someone's good —s** estar bien con uno; **to be in someone's bad —s** estar mal con uno; **to bring someone to —** pedir cuentas a uno, llamar a uno a capítulo; **to close the —s** (*Comm*) cerrar el borrador; **to go by the —** proceder según las reglas; **to make a — on** aceptar apuestas sobre; **to read someone like a —** conocer a uno a fondo; **to suit someone's —** convenir a uno; **to throw the — at someone** echar un rapapolvo a uno.

2 *vt* (*note down*) apuntar; (*Comm*) asentar (*to* en la cuenta de), *order* anotar; *room, place* reservar; *ticket* sacar; *performer* escriturar; *suspect* (*fam*) reseñar; **the hotel is —ed up** todas las habitaciones del hotel están reservadas; **we are —ed up all summer** no tenemos nada libre en todo el verano, lo tenemos todo vendido para todo el verano; **are you —ed up for tonight?** ¿tienes compromiso para esta noche?

3 *vi*: **— well in advance** es aconsejable reservar con mucha anticipación; **to — through to** sacar un billete hasta.

bookable ['bukəbl] *adj* que se puede reservar de antemano.

bookbinding ['buk,baindiŋ] *n* encuadernación *f*.

bookcase ['bukkeis] *n* librería *f*, estante *m* para libros.

book ends ['bukendz] *npl* sujetalibros *mpl*, soportalibros *mpl*.

bookie ['buki] *n* (*fam*) = **bookmaker**.

booking clerk ['bukiŋ,klɑ:k] *n* taquillero *m*.

booking office ['bukiŋ,ɔfis] *n* (*Rail*) despacho *m* de billetes; (*Theat*) taquilla *f*.

bookish ['bukiʃ] *adj* *learning* libresco; *person* estudioso, (*pej*) pedantesco.

book-keeper ['buk,ki:pə*] *n* tenedor *m* de libros.

book-keeping ['buk,ki:piŋ] *n* teneduría *f* de libros; **— by double entry** contabilidad *f* por partida doble; **— by single entry** contabilidad *f* por partida simple.

book learning ['buk,lə:niŋ] *n* (*pej*) erudición *f* adquirida en los libros, ciencia *f* libresca.

booklet ['buklit] *n* folleto *m*; (*learned*) opúsculo *m*; (*of tickets*) bono *m*.

bookmaker ['bukmeikə*] *n* corredor *m* de apuestas, apostador *m* profesional.

bookmark ['bukmɑ:k] *n* señal *f*, registro *m* (de libro).

bookplate ['bukpleit] *n* ex libris *m*.

book post ['bukpəust] *n* correo *m* de libros; tarifa *f* especial para libros.

bookrest ['bukrest] *n* atril *m*.

bookseller ['buk,selə*] *n* librero *m*; **—'s** librería *f*.

bookshelf ['bukʃelf] *n* estante *m* para libros.

bookshop ['bukʃɔp] *n* librería *f*.

bookstall ['bukstɔ:l] *n* quiosco *m* de libros.

bookworm ['bukwə:m] *n* polilla *f*; (*fig*) ratón *m* de biblioteca.

boom[1] [bu:m] *n* (*of jib*) botalón *m*, (*of mainsail*) botavara *f*; (*of crane*) aguilón *m*; (*across harbour*) barrera *f*.

boom[2] [bu:m] **1** *n* estampido *m*, trueno *m*; **sonic —** estampido *m* sónico.

2 *vi* hacer estampido, tronar; (*voice, radio, organ*) resonar, retumbar; (*gun*) retumbar.

boom[3] [bu:m] **1** *n* alza *f* rápida (*in prices* de los precios); prosperidad *f* repentina (*in an industry* de una industria); **the — started in 1968** la época de prosperidad comenzó en 1968; **there is a big — in tin** existe una gran demanda de estaño.

2 *adj*: **— town** ciudad *f* que disfruta de una prosperidad repentina; **in — conditions** en condiciones de prosperidad repentina.

3 *vi* (*prices*) estar en alza; (*commodity*) tener mucha demanda; (*industry, town*) disfrutar de gran prosperidad, estar en bonanza.

boomerang ['bu:məræŋ] **1** *n* bumerang *m*. **2** *adj* contraproducente, contrario a lo que se esperaba. **3** *vi* tener un resultado contraproducente (*on* para).

boon[1] [bu:n] *n* (*arch*) favor *m*; **it would be a — if he went** nos alegraríamos si se fuera; **the new machine is a great —** la nueva máquina representa un gran adelanto; **the servant is a — to me** la criada me ayuda muchísimo; **it should be a — to humanity** ha de ser un beneficio para el género humano.

boon[2] [bu:n] *adj*: **— companion** compañero *m* inseparable.

boor [buə*] *n* patán *m*.

boorish ['buəriʃ] *adj* palurdo, grosero.

boorishness ['buəriʃnis] *n* grosería *f*.

boost [bu:st] **1** *n* empuje *m*, empujón *m*, estímulo *m*, ayuda *f*; **to give a — to** = **2** *vt* empujar (hacia arriba); *price, sales, total* aumentar; *product* hacer publicidad por; *person* dar bombo a; *morale* reforzar; *process* estimular, fomentar, dar ímpetu a; (*Elec*) elevar.

booster ['bu:stə*] *n* (*Elec*) elevador *m* de tensión; (*Mech*) aumentador *m* de presión; (*Radio*) repetidor *m*.

booster rocket ['bu:stə,rɔkit] *n* cohete *m* secundario.

booster station ['bu:stə,steiʃən] *n* (*Radio*) repetidor *m*.

boot[1] [bu:t] **1** *n* bota *f*, (*Aut*) maleta *f*, portaequipajes *m*; **now the — is on the other foot** los papeles están trastrocados; **to die with one's —s on** morir al pie del cañón; **to get the —** (*fam*) ser despedido; **he's getting too big for his —s** tiene muchos humos; **to give someone the —** (*fam*) poner a uno en la calle; **to lick someone's —s** hacer la pelotilla a uno.

2 *vt* dar un puntapié a; **to — out** poner en la calle.

boot[2] [bu:t] *adv*: **to —** además, por añadidura.

bootblack ['bu:tblæk] *n* limpiabotas *m*.

bootee ['bu:ti:] *n* borceguí *m*, bota *f* de lana.

booth [bu:ð] *n* (*in market*) puesto *m*; (*at fair*) barraca *f*; (*Tel, voting-*) cabina *f*.

bootlace ['bu:tleis] *n* cordón *m*.

bootlegger ['bu:t,legə*] *n* (*US*) contrabandista *m* en licores.

bootlicker ['bu:t,likə*] *n* (*fam*) lameculos *m*.

boot-polish ['bu:t,pɔliʃ] *n* betún *m*.

boots [bu:ts] *n sing* limpiabotas *m* (de un hotel).

booty ['bu:ti] *n* botín *m*, presa *f*.

booze [bu:z] **1** *n* (**a**) (*in general*) bebida *f*, alcohol *m*; (*in particular*) vino *m*, cerveza *f* etc; **to go on the —** darse a la bebida.

(**b**) (*outing*) borrachera *f*; **to go on a —** ir de juerga.

2 *vt* beber.

3 *vi* beber; emborracharse.

boozer ['bu:zə*] *n* (*person*) bebedor *m*; (*pub*) bar *m*, taberna *f*.

boozy ['bu:zi] *adj* *person* borracho, aficionado a la bebida; *party* donde se bebe bastante; *song etc* tabernario.

borage ['bɔridʒ] *n* borraja *f*.

borax ['bɔ:ræks] *n* bórax *m*.

Bordeaux [bɔ:'dəu] Burdeos; **b—** (*wine*) burdeos *m*.

border ['bɔ:də*] **1** *n* borde *m*, margen *m*; (*Sew*) orla *f*, orilla *f*, cenefa *f*; (*Pol*) frontera *f*; (*Hort*) arriate *m*; **the B—** la *frontera entre Inglaterra y Escocia*.

2 *attr* *area, town, ballad* fronterizo; *guard* de la frontera.

3 *vt* (*Sew*) ribetear, orlar; **it is —ed on the north by** . . . confina en el norte con . . .

4 *vi*: **to — on** lindar con, confinar con; (*fig*) rayar en, aproximarse a.

bordering ['bɔːdəriŋ] *adj* contiguo.

borderland ['bɔːdələænd] *n* zona *f* fronteriza.

borderline ['bɔːdəlain] **1** *n* línea *f* divisoria; (*Pol and fig*) frontera *f*. **2** *adj* case etc dudoso, incierto.

bore¹ [bɔː*] **1** *n* (a) (*tool*) taladro *m*, barrena *f*; (*Geol*) sonda *f*.

(b) (*hole*) agujero *m*, barreno *m*; (*of gun*) calibre *m*, alma *f*; (*of cylinder*) alesaje *m*; (*for oil*) perforación *f*.

2 *vt* taladrar, perforar, agujerear, barrenar; **to — a hole in** practicar un agujero en; **to — one's way through** abrirse un camino por; **wood —d by insects** madera *f* carcomida.

3 *vi*: **to — for oil** hacer perforaciones en busca de petróleo.

bore² [bɔː*] **1** *n* (a) (*person*) pelmazo *m*, pesado *m*, a *f*; **what a — he is!** ¡qué hombre más pesado!

(b) (*thing*) lata *f*; **it's such a —** es una lata.

2 *vt* aburrir; fastidiar, molestar, dar la lata a; **to be —d, to get —d** aburrirse; **to be —d to death** (*or* **to tears, stiff**) aburrirse como una almeja.

bore³ [bɔː*] *pret of* **bear**².

boredom ['bɔːdəm] *n* aburrimiento *m*, fastidio *m*.

borehole ['bɔːhəul] *n* perforación *f*.

boric ['bɔːrik] *adj*: **— acid** ácido *m* bórico.

boring ['bɔːriŋ] *adj* aburrido, pesado, latoso.

born [bɔːn] **1** *ptp of* **bear**²; **to be —** nacer; **I was — in 1927** nací en 1927; **evil is — of idleness** la pereza es madre de todos los vicios; **to be — again** renacer, volver a nacer.

2 *adj* actor, artist etc nato; *llar* innato; **a Londoner — and bred** londinense de casta y cuna; **in all my — days** en mi vida.

borne [bɔːn] *ptp of* **bear**².

borough ['bʌrə] *n* municipio *m*.

borrow ['bɔrəu] *vt* pedir prestado, tomar prestado (*from, of a*); *idea etc* adoptar, apropiarse; *word* tomar (*from* de); **may I — your car?** ¿me prestas tu coche? **you can — it till I need it** te lo presto hasta que yo lo necesite.

borrower ['bɔrəuə*] *n* el (la) que toma prestado; (*in library*) usuario *m*, a *f*; (*Comm*) prestatario *m*, a *f*.

borrowing ['bɔrəuiŋ] *n* (*word*) préstamo *m* (*from* de).

Borstal ['bɔːstl] *n* reformatorio *m* de menores.

Bosch [bɔʃ] *m* El Bosco.

bosh [bɔʃ] *n* tonterías *fpl*.

bosom ['buzəm] **1** *n* seno *m*, pecho *m*; (*of garment*) pechera *f*; **in the — of the family** en el seno de la familia. **2** *attr friend* íntimo, inseparable.

Bosphorus ['bɔsfərəs] Bósforo *m*.

boss¹ [bɔs] *n* protuberancia *f*; (*stud*) clavo *m*, tachón *m*; (*of shield*) ombligo *m*; (*Archit*) llave *f* de bóveda.

boss² [bɔs] **1** *n* jefe *m*; (*owner, employer*) patrón *m*, amo *m*; (*foreman*) capataz *m*; (*manager*) gerente *m*; (*Pol*) cacique *m*; **I'm the — here** aquí mando yo.

2 *vt* regentar, dar órdenes a, dominar.

bossy ['bɔsi] *adj* mandón; tiránico.

botanic(al) [bə'tænik(əl)] *adj* botánico.

botanist ['bɔtənist] *n* botánico *mf*, botanista *mf*.

botanize ['bɔtənaiz] *vi* herborizar.

botany ['bɔtəni] *n* botánica *f*.

botch [bɔtʃ] **1** *n*: **to make a — of =** **2** *vt* chapucear, chafullar; **to — it** arruinarlo, estropearlo; **to — up** remendar (chapuceramente).

both [bəuθ] **1** *adj and pron* ambos, los dos; **I bought — books** compré ambos libros; **we — went** fuimos los dos; **— of them** los dos; **— of us** nosotros dos.

2 *adv and conj*: **— A and B** tanto A como B; **he — plays and sings** canta y toca además; **I find it — impressive and vulgar** encuentro que es impresionante y vulgar a la vez.

bother ['bɔðə*] **1** *n* (a) molestia *f*, lata *f*; **it's such a — to clean** me molesta tener que limpiarlo, es muy incómodo limpiarlo; **what a —!** ¡qué lata!

(b) **he had a spot of — with the police** se armó un lío con la policía; **do you have much — with your car?** ¿tienes muchas dificultades con el coche?

2 *vt* molestar, fastidiar, incomodar; **— it!** ¡porras!; **does the noise — you?** ¿le molesta el ruido?; **does it — you if I smoke?** ¿le molesta que fume? **stop —ing me!** ¡no fastidies!; **please don't — me about it** now te ruego no molestarme con eso ahora; **I can't be —ed** no quiero darme el trabajo (*to* + *infin* de + *infin*); **to get —ed** desconcertarse, ponerse nervioso, perder la calma.

3 *vi*: **to — about, to — with** molestarse con, preocuparse por; **to — to** + *infin* tomarse la molestia de + *infin*.

botheration [ˌbɔðə'reiʃən] *interj* ¡porras!

bothersome ['bɔðəsəm] *adj* molesto.

bottle ['bɔtl] **1** *n* botella *f*; (*of ink, scent*) frasco *m*; (*baby's*) biberón *m*; **to hit the —** (*fam*) emborracharse; **to take to the —** darse a la bebida.

2 *vt* embotellar; enfrascar; **—d beer** de botella; **to — up** embotellar; *emotion* reprimir, contener.

bottle-fed ['bɔtlfed] *adj* alimentado con biberón.

bottle-green ['bɔtl'griːn] **1** *adj* verde botella. **2** *n* verde *m* botella.

bottleneck ['bɔtlnek] *n* (*fig*) embotellamiento *m*; obstáculo *m*; (*on road*) estrangulamiento *m*.

bottle-opener ['bɔtlˌəupnə*] *n* abrebotellas *m*, destapador *m* de botellas.

bottle party ['bɔtlˌpɑːti] *n* guateque *m* al que cada invitado lleva su botella.

bottom ['bɔtəm] **1** *n* (*of cup, river, sea, box, garden*) fondo *m*; (*of stairs, hill, page*) pie *m*; (*of chair*) asiento *m*; (*of ship*) quilla *f*, casco *m*; (*Anat*) trasero *m*, culo *m*; **false —** doble fondo *m*; **—s up!** ¡salud y pesetas!; **at —** en el fondo; **at the — of the garden** en el fondo del jardín; **he's at the — of the class** es el último de la clase; **to be at the — of something** (*fig*: *thing*) ser el motivo de algo, (*person*) ser el causante oculto de algo; **from the — of one's heart** de todo corazón; **the — has fallen out of the market** se han derrumbado los precios; **to get to the — of a matter** llegar al fondo de un asunto, desentrañar un asunto; **to go to the —** (*Naut*) irse a pique; **to knock the — out of** desfondar; **to send a ship to the —** hundir un buque; **to touch —** tocar fondo, (*fig*) llegar al punto más bajo.

2 *adj part* más bajo, inferior; (*last*) último; **the — team** el colista.

bottomless ['bɔtəmlis] *adj* sin fondo, insondable.

boudoir ['buːdwɑː*] *n* tocador *m*.

bough [bau] *n* rama *f*.

bought [bɔːt] *pret and ptp of* **buy**.

bouillon ['buːjɔːŋ] *n* caldo *m*.

boulder ['bəuldə*] *n* canto *m* rodado.

boulevard ['buːləvɑː*] *n* bulevar *m*.

bounce [bauns] **1** *n* (a) (*re*)bote *m*; **to catch a ball on the —** coger una pelota de rebote.

(b) (*fig*) fanfarronería *f*, presunción *f*.

2 *vt* hacer (re)botar; (*fam*) poner en la calle.

3 *vi* (re)botar; (*cheque*) ser incobrable; **to — in** irrumpir alegremente.

bouncer ['baunsə*] *n* (*sl*) el forzudo que echa a los alborotadores de un café etc.

bouncing ['baunsiŋ] *adj* robusto, fuerte.

bouncy ['baunsi] *adj* (a) *ball* de mucho rebote, que rebota fuertemente. (b) *person* enérgico; bullicioso, muy activo.

bound¹ [baund] **1** *pret and ptp of* **bind**.

2 *with verb*: **well I'll be —!** ¡caramba!; **to be — for** (*Naut*) navegar con rumbo a, tener . . . como puerto de destino, (*fig*) dirigirse a; **where are you — for?** ¿adónde se dirige Vd?; **to be — over** ser puesto en libertad condicional; **to be — to** + *infin* (*sure*) estar seguro de + *infin*, (*must*) tener que + *infin*; **we are — to win** estamos seguros de ganar; **he's — to come** es seguro que vendrá, no puede dejar de venir; **it's — to happen** tiene forzosamente que ocurrir; **you're not — to go** no es que tengas que ir; **I am — to say** that tengo el deber de decir que; **to be — by contract to someone** estar ligado por contrato a uno; **I feel — to him by gratitude** el agradecimiento me liga a él; **to be — up with** question etc estar estrechamente relacionado con; **they are — up in each other** están absortos el uno en el otro.

bound² [baund] **1** *n* límite *m*; **out of —s** fuera de los límites; **out of —s to civilians** prohibido el paso a los civiles; **to put a place out of —s** prohibir la entrada a un lugar; **it is within the —s of possibility** cabe dentro de lo posible; **to keep something within —s** tener algo a raya; **to set —s to one's ambitions** poner límites a sus ambiciones; **his ambition knows no —s** su ambición no tiene límite.

2 *vt* limitar, deslindar; **a field —ed by woods** un campo rodeado de bosque; **on one side it is —ed by the park** por un lado confina con el parque.

bound³ [baund] **1** *n* (*jump*) salto *m*; **at a —, in one — de** un salto.

2 *vt* saltar por encima de.

3 *vi* saltar; (*ball*) (re)botar; **to — forward** avanzar a saltos; **his heart —ed with joy** su corazón daba brincos de alegría; **the number is —ing up** el número aumenta rápidamente.

boundary ['baundəri] *n* límite *m*, lindero *m*; (*Pol etc*) frontera *f*.

boundary-stone ['baundəriˌstəun] *n* mojón *m*.

bounder ['baundə*] n (fam) calavera m.
boundless ['baundlis] adj ilimitado.
bounteous ['bauntiəs] adj, **bountiful** ['bauntiful] adj abundante; person liberal, generoso.
bounty ['baunti] n munificencia f, liberalidad f; (Mil) premio m de enganche; (Comm) prima f, subvención f.
bouquet ['bukei] n (of flowers) ramo m, ramillete m; (of wine) aroma m, nariz f.
Bourbon ['buəbən] 1 n Borbón m; **b—** (US) aguardiente m de maíz. 2 adj borbónico.
bourgeois ['buəʒwɑː] 1 adj burgués. 2 n burgués m, esa f.
bourgeoisie [,buəʒwɑː'ziː] n burguesía f.
bout [baut] n (spell) turno m, rato m; (Med) ataque m; (Fencing) asalto m; (fight in general) lucha f, combate m; (boxing fixture) encuentro m, match m; (of drinking) juerga f de borrachera.
bovine ['bəuvain] adj bovino; (fig) lerdo, estúpido.
bow[1] [bəu] n (Mil, Mus) arco m; (cross-) ballesta f; (tie, knot) lazo m; **to have two strings to one's —** tener dos posibilidades.
bow[1] [bau] 1 n inclinación f, reverencia f; **to make a —** inclinarse (to delante de), hacer una reverencia (to a); **to make one's —** presentarse, debutar; **to take a —** salir a recibir aplausos.
   2 vt head etc inclinar, (in shame) bajar; (fig: also **to — down**) agobiar; **to — someone out** hacer muchas cortesías a uno que se despide; **to — one's thanks** inclinarse en señal de agradecimiento.
   3 vi inclinarse (to delante de), hacer una reverencia (to a); **to — and scrape** hacer zalamerías; **to — beneath** estar agobiado por; **to — out** retirarse; **to — to** inclinarse a, ceder ante, transigir con, someterse a; **to — to the inevitable** conformarse con lo inevitable.
bow[2] [bau] n (Naut) proa f; **—s** proa f; **on the port —** a babor; **shot across the —s** cañonazo m de advertencia.
bowdlerize ['baudləraiz] vt expurgar.
bowel [bauəl] n intestino m; **—s** intestinos mpl, vientre m, (fig) entrañas fpl.
bower ['bauə*] n emparrado m, enramada f; cenador m.
bowl[1] [bəul] n (Cook) escudilla f, tazón m; (for washing) jofaina f, palangana f; (of spoon) cuenco m; (of fountain) tazón m; (of pipe) hornillo m; (Geog) cuenca f.
bowl[2] [bəul] 1 n bola f, bocha f; **—s** juego m de las bochas, (US) boliche m.
   2 vt rodar; (Sport) arrojar; **to — over** tumbar, echar a rodar, (fig) desconcertar.
   3 vi arrojar la pelota; jugar a las bochas; **to — along** correr rápidamente, rodar.
bow-legged ['bəu,legid] adj estevado; (stance) con las piernas en arco.
bowler ['bəulə*] n (Sport) lanzador m, el que arroja la pelota; (also **— hat**) hongo m.
bowline ['bəulin] n bolina f.
bowling ['bəuliŋ] n (US game) bolos mpl, boliche m (S Am).
bowling alley ['bəuliŋ,æli] n bolera f.
bowling green ['bəuliŋ,griːn] n pista f para bochas.
bowman ['bəumən] n, pl **—men** [mən] arquero m, (cross-) ballestero m.
bowsprit ['bəusprit] n bauprés m.
bowstring ['bəustriŋ] n cuerda f de arco.
bow tie ['bəu'tai] n corbata f de lazo.
bow window ['bəu'windəu] n ventana f salediza.
bow-wow ['bau'wau] interj ¡guau!
box[1] [bɔks] 1 n caja f, (large) cajón m; (for money etc) cofre m, arca f; (for jewels etc) estuche m; (Theat) palco m; **— of matches** caja f de cerillas; **post-office —** apartado m de correos.
   2 vt encajonar, poner en una caja; (capture) encerrar en una caja; compass cuartear; **to — someone in** encerrar a uno; **to feel —ed in** (or up) sentirse encerrado.
box[2] [bɔks] n (Bot) boj m.
box[3] [bɔks] 1 n: **— on the ear** cachete m. 2 vt boxear contra; **to — someone's ear** dar un cachete a uno. 3 vi boxear.
box camera ['bɔks'kæmərə] n cámara f de cajón.
boxer ['bɔksə*] n boxeador m; (dog) boxer m.
boxing ['bɔksiŋ] n boxeo m.
Boxing Day ['bɔksiŋdei] n día en que se dan regalos a los empleados, proveedores caseros etc (26 diciembre).
boxing gloves ['bɔksiŋglʌvz] npl guantes mpl de boxeo.
boxing match ['bɔksiŋ,mætʃ] n partido m de boxeo.
boxing ring ['bɔksiŋ,riŋ] n cuadrilátero m (de boxeo).
box-number ['bɔks,nʌmbə*] n apartado m.
box office ['bɔksɔfis] 1 n taquilla f; **to be good — ser**

taquillero, estar seguro de obtener un éxito. 2 attr taquillero.
box room ['bɔksrum] n trastero m.
boxwood ['bɔkswud] n boj m.
boy [bɔi] n (small) niño m; (older, also apprentice etc, and affectionately of adult) muchacho m, chico m; (son) hijo m; (servant) criado m; (boyfriend) novio m; oh — ! ¡vaya, vaya! old — (of school) antiguo alumno m, (fam) vejete m; old — ! ¡chico!; that's the — !, that's my — ! ¡bravo el chico!; but my dear — ! ¡pero hijo!; **I have known him from a —** le conozco desde chico; **—s will be —s** eso es muy de chicos; **my husband's out with the —s** mi marido ha salido con su peña; **he's one of the —s now** ahora es un personaje; **it's all jobs for the —s** los puestos se consiguen por enchufe; **to send a — to do a man's job** subestimar los recursos que se precisan para hacer algo.
boycott ['bɔikɔt] 1 n boicoteo m. 2 vt boicotear.
boyfriend ['bɔifrend] n amigo m, novio m.
boyhood ['bɔihud] n juventud f, muchachez f.
boyish ['bɔiiʃ] adj juvenil, muchachil, de muchacho.
bra [brɑː] n (fam) sostén m.
brace [breis] 1 n (strengthening piece) abrazadera f, refuerzo m; (Archit) riostra f, tirante m; (Typ) corchete m; (Naut) braza f; (tool) berbiquí m; (pair) par m; **—s** tirantes mpl; **— and bit** berbiquí m y barrena; **in a —** of shakes en un decir Jesús.
   2 vt asegurar, reforzar.
   3 vr: **to — oneself** prepararse para resistir (una sacudida etc); (fig) fortalecer su ánimo; **we —d ourselves for bad news** nos preparamos para aguantar una noticia mala.
bracelet ['breislit] n pulsera f, brazalete m.
bracing ['breisiŋ] adj tónico, vigorizante.
bracken ['brækən] n helecho m.
bracket ['brækit] 1 n (holding) abrazadera f; (supporting) soporte m, puntal m; (angle) escuadra f; (Archit) ménsula f, repisa f; (for gas) mechero m; (sl) nariz f; (fig) clase f, categoría f; **round —s** paréntesis mpl; **square —s** corchetes mpl; **in —s** entre corchetes.
   2 vt asegurar con ménsulas (etc); (Typ) poner entre corchetes; **to — together** agrupar, poner juntos; **to — something with something else** agrupar algo con otra cosa.
brackish ['brækiʃ] adj salobre.
brad [bræd] n puntilla f, clavito m.
brae [brei] n (Scot) ladera f de monte, pendiente f.
brag [bræg] 1 n fanfarronada f, bravata f. 2 vi jactarse (about, of de; that de que), fanfarronear.
braggart ['brægət] n fanfarrón m, jactancioso m.
Brahman ['brɑːmən], **Brahmin** ['brɑːmin] n bracmán m, ana f.
braid [breid] 1 n trenza f; (Mil) galón m; **gold —** galón m de oro. 2 vt trenzar; dress galonear.
Braille [breil] n Braille m (alfabeto de los ciegos).
brain [brein] 1 n (a) cerebro m; **—s** (Anat) sesos mpl; **electronic —** cerebro m electrónico; **to blow one's —s out** levantarse la tapa de los sesos; **to blow someone's —s out** levantar la tapa de los sesos a uno.
   (b) (fig) **—s** inteligencia f, cabeza f; capacidad f; **to cudgel** (or **rack**) **one's —** devanarse los sesos; **to get something on the —** dejarse obsesionar por algo; **to have something on the —** estar obsesionado por algo, no poder quitar algo de la cabeza; **to have —s** ser muy inteligente; **to pick someone's —s** exprimir a uno, sacar a uno el jugo; **to turn someone's —** volver loco a uno.
   2 vt (fam) romper la crisma a.
brain-child ['breintʃaild] n parto m del ingenio.
brain-fag ['breinfæg] n fatiga f cerebral.
brainless ['breinlis] adj estúpido, insensato.
brainstorm ['breinstɔːm] n frenesí m.
brains trust ['breinz,trʌst] n consultorio m intelectual; grupo m de consejeros expertos.
brainwash ['breinwɔʃ] vt lavar el cerebro a.
brainwashing ['brein,wɔʃiŋ] n lavado m de cerebro.
brainwave ['breinweiv] n idea f luminosa.
brainwork ['breinwəːk] n trabajo m intelectual.
brainy ['breini] adj muy inteligente.
braise [breiz] vt cocer a fuego lento en una vasija bien tapada.
brake[1] [breik] 1 n freno m (also fig); **emergency —** freno m de auxilio; **to put the —s on** echar los frenos, frenar; **to put a — on** (fig) frenar, detener el progreso de.
   2 vti frenar.
brake[2] [breik] n (vehicle) break m; (kind of car) rubia f, combi f.
brake[3] [breik] n (Bot) helecho m; (thicket) soto m.

brake drum ['breikdrʌm] n tambor m de freno.
brake fluid ['breik,fluid] n líquido m para frenos.
brake horsepower ['breik'hɔːspauə*] n potencia f al freno.
brake lever ['breik,liːvə*] n palanca f de freno.
brake lining ['breik,lainiŋ] n forro m del freno, guarnición f del freno.
brake pedal ['breik,pedl] n pedal m de freno.
brake shoe ['breikʃuː] n zapata f del freno.
braking ['breikiŋ] 1 n frenar m, frenaje m.
2 attr de frenar, de frenaje.
braking distance ['breikiŋ,distəns] n distancia f de parada.
braking lights ['breikiŋ,laits] npl luces fpl de detención.
braking-power ['breikiŋ,pauə*] n potencia f al freno.
bramble ['bræmbl] n zarza f.
bran [bræn] n salvado m.
branch [brɑːntʃ] 1 n (Bot) rama f; (fig) ramo m, división f, sección f; (Comm) sucursal f; (road, Rail) ramal m; (of river) brazo m.
2 vt (also to — out) ramificarse, echar ramas; to — off salir, separarse (from de); we —ed off at Medina salimos de la carretera principal en Medina; to — out (fig) extenderse, ensanchar el campo de sus operaciones (etc).
branch line ['brɑːntʃlain] n ramal m, línea f secundaria.
branch-office ['brɑːntʃ,ɔfis] n sucursal f.
brand [brænd] 1 n marca f (also Comm); (iron) hierro m de marcar; (fire-) tizón m, tea f.
2 vt marcar (con hierro candente); to — someone as motejar a uno de; to — something as calificar algo de; to be —ed a liar quedar con la nota infamante de mentiroso; —ed goods artículos mpl de marca.
branding-iron ['brændiŋ,aiən] n hierro m de marcar.
brandish ['brændiʃ] vt blandir.
brand-new ['brænd'njuː] adj flamante, muy nuevo, novísimo.
brandy ['brændi] n coñac m, brandy m.
brash [bræʃ] adj (rough) inculto, tosco; (cheeky) descarado, respondón; (rash) impetuoso; (unwise) indiscreto; (know-all) presuntuoso.
brass [brɑːs] n latón m; (plate) placa f conmemorativa; (Eccl) plancha f sepulcral (de latón); (sl) pasta f; descaro m; the — (Mus) el cobre; the top — (Mil sl) los jefazos, los espadones.
brass band ['brɑːs'bænd] n banda f, charanga f.
brass hat ['brɑːs'hæt] n (Mil sl) espadón m.
brassière ['bræsieə*] n sostén m.
brassy ['brɑːsi] adj de latón; sound desapacible, metálico; person etc descarado.
brat [bræt] n mocoso m, braguillas m.
bravado [brə'vɑːdəu] n envalentonamiento m; out of sheer — queriendo mostrarse valiente.
brave [breiv] 1 adj valiente, valeroso; esforzado; sight, show magnífico, vistoso, garboso; as — as a lion valiente como un león.
2 n valiente m; (Indian) guerrero m indio.
3 vt desafiar, arrostrar; to — the storm aguantar la tempestad; to — someone's anger no temer presentarse ante una persona encolerizada; to — it out defenderse sin confesarse culpable.
bravely ['breivli] adv valientemente, con valor; (fig) vistosamente, airosamente.
bravery ['breivəri] n valor m, valentía f.
bravo ['brɑː'vəu] interj ¡bravo!
bravura [brə'vuərə] n (a) arrojo m, brío m. (b) (Mus) bravura f.
brawl [brɔːl] 1 n pendencia f, reyerta f; alboroto m.
2 vi armar pendencia, alborotar.
brawn [brɔːn] n carne f en gelatina; (fig) fuerza f muscular.
brawny ['brɔːni] adj fornido, musculoso.
bray [brei] 1 n rebuzno m; (laugh) carcajada f. 2 vi rebuznar; (trumpet) sonar con estrépito.
braze [breiz] vt soldar.
brazen ['breizn] 1 adj (fig) descarado, cínico.
2 vt: to — it out defenderse con argumentos descarados.
brazenly ['breiznli] adv descaradamente, con cinismo.
brazier ['breiziə*] n brasero m.
Brazil [brə'zil] el Brasil.
Brazilian [brə'ziliən] 1 adj brasileño.
2 n brasileño m, a f.
Brazil nut [brə'zil'nʌt] n castaña f del Brasil.
breach [briːtʃ] 1 n (gap) abertura f, brecha f; (Mil) brecha f; (fig) violación f, infracción f; (between friends) rompimiento m de relaciones, (Pol) ruptura f; — of contract infracción f de contrato; — of faith (or trust) abuso m de confianza, infidencia f; — of the

law violación f de la ley; — of the peace perturbación f del orden público; — of privilege (Parl) abuso m del privilegio parlamentario; — of promise incumplimiento m de la palabra de casamiento; to heal the — hacer las paces.
2 vt romper; (Mil) abrir brecha en.
bread [bred] n pan m (also fig); daily — (Eccl and fig) pan m de cada día; white — pan m candeal; brown — pan m moreno; to be on — and water estar a pan y agua; to break — with sentarse a la mesa con; to cast one's — on the waters hacer bien sin mirar a quién; to earn one's daily — (or one's — and butter) ganarse el pan; to know which side one's — is buttered saber dónde aprieta el zapato; to live on the — line vivir muy justo; man cannot live by — alone no sólo de pan vive el hombre; to take the — out of someone's mouth quitar el pan de la boca de uno.
bread-and-butter ['bredən'bʌtə*] 1 n pan m con mantequilla; (fam) pan m de cada día.
2 adj corriente (y moliente), normal, regular; prosaico; de uso general; — letter carta f de agradecimiento que el invitado envía al anfitrión.
breadbin ['bredbin] n caja f del pan.
breadboard ['bredbɔːd] n tablero m para cortar el pan.
bread-crumb ['bredkrʌm] n migaja f; —s (Cook) pan m rallado.
breadfruit ['bredfruːt] n fruto m del pan; — tree árbol m del pan.
breadknife ['brednaif], pl —knives [naivz] cuchillo m para cortar el pan.
bread line ['bredlain] n cola f del pan; to be on the — recibir asistencia pública, (fig) vivir en la mayor miseria.
breadth [bretθ] n anchura f; (Naut) manga f; (fig) amplitud f, extensión f; to be 2 metres in — tener 2 metros de ancho.
breadwinner ['bred,winə*] n mantenedor m de la familia.
break [breik] 1 n (a) (breakage) ruptura f, rompimiento m; (between friends) ruptura f; (in voice) gallo m; (in weather) cambio m; (at billiards) partida f; at — of day al amanecer; to make a — with cortar con; romper relaciones con.
(b) (gap) abertura f; (crack) grieta f; (on paper etc) espacio m, blanco m; (of time) intervalo m; (in process) interrupción f; (in clouds) claro m; (holiday) vacación f, asueto m; (rest) descanso m; (at school) período m de recreo; — in continuity solución f de continuidad; without a — sin interrupción, sin descansar; to take a — descansar.
(c) (vehicle) break m.
(d) (chance) oportunidad f; lucky — chiripa f, racha f de suerte; to give someone a — abrir a uno la puerta.
(e) (break-out) evasión f, fuga f; to make a — for it tratar de evadirse.
2 (irr: pret broke, ptp broken) vt (a) romper; (Elec) interrumpir, cortar; ground roturar; impact, fall amortiguar; horse domar, amansar; bank quebrar, hacer saltar; news comunicar; record batir, superar, mejorar; code descifrar; ring, conspiracy deshacer; silence, spell romper; custom romper con; journey interrumpir; appointment no acudir a; promise, word faltar a; law violar, infringir, quebrantar; rival arruinar; someone's spirit abatir, vencer.
(b) to — down (shatter) derribar, echar abajo; resistance acabar con, vencer; alibi probar la falsedad de; figures etc analizar, descomponer, desglobar; clasificar; to — in forzar, romper; recruit desbastar; to — someone of a habit inducir a uno a que renuncie a una costumbre; to — off piece separar, partir; relations, engagement romper; to — open forzar, abrir por fuerza; to — up romper; desmenuzar; ship desguazar; camp levantar; estate parcelar; organization, meeting, federation disolver; industry desconcentrar.
3 vi (a) romperse, quebrarse, hacerse pedazos; (machine) estropearse; (boil) reventar; (voice) mudar; (singing voice) cascarse; (bank) quebrar; (heart, wave) romperse; (day) apuntar; (health) cascarse, empeorar; (news) saberse, revelarse; (ball) torcerse; (boxers) separarse.
(b) to — away desprenderse, separarse; (runner) despegarse, salir del pelotón; (at games) escapar; to — away from guards evadirse de; to — down (Med) perder la salud, sufrir un colapso; (Aut etc) averiarse; (machine) estropearse; (plan) fracasar; (person) romper a llorar; to — even salir sin ganar ni perder; to — in (burglar) forzar una entrada; (in

conversation) cortar, interrumpir; **to — into a house** forzar (*or* penetrar en) una casa; **to — into a run** echar a correr; **to — off** pararse repentinamente, dejar de hablar (*etc*), suspender el trabajo (*etc*); **to — out** (*fire, war*) estallar; (*riot, argument*) producirse; (*noise*) hacerse oír; (*Med*) declararse; (*exclaim*) exclamar, gritar; (*from prison*) evadirse; **to — out in spots** salir a uno granos en la piel; **to — out into abuse** empezar a soltar injurias; **to — through** (*water etc*) abrirse un camino; (*inventor etc*) hacer un descubrimiento sensacional; **to — through to** *miners* llegar a, abrir un camino hasta; **to — up** hacerse pedazos; (*ice*) deshacerse, romperse; desmenuzarse; (*meeting*) levantarse, (*in disorder*) disolverse; (*crowd*) dispersarse; (*federation*) desmembrarse, disgregarse; (*school*) terminar, cerrarse; **to — with** romper con.

breakable ['breikəbl] *adj* frágil, quebradizo.

breakage ['breikidʒ] *n* rotura *f*.

breakaway ['breikəwei] **1** *adj* *group etc* disidente, separatista. **2** *n* (*Sport*) escapada *f*.

breakdown ['breikdaun] *n* interrupción *f*; (*failure*) fracaso *m*, mal éxito *m*; (*Med*) colapso *m*, crisis *f* nerviosa; (*Aut etc*) avería *f*, pana *f*; (*of numbers etc*) análisis *m*, descomposición *f*.

breaker ['breikə*] *n* ola *f* grande, rompiente *m*.

breakfast ['brekfəst] **1** *n* desayuno *m*. **2** *vi* desayunar(se) (*off eggs, on eggs* huevos).

breaking-point ['breikiŋpɔint] *n* punto *m* de máxima tensión tolerable; **to reach —** llegar a la crisis, llegar al límite.

breakneck ['breiknek] *adj*: **at — speed** a mata caballo.

breakout ['breikaut] *n* evasión *f*, fuga *f*.

breakthrough ['breikθru:] *n* (*Mil*) ruptura *f*; (*fig*) avance *m*, adelanto *m*, invento *m* decisivo; **to achieve a —** hacer grandes progresos, hacer un descubrimiento importante.

break-up ['breikʌp] *n* disolución *f*, desintegración *f*, desmembración *f*.

breakwater ['breik,wɔːtə*] *n* rompeolas *m*.

bream [bri:m] *n* brema *f*.

breast [brest] **1** *n* (*Anat*) pecho *m*; (*woman's*) pecho *m*, seno *m*; (*of bird*) pechuga *f*; (*fig*) corazón *m*; **to beat one's —** darse golpes de pecho; **to make a clean — of** confesar con franqueza; **to make a clean — of it** confesarlo todo. **2** *vt* hacer cara a, arrostrar.

breastbone ['brestbəun] *n* esternón *m*.

breast-feed ['brest'fiːd] (*irr: see* **feed**) *vt* criar a los pechos.

breast-high ['brest'hai] *adv* a la altura del pecho.

breastplate ['brestpleit] *n* peto *m*.

breast-pocket ['brest,pɔkit] *n* bolsillo *m* de pecho.

breast-stroke ['breststrəuk] *n* braza *f* de pecho.

breastwork ['brestwɔːk] *n* parapeto *m*.

breath [breθ] *n* aliento *m*, respiración *f*; (*visible in air*) hálito *m*; **bad —** halitosis *f*; **the first — of spring** el primer viento suave que anuncia la primavera; **the least — of scandal** la más ligera sospecha de escándalo; **there's not a — of air stirring** no hay ni un soplo de aire; **all in the same — todo** al mismo tiempo; **in the very next — a** renglón seguido; **out of —** sofocado, jadeante, sin aliento; **to get out of —** quedar sin aliento; **short of — corto** de resuello; **under one's —** en voz baja; **to draw a deep —** respirar a fondo; **to draw one's last — tomar** el último aliento; **the best that ever drew — el** mejor que se conoció jamás; **to gasp for — luchar** por respirar; **to get one's — back** tomar aliento; **to go out for a — of air** salir a tomar el fresco; **to hold one's —** contener la respiración; **to save one's —** ahorrar las palabras; **to take a deep — respirar** a fondo; **it took my — away** me dejó pasmado; **to waste one's —** perder el tiempo (*on* hablando con).

breathe [bri:ð] **1** *vt* respirar; *sigh* dar; *prayer* decir en voz baja; **to — air into a balloon** inflar un globo soplando; **it —s the spirit of** late por todas partes el espíritu de; **to — out** exhalar.
    2 *vi* respirar; (*noisily*) resollar; **to — again** respirar; **to — in** aspirar; **to — out** espirar.

breather ['bri:ðə*] *n* respiro *m*.

breathing ['bri:ðiŋ] *n* respiración *f*; **heavy — re**suello *m*.

breathing space ['bri:ðiŋspeis] *n* respiro *m*.

breathing-tube ['bri:ðiŋtju:b] *n* tubo *m* de respiración.

breathless ['breθlis] *adj* falto de aliento, jadeante.

breathlessly ['breθlisli] *adv*: **to say —** decir jadeante.

breath-taking ['breθ,teikiŋ] *adj* *sight* imponente, pasmoso; *speed* vertiginoso.

bred [bred] *pret and ptp of* **breed**.

breech [briːtʃ] *n* recámara *f*.

breeches ['britʃiz] *npl* calzones *mpl*; **riding — pantalones** *mpl* de montar; **to wear the —** llevar los pantalones.

breeches buoy ['britʃiz'bɔi] *n* boya *f* pantalón.

breechloader ['briːtʃ,ləudə*] *n* arma *f* de retrocarga.

breed [bri:d] **1** *n* raza *f*, casta *f*.
    2 (*irr: pret and ptp* **bred**) *vt* criar, engendrar; (*fig*) engendrar, producir; **town bred** criado en la ciudad.
    3 *vi* reproducirse, procrear.

breeder ['bri:də*] *n* (*person*) criador *m*, ora *f*; (*animal*) criadero *m*, paridera *f*.

breeder reactor ['bri:dəri:,æktə*] *n* reactor *m* reproductor.

breeding ['bri:diŋ] *n* (*of stock*) cría *f*; (*of person*) crianza *f*, educación *f*; **bad —**, **ill —** mala crianza *f*, falta *f* de educación; **good —** educación *f*, cultura *f*; **he has (good) —** es una persona educada; **it shows bad —** indica una falta de educación.

breeding-season ['bri:diŋ,si:zn] *n* época *f* de reproducción.

breeze [bri:z] **1** *n* brisa *f*. **2** *vi*: **to — in** entrar como Pedro por su casa.

breezily ['bri:zili] *adv* jovialmente, despreocupadamente.

breezy ['bri:zi] *adj* *day, place* de mucho viento; *person's manner* animado, jovial, despreocupado; **it is —** hace viento.

brethren ['breðrin] *npl* (*irr pl of* **brother**) hermanos *mpl*.

Breton ['bretən] **1** *adj* bretón. **2** *n* bretón *m*, ona *f*. **3** *n* (*language*) bretón *m*.

breviary ['bri:viəri] *n* breviario *m*.

brevity ['breviti] *n* brevedad *f*.

brew [bru:] **1** *n* (*hum*) poción *f*, brebaje *m*.
    2 *vt* *beer* hacer, elaborar; *tea* hacer; (*fig*) urdir, tramar.
    3 *vi* (*fig*) prepararse; (*storm*) amenazar; **there's something —ing** algo se está tramando.

brewer ['bru:ə*] *n* cervecero *m*.

brewery ['bru:əri] *n* fábrica *f* de cerveza.

briar ['braiə*] *n* (*rose*) escaramujo *m*, rosa *f* silvestre; (*hawthorn*) espino *m*; (*bramble*) zarza *f*.

bribe [braib] **1** *n* soborno *m*, cohecho *m*; **to take a — dejarse** sobornar (*from* por). **2** *vt* sobornar, cohechar.

bribery ['braibəri] *n* soborno *m*, cohecho *m*.

bric-à-brac ['brikəbræk] *n* curiosidades *fpl*.

brick [brik] **1** *n* ladrillo *m*; (*of ice cream*) bloque *m*; **a — wall** una pared de ladrillos; **Bath — piedra** *f* para limpiar cuchillos; **gold — (US sl)** estafa *f*; **he's a —** es un buen chico; **be a — and lend it to me** préstamelo como buen amigo; **he came down on us like a ton of —s** nos echó una bronca fenomenal; **to drop a —** tirarse una plancha.
    2 *vt* (*also* **to — up**) cerrar con ladrillos.

brickbat ['brikbæt] *n* trozo *m* de ladrillo; (*fig*) palabra *f* hiriente, crítica *f*.

bricklayer ['brikleiə*] *n* albañil *m*.

brick red ['brikred] **1** *adj* rojo ladrillo. **2** *n* rojo *m* ladrillo.

brickwork ['brikwɔːk] *n* enladrillado *m*, ladrillos *mpl*.

brickworks ['brikwɔːks] *n* ladrillar *m*.

bridal ['braidl] *adj* nupcial.

bride [braid] *n* novia *f*; **the — and groom** los novios.

bridegroom ['braidgrum] *n* novio *m*.

bridesmaid ['braidzmeid] *n* dama *f* de honor.

bridge[1] [bridʒ] **1** *n* puente *m* (*also Mus*) puente *m* de mando; (*of nose*) caballete *m*; **suspension — puente** *m* colgante; **much water has flowed under the —** since then mucho ha llovido desde entonces.
    2 *vt* tender un puente sobre; *gap* llenar, salvar.

bridge[2] [bridʒ] *n* (*Cards*) bridge *m*; **auction —** bridge-remate *m*; **contract —** bridge-contrato *m*.

bridgehead ['bridʒhed] *n* cabeza *f* de puente.

Bridget ['bridʒit] *f* Brígida.

bridle ['braidl] **1** *n* brida *f*, freno *m*. **2** *vi*: **to — at** picarse por, ofenderse por.

bridle path ['braidlpɑːθ] *n* camino *m* de herradura.

brief [bri:f] **1** *adj* breve, corto; (*fleeting*) fugaz, pasajero; *style* lacónico; **please be as — as possible** explíquese con la mayor brevedad.
    2 *n* (a) (*Eccl*) breve *m*.
    (b) (*Law*) escrito *m*; **in —, to be — en** resumen; **to go beyond one's —** exceder las instrucciones; **to hold a — for** representar a; **to hold a watching — for** someone representar a un cliente a quien no interesa directamente un juicio; **to hold no — for** tener en poco, no apoyar; **to stick to one's — atenerse** a las órdenes dadas.
    (c) **—s** (*man's*) calzoncillos *mpl*, (*woman's*) bragas *fpl*.
    3 *vt* (*Mil etc*) dar órdenes a.

briefcase ['bri:fkeis] n cartera f.

briefing ['bri:fiŋ] n reunión f en que se dan las órdenes (a la tripulación de un avión militar); órdenes fpl; (to press) informe m.

briefly ['bri:fli] adv brevemente; en resumen, en pocas palabras.

briefness ['bri:fnis] n brevedad f.

brier ['braiə*] n see **briar.**

brigade [bri'geid] n brigada f; **one of the old** — un veterano.

brigadier [ˌbrigə'diə*] n general m de brigada.

brigand ['brigənd] n bandido m, bandolero m.

brigandage ['brigəndidʒ] n bandidaje m, bandolerismo m.

bright [brait] adj (a) claro, brillante, luminoso; day luminoso, de sol; eyes claro; sun brillante; surface lustroso; colour subido; smile radiante.

   (b) (clever) listo, inteligente; idea luminoso; conversation, remark ingenioso; **that was** — **of you** en eso anduviste muy listo; **you're a** — **one!** ¡qué despiste tienes!; **the child's as** — **as a button** el niño es más listo que el hambre.

   (c) (cheerful) alegre, animado, optimista.

   (d) prospect etc prometedor, esperanzador.

brighten ['braitn] **1** vt (also **to** — **up**) abrillantar, lustrar; house hacer más alegre, poner colores en; (cheer) alegrar.

   2 vi (also **to** — **up**) (person) animarse, alegrarse; (weather) despejarse.

brightly ['braitli] adv brillantemente; ingeniosamente; answer con prontitud.

brightness ['braitnis] n claridad f; brillantez f, luminosidad f; lustre m; lo subido; inteligencia f; viveza f de ingenio.

brill [bril] n rodaballo m menor.

brilliance ['briljəns] n, **brilliancy** ['briljənsi] n brillo m, brillantez f.

brilliant ['briljənt] **1** adj brillante; idea genial, luminoso; student etc brillante, sobresaliente; success arrollador. **2** n brillante m.

brilliantine [ˌbriljən'ti:n] n brillantina f.

brilliantly ['briljəntli] adv brillantemente (also fig).

brim [brim] **1** n borde m; (of hat) ala f. **2** vi: **to** — **over** desbordarse, rebosar; **to** — **with** rebosar de.

brimful ['brim'ful] adj lleno hasta el borde; — **of,** — **with** rebosante de.

brimstone ['brimstəun] n azufre m.

brindled ['brindld] adj manchado, mosqueado.

brine [brain] n salmuera f.

bring [briŋ] (irr: pret and ptp **brought**) **1** vt traer; conducir; charge hacer, formular; suit entablar; **you** — **nothing but trouble** Vd no hace más que causarme molestias; **to** — **someone to do something** inducir a uno a hacer algo; **to** — **about** ocasionar, producir; change efectuar; **to** — **along** traer consigo; **to** — **away** llevarse; **to** — **back** volver a traer, thing borrowed devolver; **to** — **down** (carry down) bajar; (Mil, Hunting) abatir, derribar; price rebajar; **to** — **forth** parir, dar a luz; (fig) producir; **to** — **forward** proposal presentar; date adelantar; (Comm) pasar a otra cuenta; **to** — **someone home** traer a uno a casa; **to** — **something home to someone** hacer que uno se dé cuenta cabal de algo; **to** — **in** bill presentar; harvest recoger, recolectar; fashion introducir; meal servir; income producir; verdict dar; person hacer entrar; — **him in!** ¡que entre!; **this should** — **them in** esto lo da hacerles venir en masa; **to** — **off** lograr, conseguir; success obtener; **to** — **on** causar, acarrear; accelerar el desarrollo de; **to** — **something on oneself** atraer algo sobre sí; **to** — **out** sacar; argument sacar a relucir; book sacar a luz; aspect subrayar, recalcar; person hacer más afable, ayudar a adquirir confianza; **to** — **round** (win over) ganarse la voluntad de; convencer, convertir; (Med) hacer volver en sí; **to** — **together** reunir; enemies reconciliar; **to** — **under** someter; **to** — **up** (carry up) subir; subject sacar a colación; person criar, educar; (fam) arrojar, vomitar.

   2 vr: **to** — **oneself to** + infin resignarse a + infin, convencerse de la conveniencia de + infin, cobrar suficiente ánimo para + infin.

brink [briŋk] n borde m; **on the** — **of** (fig) + n en la antesala de, + ger a punto de + infin.

brinkmanship ['briŋkmənʃip] n arte m de conducirse en el borde de la crisis; política f del borde del abismo.

briny ['braini] **1** adj salado, salobre. **2** n (fam): **the** — el mar.

briquette [bri'ket] n briqueta f.

brisk [brisk] adj enérgico, vigoroso; pace rápido; trade etc activo.

brisket ['briskit] n carne f de pecho (para asar).

briskly ['briskli] adv enérgicamente; rápidamente; activamente.

briskness ['brisknis] n energía f; rapidez f; actividad f.

brisling ['brizliŋ] n sardina f noruega.

bristle ['brisl] **1** n cerda f. **2** vi (hair etc) erizarse; (animal) erizar las cerdas; **to** — **with** (fig) estar erizado de.

bristly ['brisli] adj cerdoso; **to have a** — **chin** tener la barba crecida.

Britain ['britən] Gran Bretaña f, (loosely) Inglaterra f.

Britannia ['bri'tæniə] figura que representa simbólicamente a Gran Bretaña.

briticism ['britisizəm] n (US) modismo (or vocablo etc) del inglés m de Inglaterra.

British ['britiʃ] adj inglés, (more formally) británico; **the** — los ingleses.

Britisher ['britiʃə*] n (US) natural mf de Gran Bretaña.

British Guiana ['britiʃgi'a:nə] Guayana f Inglesa.

British Honduras ['britiʃhɔn'djuərəs] Honduras f Británica.

British Isles ['britiʃ'ailz] pl Islas fpl Británicas.

Briton ['britən] n inglés m, esa f, (more formally) británo m, a f.

Brittany ['britəni] Bretaña f.

brittle ['britl] adj frágil, quebradizo.

broach [brəutʃ] vt cask espitar; bottle etc abrir; subject comenzar a hablar de, mencionar por primera vez, abordar.

broad [brɔ:d] **1** adj (a) ancho; extenso, amplio; **3 metres** — ancho de 3 metros.

   (b) (fig) ancho; view comprensivo; mind tolerante, liberal; hint claro, inconfundible; accent marcado, cerrado, fuerte; story verde; sense of word ancho, lato; grin, smile jovial; **it's as** — **as it is long** lo mismo da.

   2 n (US sl) fulana f.

broad-brimmed ['brɔ:d'brimd] adj hat de ala ancha.

broadcast ['brɔ:dka:st] **1** adj (Agr) sembrado a voleo; (Radio) radiodifundido, de (la) radio.

   2 adv por todas partes.

   3 n emisión f, programa m; **repeat** — retransmisión f.

   4 vt (Agr) sembrar a voleo; (fig) diseminar, divulgar; (Radio) emitir, radiar.

   5 vi hablar (or tocar etc) por la radio.

broadcaster ['brɔ:dka:stə*] n conferenciante mf (or cronista mf) de radio; (announcer) locutor m, ora f.

broadcasting ['brɔ:dka:stiŋ] **1** n radiodifusión f. **2** attr de radiodifusión.

broadcasting station ['brɔ:dka:stiŋ,steiʃən] n emisora f.

broadcloth ['brɔ:dklɔθ] n (Hist) velarte m.

broaden ['brɔ:dn] **1** vt ensanchar. **2** vi ensancharse.

broadly ['brɔ:dli] adv extensamente; claramente; con fuerte acento; de modo jovial; **it is** — **true that** es en general verdad que; — **speaking** hablando en términos generales.

broad-minded ['brɔ:d'mainded] adj tolerante, liberal; (pej) de manga ancha.

broad-mindedness ['brɔ:d'maindidnis] n tolerancia f.

broadness ['brɔ:dnis] n anchura f, extensión f; claridad f; lo fuerte etc.

broadsheet ['brɔ:dʃi:t] n hoja f suelta impresa.

broad-shouldered ['brɔ:d'ʃauldəd] adj ancho de espaldas.

broadside ['brɔ:dsaid] n (side) costado m; (shots) andanada f; — **on** de costado; **to fire a** — hacer fuego con todos los cañones.

broadways ['brɔ:dweiz] adv a lo ancho, por lo ancho; con la parte ancha por delante; — **on to the waves** con la parte ancha de cara a las olas.

brocade [brəu'keid] n brocado m.

broccoli ['brɔkəli] n brécol m.

brochure ['brəufjuə*] n folleto m.

brock [brɔk] n tejón m.

brogue[1] [brəug] n (shoe) abarca f.

brogue[2] [brəug] n acento m irlandés.

broil [brɔil] vt asar a la parrilla.

broiler ['brɔilə*] n pollo m para asar.

broiling ['brɔiliŋ] adj: **it's** — **hot** hace un calor terrible.

broke [brəuk] pret of **break; to be** — (fam) no tener un céntimo.

broken ['brəukən] **1** ptp of **break.**

   2 adj ground accidentado, quebrado; tone de desesperación; — **in health** deshecho, muy decaído; **in** — **Spanish** en castellano imperfecto.

broken-down ['brəukən'daun] adj agotado; machine descompuesto, desvencijado.

broken-hearted ['brəukən'hɑ:tid] adj traspasado de dolor; **to be —** tener el corazón partido.

brokenly ['brəukənli] adv say etc en tono angustiado.

broker ['brəukə*] n corredor m, bolsista m; agente m de negocios.

brokerage ['brəukəridʒ] n, **broking** ['brəukiŋ] n corretaje m.

bromide ['brəumaid] n bromuro m; (fig) trivialidad f.

bronchial ['brɔŋkiəl] adj bronquial.

bronchitis [brɔŋ'kaitis] n bronquitis f.

bronco ['brɔŋkəu] n (US) potro m cerril.

bronze [brɔnz] **1** n bronce m. **2** adj de bronce. **3** vt broncear. **4** vi broncearse.

bronzed [brɔnzd] adj bronceado.

brooch [brəutʃ] n alfiler m de pecho, prendedor m.

brood [bru:d] **1** n camada f, cría f; (of chicks) nidada f; (fig) familia f, progenie f, (pej) prole f.
2 adj: **— mare** yegua f de cría.
3 vi empollar; (fig) meditar tristemente; **to — on**, **to — over** meditar tristemente; **you musn't — over** it no debes dejarte obsesionar con eso; **disaster —ed over the town** se cernía el desastre sobre la ciudad.

broody ['bru:di] adj clueca; (fig) triste, melancólico.

brook[1] [bruk] n arroyo m.

brook[2] [bruk] vt aguantar, permitir.

brooklet ['bruklit] n arroyuelo m.

broom [brum] n escoba f; (Bot) hiniesta f, retama f, piorno m; **new — (person)** persona f que entra en una compañía (etc) y propugna grandes reformas.

broomstick ['brumstik] n palo m de escoba.

broth [brɔθ] n caldo m.

brothel ['brɔθl] n prostíbulo m, casa f de putas.

brother ['brʌðə*] n hermano m (also Eccl); **X and his — teachers** X y sus colegas profesionales; **they're —s under the skin** les une una fuerte simpatía.

brotherhood ['brʌðəhud] n fraternidad f; (group) hermandad f; (Hist) cofradía f.

brother-in-law ['brʌðərinlɔ:] n cuñado m.

brotherly ['brʌðəli] adj fraternal.

brought [brɔ:t] pret and ptp of **bring**.

brow [brau] n ceja f; (forehead) frente f; (of hill) cumbre f, (of cliff) borde m; **to knit one's —** fruncir las cejas.

browbeat ['braubi:t] vt intimidar (con amenazas) (into doing something para que haga algo).

brown [braun] **1** adj pardo, moreno; oscuro; hair castaño; (tanned) bronceado; bread moreno; sugar negro; shoes de color; paper de embalar, de estraza; **as — as a berry** con un magnífico bronceado.
2 n color m pardo (etc).
3 vt poner pardo (or moreno etc); skin broncear; (Cook) dorar; **to — someone off** (sl) fastidiar a uno; **to be —ed off** (sl) estar harto (with de).
4 vi ponerse moreno (etc); (skin) broncearse; (Cook) dorarse.

brownie ['brauni] n duende m; (person) miembro joven de las Girl Guides.

brownish ['brauniʃ] adj pardusco, que tira a moreno.

browse [brauz] **1** vt grass pacer, rozar; trees ramonear.
2 vi pacer; (fig) leer ociosamente; **to spend an hour browsing in a bookshop** pasar una hora hojeando los libros en una librería; **to — on** pacer.

Bruges [bru:ʒ] Brujas.

Bruin ['bru:in] n oso m.

bruise [bru:z] **1** n contusión f, cardenal m, señal f, morado m. **2** vt contundir, magullar; fruit estropear.

bruiser ['bru:zə*] n (fam) boxeador m.

brunch [brʌntʃ] n (fam) comida f ligera de media mañana.

brunette [bru:'net] **1** adj moreno. **2** n morena f.

brunt [brʌnt] n: **the — of the attack** lo más fuerte del ataque; **the — of the work** lo peor del trabajo; **to bear the —** of aguantar lo más recio de.

brush [brʌʃ] **1** n (a) (act of brushing) cepilladura f, cepillado m.
(b) (implement) cepillo m; (large) escoba f; (shaving-) brocha f; (scrubbing-) bruza f; (artist's) pincel m; (housepainter's) brocha f; (Elec) escobilla f.
(c) (fox's) rabo m, hopo m.
(d) (Bot) broza f; maleza f, monte m bajo.
(e) (Mil) escaramuza f; (fig) encuentro m; **to have a — with someone** tener un disgusto con uno.
2 vt (a)cepillar; shoes etc limpiar; (in passing) rozar al pasar; **to — aside** rechazar, no hacer caso de; **to — away**, **to — off** quitar (con un cepillo, con la mano etc); **to — down** (a)cepillar, limpiar; horse almohazar; **to — up** acicalar, (fig) repasar, refrescar.
3 vi: **to — against** rozar al pasar; **to — by**, **to — past** pasar muy cerca (de).

brush-off ['brʌʃɔf] n: **to give someone the —** desairar a uno, despedir bruscamente a uno.

brush-stroke ['brʌʃstrəuk] n pincelada f.

brush up ['brʌʃ'ʌp] n: **to have a —** lavarse y peinarse, arreglarse.

brushwood ['brʌʃwud] n maleza f, monte m bajo; (faggots) broza f, leña f menuda.

brusque [bru:sk] adj brusco, abrupto, áspero.

brusquely ['bru:skli] adv bruscamente, abruptamente, ásperamente.

Brussels ['brʌslz] Bruselas; **— sprouts** col f de Bruselas.

brutal ['bru:tl] adj brutal.

brutality [bru:'tæliti] n brutalidad f.

brutally ['bru:təli] adv de manera brutal.

brute [bru:t] **1** adj brutal; (unthinking) bruto; **by — force** a fuerza bruta.
2 n bruto m; (person) bestia f, hombre m bestial; **you —!** ¡bestia!; **it's a — of a problem** es un problema de los más difíciles.

brutish ['bru:tiʃ] adj bruto.

Brutus ['bru:təs] m Bruto.

bubble ['bʌbl] **1** n burbuja f, ampolla f; (under paint etc) ampolla f; **to blow —s** hacer pompas.
2 vi burbujear, borbotar; **to — over** desbordarse, irse; **to — over with** rebosar de.

bubble-car ['bʌblkɑ:*] n coche-cabina m, huevo m.

bubble gum ['bʌblgʌm] n chicle m de globo, chicle m de burbuja.

bubbly ['bʌbli] **1** adj burbujeante, gaseoso. **2** n (fam) champaña m.

bubonic plague [bju:'bɔnik'pleig] n peste f bubónica.

buccaneer [ˌbʌkə'niə*] **1** n bucanero m. **2** vi piratear.

buck [bʌk] **1** adj (male) macho; (US) private raso.
2 n (male) macho m; (deer) gamo m; (goat) macho m cabrío; (rabbit) conejo m macho; (US sl) dólar m; **to pass the —** (sl) echar a uno el muerto.
3 vi (horse) corcovear, ponerse de manos; **to — up** animarse, cobrar ánimo; **— up!** ¡date prisa!, ¡espabílate!

bucket ['bʌkit] n cubo m, balde m; (child's) cubito m; (of waterwheel etc) cangilón m; **to kick the —** (sl) estirar la pata.

bucketful ['bʌkitful] n cubo m (lleno), balde m (lleno); **by the — a** cubos, (fig) a montones, en grandes cantidades.

buckle ['bʌkl] **1** n hebilla f.
2 vt (a) abrochar con hebilla; **to — on one's sword** ceñirse la espada.
(b) (deform) torcer, combar, encorvar.
3 vi torcerse, combarse, doblarse; **to — down to** dedicarse con empeño a, emprender en serio.

buckram ['bʌkrəm] n bucarán m.

buckshee [bʌk'ʃi:] (sl) **1** adj gratuito. **2** adv gratis.

buckshot ['bʌkʃɔt] n perdigón m zorrero.

buckskin ['bʌkskin] n cuero m de ante.

buckthorn ['bʌkθɔ:n] n espino m cerval.

buck-tooth ['bʌk'tu:θ] n diente m saliente.

buck-toothed ['bʌk'tu:θt] adj de dientes salientes, dentón.

buckwheat ['bʌkwi:t] n alforfón m.

bucolic [bju:'kɔlik] **1** adj bucólico. **2** n: **the B—s** las Bucólicas.

bud [bʌd] **1** n brote m, yema f, (containing flower) capullo m; **in — en** brote; **to nip in the —** cortar de raíz, salir al paso a.
2 vt injertar de escudete.
3 vi brotar, echar brotes.

Buddha ['budə] m Buda.

Buddhism ['budizəm] n budismo m.

Buddhist ['budist] **1** adj budista. **2** n budista mf.

budding ['bʌdiŋ] adj (fig) en ciernes, en embrión.

buddy ['bʌdi] n (esp US) compañero m, compinche m; (in direct address) chico, hijo.

budge [bʌdʒ] **1** vt mover, hacer que se mueva; **I couldn't — him an inch** no pude hacerle cambiar de opinión en lo más mínimo.
2 vi moverse; bullir; **he didn't dare to —** no osaba bullir; **he won't — an inch** no nos ofrece la más pequeña concesión.

budgerigar ['bʌdʒərigɑ:*] n periquito m.

budget ['bʌdʒit] **1** n presupuesto m. **2** attr presupuestario. **3** vi: **to — for** presupuestar; (fig) tener en cuenta, contar con.

budgetary ['bʌdʒitri] adj presupuestario.

buff [bʌf] **1** adj color de ante. **2** n piel f de ante; **in the — en** cueros.

buffalo ['bʌfələu] n, pl **buffaloes** búfalo m.

buffer[1] ['bʌfə*] n amortiguador m (de choques); (Rail: on carriage) tope m, (fixed) parachoques m; **— state** estado m tapón.

buffer[2] ['bʌfə*] n: old **—** mastuerzo m.

buffet ['bʌfit] **1** n bofetada f; (of sea, wind etc) golpe m. **2** vt abofetear; (of sea, wind etc) golpear, llevar de aquí para allá, combatir.

buffet ['bufei] n aparador m; (Rail) cantina f, cafetería f; — **supper** cena f fría.
buffet car ['bufeikɑ:*] n coche-comedor m.
buffeting ['bʌfitiŋ] n (of sea etc) el golpear; **to get a** — **from** sufrir los golpes de.
buffoon [bə'fu:n] n bufón m, chocarrero m.
buffoonery [bə'fu:nəri] n bufonadas fpl.
bug [bʌg] 1 n chinche f (also freq m); (loosely) bicho m, sabandija f; (Med fam) microbio m, bacilo m; (US sl) estorbo m, traba f; **big** — (fam) señorón m, pez m gordo; **to get the travel** — (fam) entusiasmarse por los viajes, dedicarse furiosamente a viajar. 2 vt (Tel sl) intervenir.
bugaboo ['bʌgəbu:] n (US) espantajo m.
bugbear ['bʌgbeə*] n pesadilla f.
buggy ['bʌgi] n calesa f; (US) cochecillo m (de niño).
bughouse ['bʌghaus] n, pl —**houses** [,hauziz] (US: sl) casa f de locos, manicomio m.
bug-hunter ['bʌghʌntə*] n (fam) entomólogo m.
bugle ['bju:gl] n corneta f, clarín m.
bugler ['bju:glə*] n corneta m.
build [bild] 1 n talle m, tipo m; **of powerful** — fornido.
  2 (irr: pret and ptp **built**) vt (a) construir, edificar, hacer (in, of de); ship construir; fire preparar; nest hacer; **that's the way I'm built** yo soy así; **I'm not built that way** yo no estoy hecho para cosas así; **British-built** de construcción inglesa.
  (b) **to** — **in** empotrar, (Mech) incorporar; **to** — **a garage on to a house** añadir un garaje a una casa; **the garage is built on to the house** la casa tiene un garaje anexo; **to** — **up** (Mech etc) montar, armar; (Med) fortalecer; company etc fomentar, desarrollar; sales, numbers acrecentar; reputation crear para sí; impression crear; stocks acumular, formar.
  3 vi: **to** — **on** edificar sobre; **to** — **on a site** construir casas (etc) sobre un solar.
builder ['bildə*] n constructor m (also fig); (contracting firm) contratista m; (Archit) arquitecto m; (man on site) maestro m de obras, aparejador m.
building ['bildiŋ] n edificio m; construcción f; (at exhibition) pabellón m; **the** — **trade** la industria de la construcción.
building contractor ['bildiŋkən'træktə*] n contratista m.
building site ['bildiŋsait] n solar m (para edificaciones).
building society ['bildiŋsə'saiəti] n cooperativa f de construcciones, sociedad f inmobiliaria.
build-up ['bildʌp] n (make-up) composición f; (of forces) concentración f; (fig) propaganda f previa.
built [bilt] pret and ptp of **build**.
built-in ['bilt'in] adj (Archit) empotrado; (Mech, Radio etc) interior, incorporado.
built-up ['bilt'ʌp] adj area urbanizado.
bulb [bʌlb] n (Bot) bulbo m; (Elec) bombilla f; (of thermometer) ampolleta f.
bulbous ['bʌlbəs] adj bulboso.
Bulgaria [bʌl'geəriə] Bulgaria f.
Bulgarian [bʌl'geəriən] 1 adj búlgaro. 2 n búlgaro m, a f. 3 n (language) búlgaro m.
bulge [bʌldʒ] 1 n bombeo m, pandeo m; protuberancia f; **the** — **in the birth rate** el aumento de la natalidad.
  2 vi bombearse, pandearse; sobresalir; (pocket etc) hacer bulto; **his pockets** —**d with apples** sus bolsillos estaban totalmente llenos de manzanas; **their eyes** —**d at the sight** se les saltaron los ojos al verlo.
bulging ['bʌldʒiŋ] adj: — **eyes** ojos mpl saltones.
bulk [bʌlk] 1 n (a) bulto m, volumen m; masa f, mole f; grueso m; **the** — **of those present** la mayor parte de los que asistían; **the** — **of the army** el grueso del ejército; **the enormous** — **of the ship** la enorme mole del buque; **he set his full** — **down in a chair** dejó caer todo el peso de su cuerpo en un sillón.
  (b) (Comm) **in** — **a granel; **to buy in** — comprar en grandes cantidades.
  2 vi: **to** — **large** tener un puesto importante.
bulk-buying ['bʌlk'baiiŋ] n compra f en grandes cantidades.
bulkhead ['bʌlkhed] n mamparo m.
bulkiness ['bʌlkinis] n volumen m, lo abultado.
bulky ['bʌlki] adj voluminoso, abultado, grueso; goods de gran bulto.
bull¹ [bul] 1 n (Zool) toro m; **fighting** — toro m de lidia; **to be like a** — **in a china shop** comportarse como un elefante en una tienda de porcelana; **to take the** — **by the horns** coger el toro por los cuernos.
  2 adj macho.
bull² [bul] 1 n (Comm) alcista m. 2 adj (Comm) alcista.
bull³ [bul] n (Eccl) bula f.

bull⁴ [bul] n (sl) tonterías fpl.
bull⁵ [bul] n (Mil sl) trabajos mpl rutinarios.
bulldog ['buldɔg] n dogo m; (Univ sl) bedel m; **the** — **breed** los ingleses (bajo su aspecto heroico y porfiado).
bulldoze ['buldəuz] vt nivelar con motoniveladora; (fig) opposition arrollar.
bulldozer ['buldəuzə*] n motoniveladora f, aplanadora f.
bullet ['bulit] n bala f.
bulletin ['bulitin] n anuncio m, parte m; (journal) boletín m.
bulletin board ['bulitinbɔ:d] n (US) tablón m de anuncios.
bulletproof ['bulitpru:f] adj a prueba de balas.
bullet-wound ['bulitwu:nd] n balazo m.
bullfight ['bulfait] n corrida f de toros.
bullfighter ['bulfaitə*] n torero m.
bullfighting ['bulfaitiŋ] n toreo m; arte m de torear, tauromaquia f; **do you like** —? ¿le gustan los toros?
bullfinch ['bulfintʃ] n camachuelo m.
bullfrog ['bulfrɔg] n rana f toro.
bullion ['buljən] n oro m en barras, plata f en barras.
bull-necked ['bul'nekt] adj de cuello de toro.
bullock ['bulək] n novillo m, toro m joven, torete m.
bullring ['bulriŋ] n plaza f de toros.
bull's-eye ['bulzai] n (of target) centro m del blanco; (lantern) linterna f sorda; (Naut) ojo m de buey; (sweet) tipo de dulce; **to score a** — dar en el blanco, (fig) acertar.
bully¹ ['buli] 1 n matón m, valentón m. 2 vt intimidar, tiranizar; **to** — **someone into** + ger forzar a uno con amenazas a + infin.
bully² ['buli] 1 adj (sl) de primera. 2 interj: — **for you!** ¡bravo!
bully beef ['buli'bi:f] n carne f de vaca conservada en lata.
bulrush ['bulrʌʃ] n anea f, espadaña f.
bulwark ['bulwək] n (Mil and fig) baluarte m; (Naut) macarrón m.
bum¹ [bʌm] n (Anat: fam) culo m.
bum² [bʌm] (US) 1 n (idler) holgazán m; (tramp) vagabundo m; (scrounger) sablista m; (as term of general disapproval) vago m; **you poor** —! ¡tío tonto!; **to go on the** — vivir de gorra, vagabundear.
  2 vi holgazanear, vagabundear.
bumblebee ['bʌmblbi:] n abejorro m.
bumboat ['bʌmbəut] n bote m vivandero.
bump [bʌmp] 1 n (a) (blow) tope m, topetón m, choque m; (jolt of vehicle) sacudida f; (Aer) rebote m; (in falling) batacazo m.
  (b) (swelling) bollo m, abolladura f, protuberancia f; (on skin) chichón m, hinchazón f; (on road) bache m; **to have a** — **for** tener el don de, tener un sentido especial de.
  2 vt chocar contra, topetar; **to** — **one's head** darse un golpe en la cabeza; **to** — **one's head on a door** dar con su cabeza contra una puerta; **to** — **off** (sl) despenar, cargarse a.
  3 vi (vehicle) dar sacudidas; **to** — **against** chocar contra, topetar, dar contra; **to** — **along** avanzar dando sacudidas; **to** — **into** chocar contra, tropezar con, person topar; fancy —**ing into you!** ¡qué casualidad encontrarle a Vd!
bumper ['bʌmpə*] 1 n (Aut) parachoques m; (glass) copa f llena. 2 adj: — **crop** cosecha f abundante, cosechón m.
bumpkin ['bʌmpkin] n (gen country —) patán m.
bumptious ['bʌmpʃəs] adj engreído, presuntuoso.
bumpy ['bʌmpi] adj surface desigual; road lleno de baches; air agitado; journey de muchas sacudidas.
bun [bʌn] n bollo m; (hair) rodete m, moño m.
bunch [bʌntʃ] 1 n manojo m, puñado m; (of flowers) ramo m, ramillete m; (of grapes) racimo m, (of bananas) piña f; (of keys) manojo m; (set of people) grupo m, (pej) pandilla f.
  2 vt agrupar, juntar; **to be** —**ed together** estar muy juntos unos a otros.
bundle ['bʌndl] 1 n lío m, bulto m, fardo m; (of sticks) haz f; (of papers) legajo m.
  2 vt: **to** — **up** liar, atar, envolver; **to** — **someone out** hacer que uno salga precipitadamente; **they** —**d him out into the street** le pusieron sin ceremonia en la calle; — **it all into the case** póngalo todo en la maleta no importa cómo.
bung [bʌŋ] 1 n bitoque m.
  2 vt tapar con bitoque; (in general) cerrar, tapar; (sl: throw) tirar, lanzar; (sl: put) poner, meter; **to be** —**ed up** estar obturado, estar obstruido, (eye) estar hinchado.
bungalow ['bʌŋgələu] n casa f de un solo piso, chalet m.
bunghole ['bʌŋhəul] n piquera f, boca f (de tonel).

bungle ['bʌŋgl] vt work chapucear, hacer con los pies; **to — it** hacerlo malísimamente; desperdiciar la ocasión.
bungler ['bʌŋglə*] n chapucero m.
bungling ['bʌŋgliŋ] adj torpe, desmañado.
bunion ['bʌnjən] n juanete m.
bunk¹ [bʌŋk] n (bed) tarima f; (Naut) litera f, camastro m; (Aer, child's) litera f; (fam) cama f.
bunk² [bʌŋk] (sl) **1** n: **to do a — = 2** vi huir, poner pies en polvorosa.
bunk³ [bʌŋk] n (sl) tonterías fpl, música f celestial; **—! ¡tonterías!; history is —** la historia es un absurdo.
bunk bed ['bʌŋk'bed] n litera f.
bunker ['bʌŋkə*] **1** n (for coal) carbonera f; (Naut) pañol m del carbón; (Mil) refugio m; (Golf) bunker m, hoya f de arena, arenal m.
2 vt (Naut) proveer de carbón; **to be —ed** (fig) estar en un atolladero.
bunkum ['bʌŋkəm] n (sl) = **bunk³**.
bunny ['bʌni] n conejito m.
Bunsen burner ['bʌnsn'bə:nə*] n mechero m Bunsen.
bunting¹ ['bʌntiŋ] n (Orn) escribano m.
bunting² ['bʌntiŋ] n (decoration) banderas fpl, empavesado m; (cloth) lanilla f.
buoy [bɔi] **1** n boya f. **2** vt channel aboyar, señalar con boyas; **to — up** person mantener a flote, (fig) animar, alentar.
buoyancy ['bɔiənsi] n lo boyante, capacidad f para flotar; (Aer) fuerza f ascensional; (fig) confianza f, optimismo m.
buoyant ['bɔiənt] adj boyante, capaz de flotar; (fig) ilusionado, optimista; (Comm) con tendencia al alza.
buoyantly ['bɔiəntli] adv de modo boyante; (fig) de modo ilusionado, con optimismo.
bur(r) [bə:*] n (Bot) erizo m.
burble ['bə:bl] vi (bubble) burbujear, hervir; (talk) parlotear.
burden ['bə:dn] **1** n (a) carga f; (weight) peso m; (Naut) arqueo m.
(b) (fig) carga f; fardo m; (of speech etc) tema m principal, (of song) estribillo m; **— of proof** peso m de la prueba; **to be a — to someone** ser una responsabilidad molesta para uno; **he carries a heavy —** tiene que cargar con una gran responsabilidad; **to make someone's life a —** amargar la vida a uno.
2 vt cargar (with de); **to be —ed with** tener que cargar con.
burdensome ['bə:dnsəm] adj gravoso, oneroso.
bureau [bjuə'rəu] n (desk) escritorio m, buró m; (office) oficina f, agencia f, departamento m; **— de change** caja f de cambio; **weather —** oficina f meteorológica.
bureaucracy [bjuə'rɔkrəsi] n burocracia f.
bureaucrat ['bjuərəukræt] n burócrata mf.
bureaucratic [,bjuərəu'krætik] adj burocrático.
burgeon ['bə:dʒən] vi (lit) retoñar.
burgess ['bə:dʒis] n ciudadano m, a f; (Parl) diputado m.
burgh ['bʌrə*] n (Scot) villa f.
burglar ['bə:glə*] n ladrón m, escalador m.
burglar alarm ['bə:glərə,la:m] n alarma f de ladrones.
burglarize ['bə:gləraiz] vt (US) = **burgle**.
burglarproof ['bə:gləpru:f] adj a prueba de ladrones.
burglary ['bə:gləri] n robo m en una casa, robo m con escalonamiento, (Law) allanamiento m de morada.
burgle ['bə:gl] vt robar, escalar, allanar, desvalijar.
Burgundian [bə:'gʌndiən] **1** adj borgoñón. **2** n borgoñón m, ona f.
Burgundy ['bə:gəndi] Borgoña f; **b—** vino m de Borgoña.
burial ['beriəl] n entierro m.
burial ground ['beriəlgraund] n cementerio m.
burlap ['bə:læp] n harpillera f.
burlesque [bə:'lesk] **1** adj festivo, paródico; **— show** (US) revista f chabacana. **2** n parodia f. **3** vt parodiar.
burly ['bə:li] adj fornido, membrudo, corpulento.
Burma ['bə:mə] Birmania f.
Burmese [bə:'mi:z] **1** adj birmano. **2** n birmano m, a f.
burn¹ [bə:n] **1** n quemadura f.
2 (irr: pret and ptp burned or burnt) vt (a) quemar; house etc incendiar; corpse incinerar; plants (by sun) abrasar; almonds etc tostar; fuel funcionar con, utilizar como combustible; mouth, tongue quemar, escaldar; **to — one's hand** quemarse la mano; **to — a hole in something** hacer un agujero en algo quemándolo; **to — something to ashes** reducir algo a cenizas; **to — a house to the ground** incendiar y arrasar una casa; **to be —ed alive** ser quemado vivo; **to be —ed to death** morir en un incendio; **with a face —ed by the sun** con una cara

tostada al sol; **it has a burnt taste** sabe a quemado.
(b) to — away quemar, consumir; **to — down** incendiar; **to — off** quitar quemando; **to — out** (Elec) fundir, quemar; **to — up** quemar, consumir; crops abrasar; (fig, fam) indignar.
3 vi (a) quemar(se), arder; (catch fire) incendiarse; (light, gas) estar encendido; (smart) escocer; **to — down** quedar destruido en un incendio; **to — out** consumirse, apagarse; (Elec) fundirse; **to — to death** morir quemado; **to — up** consumirse; (burn brighter) arder más.
(b) (fig) arder (with de, en); **to — to + infin** desear ardientemente + infin; **to — with desire for** desear ardientemente; **to — with impatience** consumirse de impaciencia.
burn² [bə:n] n (Scot) arroyo m.
burner ['bə:nə*] n mechero m; (on stove etc) quemador m, fuego m.
burning ['bə:niŋ] adj ardiente (also fig); question candente, palpitante; **it's — hot** está que quema, (sun) hace muchísimo calor.
burnish ['bə:niʃ] vt bruñir.
burnt [bə:nt] pret and ptp of **burn¹**.
burp [bə:p] (fam) **1** n eructo m. **2** vi eructar.
burr [bə:*] n (Bot) erizo m.
burrow ['bʌrəu] **1** n madriguera f; (rabbit's) conejera f.
2 vt hacer madrigueras en; (and undermine) socavar, minar; **to — one's way into** abrirse camino cavando en.
3 vi amadrigarse, hacer una madriguera; **to — into** hacer madrigueras en, horadar.
bursar ['bə:sə*] n (Univ etc) tesorero m.
bursary ['bə:səri] n (Univ) beca f.
bursitis [bə:'saitis] n bursitis f.
burst [bə:st] **1** n reventón m; (explosion) estallido m, explosión f; (of shots) serie f de tiros, ráfaga f de tiros; **a — of applause** una explosión de aplausos; **a — of speed** una escapada; **a — of activity** un frenesí repentino de actividad; **in a — of anger** en un arranque de cólera.
2 (irr: pret and ptp burst) vt balloon etc reventar; bubble deshacer; tyre pinchar; banks, dam, pipe romper; **to — open a door** abrir de golpe una puerta.
3 vi (balloon, boil, boiler) reventar(se); (bubble) deshacerse; (tyre) pincharse; (dam, pipe) romperse; (bomb etc) estallar; (heart) partirse; (storm) desencadenarse; **to — forth** brotar, salir a chorro; **to — in** entrar violentamente; **to — into a room** irrumpir en un cuarto; **to — into tears** deshacerse en lágrimas; **to — into song** romper a cantar; **to — into flames** estallar en llamas; **to — open** abrirse de golpe; **to — out laughing** soltar la carcajada; **"No," he — out "¡No!"** gritó violentamente; **the sun — through the clouds** el sol brilló repentinamente por entre las nubes; **he was —ing to tell me** reventaba por decírmelo; **he was —ing with impatience** reventaba de impaciencia; **to — with laughter** reventar de risa; **London is —ing with young people** Londres está que bulle de juventud; **to be full to —ing** estar lleno a reventar; estar apretado a presión.
burthen ['bə:ðən] n arqueo m.
bury ['beri] vt enterrar (also fig); body enterrar, sepultar; memory, matter echar tierra sobre; **to — a dagger in someone's heart** clavar un puñal en el corazón de uno; **to — one's face in one's hands** ocultar el rostro en las manos; **to — oneself in the country** enterrarse en el campo; **to be buried in thought** estar absorto en la meditación.
bus [bʌs] n autobús m; **to go by —** ir en autobús; **to miss the —** (fam) perder la ocasión.
bush [buʃ] n arbusto m; (Tech) forro m de metal; **the —** (Australia) el monte, el despoblado; **to beat about the —** andarse por las ramas, ir por rodeos.
bushel ['buʃl] n medida de áridos: British = 36,36 litros, US = 35,24 litros.
bushman ['buʃmən] n, pl **—men** [mən] (African) bosquimano m.
bushranger ['buʃ,reindʒə*] n (Australia) bandido m.
bush telegraph ['buʃ'teligra:f] n (fam) medio m de comunicación clandestina; **I heard it on the —** lo llegué a saber, me lo dijo alguno, lo supe pero no te voy a decir cómo; **they have their own —** tienen sus propios métodos para comunicarse.
bushy ['buʃi] adj plant parecido a un arbusto; ground lleno de arbustos; beard poblado, espeso.
busily ['bizili] adv atareadamente, afanosamente.
business ['biznis] **1** n (a) (commerce in general; fig) comercio m, negocios mpl; **it's — el comercio** es una cosa seria; **— before pleasure** primero es la obligación que la devoción; **— as usual** los negocios

como de costumbre; **big** — comercio m en gran escala; **he's in** — se dedica al comercio; **he's in** — **in London** trabaja en una empresa comercial de Londres; **to be on** — estar (en viaje) de negocios; **to carry on** — as tener un negocio de; **to do** — **with** comerciar con; **to get down to** — ir al grano, ir derecho a lo esencial; **to go into** — dedicarse al comercio; **to mean** — hablar (etc) en serio; **to send someone about his** — echar a uno con cajas destempladas; **to set up in** — as montar un negocio de; **to set someone up in** — proveer a uno de un capital explotable.

(b) (firm) empresa f, casa f; **it's a family** — es una empresa familiar.

(c) (task, duty) **that's my** — eso me toca únicamente a mí; **it is my** — **to** + infin me corresponde + infin; **it's no** — **of mine** yo no tengo nada que ver con eso; **you had no** — **to** + infin Vd no tuvo ningún derecho a + infin; **what** — **have you to** + infin? ¿qué derecho tiene Vd a + infin?; **I will make it my** — **to tell him** yo me propongo decírselo, yo les aseguro que se lo diré; **mind your own** — no se meta Vd donde no le llaman.

(d) (one's trade, profession) oficio m, ocupación f; **what** — **are you in?** ¿a qué se dedica Vd?; **he's got the biggest laugh in the** — tiene la risa más fuerte que hay por aquí.

(e) (affair) cosa f, asunto m, cuestión f; **the Suez** — aquello de Suez; **the** — **before the meeting** los asuntos a tratar; **I have** — **with the minister** tengo asuntos que tratar con el ministro; **it's a nasty** — es un asunto desagradable; **did you hear about that** — **yesterday?** ¿le dijeron algo de lo que pasó ayer?; **what a** — **this is!** ¡qué lío!; **I can't stand this** — **of doing nothing** no puedo con este plan de no hacer nada.

(f) (Theat) acción f.

2 attr: deal, connection, quarter comercial; house de comercio; cycle económico; trip de negocios; hours de oficina.

businesslike ['biznislaik] adj formal, metódico, serio, práctico.

businessman ['biznismæn] n, pl **—men** [men] hombre m de negocios.

busload ['bʌsləud] n autobús m (lleno, completo); **they came by the** — (fig) vinieron en masa, vinieron en tropel.

busman ['bʌsmən] n, pl **—men** [mən] conductor m or cobrador m de autobús; **—'s holiday** día de fiesta en el cual uno hace el mismo trabajo que siempre.

bus-stop ['bʌsstɔp] n parada f de autobús.

bust¹ [bʌst] n (Anat: Art) busto m; (bosom) pecho m, pechos mpl.

bust² [bʌst] 1 ptp (fam) of **burst**; **to go** — (Comm) quebrar. 2 vt romper, estropear. 3 vi romperse, estropearse.

bustard ['bʌstəd] n avutarda f.

bustle¹ ['bʌsl] n (dress) polisón m.

bustle² ['bʌsl] 1 n movimiento m, actividad f; bullicio m, animación f; (haste) prisa f. 2 vi menearse, apresurarse, ir y venir.

bustler ['bʌslə*] n bullebulle mf.

bustling ['bʌsliŋ] adj activo, hacendoso; crowd apresurado, animado.

bust-up ['bʌstʌp] n (fam) riña f.

busy ['bizi] 1 adj (a) person ocupado; atareado; activo;| (pej) entrometido; **as** — **as a bee** muy activo, ocupadísimo; **are you** — ? ¿está ocupado?; **to be** — **at** (or **on, with**) estar ocupado en; **to be** — **doing something** estar ocupado en hacer algo; **to get** — empezar a trabajar, (hurry) menearse, darse prisa; **let's get** — ! ¡vamos!; **to keep** — estar siempre ocupado; **to keep someone** — ocupar a uno.

(b) day de muchas ocupaciones; **the busiest season is the autumn** la época de mayor actividad es el otoño.

(c) place (muy) concurrido, de mucho movimiento; scene animado, lleno de movimiento.

2 vt ocupar.

3 vr: **to** — **oneself at** (or **in, with**) ocuparse en, estar ocupado con; **she busied herself with the children** ella se ocupó de los niños.

busybody ['bizibɔdi] n entrometido m, a f.

but [bʌt] 1 adv (only) sólo, solamente, no más que; **all** — casi; **nothing** — nada más que; **he is** — **a servant** no es más que un criado; **he talks** — **little** habla muy poco; **if I could** — **speak to him** si solamente pudiese hablar con él; **had I** — **known** si lo hubiera sabido.

2 prep and conj (except) excepto, menos; **all** — **him** todos excepto él; **the last** — **one** el penúltimo; **the last** — **three** el tercero antes del último; — **for**

a no ser por, si no fuera por; **there is nothing for it** — **to pay up** no hay más remedio que pagar; **I'll do anything** — **sing** lo hago todo menos cantar.

3 conj (a) pero; **she was poor** — **she was honest** era pobre pero honrada; — **it does move!** ¡pero sí se mueve!; **it never rains** — **it pours** no llueve sin hacerlo en exceso; **I never go there** — **I think of you** nunca voy allá sin pensar en ti.

(b) (in statements of direct contradiction) sino, eg **he's not English** — **Irish** no es inglés sino irlandés; **he didn't sing** — **he shouted** no cantó sino que gritó.

4 n pero m, objeción f; **there are no** —**s about it** no hay pero que valga.

butane ['bju:tein] n butano m; — **gas** gas m butano.

butcher ['butʃə*] 1 n carnicero m (also fig); —**'s (shop)** carnicería f. 2 vt matar; (fig) dar muerte a, hacer una carnicería con.

butchery ['butʃəri] n matanza f, carnicería f.

butler ['bʌtlə*] n mayordomo m.

butt¹ [bʌt] n tonel m; (for rainwater) tina f.

butt² [bʌt] n (end) cabo m, extremo m; extremo m más grueso; (of gun) culata f; (of cigarette) colilla f; (US fam) culo m.

butt³ [bʌt] n (target) blanco m; —**s** campo m de tiro al blanco; **to be a** — **for** ser el blanco de, ser el objeto de.

butt⁴ [bʌt] 1 n (push with head) cabezada f, topetada f. 2 vt dar cabezadas contra, topetar; **to** — **one's head against** dar con la cabeza contra. 3 vi: **to** — **in** interrumpir; (meddle) entrometerse.

butt-end ['bʌtend] n = **butt²**.

butter ['bʌtə*] 1 n mantequilla f; — **wouldn't melt in his mouth** es una mosquita muerta. 2 vt untar con mantequilla; **to** — **someone up** (fam) dar coba a uno.

buttercup ['bʌtəkʌp] n ranúnculo m.

butter-fingered ['bʌtə.fiŋgəd] adj desmañado en coger la pelota (etc).

butterfly ['bʌtəflai] n mariposa f.

butterfly-stroke ['bʌtəflai.strəuk] n estilo m mariposa.

buttermilk ['bʌtəmilk] n leche f de manteca.

butterscotch ['bʌtəskɔtʃ] n dulce de azúcar terciado con mantequilla.

buttery ['bʌtəri] n despensa f.

buttocks ['bʌtəks] npl nalgas fpl, cachas fpl.

button ['bʌtn] 1 n (all senses) botón m; —**s** (person) botones m. 2 vt (also **to** — **up**) abotonar, abrochar. 3 vi: **it** —**s in front** se abrocha por delante.

buttonhole ['bʌtnhəul] 1 n ojal m; (flower) flor f que se lleva en el ojal. 2 vt obligar a escuchar, abordar; **I was** —**d by X** me vi obligado a detenerme en conversación con X.

buttonhook ['bʌtnhuk] n abotonador m.

buttress ['bʌtris] 1 n contrafuerte m (also Geog); (fig) apoyo m, sostén m; **flying** — arbotante m. 2 vt poner contrafuerte a; (fig) apoyar, reforzar.

buxom ['bʌksəm] adj rollizo, frescachón.

buy [bai] 1 n compra f; **a good** — un buen negocio, una ganga.

2 (irr: pret and ptp **bought**) vt comprar (from, of a); **money couldn't** — **it** no se puede comprar con dinero; **all right, I'll** — **it** bien, dime; **to** — **back** volver a comprar; **to** — **off** comprar la benevolencia de, (bribe) sobornar; **to** — **out** partner comprar la parte de; **to** — **up** comprar todas las existencias de, acaparar.

buyer ['baiə*] n comprador m, ora f; (in store) encargado m de compras.

buzz [bʌz] 1 n zumbido m; (fam) rumor m.

2 vt (call) llamar; (Aer) avisar; (throw, fam) lanzar, tirar.

3 vi zumbar; **to** — **about** ser muy activo, ir por todas partes; **to** — **off** (fam) largarse, najarse.

buzzard ['bʌzəd] n ratonero m común, águila f ratonera.

buzzer ['bʌzə*] n zumbador m, vibrador m.

by [bai] 1 adv: — **and** — más tarde, luego; — **and large** en general, por lo general.

2 prep (a) (agent, by means of) por; **a house built** — **X** una casa construida por X; — **one's own efforts** por sus propios esfuerzos; — **God** por Dios; **made** — **hand** hecho a mano; **to divide** — **5** dividir por 5; **he had 3 children** — **his first wife** tuvo 3 hijos con su primera mujer; **he is known** — **the name of** se le conoce con (of pseudonym: bajo) el nombre de; **he did it** — **himself** lo hizo por sí solo, lo hizo por sí mismo.

(b) (manner) — **cheque** por cheque; — **air** en avión; — **train** (come) en tren, (send) por ferrocarril; — **easy stages** en cortas etapas; — **moonlight** a la luz de la luna; — **leaps and bounds** a pasos agigantados; **to be** — **oneself** estar solo.

(c) (*rate*) **hour** — **hour** hora tras hora, cada hora; — **the dozen** a docenas; **2** — **2** de 2 en 2; **little** — **little** poco a poco; **to buy something** — **the kilo** comprar algo por kilos; **to reduce something** — **a third** reducir algo en una tercera parte; **we pay** — **the month** pagamos cada mes.

(d) (*in accordance with*) según, de acuerdo con; — **what you say** según lo que dices; **to be cautious** — **nature** ser de naturaleza cauteloso.

(e) (*time*) — **2 o'clock** para las 2; — **nightfall** antes del anochecer; — **then** para entonces, antes de eso; — **day** de día.

(f) (*place*) junto a, cerca de, al lado de; — **me** a mi lado; **north** — **west** norte por oeste; (*through, along*) por; **he came in** — **the window** entró por la ventana.

(g) (*measurement*) **6 metres** — **4** 6 metros por 4; **it's too short** — **a foot** falta un pie; **he missed** — **an inch** erró el tiro en una pulgada.

(h) (*with gerund*) — **working hard** trabajando mucho; **he ended** — **saying that** terminó diciendo que. **3** *n*: — **the** — a propósito, por cierto.

bye [bai] *n*: **to have a** — pasar a la segunda eliminatoria por sorteo.

bye-bye ['bai'bai] *interj* ¡adiós!, ¡hasta luego!
by-election ['baii,lekʃən] *n* elección *f* complementaria.
bygone ['baigɔn] **1** *adj* pasado. **2** *n*: **let** —**s be** —**s** olvidemos lo pasado.
by-law ['bailɔː] *n* estatuto *m*, reglamento *m*.
by-name ['baineim] *n* sobrenombre *m*; (*nickname*) apodo *m*, mote *m*.
bypass ['baipɑːs] **1** *n* carretera *f* de circunvalación. **2** *vt* evitar, evitar el contacto con; *town* evitar entrar en.
by-play ['baiplei] *n* (*Theat*) acción *f* aparte, escena *f* muda.
by-product ['bai,prɔdəkt] *n* subproducto *m*; (*Chem*) derivado *m*.
by-road ['bairəud] *n* camino *m* vecinal.
bystander ['bai,stændə*] *n* espectador *m*, ora *f*, circunstante *mf*, curioso *m*, a *f*, mirón *m*, ona *f*.
byway ['baiwei] *n* camino *m* apartado, camino *m* poco frecuentado; **the** —**s of history** los aspectos poco conocidos de la historia.
byword ['baiwɔːd] *n*: **to be a** — **for** ser conocidísimo por.
Byzantine [bai'zæntain] **1** *adj* bizantino. **2** *n* bizantino *m*, a *f*.
Byzantium [bai'zæntiəm] Bizancio *m*.

C

cab [kæb] n taxi m; (arch) cabriolé m, coche m de alquiler; (of lorry etc) cabina f, casilla f.
cabal [kə'bæl] n cábala f, cabildeo m.
cabaret ['kæbərei] n cabaret m.
cabbage ['kæbidʒ] n col f, berza f; — white (butter-fly) mariposa f de la col.
cab(b)ala [kə'bɑːlə] n cábala f.
cabbalistic [‚kæbə'listik] adj cabalístico.
cabby ['kæbi] n (fam), **cabdriver** ['kæbdraivə*] n taxista m; (arch) cochero m.
cabin ['kæbin] n (hut) cabaña f; (Naut) camarote m; (of lorry, plane) cabina f.
cabin boy ['kæbinbɔi] n grumete m.
cabin cruiser ['kæbin‚kruːzə*] n yate m de motor, motonave f para viajes de placer.
cabinet ['kæbinit] n (a) (cupboard) armario m; (for display) vitrina f; (casing) caja f; **medicine** — botiquín m.
(b) (Pol) consejo m de ministros; — **crisis** crisis f del gobierno; — **minister** ministro m que es miembro del consejo.
cabinetmaker ['kæbinit‚meikə*] n ebanista m.
cabinetmaking ['kæbinit‚meikiŋ] n ebanistería f.
cable ['keibl] **1** n (Naut, Elec, Tel) cable m; (message) cablegrama m; **overhead** — (Elec) línea f eléctrica aérea. **2** vti cablegrafiar.
cable-car ['keiblkɑː*] n coche m de teleférico.
cablegram ['keiblgræm] n cablegrama m.
cable railway ['keibl'reilwei] n teleférico m, funicular m aéreo.
cable ship ['keiblʃip] n barco m cablero.
cable stitch ['keiblstitʃ] n punto m en cruz.
cableway ['keiblwei] n teleférico m, funicular m aéreo.
cabman ['kæbmən] n, pl —**men** [mən] taxista m; (arch) cochero m.
caboodle [kə'buːdl] n (sl): **the whole** — todo el negocio.
caboose [kə'buːs] n (US: Rail) furgón m de cola.
cabrank ['kæbræŋk] n parada f de taxis, punto m de taxis.
cabstand ['kæbstænd] n parada f de taxis, punto m de taxis.
cacao [kə'kɑːəu] n cacao m.
cache [kæʃ] n (hiding place) escondite m, escondrijo m; (stores) víveres mpl (etc) escondidos; (of contraband, arms) alijo m.
cachet ['kæʃei] n sello m, marca f de distinción.
cackle ['kækl] **1** n cacareo m; (laughter) risa f aguda; (talk) cháchara f; **cut the** —! (fam) ¡callarse!, ¡basta ya de palabras!
2 vi cacarear; (laugh) reírse agudamente, (fam) desternillarse de risa; (talk) chacharear.
cacophony [kæ'kɔfəni] n cacofonía f.
cactus ['kæktəs] n cacto m.
cad [kæd] n sinvergüenza m, caradura m, canalla m; **you** —! ¡canalla!
cadaver [kə'deivə*] n (US) cadáver m.
cadaverous [kə'dævərəs] adj cadavérico.
caddie ['kædi] n cadi m, caddie m (el portador de los palos en el golf).
caddis fly ['kædisflai] n frígano m.
caddish ['kædiʃ] adj desvergonzado, canallesco; — **trick** canallada f.
caddy ['kædi] n cajita f para té.
cadence ['keidəns] n cadencia f; **the** —**s of prose** el ritmo de la prosa.
cadenza [kə'denzə] n cadencia f.
cadet [kə'det] m (Mil) cadete m; (younger son) hijo m menor.
cadge [kædʒ] **1** vt sacar de gorra, obtener mendigando.
2 vi gorronear, vivir de gorra, sablear; **you can't** — **off me** es inútil pedirme cosas a mí.

cadger ['kædʒə*] n gorrón m, ona f, sablista mf.
Cadiz [kə'diz] Cádiz.
cadmium ['kædmiəm] n cadmio m.
cadre ['kædri] n cuadro m.
caecum ['siːkəm] n ciego m.
Caesar ['siːzə*] m César.
Caesarean [si:'zɛəriən] adj: — **operation**, — **section** operación f cesárea.
caesura [si:'zjuərə] n cesura f.
café ['kæfei] n café m.
café au lait ['kæfeiəu'lei] n café m con leche.
café crème ['kæfei'krɛːm] n café m con nata.
café noir ['kæfei'nwɑ:*] n café m solo.
café society ['kæfeisə'saiəti] n (US) (sociedad f de la) gente f que frecuenta los cafés de moda, mundo m elegante de los cafés.
cafeteria [‚kæfi'tiəriə] n restaurante m económico.
caffein(e) ['kæfiːn] n cafeína f.
cage [keidʒ] **1** n jaula f. **2** vt enjaular; **a** —**d bird** un pájaro en jaula.
cage bird ['keidʒbəːd] n pájaro m de jaula.
cagey ['keidʒi] adj (fam) cauteloso, reservado; **he was very** — **about it** en eso anduvo con pies de plomo, habló del asunto con la mayor reserva.
cahoots [kə'huːts] n (sl): **to be in** — **with someone** obrar de acuerdo con uno; estar asociado con uno; **to go** — entrar por partes iguales.
caiman ['keimən] n caimán m.
Cain [kein] m Caín; **to raise** — armar la gorda, protestar enérgicamente.
cairn [kɛən] n mojón m, montón m de piedras (puesto en una cumbre o sobre una sepultura, etc).
Cairo ['kaiərəu] el Cairo.
caisson ['keisən] n (Mech) cajón m hidráulico; (Naut) cajón m de suspensión; (of dry-dock) puerta f de dique; (Mil) cajón m.
cajole [kə'dʒəul] vt halagar, camelar; **to** — **someone into doing something** conseguir por medio de halagos que uno haga algo.
cajolery [kə'dʒəuləri] n halagos mpl, marrullería f, engatusamiento m.
cake [keik] **1** n (large) pastel m; tarta f; (small) pasta f, pastelillo m; (sponge) bizcocho m; (of soap) pastilla f; **birthday** — tarta f de cumpleaños; **Christmas** — tarta f de Reyes; **to go** (or sell) **like hot** —**s** venderse como pan bendito; **that takes the** —! (fam) ¡es el colmo!
2 vt endurecer; **a tyre** —**d with mud** un neumático cubierto de lodo endurecido.
3 vi endurecerse, apelmazarse.
caked [keikt] **1** pret and ptp of **cake**. **2** adj endurecido.
cake shop ['keikʃɔp] n pastelería f.
calabash ['kæləbæʃ] n calabaza f.
calaboose ['kæləbuːs] n (US fam) jaula f (fam), cárcel f.
calamine ['kæləmain] n calamina f.
calamitous [kə'læmitəs] adj calamitoso.
calamity [kə'læmiti] n calamidad f.
calcareous [kæl'kɛəriəs] adj calcáreo.
calcification [‚kælsifi'keiʃən] n calcificación f.
calcify ['kælsifai] **1** vt calcificar. **2** vi calcificarse.
calcination [‚kælsi'neiʃən] n calcinación f.
calcine ['kælsain] **1** vt calcinar. **2** vi calcinarse.
calcium ['kælsiəm] n calcio m; — **carbonate** carbonato m de calcio.
calculable ['kælkjuləbl] adj calculable.
calculate ['kælkjuleit] **1** vt calcular; —**d to** + infin aprestado para + infin; **this is** —**d to give him a jolt** esto tiene el propósito de darle una sacudida; **it is hardly** —**d to help us** esto apenas tendrá consecuencias beneficiosas para nosotros.
2 vi calcular; **to** — **on** contar con.
calculated ['kælkjuleitid] adj insult etc intencionado.
calculating ['kælkjuleitiŋ] adj astuto.

calculating machine ['kælkjuleitiŋmə,ʃiːn] n máquina f de calcular, calculadora f.
calculation [,kælkju'leiʃən] n cálculo m, cómputo m.
calculus ['kælkjuləs] n: **differential —** cálculo m diferencial.
Calcutta [kæl'kʌtə] Calcuta.
calendar ['kæləndə*] n calendario m; (Law) lista f de pleitos; **— year** año m civil.
calf¹ [kɑːf] n, pl **calves** [kɑːvz] (Zool) ternero m, a f, becerro m, a f; (of seal etc) cría f; (skin) piel f de becerro; **to be in** (or **with) —** estar preñada (la vaca); **to kill the fatted —** festejar con mucho rumbo a un recién llegado, celebrar una fiesta de bienvenida.
calf² [kɑːf] n, pl **calves** [kɑːvz] (Anat) pantorrilla f.
calf love ['kɑːflʌv] n amor m juvenil.
calfskin ['kɑːfskin] n piel f de becerro.
calibrate ['kælibreit] vt calibrar.
calibre, (US) **caliber** ['kælibə*] n calibre m; (fig) capacidad f, aptitud f, carácter m, valor m; **a man of his —** un hombre que vale lo que él; **then he showed his real —** luego demostró tener un gran talento.
calico ['kælikəu] n calicó m.
calipers ['kælipəz] npl calibrador m.
caliph ['keilif] n califa m.
caliphate ['keilifeit] n califato m.
call [kɔːl] **1** n (a) (in general) llamada f (also Mil, Tel); (cry) grito m; (of bird) canto m, reclamo m; (imitating bird's cry) reclamo m, (imitating animal's cry) chilla f; (Theat) llamamiento m; (at bridge) marca f, voz f; **local —** llamada f local; **trunk —, long-distance —** conferencia f interurbana; **the — of the unknown** la atracción de lo desconocido; **on — disponible, a su disposición; money on — dinero m a la vista; within — al alcance de la voz; whose — is it?** (Bridge) ¿quién habla?; **they came at my —** acudieron a mi llamada; **please give me a — at 7** haga el favor de llamarme a las 7; **he's had a — to the Palace** le han llamado a palacio; **to have a close — escapar por un pelo, casi haber muerto.
(b) (visit) visita f; port of — puerto m de escala; the boat makes a — at Vigo** el barco hace escala en Vigo; **to pay a — on someone** hacer una visita a uno.
(c) (appeal) llamamiento m; **a — went to the fire brigade** se llamó a los bomberos; **the boat sent out a — for help** el barco emitió una llamada pidiendo socorro; **the minister sent out a — to the country to remain calm** el ministro hizo un llamamiento al país para que conservara la calma.
(d) (need etc) (Comm) demanda f (for, on de); **there isn't much — for these now** éstos tienen poca demanda ahora; **you had no — to say that** Vd no tuvo motivo alguno para decir eso; **what — was there for you to intervene?** ¿qué derecho tuvo Vd a entrometerse?
(e) (claim) **there are many —s on my attention** son muchas las cosas que reclaman mi atención.
2 vt (a) (in general) llamar; **did you —?** ¿me llamaste?; **they —ed me to see it** me llamaron para que lo viese; **please — me at 8** haga el favor de llamarme a las 8.
(b) (Tel) llamar (por or al teléfono); **London —ed you this morning** esta mañana le llamaron al teléfono desde Londres; **I'll — you again tomorrow** volveré a llamarle mañana.
(c) (name) llamar; **I'm —ed Peter** me llamo Pedro; **what are you —ed?** ¿cómo te llamas?; **what are they —ing him?** ¿qué nombre le van a poner?; **they're —ing the boy John** al niño le van a dar el nombre de Juan; **I — it an insult** yo digo que es un insulto; **I —ed him a liar** le califiqué de mentiroso; **are you —ing me a liar?** ¿dice Vd que yo soy un mentiroso?
(d) (special uses) **attention** llamar (to sobre); **meeting** convocar; **roll** pasar; **strike** declarar; (Bridge) marcar; **he —ed 3 hearts** marcó 3 corazones; **to — someone as a witness** citar a uno como testigo; see **halt, name, question** etc.
(e) **to — aside** llamar aparte; **to — back** hacer volver, (Tel) volver a llamar; **to — down blessings upon someone** pedir al cielo mil bendiciones para uno; **to — forth** sacar; remark etc inspirar; protest etc motivar, provocar; **to — in** hacer entrar; expert, police llamar, pedir la ayuda de; old notes retirar de la circulación; **to — off** cancelar; search etc dar por terminado, suspender, abandonar; dogs llamar; **to — out** workers llamar a la huelga; **to — over** llamar; names pasar la lista de; **to — together** convocar; **to — up** hacer subir; (Tel) llamar; memory evocar; (Mil) llamar al servicio militar.
3 vi (a) (cry out) llamar, dar voces, dar gritos.

(b) (Tel) **who is it —ing?** ¿de parte de quién?; (Radio) **Madrid —ing!** ¡aquí Radio Madrid!
(c) (visit) venir, hacer una visita.
(d) **to — at** house visitar, pasar por; port hacer escala en; **to — back** volver (for por); **to — for** venir por, venir a recoger; (demand) pedir, exigir; **to — for help** pedir socorro a voces; **to — in** entrar, venir; dar un vistazo; **to — on** visitar, ir a ver; (for a speech) invitar a hablar; **I now — on Mr Brown** cedo la palabra al Sr Brown; **to — on someone for help** acudir a uno para pedir ayuda; **the minister —ed on the nation to help** el ministro hizo un llamamiento a la nación para que ayudase; **to — out** gritar, dar voces; **to — to** dar voces a; **heart —s to heart** los corazones se hablan.
callbox ['kɔːlbɔks] n cabina f telefónica.
callboy ['kɔːlbɔi] n (Theat) traspunte m.
caller ['kɔːlə*] n visita f; (Tel) usuario m; **the first — at the shop** el primer cliente de la tienda.
call girl ['kɔːlgəːl] n prostituta f (que hace citas por teléfono).
calligraphic [,kæli'græfik] adj caligráfico.
calligraphy [kə'ligrəfi] n caligrafía f.
calling ['kɔːliŋ] n vocación f, profesión f.
calling card ['kɔːliŋkɑːd] n (US) tarjeta f de visita.
callipers ['kælipəz] npl calibrador m; (Med) soporte m, corrector m.
callisthenics [,kælis'θeniks] n sing calistenia f.
call letters ['kɔːl,letəz] npl (US: Tel) letras fpl de identificación.
call money ['kɔːlmʌni] n dinero m a la vista.
callosity [kæ'lɔsiti] n callosidad f.
callous ['kæləs] adj insensible, cruel; (Med) calloso.
callously ['kæləsli] adv cruelmente.
callousness ['kæləsnis] n insensibilidad f, crueldad f.
callow ['kæləu] adj inexperto, novato; youth imberbe.
call sign ['kɔːlsain] n (Radio) indicativo m.
call-up ['kɔːlʌp] n (of reserves) movilización f; (conscription) servicio m militar obligatorio; (act of calling) llamamiento m.
callus ['kæləs] n callo m.
calm [kɑːm] **1** adj person, mind tranquilo, sosegado; weather calmoso, sin viento; sea liso, en calma; **to keep —** no emocionarse, conservar la tranquilidad; **to grow —** calmarse, sosegarse.
2 n calma f, tranquilidad f; **dead —** calma f chicha.
3 vt calmar, tranquilizar (also **to — down**).
4 vi calmarse, tranquilizarse (also **to — down**); **— down!** ¡cálmese!, (to excited child) ¡tente quieto!
5 vr: **— yourself** ¡cálmese!
calming ['kɑːmiŋ] adj calmante.
calmly ['kɑːmli] adv con calma, tranquilamente.
calmness ['kɑːmnis] n calma f, tranquilidad f.
caloric ['kælərik] adj calórico.
calorie ['kæləri] n caloría f.
calorific [,kælə'rifik] adj calorífico.
calumniate [kə'lʌmnieit] vt calumniar.
calumny ['kæləmni] n calumnia f.
Calvary ['kælvəri] Calvario m.
calve [kɑːv] vi parir (la vaca).
calves [kɑːvz] npl of **calf**¹ and **calf**².
Calvin ['kælvin] m Calvino.
Calvinism ['kælvinizəm] n calvinismo m.
Calvinist ['kælvinist] **1** adj calvinista. **2** n calvinista mf.
Calvinistic [,kælvi'nistik] adj calvinista.
calypso [kə'lipsəu] n calipso m.
calyx ['keiliks] n, pl **calyces** ['keilisiːz] cáliz m.
cam [kæm] n leva f.
camaraderie [,kæmə'rɑːdəri] n compañerismo m.
camber ['kæmbə*] **1** n combadura f; convexidad f.
2 vt combar, arquear. **3** vi combarse, arquearse.
Cambodia [kæm'bəudiə] Camboya f.
Cambodian [kæm'bəudiən] **1** adj camboyano. **2** n camboyano m, a f.
cambric ['keimbrik] n batista f.
came [keim] pret of **come**.
camel ['kæməl] n camello m.
camel hair ['kæməlhɛə*] n pelo m de camello.
camel's-hair ['kæməlzhɛə*] adj de pelo de camello.
camellia [kə'miːliə] n camelia f.
cameo ['kæmiəu] n camafeo m.
camera ['kæmərə] n máquina f (fotográfica); (Cine, TV) cámara f; **aerial —** aparato m de fotografía aérea; **colour —** cámara f para hacer fotos en color; **in —** en secreto.
cameraman ['kæmərəmæn] n, pl **—men** [men] cameraman m, cámara m.
Cameroon [,kæmə'ruːn] Camerón m.
camisole ['kæmisəul] n cubrecorsé m.
camomile ['kæməumail] n camomila f; **— tea** manzanilla f.

camouflage ['kæməflɑːʒ] **1** *n* camuflaje *m*. **2** *vt* camuflar.

camp[1] [kæmp] **1** *n* campamento *m*, campo *m*; (*Pol etc*) grupo *m*, facción *f*; **concentration** — campo *m* de concentración; **internment** — campo *m* de internamiento; **holiday** — colonia *f* veraniega; **labour** — campamento *m* de trabajo; **prison** — campamento *m* para prisioneros; **summer** — (*for children etc*) colonia *f* veraniega; **to pitch** — poner el campamento, armar la tienda, acampar(se); **to strike** — levantar el campamento.

2 *vi* acampar(se); (*fam*) alojarse temporalmente; **to** — **out on the beach** pasar la noche en la playa.

camp[2] [kæmp] **1** *adj* (**a**) afectado (y divertido), (intencionadamente) teatral; sensible, elegante; (*Lit etc*) afectado, amanerado.

(**b**) afeminado; (abiertamente) homosexual.

2 *n* (**a**) afectación *f* divertida, exageración *f*, teatralidad *f* intencionada; (*Lit etc*) amaneramiento *m*.

(**b**) afeminación *f*; homosexualidad *f* (abierta).

3 *vi* parodiarse a sí mismo; comportarse ostentosamente de modo raro; guasearse, hacer el tonto; **stop** —**ing!** ¡déjate de bromas!

campaign [kæm'pein] **1** *n* campaña *f*; **election** — campaña *f* electoral.

2 *vi* (*Mil*) luchar; servir; hacer campaña; **to** — **against** hacer campaña en contra de; **to** — **for** hacer campaña a favor de.

campaigner [kæm'peinə*] *n* (*fig*) paladín *m*, partidario *m*, a *f* (*for* de), propagandista *mf* (*for* por); **old** — (*Mil*) veterano *m*.

campanile [ˌkæmpə'niːli] *n* campanario *m*.

campbed ['kæmp'bed] *n* cama *f* de campaña.

camp chair ['kæmp'tʃeə*] *n* silla *f* plegadiza.

camper ['kæmpə*] *n* acampador *m*, ora *f*, campista *mf*.

campfire ['kæmp'faiə*] *n* hoguera *f* de campamento; (*of scouts*) reunión *f* alrededor de la hoguera.

camp follower ['kæmp,fɔləuə*] *n* vivandero *m*, a *f*; (*pej*) prostituta *f*.

campground ['kæmpgraund] *n* (*US*) camping *m*.

camphor ['kæmfə*] *n* alcanfor *m*.

camphorated ['kæmfəreitid] *adj* alcanforado.

camping ['kæmpiŋ] *n* camping *m*; **to go** — hacer camping.

camping ground ['kæmpiŋgraund] *n*, **camping site** ['kæmpiŋsait] *n* (terreno *m* de) camping *m*.

campsite ['kæmpsait] *n* camping *m*; campamento *m*.

campstool ['kæmpstuːl] *n* taburete *m* plegable.

camp stove ['kæmp'stəuv] *n* hornillo *m* de campista.

campus ['kæmpəs] *n* (*Univ*) recinto *m*.

campy ['kæmpi] *adj* (*sl*) = **camp**[2] **1**.

camshaft ['kæmʃɑːft] *n* árbol *m* de levas.

can[1] [kæn] (*irr*: *pret* **could**; *defective*) *vi* (**a**) (*be able to*) poder; **if I** — si puedo; **we can't swim today** hoy no podemos ir a bañarnos.

(**b**) (*with verbs of perception, often not translated*) **I** — **hear it** lo oigo; **I couldn't see it anywhere** no lo veía en ninguna parte; **I can't understand why** no comprendo por qué.

(**c**) (*of acquired skills, know how to*) saber, *eg* — **you swim?** ¿sabes nadar?

(**d**) (*have permission to*) poder, *eg* — **I go now?** ¿puedo irme ahora?

can[2] [kæn] **1** *n* lata *f*, bote *m*; (*for petrol etc*) bidón *m*; (*US sl*) wáter *m*; **to carry the** — (*sl*) pagar el pato.

2 *vt* conservar en lata; enlatar, envasar; — **it!** (*sl*) ¡cállate!; *see also* **canned**.

Canada ['kænədə] *n* el Canadá.

Canadian [kə'neidiən] **1** *adj* canadiense. **2** *n* canadiense *mf*.

canal [kə'næl] *n* canal *m*; **alimentary** — tubo *m* digestivo.

canalization [ˌkænəlai'zeiʃən] *n* canalización *f*.

canalize ['kænəlaiz] *vt* canalizar.

canapé ['kænəpei] *n* canapé *m*.

canard [kæ'nɑːd] *n* filfa *f*, habilla *f*, noticia *f* falsa.

Canarian [kə'nɛəriən] **1** *adj* canario. **2** *n* canario *m*, a *f*.

canary [kə'nɛəri] *n* canario *m*.

Canary Isles [kə'nɛəriailz] *pl* Islas *fpl* Canarias.

canasta [kə'næstə] *n* canasta *f*.

cancan ['kænkæn] *n* cancán *m*.

cancel ['kænsəl] **1** *vt* cancelar; suprimir; *permission etc* retirar; *stamp* matar, inutilizar; **they** — **each other out** se anulan mutuamente.

2 *vi* (*Math*): **to** — **out** destruirse.

cancellation [ˌkænsə'leiʃən] *n* cancelación *f*; supresión *f*; el retirar; (*Post: mark*) matasellos *m*, (*act*) inutilización *f*.

cancer ['kænsə*] *n* cáncer *m*.

cancerous ['kænsərəs] *adj* canceroso; **to become** — cancerarse.

candelabra [ˌkændi'lɑːbrə] *n* candelabro *m*.

candid ['kændid] *adj* franco, sincero, abierto; **to be quite** — hablando con franqueza.

candidly ['kændidli] *adv* francamente, con franqueza.

candidness ['kændidnis] *n* franqueza *f*.

candidate ['kændideit] *n* (*applicant*) aspirante *mf* (*for* a), solicitante *mf* (*for* de); (*for election, examinee, Pol, etc*) candidato *m*, a *f* (*for* a); (*in competitive exams*) opositor *m*, ora *f* (*for* a).

candidature ['kændidətʃə*] *n* candidatura *f*.

candied ['kændid] *adj* azucarado.

candle ['kændl] *n* vela *f*; (*esp large*) candela *f*; (*Eccl*) cirio *m*; **to burn the** — **at both ends** consumir la vida, gastar sus fuerzas; **you can't hold a** — **to him** no llegas a la suela de su zapato.

candlelight ['kændllait] *n* luz *f* de una vela; **by** — a la luz de una vela.

Candlemas [ˌkændlmæs] *n* Candelaria *f* (2 *febrero*).

candle power ['kændl,pauə*] *n* bujía *f*.

candlestick ['kændlstik] *n* (*single*) candelero *m*; (*low*) palmatoria *f*; (*large, ornamental*) candelabro *m*; (*processional*) cirial *m*.

candlewick ['kændlwik] *n* pabilo *m*, mecha *f* (de vela).

candour, (*US*) **candor** ['kændə*] *n* franqueza *f*.

candy ['kændi] **1** *n* azúcar *m* cande; (*US*) bombón *m*, dulce *m*. **2** *vt* azucarar, garapiñar.

candy-floss ['kændiflɔs] *n* caramelo *m* americano.

candy store ['kændistɔː*] *n* (*US*) bombonería *f*, confitería *f*.

cane [kein] **1** *n* (*Bot*) caña *f*; (*sugar-*) caña *f* de azúcar; (*stick*) bastón *m*; (*for punishment*) palmeta *f*, vara *f*; (*in furnishings*) mimbre *f*.

2 *vt* castigar con palmeta.

canine ['kænain] **1** *adj* canino; — **tooth** diente *m* canino, colmillo *m*. **2** *n* (*dog*) perro *m*, can *m*; (*tooth*) canino *m*, colmillo *m*.

caning ['keiniŋ] *n* castigo *m* con palmeta; **to give someone a** — castigar a uno con la palmeta, (*fig*) cascar a uno.

canister ['kænistə*] *n* lata *f*, bote *m*.

canker ['kænkə*] **1** *n* (*Med*) llaga *f* gangrenosa; úlcera *f* en la boca; (*Bot*) cancro *m*; (*fig*) cáncer *m*. **2** *vt* ulcerar; (*fig*) corromper.

3 *vi* ulcerarse; (*fig*) corromperse.

cankerous ['kænkərəs] *adj* ulceroso.

cannabis ['kænəbis] *n* marijuana *f*.

canned [kænd] **1** *pret* and *ptp* of **can**[2]. **2** *adj* *food* en lata, de lata; *music* (*fam*) en discos, grabado; *person* (*sl*) borracho.

cannery ['kænəri] *n* fábrica *f* de conservas alimenticias.

cannibal ['kænibəl] **1** *adj* antropófago. **2** *n* caníbal *mf*, antropófago *m*.

cannibalism ['kænibəlizəm] *n* canibalismo *m*.

cannibalize ['kænibəlaiz] **1** *vt* (**a**) someter al canibalismo, practicar el canibalismo en.

(**b**) (*fig*) **to** — **an old car** desmontar un coche viejo para aprovechar sus piezas como repuestos.

2 *vi* practicar el canibalismo.

canning ['kæniŋ] *n* enlatado *m*; — **industry** industria *f* conservera.

cannon ['kænən] **1** *n* cañón *m*; (*collectively*) artillería *f*; (*Billiards*) carambola *f*.

2 *vi* (*Billiards*) hacer carambola; **to** — **into** chocar violentamente con; **to** — **off** rebotar contra.

cannonade [ˌkænə'neid] *n* cañoneo *m*.

cannonball ['kænənbɔːl] *n* bala *f* de cañón.

cannon fodder ['kænən,fɔdə*] *n* carne *f* de cañón.

cannon-shot ['kænənʃɔt] *n* cañonazo *m*, tiro *m* de cañón; (*ammunition*) bala *f* de cañón; **within** — al alcance de un cañón.

cannot ['kænɔt] *negative of* **can**[1].

canny ['kæni] *adj* (*Scot*) astuto.

canoe [kə'nuː] **1** *n* canoa *f*; (*sporting*) piragua *f*. **2** *vi* ir en canoa.

canoeing [kə'nuːiŋ] *n* piragüismo *m*.

canoeist [kə'nuːist] *n* piragüista *mf*.

canon ['kænən] *n* canon *m*; (*Typ*) gran canon *m*; (*person*) canónigo *m*; — **law** derecho *m* canónico.

canonical [kə'nɔnikəl] *adj* canónico.

canonization [ˌkænənai'zeiʃən] *n* canonización *f*.

canonize ['kænənaiz] *vt* canonizar.

canonry ['kænənri] *n* canonjía *f*.

canoodle [kə'nuːdl] *vi* (*sl*) besuquearse.

can opener ['kænəupnə*] *n* abrelatas *m*.

canopy ['kænəpi] *n* dosel *m*, toldo *m*; (*over bed*) cielo *m*; (*Archit*) baldaquín *m*; (*over tomb*) doselete *m*; **the** — **of heaven** la bóveda celeste.

cant[1] [kænt] **1** *n* (*slope*) inclinación *f*, sesgo *m*; (*of*

crystal *etc*) bisel *m*. **2** *vt* inclinar, sesgar. **3** *vi* inclinarse, ladearse; **to — over** volcar.
cant[2] [kænt] **1** *n* (*special language*) jerga *f*; (*hypocritical talk*) hipocresías *fpl*, camándulas *fpl*, gazmoñería *f*. **2** *vi* camandulear.
can't [kɑ:nt] = **cannot**.
Cantabrian [kæn'tæbrian] *adj* cantábrico.
cantaloup ['kæntəlu:p] *n* cantalupo *m*.
cantankerous [kæn'tæŋkərəs] *adj* arisco, malhumorado, irritable.
cantata [kæn'tɑ:tə] *n* cantata *f*.
canteen [kæn'ti:n] *n* (*bar*) cantina *f*; (*bottle*) cantimplora *f*; (*of cutlery*) juego *m*.
canter ['kæntə*] **1** *n* medio galope *m*; **to win in a —** (*fig*) ganar fácilmente. **2** *vi* ir a medio galope.
Canterbury ['kæntəberi] Cantórbery.
cantharides [kæn'θæridi:z] *npl* polvo *m* de cantárida.
canticle ['kæntikl] *n* cántico *m*; **the C—s** el Cantar de los Cantares.
cantilever ['kæntili:və*] *n* viga *f* voladiza; **— bridge** puente *m* voladizo.
canting ['kæntiŋ] *adj* hipócrita.
canto ['kæntəu] *n* canto *m*.
canton ['kæntɔn] *n* cantón *m*.
cantonal ['kæntənl] *adj* cantonal.
Cantonese [,kæntə'ni:z] **1** *adj* cantonés. **2** *n* cantonés *m*, esa *f*. **3** *n* (*dialect*) cantonés *m*.
cantonment [kən'tu:nmənt] *n* acantonamiento *m*.
canvas ['kænvəs] *n* lona *f*; (*Art*) lienzo *m*; (*Naut*) velamen *m*, velas *fpl*; **under —** en tiendas de campaña.
canvass ['kænvəs] **1** *n* (*inquiry*) sondeo *m*; (*for votes*) solicitación *f*; **to make a door-to-door —** ir solicitando votos de puerta en puerta.
2 *vt possibility*, *question* discutir, hacer que se discuta, someter a una discusión pública; *opinion* sondear; *votes* solicitar; *voter* solicitar el voto de.
3 *vi*: **to — for** solicitar votos por, hacer campaña a favor de.
canvasser ['kænvəsə*] *n* (*Pol*) solicitador *m*, ora *f* (de votos).
canvassing ['kænvəsiŋ] *n* solicitación *f* (de votos).
canyon ['kænjən] *n* cañón *m*.
cap [kæp] **1** *n* (a) (*hat*) gorra *f*; (*Univ*) bonete *m*; (*servant's etc*) cofia *f*; **cloth —** gorra *f* de paño; **peaked —** gorra *f* de visera; **— and gown** toga *f* y bonete; **to come — in hand to someone** venir a uno con el sombrero en la mano; **if the — fits wear it** el que se pica ajos come; **to put on one's thinking —** meditarlo bien; **to set one's — at someone** proponerse conquistar a uno como novio.
(b) (*lid*) tapa *f*, tapón *m*; (*of gun, bottle*) cápsula *f*; (*of pen*) capuchón *m*; (*on chimney*) caballete *m*; (*Mech*) casquete *m*; **polar —** casquete *m* polar.
2 *vt hill etc* coronar; *work* terminar, poner remate a; (*surpass*) exceder, superar; **see if you can — that story** a ver si cuentas un chiste mejor que ése; **I can — that** yo sé algo mejor sobre el mismo asunto; **to — it all** para colmo de desgracias.
capability [,keipə'biləti] *n* capacidad *f*, aptitud *f*.
capable ['keipəbl] *adj* capaz, competente; **to be — of** ser capaz de; **it's — of some improvement** es susceptible de ser algo mejorado.
capably ['keipəbli] *adv* competentemente.
capacious [kə'peiʃəs] *adj room* grande, extenso, espacioso; *container* grande, capaz; *dress* ancho, holgado.
capacity [kə'pæsiti] **1** *n* capacidad *f*; (*Aut*) cilindrada *f*; **carrying —** capacidad *f* de cargo; **effective —, useful —** capacidad *f* útil; **seating —** cabida *f*, número *m* de asientos; **filled to —** totalmente lleno; **in my —** as en mi calidad de.
2 *attr*: **there was a — crowd** el campo (*or* teatro *etc*) estuvo totalmente lleno.
caparison [kə'pærisn] **1** *n* caparazón *m*, gualdrapa *f*; (*harness etc*) equipo *m*.
2 *vt* engualdrapar; **gaily —ed** brillantemente enjaezado, (*fig*) brillantemente vestido.
cape[1] [keip] *n* (*Geog*) cabo *m*, promontorio *m*.
cape[2] [keip] *n* capa *f*; (*short*) capotillo *m*, esclavina *f*; (*of fur*) cuello *m*; (*oilskin*) chubasquero *m*.
Cape Horn ['keip'hɔ:n] Cabo *m* de Hornos.
Cape of Good Hope ['keipəvgud'həup] Cabo *m* de Buena Esperanza.
caper[1] ['keipə*] *n* (*Bot*) alcaparra *f*.
caper[2] ['keipə*] **1** *n* (a) (*of horse*) cabriola *f*; **to cut —s** hacer cabriolas.
(b) (*fig*) (*prank*) travesura *f*; (*fam*) lío *m*, embrollo *m*; **that was quite a —** eso sí que fue un lío; **how did your Spanish — go?** ¿qué tal el viajecito por España?

2 *vi* (*horse*) hacer cabriolas; (*other animal*) brincar, corcovear; (*child*) juguetear, correr y brincar; (*fam*) ir, correr; **to — about** brincar, juguetear; **he went —ing off to Paris** se marchó a París como si tal cosa.
capercaillie [,kæpə'keili] *n* urogallo *m*.
capeskin ['keipskin] *n* (*US*) (especie *f* de) cabritilla *f*.
Cape Town ['keiptaun] Ciudad *f* del Cabo.
Cape Verde Islands ['keip'və:d'ailəndz] *pl* Islas *fpl* de Cabo Verde.
capillarity [,kæpi'læriti] *n* capilaridad *f*.
capillary [kə'piləri] **1** *adj* capilar. **2** *n* vaso *m* capilar.
capital ['kæpitl] **1** *adj* capital; *importance* primordial; (*fam*) magnífico, estupendo; **—!** ¡magnífico!; **— city** capital *f*; **— gains** ganancias *fpl* (por venta de bienes) de capital; **— goods** bienes *mpl* de capital; **— letter** mayúscula *f*; **— punishment** pena *f* de muerte; **— ship** acorazado *m*; **— sum** capital *m*.
2 *n* **(a)** (*money*) capital *m*; **working —** capital *m* de explotación; **to make — out of** (*fig*) aprovechar, sacar partido de.
(b) (*city*) capital *f*.
(c) (*Archit*) capitel *m*.
(d) (*letter*) mayúscula *f*; **large —s** (*Typ*) versales *fpl*; **small —s** (*Typ*) versalitas *fpl*.
capitalism ['kæpitəlizəm] *n* capitalismo *m*.
capitalist ['kæpitəlist] **1** *adj* capitalista. **2** *n* capitalista *mf*.
capitalistic [,kæpitə'listik] *adj* capitalista.
capitalization [kæ,pitəlai'zeiʃən] *n* capitalización *f*.
capitalize [kə'pitəlaiz] **1** *vt* capitalizar; (*Typ*) escribir (*or* imprimir) con mayúscula. **2** *vi*: **to — on** aprovechar, sacar partido de.
capitation [,kæpi'teiʃən] *n* capitación *f*.
Capitol ['kæpitl] *n* Capitolio *m*.
capitulate [kə'pitjuleit] *vi* capitular (*to* ante), rendirse, entregarse (*to* a); (*fig*) ceder, conformarse.
capitulation [kə,pitju'leiʃən] *n* capitulación *f*, rendición *f*.
capon ['keipən] *n* capón *m*.
caprice [kə'pri:s] *n* capricho *m*.
capricious [kə'priʃəs] *adj* caprichoso, caprichudo.
capriciously [kə'priʃəsli] *adv* caprichosamente.
Capricorn ['kæprikɔ:n] Capricornio *m*.
capsicum ['kæpsikəm] *n* pimiento *m*.
capsize [kæp'saiz] **1** *vt* volcar; (*Naut*) hacer zozobrar, tumbar. **2** *vi* volcarse, dar una vuelta de campana; (*Naut*) zozobrar.
capstan ['kæpstən] *n* cabrestante *m*.
capsule ['kæpsju:l] *n* (*all senses*) cápsula *f*.
captain ['kæptin] **1** *n* capitán *m*; **— of industry** gran industrial *m*, magnate *m*.
2 *vt* capitanear, ser el capitán de; **a team —ed by Grace** un equipo capitaneado por Grace.
captaincy ['kæptənsi] *n* capitanía *f*.
caption ['kæpʃən] **1** *n* (*heading*) encabezamiento *m*, título *m*; (*to cartoon etc*) pie *m*; (*in film*) subtítulo *m*. **2** *vt* titular; poner un pie a.
captious ['kæpʃəs] *adj* criticón, reparón.
captivate ['kæptiveit] *vt* cautivar, encantar.
captivating ['kæptiveitiŋ] *adj* encantador, delicioso.
captive ['kæptiv] **1** *adj* cautivo. **2** *n* cautivo *m*, a *f*.
captivity [kæp'tiviti] *n* cautiverio *m*.
captor ['kæptə*] *n* apresador *m*, ora *f*.
capture ['kæptʃə*] **1** *n* **(a)** (*act*) apresamiento *m*, captura *f*; (*of city etc*) toma *f*, conquista *f*.
(b) (*thing captured*) presa *f*.
2 *vt person* prender; apresar; *specimen etc* capturar; *animal* coger; *city etc* tomar, conquistar; (*fig*) captar; *attention* llamar, atraer; *interest* ocupar; (*Art etc*) captar, reproducir, representar fielmente.
capuchin ['kæpjuʃin] *n* **(a)** (*cowl*) capucho *m*. **(b)** (*Zool*) mono *m* capuchino. **(c) C—** (*Eccl*) capuchino *m*.
car [kɑ:*] *n* (*Aut*) coche *m*, automóvil *m*; (*tramcar*) tranvía *m*; (*Rail*) vagón *m*, coche *m*; (*of cable railway*) coche *m*; (*of lift*) caja *f*; (*of balloon etc*) barquilla *f*; **racing —** coche *m* de carreras; **saloon —, touring —** turismo *m*.
carafe [kə'ræf] *n* garrafa *f*.
caramel ['kærəməl] *n* caramelo *m*.
carapace ['kærəpeis] *n* carapacho *m*.
carat ['kærət] *n* quilate *m*.
caravan ['kærəvæn] *n* (*gipsies'*) carricoche *m*, carromato *m*; (*trailer, for holidays*) caravana *f*, remolque *m*, rulota *f*, roulotte *f*; (*of camels*) caravana *f*.
caravel ['kærə'vel] *n* carabela *f*.
caraway ['kærəwei] *n* alcaravea *f*.
carbide ['kɑ:baid] *n* carburo *m*.
carbine ['kɑ:bain] *n* carabina *f*.
carbohydrate ['kɑ:bəu'haidreit] *n* hidrato *m* de carbono; (*starch in food*) fécula *f*.
carbolic [kɑ:'bɔlik] *adj*: **— acid** ácido *m* carbólico.

carbon ['kɑ:bən] carbono m; (Elec, — paper) carbón m; — **dioxide** bióxido m de carbono; — **monoxide** monóxido m de carbono.
carbonaceous [,kɑ:bə'neiʃəs] adj carbonoso.
carbonate ['kɑ:bənit] n carbonato m.
carbon copy ['kɑ:bən'kɔpi] n copia f al carbón.
carbonic [kɑ:'bɔnik] adj: — **acid** ácido m carbónico.
carboniferous [,kɑ:bə'nifərəs] adj carbonífero.
carbonization [,kɑ:bənai'zeiʃən] n carbonización f.
carbonize ['kɑ:bənaiz] 1 vt carbonizar. 2 vi carbonizarse.
carbon paper ['kɑ:bən,peipə*] n papel m carbón.
carborundum [,kɑ:bə'rʌndəm] n carborundo m.
carboy ['kɑ:bɔi] n bombona f, garrafón m.
carbuncle ['kɑ:bʌŋkl] n (ruby) carbunclo m; (Med) carbunco m, grano m.
carburettor [,kɑ:bju'retə*] n carburador m.
carcass ['kɑ:kəs] n cadáver m de animal, res f muerta; (frame) armazón f; (fam) cuerpo m.
carcinogen [kɑ:'sinədʒen] n agente m carcinogénico.
carcinogenic [,kɑ:sinə'dʒenik] adj carcinogénico.
carcinoma ['kɑ:si'nəumə] n, pl **carcinomata** [,kɑ:si'nəumətə] carcinoma m.
card¹ [kɑ:d] (Tech) 1 n carda f. 2 vt cardar.
card² [kɑ:d] n (a) (playing-) carta f, naipe m; (Post) tarjeta f, postal f; (visiting-) tarjeta f; (index-) ficha f; (member's, press-) carnet m, carné m (Acad); (piece of cardboard) cartulina f; **to play** —s jugar a las cartas; **to lose money at** —s perder el dinero jugando a las cartas.
  (b) (idioms) **isn't he a** —? es célebre ¿no?, ¡qué tipo más salado!; **like a house of** —s como un castillo de naipes; **it is quite on the** —s that . . . es perfectamente posible que . . . + subj; **to have a** — **up one's sleeve** quedar a uno todavía un recurso; **to hold all the** —s tener los triunfos en la mano; **to lay one's** —s **on the table** poner las cartas boca arriba; **if you play your** —s **properly** si obras con el debido cuidado; **to speak by the** — hablar con conocimiento de causa.
cardamom ['kɑ:dəməm] n cardamomo m.
cardboard ['kɑ:dbɔ:d] n cartón m, cartulina f; — **box** caja f de cartón.
card catalogue ['kɑ:d,kætəlɔg] n catálogo m de fichas, fichero m.
card game ['kɑ:dgeim] n juego m de naipes.
cardiac ['kɑ:diæk] adj cardíaco.
cardigan ['kɑ:digən] n rebeca f.
cardinal ['kɑ:dinl] 1 adj cardinal. 2 n cardenal m.
card index ['kɑ:d,indeks] n fichero m.
cardiological [,kɑ:diə'lɔdʒikəl] adj cardiológico.
cardiologist [,kɑ:di'ɔlidʒist] n cardiólogo m.
cardiology [,kɑ:di'ɔlədʒi] n cardiología f.
card sharper ['kɑ:d,ʃɑ:pə*] n fullero m.
card table ['kɑ:d,teibl] n mesa f de baraja, tapete m verde.
card trick ['kɑ:d,trik] n juego m de naipes, truco m de naipes.
care [kɛə*] 1 n (a) (anxiety) cuidado m; inquietud f, solicitud f; **he has many** —s son muchas las cosas que le preocupan; **he hasn't a** — **in the world** le importa todo un rábano; **the** —s **of State** las responsabilidades de un cargo oficial, las preocupaciones y fatigas del gobierno.
  (b) (carefulness) cuidado m, esmero m, atención f; **"with** — **!"** "¡atención!", "¡cuidado!"; **have a** —, **sir !** ¡mire lo que está diciendo!; **to take** — tener cuidado; **take** — **!** ¡ten cuidado!, ¡ojo!; **to take** — **of** cuidar de, valuable object guardar, custodiar, thing to be done encargarse de; **I'll take** — **of him** (fam) yo me encargo de él; **that can take** — **of itself** eso se resolverá por sí mismo; **to take good** — **of oneself** cuidarse mucho; **to take** — **to** + infin cuidar de que + subj, asegurar que + subj; **he doesn't take enough** — **to** + infin no pone bastante cuidado en + infin; **to take** — **not to** + infin guardarse de + infin; **take** — **not to drop it !** ¡ten cuidado, no lo dejes caer!
  (c) (charge) cargo m, custodia f; (Med etc) asistencia f; — **of** (on letter) en casa de; **to be in the** — **of** estar bajo la custodia de; **he is in the** — **of Dr X** le asiste el doctor X, le atiende el doctor X.
  2 vi (a) (absolute) **what do I** —? ¿qué se me da a mí?, ¡maldito lo que me importa!; **as if I** —**d !** ¡cómo si eso tuviera que ver conmigo!; **I couldn't** — **less !** eso me trae sin cuidado; **for all I** — **you can take it** me resulta indiferente que lo tomes; **I don't** — me es igual, no me importa; **I don't** — **tuppence !** (or a fig, hoot, jot, rap etc) ¡me importa un comino!; **I don't** — **either way** me resulta indiferente; **I don't** — **what people say** me trae sin cuidado lo que diga la gente.

  (b) **to** — **about** preocuparse de (or por), tener interés en; **to** — **deeply about someone's fate** preocuparse hondamente por la suerte de uno; **that's all he** —s **about** es lo único que le interesa; **to** — **for** cuidar; person querer; **I don't** — **for the idea** no me hace gracia la idea; **I don't** — **for coffee** no me gusta el café; **would you** — **for a walk?** ¿te apetece dar un paseo?; **would you** — **for a drink?** ¿quieres tomar algo?; **the kids are being** —d **for by their aunt** los niños los está cuidando su tía; **well** —d **for** bien cuidado; **to** — **to** + infin tener ganas de + infin; **if you** — **to** si Vd quiere; **would you** — **to tell me?** ¿quiere Vd decírmelo?; **would you** — **to go for a walk?** ¿te apetece dar un paseo?, ¿te gustaría dar un paseo?; **would you** — **to take off your hat?** ¿tendría inconveniente en quitarse el sombrero?
careen [kə'ri:n] vt carenar.
career [kə'riə*] 1 n carrera f; — **diplomat** (US) diplomático m de carrera. 2 vi correr a toda velocidad.
careerist [kə'riərist] n ambicioso m, a f.
carefree ['kɛəfri:] adj despreocupado, libre de preocupaciones, alegre, inconsciente.
careful ['kɛəful] adj cuidadoso; piece of work esmerado; (in acting) cauteloso, prudente; (with money) económico, ahorrativo, (pej) tacaño; —! ¡cuidado!, ¡ojo!; **to be** — tener cuidado; **be** —! ¡ten cuidado!; **one can't be too** — nunca se peca por demasiado cuidadoso; **we must be very** — **here** en esto conviene andar con pies de plomo; **be** — **what you say to him** ten cuidado con lo que le dices; **to be** — **of** tener cuidado con; **to be** — **to** + infin poner diligencia en + infin, asegurar cuidadosamente que + subj; **he was** — **to say that** . . . dijo de modo particular que . . .
carefully ['kɛəfəli] adv con cuidado, cuidadosamente; **we must go** — **here** en esto conviene andar con pies de plomo; **I have to spend** — tengo que pensar mucho en lo que gasto; **he replied** — contestó con cautela.
carefulness ['kɛəfulnis] n cuidado m; esmero m; prudencia f, cautela f; economía f, tacañería f.
careless ['kɛəlis] adj descuidado; (inattentive) poco atento; (thoughtless) irreflexivo, imprudente; stroke hecho a la ligera; appearance descuidado, desaliñado; (— **of others**) indiferente, insensible (of a); **that was very** — **of you** en eso ha sido Vd muy imprudente.
carelessly ['kɛəlisli] adv descuidadamente; a la ligera.
carelessness ['kɛəlisnis] n descuido m; falta f de atención; desaliño m; indiferencia f (of a); **through sheer** — por simple descuido, por simple falta de atención.
caress [kə'res] 1 n caricia f. 2 vt acariciar.
caressing [kə'resiŋ] adj acariciador, acariciante, seductor.
caret ['kærət] n signo m de intercalación (∧).
caretaker ['kɛə,teikə*] n vigilante m; (in museum etc) guardián m; (of flats) portero m, conserje m, casero m.
careworn ['kɛəwɔ:n] adj agobiado de inquietudes.
carfare ['kɑ:fɛə*] n pasaje m, precio m (del billete).
car-ferry ['kɑ:,feri] n transbordador m para coches.
cargo ['kɑ:gəu] n cargamento m, carga f.
cargo boat ['kɑ:gəubəut] n barco m de carga.
carhop ['kɑ:hɔp] n (US) camarero m de motel, camarera f de motel.
Caribbean [,kæri'bi:ən] adj caribe.
Caribbean Sea [,kæri'bi:ən'si:] Mar m Caribe.
caribou ['kæribu:] n caribú m.
caricature ['kærikətjuə*] 1 n caricatura f; (in newspaper) dibujo m cómico. 2 vt caricaturizar.
caricaturist [,kærikə'tjuərist] n caricaturista mf, dibujante mf.
caries ['kɛəri:z] n caries f.
carillon [kə'riljən] n carillón m.
carious ['kɛəriəs] adj cariado.
Carlism ['kɑ:lizəm] n carlismo m.
Carlist ['kɑ:list] 1 adj carlista. 2 n carl'sta mf.
Carmelite ['kɑ:məlait] 1 adj carmelita. 2 n carmelita mf.
carminative ['kɑ:minətiv] 1 adj carminativo. 2 n carminativo m.
carmine ['kɑ:main] 1 adj carmíneo. 2 n carmín m.
carnage ['kɑ:nidʒ] n carnicería f, mortandad f.
carnal ['kɑ:nl] adj carnal.
carnation [kɑ:'neiʃən] n clavel m.
carnelian [kɑ:'ni:liən] n cornalina f, cornerina f.
carnival ['kɑ:nivəl] n carnaval m; fiesta f, feria f; — **queen** reina f de la fiesta, dama f regidora.
carnivore ['kɑ:nivɔ:*] n carnívoro m.
carnivorous [kɑ:'nivərəs] adj carnívoro.

carol ['kærəl] **1** n vil ancico m. **2** vi cantar alegremente.
Carolingian [kærə'linʒiən] adj carolingio.
carotid [kə'rɔtid] n carótida f.
carousal [kə'rauzəl] n jarana f, parranda f.
carouse [kə'rauz] vi jaranear, estar de parranda.
carp[1] [kɑːp] n carpa f.
carp[2] [kɑːp] vi criticar (sin motivo); **to — at** quejarse (sin motivo) de, murmurar de.
car park ['kɑːpɑːk] n aparcamiento m, parque m.
Carpathians [kɑː'peiθiənz] pl Montes mpl Cárpatos.
carpenter ['kɑːpintə*] n carpintero m.
carpentry ['kɑːpintri] n carpintería f.
carpet ['kɑːpit] **1** n alfombra f; **to be on the —** (fam) tener que aguantar un rapapolvo; **to roll out the red — for someone** volcarse para festejar la llegada de uno.
    2 vt alfombrar; (fig) alfombrar, cubrir, revestir (with de); **to — someone** (fam) echar un rapapolvo a uno.
carpetbagger ['kɑːpit,bægə*] n (US) aventurero m político, explotador m político (venido de fuera).
carpet slippers ['kɑːpit,slipəz] npl zapatillas fpl.
carpet sweeper ['kɑːpit,swiːpə*] n aspirador m.
carping ['kɑːpiŋ] adj criticón, reparón.
carport ['kɑːpɔːt] n garaje m abierto, cobertizo m para coche.
carriage ['kæridʒ] n **(a)** (Rail) vagón m, coche m; (horse-drawn) carruaje m, coche m; (of gun) cureña f; (of typewriter etc) carro m.
    (b) (bearing) andares mpl, modo m de andar, porte m.
    (c) (act of carrying) transporte m; (Comm) porte m; **— free** franco de porte; **— paid** porte pagado.
carriage drive ['kæridʒdraiv] n calzada f.
carriage trade ['kæridʒ,treid] n (US) clientela f de gente acaudalada.
carriageway ['kæridʒwei] n carretera f; **dual —** (Aut) carretera f de dos calles, carretera f de doble calzada.
carrier ['kæriə*] n (person) trajinante m, carrero m (ordinario); (company) empresa f de transportes; (Med) portador m, ora f (de gérmenes); (on car, cycle) portaequipajes m; (Naut) portaaviones m.
carrier-bag ['kæriə'bæg] n pequeño saco m de papel (para compras).
carrion ['kæriən] n carroña f; inmundicia f.
carrion crow ['kæriən'krəu] n corneja f negra.
carrot ['kærət] n zanahoria f.
carroty ['kærəti] adj pelirrojo.
carrousel [kæru:'sel] n carusel m, tiovivo m.
carry ['kæri] **1** n alcance m.
    2 vt llevar; traer; transportar, acarrear; burden, weight sostener; (on one's person) llevar consigo, tener consigo; (Math) llevar; stock tener en existencia; meaning tener; interpretation encerrar, llevar implícito; (in the mind) retener; (extend) prolongar; (Mil) conquistar, tomar; (Parl) seat ganar, ganar las elecciones en; proposition hacer aceptar; motion aprobar; **to — the committee with one** persuadir al comité a que apruebe lo que se le propone; **to — one's audience with one** meterse al auditorio en el bolsillo; **to — about** llevar consigo, llevar de acá para allá; **to — along** llevar; (water etc) arrastrar; **to — away** llevarse; (kidnap) secuestrar; (fig) arrebatar, inspirar, entusiasmar; **to get carried away** exaltarse, entusiasmarse (demasiado), extasiarse, hacerse inconsciente de la situación real; **to — all before one** vencer todos los obstáculos, arrollarlo todo; **to — down** bajar; **to — something too far** exagerar algo, llevar algo al exceso; **to — forward** (Comm) pasar a cuenta nueva; **carried forward** suma y sigue; **to — off** llevarse; prize alzarse con, ganar; election ganar; (kill) matar; **he carried it off splendidly** salió muy airoso de la prueba, su actuación fue brillante; **to — on** work continuar, proseguir; business poseer, tener, ser dueño de; **to — out** order, threat, promise cumplir; plan llevar a cabo, poner por obra; intention realizar; repairs hacer; test verificar; **to — over** guardar para más tarde; (Comm) pasar a cuenta nueva; **to — through** llevar a cabo; person sostener hasta el fin; **to — up** subir.
    3 vi (reach) alcanzar, llegar; (sound) oírse; **to — on** (a) (continue) continuar, seguir adelante; **if you — on like that** como sigas en ese plan; **we — on somehow** vamos tirando; **— on!** ¡adelante!, ¡siga!, (in talking) ¡prosigue!
    (b) (fam: complain) quejarse, protestar; murmurar (about de).
    (c) (fam: insist) insistir, machacar (about en); **you do — on!** ¡dale que dale!; **don't — on so!** ¡no machaques!

    (d) (fam: amorously) **to be —ing on with someone** tener un plan con uno.
    4 vr: **to — oneself** andar; **to — oneself well** andar con garbo, tener buena presencia.
carryall ['kæriɔːl] n (US) cesto m grande; **= holdall.**
carrycot ['kærikɔt] n cuna f portátil, capazo m.
carrying-on ['kæriiŋ'ɔn] n **(a)** continuación f; prosecución f.
    (b) (fam) plan m, relaciones fpl amorosas (ilícitas); **I don't approve of their —** no apruebo sus relaciones.
carry-on [kæri'ɔn] n (fam) aspaviento m, conmoción f, alharaca f; lío m; riña f, pelea f; **there was a great — about the tickets** se armó un tremendo lío a causa de los billetes; **did you ever see such a —?** ¿se ha visto un embrollo igual?
carry-over ['kæri'əuvə*] n (surplus) sobrante m; (Comm) suma f anterior, suma f que pasa de una página (de cuenta) a la siguiente.
cart [kɑːt] **1** n carro m, carreta f; (heavy) carretón m; (hand-) carretilla f, carro m de mano; **to be in the —** (fam) estar en un atolladero; **to put the — before the horse** trastrocar las cosas, tomar el rábano por las hojas.
    2 vt llevar, acarrear, carretear; (fam) llevar (con gran dificultad).
cartage ['kɑːtidʒ] n acarreo m, porte m.
carte blanche ['kɑːt'blɑ̃ːnʃ] n carta f blanca; **to give someone —** dar carta blanca a uno.
cartel [kɑː'tel] n cartel m.
carter ['kɑːtə*] n carretero m.
Cartesian [kɑː'tiːziən] **1** adj cartesiano. **2** n cartesiano m.
Carthage ['kɑːθidʒ] Cartago f.
Carthaginian [kɑːθə'dʒiniən] **1** adj cartaginés. **2** n cartaginés m, esa f.
cart-horse ['kɑːthɔːs] n caballo m de tiro.
Carthusian [kɑː'θjuːziən] **1** adj cartujano. **2** n cartujo m, cartujano m.
cartilage ['kɑːtilidʒ] n cartílago m.
cartilaginous [kɑːti'lædʒinəs] adj cartilaginoso.
cartload ['kɑːtləud] n carretada f (also fig); **by the —** a carretadas, a montones.
cartographer [kɑː'tɔgrəfə*] n cartógrafo m.
cartography [kɑː'tɔgrəfi] n cartografía f.
carton ['kɑːtən] n envase m, caja f de cartón.
cartoon [kɑː'tuːn] n (newspaper) dibujo m cómico, caricatura f; (Art) cartón m; (film) dibujos mpl animados, película f de dibujos.
cartoonist [kɑː'tuːnist] n dibujante mf, caricaturista mf.
cartridge ['kɑːtridʒ] n cartucho m; **blank —** cartucho m sin bala.
cartridge belt ['kɑːtridʒbelt] n cartuchera f, canana f.
cartridge case ['kɑːtridʒkeis] n cartucho m.
cartridge paper ['kɑːtridʒ,peipə*] n papel m guarro, papel m camso.
cart-track ['kɑːttræk] n (rut) carril m, rodada f; (road) camino m (para carros).
cartulary ['kɑːtjuləri] n cartulario m.
cartwheel ['kɑːtwiːl] n rueda f de carro; (fig) salto m mortal de lado, rueda f.
cartwright ['kɑːtrait] n carretero m.
carve [kɑːv] vt meat trinchar; stone esculpir, tallar, labrar; name on tree etc grabar; **to — one's way through** abrirse a la fuerza un camino por; **to — up** country dividir, repartir entre los vencedores; person coser a puñaladas.
carver ['kɑːvə*] n (Cook) trinchador m; (Art) escultor m, ora f, tallista mf; **—s** cubierto m de trinchar.
carving ['kɑːviŋ] n (Cook) arte m de trinchar; (Art) escultura f, obra f de talla.
carving knife ['kɑːviŋnaif] n, pl **—knives** [naivz] trinchante m.
car wash ['kɑːwɔʃ] n lavado m de coches.
caryatid [kæri'ætid] n cariátide f.
cascade [kæs'keid] **1** n cascada f, salto m de agua; (fig) chorro m; torrente m. **2** vi caer.
cascara [kæs'kɑːrə] n cáscara f sagrada.
case[1] [keis] **1** n (container) caja f; (packing-) cajón m; (suitcase) maleta f; (for jewels, spectacles etc) estuche m; (for scissors etc) vaina f; (of watch) caja f; (of window) marco m, bastidor m; (of cartridge) cartucho m, cápsula f; (showcase) vitrina f; (Typ) caja f; **lower —** caja f baja; **upper —** caja f alta.
    2 vt encajonar; enfundar; **—d in concrete** revestido de hormigón.
case[2] [keis] n **(a)** caso m (also Gram, Med); asunto m; **a fever —** un caso de fiebre; **a hospital —** un caso para el hospital, un enfermo que tendrá que

ser trasladado al hospital; **a — in point** un ejemplo que hace al caso; **it's a sad** — es un caso triste; **it's a hopeless** — es un caso desahuciado; **it's a — for the police** éste es asunto para la policía; **it's a clear — of murder** es un claro caso de homicidio; **he's working on the train-robbery** — está haciendo investigaciones sobre el robo del tren; **he's a —** es una persona rarísima.

(b) **there seems to be a — for reform** parece que hay razones para reformarlo; **that alters the —** eso cambia la cosa; **I understand that is not the —** tengo entendido que no es así; **if that is the —**, such being the — si las cosas son así; **as the — may be** según el caso.

(c) (*with prep*) **in — he comes** por si viene, (en) caso de que venga; **in — of** en caso de; **in your —** en el caso de Vd; **as in the — of** como en el caso de; **in most —s** en la mayoría de los casos; **in any —** en todo caso, de todas formas; **just in —** por si acaso, por si las moscas; **in such a —** en tal caso; **in that —** en ese caso.

(d) (*Law*) causa *f*, pleito *m*, proceso *m*; **the — for the defence** la defensa, el conjunto de razones alegadas por el acusado; **the — for the prosecution** la acusación, el conjunto de acusaciones alegadas por el fiscal; **the Dreyfus —** el proceso de Dreyfus, (*more loosely*) el asunto Dreyfus; **there is no —** to answer no hay acusación que merezca la pena de rechazarse; **to have a good** (*or* strong) **—** tener argumentos fuertes (*for* para); **to make out a good —** presentar argumentos convincentes (*for* para); **to put** (*or* state) **one's —** presentar sus argumentos; **to rest one's —** terminar la presentación de argumentos.

casebook ['keisbuk] *n* diario *m*, registro *m* (*de un médico, detective etc*).

case-hardened ['keis,hɑːdnd] *adj* cementado; (*fig*) insensible, poco compasivo.

case history ['keis'histəri] *n* historia *f*, historial *m*, antecedentes *mpl*; **what is the patient's —?** ¿cuál es la historia médica del enfermo?; **I'll give you the full —** le contaré la historia con todos los detalles.

casement ['keismənt] *n* ventana *f* a bisagra; (*frame*) marco *m* de ventana.

casework ['keiswəːk] *n* asistencia *f* social individualizada, casework *m*.

caseworker ['keis,wəːkə*] *n* asistente *m* social, caseworker *mf*.

cash [kæʃ] **1** *n* dinero *m* contante; (*fam*) dinero *m*; (*cashdesk*) caja *f*; **hard —** dinero *m* contante y sonante; **petty —** (dinero *m* para) gastos *mpl* menores; **— down, for —** al contado; **— payment**, **— terms** pago *m* al contado; **— price** precio *m* al contado; **— prize** premio *m* en metálico; **— in hand** efectivo *m* en caja; **— on delivery** pagar contra recepción; **in —** en metálico; **to be out of —** estar sin blanca; **to pay — for** pagar al contado.

2 *vt* *cheque* cobrar, hacer efectivo.

3 *vi*: **to — in on** sacar partido de, aprovechar.

cash-and-carry ['kæʃən'kæri] *attr*: **— system** sistema *m* de pago al contado con el transporte pagado por el comprador.

cashbook ['kæʃbuk] *n* libro *m* de caja.

cashbox ['kæʃbɔks] *n* caja *f*.

cash crop ['kæʃkrɔp] *n* cultivo *m* que se vende inmediatamente después de la recolección (*sin almacenar*); producción *f* agrícola que tiene una salida fácil.

cashdesk ['kæʃdesk] *n* caja *f*.

cashew [kæ'ʃuː] *n* (*also* **— nut**) anacardo *m*.

cashier [kæ'ʃiə*] **1** *n* cajero *m*, a *f*. **2** *vt* separar del servicio.

cashmere [kæʃ'miə*] *n* casimir *m*, cachemira *f*.

cash register ['kæʃ,redʒistə*] *n* caja *f* registradora.

casing ['keisiŋ] *n* caja *f*, cubierta *f*, envoltura *f*, revestimiento *m*.

casino [kə'siːnəu] *n* casino *m*.

cask [kɑːsk] *n* tonel *m*, barril *m*.

casket ['kɑːskit] *n* cajita *f*, cofrecito *m*, estuche *m*, arquilla *f*; (*US*) ataúd *m*.

Caspian Sea ['kæspiən,siː] Mar *m* Caspio.

Cassandra [kə'sændrə] *f* Casandra.

cassava [kə'sɑːvə] *n* mandioca *f*.

casserole ['kæsərəul] *n* cacerola *f*.

Cassius ['kæsiəs] *m* Casio.

cassock ['kæsək] *n* sotana *f*.

cassowary ['kæsəwɛəri] *n* casuario *m*.

cast [kɑːst] **1** *n* (*throw*) echada *f*; (*shape*) forma , molde *m*; (*plaster-*) vaciado *m*; (*Metal*) pieza *f* fundida; (*Theat*) reparto *m*, personal *m*; (*in eye*) defecto *m*; **— of features** facciones *fpl*, fisonomía *f*; **— of mind** temperamento *m*; inclinación *f*.

2 (*irr*: *pret and ptp* **cast**) *vt* (*throw*) echar, lanzar, arrojar; *anchor, blame, glance, lots, net etc* echar; *eyes* volver (*on a, hacia*); *skin* mudar; (*lose*) perder; *vote* dar; (*in a mould*) vaciar; (*Metal*) fundir; *horoscope* hacer; (*Theat*) *parts in a play* repartir; *part* asignar; **to — an actor in** (*or* for) **the part of** dar a un actor el papel de; **he was — as the king** le dieron el papel del rey; **to — aside** desechar; **to — away** desechar, tirar; abandonar; **to be — away** (*Naut*) naufragar; **to be — away on a desert island** naufragar y arribar a una isla desierta; **to — down** derribar; (*fig*) desanimar; *eyes* bajar; **to be — down** estar deprimido; **to — forth** despedir; **to — loose** soltar; **to — off** abandonar; *wife* repudiar; *burden* deshacerse de, quitar de encima; (*Knitting*) terminar (la última hilera de puntadas de); **to — on** (*Knitting*) montar; **to — out** arrojar, echar fuera de sí; **to — up** echar; vomitar; *account* sumar.

3 *vi* (*Fishing*) lanzar, arrojar; **to — about for** buscar, andar buscando; **to — off** soltar las amarras, desamarrar.

castanets [,kæstə'nets] *n pl* castañuelas *fpl*.

castaway ['kɑːstəwei] *n* náufrago *m*, a *f*.

caste [kɑːst] *n* casta *f*; **to lose —** desprestigiarse.

castellated ['kæstəleitid] *adj* almenado.

caster ['kɑːstə*] *n see* **castor**.

castigate ['kæstigeit] *vt* castigar.

castigation [,kæsti'geiʃən] *n* castigo *m*.

Castile [kæs'tiːl] Castilla *f*.

Castilian [kæs'tiliən] **1** *adj* castellano. **2** *n* castellano *m*, a *f*. **3** *n* (*language*) castellano *m*.

casting ['kɑːstiŋ] **1** *adj* *vote* de calidad, decisivo. **2** *n* pieza *f* fundida, pieza *f* de fundición.

castiron ['kɑːst'aiən] **1** *adj* hecho de hierro fundido; (*fig*) fuerte, duro; *will* inflexible; *case* sólido, convincente; *excuse* inatacable. **2** *n* hierro *m* colado, hierro *m* fundido.

castle ['kɑːsl] **1** *n* castillo *m*; (*Chess*) torre *f*, roque *m*; **to build —s in the air** construir castillos en el aire; **an Englishman's home is his —** la casa de un inglés es su castillo.

2 *vi* (*Chess*) enrocar.

castling ['kɑːsliŋ] *n* (*Chess*) enroque *m*.

cast-off ['kɑːstɔf] **1** *adj* *clothing etc* de desecho.

2 *n* persona *f* (*or* cosa) abandonada, persona *f* (*or* cosa) desechada, plato *m* de segunda mesa; **—s** ropa *f* de desecho.

castor[1] ['kɑːstə*] *n* (*at table*) azucarero *m*; **—s** convoy *m*, angarillas *fpl*.

castor[2] ['kɑːstə*] *n* (*wheel*) ruedecilla *f*.

castor oil ['kɑːstər'ɔil] *n* aceite *m* de ricino.

castor sugar ['kɑːstə'ʃugə*] *n* azúcar *m* extrafino.

castrate [kæs'treit] *vt* castrar.

castration [kæs'treiʃən] *n* castración *f*.

casual ['kæʒjul] *adj* (a) (*happening by chance*) fortuito, accidental; **a — glance** una mirada al azar; **a — stroll** un paseo sin propósito fijo; **in a — conversation I had with him** en una conversación sin trascendencia que tuve con él, en una conversación que por casualidad tuve con él; **a — remark** una observación hecha a la ligera; **a — meeting** un encuentro fortuito.

(b) (*offhand*) despreocupado; **he tried to sound —** se esforzó por parecer tan tranquilo como siempre; **to assume a — air** hacer como si nada; **he was very — about it** no daba importancia a la cosa.

(c) *clothing* de estar por casa, de sport.

(d) *labour* temporero, eventual; **— worker** jornalero *m*, temporero *m*.

casually ['kæʒjuli] *adv* (a) (*by chance*) por casualidad, de manera fortuita.

(b) (*offhandedly*) de manera despreocupada; **he said —** dijo con mucha tranquilidad; **I was — watching them** los miraba con aire distraído; **I said it quite —** lo dije sin darle importancia.

casualty ['kæʒjulti] *n* (a) (*Mil*) baja *f*; **casualties** pérdidas *fpl*; **there were heavy casualties** hubo pérdidas importantes.

(b) (*in accident*) víctima *f*, herido *m*, muerto *m*; **casualties** víctimas *fpl*; **fortunately there were no casualties** por fortuna no hubo víctimas.

casualty list ['kæʒjultilist] *n* (*Mil*) lista *f* de bajas; (*in accident*) lista *f* de víctimas.

casuist ['kæʒjuist] *n* casuista *mf*; (*pej*) sofista *mf*.

casuistry ['kæʒjuistri] *n* casuística *f*; (*pej*) sofismas *mpl*, razonamiento *m* falaz.

cat [kæt] *n* gato *m*, (*she-*) gata *f*; (*whip*) azote *m* con nueve ramales; **to be like a — on hot bricks** estar como gato sobre ascuas; **to lead a — and dog life** vivir como perros y gatos; **to let the — out of the bag** revelar el secreto; **to rain —s and dogs** llover a cántaros; **to see which way the — jumps** esperar a ver qué sesgo toma el asunto; **to set the —among the pigeons** meter los perros en danza; **there isn't room to swing a —** aquí no cabe un alfiler.

cataclysm ['kætəklizəm] n cataclismo m.

catacombs ['kætəku:mz] npl catacumbas fpl.

catafalque ['kætəfælk] n catafalco m.

Catalan ['kætəlæn] 1 adj catalán. 2 n catalán m, ana f. 3 n (language) catalán m.

catalepsy ['kætəlepsi] n catalepsia f.

cataleptic [.kætə'leptik] 1 adj cataléptico. 2 n cataléptico m, a f.

catalog (US), **catalogue** ['kætələɔg] 1 n catálogo m; (of cards) fichero m. 2 vt catalogar, poner en un catálogo; **it is not —d** no consta en el catálogo.

Catalonia [kætə'ləuniə] Cataluña f.

Catalonian [.kætə'ləuniən] see **Catalan**.

catalyst ['kætəlist] n catalizador m.

catamaran [.kætəmə'ræn] n catamarán m.

cat-and-mouse ['kætn'maus]: **to play a — game with someone** jugar al gato y ratón con uno.

catapult ['kætəpʌlt] 1 n (Hist and Aer) catapulta f; (boy's) tirador m. 2 vt (Aer) catapultar.

cataract ['kætərækt] n (Geog and Med) catarata f.

catarrh [kə'tɑ:*] n catarro m.

catastrophe [kə'tæstrəfi] n catástrofe f.

catastrophic [.kætə'strɔfik] adj catastrófico.

catbird ['kætbə:d] n pájaro m gato.

cat burglar ['kætbə:glə*] n balconero m.

cat call ['kætkɔ:l] 1 n silbo m, rechifla f. 2 vi silbar, rechiflar.

catch [kætʃ] 1 n (a) (act of catching) cogida f.
    (b) (quantity caught) pesca f, cantidad f de peces cogidos; **he's a good —** es un buen partido.
    (c) (of lock, on door) pestillo m; (of box, window) cerradura f; (small flange) fiador m.
    (d) (Mus) canon m.
    (e) (trick) trampa f; **there must be a — here somewhere** aquí debe haber trampa; **the — is la** dificultad es que; **a question with a — to it** una pregunta de pega.
    (f) **with a — in one's voice** con la voz entrecortada.

    2 (irr: pret and ptp **caught**) vt (a) (capture) coger, atrapar; (grasp) asir; (arrest) prender, detener; **ball** recoger, coger, parar; **bus, train etc** coger, tomar; (catch up with) alcanzar; **—! ¡cógelo!, ¡toma!; we only just caught the train** por poco perdimos el tren; **I caught my fingers in the door** me cogí los dedos en la puerta; **I caught my coat on that nail** mi chaqueta se enganchó en ese clavo; **I caught my head on that beam** di con la cabeza contra esa viga.
    (b) **to — someone a blow** dar un golpe a uno.
    (c) (surprise) sorprender, cazar, coger en una falta; **you'll not — me doing it** yo sería incapaz de hacer eso, yo nunca haría eso.
    (d) person's meaning comprender; (manage to hear) oír, llegar a oír; **I didn't quite — you** no oí lo que Vd dijo.
    (e) **the poet has caught the mood of the times** el poeta ha hecho revivir el espíritu de la época; **the painter has caught his expression** el pintor ha sabido captar su gesto.
    (f) (Med) contagiarse de, coger; habit tomar, adoptar.
    (g) breath suspender.
    (h) (fam) **to — it** merecerse un regaño (from de); **you'll — it!** ¡las vas a pagar!
    (i) **to — someone out** sorprender a uno, cazar a uno, coger a uno en una falta; **to — up thing** asir; person alcanzar, emparejar con.

    3 vi enredarse (in en), engancharse (on en); (Tech) engranar; (fire) encenderse; **to — at tratar** de coger, asir; **to — on** (see the joke) percibir lo gracioso del cuento; (tumble to something) caer en la cuenta; (get the knack) coger el tino; (song, craze etc) hacerse popular, alcanzar gran popularidad, afirmarse en el gusto del público; **it never really caught on** nunca logró establecerse; **to — on something** prender en algo, (parts of machine) rozar, ludir con; **to — on to** comprender; **to — up** ponerse al día; hacer los atrasos de trabajo (etc); ponerse al nivel de los demás; **to — up with news** ponerse al corriente de, person alcanzar.

catcher ['kætʃə*] n (Baseball) apañador m.

catching ['kætʃiŋ] adj (Med) contagioso; (fig) pegajoso.

catchment ['kætʃmənt] n: **— area** zona f de captación; **— basin** cuenca f.

catchpenny ['kætʃ.peni] adj de pacotilla, sin valor.

catch phrase ['kætʃfreiz] n tópico m; slogan m; (Radio etc) frase f típica.

catchword ['kætʃwə:d] n (Typ) reclamo m; (Theat) pie m; (catch phrase) tópico m.

catchy ['kætʃi] adj (Mus) pegajoso, pegadizo, que se pega.

catechize ['kætikaiz] vt catequizar.

catechism ['kætikizəm] n catequismo m.

categoric(al) [.kæti'gɔrik(əl)] adj categórico, terminante; refusal rotundo.

categorically [.kæti'gɔrikəli] adv state etc de modo terminante; refuse rotundamente.

categorize ['kætigəraiz] vt clasificar; **to — something as** calificar algo de.

category ['kætigəri] n categoría f.

cater ['keitə*] vi: **to — for** abastecer a, proveer comida a; (fig) atender a, proveer a; **to — for all tastes** atender a todos los gustos.

cater-cornered ['keitə'kɔ:nəd] (US) 1 adj diagonal. 2 adv diagonalmente.

caterer ['keitərə*] n abastecedor m, ora f, proveedor m, ora f.

catering ['keitəriŋ] n abastecimiento m; servicio m de comidas, servicio m de comedor.

caterpillar ['kætəpilə*] n oruga f, gusano m; **— track, — tread** rodado m de oruga; **— tractor** tractor m de oruga.

caterwaul ['kætəwɔ:l] vi chillar.

catfish ['kætfiʃ] n siluro m, bagre m.

catgut ['kætgʌt] n cuerda f de tripa; (Med) catgut m.

Catharine ['kæθərin] f Catalina.

catharsis [kə'θɑ:sis] n catarsis f.

cathartic [kə'θɑ:tik] 1 adj (Med) catártico, purgante; (Lit) catártico. 2 n purgante m.

cathedral [kə'θi:drəl] n catedral f; **— city** ciudad f episcopal; **— church** iglesia f catedral.

Catherine ['kæθərin] f Catalina; **— wheel** (firework) rueda f catalina.

catheter ['kæθitə*] n catéter m.

cathode ['kæθəud] n cátodo m; **— ray tube** tubo m de rayos catódicos.

catholic ['kæθəlik] adj católico; (fig) liberal, de amplias miras; **a person of — tastes** una persona a quien le gusta todo.

Catholic ['kæθəlik] 1 adj católico. 2 n católico m, a f.

Catholicism [kə'θɔlisizəm] n catolicismo m.

catkin ['kætkin] n amento m.

cat-lick ['kætlik] n (fam) lavado m de gato.

catlike ['kætlaik] adj felino, gatuno.

catmint ['kætmint] n, (US) **catnip** ['kætnip] n hierba f gatera.

catnap ['kætnæp] n siesta f breve.

Cato ['keitəu] m Catón.

cat-o'nine-tails ['kætə'nainteilz] n azote m con nueve ramales.

cat's-cradle ['kæts.kreidl] n cunas fpl, pata f de gallina.

cat's-paw ['kætspɔ:] n instrumento m.

catsup ['kætsəp] n (US) salsa f de tomate.

cattle ['kætl] npl ganado m, ganado m vacuno, vacas fpl.

cattleman ['kætlmæn] n, pl **—men** [men] ganadero m.

cattle raising ['kætlreiziŋ] n ganadería f.

cattle rustler ['kætlrʌslə*] n (US) ladrón m de ganado, cuatrero m.

cattle show ['kætlʃəu] n feria f de ganado.

cattle truck ['kætltrʌk] n (Aut) camión m ganadero; (Rail) vagón m para ganado.

catty ['kæti] adj malicioso, rencoroso.

Catullus [kə'tʌləs] m Catulo.

catwalk ['kætwɔ:k] n pasadizo m, pasarela f.

Caucasian [kɔ:'keiziən] 1 adj (by race) caucásico; (Geog) caucasiano. 2 n (by race) caucásico m, a f; (Geog) caucasiano m, a f.

Caucasus ['kɔ:kəsəs] Cáucaso m.

caucus ['kɔ:kəs] n camarilla f política.

caudal ['kɔ:dl] adj caudal.

caught [kɔ:t] pret and ptp of **catch**.

caul [kɔ:l] n redaño m.

cauldron ['kɔ:ldrən] n caldera f, calderón m.

cauliflower ['kɔliflauə*] n coliflor f; **— ear** (Boxing) oreja f deformada por los golpes.

caulk [kɔ:k] vt calafatear.

causal ['kɔ:zəl] adj causal.

causality [kɔ:'zæliti] n causalidad f.

causation [kɔ:'zeiʃən] n causalidad f.

causative ['kɔ:zətiv] adj causativo.

cause [kɔ:z] 1 n causa f, motivo m, razón f; (Law) causa f; **lost —** causa f perdida, causa f imposible; **with good —** con razón; **to be the — of** ser causa de, motivar; **there's no — for alarm** no hay para

qué asustarse; **in the — of liberty** por la libertad; **it's all in a good —** todo esto tiene un propósito noble; **to die in a good —** morir por una causa noble; **to give — for complaint** dar motivo para que se queje uno; **you have — to be worried** Vd tiene buen motivo para inquietarse; **to make common — with** hacer un frente común con, hacer causa común con; **to show —** aducir argumentos convincentes; **to take up someone's —** apoyar la campaña de uno, acudir a la defensa de uno.
  2 *vt* causar, motivar, provocar; **to — an accident** causar un accidente; **to — trouble** provocar un disturbio; armar un lío; **to — someone to do something** hacer que uno haga algo.
cause célèbre [ˌkɔːzseiˈlebr] *n* caso *m* célebre.
causeway [ˈkɔːzwei] *n* calzada *f*; (*in sea*) arrecife *m*.
caustic [ˈkɔːstik] *adj* cáustico; (*fig*) cáustico, mordaz; **— soda** sosa *f* cáustica.
cauterize [ˈkɔːtəraiz] *vt* cauterizar.
cautery [ˈkɔːtəri] *n* cauterio *m*.
caution [ˈkɔːʃən] **1** *n* (**a**) cautela *f*, prudencia *f*; **"—!"** "¡atención!"
  (**b**) (*warning*) advertencia *f*, amonestación *f*.
  (**c**) (*fam*) **he's a —** es un tío muy raro, (*amusing*) es un tío divertidísimo.
  2 *vt* amonestar (*against* contra).
cautionary [ˈkɔːʃənəri] *adj* **tale** de escarmiento, aleccionador.
cautious [ˈkɔːʃəs] *adj* cauteloso, prudente, precavido; **to make a — statement** hacer una declaración prudente; **to play a — game** jugar con mucha prudencia.
cautiously [ˈkɔːʃəsli] *adv* cautelosamente, con cautela.
cautiousness [ˈkɔːʃəsnis] *n* cautela *f*, prudencia *f*.
cavalcade [ˌkævəlˈkeid] *n* cabalgata *f*; (*fig*) desfile *m*.
cavalier [ˌkævəˈliə*] **1** *adj* arrogante, desdeñoso; **treatment** sin miramientos.
  2 *n* caballero *m*; (*arch*) galán *m*; (*Hist*) *partidario del Rey en la Guerra Civil inglesa* (1641–49).
cavalierly [ˌkævəˈliəli] *adv* arrogantemente, desdeñosamente; sin miramientos.
cavalry [ˈkævəlri] *n* caballería *f*.
cavalryman [ˈkævəlrimən] *n*, *pl* **-men** [mən] soldado *m* de caballería.
cave[1] [keiv] **1** *n* cueva *f*, caverna *f*. **2** *vi*: **to — in** derrumbarse, hundirse (*also fig*).
cave[2] [ˈkeivi] *interj*: **—!** ¡ojo!, ¡ahí viene!; **to keep —** estar a la mira.
caveat [ˈkæviæt] *n* advertencia *f*; (*Law*) advertencia *f* de suspensión; **to enter a —** hacer una advertencia.
cave dweller [ˈkeivˌdwelə*] *n* cavernícola *mf*, troglodita *mf*.
cave-in [ˈkeivin] *n* (*of roof etc*) derrumbe *m*, derrumbamiento *m*; (*of pavement etc*) socavón *m*.
caveman [ˈkeivmæn] *n*, *pl* **-men** [men] hombre *m* de las cavernas; (*hum and iro*) machote *m*.
cave painting [ˈkeivˌpeintiŋ] *n* pintura *f* rupestre.
cavern [ˈkævən] *n* caverna *f*.
cavernous [ˈkævənəs] *adj* cavernoso.
caviar(e) [ˈkæviɑː*] *n* caviar *m*.
cavil [ˈkævil] **1** *n* reparo *m*. **2** *vi* sutilizar, critiquizar; **to — at** poner peros a, criticar sin motivo.
caving [ˈkeiviŋ] *n* espeleología *f*.
cavity [ˈkæviti] *n* cavidad *f*, hueco *m*, hoyo *m*; **nasal cavities** fosas *fpl* nasales.
cavort [kəˈvɔːt] *vi* dar cabriolas; (*fig*) ir de juerga, divertirse ruidosamente.
cavy [ˈkeivi] *n* conejillo *m* de Indias, cobaya *m*.
caw [kɔː] **1** *n* graznido *m*. **2** *vi* graznar.
cawing [ˈkɔːiŋ] *n* graznidos *mpl*, el graznar.
cayenne pepper [ˈkeienˌpepə*] *n* pimentón *m*.
cayman [ˈkeimən] *n* caimán *m*.
cease [siːs] **1** *vt* suspender, cesar; **to — work** suspender el trabajo, terminar de trabajar.
  2 *vi* cesar; **to — (from) +** *ger*, **to — to + *infin*** dejar de *+ infin*, cesar de *+ infin*; **to — from strife** dejar de luchar.
ceasefire [ˌsiːsˈfaiə*] *n* cese *m* de hostilidades, alto *m* el fuego; **— line** línea *f* de alto el fuego.
ceaseless [ˈsiːslis] *adj* incesante, continuo.
ceaselessly [ˈsiːslisli] *adv* incesantemente, sin cesar.
Cecil [ˈsesl] *m* Cecilio.
Cecily [ˈsisili] *f* Cecilia.
cecum [ˈsiːkəm] *n* (*US*) = **caecum**.
cedar [ˈsiːdə*] *n* cedro *m*.
cede [siːd] *vt* ceder (*to* a).
cedilla [siˈdilə] *n* cedilla *f*.
ceiling [ˈsiːliŋ] *n* techo *m* (*also Aer*); (*fig*) límite *m*, punto *m* más alto; **— price** precio *m* tope; **to fix a — for**, **to put a — on** fijar el límite de, señalar el punto más alto de; **to hit the —** (*si*) ponerse negro.

he has not yet reached his — se desarrollará todavía algo más, ha de ser mejor aún.
celandine [ˈseləndain] *n* celidonia *f*.
celebrant [ˈselibrənt] *n* celebrante *m*.
celebrate [ˈselibreit] **1** *vt* celebrar; *marriage* solemnizar; *happy event* celebrar, señalar con una fiesta; **we're celebrating his arrival** estamos celebrando su llegada; **what are you celebrating?** ¿qué motivo tiene esta fiesta?; **he —d his birthday by scoring 2 goals** celebró su cumpleaños marcando 2 goles.
  2 *vi* divertirse, estar (*or* ir) de parranda.
celebrated [ˈselibreitid] *adj* célebre, famoso (*for* por).
celebration [ˌseliˈbreiʃən] *n* celebración *f*; (*party*) fiesta *f*, guateque *m*; (*public rejoicing*) festividad *f*; **—s** (*of anniversary etc*) conmemoraciones *fpl*; **in — of** en conmemoración de.
celebrity [siˈlebriti] *n* (*all senses*) celebridad *f*.
celeriac [səˈleriæk] *n* apio-nabo *m*.
celerity [siˈleriti] *n* celeridad *f*.
celery [ˈseləri] *n* apio *m*.
celestial [siˈlestiəl] *adj* celestial.
celibacy [ˈselibəsi] *n* celibato *m*.
celibate [ˈselibit] **1** *adj* célibe. **2** *n* célibe *mf*.
cell [sel] *n* (*of prison, monastery*) celda *f*; (*Bio, Pol*) célula *f*; (*of bees*) celda *f*; celdilla *f*; (*Elec*) elemento *m*; **condemned —** celda *f* de los condenados a muerte.
cellar [ˈselə*] *n* sótano *m*; (*for wine*) bodega *f*; **to keep a good —** tener buena bodega.
'cellist [ˈtʃelist] *n* violoncelista *mf*.
'cello [ˈtʃeləu] *n* violoncelo *m*.
cellophane [ˈseləfein] *n* (*Protected Trade Name*) celofán *m*.
cellular [ˈseljulə*] *adj* celular.
celluloid [ˈseljuloid] *n* celuloide *m*.
cellulose [ˈseljuləus] *n* celulosa *f*.
Celt [kelt, selt] *n* celta *mf*.
Celtiberia [ˌkeltaiˈbiəriə] Celtiberia *f*.
Celtiberian [ˌkeltaiˈbiəriən] **1** *adj* celtibérico. **2** *n* celtíbero *m*, a *f*.
Celtic [ˈkeltik, ˈseltik] **1** *adj* celta, céltico. **2** *n* (*language*) céltico *m*.
cement [səˈment] **1** *n* cemento *m*; (*Phot*) cola *f*. **2** *vt* cementar; cubrir (*or* revestir *etc*) de cemento; (*fig*) fortalecer, reforzar, consolidar.
cementation [ˌsiːmenˈteiʃən] *n* cementación *f*.
cemetery [ˈsemitri] *n* cementerio *m*.
cenotaph [ˈsenətɑːf] *n* cenotafio *m*.
censer [ˈsensə*] *n* incensario *m*.
censor [ˈsensə*] **1** *n* censor *m*. **2** *vt* censurar; (*delete*) tachar, suprimir.
censorious [senˈsɔːriəs] *adj* hipercrítico, criticón.
censorship [ˈsensəʃip] *n* censura *f*.
censurable [ˈsenʃərəbl] *adj* censurable.
censure [ˈsenʃə*] **1** *n* censura *f*. **2** *vt* censurar.
census [ˈsensəs] *n* censo *m*; empadronamiento *m*; **to take a — of** levantar el censo de, empadronar.
cent [sent] *n* centavo *m*; **per —** por ciento, por cien; **I haven't a —** no tengo un céntimo.
centaur [ˈsentɔː*] *n* centauro *m*.
centaury [ˈsentɔːri] *n* centaura *f*.
centenarian [ˌsentiˈneəriən] **1** *adj* centenario. **2** *n* centenario *m*, a *f*.
centenary [senˈtiːnəri] *n* centenario *m*; **the — celebrations** las festividades para celebrar el centenario de . . .
centennial [senˈteniəl] **1** *adj* centenario. **2** *n* centenario *m*.
center [ˈsentə*] *n* (*US*) = **centre**.
centesimal [senˈtesiməl] *adj* centesimal.
centigrade [ˈsentigreid] *adj* centígrado; **30 degrees —** 30 grados centígrados.
centigramme, (*US*) **-gram** [ˈsentigræm] *n* centigramo *m*.
centilitre, (*US*) **-liter** [ˈsentiˌliːtə*] *n* centilitro *m*.
centime [ˈsãːntiːm] *n* céntimo *m*.
centimetre, (*US*) **-meter** [ˈsentiˌmiːtə*] *n* centímetro *m*.
centipede [ˈsentipiːd] *n* ciempiés *m*.
central [ˈsentrəl] *adj* central; (*in town etc*) céntrico.
Central America [ˈsentrəˈmerikə] Centroamérica *f*.
Central American [ˈsentrələˈmerikən] **1** *adj* centroamericano. **2** *n* centroamericano *m*, a *f*.
Central European [ˈsentrəlˌjuərəˈpiːən] **1** *adj* centroeuropeo. **2** *n* centroeuropeo *m*, a *f*.
central heating [ˌsentrəlˈhiːtiŋ] *n* calefacción *f* central.
centralization [ˌsentrəlaiˈzeiʃən] *n* centralización *f*.
centralize [ˈsentrəlaiz] *vt* centralizar; concentrar, reunir en un centro.
centre, (*US*) **center** [ˈsentə*] **1** *n* centro *m*; núcleo *m*; **city —** centro *m* de la ciudad; **civic —** conjunto *m*

de edificios municipales; **community** — centro *m* social; **dead** — el mismo centro, (*Mech*) punto *m* muerto; — **of attraction** centro *m* de atracción; — **of gravity** centro *m* de gravedad; — **of intrigue** centro *m* de intrigas.

2 *attr* central; del centro.

3 *vt* centrar; *ball* pasar al centro; (*fig*) concentrar (*on* en).

4 *vi*: **to** — **in, to** — **on** concentrarse en, estar concentrado en, tener por centro, (*hopes etc*) cifrarse en.

centre-board, (*US*) **center**— ['sentəbɔːd] *n* orza *f* de deriva.

centre-forward ['sentə'fɔːwəd] *n* delantero *m* centro.

centre-half ['sentə'hɑːf] *n*, *pl* **—halves** [hɑːvz] medio *m* centro.

centre-piece, (*US*) **center**— ['sentəpiːs] *n* centro *m* de mesa; (*fig*) atracción *f* principal, objeto *m* (*etc*) de mayor interés.

centrifugal [sen'trifjugəl] *adj* centrífugo.

centrifuge ['sentrifjuːʒ] 1 *n* centrífuga *f*. 2 *vt* centrifugar.

centripetal [sen'tripitl] *adj* centrípeto.

centuries-old ['sentjuriz,əuld] *adj* secular.

centurion [sen'tjuəriən] *n* centurión *m*.

century ['sentjuri] *n* siglo *m*; **in the 20th** — en el siglo veinte.

cephalic [si'fælik] *adj* cefálico.

ceramic [si'ræmik] *adj* cerámico.

ceramics [si'ræmiks] *n* sing cerámica *f*.

cereal ['siəriəl] 1 *adj* cereal. 2 *n* cereal *m*; **—s** (*crops*, *cornflakes*) cereales *mpl*.

cerebellum [,seri'beləm] *n* cerebelo *m*.

cerebral ['seribrəl] *adj* cerebral.

cerebrate ['seribreit] *vi* pensar, meditar.

cerebration [,seri'breiʃən] *n* meditación *f*, actividad *f* mental.

ceremonial [,seri'məuniəl] 1 *adj* ceremonial; de ceremonia, de gala. 2 *n* ceremonial *m*.

ceremonially [,seri'məuniəli] *adv* con ceremonia.

ceremonious [,seri'məuniəs] *adj* ceremonioso.

ceremoniously [,seri'məuniəsli] *adv* ceremoniosamente.

ceremony ['seriməni] *n* ceremonia *f*; **to stand on** — hacer ceremonias, estar de cumplido; **let's not stand on** — dejémonos de cumplidos.

cerise [sə'riːz] 1 *adj* (de) color de cereza. 2 *n* cereza *f*.

cert [səːt] *n* (*sl*): **it's a** — es cosa segura.

certain ['səːtən] *adj* (a) (*of things*) seguro, cierto; **it is** — **that** es seguro que, es cierto que; **it is** — **death to go there** ir allí es buscarse una muerte segura.

(b) (*of person*) seguro; **are you** —? ¿estás seguro?; **I am** — **of it** estoy seguro de ello; **I am** — **that** estoy seguro de que; **we are** — **of his support** estamos seguros de tener su apoyo; **he is** — **to be there** es seguro que él estará allí; **be** — **to call on him** no dejes de visitarle; **you don't sound very** — no pareces estar muy seguro.

(c) (*a particular*) cierto; **to quote a** — **book** citar cierto libro; **to see a** — **man** ver a cierto hombre; **a** — **Mr Smith** un tal Sr Smith; **on a** — **day in May** cierto día de mayo.

(d) (*phrases*) **we don't know for** — no sabemos a ciencia cierta; **to make** — **of** asegurarse de; **I'll make** — yo lo averiguaré; **I'll make it as** — **as I can** yo lo haré todo lo seguro que pueda ser; **this should make victory** — esto ha de asegurarnos la victoria; **you should make** — **of your facts** conviene comprobar los datos.

certainly ['səːtənli] *adv* (a) —! ¡desde luego!, ¡naturalmente!; — **madam!** ¡con mucho gusto, señora!; ¡cómo Vd quiera, señora!; — **not!** ¡de ninguna manera!, ¡ni hablar!

(b) **it is** — **true that** desde luego es verdad que; **you may** — **take the car** desde luego que puedes tomar el coche; **I shall** — **be there** es seguro que yo asistiré, yo estaré allí sin falta; **you** — **did that well** eso sí que lo hiciste bien; **the meat is** — **tough** la carne sí es dura; **and** — **the Germans had more planes** y por cierto los alemanes tuvieron más aviones.

certainty ['səːtənti] *n* certeza *f*, certidumbre *f*; seguridad *f*; **in the** — **of being able to go** con la certeza de poder ir; **there is no** — **about it** sobre esto no hay seguridad alguna; **his** — **was alarming** su convicción era desconcertante; **faced with the** — **of disaster** ante la inevitabilidad del desastre; **it's a** — esa cosa segura; **we know for a** — **that** sabemos a ciencia cierta que; **we can't know with any** — no lo podemos saber a ciencia cierta.

certifiable [,səːti'faiəbl] *adj* certificable; (*Med*)

demente, que padece tal demencia que hay que encerrarle en un manicomio.

certificate [sə'tifikit] *n* certificado *m*; (*academic etc*) título *m*; (*of birth etc*) partida *f*; **medical** — certificado *m* médico; — **of baptism** partida *f* de bautismo; — **of birth** partida *f* de nacimiento; — **of death** partida *f* de defunción; — **of marriage** partida *f* de casamiento.

certificated [sə'tifikeitid] *adj* con título, diplomado.

certify ['səːtifai] *vt* certificar; **to** — **that** declarar que; **to** — **someone insane** certificar que uno está loco.

certitude ['səːtitjuːd] *n* certidumbre *f*.

cervical ['səːvikəl] *adj* cervical.

cervix ['səːviks] *n*, *pl* **cervices** ['səːvisiːz] cerviz *f*.

cessation [se'seiʃən] *n* cesación *f*, suspensión *f*; — **of hostilities** cese *m* de hostilidades.

cession ['seʃən] *n* cesión *f*.

cesspool ['sespuːl] *n* pozo *m* negro; (*fig*) sentina *f*.

cetacean [si'teiʃən] 1 *adj* cetáceo. 2 *n* cetáceo *m*.

Ceylon [si'lɒn] Ceilán *m*.

Ceylonese [silə'niːz] 1 *adj* ceilanés. 2 *n* ceilanés *m*, esa *f*.

chafe [tʃeif] 1 *vt* rozar, raer; (*warm*) calentar frotando; (*fig*) irritar.

2 *vi* desgastarse (*against*, *on* contra); (*fig*) irritarse, impacientarse; **to** — **at, to** — **under** (*fig*) impacientarse por, irritarse debido a.

chaff [tʃɑːf] 1 *n* barcia *f*, aechaduras *fpl*; (*waste*) desperdicios *mpl*; (*fig*) zumbas *fpl*, chanzas *fpl*. 2 *vt* zumbarse de, tomar el pelo a.

chaffinch ['tʃæfintʃ] *n* pinzón *m* vulgar.

chafing dish ['tʃeifindiʃ] *n* escalfador *m*.

chagrin ['ʃægrin] 1 *n* mortificación *f*, desazón *f*, disgusto *m*; **to my** — con gran disgusto mío. 2 *vt* mortificar, disgustar.

chain [tʃein] 1 *n* cadena *f* (*also fig*); — **of mountains** cordillera *f*. 2 *vt* encadenar.

chain gang ['tʃeingæŋ] *n* (*US and Hist*) cadena *f* de presidiarios.

chain letter ['tʃein,letə*] *n* carta *f* que circula en cadena (*con promesa de una ganancia cuantiosa para los que la hacen seguir según las indicaciones*).

chain lightning ['tʃein'laitniŋ] *n* (*US*) relámpagos *mpl* en zigzag.

chain mail ['tʃein'meil] *n* cota *f* de malla.

chain pump ['tʃeinpʌmp] *n* bomba *f* de cadena.

chain reaction ['tʃeinri'ækʃən] *n* reacción *f* en cadena.

chain smoker ['tʃeinsməukə*] *n* fumador *m* que fuma un pitillo tras otro.

chain stitch ['tʃeinstitʃ] *n* cadeneta *f*.

chain store ['tʃeinstɔː*] *n* tienda *f* de una cadena.

chair [tʃɛə*] 1 *n* silla *f*; (*Univ*) cátedra *f*; (*of meeting*) presidencia *f*; **electric** — silla *f* eléctrica; **high** — silla *f* alta; **to be in the** —, **to take the** — presidir (*at a meeting* una reunión); **won't you take a** —? ¿quiere Vd sentarse?

2 *vt* (a) *person* llevar a hombros; **they** —**ed him off the ground** le sacaron a hombros del campo.

(b) *meeting* presidir.

chairlift ['tʃɛəlift] *n* telesilla *m*.

chairman ['tʃɛəmən] *n*, *pl* —**men** [mən] presidente *m*.

chairmanship ['tʃɛəmənʃip] *n* (*post*) presidencia *f*; (*art*) arte *m* de presidir reuniones.

chaise [ʃeiz] *n* calesa *f*, landó *m*.

chaise longue ['ʃeiz'lɔːŋ] *n* tumbona *f*.

chalet ['ʃælei] *n* chalet *m*, chalé *m* (*Acad*).

chalice ['tʃælis] *n* cáliz *m*.

chalk [tʃɔːk] 1 *n* (*Geol*) creta *f*; (*for writing*) tiza *f*; **French** — jaboncillo *m* de sastre, esteatita *f*; **not by a long** — ni con mucho; **it's as different as** — **from cheese** son tan diferentes como el agua y el vino.

2 *vt* marcar (*or* dibujar *etc*) con tiza; **to** — **up** apuntar.

chalkpit ['tʃɔːkpit] *n* cantera *f* de creta.

chalky ['tʃɔːki] *adj* cretoso.

challenge ['tʃælindʒ] 1 *n* (*to duel*) desafío *m*, reto *m*; (*of sentry*) quién vive *m*; (*Law*) recusación *f*; **the** — **of new ideas** el estímulo de las nuevas ideas; **the** — **of the 20th century** el incentivo (*or* estímulo) del siglo XX, las posibilidades del siglo XX; **Vigo's** — **for the league leadership** la tentativa que hace el Vigo para tomar el liderato de la liga; **this is a** — **to us all** esto nos llama a todos a la acción; **to issue a** — **to someone** desafiar a uno; **to take up a** — aceptar un desafío.

2 *vt* (*to duel*) desafiar, retar; (*sentry*) dar el quién vive a; (*Law*) recusar; *fact*, *point* poner en duda, expresar dudas acerca de; *speaker* hablar en contra de; **to** — **someone to** + *infin* desafiar a uno a que + *subj*.

challenger ['tʃælindʒə*] n desafiador m; (competitor) concursante mf; (opponent) contrincante mf.

challenging ['tʃælindʒiŋ] adj desafiante; tone de desafío; speech etc emocionante, estimulante, provocador; book sugestivo, lleno de sugestiones.

chamber ['tʃeimbə*] n cámara f; (arch) aposento m, sala f; (of gun) recámara f; —s (Law) despacho m; — of commerce cámara f de comercio.

chamberlain ['tʃeimbəlin] n chambelán m, gentilhombre m de cámara.

chambermaid ['tʃeimbəmeid] n camarera f, sirvienta f.

chamber music ['tʃeimbə‚mjuːzik] n música f de cámara.

chamberpot ['tʃeimbəpɔt] n orinal m.

chambray ['tʃæmbrei] n (US) cambray m.

chameleon [kə'miːliən] n camaleón m.

chamfer ['tʃæmfə*] 1 n chaflán m. 2 vt chaflanar.

chamois n (a) (Zool) ['ʃæmwaː] gamuza f. (b) (leather) ['ʃæmi] gamuza f.

chamois leather ['ʃæmi‚leðə*] n gamuza f.

champ[1] [tʃæmp] vt morder, mordiscar; bit tascar.

champ[2] [tʃæmp] n (fam) = champion.

Champagne [ʃæm'pein] Champaña f.

champagne [ʃæm'pein] n champán m, champaña m.

champion ['tʃæmpiən] 1 adj campeón; a — athlete un atleta campeón.
2 n campeón m, ona f; (of a cause) defensor m, ora f, paladín m; world — campeón m mundial.
3 vt defender, apoyar, abogar por.

championship ['tʃæmpiənʃip] n campeonato m.

chance [tʃɑːns] 1 adj fortuito, casual; imprevisto; (random) aleatorio.
2 n (a) (luck, fortune, fate) casualidad f; azar m; suerte f; game of — juego m de azar; the —s of war la fortuna de la guerra; — was against him la suerte le fue contraria; — ordained that la suerte quiso que; it cannot have been a matter of — esto no habrá tenido nada de casual; by — por casualidad; by sheer — por pura casualidad; do you by any — have a pen? ¿tienes por casualidad una pluma?; to leave things to — dejar las cosas al azar; to leave nothing to — obrar con la mayor previsión, comprobarlo todo hasta el más pequeño detalle.
(b) (opportunity) ocasión f, oportunidad f; now's our —! ya nos toca el turno, nos ha llegado la vez; this is my big — ésta es la oportunidad que venía esperando; you'll never get another — like this la suerte nunca le deparará otra ocasión como ésta; give me a — to show what I can do déme la oportunidad de mostrar si soy capaz; give me a — won't you? ¡déjame un momento en paz!; to give someone another — olvidar el pasado de uno, seguir empleando a uno a pesar de su insuficiencia (etc); he has had every — le hemos dado todas las oportunidades posibles; to have an eye for the main —, to look out for the main — mirar por su propio provecho; to waste one's —s desperdiciar las ocasiones.
(c) (possibility) posibilidad f, probabilidad f; the —s are that lo más probable es que + subj; there is no — of that no existe la posibilidad de que ocurra eso; it's a long — eso es poco probable; to have a fair — of + ger tener buenas probabilidades de + infin; he hasn't a — no tiene posibilidad alguna; I never had a — in life la suerte no me ha favorecido jamás en la vida; to stand a — tener posibilidades; you don't stand a — no tienes posibilidad alguna.
(d) (risk) riesgo m; to take a — arriesgarse, probar fortuna; to take no —s obrar con la mayor previsión, comprobarlo todo hasta el más pequeño detalle; that's a — we shall have to take es un peligro que no podemos soslayar.
3 vt arriesgar; probar; to — it probarlo, aventurarse; shall we — it? ¿probaremos?
4 vi: it —d that aconteció que; if it —s that si resulta que; I —d to see him le vi por casualidad; to — upon encontrar por casualidad, tropezar con.

chancel ['tʃɑːnsəl] n coro m y presbiterio.

chancellery ['tʃɑːnsələri] n cancillería f.

chancellor ['tʃɑːnsələ*] n canciller m; C— of the Exchequer Ministro m de Hacienda; Lord C— presidente de la Cámara de los Lores.

chancery ['tʃɑːnsəri] n (Law) chancillería f; ward in — pupilo m, a f bajo la protección del tribunal.

chancre ['ʃæŋkə*] n chancro m.

chancy ['tʃɑːnsi] adj (fam) arriesgado; dudoso.

chandelier [‚ʃændə'liə*] n araña f (de luces).

chandler ['tʃɑːndlə*] n velero m.

change [tʃeindʒ] 1 n cambio m; modificación f;

transformación f; (of skin etc) muda f; (small coins) moneda f suelta, calderilla f, suelto m; (for a larger coin) cambio m; (money returned) vuelta f; — of address cambio m de domicilio; — of clothes cambio m de ropa; — of front cambio m de frente; — of heart cambio m de sentimiento, conversión f; — of horses relevo m de los tiros; — of life menopausia f; — of scene (Theat) mutación f; for a — para variar un poco; it's a — for the better es un cambio beneficioso; to get no — out of someone no conseguir sacar nada a uno; you may keep the — quédese con la vuelta; to ring the —s on something hacer algo de diversas maneras.
2 vt cambiar (for por), trocar; reemplazar; modificar; transformar (into en); clothes, colour, gear, mind etc cambiar de, mudar de; can you — this note for me? ¿me hace Vd el favor de cambiar este billete?; I find him much —d le veo muy cambiado.
3 vi cambiar(se), mudar; (Rail etc) hacer transbordo, cambiar de tren (etc); all —! ¡cambio de tren!; to — over cambiar (to a); you haven't —d a bit! ¡no has cambiado en lo más mínimo!

changeability [‚tʃeindʒə'biliti] n lo cambiable, mutabilidad f; inconstancia f, lo cambiadizo; the — of the weather la mudabilidad del tiempo.

changeable ['tʃeindʒəbl] adj cambiable, mudable; inconstante, cambiadizo.

changeless ['tʃeindʒlis] adj inmutable.

changeling ['tʃeindʒliŋ] n niño m. cambiado por otro, niña f cambiada por otra.

changeover ['tʃeindʒ‚əuvə*] n cambio m.

changing ['tʃeindʒiŋ] adj cambiante.

changing-room ['tʃeindʒiŋrum] n vestuario m.

channel ['tʃænl] 1 n canal m (also TV); (of a river) cauce m; (strait) estrecho m; (fig) conducto m, medio m; irrigation — acequia f, canal m de riego; the C— el Canal (de la Mancha).
2 vt acanalar; (fig) encauzar, dirigir (into a, por).

Channel Isles ['tʃænl‚ailz] fpl Islas fpl Normandas.

chant [tʃɑːnt] 1 n canto m llano; (fig) sonsonete m.
2 vt cantar (el canto llano); praises cantar; (fig) salmodiar, recitar en tono monótono.

chaos ['keiɔs] n caos m, desorden m.

chaotic [kei'ɔtik] adj caótico, desordenado.

chap[1] [tʃæp] 1 n grieta f, hendedura f. 2 vt agrietar. 3 vi agrietarse.

chap[2] [tʃæp] n (Anat) mandíbula f; (cheek) mejilla f.

chap[3] [tʃæp] n (fam) tío m, tipo m, pájaro m; a — I know un tío que yo conozco; he's a nice — es buen chico, es buena persona; he's very deaf, poor — es muy sordo, el pobre; how are you, old —? ¿qué tal, amigo?; be a good — and say nothing sé buen chico y no digas ni pío de esto.

chapbook ['tʃæpbuk] n libreta f, librito m de cuentos (etc).

chapel ['tʃæpəl] n capilla f; (Protestant etc) templo m; (Typ) personal m de una imprenta.

chaperon ['ʃæpərəun] 1 n acompañanta f (de señorita), carabina f (fam). 2 vt acompañar (a una señorita).

chaplain ['tʃæplin] n capellán m.

chaplaincy ['tʃæplənsi] n capellanía f.

chaplet ['tʃæplit] n guirnalda f, corona f de flores; (necklace) collar m; (Eccl) rosario m.

chappy ['tʃæpi] n (fam) = chap[3].

chaps [tʃæps] npl (US) zahones mpl, chaparreras fpl.

chapter ['tʃæptə*] n capítulo m; (Eccl) cabildo m; — of accidents serie f de desgracias; with — and verse con pelos y señales; he can quote you — and verse él lo sabe citar con todos sus pelos y señales.

chapter house ['tʃæptəhaus] n sala f capitular.

char[1] [tʃɑː*] n (Fish) umbra f.

char[2] [tʃɑː*] vt carbonizar, chamuscar.

char[3] [tʃɑː*] n (sl) té m.

char[4] [tʃɑː*] n (fam) = charlady.

char-à-banc ['ʃærəbæŋ] n (arch) autocar m.

character ['kæriktə*] n (a) (nature of thing) carácter m, naturaleza f, índole f, calidad f; (moral — of person) carácter m; a man of — un hombre de carácter; to be in — ser característico, ser conforme al tipo; to be out of — no ser característico; to bear a good — tener una buena reputación; to have a bad — tener mala fama; to give someone a good — dar a uno una recomendación satisfactoria.
(b) (personage in novel, play etc) personaje m; (rôle) papel m; "Six C—s in Search of an Author" "Seis personajes en busca de autor"; the play has 8 —s la obra tiene 8 personajes; chief — protagonista mf; — actor actor m de carácter; — actress característica f; in the — of en el papel de; that is more in — eso está más en carácter.

(c) (fam) tipo m, sujeto m; **a — I know** un tipo que yo conozco; **he's quite a —** es un tipo pintoresco, es un original; **he's a very odd —** es un tipo muy raro.

(d) (Bio, Typ etc) carácter m.

characteristic [ˌkærɪktəˈrɪstɪk] **1** adj característico (of de). **2** n característica f, carácter m; distintivo m, señal f distintiva.

characteristically [ˌkærɪktəˈrɪstɪkəli] adv característicamente, de modo característico.

characterization [ˌkærɪktəraɪˈzeɪʃən] n caracterización f.

characterize [ˈkærɪktəraɪz] vt caracterizar.

characterless [ˈkærɪktəlɪs] adj sin carácter.

charade [ʃəˈrɑːd] n charada f (also fig).

charcoal [ˈtʃɑːkəul] n carbón m vegetal; (Art) carboncillo m; **— drawing** dibujo m al carbón.

charcoal burner [ˈtʃɑːkəulˌbənə*] n carbonero m.

charge [tʃɑːdʒ] **1** n (a) (explosive, electrical) carga f.

(b) (attack) carga f, ataque m, asalto m; (of bull) embestida f; (Sport) carga f; **cavalry —** carga f de caballería.

(c) (Law etc) acusación f, cargo m; **to appear on a —** of comparecer acusado de; **to bring** (or lay) **—s against** hacer acusaciones contra; **to give someone in —** entregar a uno a la policía; **to return to the —** volver al cargo, repetir la acusación.

(d) (price) precio m, coste m; **professional —s** honorarios mpl; **extra —** recargo m, suplemento m; **free of —** gratis; **— for admission** precio m de entrada; **"no — for admission"** "entrada gratis"; **to be a —** upon cargar en cuenta a; **to make a — for something** cobrar por algo; **to reverse the —s** (Tel) cobrar al número llamado.

(e) responsabilidad f; (office) cargo m; (task) encargo m, cometido m; **the person in —** la persona responsable; **to be in —** mandar; **who is in — here?** ¿quién manda aquí?; **to be in —** of estar encargado de; **to be in the —** of correr a cargo de; **to take — of** hacerse cargo de, encargarse de; **men, expedition etc** asumir el mando de.

(f) (Her) blasón m.

2 vt (a) (fill) cargar (also Mil, Elec; **with** de).

(b) (attack) atacar, cargar; (bull etc) embestir; (Sport) cargar.

(c) (Law etc) acusar (**with** de).

(d) price pedir; price, person cobrar (a); **what are they charging for it?** ¿cuánto piden por él?; **what did they — you for it?** ¿cuánto te cobraron?; **to — something** (up) **to someone, to — something to someone's account** cargar algo en cuenta a uno.

(e) (order) **to — someone to do something** ordenar a uno hacer algo; **to — someone with a mission** confiar una misión a uno; **I am —d with the task of +** ger me han encargado el deber de + infin.

3 vi (a) (Mil) atacar, cargar; (bull) embestir; **to — down upon** cargar sobre, precipitarse sobre; **to — into** chocar contra.

(b) (make pay) cobrar, (a lot) cobrar mucho.

chargeable [ˈtʃɑːdʒəbl] adj cobradero.

charge account [ˈtʃɑːdʒəˌkaunt] n (US) cuenta f corriente.

charged [tʃɑːdʒd] adj (Elec) cargado, con carga.

chargé d'affaires [ˈʃɑːʒeɪdæˈfɛə*] n encargado m de negocios.

charger [ˈtʃɑːdʒə*] n (horse) corcel m, caballo m de guerra; (Elec) cargador m.

charily [ˈtʃɛərɪli] adv cuidadosamente, cautelosamente; parcamente, con parquedad.

chariot [ˈtʃærɪət] n carro m (romano, de guerra etc).

charioteer [ˌtʃærɪəˈtɪə*] n auriga m.

charisma [kæˈrɪzmə] n carisma m.

charitable [ˈtʃærɪtəbl] adj (a) person caritativo; remark, view comprensivo, compasivo. (b) purpose, society benéfico.

charity [ˈtʃærɪti] n (a) caridad f; (sympathy) comprensión f, compasión f; **out of —** por caridad; **— begins at home** la caridad empieza por uno mismo; **to live on —** vivir de limosnas.

(b) (organization) sociedad f benéfica; **to raffle something for —** rifar algo para fines benéficos; **most of it goes to —** la mayor parte está destinada a obras de beneficencia.

charlady [ˈtʃɑːleɪdi] n asistenta f, mujer f de la limpieza.

charlatan [ˈʃɑːlətən] n charlatán m; (Med) curandero m.

Charlemagne [ˈʃɑːləmeɪn] m Carlomagno.

Charles [tʃɑːlz] m Carlos.

charleston [ˈtʃɑːlstən] n charlestón m.

charley horse [ˈtʃɑːlihɔːs] n (US fam) calambre m.

Charlie [ˈtʃɑːli] m Carlitos.

Charlotte [ˈʃɑːlət] f Carlota.

charm [tʃɑːm] **1** n (in general) encanto m, atractivo m, hechizo m; (magic spell) hechizo m; (recited spell) ensalmo m; (trinket) amuleto m, dije m; **—s** (of woman) atractivo m, hechizos mpl; **he has great —** tiene mucho encanto, tiene un fuerte atractivo; **typical Spanish —** la típica simpatía española; **to turn on the —** ponerse fino, deshacerse en finuras.

2 vt hechizar, encantar, seducir; **we were —ed by Granada** nos encantó Granada; **to — away** hacer desaparecer como por magia, llevarse misteriosamente.

charmer [ˈtʃɑːmə*] n hombre m (etc) de fuerte atractivo.

charming [ˈtʃɑːmɪŋ] adj encantador; person encantador, simpático; present, remark etc fino, gentil; **—!** (iro) ¡qué simpático!; **how — of you!** ¡qué detalle!

charmingly [ˈtʃɑːmɪŋli] adv de modo encantador; con finura; **a — simple dress** un vestido sencillo pero muy mono.

charnel-house [ˈtʃɑːnlhaus] n osario m.

chart [tʃɑːt] **1** n tabla f, cuadro m, esquema m, gráfico m; (graph) gráfica f; (Naut) carta f de navegación.

2 vt poner en una carta, (loosely) explorar; **to — a course** trazar un derrotero.

charter [ˈtʃɑːtə*] **1** n carta f; (of city, bill of rights) fuero m; (of company) carta f de privilegio; **royal —** cédula f real.

2 vt estatuir; ship fletar; bus, plane alquilar.

chartered [ˈtʃɑːtəd] adj accountant etc diplomado.

charwoman [ˈtʃɑːˌwumən] n, pl **—women** [ˌwimin] see **charlady.**

chary [ˈtʃɛəri] adj cuidadoso, cauteloso; **to be — of + n** ser avaro de + n, ser parco en + n; **to be — of + ger** evitar + infin, no prestarse de buena gana a + infin.

chase¹ [tʃeɪs] **1** n persecución f; (hunt) caza f; **to give — to** dar caza a, perseguir; **to join in the — for something** unirse a los que buscan algo.

2 vt (follow) perseguir; (hunt) cazar; **girl etc** perseguir, dar caza a; **to — away, to — off** ahuyentar; **to — out** echar fuera.

3 vi correr, precipitarse; **to — after** ir en pos de, (fig) correr tras.

4 vr: **go — yourself!** (fam) ¡vete al cuerno!

chase² [tʃeɪs] vt (Tech) grabar; jewel engastar.

chaser [ˈtʃeɪsə*] n copita f de licor.

chasm [ˈkæzəm] n (Geog) sima f, abismo m, grieta f; (fig) abismo m.

chassis [ˈʃæsi] n chasis m.

chaste [tʃeɪst] adj casto.

chastely [ˈtʃeɪstli] adv castamente.

chasten [ˈtʃeɪsn] vt castigar, corregir, escarmentar.

chastened [ˈtʃeɪsnd] **1** pret and ptp of **chasten. 2** adj (by experience etc) escarmentado; tone etc sumiso; **they seemed much —** parecían haberse arrepentido.

chasteness [ˈtʃeɪstnɪs] n castidad f.

chastening [ˈtʃeɪsnɪŋ] adj experience etc aleccionador.

chastise [tʃæsˈtaɪz] vt castigar.

chastisement [ˈtʃæstɪzmənt] n castigo m.

chastity [ˈtʃæstɪti] n castidad f.

chasuble [ˈtʃæzjubl] n casulla f.

chat [tʃæt] **1** n charla f; **to have a — with** charlar con; **I'll have a — with him** hablaré con él.

2 vt: **to — someone up** (sl) dar jabón a uno.

3 vi charlar (**to, with** con).

chatelaine [ˈʃætəleɪn] n (Hist) castellana f.

chattels [ˈtʃætlz] npl bienes mpl muebles; (loosely) cosas fpl, enseres mpl.

chatter [ˈtʃætə*] **1** n (talk) charla f, cháchara f; (of birds) parloteo m; (of teeth) castañeteo m.

2 vi (person) charlar, chacharear; (birds) parlotear; (monkeys) chillar; (teeth) castañetear; **she does — so** es muy habladora; **stop —ing!** ¡silencio!

chatterbox [ˈtʃætəbɔks] n parlanchín m, ina f, tarabilla mf.

chatty [ˈtʃæti] adj person hablador, locuaz; style familiar; letter afectuoso y lleno de noticias; article de tono familiar.

chauffeur [ˈʃəufə*] n chófer m, chofer m (S Am).

chauvinism [ˈʃəuvɪnɪzəm] n chauvinismo m.

chauvinist [ˈʃəuvɪnɪst] **1** adj chauvinista. **2** n chauvinista mf.

chauvinistic [ˌʃəuvɪˈnɪstɪk] adj chauvinista.

chaw [tʃɔː] vt (US fam) mascar; **to — someone up** (US sl) poner a uno como un trapo.

cheap [tʃiːp] **1** adj (a) barato; ticket económico; (person selling **—**) baratero; (fig) de mal gusto, cursi, chabacano; trick malo; **that's pretty —** eso es poco recto, eso se llama no jugar limpio; **on the** — barato; en plan económico; **to feel** — sentirse humillado, sentir vergüenza; **to hold** — tener en poco; **to make oneself** — hacer cosas indignas de sí, aplebeyarse; **to make a product** —**er** abaratar un producto. **2** *adv* barato.

cheapen ['tʃiːpən] **1** *vt* abaratar. **2** *vi* abaratarse. **3** *vr:* **to** — **oneself** hacer cosas indignas de sí, aplebeyarse.

cheaply ['tʃiːpli] *adv* barato; a precio económico; **to get off** — no tener que pagar (*etc*) lo que se calculaba.

cheapness ['tʃiːpnis] *n* lo barato, baratura *f.*

cheapskate ['tʃiːpskeit] *n* (*US: fam*) canalla *m.*

cheat [tʃiːt] **1** *n* (**a**) trampa *f,* fraude *m;* **it was a** — fue una decepción, hubo trampa; **there's a** — **in it somewhere** aquí hay trampa.

(**b**) (*person*) tramposo *m,* a *f,* petardista *mf;* (*at cards*) fullero *m.*

2 *vt person* defraudar, timar; **to** — **someone out of something** estafar algo a uno; **to** — **the gallows** suicidarse para no ser ejecutado.

cheating ['tʃiːtiŋ] *n* trampa *f,* fraude *m;* (*at cards*) fullerías *fpl.*

check¹ [tʃek] **1** *n* (**a**) (*halt*) parada *f* (súbita); (*Mil*) repulsa *f;* (*to plans*) contratiempo *m,* revés *m;* (*restraint*) restricción *f* (*on de*); (*obstacle*) impedimento *m* (*on para*), estorbo *m* (*on a*); —**s and balances in a constitution** frenos *mpl* y equilibrios de una constitución; **to act as a** — **on** (*restrain*) refrenar, (*impede*) ser un estorbo a; **to hold** (*or* **keep**) **in** — contener, tener a raya; **to suffer a** — sufrir un revés.

(**b**) (*Chess*) jaque *m;* **in** — **en** jaque; **continuous** — tablas *fpl* por jaque continuo.

(**c**) (*check-up*) control *m,* inspección *f,* verificación *f* (*on de*); (*Mech etc*) repaso *m;* (*Med*) reconocimiento *m* general; **they gave the rocket a final** — dieron al cohete el último repaso; **to keep a** — **on** controlar.

(**d**) (*token*) (*counterfoil*) talón *m;* (*at cloakroom*) billete *m,* boleto *m;* (*in games*) ficha *f;* (*US: invoice*) factura *f;* (*US: cheque*) cheque *m;* (*bill for food*) nota *f,* cuenta *f;* **to hand in one's** —**s** (*sl*) estirar la pata.

2 *interj* (*Chess*) ¡jaque!

3 *vt* (**a**) *motion* parar, detener; *spread etc* restringir, tener a raya, refrenar; (*be an obstacle to*) impedir, estorbar; *attack* rechazar.

(**b**) (*Chess*) dar jaque a.

(**c**) (*examine*) controlar, examinar, inspeccionar; *facts* comprobar; *document* compulsar; (*count*) llevar la cuenta de, contar; (*Mech*) revisar, repasar; *baggage* (*US*) facturar; **to** — **a copy against an original** cotejar una copia con el original; **to** — **items off on a list** marcar artículos en una lista.

4 *vi:* **to** — **in** inscribirse (en un hotel); **to** — **on something** comprobar algo, verificar algo; investigar algo; **to** — **on someone** investigar los antecedentes (*or* la lealtad *etc*) de uno; **to** — **out** pagar su cuenta (de hotel) y marcharse, (*loosely*) salir, marcharse; **to** — **up** comprobarlo; investigarlo; **to** — **up on** = **to** — **on**; **to** — **with someone** consultar con uno.

5 *vr:* **to** — **oneself** detenerse, refrenarse.

check² [tʃek] *n* (*in pattern*) cuadro *m;* (*cloth*) paño *m* a cuadros; — **suit** traje *m* a cuadros.

checkbook ['tʃekbuk] *n* (*US*) = **cheque book.**

checkerboard ['tʃekəbɔːd] *n* tablero *m* de damas.

checkers ['tʃekəz] *npl* (*US*) juego *m* de damas.

checking ['tʃekiŋ] *n* control *m,* comprobación *f.*

checkmate ['tʃek'meit] **1** *n* mate *m,* jaque *m* mate. **2** *vt* dar mate a; **to be** —**d** (*fig*) estar en un callejón sin salida.

checkpoint ['tʃekpɔint] *n* (*punto m de*) control *m.*

checkroom ['tʃekrum] *n* (*US*) guardarropa *m;* (*Rail*) consigna *f;* (*euph*) lavabo *m.*

checkup ['tʃekʌp] *n* comprobación *f,* verificación *f;* examen *m;* (*Med*) reconocimiento *m* general.

cheek [tʃiːk] **1** *n* mejilla *f,* carrillo *m;* (*fig*) descaro *m,* frescura *f,* tupé *m;* — **by jowl** lado a lado (*with con*); **what** (**a**) —**!, of all the** —**!** ¡qué cara dura!, ¡qué valor!; **to have the** — **to** + *infin* atreverse a + *infin,* tener el valor de + *infin;* **to turn the other** — volver la otra mejilla.

2 *vt* (*fig*) decir cosas descaradas a, portarse como un fresco con.

cheekbone ['tʃiːkbəun] *n* pómulo *m.*

cheekily ['tʃiːkili] *adv* descaradamente, con frescura.

cheekiness ['tʃiːkinis] *n* descaro *m,* frescura *f.*

cheeky ['tʃiːki] *adj* descarado, fresco.

cheer [tʃiə*] **1** *n* (**a**) (*applause*) grito *m* de entusiasmo; —**s** aplausos *mpl,* aclamaciones *fpl;* **there were loud** —**s at this** en esto hubo muchos aplausos; **to give**

three —**s for** vitorear a, aclamar a; **three** —**s for the general!** ¡viva el general!

(**b**) (*food*) comida *f.*

(**c**) (*state of mind*) humor *m;* **what** —**? ¿**qué tal?; —**s!** (*fam*) ¡salud y pesetas!; **be of good** —**!** ¡ánimo!

2 *vt* (**a**) (*also* **to** — **up**) alegrar, animar; **I was much** —**ed by the news** me alegró mucho la noticia.

(**b**) (*applaud*) aplaudir, aclamar, vitorear; **to** — **on** animar con aplausos.

3 *vi* aplaudir, gritar con entusiasmo; **to** — **up** cobrar ánimo, alegrarse; — **up!** ¡ánimo!, ¡anímate!

cheerful ['tʃiəful] *adj* alegre; de buen humor.

cheerfully ['tʃiəfuli] *adv* alegremente.

cheerfulness ['tʃiəfulnis] *n* alegría *f;* buen humor *m.*

cheerily ['tʃiərili] *adv* alegremente, jovialmente; de modo acogedor.

cheering ['tʃiəriŋ] **1** *adj news etc* bueno, esperanzador. **2** *n* aplausos *mpl,* aclamaciones *fpl,* gritos *mpl* de entusiasmo.

cheerio ['tʃiəri'əu] *interj* ¡hasta luego!

cheerless ['tʃiəlis] *adj* triste, sombrío.

cheery ['tʃiəri] *adj* alegre, jovial; *room etc* acogedor.

cheese [tʃiːz] **1** *n* queso *m;* **cream** — requesón *m;* **Dutch** — queso *m* de bola; **grated** — queso *m* rallado; **hard** —**!** (*sl*) ¡mala potra!

2 *vt* (*US: sl*) dejar, poner fin a; — **it!** ¡déjalo!; ¡ojo, que viene gente!; **let's** — **it** dejémoslo; vámonos.

cheesecake ['tʃiːzkeik] *n* quesadilla *f;* (*sl*) *fotos, dibujos etc de chicas atractivas en traje o actitud incitante.*

cheesecloth ['tʃiːzklɔθ] *n* estopilla *f.*

cheesedish ['tʃiːzdiʃ] *n* quesera *f.*

cheeseparing ['tʃiːz,peəriŋ] **1** *adj* tacaño. **2** *n* economías *fpl* pequeñas.

cheesy ['tʃiːzi] *adj* (**a**) caseoso, como queso; que huele (*or* sabe) a queso. (**b**) (*US: sl*) horrible, sin valor.

cheetah ['tʃiːtə] *n* leopardo *m* cazador.

chef [ʃef] *n* jefe *m* de cocina.

cheiromancy ['kaiərəmænsi] *n* quiromancia *f.*

Chekhov ['tʃekɔf] *m* Chejof.

chemical ['kemikəl] **1** *adj* químico. **2** *n* sustancia *f* química, producto *m* químico.

chemically ['kemikəli] *adv* químicamente, por medios químicos.

chemise [ʃə'miːz] *n* camisa *f* de señora.

chemist ['kemist] *n* (*scientist*) químico *m,* a *f;* (*pharmacist*) farmacéutico *m;* —'**s** (*shop*) farmacia *f;* **all-night** —'**s** farmacia *f* de guardia.

chemistry ['kemistri] *n* química *f.*

chenille [ʃə'niːl] *n* felpilla *f.*

cheque [tʃek] *n* cheque *m;* **bad** —, **rubber** — (*fam*) cheque *m* sin fondos, cheque *m* sin provisión; **crossed** — cheque *m* cruzado; **open** — cheque *m* abierto; **traveller's** — cheque *m* de viajero; **blank** — cheque *m* en blanco; **to give someone a blank** — (*fig*) dar carta blanca a uno; **to pay by** — pagar mediante cheque.

cheque book ['tʃekbuk] *n* libro *m* de cheques.

chequered ['tʃekəd] *adj cloth etc* a cuadros; (*fig*) *career* accidentado, lleno de altibajos; *collection* variado.

cherish ['tʃeriʃ] *vt* querer, apreciar; cuidar, proteger; mimar; *hope etc* abrigar, acariciar.

cheroot [ʃə'ruːt] *n* cheruto *m.*

cherry ['tʃeri] **1** *adj* (de) color rojo cereza. **2** *n* (*fruit*) cereza *f;* (*tree, wood*) cerezo *m;* (*colour*) rojo *m* cereza.

cherry brandy ['tʃeri'brændi] *n* aguardiente *m* de cerezas.

cherry-red ['tʃeri'red] *adj* (de) color rojo cereza.

cherry tree ['tʃeritriː] *n* cerezo *m.*

cherub ['tʃerəb] *n* querubín *m.*

cherubic [tʃe'ruːbik] *adj* querúbico.

chervil ['tʃəːvil] *n* cerafolio *m.*

chess [tʃes] *n* ajedrez *m.*

chessboard ['tʃesbɔːd] *n* tablero *m* de ajedrez.

chessman ['tʃesmæn] *n, pl* —**men** [men] pieza *f,* trebejo *m,* ficha *f.*

chessplayer [tʃespleiə*] *n* ajedrecista *mf.*

chest [tʃest] *n* (**a**) (*Anat*) pecho *m;* — **trouble** enfermedad *f* del pecho; **to get something off one's** — (*fam*) desahogarse, confesar algo de una vez; **to have a cold on the** — tener el pecho resfriado.

(**b**) (*box*) cofre *m,* arca *f,* cajón *m;* — **of drawers** cómoda *f.*

chest protector ['tʃestprə,tektə*] *n* pechera *f.*

chestnut ['tʃesnʌt] **1** *adj* castaño.

2 *n* (*fruit*) castaña *f;* (*tree, wood*) castaño *m;* (*horse*) caballo *m* castaño; (*joke*) chiste *m* viejo; **to pull the** —**s out of the fire for someone** sacar a uno las castañas del fuego.

chestnut tree ['tʃesnʌtriː] *n* castaño *m.*

chesty ['tʃesti] *adj* que tiene el pecho resfriado, congestionado.

cheval glass [ʃə'vælglɑːs] *n* psique *f*.

chevron ['ʃevrən] *n* (Mil) galón *m*; (Her) cheurón *m*.

chew [tʃuː] *vt* mascar, masticar; **to — something over** rumiar algo; **to — up** grass etc estropear; person (fam) dar un rapapolvo a.

chewing gum ['tʃuːiŋgʌm] *n* chicle *m*.

chiaroscuro [ki,ɑːrəs'kuərəu] *n* claroscuro *m*.

chic [ʃiːk] 1 *adj* elegante. 2 *n* chic *m*, elegancia *f*.

chicanery [ʃi'keinəri] *n* embustes *mpl*, sofismas *mpl*; **a piece of —** un sofisma, una superchería, un subterfugio.

chick [tʃik] *n* pollito *m*, polluelo *m*; (fam) chica *f*.

chicken ['tʃikin] 1 *n* gallina *f*, pollo *m*; (as food) pollo *m*; **to be —** (sl) dejarse intimidar, acobardarse, cejar; **she's no —** ya no es una pollita; **don't count your —s before they're hatched** no hagas las cuentas de la lechera.
2 *vi*: **to — out** (fam) retirarse miedoso, amedrentarse; dejarse intimidar.

chicken farmer ['tʃikin,fɑːmə*] *n* avicultor *m*.

chicken farming ['tʃikin,fɑːmiŋ] *n* avicultura *f*.

chicken feed ['tʃikinfiːd] *n* (fig) pan *m* comido.

chicken-hearted ['tʃikin,hɑːtid] *adj* cobarde, gallina.

chickenpox ['tʃikinpɔks] *n* varicela *f*.

chicken run ['tʃikinrʌn] *n* corral *m*, gallinero *m*.

chickpea ['tʃikpiː] *n* garbanzo *m*.

chickweed ['tʃikwiːd] *n* pamplina *f*.

chicory ['tʃikəri] *n* achicoria *f*.

chide [tʃaid] (irr: pret **chid**, ptp **chidden** or **chid**) *vt* (lit) reprender.

chief [tʃiːf] 1 *adj* principal, primero, mayor, capital; official en jefe, mayor.
2 *n* jefe *m* (also fam); jerarca *m*; (of tribe) jefe *m*, cacique *m*; **— of staff** jefe *m* del estado mayor; **— of state** jefe *m* de estado; **. . . in —** . . . en jefe.

chiefly ['tʃiːfli] *adv* principalmente, sobre todo.

chieftain ['tʃiːftən] *n* jefe *m*, cacique *m*.

chiffon ['ʃifɔn] *n* gasa *f*, soplillo *m*.

chignon ['ʃiːnjɔ̃ːŋ] *n* rodete *m*, moño *m*.

chilblain ['tʃilblein] *n* sabañón *m*.

child [tʃaild] *n*, *pl* **children** ['tʃildrən] niño *m*, a *f*; (as offspring) hijo *m*, a *f*; **to be with —** estar encinta; **to get someone with —** dejar a una encinta; **I have known him from a —** le conozco desde niño.

childbearing ['tʃaild,beəriŋ] 1 *attr*: **— women** las mujeres fecundas, las mujeres que producen hijos; **women of — age** las mujeres de edad para tener hijos.
2 *n* (act) parto *m*; (as statistic) natalidad *f*.

childbed ['tʃaildbed] *n* parturición *f*.

childbirth ['tʃaildbəː θ] *n* parto *m*; **to die in —** morir de sobreparto.

childhood ['tʃaildhud] *n* niñez *f*, infancia *f*; **to be in one's second —** chochear; **from —** desde niño.

childish ['tʃaildiʃ] *adj* pueril, aniñado; **don't be so —!** ¡no seas niño!

childishly ['tʃaildiʃli] *adv* de modo pueril; **she behaved —** se portó como una niña.

childishness ['tʃaildiʃnis] *n* puerilidad *f*.

childless ['tʃaildlis] *adj* sin hijos.

childlike ['tʃaildlaik] *adj* como de niño.

children ['tʃildrən] *npl of* **child**.

child's play ['tʃaildzplei] *n* (fig): **it's —** es cosa de coser y cantar (to para).

Chile ['tʃili] Chile *m*.

Chilean ['tʃilian] 1 *adj* chileno. 2 *n* chileno *m*, a *f*.

chili ['tʃili] *n* chile *m*.

chill [tʃil] 1 *adj* frío. 2 *n* frío *m*; (Med) escalofrío *m*; resfriado *m*; **a — of horror** un estremecimiento de horror; **to cast a — over a meeting** hacer que se enfríe el ambiente de una reunión; **to catch a —** resfriarse; **to take the — off** liquid, room calentar un poco.
3 *vt* enfriar; (with fear etc) helar; meat etc congelar; **to be —ed to the bone** estar helado hasta los huesos.

chill(i)ness ['tʃil(i)nis] *n* frío *m*; (fig) frialdad *f*.

chilly ['tʃili] *adj* (a) frío; **it is (very) —** hace (mucho) frío; **I am feeling —** tengo frío.
(b) (sensitive to cold) friolento, friolero; atmosphere frío, glacial.

chime [tʃaim] 1 *n* (set) juego *m* de campanas, carillón *m*; (peal) repique *m*, campanada *f*.
2 *vt* repicar; **to — six** dar las seis.
3 *vi* repicar, sonar; **to — in** hablar inesperadamente, (pej) entrometerse; **to — in with** decir inesperadamente; (harmonize) estar en armonía con.

chimera [kai'miərə] *n* quimera *f*.

chimerical [kai'merikəl] *adj* quimérico.

chimney ['tʃimni] *n* chimenea *f*; (of lamp) tubo *m* de lámpara; (Mountaineering) olla *f*, cañón *m*.

chimney pot ['tʃimnipɔt] *n* tubo *m* de chimenea.

chimney stack ['tʃimnistæk] *n* fuste *m* de chimenea.

chimney sweep ['tʃimniswiːp] *n* deshollinador *m*, limpiachimeneas *m*.

chimpanzee [,tʃimpæn'ziː] *n* chimpancé *m*.

chin [tʃin] 1 *n* barba *f*, barbilla *f*, mentón *m*; **double —** papada *f*; **to keep one's — up** no desanimarse; **keep your — up!** ¡ánimo! 2 *vi* (fam) charlar.

china ['tʃainə] *n* porcelana *f*, china *f*; (used loosely) loza *f*.

China ['tʃainə] China *f*.

china clay ['tʃainə'klei] *n* barro *m* de porcelana, arcilla *f* figulina.

Chinaman ['tʃainəmən] *n*, *pl* **—men** [mən] chino *m*.

chinatown ['tʃainətaun] *n* (US fam) barrio *m* chino.

chinch bug ['tʃintʃbʌg] *n* (US) chinche *m or f* de los cereales.

chinchilla [tʃin'tʃilə] *n* chinchilla *f*.

Chinese ['tʃai'niːz] 1 *adj* chino. 2 *n* chino *m*, a *f*. 3 *n* (language) chino *m*.

chink[1] [tʃiŋk] *n* (slit) grieta *f*, hendedura *f*, resquicio *m*; **— in one's armour** punto *m* débil.

chink[2] [tʃiŋk] 1 *n* (sound) sonido *m* metálico, tintineo *m*. 2 *vt* hacer sonar. 3 *vi* sonar (a metal), tintinear.

Chink [tʃiŋk] *n* (sl) chino *m*.

chintz [tʃints] *n* zaraza *f*.

chinwag ['tʃinwæg] 1 *n* charla *f*. 2 *vi* charlar.

chip [tʃip] 1 *n* (splinter) astilla *f*, pedacito *m*; (of stone) lasca *f*; (mark on surface) saltadura *f*, desportilladura *f*; (at poker) ficha *f*; **—s** patatas *fpl* fritas, patatas *fpl* a la española; **he's a — off the old block** de tal palo tal astilla; **to have a — on one's shoulder** ser un resentido.
2 *vt* astillar, desportillar; surface picar; sculpture cincelar; (sl) tomar el pelo a.
3 *vi* astillarse; (surface) picarse, desconcharse; **to — in** cortar, interrumpir (with diciendo).

chipboard ['tʃipbɔːd] *n* (US) cartón *m* (de baja calidad).

chipmunk ['tʃipmʌŋk] *n* ardilla *f* listada.

chiropodist [ki'rɔpədist] *n* pedicuro *m*, podólogo *m*, callista *mf*.

chiropody [ki'rɔpədi] *n* pedicura *f*.

chirp [tʃəːp] 1 *n* pío *m*, gorjeo *m*; (of cricket) chirrido *m*. 2 *vi* piar, gorjear; (cricket) chirriar.

chirpy ['tʃəːpi] *adj* (fam) alegre.

chirrup ['tʃirəp] see **chirp**.

chisel ['tʃizl] 1 *n* (for wood) formón *m*, escoplo *m*; (for stone) cincel *m*. 2 *vt* escoplear; cincelar; (sl) timar.

chiseller ['tʃizlə*] *n* (sl) timador *m*.

chit[1] [tʃit] *n*: **a — of a girl** una muchacha no muy crecida.

chit[2] [tʃit] *n* nota *f*, esquela *f*.

chitchat ['tʃittʃæt] *n* chismes *mpl*, habladurías *fpl*.

chitterlings ['tʃitəliŋz] *npl* menudos *mpl* de cerdo (comestibles).

chitty ['tʃiti] *n* = **chit**[2].

chivalresque [ʃivəl'resk] *adj*, **chivalric** [ʃi'vælrik] *adj* caballeresco.

chivalrous ['ʃivələs] *adj* caballeroso.

chivalrously ['ʃivələsli] *adv* caballerosamente.

chivalry ['ʃivəlri] *n* (institution) caballería *f*; (spirit) caballerosidad *f*.

chive [tʃaiv] *n* cebollino *m*.

chivvy ['tʃivi] *vt* (fam) perseguir, atormentar, acosar; **to — someone into doing something** no dejar en paz a uno hasta que haga algo.

chloral ['klɔrəl] *n* cloral *m*.

chloride ['klɔːraid] *n* cloruro *m*; **— of lime** cloruro *m* de cal.

chlorinate ['klɔrineit] *vt* clorinar.

chlorine ['klɔːriːn] *n* cloro *m*.

chloroform ['klɔrəfɔːm] 1 *n* cloroformo *m*. 2 *vt* cloroformizar.

chlorophyl(l) ['klɔrəfil] *n* clorofila *f*.

chock [tʃɔk] 1 *n* calzo *m*, cuña *f*. 2 *vt* calzar, acuñar, poner calzos a.

chock-a-block ['tʃɔkə'blɔk] *adj*, **chock-full** ['tʃɔk'ful] *adj* de bote en bote; **— of, — with** atestado de, totalmente lleno de.

chocolate ['tʃɔklit] *n* (in bar, for drinking) chocolate *m*; **a —** un bombón; **a box of —s** una caja de bombones.

choice [tʃɔis] 1 *adj* selecto, escogido; quality, wine etc fino.
2 *n* (act of choosing) elección *f*, selección *f*; (thing chosen) preferencia *f*; (range to choose from) surtido *m*, serie *f* de posibilidades; **for —** preferentemente; **he did it but not from —** lo hizo pero de mala gana; **the house of my —** mi casa predilecta; **the prince married the girl of his —** el príncipe se casó con

una joven que él había elegido; **it was not a free —** no estuvo libre para elegir a su gusto; **we have a wide — (***Comm***) tenemos un gran surtido; you have á wide —** Vd tiene muchas posibilidades; **to have no —** no tener alternativa; **he had no — but to go** no tuvo más remedio que ir; **to take one's —** elegir; **take your —!** ¡lo que Vd quiera!

choir ['kwaiə*] *n* coro *m*; coros *mpl*; orfeón *m*; coral *f*; (*Archit*) coro *m*.

choirboy ['kwaiəbɔi] *n* niño *m* de coro.

choirmaster ['kwaiə,mɑːstə*] *n* maestro *m* de coros.

choke [tʃəuk] **1** *n* (*Mech*) obturador *m*, cierre *m*; (*Aut*) estrangulador *m*, (*loosely*) aire *m*.
　　2 *vt* **pipe** *etc* atascar, obstruir; (*person (to death*)) estrangular, ahogar, sofocar; **in a voice —d with emotion** en una voz embargada (*or* empañada) por la emoción; **a canal —d with weeds** un canal atascado de hierbas; **to — back** contener, ahogar; **to — someone off** (*fam*) echar un rapapolvo a uno.
　　3 *vi* sofocarse (*also* **to — to death**); (*over food*) atragantarse; **no poder respirar; to — on a bone** atragantarse con un hueso; **to — with laughter** desternillarse de risa.

choker ['tʃəukə*] *n* (*Mech*) obturador *m*; (*hum*) cuello *m* alto.

choky ['tʃəuki] *n* (*sl*) trena *f*.

cholera ['kɔlərə] *n* cólera *m*.

choleric ['kɔlərik] *adj* colérico.

choose [tʃuːz] (*irr*: *pret* **chose,** *ptp* **chosen**) **1** *vt* elegir, escoger; **team** *etc* seleccionar; **he was chosen leader** fue elegido caudillo.
　　2 *vi*: **to — between** elegir entre; **there is nothing to — between them** no les veo diferencia alguna; **there are 5 kinds to — from** a elegir entre 5 tipos; **to — to + *infin*** optar por + *infin*; **I'll do it when I —** lo haré cuando me dé la gana; **if I don't — to** si no quiero; **he cannot — but (to) go** no tiene más remedio que ir; **you cannot — but admire it** Vd no puede menos de admirarlo.

choos(e)y ['tʃuːzi] *adj* (*fam*) melindroso, delicado; **he's a bit — about it** en esto es algo difícil de contentar; **I'm — about whom I go out with** yo no salgo con un cualquiera.

chop [tʃɔp] **1** *n* (*blow*) golpe *m* cortante; (*meat*) chuleta *f*; **—s** boca *f*, labios *mpl*; **—s and changes** cambios *mpl*; **to get the —** (*fam*) ser despedido.
　　2 *vt* cortar, tajar; (*also* **to — up**) desmenuzar, **meat** picar; **to — down tree** talar; **to — off** tronchar, separar.
　　3 *vi*: **to — and change** (*wind*) virar, (*person*) cambiar constantemente de opinión.

chop-chop ['tʃɔp'tʃɔp] *interj* (*sl*) ¡en seguida!, ¡ya voy!

chophouse ['tʃɔphaus] *n* restaurante *m* económico.

chopper ['tʃɔpə*] *n* hacha *f*; (*butcher's*) tajadera *f*, cuchilla *f*; (*Mil sl*) helicóptero *m*.

chopping block ['tʃɔpiŋblɔk] *n* tajo *m*.

chopping board ['tʃɔpiŋ,bɔːd] *n* tajadera *f*.

chopping knife ['tʃɔpiŋ,naif] *n* tajadera *f*.

choppy ['tʃɔpi] *adj* **sea** picado, agitado.

chopsticks ['tʃɔpstiks] *npl* palillos *mpl* (de los chinos, para comer).

choral ['kɔːrəl] *adj* coral; **— society** orfeón *m*.

chorale [kɔ'rɑːl] *n* coral *m*.

chord [kɔːd] *n* (*string, Anat, Math*) cuerda *f*; (*group of notes, sound*) acorde *m*; **to strike the right —** juzgar bien el ambiente (de una reunión *etc*).

chore [tʃɔə*] *n* faena *f*, tarea *f*, tarea *f* necesaria pero falta de interés, trabajo *m* rutinario; **—s** (*at home*) quehaceres *mpl* domésticos.

choreographer [,kɔri'ɔgrəfə*] *n* coreógrafo *m*.

choreography [,kɔri'ɔgrəfi] *n* coreografía *f*.

chorister ['kɔristə*] *n* corista *mf*.

chortle ['tʃɔːtl] **1** *n* risa *f* alegre. **2** *vi* reírse alegremente; (*pej*) reírse satisfecho (*over por*).

chorus ['kɔːrəs] **1** *n* (*Mus*) coro *m*; (*of chorus girls*) conjunto *m*; (*repeated words*) estribillo *m*; **a — of praise greeted the book** el libro recibió la aprobación de todos, el libro se mereció las alabanzas de todos; **a — of shouts greeted this** todos gritaron a la vez al oír esto; **in — en coro; to sing in —** cantar en coro; **to join in the —** cantar el estribillo.
　　2 *vi* cantar (*etc*) en coro; (*answer*) contestar todos a una voz.

chorus girl ['kɔːrəsgəːl] *n* corista *f*, viceple *f*.

chose [tʃəuz] *pret of* **choose.**

chosen ['tʃəuzn] **1** *ptp of* **choose. 2** *adj* preferido, predilecto; **the — people** el pueblo escogido; **one of the —** uno de los elegidos.

chough [tʃʌf] *n* chova *f* piquirroja.

chow¹ [tʃau] *n* (*dog*) chao *m*.

chow² [tʃau] *n* (*sl*) comida *f*.

chowder ['tʃaudə*] *n* (*US*) pescado *m* con legumbres (*etc*); (*soup*) sopa *f* de pescado.

Christ [kraist] *m* Cristo; **—!** ¡Dios mío!

christen ['krisn] *vt* bautizar (*also fig*).

Christendom ['krisndəm] *n* cristiandad *f*.

christening ['krisniŋ] *n* bautizo *m*, bautismo *m*.

Christian ['kristiən] **1** *adj* cristiano; **name** de pila. **2** *n* cristiano *m*, a *f*.

Christianity [,kristi'æniti] *n* cristianismo *m*.

Christianize ['kristiənaiz] *vt* cristianizar.

Christlike ['kraistlaik] *adj* parecido a Jesucristo.

Christmas ['krisməs] **1** *n* Navidad *f*; (**ie — period**) Navidades *fpl*; **at — por Navidades; merry —!** ¡felices Pascuas!; **Father —** Padre *m* Noel, (*Spanish equivalent bringing presents on 6 January*) Reyes *mpl* Magos.
　　2 *attr* navideño, de Navidad; **— Day** día *m* de Navidad; **— Eve** Nochebuena *f*.

Christmas box ['krisməsbɔks] *n* aguinaldo *m*.

Christmas card ['krisməskɑːd] *n* crismas *m*, tarjeta *f* de Navidad (*Acad*).

Christmas time ['krisməstaim] *n* Navidades *fpl*.

Christmas tree ['krisməstriː] *n* árbol *m* de Navidad.

Christopher ['kristəfə*] *m* Cristóbal.

chromatic [krə'mætik] *adj* cromático.

chrome [krəum] *n* cromo *m*; **— steel** acerocromo *m*; **— yellow** amarillo *m* de cromo.

chromium ['krəumiəm] *n* cromo *m*.

chromium-plated ['krəumiəm,pleitid] *adj* cromado.

chromium-plating ['krəumiəm,pleitiŋ] *n* cromado *m*.

chromosome ['krəuməsəum] *n* cromosoma *m*.

chronic ['krɔnik] *adj* crónico; (*fig*) constante, inextirpable; (*fam*) horrible, malísimo.

chronicle ['krɔnikl] **1** *n* crónica *f*; **C—s** (*Bib*) Crónicas *fpl*. **2** *vt* historiar; registrar, describir.

chronicler ['krɔniklə*] *n* cronista *mf*.

chronological [,krɔnə'lɔdʒikəl] *adj* cronológico.

chronologically [,krɔnə'lɔdʒikəli] *adv* por orden cronológico.

chronology [krə'nɔlədʒi] *n* cronología *f*.

chronometer [krə'nɔmitə*] *n* cronómetro *m*.

chrysalis ['krisəlis] *n* crisálida *f*.

chrysanthemum [kri'sænθəməm] *n* crisantemo *m*.

chub [tʃʌb] *n* cacho *m*.

chubby ['tʃʌbi] *adj* rechoncho, gordinflón; **face** mofletudo.

chuck¹ [tʃʌk] **1** *n*: **— under the chin** mamola *f*; **to get the —** (*sl*) ser despedido.
　　2 *vt* (*throw*) lanzar, arrojar; (*hand*) pasar, dar; (*give up*) abandonar; **— it!** ¡basta ya!, ¡déjalo!; **I'm thinking of —ing it** pienso en la conveniencia de dejarlo; **so I had to —** it así que tuve que abandonarlo; **to — someone under the chin** dar la mamola a uno; **to — away** tirar, **money** despilfarrar, **chance** desperdiciar; **to — out rubbish** tirar, **person** poner de patitas en la calle, **person from work** *etc* despedir, dar el pasaporte a; **to — up** abandonar, renunciar a.

chuck² [tʃʌk] = **chock.**

chucker-out ['tʃʌkər'aut] *n* (*fam*) el forzudo que echa a los alborotadores de un café *etc*.

chuckle ['tʃʌkl] **1** *n* risita *f*, risa *f* sofocada; **we had a good —** over that nos reímos bastante con eso.
　　2 *vi* reírse entre dientes, soltar una risita; **to — at, to — over** reírse con.

chuffed [tʃʌft] *adj* (*sl*) contento, alegre; **he was pretty — about it** estaba la mar de contento.

chug [tʃʌg] *vi* hacer ruidos explosivos repetidos; (*Rail*) resoplar; **to — along** (*Aut*) ir despacio, avanzar sin gran velocidad; (*fig*) ir tirando; **the train —ged past** pasó el tren resoplando.

chum [tʃʌm] *n* **1** compinche *m*, compañero *m*; (*child*) amiguito *m*, a *f*; **to be great —s** ser íntimos amigos; **to be —s with someone** ser amigo de uno.
　　2 *vi*: **to — up** hacerse amigos; **to — up with someone** hacerse amigo de uno.

chummy ['tʃʌmi] *adj* familiar, muy afable; **they're very —** son muy amigos; **he's very — with the boss** es muy amigo del jefe.

chump [tʃʌmp] *n* (*fam*) (a) (*head*) cabeza *f*; **to be off one's —** estar chiflado. (b) (*idiot*) imbécil *m*, melón *m*; **you —!** ¡imbécil!

chunk [tʃʌŋk] *n* pedazo *m*, trozo *m*.

chunky ['tʃʌŋki] *adj* (*fam*) fornido.

church [tʃəːtʃ] *n* iglesia *f*; (*esp non-Catholic*) templo *m*; **C— of England** Iglesia *f* Anglicana; **High C—** *sector de la Iglesia Anglicana de tendencia conservadora;* **Low C—** *sector de la Iglesia Anglicana de tendencia más protestante;* **Mother C—** la santa Madre Iglesia; **mother —** iglesia *f* metropolitana; **to go to —** (*Protestant*) ir al oficio, asistir al culto,

(*Catholic*) ir a misa; **to go into the —** hacerse cura (*or pastor etc*).

churchgoer ['tʃəːtʃ͵gəuə*] n fiel mf (que practica una religión).

churchman ['tʃəːtʃmən] n, pl **-men** [mən] sacerdote m, eclesiástico m.

churchwarden ['tʃəːtʃ͵wɔːdn] n capiller m.

churchy ['tʃəːtʃi] adj (*fam*) beato; que va mucho a la iglesia, que toma muy en serio las cosas de la iglesia.

churchyard ['tʃəːtʃjɑːd] n cementerio m, campo m santo.

churl [tʃəːl] n (*fig*) patán m.

churlish ['tʃəːliʃ] adj *person* poco afable, grosero, hosco; *remark* nada amistoso; **it would be — not to thank him** sería muy maleducado no darle las gracias.

churlishly ['tʃəːliʃli] adv *behave etc* groseramente, sin educación.

churlishness ['tʃəːliʃnis] n grosería f, hosquedad; conducta f (*etc*) poco amistosa; mala educación f.

churn [tʃəːn] **1** n (*for milk*) lechera f; (*for butter*) mantequera f.

2 vt *butter* batir (*or* hacer) en una mantequera; (*fig*: *also* **to — up**) revolver, agitar.

3 vi revolverse, agitarse.

chute [ʃuːt] n (*Tech*) tolva f, vertedor m, rampa f de caída; (*in playground, swimming pool*) tobogán m; (*Aer, fam*) paracaídas m.

chutney ['tʃʌtni] n salsa f picante.

cicada [si'kɑːdə] n cigarra f.

Cicero ['sisərəu] m Cicerón.

cicerone [͵tʃitʃə'rəuni] n cicerone m.

Ciceronian [͵sisə'rəuniən] adj ciceroniano.

cider ['saidə*] n sidra f.

cider-press ['saidəpres] n lagar m para hacer sidra.

cider vinegar ['saidə'vinəgə*] n vinagre m de sidra.

cigar [si'gɑː*] n puro m.

cigar case [si'gɑːkeis] n cigarrera f.

cigarette [͵sigə'ret] n cigarrillo m, pitillo m, cigarro m.

cigarette case [͵sigə'ret͵keis] n pitillera f, petaca f.

cigarette end [͵sigə'ret͵end] n colilla f de cigarrillo.

cigarette holder [͵sigə'ret͵həuldə*] n boquilla f.

cigarette lighter [͵sigə'ret͵laitə*] n mechero m, encendedor m.

cigarette paper [͵sigə'ret͵peipə*] n papel m de fumar.

cinch [sintʃ] n (*sl*): **it's a —** es muy fácil; es cosa segura.

cinder ['sində*] n carbonilla f; **—s** cenizas fpl; **to be burned to a —** quedar carbonizado.

Cinderella [͵sində'relə] f la Cenicienta.

cinder track ['sindətræk] n pista f de ceniza.

cine-camera ['sini'kæmərə] n cámara f cinematográfica.

cinema ['sinəmə] n cine m.

Cinemascope ['sinəməskəup] n (*Protected Trade Name*) cinemascopio m.

cinematograph [͵sini'mætəgrɑːf] n cinematógrafo m.

cine-projector [͵siniprə'dʒektə*] n proyector m de películas.

cinerama [͵sinə'rɑːmə] n cinerama m.

cinerary ['sinərəri] adj cinerario.

cinnabar ['sinəbɑː*] n cinabrio m.

cinnamon ['sinəmən] n canela f.

cipher ['saifə*] **1** n (o) cero m; (*any number, initials, code*) cifra f; **he's a —** es un cero a la izquierda; **in —** en cifra.

2 vt (*code*) cifrar; (*Math*) calcular.

circle ['səːkl] **1** n (a) círculo m; (*Theat*) anfiteatro m; (*set of people*) grupo m; **turning —** dirección f cerrada; **vicious —** círculo m vicioso; **an inner — of ministers** un grupo interior de ministros; **within the family —** dentro del grupo familiar; **John and his —** Juan y sus amigos, Juan y su peña; **to be one of the charmed —** formar parte del grupo especial, ser uno de los escogidos; **the wheel has come full —** la rueda ha dado una vuelta completa.

(b) **—s** (*fig*): **in certain —s** en ciertos medios; **in business —s** en medios comerciales; **to move in fashionable —s** frecuentar la buena sociedad; **to go round in small —s** perderse en detalles nimios.

2 vt (*be round*) cercar, rodear; (*move round*) girar alrededor de, dar la vuelta a; *part of body* ceñir, rodear; **the lion —d its prey** el león se movió alrededor de la presa; **the cosmonaut —d the earth** el cosmonauta dio la vuelta al mundo; **the aircraft —d the town twice** el avión dio dos vueltas sobre la ciudad.

3 vi dar vueltas.

circlet ['səːklit] n anillo m; adorno m en forma de círculo.

circuit ['səːkit] n (*Elec etc*) circuito m; (*tour*) gira f; (*track*) pista f; (*lap by runner*) vuelta f; (*Law, approx*) distrito m.

circuit breaker ['səːkit͵breikə*] n cortacircuitos m.

circuitous [səː'kjuitəs] adj tortuoso, indirecto.

circular ['səːkjulə*] **1** adj circular; *tour* redondo. **2** n circular f.

circularize ['səːkjuləraiz] vt enviar circulares a.

circulate ['səːkjuleit] **1** vt poner en circulación; *letter, papers etc* hacer circular; *news* divulgar. **2** vi circular.

circulating ['səːkjuleitiŋ] adj circulante.

circulation [͵səːkju'leiʃən] n circulación f; (*number of papers printed*) tirada f; **— of the blood** circulación f sanguínea; **to put into —** poner en circulación.

circulatory [͵səːkju'leitəri] adj circulatorio.

circum ... ['səːkəm] circun..., circum...

circumcise ['səːkəmsaiz] vt circuncidar.

circumcision [͵səːkəm'siʒən] n circuncisión f.

circumference [sə'kʌmfərəns] n circunferencia f.

circumflex ['səːkəmfleks] n circunflejo m.

circumlocution [͵səːkəmlə'kjuːʃən] n circunlocución f, circunloquio m, rodeo m.

circumnavigate [͵səːkəm'nævigeit] vt circunnavegar.

circumnavigation ['səːkəm͵nævi'geiʃən] n circunnavegación f.

circumscribe ['səːkəmskraib] vt circunscribir; limitar, restringir.

circumspect ['səːkəmspekt] adj circunspecto, prudente.

circumspectly ['səːkəmspektli] adv prudentemente.

circumspection [͵səːkəm'spekʃən] n circunspección f, prudencia f.

circumstance ['səːkəmstəns] n (a) circunstancia f; **extenuating —s** circunstancias fpl atenuantes; **in (or under) the —s** en las circunstancias; **under no —s** de ninguna manera, bajo ningún concepto; **—s alter cases** las circunstancias cambian los casos; **were it not for the — that** si no fuera por la circunstancia de que; *see* **pomp**.

(b) **—s** (ie *economic situation*) **to be in easy —s** estar acomodado; **to be in narrow (or reduced) —s** vivir muy justo, vivir al borde del hambre; **what are your —s?** ¿cuál es su situación económica?; **if the family —s allow it** si lo permite la situación económica de la familia.

circumstantial [͵səːkəm'stænʃəl] adj *report* detallado, circunstanciado; *evidence* indiciario.

circumstantiate [͵səːkəm'stænʃieit] vt probar refiriendo todos los detalles.

circumvent [͵səːkəm'vent] vt burlar; *difficulty, obstacle* salvar.

circumvention [͵səːkəm'venʃən] n acción f de burlar (*or* salvar); **the — of this obstacle will not be easy** no va a ser fácil salvar este obstáculo.

circus ['səːkəs] n circo m; (*in town*) plaza f redonda, glorieta f.

cirrhosis [si'rəusis] n cirrosis f.

cirrus ['sirəs] n, pl **cirri** ['sirai] cirro m.

Cistercian [sis'təːʃən] **1** adj cisterciense; **— Order** Orden f del Cister. **2** n cisterciense m.

cistern ['sistən] n tanque m, depósito m; (*of WC*) cisterna f, depósito m; (*for hot water*) termo m; (*for rainwater*) aljibe m.

citadel ['sitədl] n ciudadela f; (*in Spain, freq*) alcázar m; (*fig*) reducto m.

citation [sai'teiʃən] n cita f; (*Law*) citación f; (*Mil*) mención f.

cite [sait] vt citar; (*Mil*) mencionar.

citizen ['sitizn] n ciudadano m, a f; (*in counting inhabitants etc*) habitante mf, vecino m, a f; **French —** súbdito m francés.

citizenry ['sitiznri] n ciudadanos mpl, ciudadanía f.

citizenship ['sitiznʃip] n ciudadanía f.

citrate ['sitreit] n citrato m.

citric ['sitrik] adj: **— acid** ácido m cítrico.

citron ['sitrən] n (*fruit*) cidra f; (*tree*) cidro m.

citrus ['sitrəs] n cidro m; **— fruits** agrios mpl.

city ['siti] **1** n ciudad f; **open —** ciudad f abierta; **the C—** el centro bursátil y bancario de Londres; **— editor** redactor encargado de las noticias financieras; **— page** sección de información financiera (en un periódico).

2 attr municipal, de la ciudad.

civet ['sivit] n algalia f.

civic ['sivik] adj cívico; municipal.

civics ['siviks] npl ciencia de los deberes y derechos del ciudadano.

civies ['siviz] npl (*US: fam*) = **civvies**.

civil ['sivl] adj civil; *defence* pasivo; (*polite*) cortés, atento; amable; **he was very — to me** fue muy cortés conmigo; **that's very — of you** es Vd muy amable; **be more —!** ¡hable Vd con más educación!

civilian [si'viliən] **1** adj (de) paisano; civil. **2** n civil mf, paisano m, a f.

civility [si'viliti] n (a) (politeness) cortesía f; amabilidad f; **lack of** — falta f de educación. (b) (polite remark) cortesía f, cumplido m.

civilization [‚sivilai'zeiʃən] n civilización f.

civilize ['sivilaiz] vt civilizar.

civilized ['sivilaizd] adj civilizado.

civilly ['sivili] adv cortésmente, atentamente.

civism ['sivizəm] n civismo m.

civvies ['siviz] npl (fam) traje m de paisano; **in** — vestido de paisano.

clack [klæk] vi (chatter) charlar, chismear; **this will make the tongues** — esto será tema para los chismosos.

clad [klæd] (arch) **1** pret and ptp of **clothe**. **2** adj: — in vestido de.

claim [kleim] **1** n (a) (in general, demand) reclamación f; (formally stated) petición f; **to have a** — **on someone** tener derecho a pedir algo a uno; **I think this has a** — **on your attention** creo que esto merece su atención; **I have many** —**s on my time** son muchas las cosas que ocupan el tiempo de que dispongo; **to lay** — **to** reclamar; **he put in a** — **for a rise** pidió que se le subiese el sueldo.

(b) (Law) demanda f (for de); **to put in a** — **for** entablar demanda de; **to state a** — presentar demanda; **you have no legal** — Vd no tiene derecho legal alguno.

(c) (pretension) pretensión f; (stated) afirmación f, declaración f; **his** — **turned out to be untrue** su declaración resultó ser falsa; **that's a big** — **to make** eso es mucho decir; **to make large** —**s for an invention** pretender que un invento tiene grandes ventajas.

(d) (Min) pertenencia f, concesión f.

2 vt (a) (demand as one's due) reclamar, exigir; **to** — **the right to vote** reclamar (or reivindicar) el derecho de votar; **to** — **something from someone** reclamar a uno la devolución de algo; **something else** —**ed her attention** otra cosa le llamó la atención; **death** —**ed him** se lo llevó la muerte.

(b) (Law) demandar; **to** — **damages from someone** reclamar a uno por daños.

(c) (profess, assert) pretender; **to** — **kinship with someone** pretender ser pariente de uno; **he** —**s to be her son** pretende ser su hijo; **he** —**s to have seen her** afirma haberla visto; **to** — **that** sostener que, afirmar que; **that's** —**ing a lot** eso es mucho decir.

claimant ['kleimənt] n (Law) demandante mf; (to throne) pretendiente m, a f.

clairvoyance [klɛə'vɔiəns] n clarividencia f, doble vista f.

clairvoyant(e) [klɛə'vɔiənt] n clarividente mf, vidente mf.

clam [klæm] n almeja f.

clamber ['klæmbə*] vi trepar, subir gateando (over sobre, up a).

clammy ['klæmi] adj frío y húmedo.

clamorous ['klæmərəs] adj clamoroso.

clamour, (US) clamor ['klæmə*] **1** n clamor m, clamoreo m, griterío m. **2** vi clamorear, vociferar; **to** — **for** clamar por, pedir a voces.

clamp [klæmp] **1** n (brace) abrazadera f; (eg in laboratory) grapa f; (Carpentry) tornillo m de banco, cárcel f; (Agr) ensilado m, montón m.

2 vt afianzar (or sujetar etc) con abrazadera; **he** —**ed it in his hand** lo agarró con la mano; **he** —**ed his hand down on it** lo sujetó firmemente con la mano.

3 vi: **to** — **down on** (fig) tratar de acabar con, restringir, suprimir.

clan [klæn] n clan m.

clandestine [klæn'destin] adj clandestino.

clang [klæŋ] **1** n sonido m metálico fuerte, estruendo m. **2** vt hacer sonar. **3** vi sonar, hacer estruendo; **the gate** —**ed shut** la puerta se cerró ruidosamente.

clanger ['klæŋə*] n (sl) plancha f; **to drop a** — tirarse una plancha, meter la pata.

clangorous ['klæŋgərəs] adj estrepitoso, estruendoso.

clangour, (US) clangor ['klæŋgə*] n estruendo m.

clank [klæŋk] **1** n sonido m metálico seco, golpeo m metálico.

2 vt hacer sonar.

3 vi sonar, hacer estruendo, rechinar metálico; **the train went** —**ing past** pasó el tren con estruendoso rechinar metálico.

clannish ['klæniʃ] adj exclusivista, con fuerte sentimiento de tribu.

clap¹ [klæp] **1** n (on shoulder) palmoteo m; (of the hands) palmada f; — **of thunder** trueno m seco, estampido m seco de trueno.

2 vt (a) (with hands) person, play, announcement aplaudir; **to** — **one's hands** batir las manos, dar palmadas, batir palmas; **to** — **someone on the back** dar a uno una palmada en la espalda.

(b) (place) poner; (put on) ponerse; **to** — **a hand over someone's mouth** tapar a uno la boca con la mano; **to** — **something shut** cerrar algo de golpe; **to** — **someone in jail** encarcelar a uno al instante.

3 vi aplaudir.

clap² [klæp] n (Med: fam) gonorrea f.

clapboard ['klæpbɔːd] n (US) chilla f.

clapper ['klæpə*] n badajo m.

clapping ['klæpiŋ] n aplausos mpl.

claptrap ['klæptræp] n faramalla f, farfulla f.

claque [klæk] n claque f.

claret ['klærət] n clarete m.

clarification [‚klærifi'keiʃən] n aclaración f.

clarify ['klærifai] vt aclarar.

clarinet [‚klæri'net] n clarinete m.

clarion ['klæriən] n (fig) toque m de trompeta.

clarity ['klæriti] n claridad f.

clash [klæʃ] **1** n (a) (noise) estruendo m, fragor m.

(b) (conflict) choque m; (Mil) encuentro m; (of opinions etc) desacuerdo m, conflicto m; — **of dates** coincidencia f de fechas; — **of wills** lucha f de voluntades; **timetable** — incompatibilidad f de horas; **verbal** — choque m verbal.

2 vt batir, golpear.

3 vi (Mil) encontrarse, batirse; (be opposed) pugnar (con), estar en pugna, chocar; (persons) pelearse, reñir; (colours) desentonar; (dates) coincidir; (opinions) estar en desacuerdo.

clasp [klɑːsp] **1** n (fastener) broche m, corchete m; (of box, necklace etc) cierre m; (of book) broche m, manecilla f; **with a** — **of the hand** con un apretón de manos.

2 vt (fasten) abrochar; (embrace) abrazar; hand apretar, estrechar; (in one's hand) tener asido, agarrar; **to** — **someone to one's bosom** estrechar a uno contra el pecho.

clasp knife ['klɑːspnaif] n navaja f.

class [klɑːs] **1** n clase f; **cabin** — clase f de cámara; **first** — primera clase f; **lower** —**es** clase f baja; **middle** —**es** clase f media; **upper** — clase f alta; **working** — clase f obrera; **social** — clase f social; **tourist** — clase f turista, (as fare) tarifa f turística; **a good** — **novel** una novela de buena calidad; **it's just not in the same** — no hay comparación entre los dos; **it's in a** — **by itself** tiene una neta superioridad, es único en su línea; **she's certainly got** — ella sí que tiene clase.

2 attr clasista, de clase(s).

3 vt clasificar.

class-conscious ['klɑːs'kɔnʃəs] adj consciente de las distinciones de clase.

class consciousness ['klɑːs'kɔnʃəsnis] n conciencia f de las distinciones de clase.

classic ['klæsik] **1** adj clásico. **2** n (person) autor m clásico; (work) obra f clásica; **the** —**s** las obras clásicas; —**s** (Univ etc) clásicas fpl.

classical ['klæsikəl] adj clásico; — **scholar** erudito m en lenguas clásicas.

classicism ['klæsisizəm] n clasicismo m.

classifiable ['klæsifaiəbl] adj clasificable.

classification [‚klæsifi'keiʃən] n clasificación f.

classified ['klæsifaid] adj information secreto; — **advertisement** anuncio m por palabras.

classify ['klæsifai] vt clasificar (in, into en; under letter B en la B).

classmate ['klɑːsmeit] n compañero m de clase, compañera f de clase.

classroom ['klɑːsrum] n aula f, clase f.

class struggle ['klɑːs'strʌgl] n lucha f de clases.

class war ['klɑːs'wɔː*] n lucha f de clases.

classy ['klɑːsi] adj (fam) de buen tono, muy pera.

clatter ['klætə*] **1** n ruido m, estruendo m; (of plates) choque m; (of hooves) trápala f; (hammering) martilleo m.

2 vi hacer ruido, hacer estruendo; (hooves, feet) trapalear; (metal etc) guachapear; **to come** —**ing down** caer ruidosamente; **to** — **down the stairs** bajar ruidosamente la escalera.

clause [klɔːz] n cláusula f; (Gram) oración f; **saving** — cláusula f que contiene una salvedad.

claustrophobia [‚klɔːstrə'fəubiə] n claustrofobia f.

claustrophobic [‚klɔːstrə'fəubik] adj person que padece claustrofobia; feeling de claustrofobia; situation que produce claustrofobia.

clavichord ['klævikɔːd] n clavicordio m.

clavicle ['klævikl] n clavícula f.

claw [klɔː] **1** n (Zool) garra f, (of cat) uña f, (of lobster) pinza f; (Tech) garfio m, gancho m; —**s** (fam) dedos mpl, mano *f*; **to get one's —s into someone** tener inquina a uno; **get your —s off that!** ¡fuera las manos!; **to show one's —s** sacar las uñas.

2 *vt, also* **3** *vi*: **to — at** arañar; (*tear*) desgarrar.

claw-hammer [klɔ:'hæmə*] *n* martillo *m* de orejas, martillo *m* sacaclavos.

clay [kleɪ] *n* arcilla *f*; **potter's —** arcilla *f* de alfarería; **— pigeon** pichón *m* de barro.

clayey ['kleɪɪ] *adj* arcilloso.

clean [kli:n] **1** *adj* (*not dirty*) limpio; (*clear-cut*) neto, distinto, bien definido; (*shapely*) bien formado; (*unobstructed*) despejado; (*adroit*) diestro, elegante; (*pure*) decente; **as — as a new pin** como una plata; **to come —** (*sl*) confesarlo todo, desembuchar.

2 *adv* enteramente; **he cut — through it** lo cortó de un golpe; **it cuts — across tradition** esto corta netamente la tradición; **to get — away** escaparse sin dejar rastro; **the fish jumped — out of the net** el pez saltó fuera de la red.

3 *n* limpia *f*, limpiadura *f*; **to give the car a —** limpiar el coche.

4 *vt* limpiar; asear; *streets* barrer; (*dry-clean*) lavar al seco; **to — out** limpiar vaciando; **to — out a box** limpiar el interior de una caja; **it —ed us out** (*sl*) nos dejó sin blanca; **we were —ed out** quedamos limpios; **to — up** limpiar, asear; (*fig*) *play etc* suprimir los pasajes verdes de, *area of town* limpiar; **they're trying to — up television** tratan de hacer más decentes los programas de televisión; **to — up after someone** limpiar lo que ha ensuciado otro; **we —ed up £50** (*sl*) sacamos 50 libras de ganancia.

clean-cut ['kli:n'kʌt] *adj* (a) claro, bien definido, preciso; *outline* nítido. (b) *person* de buen parecer, de tipo elegante.

cleaner ['kli:nə*] *n* asistenta *f*, mujer *f* de la limpieza; **—'s** (*shop*) tintorería *f*.

cleaning ['kli:nɪŋ] *n* limpia *f*, limpiadura *f*.

cleanliness ['klenlɪnɪs] *n* limpieza *f* (*habitual*), aseo *m*.

cleanly ['klenlɪ] *adj* limpio, aseado.

cleanly ['kli:nlɪ] *adv* limpiamente; (*adroitly*) diestramente, con destreza.

cleanness ['kli:nnɪs] *n* limpieza *f*, aseo *m*.

cleanse [klenz] *vt* limpiar (*of* de).

cleanser ['klenzə*] *n* agente *m* de limpieza, producto *m* químico para la limpieza.

clean-shaven ['kli:n'ʃeɪvn] *adj* sin barba ni bigote, carilampiño.

cleanup ['kli:nʌp] *n* limpia *f*, limpiadura *f*.

clear [klɪə*] **1** *adj* (a) (*transparent, audible, distinct, unambiguous, obvious*) claro; *sky, surface* despejado; *air* transparente; *conscience* limpio, tranquilo; *mind* penetrante, despejado; *majority* absoluto, neto; *round* (*Sport*) sin penalizaciones; **as — as crystal** más claro que el agua; **as — as day** más claro que el sol; **it is — that** está claro que; **is that —?** ¿comprende?; **I wish to make it — that** quiero subrayar que; **a — case of murder** un caso evidente de homicidio.

(b) (*certain*) **I'm not — whether** yo no sé a punto fijo si; **he was perfectly — that he did not intend to go** dijo de modo tajante que no pensaba ir; **are we — that we want this?** ¿estamos seguros de que queremos esto?

(c) (*complete*) entero, completo; **3 — days** 3 días completos; **£3 — profit** una ganancia neta de 3 libras; **to win by a — head** ganar por una cabeza larga.

(d) (*free*) **— of** libre de; **to be — of debt** estar libre de deudas.

2 *adv* claramente; **I can hear you loud and — le** oigo perfectamente; **to get — away** escaparse sin dejar rastro alguno; **to get — of** deshacerse de; **when we get — of London** cuando estemos fuera de Londres; **to steer — of** evitar cualquier contacto con.

3 *n*: **to be in the —** (*of debt*) estar libre de deudas; (*of suspicion*) quedar fuera de toda sospecha; (*of danger*) estar fuera de peligro.

4 *vt* (a) *place, surface, football* despejar; *site, woodland* desmontar; *debt, stock* liquidar; *court* desocupar, desalojar de público; *profit* sacar (una ganancia de); *cheque* pasar por un banco; **to — a space for** hacer un sitio para; **to — the table** levantar la mesa; **to — one's throat** carraspear, aclarar la voz; **to — a ship for action** alistar un buque para el combate; **to — a way for** abrir camino para; **to — away** quitar; **to — out** limpiar, vaciar, quitar; **to — up** (*clean*) limpiar, asear; (*arrange*) arreglar; *food* comerse; *doubt* resolver; *difficulty* aclarar.

(b) (*jump over*) salvar, saltar por encima de; **to — 2 metres** saltar 2 metros; (*avoid touching*)

pasar sin tocar; **the plane just —ed the roof** el avión por poco no tocó el tejado.

(c) *suspect* absolver, probar la inocencia de; **you will have to be —ed by Security** será necesario que le acredite la Seguridad; **the plan will have to be —ed with the chief** el proyecto tendrá que ser aprobado por el jefe.

5 *vi* (*liquid*) aclararse; (*weather*) despejarse; (*Sport*) despejar; **to — away** (*after meal*) quitar los platos; **to — off, to — out** irse, largarse, desaparecer; **— off!** ¡fuera de aquí!

6 *vr*: **to — oneself of a charge** probar su inocencia de una acusación.

clearance ['klɪərəns] *n* (*space*) espacio *m* libre; (*distance above ground*) luz *f* libre; (*Tech*) espacio *m* muerto; (*Sport*) despeje *m*; (*by Customs*) despacho *m* de aduana; (*by Security*) acreditación *f*; **— sale** liquidación *f*.

clear-cut ['klɪə'kʌt] *adj* claro, bien definido, neto.

clear-headed ['klɪə'hedɪd] *adj* de mentalidad lógica, perspicaz, inteligente.

clear-headedness ['klɪə'hedɪdnɪs] *n* mentalidad *f* lógica, perspicacia *f*, inteligencia *f*.

clearing ['klɪərɪŋ] *n* (*in wood*) claro *m*.

clearing bank ['klɪərɪŋbæŋk] *n*, **clearing house** ['klɪərɪŋhaus] *n*, *pl* **— houses** [‚hauzɪz] cámara *f* de compensación.

clearly ['klɪəlɪ] *adv* claramente; (*at start of sentence*) desde luego; (*as answer*) sin duda, naturalmente.

clearness ['klɪənɪs] *n* claridad *f*.

clear-sighted ['klɪə'saɪtɪd] *adj* clarividente, perspicaz.

clear-sightedness ['klɪə'saɪtɪdnɪs] *n* clarividencia *f*, perspicacia *f*.

clearway ['klɪəweɪ] *n* carretera *f* principal (para velocidades altas), carretera *f* en la que está prohibido estacionar.

cleat [kli:t] *n* abrazadera *f*, listón *m*, fiador *m*.

cleavage ['kli:vɪdʒ] *n* (*fig*) escisión *f*, división *f*; (*in dress*) escote *m*.

cleave[1] [kli:v] (*irr*: *pret* **clove** *or* **cleft**, *ptp* **cloven** *or* **cleft**) *vt* partir, hender, abrir por medio; *water* surcar.

cleave[2] [kli:v] *vi*: **to — to** adherirse a, no separarse de; **to — together** ser inseparables.

cleaver ['kli:və*] *n* cuchilla *f* de carnicero.

clef [klef] *n* clave *f*; *bass* **—** clave *f* de fa; **treble —** clave *f* de sol.

cleft [kleft] **1** *pret and ptp of* **cleave**[1]. **2** *n* grieta *f*, hendedura *f*.

cleft palate ['kleft'pælɪt] *n* palatosquisis *f*.

clematis ['klemətɪs] *n* clemátide *f*.

clemency ['klemənsɪ] *n* clemencia *f*.

clement ['klemənt] *adj* clemente.

Clement ['klemənt] *n* Clemente.

clench [klentʃ] *vt teeth, fist* apretar, cerrar; **the —ed fist** el puño cerrado; *see also* **clinch.**

clergy ['klɜ:dʒɪ] *n* clero *m*.

clergyman ['klɜ:dʒɪmən] *n*, *pl* **—men** [mən] clérigo *m*; (*specifically Anglican*) sacerdote *m* anglicano; (*Protestant minister*) pastor *m*.

cleric ['klerɪk] *n* eclesiástico *m*.

clerical ['klerɪkəl] *adj* oficinista, oficinesco, de oficina; (*Eccl*) clerical; **— error** error *m* de pluma, error *m* de copia; **— work** trabajo *m* de oficina; **— worker** empleado *m*.

clerihew ['klerɪhju:] *n* estrofa inglesa de 4 versos, de carácter festivo.

clerk [klɑ:k, (US) klɜ:rk] *n* oficinista *mf*, empleado *m*, a *f*, secretario *m*, a *f*; (*in hotel*) recepcionista *mf*; (*esp US*) dependiente *m*, a *f*, vendedor *m*, ora *f*; (*Law*) escribano *m*; (*Eccl, also* **— in holy orders**) clérigo *m*; *town* **—** secretario *m* del Ayuntamiento.

clerkship ['klɑ:kʃɪp, (US) 'klɜ:rkʃɪp] *n* empleo *m* de oficinista; (*Law*) escribanía *f*.

clever ['klevə*] *adj* inteligente, listo; *move, speech etc* hábil; *invention, parody etc* ingenioso; **to be — at** ser listo en, tener aptitud para; **he is very — with his fingers** es muy hábil con los dedos, tiene mucha destreza manual; **that was — of you** lo hiciste muy bien, ¡qué habilidad!, (*you were right*) estuviste en lo cierto; **that's —, isn't it?** ¿es ingenioso, eh?; **to be too — by half** pasarse de listo; **he was too — for us** logró embaucarnos; **he tries to be too —** se esfuerza por parecer ingenioso.

cleverly ['klevəlɪ] *adv* hábilmente; ingeniosamente; con destreza.

cleverness ['klevənɪs] *n* inteligencia *f*; habilidad *f*; ingenio *m*; destreza *f*.

clew [klu:] *n* (*US*) = **clue**; (*Naut*) puño *m*.

cliché ['kli:ʃeɪ] *n* cliché *m*, tópico *m*, frase *f* hecha.

click [klik] **1** n golpecito m seco; (of gun) piñoneo m; (of heels) taconeo m; (of tongue) chasquido m.
    2 vt tongue etc chasquear; **to — one's heels** taconear.
    3 vi (gun) piñonear; sonar con un golpecito seco; (fam) tener suerte, lograrlo; (2 persons) congeniar; hacerse novios.

client ['klaiənt] n cliente mf.

clientèle [,kli:ɑ:n'tel] n clientela f.

cliff [klif] n risco m, precipicio m; (sea-) acantilado m.

cliff-hanging ['klif,hæniŋ] adj event que produce el máximo suspense, que tiene a todos pendientes de su resultado; drama de suspense.

climacteric [klai'mæktərik] **1** adj climactérico. **2** n período m climactérico.

climactic [klai'mæktik] adj culminante.

climate ['klaimit] n clima m; (fig) ambiente m; **— of opinion** opinión f general.

climatic [klai'mætik] adj climático.

climatology [,klaimə'tɔlədʒi] n climatología f.

climax ['klaimæks] n punto m culminante, colmo m, apogeo m, crisis f; (of play etc) clímax m; **to reach a —** llegar a su punto álgido, alcanzar una cima de intensidad.

climb [klaim] **1** n subida f, escalada f, ascenso m; **it was a stiff —** la subida fue penosa.
    2 vt tree, wall etc trepar a; staircase subir, subir por; mountain subir a, escalar.
    3 vi (a) subir, trepar; **the path —s higher yet** la senda sigue subiendo todavía; **to — to power** subir al poder; **to — down a cliff** bajar por un precipicio; **to — into an aircraft** trepar a un aparato; **to — out of a hole** salir trepando de un socavón; **to — over a wall** franquear una tapia; **to — up a rope** trepar por una cuerda.
    (b) (fig) **to — down** rendirse, desdecirse, retroceder.

climber ['klaimə*] n montañista mf, alpinista mf, escalador m, ora f; (fig) arribista mf; (Bot) trepadora f, enredadera f; **social —** arribista mf.

climbing ['klaimiŋ] n montañismo m, alpinismo m.

climbing irons ['klaimiŋaiənz] npl garfios mpl.

clinch [klintʃ] **1** n abrazo m; (Boxing) clincha f; **to go into a —** abrazarse.
    2 vt (secure) afianzar; nail remachar, roblar; (fig) resolver de una vez, decidir; argument remachar; deal cerrar; **to — matters** para remacharlo todavía; **that —s it** eso es concluyente; see also **clench**.

cling [kliŋ] (irr: pret and ptp **clung**) vi: **to — to** adherirse a, pegarse a, quedar pegado a; person abrazarse a, quedar abrazado a; person pursued no separarse de; opinion seguir fiel a, sostener todavía; **they clung to one another** quedaron abrazados; **a dress that —s to the figure** un vestido que se ajuste al cuerpo.

clinging ['kliŋiŋ] adj dress ceñido, muy ajustado; person pegajoso.

clinic ['klinik] n clínica f.

clinical ['klinikəl] adj clínico.

clink[1] [kliŋk] **1** n tintín m, sonido m metálico; (of glasses) choque m. **2** vt hacer sonar, hacer tintinar; glasses chocar. **3** vi tintinar.

clink[2] [kliŋk] n (sl) trena f.

clinker ['kliŋkə*] n escoria f de hulla.

clinker-built ['kliŋkə,bilt] adj (Naut) de tingladillo.

clip[1] [klip] **1** n (cut with scissors) tijeretada f; (shearing) esquileo m; (wool) cantidad f de lana esquilada; (blow) golpe m.
    2 vt (cut) cortar; (cut to shorten) acortar; wool trasquilar, esquilar; coin cercenar; ticket picar; wings cortar; words comerse, abreviar; (hit) golpear.

clip[2] [klip] **1** n (clamp) grapa f; (for papers) sujetapapeles m; (of pen) sujetador m; (for hair) prendido m; (brooch) alfiler m de pecho, clip m.
    2 vt sujetar; **to — together** unir; **to — something on to one's dress** prender algo al traje con un alfiler.

clipper ['klipə*] n (Naut) clíper m.

clippers ['klipəz] npl (for hair) maquinilla f (para el pelo); (Hort) tijeras fpl podadoras.

clippie ['klipi] n (fam) cobradora f.

clipping ['klipiŋ] n (from newspaper) recorte m.

clique [kli:k] n pandilla f, camarilla f, peña f.

cliquish ['kli:kiʃ] adj exclusivista.

cliquishness ['kli:kiʃnis] n exclusivismo m.

cloak [kləuk] **1** n capa f, manto m; (fig) pretexto m; **under the — of piety** so capa de la piedad.
    2 vt encapotar; (cover) cubrir (in, with de); (fig) encubrir, disimular.

cloak-and-dagger ['kləukən'dægə*] adj clandestino, propio de agente secreto; story de agentes secretos, de espías.

cloakroom ['kləukrum] n guardarropa m; (Rail) consigna f; (euph) aseos mpl, lavabo m.

clobber ['klɔbə*] (sl) **1** n (dress) ropa f, traje m; (gear) cosas fpl, trastos mpl. **2** vt (defeat) cascar; (beat up) aporrear.

cloche [klɔʃ] n campana f de cristal.

clock [klɔk] **1** n reloj m; (fam) (dial) esfera f, cuadrante m; (of taxi) taxímetro m; (Aut: speedometer) velocímetro m, (milometer) cuentakilómetros m; (sl) cara f; **electric —** reloj m eléctrico; **grandfather —** reloj m de pie, reloj m de caja; **against the —** contra (el) reloj; **to sleep round the —** dormir doce horas.
    2 vt registrar; **we —ed 80 m.p.h.** alcanzamos una velocidad de 80 millas por hora.
    3 vi: **to — in** fichar; (loosely) llegar (al trabajo etc).

clockwise ['klɔkwaiz] adv en la dirección de las agujas del reloj.

clockwork ['klɔkwə:k] **1** n aparato m de relojería; **to go like —** ir como un reloj. **2** attr de cuerda; **— train** tren m de cuerda.

clod [klɔd] n terrón m; (person) patán m; **you —!** ¡bestia!

clodhopper ['klɔd,hɔpə*] n patán m.

clog [klɔg] **1** n zueco m, chanclo m. **2** vt atascar. **3** vi atascarse.

cloister ['klɔistə*] n claustro m.

cloistered ['klɔistəd] adj life de ermitaño.

close [kləus] **1** adv cerca; **— by** muy cerca; **— by something, — to something** cerca de algo; **to be — together** estar muy juntos, estar muy cerca unos de otros; **to come —** acercarse; **that comes — to an insult** eso equivale casi a un insulto; **the runners finished very —** llegaron los atletas casi a la par; **to fit —** ajustarse al cuerpo (etc); **to follow — behind someone** seguir muy de cerca a uno; **to keep — to the wall** ir arrimado a la pared; **it's — on 6 o'clock** son las 6 casi; **he must be — on 50** se acercará a los 50; **according to sources — to the police** según fuentes allegadas a la comisaría.
    2 adj (near) cercano, próximo; (of objects standing — together) apretados, arrimados unos a otros, densos; weave compacto, tupido; print compacto; formation, vowel cerrado; connection, friendship estrecho, íntimo; friend íntimo; relative cercano; attention concienzudo; study, questioning, argument detallado, minucioso; election, finish, result muy reñido; scores casi iguales; resemblance casi completo; imitation arrimado; translation fiel, exacto; person's character reservado, (mean) tacaño; atmosphere sofocante; room mal ventilado; weather pesado, bochornoso.
    3 n recinto m.

close [kləuz] **1** n fin m, final m, conclusión f; **at the — al** final; **at the — of day** a la caída de la tarde; **at the — of the year** al fin del año; **to bring something to a —** terminar algo, concluir algo; **to draw to a —** tocar a su fin, estar terminando.
    2 vt (shut) cerrar; (end) concluir, terminar; hole etc tapar, obstruir; deal, list cerrar; ceremony, debate clausurar; account (Comm) saldar; bank account liquidar; ranks apretar; **"road —d"** "cerrado el paso"; **to — down** cerrar definitivamente; **to — up** cerrar (del todo).
    3 vi (shut) cerrarse; (end) concluir(se), terminar(se); **to — down** cerrarse definitivamente; (Radio) cerrar la emisión; **to — in** acercarse rodeando; **the days are closing in** los días son cada vez más cortos; **night was closing in** se cerraba ya la noche; **to — in on someone** rodear a uno, cercar a uno; **the crowd —d round him** se agolpó la multitud en torno suyo; **the clouds —d round the peak** las nubes envolvieron la cumbre; **the waters —d round it** lo rodearon las aguas; **to — up** (flower etc) cerrarse (del todo); (people etc) arrimarse más, ponerse más cerca unos de otros; (ranks) apretarse; (wound) cicatrizarse; (fall silent) callarse; **to — with someone** cerrar con uno.

close-cropped ['kləus'krɔpt] adj al rape.

closed [kləuzd] **1** pret and ptp of **close**. **2** adj car, circuit etc cerrado; mind de miras estrechas; society exclusivista.

closed-circuit ['kləuzd'sə:kit] adj: **— television** circuito m interno de televisión, televisión f por circuito cerrado.

close-down ['kləuzdaun] n (Radio) cierre m.

close-fisted ['kləus'fistid] adj tacaño.

close-fitting ['kləus'fitiŋ] adj ceñido, ajustado.

close-knit ['kləus'nit] adj muy unido, bien ensamblado, homogéneo.

closely ['kləusli] adv (exactly) fielmente, exactamente; (carefully) atentamente; **— packed** case atestado, *objects* apretados unos contra otros; — **printed** de impresión compacta; — **contested** muy reñido; — **guarded** rigurosamente guardado; — **connected with** en íntima relación con, estrechamente relacionado con.

closeness ['kləusnis] n (*nearness*) proximidad f; (*of connection*) intimidad f; (*of election*) lo muy reñido; (*of translation*) fidelidad f; (*of room*) mala ventilación f; (*of weather*) pesantez f, lo bochornoso; (*meanness*) tacañería f.

closet ['klɔzit] 1 n wáter m, lavabo m; (*US: cupboard*) armario m, (*for clothes*) ropero m. 2 *vt:* **to be —ed with** estar encerrado con.

close-up ['kləusʌp] n primer plano m.

closure ['kləuʒə*] n (*close-down*) cierre m; (*end*) fin m, conclusión f; (*Parl*) clausura f.

clot [klɔt] 1 n (a) grumo m, cuajarón m, coágulo m; (*Med*) embolia f; — **on the brain** embolia f cerebral.
(b) (*sl*) papanatas m; **you —!** ¡imbécil!
2 *vi* cuajarse, coagularse.

cloth [klɔθ] n, pl **cloths** [klɔθs] (*material*) paño m, tela f; (*for cleaning*) trapo m; (*table-*) mantel m; **the —** (*Eccl*) el clero; **bound in —** encuadernado en tela; **American —** hule m; **made out of whole —** (*US*) enteramente fabuloso; **to lay the —** poner la mesa.

clothe [kləuð] *vt* vestir (*in, with* de); (*fig*) cubrir, revestir (*in, with* de).

clothes [kləuðz] npl ropa f, vestidos mpl; **in plain —** en traje de calle, de paisano.

clothes basket ['kləuðz,bɑːskit] n cesto m de la colada.

clothes brush ['kləuðzbrʌʃ] n cepillo m para la ropa.

clothes hanger ['kləuðz,hæŋə*] n percha f.

clothes line ['kləuðzlain] n cuerda f para tender la ropa.

clothes moth ['kləuðzmɔθ] n polilla f.

clothes peg ['kləuðzpeg] n, (*US*) **clothespin** ['kləuðzpin] n pinza f.

clothespole ['kləuðzpəul] n palo m de apoyo (*para tender la ropa*).

clothesprop ['kləuðzprɔp] n palo m de apoyo.

clothier ['kləuðiə*] n pañero m, ropero m, (*tailor*) sastre m; **—'s** (*shop*) pañería f, ropería f, (*tailor's*) sastrería f.

clothing ['kləuðiŋ] 1 n ropa f, vestidos mpl; **article of —** prenda f de vestir.
2 *attr:* — **shop** pañería f, ropería f, (*tailor's*) sastrería f; **the — trade** la industria del vestido.

cloud [klaud] 1 n nube f (*also fig*); (*storm-*) nubarrón m; **to be under a —** estar desacreditado; **to leave under a —** ser despedido bajo sospecha; **to be up in the —s** estar en las nubes; **every — has a silver lining** no hay mal que por bien no venga.
2 *vt* anublar (*also fig*).
3 *vi* nublarse (*fig, also* **to — over**).

cloudberry ['klaudbəri] n (*US*) camemoro m.

cloudburst ['klaudbəːst] n chaparrón m.

cloud-capped ['klaudkæpt] adj coronado de nubes.

cloudiness ['klaudinis] n lo anublado, lo nuboso; lo turbio.

cloudless ['klaudlis] adj sin nubes, despejado.

cloudy ['klaudi] adj anublado, nuboso; *liquid* turbio; **it is —** el cielo está anublado.

clout[1] [klaut] 1 n tortazo m. 2 *vt* dar un tortazo a.

clout[2] [klaut] n: **ne'er cast a — till May be out** hasta el cuarenta de mayo no te quites el sayo.

clove[1] [kləuv] n clavo m de especia; — **of garlic** diente m de ajo.

clove[2] [kləuv] pret of **cleave**[1].

clove hitch ['kləuvhitʃ] n ballestrinque m.

cloven ['kləuvn] ptp of **cleave**[2]; see **hoof**.

clover ['kləuvə*] n trébol m; **to be in —** estar en jauja.

cloverleaf ['kləuvəliːf] n, pl **—leaves** [liːvz] hoja f de trébol; (*Aut*) cruce m en trébol.

clown [klaun] 1 n payaso m, clown m; (*boor*) patán m.
2 *vi* hacer el payaso; **stop —ing!** ¡déjate de tonterías!

clowning ['klauniŋ] n payasadas fpl.

cloy [klɔi] *vti* empalagar.

cloying ['klɔiiŋ] adj empalagoso.

club [klʌb] 1 n (a) (*stick*) porra f, cachiporra f; (*golf-*) palo m; **Indian —** maza f (*de gimnasia*); (*Cards*) **—s** tréboles mpl, (*in Spanish pack*) bastones mpl.
(b) (*association*) club m; (*for gaming etc*) casino m.
2 *vt* aporrear; **to — someone to death** matar a uno a porrazos.
3 *vi:* **to — together** hacer una colecta, pagar cada uno su escote; **we —bed together to buy it for him** entre todos se lo compramos.

club-foot ['klʌb'fut] n pie m zopo.

clubhouse ['klʌbhaus] n, pl **—houses** [,hauziz] (*Golf*) chalet m, chalé m (*Acad*).

clubman ['klʌbmən] n, pl **— men** [mən] casinista m.

clubroom ['klʌbrum] n salón m, sala f de reuniones.

cluck [klʌk] *vi* cloquear.

clue [kluː] n indicio m; (*in a crime etc*) pista f; (*of crossword*) indicación f; **I haven't a —** no tengo ni idea; **he hasn't a —** es un pobre hombre, tiene un tremendo despiste; **can you give me a —?** ¿me puedes dar algún indicio?

clump[1] [klʌmp] n (*of trees*) grupo m; (*of plant*) mata f.

clump[2] [klʌmp] 1 n (*noise of feet*) pisadas fpl fuertes.
2 *vi* andar con pisadas fuertes.

clumsily ['klʌmzili] adv torpemente; pesadamente; toscamente, chapuceramente.

clumsiness ['klʌmzinis] n torpeza f, desmaña f; tosquedad f.

clumsy ['klʌmzi] adj torpe, desmañado; (*in movement*) desgarbado, pesado; (*inartistic*) tosco, chapucero.

clung [klʌŋ] pret and ptp of **cling**.

Cluniac ['kluːniæk] 1 adj cluniacense. 2 n cluniacense m.

cluster ['klʌstə*] 1 n grupo m; (*Bot*) racimo m. 2 *vi* agruparse, apiñarse; (*Bot*) arracimarse; **to — round someone** reunirse en torno de uno.

clutch[1] [klʌtʃ] 1 n (a) (*grasp*) agarro m, apretón m; **to make a — at something** tratar de agarrar algo.
(b) **—es: to fall into someone's —es** caer en las garras de uno; **to get something out of someone's —es** hacer que uno ceda la posesión de algo.
(c) (*Aut*) embrague m; (*pedal*) pedal m de embrague; **to disengage the —** desembragar; **to let in the —** embragar.
2 *vt* tener asido en la mano; sujetar, apretar, empuñar; **he —ed her to his heart** la estrechó contra el pecho.
3 *vi:* **to — at** agarrarse a, tratar de asir; **he —ed at my hand** trató de coger mi mano; **to — at a hope** aferrarse a una esperanza.

clutch[2] [klʌtʃ] n (*of eggs*) nidada f.

clutter ['klʌtə*] 1 n desorden m, confusión f; **a — of shoes** un montón de zapatos. 2 *vt* llenar desordenadamente, atestar; **to be —ed up with** estar atestado de.

coach [kəutʃ] 1 n (a) (*in general*) coche m; (*stage-*) diligencia f; (*ceremonial*) carroza f; (*Rail*) coche m, vagón m; (*Aut*) autocar m.
(b) (*Sport*) entrenador m, preparador m, instructor m; (*tutor*) profesor m particular.
2 *vt team* entrenar, preparar; *student* enseñar, preparar; **to — someone in French** enseñar francés a uno; **to — someone in a part** hacer que uno ensaye su papel.

coachman ['kəutʃmən] n, pl **—men** [mən] cochero m.

coachwork ['kəutʃwəːk] n carrocería f.

coadjutant [kəu'ædʒutənt] n auxiliar mf.

coagulant [kəu'ægjulənt] n coagulante m.

coagulate [kəu'ægjuleit] 1 *vt* coagular. 2 *vi* coagularse.

coagulation [kəu,ægju'leiʃən] n coagulación f.

coal [kəul] 1 n carbón m; hulla f; **a —** un pedazo de carbón; **live —** ascua f, brasa f; **soft —** hulla f grasa; **to carry —s to Newcastle** ir a vendimiar y llevar uvas de postre; **to haul someone over the —s** echar un rapapolvo a uno; **to heap —s of fire on someone's head** avergonzar a uno devolviéndole bien por mal.
2 *attr:* — **industry** industria f hullera.
3 *vi* (*Naut*) tomar carbón.

coal-black ['kəul'blæk] adj negro como el carbón.

coal-burning ['kəul,bəːniŋ] adj que quema carbón.

coal cellar ['kəul,selə*] n carbonera f.

coal cutter ['kəul,kʌtə*] n excavadora-zapadora f.

coaldust ['kəuldʌst] n polvillo m de carbón.

coalesce [,kəuə'les] *vi* fundirse; unirse, incorporarse.

coalescence [,kəuə'lesəns] n fusión f; unión f, incorporación f.

coal face ['kəulfeis] n frente m de carbón.

coalfield ['kəulfiːld] n yacimiento m de carbón; (*large area*) cuenca f minera.

coalgas ['kəulgæs] n gas m de hulla.

coalition [,kəuə'liʃən] n coalición f.

coalman ['kəulmən] n, pl **—men** [mən], **coal merchant** ['kəul,məːtʃənt] n carbonero m.

coalmine ['kəulmain] n mina f de carbón.

coalminer ['kəul,mainə*] n minero m de carbón.

coalmining ['kəul,mainiŋ] n minería f de carbón.

coalpit ['kəulpit] n mina f de carbón.

coal scuttle ['kəul,skʌtl] n cubo m para carbón.

coal tar ['kəul'tɑː*] n alquitrán m mineral.

coarse [kɔːs] *adj (of texture)* basto, burdo; *sand etc* grueso; *(badly-made)* tosco, torpe; *hands* poco elegante, *skin* áspero, poco fino; *character, laugh, remark* ordinario, grosero; *joke* verde.

coarse-grained ['kɔːsgreind] *adj* de grano grueso; *(fig)* tosco, basto.

coarsely ['kɔːsli] *adv* toscamente; groseramente.

coarsen ['kɔːsn] **1** *vt person* embrutecer; *skin* curtir. **2** *vi (person)* embrutecerse; *(skin)* curtirse.

coarseness ['kɔːsnis] *n* basteza *f*; tosquedad *f*; falta *f* de finura, falta *f* de elegancia; ordinariez *f*, grosería *f*; lo verde.

coast [kəust] **1** *n* costa *f*; litoral *m*; **the — is clear** ya no hay moros en la costa.
2 *vi (Aut etc)* ir en punto muerto; *(on sledge, cycle etc)* deslizarse cuesta abajo; **to — along** avanzar sin esfuerzo.

coastal ['kəustəl] *adj* costero, costanero; **— defences** defensas *fpl* costeras; **— traffic** *(Naut)* cabotaje *m*.

coaster ['kəustə*] *n* buque *m* costero, barco *m* de cabotaje; *(US)* trineo *m*.

coastguard ['kəustɡɑːd] *n* guardacostas *m*.

coastline ['kəustlain] *n* litoral *m*.

coat [kəut] **1** *n* **(a)** *(jacket)* chaqueta *f*, americana *f*, saco *m* *(SAm)*; *(overcoat)* abrigo *m*; **white —** *(chemist's etc)* bata *f*; **— of arms** escudo *m* de armas; **— of mail** cota *f* de malla; **to cut one's — according to one's cloth** adaptarse a las circunstancias; **to turn one's —** chaquetear, cambiar de camisa.
(b) *(animal's)* pelo *m*, lana *f*.
(c) *(layer)* capa *f*; **— of paint** mano *f* de pintura.
2 *vt* cubrir, revestir *(with de)*; *(with a liquid)* bañar *(with en)*; **to — something with paint** dar una mano de pintura a algo.

coat hanger ['kəut,hæŋə*] *n* percha *f*.

coating ['kəutiŋ] *n* capa *f*, baño *m*.

coattails ['kəutteilz] *npl* faldón *m*.

co-author '[kəu,ɔːθə*] *n* coautor *m*, ora *f*.

coax [kəuks] *vt* engatusar; **to — something out of someone** sonsacar algo a uno; **to — someone into doing something** conseguir por medio de halagos que uno haga algo; **she likes to be —ed** ella se hace rogar; **to — someone along** mimar a uno.

coaxing ['kəuksiŋ] **1** *adj* mimoso. **2** *n* mimos *mpl*, halagos *mpl*.

coaxingly ['kəuksiŋli] *adv* mimosamente.

cob [kɔb] *n (swan)* cisne *m* macho; *(horse)* jaca *f* fuerte; *(loaf)* pan *m* redondo; *(nut)* avellana *f*.

cobalt ['kəubɔlt] *n* cobalto *m*; **— blue** azul *m* de cobalto.

cobber ['kɔbə*] *n (Australia: fam)* amigo *m*, compañero *m*; *(in direct address)* amigo, hombre.

cobble ['kɔbl] *vt shoes* remendar; *street* empedrar con guijarros.

cobbler ['kɔblə*] *n* zapatero *m* remendón.

cobbles ['kɔblz] *npl*, **cobblestones** ['kɔblstəunz] *npl* guijarros *mpl*, enguijarrado *m*.

cobra ['kəubrə] *n* cobra *f*.

cobweb ['kɔbweb] *n* telaraña *f*; **to blow the —s away** salir a tomar el fresco.

cocaine [kə'kein] *n* cocaína *f*.

coccus ['kɔkəs] *n*, *pl* **cocci** ['kɔkai] coco *m*.

cochineal ['kɔtʃiniːl] *n* cochinilla *f*.

cock [kɔk] **1** *n* **(a)** *(cockerel)* gallo *m*; *(other male bird)* macho *m*; **fighting —** gallo *m* de pelea; **— of the walk** gallito *m* del lugar; **old —!** *(fam)* ¡amigo!
(b) *(tap)* grifo *m*, espita *f*; *(Anat: tabu)* polla *f*.
(c) *(of gun)* martillo *m*; **to go off at half —** *(plan)* ponerse por obra sin la debida preparación.
2 *vt gun* amartillar; *head* ladear; *ears* aguzar; **to — one's eye at** mirar con intención a.

cockade [kɔ'keid] *n* escarapela *f*.

cock-a-doodle-doo [ˌkɔkəduːdl'duː] *interj* ¡quiquiriquí!

cock-a-hoop ['kɔkə'huːp] *adj*: **to be —** estar jubiloso.

cock-and-bull ['kɔkən'buil] *adj*: **— story** cuento *m*, camelo *m*.

cockatoo [ˌkɔkə'tuː] *n* cacatúa *f*.

cockchafer ['kɔk,tʃeifə*] *n* abejorro *m*.

cockcrow ['kɔkkrəu] *n*: **at —** al amanecer.

cocked [kɔkt] *adj*: **— hat** sombrero *m* de tres picos; **to knock something into a — hat** ser netamente superior a, dar quince y raya a.

cocker ['kɔkə*] *n (also* **— spaniel)** cocker *m*.

cockerel ['kɔkrəl] *n* gallito *m*, gallo *m* joven.

cockeyed ['kɔkaid] *adj (fam)* incomprensible, estúpido.

cockfight ['kɔkfait] *n*, **cockfighting** ['kɔk,faitiŋ] *n* riña *f* de gallos.

cockle ['kɔkl] *n (Zool)* berberecho *m*; **to warm the —s of someone's heart** dar grandísimo contento a uno.

cockleshell ['kɔklʃel] *n* concha *f* de berberecho; *(boat)* cascarón *m* de nuez.

cockney ['kɔkni] *n habitante de ciertos barrios bajos de Londres; dialecto de ciertos barrios bajos de Londres.*

cockpit ['kɔkpit] *n (Aer)* carlinga *f*; *(for cockfight)* cancha *f*, reñidero *m* de gallos; **the — of Europe** Bélgica *f (escenario de muchos combates).*

cockroach ['kɔkrəutʃ] *n* cucaracha *f*.

cockscomb ['kɔkskəum] *n* cresta *f* de gallo.

cocksure ['kɔk'ʃuə*] *adj* presumido, presuntuoso.

cocktail ['kɔkteil] *n* combinado *m*, copetín *m*, coctel *or* cóctel *m*.

cocktail cabinet ['kɔkteil,kæbinit] *n* mueble-bar *m*.

cocktail party ['kɔkteil,pɑːti] *n* coctel *or* cóctel *m*.

cocktail shaker ['kɔkteil,ʃeikə*] *n* coctelera *f*.

cocky ['kɔki] *adj (fam)* engreído, fresco.

cocoa ['kəukəu] *n* cacao *m*; *(drink)* chocolate *m*.

coconut ['kəukənʌt] *n* coco *m*.

coconut palm ['kəukənʌt,pɑːm] *n* cocotero *m*.

cocoon [kə'kuːn] *n* capullo *m*.

cod [kɔd] *n* bacalao *m*.

coddle ['kɔdl] *vt* mimar, hacer mimos a.

code [kəud] **1** *n* **(a)** *(Law etc)* código *m*; **highway —** código *m* de la circulación; **penal —** código *m* penal.
(b) *(cypher)* cifra *f*; **in —** en cifra; **Morse —** el alfabeto Morse.
2 *vt* cifrar, poner en cifra.

codeine ['kəudiːn] *n* codeína *f*.

codex ['kəudeks] *n*, *pl* **codices** ['kɔdisiːz] códice *m*.

codfish ['kɔdfiʃ] *n* bacalao *m*.

codger ['kɔdʒə*] *n*: **old —** sujeto *m*, vejete *m*.

codicil ['kɔdisil] *n* codicilo *m*.

codify ['kəudifai] *vt* codificar.

cod-liver oil ['kɔdlivər'ɔil] *n* aceite *m* de hígado de bacalao.

co-driver ['kəudraivə*] *n* copiloto *m*.

coed ['kəu'ed] **1** *adj (fam)* coeducacional. **2** *n* alumna *f* de un colegio coeducacional.

coeducation ['kəu,edju'keiʃən] *n* coeducación *f*.

coeducational ['kəu,edju'keiʃənl] *adj* coeducacional.

coefficient [ˌkəui'fiʃənt] *n* coeficiente *m*.

coerce [kəu'əːs] *vt* forzar, obligar *(into doing something* a hacer algo).

coercion [kəu'əːʃən] *n* coacción *f*, compulsión *f*; **under —** obligado a ello.

coercive [kəu'əːsiv] *adj* coactivo.

coeval [kəu'iːvəl] **1** *adj* coetáneo *(with* de), contemporáneo *(with* de). **2** *n* coetáneo *m*, a *f*, contemporáneo *m*, a *f*.

coexist ['kəuig'zist] *vi* coexistir *(with* con).

coexistence ['kəuig'zistəns] *n* coexistencia *f*; **peaceful —** coexistencia *f* pacífica.

coexistent ['kəuig'zistənt] *adj* coexistente.

coffee ['kɔfi] *n* café *m*; **black —** café *m* solo; **white —** café *m* con leche.

coffee bar ['kɔfibɑː*] *n* cafetería *f*.

coffee bean ['kɔfibiːn] *n* grano *m* de café.

coffee cup ['kɔfikʌp] *n* taza *f* para café.

coffee grounds ['kɔfigraundz] *heces fpl* de café.

coffee house ['kɔfihaus] *n* café *m*.

coffee mill ['kɔfimil] *n* molinillo *m* de café.

coffeepot ['kɔfipɔt] *n* cafetera *f*.

coffer ['kɔfə*] *n* cofre *m*, arca *f*; *(Archit)* artesón *m*; **—s** *(fig)* fondos *mpl*.

cofferdam ['kɔfədæm] *n* ataguía *f*.

coffin ['kɔfin] *n* ataúd *m*.

cog [kɔg] *n* diente *m*; *(wheel)* rueda *f* dentada; **to be just a — in a machine** ser solamente una pieza de un mecanismo.

cogency ['kəudʒənsi] *n* fuerza *f*, lógica *f*, convicción *f*.

cogent ['kəudʒənt] *adj* fuerte, lógico, convincente, sólido.

cogently ['kəudʒəntli] *adv* lógicamente, de modo convincente, con argumentos sólidos.

cogitate ['kɔdʒiteit] *vti* meditar.

cogitation [ˌkɔdʒi'teiʃən] *n* meditación *f*.

cognac ['kɔnjæk] *n* coñac *m*.

cognate ['kɔgneit] **1** *adj* cognado *(with* con); afín. **2** *n* cognado *m*.

cognition [kɔg'niʃən] *n* cognición *f*.

cognizance ['kɔgnizəns] *n* conocimiento *m*; **to be within one's —** ser de la competencia de uno; **to take — of** tener en cuenta.

cognizant ['kɔgnizənt] *adj*: **to be — of** saber, estar enterado de.

cognomen [kɔg'nəumen] *n* apodo *m*, sobrenombre *m*.

cogwheel ['kɔgwiːl] *n* rueda *f* dentada.

cohabit [kəu'hæbit] *vi* cohabitar.

cohabitation [ˌkəuhæbi'teiʃən] *n* cohabitación *f*.

coheir ['kəu'ɛə*] *n* coheredero *m*.

coheiress ['kəu'ɛəris] *n* coheredera *f*.

cohere [kəu'hiə*] *vi* adherirse, pegarse; (*ideas etc*) formar un conjunto sólido, ser consecuentes.

coherence [kəu'hiərəns] *n* coherencia *f*.

coherent [kəu'hiərənt] *adj* coherente; lógico, comprensible.

cohesion [kəu'hi:ʒən] *n* cohesión *f*.

cohesive [kəu'hi:siv] *adj* cohesivo; unido.

cohort ['kəuhɔ:t] *n* cohorte *f*.

coif [kɔif] *n* cofia *f*.

coiffeur [kwɔ'fə:*] *n* peluquero *m*.

coiffure [kwɔ'fjuə*] *n* peinado *m*.

coil [kɔil] **1** *n* rollo *m*; (*of rope etc*) adujada *f*; (*of snake*) anillo *m*; (*of smoke*) espiral *f*; (*of still etc*) serpentín *m*; (*Elec*) bobina *f*, carrete *m*.
2 *vt* arrollar, enrollar; *rope* (*Naut*) adujar.
3 *vi* arrollarse, enrollarse; **to — up** (*snake*) enroscarse; (*smoke*) subir en espiral.

coin [kɔin] **1** *n* moneda *f*; **to pay someone back in his own —** pagar a uno en la misma moneda; **to toss a —** echar a cara o cruz.
2 *vt money* acuñar; *word etc* inventar, idear; **he must be —ing money** está acuñando dinero, el negocio ha de ser un río de oro para él.

coinage ['kɔinidʒ] *n* (*system*) moneda *f*, sistema *m* monetario; (*act*) acuñación *f*; (*of word etc*)invención *f*.

coincide [,kəuin'said] *vi* coincidir (*with* con); (*agree*) estar de acuerdo (*with* con).

coincidence [kəu'insidəns] *n* coincidencia *f*; (*chance*) casualidad *f*; **what a —!** ¡qué casualidad!

coincidental [kəu,insi'dentl] *adj* coincidente; (*by chance*) fortuito.

coitus ['kɔitəs] *n* coito *m*.

coke[1] [kəuk] *n* coque *m*.

coke[2] [kəuk] *n* (*fam*) Coca-Cola *f*.

colander ['kʌləndə*] *n* colador *m*, escurridor *m*.

cold [kəuld] **1** *adj* frío (*also fig*); **as — as charity** más frío que el hielo; **my feet are — as ice** tengo los pies helados; **to be —** (*person*) tener frío, (*thing*) estar frío, (*weather*) hacer frío; **to be very —** (*person*) tener mucho frío, (*thing*) estar muy frío, (*weather*) hacer mucho frío; **to get —** (*thing*) enfriarse, (*weather*) empezar a hacer frío; **he's got them —** (*audience*) los tiene en el bolsillo; **he's got three tricks —** tiene tres bazas segurísimas; **to knock someone —** poner a uno fuera de combate; **it leaves me —** no me produce emoción alguna.
2 *n* (a) frío *m*; **to catch —** tomar frío; **to leave someone out in the —** dejar a uno al margen.
(b) (*Med, also* **common —**) resfriado *m*, catarro *m*; **to catch a —** resfriarse, acatarrarse; **to have a —** estar resfriado, estar acatarrado.

cold-blooded ['kəuld'blʌdid] *adj* (*Zool*) de sangre fría; (*fig*) insensible; (*cruel*) desalmado.

cold cream ['kəuld'kri:m] *n* colcrén *m*, crema *f*.

cold cuts ['kəuld'kʌts] *npl* (*US*) fiambres *mpl*.

cold-hearted ['kəuld'hɑ:tid] *adj* insensible, cruel.

coldly ['kəuldli] *adv* fríamente (*also fig*).

cold-shoulder ['kəuld'ʃəuldə*] *vt* tratar con frialdad.

cold storage ['kəuld'stɔ:ridʒ] *n* almacenaje *m* frigorífico; **to put something into —** dar carpetazo a algo.

coleslaw ['kəulslɔ:] *n* (*US*) ensalada *f* de col.

colic ['kɔlik] *n* cólico *m*.

Coliseum [,kɔli'si:əm] Coliseo *m*.

colitis [kɔ'laitis] *n* colitis *f*.

collaborate [kə'læbəreit] *vi* colaborar (*in, on* en; *with* con).

collaboration [kə,læbə'reiʃən] *n* colaboración *f*; (*Pol*) colaboracionismo *m*.

collaborator [kə'læbəreitə*] *n* colaborador *m*, ora *f*; (*Pol*) colaboracionista *mf*.

collage [kɔ'lɑ:ʒ] *n* (*Art*) collage *m*.

collapse [kə'læps] **1** *n* (*Med*) colapso *m*; (*of building*) hundimiento *m*, derrumbamiento *m*, desplome *m*; (*of roadway etc*) socavón *m*; (*of plans*) fracaso *m*.
2 *vi* (a) (*Med*) sufrir colapso; (*fig*) **to — with laughter** morirse de risa.
(b) (*building*) hundirse, derrumbarse, desplomarse; (*fig*) fracasar; **hood that —s** capota *f* plegable.

collapsible [kə'læpsəbl] *adj* plegable.

collar ['kɔlə*] **1** *n* cuello *m*; (*of animal, Tech*) collar *m*; **soft —** cuello *m* blando; **stiff —** cuello *m* duro, cuello *m* almidonado; **to get hot under the —** sulfurarse.
2 *vt* prender por el cuello; (*fam*) apropiarse, pisar.

collarbone ['kɔləbəun] *n* clavícula *f*.

collate [kɔ'leit] *vt* cotejar.

collateral [kɔ'lætərəl] **1** *adj* colateral. **2** *n* resguardo *m*, seguridad *f* colateral.

collation [kə'leiʃən] *n* (*meal*) colación *f*; (*of texts*) cotejo *m*.

colleague ['kɔli:g] *n* colega *m*.

collect ['kɔlekt] *n* (*Eccl*) colecta *f*.

collect [kə'lekt] **1** *vt* reunir, acumular; *people* reunir; *stamps etc* coleccionar; *fares, wages* cobrar; *debts, taxes* recaudar; *money for charity* colectar; (*pick up, Post*) recoger; *dust, water etc* retener; **I'll go and — the mail** voy por el correo; **I'll — you at 8** vengo a recogerte a las 8; **I must — my bags from the station** tengo que recoger mi equipaje en la estación.
2 *vi* reunirse, acumularse; (*people*) reunirse, congregarse; (*be a collector*) ser coleccionista, coleccionar; (*water*) estancarse; (*dust*) acumularse; **when do we —?** ¿cuándo cobramos?; **to — for charity** hacer una colecta con fines benéficos.
3 *vr*: **to — oneself** reponerse, sosegarse.

collected [kə'lektid] **1** *pret and ptp of* **collect**. **2** *adj* (*cool*) sosegado, tranquilo; **— works** obras *fpl* completas.

collection [kə'lekʃən] *n* acumulación *f*, montón *m*; (*of people*) grupo *m*; (*of pictures, stamps etc*) colección *f*; (*of fares, wages*) cobro *m*; (*of debts, taxes*) recaudación *f*; (*Eccl*) colecta *f*; (*for charity*) colecta *f*, cuestación *f*; (*Post*) recogida *f*; **to make a — for** hacer una colecta a beneficio de.

collective [kə'lektiv] *adj* colectivo.

collectively [kə'lektivli] *adv* colectivamente.

collectivize [kə'lektivaiz] *vt* colectivizar.

collector [kə'lektə*] *n* coleccionador *m*, ora *f*; (*of stamps etc*) coleccionista *mf*; (*tax-*) recaudador *m*.

colleen ['kɔli:n] *n* (*Ir*) muchacha *f*.

college ['kɔlidʒ] *n* colegio *m*; (*eg of Oxford*) colegio *m* mayor; (*eg of art*) escuela *f*; **commercial —** escuela *f* para secretarias; **electoral —** colegio *m* electoral; **junior —** (*US*) colegio *m* que comprende los 2 primeros años universitarios.

collegiate [kə'li:dʒiit] *adj* (a) (*Eccl*) colegial, colegiado; **— church** iglesia *f* colegial. (b) (*Univ*) que tiene colegios, organizado a base de colegios.

collide [kə'laid] *vi* chocar (*with* con; *also fig*).

collie ['kɔli] *n* perro *m* pastor.

collier ['kɔliə*] *n* minero *m* de carbón; (*boat*) barco *m* carbonero.

colliery ['kɔliəri] *n* mina *f* de carbón.

collision [kə'liʒən] *n* choque *m* (*also fig*), colisión *f*; **to come into —** with chocar con.

colloquial [kə'ləukwiəl] *adj* familiar, coloquial.

colloquialism [kə'ləukwiəlizəm] *n* palabra *f* (*or* expresión *f*) familiar; (*style*) estilo *m* familiar.

colloquy ['kɔləkwi] *n* coloquio *m*.

collusion [kə'lu:ʒən] *n* confabulación *f*; connivencia *f*; **to be in — with** conspirar con, confabular con.

collywobbles ['kɔli,wɔblz] *npl* (*fam*) rugido *m* de tripas.

Cologne [kə'ləun] Colonia.

colon[1] ['kəulən] *n* (*Anat*) colon *m*.

colon[2] ['kəulən] *n* (*Typ*) dos puntos *mpl*.

colonel ['kə:nl] *n* coronel *m*.

colonial [kə'ləuniəl] **1** *adj* colonial; *power* colonizador.
2 *n* colono *m*.

colonialism [kə'ləuniəlizəm] *n* colonialismo *m*.

colonialist [kə'ləuniəlist] *n* colonialista *mf*.

colonist ['kɔlənist] *n* colonizador *m*, colono *m*.

colonization [,kɔlənai'zeiʃən] *n* colonización *f*.

colonize ['kɔlənaiz] *vt* colonizar.

colonnade [,kɔlə'neid] *n* columnata *f*.

eolony ['kɔləni] *n* colonia *f*.

colophon ['kɔləfən] *n* colofón *m*.

Colorado [,kɔlə'rɑ:dəu]: **— beetle** escarabajo *m* de la patata.

coloration [,kʌlə'reiʃən] *n* colorido *m*, colores *mpl*.

colossal [kə'lɔsl] *adj* colosal.

colossus [kə'lɔsəs] *n* coloso *m*.

colour, (*US*) **color** ['kʌlə*] **1** *n* (a) color *m*; **fast —** color *m* sólido; **high —** color *m* subido; **local —** color *m* local; **it's a blue —**, **it's blue in —** es de color azul; **what — is it?** ¿de qué color es?; **in full —** a todo color; **to be off —** estar indispuesto; **to change —** mudar de color; **to lend — to a story** hacer que un cuento parezca más verosímil; **let's see the — of your money!** ¡a ver el dinero!; **to take all the — out of something** quitar lo pintoresco de algo, suprimir lo emocionante de algo.
(b) **—s** (*flag*) bandera *f*; **to call to the —s** llamar a filas, llamar al servicio militar; **to come out with flying —s** salir con lucimiento, salir airoso de la prueba; **to sail under false —s** encubrir su verdadera lealtad; **to show oneself in one's true —s** dejar ver su verdadero carácter.
2 *vt* color(e)ar; (*paint*) pintar, (*dye*) teñir (*red de* rojo); *drawing* iluminar.
3 *vi* (*also* **to — up**) sonrojarse.

colour bar ['kʌləbɑ:*] *n* barrera *f* racial.

colour-blind ['kʌləblaind] *adj* daltoniano.

colour blindness ['kʌlə,blaindnis] n daltonismo m.
coloured ['kʌləd] 1 pret and ptp of **colour**. 2 adj person, pencil de color; **a highly —— tale** un cuento de los más pintorescos.
colour film ['kʌləfilm] n película f en colores.
colourful ['kʌləful] adj lleno de color; scene vivo, animado; person etc pintoresco.
colouring ['kʌləriŋ] n colorido m; (substance) colorante m; (of complexion) colores mpl.
colourless ['kʌləlis] adj sin color, incoloro; (fig) soso.
colour television ['kʌlə,teli'viʒən] n televisión f en colores.
colt [kəult] n potro m.
coltish ['kəultiʃ] adj juguetón, retozón.
coltsfoot ['kəultsfut] n uña f de caballo, fárfara f.
columbine ['kɔləmbain] n aguileña f.
Columbine ['kɔləmbain] f Columbina.
Columbus [kə'lʌmbəs] m Colón.
column ['kɔləm] n (all senses) columna f; **advertisement —** sección f de anuncios; **armoured —** columna f blindada; **fifth —** quinta columna f; **spinal —** columna f vertebral; **steering —** columna f de dirección.
columnist ['kɔləmnist] n columnista mf, articulista mf.
coma ['kəumə] n (Med) coma m.
comatose ['kəumətəus] adj comatoso.
comb [kəum] 1 n peine m; (ornamental) peineta f; (for horse) almohaza f; (cock's) cresta f; (Tech) carda f; (honey-) panal m; **to give one's hair a —** peinarse (el pelo).
2 vt peinar; wool cardar; countryside etc registrar con minuciosidad (for en busca de); **to — one's hair** peinarse.
combat ['kɔmbæt] 1 n combate m; **single —** combate m singular; **— duty** servicio m de frente. 2 vt combatir, luchar contra.
combatant ['kɔmbətənt] n combatiente m.
combative ['kɔmbətiv] adj agresivo, belicoso.
combination [,kɔmbi'neiʃən] n combinación f; **— lock** cerradura f de combinación.
combine ['kɔmbain] n (Comm) asociación f, (pej) monopolio m; (Agr) cosechadora f, segadora-trilladora f.
combine [kəm'bain] 1 vt combinar; qualities etc reunir, conjugar. 2 vi combinarse; (companies etc) asociarse, fusionarse.
combined [kəm'baind] 1 pret and ptp of **combine**. 2 adj operation coordinado.
combings ['kəumiŋz] npl peinaduras fpl.
combustible [kəm'bʌstibl] 1 adj combustible. 2 n combustible m.
combustion [kəm'bʌstʃən] n combustión f; **internal — engine** motor m de explosión interna; **spontaneous —** combustión f espontánea.
come [kʌm] (irr: pret came, ptp come) vi venir; **coming!** ¡voy!; **oh —!**, **— —!**, **now!** ¡vamos!, ¡no es para tanto!; **the harvest —s in August** la recolección es en agosto; **it came as a great surprise to us** la cosa nos sorprendió muchísimo; **it —s in 3 sizes** se sirve en 3 tamaños; **recovery came slowly** el restablecimiento fue lento; **that's what —s of waiting** eso lo trae el esperar; **you could see that coming** eso se veía venir; **how —?** ¿cómo es eso?; **easy — easy go** los dineros del sacristán cantando se vienen y cantando se van; **to — across** person topar; thing dar con, encontrarse con; **to — across with** (fam) dar, proporcionar, sacar; **— again!** (fam) ¿cómo?; **to — along** venir también; **— along!** ¡vamos!, (hurrying) ¡date prisa!, (to runner etc) ¡ánimo!; **how is the book coming along?** ¿qué tal va el libro?; **to — at** solution llegar a, dar con; (attack) atacar, precipitarse sobre; **to — away** marcharse; salir de casa (etc); (part) separarse, desprenderse; **to — back** volver (for por); **to — back (into the game)** volver a tener posibilidades de ganar; **to — back with** responder diciendo; **to — between** interponerse entre; dividir, separar; **nothing can — between us** no hay nada que sea capaz de separarnos; **to — by** conseguir, adquirir, venir en posesión de; **how did you — by that name?** ¿con qué motivo te dieron ese nombre?; **to — down** bajar (from de); (roof etc) desplomarse; (be demolished) ser derribado; (Aer) aterrizar, (crashing) estrellarse, (in sea) amerizar; **it —s down to the knee** llega hasta la rodilla; **if it —s down to a sale** cara; **to — down with** (Med) enfermar de; **to — for** venir por; **to — forward** avanzar, moverse hacia adelante; presentarse; ofrecerse (to + infin a + infin); **to — from** (stem from) venir de, proceder de; **to — in** entrar; (train) llegar; (tide) crecer; (fashion) ponerse de moda, imponerse; **to —**

in last (in race) llegar el último; **— in!** ¡adelante!, ¡pase Vd!; **to — into** room entrar en; estate heredar; scheme asociarse con; **to — of** a good family ser de buena familia; **to — off** (part) desprenderse, soltarse; (take place) tener lugar, verificarse; (succeed) tener éxito; **to — off badly** salir malparado, salir perdiendo; **does this lid — off?** ¿esta tapa se puede quitar?; **— off it!** ¡no me digas!; **to — on** (adv) (advance) avanzar; (grow) crecer, desarrollarse; (actor) salir a la escena; (improve) hacer progresos; **— on!** ¡vamos!; (hurrying) ¡date prisa!, (to runner etc) ¡ánimo!; **I've a cold coming on** me va a dar un catarro; **winter was coming on** entraba el invierno; **how is the book coming on?** ¿qué tal va el libro?; **to — on** (prep) encontrar, descubrir; **to — out** salir (of de), mostrarse; (book) salir a luz; (new thing) aparecer, estrenarse; (debutante) ser presentada en sociedad; (news) revelarse, traslucirse; (flower) florecer; (workers) declararse en huelga; (stain) quitarse; **to — out against** something declararse en contra de algo; **to — out for** something declararse a favor de algo; **to — out with** desgargarse con, soltar; **to — over** (visit) venir a ver a uno; **what's — over you?** ¿te pasa algo?; **I don't know what came over me** no sé lo que me pasó; **to — round** (visit) venir a ver a uno; (agree) asentir, dejarse persuadir; (Med) volver en sí; **to — to** (adv) (Naut) fachear; (Med) volver en sí; **to — to** (prep) (sum) ascender a; **it came to me suddenly** se me ocurrió de repente; **so it —s to this** así que se reduce a esto; **I came to believe it** llegué a creerlo; **what are we coming to?** ¿adónde va a parar todo esto?; **he had it coming to him** bien merecido lo tenía; **to — together** reunirse, juntarse; **to — under** person estar bajo la jurisdicción de, ser de la competencia de; heading estar comprendido en; **to — up** subir; (sun) salir; (plant) aparecer; (difficulty) surgir; (in conversation) ser mencionado; (Univ) matricularse; **to — up before the judge** comparecer ante el juez; **to — up against** problem tropezar con; enemy tener que habérselas con; **(in height)** llegar hasta; (approach) acercarse a; (in street) abordar; (fig) estar a la altura de, corresponder a; standard satisfacer; **to — up with** person alcanzar; thing proponer, sugerir; **to — within** someone's jurisdiction estar bajo la jurisdicción de uno.
comeback ['kʌmbæk] n (fam) (a) restablecimiento m, rehabilitación f; esfuerzo m por volver a su antigua posición; **to make a —** restablecerse, rehabilitarse.
(b) reacción f; réplica f; **witty —** respuesta f aguda.
comedian [kə'mi:diən] n cómico m.
comedienne [kə,mi:di'en] n cómica f.
comedown ['kʌmdaun] n (fam) revés m, humillación f; bajón m.
comedy ['kɔmidi] n comedia f; (humour of event) comicidad f; **C— of Errors** Comedia f de las equivocaciones; **— of manners** comedia f de costumbres; **high —** alta comedia f; **low —** farsa f; **musical —** opereta f, (in Spain) zarzuela f.
come-hither ['kʌm'hiðə*] adj look incitante, provocativo.
comely ['kʌmli] adj gentil, lindo.
comer ['kʌmə*] n: **all —s** todos los contendientes; **the first —** el primero en llegar.
comestible [kə'mestibl] 1 adj comestible. 2 **—s** npl comestibles mpl.
comet ['kɔmit] n cometa m.
comfort ['kʌmfət] 1 n (a) (solace) consuelo m; (from pain) alivio m; **that's cold (or small) —, that's — at all** eso no me consuela nada; **you're a great — to me** eres un gran consuelo; **to give — to the enemy** dar aliento al enemigo.
(b) (bodily) confort m, comodidad f; bienestar m; **the —s of life** las cosas agradables de la vida diaria; **with every modern —** con todo confort; **to live in —** vivir cómodamente.
2 vt (solace) consolar; pain aliviar; (bodily) confortar; (encourage) alentar.
comfortable ['kʌmfətəbl] adj house, chair, shoes etc cómodo, confortable; income adecuado; majority suficiente, adecuado; living holgado; **to feel —** encontrarse a gusto; **I don't feel altogether — about it** la cosa me trae algo preocupado; **to have a — win** over someone vencer a uno fácilmente; **to make oneself —** acomodarse a su gusto; **make yourself —!** ¡póngase cómodamente!, ¡acomódese a su gusto!
comfortably ['kʌmfətəbli] adv sit etc cómodamente; live holgadamente; win fácilmente; **to be — off** tener una renta adecuada.

comforter ['kʌmfətə*] n (a) (person) consolador m, ora f. (b) (scarf) bufanda f; (US) colcha f, edredón m. (c) (baby's) chupete m.

comforting ['kʌmfətiŋ] adj consolador, (re)confortante.

comfortless ['kʌmfətlis] adj incómodo, sin comodidad.

comfort station ['kʌmfət,steiʃən] n (US) urinario m público.

comfy ['kʌmfi] adj (fam) = **comfortable.**

comic ['kɔmik] n (person) cómico m; (paper) tebeo m.

comic(al) ['kɔmik(əl)] adj cómico; divertido, entretenido.

comically ['kɔmikəli] adv cómicamente; divertidamente, entretenidamente.

coming ['kʌmiŋ] 1 adj year etc que viene; (future) venidero; (promising) prometedor; it's the — thing es la moda del futuro.

2 n venida f, llegada f; (of Christ) advenimiento m; — and going ir y venir m, trajín m, ajetreo m.

coming-out ['kʌmiŋ'aut] n presentación f en sociedad.

comma ['kɔmə] n coma f; inverted —s comillas fpl; in inverted —s entre comillas.

command [kə'ma:nd] 1 n (a) (order) orden f; mandato m; at the — of, by (the) — of por orden de; by royal — por real orden; to be at the — of estar a la disposición de.

(b) (control) mando m, dominio m; — of the seas dominio m de los mares; under the — of bajo el mando de; to be in — of estar al mando de; who is in — here? ¿quién manda aquí?; to have at one's —men mandar; to have at one's —, to have a good — of language dominar; to have good resources at one's — disponer de muchos recursos; to take — of asumir el mando de.

(c) (authority, Mil, Naut, territory, fleet etc) comandancia f; high — alto mando m; second in — segundo m, subjefe m, (Naut) segundo m de a bordo; bomber — jefatura f de bombardeo, sección f de bombardeo.

2 vt (give an order to) mandar, ordenar (to do hacer); men mandar; ship comandar; (have at one's disposal) disponer de; attention llamar poderosamente; price venderse a (or por); respect imponer; sympathy merecerse; view tener, dominar.

commandant [,kɔmən'dænt] n comandante m.

commandeer [,kɔmən'diə*] vt stores, ship etc requisar, expropiar; men reclutar por fuerza; (fam) tomar, apropiarse.

commander [kə'ma:ndə*] n (in general) comandante m, jefe m; (rank) capitán m de fragata.

commander-in-chief [kə'ma:ndərin'tʃi:f] n jefe m supremo, generalísimo m.

commanding [kə'ma:ndiŋ] adj position dominante; appearance imponente; lead, advantage abrumador; — officer jefe m.

commandment [kə'ma:ndmənt] n mandamiento m.

commando [kə'ma:ndəu] n (man, group) comando m.

commemorate [kə'meməreit] vt conmemorar.

commemoration [kə,memə'reiʃən] n conmemoración f; in — of en conmemoración de.

commemorative [kə'memərətiv] 1 adj conmemorativo. 2 n (stamp) conmemorativo m.

commence [kə'mens] 1 vt comenzar, empezar. 2 vi to — to + infin to — + ger empezar a + infin.

commencement [kə'mensmənt] n comienzo m, principio m; (mainly US: Univ) graduación f.

commend [kə'mend] vt (a) (praise) alabar, elogiar; to — someone for his action alabar la acción de uno.

(b) (recommend) I — him to you se lo recomiendo; I — it to your attention creo que merece su atención; the plan does not — itself to me el proyecto no me resulta aceptable; it has little to — it poco hay que decir a su favor.

(c) (entrust) encomendar (to a).

commendable [kə'mendəbl] adj recomendable, plausible, loable.

commendably [kə'mendəbli] adv de manera loable; it was — short tuvo el mérito de ser breve; you have been — prompt le felicito por la prontitud.

commendation [,kɔmen'deiʃən] n (a) (praise) elogio m, encomio m. (b) recomendación f.

commensurable [kə'menʃərəbl] adj conmensurable, comparable (with con).

commensurate [kə'menʃərit] adj proporcionado; — with equivalente a, que corresponde a.

comment ['kɔment] 1 n comentario m; observación f; no — no tengo nada que decir; it seems to call for — sobre eso conviene hacer algún comentario; to make the — that observar que.

2 vi: to — that observar que; to — on text comentar; subject etc hacer observaciones acerca de; to — unfavourably on something criticar algo.

commentary ['kɔmentəri] n comentario m.

commentator ['kɔmenteitə*] n comentador m, comentarista m (also Radio).

commerce ['kɔmə:s] n comercio m.

commercial [kə'mə:ʃəl] 1 adj comercial; law mercantil. 2 n (fam) emisión f publicitaria; (person) viajante m.

commercialism [kə'mə:ʃəlizəm] n mercantilismo m.

commercialize [kə'mə:ʃəlaiz] vt comercializar.

commiserate [kə'mizəreit] vi expresar su sentimiento; to — with compadecerse de, condolerse de.

commiseration [kə,mizə'reiʃən] n conmiseración f.

commissar ['kɔmisa:*] n comisario m.

commissariat [,kɔmi'sɛəriət] n comisariato m, comisaría f.

commissary ['kɔmisəri] n comisario m.

commission [kə'miʃən] 1 n (order, fee) comisión f; (act) perpetración f; (Mil) graduación f de oficial, despacho m de oficial, (warrant) nombramiento m; — agent comisionista m; Royal C— Comisión f Real; on — a comisión; to be out of — estar fuera de servicio; to put out of — inutilizar; to put into — poner en servicio activo.

2 vt officer nombrar (in a regiment a un regimiento); ship poner en servicio activo; architect etc nombrar, hacer un encargo a; picture encargar; to — someone to do something encargar a uno que haga algo.

commissionaire [kə,miʃə'nɛə*] n portero m, conserje m.

commissioner [kə'miʃənə*] m comisario m; high — alto comisario m; — for oaths notario m público; — of police jefe m de policía.

commit [kə'mit] 1 vt (a) crime cometer; error hacer, incurrir en.

(b) (involve) troops enviar a la batalla; resources empeñar.

(c) (entrust) entregar (to a); (Parl) bill someter a una comisión; to — something to someone's charge confiar algo a uno; to — something to the flames entregar algo a las llamas; to — something to memory aprender algo de memoria; to — someone to prison encarcelar a uno; to — someone for trial remitir a uno al tribunal; to — something to paper (or writing) poner algo por escrito.

2 vr: to — oneself hacer una promesa, declararse; to — oneself to comprometerse a, declararse a favor de; I can't — myself to that no puedo comprometerme a eso; without —ing myself sin compromiso por mi parte; I am —ted to help him me he comprometido a ayudarle; we are deeply —ted to this policy nos hemos declarado firmemente a favor de esta política.

commitment [kə'mitmənt] n compromiso m, obligación f, cometido m.

committal [kə'mitl] comisión f; compromiso m, cometido m; (burial) entierro m; — to prison (auto m de) prisión f.

committee [kə'miti] n comisión f, comité m; management — consejo m de administración; organizing — comité m organizador; to be on a — ser miembro de un comité.

commode [kə'məud] n sillico m.

commodious [kə'məudiəs] adj grande, espacioso.

commodity [kə'mɔditi] n artículo m (de consumo or de comercio), mercancía f, mercadería f, producto m; commodities mercancías fpl, géneros mpl.

commodore ['kɔmədɔ:*] n comodoro m.

common ['kɔmən] 1 adj (a) (belonging to many) común (also Math, Gram); law consuetudinario; it is — to all men es común a todos; A has nothing in — with B A no tiene nada de común con B; we have nothing in — no tenemos ningún interés en común; we have a lot in — tenemos muchos intereses en común; I, in — with everybody else yo, al igual que todos los demás; to work for a — aim cooperar todos a un mismo fin.

(b) (public) público.

(c) (frequent) común, frecuente; this butterfly is — in Spain esta mariposa es común en España.

(d) (usual, ordinary) corriente, usual; soldier raso; belief vulgar; the — man el hombre medio; in — use de uso corriente; it is no more than — courtesy to write no es más que una cortesía elemental escribir; it is — to see such things now ahora es frecuente ver tales cosas.

(e) (vulgar) ordinario; she's very — es muy ordinaria; as — as dirt de lo más ordinario; — or garden ordinario.

2 n (a) campo m común, ejido m.
   (b) —s (*Pol*) estado m llano; **the C—s** los Comunes.
   (c) **short** —s ración f escasa; **to be on short** —s comer mal.

commoner ['kɔmənə*] n plebeyo m, a f; (*Univ*) estudiante m que no tiene beca del colegio.

commonly ['kɔmənli] adv comúnmente, frecuentemente; generalmente; **it is — believed that** se cree vulgarmente que.

commonness ['kɔmənnis] n frecuencia f; (*vulgarity*) ordinariez f.

commonplace ['kɔmənpleis] **1** adj vulgar, trivial; **it is — to see that** es frecuente ver que.
   2 n (a) (*ordinary thing*) cosa f común, cosa f corriente.
   (b) (*Lit etc*) lugar m común, tópico m, perogrullada f.

commonroom ['kɔmənrum] n salón m (de un colegio etc).

commonsense ['kɔmən,sens] adj racional, lógico; **the — thing to do is** lo lógico es.

commonwealth ['kɔmənwelθ] n república f; **the (British) C—** la Mancomunidad (Británica).

commotion [kə'məuʃən] n tumulto m, confusión f; **civil —** disturbio m, perturbación f del orden público; **to cause a —** armar un lío; **there was a —** **in the crowd** se armó un lío entre los espectadores.

communal ['kɔmju:nl] adj comunal.

communally ['kɔmju:nəli] adv comunalmente; **to act — obrar** como comunidad; **the property is held —** la propiedad la posee la comunidad.

commune ['kɔmju:n] n (*Pol*) comuna f.

commune [kə'mju:n] vi (*Eccl*) comulgar; **to — with** conversar con, comunicarse con.

communicable [kə'mju:nikəbl] adj comunicable; *disease* transmisible.

communicant [kə'mju:nikənt] n comulgante mf.

communicate [kə'mju:nikeit] **1** vt comunicar. **2** vi (*Eccl*) comulgar; (*buildings etc*) mandarse; (*speak*) comunicarse (*with* con).

communication [kə,mju:ni'keiʃən] n comunicación f; **to be in — with** estar en contacto con; **to get into — with** ponerse en contacto con.

communication cord [kə,mju:ni'keiʃənkɔ:d] n (*Rail*) timbre m de alarma.

communicative [kə'mju:nikətiv] adj comunicativo.

communion [kə'mju:niən] n comunión f; **to take —** comulgar.

communiqué [kə'mju:nikei] n comunicado m, parte m; **joint —** comunicado m conjunto.

communism ['kɔmjunizm] n comunismo m.

communist ['kɔmjunist] **1** adj comunista. **2** n comunista mf.

communistic [,kɔmju'nistik] adj comunista.

community [kə'mju:niti] n comunidad f; (*people at large*) colectividad f, sociedad f; (*local inhabitants*) vecindario m; **— centre** centro m social; **— singing** canto m colectivo.

communize ['kɔmju:naiz] vt comunizar.

commutation [,kɔmju'teiʃən] n (*US*) conmutación f; (*Rail etc*) uso m de un billete de abono; **— ticket** billete m de abono.

commute [kə'mju:t] **1** vt *payment* conmutar (*into* en, *for* por); *sentence* conmutar (*to* en, por). **2** vi viajar a diario, ir y venir regularmente (*to work* al trabajo).

commuter [kə'mju:tə*] n persona f que viaja a diario (al trabajo), persona f que viaja muy a menudo.

compact ['kɔmpækt] n (a) pacto m, convenio m.
   (b) (*powder-*) polvera f.

compact [kəm'pækt] **1** adj compacto; *material* apretado, sólido; *style* breve, conciso. **2** vt *material* comprimir (*into* en); condensar; **to be —ed of** consistir en.

compactly [kəm'pæktli] adv de modo compacto; apretadamente, sólidamente; brevemente, concisamente.

compactness [kəm'pæktnis] n compacidad f, compresión f; (*of style*) concisión f.

companion [kəm'pæniən] n compañero m, a f; (*lady's*) señora f de compañía.

companionable [kəm'pæniənəbl] adj sociable, simpático.

companionship [kəm'pæniənʃip] n compañerismo m.

companionway [kəm'pæniənwei] n (*Naut*) escalera f de cámara.

company ['kʌmpəni] n (a) (*in general*) compañía f (*also Mil, Theat*); ship's — tripulación f; **he's good — es** un compañero divertido; **present — excepted** mejorando lo presente, con perdón de los presentes;

we have — tenemos visita; **to join — with** reunirse con; **to keep someone —** acompañar a uno, estar con uno; **to keep —** (*lovers*) andar en relaciones; **to keep bad —** tener amistades sospechosas; **a man is known by the —** he keeps dime con quién andas y te diré quién eres; **to part —** separarse (*with* de), (*fig*) desprenderse, soltarse.
   (b) (*Comm*) sociedad f, compañía f, empresa f; **Smith and C—** Smith y Compañía; **affiliated —** sociedad f filial; **holding —** sociedad f de control, compañía f tenedora; **joint-stock —, limited (liability) —** sociedad f anónima; **shipping —** compañía f naviera; **trust —** banco m fideicomisario.

comparable ['kɔmpərəbl] adj comparable; **a — case** un caso análogo; **they are not —** no se les puede comparar.

comparative [kəm'pærətiv] **1** adj relativo; (*Gram etc*) comparativo; *study* comparado. **2** n (*Gram*) comparativo m.

comparatively [kəm'pærətivli] adv relativamente.

compare [kəm'peə*] **1** n: **beyond —, past —, without —** sin comparación.
   2 vt comparar (*to, with* con); (*put side by side*) cotejar; **as —d with** comparado con; **they are not to be —d** no se les puede comparar.
   3 vi poderse comparar; **he can't — with you** no se le puede comparar con Vd; **it —s very favourably with the other** no pierde por comparación con el otro; **how do they —?** ¿cuáles son sus cualidades respectivas?; **how do they — for speed?** ¿cuál tiene mayor velocidad?

comparison [kəm'pærisn] n comparación f; cotejo m; **in — with** en comparación con.

compartment [kəm'pɑ:tmənt] n compartimiento m; (*Rail, of case etc*) departamento m.

compass ['kʌmpəs] **1** n (a) (*Naut etc*) brújula f.
   (b) (*range*) alcance m, extensión f; (*area*) ámbito m; **beyond my —** fuera de mi alcance; **in a small —** en un espacio reducido.
   (c) **—es** compás m; **a pair of —es** un compás.
   2 vt (*contrive*) conseguir, (*pej*) tramar; (*grasp mentally*) comprender; (*surround*) rodear; **to be —ed about by** estar rodeado de.

compassion [kəm'pæʃən] n compasión f; **to have — on** tener piedad de; **to move someone to —** mover a uno a compasión.

compassionate [kəm'pæʃənit] adj compasivo; **on — grounds** por compasión.

compatibility [kəm,pætə'biliti] n compatibilidad f.

compatible [kəm'pætibl] adj compatible, conciliable.

compatriot [kəm'pætriət] n compatriota mf.

compel [kəm'pel] vt obligar; *respect* imponer; *surrender* exigir, hacer inevitable; **to — someone to do something** forzar a uno a hacer algo; **I feel —led to** say me veo obligado a decir.

compelling [kəm'peliŋ] adj *argument* convincente; *curiosity etc* compulsivo.

compellingly [kəm'peliŋli] adv de modo convincente.

compendious [kəm'pendiəs] adj compendioso.

compendium [kəm'pendiəm] n compendio m.

compensate ['kɔmpenseit] **1** vt compensar; (*reward*) recompensar; (*for loss etc*) indemnizar, resarcir (*for* de). **2** vi: **to — for something** compensar algo.

compensation [,kɔmpen'seiʃən] n compensación f; (*reward*) recompensa f; (*for loss etc*) indemnización f, resarcimiento m.

compensatory [kəm'pensətəri] adj compensatorio.

compère ['kɔmpeə*] n presentador m.

compete [kəm'pi:t] vi (*as rivals*; *Comm*) competir, hacer competencia (*against, with* con, *for* por); (*in a race*) tomar parte (*in* en), presentarse (*in* a), concurrir (*in* a); **to — in a market** concurrir a un mercado.

competence ['kɔmpitəns] n aptitud f, capacidad f, competencia f; (*of court etc*) competencia f, incumbencia f; **that is not within my —** eso está fuera de mi competencia.

competent ['kɔmpitənt] adj competente, capaz, adecuado; **to be — to do something** ser competente para hacer algo.

competently ['kɔmpitəntli] adv de modo adecuado, competentemente.

competition [,kɔmpi'tiʃən] n (a) (*spirit*) competencia f, rivalidad f; **in — with** en competencia con; **there was keen — for the prize** se disputó reñidamente el premio.
   (b) (*Comm*) competencia f; **unfair —** competencia f desleal.
   (c) (*contest*) concurso m; (*eg for Civil Service posts*) oposiciones fpl; **60 places to be filled by —** 60 vacantes a cubrir por oposiciones.

competitive [kəm'petitiv] adj *spirit* competidor, de competencia; *exam* de concurso; *price* competitivo.

competitor [kəm'petitə*] n (a) (rival) competidor m, ora f, rival mf; (Comm) competidor m.
 (b) (in contest) concursante mf; (eg for Civil Service post) opositor m, ora f.
compilation [ˌkɔmpi'leiʃən] n compilación f, recopilación f.
compile [kəm'pail] vt compilar, recopilar.
compiler [kəm'pailə*] n compilador m, ora f, recopilador m, ora f; autor m, ora f.
complacence [kəm'pleisəns] n, **complacency** [kəm'pleisnsi] n suficiencia f, satisfacción f de sí mismo (or consigo).
complacent [kəm'pleisənt] adj suficiente, satisfecho de sí mismo (or consigo); complacido.
complacently [kəm'pleisəntli] adv suficientemente, de modo satisfecho; **he looked at me — me miró complacido.
complain [kəm'plein] vi quejarse (about, of de, that de que, to a); **I can't — yo no tengo motivo para quejarme.
complaint [kəm'pleint] n (a) queja f; (Law) querella f, demanda f; **to have cause for — tener motivo para quejarse; **to lodge** (or **make) a — formular una queja, hacer una reclamación.
 (b) (Med) enfermedad f, mal m, dolencia f.
complaisant [kəm'pleizənt] adj servicial, cortés; **husband consentido.
complement ['kɔmplimənt] n complemento m; (Naut) dotación f, personal m.
complement ['kɔmpliment] vt complementar.
complementary [ˌkɔmpli'mentəri] adj complementario; **they are — se complementan.
complete [kəm'pli:t] 1 adj entero, completo; total; (finished) acabado; (accomplished) consumado; **my happiness is — mi dicha es completa; **tell me the — story cuéntame la historia en su totalidad; **it is a — mistake to think that es totalmente erróneo pensar que; **it's a — disaster es un desastre total; **it was not a — success no obtuvo un éxito rotundo que digamos; **my report is still not quite — mi informe todavía no está terminado del todo; **are we —? ¿estamos todos?
 2 vt completar; (finish) terminar, acabar, concluir; years cumplir; form llenar; **to — my happiness para colmo de dicha.
completely [kəm'pli:tli] adv completamente, enteramente; totalmente; por completo; a fondo.
completeness [kəm'pli:tnis] n lo completo etc; **for the sake of — para completar.
completion [kəm'pli:ʃən] n terminación f, conclusión f; (of contract etc) realización f; **on — en cuanto se termine; **to be nearing — estar para terminarse.
complex ['kɔmpleks] 1 adj complejo, complicado.
 2 n (a) (Psych) complejo m; **inferiority — complejo m de inferioridad; **Oedipus — complejo m de Edipo; **he's got a — about it sobre eso tiene una idea fija, aquello le obsesiona.
 (b) (Tech) complejo m; **industrial — complejo m industrial.
complexion [kəm'plekʃən] n tez f, cutis m; (fig) aspecto m; **that puts a different — on it entonces la cosa cambia de aspecto.
complexity [kəm'pleksiti] n complejidad f, lo complicado.
compliance [kəm'plaiəns] n condescendencia f, sumisión f (with a); (agreement) conformidad f; **in — with de acuerdo con, obedeciendo a.
compliant [kəm'plaiənt] adj condescendiente, sumiso.
complicate ['kɔmplikeit] vt complicar.
complicated ['kɔmplikeitid] adj complicado.
complication [ˌkɔmpli'keiʃən] n complicación f; lo complicado; —s dificultades fpl; **it seems there are —s parece que han surgido dificultades.
complicity [kəm'plisiti] n complicidad f (in en).
compliment ['kɔmplimənt] n (a) (polite expression, of praise) cumplido m; (amorous) piropo m; **what a nice —! ¡qué detalle!; **that was meant as a — lo dije con buena intención; **to pay a — to hacer cumplidos a, woman piropear a; **I take that as a — agradezco la cortesía; **I take it as a — that para mí es un honor que + subj; **they did me the — of coming along me hicieron el honor de asistir.
 (b) —s (greetings) saludos mpl; **with the —s of Mr X de parte del Sr X; **with the —s of the season deseándole felices Pascuas (etc); **with the author's —s homenaje del autor; **to send one's —s to enviar saludos a.
compliment ['kɔmpliment] vt: **to — someone on something felicitar a uno por algo.
complimentary [ˌkɔmpli'mentəri] adj remark etc lisonjero; ticket de favor; **he was very — about the play habló en términos lisonjeros de la obra.

comply [kəm'plai] vi obedecer; **to — with conformarse con, ajustarse a, order obedecer.
component [kəm'pəunənt] 1 adj componente; **its — parts las piezas que lo integran. 2 n (Chem) componente m; (Tech) pieza f.
comport [kəm'pɔ:t] 1 vi: **to — with concordar con. 2 vr: **to — oneself comportarse.
comportment [kəm'pɔ:tmənt] n comportamiento m.
compose [kəm'pəuz] 1 vt componer; **to be —d of constar de, componerse de. 2 vr: **to — oneself tranquilizarse; **I —d myself to play me dispuse a tocar.
composed [kəm'pəuzd] adj sosegado.
composedly [kəm'pəuzidli] adv sosegadamente.
composer [kəm'pəuzə*] n compositor m.
composite ['kɔmpəzit] adj compuesto.
composition [ˌkɔmpə'ziʃən] n composición f.
compositor [kəm'pɔzitə*] n cajista m.
compos mentis ['kɔmpɔs'mentis] adj: **to be — estar en su juicio.
compost ['kɔmpɔst] n abono m compuesto.
compost heap ['kɔmpɔsthi:p] n montón m de abono compuesto.
composure [kəm'pəuʒə*] n serenidad f, calma f; **to recover one's — serenarse.
compote ['kɔmpəut] n compota f.
compound[1] ['kɔmpaund] 1 adj compuesto; fracture complicado. 2 n (Chem) compuesto m; (Gram) vocablo m compuesto.
compound[2] ['kɔmpaund] n (enclosure) recinto m.
compound [kəm'paund] 1 vt componer, mezclar; **to — a felony aceptar dinero para no entablar juicio. 2 vi: **to — with capitular con.
comprehend [ˌkɔmpri'hend] vt comprender.
comprehensible [ˌkɔmpri'hensəbl] adj comprensible.
comprehension [ˌkɔmpri'henʃən] n comprensión f; **it is past — es incomprensible; **it passes my — that para mí resulta incomprensible que.
comprehensive [ˌkɔmpri'hensiv] adj knowledge, study extenso; report global; account, view de conjunto; insurance contra todo riesgo; school integrado.
compress ['kɔmpres] n compresa f.
compress [kəm'pres] vt comprimir (into en); text etc reducir (into a).
compressed [kəm'prest] adj comprimido; **— air aire m comprimido.
compression [kəm'preʃən] n compresión f.
comprise [kəm'praiz] vt (include) comprender; (consist of) constar de, componerse de; range abarcar; **to be —d within certain limits estar incluido dentro de ciertos límites.
compromise ['kɔmprəmaiz] 1 n (spirit, art of —) transigencia f; (agreement) componenda f, avenencia f, arreglo m; (midway point) término m medio; **there can be no — with treason no transigimos con la traición; **to reach a — llegar a un arreglo.
 2 vt person comprometer, thing poner en peligro.
 3 vi transigir, ceder un poco para llegar a un acuerdo; **I agreed to — consentí en que la cosa quedase en un término medio; **to — with transigir con, avenirse con.
compromising ['kɔmprəmaizin] adj situation comprometedor; mind, spirit acomodaticio.
comptroller [kən'trəulə*] n interventor m.
compulsion [kəm'pʌlʃən] n obligación f, fuerza f mayor, coacción f; **under — por fuerza; **you are under no — nadie le obliga a ello.
compulsive [kəm'pʌlsiv] adj compulsivo.
compulsorily [kəm'pʌlsərili] adv por fuerza, forzosamente.
compulsory [kəm'pʌlsəri] adj obligatorio; purchase forzoso.
compunction [kəm'pʌŋkʃən] n remordimiento m; **without — sin escrúpulo.
computation [ˌkɔmpju'teiʃən] n cómputo m, cálculo m.
compute [kəm'pju:t] vt computar, calcular (at en).
computer [kəm'pju:tə*] n computador m, calculadora f; **digital — computador m digital.
computerize [kəm'pju:təraiz] vt reorganizar (or preparar, programar) para su tratamiento por computador.
comrade ['kɔmrid] n camarada m (also Pol), compañero m, a f.
comrade-in-arms ['kɔmridin'a:mz] n compañero m de armas.
comradeship ['kɔmridʃip] n compañerismo m.
con[1] [kɔn] vt estudiar, repasar (also to — over).
con[2] [kɔn] vt (sl) timar.
con[3] [kɔn] n see **pro.
concatenation [kɔnˌkæti'neiʃən] n concatenación f.
concave ['kɔn'keiv] adj cóncavo.
concavity [kɔn'kæviti] n concavidad f.

conceal [kən'siːl] *vt* ocultar (*from* a); *emotion* disimular; (*Law*) encubrir.
concealed [kən'siːld] *adj* oculto; *emotion* disimulado; *lighting* indirecto.
concealment [kən'siːlmənt] *n* encubrimiento *m* (*also Law*); (*of emotion*) disimulación *f*; **place of —** escondrijo *m*.
concede [kən'siːd] *vt* conceder; **I — that** confieso que; **to — victory to an opponent** reconocer que un rival ha ganado.
conceit [kən'siːt] *n* (a) presunción *f*, engreimiento *m*. (b) (*Lit*) concepto *m*.
conceited [kən'siːtid] *adj* presumido, engreído, vanidoso; **to be — about** envanecerse con.
conceivable [kən'siːvəbl] *adj* concebible: **is it — that . . . ?** ¿es posible que . . . (+ *subj*)?
conceivably [kən'siːvəbli] *adv* posiblemente; **it cannot — be true** no es posible que sea verdad.
conceive [kən'siːv] **1** *vt* (a) (*child*) concebir.
(b) (*imagine*) imaginar, formarse un concepto de; *idea* tener; *plan* idear; **I — it to be my duty** creo que es mi deber; **I cannot — why** no me explico por qué; **—d in plain terms** formulado en lenguaje sencillo.
(c) *affection, dislike etc* tomar, cobrar (*for* a).
2 *vi* concebir; **to — of** formarse un concepto de; **I cannot — of anything worse** para mí no hay nada peor.
concentrate ['kɔnsəntreit] **1** *n* (*Chem*) concentrado *m*, sustancia *f* concentrada.
2 *vt* concentrar; *troops etc* concentrar, reunir; *hopes* cifrar (*on* en).
3 *vi* concentrarse; (*troops etc*) concentrarse, reunirse; **to — on** *thing* concentrarse en, concentrar la atención en; **to — on doing something** concentrarse para hacer algo; **he can't —** no se puede concentrar.
concentration [,kɔnsən'treiʃən] *n* concentración *f*.
concentric [kən'sentrik] *adj* concéntrico.
concept ['kɔnsept] *n* concepto *m*.
conception [kən'sepʃən] *n* (a) (*of child*) concepción *f*; **the Immaculate C—** la Purísima Concepción.
(b) (*idea*) idea *f*, concepto *m*; **a bold —** un concepto grandioso; **he has not the remotest — of** no tiene la menor idea de.
conceptual [kən'septjuəl] *adj* conceptual.
concern [kən'səːn] **1** *n* (a) (*matter*) asunto *m*; **that's my —** eso es cuenta mía; **it's no — of yours** no tiene nada que ver con Vd; **that's your —!** ¡allá Vd!
(b) (*interest*) interés *m*; **it is of some —** **to us all** nos interesa a todos; **it's of no —** la cosa no tiene importancia.
(c) (*anxiety*) preocupación *f* (*for, with* con, por), inquietud *f*; **it is a matter for — that** es inquietante que; **he showed his —** se mostró preocupado; **with growing —** con creciente alarma.
(d) (*firm*) empresa *f*; **going —** empresa *f* en pleno funcionamiento; **the whole —** (*fam*) el asunto entero, todo el negocio.
2 *vt* tener que ver con, interesar, concernir; **as —s** respecto de; **that does not —** **me** eso no tiene que ver conmigo; **it —s me closely** me toca de cerca; **the book —s a family** el libro tiene por tema una familia; **my question —s money** mi pregunta se refiere al dinero; **those —ed** los interesados; **as far as I am —ed** en cuanto a mí, por lo que a mí se refiere; **to be —ed in** tomar parte en, intervenir en; **were you —ed in this?** ¿tú andabas mezclado en esto?; **to be —ed with others in a crime** estar implicado con otros en un crimen; **I am —ed to + infin** me interesa + infin; **we are —ed with facts** a nosotros nos interesan los hechos.
3 *vr*: **to — oneself with** interesarse por, ocuparse de.
concerned [kən'səːnd] *adj* inquieto, preocupado; **to be very —** inquietarse mucho (*about* por); **he sounded very —** parecía estar muy inquieto; **I am — about you** me traes preocupado; **I am — to find that** me inquieta descubrir que.
concerning [kən'səːniŋ] *prep* sobre, acerca de.
concert ['kɔnsət] *n* concierto *m*; **in — with** de concierto con; **to act in —** obrar de común acuerdo.
concert [kən'səːt] *vt* concertar; *policy* coordinar, armonizar.
concertgoer ['kɔnsət,gəuə*] *n* aficionado *m* a los conciertos, aficionada *f* a los conciertos; **we are regular —s** vamos con regularidad a los conciertos; **the —s are an odd lot** los que asisten al concierto son gente rara.
concert hall ['kɔnsəthɔːl] *n* sala *f* de conciertos.
concertina [,kɔnsə'tiːnə] *n* concertina *f*.

concertmaster ['kɔnsət,mɑːstə*] *n* (*US*) concertino *m*.
concerto [kən'tʃeətəu] *n* concierto *m*.
concession [kən'seʃən] *n* concesión *f*; privilegio *m*; **tax —** privilegio *m* fiscal.
concessionaire [kən,seʃə'nɛə*] *n* concesionario *m*.
concierge [,kɔːnsi'eəʒ] *n* conserje *m*.
conciliate [kən'silieit] *vt* conciliar.
conciliation [kən,sili'eiʃən] *n* conciliación *f*.
conciliatory [kən'siliətəri] *adj* conciliador.
concise [kən'sais] *adj* conciso.
concisely [kən'saisli] *adv* concisamente.
conciseness [kən'saisnis] *n*, **concision** [kən'siʒən] *n* concisión *f*.
conclave ['kɔnkleiv] *n* cónclave *m*.
conclude [kən'kluːd] **1** *vt* (a) (*end*) concluir, terminar; **"to be —d"** (*serial*) "continuará".
(b) (*arrange*) *treaty* hacer, firmar, pactar; *agreement* llegar a, concertar.
(c) (*infer*) **I — that** saco la consecuencia de que; **what are we to — from that?** ¿qué consecuencia se saca de eso?
2 *vi* terminar(se); **he —d with this remark** terminó haciendo esta observación; **he —d by saying** terminó diciendo; **the book —s poorly** el libro termina mal; **the judge —d in his favour** el juez decidió a su favor.
concluding [kən'kluːdiŋ] *adj* final.
conclusion [kən'kluːʒən] *n* (a) (*end*) conclusión *f*, terminación *f*; **in —** en conclusión, para terminar; **to bring something to a —** concluir algo.
(b) (*inference*) conclusión *f*, consecuencia *f*; **foregone —** resultado *m* inevitable; **to come to the —** **that** llegar a la conclusión de que; **to jump to —s** juzgar al buen tuntún; **to try —s with** participar en una contienda con.
conclusive [kən'kluːsiv] *adj* concluyente, decisivo.
conclusively [kən'kluːsivli] *adv* concluyentemente.
concoct [kən'kɔkt] *vt* confeccionar; *lie, story* inventar; *plot* tramar.
concoction [kən'kɔkʃən] *n* (*act*) confección *f*; (*of story*) invención *f*; (*substance*) mezcla *f*, (*drink*) brebaje *m*.
concomitant [kən'kɔmitənt] *adj* concomitante.
concord ['kɔŋkɔːd] *n* concordia *f*, armonía *f*; (*Mus, Gram*) concordancia *f*.
concordance [kən'kɔːdəns] *n* concordancia *f*; (*book*) concordancias *fpl*.
concordant [kən'kɔːdənt] *adj* concordante.
concordat [kɔn'kɔːdæt] *n* concordato *m*.
concourse ['kɔŋkɔːs] *n* (*of people*) concurso *m*; (*of rivers*) confluencia *f*; (*Rail*) explanada *f*.
concrete ['kɔnkriːt] **1** *adj* concreto; (*Tech*) de hormigón. **2** *n* hormigón *m*; **reinforced —** hormigón *m* armado. **3** *vt* revestir de hormigón.
concrete mixer ['kɔnkriːt,miksə*] *n* hormigonera *f*.
concretion [kən'kriːʃən] *n* concreción *f*.
concubine ['kɔŋkjubain] *n* concubina *f*.
concupiscence [kən'kjuːpisəns] *n* concupiscencia *f*.
concupiscent [kən'kjuːpisənt] *adj* concupiscente.
concur [kən'kəː*] *vi* (a) (*happen together*) concurrir.
(b) (*agree*) asentir; **to — in** convenir en; **to — with** estar de acuerdo con.
concurrent [kən'kʌrənt] *adj* concurrente.
concurrently [kən'kʌrəntli] *adv* al mismo tiempo.
concuss [kən'kʌs] *vt* producir una conmoción cerebral en.
concussion [kən'kʌʃən] *n* conmoción *f* cerebral.
condemn [kən'dem] *vt* condenar (*to* a); (*blame*) censurar; *building* declarar ruinoso; *bad food* confiscar; **the —ed man** el reo de muerte; **such conduct is to be —ed** tal conducta es censurable.
condemnation [,kɔndem'neiʃən] *n* condenación *f*; (*blaming*) censura *f*.
condensation [,kɔnden'seiʃən] *n* condensación *f*; (*of text*) forma *f* abreviada.
condense [kən'dens] **1** *vt* condensar; *text* abreviar. **2** *vi* condensarse.
condenser [kən'densə*] *n* condensador *m*.
condescend [,kɔndi'send] *vi*: **to — to + infin** dignarse + infin.
condescending [,kɔndi'sendiŋ] *adj* superior, lleno de superioridad; **he's very —** se cree muy superior, tiene aire de superioridad.
condescendingly [,kɔndi'sendiŋli] *adv* de modo superior, con aire de superioridad.
condescension [,kɔndi'senʃən] *n* aire *f* de superioridad, aire *m* protector, dignación *f*.
condiment ['kɔndimənt] *n* condimento *m*.
condition [kən'diʃən] *n* (a) (*stipulation*) condición *f*; **on this —** con esta condición; **on no —** de ninguna manera; **on — (that)** a condición que + *subj*.

(b) (*state*) condición *f*, estado *m*; **physical —** estado *m* físico; **weather —s** estado *m* del tiempo; **in a bad —** en malas condiciones; **of humble —** de clase humilde; **to be in no — to** + *infin* no estar en condiciones de + *infin*; **to be out of —** estar en mal estado; **to keep oneself in —** mantenerse en forma.

(c) —s (*circumstances*) condiciones *fpl*; **living —s** condiciones *fpl* de vida; **working —s** condiciones *fpl* de trabajo; **under existing —s** en las circunstancias actuales.

2 *vt* condicionar, determinar; **it is —ed by the size** depende del tamaño.

conditional [kən'diʃənl] **1** *adj* condicional; **to be — upon** depender de. **2** *n* (*Gram*) potencial *m*.

conditionally [kən'diʃnəli] *adv* condicionalmente, con reservas.

conditioned [kən'diʃənd] *adj* condicionado; **— reflex** reflejo *m* condicionado.

condole [kən'dəul] *vi*: **to — with someone** condolerse de uno.

condolences [kən'dəulənsiz] *npl* pésame *m*; **please accept my —** le acompaño en el sentimiento; **to send one's —** dar el pésame.

condominium [kɔndə'miniəm] *n* condominio *m*.

condone [kən'dəun] *vt* condonar.

condor ['kɔndɔ:*] *n* cóndor *m*.

conduce [kən'dju:s] *vi*: **to — to** conducir a.

conducive [kən'dju:siv] *adj*: **— to** conducente a, que conduce a, que favorece.

conduct ['kɔndʌkt] *n* conducta *f*, comportamiento *m*; (*of business etc*) manejo *m*, dirección *f*.

conduct [kən'dʌkt] **1** *vt* conducir (*also Phys*); *business, negotiations, campaign etc* llevar, dirigir; *one's case* presentar; *orchestra* dirigir; **to — a correspondence with** estar en correspondencia con; **we were —ed through a passage** nos hicieron pasar por un pasillo; **we were —ed round by Lord X** actuó de guía Lord X.

2 *vi* (*Mus*) llevar la batuta.

3 *vr*: **to — oneself** comportarse.

conducted [kən'dʌktid] *adj*: **— tour** (*of building*) visita *f* dirigida, (*of country*) viaje *m* dirigido.

conduction [kən'dʌkʃən] *n* conducción *f*.

conductivity [kɔndʌk'tiviti] *n* conductibilidad *f*.

conductor [kən'dʌktə*] *n* (*Mus*) director *m*; (*of bus*) cobrador *m*; (*US*) revisor *m*; (*lightning-*) pararrayos *m*.

conductress [kən'dʌktris] *n* cobradora *f*.

conduit ['kɔndit] *n* conducto *m*.

cone [kəun] *n* (*Geom, Bot*) cono *m*; (*ice cream*) barquillo *m*.

coney ['kəuni] *n* conejo *m*.

confab ['kɔnfæb] *n* (*fam*) = **confabulation.**

confabulate [kən'fæbjuleit] *vi* (*hum*) conferenciar.

confabulation [kən,fæbju'leiʃən] *n* conferencia *f*.

confection [kən'fekʃən] *n* confección *f*, hechura *f*.

confectioner [kən'fekʃənə*] *n* pastelero *m*, repostero *m*; **—'s** (*shop*) pastelería *f*, repostería *f*, confitería *f*.

confectionery [kən'fekʃənəri] *n* pasteles *mpl*; (*sweets*) dulces *mpl*, confites *mpl*, confitería *f*.

confederacy [kən'fedərəsi] *n* confederación *f*; (*plot*) complot *m*; **the C—** (*US*) los Estados confederados.

confederate [kən'fedərit] **1** *adj* confederado. **2** *n* confederado *m*; (*Law*) cómplice *m*.

confederate [kən'fedəreit] **1** *vt* confederar. **2** *vi* confederarse.

confederation [kən,fedə'reiʃən] *n* confederación *f*.

confer [kən'fə:*] **1** *vt* conceder, otorgar (*on* a). **2** *vi* conferenciar (*about* sobre, *with* con).

conference ['kɔnfərəns] *n* (*talk*) conferencia *f*; (*assembly*) congreso *m*.

conferment [kən'fə:mənt] *n* concesión *f*, otorgamiento *m* (*on* a).

confess [kən'fes] **1** *vt* confesar; *guilt etc* reconocer; **to — that** confesar que.

2 *vi* (*Eccl*) confesarse; **to — to a crime** confesarse culpable de un crimen; **to — to a liking for** confesar tener afición a; **I was wrong, I —** me equivoqué, lo confieso.

confessed [kən'fest] *adj* declarado.

confessedly [kən'fesidli] *adv* según se reconoce.

confession [kən'feʃən] *n* confesión *f*; **— of faith** credo *m*; **to go to —** confesarse; **to hear someone's —** confesar a uno; **to make a full —** confesarlo todo.

confessional [kən'feʃənl] *n* confesonario *m*.

confessor [kən'fesə*] *n* confesor *m*; **father —** padre *m* confesor, director *m* espiritual.

confetti [kən'feti:] *n* confeti *m*.

confidant [kɔnfi'dænt] *n* confidente *m*.

confidante [kɔnfi'dænt] *n* confidenta *f*.

confide [kən'faid] **1** *vt* confiar (*to* a, en).

2 *vi*: **to — in** confiar en, fiarse de; **please — in me** prenda.

puedes fiarte de mí; **to — to** hacer confidencias a; **he —d to me that** me dijo en confianza que.

confidence ['kɔnfidəns] *n* **(a)** (*in general*) confianza *f* (*in* en, *that* en que); **in —** en confianza; **"write in strict —"** "absoluta reserva"; **to be in someone's —**, **to enjoy someone's —** disfrutar de la intimidad de uno; **to gain —** adquirir confianza; **to give someone —** infundir confianza a uno; **we have every — in you** tenemos entera confianza en Vd; **I have every — that** estoy totalmente seguro de que; **to put one's — in** confiar en.

(b) (*revelation*) confidencia *f*.

confidence man ['kɔnfidənsmæn] *n*, *pl* **—men** [men] timador *m*.

confidence trick ['kɔnfidənstrik] *n*, (*US*) **— game** [geim] *n* timo *m*.

confident ['kɔnfidənt] *adj* seguro de sí mismo, lleno de confianza; (*over-*) confiado; **to be — about, to be — of** estar seguro de; **to be — that** estar seguro de que.

confidential [kɔnfi'denʃəl] *adj* *information, letter, report etc* confidencial; *secretary, tone* de confianza.

confidentially [kɔnfi'denʃəli] *adv* en confianza.

confidently ['kɔnfidəntli] *adv*: **he said —** dijo lleno de confianza; **we — expect that** creemos con toda confianza que.

confiding [kən'faidiŋ] *adj*: **(too) —** confiado; crédulo; **in a — tone** en tono de confianza.

configuration [kən,figju'reiʃən] *n* configuración *f*.

confine [kən'fain] **1** *vt* (*enclose*) encerrar (*to* en); (*fig*) limitar (*to* a); **to be —d** (*woman*) estar de parto; **to be —d to** limitarse a; **the damage is —d to this part** el daño afecta únicamente esta parte; **this bird is —d to Spain** esta ave existe únicamente en España; **to be —d to bed** tener que guardar cama; **to be —d to one's room** no poder dejar su cuarto.

2 *vr*: **to — oneself to** limitarse a; **please — yourself to the facts** le ruego limitarse a exponer los hechos.

confined [kən'faind] *adj* reducido.

confinement [kən'fainmənt] *n* (*enclosure*) encierro *m* (*to* en); (*imprisonment*) prisión *f*, reclusión *f*; (*Med*) parto *m*, sobreparto *m*; **— to barracks** arresto *m* en cuartel *f*; **to be in solitary —** estar incomunicado.

confines ['kɔnfainz] *npl* confines *mpl*.

confirm [kən'fə:m] *vt* confirmar.

confirmation [kɔnfə'meiʃən] *n* confirmación *f*.

confirmed [kən'fə:md] *adj* inveterado.

confiscate ['kɔnfiskeit] *vt* confiscar, incautarse de.

confiscation [kɔnfis'keiʃən] *n* confiscación *f*, incautación *f*.

conflagration [kɔnflə'greiʃən] *n* conflagración *f*.

conflict ['kɔnflikt] *n* conflicto *m*; **to be in — with** estar en pugna con; **to come into — with** chocar con.

conflict [kən'flikt] *vi* estar en pugna (*with* con).

conflicting [kən'fliktiŋ] *adj* *report* contradictorio; *interest* opuesto.

confluence ['kɔnfluəns] *n* confluencia *f*.

conform [kən'fɔ:m] *vi* conformarse; **to — to, to — with** ajustarse a, estar de acuerdo con, cuadrar con.

conformist [kən'fɔ:mist] **1** *adj* conformista. **2** *n* conformista *mf*.

conformity [kən'fɔ:miti] *n* conformidad *f*; **in — with** conforme a.

confound [kən'faund] *vt* confundir; **— it!** ¡demonio!; **— the man!** ¡maldito sea el hombre!

confounded [kən'faundid] *adj* condenado.

confront [kən'frʌnt] *vt* (*face squarely*) hacer frente a, encararse con; (*face defiantly*) enfrentarse con; *rival* confrontarse con; *texts* confrontar; **the problems which — us** los problemas que se nos plantean; **we were —ed by the river** se nos puso delante el río; **to — someone with something** confrontar a uno con algo; **to — the accused with witnesses** confrontar a los testigos con el acusado; **to — someone with the facts** exponer delante de uno los hechos.

confrontation [kɔnfrən'teiʃən] *n* confrontación *f*; **nuclear —** confrontación *f* nuclear.

Confucius [kən'fju:fəs] *m* Confucio.

confuse [kən'fju:z] *vt* **(a)** (*mix up*) confundir (*with* con); *issue etc* entenebrecer; **to — A and B** confundir A con B, equivocar A con B.

(b) (*perplex*) desconcertar, dejar confuso a, aturdir; **to get —d** desorientarse, aturrullarse, desconcertarse.

confused [kən'fju:zd] *adj* *situation etc* confuso; *person* perplejo, despistado; **my mind is —** tengo la cabeza trastornada.

confusedly [kən'fju:zidli] *adv* confusamente.

confusing [kən'fju:ziŋ] *adj* confuso, desconcertante; **it's all very —** todo ello es muy difícil de comprender.

confusion [kən'fju:ʒən] n (a) (disorder) confusión , desorden m; to be in — estar en desorden; to retire in — retirarse en desorden.
(b) (perplexity) confusión f, perplejidad f, desorientación f, despiste m; to be in — estar desorientado; to be covered in — estar avergonzado.
confute [kən'fju:t] vt confutar.
congeal [kən'dʒi:l] 1 vt congelar, cuajar, coagular; blood coagular. 2 vi congelarse, cuajarse, coagularse; (blood) coagularse.
congenial [kən'dʒi:niəl] adj simpático, agradable.
congenital [kən'dʒenitl] adj congénito.
conger eel ['kɔŋgər'i:l] n congrio m.
congested [kən'dʒestid] adj area superpoblado; building etc lleno, de bote en bote; to get — with llenarse de, atestarse de; it's getting very — in here aquí hay demasiada gente.
congestion [kən'dʒestʃən] n congestión f (also Med), aglomeración f.
conglomerate [kən'glɔmərit] n conglomerado m.
conglomerate [kən'glɔməreit] 1 vt conglomerar. 2 vi conglomerarse.
conglomeration [kən,glɔmə'reiʃən] n conglomeración f.
Congo ['kɔŋgəu]: the — el Congo.
Congolese [,kɔŋgəu'li:z] 1 adj congolés, congoleño. 2 n congolés m, esa f, congoleño m, a f.
congratulate [kən'grætjuleit] vt felicitar, dar la enhorabuena a (on por).
congratulations [kən,grætju'leiʃənz] npl felicitaciones fpl; —! ¡enhorabuena!
congratulatory [kən'grætjulətəri] adj de felicitación.
congregate ['kɔŋgrigeit] vi congregarse.
congregation [,kɔŋgri'geiʃən] n (assembly) reunión f; (Eccl: present in church) fieles mpl, (parishioners) feligreses mpl.
congregational [kɔŋgri'geiʃnl] adj congregacionalista.
congress ['kɔŋgres] n congreso m; C— (US) Congreso m.
congressional [kɔŋ'greʃənl] adj congresional, del congreso.
congressman ['kɔŋgresmən] n, pl —men [mən] diputado m.
congruent ['kɔŋgruənt] adj congruente.
congruity [kɔŋ'gru:iti] n congruencia f (with con).
congruous ['kɔŋgruəs] adj congruo (with con).
conic(al) ['kɔnik(əl)] adj cónico.
conifer ['kɔnifə*] n conífera f.
coniferous [kə'nifərəs] adj conífero.
conjectural [kən'dʒektʃərəl] adj conjetural.
conjecture [kən'dʒektʃə*] 1 n conjetura f. 2 vt conjeturar (from de, por, that que).
conjoint ['kɔn'dʒɔint] adj conjunto.
conjointly ['kɔn'dʒɔintli] adv conjuntamente, en conjunto.
conjugal ['kɔndʒugəl] adj conyugal.
conjugate ['kɔndʒugeit] vt conjugar.
conjugation [,kɔndʒu'geiʃən] n conjugación f.
conjunct [kən'dʒʌŋkt] adj conjunto.
conjunction [kən'dʒʌŋkʃən] n conjunción f; in — with this junto con esto; in — with others en unión con otros.
conjunctive [kən'dʒʌŋktiv] adj (Gram) conjuntivo.
conjunctivitis [kən,dʒʌŋkti'vaitis] n conjuntivitis f.
conjuncture [kən'dʒʌŋktʃə*] n coyuntura f.
conjure [kən'dʒuə*] vt suplicar (to do something hacer algo).
conjure ['kʌndʒə*] 1 vt: to — away conjurar; to — up hacer aparecer, (fig) evocar, hacer pensar en; a name to — with un nombre todopoderoso.
2 vi hacer juegos de manos; he —s with handkerchiefs hace un truco con pañuelos.
conjurer ['kʌndʒərə*] n ilusionista m, mago m, prestidigitador m.
conjuring ['kʌndʒəriŋ] n juegos mpl de manos, ilusionismo m, arte m de los trucos.
conjuring trick ['kʌndʒəriŋ,trik] n juego m de manos.
conk¹ [kɔŋk] n (sl) (nose) narigón m; (head) cabeza f.
conk² [kɔŋk] vi (fam): to — out parar, tener una avería.
conker ['kɔŋkə*] n (fam) castaña f.
con man ['kɔnmæn] n, pl — men [men] (fam) timador m.
connect [kə'nekt] 1 vt (join) juntar, unir (to con); (Elec) conectar (to con); (relate) relacionar, asociar (with con); to — someone with (Tel) poner a uno en comunicación con; are these matters —ed? ¿tienen alguna relación entre sí estas cuestiones?; to be well —ed estar bien relacionado; the Jones are —ed with the Smiths los Jones están emparentados con los Smith; what firm are you —ed with? ¿con qué

empresa trabaja Vd?; I never —ed you with that nunca creía que Vd tuviera que ver con eso.
2 vi (join) unirse, (Elec) conectarse; to — with (Rail etc) enlazar con.
connecting rod [kə'nektiŋrɔd] n biela f.
connection, connexion [kə'nekʃən] n (a) (joint) juntura f, unión f; (Mech, Elec) conexión f; (Rail etc) correspondencia f (with con); our —s with the town are poor son malas nuestras comunicaciones con la ciudad.
(b) (fig) relación f (between entre, with con); (relative) pariente m, a f; we have —s everywhere tenemos relaciones con todas partes; you have to have —s hay que tener buenas relaciones; no — with any other firm ésta es una firma independiente; in — with a propósito de; in this — con respecto a esto.
conning tower ['kɔniŋ,tauə*] n torreta f.
connivance [kə'naivəns] n connivencia f; (agreement) consentimiento m; with the — of con el consentimiento de.
connive [kə'naiv] vi: to — at hacer la vista gorda a; to — with someone to do something confabularse con uno para hacer algo.
connoisseur [,kɔnə'sə:*] n entendido m, a f (of en), experto m.
connotation [,kɔnəu'teiʃən] n connotación f.
connote [kɔ'nəut] vt connotar.
connubial [kə'nju:biəl] adj conyugal.
conquer ['kɔŋkə*] 1 vt territory conquistar; enemy, habit etc vencer. 2 vi triunfar.
conquering ['kɔŋkəriŋ] adj victorioso.
conqueror ['kɔŋkərə*] n conquistador m; vencedor m; William the C— Guillermo el Conquistador.
conquest ['kɔŋkwest] n conquista f.
consanguinity [,kɔnsæŋ'gwiniti] n consanguinidad f.
conscience ['kɔnʃəns] n conciencia f; in all — en verdad; with a clear — con la conciencia limpia; I have a clear — about it no creo tener culpa alguna por ello; I have a guilty — about it me está remordiendo la conciencia por ello; I would not have the — to + infin no me atrevería a + infin.
conscience money ['kɔnʃəns,mʌni] n dinero que se paga para descargar la conciencia (p. ej., atrasos de contribuciones).
conscience-stricken ['kɔnʃəns,strikən] adj lleno de remordimientos.
conscientious [,kɔnʃi'enʃəs] adj concienzudo; objector de conciencia.
conscientiously [,kɔnʃi'enʃəsli] adv concienzudamente.
conscientiousness [,kɔnʃi'enʃəsnis] n diligencia f, escrupulosidad f.
conscious ['kɔnʃəs] adj (a) (aware) to be — of ser consciente de, saber, hacerse cargo de; to be — that saber perfectamente que; to become — of darse cuenta de; to become — that darse cuenta de que.
(b) (deliberate) intencional.
(c) (Med) to be — tener conocimiento; to become — volver en sí.
consciously ['kɔnʃəsli] adv conscientemente, a sabiendas.
consciousness ['kɔnʃəsnis] n (a) consciencia f.
(b) (Med) conocimiento m; to lose — perder el conocimiento; to regain — recobrar el conocimiento, volver en sí.
conscript ['kɔnskript] n recluta m, quinto m.
conscript [kɔn'skript] vt llamar al servicio militar.
conscription [kən'skripʃən] n servicio m militar obligatorio; (act) llamada f al servicio militar.
consecrate ['kɔnsikreit] vt consagrar.
consecration [,kɔnsi'kreiʃən] n consagración f.
consecutive [kən'sekjutiv] adj sucesivo, seguido; (Gram etc) consecutivo; on 3 — days 3 días seguidos.
consecutively [kən'sekjutivli] adv sucesivamente.
consensus [kən'sensəs] n consenso m; the — of opinion la opinión general.
consent [kən'sent] 1 n consentimiento m (to en); by common — según la opinión unánime; by mutual — de común acuerdo.
2 vi consentir (to en, to + infin en + infin).
consentient [kən'senʃiənt] adj (a) anuente. (b) acorde, unánime.
consequence ['kɔnsikwəns] n consecuencia f; resultado m; in — por consiguiente; — of en de resultas de; it is of no — la cosa no tiene importancia; to put up with (or take) the —s aceptar las consecuencias.
consequent ['kɔnsikwənt] adj consiguiente.
consequential [,kɔnsi'kwenʃəl] adj (a) (resulting) consiguiente, resultante: the moves — upon this decision las medidas que resultan de esta decisión.
(b) (important) importante, de consecuencia.

consequently ['kɔnsikwəntli] *adv* por consiguiente.

conservancy [kən'səːvənsi] *n* conservación *f*; **Nature C—** (*Brit*) *autoridad pública protectora de la naturaleza (flora, fauna, terrenos de interés científico etc).*

conservation [ˌkɔnsə'veiʃən] *n* conservación *f* (*esp de* recursos naturales).

conservatism [kən'səːvətizəm] *n* (*Pol*) conservatismo *m*, conservadurismo *m*.

conservative [kən'səːvətiv] **1** *adj* (*Pol*) conservador; *estimate etc* cauteloso, moderado. **2** *n* conservador *m*, ora *f*.

conservatoire [kən'səːvətwɑː*] *n* conservatorio *m*.

conservatory [kən'səːvətri] *n* invernadero *m*.

conserve [kən'səːv] **1** *n* conserva *f*. **2** *vt* conservar; **to — one's strength** reservarse.

consider [kən'sidə*] **1** *vt* (**a**) (*deem*) considerar; **I — that** considero que; **I — it an honour** lo tengo a mucha honra; **I — him to be clever** le considero inteligente, creo que es inteligente; **I — the matter closed** para mí el asunto está concluido.

(**b**) (*realize*) **when one —s that** cuando uno se da cuenta de que.

(**c**) (*think over*) considerar, pensar, meditar; **— how much you owe him** considere cuánto le debe Vd; **all things —ed** después de meditarlo bien; considerando todos los puntos; **my —ed opinion is that** estoy convencido de que.

(**d**) (*study*) estudiar, examinar; **we are —ing the matter** estamos estudiando el asunto; **he is being —ed for the post** le están considerando para el puesto.

(**e**) (*entertain*) **have you ever —ed going by train?** ¿has pensado alguna vez en ir en tren?; **I wouldn't — it for a moment** ni quiero pensarlo siquiera; **he refused even to — it** se negó a pensarlo siquiera.

(**f**) (*take into account*) tomar en cuenta; **you must — others' feelings** hay que tomar en cuenta los sentimientos de los demás.

2 *vr*: **I — myself happy** me considero feliz; **— yourself lucky** puede creer que ha tenido suerte; **— yourself dismissed** considérese despedido.

considerable [kən'sidərəbl] *adj* considerable; *sum etc* importante; *loss* sensible; **we had — difficulty** tuvimos bastante dificultad.

considerably [kən'sidərəbli] *adv* bastante, mucho, considerablemente.

considerate [kən'sidərit] *adj* considerado.

considerately [kən'sidəritli] *adv* con consideración.

consideration [kənˌsidə'reiʃən] *n* (**a**) consideración *f*; **as a mark of my —** en señal de mi consideración; **in — of** en consideración a; **out of — for** por respeto a; **without due —** sin reflexión; **that is a — eso** hay que tenerlo en cuenta; **it is under — lo** estamos estudiando; **we are giving the matter our — estamos** estudiando la cuestión; **to take into — tener** en cuenta.

(**b**) (*payment*) retribución *f*; **for a — si** se paga el servicio.

considering [kən'sidəriŋ] **1** *adv* (*fam*) teniendo en cuenta todas las circunstancias. **2** *prep* en consideración a.

consign [kən'sain] *vt* consignar (*also Comm*); (*fig*) enviar; **to — to oblivion** sepultar en el olvido.

consignee [ˌkɔnsai'niː] *n* consignatario *m*.

consigner, consignor [kən'sainə*] *n* (*Comm*) consignador *m*.

consignment [kən'sainmənt] *n* consignación *f*; envío *m*, remesa *f*; **— note** talón *m* de expedición.

consist [kən'sist] *vi*: **to — of** consistir en, constar de.

consistency [kən'sistənsi] *n* (*of person, action*) consecuencia *f*, lógica *f*; (*density*) consistencia *f*.

consistent [kən'sistənt] *adj person, action, argument* consecuente, lógico; *pupil, results* constante; (*dense*) consistente; **to be — with** ser consecuente con, estar de acuerdo con.

consistently [kən'sistəntli] *adv* (*logically*) consecuentemente; (*all the time*) constantemente; **to act —** obrar con consecuencia.

consolation [ˌkɔnsə'leiʃən] *n* consuelo *m*; (*act*) consolación *f*; **— prize** premio *m* de consuelo; (*academic etc*) accésit *m*; **it is some — to know that** me reconforta saber que.

consolatory [kən'sɔlətəri] *adj* consolatorio.

console¹ [kən'səul] *vt* consolar.

console² ['kɔnsəul] *n* (*Mus, Tech etc*) consola *f*.

consolidate [kən'sɔlideit] **1** *vt* consolidar. **2** *vi* consolidarse.

consolidation [kənˌsɔli'deiʃən] *n* consolidación *f*.

consoling [kən'səuliŋ] *adj* consolador, reconfortante.

consols [kən'sɔlz] *npl* consolidados *mpl*.

consommé [kən'sɔmei] *n* consomé *m*.

consonance ['kɔnsənəns] *n* consonancia *f*.

consonant ['kɔnsənənt] **1** *adj* consonante; **— with** conforme a. **2** *n* consonante *f*.

consonantal [ˌkɔnsə'næntl] *adj* consonántico.

consort ['kɔnsɔːt] *n* consorte *mf*; **prince —** príncipe *m* consorte *m*.

consort [kən'sɔːt] *vi*: **to — with** ir con, asociarse con; (*agree*) concordar con.

consortium [kən'sɔːtiəm] *n* consorcio *m*.

conspectus [kən'spektəs] *n* vista *f* general, ojeada *f* general; sumario *m*, resumen *m*.

conspicuous [kən'spikjuəs] *adj* visible, que llama la atención; (*fig*) notable; **to be —** destacar(se); **to ° make oneself —** llamar la atención; *see* absence.

conspicuously [kən'spikjuəsli] *adv* visiblemente, claramente; de modo que llama la atención; (*fig*) notablemente.

conspiracy [kən'spirəsi] *n* conspiración *f*, conjuración *f*, complot *m*.

conspirator [kən'spirətə*] *n* conspirador *m*, ora *f*.

conspire [kən'spaiə*] *vi* conspirar (*against* contra, **with** con, **to +** *infin* a **+** *infin*).

constable ['kʌnstəbl] *n* policía *m*, guardia *m*; **chief —** jefe *m* de policía.

constabulary [kən'stæbjuləri] *n* policía *f*.

Constance ['kɔnstəns] *f* Constanza.

constancy ['kɔnstənsi] *n* constancia *f*; fidelidad *f*.

constant ['kɔnstənt] **1** *adj* constante; (*faithful*) fiel, leal; (*unending*) continuo, incesante; *reader* asiduo. **2** *n* constante *f*.

constantly ['kɔnstəntli] *adv* constantemente.

Constantinople [ˌkɔnstænti'nəupl] Constantinopla.

constellation [ˌkɔnstə'leiʃən] *n* constelación *f*.

consternation [ˌkɔnstə'neiʃən] *n* consternación *f*; **in —** consternado; **there was general —** se consternaron todos.

constipate ['kɔnstipeit] *vt* estreñir; **to be —d** estar estreñido.

constipation [ˌkɔnsti'peiʃən] *n* estreñimiento *m*.

constituency [kən'stitjuənsi] *n* distrito *m* electoral, circunscripción *f*.

constituent [kən'stitjuənt] **1** *adj* constitutivo, integrante; **— assembly** cortes *fpl* constituyentes. **2** *n* constitutivo *m*, componente *m*; (*Pol*) elector *m*, ora *f*.

constitute ['kɔnstitjuːt] **1** *vt* constituir; (*make up*) componer, integrar. **2** *vr*: **to — oneself a judge** constituirse en juez.

constitution [ˌkɔnsti'tjuːʃən] *n* constitución *f*.

constitutional [ˌkɔnsti'tjuːʃənl] **1** *adj* constitucional. **2** *n* paseo *m*.

constitutionally [ˌkɔnsti'tjuːʃənəli] *adv* según la constitución.

constitutive ['kɔnstitjuːtiv] *adj* constitutivo.

constrain [kən'strein] *vt*: **to — someone to do something** obligar a uno a hacer algo; **to feel —ed to do something** verse en la necesidad de hacer algo.

constraint [kən'streint] *n* (*compulsion*) fuerza *f*; (*confinement*) encierro *m*; (*restraint*) reserva *f*, (*of atmosphere*) frialdad *f*; **under —** obligado a ello; **to feel a certain —** sentirse algo cohibido.

constrict [kən'strikt] *vt* apretar, estrechar.

constriction [kən'strikʃən] *n* constricción *f*.

construct [kən'strʌkt] *vt* construir.

construction [kən'strʌkʃən] *n* construcción *f* (*also Gram*); (*fig*) interpretación *f*; **in course of —**, **under —** en construcción; **to put a wrong — on something** interpretar algo mal.

constructional [kən'strʌkʃənl] *adj* estructural; **— toy** juguete *m* con que se construyen modelos.

constructive [kən'strʌktiv] *adj* constructivo.

constructively [kən'strʌktivli] *adv* constructivamente.

constructor [kən'strʌktə*] *n* constructor *m*.

construe [kən'struː] *vt* interpretar; (*Gram*) construir.

consul ['kɔnsəl] *n* cónsul *m*.

consular ['kɔnsjulə*] *adj* consular.

consulate ['kɔnsjulit] *n* consulado *m*.

consulship ['kɔnsəlʃip] *n* consulado *m*.

consult [kən'sʌlt] **1** *vt* consultar; **one's interests** tener en cuenta. **2** *vi*: **to — together** reunirse para consultar; **to — with** consultar con, aconsejarse con.

consultant [kən'sʌltənt] *n* asesor *m*; (*Med*) especialista *mf*; **to act as —** asesorar.

consultation [ˌkɔnsəl'teiʃən] *n* (*act*) consulta *f*; (*in general*) consultación *f*.

consultative [kən'sʌltətiv] *adj* consultivo.

consulting-room [kən'sʌltiŋrum] *n* consultorio *m*.

consume [kən'sjuːm] *vt* (*eat*) comerse, (*drink*) beberse; (*use*) consumir, utilizar; (*by fire etc*) consumir;

the house was —d by fire la casa quedó arrasada por el fuego; to be —d with envy etc estar muerto de.
consumer [kən'sjuːmə*] n consumidor m, ora f; — goods bienes mpl de consumo; — protection protección f al consumidor; — resistance resistencia f por parte del consumidor.
consuming [kən'sjuːmiŋ] adj arrollador, apasionado.
consummate [kən'sʌmit] adj consumado, completo.
consummate ['kɒnsʌmeit] vt consumar.
consummation [ˌkɒnsʌ'meiʃən] n consumación f.
consumption [kən'sʌmpʃən] n consumo m; (Med) tisis f.
consumptive [kən'sʌmptiv] 1 adj tísico. 2 n tísico m, a f.
contact ['kɒntækt] 1 n contacto m; he has a lot of —s tiene muchas relaciones, (pej) tiene muchos enchufes, tiene buenas aldabas; you have to have a — in the business hay que tener un buen enchufe en el negocio; to come into — with tocar, (violently) chocar con, (fig) tener que ver con, tratar; to get into — with ponerse en contacto con; I seem to make no — with him me resulta imposible comunicar con él.
2 vt ponerse en contacto con, comunicar con.
contact lenses ['kɒntækt,lenziz] pl lentes fpl de contacto, microlentillas fpl.
contact man ['kɒntæktmæn] n, pl — men [men] intermediario m.
contagion [kən'teidʒən] n contagio m.
contagious [kən'teidʒəs] adj contagioso.
contain [kən'tein] 1 vt contener; (Math) ser exactamente divisible por. 2 vr: to — oneself contenerse, contener la risa (etc).
container [kən'teinə*] n recipiente m, continente m; (box) caja f; (wrapper etc) envase m.
contaminate [kən'tæmineit] vt contaminar; to be —d by contaminarse con (or de).
contamination [kən,tæmi'neiʃən] n contaminación f.
contemplate ['kɒntempleit] vt (a) (gaze on) contemplar; I — the future with misgiving el futuro lo veo dudoso.
(b) (expect) contar con; we had not —d this no habíamos contado con esto.
(c) (intend) pensar, intentar, proyectar; he —d suicide pensó suicidarse; we — a holiday in Spain proyectamos unas vacaciones en España; when do you — doing it? ¿cuándo se propone hacerlo?, ¿cuándo tiene intención de hacerlo?
contemplation [ˌkɒntem'pleiʃən] n contemplación f.
contemplative [kən'templətiv] adj contemplativo.
contemporaneous [kən,tempə'reiniəs] adj contemporáneo.
contemporary [kən'tempərəri] 1 adj contemporáneo, coetáneo. 2 n contemporáneo m, a f, coetáneo m, a f.
contempt [kən'tempt] n desprecio m; — of court desacato m al juez; beneath — despreciable; to bring into — desprestigiar, envilecer; to hold in — despreciar.
contemptible [kən'temptəbl] adj despreciable, vil.
contemptuous [kən'temptjuəs] adj desdeñoso, despectivo; to be — of desdeñar, menospreciar.
contemptuously [kən'temptjuəsli] adv desdeñosamente, con desprecio.
contend [kən'tend] 1 vt afirmar, sostener (that que).
2 vi contender, luchar; to — with someone for something contender con uno sobre algo; we have many problems to — with se nos plantean muchos problemas.
contender [kən'tendə*] n contendiente mf.
contending [kən'tendiŋ] adj rival, opuesto.
content [kən'tent] 1 adj contento (with con), satisfecho (with de); to be — estar contento; he was — to stay there estaba contento de seguir allí.
2 n contento m, satisfacción f; to one's heart's — a gusto, a más no poder, cuanto quisiera.
3 vt contentar, satisfacer.
4 vr: to — oneself contentarse (with something con algo, with saying con decir).
content ['kɒntent] n contenido m; —s contenido m.
contented [kən'tentid] adj satisfecho, contento.
contentedly [kən'tentidli] adv con satisfacción, contentamente.
contentedness [kən'tentidnis] n contento m.
contention [kən'tenʃən] n (a) (strife) contienda f.
(b) (point) argumento m, aseveración f, pretensión f; it is our — that pretendemos que, sostenemos que.
contentious [kən'tenʃəs] adj contencioso.
contentment [kən'tentmənt] n contento m.
contest ['kɒntest] n (struggle) contienda f, lucha f; (competition) concurso m.
contest [kən'test] 1 vt (dispute) impugnar, atacar;

legal suit defender; election ser candidato en; seat presentarse como candidato a; I — your right to do that niego que Vd tenga el derecho de hacer eso; the seat was not —ed en las elecciones se presentó un solo candidato.
2 vi: to — against contender con; they are —ing for a big prize se están disputando un premio importante.
contestant [kən'testənt] n contendiente mf; (Sport etc) concursante mf.
context ['kɒntekst] n contexto m.
contextual [kɒn'tekstjuəl] adj del contexto, relativo al contexto.
contiguous [kən'tigjuəs] adj contiguo (to a).
continence ['kɒntinəns] n continencia f.
continent ['kɒntinənt] 1 adj continente. 2 n continente m; the C— el continente europeo.
continental [ˌkɒnti'nentl] adj continental.
contingency [kən'tindʒənsi] n contingencia f; should the — arise por si acaso; to provide for every — tener en cuenta todas las posibilidades; with £5 for contingencies con 5 libras para gastos extraordinarios.
contingent [kən'tindʒənt] 1 adj contingente, eventual; to be — upon depender de. 2 n contingente m.
continual [kən'tinjuəl] adj continuo.
continually [kən'tinjuəli] adv constantemente.
continuance [kən'tinjuəns] n continuación f; (stay) permanencia f.
continuation [kən,tinju'eiʃən] n continuación f; (lengthening) prolongación f.
continue [kən'tinjuː] 1 vt continuar; seguir; story etc proseguir; (retain) mantener (in a post en un puesto); (lengthen) prolongar; —d on page 10 sigue en la página 10; "to be —d" (serial) "continuará".
2 vi continuar; seguir; (extend) prolongarse; to — talking; to — to talk seguir hablando; to — on one's way seguir su camino; to — in office seguir en su puesto; to — in a place seguir en un sitio.
continuity [ˌkɒnti'njuːiti] n continuidad f (also Cine).
continuity girl [ˌkɒnti'njuːiti,gəːl] n (Cine) secretaria f de continuidad.
continuous [kən'tinjuəs] adj continuo.
continuously [kən'tinjuəsli] adj continuamente.
continuum [kən'tinjuəm] n continuo m.
contort [kən'tɔːt] vt retorcer, deformar.
contortion [kən'tɔːʃən] n contorsión f.
contortionist [kən'tɔːʃənist] n contorsionista mf.
contour ['kɒntuə*] n contorno m; — line curva f de nivel.
contour map ['kɒntuə,mæp] n mapa m que indica las curvas de nivel, plano m acotado.
contraband ['kɒntrəbænd] 1 n contrabando m. 2 adj and attr de contrabando.
contraception [ˌkɒntrə'sepʃən] n anticoncepcionismo m.
contraceptive [ˌkɒntrə'septiv] 1 adj anticonceptivo. 2 n anticonceptivo m.
contract ['kɒntrækt] n contrato m (for de); contrata f; marriage — capitulaciones fpl matrimoniales; to enter into a — hacer un contrato (with con); to place a — with dar un contrato a.
contract [kən'trækt] 1 vt contraer.
2 vi (become smaller) contraerse, encogerse; to — to do something comprometerse por contrato a hacer algo; to — for contratar; to — out of something optar por no tomar parte en algo.
contracting [kən'træktiŋ] adj: — party contratante mf.
contraction [kən'trækʃən] n contracción f (in, of de).
contractor [kən'træktə*] n contratista mf.
contractual [kən'træktʃuəl] adj contractual.
contradict [ˌkɒntrə'dikt] vt contradecir; (deny) desmentir; don't — me! ¡no repliques!
contradiction [ˌkɒntrə'dikʃən] n contradicción f; — in terms falta f de lógica.
contradictory [ˌkɒntrə'diktəri] adj contradictorio.
contradistinction [ˌkɒntrədis'tiŋkʃən] n: in — to a diferencia de.
contralto [kən'træltəu] n (person) contralto f; (voice) contralto m.
contraption [kən'træpʃən] n dispositivo m, ingenio m, artilugio m; (vehicle) armatoste m.
contrapuntal [ˌkɒntrə'pʌntl] adj contrapuntístico.
contrarily [kən'treərili] adv tercamente.
contrariness [kən'treərinis] n terquedad f.
contrariwise [kən'treəriwaiz] adv: and — y a la inversa.
contrary ['kɒntrəri] 1 adj contrario (to a); in a — direction en dirección contraria.
2 adv: — to contrario a; — to what we had thought contra lo que habíamos pensado.

3 *n* contrario *m*; **the — seems to be the case** parece que es al revés; **he holds the —** él sostiene lo contrario; **quite the —** muy al contrario; **on the — al contrario**; **I know nothing to the —** yo no sé nada en contrario; **unless we hear to the —** a no ser que nos digan lo contrario.

contrary [kən'treəri] *adj* terco, que siempre lleva la contraria.

contrast ['kɒntrɑːst] *n* contraste *m* (*between* entre, *to*, *with* con); **in —** por contraste; **in — to** a diferencia de; **to form a — to** (*or* **with**) contrastar con.

contrast [kən'trɑːst] **1** *vt* poner en contraste (*with* con), comparar. **2** *vi* contrastar (*with* con), hacer contraste (*with* con).

contrasting [kən'trɑːstiŋ] *adj* opuesto.

contravene [,kɒntrə'viːn] *vt law* contravenir a; (*dispute*) oponerse a.

contravention [,kɒntrə'venʃən] *n* contravención *f*.

contretemps ['kɔ̃ntrətɑ̃ːŋ] *n* contratiempo *m*, revés *m*.

contribute [kən'tribjuːt] **1** *vt* contribuir (*to* a); *article* escribir (*to* para); *aid* prestar; *facts, information etc* aportar. **2** *vi* contribuir (*to, towards* a); **to — to + ger** contribuir **+ infin**; **to — to a journal** colaborar en una revista; **to — to a discussion** intervenir en una discusión; **it all —d to the muddle** todo sirvió para aumentar la confusión.

contribution [,kɒntri'bjuːʃən] *n* contribución *f*; (*to journal*) artículo *m*, colaboración *f*; (*to discussion*) intervención *f*; (*of information etc*) aportación *f*.

contributor [kən'tribjutə*] *n* contribuyente *m*; (*to journal*) colaborador *m*, ora *f* (*to* en).

contributory [kən'tribjutəri] *adj* contribuidor; *factor, negligence* que contribuye.

contrite ['kɒntrait] *adj* arrepentido, contrito.

contrition [kən'triʃən] *n* arrepentimiento *m*, contrición *f*.

contrivance [kən'traivəns] *n* (*scheme*) treta *f*, estratagema *f*; (*invention*) invención *f*; (*Mech*) aparato *m*, dispositivo *m*, artilugio *m*.

contrive [kən'traiv] **1** *vt* (*invent*) inventar, idear; (*bring about*) tramar. **2** *vi*: **to — to + infin** lograr que **+ subj**, ingeniarse a **+ infin**.

contrived [kən'traivd] *adj* artificial.

control [kən'trəul] **1** *n* (**a**) (*command*) control *m*, mando *m*, gobierno *m*, dirección *f*; (*of car etc*) manejo *m*, conducción *f*; **— of the seas** dominio *m* de los mares; **dual —** doble mando *m*; **remote —** comando *m* a distancia, telecontrol *m*; **to be in —** mandar, tener el mando; **to be out of —** estar fuera de control; **to be under —** estar bajo control; **to be under private —** estar en manos de particulares; **the circumstances are beyond our —** las circunstancias estan fuera de nuestro control; **to get out of —** desmandarse; **to get under —** conseguir dominar; **she has no — over the children** no tiene autoridad sobre los niños; **causes over which the vendor has no —** causas respecto a las cuales nada puede el vendedor, causas ajenas a la voluntad del vendedor; **to lose — of** perder control de; **to lose — of oneself** perder el control, perder los estribos.

(**b**) (*Mech*) control *m*; **—s** (*Aer etc*) aparatos *mpl* de mando, instrumentos *mpl* de mando; (*attr*) de mando, de control.

(**c**) (*check*) freno *m* (*on* para).

(**d**) (*self-restraint*) dominio *m* sobre sí mismo.

(**e**) (*in experiment*) norma *f* de comprobación.

2 *vt* (*command*) controlar, mandar, gobernar; *traffic, business* dirigir; *price* controlar; (*Mech*) regular, controlar; *car etc* manejar; *temper* dominar, refrenar.

3 *vr*: **to — oneself** dominarse, sobreponerse; **— yourself!** ¡domínese!, ¡cálmese!

control column [kən'trəul'kɔləm] *n* palanca *f* de mando.

control knob [kən'trəul,nɔb] *n* botón *m* de control.

controller [kən'trəulə*] *n* director *m*; inspector *m*; (*Comm*) interventor *m*.

controlling [kən'trəuliŋ] *adj interest* predominante.

control panel [kən'trəul,pænl] *n* tablero *m* de instrumentos.

control point [kən'trəulpɔint] *n* punto *m* de control.

control room [kən'trəulrum] *n* (*Radio, TV etc*) sala *f* de control, sala *f* de mando.

control tower [kən'trəul,tauə*] *n* torre *f* de control.

controversial [,kɒntrə'vəːʃəl] *adj* discutible.

controversy [kən'trɔvəsi] *n* controversia *f*.

controvert ['kɒntrəvəːt] *vt* contradecir.

contumacious [,kɒntju'meiʃəs] *adj* contumaz.

contumaciously [,kɒntju'meiʃəsli] *adv* contumazmente.

contumacy ['kɒntjuməsi] *n* contumacia *f*.

contusion [kən'tjuːʒən] *n* contusión *f*.

contumely ['kɒntju(ː)mli] *n* contumelia *f*.

conundrum [kə'nʌndrəm] *n* acertijo *m*; (*fig*) problema *m*.

conurbation [,kɒnəː'beiʃən] *n* conjunto *m* de centros urbanos.

convalesce [,kɒnvə'les] *vi* convalecer.

convalescence [,kɒnvə'lesəns] *n* convalecencia *f*.

convalescent [,kɒnvə'lesənt] **1** *adj* convaleciente. **2** *n* convaleciente *mf*; **— home** clínica *f* de reposo.

convection [kən'vekʃən] *n* convección *f*.

convector [kən'vektə*] *m* calentador *m* de convección.

convene [kən'viːn] **1** *vt* convocar. **2** *vi* reunirse.

convenience [kən'viːniəns] *n* (**a**) comodidad *f*; (*advantage*) ventaja *f*; **at your —** cuando le sea conveniente; **at your earliest —** con la mayor brevedad, tan pronto como le sea posible; **for your — an envelope is enclosed** para facilitar su contestación adjuntamos un sobre; **it is a great —** to be so close resulta muy práctico estar tan cerca; **to make a — of** abusar de (la amabilidad de).

(**b**) **public —(s)** aseos *mpl* públicos; **a house with all modern —s** una casa con todas las comodidades; **"all mod. cons"** "todo confort".

convenient [kən'viːniənt] *adj* (**a**) cómodo; *tool etc* práctico, útil; *place* accesible, céntrico; **it is — to live here** resulta práctico vivir aquí; **her death was certainly — for him** es cierto que su muerte resultó provechosa para él; **we looked for a — place to stop** buscamos un sitio apropiado para detenernos; **he put it on a — chair** lo puso en una silla que estaba a mano.

(**b**) (*of time*) oportuno; **at a — moment** en un momento oportuno; **when it is — for you** cuando le sea conveniente; **would tomorrow be —?** ¿le conviene mañana?

conveniently [kən'viːniəntli] *adv* con comodidad, cómodamente; oportunamente; **the house is — situated** la casa está en un sitio muy práctico; **it fell — close** cayó muy cerca; **when you — can do so** cuando Vd pueda hacerlo sin inconveniente.

convent ['kɒnvənt] *n* convento *m* (de monjas).

convention [kən'venʃən] *n* convención *f*; (*meeting*) asamblea *f*, congreso *m*.

conventional [kən'venʃənl] *adj* convencional.

converge [kən'vəːdʒ] *vi* convergir (*on* en); **to — on** (*persons*) dirigirse todos a.

convergence [kən'vəːdʒəns] *n* convergencia *f*.

convergent [kən'vəːdʒənt] *adj*, **converging** [kən'vəːdʒiŋ] *adj* convergente.

conversant [kən'vəːsənt] *adj*: **— with** versado en, enterado de; **to become — with** llegar a conocer, informarse sobre.

conversation [,kɒnvə'seiʃən] *n* conversación *f*.

conversational [,kɒnvə'seiʃənl] *adj tone* familiar; *person* locuaz, hablador; **he's not very —** no es amigo de la conversación.

conversationalist [,kɒnvə'seiʃənlist] *n*: **to be a good —** brillar en la conversación, resultar simpático charlando; **he's not much of a —** tiene poco que decir, no le gusta hablar mucho en las conversaciones.

conversationally [,kɒnvə'seiʃənli] *adv* en tono familiar.

conversation piece [,kɒnvə'seiʃənpiːs] *n* (*Lit*) (pasaje *m* de) conversación *f*, diálogo *m*.

converse ['kɒnvəːs] **1** *adj* contrario, inverso. **2** *n* (*Math, Logic*) inversa *f*; **but the — is true** pero la verdad es al revés.

converse [kən'vəːs] *vi* conversar, hablar (*with* con); **to — by signs** hablar por señas.

conversely [kɒn'vəːsli] *adv* a la inversa.

conversion [kən'vəːʃən] *n* conversión *f* (*into* en, *to* a); (*industrial*) reorganización *f*; (*Law*) apropiación *f* ilícita; (*Rugby*) transformación *f*; **— table** tabla *f* de conversión.

convert ['kɒnvəːt] *n* converso *m*, a *f*; **to become a —** convertirse.

convert [kən'vəːt] **1** *vt* convertir (*also Eccl, Fin*; *into* en, *to* a), transformar (*into* en); *industry* reorganizar; (*Law*) apropiarse ilícitamente (*to one's own use* para uso propio); (*Rugby*) transformar. **2** *vi* convertirse (*to* a).

converter [kən'vəːtə*] *n* (*Elec, Metal*) convertidor *m*; (*Radio*) conversor *m*.

convertibility [kən,vəːtə'biliti] *n* convertibilidad *f*.

convertible [kən'vəːtəbl] **1** *adj* convertible; *car* descapotable. **2** *n* descapotable *m*.

convex ['kɒn'veks] *adj* convexo.

convexity [kɒn'veksiti] *n* convexidad *f*.

convey [kən'vei] vt goods transportar, llevar; person llevar; sound, smell llevar; current transmitir; news comunicar; (Law) traspasar; meaning tener, expresar (to para); I am trying to — that quiero dar a entender que; the name —s nothing to me el nombre no me dice nada; what does this music — to you? ¿qué sentido tiene esta música para Vd?

conveyance [kən'veiəns] n (a) (act) transporte m; transmisión f (etc); (Law) traspaso m.
(b) (Law: deed) escritura f de traspaso.
(c) (vehicle) vehículo m, medio m de transporte; public — vehículo m de servicio público.

conveyancing [kən'veiənsiŋ] n (Law) preparación f de escrituras de traspaso.

conveyor [kən'veiə*] n portador m, transportador m; (belt) cinta f transportadora.

conveyor belt [kən'veiəbelt] n cinta f transportadora.

convict ['kɔnvikt] n presidiario m, penado m.

convict [kən'vikt] vt condenar; —ed murderer un asesino condenado como tal; to — someone of a crime declarar a uno culpable de un crimen; to — someone of an error coger a uno en una falta.

conviction [kən'vikʃən] n (a) (Law) condena f; there were 12 —s for drunkenness hubo 12 condenas por embriaguez; to have no previous —s no tener antecedentes penales.
(b) (belief) creencia f, convicción f, artículo m de fe; it is my — that yo creo firmemente de.
(c) I am open to — estoy dispuesto a dejarme convencer; it carries — me convence.

convince [kən'vins] vt convencer (of de, that que).

convincing [kən'vinsiŋ] adj convincente.

convincingly [kən'vinsiŋli] adv convincentemente; to prove something — probar algo de modo concluyente.

convivial [kən'viviəl] adj person sociable; evening alegre, festivo, atmosphere alegre.

conviviality [kən,vivi'æliti] n alegría f, buen humor m; compañerismo m alegre; there was a certain amount of — nos divertimos bastante, (freq) se bebió una barbaridad.

convocation [,kɔnvə'keiʃən] n (act) convocación f; (meeting) asamblea f.

convoke [kən'vəuk] vt convocar.

convolution [,kɔnvə'lu:ʃən] n circunvolución f.

convolvulus [kən'vɔlvjuləs] n convólvulo m.

convoy ['kɔnvɔi] 1 n convoy m. 2 vt convoyar.

convulse [kən'vʌls] vt (fig) convulsionar, sacudir; (joke etc) hacer morir de risa; his face was —d with pain el dolor le crispó la cara; to be —d with laughter estar muerto de risa.

convulsion [kən'vʌlʃən] n convulsión f; —s of laughter paroxismo m de risa.

convulsive [kən'vʌlsiv] adj convulsivo.

cony ['kəuni] n conejo m.

coo[1] [ku:] vi arrullar.

coo[2] [ku:] interj ¡vaya!

cooing ['ku:iŋ] n arrullos mpl.

cook [kuk] 1 n cocinero m, a f.
2 vt guisar, cocer, cocinar; meal preparar; accounts (fam) falsificar; to — up excuse inventar; plan tramar.
3 vi (food) cocer; (person) cocinar; what's —ing? (sl) ¿qué es lo que se guisa?

cookbook ['kukbuk] n (US) libro m de cocina.

cooker ['kukə*] n (a) (stove) cocina f; electric — cocina f eléctrica; gas — cocina f de (or a) gas. (b) (fruit) fruta f para cocer.

cookery ['kukəri] n arte m de cocinar; French — la cocina francesa.

cookery book ['kukəribuk] n libro m de cocina.

cookhouse ['kukhaus] n, pl —houses [,hauziz] cocina f; (Mil) cocina f móvil de campaña.

cookie ['kuki] n (US) pastelito m dulce, bizcochito m.

cooking ['kukiŋ] n cocina f.

cookout ['kukaut] n (US) comida f al aire libre.

cool [ku:l] 1 adj (a) (rather cold) fresco; (— enough to drink etc) tibio, bastante frío; it is (— weather) hace fresco, (object) está fresco; to get (—er) refrescarse; "to be kept in a — place" "guárdese en un sitio fresco".
(b) (calm) tranquilo, imperturbable; as — as a cucumber más fresco que una lechuga; to keep — no perder la calma; keep —! ¡no se alarme!; to play it — no dejarse emocionar, no exagerar.
(c) (lacking zeal) frío, indiferente; to be — towards a plan acoger un proyecto con poco entusiasmo; to be — towards someone tratar a uno con frialdad.
(d) (calmly audacious) fresco, descarado; he's a — customer es un caradura; he answered me as — as you please me contestó tan fresco.

(e) (fam) a — £100 cien libras contantes y sonantes.
2 n fresco m; in the — of the evening en el aire fresco de la tarde.
3 vt (also to — down) enfriar; refrescar; engine refrigerar; (fig) calmar, moderar el entusiasmo (etc) de.
4 vi (also to — down) enfriarse; (weather etc) refrescarse; (person) tener menos calor; (fig) calmarse; — down! ¡cálmese!; to — off (fig) perder su entusiasmo, entibiarse.

cooler ['ku:lə*] n (sl) trena f.

cool-headed ['ku:l,hedid] adj imperturbable.

coolie ['ku:li] n culi m.

cooling ['ku:liŋ] 1 adj refrescante; (Tech) refrigerante. 2 n refrigeración f.

cooling tower ['ku:liŋtauə*] n torre f de refrigeración.

coolly ['ku:li] adv (calmly) con tranquilidad; (unenthusiastically) con poco entusiasmo; (boldly) descaradamente.

coolness ['ku:lnis] n (a) (coldness) frescura f, lo fresco.
(b) (calmness) tranquilidad f, imperturbabilidad f; (in battle) sangre f fría.
(c) (lack of zeal) falta f de entusiasmo; (of welcome, between persons) frialdad f.
(d) (audacity) frescura f.

coomb [ku:m] n hondonada f.

coop [ku:p] 1 n gallinero m. 2 vt: to — up encerrar.

co-op ['kəuɔp] n cooperativa f.

cooper ['ku:pə*] n tonelero m.

cooperage ['ku:pəridʒ] n barrilería f, tonelería f.

cooperate [kəu'ɔpəreit] vi cooperar, colaborar (in en, with con, to + infin para + infin).

cooperation [kəu,ɔpə'reiʃən] n cooperación f, colaboración f.

cooperative [kəu'ɔpərətiv] 1 adj cooperativo; person servicial, dispuesto a ayudar; — society cooperativa f. 2 n cooperativa f.

coopt [kəu'ɔpt] vt: to — someone on to a committee nombrar a uno miembro de un comité por votación extraordinaria.

coordinate [kəu'ɔ:dnit] n (Math) coordenada f.

coordinate [kəu'ɔ:dineit] vt coordinar.

coordination [kəu,ɔ:di'neiʃən] n coordinación f.

coordinator [kəu'ɔ:dineitə*] n coordinador m.

coot [ku:t] n focha f común; (fam) bobo m, a f.

cop [kɔp] (sl) 1 n guili m, guindilla m; —s and robbers (game) justicias y ladrones.
2 vt (capture) coger, prender; —ped 6 months le condenaron a 6 meses de prisión; you'll — it! ¡las vas a pagar!; I —ped it from the head el director me puso como un trapo; — this! ¡hay que ver esto!

copartner ['kəu'pa:tnə*] n consocio m, copartícipe m.

copartnership ['kəu'pa:tnəʃip] n asociación f, cogestión f, coparticipación f.

cope[1] [kəup] n (Eccl) capa f pluvial.

cope[2] [kəup] vi (a) he's coping pretty well se las está arreglando bastante bien; we shall be able to — better next year podremos arreglarnos mejor el año que viene; can you —? ¿tú puedes con esto?; how are you coping? ¿cómo te va esto?
(b) to — with poder con; problem hacer frente a; difficulty contender con; situation enfrentarse con.

Copenhagen [,kəupn'heigən] Copenhague.

Copernicus [kə'pə:nikəs] m Copérnico.

copestone ['kəupstəun] n, **coping stone** ['kəupiŋstəun] n (piedra f de) albardilla f.

co-pilot ['kəu'pailət] n copiloto m.

copious ['kəupiəs] adj copioso, abundante.

copiously ['kəupiəsli] adv copiosamente, en abundancia.

copper[1] ['kɔpə*] 1 n (material) cobre m; (utensil) caldera f de lavar; (money) calderilla f, monedas fpl de poco valor; it costs a few —s vale unos peniques.
2 adj and attr de cobre, cobreño; (colour) cobrizo.

copper[2] ['kɔpə*] n (sl) guili m, guindilla m.

copper beech ['kɔpə'bi:tʃ] n haya f de hoja oscura.

copperplate ['kɔpəpleit] adj writing hermoso, bien formado.

coppersmith ['kɔpəsmiθ] n cobrero m.

coppery ['kɔpəri] adj cobreño; (colour) cobrizo.

coppice ['kɔpis] n, **copse** [kɔps] n soto m, bosquecillo m.

copra ['kɔprə] n copra f.

copulate ['kɔpjuleit] vi copularse (with con).

copulation [,kɔpju'leiʃən] n cópula f.

copulative ['kɔpjulətiv] adj (Gram) copulativo.

copy ['kɔpi] 1 n copia f; (of book, paper etc) ejemplar m; (Typ) material m, original m; author's —

ejemplar m autógrafo;¨**presentation** — ejemplar m con dedicatoria del autor; **fair** — copia f en limpio; **to make a fair** — **of something** sacar algo en limpio; **rough** — borrador m; **to make** (*or* **take**) **a** — **of a letter** sacar una copia de una carta.

2 *vt* copiar (*also* **to** — **out**); imitar; **to** — **from** copiar de; "**American papers please** —" "periódicos americanos: por favor, tomen nota".

copybook ['kɔpibuk] n cuaderno m de escritura; **to blot one's** — tirarse una plancha.

copycat ['kɔpikæt] n (*fam*) imitador m, ora f.

copy editor ['kɔpi'editə*] n corrector m de manuscritos; corrector m de artículos, corrector m de material.

copyist ['kɔpiist] n copista mf.

copyright ['kɔpirait] 1 *adj* protegido por los derechos del autor.

2 n derechos mpl del autor; propiedad f literaria; "— **reserved**" "es propiedad", "reservados todos los derechos".

3 *vt* registrar como propiedad literaria.

copywriter ['kɔpi,raitə*] n escritor m de material publicitario.

coquetry ['kɔkitri] n coquetería f.

coquette [kə'ket] n coqueta f.

coquettish [kə'ketiʃ] *adj* coqueta.

cor [kɔ:*] *interj* (*sl*) ¡caramba!

coracle ['kɔrəkl] n barquilla f de forma casi redonda y hecha de cuero.

coral ['kɔrəl] 1 n coral m. 2 *adj* coralino, de coral; — **island** isla f coralina.

cor anglais ['kɔr'ɔ̃glei] n corno m inglés.

cord [kɔ:d] 1 n (a) cuerda f; (*Elec*) cordón m; **spinal** — médula f espinal; **umbilical** — cordón m umbilical m; **vocal** —s cuerdas fpl vocales.

(b) (*cloth*) pana f; —s pantalones mpl de pana.

2 *vt* encordelar.

cordage ['kɔ:didʒ] n cordaje m, cordería f.

cordial ['kɔ:diəl] 1 *adj* cordial, afectuoso. 2 n cordial m.

cordiality [,kɔ:di'æliti] n cordialidad f, afecto m.

cordially ['kɔ:diəli] *adv* cordialmente, afectuosamente; **I** — **detest him** le odio cordialmente.

cordon ['kɔ:dn] 1 n cordón m. 2 *vt*: **to** — **off** acordonar.

cordon bleu [,kɔ:d5n'blə:] n cordón m azul; (*Cook*) cocinero m de primera clase, cocinera f de primera clase.

Cordova ['kɔ:dəvə] Córdoba.

Cordovan ['kɔ:dəvən] 1 *adj* cordobés. 2 n cordobés m, esa f; (*leather*) cordobán m.

corduroy ['kɔ:dərɔi] n pana f; —s pantalones mpl de pana; — **road** (*US*) camino m de troncos.

core [kɔ:*] n centro m, núcleo m; (*of fruit*) corazón m; (*of cable*) alma f; (*fig, of matter etc*) lo esencial, esencia f; **a hard** — **of resistance** un núcleo endurecido de resistencia; **English to the** — inglés hasta los tuétanos; **rotten to the** — (*fig*) corrompido hasta la médula.

co-religionist ['kəuri'lidʒənist] n correligionario m, a f.

co-respondent ['kəuris'pɔndənt] n *persona acusada de haber cometido adulterio con uno de los esposos, en un pleito de divorcio.*

coriander [,kɔri'ændə*] n culantro m.

Corinth ['kɔrinθ] Corinto.

Corinthian [kə'rinθiən] *adj* corintio.

Coriolanus [,kɔriə'leinəs] m Coriolano.

cork [kɔ:k] 1 n corcho m. 2 *attr* de corcho. 3 *vt* tapar con corcho (*also* **to** — **up**); **the wine is** —**ed** el vino sabe a corcho.

corkage ['kɔ:kidʒ] n precio m que se cobra en un restaurante por el descorche de las botellas.

corking ['kɔ:kiŋ] *adj* (*fam*) pistonudo, bárbaro.

corkscrew ['kɔ:kskru:] 1 n sacacorchos m. 2 *attr* **movement** en espiral. 3 *vi* subir en espiral.

cork-tipped ['kɔ:k'tipt] *adj* emboquillado.

cork tree ['kɔ:ktri:] n alcornoque m.

corm [kɔ:m] n bulbo m.

cormorant ['kɔ:mərənt] n cormorán m grande.

corn¹ [kɔ:n] (*Bot*) granos mpl, cereales mpl; (*wheat*) trigo m; (*US, also* **Indian** —) maíz m; (*fig*) cosas fpl viejas, cosas fpl rancias, cosas fpl al estilo antiguo; — **on the cob** maíz m en la mazorca; — **in Egypt**! ¡agua de mayo!

corn² [kɔ:n] n (*Med*) callo m; **to tread on someone's** —**s** herir los sentimientos de uno.

corncob ['kɔ:nkɔb] n (*US*) mazorca f de maíz.

corncrake ['kɔ:nkreik] n guión m de codornices.

cornea ['kɔ:niə] n córnea f.

corned ['kɔ:nd] *adj*: see **beef**.

cornelian [kɔ:'ni:liən] n cornalina f.

corner ['kɔ:nə*] 1 n ángulo m; (*outside* —) esquina f, (*inside* —) rincón m; (*bend in road*) curva f, recodo m; (*Sport*) córner m, esquina f; (*Comm*) monopolio m (*in* de); — **house** casa f en una esquina; **the four** —**s of the earth** las cinco partes del mundo; **out of the** — **of one's eye** con el rabillo del ojo; **it's round the** — está a la vuelta de la esquina; **to be in a tight** — estar en un aprieto; **to cut** —**s** atajar; **to drive someone into a** — (*fig*) poner a uno entre la espada y la pared; **to go round the** — doblar la esquina; **to rub the** —**s off someone** lijar a uno, cepillar a uno; **to turn the** — doblar la esquina, (*fig*) ir saliendo del apuro.

2 *vt* acorralar, arrinconar; *person* abordar, detener; *fugitive* cazar; *market* acaparar.

3 *vi* tomar una curva.

corner flag ['kɔ:nəflæg] n banderola f de esquina.

corner kick ['kɔ:nəkik] n córner m, saque m de esquina.

corner seat ['kɔ:nəsi:t] n asiento m del rincón.

cornerstone ['kɔ:nəstəun] n piedra f angular (*also fig*).

cornerways ['kɔ:nəweiz] *adv* diagonalmente.

cornet ['kɔ:nit] n (*Mus*) corneta f; (*of paper*) cucurucho m; (*ice cream*) barquillo m, cornete m.

corn exchange ['kɔ:niks'tʃeindʒ] n bolsa f de granos.

cornfield ['kɔ:nfi:ld] n trigal m, campo m de trigo; (*US*) maizal m.

cornflour ['kɔ:nflauə*] n harina f de maíz.

cornflower ['kɔ:nflauə*] n aciano m, azulina f.

cornice ['kɔ:nis] n cornisa f.

Cornish ['kɔ:niʃ] 1 *adj* córnico. 2 n córnico m.

cornstarch ['kɔ:nsta:tʃ] n (*US*) almidón m de maíz.

cornucopia [,kɔ:nju'kəupiə] n cornucopia f.

Cornwall ['kɔ:nwəl] Cornualles m.

corny ['kɔ:ni] *adj* (*fam*) viejo, gastado, rancio.

corolla [kə'rɔlə] n corola f.

corollary [kə'rɔləri] n corolario m; consecuencia f natural.

coronary ['kɔrənəri] *adj*: — **thrombosis** trombosis f coronaria.

coronation [,kɔrə'neiʃən] n coronación f.

coroner ['kɔrənə*] n (*approx*) juez m de primera instancia e instrucción.

coronet ['kɔrənit] n corona f (de marqués *etc*).

corporal ['kɔ:pərəl] 1 *adj* corporal. 2 n cabo m.

corporate ['kɔ:pərit] *adj* corporativo, colectivo.

corporation [,kɔ:pə'reiʃən] n corporación f; (*esp US Comm*) sociedad f anónima; (*of city*) ayuntamiento m; (*fam*) panza f.

corporeal [kɔ:'pɔ:riəl] *adj* corpóreo.

corps [kɔ:*] n, *pl* **corps** [kɔ:z] cuerpo m; **army** — cuerpo m de ejército; — **de ballet** cuerpo m de baile; **diplomatic** — cuerpo m diplomático; **medical** — cuerpo m de sanidad; **service** — cuerpo m de intendencia.

corpse [kɔ:ps] n cadáver m.

corpulence ['kɔ:pjuləns] n gordura f.

corpulent ['kɔ:pjulənt] *adj* gordo.

corpus ['kɔ:pəs] n cuerpo m; **C— Christi** Corpus m.

corpuscle ['kɔ:pʌsl] n (*of blood*) glóbulo m, corpúsculo m.

corral [kə'rɑ:l] (*US*) 1 n corral m. 2 *vt* acorralar.

correct [kə'rekt] 1 *adj* (a) (*accurate*) correcto, exacto, justo; —! ¡exacto!; **you are perfectly** — Vd tiene perfectamente razón, Vd está en lo cierto; **am I** — **in saying that** . . . ? ¿me equivoco al decir que . . . ?

(b) (*proper*) correcto.

2 *vt* corregir; rectificar, emendar; *exam* puntuar, calificar; **I stand** —**ed** confieso que me equivoqué.

correction [kə'rekʃən] n corrección f; rectificación f; (*erasure*) tachadura f; **I speak under** — puede que me equivoque.

corrective [kə'rektiv] 1 *adj* correctivo; — **glasses** gafas fpl correctoras. 2 n correctivo m.

correctly [kə'rektli] *adv* correctamente.

correctness [kə'rektnis] n (*accuracy*) exactitud f; (*properness*) corrección f.

correlate ['kɔrileit] 1 *vt* correlacionar. 2 *vi* tener correlación.

correlation [,kɔri'leiʃən] n correlación f.

correlative [kɔ'relətiv] 1 *adj* correlativo. 2 n correlativo m.

correspond [,kɔris'pɔnd] *vi* (a) (*agree*) corresponder (*to*, *with* a). (b) (*by letter*) escribirse; **to** — **with** estar en correspondencia con, cartearse con.

correspondence [,kɔris'pɔndəns] n (a) (*agreement*) correspondencia f.

(b) (*by letter*) correspondencia f; — **course** curso m por correspondencia; **to be in** — **with someone** estar en correspondencia con uno.

(c) (*collected letters*) epistolario m.

correspondent [ˌkɔris'pɔndənt] n correspondiente mf; (of paper) corresponsal mf; **special** — corresponsal m extraordinario.
corresponding [ˌkɔris'pɔndiŋ] adj correspondiente.
correspondingly [ˌkɔris'pɔndiŋli] adv igualmente, equivalentemente.
corridor ['kɔridɔ:*] n pasillo m (also Rail), corredor m (also Pol).
corroborate [kə'rɔbəreit] vt corroborar, confirmar.
corroboration [kəˌrɔbə'reiʃən] n corroboración f, confirmación f.
corroborative [kə'rɔbərətiv] adj corroborativo, confirmatorio.
corrode [kə'rəud] 1 vt corroer. 2 vi corroerse.
corrosion [kə'rəuʒən] n corrosión f.
corrosive [kə'rəuziv] adj corrosivo.
corrugated ['kɔrəgeitid] adj ondulado.
corrupt [kə'rʌpt] 1 adj corrompido; text viciado; taste depravado, estragado; person venal; — practices corrupción f. 2 vt corromper; (bribe) sobornar.
corruption [kə'rʌpʃən] n corrupción f.
corsage [kɔ:'sɑ:ʒ] n (dress) corpiño m; (flowers) ramillete m para la cintura.
corsair ['kɔ:sɛə*] n corsario m.
corset ['kɔ:sit] n faja f, (old-style) corsé m.
Corsica ['kɔ:sikə] Córcega f.
Corsican ['kɔ:sikən] 1 adj corso. 2 n corso m, a f.
cortège [kɔ:'tɛ:ʒ] n (procession) cortejo m, desfile m; (train) séquito m; **funeral** — cortejo m fúnebre.
cortex ['kɔ:teks] n, pl **cortices** ['kɔ:tisi:z] corteza f.
cortisone ['kɔ:tizəun] n cortisona f.
corundum [kə'rʌndəm] n corindón m.
Corunna [kə'rʌnə] La Coruña.
coruscate ['kɔrəskeit] vi brillar, fulgurar.
corvette [kɔ:'vet] n corbeta f.
cosh [kɔʃ] 1 n cachiporra f. 2 vt golpear con una cachiporra.
cosignatory ['kəu'signətəri] n cosignatario m, a f.
cosine ['kəusain] n coseno m.
cosiness ['kəuzinis] n comodidad f; lo acogedor; lo holgado.
cos lettuce ['kɔs'letis] n lechuga f Cos.
cosmetic [kɔz'metik] 1 adj cosmético. 2 n cosmético m.
cosmic ['kɔzmik] adj cósmico.
cosmogony [kɔz'mɔgəni] n cosmogonía f.
cosmographer [kɔz'mɔgrəfə*] n cosmógrafo m.
cosmography [kɔz'mɔgrəfi] n cosmografía f.
cosmology [kɔz'mɔlədʒi] n cosmología f.
cosmonaut ['kɔzmənɔ:t] n cosmonauta mf.
cosmopolitan [ˌkɔzmə'pɔlitən] 1 adj cosmopolita. 2 n cosmopolita mf.
cosmopolite [kɔz'mɔpəlait] n cosmopolita mf.
cosmos ['kɔzmɔs] n cosmos m.
Cossack ['kɔsæk] 1 adj cosaco m. 2 n cosaco m, a f.
cosset ['kɔsit] vt mimar.
cost [kɔst] 1 n (a) precio m; coste m, costo m, costa f; —s (in industry etc) costes mpl; — **of living** costo m de vida; at — a costa; at the — **of his health** a costa de su salud; at the — **of his life** pagó con la vida; at all —s, at any — a todo trance, a toda costa; at **great** — tras grandes esfuerzos, tras grandes pérdidas; at **little** — to **himself** con poco riesgo para sí mismo; to my — a mis expensas; **without counting the** — sin pensar en los riesgos. (b) (Law) —s costas fpl, litisexpensas fpl; he was ordered to pay — s se le condenó a pagar las costas.
2 vt calcular el coste de, preparar el presupuesto de; it has not been properly —ed no se ha calculado detalladamente el coste de esto.
3 (irr: pret and ptp cost) vi costar, valer; it — £2 costó 2 libras; how much does this — ? ¿cuánto vale esto?, ¿cuánto es?; what does it — to go? ¿cuánto cuesta el viaje?; — what it may cueste lo que cueste; it — him his life le costó la vida; it — him a lot of trouble le causó muchas molestias.
co-star ['kəustɑ:*] 1 n colega mf de reparto (en una producción cinematográfica).
2 vi: to — **with someone** figurar en un papel principal en compañía con uno.
Costa Rica ['kɔstə'ri:kə] Costa f Rica.
Costa Rican ['kɔstə'ri:kən] 1 adj costarriqueño. 2 n costarriqueño m, a f.
coster ['kɔstə*] n, **costermonger** ['kɔstəˌmʌŋgə*] n vendedor m ambulante.
costing ['kɔstiŋ] n cálculo m del coste.
costive ['kɔstiv] adj estreñido.
costliness ['kɔstlinis] n (dearness) alto precio m; (great value) suntuosidad f.
costly ['kɔstli] adj (dear) costoso; (valuable) suntuoso.
cost price ['kɔst'prais] 1 n precio m de coste; at — = 2 adv al precio de coste.

costume ['kɔstju:m] n traje m; (fancy-dress) disfraz m;— **jewellery** joyas fpl de fantasía.
costumier [kɔs'tju:miə*] n sastre m de teatro.
cosy ['kəuzi] 1 adj cómodo, agradable; atmosphere acogedor, amistoso; life holgado. 2 n cubierta f para tetera.
cot [kɔt] n camita f de niño, cuna f.
coterie ['kəutəri] n grupo m; (clique) peña f, camarilla f.
cottage ['kɔtidʒ] n casita f de campo; (US) vivienda f campestre, quinta f; (labourer's etc) cabaña f, barraca f; — **cheese** requesón m.
cottager ['kɔtidʒə*] n aldeano m, a f; (US) veraneante mf que vive en una casita de campo.
cotter ['kɔtə*] n chaveta f.
cotton ['kɔtn] 1 n algodón m; (plant) algodonero m. 2 attr de algodón; the — **industry** la industria algodonera.
3 vi: to — **on to** (fam) entender, caer en la cuenta de.
cotton grass ['kɔtngrɑ:s] n algodonosa f.
cotton mill ['kɔtnmil] n fábrica f de algodón.
cottonseed oil ['kɔtnsi:dɔil] n aceite m de algodón.
cottontail ['kɔtnteil] n liebre f de cola blanca.
cotton wool ['kɔtn'wul] n algodón m hidrófilo (en rama).
cotyledon [ˌkɔti'li:dən] n cotiledón m.
couch [kautʃ] 1 n canapé m, sofá m. 2 vt expresar.
couch grass ['kautʃgrɑ:s] n hierba f rastrera.
cougar ['ku:gə*] n puma f.
cough [kɔf] 1 n tos f. 2 vt: to — **up** escupir, arrojar; (sl) desembolsar, pagar. 3 vi toser; (sl) cantar; to — **up** (sl) desdinerarse, pagar.
cough drop ['kɔfdrɔp] n pastilla f para la tos.
could [kud] pret of can.
couldn't ['kudnt] = could not.
council ['kaunsl] n consejo m, junta f; (Eccl) concilio m; **city** —, **town** — concejo m municipal, ayuntamiento m; **works** — consejo m de obreros; — **of war** consejo m de guerra; **Privy C**— Consejo m Privado.
council house ['kaunslhaus] n, pl — **houses** [ˌhauziz] vivienda f protegida.
councillor ['kaunsilə*] n concejal m (also town —).
councilman ['kaunslmən] n, pl —**men** [mən] (US) concejal m.
counsel ['kaunsəl] 1 n (a) consejo m; a — **of perfection** un ideal imposible; to **keep one's own** — guardar silencio; to **take** — **with** aconsejarse con.
(b) (Law) abogado m; — **for the defence, defending** — abogado m defensor; — **for the prosecution** fiscal m.
counsellor ['kaunslə*] n consejero m, a f.
count[1] [kaunt] 1 n (a) (act of counting) cuenta f, cálculo m; (of words etc) recuento m; (of votes) escrutinio m; (Boxing) cuenta f; to **keep** — **of** contar; to **lose** — **of** perder la cuenta de.
(b) (total) suma f, total m.
(c) (Law) cargo m, acusación f.
2 vt (a) (Math) contar; calcular; to — **out** ir contando; (Boxing) declarar vencido; to — **up** contar.
(b) (include) incluir; **not** —**ing** sin contar, además de, con exclusión de; to — **out** excluir; **please** — **me out** por favor no cuente conmigo.
(c) (deem) creer, considerar; I **don't** — **him** **among my friends** no le considero como amigo.
3 vi (a) (Math) contar; to — **down** contar hacia atrás; to — **on one's fingers** contar por los dedos; he —s **as 2** él cuenta por 2.
(b) (be valid) that **doesn't** — eso no vale, (in games) eso no puntúa.
(c) (be important) every **second** —**s** cada segundo es importante; he **doesn't** — él no vale para esto; he **doesn't** — **for much** él apenas si vale; **ability** —**s for little here** aquí la aptitud sirve para muy poco.
(d) to — **on** contar con; to — **on** + ger contar con + infin.
count[2] [kaunt] n conde m.
countable ['kauntəbl] adj contable.
countdown ['kauntdaun] n cuenta f hacia atrás.
countenance ['kauntinəns] 1 n semblante m, rostro m; to **be out of** — estar desconcertado; to **give** (or **lend**) — to **news** acreditar; to **keep one's** — contener la risa; to **lose** — desconcertarse; to **put someone out of** — desconcertar a uno.
2 vt aprobar, tolerar.
counter[1] ['kauntə*] n (a) (of shop) mostrador m; **under the** — (fam) por la trastienda. (b) (in games) ficha f.
counter[2] ['kauntə*] 1 adj contrario, de sentido opuesto (to a).
2 adv: to **run** — to oponerse a, ser contrario a.

3 vt contrarrestar; blow parar; attack contestar a.
4 vi: **to — with** contestar con.
counteract [,kauntə'rækt] vt contrarrestar.
counter-attack ['kauntərə,tæk] **1** n contraataque m.
2 vt contraatacar.
counter-attraction ['kauntərə,trækʃən] n atracción f rival.
counterbalance ['kauntə,bæləns] **1** n contrapeso m.
2 vt contrapesar.
counterblast ['kauntəblɑːst] n respuesta f vigorosa (to a).
countercharge ['kauntətʃɑːdʒ] n recriminación f.
countercheck ['kauntətʃek] **1** n segunda comprobación f. **2** vt comprobar por segunda vez.
counterclaim ['kauntəkleim] n contrarreclamación f.
counter-clockwise ['kauntə'klɔkwaiz] adv en sentido contrario al de las agujas del reloj.
counter-espionage ['kauntə'respiənɑːʒ] n contraespionaje m.
counterfeit ['kauntəfiːt] **1** adj falso, falsificado. **2** n falsificación f; (coin) moneda f falsa. **3** vt falsificar, contrahacer.
counterfoil ['kauntəfɔil] n talón m.
counter-gambit ['kauntə'gæmbit] n contragambito m.
counterintelligence ['kauntərin,telidʒəns] n contrainteligencia f.
counterirritant ['kauntər'iritənt] n contrairritante m.
countermand ['kauntəmɑːnd] vt revocar, cancelar.
counter-measure ['kauntəmeʒə*] n contramedida f.
counter-move ['kauntəmuːv] n contrajugada f.
counter-offensive ['kauntərə'fensiv] n contraofensiva f.
counter-order ['kauntər,ɔːdə*] n contraorden f.
counterpane ['kauntəpein] n sobrecama m, colcha f, cobertor m.
counterpart ['kauntəpɑːt] n: **his — here is Mr X** aquí la persona que le equivale es el Sr X; **this piece has no —** a esta pieza no hay nada que le corresponda.
counterpoint ['kauntəpɔint] n contrapunto m.
counterpoise ['kauntəpɔiz] **1** n contrapeso m. **2** vt contrapesar.
Counter-Reformation ['kauntə,refə'meiʃən] n Contrarreforma f.
counter-revolution ['kauntərevə'luːʃən] n contrarrevolución f.
counter-revolutionary ['kauntərevə'luːʃənri] **1** adj contrarrevolucionario. **2** n contrarrevolucionario m.
countersign ['kauntəsain] vt refrendar.
countersink ['kauntəsiŋk] vt avellanar.
counter-stroke ['kauntəstrəuk] n contragolpe m.
counter tenor ['kauntə'tenə*] n tenor m ligero.
counterweight ['kauntəweit] n contrapeso m.
countess ['kauntis] n condesa f.
counting house ['kauntiŋ'haus] n, pl **— houses** [,hauziz] (arch) despacho m, oficina f.
countless ['kauntlis] adj incontable, innumerable; **— times** infinitas veces.
countrified ['kʌntrifaid] adj rústico.
country ['kʌntri] **1** n (political) país m; (regarded more sentimentally) patria f; (countryside) campo m; (region) región f, tierra f; **love of —** amor m a la patria; **Black C—** región minera e industrial de Birmingham y su comarca (Inglaterra); **mother —** madre f patria; **the old —** la patria, mi país natal; **there's some good — to the north** hacia el norte el paisaje es muy bonito; **this is good fishing —** ésta es buena tierra para la pesca; **to go to the —** (Pol) celebrar elecciones generales; **to live off the —** vivir del país.
2 attr: **— people** gente m del campo; **— life** vida f del campo; **— club** club m campestre; **— house** quinta f, finca f.
country dance ['kʌntri'dɑːns] n contradanza f, baile m campestre.
countryman ['kʌntrimən] n, pl **—men** [mən] campesino m; (fellow-) compatriota m.
countryside ['kʌntrisaid] n campo m.
countrywide ['kʌntriwaid] adj nacional.
countrywoman ['kʌntri,wumən] n, pl **—women** [,wimin] campesina f.
county ['kaunti] **1** n condado m; **the Home Counties** los condados alrededor de Londres. **2** attr and adj aristocrático; **— town** cabeza f de partido.
coup [kuː] n golpe m; **— d'état** golpe m de estado; **— de grâce** golpe m de gracia; **— de théâtre** golpe m de teatro; **to bring off a —** obtener un éxito inesperado.
coupé ['kuːpei] n cupé m.
couple ['kʌpl] **1** n (of things) par m; (of persons)

pareja f; **married —** matrimonio m; **young —** matrimonio m joven; **just a — of minutes** dos minutos nada más; **we had a — in a bar** (fam) tomamos algo en un bar; **when he's had a — he starts to shout** cuando ha bebido más de la cuenta se pone a gritar.
2 vt names etc unir, juntar; ideas asociar; (Mech) acoplar, enganchar.
3 vi (Zool) copularse.
couplet ['kʌplit] n pareado m.
coupling ['kʌpliŋ] n (Mech) acoplamiento m; (Rail, Aut) enganche m.
coupon ['kuːpɔn] n cupón m; (football-pool —) boleto m.
courage ['kʌridʒ] n valor m, valentía f; **—!** ¡ánimo!; **Dutch —** envalentonamiento m (del que ha bebido); **to have the — of one's convictions** obrar de acuerdo con su conciencia; **to pluck up one's —** hacer de tripas corazón; **to screw up one's — to + infin** cobrar bastante ánimo como para + infin; **we may take — from the fact that** es alentador el hecho de que.
courageous [kə'reidʒəs] adj valiente, valeroso.
courageously [kə'reidʒəsli] adv valientemente.
courier ['kuriə*] n estafeta f, correo m diplomático; (travel —) agente m de turismo.
course [kɔːs] **1** n (a) (movement, direction) dirección f, ruta f; (of bullet etc) trayectoria f; (of road) dirección f; (of river, star) curso m; (of illness) desarrollo m; (Naut) rumbo m, derrota f, (marked on chart) derrotero m; **to change —** cambiar de rumbo (also fig); **to set — for** hacer rumbo a; **to steer a — for** ir rumbo a.
(b) (fig) proceder m, camino m; **— of action** línea f de conducta, línea f de acción, proceder m; **— of conduct** línea f de conducta; **— of events** marcha f de los acontecimientos; **in the ordinary — of events** normalmente; **— of treatment** tratamiento m, cura f; **the — of true love** el camino del verdadero amor; **your best — is to say nothing** lo mejor es no decir nada; **there was no — open to me but to go** no tuve más remedio que ir; **what — do you suggest?** ¿qué es lo que me aconsejas?; **the affair has run its —** el asunto ha terminado; **we will let things take their —** dejaremos que las cosas se desarrollen normalmente, dejaremos correr los acontecimientos; **to take a middle —** evitar los extremos.
(c) (Golf) campo m; (for races) pista f, (for horse races) hipódromo m.
(d) (in meal) plato m; **main —** plato m principal; **fish —** pescado m.
(e) (Archit) hilada f.
(f) (series) curso m; (Univ etc) curso m, asignatura f; **I failed the chemistry —** me suspendieron en química; **what — do you take?** ¿qué asignatura haces?; **a French —** un curso de francés; **I bought a French grammar —** compré una gramática francesa; **a — of lectures** un ciclo de conferencias; **refresher —** curso m de repaso; **secretarial —** curso m de secretaria; **to take a — with** seguir un curso con.
(g) **in the — of** durante, en el curso de; durante el desarrollo de; **in — of construction** en vías de construcción; **it is in — of being applied** está en trance de ser aplicado; **in — of time, in due —** andando el tiempo, a su tiempo; **we shall inform you in due —** se lo comunicaremos en el momento oportuno; **of —** desde luego, naturalmente; **of —!** ¡naturalmente!, ¡claro!; **of — it's not true** claro que no es cierto; **it is of — true** that bien es verdad que; **he takes it all as a matter of —** para él todo esto no tiene nada de especial; **he took it as a matter of —** that para él era de cajón que.
2 vt cazar (con perros).
3 vi correr; **it sent the blood coursing through my veins** me hizo hervir la sangre.
coursing ['kɔːsiŋ] n caza f con perros.
court [kɔːt] **1** n (a) (Archit) patio m; (large room) sala f.
(b) (Sport) pista f, cancha f; **hard —** pista f dura.
(c) (royal) corte f; **at —** en la corte; **— circular** noticiario m de la corte.
(d) **to pay —** to hacer la corte a.
(e) (Law) tribunal m, juzgado m; **divorce —** tribunal m de pleitos matrimoniales; **high —**, **supreme —** tribunal m supremo; **juvenile —** tribunal m tutelar de menores; **police —** tribunal m de policía; **— of appeal** tribunal m de casación; **— of inquiry** comisión f de investigación; **— of justice** tribunal m de justicia; **in open —** en pleno

tribunal; **to laugh something out of** — rechazar algo poniéndolo en ridículo; **to rule something out of** — no admitir algo; **to settle out of** — arreglar una disputa de modo privado; **to take someone to** — demandar a uno; recurrir a la vía judicial.

2 *vt woman* cortejar, hacer la corte a, *(less formally)* tener relaciones con; *favour* solicitar; *danger, trouble* buscar; *disaster* correr a.

3 *vi* estar en relaciones, ser novios; **they've been —ing 3 years** llevan 3 años de relaciones; **are you —ing?** ¿tienes novio?; **—ing couple** pareja *f* de novios.

court card ['kɔːtkɑːd] *n* carta *f* de figura.
courteous ['kɜːtiəs] *adj* cortés, fino.
courteously ['kɜːtiəsli] *adv* cortésmente.
courtesan [ˌkɔːtiˈzæn] *n* cortesana *f*.
courtesy ['kɜːtisi] *n* cortesía *f*; atención *f*; gentileza *f*; **— title** título *m* de cortesía; **by — of** con permiso de; **to exchange courtesies** cambiar cumplidos de etiqueta; **I'll do it out of** — lo haré por cortesía; **you might have had the — to tell me** el no decírmelo es una falta de educación; **he did me the — of reading it** tuvo conmigo la amabilidad de leerlo.
courthouse ['kɔːthaus] *n, pl* **—houses** [ˌhauziz] palacio *m* de justicia.
courtier ['kɔːtiə*] *n* cortesano *m*.
courtly ['kɔːtli] *adj* cortés, elegante, fino; **— love** amor *m* cortés.
court-martial ['kɔːt'mɑːʃəl] **1** *n* consejo *m* de guerra. **2** *vt* someter a consejo de guerra.
court room ['kɔːtrum] *n* sala *f* de justicia.
courtship ['kɔːtʃip] *n* *(act)* cortejo *m*; *(period)* relaciones *fpl*, noviazgo *m*.
courtyard ['kɔːtjɑːd] *n* patio *m*.
cousin ['kʌzn] *n* primo *m*, a *f*; **first —** primo *m* carnal; prima *f* carnal; **second —** primo *m* segundo, prima *f* segunda; **country —** pariente *m* pueblerino, parienta *f* pueblerina.
cove[1] [kəuv] *n* *(Geog)* cala *f*, ensenada *f*.
cove[2] [kəuv] *n* *(sl)* tío *m*.
covenant ['kʌvinənt] **1** *n* pacto *m*, convenio *m*; *(Bible)* **C—** Alianza *f*. **2** *vi*: **to — with someone for something** pactar algo con uno.
covenanter ['kʌvinəntə*] *n* contratante *mf*; *(Hist)* covenantario *m*.
Coventry ['kɔvəntri]: **to send someone to —** hacer el vacío a uno.
cover ['kʌvə*] **1** *n* **(a)** *(in general)* cubierta *f*; *(lid)* tapa *f*, tapadura *f*; *(on bed)* cobertor *m*; *(of chair, typewriter)* funda *f*; **—s** *(bedclothes)* ropa *f* de cama, mantas *fpl*; **outer —** *(Aut)* cubierta *f*.
　(b) *(envelope)* sobre *m*; **first-day —** sobre *m* de primer día; **under separate —** por separado.
　(c) *(of book)* forro *m*, cubierta *f*; *(of magazine)* portada *f*; **to read a book from — to —** leer un libro desde el principio hasta el fin.
　(d) *(at table)* cubierto *m*.
　(e) *(fig)* protección *f*; *(shelter)* abrigo *m*; *(insurance)* cobertura *f*; *(pretext)* pretexto *m*; **air —** protección *f* aérea; **under —** al abrigo, *(indoors)* bajo techo; **under — of** al abrigo de, bajo, *(fig)* so capa de; **under the — of night** al amparo de la noche; **to break —** salir a campo raso; **to take —** abrigarse, ponerse al abrigo, *(Mil)* refugiarse *(from* de).
2 *vt* cubrir *(with* de); revestir *(with* de); *(with lid)* tapar *(with* con); *book* forrar; *(hide)* cubrir, ocultar; *(protect)* proteger, abrigar; *distance* recorrer, cubrir, salvar; *expenses* cubrir; *(include)* incluir, abarcar, comprender; *(Mil) person* amenazar *(with* con), *place* dominar, *retreat* cubrir, proteger; *(Journalism)* investigar, hacer un reportaje sobre, escribir una crónica de, dar cuenta de; *points in discussion* tratar, resolver, discutir; **to — one's eyes** taparse los ojos; **to be —ed in confusion** estar lleno de confusión; **to be —ed with glory** estar cubierto de gloria; **to — in** cubrir; *(roof)* poner un techo a; **to — over** cubrir, revestir *(with* de); **to — up** cubrir completamente, tapar; correr un velo sobre; *(fig)* ocultar, disimular.
3 *vi*: **to — up for someone** encubrir a uno, usar pretextos para no delatar a uno.
4 *vr*: **to — oneself** protegerse a sí mismo; **to — oneself with glory** cubrirse de gloria.
coveralls ['kʌvərɔːlz] *npl* *(US)* = **overalls**.
coverage ['kʌvəridʒ] *n* **(a)** alcance *m*; espacio *m* cubierto, cantidad *f* cubierta; **news —** alcance *m* del servicio de información *(de un periódico etc)*.
　(b) *(Fin)* conjunto *m* de los riesgos que cubre una póliza de seguros.
cover charge ['kʌvətʃɑːdʒ] *n* precio *m* del cubierto.
covergirl ['kʌvəgɜːl] *n* joven *f* cuyo retrato ha figurado en la portada de una revista.

covering ['kʌvəriŋ] *n* *(wrapping)* cubierta *f*, envoltura *f*; *(dress etc)* abrigo *m*; **a — of snow** una capa de nieve.
coverlet ['kʌvəlit] *n* sobrecama *m*, colcha *f*, cobertor *m*.
covert ['kʌvət] **1** *adj* secreto, disimulado. **2** *n* soto *m*.
covet ['kʌvit] *vt* codiciar.
covetous ['kʌvitəs] *adj* codicioso.
covetousness ['kʌvitəsnis] *n* codicia *f*.
covey ['kʌvi] *n* *(Orn)* nidada *f* (de perdices); *(fig)* grupo *m*.
cow[1] [kau] *n* vaca *f*; *(of elephant etc)* hembra *f*; **till the —s come home** hasta que la rana críe pelo.
cow[2] [kau] *vt* intimidar, acobardar.
coward ['kauəd] *n* cobarde *m*.
cowardice ['kauədis] *n*, **cowardliness** ['kauədlinis] *n* cobardía *f*.
cowardly ['kauədli] *adj* cobarde.
cowbell ['kaubel] *n* cencerro *m*.
cowboy ['kaubɔi] *n* vaquero *m*.
cowboy hat ['kaubɔi'hæt] *n* sombrero *m* de vaquero.
cowcatcher ['kauˌkætʃə*] *n* rastrillo *m* delantero, quitapiedras *m*.
cower ['kauə*] *vi* encogerse (de miedo), empequeñecerse (preso del terror); **the servants were —ing in a corner** los criados se habían refugiado medrosos en un rincón.
cowherd ['kauhɜːd] *n* pastor *m* de ganado.
cowhide ['kauhaid] *n* cuero *m*.
cowl [kaul] *n* *(hood)* capucha *f*; *(garment)* cogulla *f*; *(of chimney)* sombrerete *m*.
cowling ['kauliŋ] *n* cubierta *f*.
cowman ['kaumən] *n, pl* **—men** [mən] pastor *m* de ganado.
co-worker ['kəu'wɜːkə*] *n* colaborador *m*, ora *f*.
cowrie ['kauri] *n* cauri *m*.
cowpox ['kaupɔks] *n* vacuna *f*.
cowshed ['kauʃed] *n* establo *m*.
cowslip ['kauslip] *n* primavera *f*.
cox [kɔks] **1** *n* timonel *m*. **2** *vt* gobernar. **3** *vi* servir de timonel.
coxswain ['kɔksn] *n* timonel *m*.
coy [kɔi] *adj* tímido; *(roguish)* coquetón.
coyly ['kɔili] *adv* tímidamente; con coquetería.
coyness ['kɔinis] *n* timidez *f*; coquetería *f*.
coyote ['kɔi'əuti] *n* coyote *m*.
cozy ['kəuzi] *adj* = **cosy**.
crab [kræb] *n* cangrejo *m*; **C—** *(Astron)* Cáncer *m*; **to catch a —** *(fig)* faltar con el remo.
crabapple ['kræbˌæpl] *n* *(fruit)* manzana *f* silvestre; *(tree)* manzano *m* silvestre.
crabbed ['kræbd] *adj writing* apretado, indescifrable; *temperament* de miras estrechas, mezquino.
crabby ['kræbi] *adj* hosco, de mal genio; malhumorado.
crack [kræk] **1** *n* **(a)** *(noise)* crujido *m*; *(of whip)* chasquido *m*; *(shot)* estallido *m*.
　(b) *(blow)* golpe *m* con mano.
　(c) *(fissure)* grieta *f*, hendedura *f*; *(slit)* rendija *f*; **at the — of dawn** al romper el alba; **to open the window a —** abrir la ventana un poquito.
　(d) *(fam)* chiste *m*, chanza *f*, cuchufleta *f*; **to make —s about** *person* tomar el pelo a, burlarse de, *thing* poner en ridículo.
　(e) *(fam)* **to have a — at something** intentar algo, probar algo.
2 *adj team etc* de primera categoría; *shot* experto.
3 *vt* **(a)** *(cause to sound)* *whip, fingers* chasquear; *knuckles etc* crujir.
　(b) *(break)* agrietar, hender, romper; *nut* cascar; *safe* forzar; *bottle* abrir *(with* para festejar a); *heavy oils* craquear; **to — one's head on the wall** dar con la cabeza contra la pared.
　(c) *joke* contar.
　(d) **to — up** dar bombo a; **it's not all it's —ed up to be** no es tan bueno como la gente dice.
4 *vi* **(a)** *(make noise)* chasquear; crujir; *(shot)* estallar.
　(b) *(break)* agrietarse, henderse, rajarse, romperse; *(burst)* reventar; *(voice)* cascarse; **to — under the strain** romperse bajo el peso, *(person)* sufrir un colapso bajo la presión; **to — down on** castigar severamente, suprimir; **to — up** *(plane)* estrellarse, *(machine)* tener una avería, *(Med)* sufrir un colapso nervioso.
　(c) **to get —ing** *(fam)* ponerse a trabajar *(etc)*, poner manos a la obra; **let's get —ing!** ¡a ello!, ¡manos a la obra!
crack-brained ['krækbreind] *adj* mentecato.
cracked [krækt] *adj voice* cascado; *(mad)* chiflado.
cracker ['krækə*] *n* *(firework)* buscapiés *m*; *(biscuit)* cracker *m*.
crackers ['krækəz] *adj* *(sl)* lelo, chiflado.

crack-jaw ['krækdʒɔ:] n trabalenguas m.
crackle ['krækl] 1 n (of wood, bacon) crepitación f; (of dry leaves) crujido m; (of shots) traqueteo m. 2 vi crepitar; crujir; traquetear.
crackling ['kræklɪŋ] n (Cook) chicharrón m; (sound) see crackle.
cracknel ['kræknl] n coscarana f.
crackpot ['krækpɔt] 1 adj tonto, estrafalario. 2 n chiflado m.
cracksman ['kræksmən] n, pl —men [mən] (fam) ladrón m de cajas fuertes.
crack-up ['krækʌp] n (fam) (Aer) aterrizaje m violento; (Mech) avería f; (Med) colapso m nervioso.
cradle ['kreidl] 1 n cuna f (also fig); (for painting etc) plataforma f colgante.
2 vt: to — a child in one's arms mecer un niño en los brazos.
cradlesong ['kreidlsɔŋ] n canción f de cuna.
craft [krɑ:ft] n (a) (skill in general) destreza f, habilidad f; (special skill) arte m; (craftiness) astucia f; (trade) oficio m.
(b) (Naut) barco m, embarcación f.
craftily ['krɑ:ftili] adv astutamente.
craftiness ['krɑ:ftinis] n astucia f.
craftsman ['krɑ:ftsmən] n, pl —men [mən] artesano m; artífice m.
craftsmanship ['krɑ:ftsmənʃip] n artesanía f.
crafty ['krɑ:fti] adj astuto, taimado.
crag [kræg] n peñasco m, risco m.
craggy ['krægi] adj peñascoso, escarpado; face nudoso.
cram [kræm] 1 vt (a) hen cebar; subject empollar, aprender apresuradamente; pupil preparar apresuradamente para un examen.
(b) to — food into one's mouth llenarse la boca de comida; to — things into a case ir metiendo cosas apretadamente en una maleta; we can't — any more in es imposible meter más.
(c) to — something with llenar algo de, henchir algo de; the hall is —med la sala está de bote en bote; the room is —med with furniture el cuarto está atestado de muebles; he had his head —med with odd ideas tenía la cabeza cargada de ideas raras.
2 vi (for exam) empollar; (with food) = 3 vr: to — oneself with food darse un atracón; to — oneself with cakes atracarse de pastas.
cram-full ['kræm'ful] adj completamente lleno, de bote en bote.
crammer ['kræmə*] n (School: pupil) empollón m, ona f; (teacher) profesor m que prepara rapidísimamente a sus alumnos para los exámenes.
cramp[1] [kræmp] n (Med) calambre m; writer's — calambre m de los escribientes.
cramp[2] [kræmp] 1 n (Tech) grapa f; (Archit) pieza f de unión, abrazadera f.
2 vt (hamper) estorbar, restringir; to — someone's style cortar los vuelos a uno.
cramped [kræmpt] adj room etc estrecho; writing menudo, apretado; position violento, nada cómodo; we are very — for space tenemos muy poco espacio.
crampon ['kræmpən] n garfio m; (Mountaineering) crampón m.
cranberry ['krænbəri] n arándano m agrio.
crane [krein] 1 n (Zool) grulla f; (Tech) grúa f.
2 vt (also to — up) levantar con grúa; to — one's neck estirar el cuello.
3 vi: to — forward inclinarse estirando el cuello; to — to look at something estirar el cuello para mirar algo.
cranefly ['kreinflai] n típula f.
crane's-bill ['kreinzbil] n geranio m, pico m de cigüeña.
cranium ['kreiniəm] n cráneo m.
crank[1] [kræŋk] 1 n manivela f, manubrio m; cigüeñal m. 2 vt engine (also to — up) dar vuelta a, hacer arrancar con la manivela.
crank[2] [kræŋk] n (person) maniático m, a f, chiflado m, a f.
crankcase ['kræŋkkeis] n cárter m del cigüeñal.
crankshaft ['kræŋkʃɑ:ft] n eje m del cigüeñal, árbol m del cigüeñal.
cranky ['kræŋki] adj person maniático, chiflado; idea raro, estrafalario.
cranny ['kræni] n grieta f.
crap [kræp] n (sl) mierda f (also fig).
crape [kreip] n crespón m.
craps [kræps] npl dados mpl; to shoot — jugar a los dados.
crash ['kræʃ] 1 n (a) (noise) estruendo m, estrépito m; (explosion) estallido m.
(b) (collision) accidente m, choque m, encon-

tronazo m; (Aer) accidente m de aviación.
(c) (ruin) fracaso m; ruina f; (Comm) quiebra f; the 1929 — la crisis económica de 1929.
2 vt car, aircraft estrellar (into contra); estropear; he —ed the plate to the ground echó el plato por tierra; he —ed the plate into her face le dio con el plato en la cara; to — a party (fam) colarse, entrar de gorra.
3 vi (a) (fall noisily) caer con estrépito (also to — down, to come —ing down); (shatter) romperse, hacerse añicos.
(b) (have accident) tener un accidente; (2 cars etc) chocar; (Aer) estrellarse, caer a tierra; to — into chocar con, estrellarse contra.
(c) (fail) fracasar, hundirse; (Comm) quebrar; when the stock market —ed cuando la bolsa tuvo su crisis.
4 adv: he went — into a tree dio de lleno consigo contra un árbol.
5 interj ¡zas!, ¡pum!
6 adj: — programme programa m de urgencia; — course curso m acelerado, curso m concentrado.
crash helmet ['kræʃ,helmit] n casco m protector.
crass [kræs] adj craso.
crate [kreit] n cajón m de embalaje, jaula f; (fam) armatoste m.
crater ['kreitə*] n cráter m.
cravat(e) [krə'væt] n corbata f.
crave [kreiv] 1 vt suplicar, implorar; attention reclamar. 2 vi: to — for ansiar, anhelar.
craven ['kreivən] adj cobarde.
craving ['kreivɪŋ] n deseo m vehemente, ansia f, sed f (for de); (during pregnancy) antojo m; to get a — for something encapricharse por algo.
crawfish ['krɔ:fiʃ] n ástaco m.
crawl [krɔ:l] 1 n (action) arrastramiento m; (journey) camino m a gatas; (Swimming) crol m; the traffic went at a — la circulación avanzaba a paso de tortuga; the — to the coast el viaje a una lentitud desesperante hacia la costa.
2 vi (a) (drag oneself) arrastrarse; avanzar a rastras; (child) andar a gatas, gatear; to — in entrar a gatas; the fly —ed up the window la mosca subió despacito el cristal; the cars were —ing along los coches avanzaban a paso de tortuga.
(b) to — to someone humillarse ante uno, ir humildemente a pedir perdón a uno.
(c) to — with, to be —ing with estar cuajado de, estar plagado de.
crayfish ['kreifiʃ] n ástaco m.
crayon ['kreiən] 1 n (Art) pastel m, lápiz m de tiza; (child's) lápiz m de color. 2 vt dibujar al pastel (etc).
craze [kreiz] n manía f (for por); (fashion) moda f (for de); to be the — estar muy de moda.
crazed [kreizd] adj loco (with de), demente; half — medio loco.
crazily ['kreizili] adv locamente; lean etc de modo peligroso.
crazy ['kreizi] adj (a) person loco, chiflado; idea disparatado, estrafalario; to be — about person estar chiflado por, thing andar loco por; to be — with worry estar loco de inquietud; to drive someone — volver loco a uno; it's enough to drive you — es para volverse loco; to go — volverse loco.
(b) building destartalado; to lean at a — angle inclinarse de modo peligroso.
(c) paving en mosaico.
creak [kri:k] 1 n (of wood, shoe etc) crujido m; (of hinge etc) chirrido m, rechinamiento m. 2 vi crujir; chirriar, rechinar.
creaky ['kri:ki] adj rechinador; (fig) poco sólido, inestable, nada firme.
cream [kri:m] 1 n (a) (on milk) nata f; whipped — nata f batida; — cake pastel m de nata.
(b) (in general) crema f; foundation — crema f base; — of tartar crémor m tártaro.
(c) (fig) flor f y nata, crema f, lo mejor y más selecto; the — of society la crema de la sociedad; the — of the joke was that lo más gracioso fue que.
2 adj color de crema.
3 vt milk desnatar; butter batir; (fig) quitar lo mejor de.
4 vi formar nata.
cream puff ['kri:m'pʌf] n bollo m de crema.
creamy ['kri:mi] adj cremoso.
crease [kri:s] 1 n (fold) pliegue m; (in trousers) raya f; (wrinkle) arruga f.
2 vt plegar, doblar; arrugar; to — one's trousers hacer la raya a los pantalones.
3 vi plegarse, doblarse; arrugarse.

create [kri:'eit] **1** vt crear; (produce) producir, motivar; character inventar; rôle encarnar; (appoint) nombrar.
  2 vi (fam) protestar, armar un lío.
creation [kri:'eiʃən] n creación f; (appointment) nombramiento m.
creative [kri:'eitiv] adj creador; original, inventivo; work original.
creativity [,kri:ei'tiviti] n facultad f creadora; originalidad f inventiva.
creator [kri'eitə*] n creador m, ora f.
creature ['kri:tʃə*] n (a) (animal) criatura f; animal m, bicho m; **poor** —! ¡pobre animal!; — **comforts** bienestar m material.
  (b) (person) **to be someone's** — ser la criatura de uno; **wretched** —! ¡desgraciado!; **he's a poor** — es un infeliz; **doesn't she look a** —? ¡qué birria!
crèche [kreiʃ] n guardería f infantil.
credence ['kri:dəns] n: **to give** — to prestar fe a.
credentials [kri'denʃəlz] npl credenciales fpl.
credenza [krə'denzə] n aparador m.
credibility [,kredə'biləti] n credibilidad f; — **gap** margen m de confianza.
credible ['kredibl] adj creíble.
credit ['kredit] **1** n (a) (belief) crédito m; **to give** — to creer.
  (b) (reputation) buena fama f, reputación f.
  (c) (honour) honor m, mérito m; **to his** — **he** confessed dicho sea a su honor, confesó la verdad; **he is a great** — **to the family** le hace mucho honor a la familia; **to come out of something with** — salir airoso de algo; **the only people to emerge with any** — los únicos que salen con honor; **to pass a test with** — salir bien de una prueba; **it does you** — Vd puede enorgullecerse de ello; **he did himself great** — se honró mucho; **to take the** — atribuirse el mérito (for de).
  (d) (Comm) crédito m; (side of account) haber m; **"— terms available"** "ventas a plazos"; **on** — a crédito, al fiado; **on the** — **side** en el haber; **you have £10 to your** — Vd tiene 10 libras en el haber; **to give someone** — abrir crédito a uno; **I gave you** — **for more sense** le creía con más inteligencia.
  2 attr facility crediticio; balance positivo, acreedor.
  3 vt (a) (believe) creer, prestar fe a; **you wouldn't** — **it** parece mentira.
  (b) (Comm) **to** — **someone with £5, to** — **£5 to someone** abonar 5 libras en cuenta a uno.
  (c) (fig) **I** —**ed you with more sense** le creía con más inteligencia; **we must** — **him with charm at** least por lo menos hay que reconocer que tiene gran atractivo personal; **to be** —**ed with having done something** pasar por haber hecho algo; **he** —**ed them with the victory** les atribuyó el mérito de la victoria; **they had less drawing power than they were** —**ed with** no tenían tanta fuerza atractiva como se les suponía.
creditable ['kreditəbl] adj loable, estimable.
creditably ['kreditəbli] adv de modo loable.
credit agency ['kredit'eidʒənsi] n agencia que investiga los recursos financieros y confiabilidad de clientes que quieren abrir cuentas para compras al fiado.
credit card ['kreditka:d] n tarjeta f de crédito.
creditor ['kreditə*] n acreedor m, ora f.
credit rating ['kredit,reitiŋ] n (Comm) cifra f máxima permitida para las compras al fiado, límite m de las facilidades crediticias.
credo ['kreidəu] n credo m.
credulity [kri'dju:liti] n credulidad f.
credulous ['kredjuləs] adj crédulo.
creed [kri:d] n credo m.
creek [kri:k] n (inlet) cala f, ensenada f; (stream) riachuelo m.
creel [kri:l] n cesta f (de pescador).
creep [kri:p] **1** n (a) (sl) cobista mf, pelotillero m.
  (b) **it gives me the** —**s** me horripila.
  2 (irr: pret and ptp **crept**) vi (a) (animal etc) arrastrarse, deslizarse, moverse muy despacio por el suelo.
  (b) (person etc) arrastrarse, andar a gatas; (stealthily) ir cautelosamente; (slowly) ir despacito, ir a paso de tortuga; **to** — **about on tiptoe** andar a (or de) puntillas; **to** — **along** (traffic) avanzar a paso de tortuga; **to** — **in** entrar sin ser sentido; **to** — **out** salir silenciosamente; **to** — **up on someone** acercarse sigilosamente a uno.
  (c) (fig) **it's enough to make your flesh** — es para poner carne de gallina; **an error crept in** se deslizó un error; **old age is** —**ing on** se está acercando la vejez; **fear crept over him** le invadió el terror; **to** — **to someone** (sl) hacer la pelotilla a uno, dar jabón a uno.

creeper ['kri:pə*] n (Bot) enredadera f; —**s** (shoes) zapatillas fpl de goma.
creeping ['kri:piŋ] adj (Med etc) progresivo; barrage móvil.
creepy ['kri:pi] adj horripilante.
creepy-crawly ['kri:pi'krɔ:li] n (fam) bicho m.
cremate [kri'meit] vt incinerar.
cremation [kri'meiʃən] n incineración f (de cadáveres).
crematorium [,kremə'tɔ:riəm] n, pl **crematoria** [,kremə'tɔ:riə] horno m crematorio.
crenellated ['krenileitid] adj almenado.
crenellations [,kreni'leiʃənz] npl almenas fpl.
Creole ['kri:əul] **1** adj criollo. **2** n criollo m, a f.
creosote ['kriəsəut] n creosota f.
crêpe [kreip] n crespón m.
crept [krept] pret and ptp of **creep**.
crepuscular [kri'pʌskjulə*] adj crepuscular.
crescent ['kresnt] **1** adj creciente. **2** n (shape) media luna f; (street) calle f en forma de semicírculo.
cress [kres] n mastuerzo m, berro m.
crest [krest] n (of bird, wave) cresta f; (of turkey) moco m; (on helmet) cimera f (also Her); (of hill) cima f, cumbre f, cresta f; (Her) blasón m.
crestfallen ['krest,fɔ:lən] adj alicaído.
cretaceous [kri'teiʃəs] adj cretáceo.
Cretan ['kri:tən] **1** adj cretense. **2** n cretense mf.
Crete [kri:t] Creta f.
cretin ['kretin] n cretino m, a f.
cretinous ['kretinəs] adj cretino; (fig) imbécil.
cretonne [kre'tɔn] n cretona f.
crevasse [kri'væs] n grieta f de glaciar.
crevice ['krevis] n grieta f, hendedura f.
crew [kru:] n (Naut, Aer) tripulación f; (Mil, number of — members) dotación f; personal m, equipo m; (gang) banda f, pandilla f; **they looked a sorry** — daba lástima verlos.
crew-cut ['kru:kʌt] n corte m de pelo al rape.
crew-neck ['kru:nek] n cuello m plano; — **sweater** suéter m sin cuello.
crib [krib] **1** n (a) pesebre m.
  (b) (fam) (translation) traducción f; (thing copied) plagio m; (in exam) chuleta f.
  (c) **to crack a** — (sl) robar una casa.
  2 vt (fam) plagiar, tomar (from de).
  3 vi (fam) usar una chuleta.
crick [krik] n: — **in the neck** torticolis m.
cricket¹ ['krikit] n (Zool) grillo m.
cricket² ['krikit] n críquet m; **that's not** — eso no es jugar limpio.
cricketer ['krikitə*] n criquetero m.
crier ['kraiə*] n: **town** — pregonero m público.
crikey ['kraiki] interj (fam) ¡caramba!
crime [kraim] n crimen m, delito m.
Crimea [krai'miə] Crimea f.
Crimean War [krai'miən'wɔ:*] Guerra f de Crimea.
criminal ['kriminl] **1** adj criminal; act, intent delictivo; code, law penal; **it would be** — **to let her go out** sería un crimen dejarla salir.
  2 n criminal m, delincuente m; **war** — criminal m de guerra.
criminologist [,krimi'nɔlədʒist] n criminalista m.
criminology [,krimi'nɔlədʒi] n criminología f.
crimp [krimp] vt rizar, encrespar.
crimson ['krimzn] **1** adj carmesí. **2** n carmesí m.
cringe [krindʒ] vi agacharse, encogerse; (fig) reptar; **to** — **with fear** encogerse de miedo; **the servants were cringing in a corner** los criados se habían refugiado medrosos en un rincón.
cringing ['krindʒiŋ] adj servil, rastrero.
crinkle ['kriŋkl] **1** n arruga f; (sl) parné m. **2** vt arrugar. **3** vi arrugarse.
crinkly ['kriŋkli] adj arrugado; hair rizado.
crinoline ['krinəlin] n crinolina f, miriñaque m.
cripple ['kripl] **1** n lisiado m, a f, mutilado m, a f.
  2 vt lisiar, tullir, mutilar; ship inutilizar; (fig) paralizar, estropear.
crisis ['kraisis] n, pl **crises** ['kraisi:z] crisis f.
crisp [krisp] **1** adj duro pero frágil; (after cooking) curruscante, crujiente, tostado; hair crespo; air vigorizante; manner, tone resuelto, seco; style nervioso.
  2 —**s** npl patatas fpl a la inglesa.
criss-crossed ['kriskrɔst] adj entrelazado; — **by** surcado de.
criterion [krai'tiəriən] n, pl **criteria** [krai'tiəriə] criterio m.
critic ['kritik] n crítico m.
critical ['kritikəl] adj crítico; (hyper-) criticón; illness grave; **to be** — **of** criticar.

critically ['kritikəli] *adv* críticamente; **to be — ill** estar gravemente enfermo.
criticism ['kritisizəm] *n* crítica *f*.
criticize ['kritisaiz] *vt* criticar; censurar.
critique [kri'ti:k] *n* crítica *f*.
croak [krəuk] **1** *n* (*of raven*) graznido *m*; (*of frog*) canto *m*; (*of person*) gruñido *m*. **2** *vi* (*raven*) graznar; (*frog*) croar; (*person*) gruñir.
Croat ['krəuæt] *n* croata *mf*.
Croatia [krəu'eiʃiə] Croacia *f*.
Croatian [krəu'eiʃiən] **1** *adj* croata. **2** *n* croata *mf*.
crochet ['krəuʃei] **1** *n* croché *m*, labor *f* de ganchillo. **2** *vt* hacer en croché, hacer de ganchillo. **3** *vi* hacer croché, hacer labor de ganchillo.
crochet hook ['krəuʃihuk] *n* ganchillo *m*.
crock[1] [krɔk] *n* vasija *f* de barro; **old — (*person*)** carcamal *m*, (*car etc*) cacharro *m*; **old —s' race** rallye *m* de coches clásicos.
crock[2] [krɔk] *vt* lisiar, incapacitar.
crockery ['krɔkəri] *n* loza *f*, vajilla *f*, los platos.
crocodile ['krɔkədail] *n* cocodrilo *m*; **— tears** lágrimas *fpl* de cocodrilo.
crocus ['krəukəs] *n* azafrán *m*.
Croesus ['kri:səs] *m* Creso.
croft [krɔft] *n* (*Scot*) granja *f* pequeña, parcela *f*.
crofter ['krɔftə*] *n* (*Scot*) arrendatario *m* de una granja pequeña.
croissant [krwʌsã:ŋ] *n* croissant *m*, medialuna *f*.
crone [krəun] *n* vieja *f*.
crony ['krəuni] *n* compinche *mf*.
crook [kruk] **1** *n* (a) (*staff*) cayado *m*; (*bend*) curva *f*; **— of the arm** pliegue *m* del codo; *see* **hook**.
   (**b**) (*person*) criminal *m*, estafador *m*, ladrón *m*, maleante *m*; **you —!** (*hum*) ¡animal!
   2 *vt* encorvar.
   3 *vi* encorvarse.
crooked ['krukid] *adj* curvo, encorvado, torcido; *path* tortuoso; (*fig*) *deal*, *means* poco limpio; *person* criminal, nada honrado.
croon [kru:n] *vt* canturrear, cantar en voz baja.
crooner ['kru:nə*] *n* vocalista *mf* (sentimental), canzonetista *mf*.
crop [krɔp] **1** *n* (*species grown*) cultivo *m*; (*produce*) cosecha *f*; (*Orn*) buche *m*; (*whip*) látigo *m* mocho; (*hair style*) corte *m* a lo garçon.
   2 *vt* (*cut*) cortar; (*trim*) recortar; *animal's ears* desorejar, *tail* cortar; (*graze*) pacer.
   3 *vi*: *a tree which* **—s well** un árbol que rinde bien; **to — out, to — up** (*Geol*) aflorar; **to — up** (*fig*) surgir, producirse inesperadamente; **something must have —ped up** habrán tenido alguna dificultad; **now another problem has —ped up** ahora se ha planteado otro problema.
cropper ['krɔpə*] *n* (*fam*): **to come a — caer**; (*fig*) fracasar; tirarse una plancha.
croquet ['krəukei] *n* croquet *m*.
croquette [krəu'ket] *n* croqueta *f*.
crosier ['krəuʒə*] *n* báculo *m* pastoral.
cross [krɔs] **1** *adj* (a) (*crossed*) cruzado; (*diagonal etc*) transversal, oblicuo.
   (**b**) (*fig*) malhumorado; **to be — estar de mal** humor; **to be — with someone** estar enfadado con uno; **don't be — with me** no te vayas a enfadar conmigo; **to get — enfadarse** (*about* de, *with* con).
   2 *n* cruz *f* (*also fig*); (*Bio: in general*) cruzamiento *m*, (*hybrid*) híbrido *m*; **iron — cruz *f* de hierro; Maltese — cruz *f* de Malta; Red C— Cruz *f* Roja; Southern — Cruz *f* del Sur; it's a — between A and B** es una mezcla de A y B; **to cut something on the — cortar algo al sesgo; to make the sign of the C— hacer la señal de la cruz** (*over* sobre).
   3 *vt* (a) (*place crosswise*) cruzar; *screw* trasroscar; **to — one's arms** cruzarse de brazos; **to — someone's hand with silver** dar una moneda de plata a uno; **the lines are —ed** (*Tel*) hay un cruce en las líneas.
   (**b**) (*draw line across*) *cheque* cruzar; **to — off, to — out** tachar.
   (**c**) (*go across*) cruzar, atravesar; *river* (*as obstacle*) salvar.
   (**d**) (*meet and pass*) cruzar.
   (**e**) (*Bio*) cruzar.
   (**f**) (*thwart*) contrariar, ir contra; **to be —ed in love** tener un fracaso sentimental.
   4 *vi* (*also* **to — over**) cruzar, ir al otro lado; (*letters*) cruzarse.
   5 *vr*: **to — oneself** santiguarse.
crossbar ['krɔsbɑ:*] *n* travesaño *m*; (*Sport*) larguero *m*.
crossbeam ['krɔsbi:m] *n* viga *f* transversal.
crossbencher ['krɔs'bentʃə*] *n* (*Parl*) diputado *m* independiente.
crossbow ['krɔsbəu] *n* ballesta *f*.

crossbred ['krɔsbred] *adj* híbrido.
crossbreed ['krɔsbri:d] **1** *n* híbrido *m*, a *f*. **2** *vt* cruzar.
cross-check ['krɔstʃek] **1** *n* comprobación *f* hecha al revés, comprobación *f* adicional.
   2 *vt* comprobar al revés, comprobar una vez más (*or* por otro sistema).
cross-country ['krɔs'kʌntri] *adj route*, *walk* a campo traviesa; **— race** cross *m*.
cross-current ['krɔs'kʌrənt] *n* contracorriente *f*.
cross-examination ['krɔsig,zæmi'neiʃən] *n* (*Law*) repregunta *f*; (*fig*) interrogatorio *m* severo.
cross-examine ['krɔsig'zæmin] *vt* (*Law*) repreguntar; (*fig*) interrogar severamente.
cross-eyed ['krɔsaid] *adj* bizco.
cross-fertilize ['krɔs'fə:tilaiz] *vt* fecundar por fertilización cruzada.
crossfire ['krɔsfaiə*] *n* fuego *m* cruzado.
crossing ['krɔsiŋ] *n* (*intersection*) cruce *m*; (*Rail*) paso *m* a nivel; (*on road*) paso *m* para peatones; (*journey*) travesía *f*; (*Bio*) cruzamiento *m*.
cross-legged ['krɔs'legd] *adj* con las piernas cruzadas.
crossly ['krɔsli] *adv* con mal humor.
crossover ['krɔsəuvə*] *n* (*Aut etc*) paso *m* superior.
crosspatch ['krɔspætʃ] *n* persona *f* malhumorada.
crosspiece ['krɔspi:s] *n* travesaño *m*.
cross-pollination ['krɔs,pɔli'neiʃən] *n* polinización *f* cruzada.
cross-purposes ['krɔs'pə:pəsiz] *npl*: **to be at — no** comprenderse uno a otro; **I think we're at — creo** que aquí hay un malentendido.
cross-question ['krɔs'kwestʃən] *vt* (*Law*) repreguntar; (*fig*) interrogar.
cross-questioning ['krɔs'kwestʃəniŋ] *n* (*Law*) repregunta *f*; (*fig*) interrogación *f*.
cross-reference ['krɔs'refərəns] *n* contrarreferencia *f*.
crossroads ['krɔsrəudz] *n* cruce *m*, encrucijada *f*; (*fig*) punto *m* crítico, momento *m* decisivo.
cross section ['krɔs'sekʃən] *n* corte *m* transversal, sección *f* transversal, perfil *m*; (*fig*) sección *f* representativa.
cross-stitch ['krɔsstitʃ] *n* puntada *f* cruzada.
crosstalk ['krɔstɔ:k] *n* réplicas *fpl* agudas.
crosswind ['krɔswind] *n* viento *m* de costado.
crosswise ['krɔswaiz] *adv* al través; en cruz.
crossword ['krɔswə:d] *n*: **— puzzle** crucigrama *m*.
crotch [krɔtʃ] *n* (*Anat*) horcajadura *f*.
crotchet ['krɔtʃit] *n* (*Mus*) negra *f*.
crotchety ['krɔtʃiti] *adj* propenso a irritarse.
crouch [krautʃ] *vi* agacharse, acurrucarse, encogerse. **men —ing in trenches** hombres agazapados en trincheras.
croup [kru:p] *n* (*Med*) crup *m*.
croupier ['kru:piei] *n* crupier *m*.
croûton ['kru:tɔn] *n* cuscurro *m*.
crow [krəu] **1** *n* cuervo *m*, grajo *m*, corneja *f*; (*cry*) canto *m*, cacareo *m*; **as the — flies** en línea recta.
   2 *vi* cantar, cacarear; (*child*) gorjearse; (*fig*) jactarse, exultar; **to — over someone** triunfar de uno; **to — over something** jactarse de algo, felicitarse por algo; **it's nothing to — about** no hay motivo para sentirse satisfecho.
crowbar ['krəubɑ:*] *n* palanca *f*.
crowd [kraud] **1** *n* multitud *f*; muchedumbre *f*, gentío *m*; (*esp disorderly*) tropel *m*; (*Sport etc*) público *m*, espectadores *mpl*; (*Theat*) comparsas *mpl*; (*fam*) grupo *m*, peña *f*; **the — (*common herd*)** el vulgo; **there was quite a — había bastante gente; how big was the — ?** ¿cuántas personas había?; **— scene** (*Cine*) escena *f* con muchos comparsas; **in a — en** tropel, todos juntos; **to follow the — irse tras el hilo de la gente; to rise above the — destacar(se).**
   2 *vt* (a) (*collect*) amontonar; apretar unos contra otros.
   (**b**) **to — the streets** llenar las calles; **to — a place with** llenar un sitio de; **to — things in** ir metiendo cosas apretadamente; **to — on sail** hacer fuerza de vela; **we got —ed out** fuimos excluidos; **he was —ed off the pavement** había tanta gente que tuvo que abandonar la acera.
   3 *vi* reunirse, congregarse (*into* en); **to — around, to — together** agolparse, apiñarse; **to — round someone** apiñarse (*or* agruparse) en torno de uno; **to — in** entrar en tropel; **to — into a car** entrar todos apretadamente en un coche; **memories —ed in upon me** me invadieron muchísimos recuerdos.
crowded ['kraudid] *adj* lleno, atestado (*with* de); *meeting*, *event etc* muy concurrido; **it's very — here** aquí hay muchísima gente; **the place was — out** el local estaba de bote en bote; **the houses are — together** las casas están apretadas unas contra otras; **one — hour** una sola hora llena de actividad; **it's a**

very — **profession** es una profesión donde sobra gente.

crowfoot ['krəufut] n ranúnculo m.

crown [kraun] **1** n corona f; (of hat) copa f; (of hill) cumbre f; (of head) coronilla f; **the — of the road** el centro de la calzada; **half a —** media corona f.
2 attr: — **colony** colonia f; — **jewels** joyas fpl reales; — **lands** propiedad f de la corona; — **prince** príncipe m heredero.
3 vt coronar; (sl) golpear en la cabeza; (fig) completar, rematar; **to — it all** para completarlo todo, (misfortune) para colmo de desgracias; **to — something with success** coronar algo con éxito.

crowning ['krauniŋ] adj supremo.

crow's-foot ['krəuzfut] n (in eye) pata f de gallo.

crow's-nest ['krəuznest] n torre f de vigía.

crucial ['kru:ʃəl] adj decisivo, crítico, crucial.

crucible ['kru:sibl] n crisol m (also fig).

crucifix ['kru:sifiks] n crucifijo m, cruz f.

crucifixion [,kru:si'fikʃən] n crucifixión f.

cruciform ['kru:sifɔ:m] adj cruciforme.

crucify ['kru:sifai] vt crucificar.

crude [kru:d] adj oil etc crudo, steel etc bruto; object, workmanship tosco; (vulgar) ordinario.

crudely ['kru:dli] adv toscamente; ordinariamente.

crudeness ['kru:dnis] n, **crudity** ['kru:diti] n tosquedad f; ordinariez f.

cruel ['kruəl] adj cruel.

cruelly ['kruəli] adv cruelmente.

cruelty ['kruəlti] n crueldad f; **society for the prevention of — to animals** sociedad f protectora de los animales.

cruet ['kru:it] n vinagrera f; (stand) angarillas fpl.

cruise [kru:z] **1** n crucero m, viaje m por mar. **2** vi cruzar, navegar; (fig) ir, andar; **we were cruising along at 40 m.p.h.** íbamos a 40 millas por hora.

cruiser ['kru:zə*] n crucero m.

cruiser-weight ['kru:zəweit] n peso m medio fuerte.

cruising speed ['kru:ziŋspi:d] n velocidad f de crucero; (Aut) velocidad f económica.

cruller ['krʌlə*] n (US) buñuelo m.

crumb [krʌm] n (one) migaja f; (not crust) miga f; **a — of comfort** una migaja de consolación.

crumble ['krʌmbl] **1** vt desmenuzar, desmigajar. **2** vi (material) desmenuzarse, desmigajarse; (building etc) desmoronarse, derrumbarse.

crumbly ['krʌmbli] adj desmenuzable.

crummy ['krʌmi] adj (sl) ínfimo, de bajísima categoría.

crumpet ['krʌmpit] n bollo m blando (para tostar).

crumple ['krʌmpl] **1** vt ajar, deshacer; paper estrujar; (wrinkle) arrugar; (crease) plegar.
2 vi ajarse, deshacerse; arrugarse; plegarse; (fig, also **to — up**) hundirse, derrumbarse; (person) desplomarse.

crunch [krʌntʃ] **1** n crujido m; (fig) crisis f, punto m decisivo. **2** vt (with teeth) mascar, ronzar; ground etc hacer crujir. **3** vi crujir.

crunchy ['krʌntʃi] adj crujiente, que cruje.

crupper ['krʌpə*] n (of horse) anca f, grupa f.

crusade [kru:'seid] **1** n cruzada f. **2** vi participar en una cruzada; **to — for** hacer campaña en pro de.

crusader [kru:'seidə*] n cruzado m.

crush [krʌʃ] **1** n (a) (of people) agolpamiento m; (of cars etc) aglomeración f; **there was an awful —** hubo la mar de gente; **there's always a — in the tube** el metro va siempre atestado de gente; **I lost my handbag in the —** perdí el bolso en el tumulto; **two died in the —** dos murieron aplastados.
(b) **to have a — on someone** (fam) perder la chaveta por uno.
(c) orange — naranjada f.
2 vt (a) aplastar; paper etc estrujar; stones triturar, moler; grapes etc prensar, exprimir; dress ajar; **to — something into a case** meter algo a la fuerza en una maleta.
(b) (fig) country aplastar; enemy, opposition aniquilar, destruir; person in argument confundir, dejar planchado.
3 vi: **to — in** meterse apretadamente en.

crushing ['krʌʃiŋ] adj blow, defeat, reply aplastante; grief etc abrumador; argument decisivo; burden agobiador.

crust [krʌst] n (of bread, Geol) corteza f; (old bread) mendrugo m; (on wine, Med) costra f.

crustacean [krʌs'teiʃən] n crustáceo m.

crusty ['krʌsti] adj (fig) malhumorado, irritable.

crutch [krʌtʃ] n muleta f; (crotch) horcajadura f.

crux [krʌks] n: **the — of the matter** lo esencial del caso, el punto capital.

cry [krai] **1** n grito m; (of peddler) pregón m; **it's a far — from that** esto tiene poco que ver con aquello;

the hounds were in full — los perros seguían de cerca la presa; **the crowd was in full — after him** una multitud le perseguía con gritos; **to have a good —** llorar a mares.
2 vt gritar (also **to — out**); wares pregonar; **to — down** desacreditar; see **eye** etc.
3 vi (a) (call) gritar; **to — for** clamar por; **to — for help** pedir socorro a voces; **to — off** retirarse, rajarse; **to — out** gritar.
(b) (weep) llorar (for, with de); **to — over** lamentarse sobre.

crybaby ['krai,beibi] n llorón m, ona f.

crying ['kraiiŋ] adj atroz, enorme.

crypt [kript] n cripta f.

cryptic ['kriptik] adj misterioso, secreto.

cryptically ['kriptikəli] adv misteriosamente.

crypto-communist ['kriptəu'kɔmjunist] n criptocomunista mf.

cryptogram ['kriptəugræm] n criptograma m.

cryptographer [krip'tɔgrəfə*] n criptógrafo m.

cryptographic(al) [,kriptəu'græfik(əl)] adj criptográfico.

cryptography [krip'tɔgrəfi] n criptografía f.

crystal ['kristl] **1** n cristal m. **2** adj cristalino.

crystal-clear ['kristl'kliə*] adj transparente como el cristal; (fig) totalmente claro.

crystalline ['kristəlain] adj cristalino.

crystallize ['kristəlaiz] **1** vt cristalizar. **2** vi cristalizarse; (fig) cuajarse, resolverse.

crystallized ['kristəlaizd] adj fruit escarchado.

crystallography [,kristə'lɔgrəfi] n cristalografía f.

crystal set ['kristl'set] n (Radio) receptor m con detector de cristal.

cub [kʌb] n cachorro m; — **reporter** periodista m novato.

Cuba ['kju:bə] Cuba f.

Cuban ['kju:bən] **1** adj cubano. **2** n cubano m, a f.

cubbyhole ['kʌbihəul] n chiribitil m.

cube [kju:b] **1** n cubo m; (of sugar) terrón m. **2** vt cubicar.

cubic ['kju:bik] adj cúbico.

cubicle ['kju:bikəl] n cubículo m; (at swimming pool etc) caseta f.

cubism ['kju:bizəm] n cubismo m.

cubist ['kju:bist] **1** adj cubista. **2** n cubista mf.

cuckold ['kʌkəld] **1** n cornudo m. **2** vt poner los cuernos a.

cuckoo ['kuku:] **1** n cuco m, cuclillo m. **2** adj (sl) lelo.

cuckoo clock ['kuku:klɔk] n reloj m de cuclillo.

cucumber ['kju:kʌmbə*] n pepino m.

cud [kʌd] n: **to chew the —** rumiar (also fig).

cuddle ['kʌdl] **1** n abrazo m amoroso.
2 vt abrazar amorosamente.
3 vi (2 persons) abrazarse, estar abrazados; **to — up to someone** arrimarse amorosamente a uno.

cuddly ['kʌdli] adj mimoso; toy blando.

cudgel ['kʌdʒəl] **1** n porra f; **to take up the —s for someone** salir en defensa de uno. **2** vt aporrear.

cue [kju:] n (Billiards) taco m; (Theat) pie m, apunte m, entrada f; **that gave me my —** eso me sirvió de indicación; **to take one's — from** seguir el ejemplo de.

cuff[1] [kʌf] **1** n bofetada f. **2** vt abofetear.

cuff[2] [kʌf] n (of shirt) puño m; **to say something off the —** decir algo sin pensarlo, decir algo de improviso, sacar algo de la manga.

cufflinks ['kʌfliŋks] npl gemelos mpl.

cuisine [kwi'zi:n] n cocina f.

cul-de-sac ['kʌldə'sæk] n callejón m sin salida.

culinary ['kʌlinəri] adj culinario.

cull [kʌl] vt flowers coger; (select) entresacar.

culminate ['kʌlmineit] vi: **to — in** terminar en.

culminating ['kʌlmineitiŋ] adj culminante.

culmination [,kʌlmi'neiʃən] n (fig) culminación f, punto m culminante, colmo m; **it is the — of much effort** es la culminación de grandes esfuerzos.

culottes [kju(:)'lɔt] npl pantalón m corto (de mujer).

culpability [,kʌlpə'biliti] n culpabilidad f.

culpable ['kʌlpəbl] adj culpable.

culprit ['kʌlprit] n persona f culpable, culpado m, a f, delincuente mf.

cult [kʌlt] n culto m (of a).

cultivable ['kʌltivəbl] adj cultivable.

cultivate ['kʌltiveit] vt cultivar (also fig).

cultivated ['kʌltiveitid] adj (fig) culto.

cultivation [,kʌlti'veiʃən] n (Agr) cultivo m; (fig) cultura f.

cultivator ['kʌltiveitə*] n (Agr) cultivador m.

cultural ['kʌltʃərəl] adj cultural.

culture ['kʌltʃə*] n (Agr, Bio) cultivo m; (fig) cultura f; **physical —** cultura f física.

cultured ['kʌltʃəd] adj culto.

cultured pearl ['kʌltʃəd'pə:l] n perla f cultivada.

culture medium ['kʌltʃə,mi:diəm] n, pl — **media** [mi:diə] medio m de cultivo.
culvert ['kʌlvət] n alcantarilla f.
cumbersome ['kʌmbəsəm] adj molesto, incómodo.
cumin ['kʌmin] n comino m.
cummerbund ['kʌməbʌnd] n faja f de cintura.
cumulative ['kju:mjulətiv] adj cumulativo.
cumulonimbus ['kju:mələu'nimbəs] n cumulonimbo m.
cumulus ['kju:mələs] n cúmulo m.
cuneiform ['kju:nifɔ:m] adj cuneiforme.
cunning ['kʌniŋ] **1** adj (clever) astuto, (sly) taimado; (skilfully made) artificioso, ingenioso; (fam) precioso, mono. **2** n astucia f.
cunningly ['kʌniŋli] adv astutamente; artificiosamente.
cup [kʌp] **1** n taza f; (Eccl, Bot) cáliz m; (trophy) copa f; (in ground) hoyo m, hondonada f; **to be in one's —s** estar borracho; **his — of sorrow was full** le agobiaba el dolor; **there's many a slip twixt — and lip** de la mano a la boca desaparece la sopa; **it's not quite my — of tea** no me conviene del todo; **he's not my — of tea** no es de mi agrado, no es santo de mi devoción; **how's your —?** ¿quieres más té?
2 vt: **to — one's hands** formar bocina con las manos.
cupboard ['kʌbəd] n armario m; (on wall) alacena f.
cupboard love ['kʌbədlʌv] n amor m interesado.
cup final ['kʌpfainl] n final f de copa.
cupful ['kʌpful] n taza f, contenido m de una taza; **two —s of milk** dos tazas de leche.
Cupid ['kju:pid] m Cupido.
cupidity [kju:'piditi] n codicia f.
cupola ['kju:pələ] n cúpula f.
cup-tie ['kʌptai] n partido m de copa.
cur [kə:*] n perro m de mala raza; (person) canalla m; **you —!** ¡canalla!
curable ['kjuərəbl] adj curable.
curate ['kjuərit] n (approx) cura m.
curative ['kjuərətiv] adj curativo.
curator [kjuə'reitə*] n (of museum) director m, conservador m.
curb [kə:b] **1** n (fig) freno m, estorbo m (on para); **to put a — on** refrenar; see **kerb. 2** vt (fig) refrenar, reprimir, limitar; temper dominar.
curbstone ['kə:bstəun] n (US) = **kerbstone.**
curd [kə:d] n cuajada f.
curdle ['kə:dl] **1** vt cuajar; **to — one's blood** helar la sangre de uno. **2** vi cuajarse.
cure [kjuə*] **1** n cura f, curación f; (Eccl) curato m. **2** vt curar (of de).
cure-all ['kjuərɔ:l] n panacea f.
curfew ['kə:fju:] n toque m de queda.
curio ['kjuəriəu] n curiosidad f.
curiosity [,kjuəri'ositi] n curiosidad f.
curious ['kjuəriəs] adj curioso; **I am — to see Granada** tengo ganas de ver Granada.
curiously ['kjuəriəsli] adv curiosamente; **— made** ingenioso, artificioso; **— enough** aunque parece mentira.
curl [kə:l] **1** n (of hair) rizo m, bucle m; (of smoke etc) penacho m, espiral f.
2 vt hair rizar, ensortijar; paper etc arrollar; lip fruncir.
3 vi (hair) rizarse, ensortijarse, formar bucles; (paper etc) arrollarse; (leaf) abarquillarse; (waves) encresparse; **to — up** arrollarse; (smoke) subir en espiral; (animal) apelotonarse; (person) hacerse un ovillo; (fam) morirse de risa.
curler ['kə:lə*] n (for hair) bigudí m, chincho m.
curlew ['kə:lu:] n zarapito m.
curlicue ['kə:likju:] n plumada f, rasgo m.
curling iron ['kə:liŋ,aiən] n, **curling tongs** ['kə:liŋtɔŋz] npl tenacillas fpl de rizar.
curly ['kə:li] adj rizado, ensortijado.
currant ['kʌrənt] n (dried) pasa f de Corinto; **black —** (fruit) grosella f negra, (bush) grosellero m negro; **red —** (fruit) grosella f roja, (bush) grosellero m rojo.
currency ['kʌrənsi] n (a) (money) moneda f; **hard —** moneda f dura, moneda f fuerte; **soft —** moneda f blanda, moneda f débil.
(b) (fig) uso m; **it had a certain —** se usó bastante.
current ['kʌrənt] **1** adj corriente, actual; price, account etc corriente; **the — month** el mes que corre; **the — number of a magazine** el último número de una revista; **the — opinion is that** se cree actualmente que; **it is still quite —** se usa bastante todavía; **to be in — use** estar en uso corriente; see **event** etc.
2 n (most senses) corriente f; (Elec) flúido m, corriente f; **alternating —** corriente f alterna; **direct —** corriente f continua.

currently ['kʌrəntli] adv actualmente.
curriculum [kə'rikjuləm] n, pl **curricula** [kə'rikjulə] plan m de estudios.
curriculum vitae [kə:'rikjuləm'vi:ti:] n curriculum m vitae.
curry[1] ['kʌri] **1** n (spice) cari m, curry m. **2** vt preparar con cari.
curry[2] ['kʌri] vt see **favour.**
currycomb ['kʌrikəum] n almohaza f.
curry powder ['kʌri,paudə*] n polvo m de especias (para preparar el cari).
curse [kə:s] **1** n (a) maldición f; **—s!** ¡maldición!; **a — on it!** ¡maldito sea!
(b) (oath) palabrota f.
(c) (bane) calamidad f; azote m; **the dampness is a — here** aquí la humedad es una calamidad; **drought is the — of Spain** la sequía es el azote de España; **it's been the — of my life** me ha amargado la vida, siempre me ha afligido; **the — of it is that** lo peor es que.
2 vt maldecir; echar pestes de; **to — someone with** castigar a uno con; **to be —d with** padecer de, tener que aguantar, sufrir la aflicción de; **— it!** ¡maldito sea!
3 vi blasfemar, echar pestes, soltar palabrotas.
cursed ['kə:sid] adj maldito.
cursive ['kə:siv] adj cursivo.
cursorily ['kə:sərili] adv rápidamente, de modo superficial.
cursory ['kə:səri] adj rápido, superficial.
curt [kə:t] adj brusco, seco.
curtail [kə:'teil] vt acortar, abreviar; restringir.
curtailment [kə:'teilmənt] n acortamiento m, abreviación f; restricción f.
curtain ['kə:tn] **1** n cortina f (also Mil); (small) visillo m; (Theat) telón m; **iron —** telón m de acero; **the iron — countries** los países detrás del telón de acero; **it was —s for him** (fam) para él fue el fin.
2 vt proveer de cortina; **to — off** separar con cortinas.
curtain call ['kə:tnkɔ:l] n salida f (de un actor a la escena para recibir aplausos).
curtain raiser ['kə:tn,reizə*] n pieza f preliminar.
curtain ring ['kə:tnriŋ] n anilla f.
curtain rod ['kə:tnrɔd] n barra f de cortina.
curtly ['kə:tli] adv bruscamente, secamente.
curtness ['kə:tnis] n brusquedad f.
curtsy ['kə:tsi] **1** n reverencia f; **to drop a — = 2** vi hacer una reverencia (to a).
curvacious [kə:'veifəs] adj (fam) girl de buen tipo, de tipo muy atractivo.
curvature ['kə:vətʃə*] n curvatura f.
curve [kə:v] **1** n curva f. **2** vt encorvar, torcer. **3** vi encorvarse, torcerse; (road etc) torcerse, hacer una curva; (through air) volar en curva.
curved [kə:vd] adj curvo, encorvado.
cushion ['kuʃən] **1** n cojín m; (Billiards) banda f; (fig) colchón m. **2** vt blow etc amortiguar.
cushioned ['kuʃənd] adj surface acolchado, almohadillado.
cushy ['kuʃi] adj (sl) fácil, agradable.
cuss [kʌs] **1** n (fam) tipo m, tio m. **2** vt etc see **curse.**
cussed ['kʌsid] adj (fam) terco.
cussedness ['kʌsidnis] n (fam) terquedad f; **out of sheer —** de puro terco.
custard ['kʌstəd] n natillas fpl.
custard apple ['kʌstəd,æpl] n anona f; asimina f.
custodian [kʌs'təudiən] n custodio m.
custody ['kʌstədi] n custodia f; **protective —** custodia f preventiva; **to be in —** estar detenido; **to take someone into —** detener a uno.
custom ['kʌstəm] n **1** (a) costumbre f.
(b) (Comm) clientela f, parroquia f; (total sales) ventas fpl; **we've not had much — today** hoy hemos tenido pocos clientes.
(c) **—s** aduana f; (duty) derechos mpl de aduana; **to go through the —s** pasar por la aduana.
2 —s attr aduanero, de aduana.
customary ['kʌstəməri] adj acostumbrado, de costumbre; **it is — to + infin** es costumbre + infin, se suele + infin.
customer ['kʌstəmə*] n cliente m, a f; (fam) tipo m.
custom-made ['kʌstəm'meid] adj hecho a la medida.
customs house ['kʌstəmzhaus] n aduana f.
customs officer ['kʌstəmz,ofisə*] n aduanero m.
customs post ['kʌstəmzpəust] n puesto m aduanero.
cut [kʌt] **1** adj cortado; glass tallado; **— and dried** rutinario; seguro; preparado de antemano; convenido de antemano; **— off** aislado (from de).
2 n (a) (incision) corte m; (in skin) cortadura f.

(b) (*slash with sword*) tajo *m*, (*with knife*) cuchillada *f*, (*with whip*) latigazo *m*; **the — and thrust of politics** la esgrima política; **the unkindest — of all** el golpe más duro; **whose — is it?** (*Cards*) ¿quién corta?

(c) (*deletion*) corte *m*, supresión *f*, trozo *m* suprimido.

(d) short — atajo *m*; **there is no short — to success** no se alcanza el éxito por ningún camino fácil.

(e) (*of clothes*) corte *m*; **to be a — above the rest** ser algo superior a los demás.

(f) (*woodcut*) grabado *m*; (*US*) foto *f*, diagrama *m*, dibujo *m*.

(g) (*kind of meat*) clase *f* de carne; (*slice*) tajada *f*; (*share*) parte *f*, tajada *f*.

(h) (*reduction*) reducción *f*, rebaja *f* (*in* de); (*Elec*) apagón *m*.

3 (*irr: pret and ptp* **cut**) *vt* cortar; *cards, corn, communications etc* cortar; *corner* (*person*) cortar, (*car*) tomar muy cerrado; (*divide up*) partir, dividir (*into two* en dos); *line etc* cruzar; *stone etc* tallar; *disc* grabar; *hole* practicar, hacer; (*delete*) cortar, suprimir; (*reduce*) reducir (*by* 5% en un 5 por cien), *price* rebajar; *class* fumarse; *person* fingir no ver, fingir no reconocer, negar el saludo a; **he — his finger** se cortó el dedo; **he's —ting a tooth** le está saliendo un diente; **to get one's hair** — cortarse el pelo; **to — something across** cortar algo a través; cortar algo completamente; **to — across a field** atravesar un campo, atajar por un campo; **this —s across my ideas** esto es contrario a mis ideas; **this —s across the usual categories** esto hace desaparecer las categorías establecidas; **to — away** cortar, separar cortando; **to — back** acortar, recortar; (*reduce*) reducir (*by* en); **to — down** *tree etc* derribar, cortar, talar; *price* rebajar; *costs* aminorar; *size, majority etc* reducir (*by* en); **to — off** cortar (*also Elec, Tel etc*); *leg* amputar; *troops* copar, cercar; *retreat* impedir, imposibilitar; (*disinherit*) desheredar; **to — someone's life off in its prime** tronchar la vida de uno; **we were — off by the snow** quedamos bloqueados por la nieve; **to — someone in on a deal** permitir que uno participe en un negocio (*esp* poco limpio); **to — out** recortar; *hole etc* practicar, hacer; *competitor* excluir; (*delete*) suprimir, tachar; **— it out!** ¡basta ya!, ¡déjalo!; **— out the singing!** ¡basta ya de cantar!; **we can — that out for a start** en primer lugar podemos tachar eso; **he's not — out to be a poet** no tiene condiciones para ser poeta; **he's not — out for it** no tiene talento para ello; **to — up** cortar en pedazos; dividir; desmenuzar; *meat* picar; **to be — up** afligirse (*about* por).

4 *vi* cortar; (*two lines*) cruzarse; **to — across** atajar; **to — back** volverse; **to — in** interrumpir, cortar; (*Aut*) pasar peligrosamente; **to — into one's holiday** restar una parte de las vacaciones; **to — out** (*engine*) pararse; **to — through something** abrirse camino por algo; **the argument —s both ways** el argumento tiene doble filo.

cutaneous [kju:'teiniəs] *adj* cutáneo.

cute [kju:t] *adj* (*nice*) mono, lindo; (*shrewd*) astuto, listo.

cuticle ['kju:tikl] *n* cutícula *f*.

cuticle remover ['kju:tiklri'mu:və*] agente *m* químico para quitar la cutícula (de las uñas).

cutlass ['kʌtləs] *n* chafarote *m*.

cutler ['kʌtlə*] *n* cuchillero *m*.

cutlery ['kʌtləri] *n* cubiertos *mpl*, cuchillería *f*.

cutlet ['kʌtlit] *n* chuleta *f*.

cutoff ['kʌtɔf] *n* (*Mech*) cierre *m* de vapor, corta-vapor *m*.

cutout ['kʌtaut] *n* (*child's*) diseño *m* para recortar, recortable *m*; (*Elec*) portafusible *m*; (*Mech*) válvula *f* de escape.

cut-price ['kʌtprais] *adj* a precio reducido.

cutter ['kʌtə*] *n* (*Mech*) cortadora *f*; (*Naut*) cúter *m*.

cut-throat ['kʌtθrəut] **1** *adj competition* intenso. **2** *n* asesino *m*.

cutting ['kʌtiŋ] **1** *adj* cortante; *remark* mordaz; **— edge** filo *m*. **2** *n* (*from paper*) recorte *m*; (*Rail*) desmonte *m*, trinchera *f*; (*Bot*) esqueje *m*.

cuttlefish ['kʌtlfiʃ] *n* jibia *f*.

cyanide ['saiənaid] *n* cianuro *m*; **— of potassium** cianuro *m* de potasio.

cybernetics [ˌsaibə'netiks] *n sing and pl* cibernética *f*.

cyclamen ['sikləmən] *n* ciclamen *m*.

cycle ['saikl] **1** *n* **(a)** ciclo *m*; **life —** ciclo *m* de la vida; **menstrual —** ciclo *m* menstrual. **(b)** (*bicycle*) bicicleta *f*. **2** *vi* ir en bicicleta.

cyclic(al) ['saiklik(əl)] *adj* cíclico.

cycling ['saikliŋ] *n* ciclismo *m*.

cyclist ['saiklist] *n* ciclista *mf*; **racing —** corredor *m* ciclista.

cyclone ['saikləun] *n* ciclón *m*.

Cyclops ['saiklɔps] *n* cíclope *m*.

cyclorama [ˌsaiklə'rɑːmə] *n* ciclorama *m*.

cyclostyled ['saikləstaild] *adj* en ciclostil.

cyclotron ['saiklətrɔn] *n* ciclotrón *m*.

cygnet ['signit] *n* pollo *m* de cisne.

cylinder ['silində*] *n* cilindro *m*.

cylinder block ['silindəblɔk] *n* bloque *m* de cilindros.

cylinder capacity ['silindəkə'pæsiti] *n* cilindrada *f*.

cylinder head ['silindəhed] *n* culata *f* de cilindro.

cylindrical [si'lindrikəl] *adj* cilíndrico.

cymbals ['simbəlz] *npl* platillos *mpl*.

cynic ['sinik] *n* cínico *m*; escéptico *m*.

cynical ['sinikəl] *adj* cínico; escéptico, despreciativo.

cynically ['sinikəli] *adv* con cinismo.

cynicism ['sinisizəm] *n* cinismo *m*; escepticismo *m*, desprecio *m*.

cynosure ['sainəʃuə*] *n*: **— of every eye** blanco *m* de todas las miradas, miradero *m*.

cypress ['saipris] *n* ciprés *m*.

Cypriot ['sipriət] *n* chipriota *mf*.

Cyprus ['saiprəs] Chipre *f*.

cypher ['saifə*] *see* **cipher.**

cyst [sist] *n* quiste *m*.

cystitis [sis'taitis] *n* cistitis *f*.

czar [zɑ:*] *n* zar *m*.

czarina [zɑ:'ri:nə] *n* zarina *f*.

Czech [tʃek] **1** *adj* checo. **2** *n* checo *m*, a . **3** *n* (*language*) checo *m*.

Czechoslovak ['tʃekəu'sləuvæk] **1** *adj* checoslovaco. **2** *n* checoslovaco *m*, a *f*.

Czechoslovakia ['tʃekəuslə'vækiə] Checoslovaquia *f*.

Czechoslovakian ['tʃekəuslə'vækiən] **1** *adj* checoslovaco. **2** *n* checoslovaco *m*, a *f*.

D

dab[1] [dæb] **1** n (*blow*) golpe m ligero; (*small amount*) pequeña cantidad f; (*of paint*) brochazo m; (*of liquid*) gota f; **—s** (*sl*) huellas fpl dactilares.
2 vt (*strike*) golpear ligeramente, tocar ligeramente; (*with sponge etc*) tocar; (*moisten*) mojar ligeramente; **to — a stain off** quitar una mancha mojándola ligeramente; **to — paint on a wall** embadurnar una pared de pintura.
3 vi: **to — at one's eyes with a handkerchief** llevar repetidas veces un pañuelo a los ojos.
dab[2] [dæb] n (*Fish*) lenguado m.
dab[3] [dæb] adj: **to be a — hand at** tener buena mano para.
dabble ['dæbl] **1** vt salpicar, mojar; **to — one's feet** chapotear los pies.
2 vi: **to — in something** interesarse en algo por pasatiempo, ser ligeramente aficionado a; **I only — in it** para mí es un pasatiempo nada más; **to — in politics** meterse en la política; **to — in shares** jugar a la bolsa.
dabbler ['dæblə*] n (*pej*) aficionado m, a f (*in a*), diletante mf; **he's just a —** es un simple aficionado, para él es un pasatiempo nada más.
dabchick ['dæbtʃik] n somorgujo m menor.
dabs [dæbz] npl (*sl*) manos fpl; huellas fpl dactilares.
dace [deis] n albur m.
dachshund ['dækshund] n perro m tejonero.
dacron ['deikrɔn] n (*Protected Trade Name*) dacrón m.
dactylic [dæk'tilik] adj dactílico.
dad [dæd] n, **daddy** ['dædi] n papá m.
dadaism ['dɑ:dɑ:izəm] n dadaísmo m.
daddy-long-legs ['dædi'bɒŋlegz] n típula f.
dado ['deidəu] n dado m; friso m.
daffodil ['dæfədil] n narciso m trompón.
daffy ['dæfi] adj (*US: sl*) chiflado.
daft [dɑ:ft] adj imbécil, estúpido.
dagger ['dægə*] n puñal m, daga f; (*Typ*) cruz f, obelisco m; **to be at —s drawn** odiarse a muerte; **to look —s at** apuñalar con la mirada.
dago ['deigəu] n *término peyorativo aplicado a españoles, portugueses e italianos.*
dahlia ['deiliə] n dalia f.
Dail Eireann [dail'ɛərən] *parlamento de la República de Irlanda.*
daily ['deili] **1** adj diario, cotidiano; **bread** de cada día. **2** adv a diario, cada día. **3** n (*paper*) diario m; (*servant*) asistenta f, sirvienta f.
daintily ['deintili] adv delicadamente; elegantemente, primorosamente; melindrosamente.
daintiness ['deintinis] n delicadeza f; elegancia f, primor m; melindres mpl.
dainty ['deinti] **1** adj (*delicate*) delicado, fino; (*tasteful*) elegante, primoroso, precioso; (*fastidious*) delicado, melindroso.
2 n bocado m exquisito, golosina f.
dairy ['dɛəri] **1** n (*shop*) lechería f; (*on farm*) quesería f, vaquería f. **2** attr lechero; **— cattle** vacas fpl lecheras; **— farm** granja f especializada en producción de leche; **— produce** productos mpl lácteos.
dairymaid ['dɛərimeid] n lechera f, moza f de establo.
dairyman ['dɛərimən] n, pl **—men** [mən] lechero m.
dais ['deiis] n estrado m.
daisy ['deizi] n mayo m, margarita f.
dale [deil] n valle m.
dalliance ['dæliəns] n (*play*) juegos mpl, diversiones fpl; (*time-wasting*) frivolidad f; **amorous —** coquetería f, flirteo m.
dally ['dæli] vi (*delay*) tardar, perder el tiempo; (*amuse oneself*) divertirse; **to — with** (*amorously*) coquetear con, entretenerse en amores con; (*an idea*) entretenerse con.
Dalmatia [dæl'meiʃə] Dalmacia f.
dalmatian [dæl'meiʃən] n (*dog*) perro m dálmata.

dam[1] [dæm] **1** n presa f; (*small*) dique m. **2** vt represar; construir una presa sobre; **to — up** cerrar, tapar, *overflowing water* contener con un dique.
dam[2] [dæm] adj = **damn 3, damned.**
damage ['dæmidʒ] **1** n daño m, perjuicio m; (*Mech*) avería f; (*visible, eg on car*) desperfectos mpl; **—s** (*Law*) daños mpl y perjuicios; **what's the —?** (*fam*) ¿cuánto te debo?
2 vt dañar, perjudicar; (*Mech*) averiar, estropear; *chances, reputation* perjudicar; **to be —d in a collision** sufrir daños en un choque.
damaging ['dæmidʒiŋ] adj perjudicial.
damascene ['dæməsi:n] vt damasquinar.
Damascus [də'mɑ:skəs] Damasco.
damask ['dæməsk] **1** adj *cloth* adamascado; *steel* damasquino.
2 n (*cloth*) damasco m; (*steel*) acero m damasquino. **3** vt *cloth* adamascar; *steel* damasquinar.
dame [deim] n dama f, señora f; (*sl*) tía f.
damfool ['dæm'fu:l] adj (*fam*) estúpido, tonto; **some — driver** algún imbécil de conductor; **that's a — thing to say!** ¡qué tontería!
damn [dæm] **1** vt condenar (*also Eccl*); maldecir; **—!**, **— it!** ¡condenación!; **well I'm —ed!** ¡mecachis!; **I'll see him —ed first** antes le veré colgado.
2 n: **I don't give a —** maldito lo que me importa. **3** adj (*fam*) maldito.
damnable ['dæmnəbl] adj detestable.
damnably ['dæmnəbli] adv terriblemente.
damnation [dæm'neiʃən] n condenación f; perdición f; **—!** ¡condenación!; **to go down to —** ir a la perdición.
damned [dæmd] **1** adj condenado, maldito; (*damnable*) detestable, abominable; **that — book** ese maldito libro; **to do one's —est to** + *infin* hacer lo posible para + *infin.*
2 adv muy, extraordinariamente; **it's — awkward** es terriblemente difícil; **it's — hot** hace un calor terrible.
3 n: **the —** las almas en pena.
damning ['dæmiŋ] adj *evidence* irrecusable.
Damocles ['dæməkli:z] m Dámocles.
damp [dæmp] **1** adj húmedo; mojado.
2 n humedad f; (*Min*) mofeta f; **to cast a — on** hacer que se enfríe el ambiente de, introducir el desaliento en.
3 vt (*also* **dampen** ['dæmpən]) (**a**) (*wet*) mojar, humedecer.
(**b**) **to — down** amortiguar; *fire* cubrir; *demand* reducir.
(**c**) (*fig*) *person* desalentar; *hopes* ahogar; *zeal* enfriar, moderar.
damp-course ['dæmpkɔ:s] n hilada f de ladrillos (*etc*) que impide la subida de la humedad.
damper ['dæmpə*] n (*Mus*) apagador m, sordina f; (*of fire*) regulador m de tiro.
dampish ['dæmpiʃ] adj algo húmedo.
dampness ['dæmpnis] n humedad f.
damp-proof ['dæmpru:f] adj a prueba de humedad.
damsel ['dæmzəl] n damisela f, doncella f.
damson ['dæmzən] n (*fruit*) ciruela f damascena; (*tree*) ciruelo m damasceno.
Dan [dæn] m *nombre cariñoso de* **Daniel.**
dance [dɑ:ns] **1** n baile m; **— of death** danza f de la muerte; **to lead someone a —** crear muchísimas dificultades a uno.
2 vt bailar.
3 vi bailar, danzar; (*fig*) danzar, saltar, brincar; **to — for joy** brincar de alegría; **shall we —?** ¿quieres bailar?
dance band ['dɑ:nsbænd] n orquesta f de baile.
dance floor ['dɑ:nsflɔ:*] n pista f de baile.
dance hall ['dɑ:nshɔ:l] n salón m de baile.
dance music ['dɑ:ns‚mju:zik] n música f de baile.

dancer ['dɑːnsə*] n bailador m, ora f; (professional) bailarín m, ina f.
dancing ['dɑːnsiŋ] 1 n baile m. 2 attr de baile.
dancing-girl ['dɑːnsiŋgəːl] n bailarina f.
dancing-partner ['dɑːnsiŋ,pɑːtnə*] n pareja f de baile.
dandelion ['dændilaiən] n diente m de león.
dander ['dændə*] n: to get someone's — up enojar a uno.
dandified ['dændifaid] adj guapo, acicalado.
dandle ['dændl] vt hacer saltar sobre las rodillas.
dandruff ['dændrəf] n caspa f.
dandy ['dændi] 1 n dandy m, currutaco m. 2 adj (fam) mono, de primera.
Dane [dein] n danés m, esa f; great — gran danés m.
danger ['deindʒə*] n peligro m; riesgo m; "—!" (sign) "¡peligro de muerte!"; there is a — of hay riesgo de; to be in — estar en peligro; to be in — of + ger correr riesgo de + infin; to be out of — estar fuera de peligro.
danger area ['deindʒər,ɛəriə] n zona f de peligro.
danger list ['deindʒəlist] n: to be on the — estar de cuidado.
danger money ['deindʒə,mʌni] n prima f por trabajos peligrosos.
dangerous ['deindʒrəs] adj peligroso, arriesgado; animal peligroso; substance nocivo.
dangerously ['deindʒrəsli] adv peligrosamente; arriesgadamente; to come — close to acercarse de modo peligroso a; he likes to live — le gusta arriesgar la vida.
danger signal ['deindʒə,signl] n señal f de peligro.
dangle ['dæŋgl] 1 vt colgar, dejar colgado; to — a prospect before someone ofrecer a uno la posibilidad de + infin.
2 vi estar colgado, pender; to — after ir tras de; she kept him dangling for 3 months ella le tuvo suspenso durante 3 meses.
Daniel ['dænjəl] m Daniel.
Danish ['deiniʃ] 1 adj danés, dinamarqués. 2 n (language) danés m.
dank [dæŋk] adj húmedo y malsano, liento.
Danube ['dænjuːb] Danubio m.
Daphne ['dæfni] f Dafne.
dapper ['dæpə*] adj apuesto, pulcro.
dappled ['dæpld] adj moteado, salpicado de manchas; horse rodado.
Darby and Joan ['dɑːbiən'dʒəun] pl el matrimonio ideal, de ancianos que siguen viviendo en la mayor felicidad.
Dardanelles [,dɑːdə'nelz] pl Dardanelos mpl.
dare [dɛə*] 1 vt (attempt) arriesgar; someone's anger hacer frente a; gaze resistir; to — someone to do something desafiar a uno a hacer algo, provocar a uno a hacer algo.
2 vi: to — (to) do something atreverse a hacer algo, osar hacer algo; I — say quizá; I — say that no me sorprendería que + subj; how — you! ¡qué cinismo!, (more fam) ¡qué fresco!; just you —!, you wouldn't —! ¡ya te guardarás de hacerlo!
daredevil ['dɛə,devl] 1 adj temerario. 2 n temerario m, atrevido m.
daring ['dɛəriŋ] 1 adj atrevido, osado. 2 n atrevimiento m, osadía f.
daringly ['dɛəriŋli] adv atrevidamente, osadamente.
Darius [də'raiəs] m Darío.
dark [dɑːk] 1 adj (a) (unilluminated) oscuro; tenebroso; to get — hacerse de noche, anochecer.
(b) (in colour) oscuro.
(c) complexion, hair moreno.
(d) (cheerless) triste, sombrío; — days días mpl funestos, días mpl negros.
(e) (secret) secreto, escondido; doings misterioso, sospechoso; the D— Continent el Continente Negro; to keep something — tener algo secreto; keep it —! ¡de esto no digas ni pío!
(f) (unenlightened) ignorante.
2 n oscuridad f; tinieblas fpl; after — después del anochecer; to grope about in the — ir buscando algo a oscuras; we are all in the — about it no sabemos nada en absoluto de ello; to keep someone in the — no revelar a uno cierta noticia; to be left in the — quedar sin saber nada de algo.
darken ['dɑːkən] 1 vt oscurecer; (colour) hacer más oscuro. 2 vi oscurecerse; (sky) anublarse.
darkie ['dɑːki] n (fam) negro m, a f.
darkish ['dɑːkiʃ] adj algo oscuro; hair etc algo moreno.
darkly ['dɑːkli] adv misteriosamente.
darkness ['dɑːknis] n oscuridad f; tinieblas fpl; the house was in — la casa estaba a oscuras; to cast someone into outer — condenar a uno a las penas infernales.
dark room ['dɑːkrum] n cuarto m oscuro.

darling ['dɑːliŋ] 1 n querido m, a f; the — of the muses el querido de las musas; yes — sí querida; she's a little — (child) es una preciosidad.
darn[1] [dɑːn] excl (fam) —!, — it! ¡condenación!
darn[2] [dɑːn] 1 n zurcido m, zurcidura f. 2 vt zurcir.
darned [dɑːnd] adj (fam) condenado, maldito.
darning ['dɑːniŋ] n (act) zurcidura f; (garments) cosas fpl por zurcir.
darning needle ['dɑːniŋ,niːdl] n aguja f de zurcir.
dart [dɑːt] 1 n (a) (Mil) dardo m, saeta f.
(b) (in game) rehilete m; —s juego m de rehiletes.
(c) (Sew) sisa f.
(d) (movement) movimiento m rápido; to make a — for precipitarse hacia.
2 vt look lanzar.
3 vi lanzarse, precipitarse (for, to hacia).
dartboard ['dɑːtbɔːd] n blanco m (en el juego de rehiletes.
Darwinian [dɑː'winiən] adj darwiniano.
Darwinism ['dɑːwinizm] n darwinismo m.
dash [dæʃ] 1 n (a) (small quantity) pequeña cantidad f, poquito m; a — of colour una nota de color; with a — of soda con dos gotitas de sifón.
(b) (with pen) rasgo m, plumada f; (Typ) (hyphen) guión m, (longer) raya f.
(c) (rush) carrera f; to make a — for precipitarse hacia; to make a — for it huir precipitadamente; we shall have to make a — for it tendremos que correr.
(d) to cut a — hacer gran papel, destacar.
2 vt (a) (shatter) romper, estrellar (against contra); to — something to pieces hacer algo pedazos; to — something to the ground tirar algo al suelo.
(b) hopes defraudar, acabar con.
(c) to — off a letter escribir una carta de prisa.
(d) —!, — it! ¡porras!
3 vi ir de prisa, precipitarse; we shall have to — tendremos que correr; I must — tengo que marcharme; the waves are —ing against the rock las olas se rompen contra la roca; to — away, to — off marcharse apresuradamente; to — in entrar precipitadamente; to — out salir precipitadamente; to — past pasar como un rayo; to — up llegar corriendo, (car) llegar a toda velocidad.
dashboard ['dæʃbɔːd] n tablero m de instrumentos.
dashing ['dæʃiŋ] adj bizarro, gallardo, arrojado.
dastardly ['dæstədli] adj vil, miserable.
data ['deitə] npl datos mpl.
data processing ['deitə'prəusesiŋ] n proceso m de datos.
date[1] [deit] 1 n (a) fecha f; what's the —?, what — is it today? ¿qué día es hoy?; closing —, last — fecha f tope; at an early — en fecha próxima; out of — anticuado, (person) atrasado de noticias; to go out of — quedar anticuado; to — hasta la fecha; up to — (adv) hasta la fecha; to be up to — (building etc) tener aspecto moderno; to be up to — in one's thinking tener ideas modernas; to be up to — in one's studies estar al día en los estudios; to bring something up to — modernizar algo, poner algo al día, actualizar algo; to bring someone up to — poner a uno al corriente.
(b) (of stocks etc) plazo m.
(c) (with girlfriend etc) cita f, (with friend) compromiso m; to have a — with someone tener cita con uno; have you got a — tonight? ¿tienes compromiso para esta noche?; to make a — with someone citar a uno; they made a — for 8 o'clock se citaron para las 8.
(d) (US fam) novio m, novia f.
2 vt fechar (at, to en); (US fam) citar.
3 vi ir quedando anticuado, pasar de moda; his ideas are very —d sus ideas son anticuadas ya; to — back to remontar a; to — from datar de, ser de la época de.
date[2] [deit] n (Bot: fruit) dátil m; (tree) palmera f datilera.
date-line ['deitlain] n línea f de cambio de fecha.
date palm ['deitpɑːm] n palmera f datilera.
date stamp ['deitstæmp] n estampilla f para poner la fecha.
dative ['deitiv] n dativo m.
daub [dɔːb] 1 n (smear) mancha f; (bad painting) pintarrajo m.
2 vt (smear) manchar (with de); to — a wall with paint, to — paint on to a wall embadurnar una pared de pintura.
3 vi pintarrajear.
dauber ['dɔːbə*] n, **daubster** ['dɔːbstə*] n pintor m de brocha gorda, mal pintor m.
daughter ['dɔːtə*] n hija f.

daughter-in-law ['dɔ:tərinlɔ:] n nuera f, hija f política.
daunt [dɔ:nt] vt acobardar, intimidar, desalentar; **nothing —ed** sin inmutarse.
daunting ['dɔ:ntiŋ] adj desalentador, amedrentador.
dauntless ['dɔ:ntlis] adj impávido.
dauntlessly ['dɔ:ntlisli] adv impávidamente; **to carry on —** continuar impávido.
davenport ['dævnpɔ:t] n (desk) escritorio m pequeño; (sofa) sofá-cama m.
David ['deivid] m David.
davit ['dævit] n pescante m.
Davy Jones ['deivi'dʒəunz]: **—' locker** el fondo del mar (tumba de los marineros ahogados).
davy lamp ['deivi'læmp] n lámpara f de seguridad.
dawdle ['dɔ:dl] 1 vt: **to — away** malgastar. 2 vi perder el tiempo, holgazanear; (in walking) andar muy despacio; (Aut etc) ir muy despacio.
dawdler ['dɔ:dlə*] n holgazán m, ana f, ocioso m, a f; persona f que anda despacio, rezagada m, a f.
dawn [dɔ:n] 1 n alba f, amanecer m; (fig) aurora f, nacimiento m; **at —** al alba; **from — to dusk** de sol a sol; **to get up with the —** madrugar.
2 vi (a) amanecer, alborear, romper el día; **the day —ed rainy** el día empezó con lluvia; **a new epoch has —ed** ha nacido una época nueva.
(b) **it —ed on me that** caí en la cuenta de que, empecé a comprender que.
day [dei] n (a) día m; (working period etc) jornada f; **an 8-hour —** una jornada de 8 horas.
(b) (with prep etc) **— after —, — in — out** día tras día; **the — after** el día siguiente, al día siguiente; **the — after tomorrow** pasado mañana; **the — before** el día anterior; **the — before yesterday** anteayer; **two —s before this** dos días antes de esto; **the — before the coronation** la víspera de la coronación; **— by —** día por día; **by —** de día; **by the —** cada día, al día; **every other —** un día sí y otro no; **from — to —** de día en día; **in this — and age** en estos tiempos nuestros; **in my —** en mis tiempos; **in the —s of Queen Elizabeth, in Queen Elizabeth's —** en tiempos de la reina Isabel; **these —s** estos días; **to this —** hasta el día de hoy; **this — week** de hoy en ocho días.
(c) (with adj etc) **D— of Judgement** día m del Juicio Final; **— of reckoning** (fig) día m de la justicia; **it was a black — for the country** fué un día negro para el país; **it's early —s yet** todavía es pronto; **one fine —, one of these —s** el día menos pensado; **good —!** ¡buenos días!; **the good old —s** los buenos tiempos pasados; **working —** (weekday) día m laborable, (number of hours) jornada f.
(d) (with verb) **to call it a —** dejar de trabajar (etc), suspender el trabajo (etc); **let's call it a —** terminemos ya; **to carry the —** ganar la victoria; **it has had its —** ha dejado ya de ser útil, ya pasó aquello; **you don't look a — older** no pareces un día más viejo; **it has seen better —s** ya no vale lo que antes; **to take a — off** darse un día libre, no presentarse en el trabajo (etc).
daybook ['deibuk] n diario m.
day boy ['deibɔi] n externo m.
daybreak ['deibreik] n amanecer m; **at — al** amanecer.
daydream ['deidri:m] 1 n ensueño m. 2 vi soñar despierto.
day labourer ['dei'leibərə*] n jornalero m.
daylight ['deilait] n luz f, luz f del día; **in broad —** en (or a) pleno día; **to see —** empezar a ver el final de un trabajo (etc).
day nursery ['dei,nə:səri] n guardería f infantil.
day-old ['dei'əuld] adj chick de un día.
day-return ['deiri'tə:n] n (also **— ticket**) billete m barato de ida y vuelta en un día.
day shift ['deiʃift] n turno m de día.
daytime ['deitaim] n día m; **in the —** de día.
day-to-day ['deitə'dei] adj cotidiano, rutinario; **on a — basis** día por día.
daze [deiz] 1 n: **to be in a —** estar aturdido. 2 vt aturdir; (dazzle) deslumbrar.
dazed [deizd] adj aturdido.
dazedly ['deizidli] adv aturdidamente; **he said —** dijo aturdido.
dazzle ['dæzl] 1 n lo brillante, brillo m. 2 vt deslumbrar (also fig); **to be —d by** (fig) quedar deslumbrado por.
dazzling ['dæzliŋ] adj deslumbrante, deslumbrador.
deacon ['di:kən] n diácono m.
deaconess ['di:kənes] n diaconisa f.
dead [ded] 1 adj (a) muerto; **the — king** el difunto rey; **as — as the dodo, as — as a doornail, as — as mutton** más muerto que mi abuela; **to be — estar**

muerto; **he has been — 3 years** hace 3 años que murió; **to drop —** caer muerto, morir de repente; **drop —!** (fam) ¡vete al cuerno!
(b) town muerto, desierto; language muerto; leaf marchito, seco.
(c) (obsolete) anticuado; **all that stuff's pretty — now** todo eso ya no tiene interés.
(d) (fig) ball fuera de juego; calm profundo, (Naut) chicha; colour, fire apagado; level exacto; silence profundo; sound sordo; stop en seco, repentino; voice monótono; wire sin corriente; **the wire has gone —** (Tel) la línea está cortada.
2 adv completamente, totalmente; **— drunk** borracho como una cuba; **— slow** muy despacio; **— straight** completamente recto; **— tired** hecho polvo, muerto de cansancio; **— between the eyes** exactamente entre los ojos; **— on the target** exactamente en el blanco, en el mismo blanco; **to be — against something** estar totalmente opuesto a algo; **to be — certain** estar completamente seguro.
3 n (a) **the —** los muertos.
(b) **at — of night, in the — of night** en las altas horas; **in the — of winter** en lo más recio del invierno.
dead-and-alive ['dedənə'laiv] adj aburrido, monótono.
dead-beat 1 adj ['ded'bi:t]: **to be —** estar hecho polvo. 2 n ['dedbi:t] (fam) gorrón m, vagabundo m.
deaden ['dedn] vt noise etc amortiguar; pain aliviar.
dead end ['ded'end] n callejón m sin salida; **to reach a —** (fig) llegar a un punto muerto; **— kids** (US) chicos mpl de la calle.
dead heat ['ded'hi:t] 1 n empate m. 2 vi empatar (with con).
deadline ['dedlain] n fecha f tope, límite m, plazo m; **we cannot meet the government's —** no podemos terminarlo (etc) antes de la fecha señalada por el gobierno.
deadlock ['dedlɔk] 1 n (a) parálisis f; **the — is complete** la parálisis es total, no se ve salida alguna.
(b) punto m muerto; **to reach —** llegar a un punto muerto.
2 vt: **to be —ed** estar en un punto muerto.
deadly ['dedli] 1 adj mortal (also fig); (very bad) fatal; **with — accuracy** con la más absoluta exactitud; **it was a — play** la comedia fue fatal.
2 adv: **— dull** terriblemente aburrido, aburridísimo.
deadness ['dednis] n inercia f, falta f de vida.
deadnettle ['ded,netl] n ortiga f muerta.
deadpan ['ded,pæn] adj sin expresión.
dead reckoning ['ded'rekniŋ] n estima f.
Dead Sea ['ded'si:] Mar m Muerto.
dead weight ['dedweit] n peso m muerto; (fig) lastre m, carga f inútil.
deadwood ['ded'wud] n (fig) persona f inútil, gente f inútil, cosas fpl inútiles.
deaf [def] adj sordo (to a); **as — as a post** sordo como una tapia.
deaf-aid ['defeid] n aparato m del oído, audífono m.
deaf-and-dumb ['defən'dʌm] adj sordomudo.
deafen ['defn] vt ensordecer, asordar.
deafening ['defniŋ] adj ensordecedor.
deaf-mute ['def'mju:t] n sordomudo m, a f.
deafness ['defnis] n sordera f.
deal¹ [di:l] n madera f de pino (or abeto).
deal² [di:l] 1 n (a) (Comm) transacción f, negocio m, trato m; **business —** transacción f comercial; **it's a —!** ¡trato hecho!
(b) (agreement) pacto m, convenio m; (secret) pacto m secreto; **to do a — with** hacer un trato con; **we might do a —** podríamos llegar a un acuerdo; **we fear A might do a — with B** tememos que A pudiera ponerse de acuerdo con B.
(c) **New D—** (US) Nueva Política f, Nuevo Programa m, Nueva Distribución f; **a new — for the miners** un nuevo arreglo de salarios para los mineros; **Fair D—** (US) Política f Equitativa, Distribución f Equitativa; **raw —** injusticia f, trato m inequitativo; **he got a raw —** le trataron injustamente; **square —** justicia f, trato m equitativo; **I want a square —** yo pido justicia; **he didn't get a square —** le trataron injustamente.
(d) (Cards) reparto m; **whose — is it?** ¿a quién le toca dar?
(e) **a good —** bastante, mucho; **a great —** muchísimo; **a great — of** gran cantidad de; **to make a great — of** person estimar mucho a, thing dar importancia a.
2 (irr: pret and ptp **dealt**) vt (a) cards dar.
(b) blow dar, descargar; **to — a blow to** (fig)

destruir de un golpe; **to — a blow for freedom** librar una batalla en pro de la libertad.

(c) **to — out** repartir.

3 *vi* (*Cards*) ser mano; **to — in** tratar en, comerciar en; **to — with** (**a**) *person* tratar con, tener relaciones con; **he dealt very fairly with me** se portó muy bien conmigo; **he dealt cleverly with the ambassador** se las arregló inteligentemente con el embajador; **I'll — with him** yo me ocuparé de él; **he is used to —ing with criminals** está acostumbrado a tener que ver con criminales.

(**b**) *problem* ocuparse de; hacer frente a; **how should we — with this problem?** ¿qué hemos de hacer con este problema?; **the matter has been dealt with** el asunto está concluido; **how will the government — with coal?** ¿qué política tiene el gobierno para el carbón?

(**c**) *subject in book etc* tratar de, versar sobre, tener por tema; **he dealt with Africa in his speech** en su discurso se ocupó de África; **the book —s with war** el libro versa sobre la guerra.

(**d**) (*punish*) castigar; **the offenders will be dealt with** se castigará a los delincuentes; **they were dealt with severely** se les castigó de modo ejemplar.

(**e**) (*finish off*) *work* terminar, concluir; *person* despachar.

(**f**) (*in shop*) **which shop do you — with?** ¿en qué tienda compra Vd sus cosas?

dealer ['di:lə*] *n* comerciante *m*, tratante *m* (*in* en); (*retail*) distribuidor *m* (*in* de), proveedor *m*; (*Cards*) mano *f*.

dealings ['di:liŋz] *npl* (*Fin*) transacciones *fpl*; (*relations*) trato *m*, relaciones *fpl*; **to have — with** tratar con, tener relaciones con; **I wish to have no — with him** no quiero tener nada que ver con él.

dealt [delt] *pret and ptp of* **deal²**.

dean [di:n] *n* (*Eccl*) deán *m*; (*Univ etc*) decano *m*.

dear [diə*] **1** *adj* (**a**) *person etc* querido; **yes (my) — sí** querida; **a very — friend of mine** un amigo mío muy querido; **he was very — to all of us** fue querido de todos nosotros; **because your country is very — to me** por el amor que le tengo a vuestra patria.

(**b**) (*in letters*) **— John, — Mr White** mi querido amigo; **— Dr Green** (*from colleague*) mi querido amigo y colega; **— Sir** muy señor mío; **— Sirs** muy señores míos; **— Miss Brown** estimada Señorita, **— Madam** estimada Señora.

(**c**) (*expensive*) caro, costoso; *shop* carero.

2 *n*: **he's a —** es simpatiquísimo; **he's a little —** es un niño precioso.

3 *excl*: **oh —!**, **— me!** ¡ay!

dearie ['diəri] *n* (*fam*) queridito *m*, a *f*.

dearly ['diəli] *adv* (**a**) tiernamente; **to love someone — querer** muchísimo a uno; **I would — like to know why** quisiera muchísimo saber por qué.

(**b**) **to pay — for something** (*fig*) pagar algo caro; **it cost him —** le costó caro.

dearness ['diənis] *n* alto precio *m*, carestía *f*.

dearth [də:θ] *n* escasez *f*; falta *f*, ausencia *f*.

death [deθ] *n* muerte *f*; (*euph*) fallecimiento *m*, defunción *f*; **Black D—** peste *f* negra; **a living — una** vida peor que la muerte; **— to traitors!** ¡mueran los traidores!; **it will be the — of me** causará mi perdición; **this is — to our hopes** esto acaba con nuestras esperanzas; **it was — to the company** arruinó la sociedad; **to be in at the —** ver el final de la caza (*etc*); **to be at —'s door** estar a muerte; **to catch one's — (of cold)** coger un catarro de muerte; **to do (or put) to —** matar, dar muerte a, (*Law*) ajusticiar; **to fight to the —** luchar a muerte; **to hold on like grim —** estar firmemente agarrado, (*fig*) resistir con la mayor firmeza; **he's working himself to —** trabaja tanto que se está estropeando la salud; **he works his men to —** a sus hombres los mata trabajando.

deathbed ['deθbed] *n* lecho *m* de muerte; **— repentance** arrepentimiento *m* a última hora.

death-blow ['deθbləu] *n* golpe *m* mortal.

death certificate ['deθsə'tifikit] *n* partida *f* de defunción.

death duties ['deθ,dju:tiz] *npl* derechos *mpl* de herencia.

deathless ['deθlis] *adj* inmortal.

deathly ['deθli] *adj* mortal; de muerte; *silence* profundo; **— pale** pálido como la muerte.

death mask ['deθmɑ:sk] *n* mascarilla *f*.

death penalty ['deθ,penlti] *n* pena *f* de muerte.

death rate ['deθreit] *n* mortalidad *f*.

death rattle ['deθ,rætl] *n* estertor *m*.

death roll ['deθrəul] *n* número *m* de víctimas, lista *f* de víctimas.

death's-head ['deθshed] *n* calavera *f*.

death throes ['deθrəuz] *npl* agonía *f*.

deathtrap ['deθtræp] *n* sitio *m* muy peligroso.

death warrant ['deθ,wɔrənt] *n* sentencia *f* de muerte.

deathwatch beetle ['deθwɔtʃ'bi:tl] *n* reloj *m* de la muerte.

deb [deb] *n* (*fam*) = **débutante.**

débâcle [dei'bɑ:kl] *n* fracaso *m*; (*Mil*) derrota *f*.

debag [di:'bæg] *vt* (*hum*) quitar (violentamente) los pantalones a.

debar [di'bɑ:*] *vt* excluir (*from* de); **to — someone from doing something** prohibir a uno hacer algo.

debase [di'beis] *vt* degradar, envilecer; *coinage* alterar.

debasement [di'beismənt] *n* degradación *f*, envilecimiento *m*; alteración *f*.

debatable [di'beitəbl] *adj* discutible.

debate [di'beit] **1** *n* discusión *f*; (*Parl etc*) debate *m*. **2** *vt* discutir, debatir.

3 *vi* discutir (*with* con); **to — with oneself** pensar, deliberar; **I am debating whether to do it** estoy dudando si hacerlo o no.

debater [di'beitə*] *n* persona *f* que toma parte en un debate; polemista *mf*; **he was a brilliant —** brillaba en los debates.

debauch [di'bɔ:tʃ] *vt youth* corromper; *woman* seducir.

debauched [di'bɔ:tʃt] *adj* vicioso.

debauchee [,debɔ:'tʃi:] *n* libertino *m*, disoluto *m*.

debauchery [di'bɔ:tʃəri] *n* libertinaje *m*, corrupción *f*.

debenture [di'bentʃə*] *n* vale *m*, bono *m*, obligación *f*.

debilitate [di'biliteit] *vt* debilitar.

debility [di'biliti] *n* debilidad *f*.

debit ['debit] **1** *n* debe *m*; **— balance** saldo *m* deudor, saldo *m* negativo; **— side** debe *m*. **2** *vt*: **to — something to someone** cargar algo en cuenta a uno.

debonair [,debə'nɛə*] *adj* elegante, gallardo.

Deborah ['debərə] *f* Débora.

Debrett [də'bret] *n libro de referencia de la aristocracia del Reino Unido*, (*loosely*) anuario *m* de la nobleza.

debris ['debri:] *n* escombros *mpl*; (*Geol*) rocalla *f*.

debt [det] *n* deuda *f*; **bad —** deuda *f* incobrable; **National D—** Deuda *f* Pública; **— of honour** deuda *f* de honor; **to be in —** tener deudas (*to* con); **to be £5 in —** deber 5 libras (*to* a); **to be in someone's —** (*fig*) sentirse bajo una obligación a uno; **to run into —, to run up —s** contraer deudas.

debtor ['detə*] *n* deudor *m*, ora *f*.

debunk [di:'bʌŋk] *vt* quitar lo falso y legendario de; desacreditar, demoler; *person* desenmascarar.

début ['deibu:] *n* presentación *f*; **to make one's —** (*Theat*) hacer su presentación; (*in society*) presentarse en la sociedad, ponerse de largo.

débutante ['debju:tɑ:nt] *n* joven *f* que se presenta en la sociedad, debutante *f*.

decade ['dekeid] *n* decenio *m*.

decadence ['dekədəns] *n* decadencia *f*.

decadent ['dekədənt] *adj* decadente.

decagram(me) ['dekəgræm] *n* decagramo *m*.

decalitre, (*US*) **—liter** ['dekə,li:tə*] *n* decalitro *m*.

decametre, (*US*) **—meter** ['dekə,mi:tə*] *n* decámetro *m*.

decamp [di'kæmp] *vi* (*Mil*) decampar; (*fig*) largarse, fugarse.

decant [di'kænt] *vt* decantar.

decanter [di'kæntə*] *n* jarra *f*.

decapitate [di'kæpiteit] *vt* degollar, descabezar.

decapitation [di,kæpi'teiʃən] *n* degollación *f*.

decarbonize [di:'kɑ:bənaiz] *vt* descarbonizar.

decasyllable ['dekəsiləbl] *n* decasílabo *m*.

decay [di'kei] **1** *n* decadencia *f*, decaimiento *m*; (*rotting*) pudrición *f*; (*of teeth*) caries *f*; (*of building*) desmoronamiento *m*.

2 *vt* deteriorar, pudrir.

3 *vi* decaer, desmoronarse; (*rot*) pudrirse; (*teeth*) cariarse; (*building*) desmoronarse.

decayed [di'keid] *adj wood etc* podrido; *teeth* cariado; *family* venido a menos.

decease [di'si:s] **1** *n* fallecimiento *m*. **2** *vi* fallecer.

deceased [di'si:st] **1** *adj* difunto. **2** *n*: **the —** el difunto, la difunta.

deceit [di'si:t] *n* engaño *m*, fraude *m*; (*lying*) mentira *f*.

deceitful [di'si:tful] *adj* engañoso, falso, fraudulento; (*lying*) mentiroso.

deceitfully [di'si:tfəli] *adv* engañosamente; falsamente.

deceive [di'si:v] **1** *vt* engañar; *hopes* defraudar; **if my memory does not — me** si mal no recuerdo. **2** *vr*: **to — oneself** engañarse, equivocarse.

deceiver [di'si:və*] *n* impostor *m*, ora *f*, embustero *m*, a *f*; (*of woman*) seductor *m*.

decelerate [di:'seləreit] *vt* moderar la marcha de.

deceleration ['di:selə'reiʃən] n retardación f, disminución f de velocidad.
December [di'sembə*] n diciembre m.
decency ['di:sənsi] n (a) decencia f; **offence against —** atentado m contra el pudor; **it is no more than common — to** + infin la educación exige que + subj.
(b) **decencies** buenas fpl costumbres.
(c) (kindness) bondad f.
decent ['di:sənt] adj (a) (seemly) decente.
(b) person simpático, amable, bueno; **he's a — sort** es buena persona; **he was very — to me** fue muy amable conmigo.
(c) (passable) bastante bueno; **a — sum** una cantidad considerable.
decently ['di:səntli] adv decentemente; amablemente, con amabilidad; **he very — offered it to me** muy amablemente me lo ofreció.
decentralization [di:sentrəlai'zeiʃən] n descentralización f.
decentralize [di:'sentrəlaiz] vt descentralizar.
deception [di'sepʃən] n engaño m, fraude m.
deceptive [di'septiv] adj engañoso.
decibel ['desibel] n decibel(io) m.
decide [di'said] 1 vt decidir, determinar; **that —d me** eso me decidió.
2 vi decidir, resolver; **to — to do something** decidir hacer algo, decidirse a hacer algo, resolverse a hacer algo; **to — against something** optar por no hacer (etc) algo; **to — in favour of someone** decidir a favor de uno; **to — on something** decidir por algo, optar por algo, quedar en algo.
decided [di'saidid] adj person decidido, resuelto; (unquestionable) indudable.
decidedly [di'saididli] adv decididamente; **he said —** dijo con resolución; **it is — difficult** indudablemente es difícil.
deciding [di'saidiŋ] adj factor etc decisivo, concluyente; vote de calidad, decisivo.
deciduous [di'sidjuəs] adj de hoja caduca.
decimal ['desiməl] 1 adj decimal; **— fraction** fracción f decimal; **— point** coma f de decimales; **— system** sistema m métrico.
2 n decimal f; **recurring —** decimal f periódica pura.
decimate ['desimeit] vt diezmar (also fig).
decipher [di'saifə*] vt descifrar.
decipherable [di'saifərəbl] adj descifrable.
decision [di'siʒən] n (a) (a resolve) decisión f; (Law) fallo m; **to make (or take) a —** tomar una decisión.
(b) (resoluteness) resolución f, firmeza f.
decisive [di'saisiv] adj factor etc decisivo, concluyente; (conclusive) terminante; manner tajante.
decisively [di'saisivli] adv con decisión, con resolución; **to be — beaten** ser derrotado de modo decisivo.
deck [dek] 1 n (a) cubierta f; (of bus) piso m; (fam) suelo m, superficie f; **promenade —** cubierta f de paseo; **top —, upper —** (of bus) piso m de arriba; **to clear the —s** (fig) despejar la mesa (etc).
(b) (of cards) baraja f.
2 vt engalanar, adornar (with de).
deckchair ['dek,tʃeə*] n tumbona f, hamaca f.
deck hand ['dekhænd] n marinero m de cubierta.
deckhouse ['dekhaus] n, pl **—houses** [,hauziz] camareta f alta.
declaim [di'kleim] vt declamar.
declamation [,deklə'meiʃən] n declamación f.
declamatory [di'klæmətəri] adj declamatorio.
declaration [,deklə'reiʃən] n declaración f.
declare [di'kleə*] 1 vt declarar, afirmar; dividend repartir; war declarar; **to — something to the customs** declarar algo en la aduana; **have you anything to —?** ¿tiene Vd algo que declarar?; **nothing to —** nada de pago; **to — someone to be a traitor** dar a uno por traidor.
2 vi: **to — for, to — in favour of** pronunciarse a favor de; **well I —!** ¡vaya!
3 vr: **to — oneself** declararse; **to — oneself surprised** confesar su sorpresa; **he —d himself beaten** reconoció que había sido vencido; **to — oneself against something** afirmar su oposición a algo.
declared [di'kleəd] adj abierto, manifiesto.
declaredly [di'kleəridli] adv declaradamente, abiertamente.
déclassé [dei'klæsei] adj desprestigiado, empobrecido; que ha perdido su categoría social.
declension [di'klenʃən] n declinación f.
declinable [di'klainəbl] adj declinable.
decline [di'klain] 1 n (lessening) declinación f, descenso m, disminución f (in de); (in price) baja f; (decay) decaimiento m, decadencia f; (of sun, empire)

ocaso m; (Med) debilitación f; **to be on the —** ir disminuyendo; **to go into a —** ir debilitándose.
2 vt rehusar, negarse a aceptar; (Gram) declinar.
3 vi (a) (go down) declinar, disminuir; (in price) bajar; (decay) decaer; (Med) debilitarse; **to — in importance** ir perdiendo importancia.
(b) (refuse) rehusar; **to — to do something** rehusar hacer algo, negarse a hacer algo.
declining [di'klainiŋ] adj: **in my — years** en mis últimos años.
declivity [di'kliviti] n declive m.
declutch ['di:'klʌtʃ] vi desembragar.
decoction [di'kɔkʃən] n decocción f.
decode ['di:'kəud] vt descifrar.
décolletage [dei'kɔlətɑ:ʒ] n escote m.
décolleté(e) [dei'kɔltei] adj dress escotado; woman en traje escotado.
decompose [,di:kəm'pəuz] 1 vt descomponer. 2 vi descomponerse.
decomposition [,di:kɔmpə'ziʃən] n descomposición f.
decompression [,di:kəm'preʃən] n descompresión f; **— chamber** cámara f de descompresión.
decontaminate [,di:kən'tæmineit] vt descontaminar.
decontamination ['di:kən,tæmi'neiʃən] n descontaminación f.
decontrol [,di:kən'trəul] 1 n supresión f del control 2 vt suprimir el control de.
décor ['deikɔ:*] n decoración f; (Theat) decorado m, decoraciones fpl.
decorate ['dekəreit] vt adornar, decorar (with de); room empapelar, pintar; house pintar; (Mil etc) condecorar.
decorating ['dekəreitiŋ] n: **interior —** decoración f del hogar.
decoration [,dekə'reiʃən] n adorno m, ornato m; (act) decoración f; (Mil etc) condecoración f.
decorative ['dekərətiv] adj (in function) de adorno decorativo; (pleasant) hermoso, elegante.
decorator ['dekəreitə*] n pintor m decorador.
decorous ['dekərəs] adj decoroso, correcto.
decorously ['dekərəsli] adv decorosamente, correctamente.
decorum [di'kɔ:rəm] n decoro m, corrección f.
decoy ['di:kɔi] 1 n señuelo m; (bird) cimbel m, reclamo m; (fig) señuelo m, trampa f.
2 vt atraer con señuelo; **to — someone away** lograr mediante una estratagema que uno se aparte de un sitio.
decrease [di:'kri:s] 1 n disminución f (in de); **to be on the —** ir disminuyendo. 2 vt disminuir, reducir. 3 vi disminuirse, reducirse.
decree [di'kri:] 1 n decreto m. 2 vt decretar.
decree nisi [di'kri:'naisai] n orden f preliminar de divorcio.
decrepit [di'krepit] adj decrépito.
decrepitude [di'krepitju:d] n decrepitud f.
decry [di'krai] vt desacreditar, rebajar.
dedicate ['dedikeit] 1 vt dedicar. 2 vr: **to — oneself to** dedicarse a.
dedication [,dedi'keiʃən] n dedicación f; (in book) dedicatoria f; **to work with utter —** trabajar con la más abnegada devoción.
deduce [di'dju:s] vt deducir; **I — that** imagino que, supongo que; **what do you — from that?** ¿qué se colige de eso?
deducible [di'dju:sibl] adj deducible (from de).
deduct [di'dʌkt] vt restar, descontar, rebajar.
deductible [di'dʌktəbl] adj deducible.
deduction [di'dʌkʃən] n (a) (inference) deducción f, conclusión f; **what are your —s?** ¿cuáles son sus conclusiones? (b) (amount) descuento m, rebaja f.
deductive [di'dʌktiv] adj deductivo.
deed [di:d] n (a) (act) hecho m, acto m, acción f; (brave etc) hazaña f. (b) (Law) escritura f.
deed-poll ['di:d,pəul] n: **to change one's name by —** cambiar su apellido por escritura legal.
deem [di:m] vt juzgar, creer; **I — it a mistake** creo que es un error; **I — it to be true** creo que es verdad; **I — him a fool** considero que es tonto; **I — it to be my duty** considero que es mi deber.
deep [di:p] 1 adj profundo, hondo; (wide) ancho; (fig) profundo; breath profundo, a pleno pulmón; (Mus) bajo, grave; colour intenso, subido, (and dark) oscuro; tan intenso; mourning riguroso; mind penetrante; person insondable, (pej) astuto; **to be 6 metres —** tener una profundidad de 6 metros, tener 6 metros de hondo; **to be — in debt** estar lleno de deudas; **to be — in thought** estar absorto en la meditación; **he's pretty — in it** está muy metido en el asunto.
2 adv: **don't go in too —** no te metas en la parte profunda; **the miners are — underground** los

mineros están a una gran profundidad; **— in his heart** en lo más hondo del corazón; **he thrust his hand — into his pocket** metió la mano hasta el fondo del bolsillo; **— into the night** hasta las altas horas de la noche; **to form up 6**—formarse de 6 en fondo.
3 n: **the —** (lit) el piélago.

deep-breathing ['di:p'bri:ðiŋ] n gimnasia f respiratoria.

deep-chested ['di:p'tʃestid] adj ancho de pecho.

deepen ['di:pən] **1** vt hole etc ahondar, profundizar, hacer más profundo; voice ahuecar; colour, emotion intensificar; study ahondar en.
2 vi (water etc) hacerse más profundo; (colour, emotion) intensificarse; (gloom) aumentarse.

deep-felt ['di:p'felt] adj hondamente sentido.

deep-freeze ['di:p'fri:z] **1** n congeladora f. **2** vt congelar.

deep-fry ['di:p'frai] vt freír en aceite abundante.

deep-laid ['di:p'leid] adj plan bien preparado.

deeply ['di:pli] adv profundamente, hondamente; intensamente; **to breathe —** respirar a pleno pulmón.

deep-rooted ['di:p'ru:tid] adj profundamente arraigado.

deep-sea ['di:p'si:] adj de alta mar; **— fishing** pesca f de altura.

deep-seated ['di:p'si:tid] adj profundamente arraigado.

deep-set ['di:p'set] eyes hundido.

deer [diə*] n ciervo m; **red —** ciervo m común.

deerhound ['diəhaund] n galgo m para cazar venados; galgo m escocés de pelo lanoso.

deerskin ['diəskin] n piel f de ciervo, gamuza f.

deerstalker ['diə,stɔ:kə*] n (a) (person) cazador m de ciervos al acecho. (b) (hat) gorro m de cazador (de ciervos).

deer-stalking ['diə,stɔ:kiŋ] n caza f de venado.

deface [di'feis] vt desfigurar, mutilar.

de facto [dei'fæktəu] adj and adv de hecho.

defamation [,defə'meiʃən] n difamación f.

defamatory [di'fæmətəri] adj difamatorio.

defame [di'feim] vt difamar, calumniar.

default [di'fɔ:lt] **1** n: **in — of** a falta de, en ausencia de; **judgement by —** juicio m en rebeldía; **he won by —** ganó por no presentarse su adversario; **he must not let it go by —** no debemos permitir que lo perdamos por descuido (or sin hacer nada).
2 vi (a) (not pay) no pagar, ponerse en mora; **to — on one's payments** no pagar los plazos (etc).
(b) (Sport) dejar de presentarse.

defaulter [di'fɔ:ltə*] n (on payments) moroso m, a f; (Mil) delincuente m.

defeat [di'fi:t] **1** n derrota f. **2** vt vencer, derrotar; plan estorbar, frustrar; hopes defraudar; **this will — its own ends** esto será contraproducente.

defeatism [di'fi:tizəm] n derrotismo m.

defeatist [di'fi:tist] **1** adj derrotista. **2** n derrotista mf.

defecate ['defəkeit] vti defecar.

defecation [,defə'keiʃən] n defecación f.

defect ['di:fekt] n defecto m.

defect [di'fekt] vi desertar (from de, to a).

defection [di'fekʃən] n deserción f, defección f.

defective [di'fektiv] **1** adj defectuoso; (Gram) defectivo; child anormal. **2** n persona f anormal, retrasado m mental.

defence [di'fens] n defensa f (also Sport, Chess); **civil —** defensa f pasiva.

defenceless [di'fenslis] adj indefenso; (fig) inocente, inofensivo.

defend [di'fend] vt defender (against contra, from de).

defendant [di'fendənt] n (civil) demandado m, a f; (criminal) acusado m, a f.

defender [di'fendə*] n defensor m.

defense [di'fens] n (US) = **defence**.

defensible [di'fensibl] adj defendible; action etc justificable.

defensive [di'fensiv] **1** adj defensivo. **2** n defensiva f; **to be on the —** estar a la defensiva.

defer[1] [di'fɜ:*] vt aplazar, diferir; conscript dar una prórroga a.

defer[2] [di'fɜ:*] vi: **to — to** diferir a.

deference ['defərəns] n deferencia f, respeto m; **in — to, out of —** to por respeto a.

deferential [,defə'renʃəl] adj respetuoso.

deferment [di'fɜ:mənt] n aplazamiento m; (Mil) prórroga f.

deferred [di'fɜ:d] adj payment a plazos.

defiance [di'faiəns] n desafío m (of a); oposición f terca (of a); **in — of** en contra de, con infracción de; **to bid — to** desafiar a.

defiant [di'faiənt] adj provocativo, insolente; tone retador.

defiantly [di'faiəntli] adv de modo provocativo, insolentemente; en tono retador, en son de reto.

deficiency [di'fiʃənsi] n (lack) falta f; (defect) defecto m, deficiencia f; (Comm) déficit m, descubierto m; **— disease** mal m carencial.

deficient [di'fiʃənt] adj (in quantity) insuficiente; (incomplete) incompleto; (defective) defectuoso; (mentally) anormal; **to be — in** carecer de, estar falto de.

deficit ['defisit] n déficit m.

defile ['di:fail] n desfiladero m.

defile [di'fail] vt manchar, deshonrar; sacred thing profanar.

defilement [di'failmənt] n deshonra f; ensuciamiento m, corrupción f; profanación f.

definable [di'fainəbl] adj definible.

define [di'fain] vt definir, determinar.

definite ['definit] adj claro, categórico; positivo; concreto; date etc determinado; (Gram) definido; **he was very — about it** nos lo dijo sin dejar lugar a dudas; **we have no — record of it** no nos consta de manera clara; **the plan is not yet —** todavía el proyecto no se ha aprobado de modo definitivo.

definitely ['definitli] adv claramente, categóricamente; **oh, — !, yes, — !** sí, desde luego; **did he say so —?** ¿lo dijo claramente?; **we are — not going** es seguro que no vamos; **it is — impossible** es francamente imposible; **the plan is not yet — fixed** todavía el proyecto no se ha aprobado de modo definitivo.

definition [,defi'niʃən] n definición f; (of photo) claridad f; **by —** por definición.

definitive [di'finitiv] adj definitivo.

definitively [di'finitivli] adv en definitiva.

deflate [di:'fleit] vt desinflar; person quitar los humos a; reputation rebajar, desacreditar; (Fin) deflacionar.

deflation [di:'fleiʃən] n desinflación f; (Fin) deflación f.

deflationary [di:'fleiʃənəri] adj (Fin) deflacionista.

deflect [di'flekt] vt desviar (from de).

deflection [di'flekʃən] n desviación f.

defloration [,di:flɔ:'reiʃən] n desfloración f.

deflower [di:'flauə*] vt desflorar.

deform [di'fɔ:m] vt deformar.

deformation [,di:fɔ:'meiʃən] n deformación f.

deformed [di'fɔ:md] adj deforme, mutilado.

deformity [di'fɔ:miti] n deformidad f.

defraud [di'frɔ:d] vt estafar; **to — someone of something** estafar algo a uno, quitar fraudulentamente algo a uno.

defray [di'frei] vt sufragar, pagar.

defrost [di:'frɔst] vt deshelar, descongelar.

deft [deft] adj diestro, hábil.

deftly ['deftli] adv diestramente, hábilmente.

defunct [di'fʌŋkt] adj difunto; company etc que ya no existe; idea, theory que ya no tiene validez; scheme que no se realizó nunca.

defy [di'fai] vt (a) (challenge) desafiar; **to — someone to do something** desafiar a uno a hacer algo.
(b) (resist) oponerse tercamente a; order contravenir a; bad weather resistir a; **it defies definition** se escapa a la definición; **it defies description** resulta imposible describirlo.

degeneracy [di'dʒenərəsi] n degeneración f, depravación f.

degenerate [di'dʒenərit] **1** adj degenerado. **2** n degenerado m, a f.

degenerate [di'dʒenəreit] vi degenerar (into en); **to — into** (end up being) degenerar en, terminar siendo, terminar en; **the essay —d into jottings** el ensayo terminó siendo meros apuntes.

degeneration [di,dʒenə'reiʃən] n degeneración f.

degradation [,degrə'deiʃən] n degradación f, envilecimiento m.

degrade [di'greid] **1** vt degradar, envilecer. **2** vr: **to — oneself** degradarse, aplebeyarse.

degrading [di'greidiŋ] adj degradante.

degree [di'gri:] n (a) (Math, Astron, Gram etc) grado m; **10 —s below freezing** 10 grados bajo cero.
(b) (stage in process) etapa f, punto m; **things have reached such a —** that las cosas han llegado a tal extremo que; **by —s** poco a poco, gradualmente; **in no —** de ninguna manera; **in some —, to a certain —** hasta cierto punto; **to the highest —** en sumo grado; **he is superstitious to a —** es sumamente supersticioso.
(c) (Univ) grado m, título m; **first —** licenciatura f; **doctor's —** doctorado m; **honorary —** doctorado m "honoris causa"; **to get a —** sacar un título; **to take one's —** recibir un título; **to take a — in** licenciarse en.

(d) (*social*) rango *m*, condición *f* social; **people of —** personas *fpl* de cierto rango social.

(e) **third —** interrogación *f* brutal; **to give someone the third —** interrogar a uno brutalmente.

dehumanize [di:'hju:mənaiz] *vt* deshumanizar.

dehydrate [di:'haidreit] *vt* deshidratar.

dehydrated [ˌdi:hai'dreitid] *adj* deshidratado.

dehydration [ˌdi:hai'dreiʃən] *n* deshidratación *f*.

de-ice [di:'ais] *vt* deshelar, descongelar.

de-icer ['di:'aisə*] *n* (*Aer*) deshelador *m*.

deification [ˌdi:ifi'keiʃən] *n* deificación *f*.

deify ['di:ifai] *vt* deificar.

deign [dein] *vi*: **to — to** + *infin* dignarse + *infin*.

deism ['di:izəm] *n* deísmo *m*.

deist ['di:ist] *n* deísta *mf*.

deity ['di:iti] *n* deidad *f*; divinidad *f*; **the D—** Dios *m*.

dejected [di'dʒektid] *adj* abatido, desanimado.

dejection [di'dʒekʃən] *n* abatimiento *m*.

dekko ['dekəu] *n* (*sl*) vistazo *m*; **let's have a —** déjame verlo.

delay [di'lei] **1** *n* (*in general*) dilación *f*; (*a —*) retraso *m*, demora *f*; **without —** en seguida, sin más tardar.

2 *vt* (*postpone*) aplazar, demorar; (*person*) entretener; (*obstruct*) impedir; (*make slow, eg train*) retrasar, retardar; **what — ed you?** ¿por qué has tardado tanto?; **the train was —ed by fog** el tren se retrasó por la niebla; **—ed effect** efecto *m* demorado.

3 *vi* tardar, demorarse; **don't —!** (*in doing something*) ¡cuanto antes, mejor!; (*on the way*) ¡no te entretengas!

delayed-action [di'leid'ækʃən] *adj* de acción retardada.

delaying [di'leiiŋ] *adj*: **— tactics** tácticas *fpl* retardatorias.

delectable [di'lektəbl] *adj* delicioso.

delegate ['deligit] *n* delegado *m*, a *f*, diputado *m*, a *f* (*to a*).

delegate ['deligeit] *vt* delegar, diputar; **I was —d to do it** me dieron autoridad para hacerlo, me nombraron para hacerlo; **that task cannot be —d** ese cometido no se puede delegar a otro.

delegation [ˌdeli'geiʃən] *n* (*act*) delegación *f*; (*body*) delegación *f*, diputación *f*.

delete [di'li:t] *vt* suprimir, tachar.

deleterious [ˌdeli'tiəriəs] *adj* nocivo, perjudicial.

deletion [di'li:ʃən] *n* supresión *f*.

delft [delft] *n* porcelana *f* de Delft.

deliberate [di'libərit] *adj* (*intentional*) intencionado, premeditado; (*cautious*) prudente; (*unhurried*) pausado, lento.

deliberate [di'libəreit] **1** *vt* meditar; **I —d what to do** medité lo que debiera hacer.

2 *vi* deliberar (*on* sobre); **I —d whether to do it** dudaba si hacerlo o no.

deliberately [di'libəritli] *adv* (*intentionally*) con intención, a propósito; (*cautiously*) prudentemente; (*slowly*) pausadamente.

deliberation [diˌlibə'reiʃən] *n* (*consideration*) reflexión *f*; (*debate*) discusión *f*; (*slowness*) lentitud *f*; **the council's —s** las discusiones del consejo; **after due —** después de pensarlo bien.

deliberative [di'libərətiv] *adj* deliberativo.

delicacy ['delikəsi] *n* delicadeza *f*; fragilidad *f*; (*titbit*) manjar *m* exquisito, golosina *f*.

delicate ['delikit] *adj* delicado; *workmanship* fino, exquisito; (*fragile*) frágil; *flavour, food* exquisito; *situation* difícil; *action* considerado; (*Med*) algo débil, enfermizo.

delicately ['delikitli] *adv* delicadamente; finamente, exquisitamente; frágilmente.

delicatessen [ˌdelikə'tesn] *n* tienda *que se especializa en manjares exquisitos y exóticos.*

delicious [di'liʃəs] *adj* delicioso, exquisito, rico.

delight [di'lait] **1** *n* (*feeling*) placer *m*, deleite *m*; (*pleasurable thing*) encanto *m*, delicia *f*; **a — to the eye** un gozo para la retina; **one of the —s of Majorca** uno de los encantos de Mallorca; **it has been the — of many children** ha hecho las delicias de muchos niños; **the book is sheer —** el libro es un verdadero encanto; **to take — in something** deleitarse con algo; **to take — in** + *ger* deleitarse en + *infin*, (*pej*) gozarse en + *infin*.

2 *vt* encantar, deleitar; **the play —ed everyone** la obra encantó a todos; **I'm —ed to meet you** estoy encantado de conocerle; **we shall be —ed to come** tendremos muchísimo gusto en venir.

3 *vi*: **to — in something** deleitarse con algo; **to — in** + *ger* deleitarse en + *infin*, (*pej*) gozarse en + *infin*.

delightful [di'laitful] *adj* encantador, delicioso, precioso.

delightfully [di'laitfəli] *adv* deliciosamente; **to be — vague** tener un despiste delicioso.

delimit [di:'limit] *vt* delimitar.

delimitation [ˌdi:limi'teiʃən] *n* delimitación *f*.

delineate [di'linieit] *vt* delinear; (*portray*) bosquejar, pintar; (*delimit*) delimitar, definir.

delinquency [di'liŋkwənsi] *n* delincuencia *f*; (*guilt*) culpa *f*; **juvenile —** delincuencia *f* de menores.

delinquent [di'liŋkwənt] **1** *adj* delincuente.

2 *n* delincuente *mf*; **juvenile —** delincuente *mf* juvenil.

delirious [di'liriəs] *adj* delirante; **to be —** delirar, desvariar; **to be — with joy** estar loco de contento, estar delirante de alegría.

deliriously [di'liriəsli] *adv* con delirio; **to be — happy** estar loco de contento.

delirium [di'liriəm] *n* delirio *m*; **— tremens** delírium *m* tremens.

deliver [di'livə*] **1** *vt* (a) (*distribute*) repartir, entregar; *mail* repartir; **"we —"** (*Comm*) "servicio a domicilio".

(b) (*hand over*) entregar (*to a*; *also* **to — over**, **to — up**).

(c) *message* llevar, comunicar; *sermon, speech, judgement* pronunciar; *lecture* dar; *ball, missile* lanzar; *blow* dar.

(d) (*save*) librar (*from* de); **— us from evil** líbranos del mal.

(e) (*Med*) **she was —ed of a child** dio a luz un niño; **to — a woman** asistir a un parto; **the doctor —ed her of twins** el médico le asistió en el nacimiento de gemelos.

2 *vr*: **to — oneself of** *speech* pronunciar, *remark* hacer (con solemnidad), *opinion* expresar; **to — oneself up** entregarse (*to a*).

deliverance [di'livərəns] *n* liberación *f*, rescate *m* (*from* de).

deliverer [di'livərə*] *n* (a) (*Comm etc*) repartidor *m*; distribuidor *m*. (b) (*saviour*) libertador *m*, ora *f*, salvador *m*, ora *f*.

delivery [di'livəri] *n* (a) (*distribution*) distribución *f*, entrega *f*, repartido *m*; (*of mail*) reparto *m*.

(b) (*handing over*) entrega *f*; **forward —** (*Comm*) entrega *f* en fecha futura; *see* **cash**.

(c) (*of speech*) pronunciación *f*; (*manner of speaking etc*) modo *m* de leer, modo *m* de expresarse.

(d) (*saving*) liberación *f*, rescate *m* (*from* de).

(e) (*Med*) parto *m*, alumbramiento *m*.

delivery note [di'livərinəut] *n* nota *f* de entrega.

delivery room [di'livərirum] *n* sala *f* de alumbramiento.

delivery service [di'livəriˌsə:vis] *n* servicio *m* a domicilio.

delivery van [di'livərivæn] *n* furgoneta *f* de reparto.

dell [del] *n* vallecito *m*.

delouse ['di:'laus] *vt* despiojar, espulgar.

Delphi ['delfai] Delfos.

Delphic ['delfik] *adj* délfico.

delphinium [del'finiəm] *n* espuela *f* de caballero.

delta ['deltə] *n* (*Geog*) delta *m*; (*letter*) delta *f*.

delta-winged ['deltə'wiŋgd] *adj* con alas en delta.

delude [di'lu:d] **1** *vt* engañar. **2** *vr*: **to — oneself** engañarse.

deluded [di'lu:did] *adj* iluso, engañado.

deluge ['delju:dʒ] **1** *n* diluvio *m*; (*fig*) diluvio *m*, inundación *f*; **a — of protests** un torrente de protestas.

2 *vt* inundar (*with* de); **he was —d with gifts** quedó inundado de regalos, le llovieron los regalos encima; **we are —d with work** tenemos trabajo hasta encima de las cabezas.

delusion [di'lu:ʒən] *n* engaño *m*, error *m*, ilusión *f*; **to labour under a —** estar equivocado.

de luxe [di'lʌks] *adj* de lujo.

delve [delv] **1** *vt* cavar. **2** *vi* cavar; (*fig*) **to — into** investigar, ahondar en; **we must — deeper** tenemos que ahondar todavía más.

demagogic [ˌdemə'gɔgik] *adj* demagógico.

demagogue ['deməgɔg] *n* demagogo *m*.

demagoguery ['deməgɔgəri] *n* demagogismo *m*.

demagogy ['deməgɔgi] *n* demagogia *f*.

demand [di'ma:nd] **1** *n* (a) (*request*) petición *f*, solicitud *f* (*for* de); **by popular —** a petición del público; **on —** a solicitud.

(b) (*urgent claim*) exigencia *f*; requerimiento *m*; (*for payment*) reclamación *f*, aviso *m*, intimación *f*; **the —s of duty** las exigencias del deber; **I have many —s on my time** mis asuntos me tienen ocupadísimo; **it makes great —s on my resources** exige mucho dinero; **he resisted the pressing —s made on him** resistió a los apremiantes requerimientos que se le habían dirigido.

(c) (*Comm*) demanda *f* (*for* de); **there is a — for** existe demanda de; **to be in —** tener demanda, (*fig*) ser muy solicitado, ser muy popular.

2 *vt* **(a)** exigir (*from*, *of a*) reclamar, solicitar perentoriamente; **I — my rights** yo reclamo mis derechos; **the job —s care** el trabajo exige cuidado.

(b) I —ed to know why insistí en saber por qué.

demanding [di'mɑːndiŋ] *adj* (*person*) exigente; (*task*) absorbente; **physically —** duro, agotador.

demand note [di'mɑːndnəut] *n* apremio *m* de pago.

demarcate ['diːmɑːkeit] *vt* demarcar.

demarcation [ˌdiːmɑː'keiʃən] *n* demarcación *f*.

démarche ['deimɑːʃ] *n* gestión *f*, diligencia *f*.

demean [di'miːn] *vr*: **to — oneself** degradarse.

demeanour [di'miːnə*] *n* porte *m*, conducta *f*.

demented [di'mentid] *adj* demente; (*fig*) loco.

dementedly [di'mentidli] *adv* (*fig*) como un loco.

dementia [di'menʃiə] *n* demencia *f*.

demerit [diː'merit] *n* demérito *m*.

demesne [di'mein] *n* heredad *f*; tierras *fpl* solariegas.

demi . . . ['demi] semi . . ., medio . . .

demigod ['demigɔd] *n* semidiós *m*.

demijohn ['demidʒɔn] *n* damajuana *f*.

demilitarization ['diːˌmilitərai'zeiʃən] *n* desmilitarización *f*.

demilitarize ['diːˈmilitəraiz] *vt* desmilitarizar.

demimonde ['demi'mɔːnd] *n* mujeres *fpl* mundanas.

demise [di'maiz] *n* fallecimiento *m*.

demisemiquaver ['demisemiˌkweivə*] *n* fusa *f*.

demitasse [demitæs] *n* (US) taza *f* pequeña, tacita *f*.

demob [diː'mɔb] *vt* (*fam*) desmovilizar.

demobilization ['diːˌməubilai'zeiʃən] *n* desmovilización *f*.

demobilize [diː'məubilaiz] *vt* desmovilizar.

democracy [di'mɔkrəsi] *n* democracia *f*.

democrat ['deməkræt] *n* demócrata *mf*.

democratic [ˌdemə'krætik] *adj* democrático.

democratically [ˌdemə'krætikli] *adv* democráticamente.

democratize [di'mɔkrətaiz] *vt* democratizar.

démodé [dei'mɔdei] *adj* pasado de moda.

demography [di'mɔgrəfi] *n* demografía *f*.

demolish [di'mɔliʃ] *vt* derribar, demoler; *argument* destruir; *food* devorar, zamparse.

demolition [ˌdemə'liʃən] *n* derribo *m*, demolición *f*.

demolition squad [ˌdemə'liʃənskwɔd] *n* pelotón *m* de demolición.

demon ['diːmən] *n* demonio *m*.

demonetize [diː'mʌnitaiz] *vt* desmonetizar.

demoniacal [ˌdiːmə'naiəkəl] *adj* demoníaco.

demonstrable ['demənstrəbl] *adj* demostrable.

demonstrate ['demənstreit] **1** *vt* demostrar. **2** *vi* manifestarse, hacer una manifestación (*against* para protestar contra, *in favour of* a favor de).

demonstration [ˌdemən'streiʃən] *n* demostración *f*, prueba *f*; (*Pol*) manifestación *f*.

demonstrative [di'mɔnstrətiv] **1** *adj* (*Gram*) demostrativo; *person* exagerado, exaltado; **not very —** más bien reservado. **2** *n* demostrativo *m*.

demonstrator ['demənstreitə*] *n* (*Pol*) manifestante *mf*; (*Univ etc*) ayudante *mf* (en un laboratorio).

demoralize [di'mɔrəlaiz] *vt* desmoralizar.

demoralizing [di'mɔrəlaiziŋ] *adj* desmoralizador.

Demosthenes [di'mɔsθəniːz] *m* Demóstenes.

demote [di'məut] *vt* degradar.

demotic [di'mɔtik] *adj* demótico.

demotion [di'məuʃən] *n* degradación *f*.

demur [di'mə:*] *vi* objetar, poner pegas.

demure [di'mjuə*] *adj* grave, solemne; (*modest*) recatado; (*coy*) de una coquetería disimulada; **in a — little voice** en tono dulce y algo coqueta.

demurely [di'mjuəli] *adv* gravemente, solemnemente; recatadamente; con una coquetería disimulada; en tono dulce y algo coqueta.

demureness [di'mjuənis] *n* gravedad *f*, solemnidad *f*; recato *m*; coquetería *f* disimulada.

den [den] *n* (*animal's*) madriguera *f*, guarida *f*; (*private room*) estudio *m*, gabinete *m*; **— of iniquity, — of vice** templo *m* del vicio; **— of thieves** ladronera *f*.

denationalization ['diːˌnæʃnəlai'zeiʃən] *n* desnacionalización *f*.

denationalize [diː'næʃnəlaiz] *vt* desnacionalizar.

denial [di'naiəl] *n* (*of request*) denegación *f*, negativa *f*; (*of report etc*) desmentimiento *m*; (*self-*) abnegación *f*.

denier ['deniə*] *n* denier *m*.

denigrate ['denigreit] *vt* denigrar.

denim ['denim] *n* dril *m* de algodón; **—s** pantalón *m* de dril.

denizen ['denizn] *n* habitante *mf*.

Denmark ['denmɑːk] *n* Dinamarca *f*.

denominate [di'nɔmineit] *vt* denominar.

denomination [diˌnɔmi'neiʃən] *n* (*name*) denominación *f*; (*class*) clase *f*, categoría *f*; (*of coin etc*) valor *m*; (*Eccl*) secta *f*, confesión *f*.

denominational [diˌnɔmi'neiʃənl] *adj* (*Eccl*) sectario.

denominator [di'nɔmineitə*] *n*: **common —** denominador *m* común.

denote [di'nəut] *vt* denotar; indicar, significar; **what does this —?** ¿qué quiere decir esto?

dénouement [dei'nuːmɑːŋ] *n* desenlace *m*.

denounce [di'nauns] *vt* (*to police etc*) denunciar; *treaty* denunciar, abrogar; (*inveigh against*) censurar.

dense [dens] *adj* denso; espeso, compacto, tupido; *person* duro de mollera.

densely ['densli] *adv* densamente; espesamente; **— populated** con gran densidad de población.

denseness ['densnis] *n*, **density** ['densiti] *n* densidad *f*; lo espeso etc.

dent [dent] **1** *n* abolladura *f*; (*in edge*) mella. **2** *vt* abollar; mellar.

dental ['dentl] **1** *adj* dental; **— science** odontología *f*; **— surgeon** dentista *mf*, odontólogo *m*. **2** *n* dental *f*.

dentifrice ['dentifris] *n* dentífrico *m*.

dentist ['dentist] *n* dentista *mf*, odontólogo *m*.

dentistry ['dentistri] *n* odontología *f*.

denture ['dentʃə*] *n* dentadura *f*; (*false teeth, also* **—s**) dentadura *f* postiza.

denude [di'njuːd] *vt* (*Geol etc*) denudar; (*strip*) despojar (*of* de).

denunciation [diˌnʌnsi'eiʃən] *n* denuncia *f*, denunciación *f*; (*inveighing*) censura *f*.

deny [di'nai] **1** *vt* *possibility, truth of statement etc* negar; *request* denegar; *charge* rechazar; *report* desmentir; **he denies me his help** me niega su ayuda; **he denies that he said it, he denies having said it** niega haberlo dicho; **I don't — it** no lo niego.

2 *vr*: **to — oneself** privarse; **to — oneself something** privarse de algo, no permitirse algo.

deodorant [diː'əudərənt] *n* desodorante *m*.

deodorize [diː'əudəraiz] *vt* desodorizar.

deoxidize [diː'ɔksidaiz] *vt* desoxidar.

depart [di'pɑːt] **1** *vt*: **to — this life** partir de esta vida. **2** *vi* partir, irse, marcharse (*from* de); (*train etc*) salir (*at a*, *for* para, *from* de); **to — from** *custom, truth etc* apartarse de, desviarse de.

departed [di'pɑːtid] *n*: **the —** el difunto, la difunta.

department [di'pɑːtmənt] *n* departamento *m*; (*of business*) sección *f*; (*of learning, activity*) ramo *m*; (*US Pol*) ministerio *m*; **D— of State** (US) Ministerio *m* de Asuntos Exteriores; **in that — of the game** en ese aspecto del juego.

departmental [ˌdiːpɑːt'mentl] *adj* departamental; **— policy** política *f* del departamento; **— head** jefe *m* de sección.

department store [di'pɑːtməntˌstɔː*] *n* grandes almacenes *mpl*.

departure [di'pɑːtʃə*] *n* partida *f*, ida *f*; (*of train etc*) salida *f*; (*from norm*) desviación *f* (*from* de); **— time** hora *f* de salida; **new —** rumbo *m* nuevo; **this is a new —** for us esto es algo nuevo para nosotros; **to take one's —** marcharse.

depend [di'pend] *vi* **(a) it —s** eso depende, según; **it —s what you mean** depende de lo que Vd quiere decir.

(b) to — on *circumstances, result etc* depender de; (*rely on*) contar con, confiar en; **can we — on you?** ¿podemos contar contigo?; **can we — on you to do it?** ¿podemos contar contigo para hacerlo?, ¿podemos confiar en que tú lo hagas?; **she —s on her own resources** ella cuenta con sus propios recursos; **he has to — on his pen** tiene que vivir de su pluma; **you may — upon it** es cosa segurísima.

dependability [diˌpendə'biliti] *n* seguridad *f*; seriedad *f*, formalidad *f*.

dependable [di'pendəbl] *adj* *thing* seguro; *person* serio, formal.

dependant [di'pendənt] *n* familiar *mf* dependiente.

dependence [di'pendəns] *n* (*depending*) dependencia *f* (*on* de); (*reliance*) confianza *f* (*on* en); (*subordination*) subordinación *f* (*on* a).

dependency [di'pendənsi] *n* (*Pol*) posesión *f*.

dependent [di'pendənt] **1** *adj* dependiente (*on* de); (*subordinate*) subordinado (*on* a; *also Gram*); **to be on** depender de. **2** *n* familiar *mf* dependiente.

depersonalize [diː'pəːsənəlaiz] *vt* despersonalizar.

depict [di'pikt] *vt* representar, pintar.

depilatory [di'pilətəri] **1** *adj* depilatorio. **2** *n* depilatorio *m*.

deplete [di'pliːt] *vt* agotar; mermar, reducir.

depletion [di'pliːʃən] *n* agotamiento *m*; merma *f*, reducción *f*.

deplorable [di'plɔːrəbl] *adj* lamentable, deplorable; **it would be — if** sería lamentable que + *subj*.

deplorably [di'plɔːrəbli] *adv* lamentablemente, deplorablemente; **in — bad taste** de un mal gusto lamentable; **it has been — exaggerated** ha sido exagerado de un modo lamentable.

deplore [di'plɔː*] *vt* lamentar, deplorar; **it is to be —d** es de lamentar.

deploy [di'plɔi] **1** *vt* desplegar; *(fig)* organizar. **2** *vi* desplegarse.

deployment [di'plɔimənt] *n* despliegue *m*; *(fig)* organización *f*.

depopulate [diː'pɔpjuleit] *vt* despoblar.

depopulation ['diːˌpɔpju'leiʃən] *n* despoblación *f*.

deport [di'pɔːt] **1** *vt* deportar. **2** *vr*: **to — oneself** comportarse.

deportation [ˌdiːpɔː'teiʃən] *n* deportación *f*.

deportment [di'pɔːtmənt] *n* conducta *f*, comportamiento *m*; *(carriage)* porte *m*, modo *m* de andar.

depose [di'pəuz] **1** *vt* deponer. **2** *vi* declarar, deponer.

deposit [di'pɔzit] **1** *n* **(a)** *(Geol)* depósito *m*, yacimiento *m*; *(Chem, dregs)* poso *m*, sedimento *m*.
   (b) *(Fin etc)* depósito *m*; *(pledge)* señal *f*; *(act of —ing money in account)* imposición *f*, ingreso *m*; *(on hire purchase: on car)* depósito *m*, *(on house)* desembolso *m* inicial; **to have £50 on —** tener 50 libras en cuenta de ahorros; **to leave £50 —** hacer un desembolso inicial de 50 libras.
   2 *vt* **(a)** *(place, lay)* depositar; **eggs** poner.
   (b) *(entrust etc)* depositar *(in* en).
   (c) *(leave)* depositar *(with* en), dejar *(with* con).
   (d) *(Geol, Chem)* depositar, sedimentar.
   (e) *(Fin)* depositar; *(pledge)* dar para señal; *(money in account)* imponer, ingresar *(in* en); **to — £200 on a house** hacer un desembolso inicial de 200 libras para una casa.

deposition [ˌdiːpə'ziʃən] *n* deposición *f*; *(Law)* declaración *f*, deposición *f*.

depositor [di'pɔzitə*] *n* depositante *mf*, impositor *m*, ora *f*, imponente *mf*; cuentacorrentista *mf*.

depository [di'pɔzitəri] *n* depositaría *f*, almacén *m*; *(fig)* pozo *m*.

depot ['depəu] *n* *(storehouse)* depósito *m*, almacén *m*; *(Mil HQ)* depósito *m*; *(for vehicles)* parque *m*; *(buses, US Rail)* estación *f*.

depot ship ['depəu ʃip] *n* buque *m* nodriza.

depravation [ˌdeprə'veiʃən] *n* depravación *f*.

deprave [di'preiv] *vt* depravar.

depraved [di'preivd] *adj* depravado, perverso, vicioso.

depravity [di'præviti] *n* depravación *f*, perversión *f*.

deprecate ['deprikeit] *vt* desaprobar, lamentar.

deprecatingly ['deprikeitiŋli] *adv* con desaprobación.

deprecatory ['deprikətəri] *adj* de desaprobación.

depreciate [di'priːʃieit] **1** *vt* depreciar; *(fig)* desestimar. **2** *vi* depreciarse, perder valor, bajar de precio.

depreciation [diˌpriːʃi'eiʃən] *n* depreciación *f*.

depredations [ˌdepri'deiʃənz] *npl* estragos *mpl*.

depress [di'pres] *vt* *(push down)* presionar, deprimir; **status** rebajar; **trade** paralizar; **price** hacer bajar; *(dispirit)* deprimir, abatir, desalentar.

depressed [di'prest] *adj* **area** deprimido, de elevado paro obrero; **person** abatido, desalentado, pesimista; **to feel — about** sentirse pesimista por.

depressing [di'presiŋ] *adj* triste, deprimente.

depressingly [di'presiŋli] *adv* tristemente, en tono pesimista; **it was a — familiar story** era la triste historia de siempre.

depression [di'preʃən] *n* *(Fin, Meteorol etc)* depresión *f*; *(slump)* crisis *f* económica, depresión *f*, bache *m*; *(in ground)* hoyo *m*; *(dejection)* depresión *f*, desaliento *m*, abatimiento *m*.

depressive [di'presiv] *adj* depresivo.

deprivation [ˌdepri'veiʃən] *n* privación *f*; **a great —** una pérdida.

deprive [di'praiv] **1** *vt*: **to — someone of something** privar a uno de algo.
   2 *vr*: **to — oneself of something** privarse de algo; **don't — yourself!** ¡no te vayas a quedar sin nada!

deprived [di'praivd] *adj* **child** pobre.

depth [depθ] *n* **(a)** profundidad *f* *(also fig)*; *(of room)* fondo *m*; *(width)* ancho *m*; *(of colour, feeling)* intensidad *f*; **defence in —** defensa *f* en profundidad; **to be 5 metres in —** tener una profundidad de 5 metros.
   (b) **—s: in the —s of the sea** en los abismos del mar; **from the —s of the mine** desde lo más hondo de la mina; *(fig)* **the —s of degradation** la mayor degradación; **the —s of despair** la mayor desesperación; **in the —s of one's heart** en lo más hondo del corazón; **in the —s of winter** en lo más recio del invierno.
   (c) **he was out of his —** le cubría el agua; **I'm out of my — with physics** yo no entiendo nada de

física; **to get out of one's —** meterse donde le cubre a uno, *(fig)* meterse en honduras.

depth charge ['depθtʃɑːdʒ] *n* carga *f* de profundidad.

deputation [ˌdepju'teiʃən] *n* diputación *f*, delegación *f*.

depute [di'pjuːt] *vt* diputar; **to — someone to do something** diputar a uno para que haga algo.

deputize ['depjutaiz] *vi*: **to — for someone** sustituir a uno, desempeñar las funciones de uno.

deputy ['depjuti] **1** *adj* suplente; **— head** subdirector *m*, ora *f*. **2** *n* sustituto *m*, suplente *m*; *(Pol)* diputado *m*; *(agent)* representante *m*.

derail [di'reil] *vt* hacer descarrilar.

derailment [di'reilmənt] *n* descarrilamiento *m*.

derange [di'reindʒ] *vt* desarreglar, descomponer; **person** volver loco; **to be —d** padecer un trastorno mental.

derangement [di'reindʒmənt] *n* desarreglo *m*; *(Med)* trastorno *m* mental.

derby ['dɑːbi] *n* *(US)* hongo *m* *(sombrero)*.

derelict ['derilikt] **1** *adj* abandonado. **2** *n* *(Naut)* derrelicto *m*.

dereliction [ˌderi'likʃən] *n* abandono *m*; **— of duty** negligencia *f*.

deride [di'raid] *vt* ridiculizar, mofarse de.

de rigueur [dəri'gəː*] *adv* de rigor.

derision [di'riʒən] *n* irrisión *f*, mofas *fpl*; **this was greeted with —** en esto hubo risas.

derisive [di'raisiv] *adj* burlón, mofador, irónico.

derisory [di'raisəri] *adj* **quantity etc** irrisorio, ridículo.

derivation [ˌderi'veiʃən] *n* derivación *f*.

derivative [di'rivətiv] **1** *adj* derivado; **work** poco original. **2** *n* *(Gram, Chem)* derivado *m*.

derive [di'raiv] **1** *vt* derivar *(from* de); **profit, advantage** sacar, obtener *(from* de).
   2 *vi* derivar(se) *(from* de); **to — from, to be —d from** *(fig)* proceder de, provenir de.

dermatitis [ˌdəːmə'taitis] *n* dermatitis *f*.

dermatologist [ˌdəːmə'tɔlədʒist] *n* dermatólogo *m*.

dermatology [ˌdəːmə'tɔlədʒi] *n* dermatología *f*.

derogatory [di'rɔgətəri] *adj* despectivo.

derrick ['derik] *n* grúa *f*; *(of oil well)* torre *f* de perforación.

dervish ['dəːviʃ] *n* derviche *m*; *(fig)* salvaje *m*.

desalinate [diː'sælineit] *vt* desalinar, desalinizar.

desalination [diːˌsali'neiʃən] *n* desalación *f*, desalinización *f*.

descant ['deskænt] **1** *n* discante *m*. **2** *vi*: **to — on** disertar largamente sobre.

descend [di'send] **1** *vt* descender, bajar.
   2 *vi* descender, bajar *(from* de); **to — from** ancestors etc descender de; **to — on** caer sobre; *(as visitors)* invadir; **to — to** *(as inheritance)* pasar a; *(lower oneself)* rebajarse a; **to — to + ger** rebajarse a + *infin*.

descendant [di'sendənt] *n* descendiente *mf*; **to leave no —s** no dejar descendencia.

descent [di'sent] *n* *(Geog)* pendiente *f*, declive *m*; *(raid)* ataque *m* *(on* sobre), incursión *f*; *(coming down)* descendimiento *m* *(also Rel)*, bajada *f*; *(fall)* descenso *m* *(in* de); *(origin)* descendencia *f (from* de).

describe [dis'kraib] *vt* describir *(also Geom)*; **to — someone as** calificar a uno de.

description [dis'kripʃən] *n* descripción *f*; *(sort)* clase *f*, género *m*.

descriptive [dis'kriptiv] *adj* descriptivo.

descry [dis'krai] *vt* divisar.

desecrate ['desikreit] *vt* profanar.

desecration [ˌdesi'kreiʃən] *n* profanación *f*.

desegregate [diː'segrəgeit] *vt* **school etc** abrir libremente a todas las razas; suprimir las leyes sobre la separación racial referentes a, suprimir la separación racial en.

desegregation ['diːˌsegrə'geiʃən] *n* acto *m* *(or* política *f* etc*)* de suprimir las leyes sobre la separación racial.

desensitize [diː'sensitaiz] *vt* desensibilizar, insensibilizar; *(Phot)* hacer insensible a la luz.

desert ['dezət] **1** *n* desierto *m*. **2** *n* desierto *m*.

desert [di'zəːt] **1** *vt* *(Mil, Law etc)* desertar de; **person** abandonar, desamparar, dejar; **his luck —ed him** la suerte le abandonó.
   2 *vi* *(Mil)* desertar *(from* de, **to** a).

deserter [di'zəːtə*] *n* desertor *m*.

desertion [di'zəːʃən] *n* deserción *f* *(also Mil)*, abandono *m*.

deserts [di'zəːts] *npl* lo merecido; **to get one's (just) —** llevar su merecido.

deserve [di'zəːv] **1** *vt* merecer, ser digno de; **he got what he —ed** llevó su merecido.
   2 *vi*: **to — well of** merecer ser bien tratado por; **to — to + infin** merecer + *infin*.

deservedly [di'zəːvidli] *adv* merecidamente.

deserving [di'zə:viŋ] *adj* meritorio; **to be — of** merecer, ser digno de.

déshabillé [,deizæ'bi:ei] *n* desabillé *m*.

desiccate ['desikeit] *vt* desecar.

desiccation [,desi'keiʃən] *n* desecación *f*.

desideratum [di,zidə'ra:təm] *n* desiderátum *m*.

design [di'zain] **1** *n* **(a)** (*Tech etc*) diseño *m*; (*pattern of cloth, wallpaper etc*) dibujo *m*; (*preliminary sketch*) bosquejo *m*; (*Theat, Cine*) boceto *m*; (*of building etc*) estilo *m*; (*ground plan*) distribución *f*; (*art of —*) dibujo *m*.
　　(b) (*aim*) intención *f*, propósito *m*; (*pej*) mala intención *f*; (*plan*) plan *m*, proyecto *m*; **grand —** plan *m* general, (*Mil*) estrategia *f* general; **by — inten**cionalmente; **to have (one's) —s on** tener sus proyectos sobre, tener la mira puesta en.
　　2 *vt* (*contrive*) idear; (*plan*) proyectar; (*Tech*) diseñar, proyectar; *pattern* dibujar; (*sketch*) bosquejar; **a well —ed house** una casa bien distribuida; **to be —ed to + infin** estar diseñado para + *infin*, estar proyectado para + *infin*; (*fig*) tener la intención de + *infin*, ir encaminado a + *infin*.
　　3 *vi*: **to — to + infin** proponerse + *infin*.

designate ['dezignit] *adj* designado, nombrado.

designate ['dezigneit] *vt* (*name*) denominar; (*appoint*) nombrar (*to + infin* para que + *subj*); (*point to*) señalar; (*destine*) designar.

designation [,dezig'neiʃən] *n* (*name*) denominación *f*; (*appointment*) nombramiento *m*.

designedly [di'zainidli] *adv* de propósito.

designer [di'zainə*] *n* (*Tech*) diseñador *m*, proyectista *m*; (*draughtsman*) delineante *m*; (*Art*) dibujante *m*; (*Theat*) escenógrafo *m*.

designing [di'zainiŋ] *adj* intrigante.

desirability [di,zaiərə'biliti] *n* lo apetecible, lo atractivo, carácter *m* atractivo; deseabilidad *f*, conveniencia *f*; **the — of the plan is not in question** nadie duda de lo atractivo que es este proyecto.

desirable [di'zaiərəbl] *adj* (*arousing desire*) apetecible, atractivo; (*proper*) deseable, conveniente; **I don't think it — to + infin** no creo que sea conveniente + *infin*.

desire [di'zaiə*] **1** *n* deseo *m* (*for* de, *to + infin* de + *infin*); **sexual —** instinto *m* sexual; **I haven't the least — to go** no tengo el menor deseo de ir; **to meet someone's —** satisfacer los deseos de uno.
　　2 *vt* **(a)** desear; querer tener; **to — to do** desear hacer; **what does madam —?** ¿qué manda la señora?
　　(b) to — someone to do something (*wish*) rogar a uno hacer algo, (*order*) mandar a uno hacer algo.

desirous [di'zaiərəs] *adj*: **— of** deseoso de; **to be — that** querer que + *subj*; **to be — to + infin** desear + *infin*.

desist [di'zist] *vi*: **to — from something** desistir de algo; **to — from + ger** dejar de + *infin*; **we begged him to —** le rogamos dejarlo, le rogamos no continuar.

desk [desk] *n* (*in office, study etc*) mesa *f* de trabajo; (*School*) pupitre *m*; (*bureau*) escritorio *m*.

desolate ['desəlit] *adj* (*lonely*) solitario; (*deserted*) desierto, deshabitado; (*ruinous*) arruinado; (*barren*) yermo, desierto; (*dreary*) triste; *person* triste, afligido.

desolate ['desəleit] *vt* asolar, arrasar; *person* afligir.

desolation [,desə'leiʃən] *n* (*act*) arrasamiento *m*; (*state*) desolación *f*, lo desierto *etc*; (*of person*) aflicción *f*.

despair [dis'peə*] **1** *n* desesperación *f*; **to be in —** estar desesperado.
　　2 *vi* perder la esperanza, desesperar(se) (*of* de); **his life is —ed of** se ha perdido la esperanza de salvarle la vida; **don't —!** ¡ánimo!

despairing [dis'peəriŋ] *adj* desesperado.

despairingly [dis'peəriŋli] *adv* desesperadamente.

despatch [dis'pætʃ] *n* = **dispatch**.

desperado [,despə'ra:dəu] *n* criminal *m*, bandido *m*.

desperate ['despərit] *adj* (*hopeless*) desesperado; *plight, situation* desesperado, muy grave; *urgency* apremiante; *need* extremo; *measure* arriesgado; *resistance* heroico; *effort* furioso, violento; (*reckless from despair*) dispuesto a arriesgarlo todo; **we are getting —** empezamos a perder la esperanza; **he's a —man** es un hombre peligroso.

desperately ['despəritli] *adv* desesperadamente; *fight etc* furiosamente, heroicamente; **we — need it** lo necesitamos urgentemente; **— bad** terriblemente malo; **— ill** gravemente enfermo.

desperation [,despə'reiʃən] *n* desesperación *f*; **in —** desesperado.

despicable [dis'pikəbl] *adj* vil, despreciable.

despise [dis'paiz] *vt* despreciar, desdeñar.

despite [dis'pait] *prep* a pesar de.

despoil [dis'pɔil] *vt* despojar (*of* de).

despondency [dis'pɔndənsi] *n* abatimiento *m*, desaliento *m*.

despondent [dis'pɔndənt] *adj* abatido, deprimido; *letter etc* de tono triste, pesimista; **he was very — about our chances** discutió en términos pesimistas nuestras posibilidades.

despot ['despɔt] *n* déspota *m*.

despotic [des'pɔtik] *adj* despótico.

despotically [des'pɔtikəli] *adv* despóticamente.

despotism ['despətizəm] *n* despotismo *m*.

dessert [di'zə:t] *n* postre *m*; **what is there for —?** ¿qué hay de postre?

dessertspoon [di'zə:tspu:n] *n* cuchara *f* de postre.

destination [,desti'neiʃən] *n* destino *m* (*also Rail etc*), paradero *m*.

destine ['destin] *vt* destinar (*for, to* para); **to be —d to + infin** estar llamado a + *infin*; **it was —d to fail** estuvo condenado a fracasar; **it was —d to happen this way** tuvo forzosamente que ocurrir así.

destiny ['destini] *n* destino *m*.

destitute ['destitju:t] *adj* **(a)** indigente, desamparado; **to be —** vivir en la miseria. **(b) — of** desprovisto de.

destitution [,desti'tju:ʃən] *n* indigencia *f*, miseria *f*.

destroy [dis'trɔi] *vt* destruir; (*kill*) matar; *pet* sacrificar; *vermin* exterminar; (*finish*) aniquilar, acabar con.

destroyer [dis'trɔiə*] *n* destructor *m*.

destructible [dis'trʌktəbl] *adj* destructible.

destruction [dis'trʌkʃən] *n* destrucción *f*; (*fig*) ruina *f*, perdición *f*.

destructive [dis'trʌktiv] *adj* destructivo, destructor; *animal* dañino; **to be — of** ser nocivo a, ser peligroso para, ser perjudicial para.

destructiveness [dis'trʌktivnis] *n* espíritu *m* de destrucción.

destructor [dis'trʌktə*] *n* incinerador *m* de basuras.

desuetude [di'sjuitju:d] *n* desuso *m*; **to fall into —** caer en desuso.

desultory ['desəltəri] *adj* *way of working etc* poco metódico; *fire etc* intermitente, irregular; (*disconnected*) inconexo.

detach [di'tætʃ] *vt* separar; (*unstick*) despegar; (*Mil*) destacar.

detachable [di'tætʃəbl] *adj* separable; (*Tech*) desmontable.

detached [di'tætʃt] *adj* separado, suelto; *collar* postizo; *house* independiente; (*fig*) imparcial, objetivo; **to become —** separarse, desprenderse; **they live — from everything** viven desligados de todo; **to take a — view of something** considerar algo objetivamente.

detachment [di'tætʃmənt] *n* (*act*) separación *f*; (*Mil*) destacamento *m*; (*fig*) imparcialidad *f*, objetividad *f*.

detail ['di:teil] **1** *n* detalle *m*, pormenor *m*; (*Mil*) destacamento *m*; **in —** en detalle, detalladamente; **to go into —s** entrar en detalles, pormenorizar; **they planned it down to the last —** lo planearon todo hasta en los menores detalles.
　　2 *vt* detallar, referir con sus pormenores; (*Mil*) destacar (*to + infin* para + *infin*).

detailed ['di:teild] *adj* detallado, pormenorizado.

detain [di'tein] *vt* (*arrest*) detener; (*keep waiting*) retener; **I was —ed at the office** tuve que quedarme a trabajar en la oficina; **I was —ed by fog** el retraso se debe a la niebla.

detect [di'tekt] *vt* descubrir; (*perceive*) percibir; *crime* resolver, *criminal* identificar; (*Tech, by radar etc*) detectar.

detectable [di'tektəbl] *adj* perceptible.

detection [di'tekʃən] *n* descubrimiento *m*; percepción *f*; resolución *f*, identificación *f*; detección *f*.

detective [di'tektiv] *n* detective *m*.

detective story [di'tektiv,stɔ:ri] *n* novela *f* policiaca.

detector [di'tektə*] *n* (*Tech*) detector *m*.

détente ['deitã:nt] *n* detente *f*.

detention [di'tenʃən] *n* detención *f*, arresto *m*; **preventive —** arresto *m* preventivo.

deter [di'tə:*] *vt* (*discourage*) desalentar; (*dissuade*) disuadir (*from + ger* de + *infin*); (*prevent*) impedir (*from doing* hacer); *enemy etc* refrenar; **I was —red by the cost** el precio me hizo abandonar la idea; **a weapon which —s nobody** un arma que no refrena a nadie, un arma sin fuerza disuasoria; **don't let the weather — you** no dejes de hacerlo por el mal tiempo.

detergent [di'tə:dʒənt] **1** *adj* detergente. **2** *n* detergente *m*.

deteriorate [di'tiəriəreit] *vi* empeorar, deteriorarse.

deterioration [di,tiəriə'reiʃən] *n* deterioro *m*, empeoramiento *m* (*in* de).

determination [di.tə:mi'neiʃən] n (act) determinación f; (resolve) resolución f; **he set off with great —** partió muy resuelto; **in his — to do it** estando resuelto a hacerlo.

determine [di'tə:min] 1 vt (a) (ascertain, define) determinar; date etc señalar, fijar; scope, limits, boundary definir; future course, person's fate decidir; dispute determinar, resolver; (be the deciding factor in) determinar; **to — what is to be done** decidir lo que hay que hacer; **to — whether something is true** decidir si algo es verdad; **we couldn't — who it was** no podíamos decidir quién era; **demand —s supply** la demanda determina la oferta; **to be —d by** depender de.

(b) (impel) **this —d him to go** esto le determinó a ir.

(c) (resolve) **to — to do something** decidir hacer algo, resolverse a hacer algo.

2 vi: **to — on** optar por.

determined [di'tə:mind] adj person resuelto; effort resuelto, enérgico; **he's very — about it** está muy empeñado en ello; **to be — to do something** estar resuelto a hacer algo.

determining [di'tə:miniŋ] adj decisivo.

determinism [di'tə:minizəm] n determinismo m.

deterrent [di'terənt] 1 adj disuasivo, disuasorio.

2 n freno m, impedimento m (on, to para); medida f represiva; (Mil) fuerza f disuasiva, fuerza f disuasoria, amenaza f; **the nuclear —** la amenaza nuclear; **to act as a — to** servir como un freno para, ser una amenaza a, refrenar.

detest [di'test] vt detestar, aborrecer.

detestable [di'testəbl] adj detestable, aborrecible.

detestation [.di:tes'teiʃən] n detestación f, aborrecimiento m; **to hold in —** aborrecer.

dethrone [di:'θrəun] vt destronar.

detonate ['detəneit] 1 vt hacer detonar. 2 vi detonar, estallar.

detonation [.detə'neiʃən] n detonación f.

detonator ['detəneitə*] n detonador m, cápsula f fulminante.

detour ['deituə*] n rodeo m, vuelta f; **to make a —** desviarse, hacer un rodeo.

detract [di'trækt] vi: **to — from** quitar mérito (or atractivo etc) a, desvirtuar, restar valor a.

detractor [di'træktə*] n detractor m, ora f.

detriment ['detrimənt] n perjuicio m; **to the — of** en perjuicio de, en detrimento de.

detrimental [.detri'mentl] adj perjudicial (to a, para).

detritus [di'traitəs] n detrito m, talud m detrítico.

de trop [də'trəu] adv: **to be —** estar de más, sobrar.

deuce [dju:s] 1 adv (Tennis) a dos.

2 n: **a — of a row** un tremendo jaleo; **a — of a mess** una terrible confusión; **the — it is!** ¡qué demonio!; **what the . . .?** ¿qué demonios . . .?; **where the — . . .?** ¿dónde demonios . . .?; **to play the — with** arruinar, estropear.

deuced [dju:st] 1 adj maldito. 2 adv diabólicamente, terriblemente.

deuterium [dju:'tiəriəm] n deuterio m.

devaluate [di:'væljueit] vt desvalorizar, desvalorar.

devaluation [.di:vælju'eiʃən] n desvalorización f, devaluación f.

devalue ['di:'vælju:] vt desvalorizar, devaluar.

devastate ['devəsteit] vt devastar, asolar; person hundir en la tristeza; **we were simply —d** la noticia nos produjo una enorme tristeza.

devastating ['devəsteitiŋ] adj devastador; (fig) arrollador.

devastation [.devə'steiʃən] n (act) devastación f; (state) devastación f, ruinas fpl.

develop [di'veləp] 1 vt desarrollar (also Math); desenvolver; (encourage) fomentar; process perfeccionar; land urbanizar; resources, mine etc explotar; (Phot) revelar; engine trouble empezar a tener; disease coger, empezar a sufrir de, mostrar los síntomas de; tendency coger, dar en; liking mostrar, acusar; power rendir, producir.

2 vi (a) desarrollarse; progresar, avanzar; evolucionar; **how is the book —ing?** ¿qué tal te va el libro?

(b) (appear) aparecer, mostrarse.

developer [di'veləpə*] n (Phot) revelador m.

developing [di'veləpiŋ] adj country en vías de desarrollo.

development [di'veləpmənt] n (a) desarrollo m; progreso m; evolución f; (encouragement) fomento m; (of land) urbanización f; (of resources) explotación f; (Phot) revelado m; **— area** polo m de promoción.

(b) new — cambio m, novedad f.

deviate ['di:vieit] vi desviarse (from de).

deviation [.di:vi'eiʃən] n desviación f (also Med).

deviationism [.di:vi'eiʃənizəm] n desviacionismo m.

deviationist [.di:vi'eiʃənist] 1 adj desviacionista. 2 n desviacionista mf.

device [di'vais] n (a) (Mech) aparato m, mecanismo m, dispositivo m; **nuclear —** ingenio m nuclear.

(b) (scheme) estratagema f, recurso m.

(c) (emblem) emblema m; (motto) lema m.

(d) **to leave someone to his own —s** dejar a uno hacer lo que le dé la gana, dejar a uno divertirse con sus propias cosas.

devil ['devl] 1 n (a) diablo m, demonio m; (fire) arrojo m, energía f; little — diablillo m; printer's — aprendiz m de imprenta; **a poor —** un pobre diablo.

(b) **the —!** ¡demonio!; **the — it is!** ¡qué demonio!; **what the . . .?** ¿qué demonios . . .?; **like the —** como el demonio.

(c) **a — of a mess** una terrible confusión; **a — of a noise** un ruido de todos los demonios; **we had the — of a job** we had the **—'s own job** nos costó muchísimo trabajo (to get obtener); **it's a — of a problem** es un problema dificilísimo.

(d) **the — take it!** ¡que se lo lleve el diablo!; **go to the —!** ¡vete al diablo!; **to be between the — and the deep blue sea** estar entre la espada y la pared; **better the — we know** vale más lo malo conocido que lo bueno por conocer; **the — finds work for idle hands** cuando el diablo no tiene que hacer con el rabo mata moscas; **to give the — his due** a cada uno lo suyo; para ser justo hasta con los adversarios; **there'll be the — to pay** esto nos va a costar muy caro, ahí será el diablo; **to play the — with** arruinar, estropear; **to raise the —** armar la gorda; **talk of the —!** ¡hablando del ruin de Roma, por la puerta asoma!

2 vt meat asar con mucho picante.

3 vi: **to — for** (Law) trabajar de aprendiz para.

devilfish ['devlfiʃ] n raya f, manta f.

devilish ['devliʃ] 1 adj diabólico. 2 adv sumamente, la mar de.

devil-may-care ['devlmei'kɛə*] adj despreocupado; (rash) temerario, arriesgado.

devilment ['devlmənt] n diablura f.

devilry ['devlri] n (wickedness) maldad f, crueldad f; (mischief) diablura f.

devious ['di:viəs] adj path tortuoso; (means) intrincado, enrevesado; person taimado.

devise [di'vaiz] vt idear, inventar.

devitalize [di:'vaitəlaiz] vt debilitar, privar de vitalidad.

devoid [di'void] adj: **— of** desprovisto de.

devolution [.di:və'lu:ʃən] n (Pol etc) delegación f (de poderes).

devolve [di'vɔlv] vi: **to — upon** incumbir a, corresponder a; **it —s upon me to + infin** me toca a mí + infin.

devote [di'vəut] 1 vt dedicar (to a; to + ger a + infin); **he is —d to her** la quiere con verdadera devoción; **this room is —d to Goya** esta sala está dedicada a Goya; **this chapter is —d to politics** este capítulo trata de la política.

2 vr: **to — oneself to** dedicarse a.

devoted [di'vəutid] adj leal, fiel.

devotedly [di'vəutidli] adv con devoción.

devotee [.devəu'ti:] n devoto m, a f (of de).

devotion [di'vəuʃən] n devoción f (to a); (to studies etc) dedicación f (to a); (of friend etc) lealtad f; **—s** oraciones fpl.

devotional [di'vəuʃənl] adj piadoso, devoto.

devour [di'vauə*] vt devorar (also fig), comerse; **to be —ed with curiosity** no caber en sí de curiosidad.

devouring [di'vauəriŋ] adj (fig) absorbente.

devout [di'vaut] adj devoto, piadoso.

devoutly [di'vautli] adv con devoción, piadosamente.

dew [dju:] n rocío m.

dewdrop ['dju:drɔp] n gota f de rocío.

dewlap ['dju:læp] n papada f.

dewpond ['dju:pɔnd] n charca f formada por el rocío.

dewy ['dju:i] adj rociado; lleno de rocío; eyes húmedo.

dewy-eyed ['dju:i'aid] adj (fig) ingenuo.

dexterity [deks'teriti] n destreza f.

dextrose ['dekstrəus] n dextrosa f.

dextrous ['dekstrəs] adj diestro.

dextrously ['dekstrəsli] adv diestramente.

diabetes [.daiə'bi:ti:z] n diabetes f.

diabetic [.daiə'betik] 1 adj diabético. 2 n diabético m, a f.

diabolic(al) [.daiə'bɔlik(əl)] adj diabólico.

diacritic [.daiə'kritik] 1 adj (also —al) diacrítico. 2 n signo m diacrítico.

diadem ['daiədem] n diadema f.

diaeresis [dai'erisis] n diéresis f.

diagnose ['daiəgnəuz] vt diagnosticar.

diagnosis [.daiəg'nəusis] n diagnóstico m.
diagnostic [.daiəg'nɔstik] adj diagnóstico.
diagonal [dai'ægənl] 1 adj diagonal 2 n diagonal f.
diagonally [dai'ægənəli] adv diagonalmente.
diagram ['daiəgræm] n diagrama m, esquema m.
diagrammatic [.daiəgrə'mætik] adj esquemático.
dial ['daiəl] 1 n esfera f, cuadrante m; (Tel) disco m; (sl) cara f. 2 vt marcar.
dialect ['daiəlekt] 1 n dialecto m. 2 attr dialectal.
dialectal [.daiə'lektl] adj dialectal.
dialectic [.daiə'lektik] 1 adj dialéctico; (Gram) dialectal. 2 n (also —s) dialéctica f.
dialectical [.daiə'lektikəl] adj dialéctico; (Gram) dialectal.
dialling tone ['daiəliɲ.təun] n tono m de marcar.
dialogue ['daiəlɔg] n diálogo m.
diameter [dai'æmitə*] n diámetro m.
diametrical [.daiə'metrikəl] adj diametral.
diametrically [.daiə'metrikəli] adv: — opposed to diametralmente opuesto a.
diamond ['daiəmənd] n diamante m; —s (Cards) diamantes mpl, carreau m, (in Spanish pack) oros mpl; **rough** — diamante m bruto (also fig); — **cut** — tal para cual.
diamond-cutter ['daiəmənd,kʌtə*] n diamantista m.
diamond-shaped ['daiəmənd,ʃeipt] adj de forma de diamante.
Diana [dai'ænə] f Diana.
diaper ['daiəpə*] n (US) pañal m.
diaphanous [dai'æfənəs] adj diáfano.
diaphragm ['daiəfræm] n diafragma m.
diarist ['daiərist] n diarista mf.
diarrhoea [.daiə'riːə] n diarrea f.
diary ['daiəri] n diario m; (engagement —) agenda f, diario m.
diatonic [.daiə'tɔnik] adj diatónico.
diatribe ['daiətraib] n diatriba f.
dibble ['dibl] 1 n plantador m. 2 vt (also to — in) plantar con plantador.
dibs [dibz] n (sl) parné m.
dice [dais] 1 npl dados mpl; (shapes) cubitos mpl, cuadritos mpl. 2 vt vegetables cortar en cuadritos. 3 vi jugar a los dados; **to — with death** jugar con la muerte.
dicey ['daisi] adj (fam) incierto, dudoso; peligroso; difícil.
dichotomy [di'kɔtəmi] n dicotomía f.
Dick [dik] m nombre cariñoso de **Richard.**
dick [dik] n (US sl) detective m.
dickens ['dikinz] (euph) en muchas frases = **devil.**
dicker ['dikə*] vi (a) vacilar, titubear. (b) (Comm) regatear.
dickey, dicky¹ ['diki] n (fam) (a) (Zool) pajarito m. (b) (shirt front) pechera f postiza. (c) (Aut) asiento m trasero.
dicky² ['diki] adj (fam) poco firme, inestable; (Med) **to feel** — sentirse algo indispuesto; **to have a** — **heart** tener una debilidad cardíaca.
dictaphone ['diktəfəun] n (Protected Trade Name) dictáfono m.
dictate ['dikteit] n mandato m; —s dictados mpl.
dictate [dik'teit] 1 vt (say aloud) dictar; (order) mandar, disponer; **I will not be** —**d** to yo no estoy a las órdenes de nadie.
2 vi: **to** — **to one's secretary** dictar a su secretaria.
dictation [dik'teiʃən] n (a) dictado m; **to take** —, **to write at the** — **of** escribir al dictado de. (b) (order) mandato m.
dictator [dik'teitə*] n dictador m.
dictatorial [.diktə'tɔːriəl] adj dictatorio; manner etc dictatorial, imperioso.
dictatorship [dik'teitəʃip] n dictadura f.
diction ['dikʃən] n dicción f; lengua f, lenguaje m.
dictionary ['dikʃənri] n diccionario m.
dictum ['diktəm] n, pl **dicta** ['diktə] sentencia f, aforismo m; (Law) dictamen m.
did [did] pret of **do.**
didactic [di'dæktik] adj didáctico.
diddle ['didl] vt (fam) estafar; **to** — **someone out of something** estafar algo a uno.
didn't ['didənt] = **did not.**
die¹ [dai] vi morir (from, of de; for por); (wither) marchitarse; (disappear) desvanecerse, desaparecer; (light) palidecer, extinguirse; **to** — **like flies** morir como chinches; **we nearly died!** (fam) era para morirse de risa; **never say** —! ¡ánimo!, ¡mientras hay vida hay esperanza!; **to** — **away** acabarse gradualmente; desaparecer; (sound) cesar, dejar poco a poco de oírse; **to** — **down** (fire) apagarse; (wind) perder su fuerza, amainar; (discontent etc) sosegarse; (battle etc) hacerse menos violento; **the custom dies hard** la costumbre tarda bastante en

desaparecer; **to** — **off** morir; **to** — **out** extinguirse, desaparecer; **to be dying for something** morirse por algo, perecerse por algo; **to be dying to** + infin morirse por + infin; **to** — **a violent death** tener una muerte violenta.
die² [dai] n (a) (pl **dice** [dais]) dado m; **the** — **is cast** la suerte está echada. (b) (pl **dies** [daiz]) cuño m, troquel m; matriz f.
die-casting ['dai'kɑːstiɲ] n pieza f fundida a troquel.
diehard ['daihɑːd] 1 adj intransigente, cerrado, acérrimo. 2 n incondicional m, intransigente m.
dieresis [dai'erisis] n (US) = **diaeresis.**
diesel-electric ['diːzəli'lektrik] adj dieseleléctrico.
Diesel engine ['diːzəl,endʒin] n motor m Diesel.
Diesel oil ['diːzəl,ɔil] n gas-oil m, gasóleo m (Acad).
die-sinker ['dai,siɲkə*] n grabador m de troqueles.
diet¹ ['daiət] 1 n régimen m, dieta f; **to be on a** — estar a dieta; **to put someone on a** — poner a uno a dieta. 2 vi estar a dieta.
diet² ['daiət] n (Pol) dieta f.
dietary ['daiətəri] adj dietético.
dietetic [.daii'tetik] 1 adj dietético. 2 —s n dietética f.
dietician [.daii'tiʃən] n dietético m, dieteta mf.
differ ['difə*] vi (a) **they** — (things) son distintos, (persons) no están de acuerdo; **the texts** — los textos discrepan.
(b) **to** — **from** ser distinto de, diferenciarse de, discrepar de; **how does this** — **from that?** ¿en qué se diferencia éste de aquél?
(c) (personal subject) **I beg to** — tengo que decir que no estoy de acuerdo; **we** — **ed about it** no estábamos de acuerdo sobre ello; **I** — **from you** no estoy de acuerdo contigo; **I** — **from your opinion** discrepo de tu opinión, no comparto tu opinión.
difference ['difrəns] n diferencia f; — **of opinion** desacuerdo m, (euph) controversia f, (euph: quarrel) riña f; **a novel with a** — una novela que tiene algo distintivo; **it makes no** — lo mismo da; **it makes a lot of** — importa mucho; **what** — **does it make?** ¿qué más da?; **it will make no** — **to us** no nos afectará en lo más mínimo; **I see no** — **between them** no les veo diferencia alguna; **to split the** — partir la diferencia.
different ['difrənt] adj diferente, distinto (from de).
differently ['difrəntli] adv de modo distinto, de otro modo.
differential [.difə'renʃəl] 1 adj diferencial. 2 n (Math, Aut) diferencial f.
differentiate [.difə'renʃieit] 1 vt distinguir (from de). 2 vi diferenciarse (also Bio); **to** — **between two things** distinguir entre dos cosas.
difficult ['difikəlt] adj difícil; **to make life** — **for someone** hacer la vida imposible a uno.
difficulty ['difikəlti] n dificultad f; (jam) apuro m, aprieto m; **to get into difficulties** hacerse un lío, meterse en apuros, (eg while swimming) encontrarse sin fuerzas para continuar; (ship) encontrarse en peligro; **to have** — **in breathing** tener la respiración penosa; **he's having difficulties with his wife** está a malas con su mujer; **we have** — **in getting enough staff** es difícil encontrar bastante personal; **I find** — **in walking** encuentro difícil el ir a pie; **to make difficulties for someone** poner estorbos a uno; **I see no** — **in admitting that** no hay dificultad para reconocer que.
diffidence ['difidəns] n timidez f, falta f de confianza en sí mismo.
diffident ['difidənt] adj tímido, falto de confianza en sí mismo.
diffidently ['difidəntli] adv tímidamente, con timidez.
diffract [di'frækt] vt difractar.
diffraction [di'frækʃən] n difracción f.
diffuse [di'fjuːs] adj difuso; (long-winded) prolijo.
diffuse [di'fjuːz] 1 vt difundir. 2 vi difundirse.
diffused [di'fjuːzd] adj difuso.
diffusion [di'fjuːʒən] n difusión f.
dig [dig] 1 n (a) (archaeological etc) excavación f. (b) (prod) empujón m; (with elbow) codazo m.
(c) (remark) indirecta f, zumba f; **to have a** — **at** aludir irónicamente a, tomar el pelo a.
2 (irr: pret and ptp **dug**) vt (a) cavar, excavar; (of animals) escarbar; garden cultivar, patch of earth remover con laya; coal extraer, sacar; teeth, nails hincar (into en); **to** — **in manure** añadir abonos al suelo; **to** — **out** hole excavar; (buried object) sacar cavando, extraer; thorn in flesh extraer; (fig) sacar, buscar; **to** — **up** desenterrar (also fig), descubrir; potatoes sacar; plant desarraigar; roadway etc levantar.
(b) (prod) empujar, dar un codazo a; **to** — **someone in the ribs** dar a uno un codazo en las costillas.

(c) (sl) **I don't — jazz** no me gusta el jazz, el jazz no me dice nada.

3 vi (a) cavar; **to — deeper into a subject** ahondar en un tema; **to — for gold** cavar en busca de oro; **to — in** (Mil) atrincherarse; (fam) empezar a comer; **to — into** reserves etc consumir, devorar; **he dug into his pocket** metió la mano en el bolsillo; **to — into a meal** empezar a zamparse una comida.

(b) (fam: lodge) alojarse, estar alojado, hospedarse.

digest ['daidʒest] n resumen m; (Law) digesto m.

digest [dai'dʒest] vt food digerir; (think over) meditar; knowledge, territory asimilar; insult tragarse; opinion aceptar.

digestible [di'dʒestəbl] adj digerible; **easily —** fácil de digerir.

digestion [di'dʒestʃən] n digestión f.

digestive [di'dʒestiv] adj digestivo. ··

digger ['digə*] n cavador m; (archaeological) excavador m, ora f; (fam) australiano m.

diggings ['diginz] npl (archaeological) excavaciones fpl; (fam) pensión f, alojamiento m.

digit ['didʒit] n dígito m.

digital ['didʒitəl] adj digital.

digitalis [ˌdidʒi'teilis] n digital f.

dignified ['dignifaid] adj grave, solemne; gait etc majestuoso; action decoroso; **it's not — to +** infin no es elegante + infin.

dignify ['dignifai] vt dar un título altisonante a.

dignitary ['dignitəri] n dignatario m, dignidad f.

dignity ['digniti] n dignidad f; **it would be beneath my — to +** infin desmerecería de mi dignidad + infin; **to stand on one's —** ponerse en su lugar.

digress [dai'gres] vi hacer una digresión; **to — from** apartarse de; **but I —** pero vamos al grano.

digression [dai'greʃən] n digresión f.

digs [digz] npl (fam) pensión f, alojamiento m.

dike [daik] n (embankment) dique m (also fig); (ditch) canal m, acequia f.

dilapidated [di'læpideitid] adj building etc desmoronado, ruinoso; vehicle etc desvencijado.

dilapidation [diˌlæpi'deiʃən] n estado m ruinoso; lo desvencijado.

dilate [dai'leit] **1** vt dilatar. **2** vi dilatarse; **to — upon** dilatarse sobre.

dilation [dai'leiʃən] n dilatación f.

dilatory ['dilətəri] adj tardo, lento; **to be — in replying** tardar mucho en contestar.

dilemma [dai'lemə] n dilema m; **to be in a —** estar en un dilema.

dilettante [ˌdili'tænti] n, pl **dilettanti** [ˌdili'tænti] diletante mf.

diligence ['dilidʒəns] n diligencia f.

diligent ['dilidʒənt] adj diligente.

diligently ['dilidʒəntli] adv diligentemente.

dillydally ['dilidæli] vi (fam) vacilar; (loiter) perder el tiempo.

dilute [dai'luːt] **1** adj diluido. **2** vt diluir; (fig) adulterar.

dilution [dai'luːʃən] n dilución f; (fig) adulteración f.

dim [dim] **1** adj light débil; sight turbio; room etc oscuro, sombrío; object, outline indistinto, confuso; (fam) opinion poco favorable; person lerdo.

2 vt light reducir la intensidad de; headlamps poner a media luz; (fig) splendour ofuscar, oscurecer; memory borrar.

dime [daim] n (US) moneda de 10 centavos; **— novel** novelucha f.

dimension [di'menʃən] n dimensión f.

diminish [di'miniʃ] **1** vt disminuir. **2** vi disminuir(se).

diminishing [di'miniʃiŋ] adj menguante.

diminuendo [diˌminju'endəu] n (Mus) diminuendo m.

diminution [ˌdimi'njuːʃən] n disminución f.

diminutive [di'minjutiv] **1** adj diminuto; (Gram) diminutivo. **2** n diminutivo m.

dimly ['dimli] adv shine etc débilmente; see confusamente; **one could — make out forms** se veían indistintamente unos bultos.

dimness ['dimnis] n debilidad f; lo turbio; oscuridad f, semioscuridad f, lo sombrío; lo indistinto, lo confuso; lo lerdo.

dimple ['dimpl] **1** n hoyuelo m. **2** vt formar hoyuelos en; water rizar. **3** vi formarse hoyuelos; (water) rizarse.

dimwit ['dimwit] n (fam) imbécil mf.

dim-witted ['dim'witid] adj (fam) lerdo, imbécil.

din [din] **1** n estruendo m, estrépito m.

2 vt: **to —something into someone** hacer que uno se dé cuenta de algo a fuerza de repetírselo; **I had it —ned into me as a child** lo aprendí de niño a fuerza de repeticiones.

3 vi: **it —s in my ears** me taladra el oído.

dinar ['diːnɑː*] n dinar m.

dine [dain] **1** vt dar de cenar a; **they —d me very well** me dieron muy bien de cenar.

2 vi cenar; **to — off, to — on** cenar; **to — out** cenar fuera; **to — out on a story** ser invitado a cenar a costa de un cuento.

diner ['dainə*] n comensal m; (Rail) coche-comedor m.

dinette [di'net] n comedor m pequeño, comedorcito m.

ding-dong ['diŋ'dɔŋ] **1** n: **—!** ¡din don! **2** adj battle furioso, muy reñido.

dinghy ['diŋgi] n bote m; (Aer) **rubber —** lancha f neumática.

dinginess ['dindʒinis] n lo deslustrado, deslucimiento m; color m oscuro; lo sombrío, oscuridad f; lo sucio.

dingo ['diŋgəu] n, pl **dingoes** ['diŋgəuz] dingo m.

dingy ['dindʒi] adj (dull) deslustrado, deslucido; (dark in colour) de color oscuro; room etc sombrío, oscuro; (dirty) sucio.

dining car ['dainiŋkɑː*] n coche-comedor m.

dining room ['dainiŋrum] n comedor m.

dinky ['diŋki] adj (fam) (small) pequeñito; (nice) mono, precioso.

dinner ['dinə*] n (evening meal) cena f; (lunch) comida f; (public feast) cena f, banquete m; **can you come to —?** ¿puede venir a cenar?; **to have —** cenar, comer; **when he retired they gave him a —** cuando se jubiló le obsequiaron con una cena.

dinner jacket ['dinəˌdʒækit] n smoking m, esmoquin m (Acad).

dinner party ['dinəˌpɑːti] n cena f.

dinner service ['dinəˌsəːvis] n vajilla f.

dinner suit ['dinəsuːt] n smoking m, esmoquin m (Acad).

dinner table ['dinəˌteibl] n mesa f de comedor.

dinner time ['dinətaim] n hora f de cenar (or comer).

dinosaur ['dainəsɔː*] n dinosaurio m.

dint [dint] **1** n: **by — of** a fuerza de. **2** vt abollar.

diocesan [dai'ɔsisən] adj diocesano.

diocese ['daiəsis] n diócesis f.

dip [dip] **1** n (a) (bath, bathe) baño m; **to go for a —** ir a bañarse.

(b) (Geol) buzamiento m; (of horizon) depresión f; (slope) pendiente f; inclinación f; (to one side) ladeo m.

(c) **lucky —** (approx) tómbola f.

2 vt (a) (put into liquid) bañar, mojar (in, into en); pen mojar; (ladle, scoop etc meter; flag bajar, saludar con; headlamps poner a media luz.

(b) **to — water out with a bucket** sacar agua con un cubo.

3 vi (a) (slope down) inclinarse hacia abajo; (Geol) buzar; **the road —s into the valley** la carretera baja hacia el valle.

(b) (move down) (bird, plane) bajar; **the sun —ped below the hill** el sol desapareció tras la colina.

(c) **to — into one's pocket** meter la mano en el bolsillo; **to — into a book** hojear un libro, leer distraídamente un libro.

diphtheria [dif'θiəriə] n difteria f.

diphthong ['difθɔŋ] n diptongo m.

diphthongize ['difθəŋaiz] **1** vt diptongar. **2** vi diptongarse.

diploma [di'pləumə] n diploma m.

diplomacy [di'pləuməsi] n diplomacia f.

diplomat ['dipləmæt] n diplomático m.

diplomatic [ˌdiplə'mætik] adj diplomático.

diplomatically [ˌdiplə'mætikəli] adv diplomáticamente.

diplomatist [di'pləumətist] n diplomático m.

dipper[1] ['dipə*] n (Orn) mirlo m acuático.

dipper[2] ['dipə*] n: **big —** montaña f rusa.

dippy ['dipi] adj (sl) chiflado.

dipso ['dipsəu] (fam) **1** adj dipsomaníaco. **2** n dipsomaníaco m, a f, dipsómano m, a f.

dipsomania [ˌdipsəu'meiniə] n dipsomanía f.

dipsomaniac [ˌdipsəu'meiniæk] n dipsomaníaco m, a f, dipsómano m, a f.

dipstick ['dipstik] n varilla f para comprobar el nivel del aceite (etc).

dire ['daiə*] adj horrendo, calamitoso.

direct [dai'rekt] **1** adj directo; current continuo; answer claro, inequívoco; manner, character abierto, franco.

2 adv (in a — manner) directamente; (straight) derecho, en línea recta.

3 vt (a) letter, remark, gaze, attention, film etc dirigir (at, to a).

(b) **can you — me to the shop?** ¿me hace el favor de decirme dónde está la tienda?, ¿podría Vd indicarme la dirección de la tienda?.

(c) (control) dirigir, gobernar, controlar.

(d) (order) mandar; **to — that** mandar que; **to**

— **someone to do something** mandar a uno hacer algo.

direction [di'rekʃən] n **(a)** (act of managing) dirección f.

　(b) (course) dirección f; **in the — of** en la dirección de, hacia; **in the opposite —** en sentido contrario; **in all —s** por todos lados; **they ran off in different —s** salieron corriendo cada uno por su lado.

　(c) **—s** órdenes fpl, instrucciones fpl; **—s for use** modo m de empleo.

directional [di'rekʃənl] adj direccional.

direction finder [di'rekʃən,faində*] n radiogonió-metro m.

directive [di'rektiv] n orden f, instrucción f.

directly [di'rektli] **1** adv (in a direct manner) directa-mente; (in a straight line) derecho, en línea recta; (at once) en seguida; **— opposite** exactamente en frente (de).

　2 conj: **— you hear it** en cuanto lo oigas.

directness [dai'rektnis] n franqueza f.

director [di'rektə*] n (Comm, Cine etc) director m; **managing —** director m gerente.

directorate [dai'rektərit] n **(a)** (post) dirección f, cargo m de director. **(b)** (body) junta f directiva, consejo m de administración.

directorship [di'rektəʃip] n cargo m de director.

directory [di'rektəri] n (Tel) guía f telefónica.

dirge [də:dʒ] n endecha f.

dirigible ['diridʒəbl] **1** adj dirigible. **2** n dirigible m.

dirk [də:k] n puñal m.

dirt [də:t] n (unclean matter) suciedad f, mugre f, (litter) basura f; (earth) tierra f; (mud) lodo m; (obscenity) suciedad f, inmundicia f; (worthless stuff) porquería f; **to treat someone like —** tratar a uno como una basura.

dirt-cheap ['də:t'tʃi:p] adj tirado, muy barato.

dirt road ['də:trəud] n (US) camino m sin firme.

dirt track ['də:ttræk] n pista f de ceniza.

dirty ['də:ti] **1** adj sucio; (grubby) mugriento; (stained) manchado; (trick, play etc) sucio; (novel, story, joke) verde, indecente, sucio; (weather) horrible.

　2 n: **to do the — on someone** hacer una mala pasada a uno.

　3 vt ensuciar; (stain) manchar.

disability [,disə'biliti] n (state) incapacidad f; (feature) impedimento m, estorbo m, desventaja f.

disable [dis'eibl] vt (cripple) estropear, mutilar; ship etc inutilizar; (disqualify etc) incapacitar, inhabilitar (for para).

disabled [dis'eibld] adj person mutilado.

disablement [dis'eiblmənt] n inhabilitación f.

disabuse [,disə'bju:z] vt desengañar (of de).

disadvantage [,disəd'va:ntidʒ] n desventaja f, inconveniente m; **to be at a —** estar en una situa-ción desventajosa; **to be taken at a —** encontrarse en una situación violenta.

disadvantageous [,disædva:n'teidʒəs] adj desventa-joso.

disaffected [,disə'fektid] adj desafecto (towards hacia).

disaffection [,disə'fekʃən] n descontento m.

disagree [,disə'gri:] vi **(a)** no estar de acuerdo (about, on sobre, with con), discrepar (with de); **I — with you** no estoy de acuerdo contigo, discrepo de ti, no comparto esa opinión; **their findings —** discrepan sus conclusiones.

　(b) **I — with bullfighting** yo no apruebo el toreo.

　(c) (quarrel) reñir.

　(d) (of food etc) **to — with** sentar mal a, hacer daño a.

disagreeable [,disə'gri:əbl] adj desagradable; (bad-tempered) displicente, de mal genio; tone of voice etc malhumorado, áspero; **he was very — to me** me trató con bastante aspereza; **I'm rather — in the mornings** por la mañana estoy de bastante mal humor.

disagreement [,disə'gri:mənt] n **(a)** desacuerdo m, disconformidad f (with con); discrepancia f (with de).

　(b) (quarrel) riña f, altercado m.

disallow ['disə'lau] vt no aceptar, no sancionar; goal anular.

disappear [,disə'piə*] vi desaparecer.

disappearance [,disə'piərəns] n desaparición f.

disappoint [,disə'pɔint] vt decepcionar, desilusionar; hopes defraudar; **we were —ed with the book** el libro nos decepcionó; **we shall be —ed if you don't come** sentiremos mucho que no vengas.

disappointing [,disə'pɔintiŋ] adj decepcionante, desilusionante; **it is — that** es triste que + subj.

disappointment [,disə'pɔintmənt] n decepción f, desilusión f; (event) contratiempo m; **— in love** fracaso m sentimental; **he is a big — to us** nos ha decepcionado muchísimo.

disapproval [,disə'pru:vəl] n desaprobación f.

disapprove [,disə'pru:v] vi: **to — of** thing desaprobar; person tener poca simpatía a; **I strongly —** yo estoy firmemente en contra; **but father —d** pero papá no quiso permitirlo.

disapproving [,disə'pru:viŋ] adj look etc de desapro-bación.

disapprovingly [,disə'pru:viŋli] adv con desapro-bación.

disarm [dis'a:m] **1** vt desarmar. **2** vi desarmarse.

disarmament [dis'a:məmənt] n desarme m.

disarming [dis'a:miŋ] adj smile etc encantador; speech conciliador.

disarrange ['disə'reindʒ] vt desarreglar, descomponer.

disarray ['disə'rei] n desorden m, confusión f; **in —** desordenado.

disassemble ['disə'sembl] vt (US) desmontar.

disaster [di'za:stə*] n desastre m; **to court —** correr al desastre.

disastrous [di'za:strəs] adj catastrófico, desastroso.

disastrously [di'za:strəsli] adv catastróficamente.

disavow ['disə'vau] vt desconocer, rechazar.

disband [dis'bænd] **1** vt army licenciar; organization disolver. **2** vi desbandarse; disolverse.

disbelief ['disbə'li:f] n incredulidad f.

disbelieve ['disbə'li:v] vt no creer, desconfiar de.

disbeliever ['disbə'li:və*] n incrédulo m, a f; (Eccl) descreído m, a f.

disburden [dis'bə:dn] **1** vt descargar. **2** vr: **to — oneself of** descargarse de.

disburse [dis'bə:s] vt desembolsar.

disbursement [dis'bə:smənt] n desembolso m.

disc [disk] n disco m.

discard ['diska:d] n descarte m.

discard [dis'ka:d] **1** vt descartar (also Cards), rechazar, desechar; clothing dejar de llevar; un-wanted thing tirar; habit renunciar a.

　2 vi descartar(se).

discern [di'sə:n] vt percibir, discernir.

discernible [di'sə:nəbl] adj perceptible.

discerning [di'sə:niŋ] adj perspicaz.

discernment [di'sə:nment] n perspicacia f, discerni-miento m.

discharge [dis'tʃa:dʒ] **1** n (of weapon, Elec) descarga f; (unloading) descargue m; (of debt) pago m, descargo m; (of duty) desempeño m, ejecución f; (Mil) licenciamiento m; (of worker) despedida f; (Med) pus m.

　2 vt weapon, current, cargo, ship descargar; shot, arrow disparar; debt pagar, descargar; duty desem-peñar, cumplir; task ejecutar; troops licenciar; worker despedir; person from duty dispensar, exonerar (from de); prisoner poner en libertad; patient dar de alta; **to be —d from the army** ser licenciado del ejército; **they —d him from hospital on Monday** le dieron de alta el lunes.

　3 vi (river, Elec) descargar (into en); (Med) supurar.

disc harrow ['diskhærəu] n grada f de discos.

disciple [di'saipl] n discípulo m, a f.

disciplinarian [,disipli'nɛəriən] n ordenancista mf.

disciplinary ['disiplinəri] adj disciplinario.

discipline ['disiplin] **1** n disciplina f. **2** vt disciplinar.

disc jockey ['disk,dʒɔki] n (Radio) presentador m de discos.

disclaim [dis'kleim] vt negar, rechazar; desconocer; (Law) renunciar a; **he —ed all knowledge of it** dijo que no sabía nada en absoluto de ello.

disclaimer [dis'kleimə*] n negación f; (Law) renuncia f; **to put in a —** negarlo, rechazarlo.

disclose [dis'kləuz] vt revelar.

disclosure [dis'kləuʒə*] n revelación f.

discolour, (US) **discolor** [dis'kʌlə*] **1** vt descolorar. **2** vi descolorarse.

discolo(u)ration [dis,kʌlə'reiʃən] n descoloramiento m.

discomfit [dis'kʌmfit] vt desconcertar.

discomfiture [dis'kʌmfitʃə*] n desconcierto m, confusión f.

discomfort [dis'kʌmfət] n (lack of comfort) incomo-didad f, falta f de comodidades; (physical) malestar m; (uneasiness) inquietud f.

discomposure [,diskəm'pəuʒə*] n desconcierto m, confusión f.

disconcert [,diskən'sə:t] vt desconcertar.

disconcerting [,diskən'sə:tiŋ] adj desconcertante.

disconcertingly [,diskən'sə:tiŋli] adv de modo desconcertante; **he spoke in a — frank way** desconcertó a todos hablando con tanta franqueza.

disconnect [diskə'nekt] vt separar, desacoplar; (Elec) desconectar.

disconnected ['diskə'nektid] adj (fig) inconexo.

disconsolate [dis'kɔnsəlit] *adj* inconsolable.
disconsolately [dis'kɔnsəlitli] *adv* inconsolablemente.
discontent ['diskən'tent] *n* descontento *m*.
discontented ['diskən'tentid] *adj* descontento, disgustado.
discontentment ['diskən'tentmənt] *n* descontento *m*.
discontinue ['diskən'tinju:] *vt* descontinuar; *payment* suspender; *newspaper etc* anular el abono de.
discontinuous ['diskən'tinjuəs] *adj* discontinuo.
discord ['diskɔːd] *n* discordia *f*; (*Mus*) disonancia *f*; **to sow — among** sembrar cizaña entre.
discordant [dis'kɔːdənt] *adj* discorde; (*Mus*) disonante.
discothèque ['diskəutek] *n* discoteca *f*.
discount ['diskaunt] *n* descuento *m*, rebaja *f*; **to be at a — (***fig*) no valorarse en su justo precio.
discount [dis'kaunt] *vt* descontar, rebajar; (*leave out of account*) dejar a un lado, descartar, desechar; *report etc* considerar exagerado.
discourage [dis'kʌridʒ] *vt person* desalentar, desanimar; *development etc* oponerse a, desaprobar; *tendency* resistir; **to — someone from doing something** disuadir a uno de hacer algo.
discouragement [dis'kʌridʒmənt] *n* desaliento *m*; oposición *f*; desaprobación *f*; disuasión *f*; (*obstacle*) estorbo *m*; **it's a real — to progress** es un verdadero estorbo para el progreso.
discouraging [dis'kʌridʒiŋ] *adj* desalentador; **he was — about it** habló de ello en tono pesimista.
discourse ['diskɔːs] *n* discurso *m*; (*talk*) plática *f*; (*essay*) tratado *m*.
discourse [dis'kɔːs] *vi*: **to — upon** (*converse*) platicar sobre, (*make a speech*) disertar sobre.
discourteous [dis'kəːtiəs] *adj* descortés.
discourteously [dis'kəːtiəsli] *adv* descortésmente.
discourtesy [dis'kəːtisi] *n* descortesía *f*.
discover [dis'kʌvə*] *vt* descubrir.
discoverer [dis'kʌvərə*] *n* descubridor *m*.
discovery [dis'kʌvəri] *n* descubrimiento *m*.
discredit [dis'kredit] **1** *n* descrédito *m*. **2** *vt* desacreditar, deshonrar; **that theory is now —ed** esa teoría ya está desacreditada.
discreditable [dis'kreditəbl] *adj* deshonroso, vergonzoso.
discreet [dis'kriːt] *adj* discreto, circunspecto, prudente.
discreetly [dis'kriːtli] *adv* discretamente, prudentemente.
discrepancy [dis'krepənsi] *n* discrepancia *f*, diferencia *f*.
discrete [dis'kriːt] *adj* discreto.
discretion [dis'kreʃən] *n* discreción *f*, circunspección *f*, prudencia *f*; **at one's —** a discreción; **age of —** edad *f* de discernimiento; **to use one's own —** juzgar una cosa por sí mismo, obrar como mejor le parezca a uno; **— is the better part of valour** una retirada a tiempo es una victoria.
discriminate [dis'krimineit] **1** *vt* distinguir (*from* de). **2** *vi*: **to — against** discriminar contra, hacer una distinción en perjuicio de; **to — between** distinguir entre.
discriminating [dis'krimineitiŋ] *adj* perspicaz, discernidor; *duty* diferencial; *taste etc* fino.
discrimination [dis,krimi'neiʃən] *n* (*discernment*) discernimiento *m*, perspicacia *f*; (*good taste*) buen gusto *m*, finura *f*; (*distinction*) distinción *f* (*between* entre); (*partiality*) parcialidad *f*, discriminación *f* (*against* contra); **racial —** discriminación *f* racial.
discriminatory [dis'kriminətəri] *adj duty etc* discriminatorio.
discursive [dis'kəːsiv] *adj* divagador, prolijo.
discus ['diskəs] *n* disco *m*.
discuss [dis'kʌs] *vt* discutir, hablar de; *theme* tratar.
discussion [dis'kʌʃən] *n* discusión *f*; **to be under —** estar siendo discutido.
disdain [dis'dein] **1** *n* desdén *m*. **2** *vt* desdeñar. **3** *vi*: **to — to +** *infin* no dignarse **+** *infin*.
disdainful [dis'deinful] *adj* desdeñoso.
disdainfully [dis'deinfəli] *adv* desdeñosamente.
disease [di'ziːz] *n* enfermedad *f*; (*fig*) mal *m*; **infectious —** enfermedad *f* contagiosa; **occupational —** enfermedad *f* profesional; **venereal —** enfermedad *f* venérea; **virus —** enfermedad *f* por virus.
diseased [di'ziːzd] *adj person* enfermo; *tissue* contagiado; *mind* enfermo, morboso.
disembark [,disim'baːk] *vti* desembarcar.
disembarkation [,disimbaː'keiʃən] *n* (*goods*) desembarque *m*; (*person*) desembarco *m*.
disembodied ['disim'bɔdid] *adj* incorpóreo.
disembowel [,disim'bauəl] *vt* desentrañar.
disenchanted ['disin'tʃaːntid] *adj*: **to be — with someone** quedar desencantado (*or* desengañado) con

uno; **to be — with New York** quedar desencantado (*or* desengañado) de Nueva York.
disengage [,disin'geidʒ] **1** *vt* (*free*) soltar, desasir; (*Mech*) desacoplar, desenganchar; *clutch* desembragar. **2** *vi* (*Mil*) retirarse.
disengaged [,disin'geidʒd] *adj* libre, desocupado.
disentangle ['disin'tæŋgl] **1** *vt* desenredar, desenmarañar (*also fig*; *from* de). **2** *vr*: **to — oneself** desenredarse (*from* de).
disestablish ['disis'tæbliʃ] *vt* (*Eccl*) separar del Estado.
disestablishment [,disis'tæbliʃmənt] *n* (*Eccl*) separación *f* del Estado.
disfavour [dis'feivə*] *n* desaprobación *f*; **to fall into — (***custom*) dejar de usarse, caer en desuso, (*person*) caer en desgracia; **to look with — on something** desaprobar algo.
disfigure [dis'figə*] *vt* desfigurar; afear.
disfigurement [dis'figəmənt] *n* desfiguración *f*; afeamiento *m*.
disfranchise ['dis'fræntʃaiz] *vt* privar de los derechos civiles, (*esp*) privar del derecho de votar.
disgorge [dis'gɔːdʒ] *vt* vomitar, arrojar; (*bird*) desembuchar; (*fig*) devolver, restituir.
disgrace [dis'greis] **1** *n* (**a**) (*state of shame*) ignominia *f*, deshonra *f*; **to be in —** estar desacreditado, (*pet*, *child*) tener que sufrir un castigo; **to bring — on** deshonrar; **to fall into —** caer en desgracia.
(**b**) (*downfall*) caída *f*.
(**c**) (*shameful thing*) vergüenza *f*; escándalo *m*; **it's a — es una vergüenza; what a —!** ¡qué vergüenza!
2 *vt* deshonrar, desacreditar; **he was —d and banished** le destituyeron de sus cargos y le desterraron.
3 *vr*: **to — oneself** deshonrarse.
disgraceful [dis'greisful] *adj* vergonzoso, deshonroso; *behaviour* escandaloso; **—!** ¡qué vergüenza!
disgracefully [dis'greisfəli] *adv* vergonzosamente; escandalosamente.
disgruntled [dis'grʌntld] *adj* disgustado (*at*, *with* de), malhumorado; **to look —** poner mala cara.
disguise [dis'gaiz] **1** *n* disfraz *m*. **2** *vt* disfrazar (*as* de). **3** *vr*: **to — oneself as** disfrazarse de.
disgust [dis'gʌst] **1** *n* repugnancia *f*, aversión *f*; **it fills me with —** me da asco.
2 *vt* repugnar, inspirar aversión a, dar asco a; (*disappointment etc*) disgustar; **the thought —s me** el pensamiento me repugna; **you — me** me das asco; **he was —ed by his failure** se enfureció contra sí mismo por su fracaso; **I am —ed with you** me das vergüenza; **I was —ed with the referee** el árbitro me dio asco.
disgusted [dis'gʌstid] *adj*: **in a — voice** en tono disgustado.
disgusting [dis'gʌstiŋ] *adj* repugnante, asqueroso; **—!** ¡qué asco!
disgustingly [dis'gʌstiŋli] *adv* asquerosamente; **they are — rich** son tan ricos que da asco.
dish [diʃ] **1** *n* (**a**) plato *m*; (*large, for serving etc*) fuente *f*; (*food*) plato *m*; **a typical Spanish —** un plato típico español; **to wash the —es** fregar los platos.
(**b**) (*fam*) chica *f* atractiva.
2 *vt* (*fig*) confundir, burlar; **to — out** repartir; **to — up** servir; **he —ed up the same old arguments** repitió los argumentos de siempre.
dishabille [,disæ'biːl] *n* desabillé *m*.
disharmony ['dis'haːməni] *n* discordia *f*; (*Mus*) disonancia *f*.
dish cloth ['diʃklɔθ] *n* paño *m* de cocina, bayeta *f*.
dishearten [dis'haːtn] *vt* desalentar; **don't be —ed!** ¡ánimo!
disheartening [dis'haːtniŋ] *adj* desalentador.
dishevelled [di'ʃevəld] *adj* despeinado, desmelenado.
dishonest [dis'ɔnist] *adj person* nada honrado, falso, tramposo; *means* fraudulento.
dishonestly [dis'ɔnistli] *adv* fraudulentamente.
dishonesty [dis'ɔnisti] *n* falta *f* de honradez, falsedad *f*; (*of means*) fraude *m*.
dishonour, (*US*) **dishonor** [dis'ɔnə*] **1** *n* deshonra *f*, deshonor *m*.
2 *vt* deshonrar; *cheque etc* negarse a aceptar, no pagar; *promise* faltar a, no cumplir.
dishonourable, (*US*) **dishonorable** [dis'ɔnərəbl] *adj* deshonroso.
dishrack ['diʃræk] *n* estante *m* para secar los platos.
dishwasher ['diʃ,wɔʃə*] *n* (*person*) friegaplatos *mf*; (*machine*) lavaplatos *m*.
dishy ['diʃi] *adj* (*fam*) atractivo, mono.
disillusion [,disi'luːʒən] **1** *n* desilusión *f*. **2** *vt* desilusionar; **to be — with someone** quedar desilusionado con uno; **to be —ed with Paris** quedar desilusionado de París.

disillusionment [‚disi'luːʒənmənt] n desilusión f.
disincentive [‚disin'sentiv] n freno m (to sobre).
disinclination [‚disinkli'neiʃən] n aversión f (for a, hacia, por).
disinclined ['disin'klaind] adj: **to be — to do something** estar poco dispuesto a hacer algo.
disinfect [‚disin'fekt] vt desinfectar.
disinfectant [‚disin'fektənt] n desinfectante m.
disinfection [‚disin'fekʃən] n desinfección f.
disinflation [‚disin'fleiʃən] n desinflación f.
disinflationary [‚disin'fleiʃənəri] adj desinflacionista.
disingenuous [‚disin'dʒenjuəs] adj doble, poco sincero.
disinherit ['disin'herit] vt desheredar.
disintegrate [dis'intigreit] vi disgregarse, desagregarse, desintegrarse.
disintegration [dis‚inti'greiʃən] n disgregación f, desagregación f, desintegración f.
disinter ['disin'təː*] vt desenterrar.
disinterested [dis'intristid] adj desinteresado.
disjointed [dis'dʒɔintid] adj (fig) inconexo, descosido.
disjunctive [dis'dʒʌŋktiv] adj disyuntivo.
disk [disk] n see **disc**.
dislike [dis'laik] **1** n aversión f, antipatía f (for, of a, hacia); **to take a — to** coger antipatía a, tomar hincha a (fam).
  2 vt (a) (object: person) tener aversión a, tener antipatía a; **I — him** me resulta antipático; **it's not that I — him** no es que yo le tenga aversión.
  (b) (object: thing) **I — that** eso no me gusta; **I — flying** no me gusta ir en avión.
dislocate ['disləukeit] vt bone dislocarse; traffic interceptar, interrumpir; plans dar al traste con.
dislocation [‚disləu'keiʃən] n dislocación f; interceptación f; confusión f.
dislodge [dis'lɔdʒ] vt enemy etc desalojar (from de); object etc hacer caer.
disloyal ['dis'lɔiəl] adj desleal.
disloyalty ['dis'lɔiəlti] n deslealtad f.
dismal ['dizməl] adj (dark) sombrío, tenebroso; (depressing) triste, tétrico; (depressed) abatido; tone lúgubre; failure catastrófico; (very bad) malísimo, fatal.
dismally ['dizməli] adv (sadly) tristemente; **to fail —** tener un fracaso catastrófico; **the play was — bad** la obra fue fatal.
dismantle [dis'mæntl] vt machine desmontar, desarmar; fort, ship desmantelar.
dismast [dis'mɑːst] vt desarbolar.
dismay [dis'mei] **1** n consternación f; **there was general —** se consternaron todos; **in —** consternado; **to fill someone with —** consternar a uno. **2** vt consternar; **I am —ed to hear that** me da pena saber que; **don't look so —ed!** ¡no te aflijas!
dismember [dis'membə*] vt desmembrar.
dismemberment [dis'membəmənt] n desmembramiento m, desmembración f.
dismiss [dis'mis] **1** vt (a) (discharge) worker despedir, official destituir (from de), (Mil) licenciar; **to be —ed the service** ser separado del servicio.
  (b) (send away) mandar ir, dar permiso a . . . para irse; parliament disolver.
  (c) thought rechazar, apartar de sí; possibility descartar, desechar.
  (d) **to — a subject briefly** hablar brevemente de un asunto; **with that he —ed the matter** con eso dio por concluido el asunto.
  (e) (Law) appeal rechazar; **the case was —ed** el tribunal absolvió al acusado.
  2 vi (Mil) romper filas.
dismissal [dis'misəl] n despedida f; destitución f.
dismount [dis'maunt] **1** vt desmontar. **2** vi desmontarse, apearse, bajar (from de).
disobedience [‚disə'biːdiəns] n desobediencia f.
disobedient [‚disə'biːdiənt] adj desobediente.
disobey ['disə'bei] vti desobedecer.
disobliging ['disə'blaidʒiŋ] adj poco servicial.
disorder [dis'ɔːdə*] **1** n (a) (confusion) desorden m; **to be in —** estar en desorden; **to retreat in —** retirarse a la desbandada.
  (b) (commotion) disturbio m, tumulto m; **there were —s in the streets** hubo disturbios en las calles.
  (c) (Med) (upset) trastorno m, (illness) enfermedad f; **mental —** trastorno m mental.
  2 vt desordenar; (Med) trastornar.
disordered [dis'ɔːdəd] adj desordenado; (Med) trastornado.
disorderly [dis'ɔːdəli] adj (a) (untidy) desordenado; person poco metódico.
  (b) (unruly) turbulento, indisciplinado; youth revoltoso; meeting alborotado; **the meeting became —** la reunión se alborotó.
  (c) conduct escandaloso.

disorganization [dis‚ɔːgənai'zeiʃən] n desorganización f; confusión f, falta f de organización.
disorganize [dis'ɔːgənaiz] vt desorganizar; communications etc interrumpir.
disorientate [dis'ɔːrienteit] vt desorientar.
disown [dis'əun] vt rechazar, desconocer; belief etc renegar de.
disparage [dis'pæridʒ] vt menospreciar, denigrar, hablar mal de.
disparagement [dis'pæridʒmənt] n denigración f.
disparaging [dis'pæridʒiŋ] adj despreciativo.
disparagingly [dis'pæridʒiŋli] adv: **to speak — of** hablar en términos despreciativos de.
disparate ['dispərit] adj dispar.
disparity [dis'pæriti] n disparidad f.
dispassionate [dis'pæʃnit] adj desapasionado, imparcial.
dispassionately [dis'pæʃnitli] adv de modo desapasionado.
dispatch [dis'pætʃ] **1** n (a) (act of sending) (of person) envío m, (of goods) consignación f, envío m; (killing) muerte f.
  (b) (speed) prontitud f.
  (c) (message) mensaje m, despacho m, informe m; (Mil) parte m, comunicado m.
  2 vt (a) (send) person enviar, goods consignar, enviar, remitir.
  (b) (kill) despachar.
  (c) (transact) despachar.
  (d) food despabilar.
dispatch box [dis'pætʃbɔks] n cartera f.
dispatcher [dis'pætʃə*] n despachador m, ora f.
dispatch rider [dis'pætʃ‚raidə*] n correo m.
dispel [dis'pel] vt disipar, dispersar; (fig) desvanecer.
dispensable [dis'pensəbl] adj prescindible.
dispensary [dis'pensəri] n dispensario m, farmacia f.
dispensation [‚dispen'seiʃən] n (distribution, exemption) dispensación f; (of justice) administración f; (Eccl) dispensa f; (ruling) decreto m; (by Providence) designio m divino.
dispense [dis'pens] **1** vt (a) (issue) dispensar, repartir; (Pharm) preparar; justice administrar.
  (b) **to — someone from** dispensar a uno de, eximir a uno de.
  2 vi: **to — with** prescindir de.
dispenser [dis'pensə*] n (Pharm) farmacéutico m, a f.
dispersal [dis'pəːsəl] n dispersión f; (of light) descomposición f.
disperse [dis'pəːs] **1** vt dispersar; light descomponer.
  2 vi dispersarse; **they —d to their homes** fue cada uno a su casa.
dispersion [dis'pəːʃən] n dispersión f.
dispirit [dis'pirit] vt desalentar.
dispirited [dis'piritid] adj abatido, deprimido.
displace [dis'pleis] vt (shift) sacar de su sitio; (remove from office) destituir; (oust) quitar el puesto a, reemplazar; (Phys, Naut) desplazar; (Chem) reemplazar.
displaced [dis'pleist] adj: **— person** desplazado m, a f.
displacement [dis'pleismənt] n (shift) cambio m de sitio; (removal from office) destitución f; (ousting) reemplazo m; (Phys, Naut) desplazamiento m; (Chem) reemplazo m.
display [dis'plei] **1** n (a) (act of —ing) exhibición f; (showing) exposición f; (of goods for sale) exposición f, presentación f; (of emotion) manifestación f, demostración f; (of energy) despliegue m; (Mil) alarde m, demostración f militar.
  (b) (showiness) aparato m, pompa f, ostentación f.
  2 vt (put on view) exponer, presentar; emotion etc acusar, manifestar, demostrar; quality revelar; energy desplegar; (show ostentatiously) hacer ostentación de, lucir.
displease [dis'pliːz] vt (be disagreeable to) desagradar; (offend) ofender; (annoy) enojar, enfadar; **to be —d at** (or with) estar disgustado con (or de).
displeasing [dis'pliːziŋ] adj desagradable.
displeasure [dis'pleʒə*] n enojo m, indignación f, disgusto m; **to incur someone's —** ofender a uno.
disport [dis'pɔːt] vr: **to — oneself** retozar, jugar, divertirse.
disposable [dis'pəuzəbl] adj napkin etc de usar y tirar.
disposal [dis'pəuzəl] n (a) (placing, arrangement) disposición f, colocación f, orden m.
  (b) (sale) venta f; (of house etc) traspaso m; (of rights) enajenación f; (of rubbish) recogida f de basuras.
  (c) **to have at one's —** disponer de, tener a su disposición; **I am at your —** estoy a su disposición.

dispose [dis'pəuz] **1** *vt* (a) (*place, arrange*) disponer, colocar, poner en orden.
   (b) (*determine*) determinar, decidir.
   (c) (*persuade*) inclinar, mover; **to — someone to help** mover a uno a ayudar; **to be —d to do something** estar dispuesto a hacer algo; **to be well —d towards something** estar bien dispuesto hacia algo.
   2 *vi:* **to — of** (a) (*have at one's command*) disponer de. (b) (*get rid of*) deshacerse de; *rubbish* tirar, depositar; *rights* enajenar, ceder; (*sell*) vender; *house etc* traspasar; (*give away*) regalar; *food* comerse, despabilar; (*finish*) terminar, concluir; *problem* resolver; *business* despachar; (*kill*) matar.
disposition [,dispə'ziʃən] *n* (a) (*placing*) disposición *f*, colocación *f*; orden *m*.
   (b) **—s** preparativos *mpl*; plan *m*; **to make one's —s** hacer preparativos.
   (c) **to be at the — of** estar a la disposición de.
   (d) (*dispensation*) disposición *f*.
   (e) (*temperament*) natural *m*, temperamento *m*.
   (f) (*inclination*) propensión *f* (*to* a); **I have no — to help him** no estoy dispuesto a ayudarle.
dispossess ['dispə'zes] *vt tenant* desahuciar; **to — someone of** desposeer a uno de, privar a uno de.
disproportion [,disprə'pɔ:ʃən] *n* desproporción *f*.
disproportionate [,disprə'pɔ:ʃnit] *adj* desproporcionado.
disproportionately [,disprə'pɔ:ʃnitli] *adv* desproporcionadamente.
disprove [dis'pru:v] *vt* refutar, confutar.
disputable [dis'pju:təbl] *adj* discutible.
disputation [,dispju:'teiʃən] *n* disputa *f*.
disputatious [,dispju:'teiʃəs] *adj* discutidor.
dispute [dis'pju:t] **1** *n* disputa *f*; (*spoken*) discusión *f*, altercado *m*; **labour —** conflicto *m* laboral; **beyond — indiscutible, incuestionable; it is beyond — that** es indudable que; **territory in — territorio *m* disputado.
   2 *vt* disputar; cuestionar, expresar dudas acerca de; protestar de; **a —d matter** un asunto contencioso, un asunto en litigio; **a —d decision** una decisión discutida; **I — that** no lo dudo.
   3 *vi* discutir (*about, over* sobre, *whether* si).
disqualification [dis,kwɔlifi'keiʃən] *n* (*act, effect*) inhabilitación *f*; (*Sport*) descalificación *f*; (*thing that disqualifies*) impedimento *m*, desventaja *f*.
disqualify [dis'kwɔlifai] *vt* inhabilitar, incapacitar (*for* para); (*Sport*) descalificar.
disquiet [dis'kwaiət] **1** *n* inquietud *f*. **2** *vt* inquietar.
disquieting [dis'kwaiətiŋ] *adj* inquietante.
disquisition [,diskwi'ziʃən] *n* disquisición *f*.
disregard ['disri'gɑ:d] **1** *n* indiferencia *f* (*for* a); (*neglect*) descuido *m* (*of* de); **with complete — for** sin atender en lo más mínimo a; **with complete — for his own safety** sin considerar un momento su propia salvación.
   2 *vt* desatender, descuidar; (*ignore*) no hacer caso de.
disrepair ['disri'pɛə*] *n* mal estado *m*; **to fall into — desmoronarse.
disreputable [dis'repjutəbl] *adj* de mala fama; (*shameful*) vergonzoso, escandaloso; *clothing etc* horrible, asqueroso.
disreputably [dis'repjutəbli] *adv* vergonzosamente.
disrepute ['disri'pju:t] *n*: **to bring something into — desacreditar algo.
disrespect ['disris'pekt] *n* falta *f* de respeto, desacato *m*; **I meant no — no quería ofenderle.
disrespectful [,disris'pektful] *adj* irrespetuoso.
disrobe ['dis'rəub] *vi* desnudarse.
disrupt [dis'rʌpt] *vt* romper; (*fig*) *communications etc* desorganizar, interrumpir; *plans* desbaratar, dar al traste con.
disruption [dis'rʌpʃən] *n* rompimiento *m*; (*fig*) desorganización *f*, interrupción *f*; desbaratamiento *m*.
disruptive [dis'ruptiv] *adj* que tiende a romper la unidad; destructivo, subversivo, perjudicial (para la unidad).
dissatisfaction ['dis,sætis'fækʃən] *n* descontento *m*, insatisfacción *f*; disgusto *m*.
dissatisfied ['dis'sætisfaid] *adj* descontento, insatisfecho; **everyone was — with the result** el resultado no gustó a nadie, el resultado dejó insatisfechos a todos.
dissect [di'sekt] *vt* disecar; (*fig*) analizar minuciosamente.
dissection [di'sekʃən] *n* disección *f*; (*fig*) análisis *m* minucioso.
dissemble [di'sembl] **1** *vt* disimular, encubrir. **2** *vi* ser hipócrita.
disseminate [di'semineit] *vt* diseminar, difundir.

dissemination [di,semi'neiʃən] *n* diseminación *f*, difusión *f*.
dissension [di'senʃən] *n* disensión *f*, discordia *f*.
dissent [di'sent] **1** *n* disentimiento *m*; (*Eccl*) disidencia *f*. **2** *vi* disentir (*from* de); (*Eccl*) disidir.
dissenter [di'sentə*] *n* (*Eccl*) disidente *m*.
dissentient [di'senʃiənt] **1** *adj* disidente, desconforme, discrepante; **there was one — voice** hubo uno que no estaba conforme. **2** *n* disidente *m*.
dissertation [,disə'teiʃən] *n* disertación *f*; (*Univ*) tesis *f*.
disservice ['dis'sə:vis] *n* deservicio *m*; **to do a — to** perjudicar a.
dissidence ['disidəns] *n* disidencia *f*.
dissident ['disidənt] **1** *adj* disidente. **2** *n* disidente *m*.
dissimilar ['di'similə*] *adj* desemejante (*to* de).
dissimilarity [,disimi'læriti] *n* desemejanza *f*.
dissimulate [di'simjuleit] *vt* disimular.
dissimulation [di,simju'leiʃən] *n* disimulación *f*.
dissipate ['disipeit] *vt* dispar; *fear, doubt etc* desvanecer; (*waste*) derrochar, desperdiciar.
dissipated ['disipeitid] *adj* disoluto.
dissipation [,disi'peiʃən] *n* (*act*) disipación *f*; (*waste*) derroche *m*, desperdicio *m*; (*moral*) disipación *f*, disolución *f*, libertinaje *m*, vicio *m*.
dissociate [di'səuʃieit] **1** *vt* disociar (*from* de). **2** *vr:* **to — oneself from** hacerse insolidario de, separarse de, disociarse de.
dissociation [di,səusi'eiʃən] *n* disociación *f*.
dissoluble [di'sɔljubl] *adj* disoluble.
dissolute ['disəlu:t] *adj* disoluto.
dissolution [,disə'lu:ʃən] *n* disolución *f* (*also Pol*).
dissolvable [di'zɔlvəbl] *adj* soluble.
dissolve [di'zɔlv] **1** *vt* disolver (*also fig, Pol etc*). **2** *vi* disolverse; (*fade*) desvanecerse; **to — into tears** deshacerse en lágrimas.
dissonance ['disənəns] *n* disonancia *f*.
dissonant ['disənənt] *adj* disonante.
dissuade [di'sweid] *vt* disuadir (*from* de); **to — someone from doing something** disuadir a uno de hacer algo.
distaff ['distɑ:f] *n* rueca *f*; **on the — side** por parte de madre.
distance ['distəns] *n* distancia *f*; (*fig*) reserva *f*; (*difference*) diferencia *f*; **it's a good —** está bastante lejos, (*journey*) es mucho camino; **what — is it to London?** ¿cuánto hay de aquí a Londres?; **— race** carrera *f* de larga distancia; **focal — distancia *f* focal; **within easy — a poca distancia, no muy lejos (*of* de); **to be within striking — of** estar al alcance de; **at a — a distancia; at a — of 60 km** a una distancia de 60 km; **at this — a esta distancia; at this — of time** después de tanto tiempo; **from a — desde lejos; in the — a lo lejos; in the middle — en segundo término; to keep one's — mantenerse a distancia, (*fig*) guardar las distancias; **to keep someone at a — guardar las distancias con uno.
distant ['distənt] *adj* (a) distante, lejano, remoto (*from* de); **it is 12 km — dista 12 km, está a 12 km; is it very —? ¿dista mucho?, ¿está muy lejos?; **in some far — land** en algún país lejano.
   (b) *relation, resemblance* lejano.
   (c) (*fig*) reservado, frío; **to be — with someone** tratar a uno con frialdad.
distantly ['distəntli] *adv:* **we are — related** somos parientes lejanos; **it — resembles the one we had before** tiene una ligera semejanza con el que teníamos antes; **he treated me — me trató con frialdad.
distaste ['dis'teist] *n* aversión *f*, repugnancia *f* (*for* por).
distasteful [dis'teistful] *adj* desagradable, repugnante; *task* nada grato; **it is — to me to have to + *infin*** me es poco grato tener que + *infin*.
distemper[1] [dis'tempə*] **1** *n* pintura *f* al temple. **2** *vt* pintar al temple.
distemper[2] [dis'tempə*] *n* (*Vet*) moquillo *m*; (*fig*) mal *m*, destemplanza *f*.
distend [dis'tend] **1** *vt* dilatar, hinchar. **2** *vi* dilatarse, hincharse.
distension [dis'tenʃən] *n* distensión *f*, dilatación *f*, hinchazón *f*.
distil, (*US*) **distill** [dis'til] *vt* destilar.
distillation [disti'leiʃən] *n* destilación *f*.
distiller [dis'tilə*] *n* destilador *m*.
distillery [dis'tiləri] *n* destilería *f*.
distinct [dis'tiŋkt] *adj* (*different*) distinto (*from* de); (*clearly perceptible*) claro, inconfundible, visible; (*unmistakable*) inequívoco; **as — from** a diferencia de; **a — French accent** un marcado acento francés; **there is a — chance that** existe una clara posibilidad de que + *subj*.

distinction [dis'tiŋkʃən] n distinción f; (exam mark) sobresaliente m, matrícula f de honor; **to draw a — between** hacer una distinción entre; **you have the — of being the first** Vd se señala por ser el primero.

distinctive [dis'tiŋktiv] adj distintivo, característico.

distinctly [dis'tiŋktli] adv claramente; inconfundiblemente; **it is — possible** bien podría ser (that que + subj); **it is — awkward** es sumamente difícil.

distinguish [dis'tiŋgwiʃ] 1 vt distinguir (between entre, from de). 2 vr: **to — oneself** distinguirse (as como); (iro) señalarse, lucirse.

distinguishable [dis'tiŋgwiʃəbl] adj distinguible.

distinguished [dis'tiŋgwiʃt] adj distinguido (for por), eminente, de categoría.

distinguishing [dis'tiŋgwiʃiŋ] adj distintivo.

distort [dis'tɔːt] vt torcer, deformar; (fig) torcer, falsear.

distortion [dis'tɔːʃən] n torcimiento m, deformación f; (of sound) distorsión f; (fig) torcimiento m, falseamiento m.

distract [dis'trækt] vt distraer; attention apartar (from de); (bewilder) aturdir, confundir.

distracted [dis'træktid] adj alocado, aturdido; **like one — como** un loco; **she is easily —** se distrae fácilmente; **to be — with anxiety** estar loco de inquietud.

distractedly [dis'træktidli] adv locamente, como un loco.

distracting [dis'træktiŋ] adj que distrae la atención, molesto.

distraction [dis'trækʃən] n (being distracted) distracción f; (bewilderment) aturdimiento m, confusión f; (amusement) diversión f; (madness) locura f; **to drive someone to —** volver loco a uno.

distrain [dis'trein] vi: **to — upon** secuestrar, embargar.

distraint [dis'treint] n secuestro m, embargo m.

distrait [dis'trei], **distraite** [dis'treit] adj distraído.

distraught [dis'trɔːt] adj muy turbado, loco de inquietud (etc); **in a — voice** en una voz embargada por la emoción.

distress [dis'tres] 1 n (pain) dolor m; (mental anguish) angustia f, pena f, aflicción f; (misfortune) desgracia f; (want) miseria f; (danger) peligro m; (Med) agotamiento m; **to be in —** estar en un apuro, (Med) estar con dolor, (ship etc) estar en peligro; **to be in financial —** pasar apuros.
2 vt (pain) doler; (cause anguish to) apenar, afligir; (Med) agotar, fatigar; **I am —ed to hear that** me da pena saber que; **I am very —ed about it** esto me inquieta muchísimo.

distressing [dis'tresiŋ] adj doloroso, penoso, que da pena.

distress signal [dis'tres,signəl] n señal f de socorro.

distribute [dis'tribjuːt] vt distribuir, repartir.

distribution [,distri'bjuːʃən] n distribución f, reparto m, repartimiento m.

distributive [dis'tribjutiv] adj distributivo; **— trade** comercio m de repartimiento.

distributor [dis'tribjutə*] n (Mech, Elec etc) distribuidor m; (Comm, Cine etc) distribuidora f.

district ['distrikt] n zona f, región f; (of town) barrio m; (of country) comarca f; (Pol) distrito m; **postal —** distrito m postal.

distrust [dis'trʌst] 1 n desconfianza f, recelo m. 2 vt desconfiar de, recelar.

distrustful [dis'trʌstful] adj desconfiado, receloso.

disturb [dis'təːb] vt peace, order, meeting etc perturbar, alterar; process, course interrumpir; balance of mind trastornar; (disarrange) desordenar; person (disquiet) perturbar, inquietar, (bother) molestar; **don't — yourself!** ¡no se moleste!; **I am seriously —ed** estoy muy preocupado.

disturbance [dis'təːbəns] n (act, state) perturbación f; (outbreak of violence) tumulto m, alboroto m, (Pol) disturbio m; (of mind) trastorno m; **there was a — in the crowd** se alborotaron algunos de los espectadores; **the —s in the Congo** los disturbios en el Congo.

disturbed [dis'təːbd] adj state alborotado, nada tranquilo; **to have a — night** dormir mal.

disturbing [dis'təːbiŋ] adj influence, thought perturbador; event inquietante; **it is — that** es inquietante que.

disunited ['disju'naitid] adj desunido.

disuse ['dis'juːs] n: **to fall into —** caer en desuso.

disused ['dis'juːzd] adj abandonado.

disyllabic [,disi'læbik] adj disílabo.

ditch [ditʃ] 1 n zanja f; (at roadside) cuneta f, arroyo m; (irrigation channel) acequia f; (defensive) foso m; **to die in the last —** luchar hasta quemar el último cartucho.

2 vt (fam) (get rid of) deshacerse de, zafarse de; plane amerizar; car estropear.

dither ['diðə*] 1 n: **to be all of a —, to be in a —** = 2 vi estar nerviosísimo; (be undecided) no saber qué hacer, vacilar.

dithery ['diðəri] adj nervioso; indeciso, vacilante.

ditto ['ditəu] adj ídem, lo mismo; **I say —** yo digo lo mismo; **"—", he said** dijo "yo también".

ditty ['diti] n cancioneta f.

diuretic [,daijuə'retik] 1 adj diurético. 2 n diurético m.

diurnal [dai'əːnl] adj diurno.

divan [di'væn] n diván m, cama f turca.

dive [daiv] 1 n (a) zambullida f, (artistic, from board etc) salto m; **springboard —** salto m de trampolín.
(b) (by professional diver, of submarine) inmersión f.
(c) (Aer) picado m.
(d) (fam) tasca f (also low —).
2 vi (a) (duck etc) zambullirse; (from bank etc) tirarse al agua, saltar al agua, zambullirse; (artistically) saltar; (professional diver) bucear, sumergirse; (submarine) sumergirse; **to — into the water** tirarse al agua.
(b) (Aer) picar.
(c) **to — for cover** meterse precipitadamente en un abrigo, buscar cobijo precipitadamente; **to — into the undergrowth** meterse en la maleza; **to — into one's pocket** meter la mano en el bolsillo; **to — into a bar** entrar de prisa en un bar.

dive-bomb ['daivbɔm] vt bombardear en picado.

dive bomber ['daiv,bɔmə*] n bombardero m en picado.

dive bombing ['daiv,bɔmiŋ] n bombardeo m en picado.

diver ['daivə*] n (professional) buzo m; (sporting) saltador m, ora f; (Orn) colimbo m.

diverge [dai'vəːdʒ] vi divergir (from de); **to — from** apartarse de.

divergence [dai'vəːdʒəns] n divergencia f.

divergent [dai'vəːdʒənt] adj divergente.

divers ['daivəːz] adj pl diversos, varios.

diverse [dai'vəːs] adj diverso, variado.

diversification [dai,vəːsifi'keiʃən] n diversificación f.

diversify [dai'vəːsifai] vt diversificar, variar.

diversion [dai'vəːʃən] n (pastime, Mil) diversión f; (of route) desviación f.

diversity [dai'vəːsiti] n diversidad f.

divert [dai'vəːt] vt (amuse) divertir; (turn aside) desviar.

diverting [dai'vəːtiŋ] adj divertido.

divest [dai'vest] 1 vt: **to — someone of something** despojar a uno de algo. 2 vr: **to — oneself of something** renunciar a algo.

divide [di'vaid] 1 n (Geog) divisoria f.
2 vt dividir (by por, from de, into en); partir; separar; **to — the House** hacer que la Cámara proceda a la votación; **to — out** repartir; **to — up** dividir, partir.
3 vi dividirse (into en); separarse; (road etc) bifurcarse; **the House —d** la Cámara procedió a la votación.

dividend ['dividend] n dividendo m; (fig) beneficio m; **this should pay handsome —s** (fig) esto ha de proporcionar grandes beneficios.

dividers [di'vaidəz] npl compás m de puntas.

dividing line [di'vaidiŋlain] n línea f divisoria.

divination [,divi'neiʃən] n adivinación f.

divine [di'vain] 1 adj divino; (fig) sublime; (fam) estupendo, maravilloso. 2 n teólogo m. 3 vt adivinar.

divinely [di'vainli] adv divinamente; (fig) sublimamente; (fam) divinamente, maravillosamente.

diviner [di'vainə*] n adivinador m, ora f; (water —) zahorí m.

diving ['daiviŋ] n (professional) el bucear, buceo m; (sporting) salto m.

diving bell ['daiviŋbel] n campana f de bucear.

diving board ['daiviŋbɔːd] n trampolín m.

diving suit ['daiviŋsuːt] n escafandra f, traje m de buceo.

divining rod [di'vainiŋrɔd] n varilla f de zahorí.

divinity [di'viniti] n divinidad f; (as study) teología f.

divisible [di'vizəbl] adj divisible.

division [di'viʒən] n división f (also Math, Mil); separación f; (sharing out) repartimiento m; (within company etc) sección f; (disagreement) discordia f; (Parl) votación f; **without a —** por unanimidad; **there is a — of opinion about this** sobre esto hay diversos pareceres.

divisive [di'vaisiv] adj divisivo.

divisor [di'vaizə*] n divisor m.

divorce [di'vɔːs] **1** n divorcio m; (fig) separación f (from de); to get a — divorciarse (from de). **2** vt divorciarse de; (fig) divorciar, separar (from de).
divorcee [di‚vɔː'siː] n divorciado m, a f.
divulge [dai'vʌldʒ] vt divulgar, revelar.
dixie ['diksi] n (Mil) olla f.
Dixie ['diksi] el sur de los Estados Unidos.
dizzily ['dizili] adv vertiginosamente.
dizziness ['dizinis] n vértigo m, vértigos mpl.
dizzy ['dizi] adj speed vertiginoso; height que produce vértigo; feeling de vértigo; (dazed) mareado, aturdido; **to feel —, to get —** marearse, estar mareado, tener vértigos; **I'm feeling rather —** me está dando vueltas la cabeza.
do [duː] (irr: pret **did**, ptp **done**) **1** vt (a) hacer; (Cook) guisar, preparar; (Theat) play representar, poner, rôle hacer, personage hacer de, hacer el papel de; duty cumplir, hacer; homage rendir, tributar (to a); problem resolver; dishes lavar; room limpiar; hair peinar, (wash and set) arreglar; subject (Univ etc) estudiar, cursar; distance cubrir, recorrer, salvar; speed alcanzar, ir a; town etc (fam) hacer la visita de, visitar los monumentos de; (sl: cheat) estafar, timar; **they — you very well in this hotel** en este hotel la comida es muy buena; **what's to —?** ¿qué pasa?; **to have one's hair done** arreglarse el pelo.
(b) (with adv or prep) **to — again** rehacer, repetir, volver a hacer; **to — down** (cheat) estafar, (play someone under) hacer una mala pasada a; **to — in** (sl) apiolar, cargarse a; **to — a book into English** traducir un libro al inglés; **to — out** room pintar, renovar; **to — someone out of something** estafar algo a uno, (chance etc) pisar algo a uno, hacer que uno pierda algo; **to — something over** (again) rehacer algo; **to — up** laces etc liar, atar, parcel envolver, room renovar; see also **doing**, **done**.
2 vi (a) (act, proceed) hacer; obrar, actuar, proceder; **you did well** hiciste muy bien; **you would — well to draw with him** sería muy honroso lograr un empate con él; **to — better** mejorar, hacer progresos; **you can — better than that** eres capaz de hacerlo mejor; **you would — better to accept** sería aconsejable aceptar; **— as you are told!** ¡haz lo que te digo!; **— as you think best** haga lo que mejor le parezca; **— as you would be done by** trata como quieres ser tratado.
(b) (fare) **how is he —ing?** ¿qué tal le va esto?; **how did you — at school?** ¿qué tal le fue en el colegio?; **how do you —?** tengo mucho gusto en conocerle, (less formally) encantado, mucho gusto; **to — badly** sufrir reveses, ir perdiendo, fracasar, (in exam) salir mal; **you didn't — so badly** no le fue del todo mal; **to — well** tener éxito, prosperar, (in exam) salir bien; **her son's —ing well** su hijo tiene una buena posición; **business is —ing well** los negocios van bien; **the crops are —ing well** la cosecha se muestra espléndida.
(c) (cook) cocer.
(d) (answer purpose) servir; (be suitable) convenir, venir al caso, ser a propósito; **this one will — me** me quedo con éste; **will this —?** ¿qué te parece éste?; (suffice) bastar; **will that —?** ¿te basta eso?; **that will —** con eso basta; está bien así; **that will —!** ¡basta ya!, ¡cállese!, ¡déjese de eso!; **that won't — eso no vale; eso no se hace; **that will never — eso no puede ser, eso no se puede consentir; **it would never — to + infin** sería inconcebible + infin, sería intolerable que + subj; **to make — arreglárselas por su cuenta; **to make — with** contentarse con, conformarse con.
(e) (with adv or prep) **to — away with** suprimir, eliminar, poner fin a; pet sacrificar; pest exterminar; **to — for** (sl) acabar con; (fam: as servant) ser cocinera de, ser asistenta de, llevar la casa a; **to — with: I could — with a beer** ¡ojalá tuviera una cerveza!, ¡cuánto me gustaría beberme una cerveza!; **I could really — with another** en realidad necesito otro además; **we could — with more money** no nos vendría mal más dinero; **it can — with a wash** no le vendría mal un lavado; **to have nothing to — with** no tener (nada) que ver con; **she won't have anything to — with him** ella no quiere tener nada que ver con él; **we have nothing to — with the neighbours** no tenemos contacto alguno con los vecinos; **to — without** pasarse sin, prescindir de; **you can't — without money** es imprescindible tener dinero.
3 v aux (a) (emphatic) **tell me** dígamelo, por favor; **I — feel better** ciertamente me encuentro mejor; **I — hope so** así lo espero; **I — so wish I could** ¡ojalá pudiera!; **but I did —** it pero yo sí lo hice.
(b) (with inversion) **rarely does it happen that** rara vez ocurre que.

(c) (in questions) — **you know him?** ¿le conoces?
(d) (negation with not) **you — not earn enough** Vd no gana bastante.
4 verb substitute: **I spoke before you did** yo hablé antes que Vd; **he talks to servants as others — to their dogs** habla a los criados como otros a sus perros; — **as I —** haga Vd como yo; **so — I** yo también, yo hago lo mismo; **did you see him?** ... **I did** ¿le viste? ... yo sí; **but I didn't** pero yo no; **he spoke as he often did** habló como lo había hecho muchas veces.
5 vr: **to — oneself proud** (or well) darse buena vida; permitirse cosas de lujo.
6 n (fam) (a) (gathering) reunión f; (ceremony) ceremonia f, acto m; (party) fiesta f, guateque m.
(b) (trouble) lío m; **that was quite a —** eso sí que fue un lío; **he had a — with the police** tuvo un lío con la policía.
doc [dɔk] n (fam) = **doctor**.
docile ['dəusail] adj dócil.
docility [dəu'siliti] n docilidad f.
dock[1] [dɔk] n (Bot) acedera f, ramaza f.
dock[2] [dɔk] vt animal descolar; hair, tail recortar; pay etc reducir, rebajar; **I've been —ed £1** me han rebajado la paga en una libra.
dock[3] [dɔk] **1** n (Naut) dársena f, muelle m; (with gates) dique m; **—s** muelles mpl, puerto m; **dry — dique m seco; **floating — dique m flotante; **to be in — (fam: car) estar averiado, tener averías.
2 vt poner en dique, hacer entrar en dique.
3 vi entrar en dique, atracar al muelle, (loosely) llegar; **we —ed at 5** llegamos a las 5, entramos en el puerto a las 5; **when we —ed at Vigo** cuando llegamos a Vigo.
dock[4] [dɔk] n (Law) banquillo m de los acusados.
docker ['dɔkə*] n trabajador m portuario, estibador m.
docket ['dɔkit] n certificado m; (label) etiqueta f, marbete m.
dockyard ['dɔkjɑːd] n astillero m, (naval) arsenal m.
doctor ['dɔktə*] **1** n (Med) médico m, a f; (Univ) doctor m, ora f (of en); **family — médico m de cabecera; **lady —, **woman — médica f; **to be under the — ser atendida por el médico.
2 vt (Med) medicinar, tratar, curar; cat etc castrar; drink adulterar; food mezclar drogas con; **to — up** machine etc componer.
3 vr: **to — oneself** tomar medicinas, curarse.
doctorate ['dɔktərit] n doctorado m.
doctrinaire [‚dɔktri'nɛə*] **1** adj doctrinario. **2** n doctrinario m, a f.
doctrinal [dɔk'trainl] adj doctrinal.
doctrine ['dɔktrin] n doctrina f.
document ['dɔkjumənt] n documento m.
document ['dɔkjumənt] vt documentar.
documentary [‚dɔkju'mentəri] **1** adj documental. **2** n documental m.
documentation [‚dɔkjumen'teiʃən] n documentación f.
dodder ['dɔdə*] vi chochear.
doddering ['dɔdəriŋ] adj, **doddery** ['dɔdəri] adj chocho.
dodge [dɔdʒ] **1** n (of body) regate m, esguince m, evasión f; (fig) truco m, maniobra f; (Mech) dispositivo m.
2 vt (elude) evadir, blow esquivar, pursuer dar esquinazo a; **to — the issue** evadir el tema; **to — work** gandulear.
3 vi hurtar el cuerpo, dar un esguince; (fig) escurrir el bulto; **to — into a shop** entrar de repente en una tienda; **to — round a corner** doblar una esquina (y desaparecer); **to — behind a tree** ocultarse tras un árbol.
dodgems ['dɔdʒəmz] npl coches mpl de choque.
dodger ['dɔdʒə*] n gandul mf; **artful — trampista mf.
dodo ['dəudəu] n dodo m, dodó m.
doe [dəu] n (deer) gama f; (rabbit) coneja f; (hare) liebre f.
doer ['du(ː)ə*] n hacedor m, ora f; agente m.
does [dʌz] see **do**.
doeskin ['dəuskin] n ante m, piel f de ante.
doesn't ['dʌznt] = **does not**.
doff [dɔf] vt quitarse.
dog [dɔg] **1** n (a) perro m; (fox) zorro m; **the —s** (greyhounds) carreras fpl de galgos, canódromo m.
(b) (term of abuse) tunante m, bribón m; **you —!** ¡canalla!, (hum) ¡tunante!; **gay — tío m alegre; **you lucky —!** ¡qué chorra tienes!; **he's a lucky — es un tío con suerte.
(c) **hot — perro m caliente.
(d) **to be a — in the manger** ser el perro del

hortelano; **to be top** — ser el gallo del lugar, triunfar; **to go to the** —**s** echarse a perder, arruinarse; **you haven't a** —**'s chance** no tienes la más remota posibilidad; **to lead a** —**'s life** tener una vida de perros; **let sleeping** —**s lie** vale más no meneallo; **love me, love my** — quien quiere a Beltrán quiere a su can.

2 *vt* seguir los pasos de, seguir la pista de; **he was** —**ged by ill luck** le persiguió la mala suerte.

dog biscuit ['dɔg͵biskit] *n* galleta *f* de perro.
dogcart ['dɔgkɑːt] *n* dócar *m*.
dog collar ['dɔg͵kɔlə*] *n* collar *m* de perro.
dog days ['dɔgdeiz] *npl* canícula *f*, caniculares *mpl*.
doge [dəudʒ] *n* dux *m*.
dog-eared ['dɔgiəd] *adj* sobado, muy manoseado.
dogfight ['dɔgfait] *n* (*Aer*) combate *m* aéreo (reñido y confuso); (*fig*) batalla *f* muy reñida.
dogfish ['dɔgfiʃ] *n* perro *m* marino, cazón *m*.
dogged ['dɔgid] *adj* tenaz, obstinado.
doggedly ['dɔgidli] *adv* tenazmente.
doggedness ['dɔgidnis] *n* tenacidad *f*.
doggerel ['dɔgərəl] *n* versos *mpl* ramplones, malos versos *mpl*, coplas *fpl* de ciego.
doggo ['dɔgəu] *adv* (*fam*): **to lie** — no bullir; estar escondido.
doggy ['dɔgi] *n* perrito *m*.
doghouse ['dɔghaus] *n*, *pl* —**houses** [͵hauziz] (*US*) perrera *f*; **to be in the** — estar en desgracia.
dog Latin ['dɔg'lætin] *n* latín *m* macarrónico, latinajo *m*.
doglike ['dɔglaik] *adj* canino; de perro.
dogma ['dɔgmə] *n* dogma *m*.
dogmatic [dɔg'mætik] *adj* dogmático.
dogmatically [dɔg'mætikəli] *adv* dogmáticamente.
dogmatism ['dɔgmətizəm] *n* dogmatismo *m*.
dogmatize ['dɔgmətaiz] *vi* dogmatizar.
do-gooder ['duː'gudə*] *n* (*fam*) *persona que apoya constantemente las obras benéficas etc, persona candorosa y abnegada.*
dog rose ['dɔgrəuz] *n* escaramujo *m*, rosal *m* silvestre.
dogsbody ['dɔgzbɔdi] *n* (*sl*): **to be a** — cargar con la culpa de todo, ser el pagano; **to be the general** — hacer todo el trabajo rutinario, ocuparse en cosas que no quieren hacer los demás.
dog-tired ['dɔg'taiəd] *adj*: **to be** — estar rendido.
dog track ['dɔgtræk] *n* canódromo *m*.
dog-watch ['dɔgwɔtʃ] *n* (*Naut*) guardia *f* de cuartillo.
doily ['dɔili] *n* pañito *m* de adorno.
doing ['duːiŋ] **1** *pres part of* do; **there's not much** — hay poca animación; **nothing** —! ¡de ninguna manera!, ¡ni hablar!

2 —**s** *npl* (**a**) (*deeds*) hechos *mpl*; (*conduct*) conducta *f*, actuación *f*; (*happenings*) sucesos *mpl*; **there were great** —**s in the house** hubo muchísima actividad en la casa.

(**b**) (*Mech etc*) chisme *m*; **that** —**s with two knobs** aquel chisme con dos botones.
do-it-yourself ['duːitjə'self] *attr etc* hágalo Vd mismo; **a** — **kit** un equipo para hacerlo uno mismo; **he's a** — **enthusiast** le entusiasma hacer trabajos técnicos para sí mismo.
doldrums ['dɔldrəmz] *npl* (*Naut*) zona *f* de las calmas ecuatoriales; **to be in the** — (*fig*: *person*) estar abatido, (*business*) estar encalmado, (*stock exchange*) estar en calma.
dole [dəul] **1** *n* limosna *f*; (*of unemployed*) subsidio *m* de paro; **to be on the** — estar parado; **love on the** — el amor en la miseria.

2 *vt*: **to** — **out** repartir, distribuir.
doleful ['dəulful] *adj* triste, lúgubre.
dolefully ['dəulfəli] *adv* tristemente.
doll [dɔl] **1** *n* muñeca *f*; (*sl*) chica *f*. **2** *vt*: **to** — **up** adornar, ataviar. **3** *vr*: **to** — **oneself up** emperejilarse, ataviarse.
dollar ['dɔlə*] *n* dólar *m*; **you can bet your bottom** — **that** es completamente seguro que.
dollop ['dɔləp] *n* porción *f*, masa *f*.
doll's house ['dɔlzhaus] *n*, *pl* — **houses** [͵hauziz] casa *f* de muñecas.
dolly ['dɔli] *n* muñequita *f*.
dolomite ['dɔləmait] *n* dolomita *f*.
Dolomites ['dɔləmaits] *pl* Alpes *mpl* Dolomíticos.
dolphin ['dɔlfin] *n* delfín *m*.
dolt [dəult] *n* imbécil *m*, mastuerzo *m*; **you** —! ¡imbécil!
domain [dəu'mein] *n* (*lands*) heredad *f*, propiedad *f*; (*empire*) dominio *m*; (*sphere*) campo *m*, competencia *f*.
dome [dəum] *n* cúpula *f*; bóveda *f* (*also fig*); (*Geog*) colina *f* redonda.
domestic [də'mestik] **1** *adj* doméstico; *appliance* de uso doméstico; *industry, product* nacional; *trade*

interior; *strife* interno, intestino; (*home-loving*) casero, hogareño.

2 *n* doméstico *m*.
domesticate [də'mestikeit] *vt* domesticar.
domesticated [də'mestikeitid] *adj* domesticado; *person* casero, hogareño.
domesticity [͵dəumes'tisiti] *n* domesticidad *f*.
domicile ['dɔmisail] **1** *n* domicilio *m*. **2** *vt*: **to be** —**d in** tener su domicilio en.
domiciliary [͵dɔmi'siliəri] *adj* domiciliario.
dominance ['dɔminəns] *n* dominación *f*.
dominant ['dɔminənt] *adj* dominante.
dominate ['dɔmineit] *vti* dominar.
domination [͵dɔmi'neiʃən] *n* dominación *f*.
domineer [͵dɔmi'niə*] *vi* dominar, tiranizar (*over someone* a alguien).
domineering [͵dɔmi'niəriŋ] *adj* dominante, dominador, tiránico.
Dominica [͵dɔmi'niːkə] Dominica *f*.
Dominican [də'minikən] **1** *adj* dominicano. **2** *n* (*Pol*) dominicano *m*, a *f*; (*Eccl*) dominico *m*.
Dominican Republic [də'minikənri'pʌblik] República *f* Dominicana.
dominion [də'miniən] *n* dominio *m*.
domino ['dɔminəu] *n*, *pl* **dominoes** ['dɔminəuz] (*dress*) dominó *m*; (*in game*) ficha *f* de dominó.
dominoes ['dɔminəuz] *npl* dominó *m*.
Domitian [də'miʃiən] *m* Domiciano.
don[1] [dɔn] *vt* ponerse.
don[2] [dɔn] *n* (*Univ*) catedrático *m*; (*strictly*) socio (*fellow*) *un colegio de las Universidades de Oxford y de Cambridge.*
donate [dəu'neit] *vt* donar.
donation [dəu'neiʃən] *n* donativo *m*.
done [dʌn] *ptp of* do; (**a**) —! ¡trato hecho!; **well** —! ¡muy bien!, ¡bravo!

(**b**) (*Cook*) **I like my meat well** — me gusta la carne muy hecha; **is it** — **yet**? ¿está hecho ya?

(**c**) **it is not** — **to** + *infin* no es elegante + *infin*.

(**d**) **have you** —? ¿has terminado?; **I've** — **with travelling** he terminado de viajar, he renunciado a los viajes; **I've** — **with him** he roto con él.

(**e**) **I'm** — **for** (*tired*) estoy rendido; **if we don't leave now we shall be** — **for** si no nos vamos ahora estamos perdidos; **the car is** — **for** el coche está estropeado del todo; **as a musician he's** — **for** ya no vale para músico.

(**f**) **to be** — **up** (*fam*) estar rendido.
Don Giovanni ['dɔndʒiəu'vɑːni] *m* Don Juan.
donkey ['dɔŋki] *n* burro *m*, burra *f*; **for** —**'s years** durante tantísimos años.
donkey-engine ['dɔŋki͵endʒin] *n* pequeña máquina *f* de vapor, motor *m* auxiliar.
donnish ['dɔniʃ] *adj* de erudito, de profesor; de aspecto erudito; (*pej*) pedantesco; **he looks very** — tiene aspecto de muy erudito.
donor ['dəunə*] *n* donante *mf*.
Don Quixote [dɔn'kwiksət] *m* Don Quijote.
don't [dəunt] **1** = **do not**. **2** *n* prohibición *f*, consejo *m* negativo.
doodle ['duːdl] **1** *n* garabatos *mpl* (*or* dibujos *etc*) que hace uno para distraerse. **2** *vi* hacer garabatos (*or* dibujos *etc*) para distraerse.
doom [duːm] **1** *n* (*fate*) suerte *f*, hado *m*; (*death*) perdición *f*, muerte *f*; (*Rel*) juicio *m* final.

2 *vt* condenar (*a muerte etc*); predestinar (a la perdición *etc*); **to be** —**ed to die** ser condenado a muerte; **the plan was** —**ed to fail** el proyecto tuvo fatalmente que fracasar, el proyecto estuvo llamado a fracasar; **the** —**ed ship** el buque condenado.
doomsday ['duːmzdei] *n* día *m* del juicio final.
door [dɔː*] *n* puerta *f*; entrada *f*; (*of vehicle*) portezuela *f*; **back** — puerta *f* de servicio; **front** — puerta *f* principal, puerta *f* de entrada; **revolving** — puerta *f* giratoria; **side** — puerta *f* accesoria; **sliding** — puerta *f* de corredera; **behind closed** —**s** a puerta cerrada; **next** — en la casa de al lado; **this is next** — **to lunacy** esto raya en la locura; **to be out of** —**s** estar al aire libre; **to be at death's** — estar a la muerte; **never darken my** — **again** no vuelva Vd nunca por aquí; **to lay the blame at someone's** — echar a uno la culpa; **to leave the** — **open for** dar libre paso a, no excluir; **to show someone to the** — acompañar a uno a la puerta; **to show someone the** — enseñar la puerta a uno; **to slam the** — dar un portazo; **to slam the** — **in someone's face** dar con la puerta en las narices de uno; **to slam the** — **on negotiations** terminar de modo concluyente las negociaciones.
doorbell ['dɔːbel] *n* timbre *m* de llamada.
door-handle ['dɔː͵hændl] *n* tirador *m* de puerta; (*of car*) manija *f*.

doorkeeper ['dɔːˌkiːpə*] *n* conserje *m*, portero *m*.
door knob ['dɔːnɔb] *n* pomo *m* de puerta, tirador *m* de puerta.
door-knocker ['dɔːˌnɔkə*] *n* aldaba *f*, llamador *m*.
doorman ['dɔːmən] *n*, *pl* **-men** [mən] portero *m*.
doormat ['dɔːmæt] *n* felpudo *m*, estera *f*.
doornail ['dɔːneil] *n see* **dead**.
doorpost ['dɔːpəust] *n* jamba *f* (de puerta).
doorstep ['dɔːstep] *n* umbral *m*, peldaño *m* de la puerta.
doorway ['dɔːwei] *n* puerta *f*, entrada *f*; portal *m*.
dope [dəup] **1** *n* (*varnish*) barniz *m*; (*drug*) narcótico *m*, droga *f*; (*information*, *sl*) informes *mpl*, información *f*; (*person*, *sl*) imbécil *m*; **you —** ! ¡imbécil!
2 *vt* (*sl*) narcotizar, drogar.
dopey ['dəupi] *adj* (*sl*) aturdido, mareado; (*silly*) imbécil.
doping ['dəupiŋ] *n* drogado *m*.
dormant ['dɔːmənt] *adj* (**a**) inactivo; **to be —**, **to lie —** dormir. (**b**) (*fig*) inactivo, latente, en estado latente.
dormer window ['dɔːmə'windəu] *n* buhardilla *f*.
dormitory ['dɔːmitri] *n* dormitorio *m*.
dormouse ['dɔːmaus] *n*, *pl* **dormice** ['dɔːmais] lirón *m*.
Dorothy ['dɔrəθi] *f* Dorotea.
dorsal ['dɔːsl] *adj* dorsal.
dory ['dɔːri] *n* (*Fish*) gallo *m*, pez *m* de San Pedro.
dosage ['dəusidʒ] *n* dosificación *f*, dosis *f*.
dose [dəus] **1** *n* dosis *f*. **2** *vt* administrar una dosis a; medicinar; *wine* adulterar. **3** *vr*: **to — oneself** medicinarse (*with* de).
doss [dɔs] *vi* (*sl*) dormir; **to — down** echarse.
doss house ['dɔshaus] *n*, *pl* **— houses** [ˌhauziz] (*sl*) pensión *f* de bajísima categoría.
dossier ['dɔsiei] *n* expediente *m*; (*police etc*) ficha *f*; (*fig*) antecedentes *mpl*.
dot [dɔt] **1** *n* punto *m*; **three —s** (*Typ*) puntos *mpl* suspensivos; **—s and dashes** puntos *mpl* y rayas; **at 7 o'clock on the —** a las 7 en punto; **to pay on the —** pagar puntualmente.
2 *vt* (**a**) *letter* poner el punto sobre; **to — the i's and cross the t's** (*fig*) poner los puntos sobre las íes, completar los detalles; terminar de aclarar un asunto.
(**b**) (*speckle*) puntear, motear, salpicar de puntos.
(**c**) (*scatter*; *also* **to — about**) esparcir, desparramar; **to be —ted with** estar salpicado de; **they are —ted about the country** se encuentran esparcidos por el país.
(**d**) (*fam*) **to — someone a blow** dar un golpe a uno; **he —ted him one** le dio un golpe.
dotage ['dəutidʒ] *n* chochez *f*; **to be in one's —** chochear.
dote [dəut] *vi*: **to — on** adorar, idolatrar.
doting ['dəutiŋ] *adj* chocho, tontamente cariñoso; **her — parents** sus padres que le querían con exceso.
dotty ['dɔti] *adj* (*fam*) chiflado; *idea*, *scheme* estrafalario, tonto.
double ['dʌbl] **1** *adj* doble; *sense* doble, ambiguo; *bed* de matrimonio; *room* para dos; **the — 6** el 6 doble; **— 9** (*Tel*) nueve nueve; **— the sum, a — sum** una cantidad doble, el doble; **it is — what it was** es el doble de lo que era; **my income is — that of my neighbour** mis ingresos son dobles que los de mi vecino; **to be bent —** estar encorvado.
2 *adv*: **— or quits** doble o nada; **to fold something —** doblar algo; **to pay —** pagar el doble; **to see —** tener doble vista.
3 *n* (**a**) doble *mf*, (*person*) doble *mf*, (*Cine*) doble *mf*.
(**b**) **—s** (*Tennis*) juego *m* de dobles; **men's —s** dobles *mpl* masculinos; **women's —s** dobles *mpl* de damas; **mixed —s** dobles *mpl* mixtos.
(**c**) (*Bridge*) doble *m*; **asking — doble** *m* de llamada; **penalty — doble** *m* de castigo.
(**d**) **at the —** corriendo, (*Mil*) a paso ligero.
4 *vt* doblar; *money*, *quantity etc* doblar, duplicar; *efforts* redoblar; (*Theat*, *Bridge*) doblar; **to be —d up with pain** retorcerse de dolor; **to be —d up with laughter** mondarse de risa.
5 *vi* doblarse; (*quantity etc*) doblarse, duplicarse; **to — back** volver sobre sus pasos; **to — for** sustituir a (*also Theat*), hacer las veces de; **to — up** (*with pain*) desplomarse, encogerse, retorcerse; (*lodgers*) compartir la misma habitación.
double-barrelled ['dʌblˌbærəld] *adj* de dos cañones; *name* de dos apellidos (unidos con guión).
double bass ['dʌbl'beis] *n* contrabajo *m*.
double-breasted ['dʌbl'brestid] *adj* cruzado, con botonadura doble.

double-cross ['dʌbl'krɔs] **1** *n* engaño *m*, trampa *f*, traición *f*. **2** *vt* engañar, traicionar.
double-dealing ['dʌbl'diːliŋ] *n* trato *m* doble, duplicidad *f*.
double-decker ['dʌbl'dekə*] *n* autobús *m* de dos pisos.
double-edged ['dʌbl'edʒd] *adj* de doble filo.
double entendre ['duːblãːn'tãːndr] *n* equívoco *m*, frase *f* ambigua.
double entry ['dʌbl'entri] *n* partida *f* doble.
double-jointed ['dʌbl'dʒɔintid] *adj* con articulaciones dobles.
double-quick ['dʌbl'kwik] *adv* rapidísimamente, con toda prontitud, (*Mil*) a paso ligero.
double-spaced ['dʌbl'speist] *adv* (*Typ*) a doble espacio.
doublet ['dʌblit] *n* jubón *m*; (*Gram*) doble etimología *f*.
double-talk ['dʌblˌtɔːk] *n* palabras *fpl* insinceras.
doubleton ['dʌbltən] *n* dubletón *m*.
doubly ['dʌbli] *adv* doblemente.
doubt [daut] **1** *n* (*a* **—**) duda *f*; (*state*) duda *f*, incertidumbre *f*; **no —** ! ¡sin duda!; **beyond —**, **past all —**, **without (a) —** fuera de toda duda, indudablemente; **when in —** en caso de duda; **the matter is in some —** el caso sigue dudoso; **there is some — about it** sobre esto existen dudas; **there is no — that** es indudable que, no cabe duda de que; **to begin to have one's —s** empezar a dudar.
2 *vt* dudar; (*distrust*) dudar de; **I — it** lo dudo; **to — someone's loyalty** dudar de la lealtad de uno.
3 *vi* dudar; **he —ed whether to go** dudaba si iría.
doubter ['dautə*] *n* escéptico *m*, a *f*.
doubtful ['dautful] *adj* dudoso, incierto; *character*, *place* sospechoso; **I am — whether** dudo si; **he remained — about it** tenía todavía sus dudas sobre ello; **of — efficacy** de eficacia incierta.
doubtfully ['dautfəli] *adv* inciertamente; **he said —** dijo nada convencido.
doubtless ['dautlis] *adv* sin duda.
douche [duːʃ] **1** *n* ducha *f*; (*Med*) jeringa *f*. **2** *vt* duchar. **3** *vi* ducharse.
dough [dəu] *n* masa *f*, pasta *f*; (*sl*) pasta *f*.
doughboy ['dəubɔi] *n* (*US fam*) soldado *m* de infantería.
doughnut ['dəunʌt] *n* buñuelo *m*.
doughty ['dauti] *adj* *person* valiente, esforzado; *deed* hazañoso.
doughy ['dəui] *adj* pastoso.
dour ['duə*] *adj* austero, severo; (*obstinate*) terco; **a — Scot** un escocés cerrado; **a — struggle** una batalla muy reñida.
Douro ['duərəu] Duero *m*.
douse [daus] *vt* *light* apagar; (*with water*) mojar, lavar (*with* de).
dove [dʌv] *n* paloma *f*.
dovecote ['dʌvkɔt] *n* palomar *m*.
dovetail ['dʌvteil] **1** *n* cola *f* de milano. **2** *vt* ensamblar a cola de milano. **3** *vi* (*fig*) encajar (con), ajustarse; **to — in with** encajar perfectamente con.
dowager ['dauədʒə*] *n* viuda *f* de un titulado; **— duchess** duquesa *f* viuda.
dowdy ['daudi] *adj* poco elegante, poco atractivo.
dowel ['dauəl] *n* clavija *f*.
down[1] [daun] *n* (*Orn*) plumón *m*, flojel *m*; (*fluff*) pelusa *f*; (*on face*) bozo *m*; (*on body*) vello *m*; (*on fruit*) pelusilla *f*; (*Bot*) vilano *m*.
down[2] [daun] *n* (*Geog*) colina *f*.
down[3] [daun] **1** *adv* (**a**) (*downwards*) abajo, hacia abajo, para abajo; (*to the ground*) por tierra, en tierra; (*to the south*) hacia el sur; **I ran all the way —** bajé toda la distancia corriendo; **there was snow all the way —** estaba nevando durante todo el recorrido.
(**b**) **— below** allá abajo; **— by the river** abajo en la ribera; **— on the shore** abajo en la playa; **— to** hasta; **— under** en Australia *or* en Nueva Zelanda; **to go — under** ir a Australia *etc*.
(**c**) **to be —** (*price*, *temperature*, *etc*) haber bajado; (*Aer*) haber aterrizado, estar en tierra; (*person*) haber caído, estar en tierra; **to be — from college** haber terminado el curso universitario; **he's not — yet** todavía no ha bajado, sigue en cama; **to be — and out** no tener nada en absoluto, estar sin un cuarto, ser pobrísimo; **to be 3 goals —** tener 3 goles menos; **I'm £2 —** he perdido 2 libras, me faltan 2 libras; **to be — on someone** tener inquina a uno; **I'm — to my last cigarette** me queda un cigarrillo nada más.
2 *prep*: **— the hill** cuesta abajo; **— river** río abajo (*from* de); **to walk — the street** bajar la calle, ir por

la calle; **the rain was running — the trunk** la lluvia corría por el tronco.

3 *interj* —! ¡abajo!; —!, —, **boy!** (*to dog*) ¡quieto!; **— with the tyrant!** ¡abajo el tirano!, ¡muera el tirano!

4 *adj train, stroke* descendente; *payment* al contado.

5 *vt food* devorar; *drink* beberse (de un trago); *person* derribar, echar por los suelos; *plane* derribar, abatir; *see* **tool**.

6 n: **to have a — on someone** (*fam*) tener inquina a uno; *see* **up**.

down-and-out ['daunən'aut] **1** *adj* derrotado, pobrísimo. **2** n pobre *mf*, vagabundo m.

down-at-heel ['daunət'hi:l] *adj* decaído, venido a menos; *appearance* desastrado.

downcast ['daunkɑ:st] *adj* abatido, alicaído.

downfall ['daunfɔ:l] n caída f, ruina f.

downgrade ['daungreid] n: **to be on the —** ir cuesta abajo, estar en plena decadencia.

downgrade [daun'greid] *vt* degradar, asignar a un grado más bajo.

downhearted ['daun'hɑ:tid] *adj* desanimado; **don't be —** no te dejes desanimar.

downhill ['daun'hil] **1** *adv* cuesta abajo; **to go —** (*fig*) ir cuesta abajo, estar en franca decadencia. **2** *adj* en declive.

downpour ['daunpɔ:*] n aguacero m, chaparrón m.

downright ['daunrait] **1** *adj person* franco; *lie* abierto, manifiesto; (*obvious*) notorio, evidente; (*out-and-out*) abierto, declarado. **2** *adv* completamente.

down-river ['daun'rivə*] *adv* = **downstream**.

downstairs ['daun'stɛəz] **1** *adv* abajo; (*in lower flat*) en el piso de abajo; **to fall —** caer escaleras abajo; **he went slowly —** bajó despacio la escalera. **2** *adj* de abajo; **a — window** una ventana de la planta baja.

downstream ['daun'stri:m] *adv* aguas abajo, río abajo (*from de*); **to go —** ir río abajo; **to swim —** nadar con la corriente; **a town — from Soria** una ciudad más abajo de Soria; **about 5 km — from Zamora** unos 5 km más abajo de Zamora.

downstroke ['daunstrəuk] n (*with pen*) palote m, pierna f; (*Mech*) carrera f descendente.

down-to-earth ['dauntu'ə:θ] *adj* práctico, realista.

downtown ['daun'taun] **1** *adv* **go** hacia el centro de la ciudad, **be** en el centro de la ciudad. **2** *adj* del centro de la ciudad, céntrico.

downtrodden ['daun,trɔdn] *adj* oprimido.

downturn ['dauntə:n] n descenso m, bajada f, disminución f.

downward ['daunwəd] *adj curve, movement etc* descendente; *slope* en declive; *tendency* a la baja.

downward(s) ['daunwəd(z)] *adv* hacia abajo.

downy ['dauni] *adj* velloso; (*and soft*) blando, suave.

dowry ['dauri] n dote f.

dowse [dauz] *vt see* **douse**.

dowser ['dauzə*] n zahorí m.

doxy ['dɔksi] n querida f.

doyen ['dɔiən] n decano m.

doze [dəuz] **1** n sueño m ligero; sueño m breve; **to have a —** (*after meal*) echar una siestecita. **2** *vi* dormitar; **to — off** quedarse medio dormido, dormirse.

dozen ['dʌzn] n docena f; **baker's —** docena f del fraile; **daily —** pequeña serie f de ejercicios físicos para mantenerse en forma cada día; **to talk nineteen to the —** hablar más que siete.

dozy ['dəuzi] *adj* (*fam*) amodorrado.

drab [dræb] *adj* (*fig*) gris, monótono, triste.

drachm [dræm] n, **drachma** ['drækmə] n dracma f.

draconian [drə'kəuniən] *adj* draconiano, severo, riguroso.

draft [drɑ:ft] **1** n (*Comm*) giro m, letra f de cambio; (*Mil*) destacamento m; (*reinforcements*) refuerzos *mpl*; (*conscription*) quinta f; (*preliminary study*) borrador m (*also* **first —, rough —**); **third —** tercera versión f; *see* **draught**.

2 *vt document* redactar; *scheme* preparar; (*rough out*) hacer un borrador de, preparar una versión de; (*Mil*) destacar, (*send*) mandar (*to* a); (*conscript*) quintar, llamar al servicio militar; (*fig*) forzar, obligar.

drag [dræg] **1** n (*net etc*) rastra f, red f barredera; (*sledge*) narria f; (*Aer etc*) resistencia f al avance; (*fig*) obstáculo m, estorbo m (*on* a, *para*); (*boring thing*) cosa f pesada, lata f; **the film is a —** la película es pesadísima.

2 *vt object* arrastrar, llevar arrastrado; *sea bed, river etc* dragar, rastrear, efectuar obras de dragado en; **to — the anchor** garrar; **to — something along** arrastrar algo tras sí, arrastrar algo con mucha

dificultad; **to — in** *reference* traer por los pelos; **to — out** *story* contar de una manera aburridísima.

3 *vi* arrastrarse por el suelo; (*go very slowly*) moverse muy despacio; (*time*) pasar lentamente; **the book begins to —** el libro empieza a perder su interés; **how that afternoon —ged!** ¡cómo nos aburrimos aquella tarde!; **to — for** rastrear en busca de; **to — on** and **on** continuar como si nunca fuera a acabarse, ser interminable.

4 *vr*: **to — oneself along** arrastrarse.

dragnet ['drægnet] n rastra f, red f barredera.

dragoman ['drægəumən] n, *pl* **-mans** [mənz] or **-men** [mən] dragomán m.

dragon ['drægən] n dragón m; (*woman*) fiera f.

dragonfly ['drægənflai] n libélula f, caballito m del diablo.

dragoon [drə'gu:n] **1** n dragón m. **2** *vt* tiranizar; **to — someone into doing something** obligar a uno por intimidación a hacer algo.

drain [drein] **1** n (a) (*outlet*) desaguadero m; (*in street*) boca f de alcantarilla, sumidero m; (*Agr*) zanja f de drenaje; **the —s** (*sewage system*) las alcantarillas, el alcantarillado.

(b) (*fig*) (*source of loss*) desaguadero m, sumidero m, desagüe m; (*loss*) pérdida f, disminución f; **to be a — on** *energies, resources* consumir, agotar; **they are a great — on our gold reserves** constituyen el gran sumidero de nuestras reservas de oro; **the brain —** la pérdida (por emigración) de gente de formación universitaria.

(c) there's just a — left quedan unas gotitas.

2 *vt* (a) desaguar; (*Agr, Med*) drenar; (*Mech*) purgar, drenar; *glass* apurar; *last drops* beberse, tragarse; *lake* desangrar, desecar; **to — away** vaciar; **to — off** desangrar.

(b) (*fig*) agotar, consumir; **the country is being —ed of wealth** el país está siendo empobrecido; **to feel —ed of energy** estar agotado, sentirse sin fuerzas.

3 *vi* (*washed dishes*) escurrirse; **to — away** irse; **to — into** (*river etc*) desaguar en.

drainage ['dreinidʒ] **1** n (a) (*act*) desagüe m; (*Agr, Med*) drenaje m; (*of lake*) desecación f.

(b) (*sewage*) aguas *fpl* de alcantarillado; (*sewage system*) alcantarillado m.

drainage channel ['dreinidʒ,tʃænl] n zanja f de drenaje.

draining board ['dreiniŋ,bɔ:d], (US) **drainboard** ['dreinbɔ:d] n escurreplatos m, escurridera f, escurridor m.

drainpipe ['dreinpaip] n tubo m de desagüe; **— trousers** pantalones *mpl* muy estrechos.

drake [dreik] n pato m macho.

dram [dræm] n (*Pharm*) dracma f; (*of drink*) trago m.

drama ['drɑ:mə] n drama m.

dramatic [drə'mætik] *adj* dramático.

dramatist ['dræmətist] n dramaturgo m.

dramatize ['dræmətaiz] *vt* dramatizar; **X —d by Y** X en versión dramática de Y.

drank [dræŋk] *pret of* **drink**.

drape [dreip] **1** n colgadura f, cortina f.

2 *vt object* adornar con colgaduras, cubrir (*in, with* de), vestir (*with* de); *cloth, clothing* arreglar los pliegues de; **— this round your shoulders** ponte esto sobre las espaldas; **he —d a towel about himself** se cubrió con una toalla; **he —d an arm about my shoulders** me ciñó el hombro con su brazo.

draper ['dreipə*] n pañero m, lencero m.

drapery ['dreipəri] n (*hangings*) colgaduras *fpl*, ropaje m; (*as merchandise*) pañería f.

drastic ['dræstik] *adj* drástico; enérgico, fuerte; *measure* draconiano, severo; *reduction etc* importante; *change* radical.

drastically ['dræstikəli] *adv* enérgicamente; severamente; **to be — reduced** sufrir una reducción importante; **he — revised his ideas** cambió radicalmente de ideas.

drat [dræt] *vt*: **—!**, **— it!** ¡maldición!

draught [drɑ:ft] **1** n (a) (*drink*) trago m; (*Med*) dosis f; **at one —** de un trago.

(b) (*Naut*) calado m.

(c) (*of air*) corriente f de aire; (*breeze*) viento m, brisa f; **to feel the —** (*fig*) tener dificultades, sufrir las consecuencias, resentirse de los efectos.

(d) **—s** (*game*) juego m de damas.

2 *attr horse* de tiro; *beer* de barril; *see* **draft**.

draughtboard ['drɑ:ftbɔ:d] n tablero m de damas.

draught excluder [drɑ:ftiks'klu:də*] n burlete m.

draught horse ['drɑ:fthɔ:s] n caballo m de tiro.

draughtsman ['drɑ:ftsmən] n, *pl* **-men** [mən] delineante m, proyectista m.

draughtsmanship ['drɑːftsmənʃip] n arte m del delineante.

draughty ['drɑːfti] adj room que tiene corrientes de aire, lleno de corrientes de aire; day, place de mucho viento.

draw [drɔː] 1 n (a) (Sport) empate m, (Chess) tablas fpl.

(b) (lottery) sorteo m (for de).

(c) (attraction) atracción f; (Theat) función f taquillera, obra f de mucho éxito.

2 (irr: pret **drew**, ptp **drawn**) vt (a) (drag) arrastrar, tirar de; vehicle tirar; (attract) atraer; (take out) sacar; (extract) extraer; (pluck out) arrancar; (lengthen) alargar; attention llamar (to sobre); audience, crowd atraer; blood hacer manar, derramar; bow tender; breath tomar, aspirar; cards robar; cheque girar (on a cargo de, for por); comparison hacer; conclusion sacar; curtains correr; distinction hacer; drawing, model, scene dibujar; fowl destripar; line etc trazar, tirar; lots echar; money from bank retirar; number, prize sacarse; salary ganar, percibir, cobrar; tooth sacar, extraer; wages cobrar; water (draught) calar, tener un calado de; to — a game lograr el empate, empatar (with con), (Chess) entablar.

(b) **drawn: to be —n against** tener que jugar contra; **to feel —n to** subject sentir la atracción de, person tener simpatía a.

(c) **to — someone aside** apartar a uno, llamar a uno aparte; **to — back** retirar; curtain descorrer; **to — forth** hacer salir; comment motivar, suscitar; **to — in** tirar hacia dentro; atraer; **to — off** quitar; liquid vaciar, trasegar; pursuers desviar, apartar; **to — on** gloves ponerse; person engatusar; **to — out** (take out) sacar; (lengthen) alargar; wire tirar, trefilar; person hacer hablar, hacer menos reservado, (deceitfully) sonsacar; **to — together** reunir, juntar; **to — up** (raise) levantar, alzar; chair acercar; men formar; army ordenar para el combate; document redactar, preparar.

3 vi (a) (chimney) tirar (bien); (attract) atraer; (as artist) dibujar; (in game) empatar, (Chess) entablar.

(b) **to — aside** ir aparte, apartarse; **to — away** alejarse (from de); **to — back** dar un paso hacia atrás, retroceder; (fig) cejar, volverse atrás; **to — in** (evenings) hacerse más cortos; **to — near** acercarse (to a); **to — on** source inspirarse en; knowledge aprovechar; bank account retirar fondos de; supporters contar con el apoyo de; **to — out** (train etc) arrancar, ponerse en marcha, salir de la estación; **to — together** reunirse, juntarse, (fig) hacerse más unidos; **the family has —n together** la familia se ha unido más; **to — up** pararse; see **close** etc.

4 vr: **to — oneself up** erguirse, ponerse en su lugar.

drawback ['drɔːbæk] n inconveniente m, desventaja f (of, to de).

drawbridge ['drɔːbridʒ] n puente m levadizo.

drawee [drɔː'iː] n (Comm) girado m.

drawer[1] ['drɔːə*] n (Comm) girador m.

drawer[2] [drɔː*] n cajón m; **out of the top —** de primera calidad, de categoría superior.

drawers [drɔːz] npl (man's) calzoncillos mpl, (woman's) bragas fpl.

drawing ['drɔːiŋ] n dibujo m.

drawing board ['drɔːiŋbɔːd] n tablero m de delineante; (Art) tablero de dibujo.

drawing pin ['drɔːiŋpin] n chinche f.

drawing room ['drɔːiŋrum] n salón m.

drawl [drɔːl] 1 n habla f lenta y pesada. 2 vt pronunciar lenta y pesadamente, arrastrar. 3 vi hablar lenta y pesadamente.

drawn [drɔːn] 1 ptp of **draw**. 2 adj game empatado; face cansado, ojeroso; long — out larguísimo, interminable; **with — sword** con la espada en la mano.

dray [drei] n carro m pesado.

dread [dred] 1 n pavor m, terror m; **to go in — of** tener miedo a; **to fill someone with —** infundir pavor a uno.

2 adj espantoso.

3 vt tener miedo a, temer; **I — what may happen when he comes** me horroriza lo que pueda pasar cuando venga; **I — to think of it** el pensamiento me horroriza.

dreadful ['dredful] 1 adj terrible, espantoso; (fig) horrible, fatal, malísimo; **how —!** ¡qué barbaridad!; **I feel —** me siento muy mal; **I feel — about it** la cosa me da vergüenza.

2 n: penny — novelita f (etc) de bajísima categoría.

dreadfully ['dredfəli] adv terriblemente; (fig) malísimamente; **I'm — sorry** lo siento muchísimo; **it's — difficult** es terriblemente difícil.

dreadnought ['drednɔːt] n (Hist) acorazado m.

dream [driːm] 1 n sueño m; (daydream) ensueño m; (ideal) ideal m; (fond hope) ilusión f; **bad —** pesadilla f; **sweet —s!** ¡duerme bien!; **the house of my —s** mi casa ideal, la casa soñada, la casa de mis ilusiones; **isn't he a —?** ¡qué despiste tiene!; **to see something in a —** ver algo en sueños; **she goes about in a —** parece que está soñando; **my fondest — is to** + infin mi mayor ilusión es + infin; **to be rich beyond one's —s** ser más rico de lo que jamás se soñara; **to succeed beyond one's wildest —s** tener muchísimo más éxito de lo que se esperaba.

2 attr ideal; **my — house** mi casa ideal; **to live in a — world** vivir en un mundo de sueños, vivir de pura fantasía.

3 (pret and ptp **dreamed** or **dreamt**) vti soñar (of con, that que); **to — away the day** pasar el día soñando; **to — up** inventar, idear; **you must have —ed it** lo habrás imaginado; **I wouldn't — of it!** ¡ni hablar!; **I wouldn't — of going** no se me ocurriría nunca ir.

dreamer ['driːmə*] n soñador m, ora f, fantaseador m, ora f; visionario m, a f.

dreamily ['driːmili] adv distraídamente, como si estuviera soñando.

dreamland ['driːmlænd] n reino m del ensueño, país m de los sueños; utopía f.

dreamt [dremt] pret and ptp of **dream**.

dreamy ['driːmi] adj character soñador, distraído, muy en las nubes; tone etc del que fantasea, distraído; music soñador, de sueño.

dreariness ['driərinis] n tristeza f, monotonía f; lo aburrido.

dreary ['driəri] adj triste, monótono; book etc aburrido.

dredge [dredʒ] 1 n draga f, rastra f. 2 vt channel dragar, limpiar (etc) con draga; mud etc dragar; **to — up** pescar (also fig).

dredger ['dredʒə*] n draga f.

dredging ['dredʒiŋ] n dragado m, obras fpl de dragado.

dregs [dregz] npl heces fpl, sedimento m; (fig) hez f; **the — of society** la hez de la sociedad; **to drain a glass to the —** apurar un vaso hasta las heces.

drench [drentʃ] 1 n (Vet) poción f. 2 vt mojar (in, with de), empapar (in, with en); **to get —ed** mojarse hasta los huesos.

drenching ['drentʃiŋ] adj torrencial.

Dresden ['drezdən] Dresde; **— china** loza f de Dresde.

dress [dres] 1 n (in general) vestido m, indumentaria f; (clothing) ropa f; (frock) vestido m; **evening —** (man's) traje m de etiqueta, (woman's) traje m de noche; **full —** traje m de etiqueta; **morning —** chaqué m.

2 vt vestir (in de, in green de verde); (Cook) aderezar, aliñar; (Agr) abonar (with de); (Mil) formar, alinear; hair peinar; skins adobar, curtir; shop window poner; Christmas tree arreglar, adornar; stone labrar; wood desbastar; wound curar, vendar; **to be —ed in** vestir, llevar, ir vestido de; **to get —ed** vestirse; **to — someone down** poner a uno como un trapo; **to — up** ataviar (in de); **to — someone up as** disfrazar a uno de.

3 vi vestirse; (Mil) alinearse; **to — well** vestir bien; **to — up** vestirse de etiqueta; **have we to get —ed up?** ¿tenemos que ir de etiqueta?; **to — up as** disfrazarse de.

dress circle ['dres'səːkl] n principal m.

dress coat ['dres'kəut] n frac m.

dress designer ['dresdi'zainə*] n modisto m.

dresser ['dresə*] n aparador m (con estantes), rinconera f; (US) cómoda f con espejo.

dressing ['dresiŋ] n (act) el vestir(se); (Med) vendaje m; (Cook) salsa f, aliño m; (Agr) abono m.

dressing case ['dresiŋkeis] n neceser m.

dressing-down ['dresiŋ'daun] n rapapolvo m; **to give someone a —** echar un rapapolvo a uno.

dressing gown ['dresiŋgaun] n (woman's) bata f, salto m de cama; (man's) batín m.

dressing room ['dresiŋrum] n vestidor m; (Theat) camarín m, camerino m.

dressing station ['dresiŋ,steiʃən] n puesto m de socorro.

dressing table ['dresiŋ,teibl] n tocador m.

dressmaker ['dresmeikə*] n costurera f, modista f.

dressmaking ['dresmeikiŋ] n costura f.

dress rehearsal ['dresri'həːsəl] n ensayo m general.

dress shirt ['dres'ʃəːt] n camisa f de frac.

dress suit ['dres'suːt] n traje m de etiqueta.

dressy ['dresi] adj person aficionado a los trajes muy elegantes; clothing de mucho vestir, muy elegante.

drew [druː] pret of **draw**.

dribble ['dribl] 1 n (Sport) regate m.

2 vt dejar caer gota a gota; (Sport) regatear, driblar.

3 *vi* gotear, caer gota a gota (*down* por); (*from mouth*) babear; (*Sport*) regatear, driblar.

driblet ['driblit] *n* adarme *m*; **in** —*s* por adarmes.

dribs [dribz] *npl*: — **and drabs** cantidades *fpl* pequeñísimas; **the money came in in** — **and drabs** el dinero llegó por adarmes, el dinero llegó lentamente y en pequeñas cantidades.

dried [draid] *adj* seco; *fruit* paso.

drift [drift] **1** *n* (**a**) (*Naut*) impulso *m* de la corriente, velocidad *f* de la corriente; (*amount off course*) deriva *f*; (*fig*) tendencia *f*, movimiento *m*; **the** — **from the land** la despoblación del campo, el éxodo rural; **the** — **to the city** el movimiento hacia la ciudad.

(**b**) (*fig: lack of drive*) inacción *f*.

(**c**) (*of sand, snow*) montón *m*; (*Geol*) terrenos *mpl* de acarreo.

(**d**) (*fig*) (*sense*) significado *m*; (*purpose*) intención *f*, propósito *m*; **to catch someone's** — caer en la cuenta de lo que uno quiere decir.

2 *vt* (*carry*) impeler, llevar; (*pile up*) amontonar.

3 *vi* (*Naut*) ir a la deriva; (*on water, in air etc*) flotar, dejarse llevar por la corriente (*or* el viento), ir arrastrado por la corriente (*or* el viento); (*be off course*) derivar; (*snow*) amontonarse; (*fig*) vivir sin rumbo, no tener propósito fijo; **to** — **into war** dejarse llevar a la guerra, entrar sin realmente quererlo en la guerra; **to** — **from job to job** cambiar a menudo de trabajo sin propósito fijo.

drifter ['driftə*] *n* trainera *f*.

drift ice ['driftais] *n* hielo *m* flotante.

drift-net ['driftnet] *n* traína *f*.

driftwood ['driftwud] *n* madera *f* de deriva.

drill [dril] **1** *n* (**a**) (*Mech*) taladro *m*; (*part of brace and bit*) broca *f*; (*bench machine*) fresadora *f*; (*dentist's*) fresa *f*; (*in mining*) perforadora *f*, barrena *f*; (*in roadmending, also* **pneumatic** —) martillo *m* picador, taladradora *f*.

(**b**) (*Agr: machine*) sembradora *f*.

(**c**) (*Agr: row*) hilera *f*, surco *m*.

(**d**) (*Mil etc*) instrucción *f*; (*School*) ejercicios *mpl*, educación *f* física; **grammar** — ejercicios *mpl* de gramática; **oral** — práctica *f* oral; **you all know the** — (*fam*) todos sabéis lo que habéis de hacer; **what's the** —? (*fam*) ¿qué es lo que hemos de hacer?

2 *vt* (**a**) *metal etc* perforar, taladrar, barrenar; *hole* practicar.

(**b**) (*Agr*) sembrar con sembradora.

(**c**) (*Mil*) enseñar instrucción a; (*Sport etc*) entrenar, adiestrar; **to** — **a class in French** hacer ejercicios de francés con una clase; **to** — **someone to do something** enseñar metódicamente a uno a hacer algo.

3 *vi* (**a**) perforar (*for* en busca de).

(**b**) (*Mil*) hacer instrucción; (*Sport etc*) entrenarse, adiestrarse.

drilling ['driliŋ] *n* (*for oil etc*) perforación *f*.

drilling rig ['driliŋ‚rig] *n* plataforma *f* de perforación submarina.

drily ['draili] *adv* secamente; **he said** — dijo guasón, dijo con su humorismo peculiar.

drink [driŋk] **1** *n* (*in general, alcohol*) bebida *f*; (*a draught*) trago *m*; **soft** — bebida *f* no alcohólica; **the** — (*sl*) el mar, el agua; **I need a** — **of water** necesito un trago de agua; **could I have a** — **of water**? ¿puede Vd darme un poco de agua?; **to have a** — tomar algo; **will you have a** —? ¿quieres tomar algo?; **we had a** — **or two** tomamos unas copas; **to take to** — darse a la bebida.

2 (*irr: pret* **drank**, *ptp* **drunk**) *vt* beber; tomar; **what will you** —? ¿qué quieres tomar?; **to** — **someone under the table** beber hasta tumbar a uno; **to** — **down, to** — **off** beber de un trago; **to** — **in** (*fig*) beberse, *words* estar pendiente de; **to** — **out of** beber de; **to** — **up** beberse, terminar de beber.

3 *vi* (*ie* — *alcohol*) beber; **thanks, I don't** — gracias, yo no bebo; **to** — **like a fish** beber como una esponja; **to** — **to someone** brindar por uno, beber a la salud de uno; **to** — **to the success of** brindar por el éxito de; **to** — **up** terminar de beber.

4 *vr*: **to** — **oneself to death** morir alcoholizado; **to** — **oneself silly** beber hasta emborracharse.

drinkable ['driŋkəbl] *adj* potable, bebible; **it's quite a** — **wine** es un vino nada malo.

drinker ['driŋkə*] *n* bebedor *m*, ora *f*; **hard** — bebedor *m* empedernido.

drinking bout ['driŋkiŋbaut] *n* juerga *f* de borrachera.

drinking fountain ['driŋkiŋ‚fauntin] *n* fuente *f* (de agua potable).

drinking song ['driŋkiŋsɔŋ] *n* canción *f* de taberna.

drinking trough ['driŋkiŋtrɔf] *n* abrevadero *m*, camellón *m*.

drinking water ['driŋkiŋ‚wɔːtə*] *n* agua *f* potable.

drip [drip] **1** *n* (*act*) goteo *m*, el gotear; (*one drop*) gota *f*; (*bore, sl*) pelmazo *m*; (*fool, sl*) tonto *m*.

2 *vt* dejar caer gota a gota.

3 *vi* gotear, caer gota a gota (*down* por).

drip-dry ['drip'drai] *adj* de lava y pon.

dripping ['dripiŋ] **1** *adj* *tap etc* que gotea; *clothes* chorreantes, que chorrean agua; **to be** — **wet** estar calado. **2** *n* pringue *m*.

drive [draiv] **1** *n* (**a**) (*outing*) paseo *m* (en coche *etc*); (*journey*) viaje *m* (en coche *etc*); **to go for a** — dar un paseo en coche; **to take someone for a** — llevar a uno de paseo en coche; **it's a long** — es mucho viaje.

(**b**) (*Hunting*) batida *f*; (*Mil*) ataque *m*, avance *m*; (*fig*) campaña *f* (*against, on* contra, para suprimir).

(**c**) (*stroke*) golpe *m* fuerte, golpe *m* directo; (*Tennis*) golpe *m* a ras de la red.

(**d**) (*energy*) energía *f*, vigor *m*; (*driving force*) impulso *m*.

(**e**) (*carriageway*) calzada *f*, avenida *f*.

(**f**) (*Mech*) mecanismo *m* de transmisión; **front-wheel** — tracción *f* delantera; **left-hand** — conducción *f* a la izquierda.

2 (*irr: pret* **drove**, *ptp* **driven**) *vt* (**a**) (*urge in a direction*) empujar, impeler; *game* batir; *cattle* guiar, llevar; **to** — **away** ahuyentar, *person* alejar, *cares etc* quitarse de encima, alejar; **to** — **back** rechazar, *defenders* obligar a ceder terreno, *crowd* obligar a retroceder; **to** — **off** = **to** — **away**; **to** — **an actor off the stage** hacer que un actor abandone la escena; **to** — **out** obligar a salir (*of* de); expulsar.

(**b**) (*urge on*) hacer trabajar, hacer sudar; **he drove us to victory** él nos condujo a la victoria.

(**c**) (*steer*) *car, carriage etc* conducir, pilotar, guiar; *plough* manejar.

(**d**) (*power*) mover, actuar; *vehicle etc* impulsar; **the wind** —**s the boat along** el viento empuja el barco; **a car** —**n by steam** un coche impulsado por vapor, un coche que funciona con vapor; **to** — **on** empujar, llevar adelante.

(**e**) *ball etc* golpear con fuerza; *furrow* hacer; *hole* perforar, practicar; *tunnel* abrir, construir; *road* construir; *nail* clavar (*into* en); *teeth etc* hincar (*into* en); *object* introducir a la fuerza (*into* en); (*fig*) *bargain* hacer; **to** — **a way through** abrirse paso por.

(**f**) (*carry*) *passenger* llevar en coche.

(**g**) (*force*) **to** — **someone to do something, to** — **someone into doing something** forzar a uno a hacer algo; **to** — **someone mad** volver a uno loco.

3 *vi* (**a**) (*steer*) conducir, manejar (*SAm*); **"drive slowly"** "marcha moderada"; **to** — **on the left** circular por la izquierda.

(**b**) (*go etc*) pasearse en coche, dar un paseo en coche; **to** — **to London** ir en coche a Londres; **he drove alone** hizo el viaje solo; **he drove 50 miles in an hour** recorrió 50 millas en una hora; **to** — **off** irse en coche, marcharse; (*car*) arrancar y alejarse; **to** — **on** seguir adelante; **to** — **past** pasar delante de; **to** — **up** llegar en coche; **to** — **up to town** ir en coche a la ciudad.

(**c**) **the rain is driving down** está lloviendo a chuzos.

(**d**) **to let** — **at** asestar un golpe a; (*fig*) denunciar.

(**e**) **to** — **at** insinuar, querer decir; **what are you driving at?** ¿qué quiere Vd decir?, ¿qué pretende Vd?

drive-in ['draiv‚in] *n* (*US*) parador *m* (de carretera); (*cinema*) motocine *m*.

drivel ['drivl] **1** *n* tonterías *fpl*. **2** *vi* decir tonterías.

driven ['drivn] *ptp of* **drive**.

driver ['draivə*] *n* (*Aut*) conductor *m*, ora *f*; chófer *m*, chofer *m* (*SAm*); (*Rail*) maquinista *m*; (*of coach*) cochero *m*; **racing** — corredor *m* automovilista.

driveway ['draivwei] *n* calzada *f*, avenida *f*.

drive-yourself ['draivjɔː'self] *attr*: — **service** servicio *m* de alquiler sin chófer.

driving ['draiviŋ] **1** *adj* *rain* torrencial. **2** *attr* *power* motor; (*fig*) impulsor; (*Aut*) de conducción para conductor etc. **3** *n* el conducir; automovilismo *m*.

driving belt ['draiviŋbelt] *n* correa *f* de transmisión.

driving instructor ['draiviŋin'strʌktə*] *n* instructor *m* de conducción.

driving lesson ['draiviŋ‚lesn] *n* clase *f* de conducción.

driving licence ['draiviŋ‚laisəns] *n* permiso *m* de conductor, carnet *m* de conductor.

driving mirror ['draiviŋ‚mirə*] *n* retrovisor *m*.

driving school ['draiviŋskuːl] n autoescuela f, escuela f automovilista, academia f de conductores.
driving test ['draiviŋtest] n examen m de conducción.
drizzle ['drizl] 1 n llovizna f. 2 vi lloviznar.
droll [drəul] adj (funny) divertido, gracioso; (odd) raro.
dromedary ['drɔmidəri] n dromedario m.
drone [drəun] 1 n (a) (Ent, fig) zángano m.
   (b) (noise) zumbido m; (of voice) tono m monótono.
   2 vi zumbar; (voice) hablar monótonamente; he —d on and on hablaba interminablemente en tono monótono.
drool [druːl] vi babear; to — over (fig) extasiarse como un tonto ante.
droop [druːp] 1 vt inclinar; dejar caer (over por).
   2 vi (slope) inclinarse; (fall) caer, colgar; (flower) marchitarse; (fig: spirit) decaer, (person) desanimarse.
drooping ['druːpiŋ] adj caído; flower marchito; ears gacho; movement lánguido, desmayado.
drop [drɔp] 1 n (a) (of liquid) gota f (also Med); (sweet) pastilla f; just a — dos gotitas nada más; there's just a — left quedan unas gotas; with a — of soda con un poquitín de sifón; I haven't touched a — no he bebido una sola gota; in 3 weeks we didn't have a — of rain no cayó ni una gota en 3 semanas; it's a — in the ocean es tan poco que no tiene importancia; he's had a — too much lleva una copa de más.
   (b) (fall) caída f; (by parachute) lanzamiento m; (in price) baja f; (of temperature etc) descenso m; (in number, demand) disminución f, reducción f (in de); at the — of a hat con cualquier pretexto.
   (c) (slope) bajada f, declive m, pendiente f; (cliff) precipicio m; there's a — of 6 metres esto está a una altura de 6 metros sobre el suelo; to have the — on someone (fam) llevar la delantera a uno.
   (d) (Theat) telón m de boca.
   2 vt (a) (let fall) dejar caer; (let go of) soltar; bomb, parachutist lanzar; anchor echar; letter in pillar box echar; note poner (to a); curtsy hacer; hint soltar; passenger dejar (at en); eyes, voice bajar; price reducir; charge retirar; (allow to drip) verter a gotas.
   (b) game, enemy derribar, tumbar.
   (c) (lose) perder.
   (d) (lengthen) alargar, extender hacia abajo.
   (e) (omit) omitir; letter H no pronunciar; syllable comerse; claim, plan renunciar a, abandonar; condition etc suprimir; habit dejar; subject dejar, cambiar de; friend romper con; — that! ¡déjese de eso!; we had to — what we were doing tuvimos que dejar lo que estábamos haciendo; they —ped him like a hot brick le abandonaron como a perro sarnoso; I've been —ped from the team ya no formo parte del equipo.
   3 vi (fall) caer; caer a tierra; (terrain) bajar; (price) bajar; (temperature etc) descender; (number, demand) disminuir; (wind) calmarse, amainar; (drip) gotear; (crouch) agacharse; to — with fatigue caer rendido; I feel ready to — estoy que no me tengo; so we let the matter — así que dejamos el asunto; to — behind quedarse atrás, rezagarse; to — down caer; (crouch) agacharse; we —ped down to the coast bajamos hacia la costa; to — in entrar de sopetón, entrar de paso; to — in on someone visitar a uno inesperadamente; do — in any time ven a vernos sin ceremonias y cuando quieras; to — off (part) desprenderse, separarse; (passenger) bajar (at en); (go to sleep) quedarse dormido; to — out (part) desprenderse, separarse; (person) darse de baja, retirarse (of de); he —ped out of my life no volví a saber nada de él; see sight.
droplet ['drɔplit] n gotita f.
dropper ['drɔpə*] n (Med etc) cuentagotas m.
droppings ['drɔpiŋz] npl excremento m (de animales).
dropsical ['drɔpsikəl] adj hidrópico.
dropsy ['drɔpsi] n hidropesía f.
dross [drɔs] n escoria f (also fig).
drought [draut] n sequía f.
drove [drəuv] 1 pret of **drive**. 2 n (Agr) rebaño m, manada f; (of people) multitud f; people came in —s la gente acudió en tropel.
drover ['drəuvə*] n boyero m, pastor m.
drown [draun] 1 vt (kill) anegar; kittens etc ahogar; (inundate) anegar, inundar; sound apagar; cry ahogar; sorrows olvidar emborrachándose; his cries were —ed by the noise of the waves sus gritos se perdieron en el estruendo de las olas.
   2 vi (also to be —ed) perecer ahogado.
   3 vr: to — oneself ahogarse.
drowse [drauz] vi dormitar, quedar medio dormido; to — off adormecerse.

drowsiness ['drauzinis] n somnolencia f; (sluggishness) modorra f.
drowsy ['drauzi] adj (sleepy) soñoliento; (sluggish) amodorrado; (lulling) soporífero; to be —, to feel — tener sueño.
drub [drʌb] vt apalear, vapulear; (fig) derrotar, cascar.
drubbing ['drʌbiŋ] n paliza f; (fig) paliza f, derrota f.
drudge [drʌdʒ] 1 n esclavo m del trabajo; (in home) esclava f de la cocina. 2 vi trabajar como un esclavo.
drudgery ['drʌdʒəri] n trabajo m penoso, faena f monótona; to take the — out of work hacer el trabajo menos penoso.
drug [drʌg] 1 n (Med) droga f, medicamento m, fármaco m; (eg heroin) droga f, narcótico m, estupefaciente m; to be a — on the market ser invendible.
   2 vt person narcotizar, drogar, administrar narcóticos a; wine etc echar un narcótico a; to be —ged with sleep estar muerto de sueño.
   3 vr: to — oneself drogarse.
drug addict ['drʌgˌædikt] n toxicómano m, a f, morfinómano m, a f.
drug addiction ['drʌgəˈdikʃən] n toxicomanía f, morfinomanía f.
druggist ['drʌgist] n farmacéutico m; —'s (shop) farmacia f.
drugstore ['drʌgstɔː*] n (US) farmacia f, droguería f.
drug traffic ['drʌgˌtræfik] n contrabando m de narcóticos.
druid ['druːid] n druida m.
drum [drʌm] 1 n (Mus) tambor m, (large) timbal m, bombo m; (Mech) tambor m; (for oil) bidón m; (of ear) tímpano m; —s (in band) batería f; bass — bombo m.
   2 vt: to — one's fingers on the table tabalear, tamborilear con los dedos en la mesa; to — something into someone hacer que uno aprenda algo a fuerza de repetírselo; to — someone out expulsar a uno; to — up support reunir, organizar; trade fomentar.
   3 vi (Mus) tocar el tambor; (with fingers) tabalear, tamborilear, teclear; (with heels) zapatear; the noise is —ming in my ears el ruido me está taladrando los oídos; his words —med in my mind sus palabras se repetían incansablemente en mi cabeza.
drumhead ['drʌmhed] n parche m de tambor; court-martial consejo m de guerra sumarísimo.
drummer ['drʌmə*] n tambor m.
drumstick ['drʌmstik] n palillo m, baqueta f.
drunk [drʌŋk] 1 ptp of **drink**.
   2 adj: to be — estar borracho; to get — emborracharse; to get someone — emborrachar a uno; as — as a lord más borracho que una cuba; to be — with joy estar ebrio de alegría.
   3 n (fam) borracho m; to go on a — ir a emborracharse.
drunkard ['drʌŋkəd] n borracho m, a f.
drunken ['drʌŋkən] adj borracho; a — brawl una reyerta de borrachos; in a — voice en una voz turbada por el alcohol; charged with — driving acusado de conducir en estado de embriaguez.
drunkenness ['drʌŋkənnis] n embriaguez f.
dry [drai] 1 adj seco; climate árido, seco; bread sin mantequilla, (stale) viejo; measure para áridos; book, speech aburrido; wit peculiar; state (US) prohibicionista; as — as a bone completamente seco; as — as dust de lo más aburrido; I'm very — tengo mucha sed.
   2 n: we are in the — estamos bajo techo.
   3 vt secar (also to — off, to — up); (wipe) enjugar; tears enjugarse; to — up deshidratar.
   4 vi secarse (also to — off); to — up (spring etc) secarse, agotarse; (Meteorol) dejar de llover; (fam) callarse, (in speech) atascarse; oh do — up! ¡cállese por Dios!
dry-as-dust ['draiəzˌdʌst] adj de lo más seco, de lo más aburrido.
dry-clean ['draiˈkliːn] vt limpiar en seco.
dry cleaner's ['draiˈkliːnəz] n tintorería f.
dry cleaning ['draiˈkliːniŋ] n limpieza f en seco.
dryer ['draiə*] n (for hair) secador m.
dry-eyed ['draiˈaid] adj sin lágrimas.
dry goods ['draigudz] n (US): — store mercería f.
drying ['draiiŋ] adj wind secante.
drying-up ['draiiŋˈʌp] n secamiento m; deshidratación f.
dryness ['drainis] n sequedad f, lo seco; (of climate) aridez f; (of wit) lo peculiar.
dry rot ['draiˈrɔt] n putrefacción f fungoide.
dry-shod ['draiˈʃɔd] adj a pie enjuto.
dual ['djuəl] adj doble; (Gram) dual.
dualism ['djuəlizəm] n dualismo m.
duality [djuˈæliti] n dualidad f.

dual-purpose ['djuəl'pəːpəs] *adj* que sirve para dos cosas, de doble finalidad.
dub[1] [dʌb] *vt knight* armar caballero a; (*with name*) apodar.
dub[2] [dʌb] *vt film* doblar.
dubbin ['dʌbin] *n* adobo *m* impermeable.
dubbing ['dʌbin] *n* (*of film*) doblaje *m*.
dubiety [djuː'baiəti] *n* incertidumbre *f*.
dubious ['djuːbiəs] *adj* dudoso; *compliment* equívoco; *character* sospechoso; **to be — about** tener dudas sobre; **I am — whether** dudo si.
dubiously ['djuːbiəsli] *adv look etc* con duda; *act* de manera sospechosa.
Dublin ['dʌblin] Dublin.
ducal ['djuːkəl] *adj* ducal.
ducat ['dʌkit] *n* ducado *m* (*moneda*).
duchess ['dʌtʃis] *n* duquesa *f*.
duchy ['dʌtʃi] *n* ducado *m* (*territorio*).
duck[1] [dʌk] *n* (*Orn*) pato *m*, ánade *m*; (*domestic*) pato *m*; **yes, —(s)** (*fam*) sí, querido; **lame —** persona *f* incapacitada, (*Comm*) persona *f* insolvente, (*US*) político *m* derrotado; **like water off a —'s back** sin producir efecto alguno; **to play —s and drakes** hacer saltar una piedra plana sobre el agua; **to play —s and drakes with** despilfarrar; **to take to something like a — to water** aprender a hacer algo con la mayor facilidad.
duck[2] [dʌk] **1** *n* (**a**) (*under water*) chapuz *m*. (**b**) (*to escape*) agachada *f*, (*Boxing*) esquiva *f*. **2** *vt* (**a**) (*in water*) chapuzar. (**b**) (*to escape*) agachar (la cabeza *etc*), bajar. **3** *vi* (**a**) (*in water*) chapuzarse, sumergirse. (**b**) (*to escape*) agachar la cabeza, agacharse, hurtar el cuerpo.
ducking ['dʌkiŋ] *n* chapuz *m*, inmersión *f*.
duckling ['dʌkliŋ] *n* patito *m*, anadón *m*.
duckweed ['dʌkwiːd] *n* lenteja *f* de agua.
ducky ['dʌki] *n* (*fam*): **—!** ¡querido!
duct [dʌkt] *n* conducto *m*, canal *m*.
ductile ['dʌktail] *adj* dúctil.
ductless ['dʌktlis] *adj*: **— gland** glándula *f* cerrada, glándula *f* de secreción interna.
dud [dʌd] **1** *adj coin etc* falso; *shell* que no estalla, que está sin estallar. **2** *n* (*coin*) moneda *f* falsa; (*shell*) obús *m* que no estalla, granada *f* que está sin estallar; (*machine*) filfa *f*; (*person*) persona *f* inútil.
dude [djuːd] *n* (*US*) petimetre *m*, gomoso *m*; **— ranch** rancho *m* para turistas.
dudgeon ['dʌdʒən] *n*: **in high —** enojadísimo.
duds [dʌdz] *npl* (*US: fam*) prendas *fpl* de vestir, trapos *mpl*; pertenencias *fpl*.
due [djuː] **1** *adj* debido; conveniente, oportuno; **to be —** (*Comm*) ser pagadero; **I have £5 — to me** me deben 5 libras; **our thanks are — to him** le estamos muy agradecidos; **it is — to** esto es debido a, esto se debe a; **it is — to the car breaking down** esto es debido a que el coche tuvo una avería; **the train is — at 8** el tren debe llegar a las 8; **I'm — in London tomorrow** tengo que ir a Londres mañana, mañana me esperan en Londres; **it was — to happen yesterday** esto se esperaba para ayer; **when is it — to happen?** ¿para cuándo se prevé esto?; **it is — to be demolished** se prevé su demolición; **to fall —** (*Comm*) vencer. **2** *adv*: **— to** debido a, por causa de; **to go — east** ir derecho hacia el este. **3** *n* (*debt*) deuda *f*; (*desert*) lo que merece uno; **—s** derechos *mpl*; **to get one's —** recibir lo que merece uno, (*in bad sense*) llevar su merecido; **to give him his —** hay que reconocer la razón (*or* las cualidades *etc*) que tiene; **to give him his —, I ...** para evitar cualquier posibilidad de ser injusto con él, yo ...
duel ['djuəl] **1** *n* duelo *m*; **to fight a — = 2** *vi* batirse en duelo.
duellist, (*US*) **duelist** ['djuəlist] *n* duelista *m*.
duet [djuː'et] *n* dúo *m*.
duff[1] [dʌf] *adj* (*fam*) soso, insípido.
duff[2] [dʌf] *vt* (*sl*): **to — someone up** dar una paliza a uno.
duffel bag ['dʌfəlbæg] *n* (*Mil*) talego *m* para efectos de uso personal.
duffel coat ['dʌfəlkəut] *n* comando *m*, abrigo *m* tres cuartos.
duffer ['dʌfə*] *n* zoquete *m*.
dug[1] [dʌg] *n* (*Zool*) teta *f*, ubre *f*.
dug[2] [dʌg] *pret* and *ptp* of **dig**.
dugout ['dʌgaut] *n* refugio *m* subterráneo.
duke [djuːk] *n* duque *m*.
dukedom ['djuːkdəm] *n* ducado *m* (*título*).
dulcet ['dʌlsit] *adj* dulce, suave.
dulcimer ['dʌlsimə*] *n* dulcémele *m*.

dull [dʌl] **1** *adj colour, gleam* apagado; *light* sombrío, pálido; *surface* deslustrado, mate; *sound, pain* sordo; *edge* embotado; *day, weather* gris; *stock market* inactivo, flojo; *person* (*slow*) lerdo, torpe; (*uninteresting*) soso, insípido, pesado; **as — as ditchwater** de lo más aburrido; **I feel — today** hoy me siento desanimado, hoy me encuentro sin fuerzas. **2** *vt edge* embotar; *surface* deslustrar; *pain* aliviar; *person* entorpecer; *enthusiasm etc* enfriar.
dullard ['dʌləd] *n* zoquete *m*.
dullness ['dʌlnis] *n* lo deslustrado; lo sombrío; inactividad *f*, flojedad *f*; torpeza *f*; lo soso, insipidez *f*.
dully ['dʌli] *adv* de modo apagado, con brillo apagado; pálidamente; sordamente, con ruido sordo.
duly ['djuːli] *adv* (*properly*) debidamente; (*punctually*) a su debido tiempo; **he — arrived at 3** llegó en efecto a las 3; **he — protested** protestó de la manera que se había previsto; **everybody was — shocked** se escandalizaron todos según era de esperar.
dumb [dʌm] *adj* mudo; (*fam*) estúpido, soso; **the — millions** los millones que no tienen voz; **— animal** bruto *m*; **to become —** quedar mudo; **to strike someone —** dejar a uno sin habla.
dumbbell ['dʌmbel] *n* pesa *f*.
dumbfound [dʌm'faund] *vt* dejar sin habla, pasmar; **we were —ed** quedamos mudos de asombro.
dumbness ['dʌmnis] *n* mudez *f*; (*fam*) estupidez *f*.
dumb show ['dʌm'ʃəu] *n* pantomima *f*; **in — por** señas.
dumbwaiter ['dʌm'weitə*] *n* estante *m* giratorio; (*US*) montaplatos *m*.
dum-dum ['dʌmdʌm] *adj*: **— bullet** bala *f* dumdum.
dummy ['dʌmi] **1** *adj* falso, postizo. **2** *n* (*life-size figure*) muñeco *m*; (*tailor's*) maniquí *m*; (*packet*) envase *m* vacio; (*baby's*) chupete *m*; (*Bridge*) muerto *m*.
dump [dʌmp] **1** *n* (*heap*) montón *m*; (*rubbish tip*) basurero *m*, vaciadero *m*; (*Mil*) depósito *m*; (*fam*) pueblucho *m*, poblachón *m*; **to be down in the —s** (*fam*) tener murria. **2** *vt rubbish etc* descargar, verter, vaciar; (*get rid of*) deshacerse de, dejar; *goods* inundar el mercado con; **to — something down** (*fam*) poner algo (con mucho ruido); **can I — this here?** ¿puedo dejar esto aquí?
dumping ['dʌmpiŋ] *n* (*Comm*) dumping *m*.
dumpling ['dʌmpliŋ] *n* bola *f* de masa hervida.
dumpy ['dʌmpi] *adj* regordete, culibajo.
dun[1] [dʌn] *adj* pardo.
dun[2] [dʌn] *vt*: **to — someone** apremiar a uno para que pague lo que debe; (*fig*) dar la lata a uno.
dunce [dʌns] *n* zopenco *m*, a *f*.
dunderhead ['dʌndəhed] *adj* zoquete *m*.
dune [djuːn] *n* duna *f*.
dung [dʌŋ] *n* excremento *m*; (*as manure*) estiércol *m*.
dungarees [,dʌŋgə'riːz] *npl* mono *m*.
dungeon ['dʌndʒən] *n* mazmorra *f*, calabozo *m*.
dunghill ['dʌŋhil] *n* estercolero *m*.
dunk [dʌŋk] *vt* (*US*) mojar, remojar.
Dunkirk [dʌn'kəːk] Dunquerque.
duo ['djuːəu] *n* dúo *m*.
duodecimal [,djuːəu'desiməl] *adj* duodecimal.
duodenum [,djuːəu'diːnəm] *n* duodeno *m*.
dupe [djuːp] **1** *n* primo *m*, inocentón *m*; **to be the — of** ser víctima de. **2** *vt* engañar, embaucar; (*swindle*) timar.
duplicate ['djuːplikit] **1** *adj* duplicado. **2** *n* duplicado *m*; (*copy of letter etc*) copia *f*, doble *m*; **in —** por duplicado.
duplicate ['djuːplikeit] *vt* duplicar; *text* hacer a multicopista.
duplicating machine ['djuːplikeitiŋmə'ʃiːn] *n* multicopista *m*.
duplication [,djuːpli'keiʃən] *n* duplicación *f*; pluralidad *f*.
duplicator ['djuːplikeitə*] *n* multicopista *m*.
duplicity [djuː'plisiti] *n* duplicidad *f*, doblez *f*.
durability [djuərə'biliti] *n* lo duradero, durabilidad *f*.
durable ['djuərəbl] *adj* duradero.
duration [djuə'reiʃən] *n* duración *f*; **for the —** (*fam*) mientras dure la noche.
Dürer ['djuərə*] *m* Durero.
duress [djuə'res] *n* compulsión *f*; **under —** por compulsión.
during ['djuəriŋ] *prep* durante.
durst [dəːst] (*arch*) *pret* of **dare**.
dusk [dʌsk] *n* crepúsculo *m*, anochecer *m*; **at — al** atardecer; **in the gathering —** en la oscuridad casi de la noche.
dusky ['dʌski] *adj* oscuro; *complexion* moreno.
dust [dʌst] **1** *n* polvo *m*; (*sweepings*) barreduras *fpl*;

(*rubbish*) basura *f*; (*of coal*) cisco *m*; **to bite the —** morder el polvo; **to kick up the —** levantar una polvoreda; **to raise a —** armarla; **to shake the — of a place off one's feet** salir muy ofendido de un lugar; **to throw — in someone's eyes** engañar a uno.

2 *vt* (**a**) (*take — off*) quitar el polvo a, desempolvar, (*by beating*) sacudir el polvo a; (*clean*) limpiar.

(**b**) **to — something with** salpicar algo de, (*Cook etc*) espolvorear algo de; **— the insecticide on the surface** espolvoree el insecticida sobre la superficie.

dustbin ['dʌstbin] *n* cubo *m* de la basura.

dustbowl ['dʌstbəul] *n* terreno *m* inutilizado por la erosión.

dustcart ['dʌstkɑ:t] *n* camión *m* de la basura.

dustcloud ['dʌstklaud] *n* polvoreda *f*.

dust cover ['dʌst,kʌvə*] *n* guardapolvo *m*; (*of book*) sobrecubierta *f*, camisa *f*.

duster ['dʌstə*] *n* (*cloth*) paño *m*, trapo *m*, sacudidor *m*, bayeta *f*; (*of feathers*) plumero *m*; (*for blackboard*) borrador *m*.

dusting ['dʌstiŋ] *n* (*fam*) paliza *f*.

dust jacket ['dʌst,dʒækit] *n* sobrecubierta *f*, camisa *f*.

dustman ['dʌstmən] *n*, *pl* **—men** [mən] basurero *m*.

dustpan ['dʌstpæn] *n* cogedor *m*.

dust sheet ['dʌstʃiːt] *n* guardapolvo *m*.

dust storm ['dʌststɔːm] *n* vendaval *m* de polvo.

dustup ['dʌstʌp] *n* (*fam*) pelea *f*, reyerta *f*.

dusty ['dʌsti] *adj* polvoriento, empolvado; **to get —** cubrirse de polvo; **not so —** nada malo; **to give someone a — answer** dar a uno una respuesta equívoca.

Dutch [dʌtʃ] **1** *adj* holandés.

2 *npl*: **the —** los holandeses.

3 *n* (*language*) holandés *m*; **double —** galimatías *m*; **to talk double —** hablar chino; **to go —** pagar cada uno su cuota, ir a escote.

Dutchman ['dʌtʃmən] *n*, *pl* **—men** [mən] holandés *m*; **it's him or I'm a —** que me maten si no es él.

Dutchwoman ['dʌtʃ,wumən] *n*, *pl* **—women** [,wimin] holandesa *f*.

dutiable ['djuːtiəbl] *adj* sujeto a derechos de aduana.

dutiful ['djuːtiful] *adj* obediente, sumiso.

dutifully ['djuːtifəli] *adv* obedientemente, sumisamente.

duty ['djuːti] *n* deber *m*, obligación *f*; (*customs —*) derechos *mpl* de aduana; **entertainments —** impuesto *m* sobre los espectáculos; **protective —** impuesto *m* proteccionista; **stamp —** impuesto *m* del timbre; **succession —** derechos *mpl* de sucesión; **— call** visita *f* molesta pero obligatoria; **out of a**

sense of — por compromiso, cumpliendo con su deber; **to be in — bound to** + *infin* estar obligado a + *infin*; **to be off —** estar libre, (*Mil*) estar libre de servicio; **to be on —** estar de servicio; **to be on sentry —** estar de guardia; **it is no part of my — to** + *infin* no me corresponde a mí + *infin*; **to do — as** servir de; **to do — for** servir en lugar de; **to do one's —** cumplir con su deber; **to do one's — by** ser justo con; **I feel it to be my —** creo que es mi deber; **to take up one's duties** entrar en funciones.

duty-free ['djuːti'friː] *adj* libre de derechos de aduana.

dwarf [dwɔːf] **1** *adj* enano; diminuto, pequeñito. **2** *n* enano *m*, a *f*. **3** *vt* achicar, empequeñecer, hacer que parezca pequeño; (*stunt*) impedir el crecimiento de.

dwell [dwel] (*irr*: *pret and ptp* **dwelt**) *vi* morar; **to — on** *subject* explicar largamente, explayarse en; *thought* meditar; *note, syllable* dar énfasis a, alargar.

dweller ['dwelə*] *n*: **— in** habitante *mf* de; inquilino *m* de, inquilina *f* de.

dwelling ['dweliŋ] *n* morada *f*, vivienda *f*.

dwelling house ['dweliŋhaus] *n*, *pl* **— houses** [,hauziz] casa *f*.

dwelt [dwelt] *pret and ptp of* **dwell**.

dwindle ['dwindl] *vi* disminuir, menguar; **to — to** quedar reducido a.

dwindling ['dwindliŋ] **1** *adj* que va disminuyendo, menguante. **2** *n* disminución *f*.

dye [dai] **1** *n* tinte *m*; (*hue*) matiz *m*, color *m*; **of deepest —** de lo más vil. **2** *vt* teñir (*green de* verde).

dyeing ['daiiŋ] *n* tinte *m*, tintura *f*.

dyer ['daiə*] *n* tintorero *m*; **—'s** tintorería *f*.

dyestuff ['daistʌf] *n* tinte *m*, materia *f* colorante.

dye works ['daiwɜːks] *npl* tintorería *f*.

dying ['daiiŋ] **1** *present participle of* **die**. **2** *adj* *man* moribundo, agonizante; *moments* final; *words* último.

dyke [daik] *n* = **dike**.

dynamic [dai'næmik] **1** *adj* dinámico. **2** *n* dinámica *f*.

dynamics [dai'næmiks] *n* dinámica *f*.

dynamite ['dainəmait] **1** *n* dinamita *f*; **that issue is —** ese asunto es dinamita; **the book is —** el libro es explosivo. **2** *vt* dinamitar, volar con dinamita.

dynamo ['dainəməu] *n* dínamo *f*.

dynastic [dai'næstik] *adj* dinástico.

dynasty ['dinəsti] *n* dinastía *f*.

dysentery ['disntri] *n* disentería *f*.

dyspepsia [dis'pepsiə] *n* dispepsia *f*.

dyspeptic [dis'peptik] *adj* dispéptico.

dystrophy ['distrəfi] *n* distrofia *f*; **muscular —** distrofia *f* muscular.

E

each [iːtʃ] **1** adj cada (invariable); (— and every, any) todo.

   2 pron cada uno; **they help — other** (2 persons) se ayudan (mutuamente), se ayudan uno a otro, se ayudan el uno al otro, (more than 2 persons) se ayudan unos a otros.

   3 adv: **two sweets — dos dulces por persona, dos dulces para cada uno.

eager ['iːgə*] adj impaciente; desire etc apremiante, vehemente; (hopeful) ilusionado; (ambitious) ambicioso; **to be — for** ansiar, anhelar, tener vivo deseo de; **to be — to** + infin ansiar + infin, impacientarse por + infin; **don't be so —** ¡ten paciencia!

eagerly ['iːgəli] adv con impaciencia, con ansia; con ilusión.

eagerness ['iːgənis] n impaciencia f; ansia f, deseo m (for de); (hopefulness) ilusión f; **in his — to get there first** en su ansia por llegar allí el primero.

eagle ['iːgl] n águila f; **golden —** águila f real.

eagle-eyed ['iːgl'aid] adj de ojos de lince.

ear[1] [iə*] n (Anat) oreja f; (sense, Mus) oído m; **inner —** oído m interno; **middle —** oído m medio; **to be all —** ser todo oídos; **he could not believe his —s** no daba crédito a sus oídos; **to give —** to prestar oído a; **it goes in at one — and out at the other** por un oído le entra y por otro le sale; **to have a good —** tener buen oído; **to have the minister's —** poder contar con el interés del ministro; **to play by —** tocar de oído; **we're playing it by —** (fig) obramos por instinto, avanzamos a tientas y sin saber a dónde; **to prick up one's —s** aguzar el oído; **he set them by the —s** sembró la discordia entre ellos, hizo que se enfadasen unos con otros; **to turn a deaf —** to hacer oídos sordos a.

ear[2] [iə*] n (Bot) espiga f; **to come into —** espigar.

earache ['iəreik] n dolor m de oídos.

eardrum ['iədrʌm] n tímpano m.

earl [əːl] n conde m.

earldom ['əːldəm] n condado m.

early ['əːli] **1** adj temprano (also Bot); (first) primero, primitivo; age tierno; death prematuro, temprano; reply pronto; season avanzado; book, work etc juvenil, de primera época; **an — Victorian table** una mesa victoriana de primera época; **— Christian art** arte m cristiano primitivo; **to be in one's — forties** tener poco más de 40 años; see date, life etc.

   2 adv **(a)** temprano; **as — as possible** lo más pronto posible, cuanto antes; **earlier on** antes; **— in the morning** muy de mañana, de madrugada; **— in the afternoon** a primera hora de la tarde; **— in the week** en los primeros días de la semana; **— last century** a principios del siglo pasado; **— in his life** en su juventud; **— in the twenties** en los primeros años veinte, al principio de los años veinte; **— in the book** en las primeras páginas del libro.

   (b) (in good time) con tiempo, con anticipación; **to book —** reservar con mucha anticipación; **to come an hour —** llegar con una hora de anticipación; **he took his summer holiday —** anticipó el veraneo, salió en fecha temprana para veranear.

Early Bird ['əːlibəːd] n: **— (satellite)** satélite m "Pájaro del Alba".

early warning ['əːli'wɔːniŋ] attr: **— system** sistema m de aviso inmediato (contra los ataques por misiles).

earmark ['iəmaːk] vt (fig) reservar (for para), destinar (for a); **an —ed grant** una subvención destinada a fines especiales.

earn [əːn] vt salary etc ganar(se), percibir; interest devengar; (win for oneself) merecer(se); adquirir, obtener; **it —ed him the nickname of X** le valió el apodo de X.

earnest[1] ['əːnist] adj person, character etc serio, formal; wish etc fervoroso; **it is my — wish that** deseo con fervor que + subj; **to be in —** hablar con la mayor seriedad; **are you in — ?** ¿esto va de veras?, ¿me lo dices en serio?

earnest[2] ['əːnist] n prenda f, señal f; **as an — of** en señal de.

earnestly ['əːnistli] adv speak etc con la mayor seriedad; **I — entreat you** se lo suplico de todo corazón.

earnestness ['əːnistnis] n seriedad f, formalidad f.

earnings ['əːniŋz] npl (of individual) sueldo m, ingresos mpl; (of company etc) ganancias fpl, beneficios mpl, utilidades fpl.

earphones ['iəfəunz] npl auriculares mpl.

earpiece ['iəpiːs] n auricular m.

earring ['iəriŋ] n (long) pendiente m; (round) arete m, zarcillo m.

earshot ['iəʃɔt] n: **to be within —** estar al alcance del oído.

ear-splitting ['iə,splitiŋ] adj que rompe el tímpano, que taladra el oído.

earth [əːθ] **1** n **(a)** tierra f; **scorched —** tierra f quemada; **here on —** en este mundo; **to come down to —,** to get back to — volver a la realidad; **it must have cost the —** habrá costado un potosí; **to promise the —** prometer el oro y el moro.

   (b) nothing on — will stop me now no lo dejo ahora por nada del mundo; **what on — . . . ?** ¿qué demonios . . . ?; **why on — do it now?** ¿por qué demonios hacerlo ahora?

   (c) (Zool) madriguera f; **to run to —** encontrar finalmente.

   (d) (Elec) cable m de toma de tierra.

   2 vt (Elec) conectar a tierra; **to — up** (Agr) acollar.

earthen ['əːθən] adj de tierra; pot de barro.

earthenware ['əːθənwɛə*] **1** n loza f de barro. **2** attr de barro.

earthly ['əːθli] adj terrenal, mundano; **to be of no — use** no servir para nada en absoluto; **there is no — reason why** not no hay la más pequeña razón en contra; **he hasn't an —** no tiene posibilidad alguna.

earthquake ['əːθkweik] n terremoto m, seísmo m.

earthward(s) ['əːθwəd(z)] adv hacia la tierra.

earthwork ['əːθwəːk] n terraplén m.

earthworm ['əːθwəːm] n lombriz f.

earthy ['əːθi] adj terroso; character telúrico, (coarse) grosero.

ear trumpet ['iə,trʌmpit] n trompetilla f acústica.

earwax ['iəwæks] n cerumen m, cera f de los oídos.

earwig ['iəwig] n tijereta f.

ease [iːz] **1** n **(a)** (easiness) facilidad f; **with —** con facilidad, fácilmente.

   (b) (relief from pain) alivio m.

   (c) (freedom from worry) tranquilidad f; **a life of —** una vida desahogada; **to live a life of —** vivir con desahogo.

   (d) (relaxed state) comodidad f; **to be at (one's) —** sentirse cómodo, encontrarse a gusto; **to be ill at —** sentirse molesto; **to put someone at his —** lograr que uno se sienta como en su casa; **to set someone's mind at —** tranquilizar el ánimo de uno; **stand at —!** en su lugar ¡descanso!; **to take one's —** descansar.

   (e) (of manner) naturalidad f.

   2 vt **(a)** task facilitar.

   (b) pain aliviar; mind tranquilizar; (slacken) aflojar; pressure aflojar; (free) soltar, librar; **to — off** levantar una tapa poco a poco; **to — a weight up** levantar un peso con cuidado; **to — a table along** mover una mesa con cuidado.

   3 vi (wind) amainar, calmarse; (rain) moderarse; **to — off,** to **— up** suavizarse, aligerarse; (at work) dejar de trabajar tanto; **to — up on someone** tratar a uno con menos rigor; **prices have —d** han bajado ligeramente los precios.

4 *vr:* **to — oneself of a burden** quitarse un peso de encima.

easel ['i:zl] *n* caballete *m.*

easily ['i:zili] *adv* fácilmente, con facilidad; **to win —** ganar fácilmente; **it could — be** bien podría ser; **the engine is running —** el motor funciona bien; **it holds 4 litres —** caben 4 litros largos; **it's — the best** es con mucho el mejor, seguramente es el mejor; **to take life —** darse buena vida.

easiness ['i:zinis] *n* facilidad *f.*

east [i:st] **1** *n* este *m*, oriente *m*; **the E—** el Oriente; **Far E—** Extremo Oriente *m*, Lejano Oriente *m*; **Middle E—** Oriente *m* Medio; **Near E—** Próximo Oriente *m.*
2 *adj* del este, oriental; *wind* del este.
3 *adv* al este, hacia el este.

Easter ['i:stə*] *n* Pascua *f* de Resurrección; *(period, loosely)* Semana *f* Santa; **— Monday** Lunes *m* de Pascua de Resurrección; **— Sunday** Domingo *m* de Resurrección; **— egg** huevo *m* de Pascua.

easterly ['i:stəli] *adj point, direction* este; *wind* del este.

eastern ['i:stən] *adj* del este, oriental.

easterner ['i:stənə*] *n* habitante *mf* del este.

easternmost ['i:stənməust] *adj* (el) más oriental, situado más al este.

East Indies ['i:st'indiz] *pl* Indias *fpl* Orientales.

eastward(s) ['i:stwədz] *adv* hacia el este.

easy ['i:zi] **1** *adj* **(a)** *(simple)* fácil; sencillo; **it's — to see why** es fácil comprender por qué; **he's — to get on with** es muy simpático; **I'm — *(fam)*** me es igual; **an — house** una casa de fácil manejo.
    (b) **to feel — in one's mind** estar tranquilo; **you can rest —** puedes dormir tranquilo.
    (c) *life, conditions* holgado, cómodo.
    (d) *manners* natural, sin afectación; *style* llano, corriente; *movement* suelto.
    (e) *money, credit* abundante; **steel is easier** el acero tiene menos demanda; **prices are easier** los precios han bajado ligeramente.
    (f) *pace* lento, pausado; *woman* fácil; **to come in an — first** llegar fácilmente el primero.
2 *adv (fam)* fácilmente; **— there!** ¡despacio!; **to go — on someone** tratar a uno con menos rigor; **to go — with** moderar; emplear más cuidado con; economizar en; **go — with the sugar!** conviene poner menos azúcar; **to take it —** *(rest)* descansar; *(idle)* perder el tiempo; *(go slow)* ir despacio; **take it —!** ¡cálmese!, ¡no se ponga nervioso!

easy chair ['i:zi'tʃeə*] *n* butaca *f*, sillón *m.*

easy-going ['i:zi'gəuiŋ] *adj* acomodadizo, nada severo; *(morally)* de manga ancha; *(lazy)* indolente.

eat [i:t] *(irr: pret* **ate,** *ptp* **eaten) 1** *vt* comer; *meal* tomar; *(with envy etc)* consumir; **to — one's way through the menu** pedir todos los platos que figuran en la lista; **I thought he was going to — me** creía que iba a comerme vivo; **what's —ing you?** *(fam)* ¿qué mosca te ha picado?; **to — away** corroer; desgastar; **to — up** comerse, acabar; **to — up the miles** devorar los kilómetros; **the fire —s up coal** el fuego devora el carbón; **to be —en up with envy** consumirse de envidia.
2 *vi* comer; **he always —s well** siempre tiene buen apetito; **this fish —s well** este pescado es muy sabroso; **to — into** *metal* corroer; *surface etc* desgastar; *reserves etc* mermar; *leisure time etc* reducir; **to — out** comer fuera, comer en un restaurante.

eatable ['i:təbl] **1** *adj* comestible; **2** **—s** *npl* comestibles *mpl.*

eaten ['i:tn] *ptp of* **eat.**

eater ['i:tə*] *n:* **to be a big —** tener siempre buen apetito, ser comilón; **I'm not a big —** yo como bastante poco.

eating ['i:tiŋ] *n* el comer; **to be good —** ser sabroso.

eating house ['i:tiŋhaus] *n, pl* **— houses** [hauziz] restaurante *m.*

eats ['i:ts] *npl (fam)* comida *f*, comestibles *mpl.*

eau de Cologne ['əudəkə'ləun] *n* agua *f* de colonia, colonia *f.*

eaves ['i:vz] *npl* alero *m.*

eavesdrop ['i:vzdrɔp] *vi* escuchar a escondidas *(on a conversation* una conversación.

eavesdropper ['i:vz,drɔpə*] *n* escuchador *m* escondido.

ebb [eb] **1** *n* reflujo *m*; **the — and flow** el flujo y reflujo; **to be at a low —** estar decaído; **at a low — in his fortunes** en un punto bien bajo de su fortuna.
2 *vi* bajar; menguar; *(fig)* decaer; **to — and flow** fluir y refluir; **life is —ing from him** le están abandonando sus últimas fuerzas.

ebb tide ['eb'taid] *n* marea *f* menguante.

ebonite ['ebənait] *n* ebonita *f.*

ebony ['ebəni] **1** *n* ébano *m.* **2** *attr* de ébano.

ebullience [i'bʌliəns] *n* exaltación *f*, entusiasmo *m*, exuberancia *f*, animación *f.*

ebullient [i'bʌliənt] *adj* exaltado, entusiasta, exuberante, animado.

eccentric [ik'sentrik] **1** *adj* excéntrico. **2** *n* excéntrico *m*, a *f.*

eccentrically [ik'sentrikəli] *adv* de manera excéntrica.

eccentricity [,eksən'trisiti] *n* excentricidad *f.*

ecclesiastic [i,kli:zi'æstik] *n* eclesiástico *m.*

ecclesiastical [i,kli:zi'æstikəl] *adj* eclesiástico.

echelon ['eʃələn] **1** *n* escalón *m.* **2** *vt* escalonar.

echo ['ekəu] **1** *n (pl* **echoes** ['ekəuz]) eco *m*; **to cheer someone to the —** aplaudir a uno repetidas veces.
2 *vt sound* repetir; *(imitate)* imitar; *opinion etc* hacerse eco de.
3 *vi* resonar, hacer eco; **the valley —ed with shouts** resonaban los gritos por el valle.

echo-sounder ['ekəu,saundə*] *n* sonda *f* acústica.

éclair ['eikleə*] *n* relámpago *m* de chocolate.

éclat ['eiklɑ:] *n* brillo *m*; *(success)* éxito *m* brillante; **with great —** brillantemente.

eclectic [i'klektik] **1** *adj* ecléctico. **2** *n* ecléctico *m*, a *f.*

eclecticism [i'klektisizəm] *n* eclecticismo *m.*

eclipse [i'klips] **1** *n* eclipse *m.* **2** *vt* eclipsar.

eclogue ['eklɔg] *n* égloga *f.*

ecological [,i:kəu'bdʒikəl] *adj* ecológico.

ecologist [i'kɔlədʒist] *n* ecólogo *m.*

ecology [i'kɔlədʒi] *n* ecología *f.*

econometrics [i,kɔnə'metriks] *n* econometría *f.*

economic(al) [,i:kə'nɔmik(əl)] *adj* económico; *rent* equitativo; (**— to operate, to run)** rentable.

economically [,i:kə'nɔmikəli] *adj* económicamente; de modo rentable.

economics [,i:kə'nɔmiks] *npl* economía *f* política; **home —** *(US)* economía *f* doméstica.

economist [i'kɔnəmist] *n* economista *mf.*

economize [i'kɔnəmaiz] **1** *vt* economizar, ahorrar.
2 *vi* economizar *(on* en).

economy [i'kɔnəmi] *n* economía *f*; **planned —** economía *f* dirigida; **political —** economía *f* política; **to practise —** economizar; **he writes with great —** escribe con gran economía.

ecstasy ['ekstəsi] *n* éxtasis *m*; **in an — of passion** en un arrebato de pasión, arrebatado por la pasión; **to be in ecstasies** estar en éxtasis; **to go into ecstasies over something** extasiarse ante algo.

ecstatic [eks'tætik] *adj* extático.

ecstatically [eks'tætikəli] *adv* con éxtasis.

ectoplasm ['ektəuplæzəm] *n* ectoplasma *m.*

Ecuador [,ekwə'dɔ:*] El Ecuador.

Ecuador(i)an [,ekwə'dɔ:r(i)ən] **1** *adj* ecuatoriano. **2** *n* ecuatoriano *m*, a *f.*

ecumenical [,i:kju'menikəl] *adj* ecuménico; **— council** concejo *m* ecuménico; **— movement** movimiento *m* ecuménico.

eczema ['eksimə] *n* eczema *m (Acad: f).*

Ed [ed], **Eddie** ['edi] *m nombres cariñosos de* **Edward.**

eddy ['edi] **1** *n* remolino *m.* **2** *vi* arremolinarse.

edema [i'di:mə] *m (esp US)* edema *m.*

Eden ['i:dn] Edén *m.*

edge [edʒ] **1** *n (cutting)* filo *m*, corte *m*; *(border: of chair, cliff, wood etc)* borde *m*; *(of paper)* margen *m*; *(of coin, table etc)* canto *m*; *(of town)* afueras *fpl*; *(of lake etc)* margen *f*, orilla *f*; *(end)* extremidad *f*; **leading —** *(Aer)* borde *m* de ataque; **milled —** cordoncillo *m*; **to be on —** estar de canto, *(fig)* tener los nervios de punta; **my nerves are on —** tengo los nervios de punta; **to be on the — of disaster** estar al borde del desastre; **to have the — on** llevar ventaja a; **to put an —** on afilar; **to set someone's teeth on —** dar dentera a uno; **to take the — off** embotar; **to take the — off one's appetite** engañar el hambre.
    2 *vt* **(a)** *(Sew)* ribetear, orlar *(with* de); *path etc* poner un borde a; **—d in, —d with** ribeteado de; bordeado de.
    (b) **to — something in** introducir algo de canto; **to — something along** mover algo de canto *(poco a poco)*; **to — one's way into a room** introducirse con dificultad en un cuarto *(atestado de gente).*
    3 *vi:* **to — along** avanzar poco a poco de lado; **to — away** alejarse poco a poco; **to — in** abrirse paso poco a poco; **to — up to someone** acercarse con cautela a uno.

edgeways ['edʒweiz] *adv* de lado, de canto; *see* **word.**

edging ['edʒiŋ] *n (Sew)* ribete *m*, orla *f*; *(of path etc)* borde *m.*

edgy ['edʒi] *adj* nervioso, inquieto.

edible ['edibl] *adj* comestible.

edict ['i:dikt] n edicto m.
edification [ˌedifi'keiʃən] n edificación f.
edifice ['edifis] n edificio m (esp grande, imponente).
edify ['edifai] vt edificar.
edifying ['edifaiiŋ] adj edificante.
Edinburgh ['edinbərə] Edimburgo.
edit ['edit] vt newspaper, magazine, series dirigir, ser director de; text, book preparar una edición de; script preparar para la imprenta, (correct) corregir; —ed by (newspaper etc) bajo la dirección de, (text, book) prólogo y notas de, a cargo de, (en) edición de.
edition [i'diʃən] n edición f; (Typ: no of copies) tirada f; **first** — edición f príncipe; **limited** — edición f limitada; **pirated** — edición f pirata.
editor ['editə*] n (of newspaper, magazine, series) director m; (staff —) redactor-jefe m; (of a book) autor m de la edición; —'s **note** nota f de la redacción.
editorial [ˌedi'tɔːriəl] 1 adj editorial; de la dirección; — **staff** redacción f. 2 n artículo m de fondo, editorial m.
editor-in-chief ['editərin'tʃi:f] n jefe m de redacción.
editorship ['editəʃip] n dirección f; **under the** — **of** bajo la dirección de.
educable ['edjukəbl] adj educable.
educate ['edjukeit] vt educar; formar; instruir; **where were you —d?** ¿dónde cursó Vd sus estudios?; **the prince is being privately** —d el príncipe tiene un preceptor particular.
educated ['edjukeitid] adj culto.
education [ˌedju'keiʃən] n educación f; enseñanza f; instrucción f; formación f cultural, cultura f; (as Univ department etc) pedagogía f; **I never had much** — pasé poco tiempo en la escuela; **they paid for his** — le pagaron los estudios; **elementary** —, **primary** — primera enseñanza f; **secondary** — segunda enseñanza f; **higher** — enseñanza f superior; **Minister of E**— (Spain) Ministro m de Educación Nacional; **physical** — educación f física.
educational [ˌedju'keiʃənl] adj policy etc educacional, relativo a la educación; function etc, centre docente; film etc instructivo, educativo.
education(al)ist [ˌedju'keiʃn(əl)ist] n especializado m en pedagogía.
educative ['edjukətiv] adj educativo.
educator ['edjukeitə*] n educador m, ora f.
educe [i'djuːs] vt educir, sacar.
Edward ['edwəd] m Eduardo; — **the Confessor** Eduardo el Confesor.
Edwardian [ed'wɔːdiən] adj eduardiano.
eel [i:l] n anguila f.
e'en [i:n] = **even**.
e'er [eə*] = **ever**.
eerie ['iəri] adj misterioso; sound, experience extraño, fantástico, horripilante.
efface [i'feis] 1 vt borrar. 2 vr: **to** — **oneself** retirarse modestamente, lograr pasar inadvertido.
effect [i'fekt] 1 n (result) efecto m, consecuencia f, resultado m; (impression) efecto m, impresión f; —s efectos mpl; **pleasing** — impresión f agradable; **side** — efecto m secundario; **striving after** — efectismo m; **just for** — sólo por impresionar; **in** — en realidad; **to be in** — (Law) estar vigente; **of no** — inútil; **to be of no** — no tener efecto, no hacer mella; **to no** — inútilmente; **to the same** — del mismo tenor, a este tenor, en el mismo sentido; **to this** — con este propósito; **or words to that** — o algo parecido; **to feel the** —(s) **of** sentir los efectos de, estar resentido de; **to give** — **to** poner en efecto, hacer efectivo; **to have an** — dejarse sentir, surtir efecto (on en); **to put into** — poner en vigor; **to take** — (remedy) surtir efecto, (law) ponerse en vigor (from a partir de). 2 vt efectuar, llevar a cabo; sale efectuar; saving hacer.
effective [i'fektiv] 1 adj eficaz; (striking) impresionante, llamativo, logrado; (real) efectivo, verdadero; capacity (Tech) útil; (Mil) útil para todos los servicios; **to become** — entrar en vigor (from, on a partir de). 2 —s npl efectivos mpl.
effectively [i'fektivli] adv eficazmente; (strikingly) de manera impresionante, acertadamente; (in fact) en efecto.
effectiveness [i'fektivnis] n eficacia f.
effectual [i'fektjuəl] adj eficaz.
effectuate [i'fektjueit] vt efectuar, lograr.
effeminacy [i'feminəsi] n afeminación f.
effeminate [i'feminit] adj afeminado.
effervesce [ˌefə'ves] vi estar en efervescencia, (begin to —) entrar en efervescencia; bullir, hervir; (fig) ser muy alegre, ser muy vivo.
effervescence [ˌefə'vesns] n efervescencia f.

effervescent [ˌefə'vesnt] adj efervescente (also fig).
effete [i'fiːt] adj decadente, cansado.
efficacious [ˌefi'keiʃəs] adj eficaz.
efficacy ['efikəsi] n eficacia f.
efficiency [i'fiʃənsi] n eficiencia f, eficacia f; (Mech) rendimiento m.
efficient [i'fiʃənt] adj eficiente; remedy, product eficaz; (Mech) de buen rendimiento; person eficiente, eficaz, competente, capaz.
efficiently [i'fiʃəntli] adv eficientemente, eficazmente.
effigy ['efidʒi] n efigie f; **to burn someone in** — quemar a uno en efigie.
efflorescent [ˌeflɔː'resnt] adj eflorescente.
effluent ['efluənt] 1 adj efluente. 2 n corriente f efluente.
effluvium [e'fluːviəm] n, pl **effluvia** [e'fluːviə] efluvio m, emanación f, tufo m.
effort ['efət] n (a) esfuerzo m; **all his** — **was directed to** todos sus esfuerzos iban dirigidos a; **to make an** — **to** + infin esforzarse por + infin, hacer un esfuerzo por + infin; **to make every** — **to** + infin, **to spare no** — **to** + infin no regatear medio para + infin.
(b) (fam) resultado m, producto m; obra f; **it was a pretty poor** — fue una exhibición pobre; **what did you think of his latest** —? ¿qué opinas de su nueva obra?; **it's not bad for a first** — siendo su primer intento no es nada malo.
effortless ['efətlis] adj sin esfuerzo alguno, fácil.
effortlessly ['efətlisli] adv sin esfuerzo alguno, fácilmente.
effrontery [i'frʌntəri] n descaro m; **what** —! ¡qué frescura!; **he had the** — **to say** llegó su cinismo hasta decir.
effusion [i'fjuːʒən] n efusión f.
effusive [i'fjuːsiv] adj efusivo.
effusively [i'fjuːsivli] adv con efusión.
eft [eft] n tritón m.
egalitarian [iˌgæli'teəriən] adj igualitario.
egg¹ [eg] n (a) huevo m; **hard-boiled** — huevo m cocido, huevo m duro; **soft-boiled** — huevo m pasado por agua; **fried** — huevo m frito, huevo m al plato; **poached** — huevo m escalfado; **scrambled** —s huevos mpl revueltos; **as sure as** —s (is —s) sin ningún género de dudas; **don't put all your** —s **in one basket** no pongas toda la carne en el asador.
(b) (fam) tío m; **bad** — sinvergüenza m.
egg² [eg] vt: **to** — **someone on** dar pie a uno; **to** — **someone on to do something** incitar a uno a hacer algo.
eggbeater ['egˌbiːtə*] n batidor m de huevos.
eggcup ['egkʌp] n huevera f.
egg flip ['egflip] n yema f mejida.
egghead ['eghed] n (fam) intelectual m.
eggnog ['egnɔg] n yema f mejida, ponche m de huevo.
eggplant ['egplaːnt] n berenjena f.
egg-shaped ['egʃeipt] adj oviforme.
eggshell ['egʃel] n cáscara f de huevo.
eglantine ['egləntain] n eglantina f.
ego ['iːgəu] n el yo.
egocentric(al) [ˌegəu'sentrik(əl)] adj egocéntrico.
egoism ['egəuizəm] n egoísmo m.
egoist ['egəuist] n egoísta mf.
egoistical [ˌegəu'istikəl] adj egoísta.
egotism ['egəutizəm] n egotismo m.
egotist ['egəutist] n egotista mf.
egotistic(al) [ˌegəu'tistik(əl)] adj egotista.
egregious [i'griːdʒəs] adj atroz, enorme; liar etc notorio.
egret ['iːgret] n garceta f.
Egypt ['iːdʒipt] Egipto m.
Egyptian [i'dʒipʃən] 1 adj egipcio. 2 n egipcio m, a f.
Egyptology [ˌiːdʒip'tɔlədʒi] n egiptología f.
eh [ei] interj (please repeat) ¿cómo?, ¿qué?; (inviting assent) ¿no?, ¿verdad?; ¿no es así?
eider ['aidə*] n, **eider duck** ['aidə'dʌk] n eider m.
eiderdown ['aidədaun] n edredón m.
eight [eit] 1 adj ocho. 2 n ocho m; (Rowing) bote m de a ocho; **to have had one over the** — llevar una copa de más.
eighteen ['ei'tiːn] adj dieciocho.
eighteenth ['ei'tiːnθ] adj decimoctavo.
eighth [eitθ] 1 adj octavo. 2 n octavo m.
eightieth ['eitiiθ] adj octogésimo.
eighty ['eiti] adj ochenta; **the eighties** (eg 1980s) los años ochenta; **to be in one's eighties** tener más de ochenta años.
Eire ['eərə] Eire m.
either ['aiðə*] 1 adj cualquier ... de los dos; **you can do it** — **way** puedes hacerlo de este modo o del otro; **on** — **side** en ambos lados; (neg sense) **I don't like**

— **book** no me gusta ninguno de los dos libros, no me gusta ni uno ni otro.

2 *pron* cualquiera de los dos, uno u otro; — **of us** cualquiera de nosotros; (*neg sense*) **I don't want** — **of them** no quiero ninguno de los dos, no quiero ni uno ni otro.

3 *conj:* — **come in or stay out** o entras o quedas fuera.

4 *adv* tampoco; **I won't go** — yo no voy tampoco.

ejaculate [i'dʒækjuleit] *vt* exclamar; proferir (de repente), lanzar; (*Med*) eyacular.

ejaculation [i,dʒækju'leiʃən] *n* exclamación *f*; (*Med*) eyaculación *f*.

eject [i'dʒekt] *vt* expulsar, echar; *tenant* desahuciar.

ejection [i'dʒekʃən] *n* expulsión *f*; desahucio *m*.

ejector [i'dʒektə*] *n* expulsor *m*; — **seat** asiento *m* proyectable.

eke [i:k] *vt:* **to** — **out** suplir las deficiencias de; *money etc* hacer que llegue; *livelihood* ganar a duras penas.

elaborate [i'læbərit] *adj* complicado; detallado; *meal* de muchos platos; *work of art* primoroso, rebuscado; *courtesy* exquisito, estudiado.

elaborate [i'læbəreit] **1** *vt* elaborar.

2 *vi* explicarse con muchos detalles; **to** — **on** ampliar, dar más explicaciones acerca de; **he refused to** — se negó a dar más detalles.

elaborately [i'læbəritli] *adv* de manera complicada; con muchos detalles; primorosamente.

elaboration [i,læbə'reiʃən] *n* elaboración *f*.

elapse [i'læps] *vi* pasar, transcurrir.

elastic [i'læstik] **1** *adj* elástico (*also fig*). **2** *n* elástico *m*; (*Sew*) goma *f*.

elastic band [i'læstik'bænd] *n* gomita *f*.

elasticity [,i:læs'tisiti] *n* elasticidad *f*.

elated [i'leitid] *adj:* **to be** — alegrarse, regocijarse (*at, with* de).

elation [i'leiʃən] *n* alegría *f*, regocijo *m*, júbilo *m*.

elbow ['elbəu] **1** *n* codo *m*; (*of road etc*) recodo *m*; **at one's** — a la mano, muy cerca; **out at the** —**s** raído; **more power to your** —! ¡que tenga éxito en la campaña!

2 *vt* empujar con el codo; **to** — **someone aside** apartar a uno a codazos; **to** — **one's way through** abrirse paso codeando (por).

elbow grease ['elbəugri:s] *n* (*fam*) codo *m*.

elbowroom ['elbəurum] *n* espacio *m* (suficiente); espacio *m* para moverse; libertad *f* de acción.

elder[1] ['eldə*] **1** *adj* mayor; **Pliny the E—** Plinio el Viejo. **2** *n* (*Eccl*) anciano *m*; **my** —**s** mis mayores; **the** —**s of the tribe** los jefes de la tribu.

elder[2] ['eldə*] *n* (*Bot*) saúco *m*.

elderberry ['eldə,beri] *n* baya *f* del saúco.

elderly ['eldəli] *adj* de edad, mayor; **to be getting** — ir para viejo.

eldest ['eldist] *adj* (el, la) mayor; **my** — **son** mi hijo mayor; **the** — **of the four** el mayor de los cuatro.

Eleanor ['elinə*] *f* Leonor.

elect [i'lekt] **1** *vt* elegir; **to** — **someone a member** elegir a uno socio; **to** — **to** + *infin* optar por + *infin*, decidir + *infin*.

2 *adj* electo; **president** — presidente *m* electo.

3 *n:* **the** — los elegidos.

election [i'lekʃən] *n* elección *f* (*for* a); **general** — elecciones *fpl* generales.

electioneer [i,lekʃə'niə*] *vi* hacer su campaña electoral; (*pej*) hacer propaganda a favor de su partido.

electioneering [i,lekʃə'niəriŋ] *n* campaña *f* electoral; (*pej*) maniobras *fpl* electorales.

elective [i'lektiv] *adj* electivo.

elector [i'lektə*] *n* elector *m*, ora *f*.

electoral [i'lektərəl] *adj* electoral.

electorate [i'lektərit] *n* electorado *m*; número *m* de votantes; censo *m*.

electric [i'lektrik] *adj* eléctrico; **the atmosphere was** — la atmósfera estaba cargada de electricidad.

electrical [i'lektrikəl] *adj* eléctrico.

electrically [i'lektrikəli] *adv* por electricidad.

electrician [ilek'triʃən] *n* electricista *m*.

electricity [ilek'trisiti] *n* electricidad *f*.

electrification [i'lektrifi'keiʃən] *n* electrificación *f*.

electrify [i'lektrifai] *vt* electrificar; (*fig*) electrizar.

electrifying [i'lektrifaiiŋ] *adj* electrizante.

electro . . . [i'lektrəu] electro . . .

electrocardiogram [i'lektrəu'ka:diəgræm] *n* electrocardiograma *m*.

electrocute [i'lektrəukju:t] *vt* electrocutar.

electrocution [i,lektrəu'kjuʃən] *n* electrocución *f*.

electrode [i'lektrəud] *n* electrodo *m*.

electrodynamics [i'lektrəudai'næmiks] *n* electrodinámica *f*.

electrolysis [ilek'trɔlisis] *n* electrólisis *f*.

electromagnet [i'lektrəu'mægnit] *n* electroimán *m*.

electromagnetic [i'lektrəumæg'netik] *adj* electromagnético.

electron [i'lektrɔn] *n* electrón *m*.

electronic [ilek'trɔnik] *adj* electrónico.

electronics [ilek'trɔniks] *n* electrónica *f*.

electroplate [i'lektrəupleit] *vt* galvanizar, electrochapar.

electroplated [i'lektrəupleitid] *adj* galvanizado, electrochapado.

elegance ['eligəns] *n* elegancia *f*.

elegant ['eligənt] *adj* elegante.

elegantly ['eligəntli] *adv* elegantemente.

elegiac [,eli'dʒaiək] *adj* elegíaco.

elegy ['elidʒi] *n* elegía *f*.

element ['elimənt] *n* elemento *m* (*also Chem, Elec etc*); —**s** (*rudiments*) elementos *mpl*, primeras nociones *fpl*; **to be in one's** — estar en su elemento; **to be out of one's** — estar como pez fuera del agua; **to brave the** —**s** arrostrar la tempestad, (*go out*) salir a la intemperie; **it's the personal** — **that counts** es el factor personal el que cuenta.

elemental [,eli'mentl] *adj* elemental.

elementary [,eli'mentəri] *adj* elemental; (*primitive*) rudimentario; *school* primario, de primera enseñanza; —, **my dear Watson** es muy sencillo, querido Watson.

elephant ['elifənt] *n* elefante *m*, a *f*; **white** — maula *f*.

elephantine [,eli'fæntain] *adj* (*fig*) mastodóntico.

elevate ['eliveit] *vt* elevar; (*Eccl*) alzar; *person* exaltar; (*in rank*) ascender (*to* a).

elevated ['eliveitid] *adj* elevado, sublime.

elevation [,eli'veiʃən] *n* (*act*) elevación *f*; (*of person*) exaltación *f*; (*in rank*) ascenso *m*; (*of style*) sublimidad *f*; (*hill*) altura *f*; (*Aer etc*) altitud *f*.

elevator ['eliveitə*] *n* (*Agr*) almacén *m* de granos, elevador *m* de granos; (*Aer*) timón *m* de profundidad; (*US*) ascensor *m*, (*for goods*) montacargas *m*.

eleven [i'levn] **1** *adj* once. **2** *n* once *m*.

elevenses [i'levnziz] *npl* (*fam*): **to have** — tomar las once.

eleventh [i'levnθ] *adj* undécimo, onceno.

elf [elf] *n*, *pl* **elves** [elvz] elfo *m*, duende *m*.

elfin ['elfin] *adj* de elfo, como elfo; que tiene la magia (*or* la gracia *etc*) de los elfos; mágico.

elicit [i'lisit] *vt* sacar, (*lograr*) obtener.

elide [i'laid] *vt* elidir.

eligibility [,elidʒə'biliti] *n* elegibilidad *f*.

eligible ['elidʒəbl] *adj* elegible; (*desirable*) deseable, atractivo; *bachelor* de partido; **he's the most** — **bachelor in town** es el mejor partido de la ciudad; **to be** — **for** llenar los requisitos para.

eliminate [i'limineit] *vt* eliminar; suprimir; *suspect, possibility etc* descartar; *person* (*in purge*) eliminar.

elimination [i,limi'neiʃən] *n* eliminación *f*; supresión *f*.

elision [i'liʒən] *n* elisión *f*.

élite [ei'li:t] *n* élite *f*, minoría *f* selecta.

elixir [i'liksə*] *n* elixir *m*.

Elizabeth [i'lizəbəθ] *f* Isabel.

Elizabethan [i,lizə'bi:θən] **1** *adj* isabelino. **2** *n* isabelino *m*, a *f*.

elk [elk] *n* alce *m*.

ellipse [i'lips] *n* elipse *f*.

ellipsis [i'lipsis] *n*, *pl* **ellipses** [i'lipsi:z] elipsis *f*.

elliptic(al) [i'liptik(əl)] *adj* elíptico.

elm [elm] *n* olmo *m* (*also* — **tree**).

elocution [,elə'kju:ʃən] *n* elocución *f*.

elocutionist [,elə'kju:ʃənist] *n* profesor *m* de elocución.

elongate ['i:lɔŋgeit] *vt* alargar, extender.

elongated ['i:lɔŋgeitid] *adj* alargado, estirado.

elongation [,i:lɔŋ'geiʃən] *n* alargamiento *m*, estiramiento *m*.

elope [i'ləup] *vi* (1 *person*) fugarse con su amante, (2 *persons*) fugarse para casarse; **to** — **with** fugarse con.

elopement [i'ləupmənt] *n* fuga *f*.

eloquence ['eləkwəns] *n* elocuencia *f*.

eloquent ['eləkwənt] *adj* elocuente.

eloquently ['eləkwəntli] *adv* elocuentemente.

else [els] *adv* (**a**) (*after pron*) **all** —, **everything** — todo lo demás; **everyone** — todos los demás; **anyone** — **would do it** cualquier otra persona lo haría; **anything** — **is impossible** cualquier otra cosa es imposible; **have you anything** — **to tell me?** ¿tiene algo más que decirme?; **anything** —, **madam?** (*in shop*) ¿algo más, señora?, ¿alguna cosita más, señora?; **that was somebody** — eso fue otro; **there's somebody** —, **isn't there?** hay otro hombre ¿verdad?; **somewhere** — en otra parte.

(b) (*after pron, neg*) **I don't know anyone — here** aquí no conozco a ninguna otra persona; **nobody — knows** no lo sabe ningún otro; **there's nothing — I can do** no hay nada más que pueda hacer; **nothing —, thanks** nada más, gracias.

(c) (*adv of quantity*) **there was little — to do** apenas quedaba otra cosa que hacer; **and much —** besides y otras muchas cosas además.

(d) (*after interrog*) **how —?** ¿de qué otra manera?; **what —?** ¿qué más?; **where —?** ¿en qué otro sitio?; **where — can he have gone?** ¿a qué otro sitio habrá podido ir?; **who —?** ¿quién más?; **who — could do it as well as you?** ¿qué otra persona podría hacerlo tan bien como Vd?

(e) (*standing alone*) **how could I have done it —?** ¿de qué otro modo hubiera podido hacerlo?; **red or — black** rojo o bien negro; **or — I'll do it** si no, lo hago yo; **do this, or — . . .** hágalo, pues si no . . .

elsewhere ['els'wɛə*] *adv* be en otra parte, go a otra parte.

elucidate [i'luːsideit] *vt* aclarar, elucidar.

elucidation [i‚luːsi'deifən] *n* aclaración *f*, elucidación *f*.

elude [i'luːd] *vt blow etc* eludir, esquivar, evitar; *grasp* escapar de; *pursuer* escaparse de, burlar, zafarse de; *obligation* zafarse de; **the name —s me** se me escapa el nombre; **the answer has so far —d us** hasta ahora no hemos encontrado la solución.

elusive [i'luːsiv] *adj* difícil de encontrar, esquivo.

elver ['elvə*] *n* anguila *f* joven.

elves [elvz] *pl of* **elf**.

Elysium [i'liziəm] Elíseo *m*.

emaciated [i'meisieitid] *adj* demacrado; **to become —** demacrarse.

emaciation [i‚meisi'eifən] *n* demacración *f*.

emanate ['eməneit] *vi* emanar, proceder (*from* de).

emanation [‚emə'neifən] *n* emanación *f*.

emancipate [i'mænsipeit] *vt* emancipar.

emancipated [i'mænsipeitid] *adj* emancipado; (*fig*) libre.

emancipation [i‚mænsi'peifən] *n* emancipación *f*; (*fig*) libertad *f*.

emasculate [i'mæskjuleit] *vt* (*fig*) mutilar, estropear.

emasculated [i'mæskjuleitid] *adj* mutilado, estropeado; *style* empobrecido.

embalm [im'baːm] *vt* embalsamar.

embankment [im'bæŋkmənt] *n* terraplén *m*.

embargo [im'baːgəu] *n* prohibición *f* (*on* de); **to be under an —** estar prohibido; **there is an — on arms** está prohibido comerciar en armas; **there is an — on that subject** está prohibido discutir ese asunto; **to put an — on something** prohibir el comercio de algo, (*fig*) prohibir el uso de algo.

embark [im'baːk] **1** *vt* embarcar. **2** *vi* embarcarse (*for* con rumbo a, *on* en); **to — upon** emprender, lanzarse a.

embarkation [‚embaː'keifən] *n* (*of persons*) embarco *m*; (*of goods*) embarque *m*.

embarrass [im'bærəs] *vt* desconcertar, turbar, azorar; (*deliberately*) poner en un aprieto; (*financially*) crear dificultades económicas a; **to be —ed** sentirse violento, sentirse molesto, estar azorado; **to be financially —ed** tener dificultades económicas; **I was —ed by the question** la pregunta me desconcertó; **I feel —ed about it** me siento algo avergonzado por eso.

embarrassing [im'bærəsiŋ] *adj experience etc* embarazoso, desconcertante; *moment, situation* violento.

embarrassment [im'bærəsmənt] *n* (a) (*state*) desconcierto *m*, turbación *f*, azoramiento *m*; *financial —* apuros *mpl*, dificultades *fpl* económicas; **I am in a state of some —** estoy algo perplejo.

(b) (*object*) estorbo *m*; **you are an — to us all** eres un estorbo para todos nosotros.

embassy ['embəsi] *n* embajada *f*.

embattled [im'bætld] *adj army* en orden de batalla; *city* sitiado.

embed [im'bed] **1** *vt* empotrar; *weapon, teeth etc* clavar, hincar (*in* en). **2** *vr*: **to — itself in** empotrarse en.

embellish [im'belif] *vt* embellecer; (*fig, story etc*) adornar (*with* de).

embellishment [im'belifmənt] *n* embellecimiento *m*; (*fig*) adorno *m*.

embers ['embəz] *npl* rescoldo *m*, ascua *f*.

embezzle [im'bezl] *vt* malversar, desfalcar.

embezzlement [im'bezlmənt] *n* malversación *f*, desfalco *m*.

embezzler [im'bezlə*] *n* malversador *m*, desfalcador *m*.

embitter [im'bitə*] *vt* amargar; *relations etc* envenenar.

embittered [im'bitəd] *adj* resentido, rencoroso; **to be very —** estar muy amargado (*about* por, *against* contra).

emblazon [im'bleizən] *vt* engalanar (*or* esmaltar) con colores brillantes; (*fig*) escribir de modo llamativo, adornar de modo llamativo.

emblem ['embləm] *n* emblema *m*.

emblematic [‚embli'mætik] *adj* emblemático.

embodiment [im'bɔdimənt] *n* encarnación *f*, personificación *f*; **to be the very — of virtue** ser la misma virtud.

embody [im'bɔdi] *vt* (a) encarnar, personificar; *idea etc* expresar. (b) (*include*) incorporar.

embolden [im'bəuldən] *vt* envalentonar (*to* + *infin* para que + *subj*).

embolism ['embəlizəm] *n* embolia *f*.

emboss [im'bɔs] *vt* realzar; estampar en relieve; **—ed with the royal arms** con el escudo real en relieve.

embrace [im'breis] **1** *n* abrazo *m*.

2 *vt* (a) (*clasp*) abrazar, dar un abrazo a.

(b) (*include*) abarcar.

(c) *offer* aceptar; *opportunity* aprovechar; *course of action* adoptar; *doctrine, party* adherirse a; *profession* dedicarse a; *religion* convertirse a.

3 *vi* abrazarse.

embrasure [im'breizə*] *n* (*Archit*) alféizar *m*; (*Mil*) tronera *f*, cañonera *f*.

embrocation [‚embrəu'keifən] *n* embrocación *f*.

embroider [im'brɔidə*] *vt* bordar, recamar; (*fig*) adornar con detalles ficticios.

embroidery [im'brɔidəri] *n* bordado *m*.

embroil [im'brɔil] *vt* embrollar, enredar; **to — someone with** indisponer a uno con; **to get —ed in** enredarse en, hacerse un lío con.

embroilment [im'brɔilmənt] *n* embrollo *m*.

embryo ['embriəu] **1** *n* embrión *m*; (*fig*) germen *m*; **in —** en embrión. **2** *attr* embrionario.

embryonic [‚embri'ɔnik] *adj* embrionario.

emend [i'mend] *vt* enmendar.

emendation [‚iːmen'deifən] *n* enmienda *f*.

emerald ['emərəld] **1** *n* esmeralda *f*. **2** *adj* de color de esmeralda, esmeraldino; **the E— Isle** la verde Irlanda.

emerge [i'məːdʒ] *vi* salir (*from* de; *also fig*), aparecer, dejarse ver; (*problem etc*) surgir; **it —s that** resulta que; **what has —d from this inquiry?** ¿qué se saca de esta investigación?

emergence [i'məːdʒəns] *n* salida *f*, aparición *f*.

emergency [i'məːdʒənsi] **1** *n* crisis *f*; necesidad *f* urgente; situación *f* imprevista; **there is a national —** existe una crisis nacional; **in an —, in case of —** en caso de urgencia; **to provide for emergencies** tomar precauciones contra los peligros imprevisibles.

2 *attr brake* de auxilio; *exit* de urgencia, de emergencia; *landing* forzoso; *measure* de urgencia; *meeting* extraordinario.

emergent [i'məːdʒənt] *adj nation* naciente.

emeritus [i'meritəs] *adj* emeritus, honorario.

emery ['eməri] *n* esmeril *m*.

emery cloth ['eməri‚klɔθ] *n* tela *f* de esmeril.

emery paper ['eməri‚peipə*] *n* papel *m* de esmeril.

emetic [i'metik] **1** *adj* emético. **2** *n* emético *m*.

emigrant ['emigrənt] **1** *adj* emigrante. **2** *n* emigrante *mf*.

emigrate ['emigreit] *vi* emigrar.

emigration [‚emi'greifən] *n* emigración *f*.

émigré(e) ['emigrei] *n* emigrado *m*, a *f*.

Emily ['emili] *f* Emilia.

eminence ['eminəns] *n* eminencia *m*; **His E— Su** Eminencia; **Your E— Vuestra Eminencia.

eminent ['eminənt] *adj* eminente.

eminently ['eminəntli] *adv* sumamente.

emir [e'miə*] *n* emir *m*.

emissary ['emisəri] *n* emisario *m*.

emission [i'mifən] *n* emisión *f*.

emit [i'mit] *vt light, signals etc* emitir; *smoke etc* arrojar; *smell* despedir; *cry* dar; *sound* producir.

Emmanuel [i'mænjuəl] *m* Manuel.

emolument [i'mɔljumənt] *n* emolumento *m*.

emote [i'məut] *vi* (*fam*) actuar de una manera muy emocionada.

emotion [i'məufən] *n* emoción *f*.

emotional [i'məufənl] *adj* emocional; *moment* de honda emoción; *person* (*warm-hearted*) sentimental, (*taking things too hard*) demasiado sensible, (*showing excessive emotion*) exaltado, exagerado; **— tension** tensión *f* emocional.

emotionalism [i'məufnəlizəm] *n* sentimentalismo *m*; (*in newspaper etc*) sensacionalismo *m*.

emotionally [i'məuʃnəli] *adv* con emoción; — **unstable** poco estable en cuanto a las emociones.
emotionless [i'məuʃənlis] *adj* sin emoción.
emotive [i'məutiv] *adj* emotivo.
empanel [im'pænl] *vt jury* inscribir.
empathy ['empəθi] *n* empatía *f*.
emperor ['empərə*] *n* emperador *m*.
emphasis ['emfəsis] *n* énfasis *m*; **to lay** (*or* put) — **on** subrayar; **the** — **is on sport** se le concede mucha importancia al deporte; **this year the** — **is on femininity** este año las modas hacen resaltar la feminidad.
emphasize ['emfəsaiz] *vt* (*Gram*) acentuar; (*fig*) subrayar, recalcar; **I must** — **that** tengo que subrayar que.
emphatic [im'fætik] *adj* enfático; *speech, condemnation etc* enérgico; *person* decidido; **he was most** — **that** dijo de modo tajante que.
emphatically [im'fætikəli] *adv* con énfasis; **yes,** — sí, sin ningún género de dudas; **the answer is** — **no** bajo ningún concepto.
empire ['empaiə*] *n* imperio *m*.
empiric(al) [em'pirik(əl)] *adj* empírico.
empiricism [em'pirisizəm] *n* empirismo *m*.
empiricist [em'pirisist] *n* empírico *m*.
emplacement [im'pleismənt] *n* (*Mil*) emplazamiento *m*.
employ [im'plɔi] **1** *n*: **to be in the** — **of** trabajar por, (*as servant etc*) estar al servicio de.
 2 *vt person* emplear; *thing* emplear, usar; *time* ocupar; **to be** —**ed in** emplearse en.
employee [,emplɔi'i:] *n* empleado *m*, a *f*, dependiente *m*, a *f*.
employer [im'plɔiə*] *n* patrón *m*, ona *f*.
employment [im'plɔimənt] *n* (**a**) (*act*) empleo *m*; uso *m*.
 (**b**) (*job*) empleo *m*, colocación *f*, puesto *m*; ocupación *f*; **to be in** — tener trabajo; **to give** — **to** emplear a; **to look for** — buscar colocación; — **agency** agencia *f* de colocaciones; — **exchange** bolsa *f* de trabajo.
 (**c**) (*jobs collectively*) empleo *m*; **full** — pleno empleo *m*; **a high level of** — un alto nivel de trabajo.
emporium [em'pɔ:riəm] *n* emporio *m*.
empower [im'pauə*] *vt*: **to** — **someone to do something** autorizar a uno a hacer algo.
empress ['empris] *n* emperatriz *f*.
emptiness ['emptinis] *n* vacío *m*, lo vacío; (*of person's life*) vaciedad *f*, vacuidad *f*; **its** — **of moral content** lo desierto de todo contenido moral.
empty ['empti] **1** *adj* vacío; *house* desocupado; *place* desierto; *vehicle* vacío, sin carga; *post* vacante; *threat, words* vano, inútil; *phrase* sin significado real; **I'm** — tengo hambre.
 2 *n* (*gen pl*) botella *f* (*etc*) vacía; **returnable empties** envases *mpl* a devolver.
 3 *vt contents* vaciar, verter; *container* vaciar, descargar; *place, room* dejar vacío.
 4 *vi* vaciarse; (*vehicle*) quedar vacío; (*room etc*) quedar desocupado; (*place*) quedar desierto; **to** — **into** (*river*) desembocar en.
empty-handed ['empti'hændid] *adj* con las manos vacías, manivacío.
empty-headed ['empti'hedid] *adj* casquivano.
emu ['i:mju:] *n* dromeo *m*, emú *m*.
emulate ['emjuleit] *vt* emular.
emulation [,emju'leiʃən] *n* emulación *f*.
emulsify [i'mʌlsifai] *vt* emulsionar.
emulsion [i'mʌlʃən] *n* emulsión *f*.
enable [i'neibl] *vt*: **to** — **someone to do something** permitir a uno hacer algo, poner a uno en condiciones para hacer algo; **I am now** —**d to go** ahora puedo ir.
enact [i'nækt] *vt* decretar (*that* que); *law* promulgar; *play, scene* representar; *part* hacer.
enamel [i'næməl] **1** *n* esmalte *m*. **2** *vt* esmaltar, pintar al esmalte.
enamelled [i'næməld] *adj* esmaltado.
enamelware [i'næməlweə*] *n* utensilios *mpl* de hierro esmaltado.
enamour [i'næmə*] *vt*: **to be** —**ed of** *person* estar enamorado de, *thing* tener gran afición a, *idea* aferrarse a.
encamp [in'kæmp] *vi* acamparse.
encampment [in'kæmpmənt] *n* campamento *m*.
encase [in'keis] *vt* encerrar; **to be** —**d in** estar revestido de.
encash [in'kæʃ] *vt* cobrar, hacer efectivo.
encephalitis [,ensefə'laitis] *n* encefalitis *f*.
enchain [in'tʃein] *vt* encadenar.
enchant [in'tʃɑ:nt] *vt* encantar (*also fig*); **we were** —**ed with the place** el sitio nos encantó.
enchanter [in'tʃɑ:ntə*] *n* hechicero *m*.

enchanting [in'tʃɑ:ntiŋ] *adj* encantador.
enchantingly [in'tʃɑ:ntiŋli] *adv* de manera encantadora, deliciosamente.
enchantment [in'tʃɑ:ntmənt] *n* (*act*) encantamiento *m*; (*charm*) encanto *m*; **it lent** — **to the scene** aumentó el encanto de la escena.
enchantress [in'tʃɑ:ntris] *n* hechicera *f*.
encircle [in'sə:kl] *vt* rodear (*with* de); (*Mil*) envolver; *waist, shoulders etc* ceñir; **it is** —**d by a wall** está rodeado de una tapia.
encirclement [in'sə:klmənt] *n* (*Mil*) envolvimiento *m*.
encircling [in'sə:kliŋ] *adj movement* envolvente.
enclave ['enkleiv] *n* enclave *m*.
enclitic [in'klitik] *adj* enclítico.
enclose [in'kləuz] *vt land, garden* cercar (*with* de); (*put in a receptacle*) meter, encerrar; (*include*) encerrar; (*with letter*) remitir adjunto, adjuntar; —**d herewith please find** ... le mandamos adjunto ...; **the** —**d letter** la carta adjunta.
enclosure [in'kləuʒə*] *n* (*act*) cercamiento *m*; (*place*) cercado *m*, recinto *m*; (*in letter*) carta *f* adjunta, carta *f* inclusa.
encompass [in'kʌmpəs] *vt* (*surround*) cercar, rodear (*with* de); (*include*) abarcar; (*bring about*) lograr.
encore [ɔŋ'kɔ:*] **1** *interj* ¡bis!
 2 *n* bis *m*, repetición *f*; **to give an** — repetir algo a petición del público; **to sing a song as an** — bisar una canción.
 3 *vt song* pedir la repetición de, *person* pedir una repetición a.
encounter [in'kauntə*] **1** *n* encuentro *m*. **2** *vt* encontrar, encontrarse con; *difficulty etc* tropezar con.
encourage [in'kʌridʒ] *vt person* animar, alentar, dar aliento a; *industry* fomentar, estimular; *growth* estimular; (*in a belief*) fortalecer, reforzar; **to** — **someone to do something** animar a uno a hacer algo.
encouragement [in'kʌridʒmənt] *n* (*act*) estímulo *m*, (*of industry*) fomento *m*; (*support*) aliento *m*, aprobación *f*; **to give** — **to** infundir ánimos a, dar aliento a; **to give** — **to the enemy** ayudar al enemigo.
encouraging [in'kʌridʒiŋ] *adj* alentador, esperanzador; *favorable,* halagüeño; **it is not an** — **prospect** es una perspectiva nada halagüeña; **he was always very** — siempre me daba aliento.
encouragingly [in'kʌridʒiŋli] *adv speak etc* en tono alentador.
encroach [in'krəutʃ] *vi*: **to** — **on** *rights* usurpar; *land* (*of neighbour*) invadir, pasar los límites de; *land* (*by sea*) hurtar, comerse; *person's subject* invadir; *time* ocupar, llevar (una parte cada vez mayor de).
encroachment [in'krəutʃmənt] *n* usurpación *f* (*on* de); invasión *f* (*on* de); abuso *m* (*on* de); **this new** — **on our liberty** esta nueva usurpación de nuestra libertad.
encrusted [in'krʌstid] *adj*: — **with** incrustado de.
encumber [in'kʌmbə*] *vt person, movement* estorbar; (*with debts*) gravar, cargar; *place* llenar (*with* de); **to be** —**ed with** tener que cargar con, (*debts*) estar gravado de.
encumbrance [in'kʌmbrəns] *n* estorbo *m*; (*of debt*) carga *f*, gravamen *m*; **without** — sin familia.
encyclical [en'siklikəl] *n* encíclica *f*.
encyclopaedia, —**pedia** [en,saikləu'pi:diə] *n* enciclopedia *f*.
encyclopaedic, —**pedic** [en,saikləu'pi:dik] *adj* enciclopédico.
end [end] **1** *n* (**a**) (*in physical sense*) (*of street etc*) final *m*; (*of line, table etc*) extremo *m*; (*of rope etc*) cabo *m*; (*point*) punta *f*; (*of estate etc*) límite *m*; (*Sport*) lado *m*; (*of town*) barrio *m*; **the** —**s of the earth** las partes más remotas del mundo; **big** — (*Mech*) cabeza *f* de biela; **deep** — (*of pool*) parte *f* honda; **loose** — cabo *m* suelto; **at the** — **of** al cabo de, en el extremo de; **al final de; from one** — **to the other, from** — **to** — de un extremo a otro; **on** — de punta, de cabeza, de canto; — **to** — juntando los dos extremos; **to be at a loose** — estar desocupado, no tener qué hacer; **to be at the** — **of one's tether** estar casi completamente agotado; **estar para perder la paciencia; to change** —**s** (*Sport*) cambiar de lado; **to get hold of the wrong** — **of the stick** tomar el rábano por las hojas; **to go off the deep** — ponerse furioso (*about* por); **to keep one's** — **up** defenderse bien; **to make both** —**s meet** hacer llegar el dinero; **to read a book to the very** — leer un libro hasta el mismo final; **to stand on** — (*hair*) erizarse, *object* poner de punta; **to start at the wrong** — empezar por el fin; **to tie up the loose** —**s** atar cabos.

(b) (*of time, process, resources*) fin m, final m; término m, conclusión f; límite m; (*of book etc*) desenlace m, conclusión f; **the — of the empire** el fin del imperio; **that was the — of him** así terminó él; **latter —** muerte f; **at the — of 3 months** al cabo de 3 meses; **at the — of the century** a fines del siglo; **in the —** al fin, por fin, finalmente; **no — of la mar de; no — of an expert** sumamente experto, más experto que nadie; **3 days on —** 3 días seguidos; **for days on —** durante una infinidad de días; **to the bitter —** hasta que se terminara del todo; **towards the — of** hacia el final de, *century etc* hacia fines de; **to be at an —** estar terminando, (*be all over*) haber terminado ya; **to be at the — of one's resources** haber agotado los recursos; **there's no — to it all** esto no tiene fin, esto es inacabable; **to come** (*or* **draw**) **to an —** terminarse; **to come to a bad —** tener mal fin, ir a acabar mal; **you'll never hear the — of it** esto no se olvidará pronto, esto no es fácil que se olvide; **to make an — of, to put an — to** acabar con, poner fin a; **to think no — of someone** tener un muy alto concepto de uno.

(c) (*aim*) fin m, objeto m, propósito m, intención f; **to this —, with this —** in view con este propósito; **to the — that** a fin de que + *subj*; **with what —?** ¿para qué?; **the — justifies the means** el fin justifica los medios; **to gain one's —s** salirse con la suya.

2 *adj* final.

3 *vt* terminar, acabar; *abuse etc* acabar con; *book* concluir.

4 *vi* terminar, acabar; **to — by saying** terminar diciendo; **to — in** terminar en; **to — up** terminar, acabar; **to — up at** ir a parar en; **to — with** terminar con.

endanger [in'deindʒə*] *vt* poner en peligro.
endear [in'diə*] **1** *vt*: **this did not — him to the public** esto no le granjeó las simpatías del público.
2 *vr*: **to — oneself to** hacerse querer de (*or* por).
endearing [in'diəriŋ] *adj* simpático, atractivo.
endearment [in'diəmənt] *n* palabra f cariñosa, ternura f.
endeavour [in'devə*] **1** *n* (*attempt*) esfuerzo m (*to do* por hacer), tentativa f (*to do de* hacer); (*striving*) empeño m, esfuerzos mpl; **to use every — to** + *infin* no regatear medio para + *infin*.
2 *vi*: **to — to do** esforzarse por hacer, procurar hacer.
endemic [en'demik] *adj* endémico.
ending ['endiŋ] *n* fin m, conclusión f; (*of book etc*) desenlace m; (*Gram*) terminación f, desinencia f; **the tale has a happy —** el cuento tiene un fin feliz.
endive ['endaiv] *n* escarola f, endibia f.
endless ['endlis] *adj* interminable, inacabable; *screw etc* sin fin.
endlessly ['endlisli] *adv* interminablemente, sin parar.
endocrine ['endəukrain] **1** *adj* endocrino; **— gland** glándula f endocrina. **2** *n* endocrina f.
endorse [in'dɔːs] *vt* endosar; *licence* poner nota de inhabilitación en; (*fig*) aprobar, confirmar.
endorsement [in'dɔːsmənt] *n* endoso m; (*in licence*) nota f de inhabilitación; (*fig*) aprobación f, confirmación f.
endow [in'dau] *vt* dotar (*with* con, (*fig*) de); *institution* fundar, crear; **to be —ed with** (*fig*) estar dotado de.
endowment [in'daumənt] *n* (a) (*act*) dotación f; (*creation*) fundación f, creación f. (b) (*amount*) dote f. (c) (*fig*) dote f, cualidad f.
endpaper ['endpeipə*] *n* hoja f de encuadernador.
end product ['end.prɔdəkt] *n* producto m final.
endue [in'djuː] *vt* dotar (*with* de).
endurable [in'djuərəbl] *adj* tolerable, soportable.
endurance [in'djuərəns] *n* resistencia f, aguante m; **beyond —, past —** intolerable; **to have great powers of —** tener gran resistencia; **— race** carrera f de resistencia; **— test** prueba f de resistencia.
endure [in'djuə*] **1** *vt* aguantar, soportar, tolerar; resistir; **I can't — him** no le puedo ver; **I can't — it a moment longer** no lo aguanto un momento más; **I can't — being corrected** no puedo sufrir que me corrijan; **I can't — being too hot** no resisto el calor excesivo.
2 *vi* (*last*) durar, perdurar; (*not give in*) resistir, sufrir sin rendirse.
enduring [in'djuəriŋ] *adj* permanente, perdurable.
endways ['endweiz] *adv* de punta; de lado, de canto.
enema ['enimə] *n* enema f.
enemy ['enimi] **1** *adj* enemigo. **2** *n* enemigo m, a f; **public —** enemigo m público; **to be one's own worst —** ser enemigo de sí mismo.
energetic [.enə'dʒetik] *adj* enérgico; *person etc* enérgico, activo; *protest* vigoroso.

energetically [.enə'dʒetikəli] *adv* enérgicamente; activamente; vigorosamente.
energize ['enədʒaiz] *vt* activar, dar energía a.
energy ['enədʒi] *n* energía f; vigor m; **atomic —** energía f atómica.
enervate ['enəːveit] *vt* enervar, debilitar.
enervating ['enəːveitiŋ] *adj* enervador; deprimente.
enfeeble [in'fiːbl] *vt* debilitar.
enfeeblement [in'fiːblmənt] *n* debilitación f.
enfilade [.enfi'leid] *vt* enfilar.
enfold [in'fəuld] *vt* envolver; (*in arms*) abrazar, estrechar (*in* los brazos).
enforce [in'fɔːs] *vt law* hacer cumplir, (*from a date*) poner en vigor; *claim* hacer valer; *rights* hacer respetar; *demand* insistir en; *obedience, will* imponer (*on* a).
enforced [in'fɔːst] *adj* inevitable; forzoso, forzado.
enfranchise [in'fræntʃaiz] *vt* (*free*) emancipar; *voter* conceder el derecho de votar a.
enfranchisement [in'fræntʃizmənt] *n* emancipación f (*of* de); concesión f del derecho de votar (*of* a).
engage [in'geidʒ] **1** *vt attention* llamar, atraer; ocupar; *taxi etc* alquilar; *servant* tomar a su servicio; *person in conversation* abordar, (*and delay*) entretener; *workmen* apalabrar, ajustar; *lawyer etc* requerir los servicios de; *enemy* atacar, trabar batalla con; (*Mech*) *cog etc* engranar con, *coupling* acoplar.
2 *vi* (*Mech*) engranar; **to — in** dedicarse a, ocuparse en; *sport etc* tomar parte en; **to — to do something** comprometerse a hacer algo; **to — with** (*Mech*) engranar con.
3 *vr*: **to — oneself to do something** comprometerse a hacer algo.
engaged [in'geidʒd] **1** *ptp of* **engage**; **(a) to be —** (*seat*) estar ocupado; (*person*) estar ocupado; tener compromiso; no estar libre.
(b) **to be —** (*Tel*) estar comunicando.
(c) **to be — in** estar ocupado en, dedicarse a; **what are you — in?** ¿a qué se dedica Vd?
(d) **to be — (to be married)** estar prometido, (*2 persons*) estar prometidos, ser novios, tener relaciones formales; **they've been — for 2 years** llevan 2 años de relaciones formales; **to get —** prometerse (*to* con).
2 *adj writer etc* comprometido; **the — couple** los novios.
engagement [in'geidʒmənt] *n* (a) (*contract*) contrato m; obligación f; **to enter into an — to** + *infin* comprometerse a + *infin*.
(b) (*appointment*) compromiso m, cita f; **have you an — tonight?** ¿tienes compromiso para esta noche?; **I have an — at 10** tengo una cita a las 10; **owing to a previous —** por tener compromiso anterior.
(c) (*Mil*) combate m, acción f.
(d) (*to marry*) compromiso m; (*period etc*) noviazgo m; **they have announced their —** se han dado palabra de casamiento; **the — is announced of Miss A to Mr B** por los señores de B ha sido pedida la mano de su encantadora hija Isabel para su hijo Juan.
engagement ring [in'geidʒmənt.riŋ] *n* alianza f, anillo m de prometida, anillo m de compromiso.
engaging [in'geidʒiŋ] *adj* atractivo, simpático.
engender [in'dʒendə*] *vt* engendrar; (*fig*) engendrar, suscitar, motivar.
engine ['endʒin] *n* (a) motor m; **air-cooled —** motor m refrigerado por aire; **radial —** motor m radial.
(b) (*Rail*) máquina f, locomotora f; **back to the —** de espaldas a la máquina; **facing the —** de frente a la máquina.
-engined ['endʒind] *adj* de . . . motores; *eg* **four-engined** cuatrimotor, tetramotor; **petrol-engined** propulsado por gasolina.
engine driver ['endʒin.draivə*] *n* maquinista m.
engineer [.endʒi'niə*] **1** *n* ingeniero m; mecánico m; (*US Rail*) maquinista m; **civil —** ingeniero m civil, ingeniero m de caminos, canales y puentes; **electrical —** ingeniero m electricista; **mining —** ingeniero m de minas; **Royal E—s** Cuerpo m de Ingenieros.
2 *vt* lograr, gestionar, agenciar.
engineering [.endʒi'niəriŋ] *n* ingeniería f; **civil —** ingeniería f civil; **electrical —** electrotecnia f; **mechanical —** ingeniería f mecánica; **radio —** técnica f radiofónica.
engine room ['endʒinrum] *n* sala f de máquinas.
England ['iŋglənd] Inglaterra f.
English ['iŋgliʃ] **1** *adj* inglés.
2 *n*: **the —** los ingleses.
3 *n* (*language*) inglés m; **Old —** inglés m antiguo; **King's —** inglés m correcto; **to speak the King's —** hablar en cristiano.

English Channel ['ɪŋglɪʃ'tʃænl] Canal *m* de la Mancha.
Englishman ['ɪŋglɪʃmən] *n, pl* —**men** [mən] inglés *m*.
Englishwoman ['ɪŋglɪʃˌwumən] *n, pl* —**women** [ˌwɪmɪn] inglesa *f*.
engraft [in'grɑːft] *vt* (*Agr, Med*) injertar; (*fig*) implantar (*on to* en).
engrave [in'greiv] *vt* grabar (*also fig: on* en); burilar.
engraver [in'greivə*] *n* grabador *m*.
engraving [in'greiviŋ] *n* grabado *m*.
engross [in'grəus] *vt* absorber; **to be** —**ed in** estar absorto en; **to become** —**ed in** dedicarse por completo a.
engrossing [in'grəusiŋ] *adj* absorbente.
engulf [in'gʌlf] *vt* tragar; sumergir, hundir; **to be** —**ed by** quedar sumergido bajo.
enhance [in'hɑːns] *vt* realzar, intensificar, aumentar; *price etc* aumentar.
enigma ['inigmə] *n* enigma *m*.
enigmatic [ˌenig'mætik] *adj* enigmático.
enigmatically [ˌenig'mætikəli] *adv* enigmáticamente.
enjambement [in'dʒæmmənt] *n* encabalgamiento *m*.
enjoin [in'dʒɔin] *vt*: **to** — **something on someone** imponer algo a uno; **to** — **someone to do something** ordenar a uno hacer algo; **to** — **someone from doing something** (*US*) prohibir a uno hacer algo.
enjoy [in'dʒɔi] 1 *vt* (**a**) (*have use of*) *health, possession etc* disfrutar de, gozar de; *income, someone's confidence* tener; *advantage* poseer.
  (**b**) (*take delight in*) *meal* comer con gusto; *pipe* fumar con fruición; **I** —**ed the book** me gustó el libro; **did you** — **the game?** ¿te gustó el partido?, ¿qué tal el partido?; **I** — **reading** me gusta leer, me gusta la lectura; **I hope you** — **your holiday** que lo pases muy bien en las vacaciones, que te diviertas mucho en las vacaciones, espero que tendrás unas vacaciones de lo más agradables; **the author did not mean his book to be** —**ed, exactly** el autor no quería que su libro resultase meramente divertido.
  2 *vr*: **to** — **oneself** pasarlo bien, divertirse; — **yourselves!** ¡que lo paséis bien!; **we** —**ed ourselves tremendously** lo pasamos en grande, nos divertimos muchísimo; **he** —**ed himself chasing the girls** se divirtió persiguiendo a las chicas.
enjoyable [in'dʒɔiəbl] *adj* agradable; (*amusing*) divertido.
enjoyment [in'dʒɔimənt] *n* (**a**) (*use*) disfrute *m*; posesión *f*. (**b**) (*delight*) placer *m*, fruición *f*; **he listened with real** — escuchó con verdadera fruición.
enlarge [in'lɑːdʒ] 1 *vt* extender, aumentar, ensanchar; (*Phot*) ampliar; (*Med*) dilatar; —**d heart** dilatación *f* del corazón.
  2 *vi* extenderse, aumentarse; **to** — **upon** tratar con más extensión, explicar con más detalles.
enlargement [in'lɑːdʒmənt] *n* extensión *f*, aumento *m*, ensanche *m*; (*Phot*) ampliación *f*.
enlarger [in'lɑːdʒə*] *n* (*Phot*) ampliadora *f*.
enlighten [in'laitn] *vt* (**a**) (*inform*) informar, instruir; **can you** — **me?** ¿puede Vd ayudarme?; **I was able to** — **him about it** pude darle informes sobre este asunto.
  (**b**) (*civilize*) ilustrar, iluminar.
enlightened [in'laitnd] *adj* ilustrado, culto; bien informado; *despot* ilustrado; *attitude etc* comprensivo, inteligente.
enlightening [in'laitniŋ] *adj* informativo, lleno de datos útiles; *experience etc* instructivo.
enlightenment [in'laitnmənt] *n* ilustración *f*; *see* **age**.
enlist [in'list] 1 *vt* (*Mil*) alistar, reclutar; *support etc* conseguir. 2 *vi* alistarse (*in* en).
enlistment [in'listmənt] *n* alistamiento *m*.
enliven [in'laivn] *vt* avivar, animar.
en masse [ɑ̃ːŋ'mæs] *adv* en masa.
enmesh [in'meʃ] *vt* coger en una red; **to get** —**ed in** enredarse en.
enmity ['enmiti] *n* enemistad *f*.
ennoble [i'nəubl] *vt* ennoblecer.
ennui [ɑ̃ː'nwiː] *n* tedio *m*, aburrimiento *m*.
enormity [i'nɔːmiti] *n* enormidad *f*.
enormous [i'nɔːməs] *adj* enorme.
enormously [i'nɔːməsli] *adv* enormemente.
enough [i'nʌf] 1 *adv* bastante, suficientemente; **not big** — no suficientemente grande; **she sings well** — canta bastante bien; *see* **good, sure** etc.
  2 *adj* bastante, suficiente; **I hadn't** — **money to buy it** no tuve bastante dinero para comprarlo.
  3 *n*: **that's** —, **thanks** con eso basta, gracias; **that's** — **now!** ¡basta ya!; **it is** — **for us to know that** nos basta saber que; **there's more than** — **for all** hay más que suficiente para todos; — **is** — basta y sobra; **is as good as a feast** rogar a Dios

por santos mas no por tantos; **it was** — **to drive you mad** era para volverse loco; **we have** — **to live on** tenemos bastante para vivir, tenemos con qué vivir; **one can never have** — **of his music** es imposible escuchar demasiado su música; **I've had** — **of him** estoy harto de él; **tell me when you've had** — dime en cuanto te empieces a cansar; **I had** — **to do to find one** me costó trabajo encontrar uno.
  4 *interj*: — **of this!** ¡basta ya!, ¡concluyamos de una vez!
enquire [in'kwaiə*] *etc see* **inquire**.
enrage [in'reidʒ] *vt* enfurecer, hacer rabiar; **to be** —**d with pain** rabiar de dolor.
enrapture [in'ræptʃə*] *vt* encantar, embelesar.
enrich [in'ritʃ] *vt* enriquecer; *food* aumentar el valor alimenticio de; *soil* fertilizar.
enrichment [in'ritʃmənt] *n* enriquecimiento *m*; aumento *m* del valor alimenticio; fertilización *f*.
enrol [in'rəul] 1 *vt member* inscribir; *student* matricular; (*Mil*) alistar.
  2 *vi* inscribirse; matricularse; alistarse; **to** — **for a course** matricularse para un curso.
enrolment [in'rəulmənt] *n* inscripción *f*; matrícula *f*; alistamiento *m*.
en route [ɑ̃ːn'ruːt] *adv*: **to be** — **for** ir camino de, ir con rumbo a, dirigirse a; **it was stolen** — lo robaron durante el viaje.
ensconce [in'skɔns] *vr*: **to** — **oneself** instalarse cómodamente, acomodarse; **to be** —**d in** estar cómodamente instalado en.
ensemble [ɑ̃ːnsɑ̃ːmbl] *n* (*whole*) conjunto *m*; (*general effect*) impresión *f* de conjunto; (*dress*) conjunto *m*; (*Mus*) conjunto *m*, agrupación *f*.
enshrine [in'ʃrain] *vt* (*fig*) encerrar.
ensign ['ensain] *n* (**a**) (*flag*) bandera *f*; **Red E**— Enseña *f* Roja (*bandera de la marina mercante británica*); **White E**— Enseña *f* Blanca (*bandera de la marina de guerra británica*).
  (**b**) (*rank*) alférez *m*.
enslave [in'sleiv] *vt* esclavizar; (*fig*) dominar.
enslavement [in'sleivmənt] *n* esclavitud *f*.
ensnare [in'snɛə*] *vt* entrampar, coger en una trampa (*also fig*).
ensue [in'sjuː] *vi* (*follow*) seguirse; (*happen*) sobrevenir; (*result*) resultar (*from* de).
ensuing [in'sjuːiŋ] *adj* consiguiente, subsiguiente.
ensure [in'ʃuə*] *vt* asegurar.
entail [in'teil] 1 *n* vínculo *m*.
  2 *vt* (*necessitate*) imponer; (*imply*) suponer; (*bring in its train*) acarrear; (*Law*) vincular; **it** —**s a lot of work** supone mucho trabajo para nosotros, nos causa mucho trabajo; **it** —**ed buying a new car** ello nos obligó a comprar un nuevo coche.
entangle [in'tæŋgl] *vt* enredar, enmarañar; **to get** —**d in an affair** quedar enredado en un asunto; **to get** —**d with someone** meterse en un lío con uno.
entanglement [in'tæŋglmənt] *n* enredo *m*, embrollo *m*; (*love affair*) intriga *f* amorosa; (*Mil*) alambrada *f*; **to keep out of** —**s** no meterse en líos.
entente [ɑ̃ːn'tɑ̃ːnt] *n* entente *f*, trato *m* secreto.
enter ['entə*] 1 *vt* (**a**) (*go into*) entrar en; penetrar en; **it never** —**ed my head** jamás se me pasó por la cabeza.
  (**b**) (*fig*) *society* ingresar en, hacerse socio de; *army* alistarse en; *college, school* matricularse en.
  (**c**) (*write down*) *note* anotar, apuntar; *name etc* escribir; *member* inscribir, matricular; *record* asentar, anotar, dar entrada a, registrar; *order* (*Comm*) asentar; *protest* formular; **to** — **a horse for a race** presentar un caballo para una carrera; **to** — **one's son for Eton** inscribir a su hijo como futuro alumno de Eton; **to** — **a dog for a show** inscribir un perro en un concurso canino; **to** — **up** *entry* asentar; *ledger* hacer, llevar; *diary* poner al día.
  2 *vi* entrar; (*Theat*) entrar en escena; —**Macbeth** sale Macbeth; **to** — **for** *competition, race* participar en, tomar parte en, presentarse para; *post* presentarse como candidato a, oponerse a; **to** — **into** *agreement* llegar a, firmar; *bargain* cerrar; *contract* hacer, firmar; *obligation* contraer; *explanations* dar; *argument* meterse en, tomar parte en; *conversation* entablar; *negotiations* iniciar; *relations* establecer (*with* con); *plans* formar parte de; *feelings* afectar (en lo más mínimo); **that doesn't** — **into it at all** eso no figura aquí para nada, eso no afecta la cosa en lo más mínimo; **to** — **upon** *career* emprender; *office* tomar posesión de; *term of office* empezar; *one's 20th year* empezar.
enteric [en'terik] *adj* entérico; — **fever** fiebre *f* entérica.
enteritis [ˌentə'raitis] *n* enteritis *f*.

enterprise ['entəpraiz] n (a) (firm, undertaking) empresa f.
(b) (spirit) iniciativa f; espíritu m emprendedor, empuje m; **free** — libre empresa f, libertad f de empresa; **private** — iniciativa f privada.
enterprising ['entəpraiziŋ] adj person, spirit emprendedor; **an** — **thing to do** una cosa que muestra mucha iniciativa; **that was** — **of you** en eso ha mostrado Vd tener iniciativa.
enterprisingly ['entəpraiziŋli] adv de modo emprendedor, con mucha iniciativa.
entertain [,entə'tein] vt (a) (amuse) divertir, entretener.
(b) guest (at home) recibir, recibir en casa, alojar consigo; (make a fuss of) festejar, agasajar; **they** — **a good deal** reciben mucho en casa; **they** —**ed him with a dinner** le obsequiaron con una cena.
(c) idea, hope abrigar, acariciar; proposal estudiar, considerar; **I wouldn't** — **it for a moment** tal idea es totalmente inconcebible para mí.
entertainer [,entə'teinə*] n actor m, actriz f, músico m (etc).
entertaining [,entə'teiniŋ] adj divertido, entretenido.
entertainingly [,entə'teiniŋli] adv de manera divertida, graciosamente.
entertainment [,entə'teinmənt] n (a) (amusement) diversión f; **for your** — para divertiros.
(b) (show) función f, espectáculo m, fiesta f; **musical** — concierto m; **to put on an** — organizar un espectáculo.
enthrall [in'θrɔːl] vt (fig) encantar, cautivar, captar la atención de; **we listened** —**ed** escuchamos embelesados.
enthrone [in'θrəun] vt entronizar.
enthuse [in'θuːz] vi: **to** — **over** entusiasmarse muchísimo por, extasiarse ante.
enthusiasm [in'θuːziæzəm] n entusiasmo m (for por).
enthusiast [in'θuːziæst] n entusiasta mf (for por).
enthusiastic [in,θuːzi'æstik] adj person entusiasta; cry etc entusiástico; **to be** — **about** entusiasmarse por, estar lleno de entusiasmo por.
enthusiastically [in,θuːzi'æstikəli] adv con entusiasmo; **he shouted** —**ly** gritó entusiasmado.
entice [in'tais] vt tentar, atraer (con maña); (in bad sense) seducir; **to** — **someone away from someone** persuadir mañosamente a uno a dejar a una persona; **to** — **someone away from a place** persuadir mañosamente a uno a abandonar un sitio; **to** — **someone into a room** persuadir mañosamente a uno a entrar en un cuarto; **to** — **someone to do something** tentar a uno a hacer algo.
enticement [in'taismənt] n (a) (act) tentación f, atracción f; seducción f; persuasión f mañosa.
(b) (bait) atractivo m, aliciente m, cebo m.
enticing [in'taisiŋ] adj atractivo, tentador, seductor.
enticingly [in'taisiŋli] adv atractivamente, seductoramente.
entire [in'taiə*] adj entero, completo; total; todo; **the** — **world** el mundo entero; **the** — **trip** todo el viaje; **the** — **stock** todas las existencias.
entirely [in'taiəli] adv enteramente, totalmente; **that is not** — **true** eso no es del todo verdad.
entirety [in'taiərəti] n: **in its** — en su totalidad, enteramente.
entitle [in'taitl] vt (a) book etc titular; **the book is** —**d X** el libro se titula X.
(b) **to** — **someone to do something** dar a uno el derecho a hacer algo; **to be** —**d to do something** tener derecho a hacer algo; **to** — **someone to something** dar a uno derecho a algo; **I think I am** —**d to some respect** creo que se me debe cierto respeto.
entity ['entiti] n entidad f, ente m; **legal** — persona f jurídica.
entomb [in'tuːm] vt sepultar.
entomologist [,entə'mɔlədʒist] n entomólogo m.
entomology [,entə'mɔlədʒi] n entomología f.
entourage [,ɔntu'raːʒ] n séquito m.
entr'acte ['ɔntrækt] n descanso m; intermedio m.
entrails ['entreilz] npl entrañas fpl, tripas fpl.
entrain [in'trein] vi tomar el tren (for a).
entrance ['entrəns] n (place) entrada f; (act) entrada f (into en); (into profession etc) ingreso m; (Theat) entrada f en escena; — **examination** examen m de ingreso; **to make one's** — hacer su entrada.
entrance [in'trɑːns] vt encantar, hechizar; **we listened** —**d** escuchamos extasiados.
entrance fee ['entrənsfiː] n cuota f.
entrance hall ['entrəns,hɔːl] n hall m de entrada.
entrancing [in'trɑːnsiŋ] adj encantador, cautivador, delicioso.

entrancingly [in'trɑːnsiŋli] adv play etc maravillosamente, deliciosamente; **it was** — **beautiful** contemplamos extasiados aquella belleza.
entrant ['entrənt] n participante mf, concurrente mf.
entreat [in'triːt] vt rogar, suplicar; **to** — **someone to do something** suplicar a uno hacer algo.
entreatingly [in'triːtiŋli] adv de modo suplicante.
entreaty [in'triːti] n ruego m, súplica f.
entrée ['ɔntrei] n entrada f.
entrench [in'trentʃ] 1 vt atrincherar; **to be** —**ed** estar atrincherado (also fig). 2 vr: **to** — **oneself** atrincherarse.
entrenchment [in'trentʃmənt] n trinchera f.
entrepôt ['ɔntrəpəu] n centro m comercial, centro m de distribución.
entrepreneur [,ɔntrəprə'nə:*] n (Comm) patrón m, dueño m; contratista m; (Fin) capitalista m.
entrust [in'trʌst] vt: **to** — **something to someone**, **to** — **someone with something** confiar algo a uno.
entry ['entri] n (a) (place) entrada f; (passage) callejuela f; (of street) bocacalle f; **"no** —**"** "prohibido el paso", (Aut) "dirección prohibida".
(b) (act) entrada f (into en); acceso m (into a); (into profession etc) ingreso m (into en); (into office) toma f de posesión (into, on de); — **into the hall had been forbidden** se había prohibido el acceso a la sala; **to make one's** — hacer su entrada.
(c) (Sport etc) (total) participación f, participantes mpl; (competitor) participante mf, concurrente mf.
(d) (in reference book) artículo m; (in diary) apunte m; (in account) partida f; (in record) apunte m, apuntación f, entrada f.
entry form ['entrifɔːm] n boleto m de inscripción.
entwine [in'twain] vt entrelazar, entretejer.
enumerate [i'njuːməreit] vt enumerar.
enumeration [i,njuːmə'reiʃən] n enumeración f.
enunciate [i'nʌnsieit] vt words pronunciar, articular; principle enunciar.
enunciation [i,nʌnsi'eiʃən] n pronunciación f, articulación f; enunciación f.
envelop [in'veləp] vt envolver (in en).
envelop(e) ['envələup] n sobre m; (Aer) envoltura f.
enveloping [in'veləpiŋ] adj movement envolvente.
envelopment [in'veləpmənt] n envolvimiento m.
envenom [in'venəm] vt envenenar.
enviable ['enviəbl] adj envidiable.
envious ['enviəs] adj envidioso; look etc de envidia; **to be** — **of** tener envidia de; **to make someone** — **of something** hacer que uno tenga envidia de algo.
enviously ['enviəsli] adv con envidia.
environment [in'vaiərənmənt] n medio m ambiente, ambiente m.
environmental [in,vaiərən'mentl] adj ambiental.
environs [in'vaiərənz] npl alrededores mpl, inmediaciones fpl.
envisage [in'vizidʒ] vt (a) prever; **it is** —**d that se** prevé que; **an increase is** —**d next year** está previsto que se aumentará el año que viene.
(b) concebir, formarse una idea de, representarse; **it is hard to** — **such a situation** es difícil formarse una idea de tal situación.
envoy ['envɔi] n enviado m.
envy ['envi] 1 n envidia f; **it was the** — **of all the neighbours** nos lo envidiaban todos los vecinos; **to be green with** — estar verde de envidia.
2 vt: **to** — **someone** tener envidia a uno; **to** — **someone something** envidiar algo a uno.
enzyme ['enzaim] n enzima f.
epaulette ['epɔːlet] n charretera f.
ephemeral [i'femərəl] adj efímero.
epic ['epik] 1 adj épico. 2 n épica f, epopeya f.
epicentre ['episentə*] n epicentro m.
epicure ['epikjuə*] n gastrónomo m, sibarita m.
epicurean [,epikju'riːən] 1 adj epicúreo. 2 n epicúreo m.
epicureanism [,epikjuə'riənizəm] n epicureísmo m.
epidemic [,epi'demik] 1 adj epidémico. 2 n epidemia f.
epidermis [,epi'dəːmis] n epidermis f.
epiglottis [,epi'glɔtis] n epiglotis f.
epigram ['epigræm] n epigrama m.
epigrammatic(al) [,epigrə'mætik(əl)] adj epigramático.
epigraph ['epigrɑːf] n epígrafe m.
epilepsy ['epilepsi] n epilepsia f.
epileptic [,epi'leptik] 1 adj epiléptico. 2 n epiléptico m, a f.
epilogue ['epilɔg] n epílogo m.
Epiphany [i'pifəni] n Epifanía f.
episcopal [i'piskəpəl] adj episcopal.

episcopalian [i.piskə'peiliən] **1** *adj* episcopalista. **2** *n* episcopalista *mf*.
episode ['episəud] *n* episodio *m*.
episodic [.epi'sɔdik] *adj* episódico.
epistle [i'pisl] *n* epístola *f*.
epistolary [i'pistələri] *adj* epistolar.
epitaph ['epitɑːf] *n* epitafio *m*.
epithet ['epiθet] *n* epíteto *m*.
epitome [i'pitəmi] *n* epítome *m*, compendio *m*, resumen *m*; (*fig*) representación *f* en miniatura; **to be the — of virtue** ser la misma virtud.
epitomize [i'pitəmaiz] *vt* epitomar, compendiar, resumir; (*fig*) representar en miniatura; **he —d resistance to the enemy** se cifraba en él la resistencia al enemigo; **he —d virtue** era la misma virtud.
epoch ['iːpɔk] *n* época *f*; **to mark an —** hacer época.
epoch-making ['iːpɔk.meikiŋ] *adj* que hace época.
Epsom salts ['epsɔm.sɔːltz] *npl* sal *f* de La Higuera.
equable ['ekwəbl] *adj* *climate etc* uniforme, igual; *person, tone* tranquilo, afable.
equal ['iːkwəl] **1** *adj* igual (*to* a); *treatment* equitativo; **— in value** de igual valor; **with — ease** con la misma facilidad; **— sign** signo *m* de igualdad; **other things being —** si no cambian las circunstancias; **to be — to** *task* tener fuerzas para, *situation* estar a la altura de; **I don't feel — to it** no me siento con fuerzas para ello; **he is — to every demand made upon him** hace bien cuanto se le pide; **to be — to doing something** tener fuerzas para hacer algo.
2 *n* igual *mf*; **without —** sin igual, sin par; **to treat someone as an —** tratar a uno de igual a igual.
3 *vt* ser igual a; **to — out** igualar; **6 + 4 —s 10** 6 más 4 son 10.
equality [iː'kwɔliti] *n* igualdad *f*.
equalize ['iːkwəlaiz] **1** *vt* igualar. **2** *vi* (*Sport*) lograr el empate, lograr la igualada.
equalizer ['iːkwəlaizə*] *n* (*Sport*) igualada *f*.
equally ['iːkwəli] *adv* igualmente; *share etc* por igual; *treat etc* equitativamente.
equanimity [.ekwə'nimiti] *n* ecuanimidad *f*.
equate [i'kweit] *vt* considerar equivalente (*to, with* a), comparar (*to, with* con).
equation [i'kweiʒən] *n* ecuación *f*; **quadratic —** cuadrática *f*.
equator [i'kweitə*] *n* ecuador *m*.
equatorial [.ekwə'tɔːriəl] *adj* ecuatorial.
equerry ['ekwəri] *n* caballerizo *m* del rey.
equestrian [i'kwestriən] **1** *adj* ecuestre. **2** *n* jinete *m*, a *f*.
equidistant ['iːkwi'distənt] *adj* equidistante.
equilateral [.iːkwi'lætərəl] *adj* equilátero.
equilibrium [.iːkwi'libriəm] *n* equilibrio *m*.
equine ['ekwain] *adj* equino.
equinox ['iːkwinɔks] *n* equinoccio *m*.
equip [i'kwip] *vt* equipar (*with* de); *person* proveer (*with* de); **to be —ped with** (*person*) estar provisto de, (*machine etc*) estar dotado de; **to be well —ped to + infin** estar bien dotado para + infin.
equipment [i'kwipmənt] *n* equipo *m*, material *m*; (*tools*) avíos *mpl*; (*mental*) aptitud *f*, dotes *fpl*.
equitable ['ekwitəbl] *adj* equitativo.
equitably ['ekwitəbli] *adv* equitativamente.
equity ['ekwiti] *n* equidad *f*; **equities** (*Comm*) acciones *fpl* de dividendo no fijo.
equivalence [i'kwivələns] *n* equivalencia *f*.
equivalent [i'kwivələnt] **1** *adj* equivalente (*to* a); **to be — to** equivaler a. **2** *n* equivalente *m*.
equivocal [i'kwivəkəl] *adj* equívoco, ambiguo.
equivocate [i'kwivəkeit] *vi* no dar una respuesta clara, soslayar el problema.
era ['iərə] *n* época *f*, era *f*; **to mark an —** hacer época.
eradicate [i'rædikeit] *vt* desarraigar, extirpar.
eradication [i.rædi'keiʃən] *n* desarraigo *m*, extirpación *f*.
erase [i'reiz] *vt* borrar (*also fig*).
eraser [i'reizə*] *n* goma *f* de borrar.
Erasmism [i'ræzmizəm] *n* erasmismo *m*.
Erasmist [i'ræzmist] **1** *adj* erasmista. **2** *n* erasmista *mf*.
Erasmus [i'ræzməs] *m* Erasmo.
erasure [i'reiʒə*] *n* borradura *f*, raspadura *f*.
ere [eə*] (*arch*) **1** *prep* antes de; **— long** dentro de poco. **2** *conj* antes de que.
erect [i'rekt] **1** *adj* erguido, derecho; vertical.
2 *vt* (*build*) erigir, construir, levantar; (*assemble*) montar; **to — something into a principle** constituir algo en principio.
erection [i'rekʃən] *n* (*act*) erección *f*, construcción *f*; (*assembly*) montaje *m*; (*structure*) edificio *m*, construcción *f*; (*fig*) constitución *f*.
erg [əːg] *n* ergio *m*.

ergonomics [.əːgəu'nɔmiks] *n* ergonómica *f*.
ergot ['əːgət] *n* cornezuelo *m*.
Eric ['erik] *m* Erico.
Erin ['iərin] *nombre antiguo y sentimental de Irlanda.*
ermine ['əːmin] *n* armiño *m*.
Ernest ['əːnist] *m* Ernesto.
erode [i'rəud] *vt* (*Geol*) causar erosión en, erosionar; *metal* corroer, desgastar; (*fig*) erosionar, mermar, perjudicar.
erosion [i'rəuʒən] *n* (*Geol*) erosión *f*; (*of metal*) desgaste *m*.
erosive [i'rəuziv] *adj* erosivo.
erotic [i'rɔtik] *adj* erótico; erotómano; (*obscene*) sicalíptico.
eroticism [i'rɔtisizəm] *n* erotomanía *f*; (*obscenity*) sicalipsis *f*.
err [əː*] *vi* errar, equivocarse; (*sin*) pecar; **to — is human** de los hombres es errar; **to — on the side of** pecar por exceso de.
errand ['erənd] *n* recado *m*, mandado *m*; misión *f*; **— of mercy** tentativa *f* de salvamento; **what — brings you here?** ¿qué le trae por aquí?; **to run an —** llevar un recado.
errand boy ['erəndbɔi] *n* recadero *m*, mandadero *m*.
errant ['erənt] *adj* errante; *knight* andante.
erratic [i'rætik] *adj* (*uncertain*) irregular, poco constante; *conduct* excéntrico; *person* voluble; *record, results etc* desigual, poco uniforme; (*Geol, Med*) errático.
erratically [i'rætikəli] *adv* de modo irregular (*etc*).
erratum [e'rɑːtəm] *n*, *pl* **errata** [e'rɑːtə] errata *f*.
erroneous [i'rəuniəs] *adj* erróneo.
erroneously [i'rəuniəsli] *adv* equivocadamente.
error ['erə*] *n* error *m*, equivocación *f*; **by —** por equivocación; **—s and omissions excepted** salvo error u omisión; **to be in —** estar equivocado; **to see the — of one's ways** reconocer las faltas en que uno ha incurrido.
ersatz ['eəzæts] **1** *adj* sucedáneo, sustituto. **2** *n* sucedáneo *m*, sustituto *m*.
erstwhile ['əːstwail] *adj* antiguo.
erudite ['erudait] *adj* erudito.
erudition [.eru'diʃən] *n* erudición *f*.
erupt [i'rʌpt] *vi* (*volcano*) estar en erupción, (*begin to —*) entrar en erupción; (*Med*) hacer erupción; (*anger, war etc*) estallar; **to — into a room** irrumpir en un cuarto.
eruption [i'rʌpʃən] *n* (*Geol, Med*) erupción *f*; (*fig*) explosión *f*.
erysipelas [.eri'sipiləs] *n* erisipela *f*.
Esau ['iːsɔː] *m* Esaú.
escalate ['eskəleit] **1** *vt* extender, intensificar. **2** *vi* extenderse, intensificarse.
escalation [.eskə'leiʃən] *n* extensión *f*, intensificación *f*, escalamiento *m*.
escalator ['eskəlcitə*] *n* escalera *f* móvil.
escapade [.eskə'peid] *n* aventura *f*, travesura *f*.
escape [is'keip] **1** *n* escape *m*, fuga *f*, huida *f*, evasión *f*; (*leak*) fuga *f*; (*from duties etc*) escapatoria *f*; **it was a lucky — for him** tuvo suerte al poderse escapar; **to have a narrow —** escapar por los pelos; **to make one's —** escapar; **to make good one's —** escapar y desaparecer.
2 *vt* (*avoid*) evitar, eludir; *consequences, death* escapar a; *vigilance* burlar; **the meaning —s me** se me escapa el significado; **the fact had —d me for the moment** por el momento el hecho se me escapó; **a cry —d him** no pudo contener un grito; *see* **notice**.
3 *vi* escapar(se); evadirse, huir; (*leak*) fugarse; **to — from** *person* escaparse a, *prison* escaparse de, *clutches* librarse de; **to — to France** huir a Francia, refugiarse en Francia; **to — with a fright** escapar llevándose un susto; **he just —d being run over** por poco murió atropellado, en poco estuvo que no muriese atropellado.
escapism [is'keipizəm] *n* escapismo *m*.
escapist [is'keipist] **1** *adj* escapista. **2** *n* escapista *mf*.
escapologist [.eskei'pɔlədʒist] *n* rey *m* de la evasión.
escarpment [is'kɑːpmənt] *n* escarpa *f*.
eschatology [.eskə'tɔlədʒi] *n* escatología *f*.
eschew [is'tʃuː] *vt* evitar, renunciar a.
escort [is'kɔːt] *n* (*suite*) acompañamiento *m*; (*lady's*) acompañante *m*; (*Mil*) escolta *f*; (*Naut*) convoy *m*, buque *m* de escolta.
escort [is'kɔːt] *vt* acompañar; (*Mil*) escoltar; (*Naut*) convoyar, escoltar; **to — someone home** acompañar a uno a su casa.
escutcheon [is'kʌtʃən] *n* blasón *m*; (*fig*) honor *m*.
Eskimo ['eskiməu] **1** *adj* esquimal. **2** *n* esquimal *mf*. **3** *n* (*language*) esquimal *m*.
esoteric [.esəu'terik] *adj* esotérico.

especial [is'peʃəl] *adj* especial, particular.
especially [is'peʃəli] *adv* especialmente; sobre todo, ante todo; en particular; **it is — awkward** es especialmente difícil; **you — ought to know** Vd debiera saberlo más que nadie; **why me —?** ¿por qué yo y no otro?; **— when it rains** sobre todo cuando llueve.
Esperanto [ˌespəˈræntəu] *n* esperanto *m*.
espionage [ˌespiəˈnɑːʒ] *n* espionaje *m*.
esplanade [ˌespləˈneid] *n* paseo *m*; (*by sea*) paseo *m* marítimo.
espouse [is'pauz] *vt cause* adherirse a.
espresso [es'presəu] *adj*: **— bar** café *m* donde se sirve café expreso; **— coffee** café *m* expreso.
esprit de corps ['espriːdəˈkɔː*] *n* espíritu *m* de cuerpo, lealtad *f*.
espy [is'pai] *vt* divisar.
esquire [is'kwaiə*] *n*: (*on envelope*) **Colin Smith E—** Sr don Colin Smith.
essay ['esei] *n* ensayo *m*.
essay [e'sei] *vt* probar, ensayar; *task* intentar; **to — to** + *infin* intentar + *infin*.
essayist ['eseiist] *n* ensayista *mf*.
essence ['esəns] *n* esencia *f*; **the — of the matter is** lo esencial es; **speed is of the —** es esencial hacerlo con la mayor prontitud.
essential [i'senʃəl] **1** *adj* esencial; indispensable, imprescindible; **it is — to** + *infin* es imprescindible + *infin*; **it is — that** es necesario que + *subj*.
  2 *n* esencial *m*; elemento *m* necesario, factor *m* imprescindible.
essentially [i'senʃəli] *adv* esencialmente, en su esencia.
establish [is'tæbliʃ] **1** *vt* establecer, fundar, crear; *facts* verificar; *proof* demostrar, probar; *relations* entablar; *precedent* crear; **we have —ed that** hemos comprobado que; **his father —ed him in business** su padre compró el negocio para él; **he —ed her in a flat** la instaló en un piso.
  2 *vr*: **to — oneself** crearse una reputación, hacerse un negocio sólido; **to — itself** establecerse, consolidarse, (*custom*) arraigar.
established [is'tæbliʃt] *adj person, business* de buena reputación, sólido; *custom* arraigado; *fact* conocido; *church* oficial, del Estado; *staff* fijo, de plantilla.
establishment [is'tæbliʃmənt] *n* (a) (*act, body*) establecimiento *m*, fundación *f*; (*business house*) establecimiento *m*, casa *f*.
  (b) (Mil) fuerzas *fpl*, efectivos *mpl*; (*servants*) servidumbre *f*; (*staff of company etc*) plantel *m*, personal *m*; **to be on the —** ser de plantilla.
  (c) (*Britain*) **the E—** las clases directoras, el centro del poder efectivo en Gran Bretaña.
estate [is'teit] *n* (a) (*land*) finca *f*, hacienda *f*.
  (b) (*property, assets*) propiedad *f*; **real —** bienes *mpl* raíces.
  (c) (*inheritance*) bienes *mpl* relictos; herencia *f*, heredad *f*; testamentaría *f*; **he left a large —** dejó una inmensa fortuna.
  (d) (*Pol*) estado *m*; **third —** estado *m* llano; **fourth —** la prensa.
estate agent [is'teit͵eidʒənt] *n* corredor *m* de fincas, agente *m* inmobiliario.
estate car [is'teitkɑː*] *n* furgoneta *f*, rubia *f*.
estate duty [is'teit͵djuːti] *n* impuesto *m* de sucesión, impuesto *m* sobre los bienes heredados.
esteem [is'tiːm] **1** *n* estima *f*, estimación *f*; consideración *f*; **to hold someone in high —** estimar en mucho a uno, tener un alto concepto de uno; **to hold someone in low —** estimar en poco a uno; **to rise in someone's —** merecer que uno le estime más.
  2 *vt* estimar, apreciar.
esthete ['iːsθiːt] *n* (*etc*) = **aesthete** (*etc*).
Esthonia [es'təuniə] Estonia *f*.
Esthonian [es'təuniən] **1** *adj* estonio. **2** *n* estonio *m*, a *f*. **3** *n* (*language*) estonio *m*.
estimable ['estiməbl] *adj* estimable.
estimate ['estimit] *n* (*judgement*) estimación *f*, apreciación *f*; (*approximate assessment*) tasa *f*, cálculo *m*; (*for work etc*) presupuesto *m*; **rough —** cálculo *m* aproximativo; **E—s** (*Parl*) presupuesto m.
estimate ['estimeit] **1** *vt* (*judge*) estimar, apreciar; (*assess*) calcular, computar, tasar (*at* en); **to — that** calcular que. **2** *vi*: **to — for** presupuestar, hacer un presupuesto de.
estimation [ˌestiˈmeiʃən] *n* (a) (*judgement*) opinión *f*; juicio *m*; **in my —** a mi juicio; **what is your — of him?** ¿qué concepto tiene Vd de él?
  (b) (*esteem*) estima *f*, aprecio m.
estrange [is'treindʒ] *vt* enajenar, apartar (*from* de); **to become —d** enemistarse (*from* con).
estrangement [is'treindʒmənt] *n* enajenación *f*; separación *f*.

estuary ['estjuəri] *n* estuario *m*, ría *f*.
etcetera [it'setrə] **1** *as adv* etcétera. **2 —s** *npl* extras *mpl*, adornos *mpl*.
etch [etʃ] *vt* grabar al agua fuerte.
etching ['etʃiŋ] *n* aguafuerte *f*.
eternal [i'təːnl] *adj* eterno; sempiterno; de siempre.
eternally [i'təːnəli] *adv* eternamente; sempiternamente; siempre.
eternity [i'təːniti] *n* eternidad *f*; **it seemed like an —** parecía un siglo, parecía que no iba a acabar (*etc*) nunca.
ether ['iːθə*] *n* éter *m*.
ethereal [i'θiəriəl] *adj* etéreo (*also fig*).
ethical ['eθikəl] *adj* ético; (*honourable*) honrado.
ethics ['eθiks] *n* ética *f*; (*honourableness*) moralidad *f*.
Ethiopia [ˌiːθiˈəupiə] Etiopía *f*.
Ethiopian [ˌiːθiˈəupiən] **1** *adj* etíope. **2** *n* etíope *mf*.
ethnic ['eθnik] *adj* étnico.
ethnography [eθˈnɔgrəfi] *n* etnografía *f*.
ethnology [eθˈnɔlədʒi] *n* etnología *f*.
ethos ['iːθɔs] *n* genio *m*, carácter *m* (nacional), rasgo *m* distintivo (de una colectividad).
ethyl ['iːθail] *n* etilo *m*.
etiquette ['etiket] *n* etiqueta *f*; (*of profession*) honor *m* profesional; **it is not — to** + *infin* no es elegante + *infin*, está mal visto + *infin*.
Eton crop ['iːtnˈkrɔp] *n* corte *m* a lo garçon.
Etruscan [i'trʌskən] **1** *adj* etrusco. **2** *n* etrusco *m*, a *f*. **3** *n* (*language*) etrusco m.
etymological [ˌetiməˈlɔdʒikəl] *adj* etimológico.
etymology [ˌetiˈmɔlədʒi] *n* etimología *f*.
eucalyptus [ˌjuːkəˈliptəs] *n* eucalipto *m*.
Eucharist ['juːkərist] *n* Eucaristía *f*.
Euclid ['juːklid] *m* Euclides.
Eugene [juːˈʒein] *m* Eugenio.
eugenics [juːˈdʒeniks] *n* eugenismo *m*, eugenesia *f*.
eulogize ['juːlədʒaiz] *vt* elogiar, encomiar.
eulogy ['juːlədʒi] *n* elogio *m*, encomio *m*.
eunuch ['juːnək] *n* eunuco m.
euphemism ['juːfimizəm] *n* eufemismo *m*.
euphemistic [ˌjuːfiˈmistik] *adj* eufemístico.
euphonic [juːˈfɔnik] *adj*, **euphonious** [juːˈfəuniəs] *adj* eufónico.
euphony ['juːfəni] *n* eufonía *f*.
euphoria [juːˈfɔːriə] *n* euforia *f*.
euphoric [juːˈfɔrik] *adj* eufórico.
Euphrates [juːˈfreitiːz] Eufrates *m*.
Eurasian [juəˈreiʒən] **1** *adj* eurasiano. **2** *n* eurasiano *m*, a *f*.
eureka [juəˈriːkə] *interj* ¡eureka!
eurhythmics [juːˈriθmiks] *n* euritmia *f*.
Euripides [juˈripidiːz] *m* Eurípides.
Europe ['juərəp] *n* Europa *f*.
European [ˌjuərəˈpiːən] **1** *adj* europeo. **2** *n* europeo *m*, a *f*.
Eurovision ['juərəviʒən] Eurovisión *f*.
Eurydice [juˈridisiː] *f* Eurídice.
euthanasia [ˌjuːθəˈneiziə] *n* eutanasia *f*.
evacuate [i'vækjueit] *vt* evacuar; *building etc* desocupar.
evacuation [iˌvækjuˈeiʃən] *n* evacuación *f*.
evacuee [iˌvækjuˈiː] *n* evacuado *m*, a *f*.
evade [i'veid] *vt* evadir, eludir; *grasp* escaparse de; **to — taxes** defraudar impuestos; *see* issue.
evaluate [i'væljueit] *vt* evaluar, calcular (el valor de); tasar; *evidence* interpretar.
evaluation [iˌvæljuˈeiʃən] *n* evaluación *f*, cálculo *m*; (*of evidence*) interpretación *f*.
evanescent [ˌiːvəˈnesnt] *adj* efímero, evanescente.
evangelic(al) [ˌiːvænˈdʒelik(əl)] *adj* evangélico.
evangelist [i'vændʒəlist] *n* evangelizador *m*, misionero *m*; **St John the E—** San Juan Evangelista.
evangelize [i'vændʒilaiz] *vt* evangelizar.
evaporate [i'væpəreit] **1** *vt* evaporar. **2** *vi* evaporarse; (*fig*) desvanecerse.
evaporation [iˌvæpəˈreiʃən] *n* evaporación *f*.
evasion [i'veiʒən] *n* evasiva *f*, evasión *f*; **tax —** evasión *f* fiscal.
evasive [i'veiziv] *adj* evasivo; **he was very —** contestó de manera evasiva.
evasively [i'veizivli] *adv* de manera evasiva.
Eve [iːv] *f* Eva.
eve [iːv] *n* víspera *f*; **on the — of** la víspera de, (*fig*) en vísperas de.
even ['iːvən] **1** *adj* (a) (*level*) llano; (*smooth*) liso, igual, uniforme; (*on same level*) a nivel; *speed* uniforme; *temperature etc* uniforme, constante; *score, match, teams* igual; *number* par; *treatment* equitativo; *temper* ecuánime, apacible; *tone* imperturbable.
  (b) **to be — with** (*at game*) tener igual número de tantos que; (*fig*) estar en paz con; **to break —** salir sin ganar ni perder; **to get — with** ajustar

cuentas con, desquitarse con; **I'll get —— with you yet!** ¡me las pagarás!; **that makes us ——** (at game) eso iguala el tanteo, (fig) tal para cual.

2 adv **(a) —— the priest was there** hasta el cura estuvo allí; **pick them all, —— the little ones** cógelos todos incluso los pequeños; **—— on Sundays** incluso los domingos; **and he —— sings** e incluso canta.

(b) —— more curious aun más curioso, más curioso aun; **—— faster** aun más rápidamente.

(c) —— I yo también; **—— as you tricked me** del mismo modo que Vd me engañó; **—— as I went in** en el mismo momento en que yo entraba; **—— if, —— though** aunque + subj, aun cuando + subj, si bien + indic; **—— so** aun así; sin embargo.

(d) not —— ni siquiera; **not —— a look** ni una mirada siquiera; **he didn't —— kiss me** ni me besó siquiera; **without —— reading it** sin leerlo siquiera.

3 vt surface allanar, nivelar; **to —— out inequalities** igualar, allanar, distribution hacer uniforme, thing distributed repartir equitativamente; **to —— up = to —— out**; score etc igualar, nivelar.

4 vi: **to —— up with someone** ajustar cuentas con uno.

even-handed ['iːvən'hændid] adj imparcial.

evening ['iːvniŋ] **1** n (early) tarde f, (at sunset) atardecer m, (after dark) noche f; **—— was coming on** atardecía, anochecía; **good ——!** ¡buenas tardes!, ¡buenas noches!; **musical ——** velada f musical.

2 attr dress (man's) de etiqueta, (woman's) de noche; class, institute nocturno; paper de la tarde; light, star vespertino.

evenly ['iːvənli] adv (smoothly) lisamente; (uniformly) de modo uniforme; distribute etc igualmente, equitativamente; speak etc en el mismo tono, apaciblemente; look etc sin alterarse.

evenness ['iːvənnis] n lisura f; uniformidad f; igualdad f; (of treatment) imparcialidad f; (of temper) serenidad f, ecuanimidad f.

evensong ['iːvənsɔŋ] n vísperas fpl.

event [i'vent] n suceso m, acontecimiento m; (in a programme) número m; (Sport) prueba f; **current ——s** actualidades fpl; **this is quite an ——!** ¡esto sí es un acontecimiento!; **the —— will show** ya lo veremos, ello dirá, veremos qué consecuencias tendrá esto; **at all ——s, in any ——** en todo caso; **in either ——** en cualquiera de los dos casos; **in the —— of** tal como resultó después; **in the —— of** en caso de; **in the —— of his dying** en caso de que muriese; **to be expecting a happy ——** estar en estado de buena esperanza; **to be wise after the ——** mostrar sabiduría cuando ya no hay remedio.

even-tempered ['iːvən'tempəd] adj ecuánime, apacible.

eventful [i'ventful] adj life, journey etc accidentado, azaroso; match etc lleno de incidentes, lleno de emoción.

eventual [i'ventʃuəl] adj final, definitivo; consiguiente.

eventuality [i,ventʃu'æliti] n eventualidad f; **in that —— en esa eventualidad; in the —— of en la eventualidad de; to be ready for any ——** estar dispuesto a aguantar cualquier posibilidad.

eventually [i'ventʃuəli] adv (at last) finalmente, al fin y al cabo; (given time) con el tiempo, a la larga.

ever ['evə*] adv **(a)** (always): **—— since** desde entonces, (conj) después de que; **as —— como siempre; as ——, yours** (ending letter) recibe un abrazo de tu amigo . . .; **for —— para siempre; for —— and ——, for —— and a day por siempre jamás.

(b) (at no time) nunca, jamás; **hardly —— casi nunca; better than —— mejor que nunca; more than —— más que nunca; nothing —— happens no pasa nunca nada; not often if —— rara vez y creo que nunca.

(c) (at any time) **if you —— go there** si vas allí alguna vez; **did you —— find it?** ¿lo encontraste por fin?; **did you —— meet him?** ¿llegó Vd a conocerle?; **did you ——?** (fam) ¿se vio jamás tal cosa?

(d) (emphasizing question) **what —— did he want?** ¿qué demonios quería?; **why —— did you do it?** ¿por qué demonios lo hiciste?

(e) so: **he's —— so nice** es simpatiquísimo; **it's —— so cold** hace un frío terrible; **we're —— so grateful** le estamos profundamente agradecidos; **—— so much** muchísimo; **—— so little** muy poco; **—— so many things** tantísimas cosas, la mar de cosas.

(f) (after superl) **the best —— el mejor que se ha visto jamás; the coldest night —— la noche más fría que hemos conocido; as soon as —— I can** en cuanto pueda.

everglade ['evəgleid] n (US) tierra f baja pantanosa cubierta de altas hierbas.

evergreen ['evəgriːn] **1** adj de hoja perenne. **2** n árbol m (etc) de hoja perenne.

evergreen oak ['evəgriːn,əuk] n encina f.

ever-growing ['evə'grəuiŋ] adj que va en continuo aumento.

everlasting [,evə'lɑːstiŋ] adj eterno, perdurable, perpetuo; (pej) interminable.

everlastingly [,evə'lɑːstiŋli] adv eternamente; (pej) interminablemente.

evermore ['evə'mɔː*] adv eternamente; **for —— por siempre jamás.

every ['evri] adj cada (invariable); (each and every, any) todo; **—— man** cada hombre, todo hombre, todos los hombres; **—— one** cada uno; **—— one of them** todos ellos; **his —— effort** todos sus esfuerzos; **I gave you —— assistance** te ayudé en lo que podía; **—— day** cada día; **—— other month** un mes sí y otro no, cada dos meses; **—— 5 years** cada 5 años; **—— now and then, —— now and again** de vez en cuando; **—— so often** cada cierto tiempo; see bit etc.

everybody ['evribɔdi] pron todos, todo el mundo.

everyday ['evridei] adj (occurring daily) diario, cotidiano, de todos los días; (usual) corriente, acostumbrado; (commonplace) vulgar; (routine) rutinario; **for —— (use)** de diario; **in —— use** de uso corriente; **—— clothes** ropa f para todos los días; **it's an —— event** es un suceso ordinario.

everything ['evriθiŋ] pron **(a)** (as subject etc) todo; **—— is ready** todo está dispuesto; **—— nice had been sold** se había vendido todo lo deseable; **time is ——** el tiempo lo es todo; **money isn't ——** el dinero no es la única cosa que cuenta.

(b) (as object) **he sold ——** lo vendió todo.

everywhere ['evriwɛə*] adv **be ——** en todas partes, **go ——** a todas partes, por todas partes; **I looked ——** busqué por todas partes; **—— in Spain** en todas partes de España; **—— you go you'll find the same** en todas partes encontrarás lo mismo.

evict [i'vikt] vt desahuciar.

eviction [i'vikʃən] n desahucio m.

evidence ['evidəns] **1** n **(a)** (obviousness) evidencia f; **in —— bien visible, manifiesto.

(b) (sign) prueba f, indicios mpl; (testimony) testimonio m; (facts) hechos mpl, datos mpl; **circumstantial ——** prueba f indiciaria; **documentary —— prueba f documental; internal —— indicios mpl internos; there is —— to show that** hay indicios que demuestran que; **what —— is there for this belief?** ¿qué hechos se alegan a favor de tal creencia?

(c) (Law) testimonio m, declaración f, deposición f; **there is no —— against him** no hay evidencia en contra suya; **to call someone in ——** llamar a uno para que deponga como testigo; **to give ——** prestar declaración, (more formally) deponer, dar testimonio; **to turn Queen's** (or King's) **——, to turn state's ——** (US) delatar a los cómplices.

2 vt patentizar, probar; emotion dar muestras de; **as is ——d by the fact that** según lo demuestra el hecho de que.

evident ['evidənt] adj evidente, manifiesto, claro; **it is —— that** es evidente que; **to be —— in** manifestarse en; **to be —— from** quedar bien claro de.

evidently ['evidəntli] adv: **——!** ¡naturalmente!; **it is —— difficult** por lo visto es difícil; **he cannot come ——** por lo visto no puede venir.

evil ['iːvl] **1** adj malo, pernicioso; person malo, malvado, perverso; (unlucky) aciago; spirit diabólico; influence funesto; smell horrible.

2 n mal m, maldad f; **the lesser of two ——s** el menor de los males; **to do ——** hacer mal; **to speak —— of** hablar mal de.

evildoer ['iːvlduːə*] n malhechor m.

evil-minded ['iːvl'maindid] adj malintencionado, mal pensado.

evil-smelling ['iːvl'smeliŋ] adj fétido, maloliente, hediondo.

evince [i'vins] vt dar señales de, mostrar.

eviscerate [i'visəreit] vt destripar.

evocative [i'vɔkətiv] adj sugestivo, evocador.

evoke [i'vəuk] vt evocar.

evolution [,iːvə'luːʃən] n evolución f (also Bio); desarrollo m.

evolutionary [,iːvə'luːʃnəri] adj evolutivo.

evolve [i'vɔlv] **1** vt desarrollar, producir; heat etc desprender. **2** vi evolucionar, desarrollarse.

ewe [juː] n oveja f.

ewer ['juːə*] n aguamanil m.

ex [eks] prep **(a) —— dividend** sin participación en el dividendo; **price —— factory** precio m en fábrica; **—— officio** de oficio.

(b) —— leader of antiguo jefe de; **—— ambassador**

in Moscow ex embajador en Moscú; **—— minister** ex ministro.

exacerbate [eks'æsəbeit] *vt* exacerbar.

exact [ig'zækt] **1** *adj* exacto; **99, to be ——** concretamente 99, en concreto 99. **2** *vt* exigir *(from* a); *obedience etc* imponer *(from* a).

exacting [ig'zæktiŋ] *adj* exigente; *conditions* severo, arduo.

exaction [ig'zækʃən] *n* exacción *f.*

exactitude [ig'zæktitjuːd] *n* exactitud *f.*

exactly [ig'zæktli] *adv* exactamente; *(of time)* en punto; **——! ¡exacto!; what did you tell him ——?** ¿qué le dijiste, en concreto?; **he is not —— an actor** no es un actor que digamos; **and I'm not —— a dwarf** y yo tampoco soy un enano precisamente.

exactness [ig'zæktnis] *n* exactitud *f.*

exaggerate [ig'zædʒəreit] *vt* exagerar.

exaggerated [ig'zædʒəreitid] *adj* exagerado.

exaggeration [ig'zædʒəreiʃən] *n* exageración *f.*

exalt [ig'zɔːlt] *vt (elevate)* exaltar, elevar; *(praise)* ensalzar.

exaltation [ˌegzɔːl'teiʃən] *n* exaltación *f*, elevación *f*; ensalzamiento *m.*

exalted [ig'zɔːltid] *adj* exaltado, elevado.

exam [ig'zæm] *n (fam)* = **examination.**

examination [igˌzæmi'neiʃən] *n* examen *m*; *(Law)* interrogación *f*; *(inquiry)* investigación *f (into* de); *(by Customs etc)* registro *m*; *(of account)* revisión *f*; **final ——** examen *m* de fin de curso; **medical ——** reconocimiento *m* médico; **oral ——** examen *m* oral; **qualifying ——** examen *m* eliminatorio; **the matter is under ——** el asunto está examinándose; **to enter** *(or* **go in for, sit) an ——** presentarse a un examen; **to take an —— in** examinarse en.

examine [ig'zæmin] *vt* examinar; inspeccionar, escudriñar; *(Law)* interrogar; *baggage etc* registrar; *(Med)* examinar, hacer un reconocimiento médico de; **we are examining whether** estamos pensando si; **we are examining the question** estamos estudiando la cuestión.

examinee [igˌzæmi'niː] *n* examinando *m*, a *f*; **to be a bad ——** hacer siempre mal los exámenes.

examiner [ig'zæminə*] *n* examinador *m*, ora *f*; inspector *m.*

example [ig'zɑːmpl] *n* ejemplo *m*; *(copy, specimen)* ejemplar *m*; *(Math)* problema *m*; **for ——** por ejemplo; **following the —— of** siguiendo el ejemplo de; **to make an —— of someone** castigar a uno de modo ejemplar; **to set an ——** dar ejemplo.

exasperate [ig'zɑːspəreit] *vt* exasperar, irritar, sacar de quicio; **to get ——d** irritarse.

exasperating [ig'zɑːspəreitiŋ] *adj* irritante, que le saca a uno de quicio; **it's so ——!** es para volverse loco; **you're an —— person** Vd es un hombre imposible.

exasperation [igˌzɑːspə'reiʃən] *n* exasperación *f*, irritación *f.*

excavate ['ekskəveit] *vt* excavar.

excavation [ˌekskə'veiʃən] *n* excavación *f.*

excavator ['ekskəveitə*] *n (person)* excavador *m*, ora *f*; *(machine)* excavadora *f.*

exceed [ik'siːd] *vt* exceder *(by* en); *number* pasar de, exceder de; *limit* rebasar; *speed limit* sobrepasar; *rights* ir más allá de, abusar de; *powers, instructions* excederse en; *hopes, expectations* superar; **a fine not ——ing £50** una multa que no pasa de 50 libras.

exceedingly [ik'siːdiŋli] *adv* sumamente, sobremanera.

excel [ik'sel] **1** *vt* aventajar, superar. **2** *vi* sobresalir *(at, in* en). **3** *vr*: **to —— oneself** *(often iro)* lucirse.

excellence ['eksələns] *n* excelencia *f.*

Excellency ['eksələnsi] *n* Excelencia *f*; **His ——** su Excelencia; **yes, Your ——** sí, Excelencia.

excellent ['eksələnt] *adj* excelente.

except [ik'sept] **1** *vt* exceptuar, excluir. **2** *prep (also* **—— for)** excepto, con excepción de, salvo; sin contar; menos; dejando aparte; **all —— me** todos menos yo; **—— that** salvo que.

excepting [ik'septiŋ] *prep* = **except.**

exception [ik'sepʃən] *n* excepción *f*; **with the —— of** a excepción de; **without ——** sin excepción; **to be an —— to the rule** ser excepción de la regla; **the —— proves the rule** la excepción confirma la regla; **to make an ——** hacer una excepción; **to take —— to** desaprobar, *(feel offended)* ofenderse por.

exceptional [ik'sepʃənl] *adj* excepcional.

exceptionally [ik'sepʃənəli] *adv*: **—— good** excepcionalmente bueno; **it happens —— that** ocurre en casos excepcionales que.

excerpt ['eksəːpt] *n* extracto *m.*

excess [ik'ses] **1** *n* exceso *m (also fig); (Comm)*

excedente *m*; **in —— de** sobra; **in —— of** superior a; **to carry to ——** llevar al exceso; **to drink to ——** beber en exceso.

2 *attr* excedente, sobrante; **—— fare** suplemento *m*; **—— luggage** exceso *m* de equipaje; **—— profits tax** impuesto *m* sobre las ganancias excesivas.

excessive [ik'sesiv] *adj* excesivo; **with —— courtesy** con exagerada cortesía.

excessively [ik'sesivli] *adv* excesivamente; exageradamente; **you are —— kind** es Vd amable en exceso.

exchange [iks'tʃeindʒ] **1** *n* **(a)** *(act)* cambio *m*; *(of prisoners, publications, stamps etc)* canje *m*; *(of ideas, information)* intercambio *m*; **—— of shots** tiroteo *m*; **in —— for** a cambio de.

 (b) foreign —— divisas *fpl*; **—— control** control *m* de divisas; **rate of ——** tipo *m* de cambio.

 (c) *(building) (of corn, cotton etc)* lonja *f*; *(labour* **——)** bolsa *f* de trabajo; *(stock* **——)** bolsa *f*; *(Tel)* central *f* telefónica.

2 *vt* cambiar *(for* por); *prisoners, publications, stamps etc* canjear *(for* por, *with* con); *greetings, shots* cambiar; *courtesies* hacerse; *blows* darse; **we ——d glances** nos miramos el uno al otro, cruzamos una mirada.

exchangeable [iks'tʃeindʒəbl] *adj* cambiable; canjeable.

exchequer [iks'tʃekə*] *n* hacienda *f*, tesoro *m*, erario *m.*

excise ['eksaiz] *n* impuestos *mpl* sobre artículos de comercio interior.

excise [ek'saiz] *vt (cut)* cortar, quitar; *(fig)* suprimir, eliminar.

exciseman ['eksaizmæn] *n, pl* **——men** [men] *(Hist)* recaudador *m* de impuestos interiores.

excision [ek'siʒən] *n* corte *m*; supresión *f.*

excitable [ik'saitəbl] *adj* exaltado, nervioso, excitable.

excite [ik'sait] *vt (move to emotion)* emocionar, llenar de emoción, entusiasmar; *(stimulate)* excitar, estimular; provocar; *revolt* instigar; *interest* despertar, suscitar; **to —— someone to action** provocar a uno a la acción.

excited [ik'saitid] *adj voice etc* lleno de emoción; **to be ——** *(person)* estar muy emocionado, *(and upset)* estar agitado; **I'm so —— about the new house** la nueva casa me hace mucha ilusión; **to get ——** emocionarse, entusiasmarse *(about, over* por); *(crowd etc)* alborotarse; *(discussion)* acalorarse; *(get upset)* agitarse; **don't get so ——!** ¡no te emociones tanto!

excitedly [ik'saitidli] *adv* con emoción, con entusiasmo; **he said ——** dijo entusiasmadísimo, dijo excitadísimo.

excitement [ik'saitmənt] *n* emoción *f*, entusiasmo *m*; excitación *f*; ilusión *f*; agitación *f*; alboroto *m*; **his arrival caused great ——** su llegada produjo una enorme emoción; **why all the ——?, what's all the —— about?** ¿a qué se debe tanta conmoción?

exciting [ik'saitiŋ] *adj* emocionante, apasionante; excitante; **how ——!** ¡qué ilusión!; **it's a most —— film** es una película llena de emoción.

exclaim [iks'kleim] *vi* exclamar.

exclamation [ˌeksklə'meiʃən] *n* exclamación *f*; **—— mark** punto *m* de admiración.

exclamatory [eks'klæmətəri] *adj* exclamatorio.

exclude [iks'kluːd] *vt* excluir; exceptuar; *possibility of error etc* evitar; **everything excluding coal** todo excepto el carbón.

exclusion [iks'kluːʒən] *n* exclusión *f*; **to the —— of** con exclusión de.

exclusive [iks'kluːsiv] *adj* exclusivo; *(sole)* único; *policy* exclusivista; *shop, area, club etc* selecto; *offer* de privilegio; **—— of** fuera de, sin contar; **—— to** privativo de.

exclusively [iks'kluːsivli] *adv* únicamente.

excommunicate [ˌekskə'mjuːnikeit] *vt* excomulgar.

excommunication ['ekskəˌmjuːni'keiʃən] *n* excomunión *f.*

excrement ['ekskrimənt] *n* excremento *m.*

excrescence [iks'kresns] *n* excrecencia *f.*

excrete [eks'kriːt] *vt* excretar.

excretion [eks'kriːʃən] *n* excreción *f.*

excruciating [iks'kruːʃieitiŋ] *adj pain* agudísimo, atroz; *(very bad)* horrible, fatal.

excruciatingly [iks'kruːʃieitiŋli] *adv* atrozmente; *(very badly)* horriblemente, fatal; **it was —— funny** era para morirse de risa.

exculpate ['ekskʌlpeit] *vt* exculpar.

excursion [iks'kəːʃən] *n* excursión *f.*

excursion ticket [iks'kəːʃənˌtikit] *n* billete *m* de excursión.

excusable [iks'kjuːzəbl] *adj* perdonable, disculpable.

excuse [iks'kjuːs] n disculpa f, excusa f; razón f, defensa f, justificación f; (insincere) pretexto m; **there's no — for this** esto no admite disculpa; **it's only an —** es un pretexto nada más; **to make —s for someone** presentar excusas de uno; **he's only making —s** está buscando pretextos; **he gives poverty as his —** alega su pobreza; **what's your — this time?** ¿qué razón me da Vd esta vez?

excuse [iks'kjuːz] 1 vt disculpar, perdonar; **to — someone something** perdonar algo a uno; **to — someone from doing something** dispensar a uno de hacer algo, eximir a uno de hacer algo; **that does not — your conduct** eso no justifica su conducta; **— me!** (in passing someone) ¡perdón!, por favor; (on interrupting someone) perdone Vd; (on leaving table) ¡con permiso!; **if you will — me I must go** con permiso de Vds tengo que marcharme; **I must ask to be —d this time** esta vez les ruego dispensarme; **may I be —d for a moment?** ¿puedo salir un momento?
2 vr: **to — oneself from doing something** dispensarse de hacer algo; **after 10 minutes he —d himself** después de 10 minutos pidió permiso y se fue.

execrable ['eksikrəbl] adj execrable, abominable.
execrate ['eksikreit] vt execrar, abominar (de).
execration [‚eksi'kreiʃən] n execración f, abominación f.
executant [ig'zekjutənt] n ejecutante mf.
execute ['eksikjuːt] vt ejecutar (also Art, Mus); order cumplir; scheme llevar a cabo, realizar; document otorgar; man ejecutar, ajusticiar.
execution [‚eksi'kjuːʃən] n ejecución f; cumplimiento m; realización f; otorgamiento m.
executioner [‚eksi'kjuːʃnə*] n verdugo m.
executive [ig'zekjutiv] 1 adj ejecutivo. 2 n (power) poder m ejecutivo, autoridad f suprema; (person) gerente m, directivo m, director m, administrador m.
executor [ig'zekjutə*] n albacea m, testamentario m.
exegesis [‚eksi'dʒiːsis] n exégesis f.
exemplary [ig'zempləri] adj ejemplar.
exemplify [ig'zemplifai] vt ejemplificar; ilustrar, demostrar; **as exemplified by X** según lo demuestra X.
exempt [ig'zempt] 1 adj exento, libre (from de); **to be — from paying** estar dispensado de pagar. 2 vt exentar, eximir, dispensar (from de).
exemption [ig'zempʃən] n exención f (from de); inmunidad f (from de).
exercise ['eksəsaiz] 1 n ejercicio m; **to take — hacer ejercicio; in the — of my duties** en el ejercicio de mi cargo.
2 vt (a) (use) authority, influence, power ejercer; patience, restraint usar de, emplear; right valerse de; **to — care** tomar cuidado de, proceder con cautela; tomar precaución.
(b) mind preocupar; **I am much —d about it** esto me tiene preocupadísimo.
(c) horse, team entrenar; dog llevar de paseo; muscle ejercitar, hacer ejercicios con.
3 vi ejercitarse, hacer ejercicios.
exercise book ['eksəsaizbuk] n cuaderno m.
exert [ig'zəːt] 1 vt ejercer, emplear.
2 vr: **to — oneself** esforzarse, afanarse (to do por hacer); (overdo things) trabajar demasiado; **he doesn't — himself at all** no hace el más mínimo esfuerzo.
exertion [ig'zəːʃən] n esfuerzo m; (overdoing things) esfuerzo m excesivo, trabajo m excesivo.
exeunt ['eksiʌnt] vi éxeunt.
exhale [eks'heil] 1 vt air espirar; fumes despedir. 2 vi espirar.
exhaust [ig'zɔːst] 1 n (fumes) gases mpl de escape; 2 attr de escape. 3 vt (all senses) agotar; **to be —ed** estar agotado.
exhausting [ig'zɔːstiŋ] adj agotador.
exhaustion [ig'zɔːstʃən] n agotamiento m; **nervous —** postración f nerviosa.
exhaustive [ig'zɔːstiv] adj exhaustivo; inquiry minucioso.
exhaustively [ig'zɔːstivli] adv de modo exhaustivo (or minucioso).
exhaust pipe [ig'zɔːstpaip] n tubo m de escape.
exhibit [ig'zibit] 1 n objeto m expuesto; pieza f de museo; (painting etc) obra f expuesta; (Law) documento m; **to be on —** estar expuesto.
2 vt signs etc mostrar, manifestar; emotion acusar; exhibit exponer, presentar al público; film presentar.
3 vi (painter etc) presentar sus obras, organizar una exposición.
exhibition [‚eksi'biʃən] n demostración f, manifestación f; (by painter, sport etc) exposición f; (Univ)

beca f; **an — of bad temper** una demostración de mal genio; **to be on —** estar expuesto; **to make an — of oneself** ponerse en ridículo.
exhibitionism [‚eksi'biʃənizəm] n exhibicionismo m.
exhibitionist [‚eksi'biʃənist] 1 adj exhibicionista. 2 n exhibicionista mf.
exhibitor [ig'zibitə*] n expositor m, ora f.
exhilarate [ig'ziləreit] vt levantar el ánimo de, estimular, vigorizar; **to feel —d** sentirse más optimista, estar alegre.
exhilarating [ig'ziləreitiŋ] adj tónico, vigorizador, estimulador.
exhilaration [ig‚zilə'reiʃən] n (effect) efecto m tónico, efecto m vigorizador; (mood) optimismo m, alegría f; **the — of speed** lo emocionante de la velocidad.
exhort [ig'zɔːt] vt exhortar (to do a hacer).
exhortation [‚egzɔː'teiʃən] n exhortación f.
exhume [eks'hjuːm] vt exhumar; (fig) desenterrar.
exigence ['eksidʒəns] n, **exigency** [ig'zidʒənsi] n (need) exigencia f, necesidad f; (emergency) caso m de urgencia.
exigent ['eksidʒənt] adj exigente; urgente.
exiguous [eg'zigjuəs] adj exiguo.
exile ['eksail] 1 n (a) (state) destierro m, exilio m.
(b) (person) exilado m, a f, exiliado m, a f (Acad); desterrado m, a f.
2 vt desterrar, poner en el exilio, exilar, exiliar (Acad).
exist [ig'zist] vi existir; vivir.
existence [ig'zistəns] n existencia f; vida f; **to be in —** existir; **to come into —** formarse, nacer, fundarse, empezar a tener existencia.
existent [ig'zistənt] adj existente, actual.
existential [‚egzis'tenʃəl] adj existencial.
existentialism [‚egzis'tenʃəlizəm] n existencialismo m.
existentialist [‚egzis'tenʃəlist] 1 adj existencialista. 2 n existencialista mf.
existing [ig'zistiŋ] adj existente, actual.
exit ['eksit] 1 n salida f; (Theat) mutis m; **emergency —** salida f de urgencia; **to make one's —** salir, marcharse.
2 vi (Theat) hacer mutis; **— Hamlet** váse Hamlet.
exodus ['eksədəs] n éxodo m; **there was a general —** salieron todos.
exonerate [ig'zɔnəreit] vt exculpar, disculpar (from de).
exoneration [ig‚zɔnə'reiʃən] n exculpación f.
exorbitant [ig'zɔːbitənt] adj excesivo, exorbitante.
exorcise ['eksɔːsaiz] vt exorcizar, conjurar.
exorcism ['eksɔːsizəm] n exorcismo m.
exotic [ig'zɔtik] 1 adj exótico. 2 n planta f exótica.
exoticism [eg'zɔtisizəm] n exotismo m.
expand [iks'pænd] 1 vt extender; ensanchar; dilatar; number aumentar; chest expandir; market, operations etc expandir, expansionar; wings abrir, desplegar; (Math) desarrollar.
2 vi extenderse; ensancharse; dilatarse; (number) aumentarse; (market etc) expandirse; (person) ponerse más expansivo.
expanse [iks'pæns] n extensión f; (of wings) envergadura f.
expansion [iks'pænʃən] n extensión f; dilatación f; (of town etc) ensanche m; (of trade etc) expansión f; (of number) aumento m; (Math etc) desarrollo m.
expansionism [iks'pænʃənizəm] n (Pol etc) expansionismo m.
expansionist [iks'pænʃənist] adj (Pol etc) expansionista.
expansive [iks'pænsiv] adj expansivo (also fig).
expatiate [eks'peiʃieit] vi: **to — on** extenderse en un análisis de, extenderse en alabanzas (etc) de.
expatriate [eks'pætrieit] 1 adj expatriado. 2 n expatriado m, a f. 3 vt desterrar. 4 vr: **to — oneself** expatriarse.
expect [iks'pekt] 1 vt (a) (with n) storm, defeat, baby etc esperar; fun, good time prometerse; **it's not what I —ed** no es lo que yo esperaba; **I —ed as much, just what I —ed** ya me lo figuraba; **difficulties are only to be —ed** es natural que haya dificultades; **as might have been —ed, as one might —, as was to be —ed** como era de esperar, como podía esperarse; **we — your help** contamos con su ayuda; **I —ed nothing less of you** no esperaba menos de Vd; **it was not so tough as I —ed (it to be)** era menos severo de lo que yo esperaba; **when least —ed** el día menos pensado, a lo mejor; **we — you tomorrow** le esperamos mañana; **don't — me till you see me** no contéis conmigo hasta verme llegar; **you know what to —** ya sabe Vd a qué atenerse.
(b) (with verb) **I — to see him** espero verle; **we — he will come** contamos con que venga; **I — you to be punctual** cuento con que Vd sea puntual;

so you — me to pay? ¿así que esperas que pague yo?; **what do you — me to do about it?** ¿qué pretende Vd que haga yo?; **how do you — me to go out like this?** ¿cómo pretendes que salga así?; **it is —ed that** se espera que + *subj*; **it is hardly to be** —ed that apenas cabe esperar que + *subj*.
(c) (*think, suppose*) imaginar, suponer; **I — so** supongo que sí; **I — he's there by now** imagino que ya estará allí.
2 *vi*: **to be** —ing estar encinta, estar en estado (de esperanza).
expectancy [iks'pektənsi] *n* (*state*) expectación *f*; (*hope, chance*) expectativa *f* (*of* de).
expectant [iks'pektənt] *adj* expectante; (*hopeful*) ilusionado; — **mother** mujer *f* encinta, futura madre *f*.
expectantly [iks'pektəntli] *adv* con expectación; **to wait** — esperar a ver qué sale.
expectation [.ekspek'teiʃən] *n* (a) (*state*) expectación *f*; **in — of** en expectación de, esperando.
(b) (*hope*) esperanza *f*, expectativa *f*; —**s** (*in will*) esperanzas *fpl* de heredar; — **of life** probabilidades *fpl* de vida, índice *m* vital; **our — is that** esperamos que; **contrary to** —**s** contra lo que se venía esperando; **it is beyond our** —**s** es mejor de lo que esperábamos; **to come up to one's** —**s** resultar tan bueno como se esperaba; **to exceed one's** —**s** sobrepasar lo que se esperaba; **to fall below one's** —**s** no llegar a lo que se esperaba.
expectorate [eks'pektəreit] *vt* expectorar.
expedience [iks'piːdiəns] *n*, **expediency** [iks'piːdiənsi] *n* conveniencia *f*, oportunidad *f*.
expedient [iks'piːdiənt] 1 *adj* conveniente, oportuno. 2 *n* expediente *m*, recurso *m*.
expedite ['ekspidait] *vt* (*speed up*) acelerar; *business* despachar (con prontitud); *progress* facilitar.
expedition [.ekspi'diʃən] *n* expedición *f*.
expeditionary [.ekspi'diʃənri] *adj* expedicionario.
expeditious [.ekspi'diʃəs] *adj* expeditivo, pronto.
expeditiously [.ekspi'diʃəsli] *adv* con toda prontitud.
expel [iks'pel] *vt* arrojar, echar; *person* expulsar.
expend [iks'pend] *vt* *money* expender, gastar; *ammunition* usar; *resources* consumir, agotar; *time* pasar; *effort* dedicar (*on* a); *care* poner (*on* en).
expendable [iks'pendəbl] *adj* que se puede sacrificar, prescindible.
expenditure [iks'penditʃə*] *n* (*of money etc*) gasto *m*, desembolso *m*; **after a great — of time on it** después de haberle dedicado gran parte de su tiempo.
expense [iks'pens] *n* gasto *m*, gastos *mpl*; costa *f*; —**s** gastos *mpl*; **business —s** gastos *mpl* comerciales; **operating —s, working —s** gastos *mpl* de explotación; **overhead —s** gastos *mpl* generales; **travelling —s** gastos *mpl* de viaje; **at great —** gastándose muchísimo dinero; **at my —** a mi costa, corriendo yo con los gastos; **at the — of** (*fig*) a costa de, a expensas de; **regardless of —** sin parar en gastos, sin escatimar gastos; **to be a great — to someone** costar a uno mucho dinero; **to go to — meterse** en gastos (*over* por); **to pay someone's —s** pagar los gastos a uno; **to put someone to —** hacer que uno gaste dinero.
expense account [iks'pensə'kaunt] *n* cuenta *f* de gastos.
expensive [iks'pensiv] *adj* caro, costoso; *shop etc* carero.
experience [iks'piəriəns] 1 *n* experiencia *f*; **to know from bitter —** *that* saber por amargas experiencias personales que; **to learn by —, to profit from —** aprender por la experiencia.
2 *vt* experimentar; *fate, loss* sufrir; *difficulty* tener, tropezar con.
experienced [iks'piəriənst] *adj* experimentado, perito, experto (*in* en).
experiment [iks'perimənt] *n* experimento *m*; prueba *f*, ensayo *m*; **as an —, by way of —** como experimento.
experiment [iks'periment] *vi* experimentar, hacer experimentos (*on* en, *with* con).
experimental [eks,peri'mentl] *adj* experimental.
experimentally [eks,peri'mentəli] *adv* experimentalmente, como experimento.
experimentation [eks,perimen'teiʃən] *n* experimentación *f*.
expert ['ekspəːt] 1 *adj* experto, perito (*at, in* en); *touch etc* hábil; *witness, evidence* pericial. 2 *n* experto *m*, perito *m* (*at, in* en); técnico *m*; especialista *mf*.
expertise [.ekspəː'tiːz] *n* pericia *f*; (*of touch etc*) habilidad *f*.
expertly ['ekspəːtli] *adv* expertamente.
expiate [ek'spieit] *vt* expiar.

expiation [.ekspi'eiʃən] *n* expiación *f*.
expiatory ['ekspiətəri] *adj* expiatorio.
expiration [.ekspaiə'reiʃən] *n* (*ending*) terminación *f*; expiración *f*; (*Comm*) vencimiento *m*.
expire [iks'paiə*] *vi* (*end*) terminar; (*die*) expirar; (*reach its term*) expirar, cumplirse, (*Comm*) vencer, (*ticket*) caducar.
expiry [iks'paiəri] *n see* **expiration**.
explain [iks'plein] 1 *vt* explicar; *plan* exponer; *mystery* aclarar; *conduct* explicar; justificar; **that —s it** con eso todo queda aclarado; **to — something away** justificar algo hábilmente, dar razones convincentes de algo, *difficulty* salvar hábilmente; **just you — that away!** ¡a ver si logras dar razón de eso!
2 *vr*: **to — oneself** (*clearly*) hablar más claro, explicarse con más detalles; (*morally*) justificar su conducta; **kindly — yourself!** ¡explíquese Vd!
explainable [iks'pleinəbl] *adj* explicable.
explanation [.eksplə'neiʃən] *n* explicación *f*; aclaración *f*; **what is the — of this?** ¿cómo se explica esto?; **there must be some —** ha de haber alguna razón.
explanatory [iks'plænətəri] *adj* explicativo; aclaratorio.
expletive [eks'pliːtiv] *n* (*oath*) palabrota *f*.
explicable [eks'plikəbl] *adj* explicable.
explicit [iks'plisit] *adj* explícito.
explicitly [iks'plisitli] *adv* explícitamente.
explode [iks'pləud] 1 *vt* volar, hacer saltar, explotar, explosionar; *rumour* desmentir; *belief, theory* desacreditar, refutar.
2 *vi* estallar, hacer explosión, explotar, explosionar; (*with anger etc*) reventar (*with* de); **the town —d in revolt** estalló la rebelión en la ciudad; **when I said that he —d** cuando dije eso se puso furioso.
exploit ['eksplɔit] *n* hazaña *f*, proeza *f*.
exploit [iks'plɔit] *vt* explotar.
exploitation [.eksplɔi'teiʃən] *n* explotación *f*.
exploration [.eksplɔː'reiʃən] *n* exploración *f*.
exploratory [eks'plɔrətəri] *adj* exploratorio, preparatorio, de sondaje.
explore [iks'plɔː*] *vt* explorar; (*fig*) examinar, sondar, investigar.
explorer [iks'plɔːrə*] *n* explorador *m*, ora *f*.
explosion [iks'pləuʒən] *n* explosión *f* (*also fig*).
explosive [iks'pləuziv] 1 *adj* explosivo (*also fig*). 2 *n* explosivo *m*; **high —** alto explosivo *m*, explosivo *m* de gran potencia.
exponent [eks'pəunənt] *n* exponente *mf*, partidario *m*, a *f* (*of* de), intérprete *mf* (*of* de).
export ['ekspɔːt] *n* exportación *f*, artículo *m* de exportación; — **licence** permiso *m* de exportación; — **trade** comercio *m* de exportación.
export [eks'pɔːt] *vt* exportar.
exportable [eks'pɔːtəbl] *adj* exportable.
exportation [.ekspɔː'teiʃən] *n* exportación *f*.
exporter [eks'pɔːtə*] *n* exportador *m*.
expose [iks'pəuz] 1 *vt* exponer (*also Phot*); *weakness* descubrir; *falsity* demostrar; *ignorance* revelar, descubrir; *fake, plot, impostor* desenmascarar; **to — someone to ridicule** exponer a uno al ridículo.
2 *vr*: **to — oneself** to exponerse a.
exposed [iks'pəuzd] *adj* expuesto; *position* desabrigado; *flank* desguarnecido; **to be —** (*thing normally hidden*) estar al descubierto; **to be —** to estar expuesto a.
exposition [.ekspə'ziʃən] *n* exposición *f*, explicación *f*.
expostulate [iks'pɔstjuleit] *vi* protestar; **to — with** reconvenir a, discutir con, tratar de convencer a.
expostulation [iks,pɔstju'leiʃən] *n* protesta *f*, reconvención *f*.
exposure [iks'pəuʒə*] *n* exposición *f* (*also Phot*); revelación *f*; desenmascaramiento *m*; **a house with a southerly —** una casa orientada hacia el sur; **to die from —** morir de frío, morir por estar a la intemperie.
exposure meter [iks'pəuʒə,miːtə*] *n* fotómetro *m*, exposímetro *m*.
expound [iks'paund] *vt* exponer, explicar; *text* comentar.
express [iks'pres] 1 *adj* (*clear*) expreso, explícito, categórico; *train* rápido; *letter* urgente; *service etc* rápido.
2 *n* rápido *m*.
3 *adv*: **to send something —** enviar algo por carta urgente(*).
4 *vt* expresar; *juice* exprimir.
5 *vr*: **to — oneself** expresarse.
expression [iks'preʃən] *n* expresión *f*; **as an — of thanks** en señal de agradecimiento.

expressionism [eks'preʃənizəm] *n* expresionismo *m.*
expressionless [iks'preʃənlis] *adj* sin expresión.
expressive [iks'presiv] *adj* expresivo.
expressively [iks'presivli] *adv* expresivamente.
expressiveness [iks'presivnis] *n* expresividad *f.*
expressly [iks'presli] *adv* expresamente; *deny, prohibit etc* terminantemente.
expropriate [eks'prəuprieit] *vt* expropiar.
expropriation [eks,prəupri'eiʃən] *n* expropiación *f.*
expulsion [iks'pʌlʃən] *n* expulsión *f.*
expunge [iks'pʌndʒ] *vt* borrar, tachar.
expurgate ['ekspə:geit] *vt* expurgar.
exquisite [eks'kwizit] **1** *adj* exquisito, primoroso; *pain etc* intenso. **2** *n* elegante *m.*
exquisitely [eks'kwizitli] *adv* primorosamente, con primor.
ex-serviceman ['eks'sə:vismən] *n*, *pl* —**men** [mən] excombatiente *m.*
extant [eks'tænt] *adj* existente.
extemporary [iks'tempərəri] *adj* improvisado, hecho sin preparación.
extempore [eks'tempəri] **1** *adv* de improviso, sin preparación. **2** *adj* improvisado, hecho sin preparación.
extemporize [iks'tempəraiz] *vti* improvisar.
extend [iks'tend] **1** *vt* extender; *hand* tender, alargar; *building etc* ensanchar, ampliar; *road, term etc* prolongar; (*increase*) aumentar; *thanks, welcome* dar, ofrecer; *invitation* enviar; *athlete* pedir el máximo esfuerzo a.
2 *vi* extenderse; prolongarse; **to — over** abarcar, incluir; **to — to** extenderse a, llegar hasta, (*fig*) abarcar, incluir; **does that — to me?** ¿eso me incluye a mí?
3 *vr*: **to — oneself** trabajar (*etc*) al máximum.
extensible [iks'tensibl] *adj* extensible.
extension [iks'tenʃən] *n* extensión *f*; (*of building etc*) ensanche *m*, ampliación *f*; (*of road, term etc*) prolongación *f*; (*Comm*) prórroga *f*; (*increase*) aumento *m*; (*Tel*) línea *f* derivada; — **ladder** escalera *f* extensible.
extensive [iks'tensiv] *adj* extenso; vasto, ancho, dilatado; *use etc* frecuente, general, común.
extensively [iks'tensivli] *adv* extensamente; **to travel** — viajar por muchos países; **he travelled** — **in Mexico** viajó por muchas partes de Méjico; **it is used** — se usa comúnmente.
extent [iks'tent] *n* (*space*) extensión *f*; (*scope*) alcance *m*; **to the** — **of** + *ger* hasta el punto de + *infin*; **to a certain** —, **to some** — hasta cierto punto; **to the full** — en toda su extensión; (*fig*) completamente; **to a great** (*or* **large**) — en gran parte, en alto grado; **to such an** — **that** hasta tal punto que; **to that** — hasta ahí; **to what** —? ¿hasta qué punto?
extenuate [eks'tenjueit] *vt* atenuar, mitigar, disminuir (la gravedad de).
extenuating [eks'tenjueitiŋ] *adj* *circumstance* atenuante.
exterior [eks'tiəriə*] **1** *adj* exterior, externo. **2** *n* exterior *m*; (*appearance*) aspecto *m.*
exterminate [eks'tə:mineit] *vt* exterminar.
extermination [eks,tə:mi'neiʃən] *n* exterminio *m.*
external [eks'tə:nl] **1** *adj* externo, exterior. **2** —**s** *npl* exterioridad *f*, aspecto *m* exterior.
externally [eks'tə:nəli] *adv* externamente, exteriormente; por fuera.
extinct [iks'tiŋkt] *adj* *volcano* extinto, apagado, extinguido; *animal* extinto, desaparecido.
extinction [iks'tiŋkʃən] *n* extinción *f.*
extinguish [iks'tiŋgwiʃ] *vt* extinguir, apagar; *title etc* suprimir.
extinguisher [iks'tiŋgwiʃə*] *n* extintor *m.*
extirpate ['ekstə:peit] *vt* extirpar.
extol [iks'təl] *vt* ensalzar, alabar.
extort [iks'tə:t] *vt* obtener por fuerza (*from* de), exigir por amenazas (*from* a).
extortion [iks'tə:ʃən] *n* exacción *f.*
extortionate [iks'tə:ʃənit] *adj* *price etc* excesivo, exorbitante.
extortioner [iks'tə:ʃənə*] *n* desollador *m*; (*official*) concusionario *m.*
extra ['ekstrə] **1** *adj* adicional; de más, de sobra; *charge, pay etc* extraordinario; *part* de repuesto; **we need 2** — **chairs** necesitamos 2 sillas más; **we seem to have 2** — **men** parece que tenemos 2 hombres de sobra; **postage** — gastos de franqueo aparte; **postage and packing** — gastos de envío aparte; **5 tons** — **to requirements** un excedente de 5 toneladas; *see* **time** *etc.*
2 *adv* (**a**) (*with adj, adv, verb*) especialmente, extraordinariamente; — **big** más grande que lo normal; — **smart** más elegante que de costumbre;

this is — **difficult** esto es extraordinariamente difícil; **to sing** — **loud** cantar extraordinariamente fuerte.
(**b**) (*after verb, fam*) **we shall have to work** — tendremos que trabajar más.
3 *n* (**a**) (*on bill*) extra *m*, suplemento *m*; (*Theat*) extra *mf*, comparsa *mf*; (*of paper*) edición *f* extraordinaria; (*spare part, US*) repuesto *m.*
(**b**) **what shall we do with the** —? ¿qué hacemos con el exceso?, ¿qué hacemos con lo que sobra?
extract ['ekstrækt] *n* (*Lit*) cita *f*, trozo *m*; (*Pharm*) extracto *m*; **beef** — concentrado *m* de carne; **malt** — extracto *m* de malta; —**s from "Don Quijote"** (*as book*) selecciones *fpl* del "Quijote".
extract [iks'trækt] *vt* sacar (*from* de); extraer (*also Math*); *confession etc* arrancar, sacar, obtener.
extraction [iks'trækʃən] *n* extracción *f*; obtención *f.*
extractor [iks'træktə*] *n* extractor *m.*
extraditable ['ekstrədaitəbl] *adj* sujeto a extradición.
extradite ['ekstrədait] *vt* (*holding country*) entregar, permitir la extradición de; (*claiming country*) extradicionar, obtener la extradición de.
extradition [,ekstrə'diʃən] *n* extradición *f.*
extramural ['ekstrə'mjuərəl] *adj* *jurisdiction etc* de extramuros; *activities* de carácter privado; *course* para externos.
extraneous [eks'treiniəs] *adj* extraño; — **to** ajeno a.
extraordinarily [iks'trɔ:dnrili] *adv* extraordinariamente.
extraordinary [iks'trɔ:dnri] *adj* extraordinario; (*odd*) raro; (*incredible*) increíble; **how** —! ¡qué raro!; **it is** — **that** es increíble que + *subj.*
extrasensory ['ekstrə'sensəri] *adj* *perception etc* extrasensorial.
extraterritorial ['ekstrə,teri'tɔ:riəl] *adj* extraterritorial.
extravagance [iks'trævəgəns] *n* prodigalidad *f*; derroche *m*; despilfarro *m*; lujo *m* desmedido; exorbitancia *f*; lo excesivo; rareza *f.*
extravagant [iks'trævəgənt] *adj* (*lavish*) pródigo; (*wasteful*) derrochador, despilfarrador; (*luxurious*) muy lujoso; *price* exorbitante; *praise* excesivo; (*odd*) raro, estrafalario.
extravagantly [iks'trævəgəntli] *adv* *spend etc* profusamente, con gran despilfarro; (*luxuriously*) muy lujosamente; *praise* excesivamente; *behave* de modo raro.
extravaganza [eks,trævə'gænzə] *n* obra *f* extravagante y fantástica.
extreme [iks'tri:m] **1** *adj* extremo; *care, poverty etc* extremado; *case* excepcional.
2 *n* extremo *m*, extremidad *f*; —**s of temperature** temperaturas *fpl* extremas; **in the** — en sumo grado; **to go from one** — **to the other** pasar de un extremo a otro; **to go to** —**s** ir muy lejos, tomar medidas extremas.
extremely [iks'tri:mli] *adv* sumamente, extremadamente; **it is** — **difficult** es sumamente difícil, es dificilísimo; **we are** — **glad** nos alegramos muchísimo.
extremism [iks'tri:mizəm] *n* extremismo *m.*
extremist [iks'tri:mist] **1** *adj* extremista. **2** *n* extremista *mf.*
extremity [iks'tremiti] *n* (**a**) (*end*) extremidad *f*, punta *f.*
(**b**) (*want*) apuro *m*, necesidad *f*; **in this** — en tal apuro; **to be driven to** — estar muy apurado.
(**c**) **extremities** (*Anat*) extremidades *fpl*; (*measures*) medidas *fpl* extremas.
extricate ['ekstrikeit] **1** *vt* (*disentangle*) desenredar, soltar; (*fig*) librar, sacar (*from* de). **2** *vr*: **to** — **oneself from** (*fig*) lograr sacarse de.
extrinsic [eks'trinsik] *adj* extrínseco.
extrovert ['ekstrəuvə:t] **1** *adj* extrovertido. **2** *n* extrovertido *m*, a *f.*
extrude [eks'tru:d] *vt* sacar.
exuberance [ig'zu:bərəns] *n* euforia *f*; exuberancia *f.*
exuberant [ig'zu:bərənt] *adj* *person, spirit etc* eufórico; *growth, style etc* exuberante.
exude [ig'zju:d] **1** *vt* rezumar, destilar, sudar. **2** *vi* rezumarse.
exult [ig'zʌlt] *vi* exultar; **to** — **in, to** — **at** regocijarse por; **to** — **over** triunfar sobre; **to** — **to find** regocijarse al encontrar.
exultant [ig'zʌltənt] *adj* regocijado, jubiloso.
exultation [,egzʌl'teiʃən] *n* exultación *f*, júbilo *m.*
eye [ai] **1** *n* ojo *m* (*also of needle*); (*Bot*) yema *f*; **black** — ojo *m* amoratado; **evil** — aojo *m*, mal *m* de ojo; **private** — detective *m*; —**s right!** ¡vista a la derecha!; **as far as the** — **can see** hasta donde alcanza la vista; **it happened before my very** —**s** ocurrió delante de mis propios ojos; **the grass grows before your very** —**s** crece la hierba a ojos

vistas; **in the —s of** a los ojos de; **with an — to** + *infin* con la intención de + *infin*; **with the naked — a simple** vista; **it's all my —** ! (*fam*) ¡es puro cuento!; **to be all —s** ser todo ojos; **that's one in the — for him**! ese golpe va dirigido a él; **to be up to one's —s** (*in work*) estar hasta los ojos de trabajo; **to catch the —** llamar la atención; **to catch someone's —** atraer la atención de uno; **to clap —s on** clavar la vista en; **to cock one's — at** mirar con intención a; **to cry one's —s out** llorar a moco tendido; **to feast one's —s on something** recrear la vista mirando algo, mirar algo con fruición; **to give someone the glad —** lanzar una mirada incitante a uno; **to have an — for something** tener afición a algo, saber apreciar algo; **to have an — to something** tener algo en cuenta; **to have good —s** tener buena vista; **to have one's —s on** (*watch*) vigilar, echar una mirada a; (*covet*) echar el ojo a; **it hits you in the —** salta a la vista; **to keep an — on something** (*watch*) vigilar, echar una mirada a; (*bear in mind*) tener algo en cuenta; (*follow*) no perder algo de vista; **he couldn't keep his —s off the girl** se le fueron los ojos tras la chica; **to make —s at someone** lanzar una mirada incitante a uno; **there's more in this than meets the —** esto tiene su miga; **to open someone's —s to something** abrir los ojos de uno; **to rub one's —s** restregarse los párpados; **to run one's — over something** recorrer algo con la vista; **I don't see — to — with him over that** en eso no estoy completamente de acuerdo con él; **when I first set —s on him** la primera vez que le puse los ojos encima; **it's 5 years since I set —s on him** hace 5 años que no le veo; **to shut one's —s to something** cerrar los ojos a algo, hacer la vista gorda a (*or* ante) algo; **we must not shut our —s to this** importa que nos demos cuenta de esto; **to turn a blind — to something** fingir no ver algo, hacer la vista gorda a (*or* ante) algo.

2 *vt* ojear, mirar (detenidamente, sospechosamente *etc*).

eyeball ['aibɔːl] *n* globo *m* del ojo.

eyebath ['aibɑːθ] *n*, *pl* **—baths** [bɑːðz] ojera *f*.

eyebrow ['aibrau] *n* ceja *f*; **— pencil** lápiz *m* de cejas; **to raise one's —s** levantar las cejas; **he never raised an — at it** no se sorprendió en lo más mínimo.

eye-catcher ['ai‚kætʃə*] *n* cosa *f* que llama la atención.

eye-catching ['ai‚kætʃiŋ] *adj* llamativo, vistoso.

-eyed [aid] *adj* de ojos . . . , *eg* **green-eyed** de ojos verdes; **two-eyed** de dos ojos.

eyeful ['aiful] *n* (*fam*): **he got an — of mud** el lodo le dio de lleno en el ojo; **get an — of this** ! ¡echa un vistazo a esto!, ¡mírame esto!

eyeglass ['aiglɑːs] *n* lente *m*; (*worn in the eye*) monóculo *m*.

eyelash ['ailæʃ] *n* pestaña *f*.

eyelet ['ailit] *n* (*Sew*) ojete *m*.

eyelid ['ailid] *n* párpado *m*.

eye-opener ['ai‚əupnə*] *n* revelación *f*, sorpresa *f* grande; **it was an — to me** fue una revelación para mí.

eyepiece ['aipiːs] *n* ocular *m*.

eyeshade ['aiʃeid] *n* visera *f*.

eyeshadow ['ai‚ʃædəu] *n* sombreador *m* de ojos.

eyesight ['aisait] *n* vista *f*; (*extent of —*) alcance *m* de la vista.

eyesore ['aisɔː*] *n* monstruosidad *f*, cosa *f* antiestética.

eyestrain ['aistrein] *n* vista *f* fatigada; **to get —** cansar los ojos, cansar la vista; **to suffer from —** padecer de los ojos.

eye tooth ['aituːθ] *n* colmillo *m*.

eyewash ['aiwɔʃ] *n* (*sl*) música *f* celestial; **it's a lot of —**! ¡es puro cuento!

eyewitness ['ai‚witnis] *n* testigo *mf* presencial, testigo *mf* ocular.

eyrie ['aiəri] *n* aguilera *f*.

F

fab [fæb] *adj* (*sl*) = **fabulous**.
fable ['feibl] *n* fábula *f*.
fabric ['fæbrik] *n* (*cloth*) tejido *m*, tela *f*; (*Archit*) fábrica *f*; **the upkeep of the —** la manutención de los edificios; **the — of society** la estructura de la sociedad.
fabricate ['fæbrikeit] *vt* (*fig*) inventar; *document, evidence* falsificar.
fabrication [,fæbri'keiʃən] *n* invención *f*, ficción *f*; **the whole thing is a —** todo es mentira.
fabulous ['fæbjuləs] *adj* fabuloso; (*fam*) fabuloso, estupendo, macanudo.
façade [fə'sɑːd] *n* fachada *f*; (*fig*) apariencia *f*, barniz *m*; **to keep up a —** of sostener una apariencia de, guardar las apariencias de.
face [feis] **1** *n* (a) (*Anat etc*) cara *f*, rostro *m*, semblante *m*; (*of dial, watch*) esfera *f*, cuadrante *m*; (*surface*) superficie *f*; (*Min*) cara *f* de trabajo; (*of building*) frente *f*, fachada *f*; **— of the earth** faz *f* de la tierra; **— downwards** boca abajo; **— upwards** boca arriba; **— to —** cara a cara; **to bring A — to — with B** confrontar A con B; **to bring two people — to —** poner a dos personas cara a cara; **in the — of** ante, en presencia de; **in the — of this threat** ante esta amenaza; **in the — of such difficulties** vistas tantas dificultades; **courage in the — of the enemy** valor en presencia del enemigo; **the wind was blowing in our —s** el viento nos daba de cara.
(b) **to fly in the — of reason** oponerse abiertamente a la razón; **to laugh in someone's —** reírse en la cara de uno; **he didn't dare to look me in the —** no osaba mirarme a la cara; **I could never look him in the — again** yo no tendría valor para mirarle a la cara; **to say something to someone's —** decir algo en la cara de uno; **to set one's — against something** oponerse resueltamente a algo; **to show one's —** asomar la cara, dejarse ver; **to struggle to keep a straight —** esforzarse por contener la risa.
(c) (*expression*) wry — mueca *f*; **to go about with a long —** andar cariacontecido; **to make —s, to pull —s** hacer muecas, hacer carantoñas (*at a*).
(d) (*effrontery*) descaro *m*, caradura *f*; **to have the — to do something** ser bastante descarado para hacer algo.
(e) (*dignity*) prestigio *m*; **to lose —** desprestigiarse, perder prestigio; **to save (one's) —** salvar las apariencias.
(f) (*outward show*) **on the — of it** a primera vista, según las apariencias; **to put a brave — on something** hacer buena cara a algo.
2 *vt* (a) (*look towards: of person, object*) estar de cara a; ponerse de cara a; volver la cara hacia; **— the wall!** ¡póngase de cara a la pared!; **turn it to — the fire** gírelo para que esté de cara a la lumbre; **they sat facing each other** estaban sentados uno frente al otro; **to sit facing the engine** estar sentado de frente a la máquina; **the picture facing page 19** el grabado en la página opuesta a la 19.
(b) (*of building*) mirar hacia, estar enfrente de, dar a; **the flat —s the Town Hall** el piso está enfrente del Ayuntamiento; **the house —s the sea** la casa tiene vistas al mar; **the house —s the south** la casa está orientada hacia el sur.
(c) (*fig*) *person, enemy, electorate* encararse con, enfrentarse con; *consequences, danger* arrostrar, hacer cara a; *facts* reconocer; *situation* hacer frente a; *problem* afrontar; **we — grave problems** afrontamos unos problemas graves; **we are —d with grave problems** se nos plantean graves problemas; **we will — him with the facts** le expondremos los hechos; **let's — it!** ¡seamos realistas!; **we're poor, let's — it!** ¡reconozcamos lo pobres que somos!
(d) **to — it out** insistir descaradamente en ello.
(e) (*Tech*) revestir, forrar (*with de*).

3 *vi*: **to — in a direction** estar orientado en una dirección; **which way does it —?** ¿en qué dirección está orientado?; **— this way!** ¡vuélvase hacia aquí!; **to — about** dar media vuelta, (*fig*) cambiar de postura; **to — on to** mirar hacia, dar a; **to — up to something** reconocer la realidad de algo, arrostrar algo; **she —d up to it bravely** lo aguantó con mucha resolución.
face cream ['feiskriːm] *n* crema *f* (de belleza).
-faced [feist] *adj* de cara ..., *eg* **brown-faced** de cara morena, **long-faced** de cara larga.
face flannel ['feis,flænl] *n* manopla *f*, paño *m*.
faceless ['feislis] *adj* sin cara.
face lift ['feislift] *n* (operación *f* de) cirugía *f* estética.
face powder ['feis,paudə*] *n* polvos *mpl*.
facer ['feisə*] *n* (*fam*) problema *m* desconcertante.
face-saving ['feis,seiviŋ] **1** *adj*: **— operation** maniobra *f* para salvar las apariencias.
2 *n*: **— is important** importa salvar las apariencias; **this is a piece of blatant —** esto es una maniobra transparente para salvar las apariencias.
facet ['fæsit] *n* faceta *f* (*also fig*).
facetious [fə'siːʃəs] *adj person* chistoso; *remark* festivo, gracioso; *speech* divertido, lleno de chistes.
facetiously [fə'siːʃəsli] *adv* chistosamente; **he said —** dijo guasón.
face value ['feis'væljuː] *n* valor *m* nominal; (*of stamp etc*) valor *m* facial; (*fig*) valor *m* aparente, significado *m* literal; **you can't take it at its —** no se deje engañar por las apariencias; **I took his statement at its —** yo entendí su declaración en su significado literal.
facial ['feiʃəl] **1** *adj* de la cara, facial. **2** *n* masaje *m* facial.
facile ['fæsail] *adj* fácil, superficial, ligero.
facilitate [fə'siliteit] *vt* facilitar.
facility [fə'siliti] *n* facilidad *f*; **facilities** (*all senses*) facilidades *fpl*; **credit facilities** facilidades *fpl* de crédito; **they gave me every —** me ayudaron en lo posible.
facing ['feisiŋ] **1** *prep* de cara a, frente a.
2 *as adj* opuesto, de enfrente; **the houses —** las casas de enfrente.
3 *n* (*Tech*) paramento *m*, revestimiento *m*; (*Sew*) vuelta *f*, guarnición *f*; **—s** (*Sew*) vueltas *fpl*.
facsimile [fæk'simili] **1** *adj* facsímil. **2** *n* facsímil *m*.
fact [fækt] *n* hecho *m*; (*real world*) realidad *f*; **— and fiction** lo real y lo ficticio; **the —s of life** los hechos de la vida, (*esp*) los detalles de la reproducción humana; **hard —s** hechos *mpl* innegables; **a film based on —** una película que tiene una base de realidad histórica; **it has no basis in —** carece de base real; **as a matter of —, in —, in point of —** en realidad; **the — of the matter is** la pura verdad es; **the — is that** el hecho es que, ello es que; **it is a — that** se ha comprobado que; **the — that I am here** el hecho de que estoy aquí; **to bow to the —s** reconocer que las cosas son así; **I don't dispute your —s** yo no niego los hechos que alega Vd; **to know for a — that** saber a ciencia cierta que; **to stick to the —s** atenerse a los hechos; *see* **accessory**.
fact-finding ['fækt,faindiŋ] *adj* de investigación, de indagación.
faction ['fækʃən] *n* facción *f*.
factious ['fækʃəs] *adj* faccioso.
factitious [fæk'tiʃəs] *adj* facticio.
factor ['fæktə*] *n* (a) (*fact*) factor *m*, hecho *m*, elemento *m*; **determining —** factor *m* determinante; **human —** factor *m* humano; **safety —** factor *m* de seguridad.
(b) (*Math*) factor *m*; **highest common —** máximo común divisor *m*.
(c) (*Comm*) agente *m*.
factory ['fæktəri] *n* fábrica *f*.

factotum [fæk'təutəm] *n* factótum *m*.

factual ['fæktjuəl] *adj* objetivo, que consta de hechos, basado en datos; — **error** error *m* de hecho.

faculty ['fækəlti] *n* facultad *f* (*also Univ*); (*US Univ*) profesorado *m*.

fad [fæd] *n* manía *f*; novedad *f*; **it's just a** — es una novedad nada más, es una moda pasajera; **he has his** —**s** tiene sus caprichos; **the** — **for Italian clothes** la manía de los trajes italianos.

faddy ['fædi] *adj* caprichoso, dengoso, que tiene sus manías, difícil de contentar.

fade [feid] **1** *vt colour, dress* descolorar, desteñir; *flower* marchitar; **to** — **in, to** — **up** (*Cine*) hacer aparecer gradualmente.

  2 *vi* (*colour, dress*) descolorarse, desteñirse, perder su color; (*flower*) marchitarse; (*light*) apagarse gradualmente; (*sound*) desvanecerse; **the daylight was fading fast** anochecía rápidamente; **he saw his chances fading** veía como se estaban acabando sus posibilidades; **guaranteed not to** — no se descolora; **to** — **away, to** — **out** (*visually*) desdibujarse, desvanecerse; (*sound*) apagarse, dejar poco a poco de oírse; **to be fading away** (*dying*) consumirse lentamente, (*slimming*) adelgazar muchísimo; **this season the team has just** —**d away** en esta temporada el equipo ha dejado casi de figurar; **to** — **to** (*Cine*) fundir a.

faded ['feidid] *adj plant* marchito, seco; *colour, dress* descolorido.

faeces ['fi:si:z] *npl* excrementos *mpl*.

fag [fæg] **1** *n* (a) (*job*) faena *f*, trabajo *m* penoso; **what a** —! ¡qué faena!; **it's just too much** — es mucho trabajo.
  (b) (*School*) alumno *m* joven que trabaja por otro mayor.
  (c) (*sl*) pitillo *m*.
  2 *vt* fatigar, cansar; **to be** —**ged out** estar rendido.
  3 *vi* trabajar como un negro; **to** — **for** (*School*) trabajar por.

fag end ['fægend] *n* colilla *f*.

faggot, (*mainly US*) **fagot** ['fægət] *n* haz *m* de leña, astillas *fpl*.

Fahrenheit ['færənhait]: — **thermometer** termómetro *m* de Fahrenheit (*grados Fahrenheit menos* $32 \times \frac{5}{9} = grados$ *centígrados*).

fail [feil] **1** *n* (*Univ fam*) suspenso *m* (*in* en); **without** — sin falta.
  2 *vt person* faltar a, faltar en sus obligaciones a; decepcionar; *exam* no aprobar, salir mal en; *candidate* suspender; **his strength** —**ed him** se sintió desfallecer, le abandonaron sus fuerzas; **his heart** —**ed him** se encontró sin ánimo; **words** — **me** no encuentro palabras para expresarme; **you have** —**ed me** me has decepcionado.
  3 *vi* (a) (*run short: supply, strength*) acabarse; (*engine*) fallar; (*voice*) desfallecer; (*eyes*) debilitarse; (*light*) acabarse; (*crop*) fallar; (*electricity supply etc*) tener una avería, averiarse; (*patient*) debilitarse, hacerse más débil; **the light was** —**ing** iba anocheciendo.
  (b) (*neglect*) **to** — **to do something** dejar de hacer algo; **he** —**ed to appear** no se presentó, dejó de presentarse; **don't** — **to visit her** no deje de visitarla; **to** — **to keep one's word** faltar a su palabra.
  (c) (*be unable*) **I** — **to see how** no veo cómo; **I** — **to understand why** no puedo comprender por qué.
  (d) (*not succeed*) fracasar, no tener éxito; (*remedy*) no surtir efecto; (*hopes*) frustrarse, malograrse; (*Fin*) quebrar; (*Univ etc*) ser suspendido (*in* en); **a** —**ed painter** un pintor fracasado; **to** — **to be elected** no lograr ser elegido; **to** — **to win a prize** no obtener un premio; **to** — **by 5 votes** perder por 5 votos.
  (e) **to** — **in one's duty to someone** faltar a uno, faltar en sus obligaciones a uno.

failing ['feiliŋ] **1** *prep* a falta de; — **that** si eso no es posible.
  2 *n* falta *f*, defecto *m*; (*moral*) flaqueza *f*; **the plan has numerous** —**s** el plan tiene muchos defectos; **it is his only** — es su único punto débil.

failure ['feiljə*] *n* (a) (*ill success*) fracaso *m*; (*of hopes*) malogro *m*; (*failed thing*) fracaso *m*, (*person*) fracasado *m*, a *f*; (*Mech*) fallo *m*, avería *f*; (*Elec*) corte *m*, interrupción *f*; (*Univ etc*) suspenso *m* (*in* en); **the crop was a total** — el cultivo se perdió por completo.
  (b) **your** — **to come** el que Vd dejara de venir, el dejar de venir Vd.

faint [feint] **1** *adj* débil; *colour* pálido; *line* tenue; *outline* borroso, indistinto; *trace* apenas perceptible;

sound casi imperceptible, débil; *voice* débil; *smell* tenue; *hope* nada firme; *idea, memory* vago; *resemblance* ligero; *heart* medroso; **to feel** — estar mareado, tener vahídos; **I haven't the** —**est (idea)** no tengo la más remota idea.
  2 *n* desmayo *m*; **to be in a** — estar desmayado, estar sin conocimiento; **to fall down in a** — desmayarse.
  3 *vi* desmayarse, perder conocimiento (*also to* — **away**); **to be** —**ing with tiredness** estar rendido.

fainthearted ['feint'ha:tid] *adj* medroso, pusilánime.

faintly ['feintli] *adv* débilmente; indistintamente; vagamente; ligeramente; **she said** — dijo en voz débil.

faintness ['feintnis] *n* debilidad *f*; tenuidad *f*; lo indistinto; (*Med*) desmayo *m*, desfallecimiento *m*.

fair[1] [fɛə*] **1** *adj* (a) (*beautiful*) bello, hermoso; **the** — **sex** el bello sexo.
  (b) (*blond*) *hair* rubio; *skin* blanco.
  (c) (*clean*) *copy* en limpio; *name* honrado; *reputation* bueno.
  (d) (*just*) justo, equitativo; *hearing, report, summary* imparcial; *comment* acertado; *means* recto; *play* limpio; *competition* leal; *chance, price, warning* razonable; — **enough!** ¡muy bien!; **as is only** — como es justo; **but to be** — pero en honor a la verdad; **it's not** —! ¡no hay derecho!; **it's not** — **on the old** afecta injustamente a los viejos.
  (e) (*middling*) regular, mediano.
  (f) (*promising*) prometedor, favorable, bastante bueno.
  (g) (*Meteorol*) *sky* sereno, despejado; *day, weather* bueno; **if it's** — **tomorrow** si hace buen tiempo mañana.
  2 *adv* (a) **to play** — jugar limpio.
  (b) **it hit the target** — **and square** dio en el centro del blanco.
  (c) (*fam*) **we were** — **terrified** nos asustamos bastante; **then it** — **rained** entonces sí que llovió.

fair[2] [fɛə*] *n* (a) feria *f*; **trade** — feria *f* de muestras; **world** — feria *f* mundial, exposición *f* internacional.
  (b) (*fun-*) parque *m* de atracciones; verbena *f*.

fairground ['fɛəgraund] *n* real *m* (de la feria); parque *m* de atracciones.

fair-haired ['fɛə'hɛəd] *adj*, **fair-headed** ['fɛə'hedid] *adj* pelirrubio.

fairly ['fɛəli] *adv* (a) justamente, equitativamente, con imparcialidad; rectamente; limpio, limpiamente.
  (b) — **good** bastante bueno.
  (c) (*utterly*) completamente.

fair-minded ['fɛə'maindid] *adj* imparcial.

fairness ['fɛənis] *n* (a) hermosura *f*. (b) lo rubio; blancura *f*. (c) justicia *f*, imparcialidad *f*; **in all** — para ser justo (*to him* con él).

fair-sized ['fɛəsaizd] *adj* bastante grande.

fairway ['fɛəwei] *n* (*Naut*) canalizo *m*; (*Golf*) calle *f*.

fair-weather ['fɛə,weðə*] *adj*: — **friend** amigo *m* en la prosperidad.

fairy ['fɛəri] **1** *n* hada *f*; (*sl*) maricón *m*. **2** *adj and attr* feérico, mágico; *story etc* de hada(s).

fairyland ['fɛərilænd] *n* tierra *f* de las hadas.

fairy lights ['fɛərilaits] *npl* bombillas *fpl* de colorines.

fairy tale ['fɛəriteil] **1** *n* cuento *m* de hadas; (*fig*) cuento *m*, patraña *f*. **2** *adj* fantástico, de ensueño.

fait accompli [,feitə'kɔmpli] *n* hecho *m* consumado.

faith [feiθ] *n* fe *f* (*also Eccl*); (*trust*) confianza *f* (*in* en); (*doctrine*) creencia *f*; (*sect, confession*) religión *f*; **bad** — mala fe *f*; **in good** — de buena fe; **what** — **does he belong to?** ¿qué religión tiene?; **to break** — faltar a su palabra (*with* dada a); **to have** — in tener fe en; **to keep** — cumplir su palabra (*with* dada a); **to pin one's** — **to** cifrar sus esperanzas en.

faithful ['feiθful] *adj* fiel (*also Eccl*); *friend, servant* leal; *translation* fiel; *account* exacto; **the** — los fieles.

faithfully ['feiθfəli] *adv* fielmente; lealmente; con exactitud; **yours** — le saluda atentamente.

faithfulness ['feiθfulnis] *n* fidelidad *f*; lealtad *f*; exactitud *f*.

faith healing ['feiθ,hi:liŋ] *n* curación *f* por fe.

faithless ['feiθlis] *adj* desleal, pérfido.

fake [feik] **1** *n* (*thing*) falsificación *f*, impostura *f*; imitación *f*; (*person*) impostor *m*, embustero *m*, (*as term of abuse*) farsante *m*.
  2 *adj* falso, fingido, contrahecho.
  3 *vt* (*also to* — **up**) contrahacer, falsificar, fingir.

fakir ['fa:kiə*] *n* faquir *m*.

falcon ['fɔ:lkən] *n* halcón *m*.

falconry ['fɔ:lkənri] *n* halconería *f*, cetrería *f*.

Falkland Isles ['fɔ:lklənd,ailz] *pl* Islas *fpl* Malvinas.

fall [fɔ:l] **1** *n* caída *f*; (*Fin*) baja *f*; (*decrease*) disminución *f*; (*in price, demand, temperature*) descenso *m* (*in* de); (*Mil*) caída *f*, toma *f*, rendición *f*; (*of* *ground*) declive *m*, desnivel *m*; (*of water*; *also* —s) salto *m* de agua, catarata *f*, cascada *f*; (US) otoño *m*; the F— la Caída; — of earth corrimiento *m* de tierras; — of rocks derrumbamiento *m* de piedras; — of snow nevada *f*; to have a — sufrir una caída; to be riding for a — presumir demasiado.

2 (*irr*: *pret* fell, *ptp* fallen) *vi* caer; caerse; (*fig*: *empire, government, night, hair, drapery, morally etc*) caer; (*decrease*) disminuir; (*price, level, demand, temperature etc*) bajar, descender; (Mil) caer, rendirse; (*ground*) estar en declive; (*wind*) amainar; his face fell se inmutó; night was —ing anochecía, se hacía de noche; to — among thieves ir a parar entre ladrones; to — apart romperse, deshacerse, (*empire etc*) desmoronarse; to — away (*plaster etc*) desconcharse; (*cliff etc*) desmoronarse; (*ground*) estar en declive (*lo hacia*); (Med) enflaquecer; (*Eccl etc*) ir perdiendo su fe; to — back retroceder, (Mil) replegarse (*on* sobre); to — back on *remedy etc* recurrir a; to — backwards caer de espaldas; to — behind quedarse atrás, rezagarse; to — down caer, caerse; (*person*) caerse, dar consigo en el suelo; (*building*) hundirse, derrumbarse; venirse abajo; (*fail*) fracasar, ser frustrado; the rain was —ing down llovía a cántaros; to — down and worship arrodillarse ante; to — for *person* enamorarse de, *thing* tomar afición a; *trick* dejarse engañar por; he fell for it picó; to — in (*roof*) desplomarse; (*lease*) vencer; (Mil *etc*) alinearse; — in! ¡en filas!; to — in with *person* encontrarse con, juntarse con; *idea* convenir en, aprobar; to — into (*river*) desembocar en; *error* incurrir en; *conversation* entablar; *habit* adquirir; *category* estar incluido en; it —s into 4 parts puede dividirse en 4 partes; to — off caerse; (*part*) desprenderse; (*leaf*) separarse; (*in quality*) empeorar; (*in quantity*) disminuir; (*zeal etc*) enfriarse; to — on (*tax burden etc*) incidir en; (*accent*) cargar sobre, caer sobre; (Mil) caer sobre; to — on one's knees arrodillarse; to — on one's food tirarse a la comida como un león; my birthday —s on a Monday mi cumpleaños cae en lunes; the choice —s on X la elección recae en X; to — out caer; (*quarrel*) reñir, pelearse, tener un disgusto (*with* con); (Mil) romper filas; it fell out that resultó que; to — over caer, caerse; *obstacle* tropezar con; they were —ing over each other to buy it se estaban pegando por comprarlo; to — through (Aut) fracasar; to — to (*adv*) empezar a comer, ponerse a trabajar (*etc*); to — to (*prep*) (*of a duty*) corresponder a, incumbir a, tocar a; to — to temptation sucumbir a la tentación; to — to + *ger* empezar a + *infin*.

fallacious [fə'leiʃəs] *adj* erróneo, engañoso.
fallacy ['fæləsi] *n* error *m*; sofisma *m*; mentira *f*; pathetic — patética falacia *f*, engaño *m* sentimental.
fallen ['fɔːlən] 1 *ptp of* fall; the — los caídos. 2 *adj* (*morally*) perdido.
fall guy ['fɔːlgai] *n* (US *fam*) cabeza *f* de turco.
fallibility [,fæli'biliti] *n* falibilidad *f*.
fallible ['fæləbl] *adj* falible.
falling-off ['fɔːlin'ɔf] *n* (*in quantity*) disminución *f*; (*of price etc*) baja *f*, descenso *m*; (*in quality*) empeoramiento *m*.
falling star ['fɔːlin'stɑː*] *n* estrella *f* fugaz.
fallout ['fɔːlaut] *n* polvillo *m* radiactivo, lluvia *f* radiactiva; — shelter refugio *m* contra ataques nucleares.
fallow ['fæləu] 1 *adj* barbecho; to lie — estar en barbecho. 2 *n* barbecho *m*.
fallow deer ['fæləu'diə*] *n* gamo *m*.
false [fɔːls] *adj* falso; *person* desleal, pérfido; *hair, jewel, teeth etc* postizo; *bottom* doble; to be — to someone, to play someone — traicionar a uno.
falsehood ['fɔːlshud] *n* (*falseness*) falsedad *f*; (*lie*) mentira *f*.
falsely ['fɔːlsli] *adv* falsamente.
falseness ['fɔːlsnis] *n* falsedad *f*; (*of person*) perfidia *f*.
falsification [,fɔːlsifi'keiʃən] *n* falsificación *f*.
falsify ['fɔːlsifai] *vt* falsificar.
falsity ['fɔːlsiti] *n* falsedad *f*.
falter ['fɔːltə*] 1 *vt* decir titubeando. 2 *vi* (*waver*) vacilar, titubear; (*voice*) desfallecer, empañarse; without —ing sin vacilar.
faltering ['fɔːltəriŋ] *adj* *step* vacilante; *voice* entrecortado.
falteringly ['fɔːltəriŋli] *adv* *say* en voz entrecortada.
fame [feim] *n* fama *f*; ill — mala reputación *f*; Bader, of 1940 — Bader, famoso por lo que hizo en 1940.
famed [feimd] *adj* famoso.
familiar [fə'miliə*] *adj* familiar; (*well-known*) conocido, consabido; (*common*) corriente, común; *tone of voice* íntimo, de confianza; (*pej*) fresco, que

presume de amigo; to be — with estar familiarizado con, conocer, estar enterado de; to be on — terms with tener confianza con; to make oneself — with familiarizarse con; his voice sounds — me parece que conozco su voz; it doesn't sound — no me suena; he got much too — se tomó muchas confianzas.
familiarity [fə,mili'æriti] *n* familiaridad *f*; (*knowledge*) conocimiento *m* (*with* de); (*of tone*) intimidad *f*; (*pej*) frescura *f*; familiarities familiaridades *fpl*; — breeds contempt lo conocido no se estima.
familiarize [fə'miliəraiz] *vr*: to — oneself with familiarizarse con.
family ['fæmili] 1 *n* familia *f*; to be one of the — ser como de la familia; to be in the — way estar en estado de buena esperanza; to run in the — venir de familia.
  2 *attr* *allowance, gathering etc* familiar; *butcher* doméstico; *doctor* de cabecera; *business* de familia; *see* tree *etc*.
famine ['fæmin] *n* hambre *f*; (*of goods*) escasez *f*, carestía *f*.
famished ['fæmiʃt] *adj* hambriento, famélico; I'm simply — tengo un hambre canina.
famous ['feiməs] *adj* famoso, célebre (*for* por).
famously ['feiməsli] *adv* (*fig*) estupendamente bien, a las mil maravillas.
fan[1] [fæn] 1 *n* abanico *m* (*also fig*); (Agr) aventador *m*; (*machine*) ventilador *m*; electric — abanico *m* eléctrico, ventilador *m*.
  2 *vt* *face* abanicar; (*mechanically*) ventilar; (Agr) aventar; *fire* soplar; (*fig*) excitar, atizar.
  3 *vi*: to — out desparramarse (en abanico), avanzar separados.
  4 *vr*: to — oneself abanicarse.
fan[2] [fæn] *n* (*fam*) aficionado *m*, a *f*, admirador *m*, ora *f*, entusiasta *mf*, partidario *m*; radio — radio-experimentador *m*; the boxer's —s los partidarios del boxeador; thousands of Real Madrid —s miles de hinchas del Real Madrid; I am not one of his —s yo no soy de sus admiradores, yo no soy de los que le admiran.
fanatic [fə'nætik] *n* fanático *m*, a *f*.
fanatic(al) [fə'nætik(əl)] *adj* fanático.
fanaticism [fə'nætisizəm] *n* fanatismo *m*.
fan belt ['fænbelt] *n* (Aut) correa *f* de ventilador.
fancied ['fænsid] *adj* (*imaginary*) imaginario; (*preferred*) favorito; selecto.
fanciful ['fænsiful] *adj* *temperament* caprichoso; *construction, explanation etc* fantástico; (*unreal*) imaginario.
fan club ['fænklʌb] *n* club *m* de admiradores.
fancy ['fænsi] 1 *n* (a) (*delusion*) quimera *f*, suposición *f* arbitraria; it's just your — lo habrás soñado; it's one of her fancies son cosas de ella.
  (b) (*imaginative capacity*) fantasía *f*, imaginación *f*; in the realm of — en el mundo de la fantasía.
  (c) (*whim*) capricho *m*, antojo *m*; passing — capricho *m*; to have a — for something antojarse algo a uno; as the — takes her según su capricho.
  (d) (*taste*) afición *f*, gusto *m*; to take a — to something tomar afición a algo, encapricharse por algo; to take a — to someone tomar cariño a uno, (*amorously*) prendarse de uno; to take (*or* tickle) someone's — atraer a uno, cautivar a uno, (*amuse*) caer en gracia a uno.
  2 *attr* (*ornamental*) de adorno, de lujo; *goods, jewels etc* de fantasía; *price* excesivo; *idea* fantástico, estrafalario.
  3 *vt* (a) (*picture to oneself*) imaginarse, figurarse.
  (b) (*rather think*) creer, suponer; I — he is away creo que está fuera; he fancies he knows it all se cree un pozo de sabiduría.
  (c) —!, — that!, just —! ¡fíjate!, (*doubting*) ¡parece mentira!; — meeting you! ¡qué casualidad encontrarle a Vd!; — him winning! ¡qué raro que lo ganara él!
  (d) (*take a — to*) aficionarse a, encapricharse por; I don't — the idea no me gusta la idea; what do you —? ¿qué quieres tomar?; do you — a stroll? ¿te apetece dar un paseo?; he fancies her ella le interesa bastante, él se siente atraído por ella.
  (e) (*have high opinion of*) tener un alto concepto de; he fancies his game cree tener muchísima habilidad; I don't — his chances of winning no creo que tenga muchas posibilidades de ganar.
  4 *vr*: to — oneself (a) (*imagine oneself*) creerse, soñar que uno es *etc*; he fancied himself in Spain soñó que estaba en España.
  (b) presumir; you — yourself! ¡eres un presumido!; he fancies himself as a footballer las echa de futbolista.

fancy dress ['fænsi'dres] n disfraz m; **fancy-dress ball** baile m de trajes.
fancy-free ['fænsi'fri:] adj libre de amores.
fancy woman ['fænsi'wumən] n, pl — **women** [,wimin] (hum) querida f.
fancy work ['fænsiwə:k] n (Sew) labor f.
fanfare ['fænfɛə*] n toque m de trompeta, fanfarria f.
fang [fæŋ] n colmillo m.
fanlight ['fænlait] n abanico m.
fanmail ['fænmeil] n cartas fpl escritas por admiradores.
fantastic [fæn'tæstik] adj fantástico.
fantastically [fæn'tæstikəli] adv fantásticamente; — **learned** enormemente erudito.
fantasy ['fæntəzi] n fantasía f.
far [fɑ:*] 1 adv (a) (distance, literal) lejos, a lo lejos (also — away, — off); not — from Dover no muy lejos de Dover; is it —? ¿está lejos?, ¿dista mucho?; how — is it to Irún? ¿cuánto hay de aquí a Irún?; — and near, — and wide por todas partes; as — as hasta; so — hasta aquí; to walk — into the hills penetrar profundamente en las montañas.
　　(b) (distance, fig) how — . . .? ¿hasta qué punto . . .?; how — have you gone in your work? ¿a qué punto han llegado sus trabajos?; — into the night hasta las altas horas de la noche; he's not — off 70 tiene casi 70 años, frisa con los 70 años; she was not — off tears estaba al borde de las lágrimas; as — back as we can recall hasta donde alcanza la memoria; so — hasta aquí, (in time) hasta ahora; so — this year en lo que va del año; so — so good hasta aquí, bien; so — and no further hasta aquí pero ni un paso más.
　　(c) (fig) as — as I know, as — as I can tell que yo sepa; I will help you as — as I can te ayudaré en lo que pueda; as — as I am concerned en cuanto a mí, por lo que a mí se refiere; in so — as en tanto que.
　　(d) — from approving it, I . . . lejos de aprobarlo, yo . . .; — from it! ¡nada de eso!; — be it from me to + infin no permita Dios que yo + subj.
　　(e) (with adj or adv) — better mucho mejor; it is — better not to go más vale no ir; — and away the best, the best by — con mucho el mejor; — superior to muy superior a; — faster than mucho más rápidamente que.
　　(f) (with go) to go — (plan etc) ir lejos; that young man will go — ese joven irá lejos, ese joven tiene un brillante porvenir; it doesn't go — enough no va bastante lejos, no tiene todo el alcance que quisiéramos; he's gone too — to back out now ha ido demasiado lejos para retirarse ahora; to go — to + infin contribuir mucho a + infin; to go so — as to + infin llegar a + infin.
　　2 adj lejano, remoto; at the — end en el otro extremo, (of room) en el fondo; at the — side en el lado opuesto.
faraway ['fɑːrəwei] adj remoto; look preocupado, distraído.
farce [fɑːs] n (Theat) farsa f; (fig) absurdo m, tontería f; this is a — esto es absurdo; what a — this is! ¡qué follón!; the trial was a — el proceso fue una parodia de la justicia.
farcical ['fɑːsikəl] adj absurdo, ridículo.
fare [fɛə*] 1 n (a) (cost) precio m (del viaje, del billete); (ticket) billete m; (Naut) pasaje m; —s please! ¡billetes, por favor!; excess — suplemento m.
　　(b) (person) pasajero m, a f.
　　(c) (food) comida f.
　　2 vi: to — well pasarlo bien, irle bien a uno; how did you —? ¿qué tal le fue?; to — alike correr la misma suerte.
Far East ['fɑːr'iːst] Extremo Oriente m, Lejano Oriente m.
farewell [fɛə'wel] 1 interj ¡adiós!; it's — to all that ya se acabó todo eso; you can say — to your wallet puedes considerar tu cartera como perdida.
　　2 n adiós m; (ceremony) despedida f; to bid — to despedirse de.
　　3 attr de despedida.
far-fetched ['fɑː'fetʃt] adj inverosímil, poco probable; comparison traído por los pelos.
far-flung ['fɑː'flʌŋ] adj extenso.
farinaceous [,færi'neiʃəs] adj farináceo.
farm [fɑːm] 1 n granja f; cortijo m, quinta f, estancia f (SAm); (of mink, oysters etc) criadero m; (house) cortijo m, alquería f, casa f de labranza; collective — granja f colectiva.
　　2 vt (till) cultivar, labrar; he —s 300 acres tiene una finca de 300 acres; to — out arrendar, dar en arriendo.
　　3 vi (till) cultivar la tierra; (as profession) ser

agricultor; he —s in Devon tiene una finca (or tierras) en Devon.
farmer ['fɑːmə*] n agricultor m, cultivador m, granjero m; (peasant —) labrador m; estanciero m (SAm).
farmhand ['fɑːmhænd] n labriego m, mozo m de labranza, peón m.
farmhouse ['fɑːmhaus] n, pl —houses [,hauziz] cortijo m, alquería f, casa f de labranza.
farming ['fɑːmiŋ] 1 n (tilling) cultivo m, labranza f; (in general) agricultura f. 2 attr agrícola; the — community los agricultores.
farmland ['fɑːmlænd] n tierras fpl de labrantío.
farmstead ['fɑːmsted] n alquería f.
farmyard ['fɑːmjɑːd] n corral m.
far-off ['fɑːr'ɔf] adj lejano, remoto.
farrago [fə'rɑːgəu] n fárrago m.
far-reaching ['fɑː'riːtʃiŋ] adj trascendental, de mucho alcance, de ancha repercusión.
farrow ['færəu] 1 n lechigada f de puercos. 2 vt parir. 3 vi parir (la cerda).
far-seeing ['fɑː'siːiŋ] adj clarividente, previsor.
far-sighted ['fɑː'saitid] adj clarividente, previsor.
far-sightedly ['fɑː'saitidli] adv de modo clarividente, con previsión.
far-sightedness ['fɑː'saitidnis] n clarividencia f, previsión f.
fart [fɑːt] (tabu) 1 n pedo m. 2 vi peer.
farther ['fɑːðə*] comp of far; see **further**.
farthest ['fɑːðist] superl of far; see **furthest**.
farthing ['fɑːðiŋ] n cuarto m de penique; it's not worth a brass — no vale un céntimo.
fascinate ['fæsineit] vt fascinar, encantar.
fascinating ['fæsineitiŋ] adj fascinador, encantador, sugestivo.
fascination [,fæsi'neiʃən] n fascinación f, encanto m, sugestión f; his — with the cinema la atracción que tuvo para él el cine.
fascism ['fæʃizəm] n fascismo m.
fascist ['fæʃist] 1 adj fascista. 2 n fascista mf.
fashion ['fæʃən] 1 n (a) (usage, manner) uso m, manera f, estilo m; it is not my — to pretend yo no acostumbro fingir; after a — en cierto modo; I play after a — toco algo; after the — of a la manera de; in the French — a la francesa, a lo francés, al estilo francés; in one's own — a su propio modo.
　　(b) (vogue) moda f; it's all the — now ahora está muy de moda; it's the — to say that es un tópico decir que; to be in — estar de moda; to be out of — haber pasado de moda; to come into — empezar a estar de moda; to dress in the latest — vestirse a la última moda; to go out of — pasar de moda; to set the — imponer la moda (for de).
　　(c) (good taste) buen tono m, buen gusto m; what — demands lo que impone el buen gusto; a man of — un hombre elegante.
　　2 vt formar, labrar, forjar (on sobre).
fashionable ['fæʃnəbl] adj dress etc de moda, elegante; place, restaurant de buen tono, elegante; in — society en la buena sociedad; it is — to + infin está de moda + infin; he is hardly a — painter now es un pintor que no está ahora muy de moda.
fashionably ['fæʃnəbli] adv: to be — dressed estar vestido muy elegantemente, ir vestido de acuerdo con la moda actual.
fashion designer ['fæʃəndi'zainə*] n modisto m.
fashion model ['fæʃən,mɔdl] n modelo mf.
fashion parade ['fæʃənpə'reid] n desfile m de modelos.
fashion plate ['fæʃənpleit] n figurín m de moda.
fashion show ['fæʃənʃəu] n presentación f de modelos.
fast[1] [fɑːst] 1 adj (a) (speedy) rápido, veloz; ligero; pitch seco y firme; my watch is 5 minutes — mi reloj adelanta 5 minutos; he was too — for me corrió más que yo; to pull a — one on someone jugar una mala pasada a uno, embaucar a uno.
　　(b) woman lanzada, cachonda, fresca; life, set disoluto.
　　(c) (firm) fijo, firme; friend leal; colour sólido, inalterable.
　　2 adv (a) (speedily) rápidamente; de prisa; not so —! ¡un momento!
　　(b) to play — and loose with jugar con.
　　(c) (firmly) firmemente; — asleep profundamente dormido; to hold — agarrarse bien, (fig) mantenerse firme; hold —! ¡agarraos!, (stop) ¡para!; to make something — sujetar algo; to make a rope — atar firmemente una cuerda; to make a boat — amarrar una barca; to rain — llover a cántaros; to stand — mantenerse firme; to stick — quedar

bien pegado; **to be stuck — in the mud** quedar atascado en el lodo; **to be stuck — in a doorway** estar metido por una puerta sin poderse mover.

fast[2] [fɑːst] **1** n ayuno m. **2** vi ayunar.

fast day [ˈfɑːstdei] n día m de ayuno.

fasten [ˈfɑːsn] **1** vt (a) asegurar, sujetar, fijar; (with rope) atar; (with paste) pegar; box, door, window cerrar; (with bolt) echar el cerrojo a; belt, dress abrochar; **to — two things together** pegar dos cosas.

(b) **to — the blame on someone** echar (or achacar) la culpa a uno; **to — the responsibility on someone** atribuir a uno la responsabilidad; **they're trying to — the crime on me** tratan de demostrar que yo fui autor del crimen.

2 vi (box etc) cerrarse; **to — on to** agarrarse de, pegarse a, (fig) fijarse en; **he —ed on to me at once** se fijó en mí en seguida, (as companion) se me pegó a mí en seguida; **to — on to a pretext** echar mano de un pretexto.

fastener [ˈfɑːsnə*] n, **fastening** [ˈfɑːsniŋ] n (of door etc) cerrojo m, pestillo m; (on box) cierre m; (on dress) broche m, corchete m; (for papers) grapa f; (zip-) cremallera f.

fastidious [fæsˈtidiəs] adj delicado, quisquilloso; (about cleanliness etc) exigente; taste fino; mind refinado.

fastness [ˈfɑːstnis] n (Mil) fortaleza f; (of mountain etc) lo más intrincado; **in their Cuban mountain —** en las espesuras serranas de Cuba.

fat [fæt] **1** adj (a) person gordo; (thick) grueso; **to get — engordar.

(b) meat poco magro, que tiene mucha grasa; (greasy) grasiento, graso.

(c) land fértil; living lujoso; profit pingüe; salary muy grande.

(d) (fam) **a — lot he knows!** ¡maldito lo que él sabe!; **a — chance he's got** tiene poquísimas posibilidades; **a — lot of good that is!** y eso ¿para qué sirve?

2 n (on person) carnes fpl; (of meat) grasa f; (for cooking) manteca f, (lard) lardo m; **to live on the — of the land** darse buena vida, comer lo mejor y más rico de la tierra; **now the — is in the fire** aquí se va a armar la gorda.

fatal [ˈfeitl] adj fatal; consequences funesto (to para); injury mortal; **that was — eso fue el colmo; **it's — to say that es peligrosísimo decir eso.

fatalism [ˈfeitəlizəm] n fatalismo m.

fatalist [ˈfeitəlist] n fatalista mf.

fatalistic [feitəˈlistik] adj fatalista.

fatality [fəˈtæliti] n fatalidad f; (victim) víctima f, muerto m; **luckily there were no fatalities** por fortuna no hubo víctimas.

fatally [ˈfeitəli] adv fatalmente; injure etc mortalmente, a muerte.

fate [feit] **1** n (a) (force) hado m, destino m, sino m; **the F—s** las Parcas; **what — has in store for us** lo que la suerte nos va a deparar.

(b) (person's lot) suerte f; **to leave someone to his — dejar a uno a su suerte; **to meet one's — encontrar la muerte; **this sealed his — esto acabó de perderle.

2 vt: **to be —d to + infin** estar predestinado a + infin, tener fatalmente que + infin.

fateful [ˈfeitful] adj fatal, fatídico; decisivo.

fathead [ˈfæthed] n (fam) imbécil mf; **you —!** ¡imbécil!

fat-headed [ˈfæt,hedid] adj (fam) imbécil.

father [ˈfɑːðə*] **1** n padre m; **F—s of the Church** Santos Padres mpl; **Our F—** Padre Nuestro; **Holy — Santo Padre m; **city —s** concejales mpl; **my — and mother** mis padres; **like — like son** de tal palo tal astilla; **a — and mother of a row** una bronca fenomenal; **to talk to someone like a — hablar a uno en tono paternal.

2 vt child engendrar; (fig) inventar, producir; **to — something on someone** atribuir algo a uno.

father-figure [ˈfɑːðəˌfigə*] n figura f que sirve de padre, persona f que se finge (or cree etc) dotada de las cualidades paternales.

fatherhood [ˈfɑːðəhud] n paternidad f.

father-in-law [ˈfɑːðərinlɔː] n suegro m.

fatherland [ˈfɑːðəlænd] n patria f.

fatherless [ˈfɑːðəlis] adj huérfano de padre.

fatherly [ˈfɑːðəli] adj paternal.

fathom [ˈfæðəm] **1** n braza f; **5 —s deep** de (or a etc) una profundidad de 5 brazas.

2 vt (Naut) sond(e)ar; (fig) profundizar, penetrar; mystery desentrañar; **we couldn't — it out** no logramos sacar nada en claro; **I can't — why** no comprendo por qué.

fathomless [ˈfæðəmlis] adj insondable.

fatigue [fəˈtiːg] **1** n fatiga f, cansancio m; (Mil) faena f; **metal — fatiga f del metal.

2 vt fatigar, cansar.

fatigue party [fəˈtiːg,pɑːti] n destacamento m de trabajo.

fatiguing [fəˈtiːgiŋ] adj fatigoso.

fatness [ˈfætnis] n gordura f.

fatten [ˈfætn] **1** vt animal engordar, cebar. **2** vi engordar.

fatty [ˈfæti] **1** adj graso; tissue, degeneration etc grasoso. **2** n (fam) gordinflón m, ona f.

fatuity [fəˈtjuːiti] n fatuidad f, necedad f.

fatuous [ˈfætjuəs] adj fatuo, necio.

faucet [ˈfɔːsit] n (US) grifo m.

faugh [fɔː] interj ¡bah!

fault [fɔːlt] **1** n (a) (defect: in character) defecto m; (in manufacture) desperfecto m, imperfección f; (in supply, machine) avería f; **with all his —s** con todos sus defectos; **her — is excessive shyness** peca de demasiado reservada; **generous to a — excesivamente generoso, generoso hasta el exceso; **to find — with criticar, poner peros a.

(b) (Geol) falla f.

(c) (blame) culpa f; **it's all your — Vd tiene toda la culpa; **it's not my — yo no tengo la culpa; **whose — is it if . . .?** ¿quién tiene la culpa si . . .?; **you were not at — Vd no tuvo la culpa; **you were at — in not telling me** Vd hizo mal en no decírmelo; **your memory is at — Vd recuerda mal.

(d) (mistake) falta f (also Tennis etc); **double service — doble falta f de saque.

2 vt tachar, encontrar defectos en; **it cannot be —ed** es intachable.

faultfinder [ˈfɔːltˌfaində*] n criticón m, ona f.

faultfinding [ˈfɔːltˌfaindiŋ] **1** adj criticón, reparón. **2** n manía f de criticar.

faultless [ˈfɔːltlis] adj impecable, intachable.

faulty [ˈfɔːlti] adj defectuoso, imperfecto.

faun [fɔːn] n fauno m.

fauna [ˈfɔːnə] n fauna f.

Faust [faust] m Fausto.

faux pas [ˈfəuˈpɑː] n (false move) paso m en falso; (gaffe) plancha f.

favour, (US) **favor** [ˈfeivə*] **1** n (a) (approval, regard) favor m; aprobación f; (protection) amparo m; **to be in — (thing) tener mucha aceptación, (dress etc) estar de moda; **to be in — with (person) tener el apoyo de, (at court etc) gozar de favor cerca de; **to be out of — (thing) no estimarse, (dress etc) estar fuera de moda; **to curry — buscar favores; **to curry — with someone** tratar de congraciarse con uno; **to find — with someone** caer en gracia a uno; **to look with — on** favorecer; **to stand high in someone's — ser tenido en mucho por uno.

(b) (kindness) favor m; **—s (of woman) favores mpl; **to ask a — of** pedir un favor a; **to do someone a — hacer un favor a uno; **please do me the — of + ger** haga el favor de + infin; see esteem.

(c) (Comm) **your — of the 5th inst** su atenta del 5 del corriente.

(d) (partiality) parcialidad f; **by your — con permiso de Vd; **to show — to someone** favorecer a uno.

(e) (aid, support) apoyo m; **in — of** a favor de; **balance in your — saldo m a su favor; **that's a point in his — es un punto a su favor; **to be in — of person apoyar, estar por; thing aprobar, ser partidario de; **to be in — of + ger** apoyar la idea de + infin, ser partidario de + infin.

(f) (token) prenda f.

2 vt person favorecer, (unjustly) mostrar parcialidad hacia; idea, scheme aprobar, ser partidario de; party apoyar, (choose to wear) elegir; progress ser propicio a, ayudar; team, horse preferir; **fortune —s the brave** la fortuna ayuda a los valientes; **he eventually —ed us with a visit** por fin se dignó visitarnos; **most —ed nation treatment** régimen m de nación más favorecida.

favourable, (US) **favorable** [ˈfeivərəbl] adj favorable; conditions etc propicio.

favourably, (US) **favorably** [ˈfeivərəbli] adv favorablemente.

favoured, (US) **favored** [ˈfeivəd] adj favorecido; (favourite) predilecto; **— by nature** dotado por la naturaleza (with de); **one of the — few** uno de los pocos afortunados.

favourite, (US) **favorite** [ˈfeivərit] **1** adj favorito, predilecto. **2** n favorito m, a f (also Sport); (at court) valido m, privado m; (mistress) querida f.

favouritism, (US) **favoritism** [ˈfeivəritizəm] n favoritismo m.

fawn[1] [fɔːn] **1** n (Zool) cervato m. **2** n (colour) color m de cervato. **3** adj color de cervato.

fawn[2] [fɔːn] vi: to — on (animal) acariciar; (fig) adular, lisonjear.

fawning ['fɔːniŋ] adj adulador, servil.

fealty ['fiːəlti] n lealtad f.

fear [fiə*] **1** n miedo m (of a, de), temor m; aprensión f; for — of temiendo, por miedo de; for — that por miedo de que + subj; no — ! ¡ni hablar!; there's no — of that happening no hay peligro de que ocurra eso; without — or favour imparcialmente; to go in — of one's life temer por su vida; to put the — of God into someone dar un susto mortal a uno.
2 vt temer; person tener miedo a, thing tener miedo de.
3 vi: to — for temer por; to — to + infin tener miedo de + infin; never —! ¡no hay cuidado!

fearful ['fiəful] adj (frightened) temeroso (of de); aprensivo; (cowardly) tímido; (frightening) pavoroso, horrendo; (fam) tremendo, terrible.

fearfully ['fiəfəli] adv cower etc con miedo; say tímidamente; (fam) terriblemente.

fearless ['fiəlis] adj intrépido, audaz;‖— of sin temor a.

fearlessly ['fiəlisli] adv intrépidamente, audazmente; he went on — siguió impertérrito.

fearlessness ['fiəlisnis] n intrepidez f.

fearsome ['fiəsəm] adj temible, espantoso.

fearsomely ['fiəsəmli] adv espantosamente.

feasibility [ˌfiːzəˈbiliti] n carácter m factible, viabilidad f; to doubt the — of a scheme dudar si un proyecto es factible.

feasible ['fiːzəbl] adj factible, hacedero, posible; to make something — posibilitar algo.

feast [fiːst] **1** n (meal) banquete m, festín m; (Eccl) fiesta f. **2** vt banquetear. **3** vi banquetear; to — on regalarse con.

feast day ['fiːstdei] n fiesta f.

feat [fiːt] n hazaña f, proeza f.

feather ['feðə*] **1** n pluma f; in fine — de excelente humor; that is a — in his cap es un triunfo para él; you could have knocked me down with a — me pasmó la noticia; to show the white — mostrarse cobarde.
2 vt emplumar; oar volver horizontal.

feather bed ['feðə'bed] **1** n plumón m. **2** feather-bed vt subvencionar (demasiado), dar primas (excesivas) a.

featherbrained ['feðəbreind] adj cascabelero.

featherweight ['feðəweit] n peso m pluma.

feathery ['feðəri] adj texture plumoso; (light) ligero como pluma.

feature ['fiːtʃə*] **1** n rasgo m distintivo, característica f; (of face) facción f; (Theat) número m, (Cine) película f de largo metraje, atracción f principal; (in paper) artículo m, crónica f.
2 vt (portray) delinear, representar; (in paper etc) presentar, ofrecer (como atracción principal); actor presentar; a film featuring Garbo as . . . una película que presenta a Garbo en el papel de . . .
3 vi existir, constar, figurar.

featureless ['fiːtʃəlis] adj sin rasgos distintivos, monótono.

feature writer ['fiːtʃəˌraitə*] n cronista mf.

febrile ['fiːbrail] adj febril.

February ['februəri] n febrero m.

feces ['fiːsiːz] npl (US) = **faeces**.

feckless ['feklis] adj irreflexivo; casquivano.

fecundity [fiˈkʌnditi] n fecundidad f.

fed [fed] pret and ptp of **feed**.

federal ['fedərəl] adj federal.

federalism ['fedərəlizəm] n federalismo m.

federalist ['fedərəlist] n federalista mf.

federation [ˌfedəˈreiʃən] n federación f.

fee [fiː] n (professional) derechos mpl, honorarios mpl; (to club etc) cuota f; membership — cuota f de socio; registration — derechos mpl de matrícula; retaining — ajuste m, anticipo m; school —s cuota f de enseñanza, (at boarding school) precio m de la pensión.

feeble ['fiːbl] adj débil (also Med); flojo; light, sound tenue; effort irresoluto, débil.

feeble-minded ['fiːbl'maindid] adj imbécil.

feebleness ['fiːblnis] n debilidad f (also Med); flojedad f; tenuidad f; irresolución f.

feebly ['fiːbli] adv débilmente; flojamente.

feed [fiːd] **1** n (a) (food) comida f; (Agr) pienso m; to be off one's — no tener apetito.
(b) (fam) cuchipanda f, comilona f; to have a good — darse un atracón.
(c) (Mech) tubo m de alimentación.
2 (irr: pret and ptp **fed**) vt (nourish) alimentar,

nutrir; (give meal to) dar de comer a; baby dar el pecho a, dar de mamar a, (with bottle) dar el biberón a; fire cebar; (fig) alimentar; they fed us well at the hotel nos dieron bien de comer en el hotel; to — something into a machine ir metiendo algo en una máquina; to — someone on something dar algo de comer a uno; to — up animal cebar; it —s me up (fam) me fastidia, me saca de quicio; to be fed up estar harto (with de).
3 vi comer; (Agr) pacer; to — on comer, alimentarse de (also fig).

feedback ['fiːdbæk] n realimentación f.

feeder ['fiːdə*] n (Mech) alimentador m, tubo m de alimentación; (Geog) afluente m; (Rail) ramal m tributario.

feeding bottle ['fiːdiŋˌbɔtl] n biberón m.

feeding stuffs ['fiːdiŋˌstʌfs] npl (Agr) piensos mpl.

feedpipe ['fiːdpaip] n tubo m de alimentación.

feel [fiːl] **1** n (sense of touch) tacto m; (sensation) sensación f; at the — of his skin al contacto con su piel; to be rough to the — ser áspero al tacto; to know silk by its — conocer la seda al tocarla; to get the — of acostumbrarse a, (knack) coger el tino a.
2 (irr: pret and ptp **felt**) vt (a) (explore) tocar, palpar, tentar; pulse tomar; (caress) acariciar, palpar; to — out the ground tantear el terreno, reconocer el terreno.
(b) (perceive) blow, pain, heat, need sentir; experimentar; I felt it move lo sentí moverse, sentí que se movió; I felt it getting hot sentí como se estaba calentando.
(c) (be conscious of) estar consciente de, darse cuenta de; I — my position very much me doy plenamente cuenta de mi situación.
(d) (experience) sentir, experimentar; (be affected by) resentirse de; I — no interest in it no me interesa; we are beginning to — the effects empezamos a resentirnos de los efectos.
(e) (think, believe) I — that creo que, me parece que; I — strongly that estoy convencido de que.
3 vi (a) (explore) to — about in the dark buscar a tientas en la oscuridad; to — in one's pocket for a key buscar una llave en el bolsillo.
(b) (be) sentirse; to — bad, to — ill sentirse mal; to — old sentirse viejo; to — cold (person) tener frío; to — hungry tener hambre; how do you —? ¿qué tal te encuentras?; she's not —ing quite herself no se encuentra del todo bien; to — all the better for something sentirse mucho mejor después de algo; I don't — up to it no me siento con fuerzas para ello; I — sure that estoy seguro de que.
(c) (think) how do you — about this? ¿qué opinas de esto?; how does it — to go hungry? ¿cómo le gusta pasar hambre?
(d) (give impression of) it —s rough es áspero al tacto; it —s like silk es como la seda al tacto, parece ser seda; it —s cold está frío (al tacto); it —s colder out here aquí fuera hace más frío; it —s like rain parece que va a llover.
(e) (sympathize) I — for you lo siento en el alma, te compadezco.
(f) to — like doing something tener ganas de hacer algo; I — like an apple me apetece una manzana; do you — like a walk? ¿quieres dar un paseo?, ¿te apetece dar un paseo?

feeler ['fiːlə*] n (Zool) antena f; tentáculo m; (Pol etc) sondeo m, tentativa f; to put out a — hacer un sondeo.

feeling ['fiːliŋ] n (a) (sensation) sensación f; a cold — una sensación de frío; to have no — in one's arm no tener sensibilidad en un brazo.
(b) (emotion) sentimiento m, emoción f; (tenderness) ternura f; bad — rencor m, envidia f, hostilidad f; a man of — un hombre sensible; to speak with — hablar con convicción, (angrily) hablar con pasión; —s sentimientos mpl; you can imagine my —s Vd puede suponer cuáles serían mis sentimientos; to appeal to someone's finer —s hablar a los sentimientos nobles de uno; to hurt someone's —s herir los sentimientos de uno; to relieve one's —s desahogarse.
(c) (appreciation) he has no — for music no sabe apreciar la música.
(d) (opinion) opinión f, parecer m; our —s do not matter nuestras opiniones no valen para nada; my — is that creo que; what is your —? ¿que opina Vd? the general — was that en general se creía que.
(e) (foreboding) presentimiento m; I have a — that presiento que, se me antoja que.

feelingly ['fiːliŋli] adv con honda emoción.

feet [fiːt] npl of **foot**.

feign [fein] vt fingir, aparentar; excuse etc inventar; **to — mad(ness)** fingirse loco; **to — sleep** fingirse dormido; **to — dead** fingirse muerto; **to — not to know** fingir no saber.

feigned [feind] adj fingido.

feint [feint] **1** n treta f, estratagema f; (Fencing) finta f. **2** vi hacer una finta.

felicitous [fi'lisitas] adj feliz, oportuno.

felicity [fi'lisiti] n felicidad f; (phrase) ocurrencia f oportuna.

feline ['fi:lain] adj felino.

fell[1] [fel] pret of **fall**.

fell[2] [fel] vt derribar (with a blow de un golpe); tree talar, cortar; cattle acogotar.

fell[3] [fel] n (Geog: hill) montaña f; (moor) brezal m, páramo m.

fell[4] [fel] adj cruel, feroz; (fatal) funesto; **at one — swoop** de un solo golpe.

fellow ['feləu] n **(a)** (comrade) compañero m, a f; (-being) prójimo m; **one's — animals** sus prójimos los animales.
  (b) (other half) pareja f; (equal) igual mf; **it has no —** no tiene par.
  (c) (Univ etc) miembro de la junta de gobierno de un colegio; (of society) socio m, miembro m; **research —** becario m investigador.
  (d) (chap) tipo m, sujeto m, tío m; **he's an odd —** es un tipo raro; **well, this journalist —** bueno, el tal periodista; **those journalist —s** los periodistas esos; **a — gets no peace** no le dejan a uno en paz; **my dear —!** ¡hombre!; **nice — buen chico m, buena persona f; old — viejo m; look here, old — mira, amigo; poor —!** ¡pobrecito!; **some poor —** algún pobre diablo; **young —** chico m; **I say, young —** oiga Vd, joven.

fellow being ['feləu'bi:iŋ] n prójimo m.

fellow citizen ['feləu'sitizən] n conciudadano m.

fellow countryman ['feləu'kʌntrimən] n, pl —men [mən] compatriota mf.

fellow creature ['feləu'kri:tʃə*] n prójimo m.

fellow feeling ['feləu'fi:liŋ] n simpatía f, afinidad f.

fellow member ['feləu'membə*] n consocio m.

fellow men ['feləu'men] n prójimos mpl.

fellow passenger ['feləu'pæsindʒə*] n compañero m de viaje.

fellowship ['feləuʃip] n (companionship) compañerismo m; (society) asociación f; (Univ) dignidad f del fellow; (grant) beca f.

fellow traveller ['feləu'trævlə*] n compañero m de viaje; (Pol) filocomunista mf, comunizante mf.

fellow worker ['feləu'wə:kə*] n colega m.

felon ['felən] n criminal m, delincuente mf (de mayor cuantía).

felonious [fi'ləuniəs] adj criminal, delincuente.

felony ['feləni] n crimen m, delito m (de mayor cuantía).

felspar ['felspɑ:*] n feldespato m.

felt[1] [felt] pret and ptp of **feel**.

felt[2] [felt] n fieltro m.

female ['fi:meil] **1** adj hembra; (of character) femenino. **2** n hembra f.

feminine ['feminin] adj femenino.

femininity [femi'niniti] n feminidad f.

feminism ['feminizəm] n feminismo m.

feminist ['feminist] n feminista mf.

femur ['fi:mə*] n fémur m.

fen [fen] n pantano m.

fence [fens] **1** n cerca f, cercado m, valla f; (person) receptor m de cosas robadas; **to sit on the —** ver los toros desde la barrera; no resolverse, estar a ver venir.
  2 vt cercar; machinery etc cubrir, proteger; **to — in** encerrar con cerca; **to — off** separar con cerca.
  3 vi (Sport) esgrimir; (fig) defenderse con evasivas.

fencer ['fensə*] n esgrimidor m, ora f.

fencing ['fensiŋ] n esgrima f.

fend [fend] **1** vt: **to — off** attack defenderse de, rechazar; blow apartar. **2** vi: **to — for oneself** apañárselas por su cuenta.

fender ['fendə*] n (round fire) guardafuego m; (US Aut) parachoques m; guardafango m; (US Rail) trompa f; (Naut) defensa f.

fennel ['fenl] n hinojo m.

Ferdinand ['fə:dinænd] m Fernando.

ferment ['fə:ment] n (leaven) fermento m; (process) fermentación f; (fig) agitación f, conmoción f; **to be in a —** estar en conmoción.

ferment [fə'ment] **1** vt hacer fermentar. **2** vi fermentar.

fermentation [ˌfə:men'teiʃən] n fermentación f.

fern [fə:n] n helecho m.

ferocious [fə'rəuʃəs] adj feroz.

ferociously [fə'rəuʃəsli] adv ferozmente.

ferocity [fə'rɔsiti] n ferocidad f.

ferret ['ferit] **1** n hurón m. **2** vi: **to — about** buscar revolviéndolo todo; **to — out** person encontrar por fin; secret descubrir, lograr saber.

ferroconcrete ['ferəu'kɔŋkri:t] n ferrohormigón m.

ferrous ['ferəs] adj ferroso.

ferry ['feri] **1** n (small boat) balsa f, barca f (de pasaje); (large, for cars, trains etc) transbordador m.
  2 vt: **to — someone across** llevar a uno a la otra orilla; **to — something across** transportar (or pasar) algo a través del río (etc).

ferryboat ['feribəut] n = **ferry**.

ferryman ['ferimən] n, pl —men [mən] balsero m, barquero m.

fertile ['fə:tail] adj (Agr) fértil (of, in en; also fig); (Bio) fecundo.

fertility [fə'tiliti] n fertilidad f; fecundidad f.

fertilize ['fə:tilaiz] vt fecundar, fertilizar; (Agr) abonar.

fertilizer ['fə:tilaizə*] n fertilizante m, abono m.

fervent ['fə:vənt] adj, **fervid** ['fə:vid] adj fervoroso, ardiente, apasionado.

fervour, (US) **fervor** ['fə:və*] n fervor m, ardor m, pasión f.

fester ['festə*] vi ulcerarse, enconarse; (fig) amargarse.

festival ['festivəl] n fiesta f; (Mus etc) festival m.

festive ['festiv] adj festivo, regocijado; **the — season** las Navidades; **to be in a — mood** estar muy alegre.

festivity [fes'tiviti] n (celebration) fiesta f, festividad f; (joy) regocijo m; **festivities** regocijos mpl, festejos mpl, fiestas fpl.

festoon [fes'tu:n] **1** n adorno m; (Sew) festón m. **2** vt adornar, engalanar, enguirnaldar (with de); **to be —ed with** estar adornado de.

fetch [fetʃ] **1** vt **(a)** (bring) traer; ir por, ir a buscar; (fam) atraer; **I'll go and — it for you** te lo voy a buscar; **please — my coat** ¿me trae el abrigo, por favor?; **they're —ing the doctor** han ido por el médico; **please — the doctor** llame al médico, por favor; **they —ed him all that way** le hicieron venir desde tan lejos; **to — someone back from Spain** hacer que uno vuelva de España; **to — out** sacar; **to — up** (fam) arrojar, vomitar.
  (b) blow, sigh dar; price venderse por, venderse a; **how much did it —?** ¿cuánto dieron por él?
  2 vi: **to — and carry** ir de acá para allá, trajinar; ocuparse en oficios humildes; **to — and carry for someone** ser como el esclavo de uno; **to — up at** ir a parar a.

fetching ['fetʃiŋ] adj atractivo.

fête [feit] **1** n fiesta f; **to be en —** estar en fiestas. **2** vt festejar.

fetid ['fetid] adj fétido.

fetish ['fi:tiʃ] n fetiche m.

fetishism ['fi:tiʃizəm] n fetichismo m.

fetishist ['fi:tiʃist] n fetichista mf.

fetlock ['fetlɔk] n (spur) espolón m; (hair) cernejas fpl.

fetter ['fetə*] vt poner grillos a, encadenar; trabar; (fig) estorbar.

fetters ['fetəz] npl grillos mpl; (fig) trabas fpl.

fettle ['fetl] n: **in fine —** en buenas condiciones; (of mood) de excelente humor.

fetus ['fi:təs] n (US) = **foetus**.

feud [fju:d] **1** n enemistad f heredada (entre dos familias etc), odio m de sangre; disputa f. **2** vi reñir, pelear.

feudal ['fju:dl] adj feudal.

feudalism ['fju:dəlizəm] n feudalismo m.

fever ['fi:və*] n (disease) fiebre f; (high temperature) fiebre f, calentura f; **scarlet —** escarlatina f; **yellow —** fiebre f amarilla; **a — of excitement** una emoción febril; **the gambling —** la fiebre del juego; **to be in a —** tener fiebre.

feverish ['fi:vəriʃ] adj **(a)** (Med) febril, calenturiento; **to be —** tener fiebre. **(b)** (fig) febril.

feverishly ['fi:vəriʃli] adv febrilmente.

few [fju:] adj pocos; algunos, unos; **a —,** some unos pocos, unos cuantos; **a — of us** algunos de nosotros; **quite a —,** not a — no pocos, algunos; **a good —** un buen número (de); **every — minutes** cada pocos minutos; **in the next — days** un día de éstos que vienen; **the —** los pocos, la minoría; **the lucky —** los pocos afortunados; **such men are — and far between** son poquísimos, son contadísimos; **they are —** los hombres así son muy pocos; **they are — and far between** son poquísimos, son contadísimos.

fewer ['fju:ə*] adj comp menos; **— than 10** menos de 10; **— than I** menos que yo; **the — the better** cuantos menos mejor.

fewest ['fju:ist] *adj superl* los menos, las menos, el menor número (de).

fewness ['fju:nis] *n* corto número *m*.

fiancé [fi'ã:nsei] *n* novio *m*, prometido *m*.

fiancée [fi'ã:nsei] *n* novia *f*, prometida *f*.

fiasco [fi'æskəu] *n* fiasco *m*.

fiat ['faiæt] *n* fíat *m*, autorización *f*.

fib [fib] **1** *n* mentirilla *f*, bola *f*. **2** *vi* decir mentirillas.

fibber ['fibə*] *n* mentirosillo *m*, a *f*.

fibre, (US) **fiber** ['faibə*] *n* fibra *f*; (*fig*) nervio *m*, carácter *m*.

fibre-glass, (US) **fiberglass** ['faibəgla:s] *n* fibra *f* de vidrio.

fibrous ['faibrəs] *adj* fibroso.

fibula ['fibjulə] *n* (*Anat*) peroné *m*.

fickle ['fikl] *adj* inconstante, veleidoso, voluble.

fickleness ['fiklnis] *n* inconstancia *f*, veleidad *f*, volubilidad *f*.

fiction ['fikʃən] *n* (*invention*) ficción *f*, invención *f*; (*Lit*) novelas *fpl*, novelística *f*, género *m* novelístico.

fictional ['fikʃnl] *adj* novelesco; relativo a la novela (*etc*).

fictitious [fik'tiʃəs] *adj* ficticio.

fiddle ['fidl] **1** *n* (a) (*Mus*) violín *m*; **to play second —** desempeñar un papel secundario (*to* después de), ser plato de segunda mesa.
(b) (*fam*) trampa *f*, superchería *f*; **tax —** defraudación *f* fiscal, evasión *f* fiscal; **it's a —** aquí hay trampa, son unos tramposos.
2 *vt* (*fam*) *results* falsificar; *job etc* agenciarse, obtener por enchufe; **to — one's income tax** defraudar impuestos.
3 *vi* (*Mus*) tocar el violín; **to — about** perder el tiempo; **to — with** jugar con, manosear; **someone's been fiddling with it** alguno lo ha estropeado.

fiddler ['fidlə*] *n* violinista *mf*.

fiddlesticks ['fidlstiks] *interj* ¡tonterías!

fiddling ['fidliŋ] *adj* trivial, insignificante.

fidelity▮[fi'deliti] *n* fidelidad *f*; **high — (** *abbr*: **hi-fi)** alta fidelidad *f*.

fidget ['fidʒit] **1** *n* persona *f* inquieta, azogado *m*, a *f*; **—s** agitación *f* nerviosa; **to have the —s** tener azogue, no poder estar quieto.
2 *vt* poner nervioso.
3 *vi* tener azogue, agitarse nerviosamente; **don't —!, stop —ing!** ¡estáte quieto!; **to — about** revolverse nerviosamente; **to — with** jugar con.

fidgety ['fidʒiti] *adj* azogado, nervioso; **to be —** tener azogue.

fiduciary [fi'dju:ʃiəri] *adj* fiduciario.

fief [fi:f] *n* feudo *m*.

field [fi:ld] **1** *n* (a) (*Agr*) campo *m* (*also Elec, Her, Mil, Sport*), prado *m*; (*Geol*) yacimiento *m*; **— of battle** campo *m* de batalla; **— of vision** campo *m* visual; **magnetic —** campo *m* magnético; **to be the first in the —** ser el primero en inventar algo (*etc*); **to take the —** salir a palestra.
(b) (*fig*) esfera *f*; especialidad *f*; **— of activity** esfera *f* de actividades, ámbito *m* de acción; **what's your —?** ¿qué especialidad tiene Vd?; **it's not my —** no es de mi competencia.
(c) (*in race etc*) competidores *mpl*, (*in competition*) concurrentes *mpl*, (*for post*) opositores *mpl*, candidatos *mpl*; **is there a strong —?** ¿se ha presentado gente buena?
2 *vt ball* parar, recoger; *team* presentar.

field day ['fi:lddei] *n* (*Mil*) día *m* de maniobras; **to have a —** (*fig*) obtener un gran éxito, triunfar; divertirse muchísimo.

field glasses ['fi:ld,gla:siz] *npl* gemelos *mpl* (de campo), prismáticos *mpl*.

field gun ['fi:ldgʌn] *n* cañón *m* de campaña.

field kitchen ['fi:ld'kitʃin] *n* cocina *f* de campaña.

field marshal ['fi:ld'ma:ʃəl] *n* mariscal *m* de campo; (*Spain*) capitán *m* general del ejército.

field mouse ['fi:ldmaus] *n*, *pl* **— mice** [mais] ratón *m* de campo.

field sports ['fi:ldspɔ:ts] *npl* caza *f*.

fieldwork ['fi:ldwə:k] *n* trabajo *m* en el propio campo.

fiend [fi:nd] *n* demonio *m*, diablo *m*; (*fig*) desalmado *m*; (*for hobby etc*) fanático *m*, a *f*, entusiasta *mf* (*for* de).

fiendish ['fi:ndiʃ] *adj* diabólico.

fierce [fiəs] *adj animal etc* feroz, salvaje; cruel; *look* feroz; *attack* furioso; *wind* violento; *heat*, *competition* intenso; *supporter* acérrimo.

fiercely ['fiəsli] *adv* ferozmente; furiosamente; intensamente.

fierceness ['fiəsnis] *n* ferocidad *f*; furia *f*; intensidad *f*.

fiery ['faiəri] *adj* (*burning*) ardiente; (*red*) rojo; *taste*

muy picante; *temperament*, *speech* apasionado, vehemente; *horse* fogoso; *liquor* muy fuerte.

fife [faif] *n* pífano *m*.

fifteen [fif'ti:n] **1** *adj* quince. **2** *n* quince *m*.

fifteenth [fif'ti:nθ] *adj* decimoquinto.

fifth [fifθ] **1** *adj* quinto. **2** *n* quinta parte *f*, quinto *m*; (*Mus*) quinta *f*.

fiftieth ['fiftiiθ] *adj* quincuagésimo.

fifty ['fifti] *adj* cincuenta; **the fifties** (*eg* 1950s) los años cincuenta; **to be in one's fifties** tener más de cincuenta años; **to go fifty-fifty** ir a medias.

fiftyish ['fiftiiʃ] *adj* cincuentón.

fig [fig] *n* higo *m*; (*early*) breva *f*; (*tree*) higuera *f*.

fight [fait] **1** *n* (a) (*Mil*) combate *m*; (*between* 2 *persons*) pelea *f*; (*struggle*, *campaign*) lucha *f* (*for* por); **in fair —** en buena lid; **to make a — of it** no dejarse vencer fácilmente; **to put up a good —** dar buena cuenta de sí.
(b) (*argument*) disputa *f* (*over* sobre); (*quarrel*, *esp US*) riña *f*, pelea *f*; **to have a — with someone** tener una pelea con uno; **to pick a — with someone** meterse con uno.
(c) (*fighting spirit*) combatividad *f*, ánimo *m* (de pelear), brío *m*; **to show —** enseñar los dientes, mostrarse dispuesto a resistir; **there was no — left in him** no le quedaba ningún ánimo de luchar más.
2 (*irr*: *pret and ptp* **fought**) *vt* (*Mil*) *enemy* batirse con, luchar con (*or* contra); *battle* dar, librar; *bull* lidiar; *fire* luchar por sofocar, combatir; *proposal*, *urge*, *tendency* combatir, resistir, luchar contra; **to — a case** negar una acusación; **we shall — this case all the way** seguiremos luchando por cambiar esta decisión, no nos conformaremos nunca con esta decisión; **to — one's way out** lograr salir luchando; **to — one's way to the sea** abrirse paso luchando hacia el mar; **to — down** reprimir; **to — it out** decidirlo luchando; **to — off** *attack* rechazar, *sleep* sacudirse, *illness etc* luchar por no sucumbir ante.
3 *vi* pelear, luchar (*against* contra, *for* por, *with* con); batirse; **did you — in the war?** ¿fue Vd soldado cuando la guerra?, ¿desempeñó Vd algún papel en la guerra?; **they were —ing over it** lo estaban disputando a golpes; **we shall have to —** tendremos que luchar; **to — back** defenderse, resistir; **to go down —ing** seguir luchando hasta el fin.

fighter ['faitə*] *n* combatiente *mf*; luchador *m*, ora *f* (*for* por); (*warrior*) guerrero *m*, soldado *m*; (*boxer*) boxeador *m*; (*Aer*) caza *m*; **a bonny —** un valiente guerrero.

fighter-bomber ['faitə'bɔmə*] *n* caza-bombardero *m*.

fighter pilot ['faitə'pailət] *n* piloto *m* de caza.

fighting ['faitiŋ] **1** *n* (*in general*) el luchar, el pelear; (*battle*) combate *m*; **the street — lasted all day** se luchó todo el día en las calles; **there has been — in the colony** ha estallado la guerra en la colonia, ha habido disturbios sangrientos en la colonia; **we want no — here** aquí nada de pendencias; **the Irish are fond of —** a los irlandeses les gusta pelearse.
2 *attr*: **— man** guerrero *m*; **— forces** fuerzas *fpl* militares; **— line** frente *m* de combate; **— spirit** combatividad *f*; *see* **cock** *etc*.

fig leaf ['figli:f] *n* (*fig*) hoja *f* de parra.

figment ['figmənt] *n*: **— of the imagination** quimera *f*.

fig tree ['figtri:] *n* higuera *f*.

figurative ['figərətiv] *adj* figurado.

figure ['figə*] **1** *n* (a) (*statue*) figura *f*, estatua *f*.
(b) (*form of body*) tipo *m*, línea *f*, talle *m*, silueta *f*; **a fine — of a man** un hombre de físico imponente; **a fine — of a woman** una real hembra; **she's got a nice —** tiene buen tipo; **to keep one's —** guardar la línea.
(c) (*person*) figura *f*; **public —** figura *f* pública; **the central — in the crisis** la figura más importante de la crisis; **to cut a —** hacer papel; **to cut a sorry —** parecer ridículo, salir desairado.
(d) (*diagram*) figura *f*, dibujo *m*.
(e) (*Math*) (*numeral*) cifra *f*, número *m*, guarismo *m*; (*quantity*) cifra *f*, cantidad *f*; (*price*) precio *m*, (*sum*) suma *f*; **in round —s** en números redondos; **to be good at —s** ser fuerte en aritmética; **to have a five — income** ganar más de 10.000 libras al año; **to reach double —s** llegar a 10, to **reach 3 —s** ascender a 100.
(f) (*Geom*, *Dancing*, *Skating*) figura *f*.
(g) (*Gram*) **— of speech** figura *f*, tropo *m*.
2 *vt* (*in diagram*) representar; (*picture mentally*) representarse, figurarse; (*esp US*) imaginar; **I — it**

like this (US) yo lo veo del modo siguiente; **to —
out** problem resolver; writing descifrar; sum calcular;
I can't — it out at all no me lo explico, no lo
comprendo; **to — up** (US) calcular.
   3 vi (appear) figurar (among entre, as como); constar; **it doesn't —** (US) no tiene sentido; **to — on**
(US) contar con; proyectar; esperar; **to — out** at
venir a ser.
figurehead ['figəhed] n mascarón m de proa; (fig)
figura f decorativa.
figure skating ['figə‚skeitiŋ] n patinaje m de figuras.
filament ['filəmənt] n filamento m.
filch [filtʃ] vt sisar, ratear.
file[1] [fail] **1** n (tool) lima f. **2** vt limar (also **to — away,
to — down, to — off**).
file[2] [fail] **1** n (folder) carpeta f; (dossier) expediente
m; (eg loose-leaf —) archivador m, clasificador m;
(bundle of papers) legajo m; (cabinet) fichero m,
archivo m; **the —s** los archivos; **police —s** archivos
mpl policíacos; **to close the —s** cerrar la carpeta;
to have something on — tener algo archivado.
   2 vt archivar (also **to — away**); clasificar;
registrar; **to — a claim** presentar una reclamación;
to — a petition for divorce entablar pleito de
divorcio.
file[3] [fail] **1** n (row) fila f, hilera f; **Indian — fila** f
india; **in single —** en fila de a uno. **2** vi: **to — in**
entrar en fila; **to — past** desfilar ante.
filial ['filiəl] adj filial.
filiation [‚fili'eiʃən] n filiación f.
filibuster ['filibʌstə*] **1** n (Parl: person) obstruccionista m; (act) maniobra f obstruccionista. **2** vi
usar de maniobras obstruccionistas.
filigree ['filigriː] n filigrana f.
filing cabinet ['failiŋ‚kæbinit] n fichero m, archivo m.
filing clerk ['failiŋ‚klɑːk] n archivero m, a f.
filings ['failiŋz] npl limaduras fpl.
fill [fil] **1** vt llenar (with de); (stuff) rellenar; (charge,
fuel, load) cargar; space llenar completamente,
ocupar completamente; tooth obturar, empastar;
tyre inflar; sail hinchar; post, chair ocupar; vacancy
cubrir; requirement llenar; order despachar; **he —ed
the post very well** desempeñó muy bien el cargo;
to — in llenar; depression terraplenar; form llenar;
details añadir; outline completar; **to — out** (fatten)
engordar; form (US) llenar; **to — up** llenar (hasta
el borde), colmar; form llenar.
   2 vi llenarse (with de; also **to — up**); (sail)
hincharse; **to — in for someone** hacer las veces de
uno, suplir a uno; **to — out** echar carnes, (face)
redondearse; **to — up with fuel** repostar combustible.
   3 n: **to eat one's —** comer bastante; **to have a —
of tobacco** cargar la pipa; **I've had my — of that**
estoy harto ya de eso.
fillet ['filit] **1** n (all senses) filete m. **2** vt fish quitar la
raspa de, cortar en filetes.
filling ['filiŋ] n relleno m; (Mech) empaquetadura f;
(of tooth) obturación f, empaste m.
filling station ['filiŋ‚steiʃən] n estación f de servicio.
fillip ['filip] n (fig) estímulo m; **to give a — to**
estimular.
filly ['fili] n potra f.
film [film] **1** n (thin skin) película f; (of dust) capa f;
(fig) velo m; (Phot, Cine) película f, film m, filme
m (Acad); **the —s** el cine; **silent —** película f muda;
talking — película f sonora; **to make a — of** book
hacer una película de, event filmar.
   2 vt book hacer una película de, event filmar;
scene rodar (at, in en).
   3 vi: **to — over** empañarse, cubrirse con película.
film fan ['filmfæn] n aficionado m, a f, al cine,
cineasta mf.
film library ['film'laibrəri] n cinemateca f.
film star ['filmstɑː*] n astro m, estrella f (de cine).
filmstrip ['filmstrip] n tira f de película.
film studio ['film‚stjuːdiəu] n estudio m (de cine).
filmy ['filmi] adj transparente, diáfano.
filter ['filtə*] **1** n filtro m.
   2 vt filtrar.
   3 vi filtrarse; **to — in, to — through** infiltrarse,
(person etc) introducirse; **to — out** (news) trascender,
llegar a saberse.
filter paper ['filtə‚peipə*] n papel m de filtro.
filter tip ['filtə‚tip] n boquilla f de filtro; **— cigarette**
cigarrillo m emboquillado.
filter-tipped ['filtə‚tipt] adj con filtro, emboquillado.
filth [filθ] n inmundicia f, suciedad f, porquería f;
(fig) inmundicias fpl.
filthy ['filθi] adj inmundo, sucio, puerco; (fig)
inmundo, obsceno.
fin [fin] n (all senses) aleta f.

final ['fainl] **1** adj (last) último, final; (conclusive)
terminante, decisivo, definitivo; exam de fin de
curso; **and that's —** y no hay más que decir.
   2 n (Sport) final f; **—s** (Univ) examen m de fin
de curso.
finale [fi'nɑːli] n (Mus) final m; **grand — final** m
impresionante, final m triunfal.
finalist ['fainəlist] n (Sport) finalista mf.
finality [fai'næliti] n finalidad f; (decision) resolución
f; **he said with —** dijo de modo terminante.
finalize ['fainəlaiz] vt ultimar, completar, concluir,
aprobar de modo definitivo.
finally ['fainəli] adv (lastly) por último, finalmente;
(eventually) por fin; (irrevocably) de modo definitivo.
finance [fai'næns] **1** n (in general) finanzas fpl,
asuntos mpl financieros; (funds) finanzas fpl,
fondos mpl (also **—s**); **the country's —s** la situación
económica del país; **Minister of F—** Ministro m de
Hacienda; **— company** sociedad f financiera.
   2 vt financiar, proveer fondos para.
financial [fai'nænʃəl] adj financiero; policy, resources, year económico.
financier [fai'nænsiə*] n financiero m.
find [faind] (irr: pret and ptp **found**) **1** vt (a) (general
sense) encontrar, hallar; descubrir; (stumble on) dar
con, tropezar con; **where did you — it?** ¿dónde lo
encontraste?; **how did you — him?** (in health)
¿qué tal le encontraste?; **it's found all over Spain**
se encuentra (or existe) en todas partes de España;
it's not to be found no se encuentra en ninguna
parte; **I now — it is not so** ahora descubro que no
es así; **it has been found that** se ha comprobado
que; **to — out** averiguar, (llegar a) saber; **to —
someone out** conocer el juego de uno, calar a uno;
his pride found him out su orgullo le traicionó.
   (b) (supply, obtain) facilitar, proporcionar,
proveer; **we found him a car** le facilitamos un
coche; **if you can — the time** si Vd tiene el tiempo;
can you — the money? ¿podrás reunir el dinero?;
they found half the cost lograron hacerse con la
mitad del precio; **all found** todo incluido.
   (c) (with adj) **you will not — it easy** no le será
fácil (to do hacer); **I found it impossible** me fue
imposible (to go ir); **I — the house small** la casa me
resulta pequeña; (Law) see **guilty.**
   2 vi: **to — for the defendant** fallar a favor del
demandado; **to — out about** informarse sobre,
buscar detalles acerca de; **we didn't — out about
it in time** no nos enteramos a tiempo.
   3 vr: **to — oneself** encontrarse; verse; **I found
myself alone** me encontré solo; **I — myself at a loss**
me encuentro perplejo; **he found himself** descubrió
su verdadera vocación (or identidad etc).
   4 n hallazgo m.
finder ['faində*] n descubridor m, ora f, el (la) que
encuentra algo.
finding ['faindiŋ] n descubrimiento m; **—s** (Law etc)
fallo m; (of report etc) recomendaciones fpl.
fine[1] [fain] **1** adj (a) (delicate, small) thread fino, sutil;
particle, print menudo; line tenue; pencil, nib
delgado; edge muy afilado; distinction delicado, sutil.
   (b) (good) bueno; (beautiful) bello, hermoso;
(exquisitely made) fino, delicado, primoroso; dress
elegante; (showy) vistoso; (imposing) magnífico,
imponente; (selected) escogido; (pure) refinado, puro;
ideal bello; day bueno; feeling elevado, noble;
person admirable; (accomplished) excelente, experto;
—! ¡magnífico!, ¡estupendo!; to be — (weather)
hacer buen tiempo; **it's a — thing to +** infin es
admirable + infin.
   (c) (iro) bueno, lindo, valiente; **that's all very
—, but . . .** todo eso está muy bien, pero . . .; **a —
friend you are!** ¡valiente amigo!; **you're a — one!**
¡estás tú bueno!, ¡qué tío!
   2 adv (a) (fam) muy bien; **you're doing —** lo estás
haciendo la mar de bien; **to feel —** estar como un
reloj.
   (b) to chop something up — cortar algo en
trozos menudos; **to cut (or run) it —** llegar con
muy poco tiempo, dejarse muy poco tiempo.
   3 vi: **to — down** adelgazar.
fine[2] [fain] **1** n multa f. **2** vt multar.
fine-drawn ['fain'drɔːn] adj estirado en un hilo muy
delgado; wire muy delgado; distinction etc sutil, fino.
fine-grained ['fain'greind] adj de grano fino.
finely ['fainli] adv (a) sutilmente; menudamente.
(b) hermosamente; primorosamente; elegantemente;
vistosamente. **(c)** (iro) lindamente.
finery ['fainəri] n galas fpl, adornos mpl, trajes mpl
vistosos.
finesse [fi'nes] **1** n (in judgement) discriminación f
sutil, discernimiento m; (in action) diplomacia f,

tino *m*, sutileza *f*; (*cunning*) astucia *f*; (*Cards*) impase m. **2** *vt* hacer el impase a.

finger ['fiŋgə*] **1** *n* dedo *m*; **first —, index —** dedo *m* índice; **little —** dedo *m* meñique; **middle —** dedo *m* del corazón; **ring —** dedo *m* anular; **his —s are all thumbs** es terriblemente desmañado; **to burn one's —s, to get one's —s burned** (*fig*) cogerse los dedos; **to have green —s** tener mucha habilidad en jardinería; **to have a —** in the pie meter su cucharada; **they never laid a — on her** no la tocaron en absoluto; **he didn't lift a — to help** no movió un dedo para ayudarnos; **to point the — of scorn at someone** señalar a uno con el dedo; **to put one's — on** (*fig*) concretar, señalar acertadamente; **to put one's — on it** (*or* **on the spot**) poner el dedo en la llaga; **there was nothing you could put your —** on no habia nada concreto; **he slipped through their —s** se les escapó entre los dedos; **to snap one's —s at someone** (*fig*) tratar a uno con desprecio; **to twist someone round one's little —** hacer con uno lo que le da la gana.

2 *vt* manosear, tocar; (*Mus*) tocar (distraídamente).

fingering ['fiŋgəriŋ] *n* (*Mus*) digitación *f*.

fingernail ['fiŋgəneil] *n* uña *f*.

fingerprint ['fiŋgəprint] **1** *n* huella *f* dactilar. **2** *vt* tomar las huellas dactilares a.

fingerstall ['fiŋgəstɔ:l] *n* dedil *m*.

fingertip ['fiŋgətip] *n* punta *f* (*or* yema *f*) del dedo; **to have something at one's —s** saber algo al dedillo.

finicky ['finiki] *adj* delicado, melindroso, superferolítico.

finish ['finiʃ] **1** *n* (a) (*end*) fin *m*, final *m*, conclusión *f*; remate *m*; (*Sport*) poste *m* de llegada; **to be in at the —** estar presente en la conclusión; **to fight to a —** seguir luchando hasta decidir la victoria.

(b) (*of manufactured article*) acabado *m*; **gloss(y) —** acabado *m* brillo; **to have a rough —** estar sin pulir.

2 *vt* (a) (*also* **to — off, to — up**) terminar, acabar, concluir; completar, llevar a cabo, rematar; dar la última mano a; **I'm —ed** (*tired*) estoy rendido; **he's —ed now** (*fig*) se acabó para él, ahora no vale para nada; **as a film star she's —ed** como estrella está acabada; **to — off** (*kill*) despachar, (*destroy*) acabar con; **to — up** *food* terminar de comer, *drink* terminar de beber.

(b) (*Tech*) acabar; **—ed goods** productos *mpl* acabados.

3 *vi* (a) terminar, acabar; **to — doing something** terminar de hacer algo; **to — by saying that** terminar diciendo que; **to — up at** ir a parar a; **to — with** terminar con; **she —ed with him** rompió con él; **wait till I've —ed with him!** ¡a ver lo que le voy a hacer!

(b) (*Sport*) llegar; **to — third** llegar el tercero.

finishing line ['finiʃiŋ lain] *n* línea *f* de meta.

finishing school ['finiʃiŋ sku:l] *n* escuela *f* particular de educación social para señoritas.

finite ['fainait] *adj* finito (*also Gram*), que tiene fin.

Finland ['finlənd] Finlandia *f*.

Finn [fin] *n* finlandés *m*, esa *f*.

Finnish ['finiʃ] **1** *adj* finlandés. **2** *n* (*language*) finlandés *m*.

fiord [fjɔ:d] *n* fiordo *m*.

fir [fə:*] *n* abeto *m*.

fir cone ['fə:kəun] *n* piña *f* (de abeto).

fire [faiə*] **1** *n* (a) (*in general*) fuego *m*; (*accidental*, *damaging*) incendio *m*; (*in grate*) fuego *m*, lumbre *f*; **electric —** estufa *f* eléctrica; **to be on —** estar ardiendo, estar en llamas; **to catch —** encenderse; **to cook something on a slow —** cocer algo a fuego lento; **to hang —** demorarse, estar en suspenso; **to make up a —** echar carbón a la lumbre; **to play with —** jugar con fuego; **to set on —, to set — to** pegar (*or* prender) fuego a, incendiar; **to sit by** (*or* **round**) **the —** estar sentado al lado de la chimenea; **to take —** encenderse.

(b) (*Mil*) **to open —** abrir fuego, romper el fuego; **to be under —** (*fig*) ser criticado.

(c) (*fig*) ardor *m*, pasión *f*; entusiasmo *m*; **the — of youth** el ardor de la juventud; **men with — in their bellies** hombres llenos de celo idealista.

2 *vt* (a) (*set — to*) encender, incendiar, pegar fuego a, quemar; *bricks*, *pottery* cocer.

(b) *gun*, *shot*, *salute* disparar; *torpedo*, *rocket* lanzar; *person* (*fam*) despedir; **to — a question at someone** disparar una pregunta inesperada a uno.

(c) (*fig*) *imagination* excitar, enardecer, exaltar; *interest* despertar; (*inspire*) inspirar.

3 *vi* (a) (*catch —*) encenderse; **to — up** (*fig*) ponerse furioso.

(b) (*Mil*) hacer fuego; **to — at, to — on** hacer fuego sobre, tirar a; **they were firing at each other all day** se estaban tiroteando todo el día; **—! ¡fuego!; — away!** (*fig*) ¡adelante!

(c) (*Aut*) dar explosiones; **the engine is not firing on one cylinder** uno de los cilindros del motor no se enciende.

fire alarm ['faiər͵lɑ:m] *n* alarma *f* de incendios.

firearm ['faiərɑ:m] *n* arma *f* de fuego.

fireball ['faiəbɔ:l] *n* bola *f* de fuego.

firebrand ['faiəbrænd] *n* tea *f*; (*fig*) partidario *m* violento, revoltoso m.

firebrick ['faiəbrik] *n* ladrillo *m* refractario.

fire brigade ['faiəbri͵geid] *n* cuerpo *m* de bomberos.

fire curtain ['faiə͵kə:tn] *n* (*Theat*) telón *m* a prueba de incendios.

firedamp ['faiədæmp] *n* grisú m.

fire engine ['faiər͵endʒin] *n* bomba *f* de incendios, coche *m* de bomberos.

fire escape ['faiəris͵keip] *n* escalera *f* de incendios.

fire extinguisher ['faiəriks'tiŋgwiʃə*] *n* extintor *m*.

firefly ['faiəflai] *n* luciérnaga *f*.

fireguard ['faiəgɑ:d] *n* alambrera *f*, guardafuego *m*.

fire insurance ['faiərin͵ʃuərəns] *n* seguro *m* contra incendios.

fire irons ['faiər͵aiənz] *n* útiles *mpl* de chimenea.

firelighter ['faiə͵laitə*] *n* astillas *fpl* (para encender el fuego), tea *f*.

fireman ['faiəmən] *n*, *pl* **—men** [mən] bombero *m*; (*Rail*) fogonero m.

fireplace ['faiəpleis] *n* chimenea *f*; (*hearth*) hogar *m*.

fireproof ['faiəpru:f] *adj* incombustible, a prueba de fuego.

fire-raiser ['faiə͵reizə*] *n* incendiario *m*.

fire-raising ['faiə͵reiziŋ] *n* (delito *m* de) incendiar *m*, incendio m.

fireside ['faiəsaid] **1** *n* hogar m. **2** *attr* hogareño, doméstico, familiar.

fire station ['faiə͵steiʃən] *n* parque *m* de bomberos.

firewood ['faiəwud] *n* leña *f*, astillas *fpl*.

fireworks ['faiəwə:ks] *npl* fuegos *mpl* artificiales; (*fig*) explosión *f* (de cólera *etc*); **there will be — at the meeting** (*fig*) en la reunión se va a armar la gorda.

firing ['faiəriŋ] *n* (*Mil*) disparo *m*, (*continuous*) tiroteo *m*, cañoneo *m*; (*Aut*) encendido *m*; (*of bricks etc*) cocción f.

firing line ['faiəriŋlain] *n* línea *f* de fuego.

firing squad ['faiəriŋskwɔd] *n* pelotón *m* de ejecución.

firm[1] [fə:m] *adj* firme; (*Comm*) *offer*, *order* en firme; **as — as a rock** tan firme como una roca; **he was very — about it** se mostró muy decidido, lo dijo de modo terminante; **to stand —** mantenerse firme.

firm[2] [fə:m] *n* firma *f*, empresa *f*, casa *f* de comercio.

firmament ['fə:məmənt] *n* firmamento *m*.

firmly ['fə:mli] *adv* firmemente; con firmeza.

firmness ['fə:mnis] *n* firmeza *f*.

first [fə:st] **1** *adj* primero; primitivo, original; *edition* príncipe.

2 *adv* primero; (*firstly*) en primer lugar; (*for the first time*) por primera vez; **— of all, — and foremost** ante todo; **head —** de cabeza; **stern —** la popa por delante; **ladies —** las señoras pasan primero; **women and children —!** ¡primero las mujeres y los niños!; **to get in —** (*fig*) madrugar; **to go —** entrar (*etc*) el primero, (*Rail*) viajar en primera; **you go —!** ¡Vd primero!, ¡pase Vd!

3 *n* primero *m*, a *f*; (*Univ*) primera clase *f*, sobresaliente *m*; **at —** al principio; **I didn't see them at —** no les vi de momento; **from the —** desde el principio; **from — to last** desde el principio hasta el fin; **to be the — to do something** ser el primero en hacer algo; **he came in an easy —** llegó con mucho el primero, obtuvo fácilmente la victoria.

first aid ['fə:st'eid] **1** *n* primera curación *f*, primeros auxilios *mpl*. **2** *attr* **first-aid: — box, — kit** botiquín *m*; **— post** puesto *m* de socorro.

first-born ['fə:stbɔ:n] *n* primogénito *m*, a *f*.

first-class ['fə:stklɑ:s] *adj* de primera clase.

first-hand ['fə:st'hænd] *adj* de primera mano; directo, personal; **at —** directamente.

firstly ['fə:stli] *adv* en primer lugar.

first-nighter ['fə:st'naitə*] *n* estrenista *mf*.

first-rate ['fə:st'reit] *adj* de primera clase.

firth [fə:θ] *n* estuario *m*, ría *f*.

fir tree ['fə:tri:] *n* abeto *m*.

fiscal ['fiskəl] *adj* fiscal; monetario; *policy*, *year* económico.

fish [fiʃ] **1** *n* pez *m*, (*as food*) pescado *m*; (*fam*) tío *m*; **queer —** tipo *m* raro; **he's a poor —** es un pobre hombre; **to be like a — out of water** estar como pez fuera del agua; **to have other — to fry** tener cosas más importantes que hacer.

2 *vt river* pescar en; **to — out, to — up** sacar.

3 *vi* pescar; **to — for** (tratar de) pescar; *compliment etc* andar a la pesca de; **he —ed in his pocket for it** lo buscó en el bolsillo; **to go —ing** ir de pesca.

fishbone ['fiʃbəun] *n* raspa *f*, espina *f* de pez.

fishbowl ['fiʃbəul] *n* pecera *f*.

fisherman ['fiʃəmən] *n*, *pl* **—men** [mən] pescador *m*.

fishery ['fiʃəri] *n* pesquería *f*, pesquera *f*.

fish glue ['fiʃglu:] *n* cola *f* de pescado.

fish hook ['fiʃhuk] *n* anzuelo *m*.

fishing ['fiʃiŋ] *n* pesca *f*.

fishing boat ['fiʃiŋbəut] *n* barca *f* pesquera.

fishing grounds ['fiʃiŋgraundz] *npl* pesquería *f*.

fishing line ['fiʃiŋlain] *n* sedal *m*.

fishing net ['fiʃiŋnet] *n* red *f* de pesca.

fishing rod ['fiʃiŋrɔd] *n* caña *f* de pescar.

fishing tackle ['fiʃiŋ,tækl] *n* aparejo *m* de pescar.

fish manure ['fiʃmə,njuə*] *n* abono *m* de pescado.

fish market ['fiʃmɑːkit] *n* mercado *m* de pescado, pescadería *f*.

fishmonger ['fiʃmʌŋgə*] *n* pescadero *m*; **—'s (shop)** pescadería *f*.

fishplate ['fiʃpleit] *n* (*Rail*) eclisa *f*.

fishpond ['fiʃpɔnd] *n* piscina *f*, vivero *m*.

fish slice ['fiʃslais] *n* pala *f* para el pescado.

fishwife ['fiʃwaif] *n*, *pl* **—wives** [waivz] pescadera *f*; (*pej*) verdulera *f*.

fishy ['fiʃi] *adj eye* como de pez; (*of taste*) que sabe a pescado, (*of smell*) que huele a pescado; (*fam*) sospechoso; **it's —** me huele a camelo; **there's something — going on here** aquí hay gato encerrado.

fissile ['fisail] *adj* físil.

fission ['fiʃən] *n* (*Phys*) fisión *f*; (*Bio*) escisión *f*; **nuclear —** fisión *f* nuclear.

fissionable ['fiʃnəbl] *adj* fisionable.

fissure ['fiʃə*] *n* grieta *f*, hendedura *f*; (*Anat, Geol, Metal*) fisura *f*.

fissured ['fiʃəd] *adj* agrietado.

fist [fist] *n* puño *m*; (*writing*) letra *f*; **to shake one's — at someone** amenazar a uno con el puño.

fistful ['fistful] *n* puñado *m*.

fisticuffs ['fistikʌfs] *npl* puñetazos *mpl*.

fit¹ [fit] **1** *adj* (**a**) adecuado, conveniente, apto, a propósito, apropiado (*for* para); hábil, capaz; **the —test** (*Bio*) los mejor dotados; **— for duty** apto para servicio; **a meal — for a king** una comida digna de un rey; **to be — for** ser adecuado para; **he's not — for the job** no es adecuado para el puesto, no merece que se le dé el puesto; **he's not — to teach** no tiene madera de profesor; **he is not — to drive** no es apto para conducir; **— to eat** bueno de comer; **it's not — to eat** no se puede comer, es incomible; **it's not — to be seen** es indigno de que lo vean las gentes; **is this — to wear?** ¿puedo ponerme esto?; **I felt — to drop** tuve ganas de caerme rendido; **to see** (*or* **think**) **— to** + *infin* estimar conveniente + *infin*; **he saw — to** + *infin* (*iro*) se vio en el caso de + *infin*; **do as you think —** haga lo que mejor le parezca.

(**b**) (*Med*) sano, bien de salud; en buen estado físico, (*Sport*) en forma; **3 players are not —** 3 jugadores están lesionados; **come when you're — again** ven cuando te hayas repuesto del todo; **to be as — as a fiddle** andar como un reloj; **are you —?** (*fam*) ¿estás listo?, ¿vamos?; **to get —** (*Sport*) entrenarse, (*Med*) reponerse; **to keep —** mantenerse en forma, mantenerse en buen estado físico.

2 *as adv*: **to laugh — to burst** desternillarse de risa.

3 *vt* (**a**) (*make suitable*) ajustar, acomodar, adaptar (*to* a); **to — someone for a post** capacitar a uno para un puesto.

(**b**) (*suit*) *description, facts* cuadrar con, corresponder con, estar de acuerdo con; *colour scheme etc* hacer juego con; (*of dress etc*) sentar bien a, ir bien a.

(**c**) (*try on*) *clothes* probar (*on* a).

(**d**) (*fill up, exactly correspond to*) encajar en; **it —s the space perfectly** encaja perfectamente en el espacio; **the key does not — the lock** la llave no entra en la cerradura.

(**e**) (*put*) **to — two things together** unir dos cosas; **I —ted A into B** encajé A en B; **you — it in here** se encaja aquí, se coloca aquí; **to — the key into the lock** introducir la llave en la cerradura; **can you — me in?** ¿puede incluirme?; **I'll see if the director can — you in** voy a ver si el director tiene tiempo para verle; **I —ted in a trip to Ávila** logré hacer una excursión a Ávila.

(**f**) (*supply*) **to — something with** proveer algo de; **to — someone out** (*or* **up**) **with** proveer a uno de, equipar a uno con; **—ted with a heater** provisto de un calentador, dotado de un calentador; **I'm having a new door —ted** me van a colocar una nueva portezuela; **to — out a ship** armar un buque; **to — up** montar, instalar; *see also* **fitted**.

4 *vi* (**a**) (*correspond*) corresponder, estar de acuerdo; **the facts don't —** los datos no tienen sentido; **it all —s** todo hace un conjunto lógico.

(**b**) (*of clothes etc*) entallar; **the suit —s well** el traje le sienta bien.

(**c**) (*of person*) **he —s in well here** aquí se lleva bien con todos; **I don't — in here** aquí no estoy bien.

(**d**) (*of space*) encajarse; caber; **it —s in here, it —s on here** se encaja aquí; **do they —?** ¿se encajan uno en otro?; **does it —?** ¿cabe?; **it won't — in here** aquí no cabe; **the key doesn't —** la llave no sirve; **the key —s into the lock** la llave se ajusta a la cerradura.

5 *n* ajuste *m*, corte *m*; **it's a good —** le sienta bien; **the suit is a tight —** el traje me viene bastante estrecho.

fit² [fit] *n* (*Med*) acceso *m*, ataque *m*; **— of anger** arranque *m* de cólera; **— of coughing** acceso *m* de tos; **fainting —** síncope *m*; **by —s and starts a** rachas, a empujones; **we were in —s (of laughter)** moríamos de risa; **he'd have a — if he knew** le daría un ataque si lo supiera.

fitful ['fitful] *adj* espasmódico, caprichoso.

fitfully ['fitfəli] *adv* espasmódicamente, a rachas, por intervalos.

fitment ['fitmənt] *n* mueble *m*.

fitness ['fitnis] *n* (*suitability*) conveniencia *f*, oportunidad *f*; (*for post etc*) idoneidad *f*, capacidad *f*; (*Med*) (buena) salud *f*, (buen) estado *m* físico.

fitted ['fitid] *adj suit, carpet* hecho a medida; *cupboard* empotrado; **to be — for something** tener talento para algo, ser idóneo para algo.

fitter ['fitə*] *n* (*Mech*) (mecánico *m*) ajustador *m*.

fitting ['fitiŋ] **1** *adj* (*suitable*) conveniente, adecuado; (*worthy*) digno; **it is — that** es propio que + *subj*, es justo que + *subj*; **it is not — that** no está bien que + *subj*.

2 *n* (*of dress*) prueba *f*; (*size*) medida *f*; **—s** guarniciones *fpl*; **bathroom —s** aparatos *mpl* sanitarios; **electrical —s** accesorios *mpl* eléctricos; **furniture and —s** muebles *mpl* y enseres.

fittingly ['fitiŋli] *adv* convenientemente, adecuadamente; dignamente; **—, it was he who . . .** según cabía razonablemente esperar, era él quien . . .

five [faiv] **1** *adj* cinco. **2** *n* cinco *m*.

fiver ['faivə*] *n* (*fam*) billete *m* de 5 libras.

five-year ['faiv'jiə*] *adj*: **— plan** plan *m* quinquenal.

fix [fiks] **1** *vt* (**a**) (*secure*) fijar, asegurar, sujetar; *bayonet* calar; (*Phot*) fijar; **to — something in one's memory** grabar algo en la memoria.

(**b**) (*direct*) *attention* fijar (*on* en); *eyes* clavar (*on* en); *hopes* poner (*on* en); *blame* echar (*on* a).

(**c**) **to — someone with one's eyes** fijar los ojos en uno.

(**d**) (*place*) fijar (*at* en).

(**e**) (*determine position of*) fijar, precisar.

(**f**) (*determine*) *author, date etc* fijar, señalar; *price* fijar, determinar.

(**g**) (*arrange, prepare; also* **to — up**) arreglar; decidir; organizar, preparar; **it's all —ed up** todo está arreglado; **there is nothing —ed yet** todavía no se ha decidido nada.

(**h**) (*US*) dar, servir, preparar; **can I — you a drink?** ¿le traigo algo de beber?; **I'll — you some supper** te prepararé una cena.

(**i**) (*repair*) componer, arreglar.

(**j**) **he —ed it with the police** se las arregló con la policía.

(**k**) **I'll — him!** ¡me lo cargaré!; **that ought to — him** eso ha de acabar con él.

(**l**) **to — someone up with something** proveer a uno de algo.

(**m**) (*Sport etc*) *game, jury* amañar; **it's been —ed!** ¡hay tongo!

(**n**) **how are we —ed for time?** ¿tenemos tiempo?; **how are we —ed for money?** ¿qué tal andamos de dinero?

2 *vi*: **to — on** escoger; *date etc* fijar, señalar; **to — up with someone** arreglarlo con uno; **to — up with someone to** + *infin* convenir con uno en + *infin*.

3 *n* (*Aer etc*) posición *f*; (*fam*) aprieto *m*; **to be in a —** estar en un aprieto.

fixation [fik'seiʃən] *n* fijación *f*.

fixative ['fiksətiv] *n* fijativo *m*.

fixed [fikst] *adj* (*all senses*) fijo.

fixedly ['fiksidli] *adv* fijamente.

fixings ['fiksiŋz] *npl* (*US*) accesorios *mpl*, guarniciones *fpl*.

fixture ['fikstʃə*] *n* cosa *f* fija; (*furniture etc*) mueble *m* fijo, instalación *f* fija; (*Sport*) partido *m*, encuentro *m*; (*person*) cliente *m* fijo; **lighting —s** (*US*) guarniciones *fpl* de alumbrado.

fizz [fiz] **1** *n* efervescencia *f*; (*noise*) ruido *m* sibilante; (*fam*) gaseosa *f*. **2** *vi* estar (*or* entrar) en efervescencia; hacer un ruido sibilante.

fizzle ['fizl] = **fizz**; (*vi*) **to — out** apagarse; (*fig*) no dar resultado, fracasar.

fizzy ['fizi] *adj* gaseoso, espumoso, efervescente.

flabbergast ['flæbəgɑːst] *vt* pasmar, dejar sin habla; **I was —ed by the news** la noticia me causó estupor.

flabby ['flæbi] *adj* flojo, fofo, blanducho; (*fat*) gordo; (*fig*) débil, soso.

flaccid ['flæksid] *adj* fláccido.

flaccidity [flæk'siditi] *n* flaccidez *f*.

flag¹ [flæg] *n* (*Bot*) lirio *m*.

flag² [flæg] *n* (*stone*) losa *f*.

flag³ [flæg] **1** *n* bandera *f*, pabellón *m*; (*small, charity etc*) banderita *f*; (*small, as souvenir, also Sport*) banderín *m*; **— of convenience** bandera *f* de conveniencia; **— of truce, white —** bandera *f* de parlamento; **red —** bandera *f* roja; **to keep the — flying** seguir defendiéndose, resistir, no rendir la bandera; **to show the —** hacer acto de presencia.
2 *vt* hacer señales con una bandera a; **to — someone down** hacer señales a uno para que se detenga.

flag⁴ [flæg] *vi* (*strength*) acabarse, flaquear, decaer; (*enthusiasm etc*) enfriarse; (*conversation*) languidecer.

flag day ['flægdei] *n* día *m* de la banderita.

flagellate ['flædʒəleit] *vt* flagelar.

flagellation [ˌflædʒə'leiʃən] *n* flagelación *f*.

flagon ['flægən] *n* (*approx*) jarro *m*; (*as measure*) botella *de unos 2 litros*.

flagpole ['flægpəul] *n* asta *f* de bandera.

flagrant ['fleigrənt] *adj* notorio, escandaloso.

flagship ['flægʃip] *n* buque *m* insignia, buque *m* almirante, buque *m* escuadra, (*arch*) capitana *f*.

flagstaff ['flægstɑːf] *n* asta *f* de bandera.

flagstone ['flægstəun] *n* losa *f*.

flail [fleil] **1** *n* mayal *m*. **2** *vt* (*fig*) golpear, azotar. **3** *vi*: **to — about** debatirse.

flair [fleə*] *n* instinto *m*, aptitud *f* especial (*for* para).

flak [flæk] *n* fuego *m* antiaéreo.

flake [fleik] **1** *n* escama *f*, hojuela *f*; (*of snow*) copo *m*.
2 *vt* separar en escamas; **to be —d out** (*fam*) estar rendido.
3 *vi* (*also* **to — away, to — off**) desprenderse en escamas; **to — out** (*fam*) caer rendido.

flaky ['fleiki] *adj* escamoso; desmenuzable.

flamboyant [flæm'bɔiənt] *adj* (*Archit etc*) flameante; *dress etc* vistoso, llamativo; *character, speech* extravagante; *style* rimbombante.

flame [fleim] **1** *n* llama *f*; (*fam*) novio *m*, a *f*; **to be in —s** arder en llamas; **to burst into —s** estallar en llamas; **to commit something to the —s** entregar algo a las llamas; **to fan the —s** soplar el fuego.
2 *vi* (*burn*) llamear; (*shine*) brillar; **to — up** (*fig*) estallar, (*person*) inflamarse.

flamethrower ['fleimˌθrəuə*] *n* lanzallamas *m*.

flaming ['fleimiŋ] *adj* (*fam*) condenado.

flamingo [flə'miŋgəu] *n* flamenco *m*.

flan [flæn] *n* tarta *f*, tarteleta *f* de fruta.

Flanders ['flɑːndəz] Flandes *m*.

flange [flændʒ] *n* pestaña *f*, reborde *m*.

flanged [flændʒd] *adj* con pestaña.

flank [flæŋk] **1** *n* (*of person*) costado *m*; (*of animal*) ijada *f*; (*of hill*) lado *m*, falda *f*; (*Mil*) flanco *m*.
2 *vt* lindar con, estar contiguo a; (*Mil etc*) flanquear; **it is —ed by hills** tiene unas colinas a su lado; **he was —ed by two policemen** iba escoltado por dos guardias.

flannel ['flænl] **1** *n* (*cloth*) franela *f*; (*face-*) manopla *f*, paño *m*; (*sl*) jabón *m*, coba *f*, (*waffle*) paja *f*; **—s** (*trousers*) pantalones *mpl* de franela, (*underclothes*) ropa *f* interior de lana.
2 *adj* de franela.
3 *vt* (*sl*) dar coba a.
4 *vi* (*sl*) llenar muchos renglones (*etc*) sin decir nada de valor.

flannelette [ˌflænə'let] *n* moletón *m*.

flap [flæp] **1** *n* (*a*) (*on dress*) faldilla *f*; (*of pocket*) cartera *f*; (*of envelope*) solapa *f*; (*of table*) hoja *f* plegadiza; (*of counter*) trampa *f*; (*of skin*) colgajo *m*; (*Aer*) flap *m*.
(b) (*of wing*) aletazo *m*, movimiento *m*.
(c) (*fam*) (*crisis*) crisis *f*; (*row*) lío *m*; **there's a big — on** hay una crisis; **se ha armado un lío**

imponente; **to get into a —** ponerse nervioso, inquietarse.
2 *vt wings* batir; (*shake*) sacudir; *arms* agitar.
3 *vi* (*wings*) aletear; (*sail*) sacudirse; (*flag etc*) ondear, agitarse; (*fam*) ponerse nervioso, inquietarse; **don't —!** ¡con calma!

flapjack ['flæpdʒæk] *n* hojuela *f*.

flare [fleə*] **1** *n* (*a*) (*blaze*) llamarada *f*; (*signal*) cohete *m* de señales, (*Mil*) bengala *f*, proyectil *m* de iluminación; **landing —** bengala *f* de aterrizaje; **solar —** erupción *f* solar.
(b) (*Sew*) vuelo *m*.
2 *vt* (*Sew*) abocinar, acampanar.
3 *vi* (*a*) (*blaze*) llamear, resplandecer, fulgurar; (*shine*) brillar; **to — up** encenderse.
(b) to — up (*fig: person*) encolerizarse; (*revolt etc*) estallar; (*epidemic*) declararse.
(c) (*skirt*) acampanarse.

flare path ['fleəpɑːθ] *n, pl* **paths** [pɑːðz] baliza *f*.

flare-up ['fleərʌp] *n* (*fig: of anger*) arranque *m* de cólera; (*quarrel*) riña *f*; (*of trouble*) manifestación *f* súbita, estallido *m*.

flash [flæʃ] **1** *n* (*a*) (*of light*) relámpago *m*; destello *m*, ráfaga *f*; (*of gun*) fogonazo *m*; **— of lightning** relámpago *m*; **like a —** como un relámpago.
(b) (*moment*) instante *m*; **in a —** en un instante.
(c) — of inspiration ráfaga *f* de inspiración; **— of wit** rasgo *m* de ingenio; **— in the pan** esfuerzo *m* abortado, éxito *m* único; **it was just a — in the pan** eso fue un éxito excepcional que no se puede repetir.
(d) (*news-*) flash *m*, noticia *f* de última hora; mensaje *m* urgente.
(e) (*Phot*) flash *m*, magnesio *m*.
2 *vt* (*a*) *light* despedir, lanzar; *look* dirigir, lanzar (*rápidamente*); *message* transmitir por heliógrafo, transmitir por radio, (*fig*) transmitir rápidamente.
(b) (*torch*) encender; **— it this way** proyéctala por aquí; **he —ed the light in my eyes** hizo brillar la luz delante de mis ojos.
(c) to — something about sacar algo a relucir, hacer ostentación de algo.
3 *vi* relampaguear, destellar; (*window, reflection*) brillar; **to — past** pasar como un rayo.

flashback ['flæʃbæk] *n* escena *f* retrospectiva.

flash bulb ['flæʃbʌlb] *n* bombilla *f* fusible.

flashlight ['flæʃlait] *n* (*Phot*) flash *m*; (*torch*) linterna *f* eléctrica.

flash point ['flæʃpɔint] *n* punto *m* de inflamación.

flashy ['flæʃi] *adj jewel etc* de relumbrón; *car etc* ostentoso; *person* charro, chulo.

flask [flɑːsk] *n* frasco *m*; redoma *f*; (*vacuum-*) termo *m*, termos *m*; (*Chem*) matraz *m*.

flat [flæt] **1** *adj* (*a*) (*level*) *countryside etc* llano; *object* plano; horizontal; (*smooth*) liso, igual; *tyre* desinflado; *foot* plano; *nose* chato; *finish, surface* mate; *rate* uniforme, igual; **400 metres —** 400 metros lisos; **as — as a pancake** *countryside* totalmente llano, (*after bombing*) desnudo como la palma de la mano; **the town was just —** la ciudad quedó totalmente arrasada.
(b) (*downright*) terminante, categórico; **and that's —** no hay más que decir.
(c) (*Mus*) *voice, instrument* desafinado; *key* bemol; **E — major** mi bemol mayor.
(d) (*dull, lifeless*) *taste, style* insípido, soso; *drink* muerto; *battery* descargado; *tone* monótono; *lecture etc* aburrido, pesado; *business* flojo; *feeling* de abatimiento; **to be feeling rather —** sentirse algo deprimido.
2 *adv* (*a*) **to fall —** (*on one's face*) caer de bruces, caer de boca; **to fall —** (*joke*) caer mal, no hacer gracia a uno, (*suggestion*) caer en el vacío; **to be lying down —** estar tendido; **to put something — on the table** extender algo sobre la mesa.
(b) (*Mus*) **to sing —, to play —** desafinar.
(c) to be — broke no tener ni un céntimo; **to go — out** ir a máxima velocidad; **to go — out for something** tratar de conseguir algo por todos los medios; **to turn something down —** rechazar algo de plano.
3 *n* (*rooms*) piso *m*, apartamento *m*; (*of hand*) palma *f*; (*of sword*) plano *m*; (*Mus*) bemol *m*; (*Aut, esp US*) pinchazo *m*, neumático *m* pinchado.

flat-chested ['flæt'tʃestid] *adj* de pecho plano.

flatfish ['flætfiʃ] *n* pez *m* pleuronecto (*eg platija, lenguado*).

flatfooted ['flæt'futid] *adj* que tiene los pies planos; (*fig*) torpe, desmañado.

flatiron ['flætˌaiən] *n* plancha *f*.

flatlet ['flætlit] *n* piso *m* pequeño.

flatly ['flætli] *adv refuse etc* de plano; *deny* terminantemente; **we are — opposed to** quedamos totalmente opuestos a.

flatness ['flætnis] *n* llanura *f*, lo llano; *(fig)* insipidez *f*, monotonía *f*, aburrimiento *m*.

flatten ['flætn] 1 *vt (also* **to — out)** allanar, aplanar; *(smoothe)* alisar; *map etc* extender; *house, city* aplastar; *(fig)* desconcertar, aplastar.
2 *vi:* **to — out** *(Aer)* enderezarse.
3 *vr:* **to — oneself against a wall** aplanarse contra una pared.

flatter ['flætə*] 1 *vt* adular, lisonjear, halagar; *(photo, clothes etc)* favorecer.
2 *vr:* **to — oneself** felicitarse, congratularse *(on de, that* de que); **you — yourself!** ¡presumido!

flatterer ['flætərə*] *n* adulador *m*, ora *f*.

flattering ['flætəriŋ] *adj* lisonjero; halagüeño; *photo, clothes etc* que favorece.

flatteringly ['flætəriŋli] *adv speak etc* en términos lisonjeros.

flattery ['flætəri] *n* adulación *f*, lisonja *f*.

flatulence ['flætjuləns] *n* flatulencia *f*; *(fig)* hinchazón *f*.

flatulent ['flætjulənt] *adj* flatulento; *(fig)* hinchado.

flaunt [flɔːnt] 1 *vt* ostentar, lucir; hacer gala de. 2 *vr:* **to — oneself** pavonearse.

flautist ['flɔːtist] *n* flautista *mf*, flauta *m*.

flavour, (US) flavor ['fleivə*] 1 *n* sabor *m* *(of* a), gusto *m*; *(flavouring)* condimento *m*; **with a banana —** con sabor a plátano.
2 *vt* sazonar, condimentar *(with* con); *(fig)* dar un sabor característico a; **—ed with** con sabor a.

flavouring, (US) flavoring ['fleivəriŋ] *n* condimento *m*.

flavourless, (US) flavorless ['fleivəlis] *adj* insípido, soso.

flaw [flɔː] *n* desperfecto *m*, imperfección *f*; *(crack)* grieta *f*; *(in character, scheme, case etc)* defecto *m*.

flawless ['flɔːlis] *adj* intachable, impecable.

flax [flæks] *n* lino *m*.

flaxen ['flæksən] *adj hair* muy rubio.

flay [flei] *vt* desollar; *(fig: beat)* azotar, *(defeat)* cascar, *(criticize)* despellejar.

flea [fliː] *n* pulga *f*; **to send someone away with a — in his ear** echar a uno con cajas destempladas.

fleabite ['fliːbait] *n* picadura *f* de pulga; *(fig)* pérdida *f* insignificante.

flea-pit ['fliːpit] *n (fam)* cine *m* de bajísima categoría.

fleck [flek] 1 *n* punto *m*, mancha *f*. 2 *vt* puntear, salpicar *(with* de).

fled [fled] *pret and ptp of* **flee**.

fledged [fledʒd] *adj* plumado; **fully —** *(fig)* hecho y derecho.

fledgeling ['fledʒliŋ] *n* volantón *m*, pajarito *m*.

flee [fliː] *(irr: pret and ptp* **fled)** 1 *vt (escape from)* huir de, abandonar; *(shun)* evitar. 2 *vi* huir *(from* de), fugarse *(to* a); *(vanish)* desaparecer.

fleece [fliːs] 1 *n* vellón *m*; lana *f*; **Golden F—** Vellocino *m* de Oro. 2 *vt* esquilar; *(fig)* pelar, mondar.

fleecy ['fliːsi] *adj* lanudo; *cloud* aborregado.

fleet[1] [fliːt] *n (Naut, Aer)* flota *f*; *(of cars)* escuadra *f*; **the British —** la armada inglesa.

fleet[2] [fliːt] *adj*, **fleet-footed** ['fliːt'futid] *adj* veloz, ligero.

fleeting ['fliːtiŋ] *adj* fugaz, efímero, pasajero; *moment* breve.

Fleming ['flemiŋ] *n* flamenco *m*, a *f*.

Flemish ['flemiʃ] 1 *adj* flamenco. 2 *n (language)* flamenco *m*.

flesh [fleʃ] *n* carne *f (also fig)*; *(of fruit)* pulpa *f*; **in the —** en persona; **of — and blood** de carne y hueso; **my own — and blood** mi familia, mis parientes; **it was more than — and blood could stand** era inaguantable; **to go the way of all —** acabar como todo el género humano; **to put on —** echar carnes; *see* **creep.**

flesh colour ['fleʃ,kʌlə*] *n* color *m* de carne.

flesh-coloured ['fleʃ,kʌləd] *adj* encarnado, color de carne.

fleshpots ['fleʃpɔts] *npl* ollas *fpl*.

flesh wound ['fleʃwuːnd] *n* herida *f* superficial.

fleshy ['fleʃi] *adj (fat)* gordo; *(Bot etc)* carnoso.

flew [fluː] *pret of* **fly.**

flex [fleks] 1 *n* flexible *m*, hilo *m*, cordón *m* (de la luz). 2 *vt* doblar. 3 *vi* doblarse.

flexibility [,fleksi'biliti] *n* flexibilidad *f (also fig)*.

flexible ['fleksəbl] *adj* flexible *(also fig)*.

flexion ['flekʃən] *n* flexión *f*.

flibbertigibbet ['flibəti'dʒibit] *n* casquivano *m*, a *f*.

flick [flik] 1 *n (blow)* golpecito *m* rápido; *(with finger)* capirotazo *m*; *(of whip)* chasquido *m*; *(sl)* película *f*; **—s** *(sl)* cine *m*; **with a — of the wrist** con un movimiento rápido de la muñeca.

2 *vt (strike)* dar un golpecito a; *(touch in passing)* rozar levemente; *(with finger)* dar un capirotazo a; *whip* chasquear; **to — something with a whip** dar algo ligeramente con el látigo; **to — something away** quitar algo con un movimiento rápido; **to — over the pages** hojear rápidamente las páginas.

flicker ['flikə*] 1 *n* parpadeo *m*; **without a — of** sin la menor señal de.
2 *vi (light)* parpadear, *(on going out)* brillar con luz mortecina; *(flame)* vacilar; *(snake's tongue etc)* vibrar.

flier ['flaiə*] *n* aviador *m*, ora *f*.

flight [flait] *n* **(a)** *(flying)* vuelo *m*; *(of bullet)* trayectoria *f*; *(distance flown)* recorrido *m*; *(group of birds)* bandada *f*; *(unit)* escuadrilla *f*; **orbital —** vuelo *m* orbital; **reconnaissance —** vuelo *m* de reconocimiento; **— of fancy** sueño *m*, ilusión *f*; **to be in the first —** ser de primera categoría; **to take —** alzar el vuelo.
(b) *(escape)* huida *f*, fuga *f*; **— of capital** evasión *f* de capitales; **to be in full —** huir en desorden; **to put to —** ahuyentar, *(Mil)* poner en fuga; **to take —** darse a la fuga.
(c) **— of steps** tramo *m*, escalera *f*; **we live 3 —s up** vivimos 3 pisos más arriba.

flight deck ['flaitdek] *n* cubierta *f* de vuelo.

flighty ['flaiti] *adj* frívolo, poco serio; caprichoso, inconstante; travieso; coqueta.

flimsily ['flimzili] *adv* débilmente; muy delgadamente, muy ligeramente; de modo diáfano; **— covered** ligeramente cubierto.

flimsiness ['flimzinis] *n* debilidad *f*, endeblez *f*; delgadez *f*, ligereza *f*; diafanidad *f*; lo baladí.

flimsy ['flimzi] *adj (weak)* débil, endeble; *(thin)* muy delgado, muy ligero; *cloth* diáfano; *excuse* baladí.

flinch [flintʃ] *vi* acobardarse, arredrarse, retroceder *(from* ante), encogerse de miedo; **without —ing** sin vacilar.

fling [fliŋ] 1 *n* **(a)** **to go on a —** echar una cana al aire; **to have one's —** correrla; **youth will have its —** los jóvenes se rebelan de vez en cuando; **to have a — at something** intentar algo.
(b) **highland —** cierto baile escocés.
2 *(irr: pret and ptp* **flung)** *vt* arrojar, tirar, lanzar; *rider* tirar al suelo; **to — someone into jail** echar a uno; **to — one's arms round someone** echar los brazos encima a uno; **to — about** esparcir; **to — away** tirar, *opportunity etc* desperdiciar; **to — back** *ball* devolver, *head* echar atrás; **to — down** tirar al suelo, *building etc* derribar; **to — off** *dress* quitarse de golpe; **to — open** abrir de golpe; **to — out** echar; **to — out an arm** extender repentinamente un brazo; **to — over** tirar; **to — up** *(fig)* renunciar a.
3 *vi:* **to — out** salir muy enfadado.
4 *vr:* **to — oneself** arrojarse, precipitarse; **to — oneself down** tirarse al suelo; **to — oneself on someone** echarse sobre uno; **to — oneself over a cliff** despeñarse por un precipicio.

flint [flint] *n* pedernal *m* *(of lighter)* piedra *f*; **— axe** hacha *f* de sílex.

flinty ['flinti] *adj (fig)* empedernido.

flip [flip] 1 *n* capirotazo *m*; *(Aer: fam)* vuelo *m*.
2 *vt (with fingers)* echar de un capirotazo; *(jerk)* mover de un tirón; *coin* echar a cara o cruz; **to — open** abrir con un movimiento rápido.

flippancy ['flipənsi] *n* falta *f* de seriedad, ligereza *f*.

flippant ['flipənt] *adj* poco serio, ligero.

flippantly ['flipəntli] *adv* con poca seriedad, ligeramente.

flipper ['flipə*] *n* aleta *f (also sl)*.

flirt [flɜːt] 1 *n* mariposón *m*, coqueta *f*; **she's a great —** es terriblemente coqueta.
2 *vi* flirtear, coquetear *(with* con), mariposear; **to — with** *(fig)* jugar con, entretenerse con; **to — with death** jugar con la muerte; **to — with an idea** acariciar una idea con poca seriedad.

flirtation [flɜː'teiʃən] *n* flirteo *m*; **to have a — with someone** tener un amorío con uno.

flirtatious [flɜː'teiʃəs] *adj man* mariposón, coqueta; *glance etc* coqueta.

flit [flit] *vi* revolotear, volar con vuelo cortado; *(before eyes etc)* pasar rápidamente; *(fam)* mudarse a la chita callando.

flitch [flitʃ] *n:* **— of bacon** hoja *f* de tocino.

float [fləut] 1 *n (Fishing)* corcho *m*; *(of seaplane etc)* pontón *m*, flotador *m*; *(in procession)* carroza *f*.
2 *vt* hacer flotar; *(refloat)* poner a flote; *company* lanzar, fundar; *share issue, loan* emitir.
3 *vi* flotar; *(bather)* hacer la plancha; *(flag, hair)* ondear; **it —ed to the surface** salió a la superficie.

floating ['fləutiŋ] *adj object, population etc* flotante; *voter* indeciso.

flock [flɔk] **1** n (Agr etc) rebaño m; (of birds) bandada f; (Eccl) grey f; (of people) multitud f, tropel m; **they came in** —s acudieron en tropel.
2 vi congregarse, reunirse (also **to — together**); **to — about someone** reunirse en torno de uno; **to — to** acudir en tropel a.
floe [fləu] n témpano m de hielo.
flog [flɔg] vt azotar.
flogging ['flɔgiŋ] n azotaina f, paliza f.
flood [flʌd] **1** n inundación f; (in river) avenida f; (tide) pleamar f, flujo m; (fig) torrente m, diluvio m; **the F**— el Diluvio; **a — of letters** una riada de cartas; **a — of light** un torrente de luz; **to be in —** estar crecido; **to weep —s of tears** llorar a mares.
2 vt inundar, anegar; **to — the market with something** inundar el mercado de algo; **we are —ed with applications** tenemos montones de solicitudes; **ten families were —ed out** diez familias tuvieron que abandonar sus casas debido a la inundación.
3 vi desbordar; **to come —ing in** (people) entrar a raudales, (applications) llegar a montones.
floodgate ['flʌdgeit] n compuerta f, esclusa f.
flooding ['flʌdiŋ] n inundación f.
floodlight ['flʌdlait] **1** n foco m. **2** vt iluminar con focos.
floodlighting ['flʌdlaitiŋ] n iluminación f con focos.
floodtide ['flʌdtaid] n pleamar f, marea f creciente.
floor [flɔ:*] **1** n (a) suelo m; (of sea etc) fondo m; (dance-) pista f; **to cross the —** (of the House) atravesar la sala; **to have the —** tener la palabra; **to take the —** salir a bailar, (fig) salir a palestra; **to wipe the — with** (fam) cascar.
(b) (storey) piso m; **ground —** planta f baja; **first —** primer piso m, (US) planta f baja; **second —** segundo piso m, (US) primer piso m; **top —** piso m alto.
2 vt (a) room solar, entarimar (with de).
(b) person derribar; (fig) dejar sin réplica posible, confundir.
floorboard ['flɔ:bɔ:d] n tabla f (del suelo).
floorcloth ['flɔ:klɔθ] n bayeta f.
floor polish ['flɔ:ˌpɔliʃ] n cera f (para suelos).
floor show ['flɔ:ʃəu] n espectáculo m de cabaret, atracciones fpl (en la pista de baile).
floorwalker ['flɔ:ˌwɔ:kə*] n (Comm) superintendente m de división.
flop [flɔp] **1** n (fam) fracaso m; (Theat) caída f; **it was an awful —** fue un rotundo fracaso.
2 vi dejarse caer pesadamente (into en); (fam) fracasar, (Theat) venirse al foso.
flophouse ['flɔphaus] n, pl **-houses** [ˌhauziz] (US) pensión f de bajísima categoría.
floppy ['flɔpi] adj flojo, colgante.
flora ['flɔ:rə] n flora f.
floral ['flɔ:rəl] adj floral; tribute etc de flores.
Florence ['flɔrəns] Florencia.
Florentine ['flɔrəntain] **1** adj florentino. **2** n florentino m, a f.
florescence [flɔ:'resns] n florescencia f.
florid ['flɔrid] adj florido (also Liᵗ etc); complexión rojizo, subido de color.
florin ['flɔrin] n florín m; (British) moneda de 2 chelines.
florist ['flɔrist] n florista mf; —'s (shop) floristería f, florería f.
floss [flɔs] n (also — silk) cadarzo m; seda f floja.
flotilla [flə'tilə] n flotilla f.
flotsam ['flɔtsəm] n pecios mpl, restos mpl flotantes; — **and jetsam** (fig) restos mpl, desechos mpl.
flounce¹ [flauns] n (Sew) volante m.
flounce² [flauns] vi: **to — about** moverse violentamente; **to — away, to — off** alejarse exagerando los movimientos del cuerpo; **to — out** salir enfadado.
flounced [flaunst] adj dress guarnecido con volantes.
flounder¹ ['flaundə*] n (Fish) (especie de) platija f.
flounder² ['flaundə*] vi (in a speech etc) tropezar, perder el hilo, no saber qué decir; **to — about** revolcarse, debatirse, forcejear.
flour ['flauə*] **1** n harina f. **2** vt enharinar.
flour-bin ['flauəbin] n harinero m.
flourish ['flʌriʃ] **1** n (a) (with pen) rasgo m, plumada f; (on signature) rúbrica f; (of hand) movimiento m, ademán m; **to do something with a —** hacer algo con un ademán triunfal.
(b) (Mus: on guitar) floreo m, (fanfare) toque m de trompeta.
2 vt weapon etc blandir; stick etc agitar, menear; (fig) hacer gala de, mostrar orgullosamente.
3 vi florecer, prosperar; (plant etc) crecer rápidamente.
flourishing ['flʌriʃiŋ] adj floreciente, próspero; (Bot) lozano; (healthy) como un reloj.
floury ['flauəri] adj harinoso.
flout [flaut] vt mofarse de, no hacer caso de.

flow [fləu] **1** n (stream) corriente f; (jet) chorro m; (movement) flujo m, movimiento m; (quantity flowing) caudal m, cantidad f; (direction of —) curso m; (of words etc) torrente m; (of dress etc) movimiento m suave, movimiento m elegante; (of music) lo corriente, lo suave; **to have a ready — of words** hablar con soltura; **to maintain a steady —** mantener un movimiento constante.
2 vi fluir, correr (along, down por); (tide) subir, crecer; (hair) ondear (in the wind al viento); (blood, being shed) derramarse, (from wound) manar, correr; **to — away** irse; **to — back** refluir; **tears were —ing down her cheeks** le corrían las lágrimas por las mejillas; **to — from** provenir de; **money is —ing in** entra el dinero en grandes cantidades; **people are —ing in** entra la gente a raudales; **to — into** river desaguar en, desembocar en; **to — over** desbordarse; **to — past** pasar (delante de); **to — with** abundar en.
flower ['flauə*] **1** n flor f; (fig) flor f, flor f y nata; **in — en** flor; **to say something with —s** comunicar algo a uno enviando flores. **2** vi florecer.
flower bed ['flauəbed] n cuadro m, macizo m.
flowerpot ['flauəpɔt] n tiesto m, maceta f.
flower shop ['flauəʃɔp] n floristería f, florería f.
flower show ['flauəʃəu] n exposición f de flores.
flowery ['flauəri] adj florido (also fig).
flowing ['fləuiŋ] adj movement, stream corriente; hair suelto; style fluido, corriente.
flown [fləun] ptp of **fly**.
flu [flu:] n (fam) gripe f.
fluctuate ['flʌktjueit] vi fluctuar; variar.
fluctuation [ˌflʌktju'eiʃən] n fluctuación f; variación f.
flue [flu:] n humero m, cañón m de chimenea; (of lamp, boiler) tubo m.
fluency ['flu:ənsi] n fluidez f; elocuencia f, facundia f; **his — in Russian** su dominio del ruso.
fluent ['flu:ənt] adj style fluido, corriente; speaker elocuente, facundo; **he is — in Russian, his Russian is —** domina el ruso.
fluently ['flu:əntli] adv con fluidez, corrientemente; elocuentemente; **he speaks Russian —** domina el ruso.
fluff [flʌf] n pelusa f, lanilla f.
fluffy ['flʌfi] adj velloso, lanudo; hair encrespado; (feathered) plumoso; surface que tiene mucha pelusa.
fluid ['flu:id] **1** adj fluido, líquido; situation inestable; plan flexible. **2** n fluido m, líquido m.
fluidity [flu:'iditi] n fluidez f; inestabilidad f.
fluke¹ [flu:k] n (Zool) trematodo m; (Fish) (especie de) platija f.
fluke² [flu:k] n chiripa f, racha f de suerte; **to win by a —** ganar por chiripa.
fluky ['flu:ki] adj afortunado.
flummox ['flʌməks] vt (disconcert) desconcertar, confundir; (startle) asombrar; **I was completely —ed** quedé totalmente despistado.
flung [flʌŋ] pret and ptp of **fling**.
flunk [flʌŋk] (US) **1** vt student suspender; course perder; exam no aprobar, salir mal en.
2 vi se suspende; **I —ed me suspendieron; to — out** salir del colegio (etc) sin recibir un título.
flunk(e)y ['flʌŋki] n lacayo m (also fig).
fluorescence [fluə'resns] n fluorescencia f.
fluorescent [fluə'resnt] adj fluorescente.
fluoridation [ˌfluəri'deiʃən] n fluorización f.
fluoride ['fluəraid] n fluoruro m.
flurry ['flʌri] **1** n (a) (nervous haste) agitación f, estado m nervioso; **a — of activity** un frenesí de actividad; **to be in a —** estar agitado, estar aturrullado.
(b) (of snow etc) ráfaga f.
2 vt agitar, hacer nervioso; **to get flurried** aturrullarse.
flush¹ [flʌʃ] vt game levantar; **to — someone out** hacer que uno salga.
flush² [flʌʃ] **1** vt (also **to — out**) limpiar con un chorro de agua; WC hacer funcionar. **2** vi (WC) funcionar.
flush³ [flʌʃ] **1** n (on face) rubor m; (in sky) arrebol m; (abundance) abundancia f repentina, plenitud f; (of fever) calor m súbito; **in the first — of success** en el momento emocionado del triunfo.
2 vt: **to be —ed with success** estar muy emocionado con el triunfo; **a face —ed with drink** una cara encendida por el alcohol.
3 vi ruborizarse, sonrojarse; (with anger) sofocarse.
flush⁴ [flʌʃ] adj (a) (Tech) nivelado, igual, parejo, a ras; **to make two things —** nivelar dos cosas. (b) **to be —** (sl) tener dinero.
flush⁵ [flʌʃ] n (Cards) flux m.
Flushing ['flʌʃiŋ] Flesinga.

fluster ['flʌstə*] **1** n confusión f, aturdimiento m; conmoción f; **to be in a** — estar azacaneado.
2 vt aturdir, poner nervioso, aturrullar; **to get —ed** aturrullarse.
flute [fluːt] n flauta f.
fluted ['fluːtid] adj (Archit) estriado, acanalado.
flutter ['flʌtə*] **1** n (of wings) revoloteo m, aleteo m, movimiento m; (of eyelashes) pestañeo m; (excitement) emoción f, agitación f, conmoción f; (fam) apuesta f; **to cause a** — agitar los espíritus.
2 vt agitar, menear, mover ligeramente; (fig) agitar.
3 vi (bird etc) revolotear, aletear; (butterfly) mover ligeramente las alas; (flag) ondear; (heart) palpitar; **a leaf came —ing down** cayó balanceándose una hoja.
fluty ['fluːti] adj tone aflautado.
flux [flʌks] n (flow) flujo m; **to be in a state of** — estar continuamente cambiando.
fly [flai] **1** n mosca f; (of trousers, also **flies**) bragueta f; (carriage) calesa f; **flies** (Theat) bambalinas fpl; **Spanish** — cantárida f; **there's a** — **in the ointment** existe una dificultad; **he's the** — **in the ointment** él es el estorbo; **there are no flies on him** es muy listo; **to fish with a** — pescar a mosca.
2 adj avispado, despabilado.
3 (irr: pret **flew**, ptp **flown**) vt hacer volar; plane pilotar, dirigir; passengers, goods etc transportar (en avión); ocean etc atravesar (en avión); distance recorrer (en avión); flag llevar, tener izado; danger huir (de); country abandonar, salir de.
4 vi (a) volar; (travel by air) ir en avión; (fly a plane) pilotar un avión; (flag) estar izado, ondear; **to send something —ing** echar algo a rodar; **to** — **into pieces** hacerse pedazos; **to** — **away** irse volando; **to** — **in** llegar (en avión); **to** — **into London Airport** llegar en avión al aeropuerto de Londres; **to** — **off** (bird, insect) alejarse volando, (in plane) partir en avión, (part) desprenderse, separarse; **to** — **open** abrirse de repente; **to** — **over Rome** sobrevolar Roma; **to let** — (shoot) tirar, disparar, hacer fuego; (emotionally) desahogarse; (verbally) empezar a proferir insultos (etc); **to let** — **at** (shoot) tirar sobre, disparar contra, (emotionally) desahogarse criticando, (verbally) empezar a llenar de injurias.
(b) (rush) lanzarse, precipitarse; **I must** — tengo que darme prisa; **to** — **at someone** lanzarse sobre uno; **to** — (fig) ponerse furioso con uno; **to** — **in a rage** encolerizarse; **to** — **to someone's help** correr a socorrer a uno; **to** — **to someone's side** volar hacia el lado de uno.
(c) (escape) evadirse, huir (from de); (vanish) desaparecer; **to** — **for one's life** salvar la vida huyendo.
fly-by-night ['flaibainait] **1** adj frívolo; poco serio, nada confiable. **2** n persona f frivola, casquivano m, a f; persona f nada confiable.
flycatcher ['flai‚kætʃə*] n papamoscas m.
fly fishing ['flai‚fiʃiŋ] n pesca f a mosca.
flying ['flaiiŋ] adj volante, volador; (swift) rápido, veloz; visit muy breve.
flying boat ['flaiŋbəut] n hidroavión m.
flying bomb ['flaiŋ‚bɔm] n bomba f volante.
Flying Dutchman ['flaiŋ‚dʌtʃmən] el Buque fantasma.
flying fish ['flaiŋ‚fiʃ] n pez m volador.
flying machine ['flaiŋmə‚ʃiːn] n avión m.
flying time ['flaiŋ‚taim] n horas fpl de vuelo, duración f del vuelo.
flyleaf ['flailiːf] n, pl —**leaves** [liːvz] hoja f de guarda.
flyover ['flai‚əuvə*] n paso m superior.
flypaper [flai‚peipə*] n papel m matamoscas.
flyswat(ter) ['flaiswɔt(ə*)] n palmeta f matamoscas.
flyweight ['flaiweit] n peso m mosca.
flywheel ['flaiwiːl] n volante m (de motor).
foal [fəul] **1** n potro m, a f. **2** vi parir (la yegua).
foam [fəum] **1** n espuma f. **2** vi espumar, echar espuma; **to** — **at the mouth** espumajear.
foam rubber ['fəum'rʌbə*] n espuma f de caucho.
foamy ['fəumi] adj espumoso.
fob [fɔb] vt: **to** — **someone off** apartar a uno de un propósito con excusas; **to** — **someone off with something** persuadir a uno a aceptar algo (de modo fraudulento).
focal ['fəukəl] adj focal.
focus ['fəukəs] **1** n foco m; (of attention etc) centro m; **to be in** — estar enfocado; **to be out of** — estar desenfocado.
2 vt enfocar (on a); attention etc fijar, concentrar (on en); **all eyes were —sed on him** todos le miraban fijamente.
3 vi enfocar(se); **to** — **on** enfocar a.

fodder ['fɔdə*] n pienso m, forraje m.
foe [fəu] n (lit) enemigo m.
foetus ['fiːtəs] n feto m.
fog [fɔg] **1** n niebla f; (fig) confusión f. **2** vt (fig) matter entenebrecer; person ofuscar; (Phot) velar.
fogbound ['fɔgbaund] adj inmovilizado por la niebla.
fogey ['fəugi] n: **old** — persona f de ideas anticuadas, persona f chapada a la antigua.
foggy ['fɔgi] adj nebuloso, brumoso; day de niebla; (Phot) velado; **it is** — hay niebla; **I haven't the foggiest** (idea) no tengo la más remota idea.
foghorn ['fɔghɔːn] n sirena f (de niebla).
foible ['fɔibl] n flaco m; manía f.
foil [fɔil] n (metal) hoja f, hojuela f; (fig) contraste m (to con); **to act as a** — **to something** servir de contraste con algo, hacer resaltar algo.
foil² [fɔil] vt frustrar.
foil³ [fɔil] n (Fencing) florete m.
foist [fɔist] **1** vt: **to** — **something off on someone** encajar algo a uno, lograr con engaño que uno acepte algo; **the job was —ed on to me** lograron mañosamente que yo me encargara de ello.
2 vr: **to** — **oneself on someone** insistir en acompañar a uno, pegarse a uno.
fold¹ [fəuld] n (Agr) redil m, aprisco m; **to return to the** — (Eccl) volver al redil de la Iglesia.
fold² [fəuld] **1** n pliegue m, doblez m, arruga f; (Geol) pliegue m.
2 vt plegar, doblar; wings recoger; **to** — **one's arms** cruzar los brazos; **to** — **back**, **to** — **down** doblar hacia abajo; **to** — **someone in one's arms** abrazar a uno tiernamente, estrechar a uno contra el pecho; **to** — **something in a wrapper** envolver algo en una envoltura; **to** — **up** doblar, chair etc plegar.
3 vi plegarse, doblarse; **it —s down at night** de noche se dobla hacia abajo; **to** — **up** doblarse, plegarse; (fig) fracasar, terminar; (Comm) quebrar, entrar en liquidación.
folder ['fəuldə*] n (file) carpeta f; (brochure) folleto m; (of matches) carterita f.
folding ['fəuldiŋ] adj plegable, plegadizo; de tijera.
folding chair ['fəuldiŋ'tʃɛə*] adj silla f de tijera.
folding doors ['fəuldiŋ'dɔːz] npl puertas fpl plegadizas.
folding table ['fəuldiŋ'teibl] n mesa f plegable.
foliage ['fəuliidʒ] n hojas fpl, follaje m.
foliation [‚fəuli'eifən] n foliación f.
folio ['fəuliəu] n folio m; (book) infolio m, libro m en folio.
folk [fəuk] n (a) (tribe) nación f, tribu f, pueblo m.
(b) (people in general; also —**s**) gente f; **my** —**s** mi familia, mis parientes; **the old** —**s** los viejos; **hullo** —**s!** ¡hola, amigos!; **they're strange** — **here** aquí la gente es algo rara.
folk dance ['fəukdɑːns] n baile m popular, danza f tradicional.
folklore ['fəuklɔ:*] n folklore m.
folk singer ['fəuk‚siŋə*] n cantante mf folklorista.
folksong ['fəuksɔŋ] n canción f popular, canción f tradicional.
folksy ['fəuksi] adj (fam) afectadamente folklorista; que finge ser popular (or tradicional etc), que se esfuerza por parecer que es del pueblo.
folk tale ['fəukteil] n cuento m popular.
follow ['fɔləu] **1** vt (a) (general sense) seguir; suspect etc seguir la pista a; (pursue) perseguir; **there's someone —ing us** alguien nos viene siguiendo; **the road** —**s the coast** la carretera va por la costa; **to** — **someone into a room** entrar en una habitación detrás de uno; **they —ed this with threats** tras esto empezaron a amenazarnos; **to** — **someone about** seguir a uno por todas partes; **to** — **through**, **to** — **up** shot terminar, completar; plan llevar hasta el fin; clue investigar; matter perseguir; suggestion adoptar.
(b) advice, example seguir; person imitar el ejemplo de; instructions seguir; news estar al corriente de, estar enterado de; **do you** — **football?** ¿le interesa el fútbol?
(c) profession ejercer.
(d) (understand) person comprender, argument seguir el hilo de.
2 vi (a) seguir; **we'll** — **on behind** vendremos después.
(b) seguirse; resultar; **as** —**s** como sigue, a saber; **it** —**s that** síguese que, resulta que; **it doesn't** — **at all that** ... no es lógico que ... + subj; **it** —**s on from what I said** es la consecuencia lógica de lo que dije.
follower ['fɔləuə*] n (Pol etc) partidario m, a f, adherente mf; (Sport) seguidor m, hincha m; (pej)

secuaz *mf*; (*Philos etc*) discípulo *m*; (*imitator*) imitador *m*, ora *f*; —s (*of prince etc*) séquito *m*; **all the —s of football** todos los que se interesan por el fútbol; **the —s of fashion** los que siguen la moda.

following ['foləuiŋ] **1** *adj* siguiente; *wind* en popa; **the —** lo siguiente.

   2 *n* (*Pol etc*) partidarios *mpl*, (*pej*) secuaces *mpl*; (*of prince etc*) séquito *m*; **football has no — here** aquí nadie se interesa por el fútbol.

follow-through ['foləu'θru:] *n* continuación *f*.

follow-up ['foləu'ʌp] *adj*: **— interview** entrevista *f* complementaria; **— letter** carta *f* recordativa.

folly ['foli] *n* locura *f*.

foment [fəu'ment] *vt* fomentar (*also Med*); *revolt etc* provocar, instigar.

fomentation [,fəumen'teiʃən] *n* fomentación *f*; fomento *m*.

fond [fond] *adj* (*loving*) cariñoso, afectuoso; (*doting*) demasiado indulgente; *hope* fervoroso; **to be — of** *thing* ser aficionado a, tener afición a; *person* tener mucho cariño a; **to be — of** + *ger* ser aficionado a + *infin*; **to become** (*or* **grow**) **— of** *thing* aficionarse a, *person* tomar cariño a.

fondle ['fondl] *vt* acariciar.

fondly ['fondli] *adv* con cariño, afectuosamente; *hope* fervorosamente; *imagine* inocentemente.

fondness ['fondnis] *n* cariño *m*; afición *f* (*for* a).

font [font] *n* pila *f* (bautismal); (*Typ*) fundición *f*.

food [fu:d] *n* alimento *m*, comida *f*; (*edible matter*) comestible *m*; (*for animals*) pasto *m*, pienso *m*; **to buy —** comprar víveres, comprar provisiones; **the — is good here** aquí se come bien; **the cost of —** el coste de la alimentación; **she gave him —** le dio de comer; **he likes plain —** le gustan las comidas sencillas; **to send — and clothing** enviar comestibles y ropa; **to be off one's —** no tener apetito; **to give someone — for thought** dar a uno en qué pensar, dar a uno un tema de meditación.

food poisoning ['fu:d,poizniŋ] *n* botulismo *m*, intoxicación *f* alimenticia.

foodstuffs ['fu:dstʌfs] *npl* comestibles *mpl*, artículos *mpl* alimenticios.

food value ['fu:d,vælju:] *n* valor *m* alimenticio.

fool [fu:l] **1** *n* tonto *m*, a *f*, imbécil *mf*; (*jester*) bufón *m*; **you —!** ¡imbécil!; **some — of a minister** algún ministro imbécil; **he's nobody's —** no se deja engañar por nadie; **to be — enough to** + *infin* ser bastante tonto como para + *infin*; **don't be a —!** ¡no seas tonto!, ¡déjate de tonterías!; **to act** (*or* **play**) **the —** hacer el tonto; **to live in a —'s paradise** vivir en un mundo de sueños, imaginarse una novela; **to make a — of someone** poner a uno en ridículo, engañar a uno; **to make a — of oneself** ponerse en ridículo; **to send someone on a —'s errand** enviar a uno a una misión inútil.

   2 *adj* (*US*) tonto.

   3 *vt* (*deceive*) engañar, embaucar; (*puzzle*) confundir, dejar perplejo; **you can't — me** a mí no me engaña nadie; **you had me properly —ed there** eso sí que me despistó; **that —ed nobody** no se dejó engañar nadie por eso; **to — away** *time* perder ociosamente, *money* despilfarrar.

   4 *vi* chancear, bromear; **no —ing** en serio; **I was only —ing** lo dije en broma; **quit —ing!** ¡déjate de tonterías!; **to — about** divertirse, juguetear; hacer el tonto; **to — about with** jugar con, (*and damage*) estropear; **to — around** perder el tiempo neciamente.

foolery ['fu:ləri] *n* bufonadas *fpl*; (*nonsense*) tonterías *fpl*.

foolhardy ['fu:l,ha:di] *adj* temerario.

foolish ['fu:liʃ] *adj* tonto, necio; imbécil; ridículo; absurdo; estúpido; imprudente; **— thing** tontería *f*; **don't be —** no seas tonto; **that was very — of you** en eso fuiste muy imprudente; **I felt very —** creí haberme puesto en ridículo; **to make someone look —** hacer que uno parezca ridículo.

foolishly ['fu:liʃli] *adv* tontamente, neciamente; **—, I agreed** como un tonto consentí.

foolishness ['fu:liʃnis] *n* tontería *f*, necedad *f*; imbecilidad *f*; ridiculez *f*; estupidez *f*; imprudencia *f*.

foolproof ['fu:lpru:f] *adj* (*Tech*) a prueba de impericia; *scheme etc* de éxito seguro, infalible.

foolscap ['fu:lskæp] *n* (*approx*) papel *m* tamaño folio.

foot [fut] **1** *n*, *pl* **feet** [fi:t] pie *m*; (*of animal, furniture*) pata *f*; (*of hill, page, stairs etc*) pie *m*; (*measure*) pie *m*; **at the — of the hill** al pie de la colina; **he's on his feet all day long** está trajinando todo el santo día, no descansa en todo el día; **he's on his feet again** ha vuelto a levantarse y a salir; **it's wet under —** el suelo está mojado; **to come** (*or* **go**) **on —** venir (*or* ir) a pie, venir (*or* ir) andando; **to drag one's feet** (*fig*)

echarse atrás, hacerse el roncero; **to fall on one's feet** (*fig*) caer de pie; **to find one's feet** acostumbrarse al ambiente; **to get cold feet** encogerse a uno el ombligo; **to get one's — in the door** abrirse una brecha; **to have one — in the grave** estar con un pie en la sepultura; **to keep one's feet** mantenerse en pie; **to put one's — down** (*Aut*) acelerar, (*fig*) adoptar una actitud firme; **to put one's — in it** meter la pata; **to put one's best — forward** animarse a continuar; hacer lo posible por hacer una buena impresión; **to rise to one's feet** ponerse de pie, levantarse; **to set — inside someone's door** poner los pies en la casa de uno, pasar el umbral de uno; **to set something on —** promover algo, poner algo en marcha; **to set — on dry land** poner el pie en tierra firme; **to sit at someone's feet** ser discípulo de uno; **to stand on one's own two feet** ser independiente; **to sweep a girl off her feet** enamorar perdidamente a una chica; **to trample something under —** pisotear algo.

   2 *vt bill* pagar; **to — it** (*walk*) ir andando, (*dance*) bailar.

foot-and-mouth (**disease**) ['futən'mauθ(di'zi:z)] *n* fiebre *f* aftosa, glosopeda *f*.

football ['futbo:l] *n* (*game*) fútbol *m*; (*ball*) balón *m*; **association —** fútbol *m* asociación.

footballer ['futbo:lə*] *n* futbolista *m*.

football pool ['futbo:l,pu:l] *n* quinielas *fpl*.

footboard ['futbo:d] *n* estribo *m*.

footbrake ['futbreik] *n* pedal *m* del freno; freno *m* de pie.

footbridge ['futbridʒ] *n* puente *m* para peatones.

-footed ['futid] *adj* de . . . patas, *eg* **four-footed** de cuatro patas; **light-footed** ligero (de pies).

footfall ['futfo:l] *n* paso *m*, pisada *f*.

foothills ['futhilz] *npl* estribaciones *fpl*.

foothold ['futhəuld] *n* pie *m* firme, asidero *m* para el pie; **to gain a —** ganar pie, lograr establecerse.

footing ['futiŋ] *n* (a) pie *m*; **to lose** (*or* **miss**) **one's —** perder el pie.

   (b) pie *m*, posición *f*; **on an equal —** en un mismo pie de igualdad (*with* con); **on a friendly —** en relaciones amistosas; **on a war —** en pie de guerra; **to gain a —** ganar pie, lograr establecerse.

footle ['fu:tl] **1** *vt*: **to — away** malgastar. **2** *vi* perder el tiempo, hacer el tonto.

footlights ['futlaits] *npl* candilejas *fpl*.

footling ['fu:tliŋ] *adj* trivial, insignificante.

footloose ['futlu:s] *adj* libre; (*wandering*) andariego.

footman ['futmən] *n*, *pl* **-men** [mən] *n* lacayo *m*.

footmark ['futma:k] *n* huella *f*.

footnote ['futnəut] *n* nota *f* (al pie de la página).

footpath ['futpɑ:θ] *n*, *pl* **-paths** [pɑ:ðz] senda *f*, sendero *m*; (*pavement*) acera *f*.

footplate ['futpleit] *n* plataforma *f* del maquinista.

footprint ['futprint] *n* huella *f*.

footrest ['futrest] *n* apoyapié *m*.

footslogger ['futslogə*] *n* (*fam*) peatón *m*; (*Mil*) soldado *m* de infantería.

footsore ['futso:*] *adj*: **to be —** tener los pies cansados.

footstep ['futstep] *n* paso *m*, pisada *f*; **to follow in someone's —s** seguir los pasos de uno.

footstool ['futstu:l] *n* escabel *m*.

footwear ['futweə*] *n* calzado *m*.

footwork ['futwɜ:k] *n* (*Sport*) juego *m* de piernas.

fop [fop] *n* petimetre *m*, currutaco *m*.

foppish ['fopiʃ] *adj* currutaco.

for [fo:*] **1** *prep* (a) (*destined for*) para; **hats — women** sombreros para mujeres; **is this — me?** ¿es esto para mí?; **a job — next week** un trabajo para la semana que viene; **we went to Tossa — our holidays** fuimos a pasar nuestras vacaciones a Tossa, las vacaciones las pasamos en Tossa; **it's time — dinner** es hora de comer; **to write — the papers** escribir en los periódicos; **I have news — you** tengo que darle una noticia; **it was — your good** era para bien (*or* **por**) su bien.

   (b) (*as, representing*) por; **member — Hove** diputado por Hove; **M — Madrid** M de Madrid; **agent — Ford cars** distribuidor de automóviles Ford; **will you write — me?** ¿quieres escribir en mi nombre?; **I'll go — you** yo iré en tu lugar; **if not the government will do it — them** si no lo gobierno lo hará en su lugar; **they shot him — a traitor** le fusilaron por traidor.

   (c) (*in exchange for*) por; **I'll give you this — that** te doy éste por ése; **I sold it — £5** lo vendí por 5 libras; **to exchange one's hat — another** cambiar el sombrero por otro; **word — word** palabra por palabra; **1 dead — every 5 injured** 1 muerto por cada 5 lisiados; **what's the German — "hill"?** ¿cómo se dice en alemán "colina"?

(**d**) (*in favour of*) **I'm — the government** yo soy partidario del gobierno; **a collection — the poor** una colecta a beneficio de los pobres; **the campaign — education** la campaña pro (*or* en pro de la) enseñanza; **I'm all — it** lo apruebo sin reserva.

(**e**) (*because of*) por, a causa de, con motivo de, debido a; **— this reason** por esta razón; **famous — its church** famoso por su iglesia; **the reason — not doing it** la razón por no hacerlo; **we chose it — its climate** lo escogimos por su clima; **if it were not — him** si no fuera por él; **to shout — joy** gritar de alegría.

(**f**) (*purpose*) **what —?** ¿para qué?, ¿por qué?; **what's this —?** ¿para qué sirve esto?

(**g**) (*bound for*) **he left — Ohio** partió para Ohio; **the ship left — Vigo** el buque partió (con) rumbo a Vigo; **the train — Madrid** el tren de Madrid; **where are you —?** ¿adónde se dirige Vd?

(**h**) (*considering*) **tall — his age** alto para su edad.

(**i**) (*in spite of*) **he's nice — a policeman** para policía es muy simpático, a pesar de ser policía es muy simpático; *see* all.

(**j**) **oh — a horse!** ¡quién tuviera un caballo!

(**k**) (*distance*) **there was nothing to be seen — miles** no había nada que ver en muchos kilómetros.

(**l**) (*time: past*) **he was away — 2 years** estuvo ausente (durante) 2 años; **was he away — long?** ¿estuvo fuera mucho tiempo?; **it has not rained — 3 weeks** hace 3 semanas que no llueve, desde hace 3 semanas no llueve; **we went to the seaside — the day** fuimos a pasar el día en la playa; (*future*) **I'm going — 3 weeks** voy por 3 semanas; **will it be — long?** ¿será mucho tiempo?

(**m**) **now — it!** ¡ahora!; ¡ya viene!; **he'll be — it!** ¡le va a tocar la gorda!; **there's nothing — it** no hay más remedio; *see* but.

(**n**) (*with which clause*) **it is — you to decide** le toca a Vd decidir; **it is best — you to go** más vale que vaya Vd; **it is right — you to go** es justo que vaya Vd; **it's bad — you to smoke so much** te hace daño fumar tanto; **— this to be possible** para que esto sea posible; **— him to fail now would be disastrous** sería terrible que fracasara ahora; **he gave orders — it to be done** mandó que se hiciera, dio instrucciones para que se hiciera.

2 *conj* pues, ya que.

forage ['fɔridʒ] **1** *n* forraje *m*. **2** *vi* forrajear; **to — for** buscar.

foray ['fɔrei] *n* correría *f*, incursión *f* (*into* en).

forbad(e) [fə'bæd] *pret of* **forbid**.

forbear [fɔː'beə*] (*irr: see* bear) *vi* contenerse; tener paciencia; **to — to +** *infin* abstenerse de **+** *infin*.

forbearance [fɔː'beərəns] *n* paciencia *f*, dominio *m* sobre sí mismo.

forbears ['fɔːbeəz] *npl* antepasados *mpl*.

forbid [fə'bid] (*irr: pret* **forbad(e)**, *ptp* **forbidden**) *vt* prohibir; **to — something to someone, to — someone something** prohibir algo a uno; **to — someone to do something** prohibir a uno hacer algo; **that's —den** eso está prohibido; **"smoking —den"** "prohibido fumar"; *see* God.

forbidden [fə'bidn] **1** *ptp of* **forbid**. **2** *adj* prohibido.

forbidding [fə'bidiŋ] *adj appearance etc* formidable; (*dismal*) lúgubre; *person's manner* severo.

forbore [fɔː'bɔː*] *pret of* **forbear**.

forborne [fɔː'bɔːn] *ptp of* **forbear**.

force [fɔːs] **1** *n* (**a**) fuerza *f*; **brute —** fuerza *f* bruta; **— of gravity** fuerza *f* de gravedad; **I can see the — of that** comprendo la fuerza de ese argumento; **to resort to —** recurrir a la fuerza; **to yield to —** rendirse a la fuerza; **by — a** la fuerza; **by — of a** fuerza de; **by — of circumstances** debido a las circunstancias; **by — of habit** por la fuerza de la costumbre; **by sheer —** por fuerza mayor; **to be in — (Law)** ser vigente, estar en vigor, (*price*) regir, imperar; **to come in —** venir en gran número.

(**b**) (*persons*) personal *m*, (*Mil*) cuerpo *m*; **the —** la policía; **a strong — of police** un numeroso cuerpo de policía; **—s (Mil)** fuerzas *fpl* armadas; **allied —s** fuerzas *fpl* aliadas; **land —s** fuerzas *fpl* terrestres; **police —** la policía; **sales —** personal *m* de ventas; **to join —s** juntar meriendas.

2 *vt* (**a**) (*compel*) forzar, obligar; *door* forzar, violentar, descerrajar; *pace* apresurar; *plant* hacer madurar temprano; (*cause*) hacer; **to — a smile** sonreír forzadamente; **to — a country into war** empujar a un país a que declare la guerra; **to — someone into a corner** arrinconar a uno, hacer que uno quede arrinconado; **to — a car off the road** hacer

que un coche salga de la calzada; **to — someone into bankruptcy** hacer que uno quiebre.

(**b**) **to — someone to do something** forzar a uno a hacer algo; **I am —d to say** me veo obligado a decir.

(**c**) **to — back** hacer retroceder; **to — down** hacer bajar; (*Aer*) obligar a aterrizar; *food* tragar por fuerza; **can you — a bit more down?** ¿cabe todavía un poco más?; **to — in** introducir por fuerza; **to — something on someone** imponer algo a uno, forzar a uno a aceptar algo; **the decision was —d on him** se le impuso la decisión; **to — open** forzar, abrir por fuerza; **to — out** hacer salir; empujar hacia fuera; *words* pronunciar con dificultad; **we —d the secret out of him** logramos por fuerza que nos dijera el secreto; **to — a bill through parliament** hacer aprobar por el parlamento un proyecto de ley.

3 *vr*: **to — oneself to +** *infin* hacer un esfuerzo por **+** *infin*.

forced [fɔːst] *adj smile* que no le sale a uno; *laughter* forzado; *landing* forzoso; *march, sale, loan* forzado.

forceful ['fɔːsful] *adj* enérgico, vigoroso.

forcefully ['fɔːsfuli] *adv* enérgicamente, vigorosamente.

force majeure ['fɔːsmæ'ʒəː*] *n* fuerza *f* mayor.

forcemeat ['fɔːsmiːt] *n* relleno *m* (de carne picada).

forceps ['fɔːseps] *n sing and pl* fórceps *m*; pinzas *fpl*, tenacillas *fpl*.

forcible ['fɔːsəbl] *adj* (*done by force*) a la fuerza, a viva fuerza, por fuerza; *feeding* forzoso; (*telling*) enérgico, vigoroso.

forcibly ['fɔːsəbli] *adv* a la fuerza; enérgicamente.

ford [fɔːd] **1** *n* vado *m*. **2** *vt* vadear.

fordable ['fɔːdəbl] *adj* vadeable.

fore [fɔː*] **1** *adv*: **— and aft** de popa a proa, por todas partes.

2 *adj* anterior, delantero; (*Naut*) de proa.

3 *n*: **to be at the —** ir delante; **to come to the —** empezar a destacar.

forearm ['fɔːrɑːm] *n* antebrazo *m*.

forebode [fɔː'bəud] *vt* presagiar, anunciar.

foreboding [fɔː'bəudiŋ] *n* presagio *m*; presentimiento *m*; **to have a —** tener un presentimiento; **to have —s that** presentir que; **to have —s** tener una corazonada.

forecast ['fɔːkɑːst] **1** *n* pronóstico *m*; previsión *f*; (*in betting*) acierto *m*; **according to all the —s** según todas las previsiones; **what is the — for the weather?** ¿qué pronóstico hacen del tiempo?

2 (*irr: see* cast) *vt* pronosticar, prever.

forecastle ['fəuksl] *n* castillo *m* de proa.

foreclose [fɔː'kləuz] *vti* (*Law*) extinguir el derecho de redimir (una hipoteca).

foredoomed [fɔː'duːmd] *adj*: **to be — to +** *infin* estar condenado a **+** *infin*.

forefathers ['fɔːfɑːðəz] *npl* antepasados *mpl*.

forefinger ['fɔːfiŋgə*] *n* dedo *m* índice.

forefoot ['fɔːfut] *n*, *pl* **—feet** [fiːt] pata *f* delantera.

forefront ['fɔːfrʌnt] *n*: **to be in the —** estar en la vanguardia (*of* de).

foregoing ['fɔːgəuiŋ] *adj* anterior, precedente.

foregone ['fɔːgɔn] *adj see* **conclusion**.

foreground ['fɔːgraund] *n* primer plano *m*, primer término *m*; **in the —** en primer término.

forehand ['fɔːhænd] **1** *n* directo *m*, derechazo *m*. **2** *attr* directo.

forehead ['fɔrid] *n* frente *f*.

foreign ['fɔrin] *adj* (**a**) extranjero; *policy, trade etc* exterior; **F— Minister, F— Secretary** Ministro *m* de Asuntos Exteriores; **F— Ministry, F— Office** Ministerio *m* de Asuntos Exteriores.

(**b**) *body* extraño; (*belonging to someone else*) ajeno (*to* a); **deceit is — to his nature** no cabe en él el engaño.

foreigner ['fɔrinə*] *n* extranjero *m*, a *f*.

foreknowledge ['fɔː'nɔlidʒ] *n* presciencia *f*; **to have — of something** saber algo de antemano.

foreland ['fɔːlənd] *n* cabo *m*, promontorio *m*.

foreleg ['fɔːleg] *n* pata *f* delantera.

forelock ['fɔːlɔk] *n* guedeja *f*; **to take time by the —** tomar la ocasión por los cabellos.

foreman ['fɔːmən] *n*, *pl* **—men** [mən] (*of workers*) capataz *m*; (*in building*) maestro *m* de obras; (*Law*) presidente *m* (del jurado).

foremast ['fɔːmɑːst] *n* trinquete *m* (*palo*).

foremost ['fɔːməust] *adj* primero, delantero; (*outstanding*) primero, principal.

forename ['fɔːneim] *n* nombre *m*, nombre *m* de pila.

forenoon ['fɔːnuːn] *n* mañana *f*.

forensic [fə'rensik] *adj* forense; *medicine* legal.

forerunner ['fɔːrʌnə*] *n* precursor *m*, ora *f*.

foresail ['fɔːseil] *n* trinquete *m* (*vela*).

foresee [fɔː'siː] (*irr: see* see) *vt* prever.

foreseeable [fɔː'siːəbl] *adj* previsible; **in the — future** hasta donde se pueda ver.

foreshadow [fɔː'ʃædəu] *vt* prefigurar, anunciar; (*person*) prever.

foreshore ['fɔːʃɔː*] *n* playa *f* (entre los límites de pleamar y bajamar).

foreshorten [fɔː'ʃɔːtn] *vt* escorzar.

foreshortening [fɔː'ʃɔːtniŋ] *n* escorzo *m*.

foresight ['fɔːsait] *n* previsión *f*; **lack of — impre-** visión *f*.

foreskin ['fɔːskin] *n* prepucio *m*.

forest ['fɔrist] **1** *n* bosque *m*; (*large, dense*) selva *f*. **2** *attr* forestal, del bosque.

forestall [fɔː'stɔːl] *vt event* anticipar, prevenir, impedir; *person* anticipar (e impedir).

forester ['fɔristə*] *n* (*expert*) ingeniero *m* de montes; (*keeper*) guardabosques *m*.

forestry ['fɔristri] *n* silvicultura *f*.

foretaste ['fɔːteist] *n* anticipo *m*, muestra *f*.

foretell [fɔː'tel] (*irr: see* **tell**) *vt* (*predict*) predecir, pronosticar; (*presage*) presagiar.

forethought ['fɔːθɔːt] *n* prevención *f*, previsión *f*; (*pej*) premeditación *f*.

forewarn [fɔː'wɔːn] *vt* prevenir; **to be — ed** estar prevenido, precaverse; **— ed is forearmed** hombre prevenido vale por dos.

foreword ['fɔːwəːd] *n* prefacio *m*.

forfeit ['fɔːfit] **1** *n* (*loss*) pérdida *f*; (*fine*) multa *f*; (*penalty*) pena *f*; (*in games*) prenda *f*; **—s** juego *m* de prendas. **2** *vt* perder (el derecho a).

forfeiture ['fɔːfitʃə*] *n* pérdida *f*.

forgather [fɔː'gæðə*] *vi* reunirse.

forgave [fə'geiv] *pret of* **forgive**.

forge[1] [fɔːdʒ] **1** *n* (*fire*) fragua *f*; (*smithy*) herrería *f*; (*ironworks*) fundición *f*. **2** *vt metal* forjar, fraguar; *friendship, plan, unity etc* fraguar; (*falsify*) falsificar, falsear, contrahacer.

forge[2] [fɔːdʒ] *vi:* **to — ahead** avanzar constantemente; adelantarse muchísimo (*of* a).

forger ['fɔːdʒə*] *n* falsificador *m*, falsario *m*.

forgery ['fɔːdʒəri] *n* falsificación *f*.

forget [fə'get] (*irr: pret* **forgot**, *ptp* **forgotten**) **1** *vt* olvidar, olvidarse de; **I forgot my umbrella in a train** dejé el paraguas en un tren; **— it!** ¡no se preocupe!; **and don't you — it!** ¡y que no se te olvide esto!; **never to be forgotten** inolvidable.

2 *vi* olvidarse; **I — no recuerdo, me he olvidado; but I forgot pero se me olvidó; to — about** olvidarse de; **let's — about it!** ¡pelillos a la mar!; **to — to do something** olvidarse de hacer algo; **I forgot to tell you why** se me olvidó decirle por qué.

3 *vr:* **to — oneself** propasarse, olvidar los buenos modales; **you — yourself, sir!** ¡prudencia, caballero!

forgetful [fə'getful] *adj character* olvidadizo, desmemoriado; descuidado; **— of all else** olvidando todo lo demás, sin hacer caso de todo lo demás; **he's terribly —** tiene un tremendo despiste.

forgetfulness [fə'getfulnis] *n* olvido *m*, falta *f* de memoria; descuido *m*; (*absentmindedness*) despiste *m*.

forget-me-not [fə'getminɔt] *n* nomeolvides *f*.

forgivable [fə'givəbl] *adj* perdonable.

forgive [fə'giv] (*irr: see* **give**) *vt* perdonar; **to — someone (for) something** perdonar algo a uno, perdonar a uno por algo.

forgiven [fə'givn] *ptp of* **forgive**.

forgiveness [fə'givnis] *n* (*pardon*) perdón *m*; (*compassion*) misericordia *f*.

forgiving [fə'giviŋ] *adj* perdonador, misericordioso; **to feel —** estar dispuesto a perdonar.

forgo [fɔː'gəu] (*irr: see* **go**) *vt* renunciar a, privarse de.

forgot [fə'gɔt] *pret of* **forget**.

forgotten [fə'gɔtn] *ptp of* **forget**.

fork [fɔːk] **1** *n* (*at table*) tenedor *m*; (*Agr*) horca *f*, horquilla *f*; (*Mech etc*) horquilla *f*; (*in road*) bifurcación *f*; (*Anat*) horcajadura *f*, entrepierna *f*; (*in river*) horcajo *m*; (*of tree*) horcadura *f*.

2 *vt* (*also to — over*) cultivar con horquilla; **to — out** (*fam*) desembolsar (de mala gana); **to — over** (*fam*) entregar.

3 *vi* (*road*) bifurcarse; **— right for Oxford** tuerza a la derecha para ir a Oxford.

forked [fɔːkt] *adj* ahorquillado, bifurcado; *lightning* en zigzag; *tail* hendido.

fork-lift truck ['fɔːklift'trʌk] *n* elevadora-transportadora *f* de horquilla.

forlorn [fə'lɔːn] *adj* abandonado, desamparado; *appearance* de abandono; **to look —** (*person*) tener aspecto triste; **why so —?** ¿por qué tan triste?; **— hope** empresa *f* desesperada; esperanza *f* que tiene poca probabilidad de verse realizada.

form [fɔːm] **1** *n* (a) (*shape, style, type, method etc*; *also Lit, Gram*) forma *f*; **a new — of government** un

nuevo sistema de gobierno; **the same thing in a new — la misma** cosa bajo una nueva forma; **choose another — of words** busque otra expresión; **it took the — of a cash prize** consistió en un premio en metálico; **what — will the ceremony take?** ¿cómo se organizará la ceremonia?

(**b**) (*shape vaguely seen*) figura *f*, bulto *m*.

(**c**) (*School*) clase *f*.

(**d**) (*bench*) banco *m*.

(**e**) (*document*) hoja *f*, formulario *m*; **application — (hoja *f* de) solicitud *f*; formulario *m* de inscripción; **to fill up a — llenar una hoja; has he got any — ?** (*fam*) ¿tiene antecedentes penales?

(**f**) (*customary method*) forma *f*; **in due — en la** debida forma, en la forma reglamentaria; **that is common — eso es muy corriente; what's the — ?** ¿qué es lo que hemos de hacer?

(**g**) (*formality*) **for —'s sake** por pura fórmula, para salvar las apariencias.

(**h**) (*behaviour*) **it's bad — to + infin** es de mal gusto + *infin*, es de mala educación + *infin*.

(**i**) (*condition*) estado *m* físico; **to be in good — (*Sport*) estar en forma, (*be witty*) estar de vena; **to be out of — estar** desentrenado, haber perdido el tacto.

2 *vt* formar; *habit* adquirir; *company* fundar, establecer; *plan* concebir; *idea* hacerse; *impression, opinion* formarse; *queue* hacer; **to — a government** formar gobierno; **those who — the group** los que forman parte del grupo; **to — up** *troops* formar.

3 *vi:* **to — up** alinearse, (*Mil*) formar.

formal ['fɔːməl] *adj person's manner* ceremonioso, estirado; *person's character* etiquetero; *greeting* ceremonioso; *visit* de cumplido, oficial; *function* protocolario; *dance, dress* de etiqueta; (*relating to form*) formal; **don't be so —!** ¡no te andes con tantos cumplidos!; **there was no — agreement** no hubo contrato en forma.

formaldehyde [fɔː'mældihaid] *n* formaldehido *m*.

formalin(e) ['fɔːmalin] *n* formalina *f*.

formality [fɔː'mæliti] *n* (**a**) (*of occasion*) ceremonia *f*, lo ceremonioso; (*of person*) lo etiquetero; (*of dress etc*) etiqueta *f*; **with all due — en la debida forma; it's a mere — es pura fórmula.

(**b**) **formalities** ceremonias *fpl*; formalidades *fpl*; **let's do without the formalities** prescindamos de los trámites de costumbre.

formally ['fɔːməli] *adv greet etc* ceremoniosamente; *open, visit* oficialmente; *agree etc* en forma.

format ['fɔːmæt] *n* formato *m*.

formation [fɔː'meiʃən] *n* formación *f*; **in battle — en** orden de batalla.

formative ['fɔːmətiv] *adj* formativo.

former ['fɔːmə*] *adj* (**a**) (*of two*) primero, anterior; **your — idea** su primera idea.

(**b**) (*earlier*) antiguo; **a — seat of government** una antigua sede del gobierno.

(**c**) (*of person*) ex, que fue; **— president** ex presidente *m*; **a — ambassador in Lima** embajador que fue en Lima.

(**d**) **the — (. . . the latter)** aquél *etc* (. . . éste *etc*).

formerly ['fɔːməli] *adv* antes, antiguamente.

formic ['fɔːmik] *adj:* **— acid** ácido *m* fórmico.

formidable ['fɔːmidəbl] *adj* formidable.

formless ['fɔːmlis] *adj* informe.

formula ['fɔːmjulə] *n*, *pl* **formulae** ['fɔːmjuliː] fórmula *f*.

formulate ['fɔːmjuleit] *vt* formular.

formulation [ˌfɔːmju'leiʃən] *n* formulación *f*.

fornicate ['fɔːnikeit] *vi* fornicar.

fornication [ˌfɔːni'keiʃən] *n* fornicación *f*.

forsake [fə'seik] (*irr: pret* **forsook**, *ptp* **forsaken**) *vt person etc* abandonar, dejar, desamparar; *plan* renunciar a; *belief* renegar de; **he forsook Seville for Madrid** abandonó Sevilla y se fue a vivir a Madrid.

forsaken [fə'seikən] *ptp of* **forsake**.

forsook [fə'suk] *pret of* **forsake**.

forswear [fɔː'sweə*] (*irr: see* **swear**) *vt* abjurar de, renunciar a.

forsythia [fɔː'saiθiə] *n* forsitia *f*.

fort [fɔːt] *n* fuerte *m*, fortín *m*; **to hold the — (*fig*) defenderse, seguir en su puesto, encargarse del trabajo (temporalmente).

forte [fɔːt] *n* fuerte *m*.

forth [fɔːθ] *adv:* **and so — etcétera; y así sucesivamente; from this day — de aquí en adelante; *see* **back** *etc*.

forthcoming [fɔːθ'kʌmiŋ] *adj* (**a**) (*approaching*) venidero, próximo; *book etc* de próxima aparición, en preparación.

(**b**) (*available*) disponible; **if help is — si nos mandan socorros, si nos ayudan; **if funds are — si nos dan el dinero; **no answer was** — no hubo respuesta.

(c) *character* afable, comunicativo; **he's not very** — no dice mucho; **he's not** — **with strangers** tiene poca confianza con los desconocidos.

forthright ['fɔːθrait] *adj person* directo, franco; enérgico; *answer etc* terminante; *refusal* rotundo.

forthwith ['fɔːθ'wiθ] *adv* (*then and there*) en el acto; (*without delay*) sin dilación.

fortieth ['fɔːtiiθ] *adj* cuadragésimo.

fortification [ˌfɔːtifi'keiʃən] *n* fortificación *f*.

fortify ['fɔːtifai] **1** *vt* (*Mil*) fortificar; (*strengthen*) fortalecer; *wine* encabezar; *person* vigorizar, fortalecer; **to** — **someone in a belief** confirmar la opinión que tiene uno.

2 *vr*: **to** — **oneself** (*fig*) fortalecerse.

fortitude ['fɔːtitjuːd] *n* fortaleza *f*, estoicismo *m*, valor *m*.

fortnight ['fɔːtnait] *n* quince días *mpl*, quincena *f*; **today** — de hoy en quince (días).

fortnightly ['fɔːtnaitli] **1** *adj* que sale (*etc*) cada quince días, quincenal. **2** *adv* cada quince días, quincenalmente.

fortress ['fɔːtris] *n* fortaleza *f*, plaza *f* fuerte.

fortuitous [fɔː'tjuːitəs] *adj* fortuito, casual.

fortuitously [fɔː'tjuːitəsli] *adv* fortuitamente, por casualidad.

fortunate ['fɔːtʃənit] *adj* afortunado; (*happy*) dichoso, feliz; **to be** — (*person*) tener suerte; **that was** — **for you** en eso tuviste suerte.

fortunately ['fɔːtʃənitli] *adv* afortunadamente.

fortune ['fɔːtʃən] *n* (a) (*luck, fate*) fortuna *f*, suerte *f*; **by good** — por fortuna; **the** —**s of war** las peripecias de la guerra; **we had the good** — to find him tuvimos la suerte de encontrarle; **to tell someone's** — decir a uno la buenaventura; **to try one's** — probar fortuna.

(b) (*money*) fortuna *f*, caudal *m*; **to come into a** — heredar una fortuna; **to cost a** — valer un dineral; **to make a** — enriquecerse, hacer su pacotilla (*fam*); **to marry a** — casarse con una mujer acaudalada.

fortuneteller ['fɔːtʃən,telə*] *n* adivina *f*.

forty ['fɔːti] *adj* cuarenta; **the forties** (*eg* 1940s) los años cuarenta; **to be in one's forties** tener más de cuarenta años.

fortyish ['fɔːtiiʃ] *adj* cuarentón.

forum ['fɔːrəm] *n* foro *m*; (*fig*) tribunal *m*.

forward ['fɔːwəd] **1** *adj* (a) (*front*) delantero; *position* (*Mil etc*) avanzado; *line* (*Sport*) delantero; (*Naut*) de proa; *movement* progresivo, de avance; *gears* de avance; *pass* (*Rugby*) adelantado; *delivery* (*Comm*) en fecha futura.

(b) *season, crop* adelantado; precoz; *person* atrevido, fresco, descarado.

2 *n* (*Sport*) delantero *m*.

3 *vt* (*send*) enviar; (*re-address*) hacer seguir; **"to be** —**ed", "please** —**"** "se ruega hacer seguir".

forward(s) ['fɔːwəd(z)] *adv* adelante, hacia adelante; (*Naut*) hacia la proa; —**!** ¡adelante!; — **march!** de frente ¡mar!; **the lever is placed well** — la palanca está colocada bastante hacia adelante; **from that day** — desde ese día en adelante; **to go** — ir hacia adelante, avanzar; (*fig*) progresar, hacer progresos.

forwardness ['fɔːwədnis] *n* (*of crop etc*) precocidad *f*; (*pertness*) frescura *f*, descaro *m*.

forwent [fɔː'went] *pret of* **forgo**.

fossil ['fɔsl] **1** *adj* fósil. **2** *n* fósil *m*.

fossilized ['fɔsilaizd] *adj* fosilizado.

foster ['fɔstə*] *vt* (*encourage*) fomentar, promover; (*aid*) favorecer; *hope* alentar; *child* criar.

foster brother ['fɔstə,brʌðə*] *n* hermano *m* de leche.

foster mother ['fɔstə,mʌðə*] *n* madre *f* adoptiva; (*wet-nurse*) ama *f* de leche.

fought [fɔːt] *pret and ptp of* **fight**.

foul [faul] **1** *adj* (*dirty*) sucio, puerco; (*disgusting*) asqueroso; (*of bad quality*) horrible; (*morally vile*) vil, horrible; *air* viciado; *blow, language, play* sucio; *breath* fétido; *calumny* vil; *smell* insoportable; *weather* feo, horrible; **to fall** — **of** indisponerse con, ponerse a malas con; *rule* infringir.

2 *n* (*Sport*) falta *f* (*on contra*).

3 *vt* (a) (*dirty*) ensuciar; *one's nest* manchar.

(b) (*block*) atascar, obstruir; (*catch up in*) enredarse en; (*hit*) chocar contra.

(c) (*Sport*) cometer una falta contra.

foulmouthed ['faul'mauðd] *adj* malhablado.

foul-smelling ['faul'smeliŋ] *adj* hediondo.

found[1] [faund] *pret and ptp of* **find**.

found[2] [faund] *vt* fundar, establecer; *fortune* crear; **a statement** —**ed on fact** una declaración basada en hechos.

found[3] [faund] *vt* (*Tech*) fundir.

foundation [faun'deiʃən] *n* (a) (*act*) fundación *f*, establecimiento *m*; creación *f*.

(b) (*basis*) base *f*, fundamento *m*; **statement devoid of** — declaración *f* que carece de base.

(c) —**s** (*Archit*) cimientos *mpl*; **to lay the** —**s** echar los cimientos (*of de; also fig*).

foundation stone [faun'deiʃənstəun] *n* primera piedra *f*; (*fig*) piedra *f* angular.

founder[1] ['faundə*] *n* fundador *m*, ora *f*.

founder[2] ['faundə*] *vi* irse a pique, hundirse; (*fig*) fracasar (*on debido a*).

foundling ['faundliŋ] *n* niño *m* expósito, niña *f* expósita, inclusero *m*, a *f*; — **hospital** inclusa *f*.

foundry ['faundri] *n* fundición *f*.

fount [faunt] *n* (*Typ*) fundición *f*, familia *f* (de la letra).

fountain ['fauntin] *n* (*natural*) fuente *f*, manantial *m* (*also fig*); (*artificial*) fuente *f*, surtidor *m*; (*jet*) chorro *m*.

fountainhead ['fauntinhed] *n* fuente *f*, origen *m*; **to go to the** — acudir a la propia fuente.

fountain pen ['fauntinpen] *n* estilográfica *f*, pluma-fuente *f* (*S Am*).

four [fɔː*] **1** *adj* cuatro. **2** *n* cuatro *m*; **to be on all** —**s with** estar en completa armonía con; **to go on all** —**s** ir a gatas; **to form** —**s** formar a cuatro.

four-door ['fɔː'dɔː*] *adj car* de cuatro puertas.

four-engined ['fɔːr'endʒind] *adj* cuatrimotor, tetra-motor.

fourflusher ['fɔː'flʌʃə*] *n* (*US sl*) embustero *m*.

fourfold ['fɔːfəuld] **1** *adj* cuádruple. **2** *adv* cuatro veces.

fourfooted ['fɔː'futid] *adj* cuadrúpedo.

fourposter ['fɔː,pəustə*] *n* (*also* — **bed**) cama *f* de columnas.

fourscore ['fɔː'skɔː*] *adj* ochenta.

foursome ['fɔːsəm] *n* grupo *m* de cuatro personas.

foursquare ['fɔː'skweə*] **1** *adj* firme; franco, sincero. **2** *adv*: **to stand** — **with someone** estar en completa armonía con uno, apoyar a uno incondicionalmente.

fourteen ['fɔː'tiːn] *adj* catorce.

fourteenth ['fɔː'tiːnθ] *adj* decimocuarto.

fourth [fɔːθ] **1** *adj* cuarto. **2** *n* cuarto *m*, cuarta parte *f*; (*Mus*) cuarta *f*; **to make a** — (*Cards*) unirse a otras tres personas (para que se pueda jugar).

fourthly ['fɔːθli] *adv* en cuarto lugar.

four-wheel drive ['fɔːwiːl'draiv] *n* tracción *f* a las cuatro ruedas.

fowl [faul] *n* (*bird in general*) ave *f*; (*chicken*) ave *f* de corral, gallina *f*; (*served as food*) pollo *m*; **the** —**s of the air** las aves.

fowlpest ['faulpest] *n* peste *f* aviar.

fox [fɔks] **1** *n* zorra *f*, (*dog-*) zorro *m*; (*fig*) zorro *m*. **2** *vt* confundir, dejar perplejo; **this will** — **them** esto les ha de despistar; **you had me properly** —**ed** there eso me tuvo completamente despistado. **3** *vi* disimular, fingir.

fox cub ['fɔkskʌb] *n* cachorro *m* (de zorro).

foxed [fɔkst] *adj* manchado.

foxglove ['fɔksglʌv] *n* dedalera *f*.

foxhole ['fɔkshəul] *n* (*Mil*) hoyo *m* de protección.

foxhound ['fɔkshaund] *n* perro *m* raposero.

foxhunt ['fɔkshʌnt] *n* cacería *f* de zorras.

foxhunting ['fɔks,hʌntiŋ] *n* caza *f* de zorras.

fox terrier ['fɔks'teriə*] *n* foxterrier *m*.

foxtrot ['fɔkstrɔt] *n* fox *m*.

foxy ['fɔksi] *adj* taimado, astuto.

foyer ['fɔiei] *n* hall *m*, vestíbulo *m*.

fracas ['frækaː] *n* gresca *f*, riña *f*.

fraction ['frækʃən] *n* (*Math*) fracción *f*, quebrado *m*; (*fig*) pequeña porción *f*, parte *f* muy pequeña.

fractional ['frækʃənl] *adj* fraccionario; (*fig*) muy pequeño.

fractious ['frækʃəs] *adj* (*character*) rebelón, displicente; (*mood*) malhumorado.

fracture ['fræktʃə*] **1** *n* fractura *f*; **compound** — fractura *f* complicada. **2** *vt* fracturar. **3** *vi* fracturarse.

fragile ['frædʒail] *adj* frágil, quebradizo; *person* delicado.

fragility [frə'dʒiliti] *n* fragilidad *f*.

fragment ['frægmənt] *n* fragmento *m*; trozo *m*; **to smash something to** —**s** hacer algo añicos.

fragmentary ['fræg'mentəri] *adj* fragmentario.

fragrance ['freigrəns] *n* fragancia *f*.

fragrant ['freigrənt] *adj* fragante, oloroso; *memory* dulce.

frail [freil] *adj* frágil, quebradizo; delicado; (*Med*) débil; (*morally*) flaco, endeble.

frailty ['freilti] *n* fragilidad *f*; (*Med*) debilidad *f*; (*moral*) flaqueza *f*.

frame [freim] **1** *n* **(a)** *(framework)* estructura *f*, esqueleto *m*; *(Tech)* armazón *f*, bastidor *m*; *(Sew)* bastidor *m* para bordar; *(of spectacles)* montura *f*, armadura *f*; *(of bicycle)* cuadro *m*; *(of picture, window)* marco *m*.
(b) *(body)* figura *f*, talle *m*; **his large — su** cuerpo fornido; **her whole — was shaken by sobs** los sollozos sacudían su cuerpo entero.
(c) — of mind estado *m* de ánimo; **when you're in a better — of mind** cuando estés de mejor humor.
2 *vt* *(construct)* construir; *(arrange)* disponer, arreglar; *picture* poner un marco a, *(fig)* servir de marco a; *(contrive)* idear; *sound* articular; *question etc* formular, expresar; *(fam)* incriminar por medio de una estratagema.
3 *vi* **(a) how is it framing?** ¿qué tal se está desarrollando?; **he's framing well** hace buenos progresos, promete.
(b) to — up to someone ponerse en actitud para defenderse contra uno.
frame-up ['freimʌp] *n* *(fam)* estratagema *f* para incriminar a uno; **it's a —** aquí hay trampa.
framework ['freimwə:k] *n* *(Tech)* armazón *f*, esqueleto *m*; *(fig)* sistema *m*, organización *f*, marco *m*; **within the — of the constitution** dentro del marco de la constitución.
franc [fræŋk] *n* franco *m*.
France [fra:ns] *n* Francia *f*.
Frances ['fra:nsis] *f* Francisca.
Francis ['fra:nsis] *m* Francisco.
franchise ['fræntʃaiz] *n* derecho *m* de votar, sufragio *m*.
Franciscan [fræn'siskən] **1** *adj* franciscano. **2** *n* franciscano *m*.
francophile ['fræŋkəufail] *n* francófilo *m*, a *f*.
francophobe ['fræŋkəufəub] *n* francófobo *m*, a *f*.
Frank[1] [fræŋk] *n* *(Hist)* franco *m*.
Frank[2] [fræŋk] *m* Paco.
frank[1] [fræŋk] *adj* franco.
frank[2] [fræŋk] *vt* *letter* franquear.
frankfurter ['fræŋkfə:tə*] *n* salchicha *f*.
frankincense ['fræŋkinsens] *n* incienso *m*.
Frankish ['fræŋkiʃ] **1** *adj* fráncico. **2** *n* *(language)* fráncico *m*.
frankly ['fræŋkli] *adv* francamente.
frankness ['fræŋknis] *n* franqueza *f*.
frantic ['fræntik] *adj* frenético, furioso; **to be — with** worry andar como loco de inquietud; **to drive someone —** volver a uno loco.
frantically ['fræntikəli] *adv* frenéticamente, con frenesí.
fraternal [frə'tə:nl] *adj* fraternal, fraterno.
fraternity [frə'tə:niti] *n* fraternidad *f*; *(guild)* cofradía *f*; *(US)* club *m* de estudiantes.
fraternization [,frætənai'zeiʃən] *n* fraternización *f*.
fraternize ['frætənaiz] *vi* confraternizar *(with* con).
fratricide ['frætrisaid] *n* *(act)* fratricidio *m*; *(person)* fratricida *m*.
fraud [frɔ:d] *n* fraude *m*; *(person)* impostor *m*, farsante *m*.
fraudulence ['frɔ:djuləns] *n* fraudulencia *f*, fraude *m*.
fraudulent ['frɔ:djulənt] *adj* fraudulento.
fraught [frɔ:t] *adj*: **— with** cargado de, lleno de.
fray[1] [frei] *n* combate *m*, lucha *f*; **to be ready for the — tener ganas de pelear; to gird oneself for the —** aprestarse para la lucha.
fray[2] [frei] **1** *vt* desgastar, raer. **2** *vi* deshilacharse; **to — against, to — on** ludir con, rozar.
frayed [freid] *adj* raído, dishilachado; **tempers were getting —** todos estaban a punto de perder la paciencia.
frazzle ['fræzl] *n* *(fam)*: **to beat someone to a —** *(Sport)* cascar a uno, derrotar a uno por completo; **to be worn to a —** estar rendido de cansancio.
freak [fri:k] **1** *n* **(a)** *(person)* fenómeno *m*; *(abnormal specimen)* monstruo *m*, monstruosidad *f*; curiosidad *f*; ejemplar *m* anormal; *(Bio)* mutación *f*; **the result was a —** el resultado fue totalmente fortuito, fue imposible prever tal resultado.
(b) *(whim)* capricho *m*.
2 *adj* = **freakish**.
freakish ['fri:kiʃ] *adj* **(a)** *specimen* anormal, monstruoso; *result* inesperado, imprevisible, fortuito.
(b) *person* caprichoso.
freckle ['frekl] *n* peca *f*.
freckled ['frekld] *adj* pecoso, lleno de pecas.
Fred [fred], **Freddie, Freddy** ['fredi] *m* *nombres cariñosos de* **Frederick**.
Frederick ['fredrik] *m* Federico.
free [fri:] **1** *adj* **(a)** *(at liberty etc)* libre *(from, of* de); *(not fixed)* suelto, libre; *(untied)* libre, desatado; *account, choice, translation, verse* libre; *port* franco;

— speech libertad *f* de palabra; **— of duty** libro de derechos de aduana; **a surface — from dust** una superficie libre de polvo; **the fishing is —** la pesca está autorizada; **the area is — of malaria** la región es inmune contra el paludismo; **to be — to + infin** poder libremente **+ infin**, ser libre de **+ infin**; **he is not — to act** tiene las manos atadas; **we are — of him at last** por fin nos hemos librado de él; **to break —** soltarse; **to let someone go —** poner en libertad a uno; **to set — person** poner en libertad, libertar, librar; *slave* manumitir, emancipar; *animal* soltar.
(b) *(not occupied)* libre; *post* vacante; *premises* desocupado; **is this table —?** ¿está libre esta mesa?; **are you — tomorrow?** ¿estás libre mañana?
(c) *language etc* libre, desvergonzado; *(insolent)* descarado; **— and easy** despreocupado, poco ceremonioso.
(d) to be — with ser liberal con, no regatear; dar en abundancia; **to be — with one's money** ser manirroto; **he's very — in blaming others** echa libremente la culpa a otros; **he's too — with his remarks** es demasiado libre en sus comentarios; **to be — with one's hands** *(stealing)* ser largo de uñas, *(amorously)* ser un tocotón; **to make — of** *(or* with*)* usar como si fuera cosa propia.
(e) *(for nothing)* gratuito; *ticket* de favor; **— of charge** gratis; **admission —** entrada gratis; **catalogue — on request** el catálogo se envía gratis a petición; **— on board** franco a bordo.
2 *adv* gratis.
3 *vt* *(set free)* poner en libertad, libertar; *slave* manumitir; *animal* soltar; *(untie)* desatar, soltar; *knot, tangle* desenredar; *place, surface etc* despejar, desembarazar *(of* de); *(rescue)* librar, salvar *(from* de), rescatar; *(from burden, tax etc)* eximir, exentar *(from* de).
4 *vr*: **to — oneself** desatarse, soltarse.
freebooter ['fri:bu:tə*] *n* filibustero *m*.
freedom ['fri:dəm] *n* libertad *f*; exención *f* *(from* de), inmunidad *f* *(from* contra); *(ease)* facilidad *f*, soltura *f*; **— of a city** ciudadanía *f* de honor; **— of action** libertad *f* de acción; **— of the press** libertad *f* de prensa; **— of speech** libertad *f* de palabra; **— of worship** libertad *f* de cultos.
free-fight ['fri:fait] *n*, **free-for-all** ['fri:fə'rɔ:l] *n* sarracina *f*, riña *f* general.
freehand ['fri:hænd] *adj* hecho a pulso.
freehold ['fri:həuld] **1** *adj*: **— property** = **2** *n* feudo *m* franco.
freeholder ['fri:,həuldə*] *n* poseedor *m* de feudo franco.
free kick ['fri:'kik] *n* golpe *m* franco.
freelance ['fri:la:ns] **1** *adj* independiente. **2** *n* periodista *mf* *(etc)* independiente. **3** *vi* trabajar como periodista *(etc)* independiente.
freely ['fri:li] *adv* libremente; *(generously)* liberalmente; *confess, speak etc* francamente; **you may come and go —** Vd puede ir y venir con toda libertad.
freeman ['fri:mən] *n*, *pl* **—men** [mən] *(Hist)* hombre *m* libre; *(of city)* ciudadano *m* de honor.
freemason ['fri:,meisn] *n* francmasón *m*.
freemasonry ['fri:,meisnri] *n* francmasonería *f*; *(fig)* compañerismo *m*, camaradería *f*.
freesia ['fri:ziə] *n* fresia *f*.
freestyle ['fri:stail] *adj*: **200 metres —** 200 metros libres.
freethinker ['fri:'θiŋkə*] *n* librepensador *m*, ora *f*.
freethinking ['fri:'θiŋkiŋ] *n* librepensamiento *m*.
free trade ['fri:'treid] *n* libre cambio *m*.
free trader ['fri:'treidə*] *n* librecambista *m*.
freewheel ['fri:'wi:l] **1** *n* rueda *f* libre. **2** *vi* *(cyclist)* andar a rueda libre, *(Aut)* ir en punto muerto.
free will ['fri:'wil] *n* libre albedrío *m*.
freeze [fri:z] *(irr: pret* **froze***, ptp* **frozen***)* **1** *vt* helar; *food, prices, wages etc* congelar; **the lake is frozen over** el lago está helado; **we're simply frozen** estamos francamente helados; **we're frozen up at home** en casa las cañerías están heladas; **to — out** *competitor* deshacerse de (quitándole la clientela).
2 *vi* helarse; congelarse; *(fig)* quedar helado (de miedo *etc*); *(animal)* permanecer enteramente inmóvil; **I'm freezing** estoy helado; **to — to death** morir de frío; **the smile froze on his lips** se le heló la sonrisa en los labios.
3 *vi* *(impersonal)* helar; **it will — tonight** esta noche habrá helada.
4 *n* helada *f*; *(of prices, wages etc)* congelación *f*.
freezer ['fri:zə*] *n* congelador *m*, heladora *f*.
freeze-up ['fri:zʌp] *n* helada *f*.

freezing ['fri:ziŋ] **1** adj glacial (also fig), helado. **2** n (a) (of rents etc) congelación f. (b) = freezing point.

freezing point ['fri:ziŋpɔint] n punto m de congelación; **5 degrees below** — 5 grados bajo cero.

freight [freit] n flete m; (load) carga f; (goods) mercancías fpl.

freightage ['freitidʒ] n flete m.

freight car ['freitkɑ:*] n (US) vagón m de mercancías.

freighter ['freitə*] n buque m de carga.

French [frentʃ] **1** adj francés; **the** — los franceses. **2** n (language) francés m.

French Canadian ['frentʃkə'neidiən] **1** adj francocanadiense. **2** n francocanadiense mf.

Frenchman ['frentʃmən] n, pl —**men** [mən] francés m.

Frenchwoman ['frentʃ,wumən] n, pl —**women** [,wimin] francesa f.

frenetic [fri'netik] adj frenético.

frenzied ['frenzid] adj effort etc frenético; crowd etc enloquecido.

frenzy ['frenzi] n frenesí m, delirio m.

frequency ['fri:kwənsi] n frecuencia f (also Elec); **high** — alta frecuencia f.

frequent ['fri:kwənt] adj frecuente.

frequent [fri:'kwent] vt frecuentar.

frequently ['fri:kwəntli] adv frecuentemente, con frecuencia, a menudo.

fresco ['freskəu] n, pl **fresco(e)s** ['freskəuz] fresco m.

fresh [freʃ] adj (a) (new) nuevo; **to start a** — **life** comenzar una vida nueva; **he has had a** — **attack** ha sufrido un nuevo ataque; **it is** — **in my memory** se conserva muy fresco en mi memoria; **to put** — **courage into someone** reanimar a uno.
(b) (newly come) — **from Spain** recién llegado (or importado etc) de España; — **from the oven** que acaba de salir del horno.
(c) (inexperienced) nuevo.
(d) (not stale) fruit etc fresco; air fresco, puro (and see air); water dulce; **as** — **as a daisy** tan fresco como una rosa; **to feel perfectly** — estar lleno de vigor.
(e) (cheeky) fresco, descocado; **to get** — **with someone** ponerse fresco con uno.
(f) (cool) fresco.
(g) wind recio.
(h) face, complexion de buen color.

freshen ['freʃn] **1** vt (also **to** — **up**) refrescar. **2** vi (temperature) refrescarse; (wind) soplar más recio; (person; also **to** — **up**) lavarse, arreglarse.

fresher ['freʃə*] n (fam) = **freshman**.

freshly ['freʃli] adv nuevamente, recientemente; — **made** nuevo, recién hecho, acabado de hacer.

freshman ['freʃmən] n, pl —**men** [mən] (Univ) estudiante m de primer año, pipiolo m (fam).

freshness ['freʃnis] n frescura f; (newness) novedad f; vigor m.

freshwater ['freʃ,wɔ:tə*] adj de agua dulce.

fret [fret] **1** vt (a) (wear away) corroer, raer, desgastar.
(b) person irritar, molestar.
(c) **to** — **the hours away** pasar las horas consumiéndose de inquietud.
2 vi inquietarse, apurarse; impacientarse (at por); **it's** —**ting for its mother** se está apurando por la ausencia de su madre; **don't** — ! ¡no te apuras!
3 n: **to be in a** — estar muy inquieto, apurarse.

fretful ['fretful] adj displicente, quejoso; impaciente; inquieto.

fretfully ['fretfəli] adv impacientemente; inquietamente.

fretsaw ['fretsɔ:] n sierra f de calados.

fretwork ['fretwɔ:k] n calado m.

Freudian ['frɔidiən] adj freudiano.

friable ['fraiəbl] adj desmenuzable, friable.

friar ['fraiə*] n (a) fraile m; **black** — dominico m; **grey** — franciscano m; **white** — carmelita m.
(b) (before name) fray.

fricative ['frikətiv] **1** adj fricativo. **2** n fricativa f.

friction ['frikʃən] n (Tech) fricción f, rozamiento m; (Med etc) frote m, frotamiento m; (fig) tirantez f, desavenencia f (about, over con motivo de).

Friday ['fraidi] n viernes m; **Good** — Viernes m Santo.

fridge [fridʒ] n (fam) = **refrigerator**.

fried [fraid] adj frito.

fried-fish shop ['fraid'fiʃʃɔp] n freiduría f de pescado.

friend [frend] n amigo m, a f; **F**— (Rel) cuáquero m, a f; —**s** amigos mpl, amistades fpl; — ! (Mil) ¡gente de paz!; **a** — **of mine** un amigo mío; **he's no** — **of mine** no es de mis amigos; **he is no** — **to violence** no es partidario de la violencia; **we're the best of** —**s**

somos muy amigos; **to be** —**s with someone** ser amigo de uno; **to have a** — **at court** tener el padre alcalde; **to make** —**s with someone** hacerse amigo de uno, trabar amistad con uno; **he makes** —**s easily** le es fácil trabar amistad con las personas.

friendless ['frendlis] adj sin amigos.

friendliness ['frendlinis] n simpatía f; amabilidad f; cordialidad f; lo acogedor.

friendly ['frendli] adj (a) (of person) simpático; amable; **people here are so** — aquí la gente es muy simpática; **he's a** — **soul** es simpatiquísimo; **to be** — **with ser** amigo de; **to get** — hacerse amigos.
(b) relationship, greeting, tone amistoso, cordial; shout jovial; atmosphere, place acogedor; match amistoso; nation amigo; society de socorro mutuo; **that wasn't a very** — **thing to do** eso no fue la acción de un amigo.

friendship ['frendʃip] n amistad f.

Friesland ['fri:zlənd] Frisia f.

frieze [fri:z] n friso m.

frigate ['frigit] n fragata f.

fright [frait] n (a) (sudden fear) susto m, sobresalto m; (state of alarm) terror m; **what a** — **you gave me** ! ¡qué susto me diste!; **to have a** — tener un susto, llevarse un susto; **to take** — asustarse (at de).
(b) (person) espantajo m; **doesn't she look a** —? ¡qué adefesio de mujer!

frighten ['fraitn] vt asustar, espantar, sobresaltar; alarmar; **to** — **away, to** — **off** ahuyentar, espantar; **to be** —**ed** tener miedo (of a); **don't be** —**ed** ! ¡no te asustes!; **she is easily** —**ed** es asustadiza; **to** — **someone into doing something** obligar a uno a hacer algo infundiéndole miedo.

frightening ['fraitniŋ] adj espantoso, aterrador.

frightful ['fraitful] adj espantoso, horrible, horroroso; (very bad) horrible, malísimo.

frightfully ['fraitfəli] adv (fig) terriblemente, tremendamente; **it's** — **hard** es terriblemente difícil; **it's** — **good** es la mar de bueno; **I'm** — **sorry** lo siento muchísimo.

frightfulness ['fraitfulnis] n horror m; (Mil) terrorismo m.

frigid ['fridʒid] adj frío; (Med) frígido; atmosphere, look etc glacial.

frigidity [fri'dʒiditi] n frialdad f; (Med) frigidez f.

frill [fril] n lechuga f, volante m; —**s** (fig) adornos mpl.

fringe [frindʒ] **1** n (a) (Sew) franja f, orla f, borde m; (hair) flequillo m.
(b) margen m; **the outer** —**s of the city** las partes exteriores de la ciudad; **on the** —**s of the lake** en los bordes del lago.
(c) lunatic — elementos mpl fanáticos (y estrafalarios); **to live on the** — **of society** vivir al margen de la sociedad.
2 attr: — **benefits** ventajas fpl supletorias, ingresos mpl accesorios.

frippery ['fripəri] n perifollos mpl, perejiles mpl.

frisk [frisk] **1** vt palpar, cachear. **2** vi (also **to** — **about**) retozar, juguetear, brincar.

frisky ['friski] adj retozón, juguetón; horse fogoso; **he's pretty** — **still** sigue muy activo.

fritter ['fritə*] **1** n fruta f de sartén, buñuelo m. **2** vt: **to** — **away** desperdiciar, disipar.

frivolity [fri'vɔliti] n frivolidad f, informalidad f, ligereza f.

frivolous ['frivələs] adj frívolo, poco formal, ligero.

frizz [friz] n, **frizzle** ['frizl] n rizos mpl pequeños y muy apretados.

frizz(l)y ['friz(l)i] adj muy ensortijado.

fro [frəu] adv: **to and** — de un lado a otro, de aquí para allá; **to and** — **movement** vaivén m.

frock [frɔk] n vestido m.

frock coat ['frɔk'kəut] n levita f.

frog [frɔg] n rana f; **to have a** — **in one's throat** padecer carraspera.

frogman ['frɔgmən] n, pl —**men** [mən] hombrerana m.

frog-march ['frɔgmɑ:tʃ] vt llevar codo con codo.

frolic ['frɔlik] **1** n juego m alegre; (party) fiesta f, holgorio m; (prank) travesura f. **2** vi juguetear, retozar; divertirse (with con).

frolicsome ['frɔliksəm] adj retozón, juguetón; (mischievous) travieso.

from [frɔm] prep de; — **A to Z** de A a Z, desde A hasta Z; — **door to door** de puerta en puerta; — **£2 upwards** desde 2 libras en adelante; **he had gone** — **home** se había ido de su casa; **to pick someone** — **the crowd** escoger a uno de la multitud.
(b) (time) — **Friday** a partir del viernes; — **a child** desde niño; — **that time** desde aquel momento.
(c) (deprivation) **to take something** — **someone**

quitar algo a uno; **he stole the book** — me me robó el libro; **I'll buy it** — **you** te lo compraré.

(d) (against) **to shelter** — **the rain** abrigarse de la lluvia.

(e) (distinguishing) **to know good** — **bad** saber distinguir entre el bien y el mal, saber distinguir el bien del mal.

(f) (originating) **the train** — **Madrid** el tren de Madrid, el tren procedente de Madrid; **he comes** — **Segovia** es de Segovia; **where are you** — ? ¿de dónde es Vd?; **a message** — **him** un mensaje de parte de él; **tell him that** — me dile eso de parte mía; **one of the best performances we have seen** — **him** uno de los mejores papeles que le hayamos visto; **to drink** — **a cup** beber de una taza; **we learned it** — **him** lo aprendimos de él; **we learned it** — **a book** lo aprendimos en un libro.

(g) (because of) — **what he says** por lo que dice, según lo que dice; **to act** — **conviction** obrar por convicción; — **sheer necessity** por pura necesidad; **to die** — **a fever** morir de una fiebre; **he is tired** — **overwork** está cansado por exceso de trabajo.

(h) — **above** desde encima; — **afar** desde lejos; — **among** de entre.

frond [frɔnd] n fronda f.

front [frʌnt] **1** adj (a) delantero, anterior; (first) primero; door principal, de entrada; view de frente.

(b) — **organization** organización f controlada clandestinamente por un partido político.

2 n (a) frente m (also Mil, Pol, Meteorol); (forepart) parte f delantera, parte f anterior; (of house) fachada f; (of book, start) principio m; (of shirt etc) pechera f; (Theat) auditorio m; (beach) playa f, (promenade) paseo m marítimo; **on Brighton** — en la playa de Brighton; **cold** — frente m frío; **popular** — frente m popular; **at** (or **in**) **the** — **of the book** al principio del libro; **in** — delante; **in** — of delante de; **to be in** — ir primero, ir delante, (in race) ir en cabeza; **to come to the** — empezar a destacar; **to push one's way to the** — abrirse camino a empujones hasta la primera fila (etc); **to send someone on in** — enviar a uno por delante.

(b) (fig) apariencias fpl; **it's all just** — **with him** con él no son más que apariencias; **to put on a bold** — hacer de tripas corazón.

3 vi: **to** — **on** (**to**) dar a, estar enfrente de.

frontage ['frʌntidʒ] n fachada f.

frontal ['frʌntl] adj frontal; attack de frente.

frontier ['frʌntiə*] **1** n frontera f. **2** attr fronterizo.

frontispiece ['frʌntispiːs] n (Typ) portada f.

front-page ['frʌnt'peidʒ] adj de primera página, de primera plana.

front room ['frʌnt'rum] n cuarto m que da a la calle, (freq) salón m.

front-wheel drive ['frʌntwiːl'draiv] n tracción f delantera.

frost [frɔst] **1** n helada f; (visible, also hoar-, white —) escarcha f; (sl) fracaso m; **4 degrees of** — 4 grados bajo cero.

2 vt (a) cubrir de escarcha; **the grass was** — **ed over** el césped apareció cubierto de escarcha.

(b) plant quemar.

frostbite ['frɔstbait] n congelación f.

frostbitten ['frɔst,bitn] adj congelado.

frosted ['frɔstid] adj glass deslustrado.

frosty ['frɔsti] adj (a) (Meteorol) **in** — **weather** en época de hielo; **on a** — **morning** una mañana de helada; **it was** — **last night** anoche heló.

(b) surface escarchado, cubierto de escarcha.

(c) (fig) glacial.

froth [frɔθ] **1** n espuma f; (fig) bachillerías fpl. **2** vi espumar, echar espuma; **to** — **at the mouth** espumajear.

frothy ['frɔθi] adj espumoso; (fig) superficial, de poca sustancia.

frown [fraun] **1** n ceño m; **he said with a** — dijo frunciando el entrecejo. **2** vi fruncir el entrecejo; **to** — **at** mirar con ceño; **to** — **on** desaprobar.

frowning ['fraunin] adj (fig) ceñudo, amenazador.

frowzy ['frauzi] adj (dirty) sucio; (untidy) desaliñado; (smelly) fétido, maloliente.

froze [frəuz] pret of **freeze**.

frozen ['frəuzn] **1** ptp of **freeze**. **2** adj food congelado.

frugal ['fruːgəl] adj frugal.

frugality [fruː'gæliti] n frugalidad f.

fruit [fruːt] **1** n sing and pl (on the tree etc) fruto m (also Bio, fig); (served as food) fruta f, frutas fpl; **dried** — fruta f seca; **soft** — frutas fpl blandas; **to bear** — (fig) dar resultado.

2 vi frutar, dar fruto.

fruit cup ['fruːtkʌp] n sangría f.

fruit cake ['fruːtkeik] n tarta f de frutas.

fruit dish ['fruːtdiʃ] n frutera f.

fruiterer ['fruːtərə*] n frutero m; — **'s** (**shop**) frutería f.

fruitful ['fruːtful] adj (fig) fructuoso, provechoso.

fruition [fruː'iʃən] n cumplimiento m; (of plan etc) realización f; **to bring to** — realizar; **to come to** — llegar a la madurez, (plan etc) verse logrado, realizarse, (hope) cumplirse.

fruitless ['fruːtlis] adj infructuoso.

fruit machine ['fruːtmə,ʃiːn] n máquina f tragaperras.

fruit salts ['fruːtsɔlts] npl sal f de fruta(s).

fruit tree ['fruːttriː] n árbol m frutal.

fruity ['fruːti] adj que sabe a fruta; voice pastoso; joke etc verde; style de fuerte sabor.

frump [frʌmp] n espantajo m, estantigua f.

frustrate [frʌs'treit] vt frustrar; **to feel** — **d** sentirse frustrado.

frustration [frʌs'treiʃən] n frustración f.

fry[1] [frai] n (Fish) pececillos mpl; **small** — gente f menuda.

fry[2] [frai] **1** n fritada f. **2** vt freír; **fried fish** pescado m frito. **3** vi freírse.

frying pan ['fraiin,pæn] n sartén f; **to jump out of the** — **into the fire** escaparse del trueno para dar en el relámpago.

fuchsia ['fjuːʃə] n fucsia f.

fuddled ['fʌdld] adj (drunk) borracho; (confused) aturdido; **to get** — emborracharse.

fuddy-duddy ['fʌdi,dʌdi] n (fam) persona f chapada a la antigua.

fuel [fjuəl] **1** n combustible m, carburante m; (specifically coal) carbón m, (wood) leña f; (fig) pábulo m; **to add** — **to the flames** echar leña al fuego.

2 vt aprovisionar de combustible.

3 vi aprovisionarse de combustible.

fuel oil ['fjuəloil] n aceite m combustible.

fuel tank ['fjuəltæŋk] n depósito m de combustible.

fug [fʌg] n aire m viciado (or confinado, cargado); **what a** — **!** ¡qué olor!; **there's a** — **in here** aquí huele a encerrado.

fuggy ['fʌgi] adj viciado, cargado; **it's** — **in here** aquí huele a encerrado.

fugitive ['fjuːdʒitiv] **1** adj fugitivo. **2** n fugitivo m, f; (refugee) refugiado m, a f; — **from justice** prófugo m, a f.

fugue [fjuːg] n fuga f.

fulcrum ['fʌlkrəm] n fulcro m.

fulfil [ful'fil] vt duty, promise cumplir con; ambition, norm, plan realizar; condition satisfacer, llenar; order ejecutar.

fulfilment [ful'filmənt] n cumplimiento m; realización f; satisfacción f; ejecución f; (satisfied feeling) contento m, satisfacción f.

full [ful] **1** adj (a) lleno; vehicle etc completo (also — **up**); — **of cares** lleno de cuidados; — **of hope** lleno de esperanza, ilusionado; — **to bursting** lleno de bote en bote; — **to overflowing** lleno hasta los bordes; **to be** — **of** estar lleno de; **I'm** — (of food) no puedo más; **we are** — **up for July** no tenemos nada libre para julio; **I've had a** — **day** he estado ocupado todo el día; **he's had a** — **life** ha tenido una vida llena de actividades.

(b) (fig) session pleno, plenario; member de número; authority, employment, power pleno; **in** — **colour** a todo color; **in** — **flower** en plena floración.

(c) (complete) completo; account detallado, extenso; measure colmado, exacto; meal completo; moon lleno; fare, price íntegro; sin descuento; speed, strength máximo; text íntegro; dress de etiqueta, uniform de gala; **with** — **particulars** con todos los detalles; **until we have** — **information** hasta que tengamos todos los datos; **in the** — **sense of the word** en el sentido más amplio de la palabra; **a** — **hour** una hora entera, una hora larga; **a** — **3 miles** 3 millas largas.

(d) face redondo; figure llenito; bosom abultado, (euph) importante; lips grueso; skirt amplio; see **name**, **speed** etc.

2 adv (a) — **well** perfectamente, muy bien, sobradamente.

(b) **it hit him** — **in the face** le dio de lleno en la cara.

3 n: **in** — sin abreviar, por extenso, sin quitar nada; **name in** — nombre m y apellidos; **text in** — texto m íntegro; **to pay in** — pagar la deuda entera; **to the** — completamente, al máximum.

fullback ['fulbæk] n defensa m.

full blast ['ful'blɑːst] adv work a máxima capacidad; travel a toda velocidad; play etc al máximo volumen sonoro, a toda potencia.

full-blooded ['ful'blʌdid] *adj character* viril, vigoroso; *animal* de raza.
full-blown ['ful'bləun] *adj* (*fig*) hecho y derecho.
full-bodied ['ful'bɔdid] *adj cry* fuerte; *wine* generoso.
full-dress ['ful'dres] *adj function* de etiqueta, de gala.
full-grown ['ful'grəun] *adj* crecido, maduro.
full-length ['ful'leŋθ] *adj picture* de cuerpo entero; *pool etc* de tamaño normal; — **film** cinta *f* de largo metraje.
fullness ['fulnis] *n* plenitud *f*; amplitud *f*; **in the — of time** a su debido tiempo.
full-scale ['ful'skeil] *adj study* amplio, extenso; *investigation* de gran alcance; *attack* en gran escala.
full-sized ['ful'saizd] *adj* de tamaño normal.
full stop ['ful'stɔp] *n* punto *m*; **to come to a —** (*fig*) pararse, paralizarse, quedar detenido en un punto muerto.
full-time ['ful'taim] **1** *adj professional man* en plena dedicación, *worker* que trabaja una jornada completa.
  2 *adv*: **to work —** trabajar en régimen de dedicación exclusiva, trabajar una jornada entera.
fully ['fuli] *adv* completamente, enteramente; **— dressed** completamente vestido; **I'm not — convinced** no me convenzo del todo; **he earns — as much as I do** gana sin duda tanto como yo; **it is — 3 miles** son lo menos 3 millas; **we waited — 3 hours** esperamos 3 horas largas.
fully-fashioned ['fuli'fæʃnd] *adj stocking* de costura francesa.
fully-fledged ['fuli'fledʒd] *adj* (*fig*) hecho y derecho.
fulminate ['fulmineit] *vi*: **to — against** tronar contra.
fulsome ['fulsəm] *adj* exagerado, excesivo; *person* servil.
fumble ['fʌmbl] **1** *vt* manosear, revolver (*etc*) torpemente; *ball* dejar caer; **to — one's way across a room** ir a tientas a través de un cuarto.
  2 *vi*: **to — for something** buscar algo con las manos; **to — for a word** titubear buscando una palabra; **to — in one's pockets** revolver en los bolsillos; **to — with something** manejar (*etc*) algo torpemente; **to — with a door** tratar torpemente de abrir una puerta.
fume [fjuːm] *vi* humear; (*fig*) estar furioso, rabiar; echar pestes (*at thing* contra, *at person* de).
fumes [fjuːmz] *npl* humo *m*, gas *m*, vapor *m*.
fumigate ['fjuːmigeit] *vt* fumigar.
fun [fʌn] *n* (*amusement*) diversión *f*; (*merriment*) alegría *f*; (*joke*) broma *f*; **for —, in — ** en broma; **it's great —** es muy divertido; **he's great —** es una persona divertidísima; **it's not much — for us** no nos divertimos en absoluto; **it's only his —** está bromeando, te está tomando el pelo; **to do something for the — of it** hacer algo para divertirse, hacer algo sin propósito serio; **to have —** divertirse; **have —!** ¡que os divirtáis!, ¡que lo paséis bien!; **what — we had!** ¡cómo nos divertimos!; **we had — with the passports** nos armamos un lío con los pasaportes; **to make — of, to poke — at** burlarse de, ridiculizar; **to spoil the —** aguar la fiesta.
function ['fʌŋkʃən] **1** *n* función *f*; **it is no part of my — to +** *infin* no corresponde a mi cargo + *infin*; **to exceed one's —s** excederse en sus funciones.
  2 *vi* funcionar.
functional ['fʌŋkʃnəl] *adj* funcional.
functionary ['fʌŋkʃənəri] *n* funcionario *m*.
fund [fʌnd] **1** *n* fondo *m*; **—s** fondos *mpl*; **to be in —s** estar en fondos; **to have a — of stories** saber un montón de chistes. **2** *vt debt* consolidar.
fundamental [ˌfʌndə'mentl] *adj* fundamental; **to be — to** ser esencial para.
fundamentally [ˌfʌndə'mentəli] *adv* fundamentalmente, esencialmente.
fundamentals [ˌfʌndə'mentlz] *npl* fundamentos *mpl*.
funeral ['fjuːnərəl] **1** *adj* and *attr march, procession* fúnebre; *pyre* funerario; *service* de difuntos; **— director** director *m* de funeraria.
  2 *n* entierro *m*, funerales *mpl*; **that's your —!** (*fam*) ¡allá te las compongas!, ¡allá te las apañes!, ¡con tu pan te lo comas!
funereal [fjuː'niəriəl] *adj* fúnebre, funéreo.
fun fair ['fʌnfeə*] *n* parque *m* de atracciones.
fungoid ['fʌŋgoid] *adj* fungoideo.
fungous ['fʌŋgəs] *adj* fungoso.
fungus ['fʌŋgəs] *n*, *pl* **fungi** ['fʌŋgai] *n* hongo *m*.
funicular [fjuː'nikjulə*] *n* (ferrocarril *m*) funicular *m*.
funk [fʌŋk] (*fam*) **1** *n* (a) (*state*) canguelo *m*, jindama *f*; **to be in a** (**blue**) **—** estar muerto de miedo.
  (**b**) (*person*) gallina *mf*, mandria *mf*.
  2 *vt*: **to — it** rajarse, dejar de hacer algo por

miedo, retirarse por miedo; **to — doing something** dejar de hacer algo por miedo.
funky ['fʌŋki] *adj* (*fam*) cobarde, miedoso; **you're —!** ¡cobarde!
funnel ['fʌnl] *n* embudo *m*; (*Naut, Rail etc*) chimenea *f*.
funnily ['fʌnili] *adv* de un modo divertido; **— enough** . . . cosa curiosa . . ., cosa más rara . . .
funny ['fʌni] *adj* (**a**) (*amusing*) divertido, gracioso, cómico; (*full of jokes*) chistoso; **I thought the film very —** la película me hizo mucha gracia; **that's not — ** eso no tiene gracia; **I find it — that, it strikes me as — that** me hace mucha gracia que; **he's trying to be —** quiere hacerse el gracioso.
  (**b**) (*odd*) raro, curioso; **a — feeling** una sensación rara; **the — thing about it is that** lo curioso es que; **he's — that way** tiene esa manía.
funny bone ['fʌnibəun] *n* hueso *m* de la alegría.
fur [fəː*] *n* piel *f*; (*on tongue*) saburra *f*; (*in kettle*) sarro *m*; **— coat** abrigo *m* de pieles.
furbish ['fəːbiʃ] *vt*: **to — up** renovar, restaurar.
furious ['fjuəriəs] *adj* furioso; *effort etc* frenético, violento; *pace* vertiginoso; **to be — with someone** estar muy enfadado con uno; **to get —** ponerse furioso.
furiously ['fjuəriəsli] *adv* con furia.
furl [fəːl] *vt* (*Naut*) aferrar; *wings* recoger.
furlong ['fəːlɔŋ] *n* estadio *m* (*octava parte de una milla*).
furlough ['fəːləu] *n* (*Mil etc*) licencia *f*.
furnace ['fəːnis] *n* horno *m*; **the town was like a —** la ciudad era un horno.
furnish ['fəːniʃ] *vt* (**a**) (*provide*) proveer, suministrar, proporcionar (*someone with something* algo a uno); *opportunity* dar, proporcionar, deparar; *proof* aducir; *information* facilitar; **we are —ed with all that is necessary** estamos equipados con todo lo necesario.
  (**b**) *room* amueblar (*with* de); **—ed flat** piso *m* amueblado.
furnishings ['fəːniʃiŋz] *npl* muebles *mpl*, mobiliario *m*.
furniture ['fəːnitʃə*] *n* muebles *mpl*, mobiliario *m*, mueblaje *m*; (*piece of* —) mueble *m*.
furniture van ['fəːnitʃə.væn] *n* camión *m* de mudanzas.
furrier ['fʌriə*] *n* peletero *m*.
furrow ['fʌrəu] **1** *n* surco *m*; (*on face*) arruga *f*; **to plough a lonely —** ser el único en estudiar (*etc*) algo.
  2 *vt* surcar; arrugar.
furry ['fəːri] *adj* peludo.
further ['fəːðə*] *comp of* **far**: **1** *adv* (**a**) (*place*) más lejos, más allá; **move it — away** apártalo un poco más; **— back** más atrás; **— off** más lejos; **— on** más adelante; **how much — is it?** ¿cuánto camino nos queda?; **have you much — to go?** ¿le queda mucho camino por hacer?; **I got no — with him** no logré sacar más consecuencias de él; **nothing is — from my thoughts** nada más lejos de mi intención.
  (**b**) (-*more*) además; **and I — believe that** y creo además que.
  (**c**) **to go — into a matter** estudiar una cosa más detenidamente; **they questioned us —** nos hicieron más preguntas; **he heard nothing —** no le volvieron a decir nada; **don't trouble yourself any —** no se moleste más.
  2 *adj* (**a**) (*place*) más lejano, más remoto, de más allá; *end, side* opuesto; **at the — end** en el otro extremo.
  (**b**) (*additional*) nuevo, adicional; complementario, supletorio; *education* superior; **— facts** nuevos datos *mpl*, más datos *mpl*; **after — consideration** después de considerarlo más detenidamente; **till — orders** hasta nueva orden; **without — loss of time** sin más pérdida de tiempo.
  3 *vt* promover, fomentar, adelantar.
furtherance ['fəːðərəns] *n* promoción *f*, fomento *m*.
furthermore ['fəːðəː'mɔː*] *adv* además.
furthermost ['fəːðəməust] *adj* más lejano.
furthest ['fəːðist] *superl of* **far**: **1** *adv* más lejos; **that's the —** that anyone has gone es el punto extremo a que han llegado, nadie ha ido más allá.
  2 *adj* más lejano; extremo.
furtive ['fəːtiv] *adj* furtivo.
furtively ['fəːtivli] *adv* furtivamente.
fury ['fjuəri] *n* furor *m*, furia *f*; violencia *f*; frenesí *m*; **the Furies** las Furias; **like — ** a toda furia, (*of person*) hecho una furia; **to be in a —** estar furioso; **to work oneself up into a —** montar en cólera.
furze [fəːz] *n* aulaga *f*, tojo *m*.

fuse [fjuːz] **1** n (*Elec*) plomo m, fusible m; (*Mil*) mecha f, espoleta f.

2 vt fundir; (*fig*) fusionar.

3 vi fundirse; (*fig*) fusionarse; **the lights —d** se fundieron los plomos.

fuse box ['fjuːzbɔks] n caja f de fusibles.

fuselage ['fjuːzəlɑːʒ] n fuselaje m.

fusillade [ˌfjuːzi'leid] n descarga f cerrada; (*fig*) lluvia f, torrente m.

fusion ['fjuːʒən] n fusión f (*also fig*), fundición f.

fuss [fʌs] **1** n **(a)** (*noise, bustle*) conmoción f, bulla f, alharaca f.

(b) (*dispute*) lío m; protesta f; **that — about the money** ese lío con el dinero; **to kick up** (*or* **make) a —** dar cuatro voces, armar un lío; **I think you were quite right to make a —** creo que hiciste bien en protestar.

(c) (*excessive display*) aspaviento m, hazañería f; **it's a lot of — about nothing** mucho ruido y pocas nueces; **there's no need to make such a —** no es para tanto; **to make a — of** hacer mimos a, hacer fiestas a.

(d) (*formalities*) ceremonias fpl; trámites mpl; **such a — to get a passport!** ¡tantos trámites para conseguir un pasaporte!

2 vi agitarse, preocuparse (por bagatelas); **to —** about andar azacaneado, andar de acá para allá; **to — over someone** mimar con exceso a uno.

fusspot ['fʌspɔt] n (*fam*) persona f que se preocupa por nimiedades, persona f tontamente exigente.

fussy ['fʌsi] adj person (*demanding*) exigente; (*nervous*) nervioso; details nimio; dress con muchos ringorrangos; decoration con muchos adornos.

fusty ['fʌsti] adj mohoso, rancio; air, room que huele a cerrado.

futile ['fjuːtail] adj inútil, vano, infructuoso.

futility [fjuː'tiliti] n inutilidad f, lo inútil.

future ['fjuːtʃə*] **1** adj futuro; venidero; **in — years** en los años venideros.

2 n futuro m, porvenir m; **—s** (*Comm*) futuros mpl; **in** (**the**) **—** en el futuro, en lo sucesivo; **in the near —** en fecha próxima; **there's no — in it** esto no tiene porvenir; **what does the — hold for us?** ¿qué nos tiene reservado el destino?

futurism ['fjuːtʃərizm] n futurismo m.

futuristic [ˌfjuːtʃə'ristik] adj futurístico.

fuze [fjuːz] n (*US*) = fuse.

fuzz [fʌz] n tamo m, pelusa f; (*on face*) vello m.

fuzzy ['fʌzi] adj (*hairy*) velloso; hair muy ensortijado; (*blurred*) borroso.

G

gab [gæb] (*fam*) **1** n (*chatter*) cháchara f; (*chat*) charla f; **to have the gift of the** — tener un pico de oro. **2** vi parlotear, charlar, cotorrear.

gabardine [ˌgæbəˈdiːn] n gabardina f.

gabble [ˈgæbl] **1** n torrente m de palabras ininteligibles.

   2 vt decir (*or* leer *etc*) atropelladamente, pronunciar de modo ininteligible.

   3 vi hablar atropelladamente; parlotear, cotorrear; **they were gabbling away in French** hablaban atropelladamente en francés.

gaberdine [ˌgæbəˈdiːn] n gabardina f.

gable [ˈgeibl] n aguilón m; — **roof** tejado m de dos aguas.

gad[1] [gæd] vi: **to** — **about** salir mucho, viajar mucho, ir a muchos sitios.

gad[2] [gæd] *interj* ¡caramba!

gadabout [ˈgædəbaut] n persona f aficionada a salir (*etc*) mucho.

gadfly [ˈgædflai] n tábano m.

gadget [ˈgædʒit] n artilugio m, chisme m, aparato m.

Gael [geil] n gaélico m, a f.

Gaelic [ˈgeilik] **1** adj gaélico. **2** n (*language*) gaélico m.

gaff[1] [gæf] **1** n arpón m, garfio m. **2** vt arponear, enganchar.

gaff[2] [gæf] n (*sl*): **to blow the** — descubrir el pastel.

gaffe [gæf] n plancha f; **to make a** — tirarse una plancha.

gaffer [ˈgæfə*] n vejete m, tío m; (*foreman*) capataz m; (*boss*) jefe m.

gag [gæg] **1** n mordaza f; (*Parl*) clausura f; (*Theat*) morcilla f; (*joke*) chiste m; (*hoax*) broma f; (*gimmick*) truco m publicitario; **is this a** — ? ¿es una broma esto?; **it's a** — **to raise funds** es un truco para reunir fondos.

   2 vt amordazar; (*fig*) amordazar, hacer callar; (*Parl*) clausurar; *discussion* impedir, estorbar.

   3 vi (*Theat*) meter morcillas; (*joke*) contar chistes, chunguear; **I was only** —**ging** lo dije en broma.

gaga [ˈgɑːgɑː] adj (*sl*) lelo, chocho; **to be going** — chochear.

gaiety [ˈgeiiti] n alegría f, regocijo m; (*of gathering etc*) animación f; **gaieties** diversiones fpl alegres.

gaily [ˈgeili] adv alegremente.

gain [gein] **1** n (*increase*) aumento m (*in, of* de); (*profit, earning*) ganancia f, beneficio m; **ill-gotten** —**s** ganancias fpl ilícitas; **his loss is our** — su pérdida supone nuestra ganancia; **there have been** —**s of up to 3 points** ha habido alzas de hasta 3 enteros; **I lost all my** — perdí todas mis ganancias.

   2 vt ganar; *objective* conseguir; *possession, territory etc* adquirir; *approval, respect* merecer, captar, conquistar; (*reach*) llegar a, alcanzar; *time* ganar; **my watch has** —**ed 5 minutes** mi reloj se ha adelantado 5 minutos; **I've** —**ed 3 kilos** he engordado 3 kilos; **the shares have** —**ed 4 points** las acciones han subido 4 enteros; **what have you** —**ed by it?** ¿qué has logrado con esto?; **what do you hope to** —? ¿qué provecho vas a sacar?

   3 vi (*shares etc*) aumentar en valor, subir; (*Med*) mejorar; (*in weight*) engordar, poner carnes; (*in advantage*) ganar terreno; **to** — **in popularity** resultar más popular, adquirir mayor popularidad; **it** —**s in contrast with the other picture** parece más atractivo al compararse con el otro cuadro; **to** — **on someone** ir ganando terreno a uno, ir alcanzando a uno, (*and outstrip*) ir dejando atrás a uno.

gainer [ˈgeinə*] n: **to be the** — salir ganando.

gainful [ˈgeinful] adj *employment* remunerado, retribuido.

gainsay [ˌgeinˈsei] (*irr: see* **say**) vt contradecir, negar; **it cannot be gainsaid** es innegable.

gait [geit] n modo m de andar, paso m.

gaiter [ˈgeitə*] n polaina f.

gal [gæl] n (*fam*) = **girl**.

gala [ˈgɑːlə] n fiesta f; **sports** — certamen m deportivo; **swimming** — gala f de natación.

galactic [gəˈlæktik] adj lácteo; (*Astron*) galáctico.

galaxy [ˈgæləksi] n galaxia f; (*fig*) grupo m brillante, constelación f, pléyade f.

gale [geil] n ventarrón m, vendaval m; (*storm*) tempestad f; **to blow a** — soplar una galerna.

Galen [ˈgeilən] m Galeno.

Galician [gəˈliʃiən] **1** adj gallego. **2** n gallego m, a f. **3** n (*dialect*) gallego m.

Galilee [ˈgælili] Galilea f.

gall[1] [gɔːl] **1** n (*Anat*) bilis f, hiel f; (*fig*) hiel f; (*fam*) descaro m; **she had the** — **to say that** tuvo el descaro de decir eso. **2** vt mortificar.

gall[2] [gɔːl] n (*Bot*) agalla f.

gallant [ˈgælənt] adj (**a**) (*brave*) valiente, valeroso, bizarro; (*showy*) lucido, gallardo; (*stately*) imponente; **the** — **captain** el intrépido capitán.

   (**b**) (*attentive: also* [gəˈlænt]) galante; cortés, atento.

gallantly [ˈgæləntli] adv (**a**) valientemente. (**b**) galantemente; cortésmente.

gallantry [ˈgæləntri] (**a**) (*bravery*) valentía f, valor m, heroísmo m, bizarría f. (**b**) (*courtesy*) galantería f, cortesía f; **gallantries** galanterías fpl.

gall-bladder [ˈgɔːlˌblædə*] n vesícula f biliar.

galleon [ˈgæliən] n galeón m.

gallery [ˈgæləri] n galería f (*also* Min, Theat); (*for spectators*) tribuna f; (*art*) — museo m de bellas artes; **a** — **of portraits** una colección de retratos; **to play to the** — actuar para la galería.

galley [ˈgæli] n (*ship*, Typ) galera f; (*kitchen*) cocina f, fogón m.

galley proof [ˈgælipruːf] n galerada f.

galley slave [ˈgælisleiv] n galeote m.

gallicism [ˈgælisizəm] n galicismo m.

galling [ˈgɔːliŋ] adj mortificante.

gallivant [ˌgæliˈvænt] vi = **gad**[1].

gallon [ˈgælən] n galón m (= 4,546 *litros*, US = 3,785 *litros*).

gallop [ˈgæləp] **1** n galope m; (*distance covered*) galopada f; **at a** — a galope; **at full** — a galope tendido; **to break into a** — echar a galopar.

   2 vt hacer galopar.

   3 vi galopar; **to** — **off** alejarse a galope; **to** — **past** desfilar a galope; **to** — **up** llegar a galope.

galloping [ˈgæləpiŋ] adj (*Med and fig*) galopante.

gallows [ˈgæləuz] n sing horca f.

gallstone [ˈgɔːlstəun] n cálculo m biliario.

galore [gəˈlɔː*] adv en abundancia, a porrilla.

galosh [gəˈlɔʃ] n chanclo m (de goma).

galumph [gəˈlʌmf] vi (*hum*) saltar alegremente (por una victoria *etc*).

galvanic [gælˈvænik] adj galvánico.

galvanism [ˈgælvənizəm] n galvanismo m.

galvanize [ˈgælvənaiz] vt galvanizar; **to** — **someone into life** sacudir a uno de su abstracción; **to** — **someone into doing something** sacudir a uno para que haga algo.

galvanized [ˈgælvənaizd] adj galvanizado.

gambit [ˈgæmbit] n gambito m; (*fig*) táctica f.

gamble [ˈgæmbl] **1** n jugada f (de resultado imprevisible); empresa f arriesgada; **life's a** — la vida es una lotería; **I did it as a pure** — lo hice para probar suerte nada más; **the** — **came off** la tentativa tuvo éxito, la jugada nos salió bien; **to have a** — **on horse** jugar dinero a, apostar a, *company shares* especular en.

   2 vt jugar, aventurar en el juego; **to** — **one's future** jugarse el porvenir; **to** — **away** perder en el juego.

   3 vi jugar; (*Fin*) especular; **to** — **on the Stock Exchange** jugar a la bolsa; **to** — **on something**

happening atenerse a la probabilidad de que ocurra algo, confiar en que algo vaya a suceder; **to — with others' money** especular con el dinero ajeno.

gambler ['gæmblə*] n jugador m, ora f.

gambling ['gæmbliŋ] n juego m; **— on the Stock Exchange** especulación f en la bolsa.

gambling den ['gæmbliŋden] n garito m, casa f de juego.

gambol ['gæmbəl] vi brincar, retozar, juguetear.

game¹ [geim] **1** n **(a)** (in general) juego m; deporte m; (match: with ball etc) partido m, (of cards, chess etc) partida f; (at bridge) manga f; **—, set and match** juego, set y partido; **— of chance** juego m de azar; **indoor —** diversión f de salón; **it's only a —** es un juego nada más; **this isn't a —** esto no es ninguna broma, esto va de veras; **the — is not worth the candle** la cosa no vale la pena; **to be off one's —** no estar en forma, estar desentrenado; **to go to —** (Bridge) ir a manga; **to have a — of chess** echar una partida de ajedrez; **to have a — with** (tease) tomar el pelo a, hacer una broma a; **to play the —** (fig) jugar limpio; **he plays a good — of football** juega bien al fútbol, es buen futbolista; **two can play at that —** donde las dan las toman; **to play a double —** jugar doble; **to play a waiting —** estar a ver venir, esperar hasta ver qué pasa; **to put someone off his —** hacer que uno pierda su concentración.

(b) (deception) **the — is up** todo se acabó; **they saw the — was up** comprendieron que ya no había nada que hacer; **what's the —?** ¿qué hacen Vds ahí?, ¿qué pretenden Vds con eso?; **we know his little —** le hemos calado; **I wonder what his — is?** ¿qué estará tramando?

(c) (fam) lío m; **I had such a — getting here** me hice un lío al venir aquí; **what a — this is!** ¡qué faena!

(d) (business) **how long have you been in this —?** ¿cuánto tiempo lleva Vd dedicado a esto?; **what's your —?** ¿a qué se dedica Vd?

(e) (Hunting) caza f; **big —** caza f mayor; **fair —** caza f legal; (fig) objeto m legítimo; **it is fair — for criticism** es un objeto legítimo de la crítica.

2 adj animoso, valiente; **are you —?** ¿quieres?, ¿te animas?; **to be — for anything** atreverse a todo.

3 vi jugar (por dinero).

game² [geim] adj (lame) cojo.

gamebag ['geimbæg] n morral m.

game bird ['geimbə:d] n ave f de caza.

gamecock ['geimkɔk] n gallo m de pelea.

gamekeeper ['geim,ki:pə*] n guardabosque m.

gamester ['geimstə*] n jugador m, tahur m.

gamin ['gæmɛ̃] n golfillo m.

gamine [gæ'mi:n] n chica f provocativa, joven f picaruela; **— haircut** corte m a la garçon.

gaming ['geimiŋ] n juego m.

gaming house ['geimiŋhaus] n casa f de juego.

gammon ['gæmən] n jamón m.

gamp [gæmp] n (fam) paraguas m.

gamut ['gæmət] n gama f.

gamy ['geimi] adj meat manido.

gander ['gændə*] n ganso m (macho).

gang [gæŋ] **1** n pandilla f, cuadrilla f, grupo m; (of workmen) brigada f; (criminal) pandilla f; **he's one of the —** now ya es uno de los nuestros.

2 vi **(a)** (Scot) ir; **to — agley** fracasar.

(b) **to — up** conspirar, obrar de concierto (against, on contra).

ganger ['gæŋə*] n capataz m.

gangling ['gæŋgliŋ] adj larguirucho, desgarbado.

ganglion ['gæŋgliən] n ganglio m.

gangplank ['gæŋplæŋk] n (Naut) plancha f.

gangrene ['gæŋgrin] n gangrena f.

gangster ['gæŋstə*] n pistolero m, pandillero m, gángster m.

gangsterism ['gæŋstərizm] n gangsterismo m.

gangway ['gæŋwei] n pasillo m, pasadizo m; (Naut: on ship) escalerilla f, pasarela f; (from ship to shore) plancha f, pasadera f; **—!** ¡abran paso!

gannet ['gænit] n alcatraz m.

gantlet ['gæntlit] n (US: Rail) vía f traslapada, vía f de garganta.

gantry ['gæntri] n caballete m.

gaol [dʒeil] n see **jail**.

gap [gæp] n (natural) vacío m, hueco m; (man-made) abertura f, brecha f; (in wall etc) boquete m; (in mountains) desfiladero m; (in writing) espacio m; (in text) laguna f; (of time) intervalo m; (in traffic, trees) claro m; (crack) hendedura f, resquicio m; **he left a — which it will be hard to fill** dejó un hueco difícil de llenar; **leave a — for the name** deje un espacio para poner el nombre.

gape [geip] vi **(a)** abrirse (mucho), estar muy abierto; **the chasm —d before him** se abría delante de él la sima.

(b) (person) estar boquiabierto; **to — at** mirar boquiabierto, embobarse con.

gaping ['geipiŋ] adj **(a)** abierto. **(b)** person boquiabierto, embobado.

gap-toothed ['gæp'tu:θt] adj con dientes mal formados; que ha perdido un diente (or varios dientes).

garage ['gæra:ʒ] **1** n garaje m. **2** vt dejar en garaje.

garb [ga:b] **1** n traje m, vestido m; (iro) ropaje m (also fig). **2** vt vestir (in de).

garbage ['ga:bidʒ] n basuras fpl, desperdicios mpl.

garbage can ['ga:bidʒkæn] n (US) cubo m para basuras.

garble ['ga:bl] vt mutilar, falsear (por selección).

garden ['ga:dn] **1** n jardín m; **back —,** **kitchen —** huerto m; **front —** jardín m; **G— of Eden** Edén m. **2** attr de jardín. **3** vi cultivar un huerto, trabajar en el jardín (or huerto).

gardener ['ga:dnə*] n jardinero m, a f; (professional) hortelano m; **I'm no —** no entiendo de jardines.

gardenia [ga:'di:niə] n gardenia f.

gardening ['ga:dniŋ] n jardinería f, horticultura f.

garden party ['ga:dn,pa:ti] n recepción f (al aire libre).

gargantuan [ga:'gæntjuən] adj colosal, gigantesco.

gargle ['ga:gl] **1** n (act) gárgaras fpl; (liquid) gargarismo m. **2** vi gargarizar, hacer gárgaras.

gargoyle ['ga:gɔil] n gárgola f.

garish ['gɛəriʃ] adj chillón, llamativo, charro.

garland ['ga:lənd] **1** n guirnalda f. **2** vt enguirnaldar.

garlic ['ga:lik] n ajo m.

garment ['ga:mənt] n prenda f (de vestir).

garner ['ga:nə*] **1** n troj f, granero m; (fig) acopio m, abundancia f; provisión f. **2** vt entrojar; (fig) recoger.

garnet ['ga:nit] n granate m.

garnish ['ga:niʃ] **1** n (Cook) aderezo m. **2** vt adornar (with de); (Cook) aderezar (with de).

garnishing ['ga:niʃiŋ] n (Cook) aderezo m.

Garonne [gə'rɔn] Garona m.

garret ['gærit] n guardilla f, desván m.

garrison ['gærisən] **1** n guarnición f. **2** vt guarnecer.

garrotte [gə'rɔt] vt agarrotar.

garrulity [gə'ru:liti] n garrulidad f.

garrulous ['gæruləs] adj gárrulo.

garter ['ga:tə*] n liga f; **Order of the G—** Orden f de la Jarretera.

garter belt ['ga:təbelt] n (US) portaligas m.

gas [gæs] **1** n gas m; (US) gasolina f; **natural —** gas m natural; **to step on the —** (fam) acelerar la marcha. **2** vt asfixiar con gas. **3** vi (fam) charlar, parlotear.

gasbag ['gæsbæg] n (Aer) bolsa f de gas; (fam) charlatán m, ana f.

gas bracket ['gæs,brækit] n brazo m de lámpara de gas.

gas burner ['gæs,bə:nə*] n mechero m de gas.

gas chamber ['gæs,tʃeimbə*] n cámara f de gas.

Gascon ['gæskən] **1** adj gascón. **2** n gascón m, ona f. **3** nm (dialect) gascón m.

Gascony ['gæskəni] Gascuña f.

gas cooker ['gæs'kukə*] n cocina f de (or a) gas.

gaseous ['gæsiəs] adj gaseoso.

gas fire ['gæs'faiə*] n estufa f de gas.

gas fitter ['gæs,fitə*] n empleado m del gas.

gash [gæʃ] **1** n raja f, hendedura f; (wound) cuchillada f. **2** vt rajar, hender; (wound) acuchillar.

gasholder ['gæs,həuldə*] n gasómetro m.

gas jet ['gæsdʒet] n llama f de mechero de gas.

gasket ['gæskit] n (Mech) junta f.

gaslight ['gæslait] n luz f de gas, alumbrado m de gas.

gas main ['gæsmein] n cañería f maestra de gas.

gasman ['gæsmæn] n, pl **—men** [men] empleado m del gas.

gas mantle ['gæs,mæntl] n manguito m incandescente.

gasmask ['gæsma:sk] n careta f antigás.

gas meter ['gæs,mi:tə*] n contador m de gas.

gasoline ['gæsəlin] n (US) gasolina f.

gasometer [gæ'sɔmitə*] n gasómetro m.

gas oven ['gæs,ʌvn] n cocina f de (or a) gas.

gasp [ga:sp] **1** n boqueada f; (cry) grito m sofocado; **last —** boqueada f; **to be at one's last —** dar su última boqueada; **with a — of astonishment** con un grito sofocado de asombro. **2** vt: **to — (out)** decir con voz entrecortada. **3** vi boquear, anhelar, respirar con dificultad; (pant) jadear; **to — for air** (or **breath**) luchar por respirar; **to — with astonishment** dar un grito sofocado de asombro.

gasper ['gɑːspə*] n (sl) pito m, truja m.

gas ring ['gæsriŋ] n hornillo m de gas.

gas stove ['gæs'stəuv] n cocina f de (or a) gas.

gassy ['gæsi] adj gaseoso.

gas tank ['gæstæŋk] n (US) depósito m de gasolina.

gas tap ['gæstæp] n llave f del gas.

gastric ['gæstrik] adj gástrico.

gastritis [gæs'traitis] n gastritis f.

gastronome ['gæstrənəum] n, **gastronomist** [,gæs-'trɒnəmist] n gastrónomo m, a f.

gastronomic [,gæstrə'nɒmik] adj gastronómico.

gastronomy [gæs'trɒnəmi] n gastronomía f.

gasworks ['gæswəːks] npl fábrica f de gas.

gat [gæt] n (US sl) revólver m.

gate [geit] n puerta f (also of town); (iron) verja f; (Rail) barrera f; (of sluice) compuerta f; (Sport) entrada f.

gatecrash ['geitkræʃ] **1** vt colarse de gorra en, asistir sin ser invitado a. **2** vi colarse de gorra, asistir sin ser invitado.

gatehouse ['geithaus] n, pl **—houses** [,hauziz] casa f del guarda (or del portero etc).

gatekeeper ['geit,kiːpə*] n portero m; (Rail) guarda-barrera m.

gate-legged ['geitlegd] adj: **— table** mesa f de alas abatibles.

gate money ['geit,mʌni] n ingresos mpl de entrada.

gatepost ['geitpəust] n poste m de una puerta (de cercado).

gateway ['geitwei] n = **gate**; (fig) puerta f, pórtico m (to de).

gather ['gæðə*] **1** vt (a) (assemble) reunir, recoger; acumular, acopiar; (harvest) recolectar; flowers, wood coger; (Sew) fruncir; **to — in** recoger; taxes etc recaudar; **to — together** reunir, juntar; **to — up** recoger.

(b) **to — dust** empolvarse; **to — speed** ganar velocidad, ir cada vez más rápidamente; **to — strength** cobrar fuerzas.

(c) **to — that** colegir que, sacar la consecuencia que; **I — from him that** según lo que él me dice; **what are we to — from this?** ¿qué consecuencia sacamos de esto?; **as you will have —ed** según Vd habrá comprendido; **as one —s from** según se desprende de.

2 vi (also **to — together**) reunirse, juntarse, congregarse; (clouds) amontonarse; (Med) formar pus; **to — round someone** agruparse en torno a uno; **— round!** ¡acercaos!; **the —ing storm** la tormenta que amenaza.

gathering ['gæðəriŋ] n (meeting) reunión f, asamblea f; (persons present) concurrencia f; (Med) absceso m.

gauche [gəuʃ] adj desmañado; (socially) falto de confianza, poco seguro de sí mismo.

gaudy ['gɔːdi] adj chillón, llamativo.

gauge [geidʒ] **1** n (standard measure) norma f de medida; (of gun etc) calibre m; (test) indicación f, prueba f; (instrument) indicador m, manómetro m; (Rail) ancho m, entrevía f, trocha f (SAm).

2 vt medir; calibrar; (fig) juzgar, estimar; **to — the distance with one's eye** medir la distancia con el ojo; **to — the right moment** elegir el momento propicio.

Gaul [gɔːl] **1** Galia f. **2** n (person) galo m, a f.

gaunt [gɔːnt] adj flaco, desvaído, chupado; (fig) severo, adusto.

gauntlet ['gɔːntlit] n guante m; (Hist) guantelete m; **to run the —** correr baquetas; **to run the — of** (fig) pasar por los peligros de; salir ileso de; **to throw down the —** arrojar el guante.

gauze [gɔːz] n gasa f.

gave [geiv] pret of **give**.

gavel ['gævl] n martillo m (de presidente o subastador).

gavotte [gə'vɒt] n (Hist) gavota f.

gawk [gɔːk] **1** n bobo m. **2** vi papar moscas.

gawky ['gɔːki] adj desgarbado, torpe.

gawp [gɔːp] vi (fam) papar moscas; **to — at** mirar boquiabierto.

gay [gei] adj alegre; colour, appearance brillante, vistoso; life lleno de placeres; **to have a — time** pasarlo bomba.

gaze [geiz] **1** n mirada f (fija); **his — met mine** cruzamos una mirada. **2** vi (also **to — at, to — upon**) mirar (con fijeza), contemplar.

gazelle [gə'zel] n gacela f.

gazette [gə'zet] n gaceta f.

gazetteer [,gæzi'tiə*] n diccionario m geográfico.

gear [giə*] **1** n (a) (equipment) equipo m, herramientas fpl, pertrechos mpl; (fam) cosas fpl, bártulos mpl; (clothing) ropa f, traje m.

(b) (apparatus) aparato m, mecanismo m.

(c) (Mech) engranaje m, rueda f dentada; timing — engranaje m de distribución; **in —** en juego, engranado; **to be in — with** engranar con; **to throw out of —** desengranar, (fig) dislocar.

(d) (Aut etc: speed) marcha f, velocidad f, cambio m; **there are 5 forward —s** hay 5 marchas adelante; **bottom —, low —** primera velocidad f; **second —** segunda velocidad f; **top —** tercera (or cuarta) velocidad f; **neutral —** punto m muerto; **reverse —** cambio m de marcha atrás; **to change —** cambiar de marcha.

2 vt (Mech) engranar (into, with con); **to — down** desmultiplicar; **to — up** multiplicar; **the programme is —ed in with** (or **to**) **the plan** el programa forma parte integral del plan.

3 vi engranar (into, with con); **it —s in with the plan** concuerda con el plan, se desarrolla al ritmo del plan.

gearbox ['giəbɒks] n (Aut) caja f de cambios; (Mech) caja f de engranajes; **with automatic —** con cambio de marchas automático.

gear-lever ['giə,liːvə*], (US) **gearshift** ['giə,ʃift] n palanca f de velocidades.

gearwheel ['giəwiːl] n rueda f dentada.

gee [dʒiː] interj ¡caramba!; **— up!** ¡arre!

gee-gee ['dʒiːdʒiː] n (fam) caballito m.

geese [giːs] npl of **goose**.

geezer ['giːzə*] n (sl) vejancón m, tío m.

Geiger counter ['gaigə,kauntə*] n contador m Geiger.

geisha ['geiʃə] n geisha f.

gelatin(e) ['dʒelətiːn] n gelatina f.

gelatinous [dʒi'lætinəs] adj gelatinoso.

geld [geld] vt castrar, capar.

gelding ['geldiŋ] n caballo m castrado.

gelignite ['dʒelignait] n gelignita f.

gem [dʒem] n joya f (also fig), piedra f preciosa.

Gemini ['dʒemini:] npl (Astron) Géminis m, Gemelos mpl.

gen [dʒen] n (sl) información f.

gendarme ['ʒɑːndɑːm] n gendarme m.

gender ['dʒendə*] n género m.

gene [dʒiːn] n gen m.

genealogical [,dʒiːniə'lɒdʒikəl] adj genealógico.

genealogist [,dʒiːni'ælədʒist] n genealogista mf.

genealogy [,dʒiːni'ælədʒi] n genealogía f.

genera ['dʒenərə] npl of **genus**.

general ['dʒenərəl] **1** adj general; (common) corriente, usual; cargo mixto; anaesthetic total.

2 n (Mil) general m; (servant) chica f para todo; **in —** en general, por lo general.

generality [,dʒenə'ræliti] n generalidad f.

generalization [,dʒenərəlai'zeiʃən] n generalización f.

generalize ['dʒenərəlaiz] vi generalizar.

generally ['dʒenərəli] adv generalmente, en general, por lo común; **— speaking** en términos generales.

generalship ['dʒenərəlʃip] n estrategia f, táctica f; (leadership) dirección f, don m de mando.

generate ['dʒenəreit] vt (Elec etc) generar; (fig) producir.

generating station ['dʒenəreitiŋ,steiʃən] n central f generadora.

generation [,dʒenə'reiʃən] n generación f; **the young —** los jóvenes; **the rising —** las nuevas generaciones; **the '98 —** la generación del '98.

generator ['dʒenəreitə*] n generador m.

generic [dʒi'nerik] adj genérico.

generosity [,dʒenə'rɒsiti] n generosidad f.

generous ['dʒenərəs] adj generoso; supply, quantity abundante, amplio, liberal.

generously ['dʒenərəsli] adv generosamente; abundantemente.

genesis ['dʒenisis] n génesis f; **G—** Génesis m.

genetic [dʒi'netik] adj genético, genésico.

geneticist [dʒi'netisist] n genetista mf.

genetics [dʒi'netiks] npl genética f.

Geneva [dʒi'niːvə] Ginebra f.

genial ['dʒiːniəl] adj simpático, afable.

geniality [,dʒiːni'æliti] n simpatía f, afabilidad f.

genially ['dʒiːniəli] adv afablemente.

genitals ['dʒenitlz] npl órganos mpl genitales.

genitive ['dʒenitiv] n genitivo m.

genius ['dʒiːniəs] n genio m; genialidad f; **man of —** hombre m genial; **he's a —** es un genio, es genial; **you're a —!** (iro) ¡eres un hacha!; **he has a — for propaganda** tiene genialidad para la propaganda; **you have a — for forgetting things** tienes un don especial para olvidar las cosas.

Genoa ['dʒenəuə] Génova.

genocide ['dʒenəusaid] n genocidio m.

Genoese [,dʒenəu'iːz] **1** adj genovés. **2** n genovés m, esa f.

genre [ʒãːnr] n género m.

gent [dʒent] n (fam) = **gentleman**; the —s' el wáter (de caballeros).

genteel [dʒen'tiːl] adj (iro) fino, elegante; school etc de buen tono.

gentian ['dʒenʃiən] n genciana f.

gentian violet ['dʒenʃiən'vaiəlit] n violeta f de genciana.

gentile ['dʒentail] **1** adj no judío; (pagan) gentil. **2** n no judío m, a f; (pagan) gentil mf.

gentility [dʒen'tiliti] n (iro) finura f, elegancia f; buen tono m.

gentle ['dʒentl] adj person's character benévolo, amable; apacible; breeze, heat, stop, progress, transition etc suave; rule blando; sound, voice dulce; push, touch ligero; (slow) lento, pausado; hint, reminder discreto; animal etc manso, dócil, apacible; (tender) dulce, tierno; of — birth bien nacido; — reader amado lector; the — sex el sexo débil.

gentleman ['dʒentlmən] n, pl **gentlemen** ['dʒentlmən] (man) señor m; (having gentlemanly qualities) caballero m; (at court) gentilhombre m; **young** — señorito m; **there's a — waiting to see you** te espera un señor; **to be a perfect** — ser un cumplido caballero; **he's no** — es un mal caballero; **"gentlemen"** (lavatory) "caballeros".

gentlemanly ['dʒentlmənli] adj caballeroso; cortés, fino.

gentleness ['dʒentlnis] n amabilidad f; suavidad f; dulzura f; mansedumbre f; docilidad f; ternura f.

gently ['dʒentli] adv suavemente; dulcemente; (slowly) despacio, pausadamente, poco a poco; apaciblemente; tiernamente; — !, — now !, — there ! ¡más despacio!, ¡con cuidado!

gentry ['dʒentri] n alta burguesía f, pequeña aristocracia f; (pej) familias fpl bien, gente f bien; (set of people) gente f.

genuflect ['dʒenjuflekt] vi doblar la rodilla.

genuflexion [,dʒenju'flekʃən] n genuflexión f.

genuine ['dʒenjuin] adj auténtico, legítimo, genuino; person sincero.

genus ['dʒenəs] n, pl **genera** ['dʒenərə] género m.

geodesic [,dʒi(ː)əu'desik] adj geodésico.

geodesy [dʒiːˈɔdisi] n geodesia f.

Geoffrey [dʒefri] m Geofredo, Godofredo.

geographer [dʒiˈɔgrəfə*] n geógrafo m.

geographical [dʒiəˈgræfikəl] adj geográfico.

geography [dʒiˈɔgrəfi] n geografía f.

geological [dʒiəuˈlɔdʒikəl] adj geológico.

geologist [dʒiˈɔlədʒist] n geólogo m.

geology [dʒiˈɔlədʒi] n geología f.

geometric(al) [dʒiəˈmetrik(əl)] adj geométrico.

geometry [dʒiˈɔmitri] n geometría f; **solid** — geometría f del espacio.

geophysics [dʒiəuˈfiziks] n sing geofísica f.

geopolitics [dʒiːəuˈpɔlitiks] n sing geopolítica f.

George [dʒɔːdʒ] m Jorge.

Georgian ['dʒɔːdʒiən] adj georgiano.

geranium [dʒiˈreiniəm] n geranio m.

geriatrics [,dʒeriˈætriks] n sing geriatría f.

germ [dʒəːm] n germen m (also Med); (Med) microbio m, bacilo m, bacteria f; (fig) germen m; **the — of an idea** el germen de una idea.

German ['dʒəːmən] **1** adj alemán. **2** n alemán m, ana f. **3** n (language) alemán m.

germane [dʒəːˈmein] adj relacionado (to con); **not — to the issue** inoportuno.

Germanic [dʒəːˈmænik] adj germánico.

germanophile [dʒəːˈmænəfail] n germanófilo m, a f.

germanophobe [dʒəːˈmænəfəub] n germanófobo m, a f.

Germany ['dʒəːməni] Alemania f.

germ carrier ['dʒəːm,kæriə*] n portador m de gérmenes.

germ cell ['dʒəːm'sel] n célula f germen.

germicide ['dʒəːmisaid] n germicida m, bactericida m.

germinate ['dʒəːmineit] vi germinar.

germination [,dʒəːmiˈneiʃən] n germinación f.

germ-killer ['dʒəːm,kilə*] n germicida m, bactericida m.

germ plasm ['dʒəːm'plæzəm] n germen m plasma.

germproof ['dʒəːmpruːf] adj a prueba de gérmenes.

gerrymander ['dʒerimændə*] vi falsificar elecciones.

gerund ['dʒerənd] n gerundio m.

gerundive [dʒiˈrʌndiv] n gerundio m adjetivado; (Latin) gerundino m.

Gestapo [gesˈtaːpəu] n Gestapo f.

gestate [dʒesˈteit] vt (a) (Bio) llevar en el útero. (b) (fig) idea meditar.

gestation [dʒesˈteiʃən] n gestación f.

gesticulate [dʒesˈtikjuleit] vi accionar, gesticular, manotear.

gesticulation [dʒes,tikjuˈleiʃən] n gesticulación f, manoteo m.

gesture ['dʒestʃə*] **1** n (a) ademán m, gesto m.
(b) (fig) demostración f; (small token) muestra f, detalle m; **as a — of friendship** en señal de amistad; **as a — of support** para demostrar nuestro apoyo; **empty** — pura formalidad f; **what a nice** —! ¡qué detalle!
2 vi hacer un ademán; **he —d towards the door** con la mano indicó la puerta.

get [get] (irr: pret **got**, ptp **got**, US **gotten**) **1** vt
(a) (obtain) obtener, adquirir, (after effort) lograr, conseguir; (buy) comprar; (find) encontrar; (gain) ganar; prize ganar, llevarse; reputation hacerse; credit, glory atribuirse; (receive) recibir; radio station captar, sintonizar; wage cobrar; benefit, profit sacar; goals, points marcar; **he got it for me** él me lo procuró; **he got me a job** él logró que me diesen un puesto; **that's what got him the rise** eso fue lo que le valió el aumento; **I never got an answer** no me contestaron; — **me Mr X, please** (Tel) póngame con el Sr X, por favor; **he got 6 months** le condenaron a 6 meses de prisión; **I don't** — **much from his lectures** saco poco provecho de sus clases; **we shan't** — **anything out of him** no lograremos sacarle nada, no nos dirá nada; **what are you** —**ting out of it?** ¿qué va a sacar Vd de ello?, ¿qué va a sacar Vd en beneficio propio?; **you may** — **some fun out of it** puede que le resulte divertido; **we got him on the subject of drugs** logramos que hablase de las drogas.
(b) (arrest) prender, detener; (capture, kill) cazar; **got you at last !** ¡por fin te he cazado!; **I'll** — **him one day !** ¡algún día me lo cargaré!; **I'll** — **you yet !** ¡me las pagarás!; **he got it from the teacher** el profesor le echó un rapapolvo.
(c) disease coger; **to** — **it bad** (fam) sufrir mucho; **to** — **religion** (fam) ser convertido, entusiasmarse por la religión.
(d) (irritate) **that's what** —**s me !** ¡eso es lo que más me fastidia!
(e) (attract) **this tune** —**s me** esta melodía me chifla, esta melodía me apasiona.
(f) (strike) dar en; **it got him on the head** le dio en la cabeza; **it** —**s me in the throat** afecta la garganta.
(g) (understand) comprender; (do you) — **it?** ¿comprendes?, ¿me entiendes?
(h) (move) trasladar, pasar; **we can't** — **it through the door** no lo podemos pasar por la puerta; **to** — **something past the customs** conseguir pasar algo por la aduana; **how can we** — **it home?** ¿cómo podemos llevarlo a casa?
(i) (fetch) buscar, traer, ir a buscar; person llamar, ir por; **I'll go and** — **it for you** te lo voy a buscar; **please** — **the doctor** por favor llame al médico; **can I** — **you a drink?** ¿quieres tomar algo?, ¿te traigo algo de beber?
(j) meal preparar, hacer.
(k) **to have got** tener, poseer; **what have you got there?** ¿qué tienes ahí?; **there you've got me** eso no te lo puedo decir, no sé nada de eso.
(l) **to have got to** + infin tener que + infin.
(m) **to** — **someone to do something** (persuading) conseguir que uno haga algo, persuadir a uno a hacer algo; (ordering) encargar a uno que haga algo.
(n) **to get** + ptp or adj: **to** — **something done** mandar hacer algo; **to** — **one's hair cut** hacerse cortar el pelo, cortarse el pelo; **to** — **one's feet wet** mojarse los pies; (often translated by a simple verb, eg) **to** — **something ready** preparar algo.
(o) **to** — **something going** poner algo en marcha, hacer que algo empiece a funcionar; **to** — **a plan moving** hacer que se empiece a realizar un proyecto.
(p) (with adv or prep) **to** — **across** hacer entender; **to** — **along: we'll try to** — **him along** trataremos de hacerle venir; **to** — **away** (remove) quitar de en medio; separar; **to** — **something away from someone** quitar algo a uno; **to** — **someone away** ayudar a uno a escapar; **to** — **back** recobrar; **to** — **down** (lift down) bajar; descolgar; (swallow) tragar; (note) apuntar; (put in writing) poner por escrito; **it** —**s me down** me deprime; **don't let it** — **you down** no te dejes desanimar; **to** — **in** hacer entrar; harvest recoger; word decir; blow lograr dar; **to** — **off** quitarse de encima; clothes quitarse; stain sacar, quitar; letter escribir; work despachar, terminar; (learn) aprender; **to** — **an accused person off** lograr que se absuelva a un acusado; **to** — **on** poner;

clothes ponerse; **to — out** hacer salir; (*take out*) sacar; *stain* sacar, quitar; *book* publicar, (*from library*) sacar; *problem* resolver; **to — over** hacer pasar por encima de; (*put across*) hacer comprender, comunicar; (*finish*) terminar; **let's — it over!** ¡vamos a concluir de una vez!; **to — through** conseguir pasar (por); *bill* hacer que se apruebe; **to — together** reunir, juntar; **to — up** (*lift*) levantar, alzar; (*take up*) subir; (*learn*) aprender; (*revise*) repasar; (*organize*) organizar, preparar; (*dress*) ataviar (*in de*); (*disguise*) disfrazar (*as de*).

2 *vi* (a) (*become*) ponerse, volverse, hacerse (*for usage, see* **become** 2 (c); **to — + ptp** *or adj is often translated by passive, vi or vr*) **to — beaten** ser vencido; **to — run over** ser atropellado; **to — angry** enfadarse; **to — dark** hacerse de noche, anochecer; **to — drunk** emborracharse; **to — excited** emocionarse; **to — hurt** hacerse daño; **to — married** casarse; **to — old** envejecer(se); **to — wet** mojarse.

(b) (*reach*) **to — from A to B** ir de A a B, trasladarse de A a B; **how did it — here?** ¿cómo llegó a encontrarse aquí?; **he got there late** llegó tarde allí.

(c) (*sl*) marcharse.

(d) **to — + ger** empezar a + *infin*; **we got talking** empezamos a charlar; **to — going, to — moving** ponerse en marcha; **— going!** ¡menearse!; **the idea never got going** la idea nunca tuvo consecuencias prácticas.

(e) (*with adv or prep*) **to — about** salir mucho, viajar mucho, ir a muchos sitios; (*after sickness*) levantarse y salir; (*report*) saberse, divulgarse; **to — above oneself** engreírse; **to — across** lograr cruzar; (*message*) surtir efecto, (*meaning*) ser comprendido; **to — across** to lograr comunicar con; **he did not — across to the audience** no logró ponerse en contacto con el público; **he got across the manager** se indispuso con el director; **to — along** seguir andando; (*depart*) irse; **we must be — ting along** es hora de irnos ya; **— along now!** ¡vete ya!; **we — along somehow** vamos tirando; **— along with you!** ¡no digas bobadas!; **to — along without something** pasarse sin algo; (*for other senses of* **to — along,** *see* **to — on**); **to — around = to — about; to — around to something** llegar por fin a algo; **I never seem to — around to it** parece que nunca tengo tiempo para ello; **to — at** llegar a; *facts* descubrir, averiguar; (*attack*) atacar; (*refer to*) apuntar a; (*tease*) tomar el pelo a; (*spoil*) estropear; (*bribe*) sobornar; (*intimidate*) intimidar; **what are you —ting at?** ¿qué quieres decir con eso?; **as soon as he —s at the drink** en cuanto se pone a beber; **to — away** (*leave*) conseguir marcharse; salir, ir fuera; ir de vacaciones; (*escape*) escaparse, evadirse; (*at start of race*) escapar; **— away!** ¡no digas bobadas!; **to — away from place, person** escaparse de; **to — away from it all** evadirse del bullicio; **to — away with** (*take, steal*) llevarse, alzarse con; (*go unpunished*) hacer impunemente, quedar sin castigo; **you shan't — away with it!** ¡me las pagarás!; **to — back** volver; **to — back at someone** desquitarse con uno; **to — behind** (*adv*) quedarse atrás; **to — behind** (*prep*) penetrar, ahondar en; **to — by** (*adv*) lograr pasar; **we'll — by** (*fig*) nos las apañaremos, nos las arreglaremos; **I can — by in Dutch** me defiendo en holandés; **to — by** (*prep*) *thing* lograr pasar; *person* eludir, burlar la vigilancia de; **to — down** bajar; **to — down to** llegar a; *problem* abordar, empezar a estudiar; **to — down to work** ponerse seriamente a trabajar; **to — in** (*adv*) (*lograr*) entrar; (*train etc*) llegar; (*arrive home*) volver a casa, regresar; (*Pol*) ser elegido; **to — in** (*prep*) (*lograr*) entrar en; **to — in with** congraciarse con, llegar a tener influencia con; **to — into** (*lograr*) entrar en; *vehicle* subir a; *club* ingresar en; *clothes* ponerse; **difficulties** meterse en; *habit* adquirir; **what's got into you?** ¿qué mosca te ha picado?; **to — off** (*adv*) (*from vehicle*) apearse, bajar; (*Aer*) despegar; (*go away*) marcharse; (*to sleep*) conciliar el sueño; **— off!** ¡suelta!; **he got off unharmed** salió indemne; **he got off with a fine** escapó con una multa; **to tell someone where he —s off** cantar a uno las cuarenta; **to — off with someone** enamorar a uno; **to — off** (*prep*) (*from vehicle*) apearse de, bajar de; *punishment* librarse de; **to — on** (*adv*) (*mount*) subir, ponerse encima; (*progress*) hacer progresos, tener éxito, (*continue*) seguir; (*depart*) irse; **— on, man!** ¡siga!; **he's —ting on for 70** anda cerca de los 70; **he's —ting on va para viejo; it's —ting on for 9** falta poco para las 9; **to — on with someone** llevarse bien con uno, congeniar con uno; **how are you —ting on with him?** ¿cómo te avienes con él?; **they — on well together**

se llevan bien; **I'll — on to him at once** hablaré con él en seguida; **the police have got on to him** la policía tiene una pista que le conducirá al criminal; **I can't — on with maths** no me entran las matemáticas; **to — on** (*prep*) subir a, ponerse encima de; **to — out** salir; escaparse; (*news*) saberse, hacerse público; **— out!** ¡vete!, ¡fuera de aquí!; **to — out of** *vehicle* bajar de; *duty, punishment* librarse de; *obligation* zafarse de; *habit* perder; **to — over** (*adv*) cruzar, pasar por encima; **to — over** (*prep*) vencer, superar; *illness* reponerse de; *fright* sobreponerse a; *grief* dominar; *surprise* volverse de; *resentment* olvidar; **to — round** dar la vuelta a; *difficulty* soslayar; *person* persuadir, engatusar (*see also* **to — around**); **to — through** (*adv*) lograr pasar; **to — through** (*prep*) conseguir pasar por; *time* pasar; *period, work* llegar al final de, terminar; *money* gastar; *exam* aprobar; **to — through to** comunicar con (*also Tel*); **to — to** *place* llegar a; **to — to do something** acostumbrarse a hacer algo, aprender a hacer algo; **to — to like something** tomar afición a algo; **to — together** reunirse, verse, organizar una fiesta; **to — up** (*stand*) levantarse, ponerse de pie; (*from bed*) levantarse; (*bird etc*) alzar el vuelo; (*rise*) subir; (*wind*) empezar a soplar recio; (*fire*) avivarse; (*sea*) embravecerse; **— up!** ¡levántate!, (*to horse*) ¡arre!; **what did you — up to in London?** ¿qué diabluras hiciste en Londres?

3 *vr*: **to — oneself up as** disfrazarse de; **to — oneself arrested** hacerse detener; **to — oneself drunk** emborracharse; **to — oneself lost** extraviarse.

get-at-able [get'ætəbl] *adj* accesible.

getaway ['getəwei] *n* escape *m*, fuga *f*; **to make one's — escaparse.**

Gethsemane [geθ'semənɪ] Getsemaní *m*.

get-together ['gettə,geðə*] *n* (*meeting*) reunión *f*; (*regular social gathering*) tertulia *f*; (*party*) guateque *m*.

getup ['getʌp] *n* atavío *m*.

geyser ['giːzə*] *n* (*Geog*) géiser *m*; (*heater*) calentador *m* de agua.

Ghana ['gɑːnə] Ghana.

Ghanaian [gɑːˈneiən] **1** *adj* de Ghana, ghaneano. **2** *n* natural *mf* de Ghana, ghaneano *m*, a *f*.

ghastly ['gɑːstlɪ] *adj* horrible; (*pale*) pálido; (*corpselike*) cadavérico; (*fam*) horrible, fatal, malísimo; *person* pesado.

Ghent [gent] Gante.

gherkin ['gəːkɪn] *n* pepinillo *m*.

ghetto ['getəu] *n* judería *f*.

ghost [gəust] **1** *n* fantasma *m*, espectro *m*; **Holy G—** Espíritu *m* Santo; **he hasn't the — of a chance** no tiene la más remota posibilidad; **to give up the —** entregar el alma, (*fig*) perder toda esperanza.

2 *vt book* escribir por otro; **an autobiography —ed by X** una autobiografía que escribió realmente el escritor fantasma X.

ghostly ['gəustlɪ] *adj* espectral, fantasmal.

ghost story ['gəust,stɔːrɪ] *n* cuento *m* de fantasmas.

ghost writer ['gəust,raitə*] *n* escritor *m* fantasma.

ghoul [guːl] *n* demonio *m* necrófago; (*fig*) persona *f* de gustos inhumanos.

ghoulish ['guːlɪʃ] *adj* espantosamente cruel, sádico.

giant ['dʒaiənt] **1** *n* gigante *m*. **2** *adj* gigantesco, gigante.

gibber ['dʒibə*] *vi* farfullar, hablar atropelladamente, hablar de una manera ininteligible.

gibberish ['dʒibərɪʃ] *n* galimatías *m*, guirigay *m*.

gibbet ['dʒibit] *n* horca *f*.

gibbon ['gibən] *n* gibón *m*.

gibe [dʒaib] **1** *n* pulla *f*, dicterio *m*. **2** *vi* mofarse (*at de*).

giblets ['dʒiblits] *npl* menudillos *mpl*.

Gibraltar [dʒi'brɔːltə*] Gibraltar; **Rock of —** Peñón *m* de Gibraltar; **Straits of —** Estrecho *m* de Gibraltar.

giddiness ['gidinis] *n* vértigo *m*.

giddy ['gidi] *adj speed* vertiginoso; *character* atolondrado, ligero de cascos; (*dizzy*) mareado; **to feel — sentirse mareado; it makes me — me marea, me da vértigo.**

gift [gift] *n* (a) (*present*) regalo *m*; obsequio *m*; (*Eccl*) ofrenda *f*; (*Law*) donación *f*; (*bargain*) ganga *f*; **the office is in the —** of la dignidad está en manos de; **it's a —!** (*fam*) ¡está tirado!; **I wouldn't have it as a —** no lo quiero ni regalado.

(b) (*faculty, talent*) don *m*, talento *m*, prenda *f*; **— of tongues** don *m* de las lenguas; **he has a — for administration** tiene talento para la administración; **he has artistic —s** tiene dotes artísticas.

gifted ['giftid] *adj* talentoso.

gig [gig] *n* calesín *m*; (*Naut*) lancha *f*, canoa *f*.

gigantic [dʒai'gæntik] *adj* gigantesco.

giggle ['gigl] **1** n risilla f sofocada, risilla f tonta. **2** vi reirse con una risilla sofocada (or tonta).

gigolo ['ʒigələu] n gigoló m.

gild [gild] (irr: pret **gilded**, ptp **gilded** or **gilt**) vt dorar; metal sobredorar; (fig) embellecer, adornar; pill dorar.

gilding ['gildiŋ] n doradura f, dorado m.

Giles [dʒailz] m Gil.

gill [dʒil] n cuarta parte de una pinta (= approx ⅛ litro).

gill [gil] n (Fish) agalla f, branquia f; **to look green about the —s** tener cara olivácea.

gillie ['gili] n (Scot) ayudante m de cazador (or pescador); (Scot) criado m.

gillyflower ['dʒili,flauə*] n (poet) alhelí m.

gilt [gilt] **1** ptp of **gild**. **2** adj dorado. **3** n dorado m; (fig) atractivo m.

gilt-edged ['gilt'edʒd] adj: **— securities** papel m del Estado, valores mpl de máxima confianza.

gimlet ['gimlit] n barrena f de mano.

gimmick ['gimik] n (Theat) truco m característico; (Comm) truco m publicitario; **it's just a sales —** es un truco para vender más.

gin¹ [dʒin] n (drink) ginebra f.

gin² [dʒin] n (trap) trampa f; (Mech) desmotadera f de algodón.

ginger ['dʒindʒə*] **1** n jengibre m; (fig) energía f, empuje m. **2** adj hair rojo; cat de color melado, barcino, amarillento. **3** vt: **to — up** animar, estimular.

ginger ale ['dʒindʒər'eil] n cerveza f de jengibre.

ginger beer ['dʒindʒə'biə*] n gaseosa f.

gingerbread ['dʒindʒəbred] n pan m de jengibre.

ginger group ['dʒindʒəgru:p] n grupo m de activistas.

gingerly ['dʒindʒəli] **1** adj cauteloso. **2** adv con tiento, con pies de plomo.

gipsy ['dʒipsi] **1** n gitano m, a f. **2** attr gitano.

giraffe [dʒi'rɑ:f] n jirafa f.

gird [gə:d] (irr: pret and ptp **girded** or **girt**) vt ceñir; rodear (with de); **to — on one's sword** ceñirse la espada.

girder ['gə:də*] n viga f.

girdle ['gə:dl] **1** n cinto m, ceñidor m; (belt, also fig) cinturón m; (woman's) faja f. **2** vt ceñir, rodear (also fig; with de).

girl [gə:l] n chica f, muchacha f; (small) niña f; (young woman) chica f, joven f; (servant) criada f, chica f; (girlfriend) amiguita f, novia f; **best —** novia f; **old —** (of school) antigua alumna f, (fam) vieja f.

girlfriend ['gə:lfrend] n (of girl) amiga f, amiguita f, (of boy) novia f.

girlhood ['gə:lhud] n juventud f, mocedad f.

girlish ['gə:liʃ] adj de niña; juvenil; (pej) afeminado.

girl scout ['gə:l'skaut] n (US) exploradora f, muchacha-guía f.

Gironde [dʒi'rɔnd] Gironda m.

girt [gə:t] pret and ptp of **gird**.

girth [gə:θ] n (strap) cincha f; (measure) circunferencia f; (stoutness) gordura f, obesidad f; **because of its great —** por su gran tamaño, por lo abultado.

gist [dʒist] n esencia f, lo esencial, quid m; **to get the — of a matter** entender lo esencial de una cuestión.

give [giv] (irr: pret **gave**, ptp **given**) **1** vt **(a)** (bestow free) dar; (as present) regalar; (hand over) entregar; aid prestar; life dar, sacrificar; party ofrecer, organizar (for en honor de); **to — something to someone, to — someone something** dar algo a uno; **I wouldn't want it if you gave it to me** eso no lo quiero ni regalado; **(God) — me strength!** ¡Dios me dé paciencia!; **— me the old songs!** ¡yo prefiero las canciones viejas!

(b) (deliver) entregar; regards etc dar; one's word dar, empeñar; promise hacer; **to — something into someone's hands** entregar (or confiar) algo a uno; **to — someone something to eat** dar de comer a uno.

(c) (pay) pagar, dar; **what did you — for it?** ¿cuánto pagaste por él?; **I would — a lot to know** daría un dineral por saberlo.

(d) (dedicate) energy, time etc dedicar, consagrar; **he gave his life to it** consagró su vida a ello.

(e) cry etc lanzar, proferir, dar; **to — a smile** sonreír (to a); **to — a start** sobresaltarse.

(f) (state, present, utter) particulars hacer constar; example citar; details etc dar; recitation etc ofrecer; play representar, poner; lecture dar; speech pronunciar; decision comunicar, (by judge etc) dictar; **he —s no references** no cita referencias; **he gave no name** no dijo su nombre; **it gave no sign of life** no dio señal alguna de vida; **— us a song!** ¡cántanos algo!; **I — you the Queen** brindemos por la Reina.

(g) (impart) comunicar; (pass on) transmitir; disease contagiar con; **to — someone to understand**

that dar a uno a entender que; **I was given to believe that** me hicieron creer que.

(h) (allot, grant, assign) dar; conceder, otorgar; contract, job dar; task imponer; name dar, poner; (formally) imponer; punishment condenar a, castigar con.

(i) (produce) result dar por resultado, producir, arrojar; **it —s a total of 80** arroja un total de 80, suman 80; **it —s 6% a year** rinde un 6 por cien al año; **it —s an average of 4** da un promedio de 4.

(j) (cause) ocasionar, causar; **you gave me much pain** me causaste mucha pena.

(k) (allow) permitir; **I gave myself 10 minutes to do it** me permití 10 minutos para hacerlo; **he can — you 5 years** él tiene la ventaja de ser 5 años más joven que Vd; **how long would you — that marriage?** ¿cuánto tiempo crees que durará ese matrimonio?

(l) (fam) **to — it to someone** (beat) dar una paliza a uno; (verbally) poner a uno como un trapo; **I gave him what for** le dije cuatro verdades; **I'll — him what for!** ¡me lo cargaré!

(m) to — away (give free) regalar; (get rid of) deshacerse de; (sell cheap) malvender; (disclose) revelar, descubrir; (betray) traicionar; bride conducir al altar; **to — back** devolver; **to — in** entregar; **to — off** emitir, arrojar, despedir, echar; **to — out** (hand out) distribuir, repartir; (announce) anunciar; (reveal) revelar, divulgar; smoke etc emitir, arrojar; **he gave it out that** anunció que, hizo creer que; **to — over** entregar; (transfer) traspasar; **to — up** (hand over) entregar; ceder; (renounce) renunciar a; post dejar, renunciar a, dimitir de; (sacrifice) sacrificar; problem renunciar a resolver; patient desahuciar; (for lost) dar por perdido; **she gave him up** ella riñó con él; **we wish she'd give him up** estamos deseando que ella rompa con él; **he gave up smoking** dejó de fumar; **we'd —n you up** creíamos que no ibas a venir.

2 vi **(a)** (bestow) dar; **to — and take** hacer concesiones mutuas; **to — as good as one gets** devolver golpe por golpe.

(b) (stretch) dar de sí; (break) romperse; (door etc) ceder; (floor, roof etc) hundirse.

(c) to — in ceder; rendirse, darse por vencido; (agree) consentir; **to — in to person** condescender con, ceder a las súplicas de; threats etc rendirse ante, sucumbir ante; **she always —s in to him** ella hace siempre lo que él quiere; **to — on to** dar a; **to — out** (supply) agotarse, acabarse; (engine) fallar, averiarse; **to — over** cesar; **over!** ¡basta ya!; **to — up** darse por vencido; perder la esperanza; **don't — up yet!** ¡animate!

3 vr: **to — oneself over** (or up) to entregarse a, darse a; **to — oneself up** entregarse a la policía (etc).

give-and-take ['givən'teik] n toma y daca, concesiones fpl mutuas.

giveaway ['givəwei] adj: **— price** precio m obsequio, precio m de ruina.

given ['givn] **1** ptp of **give**.

2: — money one can do anything con dinero todo es posible; **on a — day** un día determinado; **in a — time** en un tiempo dado; **— that** dado que; **to be — to something** ser dado a, ser adicto a; **to be — to + ger** ser propenso a + infin.

giver ['givə*] n donador m, ora f.

gizzard ['gizəd] n molleja f; **it sticks in my —** no lo puede tragar.

glacial ['gleisiəl] adj glacial.

glaciation [,gleisi'eiʃən] n glaciación f.

glacier ['glæsiə*] n glaciar m.

glad [glæd] adj alegre; news etc bueno; **to be — about** alegrarse de; **I'm very — for you** me alegro mucho por ti; **to be — that** alegrarse de que + subj; **I am — to hear it** me alegro de saberlo; **I shall be — to come** tendré mucho gusto en venir; **he seemed — se** mostró satisfecho.

gladden ['glædn] vt alegrar, regocijar.

glade [gleid] n claro m.

gladiator ['glædieitə*] n gladiador m.

gladiolus [,glædi'əuləs] n, pl **gladioli** [,glædi'əulai] estoque m, gladiolo m.

gladly ['glædli] adv alegremente, con satisfacción; **yes,** — sí, con mucho gusto.

gladness ['glædnis] n alegría f; satisfacción f.

glamorize ['glæməraiz] vt embellecer; hacer más atractivo; **this programme —s crime** este programa presenta el crimen bajo una luz favorable, este programa nos hace ver los atractivos de la vida criminal.

glamorous ['glæmərəs] adj encantador, atractivo, hechicero.

glamour ['glæmə*] n encanto m, atractivo m, hechizo m.

glamour-girl ['glæməgə:l] n belleza f, guapa f (oficial).

glance [glɑːns] 1 n ojeada f, vistazo m; mirada f; **at a** — de un vistazo; **at first** — a primera vista; **with many a backward** — **at** (fig) pensando con mucha nostalgia en.
  2 vi (a) (look) mirar; **she** —**d in my direction** miró hacia donde yo estaba; **to** — **at** person etc lanzar una mirada a, object echar un vistazo a, ojear; **to** — **at, to** — **over, to** — **through** book etc hojear, examinar de paso; **to** — **away** apartar los ojos.
  (b) (strike) — **off something** chocar con algo y rebotar, desviarse al chocar con algo.

glancing ['glɑːnsiŋ] adj blow oblicuo.

gland [glænd] n (Bio) glándula f; (Mech) prensaestopas m.

glandular ['glændjulə*] adj glandular; — **fever** fiebre f glandular.

glare [gleə*] 1 n (a) (of light) luz f deslumbradora, reverbero m, brillo m, luminosidad f; (dazzle) deslumbramiento m; **because of the** — **of the light in Spain** debido a lo fuerte de la luz en España.
  (b) (look) mirada f feroz.
  2 vi (a) relumbrar, deslumbrar.
  (b) mirar ferozmente (at a), echar fuego por los ojos.

glaring ['gleəriŋ] adj (dazzling) deslumbrador, fuerte; colour chillón; mistake manifiesto, notorio.

glass [glɑːs] 1 n (a) (material) vidrio m, cristal m; (glassware) artículos mpl de vidrio, cristalería f; (tumbler, also for wine) vaso m; (for beer) caña f; (for sherry, champagne etc) copa f; (for liqueur, brandy) copita f; (Meteorol) barómetro m; (spyglass) catalejo m; (mirror) espejo m; **cut** — vidrio m tallado; **frosted** — vidrio m deslustrado; **under** — (exhibit) bajo vidrio, en una vitrina, (plant) en invernáculo; **to look at oneself in the** — mirarse en el espejo.
  (b) —**es** (spectacles) gafas fpl, lentes mpl; (binoculars) gemelos mpl; **dark** —**es** gafas fpl negras.
  2 attr de vidrio, de cristal; — **case** vitrina f; — **door** puerta f vidriera, puerta f de cristales; — **eye** ojo m de cristal.

glassful ['glɑːsful] n vaso m.

glasshouse ['glɑːshaus] n, pl —**houses** [,hauziz] (Hort) invernáculo m, invernadero m; (sl) cárcel f (militar).

glassware ['glɑːsweə*] n artículos mpl de vidrio, cristalería f.

glassy ['glɑːsi] adj substance vítreo; surface liso; water espejado; eye vidrioso.

glaucoma [glɔːˈkəumə] n glaucoma m.

glaze [gleiz] 1 n vidriado m, barniz m, lustre m. 2 vt (put glass in) poner vidrios a, vidriar; (fig) lustrar.

glazed [gleizd] adj surface vidriado; paper satinado; eye vidrioso.

glazier ['gleiziə*] n vidriero m.

gleam [gliːm] 1 n (of light) rayo m, destello m; (of colour) viso m; (in one's eye) chispa f; (fig) vislumbre f; **there is a** — **of hope** hay un rayo de esperanza.
  2 vi brillar (in the sun al sol; with de), relucir, destellar.

gleaming ['gliːmiŋ] adj reluciente.

glean [gliːn] 1 vt espigar; (fig) espigar, recoger; **to** — **information about** recoger (con dificultad) datos sobre; **from what I have been able to** — de lo que yo he podido saber. 2 vi espigar.

gleaner ['gliːnə*] n espigador m, ora f.

gleanings ['gliːniŋs] npl (fig) fragmentos mpl recogidos.

glebe [gliːb] n (Eccl) terreno m beneficial.

glee [gliː] n alegría f, júbilo m, regocijo m.

glee club ['gliːklʌb] n orfeón m.

gleeful ['gliːfəl] adj alegre, regocijado.

gleefully ['gliːfəli] adv con júbilo.

glen [glen] n cañada f, valle m estrecho.

glib [glib] adj person de mucha labia, poco sincero; speech elocuente pero poco sincero; explanation fácil.

glibly ['glibli] adv con poca sinceridad; elocuentemente pero con poca sinceridad; con una facilidad sospechosa.

glibness ['glibnis] n labia f; falta f de sinceridad; facilidad f.

glide [glaid] 1 n deslizamiento m; (Aer) planeo m, vuelo m sin motor; (Mus) ligadura f.
  2 vi (a) deslizarse; **to** — **away, to** — **off** escurrirse, irse silenciosamente; **she** —**s to the door** se desliza hacia la puerta.
  (b) (Aer) planear, volar sin motor.

glider ['glaidə*] n planeador m, velero m; (towed) avión m remolcado.

gliding ['glaidiŋ] n vuelo m sin motor.

glimmer ['glimə*] 1 n luz f trémula, luz f tenue, vislumbre f; **without a** — **of understanding** sin dar el menor indicio de comprenderme; **there is a** — **of hope** hay un rayo de esperanza.
  2 vi brillar con luz trémula (or tenue).

glimpse [glimps] 1 n vislumbre f; vista f momentánea; **to catch a** — **of** vislumbrar. 2 vt vislumbrar, entrever, ver por un instante.

glint [glint] 1 n destello m, centelleo m; (in one's eye) chispa f. 2 vi destellar, centellear.

glisten ['glisn] vi relucir, brillar.

glitter ['glitə*] 1 n brillo m, resplandor m. 2 vi relucir, brillar, rutilar; **all that** —**s is not gold** no es oro todo lo que reluce.

glittering ['glitəriŋ] adj reluciente, brillante (also fig).

gloaming ['gləumiŋ] n crepúsculo m; **in the** — al anochecer.

gloat [gləut] vi relamerse; **to** — **over** money etc recrearse contemplando, sight saborear, news refocilarse con, victory manifestar satisfacción maligna por, beaten enemy triunfar jactanciosamente de.

glob [glɔb] n (US) gotita f, glóbulo m; masa f redonda, masa f pequeña; grumo m.

global ['gləubl] adj (world-wide) mundial; sum etc global.

globe [gləub] n globo m, esfera f; (spherical map) esfera f terrestre, globo m terráqueo.

globe-trotter ['gləub,trɔtə*] n trotamundos m.

globular ['glɔbjulə*] adj globular.

globule ['glɔbjuːl] n glóbulo m.

gloom [gluːm] n, **gloominess** [gluːminis] n oscuridad f, lobreguez f, tenebrosidad f; (fig) pesimismo m; melancolía f, tristeza f.

gloomily ['gluːmili] adv oscuramente, lóbregamente; de modo pesimista, con pesimismo; melancólicamente, tristemente.

gloomy ['gluːmi] adj oscuro, lóbrego, tenebroso; atmosphere, character, forecast pesimista; outlook nada prometedor; day, tone melancólico, triste.

glorification [,glɔːrifiˈkeiʃən] n glorificación f.

glorify ['glɔːrifai] vt glorificar; (praise) alabar; **it was nothing but a glorified cottage** resultó ser solamente una casita con pretensiones de palacio.

glorious ['glɔːriəs] adj glorioso; day, view, stroke etc magnífico; **it was a** — **muddle** la confusión era mayúscula.

glory ['glɔːri] 1 n gloria f; (fig) esplendor m; **Old G— bandera de EE.UU**; **to be in one's** — estar en sus glorias.
  2 vi: **to** — **in** gloriarse de; **I** — **in the name of Briton** para mí el ser inglés es motivo de orgullo; **the café glories in the name of El Dorado** el café tiene el magnífico nombre de El Dorado.

glory hole ['glɔːrihəul] n (fam) cuarto m (or cajón etc) en desorden, cuarto m (etc) que se deja sin arreglar.

gloss¹ [glɔs] (note) 1 n glosa f. 2 vt glosar, comentar.

gloss² [glɔs] 1 n lustre m, brillo m.
  2 attr: — **finish** acabado m brillo; — **paint** pintura f esmalte; — **paper** papel m satinado.
  3 vt lustrar, pulir; **to** — **over** (excuse) disculpar, (play down) paliar, colorear, (cover up) encubrir.

glossary ['glɔsəri] n glosario m.

glossy ['glɔsi] adj surface lustroso, brillante; hair liso; cloth, paper satinado; magazine etc de buen tono, elegante.

glove [glʌv] n guante m; **to fit someone like a** — sentar a uno como un guante.

gloved [glʌvd] adj hand enguantado.

glover ['glʌvə*] n guantero m, a f.

glow [gləu] 1 n (of lamp, sun etc) luz f (difusa); (of jewel) brillo m; (of fire) calor m vivo; (bright colour) color m vivo; (in sky) arrebol m; (Tech) incandescencia f; (warm feeling) sensación f de bienestar; (of satisfaction etc) sensación f grata, sentimiento m de vivo placer.
  2 vi (lamp, sun, jewel etc) brillar (con luz difusa); (fire) arder vivamente; (Tech) estar candente; **to** — **with pleasure** experimentar una sensación de bienestar; **to** — **with health** estar rebosando de salud.

glower ['glauə*] vi: **to** — **at** mirar con ceño.

glowering ['glauəriŋ] adj person, sky ceñudo.

glowing ['gləuiŋ] adj candente, incandescente; light brillante; fire vivo; cheek etc encendido; colour intenso; report etc entusiasta.

glow-worm ['gləuwəːm] n luciérnaga f.

glucose ['gluːkəus] n glucosa f.

glue [gluː] 1 n cola f, goma f (de pegar). 2 vt encolar, pegar (also **to** — **on, to** — **together**); **her face was** —**d to the window** tenía la cara pegada a la ventana.

gluey ['gluːi] adj pegajoso, viscoso.

glum [glʌm] *adj* (*by nature*) taciturno, melancólico; *mood* triste, abatido; *tone* melancólico, sombrío.

glut [glʌt] **1** *n* superabundancia *f*, exceso *m*; **to be a — on the market** abarrotar el mercado.

2 *vt person* hartar, saciar; *market* abarrotar, inundar; **to be —ted with fruit** (*person*) haberse atracado de frutas.

3 *vr*: **to — oneself** atracarse (**with** de).

gluten ['glu:tən] *n* gluten *m*.

glutinous ['glu:tinəs] *adj* glutinoso.

glutton ['glʌtn] *n* glotón *m*, ona *f*; **to be a — for work** trabajar incansablemente.

gluttonous ['glʌtənəs] *adj* glotón, goloso.

gluttony ['glʌtəni] *n* glotonería *f*, gula *f*.

glycerin(e) [,glisə'ri:n] *n* glicerina *f*.

G-man ['dʒi:mæn] *n*, *pl* **—men** [men] (*US*) agente *m* secreto federal.

gnarled [nɑ:ld] *adj* nudoso, torcido.

gnash [næʃ] *vt teeth* rechinar.

gnat [næt] *n* mosquito *m*, jején *m* (*SAm*).

gnaw [nɔ:] *vt* roer.

gneiss [nais] *n* gneis *m*.

gnome [nəum] *n* gnomo *m*.

gnu [nu:] *n* ñu *m*.

go [gəu] (*irr: pret* **went**, *ptp* **gone**) **1** *vi* (a) (*general sense*) ir; viajar; andar; **to — to London** ir a Londres; **to — to England** ir a Inglaterra; **all roads — to Rome** todos los caminos van a Roma; **to — the shortest way** tomar el camino más corto; **to — (at) 30 m.p.h.** ir a 30 m.p.h.; **the numbers that — from 6 to 12** los números que van de 6 a 12; **to — to someone for something** acudir a uno a pedir (*or* buscar) algo; **there he —es!** ¡ahí va!; **here —es!** ¡vamos a ver!, ¡a ello!; **who —es there?** ¿quién va?; **there you — again!** ¡has vuelto a la misma canción!; **there —es the bell** suena el timbre; **what shall I — in?** ¿qué traje me pongo?; **it —es by seasons** esto va por temporadas; **it —es by age** varía según la edad, depende de la edad; **promotion —es by seniority** los ascensos se hacen por orden de antigüedad.

(b) (*progress*) ir; **business is —ing well** los negocios van bien; **everything went well** todo salió bien, todo resultó perfecto; **how —es it?** ¿qué tal?, ¿cómo te va esto?; **how did the exam —?** ¿qué tal el examen?; **we'll see how things —** veremos cómo se desarrolla la situación; **to make the party —** hacer que resulte alegre la fiesta, animar la fiesta; *see get, keep etc.*

(c) (*purpose etc*) **to — and see someone, to — to see someone** ir a ver a uno; **he went and bought it** lo compró, por fin se resolvió a comprarlo; (*near future*) **I am —ing to see him** voy a verle; (*emphatic*) **I am —ing to see him** sí voy a verle.

(d) (*function*) funcionar, marchar; **it won't —** no funciona; **it —es on petrol** funciona con gasolina; **it —es on wheels** marcha sobre ruedas; **to make something —** hacer funcionar algo; **to set a machine —ing** poner en marcha una máquina.

(e) (*depart*) irse, marcharse, partir; (*train etc*) partir, salir; **let's —!** ¡vamos!, ¡vámonos!; **don't — yet** no te vayas tan pronto, quédate un poco más; **be gone!, get you gone!** ¡váyase!; **—!** (*starting race*) ¡ya!; **from the word —** desde el principio; **when does the train —?** ¿a qué hora sale el tren?

(f) (*disappear etc*) **my hat has gone** ha desaparecido mi sombrero; **my money is all gone** ya no me queda dinero; **the coffee is all gone** se acabó el café; **he'll have to —** (*be dismissed*) tendremos que deshacernos de él, tendremos que echarle; **luxuries will have to —** tendremos que prescindir de las cosas de lujo; **the trees have been gone for years** hace años que se quitaron los árboles; **his mind is —ing** está perdiendo la cabeza; **all my teeth have gone** he perdido todos mis dientes.

(g) (*be sold*) venderse; **it went next day** se vendió al día siguiente; **it went for £5** se vendió por 5 libras; **—ing, —ing, gone!** ¡a la una . . . a las dos . . . a las tres!

(h) (*of time*) pasar; **the day went slowly** el día pasó lentamente; **how is the time —ing?** ¿cuánto tiempo ha pasado ya?, ¿cuánto tiempo nos queda?

(i) (*of the hour*) **it has gone 3** ya dieron las 3, son las 3 y pico; **it has gone 8 already** son las 8 dadas.

(j) (*pass by descent*) pasar; **his books went to the college** sus libros pasaron al colegio.

(k) (*extend*) **the garden —es down to the lake** el jardín se extiende hasta el lago; **it's good as far as it —es** dentro de sus límites es bueno.

(l) (*be available*) estar disponible; **are there any houses —ing?** ¿hay casas en venta?; **are there any jobs —ing?** ¿están ofreciendo empleos?; **anything that's —ing** lo que haya.

(m) (*exist*) **as prices —** that's not dear considerando los precios que corren eso no es caro.

(n) (*of text*) decir, rezar; **the text —es . . .** reza el texto así . . .; **as the saying —es** como dice el refrán; **how does the song —?** ¿qué dice la canción?

(o) (*be acceptable*) **anything —es with him** se allana a todo; se amolda a todo; hace las cosas de cualquier modo; **what I say —es** aquí mando yo; **that —es for me too** yo de acuerdo, yo contigo.

(p) (*fit*) **it —es under the table** cabe debajo de la mesa; **where does this book —?** ¿dónde pongo este libro?; **this part —es here** esta pieza se coloca aquí; **3 into 12 —es 4** 12 entre 3 son 4.

(q) (*break etc*) romperse, estropearse; (*give way*) ceder, hundirse; (*fall*) caer; **a fuse went** se quemó un plomo; **it went at the seams** se deshizo por las juntas; **there —es another button** se ha descosido otro botón.

(r) (*help, contribute*) **the qualities that — to make a king** las cualidades que hacen a un rey; **it —es to show that** sirve para demostrar que; **the money —es to help the poor** el dinero se destina a ayudar a los pobres.

(s) (*with ger*) **to — fishing** ir de pesca; **to — hunting** ir de caza; **to — riding** montar a caballo.

(t) (*become*) hacerse, volverse, ponerse; (*ie — bad*) pasarse, (*of milk*) cortarse; **to — black** ponerse negro; **to — mad** volverse loco; **to — communist** hacerse comunista; **to — pale** palidecer ponerse pálido; *see blind etc.*

(u) (*let —*) let me **—!** ¡suelta!, ¡déjame!; **to let — of something** soltar algo; **to let oneself —** (*emotionally*) desahogarse, (*angrily*) perder los estribos, (*on a subject*) entusiasmarse; (*physically*) abandonarse, dejar de cuidarse; **they've let the house —** han dejado de cuidar la casa; **we'll let it — at that** dejémoslo ahí.

(v) (*make a noise*) **he went "psst"** dijo "psst"; **the balloon went bang** el globo estalló.

(w) **to — about** (*move about*) andar (de un sitio para otro); (*Naut*) virar; (*undertake*) emprender, intentar; **to — about one's business** ocuparse en sus asuntos; **to — about together** salir juntos; **to — about with** salir con, alternar con; **to — after** andar tras; (*follow*) seguir; (*persecute*) perseguir; **to — against principle etc** ir en contra de, oponerse a, *person* oponerse a, (*result, decision*) ser desfavorable a; **to — along** (*adv*) ir; (*go away*) marcharse; **to — along with** acompañar a; **to — along with an idea** consentir en un proyecto, aprobar una idea; **we can't — along with that** no estamos de acuerdo con eso; **to — along** (*prep*) ir por, pasar por; **to — at** (*undertake*) emprender; (*attack*) lanzarse sobre, acometer; **to — away** irse, marcharse; (*vanish*) desaparecer; **to — back** (*return*) volver, regresar; (*fall back*) retroceder; **to — back on promise** faltar a, desdecirse de; **it —es back to Elizabeth I** se remonta a Isabel I; **to — before** (*adv*) ir primero; (*in order etc*) anteceder, preceder; **all that has gone before** todo lo que ha pasado (*etc*) antes; **to — before** (*prep*) (*lead*) ir a la cabeza de; (*appear before*) comparecer ante; **to — beyond** ir más allá de, (*fig*) exceder; **to — by** (*adv*) (*of place*) pasar, (*of time*) pasar, transcurrir; **to — by** (*prep*) (*place*) pasar delante de, pasar cerca de, pasar junto a; (*be guided by*) atenerse a, guiarse por; **to — by appearances** juzgar por las apariencias; **that's nothing to — by** eso no es ningún criterio seguro; **to — down** (*adv*) bajar; (*sun*) ponerse; (*ship*) hundirse; (*be defeated*) sucumbir; (*before* ante); (*Univ*) salir de la universidad; (*be acceptable*) ser aceptable, poderse aguantar; gustar; (*in history*) pasar a la historia; **that will — down well with him** eso le va a gustar; **the play did not — down well** la obra no gustó; **Madrid went down 2-0 to Seville** el Madrid perdió 2-0 frente al Sevilla; **to — down** (*prep*) bajar, bajar por, descender; **to — for** (*fetch*) ir por, ir a buscar; (*attack*) atacar, acometer; **to — all out for** tratar por todos los medios de conseguir; **I really — for jazz** me entusiasma de verdad el jazz; **I don't much — for that** eso realmente no me gusta; **to — in** (*adv*) entrar; (*fit*) caber; (*compete*) presentarse (**for** a); **to — in** (*prep*) entrar en; (*fit*) caber en; (*have a place*) ponerse en, deber colocarse en; **to — in for** dedicarse a; tomar parte en; (*compete*) presentarse a; *exam* tomar, presentarse a; (*buy*) comprar, (*collect*) coleccionar; **we don't — in for such things here** aquí esas cosas no se hacen; **to — in with someone** asociarse con uno; **to — into** (*enter*) entrar en; (*fit*) caber en; (*study*) examinar, investigar; **to — off** (*adv*) (*away*) irse, marcharse; (*explode*) estallar, hacer explosión; (*gun*) dispararse; (*go bad*) pasarse, deteriorarse; *(lose the knack)* perder el tino; **it all went off well** todo salió perfecto; **how did it — off?** ¿qué tal resultó?; **to — off** *(prep)* perder el gusto por, *person* dejar de querer a; **to — on** *(travelling)* seguir, seguir adelante, seguir su camino; avanzar; *(Theat)* salir a escena; *(progress)* progresar, hacer progresos; *(last)* durar; *(narration)* continuar, decir después; **to — on to** + *ger* seguir + *ger*, continuar + *ger*; **— on!** ¡vamos!, *(with narration)* ¡adelante!, *(excl of surprise)* ¡anda!; **how are you —ing on?** ¿qué tal estás?; **he does — on so** habla más que siete, no acaba nunca de hablar; **don't — on so!** ¡no machaques!; **he's always —ing on about it** siempre está con la misma cantilena; **he —es on about the government** se queja siempre del gobierno, echa pestes siempre contra el gobierno; **don't — on like that!** ¡no te pongas así! **there's nothing to — on** no hay pista que podamos seguir; **that's nothing to — on** no se puede juzgar por eso; **to be gone on someone** *(fam)* andar mochales por uno; **to — on at** reñir; **it's —ing on for 7** son casi las 7; **he's —ing on for 50** va para los 50; **to — on to** + *infin* pasar luego a *infin*; **he went on to say** dijo a continuación; **to — on with** continuar, proseguir; **to — out** salir; *(light)* apagarse; *(of fashion)* pasar de moda; **to — out with** *boyfriend etc* salir con; **to — over** *(adv)* pasar por encima; **how did it — over?** ¿qué tal lo recibió el público? *(etc)*; **to — over to the opposition** pasarse a la oposición; **to — over** *(prep)* pasar por encima de; recorrer, atravesar; *(check)* revisar, repasar; **to — round** *(adv)* dar la vuelta, hacer un rodeo; *(revolve)* girar; *(suffice)* alcanzar para todos; **to — round to John's** ir a casa de Juan; **to — round** *(prep)* dar la vuelta a, hacer un rodeo para evitar; **to — through** *(adv)* pasar a través; **your promotion has gone through** se ha aprobado su ascenso; **to — through** *(prep)* pasar por, pasar a través de; penetrar; *(undergo)* sufrir, experimentar; *(examine)* examinar, estudiar; *(spend)* gastar; **to — through with** something llevar algo a cabo; **to — to** *(bequest)* pasar a; **to — together** ir juntos; *(colours etc)* armonizar, hacer juego; ser complementarios; **to — under** *(adv)* hundirse; *(ship)* hundirse; *(person)* desaparecer debajo del agua; *(fig)* fracasar; **to — under** *(prep)* *name* ser conocido por; **to — up** *(adv)* subir; *(Univ)* entrar en la universidad; *(explode)* estallar; **to — up to London** ir a Londres; **to — up to someone** acercarse a uno; **if the total —es up to 100** si el total asciende a 100; **to — with it** con, acompañar; *(match)* armonizar con, hacer juego con; *(in mixing drinks)* ligar con; **to — without** *(adv)* arreglárselas; **to — without** *(prep)* pasarse sin.

2 *vt*: **to — it** *(speed)* ir a toda velocidad; *(work hard)* obrar enérgicamente; *(live it up)* correrla; **— it!** ¡a ello!, ¡ánimo!; **to — it alone** obrar sin ayuda de nadie, seguir una política independiente; **to — one better** hacer mejor todavía *(than que)*; **to — 3 hearts** *(Cards)* marcar 3 corazones.

3 *n (mostly fam)* **(a)** *(energy)* energía *f*, empuje *m*; **there's no — about him** le falta energía.

(b) **to be on the —** trajinar, moverse, estar trabajando, estar viajando; **to have two novels on the —** tener dos novelas entre manos; **to keep someone on the —** hacer que uno siga trabajando, no dejar descansar a uno,

(c) *(attempt)* **at one —, in one —** de un solo golpe, de un tirón; **to have a —** hacer una tentativa, probar suerte; **have a —!** ¡a ello!; **to have a — at something** intentar algo; **to have a — at** + *ger* intentar + *infin*.

(d) *(turn)* **it's your —** te toca a ti; **whose — is it?** ¿a quién le toca?

(e) *(success)* **it's all the —** hace furor; **it's no —** es inútil, es imposible; **to make a — of something** tener éxito en algo.

(f) *(bargain)* **it's a —** ¡trato hecho!; **is it a —?** ¿hace?, ¿estamos de acuerdo?

goad [gəud] **1** *n* aguijada *f*, aguijón *m*; *(fig)* estímulo *m*.

2 *vt* aguijonear, picar; *(fig)* incitar, provocar, *(anger)* irritar, *(taunt)* provocar con insultos; **to — someone into fury** provocar a uno hasta la furia; **to — someone into doing something, to — someone to do something** incitar a uno a hacer algo.

go-ahead ['gəuəhed] **1** *adj* emprendedor, enérgico.

2 *n* permiso *m* (or señal *f*) para seguir adelante.

goal [gəul] *n* **(a)** *(purpose)* fin *m*, objeto *m*, meta *f*; *(ambition)* ambición *f*; **to reach one's —** llegar a la meta, realizar una ambición.

(b) *(-posts)* meta *f*, portería *f*.

(c) *(score)* gol *m*, tanto *m*; **to score a —** marcar un gol.

goal-area ['gəul,ɛəriə] *n* área *f* de meta.

goalie ['gəuli] *n (fam)* = **goalkeeper.**

goalkeeper ['gəul,ki:pə*] *n* guardameta *m*, portero *m*.

goal-kick ['gəul'kik] *n* saque *m* de portería.

goal-line ['gəullain] *n* línea *f* de portería.

goal-post ['gəulpəust] *n* poste *m* de la portería.

goat [gəut] *n* cabra *f*, macho *m* cabrío; **to get someone's —** *(fam)* sacar a uno de quicio.

goatee [gəu'ti:] *n* barba *f* de chivo.

goatherd ['gəuthə:d] *n* cabrero *m*.

goatskin ['gəutskin] *n* piel *f* de cabra.

gob [gɔb] *n* salivazo *m*; *(sl)* boca *f*.

gobble ['gɔbl] **1** *n* gluglú *m*. **2** *vt* engullir; **to — up** engullirse ávidamente. **3** *vi (turkey)* gluglutear.

gobbler ['gɔblə*] *n (Orn)* pavo *m*.

gobbledygook ['gɔbldiguːk] *n (fam)* jerga *f* burocrática.

go-between ['gəubi,twiːn] *n* medianero *m*, a *f*, mediador *m*, ora *f*; *(pimp)* alcahuete *m*, a *f*.

goblet ['gɔblit] *n* copa *f*.

goblin ['gɔblin] *n* duende *m*, trasgo *m*.

go-by ['gəubai] *n (fam)*: **to give something the —** pasar algo por alto, omitir algo; **to give a place the —** dejar de visitar un sitio; **to give someone the —** desairar a uno (no haciendo caso de él).

go-cart ['gəukɑ:t] *n* cochecito *m* de niño.

god [gɔd] *n* dios *m*; **G—** Dios *m*; **—s** *(Theat)* paraíso *m*, gallinero *m*; **for G—'s sake!** ¡por Dios!; **my G—!** ¡Dios mío!, ¡santo Dios!; **G— forbid!** ¡no lo permita Dios!; **please —!** *(arch)* ¡plegue a Dios!; **G— willing** si Dios quiere, Dios mediante; **G— only knows** sólo Dios sabe; **G— helps those who help themselves** a Dios rogando y con el mazo dando.

godchild ['gɔdtʃaild] *n*, *pl* **—children** [,tʃildrən] ahijado *m*, a *f*.

goddaughter ['gɔd,dɔ:tə*] *n* ahijada *f*.

goddess ['gɔdis] *n* diosa *f*.

godfather ['gɔd,fɑːðə*] *n* padrino *m* *(to* de).

god-fearing ['gɔd,fiərin] *adj* timorato.

godforsaken ['gɔdfə,seikn] *adj person* dejado de la mano de Dios; *place* triste, remoto, desierto.

Godfrey ['gɔdfri] *m* Godofredo.

godhead ['gɔdhed] *n* divinidad *f*.

godless ['gɔdlis] *adj* impío, descreído.

godly ['gɔdli] *adj* piadoso.

godmother ['gɔd,mʌðə*] *n* madrina *f* *(to* de); **fairy —** hada *f* madrina.

godparents ['gɔd,pɛərənts] *npl* padrinos *mpl*.

godsend ['gɔdsend] *n* cosa *f* llovida del cielo; **it was a — to us** fue un regalo celestial para nosotros.

godson ['gɔdsʌn] *n* ahijado *m*.

goes [gəuz] *see* **go.**

go-getter ['gəugetə*] *n* ambicioso *m*, a *f*, egoísta *mf*.

goggle ['gɔgl] *vi* salírsele a uno los ojos de las órbitas; **to — at** mirar con ojos desorbitados, mirar sin comprender.

goggle-eyed ['gɔgl,aid] *adj* con ojos desorbitados.

goggles ['gɔglz] *npl (Aut etc)* anteojos *mpl*; *(of skindiver)* gafas *fpl* submarinas; *(fam)* gafas *fpl*.

going ['gəuin] *n* **(a)** *(departure)* ida *f*, partida *f*.

(b) *(pace)* **good —!** ¡bien hecho!; **that was good —** eso fue muy rápido; **it was slow —** el avance fue lento.

(c) *(state of surface etc)* estado *m* del camino, *(Sport)* estado *m* de la pista; **the path is hard —** el camino está muy malo; **let's cross while the — is good** crucemos mientras podamos; **the book was heavy —** la lectura del libro resultó pesada; **it's heavy — talking to her** exige mucho esfuerzo conversar con ella.

going-over ['gəuin'əuvə*] *n* **(a)** inspección *f*; **we gave the house a thorough —** registramos la casa de arriba abajo.

(b) *(fam)* paliza *f*; **they gave him a —** le dieron una paliza.

goings-on ['gəuinz'ɔn] *npl* actividades *fpl (sospechosas)*; conducta *f* (sospechosa).

goitre, (US) goiter ['gɔitə*] *n* bocio *m*.

gold [gəuld] **1** *n* oro *m*; **rolled —** oro *m* laminado. **2** *attr* de oro.

goldbrick ['gəuld'brik] **1** *n (fam)* estafa *f*. **2** *vi (fam)* dar gato por liebre.

Gold Coast ['gəuld'kəust] *n* Costa *f* de Oro.

goldcrest ['gəuldkrest] *n* reyezuelo *m* sencillo.

gold digger ['gəuld,digə*] *n* aventurera *f*.

golden ['gəuldən] *adj* de oro; dorado; áureo; *age, voice, wedding etc* de oro; *opportunity* excelente.

goldenrod ['gəuldən'rɔd] *n (Bot)* vara *f* de oro.

goldfield ['gəuldfiːld] *n* campo *m* aurífero.

gold-filled ['gəuld,fild] *adj* lleno de oro; *(Tech)* revestido de oro, enchapado en oro; *tooth* empastado de oro.

goldfinch ['gəuldfintʃ] *n* jilguero *m*.

goldfish ['gəuldfiʃ] *n* pez *m* de colores.

goldfish bowl ['gəuldfiʃˌbəul] n pecera f.
gold mine ['gəuldmain] n mina f de oro; (fig) río m de oro, potosí m.
goldsmith ['gəuldsmiθ] n orfebre m.
gold standard ['gəuldˌstændəd] n patrón m oro.
golf [gɔlf] n golf m.
golf club ['gɔlfklʌb] n (society) club m de golf; (stick) palo m (de golf).
golf course ['gɔlfkɔːs] n campo m de golf.
golfer ['gɔlfə*] n golfista m.
golf links ['gɔlfliŋks] npl campo m de golf.
Goliath [gə'laiəθ] m Goliat.
golliwog ['gɔliwɔg] n negrito m.
golly[1] ['gɔli] n (fam) = **golliwog**.
golly[2] ['gɔli] interj (fam) ¡caramba!
golosh [gə'lɔʃ] n chanclo m, galocha f.
gonad ['gɔnæd] n gónada f.
gondola ['gɔndələ] n góndola f; (Aer) barquilla f.
gone [gɔn] ptp of **go**.
goner ['gɔnə*] n (sl): he's a — está muerto.
gong [gɔŋ] n gong m, gongo m.
gonorrhoea [ˌgɔnə'riə] n gonorrea f.
goo [guː] n (fam) cosa f muy pegajosa, sustancia f viscosa.
good [gud] 1 adj (comp **better**, superl **best**) (a) (general sense; also of — quality, right, morally sound, favourable etc) bueno, (before a sing n buen, eg) a — book un buen libro; —! ¡bueno!, ¡muy bien!; — for you! ¡muy bien Vd!; — old Peter! ¡bravo Pedro!
(b) (— enough) — enough! ¡muy bien!; that's — enough for me eso me basta; it's just not — enough! ¡esto no se puede consentir!
(c) (pleasant) it's — to see you me alegro de verte; how — it is to know that . . .! ¡cuánto me alegro de saber que . . .!; it's — to be here es agradable estar aquí; it's as — as a holiday to me esto me vale tanto como unas vacaciones.
(d) (beneficial) bueno, provechoso; (advantageous) ventajoso; (wholesome) sano, saludable; — to eat bueno de comer; it's — for you es cosa muy sana; it's — for you to swim la natación es cosa sana; oil is — for burns el aceite es bueno para las quemaduras; spirits are not — for me los licores no me sientan bien; he eats more than is — for him come más de lo razonable.
(e) (useful) bueno, útil, servible; the only — chair la única silla servible (or sana); to be — for servir para; he's — for nothing es completamente inútil; he's — for 10 years yet tiene todavía por delante 10 años de vida; he's — for £5 seguramente tiene 5 libras que prestarnos; I'm — for another mile tengo fuerzas para ir otra milla más; it'll be — for some years durará todavía algunos años; a ticket — for 3 months un billete valedero para 3 meses.
(f) (clever) to be — at ser hábil en, tener aptitud para, ser fuerte en; she's — with cats entiende de gatos.
(g) (kind) bueno, amable; he's a — sort es buena persona; he was — to me fue muy amable conmigo; he was so — as to + infin tuvo la amabilidad de + infin; please be so — as to + infin ¿me hace el favor de + infin?, (more formally) tenga la bondad de + infin; that's very — of you es Vd muy amable.
(h) (well-behaved) de buenos modales, educado; the child has been as — as gold el niño se ha portado como un ángel; be —! (morally) ¡sé bueno!, (in behaviour) ¡pórtate bien!, (at this moment) ¡estáte formal!
(i) (at least) a — 3 hours 3 horas largas; a — 4 miles 4 millas largas; a — £10 lo menos 10 libras.
(j) (practically) it's as — as new está como nuevo; it's as — as done está casi terminado; it's as — as lost puede darse por perdido; they're as — as beaten pueden darse por vencidos.
(k) to make — promise cumplir, accusation hacer bueno, probar, claim justificar, loss compensar, reparar; damage reparar, pagar; see **escape**.
2 adv: — and proper por las buenas; — and strong bien fuerte; to feel — estar satisfecho, creer haber hecho algo meritorio, (in health) estar como un reloj; to give as — as one gets devolver golpe por golpe; you never had it so — nunca habéis estado mejor; to hold — ser valedero, seguir verdadero (of con respecto a); to make — salir bien, tener éxito, demostrar tener capacidad.
3 n (a) bien m, provecho m, utilidad f; the — (abstract) lo bueno, (people) los buenos; — and evil el bien y el mal; there is much — in him tiene buenas cualidades; there is some — in him no es del todo malo; for — definitivamente, para siempre;

he's gone for — se ha ido para no volver; for the — of en bien de, a beneficio de; it's for your own — es por su propio bien; it's no — es inútil, no sirve para nada; it's no — complaining de nada sirve quejarse, no vale la pena de quejarse; what's the — of it? ¿para qué sirve?; I'm no — at such things yo no sirvo para tales cosas; he's no — (morally) es un perdido; he's up to no — está tramando algo malo; he'll come to no — tendrá mal fin; we're £2 to the — hemos ganado 2 libras; we're a spoon to the — tenemos una cuchara de sobra; to do — hacer bien; he never did any — nunca hizo nada bueno; it can't do any — es imposible que sea útil; it will do him no — esto no le aprovechará en lo más mínimo; this medicine will do you — esta medicina le sentará bien; much — may it do him! ¡buen provecho le haga!
(b) —s bienes mpl, efectos mpl; (Comm) géneros mpl, artículos mpl, mercancías fpl; canned —s conservas fpl alimenticias; capital —s bienes mpl de capital; consumer —s bienes mpl de consumo; fancy —s géneros mpl de fantasía; knitted —s géneros mpl de punto; to deliver the —s (fam) cumplir lo prometido.
4 —s attr de mercancías.
good-bye ['gud'bai] 1 interj ¡adiós! 2 n adiós m; to say — to despedirse de, (fig) dar por perdido.
good-for-nothing ['gudfə'nʌθiŋ] 1 adj inútil. 2 n perdido m.
good-humoured ['gud'hjuːməd] adj person afable, jovial; remark etc jovial; discussion de tono amistoso.
good-looking ['gud'lukiŋ] adj bien parecido, guapo.
goodly ['gudli] adj (fine) agradable, excelente; sum etc importante; number crecido.
good-natured ['gud'neitʃəd] adj person afable, bonachón; discussion de tono amistoso.
goodness ['gudnis] n (virtue, kindness) bondad f; (good quality) buena calidad f; (essence) sustancia f, lo mejor; —!, — gracious!, — me! ¡Dios mío!; for —' sake! ¡por Dios!; — only knows! ¡vaya Vd a saber!
good-tempered ['gud'tempəd] adj afable, ecuánime, de natural apacible; tone afable, amistoso; discussion sereno, sin pasión.
good-time ['gud'taim] adj: — girl chica f alegre.
goodwill ['gud'wil] n buena voluntad f; (Comm) clientela f, buen nombre m; — mission misión f de buena voluntad.
goody ['gudi] (fam: esp US) 1 adj beatuco, santurrón. 2 interj (also — —) ¡qué bien!, ¡qué estupendo! 3 n golosina f.
gooey ['guːi] adj (fam) pegajoso, viscoso; sweet empalagoso.
goof [guːf] (sl) 1 n bobo m, a f. 2 vi tirarse una plancha.
goofy ['guːfi] adj (sl) bobo.
goon [guːn] n (a) imbécil mf, idiota mf. (b) (US) gorila m contratado para sembrar el terror entre los obreros.
goose [guːs] n, pl **geese** [giːs] (domestic) ganso m, a f, oca f; (wild) ánsar m; to cook someone's — hacer la santísima a uno.
gooseberry ['guzbəri] n uva f espina; to play — hacer de carabina; I don't want to play — yo no quiero estar de más.
gooseflesh ['guːsfleʃ] n, **goosepimples** ['guːsˌpimplz] npl carne f de gallina.
goose-step ['guːsstep] 1 n paso m de ganso. 2 vi marchar a paso de ganso.
gopher ['gəufə*] n ardillón m, ardilla f de tierra; tuza f.
gore[1] [gɔː*] n sangre f (derramada).
gore[2] [gɔː*] vt cornear.
gorge [gɔːdʒ] 1 n (Geog) cañón m, barranco m, garganta f; my — rises at it me da asco. 2 vt engullir. 3 vi (also vr: to — oneself) hartarse, atracarse (on de).
gorgeous ['gɔːdʒəs] adj magnífico, brillante, vistoso; (fam) maravilloso; hullo —! (fam) ¿qué hay, ricura?
gorilla [gə'rilə] n gorila m.
gormandize ['gɔːməndaiz] vi glotonear.
gorse [gɔːs] n aulaga f, tojo m.
gory ['gɔːri] adj ensangrentado; details, story sangriento.
gosh [gɔʃ] interj (sl) ¡caray!
goshawk ['gɔshɔːk] n azor m.
gosling ['gɔzliŋ] n ansarino m.
go-slow ['gəu'sləu] 1 n huelga f de trabajo lento. 2 vi trabajar a ritmo lento, (strictly) trabajar con arreglo a las bases.

gospel ['gɔspəl] n evangelio m; **as though it were —
truth** como si fuese el evangelio.
gossamer ['gɔsəmə*] n hilos mpl de telaraña; (fabric)
gasa f sutil; — **thin** muy delgado.
gossip ['gɔsip] **1** n (a) (person: great talker) hablador
m, ora f; (pej) chismoso m, a f, murmurador m, ora f,
comadre f, mala lengua f.
    (b) (conversation) charla f; **we had a good old —
about it** charlamos un buen rato de ello.
    (c) (scandal) chismes mpl, chismorreo m,
comadreo m, habladurías fpl, murmuración f;
piece of — chisme m, hablilla f.
  2 vi (talk) charlar; (talk scandal) cotillear, contar
chismes.
gossip column ['gɔsip,kɔləm] n gacetilla f, notas fpl
de sociedad.
gossiping ['gɔsipiŋ] **1** adj chismoso. **2** n chismorreo
m.
gossipy ['gɔsipi] adj chismoso; style familiar.
got [gɔt] pret and ptp of get.
Goth [gɔθ] n godo m, a f.
Gothic ['gɔθik] **1** adj race godo; (Archit, Typ) gótico.
2 n (language) gótico m.
gotten ['gɔtn] (US) ptp of get.
gouge [gaudʒ] **1** n gubia f. **2** vt excavar con gubia;
(fig) excavar; **to — someone's eyes out** sacar los ojos
a uno.
gourd [guəd] n calabaza f.
gourmand ['guəmənd] n glotón m.
gourmet ['guəmei] n gastrónomo m.
gout [gaut] n (Med) gota f.
govern ['gʌvən] vt gobernar; dominar; (guide) guiar,
regir; (Gram) regir; **to — one's temper** contenerse,
dominarse.
governess ['gʌvənis] n institutriz f.
governing ['gʌvəniŋ] adj: — **body** junta f directiva;
— **principle** principio m rector.
government ['gʌvnmənt] **1** n gobierno m; (Gram etc)
régimen m; **local —** administración f local; **minority
—** gobierno m minoritario.
  2 attr: — **bonds** títulos mpl del Estado; — **house**
palacio m del gobernador; — **policy** política f del
gobierno.
governmental [,gʌvən'mentl] adj gubernamental,
gubernativo.
governor ['gʌvənə*] n gobernador m; (of prison)
director m, alcaide m; (Mech) regulador m; (fam:
boss) jefe m, (father) progenitor m, viejo m; **thanks,
—!** ¡gracias, caballero!
governor-general ['gʌvənə'dʒenərəl] n gobernador
m general.
governorship ['gʌvənəʃip] n gobierno m, cargo m de
gobernador.
gown [gaun] n (dress) vestido m, traje m; (Law, Univ)
toga f.
grab [græb] **1** n (a) (snatch) arrebatiña f, agarro m;
(fam) robo m; **to make a — at something** tratar de
arrebatar algo.
    (b) (Mech) cubeta f draga, cuchara f de dos
mandíbulas.
  2 vt asir, coger, arrebatar; (fig) arrebatarse,
apropiarse.
  3 vi: **to — at** (snatch) tratar de arrebatar; (in
falling) tratar de asir.
grace [greis] **1** n (a) (Rel) gracia f, gracia f divina.
    (b) (gracefulness) finura f, elegancia f; (of shape)
armonía f; (of movement) garbo m, donaire m; (of
style) elegancia f, amenidad f.
    (c) **with a good —** de buen talante; **with a bad
— a** regañadientes; **he had the — to apologize** tuvo
la cortesía de pedir perdón.
    (d) **it has the saving — that** tiene el único
mérito de que; **to get into someone's good —s**
congraciarse con uno.
    (e) (delay) demora f; **3 day's —** un plazo de 3
días.
    (f) (blessing) bendición f de la mesa; **to say —**
bendecir la mesa.
    (g) (in title: dukes) **His G— the Duke** su Ex-
celencia; **yes, Your G—** sí, Excelencia.
    (h) (in title: Eccl) **His G— Bishop X** su Ilustrí-
sima Monseñor X; **yes, your G—** sí, Ilustrísima.
  2 vt adornar (with de), embellecer; **he —d the
meeting with his presence** honró a los asistentes con
su presencia.
graceful ['greisful] adj gracioso, agraciado; movement airoso, elegante, garboso; compliment elegante;
lines grácil.
gracefully ['greisfəli] adv elegantemente, con garbo.
graceless ['greislis] adj desgarbado; (impolite) descortés, grosero.

gracious ['greiʃəs] adj (merciful) clemente; (urbane)
cortés, afable; monarch gracioso; — **(me)!** ¡Dios
mío!; **he was very — to me** estuvo muy amable
conmigo.
gradation [grə'deiʃən] n gradación f.
grade [greid] **1** n (degree) grado m; (quality) clase f,
calidad f; (mark) nota f, clase f; (US school) clase f;
(slope) pendiente f; **to make the —** alcanzar el nivel
deseado, tener éxito, ser satisfactorio.
  2 vt clasificar, graduar; (School, Univ) calificar,
dar nota a.
grade crossing ['greid,krɔsiŋ] n (US) paso m a nivel.
grade school ['greid'sku:l] n (US) escuela f primaria.
gradient ['greidiənt] n pendiente f.
gradual ['grædjuəl] adj gradual; paulatino; progresivo.
gradually ['grædjuəli] adv gradualmente; poco a
poco; paulatinamente; progresivamente.
graduate ['grædjuit] n graduado m, a f, licenciado m,
a f (in en).
graduate ['grædjueit] **1** vt graduar. **2** vi (Univ)
graduarse, licenciarse (in en); **to — as** recibirse de.
graduation [,grædju'eiʃən] n graduación f.
graft¹ [grɑ:ft] (Hort, Med) **1** n injerto m. **2** vt injertar
(in, into, on to en).
graft² [grɑ:ft] n corrupción f, chanchullos mpl; **hard
—** trabajo m muy duro.
graham flour ['greiəm,flauə*] n (US) harina f de
trigo sin cerner.
Grail [greil] n: **Holy —** Santo Grial m.
grain [grein] n (a) (single seed) grano m; (corn) granos
mpl, cereales mpl; **bread —s** granos mpl panificables.
    (b) (fig) **with a — of salt** con un grano de sal;
there's not a — of truth in it eso no tiene ni pizca de
verdad.
    (c) (in wood) fibra f, hebra f; (in stone) vena f, veta
f; (in leather) flor f; (in cloth) granilla f; **it goes
against the — with me to +** infin se me hace cuesta
arriba **+** infin; **to saw with the —** aserrar a hebra.
grammar ['græmə*] n gramática f.
grammarian [grə'meəriən] n gramático m.
grammatical [grə'mætikəl] adj gramatical; **in —
English** en buen inglés.
grammatically [grə'mætikəli] adv bien, correctamente.
gram(me) [græm] n gramo m.
gramophone ['græməfəun] n gramófono m.
gramophone record ['græməfəun,rekɔːd] n disco m
de gramófono.
grampus ['græmpəs] n orca f.
granary ['grænəri] n granero m, troj f.
grand [grænd] **1** adj (fine, splendid) magnífico,
imponente, grandioso; person distinguido, augusto;
style elevado, sublime; staircase etc principal; (fam)
magnífico, bárbaro, estupendo; **a — game** un
magnífico partido; **we had a — time** lo pasamos
estupendamente.
  2 n (piano) piano m de cola; (US sl) mil dólares
mpl.
grand(d)ad ['grændæd] n (fam) abuelito m; **yes, —**
sí, abuelo.
grandchild ['græntʃaild] n, pl **—children** [,tʃildrən]
nieto m, a f; **grandchildren** nietos mpl.
granddaughter ['græn,dɔːtə*] n nieta f.
grandee [,græn'di:] n grande m de España.
grandeur ['grændjə*] n magnificencia f, grandiosidad
f, sublimidad f.
grandfather ['grænd,fɑːðə*] n abuelo m.
grandiloquent [græn'diləkwənt] adj altisonante,
hinchado.
grandiose ['grændiəuz] adj grandioso; (pej) building
etc ostentoso, hecho para impresionar; scheme, plan
vasto, ambicioso; style exagerado, pomposo.
grandma ['grænmɑ:] n (fam) abuelita f; **yes, —** sí,
abuela.
grandmother ['græn,mʌðə*] n abuela f.
grandpa ['grænpɑ:] n (fam) abuelito m; **yes, —** sí,
abuelo.
grandparents ['græn,peərənts] npl abuelos mpl.
grandson ['grænsʌn] n nieto m.
grandstand ['grændstænd] n tribuna f.
grange [greindʒ] n (Agr) cortijo m, alquería f;
(Brit) casa f solariega, casa f de señor.
granite ['grænit] n granito m.
granny ['græni] n (fam) abuelita f, nana f; **yes, —** sí,
abuela.
grant [grɑ:nt] **1** n (act) otorgamiento m, concesión f;
(thing granted) concesión f; (Law) cesión f; (gift)
donación f; (scholarship) beca f; (subsidy) subvención f.
  2 vt (bestow, concede) otorgar, conceder; (Law)
ceder; (give) donar; proposition asentir a; **—ed that**

dado que, supuesto que; **—ing this (to) be so** dado que así sea; **to take something for —ed** dar algo por sentado, suponer algo; **we may take that for —ed** eso es indudable; **he takes her for —ed** él no le hace caso alguno a ella.

grant-in-aid ['grɑːntin'eid] n subvención f.

granulated ['grænjuleitid] adj granulado.

granule ['grænjuːl] n gránulo m.

grape [greip] n uva f; **sour —s!** ¡están verdes!; **it's just sour —s with him** es un envidioso.

grapefruit ['greipfruːt] n toronja f, pomelo m.

grape harvest ['greip,hɑːvist] n vendimia f.

grape juice ['greipdʒuːs] n mosto m; zumo m de uva.

grapeshot ['greipʃɔt] n metralla f.

grapevine ['greipvain] n vid f; (trained against wall etc) parra f; (sl) medio m de comunicación clandestina; **I hear on the — that** he llegado a saber que, me ha dicho alguno que.

graph [grɑːf] n gráfica f.

graphic ['græfik] adj gráfico.

graphite ['græfait] n grafito m.

graphology [græ'fɔlədʒi] n grafología f.

graph paper ['grɑːf,peipə*] n papel m cuadriculado.

grapnel ['græpnəl] n rezón m, arpeo m.

grapple ['græpl] 1 vt asir, agarrar; (Naut) aferrar.

2 vi (wrestlers etc) agarrarse; **to — with someone** agarrar a uno, luchar a brazo partido con uno; **to — with a problem** esforzarse por resolver un problema, tratar de vencer un problema.

grappling iron ['græpliŋ,aiən] n arpeo m, garfio m.

grasp [grɑːsp] 1 n (a) agarro m, asimiento m; (handclasp) apretón m; **to be within someone's —** estar al alcance de la mano; **he has a strong —** agarra muy fuerte; **to lose one's —** desasirse (on de).

(b) (fig) (power) garras fpl, control m; (range) alcance m; (mental hold) comprensión f, capacidad f intelectual; **it's within everyone's —** está al alcance de todos; **to have a good — of** dominar, conocer a fondo.

2 vt (hold firmly) asir, agarrar; hand estrechar, apretar; weapon etc empuñar; chance asir; power, territory apoderarse de; (get mental hold of) comprender.

3 vi: **to — at** hacer por asir, tratar de asir.

grasping ['grɑːspiŋ] adj avaro, codicioso.

grass [grɑːs] 1 n hierba f; (lawn) césped m; (grazing) pasto m; **"keep off the —"** "se prohibe pisar la hierba"; **to let the — grow under one's feet** dejar crecer la hierba; **to put a horse out to —** echar un caballo al pasto.

2 vt cubrir de hierba.

3 vi (sl) soplar.

grasshopper ['grɑːs,hɔpə*] n saltamontes m.

grassland ['grɑːslænd] n pradera f, dehesa f.

grass-roots ['grɑːs'ruːts] adj básico; popular; **— politics** política f donde se trata de los problemas corrientes de la gente.

grass widow ['grɑːs'widəu] n mujer f cuyo marido está ausente.

grass widower ['grɑːs'widəuə*] n marido m cuya mujer está ausente.

grassy ['grɑːsi] adj herboso, cubierto de hierba.

grate[1] [greit] n hogar m; (strictly) parrilla f de hogar, emparrillado m.

grate[2] [greit] 1 vt food rallar; teeth hacer rechinar.

2 vi (make a noise) rechinar; (rub on) rozar; **to — on** rozar con, (fig) molestar; **to — on the ear** herir el oído; **to — on one's nerves** destrozar los nervios a uno.

grateful ['greitful] adj agradecido, reconocido; **with — thanks** con mis más efusivas gracias; **I am — for your letter** agradezco su carta; **I am most — to you** te lo agradezco muchísimo; **I should be — if** agradecería que + subj.

gratefully ['greitfəli] adv agradecidamente, con agradecimiento; **she looked at me —** me miró agradecida.

grater ['greitə*] n rallador m.

gratification [,grætifi'keiʃən] n (a) (reward) gratificación f, recompensa f; (tip) propina f.

(b) (pleasure) placer m, satisfacción f; **to my great —** con gran satisfacción mía.

gratify ['grætifai] vt person complacer; whim etc satisfacer; **I was gratified to hear that** me alegré de saber que; **he was much gratified** estuvo muy contento.

gratifying ['grætifaiiŋ] adj satisfactorio, grato; **with — speed** con loable prontitud; **it is — to know that** me es grato saber que.

grating[1] ['greitiŋ] n reja f, enrejado m, emparrillado m.

grating[2] ['greitiŋ] adj tone etc áspero.

gratis ['grɑːtis] adv gratis.

gratitude ['grætitjuːd] n agradecimiento m, reconocimiento m.

gratuitous [grə'tjuːitəs] adj gratuito.

gratuitously [grə'tjuːitəsli] adv (free) gratis; (arbitrarily) gratuitamente.

gratuity [grə'tjuːiti] n gratificación f, propina f; (at Christmas) aguinaldo m.

grave[1] [greiv] adj grave (also Gram); serio; (anxious) preocupado; solemne.

grave[2] [greiv] n sepultura f; (with monument) tumba f, sepulcro m.

gravedigger ['greiv,digə*] n sepulturero m.

gravel ['grævəl] n grava f, cascajo m, recebo m.

gravelled ['grævəld] adj engravado, cubierto con grava.

gravelly ['grævəli] adj arenisco, cascajoso.

gravely ['greivli] adj gravemente; seriamente; **he is — ill** está grave; **he spoke —** habló en tono preocupado.

graven ['greivən] adj: **— image** ídolo m; **it is — on my memory** lo tengo grabado en la memoria.

gravestone ['greivstəun] n lápida f sepulcral.

graveyard ['greivjɑːd] n cementerio m (also fig), camposanto m.

graving dock ['greiviŋdɔk] n dique m de carena.

gravitate ['græviteit] vi gravitar; **to — towards** (fig) dejarse atraer por, tender hacia.

gravitation [,grævi'teiʃən] n gravitación f; (fig) tendencia f (towards hacia).

gravitational [,grævi'teiʃənl] adj gravitatorio.

gravity ['græviti] n gravedad f (also Phys); seriedad f; solemnidad f; **specific —** peso m específico; **the — of the situation** lo grave de la situación, los peligros de la situación; **he spoke with the utmost —** habló con la mayor solemnidad.

gravy ['greivi] n salsa f.

gravy boat ['greivi,bəut] n salsera f.

gray [grei] adj = **grey**.

graze[1] [greiz] (Agr) 1 vt grass pacer; cattle apacentar, pastar. 2 vi pacer.

graze[2] [greiz] 1 n roce m, abrasión f, desolladura f. 2 vt (touch) rozar al pasar; (scrape) raspar, raer.

grease [griːs] 1 n grasa f; (dirt) mugre f; (of candle) sebo m. 2 vt engrasar, lubricar.

grease gun ['griːsgʌn] n pistola f engrasadora, engrasadora f a presión.

greasepaint ['griːspeint] n maquillaje m.

greaseproof ['griːspruːf] adj impermeable a la grasa; paper apergaminado.

greasiness ['griːsinis] n lo grasiento; lo resbaladizo; mugre f; zalamería f.

greasy ['griːsi] adj substance, surface grasiento; road etc resbaladizo; pole ensebado; (grubby) mugriento; person adulón, cobista.

great [greit] adj (a) (large) grande, vasto, enorme; sum importante; care etc especial; age avanzado; time largo; **of — power** de gran potencia; **to my — surprise** con gran sorpresa mía; **what a — (big) dog!** ¡qué perro más grande!; **to be — friends** ser muy amigos; **it was a — joke** fue divertidísimo; **to have no — opinion of** tener un concepto mediocre de; **see deal, many** etc.

(b) (important) grande, importante, principal; **the — thing is that** lo importante es que.

(c) (outstanding) grande, famoso, destacado; **a — man** un gran hombre; **the —** los grandes; **he has a — future** tiene un brillante porvenir.

(d) (clever) **to be — at, to be — on** ser fuerte en, entender de.

(e) (keen) **he's a — angler** tiene gran afición a la pesca; **he's a — arguer** tiene la manía de discutir; **he's a — eater** tiene buen apetito, es muy comilón.

(f) (fam) magnífico, estupendo; **—!** ¡magnífico!; **it's —!** ¡es fabuloso!; **you were —!** ¡estuviste magnífico!

great-aunt ['greit'ɑːnt] n tía f abuela.

Great Britain ['greit'britn] Gran Bretaña f.

greatcoat ['greitkəut] n sobretodo m.

greater ['greitə*] adj (comp of **great**) mayor.

greatest ['greitist] adj (superl of **great**) (a) el mayor, la mayor; **with the — difficulty** con la mayor dificultad; **the — writer of his age** el mayor escritor de su época; **when the heat is at its —** cuando más aprieta el calor.

(b) (fam) **it's the —!** ¡es el colmo!, ¡es el delirio!; **he's the —!** ¡es fabuloso!

great-grandchild ['greit'græntʃaild] pl **—children** [,tʃildrən] bisnieto m, a f.

great-grandfather ['greit'grænd,fɑːðə*] n bisabuelo m.

great-grandmother ['greit'græn,mʌðə*] n bisabuela f.

great-great-grandfather ['greit'greit'grænd,fɑːðə*] n tatarabuelo m.
great-great-grandson ['greit'greit'grænsʌn] n tataranieto m.
great-hearted ['greit'hɑːtid] adj valiente.
Great Lakes ['greit'leiks] pl Grandes Lagos mpl.
greatly ['greitli] adv grandemente, mucho, muy, sumamente; **superior** muy superior; **we were — amused** nos divirtió muchísimo; **it is — to be regretted** es muy de lamentar; **not — expensive** no muy caro.
greatness ['greitnis] n grandeza f.
Great War ['greit'wɔː*] Primera Guerra f Mundial (1914-18).
grebe [griːb] n zampullín m, somormujo m.
Grecian ['griːʃən] adj griego.
Greece [griːs] Grecia f.
greed [griːd] n, **greediness** ['griːdinis] n codicia f, avaricia f; avidez f (for de); (for food) gula f, glotonería f.
greedily ['griːdili] adv con avidez; eat vorazmente.
greedy ['griːdi] adj codicioso, avaro; ávido (for de); (for food) goloso, glotón; **don't be so —!** ¡no seas glotón!
Greek [griːk] **1** adj griego.
   2 n griego m, a f.
   3 n (language) griego m; **ancient —** griego m antiguo; **it's — to me** para mí es chino, no entiendo ni palabra.
green [griːn] **1** adj verde; (fresh) fresco; (unripe, unseasoned) verde; (raw) crudo; complexion pálido; (inexperienced) nuevo, novato; (naïve) crédulo; **bright —** verdegay; **dark —** verdinegro; **to grow —, to look —** verdear.
   2 n (a) (colour) verde m.
   (b) (lawn) césped m; (field) prado m; (for bowls etc) pista f; **village —** (approx) césped m comunal.
   (c) —s verduras fpl.
greenery ['griːnəri] n verdura f.
green-eyed ['griːnaid] adj de ojos verdes.
greenfinch ['griːnfintʃ] n verderón m.
greenfly ['griːnflai] n pulgón m.
greengage ['griːngeidʒ] n claudia f.
greengrocer ['griːn,grəusə*] n verdulero m, a f; **—'s (shop)** verdulería f.
greenhorn ['griːnhɔːn] n bisoño m, novato m.
greenhouse ['griːnhaus] n, pl **—houses** [,hauziz] invernáculo m, invernadero m.
greenish ['griːniʃ] adj verdoso.
Greenland ['griːnlənd] Groenlandia f.
Greenlander ['griːnləndə*] n groenlandés m, esa f.
greenness ['griːnnis] n verdor m, lo verde; (fig) inexperiencia f; credulidad f.
greenstuff ['griːnstʌf] n verduras fpl, legumbres fpl.
greensward ['griːnswɔːd] n césped m.
greet [griːt] vt (in general) recibir; (with words etc) saludar; (welcome) dar la bienvenida a; (meet one's eyes) presentarse a; **this was —ed with relief by everybody** todos sintieron un gran alivio al saber la noticia; **the statement was —ed with laughter** al terminar la declaración hubo risas.
greeting ['griːtiŋ] n (with words etc) saludo m, salutación f; (welcome) bienvenida f; **—s!** ¡bienvenido!; **—s** (in letter) recuerdos mpl.
gregarious [gri'gɛəriəs] adj gregario.
Gregory ['gregəri] m Gregorio.
gremlin ['gremlin] n (Aer sl) duendecillo m.
grenade [gri'neid] n (hand sl) bomba f de mano.
grenadine ['grenədiːn] n granadina f.
grew [gruː] pret of **grow**.
grey [grei] **1** adj gris; horse etc rucio. **2** n gris m; (horse) rucio m. **3** vi (hair) encanecer.
greybeard ['greibiəd] n anciano m, viejo m.
grey-haired ['grei'hɛəd] adj canoso.
greyhound ['greihaund] n galgo m, lebrel m.
greyish ['greiiʃ] adj grisáceo; hair entrecano.
grid [grid] n (with bars) reja f; (Cook etc) parrilla f; (Elec) red f; (Aut) portaequipajes m, portamaletas m; (Aut sl) armatoste m, rácano m.
gridiron ['grid,aiən] n (Cook etc) parrilla f; (US) campo m de fútbol.
grief [griːf] n dolor m, pesar m, aflicción f; **good —!** ¡demonio!; **to come to —** tener un desastre, fracasar.
grievance ['griːvəns] n motivo m de queja; agravio m, injusticia f.
grieve [griːv] **1** vt dar pena a; **you — me** me das pena; **it — s one to see . . .** da pena ver . . .
   2 vi afligirse, acongojarse (about, at de, por); **to — for** llorar, llorar la pérdida (etc) de.
grievous ['griːvəs] adj loss etc cruel, doloroso, penoso; blow severo; pain fuerte; crime, offence grave; error lamentable, craso; task penoso.
griffin ['grifin] n (Myth) grifo m.

grifter ['griftə*] n (US) (a) propietario m de una caseta de feria (etc); garitero m. (b) (sl) fullero m; estafador m, timador m.
grill [gril] **1** n parrilla f; (meat) asado m a la parrilla; **mixed —** fritos mpl variados; see also **grille**. **2** vt asar a la parrilla; (fam) interrogar (sin piedad).
grille [gril] n rejilla f; (of window) reja f; (screen) verja f.
grilled [grild] adj asado a la parrilla.
grillroom ['grilrum] n parrilla f.
grilse [grils] n salmón m joven (que sólo ha estado una vez en el mar).
grim [grim] adj (a) (stern) severo; (frowning) ceñudo; (unrelenting) inexorable, inflexible; battle porfiado, muy reñido, encarnizado; humour macabro; (frightful) horrible; **with a — smile** sonriendo inexorable; **the — truth** la verdad lisa y llana; **the — facts** los hechos inexorables.
   (b) (fam) horrible.
grimace [gri'meis] **1** n mueca f, visaje m. **2** vi hacer una mueca, hacer muecas.
grime [graim] n mugre f, suciedad f.
grimly ['grimli] adv severamente; inexorablemente; encarnizadamente; **he smiled —** sonrió inexorable; **to hang on —** resistir sin cejar.
grimy ['graimi] adj mugriento, sucio.
grin [grin] **1** n sonrisa f (abierta, bonachona, burlona etc); (grimace) mueca f.
   2 vi sonreír (mostrando los dientes, bonachón, burlón etc; at a); **to — and bear it** sonreír y resignarse, poner al mal tiempo buena cara.
grind [graind] **1** n trabajo m pesado; rutina f; (boredom) lo pesado.
   2 vt (irr: pret and ptp **ground**) corn etc moler; stone pulverizar; teeth hacer rechinar; (sharpen) amolar, afinar; (oppress) agobiar, oprimir; **to — down** pulverizar; (wear away) desgastar; (oppress) agobiar, oprimir; **to — down to, to — into** reducir a; **to — out** reproducir mecánicamente (or laboriosamente etc).
   3 vi (machine etc) rechinar, funcionar con dificultad; **to — against** ludir ruidosamente con; **to — away** (Mus) tocar laboriosamente; **to — to a halt** pararse con gran estruendo de frenos.
grinder ['graində*] n (a) (person) molendero m; (Tech) amolador m; esmerilador m.
   (b) (machine) amoladora f; esmeriladora f; (for coffee etc) molinillo m.
   (c) —s (sl) muelas fpl.
grindstone ['graindstəun] n muela f, piedra f de amolar; **to keep one's nose to the —** batir el yunque.
gringo ['griŋgəu] n (US) gringo m.
grip [grip] **1** n (a) (grasp) agarre m, asimiento m; (handclasp) apretón m; **to come to —s** with luchar a brazo partido con; **to get to —s with a problem** ponerse seriamente a estudiar un problema, esforzarse por resolver un problema.
   (b) (handle) asidero m, agarradero m; (of weapon) empuñadura f.
   (c) (bag) maletín m, saco m de mano (con cremallera).
   (d) (fig: power) garras fpl; control m, dominio m; **in the — of winter** paralizado por el invierno; **in the — of a strike** paralizado por una huelga; **to lose one's —** perder las fuerzas, decaer; **get a — on yourself!** ¡cálmese!, ¡dóminese!
   2 vt (a) (hold firmly) agarrar, asir; weapon empuñar; hand apretar; **the wheels — the road** las ruedas se agarran a la carretera.
   (b) (fig) absorber la atención de, tener suspenso a.
   3 vi (wheel) agarrarse.
gripe [graip] **1** n retortijón m de tripas (also —s). **2** vt dar cólico a. **3** vi (sl) quejarse.
gripping ['gripiŋ] adj absorbente, muy emocionante.
grisly ['grizli] adj horripilante; (fam) horrible.
grist [grist] n: **it's all — to his mill** saca agua de una piedra.
gristle ['grisl] n ternilla f, cartílago m.
gristly ['grisli] adj ternilloso, cartilaginoso.
grit [grit] **1** n (a) arena f, cascajo m; (dust) polvo m.
   (b) (fig: courage) valor m; (firmness of character) firmeza f; (endurance) aguante m.
   2 vt teeth hacer rechinar; **to — one's teeth (and bear it)** apretar los dientes.
gritty ['griti] adj arenisco, arenoso.
grizzle ['grizl] vi gimotear.
grizzled ['grizld] adj gris, canoso.
grizzly ['grizli] **1** adj gris, canoso; **— bear = 2** n oso m pardo.
groan [grəun] **1** n gemido m, quejido m. **2** vi gemir, quejarse; (creak) crujirse; **to — under** sufrir bajo, (weight) crujir bajo.
groats [grəuts] npl avena f a medio moler.

grocer ['grəusə*] n tendero m (de ultramarinos), mantequero m, abacero m; —'s (**shop**) tienda f de ultramarinos, tienda f de comestibles, mantequería f, abacería f.

groceries ['grəusəriz] npl comestibles mpl, provisiones fpl.

grocery ['grəusəri] n tienda f de ultramarinos, tienda f de comestibles, mantequería f, abacería f.

grog [grɔg] n grog m.

groggy ['grɔgi] adj (unsteady) poco seguro; (after blow) aturdido, turulato; (Boxing) groggy, grogui; **I still feel a bit** — no me siento del todo bien.

groin [grɔin] n (Anat) ingle f.

grommet ['grɔmit] n ojal m; (Naut) roñada f.

groom [gru:m] **1** n mozo m de caballos; (bride-) novio m.

2 vt horse almohazar, cuidar; **to be well** —ed (person) estar muy acicalado; **she's always well** —ed siempre está muy elegante; **to** — **someone for a post** preparar a uno para un puesto.

groove [gru:v] **1** n ranura f, estría f, acanaladura f; (of record) surco m. **2** vt estriar, acanalar.

grooved [gru:vd] adj estriado, acanalado.

grope [grəup] vi ir a tientas; **to** — **for** buscar a tientas (also fig); **to** — **one's way** ir a tientas; **to** — **one's way towards** (fig) avanzar a tientas hacia.

grosgrain ['grəugrein] n gro m.

gross [grəus] **1** adj (large) grueso, enorme; (fat) muy gordo; error craso; (vulgar) grosero; earnings, profit, weight etc bruto.

2 n gruesa f; **by the** — en gruesas; **in (the)** — en grueso.

3 vt: **he** —**es £4000 a year** gana en total 4000 libras al año.

grossly ['grəusli] adv groseramente; — **exaggerated** enormemente exagerado.

grossness ['grəusnis] n gordura f; grosería f.

grotesque [grəu'tesk] adj grotesco.

grotto ['grɔtəu] n gruta f.

grouch [grautʃ] vi (fam) refunfuñar, quejarse.

grouchy ['grautʃi] adj (fam) malhumorado.

ground[1] [graund] **1** n (a) (soil) suelo m, tierra f.

(b) (surface) suelo m, tierra f; (terrain) terreno m; **above** — sobre la tierra, (fig) vivo, con vida; **on the** — sobre el terreno; **to break new** — (fig) hacer algo nuevo; **to cover a lot of** — recorrer una gran distancia, (fig) tocar muchos puntos; **to cut the** — **from under someone's feet** comer el terreno a uno; **to fall to the** — caer al suelo, (fig) venirse al suelo, caer por su base; **to get off the** — (Aer) despegar, (fig) realizarse, resultar factible; **to go to** — (fox) meterse en su madriguera, (person) esconderse, refugiarse; **to raze something to the** — arrasar algo; **to run someone to** — encontrar (por fin) a uno, averiguar el paradero de uno; **it suits you down to the** — (dress) te sienta perfectamente; **it suits me down to the** — (fig) me conviene perfectamente, me viene de perilla.

(c) (surface, fig) **there is some common** — **between us** tenemos puntos comunes; **to be on dangerous** — pisar un terreno peligroso; **to be on firm** (or **sure**) — hablar con conocimiento de causa; **to be on one's home** — tratar materia que uno conoce a fondo; **to gain** — ganar terreno; **to give** (or **lose**) — perder terreno; **to hold** (or **stand**) **one's** — mantenerse firme; **to shift one's** — cambiar de postura.

(d) (pitch) terreno m, campo m; **recreation** — campo m de deportes.

(e) (estate, property) tierras fpl.

(f) —s (gardens) jardines mpl, parque m.

(g) —s (sediment) poso m, sedimento m.

(h) (Art) fondo m; primera capa f; **on a blue** — sobre un fondo azul.

(i) (reason) causa f, motivo m, razón f; (basis) fundamento m; —(s) **for complaint** motivo m de queja; **on the** —(s) **of** con motivo de, por causa de, debido a; **on the** —(s) **that** porque, por + infin, (pej) pretextando que; **on good** —s con razón; **what** —(s) **have you for saying so?** ¿en qué se basa Vd para decir eso?

2 vt (a) ship varar.

(b) (Elec) conectar con tierra.

(c) (Aer) **he ordered the planes to be** —ed ordenó que permaneciesen los aviones en tierra; **to be** —ed **by bad weather** no poder despegar por el mal tiempo.

(d) **to** — **someone in maths** enseñar a uno los rudimentos de las matemáticas; **to be well** —ed **in** tener un buen conocimiento de, estar versado en.

3 vi (Naut) varar, encallar; (lightly) tocar (on en).

ground[2] [graund] **1** pret and ptp of **grind**. **2** adj glass deslustrado; coffee molido.

ground colour ['graund,kʌlə*] n primera capa f; fondo m.

ground crew ['graundkru:] n personal m de tierra.

ground hog ['graundhɔg] n marmota f de América.

grounding ['graundiŋ] n instrucción f en los rudimentos (in de); **to give someone a** — **in** enseñar a uno los rudimentos de.

groundless ['graundlis] adj infundado.

groundnut ['graundnʌt] n cacahuete m.

ground plan ['graundplæn] n planta f, distribución f.

groundsel ['graunsl] n hierba f cana.

groundsheet ['graundʃi:t] n tela f impermeable.

ground staff ['graundsta:f] n (Aer) personal m de tierra.

groundswell ['graundswel] n mar m de fondo.

ground-to-air ['graundtu'eə*] adj: — **missile** proyectil m tierra-aire.

groundwork ['graundwə:k] n trabajo m preliminar; **to do the** — **for** echar las bases de.

group [gru:p] **1** n grupo m, agrupación f; (Mus) conjunto m musical.

2 attr colectivo; discussion en grupo; photo de conjunto.

3 vt agrupar (also **to** — **together**).

grouper ['gru:pə*] n (Fish) mero m.

grouse[1] [graus] n: **black** — gallo m lira; **red** — lagópodo m escocés.

grouse[2] [graus] (fam) **1** n queja f; motivo m de queja. **2** vi quejarse.

grout [graut] **1** n lechada f. **2** vt enlechar.

grove [grəuv] n arboleda f, bosquecillo m; — **of pines** pineda f; — **of poplars** alameda f.

grovel ['grɔvl] vi arrastrarse; (fig) humillarse (to ante).

grovelling ['grɔvliŋ] adj rastrero, servil.

grow [grəu] (irr: pret **grew**, ptp **grown**) **1** vt (Agr) cultivar; beard etc dejar crecer; **to be** —n **over with** estar cubierto de.

2 vi (a) crecer; (be cultivated) cultivarse; (increase) aumentar; (industry, market) extenderse, desarrollarse, expandirse; **that plant does not** — **in England** esa planta no se da en Inglaterra; **will it** — **here?** ¿se puede cultivar aquí?; **she grew out of her clothes** se le hizo pequeña la ropa; **to** — **out of a habit** perder una costumbre (con el tiempo); **to** — **up** (person) crecer mucho, (become adult) hacerse hombre, hacerse mujer; (custom etc) arraigar, imponerse; — **up!** ¡no seas niño!; **hatred grew up between them** nació el odio entre ellos.

(b) (fig) **to** — **into** hacerse, llegar a ser; **the book** —s **on one** el libro gusta cada vez más; **the habit grew on him** la costumbre arraigó en él; **to** — **out of** resultar de, originarse en; **to** — **to** + infin llegar a + infin.

(c) (with adj) volverse, ponerse; (often translated by vi or vr) **to** — **angry** enfadarse; **to** — **cold** (thing) enfriarse, (person) empezar a tener frío, (weather) empezar a hacer frío; **to** — **dark** ponerse oscuro, oscurecerse, (at dusk) anochecer; **to** — **old** envejecer(se).

grower ['grəuə*] n cultivador m, ora f.

growing ['grəuiŋ] adj creciente; child crecedero.

growl [graul] **1** n gruñido m. **2** vi gruñir; rezongar; (thunder) reverberar; **"yes", he** —ed **"sí"**, refunfuñó.

grown [grəun] **1** ptp of **grow**. **2** adj crecido, adulto.

grown-up ['grəun'ʌp] **1** adj adulto; propio de persona mayor. **2** n persona f mayor.

growth [grəuθ] n (a) crecimiento m; aumento m; desarrollo m, expansión f; **to reach full** — llegar a la madurez, (fig) alcanzar su plenitud.

(b) vegetación f; (Med) tumor m; **with 3 days'** — **on his face** con barba de 3 días.

growth point ['grəuθpɔint] n polo m de desarrollo.

grub [grʌb] **1** n gusano m; (sl) comida f; — **up!** (sl) ¡la comida está servida!

2 vt: **to** — **up** arrancar, desarraigar; (discover) desenterrar.

3 vi: **to** — **about in the earth for something** remover la tierra buscando algo.

grubby ['grʌbi] adj sucio, mugriento.

grudge [grʌdʒ] **1** n motivo m de rencor; **to bear someone a** —, **to have a** — **against someone** tener inquina a uno.

2 vt (a) (give unwillingly) escatimar, dar de mala gana.

(b) **I don't** — **you your success** no te tengo envidia por tu éxito; **he** —s **us our pleasures** mira con malos ojos nuestros placeres.

grudging ['grʌdʒiŋ] adj praise etc poco generoso; **with** — **admiration** admirándolo a pesar de sí.

grudgingly ['grʌdʒiŋli] adv de mala gana.

gruel ['gruəl] *n* gachas *fpl*.
gruelling ['gruəliŋ] *adj* duro, penoso; *match etc* muy reñido.
gruesome ['gru:səm] *adj* horrible, horripilante.
gruff [grʌf] *adj voice* bronco; *manner* brusco, malhumorado.
grumble ['grʌmbl] **1** *n* queja *f*; (*noise*) ruido *m* sordo, estruendo *m* lejano.
　2 *vi* refunfuñar, quejarse; **to — about, to — at** quejarse de, murmurar de, protestar de; (*thunder etc*) retumbar (a lo lejos).
grumpy ['grʌmpi] *adj* gruñón, malhumorado.
grunt [grʌnt] **1** *n* gruñido *m*. **2** *vi* gruñir.
guano ['gwɑ:nəu] *n* guano *m*.
guarantee [.gærən'ti:] **1** *n* garantía *f*; **there is no —** **that** no es seguro que + *subj*; **I give you my —** se lo aseguro.
　2 *vt* garantizar (*against* contra, *for 3 months* por 3 meses); (*ensure*) asegurar; (*make oneself responsible for*) responder de; **I — that** les aseguro que, les prometo que; **I can't — good weather** no puedo estar seguro de tener buen tiempo.
guaranteed [.gærən'ti:d] *adj* garantizado; asegurado, seguro.
guarantor [.gærən'tɔ:*] *n* garante *mf*.
guard [gɑ:d] **1** *n* (a) (*Mil duty, Fencing*) guardia *f*; (*safeguard*) resguardo *m*; **to be on —** estar de guardia; **on —!** (*Fencing*) ¡en guardia!; **to be on one's —** estar alerta, estar prevenido (*against* contra); **to be off one's —** estar desprevenido; **to catch someone off his —** coger a uno desprevenido; **to drop (or lower) one's —** aflojar la guardia, descuidarse; **to keep —** vigilar; **to mount —** montar (la) guardia; **to put someone on his —** poner a uno en guardia, prevenir a uno (*against* contra).
　(b) (*of sword*) guarda *f*, guarnición *f*.
　(c) (*regiment, squad of men*) guardia *f*; **changing of the —** relevo *m* de la guardia; **to change —** relevar la guardia.
　(d) (*person: soldier*) guardia *m*; (*sentry*) centinela *m*; (*escort*) escolta *f*; (*Rail*) jefe *m* de tren.
　2 *vt place etc* guardar, proteger, defender (*against, from* de); *person* vigilar, (*while travelling*) escoltar.
　3 *vi*: **to — against** precaverse de; (*prevent*) impedir, estorbar, evitar; **in order to — against this** para evitar esto.
guarded ['gɑ:did] *adj* cauteloso, circunspecto.
guardedly ['gɑ:didli] *adv* cautelosamente, con circunspección.
guardhouse ['gɑ:dhaus] *n*, *pl* **-houses** [.hauziz] cuartel *m* de la guardia; cárcel *f* militar.
guardian ['gɑ:diən] *n* protector *m*, ora *f*, guardián *m*, ana *f*; (*Law*) tutor *m*, ora *f*.
guardsman ['gɑ:dzmən] *n*, *pl* **-men** [mən] guardia *m*.
guard's van ['gɑ:dzvæn] *n* furgón *m*.
Guatemala [.gwɑ:ti'mɑ:lə] Guatemala *f*.
Guatemalan [.gwɑ:ti'mɑ:lən] **1** *adj* guatemalteco. **2** *n* guatemalteco *m*, a *f*.
guava ['gwɑ:və] *n* guayaba *f*.
Guayana [gai'ɑ:nə] Guayana *f*.
gubernatorial [.gu:bənə'tɔ:riəl] *adj* de(l) gobernador.
gudgeon[1] ['gʌdʒən] *n* (*Fish*) gobio *m*.
gudgeon[2] ['gʌdʒən] *n* (*Tech*) gorrón *m*; cuello *m* de eje.
Guernsey ['gə:nzi] Guernesey *m*.
guerrilla [gə'rilə] *n* guerrillero *m*, a *f*; **— warfare** guerra *f* de guerrilleros.
guess [ges] **1** *n* conjetura *f*, suposición *f*; **rough —** estimación *f* aproximada; **at a —** a poco más o menos; **my — is that** yo conjeturo que, imagino que; **your — is as good as mine!** ¡vaya Vd a saber!; **have a —, I'll give you 3** es a ver si lo adivinas.
　2 *vti* (a) adivinar, conjeturar, suponer; **to — right** acertar; **— who!** ¡a ver si adivinas quién soy!; **¿me conoces?; you'll never —** no lo adivinarás nunca; **you've —ed it!** has acertado, estás en lo cierto; **I —ed as much ya lo suponía; I —ed him to be about 20** conjeturé que tenía unos 20 años; **to keep someone —ing** tener a uno en suspenso; **to — at** conjeturar, (*tratar de*) estimar aproximadamente.
　(b) (*esp US*) creer, imaginar, suponer; **I — we'll buy it** imagino que lo compraremos; **I — so** imagino que sí; así será, sin duda.
guesswork ['geswə:k] *n* conjeturas *fpl*; **it's all —** son meras conjeturas.
guest [gest] *n* convidado *m*, a *f*, invitado *m*, a *f*; (*at hotel etc, lodger*) huésped *m*, eda *f*; **— of honour** agasajado *m*, a *f*; **paying —** pensionista *mf*; **be my —** invito yo; **we were their —s last summer** pasamos un rato en casa de ellos el verano pasado.
guest-house ['gesthaus] *n*, *pl* **—houses** [.hauziz] casa *f* de huéspedes.
guest room ['gestrum] *n* cuarto *m* de las visitas.

guff [gʌf] *n* (*sl*) música *f* celestial.
guffaw [gʌ'fɔ:] **1** *n* risotada *f*. **2** *vi* reírse a carcajadas.
Guiana [gai'ɑ:nə] Guayana *f*.
guidance ['gaidəns] *n* (*control*) dirección *f*, gobierno *m*; (*advice*) consejos *mpl*; **vocational —** guía *f* vocacional.
guide [gaid] **1** *n* (a) (*person*) guía *mf*; **girl —** exploradora *f*. (b) (*book, Mech, fig*) guía *f*. **2** *vt* guiar; conducir; (*govern*) dirigir, gobernar.
guidebook ['gaidbuk] *n* guía *f* (del turista *etc*).
guided ['gaidid] *adj missile* teledirigido.
guide line ['gaidlain] *n* línea *f* de guía (*also fig*).
guidepost ['gaidpəust] *n* poste *m* indicador.
guild [gild] *n* gremio *m*, cofradía *f*.
guile [gail] *n* astucia *f*, maña *f*.
guileful ['gailful] *adj* astuto, mañoso.
guileless ['gaillis] *adj* inocente, candoroso.
guillemot ['gilimɔt] *n* arao *m*.
guillotine [.gilə'ti:n] **1** *n* guillotina *f*. **2** *vt* guillotinar.
guilt [gilt] *n* culpabilidad *f*.
guiltless ['giltlis] *adj* inocente, libre de culpa (*of* de).
guilty ['gilti] *adj* (a) culpable (*of* de); **verdict of —** sentencia *f* de culpabilidad; **to find someone —** declarar culpable a uno; **to find someone not —** declarar inocente a uno; **to plead —** confesarse culpable; **to plead not —** negar la acusación; **"not —", he replied** "soy inocente", contestó.
　(b) *look* lleno de confusión; *conscience* lleno de remordimiento; *thought* pecaminoso, criminal.
Guinea ['gini] Guinea *f*.
guinea ['gini] *n* guinea *f* (= 21 *chelines*).
guinea-fowl ['ginifaul] *n* gallina *f* de Guinea.
guinea-pig ['ginipig] *n* cobayo *m*, conejillo *m* de Indias.
Guinevere ['gwiniviə*] *f* Ginebra.
guise [gaiz] *n*: **in that —** de esa manera; **under the — of** bajo el disfraz de; so capa de.
guitar [gi'tɑ:*] *n* guitarra *f*.
guitarist [gi'tɑ:rist] *n* guitarrista *mf*.
gulch [gʌlʃ] *n* (*US*) barranco *m*.
gulf [gʌlf] *n* golfo *m*; (*also fig*) abismo *m*, sima *f*.
Gulf Stream ['gʌlfstri:m] Corriente *f* del Golfo.
gull [gʌl] **1** *n* gaviota *f*. **2** *vt* estafar, timar.
gullet ['gʌlit] *n* esófago *m*; garganta *f*.
gullibility [.gʌli'biliti] *n* credulidad *f*, simpleza *f*.
gullible ['gʌlibl] *adj* crédulo, simplón.
gully ['gʌli] *n* barranco *m*, torrentera *f*.
gulp [gʌlp] **1** *n* trago *m*, sorbo *m*; **at one —** de un trago; **"yes", he said with a —** "sí", dijo tragando saliva.
　2 *vt* (*also* **to — down**) tragarse, engullir.
　3 *vi* tragar saliva.
gum[1] [gʌm] *n* (*Anat*) encía *f*.
gum[2] [gʌm] *n* (*in general*) goma *f*; (*adhesive*) goma *f*, cola *f*, pegamín *m*; (*chewing*) chicle *m*; **— arabic** goma *f* arábiga.
　2 *vt* engomar, pegar con goma; **to — up** (*fig*) estropear, paralizar, parar, inutilizar.
gum[3] [gʌm] *interj*: **by —!** ¡caramba!
gumboil ['gʌmbɔil] *n* flemón *m*.
gumboots ['gʌmbu:ts] *npl* botas *fpl* altas de goma.
gumdrop ['gʌmdrɔp] *n* pastilla *f* de goma.
gummy ['gʌmi] *adj* gomoso.
gump [gʌmp] *n* (a) (*fam*) sentido *m* común. (b) tonto *m*, imbécil *mf*.
gumption ['gʌmpʃən] *n* (*fam*) seso *m*, sentido *m* común.
gum tree ['gʌmtri:] *n* eucalipto *m*; **to be up a — (**fam*) estar en un aprieto.
gun [gʌn] **1** *n* (*in general*) arma *f* de fuego; (*artillery piece*) cañón *m*; (*shot-*) escopeta *f*; (*rifle*) fusil *m*; (*pistol*) revólver *m*, pistola *f*; **a 21- salute** una salva de 21 cañonazos; **the —s** (*Mil*) la artillería; **big —** (*fam*) pez *m* gordo, espadón *m*; **to be going great —s** hacer grandes progresos, ir a las mil maravillas; **to jump the —** (*fig*) madrugar; **to stick to one's —s** mantenerse firme.
　2 *vt* disparar sobre, atacar.
　3 *vi*: **to — for** andar a la caza de, perseguir.
gunboat ['gʌnbəut] *n* (*seagoing*) cañonero *m*; (*small*) lancha *f* cañonera.
gun carriage ['gʌn.kæridʒ] *n* cureña *f*; (*at funeral*) armón *m* de artillería.
guncotton ['gʌn.kɔtn] *n* algodón *m* pólvora.
gun crew ['gʌnkru:] *n* dotación *f* de un cañón.
gunfire ['gʌnfaiə*] *n* cañoneo *m*.
gun licence ['gʌn.laisns] *n* licencia *f* de armas.
gunman ['gʌnmən] *n*, *pl* **-men** [mən] pistolero *m*, gángster *m*.
gunmetal ['gʌn.metl] *n* bronce *m* de cañón.
gunner ['gʌnə*] *n* (*Mil*) artillero *m*.
gunnery ['gʌnəri] *n* tiro *m*, puntería *f*.
gunpowder ['gʌn.paudə*] *n* pólvora *f*.

gunrunner ['gʌn,rʌnə*] n contrabandista m de armas.
gunrunning ['gʌn,rʌnɪŋ] n contrabando m de armas.
gunshot ['gʌnʃɔt] n (noise) cañonazo m, escopetazo m; — **wound** escopetazo m; **within** — a tiro de fusil.
gunsmith ['gʌnsmɪθ] n escopetero m.
gun turret ['gʌn,tʌrɪt] n torreta f.
gunwale ['gʌnl] n borde m, regala f.
gurgle ['gəːgl] **1** n (of liquid) gorgoteo m, gluglú m; (baby's) gorjeo m. **2** vi gorgotear, hacer gluglú; gorjear.
gush [gʌʃ] **1** n (of liquid) chorro m, borbotón m; (of words) torrente m; (fig) efusión f; sentimentalismo m; afectación f.
  2 vt blood etc chorrear, derramar a borbollones.
  3 vi chorrear, borbotar, salir a borbollones (from de); (person) hacer extremos; **to — over** hablar con efusión de, extasiarse ante.
gushing ['gʌʃɪŋ] adj efusivo.
gusset ['gʌsɪt] n escudete m.
gust [gʌst] n ráfaga f, racha f.
gusto ['gʌstəu] n entusiasmo m; **with —** con entusiasmo.
gusty ['gʌstɪ] adj borrascoso; wind racheado.
gut [gʌt] **1** n (a) (Anat) intestino m, tripa f; (string) cuerda f de tripa; (Naut) estrecho m.
  (b) —s (Anat) tripas fpl; (fig: content) meollo m, sustancia f; (pluck) valor m; (staying power) aguante m, resistencia f; (moral strength) carácter m; **to have —s** tener agallas.
  2 vt animal destripar; (of fire etc) destruir el interior de.
gutta-percha ['gʌtə'pəːtʃə] n gutapercha f.
gutter ['gʌtə*] n (in street) arroyo m, cuneta f; (on roof) canal m, canalón m, gotera f; **the —** (fig) los barrios bajos, (criminal) el hampa; **he rose from the —** (fig) salió de la nada.
gutter-press ['gʌtə'pres] n prensa f sensacionalista.
guttersnipe ['gʌtəsnaip] n golfillo m.
guttural ['gʌtərəl] adj gutural.
guy¹ [gai] **1** n mamarracho m; (US fam) tío m, individuo m; **wise —** sabelotodo m; **he's a nice —** es un buen chico.
  2 vt ridiculizar; (Theat etc) parodiar.
guy² [gai] n, **guy-rope** ['gairəup] n viento m, cuerda f.
Guy [gai] m Guido.
guzzle ['gʌzl] vt tragarse, engullir.
gym [dʒim] n (fam) gimnasio m.
gymkhana [dʒim'kɑːnə] n reunión f deportiva.
gymnasium [dʒim'neiziəm] n gimnasio m.
gymnast ['dʒimnæst] n gimnasta mf.
gymnastic [dʒim'næstik] adj gimnástico.
gymnastics [dʒim'næstiks] n sing and pl gimnasia f.
gynaecologist, (US) **gynecologist** [,gaini'kɔlədʒist] n ginecólogo m, a f.
gynaecology, (US) **gynecology** [,gaini'kɔlədʒi] n ginecología f.
gyp¹ [dʒip] (sl) **1** n (a) estafa f, timo m. (b) (person) estafador m, timador m. **2** vt estafar, timar.
gyp² [dʒip] n (Univ) criado m (de colegio).
gyp³ [dʒip] n (sl): **to give someone —** echar un rapapolvo de aúpa a uno; poner a uno como un trapo; **it's giving me —** me duele una barbaridad.
gypsum ['dʒipsəm] n yeso m.
gypsy ['dʒipsi] n (esp US) = **gipsy.**
gyrate [dʒai'reit] vi girar.
gyration [,dʒai'reiʃən] n giro m, vuelta f.
gyratory [,dʒai'reitəri] adj giratorio.
gyrocompass ['dʒairəu'kʌmpəs] n girocompás m.
gyroscope ['dʒairəskəup] n giróscopo m.

H

ha [hɑː] *interj* ¡ah!
habeas corpus ['heibiəs'kɔːpəs] *n* hábeas corpus *m*.
haberdasher ['hæbədæʃə*] *n* mercero *m*, a *f*, (US) camisero *m*, a *f*; —'s (*shop*) mercería *f*, (US) camisería *f*.
haberdashery [ˌhæbə'dæʃəri] *n* mercería *f*, (US) artículos *mpl* de moda para caballeros.
habiliments [hə'bilimənts] *npl* (*arch*) prendas *fpl* de vestir.
habit ['hæbit] *n* (**a**) costumbre *f*, hábito *m*; **bad** — vicio *m*, mala costumbre *f*; **from** —, **out of sheer** — por costumbre; **to be in the** — **of** + *ger* acostumbrar + *infin*, soler + *infin*; **to get into the** — **of** + *ger* acostumbrarse a + *infin*; **to get out of the** — **of** + *ger* perder la costumbre de + *infin*; **to make a** — **of something** aficionarse a algo; **let's hope he doesn't make a** — **of it** esperamos que no vuelva a hacerlo; **to make a** — **of** + *ger* adquirir la costumbre de + *infin*. (**b**) (*dress*) hábito *m*.
habitable ['hæbitəbl] *adj* habitable.
habitat ['hæbitæt] *n* habitat *m*, habitación *f*.
habitation [ˌhæbi'teiʃən] *n* habitación *f*.
habit-forming ['hæbitˌfɔːmiŋ] *adj* que conduce al hábito morboso.
habitual [hə'bitjuəl] *adj* habitual, acostumbrado, usual; *drunkard, liar etc* inveterado, empedernido.
habitually [hə'bitjuəli] *adv* por costumbre; constantemente.
habitué(e) [hə'bitjuei] *n* asiduo *m*, a *f*, parroquiano *m*, a *f*.
hacienda [ˌhæsi'endə] *n* (US) hacienda *f*.
hack[1] [hæk] **1** *n* (*blow, cut*) corte *m*, hachazo *m*, tajo *m*; (*kick*) puntapié *m* (en la espinilla); (*dent*) mella *f*.
  2 *vt* (*with knife etc*) cortar, acuchillar, tajar; (*dent*) mellar; **to** — **someone on the shin** dar a uno un puntapié en la espinilla; **to** — **something to pieces** cortar algo en pedazos (violentamente, despiadadamente *etc*); **to** — **an army to pieces** destrozar un ejército; **to** — **one's way through something** abrirse paso por algo a fuerza de tajos; **to** — **down** derribar a hachazos *etc*.
  3 *vi*: **to** — **at** tirar tajos a.
hack[2] [hæk] **1** *n* (*hired horse*) caballo *m* de alquiler; (*bad horse*) rocín *m*; (*writer*) escritorzuelo *m*, plumífero *m*, gacetillero *m*.
  2 *attr writer* mercenario, (*fig*) ínfimo; *see* **hackneyed**.
hacking ['hækiŋ] *adj cough* seco.
hackle ['hækl] *n*: **with his** —**s up** encolerizado; dispuesto a luchar; **to make someone's** —**s rise** encolerizar a uno, provocar a uno.
hackman ['hækmən] *n*, *pl* —**men** [mən] (US: Hist) cochero *m* de punto.
hackney carriage ['hækni'kærid3] *n* coche *m* de alquiler.
hackneyed ['hæknid] *adj* trillado, gastado.
hacksaw ['hæksɔː] *n* sierra *f* de arco para metales.
hackwork ['hækwɔːk] *n* trabajo *m* de rutina, trabajo *m* de poca originalidad.
had [hæd] *pret and ptp of* **have**.
haddock ['hædək] *n* eglefino *m*, merlango *m*.
Hades ['heidiːz] *n* infierno *m*.
hadn't ['hædnt] = **had not**.
Hadrian ['heidriən] *m* Adriano.
haemoglobin, (US) **hemo**— [ˌhiːməu'gləubin] *n* hemoglobina *f*.
haemophilia, (US) **hemo**— [ˌhiːməu'filiə] *n* hemofilia *f*.
haemorrhage, (US) **hemo**— ['hemərid3] *n* hemorragia *f*.
haemorrhoids, (US) **hemo**— ['hemərɔidz] *npl* hemorroides *fpl*.
haft [hɑːft] *n* mango *m*.
hag [hæg] *n* bruja *f*.

haggard ['hægəd] *adj* ojeroso, trasnochado.
haggis ['hægis] *n* (Scot) estómago de cordero relleno con el hígado, el corazón y la lengua del animal, avena etc (*plato nacional escocés*).
haggish ['hægiʃ] *adj* como de bruja.
haggle ['hægl] *vi* (**a**) discutir, disputar; **don't** —! ¡no discutas! (**b**) (*in selling*) regatear; **to** — **about** (or **over**) **the price** regatear, regatear el precio.
haggling ['hægliŋ] *n* (**a**) discusión *f*, disputa *f*. (**b**) regateo *m*.
hagiography [ˌhægi'ɔgrəfi] *n* hagiografía *f*.
hag-ridden ['hægridn] *adj* atormentado por una pesadilla; (*fam*) dominado por una mujer.
Hague [heig] *n*: **The** — La Haya.
ha-ha ['hɑː'hɑː] *interj* ¡ja, ja!
hail[1] [heil] (*Meteorol*) **1** *n* granizo *m*, pedrisco *m*; **a** — **of bullets** una lluvia de balas. **2** *vi* granizar; **to** — **down** (*fig*) llover.
hail[2] [heil] **1** *n* (*shout*) grito *m*; (*greeting*) saludo *m*; —! ¡hola!, (*more formally*) ¡salve!; **to be within** — estar al alcance de la voz.
  2 *vt* llamar a, gritar a; saludar; aclamar (*as king* rey); **within** —**ing distance** al habla, al alcance de la voz.
  3 *vi*: **to** — **from** ser natural de, ser de.
hail-fellow-well-met ['heil,feləu'wel'met] *adj* demasiado efusivo.
hailstone ['heilstəun] *n* piedra *f* de granizo.
hailstorm ['heilstɔːm] *n* granizada *f*, pedrusco *m*.
hair [heə*] *n* (**a**) (*one* —) pelo *m*, cabello *m*; —'s **breadth** (*ancho m de un*) pelo *m*; **to escape by a** —'s **breadth** escapar por un pelo; **to be within a** —'s **breadth of** estar a dos dedos de; **to split** —**s** pararse en cosas nimias, buscar tres pies al gato; **he didn't turn a** — no se inmutó.
  (**b**) (*head of* —) pelo *m*, cabello *m*, cabellera *f*; (*on legs etc*) vello *m*; **grey** —, **white** — canas *fpl*; **long** — melena *f*; **to comb one's** — peinarse; **to do one's** —, **to have one's** — **done** arreglarse el pelo; **keep your** — **on!** ¡cálmate!; **to let one's** — **down** (*fig*) echar una cana al aire; **to part one's** — hacerse la raya; **it was enough to make your** — **stand on end** era espeluznante; **to tear one's** — mesarse el pelo.
hairbrush ['heəbrʌʃ] *n* cepillo *m* para el pelo.
hair cream ['heəkriːm] *n* brillantina *f*, fijapelo *m*.
hair-curler ['heə,kəːlə*] *n* chincho *m*.
haircut ['heəkʌt] *n* corte *m* de pelo; **to get** (or **have**) **a** — hacerse cortar el pelo.
hairdo ['heəduː] *n* peinado *m*.
hairdresser ['heə,dresə*] *n* peluquero *m*, a *f*; —'s (*shop*) peluquería *f*.
hair-drier ['heədraiə*] *n* secador *m* de pelo.
-haired [heəd] *adj* de pelo . . ., *eg* **fair-haired** pelirrubio; **long-** — de pelo largo, melenudo.
hairless ['heəlis] *adj* sin pelo, pelón, calvo.
hairline ['heəlain] *n* límite *m* del pelo; (*in writing*) rayita *f*; (*Tech*) estría *f* muy delgada; — **crack** grieta *f* muy fina, grieta *f* casi imperceptible.
hairnet ['heənet] *n* redecilla *f*.
hair oil ['heərɔil] *n* brillantina *f*.
hairpiece ['heəpiːs] *n* trenza *f* postiza.
hairpin ['heəpin] *n* horquilla *f*.
hair-raising ['heə,reiziŋ] *adj* espeluznante.
hair-splitting ['heə,splitiŋ] **1** *adj* nimio; *discussion* sobre detalles nimios. **2** *n* sofismas *mpl*, sofistería *f*.
hair style ['heəstail] *n* peinado *m*.
hairy ['heəri] *adj* peludo, velloso.
Haiti ['heiti] *n* Haití *m*.
Haitian ['heiʃiən] **1** *adj* haitiano. **2** *n* haitiano *m*, haitiana *f*.
hake [heik] *n* merluza *f*.
halcyon ['hælsiən] *adj*: — **days** días *mpl* felices.
hale [heil] *adj* sano, robusto; — **and hearty** sano y fuerte.

half [hɑːf] n, pl **halves** [hɑːvz] **1** n (a) mitad f; — and — mitad y mitad; **my better** — mi cara mitad; **first** — (Sport) primer tiempo m; **return** — (of ticket) parte f de vuelta; **by** — con mucho; **better by** — con mucho el mejor; **to be too clever by** — pasarse de listo; **to do something by halves** hacer algo a medias; **to go halves with someone** ir a medias con uno; **to cut something in** — cortar algo en dos mitades.
   (b) (Sport: person) medio m.
   2 adj medio; — **an orange** media naranja; **a pound and a** —, **one and a** — **pounds** libra f y media; **3 and a** — **hours, 3 hours and a** — 3 horas y media.
   3 adv (a) medio, a medias, semi...; casi; — **asleep** medio dormido, dormido a medias, semidormido; — **done** a medio hacer; — **laughing**, — **crying** medio riendo, medio llorando; **I only** — **read it** lo leí sólo a medias; **he** — **got up** se levantó a medias; **it cost only** — **as much** costó la mitad nada más; **there were only** — **as many people as before** había solamente la mitad de los que había antes; **they paid** — **as much again** pagaron la mitad más.
   (b) (with not) **it was not** — **as bad as I had thought** no era tan malo como me lo había imaginado; **he didn't** — **run** corrió muchísimo; **it didn't** — **rain!** ¡había que ver cómo llovía!; **it wasn't** — **dear** nos resultó sumamente caro; **not** —! ¡ya lo creo!
half-back ['hɑːfbæk] n medio m.
half-baked ['hɑːf'beikt] adj a medio cocer; (fig) plan, idea incompleto, sin terminar; person soso.
half-bred ['hɑːfbred] adj mestizo.
half-breed ['hɑːfbriːd] n mestizo m, a f.
half-brother ['hɑːf͵brʌdə*] n medio hermano m.
half-caste ['hɑːfkɑːst] **1** adj mestizo. **2** n mestizo m, a f.
half-circle ['hɑːf'səːkl] n semicírculo m.
half-cock ['hɑːf'kɔk] n posición f de medio amartillado (de la escopeta etc); **to go off at** — (fig) obrar precipitadamente, obrar antes del momento propicio; (of plan) ponerse en efecto sin la debida preparación, fracasar por falta de preparación.
half-crown ['hɑːf'kraun] n media corona f.
half-dead ['hɑːf'ded] adj medio muerto, más muerto que vivo.
half-dozen ['hɑːf'dʌzn] n media docena f.
half-empty ['hɑːf'empti] adj medio vacío; hall etc semidesierto.
half-full ['hɑːf'ful] adj a medio llenar, mediado.
half-hearted ['hɑːf'hɑːtid] adj poco entusiasta, indiferente; effort débil.
half-heartedly ['hɑːf'hɑːtidli] adv con poco entusiasmo.
half-holiday ['hɑːf'hɔlidi] n medio día m festivo.
half-hour ['hɑːf'auə*] n media hora f.
half-length ['hɑːf'leŋθ] adj de medio cuerpo.
half-mast ['hɑːf'mɑːst] n: **at** — **a** media asta.
half-measure ['hɑːf'meʒə*] n medida f poco eficaz.
half-moon ['hɑːf'muːn] n media luna f.
half-naked ['hɑːf'neikid] adj semidesnudo.
half note ['hɑːf'nəut] n (Mus) nota f blanca.
half-pay ['hɑːf'pei] n media paga f.
halfpenny ['heipni] n medio penique m.
half-price ['hɑːf'prais] adv a mitad de precio.
half-seas over ['hɑːfsiːz'əuvə*] adv: **to be** — estar entre dos velas.
half-term ['hɑːf'təːm] n vacación f a mediados del trimestre.
half-time ['hɑːf'taim] n (Sport) descanso m.
half-tone ['hɑːftəun] adj: — **illustration** fotograbado m a media tinta.
half-track ['hɑːf'træk] n camión m semi-oruga.
half-truth ['hɑːf'truːθ] n, pl —**truths** [truːðz] verdad f a medias, semi-verdad f.
halfway ['hɑːf'wei] **1** adv a medio camino; **we're** — **there** estamos a medio camino; — **through the film** hacia la mitad de la película; **to meet someone** — partir el camino con uno, (fig) hacer concesiones mutuas.
   2 adj intermedio; — **house** (fig) punto m intermediario, término m medio.
half-witted ['hɑːf'witid] adj imbécil.
half-yearly ['hɑːf'jiəli] **1** adv semestralmente. **2** adj semestral.
halibut ['hælibət] n halibut m.
halitosis [͵hæli'təusis] n halitosis f.
hall [hɔːl] n (entrance-) vestíbulo m, hall m; (for concerts etc) sala f; (dining room) comedor m; (Univ: central —) paraninfo m, (hostel) residencia f, colegio m mayor; (large house) casa f solariega; **city** — palacio m municipal; **town** — ayuntamiento m.
hallelujah [͵hæli'luːjə] n aleluya f.

hallmark ['hɔːlmɑːk] n marca f del contraste; (fig) sello m.
hallo [hʌ'ləu] see **hullo.**
halloo [hə'luː] **1** interj (Hunting) ¡sus! **2** n grito m. **3** vi gritar.
hallow ['hæləu] vt santificar.
Hallowe'en ['hæləu'iːn] n (Scot, US) víspera f de Todos los Santos.
hallstand ['hɔːlstænd] n perchero m.
hallucination [hə͵luːsi'neiʃən] n alucinación f; ilusión f, fantasma m.
hallway ['hɔːlwei] n vestíbulo m, hall m.
halo ['heiləu] n aureola f, nimbo m; halo m.
halogen ['heiləudʒin] n (Chem) halógeno m.
halt [hɔːlt] **1** n alto m, parada f; interrupción f; (Rail) apeadero m; **10 minutes'** — parada f de 10 minutos; **to call a** — mandar hacer alto; **to call a** — **to parar, atajar**; **to come to a** — pararse, (process etc) interrumpirse.
   2 vt parar, detener; interrumpir.
   3 vi hacer alto; pararse; (process etc) interrumpirse; —! ¡alto!
halter ['hɔːltə*] n cabestro m, ronzal m; (noose) dogal m.
halting ['hɔːltiŋ] adj vacilante, titubeante.
halve [hɑːv] vt partir por mitad; **to** — **a game** empatar.
halves [hɑːvz] npl of **half.**
halyard ['hæljəd] n driza f.
ham [hæm] n (a) jamón m; (Anat) —**s** nalgas fpl. (b) (Theat sl) comicastro m, maleta m, racionista mf; (Radio sl) radioaficionado m.
Hamburg ['hæmbəːg] Hamburgo.
hamburger ['hæm͵bəːgə*] n hamburguesa f.
ham-handed ['hæm'hændid] adj, **ham-fisted** ['hæm'fistid] adj torpe, desmañado.
Hamitic [hæ'mitik] adj camítico.
hamlet ['hæmlit] n aldehuela f, caserío m.
hammer ['hæmə*] **1** n martillo m; (Mus) macillo m; (of firearm) percusor m; **to come under the** — ser subastado; **to go at it** — **and tongs** luchar (etc) a brazo partido.
   2 vt martillar; batir; (Fin) declarar insolvente; **to** — **a point home** subrayar repetidas veces un argumento; **to** — **some sense into someone** hacer que uno vaya comprendiendo algo a fuerza de repetírselo; **to** — **down** lid asegurar con clavos; **to** — **something in** clavar algo con martillo; **to** — **something into shape** formar algo a martillo; **to** — **out** dent quitar a martillo, extender bajo el martillo; settlement etc elaborar trabajosamente.
   3 vi: **to** — **at** (or **on**) **a door** dar golpes en una puerta; **to** — **away at** subject insistir con ahínco en, work trabajar asiduamente en; **to** — **away on the piano** tocar estrepitosamente el piano.
hammock ['hæmək] n hamaca f, (Naut) coy m.
hamper[1] ['hæmpə*] n cesto m, canasta f.
hamper[2] ['hæmpə*] vt estorbar, impedir.
hamster ['hæmstə*] n hámster m.
hamstring ['hæmstriŋ] (irr: see **string**) vt desjarretar; (fig) paralizar.
hand [hænd] **1** n (a) (general sense) mano f; —**s off!** ¡fuera las manos!; —**s up!** ¡arriba las manos!; **to be clever with one's** —**s** tener mucha destreza manual; **to go on one's** —**s and knees** ir a gatas.
   (b) (phrases with verb) **A is** — **in glove with B** A y B son uña y carne, se ha confabulado A con B; **to bear a** — arrimar el hombro; **to change** —**s** cambiar de dueño; **to clutch at an offer with both** —**s** aceptar una oferta de muy buena gana; **he never does a** —**'s turn** no da golpe; **to force someone's** — obligar a uno a hacer algo contra su voluntad; **to get one's** — **in** hacerse la mano; **to give someone a** — ayudar a uno; **to have a** — **in** tomar parte en, intervenir en; **he had no** — **in it** no tuvo arte ni parte en ello; **to hold** —**s** (children) ir cogidos de la mano, (lovers) hacer manitas; **to join** —**s** darse las manos; **to keep one's** — **in** conservar la práctica (at de), mantenerse en forma; **to keep one's** —**s off something** no tocar algo; **to lay** —**s on echar mano a, (obtain)** conseguir, (Eccl) imponer las manos a; **to lend a** — arrimar el hombro; **to lend someone a** — echar una mano a uno; **lend a** —! ¡manos a la obra!; **to make money** — **over fist** amasar una fortuna; **to put one's** — **to something** emprender algo; **to shake** —**s** estrecharse la mano, darse las manos; **to shake** —**s with someone** estrechar la mano a uno; **to take a** — tomar parte, intervenir (at, in en); **to throw up one's** —**s** (in horror) escandalizarse; **to turn one's** — **to** dedicarse a; **he can turn his** — **to anything** vale tanto para un

barrido como para un fregado; **to wash one's —s** of desentenderse de; **to win —s down** ganar fácilmente.

(c) (*phrases with adj*) **to rule with a firm —** gobernar con firmeza; **to give someone a free —** dar carta blanca a uno; **to have a free —** tener carta blanca; **to have one's —s full** estar ocupado; **with a heavy —** cruelmente, sin piedad; **with a high —** despóticamente; **to give someone a helping —** echar una mano a uno; **to get** (*or* **gain**) **the upper —** empezar a dominar; **to have the upper —** tener la ventaja.

(d) (*phrases with prep before n*) (**at**) **at — a** mano; **to be near at —** estar a la mano; estar cerca; **winter was at —** se acercaba el invierno; **at first —** de primera mano, directamente; de buena tinta; **to suffer at the —s of** sufrir a manos de; (**by**) **by — make a** mano, *raise etc* a fuerza de brazos; **to send a letter by —** enviar una carta en mano; **to take someone by the —** llevar a uno de la mano; (**from**) **to live from — to mouth** vivir al día, vivir de la mano a la boca; (**in**) **gun in —** el revólver en la mano, empuñando el revólver; **to be in someone's —s** estar en manos de uno; **to have something in —** tener algo entre manos; **to have a matter in —** estar estudiando un asunto; **the situation is in —** se ha conseguido dominar la situación; **he has them well in —** los domina perfectamente; **to put something in —** emprender algo; **to take someone in —** enseñar a uno, entrenar a uno; imponer disciplina a uno; **to take something in —** hacerse cargo de algo; **I like to have something in —** me gusta tener algo en reserva; **money in —** dinero *m* contante; **how much have we in —?** ¿cuánto tenemos en el haber?; (**into**) **to fall into enemy —s** caer en manos del enemigo; **to play into someone's —s** ceder la ventaja a un contrario; **to put something into a lawyer's —s** pedir el consejo de un abogado acerca de algo; **to take justice into one's own —s** tomar la justicia por su mano; (**off**) **to get something off one's —s** deshacerse de algo; terminar de hacer algo; (**on**) **on the left —** a la izquierda, **on the right —** a la derecha; **on every —, on all —s** por todas partes; **on the one —** por una parte, **on the other —** por otra parte; **to be on —** estar a la mano; **he's on my —s** all day está conmigo todo el día; **to have work on his —s** los géneros resultaron ser invendibles; (**out**) **to condemn someone out of —** condenar a uno sin estudiar el caso; **to shoot someone out of —** fusilar a uno sin más; **to get out of —** desmandarse; (**to**) **to come to —s** llegar a las manos; **your letter of the 3rd is to —** he recibido su carta del 3.

(e) (*of instrument*) aguja *f*; (*of clock*) manecilla *f*.

(f) (*measure*) palmo *m*.

(g) (*Cards*) mano *f*; **to have a — of bridge** echar una partida de bridge.

(h) (*writing*) escritura *f*, letra *f*; **in one's own —** de puño y letra de uno; **he writes a good —** tiene buena letra; **to put one's — to something** firmar algo.

(i) (*in marriage*) **to ask for someone's —** pedir la mano de una; **she gave him her —** se casó con él.

(j) (*person*) operario *m*, a *f*, obrero *m*, a *f*; (*Agr etc*) peón *m*; **—s** (*Naut*) tripulación *f*; **all —s on deck!** ¡todos a la cubierta!; **to be lost with all —s** desaparecer con toda la tripulación; **to be a good — at —** tener buena mano para, ser hábil en; **to be an old —** ser perro viejo.

(k) (*influence*) influencia *f*; **his — was everywhere** se notaba su influencia por todas partes.

(l) (*applause*) **they gave him a big —** le aplaudieron calurosamente.

2 *vt* dar, entregar, poner en manos de; alargar; pasar; **to — down** *object* bajar; *heirloom* pasar; *tradition* transmitir; *judgement* dictar; *person* ayudar a bajar; **to — in** entregar; *resignation* presentar; *person* ayudar a subir; **to — off** rechazar; **to — on** *tradition* transmitir; *news* comunicar; *object* pasar; **to — over** entregar; **to — round** pasar de mano en mano; (*distribute*) repartir; *chocolates etc* ofrecer; **you've got to — it to him** hay que reconocer que lo hace (*etc*) muy bien; **to — up** subir.

3 *vi*: **to — over to** ceder su puesto a.

handbag ['hændbæg] *n* bolso *m*.
handball ['hændbɔːl] *n* balonmano *m*.
handbell ['hændbel] *n* campanilla *f*.
handbook ['hændbuk] *n* manual *m*; (*guide*) guía *f*.
handbrake ['hændbreik] *n* freno *m* de mano.
handcart ['hændkɑːt] *n* carretilla *f*, carretón *m*.
handclasp ['hændklɑːsp] *n* apretón *m* de manos.
handcuff ['hændkʌf] *vt* poner las esposas a, esposar.
handcuffs ['hændkʌfs] *npl* esposas *fpl*.

-handed ['hændid] *adj* de ... mano(s); de mano(s) ...; **four-handed game** juego *m* para cuatro personas.
handful ['hændful] *n* puñado *m*, manojo *m*; **a — of people** un puñado de gente; **he's a real —** tiene el diablo en el cuerpo.
hand grenade ['hændgri,neid] *n* bomba *f* de mano.
handgrip ['hændgrip] *n* **= handle**; **= grip**.
handgun ['hændgʌn] *n* revólver *m*, pistola *f*.
handicap ['hændikæp] **1** *n* desventaja *f*, estorbo *m*, obstáculo *m*; (*Sport*) hándicap *m*.
2 *vt* perjudicar, estorbar; (*Sport*) handicapar; **he has always been —ped by his accent** su acento siempre ha sido una desventaja para él.
handicapped ['hændikæpt] *adj*: **mentally —** anormal, retrasado; **physically —** mutilado, tullido.
handicraft ['hændikrɑːft] *n* artesanía *f*; (*skill*) destreza *f* manual; **— teacher** profesor *m* de trabajos manuales.
handiness ['hændinis] *n* **(a)** proximidad *f*, lo cercano; **because of the — of the library** debido a que la biblioteca está tan cerca, porque resulta tan cómodo ir a la biblioteca.
(b) conveniencia *f*, comodidad *f*; carácter *m* manuable, facilidad *f* en el manejo.
(c) habilidad *f*, destreza *f*; **his — with a gun** su destreza con un fusil.
hand-in-hand ['hændin'hænd] *adv*: **to go —** ir cogidos de la mano; **it goes — with** está estrechamente relacionado con; **these plans should go —** estos proyectos han de realizarse al mismo ritmo.
handiwork ['hændiwɜːk] *n* obra *f*.
handkerchief ['hæŋkətʃif] *n* pañuelo *m*.
handle ['hændl] **1** *n* (*haft*) mango *m*; (*lever*) palanca *f*; (*crank*) manivela *f*; (*for winding*) manubrio *m*; (*of basket, jug etc*) asa *f*, asidero *m*; (*of door, drawer etc*) tirador *m*, manija *f*; (*fig*) pretexto *m*, asidero *m*; (*fam*) título *m*; **to have a — to one's name** (*fam*) tener título de nobleza; **to fly off the —** (*fam*) salirse de sus casillas, perder los estribos.
2 *vt* **(a)** (*touch*) tocar, (*improperly*) manosear; (*Sport*) tocar con la mano; (*delicately*) manejar, manipular; **"— with care"** "manéjese con cuidado"; **don't — the fruit** no manosees la fruta; **the police —d him roughly** la policía le trató brutalmente.
(b) (*fig*) *situation, theme, resources etc* manejar; *car* conducir, *ship* gobernar; *unruly element* saber dominar; *commodity, product* tratar en, comerciar en; **I'll — this** yo me encargo de esto; **do you — tax matters?** ¿tiene Vd que ver con las contribuciones?; **we — 2000 travellers a day** por aquí pasan 2000 viajeros cada día; **can the port — big ships?** ¿el puerto tiene capacidad para los buques grandes?
handlebar ['hændlbɑː*] *n* manillar *m*.
handler ['hændlə*] *n* (*Comm*) tratante *m*, comerciante *m*; (*Sport*) entrenador *m*; (*of dog*) amo *m*.
handling ['hændliŋ] *n* manejo *m*, manejar *m*; manipulación *f*; manoseo *m*; (*of car*) conducción *f*; (*of ship*) gobierno *m*; rough — trato *m* brutal, malos tratos *mpl*; **his — of the matter** su manejo del asunto, su modo de manejar el asunto.
hand-luggage ['hænd,lʌgidʒ] *n* bultos *mpl* de mano.
handmade ['hændmeid] *adj* hecho a mano; de artesanía.
handout ['hændaut] *n* (*act*) distribución *f*, repartimiento *m*; (*charity*) limosna *f*; (*press —*) nota *f* de prensa; (*leaflet*) folleto *m*.
hand-picked ['hænd'pikt] *adj* escogido a mano.
handrail ['hændreil] *n* pasamano *m*.
handset ['hændset] *n* (*Tel*) aparato *m*, microteléfono *m*.
handshake ['hændʃeik] *n* apretón *m* de manos; **golden —** dinero que se paga a los grandes industriales (*etc*) al jubilarse éstos.
handsome ['hænsəm] *adj* (*beautiful*) hermoso, bello; elegante; *man* guapo, bien parecido, distinguido; *gesture, salary, treatment etc* generoso; *fortune, profit* considerable; *victory* fácil, agobiador.
handsomely ['hænsəmli] *adv* elegantemente; generosamente; *win* fácilmente.
handspring ['hændspriŋ] *n* voltereta *f* sobre las manos.
handstand ['hændstænd] *n* farol *m*, puntal *m*; (*Gymnastics*) posición *f* de manos.
hand-to-hand ['hændtə'hænd] *adv, adj* cuerpo a cuerpo.
hand-to-mouth ['hændtə'mauθ] *adj* existence precario.
handwriting ['hænd,raitiŋ] *n* escritura *f*, letra *f*.
handwritten ['hænd'ritn] *adj* escrito a mano.
handy ['hændi] *adj* **(a)** (*near*) a mano; próximo, cercano; **the shop is —** la tienda está cerca; **to keep something —** tener algo listo para usar.

(b) (*convenient*) conveniente, cómodo, práctico; *machine etc* manuable, fácil de manejar; **a — little car** un coche práctico; **it's — for the shops** está muy práctico vivir aquí; **it's — for the shops** está muy cerca de las tiendas; **to come in —** venir bien, servir.

(c) (*skilful*) hábil, diestro; **to be — with one's fists** saber defenderse con los puños; **to be — with a gun** saber manejar un fusil.

handyman ['hændimən] *n*, *pl* —**men** [mən] factótum *m*; hombre *m* que tiene dotes prácticas (para hacer trabajos de carpintería en casa *etc*).

hang [hæŋ] (*irr*: *pret and ptp* **hung**, (*Law*) *pret and ptp* **hanged**) **1** *vt* **(a)** colgar, suspender; *wallpaper* pegar; **to — out** *washing etc* tender; *streamers etc* colgar, extender; **to — up** colgar.

(b) *head* bajar, inclinar.

(c) to — a room with tapestries entapizar un cuarto, adornar un cuarto con tapicerías; **balconies hung with flags** balcones *mpl* engalanados con banderas; **trees hung with lights** árboles *mpl* llenos de farolillos; **a wall hung with ivy** un muro cubierto de hiedra.

(d) *criminal* ahorcar; **— the fellow!** ¡qué tío!; **— it (all)!** ¡por Dios!; ¡demonio!; **— the expense!** ¡que no se hable de los gastos!; **I'll be —ed if I know** que me cuelguen si lo sé.

(e) to be hung up in the fog sufrir un retraso debido a la niebla; **to be hung up with a visitor** retrasarse por tener que atender a una visita; **we are hung up for lack of bricks** no podemos ir adelante por falta de ladrillos.

2 *vi* colgar, pender, estar suspendido (*from* de, *on* en); (*garment, hair*) caer; **a picture —ing on the wall** un cuadro colgado en la pared; **the hawk hung motionless in the sky** el halcón se mantenía inmóvil en el cielo; **he'll — for it** por este crimen le ahorcarán; **to — about, to — around** (*adv*) (*idle*) no hacer nada, haraganear, (*wait*) esperar; **to keep someone —ing about** hacer esperar a uno; **to — about** (*prep*) (*frequent*) frecuentar; (*haunt*) rondar; **to — about a woman** andar rondado a una mujer, andar detrás de una mujer; **the clouds hung about the summit** las nubes se pegaban a la cumbre; **to — back** quedarse atrás, resistirse a pasar adelante; (*fig*) vacilar, no resolverse; **her hair —s down her back** el pelo le cae por la espalda; **to — on** (*adv*) esperar; **— on!** ¡espera un momentito!; **they're still —ing on** siguen resistiendo; **to — on** (*prep*) colgar de; (*fig*) depender de; **we are all —ing on his decision** todos estamos pendientes de su decisión; **time —s heavy on him** se le hacen las horas siglos, para él no corre el tiempo; **to — on to** agarrarse a; (*fam*) (*keep*) guardar, quedarse con, (*preserve*) conservar; **to — on to it till I see you** guárdalo hasta que nos veamos; **to — out** colgar fuera; (*fam*) vivir; **to — out for more** esperar a que se ofrezca más; **to — out of the window** asomarse por la ventana; **to — over** (*adv*) colgar por el borde, sobresalir; **to — over** (*prep*) cernerse sobre; **a heavy silence hung over the town** se cernía sobre la ciudad un profundo silencio; **the threat —ing over us** la amenaza que se cierne sobre nosotros; **he hung over the table** se inclinó sobre la mesa; **to — together** (*person*) mantenerse unidos; (*argument etc*) ser consistente; **to — up** (*Tel*) colgar.

3 *vr*: **to — oneself** ahorcarse.

4 *n* (*of garment*) caída *f*; **to get the — of something** lograr entender algo; **I can't get the — of this machine** no entiendo el modo de manejar esta máquina; *see* care.

hangar ['hæŋə*] *n* hangar *m*.

hangdog ['hæŋdɔg] *adj* avergonzado; **he had a — look** tenía cara de pocos amigos.

hanger ['hæŋə*] *n* percha *f*, colgadero *m*.

hanger-on ['hæŋər'ɔn] *n* parásito *m*, pegote *m*.

hanging ['hæŋiŋ] **1** *adj* pendiente, colgante; *lamp* de techo; *garden* pensil; **— committee** junta *f* de una exposición; **it's not a — matter** no es cosa de vida o de muerte.

2 *n* ahorcadura *f*; **—s** colgaduras *fpl*.

hangman ['hæŋmən] *n*, *pl* —**men** [mən] verdugo *m*.

hangnail ['hæŋneil] *n* padrastro *m*.

hang-out ['hæŋaut] *n* (*fam*) guarida *f*, nidal *m*.

hangover ['hæŋ͵əuvə*] *n* (*after drinking*) resaca *f*; **it's a — from pre-war days** es algo que ha quedado de la preguerra.

hank [hæŋk] *n* madeja *f*.

hanker ['hæŋkə*] *vi*: **to — after** añorar; **to — for** anhelar, suspirar por.

hankering ['hæŋkəriŋ] *n* (*feeling*) añoranza *f*; (*wish*) anhelo *m*; **to have a — for** anhelar, suspirar por.

hankie ['hæŋki] *n* (*fam*) pañuelo *m*.

hanky-panky ['hæŋki'pæŋki] *n* trucos *mpl*, supercherías *fpl*; **there's some — going on** esto huele a camelo, aquí hay trampa; **we want no — with the girls** aquí nadie se meta en líos con las chicas.

Hannibal ['hænibəl] *m* Aníbal.

Hanover ['hænəvə*] Hanovre.

hansom ['hænsəm] *n* simón *m*.

haphazard ['hæp'hæzəd] **1** *adj* fortuito. **2** *adv* de cualquier modo, a troche y moche.

hapless ['hæplis] *adj* desventurado.

happen ['hæpən] *vi* **(a)** (*occur*) pasar, suceder, ocurrir, acontecer, acaecer; producirse; **what —ed?** ¿qué pasó?; **how did it —?** ¿cómo fue esto?; **an explosion —ed** se produjo una explosión; **these things — son** cosas que pasan; **whatever —s** suceda lo que suceda; **see it doesn't — again** y que no vuelva a ocurrir; **as it —s, it (so) —s that** da la casualidad que; **as if nothing had —ed** como si tal cosa; **how does it — that . . .?** ¿cómo es posible que . . . + *subj*?

(b) (*take place*) tener lugar, verificarse; **the match never —ed** el partido no tuvo lugar nunca.

(c) a funny thing —ed to me me pasó algo raro; **if anything should — to him** si le sobreviniera algo malo; **what —ed to him?** ¿qué fue de él?

(d) I —ed to be there me encontraba allí por casualidad; **if anyone should — to see you** si acaso te vean; **do you — to know him?** ¿le conoce Vd por ventura?; **I — to know that** pues me consta que; **it —s to be true** a pesar de todo es verdad.

(e) to — on something tropezar con algo; **to — on the solution** acertar, dar con la solución.

happening ['hæpniŋ] *n* suceso *m*, acontecimiento *m*; **there will be a beatnik "—" in the park** habrá un "acontecimiento" de los beatniks en el parque.

happenstance ['hæpənstæns] *n* (*US*) azar *m*, casualidad *f*; **by —** por casualidad.

happily ['hæpili] *adv* (*fortunately*) por fortuna, afortunadamente; (*merrily*) alegremente; **now they are living — in Seville** ahora viven muy contentos en Sevilla; **they lived — ever after** vivieron felices.

happiness ['hæpinis] *n* (*contentment*) felicidad *f*, dicha *f*; (*merriment*) alegría *f*.

happy ['hæpi] *adj* **(a)** (*fortunate*) feliz, dichoso, afortunado; **that — age** aquella época tan feliz.

(b) (*contented*) contento, satisfecho; **are you —?** ¿estás contento?; **are you — with him?** ¿eres feliz con él?; **we are not entirely — about the plan** no estamos del todo contentos con el proyecto, no nos satisface del todo el proyecto; **your success makes us all —** su éxito nos alegra a todos; **we're very — for you** nos alegramos mucho por ti; **we were — to hear it** nos alegramos de saberlo; **I am — to tell you that** tengo mucho gusto en comunicarle que.

(c) (*merry, cheerful*) alegre; (*sl*) entre dos velas; **ending of book etc** feliz; **to be as — as a lark** (*or* sandboy) estar como unas pascuas.

(d) (*apt*) feliz, oportuno; **it seems to be a — solution** parece ser una solución satisfactoria.

happy-go-lucky ['hæpigəu'lʌki] *adj* despreocupado.

Hapsburg ['hæpsbəːg] Habsburgo.

hara-kiri ['hærə'kiri] *n* haraquiri *m*.

harangue [hə'ræŋ] **1** *n* arenga *f*. **2** *vt* arengar.

harass ['hærəs] *vt* acosar, hostigar; (*Mil*) hostilizar, picar; *person* (*with worries etc*) atormentar, perseguir; **to be —ed by doubts** ser atormentado por las dudas.

harassed ['hærəst] *adj* *look* preocupado.

harbinger ['haːbindʒə*] *n* heraldo *m*, nuncio *m*; precursor *m*; presagio *m*; **— of doom** presagio *m* del desastre; **the swallow is a — of spring** la golondrina anuncia la venida de la primavera.

harbour, (*US*) **harbor** ['haːbə*] **1** *n* puerto *m*; **outer — rada** *f*.

2 *attr* portuario.

3 *vt* *fear, hope etc* abrigar; (*lodge*) hospedar; (*conceal*) esconder; **that corner —s the dust** en ese rincón se amontona el polvo.

harbour master, (*US*) **harbor master** ['haːbə͵maːstə*] *n* capitán *m* de puerto.

hard [haːd] **1** *adj* **(a)** (*unyielding, also fig*) duro; sólido, firme; *mud, snow* endurecido; *muscle* firme; *court, currency, water* duro; *drink* alcohólico; *liquor* espiritoso; *cash* contante; *look* fijo; **he's as — as nails** tiene muchísima resistencia.

(b) (*harsh, tough*) *work* arduo, penoso, agotador; *blow* duro, (*fig*) cruel, rudo; *frost* fuerte; *weather, winter* severo; *climate* áspero; *fight, match* muy reñido; *rule* severo; *decision* injusto; *fact* innegable; *word* nada amistoso; *luck, times* malo.

(c) (*of person*) severo, inflexible; **you're a — man** eres cruel; **to be — on someone** ser muy duro

con uno; **to be — on one's clothes** destrozar la ropa.
 (d) *decision* (*final*) definitivo, irrevocable.
 (e) (*difficult*) difícil; **to be — to beat** ser difícil de vencer; **I find it — to believe that** se me hace cuesta arriba creer que; **to be — to please** ser exigente, ser quisquilloso; **he's — of hearing** es duro de oído.
 2 *adv* (a) (*strenuously*) mucho; de firme; **to pull a rope** — tirar fuertemente de una cuerda; **he threw it — down** lo arrojó violentamente; **to hit someone — dar un golpe recio a uno, (*fig*) ser un golpe cruel para uno; **to be — at it** trabajar (*etc*) con ahínco; **to work —** trabajar mucho; **to rain —** llover mucho; **to beg — for something** pedir algo con insistencia; **to think —** pensar mucho, meditar profundamente; **to look —** mirar fijamente; **to drink —** beber con exceso; **hold —!** ¡tente!, ¡para!; **to try one's —est to** + *infin* esforzarse mucho por + *infin*.
 (b) **to be — up** estar a la cuarta pregunta; **to be — up for books** no tener casi libros, estar muy falto de libros; **I was — put to it** estuve en un aprieto; **to be — put to it to decide** encontrar difícil decidir; **to be — done by** ser tratado injustamente; **he took it pretty —** fue un golpe bastante rudo para él.
 (c) — **by** (*adv*) muy cerca, (*prep*) muy cerca de; **A followed — upon B** A siguió de cerca a B.
hard-and-fast ['hɑːdən'fɑːst] *adj* **rule** rígido; **decision** definitivo, irrevocable.
hard-bitten ['hɑːd'bitn] *adj* de carácter duro.
hardboard ['hɑːdbɔːd] *n* chapa *f* de madera dura.
hard-boiled ['hɑːd'bɔild] *adj* **egg** duro; **person** de carácter duro, severo.
hard-earned ['hɑːd'əːnd] *adj* ganado con el sudor de la frente.
harden ['hɑːdn] **1** *vt* endurecer (*also Comm*), solidificar; **to — someone to adversity** acostumbrar a uno a la adversidad; **to — someone to war** aguerrir a uno; **he —ed his heart** se mostró más inflexible.
 2 *vi* endurecerse (*also Comm*), solidificarse; **his voice —ed** adoptó un tono más áspero.
hardened ['hɑːdnd] *adj* **criminal** habitual.
hardening ['hɑːdniŋ] *n* endurecimiento *m* (*also Comm*); — **of the arteries** endurecimiento *m* de las arterias, arteriosclerosis *f*.
hard-fought ['hɑːd'fɔːt] *adj* muy reñido.
hard-headed ['hɑːd'hedid] *adj* práctico, realista, poco sentimental.
hard-hearted ['hɑːd'hɑːtid] *adj* duro de corazón, insensible.
hardly ['hɑːdli] *adv* (a) (*in a hard manner*) duramente; difícilmente; (*badly*) mal.
 (b) (*scarcely*) apenas; **he can — read** apenas sabe leer; **that can — be true** eso difícilmente puede ser verdad; — **anyone** casi nadie; — **ever** casi nunca; — **!** ¡nada de eso!
hardness ['hɑːdnis] *n* dureza *f*; dificultad *f*; rigor *m*; severidad *f*; — **of hearing** dureza *f* de oído; — **of heart** insensibilidad *f*.
hardship ['hɑːdʃip] *n* trabajos *mpl*, penas *fpl*; infortunio *m*; prueba *f*; (*economic etc*) apuro *m*, privación *f*; **to suffer —(s)** pasar apuros; **it is no — to him to give up smoking** él con toda facilidad puede dejar de fumar.
hardtack ['hɑːdtæk] *n* (*Naut*) galleta *f*.
hardware ['hɑːdweə*] *n* ferretería *f*, quincalla *f*; — **shop** (*or* **store**) ferretería *f*, quincallería *f*; **nuclear —** (equipo *m* de) armas *fpl* nucleares.
hard-wearing ['hɑːd'weəriŋ] *adj* resistente, duradero.
hard-won ['hɑːd'wʌn] *adj* ganado a duras penas.
hardwood ['hɑːdwud] *n* madera *f* dura; — **tree** árbol *m* de hojas caducas.
hard-working ['hɑːd'wəːkiŋ] *adj* trabajador.
hardy ['hɑːdi] *adj* fuerte, robusto; (*Bot*) resistente.
hare [heə*] **1** *n* liebre *f*; **first catch your —** no hay que empezar por el tejado. **2** *vi* (*fam*) correr, ir rápidamente; **he went haring past** pasó como un rayo.
harebell ['heəbel] *n* campánula *f*.
hare-brained ['heəbreind] *adj* casquivano.
harelip ['heə'lip] *n* labio *m* leporino.
harem ['hɑːriːm] *n* harén *m*.
haricot ['hærikəu] *n* (*also* — **bean**) alubia *f*.
hark [hɑːk] *vi*: — **!** ¡escucha!; — **at this!** ¡oye!; — **at him!** ¡qué cosas dice!; — **at him singing!** ¡cómo canta el tío!; **to — back to** *matter* volver a, *earlier occasion* recordar; **he's always —ing back to that** siempre está con la misma canción; **to — to** escuchar.
Harlequin ['hɑːlikwin] *m* Arlequín.
harlot ['hɑːlət] *n* ramera *f*.
harm [hɑːm] **1** *n* daño *m*, mal *m*; perjuicio *m*; **to be out of —'s way** estar a salvo; **to keep out of —'s way**

evitar el peligro, permanecer lejos del sitio peligroso; **there's no — in** + *ger* no hay ningún mal en + *infin*; **I see no — in** that no veo nada en contra de eso; **to do someone —** hacer daño a uno, (*fig*) perjudicar a uno; **it does more — than good** es peor el remedio que la enfermedad; **the — is done now** el mal ya está hecho; **he means no —** tiene buenas intenciones.
 2 *vt* **person** hacer daño a, hacer mal a; **crops** *etc* dañar, estropear; **interests** *etc* perjudicar.
 3 *vi*: **will it — in the rain?** ¿lo estropeará la lluvia?; **it won't — for that** eso no le hará daño.
harmful ['hɑːmful] *adj* perjudicial (*to* para), dañoso, nocivo; **pest, tobacco** *etc* dañino.
harmless ['hɑːmlis] *adj* inocuo, inofensivo.
harmonic [hɑː'mɔnik] *adj* armónico.
harmonica [hɑː'mɔnikə] *n* armónica *f*.
harmonious [hɑː'məuniəs] *adj* armonioso.
harmonium [hɑː'məuniəm] *n* armonio *m*.
harmonize ['hɑːmənaiz] *vti* armonizar (*with* con).
harmony ['hɑːməni] *n* armonía *f*; **close —** perfecta harmonía *f*.
harness ['hɑːnis] **1** *n* guarniciones *fpl*, arreos *mpl*; **to die in —** morir con las botas puestas; **to get back in —** volver al trabajo, volver a su puesto.
 2 *vt* (a) *horse* poner guarniciones a, enjaezar; **to — a horse to a cart** enganchar un caballo a un carro.
 (b) *resources etc* hacer trabajar, utilizar, aprovechar.
harp [hɑːp] **1** *n* arpa *f*. **2** *vi*: **to — on** hablar constantemente de; **stop —ing on it!** ¡no machaques!
harpist ['hɑːpist] *n* arpista *mf*.
harpoon [hɑː'puːn] **1** *n* arpón *m*. **2** *vt* arponear.
harpsichord ['hɑːpsikɔːd] *n* arpicordio *m*, clavicémbalo *m*.
harpy ['hɑːpi] *n* arpía *f*.
harquebus ['hɑːkwibəs] *n* (*Hist*) arcabuz *m*.
harridan ['hæridən] *n* bruja *f*.
harrow ['hærəu] **1** *n* grada *f*. **2** *vt* gradar.
harrowing ['hærəuiŋ] *adj* horrendo, horroroso, angustioso.
Harry ['hæri] *m* Enrique; **to play old — with** endiablar, estropear.
harry ['hæri] *vt* (*devastate*) asolar; (*Mil*) hostilizar; **person** *etc* hostigar, acosar.
harsh [hɑːʃ] *adj* **person, decision** *etc* severo, duro, cruel; **voice, cloth** *etc* áspero; **contrast** violento; **weather** severo; **colour** chillón; **taste** acerbo; **words** nada amistoso.
harshly ['hɑːʃli] *adv* severamente, duramente; ásperamente.
harshness ['hɑːʃnis] *n* severidad *f*, dureza *f*, rigor *m*; aspereza *f*.
hart [hɑːt] *n* ciervo *m*.
harum-scarum ['hɛərəm'skɛərəm] **1** *adj* tarambana. **2** *n* tarambana *mf*.
harvest ['hɑːvist] **1** *n* cosecha *f*, recolección *f*; (*time of year*) siega *f*; (*of grape*) vendimia *f*; (*fig*) cosecha *f*. **2** *vt* cosechar (*also fig*), recoger, recolectar.
harvester ['hɑːvistə*] *n* (*person*) segador *m*, ora *f*; (*machine*) cosechadora *f*, segadora-trilladora *f*.
harvest festival ['hɑːvist'festivəl] *n* fiesta *f* de la cosecha.
harvest time ['hɑːvist,taim] *n* siega *f*.
has [hæz] *see* **have**.
has-been ['hæzbiːn] *n* persona *f* que ya no sirve, vieja gloria *f*.
hash [hæʃ] **1** *n* picadillo *m*; (*fam*) embrollo *m*, lío *m*; **to make a — of something** armarse un lío con algo, estropear algo, hacer algo muy mal; **to settle someone's —** cargarse a uno, acabar con uno.
 2 *vt*: **to — something up** rehacer algo (y presentarlo como nuevo).
hashish ['hæʃiʃ] *n* hachich *m*.
hasn't ['hæznt] = **has not**.
hasp [hɑːsp] *n* pasador *m*, sujetador *m*.
hassle ['hæsl] *n* (*US: fam*) pelea *f*, riña *f*.
hassock ['hæsək] *n* (*Eccl*) cojín *m*.
haste [heist] *n* prisa *f*, precipitación *f*; **more — less speed, make — slowly** vísteme despacio que tengo prisa; **to do something in —** hacer algo de prisa; **hacer algo precipitadamente**; **to make — darse prisa; make —!** ¡date prisa!; **to make — to** + *infin* apresurarse a + *infin*.
hasten ['heisn] **1** *vt* acelerar; **to — one's steps** apretar el paso.
 2 *vi* darse prisa, apresurarse; **to — to** + *infin* apresurarse a + *infin*; **to — away, to — off** marcharse precipitadamente; **to — back** volver con toda prisa; **to — on** seguir adelante con toda prisa; **to — up** llegar apresuradamente, llegar corriendo.

hastily ['heistili] *adv* (*hurriedly*) de prisa, precipitadamente; *speak* sin reflexión, con impaciencia; *judge* a la ligera; **I —** suggested that me apresuré a sugerir que.

hasty ['heisti] *adj* (*hurried*) apresurado, precipitado; (*rash*) imprudente; (*quick-tempered*) impaciente, que tiene genio; (*superficial*) ligero; **don't be so —** hay que tomar las cosas con más calma.

hat [hæt] *n* sombrero *m*; **my —!** ¡caramba!; **that's old —** eso es de lo más anticuado; eso si lo tenemos archisabido; **I'll eat my — if** . . . que me maten si . . .; **keep it under your —** de esto no digas ni pío; **to pass the —** round pasar el platillo; **to raise** (*or* **take off**) **one's —** descubrirse; **to take one's — off to** (*fig*) quitarse el sombrero y hacer reverencia a; **to talk through one's —** decir tonterías.

hatbox ['hætbɔks] *n* sombrerera *f*.

hatch¹ [hætʃ] *n* (*hatchway*) escotilla *f*.

hatch² [hætʃ] **1** *vt chick* empollar, incubar; sacar del cascarón; (*fig*) idear; *plot* tramar.

2 *vi* (*bird*) salir del huevo; **the egg —ed** el pollo rompió el cascarón y salió; **those eggs never —ed** esos huevos resultaron ser infecundos.

hatchet ['hætʃit] *n* hacha *f* (pequeña), machado *m*; **to bury the —** echar pelillos a la mar.

hatchet-faced ['hætʃit‚feist] *adj* de cara de cuchillo.

hatching¹ ['hætʃiŋ] *n* incubación *f*; salida *f* del huevo; (*fig*) ideación *f*; preparación *f*, maquinación *f*.

hatching² ['hætʃiŋ] *n* (*Art*) sombreado *m*.

hatchway ['hætʃwei] *n* escotilla *f*.

hate [heit] **1** *n* odio *m*.

2 *vt* (**a**) odiar, detestar, aborrecer; **to — someone like poison** odiar a uno a muerte.

(**b**) **I — to see that** me da asco ver aquello; **I — to say so** lamento tener que decirlo; **I — having to do it** me repugna hacerlo; **I — to trouble you** siento muchísimo molestarle; **I should — to have to sell it** me molestaría tener que venderlo; **he —s to be corrected** se indigna si se le corrige.

hateful ['heitful] *adj* odioso, repugnante.

hatless ['hætlis] *adj* sin sombrero, descubierto.

hatpin ['hætpin] *n* agujón *m*.

hatred ['heitrid] *n* odio *m* (*for* a), aborrecimiento *m* (*for* de).

hatter ['hætə*] *n* sombrerero *m*.

hat trick ['hættrik] *n* (*fig*) tres triunfos *mpl* seguidos.

haughtily ['hɔːtili] *adv* arrogantemente.

haughtiness ['hɔːtinis] *n* altanería *f*, arrogancia *f*, altivez *f*.

haughty ['hɔːti] *adj* altanero, arrogante, altivo.

haul [hɔːl] **1** *n* (**a**) (*act of pulling*) tirón *m*, estirón *m* (*on* de).

(**b**) (*distance*) recorrido *m*, trayecto *m*; **it's a good** (*or* **long**) **—** es mucho camino.

(**c**) (*amount of fish*) redada *f*; (*fig*) cantidad *f* cazada, número *m* de piezas cazadas; (*financial*) ganancia *f*; (*stolen*) botín *m*; **the thieves made a good —** los ladrones obtuvieron un cuantioso botín.

2 *vt* (*drag*) tirar, arrastrar; (*transport*) acarrear, transportar; **to — down** *flag* arriar; **to — in** *net etc* ir recogiendo; **to — up** ir levantando.

3 *vi*: **to — on, to — at** tirar de, (*Naut*) halar.

haulage ['hɔːlidʒ] *n* (*act*) acarreo *m*, transporte *m*; (*cost*) gastos *mpl* de acarreo.

haulage contractor ['hɔːlidʒkən'træktə*] *n*, **haulier** ['hɔːliə*] *n* contratista *m* de transportes.

haunch [hɔːntʃ] *n* anca *f*; (*of meat*) pierna *f*; **to sit on one's —es** sentarse en cuclillas.

haunt [hɔːnt] **1** *n* (*animal's*) nidal *m*, guarida *f*, querencia *f*; **I know his —s** yo conozco sus sitios favoritos, yo sé dónde suele estar; **it's a — of artists** es lugar predilecto de los artistas.

2 *vt* (**a**) (*frequent*) frecuentar, rondar; **he —s the theatres** aparece constantemente en los teatros.

(**b**) (*of ghost*) aparecer en, andar por; **the house is —ed** en la casa andan fantasmas, la casa está embrujada; **—ed house** casa *f* de fantasmas.

(**c**) *person* perseguir; obsesionar; **he is —ed by memories** le persiguen sus recuerdos, le atormentan sus recuerdos; **he is —ed by the thought that** le obsesiona el pensamiento de que.

haunted ['hɔːntid] *adj look etc* obsesionado; **— house** see **haunt**.

haunting ['hɔːntiŋ] *adj* obsesionante; *melody* inolvidable.

Havana [hə'vænə] La Habana.

have [hæv] (*irr*: 3rd sing present **has**, *pret and ptp* **had**) **1** *vt* (**a**) (*possess*) tener; poseer; **all I — todo lo que tengo**; **— you any bananas?** (*in shop*) ¿hay plátanos?; **I — no words to express** . . . no encuentro palabras para expresar . . .; **I — no German** no sé alemán; **I — it!** ¡ya!; **. . . and what — you** . . . etcétera, etcétera; **the dog had him by the throat** el perro le tenía agarrado por la garganta.

(**b**) (*bear, carry*) tener, llevar; **the book has no name on it** el libro no lleva el nombre del dueño; **to — a hat on** llevar un sombrero (puesto); **do you — a shilling about you?** ¿llevas encima un chelín?

(**c**) *baby* parir, dar a luz; **she's going to — a baby** va a tener un niño.

(**d**) (*obtain, acquire, hand over*) **to — a letter from someone** recibir una carta de uno; **to — no news** no tener noticias; **I — it on good authority that** sé de buena tinta que; **it is to be had at the chemist's** se vende en la farmacia; **it's not to be had anywhere** no se puede conseguir en ninguna parte; **I must — £5 at once** necesito 5 libras en seguida; **you can — it for £2** te lo vendo por 2 libras; **let me — your pen** déme la pluma; **he let me — some money** me facilitó dinero; **I will let you — my reply tomorrow** les daré mi respuesta mañana.

(**e**) (*strike*) **let him — it!** ¡dale!; **then they let him —** it luego empezaron a pegarle, (*fig*) luego le dijeron cuatro verdades.

(**f**) (*eat, drink etc*) tomar; **I don't — anything at night** por la noche no tomo nada; **to — tea with someone** tomar el té con uno, merendar con uno; **he's having his dinner** está comiendo; **what did you — at the dinner?** ¿qué te dieron de comer en el banquete?; **will you — a drink?** ¿quieres tomar algo?; **will you — some more?** ¿quieres más?; **to — a cigarette** fumar un pitillo.

(**g**) (*for many n phrases, see the n; eg*) **to — a game** echar una partida; **to — a bath** tomar un baño; **to — a lesson** tomar lección; **to — measles** tener sarampión; **to — a good time** pasarlo bien; **did you — any trouble?** ¿tuviste alguna dificultad?; **I had a strange adventure** me pasó algo raro; **I never seem to — anything happen to me** parece que no me pasa nunca nada.

(**h**) (*wish*) **which will you —?** ¿cuál quieres?; **what more would you —?** ¿qué más quieres?; **as ill-luck would — it** desgraciadamente, como quiso la desgracia; **I would — you know that** sepa Vd que.

(**i**) (*permit*) **I won't — such behaviour** no tolero esta conducta; **I'm not having that** no puedo consentir en que se haga (*or* diga *etc*) eso; **we can't — that** eso no se puede consentir; **we don't — children here** aquí no recibimos a los matrimonios que traigan hijos.

(**j**) (*insist, say*) **he will — it that** sostiene que; **he will not — it that** no quiere reconocer que; **as rumour has it** según se dice; **as Keats has it** según (dice) Keats.

(**k**) (*deceive*) **you've been had** te han engañado; **I'm not to be had that way** no se me engaña así; **there you — me** de eso no sé nada en absoluto.

(**l**) (*obligation*) **to — to do something** tener que hacer algo; **it has to be done this way** ha de hacerse de este modo; **does it — to be ironed?** ¿hay que plancharlo?

(**m**) (*causative*) **to — something done** hacer hacer algo; **to — a suit made** mandar confeccionar un traje; **please — it repaired** por favor, mándelo componer; **he had his watch stolen** le robaron el reloj; **he had his arm broken** se rompió el brazo; **I won't — her insulted** no permito que se le insulte; **to — someone do something** hacer que uno haga algo; **he would — me do it** insistió en que yo lo hiciera; **what else would you — me do?** ¿qué más queréis que haga?

(**n**) **I — letters to write** tengo cartas que escribir; **haven't you anything to do?** ¿no tienes nada que hacer?

(**o**) (*auxiliary*) haber; **he has gone** ha ido; **he had spoken** había hablado; **it has been raining for 3 days** llueve desde hace 3 días; **I haven't seen him for 2 years** hace 2 años que no le veo; **"I — 2 cars"** . . . **"so — I"** "yo tengo 2 coches" . . . "yo también"; **"it's gone!"** . . . **"so it has!"** "¡ha desaparecido!" . . . "¡es verdad!"; *see* **just** *etc*.

(**p**) **I had better, sooner** *etc: see* **better, sooner** *etc*.

(**q**) (*with adv or prep*) **let's — him in!** ¡que pase!, ¡que entre!; **to — someone in to tea** invitar a uno a merendar; **we're having people in** tenemos invitados; **we'd better — the doctor in** será mejor llamar al médico; **to — it in for someone** tener manía a uno; **to — someone on** tomar el pelo a uno; **to — a tooth out** hacer sacar una muela; **to — it out with someone** resolver un problema discutiendo con uno, (*unfriendly*) ajustar cuentas con uno; **to — someone up** llevar a uno ante los tribunales (*for* y

acusarle de); **he was had up for larceny** le procesaron por ladrón.
2 n: **the —s and the have-nots** los ricos y los pobres.
haven ['heivn] n puerto m; (fig) refugio m, asilo m.
have-nots ['hævnɔts] npl: **the —** los pobres, los desposeídos.
haven't ['hævnt] = **have not.**
haversack ['hævəsæk] n mochila f.
havoc ['hævək] n estragos mpl, destrucción f; **to make — of, to play — with** hacer estragos en, arruinar, estropear.
haw [hɔ:] n baya f del espino.
Hawaii [hə'waii:] Islas fpl Hawai.
Hawaiian [hə'waijən] **1** adj hawaiano. **2** n hawaiano m, a f.
hawk[1] [hɔ:k] n (Orn) halcón m, gavilán m; **—s and doves** (Pol) gavilanes mpl y palomas fpl.
hawk[2] [hɔ:k] vt pregonar, vender por las calles.
hawk[3] [hɔ:k] **1** vt: **to — up** arrojar tosiendo. **2** vi carraspear.
hawker ['hɔ:kə*] n vendedor m ambulante.
hawser ['hɔ:zə*] n guindaleza f, calabrote m, maroma f.
hawthorn ['hɔ:θɔ:n] n espino m.
hay [hei] n heno m; **to hit the —** (fam) acostarse; **to make — of** enemy desbaratar, team cascar, argument destruir; **to make — while the sun shines** hacer su agosto.
haycock ['heikɔk] n montón m de heno.
hay fever ['hei.fi:və*] n fiebre f del heno.
hayloft ['heilɔft] n henil m.
haymaker ['heimeikə*] n heneador m, labrador m que trabaja en la siega (or la recolección) del heno.
haymaking ['heimeikiŋ] n henificación f; época f del heno; siega f del heno, recolección f del heno.
haystack ['heistæk] n almiar m.
haywire ['heiwaiə*] adj (fam) (confused) en desorden; (mad) loco; **to go —** (person) volverse loco, (scheme etc) embrollarse, embarrullarse; **it's all gone —** en eso existe la mayor confusión, todo está en desorden.
hazard ['hæzəd] **1** n riesgo m; **at all —s** a todo riesgo. **2** vt arriesgar, poner en peligro; guess, remark atreverse a hacer, aventurar.
hazardous ['hæzədəs] adj arriesgado, peligroso.
haze [heiz] n calina f, neblina f; (fig) confusión f; **a — of tobacco smoke filled the room** el cuarto estaba lleno de humo de tabaco.
hazel ['heizl] n avellano m.
hazelnut ['heizlnʌt] n avellana f.
haziness ['heizinis] n lo calinoso, lo brumoso; (fig) confusión f, vaguedad f.
hazy ['heizi] adj calinoso, brumoso; (fig) confuso, vago; **he's — about dates** no recuerda exactamente las fechas; **I'm — about maths** tengo solamente una idea vaga de las matemáticas; **he seemed very —** parecía no tener ninguna idea clara.
H-bomb ['eitʃbɔm] m bomba f H.
he [hi:] **1** pron él; **— who** el que, quien. **2** n macho m, varón m; **to play —** (children's game) dar la despe. **3** attr macho.
head [hed] **1** n (a) (Anat) cabeza f; **— of hair** cabellera f; **—, foremost** de cabeza; **to go — over heels** caer patas arriba; **to fall — over heels in love with someone** enamorarse perdidamente de uno; **from — to foot** de pies a cabeza; **we are banging our —s against a brick wall** todo esto es trabajo perdido; **to bite someone's — off** echar un rapapolvo a uno; **to give a horse its —** dar rienda suelta a un caballo; **now he can hold his — up again** ahora ha recuperado la propia estimación; **to keep one's — above water** (fig) ir tirando; **to nod one's —** asentir con la cabeza, mover la cabeza afirmativamente; **to shake one's —** negar algo con la cabeza, mover la cabeza negativamente; **he stands — and shoulders above the rest** los demás no le llegan a la suela del zapato; **to talk one's — off** hablar por los codos.
(b) (with prep before n) **he is taller than his brother by a —** le saca la cabeza a su hermano; **to win by a (short) —** ganar por una cabeza (escasa); **on his own —** be it sea bajo su propia responsabilidad; **to put a price on someone's —** poner la cabeza de uno a precio; **to stand on one's —** hacer el pino; **to stand an argument on its —** demostrar la falsedad de un argumento; **to give orders over someone's —** dar órdenes sin consultar a uno; **they went over my — to the mayor** hablaron con el alcalde sin hacer caso de mí; **to sell a house over someone's —** vender una casa sin darle nada a uno; **the wine goes to my —** el vino se me sube a la cabeza; **success has gone to his —** el éxito le ha hecho ser muy vanidoso.
(c) (intellect, mind) cabeza f, inteligencia f;

talento m; **two —s are better than one** cuatro ojos ven más que dos; **don't bother your —** about it no se preocupe, no se canse tratando de explicarlo (etc); **it never entered my —** jamás se me pasó por la cabeza; **to have a bad —** tener dolor de cabeza; **to have a swelled —** ser vanidoso; **to have a — for business** tener talento para los negocios; **to have a — for languages** tener aptitud para los idiomas; **to have no — for heights** no tener cabeza para las alturas; **he has a good — on him** es inteligente, tiene talento; **to keep one's —** conservar la sangre fría; **to lose one's —** perder la cabeza; **so we put our —s together** así que tratamos los dos de resolverlo; **to turn someone's —** trastornar el juicio de uno, (make vain) envanecer a uno.
(d) (as (c), with prep before n) **it was above their —s** estaba fuera de su alcance, no eran lo bastante inteligentes para comprenderlo; **to do a sum in one's —** hacer un cálculo mental; **to be soft** (or weak) **in the —** ser un poco tocado; **to get something into someone's —** meter a uno algo en la cabeza; **he has got it into his —** that cree firmemente que; **get it into your —** that dése cuenta de que; **I can't get that tune out of my —** me obsesiona esa melodía; **what put that into your —?** ¿cómo se formó Vd tal idea?, ¿de dónde colige Vd eso?; **to take it into one's — to** + infin ocurrírse a uno + infin; **to be off one's —** estar loco; **you must be off your —!** ¿estás loco?
(e) (person) (leader) jefe m, cabeza m; (of school) director m, ora f; **— of a department** jefe m de departamento; **— of state** jefe m de estado; **crowned —** testa f coronada; **£5 a —** 5 libras por persona.
(f) (on coin) cara f; **to toss —s or tails** echar a cara o cruz; **—s I win, tails you lose** cara, yo gano, cruz, usted pierde; **I couldn't make — or tail of it** no entendí palabra, no le encontré sentido alguno.
(g) **20 — of cattle** 20 reses fpl; **20 — of sheep** 20 ovejas fpl.
(h) (objects etc) (of bed) cabecera f; (of table, bridge, nail etc) cabeza f; (of arrow etc) punta f; (of stick) puño m; (of cylinder) culata f; (Naut) proa f; (Geog) punta f; (of water) altura f de caída; (on beer) espuma f; (Bot) flor f, cabezuela f; (of tree) copa f; (of corn) espigas fpl; **at the — of the valley** al final del valle; **to bring something to a —** hacer que algo llegue a su punto decisivo; **to come to a —** (abscess) supurar, (fig) llegar a la crisis.
(i) (heading) título m, encabezamiento m; (section) sección f, artículo m; **under this —** en esta sección.
(j) (front place) cabeza f; **— of the family** cabeza mf de la familia; **to be at the — of the list** encabezar la lista; **to be at the — of the league** ir en cabeza de la liga.
2 attr (a) principal, primero; **— cook** primer cocinero m; **— salesman** vendedor m en jefe.
(b) part delantero, de frente.
3 vt list etc encabezar, estar a la cabeza de; league ir en cabeza de; poll ganar; rebellion acaudillar; company dirigir; team capitanear; football cabecear; goal rematar con la cabeza; **he —ed the boat for the shore** dirigió la barca hacia la costa; **to be —ed for** ir con rumbo a; **to — off** interceptar, atajar; desviar; (fig) distraer.
4 vi: **to — for, to — towards** dirigirse a (or hacia); **to be —ing for** ir con rumbo a; **where are you —ing for?** ¿adónde se dirige Vd?; **we are —ing for ruin** vamos camino de la destrucción.
headache ['hedeik] n dolor m de cabeza; (fig) quebradero m de cabeza.
headband ['hedbænd] n cinta f (para la cabeza), venda f (para la cabeza).
headdress ['heddres] n toca f, tocado m.
-headed ['hedid] adj con cabeza . . ., de cabeza . . ., eg **small-headed** de cabeza pequeña; **fair-headed** pelirrubio.
header ['hedə*] n (fall) caída f de cabeza; (dive) salto m de cabeza; (Sport) cabezazo m.
headgear ['hedgiə*] n sombrero m; (woman's) tocado m.
headhunter ['hed.hʌntə*] n cazador m de cabezas.
heading ['hediŋ] n (title) encabezamiento m, título m; (letterhead) membrete m; (section) sección f, apartado m; **to come under the — of** clasificarse bajo, estar incluido en.
headlamp ['hedlæmp] n faro m.
headland ['hedlənd] n promontorio m.
headlight ['hedlait] n faro m.
headline ['hedlain] n titular m; **this will hit the —s** los periódicos tendrán mucho que decir sobre esto, esto es sensacional.

headlong ['hedlɔŋ] **1** adj fall de cabeza; rush etc precipitado. **2** adv de cabeza; precipitadamente.

headman ['hedmæn] n, pl —**men** [men] cacique m.

headmaster ['hed'mɑːstə*] n director m (de colegio etc).

headmistress ['hed'mistris] n directora f (de colegio etc).

head-on ['hed'ɔn] **1** adj collision de frente. **2** adv de frente.

headphones ['hedfəunz] npl auriculares mpl.

headquarters ['hed'kwɔːtəz] npl (Mil) cuartel m general; (of party, organization) sede f; (Comm) oficina f central, central f; (of revolt etc) centro m, foco m.

headrest ['hedrest] n reposa-cabezas m.

headroom ['hedrum] n espacio m para la cabeza; espacio m para estar (derecho) de pie; (under bridge etc) luz f.

headscarf ['hedskɑːf] n pañuelo m.

headship ['hedʃip] n jefatura f; dirección f; (of school) puesto m de director(a).

headsman ['hedzmən] n, pl —**men** [mən] verdugo m.

headstand ['hedstænd] n posición f de cabeza.

headstone ['hedstəun] n lápida f mortuoria.

headstrong ['hedstrɔŋ] adj voluntarioso, impetuoso.

headwaters ['hed,wɔːtəz] npl cabecera f (de un río).

headway ['hedwei] n progreso m; to make — avanzar, (fig) hacer progresos; we could make no — against the current no logramos avanzar contra la corriente, la corriente nos impidió avanzar; I didn't make much — with him no he conseguido nada de él.

headwind ['hedwind] n viento m contrario.

heady ['hedi] adj wine fuerte, cabezudo; (fig) embriagador.

heal [hiːl] **1** vt curar, sanar (of de); (fig) curar, remediar. **2** vi (also — up) cicatrizarse.

healing ['hiːliŋ] **1** adj curativo, sanativo. **2** n curación f.

health [helθ] n (a) (of person) salud f; (public —) sanidad f, higiene f; Ministry of H— (Spain) Dirección f General de Sanidad; National H— Service (Spain) Seguro m de Enfermedad; to be in good (bad) — estar bien (mal) de salud; to restore someone to — devolver la salud a uno. (b) (toast) brindis m; good —! ¡salud y pesetas!; here's a — to X! ¡vaya por X!; to drink (to) someone's — beber a la salud de uno, brindar por uno.

healthful ['helθful] adj, **health-giving** ['helθ,giviŋ] adj sano, saludable.

health officer ['helθ,ɔfisə*] n inspector m de sanidad.

health resort ['helθri,zɔːt] n balneario m.

healthy ['helθi] adj (a) (healthful) sano, saludable; place etc salubre. (b) to be — (person) tener buena salud.

heap [hiːp] **1** n montón m, pila f, rimero m; (fig) montón m; a whole — of trouble un montón de disgustos; a whole — of people muchísimas personas; —s of times muchísimas veces; we have —s tenemos montones; we have —s of time nos sobra tiempo, tenemos tiempo de sobra; the news struck him all of a — la noticia le causó estupor.
2 vt (also — up) amontonar, apilar; plate, spoon etc colmar (with de); to — together juntar en un montón; to — favours on someone colmar a uno de favores.
3 —s adv (fam) muchísimo.

hear [hiə*] (irr: pret and ptp **heard**) **1** vt oír; (perceive) sentir; (listen to) escuchar; lecture asistir a; piece of news saber; (Law) case ver; do you — me? ¿me oyes?; I — bad reports of him me dan malos informes sobre él; I never —d such rubbish! ¡en mi vida he oído tantos disparates!; I have —d it said that he oído decir que; to — someone speak oír hablar a uno; I could hardly make myself —d apenas pude hacerme entender; to — someone out escuchar a uno hasta el fin; to — that oír decir que; when I —d that ... cuando supe que ...
2 vi oír; —! ¡muy bien!; to — about, to — of oír hablar de, saber, enterarse de; when I —d of it cuando lo supe; I've never —d of him no le conozco en absoluto; he won't — of it no lo permite, no quiere autorizarlo; I won't — of it! ¡ni hablar!; to — from tener noticias de, recibir carta de; you'll be —ing from me le escribiré; let's — from you soon! ¡no deje de escribirnos pronto!, ¡mándenos noticias suyas!

heard [həd] pret and ptp of **hear**.

hearer ['hiərə*] n oyente mf.

hearing ['hiəriŋ] n (sense of —) oído m; (act of —) audición f; (Law) vista f; in my — en mi presencia, estando yo delante; to be out of — estar fuera del alcance del oído; to be within — estar al alcance del oído; to condemn someone without a — condenar a uno sin escuchar su defensa.

hearing aid ['hiəriŋeid] n aparato m del oído, audífono m.

hearken ['hɑːkən] vi: to — to escuchar.

hearsay ['hiəsei] n rumores mpl, hablillas fpl; it's just — son rumores; by — de oídas.

hearse [həːs] n coche m fúnebre.

heart [hɑːt] n (a) (Anat) corazón m; she spoke with beating — le palpitaba el corazón al decirlo; to clasp someone to one's — abrazar a uno estrechamente; to have a weak — ser cardíaco.
(b) (fig) (Cards) corazones mpl, (in Spanish pack) copas fpl; (of lettuce) cogollo m; (of place, earth etc) corazón m, seno m, centro m; in the — of the country en lo más retirado del campo; in the — of the wood en el centro del bosque; the — of the matter lo esencial, el quid.
(c) (symbol of love) corazón m; with all one's — de todo corazón, con toda el alma; affair of the — aventura f sentimental; to break someone's — (in love) partir el corazón a uno, (by behaviour etc) matar a uno a disgustos; to break one's — over partirse el corazón por; to die of a broken — morir de pena; to lose one's — to enamorarse de; to wear one's — on one's sleeve llevar el corazón en la mano; to win someone's — enamorar a uno.
(d) (seat of feeling, sympathy etc) he's a man after my own — es un hombre de los que me gustan; at — en el fondo; to have someone's interests at — tener presente el interés de uno; to be sick at — tener la muerte en el alma; from the — con toda sinceridad; in his — of —s en lo más íntimo de su corazón; with a heavy — con dolor, sintiéndolo; his — is in the right place tiene buenas intenciones; to cut someone to the — herir a uno en lo vivo; to cry one's — out llorar a mares; it would have done your — good le habría alegrado muchísimo; to eat one's — out estar muriéndose de pena; to have no — no tener entrañas; have a —! ¡ten un poco de piedad!; he has a — of gold es buenísima persona; to set someone's — at rest tranquilizar a uno; to take something to — tomar algo a pecho.
(e) (seat of desire, intention) his — was not in it no tenía fe en lo que estaba haciendo; to set one's — on poner el corazón en; see content etc.
(f) (symbol of courage) to be in good — estar lleno de confianza, (soil) estar en buen estado; I could not find it in my — to + infin, I did not have the — to + infin no tuve valor para + infin; to have one's — in one's mouth tener el alma en un hilo; to lose — descorazonarse; to put new — into someone infundir ánimo a uno; my — sank se me cayeron las alas del corazón; to take — cobrar ánimo; we may take — from the fact that que nos aliente el hecho de que.
(g) by — de memoria.

heartache ['hɑːteik] n angustia f, pena f.

heart attack ['hɑːtətæk] n ataque m cardíaco.

heartbeat ['hɑːtbiːt] n latido m del corazón.

heartbreaking ['hɑːt,breikiŋ] adj angustioso, desgarrador; it was — to see them daba lástima verlos.

heartbroken ['hɑːt,brəukən] adj angustiado, acongojado; she was — about it esto le partió el corazón.

heartburn ['hɑːtbəːn] n acedía f.

heartburning ['hɑːt,bəːniŋ] n (bad feeling) envidia f, rencor m; (regret) sentimiento m.

heart complaint ['hɑːtkəm,pleint] n, **heart disease** ['hɑːtdi,ziːz] n enfermedad f cardíaca.

-hearted ['hɑːtid] adj de corazón ...; **faint-hearted** medroso, pusilánime.

hearten ['hɑːtn] vt alentar, infundir ánimo a.

heart failure ['hɑːt,feiljə*] n fallo m de corazón, colapso m cardíaco.

heartfelt ['hɑːtfelt] adj cordial, sincero; sympathy más sentido; thanks más efusivo.

hearth [hɑːθ] n hogar m (also fig), chimenea f.

heartily ['hɑːtili] adv sinceramente, cordialmente; enérgicamente; fuertemente; laugh a carcajadas; eat con buen apetito; thank con efusión; sing con entusiasmo; to be — glad alegrarse sinceramente; to be — sick of estar completamente harto de.

heartless ['hɑːtlis] adj cruel, inhumano.

heartlessly ['hɑːtlisli] adv cruelmente, despiadadamente.

heartlessness ['hɑːtlisnis] n crueldad f, inhumanidad f.

heartrending ['hɑːt,rendiŋ] adj angustioso, desgarrador; it was — to see them daba lástima verlos.

heart-searching ['hɑːt,səːtʃiŋ] n examen m de conciencia.

heartstrings ['hɑːtstrɪŋz] npl fibras fpl del corazón.
heart-throb ['hɑːtθrɔb] n (fam) novio m, novia f.
heart-to-heart ['hɑːttə'hɑːt] adj íntimo.
hearty ['hɑːti] adj person campechano, francote; feelings sincero, cordial; effort enérgico; kick, slap etc fuerte; laugh sano, franco; appetite bueno; meal abundante; thanks efusivo; **to be a — eater** tener buen diente.
heat [hiːt] **1** n **(a)** (warmth) calor m; (heating system) calefacción f; **red — calor** m rojo; **white — candencia** f; **in the — of** the day en las horas de más calor.
　　(b) (fig) calor m, ardor m, vehemencia f, pasión f; **in the — of the moment** en el calor del momento; **he replied with some —** contestó bastante indignado; **to turn on the —** empezar a ejercer presiones, (Pol) crear un ambiente de crisis.
　　(c) (Sport) (prueba f) eliminatoria f, prueba f clasificatoria.
　　(d) (Zool) celo m; **to be on —** estar en celo.
　　2 vt (also **to — up**) calentar; (fig) acalorar.
　　3 vi (also **to — up**) calentarse; (fig) acalorarse.
heated ['hiːtid] adj acalorado; **to become —** acalorarse.
heatedly ['hiːtidli] adv con vehemencia, con pasión; **he replied —** contestó indignado.
heater ['hiːtə*] n calentador m.
heath [hiːθ] n (place) brezal m; (plant) brezo m; native — patria f chica.
heathen ['hiːðən] **1** adj pagano. **2** n pagano m, a f; (fig) bárbaro m, a f.
heathenish ['hiːðəniʃ] adj pagano, gentílico.
heathenism ['hiːðənizəm] n paganismo m.
heather ['heðə*] n brezo m.
heating ['hiːtiŋ] n calefacción f.
heatproof ['hiːtpruːf] adj termorresistente, a prueba de calor.
heatstroke ['hiːtstrəuk] n insolación f.
heatwave ['hiːtweiv] n ola f de calor.
heave [hiːv] **1** n (lift) esfuerzo m para levantar; (pull) tirón m (on de); (push) empujón m; (throw) echada f, tirada f; **with a — of his shoulders** con un fuerte movimiento de hombros; **one more — and they're out** un empujón más y los echamos fuera a todos.
　　2 vt (irr: pret and ptp **heaved**, (Naut) pret and ptp **hove**) (pull) tirar de; (push) empujar; (lift) levantar; (drag) arrastrar; (carry) llevar; (throw) tirar, lanzar; sigh exhalar.
　　3 vi (water etc) subir y bajar, agitarse; (surface) palpitar, ondular; (feel sick) basquear, tener náuseas; **it makes me —** me da asco; **to — at, to — on** tirar de, (Naut) jalar; **to — in(to) sight** aparecer; **to — to** ponerse al pairo.
heave-ho ['hiːv'həu] interj ¡ahora!, (Naut) ¡iza!
heaven ['hevn] n cielo m; **—s** cielos mpl; **(good) —s!** ¡cielos!; **thank —!** ¡gracias a Dios!; **— forbid!** ¡no lo quiera Dios!; **— forbid that I . . .** Dios me libre de + infin; **for —'s sake** ¡por Dios!; **seventh —** (fig) paraíso m; **an injustice that cries out to —** una injusticia que clama al cielo; **to move — and earth** mover cielo y tierra (to + infin para + infin); **to stink to high —** heder a perro muerto.
heavenly ['hevnli] adj celestial; (Astron) celeste; (fig) maravilloso, estupendo.
heaven-sent ['hevn'sent] adj milagroso.
heavenward(s) ['hevnwəd(z)] adv hacia el cielo.
heavily ['hevili] adv fall, move, tread pesadamente; rain fuertemente, mucho; concentrate densamente; sigh, sleep profundamente; drink con exceso; **— underlined** subrayado con línea gruesa; **to lean — on** apoyarse mucho en; **to lose —** (team) sufrir una grave derrota, (gambler) tener pérdidas cuantiosas; **it weighs — on him** pesa mucho sobre él.
heavily-built ['hevili'bilt] adj corpulento.
heaviness ['hevinis] n peso m; pesadez f (also fig); lo fuerte, fuerza f; densidad f; gravedad f; (drowsiness) letargo m, modorra f; **— of heart** tristeza f.
heavy ['hevi] adj **(a)** pesado; **to be —** ser pesado, pesar mucho; **is it —?** ¿pesa mucho?; **how — are you?** ¿cuánto pesas?
　　(b) (fig) artillery, cruiser, fall, industry, tread pesado; cloth, features, line, sea, type grueso; emphasis, expense, meal, rain, scent, shower, wine fuerte; concentration, population, traffic denso; (boring) pesado; atmosphere pesado, opresivo; blow fuerte, duro; build of person corpulento; burden (fig) grave, oneroso; crop abundante; defeat grave; feeling aletargado; fire (Mil) intenso; food indigesto; heart triste; humour laborioso; liquid espeso, viscoso; loss considerable, cuantioso; movement lento, torpe, pesado; part (Theat) serio, trágico; responsibility grave; sigh, silence, sleep profundo; sky encapotado; soil arcilloso; surface difícil; task duro, penoso; eyes

— with sleep ojos de sueño; **the air was — with scent** el aire estaba cargado de perfumes; **I've had a — day** he estado ocupadísimo todo el día; **to be a — drinker** (etc) beber (etc) mucho, beber (etc) con exceso; **to be a — sleeper** tener el sueño profundo.
heavyweight ['heviweit] n peso m pesado.
Hebrew ['hiːbruː] **1** adj hebreo. **2** n hebreo m, a f. **3** n (language) hebreo m.
Hebrides ['hebridiːz] pl Hébridas fpl.
heck [hek] interj (euph) = **hell**.
heckle ['hekl] vti interrumpir, molestar con preguntas.
heckler ['heklə*] n el (la) que interrumpe (or molesta) a un orador.
heckling ['hekliŋ] n interrupciones fpl, gritos mpl de protesta.
hectare ['hektɑː*] n hectárea f.
hectic ['hektik] adj (fig) febril; **we had 3 — days** tuvimos 3 días llenos de frenética actividad, tuvimos 3 días llenos de confusión (or incertidumbre etc); **he has a — life** tiene una vida muy agitada; **the journey was pretty —** el viaje era para volverse loco.
hectogramme, (US) **hectogram** ['hektəugræm] n hectogramo m.
hectolitre, (US) **hectoliter** ['hektəu,liːtə*] n hectolitro m.
hector ['hektə*] **1** vt intimidar con bravatas. **2** vi echar bravatas.
he'd [hiːd] = **he would**; **he had**.
hedge [hedʒ] **1** n seto m vivo.
　　2 vt **(a)** cercar con un seto; **to — off** separar con un seto.
　　(b) (fig) **to — something about, to — something in** rodear algo, encerrar algo; **to be —d about with** estar erizado de.
　　(c) **to — a bet** hacer apuestas compensatorias.
　　3 vi contestar con evasivas, no querer comprometerse a nada.
hedgehog ['hedʒhɔg] n erizo m.
hedgehop ['hedʒhɔp] vi volar a ras de tierra.
hedgerow ['hedʒrəu] n seto m vivo.
hedge sparrow ['hedʒ,spærəu] n acentor m común.
hedonism ['hiːdənizəm] n hedonismo m.
hedonist ['hiːdənist] n hedonista mf.
heed [hiːd] **1** n: **to give (or pay) — to** prestar atención a, hacer caso de; **to take no — of something** no hacer caso de algo, no tener algo en cuenta; **to take — to** + infin poner atención en + infin; **take —!** ¡atención!
　　2 vt prestar atención a, hacer caso de; tener en cuenta.
heedless ['hiːdlis] adj desatento, descuidado; **to be — of** no hacer caso de.
heedlessly ['hiːdlisli] adv sin hacer caso.
heehaw ['hiːhɔː] **1** n rebuzno m. **2** vi rebuznar.
heel[1] [hiːl] **1** n (Anat) talón m, calcañar m; (of shoe) tacón m; (sl) canalla m; **to be at (or on) someone's —s** pisar los talones a uno; **to be down at —** ir mal vestido, estar desaseado; **to be under the — of** estar bajo los talones de; **to bring someone to —** sobreponerse a uno; **to cool one's —s** hacer antesala, tener que esperar; **to kick one's —s** no tener nada que hacer; **to show someone a clean pair of —s**, **to take to one's —s** poner pies en polvorosa; **to turn on one's —** dar media vuelta.
　　2 vt shoe poner tacón a; ball talonear; **to be well —ed** (sl) ser un ricacho.
heel[2] [hiːl] vi: **to — over** ladearse, (Naut) zozobrar, escorar.
heft [heft] **1** n (US fam) influencia f; **the — of** la mayor parte de. **2** vt levantar; sopesar.
hefty ['hefti] adj object pesado; person fuerte, fornido; dose etc grande.
hegemony [hi'gemɒni] n hegemonía f.
hegira [he'dʒaiərə] n hégira f.
he-goat ['hiː'gəut] n macho m cabrío.
heifer ['hefə*] n novilla f, vaquilla f.
heigh [hei] interj ¡oye!, ¡eh!
heigh-ho ['hei'həu] interj ¡ay!
height [hait] n **(a)** altura f, elevación f, altitud f; **— above sea level** altura f sobre el nivel del mar; **at a — of 2000 m** a una altura de 2000 m; **to be 20 m in —** medir 20 m de alto, tener una altura de 20 m; **to gain —** ganar altura.
　　(b) (of person) talle m, estatura f; **of average —** de talle mediano; **he drew himself up to his full —** se irguió; **what — are you?** ¿cuánto mides de alto?
　　(c) (hill) colina f, cerro m; **the —s** las cumbres.
　　(d) (fig) (of fever) crisis f; **the — of absurdity** el colmo de lo absurdo; **it's the — of fashion** está muy de moda; **at the — of summer** en los días más calurosos del verano; **at the — of the battle** en los

momentos más críticos de la batalla; **his performance never reached the** —s su actuación distaba mucho de ser perfecta, su actuación nunca nos emocionó como debiera.

heighten ['haitn] vt (raise) elevar, hacer más alto; (increase) aumentar; (enhance) realzar, intensificar.

heinous ['heinəs] adj atroz, nefando.

heir [ɛə*] n heredero m; — **apparent**, — **at law** heredero m forzoso; **joint** — coheredero m; **universal** — heredero m único; — **to the throne** heredero m del trono; **he is** — **to a fortune** ha de heredar una fortuna.

heiress ['ɛəres] n heredera f; (fam) soltera f adinerada.

heirloom ['ɛəluːm] n reliquia f de familia.

heist [haist] (US sl) **1** n robo m (en casa). **2** vt robar (de una casa).

held [held] pret and ptp of **hold**.

Helen ['helin] f Elena, Helena.

helicopter ['helikɔptə*] n helicóptero m.

heliograph ['hiːliəgrɑːf] n heliógrafo m.

heliotrope ['hiːliətrəup] n heliotropo m.

heliport ['helipɔːt] n helipuerto m.

helium ['hiːliəm] n helio m.

helix ['hiːliks] n, pl **helices** ['helisiːz] hélice f.

hell [hel] n infierno m; **gambling** — garito m; —!, oh —! ¡demonio!; **all** — **was let loose** se desencadenó un ruido infernal; **a** — **of a lot** muchísimos, la mar de, una barbaridad de; **a** — **of a noise** un ruido de todos los demonios; **we had a** — **of a time** (bad) pasamos un rato malísimo, (good) lo pasamos en grande; **who the** — **are you?** ¿quién demonios es Vd?; **what the** — **do you want?** ¿qué demonios quiere Vd?; **like** —! ¡ni hablar!; **to run like** — correr a todo correr; **to work like** — trabajar como un demonio; **come** — **or high water** contra viento y marea; **get the** — **out of here!** ¡vete al diablo!; **let's get the** — **out of here!** ¡vámonos!; **to give someone** — poner a uno como un trapo; **to go** — **for leather** ir como el demonio; **go to** —! ¡vete al diablo!; **to raise** — armar la gorda.

he'll [hiːl] = **he will; he shall**.

hellbent ['hel'bent] adj (a) totalmente resuelto; **to be** — **on doing something** estar totalmente resuelto a hacer algo. (b) rapidísimo, velocísimo.

Hellene ['heliːn] n heleno m, a f.

Hellenic [he'liːnik] adj helénico.

hellfire ['hel'faiə*] n llamas fpl del infierno.

hellish ['heliʃ] **1** adj infernal, diabólico; (fam) horrible. **2** adv (fam) muy, terriblemente.

hello [hʌ'ləu] see **hullo**.

helm [helm] n timón m; **to be at the** — (fig) gobernar, estar en el mando.

helmet ['helmit] n casco m.

helmsman ['helmzmən] n, pl —**men** [mən] timonel m.

help [help] **1** n (a) ayuda f; auxilio m, socorro m; favor m, protección f; —! ¡socorro!; **by** (or **with**) **the** — **of** con la ayuda de; **without** — sin ayuda de nadie; **to call for** — pedir socorro; **to come to someone's** — acudir en auxilio de uno.
(b) **there's no** — **for it** no hay más remedio; **to be past** — estar desahuciado.
(c) (person: servant) criada f; (in shop etc) empleado m; **daily** — asistenta f; **mother's** — niñera f; **she has no** — **in the house** no tiene criada; **we're short of** — **in the shop** nos falta personal en la tienda; **he's a great** — me ayuda muchísimo; **you're a great** —! (iro) ¡valiente ayuda!
2 vt (a) ayudar; (esp in distress) auxiliar, socorrer; scheme etc promover; progress facilitar; pain aliviar; **so** — **me God!** bien lo sabe Dios; **to** — **someone to do something** ayudar a uno a hacer algo; **this will** — **to save it** esto contribuirá a salvarlo; **to** — **along** person ayudar, scheme etc promover, fomentar; **to** — **someone down** ayudar a uno a bajar; **to** — **someone on with a dress** ayudar a uno a ponerse un vestido; **to** — **someone out** ayudar a uno, (of vehicle) ayudar a uno a bajar; **to** — **someone out of a jam** ayudar a uno a salir de un apuro; **to** — **someone up** ayudar a uno a subir.
(b) (at table) servir; **to** — **someone to soup** servir la sopa a uno.
(c) (avoid) **he can't** — **coughing** no puede dejar de toser; **I couldn't** — (doing) **it** no pude menos de hacerlo; **it can't be** —**ed** no hay más remedio; **he won't if I can** — **it** no lo hará si puedo evitarlo; **can I** — **it if it rains?** ¿es que yo puedo impedir que llueva?; **don't spend more than you can** — no gastes más de lo necesario.
3 vi (also **to** — **out**) ayudar.
4 vr: **to** — **oneself** (at table) servirse; — **yourself!**

(to food) ¡sírvete!, (to other things) está a su disposición, tome cuanto quiera; **to** — **oneself to** food servirse, (steal) alzarse con, llevarse, robar.

helper ['helpə*] n ayudante m, asistente m, a f; (coworker) colaborador m, ora f.

helpful ['helpful] adj útil, provechoso; person servicial, atento; **he was very** — **to me** me ayudó mucho; **you have been most** — Vd ha sido muy amable.

helpfully ['helpfəli] adv amablemente.

helpfulness ['helpfulnis] n utilidad f; (of person) amabilidad f.

helping ['helpiŋ] n porción f, ración f; **will you have a second** —? ¿quiere Vd servirse más?

helpless ['helplis] adj (forsaken) desamparado; (destitute) desvalido; (powerless) impotente; (of weak character) débil, incapaz, inútil; creature indefenso; invalid que no puede hacer nada en absoluto; **we were** — **to do anything about it** nos veíamos imposibilitados para remediarlo; **to feel** — sentirse perplejo, estar indeciso.

helplessly ['helplisli] adv struggle en vano; **he said** — dijo indeciso.

helplessness ['helplisnis] n desamparo m; impotencia f; incapacidad f, inutilidad f; irresolución f.

helpmate ['helpmeit] n buen compañero m, buena compañera f; (spouse) esposo m, a f.

help-page ['help'peidʒ] n consultorio m.

helter-skelter ['heltə'skeltə*] **1** adv atropelladamente. **2** n desbandada f general.

hem [hem] **1** n dobladillo m, bastilla f; (edge) orilla f. **2** vt: **to** — **in** encerrar, cercar (also Mil).

he-man ['hiːmæn] n, pl —**men** [men] (fam) machote m.

hemiplegia [hemi'pliːdʒiə] n hemiplejía f.

hemisphere ['hemisfiə*] n hemisferio m.

hemistich ['hemistik] n hemistiquio m.

hemline ['hemlain] n (Sew) bajo m (del vestido).

hemlock ['hemlɔk] n cicuta f.

hemp [hemp] n cáñamo m; **Indian** — hachich m.

hen [hen] n gallina f; (female bird) hembra f.

henbane ['henbein] n beleño m.

hence [hens] adv (a) (place) de aquí, desde aquí; —! ¡fuera de aquí!
(b) (time) desde ahora; **5 years** — de aquí a 5 años.
(c) (therefore) por lo tanto, por eso; — **my letter de aquí que le escribiera;** — **the fact that** de aquí que.

henceforth ['hens'fɔːθ] adv, **henceforward** ['hens'fɔːwəd] adv de hoy en adelante, (of past time) en lo sucesivo.

henchman ['hentʃmən] n, pl —**men** [mən] (follower) secuaz m, partidario m; (guard) guardaespaldas m.

hendecasyllabic ['hendekəsi'læbik] adj endecasílabo.

hendecasyllable ['hendekə.siləbl] n endecasílabo m.

henhouse ['hen'haus] n gallinero m.

henna ['henə] n alheña f.

hen party ['hen.pɑːti] n (fam) tertulia f de mujeres.

henpecked ['henpekt] adj dominado por su mujer.

Henry ['henri] m Enrique.

hep [hep] adj: **to get** — (sl) enfrascarse en los encantos de la música, dejarse dominar por el ritmo de la música.

her [həː*] **1** pron (acc) la; (dat) le; (after prep) ella. **2** poss adj su(s).

herald ['herəld] **1** n heraldo m; (fig) precursor m, anunciador m. **2** vt anunciar, proclamar.

heraldic [he'rældik] adj heráldico.

heraldry ['herəldri] n heráldica f.

herb [həːb] n hierba f.

herbaceous [həː'beifəs] adj herbáceo.

herbage ['həːbidʒ] n herbaje m, vegetación f, plantas fpl.

herbal ['həːbəl] adj herbario.

herbalist ['həːbəlist] n herbolario m, a f.

herbarium [həː'bɛəriəm] n herbario m.

herbivorous [həː'bivərəs] adj herbívoro.

Herculean [.həːkjuːliːən] adj hercúleo.

Hercules ['həːkjuːliːz] m Hércules.

herd [həːd] **1** n rebaño m, hato m, manada f; (of pigs) piara f; (of people etc) multitud f, tropel m; **the common** — el vulgo; — **instinct** instinto m gregario. **2** vt (tend) guardar; (gather) reunir en manada (etc); (move) llevar en manada. **3** vi: **to** — **together** reunirse en manada, (in confusion) apiñarse unos contra otros; (people) reunirse, ir juntos.

herd-book ['həːdbuk] n libro m genealógico.

herdsman ['həːdzmən] n, pl —**men** [mən] (of cattle) vaquero m; (of sheep etc) pastor m.

here [hiə*] adv (place where) aquí; (motion to) acá; —! (at rollcall) ¡presente!, (offering something) ¡toma!, (interj) ¡oye!, ¡eh!; — **and now** ahora

mismo; — **and there** aquí y allá; —, **there and
everywhere** en todas partes; — **below** aquí abajo;
in —, **please** por aquí, por favor; **up to** — hasta
aquí; **my mate** — **will do it** este compañero mío lo
hará; **and** — **he laughed** y en este punto se rió; — **is**,
— **are he** aquí; — **it is** aquí lo tiene Vd; **that's
neither** — **nor there** eso no viene al caso; **spring is**
— ha llegado la primavera; **he's** — **at last** por fin
ha llegado; —**'s to X!** ¡vaya con X!; **come** —! ¡ven
acá!; — **he comes** ya viene; *see* go.
hereabouts ['hiərə,bauts] *adv* por aquí (cerca).
hereafter [hiər'ɑ:ftə*] **1** *adv* en el futuro. **2** *n* futuro
m; **the H**— la otra vida.
hereby ['hiə'bai] *adv* por este medio; (*with reference
to document*) por la presente.
hereditary [hi'reditəri] *adj* hereditario.
heredity [hi'rediti] *n* herencia *f*.
heresy ['herəsi] *n* herejía *f*.
heretic ['herətik] *n* hereje *mf*.
heretical [hi'retikəl] *adj* herético.
hereupon ['hiərə'pɔn] *adv* en seguida.
herewith ['hiə'wið] *adv* junto con esto; **I send
you** — . . . le mando adjunto . . .
heritage ['heritidʒ] *n* herencia *f*; (*fig*) patrimonio *m*.
hermaphrodite [həː'mæfrədait] **1** *adj* hermafrodita.
2 *n* hermafrodita *m*.
hermetic [həː'metik] *adj* hermético.
hermetically [həː'metikəli] *adv* herméticamente.
hermit ['həːmit] *n* ermitaño *m*.
hermitage ['həːmitidʒ] *n* ermita *f*.
hernia ['həːniə] *n* hernia *f*.
hero ['hiərəu] *n*, *pl* **heroes** ['hiərəuz] héroe *m*; (*Lit
etc*) protagonista *m*, personaje *m* principal.
Herod ['herəd] *m* Herodes.
heroic [hi'rəuik] *adj* heroico.
heroically [hi'rəuikəli] *adv* heroicamente.
heroin ['herəuin] *n* heroína *f*.
heroine ['herəuin] *n* heroína *f*; (*Lit etc*) protagonista *f*,
personaje *m* principal.
heroism ['herəuizəm] *n* heroísmo *m*.
heron ['herən] *n* garza *f* real.
hero worship ['hiərəu,wəː.ʃip] *n* culto *m* a los héroes.
herring ['heriŋ] *n* arenque *m*; **red** — pista *f* falsa,
ardid *m* para apartar la atención del asunto
principal.
herringbone ['heriŋbəun] *n*: — **pattern** muestra *f*
espiga; — **stitch** punto *m* de escapulario.
herring-pond ['heriŋpɔnd] *n*: (*hum*) **to cross the** —
cruzar el charco.
hers [həːz] *poss pron* (el) suyo, (la) suya *etc*.
herself [həː'self] *pron* (*subject*) ella misma; (*acc, dat*)
se; (*after prep*) sí (misma); *see* **oneself**.
he's [hiːz] = **he is**; **he has**.
hesitancy ['hezitənsi] *n* = **hesitation**.
hesitant ['hezitənt] *adj* vacilante, irresoluto, indeciso;
I am somewhat — **about accepting it** no me
resuelvo a aceptarlo.
hesitantly ['hezitəntli] *adv* con irresolución; **he said**
— dijo indeciso, dijo perplejo.
hesitate ['heziteit] *vi* vacilar, mostrarse indeciso; (*in
speech*) titubear; **to** — **about, to** — **over** no tomar
una resolución sobre; **he** —**d over his reply** tardó en
dar su respuesta; **to** — **to** + *infin* vacilar en +
infin; **I** — **to condemn him outright** no me puedo
persuadir a condenarlo del todo; **don't** — **to ask me**
no vacile en pedírmelo.
hesitation [,hezi'teiʃən] *n* vacilación *f*, irresolución *f*,
indecisión *f*; **without the slightest** — sin vacilar;
I feel a certain — **about it** tengo algunas dudas
acerca de ello.
het [het] *adj* (*fam*): **to get** — **up** acalorarse, emocionarse (*about, over* por); **don't get so** — **up!** ¡tran-
quilízate!
heterodox ['hetərədɔks] *adj* heterodoxo.
heterodoxy ['hetərədɔksi] *n* heterodoxia *f*.
heterogeneous ['hetərəu'dʒiːniəs] *adj* heterogéneo.
heterosexual ['hetərəu'seksjuəl] **1** *adj* heterosexual.
2 *n* heterosexual *mf*.
heterosexuality ['hetərəu,seksju'æliti] *n* heterosexualidad *f*.
hew [hjuː] *vt* (*irr: pret* **hewed**, *ptp* **hewed** *or* **hewn**)
cortar, tajar; (*shape*) labrar, tallar; **to** — **down**
talar; **to** — **out** excavar; *career* hacerse.
hewn [hjuːn] *ptp of* **hew**.
hex [heks] (*US fam*) **1** *n* bruja *f*. **2** *vt* embrujar.
hexagon ['heksəgən] *n* hexágono *m*.
hexagonal [hek'sægənəl] *adj* hexagonal.
hexameter [hek'sæmitə*] *n* hexámetro *m*.
hey [hei] *interj* ¡oye!, ¡eh!
heyday ['heidei] *n* auge *m*, apogeo *m*, buenos tiempos
mpl; **in the** — **of the theatre** cuando el teatro
estaba en su apogeo.

hi [hai] *interj* ¡oye!, ¡eh!; (*hullo*) ¡hola!
hiatus [hai'eitəs] *n* (*Gram*) hiato *m*; (*fig*) vacío *m*,
laguna *f*, interrupción *f*; solución *f* de continuidad.
hibernate ['haibəneit] *vi* invernar, hibernar.
hibernation [,haibə'neiʃən] *n* invernación *f*, hibernación *f*.
hiccough ['hikʌp], **hiccup** ['hikʌp] **1** *n* hipo *m*;
to have —**s** tener hipo. **2** *vi* hipar; **"yes", he** —**ed**
"sí", dijo hipando.
hick [hik] (*US*) **1** *adj* rústico, de aldea. **2** *n* palurdo *m*.
hickory ['hikəri] *n* nuez *f* dura.
hid [hid] *pret of* **hide**.
hidden ['hidn] **1** *ptp of* **hide**. **2** *adj* escondido; (*fig*)
oculto, secreto.
hide[1] [haid] *n* (*skin*) piel *f*, pellejo *m*; (*tanned*) cuero
m; (*of person*) pellejo *m*.
hide[2] [haid] **1** *n* (*Hunting*) paranza *f*, trepa *f*.
2 *vt* (*irr: pret* **hid**, *ptp* **hidden**) esconder (*from* de);
ocultar (*from* a, de); *feeling etc* ocultar, encubrir,
disimular; **he's hiding something** tiene algo que no
quiere revelar.
3 *vi* esconderse, ocultarse (*from* de); **he's hiding
behind his chief** se está buscando la protección de
su jefe.
hide-and-seek ['haidən'siːk] *n* escondite *m*; **to play**
— **with** jugar al escondite con (*also fig*).
hidebound ['haidbaund] *adj* rígido, aferrado a la
tradición.
hideous ['hidiəs] *adj* horrible.
hideously ['hidiəsli] *adv* horriblemente; — **ugly**
feísimo.
hideout ['haidaut] *n* escondrijo *m*, guarida *f*.
hiding[1] ['haidiŋ] *n* (*beating*) paliza *f*.
hiding[2] ['haidiŋ] *n*: **to be in** — estar escondido; **he is
in** — **in France** se ha refugiado en Francia; **to go
into** — ocultarse, refugiarse.
hiding place ['haidiŋpleis] *n* escondrijo *m*.
hie [hai] (*arch or hum*) **1** *vt* apresurar. **2** *vi* ir, ir con
prisa, correr. **3** *vr*: **to** — **oneself home** apresurarse a
volver a casa.
hierarchic(al) [,haiə'rɑ:kik(əl)] *adj* jerárquico.
hierarchy ['haiərɑ:ki] *n* jerarquía *f*.
hieroglyph ['haiərəglif] *n* jeroglífico *m*.
hieroglyphic [,haiərə'glifik] **1** *adj* jeroglífico. **2** *n*
jeroglífico *m*.
hi-fi ['hai'fai] (*abbr of* **high fidelity**) **1** *adj* de alta
fidelidad. **2** *n* alta fidelidad *f*.
higgledy-piggledy ['higldi'pigldi] (*fam*) **1** *adv* be *etc*
en desorden; **do** *etc* de cualquier modo. **2** *adj*
revuelto, desordenado.
high [hai] **1** *adj* (a) alto; **it's 20 feet** — tiene 20 pies de
alto; **how** — **is that tree?** ¿qué altura tiene ese
árbol?, ¿cuánto mide ese árbol de alto?; **I knew him
when he was so** — le conocí tamañito, le conocí de
niño.
(b) (*fig*) *frequency, tension, temperature, treason,
command etc* alto; *number, speed* grande; *price, rent,
stake* elevado; *official, court* superior; *post* importante; *altar, mass, street* mayor; *priest* sumo; *quality*
superior, bueno; *note* agudo; *sea* tempestuoso; *wind*
recio, fuerte; *explosive* de gran potencia; *colour*
subido; *polish* brillante; (*Cook*) *game* manido; *food*
pasado; — **and dry** en seco; **to leave someone** — **and
dry** dejar a uno plantado; — **and mighty** engreído.
2 *adv* (a) *fly etc* a gran altura; — **above my head**
muy por encima de mi cabeza; **it rose** — **in the air**
se elevó por los aires; **it sailed** — **over the house**
voló por los aires muy por encima de la casa.
(b) **to aim** — picar muy alto; **to blow** — soplar
recio; **the numbers go as** — **as 20** los números llegan
hasta 20; **I had to go as** — **as £8 for it** tuve que
pagar 8 libras nada menos por él; **the bidding went
as** — **as £5** se ofrecieron hasta 5 libras; **it went for as**
— **as £6** se vendió por 6 libras nada menos; **to hunt**
— **and low for someone** buscar a uno por todas
partes; **to run** — (*sea*) embravecerse, (*river*) estar
crecido; (*of feelings*) encenderse, exaltarse; **feelings
were running** — la gente estaba muy acalorada.
3 *n* (*Meteorol*) zona *f* de alta presión; **on** — en las
alturas, en el cielo; **exports have reached a new** —
las exportaciones han alcanzado cifras nunca
conocidas antes.
highborn ['haibɔːn] *adj* linajudo.
highbrow ['haibrau] **1** *adj* intelectual, culto, esotérico. **2** *n* intelectual *mf*, persona *f* culta.
high-class ['hai'klɑːs] *adj* de clase superior.
higher ['haiə*] **1** *adj comp of* **high**: más alto; *form,
study etc* superior; *price* más elevado; *number, speed*
mayor; **any number** — **than 6** cualquier número
superior a 6.
2 *adv comp of* **high**; **to fly** — **than the clouds** volar

encima de las nubes; **to fly — still** volar a mayor altura aun; **— up the hill** más arriba en la colina; **— up the road** más hacia el final de la calle.

highfalutin(g) ['haifə'luːtin] *adj* presuntuoso, pomposo.

high-flown ['haifləun] *adj* exagerado, altisonante.

high-grade ['hai'greid] *adj* de calidad superior.

high-handed ['hai'hændid] *adj* arbitrario, despótico.

high-hat ['hai'hæt] *adj (fam)* encopetado, esnob.

high-heeled ['hai'hiːld] *adj shoes* de tacones altos.

highjack ['haidʒæk] *(fam)* atracar.

high jump ['haidʒʌmp] *n* salto *m* de altura.

highlander ['hailəndə*] *n* montañés *m*, esa *f*.

highlands ['hailəndz] *npl* tierras *fpl* altas, montañas *fpl*; **the H—** las tierras altas de Escocia.

high-level ['hai'levl] *adj* de alto nivel.

highlight ['hailait] **1** *n (Art)* toque *m* de luz; *(fig)* aspecto *m* notable, aspecto *m* interesante; momento *m* culminante. **2** *vt* subrayar, destacar.

highly ['haili] *adv* **(a)** muy, muy bien, sumamente; **— amusing** divertidísimo; **— coloured** *(fig)* exagerado; **— paid** muy bien pagado, muy bien retribuido; **— placed official** oficial *m* de categoría, funcionario *m* importante; **— seasoned** muy picante; **— strung** muy excitable, hipertenso.
(b) to praise someone — alabar mucho a uno; **to speak — of** decir mil bienes de; **to think — of** someone tener en mucho a uno.

high-minded ['hai'maindid] *adj person* de nobles pensamientos; *act* noble, altruista.

highness ['hainis] *n* altura *f*; **H—** *(as title)* Alteza *f*; **His (or Her) Royal H—** Su Alteza Real.

high-pitched ['hai'pitʃt] *adj* de tono alto, agudo; *voice* aflautado.

high-powered ['hai'pauəd] *adj* de gran potencia; *person* enérgico, dinámico.

high-pressure ['hai'preʃə*] *adj* de alta presión; *(fig)* enérgico, dinámico, apremiante.

high-ranking ['hai'ræŋkiŋ] *adj* de categoría; *official* de alto grado, *(Mil)* de alta graduación.

highroad ['hairəud] *n* carretera *f*; *(fig)* camino *m* real *(to* de).

high-sounding ['hai'saundiŋ] *adj* altisonante.

high-speed ['hai'spiːd] *adj vehicle etc* de alta velocidad; *test etc* rápido.

high-spirited ['hai'spiritid] *adj* brioso, animoso; *horse* fogoso; *(merry)* alegre.

high-tension ['hai'tenʃən] *adj* de alta tensión.

high-test ['hai'test] *adj*: **— fuel** supercarburante *m*.

high-up ['hai'ʌp] *(fam)* **1** *adj* de categoría, importante. **2** *n* oficial *m* importante, pez *m* gordo.

highway ['haiwei] *n* carretera *f*.

highwayman ['haiweimən] *n, pl* **-men** [mən] salteador *m* de caminos.

hijack ['haidʒæk] *vt (US fam)* = **highjack**.

hike [haik] **1** *n* caminata *f*, excursión *f* a pie; **to go on a —** dar una caminata.
2 *vt*: **to — it** ir a pie.
3 *vi* dar una caminata, ir de excursión (a pie); ir a pie, ir andando.

hiker ['haikə*] *n* excursionista *mf*.

hiking ['haikiŋ] *n* excursionismo *m* a pie.

hilarious [hi'lɛəriəs] *adj scene etc* divertido, regocijante; *laughter* alegre.

hilarity [hi'læriti] *n* regocijo *m*, alegría *f*; **it caused — in the audience** provocó las carcajadas del público.

hill [hil] *n* colina *f*, cerro *m*, otero *m*; *(high)* montaña *f*; *(slope)* cuesta *f*; **to chase someone up — and down dale** perseguir a uno por todas partes; **to curse someone up — and down dale** echar mil pestes de uno; **to take to the —** echarse al monte.

hillbilly ['hil'bili] *n (US)* rústico *m* montañés.

hillock ['hilək] *n* montículo *m*, altozano *m*.

hillside ['hilsaid] *n* ladera *f*.

hilltop ['hiltɔp] *n* cumbre *f*.

hilly ['hili] *adj* montañoso, accidentado; *road* de fuertes pendientes.

hilt [hilt] *n* puño *m*, empuñadura *f*; **up to the —** hasta las cachas; **to back someone up to the —** apoyar a uno incondicionalmente; **to prove something up to the —** probar algo completamente, demostrar algo hasta la saciedad.

him [him] *pron (acc)* le, lo; *(dat)* le; *(after prep)* él.

Himalayas [.himə'leiəz] *pl* los montes Himalaya, el Himalaya.

himself [him'self] *pron (subject)* él mismo; *(acc, dat)* se; *(after prep)* sí (mismo); *see* **oneself**.

hind¹ [haind] *n* cierva *f*.

hind² [haind] *adj* trasero, posterior.

hinder ['hində*] *vt person* estorbar, impedir; *progress etc* estorbar, dificultar; *trade, traffic* entorpecer; **to**

— someone from doing something impedir a uno hacer algo.

hindmost ['haindməust] *adj* postrero, último.

hindrance ['hindrəns] *n* estorbo *m*, obstáculo *m* *(to* para).

Hindu ['hin'duː] **1** *adj* hindú. **2** *n* hindú *mf*.

Hindustan [.hindu'staːn] Indostán *m*.

Hindustani [.hindu'staːni] *n (language)* indostánico *m*, indostaní *m*.

hinge [hindʒ] **1** *n* gozne *m*, bisagra *f*; charnela *f* *(also Zool)*; *(for stamps)* fijasello *m*; *(fig)* eje *m*.
2 *vt* engoznar.
3 *vi* moverse sobre goznes; **to — on** moverse sobre, girar sobre; *(fig)* depender de.

hinged [hindʒd] *adj* con goznes, de bisagra.

hint [hint] **1** *n* **(a)** *(suggestion)* indirecta *f*, indicación *f*, insinuación *f*; *(advice)* consejo *m*; **broad —** indicación *f* inconfundible; **—s for purchasers** aviso *m* a los compradores; **—s on maintenance** instrucciones *fpl* para la manutención; **to drop** *(or* **let fall, throw out)** **a —** soltar una indirecta; **to drop a — that** insinuar que; **take a — from me** permite que te dé un consejo; **to take the —** aprovechar la indicación.
(b) *(trace)* señal *f*, indicio *m*; **without the least — of** sin la menor señal de; **with just a — of garlic** con un ligerísimo sabor a ajo; **with a — of irony** con un dejo de ironía.
2 *vt*: **to — that** insinuar que.
3 *vi* soltar indirectas; **to — at** hacer alusión a; **what are you —ing (at)?** ¿qué pretende Vd insinuar?

hinterland ['hintəlænd] *n* interior *m*, traspaís *m*.

hip¹ [hip] *n (Anat)* cadera *f*.

hip² [hip] *n (Bot)* escaramujo *m*.

hip³ [hip] *interj*: **— — hurray!** ¡viva!

hipped¹ [hipt] *adj (Archit)* a cuatro aguas.

hipped² [hipt] *adj (US: fam)* triste; enojado, resentido; **— on** obsesionado por.

hippie ['hipi] *n (fam)* hippie *mf*.

hippo ['hipəu] *n (fam)* hipopótamo *m*.

Hippocrates [hi'pɔkrətiːz] *m* Hipócrates.

hippopotamus [.hipə'pɔtəməs] *n, pl* **hippopotamuses** [.hipə'pɔtəməsiz] *or* **hippopotami** [.hipə'pɔtəmai] hipopótamo *m*.

hire ['haiə*] **1** *n* alquiler *m*; *(of person)* salario *m*, jornal *m*; **"for —"** "se alquila"; **to be on —** estar de alquiler.
2 *vt (also to — out)* alquilar; *person* contratar, emplear.

hireling ['haiəliŋ] *n* mercenario *m*.

hire purchase ['haiə'pəːtʃis] *n* compra *f* a plazos.

hirsute ['həːsjuːt] *adj* hirsuto.

his [hiz] **1** *poss adj* su(s). **2** *poss pron* (el) suyo, (la) suya *etc*.

Hispanic [his'pænik] *adj* hispánico.

hispanicism [his'pænisizəm] *n* hispanismo *m*.

hispanicize [his'pænisaiz] *vt* españolizar, hispanizar.

hispanist ['hispənist] *n* hispanista *mf*.

hispanophile [his'pænəufail] *n* hispanófilo *m*, a *f*.

hispanophobe [his'pænəufəub] *n* hispanófobo *m*, a *f*.

hiss [his] **1** *n* silbido *m*, siseo *m*; *(of protest)* silbido *m*.
2 *vt* silbar; **to — an actor off the stage** abuchear a un actor hasta que abandone la escena.
3 *vi* silbar, sisear; *(in protest)* silbar.

histology [his'tɔlədʒi] *n* histología *f*.

historian [his'tɔːriən] *n* historiador *m*, ora *f*.

historic(al) [his'tɔrik(əl)] *adj* histórico.

historiography [.histɔri'ɔgrəfi] *n* historiografía *f*.

history ['histəri] *n* historia *f*; **natural —** historia *f* natural; **that's ancient —** ésa es cosa vieja; **to go down in —** pasar a la historia *(as* como); **to know the inner — of an affair** conocer el secreto de un asunto.

histrionic [.histri'ɔnik] *adj* histriónico; *person* exagerado.

histrionics [.histri'ɔniks] *npl* histrionismo *m*.

hit [hit] **1** *n* **(a)** *(blow)* golpe *m*; *(shot)* tiro *m* certero; *(with shell etc)* impacto *m*; *(good guess)* acierto *m*; **direct —** impacto *m* directo; **we made 3 —s on the target** dimos 3 veces en el blanco; **that's a — at you** lo dijo por ti; **he made a — at the government** hizo un ataque contra el gobierno.
(b) *(Mus, Theat etc)* éxito *m*, sensación *f*; **to be a —** obtener un éxito, ser un triunfo; **the song was a big —** la canción se hizo popularísima; **to make a — with someone** caer en gracia a uno.
2 *attr (fam)* sensacional; **— songs of the twenties** las canciones más populares de los años veinte.
3 *(irr: pret and ptp* **hit**) *vt* **(a)** *(strike)* *person* golpear, pegar; *(wound)* herir; *target* alcanzar, hacer blanco en, acertar, dar en; **to — someone a blow** dar

un golpe a uno; **to — one's head against a wall** dar con la cabeza contra una pared; **the president was — by 3 bullets** el presidente fue alcanzado por 3 balas; **the house was — by a bomb** la casa fue blanco de una bomba; **I realized my plane had been —** me di cuenta de que mi avión había sido tocado; **his father used to — him** su padre le pegaba; **then it — me** (of realization) aquello fue el flechazo; en seguida me di cuenta.
(b) (collide with) chocar con, dar contra.
(c) (damage) hacer daño a, afectar; **the crops were — by the rain** las lluvias dañaron los cultivos; **the news — him hard** la noticia le afectó mucho; **the company has been hard —** la compañía ha sido afectada de mala manera, la compañía ha sufrido un rudo golpe.
(d) (find, reach) llegar a, alcanzar; problem tropezar con; **when we — the main road** cuando lleguemos a la carretera.
(e) **to — off** (imitate) imitar, remedar; resemblance coger; (describe) describir con gran acierto; **to — it off with someone** hacer buenas migas con uno; **they don't — it off** no se llevan bien.
4 vi (collide) chocar; **to — against** chocar con, dar contra; **to — at** asestar un golpe a, (fig) atacar, apuntar a, satirizar; **to — back** devolver golpe por golpe, defenderse; **to — on** dar con, tropezar con; **I — on the idea** se me ocurrió la idea; **to — out** lanzar un ataque, (wildly) repartir golpes; **to — out at someone** asestar un golpe a uno, (fig) atacar a uno; **to do something — or miss** hacer algo a la buena de Dios; **to — and run** atacar y retirarse.
hit-and-run ['hitən'rʌn] adj: **— driver** conductor m que atropella y huye.
hitch [hitʃ] **1** n (tug) tirón m; (knot) cote m, vuelta f de cabo; (fig) obstáculo m, dificultad f; **without a —** a pedir de boca; **there was a — of 15 minutes** hubo un retraso de 15 minutos; **there's been a — ha** surgido una dificultad.
2 vt (a) (shift) mover de un tirón; **he —ed a chair over** acercó una silla a tirones; **to — up** alzar.
(b) (fasten) atar, amarrar (to a); **to — a horse to a wagon** enganchar un caballo a un carro.
(c) **to — lifts** hacer autostop; **to — a lift to Rome** lograr que un automovilista le lleve a uno a Roma.
(d) **to get —ed** (sl) casarse.
hitch-hike ['hitʃhaik] vi hacer autostop.
hitch-hiker ['hitʃhaikə*] n autostopista mf.
hitch-hiking ['hitʃhaikiŋ] n autostop m.
hither ['hiðə*] adv (lit) acá; **— and thither** acá y acullá.
hitherto ['hiðə'tu:] adv hasta ahora.
Hittite ['hitait] **1** adj heteo, hitita. **2** n heteo m, a f, hitita mf. **3** n (language) hitita m.
hive [haiv] n colmena f; **a — of industry** un centro de industria, un lugar donde se trabaja muchísimo.
hoard [hɔ:d] **1** n acumulación f; provisión f; (money) tesoro m escondido.
2 vt (also **to — up**) acumular, amontonar (en secreto); money atesorar; goods in short supply retener, acaparar.
hoarding[1] ['hɔ:diŋ] n (act) acumulación f, retención f; acaparamiento m.
hoarding[2] ['hɔ:diŋ] n (fence) valla f de construcción; (for posters) cartelera f.
hoarfrost ['hɔ:'frɔst] n escarcha f.
hoarse [hɔ:s] adj ronco; **to be —** tener la voz ronca; **to shout oneself —** enronquecer a fuerza de gritar.
hoarsely ['hɔ:sli] adv en voz ronca.
hoarseness ['hɔ:snis] n (Med) ronquera f; (hoarse quality) ronquedad f.
hoary ['hɔ:ri] adj cano; joke etc viejo.
hoax [həuks] **1** n trampa f, truco m, mistificación f. **2** vt engañar, burlar, mistificar.
hobble ['hɔbl] **1** n (lameness) cojera f; (rope) maniota f; **to walk with a —** cojear.
2 vt horse manear.
3 vi (also **to — along**) cojear, andar cojeando; **to — to the door** ir cojeando a la puerta.
hobbledehoy ['hɔbldi'hɔi] n gamberro m.
hobby ['hɔbi] n pasatiempo m, afición f; **it's just a —** es sólo un pasatiempo; **he began to paint as a —** empezó a pintar como distracción.
hobby-horse ['hɔbihɔːs] n caballito m (de niño), caballo m mecedor; (fig) caballo m de batalla, tema f; **he's riding his — again** ha vuelto a la misma canción.
hobgoblin ['hɔb,gɔblin] n duende m, trasgo m.
hobnail ['hɔbneil] n clavo m (de botas).
hobnailed ['hɔbneild] adj boots con clavos, claveteado.

hobnob ['hɔbnɔb] vi tratarse con familiaridad; **to — with** codearse con, alternar con.
hobo ['həubəu] n (US) vagabundo m.
hock[1] [hɔk] n (Anat) corvejón m.
hock[2] [hɔk] n (wine) vino m del Rin.
hock[3] [hɔk] vt (fam) empeñar.
hockey ['hɔki] n hockey m.
hocus-pocus ['həukəs'pəukəs] n (jugglery) abracadabra m, pasapasa m; (deception) trampa f.
hod [hɔd] n cuezo m, capacho m.
hodgepodge ['hɔdʒpɔdʒ] n = **hotchpotch**.
hoe [həu] **1** n azada f, azadón m, sacho m. **2** vt earth azadonar; crop sachar.
hog [hɔg] **1** n cerdo m, puerco m (also fig); **to go the whole —** liarse la manta a la cabeza, poner toda la carne en el asador.
2 vt food devorar; (take for oneself) acaparar, tragarse lo mejor de; **to — all the credit** atribuirse todo el mérito de algo.
Hogmanay ['hɔgmənei] n (Scot) noche f vieja.
hogshead ['hɔgzhed] n medida de capacidad (= 52,5 galones = (approx) 225 litros).
hoist [hɔist] **1** n (lift) montacargas m; (crane) grúa f; **to give someone a — (up)** ayudar a uno a subir.
2 vt alzar, levantar (also **to — up**); flag enarbolar, (Naut) izar.
hoity-toity ['hɔiti'tɔiti] **1** adj presumido, repipi. **2** interj ¡tate!
hold [həuld] **1** n (a) (grasp) agarro m, asimiento m; (Wrestling) presa f; **to catch** (or **get, lay, seize, take) — of** agarrar, asirse de, coger; **catch —!** ¡toma!; **to get — of** (fig) (take over) adquirir, apoderarse de, (obtain) procurarse, conseguir; **where did you get — of that?** ¿dónde adquirió Vd eso?; **we're trying to get — of him** tratamos de ponernos en contacto con él; **where did you get — of that idea?** ¿de dónde colige Vd eso?; **you get — of some odd ideas** te formas unas ideas muy raras; **to have — of** estar agarrado a; **to keep — of** seguir agarrado a; (fig) guardar para sí; **to relax one's —** desasirse (on de).
(b) (place to grip) asidero m.
(c) (fig) influencia f, dominio m (over sobre); arraigo m; **to gain a firm — over someone** llegar a dominar a uno; **to have a — (thing)** estar arraigado (over en); **to have a — over (person)** dominar a uno, ejercer gran influencia sobre uno.
(d) (Naut) bodega f.
2 (irr: pret and ptp **held**) vt (a) (general sense) tener; (take — of) agarrar, coger; (bear weight of) soportar; attention mantener; belief tener; note sostener; road agarrarse a; **— him or he'll fall** sosténgale que va a caer; **he held my arm** me tuvo por el brazo; **— this for a moment** coge esto un momento; **to — something tight** agarrar algo fuertemente; **to — someone tight** abrazar a uno estrechamente; **to — something in place** sujetar algo en un lugar; **to — someone to his promise** hacer que uno cumpla su promesa; **he —s the key to the mystery** él tiene la clave del misterio; **he held us spellbound** nos tuvo embelesados; **can he — an audience?** ¿sabe mantener el interés de un público? see **hand** etc.
(b) (keep back) retener, guardar; **I will — the money for you** guardaré el dinero para ti; **the police held him for 3 days** le detuvo la policía durante 3 días; **we are —ing it pending inquiries** lo guardamos mientras se hagan indagaciones.
(c) (check, restrain) enemy, breath contener; **— it!** ¡para!; **— everything!** ¡que se pare todo!; **there was no —ing him** no había manera de detenerle.
(d) (possess) post, town, lands ocupar; shares, title tener; reserves tener en reserva, tener guardado; record ostentar, estar en posesión de.
(e) (contain) contener, tener capacidad (or cabida) para; **this —s the money** esto contiene el dinero; **this bag won't — them** all en este saco no caben todos; **a car that —s 6** un coche de 6 plazas; **what the future —s for us** lo que el futuro guarda para nosotros.
(f) interview, meeting, election celebrar; conversation tener, (formally) celebrar; **the meeting will be held on Monday** la reunión se celebrará el lunes, la reunión tendrá lugar el lunes.
(g) (consider) **to — that** creer que, sostener que; **I — that** tengo para mí que; **it is held by some that** hay quien cree que; **to — something to be true** creer que algo es verdad; **to — someone guilty** juzgar a uno culpable; **to — someone responsible** hacer a uno responsable (for de); **to — someone in respect** tener respeto a uno; **to — someone dear** tener cariño a uno.
(h) **to — back** (keep) guardar, retener; water etc retener; progress detener, refrenar; **to — down**

sujetar; *populace* oprimir; **to — down a job** (*retain*) mantenerse en su puesto, (*be equal to*) estar a la altura de su cargo; **you can't — a good man down** los realmente buenos triunfan a la larga; **to — in** contener; **to — off** *attack, enemy* rechazar; *threat* apartar; *person* defenderse contra; **to — out** *hand* tender, alargar; *arm* extender; *object* ofrecer, alargar; *possibility* ofrecer; *hope* dar; **to — over** aplazar; **to — together** *group, company* mantener la unidad de, 2 *persons* mantener unidos; **to — up** (*support*) apoyar, sostener; (*display*) mostrar, enseñar; (*delay*) atrasar; (*stop*) detener, parar; *work* interrumpir, suspender; *delivery, payments* suspender; (*rob*) atracar, asaltar; **to — something up to the light** acercar algo a la luz; **to — something up as a model** presentar algo como un modelo; **we were held up for 3 hours** no nos pudimos mover durante 3 horas; **the train was held up by fog** el tren viene con retraso debido a la niebla; **we are held up for** (*or* **by lack of**) **bricks** la escasez de ladrillos afecta el ritmo de las obras.

3 *vi* (**a**) (*stick*) pegarse; (*not give way*) mantenerse firme, resistir; (*weather*) continuar, seguir bueno.

(**b**) (*be true*) valer, ser valedero; **the objection does not** — la objeción no vale.

(**c**) **to — back** refrenarse, (*in doubt*) vacilar; **to — forth** hablar largamente (*about, on* de); **to — off** mantenerse a distancia; (*wait*) esperar; **if the rain —s off** si no llueve; **to — on** (*grip*) agarrarse bien; (*not give way*) aguantar, defenderse, resistir; **— on!** (*wait*) ¡tente!, ¡espera!, (*Tel*) ¡no cuelgue Vd!; (*giving encouragement*) ¡ánimo!; **can you — on?** ¿te animas a continuar?; **to — on to** (*clutch*) agarrarse a; (*keep back*) guardar, quedarse con; *post* retener; **to — out** resistir; **to — out for something** no cejar hasta que se conceda algo, insistir en algo; **to — to** atenerse a; **to — together** mantenerse unidos; **to — up** (*weather*) seguir bueno; **to — up under the strain** soportar bien la presión; **to — with** estar de acuerdo con, aprobar.

4 *vr*: **to — oneself back** contenerse, refrenarse; **to — oneself ready** (*or* **in readiness**) estar listo (*for* para); **to — oneself upright** mantenerse erguido.
holdall ['həʊldɔːl] *n* funda *f*, neceser *m*.
holder ['həʊldə*] *n* (**a**) (*person*) tenedor *m*, ora *f*, poseedor *m*, ora *f*; (*of property*) inquilino *m*, a *f*, arrendatario *m*, a *f*; (*of bonds*) tenedor *m*; (*of title, office, passport*) titular *m*; (*of record*) poseedor *m*, ora *f*, detentor *m*.

(**b**) (*support*) soporte *m*; (*handle*) asidero *m*; (*haft*) mango *m*; (*vessel*) receptáculo *m*; (*in compounds*) porta . . ., eg **lamp-holder** portalámparas *m*.
holding ['həʊldɪŋ] *n* (*act*) tenencia *f*; (*thing*) posesión *f*, propiedad *f*; **—s** (*Comm*) valores *mpl* en cartera.
holdup ['həʊldʌp] *n* (**a**) (*robbery*) atraco *m*; **— man** atracador *m*. (**b**) (*stoppage*) parada *f*, interrupción *f*, suspensión *f*; (*of traffic*) embotellamiento *m*.
hole [həʊl] 1 *n* (**a**) agujero *m*; (*in ground, also Golf*) hoyo *m*; (*hollow*) cavidad *f*, hueco *m*; (*in road*) bache *m*; (*in wall*) boquete *m*; (*in defences, dam*) brecha *f*; (*burrow*) madriguera *f*; (*in clothes*) roto *m*; **through a — in the clouds** a través de un agujero de las nubes; **to bore** (*or* **make**) **a — in** practicar un agujero en; **this will make a — in my salary** esto ha de agotar gran parte de mi sueldo; **to pick —s in** encontrar defectos en.

(**b**) (*fig: jam*) apuro *m*, aprieto *m*; **to be in a —** estar en un aprieto; **to get someone out of a —** sacar a uno de un aprieto.

(**c**) (*fig: room*) cuchitril *m*; (*town*) pueblo *m* muerto, pueblo *m* sin ambiente.

2 *vt* agujerear; *ball* meter en el hoyo.

3 *vi*: **to — out** (*Golf*) meter la pelota en el hoyo; **to — out in 5** terminar en 5 golpes.
hole-and-corner ['həʊlən'kɔːnə*] *adj* furtivo.
holey ['həʊli] *adj* (*fam*) lleno de rotos.
holiday ['hɔlɪdi] 1 *n* (*day*) día *m* de fiesta, día *m* festivo; (*period*) vacaciones *fpl*; **—s with pay** vacaciones *fpl* retribuidas; **tomorrow is a —** mañana es fiesta; **to be on** (*one's*) **—** estar de vacaciones; **to declare a day a —** declarar festivo un día; **to take a —** tomarse unas vacaciones.

2 *attr town* de veraneo; *mood etc* alegre, festivo; *season* de vacaciones.

3 *vi* pasar las vacaciones, (*esp*) veranear.
holiday-maker ['hɔlɪdɪˌmeɪkə*] *n* veraneante *mf*, excursionista *mf*, turista *mf*.
holiness ['həʊlinis] *n* santidad *f*; **His H—** Su Santidad.
Holland ['hɔlənd] Holanda *f*.
holler ['hɔlə*] *vti* gritar, vocear.
hollow ['hɔləʊ] 1 *adj* hueco, ahuecado; *eyes* hundido;

sound sordo; *voice* sepulcral, cavernoso; *laughter* irónico; *doctrine etc* vacío, falso; *victory* más aparente que real.

2 *adv*: **to beat someone —** cascar a uno, vencer a uno fácilmente.

3 *n* hueco *m*; concavidad *f*; (*in ground*) hoyo *m*, depresión *f*; (*small valley*) hondonada *f*; **in the — of one's back** en los riñones.

4 *vt* (*also* **to — out**) ahuecar, excavar, vaciar.
hollow-eyed ['hɔləʊ'aid] *adj* de ojos hundidos; (*with fatigue etc*) ojeroso.
holly ['hɔli] *n* acebo *m* (*also* **— tree**).
hollyhock ['hɔlihɔk] *n* malva *f* loca.
holm oak ['həʊm'əʊk] *n* encina *f*.
holocaust ['hɔləkɔːst] *n* (*fig*) incendio *m*, destrucción *f* (causada por un incendio).
holograph ['hɔləgrɑːf] 1 *adj* ológrafo. 2 *n* ológrafo *m*.
holster ['həʊlstə*] *n* pistolera *f*.
holy ['həʊli] *adj* santo; sagrado; *water etc* bendito.
Holy Land ['həʊlilænd] Tierra *f* Santa.
Holy See ['həʊli'siː] *n* Santa Sede *f*.
homage ['hɔmidʒ] *n* homenaje *m*; **to do** (*or* **pay**) **—** to rendir homenaje a.
home [həʊm] 1 *n* casa *f*; (*more officially*) domicilio *m*; (*more sentimentally*) hogar *m*; (*town*) ciudad *f* natal, (*region, native land*) patria *f*; (*Bio*) habitat *m*, (*environment*) ambiente *m* natural; (*Sport*) meta *f*; (*in children's games*) la madre; (*institution*) asilo *m*; **— for the aged** asilo *m* de ancianos; **mental —** manicomio *m*; **Jewish National H—** hogar *m* nacional judío; **we live in Madrid but my — is in Jaén** vivimos en Madrid pero nací en Jaén; **for some years he made his — in France** durante algunos años vivió en Francia; **refugees who made their — in Britain** los refugiados que se establecieron en Gran Bretaña; **Scotland is the — of the haggis** Escocia es la patria del haggis; **at — en casa**; **at — and abroad** dentro y fuera del país; **is Mr X at —?** ¿está (en casa) el Sr X?; **he is at — on any topic** puede hablar sobre cualquier materia; **to feel at —** sentirse como en su casa, estar a sus anchas; **make yourself at —!** ¡estás en tu casa!; **there's no place like —** no hay lugar como la propia casa; **that remark came near —** esa observación le hirió en lo vivo; **to have a — of one's own** tener casa propia; **to give someone a —** recibir a uno como si fuera de la familia, (*fig*) adoptar a uno, recibir a uno; **to leave —** salir de su casa.

2 *attr* (**a**) casero, doméstico, de casa; de familia; **my — address** las señas de mi casa; **— cooking** cocina *f* casera; **— journey** viaje *m* a casa, viaje *m* de vuelta; **— life** vida *f* doméstica, vida *f* de familia.

(**b**) **the — side** el equipo de casa, el equipo local.

(**c**) **the — straight** la recta de llegada; **we're on the — stretch** ésta es la última etapa del viaje.

(**d**) **natal; — area** región *f* natal; **— town** ciudad *f* natal; **— port** puerto *m* de origen.

(**e**) *defence, industry, product* nacional; *population* metropolitano; *news* del país, doméstico; *trade* interior; **H— Office** Ministerio *m* del Interior, (*Spain*) Ministerio *m* de la Gobernación; **H— Secretary** Ministro *m* del Interior, (*Spain*) Ministro *m* de la Gobernación; *see* **rule** *etc*.

3 *adv* (**a**) **to be —** estar en casa, (*return*) estar de vuelta; **to come —** volver a casa, (*from abroad*) volver a la patria; **to get —** llegar a casa; **to go —** ir a casa, (*from abroad*) volver a la patria; **to stay —** quedarse en casa.

(**b**) (*fig*) **to bring something — to someone** hacer que uno se dé cuenta cabal de algo; **it came — to me** me di cuenta cabal de ello, me llegó al alma; **to screw** (*etc*) **something —** atornillar (*etc*) algo a fondo; **to strike —** (*shell etc*) hacer blanco, dar en el blanco, (*on person*) herir en lo vivo.

4 *vi* volver a casa; (*animal*) buscar la querencia; **to — on the target** buscar al blanco.
home-baked ['həʊm'beikt] *adj* hecho en casa.
home-brewed ['həʊm'bruːd] *adj* hecho en casa.
homecoming ['həʊmkʌmiŋ] *n* regreso *m* al hogar.
home-grown ['həʊm'grəʊn] *adj* de cosecha propia.
homeland ['həʊmlænd] *n* tierra *f* natal, patria *f*.
homeless ['həʊmlis] *adj* sin casa ni hogar; **the storm left a hundred —** la tormenta dejó sin hogar a cien personas.
homely ['həʊmli] *adj* casero, doméstico, familiar; (*unpretentious*) llano, sencillo; (*US*) feo.
home-made ['həʊm'meid] *adj* casero, de fabricación casera.
Homer ['həʊmə*] *m* Homero.
Homeric [həʊ'merik] *adj* homérico.
home run ['həʊm'rʌn] *n* (*US: Baseball*) carrera *f* completa, jonrón *m* (*SAm*).

homesick ['həumsik] *adj* nostálgico; **to be —** tener morriña.
homesickness ['həumsiknis] *n* nostalgia *f*, morriña *f*.
homespun ['həumspʌn] *adj* tejido en casa, hecho en casa; (*fig*) llano.
homestead ['həumsted] *n* casa *f*, caserío *m*; (*farm*) granja *f*.
homeward(s) ['həumwəd(z)] *adv* hacia casa; (*from abroad*) hacia la patria; **— bound** (*Naut*) con rumbo al puerto de origen.
homework ['həumwə:k] *n* deberes *mpl*, ejercicios *mpl* para casa.
homicidal [,həmi'saidl] *adj* homicida.
homicide ['həmisaid] *n* (*act*) homicidio *m*; (*person*) homicida *mf*.
homily ['həmili] *n* homilía *f*; (*fig*) sermón *m*.
homoeopath, (*US*) **homeo—** ['həumiəupæθ] *n* homeópata *m*.
homoeopathy, (*US*) **homeo—** [,həumi'əpəθi] *n* homeopatía *f*.
homogeneity [,həməudʒe'ni:iti] *n* homogeneidad *f*.
homogeneous [,həmə'dʒi:niəs] *adj* homogéneo.
homograph ['həməugra:f] *n* homógrafo *m*.
homonym ['həmənim] *n* homónimo *m*.
homosexual ['həməu'seksjuəl] 1 *adj* homosexual. 2 *n* homosexual *mf*.
homosexuality ['həməuseksju'æliti] *n* homosexualidad *f*.
Honduran [hən'djuərən] 1 *adj* hondureño. 2 *n* hondureño *m*, a *f*.
Honduras [hən'djuərəs] Honduras *f*.
hone [həun] 1 *n* piedra *f* de afilar. 2 *vt* afilar.
honest ['ənist] *adj* (*upright*) honrado, recto; (*speaking openly*) franco, sincero; **by — means** por medios legales; **the — truth** is la pura verdad es; **what is your — opinion?** ¿qué piensa Vd francamente de esto?; **be —!** ¡diga la verdad!; **you were not entirely — with me** Vd no me dijo honradamente toda la verdad.
honestly ['ənistli] *adv* honradamente; francamente; **I don't — know**, **— I don't know** francamente no lo sé; **—?** ¿de veras?
honesty ['ənisti] *n* honradez *f*, rectitud *f*; franqueza *f*; **in all —** con toda franqueza.
honey ['hʌni] *n* miel *f*; **yes, —** (*US*) sí, querida; **hullo —!** (*US*) ¡oye, guapa!; **she's a —** (*US*) es un encanto.
honey-bee ['hʌnibi:] *n* abeja *f* (obrera).
honeycomb ['hʌnikoum] 1 *n* panal *m*. 2 *vt*: **the building is —ed with passages** hay un sinfín de pasillos en el edificio; **the hill is —ed with galleries** una multitud de galerías penetran por la colina.
honeyed ['hʌnid] *adj* meloso, melifluo.
honeymoon ['hʌnimu:n] 1 *n* luna *f* de miel, viaje *f* de novios. 2 *vi* pasar la luna de miel.
honeypot ['hʌnipət] *n* mielera *f*.
honeysuckle ['hʌni,sʌkl] *n* madreselva *f*.
honk [həŋk] 1 *n* (*Orn*) graznido *m*; (*Aut*) bocinazo *m*. 2 *vi* graznar; tocar la bocina, bocinar.
Honolulu [,hənə'lu:lu:] Honolulú.
honorarium [,ənə'rɛəriəm] *n* honorarios *mpl*.
honorary ['ənərəri] *adj* honorario; *president, member* de honor; (*unpaid*) no remunerado.
honour, (*US*) **honor** ['ənə*] 1 *n* (a) honor *m*; (*good name*) honra *f*; (*uprightness*) honradez *f*; **in — of** en honor de; **on my —!** ¡palabra de honor!; **it's a great — for him** es un gran honor para él; **to be on one's — to +** *infin*, **to be in — bound to +** *infin* estar moralmente obligado a **+** *infin*; **I consider it an — to +** *infin* tengo a mucha honra **+** *infin*; **I had the — to +** *infin* (*or* **of + ger**) tuve el honor de **+** *infin*; **to hold someone in high —** tener mucho respeto a uno.
(b) **Your H—** Señor Juez.
(c) (*medal etc*) condecoración *f*.
(d) **—s** honores *mpl*; **last —s** honras *fpl* fúnebres; **the —s are even** se ha logrado un empate; **to bury someone with full military —s** sepultar a uno con todos los honores militares; **to do the —s of the house** hacer los honores de la casa.
(e) (*Univ*) **—s degree** título *m* (*otorgado después de un curso de estudios superiores o especializados*); **to take —s in chemistry** graduarse en química (*con estudios superiores o especializados*).
(f) (*Bridge*) **—s** honores *mpl*; **3 —s tricks** 3 bazas *fpl* de honores.
2 *vt* honrar; *pledge, signature* hacer honor a; (*respect*) respetar, reverenciar; **I — you for it** te respeto más por esto; **to — someone with one's confidence** honrar a uno con su confianza; **I am deeply —ed** lo tengo a mucha honra; **I should be —ed if . . .** estimaría que . . . **+** *subj*.
honourable, (*US*) **honorable** ['ənərəbl] *adj* (*worthy*)

honorable; (*upright*) honrado; *title, deed etc* honroso; *mention* honorífico.
honourably, (*US*) **honorably** ['ənərəbli] *adv* honradamente.
hooch [hu:tʃ] *n* (*US fam*) licor *m*.
hood [hud] *n* (*of cloak, raincoat, Eccl*) capucha *f*; (*Univ*) muceta *f* (con capucha); (*of penitent, hawk*) capirote *m*; (*Aut*) capota *f*; (*US Aut*) capó *m*; (*US sl*) criminal *m*, gángster *m*.
hooded ['hudid] *adj* encapuchado; encapirotado.
hoodlum ['hu:dləm] *n* (*US fam*) gorila *m*, matón *m*.
hoodoo ['hu:du:] *n* vudú *m*; gafancia *f*, mala suerte *f*; **there's a — on it** quien lo toque (*etc*) tendrá mala suerte, eso no se puede tocar.
hoodwink ['hudwiŋk] *vt* burlar, engañar.
hooey ['hu:i] *n* (*sl*) música *f* celestial; **—!** ¡tonterías!
hoof [hu:f] 1 *n*, *pl* **hoofs** *or* **hooves** [hu:vz] casco *m*, pezuña *f*; (*foot*) pata *f*; **cloven —** pata *f* hendida. 2 *vt* (*fam*): **to — it** (*walk*) ir a pie, (*depart*) liar el petate.
hoofed [hu:ft] *adj* ungulado.
hook [huk] 1 *n* gancho *m*; garfio *m*; (*Fishing*) anzuelo *m*; (*hanger*) colgadero *m*; (*Boxing*) gancho *m*, crochet *m*; **—s** (*sl*) manos *fpl*; **—s and eyes** corchetes *mpl*; **—, line and sinker** totalmente, hasta las cejas; **by — or by crook** por las buenas o por las malas; **to get someone off the —** ayudar a uno a salir de un apuro; **to let someone off the —** dejar escapar a uno, permitir que uno se salve; **to sling one's —** (*sl*) suspender el trabajo.
2 *vt* (a) (*attach*) enganchar; (*Fishing*) pescar, coger, enganchar; (*sl*) birlar; **to — something to a rope** enganchar algo a una cuerda; **to — a rope round a nail** atar una cuerda a un clavo; **she finally —ed him** (*fam*) ella por fin le pescó; **to — it** (*sl*) largarse; **to get —ed on** enviciarse con, entregarse a; **to — up** enganchar, *dress* abrochar.
(b) (*curve*) encorvar.
3 *vi* (a) engancharse (*on to* a).
(b) encorvarse.
hookah ['hukɑ:] *n* narguile *m*.
hooked [hukt] *adj* ganchudo.
hookup ['hukʌp] *n* (*Elec*) acoplamiento *m*; (*Radio*) transmisión *f* en circuito; **a — with Eurovision** una emisión conjunta con Eurovisión.
hookworm ['hukwə:m] *n* anquilostoma *m*.
hooky ['huki] *n*: **to play —** hacer novillos.
hooligan ['hu:ligən] *n* gamberro *m*.
hooliganism ['hu:ligənizəm] *n* gamberrismo *m*.
hoop [hu:p] *n* aro *m*; (*in croquet*) argolla *f*.
hoopoe ['hu:pu:] *n* abubilla *f*.
hoosegow ['hu:sgau] *n* (*US sl*) trena *f* (*sl*).
hoot [hu:t] 1 *n* (*of owl*) grito *m*, ululato *m*; (*of horn*) bocinazo *m*; (*of ship, factory*) toque *m* de sirena; (*laugh*) risotada *f*; **it was a —!** ¡era para morirse de risa!; *see* **care**.
2 *vt* (*also* **to — off**) silbar, abuchear; **to — someone off the stage** abuchear a uno hasta que abandone la escena.
3 *vi* (*owl*) ulular, gritar; (*person*) silbar; (*Aut*: *person*) tocar la bocina, (*car*) dar un bocinazo; (*ship*) dar un toque de sirena; **to — with laughter** morirse de risa.
hooter ['hu:tə*] *n* (*of ship, factory*) sirena *f*; (*Aut*) bocina *f*, claxon *m*.
hooves [hu:vz] *npl of* **hoof**.
hop[1] [həp] *n* (*Bot*: *also* **—s**) lúpulo *m*.
hop[2] [həp] 1 *n* salto *m*, saltito *m*, brinco *m*; (*Aer*) vuelo *m*, etapa *f* de un vuelo; (*fam*) baile *m*; **—, skip and jump** triple salto *m*; **in one —** de un salto, (*Aer*) sin hacer escala; **to catch someone on the —** coger a uno desprevenido.
2 *vt* cruzar de un salto; **to — it** (*fam*) escabullirse, largarse; **— it!** ¡lárgate!
3 *vi* saltar, brincar; saltar con un pie; (*limp*) cojear; **to — along** avanzar a saltos; **to — off** bajar (de); **to — on** subir (a); **to — out of bed** saltar de la cama.
hope [həup] 1 *n* esperanza *f*; (*trust*) confianza *f*; (*hopefulness*) ilusión *f*; (*chance*) posibilidad *f*; **some —s!** ¡de eso ni hablar!; **my — is that** yo espero que; **there is no — of** that no hay posibilidad alguna de eso; **you are my last —** tú eres mi única salvación; **to be full of —** estar lleno de ilusión, estar muy ilusionado; **to build up —s** hacerse ilusiones; **to conceive the — that** hacerse la ilusión de **+** *infin*; **to live in — of something** vivir con la esperanza de algo; **to lose —** perder la esperanza, desesperarse; **to place — in something** poner esperanzas en algo.
2 *vt*: **to — that** esperar que **+** *subj*.
3 *vi* esperar; **to — for something** esperar algo; **to — to +** *infin* esperar **+** *infin*; **hoping to hear from**

you en espera de sus gratas noticias; **what do you —
to gain by that?** ¿qué pretende Vd con eso?; **to —
against —** esperar desesperando; **to — in** confiar en.
hopeful ['həupful] adj person lleno de esperanzas,
optimista, (falsely) ilusionado; prospect etc
esperanzador, prometedor; **he wasn't very —** no se
mostró muy optimista; **it looks —** promete mucho;
a young — un joven ilusionado.
hopefully ['həupfəli] adv con optimismo; con ilusión.
hopeless ['həuplis] adj **(a)** person (without hope)
desesperado, sin esperanza.
  (b) (impossible, useless) situation desesperado,
irremediable; task imposible; (Med) case desahuciado; drunkard etc incurable; **to give something
up as —** renunciar a algo por imposible; **I'm —** at it
yo soy inútil para eso; **it's — trying to +** infin es
inútil tratar de + infin.
hopelessly ['həuplisli] adv live etc sin esperanza; **she
looked at me —** me miró desesperada; **I'm — confused** estoy totalmente despistado; **it's — dear for
us** es excesivamente caro para nosotros.
hopper ['hɔpə*] n tolva f; (Rail) vagón m tolva.
hopscotch ['hɔpskɔtʃ] n: **to play —** jugar a la pata
coja.
Horace ['hɔris] m Horacio.
Horatian [hɔ'reiʃən] adj horaciano.
horde [hɔːd] n horda f; (fig) multitud f, muchedumbre
f.
horehound ['hɔːhaund] n (Bot) marrubio m.
horizon [hə'raizn] n horizonte m.
horizontal [,hɔri'zɔntl] adj horizontal.
horizontally [,hɔri'zɔntəli] adv horizontalmente.
hormone ['hɔːməun] n hormona f, hormón m (Acad).
horn [hɔːn] 1 n **(a)** (of bull etc) cuerno m; (of deer) asta
f; (of insect) antena f; (of snail) tentáculo m;
(material) cuerno m; **— of plenty** cuerno m de la
abundancia, cornucopia f; **to be on the —s of a
dilemma** estar entre la espada y la pared; **to draw
in one's —s** retroceder, volverse atrás, (with money)
hacer economías.
  (b) (Mus) cuerno m, trompa f; (Aut) bocina f,
claxon m; **to blow** (or **sound**) **one's —** tocar la
bocina, tocar el claxon.
  2 vi: **to — in** (fam) entrometerse (on en).
horned [hɔːnd] adj con cuernos, enastado; (in compounds) de cuernos . . .
hornet ['hɔːnit] n avispón m.
hornless ['hɔːnlis] adj sin cuernos, mocho.
hornpipe ['hɔːnpaip] n cierto baile de marineros.
horn-rimmed ['hɔːnrimd] adj spectacles de concha.
horny ['hɔːni] adj material córneo; hand calloso.
horoscope ['hɔrəskəup] n horóscopo m; **to cast a —**
sacar un horóscopo.
horrible ['hɔribl] adj horrible.
horribly ['hɔribli] adv horriblemente; **it's — difficult**
es terriblemente difícil; **he swore most —** soltó unos
tacos espantosos.
horrid ['hɔrid] adj horrible, horroroso; (fam) horrible;
person etc de lo más antipático, inaguantable; **you —
thing!** ¡bestia!; **to be — to someone** tratar a uno
muy mal, portarse muy mal con uno; **don't be —!**
¡no seas bestia!
horrendous [hɔ'rendəs] adj horrendo; (hum) horroroso.
horrific [hɔ'rifik] adj horrendo.
horrify ['hɔrifai] vt horrorizar; (shock) escandalizar,
pasmar; **they were all horrified** se escandalizaron
todos; **I was horrified to discover that** me horrorizó
descubrir que.
horrifying ['hɔrifaiiŋ] adj horroroso, horripilante.
horror ['hɔrə*] n horror m; **to have a — of** tener
horror a; **it gives me the —s** me da horror; **—s!** ¡qué
horror!; **you —!** ¡bestia!
horror-stricken ['hɔrə,strikən] adj horrorizado.
hors d'oeuvres [ɔː'dəːvr] npl entremeses mpl.
horse [hɔːs] n (Zool) caballo m; (in gymnastics) potro
m; (Tech) caballete m; (cavalry) caballería f; **dark —**
(mystery) incógnita f, figura f misteriosa, (in election)
candidato m poco conocido, (winner) ganador m
inesperado; **white —s** (waves) palomas fpl; **that's a
— of a different colour** ésa es harina de otro costal;
it's straight from the —'s mouth lo sé de buena
tinta, me lo dijo el mismo interesado; **to change —s
in midstream** cambiar de política (or personal etc) a
mitad de camino; **to eat like a —** comer como una
vaca; **to flog a dead —** machacar en hierro frío; **to
get on one's high —** darse ínfulas; **hold your —s!**
¡despacito!; **don't look a gift — in the mouth** a
caballo regalado no le mires el diente.
horse-artillery ['hɔːsɑː'tiləri] n artillería f montada.
horseback ['hɔːsbæk]: **on — or** a caballo.
horse-box ['hɔːsbɔks] n camión m para caballerías,
(Rail) vagón m para caballerías.

horse-breaker ['hɔːs,breikə*] n domador m de
caballos.
horse chestnut ['hɔːs'tʃesnʌt] n (fruit) castaña f de
Indias; (tree) castaño m de Indias.
horse-collar ['hɔːs,kɔlə*] n collera f.
horse-dealer ['hɔːs,diːlə]* n chalán m.
horse-doctor ['hɔːs,dɔktə*] n veterinario m.
horse-drawn ['hɔːsdrɔːn] adj traído por caballo(s).
horsefly ['hɔːsflai] n tábano m.
Horse Guards ['hɔːsgɑːdz] npl guardias fpl montadas.
horsehair ['hɔːsheə*] n crin m.
horsehide ['hɔːshaid] n cuero m de caballo.
horse-laugh ['hɔːslɑːf] n risotada f.
horseman ['hɔːsmən] n, pl **—men** [mən] jinete m;
caballista m.
horsemanship ['hɔːsmənʃip] n equitación f, manejo
m (del caballo).
horse opera ['hɔːs,ɔpərə] n (US) película f que se
desarrolla en el oeste de EE.UU., película f de
vaqueros.
horseplay ['hɔːsplei] n payasadas fpl, pelea f amistosa.
horsepower ['hɔːs,pauə*] n caballo m (de fuerza);
potencia f en caballos; **a 20 — engine** un motor de
20 caballos; **what is the — of this car?** ¿qué
potencia tiene este coche?
horse-race ['hɔːsreis] n carrera f de caballos.
horse-racing ['hɔːs,reisiŋ] n carreras fpl de caballos,
hipismo m.
horseradish ['hɔːs,rædiʃ] n rábano m picante.
horse-sense ['hɔːssens] n sentido m común.
horseshoe ['hɔːsʃuː] n herradura f.
horse show ['hɔːsʃəu] n concurso m hípico.
horsewhip ['hɔːswip] 1 n látigo m. 2 vt zurriagar.
horsewoman ['hɔːs,wumən] n, pl **—women** [,wimin]
amazona f, caballista f.
horsy ['hɔːsi] adj (fond of horses) aficionado a los
caballos; (fond of racing) aficionado a las carreras de
caballos, carrerista; appearance caballuno.
horticultural [,hɔːti'kʌltʃərəl] adj hortícola; **— show**
exposición f de flores y legumbres.
horticulture ['hɔːtikʌltʃə*] n horticultura f.
horticulturist [,hɔːti'kʌltʃərist] n horticultor m, ora f.
hose [həuz] 1 n **(a)** (stockings) medias fpl, (socks)
calcetines mpl; (arch) calzas fpl.
  (b) (hosepipe) manga f, manguera f.
  2 vt (also **to — down**) regar (or limpiar etc) con
manga.
hosepipe ['həuzpaip] n manga f, manguera f.
hosier ['həuʒə*] n calcetero m, a f.
hosiery ['həuʒəri] n calcetería f.
hospice ['hɔspis] n hospicio m.
hospitable [hɔs'pitəbl] adj hospitalario; atmosphere
etc acogedor.
hospitably [hɔs'pitəbli] adv de modo hospitalario.
hospital ['hɔspitl] n hospital m; **isolation —** hospital
m de contagiosos; **maternity —** casa f de maternidad; **mental —** manicomio m.
hospitality [,hɔspi'tæliti] n hospitalidad f.
hospitalize ['hɔspitəlaiz] vt hospitalizar.
hospital ship ['hɔspitl,ʃip] n buque m hospital.
host[1] [həust] n **(a)** (crowd) multitud f; **I have a — of
problems** tengo multitud de problemas; **for a whole
— of reasons** por muchísimas razones; **they came in
—s** acudieron a millares.
  (b) (arch) hueste f, ejército m.
host[2] [həust] n (to guest) huésped m, eda f; (Bio)
huésped m; (at meal) anfitrión m, ona f; (of inn)
patrón m, mesonero m; **I thanked my —s** di las
gracias a los que me habían invitado; **we were —s
for a week to a Spanish boy** recibimos en casa
durante una semana a un joven español.
host[3] [həust] n (Eccl) hostia f.
hostage ['hɔstidʒ] n rehén m.
hostel ['hɔstəl] n parador m; (youth —) albergue m;
(Univ) residencia f (de estudiantes).
hostelry ['hɔstəlri] n parador m, mesón m.
hostess ['həustes] n huéspeda f; anfitriona f (see
host[2]); (Aer) azafata f; (in night club) cabaretera f.
hostile ['hɔstail] adj (enemy) enemigo, hostil; manner,
voice etc nada amistoso; circumstances etc adverso,
desfavorable; **they were — to the plan** se opusieron
al proyecto.
hostility [hɔs'tiliti] n hostilidad f (to, towards hacia),
enemistad f, antagonismo m; **hostilities** hostilidades
fpl; **to start hostilities** romper las hostilidades; **to
call for an end to hostilities** abogar por un cese de
hostilidades.
hostler ['ɔslə*] n = **ostler.**
hot [hɔt] 1 adj **(a)** caliente; climate cálido; day,
summer caluroso, de calor; sun abrasador; spring
termal; **with running — and cold (water)** con agua

corriente caliente y fría; **to be** — (person) tener calor, (thing) estar caliente, (weather) hacer calor; **to be very** — (person) tener mucho calor, (thing) estar muy caliente, (weather) hacer mucho calor; **to get** — (thing) calentarse, (weather) empezar a hacer calor; **it was a very** — **day** fue un día de mucho calor; **it was a** — **and tiring walk** fue una caminata que nos hizo sudar y nos cansó mucho; **to get** — **and bothered** sofocarse.

(b) (fig) taste picante; contest muy reñido; dispute acalorado; temper vivo; temperament apasionado, ardiente, vehemente; situation muy difícil, apurado, de mucho peligro; pursuit enérgico; supporter acérrimo; (sexually: fam) cachondo; (stolen) robado.

(c) news — **from the press** una noticia que acaba de publicarse en la prensa; **to be** — **on someone's trail** seguir enérgicamente la pista de uno; **he's pretty** — **at maths** es un hacha para las matemáticas, es muy fuerte en matemáticas; **he's a pretty** — **player** es un jugador experto; **to make a place too** — **for someone** hacer que uno abandone un lugar; **to make things** — **for someone** amargar la vida a uno, hacer insoportable la vida a uno.

2 adv: **to blow** — **and cold** ser veleta, mudar a todos los vientos; **to give it to someone** — **and strong** no morderse la lengua; **to go at it** — **and strong** pelearse (etc) violentamente.

hotbed ['hɔtbed] n (fig) semillero m.
hot-blooded ['hɔt'blʌdid] adj apasionado, impetuoso.
hotchpotch ['hɔtʃpɔtʃ] n mezcolanza f, baturrillo m.
hotel [hɔu'tel] n hotel m.
hotfoot ['hɔt'fut] adv a toda prisa.
hothead ['hɔthed] n exaltado m, a f, fanático m, a f, extremista mf.
hotheaded ['hɔt'hedid] adj (extreme) exaltado, fanático, extremista; (rash) impetuoso.
hothouse ['hɔthaus] n invernáculo m.
hotly ['hɔtli] adv con pasión, con vehemencia.
hotplate ['hɔtpleit] n calientaplatos m.
hotpot ['hɔtpɔt] n estofado m.
hotrod ['hɔtrɔd] n (US Aut: sl) bólido m.
hotshot ['hɔtʃɔt] adj (US sl) excelente, de primera.
hot-water bottle [hɔt'wɔːtə,bɔtl] n bolsa f de agua caliente.
hound [haund] 1 n perro m (de caza), podenco m, sabueso m; (fig) canalla m.
2 vt acosar, perseguir; **to** — **someone down** perseguir a uno hasta encontrarle; **to** — **someone on** incitar a uno (to + infin a + infin); **to** — **someone out** hacer que uno abandone su puesto (etc) a fuerza de darle guerra.
hour [auə*] n hora f; **30 miles an** — 30 millas por hora; **peak** — **s** horas fpl punta; **small** — **s** altas horas fpl; **visiting** — **s** horas fpl de visita; **after** — **s** fuera de horas; **at the eleventh** — a última hora; **by the** — por horas; — **by** — hora tras hora, cada hora; **on the** — a la hora en punto; **to keep late** — **s** acostarse a altas horas de la noche; **to strike the** — dar la hora; **it takes** — **s** es cosa de muchas horas; **we waited** — **s** esperamos horas y horas; **to work long** — **s** trabajar muchas horas cada día.
hourglass ['auəglɑːs] n reloj m de arena.
hourhand ['auəhænd] n horario m.
hourly ['auəli] 1 adj de cada hora; **the** — **rate** el sueldo por hora; **there's an** — **bus** hay un autobús cada hora.
2 adv cada hora; **we expected him** — le esperábamos de un momento a otro.
house [haus] n, pl **houses** ['hauziz] 1 n casa f; (Comm) casa f, firma f; (Theat: auditorium) sala f, (audience) público m, (takings) entrada f; (Parl) cámara f; (Univ) colegio m, (part of college) pabellón m; (lineage) casa f, familia f; "— **full**" (Theat) "no hay localidades"; — **and home** hogar m; — **of cards** castillo m de naipes; **H**— **of Commons** Cámara f de los Comunes; **H**— **of Lords** Cámara f de los Lores; **H**— **s of Parliament** Parlamento m, Cámara f de los Lores y la de los Comunes; **H**— **of Representatives** (US) Cámara f de Representantes; **banking** — casa f de banca; **the big** — la casa del mayor terrateniente (de una comarca); **business** — casa f de comercio; **detached** — casa f independiente, hotelito m, chalet m, chalé m (Acad); **disorderly** — (euph) burdel m; **full** — (Theat) lleno m; **public** — taberna f; **publishing** — casa f editorial; **it's on the** — la casa invita, está pagado (por el dueño); **to bring the** — **down** (Theat) hacer venirse abajo el teatro, (speech) obtener un gran éxito, ser muy aplaudido, (joke) hacer morir de risa a todos; **to get on like a** — **afire** (progress) avanzar rapidísimamente, (2 persons) hacer buenas migas; **to keep** — llevar la casa (for a, para); **to keep open** — recibir a

todo el mundo, ser muy hospitalario; **to move** — mudarse; **to put one's** — **in order** arreglar los asuntos personales; **to set up** — poner casa, establecerse.
2 attr property inmueble; arrest domiciliario; dog etc de casa.
house [haus] vt person alojar, hospedar; population proveer viviendas para; (store) guardar, almacenar; (Mech) encajar; **the building will not** — **them all** no cabrán todos en el edificio.
house agent ['haus,eidʒənt] n corredor m de casas.
house arrest ['hausə,rest] n: **to be under** — estar bajo arresto domiciliario.
houseboat ['hausbəut] n habitación f flotante.
housebreaker ['haus,breikə*] n ladrón m de casas.
housebreaking ['haus,breikiŋ] n robo m en una casa.
housecleaning ['haus'kliːniŋ] n (US) limpieza f de la casa.
housecoat ['hauskəut] n bata f.
housedress ['hausdres] n bata f, mono m.
housefly ['hausflai] n mosca f doméstica.
household ['haushəuld] 1 n casa f, familia f; **royal** — corte f.
2 attr: — **accounts** cuentas fpl de la casa; — **chores** quehaceres mpl domésticos; — **gods** penates mpl; — **troops** guardia f real; **it's a** — **word** es un nombre conocidísimo.
householder ['haus,həuldə*] n cabeza f de familia; dueño m de una casa.
housekeeper ['haus,kiːpə*] n ama f de casa, ama f de llaves.
housekeeping ['haus,kiːpiŋ] n gobierno m de la casa, economía f doméstica; — **(money)** dinero m para gastos domésticos.
housemaid ['hausmeid] n criada f.
house painter ['haus,peintə*] n pintor m (de brocha gorda).
house party ['haus,pɑːti] n grupo m de invitados (que pasan varios días en una casa de campo).
house physician ['hausfi,ziʃən] n médico m residente.
house-proud ['hauspraud] adj: **she's very** — cuida muy bien su hogar, tiene la casa como una plata.
houseroom ['hausrum] n capacidad f de una casa; **to give something** — guardar algo en su casa; **I wouldn't give it** — no quisiera tenerlo en mi casa.
house surgeon ['haus,sə:dʒən] n cirujano m residente (en el hospital).
house-to-house ['haustə'haus] adj and adv de casa en casa.
housetop ['haustɔp] n tejado m; **to shout something from the** — **s** pregonar algo a los cuatro vientos.
house-trained ['haustreind] adj bien enseñado, limpio.
housewares ['hauswεəz] npl (US) artículos mpl de uso doméstico, utensilios mpl domésticos.
house warming ['haus,wɔːmiŋ] n fiesta f de estreno de una casa.
housewife ['hauswaif] n, pl — **wives** [waivz] ama f de casa; madre f de familia.
housewifery ['hauswifəri] n economía f doméstica.
housing ['hauziŋ] n (a) (act) alojamiento m; provisión f de vivienda.
(b) (houses) casas fpl, viviendas fpl; — **estate** bloque m de casas; — **shortage** crisis f de la vivienda; **there's a lot of new** — hay muchas casas nuevas.
(c) (Mech) caja f, cubierta f, tapa f.
hove [həuv] pret and ptp of **heave** (Naut).
hovel ['hɔvəl] n casucha f, tugurio m.
hover ['hɔvə*] vi permanecer inmóvil (en el aire), estar suspendido, flotar (en el aire); (hawk etc) cernerse; **to** — **round someone** rondar a uno, girar en torno a uno.
hovercraft ['hɔvəkrɑːft] n hidroala m, aerodeslizador m.
how [hau] adv (a) cómo; — **did you do it?** ¿cómo lo hiciste? **I know** — **you did it** yo sé cómo lo hiciste; — **are you?** ¿cómo está Vd?, ¿qué tal estás?; — **is it that . . .?** ¿cómo resulta que . . .?, ¿por qué . . .?, ¿cómo es posible que . . . + subj?; — **can that be?** ¿cómo puede ser eso?; **I see** — **it is** comprendo la situación; — **was the play?** ¿qué tal la comedia?; — **do you like your steak?** ¿cómo le gusta que se le sirva el biftec?; — **do you like the steak?** ¿qué tal le parece el biftec?; **to know** — **to do something** saber hacer algo; **to learn** — **to do something** aprender a hacer algo, aprender cómo se hace algo, aprender el modo de hacer algo; **and** —! ¡ya lo creo!
(b) (with adj or adv etc) — **beautiful!** ¡qué hermoso!; — **big it is!** ¡qué grande es!; **I know** — **hard it is** yo sé lo difícil que esto es; — **kind of you!** es Vd muy amable; — **fast?** ¿a qué velocidad?; — **big is it?** ¿cómo es de grande?, ¿de qué tamaño es?;

— **wide is this room?** ¿cuánto tiene este cuarto de ancho?; **how wide shall I make it?** ¿con qué ancho lo hago?; — **old are you?** ¿cuántos años tienes?; — **glad I am to see you!** ¡cuánto me alegro de verte!; — **sorry I am for you!** ¡cuánto te compadezco!; — **she's changed!** ¡cuánto ha cambiado!; *see* **about, else, much** *etc.*

how-d'ye-do ['haudjə'du:] *n* lío *m*.

however [hau'evə*] 1 *adv* (a) (*with verb*) — **I do it** como quiera que lo haga; — **he may want to do it** de cualquier modo que él quiera hacerlo; — **that may be** sea como ello fuere.
   (b) (*with adj or adv*) por (muy) . . . que + *subj*; — **rough it is** por (muy) tosco que sea; — **fast he runs** por rápidamente que corra; — **hot it is** por mucho calor que haga; *see* **many, much**.
   2 *conj* sin embargo, no obstante.

howitzer ['hauitsə*] *n* obús *m*.

howl [haul] 1 *n* aullido *m*, chillido *m*, grito *m*, alarido *m*; berrido *m*; bramido *m*; **with a — of rage** dando un alarido de furia; **to set up a —** (*fig*) poner el grito en el cielo.
   2 *vt:* **to — someone down** hacer callar a uno abucheándole.
   3 *vi* (*animal etc*) aullar, chillar; (*person*) gritar, dar alaridos; (*child*) berrear; (*with laughter*) reírse a carcajadas; (*wind*) bramar; **to — with rage** bramar de furia, bramar furioso.

howler ['haulə*] *n* plancha *f*, falta *f* garrafal.

howling ['haulin] *adj* **success** clamoroso.

hoy [hɔi] *interj* ¡eh!, ¡hola!

hub [hʌb] *n* cubo *m*; (*fig*) centro *m*.

hubbub ['hʌbʌb] *n* barahúnda *f*, batahola *f*; **a — of voices** un ruido confuso de voces; **when he finished a — arose** cuando terminó se armó una bronca.

hubby ['hʌbi] *n* (*fam*) marido *m*.

hub cap ['hʌbkæp] *n* tapacubos *m*.

huckster ['hʌkstə*] *n* vendedor *m* ambulante, buhonero *m*.

huddle ['hʌdl] 1 *n* (*of things*) montón *m*, grupo *m*; (*of persons*) grupo *m*, corrillo *m*; **to go into a —** ir aparte para conferenciar.
   2 *vt* (*also* **to — together**) amontonar, poner muy juntos.
   3 *vi* (*also* **to — together, to — up**) amontonarse, apretarse (unos contra otros); acurrucarse; **they were huddling together for warmth** estaban apretados unos contra otros para darse calor; **the chairs were —d in a corner** las sillas estaban amontonadas en un rincón; **we —d round the fire** nos arrimamos al fuego, nos apiñábamos junto a la lumbre.

hue[1] [hju:] *n* (*colour*) color *m*; (*shade*) matiz *m*, tono *m*; (*of opinion*) matiz *m*; **people of every political —** gente *f* de todos los matices de opinión política.

hue[2] [hju:] *n:* — **and cry** alarma *f*; (*of protest*) clamor *m*, griterío *f*; **they set up a great — and cry** protestaron clamorosamente; **there was a — and cry after him** se le persiguió enérgicamente.

huff [hʌf] *n* rabieta *f*; **to go off in a —** irse ofendido; **to get into a —** indignarse, ofenderse.

huffily ['hʌfili] *adv* malhumoradamente; **he said —** dijo malhumorado.

huffy ['hʌfi] *adj* (*of character*) enojadizo; (*in mood*) malhumorado, ofendido; **he was a bit — about it** se ofendió un tanto por ello.

hug [hʌg] 1 *n* abrazo *m*; **give me a —** dame un abrazo.
   2 *vt* (*lovingly*) abrazar; (*of bear etc*) apretar con los brazos, apretujar; *coast* no apartarse de; *prejudice etc* acariciar; *idea* aferrarse a; *belief* afirmarse en.
   3 *vr:* **to — oneself** felicitarse (*on por*).

huge [hju:dʒ] *adj* enorme, vasto, inmenso; (*over-large*) descomunal.

hugely ['hju:dʒli] *adv* enormemente; **we enjoyed ourselves —** nos divertimos una barbaridad; **he laughed —** se rió muchísimo.

hugeness ['hju:dʒnis] *n* inmensidad *f*.

hugger-mugger ['hʌgə,mʌgə*] (*fam*) 1 *n* confusión *f*; **a — of books** un montón de libros en desorden.
   2 *adv* desordenadamente.

Hugh [hju:] *m* Hugo, Ugo.

Huguenot ['hju:gənəu] 1 *adj* hugonote. 2 *n* hugonote *m*, a *f*.

hulk [hʌlk] *n* (*wreck*) barco *m* viejo; (*hull*) casco *m* (arrumbado); (*useless vessel*) carcamán *m*; (*mass*) bulto *m*, mole *f*.

hulking ['hʌlkin] *adj* grueso, pesado; **a — great brute** un hombrón.

hull [hʌl] *n* casco *m*.

hullabaloo [,hʌləbə'lu:] *n* (*fam*) (*noise*) vocería *f*, tumulto *m*; (*fuss*) lío *m*, bronca *f*; **a great — broke**

out estalló un ruido espantoso; **that — about the money** ese lío que se armó por el dinero.

hullo [hʌ'ləu] *interj* (*greeting*) ¡hola!; (*surprise*) ¡caramba!; (*Tel: calling*) ¡oiga!, (*answering*) ¡diga!; —, **what's all this?** ¡vamos a ver!

hum [hʌm] 1 *n* zumbido *m*; tarareo *m*; (*of voices etc*) ruido *m* confuso, murmullo *m*.
   2 *vt tune* tararear, canturrear.
   3 *vi* (a) (*insect, wire etc*) zumbar; (*person*) canturrear, tararear una canción; **to — with activity** bullir de actividad; **to make things —** desplegar gran actividad; avivarlo, estimular la actividad; **then things began to —** entonces sí empezaron a pasar cosas, hubo luego una actividad frenética.
   (b) (*fam: smell*) oler mal.
   (c) **to — and haw** vacilar, no resolverse.

human ['hju:mən] 1 *adj* humano. 2 *n* humano *m*, a *f*.

humane [hju:'mein] *adj* humano, humanitario.

humanism ['hju:mənizəm] *n* humanismo *m*.

humanist ['hju:mənist] *n* humanista *mf*.

humanistic [,hju:mə'nistik] *adj* humanístico.

humanitarian [hju:,mæni'tɛəriən] 1 *adj* humanitario. 2 *n* humanitario *m*, a *f*.

humanity [hju:'mæniti] *n* humanidad *f*; **the humanities** las humanidades.

humanize ['hju:mənaiz] *vt* humanizar.

humankind ['hju:mən'kaind] *n* género *m* humano.

humanly ['hju:mənli] *adv* humanamente; **all that is — possible** todo lo que pueda hacer un hombre, todo lo que cabe dentro de las posibilidades humanas.

humble ['hʌmbl] 1 *adj* humilde. 2 *vt* humillar. 3 *vr:* **to — oneself** humillarse.

humble-bee ['hʌmblbi:] *n* abejorro *m*.

humbleness ['hʌmblnis] *n* humildad *f*.

humbly ['hʌmbli] *adv* humildemente, con humildad.

humbug ['hʌmbʌg] *n* (a) (*thing*) bola *f*, embustes *mpl*, disparates *mpl*; **utter —!** ¡tonterías!; **what —!** ¡qué cinismo!
   (b) (*sweet*) caramelo *m* de menta.
   (c) (*person*) farsante *mf*, cínico *m*, charlatán *m*; **he's an old —** es un farsante.

humdinger ['hʌmdiŋə*] *n* (*sl*): **it's a —!** ¡es una auténtica maravilla!; **a real — of a car** un coche maravilloso.

humdrum ['hʌmdrʌm] *adj* monótono, aburrido; vulgar, ordinario; rutinario; mediocre, sin interés.

humerus ['hju:mərəs] *n*, *pl* **humeri** ['hju:mərai] húmero *m*.

humid ['hju:mid] *adj* húmedo.

humidifier [hju:'midifaiə*] *n* humectador *m*.

humidify [hju:'midifai] *vt* humedecer.

humidity [hju:'miditi] *n* humedad *f*.

humidor ['hju:midɔ:*] *n* (*for tobacco*) bote *m* humectativo; (*Tech*) humectador *m*.

humiliate [hju:'milieit] *vt* humillar.

humiliating [hju:'milieitin] *adj* vergonzoso, humillante.

humiliation [hju:,mili'eiʃən] *n* humillación *f*.

humility [hju:'militi] *n* humildad *f*.

hummingbird ['hʌmiŋbə:d] *n* colibrí *m*.

humming-top ['hʌmiŋtɔp] *n* trompa *f*.

hummock ['hʌmək] *n* montecillo *m*, morón *m*.

humorist ['hju:mərist] *n* persona *f* chistosa; (*writer*) humorista *mf*; **what a — you are!** ¡qué gracioso eres!

humorous ['hju:mərəs] *adj person* gracioso, chistoso, divertido; *writer, genre* festivo, cómico; *joke, event, book* divertido; *tone* festivo.

humorously ['hju:mərəsli] *adv* graciosamente, de manera divertida; en tono festivo.

humour, (US) **humor** ['hju:mə*] 1 *n* (a) (*amusingness*) humorismo *m*; (*sense of —*) sentido *m* del humor; (*creative talent*) vis *f* cómica; (*of joke, event*) gracia *f*; (*of situation*) comicidad *f*; **he has no —** no tiene sentido del humor; **I see no — in that** no encuentro nada divertido en eso; **this is no time for —** éste no es lugar para chistes; **I don't like the — in "Macbeth"** no me gustan las escenas cómicas de "Macbeth".
   (b) (*mood*) humor *m*; **to be in a good —** estar de buen humor; **to be in high good —** estar de excelente humor; **they were in no — for fighting** no estaban de humor para pelear; **to be out of —** estar de mal humor.
   (c) (*whim*) capricho *m*.
   2 *vt* complacer, seguir el humor a; (*indulge*) mimar.

-humoured, (US) **-humored** ['hju:məd] *adj* de humor . . .

humourless, (US) **humorless** ['hju:məlis] *adj person* sin sentido del humor; *joke* nada divertido.

hump [hʌ..] 1 *n* (*Anat*) joroba *f*, corcova *f*, giba *f*; (*camel's*) giba *f*; (*in ground*) montecillo *m*; **to give**

someone the — jorobar, fastidiar; **to have the —** estar de mal humor; **we're over the —** now ya hemos vencido la cuesta.
2 *vt* (a) **to — one's back** encorvarse, corcovarse. (b) (*carry*) llevar, llevar al hombro.
humpbacked ['hʌmpbækt] *adj* corcovado, jorobado; *bridge* de fuerte pendiente.
humph [mm] *interj* ¡bah!; ¡veremos!
humpy ['hʌmpi] *adj* desigual.
humus ['hjuːməs] *n* humus *m*.
Hun [hʌn] *n* (*Hist*) huno *m*; (*pej*) tudesco *m*, alemán *m*; **a —** un alemán, **the —** los alemanes.
hunch [hʌntʃ] 1 *n* (*Anat*) see **hump**; (*fig*) idea *f*; sospecha *f*; (*presentiment*) presentimiento *m*; **it's only a —** no es más que una sospecha que tengo; **I have a —** that tengo la idea de que, se me ocurre que, me da el corazón que; **—es sometimes pay off a** veces los presentimientos se cumplen.
2 *vt* (*also* **to — up**) encorvar; **to — one's back** encorvarse; **to sit —ed up** estar sentado con el cuerpo doblado.
hunchback ['hʌntʃbæk] *n* jorobado *m*, a *f*, corcovado *m*, a *f*.
hunchbacked ['hʌntʃbækt] *adj* jorobado, corcovado.
hundred ['hʌndrid] 1 *adj* ciento, (*before n*) cien; **a —** and one ciento uno; **a — and ten** ciento diez; **a — thousand** cien mil; **a — per cent** (*fig*) cien por cien.
2 *n* ciento *m*, (*less exactly*) centenar *m*, centena *f*; **—s of people** centenares *mpl* de personas; **—s of thousands of bees** centenas de miles de abejas; **in —s**, **by the —** a centenares.
hundredfold ['hʌndridfəʊld] 1 *adj* céntuplo. 2 *adv* cien veces.
hundredth ['hʌndridθ] 1 *adj* centésimo. 2 *n* centésimo *m*, centésima parte *f*.
hundredweight ['hʌndridweit] *n* (= 112 *libras* = 50,8 *kilogramos*) *approx* quintal *m*.
Hundred Years' War ['hʌndridjiəz'wɔː*] Guerra *f* de los Cien Años.
hung [hʌŋ] *pret and ptp of* hang.
Hungarian [hʌŋ'gɛəriən] 1 *adj* húngaro. 2 *n* húngaro *m*, a *f*. 3 *n* (*language*) húngaro *m*.
Hungary ['hʌŋgəri] Hungría *f*.
hunger ['hʌŋgə*] 1 *n* hambre *f* (*also fig: for* de). 2 *vi* tener hambre, estar hambriento; **to — after, to — for** tener hambre de, ansiar, anhelar.
hunger strike ['hʌŋgəstraik] *n* huelga *f* de hambre.
hungrily ['hʌŋgrili] *adv eat etc* ansiosamente, ávidamente; **to look — at something** mirar algo con ganas de comerlo.
hungry ['hʌŋgri] *adj* hambriento; *land* pobre, estéril; **to be —** tener hambre (*for* de); **to be very —** tener mucha hambre; **to go —** pasar hambre; **to make someone —** dar hambre a uno.
hunk [hʌŋk] *n* pedazo *m*, trozo *m*.
hunt [hʌnt] 1 *n* caza *f*, cacería *f* (*for* de); (*expedition*) partida *f* de caza; (*persons*) grupo *m* de cazadores; (*search*) busca *f*, búsqueda *f* (*for* de); (*pursuit*) persecución *f*; **the — for the murderer** la persecución del asesino; **to be on the — for** ir a la caza de; **the — is on, the — is up** ha comenzado la búsqueda; **we joined in the — for the missing key** ayudamos a buscar la llave perdida.
2 *vt animal* cazar; (*search for*) buscar; (*pursue*) perseguir; *hounds etc* emplear en la caza; *country* recorrer de caza, cazar en; **to — down** *person* perseguir (y encontrar), *thing* buscar hasta dar con; **to — out, to — up** (*look for*) buscar, (*find*) encontrar.
3 *vi* cazar; dedicarse a la caza; **to — for** buscar; **to — about for** buscar por todas partes; **he —ed for it in his pocket** lo buscó en el bolsillo; **to go —ing** ir de caza.
hunter ['hʌntə*] *n* cazador *m*, ora *f*; (*horse*) caballo *m* de caza.
hunting ['hʌntiŋ] 1 *n* caza *f*, montería *f*. 2 *attr* de caza; **the — fraternity** los aficionados a la caza.
hunting box ['hʌntiŋbɔks] *n* pabellón *m* de caza.
hunting ground ['hʌntiŋgraund] *n* cazadero *m*; **a happy — for** un buen terreno para.
huntress ['hʌntris] *n* cazadora *f*.
huntsman ['hʌntsmən] *n*, *pl* **—men** [mən] cazador *m*, montero *m*.
hurdle ['həːdl] *n* zarzo *m*, valla *f*; (*Sport*) valla *f*; (*fig*) obstáculo *m*.
hurdler ['həːdlə*] *n* corredor *m* en las carreras de vallas.
hurdle-race ['həːdlreis] *n* carrera *f* de vallas.
hurdy-gurdy ['həːdi,gəːdi] *n* organillo *m*.
hurl [həːl] 1 *vt* lanzar, arrojar; **to — back** *enemy* rechazar; **to — insults at someone** llenar a uno de improperios.

2 *vr*: **to — oneself at** (*or* **upon**) **someone** abalanzarse sobre uno; **to — oneself into the fray** lanzarse a la batalla; **to — oneself over a cliff** arrojarse por un precipicio.
hurly-burly ['həːli'bəːli] *n* tumulto *m*; **the — of politics** la vida alborotada de la política.
hurrah [hu'rɑː], **hurray** [hu'rei] 1 *interj* ¡viva!, ¡vítor!; **— for Brown!** ¡viva Brown! 2 *n* vítor *m*.
hurricane ['hʌrikən] *n* huracán *m*.
hurricane lamp ['hʌrikən'læmp] *n* lámpara *f* a prueba de viento.
hurried ['hʌrid] *adj* apresurado, hecho de prisa; *reading etc* superficial; **he had a — meal** comió de prisa.
hurriedly ['hʌridli] *adv* con prisa, apresuradamente; *study etc* superficialmente; *write etc* a vuela pluma; **I left —** me apresuré a salir.
hurry ['hʌri] 1 *n* prisa *f*; **to be in a —** tener prisa (*to do* por hacer), estar de prisa; **to do something in a —** hacer algo de prisa; **are you in a —** for this? ¿corre prisa esto?; **is there any —?** ¿corre prisa?; **what's all the —?, what's your —?** ¿por qué tanta prisa?; **I shan't come back here in a —** aquí no pongo los pies nunca más; **he won't do that again in a —** no volverá a hacer eso si puede evitarlo.
2 *vt work etc* apresurar, dar prisa a, acelerar (*also* **to — along, to — on, to — up**); **they hurried him to a doctor** le llevaron con toda prisa a un médico; **troops were hurried to the spot** se enviaron tropas al lugar con toda prisa; **this is a plan that cannot be hurried** éste es proyecto que no se puede realizar de prisa; **to — the work along** acelerar el ritmo del trabajo; **to — someone away, to — someone off** hacer marchar a uno de prisa; **the policeman hurried him away** el policía se le llevó apresuradamente; **to — someone out** dar prisa a uno para que salga; **to — someone up** hacer que uno se dé prisa.
3 *vi* apresurarse (*to do* a hacer), darse prisa (*to do* para hacer); **—!** ¡dése prisa!; **don't —!** ¡no hay prisa!; **I must —** tengo que darme prisa; **she hurried home** se dio prisa para llegar a casa; **to — after someone** correr detrás de uno; **to — along** correr, ir de prisa; **to — away, to — off** marcharse de prisa; **to — back** darse prisa para volver, volver de prisa; **to — in** entrar de prisa, entrar corriendo; **to — out** salir de prisa, salir corriendo; **to — over** *place* cruzar rápidamente; *work* concluir aprisa, hacer con precipitación; **to — up** darse prisa; **— up!** ¡date prisa!
hurry-scurry ['hʌri'skʌri] 1 *adv* precipitadamente, atropelladamente.
2 *n* precipitación *f*, prisa *f* grande; carrera *f* precipitada.
3 *vi* precipitarse, lanzarse, correr precipitadamente.
hurt [həːt] 1 *n* (*wound etc*) herida *f*, lesión *f*; (*harm*) daño *m*, mal *m*, perjuicio *m*.
2 (*irr*: *pret and ptp* **hurt**) *vt* (*injure, bodily*) herir, hacer mal a, hacer daño a, lastimar; (*cause pain to*) doler; (*damage*) dañar; *business, interests etc* perjudicar, afectar; *feelings* herir, ofender; (*be bad for*) hacer daño a; **he — his foot** se lastimó el pie; **where does it — you?** ¿dónde le duele?; **to get —** hacerse daño; **in such affairs someone's bound to get — en** estos asuntos siempre uno perjudicado; **wine never — anybody** el vino no hizo nunca daño a nadie; **she's feeling rather — about it** se ofendió bastante por ello.
3 *vi* (*feel pain*) doler; (*take harm*) sufrir daño, estropearse, echarse a perder; **does it — much?** ¿duele mucho?; **it won't — for being left another week** no se va a estropear si lo dejamos una semana más.
4 *vr*: **to — oneself** hacerse daño, lastimarse.
5 *adj and ptp of* **hurt**; *foot etc* lastimado, lisiado; *feelings* ofendido; **with a — look** con cara de ofendido; **in a — tone** quejoso, ofendido.
hurtful ['həːtful] *adj* dañoso, perjudicial; *remark etc* hiriente.
hurtle ['həːtl] 1 *vt* arrojar violentamente.
2 *vi*: **to — along, to — past** (*adv*) ir como un rayo; **to — down** caer con violencia; **the car —d past us** el coche cruzó como un rayo delante de nosotros; **the rock —d over the cliff** la roca cayó estrepitosamente por el precipicio.
husband ['hʌzbənd] 1 *n* marido *m*; esposo *m*; **now they're — and wife** ahora son marido y mujer. 2 *vt* economizar, ahorrar, manejar prudentemente.
husbandry ['hʌzbəndri] *n* (*Agr*) agricultura *f*, labranza *f*; (*fig*) buen gobierno *m*, manejo *m* prudente.

hush [hʌʃ] **1** n silencio m; **a — fell** se hizo un silencio.
2 vt hacer callar, acallar, imponer silencio a; **to —
up** affair encubrir, echar tierra a; person tapar la
boca a.
3 vi callar(se); —! ¡chitón!, ¡cállate!
hushed [hʌʃt] adj tone callado, muy bajo; silence
profundo; **all were —** se callaron todos.
hush-hush ['hʌʃ'hʌʃ] adj muy secreto.
hush money ['hʌʃ,mʌni] n dinero m con que se
compra el silencio de uno, dinero m por callar.
husk [hʌsk] **1** n cáscara f, vaina f; (of corn) cascabillo
m. **2** vt descascarar, desvainar.
huskily ['hʌskili] adv roncamente, en voz ronca.
huskiness ['hʌskinis] n ronquedad f.
husky[1] ['hʌski] adj voice, person ronco; (tough)
fornido.
husky[2] ['hʌski] n perro m esquimal.
hussar [hə'za:*] n húsar m.
hussy ['hʌsi] n pícara f, sinvergonzona f; **you —!**
¡lagarta!; **she's a little —** es una fresca.
hustings ['hʌstiŋz] npl (fig) elecciones fpl.
hustle ['hʌsl] **1** n actividad f febril, bullicio m;
(pushfulness) empuje m; **— and bustle** vaivén m,
actividad f bulliciosa; **to get a — on** (fam) darse
prisa.
2 vt (jostle) empujar, codear; (hurry up) person dar
prisa a, thing acelerar; **I won't be —d into anything** yo no resuelvo las cosas de prisa; **they —d him
into a car** le llevaron apresuradamente a un coche,
le hicieron entrar sin ceremonia en un coche; **to —
someone out of a room** hacer que uno salga precipitadamente de un cuarto; **they —d the job to finish
it** se apresuraron a concluir el trabajo.
3 vi darse prisa, menearse.
hut [hʌt] n casilla f; (shed) cobertizo m; (hovel)
barraca f, cabaña f; **mountain —** albergue m de
montaña.
hutch [hʌtʃ] n conejera f.
hyacinth ['haiəsinθ] n (Bot, Min) jacinto m.
hyaena [hai'i:nə] n hiena f.
hybrid ['haibrid] **1** adj híbrido. **2** n híbrido m, a f.
hybridism ['haibridizəm] n hibridismo m.
hybridization [,haibridai'zeiʃən] n hibridación f.
hybridize ['haibridaiz] vti hibridar.
hydra ['haidrə] n hidra f; **H—** (Myth) Hidra f.
hydrangea [hai'dreindʒə] n hortensia f.
hydrant ['haidrənt] n boca f de riego; **fire —** boca f
de incendios.
hydrate ['haidreit] **1** n hidrato m. **2** vt hidratar.
hydraulic [hai'drɔlik] adj hidráulico.
hydraulics [hai'drɔliks] n hidráulica f.
hydro . . . ['haidrəu] hidro . . .
hydrocarbon ['haidrəu'ka:bən] n hidrocarburo m.
hydrochloric ['haidrə'klɔrik] adj: **— acid** ácido m
clorhídrico.
hydrocyanic ['haidrəsai'ænik] adj: **— acid** ácido m
cianhídrico.
hydrodynamics ['haidrəudai'næmiks] n hidrodinámica f.
hydroelectric ['haidrəui'lektrik] adj hidroeléctrico;

— power station, — power plant central f hidro-
électrica.
hydrogen ['haidridʒən] n hidrógeno m.
hydrography [hai'drɔgrəfi] n hidrografía f.
hydrolysis [hai'drɔlisis] n hidrólisis f.
hydrolyze ['haidrəulaiz] **1** vt hidrolizar. **2** vi hidrolizarse.
hydrometer [hai'drɔmitə*] n areómetro m.
hydrophobia [,haidrə'fəubiə] n hidrofobia f.
hydrophobic [,haidrə'fəubik] adj hidrofóbico.
hydroplane ['haidrəuplein] n hidroplano m, hidroavión m.
hydroxide [hai'drɔksaid] n hidróxido m.
hyena [hai'i:nə] n hiena f.
hygiene ['haidʒi:n] n higiene f.
hygienic [hai'dʒi:nik] adj higiénico.
hymen ['haimen] n (Anat) himen m.
hymn [him] n himno m.
hymnal ['himnəl] n, **hymn book** ['himbuk] n
himnario m.
hyperacidity ['haipərə'siditi] n hiperacidez f.
hyperbola [hai'pə:bələ] n hipérbola f.
hyperbole [hai'pə:bəli] n hipérbole f.
hyperbolic(al) [,haipə'bɔlik(əl)] adj hiperbólico.
hypercritical ['haipə'kritikəl] adj hipercrítico.
hypersensitive ['haipə'sensitiv] adj extremadamente
sensible.
hypertension ['haipə'tenʃən] n hipertensión f.
hyphen ['haifən] n guión m.
hyphenate ['haifəneit] vt escribir (or unir, separar)
con guión.
hypnosis [hip'nəusis] n hipnosis f.
hypnotic [hip'nɔtik] **1** adj hipnótico. **2** n hipnótico m.
hypnotism ['hipnətizəm] n hipnotismo m.
hypnotist ['hipnətist] n hipnotista mf.
hypnotize ['hipnətaiz] vt hipnotizar.
hypo ['haipəu] n hiposulfito m sódico.
hypochondria [,haipəu'kɔndriə] n hipocondría f.
hypochondriac [,haipəu'kɔndriæk] n hipocondríaco
m, a f.
hypocrisy [hi'pɔkrisi] n hipocresía f.
hypocrite ['hipəkrit] n hipócrita mf.
hypocritical [,haipə'kritikəl] adj hipócrita.
hypocritically [,haipə'kritikəli] adv hipócritamente.
hypodermic [,haipə'də:mik] n (also **— needle**) aguja
f hipodérmica.
hypotenuse [hai'pɔtinju:z] n hipotenusa f.
hypothesis [hai'pɔθisis] n, pl **hypotheses** [hai'pɔ-
θisi:z] hipótesis f.
hypothetic(al) [,haipəu'θetik(əl)] adj hipotético.
hypothetically [,haipəu'θetikəli] adv hipotéticamente.
hysterectomy [,histə'rektəmi] n histerectomía f.
hysteria [his'tiəriə] n histerismo m, histeria f.
hysterical [his'terikəl] adj histérico; **— laughter**
risa f histérica; **to get —** ponerse histérico, excitarse
locamente.
hysterically [his'terikəli] adv histéricamente.
hysterics [his'teriks] npl histerismo m, paroxismo m
histérico; **to go into —** ponerse histérico; **we were in
— about it** nos morimos casi de risa.

I

I [ai] *pron* yo.
iambic [ai'æmbik] *adj* yámbico.
Iberia [ai'biəriə] Iberia *f*.
Iberian [ai'biəriən] 1 *adj* ibero, ibérico. 2 *n* ibero *m*, a *f*.
Iberian Peninsula [ai'biəriənpə'ninsjulə] Península *f* Ibérica.
ibex ['aibeks] *n* íbice *m*, rebeco *m*.
ibis ['aibis] *n* ibis *f*.
ice [ais] 1 *n* hielo *m*; (*ice cream*) helado *m*; (*on cake*) alcorza *f*, garapiña *f*; **my feet are like —** tengo los pies helados; **to break the —** (*fig*) romper el hielo; **he cuts no —** no pincha ni corta; **it cuts no — with me** no me convence; **to keep something on —** conservar algo en frigorífico, (*fig*) tener algo en reserva; **to skate on thin —** pisar terreno peligroso.
2 *vt* helar; *drink* enfriar, echar cubos de hielo a; *cake* alcorzar, escarchar, garapiñar.
3 *vi* (*also* **— over, to — up**) helarse.
ice age ['aiseidʒ] *n* período *m* glacial.
ice axe ['aisæks] *n* piolet *m*.
iceberg ['aisbəːg] *n* iceberg *m*.
iceboat ['aisbəut] *n* (*US Sport*) trineo *m* con vela (para deslizarse sobre el hielo).
icebound ['aisbaund] *adj* road helado, bloqueado por el hielo; *ship* preso entre los hielos.
icebox ['aisbɔks] *n* nevera *f*.
icebreaker ['ais‚breikə*] *n* rompehielos *m*.
icecap ['aiskæp] *n* casquete *m* de hielo.
ice-cold ['ais'kəuld] *adj* más frío que el hielo.
ice cream ['ais'kriːm] *n* helado *m*.
ice cube ['aiskjuːb] *n* cubito *m* de hielo.
iced [aist] *adj* cake escarchado; *drink* con hielo.
ice field ['aisfiːld] *n* campo *m* de hielo, banquisa *f*.
ice floe ['aisfləu] *n* témpano *m* de hielo.
ice hockey ['ais'hɔki] *n* hockey *m* sobre hielo.
icehouse ['aishaus] *n*, *pl* **—houses** [‚hauziz] (a) (*US*) nevera *f*. (b) (*of Eskimo*) iglú *m*.
Iceland ['aislənd] Islandia *f*.
Icelander ['aisləndə*] *n* islandés *m*, esa *f*.
Icelandic [ais'lændik] 1 *adj* islandés. 2 *n* islandés *m*.
iceman ['aismæn] *n*, *pl* **—men** [men] (*US*) vendedor *m* de hielo, repartidor *m* de hielo.
ice pick ['aispik] *n* piolet *m*.
ice rink ['aisriŋk] pista *f* de hielo, pista *f* de patinaje.
iceskate ['aisskeit] *n* patín *m* de hielo, patín *m* de cuchilla.
ice-skate ['aisskeit] *vi* patinar sobre hielo.
ice skating ['aisskeitiŋ] *n* patinaje *m* sobre hielo.
ichthyology [‚ikθi'ɔlədʒi] *n* ictiología *f*.
icicle ['aisikl] *n* carámbano *m*.
icily ['aisili] *adv* glacialmente (*also fig*).
icing ['aisiŋ] *n* formación *f* de hielo; (*on cake*) alcorza *f*, garapiña *f*.
icing sugar ['aisiŋ'ʃugə*] *n* azúcar *m* de alcorza.
icon ['aikɔn] *n* icono *m*.
iconoclast [ai'kɔnəklæst] *n* iconoclasta *mf*.
iconoclastic [ai‚kɔnə'klæstik] *adj* iconoclasta.
icy ['aisi] *adj* helado, glacial; (*fig*) glacial; **it's — cold** hace un frío glacial.
id [id] *n* id *m*.
I'd [aid] = **I would; I had.**
idea [ai'diə] *n* idea *f*; concepto *m*; ocurrencia *f*; **bright —** idea *f* luminosa, idea *f* genial; **what an —!**, **the very —!** ¡ni hablar!, ¡qué cosas dices!; **the — is to sell it** nos proponemos venderlo; **whose — was it to come this way?** ¿a quién se le ocurrió venir por aquí?; **it would not be a bad — to paint it** no le vendría mal una mano de pintura; **that's the —!** ¡eso es!; **what's the big —?** ¿que hace Vd ahí?, ¿qué pretende Vd con esto?; **to get an — of something** hacerse una idea de algo; **to get an — for a novel** encontrar la inspiración para hacer una novela; **you're getting the —** estás empezando a comprender, (*of knack*) estás cogiendo el tino; **to get an —**

into one's head meterse una idea en la cabeza; **don't go getting —s** no te hagas ilusiones; **he has some — of French** tiene algunas nociones de francés; **I've no —!** ¡ni idea!; **I haven't the foggiest** (*or remotest etc*) **—** no tengo la más remota idea; **I had no — that . . .** no tenía la menor idea de que . . .; **he hit on the — of** + ger se le ocurrió + infin; **to put —s into someone's head** sugerir cosas a uno.
ideal [ai'diəl] 1 *adj* ideal; perfecto; soñado. 2 *n* ideal *m*.
idealism [ai'diəlizəm] *n* idealismo *m*.
idealist [ai'diəlist] *n* idealista *mf*.
idealistic [ai‚diə'listik] *adj* idealista.
idealize [ai'diəlaiz] *vt* idealizar.
ideally [ai'diəli] *adv* idealmente; perfectamente; **they are — suited to each other** se convienen perfectamente uno a otra; **—, we should all go** en el mejor de los casos, debemos ir todos.
idée fixe ['iːdei'fiːks] *n* idea *f* fija.
identical [ai'dentikəl] *adj* idéntico.
identification [ai‚dentifi'keiʃən] *n* identificación *f*; **— mark** señal *f* de identificación; **— tag** chapa *f* de identificación.
identify [ai'dentifai] 1 *vt* identificar. 2 *vr*: **to — oneself** identificarse, establecer su identidad; **to — oneself with** identificarse con.
identikit [ai'dentikit] *n*: **— picture** retrato-robot *m*.
identity [ai'dentiti] *n* identidad *f*; **mistaken —** identificación *f* errónea; **— card** cédula *f* personal, carnet *m* de identidad *m*; **— disc** chapa *f* de identidad.
ideological [‚aidiə'lɔdʒikəl] *adj* ideológico.
ideologist [‚aidi'ɔlədʒist] *n* ideólogo *m*.
ideology [‚aidi'ɔlədʒi] *n* ideología *f*.
ides [aidz] *npl* idus *mpl*.
idiocy ['idiəsi] *n* imbecilidad *f*; estupidez *f*.
idiom ['idiəm] *n* (*phrase*) idiotismo *m*, modismo *m*, locución *f*; (*style of expression*) lenguaje *m*.
idiomatic [‚idiə'mætik] *adj* idiomático.
idiosyncrasy [‚idiə'siŋkrəsi] *n* idiosincrasia *f*.
idiosyncratic [‚idiəsiŋ'krætik] *adj* idiosincrásico.
idiot ['idiət] *n* idiota *mf*, imbécil *mf*, tonto *m*, a *f*; **village —** tonto *m* del lugar; **you —!** ¡imbécil!
idiotic [‚idi'ɔtik] *adj* idiota, imbécil, tonto, estúpido; *laughter* tonto; **that was — of you** has hecho el tonto.
idiotically [‚idi'ɔtikəli] *adv* tontamente, estúpidamente; **to laugh —** reírse como un tonto.
idle ['aidl] 1 *adj* ocioso; (*lazy*) holgazán; (*work-shy*) vago; *student etc* gandul; (*without work*) desocupado; *fear* vano, infundado; *speculation* inútil; *question* ocioso; *talk* frívolo; *moment* de ocio, libre; **the machine is never —** la máquina no está parada jamás; **the strike made 100 workers —** la huelga dejó sin trabajo a 100 obreros.
2 *vt*: **to — away** time perder, malgastar.
3 *vi* haraganear, gandulear; (*Mech*) marchar en vacío; **we spent a few days idling in Paris** pasamos unos días ociosos en París; **we —d over our meal** no nos dimos prisa para terminar la comida.
idleness ['aidlnis] *n* ociosidad *f*, holgazanería *f*, gandulería *f*; desocupación *f*; inutilidad *f*; frivolidad *f*; **to live in —** vivir en el ocio.
idler ['aidlə*] *n* ocioso *m*, a *f*, holgazán *m*, ana *f*, vago *m*, a *f*; (*student*) gandul *m*.
idly ['aidli] *adv* ociosamente; vanamente, inútilmente; **he glanced — out of the window** miró distraído por la ventana.
idol ['aidl] *n* ídolo *m*.
idolater [ai'dɔlətə*] *n* idólatra *mf*.
idolatrous [ai'dɔlətrəs] *adj* idólatra, idolátrico.
idolatry [ai'dɔlətri] *n* idolatría *f*.
idolize ['aidəlaiz] *vt* idolatrar.
idyll ['idil] *n* idilio *m*.

idyllic [i'dilik] *adj* idílico.

if [if] **1** *conj* (**a**) si; (*open condition*) — he comes I'll go si él viene yo iré; (*past: habit*) — it was fine we went out si hacía buen tiempo dábamos un paseo; (*past: unfulfilled*) — you were to say that you would be wrong si dijese eso se equivocaría; — you had said that you would have been wrong si hubiera dicho eso se habría equivocado.
(**b**) — I were you yo en tu lugar, yo que tú.
(**c**) (*whether*) si; I don't know — he's here no sé si está aquí.
(**d**) — anything this one is better hasta creo que éste es mejor; — not si no; — so si es así; a nice film — rather long una buena película pero algo larga.
(**e**) — only to see him si solamente para verle; — only for a few hours si solamente durante unas pocas horas; — only I could! ¡ojalá pudiera!, ¡si solamente pudiera!; — only I had known! ¡si lo hubiese sabido!; — only we had a car! ¡quién tuviera coche!; *see* **as, even** *etc*.
2 *n* hipótesis *f*; duda *f*; there are a lot of —s and buts hay muchas dudas no resueltas; it's a big — es una duda importante, es sumamente dudoso.
iffy ['ifi] *adj* (*US fam*) dudoso, incierto.
igloo ['iglu:] *n* iglú *m*.
Ignatius [ig'neiʃəs] *m* Ignacio.
igneous ['igniəs] *adj* ígneo.
ignite [ig'nait] **1** *vt* encender, incendiar, pegar fuego a. **2** *vi* encenderse, incendiarse.
ignition [ig'niʃən] *n* ignición *f*; (*Aut*) encendido *m*.
ignition key [ig'niʃən.ki:] *n* llave *f* de contacto.
ignoble [ig'nəubl] *adj* innoble, vil.
ignominious [,ignə'miniəs] *adj* ignominioso, oprobioso; *defeat* vergonzoso.
ignominiously [,ignə'miniəsli] *adv* ignominiosamente; to be — defeated sufrir una derrota vergonzosa.
ignominy ['ignəmini] *n* ignominia *f*, oprobio *m*, vergüenza *f*.
ignoramus [,ignə'reiməs] *n* ignorante *mf*.
ignorance ['ignərəns] *n* ignorancia *f*; to be in — of something ignorar algo, desconocer algo.
ignorant ['ignərənt] *adj* ignorante; to be — of ignorar, no saber, desconocer.
ignorantly ['ignərəntli] *adv* neciamente; we — went to the next house por ignorancia fuimos a la casa de al lado.
ignore [ig'nɔ:*] *vt* no hacer caso de, desatender; (*omit*) pasar por alto; *awkward fact* cerrar los ojos ante; we can safely — that eso lo podemos dejar a un lado; I smiled but she —d me le sonreí pero ella no me hizo caso.
iguana [i'gwɑ:nə] *n* iguana *f*.
ikon ['aikɔn] *n* icono *m*.
ilex ['aileks] *n* encina *f*.
Iliad ['iliæd] *n* Ilíada *f*.
ilk [ilk] *n*: and others of that — y otros de ese jaez.
ill [il] **1** *adj* (**a**) (*Med*) enfermo, malo; to be — estar enfermo; to fall (*or* take, be taken) — ponerse enfermo, enfermar; to feel — sentirse mal.
(**b**) *fame, temper, turn etc* malo.
2 *adv* mal; we can — afford to lose him mal podemos permitir que se vaya; to speak — of someone hablar mal de uno, criticar a uno; he took it very — se ofendió bastante; don't take it — no lo tome a mal.
3 *n* (*Med*) mal *m*; (*fig*) infortunio *m*, desgracia *f*; the —s of the economy la dolencia de la economía.
I'll [ail] = **I will, I shall**.
ill-advised ['iləd'vaizd] *adj*: an — plan un proyecto nada recomendable; you were very — en eso no anduvo Vd muy acertado; you would be — to + *infin* sería poco aconsejable que Vd + *subj*.
ill-at-ease ['ilət'i:z] *adj* molesto; inquieto, intranquilo.
ill-bred ['il'bred] *adj* mal educado, mal criado.
ill-considered ['ilkən'sidəd] *adj plan* nada recomendable; *act* irreflexivo.
ill-disposed ['ildis'pəuzd] *adj* malintencionado; to be — towards someone estar maldispuesto hacia uno; he is — towards the idea la idea no le hace gracia.
illegal [i'li:gəl] *adj* ilegal, ilícito.
illegality [,ili:'gæliti] *n* ilegalidad *f*.
illegally [i'li:gəli] *adv* ilegalmente, ilícitamente.
illegible [i'ledʒəbl] *adj* ilegible.
illegibly [i'ledʒəbli] *adv* de un modo ilegible.
illegitimacy [,ili'dʒitiməsi] *n* ilegitimidad *f*.
illegitimate [,ili'dʒitimit] *adj* ilegítimo.
illegitimately [,ili'dʒitimitli] *adv* ilegítimamente.
ill-fated ['il'feitid] *adj* malogrado, malhadado.
ill-favoured ['il'feivəd] *adj* feo, mal parecido.

ill-feeling ['il'fi:liŋ] *n* hostilidad *f*, rencor *m*.
ill-founded ['il'faundid] *adj claim etc* mal fundado, infundado.
ill-gotten ['il'gɔtn] *adj* mal adquirido.
ill health ['il'helθ] *n* mala salud *f*; to be in — no estar bien de salud.
ill humour, (*US*) — **humor** ['il'hju:mə*] *n* mal humor *m*.
ill-humoured, (*US*) —**-humored** ['il'hju:məd] *adj* malhumorado.
illiberal [i'libərəl] *adj* iliberal; intolerante.
illicit [i'lisit] *adj* ilícito.
illicitly [i'lisitli] *adv* ilícitamente.
illimitable [i'limitəbl] *adj* ilimitado, sin límites.
ill-informed ['ilin'fɔ:md] *adj* poco enterado, ignorante.
illiteracy [i'litərəsi] *n* analfabetismo *m*.
illiterate [i'litərit] **1** *adj* analfabeto; (*fig*) sin instrucción, poco instruido; iletrado; *style etc* inculto. **2** *n* analfabeto *m*, a *f*.
ill-judged ['il'dʒʌdʒd] *adj* imprudente.
ill-kempt ['il'kempt] *adj* desaliñado, desaseado.
ill luck ['il'lʌk] *n* mala suerte *f*; as — would have it desgraciadamente, como quiso la desgracia.
ill-mannered ['il'mænəd] *adj* mal educado, sin educación.
ill-natured ['il'neitʃəd] *adj* malévolo, malicioso.
illness ['ilnis] *n* enfermedad *f*, mal *m*.
illogical [i'lɔdʒikəl] *adj* ilógico.
illogicality [i,lɔdʒi'kæliti] *n* falta *f* de lógica.
ill-omened ['il'əumənd] *adj* de mal agüero; nefasto.
ill-starred ['il'stɑ:d] *adj* malhadado, malogrado.
ill-suited ['il'su:tid] *adj*: they are — no se convienen uno a otro; he is — to the job no conviene al puesto, no tiene las cualidades que convienen al puesto.
ill-tempered ['il'tempəd] *adj person* de mal genio; *remark, tone etc* malhumorado.
ill-timed ['il'taimd] *adj* inoportuno, intempestivo.
ill-treat ['il'tri:t] *vt* maltratar, tratar mal.
ill treatment ['il'tri:tmənt] *n* maltratamiento *m*, malos tratos *mpl*.
illuminate [i'lu:mineit] *vt* iluminar (*also Art*); (*decorate with lights*) poner luminarias en; *subject* aclarar; the castle is —d in summer en el verano el castillo está iluminado.
illuminated [i'lu:mineitid] *adj sign etc* luminoso.
illuminating [i'lu:mineitiŋ] {*adj* aclaratorio; *book, speech etc* instructivo; *remark etc* revelador, significativo.
illumination [i,lu:mi'neiʃən] *n* iluminación *f* (*also Art*), alumbrado *m*; —s (*festive etc*) luminarias *fpl*.
illuminator [i'lu:mineitə*] *n* iluminador *m*.
illumine [i'lu:min] *vt* = **illuminate**.
ill-use ['il'ju:z] *vt* maltratar, tratar mal.
illusion [i'lu:ʒən] *n* ilusión *f*; optical — ilusión *f* de óptica; to be under an — estar equivocado; I am under no —s on that score sobre ese punto no tengo ilusiones.
illusive [i'lu:siv] *adj*, **illusory** [i'lu:səri] *adj* ilusorio.
illustrate [i'ləstreit] *vt* ilustrar; *subject* aclarar; *point* ejemplificar, demostrar; *book* ilustrar; a book —d by X un libro con grabados de X; I can best — this in the following way esto quedará más claro si se explica del modo siguiente.
illustration [,iləs'treiʃən] *n* (*example*) ejemplo *m*; (*explanation*) explicación *f*, aclaración *f*; (*in book*) grabado *m*, lámina *f*, ilustración *f*.
illustrative ['iləstrətiv] *adj* ilustrativo, ilustrador, aclaratorio; to be — of something ejemplificar algo.
illustrator ['iləstreitə*] *n* ilustrador *m*.
illustrious [i'lʌstriəs] *adj* ilustre.
ill will ['il'wil] *n* mala voluntad *f*; (*spite*) rencor *m*; I bear you no — for that no le guardo rencor por eso.
I'm [aim] = **I am**.
image ['imidʒ] *n* (**a**) imagen *f* (*also Lit, Eccl*); mirror — reflejo *m* exacto; to be the very (*or* spitting) — of ser el vivo retrato de; to make someone in one's own — hacer a uno a su imagen.
(**b**) (*public face*) reputación *f*, opinión *f*; brand — reputación *f* de una marca; the company's — la reputación de la compañía; we must improve our — hemos de mejorar la opinión que el público tiene de nosotros.
imagery ['imidʒəri] *n* (*Lit*) imágenes *fpl*, metáforas *fpl*.
imaginable [i'mædʒinəbl] *adj* imaginable; the biggest surprise — la mayor sorpresa que se puede imaginar.
imaginary [i'mædʒinəri] *adj* imaginario.
imagination [i,mædʒi'neiʃən] *n* imaginación *f*;

(*capacity for* —) imaginativa *f*; (*inventiveness*) inventiva *f*; **it's all** —! ¡es pura fantasía!, ¡lo has soñado!; **have you no** —? ¿eres incapaz de imaginártelo?; **she lets her** — **run away with her** se deja llevar por la imaginación.
imaginative [i'mædʒinətiv] *adj* imaginativo.
imaginativeness [i'mædʒinətivnis] *n* imaginativa *f*.
imagine [i'mædʒin] *vt* imaginar, imaginarse, figurarse; **just** —! ¡imagínese!; **you can** — **how I felt**! ¡Vd puede suponer lo que yo sufría!; **don't** — **that** . . . no se vaya a pensar que yo + *subj*; **to fondly** — **that** . . . hacerse la ilusión de que . . ., creer inocentemente que . . .
imbalance [im'bæləns] *n* desequilibrio *m*, falta *f* de equilibrio.
imbecile ['imbəsi:l] **1** *adj* imbécil. **2** *n* imbécil *mf*; **you** —! ¡imbécil!
imbecility [,imbi'siliti] *n* imbecilidad *f*.
imbibe [im'baib] **1** *vt* (*drink*) beber; (*absorb*) embeber; (*fig*) embeberse de (*or* en), empaparse de. **2** *vi* beber.
imbroglio [im'brəuliəu] *n* embrollo *m*, lío *m*.
imbue [im'bju:] *vt*: **to** — **something with** imbuir algo de (*or* en); **to be** —**d with** estar empapado de.
imitable ['imitəbl] *adj* imitable.
imitate ['imiteit] *vt* imitar; (*pej*) remedar; (*make another copy of*) copiar, reproducir.
imitation [,imi'teiʃən] **1** *n* imitación *f*; (*pej*) remedo *m*; (*copy*) copia *f*, reproducción *f*; **in** — **of** a imitación de; **beware of** —**s** desconfíe de las imitaciones.
2 *attr*: — **jewels** joyas *fpl* de imitación.
imitative ['imitətiv] *adj* imitativo; imitador; **a style** — **of Joyce's** un estilo que imita el de Joyce.
imitator ['imiteitə*] *n* imitador *m*, ora *f*.
immaculate [i'mækjulit] *adj* (*spotless*) limpísimo, perfectamente limpio; *style etc* perfecto; (*Eccl*) inmaculado, purísimo.
immanent ['imənənt] *adj* inmanente.
immaterial [,imə'tiəriəl] *adj* inmaterial, incorpóreo; **it is** — **whether** . . . no importa si . . .; **that is quite** — eso no hace al caso; **that is** — **to me** eso me es indiferente.
immature [,imə'tjuə*] *adj* inmaturo, no maduro; *specimen* joven; *fruit* verde; *work* juvenil.
immaturity [,imə'tjuəriti] *n* inmadurez *f*, falta *f* de madurez; juventud *f*.
immeasurable [i'meʒərəbl] *adj* inmensurable, inconmensurable.
immeasurably [i'meʒərəbli] *adv* enormemente.
immediacy [i'mi:diəsi] *n* inmediatez *f*; urgencia *f*.
immediate [i'mi:diət] *adj* inmediato; (*pressing*) urgente, apremiante; (*prime*) primero, principal; **my** — **object** mi primer propósito; **the** — **area** las inmediaciones; **we must take** — **action** hay que obrar inmediatamente.
immediately [i'mi:diətli] **1** *adv* **(a)** (*of time*) inmediatamente, en seguida; sin demora; en el acto; — **following the dinner** luego de la cena; — **following this discussion** a raíz de esta discusión.
(**b**) (*of place*) — **next to the wall** muy junto a la pared.
2 *conj* así que, luego que, al instante que; **let me know** — **he comes** avíseme en cuanto venga.
immemorial [,imi'mɔ:riəl] *adj* inmemorial, inmemorable; **from time** — desde hace muchísimo tiempo.
immense [i'mens] *adj* inmenso, enorme.
immensely [i'mensli] *adv* enormemente; **we were** — **cheered** nos alegramos muchísimo; **did you enjoy yourselves?** **yes,** — ¿qué tal lo pasasteis? estupendamente; **it is** — **difficult** es enormemente difícil.
immensity [i'mensiti] *n* inmensidad *f*.
immerse [i'mə:s] **1** *vt* sumergir; hundir; **to be** —**d in** (*fig*) estar absorto en. **2** *vr*: **to** — **oneself in** (*fig*) sumergirse en.
immersion [i'mə:ʃən] *n* inmersión *f*, sumersión *f*.
immersion heater [i'mə:ʃən,hi:tə*] *n* calentador *m* de inmersión.
immigrant ['imigrənt] **1** *adj* inmigrante. **2** *n* inmigrante *mf*.
immigrate ['imigreit] *vi* inmigrar.
immigration [,imi'greiʃən] *n* inmigración *f*.
imminence ['iminəns] *n* inminencia *f*.
imminent ['iminənt] *adj* inminente.
immobile [i'məubail] *adj* inmóvil, inmoble.
immobility [,iməu'biliti] *n* inmovilidad *f*.
immobilize [i'məubilaiz] *vt* inmovilizar.
immoderate [i'mɔdərit] *adj* excesivo.
immoderately [i'mɔdəritli] *adv* excesivamente; **to drink** — beber en exceso.
immodest [i'mɔdist] *adj* (*indecent*) deshonesto, impúdico; (*impudent*) descarado.
immodestly [i'mɔdistli] *adv* impúdicamente; descaradamente.

immodesty [i'mɔdisti] *n* deshonestidad *f*, impudicia *f*; descaro *m*.
immolate ['iməuleit] *vt* inmolar.
immoral [i'mɔrəl] *adj* inmoral; *earnings* ilícito.
immorality [,imə'ræliti] *n* inmoralidad *f*.
immortal [i'mɔ:tl] **1** *adj* inmortal; *fame etc* imperecedero. **2** *n* inmortal *mf*.
immortality [,imɔ:'tæliti] *n* inmortalidad *f*.
immortalize [i'mɔ:təlaiz] *vt* inmortalizar.
immovable [i'mu:vəbl] *adj* inmoble, inmóvil; que no se puede mover; *feast etc* fijo; (*fig*) inalterable, inconmovible; **he was quite** — fue imposible convencerle.
immune [i'mju:n] *adj* inmune (*also Med*; *from, to* a, contra); **to be** — **from taxes** estar exento de impuestos.
immunity [i'mju:niti] *n* inmunidad *f* (*also Med*; *from, to* contra); exención *f* (*from* de); **diplomatic** — inmunidad *f* diplomática; **parliamentary** — inmunidad *f* parlamentaria.
immunization [,imjunai'zeiʃən] *n* (*Med*) inmunización *f*.
immunize ['imjunaiz] *vt* inmunizar.
immure [i'mjuə*] *vt* emparedar; (*fig*) encerrar; **to be** —**d in** estar encerrado en.
immutability [i,mju:tə'biliti] *n* inmutabilidad *f*, inalterabilidad *f*.
immutable [i'mju:təbl] *adj* inmutable, inalterable.
imp [imp] *n* diablillo *m* (*also fig*).
impact ['impækt] *n* impacto *m*, choque *m*; (*fig*) impacto *m*, efecto *m*, consecuencias *fpl*; **the book had a great** — **on its readers** el libro conmovió profundamente a sus lectores; **the** — **of our advertising campaign** el efecto de nuestra campaña publicitaria.
impair [im'pɛə*] *vt* perjudicar, dañar, deteriorar, debilitar.
impale [im'peil] **1** *vt* (*as punishment*) empalar; (*on sword etc*) espetar, atravesar. **2** *vr*: **to** — **oneself on** atravesarse en.
impalpable [im'pælpəbl] *adj* impalpable; (*fig*) intangible, inaprensible.
imparity [im'pæriti] *n* disparidad *f*.
impart [im'pa:t] *vt* comunicar.
impartial [im'pa:ʃəl] *adj* imparcial.
impartiality [im,pa:ʃi'æliti] *n* imparcialidad *f*.
impartially [im'pa:ʃəli] *adv* imparcialmente.
impassable [im'pa:səbl] *adj* intransitable; *river etc* invadeable; *barrier* infranqueable.
impasse [æm'pa:s] *n* callejón *m* sin salida; parálisis *f*, situación *f* sin solución; **the** — **lasted 3 months** la parálisis duró 3 meses; **the** — **is complete** la parálisis es total; **negotiations have reached an** — las negociaciones han llegado a un punto muerto, las negociaciones están en un callejón sin salida.
impassioned [im'pæʃnd] *adj* apasionado, exaltado.
impassive [im'pæsiv] *adj* impasible, imperturbable.
impassively [im'pæsivli] *adv* imperturbablemente; **he listened** — escuchó impasible.
impatience [im'peiʃəns] *n* impaciencia *f*.
impatient [im'peiʃənt] *adj* impaciente; intolerante; **to be** — **to** + *infin* impacientarse por + *infin*; **to be** — **of something** no sufrir algo con paciencia, no aguantar algo ; **to get** (*or* **become, grow**) — **about something** impacientarse ante algo, impacientarse por algo; **to get** — **with someone** perder la paciencia con uno; **to make someone** — impacientar a uno.
impatiently [im'peiʃəntli] *adv* con impaciencia, impacientemente.
impeach [im'pi:tʃ] *vt* (*accuse*) acusar (de alta traición); (*try*) procesar; (*criticize*) censurar; tachar.
impeachment [im'pi:tʃmənt] *n* acusación *f* (de alta traición); proceso *m*.
impeccable [im'pekəbl] *adj* impecable, intachable.
impecunious [,impi'kju:niəs] *adj* inope, indigente.
impede [im'pi:d] *vt* *person* estorbar; (*fig*) dificultar, estorbar, impedir.
impediment [im'pedimənt] *n* obstáculo *m*, estorbo *m* (*to* para); (*Law*) impedimento *m*; (*in speech*) defecto *m* del habla.
impedimenta [im,pedi'mentə] *npl* equipaje *m*; (*Mil*) impedimenta *f*.
impel [im'pel] *vt* impulsar, mover (*to* + *infin* a + *infin*); **I feel** —**led to say** . . . me veo obligado a decir . . .
impend [im'pend] *vi* amenazar, ser inminente.
impending [im'pendiŋ] *adj* inminente; (*near*) próximo; **his** — **fate** el hado que le amenazaba; **his** — **retirement** su jubilación que va a realizarse en breve; **our** — **removal** nuestra mudanza en fecha próxima.
impenetrability [im,penitrə'biliti] *n* impenetrabilidad *f*.

impenetrable [im'penitrəbl] *adj* impenetrable (*to* a); *mind etc* insondable, enigmático.

impenitence [im'penitəns] *n* impenitencia *f*.

impenitent [im'penitənt] *adj* impenitente, incorregible; **he was quite — about** it no tuvo el menor deseo de pedir perdón por ello.

imperative [im'perətiv] **1** *adj tone* imperioso, perentorio; (*Gram*) imperativo; (*necessary*) esencial, indispensable; (*pressing*) urgente, apremiante; **it is — that** es imprescindible que + *subj*. **2** *n* (*Gram*) imperativo *m*.

imperceptible [,impə'septəbl] *adj* imperceptible, insensible.

imperceptibly [,impə'septəbli] *adv* imperceptiblemente, insensiblemente.

imperfect [im'pə:fikt] **1** *adj* imperfecto (*also Gram*), defectuoso. **2** *n* (*Gram*) imperfecto *m*.

imperfection [,impə'fekʃən] *n* (*state*) imperfección *f*; (*blemish*) desperfecto *m*, tacha *f*.

imperfectly [im'pə:fiktli] *adv* defectuosamente.

imperial [im'piəriəl] *adj* imperial.

imperialism [im'piəriəlizəm] *n* imperialismo *m*.

imperialist [im'piəriəlist] *n* imperialista *mf*.

imperialistic [im,piəriə'listik] *adj* imperialista.

imperially [im'piəriəli] *adv* imperialmente.

imperil [im'peril] *vt* poner en peligro, arriesgar.

imperious [im'piəriəs] *adj* imperioso, arrogante; *need* apremiante.

imperiously [im'piəriəsli] *adv* imperiosamente.

imperishable [im'periʃəbl] *adj* imperecedero.

impermanent [im'pə:mənənt] *adj* impermanente.

impermeable [im'pə:miəbl] *adj* impermeable (*to* a).

impersonal [im'pə:snl] *adj* impersonal.

impersonality [im,pə:sə'næliti] *n* impersonalidad *f*.

impersonate [im'pə:səneit] *vt* hacerse pasar por; (*Theat*) imitar.

impersonation [im,pə:sə'neiʃən] *n* (*Theat*) imitación *f*.

impersonator [im'pə:səneitə*] *n* (*Theat*) imitador *m*, ora *f*.

impertinence [im'pə:tinəns] *n* impertinencia *f*, insolencia *f*, descaro *m*; **an —, a piece of —** una impertinencia; **it would be an — to** + *infin* sería inoportuno + *infin*; **what —!, the — of it!** ¡qué frescura!

impertinent [im'pə:tinənt] *adj* impertinente, insolente, descarado; **to be — to someone** decir impertinencias a uno; **don't be —!** ¡no seas fresco!

impertinently [im'pə:tinəntli] *adv* impertinentemente, descaradamente.

imperturbable [,impə'tə:bəbl] *adj* imperturbable.

impervious [im'pə:viəs] *adj* impermeable, impenetrable (*to* a); (*fig*) insensible (*to* a).

impetigo [,impi'taigəu] *n* impétigo *m*.

impetuosity [im,petju'ɔsiti] *n* impetuosidad *f*, irreflexión *f*.

impetuous [im'petjuəs] *adj* impetuoso, irreflexivo.

impetuously [im'petjuəsli] *adv* impetuosamente, irreflexivamente.

impetus ['impitəs] *n* ímpetu *m*; (*fig*) impulso *m*, incentivo *m*, fuerza *f* motriz.

impiety [im'paiəti] *n* impiedad *f*.

impinge [im'pindʒ] *vi*: **to — on** afectar a.

impious ['impiəs] *adj* impío.

impish ['impiʃ] *adj* travieso, endiablado.

implacable [im'plækəbl] *adj* implacable.

implant [im'plɑ:nt] *vt* implantar; *idea etc* inculcar.

implausible [im'plɔ:zəbl] *adj* inverosímil; poco convincente.

implement ['implimənt] *n* herramienta *f*, instrumento *m*; (*Agr*) apero *m*.

implement [im'pliment] *vt* poner por obra, llevar a cabo, hacer efectivo; realizar, ejecutar.

implementation [,implimen'teiʃən] *n* realización *f*, ejecución *f*.

implicate ['implikeit] *vt* comprometer; enredar; **he —d 3 others** acusó a 3 más (de haber tomado parte en el crimen), delató a 3 cómplices suyos; **are you —d in this?** ¿anda Vd metido en esto?

implication [,impli'keiʃən] *n* (a) (*act*) comprometimiento *m*.
(b) (*in crime*) complicidad *f*.
(c) (*consequence etc*) consecuencia *f*, inferencia *f*; **—s** consecuencias *fpl*, trascendencia *f*; **by —, then ...** de ahí se deduce, pues, . . .; **he did not realise the full —s of his words** no se dio cuenta de la trascendencia de sus palabras; **we shall have to study all the —s** tendremos que estudiar todas las consecuencias.

implicit [im'plisit] *adj* implícito; *faith etc* incondicional, absoluto.

implicitly [im'plisitli] *adv* implícitamente; sin reservas, incondicionalmente.

implied [im'plaid] *adj* implícito, tácito; **it is not stated but it is —** no se declara abiertamente pero se sobreentiende.

implore [im'plɔ:*] *vt thing* implorar, suplicar; *person* suplicar; **I — you!** ¡se lo suplico!; **to — someone to do something** suplicar a uno hacer algo.

imploring [im'plɔ:riŋ] *adj* suplicante; *look etc* lleno de suplicación.

imploringly [im'plɔ:riŋli] *adv* de modo suplicante.

imply [im'plai] *vt* (*involve*) implicar, suponer, presuponer; (*mean*) querer decir, significar; (*state indirectly*) dar a entender; (*hint*) insinuar; **that implies some intelligence** eso supone cierta inteligencia; **are you —ing that . . .?** ¿quiere Vd decir que . . .?; **what do you — by that?** ¿qué quiere Vd insinuar con eso?; **he implied he would do it** dio a entender que lo haría; **it implies a lot of work for him** esto significa que tendrá mucho trabajo.

impolite [,impə'lait] *adj* descortés, mal educado.

impolitely [,impə'laitli] *adv* con descortesía.

impolitic [im'pɔlitik] *adj* impolítico.

imponderable [im'pɔndərəbl] **1** *adj* imponderable. **2 —s** *npl* (elementos *mpl*) imponderables *mpl*.

import ['impɔ:t] **1** *n* (a) (*Comm*) importación *f*, artículo *m* importado.
(b) (*meaning*) significado *m*, sentido *m*; importancia *f*.
2 *attr*: **— duty** derechos *mpl* de entrada; **— licence** permiso *m* de importación; **— surcharge** sobrecarga *f* de importación; **— trade** comercio *m* importador.

import [im'pɔ:t] *vt* (a) (*Comm*) importar (*from* de, *into* en). (b) (*mean*) significar, querer decir.

importance [im'pɔ:təns] *n* importancia *f*; **of some —** de cierta importancia, importante; **a fact of the first —** un hecho primordial; **to attach great — to something** conceder mucha importancia a algo; **to be of —** tener importancia; **that's of no —** eso no importa; **to be full of one's own —** darse ínfulas.

important [im'pɔ:tənt] *adj* importante; de categoría; **it's not —** no importa, no tiene importancia; **to try to look —** tratar de hacer figura.

importantly [im'pɔ:təntli] *adv* say *etc* en tono rimbombante.

importation [,impɔ:'teiʃən] *n* importación *f*.

imported [im'pɔ:tid] *adj article* de importación.

importer [im'pɔ:tə*] *n* importador *m*, ora *f*.

importunate [im'pɔ:tjunit] *adj demand etc* importuno; *person* molesto, pesado.

importune [,impɔ:'tju:n] *vt* importunar, perseguir, fastidiar; (*prostitute*) abordar con fines inmorales.

importunity [,impɔ:'tju:niti] *n* importunidad *f*; pesadez *f*.

impose [im'pəuz] **1** *vt* imponer (*on* a); (*palm off*) hacer aceptar (*on* a).
2 *vi*: **to — upon** (*deceive*) embaucar; (*take advantage of*) *kindness etc* abusar de, *person* abusar de la amabilidad de; **I don't wish to — upon you** no quiero abusar, no quiero molestarle.

imposing [im'pəuziŋ] *adj* imponente, impresionante; majestuoso.

imposition [,impə'ziʃən] *n* (*act*) imposición *f*; (*burden*) carga *f*, molestia *f*; abuso *m*; (*tax*) impuesto *m*; **it's a bit of an —** me resulta bastante molesto; **I fear it's rather an — for you** me temo que le vaya a molestar bastante.

impossibility [im,pɔsə'biliti] *n* imposibilidad *f*.

impossible [im'pɔsəbl] *adj* imposible; *person* inaguantable, insufrible; **you're —!** ¡eres insufrible!, ¡no puedo contigo!; **to do the —** hacer lo imposible; **to make it — for someone to do something** quitar a uno la posibilidad de hacer algo, imposibilitar algo a uno.

impossibly [im'pɔsəbli] *adv* imposiblemente; **— difficult** de lo más difícil, tan difícil que resulta imposible.

impost ['impəust] *n* impuesto *m*.

impostor [im'pɔstə*] *n* impostor *m*, ora *f*, embustero *m*, a *f*.

imposture [im'pɔstʃə*] *n* impostura *f*, engaño *m*, fraude *m*.

impotence ['impətəns] *n* impotencia *f*.

impotent ['impətənt] *adj* impotente.

impound [im'paund] *vt goods* embargar, confiscar.

impoverish [im'pɔvəriʃ] *vt* empobrecer, reducir a la miseria; *land* agotar.

impoverished [im'pɔvəriʃt] *adj* necesitado, indigente; *land* agotado.

impoverishment [im'pɔvəriʃmənt] *n* empobrecimiento *m*; agotamiento *m*.

impracticability [im,præktikə'biliti] *n* impracticabilidad *f*, imposibilidad *f*.

impracticable [im'præktikəbl] *adj* impracticable, no factible, imposible de realizar.

impractical [im'præktikəl] *adj* falto de sentido práctico, poco práctico; desmañado.

imprecation [,impri'keiʃən] *n* imprecación *f*.

impregnable [im'pregnəbl] *adj* inexpugnable.

impregnate ['impregneit] *vt* impregnar, empapar (*with* de); (*Bio*) fecundar; **to become —d with** impregnarse de.

impregnation [,impreg'neiʃən] *n* impregnación *f*; (*Bio*) fecundación *f*.

impresario [,impre'sɑːriəu] *n* empresario *m*.

impress ['impres] *n* impresión *f*, señal *f*; (*fig*) sello *m*, huella *f*.

impress [im'pres] **1** *vt* (a) (*mark, stamp*) estampar; (*fig*) grabar, inculcar; **I must — upon you that . . .** tengo que subrayar que . . . ; **it —ed itself upon my mind** quedó grabado en mi memoria; **I tried to — the importance of the job on him** traté de convencerle de la importancia del puesto.

(b) (*affect*) impresionar; **he does it just to — people** lo hace sólo para impresionar a la gente; **he is not easily —ed** no se deja impresionar fácilmente; **I was not —ed** no me hizo buena impresión; **he —ed me quite favourably** me hizo una impresión bastante buena; **how did it — you?** ¿qué impresión te produjo?; **the play deeply —ed everyone** la obra causó honda impresión en todos.

2 *vi* hacer buena impresión.

impression [im'preʃən] *n* impresión *f*; huella *f*; señal *f*; (*Typ*) edición *f*, tirada *f*; (*fig*) impresión *f*, efecto *m*; **to be under the — that, to have the — that** tener la impresión de que; **he gives an — of knowing a lot** da la impresión de saber mucho; **to make an —** impresionar; **she's out to make an —** se dedica a impresionar, quiere causar una sensación; **to make an — on someone** impresionar a uno; **what — did it make on you?** ¿qué impresión le produjo?; **all our arguments seemed to make no — on him** todos nuestros argumentos al parecer no tuvieron efecto alguno en él; **he could make no — on his opponent's majority** no logró rebajar la mayoría de su rival.

impressionable [im'preʃnəbl] *adj* impresionable; influenciable; sensible.

impressionism [im'preʃənizəm] *n* impresionismo *m*.

impressionist [im'preʃənist] **1** *adj* impresionista. **2** *n* impresionista *mf*.

impressionistic [im,preʃə'nistik] *adj* impresionista.

impressive [im'presiv] *adj* impresionante.

impressively [im'presivli] *adv* de modo impresionante.

imprint ['imprint] *n* impresión *f*, huella *f*, señal *f*; (*Typ*) pie *m* de imprenta.

imprint [im'print] *vt* imprimir, estampar (*on* en); (*fig*) grabar (*on the mind* en la memoria).

imprison [im'prizn] *vt* encarcelar, poner en la cárcel; **the judge —ed him for 10 years** el juez le condenó a 10 años de prisión.

imprisonment [im'priznmənt] *n* encarcelamiento *m*, prisión *f*; **false —** detención *f* ilegal; **the judge sentenced him to 10 years'** — el juez le condenó a 10 años de prisión; **to escape from —** escapar de la cárcel.

improbability [im,prɔbə'biliti] *n* improbabilidad *f*; inverosimilitud *f*.

improbable [im'prɔbəbl] *adj* improbable; inverosímil; **it is — that it will happen** no es probable que ocurra eso, es poco probable que ocurra eso.

impromptu [im'prɔmptjuː] **1** *adj* performance improvisado, no preparado de antemano; utterance impremeditado.

2 *adv* perform de improviso, sin preparación; say *etc* de repente.

3 *n* improvisación *f*.

improper [im'prɔpə*] *adj* impropio, incorrecto, indebido; (*unseemly*) indecoroso; (*indecent*) indecente, deshonesto.

improperly [im'prɔpəli] *adv* impropiamente, incorrectamente, indebidamente, indecorosamente, indecentemente, deshonestamente.

impropriety [,imprə'praiəti] *n* inconveniencia *f*; incorrección *f*; falta *f* de decoro; indecencia *f*, deshonestidad *f*; (*of language*) impropiedad *f*.

improve [im'pruːv] **1** *vt* mejorar, perfeccionar; reformar; (*beautify*) embellecer; land abonar, bonificar; property aumentar el valor de; production, yield aumentar; mind ilustrar, edificar; opportunity aprovechar; wording *etc* corregir, enmendar.

2 *vi* mejorar(se); perfeccionarse; (*production, yield*) aumentar(se); (*price*) subir; (*in skill, studies etc*) hacer progresos; **the patient is improving** el enfermo está mejor; **to — on** mejorar, perfeccionar;

it cannot be —ed on es inmejorable; **to — on someone's offer** ofrecer más que otro.

3 *vr*: **to — oneself** (*in mind*) edificarse, instruirse; (*in wealth etc*) mejorar su situación.

improvement [im'pruːvmənt] *n* mejora *f*, mejoramiento *m*; perfeccionamiento *m*; reforma *f*; embellecimiento *m*; aumento *m*, subida *f* (*in* de); progreso *m*, adelantamiento *m*; (*Med*) mejoría *f*; enmienda *f*; **there has been some — in the patient's condition** el enfermo está algo mejor; **it's an — on the old one** es mejor que el antiguo; **to make —s in a text** enmendar un texto; **to make —s to a property** hacer reformas en un inmueble.

improvidence [im'prɔvidəns] *n* imprevisión *f*.

improvident [im'prɔvidənt] *adj* impróvido, imprevisor.

improvidently [im'prɔvidəntli] *adv* impróvidamente.

improving [im'pruːviŋ] *adj* edificante, instructivo.

improvisation [,imprəvai'zeiʃən] *n* improvisación *f*.

improvise ['imprəvaiz] *vti* improvisar.

imprudence [im'pruːdəns] *n* imprudencia *f*.

imprudent [im'pruːdənt] *adj* imprudente.

imprudently [im'pruːdəntli] *adv* imprudentemente.

impudence ['impjudəns] *n* descaro *m*, insolencia *f*, atrevimiento *m*; **what —!** ¡qué frescura!; **he had the — to say that** tuvo la cara dura de decir que.

impudent ['impjudənt] *adj* descarado, insolente, atrevido.

impudently ['impjudəntli] *adv* descaradamente, insolentemente.

impugn [im'pjuːn] *vt* impugnar.

impulse ['impʌls] *n* (*Mech etc*) impulso *m*; (*fig*) impulso *m*, impulsión *f*, estímulo *m*; incitación *f*; **to act on —** obrar por capricho, obrar sin reflexión; **my first — was to** + infin mi primera idea fue de + infin, primero intenté + infin; **to yield to a sudden —** dejarse llevar por un capricho.

impulsion [im'pʌlʃən] *n* impulsión *f*.

impulsive [im'pʌlsiv] *adj* person irreflexivo, que no reflexiona, impulsivo; act irreflexivo.

impulsively [im'pʌlsivli] *adv* por impulso; sin reflexión, sin pensar.

impulsiveness [im'pʌlsivnis] *n* irreflexión *f*; carácter *m* impulsivo.

impunity [im'pjuːniti] *n* impunidad *f*; **with —** impunemente.

impure [im'pjuə*] *adj* impuro; adulterado, mezclado; (*morally*) deshonesto.

impurity [im'pjuəriti] *n* impureza *f*; deshonestidad *f*.

imputation [,impju'teiʃən] *n* imputación *f*; acusación *f*.

impute [im'pjuːt] *vt* imputar, achacar, atribuir (*to* a); acusar.

in [in] **1** *adv* (a) dentro, adentro; **— here** aquí dentro; **— there** allí dentro; **day —, day out** día tras día; **£10 a week all —** 10 libras por semana todo incluido.

(b) **to be —** (*person*) estar, estar en casa, estar en la oficina (*etc*); **is Mr Cox —?** ¿está el Sr Cox?; **the train is —** ha llegado el tren; **he's — for 5 years** le condenaron a 5 años; **when the Tories were —** cuando los conservadores estaban en el poder; **when the sun is —** cuando el sol está escondido; **the harvest is —** ha terminado la recolección; **strawberries are —** las fresas están en sazón; **short skirts are —** la falda corta está de moda.

(c) **to be — for a post** ser candidato a un puesto, solicitar un puesto; **to be — for a competition** concurrir a un certamen, tomar parte en un concurso; **to be — for an exam** presentarse a un examen; **we're — for it now** aquí se va a armar la gorda; **you don't know what you're — for** no sabes lo que te pescas; **we're — for a hard time** vamos a pasar un mal rato.

(d) **to be — on the secret** estar en el secreto; **to be — on a plan** estar enterado de un proyecto.

(e) **to be well — with someone** estar muy metido con uno, tener mucha confianza con uno.

(f) **to be all —, to feel all —** estar rendido, no poder más.

2 *prep* (a) (*place*) en; dentro de; **— the house** en la casa; **— one's hand** en la mano; **— Rome** en Roma; **— Italy** en Italia; **— prison** en la cárcel; **— school** en la escuela; **— the distance** a lo lejos; **— everybody's eyes** a los ojos de todos; **it is not — him to do that** no es capaz de hacer eso, no cabe en él hacer eso; **he has it — him to succeed** es capaz de triunfar.

(b) (*in respect of*) **better — health** mejor de salud; **strong — maths** fuerte en matemáticas; **a change — policy** un cambio de política; **a rise — prices** una subida de los precios; **3 metres — length**

3 metros de largo; **long — the leg** de piernas largas; **diseased — mind** de mentalidad anormal.

(c) *(ratio)* **1 —** 7 1 sobre 7, 1 de cada 7.

(d) *(time)* **— 1972** en 1972; **— the 20th century** en el siglo XX; **—** May en mayo; **— summer** en el verano; **— the past** en el pasado; **— the reign of** bajo el reinado de; **it was built — a week** fue construido en una semana; **I'll bring it back —** a **week** lo devolveré dentro de una semana, lo devolveré de aquí a ocho días; **— a week he was back** al cabo de una semana volvió; **— the morning** por la mañana; **at 8 — the morning** a las 8 de la mañana; **— the daytime** de día, durante el día; **I haven't seen him —** years hace años que no le veo.

(e) **— tears** llorando; **— despair** desesperado; **any man — his senses** cualquier hombre sensato.

(f) *(clothed in)* **the girl — green** la chica vestida de verde; **he went out — his new raincoat** al salir se puso el impermeable nuevo; **she looks nice — that hat** con ese sombrero está guapísima.

(g) *(weather)* **— the rain** bajo la lluvia; **— the July sun** bajo el sol de julio.

(h) **he's — the tyre business** se dedica al comercio de neumáticos, tiene un negocio de neumáticos; **those — teaching** los profesores, los que se dedican a enseñar; **he travels — soap** es viajante en jabones; **she has shares — oil** tiene acciones de compañías de petróleo; **he's something — advertising** tiene un puesto en la publicidad; **the latest thing — hats** lo más nuevo en cuanto a sombreros.

(i) *(manner)* **— this way** de este modo; **— the American fashion** a la americana; **— alphabetical order** por orden alfabético; **cut — half** cortado por el medio; **— French** en francés; **written — pencil** escrito con *(or a)* lápiz; **painted — black** pintado de negro; **packed — dozens** envasados por docenas; **— hundreds** a cientos, a centenares; **— cash** en metálico; **— mourning** de luto; **— writing** por escrito; **— anger** con enojo; **lame — one foot** cojo de un pie.

(j) *(after superlative)* **the best pupil — the class** el mejor alumno de la clase; **the biggest — Europe** el mayor de Europa.

(k) *(with verb)* **— saying this** al decir esto; **— making a fortune he lost his wife** mientras se ganaba una fortuna, perdió a su mujer.

3 n: **—s and outs** recovecos *mpl*; *(fig)* detalles *mpl* nimios; interioridades *fpl*.

inability [ˌinəˈbiliti] n incapacidad f, falta f de aptitud; **my — to come** sí que yo no pueda venir.

inaccessibility [ˈinækˌsesəˈbiliti] n inaccesibilidad f.

inaccessible [ˌinækˈsesəbl] adj inaccesible.

inaccuracy [inˈækjurəsi] n inexactitud f, incorrección f.

inaccurate [inˈækjurit] adj inexacto, incorrecto, erróneo.

inaccurately [inˈækjuritli] adv erróneamente.

inaction [inˈækʃən] n inacción f.

inactive [inˈæktiv] adj inactivo.

inactivity [ˌinækˈtiviti] n inactividad f.

inadequacy [inˈædikwəsi] n insuficiencia f; *(of person)* incapacidad f.

inadequate [inˈædikwit] adj insuficiente, inadecuado; *person* incapaz.

inadequately [inˈædikwitli] adv de modo inadecuado.

inadmissible [ˌinədˈmisəbl] adj inadmisible.

inadvertence [ˌinədˈvəːtəns] n inadvertencia f; **by —** por equivocación, por descuido.

inadvertent [ˌinədˈvəːtənt] adj inadvertido; accidental.

inadvertently [ˌinədˈvəːtəntli] adv por equivocación, por descuido.

inadvisability [ˈinədˌvaizəˈbiliti] n imprudencia f, inconveniencia f.

inadvisable [ˌinədˈvaizəbl] adj no aconsejable, desaconsejable, imprudente, inconveniente.

inalienable [inˈeiliənəbl] adj inalienable.

inamorata [inˌæməˈrɑːtə] n amada f, querida f.

inane [iˈnein] adj necio, fatuo, inútil.

inanimate [inˈænimit] adj inanimado.

inanition [ˌinəˈniʃən] n inanición f.

inanity [iˈnæniti] n necedad f, fatuidad f, inutilidad f; **inanities** estupideces *fpl*, necedades *fpl*.

inapplicable [inˈæplikəbl] adj inaplicable.

inappropriate [ˌinəˈprəupriit] adj inoportuno, inconveniente, impropio.

inappropriately [ˌinəˈprəupriitli] adv inoportunamente.

inapt [inˈæpt] adj impropio; *(lacking skill)* inhábil.

inaptitude [inˈæptitjuːd] n impropiedad f; inhabilidad f.

inarticulate [ˌinɑːˈtikjulit] adj *(of character)* incapaz de expresarse, que habla poco y mal; **an — speech** un discurso mal pronunciado; **he was — with rage** la rabia le embargó la voz.

inartistic [ˌinɑːˈtistik] adj *work* antiestético, burdo, mal hecho; *person* falto de talento artístico.

inasmuch [inəzˈmʌtʃ]: **— as** conj puesto que, ya que.

inattention [ˌinəˈtenʃən] n inatención f, desatención f, distracción f.

inattentive [ˌinəˈtentiv] adj desatento, distraído.

inattentively [ˌinəˈtentivli] adv distraídamente.

inaudible [inˈɔːdəbl] adj inaudible, que no se puede oír; **he was almost —** apenas se le podía oír.

inaudibly [inˈɔːdəbli] adv de modo inaudible; **he spoke almost —** habló tan bajo que apenas se le podía oír.

inaugural [iˈnɔːgjurəl] adj inaugural; **speech** de apertura.

inaugurate [iˈnɔːgjureit] vt inaugurar.

inauguration [iˌnɔːgjuˈreiʃən] n inauguración f; ceremonia f de apertura; *(US Pol)* toma f de posesión *(de su cargo por el presidente)*.

inauspicious [ˌinɔːsˈpiʃəs] adj poco propicio, desfavorable.

inauspiciously [ˌinɔːsˈpiʃəsli] adv de modo poco propicio, en condiciones desfavorables.

in-between [ˈinbiˈtwiːn] adj intermedio; de en medio; **it's rather —** ocupa una posición más bien intermedia, no es ni lo uno ni lo otro.

inboard [ˈinbɔːd] adj *(Naut)* **engine** interior.

inborn [inˈbɔːn] adj innato; instintivo.

inbred [ˈinˈbred] adj *tendency etc* innato; instintivo; *(of race)* engendrado por endogamia; **people there are very —** allí la endogamia ha debilitado a la gente.

inbreeding [ˈinˈbriːdiŋ] n endogamia f.

Inca [ˈiŋkə] **1** n inca *mf*. **2** *attr* incaico, de los incas.

incalculable [inˈkælkjuləbl] adj incalculable; *person etc* voluble, veleidoso.

Incan [ˈiŋkən] adj inca, incaico, de los incas.

incandescence [ˌinkænˈdesns] n incandescencia f.

incandescent [ˌinkænˈdesnt] adj incandescente.

incantation [ˌinkænˈteiʃən] n conjuro m, ensalmo m.

incapability [inˌkeipəˈbiliti] n incapacidad f.

incapable [inˈkeipəbl] adj incapaz *(of de)*; *(physically)* imposibilitado; **to be — of speech** no poder hablar; **she is — of shame** no tiene vergüenza; **he was drunk and —** estaba totalmente borracho.

incapacitate [ˌinkəˈpæsiteit] vt incapacitar, inhabilitar; *(physically)* imposibilitar.

incapacity [ˌinkəˈpæsiti] n incapacidad f; insuficiencia f.

incarcerate [inˈkɑːsəreit] vt encarcelar.

incarnate [inˈkɑːnit] adj: **the devil —** el mismo diablo, el diablo en persona; **to become —** encarnar.

incarnate [inˈkɑːneit] vt encarnar.

incarnation [ˌinkɑːˈneiʃən] n encarnación f; **to be the — of vice** ser el mismo vicio.

incautious [inˈkɔːʃəs] adj incauto, imprudente.

incautiously [inˈkɔːʃəsli] adv incautamente.

incendiary [inˈsendiəri] **1** adj incendiario. **2** n *(person)* incendiario m; *(bomb)* bomba f incendiaria.

incense [ˈinsens] n incienso m.

incense [inˈsens] vt indignar, encolerizar.

incentive [inˈsentiv] n incentivo m, estímulo m; **an — to harder work** un incentivo para que se trabaje más.

inception [inˈsepʃən] n comienzo m, principio m; **from its —** desde los comienzos.

incertitude [inˈsəːtitjuːd] n incertidumbre f.

incessant [inˈsesnt] adj incesante, constante, continuo.

incessantly [inˈsesntli] adv constantemente, sin cesar.

incest [ˈinsest] n incesto m.

incestuous [inˈsestjuəs] adj incestuoso.

inch [intʃ] **1** n pulgada f (= 2,54 cm); **—es** *(of person: height)* estatura f, *(of waist)* cintura f; **not an — from** my face a dos centímetros de mi cara; **— by —** by **—es** palmo a palmo; **not an — of Spanish territory** ni un palmo de territorio español; **we searched every — of the room** registramos minuciosamente el cuarto; **every — of soil is used** se aprovecha la tierra hasta el último centímetro; **he's every — a man** es todo un hombre; **he's every — a soldier** es lo que se llama un soldado; **to be within an — of** estar a dos dedos de; **he didn't give an — no** nos ofreció la menor concesión; **give him an — and he'll take a yard** dale un dedo y se toma hasta el codo.

2 vi: **to — (one's way) forward** avanzar palmo a palmo; **prices are —ing up** los precios suben constantemente un poco.

inchoate ['inkəueit] *adj* rudimentario, incompleto, todavía no formado.

incidence ['insidəns] *n* frecuencia *f*; extensión *f*; distribución *f*; **the — of measles in children** la frecuencia del sarampión en los niños; **the — of taxation** el peso de las contribuciones.

incident ['insidənt] *n* incidente *m*, episodio *m*, suceso *m*; **the Agadir —** el episodio de Agadir; **to provoke a diplomatic —** provocar una crisis diplomática; **a life full of —** una vida azarosa, una vida llena de acontecimientos; **to arrive without —** llegar sin novedad.

incidental [,insi'dentl] **1** *adj* incidental, incidente; (*casual*) fortuito; (*inessential*) no esencial, accesorio, de importancia secundaria; **— expenses** gastos *mpl* no previsibles; **— music** música *f* de fondo; **the troubles — to any journey** las dificultades que acarrea cualquier viaje; **but that is — to my purpose** pero eso queda al margen de mi propósito. **2** *n* cosa *f* fortuita; cosa *f* accesoria, cosa *f* sin importancia.

incidentally [,insi'dentəli] *adv* incidentemente; **and —...** y a propósito...; **it was interesting only —** era interesante solamente en parte.

incinerate [in'sinəreit] *vt* incinerar.

incinerator [in'sinəreitə*] *n* incinerador *m*.

incipient [in'sipiənt] *adj* incipiente, naciente.

incise [in'saiz] *vt* cortar; (*Art*) grabar, tallar.

incision [in'siʒən] *n* incisión *f*, corte *m*.

incisive [in'saisiv] *adj mind* penetrante; *tone* mordaz; *words, criticism, speech* tajante.

incisively [in'saisivli] *adv* con penetración; mordazmente; de modo tajante.

incisiveness [in'saisivnis] *n* penetración *f*; mordacidad *f*; lo tajante.

incisor [in'saizə*] *n* incisivo *m*.

incite [in'sait] *vt* incitar, estimular, provocar; **to — someone to do something** incitar a uno a hacer algo.

incitement [in'saitmənt] *n* incitación *f*, instigación *f* (*to* de).

incivility [,insi'viliti] *n* descortesía *f*, incivilidad *f*.

inclemency [in'klemənsi] *n* inclemencia *f*; (*of weather*) intemperie *f*.

inclement [in'klemənt] *adj* inclemente, riguroso; *weather* malo, feo.

inclination [,inkli'neiʃən] *n* (a) (*slope*) inclinación *f*. (b) (*tendency*) inclinación *f*, tendencia *f*, propensión *f*; **my — is to + infin** yo prefiero la idea de + *infin*; **what are his natural —s?** ¿cuáles son sus propensiones naturales?; **to have an — to meanness** tener tendencia a ser tacaño; **I have no — to help him** no estoy dispuesto a ayudarle, tengo pocas ganas de ayudarle; **to follow one's —** seguir su capricho, hacer lo que le dé la gana.

incline ['inklain] *n* cuesta *f*, pendiente *f*.

incline [in'klain] **1** *vt* (a) (*slope*) inclinar, ladear, poner oblicuamente; **he —d his head** puso la cabeza de lado. (b) (*fig*) **to — someone to adopt a plan** inducir a uno a adoptar un plan. (c) **to be —d to + infin** (*of tendency*) inclinarse + *infin*, tener tendencia a + *infin*, ser propenso a + *infin*; (*of person's volition*) estar dispuesto a + *infin*, estar por + *infin*; **it's —d to break** tiene tendencia a romperse; **I'm —d to believe you** estoy dispuesto a creerle; **the child is —d to be left-handed** el niño tiene tendencias de zurdo; **he's that way —d** él es así; **if you feel so —d** si Vd quiere. **2** *vi* (a) (*slope, act*) inclinarse, ladearse, (*state*) estar inclinado, estar ladeado. (b) (*fig*) **I — to the belief that** yo prefiero creer que, yo creo más lógica la opinión de que; **yellow inclining to red** amarillo tirando a rojo.

inclined [in'klaind] *adj plane* inclinado.

inclose [in'kləuz] *vt see* **enclose.**

include [in'kluːd] *vt* incluir; comprender, contener, encerrar; (*with letter*) adjuntar, enviar adjunto; **your name is not —d in the list** su nombre no figura en la lista; **does that remark — me?** ¿se refiere esa observación también a mí?; **he is not —d in the team** no forma parte del equipo; **he sold the lot, books —d** lo vendió todo, incluso los libros; **everything —d** (*hotel etc*) todo comprendido.

including [in'kluːdiŋ] *as prep* incluso, inclusive, con inclusión de; **seven —, this one** siete con inclusión de éste; **everyone came, — the priest** vinieron todos, incluso (*or* hasta) el cura; **terms £15, not — service** precio 15 libras, servicio no comprendido.

inclusion [in'kluːʒən] *n* inclusión *f*.

inclusive [in'kluːsiv] **1** *adj* inclusivo, completo; **— terms** todo incluido; **to be — of** incluir.

2 *adv* inclusive; **from the 10th to the 15th —** del 10 al 15 ambos inclusive.

inclusively [in'kluːsivli] *adv* = **inclusive 2.**

incognito [in'kɔgnitəu] **1** *adv travel etc* de incógnito. **2** *n* incógnito *m*.

incoherence [,inkəu'hiərəns] *n* incoherencia *f*; ininteligibilidad *f*.

incoherent [,inkəu'hiərənt] *adj* incoherente, inconexo; ininteligible; *argument etc* sin pies ni cabeza; **his speech became —** empezó a hablar de modo ininteligible; **he was — with rage** balbuceaba de rabia.

incoherently [,inkəu'hiərəntli] *adv* de modo incoherente; de modo ininteligible.

incombustible [,inkəm'bʌstəbl] *adj* incombustible.

income ['inkʌm] *n* ingresos *mpl*, renta *f*, entrada *f*; (*profit*) rédito *m* (*from* de); **annual —** ingresos *mpl* anuales; **family —** entradas *fpl* familiares; **gross —** renta *f* bruta; **national —** renta *f* nacional; **net —** renta *f* neta; **private —** renta *f* de fuente particular; **—s policy** política *f* de rentas; **to live up to one's —** gastarse toda la renta; **to live beyond one's —** gastar más de lo que se gana; **to live within one's —** vivir con arreglo a los ingresos; **I can't live on my —** no puedo vivir con lo que gano.

incomer ['in,kʌmə*] *n* (*US*) recién llegado *m*, recién llegada *f*; persona *f* nueva (en una sociedad *etc*); inmigrante *mf*.

income tax ['inkʌmtæks] *n* impuesto *m* sobre la renta.

incoming ['in,kʌmiŋ] *adj* entrante, nuevo; *tide* ascendente.

incomings ['in,kʌmiŋz] *npl* ingresos *mpl*.

incommensurable [,inkə'menʃərəbl] *adj* inconmensurable.

incommensurate [,inkə'menʃərit] *adj* desproporcionado; **to be — with** no guardar relación con.

incommode [,inkə'məud] *vt* incomodar, molestar.

incommodious [,inkə'məudiəs] *adj* incómodo.

incomunicado [,inkəmjuni'kɑːdəu] *adj* incomunicado.

incomparable [in'kɔmpərəbl] *adj* incomparable, sin par.

incomparably [in'kɔmpərəbli] *adv* incomparablemente; **this one is — better** éste es mejor sin ningún género de dudas.

incompatibility ['inkəm,pætə'biliti] *n* incompatibilidad *f*.

incompatible [,inkəm'pætəbl] *adj* incompatible (*with* con).

incompetence [in'kɔmpitəns] *n* incompetencia *f*, inhabilidad *f*, incapacidad *f*.

incompetent [in'kɔmpitənt] *adj* incompetente, inhábil, incapaz.

incomplete [,inkəm'pliːt] *adj* incompleto, defectuoso; (*unfinished*) sin terminar, inacabado.

incompletely [,inkəm'pliːtli] *adv* incompletamente.

incompleteness [,inkəm'pliːtnis] *n* lo incompleto, estado *m* incompleto; **because of its —** debido a que no está terminado.

incomprehensible [in,kɔmpri'hensəbl] *adj* incomprensible.

incomprehensibly [in,kɔmpri'hensəbli] *adv* de modo incomprensible.

inconceivable [,inkən'siːvəbl] *adj* inconcebible.

inconclusive [,inkən'kluːsiv] *adj reasoning etc* inconcluyente, poco convincente, cuestionable; *interview, investigation* que no da resultados definitivos.

inconclusively [,inkən'kluːsivli] *adv* de modo inconcluyente, de modo poco convincente; **it ended —** terminó sin resultados definitivos.

incongruity [,inkɔn'gruːiti] *n* incongruencia *f*; desacuerdo *m*, falta *f* de lógica; lo absurdo.

incongruous [in'kɔŋgruəs] *adj* incongruo; disonante, que no concuerda, nada lógico; *appearance etc* estrafalario, absurdo; **it seems — that** parece extraño que.

inconsequent [in'kɔnsikwənt] *adj* inconsecuente.

inconsequential [in,kɔnsi'kwenʃəl] *adj* inconsecuente; (*unimportant*) sin trascendencia.

inconsiderable [,inkən'sidərəbl] *adj* insignificante.

inconsiderate [,inkən'sidərit] *adj* desconsiderado; **it was most — of you** Vd ha obrado con poca formalidad.

inconsistency [,inkən'sistənsi] *n* inconsecuencia *f*.

inconsistent [,inkən'sistənt] *adj* inconsecuente; **this is — with what you told me** esto no concuerda con lo que Vd me dijo.

inconsolable [,inkən'səuləbl] *adj* inconsolable.

inconspicuous [,inkən'spikjuəs] *adj* apenas visible, que no llama la atención; (*fig*) poco llamativo, modesto; **try to be as — as possible** procure no llamar la atención.

inconspicuously [,inkən'spikjuəsli] *adv* de modo apenas visible, sin llamar la atención; de modo poco llamativo, modestamente.

inconstancy [in'kɔnstənsi] *n* inconstancia *f*, veleidad *f*.

inconstant [in'kɔnstənt] *adj* inconstante, mudable, veleidoso.

incontestable [,inkən'testəbl] *adj* incontestable.

incontinence [in'kɔntinəns] *n* incontinencia *f* (*also Med*).

incontinent [in'kɔntinənt] *adj* incontinente.

incontrovertible [in,kɔntrə'və:təbl] *adj* incontrovertible.

inconvenience [,inkən'vi:niəns] **1** *n* incomodidad *f*, molestia *f*, inconvenientes *mpl*; **the — of living at a distance** los inconvenientes de vivir lejos; **you caused a lot of —** Vd nos creó muchas dificultades; **to put someone to —** molestar a uno.
2 *vt* incomodar, molestar, causar inconvenientes a.

inconvenient [,inkən'vi:niənt] *adj house, journey etc* incómodo, poco práctico, molesto; *time* malo, inoportuno; **it is — for me to +** *infin* me molesta tener que **+** *infin*; **it's all very —** es muy difícil.

inconveniently [,inkən'vi:niəntli] *adv* incómodamente, de modo poco práctico; a deshora, inoportunamente, en un momento inoportuno; **to come — early** venir tan temprano que crea dificultades.

inconvertibility ['inkən,və:ti'biliti] *n* inconvertibilidad *f*.

inconvertible [,inkən'və:təbl] *adj* inconvertible.

incorporate [in'kɔ:pəreit] *vt* incorporar (*in, into* a); incluir; comprender, contener; (*add*) agregar, añadir; **a product incorporating vitamin Q** un producto que contiene vitamina Q; **to — a company** constituir una compañía en sociedad anónima.

incorporated [in'kɔ:pəreitid] *adj* (*US Comm*): **Jones & Lloyd I—** Jones y Lloyd Sociedad Anónima (*abbr* S.A.).

incorporation [in,kɔ:pə'reiʃən] *n* incorporación *f*; inclusión *f*, adición *f*; (*Comm*) constitución *f* en sociedad anónima.

incorrect [,inkə'rekt] *adj* incorrecto, erróneo, inexacto; **that is —** eso no es cierto.

incorrectly [,inkə'rektli] *adv* incorrectamente, erróneamente; **a letter — addressed** una carta con las señas mal puestas.

incorrigible [in'kɔridʒəbl] *adj* incorregible; **you're —!** ¡eres un perdido!

incorruptible [,inkə'rʌptəbl] *adj* incorruptible; (*not open to bribery*) insobornable.

increase ['inkri:s] *n* aumento *m*, incremento *m* (*in* de); crecimiento *m*; (*in price*) subida *f*, alza *f*; **an — in pay** un aumento de sueldo; **to be on the — ir** en aumento.

increase [in'kri:s] **1** *vt* aumentar, acrecentar, incrementar. **2** *vi* aumentar(se), acrecentarse, tomar incremento; crecer; (*price*) subir.

increasing [in'kri:siŋ] *adj* creciente.

increasingly [in'kri:siŋli] *adv* de modo creciente; más y más, de más en más; **it becomes — difficult** se hace más y más difícil; **our — difficult task** nuestra labor cada vez más difícil.

incredible [in'kredəbl] *adj* increíble.

incredibly [in'kredəbli] *adv* increíblemente.

incredulity [,inkri'dju:liti] *n* incredulidad *f*.

incredulous [in'kredjuləs] *adj* incrédulo.

incredulously [in'kredjuləsli] *adv* con incredulidad.

increment ['inkrimənt] *n* aumento *m*, incremento *m* (*in* de); **an — in salary** un aumento de sueldo; **unearned — plusvalía** *f*.

incriminate [in'krimineit] *vt* acriminar, incriminar.

incrimination [in,krimi'neiʃən] *n* acriminación *f*, incriminación *f*.

incriminating [in'krimineitiŋ] *adj*, **incriminatory** [in'kriminətəri] *adj* acriminador.

incrust [in'krʌst] *vt* incrustar (*with* de).

incrustation [,inkrʌs'teiʃən] *n* incrustación *f*; costra *f*.

incubate ['inkjubeit] *vt* empollar, incubar.

incubation [,inkju'beiʃən] *n* incubación *f*; **— period** período *m* de incubación.

incubator ['inkjubeitə*] *n* incubadora *f*.

incubus ['inkjubəs] *n* incubo *m*.

inculcate ['inkʌlkeit] *vt* inculcar (*in* en).

incumbent [in'kʌmbent] **1** *adj*: **to be — on someone** incumbir a uno (*to do* hacer). **2** *n* ocupante *mf*, poseedor *m*, ora *f* (de un cargo o dignidad); (*Eccl*) beneficiado *m*.

incunable [in'kju:nəbl] *n* incunable *m*.

incunabula [,inkju'næbjulə] *npl* incunables *mpl*.

incur [in'kə:*] *vt* incurrir en; *debt, obligation* contraer; *expenditure* hacer.

incurable [in'kjuərəbl] **1** *adj* incurable; (*fig*) irremediable. **2** *n* incurable *mf*.

incurably [in'kjuərəbli] *adv* (*fig*) irremediablemente; **to be — optimistic** tener un optimismo indestructible.

incurious [in'kjuəriəs] *adj* poco curioso.

incursion [in'kə:ʃən] *n* incursión *f*, invasión *f*.

indebted [in'detid] *adj* (*fig*): **to be — in** estar en deuda con uno; **I am — to you for your help** agradezco su ayuda.

indebtedness [in'detidnis] *n* deuda *f*; agradecimiento *m*.

indecency [in'di:snsi] *n* indecencia *f*.

indecent [in'di:snt] *adj* indecente; *haste* nada decoroso.

indecently [in'di:sntli] *adv* indecentemente.

indecipherable [,indi'saifərəbl] *adj* indescifrable.

indecision [,indi'siʒən] *n* irresolución *f*.

indecisive [,indi'saisiv] *adj person* irresoluto, indeciso, vacilante; *result etc* inconcluyente, que no resuelve nada.

indecisively [,indi'saisivli] *adv* con irresolución, indecisamente, de modo vacilante; **it ended —** terminó sin resultados definitivos.

indeclinable [,indi'klainəbl] *adj* indeclinable.

indecorous [in'dekərəs] *adj* indecoroso.

indecorously [in'dekərəsli] *adj* indecorosamente.

indecorum [,indi'kɔ:rəm] *n* indecoro *m*, falta *f* de decoro.

indeed [in'di:d] *adv*: **—!**, **— yes!**, **yes —!** ¡claro que sí!, ¡ya lo creo!; **—?**, **is it —?**, **did you —?** ¿de veras?; **that's praise —** eso sí es una alabanza; **— you may** claro que puedes; **it is — difficult** es verdaderamente difícil, es difícil de verdad; **it is — a big house** es en efecto una casa grande, es una casa realmente grande; **I'm very glad —** me alegro muchísimo; **they're very bad —** son malísimos; **I may — be wrong** es posible que esté equivocado, claro está.

indefatigable [,indi'fætigəbl] *adj* incansable.

indefatigably [,indi'fætigəbli] *adv* incansablemente.

indefensible [,indi'fensəbl] *adj* indefendible; *theory etc* insostenible; **your conduct has been —** su conducta no tiene excusa, su conducta no admite disculpa.

indefinable [,indi'fainəbl] *adj* indefinible.

indefinite [in'definit] *adj* indefinido (*also Gram*); incierto, poco seguro; **he was very — about it all** mostró no tener ninguna idea clara sobre el asunto; **our plans are somewhat — as yet** todavía no hemos hecho ningún plan definitivo.

indefinitely [in'definitli] *adv* (**a**) indefinidamente; **it extends — into space** se prolonga indefinidamente en el espacio.
(**b**) **we can carry on —** podemos continuar hasta cuando sea (*or* por tiempo indefinido).

indelible [in'deləbl] *adj* indeleble, imborrable (*also fig*); **— pencil** lápiz *m* tinta.

indelicacy [in'delikəsi] *n* indecoro *m*, falta *f* de decoro; inoportunidad *f*.

indelicate [in'delikit] *adj* indecoroso, inoportuno.

indemnification [in,demnifi'keiʃən] *n* indemnización *f*.

indemnify [in'demnifai] *vt* indemnizar, resarcir (*against, for* de).

indemnity [in'demniti] *n* (*security*) indemnidad *f*; (*compensation*) indemnización *f*, reparación *f*.

indent ['indent] *n* (*Comm*) pedido *m*; (*Mil etc*) requisición *f*.

indent [in'dent] **1** *vt* (*cut into*) endentar, mellar; (*Typ*) sangrar.
2 *vi*: **to — for** pedir, requisar; **to — on someone for something** pedir algo a uno, requisar algo a uno.

indentation [,inden'teiʃən] *n* mella *f*, muesca *f*; (*Typ*) sangría *f*.

indenture [in'dentʃə*] *n* contrato *m* de aprendizaje.

independence [,indi'pendəns] *n* independencia *f*.

independent [,indi'pendənt] *adj* independiente (*of* de); **of — means** acomodado; **to become — independizarse** (*of* de).

independently [,indi'pendəntli] *adv* independientemente; **— of what he may decide** sin tomar en cuenta lo que él decida.

indescribable [,indis'kraibəbl] *adj* indescriptible; (*pej*) indecible, incalificable.

indescribably [,indis'kraibəbli] *adv* indescriptiblemente; (*pej*) indeciblemente, de modo incalificable; **— bad** tan malo que resulta incalificable.

indestructible [,indis'trʌktəbl] *adj* indestructible.

indeterminate [,indi'tə:minit] *adj* indeterminado.

indeterminately [,indi'tə:minitli] *adv* de modo indeterminado.

index ['indeks] **1** n, pl **indices** ['indisi:z] (finger, of book) índice m; (Math) exponente m; (fig) indicación f (to de); **I—** (Eccl) índice m expurgatorio; **cost-of-living —** índice m del coste de la vida.
   2 vt book poner índice a; entry poner en un índice; **it is —ed under Smith** está clasificado bajo Smith, está clasificado en el artículo Smith.

India ['indiə] la India.

Indian ['indiən] **1** adj indio. **2** n indio m, a f; **Red —** piel roja mf.

Indian Ocean ['indiən'əuʃən] Océano m Índico, Mar m de las Indias.

indiarubber ['indiə'rʌbə*] n caucho m; (eraser) goma f de borrar.

indicate ['indikeit] vt indicar.

indication [.indi'keiʃən] n indicación f, indicio m, señal f.

indicative [in'dikətiv] **1** adj indicativo (also Gram); **to be — of** indicar. **2** n indicativo m.

indicator ['indikeitə*] n indicador m; (Aut) indicador m de dirección.

indices ['indisi:z] npl of **index**.

indict [in'dait] vt acusar (for, on a charge of de), encausar, procesar.

indictable [in'daitəbl] adj procesable, denunciable.

indictment [in'daitmənt] n (charge) acusación f; (act) procesamiento m; **the report is an — of our whole system** el informe critica duramente todo nuestro sistema.

Indies ['indiz] pl las Indias; see **East —** etc.

indifference [in'difrəns] n indiferencia f (to ante); **it is a matter of supreme — to me** no me importa en lo más mínimo.

indifferent [in'difrənt] adj indiferente; desinteresado, imparcial; (mediocre) ordinario, regular; **it is — to me** me es igual, me es indiferente.

indifferently [in'difrəntli] adv indiferentemente; de modo desinteresado, imparcialmente; regularmente; **they go — to one or the other** van sin distinción al uno o al otro; **she performed —** su actuación fue regular nada más.

indigence ['indidʒəns] n indigencia f.

indigenous [in'didʒinəs] adj indígena (to de).

indigent ['indidʒənt] adj indigente.

indigestible [.indi'dʒestəbl] adj indigesto.

indigestion [.indi'dʒestʃən] n indigestión f, empacho m.

indignant [in'dignənt] adj indignado; **to be — about something** indignarse por algo; **to get — with someone** indignarse con uno; **it's no good getting — de** nada sirve perder la paciencia; **to make someone —** indignar a uno.

indignantly [in'dignəntli] adv con indignación, indignado.

indignation [.indig'neiʃən] n indignación f; **— meeting** mitin m de protesta.

indignity [in'digniti] n indignidad f; ultraje m, afrenta f; **to suffer the — of +** ger sufrir la indignidad de + infin.

indigo ['indigəu] **1** n añil m. **2** adj color de añil.

indirect [.indi'rekt] adj indirecto.

indirectly [.indi'rektli] adv indirectamente.

indiscernible [.indi'sə:nəbl] adj imperceptible.

indiscipline [in'disiplin] n indisciplina f.

indiscreet [.indis'kri:t] adj indiscreto, imprudente.

indiscreetly [.indis'kri:tli] adv indiscretamente.

indiscretion [.indis'kreʃən] n indiscreción f, imprudencia f.

indiscriminate [.indis'kriminit] adj indistinto, sin distinción; person falto de discernimiento; admirer ciego.

indiscriminately [.indis'kriminitli] adv indistintamente, sin distinción; admire ciegamente.

indispensable [.indis'pensəbl] adj indispensable, imprescindible.

indisposed [.indis'pəuzd] adj: **to be —** estar indispuesto.

indisposition [.indispə'ziʃən] n indisposición f, enfermedad f.

indisputable [.indis'pju:təbl] adj incontestable, incuestionable.

indisputably [.indis'pju:təbli] adv incontestablemente; **it is — the best** es el mejor sin ningún género de dudas; **oh, —** claro que sí.

indissoluble [.indi'sɔljubl] adj indisoluble; link irrompible.

indissolubly [.indi'sɔljubli] adv indisolublemente; **to be — linked** tener vínculos irrompibles.

indistinct [.indis'tiŋkt] adj indistinto; confuso.

indistinctly [.indis'tiŋktli] adv indistintamente; confusamente.

indistinguishable [.indis'tiŋgwiʃəbl] adv indistinguible (from de).

individual [.indi'vidjuəl] **1** adj individual; personal; (for one person alone) particular, propio. **2** n individuo m.

individualism [.indi'vidjuəlizəm] n individualismo m.

individualist [.indi'vidjuəlist] n individualista mf.

individuality [.indi.vidju'æliti] n individualidad f, personalidad f.

individualize [.indi'vidjuəlaiz] vt individuar, individualizar.

individually [.indi'vidjuəli] adv individualmente; particularmente; **they're all right —** cada uno de por sí es buena persona.

indivisible [.indi'vizəbl] adj indivisible.

Indo . . . ['indəu] indo . . .

Indo-China ['indəu'tʃainə] la Indochina.

indoctrinate [in'dɔktrineit] vt adoctrinar (with en).

indoctrination [in.dɔktri'neiʃən] n adoctrinamiento m.

Indo-European ['indəu.juərə'pi:ən] **1** adj indoeuropeo. **2** n indoeuropeo m, a f. **3** n (language) indoeuropeo m.

indolence ['indələns] n indolencia f, pereza f.

indolent ['indələnt] adj indolente, perezoso.

indolently ['indələntli] adv perezosamente.

indomitable [in'dɔmitəbl] adj indómito, indomable.

Indonesia [.indəu'ni:ziə] Indonesia f.

Indonesian [.indəu'ni:zion] **1** adj indonesio. **2** n indonesio m, a f.

indoor ['indɔ:*] adj interior; de casa; de puertas adentro; sport en sala, bajo cubierta, en pista cubierta; game de salón; aerial de interior; **swimming pool** cubierto.

indoors [in'dɔ:z] adv en casa; dentro; bajo techado; **to go —** entrar en la casa; **he had to spend a week —** tuvo que estar una semana sin salir de casa; **I like the outside, but what's it like —?** me gusta lo de fuera, pero ¿qué tal está por dentro?

indubitable [in'dju:bitəbl] adj indudable.

indubitably [in'dju:bitəbli] adv indudablemente, sin duda.

induce [in'dju:s] vt inducir; producir, ocasionar; sleep etc provocar; (Elec) inducir; **to — someone to do something** inducir a uno a hacer algo, persuadir a uno a hacer algo; **nothing would — me to go** nada me persuadiría a ir.

inducement [in'dju:smənt] n incentivo m, aliciente m, estímulo m; **to hold out something to someone as an —** ofrecer algo a uno como aliciente; **it offers no — to harder work** no ofrece nada que estimulara a la gente a trabajar más; **as an added — it has . . .** tiene además el atractivo de . . .

induct [in'dʌkt] vt (Eccl) instalar; new member etc iniciar (into en); (US Mil) quintar.

induction [in'dʌkʃən] n (Eccl) instalación f; (of member) iniciación f; (US Mil) quinta f; (Elec, Philos) inducción f.

induction coil [in'dʌkʃənkɔil] n carrete m de inducción.

inductive [in'dʌktiv] adj inductivo.

indulge [in'dʌldʒ] **1** vt desire etc satisfacer, dar rienda suelta a; whim condescender con; person complacer, dar gusto a; child etc consentir, mimar.
   2 vi (ie drink) beber; **to — in** darse el lujo de, permitirse; (viciously) darse a, abandonarse a.
   3 vr: **to — oneself** darse gusto, permitirse un lujo.

indulgence [in'dʌldʒəns] n (of desire etc) satisfacción f, gratificación f; (vicious) abandono m (in a), desenfreno m; (tolerance) tolerancia f, complacencia f; (Eccl) indulgencia f.

indulgent [in'dʌldʒənt] adj indulgente (towards con).

indulgently [in'dʌldʒəntli] adv indulgentemente.

industrial [in'dʌstriəl] adj industrial; accident de trabajo.

industrialism [in'dʌstriəlizəm] n industrialismo m.

industrialist [in'dʌstriəlist] n industrial m.

industrialization [in.dʌstriəlai'zeiʃən] n industrialización f.

industrialize [in'dʌstriəlaiz] vt industrializar.

industrious [in'dʌstriəs] adj trabajador, laborioso; student aplicado, diligente.

industriously [in'dʌstriəsli] adv laboriosamente; con aplicación, diligentemente.

industriousness [in'dʌstriəsnis] n laboriosidad f; aplicación f, diligencia f.

industry ['indəstri] n (a) (Tech) industria f; **basic —** industria f básica; **heavy —** industria f pesada; **the hotel —** el comercio hotelero; **the tourist —** el turismo.
   (b) (industriousness) laboriosidad f, aplicación f, diligencia f.

inebriate [i'ni:briit] n borracho m, a f.
inebriate [i'ni:brieit] vt embriagar, emborrachar.
inebriated [i'ni:brieitid] adj ebrio, borracho.
inebriation [i.ni:bri'eiʃən] n embriaguez f.
inedible [in'edibl] adj incomible, no comestible.
ineducable [in'edjukəbl] adj ineducable.
ineffable [in'efəbl] adj inefable.
ineffaceable [.ini'feisəbl] adj imborrable.
ineffective [.ini'fektiv] adj, **ineffectual** [.ini'fektjuəl] adj remedy etc ineficaz, inútil; person incapaz, inútil; he's wholly — es un cero a la izquierda; the plan proved — el proyecto no surtió efecto.
ineffectively [.ini'fektivli] adv ineficazmente, inútilmente.
inefficacious [.inefi'keiʃəs] adj ineficaz.
inefficacy [in'efikəsi] n ineficacia f.
inefficiency [.ini'fiʃənsi] n ineficacia f; incapacidad f, incompetencia f.
inefficient [.ini'fiʃənt] adj ineficaz, ineficiente; person incapaz, incompetente.
inefficiently [.ini'fiʃəntli] adv ineficazmente; de modo incompetente.
inelastic [.ini'læstik] adj inelástico; (fig) rígido, poco flexible.
inelegant [in'eligənt] adj inelegante, poco elegante.
inelegantly [in'eligəntli] adv inelegantemente.
ineligible [in'elidʒəbl] adj inelegible; to be — to vote no tener derecho a votar.
ineluctable [.ini'lʌktəbl] adj ineludible.
inept [i'nept] adj inepto; person incompetente, incapaz.
ineptitude [i'neptitju:d] n, **ineptness** [i'neptnis] n inepcia f, ineptitud f; incompetencia f, incapacidad f.
inequality [.ini'kwɒliti] n desigualdad f.
inequitable [in'ekwitəbl] adj injusto.
inequity [in'ekwiti] n injusticia f.
ineradicable [.ini'rædikəbl] adj inextirpable.
inert [i'nə:t] adj inerte, inactivo; (motionless) inmóvil; he lay — on the floor estuvo tumbado sin moverse en el suelo.
inertia [i'nə:ʃə] n inercia f (also Phys), inacción f; pereza f.
inescapable [.inis'keipəbl] adj ineludible.
inessential [.ini'senʃəl] 1 adj no esencial. 2 n cosa f no esencial.
inestimable [in'estiməbl] adj inapreciable, inestimable.
inevitability [in.evitə'biliti] n inevitabilidad f.
inevitable [in'evitəbl] adj inevitable, ineludible; forzoso; it was — it should happen tuvo forzosamente (or fatalmente) que ocurrir.
inevitably [in'evitəbli] adv inevitablemente, forzosamente.
inexact [.inig'zækt] adj inexacto.
inexactly [.inig'zæktli] adv de modo inexacto.
inexcusable [.iniks'kju:zəbl] adj imperdonable.
inexcusably [.iniks'kju:zəbli] adv imperdonablemente.
inexhaustible [.inig'zɔ:stəbl] adj inagotable.
inexorable [in'eksərəbl] adj inexorable, implacable.
inexorably [in'eksərəbli] adv inexorablemente, implacablemente.
inexpedient [.iniks'pi:diənt] adj inoportuno, inconveniente, imprudente.
inexpensive [.iniks'pensiv] adj económico, barato.
inexperience [.iniks'piəriəns] n inexperiencia f, falta f de experiencia.
inexperienced [.iniks'piəriənst] adj inexperto, falto de experiencia.
inexpert [in'ekspə:t] adj imperito, inexperto, inhábil.
inexpertly [in'ekspə:tli] adv sin habilidad, desmañadamente.
inexplicable [.iniks'plikəbl] adj inexplicable.
inexplicably [.iniks'plikəbli] adv inexplicablemente, misteriosamente.
inexpressible [.iniks'presəbl] adj inefable.
inexpressive [.iniks'presiv] adj style etc inexpresivo; person reservado, callado.
inextinguishable [.iniks'tiŋgwiʃəbl] adj inextinguible, inapagable.
inextricable [.iniks'trikəbl] adj inextricable, inseparable, imposible de desenredar (etc).
inextricably [.iniks'trikəbli] adv: — entwined entrelazados de modo inextricable.
infallibility [in.fælə'biliti] n infalibilidad f.
infallible [in'fæləbl] adj infalible; indefectible.
infallibly [in'fæləbli] adv infaliblemente; indefectiblemente.
infamous ['infəməs] adj infame.
infamy ['infəmi] n infamia f.
infancy ['infənsi] n infancia f; (Law) menor edad f; from — desde niño; it is still in its — está todavía en mantillas.

infant ['infənt] 1 adj mortality etc infantil; school de párvulos; industry etc naciente.
2 n criatura f, niño m, a f; (Law) menor mf; the — Jesus el niño Jesús.
infanta [in'fæntə] n infanta f.
infante [in'fænti] n infante m.
infanticide [in'fæntisaid] n (act) infanticidio m; (person) infanticida mf.
infantile ['infəntail] adj infantil (also Med); (pej) aniñado, pueril; don't be so —! ¡no seas niño!
infantry ['infəntri] n infantería f.
infantryman ['infəntrimən] n, pl —men [mən] soldado m de infantería.
infatuated [in'fætjueitid] adj: to be — with idea etc encapricharse por; person estar chiflado por.
infatuation [in.fætju'eiʃən] n encaprichamiento m; chifladura f.
infect [in'fekt] vt air, well, wound etc infectar, inficionar; person contagiar (with con); (fig) contagiar, comunicar; (pej) corromper, inficionar; to be —ed with (act) contagiarse de, (state) estar contagiado de; he —s everybody with his enthusiasm contagia a todos con su entusiasmo.
infection [in'fekʃən] n (Med) infección f, contagio m; (fig) contagio m; she has a slight — está ligeramente indispuesta.
infectious [in'fekʃəs] adj contagioso (also fig), infeccioso.
infectiousness [in'fekʃəsnis] n contagiosidad f.
infelicitous [.infi'lisitəs] adj infeliz, impropio.
infelicity [.infi'lisiti] n infelicidad f, impropiedad f.
infer [in'fə:*] vt deducir, colegir, inferir (from de).
inference ['infərəns] n deducción f, inferencia f, conclusión f.
inferential [.infə'renʃəl] adj ilativo, deductivo.
inferentially [.infə'renʃəli] adv por inferencia, por deducción.
inferior [in'fiəriə*] 1 adj inferior (to a). 2 n inferior mf.
inferiority [in.fiəri'ɔriti] n inferioridad f.
infernal [in'fə:nl] adj infernal (also fig).
infernally [in'fə:nəli] adv: it's — awkward es terriblemente difícil.
inferno [in'fə:nəu] n infierno m; it's like an — in there allí dentro hace un calor insufrible; in a few minutes the house was a blazing — en pocos minutos la casa estaba hecha una hoguera.
infertile [in'fə:tail] adj estéril, infecundo.
infertility [.infə:'tiliti] adj esterilidad f, infecundidad f.
infest [in'fest] vt infestar; to be —ed with estar plagado de.
infestation [.infes'teiʃən] n infestación f, plaga f.
infidel ['infidəl] 1 adj infiel, pagano, descreído. 2 n infiel mf, pagano m, a f, descreído m, a f; the I— los descreídos, la gente descreída.
infidelity [.infi'deliti] n infidelidad f (to para con); marital — infidelidad f conyugal.
in-fighting ['infaitiŋ] n lucha f cuerpo a cuerpo.
infiltrate ['infiltreit] 1 vt infiltrarse en. 2 vi infiltrarse.
infiltration [.infil'treiʃən] n infiltración f.
infinite ['infinit] 1 adj infinito; (fig) infinito, inmenso, enorme; we had — trouble finding it nos costó muchísimo trabajo encontrarlo; he took — pains over it lo hizo con el mayor esmero.
2 n: the — el infinito.
infinitely ['infinitli] adv infinitamente; this is — harder esto es muchísimo más difícil; we liked it — more the second time la segunda vez nos gustó muchísimo más; yes, — sí, muchísimo.
infinitesimal [.infini'tesiməl] adj infinitesimal.
infinitive [in'finitiv] 1 adj infinitivo. 2 n infinitivo m.
infinity [in'finiti] n (Math) infinito m; an — of infinidad de, un sinfín de.
infirm [in'fə:m] adj enfermizo, achacoso, débil; — of purpose irresoluto; the old and — los ancianos y enfermos.
infirmary [in'fə:məri] n hospital m; (at bullring etc) enfermería f.
infirmity [in'fə:miti] n (state) debilidad f; (illness) enfermedad f, achaque m, dolencia f; (moral) flaqueza f.
inflame [in'fleim] vt inflamar (also Med); to be —d with arder de, inflamarse de.
inflammable [in'flæməbl] adj inflamable; (situation etc) explosivo, de gran tirantez.
inflammation [.inflə'meiʃən] n inflamación f (also Med).
inflammatory [in'flæmətəri] adj inflamatorio; propaganda, speech incendiario.

inflate [in'fleit] *vt* hinchar, inflar (*with* de); (*fig*) hinchar (*with* de); *report etc* exagerar; *price* inflar, aumentar de modo excesivo.

inflated [in'fleitid] *adj* *report* exagerado; *price* excesivo.

inflation [in'fleiʃən] *n* inflación *f* (*also Fin*).

inflationary [in'fleiʃnəri] *adj* inflacionista, inflatorio.

inflationism [in'fleiʃənizəm] *n* inflacionismo *m*.

inflect [in'flekt] *vt* torcer, doblar; *voice* modular; (*Gram*) *noun etc* declinar, *verb* conjugar.

inflected [in'flektid] *adj* *language* flexional.

inflection [in'flekʃən] *n* inflexión *f*.

inflexibility [in,fleksi'biliti] *n* inflexibilidad *f*; (*fig*) rigidez *f*.

inflexible [in'fleksəbl] *adj* inflexible; (*fig*) rígido.

inflexion [in'flekʃən] *n* inflexión *f*.

inflict [in'flikt] 1 *vt* *wound etc* infligir, inferir (*on* a); *penalty, tax etc* imponer (*on* a); *grief, damage etc* causar (*on* a).
   2 *vr*: to — **oneself on someone** molestar a uno acompañándole (*or* visitándole *etc*).

infliction [in'flikʃən] *n* (*act*) imposición *f*; (*penalty etc*) pena *f*, castigo *m*.

inflow ['infləu] *n* afluencia *f*.

influence ['influəns] 1 *n* influencia *f*, influjo *m* (*on* sobre); ascendiente *m* (*over* sobre); valimiento *m* (*with* cerca de); **a man of** — un hombre influyente; **to be under the** — (*of drink*) estar borracho; **to drive under the** — conducir en estado de embriaguez; **to bring every** — **to bear on someone** ejercer todas las presiones posibles sobre uno; **to have** — (*person*) tener el padre alcalde, tener buenas aldabas; **you've got to have** — **to get a job** para conseguir un puesto hay que tener un buen enchufe; **to have** — **over someone** tener ascendiente sobre uno.
   2 *vt person etc* influir en, influenciar; sugestionar; *decision etc* influir en, efectar; **the novelist has been** —**d by Quevedo** el novelista ha sufrido la influencia de Quevedo, el novelista está influido por Quevedo; **what factors** —**d your decision?** ¿qué factores influyeron en su decisión?; **don't let him** — **you** no se deje persuadir por él; **to be easily** —**d** ser influenciable.

influential [,influ'enʃəl] *adj* influyente, prestigioso.

influenza [,influ'enzə] *n* gripe *f*.

influx ['inflʌks] *n* afluencia *f*; (*Mech etc*) aflujo *m*, entrada *f*.

inform [in'fɔːm] 1 *vt* informar (*about* sobre, *of* de); avisar; comunicar, participar; **I am happy to** — **you that** . . . tengo el gusto de comunicarle que . . . ; **well** —**ed** enterado, instruido; **to be** —**ed about something** estar enterado de algo, estar al corriente de algo; **why was I not** —**ed?** ¿por qué no me avisaron?; **I should like to be** —**ed as soon as he comes** que me avisen en cuanto llegue; **to keep someone** —**ed about something** tener a uno al corriente de algo.
   2 *vi* soplar; **to** — **against someone** delatar a uno, denunciar a uno.
   3 *vr*: to — **oneself about something** informarse sobre algo.

informal [in'fɔːməl] *adj* *person* desenvuelto, afable, poco ceremonioso; *occasion* sin ceremonia, sin protocolo; *dance* sin etiqueta; *visit, gathering* de confianza, íntimo; *tone, manner* familiar; (*unofficial*) extraoficial.

informality [,infɔː'mæliti] *n* afabilidad *f*; falta *f* de ceremonia; intimidad *f*; familiaridad *f*; **we liked the** — **of the occasion** nos gustó la función por su ausencia de ceremonia.

informally [in'fɔːməli] *adv*: **it was organized very** — se organizó sin ceremonia; **the president spoke** — **to the journalists** el presidente habló en tono de confianza con los periodistas; **I have been told** — **that** . . . me han dicho de modo extraoficial que . . .

informant [in'fɔːmənt] *n*: **my** — el que me lo dijo.

information [,infə'meiʃən] *n* (a) (*in general*) información *f*, informes *mpl*, datos *mpl*; (*news*) noticias *fpl*; **a piece of** — una información, un dato, una noticia; **classified** — información *f* secreta; **for your** —, **let me tell you** . . . para sacarle de duda, sepa Vd que . . . ; **to ask for** — pedir informes; **to gather** — **about something** tomar informes sobre algo, informarse sobre algo, reunir datos acerca de algo; **we have no** — **on that point** no tenemos información sobre ese particular.
   (b) (*knowledge*) conocimientos *mpl*; **he writes well but is short of** — escribe bien pero tiene escasos conocimientos.
   (c) (*Law*) denuncia *f*, delatación *f*; **to lay** — **about a crime** denunciar un crimen; **to lay** — **against someone** delatar a uno.

informative [in'fɔːmətiv] *adj* informativo.

informer [in'fɔːmə*] *n* (*Law*) denunciante *mf*, delator *m*, ora *f*; (*criminal*) soplón *m*.

infraction [in'frækʃən] *n* infracción *f*, violación *f*.

infra dig ['infrə'dig] *adj* (*fam*) deshonroso, indecoroso.

infrared ['infrə'red] *adj* infrarrojo.

infrequency [in'friːkwənsi] *n* infrecuencia *f*.

infrequent [in'friːkwənt] *adj* poco frecuente, infrecuente.

infrequently [in'friːkwəntli] *adv* rara vez.

infringe [in'frindʒ] 1 *vt* infringir, violar. 2 *vi*: to — **on** invadir, abusar de.

infringement [in'frindʒmənt] *n* infracción *f*, violación *f*; (*of rights etc*) invasión *f*, abuso *m*; (*Sport*) falta *f*.

infuriate [in'fjuərieit] *vt* enfurecer, poner rabioso; **to be** —**d** estar furioso; **this kind of thing** —**s me** estas cosas me hacen rabiar; **at times you** — **me** hay veces que me sacas de quicio.

infuriating [in'fjuərieitiŋ] *adj* enloquecedor; **it's simply** — es para volverse loco.

infuse [in'fjuːz] *vt* infundir (*into* a); **to** — **courage into someone** infundir ánimo a uno; **they were** —**d with a new hope** se les infundió una nueva esperanza.

infusion [in'fjuːʒən] *n* infusión *f*; — **of tea** infusión *f* de té.

ingenious [in'dʒiːniəs] *adj* ingenioso, inventivo, hábil; *machine etc* ingenioso; *scheme etc* genial.

ingeniously [in'dʒiːniəsli] *adv* ingeniosamente, hábilmente; con genialidad.

ingénue [,ɛ̃ːnʒei'njuː] *n* joven *f* ingenua, muchacha *f* candorosa.

ingenuity [,indʒi'njuːiti] *n* ingeniosidad *f*, inventiva *f*, habilidad *f*; genialidad *f*.

ingenuous [in'dʒenjuəs] *adj* ingenuo, candoroso.

ingest [in'dʒest] *vt* ingerir.

ingestion [in'dʒestʃən] *n* ingestión *f*.

inglenook ['iŋglnuk] *n* rincón *m* de la chimenea.

inglorious [in'glɔːriəs] *adj* ignominioso, vergonzoso.

ingot ['iŋgət] *n* lingote *m*, barra *f*; — **steel** acero *m* en lingotes.

ingrained ['in'greind] *adj* profundamente arraigado.

ingratiate [in'greiʃieit] *vr*: to — **oneself with someone** congraciarse con uno, hacerse simpático a uno, insinuarse en el favor de uno.

ingratiating [in'greiʃieitiŋ] *adj* *smile etc* insinuante, lleno de insinuación; *person* congraciador, zalamero.

ingratitude [in'grætitjuːd] *n* ingratitud *f*, desagradecimiento *m*.

ingredient [in'griːdiənt] *n* ingrediente *m*, componente *m*.

ingress ['ingres] *n* ingreso *m*, entrada *f*.

ingrowing ['in,grəuiŋ] *adj*: — **nail** uñero *m*.

inhabit [in'hæbit] *vt* habitar; vivir en; ocupar.

inhabitable [in'hæbitəbl] *adj* habitable.

inhabitant [in'hæbitənt] *n* habitante *m*.

inhabited [in'hæbitid] *adj* habitado, poblado.

inhalation [,inhə'leiʃən] *n* aspiración *f*; (*Med*) inhalación *f*.

inhalator ['inhəleitə*] *n* (*US*) inhalador *m*.

inhale [in'heil] *vt* aspirar; (*Med*) inhalar.

inhaler [in'heilə*] *n* inhalador *m*.

inharmonious [,inhɑː'məuniəs] *adj* inarmónico, disonante; (*fig*) discorde, poco armonioso.

inherent [in'hiərənt] *adj* innato, inmanente, intrínseco; — **in** inherente a; **with all the** — **difficulties** con todas las dificultades inevitables.

inherently [in'hiərəntli] *adv* intrínsecamente.

inherit [in'herit] *vt* heredar.

inheritance [in'heritəns] *n* herencia *f*; (*fig*) patrimonio *m*, legado *m*; **our national** — nuestro patrimonio nacional; **it's an** — **from the last government** es un legado del gobierno anterior.

inhibit [in'hibit] *vt* inhibir, impedir, imposibilitar; **to** — **someone from doing something** impedir a uno hacer algo; **don't let my presence** — **the discussion** no quiero que mi presencia impida la discusión; **we cannot** — **change** no podemos detener los cambios.

inhibited [in'hibitid] *adj* cohibido; **to feel rather** — sentirse algo cohibido.

inhibition [,inhi'biʃən] *n* inhibición *f*.

inhibitory [in'hibitəri] *adj* inhibitorio.

inhospitable [,inhɔs'pitəbl] *adj* *person* inhospitalario; *country* inhóspito; *attitude, remark* poco amistoso.

inhospitably [,inhɔs'pitəbli] *adv* de modo inhospitalario.

inhospitality ['in,hɔspi'tæliti] *n* inhospitalidad *f*.

inhuman [in'hjuːmən] *adj* inhumano.

inhumane [,inhju(ː)'mein] *adj* inhumano.

inhumanity [,inhju'mæniti] *n* inhumanidad *f*.

inhumation [,inhjuː'meiʃən] *n* inhumación *f*.

inimical [i'nimikəl] *adj*: — **to** opuesto a, contrario a, perjudicial para.
inimitable [i'nimitəbl] *adj* inimitable.
iniquitous [i'nikwitəs] *adj* inicuo; enorme; monstruoso; diabólico.
iniquity [i'nikwiti] *n* iniquidad *f*; perversidad *f*; injusticia *f*; enormidad *f*; **iniquities** (*of system*) injusticias *fpl*, (*of person*) excesos *mpl*, desmanes *mpl*.
initial [i'niʃəl] **1** *adj* inicial; primero; **in the — stages** al principio, en las primeras etapas; **my — reaction was to . . .** mi primer pensamiento era de . . .
   2 *n* inicial *f*, letra *f* inicial; **—s** (*of person etc*) iniciales *fpl*, (*used as abbreviation*) siglas *fpl*.
   3 *vt* marcar (*or* firmar *etc*) con las iniciales.
initially [i'niʃəli] *adv* al principio, en primer lugar.
initiate [i'niʃiit] *n* iniciado *m*, a *f*.
initiate [i'niʃieit] *vt* (**a**) (*begin*) iniciar, empezar, dar comienzo a, dar origen a; *reform etc* promover; *fashion* introducir; (*Law*) *proceedings* entablar.
   (**b**) **to — someone into a secret** iniciar a uno en un secreto; **to — someone into a society** admitir a uno a una sociedad.
initiation [i,niʃi'eiʃən] *n* iniciación *f*; principio *m*, comienzo *m*; admisión *f*; **— rite** ceremonia *f* de iniciación.
initiative [i'niʃətiv] *n* iniciativa *f*; **on one's own —** por iniciativa propia; **to take the —** tomar la iniciativa.
inject [in'dʒekt] *vt* (*Med etc*) inyectar (*into* en); (*fig*) injertar, introducir (*into* en), infundir (*into* a); **to — someone with something** inyectar algo en uno; **to — new life into a club** infundir un espíritu nuevo a un club.
injection [in'dʒekʃən] *n* inyección *f*.
injudicious [,indʒu'diʃəs] *adj* imprudente, indiscreto.
injudiciously [,indʒu'diʃəsli] *adv* imprudentemente, indiscretamente.
injunction [in'dʒʌŋkʃən] *n* mandato *m*; (*Law*) entredicho *m*; interdicto *m*.
injure ['indʒə*] **1** *vt* (**a**) (*physically*) herir, hacer daño a, lastimar, lesionar, (*permanently*) lisiar; **he —d his arm** se lesionó el brazo.
   (**b**) *chances, reputation, trade etc* perjudicar, (*offend*) ofender, agraviar; *feelings* herir.
   2 *vr*: **to — oneself** hacerse daño, lesionarse.
injured ['indʒəd] *adj*: **with an — arm** con un brazo lesionado; **an — player** un jugador lesionado; **there were 4 —** hubo 4 heridos; **in an — tone** en tono ofendido; **the — party** la persona ofendida, la persona perjudicada.
injurious [in'dʒuəriəs] *adj* (*harmful*) nocivo, dañoso, perjudicial (*to* para); (*insulting*) injurioso, ofensivo; **— to health** perjudicial para la salud.
injury ['indʒəri] *n* (**a**) (*physical*) herida *f*, lesión *f*; **3 players have injuries** 3 jugadores están lesionados; **to do someone an —** herir a uno; **to do oneself an —** hacerse daño, lesionarse.
   (**b**) (*fig*) perjuicio *m*, daño *m*; **our reputation has suffered —** nuestra reputación ha sido perjudicada.
injustice [in'dʒʌstis] *n* injusticia *f*; **you do me an —** Vd me juzga mal, Vd es injusto conmigo.
ink [iŋk] **1** *n* tinta *f*; **in —** con tinta; **Indian —** tinta *f* china; **invisible —** tinta *f* simpática; **printer's —**, **printing —** tinta *f* de imprenta.
   2 *vt* entintar; **to — in** entintar; **to — over** volver a escribir con tinta.
inkling ['iŋkliŋ] *n* (*hint*) indicio *m*; (*suspicion*) sospecha *f*; (*vague idea*) atisbo *m*; idea *f* vaga; **I had no — that** no tuve la menor idea de que; **we had some — of it** nos habíamos formado alguna idea de ello; **there was no — of the disaster to come** no había indicio alguno del desastre que había de sobrevenir.
inkpad ['iŋkpæd] *n* tampón *m* de entintar.
inkpot ['iŋkpɔt] *n* tintero *m*.
inkstand ['iŋkstænd] *n* escribanía *f*.
inkwell ['iŋkwel] *n* tintero *m*.
inky ['iŋki] *adj* (*stained*) manchado de tinta; (*black*) negro como la tinta.
inlaid ['in'leid] **1** *pret and ptp of* **inlay**. **2** *adj*: **— floor** entarimado *m*; **— work** taracea *f*.
inland ['inlænd] **1** *adj* interior; del interior; **— town** ciudad *f* del interior. **2** *adv* tierra adentro, hacia el interior. **3** *n* interior *m* (del país).
in-laws ['in,lɔːz] *npl* parientes *mpl* políticos.
inlay ['in'lei] *vt* (*irr: see* **lay**) taracear, embutir, incrustar; **a sword inlaid with jewels** una espada incrustada de joyas.
inlet ['inlet] *n* (*Geog*) ensenada *f*, cala *f*, entrante *m*; (*Mech*) admisión *f*, entrada *f*; **— pipe** tubo *m* de entrada; **— valve** válvula *f* de entrada.

inmate ['inmeit] *n* habitante *mf*, ocupante *mf*, residente *mf*; inquilino *m*, a *f*; (*of hospital*) enfermo *m*, a *f*; (*of asylum*) internado *m*, a *f*; (*of prison*) preso *m*, presidiario *m*.
inmost ['inməust] *adj* = **innermost**.
inn [in] *n* posada *f*, hostería *f*, mesón *m*; (*poor, wayside*) venta *f*; (*large, wayside*) fonda *f*; (*pub*) taberna *f*; **I—s of Court** (*London*) Colegio *m* de Abogados.
innards ['inədz] *npl* (*fam*) tripas *fpl*.
innate [i'neit] *adj* innato.
inner ['inə*] *adj* interior, interno; *thoughts etc* íntimo, secreto.
innermost ['inəməust] *adj* (más) interior, más central; *thoughts etc* más íntimo, más secreto.
innings ['iniŋz] *n sing and pl* turno *m*, entrada *f*; (*fig*) turno *m*, oportunidad *f*.
innkeeper ['inki:pə*] *n* posadero *m*, a *f*, mesonero *m*, a *f*; ventero *m*, a *f*; fondista *mf*; tabernero *m*, a *f* (*see* **inn**).
innocence ['inəsns] *n* inocencia *f*; **in all —** inocentemente; sin segunda intención, sin malicia.
innocent ['inəsnt] **1** *adj* inocente (*of* de); *amusement etc* honesto. **2** *n* inocente *mf*.
innocently ['inəsntli] *adv* inocentemente.
innocuous [i'nɔkjuəs] *adj* innocuo, inofensivo.
innovate ['inəuveit] *vi* introducir novedades.
innovation [,inəu'veiʃən] *n* innovación *f*, novedad *f*.
innovator ['inəuveitə*] *n* innovador *m*, ora *f*.
innuendo [,inju'endəu] *n* indirecta *f*, insinuación *f*.
innumerable [i'nju:mərəbl] *adj* innumerable; **there are — reasons** hay infinidad de razones; **I've told you — times** te lo he dicho muchísimas veces.
inoculate [i'nɔkjuleit] *vt* inocular (*against* contra, *with* de).
inoculation [i,nɔkju'leiʃən] *n* inoculación *f*.
inoffensive [,inə'fensiv] *adj* inofensivo; *person* apacible, pacífico.
inoperable [in'ɔpərəbl] *adj* inoperable.
inoperative [in'ɔpərətiv] *adj* inoperante.
inopportune [in'ɔpətju:n] *adj* inoportuno.
inopportunely [in'ɔpətju:nli] *adv* inoportunamente, a deshora.
inordinate [i'nɔːdinit] *adj* desmesurado, excesivo, desmedido.
inordinately [i'nɔːdinitli] *adv* desmesuradamente, excesivamente.
inorganic [,inɔː'gænik] *adj* inorgánico.
in-patient ['in,peiʃənt] *n* paciente *m* interno, paciente *f* interna.
input ['input] *n* (*Elec, Mech*) entrada *f*, potencia *f* de entrada; (*Fin*) dinero *m* invertido, inversión *f*.
inquest ['inkwest] *n* (**a**) (*Law*) investigación *f*, pesquisa *f* judicial; (*coroner's*) — encuesta *f* judicial, encuesta *f* post-mortem.
   (**b**) (*fig*) indagación *f*, encuesta *f*; **an — was held on the defeat** la derrota fue objeto de una encuesta; **he likes to hold an — on every game** le gusta discutir cada partido hasta la saciedad.
inquire [in'kwaiə*] **1** *vt* preguntar; informarse de, pedir informes sobre; **to — something of someone** preguntar algo a uno; **he —d the price** preguntó cuánto costaba.
   2 *vi*: **to — about, to — after, to — for** preguntar por, pedir informes sobre; **to — into** investigar, examinar, indagar; **to — into the truth of something** averiguar la verdad de un suceso; **to — of someone** preguntar a uno; **"— at No. 14"** "razón: núm. 14"; **"— within"** "se dan informaciones".
inquirer [in'kwaiərə*] *n* (*asker*) el (*or* la *etc*) que pregunta; (*researcher*) investigador *m*, ora *f* (*into* de).
inquiring [in'kwaiəriŋ] *adj* mind activo, penetrante, curioso; *look etc* interrogativo, de interrogación.
inquiringly [in'kwaiəriŋli] *adv look etc* interrogativamente.
inquiry [in'kwaiəri] *n* (**a**) (*question*) pregunta *f*; petición *f* de informes; **"Inquiries"** (*sign etc*) **"Información"**; **"inquiries at No. 14"** "razón: núm. 14"; **"all inquiries to the secretary"** "dirigirse al secretario"; **on — al preguntar; have you an —?** ¿quiere Vd preguntar algo?; **to make inquiries** pedir informes, tomar informes (*about, on* sobre; *of* a).
   (**b**) **a look of —** una mirada interrogativa.
   (**c**) (*Law etc*) investigación *f*, pesquisa *f*, indagación *f*, examen *m*, encuesta *f*; **there will have to be an —** esto tendrá que ser investigado; **to hold an — into something** investigar algo, examinar algo; **the police are making inquiries** la policía está investigando el asunto.
   (**d**) (*commission etc*) comisión *f* de investigación, comisión *f* investigadora; **to set up an — into the**

disaster nombrar una comisión para investigar el desastre.

inquiry office [in'kwaiəri,ɔfis] *n* oficina *f* de informaciones.

inquisition [,inkwi'ziʃən] *n* investigación *f*, inquisición *f*; the I— la Inquisición, el Santo Oficio.

inquisitive [in'kwizitiv] *adj* mind etc inquiridor, activo, curioso; (*pej*) preguntón, fisgón, curioso.

inquisitively [in'kwizitivli] *adv* con curiosidad *f*.

inquisitiveness [in'kwizitivnis] *n* curiosidad *f*.

inquisitor [in'kwizitə*] *n* inquisidor *m*.

inquisitorial [in,kwizi'tɔːriəl] *adj* inquisitorial.

inroad ['inroud] *n* incursión *f*, irrupción *f* (*into* en); (fig) invasión *f*, usurpación *f* (*into* de); to make —s into someone's savings agotar parte de los ahorros de uno.

inrush ['inrʌʃ] *n* irrupción *f*; (*of tourists etc*) afluencia *f*.

insalubrious [,insə'luːbriəs] *adj* insalubre, malsano.

insane [in'sein] *adj* person loco, demente; act etc insensato; you must be —! ¿estás loco?; to become — volverse loco; to drive someone — volver loco a uno.

insanely [in'seinli] *adv*: to laugh — reírse como un loco; to be — jealous ser terriblemente celoso.

insanitary [in'sænitəri] *adj* insalubre, antihigiénico.

insanity [in'sæniti] *n* locura *f*, demencia *f*; (*of act etc*) insensatez *f*; to drive someone to — volver loco a uno.

insatiable [in'seiʃəbl] *adj* insaciable.

inscribe [in'skraib] *vt* inscribir; book dedicar.

inscription [in'skripʃən] *n* inscripción *f*; (*in book*) dedicatoria *f*; (*label*) rótulo *m*, letrero *m*.

inscrutability [in,skruːtə'biliti] *n* inescrutabilidad *f*.

inscrutable [in'skruːtəbl] *adj* inescrutable, enigmático, insondable.

insect ['insekt] *n* insecto *m*.

insecticide [in'sektisaid] *n* insecticida *m*.

insectivorous [,insek'tivərəs] *adj* insectívoro.

insecure [,insi'kjuə*] *adj* inseguro.

insecurity [,insi'kjuəriti] *n* inseguridad *f*.

inseminate [in'semineit] *vt* inseminar.

insemination [in,semi'neiʃən] *n* fecundación *f*; artificial — fecundación *f* artificial, inseminación *f* artificial.

insensate [in'senseit] *adj* insensato.

insensibility [in,sensə'biliti] *n* (a) insensibilidad *f* (*to* a), impasibilidad *f*; inconsciencia *f* (*of* de).
　(b) (Med) estupor *m*, desmayo *m*, pérdida *f* de conocimiento.

insensible [in'sensəbl] *adj* (a) (*insensitive*) insensible (*to* a), impasible, inconmovible; (*unaware*) inconsciente (*of* de).
　(b) (Med) sin conocimiento; he fell down — cayó sin conocimiento; the blow knocked him — el golpe le hizo perder el conocimiento; to drink oneself — beber hasta perder el conocimiento.

insensitive [in'sensitiv] *adj* insensible (*to* a).

insensitivity [in,sensi'tiviti] *n* insensibilidad *f*.

inseparable [in'sepərəbl] *adj* inseparable, indisoluble; as children they were — cuando eran niños les unió la más estrecha amistad; the two questions are — los dos asuntos no se pueden considerar por separado.

inseparably [in'sepərəbli] *adv* inseparablemente, indisolublemente.

insert ['insəːt] *n* cosa *f* insertada; (*page*) hoja *f* suelta; (*section*) sección *f* añadida, materia *f* adicional.

insert [in'səːt] *vt* insertar, intercalar; object, finger etc introducir, meter dentro; (*in newspaper*) publicar; advert poner.

insertion [in'səːʃən] *n* inserción *f*; introducción *f*; publicación *f*; (*new section*) sección *f* añadida, materia *f* adicional.

inset ['inset] *n* (Typ) grabado *m* (*or* mapa, dibujo etc) que se imprime en un ángulo de otro mayor.

inshore ['in'ʃɔː*] 1 *adv* be, fish cerca de la orilla; blow, flow, go hacia la orilla. 2 *adj* cercano a la orilla; fishing cercano a la costa.

inside ['in'said] 1 *adv* dentro; hacia dentro; por dentro; (*on bus*) en el piso inferior, abajo; (*fam*) en la cárcel; he wouldn't come — no quiso entrar; please step — pase Vd, por favor; to pass the ball — pasar el balón hacia dentro.
　2 *prep* dentro de; en el interior de; — 4 hours en menos de 4 horas; — the record en tiempo inferior a la marca.
　3 *adj* interior; interno; information secreto, confidencial; it must be an — job ha de ser obra de un empleado de la casa.
　4 *n* (a) interior *m*, parte *f* interior; (*lining*) forro

m; to know the — of an affair conocer el secreto de un asunto; to see a firm from the — estudiar una empresa por dentro; on the — por dentro; ladies walk on the — of the pavement las señoras van en la parte de la acera más alejada de la calzada; the car overtook on the — (*Brit*) el coche pasó en el lado izquierdo.
　(b) to be — out estar al revés; to put a dress on — out ponerse un vestido al revés; to turn something — out volver algo al revés; they turned the whole place — out lo revolvieron todo, lo registraron todo de arriba abajo; to know a subject — out conocer un tema a fondo.
　(c) (Anat: also —s) estómago *m*, tripas *fpl*; I have a pain in my — me duele el estómago.

inside-forward ['insaid'fɔːwəd] *n* delantero *m* interior.

inside-left ['insaid'left] *n* interior *m* izquierdo.

inside-right ['insaid'rait] *n* interior *m* derecho.

insidious [in'sidiəs] *adj* insidioso; pernicioso; maligno; agitation etc clandestino, subversivo.

insidiously [in'sidiəsli] *adv* insidiosamente; perniciosamente; clandestinamente.

insight ['insait] *n* penetración *f* (psicológica), perspicacia *f*, intuición *f*; to gain (*or* get etc) an — into something formarse una idea de algo.

insignia [in'signiə] *npl* insignias *fpl*.

insignificance [,insig'nifikəns] *n* insignificancia *f*; A pales into — beside B A pierde toda su importancia al compararse con B.

insignificant [,insig'nifikənt] *adj* insignificante.

insincere [,insin'siə*] *adj* poco sincero, nada franco, doble.

insincerity [,insin'seriti] *n* falta *f* de sinceridad, doblez *f*.

insinuate [in'sinjueit] 1 *vt* insinuar; what are you insinuating? ¿qué quiere Vd insinuar?; to — that insinuar que, dar a entender que.
　2 *vr*: to — oneself into insinuarse en, introducirse en.

insinuating [in'sinjueitiŋ] *adj* insinuador; remark malintencionado, con segunda intención.

insinuation [in,sinju'eiʃən] *n* (act) insinuación *f*, introducción *f*; (hint) indirecta *f*, sugestión *f*; it carries the — that lleva implícita la noción de que; he made certain —s soltó ciertas indirectas.

insipid [in'sipid] *adj* insípido, soso, insulso.

insipidity [,insi'piditi] *n* insipidez *f*, sosería *f*, insulsez *f*.

insist [in'sist] *vi* insistir; (*obstinately*) porfiar, empeñarse, persistir; if you — si Vd lo quiere de verdad; to — on something insistir en algo, exigir algo; to — on doing something insistir en hacer algo, empeñarse en hacer algo, obstinarse en hacer algo; to — that something is so insistir en que algo es así; to — that something should be done insistir en que se haga algo.

insistence [in'sistəns] *n* insistencia *f* (*on* en); empeño *m* (*on* en); porfía *f*; I did it at his — lo hice cediendo a sus ruegos.

insistent [in'sistənt] *adj* insistente; porfiado, persistente; urgente; he was most — about it se empeñó mucho en ello; he said in — tones dijo en tono apremiante.

insistently [in'sistəntli] *adv* con insistencia; porfiadamente; urgentemente.

insole ['insoul] *n* plantilla *f*.

insolence ['insələns] *n* insolencia *f*, descaro *m*, atrevimiento *m*.

insolent ['insələnt] *adj* insolente, descarado, atrevido; don't be —! ¡qué frescura!

insolently ['insələntli] *adv* insolentemente, descaradamente.

insoluble [in'sɔljubl] *adj* insoluble.

insolvency [in'sɔlvənsi] *n* insolvencia *f*.

insolvent [in'sɔlvənt] *adj* insolvente.

insomnia [in'sɔmniə] *n* insomnio *m*.

insomniac [in'sɔmniæk] *n* insomne *mf*.

insomuch [,insəu'mʌtʃ]: — as *adv* puesto que, ya que; — that hasta tal punto que.

insouciance [in'suːsiəns] *n* despreocupación *f*.

insouciant [in'suːsiənt] *adj* despreocupado.

inspect [in'spekt] *vt* inspeccionar, examinar; (*officially*) registrar, reconocer; troops pasar revista a.

inspection [in'spekʃən] *n* inspección *f*, examen *m*; registro *m*, reconocimiento *m*; (Mil) revista *f*; customs — revisión *f* aduanera; — pit foso *m* de reconocimiento.

inspector [in'spektə*] *n* inspector *m*; (Rail) revisor *m*; customs — aduanero *m*.

inspectorate [in'spektərit] *n* inspectorado *m*.

inspiration [ˌinspə'reiʃən] n inspiración f; **to find — in** inspirarse en; **you have been an — to us all** Vd nos ha inspirado a todos.

inspire [in'spaiə*] vt inspirar; **to — something in someone, to — someone with something** inspirar algo a uno, infundir algo a uno, llenar a uno de algo; **to — someone to do something** mover a uno a hacer algo.

inspired [in'spaiəd] adj genial.

inspiring [in'spaiəriŋ] adj inspirador.

instability [ˌinstə'biliti] n inestabilidad f.

install [in'stɔːl] **1** vt instalar. **2** vr: **to — oneself** instalarse.

installation [ˌinstə'leiʃən] n instalación f.

instalment, (US) **installment** [in'stɔːlmənt] n (of story etc) entrega f; (Comm) plazo m; **payment by —s** pago m a plazos; **to pay in —s** pagar a plazos; **monthly —** mensualidad f.

instance ['instəns] **1** n **(a)** (example) ejemplo m; caso m; **for —** por ejemplo; **in that —** en ese caso; **in many —s** en muchos casos; **let's take an actual —** tomemos un caso concreto.

(b) at the — of a instancia de, a petición de.

(c) in the first — en primer lugar.

2 vt poner por caso, citar como ejemplo.

instant ['instənt] **1** adj inmediato, instantáneo; **— coffee** café m en polvo (listo para hacer); **the 3rd —** el 3 del (mes) corriente.

2 n instante m, momento m; **in an —, on the —, this —** al instante, en seguida.

3 as conj: **tell me the —** he comes avíseme en cuanto venga; **the — I heard it** luego que lo supe.

instantaneous [ˌinstən'teiniəs] adj instantáneo.

instantaneously [ˌinstən'teiniəsli] adv instantáneamente.

instantly ['instəntli] adv al instante, inmediatamente, en seguida.

instead [in'sted] adv en cambio, en lugar de eso; **— of** en lugar de, en vez de.

instep ['instep] n empeine m.

instigate ['instigeit] vt instigar.

instigation [ˌinsti'geiʃən] n instigación f; **at the — of** a instigación de.

instigator ['instigeitə*] n instigador m, ora f.

instil [in'stil] vt infundir, inculcar; **to — something into someone** infundir algo a uno, inculcar algo en uno.

instinct [in'stiŋkt] adj: **— with** lleno de, imbuido de.

instinct ['instiŋkt] n instinto m; **by —** por instinto.

instinctive [in'stiŋktiv] adj instintivo.

instinctively [in'stiŋktivli] adv instintivamente, por instinto.

institute ['institjuːt] **1** n instituto m; (for professional training) escuela f; (of professional body) colegio m, asociación f.

2 vt (found) instituir, establecer, fundar; inquiry etc iniciar, empezar; proceedings (Law) entablar.

institution [ˌinsti'tjuːʃən] n **(a)** (act) institución f, establecimiento m, fundación f; iniciación f; entablación f.

(b) (organization) instituto m, asociación f.

(c) (workhouse etc) asilo m; (madhouse) manicomio m; (Med) hospital m.

(d) (custom etc) institución f, costumbre f, tradición f; (person etc) persona f conocidísima; **it is too much of an — to abolish** es una costumbre demasiado arraigada para poder suprimirla; **tea is a British —** el té es bebida típica de los ingleses.

institutional [ˌinsti'tjuːʃənl] adj institucional.

institutionalize [ˌinsti'tjuːʃnəlaiz] vt reglamentar.

instruct [in'strʌkt] vt **(a)** (teach) instruir (about, in de, en, sobre); **to — someone in maths** enseñar matemáticas a uno.

(b) (order) **to — someone to do something** mandar a uno hacer algo.

(c) solicitor dar instrucciones a.

instruction [in'strʌkʃən] n **(a)** (teaching) instrucción f, enseñanza f; **to give someone — in fencing** enseñar esgrima a uno.

(b) (order) orden f, mandato m; **—s** instrucciones fpl; órdenes fpl; **"— for use"** (on packet etc) "modo de empleo" m; **operating —s** (of pilot etc) órdenes fpl, consigna f; **on the —s of** por orden de.

instructive [in'strʌktiv] adj instructivo, informativo, aleccionador.

instructor [in'strʌktə*] n instructor m; profesor m; (US Univ) profesor m auxiliar.

instructress [in'strʌktris] n instructora f; profesora f.

instrument ['instrumənt] n (all senses) instrumento m; **musical —** instrumento m músico; **stringed —** instrumento m de cuerda; **wind —** instrumento m

de viento; **scientific —s** instrumentos mpl científicos; **set of —s** instrumental m; **to fly on —s** volar por instrumentos.

instrumental [ˌinstru'mentl] adj instrumental; **to be — in** + ger contribuir materialmente a + infin, ser instrumento eficaz para + infin.

instrumentalist [ˌinstru'mentəlist] n instrumentista mf.

instrumentality [ˌinstrumen'tæliti] n mediación f, agencia f; **by** (or **through**) **the — of** por medio de, gracias a.

instrumentation [ˌinstrumen'teiʃən] n instrumentación f.

instrument panel ['instrumənt.pænl] n (Aer) tablero m de instrumentos.

insubordinate [ˌinsə'bɔːdənit] adj insubordinado, desobediente, rebelde.

insubordination ['insə.bɔːdi'neiʃən] n insubordinación f, desobediencia f, rebeldía f.

insubstantial [ˌinsəb'stænʃəl] adj insustancial.

insufferable [in'sʌfərəbl] adj insufrible, inaguantable.

insufferably [in'sʌfərəbli] adv de modo insufrible; **— rude** de lo más grosero.

insufficiency [ˌinsə'fiʃənsi] n insuficiencia f.

insufficient [ˌinsə'fiʃənt] adj insuficiente.

insufficiently [ˌinsə'fiʃəntli] adv insuficientemente.

insular ['insjələ*] adj insular; (fig) de miras estrechas.

insularity [ˌinsju'læriti] n insularidad f; (fig) estrechez f de miras.

insulate ['insjuleit] vt aislar (from de).

insulating tape ['insjuleitiŋ.teip] n cinta f aislante (or aisladora).

insulation [ˌinsju'leiʃən] n aislamiento m.

insulator ['insjuleitə*] n aislante m, aislador m.

insulin ['insjulin] n insulina f.

insult ['insʌlt] n insulto m, injuria f, ultraje m, ofensa f; **they are an — to the profession** son un insulto para la profesión.

insult [in'sʌlt] vt insultar, injuriar; ofender; **he felt —ed by this offer** creyó que tal oferta era deshonrosa para él; **now don't feel —ed** pues no te vayas a ofender.

insulting [in'sʌltiŋ] adj insultante, injurioso; ofensivo; deshonroso.

insultingly [in'sʌltiŋli] adv injuriosamente, ofensivamente.

insuperable [in'suːpərəbl] adj insuperable.

insuperably [in'suːpərəbli] adv: **— difficult** dificilísimo; **A is — better than B** A es con mucho mejor que B.

insupportable [ˌinsə'pɔːtəbl] adj insoportable.

insurable [in'ʃuərəbl] adj asegurable.

insurance [in'ʃuərəns] n (Comm) seguro m; **life —** seguro m sobre la vida; **mutual —** seguro m mutuo; **third-party —** seguro m contra tercera persona; **— agent** agente m de seguros; **— broker** corredor m de seguros; **— company** compañía f de seguros; **— policy** póliza f (de seguros); **— premium** prima f de seguros.

insure [in'ʃuə*] vt asegurar.

insured [in'ʃuəd] n: **the —** el asegurado, la asegurada.

insurer [in'ʃuərə*] n asegurador m, ora f.

insurgent [in'səːdʒənt] **1** adj insurrecto, insurgente. **2** n insurrecto m, insurgente mf.

insurmountable [ˌinsə'mauntəbl] adj insuperable.

insurrection [ˌinsə'rekʃən] n sublevación f, insurrección f.

insurrectionary [ˌinsə'rekʃnəri] adj rebelde, insurreccional.

intact [in'tækt] adj intacto; íntegro; ileso, entero, sano; **not a window was left —** no quedaba cristal sano (or sin romper).

intake ['inteik] n **(a)** (Mech) admisión f, toma f, entrada f; tubo m de admisión, válvula f de admisión; **air —** tubo m de admisión de aire.

(b) (quantity) cantidad f admitida, número m admitido; **what is your student —?** ¿cuántos alumnos se matriculan (cada año)?

intangible [in'tændʒəbl] adj intangible.

integer ['intidʒə*] n (número m) entero m.

integral ['intigrəl] **1** adj (whole) íntegro; part, component integrante; (Math) integral; **it is an — part of the plan** es parte esencial del proyecto. **2** n (Math) integral f.

integrate ['intigreit] **1** vt integrar (also Math); combinar en un todo, formar un conjunto con. **2** vi integrarse (into en).

integrated ['intigreitid] adj plan de conjunto, que forma un conjunto; personality armonioso, estable, sano; population, school integrado, sin separación racial.

integration [‚inti'greiʃən] n integración f; **racial —** integración f racial.
integrity [in'tegriti] n integridad f, honradez f, rectitud f.
integument [in'tegjumənt] n integumento m.
intellect ['intilekt] n intelecto m.
intellectual [‚inti'lektjuəl] **1** adj intelectual. **2** n intelectual mf.
intelligence [in'telidʒəns] n **(a)** (understanding) inteligencia f; see **test** etc.
   (b) (information) información f, informes mpl, noticias fpl; — **officer** oficial m de informaciones; — **service** (Mil) servicio m de información; **shipping —** noticias fpl navieras; **according to our latest —** según las últimas noticias.
intelligent [in'telidʒənt] adj inteligente.
intelligently [in'telidʒntli] adv inteligentemente.
intelligentsia [in‚teli'dʒentsiə] n intelectualidad f.
intelligibility [in‚telidʒə'biliti] n inteligibilidad f.
intelligible [in'telidʒəbl] adj inteligible, comprensible; **it is scarcely —** that apenas es creíble que.
intelligibly [in'telidʒəbli] adv inteligiblemente, de modo inteligible.
intemperance [in'tempərəns] n intemperancia f, inmoderación f; (drunkenness) exceso m en la bebida.
intemperate [in'tempərit] adj intemperante, inmoderado; (drunken) dado a la bebida, que bebe con exceso.
intend [in'tend] vt **(a)** (n object) **what does he — by that?** ¿qué quiere decir con eso?; **I — it as a present** pienso darlo como regalo; **it is —ed for John** está destinado a Juan, es para Juan; **no offence was —ed, he —ed** no offence no tenía la intención de ofender a nadie; **that remark was —ed for you** esa observación iba dirigida a Vd, eso lo dijo por Vd.
   (b) (with verb) **to — to + infin, to — what do you — to do about it?** ¿qué piensas hacer?; **this scheme is —ed to help** este proyecto tiene la finalidad de ayudar; **I — that he should see it** pretendo que él lo vea, quiero que él lo vea; **I fully — to punish him** tengo la firme intención de castigarle.
intended [in'tendid] **1** adj deseado. **2** n prometido m, a f.
intense [in'tens] adj intenso; interest etc muy grande, sumo, enorme; person exagerado, nervioso.
intensely [in'tensli] adv intensamente; **— difficult** sumamente difícil, terriblemente difícil, dificilísimo; **she speaks so —** habla en tono tan exagerado.
intensification [in‚tensifi'keiʃən] n intensificación f.
intensify [in'tensifai] **1** vt intensificar; aumentar, reforzar. **2** vi intensificarse; aumentar(se), reforzarse.
intensity [in'tensiti] n intensidad f; (of interest etc) fuerza f; (of person) exageración f, nerviosismo m, hipertensión f.
intensive [in'tensiv] adj intensivo; course intensivo, concentrado; study profundo, detenido.
intensively [in'tensivli] adv intensivamente; profundamente, detenidamente.
intent [in'tent] **1** adj (absorbed) absorto (on en), atento; **to be — on doing something** estar resuelto a hacer algo.
   2 n intento m, propósito m; **with — to + infin** con el propósito de + infin; **to all —s and purposes** en realidad, en efecto.
intention [in'tenʃən] n intención f; intento m, propósito m; proyecto m; **my — is to + infin** me propongo + infin, intento + infin; **I have no — of + ger** no es mi propósito + infin; **with the best —s** con buena voluntad; **what are your —s?** ¿qué piensa hacer?, ¿qué proyectos tiene Vd?; **his —s towards the girl were strictly honourable** pensaba casarse honradamente con la joven.
intentional [in'tenʃənl] adj intencional, deliberado.
intentionally [in'tenʃnəli] adv intencionalmente, de propósito, adrede.
intently [in'tentli] adv atentamente, fijamente.
inter [in'tə:*] vt enterrar, sepultar.
inter . . . ['intə*] inter . . ., entre . . .
interact [‚intər'ækt] vi obrar recíprocamente (on en); **they — se** influyen mutuamente.
interaction [‚intər'ækʃən] n interacción f, acción f recíproca, influencia f mutua.
interbreed ['intə'briːd] (irr: see **breed**) **1** vt entrecruzar. **2** vi entrecruzarse.
intercalate [in'tə:kəleit] vt intercalar.
intercalation [in‚tə:kə'leiʃən] n intercalación f.
intercede [‚intə'siːd] vi interceder (for por, with con).
intercept [‚intə'sept] vt interceptar; detener (Math) cortar; (cut off) atajar.

interception [‚intə'sepʃən] n interceptación f, detención f; atajo m.
interceptor [‚intə(:)'septə*] n interceptor m.
intercession [‚intə'seʃən] n intercesión f, mediación f.
interchange ['intə'tʃeindʒ] n intercambio m, cambio m; canje m; alternación f.
interchange [‚intə'tʃeindʒ] vt intercambiar, cambiar; prisoners, publications etc canjear; (alternate) alternar.
interchangeable [‚intə'tʃeindʒəbl] adj intercambiable.
intercollegiate ['intə(:)kə'liːdʒiit] adj interuniversitario.
intercom ['intəkəm] n (fam) sistema m de intercomunicación.
intercommunicate [‚intəkə'mjuːnikeit] vi comunicarse.
intercommunication ['intəkə‚mjuːni'keiʃən] n intercomunicación f.
intercommunion [‚intəkə'mjuːniən] n intercomunión f.
interconnect [‚intəkə'nekt] vt interconectar.
intercontinental ['intə‚kɔnti'nentl] adj intercontinental.
intercourse ['intəkɔːs] n (social) trato m, relaciones fpl, comercio m; **sexual —** comercio m sexual, trato m sexual, coito m; **to have (sexual) — with** tener comercio sexual con.
interdenominational ['intədi‚nɔmi'neiʃənl] adj interconfesional.
interdependence [‚intədi'pendəns] n interdependencia f.
interdependent [‚intədi'pendənt] adj interdependiente.
interdict ['intədikt] n entredicho m, interdicto m.
interdiction [‚intə'dikʃən] n interdicción f.
interest ['intrist] **1** n **(a)** (curiosity) interés m; **of great —** de gran interés; **questions of public —** asuntos mpl que interesan a todos; **to be of —** interesar; **it is of no — to us** no nos interesa; **to do something just for —** hacer algo como pasatiempo nada más; **to have an — in** estar interesado en, interesarse en (or por); **to take an — in something** interesarse en (or por) algo; **to take no further — in something** dejar de interesarse en algo; **no** participar más en algo.
   (b) (profit, advantage) ventaja f, provecho m, beneficio m; **in one's own —(s)** en beneficio propio; **it is in your own — to confess** hay que confesarlo en beneficio propio; **in the —s of hygiene** en interés de la higiene; **to act in someone's —s** obrar en beneficio de uno; **to promote someone's —s** fomentar los intereses de uno; **it is not in Britain's — to leave the base** le perjudicará a Inglaterra abandonar la base.
   (c) (Comm: share, stake) participación f, interés m; **—s** intereses mpl; **the coal —** la industria hullera, los propietarios de las minas de carbón; **the conservative —** los conservadores, el partido conservador; **the landed —** los terratenientes; **business —s** los negocios, el mundo de los negocios, los hombres de negocios; **vested —s** intereses mpl creados; **Switzerland is looking after British —s** Suiza se encarga de los intereses ingleses; **to have a financial — in a company** tener acciones en una compañía, ser accionista de una compañía; **to have a controlling —** tener más de la mitad de las acciones; **to give someone a joint —** admitir a uno como copartícipe.
   (d) (Comm: on loan, shares etc) interés m; rédito m; compound — interés m compuesto; **simple —** interés m simple; **at an — of 5%** con interés de 5 por ciento; **to bear —** devengar intereses; **to bear — at 5%** producir un 5 por ciento de interés; **to lend at —** dar a interés; **to put out at —** poner a interés; **to repay with — (iro)** devolver con creces; **shares that yield a high —** acciones fpl que rinden bien.
   2 vt interesar; **to be —ed in** (financially) estar interesado en, (from curiosity) interesarse en (or por); **the company is —ed in acquiring 200** la compañía está interesada en adquirir 200; **I'm not —ed in football** no me interesa el fútbol.
   3 vr: **to — oneself in** interesarse en (or por).
interested ['intristid] adj: **— party, — person** interesado m, a f.
interesting ['intristiŋ] adj interesante.
interfere [‚intə'fiə*] vi intervenir, entrometerse, mezclarse (in en); **to — with** (hinder) dificultar, impedir; (damage) manosear, estropear; (Radio etc) interferir; **who told you to —?** ¿quién le mete a Vd en esto?

interference [,intə'fiərəns] *n* intervención *f*, intromisión *f*, entrometimiento *m*; interposición *f*; (*Radio etc*) interferencia *f*.
interfering [,intə'fiəriŋ] *adj* entrometido.
interim ['intərim] **1** *n* interin *m*, intermedio *m*; **in the** — entretanto, en el interin, interinamente. **2** *attr* interino, provisional.
interior [in'tiəriə*] **1** *adj* interior, interno. **2** *n* interior *m*.
interject [,intə'dʒekt] *vt* interponer.
interjection [,intə'dʒekʃən] *n* interposición *f*; (*word*) interjección *f*, exclamación *f*.
interlace [,intə(:)'leis] **1** *vt* entrelazar. **2** *vi* entrelazarse.
interlard [,intə'lɑːd] *vt*: **to** — **with** salpicar de.
interleave [,intə(:)'liːv] *vt* interfoliar.
interline [,intə(:)'lain] *vt* (*Typ*) interlinear; (*Sew*) entretelar.
interlinear [,intə(:)'liniə*] *adj* interlineal.
interlock [,intə'lɔk] **1** *vt* trabar, unir, entrelazar; *wheels* endentar, engranar.
　2 *vi* trabarse, unirse, entrelazarse; (*wheels etc*) endentarse, engranar; **the parts of the plan** — **las partes del plan** tienen una fuerte trabazón.
interlocutor [,intə'lɔkjutə*] *n* interlocutor *m*, ora *f*.
interloper ['intələupə*] *n* intruso *m*, a *f*; (*Comm*) intérlope *m*, comerciante *m* (*etc*) no autorizado.
interlude ['intəluːd] *n* intervalo *m*, intermedio *m*; (*rest*) descanso *m*; (*Theat*: *playlet*, *interval*) intermedio *m*; (*Mus*) interludio *m*.
intermarriage [,intə'mæridʒ] *n* matrimonio *m* entre parientes; matrimonio *m* entre personas de distintas razas.
intermarry ['intə'mæri] *vi* casarse (parientes *or* personas de distintas razas); **in this village they have intermarried for centuries** en este pueblo se vienen casando los parientes desde hace siglos.
intermediary [,intə'miːdiəri] **1** *adj* intermediario. **2** *n* intermediario *m*, a *f*.
intermediate [,intə'miːdiət] *adj* intermedio, medio; intermediario; — **stop** escala *f*.
interment [in'təːmənt] *n* entierro *m*.
interminable [in'təːminəbl] *adj* inacabable, interminable.
interminably [in'təːminəbli] *adv*: **he spoke** — habló como si nunca fuera a acabar.
intermingle [,intə'miŋgl] **1** *vt* entremezclar. **2** *vi* entremezclarse.
intermission [,intə'miʃən] *n* intermisión *f*, interrupción *f*, intervalo *m*; (*Theat*) descanso *m*; **it went on without** — continuó sin interrupción.
intermittent [,intə'mitənt] *adj* intermitente.
intermittently [,intə'mitəntli] *adv* a intervalos, a ratos.
intern [in'təːn] *vt* internar, recluir, encerrar.
intern ['intəːn] *n* (*US Med*) interno *m* de hospital.
internal [in'təːnl] *adj* interno, interior.
internally [in'təːnəli] *adv* interiormente.
international [,intə'næʃənl] **1** *adj* internacional. **2** *n* **I**— Internacional *f*; (*Sport*: *game*) partido *m* internacional, (*player*) jugador *m* internacional.
internationalism [intə'næʃnəlizəm] *n* internacionalismo *m*.
internationalize [,intə'næʃnəlaiz] *vt* internacionalizar.
internecine [,intə'niːsain] *adj*: — **war** guerra *f* de aniquilación mutua.
internee [,intəː'niː] *n* internado *m*, a *f*.
internment [in'təːnmənt] *n* internamiento *m*.
interplanetary [,intə'plænitəri] *adj* interplanetario.
interplay ['intəplei] *n* interacción *f*.
interpolate [in'təːpəleit] *vt* interpolar.
interpolation [in,təːpə'leiʃən] *n* interpolación *f*.
interpose [,intə'pəuz] *vt* interponer; *remark* introducir, hacer de paso; **"never!",** —**d John** "¡jamás!", cortó Juan.
interpret [in'təːprit] *vt* interpretar; (*translate*) traducir; (*understand*) entender, explicar; **how are we to** — **that remark?** ¿cómo hemos de entender esa observación?; **if I** — **your wishes correctly** si entiendo bien sus deseos; **that is not how I** — **it** yo lo entiendo de otro modo.
interpretation [in,təːpri'teiʃən] *n* interpretación *f*; traducción *f*; (*meaning*) significado *m*; **what** — **am I to place on your conduct?** ¿cómo he de entender su conducta?; **the words bear another** — **las palabras tienen otro significado, las palabras pueden entenderse de otro modo.
interpretative [in'təːpritətiv] *adj* interpretativo, aclaratorio, explicativo.
interpreter [in'təːpritə*] *n* intérprete *mf*.
interregnum [,intə'regnəm] *n* interregno *m*.
interrelate [,intəri'leit] *vt* interrelacionar.

interrelated [,intəri'leitid] *adj* interrelacionado.
interrelation [,intəri'leiʃən] *n* interrelación *f*.
interrogate [in'terəgeit] *vt* interrogar.
interrogation [in,terə'geiʃən] *n* interrogación *f*.
interrogative [,intə'rɔgətiv] **1** *adj* interrogativo. **2** *n* interrogativo *m*.
interrogator [in'terəgeitə*] *n* interrogador *m*, ora *f*.
interrogatory [,intə'rɔgətəri] *adj* interrogante.
interrupt [,intə'rʌpt] *vti* interrumpir.
interruption [intə'rʌpʃən] *n* interrupción *f*.
intersect [,intə'sekt] **1** *vt* cruzar, cortar. **2** *vi* (*Geom*) intersecarse; (*roads etc*) cruzarse.
intersection [,intə'sekʃən] *n* intersección *f*; cruce *m*.
intersperse [,intə'spəːs] *vt* esparcir, entremezclar; **dashes** —**d with dots** rayas con puntos a intervalos (*or* a ratos); **a speech** —**d with jokes** un discurso salpicado de chistes.
interstate [,intə'steit] *adj* (*esp US*) interestatal.
interstice [in'təːstis] *n* intersticio *m*.
intertwine [,intə'twain] **1** *vt* entrelazar, entretejer. **2** *vi* entrelazarse, entretejerse.
interurban [,intəː'əːbən] *adj* interurbano.
interval ['intəvəl] *n* intervalo *m*; (*Theat*) descanso *m*, (*more formally*) entreacto *m*; (*Sport etc*) descanso *m*; **at** —**s** de vez en cuando, de trecho a trecho, a ratos, a intervalos; **at rare** —**s** muy de tarde en tarde; **at regular** —**s** con regularidad; **bright** —**s** (*Meteorol*) períodos *mpl* de sol; **lucid** — intervalo *m* lúcido; **the work went on without an** — el trabajo continuó sin interrupción; **there was an** — **for meditation** se hizo una pausa para la meditación.
intervene [,intə'viːn] *vi* intervenir (*in* en); tomar parte, participar (*in* en); (*occur*) surgir, interponerse, sobrevenir; **if nothing** —**s to prevent it** si no surge nada que lo impida.
intervening [,intə'viːniŋ] *adj* intermedio.
intervention [,intə'venʃən] *n* intervención *f*.
interview ['intəvjuː] **1** *n* entrevista *f*, (*for press, TV etc*) interviú *f*; **to have an** — **with someone** entrevistarse con uno.
　2 *vt* entrevistarse con, (*for press, TV etc*) interviuvar; **3% of those** —**ed did not know that** . . . un 3 por cien de los entrevistados ignoraban que . . .
interviewer ['intəvjuːə*] *n* interviuvador *m*, ora *f*; (*pressman*) reportero *m*, periodista *m*.
interweave [,intə'wiːv] (*irr*: *see* **weave**) *vt* entretejer.
intestate [in'testit] *adj* intestado.
intestinal [,intes'tainl] *adj* intestinal.
intestine [in'testin] *n* intestino *m*; **large** — intestino *m* grueso; **small** — intestino *m* delgado.
intimacy ['intiməsi] *n* intimidad *f*; (*euph*) relaciones *fpl* íntimas.
intimate ['intimeit] *vt* dar a entender, indicar, intimar.
intimate ['intimit] **1** *adj* íntimo; *friendship etc* estrecho; *knowledge* profundo, detallado; **they are** — **friends** son íntimos amigos; **they are very** — son muy amigos; **he was** — **with her** (*euph*) tuvo relaciones íntimas con ella; **they became** — se intimaron; **A became** — **with B** A se intimó con B. **2** *n* amigo *m* de confianza; (*pej*) compinche *m*.
intimately ['intimitli] *adv* íntimamente; a fondo, profundamente.
intimation [,inti'meiʃən] *n* (*news*) indicación *f*, intimación *f*; (*hint*) insinuación *f*, indirecta *f*; **it was the first** — **we had had of it** fue la primera indicación que habíamos tenido de ello.
intimidate [in'timideit] *vt* intimidar, acobardar, amedrentar.
intimidation [in,timi'deiʃən] *n* intimidación *f*.
into ['intu] *prep* en; a; dentro de; hacia el interior de; **to put something** — **a box** poner algo en una caja; **to go** — **the wood** penetrar en el bosque; **to go off** — **the desert** ir hacia el interior del desierto; **to go** — **town** ir a la ciudad; **it got** — **the cage** entró en la jaula; **they got** — **the plane** subieron al avión; **it fell** — **the lake** cayó al lago, cayó en el lago; **to change something** — **something else** convertir algo en otra cosa; **to translate a text** — **Latin** traducir un texto al latín; **to grow** — **a man** hacerse hombre; *see* **far, go** *etc*.
intolerable [in'tɔlərəbl] *adj* intolerable, inaguantable, insufrible; **it is** — **that** no se puede consentir que + *subj*.
intolerably [in'tɔlərəbli] *adj* insufriblemente; **he is** — **vain** es tremendamente vanidoso.
intolerance [in'tɔlərəns] *n* intolerancia *f*.
intolerant [in'tɔlərənt] *adj* intolerante (*of* con, para).
intonation [,intəu'neiʃən] *n* entonación *f*.
intone [in'təun] *vt* entonar; (*Eccl etc*) salmodiar.
intoxicant [in'tɔksikənt] **1** *adj* embriagador. **2** *n* bebida *f* alcohólica.

intoxicate [in'tɔksikeit] *vt* embriagar (*also fig*); (*Med*) intoxicar.
intoxicated [in'tɔksikeitid] *adj* ebrio, borracho; **to be — with** (*fig*) estar ebrio de.
intoxication [in.tɔksi'keiʃən] *n* embriaguez *f* (*also fig*); (*Med*) intoxicación *f*.
intra . . . ['intrə] intra . . .
intractable [in'træktəbl] *adj* person intratable; *material* difícil de trabajar; *problem* insoluble, espinoso.
intransigence [in'trænsidʒəns] *n* intransigencia *f*.
intransigent [in'trænsidʒənt] *adj* intransigente.
intransitive [in'trænsitiv] *adj* intransitivo, neutro.
intravenous [.intrə'viːnəs] *adj* intravenoso.
intrepid [in'trepid] *adj* intrépido.
intrepidity [.intri'piditi] *n* intrepidez *f*.
intrepidly [in'trepidli] *adv* intrépidamente.
intricacy ['intrikəsi] *n* lo intrincado; complejidad *f*.
intricate ['intrikit] *adj* intrincado; complejo.
intricately ['intrikitli] *adv* intrincadamente, de modo intrincado.
intrigue [in'triːg] **1** *n* intriga *f*; (*amorous*) amorío *m*, lío *m*.
  2 *vt* interesar, fascinar, despertar la curiosidad de; **she —s me** ella me fascina; **I am —d to know whether** me interesa saber si; **I am much —d by your news** me interesa muchísimo esa noticia; **we were —d by a sign** nos llamó la atención un letrero, un letrero despertó nuestra curiosidad.
  3 *vi* intrigar, andar en intrigas, meterse en líos.
intriguer [in'triːgə*] *n* intrigante *mf*.
intriguing [in'triːgiŋ] *adj* (a) (*scheming*) enredador. (b) (*fascinating*) intrigante, fascinador, curioso, interesante; seductor; misterioso; **a most — problem** un problema interesantísimo; **an — gadget** un chisme de los más curiosos; **how very —! ¡**qué raro!, ¡muy interesante!
intrinsic [in'trinsik] *adj* intrínseco.
intrinsically [in'trinsikli] *adv* intrínsecamente.
intro . . . ['intrəu, 'intrə] intro . .
introduce [.intrə'djuːs] *vt* (a) (*insert*) introducir, meter, insertar (*into* en).
  (b) (*put forward*) *new thing, reform etc* introducir; *new fashion* introducir, poner de moda, lanzar; *new product, bill* presentar; *newcomer* presentar, dar a conocer; *book* (*preface*) prologar; *subject into conversation* mencionar, sacar a colación; **be careful how you — the subject** hay que abordar el tema con mucho cuidado; **I was —d into a dark room** me hicieron entrar en un cuarto oscuro; **I was —d into his presence** me llevaron ante él; **I was —d to chess at 8** empecé a jugar al ajedrez a los 8 años; **I was —d to Milton too young** me hicieron leer a Milton demasiado temprano.
  (c) *person* presentar; **may I — Mr X?** permítame presentarle al Sr X; **I don't think we've been —d** creo que no nos han presentado oficialmente.
introduction [.intrə'dakʃən] *n* introducción *f*, inserción *f*; presentación *f*; (*to book*) prólogo *m*; **my — to life in Cadiz** mi primera experiencia de la vida en Cádiz; **my — to maths** el comienzo de mis estudios matemáticos; **to give someone an — to a person** dar a uno una carta de recomendación para una persona; **will you make the —s?** ¿quiere Vd presentarnos?
introductory [.intrə'daktəri] *adj* preliminar.
introit ['introit] *n* introito *m*.
introspection [.intrəu'spekʃən] *n* introspección *f*.
introspective [.intrəu'spektiv] *adj* introspectivo.
introversion [.intrəu'vəːʃən] *n* introversión *f*.
introvert ['intrəuvəːt] **1** *adj* introvertido. **2** *n* introvertido *m*, a *f*.
intrude [in'truːd] **1** *vt* introducir (sin derecho), meter (*in* en); imponer (*upon* a).
  2 *vi* entrometerse, encajarse (*upon* en); estorbar, molestar; **do I —?** ¿te molesto?; **to — on someone's privacy** molestar a uno cuando quiere estar a solas; **sometimes sentimentality —s** a veces se asoma el sentimentalismo; **he lets no feelings of pity —** no deja lugar a la compasión.
intruder [in'truːdə*] *n* intruso *m*, a *f*.
intrusion [in'truːʒən] *n* intrusión *f*; invasión *f*; **the — of sentimentality** la aparición del sentimentalismo; **please pardon the —** siento tener que molestarle.
intrusive [in'truːsiv] *adj* intruso.
intuition [.intjuː'iʃən] *n* intuición *f*.
intuitive [in'tjuːitiv] *adj* intuitivo.
intuitively [in'tjuːitivli] *adv* intuitivamente, por intuición.
inundate ['inʌndeit] *vt* inundar (*also fig*).
inundation [.inʌn'deiʃən] *n* inundación *f*.

inure [in'juə*] *vt* acostumbrar, habituar (*to* a), endurecer.
invade [in'veid] *vt* invadir.
invader [in'veidə*] *n* invasor *m*.
invading [in'veidiŋ] *adj* invasor.
invalid [in'vælid] *adj* inválido, nulo; **to become —** caducar.
invalid ['invəlid] **1** *adj* inválido, enfermo. **2** *n* inválido *m*, a *f*. **3** *vt*: **to — someone out of the army** licenciar a uno por invalidez.
invalidate [in'vælideit] *vt* invalidar, anular, quitar valor a; *argument* destruir.
invaluable [in'væljuəbl] *adj* inestimable, inapreciable.
invariable [in'veəriəbl] *adj* invariable, inalterable.
invariably [in'veəriəbli] *adv* invariablemente; **it — happens that** ocurre siempre que; **he is — late** siempre llega tarde.
invasion [in'veiʒən] *n* invasión *f*.
invective [in'vektiv] *n* invectiva *f*; palabras *fpl* fuertes, improperios *mpl*.
inveigh [in'vei] *vi*: **to — against** vituperar, hablar en contra de, condenar.
inveigle [in'viːgl] *vt*: **to — someone into something** inducir (engañosamente) a uno a algo; **to — someone into doing something** persuadir (mañosamente) a uno a hacer algo; **he let himself be —d into it** se dejó engatusar para que lo hiciera.
invent [in'vent] *vt* inventar; idear.
invention [in'venʃən] *n* (*gadget etc*) invención *f*, invento *m*; (*inventiveness*) inventiva *f*; (*falsehood*) ficción *f*, mentira *f*; **it's sheer — on her part** son cosas que ella ha soñado, son cosas de ella; **it's — from start to finish** todo es mentira.
inventive [in'ventiv] *adj* inventivo, ingenioso.
inventiveness [in'ventivnis] *n* inventiva *f*, ingenio *m*.
inventor [in'ventə*] *n* inventor *m*, ora *f*.
inventory ['invəntri] **1** *n* inventario *m*. **2** *vt* inventariar.
inverse ['in'vəːs] *adj* inverso.
inversely [in'vəːsli] *adv* a la inversa.
inversion [in'vəːʃən] *n* inversión *f*.
invert [in'vəːt] *vt* invertir, volver al revés, trastrocar.
invertebrate [in'vəːtibrit] **1** *adj* invertebrado. **2** *n* invertebrado *m*.
invest [in'vest] **1** *vt* (a) *money* invertir (*in* en).
  (b) (*Mil*) sitiar, cercar.
  (c) **to — someone with something** investir a uno de (*or* con) algo; **to be —ed with a dignity** revestirse con una dignidad; **he —ed it with a certain mystery** lo revistió con cierto misterio; **he seems to — it with some importance** parece que da cierta importancia a la cosa.
  2 *vi*: **to — in** *company etc* invertir dinero en; (*buy*) comprar, adquirir; (*support*) apoyar, demostrar tener confianza en; **to — with** invertir dinero en.
investigate [in'vestigeit] *vt* investigar; examinar, estudiar.
investigation [in.vesti'geiʃən] *n* investigación *f*; pesquisa *f*; examen *m*, estudio *m* (*into* de).
investigator [in'vestigeitə*] *n* investigador *m*, ora *f*.
investiture [in'vestitʃə*] *n* investidura *f*.
investment [in'vestmənt] *n* (*Comm*) inversión *f*; (*Mil*) sitio *m*, cerco *m*; (*investiture*) investidura *f*; **—s** inversiones *fpl*, fondos *mpl* invertidos, (*shares*) valores *mpl* en cartera.
investor [in'vestə*] *n* inversionista *mf*.
inveterate [in'vetərit] *adj* empedernido, habitual, incurable.
invidious [in'vidiəs] *adj* odioso, injusto.
invigilate [in'vidʒileit] *vti* vigilar (durante los exámenes).
invigilator [in'vidʒileitə*] *n* celador *m*, ora *f*.
invigorate [in'vigəreit] *vt* vigorizar; *campaign etc* avivar, estimular.
invigorating [in'vigəreitiŋ] *adj* vigorizante, vigorizador.
invincibility [in.vinsi'biliti] *n* invencibilidad *f*.
invincible [in'vinsəbl] *adj* invencible.
inviolability [in.vaiələ'biliti] *n* inviolabilidad *f*.
inviolable [in'vaiələbl] *adj* inviolable.
inviolate [in'vaiəlit] *adj* inviolado.
invisibility [in.vizə'biliti] *n* invisibilidad *f*.
invisible [in'vizəbl] *adj* invisible; *ink* simpático.
invitation [.invi'teiʃən] *n* invitación *f*; convite *m*.
invite [in'vait] *vt* (a) (*general sense*) invitar, (*esp to food and drink*) convidar; **to — someone to supper** invitar a uno a cenar; **to — someone to do something** invitar a uno a hacer algo; **to — someone to have a drink** convidar a uno a tomar algo.
  (b) (*request*) pedir, rogar; **the chairman —d me to speak** el presidente me rogó tomar la palabra; **he —s our opinions** pide nuestras opiniones.

(c) *trouble etc* correr a, buscarse; **it's just inviting trouble** esto es crear dificultades para sí; **to do so is to — defeat** hacer esto es procurar la propia derrota.

(d) *(induce)* inducir a, sugerir; **A —s comparison with B** A nos induce a compararlo con B, se impone la comparación de A con B; **she seems to — stares** según parece le gusta que la mire la gente.

invite ['invait] n *(fam)* invitación f.

inviting [in'vaitiŋ] adj atractivo, atrayente, tentador; *look* incitante, provocativo; *food* apetitoso.

invitingly [in'vaitiŋli] adv de modo atractivo *(etc)*; de modo incitante; apetitosamente.

invocation [,invǝu'keiʃǝn] n invocación f.

invoice ['invɔis] **1** n factura f; **pro forma — factura** f simulada; **as per — según factura; to send an — pasar factura**, presentar factura. **2** vt facturar.

invoke [in'vǝuk] vt invocar; *aid* suplicar, implorar; *law* recurrir a, acogerse a; *spirit* conjurar.

involuntarily [in'vɔlǝntǝrili] adv involuntariamente, sin querer.

involuntary [in'vɔlǝntǝri] adj involuntario.

involve [in'vɔlv] vt **(a)** *(physically)* enredar, enmarañar; *matter* complicar, entenebrecer.

(b) *(implicate etc)* implicar, comprometer; **to — someone in a quarrel** mezclar a uno en una disputa; **the persons —d** los interesados; **the forces —d** las fuerzas en juego; **a question of principle is —d** aquí está en juego un principio; **to be —d in** estar implicado en, estar metido en, andar envuelto en; **to be —d in a plot** estar implicado en un complot; **was he —d in it?** ¿anduvo él metido en ello?, ¿tuvo él que ver con el asunto?; **how did you come to be —d?** ¿cómo llegó Vd a estar envuelto en esto?; **to get** *(or* **become) —d in** meterse en, enredarse en, embrollarse en; **he got —d with a girl** se armó un lío con una joven; **I don't want to get —d** no quiero dejarme ir demasiado lejos, allí no entro yo.

(c) *(imply)* suponer, implicar, traer consigo, acarrear, ocasionar; **it —s moving house** ello supone que tendremos que mudar de casa; **it —d a lot of expense** nos acarreó muchos gastos; **does it — much trouble?** ¿esto supone mucho trabajo para Vd?

involved [in'vɔlvd] adj complicado; *style* enrevesado, laberíntico.

involvement [in'vɔlvmǝnt] n enredo m; compromiso m; *(difficulty)* apuro m, dificultad f; **we don't know the extent of his —** no sabemos hasta qué punto se había comprometido; **his — in the plot** su participación en el complot; **we must keep out of —s** hay que evitar los enredos.

invulnerability [in,vʌlnǝrǝ'biliti] n invulnerabilidad f.

invulnerable [in'vʌlnǝrǝbl] adj invulnerable.

inward ['inwǝd] adj interior, interno; íntimo; espiritual.

inward(s) ['inwǝd(z)] adv hacia dentro, para dentro.

inwardly ['inwǝdli] adv interiormente; *laugh etc* para sí, entre sí.

inwards ['inǝdz] npl *(fam)* tripas ʃpl, estómago m.

iodine ['aiǝdi:n] n yodo m.

iodoform [ai'ɔdǝfɔ:m] n yodoformo m.

ion ['aiǝn] n ion m.

Ionic [ai'ɔnik] adj jónico.

ionize [ai'ǝnaiz] vt ionizar.

ionosphere [ai'ɔnǝsfiǝ*] n ionosfera f.

iota [ai'ǝutǝ] n *(letter)* iota f; *(fig)* jota f, ápice m; **there's not one — of truth in it** eso no tiene ni pizca de verdad; **if he had an — of sense** si tuviera un poquito de inteligencia.

ipecacuanha [,ipikækju'ænǝ] n ipecacuana f.

Irak [i'rɑ:k] El Irak.

Iraki [i'rɑ:ki] **1** adj iraquí. **2** n iraquí mf.

Iran [i'rɑ:n] El Irán.

Iranian [i'reiniǝn] **1** adj iranio, iraní. **2** n iranio m, a f, iraní mf.

Iraq [i'rɑ:k] El Irak.

Iraqi [i'rɑ:ki] **1** adj iraquí. **2** n iraquí mf.

irascibility [i,ræsi'biliti] n irascibilidad f.

irascible [i'ræsibl] adj irascible, de prontos enojos.

irascibly [i'ræsibli] adv: **he said —** dijo colérico.

irate [ai'reit] adj colérico, enojado, indignado; **he got very —** se encolerizó mucho.

ire [aiǝ*] n ira f, cólera f; **to rouse someone's —** provocar la ira de uno; **that always rouses his —** eso siempre le saca de quicio.

Ireland ['aiǝlǝnd] Irlanda f; **Northern — Irlanda** f del Norte.

iridescence [,iri'desns] n iridescencia f, irisación f.

iridescent [,iri'desnt] adj iridescente, irisado, tornasolado.

iris ['aiǝris] n *(Anat)* iris m; *(Bot)* lirio m.

Irish ['aiǝriʃ] **1** adj irlandés. **2** n: **the —** los irlandeses. **3** n *(language)* irlandés m.

Irish Free State ['aiǝriʃ'fri:steit] Estado m Libre de Irlanda.

Irishman ['aiǝriʃmǝn] n, pl **—men** [mǝn] irlandés m.

Irish Sea ['aiǝriʃ'si:] Mar m de Irlanda.

Irishwoman ['aiǝriʃ,wumǝn] n, pl **—women** [,wimin] irlandesa f.

irk [ǝ:k] vt fastidiar, molestar.

irksome ['ǝ:ksǝm] adj molesto, pesado, fastidioso.

iron ['aiǝn] **1** n **(a)** *(Min)* hierro m; *(fig)* hierro m, acero m; *(Golf)* hierro m; *(flat-)* plancha f; **man of — hombre** m de acero; **corrugated — hierro** m ondulado; **old — chatarra** f, hierro m viejo; **wrought — hierro** m forjado, hierro m batido; **to strike while the — is hot** a hierro candente batir de repente.

(b) —s *(fetters)* hierros mpl, grillos mpl; *(at table: fam)* cuchillo m y tenedor m; **to have too many —s in the fire** tener demasiados asuntos entre manos; **to put someone in —s** aherrojar a uno, echar grillos a uno.

2 attr de hierro; *curtain, man etc* de acero; *will* férreo.

3 vt *clothes* planchar; **to — out** *unevenness* allanar; *crease* quitar; *difficulties* allanar, suprimir; *differences* nivelar.

ironclad ['aiǝnklæd] **1** adj acorazado. **2** n acorazado m.

iron foundry ['aiǝn,faundri] n fundición f de hierro.

ironic(al) [ai'rɔnik(ǝl)] adj irónico.

ironically [ai'rɔnikǝli] adv irónicamente; **say etc con ironía; — enough** paradójicamente, como quiso la suerte.

ironing ['aiǝniŋ] n *(act)* planchado m; *(clothes)* ropa f por planchar, ropa f planchada; **to give a dress an —** planchar un vestido.

ironing board ['aiǝniŋbɔ:d] n tabla f de planchar.

ironmonger ['aiǝn,mʌŋgǝ*] n ferretero m, quincallero m; **—'s (shop)** ferretería f, quincallería f.

ironmongery ['aiǝn,mʌŋgǝri] n quincalla f, ferretería f *(also fig)*.

iron ore ['aiǝnɔ:*] n mineral m de hierro.

ironwork ['aiǝnwǝ:k] n herraje m; obra f de hierro.

ironworks ['aiǝnwǝ:ks] n *sing and* pl herrería f, fundición f, fábrica f de hierro.

irony ['aiǝrǝni] n ironía f; **the — of fate** lo irónico del destino; **the — of it is that** lo irónico es que.

irradiate [i'reidieit] vt irradiar.

irradiation [i,reidi'eiʃǝn] n irradiación f.

irrational [i'ræʃǝnl] adj irracional.

irrationally [i'ræʃnǝli] adv irracionalmente.

irreconcilable [i,rekǝn'sailǝbl] adj irreconciliable, inconciliable.

irrecoverable [,iri'kʌvǝrǝbl] adj irrecuperable, incobrable.

irredeemable [,iri'di:mǝbl] adj irredimible; *(Comm)* perpetuo, no amortizable.

irreducible [,iri'dju:sǝbl] adj irreducible.

irrefutable [i'refju:tǝbl] adj irrefutable, irrebatible.

irregular [i'regjulǝ*] **1** adj irregular; anormal; *surface* desigual; *(unlawful)* ilegal, no conforme con la ley; **this is really most —** realmente esto no se debiera permitir.

2 n guerrillero m.

irregularity [i,regju'læriti] n irregularidad f; anormalidad f; desigualdad f.

irrelevance [i'relǝvǝns] n impertinencia f, inoportunidad f, inaplicabilidad f.

irrelevant [i'relǝvǝnt] adj impertinente, inoportuno, inaplicable, fuera de propósito; **that's — eso no** hace al caso.

irreligious [,iri'lidʒǝs] adj irreligioso.

irremediable [,iri'mi:diǝbl] adj irremediable.

irremediably [,iri'mi:diǝbli] adv irremediablemente.

irremovable [,iri'mu:vǝbl] adj inamovible.

irreparable [i'repǝrǝbl] adj irreparable.

irreparably [i'repǝrǝbli] adv irreparablemente.

irreplaceable [,iri'pleisǝbl] adj insustituible, irreemplazable.

irrepressible [,iri'presǝbl] adj incontrolable, irrefrenable.

irreproachable [,iri'prǝutʃǝbl] adj irreprochable, intachable.

irresistible [,iri'zistǝbl] adj irresistible.

irresistibly [,iri'zistǝbli] adv irresistiblemente.

irresolute [i'rezǝlu:t] adj irresoluto, indeciso.

irresoluteness [i'rezǝlu:tnis] n irresolución f, indecisión f.

irrespective [,iri'spektiv]: **— of** prep aparte de, sin consideración a, con independencia de.

irresponsibility [i,ris,pɔnsǝ'biliti] n irresponsabilidad f, falta f de seriedad.

irresponsible [ˌiris'pɔnsəbl] *adj* irresponsable, poco serio.
irretrievable [ˌiri'triːvəbl] *adj* irrecuperable; *error* irreparable.
irretrievably [ˌiri'triːvəbli] *adv*: — **lost** totalmente perdido, perdido sin remedio.
irreverence [i'revərəns] *n* irreverencia *f*.
irreverent [i'revərənt] *adj* irreverente, irrespetuoso.
irreverently [i'revərəntli] *adv* de modo irreverente, irrespetuosamente.
irreversible [ˌiri'vəːsəbl] *adj* decision irrevocable.
irrevocable [i'revəkəbl] *adj* irrevocable.
irrevocably [i'revəkəbli] *adv* irrevocablemente.
irrigable ['irigəbl] *adj* regadío; — **land** tierra *f* de regadío.
irrigate ['irigeit] *vt* (Agr) regar; (Med) irrigar.
irrigation [ˌiri'geiʃən] *n* (Agr) riego *m*; (Med) irrigación *f*.
irritability [ˌiritə'biliti] *n* irritabilidad *f*.
irritable ['iritəbl] *adj* (temperament) irritable, de prontos enojos; (mood) de mal humor; **to get —** ponerse nervioso.
irritably ['iritəbli] *adv*: **he said —** dijo malhumorado.
irritant ['iritənt] *n* irritante *m*.
irritate ['iriteit] *vt* irritar (also Med), sacar de quicio, molestar; **to get —d** irritarse, enfadarse.
irritating ['iriteitiŋ] *adj* person etc molesto, pesado, enojoso; thing molesto, fastidioso; **it's really most —** es para sacar a uno de quicio.
irritation [ˌiri'teiʃən] *n* irritación *f*, enojo *m*; (Med) picazón *f*, picor *m*.
irruption [i'rʌpʃən] *n* irrupción *f*.
is [iz] see **be**.
Isaac ['aizək] *m* Isaac.
Isabel ['izəbel] *f* Isabel.
isinglass ['aiziŋglɑːs] *n* cola *f* de pescado.
Islam ['izlɑːm] Islam *m*.
Islamic [iz'læmik] *adj* islámico.
island ['ailənd] **1** *n* isla *f*; (in street) refugio *m*. **2** attr isleño.
islander ['ailəndə*] *n* isleño *m*, a *f*.
isle [ail] *n* isla *f*.
islet ['ailit] *n* isleta *f*, islote *m*.
ism ['izəm] *n* ismo *m*.
isn't ['iznt] = **is not**.
iso . . . ['aisəu] iso . . .
isobar ['aisəubɑː*] *n* isobara *f*.
isolate ['aisəuleit] *vt* aislar.
isolated ['aisəuleitid] *adj* place etc aislado, apartado; case único; **to feel —** sentirse aislado.
isolation [ˌaisəu'leiʃən] *n* aislamiento *m*.
isolationism [ˌaisəu'leiʃənizəm] *n* aislacionismo *m*.
isolationist [ˌaisəu'leiʃənist] **1** *adj* aislacionista. **2** *n* aislacionista *mf*.
Isolde [i'zɔldə] *f* Iseo, Isolda.
isosceles [ai'sɔsiliːz] *adj*: — **triangle** triángulo *m* isósceles.
isotherm ['aisəuθəːm] *n* isoterma *f*.
isotope ['aisəutəup] *n* isótopo *m*.
Israel ['izreil] Israel *m*.
Israeli [iz'reili] **1** *adj* israelí. **2** *n* israelí *mf*.
Israelite ['izriəlait] *n* israelita *mf*.
issue ['iʃuː] **1** *n* (a) (outcome) resultado *m*, consecuencia *f*; **in the —** en fin; **until the — is decided** hasta que se sepa el resultado; **to await the —** esperar el resultado.
(b) (matter) cuestión *f*, asunto *m*, problema *m*, punto *m*; **an — of fact** una cuestión de hechos; **side —** cuestión *f* secundaria; **the point at — el** punto en cuestión, el asunto en litigio; **the — is whether . . .** se trata de decidir si . . .; **it's not a political —** no es una cuestión política; **to evade the —** evadir el tema, esquivar la pregunta; **to face the —** afrontar la situación; **to force the —** forzar una decisión; **to join** (or **take**) — **with someone** llevar la contraria a uno, oponerse a uno; **I feel I must take — with you over that** permítaseme disentir de esa opinión.
(c) (of shares, stamps etc) emisión *f*; (of rations) distribución *f*, repartimiento *m*.
(d) (of book: size of —) edición *f*, tirada *f*; (copy) número *m*; **back —** número *m* atrasado.
(e) (offspring) sucesión *f*, descendencia *f*; **to die without —** morir sin dejar descendencia.
(f) (Med) flujo *m*.
2 attr (Mil etc) reglamentario.
3 *vt* shares, stamps etc emitir; poner en circulación; rations etc distribuir, repartir; book publicar; order dar; decree promulgar; certificate etc expedir; cheque extender; licence facilitar; **a warrant has been —d**

for the arrest of X se ha ordenado la detención de X; **to — a rifle to each man, to — each man with a rifle** dar un fusil a cada hombre; **we were —d with 10 rounds each** nos dieron a cada uno 10 cartuchos.
4 *vi* salir (from de); **to — from** (fig) provenir de; **to — in** dar por resultado.
Istanbul [ˌistæn'buːl] Estambul.
isthmus ['isməs] *n* istmo *m*.
it¹ [it] *pron* (a) (nom) él, ella, ello; (acc) lo, la; (dat) le; (after prep) él, ella, ello.
(b) (nom pron referring to a specific noun, freq not translated) **—'s on the table** está en la mesa; **where is —?** ¿dónde está?
(c) (pron referring to "this affair", "that whole business") ello, eso, eg **— is difficult** es difícil, ello es difícil; **I have no money for —** no tengo dinero para ello; **he won't agree to —** no quiere consentir en eso.
(d) (never translated in such cases as) **— is true that** es verdad que; **— was raining** llovía; **— is 4 o'clock** son las 4; **— is not in him to do it** no es capaz de hacer eso; **— is said that** se dice que; **I have heard — said that** he oído decir que; **I do not think — (is) wise to go** creo que es más prudente no ir; **— is I, —'s me** soy yo; **—'s Jack** soy Juanito; **— was he who brought them** fue él quien los trajo.
(e) (special uses with to be) **this is —** ya llegó la hora; **ahí viene**; (before action) ¡vamos!, ¡a ello!; **that's —** (agreeing) eso es; (adjusting machine etc) ya está, está bien; (on finishing something) eso es todo, hemos terminado, está hecho, nada más; **that's — then!** ¡muy bien!; **that's just —!** ¡ahí está la dificultad!; **the worst of — is** lo peor del caso es que; **how is — that . . .?** ¿cómo resulta que . . .? (and see how (a)).
(f) (predicative) **you're —!** (children's games) ¡tú te quedas!; **she thinks she's just —** se da mucho tono, se cree la mar de elegante.
(g) (sexual attraction) aquél *m*, atracción *f* sexual; **she's got —** tiene aquél, tiene tilín; see **with**.
it² [it] *n* (fam) vermut *m* italiano.
Italian [i'tæliən] **1** *adj* italiano. **2** *n* italiano *m*, a *f*. **3** *n* (language) italiano *m*.
italic [i'tælik] *adj* (Typ) en bastardilla; (of Italy) itálico.
italicize [i'tælisaiz] *vt* poner en bastardilla, subrayar.
italics [i'tæliks] *npl* (letra) bastardilla *f*, cursiva *f*; **in —** en bastardilla, en cursiva; **my —** lo subrayado es mío.
Italy ['itəli] Italia *f*.
itch [itʃ] **1** *n* (a) (Med) (an —) picazón *f*, comezón *f*; (the —) sarna *f*.
(b) (fig) prurito *m*, deseo *m* vehemente; **to have the — to do something** tener el prurito de hacer algo, rabiar por hacer algo.
2 *vi* picar, sentir comezón; **my leg —es** me pica la pierna, siento comezón en la pierna; **to — to do something** tener el prurito de hacer algo, rabiar por hacer algo.
itching ['itʃiŋ] *n* picazón *f*, comezón *f*.
itching powder ['itʃiŋˌpaudə*] *n* polvos *mpl* de pica-pica.
itchy ['itʃi] *adj*: **to feel —** sentir comezón; **to have an — leg** sentir comezón en la pierna.
it'd ['itd] = **it would**; **it had**.
item ['aitəm] *n* artículo *m*; (detail) detalle *m*; (Comm) partida *f*; (in programme) número *m*; (on agenda) asunto *m* a tratar; (in newspaper) noticia *f*, suelto *m*; **what's the next —?** ¿qué viene después?; **it's an important — in our policy** es un punto importante de nuestra política.
itemize ['aitəmaiz] *vt* detallar, particularizar, especificar.
itinerant [i'tinərənt] *adj* ambulante.
itinerary [ai'tinərəri] *n* ruta *f*, itinerario *m*; (book, map) guía *f*.
it'll ['itl] = **it will**; **it shall**.
its [its] **1** poss adj su(s). **2** poss pron (el) suyo, (la) suya etc.
it's [its] = **it is**, **it has**.
itself [it'self] pron (nom) él mismo, ella misma, ello mismo; (acc, dat) se; (after prep) sí mismo, sí misma; see **oneself**.
I've [aiv] = **I have**.
ivory ['aivəri] **1** *n* marfil *m*; **ivories** (sl: teeth) dientes *mpl*, (Mus) teclas *fpl*, (Billiards) bolas *fpl*. **2** attr de marfil.
Ivory Coast ['aivəri'kəust] Costa *f* de Marfil.
ivy ['aivi] *n* hiedra *f*.

J

jab [dʒæb] **1** n (*poke*) pinchazo m; (*with elbow*) codazo m; (*blow*) golpe m; (*Boxing*) golpe m rápido (dado sin extender el brazo); (*prick*) pinchazo m.

2 vt hurgonear; dar un codazo a; golpear, dar un golpe rápido a; pinchar; **he —bed a gun in my back** me puso un revólver en los riñones; **I —bed the knife in my arm** me pinché el brazo con el cuchillo; **he —bed the knife into the table** clavó el cuchillo en la mesa; **he —bed a finger at the map** indicó el mapa con un movimiento brusco del dedo.

3 vi: **to — at someone with a knife** tratar de acuchillar a uno; **he —bed at the map with a finger** indicó el mapa con un movimiento brusco del dedo.

jabber ['dʒæbə*] **1** n (*also* **jabbering** ['dʒæbəriŋ]) torrente m de palabras ininteligibles; chapurreo m, farfulla f; (*of monkeys*) chillidos mpl; **a — of French** un torrente de francés; **a — of voices** un ruido confuso de voces.

2 vt decir atropelladamente.

3 vi hablar atropelladamente, hablar de modo ininteligible; chapurrear, farfullar; (*monkeys*) chillar; **they were —ing away in Russian** hablaban atropelladamente en ruso.

jacaranda [,dʒækə'rændə] n jacaranda f.

jack [dʒæk] **1** n (*Mech*) gato m; (*boot-*) sacabotas m; (*Bowls*) boliche m; (*Cards*) valet m, (*in Spanish pack*) sota f; (*Naut*) marinero m; (*Fish*) lucio m joven.

2 vt: **to — up** (*Mech*) alzar con gato; *price, production etc* aumentar.

Jack [dʒæk] m Juan, Juanito; **I'm all right, —!** ¡a mí nada!; **— Frost** personificación del hielo; **— Ketch** el verdugo; **before you can say — Robinson** en un decir Jesús; **— Tar** el marinero.

jackal ['dʒækɔ:l] n chacal m; (*fig*) paniaguado m, secuaz m.

jackanapes ['dʒækəneips] n mequetrefe m.

jackass ['dʒækæs] n burro m (*also fig*).

jackboots ['dʒækbu:ts] npl botas fpl fuertes; **under the — of the Nazis** bajo el azote de los nazis.

jackdaw ['dʒækdɔ:] n grajilla f.

jacket ['dʒækit] n chaqueta f, americana f; (*of boiler etc*) camisa f, envoltura f; (*of book*) sobrecubierta f, camisa f.

jack-in-the-box ['dʒækinðəbɔks] n caja f sorpresa, caja f de resorte.

jack-knife ['dʒæknaif] n, pl **—knives** [naivz] navaja f.

jack-of-all-trades ['dʒækəv'ɔ:ltreidz] n hombre m de muchos oficios (*and master of none* y maestro de ninguno).

jack-of-all-work ['dʒækəv'ɔ:lwə:k] n factótum m.

jack-o'-lantern ['dʒækəu'læntən] n fuego m fatuo.

jack plane ['dʒækplein] n garlopa f.

jackpot ['dʒækpɔt] n bote m; (*fig*) premio m gordo; **he hit the —** sacó el premio gordo, (*fig*) acertó, dio en el blanco.

jack rabbit ['dʒæk,ræbit] n liebre f grande (*especie norteamericana*).

jackstraw ['dʒækstrɔ:] n (*US*) pajita f.

Jacob ['dʒeikəb] m Jacob.

Jacobean [,dʒækə'bi:ən] adj de la época de Jacobo I (de Inglaterra).

Jacobin ['dʒækəbin] **1** adj jacobino. **2** n jacobino m, a f.

Jacobite ['dʒækəbait] **1** adj jacobita. **2** n jacobita mf.

jade[1] [dʒeid] n (*horse*) rocín m; (*woman*) mujerzuela f; **you —!** ¡picarona!, ¡lagarta!

jade[2] [dʒeid] n (*Min*) jade m.

jaded ['dʒeidid] adj cansado, hastiado; **to feel —** estar cansado; **to get —** cansarse, perder el entusiasmo.

jade-green ['dʒeid'gri:n] adj verde jade.

jag[1] [dʒæg] n punta f, púa f.

jag[2] [dʒæg] n (*fam*): **to go on a —** ir de juerga.

jagged ['dʒægid] adj dentado, mellado, desigual.

jaguar ['dʒægjuə*] n jaguar m.

jail [dʒeil] **1** n cárcel f; **2 years'** — 2 años de prisión, condena f de 2 años. **2** vt encarcelar.

jailbird ['dʒeilbə:d] n presidiario m.

jailbreak ['dʒeilbreik] n fuga f de la cárcel.

jailer ['dʒeilə*] n carcelero m.

jalop(p)y [dʒə'lɔpi] n cacharro m, armatoste m.

jalousie ['ʒælu(:)zi:] n celosía f.

jam[1] [dʒæm] **1** n (*food*) mermelada f; (*fig*) lo mejor, la parte más rica; **you want — on it!** ¡y un jamón con chorreras!; **look at that for —!** ¡qué chorra tiene el tío!

2 vt hacer mermelada de.

jam[2] [dʒæm] **1** n (**a**) (*blockage*) atasco m, obstrucción f; (*of people*) agolpamiento m; (*Aut*) embotellamiento m, aglomeración f, ensalada f; **there's a — in the pipe** se ha atascado el tubo, está atascado el tubo; **there was a — in the doorway** se había agolpado la gente en la puerta; **you never saw such a —!** ¡había que ver cómo se agolpaba la gente!; **a 5-mile — of cars** una cola de coches que se extiende hasta 5 millas; **there are always —s here** aquí siempre se embotella el tráfico.

(**b**) (*difficulty*) apuro m, aprieto m; **to be in a —** estar en un aprieto; **to get into a —** meterse en un apuro; **to get into a — with a problem** armarse un lío con un problema; **to get someone out of a —** ayudar a uno a salir del paso.

2 vt *pipe etc* atascar, obstruir; *wheel* trabar; *exit, road* cerrar, obstruir; *radio station* interferir; **it's got —med** se ha atascado, no se puede mover (*or* quitar, retirar *etc*); **people —med all the exits** la gente se agolpaba en todas las salidas; **if we can — 2 more books in** si podemos introducir a la fuerza 2 libros más; **there were 15 people —med in one room** había 15 personas apretadas unas contra otras en un cuarto; **the room was —med with people** el cuarto estaba atestado de gente; **to — one's fingers in the door** cogerse los dedos en la puerta; **to — something into a box** meter algo apretadamente en una caja; **to — a hat on one's head** encasquetarse un sombrero; **with his hat —med on his head** con la cabeza encasquetada en un sombrero; **to — one's brakes on** echar los frenos con violencia, frenar de repente.

3 vi (*pipe etc*) atascarse, obstruirse; (*nut, part, wheel etc*) trabarse; **this part has —med** no se puede mover esta pieza.

Jamaica [dʒə'meikə] Jamaica f.

Jamaican [dʒə'meikən] **1** adj jamaicano. **2** n jamaicano m, a f.

jamb [dʒæm] n jamba f.

jamboree [,dʒæmbə'ri:] n (*of Scouts*) congreso m de niños exploradores; (*fam*) francachela f, juerga f.

James [dʒeimz] m Jaime, Diego; (*Saint*) Santiago; (*British kings*) Jacobo.

jam-full ['dʒæm'ful] adv de bote en bote.

jamjar ['dʒæmdʒɑ:*] n pote m para mermelada.

jamming ['dʒæmiŋ] n (*Radio*) interferencia f.

jam session ['dʒæmseʃən] n (*sl*) concierto m improvisado de jazz.

Jane [dʒein] f Juana.

jangle ['dʒæŋgl] **1** n sonido m discordante (metálico), cencerrco m.

2 vt chocar, hacer sonar de manera discordante.

3 vi sonar de manera discordante, cencerrear.

jangling ['dʒæŋgliŋ] adj discordante, desapacible, ruidoso.

janitor ['dʒænitə*] n portero m, conserje m.

January ['dʒænjuəri] enero m.

Jap [dʒæp] (*fam*) = **Japanese**.

japan [dʒə'pæn] **1** n laca f japonesa. **2** vt charolar con laca japonesa.

Japan [dʒə'pæn] el Japón.

Japanese [‚dӡæpəˈniːz] **1** adj japonés. **2** n japonés m, esa f; **the —** (pl) los japoneses. **3** n (language) japonés m.
jape [dӡeip] n burla f, broma f.
japonica [dӡəˈpɔnikə] n rosal m de China, rosal m japonés.
jar¹ [dӡɑː*] n (small) tarro m, pote m; (with handles) jarra f; (large) tinaja f.
jar² [dӡɑː*] **1** n (jolt) sacudida f, choque m; vibración f; (fig) sacudida f, sorpresa f desagradable; **it gave me a bit of a —** me chocó bastante.
    2 vt (jog) tocar; mover; (shake) sacudir, hacer vibrar; **he must have —red the camera** ha debido mover ligeramente la máquina; **someone —red my elbow** alguien me hizo mover el codo.
    3 vi (grate) chirriar; (shake) vibrar; (sounds) ser discorde, sonar mal; (colours) chillar; **to — on someone** poner a uno los nervios de punta, crispar los nervios a uno.
jar³ [dӡɑː*]: **on the —** adv see **ajar**.
jargon [ˈdӡɑːgən] n (incomprehensible) jerigonza f; (specialist) jerga f.
jarring [ˈdӡɑːriŋ] adj sound discorde, desapacible; colour chillón; (fig) opuesto, adverso, discorde.
jasmin(e) [ˈdӡæzmin] n jazmín m.
jasper [ˈdӡæspə*] n jaspe m.
jaundice [ˈdӡɔːndis] n ictericia f.
jaundiced [ˈdӡɔːndist] adj (fig: envious, sour) envidioso, avinagrado, agrio; (disillusioned) desilusionado, decepcionado.
jaunt [dӡɔːnt] n excursión f (also fig); viajecito m.
jauntily [ˈdӡɔːntili] adv con garbo, airosamente; con confianza; **he replied —** contestó satisfecho.
jauntiness [ˈdӡɔːntinis] n garbo m; confianza f, satisfacción f.
jaunting car [ˈdӡɔːntiŋ‚kɑː*] n tílburi m (irlandés).
jaunty [ˈdӡɔːnti] adj garboso, airoso; alegre; desenvuelto; confiado, satisfecho.
Java [ˈdӡɑːvə] Java f.
Javanese [‚dӡɑːvəˈniːz] **1** adj javanés. **2** n javanés m, esa f.
javelin [ˈdӡævlin] n jabalina f; **to throw the —** lanzar la jabalina.
jaw [dӡɔː] **1** n (a) (Anat) quijada f, mandíbula f; (Mech) mordaza f, mandíbula f; **a blow on the —** un golpe en la mandíbula.
    (b) —s (Anat) boca f; (fig: swallowing) boca f, fauces fpl; (holding) garras fpl; **they rode into the very —s of death** entraron por entre las mismas garras de la muerte.
    (c) (fam) cháchara f; palabrería f; **we had a good old —** charlamos largo rato; **it's just a lot of —** mucho ruido y pocas nueces; **hold your —!** ¡cállate la boca!
    2 vt (sl) sermonear.
    3 vi (fam) charlar; hablar por los codos, hablar interminablemente.
jawbone [ˈdӡɔːbəun] n mandíbula f, maxilar m.
jawbreaker [ˈdӡɔː‚breikə*] n (fam) trabalenguas m, palabra f kilométrica, terminacho m.
jay [dӡei] n arrendajo m.
jaywalker [ˈdӡei‚wɔːkə*] n peatón m imprudente.
jazz [dӡæz] **1** n jazz m; **all that —** (sl) esas tonterías. **2** attr de jazz. **3** vt (also **to — up**) sincopar; (fig) animar, avivar.
jazzy [ˈdӡæzi] adj (Mus) sincopado; dress etc de colores llamativos, de colores chillones.
jealous [ˈdӡeləs] adj celoso; envidioso; **— husband** marido m celoso; **with — care** con el mayor celo; **to be —** tener celos (of someone de uno); **to make someone —** dar celos a uno.
jealously [ˈdӡeləsli] adv celosamente; envidiosamente.
jealousy [ˈdӡeləsi] n celos mpl; envidia f.
jeans [dӡiːnz] npl pantalones mpl vaqueros, pantalones mpl tejanos.
jeep [dӡiːp] n jeep m.
jeer [dӡiə*] **1** n (shout) grito m de sarcasmo, grito m de protesta; (insult) insulto m, dicterio m; (boo) abucheo m.
    2 vt mofarse de; llenar de insultos; abuchear.
    3 vi mofarse (at de), befar; gritar con sarcasmo (etc; at a), prorrumpir en gritos sarcásticos (etc).
jeering [ˈdӡiəriŋ] **1** adj mofador, sarcástico; **he was led through a — crowd** le hicieron pasar por una multitud que le llenó de insultos.
    2 n gritos mpl de sarcasmo, protestas fpl; insultos mpl; abucheo m.
Jehovah [dӡiˈhəuvə] m Jehová.
jejune [dӡiˈdӡuːn] adj árido; insípido, sin sustancia.
jell [dӡel] vi convertirse en jalea, cuajar; (fig) cuajar.

jelly [ˈdӡeli] n jalea f, gelatina f; **petroleum —** vaselina f, jalea f de petróleo.
jellyfish [ˈdӡelifiʃ] n medusa f.
jemmy [ˈdӡemi] n palanqueta f.
jeopardize [ˈdӡepədaiz] vt arriesgar, poner en peligro, comprometer.
jeopardy [ˈdӡepədi] n: **to be in —** estar en peligro, correr riesgo; **to put something in —** poner algo en peligro, hacer peligrar algo.
Jeremiad [‚dӡeriˈmaiəd] n jeremiada f.
Jeremy [ˈdӡerəmi] m Jeremías.
Jericho [ˈdӡerikəu] Jericó.
jerk [dӡɜːk] **1** n tirón m, sacudida f; espasmo m muscular; **physical —s** ejercicios mpl físicos, gimnasia f; **by —s** a sacudidas; **he sat up with a —** se incorporó de repente, se incorporó con un movimiento brusco; **to put a — in it** (fam) menearse.
    2 vt (shake etc) sacudir, dar una sacudida a; (pull) tirar bruscamente de; (throw) arrojar con un movimiento rápido; meat (US) atasajar; **to — something along** mover algo a tirones; **to — something away from someone** quitar algo a uno de un tirón.
    3 vi sacudirse, dar una sacudida; **to — along** moverse a sacudidas, avanzar a tirones.
    4 vr: **to — oneself free** librarse con un movimiento brusco; **to — oneself along** moverse a sacudidas, avanzar a tirones.
jerkily [ˈdӡɜːkili] adv move etc a tirones, a sacudidas; play, write etc de modo desigual, nerviosamente.
jerkin [ˈdӡɜːkin] n justillo m.
jerkwater [ˈdӡɜːk‚wɔːtə*] adj (US fam) de poca monta.
jerky [ˈdӡɜːki] adj (in movement) que se mueve a sacudidas, que avanza a tirones; movement espasmódico, nervioso; (uneven) desigual, nervioso.
Jerome [dӡəˈrəum] m Jerónimo.
jerry [ˈdӡeri] n (sl) orinal m.
Jerry [ˈdӡeri] n (Mil sl): **a —** un alemán; **los —** los alemanes.
jerry-builder [ˈdӡeri‚bildə*] n mal constructor m, tapa(a)gujeros m.
jerry-building [ˈdӡeri‚bildiŋ] n mala construcción f, construcción f defectuosa.
jerry-built [ˈdӡeribilt] adj mal construido, de pacotilla.
jersey [ˈdӡɜːzi] n jersey m, jersé m, jersei m (Acad).
Jerusalem [dӡəˈruːsələm] Jerusalén.
jessamine [ˈdӡesəmin] n jazmín m.
jest [dӡest] **1** n chanza f, broma f; (verbal) chiste m; **in —** en broma, de guasa. **2** vi bromear, chancearse; **he was only —ing** lo dijo en broma nada más.
jester [ˈdӡestə*] n bufón m.
jesting [ˈdӡestiŋ] **1** adj person chistoso, guasón; tone guasón; reference burlón, en broma. **2** n chanzas fpl, bromas fpl; chistes mpl.
Jesuit [ˈdӡezjuit] **1** adj jesuita. **2** n jesuita m.
Jesuitical [‚dӡezjuˈitikəl] adj jesuítico.
Jesus [ˈdӡiːzəs] m Jesús; **— Christ** Jesucristo.
jet¹ [dӡet] n (Min) azabache m.
jet² [dӡet] **1** n (a) (of liquid) chorro m, surtidor m; (gas burner) mechero m; **a — of flame** una llama.
    (b) (Aer) avión m a reacción, avión m a chorro, reactor m; **the big —s of the future** los grandes reactores del futuro.
    2 attr (Aer) a reacción, a chorro.
    3 vt lanzar en chorro, echar en chorro.
    4 vi chorrear, salir a chorro.
jet-black [ˈdӡetˈblæk] adj de azabache, negro como el azabache.
jet engine [ˈdӡetˈendӡin] n motor m a reacción, reactor m.
jet plane [ˈdӡetˈplein] n avión m a reacción, avión m a chorro, reactor m.
jet-powered [ˈdӡetˈpauəd] adj, **jet-propelled** [ˈdӡetprəˈpeld] adj a reacción, a chorro.
jet propulsion [ˈdӡetprəˈpʌlʃən] n propulsión f por reacción, propulsión f a chorro.
jetsam [ˈdӡetsəm] n echazón f.
jettison [ˈdӡetisn] vt (Naut etc) echar al mar, echar por la borda; (fig) desechar, abandonar, librarse de; **we can safely — that** bien podemos prescindir de eso.
jetty [ˈdӡeti] n malecón m, muelle m, embarcadero m.
Jew [dӡuː] n judío m, a f.
jewel [ˈdӡuːəl] n joya f (also fig), alhaja f; (of watch) rubí m.
jewel case [ˈdӡuːəlkeis] n joyero m, estuche m de joyas.
jewelled, (esp US) **jeweled** [ˈdӡuːəld] adj adornado con piedras preciosas, enjoyado; watch con rubíes.
jeweller, (esp US) **jeweler** [ˈdӡuːələ*] n joyero m; **—'s (shop)** joyería f.

jewellery, (esp US) jewelry ['dʒuːəlri] n joyas fpl, alhajas fpl.
Jewess ['dʒuːis] n judía f.
Jewish ['dʒuːiʃ] adj judío.
Jewishness ['dʒuːiʃnis] n judaísmo m.
Jewry ['dʒuəri] n judería f, los judíos.
Jew's-harp ['dʒuːz'haːp] n birimbao m.
jib¹ [dʒib] n (Naut) foque m; (Mech) aguilón m, brazo m.
jib² [dʒib] vi (horse) plantarse; (person) rehusar; I — at that no puedo consentir en eso; he —ed at it se negó a aprobarlo (etc), no quiso permitirlo, se opuso a ello.
jib boom ['dʒib'buːm] n botalón m de foque.
jibe [dʒaib] 1 n pulla f, dicterio m. 2 vi mofarse (at de).
jiffy ['dʒifi] n (fam) instante m, momento m; I'll be with you in a — un momento y estoy con vosotros; to do something in a — hacer algo en un decir Jesús.
jig [dʒig] 1 n (dance) jiga f; (Mech) plantilla f (de guía). 2 vi (dance) bailar (la jiga); to — along, to — up and down vibrarse, sacudirse, (person) moverse a saltitos; to keep —ging up and down no poderse estar quieto.
jigger ['dʒigə*] n (sl) chisme m.
jiggered ['dʒigəd] adj (sl): well I'm —! ¡caramba!; I'm — if I will que me cuelguen si lo hago.
jiggery-pokery ['dʒigəri'pəukəri] n (fam) trampas fpl, embustes mpl, maniobras fpl poco limpias; there's some — going on hay trampa; están maquinando algo.
jiggle ['dʒigl] 1 n zangoloteo m. 2 vt zangolotear. 3 vi zangolotearse.
jigsaw ['dʒigsɔː] n sierra f de vaivén; (puzzle) rompecabezas m.
jigsaw puzzle ['dʒigsɔː.pʌzl] n rompecabezas m.
jilt [dʒilt] vt dar calabazas a.
Jim [dʒim] m nombre cariñoso de James.
Jim Crow ['dʒim'krəu] 1 n el negro estadounidense. 2 attr segregado; relativo a la segregación racial; Jim-Crow law ley f racista, ley f segregacionista.
jimjams ['dʒimdʒæmz] npl (sl) delírium m tremens; it gives me the — me horripila, me da miedo.
Jimmy ['dʒimi] m nombre cariñoso de James.
jimmy ['dʒimi] n = jemmy.
jingle ['dʒiŋgl] 1 n tintineo m, retintín m, ruido m (de campanita, monedas etc); cascabeleo m; (Lit) verso m, poemita m popular, rima f infantil. 2 vt hacer sonar. 3 vi tintinear, retiñir, cascabelear.
jingo ['dʒiŋgəu] n patriotero m, a f, jingoísta mf; by —! ¡caramba!
jingoism ['dʒiŋgəuizəm] n patriotería f, jingoísmo m.
jingoistic [.dʒiŋgəu'istik] adj patriotero, jingoísta.
jinks [dʒiŋks] npl: high — jolgorio m; fiesta f animadísima; we had high — last night anoche lo pasamos bomba.
jinx [dʒiŋks] n (fam) cenizo m, gafe m; (gremlin) duendecillo m; there's a — on it esto está como encantado, esto está que da rabia.
jitney ['dʒitni] n (US sl) (a) taxi m. (b) moneda de 5 centavos.
jitterbug ['dʒitəbʌg] n persona f aficionada a bailar el jazz.
jitters ['dʒitəz] npl (sl) inquietud f, nerviosismo m; to get the — ponerse nervioso; to have the — estar nervioso.
jittery ['dʒitəri] adj (sl) muy inquieto, nervioso; to get — inquietarse, ponerse nervioso.
jiujitsu [dʒuː'dʒitsuː] n jiu-jitsu m.
jive [dʒaiv] vi (sl) bailar (el jazz), bailar con frenesí.
Joan [dʒəun] f Juana; — of Arc Juana de Arco.
job [dʒɔb] 1 n (a) (piece of work) trabajo m, tarea f; odd — tarea f suelta, chapuza f; odd- —man hombre m que hace de todo; to be on the — estar trabajando; he has done a good — with the book ha hecho un buen trabajo con el libro, en el libro ha realizado una labor muy meritoria; he never did a — in his life no ha trabajado nunca; to fall down on the — fracasar, demostrar no tener capacidad; he knows his — sabe su oficio; to make a good — of something hacer algo bien.
(b) (criminal, fam) golpe m, robo m; that warehouse — ese robo en el almacén; he did his first — at 12 dio el primer golpe a los 12 años.
(c) (piecework) destajo m; by the — a destajo.
(d) (duty) deber m, cometido m; my — is to sell them mi deber es venderlos, yo estoy encargado de venderlos; that's not his — eso no le toca a él, eso no le cumple a él; he does his — hace lo que debe; I had the — of telling him yo tuve la tarea ingrata de decírselo.
(e) (post, employment) empleo m, puesto m,

trabajo m; we shall create 1000 new —s vamos a crear 1000 puestos de trabajo más; to be in a — tener trabajo; to be out of a — estar sin trabajo, estar desocupado; to look for a — buscar un empleo; to lose one's — perder su empleo, ser despedido; automation has put them out of a — la automatización les ha quitado el trabajo, han sido despedidos debido a la automatización.
(f) (fam) it's a bad — es una situación difícil; es lamentable, es terrible; to make the best of a bad — poner a mal tiempo buena cara; that's a good —!, and a good — too! ¡menos mal!; it's a good — that menos mal que; we had quite a — getting here nos costó trabajo venir aquí, nos armamos un lío al venir aquí; he has a — to express himself le cuesta expresarse.
(g) (fam) it's just the —! ¡estupendo!; a holiday in Majorca would be just the — sería estupendo pasar unas vacaciones en Mallorca; this machine is just the — esta máquina es exactamente lo que nos hacía falta.
2 attr (a) — evaluation apreciación f del trabajo.
(b) — lot lote m suelto de mercancías, saldo m.
Job [dʒəub] n Job; —'s comforter el que, bajo pretexto de animar a otro, le desconsuela todavía más.
jobber ['dʒɔbə*] n (Stock Exchange) agiotista m; (agent) corredor m; (middleman) intermediario m.
jobbery ['dʒɔbəri] n intrigas fpl, chanchullos mpl; piece of — intriga f, chanchullo m; by a piece of — por enchufe.
jobbing ['dʒɔbiŋ] 1 adj que trabaja a destajo. 2 n agiotaje m; comercio m de intermediario.
jobless ['dʒɔblis] adj sin trabajo.
Jock [dʒɔk] m el escocés típico; the —s los escoceses.
jockey ['dʒɔki] 1 n jockey m, yoquey m (Acad). 2 vt: to — someone into doing something persuadir mañosamente a uno a hacer algo; to — someone out of doing something disuadir mañosamente a uno de hacer algo; to — someone out of a post lograr mañosamente que uno renuncie a un puesto. 3 vi : to — for a position maniobrar para conseguir una posición.
jockstrap ['dʒɔkstræp] n suspensorio m.
jocose [dʒə'kəus] adj, jocular ['dʒɔkjulə*] adj (merry) alegre, de buen humor; (humorous) guasón, zumbón, jocoso.
jodhpurs ['dʒɔdpəz] npl pantalones mpl de equitación.
Joe [dʒəu] m Pepe; (US sl) tío m; a good — un buen chico.
jog [dʒɔg] 1 n (a) (push etc) empujoncito m, sacudida f (ligera), codazo m; (encouragement) estímulo m; to give someone's memory a — refrescar la memoria de uno.
(b) (pace) trote m corto; to go at a steady — andar a trote corto.
2 vt (push etc) empujar (ligeramente), sacudir (levemente); (encourage) estimular; memory refrescar; he —ged my arm me dio ligeramente con el codo.
3 vi (also to — along) andar a trote corto, avanzar despacio; (fig) hacer algunos progresos, avanzar pero sin prisa; we keep —ging along vamos tirando.
joggle ['dʒɔgl] 1 n traqueo m. 2 vti traquear.
jog-trot ['dʒɔg'trɔt] n: at a — a trote corto.
John [dʒɔn] m Juan; — Bull personificación de Inglaterra; — Doe Fulano de Tal.
john [dʒɔn] n (US sl) water m.
Johnny ['dʒɔni] m Juanito.
johnny ['dʒɔni] n (fam) tío m, sujeto m.
joie de vivre ['ʒwɑːdə'viːvr] n goce m del vivir, alegría f vital.
join [dʒɔin] 1 n juntura f; (Sew) costura f.
2 vt (a) two things unir, juntar, poner juntos; (Tech) unir, acoplar, ensamblar; everybody —ed hands se cogieron todos de la mano; to his genius he —s humanity y su genialidad une la humanidad.
(b) society ingresar en, club hacerse socio de, party afiliarse a, hacerse miembro de; (Mil) alistarse en; to — one's regiment incorporarse a su regimiento; to — one's ship volver a su buque; where the track —s the road donde el camino empalma con la carretera.
(c) person reunirse con, unirse a, juntarse con; may I —you? ¿se permite?; will you — me in a drink? ¿quieres tomar algo conmigo?; they —ed us last Friday vinieron a estar con nosotros el viernes pasado; they will — us for the holidays vendrán a pasar las vacaciones con nosotros; to — someone in doing something acompañar a uno en hacer algo, hacer algo juntamente con uno; they —ed us in protesting se hicieron eco de nuestras protestas.

3 *vi* unirse, juntarse; (*lines*) empalmar; (*rivers*) confluir; **where the paths — donde** empalman los caminos; **to — in** (*adv*) tomar parte, participar; **he doesn't — in** much apenas participa en nuestras actividades; **to — in** (*prep*) tomar parte en, participar en; *discussion* intervenir en; *chorus etc* cantar todos; **to — together** unirse; **to — up** unirse; (*Mil*) alistarse; **to — up with someone** reunirse con uno; **to — with someone in something** acompañar a uno en algo, participar juntamente con uno en algo; **we — with you in that feeling** compartimos esa opinión, nos hacemos eco de eso; **we — with you in hoping that . . .** lo mismo que Vds esperamos que . . .

joiner ['dʒɔinə*] *n* carpintero *m* (de blanco), ensamblador *m*.

joinery ['dʒɔinəri] *n* carpintería *f*.

joint [dʒɔint] **1** *adj* (en) común; combinado; *action, effort, product etc* colectivo; *agreement* mutuo; *declaration etc* conjunto; *responsibility* solidario, que comparten todos; *committee etc* mixto; *ownership* común; *account* (*Comm*) indistinto; (*in compounds*) co . . .; *see* **company, stock** *etc*.
2 *n* **(a)** (*Tech: metal*) junta *f*, juntura *f*, unión *f*; (*wood*) ensambladura *f*; (*hinge*) bisagra *f*; (*Anat*) articulación *f*, coyuntura *f*; (*knuckle*) nudillo *m*; (*Bot*) nudo *m*; (*of meat*) cuarto *m*; **mitre —** ensambladura *f* de inglete; **universal —** junta *f* cardán, junta *f* universal; **to be out of —** (*bone*) estar descoyuntado, estar dislocado; (*fig*) estar fuera de quicio; **to put a bone out of —** dislocarse un hueso; **to put someone's nose out of —** desconcertar a uno (adelantándose a él); **to throw someone's plans out of —** estropear los planes de uno.
(b) (*sl*) garito *m*, tasca *f*, cafetucho *m*.
3 *vt* articular; *parts* juntar, unir; *wood etc* ensamblar.

jointed ['dʒɔintid] *adj* articulado; (*folding*) plegadizo, plegable.

jointly ['dʒɔintli] *adv* en común; colectivamente; mutuamente; conjuntamente.

joist [dʒɔist] *n* viga *f*, vigueta *f*.

joke [dʒəuk] **1** *n* (*hoax etc*) broma *f*, burla *f*; (*witticism, story*) chiste *m*; (*person*) hazmerreír *m*; **practical —** broma *f* pesada, mistificación *f*, trastada *f*; **he's a standing —** es un pobre hombre, es un hombre que da risa; **it's a standing —** here aquí eso siempre provoca a risa; **it's no —** no es cosa de risa, no es para reírse; **it's no — having to** + *infin* no tiene nada de divertido + *infin*; **the — is that** lo gracioso es que; **the — is on you** Vd es el aludido, eso lo dicen por Vd; **it's beyond a —** esto es el colmo, esto pasa de castaño oscuro; **what sort of a — is this?** ¿qué broma es ésta?; **is that your idea of a —?** ¿es que eso tiene gracia?; **to crack (or make) a —** hacer un chiste; **to crack —s with someone** contar chistes a uno; **they spent an evening cracking —s together** pasaron una tarde contándose chistes; **he will have his little —** le gusta tomar el pelo; **to play a — on someone** gastar una broma a uno; **I can take a —** tengo mucho aguante; **he can't take a —** no le gusta que se le tome el pelo; **to tell a —** contar un chiste; **why do you have to turn everything into a —?** ¿eres incapaz de tomar nada en serio?
2 *vi* bromear, chancearse, chungear; hablar en broma; (*tell —s*) contar chistes; **I was only joking** lo dije en broma; **I'm not joking** esto lo digo en serio; **you must be joking!** ¿pero lo dices en serio?; **to — about something** tomar algo en chunga.

joker ['dʒəukə*] *n* (*wit*) chistoso *m*, a *f*, guasón *m*, ona *f*; (*practical-*) bromista *mf*; (*Cards*) comodín *m*; (*fam*) tío *m*, sujeto *m*.

joking ['dʒəukiŋ] **1** *adj reference etc* humorístico; *tone* guasón; **I'm not in a — mood** no estoy para bromas.
2 *n* bromas *fpl*; chistes *mpl*.

jokingly ['dʒəukiŋli] *adv* humorísticamente; **he said — dijo** en broma, dijo guasón.

jollification [,dʒɔlifi'keiʃən] *n* (*merriment*) regocijo *m*, festividades *fpl*; (*party*) fiesta *f*, guateque *m*.

jollity ['dʒɔliti] *n* alegría *f*, regocijo *m*.

jolly ['dʒɔli] **1** *adj* alegre; divertido; *character* alegre, jovial; **to get —** (*fam*) achisparse; **we had a — time** lo pasamos muy bien, nos divertimos mucho; **it wasn't very — for the rest of us** los demás no nos divertimos nada.
2 *adv* (*fam*) muy, terriblemente; **it's — hard** es terriblemente difícil; **we were — glad** nos alegramos muchísimo; **you did — well** lo hiciste la mar de bien; **you've — well got to** no tienes más remedio en absoluto; **— good!** ¡estupendo!
3 *vt*: **to — someone along** engatusar a uno, seguir el humor a uno; **to — someone into doing something** persuadir mañosamente a uno a hacer algo.

jolly boat ['dʒɔlibəut] *n* esquife *m*.

jolt [dʒəult] **1** *n* sacudida *f*, choque *m*; **to give someone a —** (*fig*) dar una sacudida a uno; **it gave me a bit of a —** me dio un susto, con eso me pegué un susto.
2 *vt* sacudir; *elbow etc* empujar (ligeramente), sacudir (levemente); **to — someone into doing something** dar una sacudida a uno para animarle a hacer algo; **to — someone out of his complacency** hacer que uno se dé cuenta de la necesidad de hacer algo, destruir el optimismo de uno.
3 *vi* (*vehicle*) traquetear, dar saltos.

jolting ['dʒəultiŋ] *n* (*of vehicle*) traqueteo *m*.

jolty ['dʒəulti] *adj vehicle* que traquetea, que da saltos.

Jonah ['dʒəunə] *m* Jonás.

jonquil ['dʒɔŋkwil] *n* junquillo *m*.

Jordan ['dʒɔːdn] (*river*) Jordán *m*; (*country*) Jordania *f*.

Joseph ['dʒəuzif] *m* José.

Josephine ['dʒəuzifiːn] *f* Josefina.

josh [dʒɔʃ] *vt* (*US sl*) tomar el pelo a.

Joshua ['dʒɔʃwə] *m* Josué.

josser ['dʒɔsə*] *n* (*sl*) tío *m*, individuo *m*.

joss stick ['dʒɔsstik] *n* pebete *m*.

jostle ['dʒɔsl] **1** *n* empujón *m*, empellón *m*, codazo *m*.
2 *vt* empujar.
3 *vi* empujar, dar empellones, codear; **they were all jostling for a place** todos se estaban empujando para asegurarse un sitio.

jot [dʒɔt] **1** *n* jota *f*, pizca *f*; **there's not a — of truth in it** eso no tiene ni pizca de verdad; *see* **care. 2** *vt*: **to — down** apuntar.

jotter ['dʒɔtə*] *n* taco *m* para notas.

jottings ['dʒɔtiŋz] *npl* apuntes *mpl*.

journal ['dʒəːnl] *n* (*newspaper*) periódico *m*; (*review, magazine*) revista *f*; (*diary*) diario *m*; (*Naut*) diario *m* de navegación; (*Mech*) gorrón *m*, muñón *m*.

journal bearing ['dʒəːnl'beariŋ] *n* cojinete *m*.

journalese [,dʒəːnə'liːz] *n* lenguaje *m* periodístico.

journalism ['dʒəːnəlizəm] *n* periodismo *m*.

journalist ['dʒəːnəlist] *n* periodista *mf*.

journalistic [,dʒəːnə'listik] *adj* periodístico.

journey ['dʒəːni] **1** *n* viaje *m*; trayecto *m*; camino *m*; **outward —** viaje *m* de ida; **return —** viaje *m* de regreso; **Scott's — to the Pole** la expedición de Scott al Polo; **the capsule's — through space** el trayecto de la cápsula por el espacio; **pleasant —!** ¡buen viaje!; **to be on a —** estar de viaje; **have you much — left?** ¿le queda mucho camino?
2 *vi* viajar.

journeyman ['dʒəːnimən] *n*, *pl* **—men** [mən] oficial *m*.

joust [dʒaust] **1** *n* justa *f*, torneo *m*. **2** *vi* justar.

Jove [dʒəuv] *m* Júpiter; **by —!** ¡caramba!

jovial ['dʒəuviəl] *adj* jovial.

joviality [,dʒəuvi'æliti] *n* jovialidad *f*.

jowl [dʒaul] *n* (*Anat: jaw*) quijada *f*; (*chin*) barba *f*; (*cheek*) carrillo *m*; (*Zool*) papada *f*.

joy [dʒɔi] *n* (*gladness*) alegría *f*, júbilo *m*, regocijo *m*; (*pleasant quality*) deleite *m*, encanto *m*; **the —s of opera** los encantos de la ópera; **it's a — to hear him** da gozo escucharle; **to be a — to the eye** ser un gozo para la retina; **to be beside oneself with —** no caber en sí de gozo; **to jump for —** saltar de alegría; **I wish you —!** ¡enhorabuena! (*also iro*).

joyful ['dʒɔiful] *adj* alegre; jubiloso, regocijado; **to be — about** alegrarse de.

joyfully ['dʒɔifəli] *adv* alegremente; con júbilo, regocijadamente.

joyfulness ['dʒɔifulnis] *n* alegría *f*; júbilo *m*, regocijo *m*.

joyless ['dʒɔilis] *adj* sin alegría, triste.

joyous ['dʒɔiəs] *adj* alegre.

joy ride ['dʒɔiraid] *n* paseo *m* en coche (*etc*), excursión *f* en coche (*etc*).

joystick ['dʒɔistik] *n* (*Aer*) palanca *f* de gobierno.

jubilant ['dʒuːbilənt] *adj* jubiloso.

jubilation [,dʒuːbi'leiʃən] *n* júbilo *m*.

jubilee ['dʒuːbiliː] *n* (*Hist, Eccl*) jubileo *m*; (*anniversary: strictly*) quincuagésimo aniversario *m*; **diamond —** sexagésimo aniversario *m*; **golden —** quincuagésimo aniversario *m*; **silver —** vigésimo quinto aniversario *m*.

Judaea [dʒuː'diə] *n* Judea *f*.

Judah ['dʒuːdə] *n* Judá *f*.

Judaic [dʒuː'deiik] *adj* judaico.

Judaism ['dʒuːdeiizəm] *n* judaísmo *m*.

Judaize ['dʒuːdeiaiz] *vi* judaizar.

Judas ['dʒuːdəs] *m* Judas.

judge [dʒʌdʒ] **1** *n* (*Law*) juez *m*; (*Sport*) árbitro *m*, (*in races*) juez *m* de raya; (*connoisseur*) conocedor m, ora f (of de), (expert) perito m (of en); — of appeal juez m de alzados; he's a fine — of horses es un excelente conocedor de caballos; I'm no — of wines yo no entiendo de vinos.

2 vt person, case juzgar; question decidir, resolver; (Sport) arbitrar; (consider) juzgar, considerar; I — it to be right lo considero acertado; I — him a fool considero que es tonto; one has to — the distance hay que conjeturar la distancia; he —d the moment well acertó escogiendo tal momento; who can — this question? ¿quién puede resolver esta cuestión?

3 vi juzgar; opinar, expresar una opinión; to — by, judging by a juzgar por; to — of juzgar de, opinar sobre; who am I to —? ¿es que yo soy capaz de juzgar? only an expert can — sólo lo puede decidir un experto; to — for oneself formar su propia opinión.

judge-advocate ['dʒʌdʒ'ædvəkit] n (Mil) auditor m de guerra.

judg(e)ment ['dʒʌdʒmənt] n (a) (Law) juicio m; sentencia f, fallo m; Last J— Juicio m Final; J— Day día m del Juicio Final; — seat tribunal m; it's a — on you for lying es un castigo por haber mentido; to pass (or pronounce) — (Law) pronunciar sentencia (on en, sobre), (fig) emitir un juicio crítico sobre, dictaminar sobre.

(b) (opinion) opinión f, parecer m; juicio m; a critical — of Auden un juicio crítico de Auden.

(c) (understanding) juicio m; criterio m, entendimiento m, discernimiento m; in my — en mi opinión; to the best of my — según mi leal saber y entender; to have good (or sound) — tener buen juicio, tener buen criterio.

judicature ['dʒuːdikətʃə*] n judicatura f.
judicial [dʒuːˈdiʃəl] adj judicial; murder, separation etc legal.
judiciary [dʒuːˈdiʃiəri] 1 adj judicial. 2 n judicatura f.
judicious [dʒuːˈdiʃəs] adj juicioso; prudente, sensato, acertado.
judiciously [dʒuːˈdiʃəsli] adv juiciosamente; prudentemente, acertadamente.
Judith ['dʒuːdiθ] f Judit.
judo ['dʒuːdəu] n judo m.
Judy ['dʒuːdi] f nombre cariñoso de **Judith**.
jug [dʒʌg] 1 n jarro m; (sl) chirona f. 2 vt (sl) encarcelar; —ged hare liebre f en estofado.
juggernaut ['dʒʌgənɔːt] n monstruo m destructor de los hombres.
juggins ['dʒʌginz] n (fam) bobo m, a f.
juggle ['dʒʌgl] vi hacer juegos malabares, hacer juegos de manos (with con); to — with (fig) arreglar de otro modo, (pej) falsear, falsificar, hacer trampa con.
juggler ['dʒʌglə*] n malabarista mf.
jugglery ['dʒʌgləri] n, **juggling** ['dʒʌgliŋ] n juegos mpl malabares, malabarismo m, juegos mpl de manos; (pej) trampas fpl, fraude m.
Jugoslav ['juːgəuˈslɑːv] 1 adj yugo(e)slavo. 2 n yugo(e)slavo m, a f.
Jugoslavia ['juːgəuˈslɑːviə] Yugo(e)slavia f.
jugular ['dʒʌgjulə*] adj: — vein vena f yugular.
juice [dʒuːs] n (fruit-) jugo m, zumo m; (sl) salacidad f, lo verde, lo picante; (Aut sl) gasolina f; (Elec sl) fuerza f, corriente f; digestive —s jugos mpl digestivos.
juiciness ['dʒuːsinis] n jugosidad f; (sl) salacidad f, lo verde.
juicy ['dʒuːsi] adj jugoso, zumoso; (sl) salaz, verde, picante.
jujube ['dʒuːdʒuːb] n pastilla f.
jujutsu [dʒuːˈdʒitsu] n jiu-jitsu m.
jukebox ['dʒuːkbɔks] n tocadiscos m automático, tocadiscos m tragaperras, gramola f.
julep ['dʒuːlep] n julepe m.
Julian ['dʒuːliən] m Juliano, Julián.
Juliet ['dʒuːliet] f Julieta.
Julius ['dʒuːliəs] m Julio; — Caesar Julio César.
July [dʒuːˈlai] julio m.
jumble ['dʒʌmbl] 1 n revoltijo m, confusión f; a — of furniture un montón de muebles revueltos; a — of sounds una serie de ruidos confusos.

2 vt (also to — together, to — up) mezclar, emburujar; papers —d up together papeles mpl revueltos; they were just —d together anyhow estaban amontonados sin orden.
jumble sale ['dʒʌmblseil] n venta f de objetos usados (con fines benéficos).
jumbo ['dʒʌmbəu] n elefante m.
jump [dʒʌmp] 1 n salto m, brinco m; (fig) ascenso m, aumento m; to — give a — dar un saltito; to give someone a — dar un susto a uno; you gave me quite a —! ¡ay qué susto me diste!; to have the — on

someone (fam) llevar ventaja a uno; the temperature took a — subió rápidamente la temperatura; there has been a big — in the reserves las reservas han subido de golpe.

2 vt (a) saltar, saltar por encima de, salvar; see gun, rail etc.

(b) horse hacer saltar; presentar en un concurso hípico.

(c) (omit) pasar por alto, omitir.

3 vi (a) saltar, brincar, dar saltos; (Sport) saltar; (Aer) lanzarse (en paracaídas); (vibrate) temblar, bailar, vibrar; to — about dar saltos, brincar; moverse de un lado para otro; to — across a stream cruzar un arroyo de un salto, saltar por encima de un arroyo; to — down bajar de un salto, saltar a tierra; — in! ¡vamos!; to — into a car entrar de prisa en un coche; to — on to something ponerse encima de algo de un salto; we —ed on to the train subimos de prisa al tren; to — on someone (fam) poner verde a uno; to — on an abuse (fam) tratar de acabar con un abuso; to — out of bed saltar de la cama; I nearly —ed out of my skin! ¡vaya susto que me pegué!; he —ed out from behind a bush salió de repente de detrás de un arbusto; to — over saltar, saltar por (encima de), salvar; — to it! ¡menearse!; to — up ponerse en pie de un salto; see conclusion etc.

(b) (fig: start) asustarse, sobresaltarse, pegar un bote; to make someone — dar un susto a uno; you did make me —! ¡ay qué susto me diste!

(c) (fig: emotion) to — for joy saltar de alegría, no caber en sí de gozo.

(d) to — at a chance apresurarse a aprovechar una oportunidad; to — at an offer apresurarse a aceptar una oferta.

jumped-up ['dʒʌmpt'ʌp] adj arribista, presuntuoso.
jumper ['dʒʌmpə*] n saltador m, ora f; (dress) suéter m, jersey m.
jumping-off place ['dʒʌmpiŋ'ɔf,pleis] n base f avanzada.
jumpy ['dʒʌmpi] adj nervioso, asustadizo.
junction ['dʒʌŋkʃən] n juntura f, unión f; (of roads) cruce m; (Rail) empalme m; (of rivers) confluencia f.
junction box ['dʒʌŋkʃənbɔks] n caja f de empalmes.
juncture ['dʒʌŋktʃə*] n coyuntura f; at this — en este momento, en esta coyuntura; critical — coyuntura f crítica.
June [dʒuːn] junio m.
jungle ['dʒʌŋgl] n selva f, jungla f; (fig) maraña f, selva f.
junior ['dʒuːniə*] 1 adj (in age) menor, más joven; (on a staff) más nuevo; position, rank subalterno; section (in competition etc) juvenil, para menores; partner menor, menos antiguo; Roy Smith, J— Roy Smith, hijo.

2 n menor mf, joven mf; (British School) alumno m (or alumna f) de 8 a 11 años; (US Univ) estudiante mf de tercer año; he is my — by 3 years, he is 3 years my — tiene 3 años menos que yo, le llevo 3 años.
juniper ['dʒuːnipə*] n enebro m.
junk[1] [dʒʌŋk] n (Naut) junco m.
junk[2] [dʒʌŋk] n (lumber) trastos mpl viejos; (rubbish) basura f, desperdicios mpl; (iron) chatarra f; (cheap goods) baratijas fpl; the play is a lot of — la obra es una porquería; he talks a lot of — no habla más que tonterías.
junket ['dʒʌŋkit] 1 n dulce m de leche cuajada. 2 vi ir de juerga, ir de jira, estar de fiesta.
junketing ['dʒʌŋkitiŋ] n (also —s) festividades fpl, fiestas fpl.
junkie ['dʒʌŋki] n (fam) drogadicto m, a f.
junkshop ['dʒʌŋkʃɔp] n tienda f de trastos viejos.
junk yard ['dʒʌŋkjɑːd] n parque m de chatarra.
junta ['dʒʌntə] n junta f.
Jupiter ['dʒuːpitə*] m Júpiter.
juridical [dʒuəˈridikəl] adj jurídico.
jurisdiction [,dʒuəris'dikʃən] n jurisdicción f; to come within someone's — ser de la competencia de uno.
jurisprudence [,dʒuəris'pruːdəns] n jurisprudencia f; medical — medicina f legal.
jurist ['dʒuərist] n jurista m.
juror ['dʒuərə*] n jurado m (persona).
jury ['dʒuəri] n jurado m (conjunto de jurados); grand — (US) jurado m de acusación; to be on the — ser miembro del jurado.
jury box ['dʒuəribɔks] n tribuna f del jurado.
juryman ['dʒuərimən] n, pl —men [mən] (miembro m del) jurado m.
jury mast ['dʒuərimɑːst] n bandola f.
jury rig ['dʒuəririg] n aparejo m provisional.

just [dʒʌst] **1** *adj* (*upright*) justo, recto, imparcial; (*accurate*) exacto, correcto; (*deserved*) merecido, apropiado; (*well grounded*) justificado, lógico; **as is only** — como es justo, como es de razón; **the** — los justos.

2 *adv* (*a*) (*exactly*) exactamente, precisamente; — **here** aquí mismo; — **by the church** al lado mismo de l₂ iglesia, muy cerca de la iglesia; — **beyond the pub** un poco más allá de la tasca; **it's** — **4 o'clock** son las 4 en punto; — **so !** ¡eso es!, ¡perfectamente!, ¡precisamente!; **that's** — **it !** ¡ahí está la dificultad!; **it's** — **the same** es exactamente igual; **it's** — **what I needed** es precisamente lo que necesitaba; **we were** — **talking about it** precisamente estábamos hablando de eso; — **when he started to sing** precisamente cuando empezaba a cantar; **I was** — **going** estaba a punto de marcharme; **now** — **what did he say ?** ¿qué es lo que dijo, en concreto?; — **how many we don't know** no sabemos exactamente cuántos; **a policeman ?** **that's** — **what I am** ¿un policía? pues yo lo soy.

(*b*) (*with* as) **you sing** — **as well as I do** Vd canta tan bien como yo; — **as you wish** como Vd quiera; — **as it started to rain** en el momento en que empezó a llover; **we left everything** — **as it was** lo dejamos todo exactamente como estaba; **it's** — **as well it's insured** menos mal que está asegurado; **it would be** — **as well if he went** más vale que se vaya él.

(*c*) (*only*) solamente, sólo; — **as a joke** en broma nada más; — **for a laugh** sólo para hacer reír; — **once** una vez nada más, solamente una vez, una vez solamente; — **the two of us** nosotros dos solamente; — **a little bit** un poquito; — **a few** unos pocos; **he's** — **a lad** no es más que un chico; — **let me get at him !** ¡que me dejen llegar a él!

(*d*) (*merely*) **I** — **told him to go away** le dije que se fuera, nada más; — **wait a moment !** ¡espere un momento!; — **imagine !** ¡imagínese!; — **listen !** ¡escucha un poco!; — **look !** ¡mira!, ¡fíjate!; — **a tick !** un momentito!

(*e*) (*positively*) **it's** — **fine !** ¡es francamente maravilloso!, ¡es sencillamente maravilloso!; **it's** — **perfect !** ¡qué maravilla!

(*f*) (*barely*) **I** — **managed to catch it** por poco lo perdí; **he was only** — **saved from drowning** en poco estuvo que muriese ahogado; **you're** — **in time** llegas justamente con tiempo; — **before it rained** momentos antes de que lloviese.

(*g*) (*with* have *etc*) **I have** — **seen him** acabo de verle; **I had** — **seen him** acababa de verle; **the book is** — **out** el libro acaba de publicarse; — **appointed** recién nombrado; — **received** acabado de recibir; — **cooked** recién hecho, recién salido del horno.

(*h*) (*emphatic, fam*) **don't I** —**!** ¡ya lo creo!; *see* **now, yet** *etc.*

justice ['dʒʌstis] *n* (*a*) justicia *f*; **poetic** — justicia *f* poética; **to bring someone to** — llevar a uno ante el tribunal, hacer que uno sea procesado; **to do someone** — hacer justicia a uno, tratar debidamente a uno; **to do oneself** — quedar bien, justificarse; **to do a meal !** — hacer los debidos honores a una comida; **this work does not do your talents** — este ensayo no está a la altura de su talento.

(*b*) (*person*) juez *m*, juez *m* municipal; — **of the peace** (*approx*) juez *m* de paz; **Lord Chief J**—Justicia *m* Mayor.

justifiable ['dʒʌstifaiəbl] *adj* justificable; justificado.

justifiably ['dʒʌstifaiəbli] *adv* justificadamente; **and** — so y con razón; — **proud** orgulloso y con razón.

justification [ˌdʒʌstifi'keiʃən] *n* justificación *f*.

justify ['dʒʌstifai] *vt* justificar, vindicar; dar motivo para; (*excuse*) disculpar; **the future does not** — **the slightest optimism** el futuro no autoriza el más leve optimismo; **to be justified in** + *ger* tener motivo para + *infin*, tener plenamente razón al + *infin*; **you were not justified in that** en eso no tuviste razón; **am I justified in thinking that . . . ?** ¿hay motivo para creer que . . . ?

justly ['dʒʌstli] *adv* justamente, con justicia; con derecho; debidamente; con razón; **it has been** — **said that** se ha dicho con razón que.

justness ['dʒʌstnis] *n* justicia *f*; rectitud *f*.

jut [dʒʌt] *vi* (*also* — **out**) sobresalir.

Jute [dʒuːt] *n* juto *m*, a *f*.

jute [dʒuːt] *n* yute *m*.

juvenile ['dʒuːvənail] **1** *adj* juvenil; de (*or* para) menores; (*pej*) infantil; *court* de menores; *delinquency* de menores, *delinquent* juvenil.

2 *n* joven *mf*.

juxtapose ['dʒʌkstəpəuz] *vt* yuxtaponer.

juxtaposition [ˌdʒʌkstəpə'ziʃən] *n* yuxtaposición *f*.

K

Kaffir ['kæfə*] n cafre mf.
Kaiser ['kaizə*] n emperador m.
kale, kail [keil] n col f rizada.
kaleidoscope [kə'laidəskəup] n calidoscopio m.
kaleidoscopic [kə‚laidə'skɔpik] adj calidoscópico.
kangaroo [‚kæŋgə'ru:] n canguro m.
kaolin ['keiəlin] n caolín m.
kapok ['keipɔk] n capoc m.
kaput [kə'put] adj (sl): **it's —** está roto, está estropeado; **se acabó; it went —** se rompió, se estropeó.
karat ['kærət] n see **carat**.
Kashmir [kæʃ'miə*] Cachemira f.
Kate [keit] f nombre cariñoso de **Catherine** etc.
Katharine, Katherine ['kæθərin], **Kathleen** ['kæθli:n] f Catalina.
katydid ['keitidid] n saltamontes m (especie norteamericana).
kayak ['kaiæk] n kayac m.
kedge [kedʒ] n anclote m.
kedgeree [‚kedʒə'ri:] n plato de pescado, huevos y arroz.
keel [ki:l] **1** n quilla f; **on an even —** (Naut) en iguales calados, (fig) en equilibrio, equilibrado; **to keep something on an even —** mantener el equilibrio de algo.
2 vi: **to — over** (Naut) zozobrar, dar de quilla, (fig) volcar(se), (person) desplomarse.
keelhaul ['ki:lhɔ:l] vt pasar por debajo de la quilla (como castigo).
keen [ki:n] adj (a) edge afilado; wind penetrante, glacial; eyesight, hearing agudo; mind agudo, penetrante, perspicaz; look fijo, penetrante; price bajo, competitivo, económico; competition intenso; interest grande; emotion intenso, vivo, hondo; appetite bueno; **to have a — sense of history** tener un profundo sentido de la historia.
(b) (of person) entusiasta; celoso; **he's a — footballer** es muy aficionado a jugar al fútbol; **he's a — socialist** es un socialista acérrimo; **try not to seem too —** procura no mostrar demasiado entusiasmo; **to be as — as mustard** ser extraordinariamente entusiasta; **I'm terribly — about the new play** la nueva obra me hace muchísima ilusión; **he's very — about the programme** tiene mucho entusiasmo por el programa; **to be — on something** ser aficionado a algo; **are you — on opera?** ¿le gusta la ópera?; **I'm not all that — on grapes** no me gustan mucho las uvas; **I'm not — on the idea** no me hace gracia la idea; **he's — on her** ella le interesa bastante; **I'm not very — on him** no es santo de mi devoción; **to be — to +** infin tener vivo deseo de **+** infin, tener muchas ganas de **+** infin, ansiar **+** infin; **I'm not — to do it** no tengo ganas de hacerlo.
keenly ['ki:nli] adv (a) de modo penetrante; agudamente; intensamente, vivamente; **he felt her death —** su muerte le afectó profundamente; **he looked at me —** me miró fijamente.
(b) work etc con entusiasmo.
keenness ['ki:nnis] n (a) penetración f, agudeza f; intensidad f, viveza f.
(b) entusiasmo m, ilusión f; interés m, afición f; **there isn't much — here** aquí hay poco interés.
keep [ki:p] (irr: pret and ptp **kept**) **1** vt (a) promise cumplir; rule observar, atenerse a; appointment acudir a; festivity observar, celebrar.
(b) order mantener, imponer.
(c) (possess etc) dog, servant tener; chicken, sheep etc criar, dedicarse a criar, ocuparse en la cría de; family mantener; shop tener; business, hotel etc ser propietario de, dirigir; diary escribir; account, record, house llevar; **he —s a good cellar** tiene una buena bodega; **he doesn't — his garden neat** no mantiene en buen estado su jardín; **he —s his 3 daughters in clothes** les paga los vestidos a sus 3 hijas; **he has his parents to —** tiene que mantener a sus padres.
(d) (detain) detener; (in conversation etc) entretener; **they kept him in prison for 6 months** le tuvieron 6 meses en la cárcel; **illness kept her at home** se quedó en casa debido a la enfermedad, la enfermedad no le permitió salir de casa; **what kept you?** ¿por qué vienes tarde?, ¿a qué se debe este retraso?; **I mustn't — you** no le entretengo más.
(e) (prevent) **to — someone from doing something** impedir a uno hacer algo, no dejar a uno hacer algo.
(f) (save) poner aparte, tener guardado, reservar; **I was —ing it for you** lo tenía guardado para Vd.
(g) (retain) guardar, retener; reservar; secret, figure etc guardar; job retener, mantenerse en; (not give back) quedarse con; (in museum etc) conservar, custodiar; **— the change** quédese con la vuelta; **to — one's seat** permanecer sentado, (Parl) retener su escaño.
(h) (with adj, verb etc) **to — something clean** conservar algo limpio; **"K— Spain Clean"** (antilitter campaign) "Mantenga limpia España"; **she always —s the house very clean** tiene la casa siempre muy limpia; **to — something safe** tener algo seguro; **to — something warm** tener algo caliente, mantener el calor de algo; **to — someone talking** entretener a uno en conversación; **to — someone waiting** hacer que uno espere, hacer esperar a uno; **to — one's eyes fixed on something** tener los ojos puestos en algo; **to — someone at it** obligar a uno a seguir trabajando (etc).
(i) (with adv or prep) **to — someone away** mantener a uno a distancia, alejar a uno (from de), no dejar a uno acercarse (from a); **they kept him away from school** no le dejaron ir a la escuela; **they kept guns away from the child** no le dejaron al niño jugar con pistolas; **to — back** (retain) guardar, retener; information ocultar; emotion contener, reprimir; enemy no dejar avanzar, tener a raya; progress estorbar, cortar el paso a; **to — some money by one** guardar algún dinero para un apuro; **to — down** (hold down) sujetar; no dejar subir; price, temperature etc mantener bajo; growth etc restringir, limitar; (oppress) oprimir; **to — something from someone** ocultar algo a uno, no decir algo a uno; **to — in** fire mantener encendido; feelings contener; person, pet etc no dejar salir, tener encerrado; (in school) hacer quedar en la escuela (como castigo); **to — off** tener a raya, cerrar el paso a; no dejar entrar; alejar; **— the dog off!** ¡que no se acerque más el perro!; **to — someone off a subject** hacer que uno no discuta un tema, persuadir a uno a no tocar un tema; **to — one's hat on** no quitarse el sombrero, seguir con el sombrero puesto; **to — the light on** tener la luz puesta; **to — someone on in a job** mantener a uno en un puesto; **to — out** no dejar entrar, excluir; **to — something to oneself** guardar algo para sí; guardar algo en secreto; **to — someone to his promise** obligar a uno a cumplir su promesa; **to — together** mantener unido(s); **to — someone under** tener a uno subyugado; **to — up** (maintain) mantener; conservar; (hold up) sostener; **to — someone up (at night)** hacer que uno siga sin dormir, entretener a uno hasta muy tarde; **to — it up** mantener el nivel, seguir como antes; no cejar; **— it up!** ¡ánimo!, ¡dale!
2 vi (a) (remain) quedar(se), permanecer; seguir, continuar; **to — quiet** no hacer ruido; no decir nada, quedar callado, callarse; **— still!** ¡estáte quieto!; **to — clear of** evitar cualquier contacto con; seguir libre de; **how are you —ing?** ¿cómo está Vd?; **to — well** estar bien de salud.

(b) *(with ger)* **to —** + *ger* seguir + *ger*, continuar + *ger*; no dejar de + *infin*; **she —s talking** sigue hablando; no deja de hablar; **she —s asking me for it** me lo está pidiendo constantemente; **to —smiling** seguir con la sonrisa en los labios; **to —standing** seguir en pie; **to — going** seguir adelante, no cejar; **we — going somehow** vamos tirando; nos arreglamos para continuar; **I can — going in French** me defiendo en francés.

(c) *(continue)* seguir, continuar; **to — at work** seguir trabajando, mantenerse en su puesto; **—straight on for Madrid** para ir a Madrid vaya Vd todo seguido; **to — to the left** circular por la izquierda.

(d) *(of food)* conservarse fresco, conservarse en buen estado; **an apple that —s** una manzana que dura; **the news will — till I see you** no pierdes nada si me guardo la noticia hasta que nos veamos.

(e) *(with adv or prep)* **to — at something** trabajar sin descansar en algo, no cejar en algo, perseverar en algo; **— at it!** ¡dale!; **to — away** mantenerse alejado *(from de)*, mantenerse a distancia; *(not attend)* no venir, no acudir; no dejarse ver; **to — away from someone** no meterse en líos con uno, evitar cualquier contacto con uno; **— away from my daughter!** ¡no venga más a ver a mi hija!; **he can't — away from the subject** siempre vuelve al tema; **to — back** hacerse a un lado; **— back, please!** ¡más atrás, por favor!; **to — down** seguir acurrucado *(or tumbado etc)*, no levantar la cabeza; **to — from** + *ger* abstenerse de + *infin*, guardarse de + *infin*; **to — in with someone** mantener buenas relaciones con uno, cultivar la amistad de uno, *(pej)* asegurarse de la protección de uno; **to — off** mantenerse a distancia; **"— off"** "prohibida la entrada"; **to — off the grass** no pisar la hierba; **to — off a subject** no aludir a un tema, no discutir una cuestión; **if the rain —s off** si no llueve; **to — on** continuar; **to — on** + *ger* seguir + *ger*, continuar + *ger*; **he —s on talking** sigue hablando; no deja de hablar; **he —s on hoping** no renuncia a esperar, no pierde la esperanza; **don't — on so!** ¡no machaques!; **to — on at someone about something** insistir en discutir algo con uno; **to — on with something** continuar con algo; **to — out** permanecer fuera; **"— out!"** "¡prohibida la entrada!"; **to — out of place, organization etc** no entrar en; *affair* no meterse en; *trouble* evitar; **to — to direction** llevar; *path* seguir, no apartarse de; *promise* cumplir; *instructions* seguir al pie de la letra; **to — to one's bed** guardar cama; **to — to one's room** no salir de su habitación; **they — to themselves** evitan tener contacto con otros, permanecen aislados; **to —together** mantenerse unidos; **to — up** no rezagarse; **to — up with** *(in pace)* ir al paso de; *(rival)* emular, mantenerse a la altura de; **to — up with one's work** hacer su trabajo al ritmo apropiado, mantenerse al día en su trabajo; **to — up with the times** ir con los tiempos, mantenerse al día.

3 *vr*: **to — oneself clean** mantenerse limpio, cuidar su limpieza personal; **to — oneself from** + *ger* abstenerse de + *infin*, guardarse de + *infin*; **they — themselves to themselves** evitan tener contacto con otros, permanecen aislados.

4 *n* **(a)** comida *f*, subsistencia *f*; **to earn one's —** trabajar por la comida, pagar la comida trabajando; *(fig)* producir *(etc)* bastante; **I pay £5 a week for my —** la pensión me cuesta 5 libras a la semana; **he isn't worth his —** no trabaja como debe, no merece que sigamos empleándole.

(b) *(Hist)* torreón *m*, torre *f* del homenaje.

(c) for —s *(fam)* permanentemente, para guardar.

keeper ['kiːpə*] *n* *(game-)* guardabosque *m*; *(in art gallery, museum, library)* conservador *m*; *(in record office)* archivero *m*; *(in park, zoo)* guardián *m*; **am I my brother's —?** ¿es que yo respondo por mi hermano?

keeping ['kiːpiŋ] *n* **(a) to be in — with** estar de acuerdo con, estar en armonía con; **to be out of — with** estar en desacuerdo con.

(b) to be in the — of X estar en manos de X, estar bajo la custodia de X; **to be in safe —** estar en un lugar seguro, estar en buenas manos; **to give something to someone for safe —** dar algo a uno para mayor seguridad.

keepsake ['kiːpseik] *n* recuerdo *m*.

keg [keg] *n* barrilete *m*, cuñete *m*.

kelp [kelp] *n* quelpo *m*.

ken [ken] **1** *n*: **to be beyond someone's —** ser incomprensible para uno; **to be within someone's —** ser comprensible para uno.

2 *vt* *(know)* *person etc* conocer, *fact* saber; *(recognize)* reconocer.

kennel ['kenl] *n* *(doghouse)* perrera *f*; *(pack)* jauría *f*; *(fig)* cuchitril *m*.

Kenya ['kenjə] Kenia *f*.

kepi ['keipi] *n* quepis *m*.

kept [kept] *pret and ptp of* **keep.**

kerb [kəːb] *n*, **kerbstone** ['kəːbstəun] *n* bordillo *m*, encintado *m*.

kerchief ['kəːtʃif] *n* pañuelo *m*, pañoleta *f*.

kernel ['kəːnl] *n* almendra *f*; *(fig)* núcleo *m*, meollo *m*; **a — of truth** una parte de verdad.

kerosene ['kerəsiːn] *n* keroseno *m*, queroseno *m* *(Acad)*; **— lamp** lámpara *f* de petróleo.

kestrel ['kestrəl] *n* cernícalo *m* *(vulgar)*.

ketch [ketʃ] *n* queche *m*.

ketchup ['ketʃəp] *n* salsa *f* de tomate.

kettle ['ketl] *n* *(approx)* hervidor *m*, olla *f* en forma de cafetera *(or tetera)*, pava *f* *(SAm)*; **this is a pretty — of fish!** ¡en buen berenjenal nos hemos metido!

kettledrum ['ketldrʌm] *n* timbal *m*.

key [kiː] **1** *n* **(a)** *(door- etc)* llave *f*; *(of typewriter, piano etc)* tecla *f*; *(of wind instrument)* llave *f*, pistón *m*; *(Tel)* manipulador *m*; *(Tech)* chaveta *f*, cuña *f*; *(Elec)* llave *f*, interruptor *m*; *(Archit)* clave *f*.

(b) *(Mus)* tonalidad *f*, tono *m*; **major —** tonalidad *f* mayor; **minor —** tonalidad *f* menor; **change of —** cambio *m* de tonalidad; **to be in —** estar a tono, estar templado; **to play off —** desafinar, tocar desafinadamente.

(c) *(fig: to problem, also Bio, Chess)* clave *f* *(to de)*; **the — to the mystery** la clave del misterio.

2 *attr* clave; **— industry** industria *f* clave; **— point** punto *m* clave; **— man** hombre *m* clave; **— question** cuestión *f* principal, cuestión *f* madre.

3 *vt* *(Tech)* enchavetar, acuñar; *(Mus)* templar, afinar; **to — up** emocionar; **to be all —ed up** estar emocionadísimo, tener los nervios en punta.

keyboard ['kiːbɔːd] *n* teclado *m*.

keyhole ['kiːhəul] *n* ojo *m* (de la cerradura).

keynote ['kiːnəut] *n* tónica *f*; *(fig)* tónica *f*, piedra *f* clave, idea *f* fundamental; **— speech** discurso *m* de apertura, discurso *m* en que se sientan las bases de una política *(or programa)*.

key ring ['kiːriŋ] *n* llavero *m*.

keystone ['kiːstəun] *n* piedra *f* clave; *(fig)* piedra *f* angular.

khaki ['kaːki] **1** *n* caqui *m*. **2** *attr* de caqui.

Khartoum [kɑː'tuːm] Jartum.

kibitzer ['kibitsə*] *n* *(US)* mirón *m*, ona *f*.

kibosh ['kaibɔʃ] *n* *(sl)*: **to put the — on something** acabar con algo definitivamente.

kick [kik] **1** *n* patada *f*, puntapié *m* *(also Sport)*; *(by animal)* coz *f*; *(of firearm)* culatazo *m*; *(fig)* reacción *f*; **a drink with a —** to it una bebida muy fuerte; **to do something for —s** hacer algo sólo para disfrutar de la emoción que ello produce, hacer algo sólo para divertirse; **I get a — out of it** esto me entusiasma, encuentro placer en esto.

2 *vt ball etc* dar un puntapié a; golpear (con el pie); *goal* marcar; *person* dar una patada a; *(animal)* dar de coces a; **to — someone's bottom** dar a uno una patada en el culo; **to — a man when he's down** dar a moro muerto gran lanzada; **to — someone downstairs** echar a uno escaleras abajo; **to — someone upstairs** *(fig)* hacer que un miembro de los Comunes pase a serlo de los Lores; **to — one's legs in the air** agitar las piernas; **to — a ball about** divertirse dando patadas a un balón; **to — a ball away** apartar un balón con el pie; **to — someone out** echar a uno a puntapiés, *(fig)* poner a uno de patitas en la calle, expulsar a uno; *see dust, heel etc*.

3 *vi* *(animal)* dar coces, cocear; *(gun)* dar un culatazo, recular; *(fig)* protestar, quejarse; respingar, reaccionar; **it's —ing about somewhere** estará por ahí; **to — off** hacer el saque inicial; **to — out** repartir coces; **to — out for the shore** nadar enérgicamente hacia la playa.

4 *vr*: **I could have —ed myself** me di cuenta de que había hecho el tonto.

kickback ['kikbæk] *n* **(a)** *(Mil)* culatazo *m*. **(b)** *(fig)* reacción *f*, resaca *f*, contragolpe *m*.

kick-off ['kikɔf] *n* saque *m* inicial.

kid [kid] **1** *n* **(a)** *(Zool)* cabrito *m*, a *f*, chivo *m*, a *f*; *(meat)* carne *f* de cabrito; *(skin)* cabritilla *f*.

(b) *(child: fam)* chiquillo *m*, a *f*, chaval *m*, ala *f*; **when I was a —** cuando yo era chaval; **that's —'s stuff** eso es para chicos, son chiquilladas.

2 *attr*: **— gloves** guantes *mpl* de cabritilla; *(fig)* trato *m* muy blando.

3 *vt* *(fam)* tomar el pelo a; **you can't — me** no se me engaña así.

4 *vi* bromearse, chunguear; **I was only —ding** lo decía en broma; **no —ding!** ¡en serio!; **are you —ding?** ¿lo dices en serio?; **are you —ding!** ¡ni hablar!

5 *vr:* **to — oneself** engañarse a sí mismo, vivir engañado; **he —s himself that** se hace creer que; **it's time we stopped —ding ourselves** es hora ya de desengañarnos, es hora ya de despertar a la realidad.

kiddy ['kidi] *n (fam)* chiquillo *m,* a *f.*

kidnap ['kidnæp] *vt* secuestrar, raptar.

kidnapper ['kidnæpə*] *n* secuestrador *m,* ora *f,* raptor *m,* ora *f.*

kidnapping ['kidnæpiŋ] *n* secuestro *m,* rapto *m.*

kidney ['kidni] *n* riñón *m; (fig)* índole *f,* especie *f.*

kidney machine ['kidnimə,ʃiːn] *n* aparato *m* de riñón artificial.

kill [kil] **1** *vt* **(a)** matar; dar muerte a; asesinar; destruir; **he was —ed by savages** le mataron los salvajes, fue muerto por los salvajes; **thou shalt not —** no matarás; **to — off** matar, exterminar.

(b) *(fig) rumour, threat* acabar con; *feeling, hope etc* destruir; *flavour, taste* quitar; *(Parl) bill* ahogar; **this heat is —ing me** este calor acabará conmigo; **the pace is —ing him** se está matando trabajando *(etc)* a tal ritmo.

(c) *(fig)* hacer morir de risa; hacer una impresión irresistible en; **this will — you** vas a morir de risa; **to be dressed to —** ir vestida con muchísima elegancia.

2 *vr:* **to — oneself** matarse; suicidarse; **to — oneself with work** matarse trabajando.

3 *n (Hunting)* pieza *f,* animal *m* matado, *(collectively)* piezas *fpl,* animales *mpl* matados; *(act of —ing)* matanza *f;* **they gathered round for the —** se reunieron para dar el golpe final, cercaron el animal *(etc)* para acabar con él.

killer ['kilə*] *n* matador *m,* ora *f; (murderer)* asesino *m;* **diphtheria used to be a —** antes la difteria mataba a sus víctimas.

killer whale ['kiləweil] *n* orca *f.*

killing ['kiliŋ] **1** *adj disease etc* que mata, mortal; *burden* abrumador; *(ravishing)* irresistible; *(funny)* divertidísimo, muy cómico; **it was —** fue para morirse de risa.

2 *n* matanza *f; (murder)* asesinato *m; (Fin)* éxito *m* financiero; **to make a —** tener un gran éxito financiero.

killingly ['kiliŋli] *adv:* **— funny** divertidísimo; **it was — funny** fue para morirse de risa.

killjoy ['kildʒɔi] *n* aguafiestas *mf.*

kiln [kiln] *n* horno *m.*

kilo ['kiːləu] *n* kilo *m.*

kilocycle ['kiləu,saikl] *n* kilociclo *m.*

kilogramme, *(US)* **—gram** ['kiləugræm] *n* kilo- (gramo) *m.*

kilolitre, *(US)* **—liter** ['kiləu,liːtə*] *n* kilolitro *m.*

kilometre, *(US)* **—meter** ['kiləumiːtə*] *n* kilómetro *m.*

kilometric [,kiləu'metrik] *adj* kilométrico.

kilowatt ['kiləuwɔt] *n* kilovatio *m.*

kilowatt-hours ['kiləuwɔt,auəz] *npl* kilovatios-hora *mpl.*

kilt [kilt] *n* falda *f,* tonelete *m (de los escoceses).*

kimono [ki'məunəu] *n* quimono *m.*

kin [kin] *n* familia *f,* parientes *mpl,* parentela *f;* **next of —** parientes *mpl* más próximos.

kind [kaind] **1** *adj* **(a)** *person* bondadoso, amable, bueno; **you're very —, you're too —** es Vd muy amable; **to be — to someone** ser amable con uno; **please be so — as to** + *infin* tenga la bondad de + *infin;* **would you be so — as to** + *infin?* ¿me hace el favor de + *infin?;* **he was — enough to** + *infin* tuvo la amabilidad de + *infin;* **they were not — to the play in New York** trataron la obra algo duramente en Nueva York; **we must be — to animals** hay que tratar bien los animales.

(b) *act* bueno; *climate* bueno, benigno; *criticism, remark, word* elogioso, comprensivo, favorable; *tone of voice* cariñoso, tierno; *treatment* bueno, blando; **it's very — of you** es Vd muy amable; **that wasn't very — of you** eso me ha parecido algo injusto, en eso fuiste demasiado duro.

2 *n* **(a)** clase *f,* género *m,* especie *f;* **but not that —** pero no de ese tipo, pero no como eso; **he's the —who'll cheat you** él es de los que te engañarán; **to pay in —** pagar en especie, *(fig)* pagar en la misma moneda.

(b) *(a — of)* **a — of** uno a modo de; **he's a — of agent** es algo así como un agente; **I'm not that — of girl** yo no soy de ésas; **he's not that — of person** no es capaz de hacer eso, no es de los que hacen tales

cosas; **I felt a — of pity** sentí algo parecido a la compasión, en cierto modo sentí compasión; **and all that — of thing** y otras cosas por el estilo; **that's the — of thing I mean** eso es precisamente lo que quiero decir; **I don't like that — of talk** no me gusta ese modo de hablar; **what — of book?** ¿qué clase de libro?; **what — of man is he?** ¿qué clase de hombre es?

(c) *(of a —)* **three of a —** tres de la misma especie; **books of all —s** toda clase de libros, libros de toda clase; **it's tea of a —** es té pero bastante inferior, es lo que apenas se puede llamar té; **perfect of its —** perfecto en su línea; **something of the —** algo por el estilo; **nothing of the —!** ¡nada de eso!, ¡ni hablar!

3 *(as adv: fam)* **it's — of awkward** es bastante difícil; **it's — of blue** es más bien azul; **it's — of finished** está más o menos terminado; **aren't you pleased?** **— of** ¿no te alegras? en cierto modo.

kindergarten ['kində,gaːtn] *n* jardín *m* de la infancia.

kind-hearted ['kaind'haːtid] *adj* bondadoso, de buen corazón.

kind-heartedness ['kaind'haːtidnis] *n* bondad *f.*

kindle ['kindl] **1** *vt* encender *(also fig).* **2** *vi* encenderse *(also fig).*

kindliness ['kaindlinis] *n* bondad *f,* benevolencia *f.*

kindling ['kindliŋ] *n* leña *f* menuda, astillas *fpl.*

kindly ['kaindli] **1** *adj* bondadoso, benévolo; *climate etc* bueno, benigno; *remark etc* elogioso, comprensivo, favorable; *tone of voice* cariñoso, tierno; *treatment* bueno, blando.

2 *adv* bondadosamente, amablemente; **he very — helped me** muy amablemente me ayudó; **to take — to something** aceptar algo de buen grado; **he would take it — if you did so** le agradecería que Vd lo hiciese.

(b) **— pass the salt** por favor, pase la sal; **— wait a moment** haga el favor de esperar un momento; **"— pay here"** "se ruega pagar aquí".

kindness ['kaindnis] *n* **(a)** bondad *f,* amabilidad *f,* benevolencia *f;* atención *f,* consideración *f;* **they treated him with every —** le trataron con todo género de consideraciones; **to show — to someone** mostrarse bondadoso con uno.

(b) *(a —)* favor *m;* **to do someone a —** hacer un favor a uno; **it would be a — to tell him** decírselo sería un favor.

kindred ['kindrid] **1** *adj (related by blood)* emparentado; *(fig)* afín, semejante, análogo; **— spirits** espíritus *mpl* afines.

2 *n (relationship)* parentesco *m; (relations)* familia *f,* parientes *mpl.*

kinetic [ki'netik] *adj* cinético.

king [kiŋ] *n* rey *m, (fig, Chess, Cards)* rey *m; (Draughts)* dama *f;* **an oil —** un magnate del petróleo; **the — and queen** los reyes; **the Three K—s** los Reyes, los Reyes Magos; **— of arms** rey *m* de armas; **to live like a —** vivir a cuerpo de rey.

kingcup ['kiŋkʌp] *n* botón *m* de oro.

kingdom ['kiŋdəm] *n* reino *m;* **animal —** reino *m* animal; **plant —** reino *m* vegetal; **till K— come** hasta el Día del Juicio.

kingfisher ['kiŋfiʃə*] *n* martín *m* pescador.

kingly ['kiŋli] *adj* real, regio; digno de un rey.

kingpin ['kiŋpin] *n (Tech)* perno *m* real, perno *m* pinzote; *(fig)* piedra *f* angular, cosa *f* fundamental, persona *f* principal.

kingship ['kiŋʃip] *n* dignidad *f* real, monarquía *f;* **they offered him the —** le ofrecieron el trono.

king-size ['kiŋsaiz] *adj* de tamaño extra.

kink [kiŋk] **1** *n (in rope etc)* coca *f,* enroscadura *f; (in hair)* rizo *m; (in paper etc)* arruga *f,* pliegue *m; (fig)* peculiaridad *f,* manía *f, (sexual)* perversión *f.*

2 *vi* formar cocas *(etc).*

kinky ['kiŋki] *adj* enroscado; rizado, ensortijado; arrugado; *(fig)* peculiar; pervertido.

kinsfolk ['kinzfəuk] *npl* familia *f,* parientes *mpl.*

kinship ['kinʃip] *n (by blood)* parentesco *m; (fig)* afinidad *f,* relación *f.*

kinsman ['kinzmən] *n, pl* **—men** [mən] pariente *m.*

kinswoman ['kinz,wumən] *n, pl* **—women** [,wimin] parienta *f.*

kiosk ['kiːɔsk] *n* quiosco *m; (Tel)* cabina *f.*

kip [kip] *(sl)* **1** *n (lodging)* alojamiento *m; (bed)* cama *f; (sleep)* sueño *m;* **to have a —** dormir un rato.

2 *vi* dormir; **to — down** echarse a dormir.

kipper ['kipə*] *n* arenque *m* ahumado.

kirk [kəːk] *n (Scot)* iglesia *f;* **the K—** la Iglesia (Presbiteriana) de Escocia.

kiss [kis] **1** *n* beso *m; (light touch)* roce *m;* **to blow**

someone a — tirar un beso a uno, dar un beso volado a uno.
2 *vt* besar.
3 *vi*: they —ed se besaron, se dieron un beso; to — and be friends hacer las paces.
kisser ['kisə*] n (*sl*) cara *f*.
kissproof ['kispru:ᶠ adj indeleble.
Kit [kit] *mf nombre cariñoso de* **Catherine** *etc*, **Christopher**.
kit [kit] 1 n (*gear in general*) avíos *mpl*; (*baggage*) equipaje *m*; (*tools*) herramientas *fpl*, herramental *m*; (*first-aid*) botiquín *m*; (*Mil*) equipo *m*.
2 *vt*: to — someone out equipar a uno (*with* de).
kitbag ['kitbæg] n saco *m* de viaje; (*Mil*) saco *m*.
kitchen ['kitʃin] n cocina *f*.
kitchenette [,kitʃi'net] n cocina *f* pequeña.
kitchen garden ['kitʃin'gɑ:dn] n huerto *m*.
kitchen range ['kitʃin'reindʒ] n cocina *f* económica, fogón *m*.
kitchen sink ['kitʃin'siŋk] 1 n fregadero *m*. 2 *attr play etc* ultrarrealista, que tiene por tema la vida de los bajos fondos.
kitchenware ['kitʃinweə*] n batería *f* de cocina.
kite [kait] n (*Orn*) milano *m* real; (*toy*) cometa *f*; to fly a — (*fig*) lanzar una idea para sondear la opinión.
kith [kiθ] n: — and kin parientes *mpl* y amigos.
kitten ['kitn] n gatito *m*, a *f*.
kittenish ['kitəniʃ] adj (*fig*) picaruelo, coquetón.
kittiwake ['kitiweik] n gaviota *f* tridáctila, gavina *f*.
Kitty ['kiti] *f nombre cariñoso de* **Catherine** *etc*.
kitty ['kiti] n (*collection*) colecta *f*, fondo *m*; (*Cards*) puesta *f*, bote *m*, polla *f*; how much have we in the —? ¿cuánto tenemos en el haber?; there's nothing in the — no tenemos dinero alguno.
kiwi ['ki:wi:] n kiwi *m*.
klaxon ['klæksn] n claxon *m*.
kleptomania [,kleptəu'meiniə] n cleptomanía *f*.
kleptomaniac [,kleptəu'meiniæk] n cleptómano *m*, a *f*.
knack [næk] n tino *m*; maña *f*, destreza *f*; truco *m*; it's just a — es un truco que se aprende; to get the — of doing something aprender el modo de hacer algo; to have the — of doing something tener el don de hacer algo; he has a happy — of saying the right thing siempre acierta al escoger la palabra exacta.
knacker ['nækə*] n matarife *m* de caballos.
knapsack ['næpsæk] n mochila *f*.
knave [neiv] n bellaco *m*, bribón *m*; (*Cards*) valet *m*, (*in Spanish pack*) sota *f*.
knavery ['neivəri] n bellaquería *f*.
knavish ['neiviʃ] adj bellaco, bribón, vil.
knead [ni:d] *vt* amasar, sobar; (*fig*) formar.
knee [ni:] 1 n rodilla *f*; on bended —, on one's —s de rodillas; to bow the — to humillarse ante, someterse a; to bring someone to his — someter a uno, humillar a uno; to fall on one's —s, to go down on one's —s arrodillarse, caer de rodillas; to go down on one's —s to someone implorar a uno de rodillas.
2 *vt* dar un rodillazo a.
knee breeches ['ni:,britʃiz] *npl* calzón *m* corto.
kneecap ['ni:kæp] n rótula *f*, choquezuela *f*.
knee-deep ['ni:'di:p] adv: to be — in estar metido hasta las rodillas en; the place was — in paper (*fig*) había montones de papeles por todos lados; to go into the water — avanzar hasta que el agua llegue a las rodillas.
knee-high ['ni:'hai] 1 adv hasta las rodillas; al nivel de las rodillas. 2 adj: — grass hierba *f* que crece hasta la altura de las rodillas.
knee joint ['ni:dʒɔint] n articulación *f* de la rodilla.
kneel [ni:l] (*irr: pret and ptp* knelt) *vi* (a) (*act*) arrodillarse, ponerse de rodillas, hincarse de rodillas (*also* to — down); to — to (*fig*) hincar la rodilla ante.
(b) (*state*) estar de rodillas.
kneepad ['ni:pæd] n rodillera *f*.
knell [nel] n toque *m* de difuntos, doble *m*; it sounded the — of the empire anunció el fin del imperio, presagió el derrumbamiento del imperio.
knelt [nelt] *pret and ptp of* kneel.
knew [nju:] *pret of* know.
knickerbockers ['nikəbɔkəz] *npl* pantalones *mpl* cortos.
knickers ['nikəz] *npl* bragas *fpl*; (*old-fashioned*) pantalones *mpl* de señora.
knick-knack ['niknæk] n chuchería *f*, bujería *f*, baratija *f*.
knife [naif] 1 n, *pl* knives [naivz] cuchillo *m*; (*folding*) navaja *f*; (*Mech*) cuchilla *f*; — and fork (*at table*) cubierto *m*; war to the — guerra *f* a muerte; to have one's — into someone tener inquina a uno; before you can say — en un decir Jesús.
2 *vt* acuchillar.

knife box ['naifbɔks] n portacubiertos *m*.
knife edge ['naifedʒ] n filo *m* (de cuchillo); to be balanced on a — (*fig*) estar pendiente de un hilo.
knife-grinder ['naif,graində*] n amolador *m*, afilador *m*.
knight [nait] 1 n caballero *m*; (*Chess*) caballo *m*. 2 *vt* (*Hist*) armar caballero; (*modern British*) dar el título de Sir a.
knight-errant ['nait'erənt] n caballero *m* andante.
knight-errantry ['nait'erəntri] n caballería *f* andante.
knighthood ['naithud] n (*order*) caballería *f*; (*title*) título *m* de caballero, (*modern British*) título *m* de Sir.
knightly ['naitli] adj caballeroso, caballeresco.
knit [nit] 1 *vt dress* hacer a punto de aguja; *brows* fruncir; to — together (*fig*) juntar, unir.
2 *vi* hacer calceta, hacer media, hacer punto; (*bone*) soldarse; (*fig*) unirse.
knitted ['nitid] adj de punto; — goods géneros *mpl* de punto.
knitting ['nitiŋ] n labor *f* de punto; plain — punto *m* de media; she was doing her — estaba haciendo calceta.
knitting machine ['nitiŋmə,ʃi:n] n máquina *f* de tricotar, tricotosa *f*.
knitting needle ['nitiŋ,ni:dl] n aguja *f* de hacer calceta.
knitwear ['nitweə*] n géneros *mpl* de punto.
knives [naivz] *npl of* knife.
knob [nɔb] n (*natural*) protuberancia *f*, bulto *m*; (*Mech etc*) botón *m*; (*of door*) tirador *m*; (*of stick*) puño *m*; — of sugar terrón *m* de azúcar.
knobbly ['nɔbli] adj, **knobby** ['nɔbi] adj nudoso.
knock [nɔk] 1 n (a) (*blow*) golpe *m*; (*in collision*) choque *m*; (*on door*) llamada *f*; (*Aut*) golpeo *m*; there was a — on the door se llamó a la puerta; he got a — on the head recibió un golpe en la cabeza; to get the — (*sl*) mosquearse, ofenderse; perder la paciencia, ponerse negro.
(b) (*fig*) golpe *m*; the team took a hard — yesterday ayer el equipo recibió un rudo golpe; he can take plenty of hard —s sabe aguantar todos los reveses.
2 *vt* (a) (*strike*) golpear; (*collide with*) chocar contra; (*fam*) criticar, denigrar, hablar mal de; (*Comm*) hacer publicidad en contra de; to — a hole in something abrir a la fuerza un agujero en algo; to — the bottom out of a box desfondar una caja; to — the smile off someone's face hacer que uno deje de sonreír a fuerza de golpes; to — someone on the head golpear a uno en la cabeza; to — one's head on a beam dar con la cabeza contra una viga; to — something to the floor tirar algo violentamente al suelo.
(b) to — someone about pegar a uno, maltratar a uno, (*beat up*) aporrear a uno; the place was badly —ed about el lugar sufrió grandes estragos; the car was rather —ed about el coche sufrió algunos desperfectos; to — back (*sl*) *drink* beberse (de un trago); he can certainly — them back él sí sabe beber; to — down *building* derribar, demoler, echar por tierra; *person* derribar; *pedestrian* atropellar; *argument* destruir; *price* rebajar; to — something down to someone for £5 rematar algo a uno en 5 libras; it was —ed down to the highest bidder se adjudicó al mejor postor; to — in hacer entrar a golpes; *nail* clavar; to — off quitar (de un golpe); (*cause to fall*) hacer caer; (*steal, sl*) birlar, limpiar; (*arrest, sl*) detener; *task* ejecutar prontamente, despachar; *work* terminar, suspender; to — £2 off the price rebajar el precio en 2 libras, descontar 2 libras del precio; to — 3 minutes off the record mejorar la marca en 3 minutos; so we had to — it off (*sl*) así que tuvimos que dejarlo; — it off, will you? (*sl*) ¡déjalo, por Dios!; to — out *person* (*in accident etc*) dejar sin sentido, hacer perder el conocimiento; (*Boxing*) poner fuera de combate, dejar K.O.; *teeth* romper; (*remove*) suprimir, quitar; to — over volcar; *pedestrian* atropellar; to — together construir (*or* componer *etc*) de prisa; to — up *building* construir de prisa, construir toscamente; (*awaken*) llamar, despertar; (*tire*) agotar; (*make pregnant, sl*) dejar encinta; the work —ed him up el trabajo le agotó; he was —ed up for a month el agotamiento le duró un mes.
3 *vi* golpear; (*at door*) llamar a la puerta; (*Aut*) golpear, martillear; he's —ing on 50 (*fam*) va para los 50; to — about vagabundear, andar vagando, rodar; I've —ed about a bit he visto mucho mundo; he's —ing about somewhere estará por ahí; he —s about with some odd friends tiene unas amistades rarísimas; to — against chocar contra, dar contra;

to — into chocar contra; *person* topar; **to — off** suspender el trabajo, terminar, salir del trabajo; **he —s off at 5** sale del trabajo a las 5; **to — up** (*Tennis*) pelotear; **to — up against** chocar contra; *person* topar.

knockabout ['nɔkəbaut] *adj* bullicioso, tumultuoso, confuso; **— comedy** farsa *f* bulliciosa, (*fig*) payasadas *fpl*.

knockdown ['nɔkdaun] *adj:* **— price** precio *m* obsequio.

knocker ['nɔkə*] *n* aldaba *f*; (*fam*) detractor *m*, ora *f*, crítico *m*, a *f*.

knocker-up ['nɔkə'rʌp] *n* despertador *m*.

knocking ['nɔkiŋ] **1** *adj:* **— copy** anuncio *m* destinado a denigrar el producto de otro. **2** *n* golpes *mpl*, golpeo *m*; (*at door*) llamada *f*; (*Aut*) golpeo *m*.

knock-kneed ['nɔk'niːd] *adj* patizambo; (*fig*) débil, irresoluto.

knockout ['nɔkaut] **1** *adj:* **— blow** golpe *m* aplastante, (*Boxing*) K.O. *m*; **— competition** concurso *m* eliminatorio, eliminatoria *f*.
   2 *n* (*Boxing*) knock-out *m*, K.O. *m*; (*competition*) concurso *m* eliminador, eliminatoria *f*; **he's a —!** (*sl*) ¡es la monda!; **she's a —** (*sl*) es una chica estupenda; **it was a real —** (*sl*) fue una noticia (*etc*) sorprendente, la noticia nos pasmó.

knock-up ['nɔkʌp] *n* (*Tennis*) peloteo *m*.

knoll [nəul] *n* otero *m*, montículo *m*.

knot [nɔt] **1** *n* nudo *m* (*also Naut, in wood*); (*bow*) lazo *m*; (*of people*) grupo *m*, corrillo *m*; **Gordian —** nudo *m* gordiano; **to get tied up in —s** anudarse, enmarañarse, (*fig*) armarse un lío, crearse confusiones; **to tie a —** hacer un nudo.
   2 *vt* anudar, atar; **get —ted!** (*sl*) ¡fastídiate!
   3 *vi* anudarse.

knot-hole ['nɔthəul] *n* agujero *m* (que deja un nudo en la madera).

knotty ['nɔti] *adj* nudoso; (*fig*) difícil, complicado, espinoso.

knout [naut] *n* knut *m*.

know [nəu] (*irr: pret* **knew**, *ptp* **known**) **1** *vti* (a) (*general sense*) *fact etc* saber; **to — Japanese** saber japonés; **I —!** ¡ya sé!; **who —s?** ¿quién sabe?; **what do you —?** (*fam*) ¿qué hay de nuevo?; **well, what do you —!** ¡caramba!, ¡cosa más rara!; **how should I —?** ¿yo qué sé?; **to — what's what** saber cuántas son cinco; **it's not easy, you —** mire Vd, esto no es fácil; **there were 7% "don't knows"** un 7 por cien se abstuvo de contestar, un 7 por cien no quisieron opinar; **to — about, to — of** saber de, tener conocimiento de, estar enterado de; **I didn't — about that** no sabía nada de eso, lo ignoraba; **oh, I don't — about that** pues eso no es cierto; ¡hombre, no tanto!; **she —s about cats** ella entiende de gatos; **did you — about John?** ¿has oído lo de Juan?; **I don't — about you!** (*despairing*) ¿qué le vamos a hacer?; **to get to — something** (llegar a) saber algo, enterarse de algo; **we'll let you —** le avisaremos; **why didn't you let me —?** ¿por qué no me avisó Vd?; **afterwards they just don't want to —** después "si te vi no me acuerdo".
   (b) (*be acquainted with*) *person, book, subject etc* conocer; **do you — him?** ¿le conoces?; **do you — Spain?** ¿conoces España?; **to come to — someone**, **to get to — someone** (llegar a) conocer a uno.
   (c) **to — how to +** *infin* saber + *infin*.
   (d) (*recognize*) conocer, reconocer; **to — someone by sight** conocer a uno de vista; **to — someone by** (*or from*) **his walk** conocer a uno por su modo de andar; **I knew him at once** le reconocí en seguida.

(e) **don't I — it!** ¡y tú que me lo dices!; **not if I — it** no será, si puedo evitarlo; *see also* **known**.
   2 *n:* **to be in the —** estar enterado, estar en el secreto.

knowable ['nəuəbl] *adj* conocible.

know-all ['nəuːɔl] *n* sabelotodo *mf*.

know-how ['nəuhau] *n* habilidad *f*, destreza *f*; experiencia *f*; (*expertise*) pericia *f*; **a certain amount of technical —** algunos conocimientos *mpl* técnicos.

knowing ['nəuiŋ] **1** *adj* (*sharp*) astuto, avispado; *look etc* de complicidad, malicioso; **worth —** digno de saberse.
   2 *n:* **there's no —** no hay modo de saberlo; **there's no — what he'll do** es imposible adivinar lo que hará.

knowingly ['nəuiŋli] *adv* (*intentionally*) a sabiendas, adrede; *look etc* maliciosamente, con malicia.

know-it-all ['nəuitɔːl] *n* (*US*) sabelotodo *mf*.

knowledge ['nɔlidʒ] *n* (*knowing*) conocimiento *m*; (*person's range of information*) conocimientos *mpl*, saber *m*; (*learning*) erudición *f*, ciencia *f*; **the advance of —** el progreso de la ciencia; **his — will die with him** morirá su erudición con él; **to my —** según mi leal entender y saber, que yo sepa; **not to my —** que yo sepa; **without my —** sin saberlo yo; **that is common —** eso lo sabe todo el mundo; **his failure is common —** su fracaso es ya del dominio público; **it is common — that** se sabe perfectamente que, es notorio que; **it has come to my — that** he llegado a saber que; **to have a — of Welsh** saber algo de galés; **to have a working — of** dominar los principios esenciales de; **to have a thorough — of** conocer a fondo.

knowledgeable ['nɔlidʒəbl] *adj person* entendido, erudito (*about* en); *remark* erudito.

known [nəun] **1** *ptp* of **know**; **X, — as Y** X, conocido por el nombre de Y; **a product — everywhere** un producto conocido en todas partes; **he is — everywhere** se le conoce en todas partes; **to become —** (*fact*) llegar a saberse, (*person*) llegar a ser conocido; **it became — that** se supo que; **to make oneself —** darse a conocer (*to* a); **to make something — to someone** anunciar algo a uno, hacer que uno se entere de algo; **to make one's wishes —** hacer que se sepa lo que uno desea.
   2 *adj:* **a — thief** un ladrón conocido; **a — expert** un experto reconocido como tal; **the — facts** los hechos establecidos, los hechos ciertos.

knuckle ['nʌkl] **1** *n* nudillo *m*; **to rap someone's —s**, **to rap someone over the —s** echar un rapapolvo a uno.
   2 *vi:* **to — down to something** ponerse a hacer algo con ahínco, dedicarse a algo en serio; **to — under** someterse.

knuckleduster ['nʌkl,dʌstə*] *n* puño *m* de hierro.

knurl [nəːl] **1** *n* nudo *m*, protuberancia *f*; (*of coin*) moleteado *m*. **2** *vt coin* moletear.

knurled [nəːld] *adj* nudoso; *coin* moleteado.

koala [kəuˈɑːlə] *n* coala *f*.

Koran [kɔˈrɑːn] *n* Corán *m*, Alcorán *m*.

Koranic [kɔˈrænik] *adj* coránico, alcoránico.

Korea [kəˈriə] *n* Corea *f*.

Korean [kəˈriən] **1** *adj* coreano. **2** *n* coreano *m*, a *f*.

kosher ['kəuʃə*] *adj* autorizado por la ley judía.

kowtow ['kauˈtau] *vi* (*bow*) saludar humildemente; **to — to someone** humillarse ante uno.

kudos ['kjuːdɔs] *n* gloria *f*, mérito *m*; **he got all the — for it** se atribuyó todo el mérito; **there's no — in it for us** esto no aumentará nuestro prestigio, esto no nos dará más renombre.

L

lab [læb] n (fam) see **laboratory**.
label ['leibl] **1** n etiqueta f, rótulo m, marbete m; (on specimen etc) letrero m; (on book) tejuelo m; (fig) calificación f, designación f, descripción f, clasificación f.
2 vt (a) poner etiqueta a; rotular, poner un letrero a; **it is not clearly —led** la etiqueta no es legible, no hay etiqueta (etc) que lo describa claramente; **every case must be —led** cada maleta ha de llevar una etiqueta.
(b) (fig) calificar (as de), designar (as como), describir (as como); **to — someone as** (fig) tachar a uno de; **he got himself —led a troublemaker** se hizo una reputación de turbulento.
labial ['leibiəl] **1** adj labial. **2** n labial f.
laboratory [lə'bɒrətəri] n laboratorio m.
Labor Day ['leibədei] n (US) Día m del Trabajo (primer lunes de setiembre).
laborious [lə'bɔːriəs] adj penoso; difícil, pesado.
laboriously [lə'bɔːriəsli] adv penosamente, con dificultad.
labour, (US) labor ['leibə*] **1** n (a) (work in general) trabajo m; **Ministry of L—** Ministerio m de Trabajo.
(b) (task) trabajo m, labor f, faena f, tarea f; **a — of love** una tarea muy grata, un trabajo agradable; **—s of Hercules** trabajos mpl de Hércules.
(c) (toil) pena f, fatiga f, esfuerzo m; **after much —** tras grandes esfuerzos.
(d) (Law) **hard —** trabajos mpl forzados; **5 years' hard —** 5 años de trabajos forzados.
(e) (person) obreros mpl, mano f de obra; (as class) clase f obrera; **we are short of —** nos falta mano de obra; **capital and —** el capitalismo y los obreros.
(f) (Pol) **L—** laborismo m, Partido m Laborista.
(g) (Med) parto m, dolores mpl del parto; **to be in —** estar de parto.
2 attr (a) de trabajo; camp de trabajo; conflict, troubles laboral; exchange del trabajo; legislation, union obrero, industrial.
(b) (Pol) party laborista; movement obrero.
3 vt point etc insistir en, machacar en, desarrollar con nimiedad; **I won't — the point** me abstengo de subrayar esto, no hace falta insistir en esto.
4 vi (a) (work) trabajar (at en); **to — in vain** trabajar de balde; **to — to do something** afanarse por hacer algo; **to — under a delusion** estar equivocado; **to — under difficulties** trabajar en condiciones difíciles.
(b) (move etc) moverse penosamente, avanzar con dificultad; **to — up a hill** subir penosamente una cuesta; **the engine is —ing** el motor no funciona bien.
laboured, (US) labored ['leibəd] adj breathing fatigoso; movement torpe, lento, penoso; style pesado, premioso.
labourer, (US) laborer ['leibərə*] n (on roads etc) peón m; (farm —) labriego m, bracero m, peón m; (day —) jornalero m; **bricklayer's —** peón m de albañil.
labouring, (US) laboring ['leibəriŋ] adj class obrero.
labourite, (US) laborite ['leibərait] n (pej) laborista mf.
labour-saving, (US) labor-saving ['leibə,seiviŋ] adj que ahorra trabajo.
laburnum [lə'bɜːnəm] n lluvia f de oro, codeso m.
labyrinth ['læbərinθ] n laberinto m.
labyrinthine [,læbə'rinθain] adj laberíntico.
lac [læk] n laca f.
lace [leis] **1** n (open fabric) encaje m, (as trimming) puntilla f; (of shoe, corset) cordón m; (of gold, silver) galón m.
2 vt (Sew) guarnecer con encajes (etc); shoe etc atar, atar el cordón de (also **to — up**); drink echar

licor a; **a drink —d with brandy** una bebida reforzada con coñac.
3 vi: **to — into someone** (sl) dar una paliza a uno.
lacerate ['læsəreit] vt lacerar; feelings etc herir.
laceration [,læsə'reiʃən] n laceración f.
lachrymose ['lækriməus] adj lacrimoso, lloroso.
lack [læk] **1** n falta f, ausencia f, carencia f; escasez f; **for — of, through — of** por falta de; **there is a grave — of water** nos hace muchísima falta el agua; **there is no — of money** no es que falte dinero.
2 vt no tener; carecer de, necesitar; **we — time to do it** nos falta tiempo para hacerlo; **we're —ing 3 players to make up a team** nos hacen falta 3 jugadores para completar el equipo; **he does not — talent** no carece de aptitud, es cierto que tiene aptitud; **what is it that you —?** ¿qué es lo que necesitas?; **he —s confidence** no tiene confianza en sí mismo.
3 vi (a) **to be —ing** faltar, estar ausente, no haber; **but money is —ing** pero no hay dinero, pero falta el dinero; **nothing was —ing to make the play succeed** no faltaba nada para que la obra obtuviera un éxito; **where decency is —ing** donde falta la decencia.
(b) **he is —ing in confidence** no tiene confianza en sí mismo, le falta confianza en sí mismo; **it's not that he's —ing in good qualities** no es que le falten buenas cualidades.
lackadaisical [,lækə'deizikəl] adj lánguido, indiferente; (dreamy) ensimismado, despistado, distraído; (slow) perezoso, tardo; (careless) descuidado, informal.
lackey ['læki] n lacayo m; (fig) secuaz m servil.
lacking ['lækiŋ] as prep sin, no teniendo, en ausencia de; desprovisto de.
lacklustre, (US) lackluster ['læk,lʌstə*] adj surface deslustrado, deslucido; style etc inexpresivo; eyes apagado; person pesado, soso.
laconic [lə'kɒnik] adj lacónico.
laconically [lə'kɒnikəli] adv lacónicamente.
lacquer ['lækə*] **1** n laca f, maque m, pintura f al duco. **2** vt laquear, maquear, pintar al duco.
lacquered ['lækəd] adj barnizado con laca, laqueado, pintado al duco.
lacrosse [lə'krɒs] n lacrosse f.
lactate ['lækteit] vi lactar.
lactation [læk'teiʃən] n lactancia f.
lacteal ['læktiəl] adj lácteo.
lactic ['læktik] adj láctico.
lactose ['læktəus] n lactosa f.
lacuna [lə'kjuːnə] n, pl **lacunae** [lə'kjuːniː] laguna f.
lacustrine [lə'kʌstrain] adj lacustre.
lacy ['leisi] adj (of lace) de encaje; (like lace) parecido a encaje; (fig) transparente, diáfano.
lad [læd] n muchacho m, chico m; (country —) mozo m, zagal m; (in stable etc) mozo m; **young —** muchacho m, mozalbete m; **when I was a —** cuando yo era chaval; **he's only a —** es muy joven; **don't do that, —!** ¡no hagas eso, joven!; **come on, —s!** ¡vamos, muchachos!; **all together, —s!** ¡todos juntos, muchachos!; **he's a bit of a —** es un chico poco formal; es un tipo muy divertido; **he's a bit of a — with the girls** les da guerra a las chicas, se bromea mucho con las chicas.
ladder ['lædə*] **1** n (a) escalera f (de mano), escala f; (in stocking) carrera f; **folding —** escala f plegable; **rope —** escala f de cuerda.
(b) (fig) camino m, escalón m (to de); **social —** escala f social; **it's a first step up the —** es el primer paso hacia el éxito; **to be at the top of the —** estar en la cumbre de su profesión (etc), ocupar el rango más alto.
2 vt stocking hacer una carrera en.
3 vi (stocking) hacerse una carrera, desmallarse.

ladderproof ['lædəpruːf] *adj stocking* indesmallable.

laddie ['lædi] *n* (*fam*) = lad.

lade [leid] (*irr: pret* laded, *ptp* laden) 1 *vt* cargar (*with* de). 2 *vi* tomar cargamento.

laden ['leidn] *ptp of* lade; — with cargado de.

la-di-da ['lɑːdiˈdɑː] (*fam*) 1 *adj* afectado, repipi (*fam*). 2 *adv talk etc* de manera afectada, con afectación.

lading ['leidiŋ] *n* cargamento *m*, flete *m*.

ladle ['leidl] 1 *n* cucharón *m*, cazo *m*. 2 *vt* (*also to — out*) servir (*or* sacar *etc*) con cucharón; (*fig*) repartir generosamente, distribuir a manos llenas.

ladleful ['leidlful] *n* cucharón *m*, contenido *m* de un cucharón.

lady ['leidi] 1 *n* señora *f*; (*aged, distinguished, noble*) dama *f*; "**Ladies**" (*lavatory*) "Señoras"; **ladies and gentlemen!** ¡señoras y señores!; — **of the house** señora *f* de la casa; **the minister and his** — el ministro y su esposa; **your good** — su esposa; **First L**— (*US*) primera dama *f*; **leading** — primera actriz *f*; **Our L**— Nuestra Señora *f*; **young** — señorita *f*, joven *f*; **his young** — su novia *f*; **she's no** — esa mujer no es lo que aparenta, es una mujer que tiene historia; **shall we join the ladies?** ¿pasamos a estar con las señoras?

    2 *attr etc* (a) — **doctor** médica *f*; — **mayoress** alcaldesa *f*; —**'s cycle** bicicleta *f* de señora; **ladies' room** lavabo *m* de señoras.

    (b) **L**— **Chapel** capilla *f* de la Virgen; **L**— **Day** día *m* de la Anunciación (25 *marzo*).

ladybird ['leidibɜːd] *n*, (*US*) **ladybug** ['leidibʌg] *n* mariquita *f*, vaca *f* de San Antón.

lady-in-waiting ['leidiin'weitiŋ] *n* dama *f* de honor.

ladykiller ['leidiˌkilə*] *n* tenorio *m*, ladrón *m* de corazones.

ladylike ['leidilaik] *adj* elegante, fino, distinguido, bien educado; (*pej*) afeminado.

lady-love ['leidilʌv] *n* amada *f*.

ladyship ['leidiʃip] *n*: **Her** —, **Your L**— Su Señoría.

lag¹ [læg] 1 *n* retraso *m*.

    2 *vi* (*also to — behind*) retrasarse; (*in pace*) rezagarse, quedarse atrás; **Ruritania —s behind Slobodia** Ruritania anda a rastras detrás de Eslobodia, Ruritania no ha hecho tantos progresos como Eslobodia; **we — behind in space exploration** nos hemos retrasado en la exploración espacial, no destacamos en la exploración espacial.

lag² [læg] *vt* (*Tech*) revestir, recubrir, forrar (*with* de); *boiler* calorifugar.

lag³ [læg] (*sl*) 1 *n* (*also old* —) presidiario *m*. 2 *vt* encarcelar.

lager ['lɑːgə*] *n* cerveza *f* tipo Pilsen.

laggard ['lægəd] *n* (*having fallen behind*) rezagado *m*, a *f*; (*idler*) holgazán *m*, ana *f*.

lagging ['lægiŋ] *n* (*Tech*) revestimiento *m*, forro *m*.

lagoon [lə'guːn] *n* laguna *f*.

laicize ['leisaiz] *vt* laicizar.

laid [leid] *pret and ptp of* lay; **to be — up** (*Med*) estar enfermo, tener que guardar cama (*with* a causa de); (*car etc*) estar fuera de circulación, estar en garaje.

lain [lein] *ptp of* lie².

lair [leə*] *n* cubil *m*, guarida *f*.

laird [lɛəd] *n* (*Scot*) señor *m*; terrateniente *m*, propietario *m*.

laissez-faire ['leisei'fɛə*] *n* laissez-faire *m*.

laity ['leiiti] *n* laicado *m*, legos *mpl*.

lake¹ [leik] *n* (*colour*) laca *f*.

lake² [leik] *n* (*Geog*) lago *m*.

Lake District ['leikˌdistrikt] País *m* de los Lagos.

lake dwelling ['leikˌdweliŋ] *n* habitación *f* lacustre.

lam [læm] (*sl*) 1 *vt* pegar, dar una paliza a. 2 *vi*: **to — into someone** dar una paliza a uno.

lama ['lɑːmə] *n* lama *m*.

lamb [læm] 1 *n* cordero *m*, a *f*; (*older*) borrego *m*, a *f*; (*meat*) carne *f* de cordero; **the L**— **of God** el Cordero de Dios; **my poor** —! ¡pobrecito!; **he took it like a** — recibió la noticia con la mayor tranquilidad, no se ofendió en lo más mínimo.

    2 *vi* parir (*la oveja*).

lambast(e) [læm'beist] *vt* dar una paliza a; (*fig*) poner como un trapo.

lamb chop ['læm'tʃɔp] *n* chuleta *f* de cordero.

lamb-like ['læmlaik] *adj* manso como un cordero.

lambskin ['læmskin] *n* corderina *f*, piel *f* de cordero.

lamb's wool ['læmzwul] *n* lana *f* de cordero, añinos *mpl*.

lame [leim] 1 *adj* (a) cojo, lisiado; **to be** — (*permanently*) ser cojo, (*temporarily*) estar cojo; **to be** — **in one foot** ser cojo de un pie, cojear de un pie; **to go** — estropearse un pie, lisiarse un pie, empezar a cojear.

    (b) (*fig*) *excuse* débil, poco convincente; *argument* flojo; (*Lit*) *metre* defectuoso, que cojea.

    2 *vt* lisiar, hacer cojo; incapacitar.

lamely ['leimli] *adv walk etc* cojeando; *argue, say etc* sin convicción.

lameness ['leimnis] *n* cojera *f*; incapacidad *f*; (*fig*) falta *f* de convicción; flojedad *f*.

lament [lə'ment] 1 *n* lamento *m*; queja *f*; (*Lit etc*) elegía *f* (*for* por).

    2 *vt* lamentar, lamentarse de; **to — someone** llorar a uno, llorar la pérdida de uno; **it is much to be —ed that . . .** es de lamentar que + *subj*.

    3 *vi* lamentarse (*for, over* de).

lamentable ['læməntəbl] *adj* lamentable.

lamentably ['læməntəbli] *adv* lamentablemente.

lamentation [ˌlæmən'teiʃən] *n* lamentación *f*.

laminated ['læmineitid] *adj* laminado; *glass* inastillable; — **wood** contrachapado *m*.

lamp [læmp] *n* lámpara *f*; linterna *f*; (*in street*) farol *m*; (*Aut, Rail etc*) faro *m*; (*bulb*) bombilla *f*; (*fig*) antorcha *f*; **desk** — lámpara *f* de escritorio; **standard** — lámpara *f* de pie; **rear** — faro *m* trasero.

lampblack ['læmpblæk] *n* negro *m* de humo.

lamp bracket ['læmpˌbrækit] *n* brazo *m* de lámpara.

lamp chimney ['læmpˌtʃimni] *n*, **lamp glass** ['læmpglɑːs] *n* tubo *m* de lámpara.

lampholder ['læmpˌhəuldə*] *n* portalámpara *m*.

lamplight ['læmplait] *n* luz *f* de (la) lámpara; **by** —, **in the** — a la luz de la lámpara.

lamplighter ['læmpˌlaitə*] *n* farolero *m*.

lampoon [læm'puːn] 1 *n* pasquín *m*, sátira *f*. 2 *vt* pasquinar, satirizar.

lamppost ['læmppəust] *n* (poste *m* de) farol *m*, farola *f*.

lamprey ['læmpri] *n* lamprea *f*.

lampshade ['læmpʃeid] *n* pantalla *f* (de lámpara).

lance [lɑːns] 1 *n* lanza *f*. 2 *vt* alancear, herir con lanza; (*Med*) abrir con lanceta.

lance corporal ['lɑːns'kɔːpərəl] *n* soldado *m* de primera.

Lancelot ['lɑːnslət] *m* Lanzarote.

lancer ['lɑːnsə*] *n* lancero *m*; —**s** (*dance*) lanceros *mpl*.

lancet ['lɑːnsit] *n* lanceta *f*; — **arch** ojiva *f* aguda; — **window** ventana *f* ojival.

land [lænd] 1 *n* (*in most senses*) tierra *f*; (*nation*) país *m*; (*region*) tierra *f*, región *f*; (*soil*) tierra *f*, suelo *m*; (*as property*) tierras *fpl*, finca *f*; (*tract of* —) terreno *m*; (*Agr, fig*) campo *m*, agricultura *f*, *eg* **the drift from the** — la despoblación del campo, el éxodo rural; **he went on the** — se dedicó a la agricultura; **arable** — tierra *f* de labrantío; **cultivated** — tierras *fpl* cultivadas; **dry** — (*infertile*) tierra *f* de secano, (*not sea*) tierra *f* firme; **irrigated** — tierra *f* de regadío; **native** — patria *f*; — **of milk and honey** paraíso *m* terrenal, jauja *f*; — **of promise, promised** — tierra *f* de promisión; **back to the** —! ¡a cultivar la tierra! (*campaña de tiempos de guerra*); **by** — por tierra, por vía terrestre; **on** — en tierra; **to live off the** — (*army etc*) vivir sobre el país; **to see how the** — **lies** tantear el terreno, hacer un reconocimiento.

    2 *attr breeze etc* de tierra; *defences, forces, route* terrestre; *law, question, reform* agrario; *see agent etc*.

    3 *vt* (a) *person, goods, fish at port etc* desembarcar.

    (b) *fish on hook* pescar, coger, sacar del agua, traer a la orilla; (*fig: obtain*) conseguir, lograr; *prize* obtener, ganar, sacar; *job* conseguir.

    (c) *plane* poner en tierra.

    (d) *blow* dar, asestar (*on* en).

    (e) (*place*) **it —ed him in debt** le hizo contraer deudas; **it —ed him in jail** por ello acabó en la cárcel; **it —ed me in a mess** me puso en un apuro, me creó un lío; **I got —ed with the job** yo tuve que cargar con el cometido; **I got —ed with him for 2 hours** yo tuve que acompañarle durante 2 horas.

    4 *vi* (a) (*from ship*) desembarcar (*at* en).

    (b) (*Aer*) aterrizar, tomar tierra; (*on sea*) amerizar, amarar; (*on moon*) alunizar; (*of bird, insect*) posar(se).

    (c) (*hit, strike*) dar en, hacer blanco en; **the hat —ed in my lap** el sombrero cayó sobre mis rodillas; **it —ed square on the target** dio de lleno en el blanco; **the bomb —ed on the building** la bomba hizo blanco en el edificio; **the blow —ed on his cheek** el golpe le dio en la mejilla; **to — on one's feet** caer de pies; **to — on one's head** caer de cabeza; **where did it** —? ¿dónde fue a parar?

    (d) (*fig*) llegar; terminar; **to — up at Wigan** llegar (inesperadamente) a Wigan, ir a parar a Wigan; **to — up in a dreadful mess** terminar haciéndose un tremendo lío; **to — up with only £2** acabar con sólo 2 libras.

landau ['lændɔː] *n* landó *m*.

landed ['lændid] *adj person* hacendado, que posee tierras; *property* que consiste en tierras; — **gentry** terratenientes *mpl*, pequeña aristocracia *f* rural; — **property** bienes *mpl* raíces.

landfall ['lændfɔːl] *n (Naut)* aterrada *f*.

landholder ['lænd,həuldə*] *n* terrateniente *m*.

landing ['lændiŋ] *n* **(a)** *(Naut: of person)* desembarco *m*, *(of goods)* desembarque *m*.
(b) *(Aer)* aterrizaje *m*; *(on sea)* amerizaje *m*; *(on moon)* alunizaje *m*; *(descent)* descenso *m*; **crash** — aterrizaje *m* violento; **emergency** —, **forced** — aterrizaje *m* forzoso; **pancake** — aterrizaje *m* de panza; **hard** — aterrizaje *m* duro; **soft** — aterrizaje *m* suave.
(c) *(of stairs)* descanso *m*, rellano *m*.

landing craft ['lændiŋkrɑːft] *n* barcaza *f* (*or* lancha *f*) de desembarco.

landing gear ['lændiŋgiə*] *n* tren *m* de aterrizaje.

landing ground ['lændiŋgraund] *n* campo *m* de aterrizaje.

landing net ['lændiŋnet] *n* salabardo *m*, manga *f*, cuchara *f*.

landing run ['lændiŋrʌn] *n* recorrido *m* de aterrizaje.

landing stage ['lændiŋsteidʒ] *n* desembarcadero *m*.

landing strip ['lændiŋstrip] *n* pista *f* de aterrizaje.

landing wheels ['lændiŋwiːlz] *npl* ruedas *fpl* de aterrizaje.

landlady ['lænd,leidi] *n* *(owner)* dueña *f*; *(of boarding house)* patrona *f*; *(of flat)* propietaria *f*.

landless ['lændlis] *adj peasant etc* sin tierras, que no posee tierras.

landlocked ['lændlɒkt] *adj* cercado de tierra.

landlord ['lændlɔːd] *n (of property, land)* propietario *m*, dueño *m*; *(of boarding house)* patrón *m*; *(of flat)* casero *m*; *(of inn)* posadero *m*, mesonero *m*; *(of pub)* patrón *m*.

landlubber ['lænd,lʌbə*] *n* marinero *m* de agua dulce, hombre *m* de tierra.

landmark ['lændmɑːk] *n* **(a)** *(Naut)* marca *f*, señal *f* fija; *(boundary mark)* mojón *m*; *(high place)* punto *m* destacado; *(well-known thing)* lugar *m* muy conocido.
(b) **to be a** — *(fig)* hacer época, formar época, marcar un hito histórico.

landmine ['lændmain] *n* mina *f* terrestre.

landowner ['lænd,əunə*] *n* terrateniente *m*, hacendado *m*.

landscape ['lænskeip] **1** *n* paisaje *m*. **2** *vt park etc* reformar artísticamente, *terrain* convertir en parque.

landscape gardening ['lænskeip'gɑːdniŋ] *n* arquitectura *f* de jardines.

landslide ['lændslaid] *n* corrimiento *m* de tierras, desprendimiento *m* de tierras; *(Pol)* victoria *f* electoral arrolladora; **the Liberal** — **of 1906** la victoria arrolladora de los liberales en 1906.

landslip ['lændslip] *see* **landslide**.

land tax ['lændtæks] *n* contribución *f* territorial.

landward ['lændwəd] *adj* de hacia tierra, de la parte de la tierra; **on the** — **side** en el lado de la tierra.

landward(s) ['lændwədz] *adv* hacia tierra; **to** — en la dirección de la tierra.

lane [lein] *n (in country)* camino *m* vecinal, vereda *f*; *(in town)* callejón *m*; *(between plantations)* vereda *f*; *(Sport)* calle *f*, banda *f*; *(Aut)* senda *f*, carril *m*; **shipping** — ruta *f* de navegación.

language ['læŋgwidʒ] *n (faculty of speech, mode of speech, style)* lenguaje *m*; *(national tongue)* lengua *f*, idioma *m*; **bad** — lenguaje *m* indecente; palabrotas *fpl*, tacos *mpl*; **to use bad** — ser mal hablado; **strong** — palabras *fpl* mayores; **that's no** — **to use to your mother!** ¡así no se habla a tu madre!

languid ['læŋgwid] *adj* lánguido.

languidly ['læŋgwidli] *adv* lánguidamente.

languidness ['læŋgwidnis] *n* languidez *f*.

languish ['læŋgwiʃ] *vi* languidecer; *(in prison)* pudrirse; *(pine)* consumirse *(for* por); *(amorously)* ponerse sentimental.

languishing ['læŋgwiʃiŋ] *adj* lánguido; *look, tone etc* amoroso, sentimental.

languor ['læŋgə*] *n* languidez *f*.

languorous ['læŋgərəs] *adj* lánguido.

lank [læŋk] *adj person* alto y flaco; *hair* lacio; *grass* largo.

lanky ['læŋki] *adj* larguirucho.

lanolin(e) ['lænəulin] *n* lanolina *f*.

lantern ['læntən] *n* linterna *f* (*also Archit*); *(Naut)* faro *m*, farol *m*; *(of lighthouse)* fanal *m*; **Chinese** — farolillo *m*.

lantern-jawed ['læntən'dʒɔːd] *adj* chupado de cara.

lantern lecture ['læntən,lektʃə*] *n* conferencia *f* con proyecciones.

lantern slide ['læntənslaid] *n* diapositiva *f*.

lanyard ['lænjəd] *n* acollador *m*.

Laos [laus] Laos *m*.

Laotian ['lauʃiən] **1** *adj* laosiano. **2** *n* laosiano *m*, a *f*.

lap[1] [læp] **1** *n (Anat)* regazo *m*; *(knees)* rodillas *fpl*; *(skirt)* falda *f*; *(fig)* seno *m*; *(overlap)* traslapo *m*, solapa *f*; **to sit on someone's** — *(woman's)* estar sentado en el regazo (*or* en el halda) de una, *(man's)* estar sentado en las rodillas de uno; **it's in the** — **of the gods** está en manos de los dioses; **to live in the** — **of luxury** vivir en el mayor lujo, tener una vida muy regalada.
2 *vt (overlap)* traslapar; *(wrap)* envolver *(in* en; *also fig)*; **to** — **something about with** cercar algo de, *(fig)* envolver algo en.
3 *vi (overlap)* traslaparse.

lap[2] [læp] *(Sport)* **1** *n (round)* vuelta *f*; *(stage)* etapa *f*, fase *f*; — **of honour** vuelta *f* de honor; **we're on the last** — **now** *(fig)* ésta es la última etapa, hemos vencido la cuesta ya.
2 *vt*: **to** — **someone** aventajar a uno en una vuelta entera.
3 *vi*: **to** — **at 90 m.p.h.** hacer una vuelta a 90 m.p.h.

lap[3] [læp] **1** *n (lick)* lamedura *f*, lametada *f*; *(of waves)* chapaleteo *m*.
2 *vt* **(a)** *(lick)* lamer; **to** — **up** beber con la lengua, *(swallow)* tragar; **to** — **up** *(fig)* aceptar con entusiasmo, absorber, aprender con facilidad *(etc)*.
(b) *(of water)* estar al nivel de, correr tan alto como.
3 *vi (waves)* chapalear; **to** — **against** besar, tocar, lamer; **to** — **over** desbordarse, irse, salir fuera.

lapdog ['læpdɒg] *n* perro *m* faldero.

lapel [lə'pel] *n* solapa *f*.

lapis lazuli ['læpis'læzjulai] *n* lapislázuli *m*.

Lapland ['læplænd] Laponia *f*.

Laplander ['læplændə*] *n*, **Lapp** [læp] *n* lapón *m*, ona *f*.

lapping ['læpiŋ] *n (of water)* chapaleteo *m*.

lapse [læps] **1** *n* **(a)** *(error)* error *m*, equivocación *f*; *(moral)* desliz *m*, falta *f*; lapso *m*; *(relapse)* recaída *f* *(into* en); **a strange** — un extraño error.
(b) *(of time)* intervalo *m*, periodo *m*, lapso *m*; **after a** — **of 4 months** después de un período de 4 meses, al cabo de 4 meses.
2 *vi* **(a)** *(err)* caer en el error, equivocarse; *(morally)* cometer un desliz; *(relapse)* recaer, reincidir *(into* en); **to** — **from duty** faltar a su deber; **to** — **into one's old ways** volver a las andadas, volver a las malas costumbres; **he** —**d into the vernacular** volvió a hablar en la lengua vernácula; **he** —**d into silence** se calló, quedó callado, no dijo más.
(b) *(expire)* caducar; *(cease to exist)* dejar de existir, desaparecer.
(c) *(time)* pasar, transcurrir.

lapwing ['læpwiŋ] *n* avefría *f*.

larboard ['lɑːbəd] **1** *adj* de babor. **2** *n* babor *m*.

larceny ['lɑːsəni] *n* latrocinio *m*; **grand** — *(US)* robo *m* de cantidad importante; **petty** — robo *m* de menor cuantía *f*.

larch [lɑːtʃ] *n* alerce *m* *(also* **larch tree**).

lard [lɑːd] **1** *n* manteca *f* (de cerdo), lardo *m*. **2** *vt (Cook)* lardear, mechar; *(fig)* **to** — **something with** adornar algo de, salpicar algo de, sembrar algo de.

larder ['lɑːdə*] *n* despensa *f*.

lardy ['lɑːdi] *adj* mantecoso.

large [lɑːdʒ] **1** *adj* **(a)** grande; *packet etc* abultado, voluminoso; *interests* extenso; *powers* amplio, extenso; *sum* importante; *family* numeroso; *(main, chief)* principal; **as** — **as life** de tamaño natural; **there he was as** — **as life** ahí estaba en persona; **there it was as** — **as life** allí se nos apareció de modo inconfundible.
(b) **ambassador at** — embajador *m* volante (que no está acreditado permanentemente en ningún país); **people at** — la gente en general; **the world at** — el mundo en general; **to be at** — estar en libertad.
2 *adv see* **by**.

largely ['lɑːdʒli] *adv* en su mayor parte, en gran parte.

largeness ['lɑːdʒnis] *n* gran tamaño *m*; lo abultado *(etc)*; extensión *f*; importancia *f*; lo numeroso.

larger ['lɑːdʒə*] *adj comp of* **large**; más grande, mayor; **to grow** — crecer; aumentar(se); **to make** — hacer más grande; aumentar; *premises etc* ampliar, ensanchar.

large-scale ['lɑːdʒ'skeil] *adj* en gran escala.

large-sized ['lɑːdʒ'saizd] *adj* de gran tamaño, de tamaño extra.

largesse [lɑː'ʒes] *n* generosidad *f*, liberalidad *f*; *(gift)* dádiva *f* espléndida.

largo ['lɑːgəu] *n (Mus)* largo *m*.

lariat ['læriət] *n* lazo *m*.

lark¹ [lɑːk] *n* (Orn) alondra *f*; **to get up with the —** levantarse con las gallinas, madrugar; *see* **happy**.

lark² [lɑːk] **1** *n* (a) (*spree*) juerga *f*; **to go on a —** ir de juerga.

(b) (*joke etc*) broma *f*, travesura *f*; **that's a —!,** **what a —!** ¡qué bien!, ¡qué risa!; **that was a —!** ¡cómo nos reímos con aquello!; **isn't he a —?** ¿es célebre, no?; **to do something for a —** hacer algo para divertirse, divertirse haciendo algo; **to have a —** **with someone** gastar una broma a uno, tomar el pelo a uno.

(c) (*business, affair*) **that ice-cream —** ese asunto de los helados; **the Suez —** la fiestecita de Suez; **this dinner-jacket —** esta costumbre tan estúpida de ponerse un smoking.

2 *vi* (*be on a spree*) andar de jarana; (*amuse oneself*) divertirse; **to — about** hacer travesuras, gastarse bromas, divertirse tontamente; **stop —ing about!** ¡quieto!; **to — about with something** (*play*) divertirse con algo, jugar con algo, (*damage*) estropear algo, manosear algo.

larkspur ['lɑːkspɔː*] *n* espuela *f* de caballero.
larky ['lɑːki] *adj* (*fam*) guasón, bromista.
larva ['lɑːvə] *n*, *pl* **larvae** ['lɑːviː] larva *f*.
laryngitis [ˌlærin'dʒaitis] *n* laringitis *f*.
larynx ['læriŋks] *n* laringe *f*.
lascivious [lə'siviəs] *adj* lascivo.
lasciviously [lə'siviəsli] *adv* lascivamente.
lasciviousness [lə'siviəsnis] *n* lascivia *f*.
lash [læʃ] **1** *n* (a) (*whip*) látigo *m*, (*used for punishment*) azote *m*; (*thong*) tralla *f*; (Anat) pestaña *f*.

(b) (*stroke*) latigazo *m*, (*as punishment*) azote *m*; (*of tail*) coletazo *m*; **the — of the rain** el azote de la lluvia; **the — of the waves** el azote de las olas; **under the — of the Nazis** bajo el azote de los nazis.

2 *vt* (a) (*beat etc*) azotar, dar latigazos a, fustigar; *tail* agitar; (*of hail, rain, waves*) azotar; (*fig: criticize*) fustigar, dar una paliza a, increpar; **he was —ing the horse along** le daba duramente al caballo con el látigo; **the wind —ed the trees** el viento azotaba los árboles; **the wind —ed the sea into a fury** el viento levantaba enormes olas; **to — someone with one's tongue** increpar duramente a uno; **to — someone into a fury** provocar a uno hasta la furia.

(b) (*tie*) atar, (Naut) trincar, amarrar (*to* a); **to — down** sujetar, atar firmemente.

(c) (*fam*) **he had to — out £5** tuvo que pagar 5 libras (de mala gana), tuvo que desembolsar 5 libras; **they were —ing out the drink** estaban sirviendo las bebidas en grandes cantidades.

3 *vi* (a) **to — out** (*with fists*) repartir golpes a diestro y siniestro, dar golpes furiosos sin mirar a quién; (*with feet*) tirar coces.

(b) (*fam*) **to — out** desdinerarse, pagar; repartir dinero generosamente; **now we can really — out** ahora sí podemos gastar dinero; **he —ed out and bought himself a Rolls** dejó de economizar y se compró un Rolls.

(c) **to — out at** censurar enérgicamente, criticar duramente.

4 *vr*: **to — oneself into a fury** montar en cólera.
lashing ['læʃiŋ] *n* (a) (*beating*) azotamiento *m*, azotes *mpl*. (b) (*tie*) atadura *f*, (Naut) trinca *f*, amarradura *f*. (c) **—s** (*fam*) montones *mpl*.
lass [læs] *n* muchacha *f*, chica *f*, joven *f*; (*country-*) moza *f*, zagala *f*.
lassie ['læsi] *n* (*fam*) = **lass**.
lassitude ['læsitjuːd] *n* lasitud *f*.
lasso [læ'suː] **1** *n* lazo *m*. **2** *vt* lazar, coger con el lazo.
last¹ [lɑːst] **1** *adj* último; final; extremo; *week, month etc* pasado; **— Monday, on Monday —** el lunes pasado; **— night** anoche; **the night before —** anteanoche; **the year before —** el año antepasado; **the — trick but one** la penúltima baza; **the — trick but 3** la tercera baza antes de la última; **during the — 20 years** en los últimos 20 años; **it has not been seen these — 3 years** hace 3 años que no se le ve por aquí; **to be the — (one) to do something** ser el último en hacer algo; **to be — but not least** ser el último pero no el peor; **that's the — thing to worry about** eso es lo de menos; **that was the — thing I expected** eso era lo último que yo esperaba; **you're the — person to be entrusted with it** tú eres el menos indicado para hacerse cargo de ello.

2 *n* último *m*, a *f*, última cosa *f*, lo último; (*end*) fin *m*; **each one better than the —** cada uno mejor que el anterior (*or* precedente); **my — mi** última carta; **at — por** fin; **at long — al** fin y al cabo; **to the — hasta** el fin; **this is the — of it** éste es el último de la serie (*etc*), con éste terminamos,

después de éste no quedan más; **that was the — we saw of him** no le volvimos a ver; **I shall be glad to see the — of this** estoy deseando que termine esto; **to breathe one's — exhalar** el último suspiro; **we shall never hear the — of it** no nos dejarán en paz nunca; **to look one's — on something** ver algo por última vez, despedirse de algo (antes de su desaparición).

3 *adv* por último; en último lugar; por última vez; finalmente; **to arrive — llegar** el último; **the horse came in — el** caballo llegó el último, el caballo ocupó el último puesto en la clasificación; **when I — saw him** cuando le vi por última vez.

last² [lɑːst] **1** *vt*: **it —ed me a lifetime** me duró toda la vida; **the car has —ed me 8 years** el coche sigue siéndome útil después de 8 años; **I can — you out any time** de todos modos yo resisto mejor que tú; **he —ed all his colleagues out** sobrevivió a todos sus colegas.

2 *vi* durar; perdurar; permanecer, resistir; sostenerse, mantenerse; (*continue*) continuar, seguir; (*cloth etc*) ser duro, ser resistente; **it —s 2 hours** dura 2 horas; **it can't — no** puede seguir así; **things are too good to — las** cosas van demasiado bien para seguir así; **will this material —?** ¿es resistente este paño?; **he won't — long in this job** no resistirá mucho tiempo en este puesto; **the previous boss —ed only a week** el jefe anterior permaneció solamente una semana en el puesto; **to — out** resistir, continuar; (*money, resources*) durar, llegar; **can you — out another mile?** ¿puedes hacer una milla más?; **I can't — out** no puedo más, no resisto más; **my money doesn't — out the month** el dinero no me llega para un mes entero.

last³ [lɑːst] *n* horma *f*; **stick to your —!** ¡zapatero, a tus zapatos!
last-ditch ['lɑːst'ditʃ] *adj defence* de lo más terco, que continúa hasta quemar el último cartucho.
lasting ['lɑːstiŋ] *adj* duradero, perdurable, permanente; constante; *shame etc* eterno; *colour* sólido.
lastly ['lɑːstli] *adv* por último, finalmente.
last-minute ['lɑːst'minit] *adj decision etc* de última hora.
latch [lætʃ] **1** *n* picaporte *m*, pestillo *m*; **to be on the — estar** cerrado con picaporte; **to drop the — echar** el pestillo.

2 *vt* cerrar con picaporte; (*fig*) sujetar, asegurar. **3** *vi*: **to — on to something** fijarse en algo; **to — on to someone** pegarse a uno.
latchkey ['lætʃkiː] *n* llavín *m*.
late [leit] **1** *adj* (a) (*person*) **to be — for something** llegar tarde para algo; **I was too — for it** llegué tarde para ello; **I was — in getting up** tardé en levantarme; **I don't want to make you —** no quiero entretenerle.

(b) (*impersonal*) **it's — es** tarde; **it's — in the day to change your mind** es tarde para mudar de opinión; **it's getting — se** está haciendo tarde.

(c) tardío; *hour* avanzado; *delivery* atrasado; *entry* que se presenta después de la fecha señalada; **— frost** helada *f* tardía; **— potato** patata *f* tardía; **at a — hour** a una hora avanzada, a última hora; **in the — eighties** en los últimos años ochenta; **in the — spring** hacia fines de la primavera; **in the — morning** en la última parte de la mañana; **a — 18th century building** un edificio de fines del siglo XVIII; **L— Stone Age** período *m* neolítico; **Easter is — this year** la Semana Santa cae tarde este año.

(d) (*deceased*) fallecido, difunto, finado; **the — king** el finado rey.

(e) (*former*) antiguo, ex; **— prime minister** antiguo primer ministro *m*, ex primer ministro *m*.

2 *adv* (a) tarde; **to come — llegar** tarde; **to arrive too — llegar** tarde (*for* para); **the train arrived 8 minutes — el** tren llegó con 8 minutos de retraso; **better — than never** más vale tarde que nunca; **to sit up —, to stay up —** velar, no acostarse hasta las altas horas, seguir sin acostarse; **to work — at the office** trabajar en la oficina después de la hora acostumbrada, quedarse a trabajar en la oficina hasta una hora tardía; **— at night, — in the night** ya muy entrada la noche; **— into the night** hasta muy entrada la noche; **— in the afternoon** a última hora de la tarde; **— in the year** hacia fines del año; **— in life** a una edad avanzada; **— last century** hacia fines del siglo pasado; **of — última**mente, recientemente; **as — as 1900** todavía en 1900.

(b) **— of No. 13** que vivió hasta hace poco en el núm. 13; **— of the Diplomatic Service** hasta hace poco miembro del Cuerpo Diplomático, ex miembro del Cuerpo Diplomático.
latecomer ['leitkʌmə*] *n* recién llegado *m*, a *f*; el

(etc) que llega tarde; **the firm is a — to the industry** la compañia es nueva en la industria, la compañia acaba de establecerse en la industria.
late-lamented ['leitlə'mentid] *adj* malogrado, fallecido.
lately ['leitli] *adv* últimamente, recientemente; hace poco; **till — hasta** hace poco.
latency ['leitənsi] *n* estado *m* latente.
lateness ['leitnis] *n* lo tarde; lo tardío; lo reciente; *(of hour)* lo avanzado; *(delay)* retraso *m*; **he was fined for persistent — le** impusieron una multa por venir constantemente tarde.
latent ['leitənt] *adj* latente.
later ['leitə*] **1** *adj comp of* **late**; más tardío; *(in newness)* más reciente; *(in series)* posterior, ulterior; **hour** más avanzada; **his — symphonies** sus sinfonías más recientes, sus sinfonías posteriores; **this version is — than that one** esta versión es posterior a ésa; **it must have been painted at a — stage** debe de haberse pintado en una fase posterior; **at a — meeting** en una reunión celebrada después; **in his — years** en sus últimos años.
  2 *adv comp of* **late**; más tarde; *(afterwards)* luego, después; posteriormente; **a moment — un** momento después; **a few years — a** los pocos años; varios años después; **yes dear, — (on being interrupted)** sí querida, luego; **see you — !** ¡hasta pronto!; **no — than yesterday** no más lejos que ayer, ayer sin ir más lejos; **not — than 1980** no después de 1980; **— on** más tarde, después.
lateral ['lætərəl] *adj* lateral.
laterally ['lætərəli] *adv* lateralmente.
latest ['leitist] **1** *adj superl of* **late**; último; más reciente; *fashion, news etc* último; **his — painting** su último cuadro, su cuadro más reciente; **to be — to do something** ser el último en hacer algo; **what is the — date you can come?** ¿hastá qué fecha estás libre para venir?
  2 *adv superl of* **late**; **he came — él** vino el último.
  3 *n* (a) *(fam)* **have you seen John's —?** *(girl)* ¿has visto a la novia actual de Juan?; **have you heard John's —?** *(joke)* ¿has oído el último chiste de Juan?; **did you hear about John's —?** *(exploit)* ¿te han contado la última de Juan?, ¿has oído lo de Juan?
  (b) **at the — a** lo más tarde, a más tardar, como límite.
latex ['leiteks] *n* látex *m*.
lath [læθ] *n, pl* **laths** [lɑːðz] listón *m*.
lathe [leið] *n* torno *m*.
lather ['læðə*] **1** *n* espuma *f* (de jabón), jabonaduras *fpl*; *(of sweat)* espuma *f*; **the horse was in a — el** caballo estaba cubierto de espuma.
  2 *vt* enjabonar; *(fam)* zurrar.
  3 *vi* hacer espuma.
latifundia [,læti'fundiə] *npl* latifundios *mpl*.
Latin ['lætin] **1** *adj* latino.
  2 *n (person)* latino *m*, a *f*; **the —s** los latinos.
  3 *n (language)* latín *m*; **Late — latín** *m* tardío; **Low — bajo** latín *m*; **Vulgar — latín** *m* vulgar.
Latin America ['lætinə'merikə] América *f* Latina.
Latin-American ['lætinə'merikən] **1** *adj* latinoamericano. **2** *n* latinoamericano *m*, a *f*.
latinism ['lætinizəm] *n* latinismo *m*.
latinist ['lætinist] *n* latinista *mf*.
latinity [lə'tiniti] *n* latinidad *f*.
latinization [,lætinai'zeiʃən] *n* latinización *f*.
latinize ['lætinaiz] *vti* latinizar.
latitude ['lætitjuːd] *n* latitud *f*; *(fig)* libertad *f*.
latitudinal [,læti'tjuːdinl] *adj* latitudinal.
Latium ['leiʃiəm] Lacio *m*.
latrine [lə'triːn] *n* letrina *f*.
latter ['lætə*] *adj* (a) más reciente; posterior; último; *(of two)* segundo; **the — part of the story** la segunda mitad del cuento; **in the — part of the century** hacia fines del siglo; **the — opinion** esta (última) opinión.
  (b) **the former ... the — aquél ... éste.**
latter-day ['lætə'dei] *adj* moderno, reciente.
latterly ['lætəli] *adv* últimamente, recientemente.
lattice ['lætis] *n* enrejado *m*; *(on window)* reja *f*, celosía *f*.
latticed ['lætist] *adj* **window** con reja.
lattice work ['lætiswəːk] *n* enrejado *m*.
Latvia ['lætviə] Letonia *f*, Latvia *f*.
Latvian ['lætviən] **1** *adj* letón, latvio. **2** *n* letón *m*, ona *f*, latvio *m*, a *f*.
laud [lɔːd] *vt* alabar, elogiar.
laudable ['lɔːdəbl] *adj* loable; plausible.
laudably ['lɔːdəbli] *adv* de modo loable, laudablemente.
laudanum ['lɔːdnəm] *n* láudano *m*.
laudatory ['lɔːdətəri] *adj* laudatorio.

laugh [lɑːf] **1** *n* risa *f*; *(loud)* carcajada *f*, risotada *f*; **what a — ! ¡qué** risa!, ¡qué bien!; **just for a — sólo** para hacer reír; **to have a good — over something** reírse mucho con algo; **to have the — over someone** llevar ventaja a uno, quedar por encima de uno; **to play something for —s** representar algo con el propósito de hacer reír al público.
  2 *vt:* **to — something off** tomar algo a risa; **he —s everything off** no toma nada en serio; *see* **court, scorn.**
  3 *vi* reír, reírse; *(loud)* reírse a carcajadas, carcajearse; **to — about something, to — over something** reírse con algo; **it's nothing to — about** no es cosa de risa; **to — at someone** reírse de uno, burlarse de uno; **are you —ing at me?** ¿se ríe Vd de mí?; **we must be able to — at ourselves** hay que ver los aspectos ridículos de nosotros mismos; **to — out loud** soltar la carcajada, reírse abiertamente; **he who —s last —s longest** el último que ríe, ríe más fuerte.
laughable ['lɑːfəbl] *adj* ridículo, absurdo; cómico, divertido; **it's — that ... es** absurdo que + *subj*.
laughing ['lɑːfiŋ] **1** *adj* risueño, alegre; **it's no — matter** no es cosa de risa. **2** *n* risa *f*.
laughing gas ['lɑːfiŋgæs] *n* gas *m* hilarante.
laughingly ['lɑːfiŋli] *adv:* **he said — dijo** riendo.
laughing stock ['lɑːfiŋstɔk] *n* hazmerreír *m*.
laughter ['lɑːftə*] *n* risa *f*, risas *fpl*; **amid the — of those present** entre las risas de los asistentes; **at this there was — en** esto hubo risas; **to burst into — soltar** la carcajada.
Launcelot ['lɑːnslət] *m* Lanzarote.
launch [lɔːntʃ] **1** *n (act)* botadura *f*; *(vessel)* lancha *f*, falúa *f*.
  2 *vt (throw)* lanzar; *rocket etc* lanzar; *new vessel* botar; *lifeboat* echar al agua, largar; *offensive* emprender, comenzar; *company* crear, fundar; lanzar; *new product* lanzar, introducir en el mercado; *film, play* estrenar; *idea* lanzar; *plan* poner en operación; *share issue etc* emitir; **to — someone on his way** ayudar a uno a emprender su carrera, poner a uno en camino.
  3 *vi:* **to — forth, to — out** lanzarse, ponerse en marcha; **now we can afford to — out a bit** ahora nos podemos permitir algunas cosas de lujo, ahora podemos extender nuestras actividades *(etc)*; **to — out into** lanzarse a; engolfarse en; **to — out into a career** emprender una carrera; **he —ed out into a violent speech** pasó a pronunciar un discurso violento; **once he is —ed on this subject we shall never stop him** en cuanto se ponga a hablar de este tema no le haremos nunca callar.
launching ['lɔːntʃiŋ] *n* botadura *f*; lanzamiento *m*; inauguración *f*, iniciación *f*; estreno *m*; emisión *f*.
launching pad ['lɔːntʃiŋpæd] *n* plataforma *f* de lanzamiento.
launching site ['lɔːntʃiŋsait] *n* rampa *f* de lanzamiento.
launder ['lɔːndə*] **1** *vt* lavar (y planchar). **2** *vi* resistir el lavado (bien, mal *etc*).
launderette [,lɔːndə'ret] *n* lavandería *f* automática.
laundress ['lɔːndris] *n* lavandera *f*.
laundry ['lɔːndri] *n (establishment)* lavadero *m*, lavandería *f*; *(clothes: dirty)* ropa *f* sucia, ropa *f* por lavar, *(washed)* ropa *f* lavada, colada *f*.
laureate ['lɔːriit] *n* laureado *m*.
laurel ['lɔrəl] *n* laurel *m* (cerezo); **to look to one's —s** no dormirse sobre sus laureles; **to rest on one's —s** dormirse sobre sus laureles; **to win one's —s** cargarse de laureles, laurearse.
Laurence ['lɔrəns] *m* Lorenzo.
Lausanne [ləu'zæn] Lusana.
lav [læv] *n (fam)* = **lavatory.**
lava ['lɑːvə] *n* lava *f*.
lavatory ['lævətri] *n (utensil)* wáter *m*, excusado *m*, inodoro *m*; *(room)* lavabo *m*, aseos *mpl*; **public — urinarios** *mpl*.
lavender ['lævində*] *n—*espliego *m*, lavanda *f*, lavándula *f*.
lavish ['læviʃ] **1** *adj (abundant)* profuso, abundante; *(luxurious)* lujoso; *(of person, prodigal)* pródigo; *expenditure* pródigo, liberal; **to be — of** ser pródigo de, prodigar, no escatimar; **to be — with one's money** gastar libremente su dinero, derrochar su dinero.
  2 *vt:* **to — something on someone** colmar a uno de algo; **to — care on something** poner la máxima atención en algo; **to — attentions on someone** colmar a uno de atenciones.
lavishly ['læviʃli] *adv* profusamente, en profusión, abundantemente; lujosamente; pródigamente; **the house is — furnished** la casa está lujosamente amueblada; **he spends money —** derrocha su dinero.

lavishness ['lævi∫nis] *n* profusión *f*, abundancia *f*; lujo *m*; prodigalidad *f*.

law [lɔ:] *n* (*a* —, *the* —) ley *f*; (*study, body of* —s) derecho *m*, jurisprudencia *f*; (*Sport, games*) regla *f*; the L— (*Jewish*) la ley de Moisés, (*fam*) la policía; — **and order** orden *m* público; **the forces of** — **and order** las fuerzas del orden; — **of nature** ley *f* natural; **canon** — derecho *m* canónico; **civil** — derecho *m* civil; **commercial** — derecho *m* mercantil; **common** — derecho *m* consuetudinario; **constitutional** — derecho *m* político; **criminal** — derecho *m* penal; **international** — derecho *m* internacional, derecho *m* de gentes; **maritime** — código *m* marítimo; **martial** — ley *f* marcial, gobierno *m* militar; **Roman** — derecho *m* romano; **according to** —, **in** — según derecho; **by** — según la ley, de acuerdo con la ley; **in-law** político, *eg* **brother-in-law** hermano *m* político, cuñado *m*; **it's the** — es la ley; **his word is** — su palabra es ley; **is there a** — **against it?** ¿hay una ley que lo prohíba?; **he is above the** — está por encima de la ley; **he is outside the** — está fuera de la ley; **to be a** — **unto oneself** obrar por cuenta propia, no hacer caso alguno de los demás; **to go to** — pleitear, poner pleito (*about* sobre), recurrir a la ley; **to have the** — **on someone** denunciar a uno a la policía, llevar a uno ante el tribunal; **to keep within the** — obrar legalmente; **to lay down the** — hablar autoritariamente; **to practise** — ejercer de abogado; **to take the** — **into one's own hands** tomarse la justicia por su mano; **to take a case to** — recurrir a la vía judicial.

law-abiding ['lɔ:ə,baidiŋ] *adj* observante de la ley, que vive conforme a la ley; decente.

lawbreaker ['lɔ:,breikə*] *n* transgresor *m*, ora *f*, infractor *m* de la ley.

law court ['lɔ:kɔ:t] *n* tribunal *m* (de justicia).

lawful ['lɔ:ful] *adj* legítimo, lícito.

lawfully ['lɔ:fəli] *adv* legítimamente, lícitamente.

lawgiver ['lɔ:,givə*] *n* legislador *m*, ora *f*.

lawless ['lɔ:lis] *adj act* ilegal; *person* rebelde, violento, criminal; *country* sin leyes, ingobernable, desordenado.

lawlessness ['lɔ:lisnis] *n* desorden *m*; violencia *f*; criminalidad *f*.

lawn[1] [lɔ:n] *n* césped *m*.

lawn[2] [lɔ:n] *n* linón *m*.

lawnmower ['lɔ:n,məuə*] *n* cortacésped *m*.

lawn tennis ['lɔ:n'tenis] *n* tenis *m*.

Lawrence ['lɔrəns] *m* Lorenzo.

law school ['lɔ:sku:l] *n* escuela *f* de derecho, facultad *f* de derecho.

law student ['lɔ:,stju:dənt] *n* estudiante *mf* de derecho.

lawsuit ['lɔ:su:t] *n* pleito *m*, litigio *m*, proceso *m*.

lawyer ['lɔ:jə*] *n* abogado *m*.

lax [læks] *adj* flojo, descuidado, poco exigente; indisciplinado; (*morally*) laxo; **to be** — **in** + *ger* ser negligente en + *infin*; **things are very** — **at the school** en la escuela hay poca disciplina; **he is** — **in his approach** su actitud es poco seria.

laxative ['læksətiv] **1** *adj* laxante. **2** *n* laxante *m*.

laxity ['læksiti] *n*, **laxness** ['læksnis] *n* flojedad *f*; negligencia *f*, descuido *m*; falta *f* de disciplina; (*moral*) laxitud *f*, relajamiento *m*.

lay[1] [lei] *n* (*Mus, Lit*) trova *f*, canción *f*.

lay[2] [lei] *adj* (*not in orders*) laico, lego, seglar; (*not expert*) profano, no experto.

lay[3] [lei] *pret of* **lie**[2].

lay[4] [lei] **1** *n* (a) disposición *f*, situación *f*; **the** — **of the land** la configuración del terreno, (*fig*) la situación actual, el estado actual de las cosas.
(b) **hen in** — gallina *f* ponedora; **to come into** — empezar a poner huevos; **to go out of** — dejar de poner huevos.
(c) (*US sl*) **she's an easy** — es plan.
2 (*irr: pret, ptp* **laid**) *vt* (a) (*prostrate, etc*) corn abatir, encamar; *dust* matar; *fears* aquietar, acallar; *ghost* conjurar, exorcizar; **to** — **something flat** derribar algo, tirar algo al suelo; **to** — **a town flat** arrasar (*or* destruir) una ciudad.
(b) (*place, put*) poner, colocar; dejar; *blame* echar (*on* a); *bricks* poner, colocar; *cable, mains, track* tender; *cloth, meal, table* poner; *carpet, lino* extender; *fire* preparar; *foundations* echar; *foundation stone* colocar; *gun* apuntar; *hand etc* poner (*on* en); *mines* sembrar; *pipes etc* (*in building*) instalar; *plans* hacer, formar, preparar; *responsibility* atribuir (*on* a); *scene* poner, situar; *tax* imponer (*on* a).
(c) *egg* poner; **to** — **eggs** (*hen*) poner huevos, (*fish, insect etc*) desovar.

(d) *bet* hacer (*on* a); *money* apostar (*on* a); **I** — **you a fiver on it!** ¡te apuesto 5 libras a que es así!
(e) *accusation, charge* hacer; *complaint* formular, presentar; *information* dar.
(f) (*with adv or prep*) **to** — **aside** *book, pen etc* dejar; *work* dejar, suspender; (*keep in reserve*) poner aparte, poner a un lado; (*save*) ahorrar, guardar; (*cast away*) desechar; *plan etc* arrinconar, dar carpetazo a; **to** — **away** = **to** — **aside**; **to** — **something before someone** poner algo delante de uno; *idea, plan* exponer ante uno; *claim etc* presentar a uno; **to** — **by** = **to** — **aside**; **to** — **down** *book, pen etc* dejar; poner a un lado; (*lay flat*) acostar, poner en tierra; *arms* deponer, rendir, dejar; *burden* posar, depositar en tierra; *cards* extender sobre el tapete; *condition* asentar; *life* dar, sacrificar; *policy* asentar, trazar, marcar; *precedent* sentar, establecer; *principle* afirmar; *ruling* dictar; *ship* colocar la quilla de; **to** — **it down that** . . . asentar que . . ., afirmar que . . .; dictaminar que . . .; **to** — **in** *supplies* proveerse de; (*save*) ahorrar; (*amass*) acumular; (*buy*) comprar; **to** — **off** *workers* despedir (temporalmente, por falta de trabajo); **to** — **on** *blows* descargar (sobre); *paint* poner, pintar; *water etc* instalar; *duty, punishment, tax* imponer (a); **a house with water laid on** una casa con agua corriente; **to** — **it on someone** (*beat*) dar una paliza a uno; **to** — **it on** (*thick*) (*flatter*) adular más de la cuenta, (*exaggerate*) recargar las tintas; **to** — **out** *tender, extender*; disponer, arreglar; *corpse* amortajar; *garden, town* trazar, hacer el trazado de; *money* (*spend*) gastar, (*invest*) invertir, emplear (*on* en); **to** — **someone out** derribar a uno, poner a uno fuera de combate; (*with drink etc*) hacer perder el conocimiento a uno, (*by illness*) debilitar gravemente a uno; **the house is well laid out** la casa está bien distribuida; **the town is well laid out** la ciudad tiene un trazado elegante; **to** — **up** (*store*) guardar, almacenar; (*amass*) acumular; (*save*) ahorrar, atesorar; *ship* desarmar; *boat* amarrar; *car etc* encerrar en el garaje, dejar de usar temporalmente; (*Med*) obligar a guardar cama; *see also* **laid**.
3 *vi* (*hen*) poner, poner huevos; **to** — **that** . . . apostar a que . . .; **to** — **about one** dar palos de ciego, repartir golpes a diestro y siniestro; **to** — **down** (*Cards*) poner sus cartas sobre el tapete; **to** — **into someone** (*fam*) dar una paliza a uno (*also fig*); **to** — **off** (*Naut*) virar de bordo; **to** — **off someone** (*fam*) dejar a uno en paz; — **off, will you?** (*fam*) ¡déjalo, por Dios!; **to** — **off something** (*fam*) dejar algo; **to** — **off** + *ger* (*fam*) dejar de + *infin*; **to** — **on** arremeter, empezar a luchar, darse golpes.
4 *vr*: **to** — **oneself down** tumbarse, echarse; **to** — **oneself out** hacer un gran esfuerzo (*to* + *infin* por + *infin*), tomarse la molestia (*for someone* de ayudar a uno, *to* + *infin* de + *infin*); **to** — **oneself out to please** volcarse por complacer a uno; **to** — **oneself out with a blow** darse un golpe y ponerse fuera de combate.

layabout ['leiəbaut] *n* gandul *m*, vago *m*, a *f*.

lay brother ['lei'brʌðə*] *n* donado *m*, lego *m*.

lay-by ['leibai] *n* (*Aut*) apartadero *m*.

layer ['leiə*] **1** *n* (a) capa *f*; (*Geol*) estrato *m*. (b) (*Agr*) acodo *m*. (c) (*hen*) gallina *f* ponedora; **the best** — la más ponedora. **2** *vt* (*Agr*) acodar.

layette [lei'et] *n* canastilla *f*, ajuar *m* (de niño).

lay figure ['lei'figə*] *n* maniquí *m*.

laying ['leiiŋ] *n* (*placing*) colocación *f*; (*of cable, track etc*) tendido *m*; (*of eggs*) puesta *f*, postura *f*; — **on of hands** imposición *f* de manos.

layman ['leimən] *n, pl* —**men** [mən] (*Eccl*) seglar *m*, lego *m*; (*fig*) profano *m*, persona *f* no experta, lego *m*.

lay-off ['leiɔf] *n* paro *m* involuntario.

layout ['leiaut] *n* plan *m*, distribución *f*, trazado *m*; disposición *f*; (*Typ etc*) composición *f*.

lay sister ['lei'sistə*] *n* donada *f*, lega *f*.

Lazarus ['læzərəs] *m* Lázaro.

laze [leiz] **1** *n*: **to have a** — descansar.
2 *vi* no hacer nada, darse al ocio; (*pej*) holgazanear, gandulear; **we** —**d in the sun for a week** durante una semana tomamos el sol y nada más.

lazily ['leizili] *adv* perezosamente; lentamente.

laziness ['leizinis] *n* pereza *f*, holgazanería *f*, vaguedad *f*, indolencia *f*.

lazy ['leizi] *adj* perezoso, holgazán, vago, indolente; *movement etc* lento; **we had a** — **holiday** pasamos las vacaciones sin hacer nada, durante las vacaciones no hicimos nada sino descansar.

lazybones ['leizi,bəunz] *n* gandul *m*, vago *m*, a *f*.

lea [li:] *n* (*poet*) prado *m*.

leach [li:t∫] **1** *vt* lixiviar. **2** *vi* lixiviarse.

lead [led] n (metal) plomo m; (Naut) sonda f, escandallo m; (Typ) regleta f, interlínea f; (in pencil) mina f; — chapas fpl de plomo; red — minio m; white — albayalde m; they filled him full of — le acribillaron a balazos; to swing the — (fam) fingirse enfermo, racanear, hacer el rácano.

lead [li:d] 1 n (a) (front position) delantera f, cabeza f; (leading position, Sport) liderato m; (distance, time ahead) ventaja f; to be in the — ir en cabeza, ir primero; (in league etc) ocupar el primer puesto; to take the — tomar la delantera, tomar el mando; to have 2 minutes' — over someone llevar a uno una ventaja de 2 minutos; to have a — of half a length tener medio cuerpo de ventaja.

(b) (example) ejemplo m; iniciativa f; to follow someone's — seguir el ejemplo de uno; to give someone a — guiar a uno, dar el ejemplo a uno, mostrar el camino a uno; to take the — tomar la iniciativa (in en, in doing en hacer).

(c) (clue) pista f, indicación f; the police have a — la policía tiene una pista; it gave the police a — to the criminal puso a la policía sobre la pista del criminal; give me a — (in guessing) ¿me puedes dar alguna indicación?

(d) (Cards) it's my — yo soy mano, salgo yo; whose — is it? ¿quién sale?; if the — is in hearts si la salida es a corazones.

(e) (Theat) papel m principal; with Garbo in the — con la Garbo en el primer papel; to play the — tener el papel principal; to sing the — llevar la voz cantante.

(f) (leash) traílla f, cuerda f.

(g) (Elec) conductor m, cable m (eléctrico).

2 (irr: pret and ptp led) vt (a) (conduct) conducir; llevar; guiar; to — someone to a table conducir a uno a una mesa; to — someone along llevar a uno (por la mano etc); kindly — me to him haga el favor de conducirme a su presencia (or de llevarme donde está); each reference led me to another cada referencia me remitió a otra; what led you to Venice? ¿qué le llevó a Venecia?, ¿con qué motivo fue Vd a Venecia?; to — the way ir primero, (fig) dar el ejemplo, mostrar el camino; he is easily led es muy influenciable; to — someone into error inducir a uno a error.

(b) (be the leader of, govern) government dirigir, encabezar; party encabezar, ser el jefe de; expedition, regiment mandar; team capitanear; movement, revolution encabezar, acaudillar; orchestra dirigir; league, procession ir en cabeza de, encabezar.

(c) (be first in) ser el primero en, sobresalir en, ocupar el primer puesto en; to — the field ir el primero de todos, estar en cabeza, ganar; they led us by 30 seconds nos llevaban una ventaja de 30 segundos; Britain —s the world in textiles en la industria textil Inglaterra supera a los demás, en los textiles Inglaterra ocupa el primer puesto.

(d) card salir con.

(e) life llevar; to — a strange life llevar una vida muy rara; to — someone a wretched life amargar la vida a uno, tratar a uno como una basura; see also dance, life.

(f) to — someone to do something inducir (or inclinar, persuadir, mover) a uno a hacer algo; to — someone to believe that . . . hacer creer a uno que . . .; I am led to the conclusion that . . . llego a la conclusión de que . . .

(g) (with adv or prep) to — someone away conducir a uno a otra parte; llevarse a uno; he was led away by the police se lo llevaron los policías; we must not be led away from the matter in hand no nos apartemos del asunto que estamos tratando; to — someone back hacer volver a uno, conducir a uno a donde estaba; this road —s you back to Jaca por este camino se vuelve a Jaca; to — someone in hacer entrar a uno; they led him into the king's presence le condujeron ante el rey; to — someone off hacer marcharse a uno, llevarse a uno; to — someone on (persuade) engatusar a uno, halagar a uno; (amorously) coquetear con uno, ir dando esperanzas a uno; (morally) seducir a uno; (make someone talk) hacer hablar a uno, tirar de la lengua a uno; to — someone out conducir a uno fuera; to — someone out to dance sacar a una a bailar.

3 vi (a) (go in front) llevar la delantera, ir primero; — on! ¡adelante!; to — by 10 metres tener una ventaja de 10 metros; he easily —s sobresale, supera fácilmente a los demás.

(b) (be in command) tener el mando, ser el jefe.

(c) (Cards) ser mano, salir; who —s? ¿quién sale?; South —s Sur sale.

(d) (of street etc) to — to conducir a, llevar a,

salir a, desembocar en; this street —s to the station esta calle conduce a la estación, por esta calle se va a la estación; where does this corridor —? ¿adónde conduce este pasillo?; it —s into that room comunica con ese cuarto.

(e) (result in) dar, producir; it led to a result dio un resultado; it led to a change produjo un cambio; it led to nothing no dio resultado, no surtió efecto, no condujo a nada; it led to his arrest dio lugar a su detención; it led to war causó la guerra.

(f) (with adv or prep) to — off (begin) empezar; (Sport) abrir el juego; (Cards) salir (with con); the streets that — off the square las calles que salen de la plaza; a room —ing off another un cuarto que comunica con otro; to — up to conducir a; preparar el terreno para; the events that led up to the war los sucesos que condujeron a la guerra; the years that led up to the war los años que precedieron a la guerra; what's all this —ing up to? ¿qué propósito tiene todo esto?, ¿adónde conduce todo esto?; he led carefully up to the proposal preparó con cuidado el terreno antes de hacer la propuesta.

leaded ['ledid] adj: — lights cristales mpl emplomados.

leaden ['ledn] adj (of lead) de plomo, plúmbeo; (in colour) plomizo; (fig) pesado, triste.

leader ['li:də*] n (in general) jefe m, líder m; (Pol, of nation, union etc) dirigente m; (of party) jefe m, líder m; (esp military) caudillo m; (of gang) cuadrillero m; (of rebels) cabecilla m; (guide) guía mf, conductor m, ora f; (Sport: in league) líder m, (horse etc) caballo m (etc) delantero; (Mus: of orchestra) primer violín m, (of band) director m; (Typ) artículo m de fondo; party — jefe m de partido; — of the opposition jefe m de la oposición; a — of the masses un conductor de masas; our political —s nuestros dirigentes políticos.

leadership ['li:dəʃip] n (a) (persons, office) jefatura f, dirección f; mando m, liderato m; caudillaje m; under the — of bajo la jefatura de; a crisis in the — una crisis de dirección, una crisis en la dirigencia; to resign the — dimitir la jefatura; to take over the — asumir la dirección, tomar el mando.

(b) (quality) iniciativa f; (powers of —) dotes fpl de mando.

leader-writer ['li:də,raitə*] n editorialista mf.

lead-in ['li:d'in] n introducción f; entrada f; a useful — to a discussion una manera útil de introducir una discusión.

leading ['li:diŋ] adj (a) (front) delantero; wheel delantero, conductor; edge (Aer) de ataque.

(b) part, person, idea etc principal, importante; (outstanding) sobresaliente, destacado; (in race) primero, delantero; see article, lady etc.

leading strings ['li:diŋstriŋz] npl andaderas fpl.

lead pencil ['led'pensl] n lápiz m.

lead poisoning ['led,poizniŋ] n plumbismo m.

leaf [li:f] 1 n, pl leaves [li:vz] hoja f; gold — pan m de oro, oro m batido; — tobacco tabaco m en rama; to come into — echar hojas, cubrirse de hojas; to take a — out of someone's book seguir el ejemplo de uno; to turn over a new — reformarse, cambiar de modo de ser, hacer vida nueva.

2 vi: to — through a book hojear un libro.

leaf bud ['li:fbʌd] n yema f.

leafless ['li:flis] adj sin hojas, deshojado.

leaflet ['li:flit] n folleto m, hoja f volante; prospecto m.

leaf mould, (US) **leaf mold** ['li:fməuld] n abono m verde.

leafy ['li:fi] adj frondoso.

league¹ [li:g] n (measure) legua f.

league² [li:g] n liga f (also Sport); sociedad f, asociación f, comunidad f; L— of Nations Sociedad f de las Naciones; Hanseatic L— Liga f Hanseática; to be in — with someone estar de manga con uno, haberse confabulado con uno.

leak [li:k] 1 n (hole) agujero m; (Naut) vía f de agua; (in roof etc) gotera f; (of gas, liquid) escape m, fuga f, pérdida f, salida f; (of money) filtración f; there has been a security — se ha divulgado una noticia confidencial (or información secreta); to spring a — abrirse una vía de agua.

2 vt (a) rezumar, dejar perderse, derramar; it's —ing acid all over the place se está derramando el ácido por todas partes.

(b) to — information to a spy comunicar información secreta a un espía.

3 vi (a) (of ship) hacer agua; (of receptacle) rezumarse, tener agujeros, estar agujereado; (of pipe) tener fugas, dejar fugarse el gas (etc); (of pen) derramar tinta, derramarse.

(b) (of gas, liquid etc) escaparse, fugarse, salirse,

irse; (*ooze out*) rezumarse; (*drop by drop*) gotear; (*of money*) filtrarse; **to — away** irse, agotarse debido a una fuga; **to — out = to — away**; (*of news*) divulgarse (sin autorización), llegar a saberse, trascender; **finally it —ed out that . . .** por fin se supo que . . .
leakage ['liːkidʒ] n = **leak**; security — divulgación f (no autorizada) de información secreta.
leaky ['liːki] adj boat que hace agua, que tiene vías de agua; roof que tiene goteras; receptacle agujereado, defectuoso.
lean[1] [liːn] **1** adj (thin) flaco; face enjuto; meat magro; year difícil, de carestía; **to grow —** enflaquecer. **2** n carne f magra.
lean[2] [liːn] **1** n inclinación f.
2 (irr: pret and ptp **leaned** or **leant**) vt ladear, inclinar, poner oblicuamente; **to — a ladder against a wall** poner (or apoyar) una escala contra una pared; **to — one's head on someone's shoulder** apoyar la cabeza en el hombro de uno.
3 vi ladearse, inclinarse, estar ladeado, estar inclinado; **to — against something** apoyarse en algo; **to — back** reclinarse, echar el cuerpo atrás; **to — forward** inclinarse; **to — on something** apoyarse en algo (also fig); **to — on someone for support** contar con el apoyo de uno; **to — on someone** (fam) ejercer presión sobre uno, amenazar a uno; **to — out** asomarse (of a); **to — over** inclinarse; **to — over someone** inclinarse sobre uno; **to — over backwards to help someone** volcarse por ayudar a uno, desvivirse por ayudar a uno; **we have —ed over backwards to get agreement** hemos hecho todas las concesiones posibles para llegar a un acuerdo; **to — to the Left** (Pol) inclinarse a la izquierda; **to — towards someone's opinion** inclinarse hacia la opinión de uno.
Leander [liːˈændə*] m Leandro.
leaning ['liːniŋ] **1** adj inclinado.
2 n inclinación f (to, towards hacia); tendencia f, propensión f (to a); predilección f (to, towards por); **what are his —s?** ¿cuál es su predilección?; **he has artistic —s** se siente atraído por una carrera artística.
leanness ['liːnnis] n flaqueza f; magrez f; carestía f, pobreza f.
leant [lent] pret and ptp of **lean**[2].
lean-to ['liːntuː] n colgadizo m, alpende m.
leap [liːp] **1** n salto m, brinco m; (fig) salto m; **the great — forward** (China) el gran salto hacia adelante; **— in the dark** salto m en el vacío; **by —s and bounds** a pasos agigantados; **in one —** de un salto.
2 (irr: pret and ptp **leaped** or **leapt**) vt saltar, saltar por encima de.
3 vi saltar, brincar, dar un salto; (of fish) saltar, bañarse; **my heart —ed** mi corazón dio un vuelco; **to — about** dar saltos, brincar; **to — at a chance** apresurarse a aprovechar una oportunidad; **to — at an offer** apresurarse a aceptar una oferta; **to — down** bajar de un salto, saltar en tierra; **to — for joy** saltar de alegría; **to — out of a car** saltar de un coche; **to — over** saltar, saltar por (encima de), salvar; **to — to one's feet** saltar en pie; **to — up** ponerse de pie de un salto, (of flame) subir de repente, volver a estallar, (of figure etc) subir de punto.
leapfrog ['liːpfrɔg] **1** n pídola f; **to play —** jugar a la pídola. **2** vt saltar por encima de. **3** vi jugar a la pídola, saltar.
leapt [lept] pret and ptp of **leap**.
leap year ['liːpjiə*] n año m bisiesto.
learn [ləːn] (irr: pret and ptp **learned** or **learnt**) vti (in general) aprender; news, fact etc saber, enterarse de; (discover, find out) descubrir, averiguar; **to — to do something** aprender a hacer algo; **to — how to do something** aprender a hacer algo, aprender cómo se hace algo, aprender el modo de hacer algo; **to — about something** (hear of) saber algo, (instruct oneself) informarse sobre algo, instruirse en algo; **to — from experience** aprender por experiencia; **to — of, — of saber**, tener noticia de; **to — up** esforzarse por aprender, repasar, empollar.
learned ['ləːnid] adj person docto, sabio, erudito; remark, speech, society etc erudito; profession liberal; **to be — in** ser erudito en, ser muy entendido en.
learnedly ['ləːnidli] adv eruditamente.
learner ['ləːnə*] n principiante mf, aprendiz m, iza f; (student) estudiante mf, estudioso m, a f.
learner-driver ['ləːnəˈdraivə*] n aprendiz m de conductor, aprendiza f de conductora.
learning ['ləːniŋ] n (act) el aprender, estudio m; (fund of —) saber m, conocimientos mpl; (erudition)

saber m, erudición f; **man of —** sabio m, erudito m; **seat of —** centro m de estudios.
learnt [ləːnt] pret and ptp of **learn**.
lease [liːs] **1** n arriendo m, contrato m de arrendamiento; **to occupy a house on a 99-year —** ocupar una casa por un plazo de 99 años; **to let something out on —** dar algo en arriendo; **to give someone a new — of life** devolver la vitalidad a uno, servir de tónico a uno; **to take on a new — of life** (person) recobrar su vigor, (thing) renovarse.
2 vt (take) arrendar (from de), tomar en arriendo; (give: also **to — out**) arrendar, dar en arriendo.
leasehold ['liːshəuld] **1** n (contract) arrendamiento m; (property) inmueble m arrendado.
2 attr arrendado, alquilado; **— reform** reforma f del sistema de arriendos.
leaseholder ['liːshəuldə*] n arrendatario m, a f.
leash [liːʃ] n traílla f, cuerda f.
least [liːst] **1** adj menor; más pequeño; mínimo; menos importante, menos considerable; **the — of them** el menor de ellos; **with the — possible expenditure** gastándose lo menos posible; **that's the — of my worries** eso es lo de menos.
2 adv menos; **the — expensive car** el coche menos costoso; **he deserves it — of all** se lo merece menos que todos los demás; **she is — able to afford it** ella es quien menos puede permitírselo; **— of all would I wish to offend him** ante todo no quiero ofenderle; see **expect** etc.
3 n menos; **it's the — one can ask** es lo menos que se puede pedir; **you gave yourself the —** Vd se sirvió la ración más pequeña; **at — a lo menos**, al menos, por lo menos; **at — it's fine** por lo menos hace buen tiempo; **there were 8 at —** había a lo menos 8; **we can at — try** al menos podemos probarlo; **at the very —** lo menos; **not in the —!** ¡en absoluto!, ¡de ninguna manera!; **he was not in the — upset** no se alteró en lo más mínimo; **to say the —** para no decir más.
leastways ['liːstweiz] adv (fam) de todos modos.
leather ['leðə*] **1** n cuero m; piel f; (wash-) gamuza f; **American — cuero** m artificial; **patent — charol** m. **2** vt (fam) zurrar.
leathern ['leðə(ː)n] adj de cuero.
leathery ['leðəri] adj correoso; skin curtido.
leave [liːv] **1** n (a) (permission) permiso m; **by your — con** permiso de Vd; **without so much as a "by your —"** sin pedir permiso a nadie; **to ask — to do something** pedir permiso para hacer algo.
(b) (permission to be absent) permiso m; (Mil, brief) permiso m, (lengthy, compassionate etc) licencia f; **— of absence** permiso m para estar ausente; **compassionate — permiso** m especial; **to be on — estar** de permiso, estar de licencia; **to take French — despedirse** a la francesa.
(c) to take one's — despedirse (of de); **I must take my — tengo** que marcharme.
2 (irr: pret and ptp **left**) vt (a) (allow to remain) dejar; **to — 2 pages blank** dejar 2 páginas en blanco; **let's — it at that** dejemos las cosas así; **to — something with someone** dejar algo en manos de uno; entregar algo a uno; **to — things lying about** dejar las cosas de cualquier modo; **to — one's supper** dejar la cena sin comer; **to — one's greens** no comer las verduras; **to — a good impression on someone** producir a uno una buena impresión; **it —s much to be desired** deja mucho que desear; **take it or — it** una de dos, o esto o lo otro, como Vd quiera; see **chance, cold** etc.
(b) (person) **I'll — you at the station** te dejo en la estación; **to — a wife and 2 children** dejar una viuda y 2 hijos; **he has left his wife** ha abandonado a su mujer; **I must — you** tengo que despedirme de vosotros, con permiso de Vds me voy; **you may — us** Vd puede retirarse; **to — someone free for the afternoon** permitir a uno disfrutar de una tarde libre.
(c) (bequeath) legar; **her father left her £500** su padre le legó 500 libras.
(d) (Math) **3 from 10 —s 7** de 3 a 10 van 7, 10 menos 3 son 7.
(e) (remain, be over) quedar; sobrar; **all the money I have left** todo el dinero que me queda; **how many are there left?** ¿cuántos quedan?; **nothing was left for me but to sell it** no tuve más remedio que venderlo; **there are 3 left over** sobran 3.
(f) (entrust) **I — it to you** le toca a Vd decidir, que lo decida Vd; **— it to me** yo me encargo de eso; **I — it to you to do** no lo dejo en sus manos; que lo haga Vd; **I — it to you to judge** júzguelo Vd.
(g) (depart from, quit) salir de, abandonar; **to — a place** salir de un lugar, abandonar un lugar;

when the king left Rome cuando el rey abandonó Roma; **to — home** salir de su casa; **to — prison** salir de la cárcel; **to — school** salir del colegio; **to — the table** levantarse de la mesa; **to — one's post** dejar su puesto, dimitir su cargo, (*improperly*) abandonar su puesto; **to — the road** salir fuera de la carretera; **to — the rails** descarrilar.

(h) (*with adv or prep*) **to — aside** omitir, prescindir de, (*forgetfully*) olvidar; **to — someone behind** dejar a uno atrás; **we have left all that behind us** todo eso ha quedado a la espalda; **I left my coat behind** olvidé el abrigo; **he left the children behind** no llevó consigo a los niños, dejó allí a los niños; **to — off** *clothes* quitarse, no ponerse; *habit* renunciar a, dejar; **to — out** omitir, prescindir de; suprimir; **to — someone out in the rain** dejar a uno fuera en la lluvia; *see alone etc.*

3 *vi* irse, marcharse; salir (*for para*); (*of train etc*) salir; **to — off** terminar, cesar; suspender el trabajo; **when the rain —s off, when it —s off raining** cuando deje de llover; **to — off doing something** dejar de hacer algo, terminar de hacer algo.

leaven ['levn] 1 *n* levadura *f*; (*fig*) mezcla *f*; estímulo *m*. 2 *vt* aleudar; (*fig*) penetrar e influenciar, servir de estímulo a, ayudar a transformar.

leavening ['levniŋ] *n* levadura *f*; (*fig*) mezcla *f*, estímulo *m*.

leaves [li:vz] *npl of* **leaf**.

leave-taking ['li:v‚teikiŋ] *n* despedida *f*.

leavings ['li:viŋz] *npl* sobras *fpl*.

Lebanese [‚lebə'ni:z] 1 *adj* libanés. 2 *n* libanés *m*, esa *f*.

Lebanon ['lebənən] Líbano *m*.

lecher ['letʃə*] *n* libertino *m*.

lecherous ['letʃərəs] *adj* lascivo, lujurioso.

lecherously ['letʃərəsli] *adv* lascivamente.

lechery ['letʃəri] *n* lascivia *f*.

lectern ['lektə(:)n] *n* atril *m*; (*Eccl*) facistol *m*.

lecture ['lektʃə*] 1 *n* (*formal, by visitor etc*) conferencia *f*; (*Univ class*) clase *f*; (*fig*) sermoneo *m*; **to attend —s on** seguir un curso sobre (*or de*); **to give a —** dar una conferencia; **to read someone a —** sermonear a uno.

2 *vt* (*scold*) sermonear; **he —s us in French** nos da clases de francés.

3 *vi* dar una conferencia, dar una clase; **he —s in Law** tiene una cátedra de derecho; **he —s at 9 o'clock** da su clase a las 9; **he —s at Princeton** tiene una cátedra en Princeton; **he's lecturing at the moment** ahora está en clase; **he —s well** habla muy bien.

lecturer ['lektʃərə*] *n* (*visitor*) conferenciante *mf*, conferencista *mf*; (*Univ*) catedrático *m*; **assistant —** profesor *m* adjunto, profesora *f* adjunta.

lecture room ['lektʃə‚rum] *n* sala *f* de conferencias; (*Univ*) aula *f*.

lectureship ['lektʃəʃip] *n* cátedra *f*, cargo *m* (*or* puesto *m*) de profesor (adjunto).

led [led] *pret and ptp of* **lead**.

ledge [ledȝ] *n* repisa *f*, reborde *m*; (*along wall*) retallo *m*; (*of window*) antepecho *m*, alféizar *m*; (*shelf*) anaquel *m*; (*on mountain*) plataforma *f*, saliente *m*.

ledger ['ledȝə*] *n* libro *m* mayor.

lee [li:] 1 *adj* a sotavento, de sotavento. 2 *n* sotavento *m*; (*shelter*) socaire *m*; **in the — of** al socaire de, al abrigo de.

leech [li:tʃ] *n* sanguijuela *f* (*also fig*).

leek [li:k] *n* puerro *m*.

leer [liə*] 1 *n* mirada *f* impúdica, mirada *f* maliciosa; sonrisa *f* impúdica; **he said with a —** dijo sonriendo impúdico.

2 *vi* mirar impúdico, mirar malicioso (*at someone* a uno); sonreír impúdico (*at someone* a uno).

lees [li:z] *npl* heces *fpl*, poso *m*.

leeward ['li:wəd] 1 *adj* a sotavento, de sotavento. 2 *adv* a sotavento.

3 *n* sotavento *m*; **to — a** sotavento (*of de*).

Leeward Isles ['li:wəd‚ailz] *pl* Islas *fpl* de Sotavento.

leeway ['li:wei] *n* (*Naut*) deriva *f*; (*fig*) atraso *m*, tiempo *m* (*etc*) perdido; **to make up —** salir del atraso, recuperar el tiempo perdido; **there's a lot of — to make up** son muchas las pérdidas que tenemos que suplir.

left¹ [left] *pret and ptp of* **leave**.

left² [left] 1 *adj* izquierdo; (*Pol*) izquierdista.

2 *adv* a la izquierda, hacia la izquierda.

3 *n* (a) izquierda *f*; **on the —, to the —** a la izquierda; **to keep to the —** (*Aut*) circular por la izquierda.

(b) (*Pol*) izquierda *f*, izquierdas *fpl*; **he has always been on the —** siempre ha sido de

izquierdas; **he's further to the — than I am** es más izquierdista que yo.

left-hand ['lefthænd] *adj*: **— drive** conducción *f* a la izquierda; **— side** izquierda *f*; **— turn** vuelta *f* a la izquierda.

left-handed ['left'hændid] *adj* zurdo; (*fig*) *person* torpe, desmañado; *compliment* ambiguo, de doble filo; *marriage* de la mano izquierda; *tool* para zurdo.

leftist ['leftist] 1 *adj* izquierdista. 2 *n* izquierdista *mf*.

left-luggage ['left'lʌgidȝ] *attr*: **— office** consigna *f*.

left-overs ['left‚əuvəz] *npl* sobras *fpl*.

left-wing ['left‚wiŋ] *adj* izquierdista.

left-winger ['left'wiŋə*] *n* izquierdista *mf*.

leg [leg] 1 *n* pierna *f*; (*of animal, bird, furniture*) pata *f*; (*support*) pie *m*; (*of trousers*) pernera *f*; (*of stocking*) caña *f*; (*of pork*) pernil *m*; (*of lamb, veal*) pierna *f*; (*stage*) etapa *f*, fase *f*; **I've been on my —s all day** he estado trajinando todo el santo día; **to be on one's last —s** estar en las últimas; **to give someone a —** ayudar a uno a subir (*also fig*); **he hasn't a — to stand on** no tiene razón alguna, no hay nada que hable a su favor; **to pull someone's —** tomar el pelo a uno; **to shake a —** (*fam*) bailar; **to show a —** (*fam*) despertar, levantarse; **show a —!** ¡a levantarse!; **to stand on one's own two —s** (*fig*) ser independiente; **to stretch one's —s** estirar las piernas, (*after stiffness*) desentumecerse las piernas, (*fig*) dar un paseíto; **to take to one's —s** poner pies en polvorosa, echar a correr; **to walk someone off his —s** dejar a uno rendido tras una larguísima caminata.

2 *vt*: **to — it** ir andando.

legacy ['legəsi] *n* legado *m*; (*fig*) herencia *f*, patrimonio *m*.

legal ['li:gəl] *adj* (*lawful*) lícito, legítimo; (*relating to the law*) legal; *department, entity, inquiry* jurídico; *matter* de derecho; **— profession** abogacía *f*; *see* **advice, cost** *etc.*

legality [li'gæliti] *n* legalidad *f*.

legalization [‚li:gəlai'zeiʃən] *n* legalización *f*.

legalize ['li:gəlaiz] *vt* legalizar; autorizar, legitimar.

legally ['li:gəli] *adv* según la ley, según el derecho; legalmente.

legate ['legit] *n* legado *m*.

legatee [‚legə'ti:] *n* legatario *m*, a *f*.

legation [li'geiʃən] *n* legación *f*.

legend ['ledȝənd] *n* leyenda *f*; **the black —** la leyenda negra.

legendary ['ledȝəndəri] *adj* legendario.

legerdemain ['ledȝədə'mein] *n* juego *m* de manos; (*fig*) trapacería *f*.

-legged ['legid] *adj* de piernas . . . , *eg* **long-legged** de piernas largas, zancudo; **three-legged** de tres piernas, *stool* de tres patas.

leggings ['legiŋz] *npl* polainas *fpl*; (*baby's*) pantalones *mpl* polainas.

leggy ['legi] *adj* zanquilargo, zancudo.

Leghorn ['legho:n] Liorna.

legibility [‚ledȝi'biliti] *n* legibilidad *f*.

legible ['ledȝəbl] *adj* legible.

legibly ['ledȝəbli] *adv* legiblemente.

legion ['li:dȝən] *n* legión *f* (*also fig*); **American L—, British L—** organizaciones *de veteranos de las dos guerras mundiales*; **Foreign L—** Legión *f* Extranjera; **they are —** son legión.

legionary ['li:dȝənəri] 1 *adj* legionario. 2 *n* legionario *m*.

legionnaire [‚li:dȝə'nɛə*] *n* legionario *m*.

legislate ['ledȝisleit] 1 *vt*: **to — something out of existence** imponer tantas restricciones legales sobre algo que no puede continuar existiendo.

2 *vi* legislar; **one cannot — for every case** es imposible legislar para todo.

legislation [‚ledȝis'leiʃən] *n* legislación *f*.

legislative ['ledȝislətiv] *adj* legislativo.

legislator ['ledȝisleitə*] *n* legislador *m*, ora *f*.

legislature ['ledȝislətʃə*] *n* cuerpo *m* legislativo, asamblea *f* legislativa.

legist ['li:dȝist] *n* legista *m*.

legit [lə'dȝit] *adj* (*sl*) = **legitimate**.

legitimacy [li'dȝitiməsi] *n* legitimidad *f*.

legitimate [li'dȝitimit] *adj* legítimo; (*proper*) admisible, justo; **the — theatre** el teatro teatro, el teatro propiamente dicho, el teatro verdadero.

legitimate [li'dȝitimeit] *vt*, **legitimize** [li'dȝitimaiz] *vt* legitimar.

leg-pull ['legpul] *n* broma *f*.

leg-puller ['legpulə*] *n* bromista *mf*.

legroom ['legrum] *n* espacio *m* para las piernas.

leg-show ['legʃəu] *n* exhibición *f* de piernas.

legume ['legju:m] *n* (*species*) legumbre *f*; (*fruit*) vaina *f*.

leguminous [le'gju:minəs] *adj* leguminoso.

leisure ['leʒə*] **1** n ocio m, tiempo m libre; **people of** — gente f acomodada, (pej) gente f bien; **a life of** — una vida regalada; **to be at** — estar desocupado, no tener nada que hacer; **do it at your** — hágalo en sus ratos libres, hágalo cuando tenga tiempo; **to have the** — **to do something** disponer de bastante tiempo para hacer algo.
  2 attr: — **occupation** pasatiempo m, modo m de ocuparse durante los ratos libres; **in one's** — **time** en sus ratos libres, en los momentos de ocio.
leisured ['leʒəd] adj class acomodado.
leisurely ['leʒəli] **1** adj pausado, lento. **2** adv pausadamente, despacio, con calma.
lemming ['lemiŋ] n conejo m de Noruega.
lemon ['lemən] **1** n (fruit) limón m; (tree) limonero m. **2** attr, adj de limón; (colour) limonado.
lemonade [,lemə'neid] n limonada f.
lemon grove ['lemǝngrǝuv] n limonar m.
lemon squash ['lemǝn'skwɔʃ] n limonada f natural, zumo m de limón.
lemon squeezer ['lemǝn,skwi:zǝ*] n exprimelimones m, exprimidor m, prensalimones m.
lemur ['li:mǝ*] n lémur m.
lend [lend] (irr: pret and ptp **lent**) **1** vt prestar; (fig) prestar, dar, añadir; **to** — **out** prestar.
  2 vr: **to** — **oneself to** prestarse a; **it does not** — **itself to being filmed** no es apto para ser transformado en película.
lender ['lendǝ*] n prestador m, ora f; (professional) prestamista m.
lending ['lendiŋ] adj library circulante.
lend-lease ['lend'li:s] n: — **agreement** convenio m de préstamos y arriendos.
length [leŋθ] n (a) (in general) largo m, longitud f; (Naut) eslora f; **along the whole** — **of the river** a lo largo de todo el río; **over the** — **and breadth of England** por toda Inglaterra, en toda la extensión de Inglaterra; **the** — **of skirts** el largo de las faldas; **the** — **of this letter** la longitud de esta carta; **to be 4 metres in** —, **to have a** — **of 4 metres** tener 4 metros de largo; **what** — **is it?** ¿cuánto tiene de largo?; **what** — **do you want?** ¿cuánto quiere?; **to measure one's** — (**on the floor**) medir el suelo; **to go to any** —(**s**) no pararse en barras; **to go to any** —(**s**) **to** + infin hacer todo lo posible para + infin; **to go to great** — **s in extremarse en; to go to the** — **of** + ger llegar al extremo de + infin.
  (b) (Sport) cuerpo m; **to win by half a** — ganar por medio cuerpo; **to win by 4** —**s** ganar por 4 cuerpos.
  (c) (section: of cloth) corte m; (of road, track etc) tramo m.
  (d) (of time) espacio m, extensión f, duración f; — **of life** duración f de la vida; — **of service** duración f del servicio; — **of a syllable** cantidad f de una sílaba; **for what** — **of time?** ¿durante cuánto tiempo?; **at** — (finally) por fin, finalmente; **to speak at** — hablar largamente; **to discuss something at** — discutir algo detenidamente; **to explain something at** — explicar algo por extenso.
lengthen ['leŋθǝn] **1** vt alargar, prolongar, extender. **2** vi alargarse, prolongarse, extenderse; (days) crecer.
lengthily ['leŋθili] adv largamente, extensamente.
lengthways ['leŋθweiz], **lengthwise** ['leŋθwaiz] **1** adj longitudinal, de largo.
  2 adv longitudinalmente; a lo largo; **to measure something** — medir el largo de algo.
lengthy ['leŋθi] adj largo, extenso; (pej) larguísimo; illness etc de larga duración; meeting prolongado.
lenience ['li:niǝns] n, **leniency** ['li:niǝnsi] n lenidad f, poca severidad f; indulgencia f.
lenient ['li:niǝnt] adj poco severo, más bien blando; indulgente.
leniently ['li:niǝntli] adv con poca severidad, con indulgencia.
Leningrad ['leningræd] Leningrado.
lens [lenz] n (Opt, Phot) lente f; (of camera) objetivo m; (hand-, for stamps etc) lupa f; (Anat) cristalino m.
lent [lent] pret and ptp of **lend**.
Lent [lent] n Cuaresma f.
Lenten ['lentǝn] adj cuaresmal.
lentil ['lentil] n lenteja f.
Leon ['li:ɔn] León m.
Leonese [li:ǝ'ni:z] **1** adj leonés. **2** n leonés m, esa f. **3** n (dialect) leonés m.
leonine ['li:ǝnain] adj leonino.
leopard ['lepǝd] n leopardo m.
leper ['lepǝ*] n leproso m, a f.
leper colony ['lepǝ,kɔlǝni] n leprosería f.
lepidoptera [,lepi'dɔptǝrǝ] npl lepidópteros mpl.
leprechaun ['leprǝkɔːn] n (Ir) duende m.
leprosy ['leprǝsi] n lepra f.

leprous ['leprǝs] adj leproso.
Lesbian ['lezbiǝn] **1** adj lesbio; tortillera (fam). **2** n lesbiana f; tortillera f (fam).
Lesbianism ['lezbiǝnizǝm] n lesbianismo m.
lèse-majesté, lese-majesty ['leiz'mæʒǝsti] n lesa majestad f.
lesion ['li:ʒǝn] n lesión f.
less [les] **1** adj (a) (in size, degree etc) menor, inferior; **a sum** — **than £1** una cantidad inferior a 1 libra; **A or B, whichever is the** — la menor de las dos cantidades A o B; **it's nothing** — **than a disaster** no es sino un verdadero desastre, es un desastre y no se puede llamar de otro modo; **it's nothing** — **than disgraceful** es francamente vergonzoso; **St James the L** — Santiago el Menor; **no** — **a person than the bishop** no otro que el obispo, el obispo y no otro, el mismísimo obispo; **that was told me by the minister, no** — eso me lo dijo el mismo ministro.
  (b) (in quantity) menos; **now we eat** — **bread** ahora comemos menos pan; **of** — **importance de menos importancia; — **noise please!** ¡menos ruido, por favor!; — **of it!** ¡basta ya!; **to grow** — menguar, decrecer, disminuir.
  2 adv menos; — **and** — cada vez menos; — **than 6** menos de 6; **in** — **than an hour** en menos de una hora; **he works** — **than I** (do) él trabaja menos que yo; **it's** — **than you think** es menos de lo que piensas; **he is** — **well known** es menos conocido; **the** — **he works the** — **he earns** mientras menos trabaja menos gana; **even** — menos aun; **still** — menos todavía; **none the** — sin embargo, a pesar de todo, con todo; **there will be so much the** — **to pay** tanto menos habrá que pagar; **can't you let me have it for** —? ¿no me lo puedes ceder en menos?; **the problem is** — **one of capital than of personnel** el problema más que de capitales es de personal.
  3 prep menos; **the price** — **10%** el precio menos 10 por ciento; **a year** — **4 days** un año menos 4 días.
-less [lis] sin, eg **hatless** sin sombrero, **sunless** sin sol.
lessee [le'si:] n arrendatario m, a f.
lessen ['lesn] **1** vt disminuir, reducir, aminorar; cost, stature etc rebajar. **2** vt disminuir(se), reducirse, menguar.
lessening ['lesniŋ] n disminución f, reducción f.
lesser ['lesǝ*] adj comp of **less**; menor, más pequeño; inferior.
lesson ['lesn] n lección f; clase f; —**s** clases fpl; **a French** — una clase de francés; **to give a** — dar clase; **to have a** — tomar lección; **to learn one's** — (fig) escarmentar; **let that be a** — **to you!** ¡que te sirva de lección!, ¡para que lo aprendas!; **to teach someone a** — (fig) hacer que uno vaya aprendiendo.
lessor [le'sɔː*] n arrendador m, ora f.
lest [lest] conj para que no + subj, de miedo que + subj; — **we forget** para que no olvidemos; — **he catch me unprepared** para que no me coja desprevenido; **I feared** — **he should fall** temía que fuera a caer; **I didn't do it** — **someone should object** no lo hice por miedo de que alguien pusiera peros.
let¹ [let] n (Tennis) let m; **without** — **or hindrance** sin estorbo ni obstáculo.
let² [let] (irr: pret and ptp **let**) **1** vt (a) (permit) dejar, permitir; **to** — **someone do something** dejar a uno hacer algo, permitir a uno hacer algo, permitir que uno haga algo; — **me help you** déjeme ayudarle.
  (b) blood (surgically) sacar; **without** —**ting any blood** sin efusión de sangre.
  (c) (hire out) alquilar; **"to** —**" "se alquila"; we can't find a house to** — no encontramos una casa que alquilar.
  (d) (v aux, gen translated by subj) — **us pray** oremos; —**'s go!** ¡vamos!; —**'s get out here** bajémonos aquí; — **there be light** hágase la luz; — **there be no mistake about it** entiéndase bien que...; — **them all come!** ¡que vengan todos!; — **their need be never so great** por muy grande que sea su necesidad; — **X be 60** supongamos que X equivale a 60.
  (e) (with adv or prep) **to** — **someone by** dejar a uno pasar; **to** — **down** seat, step etc bajar; hair dejar caer, soltar; dress alargar; tyre desinflar, deshinchar; **to** — **something down on a rope** bajar algo con una cuerda; **to** — **someone down on a rope** descolgar a uno con una cuerda; **to** — **someone down** (morally) defraudar la confianza de uno, faltar a uno; dejar a uno plantado; desilusionar a uno; **it has never** — **us down yet** no nos ha fallado nunca; **the weather** — **us down** nos defraudó el tiempo; **to be** — **down** llevarse un chasco; **to** — **someone down gently** (fig) castigar a uno con poca severidad; **to** — **someone in** dejar a uno entrar, visitor hacer

a uno pasar; **shoes that — in water** zapatos *mpl* que dejan entrar el agua; **I got — in for £5** tuve que pagar 5 libras; **to — someone in for a lot of trouble** causar a uno muchas molestias, plantear a uno muchos problemas; **to — someone in on a secret** revelar a uno un secreto; **to — someone into a house** dejar a uno entrar en una casa; **to — a plaque into a wall** empotrar una lápida en una pared; **to — off** *arrow, gun* disparar; *firework* hacer estallar; *steam* dejar escapar; **to — someone off** perdonar a uno, dejar libre a uno; **to — someone off something** perdonar algo a uno; **to — someone off with a warning** dar a uno una amonestación pero sin otro castigo; **he was — off with a fine** escapó con una multa nada más; **to — on about something** revelar algo a uno; **he's not —ting on** no dice nada; **don't go and — on about this** de esto no digas ni pío; **to — out** dejar salir; *prisoner* poner en libertad; *cattle etc* soltar, echar al pasto; *secret* revelar, divulgar; *fire* dejar apagarse; *dress* ensanchar; (*hire out*) alquilar; **the dog is — out** at 8 se le deja salir al perro a las 8; **I'll — you out** te acompaño a la puerta; **the watchman — me out** el sereno me abrió la puerta para que saliese; **that —s me out** eso me deja libre; **to — the air out of a tyre** desinflar un neumático; **to — out a yell** dar un alarido; **to — out one's belt** aflojar un poco el cinturón; **to — someone through** dejar pasar a uno; *see* **alone, fly, go** *etc*.

2 *vi* (*be hired*) alquilarse (*at, for* en); **to — on** revelar el secreto, cantar; **he — on that . . .** reveló que . . .; **but he wouldn't — on** pero no dijo nada; **to — up** moderarse (*on* en el uso de, en el consumo de); trabajar (*etc*) menos; **when the rain —s up** cuando deje de llover tanto; **to — up on someone** tratar a uno con menos rigor.

3 *vr:* **to — oneself be seen** dejarse ver; **to — oneself down** (*fig*) no estar a la altura de uno; **to — oneself down by a rope** descolgarse con una cuerda; **to — oneself in** abrirse la puerta; **to — oneself in for trouble** crearse molestias, plantearse problemas; **you don't know what you're —ting yourself in for** no sabes lo que te pescas.

let-down ['letdaun] *n* decepción *f*, chasco *m*.

lethal ['li:θəl] *adj* mortífero; *wound etc, dose* mortal; *weapon* mortífero.

lethargic [le'θɑːdʒik] *adj* aletargado, letárgico.

lethargy ['leθədʒi] *n* letargo *m*.

Lethe ['li:θi:] Lete(o) *m*.

Lett [let] *see* **Latvian**.

letter ['letə*] **1** *n* (**a**) (*of alphabet*) letra *f*; **block —, capital —** mayúscula *f*; **dead —** letra *f* muerta; **small —** minúscula *f*; **the — of the law** la ley escrita; **to the —** a la letra, al pie de la letra.

(**b**) (*missive*) carta *f*; **covering —** carta *f* adjunta; **open —** carta *f* abierta; **registered —** carta *f* certificada; **— of credit** carta *f* de crédito; **— of introduction** carta *f* de recomendación (*to* para); **—s of Galdós** (*as published*) epistolario *m* de Galdós; **—s patent** patente *m* de privilegio; **by —** por carta, por escrito.

(**c**) **—s** (*learning*) letras *fpl*; **man of —s** hombre *m* de letras, literato *m*.

2 *vt* rotular, inscribir, estampar con letras.

letterbox ['letəbɔks] *n* buzón *m*.

letter-card ['letəkɑːd] *n* carta-tarjeta *f*.

lettered ['letəd] *adj person* culto; *object* rotulado, marcado con letras; **— in gold** marcado con letras doradas.

letter file ['letəfail] *n* carpeta *f*.

letterhead ['letəhed] *n* membrete *m*.

lettering ['letəriŋ] *n* letras *fpl*, inscripción *f*, rótulo *m*.

letterpress ['letəpres] *n* (*Typ*) texto *m* impreso.

letting ['letiŋ] *n* arrendamiento *m*.

lettuce ['letis] *n* lechuga *f*.

let-up ['letʌp] *n* calma *f*, respiro *m*, tregua *f*, descanso *m*; **we worked 5 hours without a —** trabajamos 5 horas sin interrupción; **there was no — no hubo ningún intervalo de calma; **if there is a — in the rain** si deja un momento de llover.

leukaemia, (*US*) **leukemia** [luː'kiːmiə] *n* leucemia *f*.

Levant [li'vænt] Levante *m*.

Levantine ['levəntain] **1** *adj* levantino. **2** *n* levantino *m, a f*.

levee ['levei] *n* besamanos *m*, recepción *f*.

levee ['levi] *n* ribero *m*, dique *m*.

level ['levl] **1** *adj* llano, plano, raso; a nivel, nivelado; igual, uniforme; *tone* ecuánime; *judgement, mind* juicioso; **to be dead —** estar completamente a nivel; **to be — with** estar a nivel con; **to be — with the ground** estar a ras de la tierra; **to be — with the**

water estar a flor del agua; **I'll do my — best** haré todo lo que pueda.

2 *adv* a nivel; ras con ras; **to draw — with someone** llegar a la altura de uno, alcanzar a uno, (*in league etc*) llegar a empatar con uno, colocarse en igual posición que uno.

3 *n* (**a**) (*instrument*) nivel *m*.

(**b**) (*altitude, degree*) nivel *m*; **dead —** superficie *f* completamente llana; **at eye —** a la altura del ojo; **at roof —** a la altura de los tejados; **speed on the —** velocidad *f* sobre superficie llana; **it's on the —** (*fam*) es un negocio honrado, es un juego perfectamente limpio; **is he on the —?** (*fam*) ¿es de fiar?, ¿es una persona honrada?; **are you telling me this on the —?** (*fam*) ¿me lo dices en serio?; **to be on a —** with estar al nivel de; **to be on a — with the ground** estar a ras de la tierra; **to be on a — with** (*fig*) estar al nivel de; ser parangonable con; **that trick is on a — with the other** esa jugada es tan vil como la otra; **to come down to someone's —** bajar al nivel en que está uno.

(**c**) (*flat place*) llano *m*.

4 *vt* (**a**) *ground etc* nivelar, allanar; *building* derribar; *site* desmontar, despejar; *quantities* igualar, nivelar; **to — down** rebajar al mismo nivel; **to — up** elevar al mismo nivel; **to — something to** (*or* **with**) **the ground** arrasar algo.

(**b**) *blow as*estar (*at* a); *weapon* apuntar (*at* a); *accusation* dirigir (*against, at* a), hacer (*against, at* contra).

5 *vi:* **to — off, to — out** nivelarse; (*of prices etc*) estabilizarse; (*Aer*) enderezarse.

level crossing ['levl'krɔsiŋ] *n* paso *m* a nivel.

level-headed ['levl'hedid] *adj* juicioso, sensato.

levelling ['levliŋ] *n* nivelación *f*; aplanamiento *m*.

lever ['liːvə*] **1** *n* palanca *f* (*also fig*). **2** *vt* apalancar; **to — something up** alzar algo con palanca.

leverage ['liːvəridʒ] *n* apalancamiento *m*; (*fig*) influencia *f*; fuerza *f*; ventaja *f*.

leveret ['levərit] *n* lebrato *m*.

leviathan [li'vaiəθən] *n* leviatán *m*; (*fig*) buque *m* enorme.

levitate ['leviteit] **1** *vt* elevar (por medios espiritistas). **2** *vi* elevarse (por medios espiritistas).

levitation [.levi'teiʃən] *n* elevación *f* (por medios espiritistas).

Levite ['liːvait] *n* levita *m*.

levity ['leviti] *n* frivolidad *f*, ligereza *f*, informalidad *f*; (*mirth*) risas *fpl*.

levy ['levi] **1** *n* (*act*) exacción *f* (de tributos); (*tax*) impuesto *m*; (*surcharge*) sobrecarga *f*, sobretasa *f*; (*Mil*) leva *f*.

2 *vt tax* exigir (*on* a), recaudar; *fine* imponer (*on* a); (*Mil*) reclutar.

lewd [luːd] *adj* impúdico, obsceno; *song, story etc* verde.

lewdly ['luːdli] *adv* impúdicamente, obscenamente.

lewdness ['luːdnis] *n* impudicicia *f*, obscenidad *f*; lo verde.

lexical ['leksikəl] *adj* léxico.

lexicographer [.leksi'kɔgrəfə*] *n* lexicógrafo *m*.

lexicographical [.leksikəu'græfikəl] *adj* lexicográfico.

lexicography [.leksi'kɔgrəfi] *n* lexicografía *f*.

lexicon ['leksikən] *n* léxico *m*.

Leyden ['laidn] Leide(n), Leida.

liability [.laiə'biliti] *n* (**a**) responsabilidad *f*; riesgo *m*; tendencia *f*; (*burden*) carga *f* onerosa, lastre *m*; desventaja *f*; **one's — for tax** la cantidad que uno puede ser llamado a pagar en impuestos; **he's a real —** es un estorbo, es absolutamente inútil.

(**b**) **liabilities** obligaciones *fpl*, compromisos *mpl*; (*Comm*) pasivo *m*, deudas *fpl*; **to meet one's liabilities** satisfacer sus deudas; *see* **company**.

liable ['laiəbl] *adj:* **to be —** ser el responsable; **to be — for** ser responsable de, responder de; **to be — for taxes** (*thing*) estar sujeto a impuestos, (*person*) tener que pagar impuestos; **to be — to +** *infin* tener tendencia a **+** *infin*, ser propenso a **+** *infin*; **he is — not to come** es capaz de no venir, tiene tendencia a no venir; **the pond is — to freeze** el estanque tiene tendencia a helarse, el estanque bien puede helarse; **the plan is — to changes** el plan bien puede sufrir cambios; **we are — to get shot at here** aquí corremos el riesgo de que disparen sobre nosotros, aquí estamos expuestos a los tiros.

liaison [liː'eizɔn] *n* (**a**) (*coordination*) enlace *m*, conexión *f*, coordinación *f*; (*Mil*) enlace *m*. (**b**) (*affair*) lío *m*, relaciones *fpl* amorosas.

liaison officer [liː'eizɔn.ɔfisə*] *n* oficial *m* de enlace.

liar ['laiə*] *n* mentiroso *m, a f*, embustero *m, a f*; **—!** ¡mentira!

libation [lai'beiʃən] *n* libación *f*.

libel ['laibəl] **1** *n* difamación *f*, calumnia *f* (*on* de); (*written*) libelo *m*; **it's a —!** (*hum*) ¡es mentira!; **it's a — on all of us!** ¡esto nos calumnia a todos! **2** *vt* difamar, calumniar.

libellous, (US) **libelous** ['laibələs] *adj* difamatorio, calumnioso.

liberal ['libərəl] **1** *adj* liberal (*also* Pol); *offer etc* generoso; *supply* abundante; (*in views*) tolerante. **2** *n* liberal *mf*.

liberalism ['libərəlizəm] *n* liberalismo *m*.

liberality [,libə'ræliti] *n* generosidad *f*, liberalidad *f*.

liberalize ['libərəlaiz] *vt* liberalizar.

liberally ['libərəli] *adv* generosamente, liberalmente; abundantemente; con tolerancia.

liberal-minded ['libərəl'maindid] *adj* tolerante.

liberal-mindedness ['libərəl'maindidnis] *n* tolerancia *f*.

liberate ['libəreit] *vt* (*free*) libertar, librar (*from* de); *prisoner* poner en libertad; *gas etc* dejar escapar.

liberation [,libə'reiʃən] *n* liberación *f*.

liberator ['libəreitə*] *n* libertador *m*, ora *f*.

libertinage ['libətinidʒ] *n* libertinaje *m*.

libertine ['libəti:n] *n* libertino *m*.

liberty ['libəti] *n* libertad *f*; **— of conscience** libertad *f* de conciencia; **— of the press** libertad *f* de prensa; **it's a dead —!** (*fam*) ¡no hay derecho!; **to be at —** estar en libertad, (*at leisure*) estar desocupado; **to be at — to** + *infin* tener permiso para + *infin*, tener el derecho de + *infin*, estar autorizado para + *infin*; **is he at — to come?** ¿está libre para venir?; **when you are at — to study it** cuando tenga tiempo para estudiarlo; **to restore someone to —** devolver la libertad a uno; **to set someone at —** poner a uno en libertad; **I have taken the — of giving your name** me he tomado la libertad de darles su nombre; **to take liberties with a text** tomarse libertades con un texto, interpretar demasiado libremente un texto; **to take liberties with someone** tratar a uno con demasiada familiaridad, (*sexually*) propasarse con una.

libidinous [li'bidinəs] *adj* libidinoso.

libido [li'bi:dəu] *n* libido *f*.

librarian [lai'brɛəriən] *n* bibliotecario *m*, a *f*.

librarianship [lai'brɛəriənʃip] *n* (a) profesión *f* de bibliotecario. (b) conocimientos *mpl* especializados del bibliotecario. (c) puesto *m* de bibliotecario.

library ['laibrəri] *n* biblioteca *f*; (*esp private*) librería *f*; **circulating —, lending —** biblioteca *f* circulante; **public —** biblioteca *f* pública; **reference —** biblioteca *f* de consulta; **university —** biblioteca *f* universitaria.

librettist [li'bretist] *n* libretista *mf*.

libretto [li'bretəu] *n* libreto *m*.

Libya ['libiə] Libia *f*.

Libyan ['libiən] **1** *adj* libio. **2** *n* libio *m*, a *f*.

lice [lais] *npl of* **louse**.

licence, (US) **license** ['laisəns] *n* (a) (*permit*) licencia *f*, permiso *m*; autorización *f*; (*Aut etc*) carnet *m*, permiso *m*; **dog —** licencia *f* para perro; **export —** permiso *m* de exportación; **import —** permiso *m* de importación; **marriage —** licencia *f* para casarse; **poetic —** licencia *f* poética; **wireless —** licencia *f* para radio; **to manufacture something under —** fabricar algo bajo licencia.
(b) (*excess*) libertinaje *m*, desenfreno *m*; (*freedom*) libertad *f*; **you can allow some — in translation** Vd puede permitirse cierta libertad al traducirlo.

licence number ['laisəns,nʌmbə*] *n* (Aut) número *m* de matrícula.

licence plate ['laisəns,pleit] *n* (Aut) placa *f* de matrícula.

license ['laisəns] *vt* licenciar, autorizar, dar permiso a; *car* sacar la patente de; **to be —d to** + *infin* tener permiso para + *infin*, estar autorizado para + *infin*.

licensee [,laisən'si:] *n* concesionario *m*, a *f*, persona *f* autorizada; (*of bar*) patrón *m*.

licentiate [lai'senʃiit] *n* (*person*) licenciado *m*; (*title*) licencia *f*, licenciatura *f*.

licentious [lai'senʃəs] *adj* licencioso.

lichen ['laikən] *n* liquen *m*.

lichgate ['litʃgeit] *n* puerta *f* de cementerio.

licit ['lisit] *adj* lícito.

lick [lik] **1** *n* lamedura *f*, lengüetada *f*; **a — of paint** una mano de pintura; **a — of polish** un poquito de cera; **to go at a good —** (*fam*) ir a buen tren, correr rápidamente.
2 *vt* (*with tongue, of flames*) lamer; (*of waves*) besar; (*fam: tan, defeat*) dar una paliza a; *see* **dust, lip** *etc*.

licking ['likiŋ] *n* lamedura *f*; (*fam*) paliza *f*; **to give someone a —** dar una paliza a uno.

lickspittle ['likspitl] *n* lameculos *m*.

licorice ['likəris] *n* regaliz *m*.

lid [lid] *n* (*of box, case, pot etc*) tapa *f*; (*of pan etc*) cobertera *f*; (Anat) párpado *m*; (*sl: hat*) techo *m*; **that puts the — on it** se acabó, eso es el fin.

lido ['li:dəu] *n* (*bathing*) establecimiento *m* de baños; (*swimming*) centro *m* de natación, piscina *f*; (*boating*) centro *m* de balandrismo.

lie¹ [lai] **1** *n* mentira *f*; **white —** mentira *f* piadosa, mentirilla *f*; **it's a —!** ¡es mentira!; **to give the — to** *person* dar el mentís a, *report* desmentir; **to tell a —** mentir.
2 *vi* mentir.

lie² [lai] (*irr: pret* **lay,** *ptp* **lain**) **1** *vi* (a) (*person etc: act*) echarse, acostarse, tenderse; (*state*) estar echado, estar tumbado, estar acostado, estar tendido; (*in grave*) yacer, estar enterrado; **here —s aquí yace;** **he lay where he had fallen** estaba tumbado donde había caído; **don't — on the grass** no te eches sobre el césped; **to — asleep** estar dormido; **to — dead** yacer muerto; **to — in bed** estar en la cama, (*lazily*) seguir en la cama; **to — helpless** estar tumbado sin poder ayudarse; **to — resting** estar descansando; **to — still** quedarse inmóvil.
(b) (*objects etc*) estar; (*be situated*) estar, estar situado, encontrarse; (*stretch*) extenderse; **the book lay on the table** el libro estaba en la mesa; **the book lay unopened** el libro quedaba sin abrir; **the snow lay half a metre deep** había medio metro de nieve; **the snow did not —** la nieve se derritió; **the money is lying in the bank** el dinero sigue en el banco; **it —s further on** está situado más adelante; **our road lay along the river** nuestro camino seguía a lo largo del río; **the road —s over the hills** el camino cruza las colinas; **the factory lay idle** la fábrica estaba parada; **obstacles — in the way** hay obstáculos por delante; **the plain lay before us** la llanura se extendía delante de nosotros; **how does the land —?** ¿cuál es el estado actual de las cosas?; **where does the difficulty —?** ¿en qué consiste la dificultad?; **the fault —s with you** la falta es tuya, tú eres el culpable; **it —s with you to reform it** te corresponde a Vd reformarlo; **it does not — with me** no depende de mí, no me toca a mí.
(c) (*evidence etc*) ser admisible.
(d) (*with adv or prep*) **— about** estar esparcido; estar en desorden; **he just —s about** pasa el tiempo sin hacer nada; **we lay about on our beds** quedamos tumbados en las camas; **it must be lying about somewhere** estará por aquí, debe de andar por aquí; **to — back** recostarse (*against, on* sobre); **to — down** (*act*) echarse, acostarse, tenderse; (*state*) estar tendido, estar echado, estar tumbado, estar acostado, estar tendido; **— down!** (*to dog*) ¡échate!; **to — down under it, to take it lying down** aceptarlo sin protestar, soportarlo sin chistar, tragarlo; **he's not one to take things lying down** no es de los que aceptan mansamente las injusticias; **to — in** seguir en la cama, no levantarse; (*at birth*) estar de parto; **to — over** quedar aplazado, quedar en suspenso; **to — to** (Naut: *act*) ponerse a la capa, (*state*) estar a la capa; **to — up** (*hide*) estar escondido; (*rest*) descansar; (Naut) estar amarrado.
2 *n* (*of ball etc*) posición *f*; **— of the land** configuración *f* del terreno, (*fig*) estado *m* de las cosas.

lie-abed ['laiəbed] *n* dormilón *m*, ona *f*.

lie detector ['laidi,tektə*] *n* detector *m* de mentiras.

lief [li:f] *adv* (*arch*): **I would as — + *infin*** preferiría + *infin*.

Liège [li'eiʒ] Lieja.

liege [li:dʒ] *n* (*lord*) señor *m* feudal; (*vassal*) vasallo *m*; **my —** señor.

liege lord ['li:dʒ,lɔ:d] *n* señor *m* feudal.

liegeman ['li:dʒmæn] *n*, *pl* **—men** [men] vasallo *m*.

lien [liən] *n* derecho *m* de retención (*on* de).

lieu [lu:] *n*: **in — of** en lugar de.

lieutenant [lef'tenənt] *n* lugarteniente *m*; (Mil) teniente *m*; (Naut) teniente *m* de navío; **second —** alférez *m*.

lieutenant-colonel [lef'tenənt'kə:nl] *n* teniente *m* coronel.

lieutenant-commander [lef'tenəntkə'mɑ:ndə*] *n* capitán *m* de corbeta.

lieutenant-general [lef'tenənt'dʒenərəl] *n* teniente *m* general.

life [laif] *n*, *pl* **lives** [laivz] **1** *n* (a) (*in general*) vida *f*; ser *m*, existencia *f*; modo *m* de vivir; (*liveliness*) vida *f*, vivacidad *f*, vitalidad *f*, animación *f*; (*of licence etc*) vigencia *f*, validez *f*; (*of battery*) vida *f*, duración *f*; **bird —** los pájaros; **plant —** vida *f* vegetal, las plantas; **there is not much insect — here** aquí hay pocos insectos.
(b) (*with adj*) **early —** juventud *f*, años *mpl* juveniles; **in her early —** en su juventud; **in later**

— más tarde, en los años posteriores; **the good** — una vida agradable, (*Rel*) la vida santa; **it's a good** — es una vida agradable; **high** — alta sociedad *f*, gran mundo *m*; **home** — vida *f* de familia; **low** — hampa *f*; **private** — vida *f* privada; **the private** — **of Henry VIII** la vida íntima de Enrique VIII; **X, known in private** — **as Z X**, conocido en la intimidad como Z; **my** —! ¡Dios mío!; **what a** —! ¡qué vida ésta!

(c) (*with* to be) **to be a matter of** — **and death** ser cosa de vida o de muerte; **to be the** — **and soul of the party** ser el alma de la fiesta; **such is** —! ¡así es la vida!; **this is the** —! ¡qué vida nos chupamos!, ¡esto es jauja!

(d) (*with prep*) **at my time of** — a mi edad, con los años que yo tengo; **for** — de por vida; **to be on trial for one's** — ser acusado de un crimen que pudiera castigarse con pena de muerte; **for one's** —, **for dear** — para salvarse la vida, desesperadamente, (*all out*) a más no poder; **run for your lives**! ¡sálvese el que pueda!; **for the** — **of me I can't see why** que me maten si comprendo por qué; **from** — del natural; **never in my** — en mi vida; **not on your** —! ¡ni hablar!; **to the** — al vivo; **true to** — conforme con la realidad, verdadero; **to come to** — resucitar(se), (*fig*) empezar a animarse.

(e) (*with verb other than* to be) **to bear a charmed** — salir milagrosamente ileso de todos los peligros; **she began** — **as a teacher** primero se dedicó a la enseñanza; — **begins at 40** la vida comienza de verdad a los 40; **to depart this** — partir de esta vida; **to lay down one's** — dar su vida, entregar su vida; **to lead a quiet** — llevar una vida tranquila; **to lead a strange** — llevar una vida muy rara; **to live the** — **of Riley** darse buena vida; **how many lives were lost?** ¿cuántas víctimas hubo?; **no lives were lost** no hubo víctimas; **to put new** — **into someone** reanimar a uno, infundir nueva vida a uno; **to see** — ver mundo; **to sell one's** — **dearly** vender muy cara la vida; **to take one's** — **in one's hands** jugarse la vida; **to take someone's** — quitar la vida a uno; **to take one's own** — suicidarse.

(f) (*fam*) = — **imprisonment**; **to do** — cumplir una condena de reclusión perpetua; **to get** — ser condenado a reclusión perpetua.

2 *attr* de vida; **annuity** *etc* vitalicio; — **president** presidente *m* de por vida; — **imprisonment** prisión *f* a perpetuidad; — **sentence** condena *f* a perpetuidad, condena *f* de reclusión perpetua; — **and death struggle** lucha *f* a muerte.

life annuity ['laifə'njuːiti] *n* renta *f* vitalicia, pensión *f* vitalicia.

life assurance ['laifəˌʃuərəns] *n* seguro *m* sobre la vida.

lifebelt ['laifbelt] *n* cinturón *m* salvavidas.

lifeblood ['laifblʌd] *n* sangre *f* vital; (*fig*) alma *f*, nervio *m*, sustento *m*.

lifeboat ['laifbəut] *n* (*from shore*) lancha *f* de socorro; (*from ship*) bote *m* salvavidas, chalupa *f*.

lifebuoy ['laifbɔi] *n* guindola *f*.

life force ['laifɔːs] *n* fuerza *f* vital.

life-giving ['laifgiviŋ] *adj* que da vida, vivificante.

lifeguard ['laifgɑːd] *n* (*on beach*) vigilante *m*; (*Mil*) guardia *m* de corps.

life interest ['laif'intərest] *n* usufructo *m* vitalicio (*in* de).

life jacket ['laif,dʒækit] *n* chaleco *m* salvavidas.

lifeless ['laiflis] *adj* sin vida, muerto, exánime; (*fig*) soso, flojo.

lifelessness ['laiflisnis] *n* (*fig*) falta *f* de vida, sosería *f*, flojedad *f*.

lifelike ['laiflaik] *adj* natural, vivo.

lifeline ['laiflain] *n* cuerda *f* salvavidas; (*fig*) alma *f*, sustento *m*.

lifelong ['laiflɔŋ] *adj* de toda la vida.

life preserver ['laifpri,zɜːvə*] *n* cachiporra *f*.

life-saving ['laifseiviŋ] **1** *n* salvamento *m*; (*training for* —) socorrismo *m*. **2** *attr* de salvamento, salvavidas; — **raft** balsa *f* salvavidas.

life-size(d) ['laif'saiz(d)] *adj* de tamaño natural.

lifetime ['laiftaim] *n* (a) vida *f*; **the** — **of a horse** el término medio de vida de un caballo; **once in a** — una vez en la vida; **in my** — durante mi vida; **the chance of a** — una oportunidad única en la vida; **the work of a** — el trabajo de una vida entera.

(b) (*fig*) eternidad *f*, mucho tiempo *m*; **it seemed a** — parecía una eternidad.

lifework ['laif'wɜːk] *n* trabajo *m* de toda la vida.

lift [lift] **1** *n* (a) (*act of* —*ing*) alzamiento *m*, levantamiento *m*, elevación *f*; (*effort*) esfuerzo *m* para levantar; (*upward push*) empuje *m* para arriba; (*help*) ayuda *f* (para levantar); (*Aer*) sustentación *f*, fuerza *f* de sustentación; (*Mech, of valve etc*) carrera

f, juego *m*; (*moral uplift*) exaltación *f* de ánimo, estímulo *m*; **give me a** — **with this trunk** ¿me ayudas a levantar este baúl?

(b) (*in car etc*) viaje *m* gratuito, viaje *m* en coche (*etc*) ajeno; **to give someone a** — llevar a uno gratis en su coche; **I can give you a** — **to Burgos** le puedo llevar a Burgos; *see* **hitch**.

(c) (*elevator*) ascensor *m*, (*for goods*) montacargas *m*.

2 *vt* (*raise*) alzar, levantar, elevar (*also* **to** — **up**); (*pick up*) coger, recoger; **child** *etc* levantar en brazos; **hat** quitarse; (*by air*) transportar en avión, transportar por puente aéreo; **restrictions** *etc* levantar, suprimir; (*fam: steal*) birlar, ratear, (*Lit etc*) plagiar (*from* de); (*morally uplift*) exaltar, estimular; **to** — **someone down** bajar a uno en brazos; **to** — **something down carefully** bajar algo con cuidado.

3 *vi* levantarse, alzarse; (*clouds*) disiparse.

lift attendant ['liftə,tendənt] *n*, **lift boy** ['liftbɔi] *n*, **liftman** ['liftmæn] *n*, *pl* —**men** [men] ascensorista *m*.

lift shaft ['liftʃɑːft] *n* hueco *m* del ascensor.

ligament ['ligəmənt] *n* ligamento *m*.

ligature ['ligətʃə*] *n* (*Med, Mus*) ligadura *f*; (*Typ*) ligado *m*.

light¹ [lait] **1** *n* (a) (*in general*) luz *f*; lumbre *f*; — **and shade** luz *f* y sombra; **electric** — luz *f* eléctrica; **northern** —**s** aurora *f* boreal; **the** — **of day** la luz del día; **in the cold** — **of day** a la luz del día; **against the** — a trasluz; **at first** — al rayar el día; **by the** — **of a candle** a la luz de una vela; **in the** — **of** a la luz de; **in the** — **of what you say** por lo que Vd nos dice; **it is** — now ahora es de día; **to bring to** — sacar a luz, descubrir; **to come to** — salir a luz, descubrirse; **to cast** (*or* **shed, throw**) — **on** aclarar, arrojar luz sobre; **it revealed him in a strange** — le reveló bajo una luz extraña; **to see the** — (*be born*) nacer; (*understand*) comprender, caer en la cuenta; (*Rel*) convertirse, darse cuenta de su error; **I don't see things in that** — yo no veo las cosas así; **to see things in a new** — ver las cosas bajo otro aspecto, ver las cosas desde otro punto de vista; **to stand in someone's** — quitar la luz a uno.

(b) (*lamp*) luz *f*, lámpara *f*; (*Aut, Naut*) faro *m*; **overhead** — lámpara *f* de techo; **blinker** — luz *f* destelladora; **pilot** — (*Aut*) luz *f* de situación; **rear** —**s** luces *fpl* traseras; **reversing** —**s** faros *mpl* de marcha atrás; —**s out** hora *f* de apagar las luces; **what time is** —**s out?** ¿a qué hora se apagan las luces?; **to hide one's** — **under a bushel** darse de menos, retirarse modestamente; **to show someone a** — alumbrar a uno.

(c) (*signal*) **the** —**s** (*Aut*) el semáforo, las luces de tráfico; **green** — luz *f* verde; **to get the green** — **from someone** (*fig*) ser autorizado por uno para pasar adelante; **to give someone the green** — (*fig*) dar a uno la señal para pasar adelante; **she was giving me the green** — me estaba incitando a ir adelante, me daba indicios favorables; **red** — luz *f* roja, (*fig*) señal *f* de peligro, aviso *m*; **to see the red** — (*fig*) ver el peligro que hay por delante.

(d) (*flame*) fuego *m*, lumbre *f*; **pilot** — (*on stove*) mechero *m*, encendedor *m*; **have you a** —? ¿tienes fuego?; **to put a** — **to something**, **to set** — **to something** pegar fuego a algo, encender algo.

(e) (*Art*) toque *m* de luz.

(f) (*Archit*) cristal *m*, vidrio *m*; **leaded** —**s** cristales *mpl* emplomados.

(g) (*person*) **leading** — figura *f* principal, figura *f* más destacada (*in* de); **shining** — lumbrera *f*, figura *f* genial.

(h) —**s** (*intelligence*) luces *fpl*, conocimientos *mpl*; **according to his** —**s** según Dios le da a entender.

2 *adj* (a) (*bright*) claro; (*illuminated*) bañado de luz, con mucha luz; **to grow** — clarear, hacerse de día.

(b) **colour** claro; **hair** rubio; **skin** blanco; **a** — **green dress** un vestido verde claro.

3 (*irr: pret and ptp* **lit** *or* **lighted**) *vt* (a) (*illuminate*) alumbrar, iluminar (*also* **to** — **up**); **a smile lit up her face** una sonrisa le iluminó la cara; **to** — **the way for someone** alumbrar a uno.

(b) **cigarette, fire** *etc* encender.

4 *vi* (a) (*begin to shine; also* **to** — **up**) alumbrarse, iluminarse; **her face lit up** se iluminó su cara.

(b) (*ignite, switch on*) encenderse; **to** — **up** (*smoke*) encender un cigarrillo (*etc*), empezar a fumar.

(c) (*sl*) **to** — **into someone** embestir a uno, empezar a pegar a uno; **to** — **out** largarse (*for* para).

light² [lait] (*irr: pret and ptp* **lit** *or* **lighted**) *vi:* to — on dar con, tropezar con, encontrar.

light³ [lait] *adj* (*in weight*) ligero; *food, gun, meal, sleep, troops, work* ligero; *soil* poco denso; (*Naut*) en lastre; *lorry, train* vacío, sin carga; *breeze, punishment, tax, wound etc* leve; *wine* suave; *task* fácil; *comedy, reading* ameno, de puro entretenimiento; (*morally*) ligero, liviano; (*cheerful*) alegre; **as — as air, as — as a feather** tan ligero como la pluma; **to be — on one's feet** ser ligero de pies, moverse con agilidad; **to make — of** no dar importancia a, restar importancia a.

light bulb ['laitbʌlb] *n* bombilla *f*.

light-coloured ['lait'kʌləd] *adj* claro, de color claro.

lighten¹ ['laitn] **1** *vt* iluminar. **2** *vi* clarear; (*Meteorol*) relampaguear.

lighten² ['laitn] **1** *vt load* aligerar, hacer menos pesado; *cares* aliviar; *heart* alegrar. **2** *vi* (*load*) aligerarse, hacerse menos pesado; (*heart*) alegrarse.

lighter¹ ['laitə*] *n* encendedor *m*, mechero *m*.

lighter² ['laitə*] *n* (*Naut*) gabarra *f*, barcaza *f*.

light-fingered ['lait'fiŋgəd] *adj* largo de uñas.

light fitting ['lait,fitiŋ] *n* guarnición *f* del alumbrado.

light-footed ['lait'futid] *adj* ligero (de pies).

light-haired ['lait'hɛəd] *adj* de pelo rubio.

light-headed ['lait'hɛdid] *adj* (*by temperament*) ligero de cascos, casquivano; (*dizzy*) mareado; (*with fever*) delirante; (*with excitement*) exaltado; **wine makes me —** el vino me hace ser muy frívolo, me aturde el vino.

light-hearted ['lait'hɑ:tid] *adj* alegre.

light-heartedly ['lait'hɑ:tidli] *adv* alegremente.

lighthouse ['laithaus] *n, pl* **—houses** [,hauziz] faro *m*.

lighthouse keeper ['laithaus,ki:pə*] *n* torrero *m*, farero *m*.

lighting ['laitiŋ] *n* (*act*) encendimiento *m*; (*system*) alumbrado *m*; **— engineering** lumino-tecnia *f*; **— fixtures** guarniciones *fpl* de alumbrado.

lighting-up ['laitiŋ'ʌp] *n:* **— time** hora *f* de encender los faros.

lightly ['laitli] *adv* ligeramente; levemente; ágilmente; alegremente; *act etc* sin pensarlo bien, a la ligera; **— clad** vistiendo ropa ligera, con muy poca ropa; **— wounded** levemente herido; **to get off —** escapar casi indemne; ser castigado con poca severidad; **to speak — of someone** hablar de uno en términos despreciativos; **to speak — of something** menospreciar algo; **to touch — on something** mencionar algo de paso.

light meter ['lait,mi:tə*] *n* fotómetro *m*.

lightness ['laitnis] *n* (a) (*brightness*) claridad *f*, luminosidad *f*; (*of colour*) claridad *f*.
(b) (*in weight etc*) ligereza *f*, poco peso *m*; levedad *f*; agilidad *f*; alegría *f*.

lightning ['laitniŋ] **1** *n* relámpago *m*, (*doing damage*) rayo *m*; **as quick as —, like (greased) —** como un relámpago; **where the — struck** donde cayó el rayo. **2** *attr* relámpago.

lightning conductor ['laitniŋkən,dʌktə*] *n*, (US) **lightning rod** [rɔd] *n* pararrayos *m*.

lights [laits] *npl* (*Anat*) bofes *mpl*, livianos *mpl*.

lightship ['laitʃip] *n* buque-faro *m*.

light wave ['laitweiv] *n* onda *f* luminosa.

lightweight ['laitweit] **1** *adj* ligero, de poco peso. **2** *n* persona *f* de poco peso; (*Boxing*) peso *m* ligero; (*fig*) cero *m* a la izquierda.

light-year ['laitjiə*] *n* año *m* luz.

ligneous ['ligniəs] *adj* leñoso.

lignite ['lignait] *n* lignito *m*.

lignum vitae ['lignəm'vi:tai] *n* palo *m* santo; (*tree*) guayacán *m*.

like [laik] **1** *adj* (a) parecido, semejante; igual; mismo; **in — cases** en casos parecidos; **on this and — subjects** sobre este tema y otros parecidos; **two birds of — genus** dos pájaros del mismo género; **the 3 divided the work into a — number of parts** los 3 se dividieron el trabajo en otras tantas porciones; **— father — son** de tal palo tal astilla; **they are as — as two peas** se parecen como dos gotas de agua.
(b) **to be — someone** parecerse a uno; **they are very — each other** se parecen mucho; **a house — mine** una casa parecida a la mía, una casa como la mía; **eyes — stars** ojos como estrellas; **I found one — it** encontré otro parecido (or igual); **people — that** las personas de esa clase; **the Russians are — that** los rusos son así; **he is rather — you** tiene bastante parecido con Vd; **who(m) is he —?** ¿a quién se parece?; **what's he —?** ¿cómo es?, ¿qué tal es?; **what's the coat —?** ¿cómo es el abrigo?; **she was — a sister to me** fue (como) una hermana

para mí; **the portrait is not — him** el retrato no le representa bien.
(c) (*idioms*) **it's not — him** no es propio de él (*to come late* venir tarde), no es característico de él; **I never saw anything — it** no he visto nunca nada igual; **isn't it — him?** ¡son cosas de él!; **that's just — a woman!** ¡eso es muy de mujeres!; **that's more — it!** ¡eso es mucho mejor!; **that hat's nothing — as nice as this one** ese sombrero es muy inferior a éste; **that's something — a fish!** ¡eso es mucho pez!; **I was thinking of something — a doll** pensaba en algo así como una muñeca, pensaba en una muñeca o algo por el estilo; *see* **feel, look** *etc*.

2 *prep* como; del mismo modo que, igual que; tal como; **— a man** como un hombre; **— mad** como un loco (*see also* **mad**); **— that** así; **he thinks — us** opina lo mismo que nosotros; **just — anybody else** igual que cualquier otro; **A, — B, thinks that . . .** A, al igual que B, considera que . . .

3 *adv* **it's nothing —** no tiene parecido alguno, no se parece ni con mucho; **very —, — enough, as — as not** a lo mejor; **I found this money, — (*fam*)** me encontré este dinero, sabe Vd.

4 *conj* como, del mismo modo que; **— we used to (do)** como hacíamos antes; **do it — I do** hágalo como yo; **it's just —** I say es como yo lo digo.

5 *n* (a) (*equal etc*) semejante *mf*; **we shall not see his — again** no volveremos a ver otro tan bueno (*etc*) como él, otro como él no le veremos nunca; **did you ever see the —?** ¿se vio jamás tal cosa?; **and the —, and such —** y otros por el estilo, y otros de ese jaez; **I've no time for the —s of him** (*fam*) los hombres así no los puedo ver.
(b) (*taste*) **—s** gustos *mpl*, simpatías *fpl*, cosas *fpl* predilectas; **—s and dislikes** predilecciones *fpl* y aversiones, simpatías *fpl* y antipatías.

6 *vt* (a) *person* querer, tener simpatía a, tener cariño a, apreciar; **I — him** me es simpático; **I don't — him at all** me resulta totalmente antipático; **don't you — me a little bit?** ¿no me quieres un poquitín?; **how do you — him?** ¿qué te parece él?; **he is well —d here** aquí se le quiere mucho.
(b) (*find pleasure in*) gustar, *eg* **I — black shoes** me gustan los zapatos negros; **I — football** me gusta el fútbol; **I — dancing** me gusta bailar; **we — it here** estamos contentos aquí, aquí disfrutamos; **your father won't — it** esto no le va a gustar a tu padre; **I — your nerve!** ¡qué frescura!
(c) (*wish, wish for*) querer; **I should — more time** quisiera tener más tiempo; **I should — to know why** quisiera saber por qué; **I should — you to do it** quiero que Vd lo haga; **I — to be obeyed** quiero que me obedezcan; **whether he —s it or not** quiera o no quiera, de buen o mal grado; **he is free to act as he —s** está libre para hacer lo que le dé la gana; **as you —** como quieras; **if you —** si quieres; **when you —** cuando quieras; **would you — a drink?** ¿quieres tomar algo?; **would you — to go to Seville?** ¿te gustaría ir a Sevilla?
(d) (*judge, find*) **how do you — Cadiz?** ¿qué te parece Cádiz?; **how do you — it here?** ¿qué te parece esto?, ¿estás contento aquí?; **how would you — a walk?** ¿te apetece dar un paseo?

likeable ['laikəbl] *adj* simpático.

likeableness ['laikəblnis] *n* simpatía *f*.

likelihood ['laiklihud] *n* probabilidad *f*; **in all —** según todas las probabilidades; **there is no — of that** eso no es probable; **there is little — that . . .** es poco probable que + *subj*.

likely ['laikli] **1** *adj* (a) (*probable*) probable; verosímil; **a — explanation** una razón verosímil, una explicación razonable; **a — story!** ¡puro cuento!, ¡qué cuento más inverosímil!; **the — outcome** el resultado más probable; **the plan most — to succeed** el plan con mejores probabilidades de éxito; **an incident — to cause trouble** un incidente que pudiera dar lugar a disturbios; **he is not — to come** no es probable que venga; **is it — that I did?** ¿es probable que lo hiciera yo?
(b) (*suitable*) apropiado; **I asked 6 — people** se lo pregunté a 6 personas apropiadas.
(c) (*promising*) prometedor; **a — youth** un joven prometedor, un joven que promete.

2 *adv* probablemente; **as — as not** a lo mejor; **very —** they've lost it a lo mejor lo han perdido.

like-minded ['laik'maindid] *adj* animado por los mismos sentimientos, que piensan del mismo modo.

liken ['laikən] *vt* comparar (*to* con), asemejar (*to* a).

likeness ['laiknis] *n* parecido *m*, semejanza *f*; (*portrait*) retrato *m*; **family —** aire *m* de familia; **speaking —** retrato *m* al vivo.

likewise ['laikwaiz] *adv* asimismo, igualmente; además; lo mismo; — **it is true that** . . . asimismo es verdad que . . . ; **he did** — él hizo lo mismo.
liking ['laikiŋ] *n* (a) (*for person*) simpatía *f* (*for* a), cariño *m* (*for* a); **to have a** — **for someone** tener simpatía a uno, tener cariño a uno; **to take a** — **to someone** tomar cariño a uno, coger simpatía a uno.
　(b) (*for thing*) gusto *m* (*for* por), afición *f* (*for* a); **to be to someone's** — ser del gusto de uno; **to have a** — **for something** ser aficionado a algo; **to take a** — **to something** tomar gusto a algo, cobrar afición a algo.
lilac ['lailək] **1** *n* lila *f*. **2** *adj* color de lila.
Lille [li:l] Lila.
Lilliputian [ˌlili'pju:ʃiən] **1** *adj* liliputiense. **2** *n* liliputiense *mf*.
lilt [lilt] *n* (*sound*) ritmo *m* marcado, compases *mpl*, armonía *f*; (*song*) canción *f*; **a song with a** — **to it** una canción de agradable ritmo.
lily ['lili] *n* lirio *m*, azucena *f*; — **of the valley** muguete *m*, lirio *m* de los valles.
lily-livered ['lili'livəd] *adj* cobarde, pusilánime.
lily pad ['lilipæd] *n* (*US*) hoja *f* de nenúfar.
lily-white ['liliwait] *adj* blanco como la azucena.
limb [lim] *n* (*Anat*) miembro *m*; (*Bot*) rama *f*; **to be out on a** — estar aislado, estar en una situación peligrosa; **to tear someone** — **from** — despedazar a uno.
limber[1] ['limbə*] **1** *adj* ágil; flexible.
　2 *vt* hacer flexible.
　3 *vi*: **to** — **up** agilitarse; (*Sport*) entrar en calor, hacer ejercicios preparatorios; (*fig*) entrenarse, prepararse.
limber[2] ['limbə*] *n* (*Mil*) armón *m* de artillería.
limbless ['limlis] *adj* que está falto de un brazo (*or* pierna).
limbo ['limbəu] *n* limbo *m*; **to be in** — (*fig*) estar olvidado, permanecer en la oscuridad.
lime[1] [laim] (*Geol*) **1** *n* cal *f*; (*bird-*) liga *f*; **slaked** — cal *f* muerta. **2** *vt* (*Agr*) abonar con cal.
lime[2] [laim] *n* (*Bot: linden*) tilo *m*.
lime[3] [laim] *n* (*Bot: citrus fruit*) lima *f*; (*tree*) limero *m*.
lime juice ['laimdʒu:s] *n* jugo *m* de lima.
lime kiln ['laimkiln] *n* horno *m* de cal.
limelight ['laimlait] *n* luz *m* de calcio; **to be in the** — estar a la vista del público, ser el centro de atención; **he had long experience of the** — tuvo una larga experiencia de estar a la luz de la publicidad; **he never sought the** — no trató nunca de llamar hacia sí la atención.
limerick ['limərik] *n especie de quintilla jocosa*.
limestone ['laimstəun] *n* piedra *f* caliza.
lime tree ['laimtri:] *n* (*linden*) tilo *m*.
limey ['laimi] *n* (*sl*) inglés *m*, esa *f*.
limit ['limit] **1** *n* límite *m*; **it's the (very)** —! ¡es el colmo!, ¡no faltaba más!; **he's the** —!, **isn't he the** —? ¿qué le vamos a hacer?, ¡qué tío!; **to be at the** — **of one's endurance** ya no poder más, estar completamente agotado; **I am at the** — **of my patience** ya no tengo más paciencia; **there is a** — **to what one can do** no es infinita la fuerza que tiene uno; **it is true within** —**s** es verdad dentro de ciertos límites; **to go to the** — **to help someone** hacer todo lo posible para ayudar a uno, volcarse por ayudar a uno; **to know no** —**s** ser infinito, no tener límites.
　2 *vt* limitar, restringir (*to* a); **that plant is** —**ed to Spain** esa planta se encuentra únicamente en España; **are you** —**ed as to time?** ¿hay restricción de tiempo?
　3 *vr*: **to** — **oneself to a few remarks** limitarse a hacer algunas observaciones; **I** — **myself to 10 cigarettes a day** me permito tan sólo 10 cigarrillos al día.
limitation [ˌlimi'teiʃən] *n* limitación *f*, restricción *f*; (*Law*) prescripción *f*; **he has his** —**s** tiene sus puntos flacos; **there is no** — **on exports** no hay restricción de artículos exportados.
limited ['limitid] *adj* limitado, restringido; *edition* limitado; *intelligence* más bien mediocre; *means* escaso, reducido; *person* de cortos alcances, de miras estrechas; *see* **company**.
limitless ['limitlis] *adj* ilimitado, sin límites.
limousine ['liməzi:n] *n* limusina *f*, limosina *f*.
limp[1] [limp] **1** *n* cojera *f*; **to walk with a** — cojear.
　2 *vi* cojear; **he** —**ed off** se marchó cojeando; **he** —**ed to the door** se fue cojeando a la puerta; **the ship managed to** — **to port** el buque llegó con dificultad al puerto.
limp[2] [limp] *adj* flojo, lacio; fláccido; flexible; *movement etc* lánguido; **I feel** — **today** hoy me

siento sin fuerzas; she felt — **all over** tenía un desmayo en todo el cuerpo; **he said in a** — **voice** dijo en tono desmayado; **let your body go** — deje que el cuerpo pierda su rigidez.
limpet ['limpit] *n* lapa *f*; (*fig*) persona *f* tenaz.
limpid ['limpid] *adj liquid* límpido, cristalino, transparente; *air* diáfano, puro; *eyes* claro.
limply ['limpli] *adv* flojamente, lánguidamente; **he said** — dijo en tono desmayado.
limpness ['limpnis] *n* flojedad *f*; languidez *f*.
limy ['laimi] *adj* calizo.
linchpin ['lintʃpin] *n* pezonera *f*; (*fig*) pivote *m*, eje *m*.
linden ['lindən] *n* tilo *m* (*also* **linden tree**).
line[1] [lain] **1** *n* (a) (*rope etc*) cuerda *f*; (*fishing-*) sedal *m*; **hard** —**s!** ¡mala suerte!; **it's hard** —**s on Joe** es mala suerte para Pepe.
　(b) (*Geom etc*) línea *f*; (*on tennis court etc*) raya *f*; (*on face, palm*) arruga *f*, (*in palmistry*) raya *f*, línea *f*; **the L** — (*Geog*) el ecuador; — **of fire** línea *f* de tiro; — **of life** línea *f* de la vida; — **of vision** visual *f*; **black** — raya *f* en negro; **dotted** — línea *f* de puntos; **straight** — línea *f* recta; — **drawing** dibujo *m* de líneas; **the** —**s of a ship** las formas de un buque; **all along the** — en toda la línea, (*fig*) completamente, cien por cien; **I draw the** — **at that** yo de ahí no paso; **I draw the** — **at blasphemy** yo no tolero la blasfemia; **one must draw the** — **somewhere** hay que fijar ciertos límites; **to know where to draw the** — tener sentido de la moderación, saber dónde conviene detenerse; **to shoot a** — (*fam*) darse bombo (*fam*); **to sign on the dotted** — (*fig*) aprobar algo maquinalmente.
　(c) (*row*) hilera *f*, (*of waiting cars etc*) cola *f*, (*of parked cars*) fila *f*; **forward** — (*Sport*) línea *f* delantera; **front** — primera línea *f*; **ship of the** — navío *m* de línea; — **of battle** línea *f* de batalla; — **of traffic** cola *f* de coches; **to fall** (*or* **get**) **into** — (*abreast*) meterse en fila, (*behind one another*) formar hilera, hacer cola; **to fall into** — **with** (*fig*) conformarse con; **to keep the party in** — mantener la disciplina del partido; **to stand in** — hacer cola.
　(d) (*in factory*) línea *f*; **production** — línea *f* de montaje.
　(e) (*Elec*) línea *f*; **high-tension** — línea *f* de alta tensión.
　(f) (*of aircraft, liners*) línea *f*.
　(g) (*of descent*) línea *f*, linaje *m*; **royal** — familia *f* real, casa *f* real; **in an unbroken** — en línea directa; **in the male** — por el lado de los varones.
　(h) (*Rail: in general*) línea *f*; (*track*) vía *f*; **down** — vía *f* descendente; **up** — vía *f* ascendente; **to cross the** — (*s*) cruzar la vía; **to leave the** —(s) descarrilar; **the** — **to Palencia** el ferrocarril de Palencia, la línea de Palencia.
　(i) (*Tel*) línea *f*; (*flex*) hilo *m*; **the hot** — el hilo rojo; **party** — línea *f* de dos (o más) abonados; **to be on the** — **to someone** estar al habla con uno; **hold the** —! ¡no cuelgue Vd!, ¡espere un momento!; **can you get me a** — **to Chicago?** ¿me puede poner con Chicago?
　(j) (*of print*) renglón *m*, línea *f*; (*Poet*) verso *m*; —**s** (*Theat*) papel *m*; **marriage** —**s** partida *f* de matrimonio; **in the very next** — a renglón seguido; **to drop someone a** — poner unas líneas a uno; **to read between the** —**s** leer entre líneas.
　(k) (*fig: course*) — **of argument** argumento *m*; — **of conduct** línea *f* de conducta; — **of inquiry** tema *m* de investigación; pista *f*; — **of thought** hilo *m* del pensamiento; **to be on the right** —**s** ir bien, ir por buen camino; **to take a strong** — **with someone** adoptar una actitud firme con uno.
　(l) (*fig: clue*) pista *f*; indicación *f*; **to give someone a** — **on something** poner a uno sobre la pista de algo; **can you give me a** — **on it?** ¿me puedes dar algunas indicaciones acerca de ello?; **the police have a** — **on the criminal** la policía tiene una pista que le conducirá al delincuente.
　(m) (*fig: notions of conformity*) **party** — línea *f* de partido, política *f* del partido; **along the** —**s of**, **on the** —**s of** de acuerdo con, conforme a, a tenor de; **something along these** —**s** algo por el estilo, algo en este sentido; **to be in** — **with** estar de acuerdo con, ser conforme a; **to bring something into** — **with** alinear algo con; **to step out of** — independizarse, mostrar su disconformidad, dejar de obedecer; **to toe the** — conformarse, someterse.
　(n) (*fig: métier, speciality*) especialidad *f*, rama *f*; profesión *f*; **the best in its** — el mejor en su línea; **what** — **are you in?** ¿a qué se dedica Vd?; **that's not in my** — eso no es de mi especialidad; **fishing's more in my** — me interesa más la pesca, de pesca

sí sé algo; **we have a good —— in spring hats** tenemos un buen surtido de sombreros para primavera; **that —— did not sell at all** ese género resultó ser invendible.

2 *vt* **(a)** (*cross with ——s*) rayar; *field etc* surcar; *face etc* arrugar.

(b) to —— up *people, objects* alinear, poner en fila.

(c) to —— the streets ocupar las aceras; **to —— the route** alinearse a lo largo de la ruta; **the streets were ——d with cheering crowds** en las calles había a cada lado multitudes que gritaban entusiastas; **portraits ——d the walls** las paredes estaban llenas de cuadros.

3 *vi*: **to —— up** (*along street etc*) alinearse, (*in queue*) hacer cola, ponerse en fila, (*Mil*) formar(se); **the teams ——d up like this . . .** los equipos formaron así **. . .**

line² [lain] *vt clothes etc* forrar (*with* de); (*Tech*) revestir (*with* de); *brakes* guarnecer; *see* **pocket.**

lineage ['liniidʒ] *n* linaje *m.*

lineal ['liniəl] *adj* lineal, en línea recta.

lineament ['liniəmənt] *n* lineamento *m.*

linear ['liniə*] *adj* lineal; *measure* de longitud.

lined [laind] *adj face etc* arrugado; *coat* forrado, con forro; (*Tech*) revestido; **to become ——** arrugarse.

linen ['linin] **1** *n* lino *m*, hilo *m*; lienzo *m*; (*table-*) mantelería *f*; (*sheets, underclothes etc*) ropa *f* blanca; **clean ——** ropa *f* limpia; **dirty ——** ropa *f* sucia, ropa *f* para lavar; **to wash one's dirty —— in public** (*fig*) lavar sus trapos sucios ante el mundo entero.

2 *adj* de lino.

linen closet ['linin,klɔzit] *n*, **linen cupboard** ['linin,kʌbəd] *n* armario *m* para ropa blanca.

linen draper ['linin,dreipə*] *n* lencero *m*, a *f*; **——'s** (*shop*) lencería *f.*

line-out ['lainaut] *n* (*Sport*) saque *m* de banda.

liner ['lainə*] *n* transatlántico *m*, vapor *m* de línea.

linesman ['lainzmən] *n*, *pl* **——men** [mən] (*Sport*) juez *m* de línea; (*Rail*) guardavía *m*; (*Elec*) celador *m*, recorredor *m* de la línea.

line-up ['lainʌp] *n* (*Sport*) alineación *f*, formación *f.*

ling¹ [liŋ] *n* (*Fish*) especie de abadejo *m.*

ling² [liŋ] *n* (*Bot*) brezo *m.*

linger ['liŋgə*] *vi* **(a)** (*also* **to —— on**; *be unwilling to go*) tardar en marcharse, permanecer por indecisión; (*in dying*) tardar en morirse; (*of doubts etc*) persistir, quedar; **won't you —— here a while?** ¿no puedes quedarte aquí un rato?

(b) (*delay on journey etc*) quedarse atrás, retardarse.

(c) to —— on a subject dilatarse en un tema; **I let my eye —— on the scene** seguía sin apartar los ojos de la escena; **to —— over a meal** comer despacio, no darse prisa por terminar de comer; **to —— over a task** hacer un trabajo despacio.

lingering ['liŋgəriŋ] *adj* lento, prolongado; *death* lento; *doubt* persistente, que no se desvanece; *look* fijo y triste.

lingerie ['lænʒəri:] *n* ropa *f* blanca, ropa *f* interior (de mujer).

lingo ['liŋgəu] *n* (*fam*) lengua *f*, idioma *m*; (*specialist jargon*) jerga *f.*

lingua franca ['liŋgwə'fræŋkə] *n* lengua *f* franca.

linguist ['liŋgwist] *n* **(a)** (*speaker of languages*) políglota *mf*; **he's a good ——** domina varios idiomas, aprende los idiomas con facilidad; **I'm no —— no** puedo con los idiomas.

(b) (*specialist in linguistics*) lingüista *mf.*

linguistic [liŋ'gwistik] *adj* lingüístico.

linguistics [liŋ'gwistiks] *n* lingüística *f.*

liniment ['linimənt] *n* linimento *m.*

lining ['lainiŋ] *n* (*of clothes etc*) forro *m*; (*Tech*) revestimiento *m*; (*of brake*) guarnición *f.*

link [liŋk] **1** *n* (*of chain*) eslabón *m*; (*fig*: *connection*) enlace *m*, conexión *f*; (*bond*) lazo *m*, vínculo *m*; **a new rail —— for Teruel** nuevo enlace *m* ferroviario para Teruel; **cultural ——s** relaciones *fpl* culturales; **the ——s of friendship** los lazos de la amistad; **missing ——** eslabón *m* perdido.

2 *vt* eslabonar; *spaceships* acoplar; (*fig*) enlazar, unir, vincular; **to —— arms** cogerse del brazo; **we are ——ed by telephone to . . .** tenemos conexión telefónica con . . .; **we hope to —— up the two space-ships** esperamos acoplar las dos naves espaciales; **we are ——ed in friendship** nos vincula la amistad; **the two companies are now ——ed** ahora están unidas las dos compañías.

3 *vi*: **to —— together** (*parts*) eslabonarse; **to —— up** (*persons*) reunirse (*with* con); (*companies etc*) unirse; (*spaceships etc*) acoplarse; (*railway lines*) empalmar.

links [liŋks] *npl* campo *m* de golf.

link-up ['liŋkʌp] *n* unión *f*; (*of spaceships*) acoplamiento *m*, atraque *m.*

linnet ['linit] *n* pardillo *m* común.

lino ['lainəu] *n*, **linoleum** [li'nəuliəm] *n* linóleo *m.*

linotype ['lainəutaip] *n* linotipia *f.*

linseed ['linsi:d] *n* linaza *f.*

linseed oil ['linsi:d'ɔil] *n* aceite *m* de linaza.

lint [lint] *n* hilas *fpl.*

lintel ['lintl] *n* dintel *m.*

lion ['laiən] *n* león *m*; (*fig*) celebridad *f*; **——'s share** parte *f* del león; **to beard the ——** in his den entrar en el cubil de la fiera; **to put one's head in the ——'s mouth** meterse en la boca del lobo.

lioness ['laiənis] *n* leona *f.*

lionize ['laiənaiz] *vt*: **to —— someone** tratar a uno como una celebridad, volcarse por agasajar a uno.

lip [lip] *n* **(a)** (*Anat and fig*) labio *m*; (*of jug*) pico *m*; (*of cup, crater*) borde *m*; **to hang on someone's ——s** estar pendiente de las palabras de uno; **to keep a stiff upper ——** no inmutarse, aguantarlo todo sin chistar; **to lick** (*or* **smack**) **one's ——s** relamerse, chuparse los dedos.

(b) (*sl: abuse*) injurias *fpl*; (*backchat*) insolencia *f*; **none of your ——!** ¡cállate la boca!

lipread ['lipri:d] (*irr: see* **read**) *vi* interpretar el movimiento de los labios (de otro que habla).

lip-reading ['lip,ri:diŋ] *n* interpretación *f* del movimiento de los labios.

lip service ['lip,sə:vis] *n* jarabe *m* de pico; **to pay —— to an ideal** alabar un ideal pero sin hacer nada práctico.

lipstick ['lipstik] *n* lápiz *m* labial, rojo *m* de labios, barra *f* de labios.

liquefaction [,likwi'fækʃən] *n* licuefacción *f.*

liquefy ['likwifai] **1** *vt* liquidar. **2** *vi* liquidarse.

liqueur [li'kjuə*] *n* licor *m*, poscafé *m.*

liquid ['likwid] **1** *adj* líquido; *measure* para líquidos; *asset* líquido, realizable; *sound* claro, puro, (*in Phonetics*) líquido; *air* diáfano.

2 *n* líquido *m*; (*Phonetics*) líquida *f.*

liquidate ['likwideit] *vt* (*all senses*) liquidar.

liquidation [,likwi'deiʃən] *n* liquidación *f*; **to go into ——** entrar en liquidación.

liquidize ['likwidaiz] **1** *vt* liquidar. **2** *vi* liquidarse.

liquor ['likə*] *n* licor *m*, bebida *f* alcohólica, bebidas *fpl* alcohólicas; **hard ——** licor *m* espiritoso; **to be in —— estar** borracho; **to be the worse for ——** haber bebido más de la cuenta, estar algo borracho.

liquorice ['likəris] *n* regaliz *m.*

Lisbon ['lizbən] *n* Lisboa.

lisle [lail] *n* hilo *m* de Escocia.

lisp [lisp] **1** *n* ceceo *m*; (*of child*) balbuceo *m*; **to speak with a ——** cecear. **2** *vt* decir ceceando; decir balbuceando. **3** *vi* cecear; balbucear.

lissom ['lisəm] *adj* ágil, ligero.

list¹ [list] **1** *n* lista *f*; relación *f*; catálogo *m*; (*of officials*) escalafón *m*; **to be on the active ——** estar en activo.

2 *attr*: **—— price** precio *m* de tarifa.

3 *vt* poner en una lista; inscribir; hacer una lista de; catalogar; (*Fin*) cotizar (*at* a); **he began to —— all he had been doing** empezó a enumerar todas las cosas que había hecho; **it is not ——ed** no consta (en la lista).

list² [list] *n* (*Naut*) **1** *n* inclinación *f*, escora *f*; **to have a bad ——** inclinarse de modo peligroso; **to have a —— of 20°** tener una inclinación de 20 grados.

2 *vi* inclinarse (*to port* a babor), escorar; **to —— badly** inclinarse de modo peligroso.

listen ['lisn] *vi* **(a)** (*hear*) escuchar, oír (*to something* algo, *to someone* a uno); (*heed*) escuchar, prestar atención, dar oídos, atender (*to* a); **——!** ¡escucha!; **—— to me!** ¡escúchame!; **he wouldn't ——** no quiso escuchar.

(b) to —— in (*eavesdrop*) escuchar a hurtadillas (*on a conversation* una conversación); (*Radio*) escuchar la radio.

listener ['lisnə*] *n* oyente *mf*; (*Radio*) radioyente *mf*; **dear ——s!** ¡queridos oyentes!; **to be a good ——** tener mucha paciencia, escuchar amablemente todo lo que se le dice a uno.

listening ['lisniŋ] *n*: **good ——!** ¡que se diviertan escuchando nuestros programas!; **we don't do much ——** now ahora escuchamos muy poco la radio.

listening post ['lisniŋpəust] *n* puesto *m* de escucha.

listless ['listlis] *adj* lánguido, desmayado, apático, indiferente.

listlessly ['listlisli] *adv* lánguidamente, con apatía, con indiferencia.

listlessness ['listlisnis] *n* languidez *f*, desmayo *m*, apatía *f*, indiferencia *f.*

lists [lists] *npl* (*Hist*) liza *f*; **to enter the —** (*fig*) salir a la palestra.

lit [lit] *pret and ptp of* **light**; **to be — up** (*sl*) estar achispado.

litany ['litəni] *n* letanía *f*.

literacy ['litərəsi] *n* capacidad *f* de leer y escribir; **— campaign** campaña *f* de alfabetización; **— is low in Slobodia** en Eslobodia son pocos los que saben leer y escribir.

literal ['litərəl] *adj* literal.

literally ['litərəli] *adv* (*in a literal way*) literalmente; (*fig*) materialmente, eg **it was — impossible to work there** era materialmente imposible trabajar allí; **it had — ceased to exist** había dejado materialmente de existir.

literal-minded ['litərəl'maindid] *adj* sin imaginación, poco imaginativo.

literary ['litərəri] *adj* literario.

literate ['litərit] *adj* que sabe leer y escribir; **highly —** (*fig*) muy culto; **not very —** (*fig*) poco culto, que tiene poca cultura.

literati [.litə'rɑːtiː] *npl* literatos *mpl*.

literature ['litəritʃə*] *n* literatura *f*; (*fam: brochures etc*) impresos *mpl*, folletos *mpl*; información *f* impresa; (*learned studies of subject*) estudios *mpl* impresos, bibliografía *f*.

lithe [laið] *adj* ágil, ligero.

lithium ['liθiəm] *n* litio *m*.

lithograph ['liθəugrɑːf] **1** *n* litografía *f*. **2** *vt* litografiar.

lithography [li'θɔgrəfi] *n* litografía *f*.

Lithuania [.liθju'einiə] *n* Lituania *f*.

Lithuanian [.liθju'einiən] **1** *adj* lituano. **2** *n* lituano *m*, a *f*. **3** *n* (*language*) lituano *m*.

litigant ['litigənt] *n* litigante *mf*.

litigate ['litigeit] *vi* litigar, pleitear.

litigation [.liti'geiʃən] *n* litigio *m*, litigación *f*.

litigious [li'tidʒəs] *adj* litigioso.

litmus ['litməs] *n* tornasol *m*.

litmus paper ['litməs.peipə*] *n* papel *m* de tornasol.

litre, (*US*) **liter** ['liːtə*] *n* litro *m*.

litter ['litə*] **1** *n* (a) (*vehicle*) litera *f*; (*Med*) camilla *f*.
    (b) (*bedding*) lecho *m*, cama *f* de paja.
    (c) (*Zool*) camada *f*, cría *f*, críos *mpl*.
    (d) (*rubbish*) basura *f*, desperdicios *mpl*; (*papers*) papeles *mpl* (viejos); (*wrappings*) envases *mpl*; **a — of books** un montón de libros en desorden, un revoltijo de libros.
    (e) (*general untidiness*) desorden *m*, confusión *f*; **in a —** en desorden.
    2 *vt* (a) *animal* dar cama de paja a.
    (b) (*give birth to*) parir.
    (c) **to — papers about a room, to — a room with papers** esparcir papeles por un cuarto, dejar los papeles esparcidos por un cuarto; **a street —ed with paper** una calle llena de trozos de papel.

litter basket ['litəbɑːskit] *n*, **litter bin** ['litəbin] *n* papelera *f*.

litterbug ['litəbʌg] *n* persona *f* que esparce papeles usados (*or envases etc*) por las calles (*or* en el campo).

little ['litl] **1** *adj* (a) pequeño, chico; poco; escaso; **a — book** un libro pequeño; **a — wine** un poco de vino; **with no — trouble** con bastante dificultad, con no poca dificultad.
    (b) (**— with noun**, *often translated by suffix*, eg **a — house** una casita, **just a — gift** (*as charity*) una limosnita, **a very — fish** un pececillo, **a — sip** un sorbito.
    2 *adv* poco; **he reads —** lee poco; **a — better** un poco mejor; **— more than a month ago** hace poco más de un mes; **we were not a — worried** nos inquietamos bastante, quedamos muy inquietos; **— does he know that . . .** no tiene la menor idea de que . . . ; **I walk as — as possible** voy a pie lo menos posible.
    3 *n* poco *m*; **he knows —** sabe poco; **to spend — or nothing** gastar poco o nada; **he had — to say** poco fue lo que tenía que decir, apenas tenía nada que decir; **there was but — we could do** apenas había nada que hacer; **give me a —** dame un poco; **— by —** poco a poco; **for a —** un rato, por un rato, durante un rato; **in —** en pequeño; **to make — of something** sacar poco en claro de algo.

littleness ['litlnis] *n* pequeñez *f*; poquedad *f*.

littoral ['litərəl] **1** *adj* litoral. **2** *n* litoral *m*.

liturgical [li'təːdʒikəl] *adj* litúrgico.

liturgy ['litədʒi] *n* liturgia *f*.

livable ['livəbl] *adj* llevadero, soportable.

livable-in ['livəbl.in] *adj* (*fam*) habitable.

livable-with ['livəbl.wið] *adj* (*fam*) tratable, simpático.

live [liv] **1** *vt* *life* llevar, tener, pasar; *experience* vivir;

to — a happy life tener una vida feliz; **to — a part** encarnar brillantemente un papel, (*pej*) convertir un papel dramático en realidad; **to — down** lograr borrar; **to — out** *period, reign* vivir hasta el fin de, sobrevivir a, **one's own life** pasar el resto de; **to — it up** (*fam*) correr las grandes juergas (*fam*); **let's go and — it up** vamos a echar una cana al aire.
    2 *vi* vivir; **long — Queen Anne!** ¡viva la reina Ana!; **to — and learn** vivir para ver; **to — and let — ser** tolerante con todos; **to — from hand to mouth** vivir al día; **to — like a king** (*or* **lord**) vivir a cuerpo de rey; **as long as I —** mientras viva; **he hasn't long to —** no le queda mucho de vida; **to — again** volver a vivir; **to — by one's pen** vivir de su pluma; **to — high, to — well** darse buena vida, vivir en el lujo; **to — in** (*adv*) estar de interno, ser interno; **to — in** (*prep*) vivir en, habitar, ocupar; **a house not fit to — in** una casa no habitable; **to — off one's estate** vivir de las rentas de su finca; **to — off one's relations** vivir a costa de sus parientes; **to — on** (*adv*) vivir, seguir viviendo; **to — on eggs** alimentarse de huevos, comer (únicamente) huevos; **to — on hope** nutrirse (*or* vivir) de esperanzas; **what does he — on?** ¿de qué vive?; **to — on a private income** vivir de unas rentas particulares; **he doesn't earn enough to — on** no gana bastante para vivir; **to — through an experience** vivir una experiencia; **to — together** (*in amity*) convivir, (*in sin*) vivir juntos; **to — up to a standard** vivir con arreglo a (*or* en conformidad con) una norma; **to — up to a promise** cumplir una promesa; **to — up to one's reputation** justificar su reputación; **to — up to one's hopes** corresponder a sus esperanzas; *see* **income, means** *etc*.

live [laiv] *adj* vivo; *coal etc* encendido, ardiente; *weight* en vivo; *cartridge* con bala, *shell* cargado; *wire* con corriente, conectado; (*Radio, TV*) en vivo; *issue* candente, de actualidad; **a real — duke** un duque en persona, un duque de verdad.

livelihood ['laivlihud] *n* vida *f*; sustento *m*; **rice is their —** el arroz es su único sustento; **to earn a —** ganarse la vida.

liveliness ['laivlinis] *n* vida *f*, vivacidad *f*, viveza *f*; energía *f*; animación *f*; alegría *f*.

livelong ['livlɔŋ] *adj*: **all the — day** todo el santo día.

lively ['laivli] *adj* *person, imagination, account etc* vivo; *campaign, effort, speech* enérgico; *conversation* animado; *interest* grande; *pace* rápido; *party, scene etc* bullicioso, alegre; *tune* alegre; **things are getting —** esto se está animando, empiezan a pasar cosas; **to have a — time of it** pasar un rato lleno de incidentes.

liven ['laivn] **1** *vt*: **to — up** animar, estimular; alegrar. **2** *vi*: **to — up** animarse; alegrarse.

liver[1] ['livə*] *n*: **fast —** calavera *f*; **good — gastrónomo** *m*; persona *f* que se da buena vida.

liver[2] ['livə*] *n* (*Anat*) hígado *m*; **— complaint** mal *m* de hígado, afección *f* hepática.

liveried ['livərid] *adj* en librea.

liverish ['livəriʃ] *adj*: **to be —, to feel —** sentirse mal del hígado.

liverwurst ['livəwəːst] *n* embutido *m* de hígado.

livery ['livəri] *n* librea *f*; (*lit*) ropaje *m*; **— company** gremio *m* (*antiguo, de la Ciudad de Londres*).

livery stable ['livəri.steibl] *n* caballeriza *f* de alquiler.

lives [laivz] *npl of* **life**.

livestock ['laivstɔk] *n* ganado *m*, ganadería *f*.

livid ['livid] *adj* (a) lívido. (b) (*fam*) **he was — estaba** furioso; **he got — se** puso negro.

living ['liviŋ] **1** *adj* vivo, viviente; *image, language* vivo; **the — los** vivos; **— or dead** vivo o muerto; **"The L— Desert"** "El desierto viviente"; **The greatest — pianist** el mejor pianista de los que ahora viven.
    2 *n* (a) vida *f*; **gracious — vida** *f* elegante; **high — vida** *f* regalada, vida *f* de lujo; **loose — vida** *f* inmoral; **to earn** (*or* **make**) **a — ganarse** la vida; **to make a bare — ganar** lo justo para vivir; **to work for one's — ganarse** la vida trabajando.
    (b) (*Eccl*) beneficio *m*.
    3 *attr* de vida; *conditions* de vida, vital; *expenses* de mantenimiento; *wage* suficiente para vivir.

living room ['liviŋrum] *n* sala *f* de estar, living *m*.

living space ['liviŋspeis] *n* espacio *m* vital (*also fig*).

Livy ['livi] *m* Livio.

lizard ['lizəd] *n* lagarto *m*, (*small*) lagartija *f*.

llama ['lɑːmə] *n* llama *f*.

lo [ləu] *interj*: **— and behold the result!** ¡he aquí el resultado!, ¡ved aquí el resultado!; **and — and behold there it was** y por milagro ahí estaba.

loach [ləutʃ] *n* locha *f*.

load [ləud] **1** *n* (a) carga *f* (*also Elec, Tech, fig*); (*weight*) peso *m*; (*quantity*) cantidad *f*; (*Agr etc: as* *measure*) carretada *f*; **dead** — carga *f* fija; **under full** — en plena carga; **peak** — carga *f* máxima; **useful** — carga *f* útil.

(b) (*fig and fam*) **—s of, a** — of gran cantidad de, montones de; **thanks, we have —s** gracias, tenemos bastante; **it's a** — of **old rubbish** es una basura, no vale para nada; **that's a** — **off my mind** ¡qué alivio!, ¡se me quita un peso de encima!; **get a** — **of this!** ¡mírame esto!, ¡escucha esto un poco!

2 *vt* cargar (*with* con, de; *also* Elec); (*burden, weigh down*) agobiar (*with* de); **to** — **someone with honours** llenar a uno de honores, colmar a uno de honores; **the branch was —ed with pears** la rama estaba cargada de peras; **the whole thing is —ed with problems** el asunto está erizado de dificultades; **we're —ed with debts** estamos agobiados de deudas; **to** — **up** cargar (*with* de).

3 *vi* **(a)** cargar, tomar carga; "**—ing and unloading**" (*street sign*) "permitido carga y descarga".

(b) (*Mil*) cargar; **—!** ¡carguen armas!; **how does this gun —?** ¿cómo se carga esta escopeta?; **to** — **again** volver a cargar.

4 *vr*: **to** — **oneself with** cargarse de.

loaded ['ləudid] *adj* cargado; *dice, gun* cargado; *question* intencionado, que sugiere una contestación; **to be —** (*sl: drunk*) estar trompa, (*rich*) estar podrido de dinero, (*carry much money*) llevar encima mucho dinero.

loader ['ləudə*] *n* cargador *m*.

load line *n* línea *f* de flotación con carga.

loadstone ['ləudstəun] *n* piedra *f* imán.

loaf[1] [ləuf] *n*, *pl* **loaves** [ləuvz] pan *m*; (*large, cottage*) hogaza *f*; (*small, French*) barra *f*; (*of sugar*) pan *m*, piión *m*; **half a** — **is better than no bread** vale más tener un poco que no tener nada; **use your —!** (*sl*) ¡despabílate!

loaf[2] [ləuf] *vi* haraganear, gandulear.

loafer ['ləufə*] *n*. vago *m*, gandul *m*; (*in street*) azotacalles *m*.

loam [ləum] *n* marga *f*.

loamy ['ləumi] *adj* margoso.

loan [ləun] **1** *n* (*thing lent between persons*) préstamo *m*; (*Comm, public*) empréstito *m*; **it's on** — está prestado; **I asked for the** — **of the book** le pedí prestado el libro; **I had it on** — **from the company** me lo prestó la compañía; **to raise a** — (*public*) procurar un empréstito.

2 *vt* prestar.

loan fund ['ləunfʌnd] *n* caja *f* de empréstitos.

loanword ['ləunwə:d] *n* préstamo *m*.

loath, loth [ləuθ] *adj*: **nothing** — de buena gana; **to be** — **to do something** estar poco dispuesto a hacer algo; **to be** — **for someone to do something** no querer en absoluto que uno haga algo.

loathe [ləuð] *vt thing* abominar, detestar, aborrecer; *person* odiar; **I** — **doing it** me repugna hacerlo; **he —s being corrected** se indigna si se le corrige.

loathing ['ləuðiŋ] *n* aversión *f* (*of* hacia, por); aborrecimiento *m* (*of* de); odio *m* (*of* hacia, por); **it fills me with** — me da asco; **the** — **which I felt for him** el odio que sentía hacia él.

loathsome ['ləuðsəm] *adj thing* asqueroso, repugnante; *person* odioso.

loathsomeness ['ləuðsəmnis] *n* lo asqueroso; lo odioso.

loaves [ləuvz] *npl* of **loaf**.

lob [lɔb] **1** *n* (*Tennis*) voleo *m* alto.

2 *vt ball* volear por alto; **to** — **something over to someone** tirar algo a uno; **it over, will you?** ¿me lo das, por favor?

3 *vi* volear por alto.

lobby ['lɔbi] **1** *n* (*entrance hall*) vestíbulo *m*; (*corridor*) pasillo *m*; (*anteroom*) antecámara *f*; (*waiting room*) sala *f* de espera; (*Parl, fig*) organización *f* de cabildeo, camarilla *f* de cabilderos; grupo *m* de presión; **the China** — el grupo de los que apoyan a la China (nacionalista).

2 *vt*: **to** — **one's member of parliament** tratar de convencer a su diputado (*yendo los electores a hablar con él en el edificio del parlamento*).

3 *vi* cabildear, ejercer presiones; **to** — **for a reform** tratar de convencer a su diputado de la necesidad de una reforma, ejercer presiones para conseguir una reforma.

lobbying ['lɔbiiŋ] *n* cabildeo *m*.

lobbyist ['lɔbiist] *n* cabildero *m*.

lobe [ləub] *n* lóbulo *m*.

lobelia [ləu'bi:liə] *n* lobelia *f*.

lobster ['lɔbstə*] *n* langosta *f*; (*large*) bogavante *m*.

lobster pot ['lɔbstəpɔt] *n* langostera *f*.

local ['ləukəl] **1** *adj* local; *authority, government, colour, anaesthetic etc* local; *radio station* comarcal,

regional; *train* de cercanías; *road* vecinal; (*in distribution, frequency*) poco común, que no se encuentra en todos los sitios, de distribución restringida; **he's a** — **man** es de aquí; **the** — **doctor** el médico del pueblo, el médico del barrio.

2 *n*: **the** — (*fam*) la taberna; **the —s** los vecinos, el vecindario, los de aquí.

locale [ləu'ka:l] *n* lugar *m*, escenario *m*.

locality [ləu'kæliti] *n* localidad *f*.

localize ['ləukəlaiz] *vt* localizar.

locally ['ləukəli] *adv*: **houses are dear** — por aquí las casas cuestan bastante; **we deliver free** — en la ciudad y sus inmediaciones la entrega a domicilio es gratuita; **the plant is common** — la planta es común en ciertas localidades.

locate [ləu'keit] *vt* (*place*) colocar, establecer; (*find*) encontrar, localizar; **to be —d at** estar situado en, estar ubicado en, radicar en; **we —d it eventually** por fin averiguamos su paradero; **where is it —d?** ¿dónde está?

location [ləu'keiʃən] *n* (a) (*place*) situación *f*, posición *f*; (*placing*) colocación *f*; (*finding*) localización *f*.

(b) (*Cine*) rodaje *m* fuera del estudio; terreno *m* para rodaje de exteriores; **to be on** — **in Mexico** estar rodando en Méjico.

locative ['lɔkətiv] *n* locativo *m* (*also* — **case**).

loch [lɔx] *n* (Scot) lago *m*; (*sea-*) ría *f*, brazo *m* de mar.

lock[1] [lɔk] *n* (*of hair*) mechón *m*, guedeja *f*; (*ringlet*) bucle *m*; **—s** cabellos *mpl*.

lock[2] [lɔk] **1** *n* (*on door, box etc*) cerradura *f*; (Mech) traba *f*; (*stop*) retén *m*; (*of gun*; *also* Wrestling) llave *f*; (*canal-*) esclusa *f*; (*pressure chamber*) cámara *f* intermedia; **—, stock and barrel** por completo, del todo; **to put something under** — **and key** encerrar algo bajo llave.

2 *vt door etc* cerrar con llave; (Mech) trabar; **to** — **something away** guardar algo bajo llave; **to** — **someone in a room** encerrar a uno en un cuarto; **the armies were —ed in combat** los ejércitos seguían luchando encarnizadamente; **they were —ed in each other's arms** quedaban estrechamente abrazados; **to** — **someone out** cerrar la puerta a uno, dejar a uno en la calle; **the workers were —ed out** los obreros quedaron sin trabajo debido al cierre por los patronos; **to find oneself —ed out** estar fuera sin llave para abrir la puerta; **to** — **up** encerrar; (*in prison*) encarcelar; *capital* inmovilizar; **you ought to be —ed up!** ¡irás a parar a la cárcel!

3 *vi* cerrarse con llave; (Mech) trabarse; **to** — **up** echar la llave.

locker ['lɔkə*] *n* armario *m* (*particular*); cajón *m* con llave.

locket ['lɔkit] *n* medallón *m*, guardapelo *m*.

lock gate ['lɔkgeit] *n* puerta *f* de esclusa.

lockjaw ['lɔkdʒɔ:] *n* trismo *m*.

lock keeper ['lɔk,ki:pə*] *n* esclusero *m*.

locknut ['lɔknʌt] *n* contratuerca *f*.

lockout ['lɔkaut] *n* cierre *m* (*or* paro *m* voluntario) por los patronos, lock-out *m*.

locksmith ['lɔksmiθ] *n* cerrajero *m*.

lock-up ['lɔkʌp] **1** *n* cárcel *f*, jaula *f*. **2** *attr* con cerradura; — **garage** jaula *f*.

loco ['ləukəu] *n* (*fam*) see **locomotive**.

locomotion [,ləukə'məuʃən] *n* locomoción *f*.

locomotive [,ləukə'məutiv] **1** *adj* locomotor. **2** *n* locomotora *f*, máquina *f*.

locum (tenens) ['ləukəm('tenenz)] *n* interino *m*, a *f*.

locus ['lɔkəs] *n*, *pl* **loci** ['lɔki:] punto *m*, sitio *m*; (*Math*) lugar *m* (*geométrico*).

locust ['ləukəst] *n* langosta *f*.

locust tree ['ləukəst,tri:] *n* acacia *f* falsa; algarrobo *m*.

locution [lə'kju:ʃən] *n* locución *f*.

locutory ['lɔkjutəri] *n* locutorio *m*.

lode [ləud] *n* filón *m*.

lodestar ['ləudsta:*] *n* estrella *f* polar; (*fig*) norte *m*.

lodestone ['ləudstəun] *n* piedra *f* imán.

lodge [lɔdʒ] **1** *n* (*in park*) casa *f* del guarda; (*porter's*) portería *f*; (Univ, *master's*) rectoría *f*; (*masonic*) logia *f*.

2 *vt person* alojar, hospedar; *object* (*place*) colocar, (*insert*) meter, introducir; *complaint* presentar (*with* a); **to** — **something with someone** dejar algo en manos de uno, entregar algo a uno; **the bullet is —d in the lung** la bala se ha alojado en el pulmón.

3 *vi* alojarse, hospedarse (*at, in* en; *with* con, en casa de); (*of object: end up*) ir a parar; (*remain*) quedarse, fijarse, quedar empotrado (*in* en); introducirse, penetrar (*in* en); **where do you —?** ¿dónde tiene Vd su pensión?, ¿en qué pensión vive Vd?; **the bullet —d in the lung** la bala se alojó en el pulmón.

lodger ['lɔdʒə*] n huésped m, eda f; **I was a — there** once hace tiempo me hospedé allí; **she takes —s** tiene una pensión.

lodging ['lɔdʒiŋ] n alojamiento m, hospedaje m; **—s** (in general) alojamiento m, pensión f; (room) habitación f; **they gave me a night's —** me recibieron en su casa esa noche; **to look for —s** buscar alojamiento, buscar una pensión; **we took —s with Mrs P** nos hospedamos en casa de la Sra de P; **are they good —s?** ¿es buena la pensión?

lodging house ['lɔdʒiŋhaus] n, pl **—houses** [‚hauziz] casa f de huéspedes, pensión f.

loft [lɔft] n desván m; (straw-) pajar m; (Eccl) galería f.

loftily ['lɔftili] adv en alto, hacia lo alto; say etc orgullosamente, arrogantemente.

loftiness ['lɔftinis] n altura f; grandiosidad f; sublimidad f; altanería f, orgullo m.

lofty ['lɔfti] adj (high) alto, elevado, encumbrado; (grandiose) grandioso; (high-flown) noble, sublime; (haughty) altanero, orgulloso.

log[1] [lɔg] **1** n leño m, tronco m; (Naut: apparatus) corredera f; see **logbook, sleep**.
    2 vt apuntar, registrar; **we —ged 50 kilometres** **that day** ese día recorrimos (or cubrimos) 50 kilómetros.
    3 vi cortar (y transportar) troncos.

log[2] [lɔg] n (Math) see **logarithm**.

loganberry ['lɔugənbəri] n (fruit) frambuesa f norteamericana; (bush) frambueso m norteamericano.

logarithm ['lɔgəriθəm] n logaritmo m.

logbook ['lɔgbuk] n (Naut) cuaderno m de bitácora, diario m de navegación, diario m de a bordo; (Aer) libro m de vuelo; (Tech) cuaderno m de trabajo.

log cabin ['lɔg‚kæbin] n cabaña f de madera.

loggerheads ['lɔgəhedz] npl: **to be at —** estar de pique (with con).

logging ['lɔgiŋ] n explotación f forestal; transporte m de troncos.

logic ['lɔdʒik] n lógica f; **in —** lógicamente.

logical ['lɔdʒikəl] adj lógico.

logically ['lɔdʒikəli] adv lógicamente.

logician [lɔ'dʒiʃən] n lógico m, a f.

logistic [lɔ'dʒistik] adj logístico.

logistics [lɔ'dʒistiks] n logística f.

log rolling ['lɔg‚rəuliŋ] n intercambio m de favores políticos, sistema m de concesiones mutuas.

logy ['lɔugi] adj (US) torpe, lerdo.

loin [lɔin] n ijada f; (of meat) lomo m; **—s** lomos mpl; **to gird up one's —s** aprestarse para la lucha.

loincloth ['lɔinklɔθ] n, pl **—cloths** [klɔðz] taparrabo m.

Loire [lwɑ:r] Loira m.

loiter ['lɔitə*] **1** vi: **to — away the time** perder el tiempo.
    2 vi (waste time) perder el tiempo; (idle) gandulear, holgazanear; (fall behind) rezagarse; (on the way) entretenerse; **don't — on the way!** ¡no te entretengas!; **to — with intent** rondar un edificio (etc) con fines criminales, merodear con fines criminales.

loll [lɔl] vi: **to — about** repantigarse; **to — against, to — back on** recostarse con indolencia contra; **to — back in a chair** repanchigarse en un asiento, estar repanchigado en un asiento; **the dog's tongue was —ing out** la lengua del perro colgaba hacia fuera.

lollipop ['lɔlipɔp] n pirulí m; (iced-) polo m.

lollop ['lɔləp] vi: **to — along** moverse torpemente, arrastrar los pies.

lolly ['lɔli] n (sl) parné m (sl); see **lollipop**.

Lombard ['lɔmbɑ:d] **1** adj lombardo. **2** n lombardo m, a f.

Lombardy ['lɔmbədi] Lombardía f.

London ['lʌndən] Londres; attr londinense.

Londoner ['lʌndənə*] n londinense mf.

lone [ləun] adj solitario, único, aislado; see **lonely**.

loneliness ['ləunlinis] n soledad f; aislamiento m.

lonely ['ləunli] adj, **lonesome** ['ləunsəm] adj solitario, solo; place etc aislado, remoto; (deserted) desierto; **to feel —** sentirse muy solo; **it's a — life** es una vida solitaria; **it's terribly — out here** aquí se siente uno terriblemente solo.

loner ['ləunə*] n solitario m.

long[1] [lɔŋ] **1** adj (a) (of size) largo; mirror de cuerpo entero; suit (Cards) fuerte; person (fam) alto; **it is 6 metres —** tiene 6 metros de largo; **how — is it?** ¿cuánto tiene de largo?; **to be — in the leg** tener piernas largas.
    (b) (of time) largo; prolongado; job de muchas horas, de muchos años (etc); **to be — in + ger** tardar en + infin; **how — is the lesson?** ¿cuánto tiempo dura la clase?; **the days are getting —er** los días se están alargando.

2 adv (a) largo tiempo, mucho tiempo; largamente; **don't be —!** ¡vuelve pronto!; **I shan't be —** (in finishing) termino pronto, en seguida concluyo, (in returning) vuelvo pronto; **we didn't stay —** no nos quedamos mucho tiempo; **he talked —** **about politics** habló largamente de política; **to live —** ser longevo; **women live —er than men** las mujeres son más longevas que los hombres; **— before** (adv) mucho antes, mucho tiempo antes; **you should have done it — before now** Vd debió hacerlo hace mucho tiempo ya; **— before** (conj) mucho antes de que + subj; **not — before** (adv) poco tiempo antes.
    (b) **—er** más tiempo; **we stayed —er than you** quedamos más tiempo que Vds; **how much —er can you stay?** ¿hasta cuándo podéis quedaros?; **how much —er do we have to wait?** ¿hasta cuándo tenemos que esperar?; **he no —er comes** ya no viene.
    (c) (in comparisons) **as — as** mientras; **as — as** the war lasted mientras duró la guerra; **as — as the** **war lasts** mientras dure la guerra; **stay as — as** **you like** quédate hasta cuando quieras, quédate el tiempo que quieras; **as — as, so — as** (provided that) con tal que + subj.
    (d) **so —!** ¡hasta luego!; see **ago**.

3 n: **the — and the short of it** en resumidas cuentas; **before —** en breve, dentro de poco, (in past contexts) poco tiempo después; **are you going for —?** ¿vas a estar mucho tiempo?; **to take — to** + infin tardar en + infin.

long[2] [lɔŋ] vi: **to — for something** anhelar algo, suspirar por algo; **to — for someone** sentir la ausencia de uno, suspirar por uno; **to — to do** **something** anhelar hacer algo, suspirar por hacer algo.

long-armed ['lɔŋ'ɑ:md] adj de brazos largos.

longboat ['lɔŋbəut] n lancha f.

longbow ['lɔŋbəu] n arco m.

long-dated ['lɔŋ'deitid] adj a largo plazo.

long-distance ['lɔŋ'distəns] adj bus para servicio interurbano; flight a distancia; call (Tel) interurbano; race de fondo, de larga distancia, de resistencia.

long-drawn-out ['lɔŋdrɔ:n'aut] adj muy prolongado, larguísimo, interminable.

long-eared ['lɔŋ'iəd] adj de orejas largas.

longed-for ['lɔŋfɔ:*] adj ansiado, apetecido.

longevity [lɔn'dʒeviti] n longevidad f.

long-forgotten ['lɔŋfə'gɔtn] adj olvidado hace mucho tiempo.

long-haired ['lɔŋ'hɛəd] adj person de pelo largo, melenudo; dog etc de pelo largo.

longhand ['lɔŋhænd] **1** adj escrito a mano. **2** n escritura f normal, escritura f sin abreviaturas; **in —** en escritura normal.

longing ['lɔŋiŋ] **1** adj anhelante. **2** n anhelo m, ansia f, deseo m vehemente (for de); nostalgia f (for de); sexual — hambre f sexual, instinto m sexual.

longish ['lɔŋiʃ] adj bastante largo.

longitude ['lɔŋgitjuːd] n longitud f.

longitudinal [‚lɔŋgi'tjuːdinl] adj longitudinal.

longitudinally [‚lɔŋgi'tjuːdinəli] adv longitudinalmente.

long jump ['lɔŋdʒʌmp] n salto m de longitud.

long-legged ['lɔŋ'legid] adj de piernas largas, zancudo.

long-lived ['lɔŋ'livd] adj longevo, de larga vida, que vive hasta una edad avanzada; **women are more —** **than men** las mujeres son más longevas que los hombres.

long-lost ['lɔŋ'lɔst] adj perdido hace mucho tiempo, desaparecido hace mucho tiempo.

long-playing ['lɔŋ'pleiiŋ] adj record microsurco, de larga duración.

long-range ['lɔŋ'reindʒ] adj gun de gran alcance; aircraft de gran autonomía, de largo radio de acción; weather forecast del próximo futuro, del mes (etc) que viene.

longshoreman ['lɔŋʃɔːmən] n, pl **—men** [mən] estibador m, obrero m portuario.

long-sighted ['lɔŋ'saitid] adj présbita; (fig) previsor, clarividente.

long-sightedness ['lɔŋ'saitidnis] n presbicia f; (fig) previsión f, clarividencia f.

long-standing ['lɔŋ'stændiŋ] adj de mucho tiempo, existente desde hace mucho tiempo, viejo.

long-suffering ['lɔŋ'sʌfəriŋ] adj sufrido.

long-term ['lɔŋ'təːm] adj a largo plazo (also fig).

long-wave ['lɔŋ'weiv] adj de onda larga.

longways ['lɔŋweiz] adv longitudinalmente, a lo largo.

long-winded ['lɔŋ'windid] adj prolijo.

long-windedly ['lɔŋ'windidli] adv prolijamente.

loo [luː] n (fam) wáter m.

loofah ['lu:fə*] n esponja f de lufa.

look [luk] **1** n **(a)** (glance) mirada f; vistazo m, ojeada f; **he gave me a furious** — me miró furioso, me lanzó una mirada furiosa; **she gave me a dirty** — me miró recelosa, me lanzó una mirada llena de recelo; **we got some very odd** —s la gente nos miró extrañada; **to have** (or take) **a** — **at something** echar un vistazo a algo; **have a** — **at this!** ¡a ver esto!; **let's have a** — déjame verlo, a ver; **do you want a** —? ¿quieres verlo?; **to take a good** — **at something** mirar algo con cuidado, examinar algo detenidamente; **take a long hard** — **before deciding** antes de decidir conviene pensar muchísimo; **we never got** (or had) **a** — in no nos dejaron participar, (of losers) nunca tuvimos posibilidades de ganar; **to have a** — **for something** buscar algo; **to have a** — **round a house** inspeccionar una casa; **shall we have a** — **round the town?** ¿visitamos la ciudad?

(b) (air, appearance) aspecto m, apariencia f; aire m; traza f; **good** —s buen parecer m; **the new** — la nueva moda; **by the** — **of things** según parece; **by the** — **of him** a juzgar por su aspecto; **you can't go by** —s **alone** es arriesgado juzgar por las apariencias nada más; **he had the** — **of a sailor** tenía aire de marinero; **I don't like the** — **of him** no me hace buena impresión; **I don't like the** — **of it at all** esto tiene traza de ser peligroso (etc), no me fío de esto.

2 vt emotion expresar con la mirada; age representar; **to** — **someone straight in the eye** mirar directamente a los ojos de uno; **to** — **something out** (search) buscar algo, (choose) escoger algo; **to** — **over** examinar; revisar; **to** — **a place over** dar un vistazo a un sitio; **to** — **up** buscar; averiguar; person ir a ver, visitar; **to** — **someone up and down** mirar a uno de arriba abajo; see last.

3 vi **(a)** (see, glance) mirar; (search) mirar, buscar; — **here!** ¡oye!; **just** —! ¡mira!, ¡fíjate!; — **before you leap** antes de que te cases mira lo que haces.

(b) (seem) parecer; tener aire de, tener traza de; mostrarse; **he** —s **happy** parece estar contento; **it** —s **all right to me** me parece que está bien; **how does it** — **to you?** ¿qué te parece?; **he** —ed **surprised** hizo un gesto de extrañeza; **she** —ed **prettier than ever** estaba más guapa que nunca; **how pretty you** —! ¡qué guapa estás!; **the corn** —s **good** el trigo se muestra espléndido; **to** — **well** (person) tener buena cara; **it** —s **well** parece muy bien, tiene buena apariencia; **it** —s **well on you** te sienta bien, te cae bien.

(c) to — **like** parecerse a; **he** —s **like his brother** se parece a su hermano; **the picture doesn't** — **like him** el retrato no se le parece, el retrato no le representa bien; **it** —s **like rain** parece que va a llover; **it** —s **like cheese to me** me parece que es queso; **the festival** —s **like being lively** el festival se anuncia animado.

(d) (with adv or prep) **to** — **about** mirar alrededor; **to** — **about one** mirar a su alrededor; (fig) considerar las cosas con calma; **to** — **about for something** andar buscando algo; **to** — **after something** (attend to) ocuparse de algo, encargarse de algo; (watch over) vigilar algo; **to** — **after someone** cuidar de uno; **to** — **at** mirar; considerar, examinar; problem enfocar, estudiar; **it depends how you** — **at it** depende de cómo se enfoca la cuestión, depende del punto de vista de uno; **to** — **away** desviar los ojos, apartar la mirada (from de); **to** — **back** mirar hacia atrás; (fig) considerar el pasado, volverse atrás; **to** — **back on something** recordar algo, evocar algo; **to** — **down** mirar hacia abajo; bajar los ojos; **to** — **down on something** dominar algo, (disdain) despreciar algo, mirar algo por encima del hombro; **to** — **for** (seek) buscar; (wait for) esperar; **to** — **forward** considerar el futuro; **to** — **forward to something** alegrarse de antemano de algo, pensar en algo con mucha ilusión, prometerse algo bueno; **I'm so** —ing **forward to the trip** el viaje me hace muchísima ilusión; **we had been** —ing **forward to it for weeks** durante semanas enteras veníamos pensando en ello con mucha ilusión; **to** — **in** (visit) hacer una breve visita (on a), pasar por casa, entrar por un instante; **I'll** — **in on Monday** pasaré por casa el lunes; **to** — **in** (TV) mirar la televisión; **to** — **into something** investigar algo; **to** — **on** mirar, (pej) estar de mirón; **to** — **on someone as a friend** considerar a uno como un amigo; **to** — **on to** dar a; **to** — **out** tener cuidado, tener ojo; — **out!** ¡ojo!; — **out for pickpockets** ojo con los carteristas; **to** — **out for** (seek) buscar, (expect) estar a la expectativa de, (await) esperar; **we'll** — **out for you in the**

station te esperamos en la estación; **to** — **out of window** mirar por, asomarse a; **to** — **out on** dar a; **to** — **round** (adv) volver la cabeza; **to** — **round** (prep) inspeccionar, visitar; **we just want to** — **round** queremos verlo nada más; **to** — **round for someone** buscar a uno con los ojos; **to** — **through** window mirar por; book hojear; (search among) registrar; **to** — **to** ocuparse de, mirar por; (look after) cuidar de; (beware of) tener cuidado con; (rely on) contar con; acudir a; tener puestas las esperanzas en; **to** — **to someone to** + infin esperar que uno + subj, contar con uno para + infin; **to** — **up** mirar hacia arriba; levantar los ojos; (improve) mejorar, ir mejor; **to** — **up to someone** respetar a uno, admirar a uno; **to** — **upon someone as** mirar a uno como; see alike etc.

looked-for ['luktfɔ:*] adj esperado, deseado.

looker ['lukə*] n (US fam) guapa f.

looker-on ['lukər'ɔn] n espectador m, ora f; (pej) mirón m, ona f.

looking-glass ['lukiŋglɑ:s] n espejo m.

look-out ['lukaut] n **(a)** (tower etc) atalaya f, puesto m de observación; (viewpoint) miradero m.
(b) (person) vigía m.
(c) (act) observación f, vigilancia f; **to be on the** — **for, to keep a** — **for** estar a la mira de; **to keep a sharp** — estar ojo avizor.
(d) (prospect) perspectiva f; **it's a poor** — **for cotton** el algodón tiene un porvenir dudoso; **it's a grim** — **for us** es una perspectiva negra para nosotros, esto no nos promete nada bueno; **that's his** —! ¡allá él!

look-see ['luksi:] n (fam) vistazo m.

loom¹ [lu:m] n telar m.

loom² [lu:m] vi (also to — **up**) surgir, aparecer, asomarse; (threaten) amenazar; **dangers** — **ahead** se vislumbran los peligros que hay por delante; **the ship** —ed **up out of the mist** el buque surgió de la niebla; **to** — **large** ser de gran importancia, ocupar un puesto importante.

loon [lu:n] n bobo m, a f.

loony ['lu:ni] (fam) **1** adj loco; **to drive someone** — volver loco a uno; **to go** — volverse loco. **2** n loco m, a f.

loony bin ['lu:nibin] n (sl) manicomio m.

loop [lu:p] **1** n (knot) lazo m, gaza f; (bend) curva f, vuelta f, recodo m; (Elec) circuito m cerrado; (fastening) presilla f; (Aer) rizo m; **to** — **the** — hacer el rizo, rizar el rizo.
2 vt rope etc hacer gaza con; (fasten) asegurar con gaza (or presilla); **to** — **something round a post** pasar algo alrededor de un poste.
3 vi (rope etc) formar lazo; (line, road etc) serpentear.

loophole ['lu:phəul] n (Mil) aspillera f, tronera f; (fig) escapatoria f; pretexto m; (in law) rendija f.

loop line ['lu:plain] n (Rail) vía f de circunvalación.

loose [lu:s] **1** adj (free) suelto; change, end suelto; (untied) suelto, desatado; (not tight) flojo; (movable) movible, movedizo; earth poco firme; bandage, button, knot, screw flojo; (Med) suelto de vientre; tooth inseguro; dress holgado, ancho; pulley, wheel (Mech) loco, flotante; connection desconectado; (unpacked) sin envase, a granel, suelto; translation libre, aproximado, (pej) poco exacto; thinking ilógico; style impreciso, vago; morals relajado; conduct, life disoluto; woman fácil; **to become** (or **come, get, work**) — (part) soltarse, desprenderse, (knot) aflojarse, desatarse; **to break** — desatarse, escaparse, (fig) desencadenarse; **to cast** (or **let, set, turn**) — soltar; **to cut** — separarse, independizarse (from de); **to hang** — caer suelto.
2 n (fam) **to be on the** — (free) estar en libertad; **to be** (or **go**) **on the** — ir de juerga, echar una cana al aire.
3 vt (free) soltar; (untie) desatar; (slacken) aflojar; storm, abuse etc desencadenar; **to** — **off gun** disparar (at sobre).
4 vi: **to** — **off at** (fire) disparar sobre; (abuse) empezar a soltar injurias contra.

loose-leaf ['lu:s'li:f] adj book de hojas sueltas, de hojas cambiables.

loose-limbed ['lu:s'limd] adj de movimientos sueltos, ágil.

loose-living ['lu:s'liviŋ] adj de vida airada, de vida inmoral.

loosely ['lu:sli] adv sueltamente; flojamente; holgadamente; libremente, aproximadamente; con poca exactitud; ilógicamente; imprecisamente; disolutamente; **it is** — **translated as** se traduce aproximadamente por; — **dressed** con vestidos holgados.

loosen ['lu:sn] **1** vt (free) soltar; (untie) desatar; (slacken) aflojar; to — up muscles desentumecer; see tongue etc.

2 vi soltarse; desatarse; aflojarse (also to — up); to — up (before game) desentumecer los músculos, entrar en calor; to — up on someone tratar a uno con menos severidad.

looseness ['lu:snis] n soltura f; flojedad f; holgura f; libertad f; imprecisión f; disolución f; relajación f; (Med) diarrea f.

loot [lu:t] **1** n botín m, presa f; (fam) ganancias fpl, (money) dinero m. **2** vt saquear.

looter ['lu:tə*] n saqueador m, ora f.

lop [lɔp] vt tree mochar, desmochar; branches podar; (esp fig) cercenar; to — away, to — off cortar.

lope [ləup] vi correr a paso largo (also to — along); to — off alejarse a paso largo.

lop-eared ['lɔp,iəd] adj de orejas caídas.

lop-sided ['lɔp'saidid] adj desproporcionado; desequilibrado; ladeado, sesgado; (fig) desequilibrado, falso.

loquacious [lə'kweiʃəs] adj locuaz.

loquacity [lə'kwæsiti] n locuacidad f.

lord [lɔːd] **1** n señor m; (British title) lord m; the L— (Eccl) el Señor; Our L— (Eccl) Nuestro Señor; the L—s (Parl) la Cámara de los Lores; the —s of England (peers) los nobles de Inglaterra; my — (to bishop) Ilustrísima, (to noble) señor, (to judge) señor juez; my — bishop of Tooting su Ilustrísima el obispo de Tooting; good L—! ¡Dios mío!; — of the manor señor m feudal; — and master dueño m; see justice, live etc.

2 vt: to — it hacer el señor, mandar despóticamente; to — it over someone dominar a uno despóticamente, mandar a uno como señor.

lordliness ['lɔːdlinis] n lo señorial, carácter m señorial; altivez f, arrogancia f.

lordly ['lɔːdli] adj house, vehicle etc señorial, señoril; manner altivo, arrogante; command imperioso.

lords-and-ladies ['lɔːdzənd'leidiz] n (Bot) aro m.

lordship ['lɔːdʃip] n (title) señoría f; (rule) señorío m; his — su señoría.

lore [lɔː*] n saber m popular; ciencia f, tradiciones fpl; in local — según la tradición local; he knows a lot about plant — sabe mucho de las plantas, es muy erudito en botánica.

lorgnette [lɔː'njet] n impertinentes mpl.

Lorraine [lɔ'rein] Lorena f.

lorry ['lɔri] n camión m.

lorry driver ['lɔri,draivə*] n camionero m, camionista m, conductor m de camión.

lose [lu:z] (irr: pret and ptp lost) **1** vt (a) perder; patient no lograr salvar la vida de; that lost us the war eso nos hizo perder la guerra; that lost us the game eso nos costó la victoria.

(b) (passive with lost) to be lost perderse, quedar perdido; to be lost at sea (person) perecer en el mar, morir ahogado; the ship was lost with all hands el buque se hundió con toda la tripulación; all is lost! ¡todo está perdido!, ¡se acabó todo!; to get lost perderse, extraviarse, errar el camino; get lost! (fam) ¡vete a la porra! (fam); to be lost in thought estar absorto en meditación; to be lost in wonder quedar asombrado; to look lost parecer estar confuso, parecer estar desorientado, tener aire perplejo; after his death I felt lost después de su muerte no sabía qué hacer; to give someone up for lost dar a uno por perdido; the motion was lost se rechazó la moción; he was lost to science se perdió para la ciencia; he is lost to all finer feelings es insensible a todos los sentimientos nobles; the joke was lost on her la observación pasó inadvertida por él; this modern music is lost on me no entiendo esta música moderna.

2 vi perder; ser vencido; you can't — tienes forzosamente que salir ganando; the story did not — in the telling el cuento no perdió en la narración; the clock is losing el reloj atrasa.

3 vr: to — oneself perderse, extraviarse, errar el camino; (in speech) padecer una confusión, perder el hilo; to — oneself in thought ensimismarse.

loser ['lu:zə*] n (person) perdedor m, ora f; (Sport etc) el que pierde, el vencido, el equipo derrotado; (card) carta f perdedora; to be a bad — irritarse al perder, quejarse al ser vencido; to come off the — salir perdiendo.

losing ['lu:ziŋ] **1** adj team vencido, derrotado; trick etc perdedor. **2** —s npl pérdidas fpl.

loss [lɔs] n (a) pérdida f; — of memory amnesia f; without — of time sin pérdida de tiempo, sin demora; there was a heavy — of life hubo muchas víctimas, perecieron muchos; the army suffered heavy —es el ejército sufrió pérdidas cuantiosas; to cut one's —es cortar por lo sano.

(b) it's your — Vd es el que pierde; he's no — no vamos a sentir su ausencia; he's a dead — es una calamidad; the book is a dead — el libro es absolutamente inútil, el libro no vale para nada en absoluto; the ship is a total — el buque puede considerarse como totalmente perdido.

(c) to be at a — estar perplejo, no saber qué hacer; to be at a — to explain something no saber cómo explicarse algo; we are at a — to know why no sabemos en absoluto por qué; to be at a — for words no encontrar palabras con que expresarse; he's never at a — (for words) tiene mucha facilidad de palabra, tiene la palabra facilísima; to sell something at a — vender algo con pérdida.

lost [lɔst] **1** pret and ptp of lose. **2** adj perdido.

lost-and-found department ['lɔstən'faunddi,pɑːtmənt] n (US), lost property office ['lɔst'prɔpəti,ɔfis] n oficina f de objetos perdidos.

lot [lɔt] n (a) (random selection) by — echando suertes; to cast —s, to draw —s echar suertes (for something para decidir quién tendrá algo, to decide something para decidir algo); the — fell on him él resultó elegido, la suerte le tocó a él; to throw in one's — with someone unirse a la suerte de uno.

(b) (share) porción f, parte f; (destiny) suerte f; his — was different su suerte fue otra; it fell to my — me cayó en suerte, me cupo en suerte; it falls to my — to + infin me incumbe + infin.

(c) (plot) solar m, terreno m; building — solar m de construcción.

(d) (at auction) lote m; he's a bad — es un mal sujeto; what a —! ¡qué tíos!; I'll send it in 3 —s se lo mando en 3 paquetes.

(e) (quantity) cantidad f; grupo m, serie f, colección f; a fine — of fish una bonita serie de peces; a fine — of students un buen grupo de estudiantes; a — of money mucho dinero; a — of books, —s of books muchos libros; quite a — of books bastantes libros; such a — of books tantos libros; an awful — of things to do la mar de cosas que hacer; we have —s of flowers (we don't want) nos sobran flores, tenemos flores de sobra; that's the — eso es todo; the whole — of them ellos todos, todos ellos sin excepción; he collared the — se los llevó todos; big ones, little ones, the —! ¡los grandes, los pequeños, todos!

(f) (as adv) I read a — leo bastante; we don't go out a — no salimos mucho; things have changed a — las cosas han cambiado mucho; there wasn't a — we could do apenas había nada que pudiéramos hacer; he drinks an awful — bebe una barbaridad; I'd give a — to know me gustaría muchísimo saberlo; I feel —s better me encuentro mucho mejor; see last.

lotion ['ləuʃən] n loción f.

lottery ['lɔtəri] n lotería f.

lotus ['ləutəs] n loto m.

loud [laud] **1** adj voice, tone etc alto; shout etc fuerte, recio; (noisy) ruidoso, estrepitoso; applause fuerte, estrepitoso; behaviour ruidoso, turbulento, maleducado; (-mouthed) gritón; colour chillón; (in bad taste) charro, cursi.

2 adv see loudly; to say something out — decir algo en alta voz.

loudhailer ['laud'heilə*] n megáfono m, bocina f.

loudly ['laudli] adv en alta voz; fuertemente; ruidosamente, estrepitosamente.

loud-mouthed ['laud'mauðd] adj gritón.

loudness ['laudnis] n lo alto; fuerza f; ruido m; lo chillón; vulgaridad f.

loudspeaker ['laud'spi:kə*] n altavoz m, altoparlante m.

Louis ['lu:i] m Luis.

Louisiana [lu,i:zi'ænə] Luisiana f.

lounge [laundʒ] **1** n (in house) salón m, sala f de estar; (on liner etc) salón m.

2 vi (saunter) pasearse despacito; (idle) gandulear, pasar un rato sin hacer nada; to — about tirarse a la bartola; to — against a wall apoyarse distraídamente en una pared; to — back in a chair repanchigarse en un asiento; we spent a week lounging in Naples pasamos una semana en Nápoles sin hacer nada.

lounger ['laundʒə*] n gandul m, haragán m, ana f; azotacalles mf.

lounge suit ['laundʒ'su:t] n traje m de calle.

louse [laus] **1** n, pl lice [lais] piojo m. **2** vt (sl): to — something up estropear algo.

lousy ['lauzi] *adj* piojoso; *(fam: very bad)* malísimo, horrible; *trick .etc* vil, asqueroso; **to be — with money** estar podrido de dinero.
lout [laut] gamberro *m*; patán *m*.
loutish ['lautiʃ] *adj* grosero, maleducado.
Louvain ['luːvein] Lovaina.
louver ['luːvə*] *n* lumbrera *f*; *(blind)* persiana *f*.
lovable ['lʌvəbl] *adj* amable, simpático.
love [lʌv] **1** *n* **(a)** amor *m* (*for, of, towards* a, de); cariño *m*; *(for hobby etc)* afición *f* (*for, of* a); **first — primer amor** *m*; **mother —** amor *m* maternal; **— in a cottage** contigo pan y cebolla; **— at first sight** amor *m* a primera vista, flechazo *m*; **for —** por amor, *(free)* gratis, *(without stakes)* sin jugarse dinero, sin apuestas; **not for — nor money** por nada del mundo; **for the — of** por el amor de; **for the — of God!** ¡por Dios!; **to marry for —** casarse por amor; **he studies history for the — of it** estudia la historia por pura afición al tema; **to be in —** estar enamorado (*with* de); **to fall in —** enamorarse (*with* de); **to make —** hacer el amor; **to make — to someone** *(court)* pretender a una, *(sexually)* hacer el amor a una, *(fig)* hacer la pelotilla a uno; **there is no — lost between them** existe entre ellos una fuerte antipatía.
(b) *(greetings, in letters etc)* **"with my —"** "besos"; **give him my —** mándale recuerdos míos; **to send one's — to someone** mandar cariñosos saludos a uno.
(c) *(person)* amado *m*, a *f*; **yes, —** sí, querida; **my —** mi amor; **the child's a little —** el niño es una monada.
(d) *(Tennis)* **—** all cero-cero; **15 —** 15 a cero.
2 *vt person etc* amar, querer; tener cariño a; *hobby etc* ser muy aficionado a; **she —s me, she —s me not** me quiere, no me quiere; **I — Madrid** me encanta Madrid, me gusta muchísimo Madrid; **I — this record** me encanta este disco; **he —s swimming, he —s to swim** le gusta muchísimo nadar, le entusiasma la natación; **I should — to come** me gustaría mucho venir, me encantaría venir; **— me — my dog** quien quiere a Beltrán quiere a su can.
love affair ['lʌvə,fɛə*] *n* amores *mpl*; aventura *f* sentimental; *(pej)* amoríos *mpl*.
lovebird ['lʌvbəːd] *n* periquito *m*; *(fig)* palomito *m*.
love child ['lʌvtʃaild] *n, pl* **— children** [,tʃildrən] hijo *m* del amor, hija *f* del amor.
loveless ['lʌvlis] *adj* sin amor.
love letter ['lʌv,letə*] *n* carta *f* de amor.
love life ['lʌvlaif] *n* vida *f* sentimental; vida *f* sexual.
loveliness ['lʌvlinis] *n* hermosura *f*, belleza *f*; encanto *m*.
lovelorn ['lʌvlɔːn] *adj* suspirando de amor, herido de amor.
lovely ['lʌvli] **1** *adj* *(beautiful)* hermoso; bello; *(delightful)* encantador, precioso, delicioso; *(pleasing, of objects etc)* mono, precioso, rico; *(US)* simpático; **isn't it —?** ¿verdad que es precioso?; ¡qué rico!, ¡qué monada!; **we had a — time** lo pasamos la mar de bien; **I hope you have a — time!** ¡que os divirtáis!; **it's been — to see you** ha sido una visita encantadora.
2 *n* belleza *f*, guapa *f*.
love-making ['lʌv,meikiŋ] *n* *(courtship)* galanteo *m*; *(sexual)* trato *m* sexual.
love match ['lʌvmætʃ] *n* matrimonio *m* por amor.
love nest ['lʌvnest] *n* nido *m* de amor.
lover ['lʌvə*] *n* **(a)** amante *mf*; *(pej)* amante *m*, querida *f*; **he became her —** se hizo amante de ella; **we were —s for 2 years** durante 2 años fuimos amantes; **so she took a —** así que tomó un amante; **the —s** los amantes, los novios.
(b) a — of *(hobby, wine etc)* un amigo de, una amiga de, un aficionado a, una aficionada a; **he is a great — of the violin** tiene muchísima afición al violín.
(c) *(in compounds) eg* **music — persona *f* aficionada a la música, football —s everywhere** los aficionados al fútbol de todas partes.
lovesick ['lʌvsik] *adj* enfermo de amor, amartelado.
lovesong ['lʌvsɔŋ] *n* canción *f* de amor.
loving ['lʌviŋ] *adj* amoroso; cariñoso, tierno.
loving cup ['lʌviŋkʌp] *n* copa *f* de la amistad.
lovingly ['lʌviŋli] *adv* amorosamente; cariñosamente, tiernamente.
low¹ [ləu] **1** *adj* bajo; *number, rate, speed, temperature, tide, voice* bajo; *blow* profundo; *dress* escotado; *card* pequeño; *gear* primero; *price* bajo; reducido, módico; *stock* escaso; *diet* deficiente; *note, tone* grave; *health* débil, malo; *birth, rank* humilde; *manners* grosero; *character* vil; *opinion* malo; *joke,*

song verde; *trick* sucio, malo; *comedian* chabacano; **5 at the —est** 5 como mínimo; **activity is at its —est** las actividades están en su punto más bajo; **to feel —** estar deprimido; **stocks are getting —** las existencias escasean; **we are getting — on fuel** tenemos poco combustible, se nos está agotando el combustible.
2 *adv swing etc* bajo, cerca de la tierra *(etc)*; *say, sing* bajo, en voz baja; **to bow —** hacer una profunda reverencia; **a dress cut — in the back** un vestido muy escotado de espalda; **to fall — *(morally)*** envilecerse, caer muy bajo; **England never fell so —** Inglaterra nunca cayó tan bajo; **to lay someone —** derribar a uno, abatir a uno, poner a uno fuera de combate; **to be laid — with 'flu** ser postrado por la gripe; **to lie —** estar escondido, no asomar la cabeza; **to play — *(Cards)*** poner pequeño; **to run —** escasear, casi agotarse; **to sink — = to fall —**.
3 *n* *(Meteorol)* área *f* de baja presión, depresión *f*; *(Aut)* primera marcha *f*; *(fig)* punto *m* más bajo; **to reach a new —** caer a su punto más bajo; **this represents a new — in deceit** ésta es la peor forma de vileza; no se ha visto cosa más vil; *see* **all-time**.
low² [ləu] **1** *n* mugido *m*. **2** *vi* mugir.
lowborn ['ləubɔːn] *adj* de humilde cuna.
lowbrow ['ləubrau] **1** *adj* nada intelectual, poco culto. **2** *n* persona *f* nada intelectual, persona *f* de poca cultura.
low-class ['ləu,klɑːs] *adj* de clase baja.
low-cost ['ləu'kɔst] *adj* económico.
Low Countries ['ləu,kʌntriz] *pl* Países *mpl* Bajos.
low-cut ['ləu'kʌt] *adj* *dress* escotado.
low-down¹ ['ləudaun] *adj* bajo, vil.
low-down² ['ləudaun] *n* *(fam)* verdad *f*; informes *mpl* confidenciales; **he gave me the — on it** me contó la verdad del caso; **come on, give us the —** ven, dinos la verdad.
lower ['ləuə*] **1** *adj comp of* **low**; más bajo, menos alto; inferior; *classes* bajo.
2 *adv comp of* **low**; más bajo.
3 *vt* bajar; *boat* lanzar; *flag, sail* arriar; *(reduce)* reducir, disminuir; *price* rebajar; *morale, resistance* debilitar; *guard* aflojar; *(in dignity)* humillar.
4 *vr:* **to — oneself** descolgarse *(by, on, with* con); *(fig)* envilecerse; **to — oneself to do something** rebajarse a hacer algo.
lower ['lauə*] *vi* *(person)* fruncir el entrecejo, mirar con ceño; *(sky)* encapotarse.
lower-class ['ləuə,klɑːs] *adj* de la clase baja.
lowering ['lauəriŋ] *adj* ceñudo; amenazador; *sky* encapotado.
low-grade ['ləu,greid] *adj* de baja calidad.
low-heeled ['ləu'hiːld] *adj* *shoes* de tacones bajos.
lowing ['ləuiŋ] *n* mugidos *mpl*.
lowland ['ləulənd] **1** *n* tierra *f* baja; **the L—s** las tierras bajas de Escocia. **2** *adj* de tierra baja.
lowlander ['ləuləndə*] *n* habitante *mf* de tierra baja.
low-level ['ləu'levl] *adj* de bajo nivel.
lowliness ['ləulinis] *n* humildad *f*.
lowly ['ləuli] *adj* humilde.
low-lying ['ləu,laiiŋ] *adj* bajo.
low-minded ['ləu'maindid] *adj* malpensado.
low-necked ['ləu'nekt] *adj* escotado.
lowness ['ləunis] *n* bajeza *f*, lo bajo; escasez *f*; gravedad *f*; humildad *f*; vileza *f*; lo verde; *(of spirits)* abatimiento *m*.
low-pressure ['ləu'preʃə*] *adj* de baja presión.
low-spirited ['ləu'spiritid] *adj* deprimido, abatido.
low-tension ['ləu'tenʃən] *adj* de baja tensión.
loyal ['lɔiəl] *adj* leal, fiel (*to* a).
loyalist ['lɔiəlist] *n* legitimista *mf*, gubernamental *mf*; *(Spain, 1936)* republicano *m*, a *f*.
loyally ['lɔiəli] *adv* lealmente.
loyalty ['lɔiəlti] *n* lealtad *f*, fidelidad *f* (*to* a); **one's loyalties** la lealtad de uno.
lozenge ['lɔzindʒ] *(Med)* pastilla *f*; *(Math)* rombo *m*; *(Her)* losange *m*.
lubricant ['luːbrikənt] **1** *adj* lubricante. **2** *n* lubricante *m*.
lubricate ['luːbrikeit] *vt* lubricar, engrasar.
lubrication [,luːbri'keiʃən] *n* lubricación *f*, engrase *m*.
lubricator ['luːbrikeitə*] *n* lubricador *m*.
lubricity [luː'brisiti] *n* lubricidad *f*.
Lucan ['luːkən] *m* Lucano.
lucerne [luː'səːn] *n* alfalfa *f*.
lucid ['luːsid] *adj* claro, lúcido.
lucidly ['luːsidli] *adv* claramente, con claridad.
Lucifer ['luːsifə*] *m* Lucifer.
luck [lʌk] *n* suerte *f*, fortuna *f*; azar *m*; **bad —, hard —** mala suerte *f*; **bad —!** ¡mala suerte!; **good —** suerte *f*; **good —!** ¡que tengas suerte!;

beginner's — suerte f del principiante; **here's** —! (toast) ¡salud!; **no such** —! ¡ojalá!; **with any** — a lo mejor; **worse** —! ¡desgraciadamente!; **better** — **next time**! ¡a la tercera va la vencida!; **and the best of** (British) —! (iro) ¡Dios te la depare buena!; **to be in** — estar de suerte, tener suerte; **to be out of** —, **to be down on one's** — estar de malas; **to bring someone bad** — traer mala suerte a uno; **as** — **would have it** quiso la suerte que . . .; **to have the devil's own** —, **to have the** — **of the devil** tener chorra, tener buena pata; **to have the** — **to** + infin tener la suerte de + infin; **to keep something for** — guardar algo porque pudiera traer suerte; **take this for** — toma esto por si trae suerte; **to do something trusting to** — hacer algo a la buena de Dios; **to try one's** — probar fortuna.

luckily ['lʌkili] adv afortunadamente, por fortuna.
luckless ['lʌklis] adj desdichado, desafortunado.
lucky ['lʌki] adj person afortunado, feliz, que tiene suerte; day de buen agüero; move, shot etc afortunado; charm que trae suerte; **third time** —! ¡a la tercera va la vencida!; — **you**! ¡qué suerte!; **to be** — (person) tener suerte; **to be a** — **sort** tener buena sombra; **to be born** — nacer de pie; **to be** — **in that** . . . tener la suerte de que . . .; **that was very** — **for you** en eso tuviste mucha suerte; **to believe in one's** — **star** creer en su buena estrella.
lucrative ['lu:krətiv] adj lucrativo, provechoso.
lucre ['lu:kə*] n: filthy — el vil metal.
Lucretia [lu:'kri:ʃə] f Lucrecia.
Lucretius [lu:'kri:ʃəs] m Lucrecio.
lucubration [,lu:kju'breiʃən] n lucubración f.
ludicrous ['lu:dikrəs] adj absurdo, ridículo.
luff [lʌf] 1 n orza f. 2 vi orzar.
lug [lʌg] 1 n (a) oreja f (also sl); agarradera f; (Tech) orejeta f.
   (b) (tug) tirón m.
   2 vt (drag) arrastrar; llevar con dificultad; (pull) tirar de; **to** — **something about with one** llevar algo consigo (con dificultad); **to** — **something along** arrastrar algo; **to** — **something in** llevar algo dentro arrastrándolo, subject sacar a colación; **they** —**ged him off to the theatre** le llevaron contra su voluntad al teatro.
luggage ['lʌgidʒ] n equipaje m.
luggage boot ['lʌgidʒ,bu:t] n (Aut) maleta f, portaequipajes m.
luggage carrier ['lʌgidʒ,kæriə*] n, **luggage grid** ['lʌgidʒ,grid] n portaequipajes m, baca f.
luggage rack ['lʌgidʒ,ræk] n (Rail etc) rejilla f, redecilla f; (Aut) portaequipajes m, baca f.
luggage van ['lʌgidʒ,væn] n furgón m de equipajes.
lugger ['lʌgə*] n lugre m.
lugsail ['lʌgsl] n vela f al tercio.
lugubrious [lu:'gu:briəs] adj lúgubre, triste.
lugubriously [lu:'gu:briəsli] adv lúgubremente, tristemente.
Luke [lu:k] m Lucas.
lukewarm ['lu:kwɔ:m] adj tibio, templado; (fig) tibio, indiferente, poco entusiasta.
lull [lʌl] 1 n tregua f, respiro m, intervalo m de calma; (in storm, wind) recalmón m.
   2 vt person calmar, (to sleep) adormecer, arrullar; fears etc aquietar, sosegar.
lullaby ['lʌləbai] n nana f, canción f de cuna.
lumbago [lʌm'beigəu] n lumbago m.
lumbar ['lʌmbə*] adj lumbar.
lumber[1] ['lʌmbə*] 1 n (timber) maderos mpl, maderas fpl (de sierra); (junk) trastos mpl viejos.
   2 vt space, room obstruir (with de); **to** — **things together** amontonar cosas, (fig) juntar cosas sin orden; **to** — **someone with something** hacer que uno cargue con algo; **he got** —**ed with the job** él tuvo que cargar con el trabajo; **I got** —**ed with the girl for the evening** tuve que pasar toda la tarde con la chica.
   3 vi cortar y aserrar árboles, explotar los bosques.
lumber[2] ['lʌmbə*] vi: **to** — **about**, **to** — **along** moverse pesadamente, avanzar con ruido sordo.
lumbering ['lʌmbəriŋ] adj pesado.
lumberjack ['lʌmbədʒæk] n, **lumberman** ['lʌmbəmən] n, pl —**men** [mən] maderero m, hachero m; trabajador m forestal.
lumber mill ['lʌmbə,mil] n aserradero m.
lumber room ['lʌmbərum] n trastera f.
lumberyard ['lʌmbəjɑ:d] n (US) almacén m de madera.
luminary ['lu:minəri] n lumbrera f.
luminescence [,lu:mi'nesns] n luminescencia f.
luminosity [,lu:mi'nɒsiti] n luminosidad f.
luminous ['lu:minəs] adj luminoso.
lummox ['lʌməks] n (US fam) bobo m.

lummy ['lʌmi] interj (fam) ¡caramba!
lump [lʌmp] 1 n (of earth, sugar etc) terrón m; (mass) masa f informe; (fragment) trozo m, pedazo m; (swelling) bulto m, hinchazón f; (on surface) protuberancia f; (in throat) nudo m; (person) zoquete m; **with a** — **in one's throat** con un nudo en la garganta; **I get a** — **in my throat** se me anuda la garganta.
   2 adj sum etc global.
   3 vt: **to** — **together** objects amontonar; persons, subjects poner juntos, agrupar, mezclar; **so we** —**ed it así que nos marchamos, así que no tomamos parte alguna en ello; **if he doesn't like it he can** — **it** si no le gusta que se fastidie.
lumpish ['lʌmpiʃ] adj torpe, pesado.
lump sugar ['lʌmp'ʃugə*] n azúcar m en terrón, azúcar m de cortadillo.
lumpy ['lʌmpi] adj aterronado; liquid etc lleno de grumos, con muchos grumos; bed etc desigual, nada cómodo.
lunacy ['lu:nəsi] n locura f; **it's sheer** —! ¡es una locura!
lunar ['lu:nə*] adj lunar.
lunatic ['lu:nətik] 1 adj loco, demente. 2 n loco m, a f.
lunch [lʌntʃ] 1 n (also more formally **luncheon** ['lʌntʃən]) almuerzo m, comida f; (snack) bocadillo m; **to have** —, **to take** — comer.
   2 vi almorzar, comer; (on fish pescado); tomar un bocadillo.
lunch hour ['lʌntʃauə*] n período m libre de mediodía.
lunchtime ['lʌntʃtaim] n hora f de comer.
lung [lʌŋ] n pulmón m; iron — pulmón m de acero.
lung cancer ['lʌŋ,kænsə*] n cáncer m de pulmón.
lunge [lʌndʒ] 1 n arremetida f, embestida f; (Fencing) estocada f.
   2 vi arremeter (at contra, with con), embestir; dar una estocada; **to** — **at someone** abalanzarse sobre uno; **he** —**d with his right** le asestó un golpe con la mano derecha.
lupin ['lu:pin] n altramuz m, lupino m.
lurch[1] [lə:tʃ] n: **to leave someone in the** — dejar a uno plantado.
lurch[2] [lə:tʃ] 1 n sacudida f, tumbo m, movimiento m repentino; (Naut) bandazo m; **to give a** — dar un tumbo (etc).
   2 vi (vehicle etc) dar sacudidas, dar tumbos, dar un tumbo; (Naut) dar un bandazo; (person) tambalearse; **to** — **along** (vehicle) ir dando tumbos, (person) avanzar tambaleándose; **to** — **in** entrar tambaleándose; **to** — **out** salir tambaleándose.
lure [ljuə*] 1 n (bait) cebo m; (decoy) señuelo m; (fig) aliciente m, atractivo m; encanto m; (deceitful) señuelo m.
   2 vt atraer (con señuelo); (person) atraer, tentar; seducir; **to** — **someone away from** apartar a uno de; **to** — **someone into a trap** hacer que uno caiga en una trampa; **to** — **someone into a house** persuadir mañosamente a uno a entrar en una casa; **to** — **someone on to destruction** hacer que uno avance ciegamente hacia su ruina; **to** — **someone out** persuadir mañosamente a uno a salir.
lurid ['ljuərid] adj light misterioso, fantástico; colour of skin lívido, cárdeno; dress etc chillón; language fuerte, pintoresco; account sensacional; detail horripilante, espeluznante.
lurk [lə:k] vi estar escondido; estar en acecho.
lurking ['lə:kiŋ] adj fear etc vago, indefinible.
luscious ['lʌʃəs] adj delicioso, suculento, riquísimo, exquisito; style empalagoso; girl delicioso, apetitoso.
lush [lʌʃ] adj lozano, exuberante; (fam) see **luscious**.
lust [lʌst] 1 n (sexual) lujuria f, lascivia f; sensualidad f; (greed) codicia f, deseo m vehemente (for de).
   2 vi lujuriar; **to** — **after**, **to** — **for** (sexually) apetecer contacto carnal con, (greedily) codiciar.
lustful ['lʌstful] adj lujurioso, libidinoso; look etc lascivo.
lustfully ['lʌstfəli] adv lujuriosamente, libidinosamente; lascivamente.
lustfulness ['lʌstfulnis] n lujuria f, lascivia f; sensualidad f.
lustre, (US) **luster** ['lʌstə*] n lustre m, brillo m.
lustreless, (US) **lusterless** ['lʌstəlis] adj deslustrado; eyes apagado.
lustrous ['lʌstrəs] adj lustroso, brillante.
lusty ['lʌsti] adj person vigoroso, fuerte, robusto; plant lozano; cry fuerte; effort etc grande.
lute [lu:t] n laúd m.
Luther ['lu:θə*] m Lutero.
Lutheran ['lu:θərən] 1 adj luterano. 2 n luterano m, a f.

Lutheranism ['lu:θərənizəm] n luteranismo m.
Luxembourg ['lʌksəmbɔ:g] Luxemburgo m.
luxuriance [lʌg'zjuəriəns] n lozanía f, exuberancia f.
luxuriant [lʌg'zjuəriənt] adj lozano, exuberante.
luxuriate [lʌg'zjuərieit] vi (plant) crecer con exuberancia; (person) disfrutar; **to — in** disfrutar de, deleitarse con, entregarse al lujo de.
luxurious [lʌg'zjuəriəs] adj lujoso.
luxuriously [lʌg'zjuəriəsli] adv lujosamente, con lujo; **he sank back —** se recostó con fruición.
luxury ['lʌkʃəri] **1** n (in general) lujo m; (article) artículo m de lujo; **to live in —** vivir en el lujo. **2** attr de lujo; tax suntuario.
lyceum [lai'si:əm] n liceo m.
lychgate ['litʃgeit] n puerta f de cementerio.
lye [lai] n lejía f.
lying ['laiiŋ] **1** adj mentiroso, falso. **2** n mentiras fpl.
lying-in ['laiiŋ'in] n (Med) parto m; **— ward** sala f de maternidad.
lymph [limf] n linfa f.

lymphatic [lim'fætik] **1** adj linfático. **2** n vaso m linfático.
lynch [lintʃ] vt linchar.
lynching ['lintʃiŋ] n linchamiento m.
lynch law ['lintʃlɔ:] n ley f de Lynch.
lynx [liŋks] n lince m.
lynx-eyed ['liŋksaid] adj de ojos de lince.
Lyons ['laiənz] Lyón, León de Francia.
lyre ['laiə*] n lira f.
lyrebird ['laiəbə:d] n ave f lira.
lyric ['lirik] **1** adj lírico. **2** n (poem) poema m lírico, poesía f lírica; (genre) lírica f; (words of song) letra f de una canción.
lyrical ['lirikəl] adj lírico; (fig) elocuente, entusiasta; **to get — about something** entusiasmarse por algo, extasiarse ante algo.
lyrically ['lirikəli] adv (fig) con entusiasmo, con éxtasis.
lyricism ['lirisizem] n lirismo m.
lysol ['laisɔl] n lisol m.

M

ma [mɑ:] *n* (*fam*) mamá *f* (*fam*).
ma'am [mæm] *n see* **madam**.
mac [mæk] *n* impermeable *m*.
macabre [mə'kɑ:br] *adj* macabro.
macadam [mə'kædəm] *n* macadán *m*.
macadamize [mə'kædəmaiz] *vt* macadamizar.
macaroni [,mækə'rəuni] *n* macarrones *mpl*.
macaronic [,mækə'rɔnik] *adj* macarrónico.
macaroon [,mækə'ru:n] *n* macarrón *m* (de almendras), mostachón *m*.
macaw [mə'kɔ:] *n* ararauna *f*.
mace[1] [meis] *n* (*Bot*) macis *f*.
mace[2] [meis] *n* maza *f*.
macebearer ['meis,beərə*] *n* macero *m*.
macerate ['mæsəreit] **1** *vt* macerar. **2** *vi* macerar(se).
machete [mə'tʃeiti] *n* machete *m*.
Machiavelli [,mækiə'veli] *m* Maquiavelo.
Machiavellian [,mækiə'veliən] *adj* maquiavélico.
machination [,mæki'neiʃən] *n* maquinación *f*.
machine [mə'ʃi:n] **1** *n* máquina *f* (*also fig*); aparato *m*; (*Aut*) coche *m*; (*cycle*) bicicleta *f*; (*Aer*) aparato *m*, avión *m*; (*Pol etc*) organización *f*.
   2 *attr* mecánico, (hecho) a máquina.
   3 *vt* (*Tech*) trabajar a máquina, acabar a máquina; (*Sew*) coser a máquina.
machine gun [mə'ʃi:ngʌn] **1** *n* ametralladora *f*. **2** *vt* ametrallar.
machine gunner [mə'ʃi:ngʌnə*] *n* ametrallador *m*.
machine-made [mə'ʃi:nmeid] *adj* hecho a máquina.
machinery [mə'ʃi:nəri] *n* (*machines*) maquinaria *f*; (*mechanism*) mecanismo *m*; (*fig*) mecanismo *m*, organización *f*, sistema *m*.
machine shop [mə'ʃi:nʃɔp] *n* taller *m* de máquinas.
machine tool [mə'ʃi:ntu:l] *n* máquina *f* herramienta.
machinist [mə'ʃi:nist] *n* (*Tech*) operario *m* de máquina, mecánico *m*; (*Sew*) costurera *f* a máquina.
mackerel ['mækrəl] *n* caballa *f*, escombro *m*; — **sky** cielo *m* aborregado.
mackintosh ['mækintɔʃ] *n* impermeable *m*.
macro . . . ['mækrəu] macro . . .
macrocosm ['mækrəukɔzəm] *n* macrocosmo *m*.
mad [mæd] **1** *adj* loco; demente; *dog* rabioso; *idea* loco, insensato, disparatado; *gallop, rush etc* loco, precipitado; (*angry*) furioso; — **as a hatter**, — **as a March hare** más loco que una cabra; **raving** —, **stark** — loco de atar; **a** — **thing (to do)** una locura; **are you** —? ¿estás loco?; **you must be** —! ¡qué locura!; **he's hopping** — está que bota; **to be** — **about something** (*keen*), **to be** — **on something** estar loco por algo, ser muy aficionado a algo, entusiasmarse por algo; **to be** — **about something** (*angry*) estar furioso por algo; **to be** — **about someone** (*angry*), **to be** — **at someone** estar furioso contra uno; **to be** — **about someone** (*in love*) estar locamente enamorado de uno; **I'm just** — **about you** ando loco por ti; **to be** — **with joy** estar loco de alegría; **to drive someone** — volver loco a uno; **to get** — enfadarse, ponerse furioso (*with* con); **it's no good getting** — **with me** de nada sirve ponerte furioso conmigo; **to go** — volverse loco, enloquecer; **this is patriotism gone** — esto es el patriotismo en grado ridículo.
   2 *adv*: **to be** — **keen on something** entusiasmarse como un loco por algo; **to be** — **keen to do something** desear con vehemencia hacer algo; **to play** (*etc*) **like** — tocar (*etc*) como un loco; **to rain like** — llover muchísimo; **the plant grows like** — la planta crece con una rapidez asombrosa.
madam ['mædəm] *n* señora *f*; **yes** — sí señora; **little** — niña *f* precoz, niña *f* repipi; *see* **dear**.
madame ['mædəm] *n*, *pl* **mesdames** ['meidæm] (**a**) madama *f*, señora *f*; **M**— **Dupont** la señora de Dupont. (**b**) (*of brothel*) ama *f*, dueña *f*.

madcap ['mædkæp] **1** *adj* atolondrado. **2** *n* locuelo *m*, a *f*, tarambana *mf*.
madden ['mædn] *vt* volver loco; (*fig*) volver loco, enfurecer, sacar de quicio; **it** —**s me es para** volverse loco.
maddening ['mædniŋ] *adj* *delay etc* desesperante, exasperante; **isn't it** —? ¡es para volverse loco!
maddeningly ['mædniŋli] *adv* de modo desesperante; — **slow** terriblemente lento.
made [meid] *pret and ptp of* **make**.
Madeira [mə'diərə] Madera *f*; (*wine*) vino *m* de Madera.
made-up ['meid ʌp] *adj* hecho; compuesto, artificial; *dress* confeccionado; *story* ficticio; *face* pintado, maquillado.
madhouse ['mædhaus] *n*, *pl* —**houses** [,hauziz] manicomio *m*, casa *f* de locos; **this is a** —! ¡esto es un guirigay!
madly ['mædli] *adv* locamente; furiosamente, como un loco; con rabia; **we were** — **gay** nos divertimos una barbaridad, nos divertimos de las maneras más raras; **to be** — **in love with someone** estar enamorado perdidamente de uno.
madman ['mædmən] *n*, *pl* —**men** [mən] loco *m*.
madness ['mædnis] *n* locura *f*; demencia *f*; furia *f*; rabia *f*; **it's sheer** —! ¡es una locura!; **what** —! ¡qué locura!
Madonna [mə'dɔnə] *n* Virgen *f*, Madona *f*.
Madrid [mə'drid] Madrid; (*attr*) madrileño, matritense.
madrigal ['mædrigəl] *n* madrigal *m*.
madwoman ['mædwumən] *n*, *pl* —**women** [,wimin] loca *f*.
maelstrom ['meilstrəum] *n* vórtice *m* (*also fig*), remolino *m*.
maestro [mɑ:'estrəu] *n* maestro *m*.
Mae West ['mei'west] *n* (*Aer: hum*) chaleco *m* salvavidas.
mag [mæg] *n* (*fam*) revista *f*.
magazine [,mægə'zi:n] *n* (*journal*) revista *f*; (*in rifle*) depósito *m* de cartuchos, recámara *f*; (*Typ*) almacén *m* de matrices; (*Mil: store*) almacén *m*, (*for powder*) polvorín *m*, (*Naut*) santabárbara *f*.
Magdalen ['mægdəlin] *f* Magdalena.
Magellan [mə'gelən] *m* Magallanes; — **Straits** Estrecho *m* de Magallanes.
magenta [mə'dʒentə] **1** *n* magenta *f*. **2** *adj* color magenta.
Maggie ['mægi] *f* *nombre cariñoso de* **Margaret**.
maggot ['mægət] *n* cresa *f*, gusano *m*.
maggoty ['mægəti] *adj* agusanado, lleno de gusanos.
Magi ['meidʒai] *npl*: **the** — los Reyes Magos.
magic ['mædʒik] **1** *adj* mágico. **2** *n* magia *f*; **by** — por arte de magia; **as if by** — como por ensalmo; **the** — **of that moment** la magia de ese momento.
magical ['mædʒikəl] *adj* mágico.
magically ['mædʒikəli] *adv* por arte de magia; (*fig*) como por ensalmo.
magician [mə'dʒiʃən] *n* mago *m*, mágico *m*, brujo *m*; (*conjuror*) mago *m*, prestidigitador *m*; **"Love the M—"** "El Amor brujo".
magic lantern ['mædʒik'læntən] *n* linterna *f* mágica.
magisterial [,mædʒis'tiəriəl] *adj* magistral.
magistracy ['mædʒistrəsi] *n* magistratura *f*.
magistrate ['mædʒistreit] *n* magistrado *m*; juez *m* (municipal).
Magna Charta ['mægnə'kɑ:tə] Carta *f* Magna.
magnanimity [,mægnə'nimiti] *n* magnanimidad *f*.
magnanimous [mæg'næniməs] *adj* magnánimo.
magnanimously [mæg'næniməsli] *adv* magnánimamente.
magnate ['mægneit] *n* magnate *m*, potentado *m*.
magnesia [mæg'ni:ʃə] *n* magnesia *f*.
magnesium [mæg'ni:ziəm] *n* magnesio *m*.

magnet ['mægnit] *n* imán *m*.
magnetic [mæg'netik] *adj* magnético; (*fig*) magnético, atractivo.
magnetically [mæg'netikəli] *adv* magnéticamente.
magnetism ['mægnitizəm] *n* magnetismo *m*; (*fig*) magnetismo *m* personal, don *m* de gentes.
magnetize ['mægnitaiz] *vt* magnetizar, iman(t)ar.
magneto [mæg'niːtəu] *n* magneto *f*.
magnification [,mægnifi'keiʃən] *n* (**a**) (*Opt*) aumento *m*; enfoque *m*; **high —** gran aumento *m*; **low —** pequeño aumento *m*. (**b**) (*fig*) exageración *f*.
magnificence [mæg'nifisəns] *n* magnificencia *f*.
magnificent [mæg'nifisənt] *adj* magnífico; **—!** ¡magnífico!
magnificently [mæg'nifisəntli] *adv* magníficamente; **you did —** lo hiciste estupendamente bien.
magnify ['mægnifai] *vt* (**a**) (*Opt*) aumentar; **to — something 7 times** aumentar algo 7 veces. (**b**) (*fig*) agrandar, exagerar; (*praise*) magnificar.
magnifying glass ['mægnifaiŋglɑːs] *n* lente *f* de aumento, lupa *f*.
magnitude ['mægnitjuːd] *n* magnitud *f*; (*fig*) magnitud *f*, envergadura *f*; **a star of the first —** una estrella de primera magnitud; **in operations of this —** en operaciones de esta envergadura.
magnolia [mæg'nəuliə] *n* magnolia *f*.
magnum ['mægnəm] *n* botella *f* de dos litros.
magpie ['mægpai] *n* urraca *f*, marica *f*.
Magyar ['mægjɑː*] **1** *adj* magiar. **2** *n* magiar *mf*.
maharajah [,mɑːhə'rɑːdʒə] *n* maharajá *m*.
mahogany [mə'hɔgəni] *n* caoba *f*.
Mahomet [mə'hɔmit] *m* Mahoma.
Mahometan [mə'hɔmitən] **1** *adj* mahometano. **2** *n* mahometano *m*, a *f*.
maid [meid] *n* (*servant*) criada *f*, doncella *f*; (*in hotel etc*) camarera *f*; (*maiden: lit*) doncella *f*; (*young girl*) muchacha *f*; **old —** solterona *f*; **she'll be an old —** quedará para vestir santos; **lady's —** doncella *f*; **— of honour** dama *f* de honor; **— of all work** criada *f* para todo.
maiden ['meidn] **1** *n* doncella *f*.
  2 *adj* virginal, intacto; soltera; *name* de soltera; *flight, voyage etc* inaugural; *speech* primero; **— aunt** tía *f* solterona.
maidenhair ['meidnhɛə*] *n* cabello *m* de Venus.
maidenhead ['meidnhed] *n* (*Anat*) himen *m*.
maidenhood ['meidnhud] *n* doncellez *f*.
maidenly ['meidnli] *adj* virginal; recatado, modesto.
maidservant ['meid,səːvənt] *n* criada *f*, sirvienta *f*.
mail¹ [meil] *n* (*Mil*) malla *f*, cota *f* de malla.
mail² [meil] **1** *n* (*in general*) correo *m*; (*letters*) cartas *fpl*, correspondencia *f*; **is there any — for me?** ¿hay cartas para mí?
  2 *vt* (*post off*) echar al correo; (*send by —*) enviar por correo.
mailbag ['meilbæg] *n* saca *f* de correos.
mailboat ['meilbəut] *n* vapor *m* correo.
mailbox ['meilbɔks] *n* (*US*) buzón *m*.
mail car ['meilkɑː*] *n* (*Rail*) furgón *m* postal, vagón-correo *m*.
mail coach ['meilkəutʃ] *n* (*Hist*) diligencia *f*, coche *m* correo; (*Rail*) furgón *m* postal, vagón-correo *m*.
mailing list ['meiliŋlist] *n* lista *f* de personas a quienes se envía (*por correo*) propaganda comercial (*etc*).
mailman ['meilmæn] *n*, *pl* **—men** [men] (*US*) cartero *m*.
mail-order ['meil,ɔːdə*] *n* pedido *m* postal; **— firm, — house** casa *f* de ventas por correo.
mail train ['meiltrein] *n* tren-correo *m*, tren *m* postal.
mail van ['meilvæn] *n* (*Rail*) furgón *m* postal, vagón-correo *m*.
maim [meim] *vt* mutilar, lisiar, estropear; **to be —ed for life** quedar lisiado de por vida.
main [mein] **1** *adj* principal, más importante; mayor; *beam, pipe etc* maestro; *floor* primero, bajo; *office* central; *course, line, road* principal; **the — thing is to + infin** lo más importante es + infin.
  2 *n* (*pipe*) cañería *f* maestra, conducción *f*; (*Elec*; *also* **—s**) red *f* eléctrica; **the —** (*poet*) el océano; **in the —** en general, en su mayoría, en su mayor parte.
mainland ['meinlənd] *n* tierra *f* firme, continente *m*.
main line ['mein'lain] **1** *n* línea *f* principal. **2 main-line** *attr train* principal.
mainly ['meinli] *adv* principalmente; en su mayoría, en su mayor parte.
mainmast ['meinmɑːst] *n* palo *m* mayor.
mainsail ['meinsl] *n* vela *f* mayor.
mainspring ['meinspriŋ] *n* (*Mech*) muelle *m* real; (*fig*) motivo *m* principal, origen *m*.
mainstay ['meinstei] *n* estay *m* mayor; (*fig*) sostén *m* principal, pilar *m*.

mainstream ['meinstriːm] (*fig*) **1** *n* corriente *f* principal, línea *f* central (de evolución *etc*); **to be in the — of modern philosophy** estar en la línea central de la evolución de la filosofía moderna.
  2 *attr* de la corriente principal,'en la línea central.
maintain [mein'tein] *vt* (**a**) *attitude, order, family, justice etc* mantener; *silence* guardar; *road* conservar en buen estado; *student* pagar los estudios de; (*Mech*) entretener; **if the improvement is —ed** si la cosa sigue mejorando.
  (**b**) **to — that ...** sostener que ..., afirmar que ...
maintenance ['meintinəns] *n* mantenimiento *m*; conservación *f*; (*Mech*) entretenimiento *m*; manutención *f*; **— costs** gastos *mpl* de conservación; **— crew** personal *m* de conservación; **— grant** consignación *f* para mantenimiento.
Mainz [maints] Maguncia.
maisonette [,meizə'net] *n* casita *f*, hotelito *m*.
maize [meiz] *n* maíz *m*.
maize field ['meizfiːld] *n* maizal *m*.
majestic [mə'dʒestik] *adj* majestuoso.
majestically [mə'dʒestikəli] *adv* majestuosamente.
majesty ['mædʒisti] *n* majestad *f*; **Her M—, His M—** Su Majestad; **Your M—** (Vuestra) Majestad.
major ['meidʒə*] **1** *adj* mayor (*also Mus*), principal; **of — interest** de máximo interés; **of — importance** de la mayor importancia; **Smith M—** Smith el mayor.
  2 *n* (*Law*) mayor *mf* de edad; (*Mil*) comandante *m*; (*US Univ*) asignatura *f* principal, especialidad *f*.
  3 *vi* (*US Univ*): **to — in French** estudiar el francés como asignatura principal, especializarse en francés.
Majorca [mə'dʒɔːkə] Mallorca *f*.
majordomo ['meidʒə'dəuməu] *n* mayordomo *m*.
major-general ['meidʒə'dʒənərəl] *n* general *m* de división.
majority [mə'dʒɔriti] **1** *n* mayoría *f*; **a four-fifths —** una mayoría de las cuatro quintas partes; **the great — of lecturers** la mayor parte de los conferenciantes; **the vast —** la inmensa mayoría; **to attain one's —** llegar a mayoría de edad; **such people are in a —** tales personas son las más, predominan tales personas; **to be in a — of 3** formar parte de una mayoría de 3.
  2 *attr*: **— rule** gobierno *m* mayoritario, gobierno *m* de la mayoría.
make [meik] (*irr*: *pret and ptp* **made**) **1** *vt* (**a**) (*general sense*) hacer; fabricar; construir; elaborar; formar; crear; componer; *bed, effort, fire, noise, peace, remark, tea, war, will* hacer; *dress* confeccionar; *meal* preparar; *speech* pronunciar; *error* cometer; *payment* efectuar; *cards* barajar; *face* poner; *sense* tener; **to — someone a judge** constituir a uno juez, nombrar a uno juez; **to — someone king** elevar a uno al trono; **they've made John secretary** han puesto a Juan por secretario; **to — a friend of someone** trabar amistad con uno; **he's as cunning as they — 'em** es de lo más astuto, es sumamente astuto; **I'm not made for running** yo no estoy hecho para correr; **to be made of** estar hecho de, estar compuesto de, consistir en, constar de; **it's made of gold** es de oro, está hecho de oro; **to show what one is made of** demostrar las cualidades que tiene uno; **what do you — of this?** ¿qué te parece esto?; **what did you — of the film?** ¿qué impresión te produjo la película?; **what do you — of him?** ¿qué piensas de él?, ¿qué impresión te has formado de él?; **I can — nothing of it** no lo entiendo, no saco nada en claro; **I don't know what to — of it** no me lo explico.
  (**b**) (*complete, constitute*) *circuit* cerrar; *trick* ganar, hacer; **2 and 2 — 4** 2 y 2 son 4; **that —s 20 con** éste hacen 20; **it still doesn't — a set** todavía no completa una serie entera; **it doesn't — a full course** no equivale a una asignatura completa, no es igual a una serie completa; **to — a contract** (*Cards*) cumplir un contrato; **South leads and —s 5 tricks** Sur sale y efectúa 5 bazas; **it made a nice surprise** fue una sorpresa agradable; **partridges — good eating** las perdices son buenas de comer; **it —s pleasant reading** da gusto leerlo; **he made a good husband** resultó ser un buen marido; **he'll — a good footballer** será buen futbolista, tiene madera de futbolista; **I made one of the party** yo era (uno) del grupo.
  (**c**) (*earn etc*) ganar; **he —s £30 a week** gana 30 libras a la semana; **how much do you —?** ¿cuánto ganas?, ¿qué sueldo cobras?; **to — a fortune** enriquecerse, hacer su pacotilla (*fam*); **what will you — by it?** ¿cuánto vas a ganar en

esto?; **how much do you stand to** —? ¿cuánto esperas ganar?

(**d**) (*assure future of*) hacer la fortuna de; asegurar el triunfo de; **this film made her** esta película fue el principio de su éxito; **he was made for life** se aseguró un porvenir brillante; **to** — **or break someone** hacer la fortuna o ser la ruina de uno; **to** — **or mar something** decidir de una vez la suerte de algo.

(**e**) (*with pred adj*) hacer; **to** — **someone happy** hacer a uno feliz; **to** — **someone angry** irritar a uno, provocar a uno, sacar a uno de quicio; **to** — **someone ashamed** dar vergüenza a uno; **to** — **someone sleepy** dar a uno ganas de dormirse; **to** — **someone rich** enriquecer a uno; **to** — **someone ill** sentar a uno mal; **to** — **something ready** preparar algo; **to** — **iron hot** calentar un trozo de hierro; **to** — **one's voice heard** hacer que se escuche la voz de uno.

(**f**) (*say, agree*) **let's** — **it 9 o'clock** citémonos para las 9, pongamos las 9.

(**g**) (*believe*) creer; **the situation is not so bad as you** — **it** la situación es menos grave de lo que Vd cree.

(**h**) (*calculate*) **what do you** — **the time?** ¿qué hora tienes?; **I** — **it 7.30** yo tengo las 7 y media; **how many do you** — **it?** ¿cuántos dices tú?, ¿cuántos tienes en total?

(**i**) (*force*) **to** — **someone do something** forzar (*or* obligar, compeler) a uno a hacer algo; (*persuade*) inclinar (*or* inducir) a uno a hacer algo; **you can't** — **me** Vd no puede forzarme a hacerlo; **what** —**s you do it?** ¿por qué te ves obligado a hacerlo?; **what made you say that?** ¿por qué dijiste eso?; **to** — **someone laugh** mover a uno a risa.

(**j**) (*reach, attain*) **we made 15 knots** alcanzamos una velocidad de 15 nudos; **we shall never** — **the shore** no llegamos nunca a la playa, será imposible alcanzar la playa; **to** — **it** (*arrive*) llegar; (*achieve something*) conseguir lo que se deseaba; (*succeed*) tener éxito, triunfar; **eventually we made it** por fin llegamos; **we just made it in time** llegamos apenas con el tiempo justo; **can you** — **it by 10?** ¿puedes llegar para las 10?; **to** — **it with someone** (*sl*) conseguir acostarse con una.

(**k**) (*with adv or prep*) **to** — **into** convertir en, transformar en; **to** — **out** *cheque, document, receipt* extender; *list* hacer, redactar; *form* llenar; **the cheque should be made out to Pérez** el cheque será nominativo a favor de Pérez; **to** — **out** (*see*) distinguir, vislumbrar, divisar; *writing* descifrar; (*understand*) entender; **I can't** — **it out at all** no me lo explico, no lo entiendo; **he made out that** ... dio a entender que ..., dio la impresión de que ..., nos hizo creer que ...; **you** — **him out to be better than he is** Vd hace creer que es mejor de lo que es en realidad; **he's not as rich as people** — **out** es menos rico de lo que dice la gente; **how do you** — **that out?** ¿cómo deduces eso?, ¿de qué se infiere eso?; **to** — **over** ceder, traspasar; **to** — **up** (*make*) hacer; fabricar; *dress* confeccionar; *medicine* preparar; *collection* reunir; *parcel* empaquetar; envolver; *list* hacer, redactar; *print, page* componer; **to** — **up** (*compose*) componer, formar, constituir; **the parts which** — **it up** las partes que lo componen; **the party was made up of 8 bishops** el grupo lo integraban 8 obispos; **to** — **up** (*invent*) inventar; **you're making it up!** ¡puro cuento!; **to** — **up** (*complete*) completar; *quantity, total* completar, hacer; **to** — **up** *loss* subsanar; *lost time etc* recuperar; *deficit* cubrir; **to** — **it up to someone** compensar a uno, indemnizar a uno; **to** — **up a fire** echar carbón a una lumbre; **to** — **up a quarrel** hacer las paces; **to** — **it up with someone** hacer las paces con uno; **to** — **up one's face** pintarse, maquillarse; **to** — **up an actor** maquillar a un actor.

2 *vi* (**a**) (*tide*) crecer, subir.

(**b**) **he made as if to** + *infin* hizo como si quisiese + *infin*, fingió que iba a + *infin*, hizo además de + *infin*.

(**c**) **to** — **away, to** — **off** largarse; huir, escaparse; **to** — **away with, to** — **off with** llevarse, alzarse con; escaparse con; **to** — **away with someone** matar a uno; **to** — **away with oneself** quitarse la vida, suicidarse.

(**d**) **to** — **after someone** seguir a uno, perseguir a uno; **to** — **for a place, to** — **towards a place** dirigirse a un lugar, encaminarse a un lugar; **where are you making for?** ¿adónde se dirige Vd?; **to** — **for someone** atacar a uno, abalanzarse sobre uno.

(**e**) **to** — **for** *result etc* contribuir a, conducir a;

it —**s for optimism** ayuda a crear el optimismo, fomenta el optimismo; **it** —**s for difficulties** tiende a crear dificultades.

(**f**) **to** — **out** arreglárselas, salir bien; **we're making out** vamos tirando; **we made out eventually** por fin nos las arreglamos; **how are you making out?** ¿cómo te va eso?

(**g**) **to** — **up** pintarse, maquillarse.

(**h**) **to** — **up for someone's losses** compensar a uno por sus pérdidas, indemnizar a uno de sus pérdidas; **to** — **up for a lack of** suplir una falta de; **to** — **up for lost time** recuperar el tiempo perdido.

(**i**) **to** — **up to someone** (*procurar*) congraciarse con uno, (procurar) ganarse la amistad de uno; halagar a uno, hacer zalamerías a uno.

3 *vr*: (**a**) **to** — **oneself an expert in** llegar a ser experto en; **to** — **oneself dictator** hacerse dictador, constituirse en dictador.

(**b**) **to** — **oneself comfortable** acomodarse a su gusto; **to** — **oneself ill with work** enfermar por exceso de trabajo; **to** — **oneself ridiculous** ponerse en ridículo; *see* **hear** *etc*.

(**c**) **to** — **oneself do something** obligarse a hacer algo; **I have to** — **myself** (do it) tengo que hacer un esfuerzo (por hacerlo).

4 *n* (**a**) (*brand*) marca *f*; (*type etc*) tipo *m*, modelo *m*; **it's a good** — es buena marca; **what** — **of car was it?** ¿qué tipo de coche fue?; **these are my own** — estos son según mi propia receta; **they have rifles of Belgian** — tienen fusiles de fabricación belga.

(**b**) **to be on the** — (*fam*) buscar el propio provecho, procurar a toda costa ir adelante; **the town is full of dealers on the** — la ciudad está llena de comerciantes que quieren enriquecerse.

make-believe ['meikbi,li:v] 1 *adj* fingido, simulado; *world etc* de ensueño, soñado.

2 *n* ficción *f*, invención *f*; imaginación *f*; **a world of** — un mundo de ensueño; **don't worry, it's just** — no te apures, es de mentirijillas.

3 *vi* fingir.

maker ['meikə*] *n* hacedor *m*, ora *f*, creador *m*, ora *f*; artífice *mf*; (*builder*) constructor *m*, ora *f*; (*manufacturer*) fabricante *m*; **the M**— el Hacedor.

makeshift ['meikʃift] 1 *adj* improvisado; provisional, temporal. 2 *n* improvisación *f*; expediente *m*; arreglo *m* provisional.

make-up ['meikʌp] *n* (*composition*) composición *f*; estructura *f*; (*of person etc*) carácter *m*, modo *m* de ser, naturaleza *f*; (*of clothes*) confección *f*; (*Typ*) imposición *f*; (*for face*) maquillaje *m*, cosméticos *mpl*; — **artist**, — **man** maquillador *m*; — **artist**, — **girl** maquilladora *f*.

makeweight ['meikweit] *n* contrapeso *m*; (*fig*) suplente *m*, sustituto *m*; tapa(gujeros *m*.

making ['meikiŋ] *n* (**a**) fabricación *f*; construcción *f*; elaboración *f*; formación *f*; creación *f*; confección *f*; preparación *f*; **in the** — en vías de formarse (*or* hacerse *etc*); **it's still in the** — está todavía en construcción, está todavía sin acabar; **while it was still in the** — mientras se estaba haciendo; **it's a civil war in the** — es una guerra civil en potencia; **it's history in the** — es la historia como proceso actual, es la historia que actualmente se está escribiendo; **the mistake was not of my** — no soy yo el responsable del error; **it was the** — **of him** fue la causa de su éxito, (*morally*) fue el motivo de su reforma moral.

(**b**) —**s** elementos *mpl* (necesarios); **he has the** —**s of an actor** es un actor que promete, tiene talento para ser actor, tiene madera de actor.

maladjusted ['mælə'dʒʌstid] *adj person* inadaptado.

maladjustment ['mælə'dʒʌstmənt] *n* inadaptación *f*.

maladministration ['mæləd,minis'treiʃən] *n* mala administración *f*.

maladroit ['mælə'drɔit] *adj* torpe.

maladroitly ['mælə'drɔitli] *adv* torpemente.

maladroitness ['mælə'drɔitnis] *n* torpeza *f*.

malady ['mælədi] *n* mal *m*, enfermedad *f*.

malaise [mæ'leiz] *n* malestar *m*.

malapropism ['mæləprɔpizəm] *n* despropósito *m* lingüístico, equivocación *f* de palabras.

malaria [mə'lɛəriə] *f* paludismo *m*, malaria *f*.

malarial [mə'lɛəriəl] *adj* palúdico.

Malay [mə'lei] 1 *adj* malayo. 2 *n* malayo *m*, a *f*. 3 *n* (*language*) malayo *m*.

Malaya [mə'leiə] *n* Malaya *f*, Malaca *f*.

Malayan [mə'leiən] 1 *adj* malayo. 2 *n* malayo *m*, a *f*.

Malaysia [mə'leiziə] *n* Malaysia *f*.

malcontent ['mælkən'tent] 1 *adj* malcontento, revoltoso. 2 *n* malcontento *m*, a *f*, revoltoso *m*, a *f*.

male [meil] **1** adj (Bio, Mech) macho; child etc varón; sex masculino; (manly) viril, masculino; attire etc de hombres, para hombre; see nurse etc.
2 n macho m (also Bio); varón m.
malediction [ˌmæli'dikʃən] n maldición f.
malefactor ['mælifæktə*] n malhechor m, ora f.
malevolence [mə'levələns] n malevolencia f.
malevolent [mə'levələnt] adj malévolo.
malevolently [mə'levələntli] adv con malevolencia.
malformation ['mælfɔː'meiʃən] n malformación f.
malfunction [mæl'fuŋkʃən] n funcionamiento m defectuoso.
malice ['mælis] n malevolencia f, mala voluntad f; (Law) intención f delictuosa; out of — por malevolencia; with — toward none sin malevolencia para nadie; to bear someone — guardar rencor a uno; I bear him no — no le guardo rencor.
malicious [mə'liʃəs] adj malévolo, maligno; rencoroso.
maliciously [mə'liʃəsli] adv con malevolencia, con malignidad; rencorosamente.
malign [mə'lain] **1** adj maligno. **2** vt calumniar, difamar; tratar injustamente, ser injusto con; you — me eso no es justo, ésa no era mi intención.
malignancy [mə'lignənsi] n malignidad f.
malignant [mə'lignənt] adj maligno (also Med).
malignity [mə'ligniti] n malignidad f.
malinger [mə'liŋgə*] vi fingirse enfermo.
malingerer [mə'liŋgərə*] n enfermo m fingido, enferma f fingida.
mall [mæl] n alameda f, paseo m de árboles.
mallard ['mæləd] n pato m real, ánade m real.
malleability [ˌmæliə'biliti] n maleabilidad f.
malleable ['mæliəbl] adj maleable.
mallet ['mælit] n mazo m.
mallow ['mæləu] n malva f.
malnutrition ['mælnju'triʃən] n desnutrición f.
malodorous [mæ'ləudərəs] adj maloliente, hediondo.
malpractice ['mæl'præktis] n procedimientos mpl ilegales; abuso m de autoridad; mala conducta f.
malt [mɔːlt] **1** n malta f. **2** vt barley hacer germinar; drink etc preparar con malta; —ed milk harina f lacteada.
Malta ['mɔːltə] Malta f.
Maltese ['mɔːl'tiːz] **1** adj maltés. **2** n maltés m esa f. **3** n (language) maltés m.
maltreat [mæl'triːt] vt maltratar, tratar mal.
maltreatment [mæl'triːtmənt] n maltrato m, maltratamiento m, malos tratos mpl.
mam(m)a [mə'mɑː] n (fam) mamá f (fam).
mammal ['mæməl] n mamífero m.
mammalian [mæ'meiliən] adj mamífero.
mammary ['mæməri] adj mamario; — gland mama f, teta f.
Mammon ['mæmən] m (Bib) Mammón.
mammoth ['mæməθ] **1** n mamut m. **2** adj gigantesco; (Comm) de tamaño extra.
mammy ['mæmi] n (fam) mamaíta f (fam); (US) nodriza f negra.
man [mæn] **1** n, pl men [men] **(a)** (general sense) hombre m; varón m; (humanity in general) el hombre, los hombres, el género humano; (servant) criado m; (workman) obrero m; (Mil) soldado m; (Naut) marinero m; (Chess etc) pieza f, ficha f, trebejo m.
(b) (with adj) best — padrino m de boda, testigo m del novio; family — padre m de familia, (home-loving) hombre m casero; — Friday criado m fiel; all good men and true todos los que merecen llamarse hombres; her — su marido; the inner — el estómago; ladies' — Perico entre ellas, hombre m de salón; leading — primer galán m; medical — médico m; old — viejo m, anciano m; my old — (fam) el pariente; red — piel roja m; the grand old — of the party el líder veterano del partido; the strong — of the government el hombre fuerte del gobierno; young — joven m; her young — su novio.
(c) (with qualifying phrase) — about town hombre m mundano, joven m amigo de los placeres, señorito m; — and boy desde pequeño; — and wife marido y mujer; — in the moon mujer f (or hombre m) de la luna; — in the street hombre m de la calle, hombre m medio; — of letters literato m; — of means, — of property hombre m acaudalado; — of parts hombre m de talento; — of the world hombre m de mundo.
(d) (used as pron etc) men say that ... se dice que ...; when a — needs a wash cuando uno necesita lavarse; any — cualquiera, cualquier hombre; no — nadie; that — Jones ese Jones; as one — unánimemente; como un sólo hombre,

todos a uno; — to — de hombre a hombre; they're communists to a — todos sin excepción son comunistas.
(e) (sort, type) I'm not a drinking — yo no bebo; I'm not a football — yo no soy aficionado al fútbol, no me gusta el fútbol; he's a 4-pint — es de los que se beben 4 pintas; he's a Leeds — es de Leeds; it's got to be a local — tiene que ser uno de aquí; then I'm your — entonces yo soy el que busca Vd.
(f) (in direct address) you can't do that, — hombre, no puedes hacer eso; —, was I startled! ¡vaya susto que me llevé!; (my) little —! ¡tirillas!; my good — buen hombre; good —! ¡bravo!, ¡muy bien!; look here, old — mire, amigo.
(g) (verb phrases) to be odd — out (different) diferenciarse de los demás, ser distinto, (left out) quedar excluido, (one too many) estar de más, sobrar; he's not the — to do it no es capaz de hacerlo; he's not the — for the job no es persona adecuada para el puesto; to make a — of someone hacer un hombre de uno; — proposes, God disposes el hombre propone y Dios dispone; to reach —'s estate llegar a la edad viril.
2 vt ship tripular; fortress guarnecer; guns servir; pumps acudir a, hacer funcionar; a fully —ned ship un buque con toda su tripulación; the telephone is —ned all day el telefonista está de servicio todo el día; see also manned.
manacle ['mænəkl] **1** n manilla f; —s esposas fpl, grillos mpl.
2 vt poner esposas a; they were —d together iban esposados juntos; his hands were —d llevaba esposas en las muñecas.
manage ['mænidʒ] **1** vt **(a)** tool etc manejar; manipular; car conducir; ship gobernar.
(b) company dirigir; organization regir, administrar; property administrar; affair manejar; election (pej) falsificar.
(c) person, child, animal manejar; she can't — children no puede con los niños; I can — him yo me encargo de él.
(d) £5 is the most I can — 5 libras es todo lo que puedo darte (or pagar etc); I shall — it lo haré; you'll — it next time lo harás la próxima vez; can you — the cases? ¿puedes llevar las maletas?; thanks, I can — them gracias, yo puedo con ellas; can you — two more in the car? ¿puedes llevar a dos más en el coche?; can you — 8 o'clock? ¿puedes venir a las 8?; can you — another cup? ¿quieres otra taza?; I can — another cake me atrevo con otra pasta; I couldn't — another thing no podría comer ni un bocado más.
2 vi **(a)** arreglárselas, ir tirando; can you —? ¿tú puedes con eso?; thanks, I can — gracias, yo puedo; she — s well enough se las arregla bastante bien; how do you —? ¿cómo se las arregla Vd?; to — without something pasarse sin algo; to — without someone prescindir de algo.
(b) to — to do something lograr hacer algo; arreglárselas para hacer algo, ingeniarse para hacer algo; how did you — to get it? ¿cómo lo conseguiste?; he —d not to get his feet wet logró no mojarse los pies.
manageable ['mænidʒəbl] adj manejable; person, animal dócil; of — size de tamaño razonable.
management ['mænidʒmənt] n **(a)** (act) manejo m; gobierno m; dirección f; gerencia f; administración f.
(b) (persons) dirección f; junta f de directores; (as a class) patronal f y directorial; (Theat) empresa f; "under new —" "nueva dirección".
manager ['mænidʒə*] n (Comm etc) director m, gerente m; (of estate etc) administrador m; (Theat) empresario m; sales — gerente m de ventas; works — gerente m de fábrica; business — (for play etc) secretario m; publicity — agente m de publicidad; she's a good — es buena administradora, es muy económica.
manageress ['mænidʒə'res] n directora f; administradora f.
managerial [ˌmænə'dʒiəriəl] adj directivo, directorial; administrativo; the — class la clase patronal y directorial; the — society la sociedad patronal y directorial.
managing ['mænidʒiŋ] adj (pej) mandón; see director.
man-at-arms ['mænət'ɑːmz] n, pl men-at-arms ['menət'ɑːmz] hombre m de armas.
manatee [ˌmænə'tiː] n manatí m.
Manchuria [mæn'tʃuəriə] Manchuria f.
Manchurian [mæn'tʃuəriən] **1** adj manchuriano. **2** n manchuriano m, a f.

mandarin ['mændərin] *n* mandarín *m*; **M—** (*language*) mandarina *f*.

mandate ['mændeit] **1** *n* mandato *m*; (*country*) territorio *m* bajo mandato. **2** *vt* asignar como mandato (*to a*).

mandated ['mændeitid] *adj territory* bajo mandato.

mandatory ['mændətəri] *adj* obligatorio; **to be — upon someone to do something** incumbir a uno como obligación hacer algo.

man-day ['mæn'dei] *n*, *pl* **man-days** ['mæn'deiz] día-hombre *m*.

mandible ['mændibl] *n* mandíbula *f*.

mandolin(e) ['mændəlin] *n* mandolina *f*.

mandrake ['mændreik] *n* mandrágora *f*.

mandrill ['mændril] *n* mandril *m*.

mane [mein] *n* (*of lion, person*) melena *f*; (*of horse*) crin *f*, crines *fpl*.

man-eater ['mæn͵i:tə*] *n* tigre *m* (*etc*) cebado, tigre *m* (*etc*) devorador de hombres.

man-eating ['mæn͵i:tiŋ] *adj* antropófago, peligroso para los hombres.

maneuver [mə'nu:və*] *etc* (US) *see* **manoeuvre.**

manful ['mænful] *adj* valiente, resuelto.

manfully ['mænfəli] *adv* valientemente, resueltamente.

manganese [͵mæŋgə'ni:z] *n* manganeso *m*.

mange [meindʒ] *n* roña *f*, sarna *f*.

mangel(-wurzel) ['mæŋgl('wə:zl)] *n* remolacha *f* forrajera.

manger ['meindʒə*] *n* pesebre *m*.

mangle[1] ['mæŋgl] **1** *n* rodillo *m*, exprimidor *m* de la ropa. **2** *vt* pasar por el exprimidor.

mangle[2] ['mæŋgl] *vt* destrozar, mutilar, magullar; *text etc* mutilar, estropear.

mango ['mæŋgəu] *n* (*fruit and tree*) mango *m*.

mangold(-wurzel) ['mæŋgl('wə:zl)] *n* remolacha *f* forrajera.

mangrove ['mæŋgrəuv] *n* mangle *m*.

mangrove swamp ['mæŋgrəuv͵swɔmp] *n* manglar *m*.

mangy ['meindʒi] *adj* roñoso, sarnoso.

manhandle ['mæn͵hændl] *vt* (*Tech*) mover a brazo; (*fig*) maltratar.

manhole ['mænhəul] *n* registro *m* de inspección, pozo *m* de visita.

manhole cover ['mænhəul͵kʌvə*] *n* tapa *f* de registro, tapadera *f* de cloaca.

manhood ['mænhud] *n* (*state*) virilidad *f*; (*age*) edad *f* viril; (*manliness*) hombradía *f*; **to reach —** llegar a la edad viril.

man-hour ['mæn'auə*] *n*, *pl* **man-hours** ['mæn'auəz] hora-hombre *f*.

manhunt ['mænhʌnt] *n* persecución *f* de un criminal, caza *f* de hombre.

mania ['meiniə] *n* manía *f*; **persecution —** manía *f* persecutoria; **to have a — for something** tener la manía de algo; **to have a — for doing something** tener la manía de hacer algo.

maniac ['meiniæk] **1** *adj* maníaco. **2** *n* maníaco *m*, a *f*; (*fig*) maniático *m*, a *f*; **these sports —s** estos fanáticos del deporte, estos entusiastas del deporte; **he drives like a —** conduce como un loco.

maniacal [mə'naiəkəl] *adj* maníaco.

manic-depressive ['mænikdi'presiv] **1** *adj* maníacodepresivo. **2** *n* maniacodepresivo *m*, a *f*.

manicure ['mænikjuə*] **1** *n* manicura *f*. **2** *vt person* hacer manicura a; *nails* limpiar, arreglar.

manicure case ['mænikjuə͵keis] *n*, **manicure set** ['mænikjuə͵set] *n* estuche *m* de manicura.

manicurist ['mænikjuərist] *n* manicuro *m*, a *f*.

manifest ['mænifest] **1** *adj* manifiesto, evidente, patente; **to make something —** poner algo de manifiesto.
 2 *n* (*Naut*) manifiesto *m*.
 3 *vt* mostrar, revelar, patentizar.

manifestation [͵mænifes'teiʃən] *n* manifestación *f*.

manifestly ['mænifestli] *adv* evidentemente.

manifesto [͵mæni'festəu] *n*, *pl* **manifestoes** [͵mæni'festəuz] manifiesto *m*.

manifold ['mænifəuld] **1** *adj* múltiple. **2** *n* (*Aut*) colector *m* de escape.

manikin ['mænikin] *n* (*dwarf*) enano *m*; (*Art*) maniquí *m*.

manioc ['mæniɔk] *n* mandioca *f*.

manipulate [mə'nipjuleit] *vt* manipular, manejar.

manipulation [mə͵nipju'leiʃən] *n* manipulación *f*, manejo *m*.

mankind [mæn'kaind] *n* humanidad *f*, género *m* humano, los hombres.

manlike ['mænlaik] *adj* varonil.

manliness ['mænlinis] *n* virilidad *f*, masculinidad *f*, hombradía *f*.

manly ['mænli] *adj* varonil, viril, masculino; (*courageous*) valiente; (*strong*) fuerte; **to be very —** ser muy hombre, ser todo un hombre.

man-made ['mæn'meid] *adj* artificial.

manna ['mænə] *n* maná *m*.

manned [mænd] *adj satellite etc* pilotado, habitado, tripulado.

mannequin ['mænikin] *n* (Art) maniquí *m*; (*fashion-*) modelo *f*.

manner ['mænə*] *n* **(a)** (*mode*) manera *f*, modo *m*; **— of payment** modo *m* de pago, forma *f* de pago; **after this —, in this —** de esta manera; **after** (*or* **in**) **the — of X** a la manera de X, en el estilo de X; **in like —** de la misma manera; **in such a — that ...** de tal manera que ...; **a painter in the grand —** un pintor de cuadros grandiosos; **in a — of speaking** (*so to speak*) por así decirlo, como si dijéramos, (*up to a point*) hasta cierto punto, en cierto modo; **it's a — of speaking** es un modo de decir; **as if to the — born** como si fuese avezado desde la cuna.
 (b) **—s** (*of society*) costumbres *fpl*; **a novel of —s** una novela de costumbres; **—s maketh man** la sociedad (*or* el medio ambiente) forma al hombre.
 (c) (*behaviour etc*) conducta *f*; aire *m*, ademán *m*, porte *m*; manera *f* de ser; **his — to his parents** su modo de comportarse con sus padres; **I don't like his —** no me gusta su actitud; **he had the — of an old man** tenía aire de viejo; **there's something odd about his —** tiene un aire algo raro.
 (d) **—s** (*good, bad etc*) modales *mpl*; educación *f*, crianza *f*; **bad —s** mala educación *f*; **good —s** educación *f*; **road —s** educación *f* en la carretera, conducta *f* en la carretera; **it's bad —s to yawn** es de mala educación bostezar; **good —s demand that ...** la educación exige que ...; **to have bad —s** ser mal criado, ser mal educado; **he has no —s** no tiene crianza, es un mal criado; **to forget one's —s** descomedirse; **to teach someone —s** enseñar crianza a uno.
 (e) (*class, type*) clase *f*, especie *f*; **all — of birds** toda clase de aves, aves de toda clase; **no — of doubt** sin ningún género de duda; **by no — of means** de ningún modo; **what — of man is he?** ¿qué tipo de hombre es?

mannered ['mænəd] *adj style* amanerado; (*in compounds*) de modales ...; *see* **bad-** *etc*.

mannerism ['mænərizəm] *n* **(a)** (*of style: Art, Lit*) manierismo *m*, (*pej*) amaneramiento *m*. **(b)** (*trick of speech, gesture*) hábito *m*, peculiaridad *f*.

mannerist ['mænərist] **1** *adj* manierista. **2** *n* manierista *mf*.

manneriness ['mænəlinis] *n* (buena) educación *f*, crianza *f*, cortesía *f*.

mannerly ['mænəli] *adj* (bien) educado, bien criado, cortés.

mannish ['mæniʃ] *adj* hombruno.

manoeuvrability [mə͵nu:vrə'biliti] *n* maniobrabilidad *f*.

manoeuvrable [mə'nu:vrəbl] *adj* maniobrable, manejable.

manoeuvre [mə'nu:və*] **1** *n* maniobra *f*.
 2 *vt* hacer maniobrar; manipular, manejar; **to — a gun into position** mover un cañón a su posición; **to — someone into doing something** lograr mañosamente que uno haga algo.
 3 *vi* maniobrar (*also fig*).

man-of-war ['mænəv'wɔ:*] *n*, *pl* **men-of-war** ['menəv'wɔ:*] *n* buque *m* de guerra.

manor ['mænə*] *n* (*feudal*) feudo *m*; señorío *m*; (*modern*) finca *f*; (*fam*) distrito *m*, barrio *m*; *see* **manor house.**

manor house ['mænəhaus] *n*, *pl* **— houses** [͵hauziz] casa *f* señorial, casa *f* solariega.

manorial [mə'nɔ:riəl] *adj* señorial.

manpower ['mænpauə*] *n* mano *f* de obra.

manqué ['mɔ:ŋkei] *adj*: **a novelist —** uno que pudiera haber sido gran novelista.

manse [mæns] *n* (*esp Scot*) casa *f* del párroco.

manservant ['mæn͵sə:vənt] *n*, *pl* **menservants** ['men͵sə:vənts] criado *m*.

mansion ['mænʃən] *n* palacio *m*, hotel *m*; casa *f* grande; (*of ancient family*) casa *f* solariega; **M— House** residencia del alcalde de Londres.

man-sized ['mænsaizd] *adj* de tamaño de hombre; (*fig*) bien grande, grandote.

manslaughter ['mæn͵slɔ:tə*] *n* homicidio *m* sin premeditación.

mantelpiece ['mæntlpi:s] *n*, **mantelshelf** ['mæntlʃelf] *n*, *pl* **—shelves** [ʃelvz] repisa *f* de chimenea.

mantilla [mæn'tilə] *n* mantilla *f*.

mantis ['mæntis] *n*: **praying —** mantis *f* religiosa.

mantle ['mæntl] **1** n manto m (also Zool), capa f (also fig); (gas-) manguito m incandescente. **2** vt cubrir, ocultar; envolver (in en).

man-to-man ['mæntə'mæn] adj, adv de hombre a hombre.

mantrap ['mæntræp] n cepo m.

manual ['mænjuəl] **1** adj manual. **2** n (book) manual m; (Mus) teclado m.

manually ['mænjuəli] adv manualmente, a mano.

manufacture [,mænju'fæktʃə*] **1** n (act) fabricación f; (product) manufactura f, producto m. **2** vt fabricar (also fig), manufacturar.

manufacturer [,mænju'fæktʃərə*] n fabricante m; industrial m.

manufacturing [,mænju'fæktʃəriŋ] **1** adj manu-facturero, fabril. **2** n fabricación f.

manure [mə'njuə*] **1** n estiércol m, abono m; artificial — abono m artificial. **2** vt estercolar, abonar.

manure heap [mə'njuəhi:p] n estercolero m.

manuscript ['mænjuskript] **1** adj manuscrito. **2** n manuscrito m; (Typ, original of article) original m.

Manx [mæŋks] **1** adj de la Isla de Man; the — los habitantes de la Isla de Man. **2** n lengua f (celta) de la Isla de Man.

Manxman ['mæŋksmən] n, pl —men [mən] habi-tante m de la Isla de Man.

many ['meni] **1** adj muchos, muchas; — people muchas personas, mucha gente, muchos; in — cases en muchos casos; — of them muchos de ellos; — a time I saw him act, —'s the time I saw him act muchas veces le vi representar; he has as — as I have tiene tantos como yo; he has 3 times as — as I have tiene 3 veces más que yo; there were as — as 20 había hasta 20; how — were there? ¿cuántos había?; however — you have por muchos que tenga Vd; so — flies tantas moscas; ever so — people la mar de gente, tantísimas personas; too — difficulties demasiadas dificultades; there's one too — hay uno de más, hay uno que sobra, sobra uno.

2 n muchos mpl, muchas fpl; gran número m; a good — houses, a great — houses muchísimas casas, un buen número de casas; the — la mayoría, las masas.

many-coloured ['meni'kʌləd] adj multicolor.

many-sided ['meni'saidid] adj figure multilátero; talent, personality polifacético; problem complicado.

map [mæp] **1** n mapa m; (of streets, town) plano m; (chart) carta f; geological — mapa m geológico; relief — mapa m en relieve; it's right off the — está muy aislado, está en el quinto infierno; this will put Cheam on the — esto ha de subrayar la importancia que tiene Cheam, ahora sí que se hablará de Cheam.

2 vt trazar el mapa (or plano) de; to — out (fig) proyectar; ordenar, organizar.

maple ['meipl] n arce m (also maple tree).

maple sugar ['meipl'ʃugə*] n azúcar m de arce.

maple syrup ['meipl'sirəp] n jarabe m de arce.

mapmaker ['mæp,meikə*] n cartógrafo m.

mapmaking ['mæp,meikiŋ] n, **mapping** ['mæpiŋ] n cartografía f.

mar [mɑ:*] vt estropear; desfigurar; echar a perder; happiness etc afectar; enjoyment aguar.

marathon ['mærəθən] **1** n (also — race) carrera f de maratón. **2** adj (fig) larguísimo, interminable.

maraud [mə'rɔ:d] vi merodear.

marauder [mə'rɔ:də*] n merodeador m; intruso m, indeseable m.

marauding [mə'rɔ:diŋ] **1** adj merodeador; intruso, indeseable. **2** n merodeo m.

marble ['mɑ:bl] **1** n (material) mármol m; (glass ball) canica f, bola f; to play —s jugar a las bolas. **2** adj marmóreo (also fig), de mármol.

marbled ['mɑ:bld] adj surface jaspeado.

March [mɑ:tʃ] marzo m.

march¹ [mɑ:tʃ] **1** n marcha f (also Mus, fig); (fig: long walk) caminata f; dead — marcha f fúnebre; forced — marcha f forzada; to steal a — on some-one madrugar, ganar por la mano a uno, sacar la delantera a uno.

2 vt soldiers hacer marchar, llevar; distance recorrer marchando, (fig) llevar andado; to — someone off llevarse a uno sin ceremonia.

3 vi marchar; (fig) andar, ir a pie; (stalk) ir resueltamente, caminar con resolución; forward —!, quick —! de frente ¡mar!; to — in entrar (resuelta-mente etc); to — into a room entrar resueltamente en un cuarto; to — on seguir marchando; to — out salir (resueltamente, airado etc); to — past desfilar; to — past someone desfilar ante uno; to — up to

someone abordar a uno tan fresco, acercarse resueltamente a uno.

march² [mɑ:tʃ] n (Hist) marca f; the Welsh —es la zona fronteriza entre Inglaterra y Gales.

marching ['mɑ:tʃiŋ] adj song etc de marcha.

marchioness ['mɑ:ʃənis] n marquesa f.

march-past ['mɑ:tʃ,pɑ:st] n desfile m.

mare [mɛə*] n yegua f.

mare's-nest ['mɛəznest] n parto m de los montes, hallazgo m ilusorio.

Margaret ['mɑ:gərit] f Margarita.

margarine [,mɑ:dʒə'ri:n] n, **marge** [mɑ:dʒ] n (fam) margarina f.

margin ['mɑ:dʒin] n margen m (also Typ); (fig) margen m; reserva f; excedente m, sobrante m; — of error margen m de error; — of profit margen m de beneficio; — of safety margen m de seguridad; to write something in the — escribir algo al margen.

marginal ['mɑ:dʒinl] adj note, profit etc marginal; land de poco valor agrícola; case etc dudoso, incierto.

marguerite [,mɑ:gə'ri:t] n margarita f.

Maria [mə'raiə] f María.

Marian ['mɛəriən] adj mariano.

Marie Antoinette [mə'ri:æntwɑ:'net] f María Antonieta.

marigold ['mærigəuld] n caléndula f, maravilla f.

marijuana [,mæri'hwɑ:nə] n marijuana f.

marina [mə'ri:nə] n centro m de deportes acuáticos, centro m de balandrismo.

marinade [,mæri'neid] **1** n escabeche m. **2** vt (also **marinate** ['mærineit]) escabechar, marinar.

marine [mə'ri:n] **1** adj marino; marítimo; — insurance seguro m marítimo; — life vida f marina. **2** n (a) (fleet) marina f; mercantile —, merchant — marina f mercante.

(b) (person) soldado m de marina; —s infantería f de marina; tell that to the —s! ¡a otro perro con ese hueso!

mariner ['mærinə*] n marinero m, marino m.

mariolatry [,mɛəri'ɔlətri] n mariolatría f.

marionette [,mæriə'net] n marioneta f, títere m.

marital ['mæritl] adj marital; matrimonial; — status estado m civil.

maritime ['mæritaim] adj marítimo.

marjoram ['mɑ:dʒərəm] n mejorana f, orégano m.

Mark [mɑ:k] m Marcos.

mark¹ [mɑ:k] n (coin) marco m.

mark² [mɑ:k] **1** n (a) (written symbol on paper etc) señal f, marca f; llamada f; (sign, indication) señal f, indicio m; (trade-) marca f; (stain) mancha f; (imprint, trace) huella f; the —s of violence las señales de la violencia; he had the —s of old age tenía los indicios de la vejez; he left the ring without a — on his body salió del cuadrilátero sin llevar en el cuerpo señal alguna de haber recibido golpe; it's the — of a gentleman así se distinguen los caballeros, es señal de caballerosidad; printer's — pie m de imprenta; as a — of my disapproval en señal de mi desaprobación; as a — of our gratitude en señal de nuestro agradecimiento; it bears the — of genius tiene el sello de la genialidad; to leave one's — dejar memoria de sí; to leave one's — on something dejar sus huellas en algo.

(b) (signature) cruz f; to make one's — firmar con una cruz, (fig) señalarse, distinguirse, destacar.

(c) (Sport) raya f; to be quick off the — ser muy listo; adelantarse a los demás; to be slow of the — ser lerdo; dejar que otros cojan la delantera a uno; to be up to the — ser satisfactorio, estar a la altura de las circunstancias; to come up to the — alcanzar el nivel que era de esperar; to overstep the — propasarse.

(d) (label) etiqueta f.

(e) — of — de categoría, de cierta distinción.

(f) (target) blanco m; to be wide of the — no dar en el blanco, (fig) no acertar, ser erróneo, alejarse de la verdad; to hit the — dar en el blanco, (fig) acertar, dar en el clavo.

(g) (in exam; also —s) puntuación f; calificación f, nota f; 52 —s 52 puntos, 52 por cien; first-class —s nota f de sobresaliente; to get high —s in French sacar buena nota en francés; you get no —s at all as a cook como cocinera no vales para nada; there are no —s for guessing las simples conjeturas no merecen punto alguno.

2 vt (a) (make a — on) señalar, marcar, poner una señal en; (stain) manchar; desfigurar; — it with an asterisk ponga un asterisco allí; he was not —ed at all no tuvo señal alguna de haber recibido golpe (or de haber sido lesionado); a bird —ed with red un pájaro manchado de rojo, un pájaro con manchas rojas.

(b) (*label*) rotular, poner un rótulo a; (*Comm*) poner una etiqueta a, indicar el precio de; **this exhibit is not** —ed este objeto no lleva rótulo; **the chair is** —ed at £2 se indica el precio de la silla como de 2 libras.

(c) (*indicate*) señalar, marcar, indicar; **stones** — **the path** unas piedras señalan el camino; **this** —s **the frontier** esto marca la frontera; **it** —s **a change of policy** ello indica un cambio de política; **this** —s **him as a future star** esto le señala como un as futuro; **it's not** —ed **on the map** no está indicado en el mapa, no consta en el mapa.

(d) (*note down*) apuntar; (*notice*) advertir, observar; (*heed*) prestar atención a; **did you** — **where it fell?** ¿vio Vd en qué sitio cayó?; — **you,** — **my words** entiéndase bien que . . .; — **you, he may have been right** de todas formas, puede haber tenido razón; — **what I say** escucha lo que te digo.

(e) *exam* puntuar, calificar; *candidate* dar nota a; **we** —ed **him (as) first class** le dimos nota de sobresaliente.

(f) to — **down** (*note*) apuntar; (*select*) escoger; (*Comm*) rebajar, rebajar el precio de; **to** — **off** señalar; distinguir, separar (*from* de); (*by stages etc*) jalonar; **to** — **out** *road etc* trazar, marcar; jalonar; **the road is** —ed **out by flags** el camino está jalonado de banderas; **he is** —ed **out for promotion** se le ha señalado para un ascenso.

marked [mɑ:kt] *adj contrast etc* acusado, fuerte; *accent* marcado; *improvement etc* notable, grande; — **man** hombre *m* que ha llamado la atención; hombre *m* que se ha señalado como futura víctima; **it is becoming more** — se acusa cada vez más.

markedly ['mɑ:kidli] *adv* marcadamente; fuertemente; notablemente; **it is** — **better than the other** es netamente superior al otro; **they are not** — **different** no son netamente distintos.

marker ['mɑ:kə*] *n* (*Billiards etc*) marcador *m*, (*in other games*) ficha *f*; (*in book*) registro *m*.

market ['mɑ:kit] **1** *n* mercado *m*; (*stock exchange*) bolsa *f*; **black** — estraperlo *m*, mercado *m* negro; **to buy something on the black** — comprar algo de estraperlo; **buyer's** — mercado *m* de signo favorable al comprador; **seller's** — mercado *m* de signo favorable al vendedor; **home** — mercado *m* nacional, mercado *m* interior; **overseas** — mercado *m* exterior; **world** — mercado *m* mundial; **Common M**— Mercado *m* Común; **open** — mercado *m* al aire libre; **free** — mercado *m* libre (*in* de); **there's no** — **for pink socks** los calcetines rosados no encuentran salida; **to be in the** — **for something** estar dispuesto a comprar algo; **to be on the** — estar de venta; **it's the dearest shirt on the** — es la camisa más cara del mercado; **to come on to the** — (empezar a) venderse, ponerse en venta, ofrecerse; **to corner the** — **in maize** acaparar el maíz; **to find a ready** — venderse fácilmente, tener fácil salida; **to flood the** — **with something** inundar el mercado de algo; **strawberries are flooding the** — las fresas inundan el mercado; **to play the** — jugar a la bolsa; **to rig the** — manipular la lonja.

2 *attr* — **price** precio *m* de mercado; — **research** análisis *m* de mercados; — **value** valor *m* en el mercado.

3 *vt* vender, poner a la venta; *new product etc* llevar al mercado.

4 *vi* ir de compras; hacer las compras.

marketable ['mɑ:kitəbl] *adj* vendible, comerciable; de valor comercial.

market day ['mɑ:kitdei] *n* día *m* de mercado.

marketeer [,mɑ:ki'tiə*] *n* (*Pol*) partidario *m* del Mercado Común; **black** — estraperlista *m*.

market garden ['mɑ:kit,gɑ:dn] *n* huerto *m*, (*large*) huerta *f*.

market gardener ['mɑ:kit,gɑ:dnə*] *n* hortelano *m*.

marketing ['mɑ:kitiŋ] *n* venta *f*, comercialización *f*.

market place ['mɑ:kitpleis] *n* mercado *m*, plaza *f* del mercado.

marking ['mɑ:kiŋ] *n* (*mark*) señal *f*, marca *f*; (*on animal*) mancha *f*, pinta *f*; (*coloration*) coloración *f*; (*of exams*) puntuación *f*, calificación *f*.

marking ink ['mɑ:kiŋ,iŋk] *n* tinta *f* de marcar, tinta *f* indeleble.

marksman ['mɑ:ksmən] *n*, *pl* —**men** [mən] tirador *m*, ora *f*.

marksmanship ['mɑ:ksmənʃip] *n* puntería *f*.

markup ['mɑ:kʌp] *n* precio *m*; aumento *m* de precio.

marl [mɑ:l] *n* marga *f*.

marlin ['mɑ:lin] *n* (*Fish*) aguja *f*.

marlinespike ['mɑ:linspaik] *n* pasador *m*.

marly ['mɑ:li] *adj* margoso.

marmalade ['mɑ:məleid] *n* mermelada *f* (de naranjas amargas).

marmoreal [mɑ:'mɔ:riəl] *adj* marmóreo.

marmoset ['mɑ:məzet] *n* tití *m*.

marmot ['mɑ:mət] *n* marmota *f*.

maroon[1] [mə'ru:n] **1** *adj* marrón. **2** *n* (*colour*) marrón *m*; (*firework*) petardo *m*.

maroon[2] [mə'ru:n] *vt* abandonar (en una isla desierta); **we were** —ed **by floods** quedamos aislados por las inundaciones.

marquee [mɑ:'ki:] *n* entoldado *m*.

marquess, marquis ['mɑ:kwis] *n* marqués *m*.

marquetry ['mɑ:kitri] *n* marquetería *f*.

marriage ['mærid3] *n* (*as institution*) matrimonio *m*; (*wedding*) boda *f*, bodas *fpl*; casamiento *m*; (*fig*) unión *f*; **civil** — matrimonio *m* civil; **shotgun** — casamiento *m* a la fuerza; — **of convenience** matrimonio *m* de conveniencia; **aunt by** — tía *f* política; **to be related by** — estar emparentados; **to become related by** — **to someone** emparentar con uno; **to give someone in** — **to** dar a una en matrimonio a.

marriageable ['mærid3əbl] *adj* casadero.

marriage bed ['mærid3bed] *n* lecho *m* nupcial, tálamo *m*.

marriage rate ['mærid3reit] *n* índice *m* de nupcialidad.

married ['mærid] *adj person* casado; *life, love, state etc* conyugal; — **man** casado *m*, — **woman** casada *f*; *see* **couple** *etc*.

marrow ['mærəu] *n* **(a)** (*Anat*) médula *f*, tuétano *m*, meollo *m*; (*fig*) meollo *m*; (*as food*) tuétano *m* de hueso; **a Spaniard to the** — español hasta los tuétanos; **to be frozen to the** — estar completamente helado.

(b) (*Bot*) calabacín *m* (*also* **vegetable** —).

marrowbone ['mærəubəun] *n* hueso *m* con tuétano; —s (*fam*) rodillas *fpl*.

marry ['mæri] **1** *vt* (*give or join in marriage*) casar (*to* con); (*take in marriage*) casarse con, casar con; (*fig*) unir; **he has 3 daughters to** — (*off*) tiene 3 hijas por casar; **to** — **money** casarse con uno (*or* una) que tiene una fortuna.

2 *vi* (*also* **to get married**) casarse; **to** — **again** volver a casarse, casarse en segundas nupcias; **to** — **beneath oneself** casarse con uno (*or* una) de rango inferior; **to** — **into a family** emparentar con una familia.

Mars [mɑ:z] *m* Marte.

Marseillaise [,mɑ:sə'leiz] *n*: **the** — la Marsellesa.

Marseilles [mɑ:'seilz] Marsella.

marsh [mɑ:ʃ] *n* pantano *m*; (*salt-*) marisma *f*.

marshal ['mɑ:ʃəl] *n* **1** (*Mil*) mariscal *m*; (*at ceremony*) maestro *m* de ceremonias; (*at sports meeting etc*) oficial *m*; (*US*) alguacil *m*, oficial *m* de justicia.

2 *vt facts etc* ordenar, arreglar; *soldiers, procession* formar.

marshalling yard ['mɑ:ʃəliŋ,jɑ:d] *n* playa *f* de clasificación.

marsh fever ['mɑ:ʃ,fi:və*] *n* paludismo *m*.

marsh gas ['mɑ:ʃgæs] *n* gas *m* de los pantanos.

marshland ['mɑ:ʃlænd] *n* pantanal *m*.

marshmallow ['mɑ:ʃ'mæləu] *n* (*Bot*) malvavisco *m*; (*sweet*) bombón *m* de merengue blando.

marsh marigold ['mɑ:ʃ'mærigəuld] *n* calta *f* palustre.

marshy ['mɑ:ʃi] *adj* pantanoso.

marsupial [mɑ:'su:piəl] **1** *adj* marsupial. **2** *n* marsupial *m*.

mart [mɑ:t] *n* (*trade centre*) emporio *m*; (*market*) mercado *m*; (*auction room*) martillo *m*; **property** — (*in newspaper*) bolsa *f* de la propiedad.

marten ['mɑ:tin] *n* marta *f*.

Martial ['mɑ:ʃəl] *m* Marcial.

martial ['mɑ:ʃəl] *adj* marcial; castrense; *law etc* marcial, militar.

Martian ['mɑ:ʃiən] **1** *adj* marciano. **2** *n* marciano *m*, a *f*.

Martin ['mɑ:tin] *m* Martín.

martin ['mɑ:tin] *n* (*Orn*) avión *m*.

martinet [,mɑ:ti'net] *n* ordenancista *mf*, rigorista *mf*.

Martinique [,mɑ:ti'ni:k] Martinica *f*.

Martinmas ['mɑ:tinməs] *n* día *m* de San Martín (11 *noviembre*).

martyr ['mɑ:tə*] **1** *n* mártir *mf*; **to be a** — **to arthritis** ser martirizado por la artritis, ser víctima de la artritis. **2** *vt* martirizar.

martyrdom ['mɑ:tədəm] *n* martirio *m*.

martyrize ['mɑ:tiraiz] *vt* martirizar.

marvel ['mɑ:vəl] **1** *n* maravilla; prodigio *m*; **if he gets there it will be a** — si llega allí será maravilla;

it's a — to me how he does it no llego a comprender cómo lo hace, me asombra el que lo pueda hacer. 2 *vi* maravillarse (*at* de, con).

marvellous, (*US*) **marvelous** ['mɑːvələs] *adj* maravilloso; —! ¡magnífico!; **isn't it** —? ¡qué bien! (*also iro*).

marvellously, (*US*) **marvelously** ['mɑːvələsli] *adv* maravillosamente; a maravilla.

Marxism ['mɑːksizəm] *n* marxismo *m*.

Marxist ['mɑːksist] **1** *adj* marxista. **2** *n* marxista *mf*.

Mary ['mɛəri] *f* María; — **Stuart** María Estuardo; **Bloody** — María la Sangrienta.

marzipan [‚mɑːziˈpæn] *n* mazapán *m*.

mascara [mæsˈkɑːrə] *n* rimel *m*.

mascot ['mæskət] *n* mascota *f*.

masculine ['mæskjulin] **1** *adj* masculino; varonil; *woman* hombruno. **2** *n* (*Gram*) masculino *m*.

masculinity [‚mæskjuˈliniti] *n* masculinidad *f*.

mash [mæʃ] **1** *n* (*mixture*) mezcla *f*; (*pulp*) pasta *f*, amasijo *m*, batiburrillo *m*; (*potatoes*) puré *m* de patatas; (*in brewing*) malta *f* remojada; (*bran*) afrecho *m* remojado. **2** *vt* mezclar; amasar, despachurrar; *potatoes* hacer un puré de.

mashed [mæʃt] *adj*: — **potatoes** puré *m* de patatas.

masher ['mæʃə*] *n* (*fam*) pisaverde *m*.

mask [mɑːsk] **1** *n* máscara *f* (*also fig*); (*disguise*) disfraz *m*; (*protective*) antifaz *m*; (*gas- etc*) careta *f*; (*surgeon's, death-*) mascarilla *f*; see **masque**. **2** *vt* enmascarar; (*fig*) encubrir, ocultar.

masked [mɑːskt] *adj* enmascarado; — **ball** baile *m* de máscaras.

masochism ['mæzəukizəm] *n* masoquismo *m*.

masochist ['mæzəukist] *n* masoquista *mf*.

masochistic [‚mæzəuˈkistik] *adj* masoquista.

mason ['meisn] *n* (*builder*) albañil *m*; (*in quarry*) cantero *m*; (*free-*) masón *m*, francmasón *m*; monumental — escultor *m* de monumentos funerarios.

masonic [məˈsɔnik] *adj* masónico.

masonry ['meisnri] *n* albañilería *f*; mampostería *f*; (*free-*) masonería *f*, francmasonería *f*.

masque [mɑːsk] *n* mascarada *f*.

masquerade [‚mæskəˈreid] **1** *n* baile *m* de máscaras, mascarada *f*; (*fig*) farsa *f*. **2** *vi*: **to** — **as** disfrazarse de, hacerse pasar por.

mass¹ [mæs] *n* (*Eccl*) misa *f*; **high** — misa *f* mayor; **low** — misa *f* rezada; **midnight** — misa *f* del gallo; **to go to** — ir a misa, oír misa; **to hear** — oír misa; **to say** — decir misa.

mass² [mæs] **1** *n* masa *f* (*also Phys*); (*vague shape*) bulto *m* informe; (*of mountains*) macizo *m*; (*great quantity*) montón *m*, gran cantidad *f*; (*of people*) muchedumbre *f*; **the** —**es** las masas; **a great** — **of people** una gran muchedumbre; **the** — **of** la mayoría de; **the great** — **of** la inmensa mayoría de; **in the** — en conjunto; **to gather in** —**es** acudir en masa, reunirse en tropel; **we have** —**es** tenemos montones; **he's a** — **of bruises** está cubierto de cardenales; **the garden is a** — **of yellow** el jardín es todo flores amarillas; **he's a** — **of nerves** es una madeja de nervios, tiene una tremenda tensión nerviosa. **2** *adj, attr production* en serie; *meeting* popular, público; *murders etc* en masa, en serie; *psychology de masas*; — **media** medios *mpl* de comunicación con las multitudes (*prensa, television etc*). **3** *vt* juntar en masa, reunir; *troops etc* concentrar. **4** *vi* juntarse en masa, reunirse; (*Mil*) concentrarse.

massacre ['mæsəkə*] **1** *n* matanza *f*, carnicería *f*, degollina *f*, masacre *f*. **2** *vt* hacer una carnicería de, matar despiadadamente, masacrar.

massage ['mæsɑːʒ] **1** *n* masaje *m*. **2** *vt* dar masaje a.

masseur [mæˈsɜː*] *n* masajista *m*.

masseuse [mæˈsɜːz] *n* masajista *f*.

massif [mæˈsiːf] *n* (*Geog*) macizo *m*.

massive ['mæsiv] *adj* (*solid*) macizo, sólido; *head etc* grande, abultado; (*imposing*) imponente, impresionante; *contribution, support, intervention* enérgico, fuerte, masivo, en gran escala.

massively ['mæsivli] *adv* macizamente, sólidamente; de modo imponente; enérgicamente, fuertemente.

massiveness ['mæsivnis] *n* macicez *f*, solidez *f*; lo grande, lo abultado; energía *f*, fuerza *f*.

mass-produce ['mæsprəˈdjuːs] *vt* fabricar en serie.

mass production ['mæsprəˈdʌkʃən] *n* fabricación *f* en serie.

mast¹ [mɑːst] *n* (*Naut*) mástil *m*, palo *m*; (*Radio etc*) torre *f*; **10 years before the** — 10 años de servicio como marinero.

mast² [mɑːst] *n* (*Bot: of oak*) bellota *f*, (*of beech*) hayuco *m*.

-**masted** ['mɑːstid] *adj* de … palos, *eg* **three-masted** de tres palos.

master ['mɑːstə*] **1** *n* (*of the house etc*) señor *m*, amo *m*; (*owner*) dueño *m*; (*Naut: of ship*) capitán *m*, (*of boat*) patrón *m*; (*expert, musician, painter etc*) maestro *m*; (*of Mil order*) maestre *m*; (*teacher*) maestro *m*, (*in secondary school*) profesor *m*; (*of college*) director *m*; **old** — (*man*) pintor *m* clásico, (*work*) obra *f* clásica, cuadro *m* de uno de los pintores clásicos; **the young** — el señorito; — **of arts** maestro *m* en artes; — **of ceremonies** maestro *m* de ceremonias; — **of foxhounds** cazador *m* mayor; **to be a past** — **at politics** ser maestro en política, ser un político consumado; **to be** — **of** poseer; **to be** — **of the situation** ser dueño de la situación, ser dueño del baile; **the** — **is not at home** el señor no está; **I am the** — **now** ahora mando yo; **to be** — **in one's own house** mandar en su propia casa; **to be one's own** — ser independiente; trabajar por cuenta propia; **to be the** — **of one's fate** decidir su propio destino; **to make oneself** — **of** apoderarse de; **to meet one's** — ser derrotado por fin, tener que sucumbir por fin. **2** *attr card, mason etc* maestro; *switch etc* principal; — **mariner** capitán *m*. **3** *vt* (*defeat*) vencer, derrotar; *difficulty etc* vencer; *situation* dominar; *one's defects* sobreponerse a; *subject* dominar; *craft* llegar a ser maestro en.

master builder ['mɑːstəˈbildə*] *n* constructor *m*; arquitecto *m*.

masterful ['mɑːstəful] *adj* imperioso, autoritario; *personality etc* dominante.

master key ['mɑːstəˌkiː] *n* llave *f* maestra.

masterly ['mɑːstəli] *adj* magistral, genial.

mastermind ['mɑːstəmaind] **1** *n* inteligencia *f* genial; (*in crime etc*) mente *f* directora, figura *f* principal. **2** *vt* *operation* dirigir, planear.

masterpiece ['mɑːstəpiːs] *n* obra *f* maestra.

Mastersingers ['mɑːstəˌsiŋəz] *pl*: "**The** —" "Los maestros cantores".

master stroke ['mɑːstəstrəuk] *n* golpe *m* maestro.

mastery ['mɑːstəri] *n* (*sway*) dominio *m*; autoridad *f*; (*skill*) maestría *f*; (*over competitors etc*) dominio *m*, superioridad *f*; **to gain the** — **of** (*take over*) hacerse el señor de, (*dominate*) llegar a dominar.

masthead ['mɑːsthed] *n* tope *m*.

masticate ['mæstikeit] *vti* masticar.

mastiff ['mæstif] *n* mastín *m*, alano *m*.

mastitis [mæsˈtaitis] *n* mastitis *f*.

mastodon ['mæstədən] *n* mastodonte *m*.

mastoid ['mæstɔid] **1** *adj* mastoides. **2** *n* mastoides *f*.

masturbate ['mæstəbeit] *vi* masturbarse.

masturbation [‚mæstəˈbeiʃən] *n* masturbación *f*.

mat¹ [mæt] **1** *n* estera *f*, (*small*) esterilla *f*; (*round*) ruedo *m*; (*at door*) felpudo *m*; (*on table*) salvamanteles *m*; (*of lace etc*) tapetito *m*; (*of hair*) greña *f*. **2** *vt* enmarañar, entretejer. **3** *vi* enmarañarse, entretejerse.

mat² [mæt] *adj* mate.

match¹ [mætʃ] *n* cerilla *f*, fósforo *m*; (*fuse*) mecha *f*.

match² [mætʃ] **1** *n* (a) (*person etc*) igual *mf*; **the two of them make a good** — los dos hacen una buena pareja; **the skirt is a good** — **for the jumper** la falda hace juego con el jersé; **to be a** — **for someone** poder competir (*etc*) con uno en pie de igualdad; **he's a** — **for anybody** puede dar quince y raya al más pintado; **A is no** — **for B** A no puede con B; **A was more than a** — **for B** A venció fácilmente a B; **to meet one's match** encontrar la horma de su zapato.

(b) (*marriage*) casamiento *m*, matrimonio *m*; **who thought up this** —? ¿quién ideó este matrimonio?; **she made a good** — hizo una buena boda; **he's a good** — es buen partido.

(c) (*Sport*) partido *m*, encuentro *m*; (*race*) carrera *f*; (*Boxing*) lucha *f*; (*Fencing*) asalto *m*; (*quiz etc*) concurso *m*; **return** — partido *m* de desquite *m*, revancha *f*; **away** — partido *m* fuera de casa; **home** — partido *m* en casa, partido *m* en casero; **they never tried to make a** — **of it** no se esforzaron en ningún momento por vencer; **let's make a** — **of it** juguemos con la intención de ganar.

2 *vt* (a) (*pair off*) emparejar, parear; **to** — **A against B** hacer que A compita con B; **they're well** —**ed** hacen una buena pareja; **the teams are well** —**ed** los equipos son muy iguales.

(b) (*equal*) igualar, ser igual a, valer lo que; **A doesn't quite** — **B in originality** en cuanto a originalidad A no vale lo que B; **the results did not** — **our hopes** los resultados no eran tan buenos como los habíamos esperado.

(c) (*of clothes, colours*) hacer juego con; **his tie**

—es his socks su corbata hace juego con los calcetines; **can you — this silk?** (*in shop etc*) ¿tiene una seda igual que ésta?

3 *vi* hacer juego, armonizar, ser a tono; **with a skirt to —** con una falda acompañada, con una falda a tono.

matchbox ['mætʃbɔks] *n* cajita *f* de cerillas.

matching ['mætʃiŋ] *adj* acompañado, a tono, del mismo estilo y color.

matchless ['mætʃlis] *adj* sin par, incomparable.

matchmaker ['mætʃ,meikə*] *n* casamentero *m*, a *f*.

matchmaking ['mætʃ,meikiŋ] **1** *n* actividades *fpl* de casamentero. **2** *adj* casamentero.

matchwood ['mætʃwud] *n* astillas *fpl*; **to smash something to —** hacer algo añicos; **to be smashed to —** ser convertido en un montón de astillas.

mate¹ [meit] **1** *n* mate *m*. **2** *vt* dar jaque mate a, matar; **white plays and —s in 2** blanco juega y mata en 2.

mate² [meit] **1** *n* (*companion*) compañero *m*, camarada *m*; (*married*) compañero *m*, a *f*; cónyuge *mf*, (*Zool*) macho *m*, hembra *f*; (*assistant*) ayudante *m*, peón *m*; (*Naut*) primer oficial *m*, pilota *m*, segundo *m* de a bordo; **John and his —s** Juan y sus compañeros; **first —** primer oficial *m*, piloto *m*; **plumber's —** ayudante *m* de fontanero, aprendiz *m* de fontanero; **look here, —** (*fam*) mire, amigo; **yes, —** (*fam*) sí, hombre.

2 *vt* (*Zool*) parear, acoplar; (*fig*) unir; **they are well —d** hacen una buena pareja.

3 *vi* (*Zool*) parearse, acoplarse; **age should not — with youth** no debe casarse el viejo con la joven.

material [mə'tiəriəl] **1** *adj* material; importante, esencial; *well-being etc* físico; *loss, damage* importante, considerable.

2 *n* (*ingredient, equipment, also fig*) material *m*; (*substance*) materia *f*; (*data*) datos *mpl*, material *m*; (*cloth*) tejido *m*, tela *f*; **—s** material *m*, materiales *mpl*; **building —s** material *m* de construcción; **raw —s** materias *fpl* primas; **war —** material *m* bélico; **writing —s** efectos *mpl* de escritorio.

materialism [mə'tiəriəlizəm] *n* materialismo *m*; **dialectical —** materialismo *m* dialéctico.

materialist [mə'tiəriəlist] **1** *adj* materialista. **2** *n* materialista *mf*.

materialistic [mə,tiəriə'listik] *adj* materialista.

materialize [mə'tiəriəlaiz] **1** *vt* materializar. **2** *vi* (*spirit*) tomar forma visible; (*idea etc*) realizarse, convertirse en hecho.

materially [mə'tiəriəli] *adv* materialmente; **that does not — alter things** eso no afecta la cosa de modo sensible; **they are not — different** no difieren en su esencia.

maternal [mə'tə:nl] *adj* *grandfather etc* materno; *affection etc* maternal.

maternity [mə'tə:niti] *n* maternidad *f*; **— dress** vestido *m* premamá; *see* **hospital** *etc*.

matey ['meiti] *adj* (*fam*) *person* afable, simpático; bonachón; *atmosphere* acogedor; *gathering* sin ceremonias, familiar, de ambiente acogedor.

math [mæθ] *n* (*US fam*) *see* **mathematics**.

mathematical [,mæθə'mætikəl] *adj* matemático; **he's a — genius** tiene un genio para las matemáticas.

mathematically [,mæθə'mætikəli] *adv* matemáticamente.

mathematician [,mæθəmə'tiʃən] *n* matemático *m*.

mathematics [,mæθə'mætiks] *n* matemáticas *fpl*; **applied —** matemáticas *fpl* aplicadas; **pure —** matemáticas *fpl* teóricas.

Mat(h)ilda [mə'tildə] *f* Matilde.

maths [mæθs] *n* (*fam*) *see* **mathematics**.

matinée ['mætinei] *n* función *f* de tarde.

mating ['meitiŋ] *n* (*Zool*) apareamiento *m*, acoplamiento *m*; (*fig*) unión *f*.

matins ['mætinz] *npl* maitines *mpl*.

matriarch ['meitria:k] *n* matriarca *f*.

matriarchal [meitri'a:kl] *adj* matriarcal.

matriarchy ['meitria:ki] *n* matriarcado *m*.

matric [mə'trik] *n see* **matriculation**.

matricide ['meitrisaid] *n* (*act*) matricidio *m*; (*person*) matricida *mf*.

matriculate [mə'trikjuleit] **1** *vt* matricular. **2** *vi* matricularse; (*Brit Univ*) cumplir los requisitos para entrar en la universidad.

matriculation [mə,trikju'leiʃən] *n* matriculación *f*; (*Brit Univ*) requisitos *mpl* para entrar en la universidad, (*loosely*) examen *m* para entrar en la universidad.

matrimonial [,mætri'məuniəl] *adj* matrimonial; conyugal.

matrimony ['mætriməni] *n* matrimonio *m*; vida *f* conyugal.

matrix ['meitriks] *n* matriz *f*.

matron ['meitrən] *n* (*married woman*) matrona *f*; (*in hospital*) enfermera *f* jefa; (*in school*) ama *f* de llaves.

matronly [meitrənli] *adj* matronal, de matrona; *figure etc* maduro y algo corpulento.

matt [mæt] *adj* mate.

matted ['mætid] *adj* enmarañado, entretejido; espeso; **— hair** greña *f*.

matter ['mætə*] **1** *n* (a) (*substance*) materia *f*; sustancia *f*; (*Typ*) material *m*; **advertising —** material *m* de publicidad; **colouring —** colorante *m*; **grey —** materia *f* gris, seso *m*; **printed —** impresos *mpl*; **vegetable —** material *f* vegetal.

(b) (*Med*) pus *m*, materia *f*.

(c) (*Lit etc*) materia *f*, tema *m*; **form and —** la forma y el contenido, la forma y la materia; **the main — of his speech** el tema principal de su discurso.

(d) (*question, affair*) asunto *m*, cuestión *f*, cosa *f*; **for that —, for the — of that** si vamos a eso, en cuanto a eso; **in this —** en este asunto; **in the — of** en materia de, en asuntos de; **there's the — of my expenses** hay aquello de mis gastos; **it will be a — of a few weeks** será cosa de varias semanas; **it's a — of a couple of hours** es cosa de dos horas; **in a — of 10 minutes** en cosa de 10 minutos; **it's a — of great concern to us** es cosa que nos tiene preocupadísimos; **es cosa que nos importa muchísimo**; **it is no great —** es poca cosa, no importa; **that's quite another —**, **that's another —** altogether, that's a very different **—** eso es harina de otro costal; **it's an easy — to + infin** es fácil + infin; **it will be no easy —** no será fácil; **it's a serious —** es cosa seria; **it's no laughing —** no es cosa de risa; **business —s** negocios *mpl*; **money —s** asuntos *mpl* financieros; **the — in hand** el asunto de que se trata; **as —s stand** tal como están las cosas; **the — is closed** el asunto está concluido; **to make —s worse** para colmo de desgracias; **he doesn't mince —s** no tiene pelos en la lengua; **he didn't mince —s with me** conmigo no se paró en barras; **well, not to mince —s** bueno, para decirlo como es; **as a — of course** por rutina; **it's a — of course with us** con nosotros es cosa de cajón (*see also* **course 1 (b)**); **as a — of fact . . .** en realidad **. . .**, el caso es que **. . .**; **as a — of fact we were just talking about you** precisamente estábamos hablando de Vd; **it's a — of form** es pura formalidad; **it's a — of taste** es cuestión de gusto.

(e) **no —, it makes no —** no importa; **what —?** ¿qué importa?; **no — how you do it** no importa cómo lo haga Vd; **no — what he says** diga lo que diga; **no — how big it is** por grande que sea; **no — how hot it is** por mucho calor que haga; **no — when** no importa cuándo; **no — who goes** quienquiera que vaya; **get one, no — how** procure uno, del modo que sea.

(f) **what's the —?** ¿qué hay?, ¿qué pasa?; **what's the — with you?** ¿te pasa algo?, ¿qué tienes?; **what's the — with John?** ¿qué le pasa a Juan?; **what's the — with my hat?** ¿qué tiene mi sombrero?; **what's the — with singing?** ¿es que está prohibido cantar?; **what's the — with smoking?** ¿qué inconveniente hay en fumar?; **something's the — with the lights** algo les pasa a las luces; **nothing's the —** no pasa nada; **as if nothing was the —** como si no hubiese pasado nada, como si tal cosa.

2 *vi* importar; **it doesn't —** no importa, lo mismo da, es igual; **what does it —?** ¿qué importa?; **does it — to you if I go?** ¿te importa que yo vaya?; **why should it — to me?** y a mí ¿qué?; **some things — more than others** algunas cosas son más importantes que otras.

matter-of-fact ['mætərəv'fækt] *adj* prosaico; práctico; flemático.

Matthew ['mæju:] *m* Mateo.

matting ['mætiŋ] *n* estera *f*.

mattock ['mætək] *n* azadón *m*.

mattress ['mætris] *n* colchón *m*.

mature [mə'tjuə*] **1** *adj* maduro; (*Comm*) vencido; **of — years** de edad madura; **to become — (Comm)** vencer. **2** *vti* madurar; (*Comm*) vencer.

maturity [mə'tjuəriti] *n* madurez *f*; (*Comm*) vencimiento *m*.

maudlin ['mɔ:dlin] *adj* (*sentimental*) sensiblero; (*weepy*) llorón, al punto de deshacerse en lágrimas.

maul [mɔ:l] *vt* destrozar, magullar, herir; *writer, play etc* maltratar; (*finger*) manosear; *text* estropear; **he got badly —ed in the press** la prensa le puso como un trapo.

Maundy ['mɔ:ndi] *n*: **— money** dinero *que reparte el monarca a los pobres el Jueves Santo*; **— Thursday** Jueves *m* Santo.

Maurice ['mɔris] *m* Mauricio.

Mauritius [mə'riʃəs] Mauricio *m*, Isla *f* de Francia.
mausoleum [ˌmɔːsə'liːəm] *n* mausoleo *m*.
mauve [məuv] **1** *adj* (de) color de malva. **2** *n* color *m* de malva.
maverick ['mævərik] *n* (*US Agr*) res *f* sin marcar; (*Pol etc*) disidente *m*, inconformista *mf*, persona *f* independiente.
maw [mɔː] *n* (*Anat*) estómago *m*; (*of cow etc*) cuajar *m*; (*of bird*) molleja *f*, buche *m*; (*fig*) fauces *fpl*.
mawkish ['mɔːkiʃ] *adj* empalagoso, sensiblero, insulso.
mawkishness ['mɔːkiʃnis] *n* sensiblería *f*, insulsez *f*.
maxim ['mæksim] *n* máxima *f*.
maximize ['mæksimaiz] *vt* llevar al máximum; extremar.
maximum ['mæksiməm] **1** *adj* máximo. **2** *n* máximo *m*, máximum *m*; (up) to the — al máximo; up to a — of £8 hasta 8 libras como máximum.
maxiskirt ['mæksiskəːt] *n* maxifalda *f*.
May [mei] **1** *n* mayo *m*; **m**— (*Bot: flower*) flor *f* del espino, (*tree*) espino *m*. **2** *vi*: to go m—ing ir a la fiesta de mayo.
may [mei] (*irr: pret* **might**) *vi* (a) (*of possibility*) poder, ser posible; it — rain es posible que llueva, puede que llueva; it — be that . . . puede ser que + *subj*, quizá + *subj*; he — not be hungry puede no tener hambre; I — have said so es posible que lo haya dicho, puedo haberlo dicho; I might have said so pudiera haberlo dicho; yes, I — sí, es posible; be that as it — sea como fuere; that's as — be eso puede ser.
(b) (*of permission*) poder, tener permiso para; yes, you — sí puedes; if I — si me lo permites; — I? ¿se permite?; — I see it? ¿me permites verlo?; — I come in? ¿se puede?; — I go now? ¿puedo irme ya?; you — smoke se permite fumar; you — not smoke se prohibe fumar; if I — advise you si me permite Vd ofrecer un consejo.
(c) I hope he — succeed espero que lo logre; I hoped he might succeed this time esperaba que lo lograra esta vez; such a policy as might bring peace una política que pudiera traernos la paz; we — as well go más vale irnos, bien podemos irnos; he might have offered to help bien pudiera habernos ofrecido su ayuda; you might shut the door! ¡podrías (*or* podías) cerrar la puerta!; you might try Smith's quizá valga la pena de buscarlo en la tienda de Smith; as you might expect como era de esperar, según cabía esperar; run as he might por mucho que corriese.
(d) (*of wishing*) — you be lucky! ¡que tengas suerte!; — you be forgiven! ¡que Dios le perdone!; long — he reign! ¡viva muchos años!; or — I never eat prawns again o que no vuelva yo nunca a comer gambas.
(e) (*in questions*) who might you be? ¿quién es Vd?; how old might you be? ¿cuántos años tendrá Vd?
Maya ['mɑːjə], **Mayan** ['mɑːjən] **1** *adj* maya. **2** *n* maya *mf*.
maybe ['meibiː] **1** *adv* quizá, tal vez. **2** *conj*: — he'll come quizá venga.
May Day ['meidei] *n* primero *m* de mayo.
mayfly ['meiflai] *n* efímera *f*.
mayhem ['meihem] *n* mutilación *f* criminal.
mayn't [meint] = **may not.**
mayonnaise [meiə'neiz] *n* mayonesa *f*.
mayor [mɛə*] *n* alcalde *m*.
mayoralty ['mɛərəlti] *n* alcaldía *f*.
mayoress ['mɛəres] *n* alcaldesa *f*.
maypole ['meipəul] *n* mayo *m*.
May queen ['meikwiːn] *n* maya *f*.
maze [meiz] *n* laberinto *m*; to be in a — (*fig*) estar perplejo.
me [miː] *pron* me; (*after prep*) mí; with — conmigo; dear — ! ¡vaya!; it's — (*fam*) soy yo; it's —, Paul (*identifying self*) soy Pablo.
mead [miːd] *n* aguamiel *f*, hidromiel *m*.
meadow ['medəu] *n* prado *m*, pradera *f*; (*esp water*-) vega *f*.
meadowsweet ['medəuswiːt] *n* reina *f* de los prados.
meagre, (*US*) **meager** ['miːgə*] *adj* escaso, exiguo, pobre.
meal¹ [miːl] *n* (*flour*) harina *f*.
meal² [miːl] *n* comida *f*; **square** — comida *f* realmente buena (*see also* square 1 (c)); to have a — comer; to have a good — comer bien; to make a — of something comer algo, contentarse con comer algo.
mealtime ['miːltaim] *n* hora *f* de comer.
mealy ['miːli] *adj* harinoso.
mealy-mouthed ['miːli'mauðd] *adj* excesivamente circunspecto; let us not be — about it hablemos claro sobre esto.

mean¹ [miːn] *adj* (*of poor quality*) inferior; birth etc humilde, pobre; (*shabby, unimpressive*) humilde, vil; (*with money*) tacaño; (*petty*) mezquino; don't be — ! ¡no seas malo!; you — thing! ¡canalla!; the — est citizen el menor ciudadano; he is no — player es un jugador nada despreciable; you were — to me me has tratado muy mal; it made me feel — me hizo sentir vergüenza.
mean² [miːn] *n* **1** *adj* medio.
2 *n* (a) (*middle term*) medio *m*, promedio *m*, término *m* medio; (*Math*) media *f*; golden —, happy — justo medio *m*.
(b) —s (*method*) medio *m*, manera *f*, método *m*; —s to an end medio *m* de conseguir un fin; there is no —s of doing it no hay modo de hacerlo; he was the —s of sending it él nos proporcionó un medio de enviarlo; by all —s por todos los medios, (*fig*) por cierto; by all —s! ¡naturalmente!, ¡claro que sí!; by all —s take one por favor tome uno; by any —s de cualquier modo, del modo que sea; by no —s, not by any —s de ningún modo; by no —s! ¡de ningún modo!; it is by no —s difficult no es nada difícil; by —s of por medio de, mediante; by this —s por este medio, de este modo; by fair —s por medios rectos; by fair —s or foul por las buenas o por las malas.
(c) —s (*Fin*) recursos *mpl*, medios *mpl*, fondos *mpl*, dinero *m*; a man of —s un hombre acaudalado; we have no —s to do it nos faltan recursos para hacerlo; to have private —s tener ingresos de fuente particular; to live beyond one's —s vivir por encima de sus posibilidades, gastar más de lo que se gana; to live within one's —s vivir con arreglo a los ingresos, vivir dentro de los medios.
mean³ [miːn] (*irr: pret and ptp* **meant**) *vt* (a) (*intend: with noun etc*) pretender, intentar; he —s well tiene buenas intenciones; I — it lo digo en serio; do you — it? ¿lo dices en serio?; you can't — it! ¡vaya!; I —t it as a joke lo dije en broma; he —s no harm tiene buenas intenciones; I — t no harm by what I said no lo dije con mala idea; he —t no offence no tenía la intención de ofender a nadie.
(b) (*intend: with verb*) to — to + *infin* pensar + *infin*, proponerse + *infin*, pretender + *infin*; what do you — to do? ¿qué piensas hacer?; I —t to help tenía la intención de ayudar; he didn't — to do it lo hizo sin querer; this photo is —t to be Anne esta foto quiere ser Ana; I — to be obeyed insisto en que se me obedezca; I — to have it quiero tenerlo, me propongo obtenerlo; if he —s to be awkward si quiere ser difícil.
(c) (*destine*) destinar (*for* a, para); this present was —t for you este regalo era para ti; do you — me? ¿es a mí?; was that remark —t for me? esa observación ¿iba dirigida contra mí?; he —t that for you lo dijo por ti.
(d) (*signify: person, statement etc*) querer decir (*by* con); (*word*) significar (*to* para); what does "ohm" —? ¿qué quiere decir "ohmio"?; what do you — by that? ¿qué quieres decir con eso?; "coger" —s something different in America en América "coger" tiene otro significado, en América "coger" significa otra cosa; the name —s nothing to me el nombre no me suena; it —s a lot of expense for us nos supone unos grandes gastos; this —s our ruin esto es nuestra ruina, esto significa nuestra ruina; a pound —s a lot to her para ella una libra es mucho dinero; the play didn't — a thing to me poca cosa saqué en claro de la obra; your friendship —s much to me tu amistad es muy importante para mí; don't I — anything to you? ¿no significo yo nada para ti?, ¿no tengo yo siquiera un poquito de importancia para ti?
meander [mi'ændə*] **1** *n* meandro *m*; —s (*fig*) meandros *mpl*. **2** *vi* (*river*) serpentear; (*person etc*) andar sin propósito fijo, vagar.
meaning ['miːniŋ] **1** *adj* look etc significativo, lleno de intención.
2 *n* (a) (*intention*) intención *f*, propósito *m*; a look full of — una mirada llena de intención; to mistake someone's — interpretar mal la intención de uno.
(b) (*sense of words etc*) sentido *m*, significado *m*; (*particular sense of word*) acepción *f*; (*general impact*) significación *f*; double — doble sentido *m*; literal — sentido *m* literal; what's the — of "hick"? ¿qué significa "hick"?, ¿qué quiere decir "hick"?; what's the — of this? (*as reprimand*) y esto ¿qué quiere decir?
meaningful ['miːniŋful] *adj* significativo, que tiene sentido.
meaningless ['miːniŋlis] *adj* sin sentido; (*rash, mad*) insensato; in this situation it is — en esta situación no tiene sentido; to write "xybj" is — escribir "xybj" carece de sentido.

meanness ['mi:nnis] n humildad f; vileza f, bajeza f; tacañería f; mezquindad f; maldad f.

means test ['mi:nztest] n averiguación f de los recursos económicos (*del que pide o recibe asistencia pública etc*).

meant [ment] *pret and ptp of* **mean**.

meantime ['mi:n'taim] *adv*, **meanwhile** ['mi:n'wail] *adv* entretanto, mientras tanto; **in the meantime** mientras tanto, en el ínterin.

measles ['mi:zlz] n sarampión m; **German** — rubéola f.

measly ['mi:zli] *adj* (*fam*) miserable, cochino, malísimo.

measurable ['meʒərəbl] *adj* mensurable, que se puede medir; (*perceptible*) apreciable, perceptible.

measure ['meʒə*] **1** n (a) (*system of* —) medida f; — **of capacity** medida f de capacidad; **cubic** — medida f cúbica; **dry** — medida f para áridos; **full** — medida f exacta, cantidad f exacta; **liquid** — medida f para líquidos; **square** — medida f cuadrada; **standard** — medida f tipo; **made to** — hecho a la medida; **I think we have his** — **now** creo que le tenemos calado ya; **to take someone's** — (*fig*) tomar las medidas a uno.

   (b) (*rule etc*) regla f; (*glass*) probeta f graduada.

   (c) (*limit*) **beyond** — hasta no más; excesivamente; **better beyond** — incomparablemente mejor; **in full** — abundantemente, como se debe, adecuadamente; **for good** — por añadidura; **in great** —, **in large** — en gran parte; **in some** — hasta cierto punto.

   (d) (*step*) medida f; (*Parl: bill*) proyecto m de ley, (*act*) ley f; **emergency** — medida f de urgencia; **preventive** — medida f preventiva; **to take** —s tomar medidas (*to* + *infin* para + *infin*); **to take extreme** —s tomar medidas extremas.

   (e) **coal** —s depósitos *mpl* de carbón.

   (f) (*Mus*) compás m.

   2 *vt* (*also to* — **off**, *to* — **out**) medir; *person* (*for height*) tallar, (*for clothes*) tomar las medidas a; *words etc* pesar, pensar bien; **to** — **out** (*issue*) repartir, distribuir; *see* **length**.

   3 *vi* medir; **it** —s **3 metres by 2 metres** mide 3 metros por 2 metros; **what does it** —? ¿cuánto mide?; **to** — **up to something** estar a la altura de algo.

measured ['meʒəd] *adj tread etc* deliberado, rítmico; *tone* mesurado; *statement etc* moderado, circunspecto, prudente.

measureless ['meʒəlis] *adj* inmensurable, inmenso.

measurement ['meʒəmənt] n (*system*) medición f; (*measure*) medida f; dimensión f; **to take someone's** —s tomar las medidas a uno.

measuring ['meʒərin] n medición f; **to take** —s **of** hacer mediciones de.

meat [mi:t] **1** n carne f; (*fig*) sustancia f, meollo m, jugo m; (*of fat etc*) parte f gruesa; **cold** — fiambre m, carne f fiambre; **a book with some** — **in it** un libro sólido, un libro jugoso; **one man's** — **is another man's poison** lo que para uno es bueno para otro es veneno; **it's** — **and drink to me** no puedo vivir sin él. **2** *attr* de carne; *industry etc*, *product* cárnico.

meatball ['mi:t'bɔːl] n albóndiga f.

meatfly ['mi:tflai] n mosca f de la carne.

meat pie ['mi:t'pai] n pastel m de carne, empanada f.

meat safe ['mi:tseif] n fresquera f.

meaty ['mi:ti] *adj* carnoso; (*fig*) sustancioso, jugoso, sólido.

Mecca ['mekə] La Meca.

mechanic [mi'kænik] n mecánico m; **motor** — mecánico m de automóviles.

mechanical [mi'kænikəl] *adj* mecánico; (*fig*) maquinal.

mechanically [mi'kænikəli] *adv* mecánicamente; (*fig*) maquinalmente.

mechanics [mi'kæniks] n mecánica f; mecanismo m, técnica f.

mechanism ['mekənizəm] n (*all senses*) mecanismo m; **defence** — mecanismo m de defensa.

mechanistic [,mekə'nistik] *adj* mecánico, maquinal.

mechanization [,mekənai'zeiʃən] n mecanización f.

mechanize ['mekənaiz] *vt* mecanizar.

medal ['medl] n medalla f.

medallion [mi'dæliən] n medallón m.

medallist, (*US*) **medalist** ['medəlist] n persona f condecorada con una medalla; (*Sport*) campeón m, ona f, titular *mf*.

meddle ['medl] *vi* entrometerse (*in* en); **to** — **with something** manosear algo, tocar algo, (*and damage*) estropear algo; **who asked you to** —? ¿quién le mete a Vd en esto?; **he's always meddling** es un entrometido.

meddler ['medlə*] n entrometido m, a f.

meddlesome ['medlsəm] *adj*, **meddling** ['medlin] *adj* entrometido.

meddlesomeness ['medlsəmnis] n entrometimiento m.

Mede [mi:d] n: **the** —s **and the Persians** los medos y los persas.

mediaeval [,medi'i:vəl] *adj* (*etc*) *see* **medieval** (*etc*).

medial ['mi:diəl] *adj* medial.

median ['mi:diən] **1** *adj* mediano. **2** n (*US*) zona f central (*entre las dos calzadas de una autopista*); (*Math*) número m medio; punto m medio.

mediate ['mi:dieit] *vi* mediar (*between* entre, *in* en).

mediation [,mi:di'eiʃən] n mediación f.

mediator ['mi:dieitə*] n mediador m, árbitro m.

medic ['medik] n (*fam*) médico m; (*Univ*) estudiante *mf* de medicina.

medical ['medikəl] **1** *adj* médico; *school*, *student etc* de medicina. **2** n reconocimiento m médico.

medically ['medikəli] *adv* médicamente; — **speaking** desde el punto de vista médico; **to be** — **examined** tener un reconocimiento médico.

medicament [me'dikəmənt] n medicamento m.

medicate ['medikeit] *vt* medicar; impregnar (*with* de).

medication [,medi'keiʃən] n medicación f.

medicinal [me'disinl] *adj* medicinal.

medicine ['medsin, 'medisin] n medicina f; medicamento m; **forensic** — medicina f legal; **patent** — específico m; **preventive** — medicina f preventiva; **to take one's** — (*fig*) sufrir las consecuencias.

medicine box ['medsinbɔks] n, **medicine chest** ['medsintʃest] n botiquín m.

medicine man ['medsinmæn] n, *pl* — **men** [men] hechizador m.

medico ['medikəu] n (*fam*) médico m.

medieval [,medi'i:vəl] *adj* medieval.

medievalism [,medi'i:vəlizəm] n medievalismo m.

medievalist [,medi'i:vəlist] n medievalista *mf*.

mediocre [,mi:di'əukə*] *adj* mediocre, mediano.

mediocrity [,mi:di'ɔkriti] n mediocridad f, medianía f (*also person*).

meditate ['mediteit] **1** *vt* meditar. **2** *vi* meditar (*on something* algo), reflexionar (*on* en, sobre).

meditation [,medi'teiʃən] n meditación f.

meditative ['meditətiv] *adj* meditabundo.

meditatively ['meditətivli] *adv* reflexivamente.

Mediterranean [,meditə'reiniən] **1** *adj* mediterráneo; — **Sea** Mar m Mediterráneo. **2** n Mediterráneo m.

medium ['mi:diəm] **1** *adj quality etc* mediano, regular; *size* mediano, intermedio; *wave* medio; **of** — **height** de estatura regular; **of** — **difficulty** de mediana dificultad.

   2 n (*pl in some senses* **media** ['mi:diə]) medio m; (*person*) médium *mf*; **happy** — justo medio m, término m medio; **advertising media** medios *mpl* de publicidad; **through the** — **of** por medio de.

medium-fine ['mi:diəm'fain] *adj* entrefino.

medium-sized ['mi:diəm'saizd] *adj* de tamaño mediano.

medlar ['medlə*] n (*fruit*) níspola f; (*tree*) níspero m.

medley ['medli] n mezcla f, mezcolanza f; miscelánea f; (*Mus*) popurrí m.

medulla [me'dʌlə] n medula f.

meek [mi:k] *adj* manso, dócil, sumiso; **to be very** — **and mild** (*person*) ser como una malva.

meekly ['mi:kli] *adv* mansamente, dócilmente, sumisamente.

meekness ['mi:knis] n mansedumbre f, docilidad f.

meerschaum ['miəʃəm] n espuma f de mar; (*pipe*) pipa f de espuma de mar.

meet[1] [mi:t] *adj* (*lit, arch*) conveniente, apropiado; **it is** — **that** . . . conviene que + *subj*; **to be** — **for** ser apto para.

meet[2] [mi:t] (*irr: pret and ptp* **met**) **1** *vt* (a) *person etc* (*encounter*) encontrar; (*accidentally*) encontrarse con; (*by arrangement*) reunirse con, (*formally*) entrevistarse con; **to arrange to** — **someone** citarse con uno, dar una cita a uno.

   (b) *difficulty* encontrar, tropezar con; *death* hallar, encontrar; *opponent, opposing team* enfrentarse con, (*in duel*) batirse con; **he met his death in 1800** halló la muerte en 1800; **to** — **death calmly** enfrentarse tranquilamente con la muerte; **to** — **death courageously** ir resueltamente a su muerte.

   (c) (*go to* —) ir a recibir, ir a buscar, esperar, ir al encuentro de; **I'll** — **you at the garage** te espero en el garaje; **we met her at the station** fuimos a recibirla en la estación; **don't bother to** — **me** no os molestéis viniendo a buscarme; **the car will** — **the train** el coche esperará la llegada del tren; **the bus** —s **the aircraft** hay correspondencia entre el autobús y el avión.

(d) (*get to know*) conocer; **I never met him** no le conocí nunca, no le llegué a conocer; **I met my wife in 1960** conocí a mi mujer en 1960; — **Mr Jones** quiero presentarle al Sr Jones; **I am very pleased to** — **you** tengo mucho gusto en conocerle; **pleased to** — **you!** ¡tanto gusto!

(e) **what a scene met my eyes!** ¡qué cosas se presentaron a mis ojos!; **I could not** — **his eye** no podía mirarle a los ojos; *see also* **eye**.

(f) *charge* refutar; *debt* pagar, honrar, satisfacer; *deficit* cubrir; *expense* sostener, correr con, hacer frente a; *liabilities* honrar; *need* satisfacer, cubrir; *objection* responder a; *obligation* atender, cumplir; *requirement* satisfacer; *demand, wish* conformarse con, condescender con, satisfacer; *scorn* tener que aguantar; **to** — **someone halfway** partir el camino con uno; **we met each other halfway** (*fig*) nos hicimos concesiones mutuas.

2 *vi* **(a)** (*encounter each other*) encontrarse, verse; (*by arrangement*) reunirse, verse; (*meeting, society*) reunirse; **the society** —**s at 8** la sociedad se reúne a las 8, la sesión de la sociedad comienza a las 8; **let's** — **at 8** citémonos para las 8; **until we** — **again!** ¡hasta la vista!; **keep it until we** — **again** guárdalo hasta que nos veamos.

(b) (*get to know*) conocerse; **we met in Seville** nos conocimos en Sevilla; **we have met before** nos conocemos ya; **have we met?** ¿nos conocimos antes?

(c) (*fight*) batirse; **Bilbao and Valencia will** — **in the final** el Bilbao se enfrentará con el Valencia en la final, Bilbao y Valencia se disputarán la final.

(d) (*join*) encontrarse; **our eyes met** cruzamos una mirada, nos miramos el uno al otro; **where the rivers** — donde confluyen los ríos; **the roads** — **at Toledo** las carreteras empalman en Toledo.

(e) **to** — **with** (*esp US*) *person* juntarse con, reunirse con; *kindness etc* encontrar; *accident* tener, sufrir; *loss* sufrir; *shock* experimentar; *success* tener; *difficulty* tropezar con; **to** — **up with someone** reunirse con uno.

3 *n* (*Sport*) reunión *f*; (*Hunting*) cacería *f*.

meeting ['miːtiŋ] *n* **(a)** (*between 2 persons: accidental*) encuentro *m*, (*arranged*) cita *f*, (*formal*) entrevista *f*; **the minister had a** — **with the ambassador** el ministro se entrevistó con el embajador.

(b) (*assembly*) reunión *f*; (*esp of legislative body*) sesión *f*; (*popular gathering*) mitin *m*; — **of creditors** concurso *m* de acreedores; **annual general** — junta *f* general anual; **special** (*or* **extraordinary**) **general** — junta *f* general extraordinaria; **mass** — mitin *m*, reunión *f* popular, manifestación *f* popular; **to address the** — tomar la palabra en la reunión, dirigirse a los asistentes; **to call a** — **of shareholders** convocar una junta de accionistas; **to adjourn** (*or* **close**) **the** — levantar la sesión; **to hold a** — celebrar una junta, (*Parl*) celebrar sesión; **to open the** — abrir la sesión.

(c) (*Sport: eg athletic*) concurso *m*; (*horse races*) reunión *f*; (*clash between teams*) encuentro *m*.

(d) (*of rivers*) confluencia *f*.

meeting house ['miːtiŋˌhaus] *n*, *pl* —**houses** [ˌhauziz] templo *m* de los cuáqueros.

meeting place ['miːtiŋpleis] *n* (*of 2 persons*) lugar *m* de cita, (*of many*) punto *m* de reunión; **this bar was their usual** — solían citarse en este bar, acostumbraban reunirse en este bar.

megacycle ['megəˌsaikl] *n* megaciclo *m*.

megalith ['megəliθ] *n* megalito *m*.

megalithic [ˌmegə'liθik] *adj* megalítico.

megalomania ['megələu'meiniə] *n* megalomanía *f*.

megalomaniac ['megələu'meiniæk] *n* megalómano *m*, a *f*.

megaphone ['megəfəun] *n* megáfono *m*.

megaton ['megətʌn] *n* megatón *m*.

megavolt ['megəvəult] *n* megavoltio *m*.

megawatt ['megəwɔt] *n* megavatio *m*.

melancholia [ˌmelən'kəuliə] *n* melancolía *f*.

melancholic [ˌmelən'kɔlik] *adj* melancólico.

melancholy ['melənkəli] **1** *adj* melancólico; *duty, sight etc* triste. **2** *n* melancolía *f*.

melanism ['melənizəm] *n* melanismo *m*.

melée ['melei] *n* pelea *f* confusa, refriega *f*; tumulto *m*; **there was such a** — **at the booking office** se apiñaba la gente delante de la taquilla; **it got lost in the** — se perdió en el tumulto.

mellifluous [me'lifluəs] *adj* melifluo.

mellow ['meləu] **1** *adj fruit etc* maduro, dulce; *wine* añejo; *colour, sound* dulce; *light* suave; *voice* suave, meloso; *instrument* melodioso; *character* maduro y tranquilo; **in** — **old age** en la vejez tranquila; **to be**

— (*fam: person*) estar entre dos luces; **to get** — (*fam*) achisparse.

2 *vt* madurar; suavizar, ablandar.

3 *vi* madurarse; suavizarse, ablandarse.

mellowing ['meləuiŋ] *n* maduración *f*.

mellowness ['meləunis] *n* madurez *f*; dulzura *f*, suavidad *f*; lo melodioso.

melodic [mi'lɔdik] *adj* melódico.

melodious [mi'ləudiəs] *adj* melodioso.

melodiously [mi'ləudiəsli] *adv* melodiosamente.

melodrama ['meləuˌdrɑːmə] *n* melodrama *m*.

melodramatic [ˌmeləudrə'mætik] *adj* melodramático.

melodramatically [ˌmeləudrə'mætikli] *adv* melodramáticamente.

melody ['melədi] *n* melodía *f*.

melon ['melən] *n* melón *m*.

melt [melt] **1** *vt metal* fundir; *snow* derretir; *chemical* disolver; (*fig*) *heart etc* ablandar; **to** — **down** fundir.

2 *vi* fundirse; derretirse; disolverse; ablandarse, enternecerse; **to** — **away** (*money, confidence etc*) esfumarse, desvanecerse, desaparecer misteriosamente; (*crowd etc*) dispersarse; (*person*) desaparecer silenciosamente, escurrirse; **to** — **into tears** deshacerse en lágrimas.

melting ['meltiŋ] **1** *adj look etc* tierno, dulce. **2** *n* fundición *f*; derretimiento *m*; disolución *f*.

melting point ['meltiŋpɔint] *n* punto *m* de fusión.

melting pot ['meltiŋpɔt] *n* crisol *m* (*also fig*); **the plan is in the** — el plan está sobre el tapete; **it is a nation in the** — es una nación en formación.

member ['membə*] *n* **(a)** (*person*) miembro *m*; (*of company, society*) miembro *m*, socio *m*; (*Parl*) miembro *m*, diputado *m*; "—**s only**" "reservado a los socios", "sólo para socios"; — **of the family** miembro *m* de la familia; — **of parliament** diputado *m*, miembro *m* del parlamento, (*Spain*) diputado *m* a Cortes; **if any** — **of the audience . . .** si cualquiera de los asistentes . . .; **the** — **for Woodford** el diputado por Woodford; **full** — miembro *m* de número; **private** — (*Parl*) miembro *m* (*que no es ministro*); **the** — **countries** los países participantes (*of* en).

(b) (*Anat*) miembro *m*; **male** — miembro *m* viril.

membership ['membəʃip] *n* calidad *f* de miembro (*or* socio); (*numerical*) número *m* de miembros (*or* socios); **Britain's** — **of the Common Market** el ingreso de Gran Bretaña en el Mercado Común; la participación de Gran Bretaña en el Mercado Común; **when I applied for** — **of the club** cuando solicité el ingreso en el club, cuando quise hacerme socio del club; — **carries certain rights** el ser miembro da ciertos derechos; — **list** relación *f* de socios; *see* **fee** *etc*.

membrane ['membrein] *n* membrana *f*.

membranous [mem'breinəs] *adj* membranoso.

memento [mə'mentəu] *n* recuerdo *m*.

memo ['meməu] *n* (*fam*) = **memorandum**.

memoir ['memwɑː*] *n* memoria *f*; biografía *f*, autobiografía *f*; nota *f* biográfica; —**s** memorias *fpl*.

memorable ['memərəbl] *adj* memorable.

memorably ['memərəbli] *adv* memorablemente.

memorandum [ˌmemə'rændəm] *n*, *pl* **memoranda** [ˌmemə'rændə] memorándum *m*, memorando *m* (*Acad*); apunte *m*, nota *f*, memoria *f*.

memorial [mi'mɔːriəl] **1** *adj* conmemorativo. **2** *n* monumento *m* (conmemorativo); (*document*) memorial *m*; **war** — monumento *m* a los caídos.

memorize ['meməraiz] *vt* aprender de memoria.

memory ['meməri] *n* (*faculty*) memoria *f*; (*recollection*) recuerdo *m*; "**Memories of life in Slobodia**" "Recuerdos *mpl* de la vida en Eslobodia"; **to speak from** — hablar fiándose de su memoria; **in** — **of** en memoria de, en conmemoración de; **the biggest flood in living** — la mayor inundación de que hay memoria, la mayor inundación que se recuerda; **of blessed** — de feliz recuerdo; **to the best of my** — que yo recuerde; **to commit something to** — aprender algo de memoria; **I have a bad** — **for faces** recuerdo mal las caras de las personas; **to have a** — **like a sieve** tener malísima memoria; **to have happy memories of** tener agradables recuerdos de; **if my** — **serves me** si mi memoria no me falla, si tengo buena memoria.

men [men] *npl of* **man**.

menace ['menis] **1** *n* amenaza *f*; (*fam*) persona *f* peligrosa, individuo *m* pesado. **2** *vt* amenazar.

menacing ['menisiŋ] *adj* amenazador.

menacingly ['menisiŋli] *adv* de modo amenazador.

ménage [me'nɑː3] *n* casa *f*, hogar *m*, menaje *m*.

menagerie [mi'nædʒəri] *n* casa *f* de fieras, colección *f* de fieras.

mend [mend] **1** n (*patch*) remiendo m; (*darn*) zurcido m; **to be on the —** ir mejorando.
2 vt (*repair*) reparar, componer; (*darn*) zurcir; (*improve*) reformar, mejorar; (*rectify*) remediar.
3 vi mejorar, reponerse.
mendacious [men'deiʃəs] adj mendaz.
mendacity [men'dæsiti] n mendacidad f.
Mendelian [men'di:liən] adj mendeliano.
Mendelianism [men'di:liənizəm] n, **Mendelism** ['mendəlizəm] n mendelismo m.
mendicant ['mendikənt] **1** adj mendicante. **2** n mendicante mf.
mendicity [men'disiti] n mendicidad f.
mending ['mendiŋ] n (*act*) reparación f, compostura f; zurcidura f; (*clothes*) ropa f de repaso, ropa f por zurcir; **invisible —** puntada f invisible.
Menelaus [,meni'leiəs] m Menelao.
menfolk ['menfəuk] npl hombres mpl.
menial ['mi:niəl] **1** adj doméstico; (*pej*) bajo. **2** n criado m, a f.
meningitis [,menin'dʒaitis] n meningitis f.
menopause ['menəpɔ:z] n menopausia f.
menses ['mensi:z] npl menstruo m.
menstrual ['menstruəl] adj menstrual.
menstruate ['menstrueit] vi menstruar.
menstruation [,menstru'eiʃən] n menstruación f.
mensuration [,mensjuə'reiʃən] n mensuración f.
mental ['mentl] adj mental; (*fam*) anormal, tocado; *see* **defective** etc.
mentality [men'tæliti] n mentalidad f.
mentally ['mentəli] adv mentalmente; **— ill** alienado.
menthol ['menθɔl] n mentol m.
mentholated ['menθəleitid] adj mentolado.
mention ['menʃən] **1** n mención f, alusión f; **honourable —** mención f honorífica.
2 vt mencionar, aludir a; hablar de; (*in dispatches*) nombrar; **not to —** sin contar ..., además de ..., amén de ...; **too numerous to —** demasiado numerosos para mencionar por nombre; **don't —** it! ¡no hay de qué!, ¡de nada!; **if I may —** it si se me permite aludir a ello; **I need hardly — that ...** excusado es decir que ...; **I will — it to him** se lo diré; **he —ed no names** no dijo los nombres; **to — someone in one's will** mencionar a uno en su testamento, legar algo a uno.
mentor ['mentɔ:*] n mentor m.
menu ['menju:] n lista f (de platos), menú m, minuta f.
meow [mi'au] **1** n maullido m. **2** vi maullar.
Mephistopheles [,mefis'tɔfili:z] m Mefistófeles.
mercantile ['mə:kəntail] adj mercantil; *marine* mercante.
mercantilism ['mə:kəntilizəm] n mercantilismo m.
mercenary ['mə:sinəri] **1** adj mercenario. **2** n mercenario m.
merchandise ['mə:tʃəndaiz] n mercancías fpl, géneros mpl.
merchant ['mə:tʃənt] **1** n comerciante m, negociante m; (*arch*) mercader m; (*fam*) sujeto m; **a diamond —** un comerciante en diamantes; **"The M— of Venice"** "El Mercader de Venecia".
2 attr etc marine, navy, ship mercante; **— prince** comerciante m rico; **— tailor** sastre m comerciante.
merchantman ['mə:tʃəntmən] n, pl **—men** [mən] buque m mercante.
merciful ['mə:siful] adj person misericordioso, compasivo, clemente; release etc afortunado, feliz.
mercifully ['mə:sifəli] adv act etc misericordiosamente, con compasión; **— it was short** gracias a Dios fue breve.
merciless ['mə:silis] adj despiadado.
mercilessly ['mə:silisli] adv despiadadamente, sin piedad.
mercurial [mə:'kjuəriəl] adj (*Chem*) mercurial; (*lively*) vivo; (*changeable*) veleidoso, voluble.
Mercury ['mə:kjuri] m Mercurio.
mercury ['mə:kjuri] n mercurio m.
mercy ['mə:si] n misericordia f, compasión f, clemencia f; **with a recommendation to —** con la recomendación de que no se aplique la sentencia en todo su rigor; **to be at the — of someone** estar a la merced de uno; **it is a — that ...** gracias a Dios que ..., menos mal que ...; **to beg for —** pedir clemencia; **to have — on someone** tener compasión de uno, apiadarse de uno; **have —!** ¡por piedad!; **to be left to the tender mercies of someone** verse abandonado en las manos nada piadosas de uno; **to show someone no —** tratar a uno con el mayor rigor; **no — was shown to the rioters** no hubo clemencia para los revoltosos; **to throw oneself on someone's —** pedir clemencia a uno (como única manera de salvarse).

mercy killing ['mə:si,kiliŋ] n eutanasia f.
mere[1] [miə*] n lago m.
mere[2] [miə*] adj mero, simple; solo, no más que; **he's a — clerk** es un simple empleado, no es más que un empleado; **it's — nonsense, it's the —st nonsense** es puro disparate; **it's — talk** son palabras al aire; **they quarrelled over a — nothing** riñeron por una friolera; **it's a — formality** es pura fórmula.
merely ['miəli] adv meramente, simplemente; sólo; **I — said that ...** sólo dije que ..., lo único que dije era que ...; **she's — a secretary** es una simple secretaria, no es más que una secretaria; **it's not — broken, it's ruined** no sólo está roto, sino que se ha estropeado del todo.
meretricious [,meri'triʃəs] adj de oropel, charro, postizo.
merge [mə:dʒ] **1** vt unir, combinar (*with* con); mezclar; fundir; (*Comm*) fusionar.
2 vi unirse, combinarse; fundirse; (*Comm*) fusionarse; **to — into** ir convirtiéndose en; **the bird —d into its background of leaves** el pájaro se hacía casi invisible contra el fondo de hojas; **this question —s into that bigger one** esta cuestión se pierde en aquélla mayor.
merger ['mə:dʒə*] n (*Comm*) fusión f.
meridian [mə'ridiən] n (*Astron*, *Geog*) meridiano m; (*fig*) cenit m, auge m.
meridional [mə'ridiənl] adj meridional.
meringue [mə'ræŋ] n merengue m.
merino [mə'ri:nəu] **1** adj merino. **2** n merino m.
merit ['merit] **1** n mérito m; **to treat a case on its —s** considerar un caso en relación con sus circunstancias. **2** vt merecer, ser digno de.
meritocracy [,meri'tɔkrəsi] n meritocracia f.
meritorious [,meri'tɔ:riəs] adj meritorio.
meritoriously [,meri'tɔ:riəsli] adv merecidamente.
merlin ['mə:lin] n esmerejón m.
mermaid ['mə:meid] n sirena f.
merman ['mə:mæn] n, pl **—men** [men] tritón m.
Merovingian [,merəu'vindʒiən] **1** adj merovingio. **2** n merovingio m, a f.
merrily ['merili] adv alegremente; regocijadamente, con alborozo.
merriment ['merimənt] n alegría f; regocijo m, alborozo m; (*laughter*) risas fpl; **at this there was much —** en esto hubo muchas risas.
merry ['meri] adj alegre; regocijado; alborozado; joke etc divertido; **to be as — as a lark** (*or* cricket) estar como unas pascuas; **to get —** (*fam*) achisparse; **to make —** divertirse, estar de juerga; *see* **Christmas**.
merry-go-round ['merigəu,raund] n tiovivo m, caballitos mpl.
merrymaking ['meri,meikiŋ] n festividades fpl.
mescalin ['meskəlin] n mescalina f.
mesentery ['mezəntri] n mesenterio m.
mesh [meʃ] **1** n malla f; (*Mech*) engrane m, engranaje m; **—es** (*fig*) red f, trampa f; **to be in —** (*Mech*) engranar, estar engranado.
2 vt: **to get —ed** enredarse (*in* en).
3 vi (*Tech*) engranar (*with* con).
mesmeric [mez'merik] adj mesmeriano.
mesmerism ['mezmərizəm] n mesmerismo m.
mesmerize ['mezməraiz] vt hipnotizar.
meson ['mi:zɔn] n (*Phys*) mesón m.
mess [mes] **1** n **(a)** (*confusion*) confusión f; (*of objects*) revoltijo m; (*dirt*) suciedad f; (*bungled affair*) lío m; **what a —!** ¡qué sucio está todo!; ¡qué asco!; ¡qué lío!; **to be in a —** (*things*) estar revuelto, (*house* etc) estar desarreglado, (*person*) estar en un aprieto; **his life is in a —** su vida es un fracaso; **to get into a —** (*person*) meterse en un lío, (*things*) desarreglarse, (*accounts* etc) enredarse; **to leave things in a —** dejar las cosas en confusión; **to leave a room in a —** dejar las cosas revueltas en un cuarto; **to make a — of** objects desordenar, job fracasar en, hacer muy mal, someone else's life llenar de confusión, arruinar, one's life fracasar en, (*dirty*) ensuciar.
(b) — of pottage plato m de lentejas.
(c) (*Mil* etc: *food*) rancho m, comida f; (*room*) comedor m del cuartel (*etc*); **officers' —** comedor m de oficiales.
2 vt: **to — someone about** fastidiar a uno, desorientar a uno (cambiando una cita etc con él); **to — up** (*disarrange*) desarreglar, desordenar; (*dirty*) ensuciar; (*ruin*) arruinar, estropear, echar a perder; affair, deal fracasar en, (*deliberately*) chafar.
3 vi **(a) to — about** perder el tiempo, ocuparse en fruslerías, trabajar (etc) con poca seriedad; **he enjoys —ing about in boats** le gusta entretener sus ocios navegando (etc) en bote; **we —ed about in Paris for two days** pasamos dos días en París haciendo

esto y lo otro; **they kept us —ing about for an hour** nos hicieron esperar una hora sin decirnos nada; **stop —ing about!** ¡déjate de tonterías!; **to — about with something** (*handle*) manosear algo, tocar algo, (*amuse oneself*) divertirse con algo, (*break*) romper algo, estropear algo.

(b) (*feed*) hacer rancho, comer (juntos).

message ['mesidʒ] *n* mensaje *m*, recado *m*; (*diplomatic etc*) comunicación *f*; (*of speech, book etc*) lección *f*, tema *m*, sentido *m*; **to get the —** (*fig*) comprender, caer en la cuenta; **do you think he got the —?** (*fig*) ¿crees que comprendió?; **to leave a —** dejar un recado.

messenger ['mesindʒə*] *n* mensajero *m*, a *f*, mandadero *m*, a *f*.

Messiah [mi'saiə] Mesías *m*.

messianic [‚mesi'ænik] *adj* mesiánico.

Messieurs ['mesəz], *abbr* **Messrs** ['mesəz] señores *mpl* (*abbr* Sres).

messmate ['mesmeit] *n* compañero *m* de rancho, comensal *m*, (*loosely*) amigo *m*.

mess tin ['mestin] *n* plato *m* de campaña.

mess-up ['mesʌp] *n* (*fam*) fracaso *m*; enredo *m*, lío *m*; **we had a — with the trains** nos hicimos un lío con los trenes; **what a —!** ¡qué lío!

messy ['mesi] *adj* (*dirty*) sucio; (*untidy*) desaseado, desaliñado, *room etc* en desorden; (*confused*) confuso, nada claro.

met [met] *pret and ptp of* **meet.**

metabolic [‚metə'bolik] *adj* metabólico.

metabolism [me'tæbəlizəm] *n* metabolismo *m*.

metacarpal [‚metə'kɑːpl] *n* metacarpiano *m*.

metal ['metl] **1** *n* metal *m*; (*on road*) grava *f*; (*fig*) temple *m*, ánimo *m*; **—s** (*Rail*) rieles *mpl*. **2** *adj* metálico, de metal. **3** *vt road* engravar.

metallic [mi'tælik] *adj* metálico.

metallurgic(al) [‚metə'lɜːdʒik(əl)] *adj* metalúrgico.

metallurgist [me'tælədʒist] *n* metalúrgico *m*.

metallurgy [me'tælədʒi] *n* metalurgia *f*.

metal polish ['metl‚poliʃ] *n* lustre *m* para metales.

metalwork ['metlwəːk] *n* metalistería *f*.

metamorphic [‚metə'mɔːfik] *adj* metamórfico.

metamorphose [‚metə'mɔːfəuz] **1** *vt* metamorfosear (*into* en). **2** *vi* metamorfosearse.

metamorphosis [‚metə'mɔːfəsis] *n*, *pl* **metamorphoses** [‚metə'mɔːfəsiːz] metamorfosis *f*.

metaphor ['metəfɔː*] *n* metáfora *f*; **mixed —** metáfora *f* disparatada.

metaphorical [‚metə'fɔrikəl] *adj* metafórico.

metaphysical [‚metə'fizikəl] *adj* metafísico.

metaphysics [‚metə'fiziks] *n* metafísica *f*.

metatarsal [‚metə'tɑːsl] *n* metatarsiano *m*.

metathesis [me'tæθəsis] *n* metatesis *f*.

mete [miːt] *vt*: **to — out** repartir; *punishment etc* dar, imponer.

meteor ['miːtiə*] *n* meteorito *m*, bólido *m*; (*esp fig*) meteoro *m*.

meteoric [‚miːti'ɔrik] *adj* meteórico (*also fig*).

meteorite ['miːtiərait] *n* meteorito *m*, bólido *m*.

meteoroid ['miːtiərɔid] *n* meteoroide *m*.

meteorological [‚miːtiərə'lɔdʒikəl] *adj* meteorológico.

meteorologist [‚miːtiə'rɔlədʒist] *n* meteorologista *mf*.

meteorology [‚miːtiə'rɔlədʒi] *n* meteorología *f*.

meter ['miːtə*] **1** *n* contador *m*; *see also* **metre. 2** *vt* medir (con contador).

methane ['miːθein] *n* metano *m*.

method ['meθəd] *n* método *m*; sistema *m*, procedimiento *m*; **there's — in his madness** no es tan loco como parece.

methodical [mi'θɔdikəl] *adj* metódico.

Methodism ['meθədizəm] *n* metodismo *m*.

Methodist ['meθədist] **1** *adj* metodista. **2** *n* metodista *mf*.

methodology [‚meθə'dɔlədʒi] *n* metodología *f*.

meths [meθs] *n* (*fam*), **methylated spirit** ['meθileitid'spirit] *n* alcohol *m* metilado, alcohol *m* desnaturalizado.

meticulous [mi'tikjuləs] *adj* meticuloso; minucioso.

meticulously [mi'tikjuləsli] *adv* con meticulosidad; minuciosamente; **— clean** limpísimo.

métier ['meitiei] *n* (*trade*) oficio *m*; (*strong point*) fuerte *m*; (*speciality*) especialidad *f*; **it's not my —** no es de mi especialidad.

metre, (*US*) **meter** ['miːtə*] *n* (*all senses*) metro *m*.

metric(al) ['metrik(əl)] *adj* métrico.

metrics ['metriks] *n* métrica *f*.

metronome ['metrənəum] *n* metrónomo *m*.

metropolis [mi'trɔpəlis] *n* metrópoli *f*.

metropolitan [‚metrə'pɔlitən] **1** *adj* metropolitano. **2** *n* (*Eccl*) metropolitano *m*.

mettle ['metl] *n* temple *m*; ánimo *m*, brío *m*; valor *m*; **to be on one's —** estar dispuesto a mostrar todo lo que uno vale; **to put someone on his —** provocar a uno a mostrar cuánto vale, picar a uno en el amor propio.

mettlesome ['metlsəm] *adj* animoso, brioso, esforzado.

Meuse [məːz] Mosa *m*.

mew [mjuː] **1** *n* maullido *m*. **2** *vi* maullar.

mewl [mjuːl] *vi* (*cat*) maullar; (*baby*) lloriquear.

mews [mjuːz] *n* caballeriza *f*.

Mexican ['meksikən] **1** *adj* mejicano, (*in Mexico*) mexicano. **2** *n* mejicano *m*, a *f*, (*in Mexico*) mexicano *m*, a *f*.

Mexico ['meksikəu] Méjico *m*, (*in Mexico*) México *m*.

mezzanine ['mezəniːn] *n* entresuelo *m*.

mezzo-soprano ['metsəusə'prɑːnəu] *n* mezzo-soprano *f*.

mezzotint ['metzəutint] *n* grabado *m* mezzotinto.

miaow [miː'au] **1** *n* miau *m*. **2** *vi* maullar.

miasma [mi'æzmə] *n*, *pl* **miasmata** [mi'æzmətə] miasma *m*.

mica ['maikə] *n* mica *f*.

mice [mais] *npl of* **mouse.**

Michael ['maikl] *m* Miguel.

Michaelangelo [‚maikəl'ændʒiləu] *m* Miguel Ángel.

Michaelmas ['miklməs] fiesta *f* de San Miguel (29 *setiembre*).

mickey ['miki] *n* (*sl*): **to take the — out of someone** tomar el pelo a uno.

micro . . . ['maikrəu] micro . . .

microbe ['maikrəub] *n* microbio *m*.

microbial [mai'krəubiəl] *adj* microbiano.

microbiologist [‚maikrəubai'ɔlidʒist] *n* microbiólogo *m*.

microbiology [‚maikrəubai'ɔlədʒi] *n* microbiología *f*.

microcosm ['maikrəukozəm] *n* microcosmo(s) *m*.

microfilm ['maikrəufilm] **1** *n* microfilm *m*, microfilme *m* (*Acad*). **2** *vt* hacer un microfilm de.

microfilm reader ['maikrəufilm‚riːdə*] *n* aparato *m* lector de microfilms.

microgroove ['maikrəugruːv] *n* microsurco *m*.

micrometer [mai'krɔmitə*] *n* micrómetro *m*.

microorganism ['maikrəu'ɔːgənizəm] *n* microorganismo *m*.

microphone ['maikrəfəun] *n* micrófono *m*.

microscope ['maikrəskəup] *n* microscopio *m*.

microscopic(al) [‚maikrə'skɔpik(əl)] *adj* microscópico.

microscopy [mai'krɔskəpi] *n* microscopia *f*.

mid [mid] **1** *adj* medio, *eg* **in — journey** a medio camino; **in — June** a mediados de junio; **in — afternoon** a media tarde; **in — course** a media carrera; **in — channel** en medio del canal. **2** *prep* (*lit, poet*) *see* **amid.**

Midas ['maidəs] *m* Midas.

midday ['mid'dei] **1** *n* mediodía *m*; **at — a** mediodía. **2** *adj* de mediodía.

midden ['midn] *n* muladar *m*.

middle ['midl] **1** *adj* (*of place*) medio, central; de en medio; intermedio; (*in quality, size etc*) mediano; *class* medio.

2 *n* medio *m*, centro *m*, mitad *f*; (*waist*) cintura *f*; **in the — of the table** en el centro de la mesa; **in the — of the field** en medio del campo; **right in the — of the room** en el mismo centro del cuarto; **in the — of nowhere** donde Cristo dio las tres voces; **in the — of summer** en pleno verano; **in** (*or* **about, towards**) **the — of May** a mediados de mayo; **in the — of the century** a mediados del siglo; **in the — of the morning** a media mañana; **I'm in the — of reading it** voy a mitad de su lectura.

middle-aged ['midl'eidʒd] *adj* de mediana edad, de edad madura.

middlebrow ['midlbrau] **1** *adj* de (*or* para) gusto medianamente culto, de gusto entre intelectual y plebeyo.

2 *n* persona *f* de gusto medianamente culto, persona *f* de cultura mediana.

middle-class ['midl'klɑːs] *adj* de la clase media.

middleman ['midlmæn] *n*, *pl* **—men** [men] intermediario *m*.

middle-of-the-road ['midləvðə'rəud] *adj* moderado, nada extremista.

middle-sized ['midl‚saizd] *adj* de tamaño mediano; *person* de estatura mediana.

middleweight ['midlweit] *n* (*Boxing*) peso *m* medio.

middling ['midliŋ] **1** *adj* mediano, regular. **2** *adv* (a) regular; **how are you? . . . —** ¿qué tal estás? . . . regular. (b) **— good** medianamente bueno.

middy ['midi] *n* (*fam*) *see* **midshipman.**

midge [midʒ] *n* mosca *f*, mosquito *m*.

midget ['midʒit] **1** n enano m, a f. **2** adj en miniatura, en pequeña escala; submarine etc de bolsillo.
midland ['midlənd] **1** adj del interior, del centro. **2** n: the M—s la región central de Inglaterra.
mid-morning ['mid'mɔːniŋ] adj: — coffee café m de media mañana.
midnight ['midnait] **1** n medianoche f. **2** adj, attr de medianoche.
midriff ['midrif] n diafragma m.
midsection ['midsekʃən] n sección f de en medio.
midshipman ['midʃipmən] n, pl —men [mən] guardia m marina.
midships ['midʃips] adv en medio del navío.
midst [midst] **1** n: in the — of entre, en medio de; in our — entre nosotros; in the — of plenty en medio de la abundancia. **2** prep see amid(st).
midstream ['mid'striːm] n: in — en medio de la corriente, en medio del río.
midsummer ['mid'sʌmə*] **1** n pleno verano m, (strictly) solsticio m estival; M— (Day) fiesta f de San Juan (24 junio); "M— Night's Dream" "El sueño de una noche de verano"; at — el día del solsticio de verano; in — en pleno verano.
 2 adj, attr de pleno verano, estival.
midway ['mid'wei] **1** adv a mitad del camino; — between X and Y a mitad del camino (or a medio camino) entre X e Y; we are now — ahora estamos a medio camino.
 2 adj situado a medio camino; a — point un punto intermedio, un punto equidistante de los dos extremos.
midweek ['mid'wiːk] **1** adv entre semana. **2** adj flight etc de entre semana.
Midwest ['mid'west] n mediooeste m (llanura central de EE.UU.).
Midwestern ['mid.westən] adj del mediooeste (de EE.UU.).
midwife ['midwaif] n, pl —wives [waivz] comadrona f, partera f.
midwifery ['mid.wifəri] n partería f.
midwinter ['mid'wintə*] **1** n pleno invierno m, (strictly) solsticio m de invierno; at — el día del solsticio de invierno; in — en pleno invierno.
 2 adj, attr de pleno invierno.
mien [miːn] n aire m, porte m, semblante m.
miff [mif] (US fam) **1** n disgusto m. **2** vt disgustar, ofender.
might[1] [mait] pret of may.
might[2] [mait] n fuerza f, poder m, poderío m; — is right es la ley del embudo; with — and main a más no poder, esforzándose muchísimo; with all one's — con todas sus fuerzas, empleándose a fondo.
might-have-been ['maitəv.biːn] n esperanza f no cumplida.
mightily ['maitili] adv fuertemente; poderosamente; I was — surprised me sorprendí muchísimo.
mightiness ['maitinis] n fuerza f; poder m, poderío m.
mightn't ['maitnt] = might not.
mighty ['maiti] **1** adj fuerte; potente, poderoso; (fam) enorme, inmenso.
 2 adv (fam) muy, terriblemente; it's — awkward es terriblemente difícil; I was — surprised me sorprendí muchísimo.
mignonette [.minjə'net] n reseda f.
migraine ['miːgrein] n jaqueca f.
migrant ['maigrənt] **1** adj migratorio. **2** n peregrino m, nómada m; (bird) ave f migratoria, ave f de paso; (insect) insecto m migratorio.
migrate [mai'greit] vi emigrar.
migration [mai'greiʃən] n migración f.
migratory [mai'greitəri] adj migratorio.
mike[1] [maik] n (sl): to have a good — no hacer nada, tirarse a la bartola; gandulear, racanear.
mike[2] [maik] n (sl: Radio) micro m (sl).
Mike [maik] m nombre cariñoso de **Michael**; for the love of —! ¡por Dios!
milady [mi'leidi] n miladi f.
Milan [mi'læn] Milán.
milch [miltʃ] n: — cow vaca f lechera.
mild [maild] adj (of character) apacible, pacífico; manso; rule etc blando; climate templado; day blando; medicine, effect, taste etc suave, dulce; (slight) leve, ligero; (Med) benigno.
mildew ['mildjuː] n moho m; (on wheat) añublo m; (on vine) mildeu m.
mildly ['maildli] adv apaciblemente, pacíficamente; blandamente; suavemente, dulcemente; levemente, ligeramente; to put it —, and that's putting it — para no decir más.
mildness ['maildnis] n apacibilidad f; blandura f; suavidad f, dulzura f; levedad f.

mile [mail] n milla f (= 1609,33 m); nautical — milla f marina; square — milla f cuadrada; —s per gallon equivalent to kilómetros por litro; not a hundred —s from here (fig) no muy lejos de aquí; we walked —s! ¡hemos andado kilómetros y kilómetros!; they live —s away viven bastante lejos de aquí; you were —s off the target no te acercaste ni con mucho al objetivo; you can tell it a — off eso se ve a la legua; it smelled for —s around olía a muchas leguas a la redonda.
mileage ['mailidʒ] n número m de millas, distancia f recorrida en millas; (Aut) kilometraje m; — per gallon equivalent to kilómetros mpl por litro; what — has this car done? ¿cuántos kilómetros tiene este coche?
mileage indicator ['mailidʒ.indikeitə*] n (Aut) indicador m de recorrido, cuentakilómetros m.
mileage ticket ['mailidʒ.tikit] n billete m kilométrico.
milepost ['mailpəust] n poste m miliar.
milestone ['mailstəun] n piedra f miliaria; (in Spain etc) mojón m kilométrico, hito m kilométrico; these events are —s in our history estos acontecimientos hacen época (or son hitos) en nuestra historia.
milieu ['miːljəː] n medio m, ambiente m, medio m ambiente.
militant ['militənt] **1** adj militante; belicoso, agresivo.
 2 n militante mf, extremista mf, partidario m vehemente.
militarism ['militərizəm] n militarismo m.
militarist ['militərist] **1** adj militarista. **2** n militarista mf.
militaristic [.militə'ristik] adj militarista.
militarize ['militəraiz] vt militarizar.
military ['militəri] **1** adj militar. **2** n: the — los militares.
militate ['militeit] vi: to — against militar contra.
militia [mi'liʃə] n milicia f.
militiaman [mi'liʃəmən] n, pl —men [mən] miliciano m.
milk [milk] **1** n leche f; condensed — leche f condensada; evaporated — leche f evaporada; powdered — leche f en polvo; skim — leche f desnatada; whole — leche f sin desnatar; — of magnesia leche f de magnesia; the — of human kindness la crema de la amabilidad humana, la humanidad; it's no good crying over spilt — ahora no sirven lamentaciones, agua pasada no mueve molino.
 2 attr de leche; diet, product etc lácteo.
 3 vt ordeñar; (fig) chupar.
 4 vi dar leche.
milk-and-water ['milkən'wɔːtə*] adj (fig) débil, flojo.
milk bar ['milkbɑː*] n cafetería f.
milk chocolate ['milk'tʃɔklit] n chocolate m con leche.
milk churn ['milktʃəːn] n lechera f.
milk float ['milkfləut] n carro m de la leche.
milking ['milkiŋ] **1** adj lechero. **2** n ordeño m.
milking machine ['milkiŋmə.ʃiːn] n ordeñadora f mecánica.
milkmaid ['milkmeid] n lechera f.
milkman ['milkmən] n, pl —men [mən] lechero m, repartidor m de leche.
milk shake ['milk'ʃeik] n batido m de leche.
milksop ['milksɔp] n marica m.
milk tooth ['milktuː θ] n, pl — teeth [tiː θ] diente m de leche.
milkweed ['milkwiːd] n (US) algodoncillo m.
milk-white ['milk'wait] adj blanco como la leche.
milky ['milki] adj lechoso.
Milky Way ['milki'wei] n Vía f Láctea.
mill [mil] **1** n (wind-) molino m; (small, for coffee etc) molinillo m; (factory) fábrica f; (spinning-) hilandería f; (weaving-) tejeduría f, fábrica f de tejidos; (steel-) acería f, fábrica f de acero; (workshop) taller m; to go through the — pasar por muchas cosas en la vida, sufrir mucho; aprender por experiencia práctica; (strain) entrenarse rigurosamente; to put someone through the — someter a uno a un entrenamiento riguroso; hacer que uno aprenda por experiencia práctica; pasar a uno por la piedra.
 2 vt (grind) moler; (Mech) fresar; coin acordonar; cloth abatanar; chocolate batir.
 3 vi: to — around circular en masa, moverse por todas partes; people were —ing around the office la gente se apiñaba impaciente delante de la taquilla; stop —ing around! ¡quietos!
milled [mild] adj grain molido; coin, edge acordonado.
millenary [mi'lenəri] **1** adj milenario. **2** n milenario m.
millennium [mi'leniəm] n milenio m, milenario m.
millennial [mi'leniəl] adj milenario.
miller ['milə*] n molinero m.
millet ['milit] n mijo m.

millhand ['milhænd] n obrero m, a f, operario m, a f.
milliard ['miliɑ:d] n mil millones mpl; a — marks mil millones de marcos.
milligram(me) ['miligræm] n miligramo m.
millilitre, (US) —**liter** ['mili,li:tə*] n mililitro m.
millimetre, (US) —**meter** ['mili,mi:tə*] n milímetro m.
milliner ['milinə*] n sombrerera f, modista f (de sombreros); —'s (shop) sombrerería f, tienda f de sombreros (de señora).
millinery ['milinəri] n sombrerería f, sombreros mpl de señora.
milling ['miliŋ] n (grinding) molienda f; (on coin) cordoncillo m.
milling machine ['miliŋmə,ʃi:n] n fresadora f.
million ['miljən] n millón m; one — fleas un millón de pulgas; 4 — dogs 4 millones de perros; she's one in a — es una verdadera joya, es un mirlo blanco.
millionaire [,miljə'neə*] n millonario m, a f.
millionth ['miljənθ] 1 adj millonésimo. 2 n millonésimo m.
millipede ['milipi:d] n miriópodo m.
millpond ['milpɔnd] n represa f de molino.
millrace ['milreis] n caz m.
millstone ['milstəun] n piedra f de molino, muela f; it's a — round his neck representa un grandísimo estorbo para él.
millwheel ['milwi:l] n rueda f de molino.
milometer [mai'lɔmitə*] n cuentakilómetros m.
milord [mi'lɔ:d] n milord m.
milt [milt] n (Fish) lecha f.
mime [maim] 1 n pantomima f, mímica f; (ancient play) mímica f, teatro m de mímica; (actor) mimo m. 2 vt hacer en pantomima, remedar; representar con gestos. 3 vi actuar de mimo.
mimeograph ['mimiəgrɑ:f] 1 n mimeógrafo m. 2 vt mimeografiar.
mimic ['mimik] 1 adj mímico; (pretended) fingido, simulado. 2 n remedador m, ora f, imitador m, ora f. 3 vt remedar, imitar.
mimicry ['mimikri] n imitación f, remedo m; (Bio) mimetismo m; protective — mimetismo m protector.
mimosa [mi'məuzə] n mimosa f.
minaret [minə'ret] n alminar m.
minatory ['minətəri] adj (lit) amenazador.
mince [mins] 1 n carne f picada. 2 vt desmenuzar; meat picar. 3 vi (in walking) andar con pasos menuditos; (in talking) hablar remilgadamente.
mincemeat ['minsmi:t] n conserva f de picadillo de fruta; to make — of (fig) vencer fácilmente, hacer pedazos.
mince pie ['mins'pai] n pastel m de picadillo de fruta.
mincer ['minsə*] n máquina f de picar carne.
mincing ['minsiŋ] adj remilgado, afectado; step menudito.
mincing machine ['minsiŋmə,ʃi:n] n máquina f de picar carne.
mind [maind] 1 n mente f; (intellect) inteligencia f, entendimiento m; (memory) memoria f; (contrasted with matter) espíritu m; (cast of —) mentalidad f; (sanity, judgement) juicio m; (intention) intención f, voluntad f; (opinion) opinión f, parecer m; (leaning) inclinación f; —'s eye imaginación f; state of — estado m de ánimo; of unsound — mentalmente incapacitado; time out of — tiempo m inmemorial; to my — en mi opinión; with one — unánimemente, with an open — con espíritu amplio, sin prejuicios, sin ideas preconcebidas; great —s think alike los sabios piensan lo mismo; to be in one's right — estar en su cabal juicio; to be in two —s dudar, no saber a qué carta quedarse (about en el asunto de); I am not clear in my — about the incident no recuerdo el incidente con entera claridad; I am not clear in my — about the plan no entiendo del todo el proyecto; to be uneasy in one's — estar algo inquieto; to be of one — ser unánimes, estar de acuerdo; I was of the same — as my brother yo compartía el criterio de mi hermano, mi hermano y yo éramos de la misma opinión; what's on your —? ¿qué es lo que te preocupa?; the child's death was much on his — le angustiaba muchísimo la muerte del niño; to be out of one's — estar fuera de juicio, estar (como) loco; you must be out of your —! ¿se te ha vuelto el juicio?; to bear something in — tener algo presente; I'll bear you in — me acordaré de Vd, no le olvidaré; we must bear (it) in — that . . . hemos de recordar que . . .; to call something to — recordar algo; that calls something else to — eso me trae otra cosa a la memoria; to change one's — cambiar de opinión, mudar de parecer; it came to my — that . . . se me ocurrió que . . .; it

crossed my — se me ocurrió (that que); yes, it had crossed my — sí, eso se me había ocurrido; it never crossed my — jamás se me pasó por la cabeza; does it ever cross your — that . . .? ¿piensas alguna vez que . . .?; I can't get it out of my — eso no lo puedo quitar de la cabeza; to give one's — to something aplicarse a algo; to give someone a piece of one's — decir cuatro verdades a uno; to go out of one's — volverse loco; I have a good — to do it, I have half a — to do it casi estoy por hacerlo, tengo ganas de hacerlo, por poco lo hago; to have something in — pensar en algo, tener algo pensado; to have it in — to + infin pensar + infin, proponerse + infin; whom have you in — for the job? ¿a quién piensas dar el puesto?; to have something on one's — estar preocupado por algo; to improve one's — edificar su espíritu, educarse, instruirse; to keep something in — see to bear something in —; to keep an open — on a subject evitar tener prejuicios acerca de un asunto; estar todavía sin decidirse acerca de un asunto; to know one's own — saber lo que uno quiere; to let one's — run on something dejar que la mente se distraiga en algo; to make up one's — resolverse, decidirse (to + infin a + infin); tomar partido; we can't make up our —s about the house no nos resolvemos a vender (etc) la casa; I can't make up my — about him todavía tengo ciertas dudas con respecto a él; to pass out of — caer en el olvido; he puts me in — of his father recuerda a su padre, me hace pensar en su padre; you can put that right out of your — conviene no pensar más en eso; to read someone's — adivinar el pensamiento de uno; to set one's — on something desear algo con vehemencia, estar resuelto a conseguir (or hacer etc) algo; it slipped my — se me olvidó; to speak one's — hablar con franqueza, hablar claro; this will take your — off it esto servirá para distraerte.

2 vti (a) (pay attention to) hacer caso de; fijarse en; preocuparse de; rules etc obedecer, guiarse por; never —! (don't worry) ¡no se preocupe!, (pay no attention) ¡no haga Vd caso!, (it makes no odds) ¡es igual!, ¡no importa!, ¡qué más da!; never — him! ¡no haga Vd caso de él!; never — that now! ¡no se preocupe con eso ya!; ¡déjate de eso!; buy it and never — the expense cómpralo sin hacer caso del precio; I don't — the cold el frío me trae sin cuidado, no me molesta el frío; — what you're doing! ¡cuidado con lo que haces!; don't — me! ¡no se ocupe Vd de mí!, (iro) ¿y yo que estoy delante?; — what I say! ¡escucha lo que te digo!; he didn't do it, — pero en realidad no lo hizo, la verdad es que no lo hizo; — you, it was raining at the time hay que confesar que en ese momento llovía.

(b) (meddle in) see business.

(c) (be put out by) sentirse molesto por, tener inconveniente en; I don't — me es igual, no tengo inconveniente; do you —? ¿se puede?; do you —! (iro) ¡por Dios!; a cigarette? I don't — (if I do) ¿un cigarrillo? pues muchas gracias; close the door, if you don't — haga el favor de cerrar la puerta; do you — the noise? ¿le molesta el ruido?; I don't — 4, but 6 is too many con 4 estoy bien, pero 6 son muchos; I shouldn't — a cup of tea no vendría mal una taza de té; do you — coming with me? ¿quiere hacer el favor de venir conmigo?; would you — opening the door? ¿me hace el favor de abrir la puerta?; do you — if I open the window? ¿le molesta que abra la ventana?; I don't — having to wait no tengo inconveniente en esperar.

(d) (beware of) tener cuidado con (or de); —! ¡cuidado!; — the stairs! ¡cuidado con la escalera!; — you don't get wet! ¡ten cuidado de no mojarte!; — you do it! ¡hágalo sin falta!, ¡no deje de hacerlo!; — your language! ¡cuida tu lengua!, ¡cuidado con lo que dices!

(e) (oversee) cuidar, vigilar, estar al cuidado de; children etc cuidar; shop ocuparse de, encargarse de; machine atender.

(f) (remember) acordarse de, recordar; I — the time when . . . me acuerdo de cuando . . .
minded ['maindid] adj: if you are so — si estás dispuesto a hacerlo, si quieres hacerlo.
-**minded** ['maindid] adj de mente . . ., de mentalidad . . .; eg fair-minded imparcial; an industrially-minded nation una nación consciente de sus industrias, una nación que se dedica a la industria; a romantically-minded girl una joven de pensamientos románticos, una joven con ideas románticas.
mindful ['maindful] adj: — of consciente de, atento a; we must be — of the risks hay que tener presentes los riesgos, acordémonos de los riesgos.

mindless ['maindlis] adj estúpido.
mine[1] [main] poss pron (el) mío, (la) mía etc; — **and thine** lo mío y lo tuyo; **this car is** — este coche es mío, **éste es mi coche; is this** —? ¿es mío esto?; **his friends and** — sus amigos y los míos; **I have what is** — tengo lo que es mío; **a friend of** — un amigo mío, uno de mis amigos; **it's no business of** — no tiene que ver conmigo.
mine[2] [main] **1** n (a) (Min) mina f; **to work a** — explotar una mina.
　(b) (Mil, Naut etc) mina f; **magnetic** — mina f magnética; **to lay** —s sembrar minas; **to sweep** —s dragar minas, barrer minas.
　(c) (fig) tesoro m, pozo m; **the book is a** — **of information** el libro es un tesoro de datos útiles.
　2 vt (a) coal, metal extraer, explotar.
　(b) (Mil, Naut) channel, road sembrar minas en; proteger con minas; ship hundir por medio de una mina.
　3 vi extraer minerales; dedicarse a la minería; **to** — **for something** buscar algo abriendo una mina; explotar los yacimientos de algo.
mine detector ['maindi,tektə*] n detector m de minas.
minefield ['mainfi:ld] n campo de minas.
minelayer ['main,leiə*] n barco m siembra-minas, buque m minador.
miner ['mainə*] n minero m.
mineral ['minərəl] **1** adj mineral. **2** n mineral m.
mineralogist [,minə'rælədʒist] n mineralogista m.
mineralogy [,minə'rælədʒi] n mineralogía f.
mineral water ['minərəl,wɔːtə*] n agua f mineral, (loosely) gaseosa f.
minesweeper ['main,swiːpə*] n dragaminas m, barreminas m.
mingle ['mingl] **1** vt mezclar (with con).
　2 vi mezclarse; (become indistinguishable) confundirse (in, with con); **he** —**d with people of all classes** se asociaba con personas de todas las clases, vivía con personas de todas las clases; **the police** —**d with the demonstrators** los policías se confundieron con los manifestantes.
mingy ['mindʒi] adj (fam) tacaño.
mini . . . ['mini] mini . . ., micro . . .
miniature ['minitʃə*] **1** n miniatura f; modelo m pequeño; **in** — en miniatura, en pequeña escala.
　2 adj (en) miniatura; — **golf** golf m miniatura; — **poodle** perro m de lanas miniatura; — **submarine** submarino m de bolsillo; — **watches** relojes mpl miniatura.
miniaturize ['minitʃəraiz] vt reducir a forma miniatura.
minibus ['minibʌs] n microbús m.
minicab ['minikæb] n microtaxi m.
minim ['minim] n (Mus) blanca f.
minimal ['miniml] adj mínimo.
minimize ['minimaiz] vt minimizar; aminorar, minorizar, empequeñecer.
minimum ['miniməm] **1** adj mínimo. **2** n mínimo m, minimum m; (down) **to the** — al mínimo; **down to a** — **of 5 degrees** hasta 5 grados como mínimo.
mining ['mainiŋ] **1** n minería f; explotación f, extracción f. **2** attr area, industry, town minero; **engineer de** minas.
minion ['minjən] n (favourite) favorito m, a f; (royal favourite) privado m, valido m; (servant) paniaguado m.
miniskirt ['miniskəːt] n minifalda f.
minister ['ministə*] **1** n (Pol etc) ministro m (for, of de); (Eccl) pastor m.
　2 vi: **to** — **to someone** atender a uno; **to** — **to someone's needs** ayudar a uno dándole lo que necesita, satisfacer las necesidades de uno; **to** — **to a result** contribuir a un resultado.
ministerial [,minis'tiəriəl] adj ministerial, de ministro; — **crisis** crisis f de gobierno.
ministration [,minis'treiʃən] n ayuda f, agencia f, servicio m; (Eccl) ministerio m.
ministry ['ministri] n ministerio m (for, of de); (Eccl) sacerdocio m; **to enter the** — hacerse sacerdote, (Protestant) hacerse pastor.
minium ['miniəm] n minio m.
mink [miŋk] n (Zool) visón m; (fur) piel f de visón; — **coat** abrigo m de visón.
minnow ['minəu] n pececillo m (de agua dulce).
minor ['mainə*] **1** adj menor (also Eccl, Mus etc); (under age) menor de edad; writer etc de segundo orden, secundario; operation pequeño, sin trascendencia; detail sin importancia; role, position secundario, de categoría inferior; **Smith** — Smith el joven; **G** — (Mus) sol m menor; — **third** tercera f menor.
　2 n menor mf de edad; (US Univ) asignatura f secundaria.
Minorca [mi'nɔːkə] Menorca f.
minority [mai'nɔriti] **1** n minoría f; (age) minoridad f, menor edad f; **to be in a** — estar en la minoría; **you are in a** — **of one** Vd es el único que piensa así.
　2 attr rule etc minoritario.
Minotaur ['mainətɔː*] Minotauro m.
minster ['minstə*] n catedral f; iglesia f de un monasterio; **York M** — la catedral de York.
minstrel ['minstrəl] n juglar m; cantor m; **nigger** — cómico m (disfrazado de negro).
minstrelsy ['minstrəlsi] n (music) música f; (song) canto m; (art of epic minstrel) juglaría f, (art of lyric minstrel) gaya ciencia f.
mint[1] [mint] **1** n casa f de moneda; **Royal M**— Real Casa f de la Moneda; **to be worth a** — (of money) valer un dineral.
　2 adj stamp etc nuevo, en nuevo, sin usar; **in** — **condition** en perfecto estado, sin estrenar.
　3 vt coin acuñar; phrase etc idear, inventar.
mint[2] [mint] n (Bot) hierbabuena f, menta f; (sweet) pastilla f de menta.
mint julep ['mint'dʒuːlep] n julepe m.
mint sauce ['mint'sɔːs] n salsa f de menta.
minuet [,minju'et] n minué m.
minus ['mainəs] **1** prep (a) menos; **9** — **6** 9 menos 6.
　(b) (without, deprived of) sin, desprovisto de, falto de; **he appeared** — **his trousers** apareció sin pantalón.
　2 adj menos; negativo.
　3 n (sign) signo m menos; (amount) cantidad f negativa.
minuscule ['minəskjuːl] adj minúsculo.
minute ['minit] **1** n (a) (of degree, time) minuto m; (fig) momento m, instante m; **at the last** — a última hora; **at 6 o'clock to the** — a las 6 en punto; **I'll come in a** — vengo al momento; **it was all over in a** — todo esto ocurrió en un instante; **this very** — ahora mismo; **to leave things until the last** — dejar las cosas hasta última hora; **up to the** — news noticias fpl de última hora; **tell me the** — **he comes** avíseme en cuanto venga; **I shan't be a** — vuelvo (or termino etc) muy pronto; **we expect him any** — le esperamos de un momento a otro; **it won't take 5** —s es cosa de pocos minutos; **wait a** —! ¡un momento!
　(b) (draft) borrador m, proyecto m, minuta f; (note) nota f, apuntación f; —**s** (of meeting) acta f, actas fpl; **to write up the** —**s of a meeting** levantar acta de una reunión.
　2 vt meeting levantar acta de; (draft) hacer el borrador de, minutar.
minute [mai'njuːt] adj (small) diminuto, menudo, pequeño; detail etc insignificante; (accurate, searching) minucioso.
minute book ['minitbuk] n libro m de actas.
minute hand ['minithænd] n minutero m.
minutely [mai'njuːtli] adv minuciosamente, con minuciosidad; **a** — **detailed account** un relato completo hasta en los más pequeños detalles; **anything** — **resembling a fish** cualquier cosa que tuviera el más ligero parecido con un pez.
minutiae [mi'njuːʃiiː] npl detalles mpl minuciosos.
minx [miŋks] n picaruela f, mujer f descarada; **you** —! ¡lagarta!
miracle ['mirəkl] n milagro m; **by a** —, **by some** — por milagro; **it will be a** — **if** . . . será un milagro si . . .
miracle play ['mirəkl,plei] n milagro m, auto m.
miraculous [mi'rækjuləs] adj milagroso.
miraculously [mi'rækjuləsli] adv milagrosamente, por milagro.
mirage ['mirɑːʒ] n espejismo m (also fig).
mire [maiə*] n fango m, lodo m.
mirror ['mirə*] **1** n espejo m; (Aut) retrovisor m; **to look at oneself in the** — mirarse al espejo. **2** vt reflejar.
mirth [məːθ] n alegría f, regocijo m; (laughter) risa f, risas fpl; **at this there was** — en esto hubo risas; **there was some unseemly** — se rieron algunos descaradamente.
mirthful ['məːθful] adj alegre.
mirthless ['məːθlis] adj triste, sin alegría.
miry ['mairi] adj fango, lodoso; — **place** lodazal m.
misadventure [,misəd'ventʃə*] n desgracia f, accidente m; **death by** — muerte f accidental.

misalliance [ˌmisə'laiəns] n casamiento m desigual.
misanthrope ['mizənθrəup] n misántropo m.
misanthropic [ˌmizən'θrɔpik] adj misantrópico.
misanthropist [mi'zænθrəpist] n misántropo m.
misanthropy [mi'zænθrəpi] n misantropía f.
misapply [ˌmisə'plai] vt aplicar mal; abusar de.
misapprehend ['mis.æpri'hend] vt comprender mal.
misapprehension ['mis.æpri'henʃən] n equivocación f, error m, concepto m erróneo; to be under a — estar equivocado; there seems to be some — parece haber algún malentendido.
misappropriate ['misə'prəuprieit] vt malversar.
misappropriation ['misə.prəupri'eiʃən] n malversación f.
misbegotten ['misbi'gɔtn] adj bastardo, ilegítimo; plan etc ineficaz, llamado a fracasar.
misbehave ['misbi'heiv] vi portarse mal; (child) ser malo.
misbehaviour, (US) misbehavior ['misbi'heivjə*] n mala conducta f.
miscalculate ['mis'kælkjuleit] vti calcular mal.
miscalculation ['mis.kælkju'leiʃən] n cálculo m erróneo; (fig) error m, desacierto m.
miscall ['mis'kɔːl] vt llamar equivocadamente.
miscarriage ['mis.kæridʒ] n (Med) aborto m, malparto m; (failure) fracaso m, malogro m; (of letter, goods) extravío m; — of justice error m judicial.
miscarry ['mis'kæri] vi (Med) malparir, abortar; (fail) fracasar, salir mal, frustrarse; (letter, goods) extraviarse.
miscegenation [ˌmisidʒi'neiʃən] n entrecruzamiento m de razas.
miscellaneous [ˌmisi'leiniəs] adj vario, diverso.
miscellany [mi'seləni] n miscelánea f.
mischance [mis'tʃɑːns] n mala suerte f; infortunio m, desgracia f; by some — por desgracia.
mischief ['mistʃif] n (harm) mal m, daño m; (naughtiness) travesura f, diablura f; (roguishness) malicia f; (person) diablillo m; he's up to some — está haciendo alguna travesura; there's some — going on están tramando algo mal; there's no — in him no es capaz de ninguna maldad; to do someone a — hacer mal a uno; to do oneself a — hacerse daño; he's always getting into — anda siempre metido en alguna travesura; to keep someone out of — impedir a uno hacer travesuras; to make — armar líos; to make — for someone crear dificultades para uno, amargar la vida a uno.
mischief-maker ['mistʃif,meikə*] n revoltoso m, a f, persona f turbulenta, persona f que anda metida en líos.
mischievous ['mistʃivəs] adj person malo, dañoso; (playful) malicioso, juguetón; child travieso; attack etc perjudicial; glance etc malicioso, lleno de malicia.
mischievously ['mistʃivəsli] adv maliciosamente, con malicia; por travesura.
misconceive ['miskən'siːv] vt entender mal, formar un concepto erróneo de.
misconception ['miskən'sepʃən] n concepto m erróneo, idea f falsa, equivocación f.
misconduct [mis'kɔndʌkt] n mala conducta f; (sexual) adulterio m.
misconduct [ˌmiskən'dʌkt] 1 vt manejar mal, dirigir mal. 2 vr: to — oneself portarse mal.
misconstruction ['miskəns'trʌkʃən] n mala interpretación f; mala traducción f; (deliberate) tergiversación f.
misconstrue ['miskən'struː] vt interpretar mal; traducir mal; (deliberately) tergiversar.
miscount ['mis'kaunt] 1 vt contar mal, equivocarse en la cuenta de. 2 vi contar mal.
miscreant ['miskriənt] n sinvergüenza mf, bellaco m, a f.
misdeal ['mis'diːl] 1 n reparto m erróneo. 2 (irr: see deal) vt cards dar mal, repartir mal.
misdeed ['mis'diːd] n delito m, crimen m, fechoría f.
misdemeanour, (US) misdemeanor [ˌmisdi'miːnə*] n ofensa f, delito m; (Law) delito m de menor cuantía.
misdirect ['misdi'rekt] vt operation etc manejar mal, dirigir mal; letter etc poner unas señas incorrectas en; person informar mal (acerca del camino a tomar), hacer perder el camino.
misdirection ['misdi'rekʃən] n mal manejo m, mala dirección f; instrucciones fpl erróneas, información f errónea.
miser ['maizə*] n avaro m, a f, avariento m, a f, tacaño m, a f.
miserable ['mizərəbl] adj (unhappy) triste, desdichado, desgraciado; abatido; (filthy, wretched) indecente, vil; (contemptible) vil, despreciable; (valueless) sin valor; show, spectacle de pena;

weather muy feo, de perros; wage raquítico; it was a — failure fue un rotundo fracaso; what are you so — about? ¿por qué estás tan triste?; I feel — today hoy me siento abatido; hoy me siento sin fuerzas para nada; to make someone — entristecer a uno, abatir a uno; to make someone's life — amargar la vida a uno.
miserably ['mizərəbli] adv say etc tristemente; it failed — fracasó rotundamente; they played — jugaron terriblemente mal.
misère [mi'zɛə*] n (Cards) nulos mpl; to go — jugar a nulos.
miserliness ['maizəlinis] n avaricia f, tacañería f.
miserly ['maizəli] adj avariento, tacaño.
misery ['mizəri] n (suffering) sufrimiento m; (sadness) pena f, tristeza f; (wretchedness) aflicción f, desdicha f; a life of — una vida desgraciada; to make someone's life a — amargar la vida a uno; to put an animal out of its — acortar la agonía a un animal; to put someone out of his — (fig) satisfacer por fin a uno (contándole una noticia or revelándole un secreto etc).
misfire ['mis'faiə*] vi fallar.
misfit ['misfit] n cosa f mal ajustada; (dress) traje m que no cae bien; (person) inadaptado m, a f, desplazado m, a f, persona f reñida con su ambiente; he's always been a — here no se ha adaptado nunca a las condiciones de aquí, en ningún momento ha estado realmente contento aquí.
misfortune [mis'fɔːtʃən] n desgracia f, infortunio m, desventura f; companion in — compañero m en la desgracia, compañero m de infortunio; it is his — that he is lame tiene la mala suerte de ser cojo; I had the — to meet him tuve la mala suerte de encontrarme con él.
misgiving [mis'givin] n (mistrust) recelo m, duda f, temor m; (apprehension) presentimiento m; not without some — no sin cierto recelo; I had —s about the scheme tuve mis dudas acerca del proyecto.
misgovern ['mis'gʌvən] vti gobernar mal; administrar mal.
misgovernment ['mis'gʌvənmənt] n desgobierno m, mal gobierno m; mala administración f.
misguided ['mis'gaidid] adj equivocado.
misguidedly ['mis'gaididli] adv equivocadamente.
mishandle ['mis'hændl] vt manejar mal.
mishap ['mishæp] n desgracia f, contratiempo m, accidente m; without — sin novedad; to have a — tener un accidente.
mishear ['mis'hiə*] (irr: see hear) vti oír mal.
mishmash ['miʃmæʃ] n masa f informe, masa f confusa; baturrillo m, ensaladilla f.
misinform ['misin'fɔːm] vt informar mal, dar informes erróneos a.
misinterpret ['misin'tə:prit] vt interpretar mal; traducir mal; (deliberately) tergiversar.
misinterpretation ['misin.tə:pri'teiʃən] n mala interpretación f; mala traducción f; tergiversación f.
misjudge ['mis'dʒʌdʒ] vt juzgar mal, equivocarse sobre.
misjudgement [ˌmis'dʒʌdʒmənt] n juicio m erróneo.
mislay [mis'lei] (irr: see lay) vt extraviar, perder.
mislead [mis'liːd] (irr: see lead) vt llevar a conclusiones erróneas, despistar; (deliberately) engañar; I fear you have been misled me temo que se lo hayan dicho mal.
misleading [mis'liːdin] adj erróneo; (deliberately) engañoso.
mismanage ['mis'mænidʒ] vt manejar mal, administrar mal.
mismanagement ['mis'mænidʒmənt] n mal manejo m, mala administración f.
mismatch ['mis'mætʃ] vt emparejar mal, hermanar mal.
misname ['mis'neim] vt llamar equivocadamente.
misnomer ['mis'nəumə*] n nombre m equivocado, nombre m inapropiado; that is a — ese nombre no es correcto.
misogamist [mi'sɔgəmist] n misógamo m, a f.
misogamy [mi'sɔgəmi] n misogamia f.
misogynist [mi'sɔdʒinist] n misógino m.
misogyny [mi'sɔdʒini] n misoginia f.
misplace ['mis'pleis] vt colocar mal; poner fuera de su lugar; (lose) extraviar, perder.
misplaced ['mis'pleist] adj equivocado; inoportuno; inmerecido.
misprint ['misprint] n errata f, error m de imprenta.
misprint [mis'print] vt imprimir mal.
mispronounce ['mispro'nauns] vt pronunciar mal.
mispronunciation ['misprə.nʌnsi'eiʃən] n mala pronunciación f.

misquotation ['miskwəu'teiʃən] n cita f equivocada.
misquote ['mis'kwəut] vt citar mal; **he was —d in the press** en la prensa interpretaron mal lo que había dicho, en la prensa no citaron correctamente lo que había dicho.
misread ['mis'ri:d] (irr: see **read**) vt leer mal; interpretar mal.
misrepresent ['mis,repri'zent] vt desfigurar, falsificar; describir engañosamente; tergiversar; **he was —ed in the papers** los informes de los periódicos falsificaron lo que había dicho.
misrepresentation ['mis,reprizen'teiʃən] n desfiguración f; falsificación f; descripción f engañosa; tergiversación f; **this report is a — of what I said** este informe falsifica lo que yo dije.
misrule ['mis'ru:l] **1** n desgobierno m, mal gobierno m. **2** vt desgobernar, gobernar mal.
miss¹ [mis] **1** n (shot) tiro m errado, tiro m perdido; (mistake) error m, desacierto m; (failure) fracaso m; **a — is as good as a mile** lo mismo da librarse por poco que por mucho; **it was a near —** el tiro me anduvo muy cerca; **it was a near — with that car** faltó poco para que ese coche chocara con nosotros; **to give something a —** (not go) dejar de asistir a algo, no asistir a algo, (not visit) dejar de visitar algo; **we're giving it a —** this year este año no vamos; **they voted the record a —** opinaron que el disco carecería de valor.
2 vt (a) (fail to hit) aim, target errar; **the shot just —ed me** por poco la bala me alcanzó, el tiro me anduvo muy cerca; **the plane just —ed the tower** faltó poco para que el avión chocara con la torre; **he narrowly —ed being run over** por poco fue atropellado, faltó poco para que se le atropellara.
(b) (fail to find, catch, use etc) vocation errar, equivocarse en la elección de; solution no acertar; thing sought no encontrar; bus, train, chance, footing etc perder; one's way equivocarse de; class, lecture perder; appointment no acudir a; meeting etc no asistir a, no poder asistir a; **you haven't —ed much!** ¡no has perdido nada!; **we —ed the tide** perdimos la pleamar; **we're afraid of —ing the market** tememos perder el momento más propicio para la venta; **she —ed her holiday last year** el año pasado no pudo tomarse las vacaciones; **I —ed you at the station** no te vi en la estación; **they —ed each other in the crowd** no lograron encontrarse entre tanta gente; **you mustn't — this film** esta película hay que verla, no dejes de ver esta película; **don't — the Prado** no dejes de visitar el Prado; **you can't — the house** es imposible equivocarse al venir a la casa.
(c) (fail to hear) **I —ed what you said** se me escapó lo que dijo Vd; **I —ed that** eso no lo entendí; **you're —ing the point** no comprendes el punto principal.
(d) (omit) omitir; (overlook) pasar por alto; **let's — the next dance** no bailemos la próxima vez; **he —ed out a word** omitió una palabra; **he was —ed out in the promotions** en los ascensos le pasaron por alto.
(e) (notice absence of, regret absence of) echar de menos; notar la falta de; **I — the old trams** echo de menos los viejos tranvías; **I — you so** te echo mucho de menos; **he is much —ed** se le echa mucho de menos; **then I —ed my wallet** luego me di cuenta de que no tenía ya cartera; **he won't be —ed** bien podemos prescindir de él; **we're —ing 8 dollars** nos faltan 8 dólares.
3 vi (shot, person) errar el blanco, errar el tiro; (motor) fallar; **he —ed** erró el tiro; **he never —es** (fam) siempre acierta; **you can't —!** ¡es imposible fallar!; **I've not —ed once in 10 years** en 10 años no he faltado ni una sola vez.
miss² [mis] n señorita f; (fam) niña f precoz, niña f repipi; **a modern —** una señorita moderna; **M— Jennie Smith** (la) Señorita Jennie Smith; **yes, M— Smith** sí, señorita; **M— Spain 1980** Miss España 1980.
missal ['misəl] n misal m.
misshapen ['mis'ʃeipən] adj deforme.
missile ['misail] n proyectil m; (javelin etc) arma f arrojadiza; **air-to-air —** proyectil m de aire a aire; **guided —** proyectil m teledirigido; **intercontinental ballistic —** proyectil m balístico intercontinental.
missing ['misiŋ] adj (also person ausente, (Mil etc) desaparecido; thing perdido, extraviado, que falta; **— in action** desaparecido en combate; **— person** desaparecido m; **supply the — letters** poner las letras que faltan; **the three — students are safe** los tres estudiantes desaparecidos están a salvo.
(b) to be — faltar; haber desaparecido; **there are 9 books —, 9 books are —** faltan 9 libros; **how many are —?** ¿cuántos faltan?; **one of our aircraft is —** uno de nuestros aviones no ha vuelto.
mission ['miʃən] n misión f; goodwill — misión f de buena voluntad; trade — misión f comercial; **her — in life is to + infin** su misión en la vida es + infin; **to send someone on a secret —** enviar a uno en misión secreta.
missionary ['miʃənri] **1** adj zeal etc misional. **2** n misionero m, a f.
missis ['misiz] n (fam) **my —, the —** la parienta; **John and his —** Juan y su costilla; **yes, — ** sí, señora; **is the — in?** ¿está la señora?
Mississippi [,misi'sipi] Misisipí m.
missive ['misiv] n misiva f.
Missouri [mi'zuəri] Misurí m.
misspell ['mis'spel] (irr: see **spell**) vt escribir mal.
misspelling ['mis'speliŋ] n error m de ortografía.
misspend ['mis'spend] (irr: see **spend**) vt malgastar, desperdiciar, perder; **a misspent youth** una juventud mal empleada, una juventud pasada en la disipación.
misstate ['mis'steit] vt declarar erróneamente; (deliberately) declarar falsamente.
misstatement ['mis'steitmənt] n declaración f errónea; declaración f falsa.
missus ['misiz] n (fam) see **missis**.
missy ['misi] n (fam) = **miss²**.
mist [mist] **1** n (fog) niebla f; (slight) neblina f; (summery; at sea) bruma f; (fig) nube f, velo m; **morning —** bruma f del alba; **Scotch —** llovizna f; **through a — of tears** por ojos llenos de lágrimas.
2 vt (fig) empañar, velar.
3 vi (also to — over, to — up) empañarse, velarse; (eyes) llenarse de lágrimas.
mistakable [mis'teikəbl] adj confundible.
mistake [mis'teik] **1** n equivocación f, error m, falta f; **by —** por equivocación, (carelessly) por descuido, (involuntarily) sin querer; **it's finished and no —!** ¡ya lo creo que está terminado!; **he took my hat in — for his** confundió mi sombrero con el suyo; **to acknowledge one's —** confesar su error; **the — is mine** la culpa es mía, la culpa la tengo yo; **there must be some —** ha de haber algún error; **there's no — about it** está muy claro, no hay que darle vueltas; **let there be no — about it** entiéndase bien que . . .; quede perfectamente claro que . . .; **to make a —** equivocarse; **you're making a big —** te equivocas gravemente, es una decisión totalmente errónea; **make no — (about it)** y que no queden dudas sobre esto; **to make the — of asking too much** cometer el error de pedir demasiado.
2 (irr: see **take**) vt (a) meaning entender mal, equivocarse sobre; road etc equivocar, equivocarse de.
(b) to — A for B equivocar A con B, confundir A con B.
(c) to be —n equivocarse, estar equivocado, engañarse; **if I am not —n** si no me equivoco; **he is often —n for Peter** se le confunde muchas veces con Pedro; **it cannot possibly be —n for anything else** es imposible confundirlo con otra cosa.
mistaken [mis'teikən] **1** ptp of **mistake**. **2** adj equivocado, erróneo; incorrecto.
mistakenly [mis'teikənli] adv equivocadamente, erróneamente.
mister ['mistə*] n (gen abbr **Mr**) señor m (gen abbr Sr).
mistime ['mis'taim] vt act etc hacer (or decir etc) a deshora, hacer en momento poco oportuno; race etc cronometrar mal.
mistle thrush ['mislθrʌʃ] n zorzal m charlo.
mistletoe ['misltəu] n muérdago m.
mistranslate ['mistræns'leit] vt traducir mal.
mistranslation ['mistræns'leiʃən] n mala traducción f.
mistreat [mis'tri:t] vt maltratar, tratar mal.
mistreatment [mis'tri:tmənt] n maltrato m, maltratamiento m, malos tratos mpl.
mistress ['mistris] n (of house etc) señora f, ama f de casa; (lover) querida f, amante f; (teacher: in primary school) maestra f, (in secondary school) profesora f; (abbr **Mrs** ['misiz]) señora f de . . .
mistrial [mis'trail] n juicio m viciado de nulidad.
mistrust [mis'trʌst] **1** n desconfianza f, recelo m. **2** vt desconfiar de, dudar de.
mistrustful [mis'trʌstful] adj desconfiado, receloso; **to be — of** recelarse de.
misty ['misti] adj nebuloso, brumoso; day de niebla; (fig) nebuloso, vaporoso; glasses, window empañado; **it's getting —** se está anieblando, está bajando la niebla; **the window is getting —** la ventana se está empañando.

misunderstand ['misʌndə'stænd] (*irr: see* **stand**) *vti* entender mal, comprender mal; tomar en sentido erróneo; interpretar mal; **you — me** no me entiendes, no entiendes lo que digo.

misunderstanding ['misʌndə'stændiŋ] *n* equivocación *f*, error *m*; concepto *m* erróneo; (*disagreement*) desavenencia *f*; (*between two persons*) malentendido *m*; **there must be some —** ha de haber algún malentendido.

misunderstood ['misʌndə'stud] *adj* no comprendido; insuficientemente estimado; **a — person** una persona incomprendida.

misuse ['mis'juːs] *n* abuso *m*, mal uso *m*; (*of word*) empleo *m* erróneo; (*of funds*) malversación *f*.

misuse ['mis'juːz] *vt* abusar de; *word* emplear mal; *funds* malversar; *person etc* maltratar.

mite¹ [mait] *n* (*Zool*) ácaro *m*.

mite² [mait] *n* (*coin*) ardite *m*, (*as contribution*) óbolo *m*; (*small quantity*) pizca *f*, poquitín *m*; (*child*) niño *m* pequeño, niña *f* pequeña, nene *m*, a *f*; **poor little —!** ¡pobrecito!; **a — of consolation** una pizca de consuelo; **there's not a — left** no queda ni una sola gota; **well, just a — then** bueno, un poquitín; **we were a — surprised** quedamos un tanto atónitos, nos sorprendimos un poquito.

Mithraic [miθ'reiik] *adj* mitraico.

Mithraism ['miθreiizm] *n* mitraísmo *m*.

Mithras ['miθræs] *m* Mitra.

mitigate ['mitigeit] *vt* mitigar.

mitigation [,miti'geiʃən] *n* mitigación *f*; **to say a word in —** decir algo para mitigar la ofensa (*etc*).

mitre, (*US*) **miter** ['maitə*] **1** *n* (*Eccl*) mitra *f*; (*Tech*) inglete *m*. **2** *vt* (*Tech*) ingletear.

mitt [mit] *n see* **mitten**; (*sl*) mano *f*.

mitten ['mitn] *n* mitón *m*, guante *m* con solo el pulgar separado; **—s** (*fam*) guantes *mpl* de boxeo; **to get the —** (*sl*) recibir calabazas; **to give someone the —** (*sl*) dar calabazas a uno.

mix [miks] **1** *vt* mezclar; combinar, unir; confundir; *concrete, flour, plaster etc* amasar; *drinks* preparar, mezclar; *salad* aderezar; **to — something in** añadir algo, echar algo; **to — sugar into something** añadir azúcar a algo; **to — it** (*fam*) venir a las manos, arreglar las cosas luchando; **to — up** mezclar, confundir; **don't — me up** no me confundas; **I've —ed you up with Michael** le he confundido (*or* equivocado) con Miguel; **to be —ed up in an affair** estar metido en un asunto; **are you —ed in this?** ¿tú andas metido en esto?, ¿tú tienes que ver con esto?; **to get —ed up in an affair** meterse en un asunto, mojar en un asunto.

2 *vi* mezclarse, poder mezclarse; (*ingredients etc*) ir bien juntos; (*persons: get on well*) llevarse bien; **to — (in) with others** asociarse con otros, ir con otros, alternar con otros, frecuentar la compañía de otros; **he's not keen to — (in)** tiene pocas ganas de alternar; **to — in high society** frecuentar la alta sociedad.

mixed [mikst] *adj* mixto; mezclado; (*assorted*) variado, surtido; *choir, doubles, bathing etc* mixto; **a — set of people** un grupo de personas variadas; **with — results** con resultados diversos, (*pej*) con resultados más bien mediocres; **we had — weather** el tiempo ha sido variable.

mixed-up ['mikst'ʌp] *adj things* mezclados; (*disordered*) revueltos, confusos; **I'm all —** estoy totalmente confuso; **a badly — youth** un joven de mentalidad gravemente confusa, un joven lleno de incertidumbre.

mixer ['miksə*] *n* (*Cook*) mezcladora *f*; licuadora *f*; (*Radio*) mezclador *m*; (*person*) persona *f* sociable; **to be a good —** tener don de gentes; **he's not much of a —** tiene pocas ganas de alternar, no tiene don de gentes.

mixture ['mikstʃə*] *n* mezcla *f*; (*Med*) medicina *f*; **the — as before** la misma receta que antes, (*fig*) lo de siempre; **freezing —** mezcla *f* refrigerante; **the family is an odd —** la familia muestra una extraña diversidad; **he's an odd — of poet and plumber** se reúnen en él de modo bastante raro el poeta y el fontanero.

mix-up ['miks'ʌp] *n* confusión *f*, lío *m*; **there was a dreadful —** hubo un tremendo lío; **we got in a — with the trains** nos hicimos un lío con los trenes.

mizzen ['mizn] *n* mesana *f*.

mizzenmast ['miznmɑːst] *n* palo *m* de mesana.

mizzle ['mizl] *vi* lloviznar.

mnemonic [ni'mɔnik] **1** *adj* mnemotécnico **2** *n* figura *f* (*or* frase *f etc*) mnemotécnica.

mnemonics [ni'mɔniks] *n* mnemotécnica *f*.

moan [məun] **1** *n* (*groan*) gemido *m*, quejido *m*; (*complaint*) queja *f*, protesta *f*.

2 *vt* lamentar.

3 *vi* gemir; quejarse, protestar; **"yes", he —ed** "sí", dijo gimiendo; **they're —ing about the food again** han vuelto a quejarse de la comida.

moaning ['məuniŋ] *n* gemidos *mpl*; quejas *fpl*; protestas *fpl*.

moat [məut] *n* foso *m*.

moated ['məutid] *adj* con foso, rodeado de un foso.

mob [mɔb] **1** *n* (**a**) multitud *f*, muchedumbre *f*, gentío *m*; (*pej*) turba *f*; (*of birds etc*) bandada *f*, multitud *f*; **the —** el populacho; **houses were burnt by the —s** unas casas fueron incendiadas por las turbas; **they went in a — to the town hall** fueron en tropel al ayuntamiento; **to join the —** echarse a las calles; **the army has become a —** el ejército se ha transformado en una turba.

(**b**) (*fam*) grupo *m*, pandilla *f*, peña *f*; **Joe and his —** Pepe y su peña, Pepe y sus amigotes; **I had nothing to do with that —** no tuve nada que ver con aquéllos; **which — were you in?** (*Mil*) ¿en qué regimiento (*etc*) estuviste?; **they're a hard-drinking —** son unos borrachos.

2 *vt* (*molest*) acosar, atropellar; (*attack*) atacar en masa; *actor etc* festejar tumultuosamente, apiñarse entusiastas en torno de; **the minister was —bed by journalists** los periodistas se apiñaban en torno del ministro; **he was —bed whenever he went out** al salir siempre se veía acosado por la gente.

mobcap ['mɔbkæp] *n* cofia *f*.

mobile ['məubail] *adj* móvil, movible; *canteen etc* ambulante; **now that we're —** (*fam*) ahora que tenemos coche.

mobility [məu'biliti] *n* movilidad *f*.

mobilization [,məubilai'zeiʃən] *n* movilización *f*.

mobilize ['məubilaiz] **1** *vt* movilizar. **2** *vi* movilizarse.

mob law ['mɔblɔː] *n* ley *f* de Lynch, ley *f* de la calle.

moccasin ['mɔkəsin] *n* mocasín *m*.

mocha ['mɔkə] *n* moca *f*.

mock [mɔk] **1** *n*: **to make a — of something** poner algo en ridículo.

2 *adj* (*sham*) fingido, simulado; (*imitated*) imitado; (*parodied*) burlesco; **in — anger** con ira simulada; **a — battle** un simulacro de combate.

3 *vt* (*ridicule*) ridiculizar; (*defy*) burlarse de; (*scoff at*) burlarse de, mofarse de; (*mimic*) remedar, imitar; *efforts, plans etc* frustrar, desbaratar.

4 *vi* mofarse (*at* de).

mocker ['mɔkə*] *n* mofador *m*, ora *f*.

mockery ['mɔkəri] *n* (*derision*) mofas *fpl*, burlas *fpl*; (*object*) parodia *f*, mal remedo *m*; **this is a — of justice** esto es una negación de la justicia; **it was a — of a trial** fue una parodia de un proceso; **what a — this is!** ¡esto es absurdo!, ¡qué tontería!; **he had to put up with a lot of —** tuvo que aguantar muchas burlas; **to make a — of something** hacer algo ridículo.

mock-heroic ['mɔkhi'rəuik] *adj* heroicocómico.

mocking ['mɔkiŋ] **1** *adj tone etc* burlón. **2** *n* burlas *fpl*.

mockingbird ['mɔkiŋbəːd] *n* sinsonte *m*.

mockingly ['mɔkiŋli] *adv* en tono burlón, con sorna.

mock orange ['mɔk'ɔrindʒ] *n* jeringuilla *f*.

mock-up ['mɔkʌp] *n* maqueta *f*, modelo *m* en escala natural.

modal ['məudl] *adj* modal.

modality [məu'dæliti] *n* modalidad *f*.

mode [məud] *n* modo *m* (*also Gram, Mus, Philos*), manera *f*; (*fashion*) moda *f*.

model ['mɔdl] **1** *n* (**a**) modelo *m*; (*architect's, town planner's etc*) maqueta *f*; **it is made on the — of X** está hecho a imitación de X.

(**b**) (*person: Fashion, Art*) modelo *mf*; **he is a — of good behaviour** es un modelo de buenas costumbres; **to hold someone out** (*or* **up**) **as a —** presentar a uno como modelo.

2 *adj* modelo; **— prison** cárcel *f* modelo; **— railway** ferrocarril *m* de juguete, ferrocarril *m* en miniatura; **— town** ciudad *f* modelo.

3 *vt* (**a**) (*make a —*) modelar; (*fig*) modelar, formar, planear; **to — something on something else** modelar algo sobre otra cosa, construir algo a imitación de otra cosa, planear algo según otra cosa.

(**b**) *dress etc* llevar, presentar.

4 *vi* servir de modelo (*for* a, para); ejercer la profesión de modelo, ser modelo.

5 *vr*: **to — oneself on** modelarse sobre.

modeller, (*US*) **modeler** ['mɔdlə*] *n* modelador *m*, ora *f*.

modelling, (*US*) **modeling** ['mɔdliŋ] *n* modelado *m*; profesión *f* de modelo.

moderate ['mɔdərit] **1** *adj* moderado (*also Pol*); (*fair, medium*) regular, mediano, mediocre; *price* módico. **2** *n* (*Pol*) moderado *m*, a *f*.
moderate ['mɔdəreit] **1** *vt* moderar; mitigar; *wind etc* calmar. **2** *vi* moderarse; mitigarse; (*wind etc*) calmarse, amainar; (*act as moderator*) arbitrar, servir de asesor.
moderately ['mɔdəritli] *adv* moderadamente; medianamente, mediocremente; módicamente; a — **expensive suit** un traje medianamente caro; **he was — successful** tuvo un razonable éxito.
moderation [,mɔdə'reiʃən] *n* moderación *f*; **in** — con moderación.
moderator ['mɔdəreitə*] *n* árbitro *m*, asesor *m*, ora *f*; **M**— (*Eccl*) *presidente de la asamblea de la Iglesia Escocesa y de otras iglesias protestantes.*
modern ['mɔdən] **1** *adj* moderno. **2** *n* moderno *m*.
modernism ['mɔdənizəm] *n* modernismo *m*.
modernist ['mɔdənist] **1** *adj* modernista. **2** *n* modernista *mf*.
modernistic [,mɔdə'nistik] *adj* modernista.
modernity [mɔ'dəːniti] *n* modernidad *f*.
modernization [,mɔdənai'zeiʃən] *n* modernización *f*; actualización *f*.
modernize ['mɔdənaiz] **1** *vt* modernizar; actualizar. **2** *vi* modernizarse; actualizarse.
modest ['mɔdist] *adj* modesto; moderado; (*chaste etc*) pudoroso, púdico; **to be — about one's successes** hablar en términos modestos de sus triunfos; **to be — in one's demands** ser moderado en sus reclamaciones.
modestly ['mɔdistli] *adv* modestamente; con moderación; pudorosamente.
modesty ['mɔdisti] *n* modestia *f*; moderación *f*; pudor *m*.
modicum ['mɔdikəm] *n*: **with a — of** con una cantidad mínima de, con un poquito de.
modification [,mɔdifi'keiʃən] *n* modificación *f*.
modifier ['mɔdifaiə*] *n* (*Gram*) modificante *m*.
modify ['mɔdifai] *vt* modificar.
modish ['məudiʃ] *adj* muy de moda, sumamente elegante.
modishly ['məudiʃli] *adv* elegantemente; **to be — dressed** ir vestido con suma elegancia.
modiste [məu'diːst] *n* modista *f*.
modulate ['mɔdjuleit] *vti* modular.
modulated ['mɔdjuleitid] *adj* modulado.
modulation [,mɔdju'leiʃən] *n* modulación *f*; **frequency** — (*Radio*) modulación *f* de frecuencia.
mogul ['məugəl] *n* magnate *m*; **the Great M**— el Gran Mogol.
mohair ['məuhɛə*] *n* moer *m*.
Mohammed [məu'hæmed] *m* Mahoma.
Mohammedan [məu'hæmidən] **1** *adj* mahometano. **2** *n* mahometano *m*, a *f*.
Mohammedanism [məu'hæmidənizəm] *n* mahometanismo *m*.
moiré ['mwɑːrei] *n* muaré *m*.
moist [mɔist] *adj* húmedo; mojado.
moisten ['mɔisn] **1** *vt* humedecer, mojar. **2** *vi* humedecerse, mojarse.
moistness ['mɔistnis] *n*, **moisture** ['mɔistʃə*] *n* humedad *f*.
moisturize ['mɔistʃəraiz] *vt* humedecer, mojar.
moke [məuk] *n* (*sl*) burro *m*.
molar ['məulə*] *n* muela *f*.
molasses [mə'læsiz] *n sing and pl* melaza *f*, melazas *fpl*.
mold [məuld] *n etc see* **mould**.
mole¹ [məul] *n* (*Anat*) lunar *m*.
mole² [məul] *n* (*Zool*) topo *m*.
mole³ [məul] *n* (*Naut*) malecón *m*, muelle *m*.
molecular [mə'lekjulə*] *adj* molecular.
molecule ['mɔlikjuːl] *n* molécula *f*.
molehill ['məulhil] *n* topera *f*.
moleskin ['məulskin] *n* piel *f* de topo.
molest [məu'lest] *vt* faltar al respeto a, meterse con, importunar; (*euph*) abordar con propósitos deshonestos.
molestation [,məules'teiʃən] *n* importunidad *f*, vejación *f*.
moll [mɔl] *n* (*sl*) querida *f*.
mollify ['mɔlifai] *vt* apaciguar, calmar; **he was somewhat mollified by this** con esto se calmó un poco.
mollusc ['mɔləsk] *n* molusco *m*.
mollycoddle ['mɔlikɔdl] **1** *n* marica *m*, niño *m* mimado. **2** *vt* mimar.
molten ['məultən] *adj* fundido, derretido; *lava etc* líquido.
molybdenum [mɔ'libdinəm] *n* molibdeno *m*.
moment ['məumənt] *n* (**a**) (*instant*) momento *m*, instante *m*; (*juncture*) momento *m*, coyuntura *f*;

man of the — hombre *m* del momento; **odd —s** momentos *mpl* de ocio (*and see* **odd**); **psychological** — momento *m* psicológico; **at any** — de un momento a otro; **at the** — de momento, por ahora; **at the last** — a última hora; **at this** — en este momento, ahora mismo; **for the** — por el momento; **not for a** — ni por pienso; **in a** — en un momento; **yes, in a** —! ¡sí, en seguida!; **I'll come in a** — vengo en seguida; **it was all over in a** — todo esto ocurrió en un instante; **to leave things until the last** — dejar las cosas hasta última hora; **one** —!, **half a** —!, **wait a** —! ¡un momento!; **I shan't be a** — vuelvo muy pronto; termino muy pronto; ahora mismo; **do it this very** —! ¡hazlo al instante!; **I have just this** — **heard of it** acabo de saberlo; **it won't take a** — es cosa de unos pocos momentos; **tell me the** — **he comes** avíseme en cuanto venga.
(**b**) (*Mech*) momento *m*; — **of inertia** momento *m* de inercia.
(**c**) (*importance*) importancia *f*, momento *m*; **of little** — de poca importancia, de poco momento; **matters of** — asuntos *mpl* de importancia.
momentarily ['məuməntərili] *adv* momentáneamente; *expect etc* de un momento a otro; (*US*) en este momento.
momentary ['məuməntəri] *adj* momentáneo.
momentous [məu'mentəs] *adj* trascendental, muy crítico, de suma importancia, decisivo.
momentousness [məu'mentəsnis] *n* trascendencia *f*, suma importancia *f*, lo decisivo.
momentum [məu'mentəm] *n* momento *m*; (*fig*) ímpetu *m*; **to gather** — cobrar velocidad.
monad ['mɔnæd] *n* mónada *f*.
Mona Lisa ['məunə'liːzə] *f* la Gioconda.
monarch ['mɔnək] *n* monarca *m*.
monarchic(al) [mɔ'nɑːkik(əl)] *adj* monárquico.
monarchism ['mɔnəkizəm] *n* monarquismo *m*.
monarchist ['mɔnəkist] **1** *adj* monárquico. **2** *n* monárquico *m*, a *f*.
monarchy ['mɔnəki] *n* monarquía *f*.
monastery ['mɔnəstri] *n* monasterio *m*.
monastic [mə'næstik] *adj* monástico.
monasticism [mə'næstisizəm] *n* monacato *m*, vida *f* monástica.
Monday ['mʌndi] *n* lunes *m*.
monetary ['mʌnitəri] *adj* monetario.
money ['mʌni] **1** *n* dinero *m*; **paper** — papel *m* moneda, billetes *mpl* de banco; **ready** — dinero *m* contante; **your** — **or your life!** ¡la bolsa o la vida!; — **talks** poderoso caballero es don Dinero; — **makes** — dinero llama dinero; **there's** — **in it** es un buen negocio; **it's a bargain for the** — a ese precio es una verdadera ganga; **that's the team for my** —, ¡ése sí es un equipo!, ¡ése es lo que se llama un equipo!; **it's** — **for jam, it's** — **for old rope** es dinero que se gana sin el menor esfuerzo; **he must be coining** — está forrándose de dinero; **to come into** — heredar una suma de dinero; **bad** — **drives out good** el dinero malo echa fuera al bueno; **to earn good** — tener un buen sueldo; **he gets his** — **on Fridays** cobra los viernes; **when do I get my** —? ¿cuándo cobro?, ¿cuándo me vas a pagar?; **to keep someone in** — proveer a uno de dinero; **he's made of** — es de oro; **do you think I'm made of** —? ¿crees que soy millonario?; **to make** — (*person*) ganar dinero, (*business*) dar dinero, rendir bien; **to make** — **hand over fist** amasar una fortuna; **to be rolling in** — nadar en oro; **to throw good** — **after bad** echar la soga tras el caldero.
2 *attr*: — **payment** pago *m* en metálico; — **prize** premio *m* en metálico; — **matters** asuntos *mpl* financieros.
moneybag ['mʌnibæg] *n* gato *m*, talega *f*; —**s** (*fig*) talegas *fpl*, riqueza *f*.
moneybox ['mʌnibɔks] *n* hucha *f*.
moneychanger ['mʌni,tʃeindʒə*] *n* cambista *mf*.
moneyed ['mʌnid] *adj* adinerado.
moneygrubber ['mʌni,grʌbə*] *n* avaro *m*, a *f*.
moneygrubbing ['mʌni,grʌbiŋ] **1** *adj* avaro, avariento. **2** *n* esfuerzo *m* por enriquecerse, afán *m* de dinero.
moneylender ['mʌni,lendə*] *n* prestamista *mf*.
moneymaker ['mʌni,meikə*] *n* artículo *m* (*or* producto *m*) que rinde grandes beneficios.
moneymaking ['mʌni,meikiŋ] **1** *adj* provechoso, lucrativo. **2** *n* ganancia *f*, lucro *m*.
money market ['mʌni,mɑːkit] *n* mercado *m* de dinero.
money order ['mʌni,ɔːdə*] *n* giro *m* postal.
money's-worth ['mʌnizwəːθ] *n*: **to get one's** — estar satisfecho, estar contento con lo que uno ha adquirido (*etc*); **to get one's** — **out of something** sacar todo el valor de algo.

-monger ['mʌŋgə*] n traficante m en ..., tratante m en ...; see fish- etc.

Mongol ['mɔŋgəl] 1 adj mogol. 2 n mogol m, ola f. 3 n (language) mogol m.

Mongolia [mɔŋ'gəuliə] la Mogolia.

Mongolian [mɔŋ'gəuliən] see **Mongol**.

mongolism ['mɔŋgəlizəm] n mogolismo m.

mongoose ['mɔŋguːs] n, pl **mongooses** ['mɔŋguːsiz] mangosta f.

mongrel ['mʌŋgrəl] 1 adj mestizo; dog mestizo, cruzado, (pej) callejero. 2 n (person) mestizo m, a f; (dog) perro m mestizo, (pej) perro m callejero.

monitor ['mɔnitə*] 1 n (School) monitor m; (Radio: person) escucha mf, monitor m; (TV set) receptor m de control. 2 vt foreign station escuchar; TV programme controlar.

monk [mʌŋk] n monje m.

monkey ['mʌŋki] 1 n mono m, a f, mico m, a f; (fig: child) diablillo m; (sl) 500 libras fpl; **to make a — out of someone** poner a uno en ridículo.

2 vi: **to — about** hacer travesuras, juguetear, hacer diabluras; **to — about with something** manosear algo, (and damage) estropear algo.

monkey business ['mʌŋki,biznis] n trampas fpl, malas mañas fpl.

monkey nut ['mʌŋkinʌt] n cacahuete m.

monkey puzzle ['mʌŋki,pʌzl] n araucaria f.

monkey tricks ['mʌŋki,triks] npl travesuras fpl, diabluras fpl.

monkey wrench ['mʌŋki,rentʃ] n llave f inglesa.

monkish ['mʌŋkiʃ] adj monacal, de monje; monástico; (pej) frailuno.

monkshood ['mʌŋkshud] n (Bot) acónito m.

mono ... ['mɔnəu] mono ...

monochrome ['mɔnəkrəum] 1 adj monocromo m. 2 n monocromo m.

monocle ['mɔnəkl] n monóculo m.

monogamous [mɔ'nɔgəməs] adj monógamo.

monogamy [mɔ'nɔgəmi] n monogamia f.

monogram ['mɔnəgræm] n monograma m.

monograph ['mɔnəgræf] n monografía f.

monolingual [,mɔnəu'liŋgwəl] adj monolingüe.

monolith ['mɔnəuliθ] n monolito m.

monolithic [,mɔnəu'liθik] adj monolítico.

monologue ['mɔnəlɔg] n monólogo m.

monomania [,mɔnəu'meiniə] n monomanía f.

monomial [mɔ'nəumiəl] 1 adj que consta de un solo término. 2 n monomio m.

monoplane ['mɔnəplein] n monoplano m.

monopolize [mə'nɔpəlaiz] vt monopolizar (also fig), acaparar.

monopoly [mə'nɔpəli] n monopolio m.

monorail ['mɔnəureil] n monorail m, monocarril m.

monosyllabic ['mɔnəusi'læbik] adj word monosílabo; utterance monosilábico.

monosyllable ['mɔnə,siləbl] n monosílabo m.

monotheism ['mɔnəu,θiːizəm] n monoteísmo m.

monotheist ['mɔnəu,θiːist] n monoteísta mf.

monotheistic [,mɔnəuθiː'istik] adj monoteísta.

monotone ['mɔnətəun] n monotonía f; **to speak in a —** hablar en un solo tono.

monotonous [mə'nɔtənəs] adj monótono.

monotony [mə'nɔtəni] n monotonía f.

monotype ['mɔnəutaip] n monotipia f; **— machine** máquina f monotipo.

monoxide [mɔ'nɔksaid] n monóxido m.

monseigneur [,mɔnsen'jə:*] n monseñor m.

monsignor [mɔn'siːnjə*] n monseñor m.

monsoon [mɔn'suːn] n monzón m or f; **the — rains** las lluvias monzónicas.

monster ['mɔnstə*] 1 adj enorme, monstruoso; (hum) grandísimo.

2 n monstruo m; **a real — of a fish** un pez verdaderamente enorme; **a — of greed** un monstruo de la avaricia.

monstrance ['mɔnstrəns] n (Eccl) custodia f.

monstrosity [mɔns'trɔsiti] n monstruosidad f.

monstrous ['mɔnstrəs] adj monstruoso, enorme; **it is — that ...** es terriblemente injusto que + subj.

monstrously ['mɔnstrəsli] adv enormemente; **— unfair** terriblemente injusto.

montage [mɔn'taːʒ] n montaje m.

month [mʌnθ] n mes m; **30 dollars a —** 30 dólares al mes, 30 dólares mensuales; **not in a — of Sundays** jamás; **it went on for —s** duró meses y meses.

monthly ['mʌnθli] 1 adj mensual.

2 adv cada mes, mensualmente; **40 dollars — 40** dólares al mes, 40 dólares mensuales.

3 n revista f mensual; **monthlies** (Med) reglas fpl.

monument ['mɔnjumənt] n monumento m (to de, que conmemora).

monumental [,mɔnju'mentl] adj monumental; ignorance terrible; error garrafal.

moo [muː] 1 n mugido m. 2 vi mugir, hacer mu.

mooch [muːtʃ] vi (fam): **to — about** no saber qué hacer, no tener nada que hacer, haraganear; **to — along** andar arrastrando los pies.

mood[1] [muːd] n (Gram) modo m; **imperative — modo** m imperativo; **subjunctive —** modo m subjuntivo.

mood[2] [muːd] n humor m; disposición f (de ánimo); capricho m; **to be in a bad —** estar de mal humor; **to be in a good —** estar de buen humor; **to be in a generous —** sentirse generoso; **to be in an ugly —** (person) estar de muy mal humor, (crowd) amenazar violencia; **to be in a forgiving —** estar dispuesto a perdonar; **to be in no laughing —**, **to be in no — for laughing** no tener ganas de reír; **are you in a — for chess?** ¿te apetece una partida de ajedrez?, ¿quieres jugar al ajedrez?; **to be in the — (for love)** sentirse amoroso; **I'm not in the —** no quiero; **he plays well when he's in the —** toca bien cuando está de vena; **he's in one of his —s** está en uno de sus momentos de mal humor; **that depends on his —** eso es según el humor que tenga; **he has —s (of anger)** tiene arranques de cólera, (of gloom) tiene sus rachas de melancolía.

moodily ['muːdili] adv answer etc malhumoradamente; melancólicamente.

moodiness ['muːdinis] n mal humor m; melancolía f; propensión f a cambiar bruscamente de humor.

moody ['muːdi] adj: **to be —** (angry) tener arranques de cólera, (gloomy) tener rachas de melancolía; (variable) ser propenso a cambiar bruscamente de humor.

moon [muːn] 1 n luna f; (poet) mes m; **crescent — media luna** f; **full —** luna f llena, plenilunio m; **new — luna** f nueva, novilunio m; **once in a blue —** de guindas a brevas, de Pascuas a Ramos; **to ask (or cry) for the —** pedir peras al olmo; **to promise the — prometer** el oro y el moro, prometer la luna.

2 vt: **to — away a couple of hours** pasar un par de horas sin hacer nada, pasar un par de horas soñando.

3 vi: **to — about** mirar a las musarañas, pasar el tiempo sin hacer nada; parecer estar soñando despierto.

moonbeam ['muːnbiːm] n rayo m de luna.

moonless ['muːnlis] adj sin luna.

moonlight ['muːnlait] 1 n luz f de la luna; **by —, in the —** a la luz de la luna; **— flit** mudanza f a la chita callando; **it was —** había luna.

2 vi (US fam) tener un empleo secundario además del principal.

moonlit ['muːnlit] adj object iluminado por la luna; night de luna.

moonrise ['muːnraiz] n salida f de la luna.

moonshine ['muːnʃain] n luz f de la luna; (fam: nonsense) pamplinas fpl, música f celestial; (US sl) licor m destilado ilegalmente; **that's just —!** ¡es puro cuento¡

moonshiner ['muːnʃainə*] n (US sl) fabricante m de licor ilegal.

moonstone ['muːnstəun] n adularia f.

moonstruck ['muːnstrʌk] adj tocado, que tiene el juicio trastornado, lunático.

Moor [muə*] n moro m, a f.

moor[1] [muə*] n páramo m, brezal m; (for game) coto m.

moor[2] [muə*] 1 vt amarrar. 2 vi echar las amarras.

moorhen ['muəhen] n polla f de agua.

moorings ['muəriŋz] npl (ropes) amarras fpl; (place) amarradero m.

Moorish ['muəriʃ] adj moro; (Archit etc) árabe; arch arábigo.

moorland ['muələnd] n páramo m, brezal m.

moose [muːs] n alce m de América.

moot [muːt] 1 n junta f, asamblea f.

2 adj point, question discutible.

3 vt proponer para la discusión; **it has been —ed whether ...** se ha discutido si ...; **when the question was first —ed** cuando se discutió la cuestión por primera vez.

mop [mɔp] 1 n (implement) fregasuelos m, lampazo m; (hair) mata f, greña f; **— of hair** pelambrera f.

2 vt fregar, limpiar; brow enjugar; **to — up floor, liquid** limpiar, enjugar; (absorb) absorber; (dry up) secar; (Mil) terrain limpiar, remnants acabar con; (fam) beberse.

mope [məup] vi estar deprimido, estar abatido; **to — about** andar alicaído; **to — for someone** resentirse de la ausencia de uno, estar triste por la pérdida de uno.

moped ['məuped] n ciclomotor m.

mopes [məups] npl depresión f, melancolía f.

moping ['məupiŋ] *adj*, **mopish** ['məupiʃ] *adj* abatido, melancólico.
moquette [mə'ket] *n* moqueta *f*.
moraine [mɔ'rein] *n* (*Geol*) morena *f*.
moral ['mɔrəl] **1** *adj* moral; *philosophy, support, victory* moral; (*chaste*) virtuoso; (*honourable*) honrado.
 2 *n* (a) (*of story*) moraleja *f*; sentido *m* moral; **to draw a — from** sacar una moraleja de; **to point the —** hacer resaltar la moraleja.
 (b) **—s** moral *f*, ética *f*; moralidad *f*; (*conduct*) costumbres *fpl*; **the —s of actors** la moralidad de los actores; **she has no —s** no tiene sentido moral, carece de toda noción de la moralidad.
morale [mɔ'rɑ:l] *n* moral *f*.
moralist ['mɔrəlist] *n* moralizador *m*, ora *f*; (*philosopher, teacher*) moralista *mf*.
morality [mə'ræliti] *n* moralidad *f*.
morality play [mə'ræliti,plei] *n* moralidad *f*.
moralize ['mɔrəlaiz] *vti* moralizar.
moralizing ['mɔrəlaiziŋ] **1** *adj* moralizador. **2** *n* instrucción *f* moral, predicación *f* sobre la moralidad.
morally ['mɔrəli] *adv* moralmente.
morass [mə'ræs] *n* cenagal *m*, pantano *m*; **a — of problems** un laberinto de problemas; **a — of figures** un mar de cifras.
moratorium [,mɔrə'tɔ:riəm] *n* moratoria *f*.
moray ['mɔrei] *n* morena *f*.
morbid ['mɔ:bid] *adj* insano, malsano; *mind* enfermizo; (*Med*) mórbido; (*depressed*) pesimista, melancólico; **don't be so —!** ¡no digas esas cosas horribles!
morbidity [mɔ:'biditi] *n*, **morbidness** ['mɔ:bidnis] *n* lo insano, lo malsano; lo enfermizo; (*Med*) morbosidad *f*; pesimismo *m*.
morbidly ['mɔ:bidli] *adv* talk *etc* en tono pesimista; *think etc* con pesimismo.
mordacity [mɔ:'dæsiti] *n* mordacidad *f*.
mordant ['mɔ:dənt] *adj* mordaz.
more [mɔ:*] **1** *adj* (a) más; **you have — money than I** Vd tiene más dinero que yo; **— light, please!** ¡más luz, por favor!; **a few — weeks** algunas semanas más; **do you want some — tea?** ¿quieres más té?; **is there any — wine in the bottle?** ¿queda vino en la botella?; **many — people** muchas más personas; **much — butter** mucha más mantequilla.
 (b) (*numerals*) **— than half** más de la mitad; **— than one** más de uno; **— than 15** más de 15; **not — than one** no más de uno; **not — than 15** no más de quince.
 2 *n and pron* más; **we can't afford —** no podemos pagar más; **this house cost — than ours** esta casa costó más que la nuestra; **it cost — than we had expected** costó más de lo que esperábamos; **I shall have — to say about this** volveré a hablar de esto; **and what's —** . . . y además . . .
 3 *adv* más; **— easily** más fácilmente, con mayor facilidad (*than* que); **— and —** más y más, cada vez más; **— or less** más o menos; **neither — nor less** ni más ni menos; **once —** otra vez, una vez más; **never — nunca** más; **if he comes here any —** si vuelve por aquí; **if he says that any —** si dice eso otra vez; **the house is — than half built** la casa está más que medio construida; **I had — than carried out my obligation** había cumplido con creces mi obligación; **it will — than meet the demand** satisfará ampliamente la demanda; **he was — surprised than angry** más que enfadarse se sorprendió; **it's — a short story than a novel** más que novela es un cuento.
 4 (*the —*) **the — you give him the — he wants** cuanto más se le da tanto más quiere; **the — he drank the thirstier he got** cuanto más bebía más sed tenía; **it makes me** (*all*) **the — ashamed** tanto más vergüenza me da; **all the — so because** . . . tanto más cuanto que . . .; **the — the merrier** cuantos más mejor.
 5 (*no — etc*) **I have no — pennies** no tengo más peniques; **no — singing, I can't bear it!** ¡que no se cante más, no lo aguanto!; **let's say no — about it** no se hable más de esto; **he doesn't live here any —** ya no vive aquí; **Queen Anne is no —** la reina Ana ya no existe; **we shall see her no —** no la volveremos a ver; **"I don't understand it"** . . . **"no — do I"** "no lo comprendo" . . . **"ni yo tampoco"**; **she's no — a duchess than I am** tan duquesa es como mi padre; **he no — thought of paying me than of flying to the moon** antes iría volando a la luna que pensar pagarme a mí.
moreover [mɔ:'rəuvə*] *adv* además, por otra parte.
mores ['mɔ:reiz] *npl* costumbres *fpl*, tradiciones *fpl*; moralidad *f*.
morganatic [,mɔ:gə'nætik] *adj* morganático.

morganatically [,mɔ:gə'nætikəli] *adv*: **he married her —** se casó con ella en casamiento morganático.
morgue [mɔ:g] *n* depósito *m* de cadáveres.
moribund ['mɔribʌnd] *adj* moribundo (*also fig*).
Mormon ['mɔ:mən] **1** *adj* mormónico. **2** *n* mormón *m*, ona *f*.
Mormonism ['mɔ:mənizəm] *n* mormonismo *m*.
morn [mɔ:n] *n* (*poet*) see **morning**; (*dawn*) alborada *f*.
morning ['mɔ:niŋ] **1** *n* mañana *f*; (*before dawn*) madrugada *f*; **good —!** ¡buenos días!; **the — after** (*hum*) la mañana después de la juerga; **the next —** la mañana siguiente, a la mañana; **early in the —** muy de mañana; **in the —** por la mañana; **at 7 o'clock in the —** a las 7 de la mañana; **at 3 in the —** a las 3 de la madrugada; **tomorrow —** mañana por la mañana; **yesterday —** ayer por la mañana.
 2 *adj*, *attr* de (la) mañana; *light, star* del alba; *newspaper, train etc* de la mañana.
morning coat ['mɔ:niŋ,kəut] *n* chaqué *m*.
morning-glory ['mɔ:niŋ'glɔ:ri] *n* dondiego *m* de día.
morning sickness ['mɔ:niŋ'siknis] *n* vómitos *mpl* del embarazo, achaques *mpl* mañaneros.
Moroccan [mə'rɔkən] **1** *adj* marroquí. **2** *n* marroquí *mf*.
Morocco [mə'rɔkəu] Marruecos *m*.
morocco [mə'rɔkəu] *n* (*also — leather*) marroquí *m*, tafilete *m*.
moron ['mɔ:rɔn] *n* imbécil *mf*.
moronic [mə'rɔnik] *adj* imbécil.
morose [mə'rəus] *adj* malhumorado, hosco, taciturno.
morpheme ['mɔ:fi:m] *n* morfema *m*.
morphia ['mɔ:fiə] *n*, **morphine** ['mɔ:fi:n] *n* morfina *f*.
morphological [,mɔ:fə'lɔdʒikəl] *adj* morfológico.
morphology [mɔ:'fɔlədʒi] *n* morfología *f*.
morrow ['mɔrəu] *n* (*lit*): **on the —** al día siguiente.
Morse [mɔ:s] *n*: **— code** alfabeto *m* Morse.
morsel ['mɔ:sl] *n* (*small piece*) pedazo *m*, fragmento *m*; (*of food*) bocado *m*.
mortal ['mɔ:tl] **1** *adj* mortal. **2** *n* mortal *mf*.
mortality [mɔ:'tæliti] *n* mortalidad *f*; (*number killed in war, accident*) mortandad *f*, número *m* de víctimas; **infantile —** mortalidad *f* infantil; **there was heavy —** hubo numerosas víctimas, murieron muchos.
mortally ['mɔ:təli] *adv* mortalmente; **— wounded** herido de muerte; **— offended** mortalmente ofendido.
mortar ['mɔ:tə*] **1** *n* (*Tech, Mil*) mortero *m*. **2** *vt* bombardear con morteros.
mortarboard ['mɔ:tɔ:bɔ:d] *n* (*Univ*) birrete *m*.
mortgage ['mɔ:gidʒ] **1** *n* hipoteca *f*; **to pay off a —** redimir una hipoteca; **to raise a —, to take out a —** obtener una hipoteca (*on* sobre).
 2 *vt* hipotecar; (*fig*) vender, poner en manos ajenas.
mortgagee [,mɔ:gə'dʒi:] *n* acreedor *m* hipotecario, acreedora *f* hipotecaria.
mortgagor ['mɔ:gədʒə*] *n* deudor *m* hipotecario, deudora *f* hipotecaria.
mortification [,mɔ:tifi'keiʃən] *n* mortificación *f*; humillación *f*; (*Med*) gangrena *f*.
mortify ['mɔ:tifai] **1** *vt* mortificar; humillar; **I was mortified to find that** . . . me avergoncé al descubrir que . . . **2** *vi* (*Med*) gangrenarse.
mortifying ['mɔ:tifaiiŋ] *adj* humillante.
mortise, mortice ['mɔ:tis] *n* muesca *f*, mortaja *f*.
mortuary ['mɔ:tjuəri] **1** *adj* mortuorio. **2** *n* depósito *m* de cadáveres.
Mosaic [məu'zeiik] *adj* mosaico.
mosaic [məu'zeiik] *n* mosaico *m*.
Moscow ['mɔskəu] Moscú *m*.
Moselle [məu'zel] Mosela *m*.
Moses ['məuzis] *m* Moisés.
Moses basket ['məuzis,bɑ:skit] *n* moisés *m*.
Moslem ['mɔzlem] **1** *adj* musulmán. **2** *n* musulmán *m*, ana *f*.
mosque [mɔsk] *n* mezquita *f*.
mosquito [mɔs'ki:təu] *n*, *pl* **—oes** [əuz] mosquito *m*.
mosquito net [mɔs'ki:təu,net] *n* mosquitero *m*.
moss [mɔs] *n* (*Bot*) musgo *m*; (*Geog*) pantano *m*, marjal *m*.
mossy ['mɔsi] *adj* musgoso, cubierto de musgo.
most [məust] **1** *adj superl* (a) (*with sing*) más; **who has — money?** ¿quién tiene más dinero?
 (b) (*with pl*) **— men** la mayor parte de los hombres, la mayoría de los hombres, los más hombres, casi todos los hombres.
 2 *n and pron*: **do the — you can** haga todo lo que pueda; **— of them** casi todos ellos; **— of those present** la mayor parte de los asistentes; **— of the time** la mayor parte del tiempo; **at —, at the —, at the very —** a lo más, a lo sumo, todo lo más; **it's the**

—! (*sl*) ¡es fenomenal! (*fam*); **this group is the** —! (*sl*) ¡este conjunto es fabuloso! (*fam*); **the girl with the** — (*sl*) la chica más atractiva; **to make the** — **of an affair** sacar el mejor partido de un asunto; **to make the** — **of one's advantages** aprovechar bien sus ventajas; **he made the** — **of the story** explotó todas las posibilidades del cuento, exageró los detalles del cuento.

3 *adv* (**a**) *superl* **he spent** — él gastó más; **the** — **attractive girl there** la chica más atractiva allí; **the** — **difficult of our problems** el más difícil de nuestros problemas; **which one did it** — **easily?** ¿quién lo hizo con la mayor facilidad?

(**b**) (*intensive*) muy, sumamente; — **likely** muy probable; **a** — **expensive toy** un juguete de los más caros, un juguete carísimo; **a** — **interesting book** un libro de lo más interesante, un libro interesantísimo; **you have been** — **kind** Vd ha sido muy amable; — **holy** santísimo; — **reverend** reverendísimo; *see* **all**, **part** *etc*.

-most [məust] más, *eg* **centremost** más central, **furthermost** más lejano.

mostly ['məustli] *adv* en su mayor parte; principalmente; en su mayoría; en general; **they are** — **women** en su mayoría son mujeres, casi todas son mujeres; — **because** . . . principalmente porque . . . ; **we** — **sell retail** en general vendemos al detalle, principalmente vendemos al por menor; **it's** — **finished** está casi terminado.

mote [məut] *n* átomo *m*, mota *f*; **to see the** — **in our neighbour's eye and not the beam in our own** ver la paja en el ojo ajeno y no la viga en el propio.

motel [məu'tel] *n* motel *m*.

motet [məu'tet] *n* motete *m*.

moth [mɔθ] *n* mariposa *f* (nocturna); (*clothes-*) polilla *f*.

mothball ['mɔθbɔːl] *n* bola *f* de naftalina; **in** —**s** (*Naut etc*) en la reserva.

moth-eaten ['mɔθ,iːtn] *adj* apolillado, comido de la polilla.

mother ['mʌðə*] **1** *n* madre *f*; **M**— **of God** Madre *f* de Dios; **M**— **Superior** superiora *f*, madre *f* superiora; **to be a** — **to someone** ser como una madre para uno.

2 *adj*, *attr* madre; *tongue etc* materno; *love etc* maternal; *see* **country** *etc*.

3 *vt* (*give birth to*) parir, dar a luz; (*act as* — *to*) servir de madre a; (*spoil*) mimar; *young animal* prohijar.

mothercraft ['mʌðəkrɑːft] *n* arte *m* de cuidar a los niños pequeños, arte *m* de ser madre.

motherhood ['mʌðəhud] *n* maternidad *f*; **to prepare for** — prepararse para ser madre.

mother-in-law ['mʌðərinlɔː] *n*, *pl* **mothers-in-law** ['mʌðəzinlɔː] suegra *f*.

motherland ['mʌðəlænd] *n* patria *f*, (*more sentimentally*) madre patria *f*.

motherless ['mʌðəlis] *adj* huérfano de madre, sin madre.

motherly ['mʌðəli] *adj* maternal.

mother-of-pearl ['mʌðərəv'pəːl] **1** *n* nácar *m*. **2** *adj* nacarado.

mother ship ['mʌðəʃip] *n* buque *m* nodriza.

mother-to-be ['mʌðətə'biː] *n*, *pl* **mothers-to-be** ['mʌðəztə'biː] futura madre *f*.

moth-hole ['mɔθhəul] *n* apolilladura *f*.

mothproof ['mɔθpruːf] *adj* a prueba de polillas.

motif [məu'tiːf] *n* (*Art*, *Mus*) motivo *m*; (*of speech etc*) tema *m*; (*Sew*) adorno *m*.

motion ['məuʃən] **1** *n* (**a**) (*movement*) movimiento *m*; (*of parts of machine*) marcha *f*, operación *f*, funcionamiento *m*; **perpetual** — movimiento *m* perpetuo; **to be in** — estar en movimiento; **to go through the** —**s** hacer algo en la debida forma, obrar de acuerdo con las reglas (pero sin creer que se vaya a conseguir nada); obrar por pura fórmula; **to set something in** — poner algo en marcha.

(**b**) (*sign*) ademán *m*, señal *f*; **he made a** — **with his hand** hizo una señal con la mano.

(**c**) (*Parl etc*) moción *f*, proposición *f*; **to bring forward** (*or propose*, *US* **make**) **a** — presentar una moción; **to carry a** — (*person*) hacer adoptar una moción, (*meeting*) adoptar una moción, aprobar una moción; **to vote on a** — votar una moción; **the** — **is carried** se ha aprobado la moción; **the** — **is lost** se ha rechazado la moción.

(**d**) (*Mech*, *moving part*) mecanismo *m*.

(**e**) (*Med*) movimiento *m* del vientre.

2 *vti*: **to** — (**to**) **someone to do something** hacer señas a uno para que haga algo, indicar a uno con la mano (*etc*) que haga algo; **he** —**ed me to a chair** indicó con la mano que me sentara.

motionless ['məuʃənlis] *adj* inmóvil.

motion picture ['məuʃən,piktʃə*] (*US*) **1** *n* película *f*.

2 *attr* **motion-picture** cinematográfico; — **camera** cámara *f* cinematográfica; — **industry** industria *f* del cine; — **theatre**, (*US*) **theater** cine *m*.

motivate ['məutiveit] *vt* motivar.

motivation [,məuti'veiʃən] *n* motivación *f*.

motive ['məutiv] **1** *adj* (*f*: motora, motriz).

2 *n* motivo *m* (**for** de); móvil *m*; **profit** — afán *m* de lucro; **ulterior** — motivo *m* oculto; **what can his** — **have been?** ¿cuál habrá sido su motivo?, ¿qué motivo habrá tenido?; **my** —**s were of the purest** lo hice con la mejor intención.

motiveless ['məutivlis] *adv* sin motivo, inmotivado.

motley ['mɔtli] **1** *adj* (*many-coloured*) abigarrado, multicolor; (*diversified*) vario, compuesto de elementos muy diversos.

2 *n* botarga *f*, traje *m* de colores; **on with the** — vistámonos de payaso.

motor ['məutə*] **1** *adj* (*giving motion*) motor; (*motorized*) automóvil.

2 *n* (*engine*) motor *m*; (*car*) coche *m*, automóvil *m*.

3 *vi* ir en coche, viajar en automóvil; **we** —**ed down to Ascot** fuimos en coche a Ascot; **we** —**ed over to see them** fuimos a visitarles (en coche).

motorbike ['məutəbaik] *n* (*fam*) moto *f*.

motorboat ['məutəbəut] *n* motora *f*, motorbote *m*, lancha *f* rápida, lancha *f* automóvil.

motor bus ['məutəbʌs] *n* autobús *m*.

motorcade ['məutəkeid] *n* caravana *f* de automóviles.

motorcar ['məutəkɑː*] *n* coche *m*, automóvil *m*.

motor coach ['məutəkəutʃ] *n* autocar *m*.

motorcycle ['məutə,saikl] *n* motocicleta *f*; —**combination** motocicleta *f* con sidecar.

motorcycling ['məutə,saikliŋ] *n* motorismo *m*.

motorcyclist ['məutə,saiklist] *n* motorista *mf*.

motor-driven ['məutə'drivn] *adj* automóvil, propulsado por motor.

-motored ['məutəd] *adj*: *eg* **four-motored** cuatrimotor, tetramotor; **petrol-motored** propulsado por gasolina.

motoring ['məutəriŋ] **1** *adj* *accident etc* de automóvil, automovilístico, de carretera; **the** — **public** el público aficionado al automovilismo.

2 *n* automovilismo *m*.

motoring school ['məutəriŋ,skuːl] *n* autoescuela *f*, escuela *f* automovilista.

motorist ['məutərist] *n* automovilista *mf*; conductor *m*, ora *f* (de coche), chófer *m*; — **racing** — corredor *m* automovilista.

motorization [,məutərai'zeiʃən] *n* motorización *f*.

motorize ['məutəraiz] *vt* motorizar; **to get** —**d** (*fam*) adquirir un coche; **now that we're** —**d** (*fam*) ahora que tenemos coche.

motorized ['məutəraizd] *adj* motorizado.

motor launch ['məutələːntʃ] *n* lancha *f* automóvil, lancha *f* motora.

motor lorry ['məutə,lɔri] *n* camión *m*.

motorman ['məutəmən] *n*, *pl* —**men** [mən] *n* conductor *m* (de locomotora eléctrica *etc*), maquinista *m*.

motor oil ['məutər,ɔil] *n* aceite *m* para motores.

motor racing ['məutə,reisiŋ] *n* automovilismo *m* deportivo, carreras *fpl* de coches.

motor road ['məutə,rəud] *n* autopista *f*.

motor scooter ['məutə,skuːtə*] *n* motosilla *f*, escúter *m*, moto *f*.

motor ship ['məutəʃip] *n* motonave *f*.

motor show ['məutə,ʃəu] *n* exposición *f* de automóviles; **the Paris** — el salón del automóvil de París.

motor spirit ['məutə,spirit] *n* bencina *f*, gasolina *f* (de auto).

motor vehicle ['məutə,viːikl] *n* automóvil *m*.

motor vessel ['məutə,vesl] *n* motonave *f*.

motorway ['məutəwei] *n* autopista *f*.

mottled ['mɔtld] *adj* abigarrado, multicolor; *marble etc* jaspeado; *complexion* con manchas; *animal*, *bird* con manchas, moteado; — **with** manchado de, pintado de.

motto ['mɔtəu] *n*, *pl* **mottoes** ['mɔtəuz] lema *m*; (*Heraldry*) divisa *f*; (*watchword*) consigna *f*; (*in cracker*: *verse*) versos *mpl*, (*joke*) chiste *m*.

mould¹, (*US*) **mold** [məuld] *n* (*soil*) mantillo *m*.

mould², (*US*) **mold** [məuld] **1** *n* (*hollow form*) molde *m*; (—*ed object*) cosa *f* moldeada; (*fig*) carácter *m*, índole *f*, temple *m*; **cast in a heroic** — de carácter heroico.

2 *vt* (*fashion*) moldear; (*cast*) vaciar; (*Carpentry*) moldurar; (*fig*) amoldar (**on** a), formar; **it is** —**ed on** . . . está hecho según . . .

3 *vr*: **to** — **oneself on someone** amoldarse por uno, modelarse sobre uno, tomar a uno como ejemplo.

mould³, (US) **mold** [məuld] n (fungus) moho m; (iron-) mancha f de orín.

moulder¹, (US) **molder** ['məuldə*] n (Tech) moldeador m, ora f.

moulder², (US) **molder** ['məuldə*] vi (also to — away) desmoronarse, convertirse en polvo; (fig) desmoronarse, decaer.

mouldiness, (US) **moldiness** ['məuldinis] n moho m, lo mohoso, enmohecimiento m.

moulding, (US) **molding** ['məuldiŋ] n (act) amoldamiento m; (cast) vaciado m; (Archit) moldura f; (fig) amoldamiento m, formación f.

mouldy, (US) **moldy** ['məuldi] adj mohoso, enmohecido; (sl) horrible, malísimo; miserable, cochino; **the play was —** la obra fue horrible; **all he gave me was a — old penny** lo único que me dio fue un cochino penique.

moult, (US) **molt** [məult] **1** n muda f. **2** vt mudar. **3** vi (snake etc) mudar la piel, (bird) mudar la pluma.

mound [maund] n (pile) montón m; (earthwork) terraplén m; (burial-) túmulo m; (hillock) montículo m.

mount [maunt] **1** n (a) (hill) montón m, (hillock) montículo m.
(b) (horse etc) montura f, caballería f.
(c) (of machine etc) base f, soporte m; (of jewel) engaste m; (of photo etc) borde m, marco m: (stamp-) fijasello m.
2 vt (a) horse montar, subir a; platform etc subir a, subir en; ladder subir; throne subir a.
(b) machine etc montar, armar; play poner en escena; exhibition organizar; attack lanzar, hacer.
(c) picture poner un borde a, poner un marco a; stamp pegar, fijar; jewel engastar.
(d) guard montar.
(e) (provide with horse) proveer de caballo.
3 vi (climb) subir; (get on horse) montar; (of quantity, price etc; also to — up) subir, aumentar.

mountain ['mauntin] **1** n montaña f; (pile) montón m; **to make a — out of a molehill** hacer de una pulga un elefante.
2 adj, attr montañés, de montaña; montañero, serrano.

mountain ash ['mauntin'æʃ] n serbal m.

mountaineer [,maunti'niə*] **1** n montañero m, a f, alpinista mf. **2** vi dedicarse al montañismo, hacer alpinismo.

mountaineering [,maunti'niəriŋ] **1** n montañismo m, alpinismo m. **2** adj, attr montañero, alpinista; **in — circles** en los medios montañeros.

mountainous ['mauntinəs] adj montañoso; (fig) enorme, colosal.

mountainside ['mauntin,said] n ladera f de montaña, falda f de montaña.

mountebank ['mauntibæŋk] n saltabanco m, saltimbanqui m.

mounted ['mauntid] adj montado.

mounting ['mauntiŋ] n (of machine: act) montaje m; (frame, base) armadura f, base f, soporte m; (of jewel) engaste m; (of photo etc) marco m.

mourn [mɔːn] **1** vt llorar, llorar la muerte de, lamentar; (wear —ing for) llevar luto por.
2 vi afligirse, lamentarse; (wear —ing) estar de luto; **to — for someone** llorar la muerte de uno; **to — for something** llorar la pérdida (or desaparición etc) de algo; **it's no good —ing over it** de nada sirve afligirse por eso.

mourner ['mɔːnə*] n doliente mf; (hired) plañidero m, a f; **the —s** los que acompañan el féretro.

mournful ['mɔːnful] adj person triste, afligido; tone, sound triste, lúgubre, lastimero; occasion triste, melancólico.

mournfully ['mɔːnfəli] adv tristemente.

mournfulness ['mɔːnfulnis] n tristeza f; aflicción f; melancolía f.

mourning ['mɔːniŋ] **1** n (act) lamentación f; (period etc) luto m, duelo m; (dress) luto m; **deep —** luto m riguroso; **half —** medio luto m; **to be in —** estar de luto; **to be in — for** llevar luto por; **to come out of —** dejar el luto; **to go into —** ponerse de luto; **to plunge a town into —** enlutar una ciudad.
2 attr de luto.

mouse [maus] **1** n, pl **mice** [mais] ratón m. **2** vi cazar ratones.

mousehole ['maushəul] n ratonera f.

mouser ['mausə*] n cazador m de ratones.

mousetrap ['maustræp] n ratonera f.

moustache [məs'taːʃ, US 'mʌstæʃ] n bigote m, bigotes mpl, mostacho m; **walrus —** bigotes mpl de foca; **to wear a —** tener bigote.

mousy ['mausi] adj person tímido, de personalidad poco fuerte; colour pardusco.

mouth [mauθ] n, pl **mouths** [mauðz] boca f; (fig, of bottle, cave etc) boca f; (of river) desembocadura f; (of channel) embocadero m; (of wind instrument) boquilla f; **to be down in the —** estar deprimido, andar alicaído; **to foam** (or froth) **at the —** espumajear; **to keep one's — shut** (fig) tener la boca cerrada, guardar un secreto; **he never opened his — at the meeting** en la reunión no abrió la boca; **she didn't dare to open her —** no se atrevió a decir ni pío; **to put words into someone's —** atribuir (falsamente) una declaración a uno; **to shoot off one's —** hablar inoportunamente, hablar más de la cuenta; **to stop someone's —** hacer callar a uno; see **water** etc.

mouth [mauð] **1** vt (affectedly) pronunciar con afectación, articular con rimbombancia; (soundlessly) formar con los labios.
2 vi hablar exagerando los movimientos de la boca.

mouthed [mauðd] adj de boca . . ., que tiene la boca . . ., eg **big-mouthed** de boca grande.

mouthful ['mauθful] n bocado m; (of smoke, air) bocanada f; **the name is a proper —** es un nombre kilométrico.

mouth organ ['mauθ,ɔːgən] n armónica f.

mouthpiece ['mauθpiːs] n (Mus) boquilla f; (of bridle) embocadura f; (Tel) micrófono m; (fig, person) portavoz m.

mouthwash ['mauθwɔʃ] n enjuague m.

mouth-watering ['mauθ'wɔːtəriŋ] adj sumamente apetitoso.

movable ['muːvəbl] **1** adj movible; **not easily —** nada fácil de mover. **2 —s** npl muebles mpl, mobiliario m; (Law) bienes mpl muebles.

move [muːv] **1** n (a) (movement) movimiento m; **Spain is a country on the —** España es país en marcha; **to be always on the —** estar siempre en movimiento; (travelling) estar siempre de viaje, (of animal, child) no saber estar quieto; **to get a — on** (person) menearse, darse prisa; (process etc) hacer grandes progresos, avanzar rápidamente; **get a — on!** ¡menéarse!, ¡espabílate!; **they're getting a — on with the bridge now** ahora la construcción del puente avanza rápidamente; **to make a — (to go)** ponerse en marcha; **it's time we made a —** es hora de irnos; **it was midnight and no-one had made a —** era medianoche pero nadie se había ido.
(b) (in game) jugada f; (at chess) jugada f, movida f; **key —** movida f clave; **it's my — yo juego**; **whose — is it?** ¿a quién le toca jugar?; **he's up to every — in the game** se las sabe todas; **to have first —** empezar, salir, jugar primero; **to make a —** hacer una jugada, jugar.
(c) (step) paso m, acción f; gestión f; maniobra f; **the government's first —** la primera gestión del gobierno; **false —** paso m en falso; **what's the next —?** ¿qué hacemos ahora?, y ahora ¿qué?; **to make a — dar** un paso; tomar medidas; **it's up to him to make the first —** le toca a él dar el primer paso; **without making the least —** + infin sin hacer la menor intención de + infin; **to watch someone's every —** observar a uno sin perder detalle.
(d) (of house) mudanza f; **it's our third — in two years** ésta es la tercera vez en dos años que nos mudamos; **then he made a — to Buenos Aires** luego se trasladó a Buenos Aires.
2 vt (a) (change place of) mover; cambiar de sitio, trasladar; (transport) transportar; (propel) propulsar, impeler; **he was —d to Quito** le trasladaron a Quito; **if we can — the table a few inches** si podemos mover la mesa unos centímetros; **to — a piece** (Chess) jugar una pieza.
(b) **to — house** mudarse; **to — one's job** cambiar de empleo.
(c) (cause to —) remover, agitar, sacudir, menear; **the breeze —d the leaves gently** la brisa agitaba dulcemente las hojas; **to — the bowels** desocupar el vientre.
(d) (person, from opinion) hacer cambiar de opinión; **he will not be easily —d** no será fácil hacerle cambiar de idea.
(e) (emotionally) conmover, enternecer; impresionar; **to be easily —d** ser impresionable, ser sensible; **to — someone to do something** mover a uno a hacer algo; **when I feel so —d** cuando estoy de humor para ello; **to — someone to anger** encolerizar a uno; **to — someone to tears** hacer que uno llore; see **pity**.
(f) (Parl) **to — a resolution** proponer una resolución, hacer una moción; **to — that . . .** proponer que + subj.
(g) (with adv or prep) **to — something aside**

apartar algo; **to — something away** alejar algo, apartar algo; quitar algo de en medio; **to — back** mover hacia atrás; (*postpone*) aplazar; **to — forward** mover hacia adelante; (*help progress*) avanzar, adelantar, promover; *meeting etc* adelantar la fecha de; **to — people on** hacer circular la gente; **to — someone out** desalojar a uno, trasladar a uno a otra parte; **to — up troops** mover las tropas hacia el frente; **we'll — your luggage up** le subiremos el equipaje; **to — a child up a class** trasladar a un niño a una clase superior; **he was —d up into the next grade** le ascendieron al grado superior.

3 *vi* **(a)** (*in general*) moverse; (*to a place*) trasladarse (*to a*); (*shake*) moverse, agitarse, temblar; —! ¡meneárse!; **she —d to the next room** fue a la habitación inmediata; **let's — into the garden** vamos al jardín; **she —s beautifully** anda con garbo; **I'll not — from here** no me muevo de aquí; **to —** freely (*part, Mech*) moverse libremente, (*person, traffic*) circular libremente; **to keep the traffic moving** mantener fluida la circulación; **keep moving!** ¡circulen!, ¡vayan pasando por delante!; **to — in high society** frecuentar la buena sociedad, alternar con personas de la buena sociedad.

(b) (*depart*) irse, marcharse; **it's time we were moving** es hora de irnos.

(c) (*travel*) ir; estar en movimiento; **we —d 100 miles that day** ese día cubrimos 100 millas; **the car was not moving** el coche no estaba en movimiento; **the bus was moving at 30 mph** el autobús iba a 30 mph; **the capsule is moving at 18,000 mph** la cápsula se desplaza a 18.000 mph; **he was certainly moving!** ¡iba como el demonio!

(d) (*progress*) ir adelante, avanzar, hacer progresos; (*of plants*) crecer; **things are moving at last** por fin se están haciendo progresos.

(e) (*— house*) mudarse, mudar de casa; **the family —d to a new house** la familia se mudó a una casa nueva.

(f) (*in games*) jugar, hacer una jugada; **who —s next?** ¿a quién le toca jugar?; **white —s** (*Chess*) blanco juega.

(g) (*take steps*) dar un paso, hacer una gestión, tomar medidas; **the government must — first** el gobierno ha de dar el primer paso; **the council —d to stop the abuse** el consejo hizo gestiones para corregir el abuso.

(h) (*with adv or prep*) **to — about** ir y venir, ir de acá para allá, desplazarse; moverse; **to — about** freely circular libremente; **to — along** avanzar por; **to — aside** ponerse a un lado, apartarse, quitarse de en medio; **to — away** alejarse, apartarse (*from* de); (*depart*) marcharse; (*— house*) mudar de casa; **to — back** retroceder; **to — down** bajar; **to — forward** avanzar; **to — in** tomar posesión de una casa (*etc*), instalarse en una casa (*etc*); **to — in on someone** invadir a uno; **to — off** alejarse; (*depart*) marcharse, ponerse en marcha, ponerse en camino; **to — on** (*go on*) seguir, seguir andando; reanudar el viaje; (*go forward*) avanzar; (*of time*) pasar; (*depart*) marcharse; **to — out** salir, abandonar la casa (*etc*); **we are moving out tomorrow** nos vamos mañana; **when the army —d out** cuando el ejército abandonó la ciudad (*etc*); **to — up** subir; (*in rank*) ser ascendido.

movement ['muːvmənt] *n* **(a)** (*act*) movimiento *m*; (*of part*) juego *m*, movimiento *m*; (*of traffic etc*) circulación *f*; (*on stock exchange*) actividad *f*, (*change of price*) cambio *m* de precio; (*Med*) evacuación *f*; **encircling —** movimiento *m* envolvente; **upward —** movimiento *m* ascensional; **to be in —** estar en movimiento; **there was a — towards the door** se dirigieron algunos hacia la puerta.

(b) (*Pol*) movimiento *m*; **he founded the M— in 1936** fundó el Movimiento en 1936.

(c) (*Mus*) tiempo *m*.

(d) (*Mech, part*) mecanismo *m*.

mover ['muːvə*] *n* (*of motion*) autor *m*, ora *f*; **prime —** (*Mech*) máquina *f* motriz; (*Philos*) primer motor *m*; (*person*) promotor *m*, ora *f*.

movie ['muːvi] *n* (*US*) película *f*; **the —s** el cine; **to go to the —s** ir al cine.

movie camera ['muːviˌkæmərə] *n* (*US*) cámara *f* cinematográfica.

moviegoer ['muːviˌgəuə*] *n* (*US*) aficionado *m* al cine, aficionada *f* al cine.

movie house ['muːviˌhaus] *n*, *pl* **— houses** [ˌhauziz] (*US*) cine *m*.

movieland ['muːviˌlænd] *n* (*US*) (*dreamworld*) mundo *m* de ensueño creado por el cine; (*eg Hollywood*) centro *m* de la industria cinematográfica.

moving ['muːviŋ] *adj* (*that moves*) movedor; movedizo; *part, staircase etc* móvil; (*motive*) motor; (*fig*) conmovedor; emocionante.

movingly ['muːviŋli] *adv* de modo conmovedor; **he spoke most —** conmovió profundamente a los que le escuchaban.

mow [məu] (*irr: pret* **mowed**, *ptp* **mown** *or* **mowed**) *vt corn etc* segar; *grass* cortar; **to — down** segar.

mower ['məuə*] *n* segador *m*, ora *f*; (*lawn-*) cortacésped *m*.

mowing ['məuiŋ] *n* siega *f*.

mowing machine ['məuiŋməˌʃiːn] *n* segadora *f* (mecánica).

mown [məun] *ptp of* **mow**.

Mozarab [mɔzˈærəb] *n* mozárabe *mf*.

Mozarabic [mɔzˈærəbik] **1** *adj* mozárabe. **2** *n* (*dialect*) mozárabe *m*.

much [mʌtʃ] **1** *adj* mucho; **— money** mucho dinero; **how — money?** ¿cuánto dinero?

2 *adv* **(a)** mucho; (*before ptp*) muy; **— better** mucho mejor; **— pleased** muy satisfecho; **it doesn't — matter** no importa mucho; **he's — richer than I (am)** es mucho más rico que yo; **ever so — muchísimo; not — no mucho, poco; — to my astonishment** con gran sorpresa mía.

(b) (*by far*) con mucho; **— the biggest** con mucho el más grande; **I would — rather stay** prefiero con mucho quedarme.

(c) (*almost*) casi, más o menos; **they are — of an age** tienen casi la misma edad; **they're — the same size** tienen más o menos el mismo tamaño.

(d) **how — is it?** ¿cuánto es?, ¿cuánto vale?; **how — is it a kilo?** ¿cuánto vale el kilo de esto?

(e) **however — he tries** por mucho que se esfuerce.

3 *n*: **but — remains** pero queda mucho; **— of this is true** gran parte de esto es verdad; **we don't see — of each other** nos vemos poco; **there's not — to do** no hay mucho que hacer; **it's not up to — no vale gran cosa; I'm not — of a musician** yo sé muy poco de música, entiendo poco de música, como músico no sirvo para nada; **he's not — of a player** como jugador no vale mucho; **that wasn't — of a dinner** eso apenas se podía llamar cena; **to make — of someone** mimar a uno, hacer fiestas a uno; agasajar a uno; **to make — of something** dar mucha importancia a algo; subrayar la importancia de algo.

4 (*with as, so, too*) **(a)** — **as I should like to** por más que yo quisiera; — **as I would like to go** por mucho que me gustara ir; — **as I like him** aunque le quiero mucho.

(b) (*as —*) **as — again** otro tanto; **three times as — tea** tres veces la cantidad de té; **I thought as — ya** me lo figuraba, lo había previsto ya.

(c) (*as — as, so — as*) **he has as — money as you** tiene tanto dinero como Vd; **he spends as — as he** earns gasta tanto como gana; **I have three times as — as I can eat** tengo tres veces más de lo que puedo comer; **it's as — as I can do to stand up** apenas puedo ponerme de pie; **as — as to say . . .** como si dijera . . .; **the problem is not so — one of modernization as of investment** el problema más que de modernización es de inversión; **he went without saying so — as a single word** se fue sin decir una sola palabra siquiera; **I haven't so — as a penny** no tengo ni un solo penique.

(d) (*so —*) **so — bad weather** tanto mal tiempo; **it has been so — exaggerated** se ha exagerado tanto; **we don't go out so — now** ahora no salimos tanto; **so — the better** tanto mejor; **so — for that!** ¡allá eso!; ¡ya se acabó aquello!; **that's so — the less to pay** tanto menos habrá que pagar; **at so — a pound** a tantas pesetas (*etc*) la libra; **so — so that . . .** tanto que . . .

(e) **too — demasiado**; **he talks too — habla** demasiado; **too — jam** demasiada mermelada *f*, exceso *m* de mermelada; **you gave me sixpence too — Vd** me dio seis peniques de más; **that's too — by half** de eso sobra la mitad; **don't make too — of it** no exageres la importancia de esto.

muchness ['mʌtʃnis] *n*: **they're much of a — son** casi lo mismo.

mucilage ['mjuːsilidʒ] *n* mucílago *m*.

mucilaginous [ˌmjuːsiˈlædʒinəs] *adj* mucilaginoso.

muck [mʌk] **1** *n* **(a)** (*dung*) estiércol *m*; (*dirt*) suciedad *f*, inmundicias *fpl*, mierda *f*; **to be in a — estar** sucio.

(b) (*fig*) porquería *f*; **the article is just — el** artículo es una porquería.

2 *vt* **(a)** **to — out a stable** limpiar una cuadra; **to — up** (*dirty*) ensuciar.

(b) **to — someone about** fastidiar a uno, desorientar a uno (cambiando una cita *etc* con él); **to —**

up (*disarrange*) desarreglar, desordenar; (*ruin*) arruinar, estropear, echar a perder; *affair, deal* fracasar en, (*deliberately*) chafar.
3 *vi*: to — about perder el tiempo, ocuparse en fruslerías, trabajar (*etc*) con poca seriedad; he enjoys —ing about in boats le gusta entretener sus ocios navegando (*etc*) en bote; stop —ing about! ¡déjate de tonterías!; to — about with something (*handle*) manosear algo, tocar algo, (*amuse oneself*) divertirse con algo, (*break*) romper algo, estropear algo.

muckiness ['mʌkinis] *n* suciedad *f*.

muckrake ['mʌkreik] *vi* remover el pasado; buscar y revelar cosas vergonzosas en la vida de otros, escarbar vidas ajenas.

muckraker ['mʌk,reikə*] *n* escarbador *m* de vidas ajenas, escarbadora *f* de vidas ajenas.

muck-up ['mʌkʌp] *n* (*fam*) lío *m* grande; fracaso *m* total; what a —! ¡qué faena! (*fam*); that — with the timetable ese lío que nos armamos con el horario.

mucky ['mʌki] *adj* sucio; puerco; asqueroso; to get oneself all — ensuciarse; to get one's dress all — ensuciar el vestido.

mucous ['mju:kəs] *adj* mucoso; — membrane mucosa *f*.

mucus ['mju:kəs] *n* moco *m*, mocosidad *f*.

mud [mʌd] 1 *n* lodo *m*, barro *m*, fango *m*; (*fig*) fango *m*; to stick in the — (*cart*) atascarse, atollarse, (*ship*) embarrancarse; — in your eye! ¡salud y pesetas!; his name is — tiene una reputación malísima, no se le estima en nada; if people hear this my name will be — si esto llega a saberse estoy perdido; to drag someone's name through the — llenar a uno de fango; to sling (*or* throw) — at someone vilipendiar a uno.
2 *attr*: — hut choza *f* de barro; — wall tapia *f*.

mudbank ['mʌdbæŋk] *n* banco *m* de arena.

mudbath ['mʌdbɑ:θ] *n*, *pl* —baths [bɑ:ðz] baño *m* de lodo, lodos *mpl*.

muddle ['mʌdl] 1 *n* (a) (*disorder*) desorden *m*, confusión *f*; you should have seen what a — there was in the room! ¡había que ver el desorden que había en el cuarto!; what a —! ¡qué confusión!; how did things get into such a —? ¿cómo se produjo tanta confusión?
(b) (*perplexity*) perplejidad *f*, confusión *f*; now I'm all in a — ahora estoy totalmente confuso.
(c) (*mix-up*) embrollo *m*, lío *m*; there was a — over the seats hubo un lío con las entradas; to get into a — embrollarse; to get into a — with one's accounts armarse un lío con las cuentas; what a —! ¡qué lío!, ¡qué faena!
2 *vt* (*also* to — up) (a) *things* embrollar, confundir; introducir el desorden en; you've —d up A and B has confundido A con B.
(b) *person* aturdir, dejar perplejo, confundir; I was properly —d estaba totalmente confuso; to get —d aturdirse; armarse un lío.
3 *vi*: to — along, to — through salir del paso sin saber cómo; I expect we shall — through espero que lo logremos de algún modo u otro.

muddle-headed ['mʌdl,hedid] *adj* *person* atontado, de ideas nada claras; *ideas* confuso.

muddy ['mʌdi] 1 *adj* *place* lodoso, fangoso; *hands, dress etc* cubierto de lodo; *liquid* turbio; *complexion* cetrino.
2 *vt* enlodar; cubrir de lodo; *hands, dress etc* manchar de lodo; *liquid* enturbiar.

mud flats ['mʌdflæts] *npl* marisma *f*.

mudguard ['mʌdgɑ:d] *n* guardabarros *m*.

mudlark ['mʌdlɑ:k] *n* galopín *m*.

mudpack ['mʌdpæk] *n* mascarilla *f* facial de barro.

mud-slinging ['mʌd,sliŋiŋ] *n* injurias *fpl*, vilipendio *m*.

muezzin [mu:'ezin] *n* almuecín *m*, almuédano *m*.

muff¹ [mʌf] *n* manguito *m* (*also* Tech).

muff² [mʌf] *vt* *ball* dejar escapar; *catch, stop* no lograr por torpeza; *shot* errar; *chance* perder, desperdiciar; *entrance, lines* (*Theat*) estropear; to — it fracasar, hacerlo malísimamente, no lograrlo por torpeza.

muffin ['mʌfin] *n* (*approx*) mollete *m*.

muffle ['mʌfl] 1 *vt* (a) (*also* to — up) envolver; *person etc* embozar, tapar (*with* de); —d up in embozado de.
(b) *noise* amortiguar, apagar; *noisy thing* amortiguar el ruido de; *bells, oars* envolver con tela; *drum* enfundar.
2 *vi* = 3 *vr*: to — oneself up embozarse, taparse.

muffled ['mʌfld] *adj* *sound* sordo, apagado.

muffler ['mʌflə*] *n* (*scarf*) bufanda *f*; (*Mus*) sordina *f*; (*Mech*) silenciador *m*.

mufti ['mʌfti] *n* traje *m* de paisano; in — vestido de paisano.

mug [mʌg] 1 *n* (a) (*cup*) taza *f* (alta, sin platillo); (*for beer*) pichel *m*, barro *m*, jarra *f*.
(b) (*person*: sl) bobo *m*, primo *m*; what a — I've been! ¡he sido un tonto!
(c) (*face*: sl) jeta *f* (sl), hocico *m* (sl); what a — she's got! ¡qué jeta tiene!; he hit him in the — le pegó un tortazo en el hocico.
2 *vt* (US sl) asaltar, pegar; to — up (sl) aprender (*or* estudiar *etc*) sin interés.

mugging ['mʌgiŋ] *n* (US sl) asalto *m*, vapuleo *m*.

muggins ['mʌginz] *n* *sing* (sl) tonto *m*, primo *m*; — will pay for it este pobre hombre lo pagará.

muggy ['mʌgi] *adj* húmedo y sofocante, bochornoso.

mugwump ['mʌgwʌmp] *n* (US Pol) votante que no es miembro de ningún partido.

mulatto [mju:'lætəu] 1 *adj* mulato. 2 *n*, *pl* **mulattoes** [mju:'lætəuz] mulato *m*, a *f*.

mulberry ['mʌlbəri] *n* (*fruit*) mora *f*; (*tree*) morera *f*, moral *m*.

mulch [mʌltʃ] 1 *n* capa *f* de hierba, paja, hojas (*etc*).
2 *vt* cubrir con una capa de hierba, paja, hojas (*etc*).

mulct [mʌlkt] *vt* multar; to — someone of something quitar algo a uno, privar a uno de algo.

mule¹ [mju:l] *n* mulo *m*, a *f*; (*person*) testarudo *m*, a *f*; (Tech) máquina *f* de hilar intermitente, selfactina *f*.

mule² [mju:l] *n* (*slipper*) babucha *f*.

muleteer [,mju:li'tiə*] *n* mulatero *m*, arriero *m*.

mule track ['mju:ltræk] *n* camino *m* de herradura.

mulish ['mju:liʃ] *adj* terco, testarudo.

mulishness ['mju:liʃnis] *n* terquedad *f*, testarudez *f*.

mull¹ [mʌl] *vt* *wine* calentar con especias.

mull² [mʌl] *vt*: to — something over meditar algo, reflexionar sobre algo.

mullet ['mʌlit] *n*: grey — mújol *m*; red — salmonete *m*.

mullion ['mʌliən] *n* parteluz *m*.

mullioned ['mʌliənd] *adj* *window* dividido con parteluz.

multi ... ['mʌlti] multi ...

multichannel ['mʌlti'tʃænl] *adj* (TV) multicanal.

multicoloured, (US) —**colored** ['mʌlti'kʌləd] *adj* multicolor.

multifarious [,mʌlti'feəriəs] *adj* múltiple.

multiform ['mʌltifɔ:m] *adj* multiforme.

multilateral ['mʌlti'lætərəl] *adj* multilátero.

multimillionaire ['mʌltimiljə'neə*] *n* multimillonario *m*, a *f*.

multiple ['mʌltipl] 1 *adj* (*of many parts*) múltiplo; (*in pl, many and various*) múltiple; *firm* con muchas sucursales; — stores cadena *f* de grandes almacenes.
2 *n* múltiplo *m*; lowest common — mínimo común múltiplo *m*.

multiplicand [,mʌltipli'kænd] *n* multiplicando *m*.

multiplication [,mʌltipli'keiʃən] *n* multiplicación *f*.

multiplicity [,mʌlti'plisiti] *n* multiplicidad *f*; for a — of reasons por múltiples razones; a — of solutions una gran diversidad de soluciones.

multiply ['mʌltiplai] 1 *vt* multiplicar; to — 8 by 7 multiplicar 8 por 7. 2 *vi* multiplicarse.

multiracial ['mʌlti'reiʃəl] *adj* multirracial.

multitude ['mʌltitju:d] *n* multitud *f*; the — (*pej*) las masas, la plebe; for a — of reasons por múltiples razones; they came in —s acudieron en tropel.

multitudinous [,mʌlti'tju:dinəs] *adj* multitudinario; muy numeroso, numerosísimo.

mum¹ [mʌm] *adj*: —'s the word! ¡punto en boca!; to keep — callarse; see that you keep — about it de esto no digas ni pío; everybody is keeping very — about it esto lo tienen todos muy secreto.

mum² [mʌm] *n* (*fam*) mamá *f* (*fam*).

mumble ['mʌmbl] 1 *n*: he said in a — dijo refunfuñando, dijo entre dientes. 2 *vt* decir entre dientes. 3 *vi* musitar, refunfuñar, hablar entre dientes.

mumbo jumbo ['mʌmbəu'dʒʌmbəu] *n* (*cult*) fetiche *m*; (*spell*) conjuro *m*; (*empty ritual*) mistificación *f*, farsa *f*.

mummer ['mʌmə*] *n* máscara *mf*.

mummery ['mʌməri] *n* (*fig*) mistificación *f*; ceremonia *f* ridícula, farsa *f*.

mummification [,mʌmifi'keiʃən] *n* momificación *f*.

mummify ['mʌmifai] 1 *vt* momificar. 2 *vi* momificarse.

mummy¹ ['mʌmi] *n* (Hist) momia *f*.

mummy² ['mʌmi] *n* (*fam*) mamá *f* (*fam*).

mumps [mʌmps] *n* *sing* paperas *fpl*, parótidas *fpl*.

munch [mʌntʃ] *vt* mascar, ronzar.

mundane ['mʌn'dein] *adj* mundano; (*humdrum*) vulgar, trivial.

municipal [mju:'nisipəl] *adj* municipal.

municipality [mju:,nisi'pæliti] *n* municipio *m*.

munificence [mju:'nifisns] *n* munificencia *f*.

munificent [mju:'nifisnt] *adj* munífico.

muniments ['mju:nimənts] *npl* documentos *mpl* (probatorios); (*also* — **room**) archivos *mpl*.

munitions [mju:'niʃənz] *npl* municiones *fpl*; — **dump** depósito *m* de municiones.

mural ['mjuərəl] **1** *adj* mural. **2** *n* pintura *f* mural, mural *m*.

murder ['mə:də*] **1** *n* (a) asesinato *m*, (*as Law term*) homicidio *m*; **accused of** — acusado de homicidio; **wilful** —, — **in the first degree** homicidio *m* premeditado.

(b) (*fam*) **it was** — ! ¡un horror!; **to cry** —, **to shout blue** — protestar enérgicamente, poner el grito en el cielo; **she could get away with** — hace lo que quiere y siempre sale impune.

2 *vt* asesinar; matar, dar muerte a; *song etc* arruinar, estropear; *play* degollar.

murderer ['mə:dərə*] *n* asesino *m*, (*as Law term*) homicida *m*.

murderess ['mə:dəris] *n* asesina *f*, (*as Law term*) homicida *f*.

murderous ['mə:dərəs] *adj* homicida; (*fig*) cruel, feroz, sanguinario; (*fam*) fatal, horroroso.

murk [mə:k] *n* oscuridad *f*, tinieblas *fpl*.

murkiness ['mə:kinis] *n* oscuridad *f*, lobreguez *f*; (*fig*) lo tenebroso, lo turbio.

murky ['mə:ki] *adj* oscuro, lóbrego; (*fig*) tenebroso, turbio.

murmur ['mə:mə*] **1** *n* (*soft speech*) murmullo *m*; (*of water*) murmullo *m*, murmurio *m*; (*of leaves etc*) susurro *m*; (*of distant traffic etc*) rumor *m*; (*complaint*) queja *f*, murmurio *m*; **there were** —**s of disagreement** hubo murmurios de disconformidad.

2 *vt* murmurar, decir en voz baja.

3 *vi* murmullar, murmurar; susurrar; quejarse; **to** — **about, to** — **against** murmurar de, quejarse de.

muscatel [,mʌskə'tel] **1** *adj* moscatel. **2** *n* moscatel *m*.

muscle ['mʌsl] **1** *n* músculo *m*; (*fig*) fuerza *f* muscular; **he never moved a** — se mantuvo inmóvil, no se inmutó en absoluto; **to flex one's** —**s** preparar su musculatura.

2 *vi*: **to** — **in** (*sl*) introducirse por fuerza (*on a deal* en un negocio).

musclebound ['mʌslbaund] *adj* envarado por exceso de ejercicio, con calambre en los músculos.

Muscovite ['mʌskəvait] **1** *adj* moscovita. **2** *n* moscovita *mf*.

muscular ['mʌskjulə*] *adj* *tissue etc* muscular; (*having muscles*) musculoso; (*brawny*) fornido, membrudo.

musculature ['mʌskjulətjuə*] *n* musculatura *f*.

Muse [mju:z] *n* musa *f*; **the** — las Musas.

muse [mju:z] *vi* meditar, reflexionar, rumiar; **to** — **about something, to** — **on something** meditar algo, reflexionar sobre algo; **to** — **on a scene** contemplar distraído una escena; "**yes**", **he** —**d** "sí", dijo distraído.

museum [mju:'ziəm] *n* museo *m*; **archaeological** — museo *m* arqueológico; **the British M**— el Museo Británico.

museum piece [mju:'ziəm,pi:s] *n* (*fig*) cosa *f* anticuada, antigualla *f*; **the car is a real** — el coche realmente es digno de estar en un museo.

mush [mʌʃ] *n* gachas *fpl*; masa *f* blanda y espesa; (*fig*) sensiblería *f*, sentimentalismo *m*.

mushroom ['mʌʃrum] **1** *n* seta *f*, hongo *m*; (*as food*) champiñón *m*; **a great** — **of smoke** un enorme hongo de humo; **to grow like** —**s** surgir como hongos, crecer de la noche a la mañana.

2 *adj*: — **town** ciudad *f* que aparece de la noche a la mañana.

3 *vi* (*town etc*) surgir como hongos, crecer de la noche a la mañana, crecer rapidísimamente; **the cloud of smoke went** —**ing up** subió el humo en forma de hongo; **to** — **into** convertirse rapidísimamente en.

mushy ['mʌʃi] *adj* pulposo, mollar, como gachas; (*fig*) sensiblero, muy sentimental.

music ['mju:zik] *n* música *f*; — **of the spheres** música *f* mundana, armonía *f* celestial; **to face the** — pagar el pato; **to set a work to** — poner música a una obra.

musical ['mju:zikəl] **1** *adj* (a) musical; *instrument, composition etc* músico; *sound, voice* armonioso, melodioso.

(b) **he's very** — tiene mucho talento para la música; **he comes from a** — **family** es de familia de músicos.

2 *n* comedia *f* musical.

musical box ['mju:zikəlbɔks] *n* caja *f* de música.

musicale [,mju:zi'ka:l] *n* velada *f* musical.

musically ['mju:zikəli] *adv* armoniosamente, melodiosamente.

music hall ['mju:zikhɔ:l] *n* teatro *m* de variedades.

musician [mju:'ziʃən] *n* músico *m*, a *f*.

musicianship [mju:'ziʃənʃip] *n* maestría *f* musical.

music lover ['mju:zik,lʌvə*] *n* persona *f* aficionada a la música.

musicologist [,mju:zi'kɔlədʒist] *n* musicólogo *m*.

musicology [,mju:zi'kɔlədʒi] *n* musicología *f*.

music paper ['mju:zik,peipə*] *n* papel *m* de música.

music stand ['mju:zikstænd] *n* atril *m*.

musingly ['mju:ziŋli] *adv* say *etc* con aire distraído, pensativamente.

musk [mʌsk] *n* (*substance*) almizcle *m*; (*scent*) perfume *m* de almizcle; (*smell*) olor *m* a almizcle; (*Bot*) almizcleña *f*.

musket ['mʌskit] *n* mosquete *m*.

musketeer [,mʌski'tiə*] *n* mosquetero *m*.

musketry ['mʌskitri] *n* (*muskets*) mosquetes *mpl*; (*troops*) mosquetería *f*; (*firing*) fuego *m* de mosquetes, tiros *mpl*.

muskmelon ['mʌskmelən] *n* melón *m*.

musk ox ['mʌskɔks] *n*, *pl* — **oxen** [ɔksən] buey *m* almizclado.

muskrat ['mʌskræt] *n* rata *f* almizclera.

musk rose ['mʌskrəuz] *n* rosa *f* almizcleña.

musky ['mʌski] *adj* almizcleño, almizclado; *smell* a almizcle.

Muslim ['muslim] *see* **Moslem**; **Black** — musulmán *m* negro.

muslin ['mʌzlin] **1** *n* muselina *f*. **2** *adj*, *attr* de muselina.

musquash ['mʌskwɔʃ] *n* rata *f* almizclera; (*fur*) piel *f* de rata almizclera.

muss [mʌs] *vt* (*also* **to** — **up**) *hair* desarreglar, despeinar; *dress* ajar, chafar.

mussel ['mʌsl] *n* mejillón *m*.

mussel bed ['mʌslbed] *n* criadero *m* de mejillones.

Mussulman ['mʌslmən] *see* **Moslem**.

must[1] [mʌst] *n* (*of wine*) mosto *m*.

must[2] [mʌst] *n* *see* **mustiness**.

must[3] [mʌst] *v aux* (*present tense only*) **1** (a) (*obligation*) **I** — **do it** debo hacerlo, tengo que hacerlo, he de hacerlo; **one** — **be careful** hay que tener cuidado; **one** — **not be too hopeful** no hay que ser demasiado optimista; **the patient** — **have complete quiet** el enfermo precisa silencio absoluto; **but you** — **come** pero es imprescindible que vengas; **do it if you** — hágalo si es necesario, hágalo si no hay más remedio; **there** — **be a reason** debe haber una razón, ha de haber una razón.

(b) (*probability*) **he** — **be there by now** ya debe de estar allí, ya estará allí; **it** — **be cold up there** hará frío allá arriba; **it** — **be about 3 o'clock** serán las 3; **it** — **have been about 5** serían alrededor de las 5; **but you** — **have seen him!** ¡pero debes haberle visto!; **he** — **be a Mexican** debe de ser mejicano.

2 *n* (*fam*) **this programme is a** — **for everybody** este programa no lo ha de perder ningún oyente, es imprescindible que todos los oyentes escuchen este programa.

mustache ['mʌstæʃ] *n* (*US*) *see* **moustache**.

mustang ['mʌstæŋ] *n* potro *m* mesteño.

mustard ['mʌstəd] *n* mostaza *f*.

mustard gas ['mʌstədgæs] *n* gas *m* mostaza.

mustard plaster ['mʌsted'plɑ:stə*] *n* sinapismo *m*, cataplasma *f* de mostaza.

mustard pot ['mʌstədpɔt] *n* mostacera *f*.

muster ['mʌstə*] **1** *n* (*gathering*) asamblea *f* (*also* Mil), reunión *f*; (*review*) revista *f*; (*list*) lista *f*, matrícula *f*, (*Naut*) rol *m*; **to pass** — pasar revista, (*fig*) ser aceptable, ser satisfactorio.

2 *vt* (*call together for inspection*) llamar a asamblea, juntar para pasar revista; (*collect*) juntar, reunir; (*also* **to** — **up**) *courage, strength* cobrar; **the club can** — **20 members** el club cuenta con 20 miembros, el club consiste en 20 miembros.

3 *vi* juntarse, reunirse.

mustiness ['mʌstinis] *n* moho *m*; ranciedad *f*; (*of room etc*) olor *m* a humedad, olor *m* a cerrado.

mustn't ['mʌsnt] = **must not**.

musty ['mʌsti] *adj* mohoso; rancio; *room etc* que huele a humedad, que huele a cerrado; *joke etc* viejo, gastado.

mutability [,mju:tə'biliti] *n* mutabilidad *f*.

mutable ['mju:təbl] *adj* mudable.

mutant ['mju:tənt] *n* mutante *m*.

mutate [mju:'teit] **1** *vt* mudar. **2** *vi* sufrir mutación.

mutation [mju:'teiʃən] *n* mutación *f*.

mute [mju:t] **1** *adj* mudo, silencioso; **with H** — con hache muda; **to become** — enmudecer.

2 *n* (*person*) mudo *m*, a *f*; (*Mus*) sordina *f*; (*Gram*) letra *f* muda.

3 *vt* (*Mus*) poner sordina a; *noise* amortiguar, apagar.

muted ['mju:tid] *adj noise* sordo, apagado; *criticism* callado.
mutilate ['mju:tileit] *vt* mutilar.
mutilation [,mjuti'leiʃən] *n* mutilación *f*.
mutineer [,mju:ti'niə*] *n* amotinado *m*, amotinador *m*.
mutinous ['mju:tinəs] *adj* amotinado; *(fig)* turbulento, rebelde; **we were feeling pretty** — estábamos hartos ya, estábamos dispuestos a rebelarnos.
mutiny ['mju:tini] **1** *n* motín *m*, sublevación *f*. **2** *vi* amotinarse, sublevarse.
mutt [mʌt] *n (sl)* bobo *m*.
mutter ['mʌtə*] **1** *n* murmullo *m*; **a** — **of voices** un rumor de voces.
 2 *vt* murmurar, decir entre dientes; **"yes", he** —**ed "sí"**, refunfuñó.
 3 *vi* murmurar; *(guns, thunder)* retumbar a lo lejos.
mutton ['mʌtn] *n* carne *f* de cordero.
mutton chop ['mʌtn'tʃɒp] *n* chuleta *f* de cordero.
mutual ['mju:tjuəl] *adj* mutuo; *(loosely)* común; **the feeling is** — yo comparto esa opinión, lo mismo digo yo; **our** — **friend** nuestro amigo; **their** — **friend** el amigo de los dos, el amigo que tienen en común.
mutuality [,mju:tju'æliti] *n* mutualidad *f*.
mutually ['mju:tjuəli] *adv* mutuamente.
muzzle ['mʌzl] **1** *n (snout)* hocico *m*; *(for dog)* bozal *m*; *(of gun)* boca *f*. **2** *vt dog* abozalar; *criticism etc* estorbar; *critic* amordazar, imponer silencio a.
muzzle loader ['mʌzl,ləudə*] *n* arma *f* que se carga por la boca.
muzzy ['mʌzi] *adj (from drinking)* confuso, atontado; *outline* borroso.
my [mai, mi] **1** *poss adj* mi. **2** *interj* ¡caramba!
mycology [mai'kɒlədʒi] *n* micología *f*.
myopia [mai'əupiə] *n* miopía *f*.
myopic [mai'ɒpik] *adj* miope.
myriad ['miriəd] **1** *n* miríada *f*. **2** *adj*: **a** — **flies** miríadas de moscas.

myrmidon ['məːmidən] *n* secuaz *m* fiel, satélite *m*, esbirro *m*.
myrrh [məː*] *n* mirra *f*.
myrtle ['məːtl] *n* arrayán *m*, mirto *m*.
myself [mai'self] *pron (subject)* yo mismo, yo misma; *(acc, dat)* me; *(after prep)* mí (mismo, misma); *see* oneself.
mysterious [mis'tiəriəs] *adj* misterioso.
mysteriously [mis'tiəriəsli] *adv* misteriosamente.
mystery ['mistəri] *n* misterio *m*; *(Theat)* auto *m*, misterio *m*; **he's a** — **man** es un hombre misterioso; **there's no** — **about it** aquí no hay misterio; **it's a** — **to me where it can have gone** no tengo la menor idea de dónde se habrá metido; **to make a great** — **out of a matter** envolver un asunto en un ambiente de misterio.
mystery play ['mistəri,plei] *n* auto *m*, misterio *m*.
mystic ['mistik] **1** *adj* místico. **2** *n* místico *m*, a *f*.
mystical ['mistikəl] *adj* místico.
mysticism ['mistisizəm] *n* misticismo *m*; *(doctrine, literary genre)* mística *f*.
mystification [,mistifi'keiʃən] *n* misterio *m*; confusión *f*, perplejidad *f*; **why all the** — ? ¿por qué tanto misterio?; **my** — **increased** creció mi perplejidad.
mystify ['mistifai] *vt* dejar perplejo, desorientar, desconcertar; **I am mystified** estoy perplejo; **it completely mystified him** le desorientó por completo, le despistó por completo.
mystique [mis'ti:k] *n* misterio *m* (profesional *etc*), técnica *f* (al parecer) misteriosa, pericia *f* impresionante.
myth [miθ] *n* mito *m*.
mythic(al) ['miθik(əl)] *adj* mítico.
mythological [,miθə'lɒdʒikəl] *adj* mitológico.
mythology [mi'θɒlədʒi] *n* mitología *f*.
myxomatosis [,miksəumə'təusis] *n* mixomatosis *f*.

N

nab [næb] *vt* coger, echar el guante a; (*arrest*) prender.
nabob ['neibɔb] *n* nabab *m*.
nacelle [næ'sel] *n* (*Aer*) barquilla *f*, góndola *f*.
nacre ['neikə*] *n* nácar *m*.
nacreous ['neikriəs] *adj* nacarino, nacarado, de nácar.
nadir ['neidiə*] *n* nadir *m*; (*fig*) punto *m* más bajo.
nag[1] [næg] *n* jaca *f*; (*pej*) rocín *m*.
nag[2] [næg] **1** *vt* (*scold*) regañar; (*annoy*) importunar, fastidiar; criticar; **don't — me so!** ¡no machaques!; **his conscience —ged him** le remordía la conciencia; **he was —ged by doubts** le asaltaron dudas; **she —s him all day long** ella le importuna con sus quejas todo el día.
2 *vi* ser regañón, ser importuno, criticar, quejarse; **to — at someone** importunar a uno, criticar a uno; **don't —, woman!** ¡no machaques, mujer!
nagging ['nægiŋ] **1** *adj person* regañón, criticón; *pain* continuo; *conscience* nada tranquilo; *doubt, fear etc* persistente, que no se desvanece.
2 *n* importunar *m*; críticas *fpl*; quejas *fpl*.
naiad ['naiæd] *n* náyade *f*.
nail [neil] **1** *n* (a) (*Anat*) uña *f*; (*of animal*) garra *f*; **to bite one's —s** comerse las uñas.
(b) (*metal*) clavo *m*; **to hit the — on the head** dar en el clavo, acertar; **to pay on the —** pagar a toca teja.
2 *vt* clavar, enclavar; adornar con clavos, clavetear; (*catch, get hold of*) coger; *lie* acabar con; *rumour etc* desmentir, demostrar la falsedad de; **to — something down** clavar algo, sujetar algo con clavos; **to — someone down** poner a uno entre la espada y la pared; **we —ed him down to come tomorrow** le comprometimos a que viniera mañana; **you can't — him down** es imposible hacerle concretar; **to — two things together** fijar (*or* unir) dos cosas con clavos; **to — something up** cerrar algo con clavos.
nail-biting ['neil,baitiŋ] *n* mala costumbre *f* de comerse las uñas.
nailbrush ['neilbrʌʃ] *n* cepillo *m* para las uñas.
nailfile ['neilfail] *n* lima *f* para las uñas.
nail polish ['neil,pɔliʃ] *n*, **— varnish** [,vɑːniʃ] *n* esmalte *m* para las uñas, laca *f* para las uñas; **— remover** quita-esmalte *m*.
nail scissors ['neil,sizəz] *npl* tijeras *fpl* para las uñas.
naïve [nai'iːv] *adj* ingenuo, cándido, sencillo.
naïvely [nai'iːvli] *adv* ingenuamente.
naïveté *n*, **naïvety** [nai'iːvti] *n* ingenuidad *f*, candor *m*, sencillez *f*.
naked ['neikid] *adj* desnudo; (*fig*) desabrigado, indefenso; *flame* expuesto al aire; *lamp* sin pantalla; *sword* desenvainado; *attempt* abierto, manifiesto; **the — truth** la verdad lisa y llana; **stark —** en cueros, en pelota, como le parió su madre; **to go —** ir desnudo; **to strip someone —** desnudar a uno completamente, dejar a uno en cueros.
nakedness ['neikidnis] *n* desnudez *f*.
namby-pamby ['næmbi'pæmbi] **1** *adj* soso, ñoño.
2 *n* persona *f* sosa, ñoño *m*, a *f*.
name [neim] **1** *n* (a) nombre *m*; designación *f*; (*surname*) apellido *m*; (*nickname*) apodo *m*; (*of book etc*) título *m*; **Christian —**, **first —** nombre *m* de pila; **full —** (*in Spain*) nombre *m* y apellidos; **maiden —** apellido *m* de soltera; **married —** apellido *m* de casada; **pet —** nombre *m* cariñoso, (*short form*) diminutivo *m* afectuoso; **proper —** nombre *m* propio; **by —** de nombre; **Pérez by —** de nombre Pérez, llamado Pérez; **a lady by the — of Dulcinea** una señora llamada Dulcinea; **I know him by —** only le conozco solamente de nombre; **we know it by** (*or* **under**) **another —** lo conocemos bajo otro nombre; **to go by** (*or* **under**) **the — of** ser conocido por el nombre de, vivir bajo el nombre de; **in — only** era rey tan sólo de

nombre, de rey no tenía más que el nombre; **it exists in — only** no existe sino de nombre; **at least in —** al menos nominalmente; **in the — of peace** en nombre de la paz; **I thank you in the — of all those present** le doy las gracias en nombre de todos los asistentes; **open up, in the — of the law!** ¡abran a la justicia!, ¡abran en nombre de la ley!; **what's in a —?** ¿qué importa el nombre?; **he hasn't a penny to his —** no tiene donde caerse muerto; **what's your —?** ¿cómo se llama?; **my — is Peter** me llamo Pedro; **I'll do it, or my —'s not Bloggs!** ¡como me llamo Bloggs, que lo haré!; **to call someone —s** poner motes a uno, llenar a uno de injurias; **what — are they giving the child?** ¿qué nombre le van a poner al niño?; **they married to give the child a —** se casaron para legitimizar al niño; **to mention no —s** no mencionar nombres; **to put one's — down for a car** solicitar un coche; **what — shall I say?** (*Tel*) ¿ de parte de quién?; (*announcing arrival*) ¿qué nombre quiere que diga?; **to send in one's —** presentarse; **to take someone's — and address** apuntar las señas de uno.
(b) (*reputation*) nombre *m*; reputación *f*, fama *f*; **the firm has a good —** la casa tiene buena reputación; **he has a — for carelessness** es sabido que es bastante descuidado, tiene fama de poco cuidadoso; **his middle — is "lover"** le han apodado "el enamorado"; **to get** (*oneself*) **a bad —** crearse una mala reputación, empezar a ser conocido (*as* como); **to make a — for oneself** darse a conocer, empezar a ser conocido (*as* como); **to make one's —** llegar a ser famoso.
(c) (*person*) **big —** gran figura *f*, personaje *m* de relieve; **he's one of the big —s in the business** es uno de los personajes importantes en ese campo.
2 *vt* (*call: thing*) llamar, designar, denominar; (*person*) llamar, (*at birth*) bautizar, poner de nombre a; (*surname*) apellidar; (*mention*) mencionar, mentar; (*nominate*) nombrar; (*date, price etc*) fijar, señalar; **a man —d Jack** un hombre llamado Juanito; **they —d the child Mary** a la niña le pusieron María; **you — it, we have it** cualquier cosa que pida Vd la tenemos; **he is not —d in this list** no figura en esta lista; **you were not —d in the speech** no se le mencionó a Vd en el discurso; **— the third president of the USA** diga el nombre del tercer presidente de EE.UU.; **to — someone after his grandfather** poner a uno el nombre de su abuelo; **they —d him Winston after Churchill** le pusieron (el nombre de) Winston por Churchill; **he was —d ambassador to Warsaw** le nombraron embajador en Varsovia.
name day ['neim'dei] *n* fiesta *f* onomástica.
name dropping ['neim'drɔpiŋ] *n* vicio de procurar impresionar a la gente mencionando las personas importantes que uno conoce (*o* finge haber conocido.)
nameless ['neimlis] *adj* anónimo, sin nombre, innomado; *vice* nefando; *dread etc* vago, indecible; **a person who shall be —** una persona cuyo nombre no digo.
namely ['neimli] *adv* a saber.
nameplate ['neimpleit] *n* letrero *m* con nombre (del dueño *etc*); placa *f* del fabricante.
namesake ['neimseik] *n* tocayo *m*, a *f*, homónimo *m*, a *f*.
nance [næns] *n*, **nancy-boy** ['nænsibɔi] *n* (*fam*) maricón *m* (*fam*).
nanny ['næni] *n* niñera *f*, chacha *f*.
nanny-goat ['nænigəut] *n* cabra *f*.
nap[1] [næp] **1** *n* sueñecito *m*, dormirela *f*; (*in afternoon*) siesta *f*; **to have a —**, **to take a —** descabezar un sueño, echar una siesta, dormir la siesta.
2 *vi* dormitar; dormir la siesta; **to catch someone —ping** coger a uno desprevenido; **to be caught —ping** estar desprevenido.
nap[2] [næp] *n* (*on cloth*) lanilla *f*, flojel *m*.

nap³ [næp] (*Cards: game*) napolitana *f*; **to go —** jugarse el todo (*on a*).

napalm ['neipɑ:m] *n* jalea *f* de gasolina.

nape [neip] *n* (*also* — **of the neck**) nuca *f*, cogote *m*.

naphtha ['næfθə] *n* nafta *f*.

naphthalene ['næfθəli:n] *n* naftalina *f*.

napkin ['næpkin] *n* (*table-*) servilleta *f*; (*baby's*) pañal *m*.

napkin ring ['næpkinriŋ] *n* servilletero *m*.

Naples ['neiplz] Nápoles.

Napoleon [nə'pəuliən] *m* Napoleón.

Napoleonic [nə,pəuli'ɔnik] *adj* napoleónico.

nappy ['næpi] *n* pañal *m*.

Narbonne [nɑ:'bɔn] Narbona.

narcissism [nɑ:'sisizəm] *n* narcisismo *m*.

narcissistic [,nɑ:si'sistik] *adj* narcisista.

narcissus [nɑ:'sisəs] *n*, *pl* **—i** [ai] narciso *m*.

narcosis [nɑ:'kəusis] *n* narcosis *f*, narcotismo *m*.

narcotic [nɑ:'kɔtik] **1** *adj* narcótico. **2** *n* narcótico *m*.

narcotize ['nɑ:kətaiz] *vt* narcotizar.

nard [nɑ:d] *n* nardo *m*.

nark¹ [nɑ:k] *n* (*sl*) soplón *m*.

nark² [nɑ:k] *vt* (*sl*): **it —s me** me fastidia terriblemente; **he got properly —ed** se puso negro (*fam*); **— it!** (*stop it*) ¡déjalo!, (*go away*) ¡lárgate! (*fam*).

narrate [nə'reit] *vt* narrar, referir, contar.

narration [nə'reiʃən] *n* narración *f*, relato *m*.

narrative ['nærətiv] **1** *adj* narrativo. **2** *n* narrativa *f*, narración *f*.

narrator [nə'reitə*] *n* narrador *m*, ora *f*.

narrow ['nærəu] **1** *adj* estrecho, angosto; *trousers etc* estrecho; *advantage*, *majority* pequeño; *restricted* reducido, corto, restringido; *escape* de milagro, por los pelos; (*person*) de miras estrechas, intolerante; **in the — sense of the word** en el sentido estricto de la palabra; **on — resources** con escasos recursos.
2 *vt* estrechar, angostar; reducir; **we have —ed it down to 3 possibilities** lo hemos reducido a 3 posibilidades; **the police have —ed the search down to Bristol** la policía ha podido limitar sus pesquisas a Bristol.
3 *vi* estrecharse, angostarse, hacerse más angosto; reducirse; **the passage —s at the end** el pasillo se hace más estrecho hacia el final; **the search has now —ed to Soho** se ha podido restringir las pesquisas a Soho; **so the question —s down to this ...** así que la cuestión se reduce a esto ...

narrow-gauge ['nærəugeidʒ] *adj* de vía estrecha.

narrowly ['nærəuli] *adv* estrechamente; por poco; **the slate — missed him** por poco la pizarra le alcanzó, faltó poco para que la pizarra le diese; **he — missed being elected** no fué elegido por unos pocos votos.

narrow-minded ['nærəu'maindid] *adj* de miras estrechas, intolerante.

narrow-mindedness ['nærəu'maindidnis] *n* estrechez *f* de miras, intolerancia *f*.

narrows ['nærəuz] *npl* (*Naut*) estrecho *m*.

narwhal ['nɑ:wəl] *n* narval *m*.

nasal ['neizəl] **1** *adj* nasal; (*twanging*) gangoso. **2** *n* nasal *f*.

nasality [nei'zæliti] *n* nasalidad *f*.

nasalize ['neizəlaiz] *vt* nasalizar; (*twangingly*) pronunciar con timbre gangoso.

nasally ['neizəli] *adv* nasalmente; con timbre nasal; **to speak —** hablar por las narices, ganguear.

nascent ['næsnt] *adj* naciente.

nastily ['nɑ:stili] *adv* suciamente; horriblemente; groseramente; gravemente; peligrosamente; **he said — dijo groseramente; it was raining quite —** llovía de muy mala manera.

nastiness ['nɑ:stinis] *n* suciedad *f*; cosas *fpl* horribles; indecencia *f*; lo asqueroso, lo horrible; lo malo; gravedad *f*; lo peligroso; grosería *f*; rencor *m*.

nasturtium [nəs'tə:ʃəm] *n* capuchina *f*.

nasty ['nɑ:sti] *adj* (a) (*dirty*) sucio, puerco; (*obscene*) sucio, indecente, obsceno; (*disagreeable*) asqueroso, horrible, repugnante; *smell*, *taste* horrible; *remark* feo, horrible; (*rude*) grosero; *weather* feo, malo; *accident* grave; *wound etc* peligroso, de gravedad; *corner*, *turn etc* peligroso; *temper* vivo; *trick* malo; *habit* feo; **a very — film** una película asquerosa, un film de lo más horrible; **a — mess** un lío imponente; **what a — mind you have!** ¡qué mal pensado es Vd!; **to smell —** tener un olor desagradable; **to taste —** tener un sabor desagradable; **to turn —** *situation* ponerse difícil, *weather* volverse malo.
(b) (*of person*) antipático; poco afable; (*rude*) grosero; (*malicious*) rencoroso, malévolo; **what a — man!** ¡qué hombre más horrible!; **to be — to someone** tratar muy mal a uno, portarse mal con uno; **they were — to her in the shop** se portaron groseramente con ella en la tienda; **don't be —!** ¡no

digas esas cosas horribles!; ¡no seas mal pensado!; **to turn —** ponerse negro.

natal ['neitl] *adj* natal.

natality [nə'tæliti] *n* natalidad *f*.

nation ['neiʃən] *n* nación *f*.

national ['næʃənl] **1** *adj* nacional. **2** *n* nacional *mf*.

nationalism ['næʃnəlizəm] *n* nacionalismo *m*.

nationalist ['næʃnəlist] **1** *adj* nacionalista. **2** *n* nacionalista *mf*.

nationalistic [,næʃnə'listik] *adj* nacionalista.

nationality [,næʃə'næliti] *n* nacionalidad *f*; **dual —** nacionalidad *f* doble.

nationalization [,næʃnəlai'zeiʃən] *n* estatificación *f*; nacionalización *f*.

nationalize ['næʃnəlaiz] *vt* (*bring under public ownership*) estatificar; (*foreign property etc*) nacionalizar.

nationally ['næʃnəli] *adv* en escala nacional; por toda la nación; nacionalmente, como nación; desde el punto de vista nacional.

nationhood ['neiʃənhud] *n* carácter *m* de nación; **to achieve —** llegar a constituir una nación, llegar a tener categoría de nación.

nation-wide ['neiʃənwaid] *adj* por toda la nación, a escala nacional; de toda la nación.

native ['neitiv] **1** *adj* (a) (*innate*) natural, innato.
(b) (*artless*) sencillo.
(c) (*of one's birth*) natal; *land*, *town* natal; *language* materno, nativo.
(d) (*Min*) nativo.
(e) (*indigenous*) indígena; *product*, *resources etc* natural, nacional, del país; **the animal is — to Africa** el animal es indígena de África, el animal es originario de África.
(f) (*of natives*) indígena, nativo; **the — customs** las costumbres de los indígenas; **Minister for N— Affairs** Ministro *m* de Asuntos Indígenas; **to learn the — language** aprender el idioma de los indígenas; **to go —** vivir como los indígenas; *see land etc*.
2 *n* (a) (*with reference to birth or nationality*) natural *mf*; nacional *mf*; **he was a — of Seville** nació en Sevilla, era natural de Sevilla, era sevillano; **the plant is a — of China** la planta es originaria de China; **he speaks German like a —** habla alemán como un alemán, habla alemán como si hubiera nacido allí.
(b) (*primitive*) nativo *m*, a *f*, indígena *mf*.

nativity [nə'tiviti] *n* natividad *f*; **the N—** Navidad *f*; (*Art*) nacimiento *m*; (*crib etc*) belén *m*; **— play** auto *m* del nacimiento.

natter ['nætə*] (*fam*) **1** *n* charla *f*; **to have a —** charlar (*with con*).
2 *vi* (*chat*) charlar; (*chatter*) parlotear, hablar mucho; (*keep on*) machacar; (*complain*) quejarse.

natty ['næti] *adj* (*spruce*) majo, elegante, acicalado; (*deft*) diestro; (*gadget etc*) ingenioso.

natural ['nætʃrəl] **1** *adj* (*in most senses*) natural; instintivo; *person* inafectado, sin afectación; *child* ilegítimo; **it is — that ...** es natural que ..., es lógico que ...; **it seems — enough to me** me parece totalmente normal; **he's a — painter** es un pintor nato, nació para pintor.
2 *n* (*person*) imbécil *mf*; (*Mus*) nota *f* natural; (*sign*) becuadro *m*; (*key*) tecla *f* blanca; (*fam*) cosa *f* de éxito seguro, persona *f* segura de tener éxito.

naturalism ['nætʃrəlizəm] *n* naturalismo *m*.

naturalist ['nætʃrəlist] *n* naturalista *mf*.

naturalistic [,nætʃrə'listik] *adj* naturalista.

naturalization [,nætʃrəlai'zeiʃən] *n* naturalización *f*.

naturalize ['nætʃrəlaiz] **1** *vt* (*person*) naturalizar; **to become —d** naturalizarse. **2** *vi* (*person*) naturalizarse; (*plant etc*) aclimatarse, establecerse.

naturally ['nætʃrəli] *adv* (a) (*in a natural way*) naturalmente; sin afectación, con naturalidad; instintivamente, por instinto; **a — optimistic person** una persona optimista por naturaleza; **to write —** escribir con naturalidad.
(b) (*of course*) naturalmente; desde luego ..., claro que ...; **—!** ¡naturalmente!; **— it is not true** desde luego no es cierto.

naturalness ['nætʃrəlnis] *n* naturalidad *f*.

nature ['neitʃə*] *n* (a) (*essential quality*, *character*) naturaleza *f*; modo *m* de ser; esencia *f*; (*of person*) natural *m*, carácter *m*, temperamento *m*, genio *m*; **good — afabilidad *f*, amabilidad *f*; **to abuse someone's good —** abusar de la amabilidad de uno; **he has a nice —** tiene un carácter simpático; **it is not in his —** to say that no cabe en él decir tal cosa; **that's very much in his —** eso es muy de él; **the — of birds is to fly** las aves vuelan naturalmente; **outspokenness is second — with him** la franqueza le es completamente natural; **to be cautious by —** ser de naturaleza cauteloso; **it's against —, it's**

contrary to — es contrario a la naturaleza; **in the — of things it's impossible** lógicamente es imposible.

(**b**) (*kind*) género *m*, clase *f*; **something of that —** algo por el estilo; **of quite another —** de otra índole; **some conclusions of a — to amaze one** unas conclusiones de tipo sorprendente; **in the — of** del género de, algo así como.

(**c**) (*Bio, Phys etc*) naturaleza *f*; **the laws of N—** las leyes de la Naturaleza; **a keen student of —** un estudiante entusiasta de la naturaleza (*or* de la historia natural); **in a state of —** en su estado natural; **to draw from —** dibujar del natural; **to return to —** volver a su estado natural.

(**d**) **to relieve —** hacer del cuerpo.

natured ['neitʃəd] *adj* de carácter . . ., de condición . . .; **ill-natured** malévolo, malicioso; *see* **good-natured** *etc*.

nature lover ['neitʃə,lʌvə*] *n* amigo *m* de la naturaleza, amiga *f* de la naturaleza.

nature study ['neitʃə,stʌdi] *n* historia *f* natural.

nature worship ['neitʃə,wə:ʃip] *n* culto *m* de la naturaleza; (*ancient*) panteísmo *m*.

naturism ['neitʃərizəm] *n* naturismo *m*.

naturist ['neitʃərist] *n* naturista *mf*.

naught [nɔ:t] *n* nada; **there's — I can do about it** no hay nada que yo pueda hacer; **all for —** todo en balde; **to bring to —** *attempt, plan* frustrar, *hope* destruir; **to come to —** fracasar, malograrse, no dar resultado; **to set at —** no hacer caso de, despreciar; *see also* **nought**.

naughtily ['nɔ:tili] *adv* traviesamente, mal; escabrosamente; con picardía, con malicia.

naughtiness ['nɔ:tinis] *n* travesuras *fpl*, mala conducta *f*, picardía *f*; desobediencia *f*; lo verde, lo escabroso; malicia *f*.

naughty ['nɔ:ti] *adj* (**a**) *child etc* travieso, malo, pícaro; desobediente, revoltoso; **you've been very —, that was very — of you, that was a — thing to do** has sido muy malo; **—!** ¡malo!; **don't be —!** ¡no seas malo!; **you — boy!** ¡pillo!, **you — girl!** ¡picaruela!

(**b**) *joke, song etc* verde, escabroso; **that — jealousy of yours** esos pícaros celos tuyos; **she gave me a — look** me miró picaruela; **what — times we live in!** ¡qué tiempos más inmorales éstos!

nausea ['nɔ:siə] *n* náusea *f*, bascas *fpl*; (*fig*) asco *m*, repugnancia *f*.

nauseate ['nɔ:sieit] *vt* dar náuseas a; (*fig*) dar asco a, repugnar; **your conduct —s me** me repugna su conducta; **that cheese —s me** ese queso me da asco.

nauseating ['nɔ:sieitiŋ] *adj* repugnante, asqueroso.

nauseatingly ['nɔ:sieitiŋli] *adv* asquerosamente; **— virtuous** tan virtuoso que da asco.

nauseous ['nɔ:siəs] *adj* nauseabundo.

nautical ['nɔ:tikəl] *adj* náutico, marítimo; **mile** marino.

nautilus ['nɔ:tiləs] *n* nautilo *m*.

naval ['neivəl] *adj* naval, de marina; de la marina de guerra; naval militar; *base, engagement* naval; *hospital, officer* de marina; *forces* de la marina; *college* naval militar; *power* marítimo.

Navarre [nə'vɑ:*] Navarra *f*.

Navarrese [,nævə'ri:z] **1** *adj* navarro. **2** *n* navarro *m*, a *f*. **3** *n* (*dialect*) navarro *m*.

nave [neiv] *n* (*Archit*) nave *f*.

navel ['neivəl] *n* ombligo *m*.

navigable ['nævigəbl] *adj* *river etc* navegable; (*steerable*) governable, dirigible.

navigate ['nævigeit] **1** *vt ship* marear, gobernar; *river etc* navegar por; (*fig*) conducir, guiar. **2** *vi* navegar.

navigation [,nævi'geiʃən] *n* navegación *f*; (*science of* —) náutica *f*.

navigator ['nævigeitə*] *n* (*Naut*) navegador *m*, navegante *m*; (*Aer*) navegante *m*.

navvy ['nævi] *n* peón *m* caminero, peón *m* zapador, bracero *m*.

navy ['neivi] *n* marina *f* de guerra, armada *f*, flota *f*.

navy-blue ['neivi'blu:] **1** *n* azul *m* marino. **2** *adj* azul marino.

nay [nei] **1** *adv* (*arch or prov*) no; (*or rather*) más aún, mejor dicho, más bien; **bad, — terrible** malo, mejor dicho, horrible; **dozens, — hundreds** docenas, digo centenares.

2 *n* (*refusal*) negativa *f*; (*in voting*) voto *m* negativo, voto *m* en contra; **to say someone —** dar una respuesta negativa a uno.

Nazarene [,næzə'ri:n] **1** *adj* nazareno. **2** *n* nazareno *m*, a *f*.

Nazareth ['næzərəθ] Nazaret *m*.

Nazi ['nɑ:tsi] **1** *adj* nazi, nazista. **2** *n* nazi *mf*.

Nazism ['nɑ:tsizəm] *n* nazismo *m*.

neap [ni:p] *n* (*also* **—tide**) marea *f* muerta.

Neapolitan [niə'pɔlitən] **1** *adj* napolitano. **2** *n* napolitano *m*, a *f*.

near [niə*] **1** *adv* cerca; **as — as I can recall** que yo recuerde; **— on 30 books** (*fam*) casi 30 libros; **that's — enough** (*fig*) está bien, basta ya; no vale la pena hacerlo más exacto; **to bring something —** acercar algo; **to come —, to draw —** acercarse.

2 *prep* (*also* **— to**) (*of place*) cerca de; junto a, próximo a, al lado de; (*of time*) cerca de, casi; (*of numbers*) casi; **— here** aquí cerca; **to be — (to) the fire** estar cerca del fuego; **the passage is — the end of the book** el trozo está hacia el final del libro; **— the end of the century** hacia fines del siglo; **she was — her end** tocaba a su fin, estaba cerca de la muerte; **she was — to crying** estaba a punto de llorar; **we were — to being drowned** por poco nos morimos ahogados.

3 *adj place etc* cercano; próximo, inmediato, vecino; (*of time*) próximo; *relationship* estrecho, íntimo; *relative* cercano; *resemblance* grande; *guess* casi acertado; *translation etc* aproximativo; *side* (*Aut etc: Brit*) izquierdo, (*US, Spain etc*) derecho; **the —est way** el camino más corto; **work it out to the —est pound** calcúlalo en libras enteras; **one's —est and dearest** los más allegados y queridos.

4 *vt* acercarse a, aproximarse a; **the building is —ing completion** el edificio está casi terminado, el edificio se terminará dentro de poco; **he is —ing 50** tiene casi 50 años; **the country is —ing disaster** el país está al borde de la catástrofe.

nearby ['niə'bai] *adv* cerca.

nearby ['niəbai] *adj* cercano, próximo, inmediato.

Near East ['niər'i:st] Próximo Oriente *m*.

nearly ['niəli] *adv* (**a**) **it touches me —** me toca de cerca.

(**b**) **it's — 3 o'clock** son casi las 3; **she's — 40** tiene casi 40 años, frisa en los 40.

(**c**) (*with adj etc*) **— finished** casi terminado; **— black** casi negro, más o menos negro; **very —!** ¡casi casi!; **it's pretty — dead** está casi muerto; **the same number or —** so el mismo número o casi.

(**d**) (*with negative*) **it's not — ready** no está listo ni con mucho; **it's not — good enough** no es lo suficientemente bueno (*to + infin* para + *infin*); **she is not — so poor as she says** no es, ni con mucho, tan pobre como ella dice.

(**e**) (*with verb*) **I — lost it** por loco lo perdí; **I very — caught it** por poco lo cogí.

nearness ['niənis] *n* proximidad *f*, cercanía *f*, lo cercano; intimidad *f*; **because of its — to the station** por estar tan cerca de la estación.

near-sighted ['niə'saitid] *adj* corto de vista, miope.

near-sightedness ['niə'saitidnis] *n* miopía *f*.

neat [ni:t] *adj* (*of person's appearance, etc*) pulcro, esmerado, acicalado; *figure* atractivo, esbelto; (*shapely*) bien proporcionado; *garden, room etc* bien cuidado, bien arreglado; *work* primoroso; *writing, phrase* elegante; *plan* hábil, ingenioso; (*skilful*) diestro; *drink* puro, solo, sin mezcla; **to make a — job of something** hacer algo con esmero.

neatly ['ni:tli] *adv* pulcramente, esmeradamente, con esmero; con primor, primorosamente; elegantemente; hábilmente, ingeniosamente; diestramente.

neatness ['ni:tnis] *n* pulcritud *f*, esmero *m*; esbeltez *f*; buena proporción *f*; lo arreglado, lo cuidado; primor *m*; elegancia *f*; habilidad *f*; destreza *f*.

Nebuchadnezzar [,nebjukəd'nezə*] *m* Nabucodonosor.

nebula ['nebjulə] *n* nebulosa *f*.

nebulous ['nebjuləs] *adj* nebuloso; (*fig*) vago, confuso, impreciso.

necessarily ['nesisərili] *adv* necesariamente; forzosamente; **not —** cabe otra posibilidad, eso no es cierto del todo; **it is not — true that . . .** no es necesariamente cierto que . . .

necessary ['nesisəri] **1** *adj* necesario; preciso, esencial, indispensable, imprescindible; **with the — enthusiasm** con el debido entusiasmo; **all the — ceremonies** todas las ceremonias obligatorias; **if —** si es necesario, si es preciso; **it is — that . . .** es necesario que + *subj*, es preciso que + *subj*; **it is — for us to go** es preciso que vayamos; **it made it — for us to sell them** hizo inevitable que los vendiésemos; **I shall do everything —** haré todo lo necesario; **to do the —** hacer lo que hace falta, hacer lo que hay que hacer; **don't do more than is —** no haga más de lo necesario.

2 *n* cosa *f* necesaria, requisito *m* indispensable; (*also* **necessaries** *pl*) lo necesario; (*fam: money*) cónquibus *m*.

necessitate [ni'sesiteit] *vt* necesitar, exigir.

necessitous [ni'sesitəs] *adj* necesitado, indigente.

necessity [ni'sesiti] *n* (a) necesidad *f*; inevitabilidad *f*; **— is the mother of invention** la necesidad estimula la invención, el hambre aguza el ingenio; **the — for care** la necesidad del cuidado; **of —** por necesidad, forzosamente; **out of sheer —** por fuerza; **in case of —** si fuese necesario, en caso de urgencia; **it's a case of sheer —** es un caso de la mayor necesidad; **dire — leads me to ask** la más apremiante necesidad me obliga a pedirlo; **there is no — for you to do it** no es necesario que Vd lo haga; **to be under the — of** + *ger* verse obligado a + *infin*.
(b) (*article*) cosa *f* necesaria, requisito *m* indispensable; **necessities** artículos *mpl* de primera necesidad; **the necessities of life** las cosas necesarias para la vida; **a fridge is a — nowadays** es indispensable ahora tener nevera.
(c) (*poverty*) indigencia *f*; **to be in —** estar necesitado.

neck [nek] **1** *n* (a) (*Anat*) cuello *m*; garganta *f*; (*of animal*) pescuezo *m*; (*of bottle*) cuello *m*, gollete *m*; (*Geog*) istmo *m*; (*Sew*) escote *m*; (*Mus: of guitar*) cuello *m*, (*of violin*) mástil *m*; **to race — and — ir** a las parejas; **— or nothing** todo o nada; **to fall — and crop** caer de cabeza; **to beat someone — and crop** vencer a uno fácilmente; **to be up to one's —** (*in work*) tener trabajo hasta por encima de las cejas; **to be in something up to one's —** estar muy metido en un asunto; **to break one's —** desnucarse; **to break someone's —** romper el pescuezo a uno; **she fell on his —** ella se colgó de su cuello; **to get it in the —** (*fam*) pagarlas, cargárselas (*fam*), (*be told off*) recibir una peluca (*fam*); **to have someone breathing down one's —** ser seguido de cerca por uno, tener a uno sobre sus talones; **to stick one's — out** arriesgarse, exponerse a un ataque posible, atreverse a expresar una opinión; **to win by a —** ganar por un cuello; **to wring a rabbit's —** torcer el pescuezo a un conejo.
(b) (*fam*) = **nerve** 1(d).
2 *vi* (*fam*) acariciarse, abrazarse amorosamente.

neckband ['nekbænd] *n* tirilla *f*.
neckerchief ['nekətʃi:f] *n* (*arch*) pañuelo *m* de cuello.
necking ['nekiŋ] *n* (*fam*) caricias *fpl*, abrazos *mpl* amorosos.
necklace ['neklis] *n*, **necklet** ['neklit] *n* collar *m*.
neckline ['neklain] *n* escote *m*; **plunging —** escote *m* muy bajo.
necktie ['nektai] *n* corbata *f*.
necrological [‚nekrəu'lɔdʒikəl] *adj* necrológico.
necrology [ne'krɔlədʒi] *n* necrología *f*.
necromancer ['nekrəumænsə*] *n* nigromante *m*.
necromancy ['nekrəumænsi] *n* nigromancia *f*, nigromancia *f*.
necropolis [ne'krɔpəlis] *n* necrópolis *f*.
nectar ['nektə*] *n* néctar *m*.
nectarine ['nektəri:n] *n* nectarina *f*.
née [nei]: **Mary Green, — Smith** Mary Smith de Green.

need [ni:d] **1** *n* (a) necesidad *f* (*for, of* de); **if —(s) be, in case of —** si fuera necesario, en caso de urgencia; **there is every —** es totalmente indispensable; **I see no —** no veo la necesidad; **there is no — to** + *infin* no hace falta + *infin*; **there's no — to worry** no hay para qué inquietarse; **what — is there to buy it?** ¿qué necesidad hay de comprarlo?; **no — to say that . . .** excusado es decir que . . .; **no — to tell him what to do** no hace falta decirle qué hacer; **to be in — of, to have — of, to stand in — of** necesitar; **I have no — of advice** no necesito consejos, no me hacen falta consejos; **you have no — to go** no es preciso que vayas; **when I'm in — of a drink** cuando siento la necesidad de beber algo; **a house in — of painting** una casa que hay que pintar, una casa que convendría pintar.
(b) (*want, lack*) adversidad *f*; apuro *m*; (*absence*) carencia *f*; falta *f*, escasez *f*; **in times of —** en tiempos de adversidad, en tiempos de carestía; **there is much — of food** hay una gran escasez de alimentos.
(c) (*poverty*) necesidad *f*, indigencia *f*; **my — is great** es grande mi necesidad; **to be in —** estar necesitado.
(d) (*thing needed*) cosa *f* necesaria, requisito *m*; **bodily —s** necesidades *fpl* corporales; **the —s of industry** las necesidades de la industria; **my —s are few** soy poco exigente; **to supply someone's —s** proveer lo que necesita uno.
2 *vt* (a) (*of person*) necesitar; **I — it** lo necesito, me hace falta; **it's just what I —ed** es precisamente lo que necesitaba; **I — two more to make up the series** me faltan dos para completar la serie; **he —ed no**

bidding no se hizo de rogar; **he —s watching** hay que vigilarle, conviene vigilarle.
(b) (*of thing*) exigir, requerir, reclamar; **it —s care** requiere cuidado, exige cuidado; **a visa is —ed** se exige visado; **the report —s no comment** el informe no tiene necesidad de comentarios; **a much —ed holiday** unas vacaciones muy necesarias; **I gave it a much —ed wash** lo lavé pues le hacía mucha falta; **this will — some explaining** no va a ser fácil explicar esto.
(c) (**to —** to + *infin*) **I — to do it** tengo que hacerlo, debo hacerlo; **he —s to be told twice** hay que decírselo todo dos veces; **they don't — to be told all the details** no es preciso contarles todos los detalles; **you will hardly — to be reminded that . . .** apenas es necesario recordarles que . . .; **you only —ed to ask** no había sino pedir; **this room —s to be painted** hay que pintar este cuarto, conviene pintar este cuarto.
(d) (*v aux*) **— I go?** ¿he de ir?; **he —n't do it, — he?** ¿es esencial que lo haga?; **I — hardly add that . . .** apenas hay que añadir que . . .; **it — not be done now** no es preciso hacerlo ahora.
(e) (*impersonal*) **it —ed a war to alter that** fue necesaria una guerra para cambiar eso; **it doesn't — me to tell him** no hace falta que yo se lo diga.

needful ['ni:dful] **1** *adj* necesario. **2** *n* (*fam*) **the —** el cónquibus (*fam*).
neediness ['ni:dinis] *n* necesidad *f*, pobreza *f*.
needle ['ni:dl] **1** *n* aguja *f* (*all senses*); **to look for a — in a haystack** buscar una aguja en un pajar.
2 *adj*: **— match** partido *m* importantísimo, partido *m* muy emocionante, partido *m* muy reñido.
3 *vt* (*fam*) *person* picar, provocar, fastidiar; *drink* (*US*) añadir alcohol a.
needle case ['ni:dlkeis] *n* alfiletero *m*.
needlecraft ['ni:dlkrɑ:ft] *n* arte *m* de la costura.
needless ['ni:dlis] *adj* innecesario, superfluo, inútil; **— to say . . .** excusado es decir que . . ., está de más decir que . . ., huelga decir que . . .; **he was, — to say, drunk** estaba borracho, claro (está).
needlessly ['ni:dlisli] *adv* innecesariamente, inútilmente, en vano; **you worry quite —** te inquietas sin motivo alguno.
needlewoman ['ni:dl‚wumən] *n*, *pl* **—women** [‚wimin] costurera *f*; **to be a good —** coser bien.
needlework ['ni:dlwə:k] *n* labor *f* de aguja, costura *f*, bordado *m*; **to do —** hacer costura, coser.
needs [ni:dz] *adv* necesariamente, forzosamente; **if — must** si hace falta; **we must — walk** no tenemos más remedio que ir andando.
needy ['ni:di] *adj* necesitado, pobre, indigente.
ne'er [neə*] *adv* (*poet*) nunca.
ne'er-do-well ['neədu‚wel] **1** *adj* perdido. **2** *n* perdido *m*, perdulario *m*.
nefarious [ni'feəriəs] *adj* nefario, vil, inicuo.
negate [ni'geit] *vt* anular, invalidar.
negation [ni'geiʃən] *n* negación *f*.
negative ['negətiv] **1** *adj* negativo.
2 *n* (*answer*) negativa *f*; (*Gram*) negación *f*; (*Phot*) negativo *m*, prueba *f* negativa; (*Elec*) polo *m* negativo; **double —** negación *f* doble; **to answer in the —** dar una respuesta negativa.
3 *vt* (*veto*) poner veto a; (*vote down*) rechazar, desaprobar; *statement* negar, desmentir; *effect* anular.
negatively ['negətivli] *adv* negativamente.
neglect [ni'glekt] **1** *n* (*carelessness*) negligencia *f*, descuido *m*; (*of rule etc*) inobservancia *f*; (*of duty*) incumplimiento *m*; (*neglected state*) abandono *m*; (*of oneself*) dejadez *f*; (*towards others*) desatención *f*; **to die in —** morir abandonado.
2 *vt obligations etc* descuidar, desatender; *duty etc* no cumplir, faltar a; *friends* dejar de ver; desairar; *advice etc* no hacer caso de; (*omit*) omitir, olvidar; *opportunity* no aprovechar; *garden etc* no cuidar; *wife* dejar sola; **to — to** + *infin* olvidarse de + *infin*.
neglected [ni'glektid] *adj appearance* descuidado, desaliñado; *garden etc* sin cuidar; *wife* abandonada.
neglectful [ni'glektful] *adj* negligente, descuidado; **to be — of** descuidar, desatender.
negligée ['negliʒei] *n* (*nightdress etc*) salto *m* de cama; (*housecoat*) bata *f*.
negligence ['neglidʒəns] *n* negligencia *f*, descuido *m*; **through —** por descuido.
negligent ['neglidʒənt] *adj* negligente, descuidado; **to be — of** descuidar, desatender.
negligently ['neglidʒəntli] *adv* negligentemente, con descuido.
negligible ['neglidʒəbl] *adj* insignificante; despreciable; **a — quantity** una cantidad insignificante; **a by no means — opponent** un adversario nada despreciable.

negotiable [ni'gəuʃiəbl] *adj* negociable; *road etc* transitable; **not —** que no puede negociarse.
negotiate [ni'gəuʃieit] **1** *vt* (a) *treaty* negociar; *loan, deal etc* negociar, gestionar, agenciar.
(b) *obstacle* salvar, franquear; *river etc* pasar, cruzar; *bend* tomar.
2 *vi* negociar; **to — for** negociar para obtener; **— for peace** pedir la paz; **to — with someone** negociar con uno.
negotiation [ni,gəuʃi'eiʃən] *n* negociación *f*; gestión *f*; **to be in — with someone** estar negociando con uno; **the treaty is under —** el tratado está siendo negociado; **that will be a matter for —** eso tendrá que ser discutido, eso tendrá que someterse a discusión; **to enter into —s with someone** entrar en negociaciones con uno.
negotiator [ni'gəuʃieitə*] *n* negociador *m*, ora *f*.
Negress [ni:gres] *n* negra *f*.
Negro ['ni:grəu] **1** *adj* negro. **2** *n, pl* **Negroes** ['ni:grəuz] negro *m*.
negroid ['ni:grɔid] *adj* negroide.
neigh [nei] **1** *n* relincho *m*. **2** *vi* relinchar.
neighbour, (US) **neighbor** ['neibə*] **1** *n* vecino *m*, a *f*; *(fellow being)* prójimo *m*, a *f*; **Good N— Policy** (US) Política *f* del Buen Vecino.
2 *vt, also vi*: **to — upon** *(adjoin)* colindar con, estar contiguo a; *(be almost)* rayar en.
neighbourhood, (US) **neighborhood** ['neibəhud] *n*
(a) *(area)* vecindad *f*; barrio *m*, sección *f*, sector *m*; **all the girls of the —** todas las jóvenes del barrio; **not a very nice —** un barrio poco atractivo; **somewhere in the —** por allí, cerca de allí; **anyone in the — of the crime** cualquier persona que estuviera cerca del lugar del crimen; **the soil in that —** el suelo de aquel sector; **in the — of £80** alrededor de 80 libras.
(b) *(surrounding area)* alrededores *mpl*, cercanías *fpl*; **Málaga and its —** Málaga y su región.
(c) *(persons)* vecinos *mpl*, vecindario *m*.
neighbouring, (US) **neighboring** ['neibəriŋ] *adj* vecino; cercano, inmediato.
neighbourly, (US) **neighborly** ['neibəli] *adj* de buen vecino, amable, amistoso.
neighing ['neiiŋ] *n* relinchos *mpl*.
neither ['naiðə*] **1** *adv and conj*: **— he nor I** ni él ni yo; **he — smokes nor drinks** no bebe ni fuma.
2 *conj*: **if you aren't going, — am I** si tú no vas, yo tampoco; **— will he agree to sell it** ni consiente en venderlo tampoco.
3 *pron*: **— of them has any money** ninguno de los dos tiene dinero, ni el uno ni el otro tiene dinero; **— of them saw it** ni el uno ni el otro lo vio.
4 *adj*: **on — side** por ninguno de los dos lados, en ningún lado; **— car is for sale** no se vende ninguno de los dos coches.
nemesis ['nemisis] *n (fig)* justo castigo *m*, justicia *f*.
neoclassical ['ni:əu'klæsikəl] *adj* neoclásico.
neoclassicism ['ni:əu'klæsisizəm] *n* neoclasicismo *m*.
neofascism ['ni:əu'fæʃizəm] *n* neofascismo *m*.
neofascist ['ni:əu'fæʃist] **1** *adj* neofascista. **2** *n* neofascista *mf*.
neolithic [,ni:əu'liθik] *adj* neolítico.
neologism [ni'ɔlədʒizəm] *n* neologismo *m*.
neon ['ni:ɔn] *n* neón *m*, neo *m*; **— lamp, — light** lámpara *f* de neón.
neonazi ['ni:əu'nɑ:tsi] **1** *adj* neonazi, neonazista. **2** *n* neonazi *mf*.
neophyte ['ni:əufait] *n* neófito *m*, a *f*.
neoplatonic ['ni:əuplə'tɔnik] *adj* neoplatónico.
neoplatonism ['ni:əu'pleitənizəm] *n* neoplatonismo *m*.
neoplatonist ['ni:əu'pleitənist] *n* neoplatonista *mf*.
Nepal [ni'pɔːl] Nepal *m*.
Nepalese [,nepɔ:'li:z] **1** *adj* nepalés. **2** *n* nepalés *m*, esa *f*.
nephew ['nevju:] *n* sobrino *m*.
nephritis [ne'fraitis] *n* nefritis *f*.
nepotism ['nepətizəm] *n* nepotismo *m*.
Neptune ['neptju:n] *m* Neptuno.
nereid ['niəriid] *n* nereida *f*.
Nero ['niərəu] *m* Nerón.
nerve [nə:v] **1** *n* (a) *(Anat, Bot)* nervio *m*; *(Ent)* nervadura *f*; **my —s are on edge** tengo los nervios de punta; **it gets on my —s** me pone los nervios de punta, me crispa los nervios, me saca de quicio; **he gets on my —s** me fastidia terriblemente; **to strain every — to + infin** hacer un esfuerzo supremo por + *infin*.
(b) **—s** nerviosidad *f*, nerviosismo *m*; excitabilidad *f* nerviosa; **a fit of —s** un ataque de excitabilidad nerviosa; **to be in a state of —s** estar nervioso, estar

hipertenso; **she suffers from —s** padece una hipertensión nerviosa.
(c) *(courage)* valor *m*, sangre *f* fría; **I hadn't the — to do it** no tuve el valor de hacerlo; **to lose one's —** perder el valor; **it takes some — to do that** hacer eso exige mucha sangre fría.
(d) *(cheek)* descaro *m*, tupé *m*, frescura *f*, caradura *f*; **of all the —!, the — of it!, what a —!** ¡qué frescura!, ¡qué caradura!; **you've got a —!** ¡eres un caradura!, ¡eres un fresco!; **to have the — to + infin** ser bastante descarado como para + *infin*.
2 *vt*: **to — someone to do something** animar a uno a hacer algo, infundir a uno bastante ánimo para hacer algo.
3 *vr*: **to — oneself to do something** animarse a hacer algo, esforzarse por hacer algo.
nerve cell ['nə:vsel] *n* neurona *f*.
nerve centre, (US) **— center** ['nə:v,sentə*] *n (Anat)* centro *m* nervioso; *(fig)* punto *m* neurálgico.
nerveless ['nə:vlis] *adj (fig)* grasp flojo; *person* enervado, débil, soso.
nerve-racking ['nə:v,rækiŋ] *adj* que crispa los nervios; horripilante, espantoso.
nerviness ['nə:vinis] *n* nerviosidad *f*, nerviosismo *m*.
nervous ['nə:vəs] *adj person* nervioso; *(by nature)* tímido; miedoso, asustadizo; *breakdown, system etc* nervioso; **to be — of** tener miedo a; **to be — of + ger** tener miedo a + *infin*; **I was — on his account** estaba inquieto por él; **I was — about speaking to her** me daba miedo la noción de hablar con ella; **to get —** ponerse nervioso, sentir miedo; **I get — when I'm alone** me entra cierto miedo estando a solas; **it makes me —** me da miedo.
nervously ['nə:vəsli] *adv* nerviosamente; tímidamente.
nervousness ['nə:vəsnis] *n* nerviosidad *f*, nerviosismo *m*, timidez *f*, miedo *m*.
nervy ['nə:vi] *adj* nervioso.
nest [nest] **1** *n (of bird)* nido *m*; *(of hen)* nidal *m*; *(of animal)* madriguera *f*; *(of wasps)* avispero *m*; *(of ants)* hormiguero *m*; *(clutch of eggs, young birds)* nidada *f*; *(person's house)* casita *f*, hogar *m*; *(of thieves etc)* nido *m*, cueva *f*, guarida *f*; *(of boxes, drawers)* juego *m*; **to feather one's —** ponerse las botas, hacer su agosto; **to foul one's own —** manchar el proprio nido.
2 *vi (bird)* anidar, hacer su nido; *(collector)* buscar nidos.
nest egg ['nesteg] *n* nidal *m*; *(fig)* ahorros *mpl*, cantidad *f* ahorrada, buena hucha *f*.
nesting box ['nestiŋbɔks] *n* nidal *m*, ponedero *m*.
nestle ['nesl] *vi* (a) **to — among leaves** hacerse un nido entre las hojas; **to — down among the blankets** hacerse un ovillo entre las mantas; **to — up to someone** arrimarse cómodamente a uno, apretarse contra uno.
(b) **a house nestling beside a wood** una casa situada al abrigo de un bosque; **a village nestling among hills** un pueblecito protegido por las colinas.
nestling ['nesliŋ] *n* pajarito *m*.
net¹ [net] **1** *n* red *f (also fig)*; *(mesh)* malla *f*; *(fabric)* tul *m*; *(for hair etc)* redecilla *f*. **2** *vt* coger con red.
net² [net] *(Comm)* **1** *adj* neto, líquido; *income, price, weight etc* neto; **at a — profit of 5%** con un beneficio neto de 5 por cien; **"terms strictly —"** "sin descuento". **2** *vt* ganar en limpio, producir en limpio; **he —s £3000 a year** gana una renta neta de 3000 libras al año.
nether ['neðə*] *adj* inferior, más bajo, de abajo; **— lip** labio *m* inferior; **— regions** infierno *m*.
Netherlands ['neðələndz] *pl* Países *mpl* Bajos.
nethermost ['neðəməust] *adj superl* (el *etc*) más bajo.
netting ['netiŋ] *n* red *f*, redes *fpl*; *(obra f de)* malla *f*.
nettle ['netl] **1** *n* ortiga *f*. **2** *vt* provocar, irritar, molestar; **somewhat —d by this** algo molesto por eso.
nettle rash ['netlræʃ] *n* urticaria *f*.
network ['netwə:k] *n (fig)* red *f*; **radio —** red *f* de emisoras; **the national railway —** la red nacional de ferrocarriles; **a — of spies** una red de espías.
neural ['njuərəl] *adj* neural.
neuralgia [njuə'rældʒə] *n* neuralgia *f*.
neurasthenia [,njuərəs'θi:niə] *n* neurastenia *f*.
neurasthenic [,njuərəs'θenik] *adj* neurasténico.
neuritis [njuə'raitis] *n* neuritis *f*.
neurologist [njuə'rɔlədʒist] *n* neurólogo *m*.
neurology [njuə'rɔlədʒi] *n* neurología *f*.
neuron ['njuərɔn] *n* neurona *f*.
neuropath ['njuərəpæθ] *n* neurópata *mf*.
neurosis [njuə'rəusis] *n pl* **neuroses** [njuə'rəusi:z] neurosis *f*.

neurotic [njuə'rɔtik] **1** *adj* neurótico. **2** *n* neurótico *m*, a *f*.

neuter ['nju:tə*] **1** *adj* (*Gram*) neutro; *cat etc* sin sexo, castrado.
2 *n* (*Gram*) género *m* neutro; (*cat etc*) macho *m* castrado, animal *m* sin sexo.
3 *vt cat etc* castrar, capar.

neutral ['nju:trəl] **1** *adj person*, *country*, *opinion* neutral; (*Zool, Bot, Elec, Chem etc*) neutro; *colour* indeciso, indeterminado; **to remain** — seguir siendo neutral, no tomar partido.
2 *n* neutral *mf*; país *m* neutral; **in** — (*Mech*) en punto muerto.

neutralism ['nju:trəlizəm] *n* neutralismo *m*.

neutralist ['nju:trəlist] **1** *adj* neutralista. **2** *n* neutralista *mf*.

neutrality [nju:'træliti] *n* neutralidad *f*.

neutralization [,nju:trəlai'zeifən] *n* neutralización *f*.

neutralize ['nju:trəlaiz] *vt* neutralizar.

neutron ['nju:trɔn] *n* neutrón *m*.

never ['nevə*] *adv* (**a**) nunca, jamás; —! ¡jamás!; **I** — went no fui nunca, no fui jamás; **you** — saw anything like it nunca se ha visto nada parecido; **I have** — yet seen anything so horrible en mi vida he visto nada más horrible; — **in all my life** jamás en la vida; **it had** — **been tried before** no se había intentado antes.
(**b**) (*emphatic negative*) —!, **you** — did! ¿de veras?; — **a one** ni uno siquiera; — **a word did he say** no dijo ni una sola palabra; **I** — **expected it** no contaba con eso de ningún modo; **surely you** — **bought it?** ¿pero lo has comprado de veras?; **well I** —! ¡caramba!

never-ending ['nevər'endiŋ] *adj* inacabable, interminable.

never-failing ['nevə'feiliŋ] *adj* infalible.

nevermore ['nevə'mɔ:*] *adv* nunca más.

never-never ['nevə'nevə*] *n* (*fam*): **to buy something on the** — comprar algo a plazos.

nevertheless [,nevəðə'les] *adv* sin embargo, no obstante, con todo; **it is** — **true that** . . . con todo es verdad que . . .

never-to-be-forgotten ['nevətəbi:,fə'gɔtn] *adj* inolvidable.

new [nju:] *adj* nuevo; reciente; (*fresh*) fresco, nuevo; *bread* tierno; (*different*) nuevo, distinto; **a** — **car** (*different*) un nuevo coche, (*brand new*) un coche nuevo; **the** — **students** los nuevos estudiantes; **the** — **people in No. 5** la nueva familia del núm 5, la familia que acaba de establecerse en el núm 5; **she's very** —, **poor girl** no está habituada, la pobre; **are you** — **here?** ¿eres nuevo aquí?; **are you** — **to this?** ¿esto es nuevo para ti?; **he came** — **to us last year** empezó a trabajar con nosotros el año pasado nada más; **what's** —? (*fam*) ¿qué hay de nuevo? (*fam*); **it's as good as** — está como nuevo; **there's nothing** — **under the sun** no hay nada nuevo bajo las estrellas.

new- [nju:] (*in compounds*) recién . . .

newborn ['nju:bɔ:n] *adj* recién nacido.

newcomer ['nju:,kʌmə*] *n* recién llegado *m*, a *f*, nuevo *m*, a *f*.

New England [,nju:'iŋglənd] la Nueva Inglaterra.

new-fangled ['nju:,fæŋgld] *adj* (*pej*) recién inventado, modernísimo; que está tan de moda.

new-found ['nju:,faund] *adj* recién descubierto; **his** — **zeal** el entusiasmo que acaba de mostrar.

Newfoundland [,nju:fənd'lænd] Terranova *f*; — **dog** perro *m* de Terranova.

New Guinea [,nju:'gini:] Nueva Guinea *f*.

newish ['nju:if] *adj* bastante nuevo.

new-laid ['nju:'leid] *adj egg* recién puesto, fresco.

newly ['nju:li] *adv* nuevamente, recién . . .; — **made** recién hecho, acabado de hacer; **those** — **arrived** los recién llegados; **those** — **arrived from France** los que acaban de llegar de Francia.

newly-weds ['nju:liwedz] *npl* recién casados *mpl*.

New Mexico [,nju:'meksikəu] Nuevo Méjico *m*.

new-mown ['nju:'məun] *adj* recién segado.

newness ['nju:nis] *n* novedad *f*; (*in a job etc*) inexperiencia *f*, falta *f* de práctica.

New Orleans [nju:'ɔ:liənz] Nueva Orleáns *f*.

news [nju:z] *n sing* noticias *fpl*; nuevas *fpl*; **a piece of** — una noticia, una nueva; "**N**— **in Brief**" (*newspaper*) "Brevedades"; **a sad piece of** — una triste noticia; **that's good** — es buena noticia; **no** — **is good** — falta de noticias: buena señal; **it was** — **to me** me cogió de nuevas; **what** —?, **what's the** —? ¿qué hay de nuevo?; **they're in the** — se oye hablar mucho de ellos, figuran mucho en los periódicos (*etc*); **to break the** — **to someone** dar una noticia a uno; **when the** — **broke** al saberse la noticia; **I have** — **for you** tengo que darte una noticia.

newsagent ['nju:z,eidʒənt] *n* vendedor *m* de periódicos.

newsboy ['nju:zbɔi] *n* chico *m* que reparte periódicos.

news bulletin ['nju:z,bulitin] *n* (*Radio*) noticiario *m*, diario *m* hablado; (TV) telediario *m*.

newscast ['nju:zka:st] *n* telediario *m*.

newscaster ['nju:z'ka:stə*] *n* locutor *m* de telediario, locutora *f* de telediario.

newsdealer ['nju:z,di:lə*] *n* vendedor *m* de periódicos.

news flash ['nju:zflæf] *n* flash *m*, noticia *f* de última hora.

news item ['nju:z,aitəm] *n* noticia *f*.

newsletter ['nju:z,letə*] *n* hoja *f* informativa, informe *m*.

newsman ['nju:zmæn] *n*, *pl* —**men** [men] periodista *m*, reportero *m*.

news sheet ['nju:zfi:t] *n* hoja *f* informativa; periódico *m*.

New South Wales ['nju:sauθ'weilz] Nueva Gales *f* del Sur.

newspaper ['nju:z,peipə*] **1** *n* periódico *m*, diario *m*. **2** *attr* de periódico, periodístico.

newspaperman ['nju:zpeipəmæn] *n*, *pl* —**men** [men] periodista *m*.

newsprint ['nju:zprint] *n* papel *m* prensa.

newsreel ['nju:zri:l] *n* noticiario *m*, película *f* de actualidades, (*in Spain*) Nodo *m* (*noticiario m documental*).

newsroom ['nju:zrum] *n* gabinete *m* de lectura.

news stand ['nju:zstænd] *n* quiosco *m* de periódicos.

news theatre ['nju:z,θiatə*] *n* cine *m* de actualidades.

newsworthy ['nju:z,wə:ði] *adj* periodístico, sensacional.

newsy ['nju:zi] *adj* lleno de noticias.

newt [nju:t] *n* tritón *m*.

New York ['nju:'jɔ:k] Nueva York; (*attr*) neoyorquino.

New Yorker ['nju:'jɔ:kə*] *n* neoyorquino *m*, a *f*.

New Zealand [nju:'zi:lənd] Nueva Zelanda *f*, Nueva Zelandia *f*; (*attr*) neozelandés.

New Zealander [nju:'zi:ləndə*] *n* neozelandés *m*, esa *f*.

next [nekst] **1** *adj* (**a**) (*of place*) próximo, inmediato, contiguo, vecino; **the** — **room** la habitación al lado de ésta; **the** — **house** la casa vecina, la casa de al lado; **on the** — **page** a la vuelta, a la página siguiente; **I get out at the** — **stop** yo salgo en la próxima parada.
(**b**) (*of order*) próximo, siguiente; primero; **the** — **in order is** . . . el próximo siguiendo el orden es . . ., el primero según el orden es . . .; **in the** — **volume** en el tomo siguiente, en el tomo después de éste; **the** — **life** la otra vida; — **time** la próxima vez; — **time you see him** la próxima vez que le veas; **the** — **but one** el segundo después de éste; "**see** — **page**" "véase a la página siguiente"; "**continued in the** — **column**" "sigue en la columna inmediata"; "**to be continued in our** —" "continuará"; **he's** — **after me** es el primero después de mí; — **please!** ¡el siguiente!; **what** —? y ahora ¿qué?; **what** —, **madam?** (*in shop*) ¿algo más, señora?; **who's** —? ¿quién es el siguiente?; **whatever** —! ¡qué horror!
(**c**) (*of time*) próximo, siguiente; *week, month, year* próximo, que viene; — **year** (*looking to future*) el año que viene, (*in past time*) el año siguiente; — **day** el día siguiente; **the** — **day but one** el segundo día después de éste; **the** — **5 days** los 5 días que vienen; — **morning** la mañana siguiente, a la mañana; **on 4th May** — el próximo 4 de mayo; **the year after** — el segundo año después de éste; **by this time** — **year** por estas fechas del año que viene.
2 *adv* (**a**) (*of place, order*) inmediatamente después; **who comes** —? ¿quién sigue?, ¿a quién le toca?; **what do we do** —? ¿qué hacemos ahora?; **the** — **smaller size** el tamaño más pequeño después de éste; **the** — **best thing would be to** + *infin* lo mejor después de esto sería + *infin*; **to take the** — **best** tomar el segundo.
(**b**) (*of time*) luego, después; inmediatamente; la próxima vez; — **we put the salt in** luego echamos la sal; **what did he do** —? ¿qué hizo después?, ¿qué hizo entonces?; **when you** — **see him** cuando le veas la próxima vez; **when I** — **saw him** cuando le volví a ver.
3 *prep* (**a**) (*also* — **to**) junto a, al lado de; **the car** — **to the door** el coche que está junto a la puerta; **his room is** — **to mine** su habitación está al lado de la mía; **to wear silk** — (**to**) **one's skin** llevar seda sobre la piel.
(**b**) (*fig*) casi; **we got it for** — **to nothing** lo adquirimos por casi nada; **there was** — **to nobody**

there no había casi nadie; **there is — to no news** apenas hay noticias, no hay noticias casi; *see* **door, kin** *etc*.

next-door ['neks'dɔ:*] *adj* de al lado.

nexus ['neksəs] *n* nexo *m*.

Niagara [nai'ægrə] Niágara *m*; **— Falls** Cataratas *fpl* de Niágara.

nib [nib] *n* punta *f*; (*of fountain pen*) plumilla *f*, plumín *m*.

nibble ['nibl] 1 *n* mordisco *m*; **I never had a — all day** (*Fishing*) el corcho no se movió en todo el día; **at £3000 he never got a —** a las 3000 libras nadie le echó un tiento.
2 *vt* mordiscar; (*rat etc*) roer; (*horse*) rozar; (*fish*) picar; **the cheese is all —d** el queso está lleno de roeduras.
3 *vi*: **to — at** mordiscar *etc* (*as vt*); **to — at an offer** considerar una oferta, mostrar cierto interés por una oferta.

nibs [nibz] *n* (*fam*): **his —** su señoría.

Nicaragua [ˌnikə'rægjuə] Nicaragua *f*.

Nicaraguan [ˌnikə'rægjuən] 1 *adj* nicaragüense. 2 *n* nicaragüense *mf*.

Nice [ni:s] Niza.

nice [nais] *adj* (a) (*of person: likeable*) simpático; **he's a — man** es un hombre simpático.
(b) (*of person: kind*) amable; **he was very — about it** estuvo muy amable; **it is — of you to help Vd** es muy amable ayudándome; **try to be — to him** procura ser amable con él; **I find it hard to be — to him** encuentro difícil hablar amistosamente con él.
(c) (*of person: attractive*) guapo, mono, bonito; **how — you look!** ¡qué guapa estás!
(d) (*of thing: pleasant*) agradable, ameno; (*attractive*) mono, bonito, precioso; *weather etc* bueno; **a — photo** una bonita foto; **that's a — ring** ¡qué anillo más mono!; **what a — idea that was!** ¡ésa sí fue una idea genial!; **it's — here** aquí se está bien; **we had a very — holiday in Ibiza** lo pasamos muy bien en Ibiza, hemos pasado unas vacaciones excelentes en Ibiza; **it smells —** huele bien, tiene un olor agradable; **it doesn't taste at all —** tiene un sabor nada agradable; **they give you — things to do** le dan cosas interesantes que hacer; **they give you — things to eat** le dan cosas deliciosas que comer; **it's not very — to have to + infin** no es muy agradable tener que + *infin*.
(e) (*of things, persons: refined*) fino, culto; bien; **he has — manners** tiene modales muy finos; **where are all the — girls?** ¿adónde se habrán metido todas las chicas finas?; **only — people live here** aquí no vive sino gente culta, (*pej*) aquí no vive sino gente bien; **a — district** un barrio elegante; **that's not — aquello** es feo, eso no es fino.
(f) (*intensive*) muy, bastante, bien; **— and sweet** bien dulce; **— and early** tempranito; **it's — and warm here** aquí hace un calor agradable; **my feet are — and warm** tengo los pies a gusto y calientes; **a — long holiday** unas vacaciones bien largas; **a — cold drink** una bebida bien fría.
(g) (*fastidious*) melindroso, delicado; difícil de contentar; (*exacting*) exigente; (*precise*) exacto, meticuloso; (*scrupulous*) escrupuloso; **he's not too — about his methods** no es demasiado escrupuloso en cuanto a sus métodos.
(h) (*requiring care etc*) fino, delicado, sutil; **a — distinction** una distinción sutil; **a — point** un punto delicado; **it's a — question whether . . .** es difícil determinar si . . .
(i) (*discriminating*) fino, discernidor; **he has a — ear** tiene un oído fino.
(j) (*iro*) bonito, valiente; **a — friend you are!** ¡valiente amigo!; **that's a — thing to say!** ¡qué cosas más bonitas me dices!; **a — mess** ¡un lío imponente!

nice-looking ['nais'lukiŋ] *adj* atractivo; *person* mono, guapo.

nicely ['naisli] *adv* amablemente; agradablemente; con finura, bien; **very —,** thanks muy bien, gracias; **a — situated house** una casa bien situada; **that will do —** eso está muy bien; **he's getting on —** hace buenos progresos; **she thanked me very —** muy amablemente me dio las gracias; **the child behaves quite —** el niño tiene modales bastante buenos.

niceness ['naisnis] *n* simpatía *f*, lo simpático; amabilidad *f*; lo agradable, amenidad *f*; finura *f*, lo culto; delicadeza *f*; meticulosidad *f*; escrupulosidad *f*; sutileza *f*; discernimiento *m*.

nicety ['naisiti] *n* = **niceness**; **to judge something to a —** juzgar algo con toda precisión; **niceties** detalles *mpl*, puntos *mpl* sutiles.

niche [ni:ʃ] *n* nicho *m*; hornacina *f*; (*fig*) colocación *f*

conveniente, buena posición *f*; **to find a — for oneself** encontrarse una buena posición.

Nicholas ['nikələs] *m* Nicolás.

Nick [nik] *nombre cariñoso de* **Nicholas; Old —** Patillas.

nick¹ [nik] 1 *n* mella *f*, muesca *f*, corte *m*; **in the — of time** a última hora, en el momento crítico.
2 *vt* (a) mellar, hacer muescas en, hacer cortes en; cortar; (*with sword etc*) pinchar.
(b) (*sl: steal*) robar, birlar; (*sl: arrest*) trincar.

nick² [nik] *n* (*sl: prison*) jaula *f*.

nickel ['nikl] *n* níquel *m*; (*US*) *moneda de 5 centavos*.

nickel-plated ['nikl'pleitid] *adj* niquelado.

nickname ['nikneim] 1 *n* apodo *m*, mote *m*. 2 *vt* apodar; **they —d him Nobby** le dieron el apodo de Nobby; **Clark —d Nobby** Clark apodado Nobby.

nicotine ['nikəti:n] *n* nicotina *f*.

niece [ni:s] *n* sobrina *f*.

niff [nif] *n* (*sl*) olorcito *m* (*of* a); tufillo *m*.

niffy ['nifi] *adj* (*sl*) maloliente.

nifty ['nifti] *adj* (*fam*) (*smart*) elegante, muy pena; (*skilful*) diestro, hábil, experto.

Nigeria [nai'dʒiəriə] Nigeria *f*.

Nigerian [nai'dʒiəriən] 1 *adj* nigeriano. 2 *n* nigeriano *m*, a *f*.

niggardliness ['nigədlinis] *n* tacañería *f*.

niggardly ['nigədli] *adj person* tacaño, avariento; *allowance etc* miserable.

nigger ['nigə*] *n* (*pej*) negro *m*, a *f*; **to be the — in the woodpile** ser el obstáculo, ser la cosa que estropea el todo.

niggle ['nigl] *vi* (*worry*) inquietarse por pequeñeces; (*fuss*) perder el tiempo con detalles nimios; (*complain*) quejarse, murmurar.

niggling ['nigliŋ] *adj detail* nimio, insignificante; (*small-minded*) de miras estrechas.

nigh [nai] (*arch or prov*) 1 *adv* cerca; casi, **it's — on finished** está casi terminado. 2 *prep* cerca de.

night [nait] 1 *n* noche *f*; **a Beethoven —** un concierto dedicado a la música de Beethoven; **first —** (*Theat*) estreno *m*; **good —!** ¡buenas noches!; **last — anoche; the — before last** anteanoche; **to-morrow —** mañana por la noche; **the — before the ceremony** la víspera de la ceremonia; **all —** toda la noche; **at —, by —, in the —** de noche, por la noche; **11 o'clock at —** las 11 de la noche; **it is — es de noche; it's the servant's — out** es la tarde libre de la criada; **to have a — out** salir de juerga por la noche; **to have a bad —** dormir mal, pasar una mala noche; **to have a late —** no acostarse hasta muy tarde; **she's used to late —s** ella está acostumbrada a acostarse muy tarde; **to make a — of it** estar de juerga hasta muy entrada la noche.
2 *attr* nocturno, de noche; **— work** trabajo *m* nocturno.

night-bird ['naitbə:d] *n* pájaro *m* nocturno; (*person*) trasnochador *m*, ora *f*.

nightcap ['naitkæp] *n* gorro *m* de dormir; (*drink*) resopón *m*.

night club ['naitklʌb] *n* cabaret *m*.

nightdress ['naitdres] *n* camisón *m* (de noche).

nightfall ['naitfɔ:l] *n* anochecer *m*; **at —** al anochecer; **by —** antes del anochecer.

night-fighter ['naitfaitə*] *n* (*Aer*) caza *m* nocturno.

nightgown ['naitgaun] *n*, **nightie** ['naiti] *n* (*fam*) camisón *m* (de noche).

nightingale ['naitiŋgeil] *n* ruiseñor *m*.

nightjar ['naitdʒa:*] *n* chotacabras *m*.

night life ['naitlaif] *n* vida *f* nocturna.

night light ['naitlait] *n* mariposa *f*.

nightly ['naitli] 1 *adv* todas las noches. 2 *adj* de noche, nocturno; (*regular*) de todas las noches.

nightmare ['naitmɛə*] *n* pesadilla *f* (*also fig*).

nightmarish ['naitmɛəriʃ] *adj* de pesadilla.

night school ['naitsku:l] *n* escuela *f* nocturna.

nightshade ['naitʃeid] *n* dulcamara *f*, hierba *f* mora; **deadly —** belladona *f*.

nightshift ['naitʃift] *n* turno *m* de noche.

nightshirt ['naitʃə:t] *n* camisa *f* de dormir (*de caballero*).

night-time ['naitaim] *n* noche *f*; **in the —** de noche, durante la noche.

night watchman ['nait'wɔtʃmən] *n*, *pl* **—men** [mən] sereno *m*; vigilante *m* de noche, vigilante *m* nocturno.

nihilism ['naiilizəm] *n* nihilismo *m*.

nihilist ['naiilist] *n* nihilista *mf*.

nihilistic [ˌnaii'listik] *adj* nihilista.

nil [nil] *n* cero *m*, nada *f*; **Granada beat Murcia two — nil** el Granada venció al Murcia dos-cero.

Nile [nail] Nilo *m*.

nimble ['nimbl] *adj* (*in moving*) ágil, ligero; (*in wit*) listo; *fingers etc* diestro, experto.
nimbly ['nimbli] *adv* ágilmente, ligeramente; diestramente.
nimbus ['nimbəs] *n* nimbo *m*.
nincompoop ['niŋkəmpuːp] *n* bobo *m*, a *f*, papirote *m*.
nine [nain] *adj* nueve; **to be dressed up to the —s** estar hecho un brazo de mar.
ninepins ['nainpinz] *npl* (*objects*) bolos *mpl*; (*game*) juego *m* de bolos; **to go down like —** caer como bolos en bolera.
nineteen ['nain'tiːn] *adj* diecinueve; *see* **dozen**.
nineteenth ['nain'tiːnθ] *adj* decimonoveno, decimonono.
ninetieth ['naintiiθ] *adj* nonagésimo.
ninety ['nainti] *adj* noventa; **the nineties** (*eg* 1990s) los años noventa; **the naughty nineties** los alegres años noventa (del siglo XIX); **to be in one's nineties** tener más de noventa años.
ninny ['nini] *n* bobo *m*, a *f*.
ninth [nainθ] *adj* noveno, nono.
nip[1] [nip] **1** *n* pellizco *m*; mordisco *m*; **there's a — in the air** hace un poco frío, hay helada.
  2 *vt* (*with fingers*) pellizcar, pinchar; (*bite*) mordiscar; (*cut*) cortar; *plant* helar; (*wind*) picar, helar; (*sl*) coger, birlar; **to — one's fingers in a door** cogerse los dedos en una puerta; **to — off** cortar.
  3 *vi* correr, ir a toda velocidad; **we were —ping along at 80 mph** corríamos a 80 mph; **to — in** entrar, entrar un momento; entrar sin ser visto; **to — in and out of the traffic** colarse por entre el tráfico; **to — off** pirarse, largarse; **I must — out for a moment** salgo un momento; **I —ped round to the shop** fui en dos patadas a la tienda.
nip[2] [nip] *n* (*of drink*) trago *m*.
nipper ['nipə*] *n* chiquillo *m*, a *f*.
nipple ['nipl] *n* (*Anat*) pezón *m*; (*of man, bottle*) tetilla *f*; (*Mech*) boquilla *f* roscada, manguito *m* de unión; (*for greasing*) engrasador *m*, pezón *m* de engrase.
nippy ['nipi] *adj person* ágil, listo; *car etc* rápido, veloz; **be — about it!** ¡corre!, ¡menearse!; **we shall have to be —** tendremos que darnos prisa.
nit [nit] *n* (*Zool*) liendre *f*; (*sl*) imbécil *mf*, idiota *m*; **you —!** ¡imbécil!
nitrate ['naitreit] *n* nitrato *m*.
nitre, (US) **niter** ['naitə*] *n* nitro *m*.
nitric ['naitrik] *adj*: **— acid** ácido *m* nítrico.
nitrogen ['naitrədʒən] *n* nitrógeno *m*.
nitrogenous [nai'trɔdʒinəs] *adj* nitrogenado.
nitroglycerin(e) ['naitrəu'glisəriːn] *n* nitroglicerina *f*.
nitrous ['naitrəs] *adj* nitroso.
nitwit ['nitwit] *n* (*sl*) imbécil *mf*, idiota *m*; **you —!** imbécil!
nix [niks] *n* (*sl*) nada.
no [nəu] **1** *adv* (a) no; **whether he comes or —** si viene o no.
  (b) (*comp*) **I am — taller than you** yo no soy más alto que tú.
  2 *adj* (a) ninguno, no . . . alguno; **no-one** *see* **nobody**; (*often not translated, eg*) **I have — money** no tengo dinero, no tengo dinero alguno; **he made — reply** no contestó, no dio respuesta alguna; **— two of them are alike** no hay dos iguales; **it's — distance** no está lejos; **it's — trouble** no es molestia; **— surrender!** ¡no nos rendimos! **"— smoking"** "se prohibe fumar"; **details of little or — interest** detalles *mpl* de poco o ningún interés.
  (b) **problems of — easy solution** problemas que no tienen soluciones fáciles, problemas que no se resolverán fácilmente; **it is — easy task** es una tarea nada fácil; **he's — poet** de poeta no tiene nada; **he was — general** no era lo que se llama un general, no merecía el nombre de general; **judge or — judge, he's a fool** no importa que sea juez, es un tonto.
  (c) **there's — denying it** es imposible negarlo; **there's — getting out of it** no hay posibilidad de evitarlo; **there's — pleasing him** resulta imposible contentarle.
  3 *n* (*pl* **noes** [nəuz]) (a) no *m*; **I won't take — for an answer** no permito que lo rechaces, no acepto una respuesta negativa.
  (b) (*Parl*) voto *m* negativo, voto *m* en contra; **there were 7 —es** votaron 7 en contra; **the —es have it** se ha rechazado la moción.
Noah ['nəuə] *m* Noé.
nob[1] [nɔb] *n* (*sl*: *Anat*) cabeza *f*.
nob[2] [nɔb] *n* (*sl*: *person of importance*) personaje *m*, pájaro *m* de cuenta; (*toff*) majo *m*, currutaco *m*.
nobble ['nɔbl] *vt* (*sl*) *person* sobornar; ejercer presión sobre, persuadir por medios nada rectos; *horse* narcotizar, estropear; (*arrest*) coger; (*steal*) birlar, pisar.

nobility [nəu'biliti] *n* (*all senses*) nobleza *f*.
noble ['nəubl] **1** *adj* noble; *title* de nobleza. **2** *n* noble *m*, aristócrata *m*, (*Spanish Hist*) hidalgo *m*.
nobleman ['nəublmən] *n*, *pl* **—men** [mən] noble *m*, aristócrata *m*, (*Spanish Hist*) hidalgo *m*.
nobleness ['nəublnis] *n* nobleza *f*.
noblesse oblige [nəu'blesəu'bliːʒ] nobleza obliga.
noblewoman ['nəublwumən] *n*, *pl* **—women** [wimin] dama *f* noble, aristócrata *f*, (*Spanish Hist*) hidalga *f*.
nobly ['nəubli] *adv* noblemente, con nobleza; (*fig*) generosamente.
nobody ['nəubədi] **1** *pron* nadie; **— spoke** nadie habló, no habló nadie; **who spoke? . . . —** ¿quién habló? . . . nadie; **— has more right to it than she has** no hay nadie que tenga más derecho a ello que ella; **would — buy it?** ¿no había quién lo comprara?
  2 *n*: **a mere —** un don nadie, un cero a la izquierda; **I knew him when he was a —** le conocí cuando no era nadie.
nocturnal [nɔk'təːnl] *adj* nocturno.
nocturne ['nɔktəːn] *n* nocturno *m*.
nod [nɔd] **1** *n* (*sleepy etc*) cabezada *f*; (*sign*) señal *f* hecha con la cabeza, inclinación *f* de cabeza; **a — is as good as a wink** a buen entendedor con pocas palabras basta; **he gave me a —** me saludó inclinando la cabeza; **he agreed with a —** asintió con la cabeza; **to go through on the —** ser aprobado sin discusión, ser aprobado sin someterse a votación.
  2 *vt head* inclinar, mover, hacer una señal con; **he —ded his agreement** asintió con la cabeza; **he —ded a greeting** me saludó inclinando la cabeza; **he —ded his head** (*ie saying yes*) asintió con la cabeza, movió la cabeza afirmativamente.
  3 *vi* (*sleepily*) dar cabezadas, cabecear; (*say yes*) decir que sí con la cabeza, asentir con la cabeza; (*trees*) mecerse, inclinarse; **Homer —s** incluso Homero se duerme a veces.
noddle ['nɔdl] *n* (*fam*) mollera *f*.
node [nəud] *n* (*Anat, Astron, Phys*) nodo *m*; (*Bot*) nudo *m*.
nodular ['nɔdjulə*] *adj* nodular.
nodule ['nɔdjuːl] *n* nódulo *m*.
noggin ['nɔgin] *n* (a) vaso *m* pequeño, (*loosely*) vaso *m*, caña *f* (de cerveza); **let's have a —** tomemos algo.
  (b) (*measure*) medida de licor (= 1,42 *decilitros*).
no-good ['nəugud] *adj* (US *fam*) malísimo, malvado.
nohow ['nəuhau] *adv* (*fam*) de ninguna manera, por ningún medio que sea.
noise [nɔiz] **1** *n* (a) ruido *m*; estrépito *m*; estruendo *m*; clamor *m*; tumulto *m*; alboroto *m*; (*fig*) escándalo *m*; **to make a —** hacer ruido; **the book made a lot of — when it came out** el libro causó un escándalo cuando apareció, al aparecer se armó un escándalo en torno al libro.
  (b) **big —** (*person: fam*) pez *m* gordo, pájaro *m* de cuenta; **he's a big —** now ahora es un personaje.
  2 *vt*: **to — something abroad** divulgar la noticia de algo, hacer correr la voz de algo; **we don't want it —d abroad** no queremos que se publique.
noiseless ['nɔizlis] *adj* silenciosamente, sin ruido.
noisily ['nɔizili] *adv* ruidosamente, estrepitosamente, clamorosamente; escandalosamente.
noisiness ['nɔizinis] *n* ruido *m*, estrépito *m*; lo ruidoso, lo estrepitoso.
noisome ['nɔisəm] *adj* (*disgusting*) asqueroso; (*smelly*) fétido, maloliente; (*harmful*) nocivo.
noisy ['nɔizi] *adj* ruidoso, estrepitoso, clamoroso; *child etc* escandaloso; *protest* ruidoso.
nomad ['nəumæd] *n* nómada *mf*.
nomadic [nəu'mædik] *adj* nómada.
nomadism ['nəumədizəm] *n* nomadismo *m*.
no-man's land ['nəumænzlænd] *n* tierra *f* de nadie.
nom de plume ['nɔmdə'pluːm] *n* seudónimo *m*, nombre *m* artístico.
nomenclature [nəu'menklətʃə*] *n* nomenclatura *f*.
nominal ['nɔminl] *adj* nominal; *sum, rent etc* nominal; **he's only the — head** es el jefe solamente en nombre.
nominalism ['nɔminəlizəm] *n* nominalismo *m*.
nominally ['nɔminəli] *adv* nominalmente.
nominate ['nɔmineit] *vt* nombrar; **to — someone as chairman** proponer a uno como candidato a la presidencia, nombrar a uno para presidente; **to — someone for a job** nombrar a uno para un cargo.
nomination [.nɔmi'neiʃən] *n* nombramiento *m*; propuesta *f*.
nominative ['nɔminətiv] *n* nominativo *m*.
nominee [.nɔmi'niː] *n* candidato *m*; **the — of someone** el candidato propuesto por uno, el candidato que apoya uno.

non . . . [nɔn] *in compounds*: no . . ., des . . ., in . . .
non-acceptance ['nɔnək'septəns] *n* rechazo *m*.
nonagenarian [ˌnɔnədʒi'neəriən] **1** *adj* nonagenario, noventón. **2** *n* nonagenario *m*, a *f*, noventón *m*, ona *f*.
non-aggression ['nɔnə'greʃən] *n* no agresión *f*; — **pact** pacto *m* de no agresión.
non-alcoholic ['nɔnælkə'hɔlik] *adj* no alcohólico, analcohólico.
non-aligned ['nɔnə'laind] *adj* neutral, no comprometido.
non-alignment ['nɔnə'lainmənt] *n* neutralismo *m*; no comprometimiento *m*.
non-appearance ['nɔnə'piərəns] *n* ausencia *f*; (*Law*) no comparecencia *f*.
non-arrival ['nɔnə'raivəl] *n* ausencia *f*.
non-attendance ['nɔnə'tendəns] *n* ausencia *f*, falta *f* de asistencia.
nonbelligerent ['nɔnbi'lidʒərənt] **1** *adj* no beligerante. **2** *n* no beligerante *mf*.
non-breakable ['nɔn'breikəbl] *adj* irrompible.
non-Catholic ['nɔn'kæθlik] **1** *adj* no católico, acatólico. **2** *n* no católico *m*, no católica *f*.
nonce [nɔns] *adv*: **for the** — por el momento.
nonce-word ['nɔnswəːd] *n* palabra *f* creada para un caso especial.
nonchalance ['nɔnʃələns] *n* indiferencia *f*; negligencia *f*; aplomo *m*; sangre *f* fría, calma *f*.
nonchalant ['nɔnʃələnt] *adj* indiferente, impasible; negligente; **to be — about something** no prestar atención a algo, no tomar algo en serio; **with — ease** con aplomo y facilidad.
nonchalantly ['nɔnʃələntli] *adv* con indiferencia; negligentemente; con aplomo, con calma; **a — knotted tie** una corbata negligentemente anudada.
noncom ['nɔnkɔm] *n* (*Mil fam*) suboficial *m*.
non-combatant ['nɔn'kɔmbətənt] **1** *adj* no combatiente. **2** *n* no combatiente *mf*.
non-commissioned ['nɔnkə'miʃənd] *adj*: **— officer** suboficial *m*, sargento *m* *or* cabo *m*; **— officers** (*approx*) clases *fpl* de tropa.
non-committal ['nɔnkə'mitl] *adj statement etc* que no compromete a nada; (*pej*) evasivo, equívoco; **he was very — about it** se abstuvo de comprometerse a nada, no quiso concretar, eludió tomar una resolución definitiva.
non-compliance ['nɔnkəm'plaiəns] *n* incumplimiento *m*, infracción *f* (*with* de); desobediencia *f* (*with* de).
non-conductor ['nɔnkən'dʌktə*] *n* (*Elec*) no conductor *m*, mal conductor *m*.
nonconformism ['nɔnkən'fɔːmizəm] *n* inconformismo *m*.
nonconformist ['nɔnkən'fɔːmist] **1** *adj* inconformista. **2** *n* inconformista *mf*.
nonconformity ['nɔnkən'fɔːmiti] *n* inconformismo *m*, disidencia *f*.
non-cooperation ['nɔnkəuˌɔpə'reiʃən] *n* (*Pol*) no cooperación *f*.
nondescript ['nɔndiskript] *adj* indeterminado, inclasificable; (*pej*) mediocre.
none [nʌn] **1** *pron* (*person*) nadie; (*person, thing*) ninguno; (*thing*) nada; — **of them** ninguno de ellos; — **of you can tell me** ninguno de vosotros sabe decirme; **we have — of your books** no tenemos ninguno de sus libros; — **can tell** nadie lo sabe; **but he knows of this** nadie sino él está enterado de esto; — **of this is true** ninguna parte de esto es verdad; **any news?** . . . — ¿alguna noticia? . . . **nada; I'm sorry, there are** — lo siento, pero no hay; **there are — left** no queda ninguno; — **of that, now!** ¡déjese de eso!; **I want — of your lectures!** ¡basta ya de sermones!; **he is aware, — better, that . . .** se da cuenta, cómo no, de que . . .; **it was — other than the bishop** fue el obispo en persona, fue el propio obispo.
   2 *adj*: **riches have I** — riqueza no la tengo; **reply came there** — no hubo respuesta.
   3 *adv* de ningún modo; **I was — too comfortable** no me sentía muy cómodo; **they get on — too well** no se llevan del todo bien; **it was — too soon** ya era tiempo; **it's — the worse for that** no es peor por eso (*and see worse*); **he was still — the better off** aun así no había mejorado su posición en lo más mínimo.
nonentity [nɔ'nentiti] *n* nulidad *f*, cero *m* a la izquierda.
non-essential ['nɔni'senʃəl] **1** *adj* no esencial. **2** *n* cosa *f* no esencial.
non-existence ['nɔnig'zistəns] *n* inexistencia *f*.
non-existent ['nɔnig'zistənt] *adj* inexistente.
non-ferrous ['nɔn'ferəs] *adj* no ferroso, no férreo.
non-fiction ['nɔn'fikʃən] *n* literatura *f* no novelesca.

non-fulfilment ['nɔnful'filmənt] *n* incumplimiento *m*.
non-inflammable ['nɔnin'flæməbl] *adj* ininflamable.
non-intervention ['nɔnˌintə'venʃən] *n* no intervención *f*.
non-iron ['nɔn'aiən] *adj* de no planchar, que no necesita planchado.
non-laddering ['nɔn'lædəriŋ] *adj* (*stocking*) indesmallable.
non-member ['nɔnˌmembə*] *n* no miembro *m*, visitante *mf*.
nonpareil ['nɔnpərəl] **1** *adj* sin par. **2** *n* persona *f* sin par, cosa *f* sin par; (*Typ*) nomparell *m*.
nonpartisan ['nɔnˌpɑːti'zæn] *adj* independiente, imparcial.
non-party ['nɔn'pɑːti] *adj* (*Pol*) independiente.
non-payment ['nɔn'peimənt] *n* impago *m*; **sued for — of debts** demandado por no pagar sus deudas.
nonplus ['nɔn'plʌs] *vt* dejar perplejo, confundir; **he was completely —sed** estaba totalmente perplejo; **I confess myself —sed** confieso que estoy perplejo.
non-professional ['nɔnprə'feʃnəl] *adj* no profesional, aficionado.
non-profitmaking ['nɔn'prɔfitmeikiŋ] *adj* no lucrativo, no comercial.
non-resident ['nɔn'rezidənt] **1** *adj* no residente, no fijo, transeúnte. **2** *n* no residente *mf*, huésped *m* no fijo, transeúnte *mf*.
nonsectarian ['nɔnsek'teəriən] *adj* no sectario.
nonsense ['nɔnsəns] *n* disparates *mpl*, tonterías *fpl*, desatinos *mpl*; **a —, a piece of —** una tontería; —! ¡tonterías!; **what —!** ¡qué ridículo!; **but that's —!** ¡eso es absurdo!; **it is — to say that . . .** es absurdo decir que . . .; **this passage makes —** este pasaje no tiene sentido; **this makes a — of our policy** esto es volver de arriba abajo nuestra política; **to talk —** no decir más que tonterías; **it's just his —** son cosas de él; **we don't want any of your —** no queremos escuchar esas tonterías tuyas.
nonsensical [nɔn'sensikəl] *adj* disparatado, absurdo, tonto.
non-shrink ['nɔn'ʃriŋk] *adj* inencogible.
non-skid ['nɔn'skid] *adj* antideslizante, antirresbaladizo.
non-smoker ['nɔn'sməukə*] *n* (*person*) no fumador *m*; (*Rail*) departamento *m* de no fumadores; **I've always been a —** no he fumado nunca.
non-smoking ['nɔn'sməukiŋ] *adj person* que no fuma; (*Rail*) para no fumadores.
non-stop ['nɔn'stɔp] **1** *adv* sin parar; (*Rail*) directamente; (*Aer etc*) sin escalas; **he talks —** no para de hablar. **2** *adj* continuo, incesante; (*Rail*) directo; (*Aer*) sin escalas.
non-taxable ['nɔn'tæksəbl] *adj* no sujeto a impuestos.
non-union ['nɔn'juːnjən] *adj shop etc* no sindicalizado.
non-violence ['nɔn'vaiələns] *n* no violencia *f*.
non-violent ['nɔn'vaiələnt] *adj* no violento, pacífico.
noodle ['nuːdl] *n* (*fam: head*) cabeza *f*; (*fool*) bobo *m* a *f*.
noodles ['nuːdlz] *npl* tallarines *mpl*; — **soup** sopa *f* de pastas.
nook [nuk] *n* rincón *m*; escondrijo *m*.
noon [nuːn] (*also* **noonday** ['nuːndei]) **1** *n* mediodía *m*; **at — a** mediodía; **high —** (*fig*) apogeo *m*, punto *m* culminante. **2** *attr* de mediodía.
no-one ['nəuwʌn] *pron* = **nobody**.
noose [nuːs] **1** *n* lazo *m* corredizo; (*hangman's*) dogal *m*. **2** *vt* coger con lazo.
nope [nəup] *interj* (*esp US fam*) ¡no!
nor [nɔː*] *conj* ni; **neither A — B** ni A ni B; — **I** yo, ni yo tampoco; **I don't know, — can I guess** no lo sé, ni puedo conjeturarlo; — **does it seem likely** ni tampoco parece probable; — **was this all** y esto no fue todo.
Nordic ['nɔːdik] *adj* nórdico.
norm [nɔːm] *n* norma *f*; pauta *f*; modelo *m*; (*Bio etc*) tipo *m*; **larger than the —** más grande que lo normal, (*Bio*) más grande que el tipo; **to exceed one's —** exceder de la norma.
normal ['nɔːməl] **1** *adj* normal; regular, corriente; **the child is not —** el niño es anormal; **it is perfectly — to + infin** es muy normal + infin.
   2 *n* estado *m* normal; nivel *m* normal; normalidad *f*; **the — is 20 degrees** lo normal es 20 grados; **things are returning to —** la situación vuelve a la normalidad.
normalcy ['nɔːməlsi] *n* normalidad *f*.
normality [nɔː'mæliti] *n* normalidad *f*.
normalize ['nɔːməlaiz] *vt* normalizar.
normally ['nɔːməli] *adv* normalmente.
Norman ['nɔːmən] **1** *adj* normando; (*Archit*) normánico. **2** *n* normando *m*, a *f*.

Normandy ['nɔːməndi] Normandía f.
Norman-French ['nɔːmən'frentʃ] 1 adj normando francés. 2 n normando francés m.
Norse [nɔːs] 1 adj nórdico, noruego, escandinavo. 2 n (language) nórdico m.
Norseman ['nɔːsmən] n, pl —men [mən] vikingo m, escandinavo m.
north [nɔːθ] 1 n norte m. 2 adj del norte, septentrional. 3 adv al norte, hacia el norte.
North Africa ['nɔːθ'æfrikə] África f del Norte.
North America ['nɔːθə'merikə] América f del Norte, Norteamérica f.
North American ['nɔːθə'merikən] 1 adj norteamericano. 2 n norteamericano m, a f.
north-east ['nɔːθ'iːst] 1 n nor(d)este m. 2 adj point, direction nor(d)este; wind del nor(d)este.
north-easterly ['nɔːθ'iːstəli] adj point, direction nor(d)este; wind del nor(d)este.
north-eastern ['nɔːθ'iːstən] adj nor(d)este.
north-eastward(s) ['nɔːθ'iːstwəd(z)] adv hacia el nor(d)este.
northerly ['nɔːðəli] adj point, direction norte; wind del norte; **the most — point in Europe** el punto más septentrional de Europa, el punto más nórdico de Europa.
northern ['nɔːðən] adj del norte, septentrional, norteño.
northerner ['nɔːðənə*] n habitante mf del norte; nórdico m, a f; **he's a —** es del norte; **the —s are kindly people** los nórdicos son gente amable.
Northern Ireland ['nɔːðən'aiələnd] Irlanda f del Norte.
northernmost ['nɔːðənməust] adj (el) más norte, situado más al norte; **the — town in Europe** la ciudad más septentrional de Europa.
North Korea ['nɔːθkə'riə] Corea f del Norte.
North Korean ['nɔːθkə'riən] 1 adj norcoreano. 2 n norcoreano m, a f.
northland ['nɔːθlənd] n (US) región f septentrional.
Northman ['nɔːθmən] n, pl —men [mən] vikingo m, escandinavo m.
North Sea ['nɔːθ'siː] Mar m del Norte.
North Vietnam ['nɔːθviet'næm] Vietnam m del Norte.
North Vietnamese ['nɔːθvietnə'miːz] 1 adj norvietnamita. 2 n norvietnamita mf.
northward(s) ['nɔːθwəd(z)] adv hacia el norte.
north-west ['nɔːθ'west] 1 n noroeste m. 2 adj point, direction noroeste; wind del noroeste.
north-westerly ['nɔːθ'westəli] adj point, direction noroeste; wind del noroeste.
north-western ['nɔːθ'westən] adj noroeste.
north-westward(s) ['nɔːθ'westwəd(z)] adv hacia el noroeste.
Norway ['nɔːwei] Noruega f.
Norwegian [nɔː'wiːdʒən] 1 adj noruego. 2 n noruego m, a f. 3 n (language) noruego m.
nose [nəuz] 1 n (Anat) nariz f; (pej) narizota f, narices fpl; (of animal) hocico m; (sense of smell) olfato m; (Aer) morro m, proa f; (Naut) proa f; **flat —** nariz f chata; **snub —** nariz f respingona; **Roman —** nariz f aguileña; **right under one's —** a ojos vistas, en las barbas de uno, bajo las narices de uno; **to bleed at the —** echar sangre por las narices; **to blow one's —** sonarse (las narices); **to follow one's —** (go straight) ir todo seguido, (by instinct) dejarse guiar por el instinto; **to get one's — in front** conseguir una pequeña ventaja; **to have a good — for something** tener buen olfato para algo; **to hold one's —** taparse las narices; **to lead someone by the —** tener a uno agarrado por las narices; **to look down one's — at something** desdeñar algo, mirar algo con desprecio; **to make someone pay through the —** desollar a uno, cobrar a uno un precio elevadísimo; **to pay through the —** dejarse desollar (for something al comprar algo); **to talk through one's —** hablar por las narices; **to poke** (or stick) **one's — into something** meterse en algo; **who asked you to poke your — in?** ¿quién le manda a Vd meter su nariz en esto?; **to turn up one's — at something** hacer un gesto de desprecio al ver algo, desdeñar algo; see grindstone, joint.
2 vt: **to — something out** husmear algo, olfatear algo; secret lograr descubrir; **to — one's way forward** avanzar con precaución.
3 vi: **to — about** curiosear.
nosebag ['nəuzbæg] n morral m, cebadera f.
nosebleed ['nəuzbliːd] n hemorragia f nasal.
-nosed [nəuzd] adj de nariz . . ., eg **red-nosed** de nariz coloradota.

nose-dive ['nəuzdaiv] 1 n picado m vertical; (involuntary) caída f de narices. 2 vi descender en picado; (involuntarily) caer de morro (into en).
nosegay ['nəuzgei] n ramillete m.
nosey ['nəuzi] adj curioso, fisgón.
nosey-parker ['nəuzi'pɑːkə*] n fisgón m, ona f.
nosh [nɔʃ] n (sl) comida f; **— up!** ¡la comida está servida!
nostalgia [nɔs'tældʒiə] nostalgia f.
nostalgic [nɔs'tældʒik] adj nostálgico.
nostril ['nɔstril] n nariz f, ventana f de la nariz; **—s** narices fpl.
nostrum ['nɔstrəm] n panacea f (also fig); remedio m secreto.
not [nɔt] adv (a) no; **he is — here** no está aquí; **fear —!** ¡no temas!; **is it — so?** ¿no es verdad?; **you owe me money, do you —?** me debes algo, ¿no es verdad?; **he is a doctor, is he —?** es (un) médico, ¿no?; **he asked me — to do it** me rogó no hacerlo.
(b) **I wish it were — so** ¡ojalá no fuera así!; **whether you go or —** vayas o no; **let me know if —** avíseme en caso contrario; si no, me avisa; **I think — **creo que no; **— thinking that . . .** sin pensar que . . .; **— that I don't like him** no es que me resulte antipático; **big, — to say enormous** grande, por no decir enorme; **why —?** ¿por qué no?, ¿cómo no?; **— without some regrets** no sin cierto sentimiento.
(c) **absolutely —!** ¡en absoluto!; **certainly —!**, **— likely!** ¡de ninguna manera!, ¡ni hablar!; **of course —!** ¡claro que no!
(d) (with pron etc) **— I!** ¡yo no!; **— one ni uno;** **— him either** él tampoco, ni él tampoco; **— everybody can do it** no es cosa que todos sepan hacer; **— any more** ya no.
(e) (understatement) **with — a little surprise** con no poca sorpresa; **there were — a few lions** hubo no pocos leones; see even, much etc.
notability [nəutə'biliti] n notabilidad f; (person) notabilidad f, personaje m.
notable ['nəutəbl] 1 adj notable; señalado, memorable; **it is — that . . .** es notable que . . . 2 n notabilidad f, personaje m; **—s** notables mpl.
notably ['nəutəbli] adv notablemente, señaladamente.
notarial [nəu'teəriəl] adj notarial.
notary ['nəutəri] n notario m (also **public —**).
notation [nəu'teiʃən] n notación f.
notch [nɔtʃ] 1 n muesca f, mella f, corte m. 2 vt cortar muescas en, mellar; **to — up** apuntar.
note [nəut] 1 n (a) (Mus etc) nota f; **false — nota f falsa**; **with a — of anxiety in his voice** con una nota de inquietud en la voz; **to hit the right — ** (fig) acertar, elegir acertadamente el tono (de un discurso etc); **to strike quite the wrong — ** (fig) desentonar, ser como perro en misa, ser como guitarra en un entierro.
(b) (sign, stigma) marca f, señal f; **— of infamy** nota f de infamia.
(c) (annotation) nota f, apunte m; apuntación f; (foot—) nota f (en pie de página); **"N—s on Lucan"** "Apuntes mpl sobre Lucano"; **"editor's —"** (in newspaper) "nota de la redacción"; **to compare —s** cambiar impresiones, discutir los resultados; **to make a — of something** apuntar algo, tomar nota de algo; **to speak from —s** pronunciar un discurso a base de apuntes; **to take a — of something** tomar nota de algo; **to take down —s** tomar apuntes.
(d) (letter etc) nota f, carta f; recado m; esquela f; **take a —, Miss Jones** tome nota, señorita.
(e) (Comm) vale m; (bank—) billete m; **promissory —** pagaré m.
(f) (eminence) of — notable, eminente, de importancia; **man of —** hombre m notable.
(g) (notice) **worthy of —** digno de atención; **nothing of —** nada de particular, sin novedad; **to take — of** prestar atención a, ocuparse de; **only the critics took — of the book** sólo se ocuparon del libro los críticos.
2 vt (observe) notar, observar, advertir; (write down) apuntar, anotar (also **to — down**); **we duly —that . . .** nos hacemos cuenta de que . . .; **your remarks have been —d** hemos leído con atención sus observaciones.
notebook ['nəutbuk] n libro m de apuntes, libreta f; (student's etc) cuaderno m.
note-case ['nəutkeis] n cartera f, billetero m.
noted ['nəutid] adj célebre, conocido, famoso (for por).
notepaper ['nəut.peipə*] n papel m para cartas.
noteworthy ['nəut.wɔːði] adj notable, digno de notarse; **it is — that . . .** es notable que . . .

nothing ['nʌθiŋ] **1** n (**a**) nada; (*nought*) cero m; **I have — to give you** no tengo nada que darte, nada tengo que darte; **I see — that I like** no veo nada que me guste; **— else** nada más; **— much** poca cosa; **there's — much to be said** poco es lo que hay que decir; **next to —** casi nada; **there is — mean about him** no tiene nada de tacaño; **there's — special about it** no tiene nada de particular; **it's — to be proud of** no hay motivo para enorgullecerse; **there's — to fear** no hay de qué tener miedo.

(**b**) **there is — in the rumours** los rumores no tienen ni pizca de verdad; **there's — in it** (*in race*) van muy iguales; **there's — in it for us** de esto no vamos a sacar nada útil; **there's — for it but to pay** no hay más remedio que pagar; **there's — to it!** ¡es facilísimo!; **she is — to him** ella le es indiferente; **it is — to me whether he comes or not** no me importa que venga o no; **he is — if not careful** es prudente por encima de todo; **I'm — of a swimmer** yo nado bastante mal.

(**c**) **for —** (*free*) gratis, (*unpaid*) gratuitamente, sin sueldo, (*in vain*) en vano, en balde; **it is not for — that . . .** no es sin motivo que . . .

(**d**) **to build up a business from —** crear un negocio de la nada; **to come to —** fracasar, parar en nada, no dar resultado; **to make — of** (*not understand*) no entender, no sacar nada en claro de; (*not use*) no aprovechar; (*not esteem*) no dar importancia a; **to say — of . . .** sin mencionar . . ., amén de . . .; **to think — of** tener en poco, *task* tener por fácil; **he thinks — of walking 20 miles** para él no tiene importancia recorrer 20 millas a pie; **he thinks — of borrowing a fiver** con la mayor frescura pide prestado un billete de 5 libras; **think — of it!** ¡no hay de qué!

(**e**) **a mere —** una friolera, una bagatela; **a mere —!** ¡una bagatela!; **to say sweet ₋—s to someone** decir mil ternezas a una; *see do, doing, kind etc.*

2 adv de ninguna manera; **it's — like him** el retrato no se le parece en nada; **it was — like so big as we thought** era mucho menos grande de lo que nos imaginábamos; **pretty girl —!** (*fam*) ¡guapa, ni háblar! (*fam*); **— daunted** sin inmutarse; *see less.*

nothingness ['nʌθiŋnis] n nada f.

notice ['nəutis] **1** n (**a**) (*intimation, warning*) aviso m; **at short —** a corto plazo, con poco tiempo de anticipación; **at a moment's —** en el acto, inmediatamente, casi sin aviso; **you must be ready to leave at a moment's —** has de estar listo para partir luego de recibir el aviso; **until further —** hasta nuevo aviso; **without previous —** sin previo aviso; **he went without —** se fue sin avisar a nadie; **to give someone at least a week's —** avisar a uno lo menos con una semana de anticipación; **to give someone — that . . .**, **to serve — on someone that . . .** avisar a uno que . . ., hacer saber a uno que . . .; **— is hereby given that . . .** se pone en conocimiento del público que . . .; **to give someone — to do something** avisar a uno que haga algo; **I must have — es** imprescindible avisarme con anticipación; **we had no — of it** no nos habían avisado de ello; **final — aviso** m definitivo (*or* final); **— to quit** aviso m de desalojo.

(**b**) (*order to leave job etc: by employer*) despido m, (*by employee*) dimisión f; (*period*) plazo m; **to be under —** estar dimitido; **to dismiss someone without —** despedir a uno sin aviso; **to get one's —** ser despedido; **to give someone —** despedir a uno; **to give someone a week's —** despedir a uno con una semana de plazo; **to hand in one's —** dimitir; **a week's wages in lieu of —** el salario de una semana como despido.

(**c**) (*announcement*) anuncio m; (*in press*) anuncio m, nota f; (*sign*) letrero m; (*poster*) cartel m: **the — says "Keep out"** el letrero dice "Prohibida la entrada"; **— of a meeting** convocatoria f, llamada f; **to give out a —** leer un anuncio; **to put a — in the papers** poner un anuncio en los periódicos.

(**d**) (*review*) reseña f, crítica f.

(**e**) (*attention*) atención f; interés m; **to be beneath one's —** no merecer atención; **to attract one's —** atraer la atención de uno, llamar la atención de uno; **it has attracted a lot of —** ha suscitado gran interés; **to avoid —** procurar pasar inadvertido; **to bring a matter to someone's —** llamar la atención de uno sobre un asunto; **to come to someone's —** llegar al conocimiento de uno; **it has come to my — that . . .** ha llegado a mi conocimiento que . . ., ha llegado a saber que . . .; **to escape —** pasar inadvertido; **to take — of someone** hacer caso a uno; **a fat lot of — he takes of me!** ¡maldito el caso que

me hace!; **to take — of something** hacer caso de algo, prestar atención a algo; **to take no — of something** no hacer caso de algo; **he took no —** no hizo caso; **take no —!** ¡no haga Vd caso!, ¡no importa!; **I was not taking much — at the time** en ese momento iba yo algo distraído; **to sit up and take —** despertar y prestar atención.

2 vt (**a**) (*perceive*) notar, observar, reparar en, fijarse en; **I never —d** no me había fijado; **I don't — such things** no me fijo en tales cosas.

(**b**) (*heed*) hacer caso de.

(**c**) (*recognize*) ver, reconocer; **eventually he deigned to — me** por fin se dignó reconocerme.

(**d**) (*review*) reseñar, escribir una reseña de.

noticeable ['nəutisəbl] adj evidente, obvio; sensible, perceptible; notable; **it was — that . . .** era evidente que . . ., se echaba de ver que . . .; **there has been a — increase in . . .** ha habido un aumento sensible de . . .

noticeably ['nəutisəbli] adv evidentemente, obviamente; sensiblemente; notablemente; **it has — improved** ha mejorado sensiblemente.

notice board ['nəutisbɔ:d] n tablón m de anuncios.

notifiable ['nəutifaiəbl] adj de declaración obligatoria.

notification [ˌnəutifi'keiʃən] n notificación f, aviso m.

notify ['nəutifai] vt notificar, comunicar, avisar; **to — someone of something** comunicar algo a uno, hacer saber algo a uno.

notion ['nəuʃən] n (*idea*) noción f, idea f; concepto m; (*view*) opinión f; (*whim*) capricho m; inclinación f; **what an odd —!** ¡qué idea más rara!; **I have a — that . . .** tengo la idea de que . . ., se me ocurre pensar que . . .; **to have no — of something** no tener concepto alguno de algo; **you have no —!** ¡no te lo puedes imaginar!; **I haven't the slightest —** no tengo la más remota idea; **it's a —** she has es un capricho suyo, son cosas de ella; **to have a — to do something** tener la intención de hacer algo, estar inclinado a hacer algo, estar dispuesto a hacer algo.

notional ['nəuʃənl] adj nocional; especulativo; imaginario; **it is purely —** existe en el pensamiento nada más, es teórico nada más.

notoriety [ˌnəutə'raiəti] n notoriedad f; (*pej*) mala fama f; escándalo m; **such was his — that . . .** tan mala fama tuvo que . . .; **to seek —** buscarse la publicidad, tratar de darse a conocer, hacer que se hable de uno.

notorious [nəu'tɔ:riəs] adj muy conocido, notorio; célebre (*for* por); (*pej*) de mala fama; escandaloso; **a — crime** un crimen muy sonado; **it is — that . . .** es sabido que . . ., es voz pública que . . .; **he is — for his affairs** es archiconocido por sus amoríos.

notoriously [nəu'tɔ:riəsli] adj notoriamente; **it is — difficult to + infin** se sabe perfectamente que es difícil + infin; **he is — unreliable** tiene fama de informal.

no-trumps ['nəu'trʌmps] n: **to bid 4 —** marcar 4 sin triunfo.

notwithstanding [ˌnɔtwið'stændiŋ] **1** adv no obstante, sin embargo; **this —** no obstante esto, a pesar de esto; **this rule —** no obstante esta regla; **I shall go —** sin embargo iré, de todas formas iré.

2 prep a pesar de.

3 conj (*also — that*) a pesar de que, por más que + subj.

nougat ['nu:ga:] n (*approx*) turrón m.

nought [nɔ:t] n nada f; (*Math etc*) cero m; **Murcia beat Granada two —** el Murcia venció al Granada dos-cero; *see also* **naught.**

noun [naun] n nombre m, sustantivo m.

nourish ['nʌriʃ] vt nutrir, alimentar, sustentar; (*fig*) fomentar, nutrir; **to — someone on something** alimentar a uno con algo, dar a uno algo de comer.

nourishing ['nʌriʃiŋ] adj nutritivo, rico; de gran valor alimenticio.

nourishment ['nʌriʃmənt] n alimento m, sustento m; nutrición f; **to derive — from** sustentarse de.

nouveau riche ['nu:vəu'ri:ʃ] n nuevo rico m.

Nova Scotia ['nəuvə'skəuʃə] Nueva Escocia f.

novel ['nɔvəl] **1** adj nuevo; original; insólito; **this is something —** esto es nuevo. **2** n novela f; **picaresque —** novela f picaresca.

novelette [ˌnɔvə'let] n novela f corta; (*pej*) novela f sentimental, novela f sin valor.

novelettish [ˌnɔvə'letiʃ] adj novelero; sentimental, romántico.

novelist ['nɔvəlist] n novelista mf.

novelty ['nɔvəlti] n (*newness*) novedad f; (*new thing*) novedad f, innovación f; (*Comm*) novedad f; **once the — has worn off** cuando deja de parecer tan nuevo.

November [nəu'vembə*] n noviembre m.
novice ['nɔvis] n principiante mf, novato m, a f;
(Eccl) novicio m, a f; a — **painter** un pintor principiante, un aspirante a pintor; **he's no** — no es
ningún principiante; **to be a** — **at a job** ser nuevo
en un oficio.
noviciate, **novitiate** [nəu'viʃiit] n período m de
aprendizaje; (Eccl) noviciado m.
now [nau] **1** adv (a) ahora; actualmente, al presente,
hoy día; (in past time) luego, entonces; **just** —
(right —) ahora mismo, (lately) hace poco; **right** —
ahora mismo; **even** — aun ahora; **even** — **we have
no rifles** no tenemos todavía fusiles; **not** —, **dear**
dejémoslo para después, querido; ahora no quiero,
querido; **I must be off** — me tengo que marchar ya;
they won't be long — ya no tardarán en venir; — **I
am committed** me he comprometido ya; — **I'm
ready** ya estoy listo; **(every)** — **and again, (every)** —
and then de vez en cuando.
　(b) — **she dances,** — **she sings** ya baila, ya
canta; — **in France,** — **in Spain** ora en Francia, ora
en España.
　(c) (with prep) **before** — (already) antes, ya; (at
other times) en otras ocasiones; **long before** — hace
tiempo ya, mucho tiempo ha; **between** — **and next
Tuesday** entre hoy y el martes que viene; **by** —
ahora, ya; **they must be there by** — habrán llegado
ya allí; **by** — **everybody was tired** antes de eso
todos se habían cansado; **3 weeks from** — de hoy
en 3 semanas; **from** — **on** a partir de ahora, de aquí
en adelante; **until** —, **up to** — hasta ahora.
　(d) (without temporal force) — ! ¡a ver!; **come**
—! ¡vamos!, ¡no es para tanto!; **well** — ahora bien;
— **then!** ¡vamos a ver!; — **then, what's all this?**
¡eh! ¿qué hacéis aquí?, ¡eh! ¿qué es esto?; — **Johnny!**
(warning) ¡oye, Juanito!
　2 conj (a) — **(that) you are 16** ahora que tienes
16 años; **take it,** — **that I've got 2** tómalo, pues
tengo dos.
　(b) (without temporal force) ahora bien, pues; —
as you all know . . . pues como saben todos Vds . . .;
— **Peter was a fisherman** ahora bien, Pedro era
pescador.
nowadays ['nauədeiz] adv hoy día, actualmente.
noways ['nəuweiz] adv (US fam) de ninguna manera.
nowhere ['nəuwɛə*] adv (a) **I see it** — no lo veo en
ninguna parte; **you're going** — no vas a ninguna
parte; — **in Europe** en ninguna parte de Europa; —
else en ninguna otra parte; **it's** — **you know** no es
ningún sitio de los que conoce Vd; **it's** — **you'll ever
find it** está en un sitio donde no lo encontrará Vd
nunca; **they seemed to come from** — parecían
haber salido de la nada.
　(b) (fig) **it's** — **near as good** no es tan bueno ni
con mucho, dista mucho de ser tan bueno; **A is** —
near as big as B A no es tan grande como B ni con
mucho; **the rest of the runners came** — los demás
atletas quedaron muy atrás; **in my opinion the rest
come** — en mi opinión los demás son muy inferiores.
nowise ['nəuwaiz] adv (US) de ninguna manera.
noxious ['nɔkʃəs] adj nocivo, dañoso.
nozzle ['nɔzl] n (Mech) tobera f, inyector m; (of hose,
vacuum cleaner etc) boquilla f; (of spray) pulverizador
m.
nuance ['nju:ã:ns] n matiz m.
nub [nʌb] n pedazo m, trozo m; protuberancia f; (fig)
lo esencial, parte f esencial; **that's the** — **of the
question** eso es lo esencial, eso es lo que más
importa.
nubile ['nju:bail] adj núbil.
nuclear ['nju:kliə*] adj nuclear.
nucleus ['nju:kliəs] n, pl **nuclei** ['nju:kliai] núcleo m;
atomic — núcleo m atómico; **the** — **of a library** el
núcleo indispensable de una biblioteca; **we have the**
—- **of a crew** tenemos los elementos indispensables
para formar una tripulación.
nude [nju:d] **1** adj desnudo. **2** n (Art) desnudo m; a —
of Goya un desnudo de Goya. (b) (person) desnudo
m; mujer f desnuda. (c) **in the** — desnudo.
nudge [nʌdʒ] **1** n codazo m (ligero). **2** vt dar un
codazo a; empujar (ligeramente); **to** — **someone's
memory** refrescar la memoria de uno.
nudism ['nju:dizəm] n desnudismo m.
nudist ['nju:dist] n desnudista mf, nudista mf; —
colony colonia f de desnudistas.
nudity ['nju:diti] n desnudez f.
nugatory ['nju:gətəri] adj (trivial) insignificante;
(useless) ineficaz.
nugget ['nʌgit] n (Min) pepita f; **gold** — pepita f de
oro.
nuisance ['nju:sns] **1** n (a) molestia f, incomodidad

f; **the** — **of having to shave** la incomodidad de tener
que afeitarse.
　(b) molestia f, fastidio m, lata f; **what a** —! ¡qué
lata!, ¡qué fastidio!; **this hat is a** — este sombrero
me está fastidiando; me estoy armando un lío con
este sombrero; **it's a** — **having to shave** es una
molestia tener que afeitarse, es incómodo tener que
afeitarse; **"commit no** —**"** "mantenga limpio este
sitio", (more specifically) "prohibido hacer aguas".
　(c) (person) moscón m, pelmazo m; pesado m;
what a — **you are!** ¡eres un pesado!; **you're being a**
— me estás dando la lata; **to make a** — **of oneself**
dar la lata.
　2 attr: — **value** valor m como irritante.
null [nʌl] adj nulo, inválido; — **and void** nulo y sin
efecto; **to render someone's efforts** — hacer que los
esfuerzos de uno resulten infructuosos.
nullification [.nʌlifi'keiʃən] n anulación f, invalida-
ción f.
nullify ['nʌlifai] vt anular, invalidar.
nullity ['nʌliti] n nulidad f.
numb [nʌm] **1** adj entumecido; (fig) insensible; **my
leg has gone** — se me ha dormido la pierna; **to be** —
with cold estar entumecido de frío, (fig) estar
helado; **to be** — **with fright** estar paralizado de
temor. **2** vt entumecer, entorpecer.
number ['nʌmbə*] **1** n (a) (Math) número m;
(figure) número m, cifra f; (Gram, Tel, Theat, of
journal etc) número m; —**s** (Poet) versos mpl;
cardinal — número m cardinal; **ordinal** — número
m ordinal; **whole** — número m entero; **round** —
número m redondo; **in round** —s en números
redondos; **rational** — número m racional; **a**
— **of** algunos, varios, una porción de; **a** —
of people have protested varias personas han
protestado; **a large** — **of people** buen número de
personas, muchísimas personas; **in a small** — **of
cases** en unos pocos casos, en contados casos; **on a** —
of occasions en diversas ocasiones, varias veces; **any**
— **of** a la mar de; **any** — **of times** muchísimas veces;
to be few in — ser pocos; **to be 8 in** — ser 8; **to
come in** —s venir en tropel, venir en masa; **they
exist in** —s **in Africa** en África hay muchos, en
África son frecuentes; **one of their** — uno de ellos;
he is not of that — no es de ésos, no forma parte de
ese grupo; **to the** — **of some 200** en número de unos
200; **times without** — muchísimas veces; **his** — **is**
up todo se acabó para él; **I've got his** — **now** le
tengo calado ya.
　(b) (of house etc) número m; **we live at No. 15**
vivimos en el núm. 15; **reference** — número m de
referencia; **registration** — (Aut etc) matrícula f; **the**
— **one Spanish player** el jugador número uno de
España; **to look after** — **one** mirar por sí, cuidar de
sí mismo.
　(c) (person) **a nice little** — (sl) una chica
monísima; **my opposite** — **in France** el que ocupa el
puesto equivalente en Francia.
　2 vt (a) (count) contar; **the library** —s **30,000
books** la biblioteca cuenta con 30.000 libros, la
biblioteca posee 30.000 libros; **to** — **someone**
among one's friends contar a uno entre sus amigos;
to be —**ed among friends** figurar entre, ser de; **his days are**
—**ed** tiene los días contados; **his days seem to be**
—**ed** sus días parecen contados.
　(b) (amount to) ascender a, sumar; **they** — **187**
hay 187, ascienden a 187, suman 187; **they** — **several
hundreds** hay varios centenares.
　(c) (assign — to) numerar, poner número a;
MS **pages** foliar; **the houses are not** —**ed** las casas,
no están numeradas, las casas no tienen número.
　3 vi: **to** — **off** numerarse (from the right por la
derecha).
numberless ['nʌmbəlis] adj innumerable, sin número.
number plate ['nʌmbəpleit] n (Aut etc) placa f de
matrícula.
numbness ['nʌmnis] n entumecimiento m; (fig)
insensibilidad f; parálisis f.
numeral ['nju:mərəl] **1** adj numeral. **2** n número m,
cifra f, guarismo m; **Arabic** — número m arábigo;
Roman — número m romano.
numeration [.nju:mə'reiʃən] n numeración f.
numerator ['nju:məreitə*] n numerador m.
numerical [nju:'merikəl] adj numérico.
numerically [nju:'merikəli] adv numéricamente; —
superior con superioridad numérica a, superiores
en cuanto a su número a.
numerous ['nju:mərəs] adj numeroso; muchos; **a** —
family una familia numerosa; **in** — **cases** en muchos
casos; — **people believe that** . . . mucha gente cree
que . . .

numismatic [ˌnjuːmiz'mætik] *adj* numismático.
numismatics [ˌnjuːmiz'mætiks] *n* numismática *f*.
numismatist [njuː'mizmətist] *n* numismático *m*.
numskull, numbskull ['nʌmskʌl] *n* zote *m*, majadero *m*; you — ! ¡majadero!
nun [nʌn] *n* monja *f*, religiosa *f*; **to become a** — tomar el hábito, meterse monja.
nunciature ['nʌnʃiətjuə*] *n* nunciatura *f*.
nuncio ['nʌnʃiəu] *n* (*also* **papal** —) nuncio *m* apostólico.
nunnery ['nʌnəri] *n* convento *m* de monjas.
nuptial ['nʌpʃəl] *adj* nupcial.
nuptials ['nʌpʃəlz] *npl* (*hum or US*) nupcias *fpl*.
nurse [nəːs] **1** *n* (*Med*) enfermera *f*; (*wet-*) nodriza *f*, ama *f* de leche; (*children's*) niñera *f*; **male** — enfermero *m*; **practical** — (*US*) enfermera *f* práctica.
  2 *vt patient* cuidar, atender, asistir; (*suckle*) criar, amamantar; (*in arms*) mecer; **to** — **someone back to health** cuidar a uno hasta que se reponga; **to** — **a cold** tratar de curarse de un resfriado; **to** — **a constituency** (*Parl*) establecerse como candidato en un distrito electoral, hacerse conocer por los electores de un distrito; **to** — **a business along** fomentar un negocio, promover un negocio.
nursemaid ['nəːsmeid] *n* niñera *f*, chacha *f*.
nursery ['nəːsri] *n* (**a**) cuarto *m* de los niños; **from the** — desde la niñez, desde niño.
  (**b**) (*Agr etc*) criadero *m*, semillero *m*, plantel *m*; (*fig*) plantel *m*; **a** — **for new players** un plantel de jóvenes jugadores.
nurseryman ['nəːsrimən] *n, pl* —**men** [mən] horticultor *m*.
nursery rhyme ['nəːsriraim] *n* canción *f* infantil.
nursery school ['nəːsri̩skuːl] *n* jardín *m* de la infancia.
nursing ['nəːsiŋ] **1** *adj*: — **mother** madre *f* lactante; — **staff** enfermeras *fpl*, personal *m* del hospital.
  2 *n* (*of patient*) asistencia *f*, cuidado *m*; (*profession*) profesión *f* de enfermera; (*suckling*) lactancia *f*; **to go in for** — hacerse enfermera.
nursing home ['nəːsiŋ̩həum] *n* clínica *f* de reposo, clínica *f* particular.
nurture ['nəːtʃə*] **1** *n* (*nourishment*) nutrición *f*; (*bringing-up*) educación *f*, crianza *f*. **2** *vt* alimentar, nutrir (*on* de); educar, criar.

nut [nʌt] *n* (**a**) nuez *f*; (*Mech*) tuerca *f*; (*sl: head*) cabeza *f*; (*sl: person*) loco *m*, a *f*, bobo *m*, a *f*; excéntrico *m*; **it's a hard** — **to crack** es un hueso duro de roer; **to do one's** — (*sl*) echar el resto (*fam*); **to be off one's** — (*sl*) faltarle a uno un tornillo (*fam*); **you must be off your** —! (*sl*) ¿estás grillado? (*sl*).
  (**b**) —**s** (*sl*): **to be** —**s** estar loco; **to be** —**s about** (*or* **on**) **something** estar loco por algo; **I'm** —**s about you** estoy chalado por ti (*fam*); **to drive someone** —**s** volver loco a uno; **to go** —**s** volverse loco.
  (**c**) —**s** (*sl: Anat*) cojones *mpl*; —**s**! ¡narices! (*fam*); **he can't play for** —**s** no tiene talento en absoluto para el juego, como jugador no vale para nada.
nutcase ['nʌtkeis] *n* (*sl*) loco *m*, a *f*.
nutcrackers ['nʌtˌkrækəz] *npl* cascanueces *m*; **a pair of** — un cascanueces.
nuthatch ['nʌthætʃ] *n* trepador *m*.
nuthouse ['nʌthaus] *n, pl* —**houses** [ˌhauziz] (*sl*) manicomio *m*.
nutmeg ['nʌtmeg] *n* nuez *f* moscada.
nutrient ['njuːtriənt] **1** *adj* nutritivo. **2** *n* nutrimento *m*.
nutriment ['njuːtrimənt] *n* nutrimento *m*, alimento *m*.
nutrition [njuː'triʃən] *n* nutrición *f*, alimentación *f*.
nutritional [njuː'triʃənl] *adj value etc* nutritivo.
nutritious [njuː'triʃəs] *adj*, **nutritive** ['njuːtritiv] *adj* nutritivo, rico.
nutshell ['nʌtʃel] *n* cáscara *f* de nuez; **in a** — en resumidas cuentas; **to put it in a** — para decirlo brevemente; **that puts it in a** — eso lo dice en pocas palabras.
nut-tree ['nʌttriː] *n* (*hazel*) avellano *m*, (*walnut*) nogal *m*.
nutty ['nʌti] *adj* (**a**) *colour* de nuez; *cake* con nueces; *taste* a nueces, que sabe a nueces.
  (**b**) (*sl*) loco; **to be** — estar loco; **to be** — **about something** estar loco por algo.
nuzzle ['nʌzl] **1** *vt* acariciar con el hocico. **2** *vi* = **snuggle, nestle**.
nylon ['nailən] **1** *n* nilón *m*; —**s** medias *fpl* de nilón. **2** *adj* de nilón.
nymph [nimf] *n* ninfa *f*.
nymphet [nim'fet] *n* ninfita *f*, ninfilla *f*.
nymphomania [ˌnimfəu'meiniə] *n* ninfomanía *f*.
nymphomaniac [ˌnimfəu'meiniæk] **1** *adj* ninfómano. **2** *n* ninfómana *f*.

O

O [əu] *see* **oh.**

oaf [əuf] *n* zoquete *m*, patán *m*.

oafish ['əufiʃ] *adj* lerdo, zafio.

oak [əuk] **1** *n* roble *m*; **to sport one's —** (*Univ*) cerrar la puerta (para no recibir visitas). **2** *adj*, *attr* de roble.

oak apple ['əuk.æpl] *n* agalla *f* (de roble).

oaken ['əukən] *adj* de roble.

oakum ['əukəm] *n* estopa *f* (de calafatear).

oakwood ['əukwud] *n* robledo *m*.

oar [ɔ:*] *n* (a) remo *m*; **to lie** (*or* **rest**) **on one's —s** dejar de remar, (*fig*) descansar, dormir sobre sus laureles; **to put** (*or* **shove**) **one's — in** entrometerse; **to ship the —s** desarmar los remos.
(b) (*person*) remero *m*, a *f*; **to be a good —** ser buen remero, remar bien.

oared [ɔ:d] *adj* provisto de remos; **de . . . remos**, *eg* **eight-oared** de ocho remos.

oarlock ['ɔ:lɔk] *n* escalamera *f*.

oarsman ['ɔ:zmən] *n*, *pl* **—men** [mən] remero *m*.

oarsmanship ['ɔ:zmənʃip] *n* arte *m* de remar.

oasis [əu'eisis] *n*, *pl* **oases** [əu'eisi:z] oasis *m*; (*fig*) oasis *m*; remanso *m*; **an — of peace** un remanso de paz.

oast-house ['əusthaus] *n*, *pl* **—houses** [hauziz] secadero *m* para lúpulo.

oatcake ['əutkeik] *n* torta *f* de avena.

oaten ['əutn] *adj* de avena.

oatfield ['əutfi:ld] *n* avenal *m*.

oath [əuθ] *n*, *pl* **oaths** [əuðz] (a) (*solemn promise etc*) juramento *m*; **under —, on —,** bajo juramento; **to administer an — to someone** tomar juramento a uno; **to break one's —** violar su juramento; **to put someone on —** hacer prestar juramento a uno; **to take the** (*or* **an**) **—** prestar juramento (*on* sobre); **to take an — that . . .** jurar que . . .; **to take the — of allegiance** (*Mil*) jurar la bandera.
(b) (*curse*) blasfemia *f*, reniego *m*, palabrota *f*.

oatmeal ['əutmi:l] *n* harina *f* de avena.

oats [əuts] *npl* avena *f*; **rolled —** copos *mpl* de avena; **wild oat** avena *f* silvestre; **to be off one's —s** no tener ganas de comer, haber perdido el apetito; **to sow one's wild —** correrla, pasar las mocedades.

obbligato [.ɔbli'ga:təu] *n* (*Mus*) obligado *m*.

obduracy ['ɔbdjurəsi] *n* obstinación *f*, terquedad *f*; inflexibilidad *f*.

obdurate ['ɔbdjurit] *adj* obstinado, terco; (*in refusing etc*) inflexible.

obedience [ə'bi:diəns] *n* obediencia *f*; sumisión *f*; docilidad *f*; **in — to** conforme a, de acuerdo con; **in — to your wishes** accediendo a sus deseos; **blind —** obediencia *f* ciega; **to compel —** exigir obediencia (*from* a).

obedient [ə'bi:diənt] *adj* obediente; sumiso, dócil; **to be — to** ser obediente a, obedecer a.

obediently [ə'bi:diəntli] *adv* obedientemente; sumisamente, dócilmente; **yours —** su atento servidor.

obeisance [əu'beisəns] *n* (*bow etc*) reverencia *f*; (*salutation*) saludo *m*; (*homage*) homenaje *m*; **to do** (*or* **make, pay**) **— to** tributar homenaje a.

obelisk ['ɔbilisk] *n* obelisco *m*.

obese [əu'bi:s] *adj* obeso.

obeseness [əu'bi:snis] *n*, **obesity** [əu'bi:siti] *n* obesidad *f*.

obey [ə'bei] *vt* (*person etc*) obedecer; (*pay heed to*) hacer caso a; *need, controls* responder; *summons* acudir a; *law* cumplir, observar, obrar de acuerdo con; *instruction* cumplir; **the machine was no longer —ing the controls** la máquina ya no respondía a los mandos; **I like to be —ed** quiero que se me obedezca.

obfuscate ['ɔbfəskeit] *vt* ofuscar.

obituary [ə'bitjuəri] **1** *adj* necrológico; **— column** sección *f* necrológica; **— notice** necrología *f*; esquela *f* de defunción. **2** *n* necrología *f*, obituario *m*.

object ['ɔbdʒikt] *n* (a) (*thing in general*) objeto *m*; cosa *f*, artículo *m*; (*pej: thing*) mamarracho *m* (*person*) espantajo *m*, estantigua *f*; **she was an — of pity to all** daba lástima a cuantos la veían; **he became an — of ridicule** se puso en ridículo.
(b) (*aim*) objeto *m*, propósito *m*, intento *m*; **with this — in view** con este propósito; **with the — of** con el propósito de, al objeto de; **what is the — of the plan?** ¿qué finalidad tiene el plan?; **expense is no —** no importan los gastos; **salary no —** el sueldo no es de primera importancia.
(c) (*Gram*) complemento *m*.

object [əb'dʒekt] **1** *vt*: **to — that . . .** objetar que . . .; **to this it was —ed that . . .** a esto se objetó que . . .
2 *vi* hacer objeciones, oponerse; poner reparos; **I —!** ¡yo protesto!; **I — most strongly!** ¡yo me opongo rotundamente a ello!; **if you don't —** si Vd no tiene inconveniente; **I — to that remark!** ¡protesto contra esa observación!; **to — to someone doing something** oponerse a que uno haga algo; **do you — to my going?** ¿se opone Vd a que vaya yo?; **do you — to my smoking?** ¿le molesta que fume?; **I don't — to an occasional drink** no me opongo a que se tome algo de vez en cuando.

objection [əb'dʒekʃən] *n* objeción *f*, reparo *m*; protesta *f*; (*obstacle*) inconveniente *m*; obstáculo *m*, dificultad *f*; **—!** ¡yo protesto!; **what are the —s?** ¿qué obstáculo hay?, ¿cuáles son las dificultades?; **there is no —** no hay inconveniente; **there is no — to your going** no hay inconveniente en que vaya Vd; **I can find no —** to it no le encuentro ninguna dificultad; **I have no —** no tengo inconveniente; **if you have no —** si no tiene inconveniente; **have you any — to my smoking?** ¿le molesta que fume?; **have you any — to my going?** ¿tiene Vd algún inconveniente en que vaya yo?; **he made no —** no hizo ninguna objeción, no protestó, no se opuso a ello; **to raise —s** poner reparos (*to* a), protestar (*to* contra); **I see no —** no veo inconveniente.

objectionable [əb'dʒekʃnəbl] *adj* desagradable; *person* molesto, pesado; indeseable; *conduct etc* censurable; **a most — person** una persona inaguantable.

objective [əb'dʒektiv] **1** *adj* objetivo. **2** *n* objetivo *m*.

objectively [əb'dʒektivli] *adv* objetivamente.

objectivism [əb'dʒektivizəm] *n* objetivismo *m*.

objectivity [.ɔbdʒik'tiviti] *n* objetividad *f*.

object lens ['ɔbdʒikt.lenz] *n* objetivo *m*.

object lesson ['ɔbdʒikt.lesn] *n* lección *f* práctica, ejemplo *m*; **it was an — in good manners** fue una perfecta demostración de cortesía.

objector [əb'dʒektə*] *n* objetante *mf*; **conscientious — objetor** *m* de conciencia, pacifista *m* que se niega a tomar las armas.

objurgate ['ɔbdʒə:geit] *vt* increpar, reprender.

objurgation [.ɔbdʒə:'geiʃən] *n* increpación *f*, reprensión *f*.

oblation [əu'bleiʃən] *n* oblación *f*; (*gift*) oblata *f*, ofrenda *f*.

obligate ['ɔbligeit] *vt*: **to — someone to do something** obligar a uno a hacer algo; **to be —d to** + *infin* estar obligado a + *infin*.

obligation [.ɔbli'geiʃən] *n* obligación *f*; deber *m*; compromiso *m*; **of —** (*Eccl*) de precepto; **without —** (*in advert*) sin compromiso; **it is your — to see that . . .** le cumple a Vd comprobar que + *subj*, es su deber comprobar que + *subj*; **to be under an — to someone** deber favores a uno; **to be under an — to** + *infin* deber + *infin*, haberse comprometido a + *infin*, tener obligación de + *infin*; **to lay** (*or* **put**) **someone under an —** poner a uno bajo una obligación; **to meet one's —s** (*Comm*) cumplir sus compromisos; **to fail to meet one's —s** no poder cumplir sus compromisos.

obligatory [ɔ'bligətəri] *adj* obligatorio; **to make it —
for someone to do something** imponer a uno la
obligación de + *infin*.
oblige [ə'blaidʒ] *vt* (**a**) (*force*) obligar, forzar; **to —
someone to do something** obligar a uno a hacer algo,
forzar a uno a hacer algo; **to be —d to do something**
verse obligado a hacer algo; **you are not —d to do it**
nada le obliga a hacerlo.
(**b**) (*gratify*) complacer, hacer un favor a; **you
would greatly — me if** . . . agradecería mucho que
+ *subj*; **anything to — a friend!** ¡lo que sea por
complacer a un amigo!; **he did it to —** us lo hizo
como favor, lo hizo para complacernos; **to — someone with a match** hacer a uno el favor de (prestarle,
darle) una cerilla.
(**c**) (*obliged*) **much —d!** ¡muchísimas gracias!, ¡se
agradece!; **I should be much —d if** . . . agradecería
que + *subj*; **I am —d to you for your help** agradezco su ayuda; **to be —d to someone** estar reconoci-
cido a uno, deber favores a uno.
obliging [ə'blaidʒiŋ] *adj* servicial, atento, obsequioso.
obligingly [ə'blaidʒiŋli] *adv* atentamente; **he very —
helped us** muy amablemente nos ayudó.
oblique [ə'bliːk] *adj* oblicuo; *reference etc* indirecto,
tangencial.
obliquely [ə'bliːkli] *adv* oblicuamente; indirectamente, tangencialmente.
obliqueness [ə'bliːknis] *n*, **obliquity** [ə'blikwiti] *n*
oblicuidad *f*; lo indirecto, lo tangencial.
obliterate [ə'blitəreit] *vt* borrar, eliminar, destruir
toda huella de; *town etc* arrasar, destruir; (*Med*)
obliterar.
obliteration [ə,blitə'reiʃən] *n* borradura *f*, eliminación *f*; arrasamiento *m*, destrucción *f*; (*Med*)
obliteración *f*.
oblivion [ə'bliviən] *n* olvido *m*; **to cast into —** echar
al olvido; **to fall** (*or* **sink**) **into —** sumirse en el
olvido.
oblivious [ə'bliviəs] *adj*: **to be — of, to be — to**
estar inconsciente de; **he, totally — of what was
happening** . . . él, totalmente inconsciente de lo que
pasaba . . .
oblong [ɔblɔŋ] **1** *adj* rectangular, cuadrilongo. **2** *n*
rectángulo *m*, cuadrilongo *m*.
obloquy ['ɔbləkwi] *n* (*abuse*) injurias *fpl*, calumnia *f*;
(*shame*) deshonra *f*; **to cover someone with —** llenar
a uno de injurias.
obnoxious [əb'nɔkʃəs] *adj* detestable, repugnante,
odioso; *fumes etc* nocivo, desagradable; **it is — to
me to** + *infin* me repugna + *infin*, me es repugnante + *infin*.
oboe ['əubəu] *n* oboe *m*.
oboist ['əubəuist] *n* oboe *m* (*persona*).
obscene [əb'siːn] *adj* obsceno, indecente, escabroso.
obscenely [əb'siːnli] *adv* obscenamente, escabrosamente.
obscenity [əb'seniti] *n* obscenidad *f*, indecencia *f*,
escabrosidad *f*; **to utter obscenities** proferir
obscenidades.
obscurantism [,ɔbskjuə'ræntizəm] *n* oscurantismo *m*.
obscurantist [,ɔbskjuə'ræntist] **1** *adj* oscurantista.
2 *n* oscurantista *mf*.
obscure [əb'skjuə*] **1** *adj* oscuro (*also fig*).
2 *vt* oscurecer; (*eclipse*) eclipsar; (*hide*) esconder;
issue entenebrecer, confundir; *memory, glory etc*
oscurecer; **the house is —d by the trees** la casa está
escondida detrás de los árboles; **it served only to —
the matter further** sirvió para entenebrecer aun más
el asunto.
obscurely [əb'skjuəli] *adv* oscuramente.
obscurity [əb'skjuəriti] *n* oscuridad *f* (*also fig*); **to live
in —** vivir en la oscuridad.
obsequies ['ɔbsikwiz] *npl* exequias *fpl*.
obsequious [əb'siːkwiəs] *adj* servil.
obsequiously [əb'siːkwiəsli] *adj* servilmente.
obsequiousness [əb'siːkwiəsnis] *n* servilismo *m*.
observable [əb'zəːvəbl] *adj* observable, visible; **as is
— in rabbits** según se puede apreciar en los conejos;
no — difference ninguna diferencia perceptible.
observance [əb'zəːvəns] *n* (*of rule etc*) observancia *f*
(*of* de), cumplimiento *m* (*of* con); (*rite etc*) práctica *f*;
costumbre *f*.
observant [əb'zəːvənt] *adj* observador, perspicaz;
(*watchful*) vigilante; (*attentive*) atento; **the child is
very —** el niño es muy observador.
observation [,ɔbzə'veiʃən] *n* (*in most senses*) observación *f*; (*of rule etc*) observancia *f*; **"O—s on
Petrarch" "Apuntes** *mpl* **sobre Petrarca"; to be
under —** estar vigilado; **we can keep the valley
under — from here** desde aquí dominamos el valle;
the police are keeping him under — la policía le
está vigilando; **he is under — in hospital** le están

examinando en el hospital; **to escape —** pasar
inadvertido.
observation car [,ɔbzə'veiʃənkɑː*] *n* (*Rail*) vagón-
mirador *m*.
observation post [,ɔbzə'veiʃənpəust] *n* puesto *m* de
observación.
observatory [əb'zəːvətri] *n* observatorio *m*.
observe [əb'zəːv] *vt* rule etc observar, cumplir; (*watch,
examine*; *also Astron*) observar; (*remark*) observar,
decir; (*care*) usar de, emplear; *Sabbath, silence etc*
guardar; *suspect etc* vigilar; **I —d to him that** . . . le
hice observar que . . .; **as Eliot has —d** . . . según ha
dicho Eliot . . .; **I —d him steal the duck** le vi robar
el pato; **now — this closely** fíjense bien en esto.
observer [əb'zəːvə*] *n* observador *m*, ora *f*.
obsess [əb'ses] *vt* obsesionar, causar obsesión a; **to be
—ed by** (*or* **with**) **an idea** estar obsesionado por una
idea.
obsession [əb'seʃən] *n* obsesión *f*; idea *f* fija, manía *f*;
the — about cleanliness la obsesión de la limpieza,
la manía de la limpieza; **to have an — about an
idea** estar obsesionado por una idea; **it's an — with
him** es una manía que tiene.
obsessive [əb'sesiv] *adj* obsesionante.
obsessively [əb'sesivli] *adv* de modo obsesionante.
obsidian [ɔb'sidiən] *n* obsidiana *f*.
obsolescence [,ɔbsə'lesns] *n* caída *f* en desuso.
obsolescent [,ɔbsə'lesnt] *adj* algo anticuado; **to be —**
irse haciendo anticuado, estar cayendo en desuso.
obsolete ['ɔbsəliːt] *adj* anticuado, desusado; obsoleto;
(*Bio*) rudimentario.
obstacle ['ɔbstəkl] *n* obstáculo *m*; estorbo *m*, impedimento *m*, inconveniente *m*; **—s to independence** los
factores que dificultan la independencia; **one of the
—s is money** uno de los obstáculos es el dinero; **to
be an — to something** ser un estorbo para algo; **that
is no — to our doing it** eso no impide que lo hagamos; **to put —s in someone's way** crear dificultades
a uno, dificultar el camino a uno.
obstacle race ['ɔbstəkl,reis] *n* carrera *f* de obstáculos.
obstetric(al) [ɔb'stetrik(əl)] *adj* obstétrico.
obstetrician [,ɔbstə'triʃən] *n* obstétrico *m*.
obstetrics [ɔb'stetriks] *n* obstetricia *f*.
obstinacy ['ɔbstinəsi] *n* obstinación *f*, terquedad *f*,
porfía *f*; tenacidad *f*.
obstinate ['ɔbstinit] *adj* obstinado, terco, porfiado;
pursuit etc tenaz; **as — as a mule** tan terco como una
mula; **to be — about something** insistir con tesón en
algo.
obstinately ['ɔbstinitli] *adv* obstinadamente, tercamente, porfiadamente; tenazmente.
obstreperous [əb'strepərəs] *adj* (*noisy*) ruidoso,
estrepitoso; (*unruly*) turbulento, desmandado; **he
became —** empezó a desmandarse.
obstreperously [əb'strepərəsli] *adv* ruidosamente,
estrepitosamente; de modo turbulento.
obstruct [əb'strʌkt] **1** *vt* obstruir; (*Parl, Sport*)
obstruir; *plan, progress etc* estorbar; *person* estorbar,
impedir; *road* cerrar, bloquear, obstruir; *pipe etc*
obstruir, atascar, atorar.
2 *vi* estorbar.
obstruction [əb'strʌkʃən] *n* obstrucción *f* (*also Parl*)
estorbo *m*, obstáculo *m*; **to cause an —** ser un
estorbo, (*Aut etc*) obstruir el tráfico.
obstructionism [əb'strʌkʃənizəm] *n* obstruccionismo
m.
obstructionist [əb'strʌkʃənist] **1** *adj* obstruccionista.
2 *n* obstruccionista *mf*.
obstructive [əb'strʌktiv] *adj* obstructivo, estor-
bador; **you're being —** Vd nos está estorbando.
obtain [əb'tein] **1** *vt* obtener; adquirir; lograr, conseguir; **oil can be —ed from coal** el aceite se puede
extraer del carbón; **his uncle —ed the job for him**
su tío le consiguió el puesto; **a work for which he
—ed a prize** un trabajo que le valió un premio, un
trabajo por el que le dieron un premio.
2 *vi* prevalecer, predominar; privar; regir; **the
price which —s now** el precio que es normal ahora;
in the conditions then —ing en las condiciones que
existían entonces; **that did not — in my day** en mis
tiempos no existía eso, en mis tiempos no era así.
obtainable [əb'teinəbl] *adj*: **to be —** ser asequible,
poderse adquirir; (*in shop*) estar a la venta; **"— at
all chemists'" "de venta en todas las farmacias";
it is no longer —** ya no se puede conseguir.
obtrude [əb'truːd] **1** *vt* tongue etc sacar, extender; **to
— something on someone** imponer algo a uno.
2 *vi* (*person*) entrometerse; **he does not let his
opinions —** no hace gala de sus opiniones, no
impone sus opiniones a los demás.
obtrusion [əb'truːʒən] *n* imposición *f*; importunidad
f; entrometimiento *m*.

obtrusive [əb'truːsiv] *adj* importuno, molesto; indiscreto; *building etc* demasiado visible, que salta a la vista; *smell* penetrante; *person* entrometido, intruso.

obtrusively [əb'truːsivli] *adv* importunamente; indiscretamente; de modo demasiado visible; de modo penetrante.

obtuse [əb'tjuːs] *adj* (*Math etc*) obtuso; *person* obtuso, estúpido, duro de mollera; *remark* poco inteligente; **now you're just being — te has empeñado en no comprender; he can be very — at times** a veces puede ser muy obtuso.

obtuseness [əb'tjuːsnis] *n* (*fig*) estupidez *f*, torpeza *f*.

obverse ['ɔbvəːs] **1** *adj* del anverso. **2** *n* anverso *m*.

obviate ['ɔbvieit] *vt* obviar, evitar, eliminar.

obvious ['ɔbviəs] *adj* (*clear, perceptible*) evidente, obvio, manifiesto, patente; (*expected*) obvio, natural; (*unsubtle*) poco sutil, transparente; (*suitable*) indicado; **the — thing to do is . . .** lo lógico es . . .; **he's the — man for the job** es el hombre más indicado para el puesto; **it's —, isn't it?** ¿es obvio, no?; **it's not — to me** para mí no está tan claro; **we must not be too — about it** en esto conviene ser algo astuto.

obviously ['ɔbviəsli] *adv* evidentemente; —! ¡naturalmente!; **it's — the best** evidentemente es el mejor; **he was not — drunk** no estaba tan borracho como para que no quedase lugar a dudas.

ocarina [ˌɔkə'riːnə] *n* ocarina *f*.

occasion [ə'keiʒən] **1** *n* (a) (*suitable juncture*) coyuntura *f*; oportunidad *f*, ocasión *f*; **he was awaiting a suitable —** aguardaba una coyuntura favorable, esperaba un momento propicio; **to take — to +** *infin* aprovechar la oportunidad de + *infin*.

(b) (*reason*) razón *f*, motivo *m*; **there is no — for alarm** no hay motivo para inquietarse, no hay por qué inquietarse; **there was no — for it** no había necesidad de ello; **to give — for scandal** provocar el escándalo; **he has given me no — for saying so** no me ha dado ocasión para decirlo; **I had — to reprimand him** tuve que reprenderle; **if you have — to use it** si se ve en el caso de usarlo.

(c) **to go about one's lawful —s** ir a sus negocios legítimos.

(d) (*time, occurrence*) ocasión *f*, vez *f*; **on the — of the cup final** cuando la final de copa; **on the — of his retirement** con motivo de su jubilación, para festejar su jubilación, para conmemorar su jubilación; **on —** de vez en cuando; **on one —** una vez; **on other —s** otras veces; **on just such an —** ótra vez exactamente igual que ésta; **on that —** esa vez, en aquella ocasión; **as the — requires** según el caso; **if the — arises** si se da el caso; **should the — so demand** si lo exigen las circunstancias; **to rise to the —** ponerse a la altura de las circunstancias.

(e) (*event, function*) función *f*, acontecimiento *m*; **this is an important —** esto es un acontecimiento importante; **it will be a big —** será una función impresionante; **the three big —s of the university year** las tres grandes funciones del año universitario; **it was quite an —** realmente fue un acontecimiento; **music written for the —** música *f* compuesta para la función.

2 *vt* ocasionar, causar.

occasional [ə'keiʒənl] *adj* (a) **an — event** algo que pasa de vez en cuando, un acontecimiento poco frecuente; **we have an — visitor** recibimos de vez en cuando una visita; **we're just — visitors** estamos de visita nada más.

(b) *music etc* de circunstancia, compuesto para una función determinada.

occasionally [ə'keiʒnəli] *adv* de vez en cuando, a veces; **very —** muy de tarde en tarde.

occident ['ɔksidənt] *n* occidente *m*.

occidental [ˌɔksi'dentl] *adj* occidental.

occiput ['ɔksipʌt] *n* occipucio *m*.

occluded [ɔ'kluːdid] *adj*: **— front** oclusión *f*.

occlusion [ə'kluːʒən] *n* oclusión *f*.

occlusive [ɔ'kluːsiv] (*Ling*) **1** *adj* oclusivo. **2** *n* oclusiva *f*.

occult [ɔ'kʌlt] **1** *adj reason etc* oculto, misterioso; (*mystic*) oculto, sobrenatural, mágico.

2 *n*: **the —** lo oculto, lo sobrenatural; **to study the —** dedicarse al ocultismo, estudiar las ciencias ocultas.

occultism ['ɔkəltizəm] *n* ocultismo *m*.

occultist ['ɔkəltist] *n* ocultista *mf*.

occupancy ['ɔkjupənsi] *n* ocupación *f*, tenencia *f*.

occupant ['ɔkjupənt] *n* (*of boat, car etc*) ocupante *mf*; (*of house*) habitante *mf*, inquilino *m*, a *f*; **all the —s were killed** perecieron todos los viajeros; **the —s could not be reached** resultó imposible socorrer a los que iban dentro.

occupation [ˌɔkju'peiʃən] *n* (a) (*of house etc*) tenencia *f*, inquilinato *m*; (*of country*) ocupación *f*; (*of office*) tenencia *f*; **military —** ocupación *f* militar; **a house unfit for —** una casa inhabitable; **to be in — of** ocupar; **we found them already in —** encontramos que ya se habían instalado allí.

(b) (*act of taking*) ocupación *f*; **the — of Paris in 1940** la ocupación de París en 1940; **the house is ready for —** la casa está lista para su ocupación.

(c) (*work*) trabajo *m*; (*employment*) empleo *m*; oficio *m*; (*calling*) oficio *m*; profesión *f*; (*pastime*) pasatiempo *m*; **a harmless enough —** un pasatiempo inocente; **a tailor by —** de oficio sastre; **what is he by —?, what is his —?** ¿qué oficio tiene?; **it gives — to 50 men** emplea a 50 hombres, da trabajo a 50 hombres; **this will give some — to your mind** esto le servirá para entretener la inteligencia.

occupational [ˌɔkju'peiʃənl] *adj* de oficio, relativo al oficio, profesional; *disease* profesional; *therapy* laboral; *see* **risk** *etc*.

occupier ['ɔkjupaiə*] *n* inquilino *m*, a *f*.

occupy ['ɔkjupai] *vt* ocupar (*also Mil*); *house* habitar, vivir en; *time* emplear, pasar; *attention, mind* entretener; **to be occupied in** (*or* **with**) ocuparse de (*or* en, con); **he is occupied in research** se dedica a la investigación; **he is very occupied at the moment** de momento está muy ocupado.

occur [ə'kəː*] *vi* (a) (*happen*) ocurrir, suceder, acontecer, pasar; **to — again** volver a suceder, producirse de nuevo; **if a vacancy —s** si se produce una vacante; **if the opportunity —s** si se presenta la oportunidad; **don't let it ever — again** y que esto no vuelva a ocurrir nunca.

(b) (*be found*) encontrarse, existir; **the plant —s all over Spain** la planta existe en todas partes en España.

(c) (*come to mind*) **it —s to me that . . .** se me ocurre que . . .; **it —red to me to ask him** se me ocurrió preguntárselo a él; **such an idea would never have —red to her** tal idea no se le hubiera ocurrido nunca.

occurrence [ə'kʌrəns] *n* (a) (*happening*) acontecimiento *m*; incidente *m*; caso *m*; **a common —** un caso frecuente; **an everyday —** un suceso de todos los días; **that is a common —** eso sucede a menudo, ese caso se da con frecuencia.

(b) (*existence*) existencia *f*; aparición *f*; **its — in the south is well known** se sabe que existe en el sur, es conocida su existencia en el sur; **its — here is unexpected** su aparición aquí es inesperada.

ocean ['əuʃən] *n* océano *m*; **—s of** (*fig*) la mar de.

ocean-going ['əuʃən,gəuiŋ] *adj* de alta mar.

Oceania [ˌəuʃi'einiə] Oceanía *f*.

oceanic [ˌəuʃi'ænik] *adj* oceánico.

oceanography [ˌəuʃə'nɔgrəfi] *n* oceanografía *f*.

ocelot ['əusilɔt] *n* ocelote *m*.

ochre ['əukə*] *n* ocre *m*; **red —** ocre *m* rojo, almagre *m*; **yellow —** ocre *m* amarillo.

ochreous ['əukriəs] *adj* de color ocre.

o'clock [ə'klɔk] *adv* (= *of the clock*) **it is 1 —** es la una; **it is 3 —** son las 3; **at 9 —** a las 9; **at exactly 9 —** a las 9 en punto; **it is just after 2 —** son un poco más de las 2; **it is nearly 8 —** son casi las 8.

octagon ['ɔktəgən] *n* octágono *m*.

octagonal [ɔk'tægənl] *adj* octagonal.

octahedron ['ɔktə'hiːdrən] *n* octaedro *m*.

octane ['ɔktein] *n* octano *m*; **high- — petrol** gasolina *f* de alto octanaje.

octave ['ɔktiv] *n* (*Mus, Poet*) octava *f*.

Octavian [ɔk'teiviən] *m* Octavio.

octavo [ɔk'teivəu] **1** *adj* en octavo. **2** *n* libro *m* en octavo.

octet(e) [ɔk'tet] *n* octeto *m*.

October [ɔk'təubə*] *n* octubre *m*.

octogenarian [ˌɔktəudʒi'neəriən] **1** *adj* octagenario. **2** *n* octagenario *m*, a *f*.

octopus ['ɔktəpəs] *n* pulpo *m*.

octosyllabic ['ɔktəusi'læbik] *adj* octosílabo.

octosyllable ['ɔktəu'siləbl] *n* octosílabo *m*.

ocular ['ɔkjulə*] *adj* ocular.

oculist ['ɔkjulist] *n* oculista *mf*.

odalisque ['əudəlisk] *n* odalisca *f*.

odd [ɔd] *adj* (a) (*extra, left over*) sobrante, de más; (*isolated*) suelto; (*unpaired*) sin pareja, desparejado; **the — shilling** el chelín que sobra *or* el chelín que hace falta; **to be — man out** estar de más, sobrar (*see also* **man** 1(g)); **we might pick up the — trick** pudiéramos ganar alguna baza más.

(b) (*Math*) impar; **— or even** par o impar.

(c) (*and a few more*) **30 —** treinta y pico, treinta y tantos; **£20 —** unas 20 libras.

(d) (*casual*) **at — moments** a ratos perdidos; hay

veces cuando . . .; **at — times** de vez en cuando; **he has written the — article** ha escrito algún que otro artículo; **he has done the — job for us** ha trabajado para nosotros de vez en cuando.

(e) (*strange*) raro, extraño, singular; misterioso; estrambótico; **how —!**, **very —!**, **most —!** ¡qué raro!; **the — thing about it is** . . . lo raro es que . . .; **he's very —** in his ways tiene manías; **he's got rather —** lately recientemente se ha vuelto algo raro.

oddball ['ɔdbɔ:l] (*US*) **1** *adj* raro, excéntrico. **2** *n* tipo *m* raro, excéntrico *m*.

oddity ['ɔditi] *n* (*strangeness*) rareza *f*, singularidad *f*, excentricidad *f*; (*peculiar trait*) rareza *f*, manía *f*; (*odd person*) individuo *m* singular; (*odd thing*) cosa *f* rara; **he has his oddities** tiene sus manías; **one of the oddities of the situation** uno de los aspectos raros que tiene la situación.

oddly ['ɔdli] singularmente, extrañamente; **they are — similar** tienen un extraño parecido; **— attractive** extrañamente atractivo; **— enough,** . . . aunque parezca mentira, . . .; **he is behaving most — se está** comportando de una manera muy rara.

oddment ['ɔdmənt] *n* artículo *m* suelto, artículo *m* que sobra; (*pej*) bagatela *f*, baratija *f*; (*Comm*) retal *m*.

oddness ['ɔdnis] *n* rareza *f*, singularidad *f*.

odds [ɔdz] *npl* (a) (*difference*) **what's the —?** ¿qué importa?, ¿qué más da?; **it makes no —** no importa, lo mismo da; **it makes no — to me** me es igual.

(b) (*variance, strife*) **to be at —** estar reñidos, estar de punta; **to be at — with someone** estar reñido con uno (*about, over* con motivo de); **estar incomodado con uno; to set 2 people at —** enemistar a 2 personas, hacer que riñan 2 personas.

(c) (*balance of advantage*) ventaja *f*, superioridad *f*; **the — are in his favour** él parece tener la ventaja; **the — are too great** nuestra desventaja es demasiado grande, los peligros son demasiado grandes; **to fight against overwhelming —s** luchar contra fuerzas abrumadoras.

(d) (*equalizing allowance*) ventaja *f*; **to give someone —** dar ventaja a uno.

(e) (*in betting*) puntos *mpl* de ventaja; **the — on the horse are 5 to 1** los puntos de ventaja del caballo son de 5 a 1; **to give — of 3 to 1** ofrecer 3 puntos de ventaja a 1; **what — will you give me?** ¿cuánta ventaja me da?

(f) (*chances*) probabilidades *fpl*; **the — are that** . . . lo más probable es que + *subj*; **the — are against it** es poco probable.

(g) **— and ends** (*of cloth etc*) retazos *mpl*, materiales *mpl* sobrantes; (*trinkets*) baratijas *fpl*, chucherías *fpl*; (*things in disorder*) cosas *fpl* sin arreglar; (*possessions*) chismes *mpl*; **there were — and ends of machinery** había piezas sueltas de máquinas.

odds-on ['ɔdz'ɔn] *adj:* **— favourite** caballo *m* favorito, caballo *m* con puntos de ventaja; **he's — favourite for the job** él tiene las mejores posibilidades de ganar el puesto.

ode [əud] *n* oda *f*.

odious ['əudiəs] *adj* odioso, detestable.

odium ['əudiəm] *n* odio *m*; oprobio *m*; **to bring — on someone** hacer que uno sea odiado; **to incur the — of having** + *ptp* suscitar el odio de la gente por haber + *ptp*.

odometer [ɔ'dɔmitə*] *n* odómetro *m*.

odontologist [ɔdɔn'tɔlədʒist] *n* odontólogo *m*.

odontology [ɔdɔn'tɔlədʒi] *n* odontología *f*.

odoriferous [əudə'rifərəs] *adj* odorífero.

odorous ['əudərəs] *adj* oloroso.

odour, (*US*) **odor** ['əudə*] *n* olor *m* (*of* a); fragancia *f*, perfume *m*; (*fig*) sospecha *f*; **— of sanctity** olor *m* de santidad; **bad — mal** olor *m*; **to be in bad —** tener mala fama, estar bajo sospecha; **to be in bad — with someone** llevarse mal con uno.

odourless, (*US*) **odorless** ['əudəlis] *adj* inodoro.

Odysseus [ə'disju:s] *m* Odiseo.

Odyssey ['ɔdisi] *n* Odisea *f*; **o—** (*fig*) odisea *f*.

oecology *n etc see* **ecology** *etc*.

oecumenical, (*US*) **ecumenical** [ˌi:kju:'menikəl] *adj* ecuménico.

Oedipus ['i:dipəs] *m* Edipo; **— complex** complejo *m* de Edipo.

o'er ['əuə*] (*poet*) = **over**.

oesophagus, (*US*) **esophagus** [i:'sɔfəgəs] *n* esófago *m*.

of [ɔv, əv] *prep* (a) (*possession*) de; **the pen — my aunt** la pluma de mi tía; **a friend — mine** un amigo mío; **love — country** el amor a la patria; **the love — God** el amor de Dios; **it's no business — yours** aquí no se meta Vd, Vd no tiene que ver con esto.

(b) (*partitive etc*) de; **how much — this** do you want? ¿cuánto quieres de esto?; **there were 4 — us** éramos 4; **all — them** todos ellos; **the 12 two were bad** de los 12, dos estaban pasados; **most — all** más que nada; **you — all people ought to know** Vd debiera saberlo más que nadie; **the best — friends** el mejor amigo; **the book — books** el libro de los libros; **king — kings** rey de reyes.

(c) (*descriptive genitive*) **the city — Burgos** la ciudad de Burgos; **a boy — 8** un muchacho de 8 años; **cakes — her making** pasteles que ella había hecho; **by the name — Green** llamado Green; **bright — eye** de ojos claros; **hard — heart** duro de corazón; **that idiot — a minister** ese idiota de ministro.

(d) (*origin, cause etc*) **to buy something — someone** comprar algo a uno; **"— all chemists"** "de venta en todas las farmacias"; **— necessity** por necesidad, forzosamente; **— itself** de por sí; **to die — a disease** morir de una enfermedad.

(e) (*material*) de; **made — metal** hecho de metal.

(f) (*agent*) **beloved — all** querido de todos; **it was very harsh — him to** + *infin* ha sido durísimo en + *infin*; **it is kind — you** es Vd muy amable.

(g) (*with certain verbs*) **to dream — something** soñar con algo; **to judge — something** juzgar algo, opinar sobre algo; **to smell — something** oler a algo; **he was robbed — his watch** le robaron el reloj, se le robó el reloj.

(h) (*fam*) **he died — a Friday** murió un viernes; **it was fine — a morning** por la mañana hacía buen tiempo.

(i) (*with hours: US*) **it is 10 minutes — 4** son las 4 menos 10.

off [ɔf] **1** *adv* (a) (*away*) **a place 2 miles —** un lugar a 20 millas (de distancia); **it landed not 50 metres —** cayó a solamente 50 metros de nosotros; **noises — ruidos** *mpl* de fondo; **a voice — voz** de fondo, (*Cine*) voz en off.

(b) (*of removal*) **with his hat — sin** sombrero, llevando el sombrero en la mano; **with his shoes — sin** zapatos, descalzo; **hats —!** ¡descúbranse!; **with those wet socks!** ¡quítate esos calcetines mojados!; **— with his head!** ¡que le corten la cabeza!; **hands —!** ¡fuera las manos!; **the lid is — la** tapa está quitada; **— with you!** ¡fuera de aquí!, (*tenderly*) ¡vete ya!; **— we go!** ¡vamos!; **"10 % —" "descuento** de 10 por cien"; **I'll give you 5 % — te** doy un descuento de 5 por cien; **to have a day — tomarse** un día de asueto.

(c) **— and on** de vez en cuando, a intervalos; ya bien ya mal; **right —, straight — sin** parar, sin interrupción; **3 days straight — 3** días seguidos.

2 *adv* (*with* to be) (a) (*of distance, time*) **it's some way — está** algo lejos, dista varios kilómetros de aquí; **the game is 3 days — faltan** 3 días para el partido.

(b) (*depart*) **to be — irse; I'm — me** voy; **I must be — tengo** que marcharme; **I'm — to Paris** voy a París, salgo para París; **be —!** ¡fuera de aquí!, ¡lárgate!; **they're —!** ¡ya!; **he's — fishing** every Sunday todos los domingos sale a pescar, todos los domingos va de pesca.

(c) (*be absent*) **to be — estar** fuera, no estar; **he's — fishing** ha ido a pescar; **she's — on Tuesdays** los martes no viene (a trabajar); **are you — this weekend?** ¿vas a estar fuera este fin de semana?; **salmon is — (***on menu***)** no hay salmón ya, se acabó el salmón; **there are 2 buttons — faltan** 2 botones; **the game is — se** ha cancelado el partido; **sorry, but the party's — lo** siento, pero no hay guateque; **the talks are — se** han cancelado las conversaciones.

(d) (*of switches etc*) **to be — estar** en posición de desconectado; (*apparatus, radio, TV*) estar desenchufado, estar desconectado; (*light*) estar apagado; (*tap*) estar cerrado; (*Mech*) estar parado; (*water etc*) estar cortado; (*brake*) estar desapretado.

(e) (*be bad*) **to be — estar** pasado; (*milk*) estar cortado.

(f) (*fig*) **it's a bit —, isn't it?** esto no lo apruebo, ¿sabes?; **I thought his behaviour was rather — me** pareció que su conducta era bastante censurable.

(g) **to be well — estar** acomodado, tener dinero; **he's better — where he is** está mejor allí donde está ahora; **we should be no better — no** ganaríamos nada; **to be badly — andar** mal de dinero; **to be badly — for potatoes** andar escaso de patatas, tener escasez de patatas; *see* **well-off**, **worse 2** *etc*.

3 *prep* (a) de; **height — the ground** altura *f* del suelo, altura *f* sobre el suelo; **to fall — a table** caer de una mesa; **to fall — a cliff** caer por un precipicio; **to eat — a dish** comer en un plato; **to dine — fish**

cenar pescado; **to allow 5%** — **the price** rebajar el precio en un 5 por cien.

(b) a street — **the square** una calle que sale de la plaza; **a house** — **the main road** una casa algo apartada de la carretera.

(c) (*Naut*) — **Portland Bill** a la altura de Portland Bill, frente a Portland Bill.

(d) there are 2 buttons — **my coat** le faltan 2 botones a mi chaqueta; **to be** — **one's food** no tener apetito; **he was** — **work for 3 weeks** durante 3 semanas no pudo trabajar; **to take 3 days** — **work** tomarse 3 días de vacaciones.

4 *adj:* — **side** (*Aut etc: British*) lado *m* derecho, (*US, Spain etc*) lado *m* izquierdo; **to have an** — **day** tener un día malo; **in the** — **season** fuera de temporada; **in the** — **position** en posición de cerrado (*etc*).

offal ['ɔfəl] *n* asadura *f*, menudencias *fpl*.

offbeat ['ɔf,bi:t] *adj* excéntrico, original; inconformista, nada convencional.

off-centre, (*US*) **off-center** ['ɔf'sentə*] *adj:* **to be** — estar descentrado.

off chance ['ɔftʃɑ:ns] *n* posibilidad *f* remota; **we'll go on the** — iremos por si acaso, iremos aunque hay poca posibilidad; **he bought it on the** — **that it would come in useful** lo compró pensando que tal vez resultaría útil algún día.

off-colour, (*US*) **off-color** ['ɔf'kʌlə*] *adj fabric etc* desteñido; (*ill*) indispuesto, (*of child*) pachucho; *joke etc* verde.

offence, (*US*) **offense** [ə'fens] *n* **(a)** (*insult*) ofensa *f*; **no** — !, **no** — **meant** sin ofender a Vd; **no** — **was intended, he intended no** — no tenía la intención de ofender a nadie; **to give** — ofender; **to take** — ofenderse (*at* por), resentirse (*at* de).

(b) (*crime*) delito *m*, crimen *m*, infracción *f* de la ley; (*moral*) transgresión *f*, pecado *m*; **first** — primer delito *m*; **indictable** — delito *m* procesable; **minor** — delito *m* de menor cuantía; **political** — crimen *m* político; **second** — reincidencia *f*; **technical** — cuasidelito *m*; **it is an** — **to** + *infin* la ley castiga a los que . . .; **to commit an** — cometer un delito.

offend [ə'fend] **1** *vt* ofender; **it** —**s my sense of justice** ello ofende mi sentido de justicia; **to be** —**ed** ofenderse (*at, by* por), tomarlo a mal; **he wasn't a bit** —**ed** no se ofendió en lo más mínimo; **don't be** —**ed** no se vaya a ofender, no lo tome a mal; **he is easily** —**ed** es algo picajoso; **to become** —**ed** ofenderse.

2 *vi:* **to** — **against** pecar contra.

offender [ə'fendə*] *n* **(a)** (*insulter*) ofensor *m*, ora *f*.

(b) (*criminal*) delincuente *mf*, culpable *mf*; (*against traffic code etc*) infractor *m*, ora *f* (*against* de); **first** — delincuente *mf* sin antecedente penal.

(c) (*moral*) transgresor *m*, ora *f*, pecador *m*, ora *f*.

offending [ə'fendiŋ] *adj* delincuente, culpable.

offensive [ə'fensiv] **1** *adj warfare etc* ofensivo; (*insulting*) ofensivo, injurioso; (*disgusting*) repugnante; **don't be** — ! ¡hable con más educación; **to be** — **to someone** ser grosero con uno, decir injurias a uno.

2 *n* ofensiva *f*; **to go over to the** —, **to take the** — tomar la ofensiva.

offensively [ə'fensivli] *adv* injuriosamente; repugnantemente; groseramente.

offer ['ɔfə*] **1** *n* oferta *f*, ofrecimiento *m*; (*Comm*) oferta *f*; — **of marriage** oferta *f* de matrimonio; **peace** — ofrecimiento *m* de paz; **to be on** — estar en oferta, ofrecerse; **it was on** — **at £400** se ofrecía a 400 libras; **to make an** — **for something** hacer una oferta por algo, ofrecerse a comprar algo; **make me an** — ! ¡hágame una oferta!; **it's the best** — **I can make** no puedo ofrecer más.

2 *vt* **(a)** *help, services etc* ofrecer; *prayers* rezar, ofrecer (*also* **to** — **up**); *opportunity, prospect etc* brindar, facilitar, deparar; **to** — **something to someone** ofrecer algo a uno; **to** — **one's flank to the enemy** exponer su flanco al enemigo; **to** — **resistance** oponer resistencia (*to* a); **he** —**ed no resistance** no se resistió.

(b) to — **to do something** ofrecerse a hacer algo; **he** —**ed to strike me** hizo ademán de pegarme, hizo como si fuera a pegarme.

(c) *comment, remark* hacer; **he** —**ed no comment** no dijo nada; **I wish to** — **two comments** quiero hacer dos observaciones.

(d) the flowers — **a magnificent spectacle** las flores se muestran espléndidas.

3 *vi:* **if the opportunity** —**s** si se me da la oportunidad, si se da el caso.

4 *vr:* **to** — **oneself for a mission** ofrecerse a ir a una misión; **to** — **oneself for a post** presentarse para un puesto.

offering ['ɔfəriŋ] *n* ofrecimiento *m*; (*Eccl*) ofrenda *f*; (*gift*) regalo *m*, don *m*; (*sacrifice*) sacrificio *m*; **burnt** — holocausto *m*; **votive** — exvoto *m*.

offertory ['ɔfətəri] *n* (*Eccl*) ofertorio *m*.

offertory box ['ɔfətəri,bɔks] *n* (*Eccl*) cepillo *m*.,

offhand ['ɔf'hænd] **1** *adj* informal, brusco, descortés; poco ceremonioso; **to treat someone in an** — **manner** tratar a uno con bastante informalidad; **he was very** — **about it** lo discutió con poca seriedad.

2 *adv* de improviso, sin pensarlo; — **I couldn't tell you** así de improviso no se lo puedo decir.

offhandedly ['ɔf'hændidli] *adv* con informalidad, bruscamente, descortésmente; sin ceremonias, sin miramientos; **to treat someone** — tratar a uno con bastante informalidad; **he said** — dijo en tono brusco.

offhandedness ['ɔf'hændidnis] *n* informalidad *f*; brusquedad *f*; descortesía *f*.

office ['ɔfis] **1** *n* **(a)** (*place*) oficina *f*; (*room*) despacho *m*; (*lawyer's*) bufete *m*; (*as part of organization*) sección *f*, departamento *m*; (*ministry*) ministerio *m*; (*branch*) sucursal *f*; **head** — central *f*, sede *f*, oficina *f* principal; **manager's** — dirección *f*; **newspaper** — redacción *f*; **"usual —s"** "aseos"; **Foreign O**— Ministerio *m* de Asuntos Exteriores; *see* **home** *etc*.

(b) (*function*) oficio *m*; (*post*) cargo *m*; **it is my** — **to** + *infin* yo tengo el deber de + *infin*, me incumbe + *infin*; **to be in** —, **to hold** — (*person*) estar en funciones, desempeñar un cargo, (*govt*) estar en el poder; **he is in** — **for one year** ocupa el cargo durante un año; **to be out of** — no estar en el poder; **to come into** —, **to take** — (*person*) asumir un cargo, (*govt*) entrar en el poder; **to leave** — (*person*) dimitir un cargo, (*govt*) salir del poder; **to perform the** — **of someone** hacer las veces de uno.

(c) good —**s** buenos oficios *mpl*; **to offer one's good** —**s** ofrecer sus buenos oficios; **through the** —**s of** gracias a la mediación de.

(d) O— **for the Dead** (*Eccl*) oficio *m* de difuntos.

2 *attr hours, work etc* de oficina; **party** del personal de la oficina; — **supplies** materiales *mpl* de oficina.

office block ['ɔfisblɔk] *n* bloque *m* de oficinas.

office boy ['ɔfisbɔi] *n* mandadero *m*; botones *mpl*; mozo *m* de oficina.

officer ['ɔfisə*] **1** *n* (*Mil, Naut, Aer*) oficial *m*; (*of society*) dignatario *m*; (*of local govt*) magistrado *m*; funcionario *m*; (*of company*) director *m*; (*of police*) policía *m*, agente *m* de policía; (*form of address to policeman*) agente, guardia; — **of the watch** oficial *m* de guardia; **the** —**s of a company** los directores de una sociedad, la junta directiva de una sociedad; **commissioned** — oficial *m*; **non-commissioned** — suboficial *m*, sargento *m* or cabo *m*; **medical** — médico *m*, (*Mil*) oficial *m* médico, (*of town*) jefe *m* de sanidad municipal; **naval** — oficial *m* de marina; **orderly** — oficial *m* de día; **petty** — suboficial *m* de marina; **police** — policía *m*, agente *m* de policía; **staff** — oficial *m* del estado mayor.

2 *vt* (*command*) mandar; (*staff*) proveer de oficiales **to be well** —**ed** tener buena oficialidad.

office worker ['ɔfiswə:kə*] *n* oficinista *mf*.

official [ə'fiʃəl] **1** *adj* oficial; autorizado; *voice, style etc* ceremonioso, solemne; **in** — **circles** en círculos oficiales; **is that** — ? (*fig*) ¿es cierto eso?

2 *n* oficial *m*, oficial *m* público, funcionario *m*; **high** — oficial *m* importante; **an** — **of the ministry** un funcionario del Ministerio.

officialdom [ə'fiʃəldəm] *n* (*pej*) burocracia *f*.

officialese [ə,fiʃə'li:z] *n* lenguaje *m* burocrático, estilo *m* oficial burocrático.

officially [ə'fiʃəli] *adv* oficialmente; de modo autorizado.

officiate [ə'fiʃieit] *vi* oficiar (*as* de).

officious [ə'fiʃəs] *adj* oficioso.

officiously [ə'fiʃəsli] *adv* oficiosamente.

officiousness [ə'fiʃəsnis] *n* oficiosidad *f*.

offing ['ɔfiŋ] *n:* **to be in the** — (*Naut*) estar cerca, (*fig*) estar en perspectiva.

off-licence ['ɔf,laisəns] *n* tienda donde se venden bebidas alcohólicas (*sin permitirse su consumo en el local*).

offprint ['ɔfprint] *n* separata *f*, tirada *f* aparte.

offset ['ɔfset] **1** *n* compensación *f*; (*Typ*) offset *m*; (*Hort: layer*) acodo *m*, (*bulb*) bulbo *m* reproductor; (*Archit*) retallo *m*; — **press** prensa *f* offset.

2 *vt* (*irr: see* **set**) compensar; contrarrestar, contrapesar.

offshoot ['ɔfʃu:t] *n* (*Bot*) renuevo *m*, vástago *m*; (*fig*) ramal *m* (*from* de).

offshore ['ɔf'ʃɔ:] **1** *adv* a lo largo. **2** *adj breeze* terral, que sopla de tierra; *island etc* a poca distancia de la costa.

offside ['ɔf'said] **1** *adv*: **to be** — estar fuera de juego. **2** *adj*: **the** — **rule** la regla de fuera de juego. **3** *interj* ¡offside! (*pronounced* [or'sai]).

offspring ['ɔfsprɪŋ] *n* (*sing*) vástago *m*, descendiente *mf*; (*pl*) descendencia *f*, hijos *mpl*, prole *f*; **to die without** — morir sin dejar descendencia.

offstage ['ɔf'steidʒ] **1** *adv* entre bastidores. **2** *adj* de entre bastidores.

off-the-peg ['ɔfðə'peg] *adv*, *adj* confeccionado.

off-white ['ɔf'wait] *adj* de blanco algo oscuro, de un blanco que tira a gris.

oft [ɔft] *adv* (*poet*) = **often; many a time and** — muchísimas veces.

often ['ɔfən] *adv* muchas veces, mucho, a menudo, con frecuencia; **very** — muchísimas veces, repetidas veces, muy a menudo; **not** — pocas veces; **how** —? ¿cuántas veces?; **so** — tantas veces; **as** — as tantas veces como, siempre que; **as** — **as not, more** — **than not** las más veces; **every so** — (*of time*) cada cierto tiempo, (*of distance, spacing*) cada cierta distancia; **it is not** — **that** . . . no es frecuente que . . .; **it cannot be said too** — **that** . . . es necesario repetir que . .

oft-times ['ɔftaimz] *adv* (*lit*) a menudo.

ogival [əu'dʒaivəl] *adj* ojival.

ogive ['əudʒaiv] *n* ojiva *f*.

ogle ['əugl] *vt* echar miradas amorosas (*or* incitantes) a.

ogre ['əugə*] *n* ogro *m*.

oh [əu] *interj* **(a)** (*vocative*) — **king**! ¡oh rey!
(b) (*pain*) ¡ay!
(c) (*preceding questions and excls*) — **really**? ¿de veras?; — **is he**? ¿en serio?; — **what a surprise**! ¡qué sorpresa!; — **no you don't**! ¡eso no!

ohm [əum] *n* ohmio *m*.

oil [ɔil] **1** *n* (*in most senses*) aceite *m*, (*Geol, as mineral*) petróleo *m*; (*Art, Eccl*) óleo *m*; **an** — **by Rembrandt** un óleo de Rembrandt; **crude** — petróleo *m* bruto; **heavy** — aceite *m* pesado; **holy** — crisma *f*, santo óleo *m*; **lubricating** — aceite *m* lubricante; **sweet** — aceite *m* de oliva; **vegetable** — accite *m* vegetal; **to burn the midnight** — quemarse las cejas; **to check the** — (*Aut etc*) revisar el nivel del aceite; **to paint in** —**s** pintar al óleo; **to pour** — **on troubled waters** echar aceite sobre aguas turbulentas; **to strike** — encontrar un pozo de petróleo, (*fig*) encontrar un filón, enriquecerse de súbito.
2 *attr* industry *etc* petrolero; *lamp etc* de aceite.
3 *vt* lubricar, lubrificar, engrasar; **to be well —ed** (*sl*) ir a la vela.

oil-burning ['ɔil,bəːnɪŋ] *adj* que quema aceite combustible, que utiliza aceite combustible como combustible.

oilcake ['ɔilkeik] *n* torta *f* de borujo.

oilcan ['ɔilkæn] *n* aceitera *f*.

oilcloth ['ɔilklɔθ] *n* hule *m*, encerado *m*.

oilfield ['ɔilfiːld] *n* campo *m* petrolífero.

oil-fired ['ɔilfaiəd] *adj* = **oil-burning**.

oil gauge ['ɔilgeidʒ] *n* manómetro *m* de aceite; indicador *m* del nivel del aceite.

oiliness ['ɔilinis] *n* lo aceitoso, oleaginosidad *f*; lo grasiento; zalamería *f*.

oil lamp ['ɔilæmp] *n* velón *m*, quinqué *m*.

oil level ['ɔillevl] *n* nivel *m* del aceite.

oilman ['ɔilmæn] *n*, *pl* —**men** [men] petrolero *m*; magnate *m* del petróleo.

oil painting ['ɔil,peintɪŋ] *n* pintura *f* al óleo; **she's no** — no es tan hermosa que digamos.

oil pan ['ɔilpæn] *n* (*US Aut*) colector *m* de aceite.

oil refinery ['ɔilri,fainəri] *n* refinería *f* de petróleo

oilskin ['ɔilskin] *n* hule *m*, encerado *m*; —**s** traje *m* de encerado, chubasquero *m*.

oil stove ['ɔilstəuv] *n* (*cooking*) cocina *f* de petróleo; (*heating*) estufa *f* de petróleo.

oil tanker ['ɔiltæŋkə*] *n* petrolero *m*.

oil well ['ɔilwel] *n* pozo *m* de petróleo.

oily ['ɔili] *adj* *liquid etc* aceitoso, oleaginoso; *meal* grasiento; *person* zalamero.

ointment ['ɔintmənt] *n* ungüento *m*.

O.K., okay ['əu'kei] (*fam*) **1** *interj* ¡está bien!; sí!; ¡comprendo!; ¡vale!
2 *adj* (*agreed*) aprobado; (*satisfactory*) satisfactorio; **it's** — **with me** lo apruebo, estoy de acuerdo; **is it** — **with you if** . . .? ¿me das permiso para + *infin* . . .?, ¿me permites + *infin* . . .?; **that may have been** — **last year** eso puede haber estado de moda el año pasado; **the** — **hair-do of 1980** el peinado elegante de 1980, el peinado que está de moda en 1980.
3 *n* visto *m* bueno; **to give something one's** — dar el visto bueno a algo, aprobar algo.
4 *vt* dar el visto bueno a, aprobar.

old [əuld] *adj* **(a)** (*person: aged*) viejo; anciano; **an** — **man** un viejo; **an** — **woman** una vieja; **the** — los viejos, los ancianos; — **and young** grandes y pequeños; — **Peter** Pedro el viejo; — **Mrs Brown** la vieja señora de Brown; **he's a good** — **horse** es un buen caballo aunque bastante viejo ya; **to grow** — envejecerse; **to live to be** — llegar a una edad avanzada; **if I live to be that** — si llego a esa edad.
(b) (*ancient*) *thing* viejo; *clothes etc* viejo; usado, gastado; *bread* duro; *wine* añejo; **it's too** — **to be any use** es demasiado viejo para servir.
(c) (*with expression of years: person*) **how** — **are you**? ¿cuántos años tienes?, ¿qué edad tienes?; **I am 7 years** — tengo 7 años; **she's 3 years** — **today** hoy cumple 3 años; **she is** —**er than I** tiene más años que yo; **she is the** — **est** es la mayor; **to be 4 years** —**er than someone** tener 4 años más que uno; **she's** — **enough to go alone** tiene bastante edad para ir sola; **he's** — **enough to know his own mind** tiene bastante edad para saber lo que quiere; **he's** — **enough to know better** a la edad que él tiene conviene obrar con más juico.
(d) (*with expression of years: thing*) **the building is 300 years** — el edificio se construyó hace 300 años; **the company is a century** — la sociedad existe desde hace un siglo, la sociedad se fundó hace un siglo.
(e) (*old-established, long-standing*) viejo, antiguo; **an** — **friend of mine** un viejo amigo mío; **that's as** — **as the hills** eso es de tiempos de Maricastaña, eso es viejísimo.
(f) (*former*) antiguo; **an** — **boy of the school** un antiguo alumno del colegio; **my** — **school** mi antiguo colegio; **in the** — **days** antaño, en el pasado; **O**— **French** antiguo francés *m*; **the** — **country** la madre patria; **the O**— **World** el Viejo Mundo.
(g) (*affectionate: fam*) — **Lucas** el tío Lucas; **the** — **man** el jefe, el patrón; **my** — **man** el pariente, **my** — **woman** la parienta; **I say,** — **man** oye, chico; **any** — **thing does for me** me contento con cualquie. cosa; **any** — **thing you like** lo que quieras.
(h) **of** — antiguamente, antaño; **knights of** — los caballeros de antaño; **I know him of** — le conozco de antiguo.

old-clothes ['əuld'kləuðz] *adj*: — **dealer** ropavejero *m*, *a f*; — **shop** ropavejería *f*.

olden ['əuldən] *adj* (*arch or lit*) antiguo; **in the** — **days** antaño, en el pasado.

old-established ['əuldi'stæbliʃt] *adj* viejo.

olde-worlde ['əuldi'wəːldi] *adj* (*hum*) viejísimo, antiquísimo; de antaño, de sabor arcaico; **with** — **lettering** con letras al estilo antiguo; **a very** — **interior** un interior pintoresco de antaño; **Stratford is terribly** — Stratford tiene fuerte sabor arcaico.

old-fashioned ['əuld'fæʃnd] *adj* *thing* anticuado, pasado de moda; *person* de ideas anticuadas, chapado a la antigua.

oldish ['əuldiʃ] *adj* algo viejo, más bien viejo, que va para viejo.

old-line ['əuldlain] *adj* conservador, de mentalidad tradicionalista.

old-looking ['əuld,lukiŋ] *adj* de aspecto viejo.

old-maidish ['əuld'meidiʃ] *adj* de solterona; remilgado.

old stager ['əuld'steidʒə*] *n* veterano *m*.

oldster ['əuldstə*] *n* (*US*) viejo *m*, vieja *f*.

old-style ['əuld'stail] *adj* antiguo, al estilo antiguo, a la antigua.

old-timer [.əuld'taimə*] *n* veterano *m*.

old-world ['əuld'wəːld] *adj* (*Bio, Geog*) del Viejo Mundo; *character etc* antiguo, arcaico, rancio; **the** — **charm of Toledo** la atractiva ranciedad de Toledo, el sabor arcaico de Toledo.

oleaginous [əuli'ædʒinəs] *adj* oleaginoso.

oleander [.əuli'ændə*] *n* adelfa *f*.

oleo . . . ['əuliəu] *in compounds* oleo . . .

olfactory [ɔl'fæktəri] *adj* olfativo, olfatorio.

oligarchic(al) [.ɔli'gɑːkik(əl)] *adj* oligárquico.

oligarchy ['ɔligɑːki] *n* oligarquía *f*.

olive ['ɔliv] **1** *n* (*fruit*) aceituna *f*, oliva *f*; (*tree*) olivo *m*. **2** *adj* aceitunado, oliváceo.

olive branch ['ɔlivbrɑːntʃ] *n* ramo *m* de olivo (*also fig*); **to hold out the** — **to someone** ofrecer el ramo de olivo a uno.

olive-green ['ɔliv'griːn] *adj* verde-oliva; — **uniforms** uniformes *mpl* verde oliva.

olive grove ['ɔlivgrəuv] *n* olivar *m*.

olive oil ['ɔliv'ɔil] *n* aceite *m* de oliva.

Oliver ['ɔlivə*] *m* Oliverio.

Olympiad [əu'limpiæd] *n* olimpíada *f*.

Olympian [əu'limpiən] *adj* olímpico.

Olympic [əu'limpik] **1** adj olímpico. **2 O—s** npl Juegos mpl Olímpicos.

Olympus [əu'limpəs] Olimpo m.

omega ['əumigə] n omega f.

omelet(te) ['ɔmlit] n tortilla f.

omen ['əumen] n agüero m, presagio m; **bird of ill —** ave f de mal agüero; **it is a good — that . . .** es buena señal que. . . .

ominous ['ɔminəs] adj siniestro, de mal agüero, amenazador; **the silence was —** el silencio no auguraba nada bueno; **in an — tone** en tono amenazador; **that's —** eso es mala señal.

ominously ['ɔminəsli] adv: **the thunder rumbled —** retumbaba amenazador el trueno; **it was — familiar to us** nos era siniestramente familiar; **he spoke —** habló en tono amenazador.

omission [əu'miʃən] n omisión f; supresión f; olvido m, descuido m; **it was an — on my part** fue un descuido mío.

omit [əu'mit] vt omitir; suprimir; olvidar, descuidar; person, person's name pasar por alto; **we should — all reference to . . .** debiéramos suprimir toda mención de . . . ; **to — to do something** olvidar de + infin, dejar de + infin; **don't — to visit her** no dejes de visitarla.

omnibus ['ɔmnibəs] **1** adj general, para todo; edition completo. **2** n autobús m.

omnipotence [ɔm'nipətəns] n omnipotencia f.

omnipotent [ɔm'nipətənt] adj omnipotente.

omnipresence ['ɔmni'prezəns] n omnipresencia f.

omnipresent ['ɔmni'prezənt] adj omnipresente.

omniscience [ɔm'nisiəns] n omnisciencia f.

omniscient [ɔm'nisiənt] adj omnisciente, omniscio.

omnivorous [ɔm'nivərəs] adj omnívoro; **she is an — reader** lo lee todo con avidez, en su lectura muestra tener gustos muy diversos.

on [ɔn] **1** adv see **to put —** etc; see **further, later** etc.
(a) to be — (actor) estar en la escena; **to have one's boots —** llevar las botas puestas; **what had he got —?** ¿qué prendas llevaba puestas?
(b) to drive —, to go —, to ride —, to walk — etc seguir adelante (see also **go** etc); **to read —** seguir leyendo; **and so —** y así sucesivamente, y así los demás; etcétera; **to talk — and —** hablar sin parar, hablar incansablemente.
(c) from that time — desde entonces, a partir de entonces; **well — in June** bien entrado junio; **well — in years** entrado en años, que va para viejo.
(d) (with to be: of switches etc) **to be —** estar conectado. (apparatus, Radio, TV) estar conectado, estar puesto, estar enchufado; (light) estar encendido, estar puesto; (tap) estar abierto; (Mech) estar en marcha, estar funcionando; (brake) estar apretado.
(e) (with to be: of shows etc) **the show is now —** ha comenzado el espectáculo; **the show is now — in London** se ha comenzado el espectáculo en Londres; **— with the show!** ¡que empiece (or continúe) el espectáculo!; **— with the dancing girls!** ¡que salgan las bailarinas!; **what's — at the cinema?** ¿qué ponen en el cine?; **what's — at the theatre?** ¿qué representan en el teatro?; **"what's — in London"** "cartelera de los espectáculos londinenses"; **have you anything — this evening?** ¿tienes compromiso para esta noche?; **the deal is —** se ha cerrado el trato, ya está concertado el trato; **that's not —!** ¡eso no se hace!, ¡no hay derecho!
(f) (idioms with to be) **to be — to something** creer haber encontrado algo, seguir una pista interesante; **he's — to something good** se ha encontrado algo bueno; **he knows he's — to a good thing** sabe que ha tenido la mar de suerte; **the police are — to the villain** la policía tiene una pista que le conducirá al criminal; **they were — to him at once** le calaron en seguida, le identificaron en el acto; **he's always — to me about it** me está majando continuamente con eso.
(g) — and off de vez en cuando, a intervalos.
2 interj ¡adelante!
3 prep **(a)** (of place etc) en, sobre; encima de; **— the Continent** en el continente; **— the table** en la mesa, sobre la mesa; **a meal — the train** una comida en el tren; **— all sides** por todas partes, por todos lados; **— the ceiling** sobre el techo; **— the high seas** en alta mar; **hanging — the wall** colgado de la pared; **with her hat — her head** con el sombrero puesto; **a house — the square** una casa en la plaza; **— page 2** en la página 2; **— the right** a la derecha; **— foot** a pie; **— horseback** a caballo; **I've no money — me** no llevo dinero encima, no llevo dinero; **to drift — to the shore** flotar hacia la playa; **so they came — to me** así que los hicieron pasar a mí, así vinieron a mis manos.

(b) (fig) **a story based — fact** una historia basada en hechos; **the march — Rome** la marcha sobre Roma; **an attack — the government** un ataque contra el gobierno; **to swear — the Bible** prestar juramento sobre la Biblia; **all the children play — the piano** todos los chicos saben tocar el piano; **so he played it — the violin** así que lo tocó al violín; **he's — the committee** es miembro del comité; **he's — the staff** es de plantilla; **— average** por término medio; **— good authority** de buena tinta; **— his authority** con su autorización; **— my responsibility** bajo mi responsabilidad; **— a charge of murder** acusado de homicidio; **— pain of** so pena de; **— account of** a causa de; **— sale** de venta, en venta; **a student — a grant** un estudiante con beca; **I'm — £3,000** yo gano 3.000 libras (al año); **we're — irregular verbs** estamos estudiando los verbos irregulares; **I'm — a milk diet** sigo un régimen lácteo; **many live — less than that** muchos viven con menos; (for many expressions, eg — duty, — hand, see the noun).
(c) (of time) **— Friday** el viernes; **— Fridays** los viernes; **— the next day** al día siguiente; **— 14th May** el catorce de mayo; **— the evening of the 2nd July** el 2 de julio por la tarde; **— a day like this** un día como éste; **— some days it is** hay días cuando lo es; **— and after the 15th** el día 15 y a partir de la misma fecha; **— or about the 8th** el día 8 o por ahí; **— my arrival** al llegar yo.
(d) (on + ger) **— seeing him** al verle; **— my calling to him** al llamarle yo.
(e) (concerning) sobre, acerca de; **a book — physics** un libro de física, un libro sobre física; **an examination — maths** un examen de matemáticas; **Eden — the events of 1956** lo que dice Eden acerca de los acontecimientos de 1956; **Bentley — Horace** los comentarios de Bentley a Horacio; **have you heard the boss — the new tax?** ¿has oído lo que dice el jefe acerca de la nueva contribución?
(f) (after, according to) según; **— this model** según este modelo.
(g) (engaged in) **he's away — business** está fuera por negocios; **the company is — tour** la compañía está en gira; **to be — holiday** estar de vacaciones.
(h) (at the expense of) **this round's — me** esto corre de mi cuenta, invito yo; **it's — the house** la casa invita, está pagado (por el dueño); **the tour was — the Council** la gira la pagó el Consejo, corrió el Consejo con los gastos de la gira.
(i) woe — woe dolor sobre dolor; **snow — snow** nieve y más nieve.
4 adj: **the — side** (Aut etc; British) el lado izquierdo, el lado de la izquierda, (US, Spain etc) el lado derecho; **in the — position** en posición de abierto (etc).

onanism ['əunənizəm] n onanismo m.

once [wʌns] **1** adv **(a)** (on one occasion) una vez; **— before** una vez antes, ya . . . una vez; **— or twice** algunas veces; **— a week** una vez por semana; **— only** una vez nada más; **— again, — more** otra vez, una vez más; **— in a while** de vez en cuando; **— and for all** una vez para siempre; **just this —** esta vez nada más; **for —** por una vez; **more than —** más de una vez; **not —** ni una vez siquiera; **— a thief always a thief** los ladrones suelen ser incorregibles.
(b) (formerly) antes, antiguamente, en otro tiempo; **— when we were young** hace tiempo, cuando éramos jóvenes; **— upon a time** en tiempos de Maricastaña, (as start of story) érase una vez . . ., hubo una vez . . . ; **it had — been white** antes había sido blanco; **I knew him —** le conocía hace tiempo.
(c) at — en seguida, inmediatamente; (in one go) de una vez; **at — a food and a tonic** alimento y tónico a la vez, juntamente alimento y tónico; **all at —** (suddenly) de repente, de golpe; (in one go) de una vez; (all together) todo junto, todos juntos, a un mismo tiempo.
2 conj una vez que . . ., si . . .; **— allow this all is lost** en cuanto éste se permita se acaba todo; **— you give him the chance** una vez que le des la oportunidad, si le das la oportunidad.

once-over ['wʌns,əuvə*] n (fam): **to give something the —** dar un vistazo a algo, examinar algo (rápidamente); **they gave the house the —** registraron superficialmente la casa.

oncoming ['ɔn,kʌmiŋ] adj que se acerca.

one [wʌn] **1** adj **(a)** (numeral) uno, una; (before sing n) un, eg **one man** un hombre; **— or two people** algunas personas; **— man out of two** uno de cada dos hombres; **there is only — left** queda uno solamente; **chapter —** el primer capítulo; **the last but —** el penúltimo; **that's — way of doing it** es uno de los métodos de hacerlo; *see* **number.**

(b) (*sole*) solo, único; **the — and only difficulty** la única dificultad; **the — and only Charlie Chaplin** el único Charlot; **his — care** su único cuidado; **the — way to do it** el único método de hacerlo; **no — man could do it** ningún hombre podría hacerlo por sí sólo.

(c) (*same*) mismo; **all in — direction** todos en la misma dirección; **they are — and the same** son el mismo; **it's all — es** lo mismo; **it's all — to me** me es igual; **God is —** Dios es uno; **to be — with something** formar un conjunto con algo; **to become —** casarse.

2 *n*: **— and twopence** un chelín con dos peniques; **price of —** (*Comm*) precio *m* de la unidad; **it's made all in —** está hecho en una sola pieza; **to be at — with someone** estar completamente de acuerdo con uno; **to be — up** tener la ventaja; tener un punto (*or* gol *etc*) de ventaja; **haber ganado un partido más** que los adversarios; **to be — up on someone** llevar ventaja a uno; **that puts us — up** eso nos da punto (*or* gol *etc*) de ventaja; **to go — better than someone** quedar por encima de uno, colocarse en posición ventajosa con relación a uno; **but John went — better** pero Juan hizo más; **he dotted her —** (*fam*) le dio un golpe; **to have a quick —** beberse un trago sin pérdida de tiempo; **to have — for the road** beberse un trago antes de partir.

3 *dem pron*: **this —** éste, ésta; **that —** ése, ésa, aquél, aquélla; **this — is better than that —** éste es mejor que ése; **— or two** algunos; **which — do you want?** ¿cuál quieres?

4 *rel pron* **(a) the — on the floor** el que está en el suelo; **the — who, the — that** el que, la que; **the —s who, the —s that** los que, las que; **they were the —s who told us** ellos eran quienes nos lo dijeron.

(b) the white dress and the grey — el traje blanco y el gris; **who wants these red —s?** ¿quién quiere estos colorados?; **what about this little —?** ¿y el pequeño éste?

(c) that's a good —! ¡ésa sí que es buena!; **to pull a fast — on someone** jugar una mala pasada a uno, embaucar a uno; **that's a difficult —** eso es un problema difícil; **our dear —s** nuestros seres queridos; **the Evil O—** el Malo; **the little —s** los pequeños, los chiquillos, la gente menuda; **he's a clever —** es un taimado; **you're a fine —!** ¡estás tú bueno!, ¡qué tío!; **he's the troublesome —** él es el elemento revoltoso; **he's a great — for chess** es estupendo para el ajedrez, es un entusiasta del ajedrez; **he's — for the ladies** es Perico entre ellas; **he's not much of a — for sweets** no le gustan mucho los dulces; **he is not the — to protest** no es de los que protestan.

5 *indef adj*: **— day** un día, cierto día; **— hot July evening** una tarde de julio de mucho calor.

6 *indef pron* **(a) have you got —?** ¿tienes uno?; **the book is — which I have never read** el libro es de los que no he leído nunca; **— of them** uno de ellos; **any — of us** cualquiera de nosotros; **he's — of the group** es del grupo, forma parte del grupo; **he's — of the family now** ya es de la familia; **I for — am not going** de todas formas yo no voy.

(b) never a — ni uno siquiera; **— and all** todos sin excepción; **the — ..., the other ...** el uno ..., el otro ...; **you can't buy — without the other** no se puede comprar el uno sin el otro; **— after the other** uno tras otro; **for — reason or another** por alguna que otra razón; **— by —** uno a uno, uno tras otro.

(c) (*one another*) **they kissed — another** se besaron, se besaron el uno al otro; **they all kissed — another** se besaron unos a otros; **do you see — another much?** ¿os visitáis mucho?; **it's a year since we saw — another** hace un año que no nos vemos.

(d) he looked like — who had seen a ghost tenía el aspecto del que acababa de ver un fantasma; **a more sensitive — would have fainted** una persona de mayor sensibilidad se hubiera desmayado; **to — who can read between the lines** para el que sabe leer entre líneas; **— Pérez** un tal Pérez.

(e) (*subject etc*) **— never knows** nunca se sabe; **— must wash** hay que lavarse; **— has one's pride** uno tiene cierto amor propio.

(f) (*possessive*) **—'s life is not really safe** la vida de uno no es realmente segura; **—'s opinion does not count** la opinión de uno no vale; **to cut —'s finger** cortarse el dedo.

one- [wʌn] *in compounds*: de un ..., de un solo ..., un-, *eg* **a one-line message** un mensaje de una sola línea; **a one-celled animal** un animal unicelular;

he's a one-woman man es un hombre para el que no existe más que una mujer.

one-act ['wʌn'ækt] *adj* de un solo acto.

one-armed ['wʌn'ɑːmd] *adj* manco.

one-eyed ['wʌn'aid] *adj* tuerto.

one-handed ['wʌn'hændid] **1** *adv*: **to catch the ball —** recoger la pelota con una sola mano. **2** *adj* manco.

one-horse ['wʌn'hɔːs] *adj* insignificante, de poca monta; **— town** pueblucho *m*.

one-legged ['wʌn'legid] *adj* con una sola pierna.

one-man ['wʌn'mæn] *adj* monohombre, individual.

oneness ['wʌnnis] *n* unidad *f*.

one-party ['wʌn'pɑːti] *adj* **state** *etc* de partido único.

one-piece ['wʌn'piːs] *adj* enterizo, de una pieza.

onerous ['ɔnərəs] *adj* oneroso.

oneself [wʌn'self] *pron* (*subject*) uno mismo, una misma; (*acc, dat*) ser; (*after prep*) sí (mismo, misma); **to be by —** estar solo, estar a solas; **to do something by —** hacer algo solo, hacer algo por sí mismo; **to look out for —** mirar por sí; **to come to —** volver en sí; **to say to —** decir para sí, decir entre sí; **to talk to —** hablar consigo mismo.

one-sided ['wʌn'saidid] *adj* unilateral; (*unbalanced*) desequilibrado; *contest, game* desigual; *view etc* parcial.

one-time ['wʌntaim] *adj* antiguo; **— butler to Lord Yaxley** antiguo mayordomo de Lord Yaxley; **— prime minister** ex primer ministro *m*.

one-to-one ['wʌntə'wʌn] *adj, adv* en proporción de uno a uno.

one-track ['wʌntræk] *adj* (*Rail*) de vía única; **mind** que tiene un solo pensamiento.

one-upmanship [wʌn'ʌpmənʃip] *n* (*hum*) arte de establecerse en una posición superior con respecto a otra persona (logrando una ventaja táctica en una conversación etc).

one-way ['wʌnwei] *adj*: **— street** calle *f* de dirección única; **"— traffic"** "dirección única", "dirección obligatoria"; **— ticket** billete *m* sencillo.

ongoing ['ɔn,gəuiŋ] *adj* continuo, que continúa, que sigue funcionando.

onion ['ʌnjən] *n* cebolla *f*; (*sl*) cabeza *f*; **cocktail —** cebollita *f* perla; **to know one's —s** conocer a fondo su oficio.

onlooker ['ɔn,lukə*] *n* espectador *m*, ora *f*; observador *m*, ora *f*; (*esp pej*) mirón *m*, ona *f*; **I was a mere —** yo era un simple espectador.

only ['əunli] **1** *adv* sólo, solamente, únicamente; **no ... más que**; nada más; **we have — 5** tenemos solamente 5, tenemos 5 solamente, tenemos 5 nada más; **what, — 5?** ¿cómo, 5 nada más?; **"Ladies —"** "Señoras"; **— God can tell** sólo Dios lo sabe; **— time will show** el tiempo lo dirá; **I'm — the porter** yo soy simplemente el conserje; **I — touched it** no hice más que tocarlo; **you — have to ask** no hay sino preguntar; **I will — say that ...** diré solamente que ...; **— to think of it!** ¡sólo pensar en ello!; **— too glad!** ¡con mucho gusto!; **if — I could!** ¡ojalá!, ¡ojalá pudiese ...!; **— just** apenas; **not — A but also B** no sólo A sino tambien B; *see* **if** *etc*.

2 *adj* único, solo; **their — son** su hijo único; **your — hope** is to + *infin* tu única posibilidad es + *infin*; **his — response was to laugh** por toda respuesta se rió; **to be the — one to** + *infin* ser el único en + *infin*; **you are not the — one** Vd no es el único en hacer (*etc*) eso.

3 *conj*: **it's very good, — rather dear** es muy bueno, pero algo caro; **I would gladly do it, — I shall be away** lo haría de buena gana sólo que voy a estar fuera.

onomastic [,ɔnəu'mæstik] *adj* onomástico.

onomatopoeia [,ɔnəumætəu'piːə] *n* onomatopeya *f*.

onomatopoeic [,ɔnəumætəu'piːik] *adj* onomatopéyico.

onrush ['ɔnrʌʃ] *n* arremetida *f*, embestida *f*; fuerza *f*, ímpetu *m*.

onset ['ɔnset] *n* (*attack*) ataque *m*, arremetida *f*; (*beginning*) comienzo *m*; **the — of winter** el comienzo del invierno.

onshore ['ɔnʃɔː*] **1** *adv* hacia la tierra. **2** *adj breeze* que sopla hacia la tierra.

onslaught ['ɔnslɔːt] *n* ataque *m* violento, embestida *f* furiosa; **to make a furious — on a critic** atacar violentamente a un crítico.

onto ['ɔntu] *prep* (*fam*) = **on to.**

ontological [,ɔntə'lɔdʒikəl] *adj* ontológico.

ontology [ɔn'tɔlədʒi] *n* ontología *f*.

onus ['əunəs] *n* (*no pl*) carga *f*, responsabilidad *f*; **the — is upon the makers** la responsabilidad es de los fabricantes; **the — is upon him to** + *infin* le incumbe a él + *infin*; **the — of proof is on the prosecution** le incumbe al fiscal probar la acusación.

onward ['ɔnwəd] *adj* *march etc* progresivo, hacia
adelante.
onward(s) ['ɔnwəd(z)] **1** *adv* adelante,'hacia adelante;
from that time — desde entonces; from the 12th
century — desde el siglo XII en adelante, a partir
del siglo XII.
　2 *interj* ¡adelante!
onyx ['ɔniks] *n* ónice *m*.
oodles ['uːdlz] *npl* (*fam*): we have — tenemos
montones, tenemos muchísimo; we have — of
tenemos la mar de, tenemos montones de.
oolite ['əuəlait] *n* oolito *m*.
oolitic [ˌəuə'litik] *adj* oolítico.
oomph [umf] *n* (*sl*) aquél *m*, atracción *f* sexual,
sexy *m* (*sl*).
ooze [uːz] **1** *n* cieno *m*, lama *f*.
　2 *vt* rezumar; (*fig*) rezumar, rebosar de; he simply
—s confidence rebosa confianza.
　3 *vi* (*liquid*) rezumar, rezumarse; (*blood*) manar
suavemente; (*barrel etc*) rezumar; to — away, to
— out rezumarse; agotarse poco a poco; the wound
was oozing blood la herida sangraba lentamente.
opacity [əu'pæsiti] *n* opacidad *f*.
opal ['əupəl] *n* ópalo *m*.
opalescence [ˌəupə'lesns] *n* opalescencia *f*.
opalescent [ˌəupə'lesnt] *adj* opalescente.
opaque [əu'peik] *adj* opaco.
open ['əupən] **1** *adj* (a) (*not closed*) abierto; *book, grave,
parcel, pores, wound etc* abierto; *bottle etc* destapado;
wide — muy abierto, *door etc* abierto de par en par;
the door is — la puerta está abierta; a dress — at
the neck un vestido abierto por el cuello; with his
shirt — to the camisa desabotonada; — to the
public on Mondays se abre al público los lunes; to
break a safe — forzar una caja fuerte; to cut a
sack — abrir un saco cortándolo, abrir un saco de un
tajo; to fling (*or* throw) a door — abrir una puerta
de golpe, abrir una puerta de par en par.
　(b) (*unobstructed*) abierto, sin límites, no
limitado; *road* franco, abierto, no obstruido; —
country campo *m* raso; — sea mar *m* abierto; in
the — air al aire libre; with — views con amplias
vistas, con extensas vistas; the way to Paris lay —
ya no quedaban obstáculos en el camino de París.
　(c) (*permissible*) it is — to you to + *infin* Vd
puede perfectamente + *infin*, Vd tiene derecho a +
infin; what choices are — to me? qué posibilidades
hay?
　(d) (*exposed*) abierto, descubierto; *town* abierto;
boat, car, carriage descubierto; the map was — on
the table el mapa estaba extendido sobre la mesa;
the book was — at page 7 el libro estaba abierto por
la página 7; — to every wind expuesto a todos los
vientos; — to influence from advertisers accesible a
la influencia de los anunciantes; it is — to doubt
whether . . . es discutible si . . ., es dudoso que +
subj; it is — to criticism on several counts se le
puede criticar por diversas razones, es criticable
desde diversos puntos de vista; I am — to persuasion
estoy dispuesto a dejarme persuadir; I am — to
advice escucho de buena gana los consejos; to lay —
abrir; *secret etc* poner al descubierto; to lay oneself
— to criticism exponerse a ser criticado.
　(e) (*public, unrestricted*) abierto; para todos;
championship, competition, race etc abierto; *trial*
público; *letter* abierto; *secret* a voces; the competition
is — to all todos pueden participar en el certamen,
el certamen se abre a todos; membership is not —
to women la sociedad no admite a las mujeres.
　(f) (*declared, frank*) abierto, franco; *admiration
etc* franco; an — enemy of the Church un enemigo
declarado de la Iglesia; to be in — revolt estar en
franca rebeldía, estar en plena rebeldía; he was not
very — with us no se portó del todo honradamente
con nosotros.
　(g) (*undecided*) *mind* receptivo; imparcial, sin
prejuicios; *question* sin resolver, discutible, por
decidir; *race* abierto, muy igual; *cheque* sin cruzar,
abierto; let's leave it — dejémoslo sin decidir, no
hace falta decidirlo ahora.
　2 *n*: to be out in the — (*in the country*) estar en el
campo; (*in bare country*) estar al raso; (*out of doors*)
estar al aire libre; to sleep in the — dormir al raso,
dormir a cielo abierto; to bring a dispute into the —
hacer que una disputa llegue a ser del dominio
público; their true feelings came into the — sus
verdaderos sentimientos salieron a flor de piel;
why don't you come into the — about it? ¿por qué
no lo declara abiertamente?
　3 *vt* (a) (*general sense*) abrir; *arms, eyes, heart,
mouth, case, letter etc* abrir; (*unfold*) desplegar,

extender; *legs etc* abrir, separar; *abscess* cortar;
bottle etc destapar; *parcel* deshacer, desenvolver;
shop abrir, poner; (*tear*) romper; (*leave exposed*)
dejar al descubierto; to — a road to traffic abrir una
carretera al tráfico.
　(b) (*drive*) to — a hole in a wall practicar un
agujero en una pared; to — a road through a forest
construir una carretera a través de un bosque.
　(c) (*begin*) *conversation, debate, negotiations etc*
iniciar, empezar; to — an account in someone's
name abrir una cuenta a nombre de uno; to — the
case (*Law*) exponer los detalles de la acusación,
presentar los hechos en que se basa la acusación;
to — 3 hearts (*Bridge*) abrir de 3 corazones.
　(d) (*declare —, inaugurate*) inaugurar; the
exhibition was —ed by the Queen la exposición fue
inaugurada por la Reina.
　(e) to — out abrir; (*unfold*) desplegar, extender.
　(f) to — up abrir; *secret, new vista* revelar; *new
possibility* crear; *route, country* explorar; — up!
(*police command*) ¡abran a la autoridad!; to — up
a market abrirse un mercado, conquistar un mercado; to — up a country for trade ayudar al
comercio a penetrar en un país; to — up a country
for development fomentar el desarrollo de un país;
when the oilfield was —ed up cuando se empezó a
explotar el campo petrolífero; to — up a blocked
road franquear una carretera obstruida, hacer
transitable una carretera.
　4 *vi* (a) (*general sense*) abrirse; *flower etc* abrirse;
the door —ed se abrió la puerta; a door that —s
on to the garden una puerta por la que se sale al
jardín; this room —s into a larger one este cuarto
comunica con otro más grande; the shops — at 9
las tiendas se abren a las 9.
　(b) (*begin*) empezar, comenzar, iniciarse; (*Bridge*)
abrir la declaración; the season —s in June la
temporada comienza en junio; when we —ed in
Bradford cuando dimos la primera representación
en Bradford; the play —ed to great applause el
estreno de la obra fue muy aplaudido; to — for the
Crown (*Law*) exponer los detalles de la acusación,
presentar los hechos en que se basa la acusación;
the book —s with a long description el libro
comienza con una larga descripción; to — with
2 hearts (*Bridge*) abrir de 2 corazones.
　(c) to — out *map etc* extenderse, desplegarse;
flower etc abrirse; *passage, tunnel* hacerse más ancho;
car etc acelerar; a fine view —ed before us delante
de nosotros se extendía un magnífico panorama;
the team —ed out in the second half en el segundo
tiempo el equipo se mostró más enérgico; the
company is —ing out a bit now ahora la compañía
está ensanchando el campo de sus actividades.
　(d) to — up (*Comm etc*) empezar, comenzar;
(*Mil*) romper el fuego; (*emotionally*) franquearse,
descubrir el pecho.
open-air ['əupn'ɛə*] *adj* al aire libre.
opencast ['əupn'kaːst] *adj* a cielo abierto, de cielo
abierto.
open-ended ['əupən'endid] *adj* *discussion etc* sin
límites fijos, sin resultados previsibles, no limitado
de antemano.
opener ['əupnə*] *n* (*tin-*) abrelatas *m*.
open-eyed ['əupn'aid] *adj* con los ojos abiertos;
(*amazed*) con ojos desorbitados.
open-handed ['əupn'hændid] *adj* liberal, generoso.
open-handedness ['əupn'hændidnis] *n* liberalidad *f*;
generosidad *f*.
opening ['əupniŋ] **1** *adj* *remark etc* primero; *speech,
ceremony, price* de apertura.
　2 *n* (*gap*) abertura *f*; (*in walls etc*) brecha *f*; (*in
wood*) claro *m*; (*in clouds*) abertura *f*, claro *m*;
(*beginning*) comienzo *m*, principio *m*; (*of play*)
estreno *m*; (*of exhibition etc*) inauguración *f*; (*Chess*)
apertura *f*; (*chance*) oportunidad *f*; (*Comm*) salida
f; (*post*) puesto *m*, vacante *f*; an unusual — occurs
for . . . se ofrece un puesto interesante de . . .; it's
a fine — for a young man es una magnífica oportunidad para un joven; to give someone an — for something dar a uno la oportunidad de hacer algo.
openly ['əupənli] *adv* abiertamente, francamente;
públicamente.
open-minded ['əupn'maindid] *adj* libre de prejuicios,
imparcial; I am still — about it no me he decidido
todavía, sigo sin resolverme.
open-mouthed ['əupn'mauðd] *adj* boquiabierto.
open-necked ['əupn'nekt] *adj* sin cuello, sin corbata.
openness ['əupnnis] *n* franqueza *f*.
openwork ['əupnwəːk] *n* (*Sew*) calado *m*, enrejado *m*.

opera ['ɔpərə] n ópera f; (building) teatro m de la ópera; **comic** — ópera f bufa, (in Spain) zarzuela f; **grand** — ópera f seria; **light** — opereta f, (in Spain) zarzuela f.

operable ['ɔpərəbl] adj operable.

opera glasses ['ɔpərəglɑːsiz] npl gemelos mpl de teatro.

opera hat ['ɔpərəhæt] n clac m.

opera house ['ɔpərəhaus] n, pl — **houses** [ˌhauziz] teatro m de la ópera.

opera singer ['ɔpərəˌsiŋə*] n cantante mf de la ópera, operista mf.

operate ['ɔpəreit] 1 vt motor etc impulsar; machine hacer funcionar, (as driver etc) manejar; company etc dirigir; eg canal explotar, administrar; **a machine —d by electricity** una máquina impulsada (or accionada) por electricidad; **can you — this tool?** ¿sabes manejar esta herramienta?; **he has been operating a clever swindle** ha estado manejando una hábil estafa.
   2 vi (a) (person etc) obrar, actuar; (Mech) funcionar; drug etc surtir efecto (on en); (Mil etc) operar; **to — on** producir efecto en, afectar, influir.
   (b) (Med) **to — on someone for something** operar a uno de algo; **to — for appendicitis** operar a uno de apendicitis; **he has still not been —d on** todavía no se le ha operado; **to — on someone's liver** operar de hígado a uno.

operatic [ˌɔpə'rætik] adj de ópera, operístico.

operating ['ɔpəreitiŋ] adj operante; expenses etc de explotación.

operating theatre, (US) — **theater** ['ɔpəreitiŋˌθiətə*] n quirófano m, sala f de operaciones.

operation [ˌɔpə'reiʃən] n (a) funcionamiento m; manejo m; dirección f; explotación f, administración f; (Mil etc) operación f; (of person) actuación f; (manoeuvre) maniobra f; **the company's —s during the year** las actividades de la compañía durante el año; **military —s** operaciones fpl militares; **combined —s** operaciones fpl conjuntas; **—s of doubtful legality** maniobras fpl de dudosa legalidad; **to be in —** (Mech) estar en funcionamiento, estar funcionando; (Law) estar en vigor, ser vigente; **to be in full —** estar en pleno funcionamiento; **to bring a machine into —** poner una máquina en funcionamiento; **to come into —** (Law) entrar en vigor; **to put into —** (Law) hacer entrar en vigor, poner en obra.
   (b) (Med) operación f, intervención f quirúrgica; **a liver —** una operación de hígado; **to perform an — on someone for something** operar a uno de algo; **to undergo an —** ser operado (for something de algo).

operational [ˌɔpə'reiʃənl] adj (relating to operations) de operaciones; (fit: Mil) en condiciones de servicio, operacional; (Mech) en buen estado, capaz de funcionar; **it is not — until next year** no se pondrá en funcionamiento hasta el año que viene; **when the service is fully —** cuando el servicio esté en pleno funcionamiento.

operative ['ɔpərətiv] 1 adj (a) (Law) **to be —** estar en vigor; **to become — from the 9th** entrar en vigor a partir del 9.
   (b) (Med) operatorio.
   2 n operario m, a f.

operator ['ɔpəreitə*] n (of machine) operario m, a f; maquinista mf; (Cine, Med) operador m; (Tel) telefonista mf; (Comm) agente m, corredor m de bolsa; **a big-time —** un criminal a gran escala; **he's a very clever —** (pej) es un criminal de los más hábiles.

operetta [ˌɔpə'retə] n opereta f; (in Spain) zarzuela f.

Ophelia [ɔ'fiːliə] f Ofelia.

ophthalmia [ɔf'θælmiə] n oftalmía f.

ophthalmic [ɔf'θælmik] adj oftálmico.

ophthalmologist [ˌɔfθæl'mɔlədʒist] n oftalmólogo m.

ophthalmology [ˌɔfθæl'mɔlədʒi] n oftalmología f.

opiate ['əupiit] n opiata f, narcótico m.

opine [əu'pain] vi opinar.

opinion [ə'pinjən] n opinión f, parecer m; juicio m; concepto m; **public —** opinión f pública; **in my —** en mi opinión, a mi juicio; **in the — of those who know** en la opinión de los que saben, según los que saben; **well, that's my —** por lo menos eso digo yo; **I am of the — that . . .** soy del parecer de que; **I am entirely of your —** estoy completamente de acuerdo con Vd; **it's a matter of —** sobre eso hay diversos pareceres; **what is your — of him?** ¿qué concepto tienes de él?, ¿qué piensas de él?; **to ask someone's —** pedir el parecer de uno; **his — doesn't count** no vale su opinión; **to echo someone's —** compartir el sentir de uno; **to form an —** formarse una opinión; **to give one's —** dar su parecer; **to have a high — of someone** tener muy buen concepto de uno, tener a uno en mucho; **to have a high — of**

oneself pagarse de sí mismo; **to have a low (or poor) — of someone** tener un concepto poco favorable de uno; **I do not share your —** no comparto esa opinión.

opinionated [ə'pinjəneitid] adj porfiado, terco.

opium ['əupiəm] n opio m.

opium den ['əupiəmˌden] n fumadero m de opio.

opossum [ə'pɔsəm] n zarigüeya f.

opponent [ə'pəunənt] n adversario m, a f, contrario m, a f, contrincante m.

opportune ['ɔpətjuːn] adj oportuno, a propósito; **to be —** venir al caso, (of time etc) ser propicio; **at an — moment** en el momento oportuno; **his arrival was most —** su llegada fue muy oportuna.

opportunely ['ɔpətjuːnli] adv oportunamente, a propósito; **this comes most —** esto viene al pelo.

opportunism ['ɔpə'tjuːnizəm] n oportunismo m.

opportunist [ˌɔpə'tjuːnist] 1 adj oportunista. 2 n oportunista mf.

opportunity [ˌɔpə'tjuːniti] n oportunidad f, ocasión f; **equality of —** igualdad f de oportunidades; **to have the — to + infin** tener la oportunidad de + infin; **to make the most of one's —** aprovechar la ocasión; **to miss one's —** desperdiciar la ocasión; **I take this — to + infin** aprovecho esta ocasión para + infin.

oppose [ə'pəuz] vt oponerse a; resistir, combatir; **but he —d it pero él se opuso a ello; they —d the motion** ellos hablaron en contra de la moción; **we shall — this by all the means in our power** lucharemos contra esto por todos los medios.

opposed [ə'pəuzd] adj opuesto; **to be — to something** oponerse a algo, hablar en contra de algo, resistirse a aceptar algo; **it is — to all our experience** es contrario a toda nuestra experiencia; **savings as — to investments** los ahorros y no las inversiones, los ahorros en comparación con las inversiones.

opposing [ə'pəuzin] adj opuesto, contrario.

opposite ['ɔpəzit] 1 adv en frente; **they sat —** se sentaron uno enfrente del otro; **it is immediately —** está exactamente en frente; **they are directly —** están frente por frente.
   2 prep (also — to) enfrente de, frente a; **a house —** the school una casa enfrente de la escuela; **— the bus stop** frente a la parada del autobús; **— the setting sun** de cara al sol que se ponía; **to sit — someone** sentarse enfrente de uno; **we were — Calais at the time** (Naut) a la sazón estábamos a la altura de Calais.
   3 adj (a) **on the — page** en la página de enfrente; (of position) de enfrente; opuesto; **the house —** la casa de enfrente; **on the — bank** en la ribera opuesta; **in the — direction** en sentido contrario.
   (b) (point of view etc) opuesto, contrario; (hostile) antagónico; **we take an — view** pensamos al contrario, creemos lo contrario; **of the — sex** del otro sexo; see **number**.
   4 n: **the —** is true la verdad es al contrario; **he maintains the —** él sostiene lo contrario; **it's the — of what we wanted** es totalmente distinto de lo que queríamos.

opposition [ˌɔpə'ziʃən] 1 n oposición f (also Pol); resistencia f; (Comm) competencia f; **he made his — known** indicó su disconformidad; **to advance a kilometre without —** avanzar un kilómetro sin encontrar resistencia; **to act in — to the chairman** obrar de modo contrario al presidente; **the party in —** el partido de la oposición; **to be in —** (Pol) estar en la oposición; **to start up a business in —** to another montar un negocio para hacer competencia a otro.
   2 attr member, party de la oposición.

oppress [ə'pres] vt oprimir; (of moral cause etc) agobiar; (heat etc) agobiar, ahogar.

oppression [ə'preʃən] n opresión f; agobio m.

oppressive [ə'presiv] adj (Pol etc) opresivo; tiránico, cruel; burden agobiante, oneroso; tax gravoso; heat etc agobiante, agobiador, sofocante.

oppressively [ə'presivli] adv opresivamente; cruelmente; de modo agobiante, de modo sofocante; **an — hot day** un día de calor agobiante.

oppressor [ə'presə*] n opresor m, ora f.

opprobrious [ə'prəubriəs] adj oprobioso.

opprobrium [ə'prəubriəm] n oprobio m.

opt [ɔpt] vi: **to — for something** elegir algo, escoger algo; **to — to + infin** optar por + infin.

optative ['ɔptətiv] (Gram) 1 adj optativo. 2 n optativo m.

optic(al) ['ɔptik(əl)] adj óptico.

optician [ɔp'tiʃən] n óptico m.

optics ['ɔptiks] n óptica f.

optimism ['ɔptimizəm] n optimismo m.

optimist ['ɔptimist] n optimista mf.

optimistic [,ɔpti'mistik] *adj* optimista; **I am not —
about it** no lo veo tan fácil, no soy optimista
respecto de ello.
optimistically [,ɔpti'mistikli] *adv* con optimismo;
speak etc en tono optimista.
optimum ['ɔptiməm] **1** *adj* óptimo, mejor; más
favorable; **the — number is 8** el mejor número es 8;
in — conditions en las condiciones más favorables.
2 *n* lo óptimo, lo mejor; cantidad *f* óptima, grado
m óptimo (*etc*).
option ['ɔpʃən] *n* opción *f*; **with an — on 10 more
aircraft** con opción para la compra de 10 aviones
más; **6 months without the — (of a fine)** una condena
de 6 meses sin la posibilidad de pagar una multa;
at the — of the purchaser según lo desee el comprador; **to have the — of doing something** tener la
posibilidad de hacer algo; **I have no —** no tengo otro
recurso, no tengo más remedio; **to take out an — on
another 100** suscribir una opción para la compra de
otros 100.
optional ['ɔpʃənl] *adj* discrecional, facultativo; *part,
fitting etc* opcional, de opción, optativo; **dress —**
traje de etiqueta o de calle, traje a voluntad; **the
heater is —** el calentador es de opción, el calentador
es optativo; **that is completely —** eso es según lo
desee Vd.
optometrist [ɔp'tɔmətrist] *n* optometrista *m*.
opulence ['ɔpjuləns] *n* opulencia *f*.
opulent ['ɔpjulənt] *adj* opulento.
opus ['əupəs] *n*, *pl* **opera** ['ɔpərə] (*Mus*) opus *m*,
obra *f*; (*hum*) obra *f*.
or [ɔː*] *conj* (a) o; (*before* o—, ho—) u, *eg* 7 **— 8** siete u
ocho, **this one — another** éste u otro; **either A — B**
o A o B; **— else** o bien, si no; de otro modo; **an
hour — so** una hora más o menos; **20 — so** unos
veinte, veinte más o menos; **let me go — I'll
scream!** ¡suélteme, que voy a gritar!
  (b) (*after negative*) ni; **without relatives — friends**
sin parientes ni amigos; **without fear — favour**
imparcialmente; **he didn't write — telephone** no
escribió ni telefoneó.
oracle ['ɔrəkl] *n* oráculo *m*; **to work the —** dirigirlo
todo entre bastidores.
oracular [ɔ'rækjulə*] *adj* profético, fatídico; sentencioso; misterioso.
oral ['ɔːrəl] **1** *adj* oral; (*Anat*) bucal; *message* verbal,
hablado. **2** *n* examen *m* oral.
orally ['ɔːrəli] *adv* oralmente; *tell etc* por boca, en
palabras; (*Anat, Med*) por vía bucal.
orange ['ɔrindʒ] **1** *n* (*fruit*) naranja *f*; (*tree*) naranjo
m; (*colour*) color *m* naranja; **bitter —, Seville —**
naranja *f* amarga.
  2 *adj* naranjado, anaranjado, color naranja.
orangeade ['ɔrindʒ'eid] *n* naranjada *f*.
orange blossom ['ɔrindʒ,blɔsəm] *n* azahar *m*.
orange-coloured ['ɔrindʒ,kʌləd] *adj* = **orange 2.**
orange grove ['ɔrindʒgrəuv] *n* naranjal *m*.
Orangeman ['ɔrindʒmən] *n*, *pl* **—men** [mən]
orangista *m* (*miembro del partido protestante de
Irlanda del Norte*).
orang-outang, orang-utan ['ɔːræŋ'uːtæn] *n* orangután *m*.
orate [ɔː'reit] *vi* (*hum*) perorar.
oration [ɔː'reiʃən] *n* oración *f*, discurso *m*; **funeral —**
oración *f* fúnebre.
orator ['ɔrətə*] *n* orador *m*, ora *f*.
oratorical [,ɔrə'tɔrikəl] *adj* oratorio; retórico.
oratorio [,ɔrə'tɔːriəu] *n* (*Mus*) oratorio *m*.
oratory¹ ['ɔrətəri] *n* oratoria *f*; **parliamentary —**
oratoria *f* parlamentaria.
oratory² ['ɔrətəri] *n* (*Eccl*) oratorio *m*.
orb [ɔːb] *n* orbe *m*; esfera *f*, globo *m*.
orbit ['ɔːbit] **1** *n* órbita *f* (*also fig*); **to be in —** estar en
órbita; **to go into — round the moon** entrar en
órbita alrededor de la luna.
  2 *vt* orbitar, girar alrededor de.
  3 *vi* orbitar, girar.
orbital ['ɔːbitl] *adj* orbital.
orchard ['ɔːtʃəd] *n* huerto *m*; (*apple —*) pomar *m*.
orchestra ['ɔːkistrə] *n* orquesta *f*; (*seating part of
theatre*) platea *f*, patio *m* de butacas.
orchestral [ɔː'kestrəl] *adj* orquestal.
orchestrate ['ɔːkistreit] *vt* orquestar, instrumentar.
orchestration [,ɔːkis'treiʃən] *n* orquestación *f*,
instrumentación *f*.
orchid ['ɔːkid] *n*, **orchis** ['ɔːkis] *n* orquídea *f*.
ordain [ɔː'dein] **1** *vt* (a) (*order*) ordenar, decretar; **to
— that . . .** ordenar que + *subj*; **to — someone's
exile** decretar el destierro de uno.
  (b) (*Eccl*) ordenar; **to — someone priest** ordenar

a uno de sacerdote; **to be —ed** ordenarse de sacerdote.
  2 *vi* mandar, disponer; **as God —s** según Dios
manda, como Dios manda.
ordeal [ɔː'diːl] *n* (a) (*Hist*) ordalías *fpl*; **— by fire**
ordalías *fpl* del fuego.
  (b) (*fig*) prueba *f* rigurosa, experiencia *f* penosa;
sufrimiento *m*; **it was a terrible —** fue una experiencia terrible; **after such an —** después de tanto
sufrir; **exams are an — for me** para mí los exámenes
son una cosa horrible, sufro lo indecible con los
exámenes.
order ['ɔːdə*] **1** *n* (a) (*of society etc, Bio*) orden *m*;
clase *f*, categoría *f*; **the lower —s** la clase baja, la
plebe; **talents of the first —** talentos *mpl* de primer
orden; **of the — of 500** del orden de 500.
  (b) (*Eccl*) **holy —s** órdenes *fpl* sagradas; **minor
—s** órdenes *fpl* menores; **to be in holy —s** estar en
órdenes sagradas, ser sacerdote; **to take (holy) —s**
ordenarse de sacerdote.
  (c) (*society, decoration*) (*Eccl*) orden *f*; (*secular*)
orden *f*, sociedad *f*; (*worn on dress*) condecoración *f*,
insignia *f*; **Benedictine O—** Orden *f* de San Benito;
monastic — orden *f* monástica; **— of knighthood**
orden *f* de caballería; **O— of the British Empire**
Orden *f* del Imperio Británico; **O— of the Garter**
Orden *f* de la Jarretera; **to be wearing all one's —s**
vestir todas sus condecoraciones.
  (d) (*Archit*) orden *m*; **Doric —** orden *m* dórico.
  (e) (*succession, disposition*) orden *m*; clasificación *f*; método *m*; **in —** en orden, por orden, por su
orden; **in alphabetical —** por orden alfabético; **in
chronological —** por orden cronológico; **in — of
seniority** por orden de antigüedad; **to be out of —**
estar mal arreglados; estar fuera de serie; **to get out
of —** desarreglarse; **to put in —** poner en orden,
arreglar, ordenar; clasificar.
  (f) (*Mil*) **in close —** en filas apretadas; **in
battle —** en orden de batalla; **in marching —** en
orden de marchar.
  (g) (*good —*) estado *m*; **in —** en regla; **in good —**
en buen estado, en buenas condiciones; **his papers
are in —** tiene los papeles en regla; **everything is in
—** todo está en regla; **is this passport in —?** ¿este
pasaporte está en regla?; **what sort of an — is it in?**
¿en qué estado está?; **to put a matter in —** arreglar
un asunto; **a machine in working —** una máquina
en funcionamiento; **is it in — for me to go to Rome?**
¿tengo permiso para ir a Roma?; **"out of —" "no
funciona"; to be out of —** estar desarreglado;
(*Mech*) no funcionar, estar descompuesto; **my
liver is out of —** no estoy bien del hígado; **to get
out of —** (*Mech*) descomponerse, estropearse.
  (h) (*Parl*) **—!** ¡orden! **to be out of —** estar fuera
de orden, estar fuera de la cuestión; **it is not in —
to discuss the Congo** el Congo está fuera de la
cuestión; **to call someone to —** llamar a uno al
orden; **to rise to a point of —** levantarse para
discutir una cuestión de procedimiento; **to rule a
matter out of —** decidir que un asunto no se puede
discutir.
  (i) (*peace*) orden; **law and —** orden *m* público;
the forces of — las fuerzas del orden; **to keep —**
mantener el orden; **she can't keep —** es incapaz de
imponer la disciplina, no puede hacerse obedecer;
to keep children in — mantener a los niños en orden.
  (j) in — to + *infin* para + *infin*; **in — that . . .**
para que + *subj*.
  (k) (*command*) orden *f*; decreto *m*, mandato; (*of
court etc*) sentencia *f*, fallo *m*; **— of the day** orden *f*
del día; (*fig*) moda *f*, lo que es de rigor; **strikes are
the — of the day** las huelgas están a la orden del día;
O— in Council Orden *f* Real; **— of the court**
sentencia *f* del tribunal; **judge's —** mandamiento *m*
del juez; **sailing —s** últimas instrucciones *fpl* (dadas
al capitán de un buque); **sealed —s** órdenes *fpl*
secretas; **standing —** reglamento *m*, estatuto *m*;
by — of por orden de; **by — of the king** por Real
Orden; **on the —s of** por orden de; **till further —s**
hasta nueva orden; **that's an —!** ¡es una orden!;
—s are —s las órdenes no se discuten; **to be under
the —s of** estar bajo el mando de; **to be under
starter's —s** estar listo para la salida; **to get one's
marching —s** (*fig*) ser despedido; **to give an —** dar
una orden; **to give someone —s to do something**
ordenar a uno hacer algo; **to give —s that something
should be done** mandar que se haga algo; **to obey —s**
cumplir las órdenes; **I don't take —s from anyone**
a mí no me da órdenes nadie.
  (l) (*Comm*) pedido *m*, encargo *m*; **repeat —**
pedido *m* de repetición; **rush —** pedido *m* urgente;

unfilled —s pedidos *mpl* pendientes; **standing** — pedido *m* permanente, pedido *m* regular; **made to the** — **of** a la orden de; **we can't do things to** — no podemos proveer en seguida todo cuanto se nos pide; **to give an** — **for something** pedir algo, hacer un pedido de algo; **to place an** — **for something with someone** pedir algo a uno; **we have it on** — **for you** está pedido para Vd; **we will put it on** — **for you** se lo pediremos para Vd al fabricante; **that's rather a tall** — eso es much pedir.

(m) *(Fin)* libranza *f*; giro *m*; **banker's** — orden *f* bancaria; *see* **money, postal.**

2 *vt* (a) *(put in* —) disponer, arreglar, poner en orden; clasificar; **to** — **one's life properly** organizar bien su vida, vivir con arreglo a cierto método.

(b) **to** — **someone to do something** mandar a uno hacer algo, ordenar a uno hacer algo; **to** — **someone a new drug** recetar un nuevo fármaco para uno; **to** — **someone a complete rest** mandar a uno reposo absoluto; **to be** —**ed to pay costs** ser condenado a pagar las costas.

(c) *(Comm)* pedir, encargar; *meal, taxi* encargar; **to** — **a suit of clothes** mandar hacer un traje; **have you** —**ed yet?** ¿has encargado la comida ya?

(d) *(with adv or prep)* **to** — **someone about** mandar a uno de acá para allá, ser muy mandón con uno; **to** — **a regiment abroad** mandar un regimiento al extranjero; **to** — **someone back** mandar a uno volver; **to** — **someone in** mandar a uno entrar; **to** — **someone off** despedir a uno, echar a uno, decir a uno que se vaya; **the referee** —**ed him off (the field)** el árbitro le expulsó; **to** — **someone out** mandar a uno salir; **to** — **the troops out** llamar a las tropas, enviar a las tropas.

order book ['ɔːdəbuk] *n* libro *m* de pedidos.
order form ['ɔːdəfɔːm] *n* hoja *f* de pedido.
orderly ['ɔːdəli] **1** *adj (methodical)* ordenado, metódico; *(tidy)* aseado, en orden, en buen estado; *(well-behaved)* formal; *crowd etc* pacífico, obediente; disciplinado.

2 *n (Mil)* ordenanza *m*, asistente *m*; *(Med)* enfermero *m*.
orderly room ['ɔːdəli,rum] *n (Mil)* oficina *f*.
order paper ['ɔːdə,peipə*] *n (Parl etc)* lista *f* de asuntos a tratar.
ordinal ['ɔːdinl] **1** *adj* ordinal. **2** *n* ordinal *m*.
ordinance ['ɔːdinəns] *n* ordenanza *f*, decreto *m*.
ordinarily ['ɔːdnrili] *adv* ordinariamente, de ordinario; — **we buy 6 at a time** generalmente compramos 6 a la vez; **more than** — **polite** más cortés de lo común.
ordinary ['ɔːdnri] **1** *adj* (a) corriente, común, normal; **the** — **Frenchman** el francés corriente; **an** — **citizen** un simple ciudadano; **for the** — **reader** para el lector medio; **it's not what you'd call an** — **present** no es lo que se diría un regalo de todos los días.

(b) *seaman* simple; *share* ordinario.

(c) *(pej)* vulgar, ordinario; mediocre; **just an** — **man** un hombre vulgar; **they're very** — **people** son gente muy ordinaria; **neither good nor bad, just** — ni bueno ni malo, solamente mediocre.

2 *n*: **a man above the** — un hombre destacado, un hombre que no es del montón; **something out of the** — algo fuera de lo común, algo extraordinario.
ordination [,ɔːdi'neiʃən] *n (Eccl)* ordenación *f*.
ordnance ['ɔːdnəns] *n (guns)* artillería *f*, cañones *mpl*; *(supplies)* pertrechos *mpl* de guerra; **O**— **Corps** Cuerpo *m* de Armamento y Material; **O**— **Survey** servicio oficial de topografía; **O**— **Survey map** = mapa *m* del Estado Mayor.
ordure ['ɔːdjuə*] *n* inmundicia *f (also fig)*.
ore [ɔː*] *n* mineral *m*, mena *f*; **copper** — mineral *m* de cobre.
organ ['ɔːgən] *n (all senses)* órgano *m*; **sexual** —**s** órganos *mpl* sexuales; **vocal** —**s** órganos *mpl* de la voz.
organdie ['ɔːgəndi] *n* organdí *m*.
organ-grinder ['ɔːgən,graində*] *n* organillero *m*.
organic [ɔː'gænik] *adj* orgánico.
organically [ɔː'gænikəli] *adv* orgánicamente; **there's nothing** — **wrong with you** Vd está en buen estado en cuanto a lo físico.
organism ['ɔːgənizm] *n* organismo *m*.
organist ['ɔːgənist] *n* organista *mf*.
organization [,ɔːgənai'zeiʃən] *n (act)* organización *f*; *(body)* organización *f*, organismo *m*.
organize ['ɔːgənaiz] **1** *vt* organizar; *(sl)* agenciarse; **to get** —**ed** organizarse, arreglárselas; **you must give**

us **time to get** —**d** hay que darnos tiempo para que nos las arreglemos.

2 *vi* organizarse *(for* para).
organizer ['ɔːgənaizə*] *n* organizador *m*, ora *f*.
organ loft ['ɔːgənlɔft] *n* tribuna *f* del órgano.
organ pipe ['ɔːgənpaip] *n* cañón *m* de órgano.
organ stop ['ɔːgənstɔp] *n* registro *m* de órgano.
orgasm ['ɔːgæzəm] *n* orgasmo *m*.
orgiastic [,ɔːdʒi'æstik] *adj* orgiástico.
orgy ['ɔːdʒi] *n* orgía *f*; **an** — **of destruction** una orgía de destrucción; **the flowers were an** — **of colour** las flores eran una explosión de colores.
oriel ['ɔːriəl] *n* mirador *m*.
Orient ['ɔːriənt] Oriente *m*.
oriental [,ɔːri'entəl] **1** *adj* oriental. **2** *n* oriental *mf*.
orientate ['ɔːrienteit] **1** *vt* orientar. **2** *vr*: **to** — **oneself** orientarse.
orientation [,ɔːrien'teiʃən] *n* orientación *f*.
orifice ['ɔrifis] *n* orificio *m*.
origin ['ɔridʒin] *n* origen *m*; *(point of departure)* procedencia *f*; **country of** — país *m* de procedencia; **to be of humble** —, **to have humble** —**s** ser de nacimiento humilde.
original [ə'ridʒinl] **1** *adj* original; *idea, meaning, sin etc* original; *(first)* primero; *(earlier)* primitivo; **the** — **sense was** ... el sentido primitivo era ...; **one of the** — **members** uno de los primeros miembros, uno de los socios fundadores; **its** — **inventor** su inventor primitivo.

2 *n (MS, painting etc)* original *m*; *(archetype)* prototipo *m*; *(person)* original *m*, excéntrico *m*; **the** — **is lost** el original está perdido; **he reads Cervantes in the** — lee a Cervantes en su idioma original, lee a Cervantes en su propia lengua.
originality [ə,ridʒi'næliti] *n* originalidad *f*.
originally [ə'ridʒənəli] *adv* (a) *(at first)* al principio, en sus orígenes; originariamente; **as they were** — **written** tal como fueron escritas originariamente; — **they were in Athens** al principio estuvieron an Atenas, antiguamente estuvieron en Atenas.

(b) *(in an original manner)* **it is quite** — **written** está escrito con bastante originalidad; **he deals with the subject** — trata el asunto con inventiva.
originate [ə'ridʒineit] **1** *vt* producir, originar, dar lugar a; *(of person)* idear, inventar, crear.

2 *vi* originarse, nacer, surgir; **to** — **from, to** — **in** traer su origen de; **to** — **with someone** ser obra de uno, ser invento de uno; **where did the fire** —? ¿dónde empezó el incendio?; **with whom did the idea** —? ¿quién tuvo la idea primero?
originator [ə'ridʒineitə*] *n* inventor *m*, ora *f*, autor *m*, ora *f*.
oriole ['ɔːriəul] *n*: **golden** — oropéndola *f*.
Orkney Islands ['ɔːkni,ailəndz] *pl*, **Orkneys** ['ɔːkniz] *pl* Órcadas *fpl*.
ormolu ['ɔːməluː] *n* oro *m* molido.
ornament ['ɔːnəmənt] *n* adorno *m*, ornato *m*, ornamento *m*; *(trinket)* chuchería *f*; *(vase etc)* objeto *m* de adorno; **he is the chief** — **of his country** es el máximo valor de su patria; —**s** *(Eccl)* ornamentos *mpl*.
ornament ['ɔːnəment] *vt* adornar, ornamentar *(with* de).
ornamental [,ɔːnə'mentl] *adj* ornamental *(also Bot)*; decorativo, de adorno.
ornamentation [,ɔːnəmen'teiʃən] *n* ornamentación *f*.
ornate [ɔː'neit] *adj* muy ornado, vistoso; *style* florido.
ornately [ɔː'neitli] *adv* vistosamente; en estilo florido.
ornateness [ɔː'neitnis] *n* vistosidad *f*; estilo *m* florido *m*; lo florido.
ornithological [,ɔːniθə'lɔdʒikəl] *adj* ornitológico.
ornithologist [,ɔːni'θɔlədʒist] *n* ornitólogo *m*.
ornithology [,ɔːni'θɔlədʒi] *n* ornitología *f*.
orphan ['ɔːfən] **1** *adj* huérfano.

2 *n* huérfano *m*, a *f*.

3 *vt* dejar huérfano a; **the children were** —**ed by the accident** el accidente dejó huérfanos a los niños; **she was** —**ed at the age of 9** quedó huérfana a los 9 años.
orphanage ['ɔːfənidʒ] *n* orfanato *m*.
Orpheus ['ɔːfiuːs] *n* Orfeo *m*.
orthodontics [,ɔːθəu'dɔntiks] *n* ortodoncia *f*.
orthodox ['ɔːθədɔks] *adj* ortodoxo.
orthodoxy ['ɔːθədɔksi] *n* ortodoxia *f*.
orthographic(al) [,ɔːθə'græfik(əl)] *adj* ortográfico.
orthography [ɔː'θɔgrəfi] *n* ortografía *f*.
orthopaedic, |(US) —**pedic** [,ɔːθəu'piːdik] *adj* ortopédico.
orthopaedics, (US) —**pedics** [,ɔːθəu'piːdiks] *n* ortopedia *f*.

orthopaedist, (US) **—pedist** [ˌɔːθəʊ'piːdist] n ortopedista mf.

oscillate ['ɔsileit] **1** vt hacer oscilar.
2 vi **(a)** oscilar (between entre; from A to Z de A a Z); fluctuar, variar.
(b) (person) vacilar; **he —s between boredom and keenness** pasa del aburrimiento al entusiasmo.

oscillating ['ɔsileitiŋ] adj oscilante.

oscillation [ˌɔsi'leiʃən] n oscilación f; fluctuación f, variación f; vacilación f.

oscillator ['ɔsileitə*] n oscilador m.

oscillatory [ˌɔsi'leitəri] adj oscilatorio.

osculate ['ɔskjuleit] (hum) **1** vt oscular. **2** vi oscularse.

osculation [ˌɔskju'leiʃən] n (hum) ósculo m.

osier ['əuʒə*] n mimbre f.

osier bed ['əuʒəbed] n mimbrera f.

osmosis [ɔz'məusis] n ósmosis f.

osmotic [ɔz'mɔtik] adj osmótico.

osprey ['ɔsprei] n águila f pescadora.

osseous ['ɔsiəs] adj óseo.

ossification [ˌɔsifi'keiʃən] n osificación f.

ossify ['ɔsifai] **1** vt osificar. **2** vi osificarse.

ossuary ['ɔsjuəri] n osario m.

Ostend [ɔs'tend] Ostende.

ostensible [ɔs'tensəbl] adj pretendido, aparente.

ostensibly [ɔs'tensəbli] adv aparentemente, en apariencia.

ostentation [ˌɔsten'teiʃən] n ostentación f; aparato m, boato m; fausto m.

ostentatious [ˌɔsten'teiʃəs] adj ostentoso; aparatoso; person ostentativo.

ostentatiously [ˌɔsten'teiʃəsli] adv ostentosamente, con ostentación; aparatosamente; con boato; **he remained — silent** permaneció ostentosamente silencioso.

osteoarthritis ['ɔstiəuɑː'θraitis] n osteoartritis f.

osteopath ['ɔstiəpæθ] n osteópata m.

osteopathy [ˌɔsti'ɔpəθi] n osteopatía f.

ostler ['ɔslə*] n mozo m de cuadra.

ostracism ['ɔstrəsizəm] n ostracismo m.

ostracize ['ɔstrəsaiz] vt condenar al ostracismo, excluir de la sociedad (or del trato, del grupo etc); **he was —d** vivió en el ostracismo.

ostrich ['ɔstritʃ] n avestruz m.

Othello [ə'θeləu] m Otelo.

other ['ʌðə*] **1** adj otro; **the — one** el otro; **the — five** los otros cinco; **the — day** el otro día; **come some — day** venga otro día; **all the — books have been sold** todos los otros libros se han vendido, todos los demás libros se han vendido; **— people have done it** otros lo han hecho; **— people's property** la propiedad ajena; **— people's ideas** las ideas ajenas; **I do not wish him — than he is** no quiero que sea distinto de lo que es.
2 pron: **the —** el otro; **the —s** los otros, los demás; **one after the —** uno tras otro; **some do, —s don't** los hay que sí, otros no; **are there any —s?** ¿hay otros?; **and these 5 —s** y estos otros 5; **she and no — ella** y no otra; **some fool or —** algún tonto; **somebody or —** alguien; **one or — of us** uno de nosotros; **no —** ningún otro; **our happiness depends on that of —s** nuestra felicidad depende de la de otros; **we must respect —s' rights** hay que respetar los derechos ajenos; see **each**.
3 adv: **— than** de otra manera que; otra cosa que; **he could not act — than as he did** no podía hacer otra cosa que la que hizo; **I did not read it — than cursorily** no le di sino una lectura superficial.

otherwise ['ʌðəwaiz] adv **(a)** (in another way) de otra manera; **it cannot be —** no puede ser de otra manera.
(b) (in other respects) por lo demás, por otra parte; **— it's a very good car** por lo demás es un coche muy bueno, aparte de esto es un coche muy bueno.
(c) (if not) si no; **— we shall have to walk** pues si no, tendremos que ir a pie.

other-worldly ['ʌðə'wəːldli] adj person espiritual, poco realista.

otiose ['əuʃiəus] adj ocioso, inútil.

otter ['ɔtə*] n nutria f.

Otto ['ɔtəu] m Otón.

Ottoman ['ɔtəmən] **1** adj otomano. **2** n otomano m, a f.

ottoman ['ɔtəmən] n otomana f.

ought[1] ['ɔːt] n = aught.

ought[2] [ɔːt] v aux **(a)** (obligation) deber; **I — to do it** debo hacerlo, debiera hacerlo; **I — to have done it** debiera haberlo hecho; **one — not to do it** conviene no hacerlo, sería mejor no hacerlo; **to behave as one — comportarse** como se debe; **one — to be able to find it** ha de ser posible encontrarlo; **I thought I — to tell you** me creí en el deber de decírselo.

(b) (vague desirability) **you — to go and see it** vale la pena ir a verlo; **you — to have seen it!** ¡era de ver!; **you — to have seen him!** ¡había que verle!
(c) (probability) **that car — to win** ese coche tiene más probabilidades de ganar; **that — to be enough** eso ha de bastar; **he — to have arrived by now** debe de haber llegado ya.

ounce [auns] n **(a)** onza f (= 28,35 gr).
(b) (fig) pizca f; **there's not an — of truth in it** eso no tiene ni pizca de verdad; **if you had an — of common sense** si tuvieras una pizca de sentido común.

our [auə*] poss adj nuestro(s), nuestra(s).

ours [auəz] poss pron (subject) (el) nuestro, (la) nuestra etc.

ourselves [ˌauə'selvz] pron (subject) nosotros mismos, nosotras mismas; (acc, dat) nos; (after prep) nosotros (mismos), nosotras (mismas); see **oneself.**

oust [aust] vt desalojar; expulsar, echar; (from house etc) desahuciar; **to — someone from a post** lograr que uno renuncie a un puesto; **we —ed them from the position** les hicimos abandonar la posición; **"fabulous" has —ed "smashing"** "fabuloso" ha sustituido a "pistonudo".

out [aut] **1** adv **(a)** (general sense) fuera, afuera; hacia fuera; **"—"** (notice) "salida"; **— you go!** ¡fuera!; **with him!** ¡fuera con él!, ¡que le echen fuera!; **— with it!** ¡desembucha!; **the voyage —** el viaje de ida; **murder will —** el asesinato se descubrirá; **— here** aquí fuera; aquí, aquí en este sitio tan remoto; **— there** allí fuera; allí, allí en ese sitio tan remoto; **it carried us —** to sea nos llevó mar afuera; **to have a day —** pasar un día fuera de casa, pasar un día en el campo, pasar un día al aire libre; **it's her evening —** es su tarde libre; **to have a night —** salir de juerga por la noche.
(b) see other verbs, eg **to come —,** **to go —** salir; **to run —** salir corriendo.
(c) **to be —** (person): no estar (en casa), estar fuera; haber salido; **Mr Green is —** el Sr Green no está; **he's — a good deal** pasa bastante tiempo fuera; **to be — and about again** estar levantado y salir (después de una enfermedad etc); **now that the Liberals are —** ahora que los liberales están fuera del poder; **the railwaymen are —** los ferroviarios están en huelga; **I was — for some minutes** estuve varios minutos sin conocimiento; **he was — cold** estuvo completamente sin conocimiento; **I'm 2 shillings —** he perdido 2 chelines en el cálculo; **he was — in his reckoning** había hecho mal el cálculo, había calculado mal; **I was not far —** lo acerté casi; **and he was not far — either** y su conjetura resultó ser casi exacta.
(d) **to be —** (things): **when the sun is —** cuando brilla el sol; **the dahlias are —** las dalias están en flor; **the book is —** se ha publicado el libro, ha salido el libro; **the secret is —** el secreto ha salido a luz; **the ball is —** el balón está fuera del terreno; **the tide is —** la marea está baja; **long dresses are —** los vestidos largos ya no están de moda; **your watch is 5 minutes —** su reloj lleva 5 minutos de atraso (or de adelanto); **before the week is —** antes del fin de la semana; **to be — fire, light, gas** estar apagado; **"lights — at 10 pm"** "se apagan las luces a las 10"; **my pipe is —** se me ha apagado la pipa.
(e) **to be — to** be buscar; ambicionar, aspirar a; **he's — for all he can get** quiere apoderarse de todo cuanto se le ofrezca; **we're — for a quick decision** queremos que la cosa se decida cuanto antes; **they're — for trouble** quieren armar un escándalo; **we are — after duck** salimos a cazar ánades; **she's — to find a husband** se propone pescar un marido, tiene intención de buscarse un marido, se está esforzando por encontrar un marido.
(f) **the coat is — at the elbows** la chaqueta está rota por los codos.
(g) (intensive) **it's the biggest swindle —** es la mayor estafa que hay; **he's the best footballer —** es el mejor futbolista que se ha visto, es el mejor futbolista que se ha conocido jamás.
(h) **— loud** en alta voz; **right —, straight —** a quemarropa, sin rodeos.
2 prep: **— of (a)** (outside, beyond) fuera de; **to be — of range** estar fuera de alcance; **to be — of danger** estar fuera de peligro; **to be — of sight** estar invisible, no estar a la vista, no poderse ver; **to be — of season** estar fuera de temporada; **we're well — of it** de buena nos hemos librado; **to feel — of it** sentirse aislado, no tomar parte en las actividades sociales (etc).
(b) (incompatible with) **to be — of proportion**

with no guardar proporción con; — **of measure** fuera de medida; **times** — **of number** innumerables veces; *see* **mind, sort** *etc.*

(c) (*verbs of motion etc*) **to go** — **of the house** salir de la casa; **to go** — **of the door** salir por la puerta; **to throw something** — **of a window** tirar algo por una ventana; **we looked** — **of the window** nos asomamos a la ventana, miramos por la ventana; **to turn someone** — **of the house** echar a uno de la casa.

(d) (*origin*) de; **a chapter** — **of a novel** un capítulo de una novela; **like a princess** — **of a fairy tale** como una princesa de un cuento de hadas; **to drink** — **of a glass** beber de un vaso; **to eat** — **of the same dish** comer del mismo plato; **to take something** — **of a drawer** sacar algo de un cajón; **to read** — **of a novel** leer en una novela; **to copy something** — **of a book** copiar algo de un libro; **1** — **of 10 de** cada 10, 1; **1** — **of every 3 smokers** 1 de cada 3 fumadores.

(e) (*material*) de; **a box made** — **of wood** una caja hecha de madera.

(f) (*because of*) por; — **of respect for you** por el respeto que le tengo; — **of spite** por despecho; — **of necessity** por necesidad; **to do something** — **of sympathy** hacer algo movido por la compasión.

(g) (**to be** — **of:** *lacking*) **we're** — **of petrol** no hay gasolina, se acabó la gasolina, nos hemos quedado sin gasolina; **it's** — **of stock** no hay, no tenemos; **to be** — **of a suit** (*Bridge*) estar fallo; **to be** — **of hearts** tener fallo a corazones.

3 *n: see* **in 3.**

out-and-out ['autən'aut] *adj believer etc* firme, acérrimo, cien por cien; *de tomo y lomo; scoundrel* consumado, redomado.

outback ['autbæk] *n* (*Australia*) despoblado *m*, campo *m*.

outbid [aut'bid] (*irr: see* **bid**) *vt* licitar más que, hacer mejor oferta que; sobrepujar.

outboard ['autbɔːd] *adj* fuera de borda; — **motor** motor *m* fuera de borda, motor *m* fuera-bordo.

outbreak ['autbreik] *n* (*of spots*) erupción *f*; (*of disease*) epidemia *f*, brote *m*; (*of revolt*) estallido *m*; (*of war*) comienzo *m*, declaración *f*, (*of hostilities*) rompimiento *m*; (*of feeling, violence etc*) arranque *m*; (*of crimes etc*) ola *f*; **at the** — **of war** al declararse la guerra.

outbuilding ['aut,bildiŋ] *n* dependencia *f*, edificio *m* accesorio; (*shed*) cobertizo *m*.

outburst ['autbɜːst] *n* explosión *f*; arranque *m*, acceso *m*; **an** — **of anger** una explosión de cólera; **there was an** — **of applause** estallaron ruidosos los aplausos; **forgive my** — **last week** le ruego perdonar el que perdiera los estribos la semana pasada.

outcast ['autkɑːst] *n* paria *mf*, proscrito *m*, a *f*; **he is a social** — vive desterrado de la sociedad.

outclass [aut'klɑːs] *vt* ser netamente superior a, aventajar con mucho.

outcome ['autkʌm] *n* resultado *m*.

outcrop ['autkrɔp] **1** *n* afloramiento *m*. **2** *vi* aflorar.

outcry ['autkrai] *n* grito *m*, protesta *f* ruidosa; **to raise an** — **about something** poner el grito en el cielo por motivo de algo; **there was a great** — hubo fuertes protestas, se armó la gorda.

outdated ['aut'deitid] *adj* anticuado, fuera de moda.

outdistance [aut'distəns] *vt* dejar atrás.

outdo [aut'duː] (*irr: see* **do**) *vt* exceder, sobrepujar; **to** — **someone in something** exceder a uno en algo; **he was not be outdone** no se quedó en menos; **I, not to be outdone . . .** pues yo, para no quedar en menos . . .

outdoor ['autdɔː*] *adj* al aire libre.

outdoors ['aut'dɔːz] *adv* al aire libre; fuera de casa; **go and play** — id a jugar fuera.

outer ['autə*] *adj* exterior; externo.

outermost ['autəməust] *adj place* extremo, (el) más remoto, *cover etc* (el) más exterior, primero.

outfall ['autfɔːl] *n* desembocadura *f*.

outfield ['autfiːld] *n* (*Sport*) parte *f* exterior del campo, (*Baseball*) jardín *m*.

outfit ['autfit] *n* (**a**) (*gear*) equipo *m*; (*tools*) herramientas *fpl*, juego *m* de herramientas; (*of clothes*) traje *m*; **a complete camper's** — un equipo completo de campista; **why are you wearing that** —? ¿por qué te has trajeado así?

(**b**) (*fam: Mil*) cuerpo *m*, equipo *m*; grupo *m*; organización *f*; **when I joined this** — cuando vine a formar parte de esta unidad; **it's a rotten** — es una sección horrible.

outfitter ['autfitə*] *n* camisero *m*.

outflank [aut'flæŋk] *vt* (*Mil*) flanquear; (*fig*) superar en táctica, burlar.

outflow ['autfləu] *n* efusión *f*; desagüe *m*; pérdida *f*; (*Mech*) tubo *m* de salida.

outgeneral [aut'dʒenərəl] *vt* superar en estrategia.

outgo ['autgəu] *n* (*US*) gastos *mpl*.

outgoing ['aut,gəuiŋ] *adj* (**a**) *president etc* saliente; *ministry* que acaba de dimitir; *mail* que sale; *tide* que baja.

(**b**) (*of character*) extrovertido, vivo, bullicioso.

outgoings ['aut,gəuiŋz] *npl* gastos *mpl*.

outgrow [aut'grəu] (*irr: see* **grow**) *vt* (*person*) crecer más que; *habit etc* pasar de la edad de, ser ya viejo para; *defect, illness* curarse de . . . con la edad; *clothes* hacerse demasiado grande para; **she has —n her gloves** se le han quedado chicos los guantes; **we've —n all that** todo eso ha quedado ya a la espalda.

outhouse ['authaus] *n*, *pl* **—houses** [hauziz] = **outbuilding.**

outing ['autiŋ] *n* (*walk*) paseo *m*; (*trip*) excursión *f*, jira *f* campestre; **I took a brief** — di un pequeño paseo, di una vuelta; **everyone went on an** — **to Toledo** todos fueron de excursión a Toledo.

outlandish [aut'lændiʃ] *adj* estrafalario, extravagante.

outlast [aut'lɑːst] *vt* durar más tiempo que; (*person*) sobrevivir a.

outlaw ['autlɔː] **1** *n* proscrito *m*, forajido *m*. **2** *vt* proscribir; *practice etc* declarar ilegal, declarar fuera de la ley.

outlawry ['autlɔːri] *n* bandolerismo *m*.

outlay ['autlei] *n* desembolso *m*, inversión *f*.

outlet ['autlet] *n* salida *f* (*also fig, Comm*); (*of drain etc*) desagüe *m*, desaguadero *m*; (*of stream etc*) desembocadura *f*; (*Mech*) salida *f*, tubo *m* de salida; **to find an** — **for a product** encontrar una salida (*or* un mercado) para un producto; **it provides an** — **for his energies** es un modo de emplear útilmente su energía.

outline ['autlain] **1** *n* (*profile*) contorno *m*, perfil *m*; (*of plan*) trazado *m*; (*sketch*) esbozo *m*, bosquejo *m*; (*general idea, also* —**s**) idea *f* general, nociones *fpl* generales; "**O—s of History**" (*as title*) "Introducción a la Historia"; **in broad** — a grandes líneas, a grandes rasgos; **in broad** — **the plan is as follows . . .** el trazado general del plan es el siguiente . . .; **I'll give you a rapid** — **of the scheme** le explicaré el proyecto en términos generales.

2 *vt* (*draw profile of*) perfilar; (*sketch*) trazar, bosquejar; *policy etc* explicar en términos generales, dar una idea general de; *prefigurar*; **to be —d against** destacarse contra, dibujarse contra; **the building was —d in the distance** a lo lejos se dibujaba el edificio.

outlive [aut'liv] *vt* sobrevivir a; (*thing*) durar más tiempo que; (*live down*) hacer olvidar.

outlook ['autluk] *n* (**a**) (*view, future promise*) perspectiva *f*, perspectivas *fpl*; **the** — **for the wheat crop is good** son favorables las perspectivas de la cosecha de trigo; **it's a grim** — es una perspectiva nada halagüeña, el futuro no promete nada bueno.

(**b**) (*opinion*) punto *m* de vista; actitud *f*; **what is his** — **on the matter?** ¿cuál es su punto de vista en este asunto?; **his** — **is always pessimistic** su actitud siempre es pesimista; **a person with a broad** — una persona de amplias miras.

outlying ['aut,laiiŋ] *adj* (*distant*) remoto, lejano, aislado; *suburb etc* exterior.

outmanoeuvre, (US) outmaneuver [,autmə'nuːvə*] *vt* superar en la táctica.

outmatch [aut'mætʃ] *vt* superar, aventajar.

outmoded [aut'məudid] *adj* anticuado, pasado de moda.

outnumber [aut'nʌmbə*] *vt* exceder en número, ser más numeroso que; **we were —ed 10 to 1** ellos eran diez veces más que nosotros.

out-of-date ['autəv'deit] *adj* anticuado; *see also* **date**[1] 1.

out-of-doors ['autəv'dɔːz] *adv: see* **outdoors.**

out-of-the-way ['autəvðə'wei] *adj* (*remote*) remoto, apartado, aislado, inaccesible; (*unusual*) poco común; (*recherché*) rebuscado.

outpace [aut'peis] *vt* dejar atrás.

outpatient ['aut,peiʃənt] *n* paciente *m* externo, paciente *f* externa (del hospital).

outplay [aut'plei] *vt* (*Sport*) superar en la táctica, jugar mejor que; **we were —ed in every department** ellos resultaron ser mejores que nosotros en todos los aspectos del juego.

outpost ['autpəust] *n* avanzada *f* (*also fig*), puesto *m* avanzado.

outpouring ['aut,pɔːriŋ] *n* efusión *f*; **the —s of a sick mind** la efusión de una mente enferma; **an** — **of emotion** una efusión de emoción.

output ['autput] *n* producción *f*, volumen *m* de producción; (*of machine*) rendimiento *m*; (*Elec*) potencia *f* de salida; **to raise** — aumentar la producción.

outrage ['autreidʒ] **1** *n* atrocidad *f*; atropello *m*; (*committed during riot etc*) desmán *m*, desafuero *m*; (*public scandal*) escándalo *m*; (*suffered by someone*) indignidad *f*; **bomb** — incidente *m* en que estalla una bomba; **it's an** — ! ¡es un escándalo!, ¡qué barbaridad!, ¡no hay derecho!; **to commit an** — **against** (*or* **on**) **someone** cometer un desafuero contra uno.

2 *vt* ultrajar, violentar, atropellar; (*rape*) violar; **it** — **s justice** atropella la justicia.

outrageous [aut'reidʒəs] *adj* atroz, terrible; monstruoso; escandaloso; indignante; **your** — **conduct** su conducta escandalosa; **it is absolutely** — **that . . .** es indignante que + *subj*; **it's** — ! ¡es un escándalo!, ¡qué barbaridad!, ¡no hay derecho!

outrageously [aut'reidʒəsli] *adv behave etc* de modo escandaloso.

outrank [aut'ræŋk] *vt* ser de categoría superior a.

outré ['u:trei] *adj* extravagante, estrafalario.

outrider ['aut,raidə*] *n* motociclista *m* de escolta.

outrigger ['aut,rigə*] *n* (*beam, spar*) batanga *f*, balancín *m*; (*rowlock*) portarremos *m* exterior; (*boat*) bote *m* con batanga, bote *m* con portarremos exterior.

outright ['autrait] *adj* (*complete*) completo, entero, total; *sale etc* en su totalidad, definitivo; (*forthright*) franco; *supporter etc* incondicional, declarado; *refusal* rotundo.

outright [aut'rait] *adv* (*once and for all*) de una vez, de un golpe; (*forthrightly*) abiertamente, francamente; **to buy something** — comprar algo en su totalidad, comprar algo definitivamente; **to reject an offer** — rechazar una oferta de pleno; **to laugh** — **at** something **thing** reírse abiertamente de algo.

outrun [aut'rʌn] (*irr: see* **run**) *vt* correr más que; (*fig*) exceder, rebasar, pasar los límites de.

outset ['autset] *n* principio *m*, comienzo *m*; **at the** — al principio; **from the** — desde el principio.

outshine [aut'ʃain] (*irr: see* **shine**) *vt* brillar más que; (*fig*) eclipsar, superar en brillantez.

outside ['aut'said] **1** *adv* fuera; **to be** — estar fuera; **to leave a car** — dejar un coche fuera, (*at night etc*) dejar un coche en la calle, dejar un coche al descubierto; **to put the cat** — hacer salir al gato; **seen from** — visto desde fuera; **to ride** — (*on bus*) viajar en el piso superior; — **of** = 2.

2 *prep* fuera de; al exterior de; (*beyond*) más allá de, al otro lado de; **he's waiting** — **the door** espera a la puerta; **one could hear everything that was said** — **the door** se oía todo cuanto se estaba diciendo al otro lado de la puerta; **it's** — **the normal range** eso cae fuera del alcance normal; **it's** — **our scheme** no forma parte de nuestro proyecto; **that's** — **our terms of reference** eso no está comprendido dentro de nuestros puntos de consulta.

3 *adj* (*outer*) exterior, externo; (*outermost*) extremo; *chance etc* remoto, poco prometedor; (*relating to other people*) ajeno; (*brought from* —) traído desde fuera; *TV broadcast* exterior; *forward* (*Sport*) extremo; (*seat on bus*) del piso superior; **thanks to** — **influence** gracias a la influencia de personas ajenas al asunto, gracias a influencias exteriores; **to get an** — **opinion** buscar las opiniones de personas no comprometidas, sondear la opinión independiente.

4 *n* (*outer part*) exterior *m*; (*surface*) superficie *f*; (*outward aspect*) aspecto *m* exterior, apariencia *f*; (*of bus*) piso *m* superior; **at the** — a lo sumo, cuando más; **from the** — desde fuera, desde el exterior; **to open a window from the** — abrir una ventana desde fuera; **on the** — por fuera; **to pass someone on the** — adelantar a uno por el exterior; **the window opens to the** — la ventana se abre hacia fuera.

outside-forward ['autsaid'fɔ:wəd] *n* delantero *m* extremo.

outside-left ['autsaid'left] *n* extremo *m* izquierdo.

outsider ['aut'saidə*] *n* (*stranger*) forastero *m*, a *f*, desconocido *m*, a *f*, (*pej*) intruso *m*, a *f*; (*in racing*) caballo *m* que no figura entre los favoritos, (*in election*) candidato *m* poco conocido; (*cad*) canalla *m*, persona *f* indeseable; (*independent*) persona *f* independiente, persona *f* ajena al asunto, persona *f* no comprometida.

outside-right ['autsaid'rait] *n* extremo *m* derecho.

outsize ['autsaiz] *adj* de tamaño extraordinario; (*hum*) enorme.

outskirts ['autskə:ts] *npl* afueras *fpl*; alrededores *mpl*; barrios *mpl* exteriores.

outsmart [aut'smɑ:t] *vt* ser más listo que, vencer en perspicacia; (*deceive*) engañar, burlar.

outspoken [aut'spəukən] *adj* franco, abierto; **to be** — no tener pelos en la lengua.

outspokenly [aut'spəukənli] *adv* francamente.

outspokenness [aut'spəukənnis] *n* franqueza *f*.

outspread ['aut'spred] *adj* extendido; desplegado.

outstanding [aut'stændiŋ] *adj* (*exceptional*) destacado; excepcional, relevante, sobresaliente; *problem* pendiente, no resuelto; *account* por pagar.

outstandingly [aut'stændiŋli] *adv* excepcionalmente, extraordinariamente.

outstay [aut'stei] *vt person* quedarse más tiempo que; **to** — **one's welcome** permanecer tanto tiempo que uno resulta pesado; **I don't want to outstay my welcome** no quiero ser un pesado.

outstretched ['autstretʃt] *adj* extendido; alargado.

outstrip [aut'strip] *vt* dejar atrás, aventajar, superar.

outvote [aut'vəut] *vt person* vencer en las elecciones; *proposal* rechazar por votación; **but I was** —**d** pero en la votación perdí.

outward ['autwəd] *adj* exterior, externo; *journey* de ida.

outward(s) ['autwəd(z)] *adv* hacia fuera; exteriormente; **to be** — **bound from Vigo** haber salido de Vigo; **to be** — **bound for Gijón** ir con rumbo a Gijón.

outwardly ['autwədli] *adv* por fuera, aparentemente.

outwear [aut'wɛə*] (*irr: see* **wear**) *vt* (*last longer than*) durar más tiempo que; (*wear out*) gastar.

outweigh [aut'wei] *vt* pesar más que, tener mayor peso que; (*fig*) pesar más que; **this** —**s all other considerations** éste vale más que todos los demás factores.

outwit [aut'wit] *vt* ser más listo que, burlar.

outworn [aut'wɔ:n] *adj* gastado, cansado.

oval ['əuvəl] **1** *adj* oval, ovalado. **2** *n* óvalo *m*.

ovary ['əuvəri] *n* ovario *m*.

ovate ['əuveit] *adj* aovado.

ovation [əu'veiʃən] *n* ovación *f*; **to give someone an** — ovacionar a uno; **to receive an** — ser ovacionado; **he got a standing** — **from the delegates** fue ovacionado por los delegados puestos de pie.

oven ['ʌvn] *n* horno *m*; **Huelva was like an** — Huelva era un horno; **it's like an** — **in there** allí dentro es el mismo infierno.

ovenproof ['ʌvnpru:f] *adj* refractario.

ovenware ['ʌvnwɛə*] *n* utensilios *mpl* para horno, utensilios *mpl* termorresistentes.

over ['əuvə*] **1** *adv* (a) (*of place*) encima; por encima; **this goes under and that goes** — éste pasa por debajo y ése por encima.

(b) (*in another place*) — **here** acá; — **there** allá; — **in France** allá en Francia; **they're** — **for the day** han venido a pasar el día; **when we were** — **in the States** cuando estábamos allá en Estados Unidos; — **against the wall** contra la pared; — **against the church** al lado de la iglesia, junto a la iglesia.

(c) (**all** — *etc*) **the world** — en todo el mundo; **to search the whole country** — registrar el país de arriba abajo; **embroidered all** — todo bordado; **to tremble all** — estar todo tembloroso; **I ache all** — me duele en todas partes; **I looked for you all** — te busqué por todas partes; **it happens all** — ocurre en todas partes, ocurre por doquier; **he was all** — **flour** estaba completamente cubierto de harina, estaba cubierto de harina de pies a cabeza; **that's him all** — eso es muy de él.

(d) (*with verbs*) **to bend** — inclinarse, encorvarse; **to bend something** — doblar algo; **to boil** — irse, rebosar; **to flow** — desbordarse; *see* **fall**, **lean**, **look** etc.

(e) (*of number, quantity*) **persons of 21 and** — las personas de 21 años para arriba; **4 into 29 goes 7 and 1** — 29 dividido entre 4 son 7 y queda 1; **we have 4 pounds and a bit** — tenemos 4 libras y algo más; **there are 3** — sobran 3, quedan 3; **I have a card** — me sobra una carta, tengo una carta de más.

(f) **to be** — (*finished*) estar terminado; **when this is all** — cuando esto haya terminado, cuando se acabe esto; **as soon as the war is** — en cuanto termine la guerra; **the storm is** — ya pasó la tormenta; **it's all** —! ¡se acabó!; **it's all** — **with him** se acabó con él, (*relationship*) he roto con él.

2 *prep* (a) (*place: above*) encima de, por encima de; (*on, in contact with*) sobre; — **our heads** por encima de nuestras cabezas; **to spread a sheet** — **something** extender una sábana sobre algo; **to jump** — something **thing** saltar por encima de algo; **we looked** — **the wall** miramos por encima de la tapia; **with a sign**

— **the door** con un rótulo sobre la puerta; **it sticks out** — **the street** sobresale por encima de la calle; **to bend** — **a table** inclinarse sobre una mesa; **to fall** — **a cliff** caer por un precipicio; **to trip** — something tropezar con algo; **to sit** — **the fire** estar sentado muy junto a la lumbre; **the water came** — **her knees** el agua le cubrió las rodillas; **a change came** — **him** se operó en él un cambio.

(b) (*place: across*) **the pub** — **the road** la taberna de enfrente; **it's just** — **the road from us** está justamente enfrente de nuestra casa; **it's** — **the river** está en la otra orilla del río; **the bridge** — **the river** el puente que cruza el río.

(c) (*place: with all*) **all** — **Spain** por toda España; **known all** — **the world** conocido en el mundo entero; **he had mud all** — **himself** estaba totalmente cubierto de lodo; **they were all** — **him** le recibieron con el mayor entusiasmo, le dieron grandes testimonios de su afecto; **Zaragoza were all** — **Bilbao** (*Sport*) el Bilbao nada pudo contra el Zaragoza.

(d) (*place: fig*) **to rule** — **a people** reinar sobre un pueblo; **he's** — **me** tiene una categoría superior a la mía; **they gave me the preference** — **him** me prefirieron a él; **to have an advantage** — **someone** llevar ventaja a uno.

(e) (*numbers*) **the numbers** — **20** los números superiores a 20, los números más allá de 20; — **200** más de 200; **well** — **200** 200 y muchos más; **she's** — **21 now** tiene más de 21 años ya; **he must be** — **60** tendrá más de 60 años; — **and above last year's figure** en exceso de la cifra del año pasado; **an increase of 5 %** — **last year's total** un aumento de 5 por cien en relación con el año anterior.

(f) (*time*) — **the last few years** durante los últimos años; **payments spread** — **some years** pagos que abarcan varios años; **we stayed** — **the weekend** nos quedamos a pasar el fin de semana.

(g) (*motive*) **they fell out** — **money** riñeron por cuestión de dinero; **to pause** — **a difficulty** detenerse a considerar un punto difícil.

(h) (*means*) **I heard it** — **the radio** lo supe por la radio.

over- ['əuvə*] *in compounds:* sobre . . ., super . . .; demasiado. . . .

overabundance ['əuvərə'bʌndəns] *n* sobreabundancia *f*.

overabundant ['əuvərə'bʌndənt] *adj* sobreabundante.

overact ['əuvər'ækt] *vi* exagerar el papel.

overactive ['əuvər'æktiv] *adj* demasiado activo.

overall [,əuvər'ɔːl] *adv* en conjunto, en su totalidad.

overall ['əuvərɔːl] *adj* study, view etc de conjunto; *length etc* total; (*total*) global.

overalls ['əuvərɔːlz] *npl* guardapolvo *m*, mono *m*, bata *f*.

overambitious ['əuvəræm'biʃəs] *adj* demasiado ambicioso, superambicioso.

overanxious ['əuvər'æŋkʃəs] *adj* (a) (*worried*) demasiado preocupado, preocupado sin motivo.

(b) (*eager*) demasiado deseoso (*for* de; *to do* de hacer); **I'm not** — **to go** tengo pocas ganas de ir.

overawe [,əuvər'ɔː] *vt* intimidar; imponer respeto a; **to be** —**d by** ser fuertemente impresionado por.

overbalance [,əuvə'bæləns] **1** *vt* hacer perder el equilibrio. **2** *vi* perder el equilibrio.

overbearing [,əuvə'beəriŋ] *adj* imperioso, altivo; despótico.

overbid ['əuvəbid] *n* (*at auction*) mejor oferta *f*, mejor postura *f*; (*Bridge*) sobremarca *f*.

overbid [,əuvə'bid] (*irr: see* **bid**) **1** *vt* (*at auction*) licitar más que, hacer mejor oferta que; (*Bridge*) marcar más que.

2 *vi* (*Bridge*) hacer una sobremarca, (*foolishly*) declarar demasiado.

overblown ['əuvə'bləun] *adj* marchito, pasado.

overboard ['əuvəbɔːd] *adv:* **man** — ! ¡hombre al agua! **to fall** — caer al agua; **to throw something** — echar algo por la borda (*also fig*).

overbold ['əuvə'bəuld] *adj* demasiado atrevido.

overburden [,əuvə'bəːdn] *vt* sobrecargar; oprimir, agobiar (*with* de); **not exactly** —**ed with worries** no precisamente agobiado de preocupaciones.

overcall [,əuvə'kɔːl] *vti* = **overbid**.

overcast ['əuvəkɑːst] *adj* sky encapotado, cubierto.

overcautious ['əuvə'kɔːʃəs] *adj* demasiado cauteloso, prudente con exceso.

overcharge ['əuvə'tʃɑːdʒ] *vt* sobrecargar; (*Elec*) poner una carga excesiva a; *person* hacer pagar demasiado, cobrar un precio excesivo a.

overcoat ['əuvəkəut] *n* abrigo *m*, sobretodo *m*, gabán *m*.

overcome [,əuvə'kʌm] (*irr: see* **come**) **1** *vt* enemy, temptation etc vencer; difficulty salvar, superar;

sleep overcame him le rindió el sueño; **he was** — **by remorse** le remordió la conciencia; **he was** — **by grief** estaba postrado de dolor.

2 *vi* vencer, triunfar; **we shall** — venceremos.

overcompensation ['əuvə,kɔmpen'seiʃən] *n* compensación *f* excesiva.

overconfidence ['əuvə'kɔnfidəns] *n* confianza *f* excesiva, exceso *m* de confianza.

overconfident ['əuvə'kɔnfidənt] *adj* demasiado confiado (*of* en).

overconsumption ['əuvəkən'sʌmpʃən] *n* superconsumo *m*.

overcook ['əuvə'kuk] *vt* recocer, requemar.

overcrowd [,əuvə'kraud] *vt* atestar, llenar, congestionar.

overcrowded [,əuvə'kraudid] *adj* room etc atestado de gente, muy lleno; *suburb etc* congestionado; *country* superpoblado.

overcrowding [,əuvə'kraudiŋ] *n* superpoblación *f*, congestionamiento *m*; (*in tenement etc*) número *m* excesivo de inquilinos.

overdeveloped ['əuvədi'veləpt] *adj* demasiado desarrollado.

overdo [,əuvə'duː] (*irr: see* **do**) *vt food* recocer, requemar; (*exaggerate*) exagerar; (*use to excess*) usar demasiado; llevar a extremos, excederse en; **to** — **it, to** — **things** (*work too hard*) trabajar demasiado, fatigarse; (*exaggerate*) exagerar; (*in description, sentiment etc*) cargar la mano; **she rather** — **es the scent** se pone demasiado perfume; **see that you don't** — **it** cuidado con no fatigarte; **Espronceda** —**es the passion** Espronceda exagera la pasión.

overdone [,əuvə'dʌn] *adj* exagerado; *food* muy hecho, pasado.

overdose ['əuvədəus] *n* dosis *f* excesiva.

overdraft ['əuvədrɑːft] *n* (*Comm*) sobregiro *m*, giro *m* en descubierto; (*on account*) saldo *m* deudor; (*loan*) préstamo *m*; **to have an** — **at the bank** tener un saldo deudor con el banco, deber dinero al banco.

overdraw ['əuvə'drɔː] (*irr: see* **draw**) girar en descubierto; **your account is** —**n (by £50)** su cuenta tiene un saldo deudor (de 50 libras).

overdress ['əuvə'dres] *vi* vestirse con demasiada elegancia.

overdrive ['əuvədraiv] *n* (*Aut*) sobremarcha *f*.

overdue ['əuvə'djuː] *adj* (*Comm*) vencido y no pagado; *train etc* atrasado; **the bus is 30 minutes** — el autobús tiene 30 minutos de atraso; **that change was long** — ese cambio debió hacerse mucho tiempo antes.

overeager ['əuvər'iːgə*] *adj* demasiado deseoso (*for* de; *to do* de hacer); demasiado entusiasta, entusiasta con exceso; **she was not** — **to help** tenía pocas ganas de ayudar.

overeat ['əuvər'iːt] (*irr: see* **eat**) *vi* comer con exceso; (*at 1 meal*) atracarse, darse un atracón.

overelaborate ['əuvəri'læbərit] *adj* demasiado complicado; demasiado detallado, rebuscado; *courtesy etc* estudiado.

overemployment ['əuvərim'plɔimənt] *n* superempleo *m*.

overenthusiastic ['əuvərin,θjuːzi'æstik] *adj* demasiado entusiasta.

overestimate ['əuvər'estimit] *n* sobreestimación *f*, estimación *f* excesiva; (*Fin*) presupuesto *m* excesivo.

overestimate ['əuvər'estimeit] *vt* sobreestimar, apreciar en una cantidad (*etc*) excesiva; estimar en valor excesivo; *person* tener un concepto exagerado de; **to** — **one's strength** creerse uno más fuerte de lo que es.

overexcite ['əuvərik'sait] *vt* sobreexcitar.

overexcited ['əuvərik'saitid] *adj* sobreexcitado; **to get** — sobreexcitarse.

overexcitement ['əuvərik'saitmənt] *n* sobreexcitación *f*.

overexert ['əuvərig'zəːt] *vr:* **to** — **oneself** hacer un esfuerzo excesivo.

overexertion ['əuvərig'zəːʃən] *n* (*effort*) esfuerzo *m* excesivo; (*weariness*) fatiga *f*.

overexpose ['əuvəriks'pəuz] *vt* (*Phot*) sobreexponer.

overexposure ['əuvəriks'pəuʒə*] *n* (*Phot*) sobreexposición *f*.

overfamiliar ['əuvəfə'miliə*] *adj* demasiado familiar.

overfeed ['əuvə'fiːd] (*irr: see* **feed**) **1** *vt* sobrealimentar; dar demasiado de comer a. **2** *vi* sobrealimentarse; comer demasiado, atracarse.

overflow ['əuvəfləu] *n* (*liquid*) exceso *m* de líquido, líquido *m* derramado; (*pipe etc*) rebosadero *m*, cañería *f* de desagüe.

overflow [,əuvə'fləu] *vi* (*vessel*) rebosar, desbordarse; (*river*) desbordarse, salir de madre; — **with** (*fig*) rebosar de; **to fill a cup to** —**ing** llenar una taza hasta que se derrame el líquido.

overfly ['əuvə'flai] (*irr: see* **fly**) *vt* sobrevolar.

overfull ['əuvə'ful] *adj* demasiado lleno (*of* de), más que lleno.

overgenerous ['əuvə'dʒenərəs] *adj* demasiado generoso; **an — helping** una porción excesivamente grande; **they were — in their praise** le elogiaron con exceso.

overgrown ['əuvə'grəun] *adj* boy *etc* demasiado grande para su edad; **— with** cubierto de, revestido de; **the path is quite —** now ya no se ve senda alguna, la senda ha desaparecido bajo la vegetación.

overhand ['əuvəhænd] **1** *adj* stroke hecho (*or* dado *etc*) por lo alto. **2** *adv* por lo alto.

overhang ['əuvəhæŋ] *n* proyección *f*; (*of roof*) alero *m*; (*in rock climbing*) extraplomo *m*, panza *f* de burro.

overhang ['əuvə'hæŋ] (*irr: see* **hang**) **1** *vt* sobresalir por encima de; estar pendiente sobre, estar colgado sobre; (*fig*) amenazar.
2 *vi* sobresalir; estar pendiente, estar colgado.

overhanging ['əuvə'hæŋiŋ] *adj* sobresaliente, voladizo.

overhaul ['əuvəhɔ:l] *n* repaso *m* general, revisión *f*.

overhaul [,əuvə'hɔ:l] *vt* (a) (*check*) machine revisar, repasar, dar un repaso general a; plans *etc* volver a pensar, rehacer, examinar.
(b) (*overtake*) alcanzar, adelantarse a.

overhead [,əuvə'hed] *adv* por lo alto, en alto, por encima de la cabeza; **a bird flew —** pasó un pájaro.

overhead ['əuvəhed] *adj* de arriba, encima de la cabeza; cable *etc* aéreo; camshaft en cabeza; crane de techo; railway elevado, suspendido; expenses general.

overheads ['əuvəhedz] *npl* gastos *mpl* generales.

overhear [,əuvə'hiə*] (*irr: see* **hear**) *vt* oír, oír por casualidad; acertar a oír; **she was —d complaining** se le oyó por casualidad quejarse.

overheat [,əuvə'hi:t] **1** *vt* recalentar; **to get —ed** recalentarse. **2** *vi* recalentarse.

overindulge ['əuvərin'dʌldʒ] **1** *vt* child mimar con exceso; passion *etc* dar rienda suelta a; taste *etc* satisfacer con exceso.
2 *vi* darse demasiada buena vida; **to — in some-thing** comer (*etc*) un exceso de algo.

overindulgence ['əuvərin'dʌldʒəns] *n* (a) (*excess*) exceso *m* vicioso; **by his — in . . .** por su abandono vicioso a . . . (b) (*kindness*) exceso *m* de tolerancia (*towards* con).

overindulgent ['əuvərin'dʌldʒənt] *adj* demasiado indulgente (*towards* con).

overjoyed [,əuvə'dʒɔid] *adj*: **they were —** estuvieron llenos de alegría, se alegraron muchísimo; **he was — at the news** no cabía en sí de contento con la noticia; **she will be — to see you** se alegrará muchísimo de veros.

overkill ['əuvəkil] *n* contragolpe *m* más eficaz que el golpe del enemigo.

overland [,əuvə'lænd] *adv* por tierra, por vía terrestre.

overland ['əuvəlænd] *adj* terrestre.

overlap ['əuvəlæp] *n* traslapo *m*, solapo *m*; (*fig*) coincidencia *f* parcial.

overlap [,əuvə'læp] **1** *vt* traslapar. **2** *vi* traslaparse; (*fig*) coincidir en parte.

overlay ['əuvəlei] *n* capa *f* sobrepuesta; incrustación *f*.

overlay [,əuvə'lei] (*irr: see* **lay**) *vt* cubrir (*with* con); **to get overlaid with** formarse una capa de, cubrirse con, incrustarse de.

overleaf ['əuvə'li:f] *adv* a la vuelta; **"see —"** "véase al dorso".

overload ['əuvələud] *n* sobrecarga *f*.

overload [,əuvə'ləud] *vt* sobrecargar (*with* de); **to be —ed with** estar sobrecargado de, estar agobiado de.

overlook [,əuvə'luk] *vt* (a) (*of view*: person) dominar con la vista; (*of building*) dar a, mirar hacia, tener vista a; **the house —s the park** la casa tiene vistas al parque; **the garden is not —ed** el jardín no tiene ningún edificio al lado que lo domine.
(b) (*watch over*) vigilar; (*inspect*) inspeccionar, examinar.
(c) (*leave out*) pasar por alto, olvidar; no hacer caso de; (*tolerate*) disimular; (*forgive*) perdonar; (*wink at*) hacer la vista gorda a; **we'll — it this time** se perdona esta vez; **the plant is easily —ed** es fácil no echar de ver la planta.

overlord ['əuvəlɔ:d] *n* (*feudal etc*) señor *m*; (*leader*) jefe *m* supremo.

overlordship ['əuvəlɔ:dʃip] *n* señoría *f*; jefatura *f* suprema.

overmuch ['əuvə'mʌtʃ] *adv* demasiado.

overnice ['əuvə'nais] *adj* melindroso, remilgado.

overnight ['əuvə'nait] **1** *adv*: **it happened —** ocurrió durante la noche, ocurrió de la noche a la mañana; **to stay —** pasar la noche, pernoctar (*at* en); **we drove —** viajamos por la noche; **will it keep —?** ¿se conservará fresco hasta mañana? **we can't solve this one —** no podemos resolver este problema de la noche a la mañana. **2** *adj*: **— journey** viaje *m* de noche; **— stay** estancia *f* de una noche.

overparticular ['əuvəpə'tikjulə*] *adj* melindroso, remilgado; **he's not — about money** le importa poco el dinero, (*pej*) es poco escrupuloso en asuntos de dinero; **I'm not —** me da igual.

overpass ['əuvəpɑ:s] *n* paso *m* superior.

overpay ['əuvə'pei] (*irr: see* **pay**) *vt* pagar un sueldo excesivo a.

overpayment ['əuvə'peimənt] *n* pago *m* excesivo, sueldo *m* excesivo.

overpopulated ['əuvə'pɔpjuleitid] *adj* superpoblado.

overpower [,əuvə'pauə*] *vt* (*defeat*) sobreponerse a, vencer, subyugar; (*subdue physically*) dominar, asir y tener quieto; (*fig*) dominar; dejar estupefacto; senses embargar; **we were —ed by a sense of tragedy** se apoderó de nosotros un sentimiento de tragedia.

overpowering [,əuvə'pauəriŋ] *adj* abrumador, arrollador.

overpraise ['əuvə'preiz] *vt* elogiar demasiado.

overprint ['əuvə'print] **1** *n* sobrecarga *f*. **2** *vt* sobrecargar (*with* de).

overproduction ['əuvəprə'dʌkʃən] *n* superproducción *f*, exceso *m* de producción.

overrate ['əuvə'reit] *vt* exagerar el valor de; person tener un concepto demasiado alto de.

overreach [,əuvə'ri:tʃ] *vr*: **to — oneself** aventurarse más allá de sus fuerzas, ir demasiado lejos.

override [,əuvə'raid] (*irr: see* **ride**) *vt* (*ignore*) no hacer caso de; (*invalidate*) anular, invalidar, restar valor a; (*set aside*) poner a un lado; **this fact —s all others** este hecho domina todos los demás; **our protests were overridden** no hicieron caso de nuestras protestas; **this —s what we decided before** esto anula lo que decidimos antes.

overriding [,əuvə'raidiŋ] *adj* predominante, decisivo; importance primero, primordial; need *etc* imperioso.

overripe ['əuvə'raip] *adj* demasiado maduro, pasado.

overrule [,əuvə'ru:l] *vt* (*override*) anular; request *etc* denegar, rechazar; **but we were —d** pero rechazaron nuestra propuesta.

overrun [,əuvə'rʌn] (*irr: see* **run**) **1** *vt* cubrir enteramente, invadir; time limit *etc* rebasar, exceder; **the field is — with weeds** las malas hierbas han invadido el campo; **the town is — with tourists** la ciudad ha sido invadida por los turistas.
2 *vi* rebasar el límite; **his speech overran by 15 minutes** su discurso se excedió en 15 minutos.

overscrupulous ['əuvə'skru:pjuləs] *adj* = **overparticular.**

overseas ['əuvə'si:z] **1** *adv* en ultramar, allende el mar; **to be —** estar en el extranjero; **to go —** ir al extranjero; **to travel —** viajar por el extranjero; **visitors from —** visitantes *mpl* de ultramar; **to send a regiment to fight —** enviar un regimiento a servir en el extranjero.
2 *adj* de ultramar; **— service** (Mil *etc*) servicio *m* en el extranjero; **— trade** comercio *m* exterior.

oversee ['əuvə'si:] (*irr: see* **see**) *vt* superentender, vigilar.

overseer ['əuvəsiə*] *n* superintendente *mf*; inspector *m*; (*foreman*) capataz *m*.

oversell ['əuvə'sel] (*irr: see* **sell**) *vt* (Comm) product hacer una propaganda excesiva a favor de.

oversensitive ['əuvə'sensitiv] *adj* demasiado sensible.

overshadow [,əuvə'ʃædəu] *vt* sombrear, ensombrear; (*fig*) eclipsar; **it was —ed by greater events** fue eclipsado por sucesos de mayor trascendencia.

overshoe ['əuvəʃu:] *n* chanclo *m*.

overshoot ['əuvə'ʃu:t] (*irr: see* **shoot**) *vti*: **to — (the mark)** pasar de la raya, excederse; **to — (the target) by 40 tons** producir 40 toneladas más de lo provisto; **to — (the runway)** (Aer) ir a aterrizar más allá de la pista.

oversight ['əuvəsait] *n* (a) (*omission*) descuido *m*, equivocación *f*; **by an —** por descuido; **it was an —** ha sido una distracción.
(b) (*supervision*) superintendencia *f*, vigilancia *f*.

oversimplification ['əuvə,simplifi'keiʃən] *n* simplificación *f* excesiva, supersimplificación *f*.

oversimplify ['əuvə'simplifai] *vt* simplificar demasiado.

oversleep ['əuvə'sli:p] (*irr: see* **sleep**) *vi* dormir demasiado, no despertar; **I overslept** durmiendo se me pasó la hora.

overspend ['əuvə'spend] (*irr: see* **spend**) **1** *vt*: **to — one's allowance** gastar más de lo que permite la renta de uno.
2 *vi*: **we have overspent by 5 dollars** hemos gastado 5 dólares más de lo que debíamos.

overspill ['əuvəspil] n (act) desparramamiento m de población; (quantity) exceso m de población; an — town for Manchester una ciudad vecinal de absorción de Manchester.
overstate ['əuvə'steit] vt exagerar.
overstatement ['əuvə'steitmənt] n exageración f.
overstay ['əuvə'stei] vt: to — one's leave quedarse más tiempo de lo que la licencia permite.
overstep ['əuvə'step] vt exceder, pasar de, traspasar; see mark etc.
overstock ['əuvə'stɔk] vt: to be —ed with tener existencias excesivas de.
overstrain ['əuvə'strein] 1 n fatiga f excesiva; (nervous) hipertensión f. 2 vt person fatigar excesivamente; provocar una hipertensión en; metal deformar, torcer; resources exigir demasiado de, someter a exigencias excesivas.
overstrung ['əuvə'strʌŋ] adj sobreexcitado, hipertenso.
oversubscribe ['əuvəsəb'skraib] 1 vt (Fin): the issue was —d se pidieron más acciones de las que había; the issue was —d 4 times la solicitud de acciones rebasó 4 veces la cantidad de títulos ofrecidos. 2 vi contribuir más de lo pedido.
oversupply ['əuvəsə'plai] vt proveer en exceso (with de); we are oversupplied with cars tenemos exceso de coches.
overt [əu'vəːt] adj abierto, público.
overtake [,əuvə'teik] (irr: see take) 1 vt (a) alcanzar; (Aut) adelantar; pasar, sobrepasar; he doesn't want to be —n no quiere dejarse adelantar; we overtook a lorry near Burgos cerca de Burgos pasamos un camión; you can't — that car on the bend no puedes adelantar ese coche en la curva; X has —n Y in steel production X se ha adelantado a Y en la producción de acero.
(b) (fig) coger de improviso, sorprender; to be —n by events ser sorprendido por los sucesos. 2 vi adelantar, pasar; "no overtaking" "prohibido adelantar".
overtaking [,əuvə'teikiŋ] n adelantamiento m, paso m.
overtax ['əuvə'tæks] 1 vt (Fin) oprimir con tributos, exigir contribuciones excesivas a; (with effort) agobiar, exigir demasiados esfuerzos a. 2 vr: to — oneself fatigarse demasiado, exigirse demasiados esfuerzos a sí mismo.
overthrow ['əuvəθrəu] n derrumbamiento m, derrocamiento m.
overthrow [,əuvə'θrəu] (irr: see throw) echar abajo, derribar; (overturn) volcar; dictator, system, empire etc derrumbar, derrocar.
overtime ['əuvətaim] n horas fpl extraordinarias; pay pago m de horas extraordinarias; to do —, to work — trabajar horas extraordinarias; we shall have to work — to catch up (fig) tendremos que esforzarnos al máximo para recuperar lo que hemos perdido.
overtly [əu'vəːtli] adv abiertamente, públicamente.
overtone ['əuvətəun] n (Mus) armónico m; (fig) sugestión f; a speech with a hostile — un discurso con alguna nota de hostilidad.
overtop ['əuvə'tɔp] vt descollar sobre.
overtrick ['əuvətrik] n (Cards) baza f de más.
overtrump ['əuvə'trʌmp] vt (Cards) contrafallar.
overture ['əuvətjuə*] n (Mus) obertura f; (fig) proposición f, propuesta f; sondeo m; to make —s to someone hacer una propuesta a uno; to make —s for an armistice proponer que se acuerde un armisticio.
overturn [,əuvə'təːn] 1 vt car, saucepan etc volcar; (disarrange) trastornar; government etc derrumbar, derrocar. 2 vi car, aircraft etc volcar, capotar, dar una vuelta de campana; boat zozobrar.
overuse [əuvə'juːz] vt usar demasiado.
overvalue ['əuvə'vælju:] vt sobrevalorar.
overweening [,əuvə'wiːniŋ] adj arrogante, presuntuoso, altivo; — pride desmesurado orgullo m.
overweight ['əuvə'weit] 1 adj demasiado pesado; to be — pesar demasiado, person ser gordo, tener exceso de carnes; he is 8 kilos — tiene 8 kilos de más; the parcel is a kilo — el paquete tiene un exceso de un kilo. 2 n exceso m de peso, sobrepeso m.
overwhelm [,əuvə'welm] vt opponent, team etc arrollar, aplastar; (in argument) aplastar; (of waves etc) fundir, inundar; (of grief etc) vencer, postrar; (of work etc) abrumar, agobiar; he speedily —ed his opponent arrolló a su contrincante en muy poco tiempo; to — someone with favours colmar a uno de favores; to — someone with kindness tratar a uno con excesiva amabilidad; he was —ed with joy

rebosaba alegría, no cabía en sí de contento; we have been —ed with offers of help estamos inundados por las ofertas de ayuda; Venice just —s me Venecia deja a uno boquiabierto, Venecia es pasmosa; you — me! ¡basta ya, se lo ruego!
overwhelming [,əuvə'welmiŋ] adj defeat etc arrollador, aplastante, contundente; success arrollador; majority abrumador; pressure etc irresistible; one's — impression of heat la más fuerte impresión de todas es la del calor.
overwhelmingly [,əuvə'welmiŋli] adv de modo arrollador; abrumadoramente; irresistiblemente; they voted — for X la abrumadora mayoría de ellos votó por X; he was — defeated sufrió una derrota arrolladora.
overwind ['əuvə'waind] (irr: see wind) vt watch dar demasiada cuerda a.
overwork ['əuvə'wəːk] 1 n trabajo m excesivo; to suffer from — haberse cansado trabajando demasiado. 2 vt hacer trabajar demasiado; exigir un esfuerzo excesivo a. 3 vi trabajar demasiado, cansarse trabajando demasiado.
overwrought ['əuvə'rɔːt] adj: to be — estar nerviosísimo, haberse agotado por la emoción (etc), estar sobreexcitado.
overzealous ['əuvə'zeləs] adj demasiado entusiasta.
Ovid ['ɔvid] n Ovidio.
oviduct ['əuvidʌkt] n oviducto m.
oviform ['əuvifɔːm] adj oviforme.
ovine ['əuvain] adj ovino.
oviparous [əu'vipərəs] adj ovíparo.
ovoid ['əuvɔid] 1 adj ovoide. 2 n ovoide m.
ovulation [,əuvju'leifən] n ovulación f.
ovule ['əuvjuːl] n óvulo m.
ovum ['əuvəm] n, pl ova ('əuvə) óvulo m.
owe [əu] 1 vt deber; to — someone £2 deber 2 libras a uno; I'll — it to you te lo quedo a deber; to — allegiance to someone deber lealtad a uno; to — someone a grudge guardar rencor a uno; to — someone thanks for his help estar agradecido a uno por su ayuda, deber las gracias a uno por su ayuda; to — one's life to a lucky chance deber su vida a una casualidad; he —s his talent to his mother le debe su talento a su madre; to whom do I — this honour? ¿a quién le debo este honor?; I — it to her to confess mi deber con ella me obliga a confesarlo; you — it to yourself to come venir es un deber que Vd tiene consigo mismo. 2 vi tener deudas; to — someone for a meal estar en deuda con uno por una comida.
owing ['əuiŋ] 1 adj: the £5 — las 5 libras que debemos, las 5 libras que se me deben; how much is — to you now? ¿cuánto se le debe ahora? 2: — to prep debido a, por causa de; — to the bad weather debido al mal tiempo, por el mal tiempo; it is — to lack of time se debe a la falta de tiempo.
owl [aul] n (barn-) lechuza f; (little —) mochuelo m; (long-eared —) búho m; (tawny —) cárabo m.
owlish ['aulif] adj look etc de buho.
own [əun] 1 adj (a) propio; it's all my — money todo el dinero es el mío propio; but his — brother said so pero su propio hermano lo dijo; in her — house en su propia casa; the house has its — garage la casa tiene garaje propio.
(b) (pred) the house is her (very) — la casa es la suya propia, la casa le pertenece únicamente a ella; my time is my — dispongo de mi tiempo como quiero; the decision was his — la decisión fue de él y no otro.
2 n lo suyo etc; all my — todo lo mío; he has a style all his — tiene un estilo muy suyo; may I keep it for my (very) —? ¿me lo puedo guardar como cosa que me pertenece únicamente a mí?; she has money of her — tiene dinero particular; I'll give you a copy of your — te daré un ejemplar propio, te daré un ejemplar para guardar; for reasons of his — por motivos particulares; a place of one's — una casa propia, una casa para sí; to come into one's — entrar en posesión de lo suyo, (fig) justificarse, encontrar su plena justificación; obtener el éxito merecido; to be on one's — estar a solas, estar solo; ser independiente; now we're on our — ya estamos solos; she was all on her — for a week pasó una semana enteramente sola; if I can get him on his — si puedo hablar con él a solas; to do something on one's — hacer algo sin ayuda (de nadie); to call something one's — ser dueño de algo, disponer de algo como de cosa propia; without a chair to call my — sin una silla que pueda decir que es mía; I am so busy I can scarcely call my time my —

estoy tan ocupado que apenas dispongo de mi tiempo; **to get one's — back** tomar su revancha; **to hold one's —** no cejar, mantenerse firme; no ceder terreno; mantenerse al nivel de los demás; **he can hold his — with anybody** no le va a la zaga a nadie; **I can hold my — in German** me defiendo en alemán.

3 *vt* **(a)** (*possess*) poseer, tener; ser dueño de; **he —s 2 tractors** posee 2 tractores; **he —s 3 newspapers** es dueño de 3 periódicos; **who —s the newspaper?** ¿quién es el dueño del periódico?; **who —s this pen?** ¿a quién pertenece esta pluma?; **to come in as if one —ed the place** entrar como Pedro por su casa; **a cat nobody wants to —** un gato que no parece pertenecer a nadie.

(b) (*acknowledge, recognize*) reconocer; **he —ed the child as his** reconoció al niño como suyo; **I — my mistake** reconozco mi error.

(c) (*confess*) confesar; **I — it** lo confieso; **I — I was wrong** confieso que me equivoqué.

4 *vi*: **to — to a mistake** confesar un error, reconocer un error; **I —ed to debts of £47** confesé tener deudas de 47 libras; **to — up** confesar, confesar de plano; **— up!** ¡confiésalo!; **she —ed up to being 40** confesó tener 40 años; **they —ed up to having stolen the apples** confesaron haber robado las manzanas.

owner ['əunə*] *n* dueño m, a *f*, propietario m, a *f*, amo m, a *f*; poseedor m, ora *f*; (*Naut: fam*) capitán m; **the — of car no. NBG 999** el dueño del coche matrícula NBG 999; **is the — about?** ¿está el dueño?

ownerless ['əunəlis] *adj* sin dueño.

ownership ['əunəʃip] *n* posesión *f*; propiedad *f*;

"under new —" "nuevo propietario", "nuevo dueño"; **books in** (*or* **under**) **the — of . . .** libros que son de la propiedad de . . .; **under his — the business flourished** el negocio prosperó bajo su dirección.

ox [ɔks] *n*, *pl* **oxen** ['ɔksən] buey m.

oxalic [ɔk'sælik] *adj*: **— acid** ácido m oxálico.

oxcart ['ɔkskɑ:t] *n* carro m de bueyes.

oxhide ['ɔkshaid] *n* cuero m de buey.

oxidation [,ɔksi'deiʃən] *n* oxidación *f*.

oxide ['ɔksaid] *n* óxido m.

oxidise ['ɔksidaiz] **1** *vt* oxidar. **2** *vi* oxidarse.

oxlip ['ɔkslip] *n* prímula *f*.

Oxonian [ɔk'səunian] **1** *adj* oxoniense. **2** *n* oxoniense *mf*.

oxtail ['ɔksteil] *n*: **— soup** sopa *f* de cola de buey.

oxyacetylene [,ɔksiə'setili:n] *adj* oxiacetilénico; **— burner, — torch** soplete m oxiacetilénico; **— welding** soldadura *f* oxiacetilénica.

oxygen ['ɔksidʒən] *n* oxígeno m.

oxygenate [ɔk'sidʒəneit] *vt* oxigenar.

oxygenation [,ɔksidʒə'neiʃən] *n* oxigenación *f*.

oxygen mask ['ɔksidʒən,mɑ:sk] *n* máscara *f* de oxígeno.

oxygen tent ['ɔksidʒən,tent] *n* tienda *f* de oxígeno.

oyez [əu'jez] *interj* ¡oíd!

oyster ['ɔistə*] *n* ostra *f*.

oyster bed ['ɔistəbed] *n* criadero m de ostras, vivero m de otras.

oystercatcher ['ɔistə,kætʃə*] *n* ostrero m.

oyster farm ['ɔistəfɑ:m] *n* criadero m de ostras.

oyster shell ['ɔistəʃel] *n* concha *f* de ostra.

ozone ['əuzəun] *n* ozono m.

P

P [piː]: **to mind one's —s and Qs** cuidarse de no meter la pata.
pa [paː] n (fam) papá m.
pace [peis] **1** n (a) (step) paso m; **12 —s off** a 12 pasos; **to put a horse through its —s** ejercitar un caballo, entrenar un caballo; **to put someone through his —s** poner a uno a prueba, demostrar las cualidades de uno.
 (b) (speed) paso m, marcha f, velocidad f; ritmo m; **at a good —, at a smart —** rápidamente; **at a slow —** a paso lento; **at a walking —** a la velocidad del que camina a pie; **at a snail's —** a paso de tortuga; **we kept up a good — with the work** mantuvimos un buen ritmo de trabajo; **the present — of development** el actual ritmo del desarrollo; **to keep —** ir al mismo paso; **to keep — with someone** llevar el mismo paso que uno; **industry has not kept — with technology** la industria no ha avanzado al mismo paso que la tecnología; **I can't keep — with events** no puedo mantenerme al corriente de los sucesos; **to make the —, to set the —** establecer el paso, marcar el ritmo; **to quicken one's —** apretar el paso.
 2 vt distance medir a pasos (also **to — out**); floor, room pasearse preocupado (etc) por; competitor marcar el paso para; **to — off 10 yards** medir 10 yardas a pasos.
 3 vi: **— up and down** pasearse de un lado a otro.
pacemaker ['peisˌmeikə*] n el que marca el paso, el que abre carrera.
pacer ['peisə*] n (Sport) establecedor m del paso.
pachyderm ['pækidɔːm] n paquidermo m.
pacific [pə'sifik] adj pacífico.
pacifically [pə'sifikəli] adv pacíficamente.
pacification [ˌpæsifi'keiʃən] n pacificación f.
Pacific Ocean [pə'sifik'auʃən] Océano m Pacífico.
pacifier ['pæsifaiə*] n (US: baby's) chupete m.
pacifism ['pæsifizəm] n pacifismo m.
pacifist ['pæsifist] **1** adj pacifista. **2** n pacifista mf.
pacify ['pæsifai] vt pacificar; apaciguar, calmar; **we managed to — him eventually** por fin logramos apaciguarle.
pack [pæk] **1** n (bundle) lío m, fardo m; (on animal) carga f; (rucksack, also Mil) mochila f; (packet) paquete m; (of cigarettes: US) paquete m, cajetilla f; (wrapping) envase m; (Med) compresa f; (of cards) baraja f; (of hounds) jauría f; (of wolves) manada f; **the — (Rugby)** los delanteros; **a — of lies** un montón de mentiras; **it's a — of lies!** ¡todo es mentira!
 2 vt (a) container llenar, ir llenando; case, trunk etc hacer; things in case etc poner; fish, meat in tin enlatar; (wrap) envasar; (put into parcel) empaquetar; **to — up a tent** desarmar una tienda, plegar una tienda; **articles —ed in dozens** artículos en caja de a docena; **it comes —ed in polythene** se sirve envasado en politeno.
 (b) (excessively) container llenar, atestar (with de); articles meter apretadamente (also **to — in**); **to — down** apretar, comprimir; (with feet etc) apisonar; **to — earth round a plant** acollar una planta; **the place was —ed** el local estaba de bote en bote; **the Costa Brava is —ed with tourists** la Costa Brava está llena de turistas; **to — more people in** ir introduciendo más personas; **can you — two more in?** ¿caben dos más?; **they were —ed in like sardines** estaban como sardinas en banasta; **the show is —ing them in** el espectáculo tiene un lleno cada noche, el espectáculo es un éxito indiscutible.
 (c) meeting llenar de partidarios; jury nombrar de modo fraudulento.
 (d) to — someone off despachar a uno; despedir a uno, deshacerse de uno; **so they —ed him off to London** así que le enviaron sin más a Londres; **to — a child off to bed** mandar a un niño a la cama;

to send someone —ing despedir a uno con cajas destempladas.
 (e) to — it in (fam) dejarlo; **— it in!** ¡déjalo!; **it's time we —ed it in** es hora de dejarlo ya.
 3 vi (a) (of luggage: also **to — up**) hacer las maletas, hacer el equipaje; **a tent that —s up easily** una tienda que se desarma fácilmente.
 (b) to — up (fam) terminar; (and depart) liar el petate; **then the engine —ed up** luego se averió el motor.
 (c) to — round, to — together apiñarse; **they —ed round the president** se apiñaron en torno al presidente.
 (d) (form a mass) endurecerse, consolidarse, formar una masa compacta; **the snow had —ed round the wheels** la nieve se había endurecido junto a las ruedas.
package ['pækidʒ] **1** n paquete m; bulto m.
 2 attr: **— deal** acuerdo m que supone unas concesiones mutuas, convenio m que resuelve diversos problemas.
 3 vt empaquetar, envasar.
pack animal ['pækˌæniməl] n animal m de carga.
packer ['pækə*] n embalador m, ora f, empaquetador m, ora f.
packet ['pækit] n paquete m; (of cigarettes) paquete m, cajetilla f; (of stamps) sobre m; (Naut) paquebote m; **postal —** paquete m postal; **a whole — of trouble** la mar de disgustos; **to make a — (fam)** ganar mucho dinero; **to make one's — (fam)** hacer su pacotilla; **that must have cost a — eso** habrá costado un dineral.
packet boat ['pækitbəut] n paquebote m.
packhorse ['pækhɔːs] n caballo m de carga.
pack ice ['pækais] n témpanos mpl flotantes.
packing ['pækiŋ] n (a) (act) embalaje m, envase m; **to do one's —** hacer sus maletas, arreglar el equipaje.
 (b) (material: outer) envase m, (inner) relleno m, empaquetadura f.
packing case ['pækiŋkeis] n cajón m de embalaje.
packsaddle ['pækˌsædl] n albarda f.
pact [pækt] **1** n pacto m; **to make a — with someone** pactar con uno.
 2 vi pactar (with con); **to — with someone to +** infin llegar a un acuerdo para + infin.
pad¹ [pæd] vi: **to — about, to — along** andar, pisar (sin hacer ruido).
pad² [pæd] **1** n almohadilla f, cojinete m; (of fox etc) pata f; (for inking) tampón m, almohadilla f para entintar; (of paper) bloc m, taco m; (of blotting paper) secafirmas m; (on shoulder) hombrera f; (launching) plataforma f de lanzamiento.
 2 vt almohadillar; acolchar; rellenar, forrar; shoulders bombear; book etc (also **to — out**) meter paja en, hinchar con mucha paja; **the speech was —ded out with references to . . .** el discurso estaba hinchado con referencias a . . .
pad³ [pæd] n (sl) querencia f, guarida f.
padded ['pædid] adj shoulders bombeado; dashboard etc almohadillado; armour enguatado; cell acolchonado, de aislamiento.
padding ['pædiŋ] n relleno m, almohadilla f; (material) borra f, (fig) paja f.
paddle ['pædl] **1** n (a) (oar) canalete m, zagual m; (blade of wheel) paleta f; (wheel) rueda f de paletas.
 (b) to go for a —, to have a — ir a mojarse los pies, chapotear en el mar (etc).
 2 vt (a) boat impulsar con canalete, remar con canalete.
 (b) to — one's feet in the sea mojarse los pies en el mar, chapotear en el mar.
 3 vi (a) (in boat) remar con canalete; **they —ed to the bank** dirigieron el bote a la orilla.
 (b) (with feet) mojarse los pies, chapotear.

paddle boat ['pædlbəut] *n*, **paddle steamer** ['pædl,stiːmə*] *n* vapor *m* de ruedas.
paddle wheel ['pædlwiːl] *n* rueda *f* de paletas.
paddling pool ['pædliŋpuːl] *n* estanque *m* para chapotear, estanque *m* de juegos.
paddock ['pædək] *n* (*field*) prado *m*; (*of racecourse*) corral *m*, explanada *f* de ensillado.
Paddy ['pædi] *nombre cariñoso de* **Patrick**; *el irlandés típico*.
paddy¹ ['pædi] *n* (*rice*) arroz *m*.
paddy² ['pædi] *n* (*fam*) rabieta *f*; **to get into a —** coger una rabieta.
paddywhack ['pædiwæk] *n* (*fam*) rabieta *f*.
padlock ['pædlɔk] **1** *n* candado *m*. **2** *vt* cerrer con candado.
padre ['paːdri] *n* (*fam: Mil*) capellán *m* militár; (*Univ*) capellán *m* de colegio; (*in direct address*) padre.
paean ['piːən] *n* himno *m* de alegría; **—s of praise** alabanzas *fpl*.
paediatrician, (*US*) **ped—** [,piːdiə'triʃən] *n* pedíatra *mf*, médico *m* puericultor.
paediatrics, (*US*) **ped—** [,piːdi'ætriks] *n* pediatría *f*.
pagan ['peigən] **1** *adj* pagano. **2** *n* pagano *m*, a *f*.
paganism ['peigənizəm] *n* paganismo *m*.
page¹ [peidʒ] **1** *n* (*boy-servant*) paje *m*; (*squire*) escudero *m*.
  2 *vt*: **to — someone** buscar a uno llamando su nombre, hacer llamar a uno por el botones.
page² [peidʒ] **1** *n* página *f*; (*Typ, of newspaper*) plana *f*; **the news was on the front —** la noticia figuraba en la primera plana; **on — 14** a la página 14, en la página 14; **"see — 20"** "véase la página 20".
  2 *vt* paginar, foliar.
pageant ['pædʒənt] *n* (*show*) espectáculo *m* brillante; (*procession*) desfile *m*; **a — of Elizabethan times** una representación de la época isabelina en una serie de cuadros; **the town held a — to mark the anniversary** la ciudad organizó una serie de fiestas públicas para celebrar el aniversario.
pageantry ['pædʒəntri] *n* pompa *f*, boato *m*; **the — of the occasion** lo espectacular del acontecimiento, lo vistoso del acontecimiento; **all the — of History** toda la magnificencia de la Historia; **it was celebrated with much —** se celebró con gran boato.
page boy ['peidʒbɔi] *n* paje *m*.
page proofs ['peidʒpruːfs] *npl* pruebas *fpl* de planas.
paginate ['pædʒineit] *vt* paginar, foliar.
pagination [,pædʒi'neiʃən] *n* paginación *f*, foliación *f*; **without —** sin paginar.
pagoda [pə'gəudə] *n* pagoda *f*.
paid [peid] **1** *pret and ptp of* **pay**.
  2 *adj* bill *etc* pagado; official asalariado, que recibe un sueldo; work remunerado; **to put — to something** acabar con algo.
paid-up ['peid'ʌp], (*US*) **paid-in** ['peid'in] *adj* share liberado; **fully-—share** acción *f* totalmente liberada.
pail [peil] *n* cubo *m*, balde *m*; (*child's*) cubito *m*.
pailful ['peilful] *n* cubo *m*, contenido *m* de un cubo.
paillasse ['pæliæs] *n* jergón *m*.
pain [pein] **1** *n* (a) dolor *m*; sufrimiento *m*; **to be in —** estar con dolor; **to be in great —** tener mucho dolor, sufrir mucho; **he's a — in the neck, it gives me a — in the neck** me da cien patadas; **cucumber gives me a —** el pepino me sienta mal; **I have a — in my leg** me duele la pierna; **to put a wounded animal out of its —** acortar la agonía de un animal herido, despachar un animal herido.
  (b) **—s** (*efforts*) trabajos *mpl*, cuidados *mpl*, esfuerzos *mpl*; **to be at great —s over something, to take —s over something** esmerarse en algo, tomarse trabajo en algo; **all he got for his —s was ...** lo único que logró después de tantos trabajos fue ...; **to spare no —s** no perdonar esfuerzos (*to + infin* por + *infin*); **to take —s to + infin** poner especial cuidado en + *infin*.
  (c) (*penalty*) pena *f*; **on — of death** so pena de muerte; **with all the —s and penalties of fame** con todas las dificultades y disgustos que acarrea la fama.
  2 *vt* (*physically*) doler, (*mentally*) dar lástima a; **Spain —s me** me duele España; **you — me!** ¡me das lástima!; **where does it — you?** ¿dónde le duele?
pained [peind] *adj* expression de disgusto, afligido; voice dolorido; **he looked —** hizo una mueca, torció el gesto.
painful ['peinful] *adj* (*physically*) doloroso, dolorido; (*difficult*) difícil, penoso, angustioso; duty desagradable, nada grato; (*fam*) horrible, malísimo; **it is my — duty to tell you that ...** tengo el deber nada grato de decirle que ...; **my arm was becoming —** empezaba a dolerme el brazo; **it was — to behold**

daba lástima verlo; **—, isn't it?** ¿es horrible, no?; **she gave a — performance** hizo una malísima actuación.
painfully ['peinfəli] *adv* dolorosamente, con dolor; penosamente; (*fam*) terriblemente; **he dragged himself — along** se arrastraba penosamente por el suelo; **she's — shy** es terriblemente tímida.
painkiller ['peinkilə*] *n* quitadolores *m*, calmante *m*.
painless ['peinlis] *adj* indoloro, sin dolor.
painlessly ['peinlisli] *adv* sin causar dolor.
painstaking ['peinz,teikiŋ] *adj* person laborioso, concienzudo, esmerado; piece of work hecho con cuidado, hecho con esmero.
painstakingly ['peinz,teikiŋli] *adv* laboriosamente, concienzudamente, esmeradamente.
paint [peint] **1** *n* pintura *f*; (*for face*) colorete *m*; box of **—s** caja *f* de pinturas; **"wet —"** "¡ojo, que pinta!", "¡cuidado con la pintura!"
  2 *vt* pintar; **to — something out** tachar algo con una mano de pintura; **to — something black** pintar algo de negro; **to — one's face** pintarse, ponerse colorete.
  3 *vi* pintar; ser pintor.
paintbox ['peintbɔks] *n* caja *f* de pinturas.
paintbrush ['peintbrʌʃ] *n* (*Art*) pincel *m*; (*for decorating*) brocha *f*.
painter¹ ['peintə*] *n* (*Art*) pintor *m*, ora *f*; (*decorator*) pintor *m* de brocha gorda.
painter² ['peintə*] *n* amarra *f*; **to cut the —** (*fig*) cortar las amarras, independizarse.
painting ['peintiŋ] *n* (*as a whole*) pintura *f*; (*picture*) cuadro *m*, pintura *f*.
paintpot ['peintpɔt] *n* bote *m* de pintura.
paint roller ['peint,rəulə*] *n* rodillo *m* pintor.
paint spray ['peintsprei] *n* pistola *f* rociadora de pintura.
pair [pɛə*] **1** *n* (*of gloves, shoes, etc*) par *m*; (*of people, cards, stamps*) pareja *f*; (*of oxen*) yunta *f*; **a — of trousers** un pantalón, unos pantalones; **a carriage and —** un landó con dos caballos; **a — of scissors** unas tijeras; **the happy —** la feliz pareja, los novios; **arranged in —s** arreglados (*or* colocados) de dos en dos.
  2 *vt* aparear (*also Bio*).
  3 *vi* aparearse (*also Bio*); **to — off** aparearse, formar pareja; **to — with** (*Bio*) aparearse con, juntarse con.
pairing ['pɛəriŋ] *n* (*Bio*) apareamiento *m*.
pajamas [pə'dʒɑːməz] *npl* pijama *m*.
Pakistan [,pɑːkis'tɑːn] Pakistán *m*, Paquistán *m* (*Acad*).
Pakistani [,pɑːkis'tɑːni] **1** *adj* pakistaní, paquistaní (*Acad*). **2** *n* pakistaní *mf*, paquistaní *mf* (*Acad*).
pal [pæl] (*fam*) **1** *n* camarada *mf*, compinche *m*, compañero *m*, a *f*; **a —!** ¡vamos, pórtate como un amigo!; **you've always been a —** to me siempre has sido muy amable conmigo.
  2 *vi*: **to — up** hacerse amigos; **to — up with someone** hacerse amigo de uno.
palace ['pælis] *n* palacio *m*; **bishop's —** palacio *m* episcopal; **royal —** palacio *m* real.
palaeo- ['pæliəu] *see* **paleo-**.
palatable ['pælətəbl] *adj* sabroso, apetitoso; comible; (*fig*) aceptable (*to* a); **it may not be — to the government** puede no ser del gusto del gobierno, puede no ser del agrado del gobierno.
palatal ['pælətl] **1** *adj* palatal. **2** *n* palatal *f*.
palatalize ['pælətəlaiz] **1** *vi* palatalizar. **2** *vi* palatalizarse.
palate ['pælit] *n* paladar *m* (*also fig*); **hard —** paladar *m*; **soft —** velo *m* del paladar; **to have a delicate —** tener un paladar delicado; **to have no — for something** (*fig*) no poder tragar algo, no encontrar nada agradable en algo.
palatial [pə'leiʃəl] *adj* suntuoso, espléndido.
palatinate [pə'lætinit] *n* palatinado *m*.
palaver [pə'lɑːvə*] **1** *n* (*conference*) conferencia *f*, parlamento *m*; (*fuss*) lío *m*; (*trouble*) molestias *fpl*, trámites *mpl* engorrosos; **that — about the car** aquel lío que se armó acerca del coche; **can't we do it without a lot of —?** ¿no podemos hacerlo sin tantas molestias?, ¿no podemos hacerlo sin meternos en tantos líos? **2** *vi* parlamentar.
pale¹ [peil] **1** *adj* complexion, face pálido; colour claro; light tenue; **a — blue dress** un vestido azul claro; **she was deathly —** estaba pálida como la muerte; **to go —, to grow —, to turn —** palidecer, ponerse pálido.
  2 *vi* palidecer, ponerse pálido; **but X —s beside Y** pero X pierde al lado de Y; *see* insignificance.
pale² [peil] *n* (*stake*) estaca *f*; **to be beyond the —** estar excluido de la buena sociedad; ser inaceptable,

ser un indeseable; **to be outside the — of** quedar fuera de los límites de.

paleface ['peilfeis] n hombre m blanco, mujer f blanca.
paleness ['peilnis] n palidez f; tenuidad f.
paleo . . . ['pæliəʊ] paleo . . .
paleographer [,pæli'ɔgrəfə*] n paleógrafo m.
paleography [,pæli'ɔgrəfi] n paleografía f.
paleolithic [,pæliəʊ'liθik] adj paleolítico.
paleontology [,pæliən'tɔlədʒi] n paleontología f.
Palestine ['pælistain] Palestina f.
Palestinian [,pæləs'tiniən] **1** adj palestino. **2** n palestino m, a f.
palette ['pælit] n paleta f.
palette knife ['pælitnaif] n, pl — **knives** [naivz] espátula f.
palfrey ['pɔːlfri] n palafré m.
palimpsest ['pælimpsest] n palimpsesto m.
palindrome ['pælindrəum] n palindromo m.
paling ['peiliŋ] n (stake) estaca f; (fence) valla f, empalizada f.
palisade [,pæli'seid] n palizada f, estacada f.
pall[1] [pɔːl] n (on coffin) paño m mortuorio; (robe, Eccl) palio m; (fig) manto m, capa f; **a — of smoke** (covering) una capa de humo, (rising in air) un penacho de humo.
pall[2] [pɔːl] vi perder su sabor (on para), dejar de gustar (on a); empalagar (on a); **it —s after a time** después de cierto tiempo deja de gustar; **it never —s** nunca pierde su sabor; **I found the book —ed** encontré que el libro empezaba a aburrirme.
pallbearer ['pɔːl,beərə*] n el que ayuda a llevar a hombros el féretro.
pallet ['pælit] n (bed) jergón m.
palliasse ['pæliæs] n jergón m.
palliate ['pælieit] vt paliar, mitigar.
palliative ['pæliətiv] **1** adj paliativo. **2** n paliativo m.
pallid ['pælid] adj pálido.
pallidness ['pælidnis] n, **pallor** ['pælə*] n palidez f.
pally ['pæli] adj (fam): **he's a — sort** es una persona afable; **they're very —** son muy amigos; **to be pretty — with someone** ser muy amigo de uno.
palm[1] [pɑːm] n (Bot) palma f, palmera f; (English sallow) sauce m; (as carried at Easter) ramo m; **to bear the —** llevarse la palma; **to yield the — to someone** reconocer la superioridad de uno, reconocer a uno por vencedor.
palm[2] [pɑːm] (Anat) **1** n palma f; **to grease someone's —** untar la mano a uno; **to have an itching —** ser muy codicioso; (be bribable) estar dispuesto a dejarse sobornar.
2 vt card escamotear; **to — something off on someone** encajar algo a uno.
palmist ['pɑːmist] n quiromántico m, a f.
palmistry ['pɑːmistri] n quiromancia f.
palm oil ['pɑːmɔil] n aceite m de palma.
palm tree ['pɑːmtriː] n palma f, palmera f.
palmy ['pɑːmi] adj floreciente; próspero, feliz; **those — days** aquellos días tan felices.
palpable ['pælpəbl] adj palpable; (fig) palpable, sensible.
palpably ['pælpəbli] adv palpablemente; sensiblemente; **a — unjust sentence** una condena manifiestamente injusta; **that is — untrue** eso es a todas luces falso.
palpitate ['pælpiteit] vi palpitar.
palpitating ['pælpiteitiŋ] adj palpitante.
palpitation [,pælpi'teiʃən] n palpitación f; **to have —s** tener vahídos.
palsied ['pɔːlzid] adj paralítico.
palsy ['pɔːlzi] n perlesía f, parálisis f; **cerebral —** parálisis f cerebral.
paltry ['pɔːltri] adj insignificante, baladí; vil; miserable; **for a few — pesetas** por unas pesetillas, por unas miserables pesetas; **for some — reason** por alguna razón insignificante.
pampas ['pæmpəs] npl pampa f, pampas fpl; **the P—** (SAm) la Pampa.
pamper ['pæmpə*] vt mimar.
pampered ['pæmpəd] adj child etc mimado, consentido; life regalado; **he was — all his life** se crió entre algodones.
pamphlet ['pæmflit] n (informative, brochure) folleto m; (literary) panfleto m; (political, handed out in street) octavilla f, hoja f de propaganda.
pamphleteer [,pæmfli'tiə*] n folletista mf.
pan [pæn] **1** n (utensil) cazuela f, cacerola f; perol m; (frying —) sartén f; (of lavatory) taza f; (of firearm) cazoleta f.
2 vt gold separar en la gamella; play (sl) dar un palo a; (camera: Cine) tomar en panorámicas; **to — out** repartir.
3 vi: **to — out** salir bien, tener éxito; **if it —s**

out as we hope si sale como nosotros lo esperamos; **it didn't — out at all well** no dio ningún resultado satisfactorio; **we must wait and see how it —s out** tenemos que esperar hasta ver que éxito tiene esto.
pan . . . [pæn] in compounds: pan . . ., eg **pan-African** panafricano.
panacea [,pænə'siə] n panacea f.
panache [pə'næʃ] n: **to do something with —** hacer algo con brío, hacer algo con aire triunfal.
Panama [,pænə'mɑː] Panamá m; **— Canal** Canal m de Panamá; **— hat** sombrero m de jipijapa, panamá m.
Panamanian [,pænə'meiniən] **1** adj panameño. **2** n panameño m, a f.
Pan-American ['pænə'merikən] adj panamericano; **— Union** Unión f Panamericana.
Pan-Americanism ['pænə'merikənizəm] n pan-americanismo m.
pancake ['pænkeik] n hojuela f, tortita f, panqueque m (SAm).
pancake day ['pænkeik,dei] n martes m de carnaval (en que en Inglaterra se sirven hojuelas).
panchromatic ['pænkrəʊ'mætik] adj pancromático.
pancreas ['pæŋkriəs] n páncreas m.
pancreatic [,pæŋkri'ætik] adj pancreático.
panda ['pændə] n panda mf.
pandemonium [,pændi'məʊniəm] n ruido m de todos los diablos, estruendo m infernal; **it's sheer —!** ¡es la mondal!; **at this there was — en** esto estallaron ruidosos los gritos (etc).
pander ['pændə*] **1** n alcahuete m. **2** vi alcahuetear; **to — to someone** ser indulgente con uno, mimar a uno, desvivirse por complacer a uno; **to — to someone's desires** tratar por todos los medios de satisfacer los deseos de uno; **this is —ing to the public's worst tastes** esto es condescender con los peores gustos del público.
Pandora [pæn'dɔːrə] : **—'s box** caja f de Pandora.
pane [pein] n cristal m, hoja f de vidrio.
panegyric [,pæni'dʒirik] n panegírico m.
panel ['pænl] **1** n **(a)** panel m; (of wall) panel m; (of ceiling) artesón m; (of door) entrepaño m; (Sew) paño m; (Art) tabla f; (of instruments, switches) tablero m.
(b) (Med etc) lista f de pacientes; (of judges, in a competition) jurado m.
2 vt poner paneles (etc) a, adornar con paneles (etc).
panelist ['pænəlist] n miembro m del jurado (de un concurso etc).
panelled, (US) **paneled** ['pænld] adj con paneles, adornado de paneles; artesonado.
panelling, (US) **paneling** ['pænəliŋ] n paneles mpl; artesonado m; entrepaños mpl.
pang [pæŋ] n punzada f, dolor m súbito, dolor m agudo; **— of conscience** remordimiento m; **I felt a — of conscience** me remordió la conciencia; **—s of childbirth** dolores mpl del parto; **—s of hunger** dolores mpl del hambre.
panhandle ['pænhændl] (US) **1** n faja angosta de territorio de un estado que entra en el de otro. **2** vi (sl) mendigar, pedir limosna.
panic ['pænik] **1** n terror m pánico, pánico m; **to flee in —** huir aterrado; **the country was thrown into a —** el terror cundió en el país, el país fue preso de un terror pánico.
2 vt aterrar, infundir terror a.
3 vi llenarse de terror, aterrarse, ser preso de un terror pánico; **the crew —ked** la tripulación se abandonó al terror; **don't —!** ¡con calma!
panicky ['pæniki] adj **(a)** person asustadizo; lleno de un terror pánico; **to get —** llenarse de terror; **don't get —!** ¡con calma!
(b) act, measure etc influido por el terror.
panic-stricken ['pænik,strikən] adj preso de un terror pánico, muerto de miedo.
panjandrum [pæn'dʒændrəm] n jefazo m, mandamás m; **he's the great —** es el mandamás.
pannier ['pæniə*] n cuévano m, serón m, banasta f.
pannier bag ['pæniə,bæg] n (on motorcycle etc) cartera f, bolsa f (para equipage); (for mule etc) alforja f.
panoply ['pænəpli] n (armour) panoplia f; (fig) pompa f, esplendor m.
panorama [,pænə'rɑːmə] n panorama m.
panoramic [,pænə'ræmik] adj panorámico.
pansy ['pænzi] n (Bot) pensamiento m; (fam) maricón m.
pant [pænt] **1** n jadeo m; resuello m.
2 vi jadear; resollar; (of heart) palpitar; **to — for water** jadear sediento; **to — for breath** jadear; **to — for** (fig) suspirar por, anhelar; **to — out a few words** decir jadeando algunas palabras; **to — with desire for something** desear algo ardientemente.

pantaloons [ˌpæntəˈluːnz] npl (Hist) pantalones mpl.
pantechnicon [pænˈteknikən] n camión m de mudanzas.
pantheism [ˈpænθiːizəm] n panteísmo m.
pantheist [ˈpænθiːist] n panteísta mf.
pantheistic [ˌpænθiːˈistik] adj panteísta.
pantheon [ˈpænθiən] n panteón m.
panther [ˈpænθə*] n pantera f.
panties [ˈpæntiz] npl bragas fpl, braguitas fpl; **a pair of** — unas bragas.
panting [ˈpæntiŋ] n jadeo m; respiración f difícil.
pantograph [ˈpæntəgrɑːf] n pantógrafo m.
pantomime [ˈpæntəmaim] n (classical) pantomima f; (British) revista musical en época de Navidades, a base de cuentos de hadas etc; **what a** —! ¡qué absurdo!, ¡qué ridículo!
pantry [ˈpæntri] n despensa f.
pants [pænts] npl calzoncillos mpl; (US) pantalones mpl; **a pair of** — unos calzoncillos, (US) unos pantalones, un pantalón.
Panzer [ˈpæntsə*] **1** adj motorizado; — **division** división f motorizada. **2** n: **the —s** las tropas motorizadas.
pap [pæp] n papilla f, gachas fpl.
papa [pəˈpɑː] n papá m.
papacy [ˈpeipəsi] n papado m, pontificado m.
papal [ˈpeipəl] adj papal, pontificio.
paper [ˈpeipə*] **1** n (a) (material, in general) papel m; **a piece of** — un papel, una hoja de papel, un trozo de papel; **brown** — papel m de embalar, papel m de estraza; **corrugated** — papel m ondulado; **hand-made** — papel m de tina; **India** — papel m de China, papel m biblia; **rice** — papel m de paja de arroz; **squared** — papel m cuadriculado; **vellum** — papel m vitela; **waste** — papel m viejo, papeles mpl usados; **on** — sobre el papel, teóricamente; **to commit something to —,** to get (or put) something **down on** — poner algo por escrito.
(b) (document) papel m, documento m; **—s** (identity etc) papeles mpl, documentación f; identity **—s** documentación f personal, carnet m de identidad; **your —s, please** la documentación, por favor; **ship's —s** documentación f del barco; **Churchill's private —s** los papeles personales de Churchill.
(c) (Univ etc exercise) ejercicio m, ensayo m; (exam) cuestionario m de examen; **to do a good —** **in maths** hacer un buen examen de matemáticas; **to set a —** in physics poner un examen de física.
(d) (learned: written) artículo m, (read aloud) comunicación f, ponencia f; **we heard a good —** **on** place-names escuchamos una buena ponencia sobre toponimia.
(e) (newspaper) periódico m; **daily —, morning** — periódico m, diario m; **evening** — periódico m de la tarde; **weekly** — semanario m; **Sunday** — periódico m del domingo; **fashion** — revista f de modas; **illustrated** — revista f gráfica; **trade** — revista f comercial; **women's** — revista f para mujeres; **to write for the —s** colaborar en los periódicos, escribir artículos para los periódicos; **to write to the** — about something escribir una carta al director de un periódico.
2 attr de papel; — **money** papel m moneda, billetes mpl de banco.
3 vt wall, room empapelar.
paperback [ˈpeipəbæk] n libro m en rústica.
paperbacked [ˈpeipəbækt] adj en rústica.
paper bag [ˈpeipəˈbæg] n saco m de papel.
paperboy [ˈpeipəbɔi] n repartidor m de periódicos.
paper chain [ˈpeipətʃein] n cadeneta f de papel.
paper chase [ˈpeipətʃeis] n rallye-paper m.
paper clip [ˈpeipəklip] n clip m, sujetapapeles m.
paper fastener [ˈpeipəˌfɑːsnə*] n grapa f.
paperhanger [ˈpeipəˌhæŋə*] n empapelador m.
paper knife [ˈpeipənaif] n, pl **knives** [naivz] abrecartas m, plegadera f.
paper mill [ˈpeipəmil] n fábrica f de papel.
paperweight [ˈpeipəweit] n pisapapeles m.
paper work [ˈpeipəwəːk] n trabajo m administrativo; trabajo m de oficina; aspecto m teórico; (pej) papeleo m, trámites mpl burocráticos.
papery [ˈpeipəri] adj parecido al papel; delgado como el papel.
papier-mâché [ˈpæpieiˈmæʃei] **1** adj de cartón piedra.
2 n cartón m piedra.
papist [ˈpeipist] n papista mf.
papistry [ˈpeipistri] n papismo m.
paprika [ˈpæprikə] n pimienta f húngara.
papyrus [pəˈpaiərəs] n, pl **papyri** [pəˈpaiərai] papiro m.
par [pɑː*] **1** adj value etc nominal.
2 n (Comm) par f; (Golf) par m; **to be above** (or

over) — (Comm) estar por encima de la par; **to be** **under** (or below) — (Comm) estar por debajo de la par, (Med) estar indispuesto, sentirse mal, (fig) ser inferior a la calidad normal; **to get round in 6 under** — (Golf) hacer un recorrido con 6 por debajo del par; **to be at** — (Comm) estar a la par; **to be on a** — **with** ser equivalente a, correr parejas con; **to place something on a** — **with** parangonar algo con, equiparar algo con.
parable [ˈpærəbl] n parábola f.
parabola [pəˈræbələ] n (Math) parábola f.
parabolic [ˌpærəˈbɔlik] adj parabólico.
parachute [ˈpærəʃuːt] **1** n paracaídas m.
2 vt lanzar en paracaídas; **to** — **food to someone** suministrar víveres a uno en paracaídas.
3 vi lanzarse en paracaídas; bajar en paracaídas (also — **down**); **to** — **to safety** salvarse utilizando el paracaídas.
parachutist [ˈpærəʃuːtist] n paracaidista m.
parade [pəˈreid] **1** n (procession) desfile m; (Mil) desfile m, parada f; (road) paseo m; (fig) alarde m; **mannequin** — desfile m de modelos; **to make a** — **of** hacer alarde de, hacer ostentación de.
2 vt troops formar, formar en parada; streets recorrer, desfilar por; placard, image etc pasear (through the streets por las calles); (show off) hacer alarde de, hacer ostentación de, lucir; **to** — **one's learning** hacer alarde de su erudición.
3 vi (Mil) formar en parada, pasar revista; (group of people) desfilar; (one person) pasearse; **the strikers** —**d through the town** los huelguistas desfilaron por la ciudad; **she** —**d up and down with the hat on** se paseó de un lado a otro con el sombrero puesto, andaba de acá para allá para lucir el sombrero.
parade ground [pəˈreidgraund] n plaza f de armas.
paradigm [ˈpærədaim] n paradigma m.
paradise [ˈpærədais] n paraíso m; **an earthly** — un paraíso terrenal, un edén; **this is** —! ¡esto es jauja!; see fool.
paradox [ˈpærədɔks] n paradoja f.
paradoxical [ˌpærəˈdɔksikəl] adj paradójico.
paradoxically [ˌpærəˈdɔksikəli] adv paradójicamente.
paraffin [ˈpærəfin] n (oil) petróleo m (de alumbrado); (wax) parafina f.
paraffin lamp [ˈpærəfinˌlæmp] n quinqué m de petróleo.
paraffin oil [ˈpærəfinˌɔil] n petróleo m de alumbrado.
paraffin wax [ˈpærəfinˌwæks] n parafina f.
paragon [ˈpærəgən] n dechado m; **a** — **of virtue** un dechado de virtudes.
paragraph [ˈpærəgrɑːf] **1** n párrafo m; (Typ) suelto m; **"new —"** "(punto y) aparte". **2** vt dividir en párrafos.
Paraguay [ˈpærəgwai] el Paraguay.
Paraguayan [ˌpærəˈgwaiən] **1** adj paraguayo. **2** n paraguayo m, a f.
parakeet [ˈpærəkiːt] n perico m, periquito m.
parallel [ˈpærəlel] **1** adj paralelo; (Elec) en paralelo; (fig) semejante, análogo (to a); **in a** — **direction to** en dirección paralela a; **to run** — **to** ir en línea paralela a; **this is a** — **case to the last one** este caso es análago al anterior.
2 n (Geom) paralela f, línea f paralela; (Geog, fig) paralelo m; **the 49th** — el paralelo 49; **in** — (Elec) en paralelo; **a case without** — un caso inaudito, un caso nunca visto; **it has no** — **as far as I know** que yo sepa es único, que yo sepa no hay nada parecido; **to draw a** — **between X and Y** establecer un paralelo entre X e Y.
3 vt (fig) ser paralelo a, ser análogo a, correr parejas con; **it is** —**led by** ... corre parejas con ..., tiene su paralelo en ...
parallelism [ˈpærəlelizəm] n paralelismo m.
parallelogram [ˌpærəˈleləugræm] n paralelogramo m.
paralysis [pəˈrælisis] n parálisis f; **creeping** — parálisis f progresiva; **infantile** — parálisis f infantil.
paralytic [ˌpærəˈlitik] **1** adj paralítico. **2** n paralítico m, a f.
paralyzation [ˌpærəlaiˈzeiʃən] n paralización f.
paralyze [ˈpærəlaiz] vt paralizar (also fig); **to be** —**d** **in both legs** estar paralizado de las dos piernas; **to be** —**d with fright** estar paralizado de miedo.
paramilitary [ˌpærəˈmilitəri] adj paramilitar.
paramount [ˈpærəmaunt] adj supremo; **of** — **importance** de la mayor importancia, primordial; **solvency must be** — la solvencia es lo más importante, ante todo la solvencia.
paramour [ˈpærəmuə*] n (esp hum) amante mf, querido m, a f.
paranoia [ˌpærəˈnɔiə] n paranoia f.

paranoiac [ˌpærə'nɔiik] n paranoico m.
parapet ['pærəpit] n parapeto m; (of well etc) brocal m.
paraphernalia ['pærəfə'neiliə] n (belongings, gear) avíos mpl, chismes mpl; (adornments) arreos mpl; (fuss) molestias fpl.
paraphrase ['pærəfreiz] 1 n paráfrasis f. 2 vt parafrasear.
paraplegia [ˌpærə'pli:dʒə] n paraplejía f.
paraplegic [ˌpærə'pli:dʒik] 1 adj parapléjico. 2 n parapléjico m, a f.
parasite ['pærəsait] n parásito m (also fig: on de).
parasitic(al) [ˌpærə'sitik(əl)] adj parasítico, parasitario; **to be —** on ser parásito de.
parasitism ['pærəsitizm] n parasitismo m.
parasitology [ˌpærəsi'tɔlədʒi] n parasitología f.
parasol [ˌpærə'sɔl] n sombrilla f, quitasol m.
paratrooper ['pærətru:pə*] n paracaidista m.
paratroops ['pærətru:ps] npl paracaidistas mpl.
paratyphoid ['pærə'taifɔid] n paratifoidea f.
parboil ['pɑ:bɔil] vt sancochar.
Parcae ['pɑ:ki:] npl: **the —** las Parcas.
parcel ['pɑ:sl] 1 n paquete m; (of land) parcela f. 2 vt: **to — out** repartir; dividir; land parcelar; **to — up** empaquetar, embalar.
parcel post ['pɑ:slpəust] n servicio m de paquetes postales.
parch [pɑ:tʃ] 1 vt secar, resecar; quemar. 2 vi secarse.
parched [pɑ:tʃt] adj land etc seco; **to be —** (with thirst) morirse de sed.
parchment ['pɑ:tʃmənt] n pergamino m.
parchment-like ['pɑ:tʃmənt,laik] adj apergaminado.
pardon ['pɑ:dn] 1 n perdón m; (Law) indulto m; general — amnistía f; **to beg someone's —** pedir perdón a uno; **I beg your —, but could you . . . ?** perdone la molestia, pero ¿podría Vd . . . ?; **I beg your —!** ¡perdone Vd!, ¡ay perdone!; **—?, I beg your —?** ¿cómo?
2 vt perdonar, dispensar; (Law) indultar; **to — someone something** perdonar algo a uno; dispensar a uno de hacer (etc) algo; **— me, but could you . . . ?** perdone la molestia, pero ¿podría Vd . . . ?; **— me!** ¡perdone Vd!, ¡ay perdone!; **— my mentioning it** siento tener que decirlo, perdone que se lo diga.
pardonable ['pɑ:dnəbl] adj perdonable.
pardonably ['pɑ:dnəbli] adv: **he was — angry** es fácil disculpar su enojo, se comprende fácilmente que se encolerizara.
pare [pɛə*] vt nails cortar; fruit etc mondar; stick etc adelgazar; **to — away, to — down** (fig) reducir, ir reduciendo; **to — something down to the minimum** reducir algo al mínimo.
parent ['pɛərənt] 1 n padre m, madre f; **—s** padres mpl. 2 adj: **the — plant** la planta madre; **the — company** la casa matriz.
parentage ['pɛərəntidʒ] n familia f, linaje m; **of humble —** de nacimiento humilde.
parental [pə'rentl] adj care etc de padre y madre, de los padres; paternal; maternal.
parenthesis [pə'renθisis] n, pl **parentheses** [pə-'renθisi:z] paréntesis m.
parenthetic(al) [ˌpærən'θetik(əl)] adj entre paréntesis; explicativo.
parenthetically [ˌpærən'θetikəli] adv entre paréntesis; a modo de paréntesis.
parenthood ['pɛərənthud] n el ser padre (or madre), el tener hijos; paternidad f, maternidad f.
par excellence [pɑ:r'eksələ:ns] adv por excelencia.
pariah ['pæriə] n paria mf.
parietal [pə'raiitl] adj parietal.
pari mutuel ['pærimu:tu'el] n totalizador m.
parings ['pɛəriŋz] npl peladuras fpl, mondaduras fpl; desperdicios mpl.
pari passu ['pæri'pæsu] adv a ritmo parecido, al igual, **— with** a ritmo parecido al de, al igual que.
Paris ['pæris] París; (attr) parisiense.
parish ['pæriʃ] 1 n parroquia f. 2 attr parroquial, de la parroquia.
parishioner [pə'riʃənə*] n feligrés m, esa f.
parish-pump ['pæriʃ'pʌmp] attr (pej) de campanario, de aldea.
Parisian [pə'riziən] 1 adj parisiense, parisino, parisién. 2 n parisiense mf.
parity ['pæriti] n paridad f, igualdad f; **the — of the dollar** la paridad del dólar.
park [pɑ:k] 1 n parque m; jardines mpl; (Aut) aparcamiento m, parque m (de automóviles).
2 vt (Aut: briefly) estacionar, (for longer period) aparcar; (fam) poner, dejar, depositar; **can I — my car here?** ¿puedo aparcar mi coche aquí?
3 vi (Aut: briefly) estacionarse, (for longer period) aparcar; (fam) quedarse.

parking ['pɑ:kiŋ] n estacionamiento m; aparcamiento m; **"no —"** "prohibido estacionarse"; **"good — for cars"** "fácil aparcamiento de coches"; **"— for 50 cars"** "aparcamiento para 50 coches".
parking attendant ['pɑ:kiŋˌtendənt] n celador m.
parking lights ['pɑ:kiŋlaits] npl luces fpl de estacionamiento.
parking lot ['pɑ:kiŋlɔt] n (US) aparcamiento m.
parking meter ['pɑ:kiŋˌmi:tə*] n parquímetro m, contador m de aparcamiento.
parking place ['pɑ:kiŋpleis] n sitio m para aparcar, aparcamiento m; **to look for a —** buscar dónde aparcar.
park keeper ['pɑ:kˌki:pə*] n guardián m (de parque), guardabosque m.
parkway ['pɑ:kwei] n (US) gran vía f adornada de árboles.
parky ['pɑ:ki] adj (sl) frío; **it's pretty —** hace un frío glacial.
parlance ['pɑ:ləns] n lenguaje m; **in common —** en lenguaje corriente; **in technical —** en lenguaje técnico.
parley ['pɑ:li] 1 n parlamento m. 2 vi parlamentar (with con).
parliament ['pɑ:ləmənt] n parlamento m; (Spanish) Cortes fpl; **to get into —** llegar a ser diputado, ser elegido.
parliamentarian [ˌpɑ:ləmen'tɛəriən] 1 adj parlamentario. 2 n parlamentario m, a f.
parliamentary [ˌpɑ:lə'mentəri] adj parlamentario.
parlour, (US) parlor ['pɑ:lə*] n sala f de recibo, salón m; (Eccl) locutorio m.
parlour game, (US) parlor — ['pɑ:ləgeim] n juego m de salón.
parlourmaid, (US) parlor— ['pɑ:ləmeid] n camarera f.
parlous ['pɑ:ləs] adj state lamentable, crítico, pésimo.
Parnassus [pɑ:'næsəs] Parnaso m.
parochial [pə'rəukiəl] adj (Eccl) parroquial; (fig) estrecho, limitado, restringido; de miras estrechas.
parochialism [pə'rəukiəlizm] n (fig) estrechez f, lo limitado, lo restringido; estrechez f de miras.
parodist ['pærədist] n parodista mf.
parody ['pærədi] 1 n parodia f. 2 vt parodiar.
parole [pə'rəul] 1 n (promise) palabra f, palabra f de honor; (freedom) libertad f bajo palabra, libertad f condicional; **to be on —** estar libre bajo palabra; **to break one's —** faltar a su palabra; **to put someone on —** dejar a uno libre bajo palabra.
2 vt dejar libre bajo palabra.
paroxysm ['pærəksizm] n paroxismo m.
parquet ['pɑ:kei] n parquet m, parqué m (Acad); entarimado m de hojas quebradas.
parquetry ['pɑ:kitri] n entarimado m, obra f de entarimado.
parricide ['pærisaid] n (act) parricidio m; (person) parricida mf.
parrot ['pærət] 1 n loro m, papagayo m. 2 vt words repetir como un loro, (person) imitar como un loro.
parrot fashion ['pærət,fæʃən] adv learn etc mecánicamente.
parry ['pæri] vt (Fencing) parar, quitar; blow parar, desviar; attack rechazar, defenderse de; (fig) esquivar, eludir, desviar hábilmente.
parse [pɑ:z] vt (Gram) analizar.
Parsee [pɑ:'si:] n parsi mf.
parsimonious [ˌpɑ:si'məuniəs] adj parco; escaso, corto; frugal.
parsimoniously [ˌpɑ:si'məuniəsli] adv parcamente; escasamente; frugalmente.
parsimony ['pɑ:siməni] n parquedad f; escasez f; frugalidad f.
parsley ['pɑ:sli] n perejil m.
parsnip ['pɑ:snip] n chirivía f.
parson ['pɑ:sn] n clérigo m, cura m; (esp) párroco m.
parsonage ['pɑ:snidʒ] n casa f del cura, casa f del párroco.
parsonical [pɑ:'sɔnikəl] adj (hum) frailuno.
part [pɑ:t] 1 n (a) (portion, fragment) parte f; porción f; trozo m; **this — is blue** esta parte es azul; **the funny — of it is that . . .** lo gracioso es que . . .; **you haven't heard the best —** yet todavía no te he dicho lo mejor; **that's the awkward —** eso es lo difícil; **private —s, privy —s** partes fpl pudendas; **it is — and parcel of the scheme** es parte esencial del proyecto, es parte integrante del proyecto; **the book is good in —s** el libro es bueno solamente en parte, hay partes del libro que son buenas; **the greater — of it is done** la mayor parte está hecha; **this is in great — due to . . .** esto se debe ante todo a . . ., más que nada esto se debe a . . .; **for the better —, of the day** durante la mayor parte del día; **in the latter**

— **of the year** en los últimos meses del año; **in** —
en parte; **it is ready in** — en parte está listo; **to pay
a debt in** — pagar parte de una deuda; **5** —**s of
sand to 1 of cement** 5 partes de arena y 1 de cemento;
three —**s** tres cuartos; **it's 3** —**s gone** las tres cuartas
partes se han usado ya.

    (b) (*Mech*) pieza *f*; **moving** — pieza *f* móvil;
spare — pieza *f* de recambio, recambio *m*.

    (c) (*Gram*) parte *f*; — **of speech** parte *f* de la
oración; **principal** —**s of a verb** partes *fpl* principales
de un verbo.

    (d) (*of journal*) fascículo *m*, número *m*; (*of series*)
tomo *m*; (*of serial*) entrega *f*.

    (e) (*share*) parte *f*; **to do one's** — cumplir con
sus obligaciones; **each one did his** — cada uno
colaboró perfectamente; **to have no** — **in something**
(*not be active*) no participar en algo, (*have nothing
to do with*) no tener nada que ver con algo, ser ajeno
a algo, desentenderse de algo; **he had no** — **in stealing
it** él no ayudó a robarlo, él no intervino en el robo;
to take (a) — **in** tomar parte en, intervenir en,
participar en; **are you taking** —? ¿vas a tomar parte?

    (f) (*Theat and fig*) papel *m*; **bit** —, **small** —
papel *m* pequeño; **it is not my** — **to** + *infin* no me
toca a mí + *infin*; **to look the** — vestir el cargo;
to play a — hacer un papel, (*fig*) desempeñar un
papel; **what** — **do you play?** ¿qué papel haces?;
he's just playing a — está haciendo un papel, nada
más; **the climate has played a** — **in** + *ger* el clima
ha contribuido a + *infin*.

    (g) (*Mus*) parte *f*; **the soprano** — la parte de
soprano; **to sing in** —**s** cantar por partes.

    (h) —**s** (*Geog*) lugar *m*; comarca *f*, región *f*;
from all —**s** de todas partes; **in these** —**s** por aquí;
the biggest thief in these —**s** el mayor ladrón en
estos contornos; **in foreign** —**s** en el extranjero;
what — **are you from?** ¿de dónde es Vd?; **he's not
from these** —**s** no es de aquí; **it's a lovely** — es una
región hermosa.

    (i) (*side*) parte *f*; **for my** —, **on my** — por mi
parte; **a mistake on the** — **of** . . . un error por parte
de . . ., un error debido a . . .; **on the one** — . . ., **on
the other** . . . por una parte . . ., por otra . . .; **there
is opposition on the** — **of some** hay oposición por
parte de algunos; **to take someone's** — defender
a uno, tomar el partido de uno.

    (j) **to take something in good** — tomar algo en
buena parte.

    (k) **a man of** —**s** un hombre de talento.

  2 *adv*: — **one and** — **the other** parte esto y parte
lo otro; **it is** — **brass and** — **copper** parte es latón y
parte es cobre; **it was** — **eaten** había sido comido en
parte.

  3 *adj* parcial; **co** . . ., **con** . . ., *eg* **part-author**
coautor *m*, ora *f*; **part-owner** condueño *m*, a *f*;
copropietario *m*, a *f*.

  4 *vt* separar, dividir (*from* de); (*break*) romper,
partir; **to** — **something in two** partir algo en dos;
he —**ed the grass with his hand** con la mano apartó
la hierba; **to** — **one's hair** hacerse la raya.

  5 *vi* (a) (*of crowd etc*) apartarse; **the branches** —**ed**
se apartaron las ramas; **the people** —**ed to let her
through** la gente se hizo a un lado para dejarla
pasar.

    (b) (*of 2 persons*) separarse; **they** —**ed 5 years
ago** se separaron hace 5 años; **the best of friends
must** — los mejores amigos han de separarse alguna
vez; **to** — **from someone** separarse de uno, despedirse de uno; **when we** —**ed from Seville** cuando
nos despedimos de Sevilla.

    (c) (*roads etc*) bifurcarse.

    (d) (*snap, break*) romperse; (*fall away*) separarse,
desprenderse.

    (e) **to** — **with** ceder, entregar; (*money*) pagar,
dar; (*get rid of*) deshacerse de; **I hate** —**ing with it**
siento mucho tener que cederlo, me da pena perderlo.

partake [pɑː'teik] (*irr: see* **take**) *vti* (a) **to** — **of** *food*
comer, comer de, aceptar; *drink* tomar, beber; **do
you** —? ¿bebes vino? (*etc*); **will you** —? ¿quieres de
esto?

    (b) **to** — **of a quality** tener algo de una cualidad,
tener rasgos de una cualidad.

    (c) **to** — **in** tomar parte en, participar en; **are you
partaking?** ¿vas a tomar parte?

part exchange ['pɑːtiks'tʃeindʒ] *n*: **to offer something
in** — ofrecer algo como parte del pago; **"we take
your old car in** —**"** "admitimos su coche usado a
cambio".

parthenogenesis ['pɑːθinəu'dʒenisis] *n* partenso-
génesis *f*.

partial ['pɑːʃəl] *adj* parcial; **to be** — **to something**
ser aficionado a algo, tener gusto por algo.

partiality [,pɑːʃi'æliti] *n* parcialidad *f*; — **for,** — **to**
afición *f* a, gusto *m* por.

partially ['pɑːʃəli] *adv* (*partly*) parcialmente, en
parte; (*with bias*) con parcialidad.

participant [pɑː'tisipənt] *n* partícipe *mf*; (*in competition*) concursante *mf*; (*in fight*) combatiente *mf*.

participate [pɑː'tisipeit] *vi* participar, tomar parte
(*in* en).

participation [pɑː,tisi'peiʃən] *n* participación *f*.

participial [,pɑːti'sipiəl] *adj* participial.

participle ['pɑːtisipl] *n* participio *m*; **past** — participio *m* de pasado; **present** — participio *m* de
presente.

particle ['pɑːtikl] *n* partícula *f*; (*of dust etc*) átomo *m*,
grano *m*; (*fig*) pizca *f*; **there's not a** — **of truth in it**
eso no tiene ni pizca de verdad.

parti-coloured, (*US*) **-colored** ['pɑːti,kʌləd] *adj* de
diversos colores, abigarrado.

particular [pə'tikjulə*] **1** *adj* (a) (*special*) particular;
especial; concreto; determinado; individual; **that** —
person esa persona (y no otra); **a** — **thing** una cosa
determinada; **in** — **cases** en algunos casos; en casos
especiales; **it varies according to the** — **case** varía
según el caso individual; **in this** — **case** en este caso
concreto; **for no** — **reason** por ninguna razón
especial; **to take** — **care** tomar especial cuidado, ser
especialmente cuidadoso.

    (b) *account etc* detallado, minucioso.

    (c) (*fastidious*) exigente, quisquilloso (*about, as
to, as to what* en cuanto a, en asuntos de, para);
(*scrupulous*) escrupuloso; (*about food etc*) delicado;
he's — **about his food** es delicado para la comida;
he is very — **about cleanliness** es muy exigente para
la limpieza; **he's** — **about his car** cuida mucho del
coche; **I'm** — **about my friends** escojo mis amigos
con cierto cuidado; **I'm not too** — (**about it**) lo
mismo da, me es igual; **he was most** — **about it**
insistió mucho sobre esto; **he was very** — **to say
that** . . . subrayó que . . ., dijo con toda claridad
que . . .

  2 *n* detalle *m*, pormenor *m*, dato *m*; —**s** detalles
mpl; **in this** — en este caso particular; **correct in
every** — correcto en todos los detalles; **for further**
—**s apply to** . . . para más informes escriban a . . .;
to give —**s** citar los detalles; **please give full** —**s**
se ruega hacer constar todos los detalles, se ruega
dar un informe pormenorizado.

particularity [pə,tikju'læriti] *n* particularidad *f*.

particularize [pə'tikjuləraiz] **1** *vt* particularizar,
especificar, señalar; **he did not** — **which one he
wanted** no dijo de modo concreto cuál quería.

  2 *vi* dar todos los detalles, concretar; **he did not** —
no concretó.

particularly [pə'tikjuləli] *adv*: **this is** — **true of** . . .
esto es especialmente verdad por lo que se refiere
a . . .; **notice** — **that** . . . observen Vds sobre todo
que . . .; **he said most** — **not to do it** dijo de modo
particular que no se hiciera; **do you want it** — **for
tomorrow?** ¿lo necesita Vd especialmente para
mañana?; **he was not** — **pleased** no se puso loco de
contento que digamos; **not** —**!** ¡no mucho!

parting ['pɑːtiŋ] **1** *adj* de despedida; **a** — **present**
un regalo de despedida; **his** — **words** sus palabras al
despedirse; **he made a** — **threat** al separarse de
nosotros pronunció una amenaza.

  2 *n* separación *f*; despedida *f*; (*in hair*) raya *f*; **the**
— **of the ways** el momento de la separación, (*fig*) el
punto decisivo.

partisan [,pɑːti'zæn] **1** *adj* partidista; (*Mil*) de
partisanos, de guerrilleros; — **warfare** guerra *f* de
guerrilleros; — **spirit** partidismo *m*.

  2 *n* partidario *m*, a *f*, (*of* de); (*Mil*) partisano *m*,
guerrillero *m*.

partisanship [,pɑːti'zænʃip] *n* partidismo *m*.

partition [pɑː'tiʃən] **1** *n* (a) partición *f*, división *f*; **the**
— **of Poland** la división de Polonia.

    (b) (*wall*) tabique *m*; **glass** — tabique *m* de
vidrio; **wooden** — tabique *m* de madera.

  2 *vt* (a) *country etc* partir, dividir; (*share*) repartir
(*among* entre).

    (b) *room etc* tabicar, dividir con tabique; **to** —
a part off separar una parte con tabique.

partitive ['pɑːtitiv] *adj* partitivo.

partly ['pɑːtli] *adv* en parte; en cierto modo; **only** —
true verdad sólo en parte; **it was** — **destroyed**
quedaba destruido en parte.

partner ['pɑːtnə*] **1** *n* compañero *m*, a *f* (*also Cards*);
(*Comm*) socio *m*, a *f*; (*in dance, at tennis etc*) pareja *f*;
(*in crime*) codelincuente *mf*; (*spouse*) cónyuge *mf*;
junior — socio *m* menos antiguo; **senior** — socio *m*

más antiguo; **sleeping —, silent —** (US) socio m comanditario.

2 vt acompañar; **to be —ed by** ir acompañado de; tener a uno por pareja (etc).

partnership ['pɑːtnəʃip] n asociación f, (Comm) sociedad f; (of spouses) vida f conyugal, vida f en común; **to enter into —, to form a —** asociarse (with con); **to take someone into —** tomar a uno como socio.

part owner ['pɑːt'əunə*] n condueño m, a f, copropietario m, a f.

part payment ['pɑːt'peimənt] n: **to offer something in —** ofrecer algo como parte del pago.

partridge ['pɑːtridʒ] n perdiz f.

part song ['pɑːtsɔŋ] n canción f a varias voces.

part-time ['pɑːt'taim] **1** adv: **to work —** trabajar parte de la jornada. **2** adj person en dedicación parcial, que trabaja por horas; work por horas.

parturition [ˌpɑːtjuə'riʃən] n parturición f.

party ['pɑːti] **1** n (a) (Pol) partido m; **Communist P—** Partido m Comunista; **Conservative P—** Partido m Conservador; **Labour P—** Partido m Laborista; **Liberal P—** Partido m Liberal; **Socialist P—** Partido m Socialista; **to be a member of the —** ser miembro del partido; **to join the —** hacerse miembro del partido.

(b) (group) grupo m; (Mil) pelotón m, destacamento m; **a — of travellers** un grupo de viajeros; **boarding —** pelotón m de abordaje; **hunting —** partida f de caza; **we were a — of 5** éramos un grupo de 5; **we were only a small —** éramos pocos; **I was one of the —** yo formaba parte del grupo; **to join someone's —** unirse al grupo de uno.

(c) (gathering) reunión f; (tea— etc) tertulia f; (merry) fiesta f, guateque m; **birthday —** fiesta f para festejar el cumpleaños de uno; **bottle —** guateque m al que cada invitado contribuye una botella; **Christmas —** fiesta f en época de Navidades; **evening —** velada f; **private —** fiesta f particular; **that little — at El Alamein** (fam) la fiestecita de El Alamein; **that was quite a —!** ¡eso fue de miedo!; **to crash a —** (fam) colarse, entrar de gorra; **to give a —** ofrecer una fiesta, organizar una fiesta; **to go to a —** ir a una fiesta.

(d) (Law etc) parte f; interesado m, a f; **third —** tercera persona f, tercero m; **the parties to a dispute** las partes de una disputa, los interesados; **the high contracting parties** las altas partes contratantes; **to be a — to an agreement** firmar un acuerdo; **to be a — to a crime** ser cómplice en un crimen; **were you a — to this?** ¿tuvo Vd algo que ver con esto?; **I will not be a — to any violence** no quiero tener nada que ver con la violencia; **I will not be a — to any such attempt** yo no me presto a ninguna tentativa de ese tipo.

(e) (fam) individuo m; **a — of the name of Pérez** un individuo llamado Pérez.

2 attr (a) (Pol) de partido; **— politics** política f de partidos, (pej) partidismo m, politiqueo m.

(b) dress etc de gala, para fiestas.

parvenu ['pɑːvənjuː] n arribista mf.

pas de deux ['pɑːdə'dəː] n paso m a dos.

pasha ['pæʃə] n bajá m, pachá m.

pass[1] [pɑːs] n (Geog) puerto m; (small) desfiladero m; **the —es through the Guadarrama** los puertos del Guadarrama; **to sell the —** traicionar la causa; ceder lo que bien podría ser defendido.

pass[2] [pɑːs] **1** n (a) (permit) permiso m; (Mil etc) salvoconducto m; (of journalist, worker etc) permiso m; (Theat) entrada f de favor; (Rail etc) billete m de favor; (membership card) carnet m.

(b) (Sport, Fencing, by conjuror, mesmerist) pase m; **forward —** pase m adelantado.

(c) (in exams) aprobado m, nota f de aprobado; **to get a — in German** aprobar en alemán; **I need a — in physics still** todavía tengo que aprobar la física.

(d) **things have come to a pretty —** las cosas han llegado a una situación crítica, estamos en una situación crítica; **it came to — that ...** sucedió que.

(e) **to make a — at someone** echar un tiento a una, requebrar de amores a una.

2 vt (a) (move past) pasar; pasar por delante de; person (on street etc) cruzarse con; competitor alcanzar y dejar atrás; (Aut: overtake) pasar, adelantar a; **they —ed each other on the way** se cruzaron en el camino; **we are now —ing the Tower of London** pasamos ahora delante de la Torre de Londres.

(b) (cross) frontier etc cruzar.

(c) **it —es belief** es increíble (that que); **it —es**

my comprehension that ... para mí resulta incomprensible que ...

(d) (Univ etc) exam aprobar, ser aprobado en.

(e) censor ser aprobado por, critic merecer la aprobación de.

(f) (approve) motion, plan, candidate etc aprobar; **to — someone fit** dar a uno de alta; **to — someone for the army** declarar a uno apto para el servicio militar.

(g) ball etc pasar; **to — something from hand to hand** pasar algo de mano a mano; **— me the salt, please** ¿me hace el favor de pasar la sal?

(h) false coin pasar.

(i) **to — a cloth over something** limpiar algo con un paño, frotar algo con un trapo; **to — one's hand between two bars** introducir la mano entre dos rejas.

(j) (spend) time pasar; **we —ed the weekend pleasantly** pasamos el fin de semana de modo muy agradable; **just to — the time** para pasar el rato; **I —ed the time of day with him** me detuve un rato a charlar con él, cambié algunas palabras con él.

(k) remark hacer; opinion expresar; sentence pronunciar, dictar (on sobre, en el asunto de).

(l) (with adv or prep) **to — along** pasar de uno a otro; **to — by** no hacer caso de, no fijarse en, pasar por alto; **to — down** pasar; **to — off** coin pasar; offence disimular; **to — something off as a joke** hacer creer que algo se había dicho (etc) para hacer reír, hacer ver el aspecto gracioso de algo; **to — on** (hand down) pasar, transmitir; message dar, decir, comunicar; **to — out** distribuir; **to — over** (omit) pasar por alto, omitir; **he was —ed over again for promotion** en los ascensos volvieron a postergarle; **I think we can — that bit over** creo que podemos excusar ese trozo; **to — round** pasar de uno a otro; **to — up** claim renunciar a, opportunity no aprovechar.

3 vi (a) (come, go) pasar; **to — into a tunnel** entrar en un túnel; **to — into oblivion** ser olvidado; **to — out of sight** perderse de vista; **the funeral —ed slowly by** el entierro pasó lentamente; **— along the car please!** ¡vayan pasando por delante!; **words —ed between them** se cambiaron algunas palabras (fuertes); **no money has —ed** ningún dinero ha cambiado de dueño; **to let something —** no hacer caso de algo, no protestar contra algo; **we can't let that —!** ¡eso no lo podemos consentir!; **let it —** conviene dejarlo, conviene no protestar.

(b) (of time) pasar (also **to — by**); **how time —es!** ¡cómo pasa el tiempo!

(c) (disappear) pasar; desaparecer; (clouds etc) disiparse; **it'll —** eso pasará, eso se olvidará.

(d) (be acceptable) ser aceptable, aprobarse; **what —es in New York may not be good enough here** lo que se aprueba en Nueva York puede resultar inaceptable aquí.

(e) (be considered as) **it —es for a restaurant** pasa por ser restaurante; **in her day she —ed for a great beauty** en sus tiempos se le consideraba una gran belleza; **or what —es nowadays for a hat** o lo que se llama sombrero hoy día.

(f) (Univ etc) aprobar, ser aprobado; **I —ed!** ¡aprobé!; **did you — in chemistry?** ¿aprobaste en química?

(g) (with adv or prep) **to — away** pasar, desaparecer; olvidarse; (euph: die) fallecer; **to — by** (adv) pasar de largo; **to — by** (prep) pasar delante de, pasar cerca de; **to — off** pasar, desaparecer; **to — on** pasar adelante; (euph: die) fallecer; **to — out** salir (of de); **to — out from military college** graduarse en la escuela militar; **to — out** (fam) caer rodando, perder el conocimiento; **to — through** (adv) pasar; **to — through** (prep) pasar por.

4 vr: **to — oneself off as** hacerse pasar por.

passable ['pɑːsəbl] adj (tolerable) pasable; (usable, crossable) transitable.

passably ['pɑːsəbli] adv medianamente, pasablemente.

passage ['pæsidʒ] n (a) (act of passing) paso m, tránsito m; (voyage) viaje m, travesía f; (fare) pasaje m; (Parl: process) trámites mpl, (final) aprobación f; **the — of time** el paso del tiempo; **in the — of time** andando el tiempo, con el tiempo; see work 2 (g).

(b) (corridor) pasillo m, galería f, pasadizo m; (alley) callejón m; (Mech) tubo m, conducto m; (Anat) tubo m; **secret —** galería f secreta.

(c) **— of arms** combate m.

(d) (Lit, Mus etc) pasaje m; trozo m; episodio m, sección f; **"selected —s from Caesar"** "selecciones de César"; **purple —** trozo m de estilo hinchado, trozo m demasiado sentimental.

passage money ['pæsidʒ,mʌni] n (Naut) pasaje m.
passageway ['pæsidʒwei] n pasillo m, galería f, pasadizo m.
passbook ['pɑːsbuk] n libreta f de banco.
passé ['pæsei] adj pasado de moda.
passenger ['pæsindʒə*] 1 n pasajero m, a f; viajero m, a f; **will —s please rejoin the train?** ¡señores viajeros, al tren! **2** attr aircraft, train de pasajeros.
passenger miles ['pæsindʒə'mailz] npl millas-pasajero fpl.
passe-partout ['pæspɑːtuː] n paspartú m.
passer-by ['pɑːsə'bai] n, pl **passers-by** ['pɑːsəz'bai] transeúnte mf.
passing ['pɑːsiŋ] **1** adj (fleeting) pasajero; glance etc rápido, superficial; **a — car** un coche que pasaba.
2 n paso m; (Parl) aprobación f; (disappearance) desaparición f; (euph: death) fallecimiento m; **in —** de paso, de pasada.
passing bell ['pɑːsiŋbel] n toque m de difuntos.
passion ['pæʃən] **1** n (anger) cólera f, arranque m de cólera; **the P—** la Pasión; **ruling —** pasión f dominante; **he said with —** dijo con pasión; **political —s are strong here** aquí son muy fuertes las pasiones políticas; **to be in a —** estar encolerizado; **to burst** (or fly) **into a —** montar en cólera, encolerizarse; **to conceive a — for someone** enamorarse con verdadera pasión de uno; **I have a — for shellfish** tengo pasión por los mariscos, me apasionan los mariscos.
passionate ['pæʃənit] adj embrace, speech, temperament etc apasionado; believer, desire vehemente, ardiente; (angry) colérico.
passionately ['pæʃənitli] adv apasionadamente, con pasión; con vehemencia, ardientemente; colérica-mente; **to love someone —** amar a uno con pasión.
passionflower ['pæʃən,flauə*] n pasionaria f.
passionfruit ['pæʃənfruːt] n granadilla f.
passionless ['pæʃənlis] adj affair etc sin pasión, frío; (dispassionate) imparcial.
passion play ['pæʃən,plei] n drama m de la Pasión.
passive ['pæsiv] **1** adj passive (also Gram); inactivo, inerte. **2** n (Gram) voz f pasiva.
passively ['pæsivli] adv pasivamente.
passiveness ['pæsivnis] n, **passivity** [pæ'siviti] n pasividad f; inercia f.
passkey ['pɑːskiː] n llave f maestra.
Passover ['pɑːsəuvə*] n Pascua f (de los judíos).
passport ['pɑːspɔːt] n pasaporte m.
password ['pɑːswɜːd] n santo m y seña.
past [pɑːst] **1** adv por delante; **to fly —** pasar volando; **to rush —** pasar precipitadamente; **he went — without stopping** pasó sin detenerse; **she walked slowly —** pasó despacio.
2 prep (a) (of place: in front of) por delante de; (beyond) más allá de; **just — the town hall** un poco más allá del Ayuntamiento; **to run — someone** pasar delante de uno corriendo; alcanzar y pasar a uno corriendo.
(b) (with numbers) más de; **we're — 100 already** hemos contado más de 100 ya; **she's — 40** tiene más de 40 años.
(c) (with time) después de; **10 — 3** las 3 y 10; **half — 4** las 4 y media; **at a quarter — 9** a las 9 y cuarto; **it's — 12** dieron las 12 ya.
(d) (other expressions) **it is — belief** es increíble; **it is — endurance** es intolerable; **we're — caring** eso ya nos trae sin cuidado, ya no tenemos por qué preocuparnos de eso; **he's — it** ya no puede, ya no tiene fuerzas para eso; **I wouldn't put it — him** le creo capaz hasta de eso.
3 adj pasado (also Gram); (former) antiguo, ex . . ., que fue; master etc consumado; **for some time —** de algún tiempo a esta parte; **in times —** en otro tiempo, antiguamente; **all that is now —** todo eso ha quedado ya a la espalda; **in — years** en otros años, en estos últimos años; **— president of . . .** antiguo presidente de . . ., ex presidente de . . ., presidente que fue de . . .
4 n el pasado (also Gram), lo pasado; (early history) historia f, antecedentes mpl; **in the —** en el pasado, antes, antiguamente; **as we did in the —** como hacíamos antes; **it's a thing of the —** eso pertenece a la historia; **silent pictures are things of the —** las películas mudas han quedado anticuadas; **that belongs to my murky —** eso pertenece a mi turbio pasado; **what's his —?** ¿cuáles son sus ante-cedentes?; **a town with a —** una ciudad de abolengo histórico, una ciudad llena de historia; **she's a woman with a —** es una mujer que tiene historia.
paste [peist] **1** n (material in general) pasta f; (for sticking) engrudo m; (fish-) pasta f; (gems) diamante m de imitación, bisutería f.
2 vt (apply — to) engrudar; engomar; (affix, stick

together) pegar; (beat: sl) pegar, (Sport) cascar, dar una paliza a; **to — something to a wall** pegar algo a una pared; **to — up a notice** pegar un anuncio.
pasteboard ['peistbɔːd] **1** n cartón m, cartulina f. **2** attr de cartón, de cartulina.
pastel ['pæstəl] **1** n (material) pastel m; (drawing etc) pintura f al pastel. **2** attr: **— drawing** pintura f al pastel; **— shade** tono m pastel.
pastern ['pæstən] n cuartilla f (del caballo).
pasteurization [,pæstərai'zeiʃən] n pasteurización f.
pasteurize ['pæstəraiz] vt pasteurizar.
pasteurized ['pæstəraizd] adj pasteurizado.
pastiche [pæs'tiːʃ] n imitación f; **a Mozart —** una imitación de Mozart, una obra hecha a la manera de Mozart.
pastille ['pæstil] n pastilla f.
pastime ['pɑːstaim] n pasatiempo m.
pasting ['peistiŋ] n (sl) paliza f; **to give someone a —** dar una paliza a uno; **he got a — from the critics** los críticos le dieron una paliza.
pastor ['pɑːstə*] n pastor m.
pastoral ['pɑːstərəl] **1** adj economy pastoral; (Eccl) pastoral; (Lit) pastoril. **2** n (Eccl) pastoral f.
pastry ['peistri] n (dough) pasta f; (collectively) pastas fpl, pasteles mpl; (art) pastelería f; **pastries** pastas fpl, pasteles mpl.
pastrycook ['peistrikuk] n pastelero m, a f, repostero m, a f.
pastry shop ['peistriʃɔp] n pastelería f, repostería f.
pasturage ['pɑːstjuridʒ] n see **pasture 1.**
pasture ['pɑːstʃə*] **1** n (grass) pasto m; (land) pasto m, prado m, dehesa f. **2** vt animals apacentar, pastorear; grass comer, pacer. **3** vi pastar, pacer.
pasture land ['pɑːstʃəlænd] n pasto m, prado m, dehesa f.
pasty ['peisti] adj material pastoso; colour pálido; **to look —** estar pálido.
pasty ['pæsti] n pastel m (de carne), empanada f.
pasty-faced ['peisti,feist] adj pálido, de cara pálida.
Pat [pæt] nombre cariñoso de **Patricia, Patrick.**
pat[1] [pæt] **1** n (with hand) palmadita f, golpecito m; (on shoulder) palmada f; (caress) caricia f; (of butter) pastelillo m; **to give someone a — on the back** dar a uno una palmada en la espalda, (fig) pronunciar unas palabras elogiosas para uno, felicitar a uno; **to give oneself a — on the back** felicitarse a sí mismo.
2 vt (touch) tocar, pasar la mano por, posar la mano sobre; (tap, with hand) dar una palmadita en, shoulder dar una palmada en; dog etc acariciar; **he —ted the chair with the book** tocó la silla con el libro; **he —ted his secretary's bottom** le dio un azotito a su secretaria; **to — someone on the back** dar a uno una palmada en la espalda, (fig) pro-nunciar unas palabras elogiosas para uno, felicitar a uno.
3 vr: **to — oneself on the back** (fig) felicitarse a sí mismo.
pat[2] [pæt] **1** adv: **he knows it (off) —** lo sabe al dedillo; **he always has an excuse just —** siempre le es fácil encontrar un modo convincente de disculparse; **the answer came too —** dio su respuesta con demasiada prontitud; **to stand —** mantenerse firme.
2 adj answer etc oportuno, a propósito; pronto; convincente.
patch [pætʃ] **1** n (piece of cloth etc) pedazo m; (mend) remiendo m; (on tyre, wound) parche m; (beauty spot) lunar m postizo; (stain etc) mancha f; (small area) pedazo m, pequeña extensión f; (Agr) terreno m, parcela f; **a — of oil** una mancha de aceite; **a — of blue flowers** una masa de flores azules, una extensión de flores azules; **a — of blue sky** un pedazo de cielo azul; **purple —** trozo m de estilo hinchado, pasaje m demasiado sentimental; **the team is having a bad —** el equipo pasa por un momento difícil; **we have had our bad —es** hemos tenido nuestros momentos malos; **then we hit a bad — of road** dimos luego con un tramo de carretera bastante malo; **it's not a — on the other one** no se puede comparar con el otro, no está a la altura del otro.
2 vt remendar, poner remiendo a; **to — something up** componer algo de modo provisional; **we'll see if we can — something up for you** trataremos de arreglarlo para Vd; **to — up a quarrel** hacer las paces (with con).
patchwork ['pætʃwɜːk] n labor f de retazos; **— quilt** colchón m; **a — of fields** una confusa multitud de campos.
patchy ['pætʃi] adj desigual, poco uniforme; pattern etc manchado.
pate [peit] n mollera f.

pâté ['pɑ:teɪ] n pastel m (de carne etc); — **de foie gras** pastelillo m de hígado de ganso.

patella [pə'telə] n rótula f.

paten ['pætən] n patena f.

patent ['peitənt] 1 adj patente, evidente, palmario; (Comm) de patente, patentado; see **leather** etc.
2 n patente f; — **applied for** se ha solicitado patente; **to take out a** — obtener una patente.
3 attr de patentes; — **agent** agente m de patentes; — **office** oficina f de patentes.
4 vt patentar.

patentee [ˌpeitən'ti:] n poseedor m de patente.

patently ['peitəntli] adv evidentemente, a las claras; **a** — **untrue statement** una declaración de evidente falsedad.

pater ['peitə*] n: **the** — (fam) el páter.

paterfamilias ['peitəfə'miliæs] n padre m de familia.

paternal [pə'tə:nl] adj quality paternal; relation paterno.

paternalism [pə'tə:nəlizəm] n gobierno m paternal.

paternally [pə'tə:nəli] adv paternalmente; **he said** — dijo paternal.

paternity [pə'tə:niti] n paternidad f.

paternoster ['pætə'nɔstə*] n padrenuestro m.

path [pɑ:θ] n, pl **paths** [pɑ:ðz] senda f, sendero m, vereda f; (fig) camino m; trayectoria f, curso m; (person's track) pista f; (of bullet) trayectoria f; (of hurricane etc) rastro m, marcha f; **the** — **to power** el camino del poder; **the beaten** — el camino trillado; **to cross someone's** — tropezar con uno; crear dificultades a uno; **to keep to the straight and narrow** — ir por la vereda, no apartarse del buen camino; **to lead someone up the garden** — embaucar a uno, hacer que uno se crea ilusiones; **to smoothe someone's** — **for him** allanarle el camino a uno.

pathetic [pə'θetik] adj (a) patético, lastimoso, conmovedor; **a** — **sight** una escena lastimosa; **a** — **creature** un infeliz, un pobre hombre; **it was** — **to see it** daba pena verlo.
(b) (very bad) horrible, malísimo; —, **isn't it?** ¿es horrible, no?; **it was a** — **performance** fue una exhibición que daba pena.

pathetically [pə'θetikli] adv patéticamente, lastimosamente; **a** — **inadequate answer** una respuesta tan poco satisfactoria que daba pena.

pathfinder ['pɑ:θ,faində*] n explorador m, piloto m.

pathological [ˌpæθə'lɔdʒikəl] adj patológico.

pathologist [pə'θɔlədʒist] n patólogo m.

pathology [pə'θɔlədʒi] n patología f.

pathos ['peiθɔs] n patetismo m, lo patético.

pathway ['pɑ:θwei] n see **path**.

patience ['peiʃəns] n paciencia f; (Cards) solitario m; **my** — **is exhausted** se me acaba la paciencia, no tengo más paciencia; **you must have** — hay que tener paciencia; **I have no** — **with you** ya no aguanto más, estoy para desesperarme; **to lose one's** — perder la paciencia; **to possess one's soul in** — tener muchísima paciencia; **she taxes** (or **tries**) **my** — **very much** me cuesta no impacientarme con ella.

patient ['peiʃənt] 1 adj paciente; sufrido; **to be** — **with someone** ser paciente con uno; **you must be very** — **about it** hay que tener mucha paciencia; **we have been** — **long enough!** ¡ya no aguantamos más!
2 n paciente mf, enfermo m, a f.

patiently ['peiʃəntli] adv pacientemente, con paciencia.

patina ['pætinə] n pátina f.

patio ['pætiəu] n patio m.

patois ['pætwɑ:] n dialecto m.

patriarch ['peitriɑ:k] n patriarca m.

patriarchal [ˌpeitri'ɑ:kəl] adj patriarcal.

patriarchy ['peitriɑ:ki] n patriarcado m.

Patricia [pə'triʃə] f Patricia.

patrician [pə'triʃən] 1 adj patricio. 2 n patricio m, a f.

Patrick ['pætrik] m Patricio.

patrimony ['pætriməni] n patrimonio m.

patriot ['peitriət] n patriota mf.

patriotic [ˌpætri'ɔtik] adj patriótico.

patriotically [ˌpætri'ɔtikəli] adv patrióticamente.

patriotism ['pætriətizəm] n patriotismo m.

patrol [pə'trəul] 1 n patrulla f; **to be on** — estar de patrulla, patrullar.
2 vt (a) patrullar por; frontier etc guardar, defender; **they** — **ed the streets at night** patrullaban por las calles de noche; **the frontier is not** — **led** la frontera no tiene patrullas.
(b) (fig) rondar, pasearse por.
3 vi (a) patrullar.
(b) (fig) rondar, pasearse; **he** — **s up and down** se pasea de un lado a otro.

patrol boat [pə'trəulbəut] n patrullero m; bote m patrullero.

patrol car [pə'trəulkɑ:*] n coche m patrulla.

patrol leader [pə'trəul,li:də*] n jefe m de patrulla.

patrolman [pə'trəulmən] n, pl —**men** [mən] (US) guardia m, policía m.

patron ['peitrən] n (Comm) parroquiano m, a f, cliente mf; (of enterprise) patrocinador m; (Lit, Art) mecenas m; (Eccl, also — **saint**) patrono m, patrona f.

patronage ['pætrənidʒ] n (of enterprise) patrocinio m; (Lit, Art) mecenazgo m, protección f; (Eccl) patronato m; **under the** — **of** bajo el patronato de, patrocinado por, bajo los auspicios de.

patronize ['pætrənaiz] vt shop ser parroquiano de, comprar cosas en; services etc usar, utilizar; enterprise patrocinar, favorecer, fomentar, apoyar; (treat condescendingly) tratar con aire protector; **the shop is well** —**d** la tienda tiene mucha parroquia, la tienda está muy acreditada.

patronizing ['pætrənaiziŋ] adj protector.

patronizingly ['pætrənaiziŋli] adv protectoramente, con aire protector.

patronymic [ˌpætrə'nimik] 1 adj patronímico. 2 n patronímico m.

patten ['pætn] n zueco m, chanclo m.

patter[1] ['pætə*] 1 n (jargon) jerga f; (of salesman) jerga f publicitaria; (rapid speech) parloteo m; **the fellow has some very clever** — el tío tiene unos argumentos muy hábiles, hablando el tío es muy listo.
2 vi charlar, parlotear (also **to** — **on**; **about** de).

patter[2] ['pætə*] 1 n (of feet) pasos mpl ligeros, ruido m sordo; (taps) golpecitos mpl; golpeteo m; (of rain) tamborileo m.
2 vi andar con pasos ligeros, pisar con ruido sordo (also **to** — **about**); (rain) tamborilear; **he** —**ed over to the door** fue con pasos ligeros a la puerta.

pattern ['pætən] 1 n modelo m; (sample) muestra f; (design) diseño m, dibujo m; (Sew) patrón m; (fig) pauta f, norma f; **on the** — **of** sobre el modelo de, según el diseño de; **it set a** — **for other conferences** estableció una pauta para otros congresos; **it·is following the usual** — se está desarrollando como siempre, sigue la norma.
2 vt modelar (on sobre), diseñar (on según).

pattern book ['pætənbuk] n libro m de muestras.

pattern maker ['pætən,meikə*] n carpintero m modelista.

patty ['pæti] n empanada f.

paucity ['pɔ:siti] n escasez f, insuficiencia f, corto número m; **there is a** — **of money** hay poco dinero; **because of the** — **of new films** debido a la escasez de películas nuevas.

Paul [pɔ:l] m Pablo; (Saint) Pablo; (Pope) Paulo.

Pauline ['pɔ:lain] adj: **the** — **Epistles** las Epístolas de San Pablo.

Pauline ['pɔ:li:n] f Paulina.

paunch [pɔ:ntʃ] 1 n panza f, barriga f. 2 vt rabbit etc destripar.

paunchy ['pɔ:ntʃi] adj panzudo, barrigudo.

pauper ['pɔ:pə*] n pobre mf.

pauperism ['pɔ:pərizəm] n pauperismo m.

pauperization [ˌpɔ:pərai'zeiʃən] n empobrecimiento m.

pauperize ['pɔ:pəraiz] vt empobrecer, reducir a la miseria.

pause [pɔ:z] 1 n pausa f (also Mus); intervalo m; interrupción f; silencio m; **there was a** — **while ...** hubo un silencio mientras...; **we carried on without** — continuamos sin interrupción, seguíamos trabajando (etc) sin descansar; **to give someone** — dar que pensar a uno, hacer vacilar a uno.
2 vi hacer una pausa; (speaker etc) detenerse (brevemente), callarse (momentáneamente), interrumpirse; — **before you act** reflexione antes de obrar; **he** —**d for breath** se calló para cobrar aliento; **he spoke for 30 minutes without once pausing** habló durante 30 minutos sin interrumpirse una sola vez; **let's** — **here** detengámonos aquí un rato; **it made him** — le hizo vacilar.

pave [peiv] vt pavimentar; (with flags) enlosar; (with stones) empedrar; (with bricks) enladrillar; **to** — **the way** preparar el terreno (for a).

paved [peivd] adj pavimentado; enlosado; empedrado; enladrillado; (US) road asfaltado, afirmado.

pavement ['peivmənt] n pavimento m; (sidewalk) acera f; (US) calzada f, camino m asfaltado; **brick** — enladrillado m; **stone** — empedrado m, **to leave the** — (US Aut) salir de la calzada.

pavement artist ['peivmənt,ɑ:tist] n pintor m callejero.

pavilion [pə'viliən] *n* pabellón *m*; (*for band etc*) quiosco *m*; (*Sport*) caseta *f*, vestuario *m*.
paving ['peiviŋ] *n* pavimento *m*, pavimentación *f*, enlosado *m*, adoquinado *m*, enladrillado *m*.
paving stone ['peiviŋstəun] *n* losa *f*.
paw [pɔː] **1** *n* (*of animal*) pata *f*; (*of cat*) garra *f*; (*of lion*) zarpa *f*; (*large hand*) manaza *f*, manota *f*.
   2 *vt* tocar con la pata; (*lion*) dar zarpazos a; (*person: touch*) tocar, manosear, (*amorously*) sobar, palpar; **to — the ground** piafar; **stop —ing me!** ¡fuera las manos!, ¡manos quietas!
   3 *vi*: **to — at something** tocar algo con la pata, (*to wound*) dar zarpazos a algo.
pawky ['pɔːki] *adj* desgarbado.
pawl [pɔːl] *n* trinquete *m*.
pawn[1] [pɔːn] *n* (*Chess*) peón *m*; (*fig*) instrumento *m*.
pawn[2] [pɔːn] **1** *n*: **in —** en prenda; **to leave** (*or* **put**) **something in —** dejar algo en prenda; **the country is in — to foreigners** el país está en manos de extranjeros, el país está a merced de extranjeros.
   2 *vt* empeñar, pignorar, dejar en prenda.
pawnbroker ['pɔːn,brəukə*] *n* prestamista *m*, prendero *m*; **—'s** (**shop**) casa *f* de empeños, prendería *f*, monte *m* de piedad.
pawnshop ['pɔːnʃɔp] *n* casa *f* de empeños, prendería *f*, monte *m* de piedad.
pawn ticket ['pɔːn,tikit] *n* papeleta *f* de empeño.
pax [pæks] *n*: —! ¡me rindo!
pay [pei] **1** *n* paga *f*; remuneración *f*, retribución *f*; (*of professional man*) sueldo *m*; (*of worker*) salario *m*, sueldo *m*; (*of day labourer*) jornal *m*; **equal —** igualdad *f* de retribución (para hombres y mujeres); **extra —** sobresueldo *m*; **retirement —** jubilación *f*, (*Mil*) retiro *m*; **to be in someone's —** ser asalariado de uno, estar al servicio de uno; **agents in the enemy's —** agentes *mpl* al servicio del enemigo; **to draw** (*or* **get**) **one's —** cobrar; **the —'s not very good** el sueldo no es muy bueno, no pagan muy bien; **it comes out of my —** se descuenta de mi sueldo; **to stop £1 out of someone's —** retener una libra del sueldo de uno; **we'll stop it out of your —** lo descontaremos de su sueldo; *see* **holiday** *etc.*
   2 (*irr: pret and ptp* **paid**) *vt* (a) pagar; **to — someone £10** pagar 10 libras a uno, entregar 10 libras a uno; **to — money into an account** ingresar dinero en una cuenta; **how much is there to —?** ¿cuánto hay que pagar?; **to be** (*or* **get**) **paid on Fridays** cobrar los viernes; **when do you get paid?** ¿cuándo cobras?; **to — cash** (**down**) pagar al contado; **shares that — 5%** acciones *fpl* que producen un 5 por 100 de interés; **the company paid 12% last year** el año pasado la sociedad declaró un dividendo de 12 por 100; **to — someone to do a job** pagar a uno para que haga un trabajo; **I — you to prevent such mistakes** yo le pago un sueldo con el deber de impedir tales errores; **a badly paid worker** un obrero mal retribuido; **a badly paid job** un empleo mal remunerado; *see also* **paid.**
   (b) *account, debt* liquidar; satisfacer; *bill, duty, fee* pagar; **"paid"** (*on receipted bill*) "pagado".
   (c) (*be profitable to*) ser provechoso a; **it wouldn't — him to do it** no le saldría a cuenta hacerlo, (*fig*) no le sería aconsejable hacerlo, no le valdría la pena hacerlo; **it doesn't — you to be kind nowadays** hoy día no vale la pena mostrarse amable; **but it paid him in the long run** pero a la larga le fue provechoso.
   (d) *attention* prestar (*to* a); *homage* rendir (*to* a); *respects* ofrecer, presentar; *visit* hacer; *see also* **address** *etc.*
   (e) (*with adv or prep*) **to — away** pagar, desembolsar; **to — back** *money* devolver, restituir; reintegrar; reembolsar; *person* pagar; **to — someone back** (**in his own coin**) pagar a uno en la misma moneda; **to — £200 down** (*as cash*) pagar 200 libras al contado, (*as deposit*) pagar un desembolso inicial de 200 libras; **to — for** pagar por; **he paid £4 for it** pagó 4 libras por él, lo compró por 4 libras; **what did you — for it?** ¿cuánto pagaste por él?; **it's a service that has to be paid for** es un servicio que no se da gratis; **to — in a cheque** ingresar un cheque; **to — in £5** ingresar 5 libras (en una cuenta); **to — off** *debt etc* liquidar, saldar; *mortgage etc* amortizar, redimir; *old scores* ajustar; *workmen* pagar y despedir; **to — out** *money* pagar, desembolsar; *rope* ir dando; **to — someone out** pagar a uno en la misma moneda; **I'll — you out for this!** ¡me las pagarás!; **to — over** pagar, entregar; **to — up** pagar (de mala gana).
   3 *vi* (a) pagar; **who —s?** ¿quién paga?; **to — on account** pagar a cuenta; **to — in advance** pagar por adelantado; **to — in full** pagarlo todo, pagar la cantidad íntegra; **to — in instalments** pagar a

plazos; **"please — at the door"** "por favor: paguen a la entrada".
   (b) (*be profitable*) rendir, rendir bien, ser provechoso; **it's a business that —s** es un negocio que rinde; **it's —ing at last** por fin produce ganancias; **it —s to be courteous** vale la pena mostrarse cortés; **it doesn't — to paint it** vale más no pintarlo, es mejor no pintarlo; **it —s to advertise** compensa hacer publicidad.
   (c) **to — for something** pagar algo; **he paid for it** lo pagó él, lo costeó él, corrió él con los gastos; **they made him — dearly for it** le hicieron pagarlo muy caro; **he paid for it up to the hilt** lo pagó todo hasta el último céntimo; **she paid for it with her life** lo pagó con la vida; **he paid for his rashness with his life** su temeridad le costó la vida; **they paid for her education** le pagaron los estudios; **I'll make you — for this!** ¡me las pagarás!; **he invites people out and —s for them** invita a la gente a acompañarle sin que tengan que pagar nada; **they paid for her to go** pagaron para que fuera ella.
   (d) (*with other advs or preps*) **to — in** ingresar dinero; **he was —ing in for 20 years** llevaba 20 años pagando contribuciones; **the ruse paid off** la estratagema tuvo éxito; **it has paid off many times over** ha demostrado su valor muchísimas veces; **to — out** on a policy pagar una póliza; **to — up** pagar, pagar lo que se debe; soltar la mosca (*fam*).
payable ['peiəbl] *adj* pagadero; **— to bearer** pagadero al portador; **— on demand** pagadero a presentación; **— at sight** pagadero a vista; **to make a cheque — to someone** extender un cheque a favor de uno.
payday ['peidei] *n* día *m* de paga.
paydesk ['peidesk] *n* caja *f*.
paydirt ['peidəːt] *n* (*US*) grava *f* provechosa.
payee [pei'iː] *n* portador *m*, ora *f*, tenedor *m*, ora *f*; (*on cheque*) orden *f*, tomador *m*.
payer ['peiə*] *n* pagador *m*, ora *f*; **slow —, bad —** moroso *m*, a *f*.
paying ['peiiŋ] *adj* provechoso, que rinde bien; **it's a — proposition** es un negocio provechoso.
payload ['peiləud] *n* carga *f* útil.
paymaster ['peimɑːstə*] *n* oficial *m* pagador.
payment ['peimənt] *n* pago *m*; remuneración *f*, retribución *f*; **— on account** pago *m* a cuenta; **advance —** anticipo *m*; **cash —** pago *m* al contado; **deferred —,** **— by instalments** pago *m* a plazos; **down —** (*cash*) pago *m* al contado, (*deposit*) desembolso *m* inicial; **monthly —** mensualidad *f*; **yearly —** anualidad *f*; **gross —** íntegro *m*; **net —** líquido *m*; **as —** for, **in — for** en pago de; **as — for your services** en concepto de sus servicios; **on — of £5** pagando 5 libras, mediante el pago de 5 libras; **without —** sin remuneración; **to make a —** efectuar un pago; **to present something for —** presentar algo al cobro; **to stop —s** (*bank*) suspender los pagos; **to stop — of a cheque** detener el cobro de un cheque.
payoff ['peiɔf] *n* (*fam*) momento *m* decisivo, coyuntura *f* crítica, colmo *m*.
pay office ['pei,ɔfis] *n* caja *f*, pagaduría *f*.
pay packet ['pei,pækit] *n* sobre *m* de paga.
pay pause ['peipɔːz] *n* congelación *f* de sueldos y salarios.
payroll ['peirəul] *n* nómina *f*; **he has 1000 people on his —** tiene una nómina de 1000 personas.
paysheet ['peiʃiːt] *n* nómina *f*.
pay station ['pei,steiʃən] *n* (*US*) teléfono *m* público.
pay-television ['pei'teli,viʒən] *n* televisión *f* pagada.
pea [piː] *n* guisante *m*; **sweet —** guisante *m* de olor; *see* **like.**
peace [piːs] *n* paz *f*; (*peacefulness*) paz *f*, tranquilidad *f*, sosiego *m*; **— of mind** tranquilidad *f* de ánimo; **the (King's) —** el orden público; **—!** ¡silencio!; **to be at —** estar en paz; **to hold one's —** guardar silencio, callarse; **to keep the —** mantener la paz; **to make —** hacer las paces (*with* con).
peaceable ['piːsəbl] *adj* pacífico.
peaceably ['piːsəbli] *adv* pacíficamente; en paz.
peaceful ['piːsful] *adj* (*not warlike*) pacífico; (*quiet*) tranquilo, sosegado; *coexistence* pacífico; **it's very — here** aquí todo está perfectamente tranquilo; **on a — June evening** una tarde tranquila de junio.
peacefully ['piːsfuli] *adv* pacíficamente, en paz; tranquilamente; **to die —** morirse tranquilamente.
peacefulness ['piːsfulnis] *n* tranquilidad *f*, sosiego *m*, calma *f*; (*of nation*) carácter *m* pacífico.
peace-keeping ['piːs,kiːpiŋ] **1** *adj*: **— operation** operación *f* pacificadora; **— force** fuerzas *fpl* de pacificación. **2** *n* pacificación *f*; mantenimiento *m* de la paz.

peace-loving ['pi:s,lʌviŋ] adj nation amante de la paz.
peacemaker ['pi:s,meikə*] n pacificador m, ora f; (between 2 sides) árbitro m, conciliador m, ora f.
peace offensive ['pi:sə,fensiv] n ofensiva f de paz.
peace offering ['pi:s,ɔfəriŋ] n prenda f de paz, ramo m de olivo; (to gods) sacrificio m propiciatorio.
peach¹ [pi:tʃ] **1** n (a) (fruit) melocotón m; (tree) melocotonero m.
(b) (fam) she's a — es un bombón, es una real moza; it's a — es una monada; a — of a girl una real moza; a — of a dress un vestido monísimo.
(c) (colour) color m de melocotón.
2 adj color melocotón.
peach² [pi:tʃ] vi (sl) soplar (on contra).
peach tree ['pi:tʃtri:] n melocotonero m.
peacock ['pi:kɔk] n pavo m real, pavón m.
peagreen ['pi:'gri:n] adj verde claro.
peahen ['pi:hen] n pava f real.
pea jacket ['pi:,dʒækit] n chaqueta f de marinero.
peak [pi:k] **1** n (point) punta f; (of mountain) cumbre f, cima f; (mountain) pico m; (of cap) visera f; (fig) cumbre f; apogeo m, punto m más alto; **when the empire was at its** — cuando el imperio estaba en su apogeo; **when demand is at its** — cuando la demanda alcanza su punto más alto; **he was at the** — **of his fame** estaba en la cumbre de su fama.
2 as adj: — **hours** horas fpl punta; — **load** carga f máxima; — **season** época f más popular del año, época f de mayor afluencia turística (etc); — **traffic** movimiento m máximo de tráfico.
peaked [pi:kt] adj cap con visera.
peaky ['pi:ki] adj pálido, enfermizo; **to look** — tener la cara pálida.
peal [pi:l] **1** n (sound of bells) repique m, campanillazo m, toque m de campanas; — **of bells** (set) juego m de campanas; — **of laughter** carcajada f; — **of the organ** sonido m del órgano; — **of thunder** trueno m.
2 vt repicar, tocar a vuelo.
3 vi (bell) repicar, tocar a vuelo; (organ) sonar.
peanut ['pi:nʌt] n cacahuete m; **we're not playing for** —s (fam) esto va en serio.
peanut butter ['pi:nʌt'bʌtə*] n manteca f de cacahuete.
peapod ['pi:pɔd] n vaina f de guisante.
pear [peə*] n (fruit) pera f; (tree) peral m.
pearl [pə:l] **1** n perla f (also fig); (mother-of-pearl) nácar m; **cultivated** — perla f cultivada; **imitation** —s perlas fpl de imitación; **to cast** —s **before swine** echar margaritas a los cerdos.
2 attr necklace etc de perla, de perlas; (in colour) color de perla.
pearl barley [pə:l'ba:li] n cebada f perlada.
pearl fishery ['pə:l,fiʃəri] n pescaduría f de perlas.
pearl fishing ['pə:l,fiʃiŋ] n pesca f de perlas.
pearl grey ['pə:l'grei] adj gris perla.
pearl oyster ['pə:l,ɔistə*] n ostra f perlífera.
pearly ['pə:li] adj (made of pearl) de perla, de perlas; (in colour) color de perla, perlino; nacarado.
pear-shaped ['peəʃeipt] adj de forma de pera.
pear tree ['peətri:] n peral m.
peasant ['pezənt] **1** n campesino m, a f; labrador m, ora f. **2** attr campesino; rústico.
peasantry ['pezəntri] n campesinos mpl, gente f del campo.
peashooter ['pi:,ʃu:tə*] n cerbatana f.
pea soup ['pi:'su:p] n puré m de guisantes.
pea souper ['pi:'su:pə*] n (fam) puré m de guisantes, niebla f muy densa.
peat [pi:t] n turba f.
peat bog ['pi:tbɔg] n turbera f.
peaty ['pi:ti] adj turboso.
pebble ['pebl] n guija f, guijarro m, china f; **he's not the only** — **on the beach** no es el único en tener pretensiones, no es el único pretendiente.
pebbly ['pebli] adj guijarroso.
pecan [pi'kæn] n pacana f.
peccadillo [,pekə'diləu] n falta f leve, pecadillo m.
peccary ['pekəri] n pecarí m.
peck¹ [pek] n medida de áridos (= 9,087 litros); (fig) montón m; **a** — **of troubles** la mar de disgustos.
peck² [pek] **1** n picotazo m; (kiss) beso m no muy cariñoso, beso m dado de mala gana.
2 vt picotear; (kiss) besar con poco cariño, besar de mala gana.
3 vi picotear; **to** — **at** (of bird) intentar picotear; (in eating) comer melindrosamente.
pecker ['pekə*] n (fam): **to keep one's** — **up** no dejarse desanimar; **keep your** — **up!** ¡ánimo!
pecking order ['pekiŋ'ɔ:də*] n (Bio) orden m en que picotean las gallinas; (fig) orden m jerárquico establecido por los miembros de un grupo (al recibir algo etc).

peckish ['pekiʃ] adj (fam) hambriento, con hambre; **I'm** —, **I feel** — me anda el gusanillo.
pectin ['pektin] n pectina f.
pectoral ['pektərəl] adj pectoral.
peculation [,pekju'leiʃən] n peculado m.
peculiar [pi'kju:liə*] adj (a) (belong exclusively) peculiar; (typical) propio, característico; (marked) particular, especial; **an animal** — **to Africa** un animal autóctono de África, un animal que existe únicamente en África; **it is a phrase** — **to him** es una frase propia de él; **the region has its** — **dialect** la región tiene su dialecto especial.
(b) (strange) singular, extraño, raro; **a most** — **flavour** un sabor muy extraño; **he's a** — **chap** es un tío raro; **how very** —! ¡qué raro!; **it's really most** — es realmente extraño.
peculiarity [pi,kju:li'æriti] n (a) peculiaridad f; particularidad f; rasgo m característico; **it has the** — **that . . .** tiene la particularidad de que . . .; **"special peculiarities"** (on passport etc) "señas fpl particulares".
(b) singularidad f, rareza f; extravagancia f, manía f; **there is some** — **which I cannot quite define** hay alguna rareza que no puedo precisar; **it's a** — **he has** es una manía que tiene; **he has his peculiarities** tiene sus manías.
peculiarly [pi'kju:liəli] adv (a) particularmente, especialmente; **a** — **difficult work** una obra particularmente difícil.
(b) extrañamente, de modo raro; **he has been acting very** — se ha comportado de modo rarísimo.
pecuniary [pi'kju:niəri] adj pecuniario.
pedagogic(al) [,pedə'gɔdʒik(əl)] adj pedagógico.
pedagogue ['pedəgɔg] n pedagogo m.
pedagogy ['pedəgɔgi] n pedagogía f.
pedal ['pedl] **1** n pedal m (also Mus); **loud** — pedal m fuerte; **soft** — pedal m piano. **2** vt impulsar pedaleando. **3** vi pedalear.
pedant ['pedənt] n pedante m.
pedantic [pi'dæntik] adj person pedante; manner etc pedantesco.
pedantically [pi'dæntikəli] adv con pedantería, pedantescamente.
pedantry ['pedəntri] n pedantería f.
peddle ['pedl] vt vender como buhonero, vender por las casas, andar vendiendo de puerta en puerta; (fig: scandal etc) contar, repetir, difundir.
peddler ['pedlə*] n (US) see **pedlar**.
pederast ['pedəræst] n pederasta m.
pederasty ['pedəræsti] n pederastia f.
pedestal ['pedistl] n pedestal m, basa f; **to put someone on a** — poner a uno sobre un pedestal.
pedestal lamp ['pedistl,læmp] n lámpara f de pie.
pedestrian [pi'destriən] **1** adj pedestre. **2** n peatón m. **3** attr de peatones, para peatones; — **traffic** circulación f de peatones.
pedestrian crossing [pi'destriən'krɔsiŋ] n paso m de peatones.
pedicure ['pedikjuə*] n pedicura f, quiropedia f.
pedigree ['pedigri:] **1** n (lineage) genealogía f, linaje m; (tree) árbol m genealógico; (document) certificado m de genealogía. **2** attr de raza, de casta, de pura sangre; (fig) certificado, garantizado.
pediment ['pedimənt] n frontón m.
pedlar ['pedlə*] n vendedor m ambulante, buhonero m.
pedometer [pi'dɔmitə*] n podómetro m.
pee [pi:] see **piss**.
peek [pi:k] **1** n mirada f rápida, mirada f furtiva; **to take a** — **at** echar una mirada rápida (or furtiva) a.
2 vi mirar a hurtadillas; **to** — **at** echar una mirada rápida (or furtiva) a.
peel [pi:l] **1** n piel f; (after removal) pieles fpl, monda f, peladuras fpl; (fragment in cocktail etc) corteza f; **candied** — piel f almibarada.
2 vt fruit etc pelar, mondar, quitar la piel a; bark descortezar; layer of paper etc quitar, quitar una capa de; **to** — **off** dress etc quitarse rápidamente, quitarse lisamente.
3 vi (layer of paper etc) quitarse, despegarse, desprenderse; (paint etc) desconcharse; (bark) descortezarse; **to** — **off** (fam) desnudarse rápidamente.
peelings ['pi:liŋz] npl monda f, peladuras fpl.
peep¹ [pi:p] **1** n (of bird etc) pío m; **there hasn't been a** — **out of them** no han hecho comunicación alguna con nosotros; **we can't get a** — **out of them** no les podemos hacer contestar; **I don't want a single** — **out of you** de esto no digas ni pío.
2 vi piar.
peep² [pi:p] **1** n mirada f rápida, mirada f furtiva, ojeada f; **at** — **of day** al amanecer; **to get a** — **at something** lograr ver algo brevemente; **let's take**

a — vamos a verlo; **take a** — **at this** echa una ojeada a esto.

2 *vt* asomar; **she** —**ed her head out** asomó la cabeza.

3 *vi* (a) mirar rápidamente, mirar furtivamente; **to** — **at something** echar una mirada rápida (*or* furtiva) a algo; **to** — **from behind a tree** mirar a hurtadillas desde detrás de un árbol; **to** — **over a wall** mirar a hurtadillas por encima de una tapia, asomar cuidadosamente la cabeza por encima de una tapia para mirar; **to** — **through a window** atisbar a través de una ventana.

(b) **to** — **out** asomar; **the book is** —**ing out of his pocket** se deja ver el libro que no cabe enteramente en su bolsillo; **a head** —**ed out** se asomó una cabeza; **the sun** —**ed out from behind the clouds** apareció el sol detrás de las nubes, el sol empezó a dejarse ver.

peepers ['pi:pəz] *npl* (*sl*) ojos *mpl*.
peephole ['pi:phəul] *n* mirilla *f*, atisbadero *m*.
peep show ['pi:pʃəu] *n* (*fam*) vistas *fpl* sicalípticas, espectáculo *m* deshonesto.
peer[1] ['piə*] *n* (*noble*) par *m*; (*equal*) igual *mf*, par *mf*; — **of the realm** par *m* del reino; **as a musician he has no** — como músico no tiene par.
peer[2] [piə*] *vi* (a) (*person*) mirar con ojos de miope; **to** — **at something** mirar algo de cerca, mirar algo con ojos de miope; **to** — **into a room** mirar para ver lo que hay dentro de un cuarto; **to** — **out of a window** asomarse curioso a una ventana; **to** — **over a wall** asomar cuidadosamente la cabeza por encima de una tapia para mirar.

(b) (*fig*) **two eyes** —**ed out** aparecieron dos ojos, se asomaron dos ojos.
peerage ['piəridʒ] *n* (*person*) nobleza *f*, aristocracia *f*; (*rank*) título *m* de nobleza, dignidad *f* de par; (*book*) guía *f* de la nobleza; **to get a** — recibir un título de nobleza; **so they gave him a** — así que le dieron un título de nobleza.
peeress ['piəris] *n* paresa *f*.
peerless ['piəlis] *adj* sin par, incomparable.
peeve [pi:v] *vt* (*fam*) enojar, irritar.
peeved [pi:vd] *adj* (*fam*): **to be** — estar negro, estar enojado, estar furioso; **to get** — ponerse negro, sulfurarse; ofenderse; **he got a bit** — se puso negro; se ofendió.
peevish ['pi:viʃ] *adj* malhumorado, displicente, picajoso; impaciente.
peevishly ['pi:viʃli] *adv* malhumoradamente, con mal humor; impacientemente; **he said** — dijo malhumorado.
peevishness ['pi:viʃnis] *n* mal humor *m*, displicencia *f*; impaciencia *f*.
peewee ['pi:wi:] *see* **piss**.
peewit ['pi:wit] *n* avefría *f*.
peg [peg] 1 *n* clavija *f*, claveta *f*; (*Mus*) clavija *f*; (*in ground*) estaca *f*, estaquilla *f*; (*tent-*) estaca *f*; (*clothes-*) pinza *f*; (*for coat*) gancho *m*, colgadero *m*; (*in barrel*) estaquilla *f*; (*fig*) pretexto *m*; (*for argument etc*) punto *m* de apoyo, punto *m* de partida; **a** — **of whisky** un trago de whiskey; **to be a square** — **in a round hole** estar como pez fuera del agua, estar en un empleo (*or* ambiente *etc*) que no le va a uno; **to take someone down a** — bajar los humos a uno.

2 *vt* (a) (*fix* —*s to*) enclavijar; **to** — **down** estaquillar, fijar con estacas, sujetar con estacas; **to** — **out** *area* señalar con estacas; *clothes* tender (con pinzas).

(b) **to** — **prices** fijar los precios, estabilizar los precios a su nivel actual.

3 *vi*: **to** — **away** machacar, batir el yunque; **to** — **away at something** persistir en algo, afanarse por lograr algo; **to** — **out** (*sl*) estirar la pata (*fam*).
Pegasus ['pegəsəs] Pegaso.
pegleg ['pegleg] *n* pata *f* de palo, pierna *f* artificial.
peignoir ['peinwɑ:*] *n* bata *f* (de señora), peinador *m*.
pejorative [pi'dʒɔritiv] *adj* peyorativo (*also Gram*), despectivo.
pekinese [,pi:ki'ni:z] *n* pequinés *m*, esa *f*.
Pekin(g) ['pi:'kiŋ] Pekín.
pelagic [pi'lædʒik] *adj* pelágico.
pelican ['pelikən] *n* pelícano *m*.
pellet ['pelit] *n* bolita *f*; (*pill etc*) píldora *f*; (*shot*) perdigón *m*.
pell-mell ['pel'mel] *adv* en tropel, atropelladamente.
pellucid [pe'lu:sid] *adj* diáfano, cristalino.
pelmet ['pelmit] *n* galería *f* (para cubrir la barra de las cortinas).
pelota [pi'ləutə] *n* pelota *f* (vasca).
pelota player [pi'ləutə,pleiə*] *n* pelotari *m*.
pelt[1] [pelt] *n* (*skin*) pellejo *m*; (*fur*) piel *f*.
pelt[2] [pelt] 1 *vt* (a) (*throw*) tirar, arrojar (*at* a).

(b) **to** — **someone with eggs** tirar huevos a uno;

to — **someone with stones** apedrear a uno; **they** —**ed him with questions** le hicieron muchísimas preguntas.

2 *vi* (a) (*of rain*) llover a cántaros (*also* **to** — **with rain**); **it was** —**ing down** llovía de verdad, diluviaba.

(b) (*fam*) ir a máxima velocidad; **to go** —**ing past** pasar como un rayo; **to go** —**ing off** partir como un rayo.

3 *n*: **to go full** — ir a todo correr, ir a máxima velocidad.
pelvic ['pelvik] *adj* pélvico.
pelvis ['pelvis] *n* pelvis *f*.
pen[1] [pen] 1 *n* (*enclosure*) corral *m*; (*sheep-*) redil *m*, aprisco *m*; (*bull-*) toril *m*; (*play-*) parque *m* de niño; (*US fam*) cárcel *f*. 2 *vi* encerrar, acorralar.
pen[2] [pen] 1 *n* pluma *f*; (*fountain* —) estilográfica *f*, plumafuente *f* (*SAm*); **to put** — **to paper** escribir algo; **to wield a** — menear cálamo.

2 *vt* escribir; redactar, formular.
penal ['pi:nl] *adj* (a) *code, colony, etc* penal; *see* **servitude** *etc*. (b) *taxation etc* muy gravoso, perjudicial.
penalization [,pi:nəlai'zeiʃən] *n* castigo *m*.
penalize ['pi:nəlaiz] *vt* penar; (*accidentally, unfairly*) perjudicar; (*Sport*) castigar, penalizar; **to be** —**d for a foul** ser castigado por una falta; **we are** —**d by not having a car** somos perjudicados por no tener coche; **the decision** —**s those who . . .** la decisión perjudica a los que. . . .
penalty ['penəlti] *n* pena *f*, castigo *m*; (*fine*) multa *f*; (*Sport*) castigo *m*, (*football etc*) penalty *m*, (*golf*) penalización *f*, (*Bridge*) multa *f*, castigo *m*; "— **£5**" "la infracción se castigará con una multa de 5 libras"; **on** — **of so pena de; the** — **for this is death** esto se castiga con la muerte; **to pay the** — sufrir el castigo (*for* de).
penalty area ['penəlti,ɛəriə] *n* área *f* de castigo.
penalty kick ['penəlti,kik] *n* golpe *m* de castigo, penalty *m*.
penalty spot ['penəlti,spɔt] *n* punto *m* de ejecución del penálty.
penance ['penəns] *n* penitencia *f*; **to do** — hacer penitencia (*for* por).
pence [pens] *npl of* **penny**.
penchant [,pɑ̃'ʃã:ŋ] *n* predilección *f* (*for* por), inclinación *f* (*for* hacia); **to have a** — **for** tener predilección por.
pencil ['pensl] 1 *n* lápiz *m*; (*propelling* —) lapicero *m*; (*for eyebrows*) lápiz *m* de cejas; (*of light*) rayo *m* delgado. 2 *vt* escribir con lápiz (*also* **to** — **in**).
pencil box ['penslbɔks] *n* cajita de lápices.
pencil mark ['penslmɑ:k] *n* señal *f* hecha con lápiz.
pencil rubber ['pensl,rʌbə*] *n* goma *f* de borrar lápiz.
pencil sharpener ['pensl,ʃɑ:pnə*] *n* sacapuntas *m*.
pendant ['pendənt] *n* pendiente *m*, medallón *m*.
pending ['pendiŋ] 1 *adj* pendiente; **to be** — estar pendiente, estar en trámite; **and other matters** — y otros asuntos todavía por resolver.

2 *prep*: — **the arrival of . . .** antes de la llegada de . . ., hasta la llegada de . . ., hasta que llegue. . . .
pendulous ['pendjuləs] *adj* colgante.
pendulum ['pendjuləm] *n* péndulo *m*.
penetrable ['penitrəbl] *adj* penetrable.
penetrate ['penitreit] *vt* penetrar (*por*).
penetrating ['penitreitiŋ] *adj* penetrante (*also fig*); (*sound*) que taladra los oídos.
penetratingly ['penitreitiŋli] *adv* con penetración.
penetration [,peni'treiʃən] *n* penetración *f* (*also fig*).
penetrative ['penitrətiv] *adj* penetrante.
penfriend ['penfrend] *n* amigo *m* por correspondencia, amiga *f* por correspondencia.
penguin ['peŋgwin] *n* pingüino *m*.
penholder ['pen,həuldə*] *n* portaplumas *m*.
penicillin [,peni'silin] *n* penicilina *f*.
peninsula [pi'ninsjulə] *n* península *f*; **Iberian P**— Península *f* Ibérica.
peninsular [pi'ninsjulə*] *adj* peninsular; **the P**— **War** la Guerra de Independencia.
penis ['pi:nis] *n* pene *m*.
penitence ['penitəns] *n* penitencia *f*, arrepentimiento *m*.
penitent ['penitənt] 1 *adj* penitente (*also Eccl*); arrepentido, compungido. 2 *n* penitente *mf*.
penitential [,peni'tenʃəl] *adj* penitencial.
penitentiary [,peni'tenʃəri] *n* cárcel *f*, presidio *m*.
penknife ['pennaif] *n*, *pl* —**knives** [naivz] navaja *f*.
penman ['penmən] *n*, *pl* —**men** [mən] pendolista *m*.
penmanship ['penmənʃip] *n* caligrafía *f*.
pen name ['pen'neim] *n* seudónimo *m*, nombre *m* artístico.
pennant ['penənt] *n* banderola *f*; (*Naut*) gallardete *m*.

pen nib ['pennib] *n* punta *f* (de pluma); plumilla *f*, plumín *m* (de estilográfica).
penniless ['penilis] *adj* pobre; sin dinero; **to be** — no tener un céntimo; **to be left** — quedar completamente sin dinero.
pennon ['penən] *n* pendón *m*.
Pennsylvania [,pensil'veiniə] Pensilvania *f*.
penny ['peni] *n*, *pl* **pennies** ['peniz] *or* **pence** [pens] penique *m*; (*US*) centavo *m*; (*Spanish equivalent*) perra *f*; **for two pence I'd** ... por menos de nada yo ...; **in for a** —, **in for a pound** preso por mil, preso por mil quinientos; **I'm not a** — **the wiser** lo entiendo menos que antes; **that must have cost a pretty** — esa habrá costado un dineral; **to earn an honest** — emplearse en un oficio honrado; **he hasn't a** — **to his name** no tiene donde caerse muerto; **take care of the pennies and the pounds will take care of themselves** toda economía es buena por pequeña que sea; **he turns up like a bad** — aparece una y otra vez como la falsa moneda.
penny-a-liner ['peniə'lainə*] *n* escritorzuelo *m*.
penny dreadful ['peni'dredful] *n* tebeo *m* (*or* revista *f* juvenil) de bajísima calidad.
penny-in-the-slot machine ['peniinðə'slɔtmə,ʃi:n] *n* máquina *f* tragaperras.
pennyweight ['peniweit] *n* peso de 24 gramos.
pennyworth ['penəθ] *n* valor *m* de un penique, cantidad *f* que se compra con un penique; (*fig*) pizca *f*.
penologist [pi:'nɔlədʒist] *n* penalista *mf*.
penology [pi:'nɔlədʒi] *n* ciencia *f* penal.
penpusher ['pen,puʃə*] *n* (*Lit*) plumífero *m*; (*clerk*) empleadillo *m*, a *f*.
pension ['penʃən] **1** *n* pensión *f*; (*Mil*) retiro *m*; (*superannuation etc*) jubilación *f*; **old age** — subsidio *m* de vejez, pensión *f*; **retirement** — jubilación *f*; **to retire on a** — jubilarse.
 2 *vt* pensionar, dar una pensión a; **to** — **someone off** jubilar a uno.
pensioner ['penʃənə*] *n* pensionado *m*, a *f*, pensionista *mf*; (*Mil*) inválido *m*; **old age** — pensionista *mf*.
pension fund ['penʃənfʌnd] *n* caja *f* de jubilaciones.
pensive ['pensiv] *adj* pensativo, meditabundo; preocupado; triste.
pensively ['pensivli] *adv* pensativamente; tristemente; **he said** — dijo pensativo.
pent [pent] *adj see* **pent-up**.
pentagon ['pentəgən] *n* pentágono *m*; **the P—** (*Washington*) el Pentágono.
pentagonal [pen'tægənl] *adj* pentagonal.
pentameter [pen'tæmitə*] *n* pentámetro *m*; **iambic** — pentámetro *m* yámbico.
Pentateuch ['pentətju:k] *n* Pentateuco *m*.
pentathlon [pen'tæθlən] *n* pentatlón *m*.
pentatonic [,pentə'tɔnik] *adj* pentatónico; — **scale** escala *f* pentatónica.
Pentecost ['pentikɔst] *n* Pentecostés *m*.
Pentecostal [,penti'kɔstl] *adj* de Pentecostés.
penthouse ['penthaus] *n*, *pl* —**houses** [,hauziz] cobertizo *m*; (*flat*) ático *m*, casa *f* de azotea.
pent-up ['pentʌp] *adj* (a) **to be** —, **to feel** — (*of person etc*) estar encerrado, sentirse como enjaulado. (b) *emotion etc* reprimido.
penult [pi'nʌlt] *n* (*Gram*) penúltima *f*.
penultimate [pi'nʌltimit] *adj* penúltimo.
penumbra [pi'nʌmbrə] *n* penumbra *f*.
penurious [pi'njuəriəs] *adj* miserable, pobrísimo.
penury ['penjuri] *n* (a) (*poverty*) miseria *f*, pobreza *f*; **to live in** — vivir en la miseria. (b) (*lack*) falta *f*, escasez *f* (*of* de).
penwiper ['pen,waipə*] *n* limpiaplumas *m*.
peon ['pi:ən] *n* peón *m*.
peonage ['pi:ənidʒ] *n* condición *f* de peón; estado *m* en que viven los peones; (*fig*) servidumbre *f*, esclavitud *f*.
peony ['piəni] *n* peonía *f*.
people ['pi:pl] **1** *n* (a) (*Pol etc*) pueblo *m*; ciudadanos *mpl*; **the** — (*pej*), **the common** — el pueblo, la plebe; **the** — **at large** el pueblo en general; **a man of the** — un hombre del pueblo; **the king and his** — el rey y su pueblo, el rey y sus súbditos; **government by the** — gobierno *m* del pueblo.
 (b) (*race*) pueblo *m*, nación *f*; **English** — los ingleses; **the English** — el pueblo inglés; **the British** — la nación británica; **the Beaker P—** (*Hist*) la tribu de las copas, el pueblo de las copas.
 (c) (*parents*) padres *mpl*; (*relatives*) parientes *mpl*, familia *f*; **my** — mis padres, mi familia; **how are all your** —? ¿cómo están los de tu casa?, ¿cómo está tu familia?; **have you met his** —? ¿conoce Vd a sus padres?

 (d) (*in general*) gente *f*; **country** — gente *f* del campo; **fashionable** — gente *f* elegante, gente *f* de buen tono; **the good** —, **the little** — las hadas; **old** — los viejos; **young** — los jóvenes, la juventud; **respectable** — gente *f* de bien; **top** — la gente bien; **what do you** — **think?** y ustedes, ¿qué opinan?; **the place was full of** — el local estaba lleno de gente; **they're strange** — son gente rara; **I like the** — **here** aquí la gente es simpática, la gente de aquí me gusta.
 (e) (*inhabitants*) habitantes *mpl*; **the** — **of London** los habitantes de Londres, los londinenses; **Madrid has over 2 million** — Madrid tiene más de 2 millones de habitantes.
 (f) (*with numerals*) **20** — 20 personas; **many** — **think that** ... muchas personas creen que ..., son muchos los que creen que ...; **some** — algunos, algunas personas.
 (g) (*vague subject use*) — **say that** ... se dice que ..., la gente dice que ...; **here** — **quarrel a lot** aquí se riñe mucho; — **get worried** la gente se inquieta; **it's enough to worry** — basta para inquietar a la gente.
 2 *vt* poblar; **the country is** —**d by** ... el país está poblado por ..., el país está habitado por ...
pep [pep] (*sl*) **1** *n* empuje *m*, dinamismo *m*, ímpetu *m*, energía *f*. **2** *vt*: **to** — **up** estimular, animar, hacer más dinámico; *drink etc* fortalecer.
pepper ['pepə*] **1** *n* (*spice*) pimienta *f*; (*vegetable*) pimiento *m*; (-*plant*) pimentero *m*; **green** — pimiento *m*.
 2 *vt* (*spice*) sazonar con pimienta, añadir pimienta a; **to** — **a work with quotations** salpicar una obra de citas; **to** — **someone with shot** acribillar a uno a tiros.
pepper-and-salt ['pepərən'sɔ:lt] *adj marking* mezclado de negro y blanco.
pepperbox ['pepəbɔks] *n* pimentero *m*.
peppercorn ['pepəkɔ:n] *n* grano *m* de pimienta; — **rent** (*fig*) alquiler *m* nominal.
peppermint ['pepəmint] *n* (*plant, flavour*) menta *f*; (*sweet*) pastilla *f* de menta.
pepperpot ['pepəpɔt] *n* pimentero *m*.
peppery ['pepəri] *adj taste* picante; (*fig*) enojadizo, de malas pulgas.
pep pill ['peppil] *n* píldora *f* antifatiga.
pepsin ['pepsin] *n* pepsina *f*.
peptalk ['peptɔ:k] *n* (*sl*) (*speech*) discurso *m* de tono edificante, (*chat*) charla *f* que procura levantar los ánimos.
peptic ['peptik] *adj* péptico.
peptone ['peptəun] *n* peptona *f*.
per [pə:*] *prep* por; (*with year etc*) a; **£20** — **annum** 20 libras al año; **£7** — **week** 7 libras a la semana; **10/-** — **dozen** 10 chelines la docena; **60 miles** — **hour** 60 millas por hora; **30 miles** — **gallon** 30 millas por galón (*in Spain, eg* 15 km por litro); — **cent** por ciento, por cien; **20** — **cent** 20 por cien; **it has increased by 8** — **cent** ha aumentado en un 8 por cien; **there is a 10** — **cent discount** hay un descuento de un 10 por cien; — **capita**, — **person** por persona; — **se** de por sí; **as** — **invoice** según factura; *see* **usual**.
perambulate [pə'ræmbjuleit] **1** *vt* recorrer (para inspeccionar). **2** *vi* pasearse, deambular.
perambulation [pə,ræmbju'leiʃən] *n* visita *f* de inspección; (*stroll*) paseo *m*; (*journey*) viaje *m*.
perambulator ['præmbjuleitə*] *n* cochecito *m* de niño.
perceive [pə'si:v] *vt* percibir; (*see*) notar, observar; (*understand*) comprender; (*realize*) darse cuenta de; **now I** — **that** ... ahora veo que ...; **do you** — **anything strange?** ¿notas algo raro?; **I do not** — **how it can be done** no comprendo cómo se puede hacer.
percentage [pə'sentidʒ] **1** *n* porcentaje *m*, tanto *m* por ciento; proporción *f*; (*rake-off*: *sl*) tajada *f*; (*commission*) comisión *f*; **the figure is expressed as a** — la cifra está expresada como un tanto por ciento; **a high** — **are girls** un elevado porcentaje son chicas; **to get a** — **on all sales** recibir un tanto por ciento sobre todas las ventas.
 2 *attr* porcentual; **on a** — **basis** según un sistema porcentual; — **sign** signo *m* del tanto por ciento.
perceptible [pə'septəbl] *adj* perceptible; sensible.
perceptibly [pə'septəbli] *adv* perceptiblemente; sensiblemente; **it has improved** — ha mejorado sensiblemente.
perception [pə'sepʃən] *adj* perspicaz; penetrante, agudo.
perceptive [pə'septiv] *adj* perspicaz; penetrante, agudo; *function* perceptivo.
perch¹ [pə:tʃ] *n* (*Fish*) perca *f*.

perch² [pəːtʃ] **1** n **(a)** *medida de longitud* = 5,029 m.
(b) (*of bird*) percha f; (*fig*) posición f elevada; posición f peligrosa, posición f poco segura; **to knock someone off his** — destronar a uno, acabar con el dominio ejercido por uno.
2 vt colocar (en una posición elevada, poco segura *etc*); **he** —**ed his hat on his head** se puso el sombrero de modo no muy firme; **we** —**ed the child on the wall** pusimos al niño en lo alto de la tapia.
3 vi (*bird*) posarse (*on* en); (*person etc*) sentarse (en un sitio elevado, poco seguro *etc*); colocarse en una posición elevada; **we** —**ed in a tree to see the procession** nos subimos a un árbol para ver el desfile; **she** —**ed on the arm of my chair** se acomodó en el brazo de mi butaca.
perchance [pəˈtʃɑːns] adv (*lit*) por ventura, acaso.
percipient [pəˈsɪpɪənt] adj perspicaz; penetrante, agudo.
percolate [ˈpəːkəleɪt] **1** vt filtrar, colar; (*fig*) filtrarse en, filtrarse por; *coffee* preparar.
2 vi **(a)** filtrarse, colarse; **to** — **down to** penetrar hasta; **to** — **through** penetrar por.
(b) (*coffee*) prepararse.
percolator [ˈpəːkəleɪtə*] n cafetera f filtradora.
percussion [pəˈkʌʃən] **1** n percusión f. **2** attr *instrument etc* de percusión.
percussion cap [pəˈkʌʃənˌkæp] n cápsula f fulminante.
perdition [pəˈdɪʃən] perdición f.
peregrination [ˌperɪɡrɪˈneɪʃən] n peregrinación f; —**s** (*hum*) vagabundeo m, periplo m.
peregrine [ˈperɪɡrɪn] n halcón m común, neblí m.
peremptorily [pəˈremptərɪlɪ] adv perentoriamente; imperiosamente, autoritariamente.
peremptory [pəˈremptərɪ] adj perentorio; *person* imperioso, autoritario.
perennial [pəˈrenɪəl] **1** adj perenne (*also Bot*); eterno, perpetuo; **it's a** — **complaint** es una queja constante. **2** n (*Bot*) perenne m, planta f vivaz.
perennially [pəˈrenɪəlɪ] adv perennemente; perpetuamente, constantemente.
perfect [ˈpəːfɪkt] **1** adj perfecto (*also Gram*); **it's just** — ! ¡qué maravilla!; **with** — **assurance** con la más completa confianza; **she's a** — **terror** es una bruja, es una arpía; **he's a** — **stranger to me** me es completamente desconocido; **his Spanish is far from** — su español dista mucho de ser perfecto.
2 n (*Gram*) perfecto m.
perfect [pəˈfekt] vt perfeccionar.
perfectibility [pəˌfektɪˈbɪlɪtɪ] n perfectibilidad f.
perfectible [pəˈfektəbl] adj perfectible.
perfection [pəˈfekʃən] n perfección f; **she does it to** — lo hace a la perfección, lo hace a las mil maravillas.
perfectionist [pəˈfekʃənɪst] n perfeccionista mf, persona f que lo quiere tener todo perfecto, persona f que cuida hasta de los detalles más nimios.
perfectly [ˈpəːfɪktlɪ] adv **(a)** perfectamente; **she does it** — lo hace perfectamente.
(b) **it's** — **marvellous** es de lo más maravilloso; **it's** — **ridiculous** es completamente absurdo; **we're** — **happy about it** estamos completamente contentos con esto.
perfidious [pəˈfɪdɪəs] adj pérfido.
perfidiously [pəˈfɪdɪəslɪ] adv pérfidamente.
perfidy [ˈpəːfɪdɪ] n perfidia f.
perforate [ˈpəːfəreɪt] vt perforar, horadar, agujerear; **to** — **holes in something** practicar agujeros en algo.
perforated [ˈpəːfəreɪtɪd] adj *stamp* dentado.
perforation [ˌpəːfəˈreɪʃən] n perforación f; agujero m; (*of stamp*) trepado m.
perforce [pəˈfɔːs] adv (*lit*) forzosamente.
perform [pəˈfɔːm] **1** vt *task etc* hacer, cumplir, realizar; *duty* cumplir; *function* desempeñar; ejercer; (*Theat*) *play* representar, dar, poner, *part* interpretar, hacer; (*Mus*) ejecutar, interpretar.
2 vi (*Mus*: *play*) tocar, (*sing*) cantar; (*Theat*) representar, actuar; trabajar; hacer un papel, tener un papel; (*Mech etc*) funcionar, comportarse; (*trained animal*) hacer trucos; **to** — **on the violin** tocar el violín, interpretar una obra al violín; **how did he** — ? ¿qué tal lo hizo?; **he** —**ed brilliantly as Hamlet** interpretó brillantemente el papel de Hamlet, en el papel de Hamlet se lució; **when we** —**ed in Seville** cuando dimos una representación en Sevilla; **I'm not** —**ing this time** esta vez no hago ningún papel, esta vez no tomo parte; **the car is not** —**ing properly** el coche no funciona bien; **how does the metal** — **under pressure?** ¿cómo se comporta el metal bajo presión?
performance [pəˈfɔːməns] n **(a)** (*of task etc*) cumplimiento m, ejecución f, realización f; (*of function*)

desempeño m; ejercicio m; acción f, actuación f; **in the** — **of his duties** en el ejercicio de su cargo.
(b) (*Theat*: *of play*) representación f, (*by actor, of a part*) actuación f, desempeño m; interpretación f; (*sitting*: *Theat*) función f, (*cinema*) sesión f; **"continuous**—**" "sesión f continua"; the late**—la función de la noche, la sesión de la noche; **"no** — **tonight"** "no hay representación esta noche"; **first** — estreno m; **we didn't like his** — **as Don Juan** no nos gustó su interpretación del papel de don Juan, su modo de entender el papel de don Juan no nos gustó; **he gave a splendid** — su actuación fue estupenda; **the play had 300** —**s** la obra tuvo 300 representaciones, la obra siguió en la cartelera durante 300 representaciones; **it has not had a** — **since 1950** no se ha representado desde 1950.
(c) (*Mus*) ejecución f; interpretación f; **a fine** — **of the Ninth Symphony** una magnífica interpretación de la Novena Sinfonía.
(d) (*Mech etc*) comportamiento m; funcionamiento m; (*by motor*) rendimiento m; (*of team in match*) actuación f, desempeño m; (*of car in race*) performance f; **the team gave a poor** — el equipo tuvo una actuación nada satisfactoria; **they eventually put up a good** — por fin estuvieron a su altura; **it's a series of cars with outstanding** —**s** es una serie de coches con unas performances notables; **what a** —**!** (*iro*) ¡qué lío!, ¡vaya lío que se han armado!
performer [pəˈfɔːmə*] n (*Theat*) actor m, actriz f; artista mf; (*Mus*) intérprete mf, ejecutante mf, músico m; **a skilled** — **on the piano** un pianista experto.
performing [pəˈfɔːmɪŋ] adj *animal* amaestrado, sabio.
perfume [ˈpəːfjuːm] n perfume m.
perfume [pəˈfjuːm] vt perfumar.
perfumery [pəˈfjuːmərɪ] n (*perfumes*) perfumes mpl; (*factory*) perfumería f.
perfunctorily [pəˈfʌŋktərɪlɪ] adv superficialmente, someramente, a la ligera.
perfunctory [pəˈfʌŋktərɪ] adj superficial, somero, hecho (*etc*) a la ligera.
pergola [ˈpəːɡələ] n pérgola f.
perhaps [pəˈhæps, præps] adv tal vez, quizá(s), puede que; —**!** ¡quizá!; — **not** puede que no; — **so** quizá, quizá sea así; — **he did it** quizá lo hizo él; **he's in Segovia** puede que esté en Segovia; — **he'll come** quizá venga, puede que venga.
peril [ˈperɪl] n peligro m, riesgo m; **to be in** — estar en peligro; **to be in** — **of one's life** correr riesgo de perder la vida; **do it at your** — hágalo a su riesgo.
perilous [ˈperɪləs] adj peligroso, arriesgado; **it would be** — **to** + *infin* sería arriesgado + *infin.*
perilously [ˈperɪləslɪ] adv peligrosamente; **to come** — **close to...** acercarse de modo peligroso a..., (*fig*) rayar en....
perimeter [pəˈrɪmɪtə*] n perímetro m.
period [ˈpɪərɪəd] **1** n período m; época f, edad f; (*time limit*) plazo m; (*Gram*) período m; (*full stop*) punto m; (*School*) hora f, clase f; (*Sport*) tiempo m; — (*Med*), —**s** período m, reglas fpl; **at that** — en aquel entonces; **within a 3 month** — en 3 meses; dentro de un plazo de 3 meses; **this is a bad** — **for...** ésta es una mala época para...; **a painting of his early** — un cuadro de su primera época, un cuadro de su juventud; **the postwar** — la posguerra.
2 attr: **in** — **dress** en trajes de la época; — **furniture** muebles mpl de época, muebles mpl clásicos; — **piece** mueble m (*etc*) clásico.
periodic [ˌpɪərɪˈɒdɪk] adj periódico.
periodical [ˌpɪərɪˈɒdɪkəl] **1** adj periódico. **2** n revista f, publicación f periódica.
periodically [ˌpɪərɪˈɒdɪkəlɪ] adv periódicamente; (*from time to time*) de vez en cuando, cada cierto tiempo.
periodicity [ˌpɪərɪəˈdɪsɪtɪ] n periodicidad f.
peripatetic [ˌperɪpəˈtetɪk] adj ambulante, que no tiene residencia fija; (*Philos*) peripatético; **to lead a** — **existence** cambiar mucho de domicilio, no tener residencia fija.
peripheral [pəˈrɪfərəl] adj periférico.
periphery [pəˈrɪfərɪ] n periferia f.
periphrasis [pəˈrɪfrəsɪs] n, pl **periphrases** [pəˈrɪfrəsiːz] perífrasis f.
periphrastic [ˌperɪˈfræstɪk] adj perifrástico.
periscope [ˈperɪskəup] n periscopio m.
perish [ˈperɪʃ] **1** vt deteriorar, estropear, echar a perder; **to be** —**ed (with cold)** estar helado.
2 vi (*person*) *etc* perecer; (*material*) deteriorarse, estropearse, echarse a perder; **we shall do it or** — **in the attempt** lo conseguiremos o moriremos intentándolo; **he** —**ed at sea** murió en el mar; — **the thought!** ¡ni por pensamiento!

perishable ['periʃəbl] **1** *adj* perecedero; *fruit etc* que no se conserva bien, sujeto a putrefacción, corruptible. **2** —s *npl* mercancías *fpl* corruptibles, artículos *mpl* que no se conservan bien.

perisher ['periʃə*] *n* (*sl*) tío *m*; **little** — tunante *m*; **you little** —! ¡tunante!

perishing ['periʃiŋ] *adj* (*fam*) **it's** — (**cold**) hace un frío glacial; **I'm** — estoy helado.

peristyle ['peristail] *n* peristilo *m*.

peritoneum [,peritə'niːəm] *n* peritoneo *m*.

peritonitis [,peritə'naitis] *n* peritonitis *f*.

periwig ['periwig] *n* peluca *f*.

periwinkle ['peri,wiŋkl] *n* (*Bot*) vincapervinca *f*; (*Zool*) litorina *f*.

perjure ['pɔːdʒə*] *vt*: **to** — **oneself** perjurar, perjurarse.

perjured ['pɔːdʒed] *adj evidence* falso.

perjurer ['pɔːdʒərə*] *n* perjuro *m*.

perjury ['pɔːdʒəri] *n* perjurio *m*; **to commit** — jurar en falso, perjurar.

perk [pɔːk] **1** *vt*: **to** — **someone up** reanimar a uno, infundir nuevo vigor a uno; **this will** — **you up**! ¡anímate con esto!, ¡esto servirá para reanimarte!; **to** — **one's ears up** aguzar las orejas; **to** — **one's head up** levantar la cabeza.
2 *vi*: **to** — **up** (*person*) reanimarse, cobrar ánimo; (*in health*) sentirse mejor; **business is** —**ing up** los negocios van mejor.

perkily ['pɔːkili] *adv* alegremente; de modo despabilado; con frescura.

perkiness ['pɔːkinis] *n* alegría *f*, buen humor *m*; despejo *m*; frescura *f*.

perks [pɔːks] *npl* (*sl*) *see* **perquisite**.

perky ['pɔːki] *adj* (*gay*) alegre, de excelente humor; (*wide-awake*) despabilado; (*pert*) fresco; **to feel** — estar alegre, estar de buen humor.

perm [pɔːm] (*fam*) **1** *n* permanente *f*; **to have a** — hacerse una permanente. **2** *vt*: **to** — **someone's hair** hacer una permanente a una; **to have one's hair** —**ed** hacerse una permanente.

permanence ['pɔːmənəns] *n* permanencia *f*.

permanency ['pɔːmənsi] *n* (*permanence*) permanencia *f*; (*permanent arrangement*) arreglo *m* permanente, cosa *f* fija; **the post is not a** — no es un puesto permanente; **I hope this is now a** — espero que esto sea un arreglo definitivo.

permanent ['pɔːmənənt] *adj* permanente; estable, fijo; *finish on steel etc* inalterable; *wave* permanente; **I'm not** — **here** yo no ocupo aquí un puesto permanente; **we cannot make any** — **arrangements** no podemos arreglar las cosas de modo definitivo.

permanently ['pɔːmənəntli] *adv* permanentemente; de modo estable, de modo definitivo; **we seem to be** — **stuck here** parece que nos vamos a quedar aquí para siempre; **he is** — **drunk** está borracho todo el tiempo.

permanganate [pɔː'mæŋgənit] *n* permanganato *m*; — **of potash** permanganato *m* de potasio.

permeability [,pɔːmiə'biliti] *n* permeabilidad *f*.

permeable ['pɔːmiəbl] *adj* permeable.

permeate ['pɔːmieit] *vt* penetrar; saturar, impregnar (*with* de); **to be** —**d with** estar impregnado de.

permissible [pɔː'misəbl] *adj* permisible, lícito; **it is not** — **to** + *infin* no se permite + *infin*; **would it be** — **to say that** . . .? ¿podemos decir que . . .?, ¿sería lícito decir que . . .?

permission [pɔː'miʃən] *n* permiso *m*; licencia *f*; autorización *f*; **with your** — con permiso de Vds; **without** — sin licencia; **"by kind** — **of Pérez Ltd"** "con permiso de la Cía. Pérez"; **to give someone** — **to** + *infin* autorizar a uno para que + *subj*; **no** — **is needed** no hay que pedir permiso; **to withhold one's** — negar su permiso.

permissive [pɔː'misiv] *adj* permisivo; (*optional*) facultativo, opcional; **modern society is very** — **la** sociedad moderna lo permite todo, la sociedad moderna no pone su veto a casi nada.

permit ['pɔːmit] *n* permiso *m*, licencia *f*; (*allowing free entry etc*) pase *m*; **entry** — permiso *m* de entrada; **exit** — permiso *m* de salida; **export** — permiso *m* de exportación; **import** — permiso *m* de importación.

permit [pɔː'mit] **1** *vt* permitir; autorizar; tolerar, sufrir; **to** — **someone to do something** permitir a uno hacer algo; **is it** —**ted to smoke?** ¿se puede fumar?; **whoever** —**ted this was a fool** el que dio permiso para eso fue un tonto; **we could never** — **it to happen** no podríamos nunca tolerar eso; — **me!** ¡permítame ayudarle a Vd!
2 *vi* (**a**) permitir; **weather** —**ing** si el tiempo no lo impide.
(**b**) **to** — **of** permitir; dar lugar a; posibilitar; **it** —**s of certain changes** nos permite hacer varios

cambios; **it does not** — **of doubt** no deja lugar a dudas.

permutation [,pɔːmju'teiʃən] *n* permutación *f*.

permute [pɔː'mjuːt] *vt* permutar.

pernicious [pɔː'niʃəs] *adj* pernicioso (*also Med*); nocivo, dañoso; peligroso; funesto; **the** — **custom of** . . . la funesta costumbre de . . .

pernickety [pɔː'nikiti] *adj* (*fam*) quisquilloso, remirado; **he's very** — **about clocks** tiene ideas raras sobre los relojes; **he's terribly** — **about punctuality** tiene la manía de la puntualidad.

peroration [,perə'reiʃən] *n* peroración *f*.

peroxide [pɔː'rɔksaid] *n* peróxido *m*; **hydrogen** — peróxido *m* de hidrógeno; — **blonde** rubia *f* de bote, rubia *f* de frasco.

perpendicular [,pɔːpən'dikjulə*] **1** *adj* perpendicular. **2** *n* perpendicular *f*; **to be out of the** — salir de la perpendicular.

perpendicularly [,pɔːpən'dikjuləli] *adv* perpendicularmente.

perpetrate ['pɔːpitreit] *vt* cometer; (*Law*) perpetrar.

perpetration [,pɔːpi'treiʃən] *n* comisión *f*; (*Law*) perpetración *f*.

perpetrator ['pɔːpitreitə*] *n* autor *m*, ora *f*; responsable *mf*; (*Law*) perpetrador *m*, ora *f*.

perpetual [pɔː'petjuəl] *adj* perpetuo; incesante, constante, continuo; *motion etc* perpetuo, continuo; **these** — **complaints** este continuo quejarse.

perpetually [pɔː'petjuəli] *adv* perpetuamente; constantemente, continuamente; **we were** — **hungry** teníamos hambre siempre; **they complain** — se quejan constantemente.

perpetuate [pɔː'petjueit] *vt* perpetuar.

perpetuation [pɔː,petju'eiʃən] *n* perpetuación *f*.

perpetuity [,pɔːpi'tjuːiti] *n* perpetuidad *f*; **in** — para siempre.

Perpignan ['pɔːpiːnjɔ̃n] Perpiñán.

perplex [pɔː'pleks] *vt* dejar perplejo, confundir.

perplexed [pɔː'plekst] *adj* perplejo; confuso; **to look** — parecer estar confuso.

perplexedly [pɔː'pleksidli] *adv* perplejamente.

perplexing [pɔː'pleksiŋ] *adj* confuso, que causa perplejidad; complicado; misterioso; **it's all very** — no entiendo nada; **it's a** — **situation** es una situación complicada, es una situación que deja a todos perplejos.

perplexity [pɔː'pleksiti] *n* perplejidad *f*, confusión *f*; **to be in some** — estar algo perplejo.

perquisite ['pɔːkwizit] *n* gaje *m*; —**s** gajes *mpl*, (*tips*) propinas *fpl*; **a salary and** —**s** un sueldo y lo que cae, un sueldo y otras cosillas; **there are no** —**s in this job** en este empleo no hay nada aparte del sueldo.

perry ['peri] *n* sidra *f* de peras.

persecute ['pɔːsikjuːt] *vt* perseguir; importunar, molestar, acosar; **is this man persecuting you?** ¿le molesta este hombre?; **under the Nazis they were** —**d** bajo los nazis se les persiguió, bajo los nazis sufrieron la persecución.

persecution [,pɔːsi'kjuːʃən] *n* persecución *f*.

persecutor ['pɔːsikjuːtə*] *n* perseguidor *m*, ora *f*.

perseverance [,pɔːsi'viərəns] *n* perseverancia *f*.

persevere [,pɔːsi'viə*] *vi* perseverar, persistir (*in* en); **to** — **with** continuar con, no abandonar.

persevering [,pɔːsi'viəriŋ] *adj* perseverante.

perseveringly [,pɔːsi'viəriŋli] *adv* con perseverancia, perseverantemente.

Persia ['pɔːʃə] Persia *f*.

Persian ['pɔːʃən] **1** *adj* persa; — **cat** gato *m* de Angora, gata *f* de Angora; — **lamb** (*animal*) oveja *f* caracul, (*skin*) caracul *m*. **2** *n* persa *mf*. **3** *n* (*language*) persa *m*.

Persian Gulf ['pɔːʃən'gʌlf] Golfo *m* Pérsico.

persiflage [,pɔːsi'flɑːʒ] *n* burlas *fpl*, zumba *f*.

persimmon [pɔː'simən] *n* placaminero *m*.

persist [pɔː'sist] *vi* (**a**) persistir; continuar; **we must** — hay que persistir, tenemos que mantenernos firmes; **we shall** — **in our efforts to** + *infin* seguiremos esforzándonos por + *infin*; **it will** — **some time yet** durará todavía algún tiempo.
(**b**) (*insist*) porfiar, empeñarse, obstinarse; **if he** —**s** si se empeña en ello, si se obstina; **to** — **in doing something** empeñarse en hacer algo, obstinarse en hacer algo.

persistence [pɔː'sistəns] *n*, **persistency** [pɔː'sistənsi] *n* persistencia *f*; porfía *f*, empeño *m*; (*of disease etc*) pertinacia *f*; **as a reward for her** — en premio a sus esfuerzos.

persistent [pɔː'sistənt] *adj* persistente; continuo; porfiado; *disease etc* pertinaz; **he is most** — es muy porfiado, se porfía mucho; **despite our** — **warnings** a pesar de nuestras continuas advertencias.

persistently [pə'sistəntli] *adv* con persistencia, persistentemente; constantemente; he — **refuses to help** se niega constantemente a prestar su ayuda.

person ['pəːsn] *n* persona *f*; **private** — particular *m*; **in** — en persona; **in the** — **of** en la persona de; **he is neat in his** — es aseado en cuanto a su persona; **in the first** — (*Gram*) en primera persona; **per** — por persona; **murder by** — **or** —**s unknown** homicidio *m* por mano desconocida.

persona [pəː'səunə] *n*, *pl* **personae** [pəː'səunai] persona *f*; — **grata** persona *f* grata; — **non grata** persona *f* no grata.

personable ['pəːsnəbl] *adj* bien parecido, atractivo.

personage ['pəːsnidʒ] *n* personaje *m*.

personal ['pəːsnl] **1** *adj* personal; (*private*) privado, íntimo, particular; (*for one's sole use*) de uso personal; *cleanliness etc* corporal; *liberty etc* individual; *appearance, interview* en persona; **call** (*Tel*) de persona a persona; **column** de anuncios personales, de anuncios por palabras; **to ask** — **questions** hacer preguntas sobre asuntos íntimos; **don't be** — ! ¡Vd es un maleducado!; **to become** — pasar a hacer crítica personal, empezar a hacer referencias de tipo personal; **I have no** — **knowledge of it** no lo conozco directamente; **my** — **view is that** . . . yo creo para mí que . . .; **to make a** — **application for something** solicitar algo en persona.
2 *n* (*US fam*) nota *f* de sociedad.

personality [,pəːsə'næliti] *n* (*character*) personalidad *f*; (*person, figure*) personaje *m*; figura *f*; (*personal reference, insult*) personalismo *m*; **dual** — conciencia *f* doble; **split** — personalidad *f* desdoblada; **a well-known radio** — conocida figura *f* de la radio; **to indulge in personalities** hacer crítica personal, cambiar personalismos, hacer referencias de tipo personal.

personality cult [,pəːsə'nælitikʌlt] *n* culto *m* a la personalidad.

personally ['pəːsnəli] *adv* (a) personalmente; — **I think that** . . . creo personalmente que . . ., yo creo para mí que . . .; — **I am willing, but others** . . . en cuanto a mí digo que sí, pero otros . . .; **don't take it too** — no vaya Vd a creer que lo digo contra Vd, no se vaya Vd a ofender de modo personal.
(b) **to hand something over** — entregar algo en persona; **the manager saw her** — el gerente habló con ella en persona.

personalty ['pəːsnlti] *n* (*Law*) bienes *mpl* muebles.

personate ['pəːsəneit] *vt* (*impersonate*) hacerse pasar por; (*Theat*) hacer el papel de.

personification [pəː,sɔnifi'keiʃən] *n* personificación *f*; **he is the** — **of good taste** es el buen gusto en persona, es el mismo buen gusto, tiene un gusto exquisito.

personify [pəː'sɔnifai] *vt* personificar; representar; **he personified the spirit of resistance** encarnó el espíritu de la resistencia; **he is greed personified** es la codicia en persona, es la misma codicia.

personnel [,pəːsə'nel] **1** *n* personal *m*. **2** *attr*: — **management** relaciones *fpl* humanas; — **manager**, — **officer** jefe *m* del personal.

perspective [pə'spektiv] *n* perspectiva *f*; **in** — en perspectiva; **let's get things in** — pongamos las cosas en su sitio; **to see things in their proper** — apreciar debidamente las cosas, apreciar las cosas en su justo valor.

Perspex ['pəːspeks] (*Protected Trade Name*) *n* plexiglás *m*.

perspicacious [,pəːspi'keiʃəs] *adj* perspicaz.

perspicacity [,pəːspi'kæsiti] *n* perspicacia *f*.

perspicuous [pə'spikjuəs] *adj* perspicuo.

perspicuity [,pəːspi'kju(:)iti] *n* perspicuidad *f*.

perspiration [,pəːspə'reiʃən] *n* transpiración *f*; sudor *m*; **beads of** — gotitas *fpl* de sudor; **to be bathed in** — estar bañado en sudor, estar todo sudoroso.

perspire [pəs'paiə*] *vi* transpirar, sudar; **to** — **freely** sudar mucho.

perspiring [pəs'paiəriŋ] *adj* sudoroso.

persuadable [pə'sweidəbl] *adj* influenciable, persuasible; **he may be** — quizá le podamos persuadir.

persuade [pə'sweid] *vt* persuadir; **to** — **someone to do something** persuadir a uno a hacer algo, inducir a uno a hacer algo; **but they** —**d me not to** pero ellos me disuadieron, pero ellos me persuadieron a dejarlo; **to** — **someone that something is true** convencer a uno de que algo es verdad; **I am** — **that** . . . estoy convencido de que . . .; **to** — **someone of the truth of a theory** convencer a uno de que una teoría es verdadera; **she is easily** —**d** se deja convencer fácilmente; **it does not take much to** — **him** exige poco esfuerzo convencerle.

persuasion [pə'sweiʒən] *n* (a) (*act*) persuasión *f*. (b) (*persuasiveness*) persuasiva *f*; **he needed a lot of** — había que ejercer mucha persuasiva; **I don't need much** — **to stop working** me cuesta poco dejar el trabajo.
(c) (*creed*) creencia *f*, secta *f*; opinión *f*; **I am not of that** — no es ésa mi opinión, yo lo veo de otro modo; **the Methodist** — la secta metodista; **and others of that** — y otros que creen así.

persuasive [pə'sweisiv] *adj* persuasivo; **I had to be very** — tuve que ejercer mucha persuasión.

persuasively [pə'sweisivli] *adv* de modo persuasivo.

persuasiveness [pə'sweisivnis] *n* persuasiva *f*.

pert [pəːt] *adj* impertinente, respondón, fresco.

pertain [pəː'tein] *vi*: **to** — **to** (*concern*) tener que ver con, estar relacionado con; (*belong to*) pertenecer a; (*be the province of*) incumbir a; **and other matters** —**ing to it** y otros asuntos relacionados con eso.

pertinacious [,pəːti'neiʃəs] *adj* pertinaz.

pertinaciously [,pəːti'neiʃəsli] *adv* con pertinacia.

pertinacity [,pəːti'næsiti] *n* pertinacia *f*.

pertinence ['pəːtinəns] *n* pertinencia *f*, oportunidad *f*.

pertinent ['pəːtinənt] *adj* pertinente, oportuno, a propósito; **not very** — poco oportuno, no muy a propósito.

pertinently ['pəːtinəntli] *adv* oportunamente, a propósito, atinadamente.

pertly ['pəːtli] *adv* de modo impertinente, descaradamente, con frescura.

pertness ['pəːtnis] *n* impertinencia, *f*, frescura *f*.

perturb [pə'təːb] *vt* perturbar, inquietar; **we are all very** —**ed** todos estamos muy inquietos.

perturbation [,pəːtəː'beiʃən] *n* perturbación *f*, inquietud *f*; **she asked in some** — preguntó algo perturbada.

perturbing [pə'təːbiŋ] *adj* perturbador, inquietante.

Peru [pə'ruː] el Perú.

perusal [pə'ruːzəl] *n* lectura *f* (cuidadosa), examen *m* (detenido).

peruse [pə'ruːz] *vt* leer (con atención), examinar (con detenimiento).

Peruvian [pə'ruːviən] **1** *adj* peruano. **2** *n* peruano *m*, a *f*.

pervade [pəː'veid] *vt* extenderse por, difundirse por, impregnar, saturar; **to be** —**d with** estar impregnado de, estar saturado de.

pervasive [pəː'veisiv] *adj* penetrante; omnipresente.

perverse [pə'vəːs] *adj* (*wicked*) perverso; (*obstinate*) terco, contumaz; (*wayward*) travieso, díscolo.

perversely [pə'vəːsli] *adv* perversamente; tercamente; traviesamente.

perverseness [pə'vəːsnis] *n* perversidad *f*; terquedad *f*, contumacia *f*; lo travieso.

perversion [pə'vəːʃən] *n* perversión *f* (*also Med*); **sexual** — perversión *f* sexual.

perversity [pə'vəːsiti] *n* see **perverseness**.

pervert ['pəːvəːt] *n* (*Med*) pervertido *m*, a *f*.

pervert [pə'vəːt] *vt* pervertir (*also Med*); *taste etc* estragar, estropear; *words* torcer, forzar; *talent* emplear mal.

pervious ['pəːviəs] *adj* permeable (*to* a).

peseta [pə'setə] *n* peseta *f*.

pesky ['peski] *adj* (*US fam*) molesto, fastidioso.

pessary ['pesəri] *n* pesario *m*.

pessimism ['pesimizəm] *n* pesimismo *m*.

pessimist ['pesimist] *n* pesimista *mf*.

pessimistic [,pesi'mistik] *adj* pesimista.

pessimistically [,pesi'mistikəli] *adv* con pesimismo.

pest [pest] *n* (a) (*Zool*) plaga *f*; insecto *m* nocivo, animal *m* dañino; **the moth is a** — **of pinewoods** la mariposa es una plaga de los pinares; **rabbits are a** — **in Australia** el conejo es muy dañino en Australia; **this will kill the** —**s on your roses** esto matará los insectos nocivos de sus rosas.
(b) (*fig: person*) machaca *f*, mosca *f*, pelma *m*; (*thing*) molestia *f*, lata *f*; **what a** — **that child is!** ¡cómo me fastidia ese niño!; **it's a** — **having to go** es una lata tener que ir.

pest control ['pestkən,trəul] *n* lucha *f* contra los insectos nocivos, lucha *f* contra las plagas.

pester ['pestə*] *vt* molestar, acosar, importunar; **he** —**s me** no me deja a sol ni a sombra; **is this man** —**ing you?** ¿le molesta este hombre?; **she** —**ed me for the book** me pidió el libro repetidas veces; **she** —**s me with questions** me molesta con sus preguntas, me fastidia haciendo tantas preguntas; **stop** —**ing!** ¡no machaques!; **to** — **someone to do something** insistir constantemente en que uno haga algo, rogar repetidas veces que uno haga algo.

pesticide ['pestisaid] *n* pesticida *m*.

pestilence ['pestiləns] *n* pestilencia *f*, peste *f*.

pestilent ['pestilənt] *adj* pestilente.

pestilential [ˌpestiˈlenʃəl] adj pestilente; (fam) engorroso, latoso.

pestle ['pesl] n mano f de mortero.

pet[1] [pet] 1 adj animal doméstico, domesticado, de casa, familiar; (favourite) favorito; name etc cariñoso; a — lion un león domesticado; her two — dogs sus dos perros de casa; it's my — subject es mi tema predilecto; see aversion etc.
2 n (a) (animal) animal m doméstico, animal m de casa; perro m, gato m (etc); no —s are allowed in school no se permite llevar animales a la escuela.
(b) (person) favorito m, a f; persona f querida; persona f muy mimada; yes, my — sí, mi cielo; she's teacher's — es la favorita de la maestra; he's rather a — es simpatiquísimo, es un ángel.
3 vt acariciar; (amorously) acariciar, tocar, sobar; (spoil) mimar.
4 vi acariciarse, besuquearse, sobarse, hacerse arrumacos; —ting can go too far las caricias pueden resultar peligrosas.

pet[2] [pet] n: to be in a — estar de mal humor, estar enojado.

petal ['petl] n pétalo m.

petard [peˈtɑːd] n petardo m; he was hoist with his own — le salió el tiro por la culata.

Pete [piːt] m Perico.

Peter ['piːtə*] m Pedro; —'s pence los diezmos de San Pedro; to rob — to pay Paul desnudar a un santo para vestir a otro; — the Great Pedro el Grande.

peter ['piːtə*] vi: to — out (supply) agotarse, acabarse; (vein of metal etc) desaparecer; (plan etc) parar en nada, no dar resultado.

petite [pəˈtiːt] adj chiquita.

petition [pəˈtiʃən] 1 n petición f, memorial m; súplica f; — for divorce petición f de divorcio; to file a — presentar una petición.
2 vt person dirigir una instancia a; to — for something pedir algo, solicitar algo; to — someone to do something rogar a uno hacer algo, pedir que uno haga algo.

petitioner [pəˈtiʃnə*] n suplicante mf.

Petrarch ['petrɑːk] m Petrarca.

Petrarchan [peˈtrɑːkən] adj petrarquista.

Petrarchism ['petrɑːkizəm] n petrarquismo m.

petrel ['petrəl] n petrel m, paíño m.

petrifaction [ˌpetriˈfækʃən] n petrificación f.

petrified ['petrifaid] adj petrificado; see petrify.

petrify ['petrifai] 1 vt (a) petrificar; to become petrified petrificarse.
(b) (fig) pasmar, horrorizar; I was simply petrified! ¡vaya susto que me pegué!; to be petrified with fear estar muerto de miedo.
2 vi petrificarse.

petrol ['petrəl] n gasolina f; (for lighter) bencina f; to run out of — quedarse sin gasolina.

petrol can ['petrəlkæn] n bidón m de gasolina.

petrol engine ['petrəlˌendʒin] n motor m de gasolina.

petroleum [piˈtrəuliəm] n petróleo m.

petrol gauge ['petrəlgeidʒ] n indicador m de nivel de gasolina.

petroliferous [ˌpetrəˈlifərəs] adj petrolífero.

petrology [peˈtrɔlidʒi] n petrología f.

petrol pump ['petrəlpʌmp] n (in engine) bomba f de gasolina; (at garage) surtidor m de gasolina.

petrol station ['petrəlˌsteiʃən] n estación f de gasolina, gasolinera f.

petrol tank ['petrəltæŋk] n depósito m de gasolina.

petticoat ['petikəut] 1 n enaguas fpl; (slip) combinación f; (stiff) falda f can-can.
2 attr: — government gobierno m de mujeres, dominación f de la mujer.

pettifogging ['petifɔgiŋ] adj detail etc insignificante, pequeño, nimio; lawyer etc pedante, charlatán; suggestion etc hecho para entenebrecer el asunto.

pettiness ['petinis] n (a) insignificancia f, pequeñez f; nimiedad f; frivolidad f.
(b) mezquindad f; estrechez f de miras; rencor m; manía f de criticar; intolerancia f.

pettish ['petiʃ] adj malhumorado.

petty ['peti] adj (a) detail etc insignificante, pequeño, nimio; de poca monta; excuse frívolo, baladí; the — wars of the time las pequeñas guerras de la época; the — kings of Moslem Spain los reyezuelos de la España musulmana; some — chieftain algún jefe sin importancia.
(b) (small-minded) mezquino; de miras estrechas; (preoccupied with detail) que se para en menudencias, que se interesa por los detalles nimios; (spiteful) rencoroso; (faultfinding) reparón, criticón; (intolerant) intolerante; you're being very — about it en esto te estás mostrando poco comprensivo, en esto muestras que guardas rencor; see cash, officer etc.

petulance ['petjuləns] n mal humor m.

petulant ['petjulənt] adj malhumorado.

petulantly ['petjuləntli] adv malhumoradamente, con mal humor.

petunia [piˈtjuːniə] n petunia f.

pew [pjuː] n (Eccl) banco m (de iglesia, de los fieles); (fam) asiento m; take a —! ¡siéntate!; can you find a —? ¿puedes buscarte un asiento?

pewter ['pjuːtə*] 1 n peltre m. 2 attr de peltre.

phalange ['fælændʒ] n falange; P— (Spain) Falange f.

phalangist [fæˈlændʒist] 1 adj falangista. 2 n falangista mf.

phalanx ['fælæŋks] n falange f.

phalarope ['fælərəup] n falaropo m.

phallic ['fælik] adj fálico.

phallus ['fæləs] n falo m.

phantasm ['fæntæzəm] n fantasma m.

phantasmagoria [ˌfæntæzməˈgɔːriə] n fantasmagoría f.

phantasmagoric [ˌfæntæzməˈgɔrik] adj fantasmagórico.

phantasmal [fænˈtæzməl] adj fantasmal.

phantom ['fæntəm] 1 n fantasma m. 2 adj fantasmal; the — ship el buque fantasma.

Pharaoh ['feərəu] m Faraón.

Pharaonic [feəˈrɔnik] adj faraónico.

Pharisaic(al) [ˌfæriˈseiik(əl)] adj farisaico.

Pharisee ['færisiː] n fariseo m.

pharmaceutical [ˌfɑːməˈsjuːtikəl] adj farmacéutico.

pharmacist ['fɑːməsist] n farmacéutico m.

pharmacological [ˌfɑːməkəˈlɔdʒikəl] adj farmacológico.

pharmacologist [ˌfɑːməˈkɔlədʒist] n farmacólogo m.

pharmacology [ˌfɑːməˈkɔlədʒi] n farmacología f.

pharmacopoeia [ˌfɑːməkəˈpiːə] n farmacopea f.

pharmacy ['fɑːməsi] n farmacia f.

pharyngitis [ˌfærinˈdʒaitis] n faringitis f.

pharynx ['færiŋks] n faringe f.

phase [feiz] 1 n fase f (also Astron); etapa f; to be out of — estar fuera de fase.
2 vt plan etc proyectar en una serie de etapas; arreglar, organizar; we must — this carefully hay que organizar esto con cuidado; a —d withdrawal una retirada progresiva, una retirada por etapas.

pheasant ['feznt] n faisán m.

phenobarbitone ['fiːnəuˈbɑːbitəun] n fenobarbitona f.

phenol ['fiːnɔl] n fenol m.

phenomenal [fiˈnɔminl] adj fenomenal.

phenomenally [fiˈnɔminəli] adv de modo fenomenal; — rich rico en un grado fenomenal.

phenomenon [fiˈnɔminən] n, pl **phenomena** [fiˈnɔminə] fenómeno m.

phew [fjuː] interj ¡puf!; ¡caramba!

phial ['faiəl] n ampolla f, redoma f, frasco m.

Philadelphia [ˌfiləˈdelfiə] Filadelfia.

philander [fiˈlændə*] vi flirtear, mariposear (with con).

philanderer [fiˈlændərə*] n tenorio m, mariposón m.

philandering [fiˈlændəriŋ] 1 adj mariposón. 2 n flirteo m.

philanthropic [ˌfilənˈθrɔpik] adj filantrópico.

philanthropist [fiˈlænθrəpist] n filántropo m, a f.

philanthropy [fiˈlænθrəpi] n filantropía f.

philatelic [ˌfiləˈtelik] adj filatélico.

philatelist [fiˈlætəlist] n filatelista mf.

philately [fiˈlætəli] n filatelia f.

—phile [fail] —filo, eg francophile francófilo m, a f.

philharmonic [ˌfilɑːˈmɔnik] adj filarmónico.

Philip ['filip] m Felipe.

philippic [fiˈlipik] n filípica f.

Philippine ['filipiːn] 1 adj filipino. 2 n filipino m, a f.

Philippines ['filipiːnz] pl, **Philippine Islands** ['filipiːnˌailəndz] pl Islas fpl Filipinas.

Philistine ['filistain] 1 adj filisteo. 2 n filisteo m, a f.

philistinism ['filistinizəm] n filisteísmo m.

philological [ˌfiləˈlɔdʒikəl] adj filológico.

philologist [fiˈlɔlədʒist] n filólogo m.

philology [fiˈlɔlədʒi] n filología f.

philosopher [fiˈlɔsəfə*] n filósofo m.

philosophic(al) [ˌfiləˈsɔfik(əl)] adj filosófico.

philosophize [fiˈlɔsəfaiz] vi filosofar.

philosophy [fiˈlɔsəfi] n filosofía f; — of life filosofía f de la vida; moral — filosofía f moral; natural — filosofía f natural.

philtre, (US) **philter** ['filtə*] n filtro m.

phiz [fiz] n (fam) jeta f.

phlebitis [fliˈbaitis] n flebitis f.

phlegm [flem] n flema f (also fig).

phlegmatic [fleg'mætik] *adj* flemático.
phlegmatically [fleg'mætikəli] *adv* con flema; **he said** — dijo flemático.
phlox [flɔks] *n* flox *m*.
—phobe [fəub] —fobo, *eg* **francophobe** francófobo *m*, a *f*.
phobia ['fəubiə] *n* fobia *f*.
—phobia ['fəubiə] —fobia, *eg* **anglophobia** anglofobia *f*.
Phoebus ['fi:bəs] *m* Febo.
Phoenicia [fi'niʃiə] Fenicia *f*.
Phoenician [fi'niʃiən] **1** *adj* fenicio. **2** *n* fenicio *m*, a *f*.
phoenix ['fi:niks] *n* fénix *m*.
'phone [fəun] *see* **telephone**.
phoneme ['fəuni:m] *n* fonema *m*.
phonemic [fəu'ni:mik] *adj* fonémico.
phonetic [fəu'netik] *adj* fonético.
phonetician [ˌfəuni'tiʃən] *n* fonetista *mf*.
phonetics [fəu'netiks] *n* fonética *f*.
phoney ['fəuni] (*fam*) **1** *adj* falso, postizo; sospechoso; insincero; **the — war** la extraña guerra; **it's completely** — no es lo que parece ser en absoluto; **there's something — about it** esto huele a camelo.
  2 *n* (*person*) farsante *mf*; (*thing*) cosa *f* falsa, cosa *f* postiza; **it's a** — no tiene nada de auténtico.
phonic ['fɔnik] *adj* fónico.
phonograph ['fəunəgrɑːf] *n* (*US*) gramófono *m*, fonógrafo *m*.
phonological [ˌfəunə'lɔdʒikəl] *adj* fonológico.
phonology [fəu'nɔlədʒi] *n* fonología *f*.
phosgene ['fɔzdʒiːn] *n* fosgeno *m*.
phosphate ['fɔsfeit] *n* fosfato *m*.
phosphoresce [ˌfɔsfə'res] *vi* fosforecer.
phosphorescence [ˌfɔsfə'resns] *n* fosforescencia *f*.
phosphorescent [ˌfɔsfə'resnt] *adj* fosforescente.
phosphoric [fɔs'fɔrik] *adj* fosfórico.
phosphorous ['fɔsfərəs] *adj* fosforoso.
phosphorus ['fɔsfərəs] *n* fósforo *m*.
photo ['fəutəu] *n* foto *f*; *see* **photograph**.
photocopier ['fəutəu'kɔpiə*] *n* fotocopiador *m*.
photocopy ['fəutəuˌkɔpi] **1** *n* fotocopia *f*. **2** *vt* fotocopiar.
photoelectric ['fəutəui'lektrik] *adj* fotoeléctrico; — **cell** célula *f* fotoeléctrica.
photoengraving ['fəutəuen'greiviŋ] *n* fotograbado *m*.
photo finish ['fəutəu'finiʃ] *n* resultado *m* comprobado por fotocontrol; (*fig*) final *m* muy reñido.
photoflash ['fəutəuflæʃ] *n* flash *m*, magnesio *m*.
photogenic [ˌfəutəu'dʒenik] *adj* fotogénico.
photograph ['fəutəgræf] **1** *n* fotografía *f* (*foto*); **aerial** — aerofoto *f*; **colour** — fotografía *f* en colores; **to take a** — sacar una foto.
  2 *vt* fotografiar, hacer una fotografía de, sacar una foto de; **"—ed by X"** "fotografía de X".
  3 *vi*: **to — well** ser fotogénico, sacar buena foto.
photographer [fə'tɔgrəfə*] *n* fotógrafo *m*, a *f*.
photographic [ˌfəutə'græfik] *adj* fotográfico.
photographically [ˌfəutə'græfikəli] *adv*: **to record something** — registrar algo por medio de fotografías, hacer una historia fotográfica de algo.
photography [fə'tɔgrəfi] *n* fotografía *f* (*arte*); **aerial** — fotografía *f* aérea; **colour** — fotografía *f* en colores; **trick** — trucaje *m*.
photogravure [ˌfəutəgrə'vjuə*] *n* fotograbado *m*.
photometer [fə'tɔmətə*] *n* fotómetro *m*.
photon ['fəutɔn] *n* fotón *m*.
photostat ['fəutəustæt] (*Protected Trade Name in US*) **1** *n* fotóstato *m*. **2** *vt* fotostatar.
photosynthesis [ˌfəutəu'sinθəsis] *n* fotosíntesis *f*.
phototropism ['fəutəu'trəupizəm] *n* fototropismo *m*.
phrase [freiz] **1** *n* frase *f* (*also Mus*), expresión *f*, locución *f*; **set** — frase *f* hecha.
  2 *vt* expresar; **a carefully —d letter** una carta redactada con cuidado; **can we — that differently?** ¿podemos poner eso de otro modo?
phrasebook ['freizbuk] *n* libro *m* de frases.
phraseology [ˌfreizi'ɔlədʒi] *n* fraseología *f*.
phrasing ['freiziŋ] *n* (*act*) redacción *f*; (*style*) estilo *m*, fraseología *f*, términos *mpl*; (*Mus*) fraseo *m*; **the** — **is rather unfortunate** los términos empleados se han escogido bastante mal.
phrenetic [fri'netik] *adj* frenético.
phrenologist [fri'nɔlədʒist] *n* frenólogo *m*.
phrenology [fri'nɔlədʒi] *n* frenología *f*.
phthisis ['θaisis] *n* tisis *f*.
phut [fʌt] *adj* (*fam*): **to go** — estropearse, romperse, averiarse; (*fig*) fracasar, acabarse.
phylactery [fi'læktəri] *n* filacteria *f*.
phylloxera [ˌfilɔk'siərə] *n* filoxera *f*.

phylum ['failum] *n*, *pl* **phyla** ['failə] filo *m*, filum *m*.
physic ['fizik] *n* (*arch*) medicina *f*.
physical ['fizikəl] *adj* físico.
physically ['fizikəli] *adv* físicamente.
physician [fi'ziʃən] *n* médico *m*.
physicist ['fizisist] *n* físico *m*.
physics ['fiziks] *n* física *f*; **nuclear** — física *f* nuclear.
physiognomy [ˌfizi'ɔnəmi] *n* fisonomía *f*.
physiological ['fiziə'lɔdʒikəl] *adj* fisiológico.
physiologist [ˌfizi'ɔlədʒist] *n* fisiólogo *m*.
physiology [ˌfizi'ɔlədʒi] *n* fisiología *f*.
physiotherapist [ˌfiziə'θerəpist] *n* fisioterapeuta *mf*.
physiotherapy [ˌfiziə'θerəpi] *n* fisioterapia *f*.
physique [fi'ziːk] *n* físico *m*.
pi [pai] *adj* (*sl*) piadoso, devoto.
pianist ['piənist] *n* pianista *mf*.
piano ['pjɑːnəu] *n*, **pianoforte** [ˌpjɑːnəu'fɔːti] *n* piano *m*; **baby grand** — piano *m* de media cola; **grand** — piano *m* de cola; **upright** — piano *m* vertical.
piano-accordion ['pjɑːnəuə'kɔːdiən] *n* acordeón-piano *m*.
pianola [piə'nəulə] *n* piano *m* mecánico, aristón *m*.
piano stool ['pjɑːnəuˌstuːl] *n* taburete *m* de piano.
piano tuner ['pjɑːnəuˌtjuːnə*] *n* afinador *m* de pianos.
piastre, (*US*) **piaster** [pi'æstə*] *n* piastra *f*.
piazza [pi'ætsə] *n* (*US*) pórtico *m*, galería *f*.
pica ['paikə] *n* (*Med*, *Vet*) pica *f*; (*Typ*) cícero *m*.
Picardy ['pikədi] Picardía *f*.
picaresque [ˌpikə'resk] *adj* picaresco.
picayune [ˌpikə'juːn] (*US*) **1** *adj* de poca monta. **2** *n* (*person*) persona *f* insignificante; (*thing*) bagatela *f*.
piccalilli ['pikəˌlili] *n* legumbres *fpl* en escabeche.
piccaninny ['pikəˌnini] *n* negrito *m*, a *f*.
piccolo ['pikələu] *n* flautín *m*, píccolo *m*.
pick [pik] **1** *n* (a) (*tool*) pico *m*, zapapico *m*, piqueta *f*.
  (b) (*choice*, *right to choose*) derecho *m* de elección; **it's your** — a ti te toca elegir; **whose — is it?** ¿a quién le toca elegir?; **take your —!** ¡escoja el que quiera!
  (c) (*best*) lo mejor, lo más escogido; flor *f* y nata; **it's the — of the bunch** es el mejor del grupo.
  2 *vt* (a) (*hole etc*) picar, hacer; **teeth** mondarse, limpiarse; **nose** hurgarse; **bone** roer; **bird** desplumar; **lock** forzar, abrir con ganzúa.
  (b) (*choose*) escoger, elegir; escoger con cuidado; **team** seleccionar; (*pluck*) **flowers** coger, **fruit** coger, recoger; **to — one's way** andar con mucho tiento (*across* por), abrirse camino (*among* entre, *through* por).
  (c) **to — pockets** ratear, dedicarse a ser carterista; **to — someone's pocket** robar algo del bolsillo de uno.
  (d) (*with adv or prep*) **to — off** *paint etc* arrancar, separar; (*shoot*) matar de un tiro, matar con tiros sucesivos; **to — out** (*choose*) escoger; entresacar; (*identify*) conocer, identificar; (*discern*) lograr ver, alcanzar a ver; **to — out a tune on the piano** tocar de oído una melodía al piano; **to — out a colour** hacer resaltar un color; **to — out letters in gold** hacer resaltar unas letras pintándolas de oro; **to — some books over** ir revolviendo y examinando unos libros; **to — up** *object on floor etc* recoger; *telephone* descolgar; (*acquire*) adquirir, (*buy*) comprar, (*find*) encontrar; *prisoner* detener; *girl* conocer, encontrar; (*learn*) aprender, (*come to hear of*) saber, saber por casualidad; *radio message* interceptar, *radio station* captar; (*recover*) recobrar; **to — up a child in one's arms** levantar a un niño en los brazos; **to — up a trick** aprender un truco; **to — up some words of a language** aprender algunas palabras de un idioma; **I —ed it up cheap** lo adquirí por muy poco dinero; **the car —ed up speed** el coche se aceleró, el coche cobró velocidad; **we —ed them up at the station** fuimos a recogerles a la estación; **he —ed her up at a café** la conoció en un café; **he —s up a living selling firewood** se gana la vida vendiendo astillas; **I —ed that bit of news up yesterday** esa noticia la supe ayer.
  3 *vi*: **to — and choose** tardar en decidirse; hacer melindres al escoger, mostrarse difícil; **I like to — and choose** me gusta elegir con cuidado; **to — at one's food** comer con poco apetito, comer con poca gana; **to — at someone** (*US*), **to — on someone** perseguir a uno, criticar mucho a uno; **why — on me?** ¿por qué me lo dice a mí y no a otro?; **you're always —ing on me** me tiene manía; **to — up** (*Med etc*) reponerse; **business is —ing up** los negocios van mejor; **the team —ed up towards the end** hacia el final el equipo jugó mejor.

pickaback ['pikəbæk] *adv*: **to carry someone** — llevar a uno sobre los hombros.

pickaxe ['pikæks] *n* pico *m*, zapapico *m*, piqueta *f*.

picked [pikt] *adj* escogido, selecto.

picker ['pikə*] *n* (*of fruit etc*) recogedor *m*, ora *f*.

picket ['pikit] **1** *n* (**a**) (*stake*) estaca *f*.

(**b**) (*Mil*) piquete *m*; (*band of strikers*) guardia *f* de vigilantes huelguistas, piquete *m*; (*striker*) vigilante *m* huelguista, piquetero *m*.

2 *vt* factory piquetear, cercar con un cordón de huelguistas.

3 *vi* estar de guardia (los vigilantes huelguistas).

picket line ['pikitlain] *n* línea *f* de vigilantes huelguistas.

picking ['pikiŋ] *n* (**a**) (*of fruit etc*) recolección *f*, cosecha *f*; (*act of choosing*) elección *f*, selección *f*.

(**b**) **—s** (*leftovers*) sobras *fpl*, desperdicios *mpl*; (*profits*) ganancias *fpl*; (*stolen goods*) artículos *mpl* robados.

pickle ['pikl] **1** *n* (**a**) (*as condiment*) encurtido *m* (*also* **—s**); (*of fish, olives*) escabeche *m*; (*of meat*) adobo *m*; (*in salt solution*) salmuera *f*.

(**b**) (*plight*) apuro *m*; **to be in a** (*person*) — estar en un apuro, (*room*) estar en desorden, estar revuelto; **to get into a** — meterse en líos; **what a —!** ¡qué lío!

(**c**) (*child*) diablillo *m*, pillo *m*.

2 *vt* encurtir; escabechar; adobar; conservar, conservar en vinagre; (*Bio*) conservar en alcohol, conservar en formalina.

pickled ['pikld] *adj* (**a**) escabechado, encurtido, en conserva; **— onions** cebollas *fpl* en vinagre; **— herrings** arenques *mpl* en escabeche.

(**b**) **to be —** (*sl*) estar jumado (*sl*).

picklock ['piklɔk] *n* ganzúa *f*.

pick-me-up ['pikmiʌp] *n* (*drink*) reconstituyente *m*; (*Med*) tónico *m*.

pickpocket ['pik,pɔkit] *n* carterista *m*, ratero *m*.

pickup ['pikʌp] *n* (*of gramophone*) pick-up *m*, fonocaptor *m* (*Acad*).

picnic ['piknik] **1** *n* (**a**) jira *f*, excursión *f* campestre, merienda *f* en el campo, picnic *m*; **to go for a —**, **to go on a —** ir de jira, merendar en el campo; **we found a nice place for a —** encontramos un buen sitio para merendar.

(**b**) (*fam*) **it was no —** no tenía nada de fácil, no tenía nada de agradable.

2 *vi* ir de jira, merendar en el campo; llevar la merienda al campo; **we —ked by the river** merendamos junto al río; **we go —king every Sunday** todos los domingos vamos de jira.

picnicker ['piknikə*] *n* excursionista *mf*.

Pict [pikt] *n* picto *m*, a *f*.

Pictish ['piktiʃ] **1** *adj* picto. **2** *n* picto *m*.

pictorial [pik'tɔːriəl] **1** *adj* pictórico; *magazine* gráfico, ilustrado. **2** *n* revista *f* ilustrada.

pictorially [pik'tɔːriəli] *adv* pictóricamente; *represent etc* gráficamente, por imágenes.

picture ['piktʃə*] **1** *n* (**a**) (*Art*) cuadro *m*, pintura *f*; (*portrait*) retrato *m*; (*photo*) fotografía *f*; (*in book*) lámina *f*, estampa *f*, grabado *m*.

(**b**) (*TV*) cuadro *m*, imagen *f*; **we had a good —** la imagen era buena.

(**c**) (*Cine*) película *f*, film *m*; **the —s** el cine; **silent —** película *f* muda; **talking —** película *f* sonora; **to go to a —** ir a ver una película; **to go to the —s** ir al cine.

(**d**) (*spoken etc*) descripción *f*; (*mental*) imagen *f*; idea *f*; recuerdo *m*; (*outlook*) perspectiva *f*; (*overall view*) visión *f* de conjunto; **the other side of the —** el reverso de la medalla; **she looked a —!** ¡estaba guapísima!; **the garden is a — in June** en junio el jardín es de lo más hermoso; **his face was a —!** ¡había que ver la cara que puso!; **she looked a — of health** era la salud personificada; **he gave us a grim —** nos hizo una descripción horrorosa; **he painted a black — of the future** nos hizo un cuadro muy negro del porvenir; **I have no very clear — of it** no lo recuerdo con claridad; **these figures give the general —** estas cifras ofrecen una visión de conjunto; **are you in the —?** ¿estás enterado?; **to put someone in the —** poner a uno al corriente de algo.

2 *attr* de pinturas, de cuadros; *paper* gráfico, ilustrado; *hat* de ala ancha.

3 *vt* (*paint*) pintar; (*describe*) pintar, describir; **to — something to oneself** imaginarse algo, epresentarse algo en la imaginación; **— the scene** figuraos la escena. **— if you can a winkle** imaginaos, si podéis, una litorina.

picture book ['piktʃəbuk] *n* libro *m* de imágenes.

picture frame ['piktʃəfreim] *n* marco *m* (para cuadro).

picture gallery ['piktʃə'gæləri] *n* museo *m* de pintura, museo *m* de bellas artes; **the Prado —** el Museo del Prado.

picturegoer ['piktʃə,gəuə*] *n* aficionado *m* al cine, aficionada *f* al cine.

picture palace ['piktʃə,pælis] *n* cine *m*.

picture postcard ['piktʃə'pəustkɑːd] *n* postal *f* ilustrada.

picture rail ['piktʃəreil] *n* moldura *f* (*pegada a la pared para colgar cuadros*).

picturesque [,piktʃə'resk] *adj* pintoresco; (*quaint, of tourist interest*) típico.

picturesquely [,piktə'reskli] *adv* de modo pintoresco.

picture window ['piktʃə,windəu] *n* ventana *f* grande (de una sola hoja de vidrio).

piddle ['pidl] *see* **piss.**

piddling ['pidliŋ] *adj* (*fam*) de poca monta, insignificante.

pidgin ['pidʒin] *n* (*also* **— English**) lengua franca (inglés-chino) comercial del Lejano Oriente.

pie [pai] *n* (*of fruit etc*) pastel *m*, tarta *f*; (*of meat*) empanada *f*, pastel *m*; **it's — in the sky** es como prometer la luna; **to eat humble —** humillarse y pedir perdón.

piebald ['paibɔːld] *adj* pío, de varios colores.

piece [piːs] **1** *n* (**a**) (*fragment*) pedazo *m*, trozo *m*, fragmento *m*; (*Mech, Mil*) pieza *f*; (*coin*) moneda *f*; (*Lit, Theat, Mus*) obra *f*, pieza *f*; (*Chess*) pieza *f*, ficha *f*; **a two-shilling —** una moneda de dos chelines; **— set** (*of fireworks etc*) cuadro *m*, (*Art*) grupo *m*, (*Lit etc*) escena *f* importante, episodio *m* central; **that nice — in the third movement** aquel pasaje tan bonito del tercer tiempo; **to buy something by the —** comprar algo por piezas; **it is made all in one —** está hecho de una pieza, forma pieza única, las partes no son separables; **the back is all of a —** with the seat el respaldo forma pieza única con el asiento; **to get back all in one —** volver sano y salvo; **we got it back all in one —** nos lo devolvieron en buen estado; **this is of a — with the other** éste es de la misma clase que el otro, éste se parece al otro; **this is of a — with what he told us** esto es conforme con lo que él nos dijo, esto concuerda con lo que él nos dijo.

(**b**) (*girl: sl*) **a nice little —** una pizpireta, una chica muy mona.

(**c**) (*examples of a — of*) **a — of paper** un trozo de papel, una hoja de papel, un papel; **a — of bread** un pedazo de pan; **a — of cake** una porción de tarta; **another — of cake?** ¿quieres más tarta?; **a — of my work** una de mis obras, una muestra de mi trabajo; **a — out of a book** un trozo de un libro; **a — of advice** un consejo; **a — of carelessness** un descuido, un acto de imprudencia; **a — of clothing** una prenda (de vestir); **a — of folly** una locura, un acto de locura; **a — of furniture** un mueble; **a — of ground** un terreno, (*for building*) un solar; **by a — of good luck** por suerte; **a — of luggage** un bulto; **3 —s of luggage** 3 bultos; **a — of news** una noticia, una nueva; **a — of poetry** una poesía; *see* **mind** *etc*.

(**d**) **to be in —s** (*taken apart*) estar desmontado, (*broken*) estar hecho pedazos, estar roto; **to break something to** (*or* **in**) **—s** hacer algo pedazos; **to break** (*vi*) **in —s** hacerse pedazos; **to come to —s**, **to fall to —s** hacerse pedazos, romperse; **it comes to —s** se desmonta, es desmontable; **to go to —s** (*person*) sufrir un ataque de nervios, (*Med*) perder la salud, (*team etc*) desanimarse por completo; **to hack something to —** cortar algo en pedazos (violentamente, despiadadamente *etc*); **to pull to —s** deshacer, despedazar, hacer pedazos, *argument* deshacer, *person* criticar duramente; **to smash something to —s** destrozar algo violentamente, romper algo a golpes; **the boat was smashed to —s on the rocks** el barco se estrelló contra las rocas y se hizo pedazos; **to take something to —s** desmontar algo; **it takes to —s** se desmonta, es desmontable; **to tear something to —s** romper algo violentamente, (*prey etc*) desgarrar algo; **the crowd will tear him to —s** la gente le hará pedazos; **he tore the theory to —s** deshizo rápidamente la teoría.

2 *vt*: **— together** juntar, juntar las partes de; (*Mech*) montar, ir montando; (*fig*) atar cabos e ir comprendiendo; **we eventually —d the story together** por fin logramos saber toda la historia, por fin logramos atar todos los cabos.

pièce de résistance [,pjesdərezis'tɑːs] *n* lo principal, lo más importante; (*on menu*) plato *m* principal; (*in programme*) atracción *f* principal, número *m* más importante.

piecemeal ['piːsmiːl] **1** *adv* (*bit by bit*) poco a poco, a trozos, por etapas; (*haphazard*) sin sistema fijo. **2** *adj* poco sistemático.

piecework ['piːswəːk] *n* trabajo *m* a destajo; **to be on —, to do —** trabajar a destajo.

pieceworker ['piːswəːkə*] *n* destajista *mf*.

piecrust ['paikrʌst] *n* pasta *f* de pastel.

pied [paid] *adj* *animal* pío, de varios colores; *bird* manchado.

pied-à-terre [ˌpieidæˈtɛə*] *n* apeadero *m*.

Piedmont ['piːdmɒnt] Piamonte *m*.

Piedmontese [ˌpiːdmɒnˈtiːz] **1** *adj* piamontés. **2** *n* piamontés *m*, esa *f*.

pie-eyed ['paiˈaid] *adj* (*fam*) jumado (*fam*).

pier [piə*] *n* (*Archit*) pilar *m*, columna *f*; (*of bridge*) estribo *m*, pila *f*; (*Naut*) dique *m*, malecón *m*, embarcadero *m*, (*with amusements*) muelle *m*.

pierce [piəs] *vt* penetrar; atravesar; (*hole*) agujerear; (*bore*) horadar, perforar; (*punch*) taladrar; (*puncture*) pinchar; **the bullet —d the armour** la bala penetró en la coraza; **the bullet —d his lung** la bala le atravesó el pulmón, la bala entró en el pulmón; **to have one's ears —d** hacerse taladrar las orejas; **the rock is —d by numerous holes** la roca está agujereada (*or* horadada) en muchos sitios; **a nail —d the tyre** un clavo pinchó el neumático; **the dam had been —d in various places** se habían abierto brechas en distintas partes de la presa; **a wall —d with loopholes** un muro en el que se abrían aspilleras; **to — something through and through** perforar algo una y otra vez; **a cry —d the silence** un grito desgarró el silencio; **a light —d the darkness** una luz empezó súbitamente a brillar en la oscuridad; **the news —d him to the heart** la noticia le hirió en el alma.

piercing ['piəsiŋ] *adj* *wind* cortante; *cry* agudo, penetrante; *look* penetrante.

piercingly ['piəsiŋli] *adv* *blow* de modo cortante; *cry* agudamente, en tono penetrante.

pier glass ['piəglɑːs] *n* espejo *m* de cuerpo entero.

pierhead ['piəhed] *n* punta *f* del muelle.

pierrot ['piərəu] *n* pierrot *m*.

pietism ['paiətizəm] *n* piedad *f*, devoción *f*; (*pej*) beatería *f*, mojigatería *f*.

pietistic [paiəˈtistik] *adj* (*pej*) beato, mojigato.

piety ['paiəti] *n* piedad *f*, devoción *f*; **affected —** beatería *f*.

piffle ['pifl] *n* disparates *mpl*, tonterías *fpl*; **—!** ¡tonterías!

piffling ['pifliŋ] *adj* de poca monta, insignificante.

pig [pig] **1** *n* (a) cerdo *m*, puerco *m*, cochino *m*; **roast —** cochinillo *m* asado, lechón *m* asado; **to buy a — in a poke** cerrar un trato a ciegas; **to sell someone a — in a poke** dar gato por liebre.

(b) (*fig*: *person*) cochino *m*, marrano *m*; **you —!** (*hum*) ¡bandido!; **the boss is a —** el jefe es un bruto; **you're a —, sir!** ¡Vd es un maleducado!; **to make a — of oneself** comer demasiado; darse un atracón (*over* de).

(c) (*Metal*) lingote *m*.

2 *vt*: **to — it** vivir como cerdos.

pigeon ['pidʒən] *n* paloma *f*, palomo *m*; (*young*) palomino *m*, pichón *m*; (*as food*) pichón *m*; **carrier —, homing —** paloma *f* mensajera; **clay —** pichón *m* de barro.

pigeonhole ['pidʒənhəul] **1** *n* casilla *f*; **set of —s** casillas *fpl*, casillero *m*.

2 *vt* (*classify*) encasillar, clasificar; (*store away*) archivar; archivar en la memoria; (*shelve*) dar carpetazo a.

pigeon house ['pidʒənhaus] *n*, *pl* **— houses** [hauziz], **pigeon loft** ['pidʒənlɒft] *n* palomar *m*.

pigeon shooting ['pidʒənˌʃuːtiŋ] *n* tiro *m* de pichón.

pigeon-toed ['pidʒənˈtəud] *adj* patituerto.

piggery ['pigəri] *n* pocilga *f*, porqueriza *f*, cochiquera *f*.

piggy ['pigi] *n* cerdito *m*, cochinillo *m*, lechón *m*.

piggy bank ['pigibæŋk] *n* hucha *f* en forma de cerdito.

pigheaded ['pigˈhedid] *adj* *person* terco, testarudo; *attitude etc* obstinado; **it was a — thing to do** fue un acto que reveló su terquedad.

pigheadedly ['pigˈhedidli] *adv* tercamente; obstinadamente.

pigheadedness ['pigˈhedidnis] *n* terquedad *f*, testarudez *f*; obstinación *f*.

pig iron ['pigˌaiən] *n* hierro *m* en lingotes.

piglet ['piglit] *n* cerdito *m*, cochinillo *m*, lechón *m*.

pigman ['pigmæn] *n*, *pl* **—men** [men] porquerizo *m*, porquero *m*.

pigment ['pigmənt] *n* pigmento *m*.

pigmentation [ˌpigmənˈteiʃən] *n* pigmentación *f*.

pigmented ['pigmentid] *adj* pigmentado.

pigmy ['pigmi] **1** *adj* pigmeo; (*fig*) enano; miniatura, pequeñito. **2** *n* pigmeo *m*, a *f*, enano *m*, a *f*.

pigskin ['pigskin] *n* piel *f* de cerdo.

pigsty ['pigstai] *n* pocilga *f*, porqueriza *f*, cochiquera *f* (*also fig*).

pigtail ['pigteil] *n* (*of Chinese, bullfighter etc*) coleta *f*; (*girl's*) trenza *f*.

pigswill ['pigswil] *n* bazofia *f* (*also fig*).

pike¹ [paik] *n* (*Mil*) pica *f*, chuzo *m*.

pike² [paik] *n* (*Fish*) lucio *m*, sollo *m*.

pike³ [paik] *n* (*Geog*) pico *m*.

pikeman ['paikmən] *n*, *pl* **—men** [mən] piquero *m*.

piker ['paikə*] *n* (*US sl*) (*mean person*) cicatero *m*; (*unimportant person*) persona *f* de poco fuste; (*coward*) cobarde *m*.

pikestaff ['paikstɑːf] *n* see **plain 1**.

pilaster [piˈlæstə*] *n* pilastra *f*.

Pilate ['pailət] *m* Pilatos.

pilchard ['piltʃəd] *n* sardina *f* arenque.

pile¹ [pail] *n* (*Archit*) pilote *m*.

pile² [pail] **1** *n* (a) (*heap*) montón *m*, pila *f*, rimero *m*; **to make a — of things, to put things in a —** amontonar cosas, juntar cosas en un montón.

(b) (*fam*) fortuna *f*; **to make one's —** hacer su agosto; **he made his — in oil** se hizo una fortuna en el negocio del petróleo.

(c) (*of buildings*) mole *f*, masa *f* imponente, conjunto *m* grandioso; **the Escorial, that noble —** El Escorial, aquel edificio tan imponente.

(d) (*Phys etc*) pila *f*; **atomic —** pila *f* atómica.

2 *vt* (*also* **to — up**) amontonar, apilar, juntar en un montón; acumular: **we —d it all up high** hicimos un montón tan alto como podía ser; **a table —d high with books** una mesa cargada de libros; **he went on piling up the evidence** fue acumulando los datos, fue amontonando las pruebas; **to — on the pressure** ir aumentando la presión, (*fig*) presionar cada vez más fuerte; **to — on the agony** aumentar el dolor, añadir dolor sobre dolor; **to — coal on the fire, to — the fire up with coal** echar carbón al fuego; **to — it on** exagerar; **he does rather — it on** es un exagerado.

3 *vi* (a) (*also* **to — up**) amontonarse, apilarse; acumularse; **the evidence is piling up** las pruebas van acumulándose.

(b) **the car —d up against the wall** el coche se estrelló contra el muro; **the ship —d up on the rocks** el buque se estrelló contra las rocas.

(c) **we all —d into the car** entramos todos en el coche; **— in!** ¡dentro todos, que nos vamos!

pile³ [pail] *n* (*of carpet*) pelo *m*; (*of cloth*) pelillo *m*.

pile driver ['pailˌdraivə*] *n* martinete *m*.

piles [pailz] *npl* (*Med*) almorranas *fpl*, hemorroides *fpl*.

pileup ['pailʌp] *n* (*Aut etc*) accidente *m* múltiple; **there was a — at the corner** chocaron varios coches en la esquina, hubo un accidente múltiple en la esquina.

pilfer ['pilfə*] **1** *vt* *article* ratear; **the crate had been —ed** algunos artículos habían sido robados del cajón; **they often — the trucks** con frecuencia roban cosas de los vagones.

2 *vi* ratear, robar cosas.

pilferer ['pilfərə*] *n* ratero *m*, a *f*.

pilfering ['pilfəriŋ] *n* ratería *f*.

pilgrim ['pilgrim] *n* peregrino *m*, a *f*, romero *m*, a *f*; **the —s to Compostela** los que van en peregrinación a Compostela; **the P— Fathers** los padres peregrinos.

pilgrimage ['pilgrimidʒ] *n* peregrinación *f*, romería *f*; **to go on a —, to make a —** ir en peregrinación, ir en romería (*to* a).

pill [pil] *n* píldora *f*; (*sl*) pelota *f*; **birth-control —** píldora *f* anticonceptiva; **it was a bitter — (to swallow)** fue una píldora amarga, fue un trago amargo; **to sugar the —** dorar la píldora.

pillage ['pilidʒ] **1** *n* pillaje *m*, saqueo *m*. **2** *vt* pillar, saquear.

pillar ['pilə*] *n* pilar *m*, columna *f*; (*fig*) sostén *m*, pilar *m*; **— of salt** estatua *f* de sal; **the P—s of Hercules** las Columnas de Hércules; **to be a — of strength** ser una roca, ser una columna de sostén; **to chase someone from — to post** no dejar a uno a sol ni a sombra.

pillar box ['piləbɒks] *n* buzón *m*.

pillbox ['pilbɒks] *n* (*Med*) cajita *f* de píldoras; (*Mil*) fortín *m*.

pillion ['piljən] *n*: **— seat** asiento *m* de atrás, asiento *m* de pasajero; **to ride —** ir en el asiento de atrás.

pillory ['piləri] **1** *n* picota *f*. **2** *vt* (*fig*) poner en ridículo, satirizar; censurar duramente.

pillow ['piləu] **1** n almohada f.
2 vt apoyar sobre una almohada; apoyar, servir de almohada a; **she —ed her head on my shoulder** apoyó la cabeza en mi hombro.
pillowcase ['piləukeis] n funda f de almohada.
pilot ['pailət] **1** n (Aer) piloto m; (Naut) práctico m, piloto m; **automatic —** piloto m automático.
2 adj piloto, experimental; see **plant**.
3 vt pilotar; (fig) guiar, conducir; dirigir; **a plane —ed by . . .** un avión pilotado por . . .; **he —ed the negotiations through** él dirigió las negociaciones, él condujo las negociaciones a buen fin; **to — a bill through the House** encargarse de un proyecto de ley durante los debates parlamentarios sobre éste.
pilot boat ['pailətbəut] n bote m del práctico.
pilot house ['pailəthaus] n, pl **— houses** [hauziz] (Naut) timonera f.
pilot officer ['pailət‚ɔfisə*] n oficial m de aviación.
pimento [pi'mentəu] n pimienta f.
pimp [pimp] **1** n alcahuete m; coime m, chulo m de putas. **2** vi alcahuetear; ser coime, ser chulo de putas; **to — for somone** servir de alcahuete a uno.
pimpernel ['pimpənel] n murajes mpl, pimpinela f; **the Scarlet P—** el Pimpinela escarlata.
pimple ['pimpl] n grano m; **she came out in —s** le salieron granos.
pimply ['pimpli] adj lleno de granos, cubierto de granos; **— youth** (fig) mocoso m, mozalbete m.
pin [pin] **1** n (Sew etc) alfiler m; (Mech: bolt) perno m, (cotter) chaveta f; (wooden) clavija f; **—s** (sl) piernas fpl; **split —** chaveta f; **—s and needles** hormiguillo m, hormigueo m; **like a new —** como una patena; **for two —s I'd knock his head off** le daría una paliza por menos de nada; **you could have heard a — drop** se hizo un profundo silencio.
2 vt **(a)** prender con alfiler, prender con alfileres; (with bolt) sujetar (con perno etc); **to — a notice up** fijar un anuncio con chinches; **to — a medal to someone's uniform** prender una medalla al uniforme de uno; **to — papers together** unir unos papeles con una grapa; **to — someone's arms to his side** sujetar los brazos de uno; **to — someone against a wall** apretar a uno contra una pared; **the battalion was —ned against the river** el batallón estaba copado junto al río, el batallón quedó inmovilizado junto al río.
(b) (fig) **to — someone down** obligar a uno a que concrete; **it's impossible to — him down** es imposible hacerle concretar; **you can't — him down to a date** es imposible lograr que nos diga una fecha concreta; **there's something odd I can't quite — down** hay alguna rareza que no puedo precisar; **the idea is rather hard to — down** es un concepto inaprehensible.
(c) (fam) **to — something on someone** acusar (falsamente) a uno de algo; **you can't — it on me** no podéis lograr que yo cargue con la culpa, es imposible probar que yo lo hiciera; **they —ned a number of robberies on him** le acusaron (falsamente) de haber participado en una serie de robos.
pinafore ['pinəfɔ:*] n delantal m (de niña); **— dress** mandil m.
pince-nez ['pɛ̃:nsnei] npl quevedos mpl.
pincer ['pinsə*] adj: **— movement** (Mil) movimiento m de pinza.
pincers ['pinsəz] npl tenazas fpl, pinzas fpl; **a pair of —** unas tenazas.
pinch [pintʃ] **1** n **(a)** (with fingers) pellizco m; **to give someone a — on the arm** pellizcar el brazo a uno.
(b) (small quantity) pizca f; pulgarada f; **a — of salt** (Cook) una pizca de sal; **to take something with a — of salt** tomar algo con un grano de sal; **a — of snuff** un polvo de rapé.
(c) apuro m; **to feel the — (empezar a) pasar** apuros; **to feel the — of hunger** empezar a tener hambre; **to feel the — of poverty** saber lo que significa ser pobre; **at a —** si es realmente necesario, en caso de necesidad.
2 vt **(a)** (with fingers) pellizcar, dar un pellizcón a; (squeeze, crush) apretar, estrujar, aplastar; (of shoe) apretar; **to — one's finger in the door** cogerse el dedo al cerrar la puerta; **to — off a bud** quitar un brote con los dedos, separar un brote con la uña.
(b) (fam: steal) birlar (fam), guindar (fam), pisar (fam); (arrest) detener, coger, pescar (fam); (charge) acusar; **I had my pen —ed** me guindaron la pluma; **he —ed that idea from Shaw** esa idea la tomó de Shaw; **A —ed B's girl** A le pisó la novia a B; **the police —ed him with the stuff on him** los policías le detuvieron llevando todavía encima los géneros robados; **he got —ed for a parking offence** le pescaron en una infracción de aparcamiento.

3 vi **(a)** (shoe) apretar; **to know where the shoe —es** saber dónde aprieta el zapato.
(b) (economize) economizar; privarse de lo necesario; **we had to — and scrape** tuvimos que hacer muchas economías; **they —ed and scraped to send her to college** se privaron de muchas cosas a fin de poder enviarla a la universidad.
pinchbeck ['pintʃbek] **1** n similor m. **2** attr de similor.
pinched ['pintʃt] adj: **to look —** tener la cara pálida; **to look — with cold** estar aterido, estar chupado.
pinch-hit ['pintʃhit] vi (US) batear de suplente; (fig) sustituir a otro en un apuro.
pinchpenny ['pintʃpeni] adj tacaño.
pincushion ['pin‚kuʃən] n acerico m.
Pindar ['pində*] m Píndaro.
Pindaric [pin'dærik] adj pindárico.
pine¹ [pain] n pino m.
pine² [pain] vi (also **to — away**) languidecer, consumirse; **to — for** suspirar por, perecer por, consumirse pensando en.
pineapple ['pain‚æpl] n piña f (de las Indias), ananás m.
pinecone ['painkəun] n piña f.
pine grove ['paingrəuv] n pinar m.
pine kernel ['pain‚kə:nl] n piñón m.
pine marten ['pain‚mɑ:tin] n marta f.
pine needle ['pain‚ni:dl] n aguja f de pino.
pine tree ['paintri:] n pino m.
pinewood ['painwud] n pinar m.
ping [piŋ] **1** n (of bullet: through air) silbido m, (on striking) sonido m metálico; (of bell) tintín m.
2 vi silbar (como una bala); hacer un sonido metálico (como una bala); tintinear, hacer tintín.
ping-pong ['piŋpɔŋ] (Protected Trade Name in US) n ping-pong m.
pinion ['pinjən] **1** n (Mech) piñón m; (wing: poet) ala f. **2** vt bird cortar las alas a; person atar los brazos a; **he was —ed against the wall** estaba contra la pared sin poderse mover.
pink¹ [piŋk] **1** n **(a)** (Bot) clavel m, clavellina f.
(b) (colour) color m de rosa.
(c) hunting **—** levitín m rojo de caza.
(d) (Pol) rojillo m, a f.
(e) **to be in the —** estar en perfecta salud, estar como un reloj; **to be in the — of condition** estar en perfecto estado, estar en el mejor estado posible.
2 adj (colour) rosado, color de rosa; (Pol) rojillo; **strike me —!** (fam) ¡caray!; **to be tickled — about something** (fam) encontrar algo divertidísimo, reírse mucho con algo.
pink² [piŋk] vt (Sew) ondear, picar; **to — someone with a sword** herir a uno levemente con un florete.
pink³ [piŋk] vi (US) picar (por autoencendido).
pinkie ['piŋki] n (Pol fam) rojillo m, a f; (fam) dedo m meñique.
pinking shears ['piŋkiŋ‚ʃiəz] npl tijeras fpl grandes (de costura) de corte ondulado.
pinkish ['piŋkiʃ] adj rosáceo; (sl) rojillo.
pin money ['pin‚mʌni] n alfileres mpl.
pinnace ['pinis] n pinaza f.
pinnacle ['pinəkl] n (Archit) pináculo m, remate m; chapitel m; (of rock etc) punta f; (of mountain) cumbre f; **the — of fame** la cumbre de la fama.
pinny ['pini] n (fam) = **pinafore**.
pinpoint ['pinpɔint] **1** n punta f de alfiler; (fig) punto m muy pequeño. **2** vt indicar con toda precisión; concretar; poner el dedo en.
pinprick ['pinprik] n alfilerazo m; (fig) alfilerazo m, molestia f pequeña.
pinstripe ['pinstraip] **1** adj a rayas, rayado; **— suit** traje m a rayas. **2** n traje m (etc) a rayas.
pint [paint] n **(a)** pinta f (= 0,57 litros, US = 0,47 litros).
(b) (loosely) vaso m grande de cerveza, caña f de cerveza; **we had a — together** tomamos una caña; **he likes his —** le gusta la cerveza, es algo aficionado a la cerveza; **we had a few —s** bebimos cierta cantidad.
pin table ['pinteibl] n billar m romano, billar m automático.
pintail ['pinteil] n ánade m rabudo.
pinup ['pinʌp] n pin-up mf, foto f de muchacha guapa (or de hombre bien parecido etc); **she's my —** es mi mujer ideal.
pioneer [‚paiə'niə*] **1** n (explorer) explorador m; (early settler) colonizador m; (Mil) zapador m; (of scheme, in study) iniciador m, promotor m; **he was one of the —s** él era de los iniciadores; **he was a — in the study of bats** fue uno de los primeros en estudiar los murciélagos.
2 vt settlement etc preparar el terreno para, hacer

los preparativos para; *scheme, study* iniciar, promover; echar los cimientos de, sentar las bases de.

3 *vi* explorar, abrir nuevos caminos.

pious ['paiəs] *adj* piadoso, devoto.

piously ['paiəsli] *adv* piadosamente, devotamente.

pip¹ [pip] *n* (*Med*) pepita *f*; **it gives me the** — me fastidia terriblemente; **it's enough to give you the** — es para volverse loco; **he's got the** — está de muy mal humor.

pip² [pip] *n* (*Bot*) pepita *f*; (*on card, dice*) punto *m*, pinta *f*; (*on uniform*) estrella *f*.

pip³ [pip] **1** *vt* (*wound*) herir (levemente); (*defeat*) vencer; *exam* no aprobar, ser suspendido en; **A —ped B at the post** A alcanzó a B a la altura del mismo poste de llegada, (*fig*) A venció a B pero con muy pequeño margen; **I —ped French again** volvieron a suspenderme en francés.

2 *vi* (*lose*) perder; (*fail*) fracasar; (*in exam*) ser suspendido.

pipe [paip] **1** *n* (a) (*tube*) tubo *m*, caño *m*, conducto *m*; (*also* —s) tubería *f*, cañería *f*; (*of a hose etc*) manga *f*; (*of wine*) pipa *f*.

(b) (*Mus: of organ*) cañón *m*, tubo *m*; (*instrument*) caramillo *m*, (*boatswain's*) pito *m*; —s (*Scot*) gaita *f*, (*Pan's*) flauta *f*.

(c) (*smoker's*) pipa *f*; **— of peace** pipa *f* de la paz; **to fill one's** — cargar la pipa; **put that in your — and smoke it!** (*fam*) ¡chúpate eso!

2 *vt* (a) *water etc* conducir en cañerías; **water is —d to the farm** se conduce el agua a la granja por unas cañerías; **the oil is —d across the desert** el petroleo es conducido a través del desierto en un oleoducto.

(b) (*Mus*) *tune* tocar; **to — the admiral aboard** tocar el pito al llegar el almirante a bordo.

3 *vi* (*Mus*) tocar el caramillo, tocar la flauta; tocar la gaita; (*bird*) trinar; **to — down** (*fam*) callarse; **to — up** decir (inesperadamente), comenzar a hablar (inesperadamente).

pipeclay ['paipklei] **1** *n* albero *m*. **2** *vt* blanquear con albero.

pipe cleaner ['paip,kli:nə*] *n* limpiapipas *m*, limpiador *m* de pipa.

pipe dream ['paipdri:m] *n* esperanza *f* imposible, sueño *m* imposible.

pipeful ['paipful] *n* pipa *f*; **a — of tobacco** una pipa de tabaco.

pipeline ['paiplain] *n* tubería *f*, cañería *f*; tubería *f* de distribución; (*for oil*) oleoducto *m*; (*for gas*) gasoducto *m*; **it is in the** — (*fig*) está en trámite, se está tramitando.

piper ['paipə*] *n* flautista *mf*; (*Scot*) gaitero *m*; **the Pied P— of Hamelin** el flautista de Hamelín; **to pay the** — cargar con los gastos; **he who pays the — calls the tune** el que paga tiene derecho a escoger.

pipe tobacco ['paiptə,bækəu] *n* tabaco *m* de pipa.

pipette [pi'pet] *n* pipeta *f*.

piping¹ ['paipiŋ] *n* (a) tubería *f*, cañería *f*; (*Sew*) ribete *m*, cordoncillo *m*.

(b) (*Mus*) sonido *m* del caramillo, música *f* de flauta; (*of bird*) trinar *m*, trinos *mpl*.

piping² ['paipiŋ] **1** *adv*: **— hot** bien caliente, que casi quema. **2** *adj* voice agudo.

pipistrelle [,pipi'strel] *n* murciélago *m* pequeño.

pipit ['pipit] *n* bisbita *f*.

pipkin ['pipkin] *n* ollita *f* de barro.

pippin ['pipin] *n* camuesa *f*, manzana *f* reineta.

pipsqueak ['pipskwi:k] *n* (*fam*) persona *f* insignificante, cosa *f* trivial.

piquancy ['pi:kənsi] *n* picante *m*, lo picante.

piquant ['pi:kənt] *adj* picante.

piquantly ['pi:kəntli] *adv* de modo picante.

pique [pi:k] **1** *n* pique *m*, resentimiento *m*; **to be in a — estar** resentido; **to do something in a fit of —**, **to do something out of —** hacer algo motivado por el rencor.

2 *vt* picar, herir; **to be —d at** ofenderse por.

3 *vt*: **to — oneself on something** preciarse de algo, enorgullecerse de algo.

piquet [pi'ket] *n* séptimo *m*, juego *m* de los cientos.

piracy ['paiərəsi] *n* piratería *f*; (*of book*) publicación *f* desautorizada.

piranha ['pi'rɑ:njə] *n* piraña *f*.

pirate ['paiərit] **1** *n* pirata *m*. **2** *adj*: — **radio** emisora *f* ilegal. **3** *vt* book publicar en una edición furtiva.

pirated ['paiəritid] *adj*: — **edition** edición *f* furtiva, edición *f* desautorizada.

piratical [pai'rætikəl] *adj* pirático.

pirouette [,piru'et] **1** *n* pirueta *f*. **2** *vi* piruetear.

piss [pis] (*tabu*) **1** *n* orina *f*, meados *mpl*; **to have a —** mear. **2** *vti* mear; **to be —ed** (*sl*) estar ajumado (*sl*).

pistachio [pis'tɑ:ʃiəu] *n* pistacho *m*.

pistil ['pistil] *n* pistilo *m*.

pistol ['pistl] *n* pistola *f*, revólver *m*.

pistol shot ['pistl,ʃɔt] *n* pistoletazo *m*; **to be within —** estar a tiro de pistola.

piston ['pistən] *n* pistón *m*, émbolo *m*.

piston engine ['pistən,endʒin] *n* motor *m* de pistón.

piston-engined ['pistən,endʒind] *adj* con motor de pistón.

piston ring ['pistən,riŋ] *n* aro *m* de pistón, segmento *m* de pistón.

piston rod ['pistən,rɔd] *n* vástago *m* de émbolo.

piston stroke ['pistən,strəuk] *n* carrera *f* del émbolo.

pit¹ [pit] **1** *n* (*hole in ground*) hoyo *m*, hoya *f*, foso *m*; (*small depression in surface*) hoyo *m*; (*as trap*) trampa *f*; (*at garage*) foso *m* de inspección, foso *m* de reparación; (*for cockfighting*) cancha *f*, reñidero *m*; (*in motor racing*) box *m*; (*of stomach*) boca *f*; (*Theat*) platea *f*; (*Min*) mina *f*, (*quarry*) cantera *f*; (*fig*) abismo *m*; (*fig: hell*) el infierno; **the — of hell** lo más profundo del infierno; **the —s** (*motor racing*) los boxes.

2 *vt* (a) *surface* hacer hoyos en, marcar con hoyos; (*with smallpox*) marcar con viruelas; **the surface was —ted with . . .** en la superficie había hoyos formados por . . .

(b) **to — A against B** oponer A a B; **we —ted all our strength against him** nos opusimos a él con todas nuestras fuerzas; **he found himself —ted against the champion** encontró que tenía que habérselas con el campeón.

pit² [pit] (*US*) **1** *n* (*Bot*) hueso *m*. **2** *vt* deshuesar, quitar el hueso a.

pitapat ['pitə'pæt] *adv*: **my heart went —** mi corazón latía rápidamente, mi corazón hacía tictac.

pitch¹ [pitʃ] **1** *n* pez *f*, brea *f*. **2** *vt* embrear.

pitch² [pitʃ] **1** *n* (a) (*throw*) lanzamiento *m*; echada *f*; **it came full — into my hands** llegó a mis manos sin tocar el suelo; **it fell full — into the garden** cayó de plano en el jardín.

(b) (*Naut*) cabezada *f*.

(c) (*Sport*) campo *m*, terreno *m*; **the — is under water** el campo está inundado; **the supporters poured on to the —** los hinchas invadieron el campo.

(d) (*place in market etc*) puesto *m*; (*fig*) terreno *m*; **this is my usual —** éste es mi puesto habitual; **keep off our —!** ¡cuidado con no meteros en lo nuestro!; **to queer someone's —** crear dificultades a uno, chafar la guitarra a uno.

(e) (*slope*) grado *m* de inclinación; (*of roof*) pendiente *f*.

(f) (*height, degree*) punto *m*, extremo *m*; (*Mus*) tono *m*; (*height*) elevación *f*; (*of propeller etc*) paso *m*; **to such a — that . . .** a tal punto que . . .; **excitement is at fever —** la emoción está al rojo vivo; **matters reached such a — that . . .** las cosas llegaron a tal extremo que . . .; **to adjust the — of an instrument** ajustar el tono de un instrumento; **concert —, standard —** diapasón *m* normal.

2 *vt* (a) (*throw*) arrojar, lanzar, tirar; (*Baseball etc*) lanzar; **to — someone off** quitar a uno de encima; **he was —ed off his horse** fue desarzonado, cayó del caballo; **— it over here!** ¡tíramelo!; **to — something out** tirar algo; **to — someone out** echar a uno, expulsar a uno; **they —ed him out into the street** le pusieron de patitas en la calle.

(b) (*Mus*) *note* dar, producir, entonar; (*play*) tocar, (*sing*) cantar; *instrument* graduar el tono de; **she can't — a note properly** es incapaz de producir una nota buena; **I'll — you a note** os doy la nota para empezar; **you're —ing it too high for me** lo tocas demasiado alto para mí; **to — one's aspirations too high** picar muy alto; **it is —ed in rather high-flown terms** está redactado en términos algo retóricos; **it must be —ed at the right level for the audience** el tono ha de ajustarse al público.

(c) *tent* armar.

(d) **to — it strong** exagerar, no perdonar detalle; **to — someone a story** contar a uno un cuento (inverosímil); **he —ed me this hard-luck story** me contó esta historia tan trágica.

3 *vi* (a) (*fall*) caer, caerse; **to — forward** caer de cabeza; **he —ed off his horse** cayó del caballo; **the ball —ed in front of him** la pelota cayó delante de él, la pelota vino a parar a sus pies; **after —ing it bounced high** después de tocar el suelo rebotó muy alto; **the aircraft —ed into the sea** el avión cayó al mar.

(b) (*Naut*) cabecear.

(c) **to — on something** (*choose*) elegir algo; (*find*) encontrar algo, dar con algo; **we —ed on it by accident** dimos con él por pura casualidad.

(d) to — in empezar a hacer algo, (esp) empezar a comer; **— in!** ¡a ello!, ¡manos a la obra!; **so we all —ed in together** así que todos nos pusimos a trabajar juntos; **to — into someone** (attack) atacar a uno (vigorosamente), (verbally etc) arremeter contra uno, (scold) dar un rapapolvo a uno; **to — into the work** emprender enérgicamente el trabajo, ponerse enérgicamente a trabajar; **they —ed into the food** empezaron a comer con buen apetito.

pitch-and-toss ['pitʃən'tɔs] n juego m de cara o cruz.
pitch-black ['pitʃ'blæk] adj negro como boca de lobo.
pitchblende ['pitʃblend] n pechblenda f.
pitch-dark ['pitʃ'dɑːk] adj negro como boca de lobo.
pitched [pitʃt] adj: **— battle** batalla f campal.
pitcher[1] ['pitʃə*] n cántaro m, jarro m.
pitcher[2] ['pitʃə*] n (Baseball) lanzador m.
pitchfork ['pitʃfɔːk] **1** n horca f, bielda f.

2 vt (fig): **to — someone into a job** imponer inesperadamente a uno una tarea, hacer que uno se encargue de algo de buena o mala gana; **I was —ed into it** no me dieron la oportunidad de decir que no.

pitch pine ['pitʃpain] n pino m de tea.
piteous ['pitiəs] adj lastimero, lastimoso.
piteously ['pitiəsli] adv lastimosamente.
pitfall ['pitfɔːl] n escollo m, peligro m; trampa f; **it's a — for the unwary** es una trampa para los imprudentes; **"P—s of English"** "Escollos mpl del inglés"; **there are many —s ahead** hay muchos peligros por delante.
pith [piθ] n (Bot) médula f; (fig) meollo m, jugo m, esencia f.
pithead ['pithed] n bocamina f.
pithiness ['piθinis] n jugosidad f; lo sentencioso, lo expresivo; lo sucinto, lo lacónico.
pithy ['piθi] adj (full of sense) jugoso; sentencioso, expresivo; (terse) sucinto, lacónico; **— saying** dicho m sentencioso.
pitiable ['pitiəbl] adj lastimoso, digno de compasión; **in a — state** en un estado que da lástima; **it was most — to see** daba lástima verlo.
pitiful ['pitiful] adj (a) (moving to pity) lastimero, lastimoso; conmovedor. **(b)** (contemptible) lamentable, miserable, despreciable; **a — display** una exhibición lamentable; **it was just —** daba lástima.
pitifully ['pitifəli] adv (a) lastimosamente; de modo conmovedor; **she was crying most —** lloraba que daba lástima. **(b)** lamentablemente; **a — bad play** una comedia tan mala que da lástima.
pitiless ['pitilis] adj despiadado, implacable.
pitilessly ['pitilisli] adv despiadadamente, implacablemente.
pit prop ['pitprɔp] n puntal m, peón m.
pittance ['pitəns] n miseria f, renta f miserable; **a mere —!** ¡una miseria!; **to live on a —** vivir de una renta miserable.
pitted ['pitid] adj (US) fruit deshuesado, sin hueso.
pitter-patter ['pitə'pætə*] n etc = **patter**[2].
pituitary [pi'tjuːitəri] **1** adj pituitario; **— gland = 2** n glándula f pituitaria.
pity ['piti] **1** n (a) compasión f, piedad f; **for —'s sake!** ¡por piedad!, (less seriously) ¡por Dios!; **to do something out of —** for someone hacer algo movido por la compasión que se tiene a uno; **to feel no — for someone** no sentir compasión por uno; **to move someone to —** mover a uno a compasión, dar lástima a uno; **to take — on someone** tener piedad de uno, apiadarse de uno.
(b) lástima f; **what a —!** ¡qué lástima!, ¡qué pena!; **more's the —!** ¡desgraciadamente!; **it is a — that . . .** es una lástima que + subj, es una pena que + subj, **the — of it was that . . .** lo lamentable fue que . . ., lo peor del caso fue que . . .; **it is a thousand pities that . . .** es muy de lamentar que + subj.
2 vt compadecer(se de), tener lástima a; apiadarse de.
pitying ['pitiiŋ] adj glance etc de lástima, lleno de compasión, compasivo.
pityingly ['pitiiŋli] adv con lástima, compasivamente.
Pius ['paiəs] m Pío.
pivot ['pivət] **1** n pivote m; (fig) eje m, punto m central.
2 vt montar sobre un pivote; **he —ed it on his hand** lo hizo girar sobre la mano, lo mantuvo en equilibrio sobre la mano.
3 vi girar (on sobre); **to — on** (fig) depender de.
pivotal ['pivətl] adj (fig) central, fundamental.
pixie ['piksi] n duende m.
pixie hood ['piksihud] n caperucita f.
placard ['plækɑːd] **1** n (on wall etc) cartel m; (sign, announcement) letrero m; (carried in procession etc) pancarta f.

2 vt: **the wall is —ed all over** la pared está llena de carteles; **the town is —ed with slogans** en todas partes de la ciudad se ven carteles con slogans.
placate [plə'keit] vt aplacar, apaciguar.
place [pleis] **1** n (a) (in general) sitio m, lugar m; **this is the —** éste es el lugar; **we came to a — where . . .** llegamos a un sitio donde . . .; **any — will do** cualquier lugar será conveniente; **I don't see it any —** (US) no lo veo en ninguna parte; **it must be some — else** (US) estará en otra parte; **it's a pretty low sort of —** es un lugar no muy decente; **this is no — for you** éste no es sitio conveniente para Vd; **from — to —** de lugar en lugar; **in another —** en otra parte, (Parl) en la otra cámara; **in high —** allá arriba, en las altas esferas, en el gobierno (etc); **the furniture was all over the —** los muebles estaban en desorden; **we're all over the —** vivimos en la mayor confusión; **your work is all over the —** Vd hace su trabajo de cualquier modo; **to find one's — in a book** encontrar en un libro el pasaje que uno quiere leer; **to lose one's —** perder el hilo, padecer confusión al querer seguir su lectura (etc); **to laugh at the right —** reírse en el momento oportuno; **to go —s** (travel) viajar, visitar muchos países (etc); **we like to go —s at weekends** durante los fines de semana nos gusta salir de excursión; **he's going —s** es un ambicioso; tiene una carrera brillante por delante; es un hombre de empuje; **we're going —s at last** por fin empezamos a hacer progresos.
(b) (specific) sitio m, local m; **— of amusement** lugar m de diversión; **— of business** oficina f, (shop) comercio m; **— of refuge** refugio m, asilo m; **— of residence** residencia f, domicilio m; **— of worship** templo m, edificio m de culto.
(c) (town etc) lugar m; ciudad f (etc); **fortified —** plaza f, fortaleza f; **find a native of the —** busque a uno nacido aquí, busque a uno que sea realmente de aquí; **it's a small —** es un pueblo pequeño; **it's just a small country —** no es más que un pequeño pueblo rural.
(d) (house) casa f; **his — in the country** su casa de campo; **they have a new — now** tienen una nueva casa ya; **it's a vast great —** es una casa inmensa; **we were at Peter's —** estuvimos en casa de Pedro; **come to our —** ven a visitarnos a casa.
(e) (in street names) plaza f.
(f) (— in relation to owner etc) sitio m, lugar m, puesto m; **does this have a —?** ¿tiene esto un sitio determinado?; **to be in —** estar en su lugar; **to put something back in its —** devolver algo a su sitio; **to hold something in —** sujetar algo en un lugar; **in — of** en lugar de, en vez de; **if I were in your —** yo en tu lugar, yo que tú; **to be out of —** estar fuera de lugar; estar fuera de serie; haberse equivocado de sitio; **that remark was quite out of —** esa observación estaba fuera de propósito, no cabía tal observación; **it looks out of —** aquí no está bien, aquí parece que está fuera de su lugar; **I feel rather out of — here** aquí me siento algo desplazado; **to change —s** cambiar de sitio; **to change —s with someone** trocarse con uno; **to give — to** ceder el paso a; **to take —** tener lugar, verificarse; (meeting etc) celebrarse; **the marriage will not now take —** la boda no se celebrará.
(g) (seat) plaza f, asiento m; (at table) cubierto m; **a theatre with 2000 —s** un teatro de 2000 asientos, un teatro que tiene un aforo de 2000; **are there any —s left?** ¿quedan plazas?; **is this — taken?** ¿está ocupado este asiento?; **to lay an extra — for someone** poner otro cubierto para uno.
(h) (post) puesto m, empleo m; colocación f; **—s for 500 workers** 500 puestos mpl de trabajo; **school —** puesto m escolar; **it is not my — to + infin** no me cumple a mí + infin; **he found a —** for his nephew in the firm le dio un puesto en la compañía a su sobrino; **to seek a — in publishing** buscarse una colocación en una casa editorial.
(i) (in series, as rank etc) lugar m, puesto m; (in exam) calificación f; (rank) posición f, rango m; **in the first —** en primer lugar; **in the second —** en segundo lugar; **in the next —** luego, después; **to three —s of decimals** en milésimas; **to work something out to three —s of decimals** calcular algo hasta las milésimas; **P won, with Q in second —** ganó P, con Q en segunda posición; **to attain a high —** llegar muy alto, alcanzar un rango alto; **to back a horse for a —** apostar algo a un caballo para colocado; **to give up one's —** (in a queue) ceder la vez, ceder su turno; **to keep one's —** mantenerse en la misma posición, lograr seguir como antes; **to know one's —** ser respetuoso, guardar las distancias; **to put someone in his —** bajar los humos a uno; **if he gets**

fresh put him in his — si se pone fresco vuélvele a su sitio; **that properly put him in his** — eso sí le hizo sentirse humilde.

2 *vt* **(a)** (*in general*) poner, colocar; fijar; situar, emplazar; — **it on the table** ponlo en la mesa; **it is** —**d rather high up** está en una posición más bien alta, se ha fijado un poco alto; **the house is well** —**d** la casa está bien situada; **the shop is awkwardly** —**d** la tienda está en una posición de difícil acceso; **the town is** —**d on a hill** la ciudad está emplazada en una colina; **to** — **confidence in someone** poner confianza en uno, confiar a uno; **we should** — **no trust in that** no hay que fiarse de eso.

(b) (*of orders etc*) **to** — **a book with a publisher** lograr que un editor acepte un libro para publicarlo; **I shall** — **the book elsewhere** ofreceré el libro a otra editorial; **to** — **a contract for machinery with a French firm** firmar un contrato con una compañía francesa para adquirir unas máquinas; **to** — **money** invertir dinero; **to** — **money at interest** colocar dinero a interés; **to** — **an order** colocar un pedido (*for* de), pedir; **goods that are difficult to** — unos géneros que no encuentran salida; **Cuba was trying to** — **her sugar** Cuba trataba de colocar su azúcar.

(c) (*of jobs*) dar un puesto a, emplear, colocar; **we could** — **200 men if we had them** podríamos colocar a 200 hombres si los hubiera.

(d) (*of series, rank etc*) **to be** —**d** (*in race*) colocarse; **to be** —**d second** colocarse en segundo lugar; **Vigo is well** —**d in the League** Vigo tiene un buen puesto en la Liga; **he is well** —**d to see it all** está en una buena posición para observarlo todo; **we are better** —**d than a month ago** hemos mejorado de posición en relación con la que ocupábamos hace un mes; **we are well** —**d to attack** estamos en una buena posición para pasar a la ofensiva.

(e) (*recall etc*) recordar, traer a la memoria; (*recognize*) reconocer; (*identify*) identificar; **I can't** — **him** no le recuerdo; **I can't quite** — **it** no puedo identificarlo con precisión; **she** —**d him at once** le reconoció en seguida.

place card ['pleɪskɑːd] *n* tarjeta que *indica el puesto que uno ha de ocupar en la mesa.*

place kick ['pleɪskɪk] *n* puntapié *m* colocado.

place mat ['pleɪsmæt] *n* salvamantel *m*, reposaplatos *m*.

placement ['pleɪsmənt] *n* colocación *f*.

place-name ['pleɪsneɪm] *n* topónimo *m*; —**s** (*as study, in general*) toponimia *f*; **the** —**s of Aragon** la toponimia aragonesa.

placenta [plə'sentə] *n* placenta *f*.

placid ['plæsɪd] *adj* plácido; apacible; tranquilo, sosegado.

placidity [plə'sɪdɪtɪ] *n* placidez *f*; apacibilidad *f*; tranquilidad *f*; sosiego *m*.

placing ['pleɪsɪŋ] *n* (*act*) colocación *f*; (— *in table, rank*) puesto *m*, calificación *f*.

plagiarism ['pleɪdʒɪərɪzəm] *n* plagio *m*.

plagiarist ['pleɪdʒɪərɪst] *n* plagiario *m*, a *f*.

plagiarize ['pleɪdʒɪəraɪz] *vt* plagiar.

plague [pleɪg] 1 *n* (*Med*) peste *f*; (*fig*) plaga *f*; **what a** — **he is !** ¡es un pesado!; **to avoid something like the** — huir de algo como de la peste, evitar algo a toda costa; **to hate something like the** — detestar algo.

2 *vt* plagar, infestar; (*fig*) acosar, atormentar; fastidiar; **a thought is plaguing me** me atormenta una idea; **to** — **the life out of someone** fastidiar a uno terriblemente, amargar la vida a uno; **to** — **someone with questions** importunar a uno con preguntas.

plaguey ['pleɪgɪ] *adj* (*fam*) latoso, engorroso.

plaice [pleɪs] *n* platija *f*.

plaid [plæd] *n* (*cloth*) tela *f* a cuadros; (*cloak*) manta *f* escocesa, plaid *m*.

plain [pleɪn] 1 *adj* **(a)** (*clear*) claro, evidente; **a** — **case of jealousy** un caso evidente de celos; **it is** — **that** . . . es evidente que . . ., está claro que . . .; **it must be** — **to all that** . . . ha de ser obvio para todos que . . .; **it's as** — **as a pikestaff** está claro como la luz del día; **to make something** — **to someone** explicar algo a uno con toda claridad; decir algo a uno de modo que no quede lugar a dudas; **I must make it** — **that** . . ., conste que . . ., quede bien claro que . . ., tengo que subrayar que . . .; **to make one's meaning** — explicar lo que uno quiere decir; **do I make myself** —? ¿me entiendes?

(b) (*outspoken*) franco, abierto; **to be** — **with someone** hablar claro a uno; **let me be** — **with you** dejémonos de rodeos, pongamos las cosas en su sitio.

(c) (*unadorned*) sencillo, llano, sin adornos; *answer* franco; *dealing* honrado; *language, style*

llano; *living* sin lujo; *knitting* de media; *cooking* corriente, casero; *truth* liso y llano; **in** — **language** hablando sin rodeos; para decirlo como ello es, para llamar las cosas por su nombre; **they're very** — **people** son gente muy sencilla; **I'm a** — **man** yo soy un hombre llano; **they used to be called** — **Smith** antes se llamaban Smith sin más.

(d) (*unmixed*) natural, puro, sin mezcla; **I like** — **whisky** me gusta el whiskey sin añadidura, me gusta el whiskey sin mezcla.

(e) (*of appearance*) sin atractivo, algo feo, ordinario; **she's terribly** —, **poor girl** no tiene atractivo alguno, la pobre; **pretty girls and** — **ones** las guapas y las feas; *see* **clothes, English** *etc*.

2 *adv* claro, claramente; **so I told him pretty** — así que se lo dije con toda claridad; **I can't say it any** —**er** no lo puedo decir de modo más claro.

3 *n* llano *m*, llanura *f*; **the Great P**—**s** (*USA*) la Pradera.

plain-clothes ['pleɪn'kləʊðz] *adj*: — **man** agente *m* de policía que lleva traje de calle.

plainly ['pleɪnlɪ] *adv* **(a)** claramente, evidentemente; — **I was not welcome** evidentemente no iban a recibirme con placer; **to put something** — explicar algo con claridad; **to speak** — **to someone** hablar claro a uno.

(b) francamente, con franqueza.

(c) sencillamente, claramente.

plainness ['pleɪnnɪs] *n* **(a)** claridad *f*; evidencia *f*.

(b) franqueza *f*.

(c) sencillez *f*, llaneza *f*.

(d) (*of face*) falta *f* de atractivo, fealdad *f*, ordinariez *f*.

plainsman ['pleɪnzmən] *n*, *pl* —**men** [mən] llanero *m*.

plainsong ['pleɪnsɒŋ] *n* canto *m* llano.

plain speaking ['pleɪn'spiːkɪŋ] *n* franqueza *f*.

plain-spoken ['pleɪn'spəʊkən] *adj* franco, llano.

plaintiff ['pleɪntɪf] *n* demandante *mf*, querellante *mf*.

plaintive ['pleɪntɪv] *adj* lastimero, dolorido.

plaintively ['pleɪntɪvlɪ] *adv* lastimeramente, con dolor.

plait [plæt] 1 *n* trenza *f*; **in** —**s** trenzado, en trenzas. 2 *vt* trenzar.

plan [plæn] 1 *n* **(a)** (*Archit*) plano *m*; **to make a** — **of** trazar el plano de.

(b) (*schedule etc*) programa *m*; (*system*) sistema *m*; (*tariff, in hotel etc*) tarifa *f*; **American** — (*in hotel: US*) cuarto *m* con comidas, pensión *f* completa; **European** — (*in hotel: US*) cuarto *m* sólo; **if everything goes according to** — si todo se realiza tal como se prevé; **everything went according to** — todo salió bien, todo resultó como se había previsto.

(c) (*Pol, Econ etc*) plan *m*; — **of campaign** plan *m* de campaña; **the Badajoz P**— el Plan Badajoz; **development** — plan *m* de desarrollo; **five-year** — plan *m* quinquenal; **the Marshall P**— el Plan Marshall; **to draw up a** — hacer un plan, redactar un plan.

(d) (*personal project etc*) proyecto *m*; **the** — **is to come back later** pensamos volver más tarde, tenemos la idea de volver más tarde; **the best** — **is to** + *infin* la mejor idea es + *infin*; **to change one's** — cambiar de proyecto, cambiar de idea; **what** —**s have you for the holiday?** ¿qué proyectos tienes para las vacaciones?; **have you any** —**s for tonight?** ¿tienes compromiso para esta noche?; **I have no fixed** —**s** no he arreglado nada en definitivo; **what** —**s have you for Jim?** ¿qué proyectos hay para Jaimito?, ¿qué ideas tienes sobre el porvenir de Jaimito?; **to make** —**s** hacer proyectos; **to upset someone's** —**s** dar al traste con los proyectos de uno.

2 *vt* planear, planificar; proyectar; idear; **to** — **a robbery** planear un robo; **to** — **the future of an industry** planificar el porvenir de una industria; **the mania of** —**ning everything** la manía de planificarlo todo; **this trip was** —**ned by him** este viaje lo ideó él, fue él quien hizo los proyectos para este viaje.

3 *vi*: **to** — **for months** hacer proyectos durante meses enteros; **we are** —**ning for next April** hacemos proyectos para el abril que viene; **one has to** —**months ahead** hay que hacer los proyectos con varios meses de antelación; **to** — **to do something** proponerse hacer algo, pensar hacer algo; proyectar hacer algo; **we weren't** —**ning to** no teníamos tal intención; no se nos había ocurrido; **how long do you** — **to stay?** ¿cuánto tiempo piensas quedarte?

planchette [plɑːn'ʃet] *n* tabla *f* de escritura espiritista.

plane[1] [pleɪn] *n* (*Bot*) plátano *m*.

plane² [plein] **1** *adj* plano; — **geometry** geometría *f* plana.

2 *n* (a) (*Math*) plano *m*; **focal** — plano *m* focal; **inclined** — plano *m* inclinado.

(b) (*fig*) nivel *m*, esfera *f*; **he seems to exist on another** — parece existir en una esfera distinta; **on this** — en este nivel, a esta altura.

(c) (*tool*) cepillo *m* (de carpintero).

(d) (*Aer*) avión *m*; **to go by** — ir en avión; **to send goods by** — enviar artículos por avión.

3 *vt* acepillar; **to** — **down** acepillar, desbastar, alisar.

planet ['plænit] *n* planeta *m*.

plane table ['pleinteibl] *n* plancheta *f*.

planetarium [,plæni'teəriəm] *n* planetario *m*.

planetary ['plænitəri] *adj* planetario.

plangent ['plændʒənt] *adj* plañidero.

planish ['plæniʃ] *vt* aplanar.

plank [plæŋk] **1** *n* tabla *f* (gruesa), tablón *m*; —**s** (*planking*) tablaje *m*; **deck** —**s** (*Naut*) tablazón *f* de la cubierta; (*fig: Pol*) principio *m*, artículo *m* (de un programa político).

2 *vt* entablar, entarimar; **to** — **something down** tirar algo violentamente, arrojar algo violentamente.

3 *vr*: **to** — **oneself down** sentarse (*etc*) de modo agresivo.

planking ['plæŋkiŋ] *n* tablas *fpl*, tablaje *m*; (*Naut*) tablazón *f* de la cubierta.

plankton ['plæŋktən] *n* plankton *m*.

planned [plænd] *adj* **economy** dirigido.

planner ['plænə*] *n* planificador *m*.

planning ['plæniŋ] *n* (*Pol, Econ etc*) planificación *f*; (*personal projects*) proyectos *mpl*; **family** — control *m* de natalidad.

planning board ['plæniŋ,bɔːd] *n* comisión *f* planificadora.

plant [plɑːnt] **1** *n* (a) (*Bot*) planta *f*.

(b) (*Tech: machinery*) equipo *m*, maquinaria *f*, instalación *f*; (*factory*) fábrica *f*; **we need new** — necesitamos un nuevo equipo, hace falta renovar la instalación; **pilot** — planta *f* piloto, fábrica *f* experimental.

(c) (*sl*) estratagema *f* para incriminar a uno; **it's a** — aquí hay trampa.

2 *attr* vegetal; — **life** vida *f* vegetal, las plantas; — **kingdom** reino *m* vegetal.

3 *vt* (a) *plant* plantar; *seed* sembrar; **to** — **a field with turnips** sembrar un campo de nabos; **the field is** —**ed with wheat** el campo está sembrado de trigo.

(b) (*place*) poner, colocar; fijar; *people* establecer; *blow* plantar, asestar; *idea etc* inculcar (*in* en), imbuir (*in* con); **to** — **something on someone** ocultar algo en la ropa (*or* en la habitación *etc*) de uno para incriminarle.

4 *vr*: **to** — **oneself in the middle of the road** ponerse en medio de la calle.

plantain ['plæntin] *n* llantén *m*.

plantation [plæn'teiʃən] *n* (*of tea, sugar etc*) plantación *f*; (*large estate*) hacienda *f*; (*of trees*) arboleda *f*; (*of young trees*) plantel *m*; **coffee** — cafetal *m*; **rubber** — cauchal *m*.

planter ['plɑːntə*] *n* plantador *m*; (*loosely*) colono *m*.

plantpot ['plɑːntpɒt] *n* tiesto *m*, maceta *f*.

plaque [plæk] *n* placa *f*.

plash [plæʃ] *see* **splash**.

plasm ['plæzəm] *n*, **plasma** ['plæzmə] *n* plasma *m*.

plaster ['plɑːstə*] **1** *n* (*lime material*) yeso *m*; (*in building*) argamasa *f*, (*layer on wall*) enlucido *m*; (*Med: applied to wound*) emplasto *m*, parche *m*, (*for eg injured arm*) escayola *f*, tablilla *f* de yeso; **adhesive** — esparadrapo *m*; — **of Paris** yeso *m* mate; **with his leg in** — con la pierna escayolada; **to have one's neck in** — tener el cuello escayolado.

2 *vt* (a) *wall* enyesar, enlucir; (*Med*) emplastar, aplicar un emplasto a; **to** — **a wall with posters** llenar (*or* cubrir) una pared de carteles; **to** — **posters on a wall** pegar carteles a una pared; **to** — **over a hole** llenar un hoyo de argamasa; **the children came back** —**ed with mud** los niños volvieron cubiertos de lodo. (b) (*fam*) dar una paliza a, pegar.

plasterboard ['plɑːstəbɔːd] *n* cartón *m* de yeso y fieltro.

plaster cast ['plɑːstə,kɑːst] *n* vaciado *m*; (*death mask*) mascarilla *f* mortuoria.

plastered ['plɑːstəd] *adj* (*sl*): **to be** — estar ajumado (*fam*).

plasterer ['plɑːstərə*] *n* yesero *m*, enlucidor *m*.

plastering ['plɑːstəriŋ] *n* enlucido *m*.

plastic ['plæstik] **1** *adj* plástico. **2** *n* plástico *m*.

Plasticine ['plæstisiːn] *n* (*Protected Trade Name*) plasticina *f*.

plasticity [plæs'tisiti] *n* plasticidad *f*.

plate [pleit] **1** *n* (*dish*) plato *m*; (*of metal etc*) lámina *f*, chapa *f*, plancha *f*; (*plaque*) placa *f*; (*silver*) vajilla *f* de plata; (*for taking collection*) platillo *m*; (*Typ*) lámina *f*; (*Phot*) placa *f*; (*prize, in racing*) premio *m*; (*also* **dental** —) placa *f* de la dentadura postiza; **gold** — vajilla *f* de oro; **to hand someone something on a** — (*fig*) servir algo a uno en bandeja de plata; **to have a lot on one's** — estar muy ocupado, tener muchos asuntos entre manos, tener grandes responsabilidades.

2 *vt* (*with metal*) planchear, chapear; (*with armour*) blindar; (*with silver*) platear; (*with nickel*) niquelar.

plate armour, (*US*) — **armor** ['pleit,ɑːmə*] *n* blindaje *m*.

plateau ['plætəu] *n*, *pl* **plateaux** [plæ'təuz] meseta *f*, altiplanicie *f*.

plated ['pleitid] *adj* chapeado (*with* de); (*armoured*) blindado.

plateful ['pleitful] *n* plato *m*.

plate glass ['pleit'glɑːs] *n* vidrio *m* cilindrado.

plateholder ['pleit,həuldə*] *n* (*Phot*) portaplacas *m*.

platelayer ['pleit,leiə*] *n* obrero *m* de ferrocarriles.

platform ['plætfɔːm] *n* (a) plataforma *f*; (*at meeting*) tribuna *f*; (*for band etc*) estrado *m*; (*roughly-built*) tablado *m*; (*Pol*) programa *m* electoral, política *f*; **the** — **speakers** los oradores de la tribuna.

(b) (*Rail*) andén *m*; (*with number mentioned*) vía *f*; **arrival** — andén *m* de vacío; **departure** — andén *m* de salida; **the 5.15 is at** (*or* on)— **8** el tren de las 5.15 está en la vía número 8.

platform ticket ['plætfɔːm,tikit] *n* billete *m* de andén.

plating ['pleitiŋ] *n* enchapado *m*; capa *f* metálica; (*armour-*) blindaje *m*; (*of nickel*) niquelado *m*.

platinum ['plætinəm] *n* platino *m*.

platitude ['plætitjuːd] *n* lugar *m* común, tópico *m*, perogrullada *f*; **it is a** — **to say that . . .** es un tópico decir que . . .

platitudinous [,plæti'tjuːdinəs] *adj* *speech* lleno de lugares comunes (*etc*); *speaker* aficionado a los lugares comunes (*etc*), que peca por exceso de tópicos.

Plato ['pleitəu] *m* Platón.

Platonic [plə'tɒnik] *adj* platónico.

Platonist ['pleitənist] *n* platonista *mf*.

Platonism ['pleitənizəm] *n* platonismo *m*.

platoon [plə'tuːn] *n* pelotón *m*, sección *f*.

platter ['plætə*] *n* fuente *f*.

platypus ['plætipəs] *n* ornitorrinco *m*.

plaudits ['plɔːdits] *npl* aplausos *mpl*.

plausibility [,plɔːzə'biliti] *n* verosimilitud *f*, admisibilidad *f*, credibilidad *f*; **his** — **is such that . . .** habla tan bien que . . .

plausible ['plɔːzəbl] *adj* *argument etc* verosímil, admisible, creíble; *person* bien hablado pero no del todo confiable, que convence casi; **he's a** — **sort** tiene mucho cuento.

plausibly ['plɔːzəbli] *adv* de modo verosímil, creíblemente; **he tells it most** — lo cuenta de modo que convence casi.

play [plei] **1** *n* (a) (*amusement etc*) juego *m*, recreo *m*, diversión *f*; — **on words** juego *m* de palabras; **to be at** — estar jugando; **to make** — **of** burlarse de; **to say something in** — decir algo en broma.

(b) (*act of* —*ing*) jugada *f*; **neat** — una bonita jugada; **a clever piece of** — una hábil jugada; **fair** — juego *m* limpio; **foul** — juego *m* sucio; **to be in** — estar en juego; **to be out of** — estar fuera de juego; — **began at 3 o'clock** el partido comenzó a las 3, se empezó a jugar a las 3.

(c) (*activity etc*) juego *m*, actividad *f*; **to bring into** — poner en juego; **to come into** — entrar en juego; **to give full** — **to one's imagination** dar rienda suelta a la imaginación; **to make great** — **with something** recalcar algo, insistir en algo.

(d) (*Mech*) juego *m*, holgura *f*, movimiento *m* libre.

(e) **the** — **of light on the water** el rielar de la luz sobre el agua; **the** — **of light and dark in this picture** el efecto de luz y sombra en este cuadro.

(f) (*Theat*) obra *f*, obra *f* dramática, comedia *f*; **radio** — comedia *f* radiofónica; **the** —**s of Lope** las obras dramáticas de Lope, el teatro de Lope; **to go to the** — ir al teatro.

2 *vt* (a) (*Theat etc*) *play* representar, poner, dar; *part* hacer, hacer el papel de, (*fig*) desempeñar; **when we** —**ed "Hamlet"** cuando representamos "Hamlet"; **when I** —**ed Hamlet** cuando hice el papel de Hamlet; **what did you** — ? ¿qué papel tuvo Vd?; **we shall be** —**ing the West End** pondremos la obra en el West End; **when we last** —**ed Blackpool** cuando representamos la última vez en Blackpool; we —ed "Lear" as a comedy representamos "Lear" como comedia; we —ed "Charley's Aunt" straight representamos "Charley's Aunt" como obra seria; let's — it for laughs hagámoslo en versión burlesca; he likes to — the soldier se las echa de soldado, se da aires de militar; see fool etc.

(b) to — a joke on someone gastar una broma a uno; to — a dirty trick on someone hacer una mala pasada a uno.

(c) card jugar; ball golpear; chess piece etc mover; fish dejar que se canse, agotar; to — the market jugar a la bolsa.

(d) cards, game etc jugar a; to — a game of tennis jugar un partido de tenis; to — a game of cards with someone echar una partida de cartas con uno; do you — football? ¿juegas al fútbol?

(e) opponent jugar con, jugar contra; I —ed him at chess jugué contra él al ajedrez; I —ed him twice jugué contra él dos veces; I'll — you for the drinks el que pierda el juego que pague la cuenta.

(f) (make member of team) incluir, incluir en el equipo; are they —ing Gento? ¿juega Gento?, ¿van a incluir a Gento?

(g) to — someone false traicionar a uno.

(h) (direct) dirigir (on hacia, sobre); to — hoses on a fire utilizar unas mangueras para sofocar un incendio; — the hose this way a bit dirija la manguera más hacia este lado; to — a searchlight on an aircraft dirigir un reflector hacia un avión, hacer de un avión el blanco de un reflector.

(i) (Mus) instrument, record tocar; to learn to — the piano aprender a tocar el piano; they —ed the 5th Symphony tocaron la Quinta Sinfonía, interpretaron la Quinta Sinfonía.

(j) (with adv or prep) to — a record back repetir un disco; to — a tape back repetir lo grabado en una cinta; to — an event down quitar importancia a un suceso, tratar de minimizar un suceso; to — off A against B oponer A a B, contraponer A a B; to — a match off jugar el partido de desquite; to — a work out to the end seguir representando una obra hasta el fin; to — out time seguir jugando hasta el fin (sin hacer ningún esfuerzo para marcar otro gol etc); the organ —ed the congregation out tocaba el órgano mientras salían los fieles; the vein is —ed out la veta está agotada; I'm —ed out estoy agotado, estoy rendido; that joke is —ed out now ese chiste ya no vale; to — someone up burlarse de la autoridad de uno; the kids — the teacher up los pequeños le dan guerra a la maestra.

3 vi (a) (amuse oneself) jugar; divertirse; (frolic) jugar, juguetear; (gambol) retozar; run away and —! ¡idos a jugar!; to — with a stick jugar con un palo; to — with fire jugar con fuego; he's just —ing with you se está burlando de ti; to — with an idea acariciar una idea; this is not a question to be —ed with éste no es asunto para reírse, éste no es asunto para tomar en broma; see fast etc.

(b) (at a game etc) to — at chess jugar al ajedrez; he just —s at it lo hace con poca seriedad; the little girl —s at being a woman la niña juega a ser mujer; he's —ing at being a soldier se las echa de militar; no toma en serio la profesión militar; —! ¡listo!; who —s first? ¿quién juega primero?; are you —ing today? ¿tú juegas hoy?; I've not —ed for a long time hace mucho tiempo que no juego; to — fair jugar limpio; to — for time tratar de ganar tiempo; to — into someone's hands ceder la ventaja a un contrario.

(c) (Mus) tocar; to — on the piano tocar el piano; do you —? ¿sabe tocar?; to be —ed on two pianos para tocar en dos pianos; to — to someone tocar para uno; I —ed it specially for you lo toqué para ti sólo; the band was —ing rather loudly tocaba la orquesta algo fuerte; when the organ —s cuando suena el órgano.

(d) (light) rielar; the sun was —ing on the water rielaba el sol sobre el agua.

(e) (fountain) correr; funcionar.

(f) (act) to — in a film tener (or hacer) un papel en una película; we have —ed all over the South hemos representado en todas partes del Sur; to — ill fingirse enfermo.

(g) to — on someone's credulity explotar la credulidad de uno; to — on someone's feelings aprovecharse de los sentimientos de uno; we must — on their nerves les hemos de hacer una guerra de nervios.

(h) (with adv or prep) to — off jugar el partido de desempate; to — on seguir jugando; — on! ¡adelante!; to — up (play better) jugar con más ánimo,

reanimarse; (be naughty) dar guerra; — up! ¡ánimo!, ¡aúpa!; to — up to someone hacer la pelotilla a uno.

playact ['pleiækt] vi hacer la comedia.

playacting ['plei.æktiŋ] n comedia f, farsa f; this is mere — esto es puro teatro, no es más que una comedia.

playbill ['pleibil] n cartel m (de teatro).

playboy ['pleibɔi] n señorito m, córrelas m, joven m rico y amante de los placeres; "The P— of the Western World" "El córrelas del mundo occidental".

played-out ['pleid'aut] adj agotado.

player ['pleiə*] n (Theat) actor m, actriz f, representante mf; (Mus) músico m, a f; (Sport) jugador m, ora f; (not amateur) jugador m profesional; gentlemen versus —s los aficionados contra los profesionales.

playfellow ['plei.feləu] n compañero m de juego, compañera f de juego.

playful ['pleiful] adj person juguetón; mood alegre; remark dicho en broma.

playfully ['pleifuli] adv jugando, en juego; alegremente; en broma; he said — dijo guasón.

playfulness ['pleifulnis] n carácter m juguetón; alegría f; tono m guasón.

playgoer ['plei.gəuə*] n aficionado m al teatro, aficionada f al teatro; we are regular —s vamos con regularidad al teatro.

playground ['pleigraund] n patio m de recreo.

playhouse ['pleihaus] n, pl —houses [hauziz] teatro m; (US) casita f de muñecas.

playing card ['pleiiŋkɑ:d] n carta f.

playing field ['pleiiŋfi:ld] n campo m de deportes.

playmate ['pleimeit] n camarada mf, compañero m de juego, compañera f de juego.

play-off ['pleiɔf] n partido m de desempate.

playpen ['pleipen] n parque m de jugar, corral m (de niño).

playroom ['pleirum] n cuarto m de los niños.

plaything ['pleiθiŋ] n juguete m (also fig).

playtime ['pleitaim] n hora f de recreo.

playwright ['pleirait] n dramaturgo m.

plea [pli:] n (excuse) pretexto m, disculpa f; (entreaty) súplica f, petición f; (Law) alegato m, defensa f; contestación f a la demanda, declaración f; he made a — for mercy pidió clemencia; a — of insanity un alegato de desequilibrio mental.

plead [pli:d] 1 vt: to — someone's cause hablar po uno, interceder por uno, (Law) defender a uno en juicio; to — ignorance pretender ignorancia, pretextar que uno no sabe; he —ed certain difficulties alegó ciertas dificultades.

2 vi (a) suplicar, rogar; to — with someone suplicar a uno; to — with someone for something rogar a uno que conceda (or permita etc) algo; I —ed and —ed but it was no use le supliqué mil veces pero de nada sirvió; the village has —ed for a new bridge for 10 years durante 10 años el pueblo viene reclamando un nuevo puente.

(b) (Law: as barrister) abogar.

(c) (Law: as defendant) declarar; what do you —? ¿qué contestación hace Vd a la demanda?; to — guilty confesarse culpable; to — not guilty negar la acusación.

pleading ['pli:diŋ] n súplicas fpl; (Law) alegatos mpl; special — argumentos mpl especiosos.

pleasant ['pleznt] adj agradable; surprise etc grato; manner, style ameno; person simpático, afable, amable; we had a — time lo pasamos muy bien; it made a — change from our usual holiday fueron unas vacaciones distintas de las acostumbradas y muy agradables; it's a — surprise to find that . . . es una grata sorpresa descubrir que . . .; it did not make — reading su lectura no fue nada agradable; to make oneself — to someone procurar ser amable con uno.

pleasantly ['plezntli] adv agradablemente; gratamente; en estilo ameno; afablemente, amablemente; I am — surprised that . . . para mí es una grata sorpresa que + subj; it is — warm hace un calor agradable.

pleasantness ['plezntnis] n agrado m, lo agradable; amenidad f; simpatía f, amabilidad f.

pleasantry ['plezntri] n chiste m, dicho m gracioso.

please [pli:z] 1 vti (a) (give pleasure to) dar gusto a, dar satisfacción a, agradar, contentar; caer en gracia a; I did it just to — you lo hice únicamente para darte gusto; there's no pleasing him es imposible contentarle; he is easily —d se contenta con cualquier cosa; she's hard to — es muy exigente; the joke —d him el chiste le cayó en gracia; he is anxious to — procura dar satisfacción; a gift that is sure to — un regalo que siempre agrada; **music that —s the ear** una música grata para el oído; **to lay oneself out to — someone** desvivirse por contentar a uno; **it —d him to order that** . . . tuvo a bien ordenar que + *subj.*

(b) (*impers*) — **God!** (*arch*) ¡plegue a Dios!; — **God that . . .!** ¡plegue a Dios que + *subj!*

(c) (*expressing wish*) — **for favor!**, (*as protest*) ¡por Dios!; **my bill,** — la cuenta, por favor; **two pints** — ! ¡dos cañas, por favor!; **two to Victoria,** — a Victoria, dos, por favor; — **pass the salt, pass the salt** — ¿me hace el favor de pasar la sal?; — **tell me** haga el favor de decírmelo, dígamelo por favor; — **be seated** siéntense; — **sit down!** ¡hagan el favor de sentarse!; — **accept this book** le ruego acepte este libro; — **"not to open this door"** "se ruega no abrir esta puerta"; — **don't cry!** ¡no llores, te lo suplico!; **now** — **do let me know if** . . . no dejes de decirme si . . .; **may I?** . . . — **do!** ¿se puede? . . . ¡naturalmente!

(d) (*think fit*) **if you** — si te parece; **con tu permiso; he wanted 10, if you** — ! ¡quería llevarse 10, ¡fíjate!; **to do as one —s** hacer lo que le da la gana; **I shall do what I** — haré lo que me parezca bien; **as you** — como Vd quiera; **do as you** — haga lo que quiera.

2 *vr*: **to** — **oneself** hacer lo que le da la gana; — **yourself!** ¡como Vd quiera!; **he has always —d himself about holidays** en asunto de vacaciones siempre ha hecho únicamente lo que ha querido.

pleased [pliːzd] *adj* (a) (*happy*) alegre, contento; **to be** — **estar** contento; **to be as — as Punch** estar como unas pascuas; **to look** — estar alegre, parece estar contento; tener aire satisfecho.

(b) **to be — with something** estar satisfecho de algo; **to be — with someone** mostrarse satisfecho con uno; **to be — with oneself** estar satisfecho de sí mismo; **they were anything but — with the news** la noticia no fue de su agrado, antes todo lo contrario; **I am — at the decision** me alegro de la decisión; **I am — to hear it** me alegro de saberlo; **I am — to meet you** tengo mucho gusto en conocerle; **I am — to be able to announce that** . . . me es grato poderles anunciar que . . .; **we are — to inform you that** . . . (*Comm*) nos complacemos en comunicarles que . . ., nos es grato informarles que . . .

(c) (*royal usage*) **Her Majesty has been graciously — to accept** . . . su Majestad aceptó sumamente complacida . . .

pleasing [pliːziŋ] *adj* agradable; grato; halagüeño; **with — results** con resultados halagüeños; **a most — piece of news** una noticia muy grata.

pleasingly [pliːziŋli] *adv* agradablemente; gratamente.

pleasurable [pleʒərəbl] *adj* agradable, deleitoso.

pleasurably [pleʒərəbli] *adv* agradablemente, deleitosamente; **we were — surprised** para nosotros fue una grata sorpresa.

pleasure [pleʒə*] 1 *n* (a) (*in general*) placer *m*, gusto *m*, satisfacción *f*; **with** — con mucho gusto; **it's a — to see him** da gusto verle; **it's a — to know that** . . . es un motivo de satisfacción saber que . . . **it's a real** — es un verdadero placer; — !, **the — is mine!** (*returning thanks*) ¡no hay de qué!; **to find — in chess** divertirse jugando al ajedrez; **what — can you find in shooting partridges?** ¿qué placer encuentras en matar perdices?; **to give someone** — dar gusto a uno; **if it gives you any** — si Vd quiere; **I have much — in informing you that** . . . me es grato informarle que . . .; **may I have the —?** (*at dance*) ¿quiere Vd bailar?; **to take — in books** disfrutar leyendo; **I take great — in watching them grow** disfruto muchísimo viéndolos crecer; **to take — in doing damage** complacerse en hacer daño; **Mr and Mrs X request the — of Y's company** los señores de X solicitan el placer de su compañía.

(b) (*amusements*) placeres *mpl*; diversión *f*, recreo *m*; **all the —s of London** todos los placeres de Londres, todas las diversiones de Londres; **sexual** — placer *m* sexual; **to be fond of** — ser amante de los placeres.

(c) (*will*) voluntad *f*; **at — a** voluntad; **do it at your** — hágalo Vd cuando quiera, hágalo Vd cuando tenga tiempo; **during the royal** — todo el tiempo que quiera el monarca; **what is your —, sir?** ¿en qué puedo servirle, señor?, ¿qué manda Vd, señor?

2 *attr* de recreo, *eg* — **trip** viaje *m* de recreo.

pleasure boat [pleʒəbəut] *n* barco *m* de recreo.

pleasure cruise [pleʒəkruːz] *n* crucero *m* de recreo.

pleasure ground [pleʒəgraund] *n* parque *m* de atracciones.

pleasure-loving [pleʒəlʌviŋ] *adj* amante de los placeres.

pleasure steamer [pleʒəstiːmə*] *n* vapor *m* de recreo.

pleat [pliːt] 1 *n* pliegue *m*. 2 *vt* plegar, plisar.

pleb [pleb] *n* (*fam*) plebeyo *m*, a *f*, persona *f* ordinaria; **the —s** la plebe.

plebeian [pliˈbiːən] 1 *adj* plebeyo. 2 *n* plebeyo *m*, a *f*.

plebiscite [plebisit] *n* plebiscito *m*.

plectrum [plektrəm] *n* plectro *m*.

pled [pled] (*US, Scot*) *irr*: *pret, ptp of* **plead**.

pledge [pledʒ] 1 *n* (*given as security*) prenda *f*; (*promise*) promesa *f*, voto *m*; garantía *f*; (*between governments etc*) compromiso *m*; (*toast*) brindis *m*; **as a — of** en señal de, como garantía de; **I give you this** — os hago esta promesa; **the government will honour its** —s el gobierno hará honor a sus compromisos; **to sign the** — jurar abstenerse del alcohol.

2 *vt* (a) (*pawn*) empeñar, pignorar, dejar en prenda.

(b) (*promise*) prometer; **to — support for someone** prometer su apoyo a uno, prometer apoyar a uno; **to — one's allegiance to someone** jurar ser fiel a uno; **I am —d to secrecy** he jurado guardarlo secreto; **we are —d to go to their aid** hemos prometido ir a ayudarles, nos hemos comprometido a ayudarles.

(c) (*toast*) brindar por.

3 *vr*: **to — oneself to** + *infin* comprometerse a + *infin*.

plenary [pliːnəri] *adj* plenario.

plenipotentiary [ˌplenipəˈtenʃəri] *n* plenipotenciario *m*.

plenitude [plenitjuːd] *n* plenitud *f*.

plenteous [plentiəs] *adj*, **plentiful** [plentiful] *adj* copioso, abundante; **a — supply of** . . . una buena provisión de . . ., un buen surtido de . . .; **eggs are now** — hay abundancia de huevos, abundan los huevos.

plentifully [plentifəli] *adv* copiosamente, abundantemente.

plenty [plenti] 1 *n* (a) abundancia *f*; cantidad *f* suficiente; **land of** — tierra *f* de la abundancia; **in** — en abundancia; **it rained in** — llovió copiosamente; **it grows here in** — por aquí existe en abundancia; **to live in** — vivir en el lujo; **that's —, thanks!** ¡basta, gracias!; **we have** — tenemos bastante; **there's — to go on** hay suficientes datos, son muchas las pruebas; **we know — about you** sabemos mucho acerca de Vd.

(b) — **of** bastante; muchos, muchísimos; una cantidad suficiente de; **we have — of money** tenemos bastante dinero; **they have — of money** tienen mucho dinero; **we have — of tea** tenemos una cantidad suficiente de té; **we have — of time** tenemos tiempo de sobra; **it takes — of courage** exige bastante valor; — **of people do** hay muchos que lo hacen, son muchos los que lo hacen.

2 *adv* (*fam*): **it's — big enough** claro que es bastante grande; **they're — rich enough to pay for two** desde luego son lo bastante ricos para pagar dos de ellos; **it rained** — (*US*) y ¡como llovió!; **we like it** — (*US*) nos gusta muchísimo.

pleonasm [pliːənæzəm] *n* pleonasmo *m*.

pleonastic [pliəˈnæstik] *adj* pleonástico.

plethora [pleθərə] *n* plétora *f*.

plethoric [pleˈθɔrik] *adj* pletórico.

pleurisy [pluərisi] *n* pleuresía *f*.

plexus [pleksəs] *n* plexo *m*; **solar** — plexo *m* solar.

pliability [ˌplaiəˈbiliti] *n* flexibilidad *f*; (*fig*) docilidad *f*.

pliable [plaiəbl] *adj*, **pliant** [plaiənt] *adj* flexible; plegable; (*fig*) dócil, manejable.

pliers [plaiəz] *npl* alicates *mpl*, tenazas *fpl*; **a pair of —, some** — unos alicates, unas tenazas.

plight[1] [plait] *vt* dar, empeñar; **to — one's troth** (*arch or hum*) prometerse, dar su palabra de casamiento (*to a*).

plight[2] [plait] *n* condición *f* (inquietante), situación *f* (difícil); **the — of the shellfish industry** la situación difícil de la industria marisquera; **the country's economic** — la situación económica del país; los apuros económicos del país; **to be in a sad** (*or sorry*) — estar en un estado lamentable.

plimsolls [plimsəlz] *npl* zapatillas *fpl* de goma.

plinth [plinθ] *n* plinto *m*.

Pliny [plini] *m* Plinio; **the Elder** Plinio el Viejo; **the Younger** Plinio el Joven.

plod [plɔd] 1 *n* (a) **to go at a steady** — caminar despacio pero sin desanimarse.

(b) **it's a long — to the village** queda mucho camino para llegar al pueblo.

2 vt recorrer despacio; **we —ded the road for another hour** seguimos andando penosamente durante una hora más; **we —ded our way homeward** volvimos penosamente hacia casa.
3 vi **(a)** caminar despacio, andar penosamente, avanzar con dificultad (*also* **to — along, to — on**); **keep —ding!** ¡ánimo!, ¡no os dejéis desanimar!
(b) (*at work etc*) trabajar laboriosamente, trabajar lentamente pero sin desanimarse; **to — away at a task** dedicarse laboriosamente a un trabajo, seguir trabajando a pesar de las dificultades.

plodder ['plɔdə*] n estudiante mf más aplicado que brillante, persona f que trabaja con más aplicación que talento.

plodding ['plɔdiŋ] adj perseverante, laborioso; *student, worker* más aplicado que brillante.

plonk [plɔŋk] (*fam*) **1** n golpe m seco, ruido m seco; **it fell with a — to the floor** cayó al suelo con un ruido seco.
2 adv: **he went — into the stream** cayó aparatosamente al arroyo; **it landed — on his cheek** le dio de lleno en la mejilla.
3 vt **(a)** (*Mus*) puntear.
(b) **to — something down** arrojar algo con fuerza, dejar caer algo pesadamente.
4 vr: **to — oneself down in a chair** dejarse caer pesadamente en una silla; sentarse sin tener intención de levantarse.

plop [plɔp] **1** n paf m; **—!** ¡paf! **2** vt (*also* **to — down**) arrojar dejando oír un paf. **3** vi caer dejando oír un paf.

plosive ['pləusiv] (*Ling*) **1** adj oclusivo. **2** n oclusiva f.

plot[1] [plɔt] n (*Agr*) terreno m; parcela f; (*of vegetables, flowers etc*) cuadro m; (*for building*) solar m.

plot[2] [plɔt] **1** n **(a)** (*conspiracy*) complot m, conspiración f, conjura f.
(b) (*Lit, Theat*) argumento m; trama f, intriga f; **the — thickens** el argumento se complica, (*fig*) la cosa se complica.
2 vt **(a)** *course* (*on graph etc*) trazar; **to — A against Z** trazar A como función de Z.
(b) *downfall etc* urdir, tramar, maquinar.
3 vi conspirar, conjurarse; intrigar; **to — to do something** conspirar para hacer algo, conjurarse para hacer algo.

plotter ['plɔtə*] n conspirador m, ora f, conjurado m, a f.

plotting ['plɔtiŋ] n conspiración f, intrigas fpl, maquinaciones fpl.

plough, (US) **plow** [plau] **1** n arado m; **the P—** (*Astron*) el Carro, la Osa Mayor.
2 vt arar; (*fig*) surcar; (*Univ sl*) cargar, dar calabazas a; **I was —ed in French** me cargaron en francés; **to — back** (*Comm*) reinvertir; **to — in to — under** cubrir arando, enterrar arando; **to — up** *new ground* roturar, *bushes etc* arrancar con el arado, *pathway* hacer desaparecer arando; **the train —ed up the track for 100 metres** el tren destrozó unos 100 metros de la vía; **to — one's way through snow** abrirse con dificultad paso por la nieve; **to — one's way through a book** leer un libro con dificultad; **I —ed my way through it eventually** por fin acabé de leerlo pero resultó pesadísimo.
3 vi **(a)** arar; **to — through** *see* vt (**to — one's way**).
(b) (*sl*) **I —ed again** volvieron a suspenderme.

ploughing, (US) **plowing** ['plauiŋ] n arada f.

ploughing back, (US) **plowing —** ['plauiŋˌbæk] n (*Comm*) reinversión f.

ploughland, (US) **plow—** ['plaulænd] n tierra f de labrantío.

ploughman, (US) **plow—** ['plaumən] n, pl **—men** [mən] arador m, labrador m.

ploughshare, (US) **plow—** ['plauʃɛə*] n reja f del arado.

plover ['plʌvə*] n chorlito m.

plow [plau] (US) *see* **plough.**

ploy [plɔi] n (*fam*) truco m, estratagema f.

pluck[1] [plʌk] n (*courage*) valor m, ánimo m; (*guts*) agallas fpl; **it takes — to do that** hace falta tener agallas para conseguir eso; **he's got plenty of —** sí tiene agallas; **I didn't have the — to own up** no tuve bastante ánimo para confesar.

pluck[2] [plʌk] **1** n (*tug*) tirón m.
2 vt *fruit, flower* coger; *bird* desplumar; *guitar* puntear; **to — one's eyebrows** depilarse las cejas; **to — off, to — out, to — up** arrancar con los dedos, arrancar de un tirón; quitar de un tirón; **he —ed it up off the table** lo recogió de la mesa con un movimiento brusco; *see* **courage.**
3 vi: **to — at** tirar de, dar un tirón a; **to — at someone's sleeve** tirar de la manga de uno.

pluckily ['plʌkili] adv valientemente; con resolución.

pluckiness ['plʌkinis] n valor m, ánimo m; resolución f.

plucky ['plʌki] adj valiente, valeroso; resuelto.

plug [plʌg] **1** n **(a)** (*bung*) tapón m, taco m; (*in bath etc*) tapón m; (*Med, of cotton wool etc*) tampón m; (*of tobacco*) rollo m, tableta f; (*Aut*) bujía f; (*Elec: free, on wire, on apparatus*) clavija f, enchufe m, (*in wall*) toma f; (*Tel*) clavija f; **two-pin —** clavija f bipolar; **three-pin —** clavija f de 3 polos.
(b) (*sl*) anuncio m incidental, publicidad f incidental; **to give someone a —** permitir que uno se beneficie de la publicidad; **to put in a — for a product** lograr anunciar un producto de modo solapado.
2 vt **(a)** *hole etc* tapar, llenar, obturar; (*Archit*) rellenar; *tooth* empastar; **to — a radio** conectar una radio; **to — a lead into a socket** enchufar un hilo en una toma; **to — up** tapar, obturar; **to — the drain on the reserves** acabar con las pérdidas de divisas.
(b) (*sl: hit*) pegar, (*shoot*) pegar un tiro a.
(c) (*Comm sl*) anunciar de modo solapado, dar publicidad incidental a; (*repeat*) repetir, machacar en; **he's been —ging that line for years** hace años que viene diciendo lo mismo.
3 vi: **to — away** seguir trabajando (*etc*) a pesar de todo, batir el yunque; no dejarse desanimar.

plughole ['plʌghəul] n tubo m de salida, salida f.

plug-in ['plʌg'in] adj (*Elec*) enchufable.

plum [plʌm] n (*fruit*) ciruela f; (*tree*) ciruelo m; (*fig: the best*) lo mejor; (*post*) pingüe destino m, turrón m, breva f.

plumage ['plu:midʒ] n plumaje m.

plumb [plʌm] **1** n plomada f.
2 adj vertical, a plomo.
3 adv **(a)** verticalmente, a plomo.
(b) (*fam*) totalmente, completamente; **— crazy** completamente loco; **— in the middle** exactamente en el centro; **it hit him — on the nose** le dio de lleno en las narices.
4 vt sondar, sondear (*also fig*).

plumbago [plʌm'beigəu] n plombagina f.

plumber ['plʌmə*] n fontanero m.

plumbic ['plʌmbik] adj plúmbico, plúmbeo.

plumbing ['plʌmiŋ] n (*craft*) fontanería f; (*piping*) instalación f de cañerías; (*bathroom fittings*) aparatos mpl sanitarios.

plumbline ['plʌmlain] n cuerda f de plomada.

plume [plu:m] **1** n (*bird*) pluma f; (*on helmet*) penacho m; (*of smoke etc*) penacho m, hilo m.
2 vr: **the bird —s itself** el ave se limpia las plumas, el ave se arregla las plumas.

plumed [plu:md] adj plumado; con plumas; *helmet* empenachado.

plummet ['plʌmit] **1** n plomada f. **2** vi: **to — down, to come —ing down** caer a plomo.

plummy ['plʌmi] adj (*fam*) *voice* pastoso.

plump[1] [plʌmp] **1** adj *body* rechoncho, rollizo; *face* mofletudo; *chicken etc* gordo. **2** vt (*fatten*) engordar; (*swell*) hinchar. **3** vi engordar; hincharse.

plump[2] [plʌmp] **1** adv de lleno; **to fall — on to something** caer de lleno en algo.
2 vt: **to — something down** arrojar algo pesadamente, dejar caer algo pesadamente en el suelo.
3 vi **(a)** (*fall*) caer pesadamente, dejarse caer pesadamente; **to — down on to a chair** dejarse caer pesadamente en un sillón.
(b) **to — for** optar por; (*vote*) votar por.
4 vr: **to — oneself down** dejarse caer pesadamente.

plumpness ['plʌmpnis] n gordura f; lo rollizo.

plum pudding ['plʌm'pudiŋ] n *especie de pudín inglés de ciruela* (*esp de Navidad*).

plum tree ['plʌmtri:] n ciruelo m.

plunder ['plʌndə*] **1** n (*act*) pillaje m, saqueo m; (*loot*) botín m.
2 vt saquear, pillar; *tomb* robar; *safe* robar el contenido de, robar (las alhajas de); **they —ed my cellar** saquearon mi bodega.

plunderer ['plʌndərə*] n saqueador m.

plundering ['plʌndəriŋ] n saqueo m.

plunge [plʌndʒ] **1** n **(a)** (*dive from bank etc*) salto m; (*submersion by swimmer, bird etc*) zambullida f; (*by professional diver*) inmersión f; (*bathe*) baño m; **the diver rested after each —** el buzo descansó después de cada inmersión; **he had a — before breakfast** se fue a bañar antes de desayunar.
(b) (*bath*) baño m; (*pool*) piscina f; **cold —** baño m frío.
(c) (*fig*) **to take the —** dar el paso decisivo, resolverse; jugarse el todo; **we are about to take the —** estamos al punto de dar el paso decisivo;

I took the — and bought it por fin me resolví a comprarlo.

2 *vt* **(a)** *(immerse)* sumergir; hundir *(into* en); he —d his hands into the water hundió las manos en el agua; he —d his hand into his pocket metió la mano en el bolsillo.

(b) to — a dagger into someone's chest hundir *(or clavar)* un puñal en el pecho de uno.

(c) to — a room into darkness sumir un cuarto en la oscuridad; New York was suddenly —d into darkness Nueva York se vio de repente sumida en la oscuridad.

(d) to — someone into sadness hundir *(or* sumir, abismar) a uno en la tristeza; we were —d into gloom by the news la noticia nos sumió en la tristeza.

3 *vi* **(a)** *(dive)* saltar; zambullirse; sumergirse; *(sink)* hundirse; then the submarine —d luego se sumergió el submarino: she —d into 10 metres of water se zambulló en 10 metros de agua.

(b) *(fall)* caer; he —d to his death tuvo una caída mortal; he —d from a 5th storey window se arrojó desde una ventana del 5° piso; the aircraft —d into the sea off Dover el avión cayó al mar a la altura de Dover.

(c) *(dress: fam)* tener mucho escote, ser muy escotado.

(d) *(ship)* cabecear; *(horse)* corcovear.

(e) *(person: rush)* arrojarse, lanzarse, precipitarse; to — forward precipitarse hacia adelante; to — into one's work emprender resuelto su trabajo, engolfarse en el trabajo; to — heedlessly into danger meterse en los peligros sin hacer caso de ellos; he —d into a discussion of Plato se lanzó a una discusión de Platón.

(f) *(fam: gamble)* apostar el todo; *(Comm)* arriesgar mucho dinero.

(g) *(fam: decide)* resolverse, dar el paso decisivo.

plunger ['plʌndʒə*] *n* émbolo *m*.

plunging ['plʌndʒiŋ] *adj (fam)* neckline muy bajo.

plunk [plʌŋk] *n etc (US)* = **plonk**.

pluperfect ['pluː'pəːfikt] *n* pluscuamperfecto *m*.

plural ['pluərəl] **1** *adj* plural; the — form of the noun la forma del sustantivo en plural. **2** *n* plural *m*; in the — en el plural.

plurality [‚pluə'ræliti] *n* pluralidad *f*.

plus [plʌs] **1** *prep* más, y; además de; juntamente con; **3 — 4** 3 más 4; — what I have to do already además de lo que tengo que hacer ya.

2 *adj* **(a)** *(Math, quantity, Elec)* positivo, de signo positivo.

(b) two pounds — dos libras y algo más, más de dos libras; twenty — veinte y pico, veintitantos.

3 *n (Math: sign)* signo *m* más; *(amount)* cantidad *f* positiva.

plus fours ['plʌs'fɔːz] *npl* pantalones *mpl* de golf. pantalones *mpl* holgados de media pierna.

plush [plʌʃ] **1** *n* felpa *f*. **2** *adj* de felpa; *(fam) see* **plushy**.

plushy ['plʌʃi] *adj (fam)* lujoso, elegante, de buen tono.

Plutarch ['pluːtɑːk] *m* Plutarco.

Pluto ['pluːtəu] *m* Plutón.

plutocracy [pluːˈtɔkrəsi] *n* plutocracia *f*.

plutocrat ['pluːtəukræt] *n* plutócrata *mf*.

plutocratic [‚pluːtəu'krætik] *adj* plutocrático.

plutonium [pluːˈtəuniəm] *n* plutonio *m*.

pluviometer [‚pluːviˈɔmitə*] *n* pluviómetro *m*.

ply¹ [plai] *n: eg* three — *(wood)* de tres capas, *(wool)* de tres cordones.

ply² [plai] **1** *vt* needle, tool etc manejar, menear (vigorosamente); oars etc emplear; trade ejercer; seas, river navegar por; person no dejar descansar a; to — someone with questions importunar a uno haciéndole muchas preguntas; to — someone for information importunar a uno pidiéndole informes; to — someone with drink dar a uno repetidas veces de beber, emborrachar a uno; to — someone with cakes ofrecer repetidas veces los pastelitos a uno.

2 *vi:* to — between hacer el servicio entre, ir y venir entre; to — for hire ofrecerse para alquilar.

plywood ['plaiwud] *n* madera *f* contrachapada, madera *f* multilaminar, panel *m*.

pneumatic [njuːˈmætik] *adj* neumático.

pneumatically [njuːˈmætikəli] *adv* neumáticamente.

pneumonia [njuːˈməuniə] *n* pulmonía *f*; double — pulmonía *f* doble.

po [pəu] *n (fam)* orinal *m*; wáter *m*.

poach¹ [pəutʃ] *vt* egg escalfar.

poach² [pəutʃ] **1** *vt* cazar *(or* pescar *etc)* en vedado; cazar *(or* pescar *etc)* ilegalmente; *(fig: steal)* robar, advantage etc pisar, tomar.

2 *vi* cazar *(or* pescar *etc)* en finca ajena; to — on someone's preserves *(fig)* cazar en finca ajena, meterse en los asuntos ajenos.

poached [pəutʃt] *adj* egg escalfado.

poacher ['pəutʃə*] *n* cazador *m* furtivo.

poaching ['pəutʃiŋ] *n* caza *f* furtiva, pesca *f* furtiva.

pochard ['pəutʃəd] *n (Zool)* porrón *m*.

pock [pɔk] *n* pústula *f*.

pocket ['pɔkit] **1** *n* bolsillo *m*; *(Billiards)* tronera *f*; *(fig, Geol, Mil etc)* bolsa *f*; hoyo *m*, cavidad *f*, hueco *m*; *(Aer)* bolsa *f* de aire; trouser — bolsillo *m* del pantalón; — of resistance bolsa *f* de resistencia; to be in — salir ganando; to be £5 in — haber ganado 5 libras; to be out of — salir perdiendo; to be £5 out of — haber perdido 5 libras; he has the game in his — domina el partido, está seguro de ganar el partido; to have someone in one's — haberse cazado la voluntad de uno; to line one's —s ponerse las botas; see **pick**.

2 *attr* de bolsillo; — battleship acorazado *m* de bolsillo; — edition edición *f* de bolsillo.

3 *vt* meter en el bolsillo, guardar en el bolsillo; *(Billiards)* entronerar; *(earn, make)* ganar; *(pej)* apropiarse, alzarse con, embolsar; he —ed half the takings se embolsó la mitad de la recaudación; see **pride** etc.

pocketbook ['pɔkitbuk] *n* cartera *f*, portamonedas *m*.

pocketful ['pɔkitful] *n* bolsillo *m*; cantidad *f* que cabe en el bolsillo; a — of nuts un bolsillo lleno de nueces.

pocket-handkerchief [‚pɔkit'hæŋkətʃif] *n* pañuelo *m*.

pocket knife ['pɔkitnaif] *n, pl* — knives [naivz] navaja *f*.

pocket money ['pɔkit‚mʌni] *n* dinero *m* para pequeños gastos personales.

pocket-size ['pɔkitsaiz] *adj* de bolsillo.

pockmark ['pɔkmɑːk] *n* hoyo *m*.

pockmarked ['pɔkmɑːkt] *adj* face picado de viruelas; surface marcado de hoyos; to be — with estar marcado de, estar acribillado de.

pod [pɔd] *n* vaina *f*.

podgy ['pɔdʒi] *adj* gordinflón; face mofletudo.

podiatry [pɔˈdiːətri] *n* podiatría *f*.

podium ['pəudiəm] *n* podio *m*.

poem ['pəuim] *n* poesía *f*; *(long, narrative)* poema *m*; P— of the Cid Poema *m* de mío Cid, Cantar *m* de mío Cid; Lorca's — las poesías de Lorca, la obra poética de Lorca, las obras en verso de Lorca.

poet ['pəuit] *n* poeta *m*; — laureate poeta *m* laureado.

poetaster [‚pəui'tæstə*] *n* poetastro *m*.

poetess ['pəuites] *n* poetisa *f*.

poetic(al) [pəuˈetik(əl)] *adj* poético.

poetically [pəuˈetikəli] *adv* poéticamente.

poeticize [pəuˈetisaiz] *vt (enhance)* poetizar, adornar con detalles poéticos; *(translate into verse)* hacer un poema de, hacer una versión poética de.

poetics [pəuˈetiks] *n* poética *f*.

poetry ['pəuitri] *n* poesía *f*; see also **poem**.

pogrom ['pɔgrəm] *n* pogrom *m*, pogromo *m*, persecución *f* antisemítica.

poignancy ['pɔinjənsi] *n* patetismo *m*; intensidad *f*, profundidad *f*.

poignant ['pɔinjənt] *adj (moving)* conmovedor, patético; *(profound)* intenso, agudo, profundo.

poignantly ['pɔinjəntli] *adv* de modo conmovedor, patéticamente; intensamente, agudamente.

poinsettia [pɔin'setiə] *n* flor *f* de la Pascua.

point [pɔint] **1** *n* **(a)** *(Typ etc)* punto *m*; decimal — punto *m* decimal, coma *f*; 7.6 7,6 (siete enteros y seis décimos).

(b) *(on scale; place, time)* punto *m*; — of the compass cuarta *f*; — of departure punto *m* de partida; angular — vértice *m*; cardinal —s puntos *mpl* cardinales; focal — punto *m* focal; reference — punto *m* de referencia; see **boiling** — etc; Slough and all —s west Slough y las estaciones más hacia el oeste; at the — where the road forks donde se bifurca el camino; at this — en esto, llegado a este punto; at that — in time en aquel momento; at all —s por todas partes, en todos los sitios; matters are at such a — that ... las cosas han llegado a tal punto que . . .; to be on the — of + ger estar a punto de + infin; delivered free to all —s in Spain se entrega a porte pagado en toda España; he is severe to the — of cruelty es tan severo que hasta se puede decir que es cruel; up to a — hasta cierto punto; up to a —, Lord Copper en cierto modo, Lord Copper.

(c) *(aspect)* punto *m*, aspecto *m*; — of interest punto *m* interesante, aspecto *m* interesante; — of honour cuestión *f* de honor, punto *m* de honor; — of order cuestión *f* de procedimiento; in — of en cuanto a, por lo que se refiere a; **in** — **of fact** en realidad; **in** — **of numbers** en cuanto al número; **in** — **of sheer strength** en cuanto a la fuerza sola.

(**d**) — *of view* punto *m* de vista; **from the** — **of view of** desde el punto de vista de; **to come round to someone's** — **of view** adoptar el criterio de uno, compartir la opinión de uno; **to look at a matter from all** — **s of view** considerar una cuestión bajo todos sus aspectos; **to see** (*or* **understand**) **someone's** — **of view** comprender el punto de vista de uno.

(**e**) (*of argument etc*) punto *m*; **the** — **at issue** el punto en cuestión, el asunto en litigio; **the** — **s to remember are** . . . los puntos a retener son los siguientes . . .; **to be beside the** — no venir al caso; **it is beside the** — **that** . . . no importa que + *subj*; **it's off the** — está fuera de propósito; **to get off the** —, **to wander off the** — salirse del tema, apartarse del tema; **on this** — sobre este punto; **on that** — en cuanto a eso; **on that** — **we agree** sobre eso estamos de acuerdo; **to differ on a** — no estar de acuerdo en un particular; **an argument very much to the** — un argumento muy a propósito; **that is hardly to the** — eso apenas hace al caso; **to come to the** — ir al grano; **let's come to the** — ! ¡vamos al grano!, ¡dejémonos de historias!; **to get back to the** — volver al tema; **to keep to the** — no salirse del tema; **to carry one's** — salirse con la suya; **it gave** — **to the argument** hizo ver la importancia del argumento; **to make a** — establecer un punto, hacer aceptar una opinión; **he made the following** —s dijo lo siguiente; **to make the** — **that** . . . hacer ver que . . ., hacer comprender que . . .; **to make a** — **of** + *ger* no dejar de + *infin*, insistir en + *infin*; **to press the** — insistir (*that* en que); **to pursue one's** — seguir su tema; **to stretch a** — hacer una excepción, hacer una concesión.

(**f**) (*significant part, important thing*) lo significativo, lo importante; **this is the** — esto es lo importante; **the** — **is,** — lo importante es . . .; **the whole** — **is** . . . lo único que importa es . . .; **the** — **is that** . . . lo importante es que . . .; **that's just the** — ! ¡sí eso es lo más importante!; **that's not the** — no es eso; **the** — **of the joke is that** . . . la gracia del chiste consiste en que . . .; **to get the** — comprender; **to miss the** — no ver lo esencial.

(**g**) (*purpose*) fin *m*, finalidad *f*, objeto *m*; (*usefulness*) utilidad *f*; **what's the** — **of railways?** ¿qué utilidad tienen los ferrocarriles?, ¿de qué sirven los ferrocarriles?; **what's the** — **of trying?** ¿de qué sirve esforzarse?; **there is no** — **in** + *ger* no vale la pena + *infin*, no hay para qué + *infin*; **I don't see the** — **of doing it** no entiendo por qué sea necesario hacerlo, no creo que sea necesario hacerlo.

(**h**) (*of character*) rasgo *m*, característica *f*; **weak** — flaco *m*, punto *m* débil; —**s of a horse** características *fpl* de un caballo; **he has his** —**s** tiene algunas cualidades buenas; **it was always his strong** — siempre ha sido su punto fuerte; **maths is not a strong** — **of mine** nunca he entendido gran cosa en matemáticas; **what** —**s should I look for?** ¿qué puntos debo examinar?

(**i**) (*Games*) punto *m*, tanto *m*; —**s against** puntos *mpl* en contra; —**s for** puntos *mpl* a favor; **to give someone** —**s** dar una ventaja a uno; **to score 10** —**s** marcar 10 puntos; **to win on** —**s** ganar por puntos.

(**j**) (*unit*) **the thermometer went up 3** —**s** el termómetro subió 3 grados; **the shares went down 2** —**s** las acciones bajaron 2 enteros.

(**k**) (*sharp end: of needle etc*) punta *f*; (*of pen*) puntilla *f*; (*Geog*) punta *f*, promontorio *m*, cabo *m*; (*Elec*) enchufe *m*, toma *m*; —**s** (*Rail*) agujas *fpl*; **a five-point star** una estrella de cinco puntas; **to put a** — **on a pencil** sacar punta a un lápiz; **not to put too fine a** — **on it** para decirlo como ello es, hablando sin rodeos.

2 *vt* (**a**) (*sharpen*) afilar, aguzar; *pencil* sacar punta a.

(**b**) **to** — **a moral** inculcar una lección, subrayar una moraleja.

(**c**) *gun, telescope etc* apuntar (*at* a); **to** — **a gun at someone** apuntar a uno con un fusil; **to** — **a finger at someone** señalar a uno con el dedo.

(**d**) *path, way* indicar.

(**e**) *wall* rejuntar.

(**f**) *text* puntuar; *Hebrew etc* puntar.

(**g**) **to** — **out** indicar, señalar; **to** — **out something to someone** señalar algo a uno, enseñar algo a uno; (*in speaking*) hacer ver algo a uno, indicar algo a uno; **to** — **out someone's mistakes** señalar los errores de uno; **to** — **out to someone the advantages of a car** explicar a uno las ventajas de tener coche; **to** — **out that** . . . indicar que . . ., advertir que . . .;

may I — **out that** . . . permítaseme observar que . . .

(**h**) **to** — **up** destacar, poner de relieve.

3 *vi* (**a**) **to** — **at someone** señalar (*or* indicar) a uno con el dedo.

(**b**) (*of dog*) mostrar la caza, pararse.

(**c**) **it** —**s north** está orientado hacia el norte; **the hand** —**ed to midnight** la aguja marcaba las 12; **this** —**s to the fact that** . . . esto indica que . . .; **everything** —**s that way** todo parece indicarlo; **everything** —**s to his success** todo anuncia su éxito; **everything** —**s to the festival being a lively one** el festival se anuncia animado; **the evidence** —**s to her** las pruebas indican que ella es la culpable.

point-blank ['point'blæŋk] **1** *adv* a quemarropa (*also fig*); **to ask someone something** — preguntar algo a uno a quemarropa; **to refuse** — dar una negativa rotunda.

2 *adj question, shot* hecho a quemarropa.

point duty ['point,dju:ti] *n* control *m* de la circulación.

pointed ['pointid] *adj shape* puntiagudo; (*sharp*) afilado, agudo; (*Archit*) *window* ojival; *remark etc* lleno de intención; inequívoco, directo; enfático.

pointedly ['pointidli] *adv say etc* con intención; inequívocamente, directamente; enfáticamente.

pointer ['pointə*] *n* (*needle*) indicador *m*, aguja *f*; (*of balance*) fiel *m*; (*long stick*) puntero *m*; (*dog*) perro *m* de muestra; (*fig*) indicación *f*; pista *f*; **it is a** — **to a possible solution** es una indicación de una solución posible; **there is at present no** — **to the outcome** por ahora nada indica qué resultado tendrá; **this is a** — **to the guilty man** es una pista que conducirá al criminal.

pointillism ['pwæntilizəm] *n* puntillismo *m*.

pointless ['pointlis] *adj* (*useless*) inútil; (*motiveless*) sin motivo, inmotivado; (*meaningless*) sin sentido; insensato; **it is** — **to complain** es inútil quejarse, de nada sirve quejarse; **an apparently** — **crime** un crimen que parece carecer de motivo; **a** — **existence** una vida sin sentido, una vida que carece de propósito.

pointlessly ['pointlisli] *adv* inútilmente; sin motivo.

pointlessness ['pointlisnis] *n* inutilidad *f*; falta *f* de motivo; falta *f* de sentido; **the** — **of war** la insensatez de la guerra.

point-to-point ['pointtə'point] *n* (*also* — **race**) carrera de caballos a través del campo.

poise [poiz] **1** *n* (**a**) (*balance*) equilibrio *m*.

(**b**) (*fig: of body*) aire *m*, porte *m*; elegancia *f*; **she dances with such** — baila con tanta elegancia, baila con tal garbo.

(**c**) (*of mind*) serenidad *f*; aplomo *m*; confianza *f* en sí mismo; **she does it with great** — lo hace con el mayor aplomo; **he lacks** — le falta confianza en sí mismo.

2 *vt* equilibrar; balancear; **he** —**d it on his hand** lo puso en equilibrio sobre la mano; **to be** —**d** estar suspendido; (*hover*) cernerse, estar inmóvil (en el aire *etc*); **they are** —**d to attack, they are** —**d for the attack** están listos para atacar, están en condiciones de lanzarse al ataque.

poised [poizd] *adj* (*in temperament*) sereno, ecuánime, confiado en sí mismo; *see* **poise 2.**

poison ['poizn] **1** *n* veneno *m*; tóxico *m*; (*fig*) ponzoña *f*, veneno *m*; **to die of** — morir envenenado; **to take** — envenenarse.

2 *vt* envenenar; (*fig*) envenenar, emponzoñar; corromper.

poisoner ['poiznə*] *n* envenenador *m*, ora *f*.

poison gas ['poizn'gæs] *n* gas *m* tóxico, gas *m* asfixiante.

poisoning ['poizniŋ] *n* envenenamiento *m*.

poisonous ['poiznəs] *adj snake etc* venenoso; *substance, fumes etc* tóxico; (*fig: damaging*) pernicioso, (*very bad*) horrible, malísimo; **this** — **propaganda** esta propaganda perniciosa; **the play was** — la obra fue horrible; **he's a** — **individual** es una persona horrible.

poison-pen ['poizn'pen] *adj:* — **letter** carta *f* anónima con injurias.

poke[1] [pəuk] *n* (*sack*) saco *m*, bolsa *f*.

poke[2] [pəuk] **1** *n* (*push*) empuje *m*, empujón *m*; (*with elbow*) codazo *m*; (*jab*) pinchazo *m*; hurgonazo *m*; (*with poker*) hurgonada *f*, hurgonazo *m*; **to give the fire a** — atizar la lumbre, remover la lumbre; **to give someone a** — **in the ribs** dar a uno un codazo en las costillas; **to give someone a** — **with a bayonet** dar a uno un pinchazo con la bayoneta.

2 *vt* (*push*) empujar; *fire* hurgar, atizar, remover; **to** — **someone in the ribs** dar a uno un codazo en las costillas; **to** — **someone in the ribs with a stick** dar a uno un pinchazo con un palo en las costillas; **to** —

a stick into a crack introducir un palo en una grieta; **to — a rag into a tube** introducir un trapo en un tubo; **to — a stick into the ground** clavar un palo en el suelo; **to — someone's eye out** saltar el ojo a uno, quebrar el ojo a uno; **to — a hole in a picture** hacer un agujero en un cuadro; **to — one's head out** sacar la cabeza, asomar la cabeza; *see* **fun, nose,** *and compare* **jab.**

3 *vi* (a) **to — at something with a stick** tratar de remover (*etc*) algo con un bastón.

(b) **to — about, to — around** andar buscando (algo); (*pej*) fisgar, hacer indagaciones a hurtadillas; **we spent a day poking about in the shops** pasamos un día curioseando en las tiendas; **and now you come poking about!** ¡y ahora Vd se mete a husmear!; **to — into someone's business** meterse en los asuntos de uno.

poker[1] ['pəukə*] *n* atizador *m*, badila *f*.
poker[2] ['pəukə*] *n* (*Cards*) póquer *m*; **to have a — face** tener una cara impasible.
poker-faced ['pəukə'feist] *adj* de cara impasible; **they looked on —** miraron impasibles, miraron sin expresión.
poky ['pəuki] *adj room* estrecho, muy pequeño; **a — little room** un cuartucho.
Poland ['pəulənd] Polonia *f*.
polar ['pəulə*] *adj* polar.
polar bear ['pəulə'beə*] *n* oso *m* blanco.
polarity [pou'læriti] *n* polaridad *f*.
polarization [,pəulərai'zeiʃən] *n* polarización *f*.
polarize ['pəuləraiz] **1** *vt* polarizar. **2** *vi* polarizarse.
Pole [pəul] *n* polaco *m*, a *f*.
pole[1] [pəul] **1** *n* (a) *medida de longitud* = 5,029 *m.*
(b) palo *m*, palo *m* largo, vara *f* larga; (*flag—*) asta *f*; (*tent—*) mástil *m*; (*for fencing*) estaca *f*; (*Tel*) poste *m*; (*for gymnastics*) percha *f*; (*for vaulting*) pértiga *f*; (*for punting*) pértiga *f*; (*of cart*) vara *f*, lanza *f*; **greasy —** cucaña *f*, palo *m* ensebado; **to be up the —** (*sl*) estar chiflado (*fam*).
2 *vt punt etc* impeler con pértiga.
pole[2] [pəul] *n* (*Elec, Geog etc*) polo *m*; **negative —** polo *m* negativo; **positive —** polo *m* positivo; **North P—** Polo *m* Norte; **South P—** Polo *m* Sur; **from — to —** de polo a polo.
poleaxe ['pəulæks] *vt* desnucar.
polecat ['pəulkæt] *n* turón *m*; (*US*) mofeta *f*.
polemic [pɔ'lemik] **1** *adj* polémico. **2** *n* polémica *f*; **—s** polémica *f*.
polemical [pɔ'lemikəl] *adj* polémico.
pole star ['pəulstɑ:*] *n* estrella *f* polar.
pole vault ['pəulvɔ:lt] *n* salto *m* con pértiga.
police [pə'li:s] **1** *n* policía *f*; **mounted —** policía *f* montada; **river —** brigada *f* fluvial; **traffic —** policía *f* de tráfico.
2 *vt frontier* vigilar, patrullar por; *area* mantener servicio de policía en, mantener el orden público en; **the frontier is —d by UNO patrols** la frontera la vigilan las patrullas de la ONU; **the area used to be —d by Britain** antes Gran Bretaña mantenía la paz en la región.
police car [pə'li:skɑ:*] *n* coche *m* de policía, coche-patrulla *m*.
police constable [pə'li:s'kʌnstəbl] *n* policía *m*, guardia *m*.
police dog [pə'li:sdɔg] *n* perro *m* policía.
policeman [pə'li:smən] *n*, *pl* **—men** [mən] policía *m*, guardia *m*; **what the — are you doing?** (*sl*) ¿qué demonios haces ahí?
police state [pə'li:s'steit] *n* estado *m* policíaco.
police station [pə'li:s'steiʃən] *n* comisaría *f*.
policewoman [pə'li:s,wumən] *n*, *pl* **—women** [,wimin] policía *m* femenino, mujer *f* policía.
policy[1] ['pɔlisi] *n* (a) política *f*; (*loosely*) principios *mpl*; actitud *f*; sistema *m*; (*of party, at election*) programa *m* político; (*of newspaper*) normas *fpl* de conducta; **economic —** política *f* económica; **foreign —** política *f* exterior; **prices and incomes —** política *f* de ingresos y precios; **that's not my —** eso no es mi sistema; **to change one's —** cambiar de actitud; **it would be contrary to public — to + infin** no sería conforme con el interés nacional + *infin*.
(b) (*wisdom*) prudencia *f*; **it is — to + infin es** prudente + *infin*.
policy[2] ['pɔlisi] *n* póliza *f*; **insurance —** póliza *f* de seguros; **to take out a —** hacerse un seguro, asegurar algo.
policyholder ['pɔlisi,həuldə*] *n* tenedor *m* de una póliza, tenedora *f* de una póliza, asegurado *m*, a *f*.
polio ['pəuliəu] *n* polio *f*.
poliomyelitis [,pəuliəumaiə'laitis] *n* poliomielitis *f*.
Polish ['pəuliʃ] **1** *adj* polaco. **2** *n* polaco *m* (*idioma*).

polish ['pɔliʃ] **1** *n* (a) (*material*) (*shoe —*) betún *m*; (*floor —, furniture —*) cera *f* de lustrar; (*metal —*) líquido *m* para limpiar metales; (*nail —*) esmalte *m* para las uñas, laca *f* para las uñas.
(b) (*act*) pulimento *m*; **to give something a —** sacar brillo a algo, pulir algo; **my shoes need a —** hace falta limpiar mis zapatos.
(c) (*shine*) brillo *m*, bruñido *m*, lustre *m*; **high —** lustre *m* brillante; **the buttons have lost their —** los botones han perdido su brillo, los botones se han deslustrado; **to put a — on something** sacar brillo a algo; **the water takes the — off** el agua quita el brillo.
(d) (*fig: refinement*) finura *f*, cultura *f*, urbanidad *f*; (*of artistry etc*) elegancia *f*; perfección *f*; **his style needs —** le hace falta limar el estilo; **he lacks —** le falta finura.
2 *vt* (a) *shoes* limpiar; *floor, furniture* encerar, sacar brillo a; *pans etc* abrillantar; *metal* limpiar, *silver* pulir; (*mechanically, industrially*) pulimentar.
(b) (*also to — up*) *person* civilizar; *manners* refinar; *style etc* pulir, limar; *one's French etc* repasar, refrescar.
(c) **to — off** *work* terminar, despachar; *person etc* acabar con; *food, drink* despachar, dar cuenta de.
polished ['pɔliʃt] *adj* pulido; *style etc* limado, elegante; *person* culto, distinguido, fino; *manners* fino.
polisher ['pɔliʃə*] *n* (*person*) pulidor *m*, ora *f*; (*machine*) enceradora *f*.
polishing machine ['pɔliʃiŋmə,ʃi:n] *n* enceradora *f*.
polite [pə'lait] *adj* cortés, atento, fino; correcto; **that's not very —** eso no es fino; **he was very — to me** estuvo muy correcto conmigo; **in — society** en la buena sociedad.
politely [pə'laitli] *adv* cortésmente, atentamente; correctamente.
politeness [pə'laitnis] *n* cortesía *f*, finura *f*; corrección *f*; **with exquisite —** con la mayor finura; **to do something out of —** hacer algo por cortesía.
politic ['pɔlitik] *adj* prudente.
political [pə'litikəl] *adj* político.
politically [pə'litikəli] *adv* políticamente.
politician [,pɔli'tiʃən] *n* político *m*; (*pej*) politiquero *m*.
politics ['pɔlitiks] *npl* política *f*; **to go into —** dedicarse a la política; **to talk —** hablar de política; *see* **party 2** (a).
polity ['pɔliti] *n* gobierno *m*, forma *f* de gobierno; estado *m*.
polka ['pɔlkə] *n* polca *f*.
polka dot ['pɔlkədɔt] *n* punto *m*; diseño *m* de puntos.
poll [pəul] **1** *n* (a) (*election*) votación *f*; elección *f*; **in the — of 1945, at the —s in 1945** en las elecciones de 1945; **a — was demanded** se pidió que el asunto se sometiera a votación; **to go to the —s** acudir a las urnas; **to head the —** obtener la mayoría de los votos, ser elegido, ocupar el primer puesto en la elección; **to take a —** someter un asunto a votación; **a — was taken among those present** votaron los asistentes sobre el asunto.
(b) (*total votes*) votos *mpl*; **the candidate achieved a — of 5000 votes** el candidato obtuvo 5000 votos; **there was a — of 84%** votaron el 84 por cien; **the — has been a heavy one** ha votado un elevado porcentaje del electorado.
(c) (*public-opinion organization*) organismo *m* de sondeo; (*inquiry*) encuesta *f*, sondeo *m*; **the Gallup —** el Instituto Gallup, el sondeo Gallup; **to take a —** hacer una encuesta.
2 *vt* (a) *cattle* descornar.
(b) *votes* obtener, recibir; **he —ed only 50 votes** obtuvo solamente 50 votos.
3 *vi*: **he —ed badly** recibió pocos votos, tuvo escaso apoyo; **we shall — heavily** obtendremos muchos votos.
pollard ['pɔləd] **1** *n* árbol *m* desmochado. **2** *vt* desmochar.
pollen ['pɔlən] *n* polen *m*.
pollinate ['pɔlineit] *vt* fecundar (con polen).
pollination [,pɔli'neiʃən] *n* polinización *f*, fecundación *f*.
polling ['pəuliŋ] *n* votación *f*; **— will be on Thursday** las elecciones se celebrarán el jueves, se votará el jueves; **— has been heavy** ha votado un elevado porcentaje de los electores.
polling booth ['pəuliŋ,bu:ð] *n* cabina *f* de votar.
polling day ['pəuliŋ,dei] *n* día *m* de elecciones.
polling station ['pəuliŋ,steiʃən] *n* colegio *m* electoral, urnas *fpl* electorales.
pollster ['pəulstə*] *n* encuestador *m*, ora *f*.
poll tax ['pəultæks] *n* capitación *f*.

pollute [pə'luːt] *vt* contaminar; ensuciar; (*fig*) corromper; **to become —d** contaminarse (*with* de).
pollution [pə'luːʃən] *n* contaminación *f*; polución *f*; (*fig*) corrupción *f*; **air —** contaminación *f* del aire, polución *f* de la atmósfera.
polo ['pəuləu] *n* polo *m*.
polonaise [ˌpɔlə'neiz] *n* polonesa *f*.
poltergeist ['pɔːltəgaist] *n* espíritu *m* chocante.
poltroon [pɔl'truːn] *n* cobarde *m*.
poly . . . [pɔli] poli . . .
polyandrous [ˌpɔli'ændrəs] *adj* poliándrico.
polyandry ['pɔliændri] *n* poliandria *f*.
polyanthus [ˌpɔli'ænθəs] *n* hierba *f* de San Pablo mayor.
polychromatic [ˌpɔlikrəu'mætik] *adj* policromo.
polyethylene [ˌpɔli'eθiliːn] *n* (*US*) polietileno *m*.
polygamist [pɔ'ligəmist] *n* polígamo *m*.
polygamous [pɔ'ligəməs] *adj* polígamo.
polygamy [pɔ'ligəmi] *n* poligamia *f*.
polyglot ['pɔliglɔt] **1** *adj* poligloto. **2** *n* poligloto *m*, a *f*.
polygon ['pɔligən] *n* polígono *m*.
polygonal [pɔ'ligənl] *adj* poligonal.
polymer ['pɔlimə*] *n* polímero *m*.
polymerization ['pɔlimərai'zeiʃən] *n* polimerización *f*.
polymorphic [ˌpɔli'mɔːfik] *adj* polimorfo.
polymorphism [ˌpɔli'mɔːfizəm] *n* polimorfismo *m*.
Polynesia [ˌpɔli'niːziə] la Polinesia.
Polynesian [ˌpɔli'niːziən] **1** *adj* polinesio. **2** *n* polinesio *m*, a *f*.
polyp ['pɔlip] *n* pólipo *m*.
Polyphemus [ˌpɔli'fiːməs] *m* Polifemo.
polyphonic [ˌpɔli'fɔnik] *adj* polifónico.
polyphony [pə'lifəni] *n* polifonía *f*.
polypus ['pɔlipəs] *n* pólipo *m*.
polysyllabic ['pɔlisi'læbik] *adj* polisílabo.
polysyllable ['pɔli,siləbl] *n* polisílabo *m*.
polytechnic [ˌpɔli'teknik] *n* escuela *f* de formación profesional.
polytheism ['pɔliθiːizəm] *n* politeísmo *m*.
polytheistic [ˌpɔliθiː'istik] *adj* politeísta.
polythene ['pɔliθiːn] *n* politene *m*, politeno *m*.
pom¹ [pɔm] *n* (*sl*) see **pommy**.
pom² [pɔm] *n* (*fam*) perro *m* de Pomerania.
pomade [pə'mɑːd] *n* pomada *f*.
pomegranate ['pɔməgrænit] *n* (*fruit*) granada *f*; (*tree*) granado *m*.
pommel ['pʌml] **1** *n* pomo *m*. **2** *vt* apuñear, dar de puñetazos; aporrear.
pommy ['pɔmi] *n* (*sl*, *pej*) inglés *m*, esa *f* (*inmigrante en Australia o Nueva Zelanda*).
pomp [pɔmp] *n* pompa *f*; fausto *m*, boato *m*, ostentación *f*; **— and circumstance** pompa *f* y solemnidad.
pompadour ['pɔmpəduə*] *n* (*Hist*) copete *m*.
Pompeii [pɔm'peii] Pompeya.
Pompey ['pɔmpi] *m* Pompeyo.
pompom ['pɔmpɔm] *n* borla *f*.
pomposity [pɔm'pɔsiti] *n* pomposidad *f*; fausto *m*, ostentación *f*; ampulosidad *f*, hinchazón *f*.
pompous ['pɔmpəs] *adj* pomposo; fastuoso, ostentoso; (*language*) ampuloso, hinchado.
pompously ['pɔmpəsli] *adv* pomposamente; ampulosamente, hinchadamente.
ponce [pɔns] *n* coime *m*, chulo *m* de putas.
pond [pɔnd] *n* (*natural*) charca *f*; (*artificial*) estanque *m*; (*fish-*) vivero *m*.
ponder ['pɔndə*] **1** *vt* ponderar, meditar, considerar con especial cuidado.
2 *vi* reflexionar, pensar; **to — on something, to — over something** meditar algo.
ponderous ['pɔndərəs] *adj* (*all senses*) pesado.
ponderously ['pɔndərəsli] *adv* pesadamente; **say** *etc* en tono pesado, lentamente y con énfasis.
pondlife ['pɔndlaif] *n* fauna *f* de las charcas.
pondweed ['pɔndwiːd] *n* planta *f* acuática.
pone [pəun] *n* (*US*) pan *m* de maíz.
poniard ['pɔnjəd] *n* (*lit*) puñal *m*.
pontiff ['pɔntif] *n* pontífice *m*.
pontifical [pɔn'tifikəl] *adj* pontificio, pontifical.
pontificate [pɔn'tifikit] *n* pontificado *m*.
pontificate [pɔn'tifikeit] *vi* pontificar (*also fig*).
Pontius Pilate ['pɔnʃəs'pailət] *m* Poncio Pilato.
pontoon¹ [pɔn'tuːn] *n* pontón *m*.
pontoon² [pɔn'tuːn] *n* (*Cards*) veintiuna *f*.
pontoon bridge [pɔn'tuːn'bridʒ] *n* puente *m* de pontones.
pony ['pəuni] *n* caballito *m*, jaca *f*, poney *m*; (*sl*) 25 *libras*; (*US sl*) chuleta *f*; see **shank**.
ponytail ['pəuniteil] *n* trenza *f*, (peinado *m* de) cola *f* de caballo.
pooch [puːtʃ] *n* (*US sl*) perro *m*.
poodle ['puːdl] *n* perro *m* de lanas, caniche *m*.
pooh [puː] *interj* ¡bah!, ¡qué va!

pooh-pooh [puː'puː] *vt* *proposal etc* rechazar con desdén; *danger etc* negar la importancia de.
pool¹ [puːl] *n* (*natural*) charca *f*; (*artificial*) estanque *m*; (*swimming —*) piscina *f*; (*in river*) pozo *m*, remanso *m*; (*of spilt liquid*) charco *m*.
pool² [puːl] **1** *n* (a) (*Billiards*) trucos *mpl*; (*Cards*) polla *f*; (*football —*) quinielas *fpl*; (*Comm*) consorcio *m*, asociación *f*; mancomunidad *f*; fusión *f* de intereses; **coal and steel —** comunidad *f* de carbón y acero.
(b) (*reserve*) reserva *f*; (*source*) fuente *f*; **an untapped — of ability** una reserva de inteligencia no utilizada aún.
2 *vt* juntar, mancomunar.
poop [puːp] *n* popa *f*.
poor [puə*] *adj* (a) (*not rich*) pobre; *soil etc* pobre, estéril; **a — man** un pobre; **a — woman** una mujer pobre; **the —** los pobres; **an ore —** in metal un mineral de escaso contenido metálico; **a food — in vitamins** un alimento pobre en vitaminas; **to be as — as a church-mouse** ser más pobre que las ratas, ser pobre de solemnidad.
(b) (*bad*) malo; de baja calidad; (*in spirit*) apocado, mezquino; **my — memory** mi mala memoria; **it's — stuff** es malo; **the game was pretty —** el partido fue bastante malo; **to be in — health** estar mal (de salud); **to be — at maths** ser malo en matemáticas; **to have a — opinion of someone** tener un concepto poco favorable de uno.
(c) (*pitying*) pobre; **— me!** ¡pobre de mí!; **— you!, — old you!, you — old thing!** ¡pobrecito!; **— Mary!** ¡pobre María!; **— Mary's lost all her money** la pobre de María ha perdido todo su dinero; **he's very ill, — old chap** está grave el pobre.
poorbox ['puəbɔks] *n* cepillo *m* para los pobres.
poorhouse ['puəhaus] *n*, *pl* **—houses** [hauziz] asilo *m* de los pobres.
poor law ['puəlɔː] *n* ley *f* de asistencia pública.
poorly ['puəli] **1** *adv* (a) pobremente; **they live very —** viven en la mayor pobreza.
(b) (*badly*) mal; **the team is doing —** el equipo juega mal; **exports are doing —** las exportaciones no van bien; **I used to do — at chemistry** tenía malas notas en química.
2 *adj* (*ill*) mal, enfermo; **to be —, to look —** estar malo.
poorness ['puənis] *n* (a) pobreza *f*. (b) mala calidad *f*; **— of spirit** apocamiento *m*, mezquindad *f*.
poor-spirited ['puə'spiritid] *adj* apocado, mezquino.
pop¹ [pɔp] **1** *n* (a) ligera detonación *f*; (*of cork*) taponazo *m*; (*of fastener etc*) ruido *m* seco; (*imitative sound*) ¡pum!
(b) (*fam*: *drink*) gaseosa *f*.
2 *vt* (a) *balloon* hacer reventar; pinchar.
(b) (*place*) poner, poner rápidamente; **to — something into a drawer** poner algo (rápidamente, sin ser visto *etc*) en un cajón; **I'll just — my hat on** voy a ponerme el sombrero; **she —ped her head out** asomó de repente la cabeza.
(c) (*sl*: *pawn*) empeñar.
3 *vi* (a) (*burst etc*) estallar, reventar (con ligera detonación); pincharse; **there were corks —ping all over** por todas partes saltaban los tapones.
(b) **to — in** entrar de sopetón, dar un vistazo; **to — in to see someone** ir a saludar a uno, pasar por la casa de uno; **I just —ped in** entré a veros; no tuve la intención de quedarme; **to — out** salir un momento; **he —ped out for some cigarettes** fue a comprar cigarillos; **he —ped out from his hiding place** salió de repente de su escondite; **we —ped over to see them** fuimos a hacerles una breve visita; **let's — round to Joe's** vamos a casa de Pepe; **to — up** aparecer inesperadamente.
pop² [pɔp] *adj* (*fam*, *abbr of* **popular**) popular; moderno; **— music** música *f* de baile moderna, música *f* de ritmo moderno; **— concert** concierto *m* de música popular.
pop³ [pɔp] *n* (*fam*, *esp US*) papá *m*.
popcorn ['pɔpkɔːn] *n* rosetas *fpl*, palomitas *fpl* (de maíz).
pope [pəup] *n* papa *m*; **P— John XXIII** el Papa Juan XXIII.
popery ['pəupəri] *n* papismo *m*; **no —!** ¡abajo el papa!, ¡papa . . . no!
popeyed ['pɔp'aid] *adj* (*permanently*) de ojos saltones; **they were — with amazement** se les desorbitaron los ojos con el asombro; **they looked at me — me** miraron con los ojos desorbitados.
popgun ['pɔpgʌn] *n* fusil *m* de juguete, taco *m*.
popinjay ['pɔpindʒei] *n* pisaverde *m*.
popish ['pəupiʃ] *adj* (*pej*) papista, católico.

poplar ['pɔplə*] n (black) chopo m, álamo m; (white) álamo m blanco; **Lombardy** — chopo m lombardo.
poplin ['pɔplin] n popelina f.
poppet ['pɔpit] n: **yes, my** — sí, hija; sí, querida; **hullo,** — ! ¡oye, ricura!; **isn't she a** — ? ¡qué preciosidad!
poppy ['pɔpi] n amapola f, adormidera f.
poppycock ['pɔpikɔk] n tonterías fpl; — ! ¡tonterías!
popsy ['pɔpsi] n (sl) chica f.
populace ['pɔpjulis] n pueblo m, plebe f, populacho m.
popular ['pɔpjulə*] adj (a) popular; **to be** — (enjoy wide esteem) ser popular, (be in fashion) estar de moda; **it's a** — **work** (well-liked) es una obra popular; (for the layman) es una obra de vulgarización; **the show is proving very** — el espectáculo está muy concurrido.
(b) (fam) **he's** — **with the girls** tiene mucho éxito con las chicas; **I'm not very** — **in the office just now** ahora no me quieren mucho en la oficina.
popularity [,pɔpju'læriti] n popularidad f.
popularization ['pɔpjulərai'zeiʃən] n popularización f; vulgarización f.
popularize ['pɔpjuləraiz] vt (make popular) popularizar; (make available to laymen) vulgarizar.
popularly ['pɔpjuləli] adv: **X** — **known as Y** X conocido por regla general como Y, X al que se llama vulgarmente Y.
populate ['pɔpjuleit] vt poblar.
population [,pɔpju'leiʃən] n población f; (in numbering inhabitants) habitantes mpl; **the** — **explosion** la explosión demográfica.
populous ['pɔpjuləs] adj populoso; **the most** — **city in the world** la ciudad más poblada del mundo.
porcelain ['pɔːslin] n porcelana f.
porch [pɔːtʃ] n pórtico m; entrada f; (of house, church) portal m.
porcine ['pɔːsain] adj porcino, porcuno.
porcupine ['pɔːkjupain] n puerco m espín.
pore[1] [pɔː*] n poro m.
pore[2] [pɔː*] vi: **to** — **over something** estar absorto en el estudio de algo, estudiar algo larga y detenidamente; **we** —**d over it for hours** lo estudiamos durante horas y horas.
pork [pɔːk] n carne f de cerdo, carne f de puerco.
porker ['pɔːkə*] n cerdo m, cochino m.
porkpie ['pɔːk'pai] n pastel m de carne de cerdo.
porky ['pɔːki] adj (fam) gordo, gordinflón.
pornographic [,pɔːnə'græfik] adj pornográfico.
pornography [pɔː'nɔgrəfi] n pornografía f.
porosity [pɔː'rɔsiti] n porosidad f.
porous ['pɔːrəs] adj poroso.
porousness ['pɔːrəsnis] n porosidad f.
porphyry ['pɔːfiri] n pórfido m.
porpoise ['pɔːpəs] n marsopa f.
porridge ['pɔridʒ] n (approx) gachas fpl de avena; (baby's) papilla f.
port[1] [pɔːt] 1 n (Naut: harbour) puerto m; — **of call** puerto m de escala; — **of entry** puerto m de entrada; **home** — puerto m de origen; **naval** — puerto m naval; **trading** — puerto m comercial; **any** — **in a storm** en el peligro cualquier refugio es bueno; **to come into** —, **to put into** — entrar a puerto; **to leave** — hacerse a la mar, zarpar.
2 attr de puerto, portuario; — **authority** autoridad f portuaria; — **dues** derechos mpl de puerto; — **facilities** facilidades fpl portuarias.
port[2] [pɔːt] n (Naut: —hole) portilla f; (Mech) lumbrera f; (Mil Hist) tronera f.
port[3] [pɔːt] (Naut: side) 1 n babor m; **on the** — **side a** babor; **the sea to** — la mar a babor; **land to** — ! ¡tierra a babor!;
2 vt: **to** — **the helm** poner el timón a babor, virar a babor.
port[4] [pɔːt] n vino m de Oporto, oporto m.
portable ['pɔːtəbl] adj portátil.
portage ['pɔːtidʒ] n porteo m.
portal ['pɔːtl] n puerta f (grande, imponente).
portcullis [pɔːt'kʌlis] n rastrillo m.
portend [pɔː'tend] vt presagiar, anunciar; **what does this** — ? ¿qué quiere decir esto?
portent ['pɔːtent] n presagio m, augurio m, señal f; **a** — **of doom** un presagio de la catástrofe.
portentous [pɔː'tentəs] adj portentoso.
portentously [pɔː'tentəsli] adv portentosamente.
porter ['pɔːtə*] n (a) (of hotel, office etc) portero m, conserje m; (Rail: uniformed employee) mozo m de estación, (touting for custom) mozo m de cuerda; (eg Sherpa) porteador m; —**'s lodge** portería f, conserjería f.
(b) (beer) cerveza f negra.
porterage ['pɔːtəridʒ] n porte m.

porterhouse ['pɔːtəhaus] n (arch) mesón m; — **steak** biftec m de filete.
portfolio [pɔːt'fəuliəu] n cartera f, carpeta f; (Pol) cartera f; — **of shares** cartera f de acciones; **minister without** — ministro m sin cartera.
porthole ['pɔːthəul] n portilla f.
Portia ['pɔːʃə] f Porcia.
portico ['pɔːtikəu] n pórtico m.
portion ['pɔːʃən] 1 n porción f, parte f; (helping) ración f; (also marriage —) dote f; (quantity, in relation to a whole) porción f; sección f; porcentaje m.
2 vt (also to — out) repartir, dividir.
portliness ['pɔːtlinis] n gordura f.
portly ['pɔːtli] adj gordo.
portmanteau [pɔːt'mæntəu] n baúl m de viaje; — **word** palabra f híbrida.
Porto Rico [,pɔːtəu'riːkəu] etc see **Puerto Rico** etc.
portrait ['pɔːtrit] n retrato m; **full-length** — retrato m de cuerpo entero; **half-length** — retrato m de medio cuerpo; **to have one's** — **painted, to sit for one's** — retratarse, hacerse retratar.
portraitist ['pɔːtritist] n, **portrait painter** ['pɔːtrit,peintə*] n retratista mf.
portraiture ['pɔːtritʃə*] n (portrait) retrato m; (portraits collectively) retratos mpl; (art of —) arte m de retratar; **Spanish** — **in the 16th century** retratos mpl españoles del siglo XVI.
portray [pɔː'trei] vt (Art) retratar; (fig) pintar, describir; representar.
portrayal [pɔː'treiəl] n (Art) retrato m; (fig) descripción f, descripción f gráfica, representación f; **a most unflattering** — una representación nada halagüeña.
portress ['pɔːtris] n portera f.
Portugal ['pɔːtjugəl] Portugal m.
Portuguese [,pɔːtju'giːz] 1 adj portugués. 2 n portugués m, esa f. 3 n (language) portugués m.
pose [pəuz] 1 n (of body) postura f, actitud f; (fig) afectación f, pose f; **it's just a big** — todo esto no es más que afectación.
2 vt (a) (place) colocar; **he** —**d the model in the position he wanted** hizo que la modelo adoptara la postura que él quería.
(b) **problem** plantear; **question** hacer, formular.
3 vi (a) (place oneself) colocarse; (as model) posar; **she once** —**d for Picasso** una vez posó para Picasso.
(b) (affectedly) darse tono; tomar una postura afectada; **to** — **as** hacerse pasar por, echárselas de.
poser ['pəuzə*] n pregunta f difícil, problema m difícil.
poseur [pəu'zə:*] n persona f afectada.
posh [pɔʃ] 1 adj elegante, de lujo, lujoso; (—but in bad taste) cursi; wedding etc de mucho rumbo; accent afectado; school de buen tono; — **people** gente f bien; **a** — **car** un coche de lujo; **it's a very** — **neighbourhood** es un barrio de lo más elegante.
2 adv: **to talk** — hablar con acento afectado.
3 vt: **to** — **a place up** procurar que un local parezca más elegante, renovar la pintura (etc) de un local; **it's all** —**ed up** está totalmente renovado, se ha reformado por completo.
4 vr: **to** — **oneself up** procurar parecer más elegante; asearse, vestir mucho mejor.
posit ['pɔzit] vt proponer como principio (that que), postular.
position [pə'ziʃən] 1 n (a) (place, in physical sense) posición f, situación f; (of body, posture) posición f, postura f, actitud f; **the** — **of the shop on the high street** la posición de la tienda en la calle mayor; **to be in** — estar en posición, estar en su lugar; **to be in a dangerous** — estar en una posición peligrosa; **what** — **was the body in?** ¿cuál era la postura del cadáver?; **you are in the best** — **to see it** Vd está en la mejor posición para verlo, Vd está en el mejor sitio para verlo; **to place something in** — colocar algo, poner algo en su lugar; **put yourself in my** — póngase Vd en mi lugar; **to be out of** — estar fuera de su lugar, estar desplazado.
(b) (Naut) posición f; **to fix one's** — determinar su posición, averiguar su posición; **to take up** — **astern** ponerse a popa.
(c) (Mil) posición f; (post) puesto m; (for gun) emplazamiento m; **our** —**s before the attack** nuestras posiciones antes del ataque; **to manoeuvre for** — hacer maniobras para mejorar de posición; **to storm an enemy** — tomar una posición enemiga al asalto.
(d) (rank) posición f; (social) posición f, rango m, categoría f; (in class, league etc) puesto m; **of good social** — de buena posición social, de categoría; **to have a high social** — ocupar una posición social elevada; **to lose one's** — **at the top of the league** perder su puesto a la cabeza de la liga.

(e) (*post*) puesto *m*, empleo *m*; colocación *f*; cargo *m*; **the — of ambassador in Bogotá** el puesto de embajador en Bogotá; **to have a good — in a bank** tener un buen puesto en un banco; **to look for a** — buscar una colocación; **he took up a — in the South** se trasladó a un puesto en el Sur.

(f) (*state*) situación *f*; **the country's economic —** la situación económica del país; **the — is that . . . es que . . .,** el hecho es que . . .; **our — is improving** estamos mejorando de situación; **to be in a — to +** *infin* estar en condiciones de + *infin*; **to be in no — to +** *infin* no estar en condiciones de + *infin.*

(g) (*opinion*) opinión *f*; actitud *f*; **what is our — on Greece?** ¿cuál es nuestra actitud hacia Grecia?, ¿cuál es nuestra política con Grecia?; **to take up a — on a matter** adoptar una actitud en un asunto; **to change one's —** cambiar de opinión, cambiar de idea.

2 *vt* colocar, disponer.

positive ['pozitiv] **1** *adj* **(a)** (*definite*) positivo; definitivo; real, verdadero; **proof —** la prueba definitiva; **there are some — results at last** por fin hay unos resultados positivos; **it's a — miracle!** ¡es un auténtico milagro!; **he's a — nuisance** realmente es un pesado.

(b) (*of person: sure*) seguro; **he is — of it** está seguro de ello; **I'm quite — on that point** estoy completamente convencido de ello; **you don't sound very —** no pareces estar muy seguro.

(c) (*of things: sure*) enfático, categórico; **in a — tone of voice** con énfasis.

(d) (*of character*) de fuerte personalidad, enérgico, activo; **she's a very — sort of person** es una persona enérgica, es una persona que impresiona.

(e) (*Gram*) *degree* positivo; (*affirmative*) afirmativo.

(f) (*Elec, Math, Phot*) positivo.

2 *n* (*Phot*) positiva *f*.

positively ['pozitivli] *adv* **(a)** positivamente; definitivamente; verdaderamente; **it's — marvellous!** ¡es realmente maravilloso!

(b) con énfasis, categóricamente.

(c) con energía, enérgicamente.

positivism ['pozitivizəm] *n* positivismo *m*.

positivist ['pozitivist] **1** *adj* positivista. **2** *n* positivista *mf*.

positron ['pozitron] *n* positrón *m*.

posse ['posi] *n* (*US*) pelotón *m*, grupo *m* (*esp fuerza civil armada bajo el mando del Sheriff*).

possess [pə'zes] **1** *vt* **(a)** (*have, own, also* **to be —ed of**) poseer; **it —es many advantages** posee muchas ventajas; **they — a fortune** poseen una fortuna, tienen una fortuna.

(b) *see* **patience.**

(c) to be —ed by demons estar poseído por los demonios; **to be —ed by an idea** estar dominado por una idea; **we are —ed by many doubts** son muchas las dudas que tenemos; **whatever can have —ed you?** ¿cómo lo has podido hacer?; **what can have —ed you to think like that?** ¿cómo has podido pensar así?

2 *vr* **(a) to — oneself of** tomar posesión de, (*violently*) apoderarse de.

(b) to — oneself in patience tener paciencia, esperar con calma.

possessed [pə'zest] *adj* poseso, poseído; **like one —** como un poseso.

possession [pə'zeʃən] *n* **(a)** (*act, state*) posesión *f*; **to get — of** adquirir, (*improperly*) apoderarse de; **to take — of** tomar posesión de; *house etc* ocupar, entrar en; (*improperly*) apoderarse de, hacerse dueño de; (*confiscate*) incautarse de; **to be in — of** poseer, tener; **to be in full — of one's faculties** poseer todas sus facultades; **to be in the — of** estar en manos de, ser de la propiedad de, pertenecer a; **to come into — of** adquirir; **to come** (*or* **pass**) **into the — of** pasar a manos de; **to have something in one's —** poseer algo; **a house with vacant —** una casa desocupada, una casa lista para ocupar.

(b) (*object*) posesión *f*; **—s** posesiones *fpl*, (*as legal term*) bienes *mpl*.

possessive [pə'zesiv] **1** *adj* (*Gram*) posesivo; *love etc* dominante, tiránico, absorbente; **to be — towards someone** ser absorbente con uno.

2 *n* (*Gram*) posesivo *m*.

possessively [pə'zesivli] *adv* tiránicamente; de modo absorbente.

possessor [pə'zesə*] *n* poseedor *m*, ora *f*; dueño *m*, a *f*; **he was the proud — of . . .** se enorgullecía de poseer . . .

possibility [,posə'biliti] *n* **(a)** (*chance*) posibilidad *f*; (*outlook*) perspectiva *f*; **the — of severe losses** la posibilidad de sufrir pérdidas cuantiosas; **there is no — of his agreeing to it** no existe posibilidad alguna de que él consienta en ello; **if by any — . . .** si por casualidad . . .; **it is within the bounds of —** cabe dentro de lo posible; **it's a grim —** es una perspectiva aterradora.

(b) (*event etc*) acontecimiento *m* posible; posibilidad *f*; **to allow for the —** that it may happen tener en cuenta la posibilidad de que una cosa ocurra; **to foresee all the possibilities** prever todos los resultados posibles.

(c) (*promise*) **he has possibilities** promete, es prometedor; **the subject has possibilities** es un tema prometedor, es un tema de gran potencial.

possible ['posəbl] *adj* **(a)** posible; **a — defeat** una posible derrota; **all — concessions** todas las concesiones posibles; **one has to foresee all — outcomes** hay que prever todos los resultados posibles; **to make something —** hacer algo posible, posibilitar algo.

(b) (*with verb* **to be** *etc*) **if —** si es posible, de ser posible; **it is just — that** existe una pequeña posibilidad (*that* de que + *subj*); **it is — that . . .** es posible que + *subj*, puede que + *subj*; **it is — to + ** *infin* es posible + *infin*; **it is not — to do more** no se puede hacer más; **it will be — for you to return the same day** le será posible volver el mismo día.

(c) (*with* **as**) **we will help as far as —** ayudaremos en lo posible, ayudaremos en cuanto podamos; **as often as —** lo más frecuentemente posible; **as soon as —** cuanto antes, lo antes posible, lo más pronto posible; **as heavy as —** lo más pesado que pueda ser, todo lo pesado que pueda ser; el más pesado que haya; *see* **much** *etc*.

possibly ['posəbli] *adv* posiblemente; tal vez; **— sí, es** posible; **if I — can** si me es posible; **— they've gone already** es posible que hayan ido ya, puede que hayan ido ya, han ido ya quizá; **he did all he — could** hizo todo lo que pudo; **I come as often as I — can** vengo todas las veces que puedo, vengo lo más frecuentemente posible; **I cannot — allow it** no lo puedo permitir de ninguna manera, me es totalmente imposible autorizarlo.

possum ['posəm] *n* zarigüeya *f*; **to play —** (*sleeping*) fingir estar dormido, (*dead*) hacerse el muerto.

post¹ [pəust] **1** *n* (*of timber etc*) poste *m*; (*for fencing, marking*) estaca *f*; **the —** (*starting*) poste *m* de salida, (*finishing*) poste *m* de llegada, meta *f*; **to be left at the —** quedar muy atrasado (*also fig*); **to win on the —** ganar junto al mismo poste de llegada.

2 *vt* (*announce*) anunciar; *bills etc* (*also* **to — up**) fijar, pegar; **"— no bills"** "prohibido fijar carteles"; **to — someone missing** anunciar que uno es considerado como desaparecido.

post² [pəust] **1** *n* **(a)** (*mail*) correo *m*; (*office*) casa *f* de correos, correos *mpl*; (*numbered: collection*) recogida *f*, (*delivery*) entrega *f*; **first —** primera recogida *f*; **last —** última recogida *f*, última entrega *f*; **registered —** correo *m* certificado; **by —** por correo; **by return of —** a vuelta de correo; **the — has come** ha llegado el correo; **it came with the —** vino con el correo; **to drop a card in the —** echar una postal al buzón; **to go to the —** ir a correos, ir al buzón; **to open one's —** abrir sus cartas; **to sort the —** clasificar las cartas; **to take a parcel to the —** llevar un paquete a correos.

(b) there has been a general — among the staff muchos miembros del personal han intercambiado sus puestos.

2 *vt* **(a)** echar al buzón, llevar a correos; **this was —ed on Monday** esto se echó al buzón el lunes; **to — something to someone** mandar algo a uno por correo.

(b) to keep someone —ed tener a uno al corriente; **please keep me —ed** no dejes de decirme las noticias.

3 *vi* (*arch*) viajar en posta; **he went —ing off to India** se fue (inesperadamente, a toda prisa *etc*) a la India.

post³ [pəust] **1** *n* **(a)** (*job*) puesto *m*, empleo *m*; destino *m*; cargo *m*; **to look for a —** buscar un puesto; **there are 10 —s for women** hay 10 puestos para mujeres; **the duties of the —** las funciones del cargo; **to take up one's —** ocupar el puesto, entrar en funciones.

(b) (*Mil*) puesto *m*; **advanced —** puesto *m* avanzado, avanzada *f*; **to die at one's —** morir en su puesto.

2 *vt* **(a)** situar, apostar; **to — sentries** apostar centinelas; **to — a man at the gate** apostar un hombre a la puerta.

(b) to — someone to Buenos Aires enviar a uno

a Buenos Aires, nombrar a uno en Buenos Aires, destinar a uno para Buenos Aires; **to be —ed to a regiment** ser ordenado a incorporarse a un regimiento; **he was —ed first to a destroyer** se le mandó primero a un destructor; **to be —ed captain** ser ascendido a capitán.

post⁴ [pəust] post . . ., pos . . .

postage ['pəustidʒ] n porte m, franqueo m; **—s** (*in account*) gastos mpl de correo; **— due** a pagar; **— paid** porte pagado, franco de porte.

postage stamp ['pəustidʒ‚stæmp] n sello m (de correo), estampilla f (SAm).

postal ['pəustəl] adj postal, de correos.

postal order ['pəustl‚ɔːdə*] n giro m postal.

postbox ['pəustbɔks] n buzón m.

postcard ['pəustkɑːd] n tarjeta f postal, postal f; **reply —** tarjeta f de porte pagado.

postdate ['pəust'deit] vt poner fecha adelantada a, posfechar.

postdated ['pəust'deitid] adj cheque con fecha adelantada.

poster ['pəustə*] n cartel m.

poste restante ['pəust'restɑ̃nt] n lista f de correos.

posterior [pɔs'tiəriə*] 1 adj posterior. 2 n (*fam*) culo m, trasero m.

posterity [pɔs'teriti] n posteridad f.

postern ['pəustəːn] n postigo m.

post-free ['pəust'friː] adv porte pagado, franco de porte.

postglacial ['pəust'gleisiəl] adj postglacial.

postgraduate ['pəust'grædjuit] 1 adj postgraduado; **— course** curso m para postgraduados. 2 n postgraduado m, a f.

posthaste ['pəust'heist] adv a toda prisa, con toda urgencia.

post hole ['pəusthəul] n agujero m de poste.

posthumous ['pɔstjuməs] adj póstumo.

posthumously ['pɔstjuməsli] adv después de la muerte.

postilion [pəs'tiliən] n postillón m.

post-impressionism ['pəustim'preʃənizəm] n post-impresionismo m.

post-impressionist ['pəustim'preʃənist] 1 adj post-impresionista. 2 n postimpresionista mf.

postlude ['pəustluːd] n postludio m.

postman ['pəustmən] n, pl **—men** [mən] cartero m.

postmark ['pəustmɑːk] 1 n matasellos m. 2 vt matar (el sello de), timbrar; **it is —ed "León"** lleva el matasellos de León.

postmaster ['pəust‚mɑːstə*] n administrador m de correos, **P— General** Director m General de Correos.

postmeridian ['pəustmə'ridiən] adj postmeridiano.

postmistress ['pəust‚mistris] n administradora f de correos.

post-mortem ['pəust'mɔːtem] n autopsia f.

postnatal ['pəust'neitl] adj postnatal.

post office ['pəust‚ɔfis] n (oficina f, casa f de) correos; **General P—** Administración f General de Correos; **I was in the —** estaba en correos; **I'm going to the —** voy a correos; see **box, saving**.

post-paid ['pəust'peid] adv porte pagado, franco de porte.

postpone [pəust'pəun] vt aplazar; **to — something for a month** aplazar algo por un mes; **it has been —d till Tuesday** ha sido aplazado hasta el martes.

postponement [pəust'pəunmənt] n aplazamiento m.

postposition ['pəustpə'ziʃən] n posposición f.

postprandial ['pəust'prændiəl] adj speech, talk etc de sobremesa; walk etc que se da después de comer.

postscript ['pəusskript] n posdata f.

postulant ['pɔstjulənt] n postulante m, a f.

postulate ['pɔstjulit] n postulado m.

postulate ['pɔstjuleit] vt postular.

postulation [‚pɔstju'leiʃən] n postulación f.

posture ['pɔstʃə*] 1 n postura f, actitud f. 2 vi tomar una postura, adoptar una actitud; (*pej*) adoptar una actitud afectada.

postwar ['pəust'wɔː*] adj de pos(t)guerra, de la pos(t)guerra, posbélico; **the — period** la pos(t)-guerra.

posy ['pəuzi] n ramillete m de flores.

pot [pɔt] 1 n (*for cooking*) olla f, puchero m, marmita f; (*for preserving*) tarro m, pote m; (*fam: cup*) copa f; (*flower—*) tiesto m, maceta f; (*chamber—*) orinal m; (*sl*) marijuana f; **big —** (*fam*) pez m gordo, personaje m; **—s and kettles, the —** calls the kettle black el puchero dijo a la sartén "apártate de mí que me tiznas"; **—s and pans** cacharros mpl, (*modern*) batería f de cocina; **we have —s of it** tenemos montones; **to have —s of money** ser muy rico; **to go to —** echarse a perder, arruinarse; **to keep the —**

boiling (*earn living*) ganarse la vida, (*make things progress*) mantener las cosas en marcha.

2 vt food conservar (en botes etc); plant poner en tiesto; game derribar; abatir (a tiros); person herir, matar (a tiros).

3 vi: **to — at someone** disparar sobre uno; **to — away** seguir disparando.

potable ['pəutəbl] adj potable.

potash ['pɔtæʃ] n potasa f.

potassium [pə'tæsiəm] n potasio m; **— cyanide** cianuro m de potasio; **— nitrate** nitrato m de potasio.

potation [pəu'teiʃənz] npl libaciones fpl.

potato [pə'teitəu] n, pl **potatoes** [pə'teitəuz] patata f, papa f (SAm); **—es in their jackets** patatas fpl enteras, patatas fpl con su piel; **baked —es** patatas fpl al horno; **boiled —es** patatas fpl cocidas al agua; **chip(ped) —es,** (*US*) **French fried —es** patatas fpl fritas, patatas fpl a la española; **mashed —es** puré m de patatas; **sweet —** batata f.

potato field [pə'teitəu‚fiːld] n patatal m.

potbellied ['pɔt‚belid] adj barrigón, tripudo.

potboiler ['pɔt‚bɔilə*] n obra f (mediocre) compuesta para ganar dinero.

poteen [pɔ'tiːn] n whiskey m (*irlandés, destilado ilegalmente*).

potency ['pəutənsi] n potencia f; fuerza f; eficacia f.

potent ['pəutənt] adj potente, poderoso; drink fuerte; remedy eficaz.

potentate ['pəutənteit] n potentado m.

potential [pəu'tenʃəl] 1 adj potencial; posible, en potencia; futuro; **a — prime minister** un futuro primer ministro, un primer ministro en potencia; **a — threat** una posible amenaza.

2 n potencial m (*also Elec, Math, Phys*); potencialidad f, capacidad f; **the war — of Ruritania** el potencial bélico de Ruritania.

potentiality [pəu‚tenʃi'æliti] n potencialidad f.

potentially [pəu'tenʃəli] adv potencialmente, en potencia.

pother ['pɔðə*] n alharaca f, aspaviento m; lío m; **all this —!** ¡qué lío!; **to make a — about something** armar un lío a causa de algo.

pothole ['pɔthəul] 1 n (*in road*) bache m; (*Geol*) sima f, marmita f de gigante, (*loosely*) cueva f, caverna f profunda.

2 vi: **to —, to go potholing** dedicarse a la espeleología; ir a explorar una caverna.

potholer ['pɔthəulə*] n espeleólogo m.

potholing ['pɔthəuliŋ] n espeleología f.

pothunter ['pɔthʌntə*] n persona que toma parte en torneos (etc) con el solo propósito de ganar premios.

potion ['pəuʃən] n poción f, pócima f.

potluck ['pɔt'lʌk] n: **to take —** comer lo que haya; (*fig*) tomar lo que haya, contentarse con lo que haya.

potpourri [pəu'puri] n (*Mus*) popurrí m; (*Lit etc*) mezcla f, centón m.

potsherd ['pɔt‚ʃəːd] n tiesto m, casco m.

potshot ['pɔt‚ʃɔt] n tiro m sin apuntar, tiro m al azar; **to take a — at something** tirar a algo sin apuntar.

potted ['pɔtid] adj food en conserva, cocido y conservado en bote; plant en tiesto, en maceta.

potter¹ ['pɔtə*] n alfarero m; (*artistic*) ceramista mf.

potter² ['pɔtə*] vi ocuparse en fruslerías; no hacer nada de particular (*also to — about*); **he likes —ing about in the garden** le gusta pasar el tiempo haciendo pequeños trabajos en el jardín; **we — along** vamos tirando; **I —ed round the house all day** hice bagatelas en casa todo el día.

pottery ['pɔtəri] n (*workshop*) alfar m, alfarería f; (*craft*) alfarería f, (*art*) cerámica f; (*pots*) cacharros mpl, (*of fine quality*) loza f; (*archaeological remains*) cerámicas fpl.

potty¹ ['pɔti] n (*fam*) orinal m de niño, orinal m pequeño.

potty² ['pɔti] adj (*fam*) **(a)** (*small*) insignificante, miserable.

(b) (*mad*) chiflado; **you must be —!** ¿has perdido el juicio?; **to drive someone —** volver loco a uno; **it's enough to drive you —** es para volverse loco.

pouch [pautʃ] n bolsa f (*also Anat, Zool*); (*hunter's*) morral m, zurrón m; (*tobacco-*) petaca f; (*Mil*) cartuchera f.

pouf(fe) [puːf] n pouf m.

poulterer ['pəultərə*] n pollero m; **—'s** (*shop*) pollería f.

poultice ['pəultis] 1 n cataplasma f, emplasto m. 2 vt poner una cataplasma a, emplastar (*with* con).

poultry ['pəultri] n (*alive*) aves fpl de corral; (*dead*) pollos mpl, volatería f.

poultry dealer ['pəultri‚diːlə*] n recovero m; pollero m.

poultry farm ['pəultrifɑːm] n granja f avícola.
poultry house ['pəultrihaus] n, pl — **houses** [hauziz] gallinero m.
poultry keeper ['pəultri,kiːpə*] n avicultor m.
poultry keeping ['pəultri,kiːpiŋ] n avicultura f.
pounce [pauns] 1 n salto m; ataque m súbito; (swoop by bird) calada f.
　2 vi atacar súbitamente; saltar, precipitarse; (by bird) calarse; to — **on something** saltar sobre algo, precipitarse sobre algo, arrojarse sobre algo; to — **on someone's mistake** saltar sobre el error de uno.
pound¹ [paund] n (a) (weight) libra f (=453,6 gr); **half a** — media libra f; **two shillings a** — dos chelines la libra; **they sell it by the** — lo venden por libras.
　(b) (money) libra f; — **sterling** libra f esterlina; **it must have cost** —s habrá costado un potosí.
pound² [paund] n corral m de concejo; (police —, for cars) depósito m.
pound³ [paund] 1 vt (crush etc) machacar, majar; (with hammer) martillar; (grind) moler; (beat) golpear, aporrear; (of sea) azotar, batir; (Mil) bombardear; **he** —**ed the table with his fists** aporreaba la mesa con los puños, daba golpes en la mesa con los puños; **to** — **someone with one's fists** dar de puñetazos a uno; **he was** —**ing the piano** aporreaba el piano; **he was** —**ing out a tune on the piano** a golpes violentos tocaba una melodía al piano; **to** — **something to pieces** romper algo a martillazos; **to** — **a fort into surrender** bombardear una fortaleza hasta que se rinda.
　2 vi: **to** — **at, to** — **on** aporrear, dar golpes en, descargar golpes sobre; **to** — **away at** machacar en, seguir machacando en (also fig); **the sea was** —**ing against the rocks** las olas se rompían contra las rocas, el mar azotaba las rocas; **he was** —**ing along the road** corría pesadamente por la carretera; **the train** —**ed past us** el tren pasó estrepitosamente delante de nosotros.
poundage ['paundidʒ] n impuesto m (or comisión f etc) que se exige por cada libra.
-pounder ['paundə*]: eg four-pounder (pez m etc) de cuatro libras; **twenty-five pounder** (Mil) cañón m del veinticinco.
pounding ['paundiŋ] n (noise) martilleo m, golpeo m, el aporrear etc; (of sea) azote m, embate m; (Mil) bombardeo m; **the ship took a** — **from the waves** el barco tuvo que aguantar la violencia de las olas; **the city took a** — **last night** la ciudad sufrió terriblemente en el bombardeo de anoche.
pour [pɔː*] 1 vt (a) verter, echar; derramar; a drink, tea etc servir, echar; preparar; **he** —**ed me a drink** me sirvió un vaso; **shall I** — **the tea?** ¿sirvo el té?, ¿echo el té?; **he** —**ed himself some coffee** se sirvió café; **to** — **money into a project** invertir muchísimo dinero en un proyecto, proveer abundantes fondos para un proyecto; **he has** —**ed good ideas into the book** ha llenado el libro de excelentes ideas.
　(b) (of rain) **to** — **cats and dogs, to** — **torrents** llover a cántaros.
　(c) **to** — **in a broadside** hacer fuego con todos los cañones.
　(d) **to** — **away, to** — **off** vaciar, verter; **to** — **out** coffee etc servir, echar; unwanted remainder vaciar; smoke arrojar; **to** — **out one's feelings** expresar tumultuosamente sus sentimientos; **to** — **out one's thanks** expresar efusivamente sus gracias; **to** — **out threats against someone** desatarse en amenazas contra uno; **to** — **out one's heart to someone** abrir su pecho a uno.
　2 vi (a) (of rain) llover mucho, diluviar, llover a cántaros; (of water etc) correr, fluir (abundantemente); **it's** —**ing, it's** —**ing with rain** está lloviendo a cántaros; **it** —**ed for 4 days** llovió mucho durante 4 días; **water came** —**ing into the room** el agua entraba a raudales en el cuarto; **water** —**ed from the broken pipe** el agua salía a raudales del tubo roto; **blood** —**ed from the wound** la sangre salía a borbotones de la herida, la herida sangraba muchísimo.
　(b) (of persons etc) **to** — **in** entrar a raudales, entrar en tropel; **tourists are** —**ing in from all sides** acuden los turistas en tropel de todas partes; **they came** —**ing into the shop** entraban a raudales en la tienda; **to** — **out** salir a raudales, salir en tropel; **they** —**ed out into the streets** invadieron las calles.
pouring ['pɔːriŋ] adj: — **rain** lluvia f torrencial.
pout [paut] 1 n puchero m, mala cara f; **to say with a** — decir poniendo mala cara. 2 vt: **to** — **one's lips** = 3 vi hacer pucheros, poner mala cara.
poverty ['pɔvəti] n pobreza f, miseria f; (of ideas etc)

falta f, escasez f; — **is no crime** pobreza no es vileza; **to live in** — vivir en la miseria.
poverty-stricken ['pɔvəti,strikn] adj menesteroso, necesitado.
powder ['paudə*] 1 n polvo m; (face —) polvos mpl; (gun-) pólvora f; **to keep one's** — **dry** reservarse para mejor ocasión; **to reduce something to** — reducir algo a polvo, pulverizar algo.
　2 vt (a) (reduce to —) reducir a polvo, pulverizar.
　(b) (apply — to) polvorear, (Cook etc) espolvorear (with de); **to** — **one's face, to** — **one's nose** ponerse polvos, empolvarse.
　3 vi (a) pulverizarse, hacerse polvo.
　(b) (person) ponerse polvos, empolvarse.
　4 vr: **to** — **oneself** ponerse polvos, empolvarse.
powder blue ['paudə'bluː] 1 adj azul pálido. 2 n azul m pálido.
powder compact ['paudə,kɔmpækt] n polvera f.
powdered ['paudəd] adj milk etc en polvo.
powder keg ['paudəkeg] n (fig) polvorín m; **the country is a** — el país es un polvorín.
powder magazine ['paudəmægə,ziːn] n (Naut) santabárbara f.
powder puff ['paudəpʌf] n borla f (para empolvarse).
powder room ['paudərum] n (euph) aseos mpl.
powdery ['paudəri] adj substance en polvo, polvoriento; snow polvoriento; surface polvoriento, empolvado.
power ['pauə*] 1 n (a) (in general) poder m; (physical strength) fuerza f, vigor m; — **more** — **to your elbow!** ¡qué tenga Vd éxito!; **it is beyond his** — **to save her** no está dentro de sus posibilidades salvarla, él no puede hacer nada para salvarla; **to be in the** — **of** estar en manos de; **to do all in one's** — **to** + infin hacer lo posible por + infin; **to have someone in one's** — tener a uno en su poder; **to fall into someone's** — caer en manos de uno; **it does not lie within my** — no está dentro de mis posibilidades, eso no es de mi competencia; **as far as lies within my** — en cuanto me sea posible; **to the utmost of one's** — hasta más no poder.
　(b) (mental) facultad f (of de); (drive) empuje m, energía f; **mental** —s facultades fpl mentales; **his** —s **are failing** decaen sus facultades; **to lose the** — **of speech** perder el habla.
　(c) (Mech etc) potencia f; energía f; (output) rendimiento m; **attractive** — fuerza f atractiva; **effective** — potencia f real; **magnifying** — fuerza f de aumento; **motive** — fuerza f motriz; **engines at half** — motores mpl a medio rendimiento; **the ship returned to port under her own** — el buque volvió al puerto impulsado por sus propios motores.
　(d) (Elec) fuerza f, energía f, fluido m; **electric** — fuerza f eléctrica, energía f eléctrica; — **consumption** consumo m de energía; — **unit** (Elec) grupo m electrógeno; **they cut off the** — cortaron el fluido.
　(e) (Pol etc) poder m; poderío m; autoridad f; influencia f; **absolute** — poder m absoluto; **executive** — poder m ejecutivo; — **of life and death** poder m de vida y de muerte; **the** —s **of darkness** las fuerzas del mal; **the** —s **that be** los que mandan, las autoridades (actuales); **he's a** — **in the land** es de los que mandan en el país; **to be at the height of one's** — estar en la cumbre de su poder; **to be in** — estar en el poder; **to come to** — subir al poder, empezar a gobernar, tomar el mando; **to raise someone to** — alzar a uno al poder.
　(f) (specific —) — **of attorney** poder m; **full** —s plenos poderes mpl; **to exceed one's** —s excederse, ir demasiado lejos.
　(g) (nation) potencia f; **atomic** — potencia f atómica; **colonial** — potencia f colonial; **world** — potencia f mundial; **the Great P**—s las Grandes Potencias.
　(h) **a** — **of people** muchísima gente; **to make a** — **of money** ganar muchísimo dinero; **that did me a** — **of good!** ¡con eso me siento mucho mejor!, ¡ahora estoy mucho mejor!; **beer does you a** — **of good** la cerveza fortalece.
　(i) (Math) potencia f; **7 to the** — **of 3** 7 elevado al cubo, 7 elevado a la 3ª potencia; **to the nth** — **a** la enésima potencia.
　2 vt accionar, impulsar; **a car** —**ed by electricity** un coche impulsado por electricidad; **a plane** —**ed by 4 jets** un avión impulsado por 4 motores a reacción.
power cable ['pauəkeibl] n cable m de energía eléctrica.
power cut ['pauəkʌt] n corte m de corriente, apagón m.
power drill ['pauədril] n taladradora f de fuerza.

power-driven ['pauədrivn] *adj* con motor; *tool, saw etc* mecánico.

powered ['pauəd] *adj* con motor; mecánico.

powerful ['pauəful] *adj* *person, government etc* poderoso; *engine etc* potente; *build* fuerte, fornido; *emotion* intenso, profundo; *argument* convincente; **a — lot of people** (*fam*) muchísima gente; **it is a — film** es una película muy emocionante; **he gave a — performance** su actuación fue brillante.

powerfully ['pauəfəli] *adv* poderosamente; fuertemente; intensamente; profundamente; de modo convincente; **to be — built** ser fornido; **I was affected by the book** el libro me conmovió profundamente.

power hammer ['pauə,hæmə*] *n* martillo *m* mecánico.

powerhouse ['pauəhaus] *n*, *pl* **—houses** [hauziz] central *f* eléctrica.

powerless ['pauəlis] *adj* impotente, ineficaz; **to be — to resist** no tener fuerzas para resistir, no poder resistir; **we are — to help you** estamos sin fuerzas para ayudarle, somos incapaces de prestarle ayuda; **they are — in the matter** no tienen autoridad para intervenir en el asunto, el asunto no es de su competencia.

power line ['pauəlain] *n* línea *f* de conducción eléctrica.

power loader ['pauə,ləudə*] *n* (*Min*) rompedora-cargadora *f*.

power plant ['pauəplɑːnt] *n* grupo *m* electrógeno.

power saw ['pauəsɔː] *n* motosierra *f*, sierra *f* mecánica.

power shovel ['pauə,ʃʌvl] *n* excavadora *f*.

power station ['pauə,steiʃən] *n* central *f* eléctrica.

power tool ['pauətuːl] *n* herramienta *f* mecánica.

powwow ['pauwau] **1** *n* conferencia *f*. **2** *vi* conferenciar.

pox [pɔks] *n* (*fam*) sífilis *f*, enfermedad *f* venérea; **a — on . . .!** (*arch*) ¡maldito sea . . .!

practicability [,præktikə'biliti] *n* factibilidad *f*.

practicable ['præktikəbl] *adj* factible, practicable, hacedero.

practical ['præktikəl] *adj* práctico; *see* **joke**.

practicality [,prækti'kæliti] *n* (*of temperament*) espíritu *m* práctico; (*of scheme etc*) factibilidad *f*; (*thing*) cosa *f* práctica.

practically ['præktikli] *adv* (*in a practical way*) prácticamente; (*almost*) prácticamente, casi; **— everybody** casi todos; **— nothing** casi nada; **there has been — no rain** no ha llovido casi.

practice ['præktis] *n* (a) (*habit*) costumbre *f*, uso *m*; **corrupt —s** corrupción *f*; **restrictive —s** normas *fpl* restrictivas, prácticas *fpl* restrictivas; **sharp — trampa** *f*, maña *f*; **according to his usual —** según su costumbre; **it is not our — to + infin** no acostumbramos + *infin*; **to make a — of + ger** acostumbrar + *infin*; **to make it a — to + infin** acostumbrar + *infin*.

(b) (*exercise*) ejercicio *m*; (*training*) adiestramiento *m*, (*period*) período *m* de entrenamiento; **clase** *f* práctica; (*Sport*) entrenamiento *m*; **to be in —** estar entrenado, estar en forma; **to be out of —** estar desentrenado, no estar en forma; **to learn by —** aprender por la práctica, aprender por la experiencia; **— makes perfect** la práctica hace maestro; **it needs a lot of —** hace falta bastante experiencia.

(c) (*reality*) práctica *f*; **in —** en la práctica; **to put something into —** poner algo en obra.

(d) (*of profession etc*) práctica *f*, ejercicio *m*; **the — of medicine** el ejercicio de la medicina; **he was in — in Bilbao** ejercía en Bilbao; **he is no longer in —** ya no ejerce la profesión; **to set up in —** (*Law*) poner su bufete; (*Med*) empezar a ejercer de médico, (*fig*) poner tienda; **to set up in — as** empezar a trabajar como.

(e) (*Med: no. of patients*) clientela *f*.

practise, (*US*) **practice** ['præktis] **1** *vt* (a) (*carry out in action*) practicar; tener por costumbre; **we — this method** nosotros empleamos (*or* seguimos) este método; **to — charity** ejercitar la caridad; **to — patience** tener paciencia; **to — what one preaches** predicar con el ejemplo.

(b) *profession* ejercer; **to — medicine** practicar la medicina, ejercer de médico.

(c) (*train oneself at*) hacer ejercicios de, hacer prácticas de; **to — the piano** hacer ejercicios en el piano, estudiar el piano; **to — football** entrenarse en el fútbol; **to — a shot at golf** ensayar un golpe de golf; **to — + ger** ensayarse + *infin*.

2 *vi* (a) (*Mus*) tocar, estudiar, hacer ejercicios;

(*Sport*) ejercitarse, entrenarse, adiestrarse; ensayarse; **to — every day** hacer ejercicios todos los días; **one has to —** a lot hace falta estudiar mucho.

(b) **to — as a doctor** ejercer de médico, practicar la medicina.

practised, (*US*) **practiced** ['præktist] *adj* *eye etc* experto.

practising, (*US*) **practicing** ['præktisiŋ] *adj* activo, que ejerce, practicante; **a — Christian** un cristiano practicante.

practitioner [præk'tiʃənə*] *n* (*of an art*) practicante *mf*; (*Med*) médico *m*, a *f* (*also* **medical —**); **general — médico** *m* general, médica *f* general.

pr(a)esidium [pri'sidiəm] *n* (*Pol*) presidio *m*.

pragmatic [præg'mætik] *adj* pragmático.

pragmatism ['prægmətizəm] *n* pragmatismo *m*.

pragmatist ['prægmətist] *n* pragmatista *mf*.

Prague [prɑːg] Praga.

prairie ['preəri] *n* pradera *f*, llanura *f*, pampa *f* (*SAm*).

praise [preiz] **1** *n* alabanza *f*, elogio *m*; alabanzas *fpl*, elogios *mpl*; **in — of** en alabanza de; **all — to him!** ¡enhorabuena!; **— be!**, **— be to God!** ¡gracias a Dios!; **it's beyond —** queda por encima de todo elogio; **to be loud (*or* warm) in one's —s of something** alabar algo sinceramente, elogiar algo con entusiasmo; **he is not much given to —** no acostumbra pronunciar palabras de elogio; **I have nothing but — for him** merece todos mis elogios; **to heap —s on someone** amontonar alabanzas sobre uno; **to sing the —s of someone** cantar las alabanzas de uno, elogiar con efusión a uno; **to sound one's own —s** cantar sus propias alabanzas.

2 *vt* alabar, elogiar; **to — God** glorificar a Dios; **to — something up** poner algo por las nubes.

praiseworthily ['preiz,wəːðili] *adv* loablemente, plausiblemente, de modo digno de elogio.

praiseworthiness ['preiz,wəːðinis] *n* lo loable, lo plausible, mérito *m*.

praiseworthy ['preiz,wəːði] *adj* loable, plausible, digno de elogio.

pram [præm] *n* cochecito *m* de niño.

prance [prɑːns] *vi* (*horse*) hacer cabriolas, encabritarse; (*person*) saltar, bailar; andar con cierta afectación; **he came prancing into the room** entró haciendo cabriolas en la habitación; **to — with rage** enfurecerse.

prang [præŋ] *vt* (*sl*) (a) *town etc* bombardear, destruir.

(b) *plane* estrellar; *car etc* estropear.

prank [præŋk] *n* travesura *f*; broma *f*; **a childish —** una travesura, una diablura; **a student —** una broma estudiantil; **to play a — on someone** gastar una broma a uno.

prankish ['præŋkiʃ] *adj* travieso, pícaro.

prankster ['præŋkstə*] *n* bromista *mf*.

prate [preit] *vi* parlotear, charlar; **to — of** hablar interminablemente de.

prating ['preitiŋ] *adj* parlanchín.

prattle ['prætl] **1** *n* parloteo *m*; (*child's*) balbuceo *m*. **2** *vi* parlotear; balbucear.

prawn [prɔːn] *n* gamba *f*; (*small*) quisquilla *f*.

pray [prei] **1** *vt* rogar, suplicar; **I — you** se lo suplico; **I — you tell me . . .** le ruego decirme . . .; **to — someone to do something** rogar a uno hacer algo, rogar a uno que haga algo.

2 *vi* (a) (*say prayers*) rezar, orar; **to — to God** rogar a Dios; **to — for something** rogar algo, orar por algo; **to — for someone's soul** orar por el alma de uno; **to — for someone** orar por uno, rezar por uno; **to — that something may not happen** hacer votos para que algo no ocurra, hacer rogativas para que algo no ocurra; **he's past —ing for** ya no le valen oraciones.

(b) **— tell me . . .** dígame por favor . . ., le ruego decirme . . .; **— take a seat** siéntese por favor, haga el favor de sentarse; **what good is that, —?** ¿de qué sirve eso, pues?

prayer [preə*] *n* (a) (*to God*) oración *f*, rezo *m*; **—s** (*as service*) rezo *m*, oficio *m*; **—s for peace** oraciones *fpl* por la paz; **evening —s** vísperas *fpl*; **Lord's P— padrenuestro** *m*; **morning —s** maitines *mpl*; **Book of Common P—** liturgia de la Iglesia Anglicana; **to be at one's —s** estar en oración; **to offer up —s for** orar por, rezar por; **to say one's —s** orar, rezar.

(b) (*entreaty*) ruego *m*, súplica *f*; (*Law*) petición *f*.

prayer book ['preəbuk] *n* devocionario *m*, misal *m*.

prayer meeting ['preə,miːtiŋ] *n* reunión *f* para rezar.

pre . . . [priː] pre . . .; ante . . .

preach [priːtʃ] **1** *vt* (a) predicar; **to — a sermon** predicar un sermón; **to — the gospel** predicar el Evangelio.

(b) *advantages etc* celebrar; *patience etc* aconsejar.

2 *vi* predicar; **to — at someone** predicar a uno, dar un sermón a uno; **to — to a congregation** predicar a los fieles.

preacher ['priːtʃə*] *n* predicador *m*; *(US)* pastor *m*.

preachify ['priːtʃifai] *vi* sermonear largamente; *(fig)* disertar largamente.

preaching ['priːtʃiŋ] *n* predicación *f*; *(pej)* sermoneo *m*.

preachy ['priːtʃi] *adj (fam)* dado a sermonear.

preamble [priː'æmbl] *n* preámbulo *m*.

prearrange ['priːə'reindʒ] *vt* arreglar de antemano.

prebend ['prebənd] *n (stipend)* prebenda *f*; *(person)* prebendado *m*.

prebendary ['prebəndəri] *n* prebendado *m*.

precarious [pri'kɛəriəs] *adj* precario.

precariously [pri'kɛəriəsli] *adj* precariamente.

precaution [pri'kɔːʃən] *n* precaución *f*; **by way of —** como precaución, para mayor seguridad; **to take —s** tomar precauciones; **to take the — of + ger** tomar la cautela de + *infin*.

precautionary [pri'kɔːʃənəri] *adj* de precaución, preventivo.

precede [pri'siːd] *vti* preceder; **for a month preceding this** durante un mes antes de esto; **to — a lecture with a joke** empezar una conferencia contando un chiste.

precedence ['presidəns] *n* precedencia *f*; prioridad *f*; primacía *f*; **to take — over someone** preceder a uno, primar sobre uno.

precedent ['presidənt] *n* precedente *m*; **according to —** de acuerdo con el precedente; **against all the —s** contra todos los precedentes; **without — sin** precedentes; **to establish** *(or* lay down, set up) **a —** establecer un precedente, sentar un precedente *(for* a).

preceding [pri'siːdiŋ] *adj* precedente.

precentor [pri'sentə*] *n* chantre *m*.

precept ['priːsept] *n* precepto *m*.

preceptor [pri'septə*] *n* preceptor *m*.

precinct ['priːsiŋkt] *n* recinto *m*; *(US: area)* barrio *m*, *(US Pol)* distrito *m* electoral, circunscripción *f*; **—s** contornos *mpl*; **within the —s of** dentro de los límites de; **pedestrian —** calles *fpl* exclusivas para el tránsito de peatones.

preciosity [,presi'ɔsiti] *n* preciosidad *f*.

precious ['preʃəs] **1** *adj* **(a)** precioso; *metal, stone* precioso; *person etc* amado, querido; **my —!** ¡querida!; **the book is very — to me** para mí el libro tiene gran valor.
    (b) *style etc* preciosista, afectado, rebuscado.
    2 *adv (fam)* muy; **there are — few left** quedan muy pocos; **to take — good care to see that . . .** velar de modo muy particular para que + *subj*.

precipice ['presipis] *n* precipicio *m*, despeñadero *m*.

precipitancy [pri'sipitənsi] *n* precipitación *f*.

precipitate [pri'sipiteit] **1** *n (Chem)* precipitado *m*. **2** *vt* precipitar *(also Chem)*; *(hasten)* acelerar; *trouble etc* causar, motivar, producir.

precipitate [pri'sipitit] *adj* precipitado, apresurado.

precipitately [pri'sipititli] *adv* precipitadamente.

precipitation [pri,sipi'teiʃən] *n* precipitación *f (also Chem, Meteorol)*; **to act with —** obrar con precipitación.

precipitous [pri'sipitəs] *adj* escarpado, cortado a pico.

precipitously [pri'sipitəsli] *adv* en escarpa, en precipicio.

précis ['preisiː] *n* resumen *m*; **to make a — of** hacer un resumen de, resumir.

precise [pri'sais] *adj thing* preciso, exacto; *(clearly stated)* claro; *person* meticuloso, puntual, escrupuloso; *(over-)* afectado, pedante; **at that — moment** en ese mismo momento; **they gave me the — book** me dieron el libro exacto; **he's very — in his ways** es meticuloso en todo; **in that — voice of hers** en ese tono suyo un tanto afectado; **let's be — about this** pongamos las cosas en su punto, concretemos; **well, to be — . . .** bueno, en rigor . . .; **there were 6, to be —** había 6, para ser exacto.

precisely [pri'saisli] *adv* precisamente, con precisión, exactamente; claramente; puntualmente, escrupulosamente; afectadamente, con pedantería; **he said very —** dijo con énfasis; **—!** ¡perfectamente!, ¡eso es!; **at — 7 o'clock** a las 7 en punto.

preciseness [pri'saisnis] *n* precisión *f*, exactitud *f*; puntualidad *f*, escrupulosidad *f*; afectación *f*, pedantería *f*.

precision [pri'siʒən] **1** *n see* preciseness. **2** *attr* de precisión; **— instrument** instrumento *m* de precisión.

preclude [pri'kluːd] *vt* excluir; imposibilitar; **this does not — the possibility of . . .** esto no excluye la posibilidad de . . .; **so as to — all doubt** para disipar cualquier duda; **we are —d from + ger** nos vemos

imposibilitados para **+** *infin*; **nos está vedado + infin**.

precocious [pri'kəuʃəs] *adj* precoz.

precociously [pri'kəuʃəsli] *adv* de modo precoz, con precocidad.

precociousness [pri'kəuʃəsnis] *n* precocidad *f*.

precocity [prə'kɔsiti] *n* precocidad *f*.

precognition [,priːkɔg'niʃən] *n* precognición *f*.

pre-Columbian ['priːkə'lʌmbiən] *a* precolombino.

preconceived ['priːkən'siːvd] *adj* preconcebido.

preconception ['priːkən'sepʃən] *n* preconcepción *f*, idea *f* preconcebida.

precondition ['priːkən'diʃən] *n* condición *f* preliminar, estipulación *f* hecha de antemano.

precool ['priː'kuːl] *vt* preenfriar.

precursor [priː'kəːsə*] *n* precursor *m*, ora *f*.

predate ['priː'deit] *vt* preceder, ser anterior a.

predator ['predətə*] *n* predador *m*, animal *m (etc)* de rapiña.

predatory ['predətəri] *adj animal* rapaz, de rapiña.

predecease ['priːdi'siːs] *vt* morir antes que.

predecessor ['priːdisesə*] *n* predecesor *m*, ora *f*, antecesor *m*, ora *f*.

predestination [priː,desti'neiʃən] *n* predestinación *f*.

predestine [priː'destin] *vt* predestinar; **to be —d to + infin** ser predestinado a + *infin*.

predetermination ['priːdi,təːmi'neiʃən] *n* predeterminación *f*.

predetermine ['priːdi'təːmin] *vt* predeterminar.

predicament [pri'dikəmənt] *n* apuro *m*, situación *f* difícil; **to be in a —** estar en un apuro; **what a — to be in!** ¡qué lío!

predicate ['predikit] *n* predicado *m*.

predicative [pri'dikətiv] *adj* predicativo.

predict [pri'dikt] *vt* pronosticar, profetizar, predecir.

prediction [pri'dikʃən] *n* pronóstico *m*, profecía *f*, predicción *f*.

predictive [pri'diktiv] *adj* profético, que vale como pronóstico.

predilection [,priːdi'lekʃən] *n* predilección *f*; **to have a — for** tener predilección por.

predispose ['priːdis'pəuz] *vt* predisponer.

predisposition ['priː,dispə'ziʃən] *n* predisposición *f*.

predominance [pri'dominəns] *n* predominio *m*.

predominant [pri'dominənt] *adj* predominante.

predominantly [pri'dominəntli] *adv* de modo predominante, en un grado predominante; en su mayor parte.

predominate [pri'domineit] *vi* predominar.

pre-eminence [priː'eminəns] *n* preeminencia *f*.

pre-eminent [priː'eminənt] *adj* preeminente.

pre-eminently [priː'eminəntli] *adv* preeminentemente; por excelencia; sobre todo.

pre-empt [priː'empt] *vt*: **to — something** asegurarse de algo antes que nadie, hacer valer sus derechos sobre algo, apropiarse algo.

pre-emption [priː'empʃən] *n* preempción *f*.

pre-emptive [pri(ː)'emptiv] *adj claim etc* por derecho de prioridad.

preen [priːn] **1** *vt feather* limpiar, arreglar con el pico.
    2 *vr*: **to — oneself** *(bird)* limpiarse, arreglarse las plumas con el pico; *(person)* pavonearse, atildarse; **to — oneself on** enorgullecerse de, jactarse de.

pre-established ['priːis'tæbliʃt] *adj* establecido de antemano.

pre-exist ['priːig'zist] *vi* preexistir.

pre-existence ['priːig'zistəns] *n* preexistencia *f*.

pre-existent ['priːig'zistənt] *adj* preexistente.

prefab ['priːfæb] *n (fam)* casa *f* prefabricada.

prefabricate ['priː'fæbrikeit] *vt* prefabricar.

prefabricated ['priː'fæbrikeitid] *adj* prefabricado.

preface ['prefis] **1** *n* prólogo *m*, prefacio *m*.
    2 *vt*: **he —d this by saying that . . .** a modo de prólogo a esto dijo que . . ., introdujo este tema diciendo que . . .; **the book is —d by an essay** el libro tiene un ensayo a modo de prólogo.

prefatory ['prefətəri] *adj* preliminar, a modo de prólogo.

prefect ['priːfekt] *n* prefecto *m*; *(School)* tutor *m*, monitor *m*.

prefecture ['priːfektjuə*] *n* prefectura *f*.

prefer [pri'fəː*] *vt* **(a)** preferir; **to — coffee to tea** preferir el café al té; **to — walking to going by car** preferir ir a pie a ir en coche; **to — to + infin** preferir + *infin*; **I — not to say** me parece preferible no decirlo; **which do you —?** ¿cuál prefieres?, ¿cuál te gusta más?
    (b) *(promote)* ascender, promover; *(appoint)* nombrar; **he was —red to the see of Toledo** le nombraron al arzobispado de Toledo.
    (c) *(charge)* hacer, presentar; **to — a charge against someone** poner a uno un juicio, acusar a uno.

preferable ['prefərəbl] adj preferible (to a).
preferably ['prefərəbli] adv preferentemente, más bien.
preference ['prefərəns] 1 n preferencia f, prioridad f; for — de preferencia; A in — to B A más que B, A antes que B; to give something — preferir algo, tener preferencia por algo; to give something — over something else anteponer algo a otra cosa; what is your —? ¿cuál te gusta más?; I have no — no prefiero ni el uno ni el otro.
2 attr share preferente.
preferential [,prefə'renʃəl] adj preferente.
preferment [pri'fəːmənt] n ascenso m, promoción f; nombramiento m (to a); to get — ser ascendido.
prefiguration [,priːfigə'reiʃən] n prefiguración f.
prefigure [priː'figə*] vt prefigurar.
prefix ['priːfiks] n prefijo m.
prefix [priː'fiks] vt prefijar.
pregnancy ['pregnənsi] n embarazo m.
pregnant ['pregnənt] adj (a) embarazada; to be — estar embarazada, estar en estado, estar encinta.
(b) — with cargado de, preñado de; a — silence un silencio cargado de emoción; a — pause una pausa llena de expectación.
preheat ['priː'hiːt] vt precalentar.
prehensile [pri'hensail] adj prensil.
prehistoric ['priː'his'tɔrik] adj prehistórico.
prehistory ['priː'histəri] n prehistoria f.
preignition ['priːig'niʃən] n preignición f.
prejudge ['priː'dʒʌdʒ] vt prejuzgar.
prejudice ['predʒudis] 1 n (a) (bias) parcialidad f; (biassed view) prejuicio m; (hostility) mala voluntad f, prevención f; there are many —s about this sobre esto existen muchos prejuicios; to have a — against someone tener mala voluntad contra uno, tener prevención contra uno, estar predispuesto contra uno.
(b) (injury, detriment) perjuicio m; to the — of con perjuicio de; without — (Law) sin detrimento de sus propios derechos; without — to sin perjuicio de.
2 vt (a) (predispose, bias) prevenir, predisponer (against contra).
(b) (damage) perjudicar; to — one's chances perjudicar las posibilidades de uno.
prejudiced ['predʒudist] adj (a) view etc parcial, interesado; he's very — tiene muchos prejuicios.
(b) to be —d against someone tener mala voluntad contra uno, tener prevención contra uno, estar predispuesto contra uno.
prejudicial [,predʒu'diʃəl] adj perjudicial (to para).
prelacy ['preləsi] n (office) obispado m; (bishops collectively) episcopado m.
prelate ['prelit] n prelado m.
preliminary [pri'limineri] 1 adj preliminar. 2 n preliminar m; **preliminaries** preliminares mpl, preparativos mpl.
prelude ['preljuːd] n preludio m (also Mus; to de).
premarital ['priː'mæritl] adj premarital.
premature ['premətʃuə*] adj prematuro; baldness etc precoz; it seems — to think of it parece prematuro pensar en ello.
prematurely ['premətʃuəli] adv prematuramente; antes de su debido tiempo; — bald con calvicie precoz.
premedical ['priː'medikəl] adj premédico.
premeditate [priː'mediteit] vt premeditar.
premeditated [priː'mediteitid] adj premeditado.
premeditation [priː,medi'teiʃən] n premeditación f.
premier ['premiə*] 1 adj primero, principal. 2 n primer ministro m.
première [,premi'eə*] n estreno m; world — estreno m mundial; the film had its — se estrenó la película.
premiership ['premiəʃip] n cargo m del primer ministro; puesto m de primer ministro.
premise ['premis] n premisa f; —s local m; (house) casa f; (building) edificio m; (shop etc) tienda f, establecimiento m; (as property) local m, propiedad f; on the —s en el local (etc).
premium ['priːmiəm] n (prize) premio m; (Comm, insurance) prima f; to be at a — (Comm) estar sobre la par, (fig) tener mucha demanda, ser muy solicitado; to put a — on something estimular algo, fomentar algo; hacer que suba el valor de algo (debido a su escasez); to sell something at a — vender algo en más de su valor nominal.
premium bond ['priːmiəm'bɔnd] n bono de la caja de ahorros que participa en una especie de lotería nacional.
premonition [,priːmə'niʃən] n presentimiento m; to have a — that ... presentir que ...
prenatal ['priː'neitl] adj prenatal.

preoccupation [priːˌɔkju'peiʃən] n preocupación f.
preoccupied [priː'ɔkjupaid] adj preocupado; absorto; abstraído; to be — about estar preocupado por, inquietarse por; to be — with something estar absorto en algo; he was too — to notice estaba demasiado absorto para darse cuenta.
preoccupy [priː'ɔkjupai] vt preocupar.
preordain ['priːɔː'dein] vt predestinar.
prep [prep] (fam) see preparation, preparatory.
prepackaged ['priː'pækidʒd] adj precintado.
prepaid ['priː'peid] adj porte pagado, franco de porte.
preparation [,prepə'reiʃən] n preparación f; —s preparativos mpl (for para); to be in — (book) estar en preparación; to do something without — hacer algo sin preparación; to make one's —s hacer sus preparativos (to + infin para + infin); Latin is a good — for Greek saber latín es un buen método para iniciarse en el estudio del griego, el latín es buena preparación para el griego.
preparatory [pri'pærətəri] 1 adj preparatorio, preliminar. 2 — to as prep como preparación para; con miras a, antes de.
prepare [pri'peə*] 1 vt preparar; disponer; aparejar; how is it —d? ¿cómo se prepara?; ¿cómo se hace?; to — a surprise for someone preparar una sorpresa para uno; to — the way for a treaty preparar el terreno para un tratado; to — someone for bad news prevenir a uno para recibir una mala noticia.
2 vi prepararse; disponerse; hacer preparativos; prevenirse; to — for someone's arrival hacer preparativos para recibir a uno; to — for a storm hacer preparativos para aguantar una tempestad; to — for an examination estudiar para un examen; to — to + infin disponerse a + infin, hacer preparativos para + infin.
prepared [pri'peəd] adj (a) listo; "be —" "siempre listos", "listos para todo".
(b) to be — for anything estar dispuesto a aguantarlo todo; no dejarse sorprender por nada; we were not — for this esto no lo esperábamos, no contábamos con esto; we were — for it lo habíamos previsto; to be — to + infin estar dispuesto a + infin; he was not — to listen to us no estaba dispuesto a escucharnos.
preparedness [pri'peəridnis] n preparación f, estado m de preparación; military — preparación f militar.
prepay ['priː'pei] (irr: see pay) vt pagar por adelantado.
prepayment ['priː'peimənt] n pago m adelantado.
preponderance [pri'pɔndərəns] n preponderancia f, predominio m.
preponderant [pri'pɔndərənt] adj preponderante, predominante.
preponderantly [pri'pɔndərəntli] adv de modo predominante, en un grado predominante; en su mayor parte.
preponderate [pri'pɔndəreit] vi preponderar, predominar.
preposition [,prepə'ziʃən] n preposición f.
prepositional [,prepə'ziʃənl] adj preposicional.
prepossessing [,priːpə'zesiŋ] adj atractivo, agradable.
preposterous [pri'pɔstərəs] adj absurdo, ridículo.
preposterously [pri'pɔstərəsli] adv absurdamente.
preposterousness [pri'pɔstərəsnis] n lo absurdo.
prepuce ['priːpjuːs] n prepucio m.
pre-Raphaelite ['priː'ræfəlait] 1 adj prerrafaelista. 2 n prerrafaelista mf.
prerecord ['priːri(ː)'kɔːd] vt grabar (or registrar) de antemano.
prerequisite ['priː'rekwizit] n requisito m previo; cosa f necesaria, esencial m; —s for success las cosas necesarias para asegurar el éxito.
prerogative [pri'rɔgətiv] n prerrogativa f.
presage ['presidʒ] 1 n presagio m. 2 vt presagiar.
presbyopia ['prezbi'əupiə] n presbiopía f.
Presbyterian [,prezbi'tiəriən] 1 adj presbiteriano. 2 n presbiteriano m, a f.
presbytery ['prezbitəri] n presbiterio m.
preschool ['priː'skuːl] adj: — years los años que preceden a la entrada del niño en la escuela; — training enseñanza f recibida por el niño antes de entrar en la escuela.
prescience ['presiəns] n presciencia f.
prescient ['presiənt] adj presciente.
prescribe [pris'kraib] vti (a) prescribir (also Law); ordenar; in the —d way en el modo que ordena la ley; in the —d time dentro del plazo que fija la ley.
(b) (Med) recetar; to — a medicine for someone recetar una medicina para uno; to — for boils recetar una medicina para curar los diviesos; he —d complete rest recomendó el reposo completo; what do you —? ¿qué me recomienda Vd?

prescription [pris'krip∫ən] *n* prescripción *f* (*also Law*); precepto *m*; (*Med*) receta *f*.

prescriptive [pris'kriptiv] *adj* legal; sancionado por la costumbre.

presealed ['pri:si:ld] *adj* precintado.

presence ['prezns] *n* presencia *f*; (*attendance*) asistencia *f* (*at* a); — of mind presencia *f* de ánimo, serenidad *f*, sangre *f* fría; **saving your** — con perdón de los presentes; **in the** — of en presencia de, (*fig*) ante; **to be admitted to the P** — ser conducido ante el rey (*etc*); **to make one's** — felt imponerse, hacer que todos se den cuenta de lo que vale uno; **your** — is requested se ruega asista . . .

present ['preznt] **1** *adj* (a) (*in attendance*) presente; — ! ¡presente!; **those** — los presentes, los asistentes; **to be** — asistir (*at* a); **all were** — **to hear it** todos asistieron para oírlo, acudieron todos a oírlo; **he was** — **at the accident** fue testigo del accidente; **he was** — **at the foundation** presenció la fundación; **nobody else was** — no había nadie más; **how many others were** — ? ¿cuántos más había?

(b) (*actual*) actual; presente; *month etc* corriente; (*Gram*) *tense* presente, *participle de* presente; — **methods include** . . . los métodos actuales incluyen . . . , los métodos en uso incluyen . . . ; **the** — **Queen of England** la actual Reina de Inglaterra; **the** — **letter** la presente; **the** — **writer** el que esto escribe; **its** — **value** su valor actual; **in the** — **year** en el año que corre.

2 *n* (a) (*actuality*) presente *m*, actualidad *f*; **the** — el presente; **at** — al presente, actualmente; **for the** — por ahora, por el momento; **up to the** — hasta ahora.

(b) (*gift*) regalo *m*, presente *m*; **Christmas** — regalo *m* de Navidad; **to make someone a** — **of something** regalar algo a uno, (*fig*) dar algo a uno medio regalado.

(c) (*Gram*) (*tiempo m*) presente *m*; — **perfect** pretérito *m* perfecto.

present [pri'zent] **1** *vt* (a) (*introduce*) presentar; **to** — X **to** Y presentar a X a Y; **may I** — **Miss Blandish?** permítame presentarle a la señorita Blandish; **to be** — **ed at court** ser presentado a la corte.

(b) (*Theat*) **to** — **a play** representar una obra; **"** — **ing Garbo as Mimi"** "con Garbo en el papel de Mimí".

(c) (*expound*) *case etc* exponer; **to** — **a plan to a meeting** exponer (*or* explicar) un proyecto a una reunión.

(d) (*give*) presentar, ofrecer, dar; **to** — **something to someone, to** — **someone with something** regalar algo a uno, (*more formally*) obsequiar a uno con algo; **to** — **an account** (*Comm*) pasar factura; **to** — **a report** presentar un informe; **to** — **one's compliments to someone** cumplimentar a uno.

(e) (*provide*) ofrecer; **it** — **s a magnificent sight** ofrece un espectáculo maravilloso; **the case** — **s some odd features** el caso tiene ciertas características algo raras; **it** — **s some difficulties** nos plantea algunas dificultades; **the boy** — **s a problem** el chico nos plantea un problema.

(f) (*Mil*) **to** — **arms** presentar las armas; — **arms!** ¡presenten armas!

2 *vr*: **to** — **oneself** presentarse (*at a time* a una hora, *at a place* en un sitio); **to** — **oneself for examination** examinarse (*in* de); **when the chance** — **s itself** cuando se ofrece la ocasión; **a problem has** — **ed itself** ha surgido un problema.

presentable [pri'zentəbl] *adj* presentable.

presentation [,prezən'tei∫ən] *n* (a) (*act*) presentación *f*; (*of case etc*) exposición *f*; (*Theat*) representación *f*; **on** — **of the voucher** al presentarse el vale.

(b) (*present*) obsequio *m*; (*ceremony*) entrega *f* ceremoniosa de un regalo; **to make someone a** — **on his retirement** hacer un obsequio a uno en su jubilación.

present-day ['preznt'dei] *adj* actual.

presentiment [pri'zentimənt] *n* presentimiento *m*, corazonada *f*; **to have a** — **about something** tener un presentimiento acerca de algo; **to have a** — **that** . . . presentir que . . .

presently ['prezntli] *adv* luego, dentro de poco; (*US*) ahora, actualmente.

preservation [,prezə'vei∫ən] *n* conservación *f*; preservación *f*; **in a good state of** —, **in good** — bien conservado, en buen estado.

preservative [pri'zə:vətiv] **1** *adj* preservativo. **2** *n* preservativo *m*.

preserve [pri'zə:v] **1** *n* (a) (*Cook*) conserva *f*; confitura *f*; compota *f*.

(b) (*Hunting*) coto *m*, vedado *m*; **game** — coto *m* de caza.

2 *vt* (a) (*keep*) conservar; mantener en buen estado; (*keep from harm*) preservar (*against, from* contra), guardar, proteger (*against, from* de); **may God** — **you** que Dios os guarde.

(b) (*Cook*) hacer una conserva de; (*in syrup*) almibarar, (*in salt*) salar, salpresar.

preserved [pri'zə:vd] *adj food* en conserva.

preshrunk ['pri:'∫rʌŋk] *adj* encogido de antemano.

preside [pri'zaid] *vi* presidir; **to** — **at** (*or* over) **a meeting** presidir una reunión.

presidency ['prezidənsi] *n* presidencia *f*.

president ['prezidənt] *n* (*Pol etc*) presidente *m*; (*US Comm*) director *m*; (*US Univ*) rector *m*.

presidential [,prezi'den∫əl] *adj* presidencial.

press [pres] **1** *n* (a) (*pressure*) presión *f*; (*of hand etc*) apretón *m*, presión *f*; (*Sport*) presa *f*; **give it a** — **here** presione aquí.

(b) (*crush etc of people*) apiñamiento *m*, agolpamiento *m*; (*of affairs*) urgencia *f*; **there was such a** — **of people** había tal multitud de gente, era tal el apiñamiento; **in the** — **of the battle** en lo más reñido de la batalla.

(c) (*Mech*) prensa *f*; **hydraulic** — prensa *f* hidráulica; **linen** — prensa *f* de ropa.

(d) (*Typ*) (*printing press, publishing firm*) imprenta *f*; (*newspapers in general*) prensa *f*; **the P** — la Prensa; **rotary** — prensa *f* rotativa; **yellow** — periódicos *mpl* sensacionales; **to be in** — estar en prensa; **to get** (*or* have) **a bad** — tener mala prensa; **to get** (*or* have) **a good** — tener buena prensa; **to go to** — entrar en prensa, entrar en máquina; **to pass something for the** — aprobar algo para la prensa.

2 *vt* (a) *button, switch, doorbell etc* apretar, pulsar, presionar, empujar; *hand, trigger* apretar; *hand* (*painfully*) apretujar; *grapes* pisar, prensar; *metal, olives etc* (*Tech*) prensar; *suit* planchar; (*crush, squeeze*) estrujar; **to** — **someone's hand** apretar la mano a uno; **to** — **the juice out of an orange** exprimir el zumo de una naranja; **it** — **es me here** me aprieta aquí; **he** — **ed his face to the window** pegó la cara al cristal; **to** — **someone to one's heart** abrazar a uno estrechamente; **to** — **something down** comprimir algo; **to** — **books into a case** meter libros apretadamente en una maleta.

(b) (*put pressure on enemy*) acosar, hostigar, (*in game*) apretar, (*in pursuit*) seguir muy de cerca, pisar los talones de; **to** — **someone hard** apretar mucho a uno; **to** — **someone for payment** insistir en que uno pague algo, exigir un pago a uno; **to** — **someone for an answer** pedir insistentemente que uno conteste a algo; **to** — **a claim** insistir en una demanda; **to** — **a point** insistir en su punto de vista; **to** — **home an advantage** aprovecharse todo lo posible de una ventaja; **to** — **a gift on someone** insistir en que uno acepte un regalo; **to** — **someone to do something** instar a uno a que haga algo, apremiar a uno para que haga algo, hacer presión sobre uno para que haga algo; **he didn't need much** — **ing** no hacía falta persuadirle; **he was being** — **ed by creditors** le acosaban los acreedores; **to be** — **ed for money** andar muy escaso de dinero; **to be** — **ed for time** tener poco tiempo, tener mucha prisa; *see service etc*.

3 *vi* (a) (*in physical sense*) apretar; ejercer presión, hacer presión; **to** — **hard** apretar mucho; **to** — **close up to someone** arrimarse a uno; **to** — **down on something** apretar algo comprimiéndolo; pesar sobre algo; **to** — **on one's pen** escribir haciendo más presión con la pluma; **the people** — **ed round him** la gente se apiñó en torno a él.

(b) (*fig*) ejercer presión, hacer presión; presionar; **time** — **es** el tiempo apremia; **responsibilities** — **hard on him** las responsabilidades pesan sobre él; **to** — **forward, to** — **on** avanzar; seguir su camino; (*hasten*) apretar el paso; — **on!** ¡adelante!

(c) **to** — **for something** presionar por algo, presionar para conseguir algo; reclamar algo, exigir algo, pedir algo con urgencia; hacer propaganda a favor de algo.

press agency ['pres,eidʒənsi] *n* agencia *f* de información.

press agent ['pres,eidʒənt] *n* agente *m* de publicidad.

press baron ['pres,bærən] *n* magnate *m* de la prensa.

press box ['presbɒks] *n* tribuna *f* de la prensa.

press button ['pres'bʌtn] **1** *n* botón *m* (de control).

2 press-button *attr* mandado por botón.

press conference ['pres,kɒnfərəns] *n* rueda *f* de prensa.

press cutting ['pres,kʌtiŋ] *n* recorte *m* de periódico.

press gallery ['pres,gæləri] *n* tribuna *f* de la prensa (*esp* de la cámara, del parlamento).

press-gang ['presgæn] **1** n ronda f de enganche.
2 vt: **to — someone into something** obligar a uno muy contra su voluntad a hacer algo.
pressing ['presin] adj urgente, apremiante, acuciante.
pressman ['presmæn] n, pl **-men** [men] periodista m.
pressmark ['presmɑ:k] n signatura f.
press photographer ['presfə'tɔgrəfə*] n fotógrafo m de prensa.
press stud ['prestʌd] n botón m de presión.
pressure [preʃə*] n **(a)** (Meteorol, Phys, Tech) presión f; (weight) peso m; (strength) fuerza f; **barometric —** presión f barométrica; **tyre —** presión f de los neumáticos; **a — of X pounds to the square inch** una presión de X kilogramos al cm².
　(b) (urgency) urgencia f, apremio m; (influence) influencia f, persuasión f; (Med) tensión f nerviosa; **because of the — of business** (Comm) debido a la cantidad de negocios, (at meeting etc) por el número de los asuntos a tratar; **to act under —** obrar bajo persuasión; **to do something under —** from the **bankers** hacer algo presionado por los banqueros; **to bring — to bear on someone** hacer presión sobre uno (to do something para que haga algo); **to live at high —** tener una vida muy activa; **to work under —** trabajar con urgencia.
pressure cooker ['preʃə,kukə*] n olla f a presión.
pressure-feed ['preʃəfi:d] n tubo m de alimentación a presión.
pressure gauge ['preʃəgeidʒ] n manómetro m.
pressure group ['preʃəgru:p] n grupo m de presión.
pressure pan ['preʃəpæn] n (US) olla f a presión.
pressurized ['preʃəraizd] adj cabin a presión, altimático.
press view ['presvju:] n preestreno m.
prestidigitation ['presti,didʒi'teiʃən] n prestidigitación f.
prestige [pres'ti:ʒ] n prestigio m.
prestigious [pres'tidʒəs] adj prestigioso.
presto ['prestəu] adv: **hey —!** ¡abracadabra!
prestressed [pri:'strest] adj: **— concrete** hormigón m pretensado.
presumably [pri'zju:məbli] adv probablemente, según cabe presumir; **— he will come** imagino que vendrá; **— he did** cabe presumir que lo hizo.
presume [pri'zju:m] vti **(a)** presumir; suponer; **his death must be —d** hay que presumir que ha muerto, es de suponer que murió; **to — that . . .** suponer que . . .; **it may be —d that . . .** es de suponer que . . .; **to — someone to be innocent** suponer que uno es inocente; **Dr Livingstone, I —** Dr Livingstone según creo, cabe conjeturar que Vd es el Dr Livingstone.
　(b) **to — to +** infin atreverse a + infin; pretender + infin, tomarse la libertad de + infin; **if I may — to advise you** si se me permite ofrecerle un consejo.
　(c) **to — on someone's friendship** abusar de la amistad de uno; **you — too much** Vd no sabe lo que pide, eso es mucho pedir.
presumption [pri'zʌmpʃən] n **(a)** (arrogance) presunción f; atrevimiento m; **pardon my —** le ruego perdonar mi atrevimiento.
　(b) (thing presumed) suposición f; pretensión f; **the — is that . . .** es de suponer que . . ., puede presumirse que . . .
presumptive [pri'zʌmptiv] adj heir presunto.
presumptuous [pri'zʌmptjuəs] adj presumido, presuntuoso; atrevido; **in that I was rather —** en eso fui algo atrevido; **it would be — of me to +** infin sería atrevido + infin.
presumptuously [pri'zʌmptjuəsli] adv con presunción, presuntuosamente.
presumptuousness [pri'zʌmptjuəsnis] n presunción f, atrevimiento m.
presuppose [,pri:sə'pəuz] vt presuponer.
presupposition [,pri:sʌpə'ziʃən] n presuposición f.
pretence [pri'tens] n **(a)** (claim) pretensión f; **to make no — to learning** no pretender ser erudito.
　(b) (display) ostentación f; afectación f; **without —, devoid of all —** sin ostentación, sin afectación.
　(c) (pretext) pretexto m; **false —s** fraude m; **by false —s** fraudulentamente, con engaño; **on the — of, under the — of** so pretexto de.
　(d) (make-believe) fingimiento m; **it's all a —** todo es fingido; **to make a — of something** fingir algo.
pretend [pri'tend] **1** vt **(a)** (feign) fingir, aparentar, simular; **to — ignorance** fingir ignorar, aparentar no saber; **to — to +** infin fingir + infin, aparentar + infin; **to — to go away** fingir marcharse; **to — to be mad** fingirse loco; **to — to be asleep, to — to sleep** fingir dormir, fingirse dormido, hacerse el dormido; **he —s to be a poet** se dice poeta, se hace el poeta,

las echa de poeta; **to — not to be listening** hacerse el distraído; **to — not to understand** hacerse el desentendido.
　(b) (claim) pretender; **I do not — to know the answer** no pretendo saber qué solución pueda haber; **I don't — to understand art** no pretendo entender de arte.
2 vi **(a)** (feign) fingir; **it's just —, we're only —ing** (to child etc) es de mentirijillas; **let's — —** imaginémoslo; **let's not — to each other** no nos engañemos uno a otro.
　(b) (claim) **to — to the throne** pretender al trono; **to — to intelligence** afirmar tener inteligencia, pretender ser inteligente.
pretended [pri'tendid] adj pretendido.
pretender [pri'tendə*] n pretendiente mf; **the Young P—** el joven Pretendiente.
pretense [pri'tens] (US) see **pretence**.
pretension [pri'tenʃən] n **(a)** (claim) pretensión f; **to have —s to culture** tener pretensiones de cultura, pretender ser culto.
　(b) (pretentiousness) presunción f; afectación f.
pretentious [pri'tenʃəs] adj pretencioso; person presumido; (ostentatious) ostentoso, aparatoso, ambicioso; (and vulgar) cursi.
pretentiously [pri'tenʃəsli] adv con presunción; ostentosamente, aparatosamente.
pretentiousness [pri'tenʃəsnis] n lo pretencioso; presunción f; lo ostentoso, lo aparatoso; cursilería f.
preterite ['pretərit] n pretérito m.
preternatural [,pri:tə'nætʃrəl] adj preternatural.
pretext ['pri:tekst] n pretexto m; **under — of** so pretexto de; **it's just a —** es sólo un pretexto.
prettify ['pritifai] vt (pej) embellecer, adornar de modo ridículo; representar bajo una forma demasiado hermosa.
prettily ['pritili] adv con gracia, elegantemente; preciosamente; **— adorned with** con adornos elegantes de.
pretty ['priti] **1** adj **(a)** person guapo, bonito; dress, object etc precioso, mono; scene hermoso; **a — girl** una muchacha guapa; **a — little house** una casita preciosa; **what a — hat!** ¡qué sombrero más mono!, ¡qué monada de sombrero!; **yes, my —** sí, ricura; **she's as — as a picture** es guapísima; **he has a — wit** tiene un ingenio muy vivo, tiene mucha chispa.
　(b) sum etc importante, considerable.
　(c) (iro) bueno; **a — mess we're in!** ¡vaya lío!
2 adv bastante; casi; **— good** bastante bueno, muy bueno; **— hard** bastante difícil; **it's — much the same** es lo mismo más o menos; **he got — cross** se enfadó bastante; **it's — near ruined** está casi arruinado; **— well, thanks!** ¡regular, gracias!; **to be sitting —** estar bien, estar en una posición ventajosa.
pretzel ['pretsl] n (US) galleta tostada en forma de rosquilla, polvoreada con sal.
prevail [pri'veil] vi **(a)** (gain mastery) prevalecer, imponerse; **to — against** (or over) one's enemies triunfar sobre los enemigos; **finally good sense —ed** por fin se impuso el buen sentido; **eventually peace —ed** por fin se restableció la paz.
　(b) (be current) reinar, imperar; predominar; (be in fashion) estar de moda, estar en boga; **the conditions that now —** las condiciones que ahora imperan.
　(c) (persuade) **to — upon someone to do something** persuadir a uno a hacer algo, inducir a uno a hacer algo; **he was eventually —ed upon to +** infin por fin se dejó persuadir a + infin; **he could not be —ed upon** era imposible persuadirle, no se convenció.
prevailing [pri'veilin] adj reinante, imperante; predominante; usual, corriente; **the — fashion** la moda actual, la moda reinante; **under — conditions** bajo las condiciones actuales; **the — wind** el viento predominante.
prevalence ['prevələns] n predominio m; frecuencia f; uso m corriente, costumbre f.
prevalent ['prevələnt] adj predominante, frecuente, común, corriente; (fashionable) en boga, de moda; custom etc extendido; (present-day) actual.
prevaricate [pri'værikeit] vi buscar evasivas, usar sofismas, tergiversar.
prevarication [pri,væri'keiʃən] n evasivas fpl, sofismas mpl, tergiversación f.
prevent [pri'vent] vt person impedir, estorbar; event etc impedir, evitar; estorbar; illness etc evitar; **it was impossible to — it** fue imposible impedirlo; **to — someone +** ger, **to — someone from +** ger impedir a uno + infin.
preventable [pri'ventəbl] adj evitable.
preventative [pri'ventətiv] adj see **preventive**.

prevention [pri'venʃən] n prevención f; el impedir, el evitar; **the — of errors is not easy** no es fácil evitar los errores; **for the — of accidents** para evitar los accidentes; **a society for the — of cruelty to animals** una sociedad protectora de animales.

preventive [pri'ventiv] adj preventivo, impeditivo; (Med) profiláctico; measure, medicine preventivo.

preview ['pri:vju:] n preestreno m; (fig) anticipo m, vista f anticipada; **to have a — of something** ver algo con anticipación, lograr ver algo antes que otros.

previous ['pri:viəs] 1 adj (a) previo, anterior; **in — years** en años anteriores; **no — experience necessary** no es necesario tener conocimientos del oficio; **because of a — engagement** por tener compromiso anterior.

(b) (hasty) prematuro; **this seems somewhat —** esto parece ser algo prematuro; **you have been rather —** Vd ha obrado con cierta prisa, Vd ha obrado antes del momento justo.

2 prep: **— to** antes de; **— to doing this** antes de hacer esto.

previously ['pri:viəsli] adv (already) previamente, con anticipación, anteriormente; (in early times) antes.

prewar ['pri:'wɔ:*] adj de preguerra, de la preguerra, prebélico; **the — period** la preguerra.

prey [prei] 1 n presa f, víctima f; **bird of —** ave f de rapiña; **to be a — to** ser víctima de.

2 vi (a) **to — on** (feed on) atacar, alimentarse de, comer, devorar; (plunder) robar, pillar; (sponge on) vivir a costa de; **rabbits are —ed on by foxes** los conejos son presa de los zorros.

(b) **to — on** (mind) agobiar, remorder, pre-ocupar; **doubts —ed on him** le obsesionaban las dudas; **the tragedy so —ed on his mind that . . .** la tragedia le afectó de tal modo que . . .

price [prais] 1 n precio m; (quotation, Fin) cotización f; **asking —** precio m a que se ofrece; **cash —** precio m al contado; **closing —** (Fin) cotización f de cierre, cotización f de clausura; **cost —** precio m de coste; **fixed —** precio m fijo; **list —** precio m de lista; **market —** precio m de mercado; **net —** precio m neto; **opening —** (Fin) cotización f de apertura; **reserve —** precio m mínimo; **at a — of £500** a un precio de 500 libras; **at a reduced —** a un precio reducido, con descuento; **at any —** (fig) a toda costa; **peace at any —** paz a ultranza; **you can buy it at a —** se puede comprar pero cuesta bastante; **not at any —!** de ningún modo; **I don't want that at any — eso** no lo quiero ni regalado; **what — these pigs?** ¿cuánto se me ofrece por estos cerdos?; **what — liberty?** y la libertad, ¿qué?; **what — Joe Soap now?** ¿qué me dicen ahora sobre Joe Soap?; **what's the — of this?** ¿cuánto vale esto?; **to pay top — for something** pagar algo al precio máximo; **to rise in — subir** de precio; **houses have risen in —** ha aumentado el valor de las casas; see **head**.

2 vt (a) estimar, valuar, valorar (at en); tasar (at en), fijar el precio de; **it is —d rather high at £80** está valorado en 80 libras, lo cual es mucho; **it's not —d in the window** en el escaparate no le han puesto el precio.

(b) **to be —d out of the market** (article) alcanzar tal precio de coste que no puede concurrir a los mercados (internacionales), (producer, nation) señalar precios tan elevados a los artículos pro-ducidos que el productor (or el país) no puede con-currir a los mercados (internacionales).

price control ['praiskən,trəul] n control m de precios.

priceless ['praislis] adj (a) inapreciable, que no tiene precio. (b) (amusing) divertidísimo; **it was —!** ¡fue para morirse de risa!

price list ['praislist] n lista f de precios.

price range ['praisreindʒ] n gama f de precios, escala f de precios.

prick [prik] 1 n (a) pinchazo m, punzada f; (sting etc) picadura f; (with pin) alfilerazo m; (of spur) es-polada f; (with goad) aguijonazo m; **— of con-science** escrúpulo m de conciencia, remordimiento m; **to kick against the —s** dar coces contra el aguijón.

(b) (Anat, tabu) polla f.

2 vt (a) pinchar, punzar, picar; (sting) picar; (with spur) dar con las espuelas; (goad) aguijar; (make hole in) agujerear; (mark with holes) marcar con agujerillos; **to — out** (Hort) plantar; **to — up one's ears** aguzar el oído.

(b) **it —ed his conscience** le remordió la con-ciencia, le dio un escrúpulo de conciencia.

3 vi: **to — up** aguzar el oído, empezar a prestar atención.

prickings ['prikiŋz] npl: **— of conscience** remordi-mientos mpl.

prickle ['prikl] n (a) (Bot) espina f; (Zool) púa f. (b) (on skin etc) escozor m.

prickly ['prikli] adj espinoso, lleno de espinas; lleno de púas; person poco afable, malhumorado, difícil; **he's rather — about that** sobre ese tema es algo quisquilloso.

prickly heat ['prikli'hi:t] n salpullido m causado por exceso de calor.

prickly pear ['prikli'pɛə*] n higo m chumbo, chumbera f.

pride [praid] 1 n orgullo m; (pej) orgullo m, soberbia f, arrogancia f; **it's the — of Navarre** es el orgullo de Navarra; **he's the — of the family** es el orgullo de la familia; **— comes before a fall, — must have a fall** el orgullo excesivo conduce a la caída; **it is a source of — to us that . . .** es para nosotros un motivo de orgullo el que . . .; **to pocket one's —** olvidarse de su amor propio; tragar una afrenta; **to take (a) — in something** enorgullecerse de algo, ufanarse de algo; **to take — of place** venir primero, ocupar el primer puesto.

2 vr: **to — oneself on something** enorgullecerse de algo, ufanarse de algo; **to — oneself on** + ger enorgullecerse de + infin.

priest [pri:st] n (in general, pagan) sacerdote m; (Christian) sacerdote m, cura m; **high —** sumo sacerdote m; **parish —** párroco m.

priestess ['pri:stis] n sacerdotisa f.

priesthood ['pri:sthud] n (function) sacerdocio m; (priests collectively) clero m; **to enter the —** ordenarse de sacerdote.

priestly ['pri:stli] adj sacerdotal.

priest-ridden ['pri:st,ridn] adj dominado por el clero.

prig [prig] n presumido m, a f; pedante mf; mojigato m, a f, gazmoño m, a f; **don't be such a —!** ¡no presumas!

priggish ['prigiʃ] adj presumido; pedante; mojigato, gazmoño.

priggishness ['prigiʃnis] n presunción f; pedantería f; mojigatería f, gazmoñería f.

prim [prim] adj (formal) etiquetero, estirado; (affected) remilgado; (prudish) gazmoño.

primacy ['praiməsi] n primacía f.

prima donna ['pri:mə'dɒnə] n primadonna f, diva f.

prima facie ['praimə'feiʃi] 1 adv a primera vista.

2 adj (Law) suficiente para justificar la presunción del hecho; **there are — reasons why . . .** hay sufi-cientes razones que justifican el que + subj; **he has a — case** a primera vista parece que tiene razón.

primarily ['praimərili] adv ante todo; en primer lugar; principalmente.

primary ['praiməri] 1 adj primario; principal; colour, education primario; **that is not the — reason** ésa no es la razón principal; see **school**.

2 n (US) elección preliminar para nombrar candidatos.

primate ['praimit] n (Eccl) primado m.

primate ['praimeit] n (Zool) primate m.

prime [praim] 1 adj (a) (Math) primo.

(b) (chief) primero, principal, fundamental; **the — reason** la razón principal; **of — importance** de primera importancia; **of — necessity** de primera necesidad.

(c) (excellent) selecto, de primera clase; **— quality beef** carne f de vaca de primera calidad; **in — condition** en excelente estado.

2 n (a) flor f, lo mejor; **the — of life** la flor de la vida, la edad viril; **to be in one's —** estar en la flor de la vida; **to be past one's —** haber dado lo mejor de sí, estar en decadencia; **to be cut off in one's —** morir en la flor de la vida.

(b) (Eccl) prima f.

3 vt gun, pump cebar; surface et preparar, apres-tar; **to — someone** informar a uno de antemano, hacer que uno se entere de algo clandestinamente; **they —d him about what he should say** le dieron instrucciones acerca de lo que había de decir; **to — someone with drink** emborrachar a uno, hacer que uno beba; **he arrived well —d** llegó ya medio borracho.

prime minister [,praim'ministə*] n primer ministro m.

primer ['praimə*] n cartilla f, libro m de texto elemental; **a French —** un libro elemental de francés.

primeval [prai'mi:vəl] adj primitivo.

priming ['praimiŋ] n preparación f; (of pump etc) cebo m; (Art) primera capa f.

primitive ['primitiv] **1** *adj* (*early*; *original*, *primary*) primitivo; (*old-fashioned*) anticuado; (*simple*, *rude*) rudimentario, sencillo; (*uncivilized*) inculto; (*sordid*) sucio, miserable, asqueroso; (*Art*) primitivo.
2 *n* (*Art*) primitivo.

primly ['primli] *adv* remilgadamente; con gazmoñería.

primness ['primnis] *n* lo etiquetero, lo estirado; remilgo m; gazmoñería *f*.

primogeniture [,praiməu'dʒenitʃə*] *n* primogenitura *f*.

primordial [prai'mɔːdiəl] *adj* primordial.

primus (stove) ['praiməs(stəuv)] (*Protected Trade Name*) *n* cocinilla *f* de alcohol, cocinilla *f* de camping, infiernillo m campestre.

primrose ['primrəuz] **1** *n* (*Bot*) primavera *f*; (*colour*) color m amarillo pálido. **2** *adj* amarillo pálido. **3** *attr*: — **path** caminito m de rosas.

primula ['primjulə] *n* oreja f de oso.

prince [prins] *n* príncipe m; **P— Charming** el príncipe encantador; **the — of darkness** el príncipe de las tinieblas; — **consort** príncipe m consorte; — **regent** príncipe m regente; **P— of Wales** Príncipe m de Gales (*heredero del trono del Reino Unido*, *equivalente al* Príncipe de Asturias *en* España).

princely ['prinsli] *adj* principesco; magnífico, noble; **the — sum of two shillings** la bonita cantidad de dos chelines.

princess [prin'ses] *n* princesa *f*.

principal ['prinsipəl] **1** *adj* principal; mayor. **2** *n* principal m, jefe m; (*of school*, *college*) director m, ora *f*; (*Fin*) principal m, capital m.

principality [,prinsi'pæliti] *n* principado m.

principally ['prinsipəli] *adv* principalmente.

principle ['prinsəpl] *n* principio m; **in —** en principio; **on —** por principio; **to argue from first —s** construir su argumento sobre los principios fundamentales; **to go back to first —s** volver a los principios fundamentales; **to have high —s** tener principios nobles; **to lay it down as a — that . . .** sentar el principio de que . . .; **I make it a — never to +** *infin* me hago una regla de nunca + *infin*.

prink [priŋk] **1** *vt* acicalar, ataviar; arreglar elegantemente. **2** *vi* acicalarse, ataviarse; arreglarse elegantemente.

print [print] **1** *n* (*mark*, *imprint*) marca *f*, señal *f*, impresión *f*; (*Typ*) tipo m, letra *f* de molde; (*printed matter*) impreso m; (*fabric*, *dress*) estampado m; (*picture*) estampa *f*, grabado m; (*Phot*) positiva *f*, copia *f*; **large —** tipo m grande; **small —** tipo m menudo; **in (cold) —** en letras de molde; **to be in —** (*be published as book etc*) estar impreso, (*be available*) estar disponible, estar en existencia; **to be out of —** estar agotado; **he likes to see himself in —** se enorgullece de que se impriman sus artículos (*etc*); le agrada que le mencionen en los periódicos; **to get into —** imprimirse, publicarse; **we don't want that to get into —** no queremos que se publique la noticia en los periódicos; **I've got into — at last!** ¡por fin me van a publicar el artículo! (*etc*); **to rush into —** publicar una obra sin reflexionar.
2 *attr dress* estampado.
3 *vt* imprimir; (*on the mind etc*) grabar; *book etc* imprimir; sacar a luz, dar a la estampa, publicar; (*Phot*) imprimir; (*write plainly*) escribir en caracteres de imprenta, escribir en letras de molde; **—ed by** impreso por; **they —ed 300 copies** (*Typ*) tiraron 300 ejemplares, hicieron una tirada de 300 ejemplares.

printed ['printid] *adj* impreso; *dress* estampado; — **matter** impresos mpl.

printer ['printə*] *n* impresor m.

printing ['printiŋ] *n* (*art*) tipografía *f*, imprenta *f*; (*act*) impresión *f*; (*quantity printed*) tirada *f*; **4th —** 4ª impresión; **a — of 500 copies** una tirada de 500 ejemplares; **"16th century — in Toledo"** "la imprenta en Toledo en el siglo XVI".

printing frame ['printiŋ,freim] *n* prensa *f* de copiar.

printing machine ['printiŋmə,ʃiːn] *n* máquina *f* tipográfica.

printing office ['printiŋ,ɔfis] *n* imprenta *f*.

printing press ['printiŋ,pres] *n* prensa *f* de imprenta.

printing works ['printiŋ,wəːks] *n* imprenta *f*.

prior ['praiə*] **1** *adj* anterior, previo; *claim etc* preferente.
2 *adv*: — **to** antes de; hasta; — **to this discovery** antes de este descubrimiento.
3 *n* (*Eccl*) prior m.

prioress ['praiəris] *n* priora *f*.

priority [prai'ɔriti] *n* prioridad *f*; (*in time*) antelación *f*, precedencia *f*; **to have —** tener prioridad (*over someone* sobre uno); **they will be given out in strict order of —** serán distribuidos con arreglo a un riguroso criterio de prioridades; **we must get our priorities right** hemos de establecer un justo orden de prioridades.

priory ['praiəri] *n* priorato m.

prise [praiz] *vt*: **to — open** abrir por fuerza, abrir con una palanca; **to — a lid up** levantar una tapa con una palanca; **to — someone out of his post** lograr que uno renuncie a su puesto, desahuciar a uno.

prism ['prizm] *n* prisma m.

prismatic [priz'mætik] *adj* prismático.

prison ['prizn] **1** *n* cárcel *f*, prisión *f*; **to be in —** estar en la cárcel; **to go to — for 5 years** ser condenado a 5 años de prisión; pasar 5 años en la cárcel; **to put someone in —**, **to send someone to —** encarcelar a uno; **to send someone to — for 2 years** condenar a uno a 2 años de prisión.
2 *attr* carcelario; — **life** vida *f* en la cárcel; — **population** población *f* reclusa; — **camp** campamento m para prisioneros.

prisoner ['priznə*] *n* (*under arrest*) detenido m, a *f*; (*facing charge*, — **at the bar**) acusado m, a *f*; (*convicted*) preso m, a *f*; (*Mil*) prisionero m; **to hold someone —** detener a uno; **to take someone —** hacer prisionero a uno.

prison van ['priznvæn] *n* coche m celular.

prison yard ['priznjɑːd] *n* patio m de la cárcel.

prissy ['prisi] *adj* (*fam*) remilgado, repipi.

pristine ['pristain] *adj* prístino.

privacy ['privəsi] *n* soledad *f*, retiro m, aislamiento m; intimidad *f*; (*secrecy*) secreto m, reserva *f*; **desire for —** deseo m de estar a solas; **in search of some —** en busca de soledad; **there is no — in these flats** en estos pisos no se puede estar en privado; **in the — of one's home** en la intimidad de su casa; **in the strictest —** en el mayor secreto; **to invade someone's —** invadir la soledad de uno.

private ['praivit] **1** *adj* privado; particular; (*for — use*) propio, personal; (*confidential*) secreto, reservado, confidencial; *enterprise* privado; *life* privado, íntimo; *conversation*, *letter* íntimo, entre los dos; *opinion* personal; *arrangement*, *car*, *company*, *entrance*, *house*, *income*, *interview*, *lesson*, *room*, *school*, *secretary etc* particular; *hearing*, *sitting* secreto, a puertas cerradas; *report* secreto, confidencial; **"—"** "propiedad particular"; **"— and confidential"** "privado y confidencial"; — **person** particular mf; **my — opinion is that . . .** creo para mí que . . ., mi opinión personal es que . . .; **the wedding was —** la ceremonia se celebró en la intimidad; **to keep something —** guardar el secreto de algo; **they want to be —** quieren estar a solas; *see* **life, member, view** *etc*.
2 *n* (a) (*Mil*) soldado m raso; **P— Jones** el soldado Jones; **P— Jones!** ¡Jones!
(b) **in —** en privado; en secreto; de persona a persona, entre los dos; confidencialmente; **I have been told in — that . . .** me han dicho confidencialmente que . . . **the committee sat in —** la comisión se reunió a puerta cerrada; **the wedding was held in —** la ceremonia se celebró en la intimidad.
(c) **—s** (*Anat*) partes fpl pudendas.

privateer [,praivə'tiə*] *n* corsario m.

privately ['praivitli] *adv* privadamente, en privado; en secreto; particularmente; **the meeting was held —** la reunión fue a puerta cerrada; **the wedding took place —** la ceremonia se celebró en la intimidad; **I think that . . .** personalmente creo que . . .; **I have been told — that . . .** me han dicho confidencialmente que . . .; **but — he was very upset** pero en su corazón se sintió muy molesto; **so he spoke —** to me así que me habló de persona a persona; **he is being — educated** está en un colegio particular; tiene un profesor particular.

privation [prai'veiʃən] *n* (a) (*state*) miseria *f*, estrechez *f*; **to live in —** vivir en la miseria. (b) (*difficulty*) apuro m; **to suffer many —s** pasar muchos apuros.

privative ['privətiv] *adj* privativo.

privet ['privit] *n* ligustro m, alheña *f*.

privilege ['privilidʒ] **1** *n* privilegio m; prerrogativa *f*; (*Law*, *Parl*) inmunidad *f*; **to have parliamentary —** gozar de la inmunidad parlamentaria.
2 *vt*: **to be —d to +** *infin* tener el privilegio de + *infin*.

privileged ['privilidʒd] *adj* privilegiado; *speech* que goza de la inmunidad parlamentaria (*etc*); **for a —** **few** para unos pocos afortunados.

privily ['privili] *adv* privadamente, en privado; *tell etc* confidencialmente.

privy ['privi] **1** *adj*: **to be — to something** estar enterado secretamente de algo; *see* **council** *etc*. **2** *n* retrete m.

prize[1] [praiz] **1** n (a) premio m; **cash** — premio m en
metálico; **first** — primer premio m, (in lottery)
premio m gordo; **Nobel P**— Premio m Nobel; **to
carry off the** —, **to win the** — ganar el premio.
   (b) (Naut) presa f.
   2 adj entry, rose etc premiado; (fig) digno de
premio; excelente, de primera clase; **he's a** — **idiot**
es un tonto de capirote; **what a** — **idiot you are!**
¡imbécil!
   3 vt apreciar, estimar; **to** — **something highly**
estimar algo en mucho.
prize[2] [praiz] vt see **prise.**
prize court ['praizkɔ:t] n tribunal m de presas
marítimas.
prize fight ['praizfait] n partido m de boxeo profesional.
prize fighter ['praizfaitə*] n boxeador m profesional.
prize fighting ['praiz,faitiŋ] n boxeo m profesional.
prize giving ['praiz,giviŋ] n distribución f de
premios.
prize money ['praiz,mʌni] n (Naut) parte f de presa;
(cash) premio m en metálico; (Boxing) bolsa f.
prizewinner ['praiz,winə*] n premiado m, a f.
prize winning ['praiz,winiŋ] adj premiado.
pro[1] [prəu] prep (a) pro; en pro de.
   (b) (in compounds) pro-, eg **pro-Soviet** prosoviético; **pro-Spanish** hispanófilo; **they were
terribly pro-Franco** eran unos franquistas furi-
bundos, eran partidarios acérrimos de Franco.
   (c) **the** —**s and the cons** los pros y los contras;
we weigh up the —**s and the cons** estudiamos los
argumentos a favor y en contra.
   (d) — **forma,** — **forma invoice** factura f simulada; — **rata** a prorrateo; **the money will be shared
out** — **rata** el dinero será repartido a prorrateo, se
prorrateará el dinero; — **tempore,** — **tem** (fam) por
ahora, por el momento, interinamente.
pro[2] [prəu] n (fam) profesional mf.
probability [,prɔbə'biliti] n probabilidad f; **in all** —
según toda probabilidad; **the** — **is that** . . . es
probable que + subj.
probable ['prɔbəbl] adj probable; verosímil; **it is** —
that . . . es probable que + subj.
probably ['prɔbəbli] adv probablemente; **he will** —
come, — **he will come** es probable que venga; **he**
— **forgot** lo habrá olvidado, a lo mejor lo olvidó.
probate ['prəubit] n verificación f oficial de los testamentos; — **court** tribunal m de testamentarías; **to
value something for** — evaluar algo para la verificación oficial de testamentos.
probation [prə'beiʃən] **1** n (Law) libertad f condicional, libertad f vigilada; **to be on** — estar en
libertad condicional; **to take something on** —
tomar algo a prueba.
   2 attr: — **officer** oficial que vigila las personas que
están en libertad condicional.
probationary [prə'beiʃnəri] adj de prueba; — **period**
(Law) período m de libertad condicional.
probationer [prə'beiʃnə*] n (Law) persona f en
libertad condicional; (Med) aprendiza f de enfermera; (Eccl) novicio m, a f.
probe [prəub] **1** n (a) (Med) sonda f, tienta f; (rocket)
cohete m, proyectil m; **space** — vehículo m espacial,
vehículo m de exploración espacial.
   (b) (inquiry) investigación f, indagación f,
encuesta f; **a** — **into the drug traffic** una investigación del tráfico de narcóticos.
   2 vt (Med) sondar, tentar; ground etc sondar;
(explore) explorar; (search) registrar; (investigate)
investigar, indagar; **to** — **a mystery** investigar un
misterio.
   3 vi investigar; **to** — **into someone's past** investigar el pasado de uno; **you should have** —**d more
deeply** convenía hacer una investigación más a
fondo.
probing ['prəubiŋ] n sondeo m; investigación f;
exploración f.
probity ['prəubiti] n probidad f.
problem ['prɔbləm] **1** n problema m; **the housing** —
el problema de la vivienda; **it's a real** — realmente
es un problema.
   2 attr: — **child** niño m difícil; — **play** drama m de
tesis.
problematic [,prɔbli'mætik] adj problemático,
dudoso; **it is** — **whether** . . . es dudoso si . . .
problem page ['prɔbləm,peidʒ] n consultorio m.
proboscis [prəu'bɔsis] n probóscide f, trompa f.
procedural [prə'si:djurəl] adj procesal; relativo al
procedimiento; **a** — **question** una cuestión de
procedimiento.
procedure [prə'si:dʒə*] n procedimiento m; proceder
m; trámites mpl, tramitación f; **the usual** — **is to** +

infin lo que se hace por lo general es + infin; **the
correct** — **would be to** + infin lo correcto sería +
infin.
proceed [prə'si:d] vi (a) (go) proceder; ir; **before we**
— **any further** antes de ir más lejos; **to** — **on one's
way** seguir adelante, seguir su camino; **we** —**ed to
London** fuimos a Londres; **we** —**ed to the bar** nos
trasladamos al bar; **the ship** —**ed at 10 knots** el
barco iba a una velocidad de 10 nudos, el barco
reanudó el viaje a una velocidad de 10 nudos; **cars
should** — **slowly** los automóviles deberán ir despacio; **let us** — **with caution** avancemos con precaución.
   (b) (go on to) **how should we** —? ¿cómo hemos de
proceder?; **to** — **to blows** llegar a las manos; **to** —
to business pasar a discutir los asuntos a tratar;
let us — **to the next item** pasemos al asunto siguiente; **to** — **to do something** pasar a hacer algo,
ponerse a hacer algo, empezar a hacer algo; **he** —**ed
to drink the lot** en seguida se lo bebió todo; **he** —**ed
to say that** . . . dijo a continuación que . . .
   (c) (continue) continuar, seguir; **the text** —**s thus**
el texto sigue así; **things are** —**ing according to plan**
las cosas se están desarrollando tal como se había
previsto; **how does the story** — **after that?** ¿cómo
se desarrolla el argumento después de eso?; **they**
—**ed with their plan** prosiguieron su proyecto; —!
¡siga!
   (d) (Law etc) **to** — **against someone** proceder
contra uno, procesar a uno.
   (e) (emerge) **to** — **from** salir de; (fig) proceder de,
provenir de; **sounds** —**ed from the box** unos ruidos
salían de la caja; **this** —**s from ignorance** esto
proviene de la ignorancia.
proceeding [prə'si:diŋ] n (a) (way) procedimiento m,
modo m de proceder; proceder m; **the best** — el
mejor modo de proceder; **a somewhat dubious** — un
proceder sospechoso.
   (b) —**s** (function) acto m, actos mpl, función f; **the**
—**s began at 7 o'clock** el acto comenzó a las 7; **the**
—**s were orderly** en estos actos no sufrió alteración
el orden público.
   (c) —**s** (of learned society) actas fpl, transacciones
fpl; **P**—**s of the Royal Society** Actas fpl de la Real
Sociedad.
   (d) —**s** (measures) medidas fpl; **to take** —**s** tomar
medidas; **to take** —**s against someone** (Law)
proceder contra uno, procesar a uno; **to take legal**
—**s** entablar demanda, instruir causa.
proceeds ['prəusi:ds] npl ganancias fpl, ingresos mpl,
producto m.
process ['prəuses] **1** n (a) (proceeding) procedimiento
m; proceso m; **the** —**es of government** los trámites
gubernamentales; **the** —**es of the mind** los procedimientos de la mente; **it's a very slow** — es un
proceso muy lento.
   (b) (course) **in** — **of construction** bajo construcción, en construcción; **it is in** — **of reform** está
siendo reformado; **it is in** — **of demolition** está
siendo derribado; **in the** — **of time** con el tiempo,
andando el tiempo; **we are in** — **of removal to** . . .
estamos en vía de trasladarnos a . . .
   (c) (method) método m, sistema m; (Tech)
proceso m; **the Bessemer** — el proceso de Bessemer.
   (d) (Law) proceso m.
   (e) (Anat, Bot etc) proceso m.
   2 vt (Tech) preparar; tratar; someter a un tratamiento especial; elaborar.
process [prə'ses] vi (fam) desfilar.
processing ['prəusesiŋ] n preparación f; tratamiento
m; elaboración f.
procession [prə'seʃən] n desfile m; (Eccl) procesión f;
funeral — cortejo m fúnebre, comitiva f fúnebre;
to go (or **walk**) **in** — desfilar, (Eccl) ir en procesión.
processional [prə'seʃənl] adj procesional.
proclaim [prə'kleim] **1** vt (a) proclamar; **to** — **someone king** proclamar a uno rey.
   (b) (reveal) revelar, anunciar; **his tone** —**ed his
confidence** su tono declaraba su optimismo; **their
faces** —**ed their guilt** su culpabilidad se revelaba en
las caras.
   2 vr: **to** — **oneself king** proclamarse rey.
proclamation [,prɔklə'meiʃən] n (act) proclamación
f; (document) proclama f.
proclivity [prə'kliviti] n propensión f, inclinación f.
procrastinate [prəu'kræstineit] vi aplazar una
decisión, no resolverse; hablar (etc) con el propósito
de aplazar una decisión.
procrastination [prəu,kræsti'neiʃən] n dilación f,
falta f de resolución.
procreate ['prəukrieit] vt procrear.
procreation [,prəukri'eiʃən] n procreación f.

Procrustean [prəu'krʌstiən] *adj* de Procusto; **— bed** lecho *m* de Procusto.
Procrustes [prəu'krʌstiːz] *m* Procustes, Procusto.
proctor ['prɔktə*] *n* (*Law*) procurador *m*; (*Univ*) censor *m*, *oficial que cuida de la disciplina*.
procurable [prə'kjuərəbl] *adj* asequible; **easily —** muy asequible.
procurator ['prɔkjuəreitə*] *n* procurador *m*.
procure [prə'kjuə*] **1** *vt* obtener, conseguir; lograr; gestionar; **to — someone something, to — something for someone** obtener algo para uno; **to — some relief** conseguir cierto alivio; **to — a girl** obtener una joven para una casa de prostitución.
2 *vi* alcahuetear.
procurement [prə'kjuəmənt] *n* obtención *f*, consecución *f*.
procurer [prə'kjuərə*] *n* alcahuete *m*.
procuress [prə'kjuəris] *n* alcahueta *f*.
prod [prɔd] **1** *n* (*push*) empuje *m*; (*with elbow*) codazo *m*; (*jab*) pinchazo *m*; **to give someone a —** dar un pinchazo a uno (*also fig*); **he needs an occasional —** hay que pincharle de vez en cuando.
2 *vt* (*push*) empujar; (*with elbow*) codear, dar un codazo a; (*jab*) pinchar, punzar; (*with goad*) aguijar; **he has to be —ded along** hay que empujarle constantemente hacia adelante; **he needs to be —ded** hay que pincharle; **to — someone to do something** instar a uno a hacer algo.
3 *vi*: **he —ded at the picture with a finger** indicó el cuadro con un movimiento brusco del dedo.
prodigal ['prɔdigəl] **1** *adj* pródigo; **— of** pródigo de, pródigo en; **the — son** el hijo pródigo.
2 *n* pródigo *m*, a *f*.
prodigality [,prɔdi'gæliti] *n* prodigalidad *f*.
prodigally ['prɔdigəli] *adv* pródigamente.
prodigious [prə'didʒəs] *adj* prodigioso; enorme, vasto, ingente.
prodigiously [prə'didʒəsli] *adv* prodigiosamente, maravillosamente.
prodigy ['prɔdidʒi] *n* prodigio *m*; **child —, infant —** niño *m* prodigio.
produce ['prɔdjuːs] *n* producto *m*; (*Agr*) productos *mpl* agrícolas; **home —** productos *mpl* agrícolas nacionales.
produce [prə'djuːs] *vt* (**a**) (*bring forward, show*) presentar, mostrar; *proof* aducir, presentar; **he —d it from his pocket** lo sacó del bolsillo; **he seemed to — it out of thin air** parece que lo sacó de la nada; **how can I — £100?** ¿dónde voy yo a buscar 100 libras?; **"please — your tickets"** "se ruega mostrar los billetes"; **he could — no witnesses** no pudo nombrar ningún testigo.
(**b**) (*Theat*) *play* presentar, poner en escena; representar, dar; *actors* dirigir; **when we last —d "Hamlet"** cuando representamos "Hamlet" la última vez.
(**c**) *line* prolongar.
(**d**) (*manufacture*) producir, fabricar; (*yield*) producir; *crop, fruit* dar; *interest, profit* rendir; *offspring* dar a luz, tener; **he —s 3 novels a year** escribe (*or* publica) 3 novelas al año; **it —s 200 watts** da 200 vatios, produce 200 vatios; **the mine —s 20 tons of lead** la mina produce 20 toneladas de plomo; **Ireland does not — atomic bombs** Irlanda no fabrica bombas atómicas.
(**e**) (*cause*) causar, motivar, ocasionar, producir; acarrear; **it —d great alarm** causó mucha alarma; **this —d a sensation** esto causó una sensación; **what impression does it — on you?** ¿qué impresión te produce?
producer [prə'djuːsə*] *n* productor *m*, ora *f*; (*Theat*) director *m* de escena; (*Cine*) productor *m*; (*TV*) realizador *m*, ora *f*.
product ['prɔdʌkt] *n* (*thing produced*) producto *m*; (*result*) fruto *m*, resultado *m*, consecuencia *f*; (*Math*) producto *m*; **finished —** producto *m* terminado; **gross national —** producto *m* nacional bruto; **milk —s** productos *mpl* lácteos; **waste —s** (*Bio*) desperdicios *mpl*.
production [prə'dʌkʃən] *n* (*act*) producción *f*; (*thing produced*) producto *m*; (*Art, Theat*) producción *f*; (*Theat: performance*) presentación *f*, representación *f*; (*of actor*) dirección *f*; **the country's steel —** la producción nacional de acero; **"Peribáñez: a new — by . . ."** "Peribáñez: nueva presentación a cargo de . . ."; **the — lacked vigour** la representación carecía de vigor.
production line [prə'dʌkʃən,lain] *n* línea *f* de montaje.
productive [prə'dʌktiv] *adj* (**a**) productivo; **the factory is not yet fully —** la fábrica todavía no trabaja a plena capacidad.

(**b**) **— of** fértil en, prolífico en; **to be — of error** tener fuerte tendencia a causar errores; **it is — of nothing but trouble** no produce sino disgustos.
productivity [,prɔdʌk'tiviti] *n* productividad *f*; **when it is in full —** cuando esté trabajando a plena capacidad.
prof [prɔf] *n* (*fam*) profe *m* (*profesor*).
profanation [,prɔfə'neiʃən] *n* profanación *f*.
profane [prə'fein] **1** *adj* (**a**) (*secular, uninitiated, lay*) profano; (*irreverent*) profano, sacrílego, blasfemo.
(**b**) *language etc* fuerte, indecente; **he's very —** es un malhablado; **don't be —!** ¡no digas palabrotas!; **he became —** empezó a jurar.
2 *vt* profanar.
profanity [prə'fæniti] *n* (**a**) profanidad *f*; blasfemia *f*, impiedad *f*.
(**b**) lenguaje *m* indecente, palabrotas *fpl*; **to utter a string of profanities** soltar una serie de palabrotas.
profess [prə'fes] **1** *vt faith, belief etc* profesar; (*assent*) afirmar, declarar; *regret etc* manifestar; *ignorance etc* confesar; **I do not — to be an expert** no pretendo ser un experto; **he —es to know all about it** dice estar enterado de ello; **she —es to be 25** dice tener 25 años, afirma tener 25 años.
2 *vr*: **to — oneself satisfied** declararse satisfecho; **to — oneself unable to +** *infin* declararse incapaz de + *infin*.
professed [prə'fest] *adj* declarado; (*pej*) supuesto, ostensible; (*Eccl*) profeso.
professedly [prə'fesidli] *adv* declaradamente; (*pej*) supuestamente.
profession [prə'feʃən] *n* (**a**) (*declaration*) profesión *f*, declaración *f*; **— of faith** profesión *f* de fe.
(**b**) (*calling*) profesión *f*; oficio *m*; carrera *f*; **by — he is an engineer** es ingeniero de oficio.
professional [prə'feʃənl] **1** *adj* (**a**) profesional; de profesión, de oficio; **— man** hombre *m* profesional, hombre *m* de carrera liberal; **— diplomat** diplomático *m* de carrera; **he's a — thug** es un matón de oficio.
(**b**) (*competent*) experto, perito.
2 *n* profesional *mf*.
professionalism [prə'feʃnəlizəm] *n* (**a**) profesionalismo *m*. (**b**) pericia *f*.
professionally [prə'feʃnəli] *adv* (**a**) profesionalmente; **I never met him —** no le conocí nunca en su cargo profesional; **X, known — as Y** X conocido por Y en la profesión.
(**b**) expertamente, con pericia; **they did it most —** lo hicieron expertamente.
professor [prə'fesə*] *n* profesor *m* (universitario), profesora *f* (universitaria), catedrático *m*, a *f*; **assistant —** (*US*) profesor *m* agregado; **associate —** (*US*) profesor *m* adjunto; **full —** profesor *m* numerario, profesor *m* titular; **visiting —** profesor *m* visitante.
professorial [,prɔfə'sɔːriəl] *adj* de profesor, de catedrático; profesoral.
professorship [prə'fesəʃip] *n* cátedra *f*; **to be appointed to a —** obtener una cátedra.
proffer ['prɔfə*] *vt* ofrecer.
proficiency [prə'fiʃənsi] *n* pericia *f*, habilidad *f*.
proficient [prə'fiʃənt] *adj* perito, hábil (*at, in* en).
profile ['prəufail] *n* perfil *m*; **in —** de perfil.
profit ['prɔfit] **1** *n* (*Comm*) ganancia *f*; (*fig*) provecho *m*, beneficio *m*; utilidad *f*, ventaja *f*; **—s** ganancias *fpl*, beneficios *mpl*; **— and loss** ganancias *fpl* y pérdidas; **gross —** ganancia *f* bruta; **net —** ganancia *f* neta; **to make a — of two millions** ganar dos millones, sacar una ganancia de dos millones; **to make a — on a deal** salir ganando en un negocio; **to show (or yield) a —** dar dinero, rendir una ganancia; **to sell something at a —** vender algo con ganancia; **to turn something to —** aprovecharse de algo.
2 *vt* servir a, aprovechar a, ser de utilidad a; **what will it — him to +** *infin*? ¿qué le aprovechará + *infin*?
3 *vi* ganar; (*Comm*) sacar ganancia; **he does not seem to have —ed** no parece haber sacado provecho de ello; **to — by, to — from** aprovechar, beneficiarse de, sacar partido de; **to — by the mistakes of others** escarmentar en cabeza ajena.
profitability [,prɔfitə'biliti] *n* rentabilidad *f*.
profitable ['prɔfitəbl] *adj* provechoso, útil; ventajoso; (*Comm*) lucrativo; (*economic to run etc*) rentable; **a most — trip** un viaje sumamente provechoso; **a — investment** una inversión lucrativa; **the line is no longer —** la línea ya no es rentable; **it would be — to you to read this** Vd se beneficiará de leer esto, le sería útil leer esto.

profitably ['prɔfitəbli] *adv* con provecho, provechosamente; (*Comm*) lucrativamente, con lucro.
profiteer [,prɔfi'tiə*] **1** *n* acaparador *m*, el que hace
ganancias excesivas, (*black marketeer*) estraperlista
m. **2** *vi* hacer ganancias excesivas, cobrar más de lo
justo.
profiteering [,prɔfi'tiəriŋ] *n* ganancias *fpl* excesivas.
profitless ['prɔfitlis] *adj* inútil.
profitlessly ['prɔfitlisli] *adv* inútilmente.
profit-sharing ['prɔfit,ʃeəriŋ] *n* (*by workers*) participación *f* directa en los beneficios, (*by company*)
reparto *m* de los beneficios.
profit taking ['prɔfit,teikiŋ] *n* (*Fin*) realización *f* de
plusvalías.
profligacy ['prɔfligəsi] *n* libertinaje *m*; prodigalidad *f*.
profligate ['prɔfligit] **1** *adj* (*dissolute*) libertino,
disoluto; (*extravagant*) manirroto, pródigo. **2** *n*
libertino *m*; manirroto *m*.
profound [prə'faund] *adj* profundo.
profoundly [prə'faundli] *adv* profundamente.
profundity [prə'fʌnditi] *n* profundidad *f*.
profuse [prə'fjuːs] *adj* profuso; pródigo (*in* en); **to be
— in one's apologies** disculparse con efusión.
profusely [prə'fjuːsli] *adv* profusamente; pródigamente; **he apologized** — se disculpó con efusión; **to
sweat** — sudar muchísimo.
profusion [prə'fjuːʒən] *n* profusión *f*, abundancia *f*;
prodigalidad *f*; **a** — **of flowers** una abundancia de
flores; **trees in** — árboles *mpl* abundantes, muchísimos árboles *mpl*.
progenitor [prəu'dʒenitə*] *n* progenitor *m*.
progeny ['prɔdʒini] *n* progenie *f*, prole *f*.
prognosis [prɔg'nəusis] *n*, *pl* **prognoses** [prɔg'nəu-
siːz] (*Med*) pronóstico *m*.
prognostic [prɔg'nɔstik] *n* pronóstico *m*.
prognosticate [prɔg'nɔstikeit] *vt* pronosticar.
prognostication [prɔg,nɔsti'keiʃən] *n* (*act*, *art*)
pronosticación *f*; (*forecast*) pronóstico *m*.
programme, (*US*) **program** ['prəugræm] **1** *n* programa *m*. **2** *vt computer* programar.
programmed ['prəugræmd] *adj* programado; —
learning enseñanza *f* programada.
programmer, (*US*) **programer** ['prəugræmə*] *n*
programador *m*, ora *f*.
programme music, (*US*) **program** — ['prəugræm-
,mjuːzik] *n* música *f* de programa.
programming, (*US*) **programing** ['prəugræmiŋ] *n*
programación *f*.
progress ['prəugres] *n* progreso *m*· progresos *mpl*; (*of
events etc*) marcha *f*, desarrollo *m*; **the** — **of a student**
los progresos de un estudiante; **it is in** — está en vía
de realizarse (*etc*); **harvesting is in full** — la
cosecha está en plena marcha; **the game was
already in** — había comenzado ya el partido; **to
make** (**some**) — hacer progresos, progresar; **to make
slow** — avanzar despacio.
progress [prə'gres] *vi* hacer progresos, progresar;
avanzar; desarrollarse; **as the game** —**ed** a medida
que iba desarrollándose el partido; **matters are
—ing slowly** las cosas avanzan lentamente; **how is
the student** —**ing?** ¿qué progresos hace el estudiante?; **the patient is** —**ing favourably** el enfermo
está mejorando de modo satisfactorio.
progression [prə'greʃən] *n* progresión *f*; **arithmetical** — progresión *f* aritmética; **geometric** —
progresión *f* geométrica.
progressive [prə'gresiv] **1** *adj* progresivo; (*Pol*)
progresista. **2** *n* (*Pol*) progresista *mf*.
progressively [prə'gresivli] *adv* progresivamente;
(*Pol*) de modo progresista; **it diminishes** — disminuye progresivamente; **it's getting** — **better** se
va haciendo cada vez mejor.
progressiveness [prə'gresivnis] *n* carácter *m* progresista.
prohibit [prə'hibit] *vt* (a) (*forbid*) prohibir; **to** —
someone from doing something prohibir a uno
hacer algo; **"it is** —**ed to feed the animals"** "se
prohibe dar de comer a los animales"; **"smoking
—ed"** "se prohibe fumar", "prohibido fumar".
(b) (*prevent*) impedir; **to** — **someone from doing
something** impedir a uno hacer algo; **his health** —**s
him from swimming** su salud le impide nadar.
prohibition [,prəui'biʃən] *n* prohibición *f*; (*US*)
prohibicionismo *m*.
prohibitionism [,prəui'biʃnizəm] *n* prohibicionismo
m.
prohibitionist [,prəui'biʃnist] **1** *adj* prohibicionista.
2 *n* prohibicionista *mf*.
prohibitive [prə'hibitiv] *adj* prohibitivo; *price etc*
excesivo.
prohibitory [prə'hibitəri] *adj* prohibitorio.

project ['prɔdʒekt] *n* proyecto *m*.
project [prə'dʒekt] **1** *vt* proyectar. **2** *vi* salir, sobresalir, resaltar; **to** — **beyond** sobresalir más allá de;
to — **over** sobresalir por encima de.
projectile [prə'dʒektail] *n* proyectil *m*.
projecting [prə'dʒektiŋ] *adj* saliente.
projection [prə'dʒekʃən] *n* proyección *f*; (*overhang
etc*) saliente *m*, resalto *m*; (*knob etc*) protuberancia *f*;
(*Fin*) proyección *f*.
projectionist [prə'dʒekʃnist] *n* operador *m*, ora *f* (de
proyector).
projection room [prə'dʒekʃən,rum] *n* cabina *f* (de
proyección).
projector [prə'dʒektə*] *n* proyector *m* (de películas).
prolapse ['prəulæps] *n* prolapso *m*.
proletarian [,prəulə'teəriən] **1** *adj* proletario. **2** *n*
proletario *m*, a *f*.
proletarianism [,prəulə'teəriənizəm] *n* proletarismo
m.
proletarianize [,prəulə'teəriənaiz] *vt* proletarizar.
proletariat [,prəulə'teəriət] *n* proletariado *m*.
proliferate [prə'lifəreit] **1** *vt* multiplicar; extender.
2 *vi* proliferar, multiplicarse; extenderse.
proliferation [prə,lifə'reiʃən] *n* proliferación *f*, multiplicación *f*; extensión *f*; — **of nuclear weapons**
proliferación *f* de armas nucleares.
prolific [prə'lifik] *adj* prolífico (*of* en).
prolix ['prəuliks] *adj* prolijo.
prolixity [prau'liksiti] *n* prolijidad *f*.
prologue ['prəulɔg] *n* prólogo *m* (*to* de).
prolong [prə'lɔŋ] *vt* (*in space*) prolongar, extender;
(*in time*) alargar, extender.
prolongation [,prəulɔŋ'geiʃən] *n* prolongación *f*,
alargamiento *m*, extensión *f*.
prom [prɔm] *n* (*fam*) (a) = **promenade concert**.
(b) (*US*) baile de gala bajo los auspicios de los
alumnos de una clase universitaria.
promenade [,prɔmi'nɑːd] **1** *n* (*act*) paseo *m*; (*avenue*)
paseo *m*, avenida *f*; (*at seaside*) paseo *m* marítimo;
— **concert** concierto en el que una parte del público
permanece de pie.
2 *vt* pasear.
3 *vi* pasearse.
Prometheus [prə'miːθjuːs] *m* Prometeo.
prominence ['prɔminəns] *n* prominencia *f*; (*fig*)
eminencia *f*, importancia *f*; **to bring something into
—** hacer que algo destaque; **he came into** — **in the
Cuba affair** empezó a destacar cuando lo de Cuba;
that aspect is coming into — ese aspecto está
adquiriendo importancia.
prominent ['prɔminənt] *adj* (*jutting out*) prominente;
cheekbone, tooth etc saliente; *eye* saltón; (*fig*) eminente, importante, notable, destacado; **the most** —
article in the window el objeto que más salta a la
vista en el escaparate; **the most** — **feature of this
theory** el aspecto más notable de esta teoría; **put it
in a** — **position** ponlo muy a la vista; **to be** — **in a
deal** desempeñar un papel importante en un
negocio; **she is** — **in London society** es una figura
destacada de la buena sociedad londinense.
prominently ['prɔminəntli] *adv*: **to display something** — exponer algo muy a la vista, poner algo en
un sitio donde resulta perfectamente visible; **he
figured** — **in the case** desempeñó un papel importante en el proceso.
promiscuity [,prɔmis'kjuːiti] *n* (a) libertad *f* en las
relaciones sexuales, inmoralidad *f*, libertinaje *m*.
(b) promiscuidad *f*.
promiscuous [prə'miskjuəs] *adj* (a) *person* libre en
las relaciones sexuales, inmoral, libertino; *relationship* ilícito; *conduct* inmoral, libre.
(b) (*mixed*) promiscuo.
promiscuously [prə'miskjuəsli] *adv* (a) libremente,
de modo inmoral; ilícitamente. (b) promiscuamente.
promise ['prɔmis] **1** *n* (a) (*pledge*) promesa *f*; — **of
marriage** palabra *f* de matrimonio; **under** — **of** bajo
palabra de; **to break one's** — faltar a su palabra; **to
hold** (*or* **keep**) **someone to his** — obligar a uno a
cumplir su promesa, hacer que uno cumpla su
promesa; **to keep one's** — cumplir su promesa; **to
release someone from his** — absolver a uno de su
promesa.
(b) (*hope*) promesa *f*; esperanza *f*; porvenir *m*; **a
young man of** — un joven que promete, un joven de
porvenir; **to hold out a** — **of** dar esperanzas de; **to
show** — prometer, demostrar tener aptitudes.
2 *vti* prometer; (*forecast*) prometer, augurar,
pronosticar; **no, I** — **you** no, se lo aseguro; **to** — **to
do something** prometer hacer algo; **to** — **someone
something, to** — **something to someone** prometer
dar algo a uno; **it** —**s trouble** nos augura algo malo;
they — **us rain tomorrow** nos pronostican lluvia

para mañana; **the crop —es well** la cosecha se anuncia espléndida, la cosecha se muestra buena; **this does not — to be easy** esto me parece que no va a ser fácil.
3 *vr*: **to — oneself something** prometerse algo.
promised ['prɔmist] *adj* prometido; **land** de promisión.
promising ['prɔmisiŋ] *adj* prometedor, que promete; *future prospect* halagüeño; **a — young man** un joven que promete, un joven de porvenir; **two — candidates** dos candidatos buenos; **it doesn't look very — no** parece muy halagüeño, es una perspectiva poco atractiva.
promisingly ['prɔmisiŋli] *adv*: **it's going quite —** va bastante bien; **she plays —** toca lo bastante bien para demostrar que tiene aptitudes.
promissory ['prɔmisəri] *adj*: **— note** pagaré *m*.
promontory ['prɔməntri] *n* promontorio *m*.
promote [prə'məut] *vt* (a) *trade etc* promover, fomentar; *good feeling* fomentar; *campaign* apoyar; (*Comm*) *business* gestionar; *product* (*advertise*) dar publicidad a, hacer propaganda por, (*sell*) promover, aumentar las ventas de; *discussion etc* estimular, favorecer, facilitar; (*Parl*) *bill* presentar; *company* fundar, crear, financiar.
(b) (*in rank*) ascender; **to be —d** ser ascendido (*to the rank of colonel* a coronel); **Tarifa was —d to the first division** Tarifa fue promovida a primera división, Tarifa ascendió a primera división.
promoter [prə'məutə*] *n* promotor *m*; (*of company*) fundador *m*; (*Boxing*) empresario *m*, promotor *m*; **sales —** promotor *m* de ventas.
promotion [prə'məuʃən] *n* (a) promoción *f*, fomento *m*; apoyo *m*; gestión *f*; facilitación *f*; presentación *f*; fundación *f*, creación *f*; **sales —** promoción *f* de ventas; **"a — by Bloggs Enterprises"** "presentación de la Empresa Bloggs".
(b) (*in rank*) ascenso *m*; promoción *f*; **to get —** ser ascendido (*to* a); **to win —** (*Sport*) ser promovido, ganar la promoción, ascender.
prompt [prɔmpt] **1** *adj* pronto; *action, delivery, reply etc* pronto, inmediato; *service* rápido; *payment* puntual; *person's character* puntual; **they're very —** son muy puntuales; **"please be —"** "se ruega mucha puntualidad".
2 *adv* puntualmente; **at 6 o'clock —** a las 6 en punto.
3 *vt* (a) **to — someone to do something** mover a uno a hacer algo, incitar a uno a hacer algo; **I felt —ed to protest** me encontré en la necesidad de protestar; **what —ed you to do it?** ¿qué te movió a hacerlo?
(b) **a poem —ed by a memory** una poesía inspirada por un recuerdo; **it —s the thought that . . .** sugiere la noción de que . . ., hacer pensar que . . .
(c) (*Theat*) apuntar; **don't — her!** ¡no la ayudes a recordar!, ¡no le soples cosas al oído!; **the witness had to be —ed** fue necesario recordar unos hechos al testigo, hubo que traer ciertas cosas a la memoria del testigo.
4 *vi* (*Theat*) apuntar.
5 *n* (*Theat*) apuntador *m*, ora *f*.
prompt box ['prɔmptbɔks] *n* concha *f* (del apuntador).
prompter ['prɔmptə*] *n* apuntador *m*, ora *f*.
prompting ['prɔmptiŋ] *n*: **without —** sin ayuda de nadie, sin tener que consultar el texto (*etc*); **the —s of conscience** los escrúpulos de la conciencia; **the —s of love** los dictados del amor.
promptitude ['prɔmptitjuːd] *n see* **promptness.**
promptly ['prɔmptli] *adv* puntualmente, con prontitud; inmediatamente; rápidamente; **they do it very —** lo hacen con toda prontitud; **they left — at 6** partieron a las 6 en punto.
promptness ['prɔmptnis] *n* prontitud *f*, puntualidad *f*; rapidez *f*.
promulgate ['prɔmʌlgeit] *vt* promulgar.
promulgation [,prɔmʌl'geiʃən] *n* promulgación *f*.
prone [prəun] *adj* (a) **to be —** estar postrado (boca abajo).
(b) **to be — to** + *n* ser propenso a + *n*, estar inclinado a + *n*; **to be — to** + *infin* ser propenso a + *infin*.
proneness ['prəunnis] *n* propensión *f* (*to* a).
prong [prɔŋ] *n* punta *f*, púa *f*, diente *m*.
-pronged [prɔŋd] *adj*: *eg* **three-pronged** de tres puntas.
pronominal [prəu'nɔminl] *adj* pronominal.
pronoun ['prəunaun] *n* pronombre *m*; **personal —** pronombre *m* personal; **possessive —** pronombre *m* posesivo; **reflexive —** pronombre *m* reflexivo.

pronounce [prə'nauns] **1** *vt* (*Gram, Law*) pronunciar; (*with adj*) declarar; **they —d him unfit to** + *infin* le declararon incapaz de + *infin*.
2 *vi*: **to — in favour of something** pronunciarse en favor de algo; **to — on something** expresar una opinión sobre algo, juzgar algo.
pronounced [prə'naunst] *adj* marcado, fuerte; decidido.
pronouncement [prə'naunsmənt] *n* declaración *f*; opinión *f*; **to make a —** pronunciarse, hacer una declaración (*about* sobre).
pronto ['prɔntəu] *adv* (*US fam*) pronto.
pronunciation [prə,nʌnsi'eiʃən] *n* pronunciación *f*.
proof [pruːf] **1** *n* (a) prueba *f* (*also Math etc*); comprobación *f*; **positive —, — positive** prueba *f* concluyente; **. . ., — positive that . . .,** lo cual es prueba concluyente de que . . .; **in — of** en prueba de, en comprobación de; **como señal de**; **in — whereof** en fe de lo cual; **it is — that he is poor** es prueba de su pobreza; **to adduce — to the contrary** aducir hechos que prueban lo contrario; **to give** (*or* **show**) **— of** dar prueba de; **the onus of — lies with the accuser** le cumple al acusador probar lo que dice.
(b) (*Typ*) prueba *f*; **—s** pruebas *fpl*; **to read the —s** corregir las pruebas.
(c) (*of alcohol*) graduación *f* normal; **this drink is 70% —** esta bebida tiene una graduación de 70 por 100.
2 *adj* (a) *drink* de graduación normal.
(b) **to be — against something** ser (*or* estar) a prueba de algo; **it is — against moisture** está a prueba de la humedad; **I'm not — against temptation** yo no soy insensible a la tentación.
(c) *eg* **bullet-proof** a prueba de balas.
3 *vt* impermeabilizar.
proofread ['pruːfriːd] (*irr: see* **read**) *vt* corregir las pruebas de.
proofreader ['pruːf,riːdə*] *n* corrector *m* de pruebas.
proofreading ['pruːf,riːdiŋ] *n* corrección *f* de pruebas.
proof sheets ['pruːfʃiːts] *npl* pruebas *fpl*.
proof spirit ['pruːf'spirit] *n* licor *m* de prueba.
prop [prɔp] **1** *n* apoyo *m*; (*Archit*) puntal *m*; (*Agr*) horca *f*, rodrigón *m*; (*Min*) peón *m*, entibo *m*; (*Naut*) escora *f*; (*fig*) sostén *m*.
2 *vt* (*also* **to — up**) apoyar; apuntalar; apoyar con rodrigón (*etc*); (*fig*) apoyar, sostener; **to — a ladder against a wall** apoyar una escalera contra una pared; **the company was —ped up by a big loan** la compañía recibió el apoyo de un préstamo cuantioso.
3 *vr*: **to — oneself against a tree** apoyarse contra un árbol.
propaganda [,prɔpə'gændə] *n* propaganda *f*.
propagandist [,prɔpə'gændist] *n* propagandista *mf*.
propagate ['prɔpəgeit] **1** *vt* propagar. **2** *vi* propagarse.
propagation [,prɔpə'geiʃən] *n* propagación *f*.
propel [prə'pel] *vt* impulsar, propulsar; (*push*) empujar; **it is —led by turbines** está propulsado por turbinas.
propellent [prə'pelənt] *n* propulsor *m*.
propeller [prə'pelə*] *n* hélice *f*.
propeller shaft [prə'peləʃɑːft] *n* árbol *m* de la hélice.
propelling pencil [prə'peliŋ'pensl] *n* lapicero *m*, portaminas *m*.
propensity [prə'pensiti] *n* propensión *f* (*to* a).
proper ['prɔpə*] **1** *adj* (a) (*peculiar, characteristic*) propio, peculiar; característico; *name* propio; **the qualities which are — to it** las cualidades que le son propias, las cualidades que son propias de él.
(b) (*correct*) verdadero, exacto, apropiado; **physics — la** física propiamente dicha; **in the — sense of the word** en el sentido estricto de la palabra.
(c) (*fam*) **he's a — rogue** es un verdadero pillo; **it's a — nuisance** es una verdadera molestia; **he's a — gentleman** now ya es un caballero hecho y derecho; **we got a — beating** nos dieron una paliza de las buenas; **there was a — row** hubo un lío de todos los diablos.
(d) (*right, suitable*) apropiado, conveniente; oportuno; debido; justo, exacto; **in — condition** en buen estado; **at the — time** en el momento oportuno; **in the — way** convenientemente, del modo conveniente; **as you think —** según le parezca; **do as you think —** haga lo que le parezca bien; **to do the — thing by someone** tratar a uno con justicia; **to say the — thing** decir lo que piden las circunstancias; **it was the — thing to say** fue lo que había que decir; **in a style — to his station** en un estilo que conviene a su rango; **I think it — to** + *infin* creo hacer bien en + *infin*.

(e) (*seemly*) decente; correcto; — **behaviour** conducta *f* correcta; **what is** — lo que está bien; **it is not** — **for you to** + *infin* no está bien que Vd + *subj*; **it's not** — **with children about** no es decente si hay niños delante.

(f) (*prim and* —) etiquetero, relamido; formal.

(g) (*Her*) natural.

2 *adv* (*fam*) **it's** — **difficult** es realmente difícil, es dificilísimo; **we were** — **puzzled** quedamos totalmente perplejos.

properly ['prɔpəli] *adv* **(a)** (*correctly etc*) correctamente, apropiadamente, debidamente; **a word** — **used** una palabra correctamente empleada; — **speaking** propiamente dicho; en el sentido estricto de la palabra; **it is not** — **so called** no es correcto llamarlo así, no se llama así en propiedad, en propiedad no se dice así; **she very** — **refused** se negó a ello e hizo bien; **to do something** — hacer algo bien, hacer algo como se debe, hacer algo como Dios manda.

(b) (*in seemly fashion*) decentemente; correctamente; **not** — **dressed** incorrectamente vestido; **to behave** — portarse correctamente; **behave** —**!** ¡estáte formal!

(c) (*intensive*) **we were** — **ashamed** nos avergonzamos de verdad; **we got** — **beaten** nos dieron una paliza de las buenas; **we were** — **puzzled** quedamos totalmente perplejos.

propertied ['prɔpətid] *adj* adinerado, acaudalado.

property ['prɔpəti] *n* **(a)** (*quality*) propiedad *f*; **the properties of this substance** las propiedades de esta sustancia.

(b) (*thing owned*) propiedad *f*; bienes *mpl*; (*estate*) hacienda *f*, finca *f*, propiedad *f*; **personal** — bienes *mpl* muebles; cosas *fpl* personales; **real** — (US) bienes *mpl* raíces; **that's my** — eso es mío; **whose** — **is this?** ¿de quién es esto?; **it doesn't seem to be anyone's** — no parece que tenga dueño, no parece que pertenezca a nadie; **that news is common** — eso lo saben todos ya, esa noticia es ya del dominio público; **it is common** — **that ...** todos saben que ...; **it became the** — **of Mr Jones** pasó a ser propiedad del Sr Jones; **she left her** — **to X** dejó sus bienes a X.

(c) **properties** (*Theat*) accesorios *mpl*.

property owner ['prɔpəti,əunə*] *n* dueño *m* de una finca, dueña *f* de una finca; (*landed gentry*) terrateniente *mf*.

property tax ['prɔpəti,tæks] *n* impuesto *m* sobre la propiedad.

prophecy ['prɔfisi] *n* profecía *f*.

prophesy ['prɔfisai] *vt* profetizar; (*fig*) predecir, prever, augurar (*that* que).

prophet ['prɔfit] *n* profeta *m*.

prophetess ['prɔfitis] *n* profetisa *f*.

prophetic [prə'fetik] *adj* profético.

prophetically [prə'fetikəli] *adv* proféticamente.

prophylactic [,prɔfi'læktik] **1** *adj* profiláctico. **2** *n* profiláctico *m*.

prophylaxis [,prɔfi'læksis] *n* profilaxis *f*.

propinquity [prə'piŋkwiti] *n* propincuidad *f*; (*kinship*) consanguinidad *f*, parentesco *m*.

propitiate [prə'piʃieit] *vt* propiciar.

propitiation [prə,piʃi'eiʃən] *n* propiciación *f*.

propitiatory [prə'piʃiətəri] *adj* propiciatorio, conciliatorio.

propitious [prə'piʃəs] *adj* propicio, favorable.

propitiously [prə'piʃəsli] *adv* de modo propicio, bajo signo propicio, favorablemente.

proportion [prə'pɔːʃən] *n* **(a)** proporción *f* (*also* Math); parte *f*, porción *f*, porcentaje *m*; **the** — **of blacks to whites** la proporción entre negros y blancos; **what** — **is in private hands?** ¿qué porción queda en manos de particulares?; **in equal** —**s** por partes iguales; **in due** — en su justa medida; **in** — **as** a medida que; **in** — **to** en proporción con, a medida de; **and the rest in** — y lo demás en proporción, (*Comm*) y lo demás a prorrateo; **to be out of** — ser desproporcionado; **to be out of** — **with** (*or* to) no guardar proporción con.

(b) **sense of** — sentido *m* de la medida.

(c) —**s** dimensiones *fpl*.

proportional [prə'pɔːʃənl] *adj* proporcional; (*representation etc*) proporcional; — **to** en proporción con, a medida de; **X is not** — **to Y** X no guarda proporción con Y.

proportionally [prə'pɔːʃnəli] *adv* proporcionalmente, en proporción.

proportionate [prə'pɔːʃnit] *adj* proporcionado.

proportionately [prə'pɔːʃnitli] *adv* proporcionadamente, en proporción.

proportioned [prə'pɔːʃnd] *adj*: **well** — bien proporcionado, de forma elegante; *person* de talle elegante.

proposal [prə'pəuzl] *n* **(a)** propuesta *f*, proposición *f*; oferta *f*; (*to girl*) declaración *f* (de amor); — **of marriage** oferta *f* de matrimonio, (*formally*) petición *f* de mano; **to make a** — hacer una propuesta; **to make the** — **that ...** proponer que ...

(b) (*plan*) proyecto *m*; (*notion*) idea *f*; (*suggestion*) sugerencia *f*; **my** — **was to** + *infin* mi idea era de + *infin*; **it is a new** — **to reform the currency** es un nuevo proyecto para reformar la moneda.

propose [prə'pəuz] **1** *vt* **(a)** proponer; ofrecer; *motion* proponer; *candidate* proponer, nombrar; **to** — **marriage to someone** hacer una oferta de matrimonio a una, (*formally*) pedir la mano de una a su padre; **to** — **someone for membership of a club** nombrar a uno como socio de un club; **what course do you** —**?** ¿qué línea de acción nos recomienda Vd?

(b) **to** — **someone's health** brindar por uno.

2 *vi* **(a)** **to** — **to** + *infin* proponerse + *infin*; pensar + *infin*, tener la intención de + *infin*; **what do you** — **doing?** ¿qué piensas hacer?

(b) **Man** —**s, God disposes** el hombre propone y Dios dispone.

(c) (*to girl*) declararse (*to* a); **to** — **to someone** (*formally*) hacer una oferta de matrimonio a una, pedir la mano de una a su padre.

proposer [prə'pəuzə*] *n* (*Parl etc*) proponente *mf*.

proposition [,prɔpə'ziʃən] *n* **(a)** (*statement*, Math, Logic *etc*) proposición *f*; (*proposal*) propuesta *f*, proposición *f*; oferta *f*; (*plan*) proyecto *m*.

(b) (*job*) tarea *f*; (*enterprise*) empresa *f*, cosa *f*; (*problem*) problema *m*; (*objective*) propósito *m*; (*opponent*) adversario *m*, a *f*; (*prospect*) perspectiva *f*; **it's a tough** — es mucho pedir; **he's a tough** — es un adversario fuerte; **the journey alone is quite a** — sólo el viaje pide grandes esfuerzos; **it will be a paying** — dará dinero; **it's not an economic** — no es rentable.

propound [prə'paund] *vt* proponer, exponer, presentar.

proprietary [prə'praiətəri] *adj* propietario; *article* patentado.

proprietor [prə'praiətə*] *n* propietario *m*, dueño *m*.

proprietorship [prə'praiətəʃip] *n* propiedad *f*, posesión *f*.

proprietress [prə'praiətris] *n* propietaria *f*, dueña *f*.

propriety [prə'praiəti] *n* (*seemliness*) decoro *m*, decencia *f*, corrección *f*; (*fitness*) conveniencia *f*; **the proprieties** las convenciones, los cánones sociales, el decoro; **breach of** — ofensa *f* contra el decoro; **to observe the proprieties** atenerse a los cánones sociales; **to throw** — **to the winds** abandonar totalmente el decoro.

props [prɔps] *npl* (*Theat*: *fam*) accesorios *mpl*.

propulsion [prə'pʌlʃən] *n* propulsión *f*.

prorate ['prəureit] (US) **1** *n* prorrata *f*. **2** *vt* prorratear.

prorogation [,prəurəu'geiʃən] *n* prorrogación *f*.

prorogue [prə'rəug] *vt* prorrogar.

prosaic [prəu'zeiik] *adj* prosaico.

prosaically [prəu'zeiikəli] *adv* prosaicamente.

proscenium [prəu'siːniəm] *n* proscenio *m*.

proscribe [prəus'kraib] *vt* proscribir.

proscription [prəus'kripʃən] *n* proscripción *f*.

prose [prəuz] **1** *n* prosa *f*. **2** *attr* de prosa; **in** — en prosa.

prosecute ['prɔsikjuːt] *vt* **(a)** (Law) procesar; *claim* demandar en juicio; **to** — **someone for theft** procesar a uno por ladrón; **to be** — **d for a traffic offence** ser procesado por una infracción del código; **"trespassers will be** —**d"** "se procederá contra los intrusos".

(b) (*follow up*) proseguir, continuar, llevar adelante.

prosecution [,prɔsi'kjuːʃən] *n* **(a)** (*Law: case*) proceso *m*, causa *f*, juicio *m*; (*act*) acusación *f*, procesamiento *m*; (*side*) parte *f* actora; **counsel for the** — fiscal *m*; **to start a** — **against someone** entablar juicio contra uno.

(b) prosecución *f*; **in the** — **of his duty** en el cumplimiento de su deber.

prosecutor ['prɔsikjuːtə*] *n* acusador *m*; (*also* **public** —) fiscal *m*.

proselyte ['prɔsilait] *n* prosélito *m* a *f*.

proselytism ['prɔsilitizəm] *n* proselitismo *m*.

proselytize ['prɔsilitaiz] *vi* ganar prosélitos, convertir a las personas a la secta de uno.

prose writer ['prəuz,raitə*] *n* prosista *mf*.

prosody ['prɔsədi] *n* métrica *f*.

prospect ['prɔspekt] n (a) (view) vista f, panorama m; the — from the window la vista desde la ventana; a — of Toledo una vista de Toledo; where every — pleases donde todo deleita la vista.
(b) (outlook) perspectiva f; (hope) esperanza f; (future) porvenir m; what a —! (iro) ¡qué perspectiva más halagüeña!; future —s perspectivas fpl del futuro; —s are really good las perspectivas son francamente buenas; "good —s" (advert for job) "buenas perspectivas de mejora"; it's a grim — es una perspectiva nada atractiva; there are —s of a fine day el día se presenta muy bueno; —s for the harvest are poor la cosecha se anuncia más bien mediocre; his —s are outstandingly good le espera un gran porvenir; he has no —s no tiene porvenir; this — cheered him up se alegró con esta perspectiva; we are faced with the — of + ger nos encontramos ante la perspectiva de + infin; to have something in — esperar algo; to hold out a — of dar esperanzas de.
(c) (chance) probabilidad f, posibilidad f; the — of an early peace la posibilidad de una pronta paz; there is little — of his coming hay pocas posibilidades de que venga; to dangle a — before someone ofrecer a uno la posibilidad de + infin, tentar a uno con la posibilidad de + infin; I see no — of that eso no lo creo probable.
(d) (person) persona f en perspectiva; (Comm) cliente m posible, comprador m (etc) probable; is he a — for the team? ¿vale considerarle como posible miembro del equipo?; he's not much of a — for her no vale gran cosa como posible marido de ella.
prospect [prəs'pekt] 1 vt explorar. 2 vi: to — for buscar.
prospecting [prəs'pektiŋ] n (Min) prospección f.
prospective [prəs'pektiv] adj anticipado, esperado, probable; son-in-law etc futuro; heir presunto; legislation etc en perspectiva.
prospector [prəs'pektə*] n explorador m; gold — buscador m de oro.
prospectus [prəs'pektəs] n prospecto m; programa m; folleto m informativo.
prosper ['prɔspə*] 1 vt favorecer, fomentar. 2 vi prosperar; medrar; florecer.
prosperity [prɔs'periti] n prosperidad f.
prosperous ['prɔspərəs] adj próspero.
prosperously ['prɔspərəsli] adv prósperamente.
prostate ['prɔsteit] n próstata f.
prosthetic [prɔs'θetik] adj (Ling, Med) prostético.
prostitute ['prɔstitjuːt] 1 n prostituta f. 2 vt prostituir (also fig).
prostitution [.prɔsti'tjuːʃən] n prostitución f.
prostrate ['prɔstreit] adj postrado; (fig) postrado, abatido (with por).
prostrate [prɔs'treit] 1 vt postrar; (fig) postrar, abatir; to be —d by grief ser postrado por el dolor. 2 vr: to — oneself prostrarse.
prostration [prɔs'treiʃən] n postración f; (fig) postración f, abatimiento m.
prosy ['prəuzi] adj prosaico, aburrido.
protagonist [prəu'tægənist] n protagonista mf.
protean ['prəutiən] adj proteico.
protect [prə'tekt] vt proteger (against, from contra, de).
protection [prə'tekʃən] n protección f; (Comm) protección f, proteccionismo m; to be under someone's — estar bajo la protección de uno.
protectionism [prə'tekʃənizəm] n proteccionismo m.
protectionist [prə'tekʃənist] 1 adj proteccionista. 2 n proteccionista mf.
protective [prə'tektiv] adj protector; custody preventivo; (Comm) duty, policy proteccionista.
protectively [prə'tektivli] adv protectoramente, de modo protector.
protector [prə'tektə*] n protector m.
protectorate [prə'tektərit] n protectorado m.
protégé ['prɔteʒei] n protegido m, ahijado m.
protégée ['prɔteʒei] n protegida f, ahijada f.
protein ['prəutiːn] n proteína f.
protest ['prəutest] n protesta f; under — bajo protesta, haciendo objeciones; I'll do it but under — lo haré pero que conste mi protesta; to make a — hacer una protesta.
protest [prə'test] 1 vt (a) (complain) protestar; to — that protestar de que.
(b) (affirm) afirmar, declarar (enérgicamente, solemnemente etc).
2 vi protestar; to — against protestar de, protestar contra.
Protestant ['prɔtistənt] 1 adj protestante. 2 n protestante mf.
Protestantism ['prɔtistəntizəm] n protestantismo m.

protestation [.prɔtes'teiʃən] n (a) protesta f. (b) afirmación f, declaración f (enérgica, solemne etc).
proto ... ['prəutəu] proto ...
protocol ['prəutəkɔl] n protocolo m.
proton ['prəutɔn] n protón m.
protoplasm ['prəutəuplæzəm] n protoplasma m.
prototype ['prəutəutaip] n prototipo m.
protract [prə'trækt] vt prolongar; extender, alargar.
protracted [prə'træktid] adj largo, prolongado.
protraction [prə'trækʃən] n prolongación f; extensión f, alargamiento m.
protractor [prə'træktə*] n transportador m.
protrude [prə'truːd] 1 vt sacar fuera. 2 vi salir (fuera), sobresalir.
protruding [prə'truːdiŋ] adj saliente; eye, tooth saltón.
protrusion [prə'truːʒən] n saliente m, protuberancia f.
protuberance [prə'tjuːbərəns] n protuberancia f, saliente m.
protuberant [prə'tjuːbərənt] adj protuberante, saliente; prominente; (tooth) saltón.
proud [praud] adj (a) (of person etc) orgulloso; (pej) soberbio, arrogante, altanero; as — as a peacock más orgulloso que un pavo real; to be — of estar orgulloso de, enorgullecerse de, preciarse de, ufanarse de; to be — that ... estar orgulloso de que ...; to be — to + infin tener el honor de + infin, estar orgulloso de + infin; to do oneself — (fam) darse buena vida; permitirse cosas de lujo; to do someone — hacer muchas fiestas a uno, tratar a uno con toda clase de atenciones, (with food) dar muy bien de comer a uno.
(b) (imposing) espléndido, imponente; (glorious) glorioso; it is a — day for us es un día glorioso para nosotros; a — ship un magnífico buque.
proudly ['praudli] adv (a) orgullosamente; say etc con orgullo; arrogantemente. (b) de modo imponente.
prove [pruːv] 1 vt probar; (verify) comprobar; (show) demostrar; (confirm) confirmar; will verificar; this —s that ... esto prueba que ...; the exception —s the rule la excepción confirma la regla; can you — it? ¿tiene Vd prueba de ello?; you can't — anything against me Vd no puede demostrarme nada; it remains to be —d whether ... queda por demostrar si ...; it all goes to — that ... todo sirve para demostrar que ...; he was —d right in the end por fin quedó demostrado que había tenido razón; to — someone innocent demostrar la inocencia de uno.
2 vi resultar; if it —s useful si resulta ser útil; the news —d false resultó que la noticia era falsa; she —d unequal to the job resultó que ella no estaba al nivel del puesto; if it —s otherwise si sale al contrario, si resulta que no es así.
3 vr: to — oneself ponerse a prueba.
provenance ['prɔvinəns] n origen m, punto m de origen.
Provençal [.prɔvãːn'saːl] 1 adj provenzal. 2 n provenzal mf. 3 n (language) provenzal m.
Provence [prɔ'vãːns] Provenza f.
provender ['prɔvində*] n forraje m; (hum) provisiones fpl, comida f.
proverb ['prɔvəːb] n refrán m, proverbio m.
proverbial [prə'vəːbiəl] adj proverbial.
proverbially [prə'vəːbiəli] adv proverbialmente.
provide [prə'vaid] 1 vt (a) (supply, furnish) suministrar, surtir; dar, proporcionar; to — someone with something (supply) proveer a uno de algo, suministrar algo a uno; (give) proporcionar algo a uno; the car is —d with a heater el coche está provisto de un calentador; can you — a substitute? ¿pueden encontrar un suplente?; the government —d half the money el gobierno proporcionó la mitad del dinero; the plant will — an output of ... la fábrica permitirá una producción de ...; it —s shade for the cows da sombra para las vacas.
(b) to — that ... estipular que ..., disponer que ...
2 vi (a) God will — Dios proveerá; a husband who —s well un marido que mantiene debidamente a su familia.
(b) to — against precaverse de, tomar precauciones contra; to — for someone mantener a uno, proporcionar medios de vida a uno, (with an allowance) señalar una pensión a uno; they are well —d for tienen medios adecuados; to — for one's dependents asegurar el porvenir de su familia; to — for every contingency prevenir cualquier posibilidad; we have —d for that eso lo hemos previsto.
(c) the treaty —s for ... el tratado estipula ...; as —d for in the 1970 contract de acuerdo con lo estipulado en el contrato de 1970.
3 vr: to — oneself with something proveerse de algo.

provided [prə'vaidid] *conj*: —, — **that** con tal que + *subj*, siempre que + *subj*; a condición de que + *subj*.
providence ['prɔvidəns] *n* (*all senses*) providencia *f*; P— Divina Providencia *f*.
provident ['prɔvidənt] *adj* providente, previsor, próvido.
providential [‚prɔvi'denʃəl] *adj* providencial; (*lucky*) afortunado, milagroso.
providentially [‚prɔvi'denʃəli] *adv* providencialmente; afortunadamente, milagrosamente.
providently ['prɔvidəntli] *adv* próvidamente.
provider [prə'vaidə*] *n* proveedor *m*, ora *f*.
providing [prə'vaidiŋ] *conj* = **provided**.
province ['prɔvins] *n* (**a**) provincia *f*; **they live in the** —**s** viven en provincia.
(**b**) (*fig: field*) esfera *f*; especialidad *f*; (*jurisdiction etc*) competencia *f*; **it's not within my** — no es de mi competencia.
provincial [prə'vinʃəl] **1** *adj* provincial, de provincia; (*pej*) provinciano. **2** *n* provinciano *m*, a *f*.
provincialism [prə'vinʃəlizəm] *n* provincialismo *m*.
provision [prə'viʒən] **1** *n* (**a**) (*in general*) provisión *f*; (*supply*) provisión *f*, suministro *m*; abastecimiento *m*; **the** — **of new capital** la provisión de nuevos capitales; **the** — **of new housing** la provisión de nuevas viviendas; **to make** — **for** prevenir, prever; **to make** — **for one's family** asegurar el porvenir de su familia.
(**b**) —**s** (*food*) provisiones *fpl*, comestibles *mpl*, víveres *mpl*.
(**c**) (*stipulation*) estipulación *f*, disposición *f*; **according to the** —**s of the treaty** de acuerdo con lo estipulado en el tratado; **there is no** — **to the contrary** no hay estipulación que lo prohiba; **it comes within the** —**s of this law** está comprendido dentro de lo estipulado por esta ley.
2 *vt* aprovisionar, abastecer.
provisional [prə'viʒənl] *adj* provisional; interino.
provisionally [prə'viʒnəli] *adv* provisionalmente; con carácter provisional; interinamente.
proviso [prə'vaizəu] *n* condición *f*, estipulación *f*; **with the** — **that** . . . con la condición de que + *subj*.
provocation [‚prɔvə'keiʃən] *n* provocación *f*; **to act under** — obrar bajo provocación; **to suffer great** — sufrir una gran provocación.
provocative [prə'vɔkətiv] *adj remark etc* provocador, provocativo; *title* provocador; *book etc* sugestivo, que invita a pensar; **she's a very** — **woman** es una mujer muy provocativa; **now you're trying to be** — ahora intentas hacerme perder los estribos.
provocatively [prə'vɔkətivli] *adv* de modo provocativo.
provoke [prə'vəuk] *vt* (*cause*) causar, producir, motivar; facilitar; (*rouse, move*) provocar, incitar, mover (*to* a); (*anger*) provocar; irritar; **it** —**d us to action** nos incitó a obrar; **it** —**d the town to revolt** incitó la ciudad a sublevarse; **he is easily** —**d** se irrita con cualquier cosa.
provoking [prə'vəukiŋ] *adj* provocativo; irritante, fastidioso; **how very** —! ¡qué lata!
provost ['prɔvəst] *n* (*Univ*) rector *m*; director *m*; (*Scot*) alcalde *m*.
provost marshal [prə'vəu'mɑːʃəl] *n* capitán *m* preboste.
prow [prau] *n* proa *f*.
prowess ['prauis] *n* (*skill*) destreza *f*, habilidad *f*; (*courage*) valor *m*.
prowl [praul] **1** *n* ronda *f* (en busca de presa, botín *etc*).
2 *vt*: **to** — **the streets** rondar las calles, vagar por las calles.
3 *vi* rondar (en busca de presa, botín *etc*); **he** —**s round the house at night** (*outside*) ronda la casa de noche, (*inside*) se pasea por la casa de noche.
prowler ['praulə*] *n* rondador *m*, hombre *m* que ronda en busca de presa (*or* mujeres *etc*); ladrón *m*.
proximity [prɔk'simiti] *n* proximidad *f*; **in** — **to** cerca de, junto a.
proximo ['prɔksiməu] *adv* (*Comm*) del mes próximo.
proxy ['prɔksi] *n* (*power*) poder *m*, procuración *f*; (*person*) apoderado *m*, a *f*; sustituto *m*, a *f*; **by** — por poder, por poderes; **to be married by** — casarse por poderes.
prude [pruːd] *n* remilgada *f*, gazmoña *f*.
prudence ['pruːdəns] *n* prudencia *f*.
prudent ['pruːdənt] *adj* prudente.
prudential [pru(ː)'denʃəl] *adj* prudencial.
prudently ['pruːdəntli] *adv* prudentemente, con prudencia.
prudery ['pruːdəri] *n* remilgo *m*, gazmoñería *f*.
prudish ['pruːdiʃ] *adj* remilgado, gazmoño.
prudishness ['pruːdiʃnis] *n* see **prudery**.
prune[1] [pruːn] *n* ciruela *f* pasa.

prune[2] [pruːn] *vt* podar; (*fig*) reducir, escamondar.
pruning ['pruːniŋ] *n* poda *f*.
pruning hook ['pruːniŋhuk] *n*, **pruning knife** ['pruːniŋnaif] *n*, **pruning shears** ['pruːniŋʃiəz] *npl* podadera *f*.
prurience ['pruəriəns] *n* salacidad *f*.
prurient ['pruəriənt] *adj* salaz.
Prussia ['prʌʃə] Prusia *f*.
Prussian ['prʌʃən] **1** *adj* prusiano. **2** *n* prusiano *m*, a *f*.
prussic ['prʌsik] *adj*: — **acid** ácido *m* prúsico.
pry[1] [prai] *vi* (*watch*) fisgonear, curiosear; (*meddle*) entrometerse; **to** — **into someone's affairs** entrometerse en lo ajeno; **to** — **into someone's secrets** tratar de saber los secretos de uno.
pry[2] [prai] *vt* (*US*) see **prise**.
prying ['praiiŋ] *adj* fisgón, curioso; entrometido.
psalm [sɑːm] *n* salmo *m*.
psalmist ['sɑːmist] *n* salmista *m*.
psalmody ['sælmədi] *n* salmodia *f*.
psalter ['sɔːltə*] *n* salterio *m*.
psephologist [se'fɔlədʒist] *n* psefólogo *m* (se— *Acad*).
psephology [se'fɔlədʒi] *n* psefología *f* (se— *Acad*).
pseudo . . . ['sjuːdəu] seudo . . .; falso, fingido, *eg* **a pseudo-artist** un falso artista.
pseudo ['sjuːdəu] *adj* (*fam*) falso, fraudulento; *person* fingido; (*of person's character*) artificial, afectado.
pseudonym ['sjuːdənim] *n* seudónimo *m*.
pseudonymous [sjuːˈdɔniməs] *adj* seudónimo.
pshaw [pʃɔː] *interj* ¡bah!
psittacosis [‚psitə'kəusis] *n* psitacosis *f*.
psych . . . [saik] psic . . ., psiqu . . .; *the Academy recommends the spelling* sic . . ., siqu . . .
Psyche ['saiki] *f* Psique.
psyche ['saiki] *n* psique *f*.
psychedelic [‚saiki'delik] *adj* psiquedélico.
psychiatric [‚saiki'ætrik] *adj* psiquiátrico.
psychiatrist [sai'kaiətrist] *n* psiquiatra *mf*.
psychiatry [sai'kaiətri] *n* psiquiatría *f*.
psychic(al) ['saikik(əl)] *adj* psíquico.
psycho ['saikəu] *n* (*US fam*) caso *m* psicológico, persona *f* anormal.
psychoanalyse, (US) **psychoanalyze** [‚saikəu-'ænəlaiz] *vt* psicoanalizar.
psychoanalysis [‚saikəuə'nælisis] *n* psicoanálisis *m*.
psychoanalyst [‚saikəu'ænəlist] *n* psicoanalista *mf*.
psychological [‚saikə'lɔdʒikəl] *adj* psicológico.
psychologically [‚saikə'lɔdʒikəli] *adv* psicológicamente.
psychologist [sai'kɔlədʒist] *n* psicólogo *m*.
psychology [sai'kɔlədʒi] *n* psicología *f*.
psychoneurosis ['saikəunjuə'rəusis] *n*, *pl* **psychoneuroses** ['saikəunjuə'rəusiːz] psiconeurosis *f*.
psychopath ['saikəupæθ] *n* psicópata *mf*.
psychopathic [‚saikəu'pæθik] *adj* psicopático.
psychopathology ['saikəupə'θɔlədʒi] *n* psicopatología *f*.
psychosis [sai'kəusis] *n* psicosis *f*.
psychosomatic ['saikəusəu'mætik] *adj* psicosomático.
psychotherapy ['saikəu'θerəpi] *n* psicoterapia *f*.
psychotic [sai'kɔtik] **1** *adj* psicótico. **2** *n* psicótico *m*, a *f*.
ptarmigan ['tɑːmigən] *n* perdiz *f* blanca, perdiz *f* nival.
pterodactyl [‚terəu'dæktil] *n* pterodáctilo *m*.
Ptolemaic [‚tɔlə'meiik] *adj*: — **system** sistema *m* de Tolomeo.
Ptolemy ['tɔləmi] *m* Tolomeo.
ptomaine ['təumein] *n* ptomaína *f*; — **poisoning** envenenamiento *m* ptomaínico.
pub [pʌb] *n* (*fam*) taberna *f*, tasca *f*, bar *m*.
pub crawl ['pʌbkrɔːl] (*fam*) **1** *n* chateo *m* (de tasca en tasca); **to go on a** — = **2 pub-crawl** *vi* ir de chateo, copear, alternar.
puberty ['pjuːbəti] *n* pubertad *f*.
pubescence [pjuː'besəns] *n* pubescencia *f*.
pubescent [pjuː'besənt] *adj* pubescente.
pubic ['pjuːbik] *adj* púbico.
pubis ['pjuːbis] *n* pubis *m*.
public ['pʌblik] **1** *adj* público; **to make something** — publicar algo.
2 *n* público *m*; **in** — en público; **the general** — el gran público; **the sporting** — los aficionados al deporte; **the great British** — (*hum*) los ingleses, los súbditos de su Majestad.
publican ['pʌblikən] *n* tabernero *m*.
publication [‚pʌbli'keiʃən] *n* publicación *f*.
publicist ['pʌblisist] *n* publicista *mf*.
publicity [pʌb'lisiti] *n* publicidad *f*.
publicize ['pʌblisaiz] *vt* publicar, dar publicidad a, anunciar.
publicly ['pʌblikli] *adv* públicamente, en público.

public-spirited ['pʌblik'spiritid] *adj act* de buen ciudadano; *person* lleno de civismo, consciente del bien público.
publish ['pʌbliʃ] *vt* publicar; *banns* correr.
publisher ['pʌbliʃə*] *n* editor *m*.
publishing ['pʌbliʃiŋ] *n* publicación *f* (de libros).
puce [pju:s] **1** *n* color *m* castaño rojizo. **2** *adj* de color castaño rojizo; (*with shame etc*) colorado.
puck¹ [pʌk] *n* duende *m* (malicioso).
puck² [pʌk] *n* (*Sport*) disco *m* de caucho.
pucker ['pʌkə*] **1** *n* arruga *f*; (*Sew*) frunce *m*, fruncido *m*; (*accidentally formed*) buche *m*.
2 *vt* (*also to — up*) arrugar; (*brow, Sew*) fruncir.
3 *vi* (*also to — up*) arrugarse, formar buches.
puckish ['pʌkiʃ] *adj* malicioso, juguetón.
pud [pud] *n* (*fam*) (a) (*Cook*) = **pudding**. (b) niño *m* rollizo, niña *f* rolliza.
pudding ['pudiŋ] *n* pudín *m*; **black —** morcilla *f*.
puddingstone ['pudiŋstəun] *n* pudinga *f*.
puddle ['pʌdl] **1** *n* charco *m*. **2** *vt* (*Tech*) pudelar.
pudenda [pu:'dendə] *npl* partes *fpl* pudendas.
pudgy ['pʌdʒi] *adj* = **podgy**.
puerile ['pjuərail] *adj* pueril.
puerility [pjuə'riliti] *n* puerilidad *f*.
puerperal [pju(:)'ɜ:pərəl] *adj* puerperal; **— fever** fiebre *f* puerperal.
Puerto Rican ['pwɜ:təu'ri:kən] **1** *adj* puertorriqueño. **2** *n* puertorriqueño *m*, a *f*.
Puerto Rico ['pwɜ:təu'ri:kəu] Puerto *m* Rico.
puff [pʌf] **1** *n* (a) (*of air*) soplo *m*, (*of wind*) soplo *m*, racha *f*; (*of smoke*) humareda *f*, (*from mouth*) bocanada *f*; (*sound: of breathing, of engine*) resoplido *m*, resuello *m*, bufido *m*.
(b) (*powder —*) borla *f*; (*Cook*) pastelillo *m* de crema.
(c) (*advert*) bombo *m*.
2 *vt* (*blow*) soplar; *pipe etc* chupar; **to — out** *smoke etc* echar, arrojar, despedir; **to — out one's cheeks** hinchar los carrillos; **to — up** hinchar, inflar; (*fig*) dar bombo a.
3 *vi* (*blow*) soplar; (**— and blow**) jadear, resollar, acezar; **to — (away) at one's pipe** chupar su pipa; **the train —ed out** el tren salió bufando, el tren salió echando humo.
4 *vr*: **to — oneself up** darse bombo, engreírse.
puff adder ['pʌf,ædə*] *n* víbora *f* puff.
puffball ['pʌfbɔ:l] *n* bejín *m*, cuezco *m* de lobo.
puffed [pʌft] *adj eye* hinchado; **to be —** (*out of breath*) estar sin aliento, estar acezando; **to be — up** (*with pride*) estar engreído.
puffer [pʌfə*] *n* (*fam*) locomotora *f*.
puffin ['pʌfin] *n* frailecillo *m*.
puff pastry ['pʌf'peistri] *n*, (*US*) **— paste** [peist] *n* hojaldre *m*.
puffy ['pʌfi] *adj eye etc* hinchado.
pug [pʌg] *n* doguillo *m*.
pugilism ['pju:dʒilizəm] *n* pugilato *m*.
pugilist ['pju:dʒilist] *n* púgil *m*.
pugnacious [pʌg'neiʃəs] *adj* pugnaz, belicoso, agresivo.
pugnaciously [pʌg'neiʃəsli] *adv* con pugnacidad, agresivamente.
pugnacity [pʌg'næsiti] *n* pugnacidad *f*, belicosidad *f*, agresividad *f*.
pug-nosed ['pʌg'nəuzd] *adj* chato, braco.
puke [pju:k] *vti* vomitar; (*fam*) **it makes me — me** da asco.
pukka [pʌkə] *adj* (*fam*) auténtico, genuino, elegante, lujoso.
pulchritude ['pʌlkritju:d] *n* belleza *f*.
pull [pul] **1** *n* (a) (*tug*) tirón *m*; estirón *m*; (*with oar etc*) golpe *m*; (*of a magnet, also fig*) atracción *f*, fuerza *f* atractiva; **the — of the south** la atracción del Sur, lo atractivo del Sur; **it was a long —** fue mucho camino; **we had a long — up the hill** nos costó mucho trabajo subir la cuesta; **give the rope a —** tira de la cuerda; **suddenly it gave a —** de repente dio un tirón.
(b) (*advantage*) ventaja *f*; (*influence*) influencia *f*, poder *m*; **they have a — over us now** ahora nos llevan ventaja; **he has a slight —** tiene una pequeña ventaja; **he has — in the right places** tiene influencia donde hace falta tenerla.
(c) (*at one's pipe*) chupada *f*; (*drink*) trago *m*; **he took a — at his pipe** chupó la pipa.
(d) (*handle of drawer etc*) tirador *m*; (*of bell*) cuerda *f*.
(e) (*Typ*) primeras pruebas *fpl*.
2 *vt* (a) (*tug at*) *bell rope, hair etc* tirar de; *trigger* apretar; *oar* tirar de; *boat* remar; (*Naut*) *rope* halar, jalar; *weeds* arrancar; *muscle* torcerse, dislocarse.
(b) (*extract, take out*) sacar.

(c) (*draw along*) tirar, arrastrar; **the engine —s 6 coaches** la locomotora arrastra 6 vagones; **— your chair over** acerca la silla.
(d) (*Typ*) imprimir.
(e) *ball* (*at golf, etc*) golpear oblicuamente, *shot* ejecutar mal.
(f) *see* **face, fast** *etc*.
(g) (*with adv or prep*) **to — about** manosear, estropear; **to — along** arrastrar; **to — apart** (*separate*) separar; despegar, desunir; (*break*) romper en dos; (*take to pieces*) desmontar; **to — something away from someone** arrancar algo a uno, quitar algo a uno arrancándoselo; **to — something back** tirar algo hacia atrás; **to — down** *person etc* hacer caer, hacer bajar; (*take down*) bajar; *blinds etc* bajar; *house, fortifications* derribar, demoler; *government* derribar; *grade, price etc* rebajar; **he —ed his hat well down** se caló el sombrero, se encasquetó el sombrero; **the mark in chemistry —s her down** la nota de química es la causa de que salga mal; **to — in** tirar hacia sí; *rope* cobrar; *horse* enfrenar; *suspect* detener; **the film —s the people in** la película atrae un numeroso público; **to — off** arrancar, separar; quitar de un tirón; *clothes* quitarse (de prisa); *deal* cerrar, concluir con éxito (algo inesperadamente); *game* ganar (algo inesperadamente); **to — it off** lograrlo, llevarlo a cabo (algo inesperadamente); vencer (algo inesperadamente); **to — on** *clothes* ponerse (de prisa); **to — out** (*take out*) sacar; *teeth etc* sacar, arrancar; (*stretch*) estirar; **to — someone out of a hole** ayudar a uno a salir de un hoyo tirando de sus brazos (*etc*); **to — someone out of a river** sacar a uno de un río; **to — a car over** volcar un coche; **to — someone round** ayudar a uno a reponerse; **to — someone through** sacar a uno de un apuro (*or* enfermedad *etc*); **to — a team together** hacer que los jugadores recuperen su espíritu de equipo; **to — up** *plants* arrancar, desarraigar; *socks etc* alzar; *car* parar; *horse* refrenar; **to — someone up for shoddy work** reprender a uno por la baja calidad de su trabajo; **his mark in maths —ed him up a bit** su nota en matemáticas le ayudó a salir mejor.
3 *vi* (a) tirar (*at* de); dar un tirón; **to — at a rope** tirar de una cuerda.
(b) (*vehicle*) ir; (*oarsmen etc*) remar; **we —ed for the shore** remamos con el propósito de llegar a la orilla; **the car —ed slowly up the hill** el coche subía despacio la cuesta; **it —ed to a stop** se paró, se detuvo.
(c) **to — at one's pipe** dar chupadas a la pipa; **to — at a bottle** echar un trago de una botella.
(d) (*with adv or prep*) **they — apart easily** se separan fácilmente; **to — away from someone** apartarse bruscamente de uno; (*outdistance*) dejar a uno atrás; **to — in** (*Rail*) llegar, llegar al andén, (*Aut*) parar, parar junto a la acera; **to — on something** tirar de algo; **to — out** irse, marcharse (*from* de), (*Mil*) retirarse (*from* de); (*Rail*) salir de la estación; **we're —ing out** nos marchamos ya; **the red car —ed out from behind that black one** el coche rojo salió detrás del negro; **to — over to one side** (*Aut etc*) desviarse hacia un lado; **to — round** reponerse; **to — through** salir de un apuro, (*Med*) recobrar la salud; **to — together** trabajar con un propósito común, obrar de común acuerdo; **to — up** (*stop*) pararse, detenerse; (*restrain oneself*) contenerse; (*stop talking etc*) interrumpirse; (*improve*) mejorar su posición; **please — up at the corner** pare en la esquina, por favor; **the car —ed up suddenly** el coche se paró en seco.
4 *vr*: **to — oneself along** arrastrarse; **to — oneself in** apretarse el cinturón; **to — oneself together** sobreponerse, serenarse, recobrar la calma; reanimarse; **— yourself together!** ¡anímese!
pullet ['pulit] *n* polla *f*, pollita *f*.
pulley ['puli] *n* polea *f*.
pull-in ['pul,in] *n* (*Aut: lay-by*) apartadero *m*; (*for food*) café *m* de carretera, restaurante *m* de carretera.
Pullman ['pulmən] (*Protected Trade Name*): **— car** *n* coche *m* Pullman.
pullover ['puləuvə*] *n* jersey *m*, jersé *m*, jersei *m* (*Acad*).
pullulate ['pʌljuleit] *vi* pulular.
pulmonary ['pʌlmənəri] *adj* pulmonar.
pulp [pʌlp] **1** *n* pulpa *f*; (*Bot*) pulpa *f*, carne *f*; (*paper —, wood—*) pasta *f*; **a leg crushed to —** una pierna hecha trizas; **to beat someone to a —** dar a uno una tremenda paliza; **to reduce something to —** hacer algo pulpa, reducir algo a pulpa.
2 *vt* hacer pulpa, reducir a pulpa.
pulpit ['pulpit] *n* púlpito *m*.
pulpy ['pʌlpi] *adj* pulposo.

pulsate [pʌl'seit] vi pulsar, latir.
pulsation [pʌl'seiʃən] n pulsación f, latido m.
pulse¹ [pʌls] 1 n (Anat) pulso m; (throb) pulsación f, latido m; to feel (or take) someone's — tomar el pulso a uno. 2 vi pulsar, latir.
pulse² [pʌls] n (Bot) legumbre f, legumbres fpl.
pulsebeat ['pʌlsbiːt] n latido m del pulso.
pulverization [ˌpʌlvərai'zeiʃən] n pulverización f.
pulverize ['pʌlvəraiz] 1 vt pulverizar; (fig) hacer polvo; anonadar; (fam) cascar. 2 vi pulverizarse.
puma ['pjuːmə] n puma f.
pumice ['pʌmis] n, pumice stone ['pʌmisstəun] n piedra f pómez.
pummel ['pʌml] see pommel.
pump¹ [pʌmp] 1 n bomba f; (Naut) pompa f.
  2 vt sacar (or elevar, llevar etc) con una bomba; arm mover rápidamente de arriba para abajo; person (fam) sonsacar; to — air along a tube hacer que pase el aire por un tubo por medio de una bomba; to — a tank dry secar (or vaciar) un tanque con una bomba; to — out liquid sacar líquido con una bomba; to — up a tyre inflar un neumático con una bomba; it's no good —ing me es inútil tratar de sonsacarme.
pump² [pʌmp] n (shoe) zapatilla f.
pumpernickel ['pʌmpənikl] n (US) pan m de centeno entero.
pump house ['pʌmphaus] n, pl — houses ['hauziz] casa f de bombas.
pumping station ['pʌmpiŋˌsteiʃən] n estación f de bombeo.
pumpkin ['pʌmpkin] n (vegetable) calabaza f; (plant) calabacera f.
pump room ['pʌmprum] n pabellón m de hidroterapia.
pun [pʌn] 1 n juego m de palabras (on sobre). 2 vi hacer un juego de palabras (on sobre), jugar del vocablo.
Punch [pʌntʃ] m Polichinela; —and-Judy show teatro m de polichinelas.
punch¹ [pʌntʃ] 1 n (a) (tool) punzón m; (for tickets) taladro m.
  (b) (blow) puñetazo m, golpe m; rabbit — golpe m de nuca; he packs a — tiene mucha fuerza en los puños; to pull one's —es no emplear toda su fuerza; he didn't pull any —es (fig) no se mordió la lengua.
  (c) (fig) empuje m, vigor m, fuerza f; he has — es hombre de empuje; he's a speaker with some — es un orador de tono enérgico; think of a phrase that's got some — to it dame una frase que tenga fuerza.
  2 vt (a) (with tool) punzar, taladrar; agujerear; perforar; ticket picar; to — holes in a sheet practicar agujeros en una lámina.
  (b) (with fist) dar un puñetazo a, pegar con los puños, golpear.
punch² [pʌntʃ] n (drink) ponche m.
punchball ['pʌntʃbɔːl] n saco m de arena, punching m.
punch bowl ['pʌntʃbəul] n ponchera f.
punch card ['pʌntʃkɑːd] n tarjeta f perforada.
punch-drunk ['pʌntʃ'drʌŋk] adj: to be — estar aturdido (a causa de los muchos golpes recibidos).
punched tape ['pʌntʃt'teip] n cinta f perforada.
punch line ['pʌntʃlain] n (of joke) palabras fpl que contienen la esencia del chiste; (of speech etc) palabras fpl más significativas, declaración f impresionante.
punch-up ['pʌntʃʌp] n (fam) riña f, pendencia f.
punctilio [pʌŋk'tiliəu] n puntillo m, etiqueta f; puntualidad f.
punctilious [pʌŋk'tiliəs] adj puntilloso, etiquetero, puntual.
punctiliously [pʌŋk'tiliəsli] adv de modo puntilloso; puntualmente.
punctual ['pʌŋktjuəl] adj puntual; "please be —" "se ruega la mayor puntualidad"; will the train be —? ¿llegará el tren a la hora exacta?
punctuality [ˌpʌŋktju'æliti] n puntualidad f.
punctually ['pʌŋktjuəli] adv puntualmente; — at 6 o'clock a las 6 en punto; the bus arrived — el autobús llegó a la hora exacta.
punctuate ['pʌŋktjueit] vt puntuar; (fig) interrumpir; his speech was —d by bursts of applause su discurso fue interrumpido por salvas de aplausos.
punctuation [ˌpʌŋktju'eiʃən] n puntuación f.
punctuation mark [ˌpʌŋktju'eiʃənmɑːk] n signo m de puntuación.
puncture ['pʌŋktʃə*] 1 n perforación f; (of skin etc) puntura f, punzada f; (Aut) pinchazo m; (Med) punción f; I have a — tengo un neumático pinchado, se me ha reventado un neumático.
  2 vt perforar; punzar, pinchar; tyre pinchar.

pundit ['pʌndit] n (iro) erudito m, sabio m.
pungency ['pʌndʒənsi] n lo acre; picante m; mordacidad f, acerbidad f.
pungent ['pʌndʒənt] adj smell acre; (piquant) picante; satire etc mordaz, acerbo.
pungently ['pʌndʒəntli] adv acremente; de modo picante; mordazmente, acerbamente.
Punic ['pjuːnik] 1 adj púnico. 2 n púnico m.
punish ['pʌniʃ] vt (a) castigar; to — someone for something, to — someone for doing something castigar a uno por haber hecho algo.
  (b) (fig: maltreat) maltratar; (tax) exigir esfuerzos sobrehumanos a; (take advantage of) aprovecharse al máximo de; food devorar, no perdonar.
punishable ['pʌniʃəbl] adj punible, castigable; a — offence una infracción que castiga la ley.
punishment ['pʌniʃmənt] n (a) castigo m; capital — pena f de muerte; corporal — castigo m corporal; to make the — fit the crime señalar un castigo de acuerdo con el crimen; to take one's — like a man sufrir el castigo sin quejarse.
  (b) malos tratos mpl, tratamiento m severo.
punitive ['pjuːnitiv] adj punitivo.
punk [pʌŋk] (US sl) 1 n pobre hombre m; novato m; bobo m. 2 attr malo, baladí, de baja calidad.
punster ['pʌnstə*] n persona f aficionada a los juegos de palabras.
punt¹ [pʌnt] 1 n batea f. 2 vt impulsar con percha. 3 vi ir en batea, pasearse en batea.
punt² [pʌnt] vt ball dar un puntapié a.
punt³ [pʌnt] vi (bet) jugar, hacer apuestas.
punter ['pʌntə*] n jugador m.
punt pole ['pʌntpəul] n percha f, pértiga f (de batea).
puny ['pjuːni] adj person etc débil, encanijado; effort débil, flojo; (petty) insignificante.
pup [pʌp] n cachorro m, a f; to sell someone a — dar a uno gato por liebre. 2 vi parir (la perra).
pupa ['pjuːpə] n, pl pupae ['pjuːpiː] crisálida f.
pupate ['pjuːpeit] vi crisalidar.
pupil ['pjuːpl] n alumno m, a f; (Anat) pupila f.
puppet ['pʌpit] 1 n títere m; (fig) títere m, marioneta mf. 2 attr: — régime gobierno m títere, régimen m marioneta.
puppetry ['pʌpitri] n títeres mpl, arte m del titiritero.
puppet show ['pʌpitʃəu] n títeres mpl, teatro m de títeres.
puppy ['pʌpi] n cachorro m, a f, perrito m, a f.
purblind ['pəːblaind] adj cegato; (fig) ciego, falto de comprensión.
purchase ['pəːtʃis] 1 n (a) (act) compra f; (thing purchased) adquisición f; to make a — hacer una compra.
  (b) (on rock etc) agarre m firme, pie m firme; (Mech) apalancamiento m; to get a — on the surface tener donde agarrarse a la superficie, lograr pegarse a la superficie.
  2 vt comprar, adquirir.
purchaser ['pəːtʃisə*] n comprador m, ora f.
purchase tax ['pəːtʃistæks] n impuesto m de venta.
purchasing power ['pəːtʃisiŋˌpauə*] n poder m de compra, poder m adquisitivo.
pure [pjuə*] adj puro.
purebred ['pjuə'bred] adj de pura sangre, de raza.
purée ['pjuərei] n puré m.
purely ['pjuəli] adv puramente.
pure-minded ['pjuə'maindid] adj de mente pura.
pureness ['pjuənis] n pureza f.
purgation [pəː'geiʃən] n purgación f.
purgative ['pəːgətiv] 1 adj purgativo, purgante. 2 n purgante m.
purgatory ['pəːgətəri] n purgatorio m; it was —! ¡fue un purgatorio!
purge [pəːdʒ] 1 n (act) purga f; (medicine) purga f, purgante m; (Pol) purga f, depuración f. 2 vt purgar; purificar, depurar; offence, sin purgar; (Pol) party purgar, depurar, member liquidar.
purification [ˌpjuərifi'keiʃən] n purificación f, depuración f.
purifier ['pjuərifaiə*] n depurador m.
purify ['pjuərifai] vt purificar, depurar; metal acrisolar, refinar; town etc depurar.
purist ['pjuərist] n purista mf, casticista mf.
puritan ['pjuəritən] 1 adj puritano. 2 n puritano m, a f.
puritanical [ˌpjuəri'tænikəl] adj puritano.
puritanism ['pjuəritənizəm] m puritanismo m.
purity ['pjuəriti] n pureza f.
purl [pəːl] 1 n puntada f invertida. 2 vt hacer a puntadas invertidas; "— two" "dos puntadas invertidas".
purler ['pəːlə*] n (fam): to come a — caer pesadamente, caer aparatosamente; (fig) fracasar rotundamente.

purlieus ['pəːljuːz] npl alrededores mpl, inmediaciones fpl.
purloin [pəː'lɔin] vt robar, hurtar.
purple ['pəːpl] 1 adj purpúreo; bruise etc morado; to go — (in the face) ponerse negro. 2 n púrpura f. 3 vt purpurar.
purplish ['pəːpliʃ] adj purpurino, algo purpúreo.
purport ['pəːpət] n (meaning) significado m, sentido m; (purpose) intención f.
purport [pəː'pɔːt] vt (mean) significar; (convey meaning) dar a entender (that que); (profess) pretender (to be ser); this —s to be a statement of ... esto pretende ser una declaración de ...
purpose ['pəːpəs] 1 n (a) (intention) propósito m, intención f, objeto m; novel with a — novela f de tesis, novela f de intención seria; my — in doing this mi propósito al hacer esto; for the — al efecto; for this — para este fin; for our —s we may disregard this para nuestros fines podemos hacer caso omiso de esto; for the — of + ger con el fin de + infin, al efecto de + infin; for the —s of this meeting por lo que toca a esta reunión; on — de propósito, adrede; to good —, to some — con buenos resultados, provechosamente; to no — inútilmente, en vano; to answer (or serve) someone's — servir para el caso, servir para lo que quiere uno; it serves no useful — no tiene prácticamente utilidad; it serves a variety of —s sirve para diversos efectos.
(b) (sense of —) resolución f; infirmity of — falta f de resolución; strength of — resolución f, firmeza f.
2 vt proponerse, proyectar, intentar; to — to do something proponerse hacer algo.
purposeful ['pəːpəsful] adj resuelto, determinado.
purposefully ['pəːpəsfəli] adv resueltamente.
purposefulness ['pəːpəsfulnis] n resolución f.
purposeless ['pəːpəslis] adj person's character irresoluto; person's state indeciso; act sin propósito fijo, sin finalidad concreta.
purposely ['pəːpəsli] adv de propósito, adrede, expresamente; a — vague statement una declaración hecha adrede en términos vagos.
purr [pəː*] 1 n ronroneo m. 2 vt (say) decir suavemente, susurrar. 3 vi (cat, engine) ronronear; (person) estar satisfecho.
purse [pəːs] 1 n bolsa f; (handbag: US) bolso m; (prize) premio m; (collection) colecta f; privy — gastos mpl personales del monarca; a well-lined — una bolsa llena; it is beyond my — mis recursos no llegan a tanto, es demasiado costoso para mí. 2 vt: to — one's lips fruncir los labios.
purser ['pəːsə*] n contador m de navío.
purse strings ['pəːsstriŋz] npl: to hold the — tener las llaves de la caja.
pursuance [pə'sjuːəns] n prosecución f, cumplimiento m; in — of con arreglo a, en cumplimiento de.
pursuant [pə'sjuːənt] adv: — to de acuerdo con.
pursue [pə'sjuː] vt (hunt) seguir, seguir la pista de, perseguir, cazar, dar caza a; (chase, molest) acosar, dar caza a, asediar; line of conduct, inquiry seguir; study proseguir; profession dedicarse a, ejercer; plan proceder de acuerdo con, obrar con arreglo a; pleasures etc dedicarse a; they —d the fox into the wood siguieron la zorra al entrar ésta en el bosque; he —d the girl home siguió a la chica hasta casa; he won't stop pursuing me! ¡no me deja a sol ni a sombra!
pursuer [pə'sjuːə*] n perseguidor m, ora f.
pursuit [pə'sjuːt] n (a) (chase) caza f; perseguimiento m, persecución f; (search) busca f; in — of en busca de, en pos de; with two policemen in hot — con dos policías que le seguían muy de cerca; to go in — of someone ir en pos de uno; to set out in — of someone salir a buscar a uno.
(b) the — of happiness la busca de la felicidad; the — of wealth el afán de riqueza.
(c) (occupation) ocupación f, carrera f, empleo m; (pastime) pasatiempo m; her favourite — su pasatiempo predilecto; literary —s intereses mpl literarios, actividades fpl literarias.
pursuit plane [pə'sjuːtplein] n avión m de caza.
purulence ['pjuəruləns] n purulencia f.
purulent ['pjuərulənt] adj purulento.
purvey [pəː'vei] vt proveer, suministrar, abastecer.
purveyance [pəː'veiəns] n provisión f, suministro m, abastecimiento m.
purveyor [pəː'veiə*] n proveedor m, ora f.
purview ['pəːvjuː] n alcance m, esfera f; it comes within the — of the law está comprendido dentro de los límites de la ley.
pus [pʌs] n pus m.

push [puʃ] 1 n (a) (shove) empuje m, empujón m; (Mil) ataque m, ofensiva f; avance m; with one — de un empuje; to give someone a — dar un empujón a uno; to give someone a helping — ayudar a uno empujando su coche (etc).
(b) (fam) to get the — ser despedido; to give someone the — despedir a uno.
(c) (pushfulness) empuje m, energía f; he's got no — no tiene empuje, le falta energía; he's a man with plenty of — es hombre de empuje.
(d) (fam) at a — si es necesario, en caso de necesidad; when it comes to the — en el momento decisivo, llegado el punto crítico.
2 vt (a) (press) empujar; (down, with foot) pisar, apretar; button etc apretar, pulsar, presionar; to — a car into the garage hacer que un coche entre en el garaje empujándolo; to — one's finger into a hole introducir el dedo en un agujero; he —ed his finger into my eye me clavó el dedo en el ojo; to — one's way through a crowd abrirse paso empujando a través de una multitud.
(b) person empujar; don't — me! ¡no me empuje!; to — someone off the pavement hacer que uno abandone la acera a fuerza de empujones; they —ed me off the ball me quitaron el balón a empujones.
(c) (press) advantage aprovecharse de; claim proseguir, insistir en; enterprise promover, fomentar; person proteger, ayudar, ayudar en su carrera; product etc hacer una campaña publicitaria a favor de; to — an attack home esforzarse por asegurar el éxito de un ataque; don't — your luck no te fíes demasiado de tu buena suerte.
(d) (force) to — someone to do something obligar a uno a hacer algo; incitar a uno a hacer algo; I was —ed into it me obligaron a ello; to — someone for payment ejercer presión sobre uno para que pague; we are —ed for time tenemos poco tiempo, tenemos mucha prisa; to be —ed for money andar muy escaso de dinero; I'm rather —ed for boxes just now ahora tengo pocas cajas disponibles.
(e) (with adv or prep) to — something against something else poner algo apretadamente contra otra cosa; to — something aside apartar algo con la mano; to — someone aside apartar a uno empujándole, (fig) arrinconar a uno; to — one's plate away apartar el plato con la mano; to — back hair etc echar hacia atrás; enemy echar atrás, rechazar; crowd hacer retroceder; to — down (press down) comprimir; (make fall) hacer caer; (lower) hacer bajar; to — someone forward empujar a uno hacia adelante; to — a plan forward llevar adelante un proyecto; to — in introducir a la fuerza; empujar; clavar, hincar; to — a lid off quitar una tapa a la fuerza; to — the work on hacer que se trabaje a un ritmo acelerado; to — a door open abrir una puerta empujándola; to — out empujar hacia fuera; expulsar, hacer salir; to — a boat out desatracar un barco; the snail —ed out its horns el caracol sacó los cuernos; to — through business despachar rápidamente; (Parl) bill hacer aceptar a la fuerza; to — up window etc levantar; (make rise) empujar hacia arriba; total, thermometer etc hacer subir.
3 vi (a) empujar; dar un empujón, dar empujones; "—" (on doors) "empujad"; don't —! ¡no empujen!
(b) (fig) hacer esfuerzos, obrar con energía.
(c) (with adv or prep) to — in introducirse a la fuerza, entrar a empujones; to — off (Naut) desatracar; apartarse de la orilla; (fam) largarse, marcharse; — off! ¡lárgate!; it's time to — off es hora de marcharnos; to — off from (Naut) apartarse de, alejarse de; to — on seguir adelante, continuar (a pesar de todo); they —ed on 5 miles avanzaron 5 millas; so we —ed on to the camp así que seguimos hasta el campamento; it's time to — on es hora de ponernos otra vez en camino; the pier —es out into the sea el muelle se extiende sobre el mar; to — past someone pasar delante de uno empujándole; to — through a crowd abrirse camino a empujones por entre una multitud; the plants are —ing through están apareciendo las plantas.
4 vr: to — oneself forward ofrecer sus servicios, ofrecerse; (pej) darse demasiada importancia.
push-bike ['puʃbaik] n (fam) bici f.
push-button ['puʃ,bʌtn] 1 n pulsador m, botón m (de control etc).
2 attr dotado de pulsador, con botón (de mando etc); with — control con mando por botón.
pushcart ['puʃkɑːt] n carretilla f de mano.
push chair ['puʃtʃeə*] n sillita f de ruedas.
pusher ['puʃə*] n persona f emprendedora; (pej) persona f de ambición desmesurada.

pushful 375 **put**

pushful ['puʃful] adj emprendedor, vigoroso, enérgico; ambicioso; (pej) agresivo.
pushfully ['puʃfəli] adv de modo emprendedor, enérgicamente; ambiciosamente; (pej) agresivamente.
pushfulness ['puʃfulnis] n empuje m, pujanza f, espíritu m emprendedor; ambición f; (pej) espíritu m agresivo.
pushing ['puʃiŋ] adj see **pushful**.
pushover ['puʃ,əuvə*] n (fam) cosa f muy fácil; persona f muy fácil de vencer (or convencer etc); it's a — es facilísimo.
pusillanimity [,pju:silə'nimiti] n pusilanimidad f.
pusillanimous [,pju:si'læniməs] adj pusilánime.
puss [pus] n minino m, micho m; (sl) cara f; —, —! ¡miz, miz!; **P—in Boots** el gato con botas.
pussy ['pusi] n see **puss**.
pussyfoot ['pusifut] vi (US fam) moverse a paso de gato; andar a tientas; (fig) no decidirse, no declararse.
pustule ['pʌstjuːl] n pústula f.
put [put] (irr: pret and ptp put) **1** vt (a) (place) poner; colocar; (esp into, inside) meter; — **it here** póngalo aquí; **to — milk in one's coffee** echar (or añadir) leche a su café; **to — something to one's ear** acercar algo al oído; **to — one's signature to something** poner su firma en algo, firmar algo; **to — a field under oats** sembrar un campo de avena; **to — someone under an obligation** poner a uno bajo una obligación; **to — virtue before success** anteponer la virtud al éxito, preferir la virtud al éxito; **he —s the Italians before the Spaniards** estima a los italianos más que a los españoles.

(b) (of versions) **to — a text into verse** poner un texto en verso, versificar un texto; **to — a passage into Greek** traducir un pasaje al griego.

(c) (invest etc) **to — money into a company** invertir dinero en una sociedad; **to — money into shares** comprar acciones con su dinero; **to — one's savings into marks** cambiar sus ahorros en marcos; **to — money on a horse** apostar dinero a un caballo.

(d) (state etc) declarar; (express) expresar; (in writing) redactar; plan etc exponer, explicar (to a); problem plantear; **as Lope —s it** como lo expresa Lope; **if I may** — **it so** por así decirlo; **all that can be — in 2 sentences** todo eso se puede expresar en 2 frases; **as the Portuguese — it** como dicen los portugueses; **to — it bluntly** para decirlo como es, hablando sin rodeos; — **it to him nicely** díselo lo más amablemente que puedas; **how will you — it to him?** ¿cómo se lo vas a explicar?; **he —s a convincing case** se explica con argumentos convincentes; **I — it to you that** . . . les sugiero que . . ., me veo en el caso de decirles que . . .; **to — a question to someone** hacer una pregunta a uno; **I should like to — a resolution** quiero proponer una moción; **the chairman — it to the committee** el presidente lo sometió a votación en el comité.

(e) (estimate) calcular; computar, estimar (at en); **the population is — at 2500** se calcula la población en 2500; **what would you — it at?** ¿en cuánto lo estima Vd?

(f) (with personal object) **to — someone to bed** acostar a uno; **to — the enemy to flight** derrotar al enemigo, hacer huir al enemigo; **they — the lad to a trade** le pusieron al muchacho de aprendiz en un oficio; **to — someone to a new kind of work** poner a uno a trabajar en un nuevo oficio; **to — someone through his paces** poner a uno a prueba, demostrar las cualidades de uno; **they really — him through it** le sometieron a las pruebas más rigurosas; **to — a horse at a fence** hacer que un caballo salte una valla.

(g) (direct) **to — a bullet through someone** atravesar a uno de una bala; **to — one's pen through a word** tachar una palabra con la pluma; **to — the weight** lanzar el peso.

(h) (ptp) **to stay —** no moverse, seguir en el mismo sitio.

2 vt (with adv or prep) (a) **to — about** news, rumour etc diseminar; **to — it about that** . . . dar a entender que . . ., hacer creer que . . ., hacer correr el rumor de que . . .; **to — someone about** (anger) enojar a uno; (trouble) molestar a uno, incomodar a uno; **she was much — about by it** se enfadó mucho con ello; **to — a ship about** hacer que un barco cambie de bordada.

(b) **to — across** idea, product hacer aceptar; meaning comunicar, hacer entender; deal cerrar; **he knows his stuff but he can't — it across** domina su material pero es incapaz de comunicarlo a otros; **to — it across someone** (deceive) engañar a uno, embaucar a uno; (defeat) dar una paliza a uno;

they properly — it across us nos dieron una paliza de verdad.

(c) **to — aside** (reject) rechazar; (save) poner aparte; fears desechar.

(d) **to — away** (replace) devolver a su lugar; (in pocket, drawer etc) guardar; thought desechar, descartar; car poner en el garaje; sword envainar; food zampar; lunatic poner en un manicomio; wife repudiar; prisoner encarcelar; (banish) alejar; **to — money away** ahorrar dinero, poner el dinero aparte.

(e) **to — back** (replace) devolver a su lugar; restituir, volver a poner; (in pocket, drawer etc) guardar; (postpone) aplazar; — **that back!** ¡déjalo!; **to — a clock back an hour** retrasar un reloj una hora; **this will — us back 10 years** esto nos retrasará 10 años.

(f) **to — by** poner aparte; (save) ahorrar; (keep) guardar; **to have money — by** tener dinero ahorrado, tener ahorros; **I had it — by for you** lo tenía guardado para Vd.

(g) **to — down** (on ground) poner en tierra, poner en el suelo, deponer; blinds etc bajar; umbrella cerrar; (let go) soltar, dejar; (preserve) conservar; (put to sleep) sacrificar; (in rank) degradar; passengers dejar apearse; revolt sofocar, dominar; abuse suprimir; (note) apuntar; — **it down!** ¡déjalo!, ¡suéltalo!; **I couldn't — the book down** me era imposible dejar el libro de la mano; — **it down in writing** póngalo por escrito; **did you — the names down?** ¿apuntó Vd los nombres?; **you may — my name down on the list** puede poner (or inscribir) mi nombre en la lista; **we — it down to his account** lo hemos sentado en su cuenta; **we — £50 down** pagamos un desembolso inicial de 50 libras; **I — him down as useless** yo le creí una calamidad; **I — him down as a troublemaker** le califiqué como un revoltoso; **I should — her down as about 30** creo que tendría unos 30 años; **we — it down to nerves** lo atribuimos a los nervios; **it can be — down to his childhood** se puede achacar a su niñez.

(h) **to — forth** hand alargar; arm extender; leaves etc echar; effort etc emplear, desplegar.

(i) **to — forward** candidate proponer; idea adelantar; case, theory presentar, proponer, exponer; suggestion hacer; (date, function etc) adelantar; **to — a clock forward 1 hour** adelantar un reloj una hora.

(j) **to — in** meter, introducir, insertar; claim presentar; evidence aducir; (say) decir; remark etc interponer; **to — in a good day's work** hacer bien el trabajo del día; **I — in 2 hours reading** pasé 2 horas leyendo, leí durante 2 horas; **to — in time on a project** invertir tiempo en un proyecto, dedicar tiempo a un proyecto; **they — the liberals in** votaron a los liberales, eligieron un gobierno liberal.

(k) **to — off** quitar; (postpone) aplazar, dejar para después; (get rid of) desembarazarse de; (confuse) desconcertar; (discourage) desanimar; **he keeps —ting it off** lo aplaza siempre; **you can't — off doing it for ever** no puedes evitar hacerlo siempre, no será siempre posible dejar de hacerlo; **we shall have to — the guests off** tendremos que decir a los invitados que no vengan, tendremos que ofrecer nuestras excusas a los invitados; **to — someone off with a promise** dar a uno largas con una promesa; **he's not easily — off** no es fácil apartarle de su propósito; **he tried to — me off my stroke** se esforzó por distraerme en el golpe, trató de hacerme errar el golpe; **her face is enough to — anyone off** su cara basta para desanimar al más fuerte; **you quite — me off my meal** me has quitado todo el apetito; **what you say —s me off prawns** lo que dices me quita las ganas de las gambas; **it almost — me off opera for good** casi me hizo perder permanentemente el sabor de la ópera; **we managed to — them off the scent** logramos desviarlos de la pista.

(l) **to — on** clothes ponerse; shoes ponerse, calzarse; brake echar, aplicar; light, radio etc poner, encender; play representar, poner en escena; (add) añadir; speed aumentar; — **the coffeepot on** puso la cafetera; **so we — on lettuce instead** así que pusimos lechuga en su lugar; **to — a clock on 1 hour** adelantar un reloj 1 hora; **to — on weight** echar carnes, engordar; **to — on an extra train** poner un tren de más; **she's —ting it on** (pretending) está exagerando, (overacting) está exagerando el papel, se emociona demasiado, (affectedly) se da mucho tono; **she —s the accent on** habla con un acento afectado; **to — on an innocent air** adoptar una postura de inocencia; **Jack — us on to you** Jack nos dio su nombre; **what — you on to it?** ¿qué le hizo pensar en esto?; ¿qué le dio la pista?; **one of the thieves — the police on to the others** uno de los ladrones denunció a los otros a la policía.

(m) to — out *hand* alargar, (*Aut*) sacar; *arm* extender; *tongue* sacar; *head* asomar, sacar; *horns* sacar; *leaves etc* echar; (*dislocate*) dislocarse; (*publish*) publicar, sacar a luz; *rumour* diseminar, hacer correr; *announcement* hacer; (*eject*) echar, expulsar; poner en la calle; *tenant* desahuciar; *cat* mandar a pasearse; *fire, light* apagar; **to — clothes out to dry** tender la ropa, poner la ropa a secar; **to — out a boat** echar un bote al mar; **to — money out at interest** poner el dinero a interés; **to — someone out** (*anger*) enojar a uno, irritar a uno, (*inconvenience*) molestar a uno, incomodar a uno, (*confound*) desconcertar a uno; **I don't want to — you out at all** no quiero molestarle en lo más mínimo; **she was very — out** estaba muy enfadada; **she never seems to be — out** no parece alterarse por nada.

(n) to — over = **to — across**; **to — one over on someone** (*forestall*) ganar por la mano a uno, (*deceive*) engañar a uno.

(o) to — through *task* concluir, llevar a cabo; *proposal* hacer aprobar; *business* despachar; **— me through to Sr Negro** póngame con el Sr Negro.

(p) to — together (*place together*) poner juntos, juntar; (*add*) añadir; (*Sew*) confeccionar; (*Tech*) montar, armar; *collection* reunir, juntar, formar; **more than all the rest — together** más que todos los demás reunidos; **if all the cigars in the world are — together end to end** si se ponen uno tras otro todos los puros del mundo.

(q) to — up *hand etc* poner en alto, levantar, alzar; *window etc* levantar; *umbrella* abrir; *collar* alzar; *ladder* montar, poner; *flag, sail* izar; *picture* colgar; *poster* pegar; *notice* fijar, poner; *game* levantar; *building* construir; *sword* envainar; *price* aumentar; *petition* presentar; *prayer, prize* ofrecer; *candidate* nombrar, proponer (*for* a); *lunch, prescription* preparar; **to — one's hair up** hacerse un peinado alto; **to — something up for sale** poner algo en venta; **to — up the money for something** poner el dinero para algo; **to — someone up** hospedar a uno, alojar a uno; **can you — me up for the night?** ¿me pueden dar una habitación para esta noche?; **to — someone up free** alojar a uno gratis; **to — someone up to something** incitar a uno a hacer algo; **someone must have — him up to it** alguien ha debido sugerírselo.

3 *vi* **(a)** (*Naut*) **to — about** virar, cambiar de bordada, cambiar de rumbo; **to — back to harbour** volver a puerto; **to — in at a port, to — into a port** entrar a puerto; **the boat —s in at Vigo** el barco hace escala en Vigo; **to — off, to — out** hacerse a la mar; **we — out from Cadiz** salimos del puerto de Cádiz.

(b) to — in for a post presentarse a un puesto, solicitar un puesto; **are you —ting in?** ¿te vas a presentar?; **to — up for president** ser candidato a la presidencia; **to — up for the socialists** ser candidato socialista; **to — up for East Hull** ser candidato en el distrito electoral de East Hull.

(c) to — up at an hotel hospedarse en un hotel.

(d) to — up with someone aguantar a uno; **to — up with something** resignarse a algo; **I can't — up with her** no la puedo ver; **I can't — up with it any longer** no aguanto más; **she —s up with a lot** tiene mucho aguante.

(e) to — upon someone molestar a uno, incomodar a uno; abusar de la amabilidad de uno.

4 *vr*: **to — oneself forward** ofrecerse (con poca

modestia), ponerse en evidencia; llamar sobre sí la atención; **to — oneself out** tomarse la molestia, molestarse; **don't — yourself out!** ¡no se moleste!; **to — oneself over** impresionar con su personalidad; comunicar eficazmente lo que uno quiere decir.

putative ['pjuːtətiv] *adj* supuesto; *relation* putativo.
putrefaction [ˌpjuːtrɪ'fækʃən] *n* putrefacción *f*.
putrefy ['pjuːtrɪfai] **1** *vt* pudrir. **2** *vi* pudrirse.
putrescence [pjuːˈtresns] *n* pudrición *f*.
putrescent [pjuːˈtresnt] *adj* putrescente, podrido.
putrid ['pjuːtrɪd] *adj* podrido, putrefacto; (*fam*) horrible, malísimo.
putsch [putʃ] *n* golpe *m* de estado.
putt [pʌt] **1** *n* put *m*, golpe *m* corto, tiro *m* al hoyo. **2** *vt* golpear con poca fuerza, tirar hacia el hoyo.
puttee ['pʌtiː] *n* polaina *f*.
putter ['pʌtə*] *n* putter *m*.
putting ['pʌtiŋ] *n*: **— the weight** lanzamiento *m* del peso.
putting green ['pʌtiŋgriːn] *n* campo *m* de golf en miniatura.
putty ['pʌti] *n* masilla *f*.
putty knife ['pʌtinaif] *n*, *pl* **— knives** [naivz] espátula *f* para masilla.
put-up ['putʌp] *adj*: **— job** cosa *f* proyectada y preparada de antemano; asunto *m* fraudulento; **it was a — job to give him the post** habían decidido antes darle el puesto.
puzzle ['pʌzl] **1** *n* **(a)** (*game*) rompecabezas *m*; (*riddle*) acertijo *m*; (*crossword*) crucigrama *m*; (*jigsaw*) rompecabezas *m*.
 (b) (*mystery*) problema *m*, enigma *m*, misterio *m*; **it's a real —** es un verdadero problema; **the — of their origin** el enigma de su origen; **your friends are —s to me** no comprendo en lo más mínimo a tus amigos.
 2 *vt* dejar perplejo, confundir; **that properly —d him** eso le dejó totalmente perplejo; **I am —d to know why** no comprendo por qué; **I was —d to know what to answer** no sabía en absoluto lo que debía contestar; **to — something out** resolver algo, descifrar algo.
 3 *vi*: **to — over something** esforzarse por resolver algo, devanarse los sesos para descifrar algo.
puzzled ['pʌzld] *adj look etc* perplejo.
puzzlement ['pʌzlmənt] *n* perplejidad *f*, confusión *f*.
puzzler ['pʌzlə*] *n* problema *m*, enigma *m*, misterio *m*.
puzzling ['pʌzliŋ] *adj* enigmático, misterioso; **it is — that . . .** es curioso que . . .
pygmy ['pigmi] **1** *adj* pigmeo; (*fig*) miniatura, minúsculo. **2** *n* pigmeo *m*.
pyjamas [pi'dʒɑːməz] *npl* pijama *m*.
pylon ['pailən] *n* pilón *m*, poste *m*; (*Elec*) torre *f* de conducción eléctrica.
pyorrhoea [ˌpaiə'riə] *n* piorrea *f*.
pyramid ['pirəmid] *n* pirámide *f*.
pyramidal [pi'ræmidl] *adj* piramidal.
pyre ['paiə*] *n* pira *f*; (*fig*) hoguera *f*.
Pyrenean [ˌpirə'niːən] *adj* pirenaico, pirineo.
Pyrenees [ˌpirə'niːz] *pl* Pirineo *m*, Pirineos *mpl*.
pyrethrum [pai'riːθrəm] *n* piretro *m*.
pyretic [pai'retik] *adj* pirético.
pyrites [pai'raitiːz] *n* piritas *fpl*.
pyro- ['paiərəu] piro . . .
pyromaniac ['paiərəu'meiniæk] *n* incendiario *m*, a *f*.
pyrotechnic [ˌpaiərəu'teknik] *adj* pirotécnico.
pyrotechnics [ˌpaiərəu'tekniks] *npl* pirotecnia *f*.
Pyrrhic ['pirik] *adj*: **— victory** victoria *f* pírrica.
Pythagoras [pai'θægərəs] *m* Pitágoras *m*.
python ['paiθən] *n* pitón *m*.
pyx [piks] *n* píxide *f*.

Q

qua [kwei] *prep* como, en cuanto.
quack[1] [kwæk] **1** *n* graznido *m* (del pato). **2** *vi* graznar.
quack[2] [kwæk] **1** *n* charlatán *m*; (*Med*) curandero *m*. **2** *adj* falso, fingido; (*remedy*) de curandero; **— doctor** curandero *m*.
quackery ['kwækəri] *n* charlatanismo *m*.
quad [kwɔd] *n* (*fam*) *see* **quadrangle.**
Quadragesima [ˌkwɔdrə'dʒesimə] *n* Cuadragésima *f*.
quadrangle ['kwɔdræŋgl] *n* cuadrángulo *m*; (*court*) patio *m*.
quadrangular [kwɔ'dræŋgjulə*] *adj* cuadrangular.
quadrant ['kwɔdrənt] *n* cuadrante *m*.
quadratic [kwɔ'drætik] *adj equation* de segundo grado.
quadrature ['kwɔdrətʃə*] *n* cuadratura *f*.
quadrilateral [ˌkwɔdri'lætərəl] **1** *adj* cuadrilátero. **2** *n* cuadrilátero *m*.
quadrille [kwə'dril] *n* cuadrilla *f*.
quadripartite ['kwɔdri'pɑːtait] *adj* cuadripartido.
quadrivium [kwɔ'driviəm] *n* cuadrivio *m*.
quadroon [kwɔ'druːn] *n* cuarterón *m*.
quadruped ['kwɔdruped] *n* cuadrúpedo *m*.
quadruple ['kwɔdrupl] **1** *adj* cuádruple. **2** *n* cuádruplo *m*.
quadruple ['kwɔ'druːpl] **1** *vt* cuadruplicar. **2** *vi* cuadruplicarse.
quadruplets [kwɔ'druːplits] *npl* cuatrillizos *mpl*, cuatrillizas *fpl*.
quadruplicate [kwɔ'druːplikit] **1** *adj* cuadruplicado. **2** *n:* **in —** por cuadruplicado.
quadruplicate [kwɔ'druːplikeit] *vt* cuadruplicar.
quads [kwɔdz] *npl* (*fam*) *see* **quadruplets.**
quaestor ['kwiːstə*] *n* cuestor *m*.
quaff [kwɔf] *vt* (*arch or hum*) beber.
quagmire ['kwæɡmaiə*] *n* tremedal *m*, cenegal *m*; (*fig*) atolladero *m*.
quail[1] [kweil] *n* codorniz *f*.
quail[2] [kweil] *vi* acobardarse, amedrentarse (*before ante*).
quaint [kweint] *adj* (*odd*) curioso, original, singular; *workmanship etc* rebuscado; *person* singular; (*picturesque, of tourist interest etc*) típico, pintoresco.
quaintly ['kweintli] *adv* curiosamente; singularmente; típicamente; **he described it — as . . .** le dio la calificación curiosa de **. . .**
quaintness ['kweintnis] *n* curiosidad *f*, originalidad *f*, singularidad *f*; lo rebuscado; tipismo *m*, lo pintoresco.
quake [kweik] *vi* temblar, estremecerse; **to — at the knees** temblarle a uno las rodillas; **to — at the sight** estremecerse viendo tal cosa; **to — with fright** temblar de miedo; **the earth —d 3 times** la tierra tembló 3 veces.
Quaker ['kweikə*] **1** *adj* cuáquero. **2** *n* cuáquero *m*, a *f*.
Quakerism ['kweikərizəm] *n* cuaquerismo *m*.
qualification [ˌkwɔlifi'keiʃən] *n* (a) (*reservation*) reserva *f*; modificación *f*, restricción *f*; **to accept something without —** aceptar algo sin reserva.
(b) (*for a post etc*) requisito *m*; **the —s for the post are . . .** los requisitos del puesto son **. . .**; **the —s for membership** lo que se requiere para ser socio.
(c) (*of person*) **—s** aptitud *f*, capacidad *f*; (*paper* **—s**) títulos *mpl*; **to have the —s for a post** llenar los requisitos de un puesto, estar capacitado para ocupar un puesto; **what are his —s?** ¿qué títulos tiene?
(d) (*act*) calificación *f*; **the — of his work as useless** la calificación de su obra de inútil.
qualified ['kwɔlifaid] *adj* (a) *person* (*fit*) apto, competente (*to* + *infin* para + *infin*); (*trained*) capacitado, cualificado, habilitado; (*professionally*) titulado, que tiene título, con título; **a — engineer**

un ingeniero titulado; **to be — to do something** estar capacitado para hacer algo; ser competente para hacer algo; **to be — to vote** tener los requisitos para votar; **I don't feel — to judge that** no me creo lo bastante experto para juzgar eso.
(b) (*limited*) modificado, limitado; **he gave it his — approval** lo aprobó pero con reservas; **it was a — success** obtuvo un éxito moderado.
qualify ['kwɔlifai] **1** *vt* (a) (*describe*) calificar (*as* de); (*Gram*) calificar a.
(b) (*make competent*) habilitar, capacitar; **this should — you for the post** esto ha de darle los requisitos para el puesto; **to — someone to do something** habilitar a uno para hacer algo; **that doesn't — him to speak on this** eso no le da derecho para hablar sobre este asunto.
(c) (*modify*) modificar; restringir; **I think you should — that** creo que le conviene modificar eso.
(d) (*diminish*) atenuar, moderar, disminuir.
2 *vi* habilitarse, capacitarse; (*professionally*) cursar los estudios profesionales, estudiar; (*graduate*) obtener el título, graduarse; **to — as an engineer** estudiar para ingeniero, (*finally*) obtener el título de ingeniero; **to — for a post** llenar los requisitos para un puesto; **does he —?** ¿tiene los requisitos?; **I qualified in 1968** yo saqué el título en 1968; **we shall marry when he qualifies** nos casaremos en cuanto él termine la carrera; **he hardly qualifies as a poet** apenas se le puede calificar de poeta.
qualifying ['kwɔlifaiiŋ] *adj* (*Gram*) calificativo; *exam, round* eliminatorio.
qualitative ['kwɔlitətiv] *adj* cualitativo.
qualitatively ['kwɔlitətivli] *adv* bajo el aspecto cualitativo.
quality ['kwɔliti] **1** *n* (a) (*nature, kind*) calidad *f*; categoría *f*, clase *f*; **of the best —** de la mejor calidad; **of good —, of high —** de buena calidad **of low —** de baja calidad; **fibres of — fibras** *fpl* de calidad; **he's a man of some —** es hombre de cierta categoría; **he has real —** tiene verdadera excelencia.
(b) (*characteristic, moral — etc*) cualidad *f*; **among her qualities** entre sus cualidades; **he has many good qualities** tiene muchas buenas cualidades.
(c) **the —** la aristocracia; **people of —** la gente bien nacida, las personas cultas.
(d) (*of sound*) timbre *m*, tono *m*.
2 *adj*: **a — carpet** una alfombra de calidad.
qualm [kwɑːm] *n* (a) (*Med*) bascas *fpl*, náusea *f*; mareo *m*.
(b) (*scruple*) escrúpulo *m*, duda *f*; **to have —s about doing something** sentir escrúpulo al hacer algo; **now she's having —s about it** ahora lo está remordiendo la conciencia por ello, ahora le están asaltando las dudas; **to have no —s about doing something** no dudar en hacer algo, hacer algo sin escrúpulos, hacer algo sin remordimientos.
quandary ['kwɔndəri] *n* dilema *m*, apuro *m*; **to be in a —** estar perplejo, estar en un dilema; **to get someone out of a —** sacar a uno de un apuro.
quantitative ['kwɔntitətiv] *adj* cuantitativo.
quantitatively ['kwɔntitətivli] *adv* bajo el aspecto cuantitativo.
quantity ['kwɔntiti] *n* cantidad *f*; **unknown —** incógnita *f*; **in large quantities, in —** en grandes cantidades; **what — do you want?** ¿cuánto quiere?
quantity surveyor ['kwɔntiti,sə'veiə*] *n* aparejador *m*.
quantum ['kwɔntəm] *n:* **— theory** teoría *f* cuántica, teoría *f* de los cuanta.
quarantine ['kwɔrəntiːn] **1** *n* cuarentena *f*; **to be in —** estar en cuarentena; **to place a dog in —** poner un perro en cuarentena. **2** *vt* poner en cuarentena.

quarrel ['kwɔrəl] **1** n (argument) riña f, disputa f; (with blows) reyerta f, pendencia f, pelea f; **to have a — with someone** reñir con uno; **we had a —** reñimos; **I have no — with you** yo no tengo nada en contra de Vd, yo no tengo queja de Vd; **to pick a —** buscar camorra; **to pick a — with someone** armar pleito con uno; **to take up someone's —** ponerse de la parte de uno.
2 vi reñir; disputar; **they —led about (or over) money** riñeron por cuestión de dinero; **to — with someone** reñir con uno, pelearse con uno; **we —led and I never saw him again** reñimos y no volví a verle; **to — with someone for having done something** reñir a uno por haber hecho algo; **you can't — with that** es imposible quejarse de eso; **what we — with is . . .** nuestro motivo de queja es . . .
quarrelling, (US) **quarreling** ['kwɔrəliŋ] n disputas fpl, altercados mpl; **there was constant —** se reñía constantemente.
quarrelsome ['kwɔrəlsəm] adj pendenciero, peleador.
quarrelsomeness ['kwɔrəlsəmnis] n espíritu m pendenciero.
quarry[1] ['kwɔri] n (Hunting) presa f; (fig) presa f, víctima f.
quarry[2] ['kwɔri] **1** n cantera f; (fig) mina f, cantera f. **2** vt sacar, extraer.
3 vi explotar una cantera, extraer piedra (etc) de una cantera.
quarryman ['kwɔrimən] n, pl —**men** [mən] cantero m, picapedrero m.
quart [kwɔt] n cuarto de galón (= 1,136 litros); **we drank —s** bebimos una gran cantidad.
quarter ['kwɔtə*] **1** n (a) (fourth part) cuarto m, cuarta parte f; (weight) = 28 libras (= 12,7 kg, approx = arroba f); (Fin US) moneda f de 25 centavos; (Her) cuartel m; —**s** (of horse) anca f; **hind-—s** cuartos mpl traseros, (hum, of person) culo m; **a — mile** un cuarto de milla f; **a — of a century** un cuarto de siglo; **for a — of the price** por la cuarta parte del precio; **it's a — gone already** ya ha desaparecido la cuarta parte; **it's only a — as long** tiene solamente la cuarta parte de largo; **to divide something into —s** dividir algo en cuartos.
(b) (of moon) cuarto m; (3 months) trimestre m; **to pay by the —** pagar cada 3 meses, pagar trimestralmente.
(c) (time) **a — of an hour** un cuarto de hora; **it's a — to 3, it's a — of 3** (US) son las 3 menos cuarto; **it's a — past 3, it's a — after 3** (US) son las 3 y cuarto.
(d) (of compass) cuarta f; (region) región f; (fig) fuente f, origen m; procedencia f; dirección f; **the 4 —s of the globe** las 4 partes del mundo; **from all —s** de todas partes; **at close —s** (fight) casi cuerpo a cuerpo; **from an unknown —** de procedencia desconocida, de origen desconocido; **we may expect trouble in that —** podemos tener dificultades en esa región; **the wind is in the right —** el viento sopla en dirección favorable; **what — is the wind in?** ¿qué dirección lleva el viento?
(e) (of town) barrio m; **the business —** el barrio comercial.
(f) —**s** vivienda f; alojamiento m; (Mil) alojamiento m; (barracks) cuartel m; **to have free —s** tener alojamiento gratis; **to live in cramped —s** tener un cuarto (etc) muy estrecho; **to shift one's —s** cambiar de alojamiento; **to take up one's —s** ocupar su cuarto (etc); establecerse, alojarse.
(g) **to give no —** no dar cuartel.
2 vt (a) (divide into 4) cuartear, dividir en cuartos; meat descuartizar; (Her) cuartelar.
(b) (Mil) acuartelar, alojar; **to be —ed on someone** estar alojado en casa de uno.
quarter day ['kwɔtədei] n primer día m del trimestre; (Fin) día m en que se paga un trimestre.
quarter-deck ['kwɔtədek] n alcázar m.
quarter final ['kwɔtə,fainl] n cuarto m de final; —**s** cuartos mpl de final.
quartering ['kwɔtəriŋ] n (Her) cantón m.
quarterly ['kwɔtəli] **1** adv cada tres meses, trimestralmente, por trimestres. **2** adj trimestral. **3** n publicación f trimestral.
quartermaster ['kwɔtə,mɑːstə*] n (approx) furriel m, comisario m.
quartermaster sergeant ['kwɔtə,mɑːstə'sɑːdʒənt] n (approx) brigada m.
quartern ['kwɔtən] n cuarta f; — **loaf** pan m de 4 libras.
quarterstaff ['kwɔtəstɑːf] n (Hist) barra f.
quarter tone ['kwɔtətəun] n cuarto m de tono.

quartet(te) [kwɔ'tet] n (Mus) cuarteto m; (set of 4) grupo m de cuatro.
quarto ['kwɔtəu] **1** adj en cuarto; (paper size) tamaño m holandesa. **2** n libro m en cuarto.
quartz ['kwɔts] n cuarzo m.
quartzite ['kwɔtsait] n cuarcita f.
quash ['kwɔʃ] vt anular, invalidar.
quasi ['kwɑːzi] adv cuasi.
quatercentenary [,kwɔtəsen'tiːnəri] n cuarto centenario m.
quaternary [kwə'təːnəri] **1** adj cuaternario. **2** n cuaternario m.
quatrain ['kwɔtrein] n cuarteto m, estrofa f de cuatro versos.
quaver ['kweivə*] **1** n temblor m; vibración f; (Mus: trill) trémolo m, (note) corchea f; **with a — in her voice** con voz trémula.
2 vi temblar; vibrar; (Mus) trinar.
3 vt decir con voz temblorosa; **"yes", she —ed** "sí", dijo temblorosa.
quavering ['kweivəriŋ] adj tembloroso, trémulo; **in — tones** en tono tembloroso.
quaveringly ['kweivəriŋli] adv: **to say something —** decir algo con voz temblorosa.
quavery ['kweivəri] adj see **quavering**.
quay [kiː] n, **quayside** ['kiːsaid] n muelle m; **on the —** en el muelle.
queasiness ['kwiːzinis] n bascas fpl; propensión f a la náusea; delicadeza f, escrupulosidad f.
queasy ['kwiːzi] adj (Med) bascoso; stomach delicado; conscience delicado, escrupuloso; **I feel —** me siento mal.
queen [kwiːn] **1** n reina f; (Chess) reina f; (Cards) dama f, (in Spanish pack) caballo m; (Zool: bee) abeja f reina, (ant) hormiga f reina; **she was — to Charles II** era la reina de Carlos II.
2 vt pawn coronar; **to — it** conducirse como una reina, (fig) pavonearse.
3 vi (Chess) ser coronado.
queen bee ['kwiːn'biː] n abeja f reina.
queenly ['kwiːnli] adj regio, de reina.
queen mother ['kwiːn'mʌðə*] n reina f madre.
queer [kwiə*] **1** adj (a) (odd) raro, extraño, singular; misterioso; excéntrico; sospechoso; **it's very —** es muy raro; **there's something — going on** pasa algo raro; **what's — about it?** ¿qué tiene esto de raro?
(b) (fam: homosexual) maricón.
(c) (Med) enfermo; **he was — for 2 months** estuvo enfermo durante 2 meses; **to come over —**, **to feel —** tener vahídos, sentirse mal, sentirse indispuesto.
2 n (fam) maricón m.
3 vt estropear; see **pitch**.
queerly ['kwiəli] adv de modo raro, extrañamente; misteriosamente; **to behave —** comportarse de modo raro.
queerness ['kwiənis] n rareza f, singularidad f; lo misterioso; lo excéntrico.
quell [kwel] vt passion etc reprimir; calmar; revolt sofocar, dominar; opposition sobreponerse a; fears desechar.
quench [kwentʃ] vt (all senses) apagar.
quenchless ['kwentʃlis] adj inapagable.
quern [kwəːn] n molinillo m de mano.
querulous ['kwerʊləs] adj quejumbroso.
querulously ['kwerʊləsli] adv quejumbrosamente; en tono quejumbroso.
query ['kwiəri] **1** n (question) pregunta f; (doubt) duda f; (?) punto m de interrogación, (fig) interrogante f; **there are many queries about it** hay muchas interrogantes acerca de esto; **did you have a —?** ¿quería preguntar algo?; —: **who killed Cock Robin?** pregunta: ¿quién mató a Cock Robin?
2 vti (ask) preguntar; (doubt) dudar de, expresar dudas acerca de; (disagree with) no estar conforme con; **to — whether . . .** dudar si . . .; **I — that** dudo si eso es cierto, tengo mis dudas acerca de eso; **do you — the evidence?** ¿tiene Vd dudas acerca del testimonio?
quest [kwest] **1** n busca f, búsqueda f (for de); (Hist) demanda f (for de); **to go in — of** ir en busca de.
2 vti buscar (for something algo).
question ['kwestʃən] **1** n (a) (interrogative) pregunta f; —**s and answers** preguntas fpl y respuestas; **indirect —** (Gram) pregunta f indirecta; **leading —** (Law) pregunta f capciosa, pregunta f que sugiere la respuesta; **rhetorical —** pregunta f a la que no se espera contestación, comunicación f; **trick —** pregunta f de pega; **to ask someone a —**, **to put a — to someone** hacer una pregunta a uno; **many —s were left unanswered** muchas preguntas quedaron sin contestar; **to pop the —** declararse.

(b) (*matter*) asunto *m*, cuestión *f*; problema *m*; **the German —** el problema alemán; **burning —** cuestión *f* candente, cuestión *f* palpitante; **vexed —** cuestión *f* batallona; **open —** cuestión *f* pendiente, cuestión *f* sin resolver; **it is an open — whether . . .** queda por resolver si . . ., el tiempo dirá si . . .; **the — is, . . .** el caso es, . . .; **it is a — of** se trata de . . .; **it is a — of whether . . .** se trata de saber si . . .; **that is the —** ahí está la dificultad; **that is not the —** no se trata de eso; **it is not simply a — of money** no se trata simplemente de dinero, no es cuestión de dinero y nada más; **there is no — of outside help** no se trata de la ayuda exterior; **there can be no — of your resigning** no se puede consentir en que Vd dimita; **there was some — of John coming** se hablaba de que pudiera venir Juan; **it's out of the —** es imposible; **that begs the —** eso es una petición de principio.

(c) (*at meeting*) asunto *m*; **—!** ¡que se vuelva al tema de la discusión!; **to move the previous —** pedir pareceres sobre si se ha de someter la moción a votación; **to put the —** someter la moción a votación.

(d) (*doubt etc*) **beyond —, past —** fuera de toda duda; **in — en** cuestión; **without —** sin duda, indudablemente; **there is no — about it** no existen dudas sobre ello; **to bring** (*or* **call**) **something in —** poner algo en duda; **to come into —** empezar a discutirse; **I make no —** but that **it is so** yo no dudo que es así.

2 *vt* **(a)** (*interrogate*) hacer preguntas a; (*by police etc*) interrogar; (*by examiner etc*) examinar; **we —ed him closely to find out whether . . .** le interrogamos del modo más apremiante para saber si . . .; **I will not be —ed about it** no permito que se me interrogue sobre eso.

(b) (*doubt*) poner en duda; dudar de, desconfiar de; **I — whether it is worthwhile** me pregunto si vale la pena; **I don't — your honesty** no dudo de su honradez.

questionable ['kwestʃənəbl] *adj* cuestionable, dudoso, discutible; **it is — whether . . .** es dudoso si . . .; **in — taste** de gusto dudoso.

questionary ['kwestʃənəri] *n* cuestionario *m*.

questioner ['kwestʃənə*] *n* interrogador *m*, ora *f*.

questioning ['kwestʃəniŋ] **1** *adj* interrogativo. **2** *n* preguntas *fpl*; (*by police etc*) interrogatorio *m*.

question mark ['kwestʃənmɑːk] *n* punto *m* de interrogación; (*fig*) interrogante *f*; **a big — hangs over him** sobre él pende una interrogante mayúscula.

questionnaire [,kwestʃə'neə*] *n* cuestionario *m*.

queue [kjuː] **1** *n* cola *f*; **to form a —, to stand in a —** hacer cola; **to jump the —** salirse de su turno.

2 *vi* (*also* **to — up**) hacer cola; **to — for something** hacer cola para comprar (*etc*) algo; **to — for 3 hours** pasar 3 horas haciendo cola.

quibble ['kwibl] **1** *n* sofistería *f*, sutileza *f*; objeción *f* de poca monta; **that's just a —** eso es pura sofistería, eso es extremar demasiado con el vocablo.

2 *vi* usar sofisterías, sutilizar, buscar evasivas; hacer objeciones de poca monta; **he always —s** es un sofista; **you can't — about that** no puedes hacer objeciones acerca de eso.

quibbler ['kwiblə*] *n* sofista *mf*.

quibbling ['kwibliŋ] *n* sofistería *f*, sofismas *mpl*; sutilezas *fpl*; objeciones *fpl* de poca monta.

quick [kwik] **1** *adj* (*speedy*) rápido; veloz; (*early*) pronto; (*of foot*) ligero, veloz; (*agile*) ágil; (*in mind*) listo, inteligente; **ear** fino; **eye, wit** *etc* agudo; **temper** vivo; **a — train** un tren rápido; **the —est method** el método más rápido; **a — reply** una pronta contestación; **for a — sale** para poder venderlo pronto; **as — as a flash, as — as lightning** como un relámpago; **be —!** ¡pronto! ¡date prisa!; **and just be — about it!** ¡no te entretengas!; **you have been very — about it** lo has hecho con la mayor prontitud; **he's too — for me** (*in speech*) habla demasiado de prisa para mí, (*in escaping*) corre más que yo, (*in intelligence*) es demasiado listo para mí; **to be — to act** obrar con prontitud; **to be — to take offence** ofenderse por poca cosa; **to be — to anger** tener repentinos enojos; **to be — to pity** tener repentina compasión; **to have a — one** beberse un trago sin pérdida de tiempo; **let's have a — one** entremos a tomar algo.

2 *n* **(a)** (*Anat*) carne *f* viva; **to cut someone to the —** herir a uno en lo vivo.

(b) **the —** (*living*) los vivos; **the — and the dead** los vivos y los muertos.

3 *adv* see **quickly**.

quick-acting ['kwik'æktiŋ] *adj* extrarrápido.

quick-change ['kwik'tʃeindʒ] *adj*: **— actor** transformista *m*.

quick-eared ['kwik'iəd] *adj* de oído fino.

quicken ['kwikən] **1** *vt* acelerar, apresurar; avivar; **to — one's pace** apretar el paso. **2** *vi* acelerarse, apresurarse; avivarse; (*embryo*) empezar a moverse.

quick-eyed ['kwik'aid] *adj* de vista aguda.

quick-fire ['kwikfaiə*] *adj* **gun** de tiro rápido; **question** *etc* rápido, hecho a quemarropa.

quick-firing ['kwik,faiəriŋ] *adj* de tiro rápido.

quick-freeze ['kwikfriːz] *adj* de congelación rápida.

quickie ['kwiki] *n* (*fam*) pregunta *f* relámpago.

quicklime ['kwiklaim] *n* cal *f* viva.

quickly ['kwikli] *adv* rápidamente; de prisa; pronto; **—!** ¡pronto!; **they answered —** contestaron pronto; **the next phase followed —** la etapa siguiente empezó inmediatamente; **he talks too — for me to understand** habla demasiado rápidamente para que yo pueda entenderle; **come as — as you can** ven cuanto antes, ven lo más pronto que puedas; **the firemen were — on the spot** los bomberos se presentaron sin pérdida de tiempo.

quickness ['kwiknis] *n* rapidez *f*, velocidad *f*; prontitud *f*, presteza *f*; agilidad *f*; inteligencia *f*; penetración *f*; finura *f*; agudeza *f*; viveza *f*.

quicksand ['kwiksænd] *n* arena *f* movediza.

quickset ['kwikset] **1** *adj* compuesto de plantas vivas, (*esp*) de espinos. **2** *n* (*slip*) plantón *m*; (*hawthorn*) espino *m*; (*hedge*) seto *m* vivo (*esp* de espinos).

quick-sighted ['kwik'saitid] *adj* de vista aguda.

quicksilver ['kwik,silvə*] **1** *n* azogue *m*, mercurio *m*. **2** *adj* azogado; (*fig*) inconstante, caprichoso. **3** *vt* azogar.

quick-tempered ['kwik'tempəd] *adj* de genio vivo, de prontos enojos.

quick-witted ['kwik'witid] *adj* agudo, perspicaz; **that was very — of you** en eso has sido muy perspicaz.

quid[1] [kwid] *n* (*sl*) libra *f* esterlina; **3 —** 3 libras.

quid[2] [kwid] *n* mascada *f* (de tabaco).

quiddity ['kwiditi] *n* (*Philos*) esencia *f*; (*quibble*) sutileza *f*, sofistería *f*.

quid pro quo ['kwidprəu'kwəu] *n* compensación *f*, recompensa *f* (*for* de).

quiescence [kwai'esns] *n* quietud *f*, inactividad *f*; reposo *m*.

quiescent [kwai'esnt] *adj* quieto, inactivo; reposado.

quiet ['kwaiət] **1** *adj* **(a)** (*silent*) silencioso, callado; **person** (*by nature*) callado, reservado; **place, town** *etc* tranquilo; (*pej: of town life etc*) aburrido; (*of engine etc*) sin ruido, que no hace ruido, silencioso; (*not excited*) tranquilo, reposado; **—!, be —!** (*to people*) ¡silencio!, (*more forcefully*) ¡a callar!, (*to 1 person*) ¡cállate!; **to be —!** (*person: after speaking*) callarse, (*in moving about*) no hacer ruido; **isn't it —?** ¡qué silencio!; **it was as — as the grave** había un silencio sepulcral; **to keep —** no hacer ruido; no decir nada, quedar callado, callarse; **keep those bottles —!** ¡no haga tanto ruido con esas botellas!; **they paid £100 to keep him —** pagaron 100 libras para tenerle callado.

(b) *temperament* tranquilo, sosegado; *animal* manso.

(c) *dress etc* no llamativo, discreto; *colour* suave.

(d) (*not overt*) discreto; (*private*) más bien privado; íntimo, que se celebra en la intimidad; (*informal*) íntimo, sin ceremonias; **with — humour he said . . .** ligeramente guasón dijo . . .; **all — here** aquí sin novedad; **all — on the Western Front** sin novedad en el frente del oeste; **it was a — wedding** la boda se celebró en la intimidad; **we had a — supper** cenamos en la intimidad; **business is very —** el negocio está muy flojo; **to have a — dig at someone** burlarse discretamente de uno; **they lead a — life** llevan una vida tranquila

2 *n* silencio *m*; paz *f*; tranquilidad *f*; reposo *m*; **an hour of blessed —** una hora de paz bendita; **on the —** a la sordina, a hurtadillas; **let's have complete —** quiero que se callen completamente todos.

3 *vt* calmar; see **quieten**.

quieten ['kwaiətn] **1** *vt* (*also* **to — down**) (*calm*) calmar, tranquilizar; (*silence*) hacer callar; **he managed to — the crowd** logró tranquilizar a la multitud.

2 *vi* (*also* **to — down**) calmarse, tranquilizarse; callarse; (*after unruly youth etc*) sentar los cascos, hacerse más juicioso.

quietism ['kwaiitizəm] *n* quietismo *m*.

quietist ['kwaiitist] *n* quietista *mf*.

quietly ['kwaiətli] *adv* **(a)** silenciosamente, en silencio, calladamente; tranquilamente; sin hacer

ruido; **he said —** dijo dulcemente, dijo en tono bajo; **please play more —** procure tocar con menos ruido, por favor; **she came in —** entró sin hacer ruido.
(b) sosegadamente; mansamente.
(c) discretamente; **to be — dressed** ir vestido con discreción.
(d) discretamente; en la intimidad, en privado; sin ceremonias; **let's get married —** casémonos sin ceremonias; **we dined — at home** cenamos en la intimidad del hogar.
quietness ['kwaiətnis] *n* (a) silencio *m*; paz *f*; tranquilidad *f*; reposo *m*; **the — of her voice** lo dulce de su voz.
(b) sosiego *m*, lo sosegado; mansedumbre *f*.
(c) discreción *f*.
(d) discreción *f*; intimidad *f*.
quietude ['kwaiətjuːd] *n* quietud *f*.
quietus [kwaiˈiːtəs] *n* golpe *m* de gracia; (*death*) muerte *f*.
quiff [kwif] *n* copete *m*.
quill [kwil] *n* (*Zool*) pluma *f* de ave; (*part of feather*) cañón *m* de pluma; (*pen*) pluma *f* (de ganso); (*in fishing*) cañón *m* de pluma; (*spine*) púa *f*; (*bobbin*) canilla *f*.
quill-pen ['kwil'pen] *n* pluma *f* (de ganso).
quilt [kwilt] **1** *n* colcha *f*, edredón *m*. **2** *vt* acolchar.
quilting ['kwiltiŋ] *n* colchadura *f*.
quince [kwins] *n* (*fruit, tree*) membrillo *m*.
quince cheese ['kwins'tʃiːz] *n* carne *f* de membrillo.
quince jelly ['kwins'dʒeli] *n* conserva *f* de membrillo.
quincentenary [ˌkwinsen'tiːnəri] *n* quinto centenario *m*.
quinine [kwi'niːn] *n* quinina *f*.
Quinquagesima [ˌkwiŋkwə'dʒesimə] *n* Quincuagésima *f*.
quinquennial [kwiŋ'kweniəl] *adj* quinquenal.
quinquennium [kwiŋ'kweniəm] *n* quinquenio *m*.
quins [kwinz] *npl* (*fam*) see **quintuplets**.
quinsy ['kwinzi] *n* angina *f*.
quint [kwint] *n* (*US fam*) quintillizo *m*, a *f*.
quintessence [kwin'tesns] *n* quinta esencia *f*.
quintet(te) [kwin'tet] *n* quinteto *m*.
quintuple ['kwintjupl] **1** *adj* quíntuplo. **2** *n* quíntuplo *m*.
quintuple ['kwin'tjuːpl] **1** *vt* quintuplicar. **2** *vi* quintuplicarse.
quintuplets [kwin'tjuːplits] *npl* quintillizos *mpl*, quintillizas *fpl*.
quip [kwip] **1** *n* chiste *m*, agudeza *f*, pulla *f*. **2** *vi* hacer un chiste; **"—", he —ped "—"**, dijo humorísticamente.
quire ['kwaiə*] *n* mano *f* de papel.
quirk [kwəːk] *n* (*oddity*) peculiaridad *f*, rasgo *m* peculiar; capricho *m*; (*flourish*) rasgo *m*; (*Archit*) avivador *m*; **by some — of fate** por algún capricho de la suerte; **it's just a —** he has son cosas suyas, es un rasgo peculiar suyo.
quisling ['kwizliŋ] *n* quisling *m*, colaboracionista *m*.
quit [kwit] (*irr: pret and ptp* **quit** *or* **quitted**) **1** *vt* dejar, abandonar; *place* abandonar, salir de; *premises etc* desocupar; **to — one's job** abandonar su puesto, dimitir; **to — work** suspender el trabajo; **to — + ger** (*esp US*) dejar de + *infin*, desistir de + *infin*; **— fooling!** ¡déjate de tonterías!; **it's time to — dreaming** es hora de renunciar a los sueños.
2 *vi* (*go away*) irse, marcharse; (*withdraw*) retirarse; (*resign*) dimitir; (*give up, in game etc*) abandonar; (*stop work*) suspender el trabajo; (*be a quitter*) renunciar a una empresa, abandonar, rajarse; **I —!** ¡me rajo!
3 *adj*: **to be — of someone** estar libre de algo, haberse librado de uno.
quite [kwait] *adv* (a) (*completely*) totalmente, completamente; **— new** completamente nuevo; **— a hero** todo un héroe (*also iro*); **— so!** ¡se comprende!,

¡así es!, perfectamente; **oh, — that!** ¡lo menos eso!; **that's — enough** eso basta y sobra; **that's — enough for me** eso me basta a mí; **not — as many as last time** no tantos como la última vez; **I — understand** lo comprendo perfectamente; **that's not — right** eso no está del todo bien; **he has not — recovered yet** no se ha repuesto todavía del todo; **it was — 3 months** era lo menos 3 meses; **it's not — what we wanted** no es exactamente lo que buscábamos; **we don't — know** no sabemos exactamente; **he's — grown up now** ahora está hecho un hombre; es todo un hombre.
(b) (*rather*) bastante; **it's — good** es bastante bueno; **it was — a surprise** me sorprendió bastante; **I — believe that . . .** casi tengo la certeza de que . . .
quits [kwits] *adv*: **to be — with someone** estar en paz con uno; **now we're —!** ¡ahora no nos debemos nada!; **let's call it —** hagamos las paces; **to cry —** (*querer*) hacer las paces.
quitter ['kwitə*] *n* remolón *m*, persona *f* que deja fácilmente lo empezado; cobarde *mf*.
quiver [1] ['kwivə*] *n* carcaj *m*, aljaba *f*.
quiver [2] ['kwivə*] **1** *n* temblor *m*, estremecimiento *m*. **2** *vi* temblar, estremecerse (*with* de).
qui vive [ki'viːv]: **to be on the —** estar alerta.
Quixote ['kwiksət] *m* Quijote.
quixotic [kwik'sɔtik] *adj* quijotesco.
quixotically [kwik'sɔtikəli] *adv* quijotescamente.
quixotism ['kwiksətizəm] *n* quijotismo *m*.
quiz [kwiz] **1** *n* (*interrogation*) interrogatorio *m*; examen *m*; (*inquiry*) encuesta *f*; (*Radio etc; also* **— programme**) concurso *m* (*radiofónico etc*).
2 *vt* (*stare at*) mirar con curiosidad; (*question*) interrogar (*about* sobre).
quizzical ['kwizikəl] *adj* burlón.
quizzically ['kwizikəli] *adv*: **he looked at me —** me miró burlón.
quod [kwɔd] *n* (*sl*) chirona *f*.
quoin [kwɔin] *n* (*angle*) esquina *f*, ángulo *m*; (*stone*) piedra *f* angular; (*Typ*) cuña *f*.
quoit [kwɔit] *n* aro *m*, tejo *m*; **—s** juego *m* de aros, juego *m* de tejos.
quondam ['kwɔndæm] *adj* antiguo.
Quonset ['kwɔnsit] *n* (*Protected Trade Name in US*) cobertizo *m* de metal semicilíndrico.
quorum ['kwɔːrəm] *n* quórum *m*; **to constitute a —** constituir un quórum; **what number constitutes a —?** ¿cuántos constituyen un quórum?
quota ['kwəutə] *n* cuota *f*; (*Comm etc*) contingente *m*, cupo *m*; **import —** cupo *m* de importación.
quotable ['kwəutəbl] *adj* citable; digno de citarse; (*Fin*) cotizable.
quotation [kwəu'teiʃən] *n* (*words*) cita *f*; (*act*) citación *f*; (*Fin*) cotización *f*.
quotation marks [kwəu'teiʃən,maːks] *npl* comillas *fpl*.
quote [kwəut] **1** *vt* (a) citar; *reference number etc* expresar; *example* dar, aducir; **he —d Góngora** citó a Góngora; **he can — Góngora all day long** es capaz de seguir recitando versos de Góngora hasta cuando sea; **please — the number of the postal order** por favor exprese el número del giro postal; **can you — me an example?** ¿puede darme un ejemplo?
(b) (*Fin*) cotizar (*at* en); **it is not —d on the Stock Exchange** no se cotiza en la Bolsa.
2 *vi* citar; **to — from an author** citar versos (*etc*) de un autor; **and I —** y aquí cito sus propias palabras.
3 *n* cita *f*; **—s** (*inverted commas*) comillas *fpl*; **"—"** "comienza la cita"; **"close the —"**, **"end of —"** "fin de la cita".
quoth [kwəuθ] *vi* (*arch*): **— I** dije yo; **— he** dijo él.
quotient ['kwəuʃənt] *n* cociente *m*; **intelligence —** cociente *m* intelectual.

R

rabbi ['ræbai] n rabino m; (before name) rabí m; **chief —** gran rabino m.

rabbinical [rə'binikəl] adj rabínico.

rabbit ['ræbit] 1 n conejo m; (Sport, fam) jugador m inhábil; **Peter R—** el Conejo Peter; **Welsh —** pan m con queso tostado.
2 vi: **to go —ing** (ir a) cazar conejos.

rabbit hole ['ræbithəul] n hura f de conejos.

rabbit hutch ['ræbithʌtʃ] n conejera f.

rabbit warren ['ræbit,wɔrən] n madriguera f de conejos.

rabble ['ræbl] n (the —) canalla f, chusma f; **a — of** una multitud turbulenta de.

rabble-rouser ['ræbl,rauzə*] n agitador m, demagogo m.

rabble-rousing ['ræbl'rauziŋ] n agitación f, demagogia f.

Rabelaisian [,ræbə'leiziən] adj rabelasiano.

rabid ['ræbid] adj (Med) rabioso; (fig) rabioso, fanático.

rabies ['reibi:z] n rabia f.

raccoon [rə'ku:n] n mapache m.

race¹ [reis] 1 n (a) (contest) carrera f, (on water) regata f; **—s** carreras fpl; **the — for the moon** la carrera hacia la luna; **— against the clock** carrera f contra reloj; **arms —** carrera f de armamentos; **flat —** carrera f lisa; **long-distance —** carrera f de fondo; **relay —** carrera f de relevos; **walking —** carrera f pedestre; **to go to the —s** ir a las carreras; **to run a —** tomar parte en una carrera; **you ran a good —** corriste muy bien.
(b) (rush) carrera f, corrida f; **the — to the bus** la carrera precipitada para coger el autobús; **it was a — to finish it in time** nos dimos prisa para terminarlo a tiempo.
(c) (current) corriente f fuerte; (of mill) caz m, saetín m.
2 vt (a) horse etc hacer correr, (at race meeting) presentar.
(b) **to — someone** competir con uno en una carrera (or regata); **I'll — you!** ¡te echo una carrera!, ¡a ver quién corre más!; **I'll — you home!** ¡a ver quién llega primero a casa!
(c) (Aut etc) **to — an engine** acelerar un motor al máximo, hacer funcionar un motor a velocidad excesiva.
(d) **to — a plan through** hacer que se apruebe un proyecto de prisa; no permitir que se discuta debidamente un proyecto.
3 vi (a) (go fast) correr de prisa, (Aut etc) ir a máxima velocidad; **to — along** ir corriendo; **to — down a hill** ir cuesta abajo a máxima velocidad; **he —d past us** pasó delante de nosotros corriendo como un demonio.
(b) (pulse) latir a ritmo acelerado; (engine) girar a velocidad excesiva.
(c) (in contest) competir; presentarse; **they will — at 3 o'clock** empezarán la carrera a las 3; **we're not racing today** no tomamos parte hoy; **when did you last —?** ¿cuándo corriste (etc) la última vez?

race² [reis] n raza f; casta f, estirpe f, familia f; (pej) ralea f; (Bio) raza f; **human —** género m humano; **the white —** la raza blanca; **he comes from a — of smugglers** es de linaje de contrabandistas.

race card ['reiska:d] n programa m de carreras.

racecourse ['reiskɔ:s] n hipódromo m, cancha f (S Am).

racegoer ['reisgəuə*] n el m (or la f) que asiste a las carreras, aficionado m a las carreras (de caballos).

race hatred ['reis'heitrid] n odio m racial.

racehorse ['reishɔ:s] n caballo m de carreras.

raceme ['ræsi:m] n racimo m.

race meeting ['reis,mi:tiŋ] n reunión f; concurso m hípico.

racer ['reisə*] n corredor m; (horse) caballo m de carreras; (Aut) coche m de carreras.

race riot ['reis,raiət] n disturbio m provocado por odios raciales, motín m de carácter racista.

racetrack ['reistræk] n (horses) pista f, cancha f (S Am), hipódromo m; (Aut etc) autódromo m.

Rachel ['reitʃəl] f Raquel.

rachitic [ræ'kitik] adj raquítico.

racial ['reiʃəl] adj racial; racista.

racialism ['reiʃəlizəm] n racismo m.

racialist ['reiʃəlist] 1 adj racista. 2 n racista mf.

raciness ['reisinis] n picante m, sal f, vivacidad f.

racing ['reisiŋ] 1 n carreras fpl.
2 attr de carreras; **— calendar** calendario m de carreras (de caballos); **— car** coche m de carreras; **— driver, — motorist** corredor m automovilista.

racism ['reizizəm] n racismo m.

rack¹ [ræk] 1 n (shelf) estante m, estantería f, anaquel m; (for clothes etc) percha f, perchero m, cuelgacapas m; (Rail) rejilla f; (Mech) cremallera f; (for torture) potro m; (for arms) armero m; (for billiard cues) taquera f; **— and pinion** cremallera f y piñón.
2 vt atormentar; **to be —ed by pains** tener dolores atroces por todas partes; **to be —ed by remorse** ser atormentado por el remordimiento; see **brain**.

rack² [ræk] vt wine (also **to — off**) trasegar.

rack³ [ræk] n: **to go to — and ruin** arruinarse, echarse a perder.

racket¹ ['rækit] n, **racquet** ['rækit] n raqueta f; **—s** (game) especie de tenis jugado contra frontón.

racket² ['rækit] 1 n (a) (din) ruido m, estrépito m; (confused noise) barahúnda f, jaleo m; **you never heard such a —!** ¡no se había oído nunca tal ruido!; **to kick up (or make) a —** armar un jaleo, meter ruido.
(b) (trick) trampa f, trapacería f; (criminal) estafa f, timo m; (blackmail, protection) chantaje m; **the drug —** el negocio ilegal de los narcóticos; **the car —** (hum) el negocio del automóvil; **it's a —!** ¡aquí hay trampa!; **what — are you in?** ¿a qué se dedica Vd?; **to stand the —** pagar los platos rotos.
2 vi (make noise) hacer ruido, armar un jaleo (also **to — about**); (celebrate) jaranear.

racketeer [,ræki'tiə*] n (esp US) estafador m, timador m; chantajista m.

racketeering [,ræki'tiəriŋ] n (esp US) chantaje m sistematizado, crimen m organizado.

racking ['rækiŋ] adj pain atroz.

rack railway ['ræk'reilwei] n ferrocarril m de cremallera.

rack-rent ['rækrent] n alquiler m exorbitante.

raconteur [,rækɔn'tə:*] n narrador m, (esp) el que cuenta con gracia los chistes.

racoon [rə'ku:n] n mapache m.

racquet ['rækit] n see **racket¹**.

racy ['reisi] adj picante, salado, vivo.

radar ['reida:*] n radar m.

radar screen ['reida:skri:n] n pantalla f de radar.

radar station ['reida:,steiʃən] n estación f de radar.

raddle ['rædl] 1 n almagre m. 2 vt almagrar.

radial ['reidiəl] adj radial.

radiance ['reidiəns] n brillantez f, resplandor m.

radiant ['reidiənt] adj radiante, brillante, resplandeciente; **a — smile** una sonrisa radiante; **the bride was —** la novia estaba hermosísima; **to be — with happiness** estar radiante de felicidad.

radiantly ['reidiəntli] adv brillantemente; **to be — happy** irradiar felicidad; **to smile — at someone** echar una sonrisa radiante a uno.

radiate¹ ['reidieit] adj radiado.

radiate² ['reidieit] *vt* radiar, irradiar; *happiness etc* difundir; **lines that — from the centre** líneas *fpl* que se extienden desde el centro.

radiation [,reidi'eiʃən] *n* radiación *f*.

radiation sickness [,reidi'eiʃən,siknis] *n* enfermedad *f* de radiación.

radiator ['reidieitə*] *n* radiador *m*.

radiator cap ['reidieitə,kæp] *n* (*Aut*) tapón *m* de radiador.

radical ['rædikəl] **1** *adj* radical. **2** *n* (*all senses*) radical *m*.

radicalism ['rædikəlizəm] *n* radicalismo *m*.

radically ['rædikəli] *adv* radicalmente.

radicle ['rædikl] *n* (*Bot*) radícula *f*.

radio ['reidiəu] **1** *n* (*as science etc*) radio *f*, radiofonía *f*; (*set*) radio *f*, receptor *m* de radio, radiorreceptor *m*; **by —, on the —, over the —** por radio; **to talk on the —** hablar por radio.
2 *attr*: — **announcer** locutor *m* de radio, locutora *f* de radio; — **play** comedia *f* radiofónica; — **programme** programa *m* de radio.
3 *vt* radiar, transmitir por radio.
4 *vi*: **to — to someone** enviar un mensaje a uno por radio.

radioactive ['reidiəu'æktiv] *adj* radiactivo.

radioactivity ['reidiəuæk'tiviti] *n* radiactividad *f*.

radio astronomy ['reidiəuəs'trɔnəmi] *n* radioastronomía *f*.

radio beacon ['reidiəu,bi:kən] *n* radiofaro *m*.

radiobiology [,reidiəubai'ɔlədʒi] *n* radiobiología *f*.

radio-controlled ['reidiəukən'trəuld] *adj* teledirigido.

radiogram ['reidiəugræm] *n* (*set*) radiogramola *f*; (*message*) radiograma *m*.

radiograph ['reidiəugrɑ:f] **1** *n* radiografía *f*. **2** *vt* radiografiar.

radiographer [,reidi'ɔgrəfə*] *n* ayudante *mf* radiólogo.

radiography [,reidi'ɔgrəfi] *n* radiografía *f*.

radioisotope ['reidiəu'aisətəup] *n* radioisótopo *m*.

radiologist [,reidi'ɔlədʒist] *n* radiólogo *m*.

radiology [,reidi'ɔlədʒi] *n* radiología *f*.

radioscopy [,reidi'ɔskəpi] *n* radioscopia *f*.

radio set ['reidiəu,set] *n* radio *f*, receptor *m* de radio, radiorreceptor *m*.

radio station ['reidiəu,steiʃən] *n* emisora *f*.

radiotelephone ['reidiəu'telifəun] *n* radioteléfono *m*.

radiotelephony [,reidiəutə'lefəni] *n* radiotelefonía *f*.

radio telescope ['reidiəu'teliskəup] *n* radiotelescopia *m*.

radiotherapy [,reidiəu'θerəpi] *n* radioterapia *f*.

radish ['rædiʃ] *n* rábano *m*.

radium ['reidiəm] *n* radio *m*.

radius ['reidiəs] *n*, *pl* **radii** ['reidiai] (*all senses*) radio *m*; **within a — of 50 miles** en un radio de 50 millas.

radix ['reidiks] *n*, *pl* **radices** ['reidisi:z] (*Bot*, *Gram*) raíz *f*; (*Math*) base *f*.

raffia ['ræfiə] *n* rafia *f*.

raffish ['ræfiʃ] *adj* disipado, disoluto.

raffle ['ræfl] **1** *n* rifa *f*, sorteo *m*. **2** *vt* rifar, sortear; **10 bottles will be —d for charity** se sortearán 10 botellas con fines benéficos.

raft [rɑ:ft] *n* balsa *f*, almadía *f*; **life-saving —** balsa *f* salvavidas; **rubber —** balsa *f* neumática.

rafter ['rɑ:ftə*] *n* viga *f*, cabrio *m*.

rag¹ [ræg] *n* (a) (*piece of cloth*) trapo; (*for cleaning*) trapo *m*, paño *m*; (*shred of clothing*) andrajo *m*, harapo *m*; **—s** (*clothes: fam*) trapos *mpl*; **to be in —s** estar harapiento, estar en andrajos; **to chew the —** (*US: chat*) charlar, pasar el rato, (*argue*) discutir; **to feel like a —** estar hecho cisco; **she hasn't a — to her back** no tiene con qué vestirse; **to put on one's glad —s** endomingarse; **it's like a red — to a bull** es lo que más le provoca a cólera, no hay nada que más le enfurezca.
(b) (*newspaper: fam*) periodicucho *m* (*fam*).

rag² [ræg] **1** *n* (*practical joke*) broma *f* pesada; (*Univ*) broma *f* estudiantil, (*for charity*) función *f* estudiantil benéfica; **we did it just for a —** lo hicimos en broma nada más.
2 *vt* dar guerra a, tomar el pelo a; **they were —ging him about his new tie** le estaban tomando el pelo con motivo de la nueva corbata.
3 *vi* guasearse, bromearse; **I was only —ging** lo dije en broma.

ragamuffin ['rægə,mʌfin] *n* granuja *m*, galopín *m*.

rag-and-bone man [,rægən'bəunmæn] *n*, *pl* **— men** [men] trapero *m*.

ragbag ['rægbæg] *n* talego *m* de recortes; (*fig*)

mezcolanza *f*, cajón *m* de sastre; **it's a — of a book** es un libro hecho de muchos trozos insertos sin orden.

rag doll ['ræg'dɔl] *n* muñeca *f* de trapo.

rage [reidʒ] **1** *n* (a) (*anger*) rabia *f*, furor *m*, ira *f*; (*of wind etc*) furia *f*; **to be in a —** estar furioso (*about* por, *with someone* contra uno); **to fly into a —** encolerizarse; **to vent one's — on someone** descargar su indignación sobre uno.
(b) (*fashion*) boga *f*, moda *f* (*for* de); (*craze*) manía *f* (*for* de); **it's all the —** es la moda, es la última; **his dresses are all the — in New York** sus vestidos hacen furor en Nueva York.
2 *vi* (a) (*be angry*) estar furioso, rabiar; **to — against someone** estar furioso contra uno; culpar amargamente a uno; **to — against something** protestar furiosamente contra algo.
(b) (*of pain*) doler atrozmente; (*sea etc*) enfurecerse; (*wind*) bramar; (*fire*, *plague etc*) desencadenarse; continuar con pleno vigor; **fire —d in the building for 3 hours** durante 3 horas no se pudo apagar el incendio que consumía el edificio.

rag fair ['rægfɛə*] *n* rastro *m*, feria *f* de objetos usados.

ragged ['rægid] *adj* *dress* roto; *person* andrajoso, harapiento; *edge* desigual, mellado; *coastline etc* accidentado; *line*, *procession* confuso, desordenado, sin orden; *style* descuidado; (*Mus*) *note* poco suave.

ragged robin ['rægid'rɔbin] *n* (*Bot*) cuclillo *m*.

raging ['reidʒiŋ] *adj* rabioso, furioso; *storm etc* violento; *pain* atroz, agudo; **to be in a — temper** estar furiosísimo.

raglan ['ræglən] *n* raglán *m*.

ragman ['rægmæn] *n*, *pl* **—men** [men] trapero *m*.

ragout ['rægu:] *n* guisado *m*.

ragpicker ['rægpikə*] *n* trapero *m*.

rag tag ['rægtæg] *n* (*fam*) chusma *f* (*also* — **and bobtail**).

ragtime ['rægtaim] *n* (*Mus*) tiempo *m* sincopado; **in —** sincopado.

rag trade ['rægtreid] *n* (*fam*) industria *f* del vestido, comercio *m* del vestido.

ragwort ['rægwə:t] *n* hierba *f* lombriguera.

raid [reid] **1** *n* (*into territory across border etc*) incursión *f*, correría *f*; (*Aer*) ataque *m* (*on* contra), bombardeo *m* (*on* de); (*sweep by police*) redada *f*; (*by criminals*) asalto *m* (*on* a); **the men are away on a —** los hombres están fuera en una correría; **only 5 aircraft returned from the —** solamente 5 aviones regresaron después del ataque; **there was a — on the jeweller's last night** anoche fue asaltada la joyería.
2 *vt* (*by land*) invadir, atacar, hacer una incursión en; (*Aer*) atacar, bombardear; (*by criminals*) asaltar; **the boys —ed the orchard** los muchachos invadieron el huerto; **the police —ed the club** la policía registró el club; **shall we — the larder?** ¿asaltamos la despensa?, ¿vamos a coger algo en la despensa?; **the king's tomb had already been —ed** la tumba del rey había sido ya saqueada.

raider ['reidə*] *n* (*across frontier*) invasor *m*, incursor *m*; (*Aer*) bombardero *m*; (*Naut*) buque *m* corsario; (*criminal*) criminal *m*, asaltante *m*, ladrón *m*; **the —s got away with some diamonds** los ladrones se llevaron varios diamantes.

rail¹ [reil] **1** *n* (a) (*hand—*) baranda *f*, barandilla *f*, pasamanos *m*; (*Naut*) barandilla *f*; borda *f*; (*of bar*) apoyo *m* para los pies; **—s** (*fence*) cerca *f*, palizada *f*.
(b) (*Rail*) carril *m*, riel *m*; **—s** (*freq*) vía *f*; **—s** (*Fin*) acciones *fpl* de sociedades ferroviarias; **to come off** (*or* **run off, jump, leave**) **the —s** descarrilar; **to run off the —s** (*fig*) extraviarse; **by —** por ferrocarril.
2 *vt* (a) (*also* **to — in, to — off**) cercar con una barandilla, poner barandilla a.
(b) (*Rail*) transportar por ferrocarril, mandar por ferrocarril.

rail² [reil] *n* (*Orn*) rascón *m*.

rail³ [reil] *vi*: **to — at, to — against** protestar amargamente contra, quejarse amargamente de.

railhead ['reilhed] *n* estación *f* terminal.

railing ['reiliŋ] *n* baranda *f*, barandilla *f*, pasamanos *m*; **—s** verja *f*, enrejado *m*.

raillery ['reiləri] *n* burlas *fpl*, chanzas *fpl*.

railroad ['reilrəud] **1** *n* (*US*) *see* **railway**.
2 *vt* *person* (*sl*) encarcelar falsamente; **to — something through** llevar algo a cabo muy precipitadamente; **to — a bill through** hacer que se apruebe un decreto de ley sin discutirse.

railway ['reilwei] **1** *n* ferrocarril *m*; (*as track*) vía *f*, vía *f* férrea; (*as route*) línea *f* (de ferrocarril);

aerial — funicular m aéreo; **elevated** —, **overhead** — ferrocarril m elevado; **narrow-gauge** — ferrocarril m de vía estrecha; **scenic** — montaña f rusa; **underground** — ferrocarril m subterráneo.

2 attr ferroviario.

railway carriage ['reilwei,kærid3] n vagón m, coche m (de ferrocarril).

railway engine ['reilwei,end3in] n máquina f, locomotora f.

railway line ['reilwei,lain] n (track) vía f, vía f férrea; (route) línea f (de ferrocarril).

railwayman ['reilweimən] n, pl **-men** [mən] ferroviario m.

railway station ['reilwei,steiʃən] n estación f (de ferrocarril).

railway ticket ['reilwei,tikit] n billete m de ferrocarril.

raiment ['reimənt] n (lit) hábitos mpl, vestimenta f.

rain [rein] 1 n lluvia f (also fig); **the** —**s** la época de las lluvias; **a** — **of gifts** una lluvia de regalos; **a walk in the** — un paseo bajo la lluvia; **to be out in the** — estar fuera aguantando la lluvia; **come in out of the** —! ¡entra, que te vas a mojar!; **come** — **or shine** (fig) contra viento y marea; **if the** — **keeps off** si no llueve; **it looks like** — parece que va a llover.

2 vti llover; **to** — **blows on someone** llover golpes sobre uno; **to** — **gifts on someone** colmar a uno de regalos; **hereabouts it** —**s soot** por aquí llueve hollín; **to** — **cats and dogs** llover a cántaros; **blows** —**ed upon him** llovieron sobre él los golpes; **gifts** —**ed upon him** le llovieron regalos encima; **it** —**s on the just as well as on the unjust** la lluvia cae sobre los buenos como sobre los malos; **it never** —**s but it pours** (fig) llueve sobre mojado, una desgracia nunca viene sola.

rain belt ['reinbelt] n zona f de lluvias.

rainbow ['reinbəu] n arco m iris.

rainbow trout ['reinbəu'traut] n trucha f arco iris.

raincoat ['reinkəut] n impermeable m.

raincloud ['reinklaud] n nubarrón m.

raindrop ['reindrɔp] n gota f de agua.

rainfall ['reinfɔ:l] n (act) precipitación f; (quantity) lluvia f, cantidad f de lluvia; **the region has 3" of** — **a year** la región tiene 3 pulgadas de lluvia al año.

rain gauge ['reingeid3] n pluviómetro m.

raininess ['reininis] n lo lluvioso.

rainless ['reinlis] adj sin lluvia, seco.

rainproof ['reinpru:f] adj impermeable, a prueba de lluvia.

rainstorm ['reinstɔ:m] n tempestad f de lluvia.

rainwater ['reinwɔ:tə*] n agua f llovediza, agua f de lluvia.

rainy ['reini] adj climate, region lluvioso; — **day** día m de lluvia, (fig) tiempo m de escasez; — **season** estación f de las lluvias; **it was so** — **yesterday** llovió tanto ayer.

raise [reiz] 1 n (esp US) aumento m, subida f; (of salary) aumento m de sueldo; (Cards) sobremarca f.

2 vt (in some senses also **to** — **up**) |(a) (lift) fallen object, weight, arm, eyes etc levantar, alzar, elevar; hat quitarse; flag izar, enarbolar; dust levantar; dough fermentar; sunken ship sacar a flote; camp, siege levantar; spirits evocar; (from the dead) resucitar; (Math) elevar (a una potencia); **to** — **one's glass** alzar el vaso; **to** — **someone to power** alzar a uno al poder; **to** — **the standard of revolt** pronunciarse, sublevarse; **to** — **tribesmen in revolt** sublevar las tribus; **to** — **the people against a tyrant** hacer que el pueblo se subleve contra un tirano; **to** — **someone's hopes excessively** hacer a uno concebir esperanzas desmesuradas; **to** — **someone's spirits** infundir ánimo a uno; **to** — **someone up from poverty** ayudar a uno a salir de la miseria.

(b) (erect) building erigir, edificar; statue erigir.

(c) (increase) price, salary aumentar, subir; production aumentar; person (in rank) ascender (to a); voice levantar; **don't** — **your voice!** ¡no levantes la voz!

(d) (bring up etc) family, livestock criar; crop cultivar.

(e) (produce) causar, producir; dar lugar a; bump etc causar; laughter suscitar, provocar; doubts suscitar; problem, question plantear; objection poner, hacer; cry etc poner; outcry armar; **I'll** — **the point with them** se lo mencionaré; **it** —**s many problems for us** nos plantea muchos problemas; **this** —**s the question of whether** . . .

esto plantea el problema de si . . .; **can't you** — **a smile?** ¿no guardas una sonrisa para mí?

(f) (get together) army reclutar; funds reunir; loan lograr, obtener; new taxes imponer; **to** — **money on an estate** obtener dinero hipotecando una propiedad.

3 vr: **to** — **oneself** alzarse, levantarse; **he** —**d himself up on one elbow** se apoyó en un codo; **he has** —**d himself up from nothing** ha salido de la nada.

raised [reizd] adj (in relief) en relieve; (embossed) de realce.

raisin ['reizən] n pasa f de Corinto.

raison d'être ['reizɔ:n'dɛːtr] n razón f de ser.

raj [rɑ:d3] n: **the British** — el imperio británico (en la India); la soberanía británica.

rajah ['rɑ:d3ə] n rajá m.

rake[1] [reik] 1 n (garden —) rastrillo m; (Agr) rastro m; (fire —) hurgón m.

2 vt (Agr etc) rastrillar; fire hurgar; (with shots etc) barrer; (with eyes) examinar, escudriñar; (search, ransack) registrar, buscar en; **to** — **in** gambling chips recoger; **they** —**d in a profit of £100** se sacaron 100 libras de ganancia limpia; **he** —**s in £5 on every deal** se toma una tajada de 5 libras de cada negocio; **he must be raking it in** está acuñando dinero; **to** — **off** quitar con el rastrillo; **to** — **together** reunir (or recoger) con el rastrillo; **to** — **together** (fig) reunir (con dificultad); **we managed to** — **a team together** por fin logramos formar un equipo; **to** — **up** subject sacar a relucir; the past etc remover; **why did you have to** — **that up?** ¿con qué motivo has vuelto a mencionar eso?

rake[2] [reik] n (person) libertino m, calavera m; **old** — viejo m verde.

rake[3] [reik] 1 n (Naut) inclinación f. 2 vt inclinar.

rake-off ['reikɔf] n (fam) tajada f.

rakish[1] ['reikiʃ] adj (person) libertino, disoluto.

rakish[2] ['reikiʃ] adj ship de palos inclinados; (fast-looking) veloz, ligero; (smart) elegante, gallardo; **with his hat at a** — **angle** con el sombrero echado de lado, con el sombrero a lo chulo.

rakishly ['reikiʃli] adv (of hat etc) echado al lado, a lo chulo; elegantemente.

rally[1] ['ræli] 1 n (Pol etc) reunión f, mitin m, manifestación f; (of scouts etc) reunión f, congreso m; (Aut) rallye m; (Tennis) peloteo m; (Mil) repliegue m; (Med, Fin etc) recuperación f.

2 vt (gather) reunir; (Mil) rehacer; faculties concentrar; (encourage) reanimar, infundir ánimo a, fortalecer.

3 vi (gather) reunirse (around someone, to someone en torno a uno); (demonstrate) manifestarse; (Mil) replegarse, rehacerse; (Med, Fin etc) recuperarse, mejorar; **they rallied to him** se reunieron en torno a él, afirmaron su adhesión, acudieron a su lado; **to** — **to the call** responder a la llamada; **everyone must** — **round** todos hemos de afirmar nuestra unidad; **they have all rallied round nobly** todos han hecho maravillas en un esfuerzo común.

rally[2] ['ræli] vt tomar el pelo a.

rallying point ['ræliiŋ,pɔint] n punto m de reunión.

ram [ræm] 1 n (Zool) carnero m, morueco m, (Astron) Aries m; (Mil) ariete m; (Naut) espolón m; (Tech: rammer) pisón m, (pile driver) martillo m pilón.

2 vt (a) (tread down) apisonar; (squeeze) apretar; (fill) rellenar (with de); **to** — **a charge home** introducir una carga a fondo; **they** —**med it down his throat** se lo hicieron tragar a la fuerza; **to** — **clothes into a case** poner la ropa apretadamente en una maleta; **to** — **something into a hole** meter algo apretadamente en un agujero, introducir algo apretadamente en un agujero; **we had Campoamor** —**med into us at school** nos dimos un atracón de Campoamor en el colegio.

(b) (collide with) chocar con, dar contra; (Naut: deliberately) atacar con el espolón; **the car** —**med the lamppost** el coche chocó con el farol.

Ramadan [,ræmə'dæn] n ramadán m.

ramble ['ræmbl] 1 n paseo m por el campo, excursión f a pie, caminata f; **to go for a** — salir de excursión a pie, dar una caminata.

2 vi (a) (walk) salir de excursión a pie, dar una caminata; **we spent a week rambling in the hills** pasamos una semana explorando la montaña a pie.

(b) (in speech) divagar; (lose thread) perder el hilo, salirse del tema; (of river etc) serpentear; (of plant) extenderse como una enredadera; **he just** —**d on and on** siguió hablando confusamente.

rambler ['ræmblə*] n (person) excursionista mf (a pie); — **rose** rosal m trepador.

rambling ['ræmbliŋ] **1** *adj plant* trepador; *speech* divagador, prolijo y confuso, enmarañado; *house* laberíntico, construido sobre un plano poco lógico. **2** *n* **(a)** excursionismo *m* a pie; excursiones *fpl* a pie.
(b) (*also* —s) desvaríos *mpl*.
ramification [,ræmifi'keiʃən] *n* ramificación *f*; **in all its** —s en toda su complejidad; **with numerous** —s con innumerables ramificaciones; **we don't yet know all the** —s no conocemos todavía todos los recovecos.
ramify ['ræmifai] *vi* ramificarse.
ramjet ['ræm'dʒet] *n* postquemador *m*, tubo *m* de propulsión; — **plane** avión *m* de retropropulsión.
rammer ['ræmə*] *n* pisón *m*.
ramp[1] [ræmp] *n* (*incline*) rampa *f*.
ramp[2] [ræmp] *n* (*fam*) estafa *f*, timo *m*; **the housing** — el escándalo (del precio) de la vivienda; **it's a** —! ¡no hay derecho!, ¡esto no se puede consentir!
rampage [ræm'peidʒ] **1** *n*: **to be on the** — = **2** *vi* desbocarse, desmandarse; comportarse como un loco; **the crowd** —**d through the market** la multitud corrió alocada por el mercado.
rampancy ['ræmpənsi] *n* exuberancia *f*, lozanía *f*; furia *f*, desenfreno *m*; agresividad *f*; predominio *m*.
rampant ['ræmpənt] *adj* (*Her*) rampante; (*Bot*) exuberante, lozano; *person* furioso, desenfrenado; agresivo; **to be** — (*prevail*) cundir, predominar; **he's a** — **anarchist** es un anarquista furibundo; **anarchism is** — **here** aquí el anarquismo está muy extendido, aquí ha cundido mucho el anarquismo.
rampart ['ræmpɑːt] *n* terraplén *m*, defensa *f*; (*city wall*) muralla *f*; **the** —s **of York** la muralla de York.
ramrod ['ræmrɔd] *n* baqueta *f*, atacador *m*.
ramshackle ['ræm,ʃækl] *adj* desvencijado, destartalado.
ram's horn ['ræmzhɔːn] *n* cuerno *m* de carnero.
ran [ræn] *pret of* **run**; **also** — caballo *m* (*etc*) que no logró colocarse, (*fig*) fracasado *m*.
ranch [rɑːntʃ] *n* (*US*) hacienda *f*; estancia *f*, rancho *m* (*SAm*).
rancher ['rɑːntʃə*] *n* (*US*) ganadero *m*.
rancid ['rænsid] *adj* rancio.
rancidity [ræn'siditi] *n*, **rancidness** ['rænsidnis] *n* rancidez *f*, ranciedad *f*.
rancorous ['ræŋkərəs] *adj* rencoroso.
rancour, (*US*) **rancor** ['ræŋkə*] *n* rencor *m*; **with** — **towards none** sin rencor para nadie.
randiness ['rændinis] *n* cachondez *f*.
random ['rændəm] **1** *adj* fortuito, casual; hecho al azar, hecho sin pensar; sin orden ni concierto; *distribution* (*Math*) aleatorio; *sample* seleccionado al azar; *shot* sin apuntar.
2 *n*: **at** — al azar; sin pensar; **to choose something at** — escoger algo sin pensar; **to hit out at** — repartir golpes por todos lados; **to talk at** — hablar sin pesar las palabras.
randy ['rændi] *adj* cachondo; **to feel** — estar cachondo.
rang [ræŋ] *pret of* **ring**[2].
range [reindʒ] **1** *n* **(a)** (*row*) línea *f*, hilera *f*; (*of buildings*) grupo *m*; (*of mountains*) sierra *f*, cadena *f*, cordillera *f*.
(b) (*mostly US Agr*) dehesa *f*, terreno *m* de pasto.
(c) (*for shooting: in open*) campo *m* de tiro, (*at fair*) galería *f* de tiro, barraca *f* de tiro.
(d) (*extent*) extensión *f*; (*of voice*) extensión *f*, alcance *m*, compás *m*; (*series*) serie *f*; escala *f*, gama *f*; (*Comm*) surtido *m*; — **of action** esfera *f* de acción; — **of vision** campo *m* visual; **the present** — **of knowledge** la extensión de los conocimientos actuales; — **of variation** amplitud *f* de variación; — **of colours** gama *f* de colores; — **of prices** escala *f* de precios; — **of speeds** escala *f* de velocidades; — **of frequencies** gama *f* de frecuencias; **the** — **of someone's mind** el alcance de la inteligencia de uno; **over the whole** — **of politics** sobre todo el campo de la política; **that's outside my** — eso no pertenece a mi esfera de actividades; no sé nada de eso; **to go outside one's normal** — salir de su acostumbrada esfera de actividades; **she has a wide** — **of interests** tiene una extensa gama de intereses; **they have a new** — **of models** tienen una nueva gama de modelos.
(e) (*Bio*) distribución *f*, zona *f* de distribución; **the plant has a limited** — la planta tiene una distribución restringida; **this is outside its normal** — este sitio queda fuera de su zona acostumbrada; **its** — **extends to León** alcanza la provincia de León.

(f) (*distance attainable*: Mil) alcance *m*, alcance *m* de tiro; distancia *f*; **a gun with a** — **of 3 miles** un cañón con un alcance de 3 millas; **at a** — **of 5 miles** a una distancia de 5 millas; **at close** — de cerca, (*point-blank*) a quemarropa; **within** — al alcance, a tiro, a tiro de fusil (*etc*); **the plane is out of** — el avión está fuera de alcance; **to correct the** — corregir la puntería; **to take the** — averiguar la distancia.
(g) (*of plane, ship*) autonomía *f*, radio *m* de acción; **the** — **is 3,000 miles** la autonomía es de 3.000 millas.
(h) (*kitchen* —) cocina *f* económica, fogón *m*.
2 *vt* **(a)** (*arrange*) arreglar, ordenar; clasificar; (*line up*) alinear; (*place*) colocar; **he** —**d them along the wall** los colocó a lo largo de la pared.
(b) (*go about*) recorrer; **they** —**d the countryside** recorrieron el campo; **his eye** —**d the horizon** escudriñó el horizonte.
(c) to — **a gun** apuntar un cañón.
3 *vi* **(a)** (*extend*) extenderse; (*wander over*) recorrer; vagar por; **the insect** —s **from Andalusia to Burgos** el insecto se extiende desde Andalucía hasta Burgos; **research ranging over a wide field** investigaciones *fpl* que se extienden sobre un ancho campo; investigaciones *fpl* de gran alcance; **his mind** —s **widely** tiene una mentalidad de gran alcance; **the troops** —**d over the whole province** las tropas recorrieron toda la provincia.
(b) (*of numbers etc*) oscilar, variar, fluctuar; **temperatures** — **from 5 to 30 degrees** las temperaturas oscilan entre los 5 y 30 grados; **they** — **as high as 40 degrees at times** a veces suben hasta los 40 grados.
4 *vr*: **to** — **oneself with someone** ponerse al lado de uno; **to** — **oneself with a group** sumarse a un grupo.
rangefinder ['reindʒ,faində*] *n* telémetro *m*.
ranger ['reindʒə*] *n* guardabosques *m*.
Rangoon [ræŋ'guːn] Rangún.
rangy ['reindʒi] *adj* ágil, enérgico; fuerte, robusto.
rank[1] [ræŋk] **1** *n* **(a)** (*row*) fila *f*, hilera *f*, línea *f*; (*Mil*) fila *f*; **the** —s **of poplars** las hileras de álamos; **in serried** —s en filas apretadas; **the** —**s, the** — **and file** las masas, la gente común, (*of club*) los socios ordinarios, (*Mil*) los soldados rasos; **in the** —s **of the party** en las filas del partido; **to break** —s romper filas; **to close the** —s apretar las filas; **to join the** —s **of** (*fig*) unirse con, llegar a ser uno de; **to reduce someone to the** —s degradar a uno; **to rise from the** —s ascender desde soldado raso, llegar a oficial.
(b) (*status*) posición *f*, categoría *f*, dignidad *f*, calidad *f*; (*Mil*) graduación *f*, grado *m*, rango *m*; **persons of** — gente *f* de calidad; **a writer of the first** — un escritor de primera categoría; **4 officers of high** — 4 oficiales de alta graduación; **their** —s **range from lieutenant to colonel** sus graduaciones van de teniente a coronel; **to attain the** — **of major** ser ascendido a comandante, llegar a comandante.
(c) (*taxi* —) punto *m*.
2 *vt* clasificar, ordenar; **I** — **him 6th** yo le pongo en 6ª posición; **to** — **A with B** considerar iguales A y B, poner A y B en el mismo nivel; **where would you** — **him?** ¿qué posición le daría Vd?
3 *vi* clasificarse; figurar; **to** — **4th** ocupar el 4º puesto; **to** — **2nd to someone else** tener el segundo lugar después de otra persona; **to** — **high** ocupar una alta posición; **where does she** — **?** ¿qué posición ocupa?; **the shares will** — **for dividend** se pagará el dividendo que corresponda a estas acciones; **to** — **above** ser superior a; **to** — **among** figurar entre; estar al nivel de; **to** — **as** equivaler a, figurar como; **to** — **with** ser igual a, equipararse con, estar al nivel de.
rank[2] [ræŋk] *adj* **(a)** (*Bot*) lozano, exuberante; *soil* fértil; (*thick*) espeso, tupido.
(b) (*smelly*) maloliente, fétido, rancio; **to smell** — oler mal.
(c) (*fig*) **that's** — **nonsense!** ¡puras tonterías!; **it's a** — **bad play** es una obra francamente mala; **it's** — **injustice** es una injusticia manifiesta; **he's a** — **liar** es un mentiroso redomado.
ranker ['ræŋkə*] *n* (*Mil*) oficial *m* que ha sido ascendido de soldado raso.
ranking ['ræŋkiŋ] *n* categoría *f*, clase *f*, posición *f*; (*Mil*) graduación *f*.
rankle ['ræŋkl] *vi*: **to** — **with someone** afligir a uno, roer a uno, amargar la vida a uno; **it still** —s **duele todavía.**
rankly ['ræŋkli] *adv* lozanamente, con exuberancia; espesamente.

rankness ['ræŋknis] n lozanía f, exuberancia f; fertilidad f; espesura f; mal olor m, fetidez f, ranciedad f; (of injustice etc) enormidad f.

ransack ['rænsæk] vt (search) registrar (de arriba abajo); escudriñar (minuciosamente); (pillage) saquear; they —ed the house for arms registraron toda la casa buscando armas; the place had been —ed el local había sido saqueado.

ransom ['rænsəm] 1 n rescate m; (Rel) redención f; to hold someone to — pedir un rescate por uno, (fig) poner a uno entre la espada y la pared; the public is·being held to — by these strikers estos huelguistas amenazan al público de una manera intolerable.
2 vt rescatar; (Rel) redimir.

ransoming ['rænsəmiŋ] n rescate m; redención f.

rant [rænt] 1 n lenguaje m campanudo, lenguaje m declamatorio.
2 vi vociferar, despotricar; hablar en tono violento, hablar en un estilo hinchado; he —ed on about the Pope siguió vociferando injurias contra el papa.

ranter ['ræntə*] n fanfarrón m; orador m campanudo, orador m populachero.

ranting ['ræntiŋ] 1 adj fanfarrón; campanudo, vociferador, chillón.
2 n lenguaje m campanudo, lenguaje m declamatorio; vociferación f; for all his — por más que hable de ese modo fanfarrón.

ranunculus [rə'nʌŋkjuləs] n ranúnculo m.

rap [ræp] 1 n golpecito m, golpe m seco; (at door) llamada f, aldabada f; there was a — at the door se llamó a la puerta; to take the — pagar el pato; to take the — for something sufrir las consecuencias de algo; cargar con la culpa de algo; see care, knuckle.
2 vt golpear, dar un golpecito en, tocar; (fam) criticar severamente; to — out an order espetar una orden.
3 vi: to — at the door llamar a la puerta.

rapacious [rə'peiʃəs] adj rapaz.

rapaciously [rə'peiʃəsli] adv con rapacidad.

rapacity [rə'pæsiti] n rapacidad f.

rape¹ [reip] 1 n violación f, estupro m; (fig) destrucción f, ruina f; attempted — intento m de violación; the — of Poland la destrucción de Polonia.
2 vt violar, estuprar, forzar.

rape² [reip] n (Bio) colza f.

rape oil ['reipɔil] n aceite m de colza.

rapeseed ['reipsi:d] n rabina f.

Raphael ['ræfeiel] m Rafael.

rapid ['ræpid] adj rápido.

rapidity [rə'piditi] n rapidez f.

rapidly ['ræpidli] adv rápidamente.

rapids ['ræpidz] npl rápidos mpl, rabiones mpl.

rapier ['reipiə*] n estoque m.

rapine ['ræpain] n rapiña f.

rapist ['reipist] n (esp US) violador m.

rapping ['ræpiŋ] n golpecitos mpl, golpes mpl secos; llamadas fpl, aldabadas fpl.

rapport [ræ'pɔ:*] n (a) relación f. (b) conformidad f; to be in — with estar conforme con, estar de acuerdo con.

rapprochement [ræ'prɒʃmɑ̃ŋ] n acercamiento m, aproximación f.

rapscallion [ræp'skæliən] n bribón m.

rapt [ræpt] adj arrebatado; (absorbed) absorto, ensimismado; (enraptured) extático, extasiado; with — attention con atención fija; to be — in contemplation estar absorto en la contemplación.

rapture ['ræptʃə*] n éxtasis m, rapto m, arrobamiento m; to be in — estar extasiado, extasiarse; to go into —s extasiarse (over, about ante, con).

rapturous ['ræptʃərəs] adj extático; applause etc entusiasta.

rapturously ['ræptʃərəsli] adv extáticamente; con entusiasmo.

rare¹ [reə*] raro, poco común, nada frecuente; (Phys) ralo; at — intervals muy de tarde en tarde; in a moment of — generosity en un momento de generosidad poco frecuente en él; it is — to find that ... es poco frecuente encontrar que ...; the plant is — in Wales la planta es poco común en Gales; you gave me a — old fright! (fam) ¡qué susto me diste!

rare² [reə*] adj meat poco hecho.

rarebit ['reəbit] n: Welsh — pan m con queso tostado.

rarefaction [,reəri'fækʃən] n rarefacción f.

rarefied ['reərifaid] adj atmosphere (also fig) enrarecido.

rarefy ['reərifai] 1 vt enrarecer. 2 vi enrarecerse.

rarely ['reəli] adv raramente, con poca frecuencia; rara vez, pocas veces, casi nunca; it is — found here aquí se encuentra con poca frecuencia; that method is — satisfactory ese método no es satisfactorio casi nunca.

rareness ['reənis] n, **rarity** ['reəriti] n rareza f; it's a rarity here aquí es una rareza.

rascal ['rɑ:skəl] n pillo m, pícaro m.

rascality [rɑ:s'kæliti] n picardía f.

rascally ['rɑ:skəli] adj pícaro, truhanesco.

rash¹ [ræʃ] n (Med) erupción f (cutánea).

rash² [ræʃ] adj temerario; imprudente; precipitado; that was very — of you en eso has sido muy imprudente.

rasher ['ræʃə*] n lonja f, loncha f.

rashly ['ræʃli] adv temerariamente; imprudentemente; precipitadamente.

rashness ['ræʃnis] n temeridad f; imprudencia f; precipitación f.

rasp [rɑ:sp] 1 n escofia f. 2 vt (a) escofinar, raspar. (b) (say) decir con voz áspera. 3 vi hacer un sonido desapacible.

raspberry ['rɑ:zbəri] n (a) (fruit) frambuesa f; (bush) frambueso m.
(b) (fam: sound) sonido m grosero, sonido m despectivo, sonido m ofensivo; to blow someone a — hacer un gesto grosero a uno; to get the — recibir una bronca, sufrir una repulsa.

raspberry bush ['rɑ:zbəribuʃ] n, **raspberry cane** ['rɑ:zbərikein] n frambueso m.

rasper ['rɑ:spə*] n escofina f, raspador m.

rasping ['rɑ:spiŋ] adj voice etc áspero, desapacible.

rat [ræt] 1 n rata f; (fam: rotter) canalla m, (deserter) desertor m; —s! ¡narices!; you —! ¡bestia!; to smell a — oler el poste; I smell a — aquí hay gato encerrado, esto es sospechoso.
2 vi (a) cazar ratas, matar ratas.
(b) (fam) chaquetear, desertar; to — on someone chivarse de uno, soplar contra uno.

ratable ['reitəbl] adj (property) sujeto a contribución municipal; — value valor m (de una propiedad) sobre el que se calcula la contribución municipal.

ratcatcher ['ræt,kætʃə*] n cazarratas m.

ratchet ['rætʃit] n trinquete m.

ratchet wheel ['rætʃit,wi:l] n rueda f de trinquete.

rate¹ [reit] 1 n (a) (proportion, ratio) proporción f, relación f, razón f; tanto m por ciento; — of births (índice m de) natalidad f; at a — of 5% a un 5 por ciento; at a — of 5 in every 30 a razón de 5 por cada 30; at the — of 3 per person a razón de 3 por persona; at any — de todas formas, de todos modos; at that — de ese modo; if things go on at this — de seguir las cosas así.
(b) (price etc) precio m, tasa f; (of interest etc) tipo m; (of hotel etc) tarifa f; at a cheap — a un precio reducido; the — for the job el sueldo que corresponde al trabajo, el sueldo justo; advertising —s tarifa f de anuncios; see bank — etc; insurance —s tipo m de seguro; market —s precios mpl del mercado, (Fin) cotizaciones fpl; postage — s tarifa f de correo; — of exchange (tipo m de) cambio m; — of interest tipo m de interés; —s of pay tipos mpl de sueldo; — of taxation nivel m de impuestos.
(c) —s (local tax) contribución f municipal; —s and taxes contribuciones fpl e impuestos; we pay £90 in —s pagamos 90 libras de contribuciones.
(d) eg first-rate de primera clase; some third-rate author algún autor de baja categoría.
(e) (speed) velocidad f; (of work etc) ritmo m; — of climb (Aer) velocidad f de subida; — of flow velocidad f de flujo; — of growth ritmo m de expansión; a high — of growth un elevado ritmo de crecimiento; at a great — rápidamente, (of vehicle) a gran velocidad; at a — of 20 knots a una velocidad de 20 nudos.
2 vt (a) (estimate) estimar; (estimate value) tasar, valorar (at en); (classify) clasificar; I — it at £2 yo lo valoro en 2 libras; I — the book highly yo estimo el libro en mucho; I — him highly tengo un muy buen concepto de él; how do you — her? ¿qué opinas de ella?; I — him among my best 3 pupils le pongo entre mis 3 mejores alumnos.
(b) (Fin) imponer contribución municipal a; we are highly —d here aquí nos exigen una contribución elevada; the house is —d at £84 per annum se impone una contribución de 84 libras al año a esta casa, pagamos por esta casa una contribución de 84 libras al año.
3 vi: to — as ser considerado como, ser tenido por; to — for a grant ser de la clase que recibe un subsidio; he just doesn't — no cuenta para nada, no vale para nada.

rate² [reit] *vt* regañar, reñir.

ratepayer ['reitpeɪə*] *n* contribuyente *mf*.

rather ['rɑːðə*] **1** *adv* (a) (*used alone*) antes, más bien; mejor dicho; **or — mejor** dicho; **— it is a matter of money** antes es cuestión de dinero, es al contrario cuestión de dinero.

(b) (*somewhat*) algo, un poco, bastante; **— good** bastante bueno; **— difficult** algo difícil; **it's — wet** está un poco mojado; **I'm — tired** estoy un poco cansado; **there's — a lot** hay bastante; **I — think he won't come** me inclino a creer que no vendrá; **I — expected as much** ya lo preveía; **are you keen to go? . . . yes, I am—** ¿quieres ir en efecto? . . . sí quiero; **isn't she pretty? . . . yes, she is —** ¿es guapa, eh? . . . sí, lo es bastante.

(c) **A — than B** A antes que B, más bien A que B; **this — than that** esto antes que eso; **anything — than that!** ¡todo menos eso!; **play anything — than that** toca cualquier cosa que no sea eso; **I would — not say** prefiero no decirlo; **I would — have sherry** me gustaría más un jerez; **I would — not** más bien no quiero hacerlo (*etc*).

2 *interj* ['rɑːðə*] **would you like some? . . . —!** ¿quieres algo de esto? . . . ¡ya lo creo!

ratification [ˌrætifi'keiʃən] *n* ratificación *f*.

ratify ['rætifai] *vt* ratificar.

rating¹ ['reitiŋ] *n* (a) (*act of valuing*) tasación *f*, valuación *f*; (*value*) valor *m*; (*local tax*) contribución *f*.

(b) (*standing*) clasificación *f*; puesto *m*, posición *f*; (*of ship*) clase *f*; **what's his —?** ¿qué puesto ocupa?; ¿qué opinión hay de él?

(c) (*Naut: person*) marinero *m*.

rating² ['reitiŋ] *n* represión *f*.

ratio ['reiʃiəu] *n* razón *f*, relación *f*, proporción *f*; **in direct —** to en razón directa con; **in the —** of **5 to 2** a razón de 5 a 2; **the — of wages to raw materials** la relación entre los sueldos y las materias primas.

ratiocinate [ræti'ɔsineit] *vi* raciocinar.

ratiocination [ˌrætiɔsi'neiʃən] *n* raciocinación *f*.

ration ['ræʃən] **1** *n* ración *f*; **—s** (*Mil etc*) víveres *mpl*, suministro *m*; **emergency —, iron —** ración *f* de reserva; **it's off the —** no está racionado; **to be on short —s** andar escaso de víveres, tener poco que comer; **to draw one's —s** recibir los víveres; **when they put bread on the —** cuando racionaron el pan.

2 *vt* racionar (*also* **to — out**).

rational ['ræʃənl] *adj* racional; lógico, razonable; (*sane, of person*) sensato, cuerdo; **the — thing to do would be . . .** lo lógico sería . . .; **he seemed quite —** parecía estar perfectamente cuerdo; **a long skirt is hardly — dress for the beach** una falda larga es poco práctica en la playa; **let's be — about this** seamos razonables.

rationale [ræʃə'nɑːl] *n* razón *f* fundamental, base *f* lógica.

rationalism ['ræʃnəlizəm] *n* racionalismo *m*.

rationalist ['ræʃnəlist] **1** *adj* racionalista. **2** *n* racionalista *mf*.

rationality [ˌræʃə'næliti] *n* racionalidad *f*; lógica *f*.

rationalization [ˌræʃnəlai'zeiʃən] *n* racionalización *f*.

rationalize ['ræʃnəlaiz] *vt* hacer racional; organizar lógicamente, introducir un sistema lógico en; (*Math*) quitar los radicales a, racionalizar.

rationally ['ræʃnəli] *adv* racionalmente, lógicamente, razonablemente; **he spoke quite —** habló cuerdamente, habló de modo juicioso.

ration book ['ræʃənbuk] *n*, **ration card** ['ræʃənkɑːd] *n* cartilla *f* de racionamiento.

rationing ['ræʃniŋ] *n* racionamiento *m*.

Ratisbon ['rætizbɔn] Ratisbona.

rat poison ['rætˌpɔizn] *n* matarratas *m*.

rat race ['rætreis] *n* lucha *f* del hombre por ir adelante en su profesión, competencia *f* entre los miembros de una profesión (*or* sociedad *etc*) para aventajarse unos a otros; **it's just a —** es una lucha constante por subir.

rat-tat-tat ['rætə'tæt] *interj* ¡pum!, ¡pum! (*sonido de la aldaba*).

rattle ['rætl] **1** *n* (a) (*noise: banging*) golpeteo *m*; (*of cart, train etc*) traqueteo *m*; (*of machine gun etc*) traqueteo *m*, tableteo *m*; (*eg of stone in tin*) ruido *m*, sonsonete *m*; (*of hail, rain*) tamborileo *m*; (*of window etc*) crujido *m*; (*of teeth*) castañeteo *m*; (*in throat*) estertor *m*.

(b) (*instrument*) carraca *f*, matraca *f*; (*child's*) sonajero *m*; (*snake's*) cascabel *m*.

2 *vt* (a) (*shake*) agitar, sacudir; (*play*) hacer sonar; (*vibrate*) hacer vibrar; (*jolt*) traquetear; **the**

wind —d the window el viento hacía crujir la ventana; **he —d the tin** agitó la lata.

(b) **to — off** enumerar rápidamente.

(c) (*person*) desconcertar, confundir; poner nervioso; **he was badly —d** quedó muy desconcertado; **that —d him badly** eso le desconcertó de mala manera; **to get —d** ponerse nervioso; **he never gets —d** nunca pierda la calma.

3 *vi* (a) golpear; traquetear, tabletear; sonar, hacer ruido; tamborilear; crujir; castañetear.

(b) **we were rattling along at 50** íbamos a 50 (kilómetros por hora); **she —d on** seguía parloteando; **she was rattling on about the war** seguía hablando incansablemente de la guerra.

rattlebrained ['rætlbreind] *adj* ligero de cascos.

rattlesnake ['rætlsneik] *n* serpiente *f* de cascabel.

rattletrap ['rætltræp] **1** *adj* desvencijado. **2** *n* armatoste *m*.

rattling ['rætliŋ] **1** *adj*: **at a — pace** muy rápidamente, a gran velocidad. **2** *adv*: **— good** realmente estupendo.

rattrap ['rættræp] *n* trampa *f* para ratas.

ratty ['ræti] *adj* (*fam*): **he was pretty — about it** se picó mucho por ello; **to get —** ponerse negro.

raucous ['rɔːkəs] *adj* estridente, ronco, chillón.

raucously ['rɔːkəsli] *adv* de modo estridente, roncamente, en tono chillón.

ravage ['rævidʒ] **1** *n* estrago *m*, destrozo *m*; **—s** destrucción *f*, estragos *mpl*; **the —s of time** los estragos del tiempo.

2 *vt* estragar, destruir, destrozar; (*plunder*) pillar; **the region was —d by floods** la región fue asolada por las inundaciones; **a picture —d by time** un cuadro deteriorado por el tiempo.

rave [reiv] **1** *n* (*sl*) (a) **it's a —** es lo último, es la monda.

(b) (*Mus etc*) concierto *m* de música popular, *m*; fiesta *f* animadísima.

2 *adj*: **the play got — notices** la obra fue reseñada con el mayor entusiasmo, se escribieron reseñas entusiastas de la obra.

3 *vi* delirar, desvariar; **to — about someone** pirrarse por uno, hablar en términos entusiastas de uno; **to — about something** entusiasmarse por algo; **to — at someone** insultar frenéticamente a uno de palabra.

ravel ['rævəl] *vt* enredar, enmarañar (*also fig*).

raven ['reivn] **1** *n* cuervo *m*. **2** *adj* *hair* negro como el azabache.

ravening ['rævniŋ] *adj* rapaz, salvaje.

ravenous ['rævənəs] *adj* (*starving*) famélico, hambriento; (*voracious*) voraz; **I'm —!** ¡me comería un toro!; **he was —** tenía una hambre canina.

ravenously ['rævənəsli] *adv* vorazmente; **to be — hungry** tener una hambre canina.

ravine [rə'viːn] *n* barranco *m*, garganta *f*.

raving ['reiviŋ] *adj*: **— lunatic** loco *m* de atar.

ravings ['reiviŋz] *npl* delirio *m*, desvarío *m*.

ravioli [ˌrævi'əuli] *npl* canalones *mpl*.

ravish ['ræviʃ] *vt* (a) (*charm*) encantar, embelesar. (b) (*lit: carry off*) raptar, robar; (*rape*) violar.

ravisher ['ræviʃə*] *n* raptor *m*; violador *m*.

ravishing ['ræviʃiŋ] *adj* encantador, embelesador.

ravishingly ['ræviʃiŋli] *adv*: **— beautiful** extremadamente hermoso.

ravishment ['ræviʃmənt] *n* embeleso *m*, éxtasis *m*; rapto *m*, robo *m*; violación *f*.

raw [rɔː] **1** *adj* *food* crudo; *spirit* puro, sin mezcla; *weather* crudo, áspero; *silk, leather etc* bruto, sin refinar; *cotton* crudo; *cotton* en rama; (*inexperienced*) novato, inexperto; (*socially coarse*) tosco, grosero; **that's pretty —** eso es injusto, no hay derecho a eso; **in the — flesh** en la carne viva; *see* **deal, material** *etc*.

2 *n* carne *f* viva; **it got him on the —** le hirió en lo más vivo.

rawboned ['rɔː'bəund] *adj* huesudo.

rawhide ['rɔːhaid] *adj* de cuero crudo.

rawness ['rɔːnis] *n* crudeza *f*; inexperiencia *f*; tosquedad *f*.

ray¹ [rei] *n* rayo *m*; (*Bot*) bráctea *f*; **cathode —s** rayos *mpl* catódicos; **cosmic —s** rayos *mpl* cósmicos; **gamma —s** rayos *mpl* gama; **— of light** rayo *m* de luz; **without a — of hope** sin esperanza alguna; **I see a — of hope** (*or* **light**) hay un rayo de esperanza.

ray² [rei] *n* (*Fish*) raya *f*.

Raymond ['reimənd] *m* Raimundo, Ramón.

rayon ['reiɔn] *n* rayón *m*.

raze [reiz] *vt* (*also* **to — to the ground**) arrasar, asolar.

razor ['reizə*] n (*open*) navaja f; (*safety* —) maquinilla f de afeitar; (*electric-*) maquinilla f eléctrica, rasuradora f.

razorbill ['reizəbil] n alca f (común).

razor blade ['reizəbleid] n noja f de afeitar, cuchilla f de afeitar.

razor-sharp ['reizə'ʃɑːp] adj afiladísimo; mind agudísimo, de lo más penetrante.

razor strop ['reizəstrɔp] n suavizador m.

razzle ['ræzl] n (*sl*) borrachera f; **to go on the** — ir de juerga, ir de borrachera.

razzle-dazzle ['ræzl,dæzl] n = **razzle**.

re [riː] prep respecto a, con referencia a; — **yours of the 8th** me refiero a su carta del día 8.

reabsorb ['riːəb'zɔːb] vt resorber.

reabsorption ['riːəb'zɔːpʃən] n resorción f.

reach [riːtʃ] **1** n **(a)** alcance m; extensión f; distancia f; (*Boxing etc*) envergadura f; **to have a long** — tener brazos largos; **to be beyond someone's** —, **to be out of someone's** — estar fuera del alcance de uno; **to be within** — **of the hand** estar al alcance de la mano; **to be within (easy)** — estar al alcance, estar a la mano; **cars within the** — **of all families** coches mpl al alcance de todas las familias; **a house within easy** — **of the station** una casa a corta distancia de la estación; **it's within easy** — **by bus** es fácilmente accesible en autobús.
(b) (*of river*) extensión f entre dos recodos; (*of canal*) extensión f entre dos compuertas; **the upper** —**es of the Seine** la parte alta del Sena.
2 vt **(a)** (*stretch out*) alargar, extender; **he** —**ed out a hand** alargó la mano.
(b) (*pass*) pasar, dar; **please** — **me down that case** por favor bájeme la maleta esa; **can you** — **me (over) the oil?** ¿me da el aceite, por favor?
(c) (*arrive at, attain*) alcanzar; llegar a, llegar hasta; lograr; extenderse a, abarcar; **to** — **home** llegar a casa; **it doesn't** — **the bottom** no llega al fondo; **the child hardly** —**ed my waist** el niño apenas me llegaba a la cintura; **the door is** —**ed by a long staircase** se sube a la puerta por una larga escalera; **your letter** —**ed me this morning** su carta llegó a mis manos esta mañana; **when this news** —**ed my ears** cuando supe esta noticia; **to** — **21** cumplir los 21 años; **to** — **perfection** lograr la perfección; **to** —**a compromise** llegar a un arreglo; **production now** —**es 3,400 megawatts** la producción actual alcanza 3.400 megavatios; **the law does not** — **such cases** la ley no se extiende a tales casos.
(d) person ponerse en contacto con; **to** — **someone by telephone** hablar con uno por teléfono; **you can always** — **me at the office** me puedes llamar en todo momento en la oficina.
3 vi **(a) to** — **out (with one's hand) for something** alargar (*or* tender) la mano para tomar algo; **don't** — **over people** no alargues la mano para tomar cosas delante de otros; **to** — **for the sky** aspirar al cielo; — **for the sky!** (*sl*) ¡arriba las manos!
(b) (*stretch*) alcanzar; extenderse; llegar; **it won't** — no llega; **it** —**es to the sea** se extiende hasta el mar; **as far as the eye could** — hasta donde alcanzaba la vista; **the beer won't** — **till Friday** la cerveza no llega al viernes.

reachable ['riːtʃəbl] adj alcanzablo; accesible.

reach-me-downs ['riːtʃmi,daunz] npl ropa f hecha, traje m (etc) hecho.

react [riː'ækt] vi reaccionar (*against* contra; on sobre; to a, ante); **how did she** —? ¿cómo reaccionó?

reaction [riː'ækʃən] n reacción f; **what was your** —? ¿cómo reaccionó Vd?, ¿qué impresión le produjo?; **it produced no** — no surtió efecto.

reactionary [riː'ækʃnri] **1** adj reaccionario. **2** n reaccionario m, a f.

reactive [riː'æktiv] adj reactivo.

reactor [riː'æktə*] n reactor m; **nuclear** — reactor m nuclear.

read [riːd] (*irr*: pret and ptp **read** [red]) **1** vt **(a)** leer; (*with difficulty*) lograr leer, interpretar, descifrar; **do you** — **Russian?** ¿sabes leer el ruso?; **I** — **it differently** yo lo entiendo de otro modo.
(b) to — **something aloud** leer algo en voz alta; **to** — **the news** leer las noticias; **to** — **a report to a meeting** leer un informe a una reunión.
(c) to — **someone to sleep** leer un libro (*etc*) para dormir a uno.
(d) (*Univ*) estudiar, cursar; **to** — **Romance languages** estudiar lenguas románicas; **what are you** —**ing?** ¿qué asignatura estudias?
(e) to — **music** leer música; **to** — **someone's hand** leer la mano a uno; **she can** — **me like a book** me conoce a fondo; **to** — **the future** adivinar el porvenir; **to** — **someone's thoughts** adivinar el pensamiento de uno.
(f) (*take a reading from*) consultar; **when I** — **the thermometer** cuando consulté el termómetro; **they come to** — **the meter once a month** vienen una vez al mes a comprobar lo que marca el contador; **he wants to** — **the gas meter** quiere ver el contador de gas.
(g) you're —**ing too much into it** le atribuyes una importancia que realmente no tiene; **crees ver cosas escondidas que en realidad no hay; **to** — **into a sentence what is not there** ver en una frase un significado que no tiene.
(h) (*with adv or prep*) **to** — **something out** leer algo en alta voz, leer algo para que lo oigan todos (*etc*); **please** — **it out** por favor léanoslo; **to** — **something over, to** — **something through** repasar algo, volver a leer algo; **to** — **up a subject** estudiar un tema; repasar un tema.
2 vi **(a)** leer; **to** — **aloud** leer en alta voz; **I** — **about it in the papers** lo leí en los periódicos; **I'm** —**ing about Napoleon** me estoy documentando sobre Napoleón; leo un libro sobre Napoleón; **to** — **between the lines** leer entre líneas; **to** — **on** seguir leyendo; **"now** — **on"** "prosigue el cuento"; **to** — **to someone** leer un libro (*etc*) a uno.
(b) (*notice etc*) decir, rezar; (*of thermometer etc*) indicar, marcar; **it should** — **"Urraca"** debiera decir "Urraca".
(c) how does the letter — **now?** ¿qué tal te parece la carta ahora?; **it would** — **better if you said** . . . causaría mejor impresión si pusieras . . . , sería más elegante si escribieras . . . ; **the play acts better than it** —**s** la obra es mejor representada que leída.
3 n: **I was having a quiet** — **in the garden** leía tranquilamente un libro en el jardín; **I like a good** — me gusta la lectura; **it's a good solid** — el libro dará muchas horas de lectura amena.

read [red] pret and ptp of **read**; **well** — leído, culto, instruido; **to take the minutes as** — dar las actas por leídas; **we can take that as** — (*fig*) eso lo podemos dar por sentado.

readability [,riːdə'biliti] n legibilidad f; amenidad f, interés m.

readable ['riːdəbl] adj writing legible; book etc digno de leerse, ameno, interesante.

readdress ['riːə'dres] vt letter poner señas nuevas (*or* correctas) en; **to** — **a letter to someone** volver a dirigir una carta a uno.

reader ['riːdə*] n lector m, ora f; (*Typ*) corrector m; (*book*) libro m de lectura; (*Univ*) profesor que ocupa una cátedra sólo inferior a la del jefe de departamento; **he's a great** — lee mucho, es muy aficionado a la lectura; **I'm not much of a** — leo poco, no me interesan mucho los libros.

readership ['riːdəʃip] n número m total de lectores (de un periódico); (*Univ*) puesto del **reader.**

readily ['redili] adv (*quickly*) en seguida, pronto; (*willingly*) de buena gana; (*easily*) fácilmente.

readiness ['redinis] n prontitud f; disponibilidad f; buena disposición f, buena voluntad f; (*preparedness*) preparación f; — **of wit** viveza f de ingenio; **everything is in** — todo está listo, todo está preparado; **to hold oneself in** — **for something** estar listo para algo; **hold yourself in** — **for** . . . prepárese para . . .

reading ['riːdiŋ] **1** n (*in general*) lectura f; (*aloud*) lectura f, recitación f; (*understanding*) interpretación f; (*of thermometer etc*) indicación f, lectura f; (*Parl*) lectura f, (*in text*) lección f; **second** — (*Parl*) segunda lectura f; **to give a bill a second** — leer un proyecto de ley por segunda vez.
2 adj: **the** — **public** el público que lee; **he's a great** — **man** es un hombre que lee mucho, es hombre muy aficionado a la lectura.
3 attr de lectura.

reading glass ['riːdiŋglɑːs] n lente m para leer.

reading lamp ['riːdiŋlæmp] n lámpara f para leer (en la cama etc).

reading matter ['riːdiŋ,mætə*] n lectura f.

reading room ['riːdiŋrum] n sala f de lectura.

readjust ['riːə'dʒʌst] **1** vt reajustar; reorientar. **2** vi reajustarse; reorientarse.

readjustment ['riːə'dʒʌstmənt] n reajuste m; reorientación f.

readmit ['riːəd'mit] vt readmitir.

ready ['redi] **1** adj **(a)** (*prepared*) listo, preparado; pronto; (*available*) disponible; —?, **are you** —? ¿estás listo?, ¿vamos?; —, **steady, go!** ¡preparados, listos, ya!; — **for action** dispuesto para el combate, (*fig*) lanza en ristre; — **for use** listo para usar; — **money** dinero *m* contante; **to be — to hand** estar a la mano, estar disponible; **to be — to do something** estar listo para hacer algo; **the aircraft will be — to fly in 6 months** el avión estará listo para volar en 6 meses; **I am — to face him now** me he cobrado bastante ánimo para entrar a verle ahora; — **to serve** preparado; — **to use** listo para usar; **to get** —, **to make** — prepararse; disponerse (*to* + *infin* a + *infin*); **to get something** —, **to make something** — preparar algo, disponer algo; **to hold oneself** — estar listo (*for* para); **hold yourselves — to leave at any moment** prepárense para partir en cualquier momento.

(**b**) (*willing*) dispuesto (*to* + *infin* a + *infin*); **he's a — helper** presta su ayuda de buena gana.

(**c**) (*about*) **I was — to die of hunger** estaba para morirme de hambre; **we were — to give up there and then** estábamos a punto de abandonarlo sin más.

(**d**) *answer* fácil, pronto; *wit* agudo, vivo; **to have a — wit** ser ingenioso, tener chispa; **to have a — pen** escribir con soltura; **to have a — tongue** no morderse la lengua; **to find a — sale** venderse fácilmente, tener una salida fácil.

2 *n* (**a**) **with rifles at the** — con los fusiles listos para tirar, con los fusiles apercibidos; **pen at the** — pluma en ristre.

(**b**) **some of the** — (*fam*) algún dinero *m* contante.

ready-cooked ['redi'kukt] *adj* listo para comer.
ready-made ['redi'meid] *adj* hecho, confeccionado.
ready reckoner ['redi'reknə*] *n* libro *m* de cálculos hechos.
ready-to-wear ['reditə'wɛə*] *adj* hecho, confeccionado.
reaffirm ['ri:ə'fə:m] *vt* reafirmar, reiterar.
reaffirmation ['ri:æfə'meiʃən] *n* reafirmación *f*, reiteración *f*.
reafforest ['ri:ə'fɒrist] *vt* repoblar de árboles.
reafforestation ['ri:ə,fɒris'teiʃən] *n* repoblación *f* forestal.
reagent [ri:'eidʒənt] *n* reactivo *m*.
real [riəl] *adj* real; verdadero; auténtico; legítimo; **the — world** el mundo real; **you're a — friend** eres un verdadero amigo; **the — power is in the hands of X** el poder efectivo está en manos de X; **this is — coffee** esto es auténtico café, esto es lo que se llama café; **we have had days of — heat** hemos tenido días de auténtico calor; **is he the — king?** ¿él es el rey legítimo?; **this is the — thing at last** por fin lo tenemos sin trampa ni cartón; *see* **estate**.
realism ['riəlizəm] *n* realismo *m*; autenticidad *f*.
realist ['riəlist] *n* realista *mf*.
realistic [riə'listik] *adj* realista; auténtico.
realistically [riə'listikəli] *adv* de modo realista; auténticamente.
reality [ri:'æliti] *n* realidad *f*; **in — en realidad; the realities of power** la realidad del poder; **let's get back to —** volvamos a la realidad; **let's stick to realities** atengámonos a la realidad.
realizable ['riəlaizəbl] *adj* realizable.
realization [,riəlai'zeiʃən] *n* comprensión *f*; (*Comm etc*) realización *f*; **this — came too late** esto lo comprendió tarde; **it was a sudden —** cayó de repente en la cuenta.
realize ['riəlaiz] *vt* (**a**) (*comprehend*) darse cuenta de, hacerse cargo de, comprender; **without realizing it** sin darse cuenta; **I — that . . .** me doy cuenta de que . . ., comprendo que . . .; **once I —d how it was done** tan pronto como caí en la cuenta de cómo se hacía; **do you — what you've done?** ¿te das cuenta de lo que has hecho?

(**b**) (*carry out*) realizar, llevar a cabo, poner por obra.

(**c**) (*Comm*) *assets etc* realizar.
really ['riəli] *adv* (**a**) (*used alone*) —? ¿de veras?, ¿ah sí?; **not** —? ¿lo dices en serio? — ! ¡ca!; ¡eh!; ¡mire Vd!; **!—, whatever next!** ¡qué cosas pasan!

(**b**) (*with adj*) verdaderamente, realmente, francamente; **a — good film** una película realmente buena, una película francamente buena; **I'm — very cross with you** estoy francamente disgustado contigo; **now it's — true** ahora sí es verdad; **this time we're — done for** esta vez hemos pringado de verdad.

(**c**) (*with verb*) en realidad; realmente; **I don't — know** en realidad no lo sé; **you — must see it** realmente tienes que verlo; **can it — be expected that . . . ?** ¿cabe realmente esperar que . . . ?; **has he — gone?** ¿es cierto que se ha ido?; **how a gentleman who is — a gentleman lives** cómo vive un señor señor; **as for — talking Chinese, I can't** hablar chino, lo que se dice hablar chino, no sé.

realm [relm] *n* reino *m*; (*fig*) esfera *f*, campo *m*; **in the — of speculation** en la esfera de la especulación; **in the —s of fantasy** en el país de la fantasía.
realtor ['riəltɔ:*] *n* (*US*) corredor *m* de bienes raíces, corredor *m* de fincas.
realty ['riəlti] *n* bienes *mpl* raíces.
ream[1] [ri:m] *n* resma *f*; (*fig*) montón *m*, gran cantidad *f*.
ream[2] [ri:m] *vt* escariar (*also to — out*).
reamer ['ri:mə*] *n* escariador *m*.
reanimate ['ri:'ænimeit] *vt* reanimar.
reap [ri:p] *vt* segar; (*fig*) cosechar, recoger; **to — what one has sown** cosechar lo que ha sembrado uno; **to — no profit from something** no obtener ganancia alguna de algo, (*fig*) no sacarse ventaja alguna de algo; **who —s the reward?** ¿quién saca el premio?
reaper ['ri:pə*] *n* (*person*) segador *m*, ora *f*; (*machine*) segadora *f*, agavilladora *f*.
reaping ['ri:piŋ] *n* siega *f*.
reaping hook ['ri:piŋhuk] *n* hoz *f*.
reappear ['ri:ə'piə*] *vi* reaparecer.
reappearance ['ri:ə'piərəns] *n* reaparición *f*.
reapply ['ri:ə'plai] **1** *vt* aplicar de nuevo; *paint etc* dar otra capa de. **2** *vi* volver a presentarse, mandar una nueva solicitud (*for* pidiendo).
reappoint ['ri:ə'pɔint] *vt* volver a nombrar.
reappointment ['ri:ə'pɔintmənt] *n* nuevo nombramiento *m*.
reapportion ['ri:ə'pɔ:ʃən] *vt* volver a repartir (*among* entre).
reappraisal ['ri:ə'preizəl] *n* nueva estimación *f*, nueva apreciación *f*; **agonizing — reajuste *m* agonizante (*or* doloroso).
rear[1] [riə*] **1** *adj* trasero, posterior; de cola; (*Mil*) de retaguardia; **— wheel** rueda *f* trasera.

2 *n* parte *f* trasera, parte *f* posterior; cola *f*; (*Anat: fam*) culo *m*; (*Mil: row*) última fila *f*, (*rearguard*) retaguardia *f*; (*fam*: WC) wáter *m*; **at the — of, in (the)** — of detrás de; **in the —** (*Mil*) a retaguardia; **3 miles to the —** 3 millas a retaguardia; **to be well to the —** quedar muy atrasado; **to bring up the —** cerrar la marcha; **to take the enemy in the —** atacar al enemigo por detrás.
rear[2] [riə*] **1** *vt* (*build*) erigir; (*raise*) levantar, alzar; (*bring up*) criar. **2** *vi* encabritarse, ponerse de manos.
rear admiral ['riər'ædmərəl] *n* contraalmirante *m*.
rear-engined ['riər,endʒind] *adj* con motor trasero.
rearguard ['riəgɑ:d] **1** *n* retaguardia *f*. **2** *attr*: **— action** combate *m* para cubrir una retirada.
rearm ['ri:'ɑ:m] **1** *vt* rearmar. **2** *vi* rearmarse.
rearmament ['ri:'ɑ:məmənt] *n* rearme *m*.
rearmost ['riəməust] *adj* trasero, último de todos.
rear-mounted ['riə'mauntid] *adj*: **— engine** motor *m* trasero, motor *m* posterior.
rearrange ['ri:ə'reindʒ] *vt* volver a arreglar; ordenar de nuevo, arreglar de otro modo; (*Lit*) refundir; (*Mus*) volver a adaptar; **—d by Rossini** en versión de Rossini.
rearrangement ['ri:ə'reindʒmənt] *n* nuevo arreglo *m*, nueva disposición *f*; (*Lit*) refundición *f*; (*Mus*) nueva adaptación *f*, versión *f*.
rear-view ['riə,vju:] *attr* retrovisor; **— mirror** espejo *m* retrovisor.
rearward ['riəwəd] *adj* trasero, de atrás, posterior.
rearward(s) ['riəwəd(z)] *adv* hacia atrás.
reason ['ri:zn] **1** *n* (**a**) (*motive*) razón *f*; motivo *m*; causa *f*; **the — for my departure** el motivo de mi ida; **the — for my going** la razón por la que me marcho; **the — why** la razón por qué, el por qué; **—s of state** razón *f* de estado; **by —** a causa de; **en virtud de; for this —** por eso, por esta razón; **for that very — por esa misma razón; for no good —**, **for no — at all** sin motivo; **for —s best known to himself** por motivos que se sabe él; **with good —** con razón; **all the more — why you should not sell it** tanto más lógico me parece no venderlo; **what — can there be for it?** ¿qué razón puede haber?; **you had — to complain** Vd tuvo motivo de queja; **we have — to believe that . . .** tenemos motivo para creer que . . . ; **as I have good — to know** según ciertos indicios que tengo.

(**b**) (*faculty*) razón *f*; **to lose one's —** perder la razón.

(**c**) (*good sense*) sensatez *f*; moderación *f*; **everything in —** todo con moderación; **we cannot in — agree** no podemos razonablemente consentir;

it's out of all — está fuera de razón; **to listen to** — meterse en razón; **it stands to** — es evidente, es lógico (*that* que); **within** — dentro de lo razonable. **2** *vt* **(a) to** — **that** razonar que; calcular que, estimar que; **ours not to** — **why** no nos cumple a nosotros averiguar por qué.
(b) to — **out a problem** resolver un problema meditándolo.
(c) to — **someone out of something** disuadir a uno de algo alegando razones en contra.
3 *vi* razonar, discurrir; **to** — **about the universe** especular acerca del universo; **to** — **from data** razonar partiendo de ciertos datos; **to** — **with someone** alegar razones para convencer a uno.
reasonable ['ri:znəbl] *adj* (*in most senses*) razonable; *person* sensato, juicioso; tolerante; **be** —! ¡sé razonable!
reasonableness ['ri:znəblnis] *n* lo razonable; sensatez *f*; juicio *m*; tolerancia *f*; **in an atmosphere of sweet** — en un ambiente de moderación, en un ambiente de tolerancia.
reasonably ['ri:znəbli] *adv* razonablemente; **a** — **good price** un precio razonable; **a** — **accurate report** un informe bastante exacto; **he acted very** — obró con mucho tino.
reasoned ['ri:znd] *adj* razonado.
reasoning ['ri:zniŋ] **1** *adj* racional. **2** *n* razonamiento *m*; argumentos *mpl*; **I don't follow your** — no comprendo sus argumentos.
reassemble ['ri:ə'sembl] **1** *vt* volver a reunir; (*Tech*) montar de nuévo. **2** *vi* volver a reunirse.
reassert ['ri:ə'sə:t] *vt* reafirmar, reiterar.
reassess ['ri:ə'ses] *vt* (*Fin*) tasar de nuevo, valorar de nuevo (*at en*); *amount of tax* fijar de nuevo (*at en*); (*Lit etc*) hacer una nueva apreciación de; **we shall have to** — **the situation** tendremos que estudiar la situación de nuevo.
reassurance ['ri:ə'ʃuərəns] *n* noticia *f* tranquilizadora, promesa *f* tranquilizadora.
reassure ['ri:ə'ʃuə*] *vt* tranquilizar; alentar; **to feel** —d estar más tranquilo.
reassuring ['ri:ə'ʃuəriŋ] *adj* tranquilizador; alentador.
reassuringly ['ri:ə'ʃuəriŋli] *adv* de modo tranquilizador; **he spoke** — nos alentó con sus palabras; **a** — **strong performance** una actuación cuya fuerza nos alentó.
reawaken ['ri:ə'weikən] **1** *vt* volver a despertar. **2** *vi* (volver a) despertarse.
reawakening ['ri:ə'weikniŋ] *n* despertar *m*.
rebarbative [ri'bɑ:bətiv] *adj* repugnante.
rebate ['ri:beit] **1** *n* rebaja *f*, descuento *m*. **2** *vt* rebajar, descontar.
Rebecca [ri'bekə] *f* Rebeca.
rebel ['rebl] **1** *adj* rebelde; **the** — **government** el gobierno rebelde; — **leader** cabecilla *m*. **2** *n* rebelde *mf*.
rebel [ri'bel] *vi* rebelarse, sublevarse.
rebellion [ri'beliən] *n* rebelión *f*, sublevación *f*.
rebellious [ri'beliəs] *adj* rebelde; *child etc* revoltoso, díscolo.
rebelliousness [ri'beliəsnis] *n* rebeldía *f*; carácter *m* revoltoso, naturaleza *f* díscola.
rebind [ri:'baind] (*irr: see* **bind**) *vt* volver a atar; *book* reencuadernar.
rebirth ['ri:'bə:θ] *n* renacimiento *m*.
rebore ['ri:'bɔ:*] **1** *n* rectificado *m*. **2** *vt* rectificar.
reborn ['ri:'bɔ:n] *ptp*: **to be** — renacer.
rebound [ri'baund] *n* rebote *m*; **on the** — de rebote, de rechazo; **she married him on the** — se casó con él a consecuencia del chasco que acababa de llevarse con el otro.
rebound [ri'baund] *vi* rebotar (*off* después de chocar *con*), dar un rebote.
rebroadcast ['ri:'brɔ:dkɑ:st] **1** *n* retransmisión *f*. **2** *vt* retransmitir.
rebuff [ri'bʌf] **1** *n* repulsa *f*, desaire *m*; **to meet with a** — ser repulsado, aguantar un desaire. **2** *vt* rechazar; desairar.
rebuild ['ri:'bild] (*irr: see* **build**) *vt* reconstruir, reedificar.
rebuilding ['ri:'bildiŋ] *n* reconstrucción *f*, reedificación *f*.
rebuke [ri'bju:k] **1** *n* reprensión *f*; reprimenda *f*. **2** *vt* reprender, censurar; **to** — **someone for having done something** reprender a uno por haber hecho algo.
rebus ['ri:bəs] *n* jeroglífico *m*.
rebut [ri'bʌt] *vt* rebatir, refutar, rechazar.
rebuttal [ri'bʌtl] *n* refutación *f*.
recalcitrance [ri'kælsitrəns] *n* obstinación *f*, terquedad *f*.

recalcitrant [ri'kælsitrənt] *adj* reacio, refractorio, recalcitrante.
recall [ri'kɔ:l] **1** *n* aviso *m*, llamada *f* (*para hacer volver a uno*); retirada *f*; destitución *f*; **to be beyond** (*or past*) — ser irrevocable; (*person*) haberse ido definitivamente; **those days are gone beyond** — aquellos días pertenecen al pasado, aquellos días quedan ya a la espalda.
2 *vt* **(a)** (*call back*) *person* llamar, hacer volver; *ambassador*, *capital* retirar; (*dismiss*) destituir; **to** — **someone to his duty** recordar a uno su deber, hacer que uno se acuerde de su deber.
(b) (*remember*) recordar, traer a la memoria; **I can't quite** — **whether** . . . no recuerdo del todo si . . . ; **it** —s **the time when** . . . hace pensar en aquella ocasión cuando . . .
recant [ri'kænt] **1** *vt* retractar, desdecirse de; renunciar a. **2** *vi* retractarse, desdecirse; confesar su error.
recantation [,ri:kæn'teiʃən] retractación *f*; confesión *f* de error.
recap ['ri:kæp] (*fam*) **1** *n* recapitulación *f*, resumen *m*. **2** *vti* recapitular, resumir.
recapitulate [,ri:kə'pitjuleit] *vti* recapitular, resumir.
recapitulation ['ri:kə,pitju'leiʃən] *n* recapitulación *f*, resumen *m*.
recapture [ri:'kæptʃə*] **1** *n* recobro *m*; reconquista *f*.
2 *vt* *prisoner etc* recobrar, volver a prender; *town* reconquistar, volver a tomar; *memory*, *scene* hacer revivir, recordar (*en su totalidad*).
recast ['ri:'kɑ:st] (*irr: see* **cast**) *vt* (*Tech, Lit etc*) refundir.
recede [ri'si:d] *vi* retroceder, retirarse; (*floods, price*) bajar; (*danger etc*) alejarse, disminuir.
receding [ri'si:diŋ] *adj* *prospect* que va disminuyendo; *tide* que está bajando; *forehead* huidizo.
receipt [ri'si:t] **1** *n* **(a)** (*act of receiving*) recepción *f*, recibo *m*; **to acknowledge** — of acusar recibo de; **I am in** — **of your letter** he recibido su carta, (*more formally*) obra su carta en mi poder; **on** — **of** al recibo de; **on** — **of this news** al saber esta noticia, al recibir esta noticia.
(b) (*document*) recibo *m*; **please give me a** — haga el favor de darme un recibo.
(c) —s ingresos *mpl*; (*of function, game etc*) entrada *f*.
2 *vt* *goods* dar recibo por; *bill* poner el "recibí" en.
receipt book [ri'si:tbuk] *n* libro *m* talonario.
receivable [ri'si:vəbl] *adj* recibidero; (*Comm*) por cobrar.
receive [ri'si:v] **1** *vt* recibir; *money* recibir, (*as payment*) cobrar, (*as salary*) percibir; (*accept*) aceptar, admitir; *guests* acoger, (*to stay*) hospedar, alojar; *stolen goods* receptar; *wound* sufrir; (*stand weight of*) sufrir, aguantar; *ball* restar; (*approve*) aprobar; **"—d with thanks"** "recibí"; **to** — **someone into the Academy** recibir a uno en la Academia; **to** — **someone as a partner** admitir a uno como socio; **to** — **someone into the Church** bautizar a uno, recibir a uno en el seno de la Iglesia; **to** — **someone into one's home** hospedar a uno en su casa; **the idea was well** —d la idea tuvo buena acogida; **the book was not well** —d el libro tuvo una acogida poco entusiasta; **he** —d **a wound in the leg** sufrió una herida en la pierna; **to** — **a blank refusal** encontrar una negativa rotunda; **what treatment did you** —? ¿qué tratamiento le dieron?
2 *vi* (*Law*) receptar, ser receptador; (*Sport*) ser restador.
received [ri'si:vd] *adj* *pronunciation etc* admitido, aprobado, correcto.
receiver [ri'si:və*] *n* recibidor *m*, ora *f*; (*addressee*) destinatario *m*, a *f*; (*of stolen goods*) receptador *m*, ora *f*; (*in bankruptcy, also* official —) síndico *m*; (*Sport*) restador *m*; (*Radio*) receptor *m*, radiorreceptor *m*; (*Tel*) auricular *m*; (*Chem etc*) recipiente *m*.
receiving [ri'si:viŋ] *n* recepción *f*; (*of stolen goods*) receptar *m*.
receiving set [ri'si:viŋset] *n* (*Radio*) receptor *m*, radiorreceptor *m*.
recension [ri'senʃən] *n* recensión *f*.
recent ['ri:snt] *adj* reciente; nuevo; **in** — **years** en estos últimos años; **in the** — **past** en el pasado próximo.
recently ['ri:sntli] *adv* recientemente; (*before ptps*) recién, *eg* — **arrived** recién llegado; **as** — **as 1970** todavía en 1970; **until** — hasta hace poco.
receptacle [ri'septəkl] *n* receptáculo *m*.
reception [ri'sepʃən] *n* (*act*) recepción *f*, recibimiento *m*; (*welcome*) acogida *f*; (*social function*) recepción *f*; (*Radio etc*) recepción *f*; **to get a warm** — tener buena acogida, ser recibido con entusiasmo; **they'll get a warm** — **if they come here** (*iro*) estamos listos para recibirles si se presentan aquí.

reception centre, (US) — **center** [ri'sepʃən͵sentə*] n centro m de recepción.

rèceptionist [ri'sepʃənist] n (hotel) recepcionista f; (dentist's etc) chica f, chica f enfermera; (other) secretaria f.

reception room [ri'sepʃən͵rum] n sala f de recibo.

receptive [ri'septiv] adj receptivo.

receptiveness [ri'septivnis] n, **receptivity** [risep-'tiviti] n receptividad f.

recess [ri'ses] **1** n **(a)** (vacation) vacaciones fpl; (short rest) descanso m; (in school) recreo m; (Parl) suspensión f, (between sittings) intermedio m; **parliament is in** — la sesión del parlamento está suspendida.
    (b) (Tech) rebajo m; (Archit) hueco m; nicho m; (hiding place) escondrijo m.
    (c) —**es** (fig) seno m; lo más hondo, lo más recóndito.
    2 vi (Parl) prorrogarse, suspenderse la sesión.

recession [ri'seʃən] n retroceso m, retirada f; (fall) baja f; (lessening) disminución f; (Fin, Comm) recesión f.

recessional [ri'seʃnl] n himno m de fin de oficio.

recessive [ri'sesiv] adj (Bio) recesivo.

recharge ['riː'tʃɑːdʒ] vt recargar, volver a cargar.

recherché [rə'ʃeəʃei] adj rebuscado.

rechristen [ri'krisn] n (Eccl) rebautizar; (rename) poner nuevo nombre a; **they have —ed the machine "Fido"** han puesto a la máquina el nuevo nombre de "Fido".

recidivist [ri'sidivist] n reincidente mf.

recipe ['resipi] n receta f (for de).

recipient [ri'sipiənt] n recibidor m, ora f, recipiente mf; (addressee) destinatario m a f.

reciprocal [ri'siprəkəl] **1** adj recíproco, mutuo. **2** n (Math) recíproca f.

reciprocally [ri'siprəkəli] adv recíprocamente, mutuamente.

reciprocate [ri'siprəkeit] **1** vt good wishes etc intercambiar, devolver; corresponder a; **and this feeling is —d** y por nuestra parte nos hacemos eco de tal sentimiento; **her kindness was not —d** no correspondieron a su amabilidad.
    2 vi (Mech) oscilar, alternar; (fig) usar de reciprocidad, corresponder; **but they did not —** pero ellos no correspondieron a esto; **he —d with a short speech** pronunció un breve discurso a modo de contestación; **it is up to us to —** nos incumbe usar de reciprocidad.

reciprocation [ri͵siprə'keiʃən] n reciprocación f; reciprocidad f, correspondencia f.

reciprocity [͵resi'prɔsiti] n reciprocidad f.

recital [ri'saitl] n relación f, narración f; (Mus) recital m.

recitation [͵resi'teiʃən] n (act) recitación f; (text, piece for —) recitado m; **with humorous —s** con recitados humorísticos.

recitative [͵resitə'tiːv] n recitativo m.

recite [ri'sait] **1** vt narrar, referir; enumerar; recitation recitar; **she —d her troubles all over again** volvió a enumerar todas sus dificultades.
    2 vi dar un recitado.

reckless ['reklis] adj person temerario, imprudente; act imprudente; speed etc excesivo, peligroso; statement inconsiderado; **a — youth** un joven atolondrado.

recklessly ['reklisli] adv temerariamente, imprudentemente; **to drive —** conducir sin cuidado, conducir de modo peligroso; **to spend —** derrochar dinero.

recklessness ['reklisnis] n temeridad f, imprudencia f; inconsideración f; **the — of youth** la temeridad de la juventud; **the — of her driving** su modo peligroso de conducir.

reckon ['rekən] **1** vt (count number) contar, calcular; computar; (ascertain quantity) calcular, estimar; (believe) considerar, estimar; **to — someone among one's friends** contar a uno entre los amigos; **to — someone as** considerar a uno como; **to — something in** incluir algo; **to — that . . .** estimar que . . . , considerar que . . . , creer que . . . ; **I — he's worth more** considero que vale más; **to — up** calcular, computar; **to — up one's losses** calcular sus pérdidas.
    2 vi (do sum) calcular; hacer cálculos; (think) calcular, creer; **to learn to —** aprender a calcular; —**ing from today** contando desde hoy; **she'll come, I —** según creo vendrá, calculo que vendrá; **I — so** así lo creo; cierto; **to — on** contar con; **to — on** + ger contar con + infin; **to — with** tener en cuenta, contar con; **we didn't — with that** no contábamos con eso; **we hadn't —ed with having to walk** no habíamos tenido en cuenta la posibilidad de tener que ir a pie; **to — without someone** hacer caso omiso de uno.

reckoning ['rekniŋ] n (calculation) cálculo m, cuenta f; (bill) cuenta f; **day of —** (fig) día m de la justicia; día m del juicio final; día m decisivo; **by any —** a todas luces; en opinión de todos; **according to my —** según mis cálculos; **to be out in one's —** hacer mal el cálculo, calcular mal; see **dead —**.

reclaim [ri'kleim] **1** n: **to be beyond** (or past) — ser irremediable, no tener remedio; estar definitivamente perdido.
    2 vt (claim back) reclamar; sinner etc reformar; (tame) amansar, domesticar; land recuperar, hacer utilizable; (from sea) ganar, rescatar; swamp entarquinar; rubber etc utilizar, regenerar.

reclaimable [ri'kleiməbl] adj reclamable; utilizable.

reclamation [͵reklə'meiʃən] n reclamación f; reformación f; domesticación f; recuperación f; utilización f; **land —** rescate m de terrenos, entarquinamiento m.

recline [ri'klain] **1** vt (lean) apoyar; (lay) recostar; (rest) descansar. **2** vi reclinarse, recostarse; apoyarse; descansar; **to — upon** (fig) contar con, fiarse de.

reclining [ri'klainiŋ] adj acostado; tumbado; figure, statue yacente; — **chair** sillón m reclinable, poltrona f, (Med) silla f de extensión.

recluse [ri'kluːs] n solitario m, a f, recluso m, a f.

recognition [͵rekəg'niʃən] n reconocimiento m; **a smile of —** una sonrisa de reconocimiento; **in — of** en reconocimiento de, en premio de; en señal de; **in — of this fact** reconociendo este hecho; **to change something beyond —** cambiar algo de modo que resulta irreconocible.

recognizable ['rekəgnaizəbl] adj reconocible; identificable; **it is — as** se puede reconocer como, se puede identificar como.

recognizance [ri'kɔgnizəns] n reconocimiento m; obligación f contraída; (sum) fianza f; **to enter into —s to** + infin comprometerse legalmente a + infin.

recognize ['rekəgnaiz] vt **(a)** (know again) reconocer, identificar; conocer; **you don't — me** no me reconoce; **I —d him by his walk** le reconocí por su modo de andar; **his own mother would not have —d him** su propia madre no le hubiera reconocido; **he was —d by 2 policemen** le reconocieron 2 policías; **do you — this handbag?** ¿reconoce Vd este bolso?
    (b) (acknowledge) admitir, confesar; reconocer; **we — that . . .** reconocemos que . . . , confesamos que . . . ; **we do not — the government of Ruritania** no reconocemos el gobierno de Ruritania; **does the Academy — the word?** ¿admite la Academia la palabra?; **we do not — your claim** no admitimos (or aceptamos) su pretensión; **to — someone as king** reconocer a uno por rey.

recognized ['rekəgnaizd] adj expert etc reconocido como tal; feature conocido; agent etc acreditado, oficial; **it's the — method** es el sistema normal.

recoil [ri'kɔil] **1** n retroceso m; (of gun) retroceso m, rebufo m, culatazo m.
    2 vi recular, retroceder; (Mil) retroceder, rebufar; **to — in fear** retroceder espantado; **to — from something** retroceder ante algo, cejar ante la perspectiva de algo; **to — from doing something** sentir repugnancia por hacer algo, no animarse a hacer algo; **it —ed on him** recayó sobre él, resultó contraproducente para él.

recollect [͵rekə'lekt] vt recordar, acordarse de.

recollection [͵rekə'lekʃən] n recuerdo m; **to the best of my —** que yo recuerde.

recommence ['riːkə'mens] vti recomenzar.

recommend [͵rekə'mend] vt recomendar; **to — a candidate for a post** recomendar a un candidato para un puesto; **I — him to you most warmly** se lo recomiendo a Vd con la mayor confianza; **to — someone to do something** recomendar a uno que haga algo, aconsejar a uno hacer algo.

recommendable [͵rekə'mendəbl] adj recomendable.

recommendation [͵rekəmen'deiʃən] n recomendación f; **the —s of a report** las recomendaciones de un informe.

recommendatory [͵rekə'mendətəri] adj recomendatorio.

recompense ['rekəmpens] **1** n recompensa f. **2** vt recompensar (for por).

reconcilable ['rekənsailəbl] adj conciliable, reconciliable.

reconcile ['rekənsail] **1** vt persons reconciliar; theories etc conciliar; quarrel componer; **to become —d to something** resignarse a algo, acomodarse con algo; **what —d him to the place was the weather** lo que hizo que se conformara con vivir en el lugar fue el tiempo.
    2 vr: **to — oneself to something** resignarse a algo, acomodarse con algo, conformarse con algo.

reconciliation [ˌrekənsili'eiʃən] n reconciliación f; conciliación f; composición f.
recondite [ri'kɔndait] adj recóndito.
recondition ['ri:kən'diʃən] vt reacondicionar.
reconnaissance [ri'kɔnisəns] n reconocimiento m; — flight vuelo m de reconocimiento; to make a — reconocer el terreno, explorar el terreno.
reconnoitre, (US) **reconnoiter** [ˌrekə'nɔitə*] vti reconocer, explorar.
reconquer ['ri:'kɔŋkə*] vt reconquistar.
reconquest ['ri:'kɔŋkwest] n reconquista f; **the R—** (of Spain) la Reconquista.
reconsider ['ri:kən'sidə*] vti reconsiderar, repensar.
reconsideration ['ri:kənˌsidə'reiʃən] n reconsideración f; **on** — después de repensarlo.
reconstitute ['ri:'kɔnstitju:t] vt reconstituir.
reconstitution ['ri:ˌkɔnsti'tju:ʃən] n reconstitución f.
reconstruct ['ri:kən'strʌkt] vt reconstruir; reedificar; crime etc reconstituir.
reconstruction ['ri:kən'strʌkʃən] n reconstrucción f; reedificación f; reconstitución f.
reconvert ['ri:kən'və:t] vt reconvertir (to en); reorganizar.
record ['rekɔ:d] **1** n (a) (document, report etc) documento m; registro m, partida f; relación f; (Law) acta f; (note) nota f, apunte m; — **of attendances** registro m de asistencias; — **of a case** acta f de un proceso; **off the** — (adj) no oficial, confidencial, (adv) de modo no oficial, confidencialmente; **it is on** — **that ...**, **it is a matter of** — **that ...** consta que ...; **the fact is on** — consta el hecho; **there is no** — **of it** no hay constancia de ello, no consta en los documentos; **to keep** (or **make**) **a** — **of** apuntar, tomar nota de; **he left no** — **of it** no dejó relación de ello; **to place** (or **put**) **something on** — hacer constar algo, dejar constancia de algo; **to write something into the** — añadir algo a la relación escrita.
(b) —**s** archivos mpl; **the** —**s of a society** los archivos de una sociedad; **Public R— Office** Archivo m Nacional; **I will have the** —**s searched** buscaré en los archivos; **the** —**s** (police department) archivo m del servicio de identificación.
(c) (person's past in general) historia f; reputación f; antecedentes mpl; (as dossier) expediente m; (written with application for post) carrera f, curriculum m vitae; (of person, organization etc) historial m; (Mil) hoja f de servicios; **criminal** — antecedentes mpl penales; **her past** — su historia, su historial; **Iberia's splendid** — el brillante historial de Iberia; **his** — **is against him** su historial obra en perjuicio suyo; **has he a** —? ¿tiene antecedentes penales?; **he has a clean** — no hay nada en su historial que le perjudique; **he left behind a splendid** — **of achievements** dejó una magnífica historia de éxitos.
(d) (Sport etc) récord m, marca f; **the** — **for this distance is 4 minutes** el tiempo mínimo para esta distancia es de 4 minutos; **is this a** —? ¿es esto un récord?; ¿es excepcional esto?; **to beat** (or **break**) **the** — batir el récord, superar la marca; **to establish** (or **set up**) **a** — establecer un récord; **to hold the** — **for the 100 metres** ostentar el récord de los 100 metros.
(e) (Mus etc) disco m; **long-playing** — disco m microsurco, disco m de larga duración; **to make a** — grabar un disco.
2 adj sin precedentes, máximo, nuevo; **a** — **output** una producción sin precedentes; **in a** — **time** en un tiempo récord; **in the** — **time of 12 seconds** en el tiempo récord de 12 segundos
record [ri'kɔ:d] vt (a) (set down) registrar; inscribir; apuntar; hacer constar, dejar constancia de, consignar; **it is not** —**ed anywhere** no consta en ninguna parte; **I will** — **your order** apuntaré su pedido.
(b) (on dial etc) indicar, marcar.
(c) (Mus etc) grabar, registrar; **she** —**ed the song in 1969** grabó la canción en 1969; **to have one's voice** —**ed** hacer grabar su voz.
record breaker ['rekɔ:dˌbreikə*] n recordman m, plusmarquista mf.
record-breaking ['rekɔ:dˌbreikiŋ] adj person, team brillante, excepcional; que tantos récords ostenta; effort, run récord.
record cabinet ['rekɔ:dˌkæbinit] n armario m para discos, discoteca f.
record card ['rekɔ:dˌkɑ:d] n ficha f.
record changer ['rekɔ:dˌtʃeindʒə*] n cambiadiscos m.
recorded [ri'kɔ:did] adj: — **music** música f grabada; **never in** — **history** nunca en la historia escrita; **it is a** — **fact that** — consta el hecho de que ...
recorder [ri'kɔ:də*] n (a) (person) registrador m;

archivero m; **he was a faithful** — **of the facts** registró puntualmente los hechos.
(b) (Law) juez m municipal.
(c) (Mus) flauta f dulce, flauta f de pico.
(d) (Mech) contador m, indicador m.
record holder ['rekɔ:dˌhəuldə*] n recordman m; **the 100 metres** — el que ostenta el récord de los 100 metros.
recording [ri'kɔ:diŋ] n grabación f; registro m; **this** — **of "Ave Maria"** esta grabación del "Ave María"; **it's a good** — el registro es bueno, tiene buen registro.
recording tape [ri'kɔ:diŋˌteip] n cinta f de grabación, cinta f magnetofónica.
recording van [ri'kɔ:diŋˌvæn] n camión m de grabación.
record library ['rekɔ:dˌlaibrəri] n discoteca f.
record player ['rekɔ:dˌpleiə*] n tocadiscos m.
recount [ri'kaunt] vt contar, referir.
re-count ['ri:'kaunt] **1** n (Parl) segundo escrutinio m; **to have a** — someter los votos a un segundo escrutinio. **2** vt volver a contar.
recoup [ri'ku:p] vt recobrar, recuperar; indemnizarse por.
recourse [ri'kɔ:s] n recurso m; **to have** — **to** recurrir a.
recover [ri'kʌvə*] **1** vt recobrar, recuperar; money reembolsarse; stolen property recuperar; (rescue) rescatar; **to** — **lost time** recuperar el tiempo perdido; **to** — **consciousness** recobrar el conocimiento, volver en sí; **to** — **one's health** recobrar la salud, reponerse; **to** — **something from someone** hacer que uno devuelva algo; **to** — **one's property** (Law) reivindicar su propiedad; **to** — **damages from someone** ser indemnizado por daños y perjuicios por uno.
2 vi (Med, Fin etc) restablecerse, reponerse; **to** — **from an illness** reponerse de una enfermedad; **has she quite** —**ed?** ¿se ha curado del todo?; **shares have** —**ed** las acciones han vuelto a subir; **when I had** —**ed from my astonishment** cuando me hube sobrepuesto a mi asombro.
3 vr: **to** — **oneself** reponerse, sobreponerse.
re-cover ['ri:'kʌvə*] vt recubrir.
recoverable [ri'kʌvərəbl] adj recuperable; (at law) reivindicable.
recovery [ri'kʌvəri] n recobro m, recuperación f; (rescue) rescate m; (Med etc) restablecimiento m, mejoría f; (Law) reivindicación f; **an action for** — **of damages** una demanda del pago de daños y perjuicios; **to be past** — haberse perdido definitivamente, ser irrecuperable, (Med) estar desahuciado; **to make a rapid** — restablecerse rápidamente; **to make a slow** — restablecerse lentamente; **prices made a slow** — las cotizaciones tardaron en restablecerse.
recreate ['rekrieit] vt recrear.
re-create ['ri:kri'eit] vt (create again) recrear.
recreation [ˌrekri'eiʃən] n (act) recreación f; (play, amusement) recreo m; (School) recreo m, hora f de recreo.
recreational [ˌrekri'eiʃənəl] adj: — **facilities** facilidades fpl de recreo; **this is only** — esto es sólo un pasatiempo.
recreation room [ˌrekri'eiʃənrum] n salón m de recreo.
recreative ['rekri.eitiv] adj recreativo.
recriminate [ri'krimineit] vi recriminar.
recrimination [riˌkrimi'neiʃən] n recriminación f; **mutual** — recriminación f mutua.
recross ['ri:'krɔs] vti volver a cruzar.
recrudesce [ˌri:kru'des] vi recrudecer.
recrudescence [ˌri:kru'desns] n recrudescencia f, recrudecimiento m.
recrudescent [ˌri:kru'desnt] adj recrudescente.
recruit [ri'kru:t] **1** n recluta m; **raw** — (Mil) soldado m bisoño, quinto m, (fig) novicio m. **2** vt (Mil) reclutar; strength etc restablecer. **3** vi alistar reclutas.
recruiting [ri'kru:tiŋ] n reclutamiento m.
recruiting office [ri'kru:tiŋˌɔfis] n caja f de reclutas.
recruitment [ri'kru:tmənt] n reclutamiento m.
rectal ['rektəl] adj rectal.
rectangle ['rekˌtæŋgl] n rectángulo m.
rectangular [rek'tæŋgjulə*] adj rectangular.
rectifiable ['rektifaiəbl] adj rectificable.
rectification [ˌrektifi'keiʃən] n rectificación f.
rectifier ['rektifaiə*] n (Elec, Chem etc) rectificador m; (Mech) rectificadora f.
rectify ['rektifai] vt (all senses) rectificar.
rectilinear ['rekti'liniə*] adj rectilíneo.
rectitude ['rektitju:d] n rectitud f.
rector ['rektə*] n (Eccl) párroco m; (Univ etc) rector m.
rectorship ['rektəʃip] n rectorado m.
rectory ['rektəri] n (Eccl) casa f del cura.
rectum ['rektəm] n recto m.

recumbent [ri'kʌmbənt] *adj* recostado, acostado; *statue* yacente.
recuperate [ri'ku:pəreit] **1** *vt* recuperar. **2** *vi* restablecerse, reponerse; **to — after an illness** reponerse de una enfermedad.
recuperation [ri,ku:pə'reiʃən] *n* recuperación *f*; (*Med*) restablecimiento *m*.
recuperative [ri'ku:pərətiv] *adj* recuperativo.
recur [ri'kə:*] *vi* repetirse, producirse de nuevo, volver a producirse; (*revert to*) volver a; (*come to mind again*) volver a la mente; **the idea —s constantly in his work** la idea se repite constantemente en su obra.
recurrence [ri'kʌrəns] *n* repetición *f*, reaparición *f*.
recurrent [ri'kʌrənt] *adj* repetido; constante; (*Anat, Med*) recurrente; **it is a — theme** es un tema constante, es un tema que se repite a menudo.
recurring [ri'kə:riŋ] *adj see* **decimal.**
recusant ['rekjuzənt] **1** *adj* recusante. **2** *n* recusante *mf*.
red [red] **1** *adj* rojo, colorado; *face* (*high-coloured*) encarnado, (*with anger*) encendido, (*with shame*) ruboroso; *hair* rojo; *wine* tinto; *ink* colorado; (*Pol*) rojo; **to be — in the face** tener la cara encendida, tener el rostro sofocado; **was my face — !** ¡cómo me avergoncé!; **to go** (*or* **turn**) **as — as a beetroot** (*or* **lobster, tomato**) ponerse como un tomate; **to go** (*or* **turn**) **— with shame** ponerse colorado, ruborizarse.

  2 *n* rojo *m*, color *m* rojo; (*Pol*) rojo *m*, a *f*; **to be in the —** deber dinero, estar en el libro de los morosos; **to be £1000 in the —** deber 1000 libras; **to get into the —** contraer deudas; **to get out of the —** pagar las deudas; **to see —** sulfurarse, salirse de sus casillas; **this makes me see —** esto me saca de quicio.
redact [ri'dækt] *vt* redactar.
redaction [ri'dækʃən] *n* redacción *f*.
Red Army ['red'ɑ:mi] *n* Ejército *m* Rojo.
red-berried ['red'berid] *adj* con bayas rojas.
red-blooded ['red'blʌdid] *adj* viril, vigoroso, enérgico.
redbreast ['redbrest] *n* (*also* **robin —**) petirrojo *m*.
redcap ['redkæp] *n* (*Mil sl*) policía *m* militar; (*US*) mozo *m* de estación.
redcoat ['redkəut] *n* soldado *m* inglés (del siglo XVIII *etc*).
redden ['redn] **1** *vt* enrojecer, teñir de rojo. **2** *vi* enrojecerse, ponerse rojo; (*person: with anger*) enrojecerse, (*with shame*) ponerse colorado, ruborizarse.
reddish ['rediʃ] *adj* rojizo.
redecorate ['ri:'dekəreit] *vt room* renovar, pintar de nuevo, volver a decorar.
redecoration [ri:,dekə'reiʃən] *n* renovación *f*.
redeem [ri'di:m] **1** *vt* redimir (*also Rel*), rescatar; *mortgage, bonds* amortizar; (*from pawn*) desempeñar; *promise* cumplir; *fault* expiar. **2** *vr*: **to — oneself** salvarse, expiar su falta.
redeemable [ri'di:məbl] *adj* redimible; (*Fin*) amortizable.
Redeemer [ri'di:mə*] *n* Redentor *m*.
redeeming [ri'di:miŋ] *adj*: **— feature** rasgo *m* bueno, (*fig*) punto *m* favorable; **— virtue** virtud *f* compensadora; **I see no — feature in it** no le encuentro ningún aspecto bueno.
redemption [ri'dempʃən] *n* redención *f* (*also Rel*), rescate *m*; (*Fin*) amortización *f*; desempeño *m*; cumplimiento *m*; expiación *f*; **to be beyond** (*or* **past**) **—** no tener remedio, ser irremediable.
redemptive [ri'demptiv] *adj* redentor.
redeploy ['ri:di'plɔi] *vt resources, men* disponer de otro modo, reorganizar; utilizar de modo distinto.
redeployment ['ri:di'plɔimənt] *n* nueva disposición *f*, reorganización *f*; utilización *f* más económica (*or* lógica).
red-eyed ['red'aid] *adj* con los ojos inyectados en sangre, con los ojos en sangre.
red-faced ['red'feist] *adj* (*with anger*) con la cara encendida; (*with shame*) colorado, ruboroso, avergonzado.
red-haired ['red'hεəd] *adj* pelirrojo.
red-handed ['red'hændid] *adj*: **to catch someone —** coger a uno con las manos en la masa, coger a uno en flagrante delito.
redhead ['redhed] *n* pelirroja *f*.
red-headed ['red'hedid] *adj* pelirrojo.
red-hot ['red'hɔt] *adj* candente; (*fig*) *news* de última hora; *issue* peligrosísimo; de máxima importancia, de la mayor actualidad; *supporter etc* vehemente, acérrimo.
redirect ['ri:dai'rekt] *vt letter* reexpedir.
rediscover ['ri:dis'kʌvə*] *vt* volver a descubrir.

rediscovery ['ri:dis'kʌvəri] *n* segundo descubrimiento *m*; **its — was the work of . . .** el que se haya vuelto a descubrir se debe a . . .
redistribute ['ri:dis'tribju:t] *vt* distribuir de nuevo, hacer una nueva distribución de.
redistribution ['ri:,distri'bju:ʃən] *n* nueva distribución *f*.
red-letter ['red'letə*] *adj*: **— day** día *m* señalado, día *m* especial.
red-light ['red'lait] *adj*: **— district** barrio *m* chino.
redness ['rednis] *n* rojez *f*, lo rojo, lo encarnado.
redo ['ri:'du:] (*irr: see* **do**) *vt* rehacer, volver a hacer.
redolence ['redəuləns] *n* fragancia *f*, perfume *m*.
redolent ['redəulənt] *adj*: **— of** perfumado como, con perfume como el de; **to be — of** (*fig*) recordar, hacer pensar en.
redouble [ri'dʌbl] **1** *vt* redoblar, intensificar; (*Bridge*) redoblar. **2** *vi* redoblarse, intensificarse; (*Bridge*) redoblar.
redoubt [ri'daut] *n* reducto *m*; **the last — of . . .** el último reducto de . . .
redoubtable [ri'dautəbl] *adj* terrible, formidable.
redound [ri'daund] *vi*: **to — to** redundar en, redundar en beneficio de.
redraft ['ri:'drɑ:ft] *vt* volver a redactar, hacer un nuevo borrador de, rehacer.
redraw ['ri:'drɔ:] (*irr: see* **draw**) *vt* volver a dibujar; *map, plan* volver a trazar.
redress [ri'dres] **1** *n* reparación *f*, compensación *f*; remedio *m* (legal), derecho *m* a satisfacción; **in such a case you have no —** en tal caso Vd no tiene ningún derecho a satisfacción.
  2 *vt* (*readjust*) reajustar; *balance etc* rectificar, corregir; (*make up for*) reparar, compensar; *fault* remediar; *offence* desagraviar, enmendar.
Red Riding Hood ['red'raidiŋhud] *f* Caperucita Roja.
Red Sea ['red'si:] Mar *m* Rojo.
redshank ['redʃæŋk] *n* archibebe *m*.
redskin ['redskin] *n* piel roja *mf*.
redstart ['redstɑ:t] *n* colirrojo *m* real.
reduce [ri'dju:s] **1** *vt* reducir (*to* a; *also Math etc*), disminuir; *price* rebajar; (*in rank*) degradar; (*Mil*) reducir, tomar, conquistar; **to — an article by a quarter** abreviar un artículo en la cuarta parte; **to — everything to simple terms** expresarlo todo en términos sencillos; **to — something to ashes** hacer algo cenizas, convertir algo en cenizas; **to — speed** reducir la velocidad; **this —d him to silence** esto le hizo callar; **we were —d to begging in the streets** nos vimos sin otro recurso que el de pedir por las calles.
  2 *vi* reducirse, disminuir; (*slim*) adelgazar.
reduced [ri'dju:st] *adj*: **a — income** una renta mermada, unos ingresos disminuidos; **at a — price** con rebaja, con descuento; **"greatly — prices"** "grandes rebajas"; *see* **circumstance.**
reducible [ri'dju:səbl] *adj* reducible.
reduction [ri'dʌkʃən] *n* reducción *f* (*in, of* de), disminución *f*; (*in price*) rebaja *f*; (*in rank*) degradación *f*; (*Mil*) reducción *f*, toma *f*, conquista *f*; (*shortening*) abreviación *f*; **"great —s"** (*Comm*) "grandes rebajas"; **there has been no — in demand** no ha disminuido la demanda.
redundance [ri'dʌndəns] *n* (*Gram*) redundancia *f*.
redundancy [ri'dʌndənsi] *n* exceso *m*, superfluidad *f*; (*among workers*) desempleo *m*; **the problems of —** los problemas del exceso de mano de obra.
redundant [ri'dʌndənt] *adj* excesivo, superfluo; (*Gram*) redundante; **to be —** estar de más; **the workers now made —** los obreros que quedan ahora sin trabajo; **automation may make some workers —** la automatización puede hacer que varios obreros pierdan sus puestos.
reduplicate [ri'dju:plikeit] *vt* reduplicar.
reduplication [ri,dju:pli'keiʃən] *n* reduplicación *f*.
redwood ['redwud] *n* secoya *f*.
redye ['ri:'dai] *vt* reteñir.
re-echo ['ri:'ekəu] **1** *vt* repetir, resonar con. **2** *vi* resonar, repercutirse.
reed [ri:d] *n* (*Bot*) carrizo *m*, junco *m*, caña *f*; (*Mus: in mouthpiece*) lengüeta *f*, (*pipe*) caramillo *m*; **broken —** persona *f* (*or* cosa *f*) que no es de fiar, persona *f* débil.
reedbed ['ri:dbed] *n* carrizal *m*, juncal *m*, cañaveral *m*.
re-edit ['ri:'edit] *vt* reeditar.
reedmace ['ri:dmeis] *n* anca *f*, enca *f*.
re-educate ['ri:'edjukeit] *vt* reeducar.
re-education ['ri:,edju'keiʃən] *n* reeducación *f*.
reedy ['ri:di] *adj place* lleno de cañas, cubierto de carrizos (*etc*); (*Mus*) agudo, alto y delgado.

reef[1] [riːf] (*Naut*) **1** n rizo m; **to let out a —** largar rizos, (*fig*) aflojar el cinturón (*etc*); **to take in a —** tomar rizos, (*fig*) apretar el cinturón (*etc*).
   2 vt arrizar.

reef[2] [riːf] n (*Geog*) escollo m, arrecife m; **coral —** barrera f coralina.

reefer[1] ['riːfə*] n chaquetón m.

reefer[2] ['riːfə*] n (*sl*) pitillo m de marijuana.

reef knot ['riːfnɔt] n nudo m de marino.

reek [riːk] **1** n mal olor m, hedor m (*of* a).
   2 vi (*smoke*) humear, vahear; (*smell*) oler, heder (*of* a); trascender (*of* a); **this —s of treachery** esto huele a traición; **she —s with affectation** su afectación es inaguantable; **he comes home simply —ing** vuelve a casa oliendo a vino de muy mala manera.

reel [riːl] **1** n (*in fishing etc*) carrete m; (*for tape recorder etc*) carrete m, bobina f; (*Sew*) broca f, devanadera f; (*Phot: for small camera*) carrete f, película f, rollo m, (*of cine film*) bobina f, cinta f; (*Mus*) baile escocés muy vivo; **about 20 right off the —** unos 20 seguidos, unos 20 sin parar.
   2 vt (*Sew*) devanar; **to — in one's line** ir cobrando el sedal; **to — in a fish** tirar de un pez haciendo girar el carrete; **to — off** enumerar rápidamente, recitar de una tirada, ensartar.
   3 vi tambalear, tambalearse; (*retreat*) cejar, retroceder; **he was —ing about drunkenly** andaba haciendo eses; **the boxer —ed to his corner** el boxeador se fué tambaleando a su rincón; **the mind —s** la mente queda atolondrada; **to make someone's mind —** atolondrar a uno; **my head is —ing** mi cabeza está dando vueltas.

re-elect ['riːi'lekt] vt reelegir.

re-election ['riːi'lekʃən] n reelección f.

re-eligible ['riː'elidʒəbl] adj reelegible.

re-emerge ['riːi'məːdʒ] vi volver a salir, reaparecer.

re-enact ['riːi'nækt] vt (*Parl*) volver a promulgar; decretar de nuevo; (*Theat etc*) volver a representar; *crime* reconstituir.

re-engage ['riːin'geidʒ] vt contratar de nuevo.

re-enlist ['riːin'list] vi reengancharse, alistarse de nuevo.

re-enter ['riː'entə*] vt reingresar en, volver a entrar en.

re-entry ['riː'entri] n reingreso m, segunda entrada f; (*of spacecraft*) reentrada f, reingreso m.

re-equip ['riːi'kwip] vt equipar de nuevo (*with* con).

re-establish ['riːis'tæbliʃ] vt restablecer.

re-establishment ['riːis'tæbliʃmənt] n restablecimiento m.

reeve [riːv] vt (*Naut*) asegurar (con cabo); pasar por un ojal.

re-examination ['riːig,zæmi'neiʃən] n reexaminación f.

re-examine ['riːig'zæmin] vt reexaminar.

re-export ['riː'ekspɔːt] vt reexportar.

ref [ref] n (*fam*) árbitro m.

reface ['riː'feis] vt revestir de nuevo, forrar de nuevo (*with* de), poner un nuevo revestimiento a.

refashion ['riː'fæʃən] vt formar de nuevo.

refection [ri'fekʃən] n refacción f.

refectory [ri'fektəri] n refectorio m.

refer [ri'fəː*] **1** vt (a) (*send, direct*) remitir; **to — something to someone** remitir algo a uno; **to — someone to something** remitir a uno a algo; **the reader is —red to page 15** remito al lector a la página 15; **it is —red to us for decision** se remite a nosotros para que decidamos; **to — a matter to a lawyer** entregar un asunto a un abogado; **a cheque —red to drawer** (*R/D*) un cheque protestado por falta de fondos.
   (b) (*ascribe*) atribuir, referir (*to* a); relacionar (*to* con); **he —s his mistake to tiredness** el error lo achaca a su cansancio; **he —s the painting to the 14th century** atribuye el cuadro al siglo XIV; **this insect is to be —red to the genus Pieris** este insecto ha de clasificarse en el género Pieris.
   2 vi: **to —** to referirse a, aludir a, mencionar, hacer referencia a; **I — to our worthy president** me refiero a nuestro benemérito presidente; **we will not — to it again** no lo volveremos a mencionar; **—ring to yours of the 5th** me refiero a su carta del 5; **please — to section 3** véase la sección 3; **you must — to the original** hay que recurrir al original.

referable [ri'fəːrəbl] adj: **— to** referible a; atribuible a; que ha de clasificarse en.

referee [,refə'riː] **1** n (*in dispute, Sport etc*) árbitro m; (*for application, post*) persona f a quien se puede acudir para pedir una recomendación. **2** vti arbitrar.

reference ['refrəns] **1** n (a) (*act of referring*) remisión f; **terms of —** puntos mpl de consulta; **it was agreed without —** to me se acordó sin consultarme, se decidió sin que se pidiera mi parecer.
   (b) (*bearing*) relación f (*to* con); **with — to en** cuanto a, respecto de; **with — to yours of the 8th** me refiero a su carta del 8; **without — to any particular case** sin referirme (*etc*) a ningún caso concreto; **what — has A to B?** ¿qué tiene que ver A con B?; **it has no — to what I asked** no tiene que ver con lo que yo pregunté.
   (c) (*allusion*) referencia f, alusión f, mención f; **he spoke without any — to you** habló sin mencionar para nada a Vd; **to make — to** referirse a, hacer referencia de.
   (d) (*directive*) referencia f; número m de referencia f; sigla f; (*Typ: also* **— mark**) llamada f; **"— XYZ2"** "número de referencia: XYZ2"; **a — in the margin** una referencia al margen.
   (e) (*testimonial*) referencia f; (*person*) persona f a quien se puede acudir para pedir una referencia; **to have good —s** tener buenas referencias; **to take up someone's —s** pedir referencias (*or* informes) acerca de uno.
   2 attr number, point de referencia; book, library de consulta.

referendum [,refə'rendəm] n referéndum m.

refill ['riːfil] n repuesto m, recambio m; (*for pencil*) mina f.

refill ['riː'fil] vt rellenar, volver a llenar.

refine [ri'fain] **1** vt refinar; purificar; refinar, educar, hacer más culto; *methods* refinar; *style* limar, purificar; *oil etc* refinar; *metal* acrisolar, acendrar; *fats* clarificar.
   2 vi: **to — upon something** refinar algo, mejorar algo; (*discuss*) discutir algo con mucha sutileza.

refined [ri'faind] adj refinado; society, person fino, culto; (*pej: often pronounced* [ri'fiːnd]) redicho, afectado; *style* elegante, pulido.

refinement [ri'fainmənt] n refinamiento m; (*act, Tech*) refinación f; purificación f; (*of society, person*) finura f, cultura f, educación f; (*pej*) afectación f; (*of style*) elegancia f, urbanidad f; **a person of some —** una persona fina; **that is a — of cruelty** eso es ser más cruel todavía; **with every possible — of cruelty** con las formas más sutiles de la crueldad.

refiner [ri'fainə*] n refinador m.

refinery [ri'fainəri] n refinería f.

refit ['riː'fit] **1** n reparación f, compostura f; (*Naut*) embonada f.
   2 vt reparar, componer; (*Naut*) reparar, embonar; **to — something with a device** volver a equipar algo con un dispositivo.
   3 vi (*Naut*) repararse, embonarse.

refitting ['riː'fitiŋ] n, **refitment** ['riː'fitmənt] n reparación f, compostura f; (*Naut*) embonada f.

reflect [ri'flekt] **1** vt (a) reflejar; **plants —ed in the water** plantas fpl reflejadas en el agua; **the difficulties —ed in his report** el informe se hace eco de las dificultades, las dificultades se reflejan en su informe.
   (b) **the speech —s credit on him** el discurso le hace honor.
   2 vi (a) (*think*) reflexionar, pensar; meditar; **— before you act** reflexione antes de obrar; **if we but — a moment** sí sólo reflexionamos un instante; **I —ed that ... pensé que ...; — on it!** ¡medítelo!
   (b) **that —s well on him** eso le hace honor; **that —s ill on him** eso le muestra bajo una luz poco favorable; **it — on all of us** eso tiende a perjudicarnos (*or* desprestigiarnos) a todos; **it —s on her reputation** eso pone en tela de duda su fama.

reflection [ri'flekʃən] n (a) (*of light: act*) reflexión f, (*image*) reflejo m; **the — of the light in the mirror** el reflejo de la luz en el espejo; **a pale — of former glories** un pálido reflejo de glorias pretéritas; **to see one's — in a shop window** verse reflejado en una vitrina.
   (b) (*aspersion*) reproche m (*on* a), crítica f; **this is no — on your honesty** esto no dice nada en contra de su honradez, esto no es ningún reproche a su honradez; **to cast —s on someone** reprochar a uno.
   (c) (*reconsideration*) **on —** después de volver a pensarlo, pensándolo bien; **without due —** sin pensarlo bastante; **mature — suggests that ...** una meditación más profunda indica que ...
   (d) (*idea*) pensamiento m, idea f; **"R—s on Ortega"** "Meditación f sobre Ortega".

reflective [ri'flektiv] adj pensativo, meditabundo.

reflectively [ri'flektivli] adv pensativamente; **he said — dijo** pensativo; **she looked at me —** me miró pensativa.

reflector [ri'flektə*] n reflector m; (Aut: also **rear**
—) captafaros m, placa f de captafaros.
reflex ['ri:fleks] 1 adj reflejo. 2 n reflejo m.
reflexive [ri'fleksiv] adj reflexivo.
refloat ['ri:'fləut] vt sacar a flote.
reforestation ['ri:,fɔris'teiʃən] n repoblación f
forestal.
reform [ri'fɔ:m] 1 n reforma f; **agrarian** —, **land** —
reforma f agraria; **monetary** — reforma f monetaria.
2 vt reformar. 3 vi reformarse.
re-form ['ri:'fɔ:m] 1 vt formar de nuevo; reorganizar,
reconstituir. 2 vi formarse de nuevo; reconstituirse;
(Mil) rehacerse.
reformation [,refə'meiʃən] n reformación f; **R—**
(Eccl) Reforma f.
reformatory [ri'fɔ:mətəri] n reformatorio m.
reformed [ri'fɔ:md] adj reformado.
reformer [ri'fɔ:mə*] n reformador m, ora f.
reformist [ri'fɔ:mist] 1 adj reformista. 2 n reformista
mf.
refract [ri'frækt] vt refractar.
refracting [ri'fræktiŋ] adj: — **telescope** telescopio
m de refracción.
refraction [ri'frækʃən] n refracción f.
refractive [ri'fræktiv] adj refractivo.
refractor [ri'fræktə*] n refractor m.
refractoriness [ri'fræktərinis] n obstinacia f.
refractory [ri'fræktəri] adj refractario, obstinado;
(Tech) refractario.
refrain¹ [ri'frein] n estribillo m; **his constant** —
is . . . siempre está con la misma canción . . .
refrain² [ri'frein] vi: to — **from something**
abstenerse de algo; to — **from** + **ger** abstenerse
de + infin; **I couldn't** — **from laughing** no pude
menos de reír, no pude contener la risa.
refresh [ri'freʃ] vt refrescar.
refresher [ri'freʃə*] 1 n (fam) refresco m. 2 attr
course de repaso.
refreshing [ri'freʃiŋ] adj refrescante; (fig) interesante,
estimulante; **it's a** — **change to find this** es
interesante encontrar esta novedad, es alentador
encontrar esto; **it's** — **to hear some new ideas**
escuchar nuevas ideas estimula la imaginación.
refreshment [ri'freʃmənt] n refresco m; "**R—s**"
"Refrescos"; **to take some** — tomar algo, comer
(or beber etc).
refreshment room [ri'freʃmənt,rum] n (Rail etc)
cantina f.
refreshment stall [ri'freʃmənt,stɔ:l] n puesto m de
refrescos.
refrigerant [ri'fridʒərənt] n refrigerante m.
refrigerate [ri'fridʒəreit] vt refrigerar.
refrigeration [ri,fridʒə'reiʃən] n refrigeración f.
refrigerator [ri'fridʒəreitə*] n nevera f, frigorífico
m, refrigerador m.
refrigerator lorry [ri'fridʒəreitə,lɔri] n camión m
frigorífico.
refrigerator ship [ri'fridʒəreitə,ʃip] n buque m
frigorífico.
refuel ['ri:'fjuəl] 1 vt reabastecer (or rellenar) de
combustible. 2 vi repostar, reabastecer combustible.
refuelling ['ri:'fjuəliŋ] n reabastecimiento m (or
rellenado m) de combustible.
refuge ['refju:dʒ] n refugio m, asilo m; (resort)
recurso m; (hut) albergue m; **God is my** — Dios
es mi amparo; **to seek** — buscar dónde guarecerse;
to take — ponerse al abrigo, guarecerse; **to take** —
in refugiarse en, (fig) acogerse a, recurrir a.
refugee [,refju'dʒi:] n refugiado m, a f.
refulgence [ri'fʌldʒəns] n refulgencia f.
refulgent [ri'fʌldʒənt] adj refulgente.
refund ['ri:fʌnd] n (act) devolución f; (amount)
reembolso m.
refund [ri'fʌnd] vt devolver, reintegrar, reembolsar.
refurbish ['ri:'fɔ:biʃ] vt restaurar; (decorate) renovar;
literary work refundir.
refurnish ['ri:'fɔ:niʃ] vt amueblar de nuevo.
refusal [ri'fju:zəl] n (a) negativa f, denegación f;
a blank (or **flat**) — una rotunda negativa; **the
offer met a flat** — rechazaron la oferta de plano.
(b) (Comm etc) opción f, opción f exclusiva; **you
have first** — Vd tiene opción al artículo, lo ofreceré
primero a Vd.
refuse ['refju:s] n basura f, desperdicios mpl, desecho
m; **household** — basura f doméstica; **garden** —
basura f de jardín.
refuse [ri'fju:z] 1 vt rehusar, rechazar, denegar; **no
querer aceptar; negar; to** — **someone something**
negar algo a uno; **they can** — **her nothing son**
incapaces de privarla de nada; **I have never been
—d here** aquí no se han negado nunca a servirme;
she —d my offer rechazó mi oferta; **I regret to**

have to — **your invitation** siento no poder aceptar
su invitación.
2 vi (a) **he —d se** negó a hacerlo; **to** — **to do
something** negarse a hacer algo, rehusar hacer algo.
(b) (of horse) rehusar, plantarse, resistirse a
saltar.
3 vr: **to** — **oneself something** privarse de algo.
refuse bin ['refju:sbin] n cubo m de la basura.
refuse dump ['refju:sdʌmp] n vertidero m, basurero
m.
refuse lorry ['refju:s,lɔri] n camión m de la basura.
refutable [ri'fju:təbl] adj refutable.
refutation [,refju'teiʃən] n refutación f.
refute [ri'fju:t] vt refutar, rebatir.
regain [ri'gein] vt cobrar, recobrar, recuperar;
(breath) cobrar; **to** — **consciousness** recobrar el
conocimiento, volver en sí.
regal ['ri:gəl] adj regio, real.
regale [ri'geil] 1 vt agasajar, festejar; **to** — **someone
on oysters** agasajar a uno dándole ostras de comer;
he —d the company with a funny story para
divertirles les contó a los comensales un chiste.
2 vr: **to** — **oneself on something** regalarse con algo.
regalia [ri'geilià] n insignias fpl (esp reales).
regally ['ri:gəli] adv regiamente; con pompa (etc) regia.
regard [ri'gɑ:d] 1 n (a) (gaze) mirada f.
(b) (aspect, point) respecto m; aspecto m;
in — **to, with** — **to** con respecto a, en cuanto a,
por lo que se refiere a; **in this** — con respecto a esto.
(c) (attention, care) atención f; **without** — **to**
sin hacer caso de, sin considerar; **having** — **to en
atención a**, considerando, teniendo en cuenta; **to
have no** — **to** (of person) no prestar atención a,
no tener en cuenta; (of relationship) no guardar
relación con, no tener que ver con; — **must be
had to this matter** hay que tener en cuenta este
asunto.
(d) (esteem) respeto m, consideración f,
estimación f; **my** — **for him** el respeto que le tengo;
out of — **for** por respeto a; **to have a high** — **for
someone, to hold someone in high** — tener buen
concepto de uno, respetar mucho a uno; **to show
— for someone** mostrar tener respeto a uno; **he
shows little** — **for their feelings** le importan poco
sus susceptibilidades.
(e) —s recuerdos mpl; —s **to X, please give
my** —s to X recuerdos a X, salude de mi parte a X;
with kind —s con muchos recuerdos.
2 vt (a) (look at) mirar; observar; **she —ed me
with astonishment** me miró atónita.
(b) (consider) considerar; **we** — **it as worth
doing** consideramos que vale la pena hacerlo;
we don't — **it as necessary** no creemos que sea
necesario; **they** — **it with horror** lo ven con horror;
to — **someone with suspicion** recelarse de uno.
(c) **as** —s en cuanto a, por lo que se refiere a.
regardful [ri'gɑ:dful] adj: — **of** atento a.
regarding [ri'gɑ:diŋ] prep en cuanto a, por lo que
se refiere a; **and other things** — **money** y otras
cosas relativas al dinero.
regardless [ri'gɑ:dlis] 1 adj: — **of** indiferente a;
insensible a; sin hacer caso de, sin pensar para
nada en, sin miramientos de; **buy it** — **of the cost**
cómprelo a no importa qué precio; **they shot them
all** — **of rank** los fusilaron a todos sin miramientos
a su graduación; **we did it** — **of the consequences**
lo hicimos sin inquietarnos por las consecuencias.
2 adv (fam) a pesar de todo; pese a quien pese;
he went on — continuó sin prestar atención a esto,
a pesar de esto siguió adelante; **press on** —!
¡adelante sin contemplaciones!, ¡adelante pase lo
que pase!
regatta [ri'gætə] n regata f.
regency ['ri:dʒənsi] n regencia f.
regenerate [ri'dʒenərit] adj regenerado.
regenerate [ri'dʒenəreit] vt regenerar.
regeneration [ri,dʒenə'reiʃən] n regeneración f.
regenerative [ri'dʒenərətiv] adj regenerador.
regent ['ri:dʒənt] 1 adj: **prince** — príncipe m regente.
2 n regente mf.
regicide ['redʒisaid] n (act) regicidio m; (person)
regicida mf.
régime [rei'ʒi:m] n régimen m; **ancien** — antiguo
régimen m; **under the Nazi** — bajo el régimen de
los nazis.
regimen ['redʒimen] n régimen m.
regiment ['redʒimənt] n (Mil) regimiento m; **a
whole** — **of mice** todo un ejército de ratones.
regiment ['redʒiment] vt organizar muy estrictamente; reglamentar; **we are very —ed at the college**
en el colegio nuestra vida está organizada muy
estrictamente.

regimental [.redʒi'mentl] *adj* de regimiento, del regimiento; (*fig*) militar; **with — precision** con precisión militar.
regimentals [.redʒi'mentlz] *npl* uniforme *m*.
regimentation [.redʒimen'teiʃən] regimentación *f*, organización *f* estricta.
Reginald ['redʒinld] *m* Reinaldos, Reginaldo.
region ['ri:dʒən] *n* región *f*; comarca *f*; zona *f*; **a fertile —** una región fértil; **the lower —s** (*fig*) el infierno; **in the — of 40** alrededor de 40, unos 40; **I felt a pain in the kidney —** sentí un dolor de riñones.
regional ['ri:dʒənl] *adj* regional; **— development** desarrollo *m* regional.
regionalism ['ri:dʒənəlizəm] *n* regionalismo *m*.
regionalist ['ri:dʒənəlist] **1** *adj* regionalista. **2** *n* regionalista *mf*.
register ['redʒistə*] **1** *n* registro *m*; (*Mus*, *Typ*, *of hotel*) registro *m*; (*in school*) lista *f*; (*of members*) lista *f*, padrón *m*; (*Univ*, *Naut*) matrícula *f*; (*Tech*) indicador *m*; **parish —** libro *m* parroquial, registro *m* parroquial; **— of births** registro *m* de nacimientos; **— of deaths** registro *m* de defunciones; **— of marriages** registro *m* de casamientos; **— of voters, voting —** registro *m* electoral; **to be in —** (*Typ*) estar en registro; **to call the —** (*School*) pasar lista; **to sign the —** (*in hotel*) firmar el registro; *see* **ton**.
2 *vt* (a) registrar; *birth etc* declarar; *trademark etc* registrar; (*record*) apuntar, registrar, hacer constar; (*Univ*, *Naut*) matricular; (*by post*) certificar, (*by rail*) facturar.
(b) (*of instruments*) marcar, indicar; *emotion* acusar, mostrar, manifestar; **the thermometer —s 40 degrees** el termómetro marca 40 grados; **he —d no surprise** no acusó sorpresa alguna; **the patient has —d a marked improvement** el enfermo ha acusado una notable mejoría; **production has —d a big fall** la producción ha experimentado un descenso considerable.
3 *vi* (a) (*sign on etc*) inscribirse, matricularse; **to — at an hotel** registrarse en un hotel; **to — for a course** matricularse en un curso.
(b) (*Typ*) estar en registro.
(c) producir impresión (*with* en); **it doesn't seem to have —ed with her** parece no haber producido impresión en ella; **when it finally —ed** cuando se dio cuenta de ello, cuando por fin comprendió; **things like that just don't —** las cosas así pasan inadvertidas.
registered ['redʒistəd] *adj letter* certificado, *baggage* facturado; *design*, *trademark etc* registrado; *student etc* matriculado.
register office ['redʒistər.ɔfis] *n see* **registry office**.
registrar [.redʒis'trɑ:*] *n* registrador *m*, archivero *m*; (*of society*) secretario *m*; (*Univ*) secretario *m* géneral; (*of births etc*) secretario *m* del registro civil.
registration [.redʒis'treiʃən] *n* (*act*) registro *m*; inscripción *f*; matrícula *f*; declaración *f*; certificación *f*, facturación *f*; (*number*: *Aut*, *Naut*, *Univ etc*) matrícula *f*; **the ship's Panamanian — has been withdrawn** se ha cancelado la matrícula panameña del buque.
registration fee [.redʒis'treiʃənfi:] *n* derechos *mpl* de matrícula.
registration tag [.redʒis'treiʃəntæg] *n* (*US Aut*) placa *f* de matrícula, matrícula *f*.
registry ['redʒistri] *n* registro *m*, archivo *m*; (*Univ etc*) secretaría *f* general; **servants' —** agencia *f* de colocaciones.
registry office ['redʒistri.ɔfis] *n* (*approx*) juzgado *m* municipal; **to get married at a —** casarse por lo civil, casarse por el juzgado.
regression [ri'greʃən] *n* regresión *f*.
regressive [ri'gresiv] *adj* regresivo.
regret [ri'gret] **1** *n* (a) sentimiento *m*, pesar *m*; remordimiento *m*; **much to my —, to my great —** con gran pesar mío; **to express one's —** **to someone** (*for act*) expresar su sentimiento a uno, disculparse con uno, (*for death etc*) enviar el pésame a uno; **to feel —** sentirlo, sentir pesar; **I have no —s** no me arrepiento de ello; **I say it with —** lo digo con pesar.
(b) **—s** (*excuses*) excusas *fpl*; **to send one's —s for not being able to come** mandar sus excusas por no poder venir.
2 *vt* sentir, lamentar; arrepentirse de; **I — the error** lamento el error; **it is to be —ted** es de sentir, es de lamentar; **to — that . . .** sentir que + *subj*, lamentar que + *subj*; **we — to inform you that . . .** lamentamos tener que informarle que . . .; **he —s having said it** lamenta haberlo dicho, se arrepiente de haberlo dicho.

regretful [ri'gretful] *adj* pesaroso; arrepentido; **to be — that . . .** lamentar que + *subj*; **he was most — about it** lo lamentó profundamente; **we are not — about leaving** no nos pesa tener que partir.
regretfully [ri'gretfəli] *adv* con pesar, sentidamente; **she spoke —** habló con sentimiento; **— I have to tell you that . . .** siento tener que decirles que . . .
regrettable [ri'gretəbl] *adj* lamentable, deplorable; *loss etc* sensible.
regrettably [ri'gretəbli] *adv* lamentablemente; sensiblemente.
regroup [ri:'gru:p] **1** *vt* reagrupar; (*Mil etc*) reorganizar. **2** *vi* reagruparse; (*Mil etc*) reorganizarse.
regrouping [ri:'gru:piŋ] *n* reagrupación *f*; reorganización *f*.
regular ['regjulə*] **1** *adj* (a) regular; (*Eccl*, *Mil*, *Gram etc*) regular; uniforme; normal, corriente, constante; *attender*, *customer*, *reader etc* habitual, asiduo; **our — waiter** el camarero que suele servirnos; **the — travellers on a train** los que siempre viajan en un tren; **the — staff** los empleados permanentes; **— troops** tropas *fpl* regulares; **as a — reader of your journal, may I . . .** como lector habitual de su revista, me permito . . .; **as — as clockwork** con la regularidad de una máquina; **to have a — time for doing something** hacer algo siempre a la misma hora; **to make — use of something** usar algo con regularidad.
(b) (*systematic*) sistemático, regular; (*consistent*) constante; **— features** facciones *fpl* correctas; **a man of — habits** un hombre ordenado (en sus costumbres).
(c) (*normal*) normal, corriente; **the — word is "looking glass"** la palabra corriente es "espejo"; **it's perfectly —** es completamente normal; **it's quite — to see deer here** es corriente ver ciervos por aquí.
(d) (*intensive*) cabal, verdadero; **a — feast** un verdadero banquete; **there was a — quarrel** se riñó de verdad; **he's a — guy** es buen chico, es un verdadero amigo.
2 *n* (*Eccl*) regular *m*; (*Mil*) soldado *m* de línea; (*client etc*) parroquiano *m*, cliente *m* habitual; **one of the café —s** un asiduo del café; **we keep the best goods for our —s** guardamos lo mejor para nuestros clientes habituales.
regularity [.regju'læriti] *n* regularidad *f*; **with great — con** la mayor regularidad.
regularize ['regjuləraiz] *vt* regularizar; arreglar, poner en orden; **in order to — your position** para arreglar su situación.
regularly ['regjuləli] *adv* regularmente, con regularidad; **"use brand X —"** "use la marca X con regularidad"; **he's — late** siempre llega con retraso; **a — declined noun** un sustantivo de declinación regular; **this ground has been — fought over** sobre este terreno se ha luchado constantemente.
regulate ['regjuleit] *vt* regular (*also Mech etc*); arreglar, ajustar; (*make regulations for*) reglamentar; **to — one's life by . . .** vivir según las normas establecidas por . . ., vivir con arreglo a . . .; **to — prices** regular los precios.
regulation [.regju'leiʃən] **1** *n* (*act*) regulación *f*; arreglo *m*; (*rule*) regla *f*; reglamento *m*; **the —s are very strict** los reglamentos son muy estrictos; **to introduce new traffic —s** introducir un nuevo reglamento de la circulación.
2 *adj*, *attr* reglamentario, de reglamento; normal; **it's — wear in school** es el uniforme del reglamento en la escuela.
regulator ['regjuleitə*] *n* regulador *m*.
regurgitate [ri'gə:dʒiteit] **1** *vt* volver a arrojar, vomitar (sin esfuerzo); (*fig*) reproducir maquinalmente. **2** *vi* regurgitar.
regurgitation [ri'gə:dʒi'teiʃən] *n* regurgitación *f*; (*fig*) reproducción *f* maquinal.
rehabilitate [.ri:ə'biliteit] *vt* rehabilitar.
rehabilitation ['ri:ə,bili'teiʃən] *n* rehabilitación *f*.
rehash ['ri:'hæʃ] **1** *n* refundición *f*. **2** *vt* refundir.
rehearsal [ri'hə:səl] *n* enumeración *f*, repetición *f*; (*Mus*, *Theat etc*) ensayo *m*; **it was just a — for bigger things to come** fue a modo de ensayo para las empresas mayores que habían de venir después.
rehearse [ri'hə:s] *vt* enumerar, repetir; (*Mus*, *Theat etc*) ensayar.
rehouse [ri:'hauz] *vt family* dar nueva vivienda a, proveer de vivienda nueva; trasladar a otra casa; **200 families have been —d** 200 familias tienen vivienda nueva ya.
reign [rein] **1** *n* reinado *m*; (*fig*) dominio *m*, predominio *m*; **the — of the miniskirt** la moda de la minifalda; **in** (*or* **under**) **the — of** bajo el reinado de. **2** *vi* reinar; (*fig*) predominar, imperar, prevalecer.

reigning ['reiniŋ] *adj monarch* reinante, actual; *(fig)* predominante, que impera.
reimburse [‚ri:im'bə:s] *vt* reembolsar; **to — someone for something** pagar *(or* reembolsar) a uno por algo.
reimbursement [‚ri:im'bə:smənt] *n* reembolso *m.*
reimpose ['ri:im'pəuz] *vt* volver a imponer, reimponer.
rein [rein] **1** *n* rienda *f*; **to draw —** detenerse *(also fig)*; **to give —** to dar rienda suelta a; **to keep a tight — on someone** vigilar mucho a uno, mantener una estrecha vigilancia sobre uno.
　2 *vt*: **to — back, to — in** refrenar.
　3 *vi*: **to — in** detenerse.
reincarnate [‚ri:in'ka:neit] *vt* reencarnar; **to be —d** reencarnar, volver a encarnar.
reincarnation ['ri:inka:'neiʃən] *n* reencarnación *f.*
reindeer ['reindiə*] *n* reno *m.*
reinforce [‚ri:in'fɔ:s] *vt* reforzar *(also fig)*; *concrete etc* armar.
reinforced [‚ri:in'fɔ:st] *adj* reforzado; *concrete* armado.
reinforcement [‚ri:in'fɔ:smənt] *n (act)* reforzamiento *m*; **—s** refuerzos *mpl.*
reinsert ['ri:in'sə:t] *vt* volver a insertar; volver a introducir.
reinstate ['ri:in'steit] *vt suppressed passage etc* reintegrar *(in* a), volver a incluir; *(rehabilitate)* rehabilitar; *dismissed worker* volver a emplear; *dismissed official* restituir a su puesto.
reinstatement ['ri:in'steitmənt] *n* reintegración *f (in* a); rehabilitación *f*; vuelta *f* a su empleo; restitución *f* a su puesto.
reinsurance ['ri:in'ʃuərəns] *n* reaseguro *m.*
reinsure ['ri:in'ʃuə*] *vt* reasegurar.
reintegrate ['ri:'intigreit] *vt* reintegrar.
reintegration ['ri:‚inti'greiʃən] *n* reintegración *f.*
reinter ['ri:in'tə:*] *vt* enterrar de nuevo.
reinvest ['ri:in'vest] *vt* reinvertir.
reinvestment ['ri:in'vestmənt] *n* reinversión *f.*
reinvigorate ['ri:in'vigəreit] *vt* infundir nuevo vigor a; **to feel —d** sentirse con nuevas fuerzas.
reissue ['ri:'iʃju:] **1** *n* nueva emisión *f*; reimpresión *f*; reexpedición *f*; reestreno *m.*
　2 *vt stamp* volver a emitir; *book* reimprimir; *patent etc* reexpedir; *film* reestrenar.
reiterate [ri:'itəreit] *vt* reiterar, repetir; subrayar; **I must — that ...** tengo que subrayar que ...
reiteration [ri:‚itə'reiʃən] *n* reiteración *f*, repetición *f.*
reiterative [ri:'itərətiv] *adj* reiterativo.
reject ['ri:dʒekt] *n* cosa *f* rechazada, cosa *f* defectuosa; persona *f* rechazada.
reject [ri'dʒekt] *vt offer etc* rechazar; *application* denegar; *motion* rechazar, desestimar; *plan etc* desechar; *solution* descartar; *advance* repulsar; *(of stomach etc)* arrojar.
rejection [ri'dʒekʃən] *n* rechazamiento *m*; denegación *f*; desestimación *f*; **to meet with a —** sufrir una repulsa; **the novel has already had 3 —s** la novela ya ha sido rechazada 3 veces.
rejoice [ri'dʒɔis] **1** *vt* alegrar, regocijar, causar alegría a.
　2 *vi* **(a)** alegrarse, regocijarse *(at, about, over* de); **let us not — too soon** es aconsejable no alegrarse demasiado pronto; **I — that it should be so** me alegro de que sea así.
　(b) **to — in the name of Anastasius** ser el afortunado poseedor del nombre de Anastasio.
rejoicings [ri'dʒɔisiŋz] *npl* regocijo *m*, júbilo *m*, alegría *f*; fiestas *fpl*; **the — lasted far into the night** continuaron las fiestas hasta una hora avanzada.
rejoin [ri'dʒɔin] *vt* replicar, contestar.
rejoin ['ri:'dʒɔin] *vt* reunirse con, volver a juntarse con; *regiment etc* reincorporarse a.
rejoinder [ri'dʒɔində*] *n* réplica *f*; **as a — to ...** como contestación a ...
rejuvenate [ri'dʒu:vineit] *vt* rejuvenecer.
rekindle ['ri:'kindl] *vt* reencender; *(fig)* despertar, reavivar.
relapse [ri'læps] **1** *n (Med)* recaída *f*, recidiva *f*; *(into crime, error)* reincidencia *f*; **to have a —** *(Med)* recaer, tener una recaída.
　2 *vi (Med)* recaer; *(into crime, error)* reincidir *(into* en).
relate [ri'leit] **1** *vt* **(a)** *(tell)* contar, narrar, relatar; **strange to —** aunque parece mentira, por raro que parezca.
　(b) *(establish relation between)* relacionar *(to, with* con), establecer una conexión entre.
　2 *vi*: **to —** to relacionarse con, tener que ver con, referirse a; **this —s to what I said yesterday** esto se refiere a lo que dije ayer.

related [ri'leitid] *adj* **(a)** *subject* afín, conexo; **they are — subjects** son temas afines; **this murder is not — to the other** éste asesinato no tiene que ver con el otro, no hay relación entre este asesinato y el otro.
　(b) *person* emparentado; **they are —** son parientes, están emparentados; **they are closely —** entre ellos hay un estrecho parentesco; **we are — but only distantly** somos parientes pero lejanos; **are you — to the prisoner?** ¿es Vd pariente del acusado?; **they became — by marriage to the Borgias** emparentaron con los Borja.
relating [ri'leitiŋ] *as prep*: **details — to X** detalles *mpl* acerca de X; **and other matters — to Y** y otros asuntos concernientes a Y.
relation [ri'leiʃən] *n* **(a)** *(narration)* narración *f*; relato *m*, relación *f.*
　(b) *(relationship)* conexión *f*, relación *f (to, with* con); *(between persons)* parentesco *m*; **the — between A and B** la relación entre A y B; **in — to** respecto de, con relación a; **Proust in — to the French novel** Proust en relación con la novela francesa; **to bear a certain — to ...** guardar cierta relación con ...; **it bears no — to the facts** no tiene que ver con los hechos, se desentiende por completo de los hechos.
　(c) *(correspondence)* **—s** relaciones *fpl*; **good —s** buenas relaciones *fpl*; **public —s** relaciones *fpl* públicas; **public —s officer** (PRO) encargado *m* de relaciones públicas; **—s are rather strained** las relaciones están algo tirantes; **to break off —s with someone** romper con uno; **we have broken off —s with Ruritania** hemos roto las relaciones con Ruritania; **to enter into —s with someone** establecer relaciones con uno; **we have business —s with them** tenemos relaciones comerciales con ellos; **to have sexual —s with someone** tener relaciones carnales con uno.
　(d) *(relative)* pariente *m*, a *f*, familiar *mf*; **friends and —s** amigos *mpl* y familiares; **close —** pariente *m* cercano, parienta *f* cercana; **two distant —s** dos parientes lejanos; **all my —s** todos mis parientes, toda mi familia; **what — is she to you?** ¿qué parentesco hay entre ella y Vd?; **she's no —** no es parienta mía.
relationship [ri'leiʃənʃip] *n* relación *f*, conexión *f (to, with* con); afinidad *f*; *(kinship)* parentesco *m*; *(between persons)* relaciones *fpl*; amistad *f*; trato *m*; **— by marriage** parentesco *m* por enlace matrimonial; **blood —** lazo *m* de parentesco; **our — lasted 5 years** nuestras relaciones continuaron durante 5 años; **they have a beautiful —** (US) les unen los lazos de la más fina amistad; **what is your — to the prisoner?** ¿qué parentesco hay entre Vd y el acusado?; **the — of A to B, the — between A and B** la relación entre A y B.
relative ['relətiv] **1** *adj* relativo *(to* a); **with — ease** con relativa facilidad.
　2 *n* **(a)** *(Gram)* relativo *m.*
　(b) *(person)* pariente *m*, a *f*, familiar *mf*; *see* **relation (d).**
relatively ['relətivli] *adv* relativamente; **there are — few** hay relativamente pocos.
relativism ['relətivizəm] *n* relativismo *m.*
relativist ['relətivist] *n* relativista *mf.*
relativistic [‚reləti'vistik] *adj* relativista.
relativity [‚relə'tiviti] *n* relatividad *f.*
relax [ri'læks] **1** *vt grip etc* relajar, aflojar; *restrictions, severity* mitigar, suavizar; **to — one's muscles** aflojar los músculos; **to — one's hold on something** dejar de agarrarse de *(or* a) algo tan apretadamente, soltar algo.
　2 *vi* **(a)** *(grip etc)* relajarse, aflojarse; *(restrictions, severity)* mitigarse, suavizarse; **his face —ed into a smile** se le aflojaron los músculos de la cara y empezó a sonreír; **we must not — in our efforts** es necesario no renunciar en lo más mínimo a nuestros esfuerzos *(to + infin* por *+ infin*).
　(b) *(rest)* descansar; *(amuse oneself)* esparcirse, expansionarse; **—!** ¡cálmate!; ¡no te apures!; **now there is time to — a little** ahora hay tiempo para esparcirse un poco; **we —ed in the sun of Majorca** nos expansionamos bajo el sol de Mallorca.
relaxant [ri'læksənt] *n* relajante *m.*
relaxation [‚ri:læk'seiʃən] *n* **(a)** *(act)* relajación *f*, aflojamiento *m*; mitigación *f.*
　(b) *(rest)* descanso *m*; *(amusement)* esparcimiento *m*, recreo *m*; **to seek — in painting** esparcirse dedicándose a la pintura; **to take some —** esparcirse, expansionarse.
　(c) *(pastime)* pasatiempo *m*, recreo *m*, diversión *f*; **a favourite — of the wealthy** un pasatiempo favorito de los ricos.

relaxed [ri'lækst] *adj* tranquilo, sosegado, ecuánime; **he always seems so** — siempre parece tan sosegado; **try to be more** — procure ser más tranquilo.

relaxing [ri'læksiŋ] *adj climate etc* enervante.

relay ['ri:lei] **1** *n* **(a)** (*of workmen*) tanda *f*; (*of horses*) parada *f*, posta *f*; (*Elec*) relai *m*, relais *m*, relé *m* (*Acad*); **to work in** —**s** trabajar por tandas.
(b) (*Sport*) — **race** carrera *f* de relevos; **the 400 metres** — los 400 metros relevos.
2 *vt* (*Radio etc*) retransmitir; **to** — **a message to someone** pasar un mensaje a uno, hacer llegar un mensaje a uno.

re-lay ['ri:'lei] *vt* volver a colocar; *cable, rail etc* volver a tender.

relay station ['ri:lei,steiʃən] *n* transmisora *f*.

release [ri'li:s] **1** *n* **(a)** liberación *f*; excarcelación *f*; libertad *f*; emisión *f*; lanzamiento *m*; disparo *m*; aflojamiento *m*; descargo *m*, absolución *f*; estreno *m*; publicación *f*; divulgación *f*; **a sudden** — **of gas** un súbito escape de gas; **a sudden** — **of creative energy** un repentino estallar de energía creadora; **death came as a merciful** — la muerte fue una liberación piadosa; **a film on general** — una película que se está estrenando en muchas partes; **his** — **came through on Monday** se aprobó su excarcelación el lunes.
(b) (*Mech, Phot etc*) disparador *m*.
2 *vt* (*set free*) soltar, libertar; *prisoner* poner en libertad, *convict* excarcelar; *gas, smoke etc* despedir, arrojar, emitir; *bomb* lanzar; *brake* soltar; (*Mech*) desenganchar, disparar; (*Phot*) disparar; *grip, hold* soltar, aflojar; *pressure* aflojar; *person from obligation* descargar, absolver (*from* de); *film* estrenar; *report etc* publicar, dar a conocer; *news* divulgar; — **me, sir!** ¡suéltame, señor!; **to** — **someone on bail** poner a uno en libertad bajo fianza; **they** —**d him to go to a new post** permitieron que se fuera a ocupar un nuevo puesto; **can you** — **him for a few hours each week?** ¿nos lo ceden para trabajar con nosotros algunas horas cada semana?

relegate ['religeit] *vt* relegar (*to* a); **Mérida is** —**d to the second division** (*Sport*) Mérida pasa a la segunda división, Mérida desciende a la segunda división.

relegation [,reli'geiʃən] *n* relegación *f*; (*Sport*) descenso *m*.

relent [ri'lent] *vi* ablandarse, apiadarse, ceder.

relentless [ri'lentlis] *adj* implacable, inexorable; despiadado; **with** — **severity** con implacable severidad; **he is quite** — **about it** en esto se muestra totalmente implacable.

relentlessly [ri'lentlisli] *adv* implacablemente, inexorablemente; **he presses on** — **avanza** implacable.

relet ['ri:'let] *vt* realquilar.

relevance ['reləvəns] *n* pertinencia *f*; conexión *f*, relación *f*; aplicabilidad *f*; **matters of doubtful** — asuntos *mpl* de dudosa pertinencia; **what is the** — **of that?** y eso ¿tiene que ver con lo que estamos discutiendo?

relevant ['reləvənt] *adj* **(a)** (*related*) pertinente; conexo, relacionado (*to* con); aplicable; **details** — **to this affair** detalles *mpl* relacionados con este asunto, detalles *mpl* concernientes a este asunto; **that is hardly** — eso apenas tiene que ver con lo que estamos discutiendo.
(b) (*fitting*) apropiado, oportuno, adecuado; **bring the** — **papers** traiga los documentos oportunos; **we have all the** — **data** tenemos todos los datos que hacen al caso.

reliability [ri,laiə'biliti] *n* exactitud *f*, veracidad *f*; seguridad *f*; confianza *f*; confiabilidad *f*; formalidad *f*, seriedad *f*.

reliable [ri'kaiəbl] *adj news etc* fidedigno, fehaciente, digno de crédito; *account* exacto, veraz; *machine etc* seguro; (*person: trustworthy*) de confianza, de fiar, confiable, (*businesslike*) formal, serio; **it's a most** — **firm** es una casa perfectamente seria; **I have it from a** — **source** lo sé de fuente fidedigna; **he's not very** — no es de fiar, no hay que fiarse de él; **I've always found him very** — siempre me ha parecido de mucha formalidad.

reliably [ri'kaiəbli] *adv*: **I am** — **informed that . . .** sé de fuente fidedigna que . . .

reliance [ri'laiəns] *n* confianza *f* (*on* en); dependencia *f* (*on* de); **our excessive** — **on him** nuestra excesiva dependencia con respecto de él, el que dependamos tanto de él; **you can place no** — **on that** eso no es de fiar, no hay que tener confianza en eso.

reliant [ri'laiənt] *adj* confiado; **to be** — **on something** confiar en algo, tener confianza en algo.

relic ['relik] *n* reliquia *f*, vestigio *m*; (*Eccl*) reliquia *f*.

relict ['relikt] *n* viuda *f*.

relief [ri'li:f] **1** *n* **(a)** (*alleviation*) alivio *m*; desahogo *m*; consuelo *m*; aligeramiento *m*; (*of taxation*) desgravación *f*; **by way of light** — a modo de diversión; **there is a comic scene by way of** — para aliviar la tensión sigue una escena cómica; **that's a** —! ¡menos mal!; **it is a** — **to find that . . .** me consuela encontrar que . . . , me alegro de encontrar que . . . ; **the medicine brings** — la medicina alivia; **it came as a** — **when they left** se aliviaron todos cuando ellos se marcharon; **to heave a sigh of** — dar un suspiro de alivio.
(b) (*aid*) socorro *m*, ayuda *f*; **poor** — socorro *m*, beneficencia *f*; **to be on** — vivir de la beneficencia; **to go to someone's** — acudir a socorrer a uno.
(c) (*Mil: of town*) descerco *m*, socorro *m*; (*party*) relevo *m*.
(d) (*Law*) satisfacción *f*, remedio *m*.
(e) (*Art*) relieve *m*, realce *m*; **high** — alto relieve *m*; **low** — bajo relieve *m*; **to stand out in** — destacar; **to throw something into** — hacer resaltar algo, (*fig*) servir para destacar (*or* subrayar) algo.
2 *attr* **(a)** — **work** trabajos *mpl* de socorro; — **works** obras *fpl* públicas; — **party**, — **troops** relevo *m*; — **train** tren *m* suplementario.
(b) — **map** mapa *m* en relieve.

relieve [ri'li:v] **1** *vt* **(a)** *sufferings etc* aliviar, mitigar; *person's mind* tranquilizar; *feelings* desahogar; *burden* aligerar, *pain, headache etc* quitar, suprimir, aliviar; **to** — **one's feelings** desahogarse; **I** —**ed my feelings in a letter** me desahogué escribiendo una carta; **to** — **nature** hacer del cuerpo; **to** — **the boredom of the journey** para aliviar el aburrimiento del viaje; **the plain is** —**d by an occasional hill** de vez en cuando una colina alivia la monotonía de la llanura.
(b) **to** — **the poor** socorrer a los pobres.
(c) **to** — **someone from doing something** librar a uno de la necesidad de hacer algo; **to** — **someone of anxiety** tranquilizar a uno; **this** —**s us of financial worries** esto acaba con nuestras preocupaciones económicas; **to** — **someone of a duty** exonerar a uno de un deber; **to** — **someone of a post** destituir a uno; **he was** —**d of his command** fue relevado de su mando; **to** — **someone of his wallet** quitar la cartera a uno, robar la cartera a uno; **let me** — **you of your coat** permítame tomarle el abrigo.
(d) (*Mil*) *city* descercar, socorrer; *troops* relevar.
2 *vr* **(a)** **to** — **oneself** hacer del cuerpo.
(b) **to** — **oneself of a burden** quitarse un peso de encima.

relievo [ri'li:vəu] *n* relieve *m*.

religion [ri'lidʒən] *n* religión *f*; **to get** — (*fam*) darse a la religión.

religiosity [ri,lidʒi'ɔsiti] *n* religiosidad *f*.

religious [ri'lidʒəs] **1** *adj* religioso; (*fig*) puntual, exacto, fiel; — **instruction** enseñanza *f* religiosa; — **toleration** libertad *f* de cultos.
2 *n* religioso *m*, a *f*.

religiously [ri'lidʒəsli] *adv* religiosamente; (*fig*) puntualmente, exactamente, fielmente.

religiousness [ri'lidʒəsnis] *n* religiosidad *f*.

reline ['ri:'lain] *vt* reforrar, poner nuevo forro a.

relinquish [ri'liŋkwiʃ] *vt* abandonar, renunciar a; *grip* soltar; *post* renunciar a, dimitir de.

relinquishment [ri'liŋkwiʃmənt] *n* abandono *m*, renuncia *f*; dimisión *f*.

reliquary ['relikwəri] *n* relicario *m*.

relish ['reliʃ] **1** *n* (*flavour*) sabor *m*, gusto *m*; (*smack*) dejo *m* (*of* de), sabor *m* (*of* a); (*attractive quality*) apetencia *f*; (*appetite*) apetito *m*; (*zest*) entusiasmo *m*; (*liking*) afición *f*; (*sauce*) salsa *f*, condimento *m*; **to eat something with** — comer algo con apetito; **to do something with** — hacer algo de buena gana, hacer algo con entusiasmo; **to have a** — **for something** apetecer algo, gustar de algo, ser aficionado a algo; **hunting has no** — **for me now** ya no me apetece la caza; **the** — **for hunting does not seem to be so strong** no parece que la caza atraiga tanto, parece que hay menos afición a la caza.
2 *vt taste, savour* paladear, saborear; (*like*) gustar de, tener buen apetito para; **I don't** — **the idea** no me gusta la idea; **I** — **a day's fishing** apetece salir de pesca un día, me gusta pasar el día pescando; **do you** — **some fishing?** ¿quieres ir a pescar?; **I don't** — **the idea of staying up all night** no me hace gracia la idea de estar levantado toda la noche.

relive ['ri:'liv] *vt* vivir de nuevo, volver a vivir.

reload ['ri:'ləud] *vt* recargar, volver a cargar.

relocate ['ri:ləu'keit] *vt* volver a colocar, volver a situar.

reluctance [ri'lʌktəns] *n* desgana *f*, renuencia *f*, repugnancia *f*; **with —** a desgana, de mala gana; **to affect —** aparentar no querer.

reluctant [ri'lʌktənt] *adj* (a) **he was —** no quiso, se mostró poco dispuesto a hacerlo; **to be — to do something** estar poco dispuesto a hacer algo, tener pocas ganas de hacer algo; **he was — to decide** vaciló en decidirse; **I should be most — to let you go** me resistiría a permitirle ir, no consentiría de buena gana en que fuera Vd.

(b) **it had his — agreement** consintió pero de mala gana; **the — dragon** el dragón que no quiso; **I should make a — secretary** no quiero en absoluto ser secretario.

reluctantly [ri'lʌktəntli] *adv* de mala gana, a regañadientes; **she went —** se fue pero de mala gana; **I — agree** consiento pero contra mi voluntad.

rely [ri'lai] *vi*: **to — on** confiar en, fiarse de, contar con; **you can't — on the trains** es imposible fiarse de los trenes; **one can't — on the weather** no puede uno fiarse del tiempo; **we are —ing on you to do it** contamos con Vd para hacerlo, confiamos en que Vd lo haga.

remain [ri'mein] *vi* (a) (*be left over*) sobrar; (*survive*) quedar; **if any —** si sobra alguno; **few —** quedan pocos; **the few pleasures that — to me** los pocos placeres que me quedan; **nothing —s but to sell up** no queda otro remedio sino venderlo todo; **it —s to be done** queda por hacer; **it —s to be seen whether...** queda por descubrir si...; **more than half —s to be built** queda por construir más de la mitad.

(b) (*continue*) quedar, quedarse, permanecer; seguir, continuar; **we —ed there 3 weeks** nos quedamos allí 3 semanas; **how long do you expect to —?** ¿cuánto tiempo piensa quedarse aquí?; **that objection —s** queda (en pie) esa objeción; **it will — in my memory** quedará grabado en mi memoria; **the fact —s that...** sigue siendo un hecho que..., no es menos cierto que...; **to — behind** quedarse; **to — seated, to — sitting** permanecer sentado; **to — standing** permanecer de pie.

(c) (*with adj complement*) **to — faithful to** seguir fiel a; **the problem —s unsolved** el problema sigue sin solucionar; **it —s true that...** no es menos cierto que...; **it —s the same** sigue siendo lo mismo; **if the weather —s fine** si el tiempo sigue bueno.

(d) (*in letters*) **I — yours faithfully** le saluda atentamente.

remainder [ri'meində*] **1** *n* resto *m*; **the —** lo que sobra, lo que queda; los (*etc*) demás; (*Math*) residuo *m*, resta *f*; (*books*) restos *mpl* de edición; **the — of the debt** el resto de la deuda; **during the — of the day** durante el resto del día; **the — would not come** los otros (*or* los demás) no quisieron venir.

2 *vt books etc* saldar.

remaining [ri'meiniŋ] *adj* que queda; **the 3 — possibilities** las 3 posibilidades que quedan; **the — passengers** los otros pasajeros, los demás pasajeros.

remains [ri'meinz] *npl* (*human, archaeological etc*) restos *mpl*; (*left-overs*) sobras *fpl*, desperdicios *mpl*; **human —** restos *mpl* humanos; **literary —** obras *fpl* póstumas; **mortal —** restos *mpl* mortales.

remake ['ri:'meik] (*irr: see* **make**) *vt* rehacer.

remand [ri'mɑ:nd] **1** *n*: **to be on —** estar detenido (mientras se investiga una acusación *or* se prepara el proceso).

2 *vt* reencarcelar (para que se investigue una acusación *or* se prepare el proceso); **to — someone for a week** reencarcelar a uno durante una semana; **he was —ed to Brixton** volvieron a encarcelarle en Brixton.

remand home [ri'mɑ:nd,həum] *n* reformatorio *m* de menores.

remark [ri'mɑ:k] **1** *n* (a) (*notice*) **worthy of —** notable, digno de notar; **to let something pass without —** dejar pasar algo sin hacer ningún comentario acerca de ello.

(b) (*comment*) observación *f*; comentario *m*; **"R—s on the Press"** "Observaciones *fpl* sobre la Prensa"; **after some introductory —s** después de hacer algunas observaciones a modo de prefacio; **to make a —** hacer una observación; **to make the — that...** observar que...; **to pass —s on someone** hacer observaciones acerca de uno, (*freq*) hacer un comentario desfavorable sobre uno.

2 *vt* observar, notar.

3 *vi*: **to — on something** hacer una observación sobre algo, comentar algo.

remarkable [ri'mɑ:kəbl] *adj* notable, singular; extraordinario; **—!, most —!** ¡qué raro!; **with — skill** con singular habilidad; **it is in no way —** no tiene nada que sea digno de notar; **what's — about that?** ¿es que eso le parece singular?; **he's a most — man** es un hombre extraordinario.

remarkably [ri'mɑ:kəbli] *adv* extraordinariamente.

remarriage ['ri:'mærɪdʒ] *n* segundas nupcias *fpl*, segundo casamiento *m*.

remarry ['ri:'mæri] *vi* volver a casarse, casarse en segundas nupcias.

remediable [ri'mi:diəbl] *adj* remediable.

remedial [ri'mi:diəl] *adj* remediador; (*Med*) curativo, terapéutico; **— teaching** enseñanza *f* de los niños (*etc*) atrasados; **— exercises** gimnasia *f* terapéutica.

remedy ['remədi] **1** *n* remedio *m* (*for* para curar); (*Law etc*) recurso *m*; **there's no — for that** eso no tiene remedio; **the best — for that is to protest** eso se remedia protestando; **to have no — at law** no tener recurso legal.

2 *vt* remediar; curar; **that's soon remedied** eso es fácil remediarlo, eso fácilmente queda arreglado.

remember [ri'membə*] **1** *vt* (a) (*recall*) acordarse de, recordar; **I — seeing it, I — having seen it** recuerdo haberlo visto; **she —ed to do it** se acordó de hacerlo; **don't you — me?** ¿no se acuerda Vd de mí?; **it is worth —ing that...** vale la pena recordar que...; **give me something to —you by** dame algún recuerdo tuyo; **so I gave him something to — me by** (*fig*) así que le di algo para que no me olvidara; **to — someone in one's will** mencionar a uno en su testamento.

(b) (*bear in mind*) tener presente, no olvidar; **— that he carries a gun** tenga presente que lleva revólver; **— what happened before** no se olvide de lo que pasó antes, acuérdese de lo que pasó antes; **— to turn out the light** no te olvides de apagar la luz; **— who you're with!** ¡piensa con quién estás!

(c) (*with wishes*) **— me to him!** ¡dale recuerdos míos!; **she asks to be —ed to you all** ella les manda recuerdos para todos.

2 *vi*: **yes, I —** sí, me acuerdo; **if I — aright** si bien me acuerdo; **as far as I can —** que yo recuerde.

remembrance [ri'membrəns] *n* (*remembering*) recordación *f*; memoria *f*; (*souvenir*) recuerdo *m*; **—s** recuerdos *mpl*; **in — of** en conmemoración de, para conmemorar; **I have no — of it** no lo recuerdo en absoluto; **R— Day** conmemoración *f* del fin de la guerra en 1918 (*y de las dos guerras mundiales*), 11 de noviembre.

remind [ri'maind] **1** *vt* recordar; **to — someone of something** recordar algo a uno; **that —s me of last time** eso me recuerda la vez pasada; **she —s me of Anne** me recuerda a Ana, me hace pensar en Ana, tiene mucho parecido con Ana; **that —s me!** y a propósito...; **to — someone to do something** recordar a uno que haga algo; **you have to keep —ing him to do it** hay que traérselo constantemente a la memoria.

2 *vr*: **to — oneself that...** recordarse que...; **I — myself about it all the time** me lo recuerdo constantemente.

reminder [ri'maində*] *n* (a) recordatorio *m*; advertencia *f*; **it's a gentle —** es una advertencia amistosa; **we will send a —** le enviaremos un recordatorio.

(b) (*memento*) recuerdo *m*; **it's a — of the good old days** recuerda los buenos tiempos pasados.

reminisce [,remi'nis] *vi* contar los recuerdos, recordar viejas historias (*about* de).

reminiscence [,remi'nisəns] *n* reminiscencia *f*, recuerdo *m*; **"R—s of life in the Congo"** "Recuerdos *mpl* de la vida en el Congo"; **the symphony has —s of Mozart** la sinfonía tiene reminiscencias de Mozart.

reminiscent [,remi'nisənt] *adj* (a) **it's a — work** es una obra sugestiva; **to be in a — mood** estar de humor para contar los recuerdos, estar de humor para evocar el pasado.

(b) **to be — of something** recordar algo, (*pej*) oler a algo, sonar a algo; **that bit is — of Rossini** ese trozo recuerda a Rossini, ese trozo tiene reminiscencia de Rossini; **that's — of another old joke** eso suena a otro chiste viejo.

reminiscently [,remi'nisəntli] *adv*: **he spoke —** habló pensando en el pasado.

remiss [ri'mis] *adj* negligente, descuidado; **I have been very — about it** he sido muy descuidado en eso; **you have been — in not attending to it** Vd merece que se le censure por no atenderlo, el no atenderlo ha sido por descuido suyo.

remission [ri'miʃən] n remisión f; — **of sins** remisión f de los pecados; **to earn 6 months'** — merecer que se le perdonen 6 meses de la condena.
remissness [ri'misnis] n negligencia f, descuido m.
remit [ri'mit] vt (a) (send) remitir, enviar. (b) (excuse) perdonar; **3 months of the sentence were** —**ted** se le perdonaron 3 meses de la condena.
remittance [ri'mitəns] n remesa f, envío m.
remittance man [ri'mitənsmæn] n, pl — **men** [men] persona f a quien se paga una pensión a condición de que viva alejado de la patria.
remittee [remi'ti:] n consignatario m, a f.
remittent [ri'mitənt] adj fever etc remitente.
remitter [ri'mitə*] n remitente mf.
remnant ['remnənt] n (remainder) resto m, residuo m; (of cloth) retazo m; (relic) vestigio m, resto m.
remodel ['ri:'mɔdl] vt modelar de nuevo, remodelar; rehacer; reorganizar; (Lit etc) refundir.
remonstrance [ri'mɔnstrəns] n protesta f, reconvención f.
remonstrate ['remənstreit] vi protestar, objetar; **to** — **about something** protestar contra algo, poner reparos a algo; **to** — **with someone** reconvenir a uno.
remorse [ri'mɔ:s] n remordimiento m; **to feel** — arrepentirse, compungirse.
remorseful [ri'mɔ:sful] adj arrepentido, compungido; **now he's** — ahora está lleno de remordimientos, ahora le remuerde la conciencia.
remorsefully [ri'mɔ:sfəli] adv con remordimiento; **he said** — dijo compungido.
remorsefulness [ri'mɔ:sfulnis] n remordimiento m.
remorseless [ri'mɔ:slis] adj implacable, despiadado, inexorable.
remorselessly [ri'mɔ:slisli] adv implacablemente, despiadadamente, inexorablemente.
remorselessness [ri'mɔ:slisnis] n inexorabilidad f.
remote [ri'məut] adj (a) remoto; distante, lejano; aislado; (slight) ligero, leve; **in a** — **spot** en un lugar remoto; **in a** — **farmstead** en una alquería aislada, en una alquería apartada; **it's** — **from the town** está lejos de la ciudad; **she is** — **from such things** queda alejada de tales cosas, tales cosas le son ajenas; **in some** — **future** en un futuro lejano; **it's a** — **prospect** es poco probable, de eso existe poca probabilidad; **there is a** — **resemblance** hay un ligero parecido; **he hasn't the** —**st chance** no tiene la más remota posibilidad; **I haven't the** —**st idea** no tengo la más remota idea.
(b) — **control** comando m a distancia, telecontrol m.
remote-controlled [ri'məutkən'trəuld] adj dirigido a distancia, teledirigido.
remotely [ri'məutli] adv remotamente; **it is** — **situated** está situado en un lugar remoto; **they are** — **related** hay un parentesco lejano entre ellos; **it's not even** — **likely** de eso no hay la más remota posibilidad.
remoteness [ri'məutnis] n distancia f; aislamiento m, alejamiento m; **her** — **from everyday life** su alejamiento de la vida diaria.
remould, (US) **remold** ['ri:'məuld] vt tyre recauchutar.
remount ['ri:'maunt] 1 n (Mil etc) remonta f. 2 vt volver a subir (a), subir de nuevo (a); (on horse) montar de nuevo. 3 vi subir de nuevo.
removable [ri'mu:vəbl] adj separable, amovible; collar etc de quita y pon.
removal [ri'mu:vəl] n remoción f, el quitar (etc); supresión f; separación f; eliminación f; extirpación f; destitución f; el tachar; solución f; disipación f; apartamiento m, alejamiento m; (of house) mudanza f; **his** — **to a new post** su traslado a un nuevo puesto; **the** — **of this threat** la eliminación de esta amenaza.
removal van [ri'mu:vəlvæn] n camión m de mudanzas.
remove [ri'mu:v] 1 n: **this is but one** — **from disaster** esto raya en la catástrofe; **this is several** —**s from our official policy** en esto nos apartamos bastante de nuestra política oficial.
2 vt (take away) quitar; llevarse; (take off) quitar, clothes etc quitarse; (steal) llevarse, robar; (get out of the way) quitar de en medio; letter, passage, tax etc suprimir; name from list tachar, borrar (from de); (Mech) part etc separar, retirar, quitar; obstacle, threat, waste eliminar; (Med) appendix etc extirpar; person from post destituir; problem solucionar; doubt disipar; fear acabar con; (do away with) person quitar de en medio, eliminar; competitor apartar, alejar, deshacerse de; — **hats on entering** se ruega descubrirse al entrar; **he** —**d his hat** se descubrió, se quitó el sombrero; **first** — **the lid** primero quite la tapa; — **that bauble** que se

quite esa chuchería de en medio; **this effectively** —**d him from the scene** esto terminó de alejarle de allí; **illness** —**d him from politics** una enfermedad le hizo abandonar la política; **to** — **something to another place** trasladar algo a otro sitio, cambiar algo de sitio.
3 vi mudarse, trasladarse (to a).
4 vr: **to** — **oneself** irse, marcharse; quitarse de en medio; **kindly** — **yourself at once** haga el favor de irse inmediatamente; **to** — **oneself to another place** irse a otro sitio; **I must** — **myself** tengo que marcharme.
remover [ri'mu:və*] n (owner) agente m de mudanzas; (workman) carrero m.
remunerate [ri'mju:nəreit] vt remunerar.
remuneration [ri,mju:nə'reiʃən] n remuneración f.
remunerative [ri'mju:nərətiv] adj remunerador.
Renaissance [rə'nesã:ns] 1 n Renacimiento m; **the 12th century** — el Renacimiento del siglo XII.
2 adj, attr renacentista, del Renacimiento.
renal ['ri:nl] adj renal.
rename ['ri:'neim] vt poner nuevo nombre a; **they have** —**d it "Mon Repos"** le han puesto el nuevo nombre de "Mon Repos".
renascence [ri'næsns] n renacimiento m; **a spiritual** — un renacimiento espiritual, un despertar espiritual.
renascent [ri'næsnt] adj renaciente, que renace.
renationalization ['ri:,næʃnəlai'zeiʃən] n reestatificación f.
renationalize ['ri:'næʃnəlaiz] vt reestatificar.
rend [rend] (irr: pret and ptp **rent**) vt (lit) (tear) rasgar, desgarrar; (split) hender, rajar; **to** — **something in twain** partir algo por medio, hender algo; **to** — **one's dress** rasgar su ropa; **to turn and** — **someone** perder por fin la paciencia y arremeter contra uno; **a cry rent the air** un grito desgarró los aires; **the air was rent with cries** los aires se llenaron súbitamente de gritos.
render ['rendə*] vt (a) (return) **to** — **good for evil** devolver bien por mal; **to** — **thanks to someone** dar las gracias a uno.
(b) (hand over) entregar; **to** — **up** ceder, entregar; **the earth** —**s up its treasures** la tierra rinde sus tesoros; — **unto Caesar . . . a Dios lo que es de Dios y al César lo que es del César.**
(c) (give) service hacer, prestar; assistance dar, prestar; honour dar.
(d) (send in) **to** — **an account** (Comm) pasar factura; **to account** —**ed** según factura anterior; **to** — **an account of one's stewardship** dar cuenta de su gobierno, justificar su conducta durante su mando; **to** — **an account to God** dar cuenta de sí ante Dios.
(e) (reproduce) reproducir, representar; (Mus) interpretar, ejecutar; (translate) traducir, vertir (into a); **no photograph could adequately** — **the scene** ninguna fotografía pudiera representar adecuadamente la escena; **how does one** — **"cursi"?** ¿cómo se traduce "cursi"?
(f) (make) hacer, volver; **this** —**s it impossible** esto lo hace imposible, esto lo imposibilita; **you have** —**ed our efforts useless** Vd ha hecho inútiles nuestros esfuerzos.
(g) fat (also to — **down**) derretir.
rendering ['rendəriŋ] n reproducción f, representación f; (Mus) interpretación f; traducción f, versión f; **her** — **of the sonata** su interpretación de la sonata; **an elegant** — **of Machado** una elegante versión de Machado.
rendez-vous ['rɔndivu:] 1 n cita f; lugar m de una cita; — **in space** cita f espacial; **to have a** — **with someone** tener cita con uno; **to make a** — **with another ship at sea** efectuar un enlace con otro buque en el mar.
2 vi reunirse, verse; **we will** — **at 8** nos reuniremos a las 8; **the ships will** — **off Vigo** los buques efectuarán el enlace a la altura de Vigo.
rendition [ren'diʃən] n (Mus) interpretación f, ejecución f.
renegade ['renigeid] 1 adj renegado. 2 n renegado m, a f.
renew [ri'nju:] vt renovar; (resume) reanudar; lease, loan etc extender, prorrogar; subscription renovar; promise reafirmar; attack etc volver a; effort etc volver a hacer, redoblar; **to** — **an acquaintance with someone** volver a trabar amistad con uno; **to** — **the attack on someone** volver a arremeter contra uno; **to** — **the attack on a town** volver a atacar una ciudad; **to** — **one's strength** restablecer sus fuerzas, cobrar nuevo vigor.
renewable [ri'nju:əbl] adj renovable.

renewal [ri'njuːəl] n renovación f; reanudación f; extensión f; prorrogación f; reafirmación f; — **of subscriptions** renovación f de suscripciones; **the — of the attack** el nuevo ataque; **a spiritual —** una renovación espiritual.

renewed [ri'njuːd] adj renovado; nuevo; **with — vigour** con nuevo vigor, con redoblado vigor; **to feel spiritually —** sentirse con nuevas fuerzas espirituales.

rennet ['renit] n cuajo m.

renounce [ri'nauns] 1 vt right, inheritance, offer etc renunciar; plan, post, the world etc renunciar a. 2 vi (Cards) renunciar.

renouncement [ri'naunsmənt] n renuncia f.

renovate ['renəuveit] vt renovar.

renovation [‚renəu'veiʃən] n renovación f.

renown [ri'naun] n renombre m, nombradía f.

renowned [ri'naund] adj renombrado; **it is — for ...** es famoso por ..., es célebre por ...

rent[1] [rent] 1 pret and ptp of **rend**. 2 n (tear) rasgón m, rasgadura f; (split) abertura f, raja f, hendedura f; (fig) escisión f, cisma m.

rent[2] [rent] 1 n alquiler m, arriendo m; **we pay £3 in —** pagamos 3 libras de alquiler; **to build flats for —** construir pisos para alquilarlos; **"for —"** (US) "se alquila".

2 vt: **to — a flat from someone** alquilar un piso de uno; **to — a house (out) to someone** alquilar una casa a uno; **it is —ed out at £4 a week** está alquilado a 4 libras por semana.

rental ['rentl] n alquiler m, arriendo m; **fixed —** alquiler m fijo; **yearly —** alquiler m anual.

rent collector ['rentkə‚lektə*] n recaudador m de alquileres.

rent control ['rentkən‚trəul] n control m de alquileres.

rent-controlled ['rentkən‚trəuld] adj: **a — flat** un piso de alquiler controlado.

rent-free ['rent'friː] 1 adj house etc exento de alquiler, gratuito. 2 adv: **to live —** ocupar una casa (etc) sin pagar alquiler.

rentier ['rɔntiei] n rentista m.

rent-roll ['rentrəul] n lista f de alquileres.

renumber ['riː'nʌmbə*] vt volver a numerar; corregir la numeración de.

renunciation [ri‚nʌnsi'eiʃən] n renuncia f.

reoccupy ['riː'ɔkjupai] vt volver a ocupar.

reopen ['riː'əupən] 1 vt volver a abrir, reabrir; **to — a case** (Law) rever un pleito, rever un proceso, (fig) reconsiderar un asunto.

2 vi volver a abrirse, reabrirse; **school —s on the 8th** el nuevo curso comienza el día 8.

reopening ['riː'əupniŋ] n reapertura f; (Law) revisión f; reconsideración f.

reorder ['riː'ɔːdə*] vt (a) objects ordenar (or arreglar etc) de nuevo, volver a poner en orden. (b) (Comm) volver a pedir, repetir el pedido de.

reorganization ['riː‚ɔːgənai'zeiʃən] n reorganización f.

reorganize ['riː'ɔːgənaiz] 1 vt reorganizar. 2 vt reorganizarse.

rep[1] [rep] n (fabric) reps m.

rep[2] [rep] n (Comm, fam) viajante m, agente m.

rep[3] [rep] n (fam) =**repertory**.

repack ['riː'pæk] vt object reembalar, reenvasar, devolver a su caja (etc); case volver a hacer.

repaint ['riː'peint] vt repintar; **to — something blue** repintar algo de azul.

repair[1] [ri'pɛə*] vi: **to — to** (move to) trasladarse a, dirigirse a; (go regularly to) acudir a, reunirse en.

repair[2] [ri'pɛə*] 1 n (act) reparación f, compostura f; (patch etc) remiendo m; —s reparaciones fpl, (Archit) obras fpl, reformas fpl; **"closed for —s"** "cerrado por reformas"; **cost of —s** coste m de las reparaciones; **to be in (good) —** estar en buen estado; **to keep a house in (good) —** mantener una casa en buen estado; **to be under —** estar siendo reparado, (Archit) estar en obras; **it is beyond —** es irreparable, no se puede reparar, (fig) no tiene remedio; **it is damaged beyond —** ha sufrido tantos desperfectos que no se puede reparar.

2 vt reparar, componer; shoes etc remendar.

repairable [ri'pɛərəbl] adj que se puede reparar.

repair kit [ri'pɛəkit] n caja f de herramientas para reparaciones.

repairman [ri'pɛəmæn] n, pl **—men** [men] (US) reparador m, mecánico m.

repair shop [ri'pɛəʃɔp] n taller m de reparaciones.

repaper ['riː'peipə*] vt empapelar de nuevo.

reparable ['repərəbl] adj reparable.

reparation [‚repə'reiʃən] n reparación f; satisfacción f; —s (Fin) indemnizaciones fpl; **to make —s** dar satisfacción (for por).

repartee [‚repɑː'tiː] n réplicas fpl agudas; (between 2 persons) dimes mpl y diretes.

repass ['riː'pɑːs] vt repasar.

repast [ri'pɑːst] n comida f.

repatriate [riː'pætriət] n repatriado m, a f.

repatriate [riː'pætreit] vt repatriar.

repatriation [riː‚pætri'eiʃən] n repatriación f.

repay [riː'pei] (irr: see **pay**) vt money devolver, reembolsar; person pagar; debt pagar, liquidar; person (in compensation) resarcir, compensar; person (pej) pagar en la misma moneda; kindness etc devolver, corresponder a; visit pagar; **to — someone in full** pagar a uno todo lo que se le debe, devolver a uno la suma entera; **how can I ever — you?** ¿cómo podré corresponder dignamente a tanta amabilidad?; **it —s a visit** vale la pena visitarlo; **it —s study** merece que se le estudie; **it —s reading** vale la pena leerlo.

repayable [riː'peiəbl] adj reembolsable; **£5 deposit, not —** desembolso m inicial de 5 libras, no reembolsable; **— on demand** reembolsable a petición; **the money is — on the 5th of June** el dinero ha de ser devuelto el 5 de junio.

repayment [riː'peimənt] n devolución f, reembolso m; pago m; **now he asks for —** ahora pide que se le devuelva el dinero; **in 6 —s of £8** en 6 plazos de 8 libras cada uno.

repeal [ri'piːl] 1 n revocación f, abrogación f. 2 vt revocar, abrogar.

repeat [ri'piːt] 1 n repetición f; (Radio etc) retransmisión f.

2 vt repetir; thanks etc reiterar, volver a dar; (aloud) recitar; **she went and —ed it to the boss** fue a contárselo al jefe; **don't — it to anybody** no se lo digas a nadie; **this offer cannot be —ed** no se volverá a ofrecer nada igual; **can you — the design of this house?** ¿puede Vd construir otra casa igual que ésta?

3 vi repetirse; (clock, rifle, taste) repetir; **the radish —s on me** vuelvo a percibir el sabor del rábano.

repeated [ri'piːtid] adj repetido; reiterado; **in spite of — reminders** a pesar de habérselo recordado infinitas veces.

repeatedly [ri'piːtidli] adv repetidamente, repetidas veces; reiteradamente; **I have told you so —** te lo he dicho repetidas veces.

repeater [ri'piːtə*] n reloj m de repetición; rifle m de repetición.

repel [ri'pel] vt rechazar, repeler; (fig) repugnar; **he —s me** me da asco; **it —s me to have to + infin** me repugna tener que + infin.

repellent [ri'pelənt] 1 adj repugnante; **it is — to insects** ahuyenta los insectos. 2 n: **insect —** loción f para ahuyentar los insectos.

repent [ri'pent] 1 vt arrepentirse de. 2 vi arrepentirse.

repentance [ri'pentəns] n arrepentimiento m.

repentant [ri'pentənt] adj arrepentido; contrito, compungido.

repeople ['riː'piːpl] vt repoblar.

repercussion [‚riːpə'kʌʃən] n repercusión f; —s (fig) repercusiones fpl; resonancia f; **as for the political —s** en cuanto a las repercusiones políticas; **it had great —s in Ruritania** tuvo gran resonancia en Ruritania.

repertoire ['repətwɑː*] n, **repertory** ['repətəri] n 1 repertorio m; **he has an immense — of jokes** tiene un inmenso repertorio de chistes.

2 attr: **— theatre, — company** teatro m de repertorio.

repetition [‚repi'tiʃən] n repetición f; recitación f.

repetitious [‚repi'tiʃəs] adj repetidor, que se repite; monótono.

repetitive [ri'petitiv] adj reiterativo; **the book is a bit —** los incidentes del libro tienen cierta tendencia a repetirse, se repite el autor varias veces en el libro.

repine [ri'pain] vi apurarse, quejarse (at de), afligirse (at por).

repining [ri'painiŋ] n quejas fpl, aflicción f, descontento m.

replace [ri'pleis] vt (a) (put back) reponer, poner en su lugar, devolver a su sitio, colocar nuevamente; **kindly — the receiver** se ruega reponer el auricular.

(b) (take the place of) reemplazar, sustituir; **to — something by (or with) something else** sustituir a algo por otra cosa; **the Matisse was —d by a Klee** el cuadro de Matisse fue sustituido por uno de Klee, un cuadro de Klee sustituyó al de Matisse; **nobody could ever — him in my heart** sería imposible que nadie llenara el hueco que él dejó en mi corazón; **he asked to be —d** rogó que se le sustituyera; **he had to be —d** tuvo que ser destituido; **we will — the broken glasses** nosotros pagaremos los vasos rotos.

replaceable [ri'pleisəbl] *adj* reemplazable, sustituible; **it will not easily be —** no será fácil encontrar un repuesto; **he will not easily be —** no será fácil encontrar un sustituto.

replacement [ri'pleismənt] *n* (*act*) reposición *f*; devolución *f*; reemplazo *m*, sustitución *f*; (*substitute: thing*) reemplazo *m*, repuesto *m*, (*person*) sustituto *m*, suplente *mf*; **his — has still not arrived** el que le sustituye no ha llegado todavía; **it took 3 days to find a —** se tardó 3 días en encontrar un repuesto.

replant ['ri:'plɑ:nt] *vt* replantar.

replay ['ri:'plei] *vti* volver a jugar.

replenish [ri'pleniʃ] *vt* (*refill*) rellenar; (*with supplies*) reaprovisionar (*with* de); *stocks* reponer; (*with fuel*) repostar.

replenishment [ri'pleniʃmənt] *n* rellenado *m*; reaprovisionamiento *m*; reposición *f*.

replete [ri'pli:t] *adj* repleto, totalmente lleno (*with* de).

repletion [ri'pli:ʃən] *n* repleción *f*; **to eat to —** darse un atracón, comer realmente bien.

replica ['replikə] *n* (*Art etc*) copia *f*, reproducción *f* (*exacta*); (*fig: person etc*) segunda edición *f*.

reply [ri'plai] **1** *n* respuesta *f*, contestación *f*; **— coupon** cupón-respuesta *m*; **" — paid"** "porte pagado"; **in —** he said . . . contestando a esto dijo que . . .; **what is your — to this?** ¿qué contesta Vd a esto?; **we await your —** (*ending letter*) en espera de sus noticias.

2 *vi* responder, contestar; **to — to someone** contestar a uno; **to — to a letter** contestar una carta.

repopulate ['ri:'pɒpjuleit] *vt* repoblar.

repopulation ['ri:,pɒpju'leiʃən] *n* repoblación *f*.

report [ri'pɔ:t] **1** *n* (**a**) (*account*) relato *m*, relación *f*; (*Mil etc*) parte *m*; (*official*) informe *m*; (*piece of news*) noticia *f*; (*in newspaper*) reportaje *m*, crónica *f*, información *f*; (*school*) papeleta *f*, nota *f*, certificado *m* escolar; **annual —** memoria *f* anual; **chairman's —** informe *m* del presidente; **law —s** actas *fpl* de procesos; **weather —** boletín *m* meteorológico; **the Robbins R—** el Informe Robbins; **"R— on the Motor Industry"** "Informe *m* sobre la Industria del Automóvil"; **the — of his death upset us** la noticia de su muerte nos causó pesar; **to present a —** presentar un informe; **we are drawing up the — now** ahora estamos redactando el informe.

(**b**) (*rumour*) rumor *m*, voz *f*; **there is a — that** . . . corre la voz de que . . ., se rumorea que . . .; **I only know of it by —** lo sé de oídas nada más.

(**c**) (*reputation*) reputación *f*, fama *f*; **a person of good —** una persona de buena fama; **such things as are of good —** las cosas que sean estimables.

(**d**) (*bang*) estampido *m*, estallido *m*; explosión *f*; **there was a —** se oyó una explosión.

2 *vt* (*recount*) relatar, narrar, dar cuenta de; (*Mil*) dar parte de; *event etc* informar acerca de; *crime etc* denunciar (*to* a); *meeting* (*as secretary*) levantar las actas de, (*as reporter*) escribir la crónica de; **to — that** . . . informar que . . ., comunicar que . . .; **it is —ed from Berlin that** . . . se informa desde Berlín que . . ., comunican desde Berlín que . . .; **what have you to —?** ¿qué tiene Vd que decirnos?; **nothing to —** sin novedad; **nothing to — from the front** sin novedad en el frente; **to — progress** dar cuenta de los progresos; **I shall have to — this** tendré que denunciar esto; **you have been —ed for idleness** Vd ha sido denunciado por vago, le han acusado de ser holgazán; **he was —ed for swearing at the referee** se le denunció por dirigir palabrotas al árbitro.

3 *vi* (**a**) (*make report*) hacer un informe, presentar un informe (*on* acerca de); **to — back to someone** rendir cuentas a uno; pedir consejos a uno; **a committee was set up to — on the pill** se creó una comisión para investigar la píldora; **Professor X —s on his discovery in the next issue** el Profesor X informará de su descubrimiento en el próximo número; **the committee will — to the cabinet** la comisión elevará su informe al consejo de ministros.

(**b**) (*as reporter*) ser reportero; **he —ed for the "Daily Echo" for 40 years** durante 40 años fue reportero del "Daily Echo".

(**c**) (*present oneself*) presentarse; **to — at a place at 18.00 hours** presentarse en un sitio a las 18.00 horas; **— to me when you are better** venga a

verme cuando se haya repuesto; **to — sick** darse de baja por enfermo; **to — fit** darse de alta.

reportage [,repɔ:'tɑ:ʒ] *n* reportaje *m*.

reporter [ri'pɔ:tə*] *n* reportero *m*.

repose [ri'pəuz] **1** *n* reposo *m*.

2 *vt* (*lay etc*) reposar, descansar; recostar; **to — confidence in someone** poner confianza en uno.

3 *vi* reposar, descansar; **to — on** descansar sobre, (*fig*) estribar en, estar basado en.

repository [ri'pɒzitəri] *n* depósito *m*, almacén *m*; (*furniture —*) guardamuebles *m*; (*person*) depositario *m*, a *f*.

repossess ['ri:pə'zes] *vt*: **to — oneself of something** recobrar algo, volver a tomar algo.

reprehend [,repri'hend] *vt* reprender.

reprehensible [,repri'hensibl] *adj* reprensible, censurable.

reprehensibly [,repri'hensibli] *adv* de modo reprensible, de modo censurable.

reprehension [,repri'henʃən] *n* reprensión *f*.

represent [,repri'zent] *vt* representar; (*Law*) ser apoderado de, (*fig*) hablar en nombre de; (*Comm*) ser agente de; **the goods are not as —ed** las mercancías no son las que se nos describieron; **you —ed it falsely to us** Vd nos lo describió falsamente; **it has been —ed to us that** . . . se ha pretendido que . . ., se nos ha dicho que . . .; **he —s nobody but himself** no representa a nadie sino a sí mismo.

re-present ['ri:pri'zent] *vt* volver a presentar.

representation [,reprizen'teiʃən] *n* (**a**) representación *f*; **proportional —** representación *f* proporcional; **they have no — in Parliament** no tienen representante en el parlamento.

(**b**) petición *f*; **to make —s to someone** presentar una petición a uno, dirigir un memorial a uno, (*complain*) quejarse ante uno; **to make —s about something** quejarse de algo.

(**c**) **to make false —s** describir algo falsamente.

representational [,reprizen'teiʃənəl] *adj* (*Art*) figurativo.

representative [,repri'zentətiv] **1** *adj* representativo; **these figures are more —** estas cifras son más representativas; **a person not fully — of the group** una persona que no representa adecuadamente el grupo.

2 *n* representante *mf* (*also Comm, US Pol*); (*Law*) apoderado *m*.

repress [ri'pres] *vt* reprimir.

repressed [ri'prest] *adj* reprimido.

repression [ri'preʃən] *n* represión *f*.

repressive [ri'presiv] *adj* represivo.

reprieve [ri'pri:v] **1** *n* (*breathing space*) respiro *m*, alivio *m* temporal; (*Law*) indulto *m*, suspensión *f* (*esp* de la pena de muerte); **to win a last-minute —** ser indultado a última hora; **the wood got a —** se retiró la orden de talar el bosque.

2 *vt* indultar, suspender la pena de; **to — someone from death** indultar a uno de muerte, suspender la pena de muerte de uno.

reprimand ['reprimɑ:nd] **1** *n* reprimenda *f*, reprensión *f*. **2** *vt* reprender, reconvenir.

reprint ['ri:print] *n* reimpresión *f*; (*offprint*) tirada *f* aparte, separata *f*.

reprint ['ri:'print] *vt* reimprimir; **"—ed from the Transactions of** . . .**"** "tirada aparte de las Actas de . . ."

reprisal [ri'praizəl] *n* represalia *f*; **as a — for** como represalia por; **to take —s** tomar represalias.

reproach [ri'prəutʃ] **1** *n* (*spoken etc*) reproche *m*, censura *f*; (*stain, disgrace*) tacha *f*, baldón *m*, aprobio *m*; **beyond —** por encima de toda crítica, intachable; **term of —** término *m* oprobioso; **this is a — to us all** esto es deshonroso para todos nosotros; **poverty is a — to civilization** la pobreza es una vergüenza para la civilización.

2 *vt*: **to — someone for something, to — someone with something** reprochar algo a uno, censurar algo a uno, echar algo en cara a uno.

3 *vr*: **to — oneself for something** atribuirse la culpa de algo; **you have no reason to — yourself** Vd no tiene motivo para creerse culpable, la culpa no ha sido de Vd.

reproachful [ri'prəutʃful] *adj look etc* acusador, lleno de reproches; **next day she was —** el día siguiente me reprochó.

reproachfully [ri'prəutʃfəli] *adv look etc* con reproche; *speak etc* en tono acusador.

reprobate ['reprəubeit] *n* réprobo *m*, a *f*.

reprobation [,reprəu'beiʃən] *n* reprobación *f*.

reproduce [,ri:prə'dju:s] **1** *vt* reproducir. **2** *vi* reproducirse.

reproduction [,ri:prə'dʌkʃən] *n* reproducción *f*.

reproductive [ˌriːprə'dʌktɪv] *adj* reproductor.

reproof [ri'pruːf] *n* reprensión *f*, reconvención *f*; **to administer a** — **to someone** reprender a uno.

reproval [ri'pruːvəl] *n* reprobación *f*.

reprove [ri'pruːv] *vt* reprender, reconvenir; **to** — **someone for something** reprender algo a uno.

reproving [ri'pruːvɪŋ] *adj* reprobador, lleno de reproches.

reprovingly [ri'pruːvɪŋli] *adv* en tono reprobador, reprobadoramente, con reprobación; **she looked at me** — me miró severa, me reprendió con la mirada.

reptile ['reptail] *n* reptil *m*.

reptilian [rep'tilian] **1** *adj* reptil. **2** *n* reptil *m*.

republic [ri'pʌblik] *n* república *f*.

republican [ri'pʌblikən] **1** *adj* republicano. **2** *n* republicano *m*, a *f*.

republicanism [ri'pʌblikənizəm] *n* republicanismo *m*.

republication ['riːˌpʌbli'keiʃən] *n* reedición *f*.

republish ['riː'pʌbliʃ] *vt* reeditar.

repudiate [ri'pjuːdieit] *vt charge etc* rechazar, negar, desechar; *possibility* descartar; *obligation etc* rechazar, desconocer; *wife* repudiar; *debt*, *treaty* anular, cancelar.

repudiation [riˌpjuːdi'eiʃən] *n* rechazamiento *m*; desconocimiento *m*; repudio *m*; anulación *f*, cancelación *f*.

repugnance [ri'pʌgnəns] *n* repugnancia *f*.

repugnant [ri'pʌgnənt] *adj* repugnante; **it is** — **to me** me repugna.

repulse [ri'pʌls] **1** *n* repulsa *f*, repulsión *f*; rechazo *m*; **to suffer a** — ser repulsado, ser rechazado. **2** *vt* rechazar, repulsar.

repulsion [ri'pʌlʃən] *n* repulsión *f*, repugnancia *f*; (*Phys*) repulsión *f*.

repulsive [ri'pʌlsiv] *adj* repulsivo, repelente.

repulsively [ri'pʌlsivli] *adv* de modo repulsivo; — **ugly** terriblemente feo.

repulsiveness [ri'pʌlsivnis] *n* lo repulsivo; lo repelente; **of such** — tan repelente.

repurchase ['riː'pəːtʃis] *vt* readquirir, volver a comprar.

reputable ['repjutəbl] *adj firm*, *brand etc* acreditado, de toda confianza; *person* honroso, formal, estimable.

reputation [ˌrepju'teiʃən] *n* reputación *f*, fama *f*; **of good** — de buena fama; **to have a bad** — tener mala fama; **to have a** — **for meanness** tener fama de tacaño; **the hotel has a** — **for good food** el hotel es célebre por su buena comida; **he has the** — **of being awkward** se dice que es difícil, tiene fama de difícil; **to ruin a girl's** — acabar con la buena fama de una joven.

repute [ri'pjuːt] **1** *n* reputación *f*, fama *f*; **by** — según la opinión común, según se dice; **a firm of good** — una casa acreditada; **a café of ill** — un café de mala fama; **a house of ill** — (*euph*) una casa de prostitución; **to hold someone in high** — estimar a uno en mucho; **to know someone by** — **only** conocer a uno sólo por su reputación, conocer a uno de oídas nada más.

2 *vt reputar*; **to be** —**d as** tener fama de, pasar por; **to be** —**d to be clever** tener fama de inteligente, pasar por ser inteligente; **he is** —**d to be a millionaire** se dice que es millonario.

reputed [ri'pjuːtid] *adj* supuesto.

reputedly [ri'pjuːtidli] *adv* según se dice, según la opinión común.

request [ri'kwest] **1** *n* ruego *m*, petición *f*; instancia *f*; (*formal*) solicitud *f*; (*Comm*) demanda *f*; **a** — **for help** una petición de socorro; **at the** — **of** a petición de, a instancia de; **at the urgent** — **of X I have decided to** + *infin* accediendo al ruego insistente de X he decidido + *infin*; **by** — a petición; **to play a record by** — tocar un disco a petición de un oyente; **it is much in** — tiene mucha demanda, está muy solicitado; **on** — a solicitud; **to grant someone's** — acceder al ruego de uno; **to make a** — **for something** pedir algo, hacer una petición de algo.

2 *attr programme* a petición de los radioyentes; *stop* discrecional.

3 *vt* pedir, rogar; solicitar; **to** — **something of someone** pedir algo a uno; **to** — **someone to do something** rogar a uno hacer algo, pedir que uno haga algo; **"visitors are** —**ed not to talk"** "se ruega a los visitantes respetar el silencio."

requiem ['rekwiem] *n* réquiem *m*.

require [ri'kwaiə*] *vt* (a) necesitar; exigir; pedir, requerir; **we** — **another chair** necesitamos otra silla más; **it** —**s great care** exige mucho cuidado; **the lock** —**s attention** hace falta reparar la cerradura; **the battery** —**s regular attention** hay que comprobar la pila con regularidad; **no maintenance** —**d**

no necesita manutención alguna; **it** —**d all his strength to lift it** hacía falta que empleáse todas sus fuerzas para levantarlo; **this plant** —**s watering frequently** esta planta hay que regarla con frecuencia; **is my presence** —**d?** ¿es necesario que asista yo?; **your presence is** —**d** se exige que asista Vd; **if** —**d** en caso de necesidad, si es necesario; **as the situation may** — según lo exija la situación; **we will do all that is** —**d** haremos todo lo que haga falta; **what qualifications are** —**d?** ¿qué títulos se requieren?

(b) **to** — **something of someone** pedir algo a uno; **what do you** — **of me?** ¿qué piden Vds que haga?

(c) **to** — **that** ... exigir que + *subj*, requerir que + *subj*, insistir en que + *subj*; **the law** —**s that it should be done** la ley exige que se haga.

required [ri'kwaiəd] *adj* necesario, obligatorio, que hace falta; **a pipe of the** — **length** un tubo del largo que hace falta; **by the** — **date** antes de la fecha tope; **within the** — **time** dentro de los límites de tiempo que se han señalado; **has he got the** — **qualities?** ¿tiene las cualidades necesarias?; **the qualities** — **for the job** las cualidades que se requieren para el puesto; **it is a** — **course for the degree** es una asignatura obligatoria para el grado.

requirement [ri'kwaiəmənt] *n* requisito *m*; estipulación *f*; necesidad *f*; —**s** requisitos *mpl*, requerimientos *mpl*; **our** —**s are few** nuestras necesidades son pocas, necesitamos poco; **Latin is a** — **for the course** para este curso se exige un dominio del latín; **it is one of the** —**s of the contract** es una de las estipulaciones del contrato; **to meet all the** —**s for something** llenar todos los requisitos para algo.

requisite ['rekwizit] **1** *adj* preciso, indispensable, imprescindible. **2** *n* requisito *m*; **office** — **material** *m* de oficina; **toilet** —**s** artículos *mpl* de limpieza.

requisition [ˌrekwi'ziʃən] **1** *n* pedido *m*, solicitud *f* (*for* de); (*Mil*) requisa *f*, requisición *f*. **2** *vt* (*Mil*) requisar.

requital [ri'kwaitl] *n* compensación *f*, satisfacción *f*; desquite *m*.

requite [ri'kwait] *vt* (*make return for*) compensar, recompensar, pagar; (*get even with*) desquitarse con; **to** — **someone's love** corresponder al amor de uno; **that love was not** —**d** ese amor no fue correspondido.

reread ['riː'riːd] (*irr: see* **read**) *vt* releer, volver a leer.

reredos ['riədɔs] *n* retablo *m*.

reroute ['riː'ruːt] *vt* desviar; **the train was** —**ed through Burgos** el tren se desvió de la ruta normal y pasó por Burgos.

rerun ['riː'rʌn] (*irr: see* **run**) *vt race* correr de nuevo.

resale ['riː'seil] *n* reventa *f*.

rescind [ri'sind] *vt* rescindir.

rescission [ri'siʒən] *n* rescisión *f*.

rescue ['reskju:] **1** *n* salvamento *m*, rescate *m*; liberación *f* (*from* de); **the hero of the** — **was** ... el héroe del salvamento fue ...; **to come** (*or* **go**) **to the** — **of** ir al socorro de, acudir al rescate de; **to the** — **!** ¡al socorro!; **Batman to the** — **!** ¡Batman acude a la llamada!

2 *attr*: — **operations** operaciones *fpl* de salvamento, operaciones *fpl* de rescate; **the** — **vessel** el buque de salvamento.

3 *vt* salvar, rescatar; librar, libertar (*from* de); **three men were** —**d** tres hombres fueron salvados; **they waited 3 days to be** —**d** esperaron 3 días su rescate; **to** — **someone from death** librar a uno de la muerte; **the** —**d man is in hospital** el hombre rescatado está en el hospital.

rescuer ['reskjuə*] *n* salvador *m*, ora *f*.

rescue party ['reskjuːˌpɑːti] *n* expedición *f* de salvamento.

rescue work ['reskjuːwəːk] *n* trabajos *mpl* de salvamento, trabajos *mpl* de rescate.

research [ri'səːtʃ] **1** *n* investigación *f*, investigaciones *fpl* (*in*, *into* de); **atomic** — investigaciones *fpl* atómicas; **our** — **shows that** ... nuestras investigaciones demuestran que ...; **a piece of** — una investigación.

2 *attr*: — **establishment** instituto *m* de investigaciones; — **work** investigaciones *fpl*, trabajos *mpl* de investigación; — **worker** investigador *m*, ora *f*.

3 *vi* investigar; **to** — **into something** investigar algo, hacer investigaciones de algo.

4 *vt* (*US*) investigar; **to** — **an article** preparar el material para un estudio, reunir datos para escribir un artículo.

researcher [ri'səːtʃə*] *n* investigador *m*, ora *f*.

reseat ['riː'siːt] *vt valves* reasentar.

resection [riː'sekʃən] *n* resección *f*.

resell ['riː'sel] (*irr: see* **sell**) *vt* revender, volver a vender.

resemblance [ri'zembləns] *n* semejanza *f*, parecido *m*; **to bear a strong — to someone** parecerse mucho a uno; **to bear no — to someone** no parecerse en absoluto a uno; **there is no — between them** los dos no se parecen en absoluto; **there is hardly any — between this version and the one I gave you** apenas existe relación entre esta versión y la que le di.

resemble [ri'zembl] *vt* parecerse a; **he doesn't — his father** no se parece a su padre; **they do — one another** sí se parecen uno a otro.

resent [ri'zent] *vt* ofenderse por, tomar a mal, resentirse de (*or* por); **I — that!** ¡protesto contra esa observación!, ¡no permito que se diga eso!, ¡eso no!; **he —s my being here** se ofende por mi presencia aquí, no está conforme con mi presencia aquí; **I don't — your saying it** no me ofende que Vd lo diga.

resentful [ri'zentful] *adj* (**a**) *person* resentido, ofendido, agraviado; **to be** (*or* **feel**) **— of** ofenderse por, sentirse agraviado por; **no wonder she feels —** no me extraña que se sienta ofendida; **he is still — about it** todavía guarda rencor por ello.
(**b**) *tone etc* resentido, ofendido.

resentfully [ri'zentfəli] *adv* con resentimiento; **he said —** dijo resentido.

resentment [ri'zentmənt] *n* resentimiento *m* (*about, at* por).

reservation [,rezə'veiʃən] *n* (*act*) reservación *f*, reserva *f*; (*mental*) reserva *f*, (*in contract etc*) salvedad, *f* (*in argument*) distingo *m*; (*reserved seat*) plaza *f* reservada; (*US*) reserva *f* (de indios *etc*); **with certain —s** con ciertas reservas; **to accept something without —** aceptar algo sin reserva; **I had —s about it** tenía ciertas dudas sobre ese punto; **did you make the —s?** ¿has reservado las plazas?

reserve [ri'zəːv] **1** *n* (**a**) (*of money etc*) reserva *f*; **cash —s** *fpl* en metálico; **gold —** reserva *f* de oro; **to have something in —** tener algo de reserva; **to have a — of strength** tener una reserva de fuerzas; **there are untapped —s of energy** hay reservas de energía que quedan sin explotar; **Spain possesses half the world's —s of pyrites** España tiene la mitad de las reservas mundiales de piritas.
(**b**) (*Mil*) **the —** la reserva.
(**c**) (*Sport etc*) suplente *mf*.
(**d**) (*land*) reserva *f*; **game —** coto *m*, (*large*) parque *m*; **nature —** reserva *f* natural.
(**e**) **without —** sin reserva.
(**f**) (*shyness*) reserva *f*.
2 *adj, attr:* **— fund** fondo *m* de reserva; **— petrol tank** depósito *m* de gasolina de reserva; **— price** precio *m* mínimo (fijado en una subasta).
3 *vt* (**a**) reservar; **that's being —d for me** eso está reservado para mí; **did you — the seats?** ¿has reservado las plazas?
(**b**) (*Law*) aplazar, diferir; **the judge —d sentence** el juez difirió la sentencia.
4 *vr:* **I'm reserving myself for later** me reservo para más tarde.

reserved [ri'zəːvd] *adj* (*all senses*) reservado.

reservedly [ri'zəːvidli] *adv* con reserva.

reservist [ri'zəːvist] *n* reservista *m*.

reservoir ['rezəvwɑː*] *n* (*small*) depósito *m*, represa *f*; (*tank*) depósito *m*, cisterna *f*; (*large, for irrigation, hydroelectric power*) pantano *m*, embalse *m*.

reset ['riː'set] (*irr: see* **set**) *vt machine etc* reajustar; (*Typ*) recomponer; *bone* volver a encajar; *jewel* reengastar.

resettle ['riː'setl] **1** *vt persons* restablecer; *land* volver a colonizar, volver a poblar; **the lands were —d by the Poles** las tierras fueron nuevamente colonizadas por los polacos.
2 *vi* restablecerse.

resettlement ['riː'setlmənt] *n* restablecimiento *m*; nueva colonización *f*, repoblación *f*.

reshape ['riː'ʃeip] *vt* reformar, formar de nuevo, rehacer; reorganizar.

reshuffle ['riː'ʃafl] **1** *n* (*Pol*) reconstrucción *f*. **2** *vt cards* volver a barajar; (*Pol*) reconstruir.

reside [ri'zaid] *vi* residir, vivir; **to — in** (*fig*) residir en.

residence ['rezidəns] **1** *n* residencia *f*; (*stay, in official parlance*) permanencia *f*; (*home, in official parlance*) domicilio *m*; (*Univ, also* **hall of —**) residencia *f*; **after 6 months'** — después de 6 meses de permanencia; **it is the prime minister's official —** es la residencia oficial del primer ministro; **"town and country —s for sale"** "se ofrecen fincas urbanas y rurales"; **to take up one's —** establecerse.
2 *attr:* **— permit** visado *m* de permanencia.

residency ['rezidənsi] *n* residencia *f*.

resident ['rezidənt] **1** *adj* residente; *population etc* fijo, permanente; *doctor etc* interno; *servant* que duerme en casa; *bird* no migratorio; **to be — in a town** residir en una ciudad, tener domicilio fijo en una ciudad; **we were — there for some years** residimos allí durante varios años.
2 *n* residente *mf*; vecino *m*, a *f*; (*in hotel etc*) huésped *m*, a *f*; **the —s got together to protest** los vecinos se reunieron para protestar.

residential [,rezi'denʃəl] *adj* residencial; **— area** barrio *m* residencial.

residual [ri'zidjuəl] *adj* residual.

residuary [ri'zidjuəri] *adj* restante, remanente, residual; **— legatee** legatario *m* universal, legataria *f* universal.

residue ['rezidjuː] *n* resto *m*, residuo *m*; (*Fin etc*) saldo *m*, superávit *m*; **a — of bad feeling** un residuo de rencor, el rencor que queda.

residuum [ri'zidjuəm] *n* residuo *m*.

resign [ri'zain] **1** *vt office etc* dimitir, renunciar a; *claim, task etc* renunciar a; **to — a task to others** ceder un cometido a otros; **when he —ed the leadership** cuando dimitió la jefatura.
2 *vi* dimitir; renunciar; **to — in favour of someone else** renunciar en favor de otro.
3 *vr:* **to — oneself** resignarse; **to — oneself to** resignarse a, conformarse con; **I —ed myself to never seeing her again** me resigné a no volverla a ver jamás.

resignation [,rezig'neiʃən] *n* (**a**) (*act*) dimisión *f* (*from* de), renuncia *f*; **to offer** (*or* **send in, submit, tender**) **one's —** dimitir, presentar su dimision.
(**b**) (*state*) resignación *f* (*to* a), conformidad *f* (*to* con); **to await something with —** esperar algo resignado, esperar algo con resignación.

resigned [ri'zaind] *adj* resignado.

resignedly [ri'zainidli] *adv* con resignación.

resilience [ri'ziliəns] *n* elasticidad *f*; (*fig*) resistencia *f*; poder *m* de recuperación; capacidad *f* para adaptarse.

resilient [ri'ziliənt] *adj* elástico; (*fig*) resistente; que tiene poder de recuperación; que tiene capacidad para adaptarse.

resin ['rezin] *n* resina *f*.

resinous ['rezinəs] *adj* resinoso.

resist [ri'zist] **1** *vt* resistir (a); oponerse a; oponer resistencia a; **to — temptation** resistir la tentación; **they —ed the attack vigorously** resistieron vigorosamente el ataque; **we — this change** nos oponemos a este cambio; **I can't — squid** me apasionan los calamares; **I couldn't — buying it** no me resistí a comprarlo, no pude menos de comprarlo, me fue imposible dejar de comprarlo; **I can't — saying that . . .** no resisto al impulso de decir que . . .
2 *vi* resistirse, oponer resistencia.

resistance [ri'zistəns] *n* (*all senses*) resistencia *f*; **the R—** (*Pol*) la Resistencia; **passive —** resistencia *f* pasiva; **to offer —** oponer resistencia (*to* a); **to have good — to disease** tener mucha resistencia a la enfermedad; **to take the line of least —** optar por no resistirse, allanarse a todo; adoptar una actitud realista.

resistant [ri'zistənt] *adj* resistente.

resistible [ri'zistibl] *adj* resistible.

resole ['riː'səul] *vt* solar, sobresolar.

resolute ['rezəluːt] *adj* resuelto.

resolutely ['rezəluːtli] *adv* resueltamente.

resoluteness ['rezəluːtnis] *n* resolución *f*.

resolution [,rezə'luːʃən] *n* (**a**) (*resoluteness*) resolución *f*; **to show —** mostrarse resuelto.
(**b**) (*separation, solving*) resolución *f*.
(**c**) (*motion*) resolución *f*, proposición *f*; (*Parl*) acuerdo *m*; **to pass a —** tomar un acuerdo; **to put a — to a meeting** someter una moción a votación.
(**d**) (*resolve*) propósito *m*; **good —s** buenos propósitos *mpl*; **New Year —s** buenos propósitos *mpl* de fin de año.

resolvable [ri'zɔlvəbl] *adj* soluble.

resolve [ri'zɔlv] **1** *n* (**a**) (*resoluteness*) resolución *f*; **unshakeable —** resolución *f* inquebrantable.
(**b**) (*decision*) propósito *m*; **to make a — to +** *infin* resolverse a + *infin*.
2 *vt* (*all senses*) resolver (*into* en); **this will — your doubts** esto ha de resolver sus dudas; **the problem is still not —d** el problema queda por resolver.
3 *vi* (**a**) (*separate*) resolverse (*into* en); **the question —s into 4 parts** la cuestión se resuelve en 4 partes.
(**b**) **to — on something** optar por algo, resolverse por algo; **to — on +** *ger* acordar + *infin*; **to — to +** *infin* resolverse a + *infin*; **to — that . . .** acordar que . . .; **it was —d that . . .** se acordó que . . .

resolved [ri'zɔlvd] *adj* resuelto; **to be — to** + *infin* estar resuelto a + *infin*.

resonance ['rezənəns] *n* resonancia *f*.

resonant ['rezənənt] *adj* resonante.

resonator ['rezəneitə*] *n* resonador *m*.

resorption [ri'zɔːpʃən] *n* resorción *f*.

resort [ri'zɔːt] **1** *n* (a) (*recourse*) recurso *m*; **as a last —, in the last —** en último caso; **without — to force** sin recurrir a la fuerza.

(b) (*place*) punto *m* de reunión, lugar *m* de reunión; **it is a —** of thieves es lugar frecuentado por los ladrones, es donde se reúnen los ladrones; **holiday —** punto *m* de veraneo; **seaside —** playa *f*, punto *m* marítimo de veraneo; **summer —** punto *m* de veraneo; **winter-sports —** punto *m* donde se practican los deportes de invierno.

2 *vi*: **to — to** (a) *place* frecuentar, concurrir a, acudir a.

(b) (*have recourse to*) recurrir a; acudir a; hacer uso de; **to — to violence** recurrir a la violencia; **then they —ed to throwing stones** pasaron luego a tirar piedras; **then you — to me for help** así que acudes a mí a pedir ayuda.

resound [ri'zaund] *vi* resonar, retumbar; **the valley —ed with shouts** resonaron los gritos por el valle; **the whole house —s with laughter** resuenan las risas por toda la casa.

resounding [ri'zaundiŋ] *adj* sonoro; (*fig*) clamoroso, resonante.

resoundingly [ri'zaundiŋli] *adv*: **to defeat someone —** obtener una victoria resonante sobre uno.

resource [ri'sɔːs] *n* (*expedient*) recurso *m*, expediente *m*; (**—fulness**) inventiva *f*; **—s** recursos *mpl*; **financial —s** recursos *mpl* financieros; **natural —s** recursos *mpl* naturales: **to be at the end of one's —s** haber agotado sus recursos; **he has great —s of energy** tiene una gran reserva de energía; **those —s are as yet untapped** esos recursos quedan todavía sin explotar.

resourceful [ri'sɔːsful] *adj* inventivo, ingenioso.

resourcefully [ri'sɔːsfəli] *adv* ingeniosamente, mostrando tener inventiva.

resourcefulness [ri'sɔːsfulnis] *n* inventiva *f*, iniciativa *f*, ingeniosidad *f*.

respect [ris'pekt] **1** *n* (a) (*relation*) respecto *m*; **in every —** desde todos los puntos de vista; **in many —s** desde muchos puntos de vista; en cierto modo; **in other —s** por lo demás; **in some —s** desde varios puntos de vista; **in this —** por lo que se refiere a esto; en cuanto a esto; **in — of** respecto a, respecto de; **with — to** con respecto a; **with — to possible candidates, there are 3** en cuanto al número de candidatos que se pueden presentar, son 3.

(b) **without — of persons** sin distinción de personas.

(c) (*consideration*) respeto *m*, consideración *f*; **— for one's parents** respeto *m* a sus padres; **— for the truth** respeto *m* por la verdad; **out of — for someone** por consideración a uno; **out of — for the truth** en atención a la verdad; **with all — to you** sin menoscabo del respeto que se le debe a Vd; **if I may say so with —** si puedo decirlo con el mayor respeto; **worthy of —** digno de respeto, respetable; **to command —** imponer respeto, hacerse respetar; **to have — for someone, to hold someone in —** tener respeto a uno, respetar a uno; **we have the greatest — for him** le respetamos muchísimo; **to pay — to someone** respetar a uno; **to show no — to someone** faltar al respeto debido a uno; **he shows scant — for our opinions** desprecia nuestras opiniones; **to win someone's —** ganarse el respeto de uno.

(d) **—s** recuerdos *mpl*, saludos *mpl*; **to pay one's —s to someone** cumplimentar a uno; **to send one's —s to someone** mandar recuerdos a uno.

2 *vt* respetar; **to — someone's opinions** respetar las opiniones de uno; **to — someone's wishes** atenerse a los deseos de uno; **to make oneself —ed** hacerse respetar.

respectability [ris,pektə'biliti] *n* respetabilidad *f*.

respectable [ris'pektəbl] *adj* (a) (*deserving respect*) respetable; **for perfectly — reasons** por motivos perfectamente respetables.

(b) (*of fair social standing, decent*) respetable, decente, honrado; **in — society** en la buena sociedad, entre personas educadas; **that's not —** eso no se hace, eso no es decente, eso es de mala educación; **that skirt isn't —** esa falda no es decente.

(c) *amount etc* respetable; apreciable, importante; **at a — distance** a respetable distancia; **she lost a — sum** perdió una cantidad importante.

(d) (*passable*) pasable, tolerable; **we made a —**

showing lo hicimos pasablemente; **his work is — but not brilliant** su obra es pasable pero no brillante.

respectably [ris'pektəbli] *adv* respetablemente; decentemente; pasablemente.

respected [ris'pektid] *adj* respetado, estimado; **a much — person** una persona muy respetada.

respecter [ris'pektə*] *n*: **to be no — of persons** no hacer distinción de personas.

respectful [ris'pektful] *adj* respetuoso.

respectfully [ris'pektfəli] *adv* respetuosamente; **Yours —** le saluda atentamente.

respectfulness [ris'pektfulnis] *n* respetuosidad *f*, acatamiento *m*.

respecting [ris'pektiŋ] *prep* con respecto a; en cuanto a; por lo que se refiere a.

respective [ris'pektiv] *adj* respectivo.

respectively [ris'pektivli] *adv* respectivamente.

respiration [,respi'reiʃən] *n* respiración *f*.

respirator ['respireitə*] *n* careta *f* antigás.

respiratory [ris'paiərətəri] *adj* respiratorio.

respire [ris'paiə*] *vti* respirar.

respite ['respait] *n* respiro *m*, respiradero *m*; (*Law*) plazo *m*, prórroga *f*; **without —** sin tregua, sin respirar; **to get no —** no tener alivio, no poder descansar; **we got no — from the heat** el calor apenas nos dejó respirar ni de día ni de noche; **they gave us no —** nos hicieron trabajar (*etc*) sin tregua, no nos dejaron respirar.

resplendence [ris'plendəns] *n* resplandor *m*, refulgencia *f*.

resplendent [ris'plendənt] *adj* resplandeciente, refulgente; **to be —** resplandecer, refulgir; **to be — in a new dress** lucir un nuevo vestido; **the car is — in green** luce el coche su pintura verde.

respond [ris'pɔnd] *vi* (*answer*) responder; (*be responsive*) reaccionar, ser sensible (*to* a); **it —s to sunlight** reacciona a la luz solar, es sensible a la luz solar; **it is —ing to treatment** está mejorando con el tratamiento; **it does not seem to — to treatment** no parece que el tratamiento efectúe ningún cambio; **the cat —s to kindness** el gato es sensible a los buenos tratos.

respondent [ris'pɔndənt] *n* (*Law*) demandado *m*, a *f*.

response [ris'pɔns] *n* (*answer*) respuesta *f*, (*Eccl*) responsorio *m*; (*reaction*) reacción *f*, correspondencia *f* (*to* a); **in — to many requests . . .** accediendo a muchos ruegos . . .; **the — was not favourable** la reacción no fue favorable; **his only — was to yawn** por toda respuesta dio un bostezo; **we had hoped for a bigger —** habíamos esperado más correspondencia; **it found no —** no tuvo correspondencia alguna, no encontró eco alguno; **it met with a generous —** tuvo una generosa acogida.

responsibility [ris,pɔnsə'biliti] *n* (a) responsabilidad *f* (*for* de); **joint —** responsabilidad *f* solidaria; **on one's own —** bajo su propia responsabilidad; **to accept — for something** hacerse responsable de algo; **that's his —** eso le incumbe a él, eso le toca a él; **it is my — to decide** me toca a mí decidir.

(b) seriedad *f*; formalidad *f*; **try to show some —** procure tener un poco de seriedad.

responsible [ris'pɔnsəbl] *adj* (a) responsable (*for* de); **to be — to someone for something** ser responsable ante uno de algo; **those — will be punished** se castigará a las personas responsables, se castigará a los autores del crimen; **who was — for the delay?** ¿a quién se debe el retraso?; **the fog was not — this time** la niebla no tuvo la culpa esta vez; **she is — for 40 children** tiene a su cargo a 40 niños; **the committee is — to the council** la comisión depende del consejo; **he is not — for his actions** no responde de sus actos; **to hold someone — for an accident** echar a uno la culpa de un accidente, hacer a uno responsable de un accidente; **to make oneself —** responsabilizarse, tomar sobre sí la responsabilidad.

(b) (*of character*) serio, formal; **he is a fully — person** es una persona de toda formalidad; **to act in a — fashion** obrar con seriedad.

(c) *post etc* de confianza, de gran responsabilidad.

responsibly [ris'pɔnsəbli] *adv*: **to act —** obrar con seriedad.

responsive [ris'pɔnsiv] *adj*: **he was not very —** apenas dio indicio de interés, apenas parecía interesarle la cosa; **to be — to something** ser sensible a algo.

responsiveness [ris'pɔnsivnis] *n* interés *m*; sensibilidad *f* (*to* a).

rest¹ [rest] **1** *n* (a) (*repose*) descanso *m*, reposo *m*; (*fig*) paz *f*; **day of —** día *m* de descanso, asueto *m*, (*as calendar item*) día *m* festivo; **to be at —** estar en reposo, descansar, (*of insect etc*) estar posado, (*of* *the dead*) estar en paz; **to come to —** (*vehicle*) pararse, detenerse, (*machine*) pararse, (*insect etc*) posarse; **to go to** (*one's*) — ir a acostarse; **to have a 10-minute —** descansar durante 10 minutos; **to have a good night's —** dormir profundamente; **to lay someone to —** enterrar a uno; **to set someone's mind at —** tranquilizar a uno; **to take a —** descansar, descansar un rato.

(b) (*Mus*) silencio *m*, pausa *f*.

(c) (*support*) apoyo *m*, soporte *m*; (*base*) base *f*; (*Tel*) horquilla *f*; (*for lance etc*) ristre *m*.

2 *vt* (a) (*give — to*) descansar; dejar descansar; **to — one's men** dejar descansar a sus hombres; **horses have to be —ed** hay que dejar descansar a los caballos; **these colours — your eyes** estos colores descansan la vista; **God — his soul!** ¡Dios le acoja en su seno!

(b) (*support*) descansar, apoyar (*against* contra, *on* sobre); **— your head on the pillow** apoye la cabeza en la almohada; **— the ladder against the tree** apoya la escalera contra el árbol; **she —ed her eyes on the picture** clavó la vista en el cuadro; **to — one's case** terminar la presentación de argumentos.

3 *vi* (a) (*repose*) descansar (*from* de), reposar; (*stop*) detenerse, pararse; (*Theat: euph*) no tener trabajo, estar sin trabajo; **where my caravan has —ed** donde se ha detenido mi carricoche; **he never —s** no descansa nunca; **the waves never —** las olas están en continuo movimiento; **may he — in peace** descanse en paz; **we shall never — until it is settled** no nos tranquilizaremos hasta que se arregle el asunto; **let us not — until he is avenged** no descansemos hasta vengarle; **and there the matter —s** así que ahí queda el asunto; **we cannot let the matter — there** no podemos permitir que las cosas sigan en ese punto, no podemos dejar el asunto sin resolver.

(b) **to — on** (*perch*) posar en, posarse en; (*be supported*) descansar sobre, apoyarse en; (*fig*) estribar en, estar basado en; **her arm —ed on my chair** su brazo estaba apoyado en mi silla; **her head —ed on her hand** su cabeza se apoyaba en la mano; **the case —s on the following facts** la teoría está basada en los siguientes datos; **his eye —ed on me** su mirada se clavó en mí, clavó su mirada en mí; **a heavy responsibility —s on him** pesa sobre él una grave responsabilidad; **please — assured that...** tenga Vd la seguridad de que...

(c) **to — with** depender de; residir en; **it does not — with me** no depende de mí; **the authority —s with him** la autoridad reside en él.

rest² [rest] *n* resto *m*; **the —** el resto, lo demás, los demás (*etc*); **for the —** por lo demás; **the — stayed outside** los demás quedaron fuera; **what shall we give the — of them?** ¿qué daremos a los otros?; **the — of them couldn't care less** a los otros les trae sin cuidado; **the — of the soldiers** los otros soldados, los demás soldados.

restart ['riː'staːt] *vt* empezar de nuevo, volver a empezar; (*engine*) volver a arrancar.

restate ['riː'steit] *vt* repetir, reafirmar; *case* volver a exponer; *problem* volver a plantear.

restatement ['riː'steitmənt] *n* repetición *f*, reafirmación *f*; nueva exposición *f*; nuevo planteamiento *m*.

restaurant ['restərɔ̃:ŋ] *n* restaurante *m*, restorán *m*.

restaurant car ['restərɔ̃:ŋ,kaː*] *n* (*Rail*) coche-comedor *m*.

restaurateur [,restərəˈtɔː*] *n* propietario *m* de un restaurante.

rest cure ['restkjuə*] *n* cura *f* de reposo.

restful ['restful] *adj* descansado, reposado, sosegado.

restfully ['restfəli] *adv* reposadamente, sosegadamente.

rest home ['resthəum] *n* residencia *f* para jubilados.

resting place ['restiŋpleis] *n* (*also last —*) última morada *f*.

restitution [,restiˈtjuːʃən] *n* restitución *f*; **to make — for something** indemnizar a uno por algo.

restive ['restiv] *adj* inquieto, intranquilo; *horse* rebelón; **to get —** agitarse, impacientarse.

restiveness ['restivnis] *n* inquietud *f*, intranquilidad *f*; agitación *f*, impaciencia *f*.

restless ['restlis] *adj* inquieto, intranquilo, desasosegado; descontentadizo; (*sleepless*) insomne, desvelado; (*Pol etc*) turbulento, (*roving*) andariego, de mal asiento; **the poet's — genius** el genio inquieto del poeta; **he's the — sort** es una persona de mal asiento; **he is — to be gone** se impacienta por partir; **he's been — in the job** no ha estado contento en el puesto; **the spectators were getting —** los

espectadores se estaban impacientando; **the unions are getting —** se están agitando los sindicatos; **I had a — night** pasé una mala noche, me quedé la mayor parte de la noche sin dormir.

restlessly ['restlisli] *adv* inquietamente, desasosegadamente; turbulentamente; **she moved — in her sleep** se movió inquieta mientras dormía.

restlessness ['restlisnis] *n* inquietud *f*, intranquilidad *f*, desasosiego *m*; agitación *f*, impaciencia *f*; descontento *m*; insomnio *m*, desvelo *m*; turbulencia *f*; lo andariego; **there is much — in the provinces** existe gran descontento en las provincias.

restock ['riː'stɔk] *vt larder etc* reaprovisionar; *pond etc* repoblar (*with* de); **we —ed with Brand X** renovamos las existencias de Marca X.

restoration [,restəˈreiʃən] *n* restauración *f*; devolución *f*; restablecimiento *m*; **the R—** (*Hist*) la Restauración.

restorative [risˈtɔːrətiv] **1** *adj* reconstituyente. **2** *n* reconstituyente *m*.

restore [risˈtɔː*] *vt building etc* restaurar; *object to owner etc* devolver (*to* a); *strength etc* restablecer; **to — something to someone** devolver algo a uno; **to — something to its place** devolver algo a su lugar; **to — someone to health** devolver la salud a uno; **to — someone to liberty** devolver la libertad a uno; **to — someone's sight** devolver la vista a uno; **to — someone's strength** restaurar las fuerzas a uno, reconstituir las fuerzas de uno; **to — the strength of the pound** restablecer el valor de la libra; **they —d the king to his throne** volvieron a poner al rey sobre su trono; **order was soon —d** pronto se restableció el orden, se volvió pronto a la normalidad.

restorer [risˈtɔːrə*] *n* restaurador *m*, ora *f*; **hair —** loción *f* capilar.

restrain [risˈtrein] **1** *vt* contener, refrenar, reprimir; moderar; tener a raya; **to — someone from +** *ger* disuadir a uno de **+** *infin*, (*physically etc*) impedir a uno **+** *infin*; **kindly — your friend** haga el favor de refrenar a su amigo; **I managed to — my anger** logré contener mi enojo.

2 *vr*: **to — oneself** contenerse, dominarse; **but I —ed myself** pero me contuve, pero me dominé; **please — yourself!** ¡por favor, cálmese!; **to restrain oneself from +** *ger* dominarse para que no **+** *subj*.

restrained [risˈtreind] *adj* moderado, comedido; *style etc* refrenado, moderado; **he was very — about it** estuvo muy comedido.

restraint [risˈtreint] *n* (a) (*check, control*) freno *m*, control *m*; restricción *f*, limitación *f*; **a — on trade** una restricción del comercio, (*on free enterprise*) una limitación de la libre competencia; **without —** sin restricción, libremente; **to be under a —** estar cohibido; **to fret under a —** impacientarse por una restricción; **to put someone under a —** refrenar a uno, (*Law*) imponer una restricción legal a uno.

(b) (*constraint: of manner*) reserva *f*, (*of character*) moderación *f*, comedimiento *m*; (*self-control*) autodominio *m*; **to cast aside all —** abandonar toda moderación, abandonar toda reserva; **he showed great —** mostró poseer gran autodominio, se mostró muy comedido.

restrict [risˈtrikt] **1** *vt* restringir, limitar (*to* a).

2 *vr*: **I — myself to the facts** me limito a exponer los hechos; **nowadays I — myself to a litre a day** hoy día me limito a beber un litro diario.

restricted [risˈtriktid] *adj area, circulation etc* reducido; *distribution etc* restringido; *horizon* limitado; **he has rather a — outlook** tiene miras más bien estrechas; **the plant is — to Andalusia** la planta está restringida a Andalucía; **his output is — to novels** su producción consiste únicamente en novelas.

restriction [risˈtrikʃən] *n* restricción *f*, limitación *f*; **without — as to...** sin restricción de...; **to place — on the sale of a drug** restringir la venta de una droga; **to place —s on someone's liberty** restringir la libertad de uno.

restrictive [risˈtriktiv] *adj* restrictivo.

rest room ['restrum] *n* cuarto *m* de descanso; (*US euph*) aseos *mpl*.

result [riˈzʌlt] **1** *n* resultado *m*; **—s** (*of election, exam etc*) resultados *mpl*; **as a — por** consiguiente; **as a — of** de resultas de, a consecuencia de; **as a — of a misunderstanding** debido a un malentendido; **in the — finalmente; with the — that...** resultando que...; **without — sin** resultado; **the — is that...** el resultado es que...; **what will be the — of it all?** ¿en qué va a parar todo esto?

2 *vi*: **to — from** resultar de; **to — in** producir, motivar, terminar en, dar por resultado; **it —ed in his death** causó su muerte, condujo a su muerte;

it —ed in a large increase produjo un aumento apreciable; it didn't — in anything useful no produjo nada útil, no dio ningún resultado útil.

resultant [ri'zʌltənt] adj consiguiente, resultante.

resume [ri'zjuːm] 1 vt (continue) reanudar, continuar; office etc reasumir; (summarize) resumir; to — one's seat volver a sentarse; to — one's work reanudar su trabajo; "Now then", he —d "Ahora bien", dijo reanudando la conversación.
2 vi continuar; comenzar de nuevo.

résumé ['reizjuːmei] n resumen m.

resumption [ri'zʌmpʃən] n reanudación f, continuación f; reasunción f; on the — of the sitting al reanudarse la sesión.

resurface ['riːsəːfis] 1 vt poner nueva superficie a; volver a allanar; road rehacer el firme de.
2 vi (of submarine) volver a emerger, volver a salir a la superficie.

resurgence [ri'səːdʒəns] n resurgimiento m.

resurgent [ri'səːdʒənt] adj renaciente, que está en trance de renacer.

resurrect [,rezə'rekt] vt resucitar.

resurrection [,rezə'rekʃən] n resurrección f.

resuscitate [ri'sʌsiteit] vti resucitar.

resuscitation [ri,sʌsi'teiʃən] n resucitación f.

retail ['riːteil] 1 n venta f al por menor, venta f al detalle.
2 attr, adj: — dealer, — trader comerciante mf al por menor, detallista mf; — price precio m al por menor, precio m al detalle; — trade comercio m al por menor, comercio m detallista.
3 adv: to sell something — vender algo al por menor, vender algo al detalle.

retail [ri'teil] 1 vt (Comm) vender al por menor, vender al detalle; gossip repetir, story contar. 2 vi venderse al por menor (at a).

retailer [riː'teilə*] n comerciante mf al por menor, detallista mf.

retain [ri'tein] vt retener; conservar; (keep in one's possession) guardar, quedarse con; (in memory) retener; (sign up) lawyer ajustar, player contratar, fichar; the sponge —s the water la esponja retiene el agua; it —s something of its past glories conserva una parte de sus viejas glorias; the customer —s that part el cliente se queda con esa porción.

retainer [ri'teinə*] n (a) (follower) secuaz m; adherente m, partidario m, a f; (servant) criado m; family —, old — viejo criado m (que lleva muchos años sirviendo en la misma familia).
(b) (Law) ajuste m, anticipo m.

retake ['riːteik] (irr: see take) vt volver a tomar, reconquistar.

retaliate [ri'tælieit] vi desquitarse, tomar represalias, tomar su revancha; to — by + ger vengarse + ger; to — on someone tomar represalias contra uno; vengarse de uno.

retaliation [ri,tæli'eiʃən] n desquite m, represalias fpl, revancha f; venganza f; by way of —, in — para desquitarse, para vengarse.

retaliatory [ri'tæliətəri] adj: — raid ataque m vengativo, ataque m de desquite; to take — measures tomar medidas para desquitarse, tomar represalias.

retard [ri'tɑːd] vt retardar, retrasar.

retarded [ri'tɑːdid] adj retardado, retrasado.

retch [retʃ] vi vomitar; esforzarse por vomitar.

retching ['retʃiŋ] n esfuerzo m por vomitar; náusea f, bascas fpl.

retell ['riː'tel] (irr: see tell) vt recontar, volver a contar.

retention [ri'tenʃən] n retención f (also Med); conservación f.

retentive [ri'tentiv] adj retentivo.

retentiveness [ri'tentivnis] n retentiva f, poder m de retención.

rethink ['riː'θiŋk] (irr: see think) vt repensar.

reticence ['retisəns] n reticencia f, reserva f.

reticent ['retisənt] adj reticente, reservado; he has been very — about it no ha querido decirnos nada acerca de ello, ha tratado el asunto con la mayor reserva.

reticently ['retisəntli] adv con reserva.

reticle ['retikl] n retículo m.

reticulate [ri'tikjulit] adj, **reticulated** [ri'tikjuleitid] adj reticular.

reticule ['retikjuːl] n (Opt etc) retículo m; (bag) ridículo m.

retina ['retinə] n retina f.

retinue ['retinjuː] n séquito m, comitiva f.

retire [ri'taiə*] 1 vt jubilar; he was compulsorily —d le obligaron a jubilarse.
2 vi (a) (withdraw) retirarse; to — to bed to

— for the night ir a dormir, ir a acostarse, recogerse; to — from the world retirarse del mundo; to — into oneself encerrarse en sus pensamientos, huir del mundo exterior.
(b) (of age limit) jubilarse, (Mil) retirarse; to — from business dejar los negocios; to — from a post dimitir un cargo, renunciar a un puesto; to — on a pension jubilarse; they —d to the countryside se jubiló él y fueron a vivir en el campo.
(c) (Mil) retirarse; to — to prepared positions retirarse a ocupar posiciones preparadas de antemano.
(d) (Sport) abandonar; he had to — in the 5th lap tuvo que abandonar en la 5ª vuelta.

retired [ri'taiəd] adj jubilado, (Mil) retirado; a — person un jubilado; to place someone on the — list (Mil) dar el retiro a uno.

retirement [ri'taiəmənt] n (a) (state of being retired) retiro m; to live in — vivir en el retiro; to spend one's — growing roses ocuparse después de la jubilación cultivando rosas; how will you spend your —? ¿qué piensa Vd hacer después de jubilarse?
(b) (act of retiring) jubilación f, (Mil) retiro m; compulsory — jubilación f forzosa; see pay etc.
(c) (Mil: withdrawal) retirada f.

retiring [ri'taiəriŋ] adj (a) member etc saliente, dimitente; the — members of staff los miembros que se jubilan.
(b) (of character) reservado, retraído.

retort [ri'tɔːt] 1 n (answer) réplica f; (Chem) retorta f. 2 vt (insult etc) devolver; he —ed that . . . contestó secamente que . . ., contestó ásperamente que . . .

retouch ['riː'tʌtʃ] vt retocar.

retrace [ri'treis] vt volver a trazar; (in memory) recordar, rememorar; someone's journey etc seguir las huellas de.

retract [ri'trækt] 1 vt retractar, retirar; (draw in) retraer, encoger; (Tech) replegar.
2 vi retractarse; (be drawn in) retraerse; (Tech) replegarse; he refuses to — se niega a retractarse.

retractable [ri'træktəbl] adj retractable; (Aer etc) replegable, retráctil.

retractation [,riːtræk'teiʃən] n, **retraction** [ri'trækʃən] n retractación f, retracción f.

retrain ['riː'trein] vt workers reeducar, enseñar una nueva técnica a.

retraining ['riː'treiniŋ] n reeducación f profesional, readaptación f profesional.

retransmit ['riːtrænz'mit] n retransmitir.

retread ['riː'tred] vt tyre recauchutar.

retreat [ri'triːt] 1 (n) (a) (place) retiro m (also Eccl); refugio m, asilo m; (state) retraimiento m, apartamiento m.
(b) (Mil) retirada f; the — from Mons la retirada de Mons; to beat the — (Mil) dar el toque de retreta; to beat a — (Mil) retirarse, batirse en retirada; (fig) emprender la retirada; to beat a hasty — retirarse con toda prisa; to be in full — retirarse en masa, retirarse en todo el frente.
2 vi retirarse, batirse en retirada; they —ed to Dunkirk se retiraron a Dunquerque; the waters are —ing las aguas están bajando.

retrench [ri'trentʃ] 1 vt reducir, cercenar. 2 vi economizar, hacer economías.

retrenchment [ri'trentʃmənt] n reducción f, cercenadura f; economías fpl.

retrial ['riː'traiəl] n (of person) nuevo proceso m; (of case) revisión f.

retribution [,retri'bjuːʃən] n justo castigo m, pena f merecida; desquite m.

retributive [ri'tribjutiv] adj castigador, de castigo.

retrievable [ri'triːvəbl] adj recuperable; reparable.

retrieval [ri'triːvəl] n recuperación f; (Hunting) cobra f; resarcimiento m; reparación f; subsanación f; rescate m.

retrieve [ri'triːv] vt (recover) cobrar, recobrar, recuperar; (Hunting) cobrar; loss recuperar; resarcirse de; fortunes reparar; error subsanar; to — something from the water rescatar algo del agua; she —d her handkerchief recogió su pañuelo, volvió a tomar su pañuelo; we shall — nothing from this disaster no salvaremos nada de esta catástrofe.

retriever [ri'triːvə*] n perro m cobrador, perdiguero m.

retro . . . ['retrəu] retro . . .

retroactive [,retrəu'æktiv] adj retroactivo.

retroflex ['retrəufleks] adj vuelto hacia atrás.

retrograde ['retrəu'greid] adj retrógrado; **a — step** un paso hacia atrás, una medida reaccionaria.

retrogress [ˌretrəu'gres] vi retroceder; (fig) empeorar, degenerar, decaer.

retrogression [ˌretrəu'greʃən] n retrogradación f.

retrogressive [ˌretrəu'gresiv] adj retrógrado.

retrorocket ['retrəu'rɔkit] n retrocohete m.

retrospect ['retrəuspekt] n: **in —** retrospectivamente; mirando hacia atrás, volviendo a considerar el pasado; **in — it seems a happy time** visto desde esta altura parece haber sido un período feliz.

retrospection [ˌretrəu'spekʃən] n retrospección f, consideración f del pasado.

retrospective [ˌretrəu'spektiv] adj retrospectivo; law etc retroactivo.

retrospectively [ˌretrəu'spektivli] adv retrospectivamente; de modo retroactivo.

retroussé [rə'truːsei] adj nose respingado.

retry ['riː'trai] vt person procesar de nuevo, volver a procesar; case rever.

return [ri'təːn] **1** n (a) (going back) vuelta f, regreso m; (Med etc) reaparición f; **the — home** la vuelta a casa; **the — to school** la vuelta al colegio; **the — of King Kong** la vuelta de King Kong; **by —** (of post) a vuelta de correo; **on my —** al volver yo, a la vuelta; **many happy —s (of the day)!** ¡que los cumplas muy felices!, ¡feliz cumpleaños!

(b) (Comm) ganancia f; ingresos mpl; (interest) rédito m; **the — on investments is only 2%** las inversiones rinden sólo el 2 por ciento; **law of diminishing —s** ley f de rendimientos decrecientes; **to bring in a good —** rendir bien, dar un buen rédito.

(c) (of thing borrowed, of merchandise) devolución f; restitución f; **3 dozen on a sale or — basis** 3 docenas a devolver si no se venden.

(d) (Tennis etc) golpe m con que se resta la pelota.

(e) (reward) recompensa f; **in — en** cambio; **in — for** en cambio de, en recompensa de; **in — you . . .** en cambio Vd . . .; **in — for this service** en recompensa de este servicio.

(f) (report) informe m, relación f; (answer) respuesta f; (figures) estadística f; **—s** estadísticas fpl, tablas fpl de estadísticas (for de); **quarterly —** informe m trimestral; declaración f trimestral; **— of income** declaración f de renta.

(g) (Parl etc: of member) elección f; (voting) resultado m (del escrutinio).

2 attr (a) **— flight** vuelo m de regreso; **— journey** viaje m de regreso; **— ticket** billete m de ida y vuelta.

(b) **— match** (partido m de) desquite m, revancha f.

(c) **— address** señas fpl del remitente.

3 vt (a) (give back) devolver; restituir; (send back) light reflejar; ball restar; suit of cards devolver; answer, thanks dar; favour, kindness, love corresponder a; visit pagar; **to — something** devolver algo a su lugar; **to — partner's lead** devolver el palo que sirvió el compañero; **"— to sender"** "devuélvase al remitente"; **to — blow for blow** devolver golpe por golpe; **to — like for like** pagar a uno en la misma moneda; **I hope to — your kindness** espero poder corresponder a su amabilidad; **her love was not —ed** su amor no fue correspondido.

(b) (declare) declarar; **to — an income of £3,000** declarar tener una renta de 3.000 libras; **to — a verdict** pronunciar una sentencia, dar un fallo; **to — a verdict of guilty on someone** declarar culpable a uno.

(c) (Parl etc) elegir, votar a; **he was —ed by an overwhelming majority** resultó elegido por una abrumadora mayoría; **Old Sarum used to — two members to Parliament** Old Sarum tenía antes el derecho a dos escaños en el Parlamento.

4 vi (a) (go back) volver, regresar (to a); (Law) revertir (to a); **to — home** volver a casa; **to — from town** volver de la ciudad; **to — from a journey** volver de un viaje, regresar después de un viaje; **his good spirits —ed** renació su alegría, se restableció su buen humor.

(b) **to — to a task** volver a una tarea, emprender de nuevo una tarea; **to — to a theme** volver a un asunto.

(c) (Med: of symptoms etc) reaparecer.

returnable [ri'təːnəbl] adj restituible; (Law) devolutivo; (on approval) a prueba; **empties —** envases mpl a devolver; **the book is — on the 14th** el libro ha de ser devuelto el 14; **the deposit is not —** no se reembolsa el depósito.

returning officer [ri'təːniŋ ˌɔfisə*] n escudriñador m.

reunification ['riːˌjuːnifi'keiʃən] n reunificación f.

reunify ['riː'juːnifai] vt reunificar.

reunion [ri'juːnjən] n reunión f.

reunite ['riːju'nait] **1** vt reunir; (in friendship etc) reconciliar; **eventually the family was —d** por fin la familia volvió a verse unida; **she was —ed with her husband** volvió a verse al lado de su marido.

2 vi reunirse; reconciliarse; volver a verse unido.

rev [rev] (Aut etc, fam) **1** n revolución f.

2 vt (also to — up) girar (el motor de); acelerar (la marcha de).

3 vi (also to — up) girar (rápidamente); acelerarse; **the plane was —ving up** giraban los motores del avión.

revaluation [riːˌvælju'eiʃən] n revaloración f, revalorización f.

revalue ['riː'vælju:] vt revalorizar.

revamp ['riː'væmp] vt shoe poner nueva empella a; remendar; engine volver a componer; (fig) rehacer, renovar.

reveal [ri'viːl] vt revelar.

revealing [ri'viːliŋ] adj revelador.

revealingly [ri'viːliŋli] adv de modo revelador.

reveille [ri'væli] n diana f, toque m de diana.

revel ['revl] vi jaranear, estar de parranda, divertirse tumultuosamente; **to — in** deleitarse en, deleitarse con; **to — in + ger** deleitarse en + infin.

revelation [ˌrevə'leiʃən] n revelación f; **(Book of) R—s** el Apocalipsis; **it was a — to me** fue una revelación para mí.

reveller ['revlə*] n jaranero m, juerguista mf; (drunk) borracho m; (guest) convidado m, a f.

revelry ['revlri] n jolgorio m, jarana f, diversión f tumultuosa; (organized) fiestas fpl, festividades fpl; **the spirit of —** el espíritu de carnaval.

revels ['revlz] npl jolgorio m, jarana f, diversión f tumultuosa; (organized) fiestas fpl, festividades fpl; **let the — begin!** ¡que comience la fiesta!; **the — lasted for 3 days** continuaron las fiestas durante 3 días.

revenge [ri'vendʒ] **1** n venganza f; **in — para** vengarse; **in — for something** para vengarse de algo; **to have one's —** vengarse; **to take — on someone for something** vengarse de algo en uno.

2 vt vengar; **to be —d on someone** vengarse en uno.

3 vi: **to — oneself** vengarse (on someone en uno, for something de algo).

revengeful [ri'vendʒful] adj vengativo.

revengefully [ri'vendʒfəli] adv vengativamente.

revenger [ri'vendʒə*] n vengador m, ora f.

revenue ['revənju:] n (a) (income: also —s) ingresos mpl; renta f; (on investments) rédito m; (profit) ganancia f, beneficio m (from de).

(b) (of state) rentas fpl públicas; **Inland R—,** (US) **Internal R—** Delegación f de Contribuciones.

revenue cutter ['revənju:ˌkʌtə*] n guardacostas m.

revenue officer ['revənju:ˌɔfisə*] n agente m fiscal.

revenue stamp ['revənju:ˌstæmp] n sello m fiscal.

reverberate [ri'vəːbəreit] vi (a) (of sound) resonar, retumbar; **the sound —d in the distance** el sonido retumbaba a lo lejos; **the valley —d with the sound** el ruido resonaba por el valle.

(b) (Tech: of light) reverberar.

reverberation [riˌvəːbə'reiʃən] n (a) retumbo m, el retumbar, eco m. (b) reverberación f.

reverberator [ri'vəːbəreitə*] n reverberador m.

revere [ri'viə*] vt reverenciar, venerar.

reverence ['revərəns] **1** n reverencia f; **Your R—** Reverencia. **2** vt reverenciar.

reverend ['revərənd] **1** adj reverendo; **right —** reverendísimo. **2** n (fam: Catholic) padre m, cura m; (Protestant) pastor m.

reverent ['revərənt] adj reverente.

reverential [ˌrevə'renʃəl] adj reverencial.

reverently ['revərəntli] adv reverentemente, con reverencia.

reverie ['revəri] n ensueño m; **to be lost in —** estar absorto, estar ensimismado.

revers [ri'viə*] n (Sew) solapa f.

reversal [ri'vəːsəl] n (of order) inversión f; (of direction, policy) cambio m completo; (of decision) revocación f.

reverse [ri'vəːs] **1** adj (a) (of order) inverso, invertido; (of direction) contrario, opuesto; **in the — order** en orden inverso, al revés; **in the — direction** en sentido contrario; **— turn** vuelta f al revés.

(b) (Mech) gear de marcha atrás.

2 n (a) (opposite) **the —** lo contrario; **quite the —** todo lo contrario; **but the — is true** pero es al contrario; **it was the — of what we had expected**

fue todo lo contrario de lo que habíamos esperado; his **remarks were the** — **of flattering** sus observaciones eran poco halagüeñas, todo lo contrario.

(**b**) (*face: of coin*) reverso *m*; (*of cloth*) revés *m*; (*of paper etc*) dorso *m*.

(**c**) (*Mech*) marcha *f* atrás, contramarcha *f*; **to go into** — dar marcha atrás; **to put a car into** — dar marcha atrás a un coche.

3 *vt* (**a**) (*invert order of*) invertir, invertir el orden de; trastrocar; (*turn other way round*) volver al revés; *arms* llevar a la funerala; **to** — **A and B** invertir el orden de A y B, anteponer B a A.

(**b**) (*change*) *opinion* cambiar completamente de; *decision* revocar, anular, cancelar.

(**c**) (*Mech*) poner en marcha atrás; invertir la marcha de; (*Tel*) **to** — **the charges** cobrar al número llamado; **he** —**d the car into the garage** dio marcha atrás al coche y entró en el garaje; **she** —**d the car into a pillarbox** al dar marcha atrás al coche chocó con un buzón.

4 *vi* dar marcha atrás; **I** —**d into a van** al dar marcha atrás choqué con una furgoneta.

reversible [ri'və:səbl] *adj* reversible.

reversion [ri'və:ʃən] *n* reversión *f* (*also Bio, Law*); — **to type** reversión *f* al tipo, salto *m* atrás.

reversionary [ri'və:ʃnəri] *adj* reversionario, reversible.

revert [ri'və:t] *vi* (*Law*) revertir (*to* a); (*Bio*) saltar atrás; **to** — **to a subject** volver a un tema; —**ing to the matter under discussion . . .** volviendo al tema de la discusión . . .; **to** — **to type** saltar atrás en la cadena natural.

revetment [ri'vetmənt] *n* revestimiento *m*.

revictual ['ri:'vitl] **1** *vt* reabastecer. **2** *vi* reabastecerse.

review [ri'vju:] **1** *n* (**a**) (*revision: Law*) revisión *f*; (*examination*) repaso *m*; examen *m*; análisis *m*; **the annual** — **of expenditure** el examen anual de los gastos; **the sentence is subject to** — **in the high court** la sentencia volverá a ser vista en el tribunal supremo.

(**b**) (*Mil etc*) revista *f*; **the Spithead R**— la revista de Spithead; **the general passed the troops in** — el general pasó revista a las tropas; **the troops passed in** — **before the general** las tropas desfilaron en revista ante el general.

(**c**) (*critique*) reseña *f*; — **copy** ejemplar *m* para reseñar.

(**d**) (*journal*) revista *f*; **weekly** — revista *f* semanal; **literary** — revista *f* literaria.

(**e**) (*show*) revista *f*.

2 *vt* (**a**) (*Law*) rever; (*take stock of*) repasar; examinar, analizar, estudiar; **we will** — **the position in a month** volveremos a estudiar la situación dentro de un mes; **we shall have to** — **our policy** tendremos que reconsiderar nuestra política.

(**b**) (*Mil etc*) pasar revista a, revistar.

(**c**) (*write* — *of*) reseñar; **he** —**ed it for the "Journal"** él lo reseñó en el "Boletín".

reviewer [ri'vju:ə*] *n* crítico *m*, a *f*.

revile [ri'vail] *vt* injuriar, llenar de injurias, vilipendiar.

revise [ri'vaiz] **1** *vt* (*look over*) revisar, volver a examinar, volver a estudiar; *lesson etc* repasar; (*amend*) modificar, corregir; *proofs* corregir; *text* refundir; *decision* modificar.

2 *vi*: **to** — **for exams** repasar los libros (*etc*) para los exámenes.

revised [ri'vaizd] *adj text* refundido; **R**— **Version** (*of Bible*) Versión *f* Enmendada.

reviser [ri'vaizə*] *n* revisor *m*, ora *f*; refundidor *m*, ora *f*; (*Typ*) corrector *m*.

revision [ri'viʒən] *n* revisión *f*; repaso *m*; modificación *f*, corrección *f*; refundición *f*; **I need 2 weeks for** — necesito 2 semanas para repasar mis libros (*etc*).

revisionism [ri'viʒənizəm] *n* revisionismo *m*.

revisionist [ri'viʒənist] **1** *adj* revisionista. **2** *n* revisionista *m*.

revisit ['ri:'vizit] *vt* volver a visitar; **"Brideshead R**—**ed"** "Retorno *m* a Brideshead".

revitalize ['ri:'vaitəlaiz] *vt* revivificar, vigorizar; infundir fuerzas a.

revival [ri'vaivəl] *n* resucitación *f*; reanimación *f*; restablecimiento *m*; despertamiento *m*; (*Theat*) reposición *f*, reestreno *m*; (*of learning, art*) renacimiento *m*; (*Pol etc*) resurgimiento *m*; **the R**— **of Learning** el Renacimiento.

revivalist [ri'vaivəlist] *n* predicador *m* evangelista.

revive [ri'vaiv] **1** *vt* (*restore to life*) resucitar; (*fig*) reanimar; restablecer; *fire* avivar; *accusation* volver a, volver a hacer; *hopes* despertar; *suspicion* hacer revivir; *play* reponer, reestrenar; **this will** — **you**

esto te reanimará; **to** — **someone's courage** infundir nuevo ánimo a uno.

2 *vi* (*come back to life*) resucitar; (*recover*) reponerse, restablecerse; cobrar fuerzas; (*after unconsciousness*) revivir; **the pound has** —**d** la libra se ha repuesto; **interest in Góngora has** —**d** ha renacido el interés por Góngora; **his courage** —**d** se sintió con nuevo ánimo.

revivify [ri:'vivifai] *vt* revivificar.

revocation [ˌrevə'keiʃən] *n* revocación *f*.

revoke [ri'vəuk] **1** *n* (*Cards*) renuncio *m*. **2** *vt* revocar. **3** *vi* (*Cards*) renunciar.

revolt [ri'vəult] **1** *n* rebelión *f*, sublevación *f*; **to be in open** — estar en franca (*or* plena) rebeldía; **to rise in** — rebelarse, sublevarse.

2 *vt* repugnar, dar asco a; **thc book** —**ed me** el libro me dio asco.

3 *vi* rebelarse, sublevarse (*against* contra).

revolting [ri'vəultiŋ] *adj* asqueroso, repugnante.

revoltingly [ri'vəultiŋli] *adv* asquerosamente, de modo repugnante; **they're** — **rich** son tan ricos que da asco.

revolution [ˌrevə'lu:ʃən] *n* (**a**) (*Pol*) revolución *f*; **the Russian R**— la Revolución rusa.

(**b**) (*turn*) revolución *f*; vuelta *f*, rotación *f*; **600** —**s per minute** 600 revoluciones por minuto.

revolutionary [ˌrevə'lu:ʃnəri] **1** *adj* revolucionario. **2** *n* revolucionario *m*, a *f*.

revolutionize [ˌrevə'lu:ʃnaiz] *vt* revolucionar.

revolve [ri'vəlv] **1** *vt* girar, hacer girar; (*in the mind*) revolver, meditar.

2 *vi* (**a**) (*Mech etc*) girar (*on* sobre, *round* alrededor de); dar vueltas; (*Astron*) revolverse.

(**b**) (*fig*) **everything** —**s round him** todo depende de él, todo se centra en él.

revolver [ri'vəlvə*] *n* revólver *m*.

revolving [ri'vəlviŋ] *adj* giratorio.

revue [ri'vju:] *n* (*Theat*) revista *f*.

revulsion [ri'vʌlʃən] *n* (*disgust*) asco *m*, repugnancia *f*; (*Med*) revulsión *f*; (*change*) reacción *f*, cambio *m* repentino.

reward [ri'wɔ:d] **1** *n* recompensa *f*, premio *m*; (*for finding something*) hallazgo *m*; **as a** — **for** en recompensa de, como premio a; **"£50** —**" "50 libras de recompensa"**; **"a** — **will be paid for information acerca de . . ."** "se recompensará al que dé informes acerca de . . ."

2 *vt* recompensar, premiar; **to** — **someone for his services** recompensar a uno por sus servicios; **she** —**ed me with a smile** me premió con una sonrisa.

rewarding [ri'wɔ:diŋ] *adj* remunerador; (*fig*) provechoso, útil, valioso.

rewind ['ri:'waind] (*irr: see* **wind**) *vt watch* dar cuerda a; *wool etc* devanar; (*Elec*) rebobinar.

rewinding ['ri:'waindiŋ] *n* (*Elec*) rebobinado *m*.

rewire ['ri:'waiə*] *vt house* renovar completamente el alambrado de.

reword ['ri:'wɔ:d] *vt* expresar en otras palabras.

rewrite ['ri:'rait] (*irr: see* **write**) *vt* volver a escribir, escribir de nuevo; *text* rehacer, refundir; redactar en otras palabras.

rhapsodic [ræp'sɔdik] *adj* rapsódico; (*fig*) extático, locamente entusiasmado.

rhapsodize ['ræpsədaiz] *vi*: **to** — **over something** extasiarse ante algo, entusiasmarse por algo; discutir algo en términos elogiosos.

rhapsody ['ræpsədi] *n* rapsodia *f*; (*fig*) transporte *m* de admiración (*etc*); **to be in rhapsodies** estar extasiado; **to go into rhapsodies over something** extasiarse ante algo, entusiasmarse por algo; discutir algo en términos elogiosos.

rhea ['ri:ə] *n* avestruz *m* de la pampa.

Rhenish ['reniʃ] **1** *adj* renano. **2** *n* vino *m* del Rin.

rheostat ['ri:əustæt] *n* reóstato *m*.

rhesus ['ri:səs] *n* macaco *m* de la India.

rhetoric ['retərik] *n* retórica *f*.

rhetorical [ri'tɔrikəl] *adj* retórico.

rhetorically [ri'tɔrikəli] *adv* retóricamente; **I speak** — hablo en metáfora.

rhetorician [ˌretə'riʃən] *n* retórico *m*.

rheumatic [ru:'mætik] *adj* reumático.

rheumatics [ru:'mætiks] *npl* (*fam*), **rheumatism** ['ru:mətizəm] *n* reumatismo *m*.

rheumatoid ['ru:mətɔid] *adj* reumatoideo; — **arthritis** artritis *f* reumatoidea.

rheumy ['ru:mi] *adj eyes* legañoso, pitañoso.

Rhine [rain] Rin *m*.

Rhineland ['rainlənd] Renania *f*.

rhino ['rainəu] *n* (*fam*), **rhinoceros** [rai'nɔsərəs] *n* rinoceronte *m*.

rhizome ['raizəum] *n* rizoma *m*.

Rhodes [rəudz] Rodas *f*.

Rhodesia [rəu'di:ʒə] Rodesia *f*.

Rhodesian [rəu'diːʒən] 1 adj rodesiano. 2 n rodesiano m, a f.

rhododendron [‚rəudə'dendrən] n rododendro m.

rhomb [rɔm] n rombo m.

rhombic ['rɔmbik] adj (Geom) rombal.

rhomboid ['rɔmbɔid] 1 adj romboidal. 2 n romboide m.

rhombus ['rɔmbəs] n rombo m.

Rhône [rəun] Ródano m.

rhubarb ['ruːbɑːb] n ruibarbo m.

rhyme [raim] 1 n rima f; (poem) poesía f, versos mpl; **in —** en verso; **without —** or **reason** sin ton ni son. 2 vti rimar.

rhymer ['raimə*] n, **rhymester** ['raimstə*] n rimador m, ora f.

rhythm ['riðəm] n ritmo m; **— method** (Med) método m de continencia periódica.

rhythmic(al) ['riðmik(əl)] adj rítmico.

rhythmically ['riðmikəli] adv rítmicamente, de modo rítmico.

rib [rib] 1 n (Anat) costilla f; (Bot) nervio m, nervadura f; (Archit) nervadura f; (of umbrella) varilla f; (Naut) costilla f, cuaderna f.
2 vt (fam): **to — someone** tomar el pelo a uno (fam).

ribald ['ribəld] adj verde, obsceno, escabroso; irreverente y regocijado.

ribaldry ['ribəldri] n (character) lo verde, obscenidad f, escabrosidad f; (jokes etc) cosas fpl verdes, cosas fpl obscenas.

riband ['ribənd] n = **ribbon**.

ribbed [ribd] adj (Bot) nervudo, con nervaduras.

ribbon ['ribən] 1 n cinta f; (Mil) galón m; type-**writer —** cinta f para máquina de escribir; **to tear something to —s** hacer algo trizas; **with his jacket torn to —s** con su chaqueta hecha trizas.
2 attr: **— development** desarrollo m en línea.

rice [rais] n arroz m.

ricefield ['raisfiːld] n arrozal m.

rice pudding ['rais'pudiŋ] n arroz m con leche.

rich [ritʃ] adj rico; (in price, workmanship) costoso, precioso, exquisito; colour vivo, brillante; profit pingüe; soil fértil; voice sonoro; banquet suntuoso, opíparo; food sabroso, suculento, (pej) pesado, fuerte, muy dulce, empalagoso; wine generoso; style copioso; (funny: fam) muy divertido; **that's —!** ¡qué gracioso!; **the —** los ricos; **to be — in** abundar de, abundar en; **a gallery — in im-pressionists** un museo que posee gran caudal de impresionistas; **a style — in metaphors** un estilo en el que abundan las metáforas; **the soil is — in nitrates** el suelo tiene abundantes nitratos; **to become** (or **get**, **grow**) **—** enriquecerse (on con); **to get — quick** enriquecerse pronto.

Richard ['ritʃəd] m Ricardo.

riches ['ritʃiz] npl riqueza f, riquezas fpl.

richly ['ritʃli] adv ricamente; preciosamente; ex-quisitamente; suntuosamente; sabrosamente; copio-samente; **a — adorned chair** una silla de exquisitos adornos; **a — humorous situation** una situación divertidísima; **she — deserves it** muy bien merecido lo tiene.

richness ['ritʃnis] n riqueza f; preciosidad f, exquisitez f; viveza f, brillantez f; fertilidad f; sonoridad f; suntuosidad f; suculencia f; lo pesado, lo fuerte; copia f; abundancia f.

rick[1] [rik] 1 n niara f, almiar m, montón m de paja (or heno, trigo etc). 2 vt recoger en niaras (etc), amontonar.

rick[2] [rik] vt see **wrick**.

rickets ['rikits] n raquitismo m, raquitis f.

rickety ['rikiti] adj (a) (Med) raquítico. (b) des-vencijado; (unsteady) tambaleante, inseguro.

rickshaw ['rikʃɔː] n jinrikisha f, rikisha f.

ricochet ['rikəʃei] 1 n rebote m. 2 vi rebotar (off de).

rid [rid] (irr: pret **rid**, **ridded**, ptp **rid**) 1 vt (a) **to — a place of rats** librar un lugar de ratas, eliminar las ratas de un lugar; **to — someone of a difficulty** librar a uno de una dificultad; **the medicine — me of the cough** la medicina me curó la tos.
(b) **to be — of** estar libre de; **we're — of him at last!** ¡por fin nos vemos libres de él!
(c) **to get — of** deshacerse de, desembarazarse de; **the body gets — of waste** el cuerpo elimina los desechos; **to get — of someone** deshacerse de uno, (euph) eliminar a uno matándole.
2 vr: **to — oneself of** librarse de, desembarazarse de; **to — oneself of evil thoughts** librarse de los malos pensamientos.

riddance ['ridəns] n: **good —!** (iro) ¡enhoramala!; ¡vete con viento fresco!; **it was a good —** de buena nos libramos; **and good — to him** que se pudra.

ridden ['ridn] ptp of **ride**; **a horse — by ...** un caballo montado por ...

riddle[1] ['ridl] n (conundrum) acertijo m, adivinanza f; (mystery) enigma m, misterio m; (person etc) enigma m; **the — of the assassination** el misterio del asesinato; **to ask someone a —** proponer un acertijo a uno; **to speak in —s** hablar en términos nada claros.

riddle[2] ['ridl] 1 n (sieve) criba f, criba f gruesa; (potato sorter etc) escogedor m.
2 vt (sieve) cribar; potatoes etc pasar por el escogedor; **to — a door with bullets** acribillar una puerta a balazos; **the organization is —d with communists** el organismo está plagado de comunistas; **the army is —d with subversion** el ejército está lleno de subversionismo.

ride [raid] 1 n (a) (on horse) cabalgata f, paseo m a caballo; (in car etc) paseo m en coche, viaje m en coche (or bicicleta etc); (distance ridden) viaje m, recorrido m; **the — of the Valkyries** la cabalgata de las valquirias; **"2 shillings a —"** "2 chelines por persona", "2 chelines la vuelta"; **it was a rough —** fue un viaje nada cómodo; **it's only a short —** es poco camino, es poca distancia; **it's a 10-minute — by bus** el viaje dura 10 minutos en autobús; **it's a 7d — from the station** el viaje desde la estación cuesta 7 peniques; **they gave me a — into town** me llevaron en coche a la ciudad; **I got a — all the way to Bordeaux** un automovilista me llevó hasta Burdeos; **to go for a — over the fields** pasearse a caballo por los campos; **to go for a — in a car** dar un paseo en coche; **it's my first — in a Rolls** es la primera vez que viajo en un Rolls; **to take a — in a helicopter** dar un paseo en helicóptero; **to take someone for a —** (fam) engañar a uno, embaucar a uno, (US sl) dar el paseo a uno (sl).
(b) (in a wood) vereda f.
2 (irr: pret **rode**, ptp **ridden**) vt (a) **to — a horse** montar a caballo; **to — a bicycle** ir en bicicleta; **to — an elephant** ir montado en un elefante; **he rode his horse up the stairs** hizo que el caballo subiese la escalera; **he rode his horse into the shop** entró a caballo en la tienda; **it has never been ridden** hasta ahora nadie ha montado en él; **he rode it in two races** lo hizo correr en dos carreras; **to — a horse hard** castigar mucho a un caballo; **can you — a bicycle?** ¿sabes montar en bicicleta?
(b) (fig) **to — someone** tiranizar a uno, dominar a uno; **don't — him too hard** no seas demasiado severo con él; **to — an idea to death** explotar una idea con demasiado entusiasmo, acabar con una idea a fuerza de repetirla demasiado.
(c) (Naut) waves hender, surcar.
(d) **to — a good race** hacer bien una carrera, dar buena cuenta de sí en una carrera; ser adversario digno de estimación.
(e) **to — someone down** atropellar a uno; **to — out a storm** capear un temporal, hacer frente a un temporal.
3 vi (a) (an animal) montar, cabalgar; (on a bicycle, in a car) ir; pasearse, viajar; **to — on an elephant** ir montado en un elefante; **to — in a car** ir en coche; **some rode but I had to walk** algunos fueron en coche pero yo tuve que ir a pie; **to — astride** montar a horcajadas; **to — like mad** correr como el demonio; **to — home on someone's shoulders** ser llevado a casa en los hombros de uno; **she —s every day** monta a diario; **he —s for a different stable** monta para otra cuadra.
(b) (with expressions of distance and time, often not translated) **to — to Jaén** ir (a caballo) a Jaén; **we'll — over to see you** vendremos a verle; **he rode straight at me** arremetió contra mí; **he rode 12 miles** recorrió 12 millas, hizo 12 millas.
(c) (fig) **to — at anchor** estar al ancla, estar anclado; **the moon was riding high in the sky** la luna estaba en lo alto del cielo; **to be riding high** (person) estar alegre, estar en la cumbre de la felicidad; **when I'm riding high** cuando mis cosas van bien, cuando todo me va bien.
(d) (with adv or prep) **to — away**, **to — off** alejarse, irse; **to — back** volver (a caballo); volver (en bicicleta, en coche etc); **to — behind** ir después, caminar a la zaga; (in rear seat) ir en el asiento de atrás; (on same horse) cabalgar a la grupa; **to — by** pasar (a caballo); **to — on** seguir adelante; **to — up** llegar, acercarse; (of dress etc) subir.

rider ['raidə*] n (a) (horse-) jinete m, a f; caballero m; (cyclist) ciclista mf; (motorcyclist) motociclista mf; **I'm not much of a —** apenas sé montar; **he's a fine —** es un jinete destacado.
(b) (clause) aditamento m; corolario m; **I must add the — that ...** tengo que añadir que ...

ridge [ridʒ] *n* (*of hills*) cadena *f*, sierra *f*; (*of hill*) cresta *f*; (*of nose, roof*) caballete *m*; (*on cloth etc*) cordoncillo *m*; (*wrinkle*) arruga *f*; (*Agr*) caballón *m*, camellón *m*; **Vimy R—** la cresta de Vimy.

ridge pole ['ridʒpəul] *n* parhilera *f*, cumbrera *f*.

ridge tile ['ridʒtail] *n* teja *f* de caballete.

ridicule ['ridikjuːl] **1** *n* irrisión *f*; burlas *fpl*, mofa *f*; **to expose someone to public —** exponer a uno a la mofa pública; **to hold someone up to —** ridiculizar a uno, mofarse de uno; **to lay oneself open to —** exponerse al ridículo.
  2 *vt* ridiculizar, poner en ridículo, mofarse de.

ridiculous [ri'dikjuləs] *adj* ridículo, absurdo; **—!, how —!** ¡qué ridículo!; **to make oneself —** ponerse en ridículo.

ridiculously [ri'dikjuləsli] *adv* ridículamente, absurdamente; de modo ridículo; **it is — easy** es ridículamente fácil.

riding ['raidiŋ] **1** *n* equitación *f*, montar *m* a caballo. **2** *attr* de montar; de equitación.

riding boots ['raidiŋbuːts] *npl* botas *fpl* de montar.

riding breeches ['raidiŋˌbritʃiz] *npl* pantalones *mpl* de montar.

riding habit ['raidiŋˌhæbit] *n* traje *m* de montar.

riding master ['raidiŋˌmɑːstə*] *n* profesor *m* de equitación.

riding school ['raidiŋskuːl] *n* picadero *m*, escuela *f* de equitación.

riding whip ['raidiŋwip] *n* látigo *m* de montar.

rife [raif] *adj* (a) **to be —** abundar, ser muy común; ser endémico; **corruption is —** la corrupción existe en todas partes; **measles is —** hay mucho sarampión; **the abuse has become — of late** recientemente ha cundido el abuso, recientemente se ha extendido mucho el abuso.
  (b) **to be — with** estar lleno de, abundar de (*or* en).

riffraff ['rifræf] *n* gentuza *f*, chusma *f*; **and all the — of the neighbourhood** y todos los sinvergüenzas del barrio.

rifle¹ ['raifl] *vt* robar, saquear; desvalijar; **to — a case** desvalijar una maleta; **the house had been —d** habían saqueado la casa; **they —d the house in search of money** saquearon la casa buscando dinero.

rifle² ['raifl] **1** *n* rifle *m*, fusil *m*; **—s** (*as regiment etc*) rifleros *mpl*. **2** *vt* rayar.

rifle butt ['raiflbʌt] *n* culata *f* de rifle.

rifled ['raifld] *adj* (*Tech*) rayado.

rifleman ['raiflmən] *n*, *pl* **—men** [mən] riflero *m*.

rifle range ['raiflreindʒ] *n* campo *m* de tiro; (*at fair*) barraca *f* de tiro al blanco.

rifle shot ['raiflʃɔt] *n* tiro *m* de fusil; **within — a** tiro de fusil.

rifling ['raifliŋ] *n* (*Tech*) rayado *m*.

rift [rift] *n* hendedura *f*, grieta *f*, rendija *f*; (*in clouds etc*) claro *m*, abertura *f*; (*in relations etc*) grieta *f*; (*between friends*) desavenencia *f*; (*in party*) escisión *f*.

rig¹ [rig] **1** *n* (*Naut*) aparejo *m*; (*dress, fam*) atuendo *m*.
  2 *vt* (*Naut*) aparejar, enjarciar; **to — out** (*Naut*) proveer (*with* de), equipar (*with* con); **to — someone out in something** ataviar a uno de algo; **to be —ed out in a new dress** lucir un vestido nuevo; **to — up** (*fam: build*) armar, construir; (*arrange*) arreglar; (*improvise*) improvisar; **we'll see what we can — up** veremos si podemos arreglar algo.

rig² [rig] *vt*: **to — an election** falsificar los resultados de unas elecciones; **the government had got it all —ged** el gobierno lo había arreglado de modo fraudulento; **to — the market** (*Comm*) manipular la lonja; **it's been —ged!** ¡aquí hay tongo!

rigger ['rigə*] *n* (*Naut*) aparejador *m*; (*Aer*) mecánico *m*.

rigging ['rigiŋ] *n* jarcia *f*, cordaje *m*, aparejo *m*.

right [rait] **1** *adj* (a) (*just*) justo; equitativo; (*suitable*) debido, indicado; (*proper*) apropiado, propio, conveniente; (*reasonable*) razonable; **it is — that . . .** es justo que . . .; **it is only — to add that . . .** es de justicia añadir que . . .; **it is only — and proper to +** *infin* la justicia exige que *+ subj*; **it cannot be — for you to +** *infin* no puede ser justo que Vd *+ subj*; **would it be — for me to ask him?** ¿conviene que yo se lo pregunte?; **it's not —!** ¡no hay derecho!; **I thought it — to +** *infin* me pareció conveniente *+ infin*; **to do the — thing** hacer lo que hay que hacer.
  (b) (*correct*) correcto, exacto; (*true*) verdadero; *conditions etc* favorable, propicio; *thing sought etc* que hace falta, que se busca; **Mr R—** el novio

soñado, el marido ideal; **—!** ¡conforme!, ¡bueno!, ¡muy bien!; (*US*) sí, eso es; ¡justo!; (*answering call*) ¡voy!; **— you are!** ¡bueno!; **quite —!** ¡perfectamente!; **that's —** eso es; **the — answer** la respuesta correcta, (*Math: to problem etc*) la solución correcta; **the — word** la palabra exacta, la palabra apropiada; **the — time** la hora exacta; **have you the — time?** ¿tiene Vd la hora exacta?; **— side of cloth** el lado derecho *m* de un paño, haz *f* de un paño; **to choose the — moment** elegir el momento oportuno (*or* favorable); **is this the — house?** ¿es ésta la casa?; **is this the — road for Segovia?** ¿es éste el camino de Segovia?, ¿por aquí se va a Segovia?; **are we on the — road?** ¿vamos por buen camino?; **am I — for the station?** ¿por aquí se va a la estación?; **he's the — man for the job** es el hombre más indicado para el cargo, es el hombre que hace falta para el puesto; **it's not the — length** de largo no mide lo que debiera; **he's one of the — sort** es buen chico, es un tío simpático; **he's clever but not the — sort for us** es inteligente pero no nos conviene; **to say the — thing** decir lo que conviene, decir lo que se debe decir; **to put a clock —** poner un reloj en hora; **to put (*or* set) something —** arreglar algo, poner algo en orden; **that's soon put —** eso se corrige fácilmente; **to put a mistake —** corregir un error, rectificar un error; **to put someone —** corregir a uno, señalar a uno su error, (*unpleasantly*) enmendar la plana a uno.
  (c) **to be —** (*person*) tener razón; **you're dead —,** **you're quite —** estás en lo cierto; **to be — to +** *infin* hacer bien en *+ infin*; **am I — in thinking that . . .?** ¿me equivoco al afirmar que . . .?
  (d) (*in mind*) cuerdo; **to be in one's — mind** estar en su cabal juicio; **she's not — in the head** le falta un tornillo.
  (e) (*in order, settled*) **all's — with the world** todo le va bien al mundo; **to be as — as rain** estar perfectamente bien, estar en su estado normal; **I'm as — as rain,** thanks gracias, estoy perfectamente bien; **she'll be as — as rain in a few days** en unos pocos días se repondrá completamente de esto; **it all came — in the end** al fin todo se arregló, al fin todo salió bien; **it will all come — in the end** todo se arreglará.
  (f) (*all — etc*) **all —!** ¡bueno!; ¡conforme!, ¡está bien!; (*that's enough*) ¡basta ya!; **it's all —** está bien; **yes, that's all —** sí, de acuerdo; sí, vale; **it's all — for you** Vd no tiene de qué quejarse; **it's all — for you to smile** Vd bien puede sonreír; **is it all — for me to go at 4?** ¿me da su permiso para irme a las 4?; **is it all — for me to smoke?** ¿se puede fumar?; **it will be all — on the night** todo estará listo para el estreno; **I made it all — with the cabby** lo arreglé con el taxista, quedé bien con el taxista; **to be all —** (*person*) estar bien (de salud); **I'm all —** now ahora estoy bien, ahora me siento mejor; **Joe's all —!** ¡te digo que Pepe es persona de toda confianza!; **is he all — with the girls?** ¿se comporta bien con respecto a las chicas?
  (g) (*not left*) derecho; (*Pol*) derechista.
  (h) (*Math*) angle recto.
  (i) (*fam*) **he's a — idiot** es un puro idiota; **a — twit I should feel if . . .** bien tonto me creería si . . .
  2 *adv* (a) (*straight etc*) derecho; directamente; **— away** en seguida; **— away!** (*Rail etc*) ¡en marcha!; **— here** aquí mismo; **— now** ahora mismo; **to go — on** ir adelante; **he just went — on talking** siguió hablando sin hacerme caso, siguió hablando tan fresco; **to speak — out** hablar con toda franqueza, hablar enteramente sin rodeos.
  (b) (*quite, exactly*) completamente; exactamente; **— in the middle** exactamente en el centro; **— at the top** en lo alto del todo, en el punto más alto de todos; **it hit him — on the chest** le dio de lleno en el pecho; **the wind is — behind us** sopla el viento precisamente detrás de nosotros; **— at the end of his speech** precisamente al fin de su discurso; **there is a fence — round the house** hay una valla que rodea la casa por completo; **it goes — to the end** llega hasta el final (sin dejar espacio etc); **he put his hand in — to the bottom** introdujo la mano hasta el mismo fondo.
  (c) (*rightly*) bien; correctamente; **to do —** obrar bien, obrar correctamente; **you did —** hiciste bien; **if I remember —** si bien me acuerdo; **nothing goes — with them** nada les sale bien; **it was him all —** fue él sin sombra de duda; **it's a big one all —** ya lo creo que es grande; **— enough!** ¡muy bien!; **it was there — enough** sí estaba allí; *see* **serve.**

(d) (*not left*) a la derecha, hacia la derecha; — **turn**! ¡media vuelta a la derecha!; **to turn** — torcer a la derecha; **he looked neither** — **nor left** no miró a ningún lado; **they owe money** — **and left** deben dinero a todos, tienen deudas por doquier.

3 *n* **(a)** (*what is lawful*) derecho *m*; (*what is just*) justicia *f*; (*what is morally* —) bien *m*; — **and wrong** el bien y el mal; **might and** — la fuerza y el derecho; **to be in the** — tener razón; **to fight for the** — luchar por la justicia; **to have** — **on one's side** tener la razón de su parte; **to know** — **from wrong** saber distinguir el bien del mal.

(b) (*title, claim*) derecho *m*; título *m*; privilegio *m*; — **of assembly** derecho *m* de reunión; —**s of the citizen** derechos *mpl* del ciudadano; —**s of man** derechos *mpl* del hombre; — **of way** derecho *m* de paso, (*Law*) servidumbre *f* de paso, (*Aut etc*) prioridad *f*; **divine** — derecho *m* divino; **sole** — (*Comm*) exclusiva *f*; **by** — según derecho, en justicia; **by** — **of** por razón de; **by what** —? ¿con qué derecho . . .?; **to be within one's** —**s** estar en su derecho; **to exercise one's** — usar de su derecho (*to* + *infin* de + *infin*); **to have a** — **to something** tener derecho a algo; **to have the** — **to** + *infin* tener el derecho de + *infin*; **you had no** — **to** + *infin* no le correspondía a Vd + *infin*; **to own something in one's own** — poseer algo por derecho propio.

(c) (*of authorship etc*) derechos *mpl*; propiedad *f*; **film** —**s** derechos *mpl* cinematográficos; "**all** —**s reserved**" "es propiedad", "reservados todos los derechos".

(d) —**s**: **I don't know the** —**s of the matter** no sé quién tiene razón en el asunto; **to set something to** —**s** arreglar algo; componer algo.

(e) (*not left*) derecha *f* (*also Pol*); (*blow*) derechazo *m*; **on the** —, **to the** — a la derecha; **to keep to the** — (*Aut*) circular por la derecha; **reading from** — **to left** leyendo de derecha a izquierda; **he is of the** — es de derechas; **he's further to the** — **than I am** él es más derechista que yo.

4 *vt* (*set upright etc*) enderezar; (*correct*) corregir, rectificar; **to** — **a wrong** deshacer un agravio, acabar con un abuso.

right angle ['rait‚æŋgl] *n* ángulo *m* recto.

right-angled ['rait‚æŋgld] *adj* rectangular; *triangle* rectángulo; *bend etc* en ángulo recto.

righteous ['raitʃəs] *adj* justo, honrado, recto; *indignation etc* virtuoso, justificado.

righteously ['raitʃəsli] *adv* honradamente, rectamente; virtuosamente; con justicia.

righteousness ['raitʃəsnis] *n* honradez *f*, rectitud *f*; virtud *f*; justicia *f*.

rightful ['raitful] *adj* legítimo; verdadero.

rightfully ['raitfəli] *adv* legítimamente; verdaderamente.

right-hand ['raithænd] *adj*: — **drive** conducción *f* por la derecha; — **man** brazo *m* derecho, hombre *m* de confianza; — **side** derecha *f*; — **turn** vuelta *f* a la derecha.

right-handed ['rait'hændid] *adj* que usa la mano derecha; *tool* para persona que usa la mano derecha.

rightist ['raitist] **1** *adj* derechista. **2** *n* derechista *mf*.

rightly ['raitli] *adv* correctamente; debidamente; bien; — **or wrongly** mal que bien; **and** — **so** y con razón, a justo título; **to act** — obrar correctamente, obrar bien; **as he** — **believed** según creía correctamente; **he was** — **dismissed** con toda corrección le despidieron.

right-minded ['rait'maindid] *adj* (*sensible*) prudente; (*decent*) honrado.

rightness ['raitnis] *n* (*correctness*) exactitud *f*; (*justice*) justicia *f*.

right-thinking ['rait'θiŋkiŋ] *adj* juicioso, sensato.

right-wing ['rait'wiŋ] *adj* derechista.

right-winger ['rait'wiŋə*] *n* derechista *mf*.

rigid ['ridʒid] *adj* rígido; yerto; (*in attitude*) inflexible, severo; **he is quite** — **about it** es inflexible sobre ese punto; **we were** — **with fear** quedamos helados de miedo; **to shake someone** — sorprender muchísimo a uno, sobresaltar a uno.

rigidity [ri'dʒiditi] *n* rigidez *f*; inflexibilidad *f*, severidad *f*.

rigidly ['ridʒidli] *adv* rígidamente; inflexiblemente, severamente; **he is** — **opposed to it** está totalmente en contra de esto.

rigmarole ['rigmərəul] *n* galimatías *m*, relación *f* disparatada.

rigor mortis ['rigə'mɔːtis] *n* rigidez *f* cadavérica.

rigorous ['rigərəs] *adj* riguroso.

rigorously ['rigərəsli] *adv* rigurosamente.

rigour, (*US*) **rigor** ['rigə*] *n* rigor *m*, severidad *f*; **the full** — **of the law** el máximo rigor de la ley; **the** —**s of the climate** los rigores del clima.

rig-out ['rigaut] *n* (*fam*) atuendo *m*.

rile [rail] *vt* (*fam*) sulfurar, reventar, sacar de quicio a; **it** —**s me terribly** me irrita muchísimo; **there's nothing that** —**s me more** no hay nada que me reviente más.

rill [ril] *n* arroyo *m*, riachuelo *m*.

rim [rim] *n* (*of cup etc*) borde *m*, canto *m*; (*of wheel*) llanta *f*, (*of car wheel*) aro *m*; (*of spectacles*) aro *m*; **the** — **of the sun** el borde del sol.

rime[1] [raim] *n* (*poet*) rima *f*.

rime[2] [raim] *n* (*frost*) escarcha *f*.

rimless ['rimlis] *adj glasses* sin aros.

rimmed [rimd] *adj*: — **with . . .** con un borde de . . ., bordeado de . . .; **glasses** — **with gold** gafas *fpl* con aros de oro.

rind [raind] *n* (*of fruit etc*) corteza *f*, cáscara *f*, piel *f*; (*of cheese*) costra *f*; (*of bacon*) piel *f*.

ring[1] [riŋ] **1** *n* **(a)** (*circle: of metal etc*) aro *m*; argolla *f*; (*on finger*) anillo *m*, sortija *f*; (*on bird's leg, for curtain*) anilla *f*; (*ear*—) arete *m*; —**s** (*Gymnastics*) anillas *fpl*; — **of smoke** anillo *m* de humo, (*from mouth*) bocanada *f* de humo; —**s of Saturn** anillos *mpl* de Saturno; **annual** — (*Bot*) cerco *m*; **to have** —**s round one's eyes** tener ojeras.

(b) (*of people*) círculo *m*, grupo *m*; (*of children, gossips etc*) corro *m*; (*coterie*) camarilla *f*; (*gang*) pandilla *f*; (*Comm*) confabulación *f*, (*on large scale*) cartel *m*; **there was a** — **of children round her** los niños estaban reunidos en torno suyo, ella estaba rodeada de niños; **they were sitting in a** — estaban sentados en círculo; **to make** (*or* **run**) —**s round someone** vencer fácilmente a uno.

(c) (*arena etc: Boxing*) cuadrilátero *m*; (*at circus*) pista *f*; (*bull*—) ruedo *m*, redondel *m*, plaza *f*; (*at horse race*) cercado *m*; **the** — (*fig*) el boxeo.

2 *vt* cercar, rodear (*by, with* de); *bird* anillar, poner anilla a; **the town is** —**ed by hills** la ciudad está rodeada de colinas; **we are** —**ed by enemies** estamos rodeados de enemigos, nos cercan los enemigos.

ring[2] [riŋ] **1** *n* **(a)** (*metallic sound*) sonido *m* metálico; (*resonance*) resonancia *f*; (*tinkle*) retintín *m*; (*of voice*) timbre *m*; (*tone*) tono *m*, entonación *f*; (*of large bell*) repique *m*, tañido *m*; (*of handbell*) campanilleo *m*; (*of electric bell*) toque *m* de timbre; (*at door*) llamada *f*; **there was a** — **at the door** llamaron a la puerta; **with a** — **of defiance** en son de reto; **with a sarcastic** — **in his voice** con retintín, con énfasis sarcástico; **that has the** — **of truth about it** eso tiene traza de ser verdad.

(b) (*set*) **a** — **of bells** un juego de campanas.

(c) (*Tel*) llamada *f* telefónica, telefonazo *m*; **I'll give you a** — te llamaré por teléfono.

2 (*irr: pret* **rang**, *ptp* **rung**) *vt* **(a)** (*strike, make sound*) hacer sonar; *large bell* repicar, tañer; *electric bell* tocar; — **the bell, please** por favor toque el timbre.

(b) (*Tel*) **to** — **someone** (**up**) llamar a uno al (*or* por) teléfono, telefonear a uno.

(c) **to** — **down the curtain** bajar el telón; **to** — **up the curtain** levantar el telón; **to** — **up the curtain on something** (*fig*) dar comienzo a algo; **to** — **out the old year** tañer las campanas para señalar el fin del año.

3 *vi* (*sound*) sonar; resonar (*with* con); *large bell* repicar; (*small bell*) sonar; (*tinkle*) campanillear, tintinear; (*at door*) llamar; (*ears*) zumbar; **the telephone rang** sonó el teléfono; **the valley rang with cries** resonaron los gritos por el valle; **you rang, madam?** ¿me llama Vd, señora?; **we'll** — **for some sugar** llamaremos para pedir azúcar; **to** — **off** (*Tel*) colgar; **a cry rang out** se oyó un grito; **a shot rang out** se oyó un tiro; **to** — **up** (*Tel*) llamar (al teléfono).

ring-a-ring-a-roses ['riŋə'riŋə'rəuziz] *n* corro *m*; **to play** — jugar al corro.

ring binder ['riŋbaində*] *n* carpeta *f* de anillos.

ringbolt ['riŋbəult] *n* perno *m* con anillo, (*Naut*) cáncamo *m*.

ringdove ['riŋdʌv] *n* paloma *f* torcaz.

ringer ['riŋə*] *n* campanero *m*.

ringing ['riŋiŋ] **1** *adj* resonante, sonoro; **in** — **tones** en tono vibrante, en tono enérgico.

2 *n* (*of large bell*) repique *m*, tañido *m*; (*of handbell*) campanilleo *m*; (*of electric bell*) toque *m* de timbre; (*in ears*) zumbido *m*.

ringleader ['riŋ‚liːdə*] *n* cabecilla *m*.

ringlet ['riŋlit] *n* rizo *m*, bucle *m*, tirabuzón *m*.

ringmaster ['riŋ,mɑːstə*] n director m de circo; (trainer) domador m.

ring road ['riŋ'rəud] n carretera f de circunvalación, carretera f perimetral.

ringside ['riŋsaid] n: **to be at the** — estar junto al cuadrilátero; **a** — **seat** una butaca de primera fila (en el boxeo); **to have a** — **seat** (fig) verlo todo desde muy cerca.

ring spanner ['riŋ,spænə*] n llave f dentada.

ringworm ['riŋwəːm] n tiña f.

rink [riŋk] n pista f.

rinse [rins] 1 n (of dishes etc) enjuague m; (of clothes) aclarado m; (hair-colouring) reflejo m; **to give one's stockings a** — aclarar las medias; **to give one's hair a blue** — dar reflejos azules a su pelo.
2 vt enjuagar; aclarar; dar reflejos a.

riot ['raiət] 1 n motín m, disturbio m; tumulto m; (fig) orgía f; **the** —**s in Harlem** los disturbios de Harlem; **it was a** — **of colour** había una exhibición brillante de colores; **there was nearly a** — hubo casi un motín; **it was a** —! (fig) ¡fue divertidísimo!, ¡fue la monda!; **to read the** — **act** mandar que cese el disturbio, imponer la paz; **to read the** — **act to someone** reprender severamente a uno; **to run** — desmandarse, cometer excesos, librarse de toda traba; (spread) extenderse por todas partes, cubrirlo todo; **to let one's imagination run** — dejar volar la imaginación.
2 vi amotinarse.

rioter ['raiətə*] n amotinado m, a f, manifestante mf, revoltoso m.

riotous ['raiətəs] adj person, populace amotinado; assembly desordenado, alborotado; party bullicioso, ruidoso; life desenfrenado; **it was a** — **success** obtuvo un tremendo éxito; **we had a** — **time** nos divertimos una barbaridad.

riotously ['raiətəsli] adv con desorden, alborotadamente; bulliciosamente, ruidosamente; desenfrenadamente; **a** — **funny play** una comedia tremendamente divertida.

rip¹ [rip] n calavera m; (young rascal) tunante m; **you young** —! ¡tunante!; **he's a bit of a** — es algo cascabelero.

rip² [rip] 1 n rasgón m, rasgadura f.
2 vt rasgar, desgarrar; **to** — **off** arrancar, quitar (de un tirón); **to** — **a box open** abrir una caja rompiéndola, quitar violentamente la tapa de una caja; **to** — **an envelope open** abrir un sobre rompiéndolo; **to** — **out** arrancar; **to** — **up** (tear) desgarrar, romper; **the train** —**ped up 100 metres of track** el tren destrozó 100 metros de la vía.
3 vi (fig) **to** — **along** correr rápidamente, ir a buen tren; **let her** —! ¡más rápido!, ¡acelera!

riparian [rai'pɛəriən] adj ribereño.

ripcord ['ripkɔːd] n (Aer) cabo m de desgarre.

ripe [raip] adj (a) fruit etc maduro; **to be** — **for picking** estar bastante maduro para poderse coger; **to grow** — madurar.
(b) (fig) listo; perfecto, en su punto; **a plan** — **for execution** un plan listo para ponerse en obra; **to be** — **for mischief** estar dispuesto a emprender cualquier diablura; **that's pretty** —! ¡eso no se puede consentir!; **to live to a** — **old age** llegar a muy viejo; **when the time is** — cuando se nos depare la oportunidad, cuando llegue el momento propicio.

ripen ['raipən] vti madurar.

ripeness ['raipnis] n madurez f.

riposte [ri'pɔst] 1 n (Fencing) estocada f; (reply) respuesta f aguda, réplica f. 2 vi replicar, responder con viveza.

ripper ['ripə*] n: **Jack the R**— Juanito el Destripador.

ripping ['ripiŋ] adj (fam) estupendo, bárbaro.

ripple ['ripl] 1 n (wave) rizo m, onda f; (sound) murmullo m; **a** — **of excitement** un susurro de emoción; **a** — **of applause** unos cuantos aplausos.
2 vt rizar.
3 vi rizarse; correr con rizos; murmurar; **the crowd** —**d with excitement** el público se estremeció emocionado.

rip-roaring ['rip,rɔːriŋ] adj party etc bullicioso, animadísimo, de lo más ruidoso; speech apasionado, violento; success apoteósico.

rise [raiz] 1 n (a) (act of rising) subida f, ascensión f, elevación f; (of sun, moon) salida f; (of river) crecida f; **a** — **in the voice** una elevación de tono; — **and fall** (of water etc) subida f y bajada; (of music, voice) cadencia f.
(b) (act of rising, fig) **the** — **of the middle class** el desarrollo de la clase media; **the** — **of Bristol** el crecimiento de Bristol; **Napoleon's** — **to power** la subida de Napoleón al poder; **the** — **and fall**

of the Roman Empire la grandeza y decadencia del imperio romano; **to take a** — **out of someone** burlarse de uno; poner a uno en ridículo; **nobody takes a** — **out of me** a mí nadie me tose.
(c) (in price, temperature) subida f, alza f; (in value) aumento m; (in salary) aumento m, subida f; (promotion) ascenso m; **to ask for a** — pedir un aumento de sueldo; **they got a** — **of 50 pesetas** les aumentaron el sueldo en 50 pesetas; **a** — **of 5 degrees in temperature** una subida de temperatura de 5 grados.
(d) (of spring, river) nacimiento m; (fig) origen m; **the river takes its** — **in the mountains** el río nace en las montañas; **to give** — **to** dar origen a, motivar, ocasionar, (doubts etc) suscitar, dar lugar a.
(e) (high ground) altura f, eminencia f; (slope) cuesta f, pendiente f.
2 (irr: pret **rose**, ptp **risen**) vi (a) (of person: to one's feet etc) levantarse, ponerse en pie; **he rose to greet us** se levantó para recibirnos; **to** — **from table** levantarse de la mesa; **to** — **at 6** levantarse a las 6; **to** — **early** levantarse temprano, madrugar; **to** — **(again) from the dead** resucitar; **France shall** — **again** Francia renacerá; **when the House** —**s** cuando se suspenda la sesión.
(b) **to** — **(in revolt)** sublevarse, rebelarse (against contra); **to** — **(up) in arms** alzarse en armas.
(c) (of sun, moon) salir; (smoke etc) subir, elevarse, alzarse; (building, mountain) elevarse; **it rose 3 metres off the ground** se elevó 3 metros sobre el suelo; **the mountain** —**s to 3,500 metres** la montaña alcanza 3.500 metros, la montaña se eleva a 3.500 metros; **to** — **to the surface** salir a la superficie; **the partridge rose** se levantó la perdiz, la perdiz alzó el vuelo; **to** — (of fish) picar; **to** — **to the bait** picar, morder el anzuelo (also fig); **he wouldn't** — **(to the bait)** no quería picar.
(d) (of ground) subir (en pendiente); (dough) leudarse; (of barometer, temperature, sea etc) subir; (of river) crecer; (of wind) hacerse más fuerte, soplar más fuerte; (swell) hincharse, crecer; (of price) subir, avanzar; (Stock Exchange) estar en alza, cotizarse en alza; (of number) subir, aumentar; **prices are rising** suben los precios; **it has risen 20% in price** su precio ha subido en un 20 por cien; **a thought rose in my mind** se me ocurrió algo; **our spirits rose** volvimos a animarnos, nos reanimamos.
(e) **to** — **above petty rancour** mostrarse superior a los pequeños rencores; **to** — **to the occasion** ponerse a la altura de las circunstancias.
(f) (in rank) ascender, avanzar; **he rose to colonel** ascendió a coronel; **he rose from nothing** salió de la nada; **to** — **in the world** hacer carrera, avanzar en su carrera; **to** — **in someone's ópinion** ganar en la opinión de uno.
(g) (river) nacer.

risen ['rizn] ptp of **rise**.

riser ['raizə*] n: **to be an early** — madrugar, ser madrugador; **to be a late** — levantarse tarde.

risibility [,rizi'biliti] n risibilidad f.

risible ['rizibl] adj risible.

rising ['raiziŋ] 1 adj number, quantity creciente; tide creciente; sun etc naciente; ground en pendiente, que sube; generation nuevo; (promising) prometedor, que promete, de porvenir; **the** — **numbers of murders** el creciente número de homicidios; **with** — **alarm** con creciente alarma.
2 n (rebellion) sublevación f, rebelión f; (of river) nacimiento m; (of sun etc) salida f; **on the** — **of the House** al suspenderse la sesión.

risk [risk] 1 n riesgo m, peligro m; **occupational** —**s** gajes mpl del oficio; **security** — (person) persona f de dudosa lealtad, persona f no enteramente confiable (desde el punto de vista de la seguridad nacional etc); **at the** — **of a riesgo de**; **at the** — **of one's life** con peligro de la vida, arriesgando la vida; **at one's own** — bajo su propia responsabilidad; **at owner's** — bajo la responsabilidad del dueño; **there is a fire** — hay peligro de provocar un incendio; **it's not worth the** — no vale la pena correr tanto peligro; **to run the** — **of defeat** correr riesgo de ser derrotado; **to run the** — **of + ger** correr el riesgo de + infin; **to take** —**s** arriesgarse; **he takes a lot of** —**s** se arriesga mucho; **will you take the** —? ¿te atreves?; **I can't take the** — no me puedo exponer a eso.
2 vt arriesgar; atreverse a, exponerse a; **I'll** — **it** acepto; **I can't** — **it** no me puedo exponer a eso; **shall we** — **it?** ¿nos atrevemos?; **to** — **defeat** correr riesgo de ser derrotado, exponerse a una posible derrota; **to** — **+ ger** arriesgarse a + infin;

I can't — **going alone** no puedo arriesgarme a ir solo, no me atrevo a ir solo.

riskiness ['riskinis] n peligro m, lo peligroso, lo arriesgado; **in view of the — of the plan** visto lo peligroso del plan.

risky ['riski] adj **(a)** peligroso, arriesgado, aventurado; **a — enterprise** una empresa arriesgada; **it is — to suppose that** ... es arriesgado suponer que ... **(b) =risqué**.

risqué ['ri:skei] adj verde, indecente, escabroso.

rissole ['risəul] n (approx) croqueta f, albóndiga f.

rite [rait] n rito m; **funeral —s, last —s** exequias fpl; **"The R— of Spring"** (Mus) "La Consagración de la Primavera".

ritual ['ritjuəl] **1** adj ritual; (fig) consagrado; **in the — phrase** en la expresión consagrada. **2** n ritual m, ceremonia f.

ritualism ['ritjuəlizəm] n ritualismo m.

ritualist ['ritjuəlist] n ritualista mf.

ritualistic [,ritjuə'listik] adj ritualista; (fig) consagrado, sacramental.

ritzy ['ritsi] adj (US sl) muy pera, lujoso.

rival ['raivəl] **1** adj rival, opuesto; **a — firm** una firma competidora. **2** n rival mf, competidor m, ora f. **3** vt rivalizar con, competir con.

rivalry ['raivəlri] n rivalidad f; competencia f; **to enter into — with someone** empezar a competir con uno.

riven ['rivən] adj rajado, hendido.

river ['rivə*] **1** n río m; **down —** río abajo; **up —** río arriba; **up — from Toledo** aguas arriba de Toledo. **2** attr de río, del río; fluvial; **— fish** pez m de río; **— police** brigada f fluvial.

riverbank ['rivəbæŋk] n orilla f del río, margen f del río.

riverbasin ['rivə,beisn] n cuenca f de río.

riverbed ['rivəbed] n lecho m, cauce m (del río).

rivermouth ['rivəmauθ] n, pl **—mouths** [mauðz] estuario m, ría f.

riverside ['rivəsaid] **1** n ribera f, orilla f (del río). **2** attr ribereño.

rivet ['rivit] **1** n roblón m, remache m. **2** vt remachar; (fig) clavar (on, to en); **to — one's eyes on something** clavar la vista en algo; **it —ed our attention** nos llamó fuertemente la atención.

riveter ['rivitə*] n remachador m.

Riviera [,rivi'eərə] Costa f Azul.

rivulet ['rivjulit] n riachuelo m, arroyuelo m.

roach [rəutʃ] n (Fish) escarcho m; (US) cucaracha f.

road [rəud] **1** n camino m (to de; also fig); (main —) carretera f; (in town) calle f; **—s** (Naut) rada f; **"— up"** "cerrado por obras"; **the — to Teruel** el camino de Teruel; **at the 23rd kilometre on the Valencia —** en el kilómetro 23 de la carretera de Valencia; **the — to success** el camino del éxito; **arterial —, trunk —** carretera f principal, autopista f; **country —** camino m vecinal; **main — carretera** f; **across the —** al otro lado de la calle, enfrente; **she lives across the — from us** vive en frente de nosotros; **by —** por carretera; **to be on the —** estar en camino; (Comm) ser viajante; **to be on the right —** ir por buen camino (also fig); **to get out of the —** (fig) quitarse de en medio; **to hold the —** (Aut) agarrarse al camino; **to take the —** ponerse en camino (to X para ir a X). **2** attr: **— accident** accidente m de carreteras; **— construction** construcción f de carreteras; **— traffic** tránsito m rodado; **— transport** transportes mpl por carretera; **— vehicle** vehículo m carretero.

roadbed ['rəudbed] n (US) firme m; (Rail) capa f de balasto.

roadblock ['rəudblɔk] n barricada f.

road book ['rəudbuk] n (Aut) libro m de mapas e itinerarios (etc).

roadbridge ['rəudbridʒ] n puente m de carretera.

roadhog ['rəudhɔg] n conductor m poco considerado, criminal m de carretera.

roadhouse ['rəudhaus] n, pl **—houses** [hauziz] albergue m de carretera.

roadmaking ['rəud,meikiŋ] n construcción f de carreteras.

roadman ['rəudmæn] n, pl **—men** [men], **road-mender** ['rəud,mendə*] n peón m caminero.

roadmap ['rəudmæp] n mapa m de carreteras.

road metal ['rəudmetl] n grava f.

roadrace ['rəudreis] n carrera f sobre carretera.

roadroller ['rəud,rəulə*] n apisonadora f.

roadsense ['rəudsens] n instinto m del automovilista.

roadside ['rəudsaid] **1** n borde m del camino, borde m de la carretera. **2** attr de camino, de carretera.

roadsign ['rəudsain] n señal f de carretera, indicador m.

roadstead ['rəudsted] n (Naut) rada f.

roadster ['rəudstə*] n (car) coche m de turismo; (cycle) bicicleta f de turismo.

roadsweeper ['rəud,swi:pə*] n barrendero m.

roadtrial ['rəudtraiəl] n prueba f por carretera.

roaduser ['rəud,ju:zə*] n usuario m de la vía pública.

roadway ['rəudwei] n calzada f.

roam [rəum] **1** vt vagar por, errar por, recorrer. **2** vi vagar; **to — about** andar sin propósito fijo.

roamer ['rəumə*] n hombre m errante, andariego m; (tramp) vagabundo m.

roaming ['rəumiŋ] n vagabundeo m; (as tourist etc) excursiones fpl, paseos mpl.

roan [rəun] **1** adj ruano. **2** n caballo m ruano.

roar [rɔ:*] **1** n (of animal) rugido m, bramido m; (of person) rugido m; (loud noise) estruendo m, fragor m; (of fire) crepitación f; (of river, storm etc) estruendo m; (of laughter) carcajada f; **with great —s of laughter** con grandes carcajadas; **he said with a —** dijo rugiendo; **to set the room in a —** hacer reír a todo el mundo a carcajadas. **2** vt rugir, decir a gritos; **to — one's disapproval** manifestar su disconformidad a gritos; **he —ed out an order** lanzó una orden a voz en grito. **3** vi rugir, bramar; hacer estruendo; (of guns, thunder) retumbar; (with laughter) reírse a carcajadas; **to — with pain** rugir de dolor; **the lorry —ed past** el camión pasó ruidosamente; **this will make you —** esto os hará moriros de risa. **4** vr: **to — oneself hoarse** ponerse ronco gritando.

roaring ['rɔ:riŋ] adj: **in front of a — fire** junto a la lumbre que arde furiosamente; **it was a — success** fue un tremendo éxito; **to do a — trade** hacer un buen negocio.

roast [rəust] **1** n carne f asada, asado m. **2** adj asado; **coffee** tostado. **3** vt **meat** asar; **coffee** tostar; **the sun which was —ing the city** el sol que achicharraba la ciudad; **to — one's feet by the fire** calentarse los pies junto al fuego; **to — someone** (mock) mofarse de uno, (scold) desollar vivo a uno. **4** vi asarse; tostarse; **we —ed there for a whole month** nos asamos allí durante un mes entero.

roaster ['rəustə*] n (implement) asador m; (bird) pollo m para asar.

roasting jack ['rəustiŋdʒæk] n, **roasting spit** ['rəustiŋspit] n asador m.

rob [rɔb] vt robar; **to — someone of something** robar algo a uno; **I've been —bed!** ¡me han robado!

robber ['rɔbə*] n ladrón m; (footpad) salteador m (de caminos); (brigand) bandido m.

robbery ['rɔbəri] n robo m; **— with violence** robo m a mano armada; **highway —** salteamiento m; **it's daylight —!** ¡es un robo descarado!

robe [rəub] **1** n (arch) manto m, túnica f; (monk's) hábito m; (priest's) sotana f; (lawyer's, Univ) toga f, traje m talar; (bath—) albornoz m; (christening —) mantillas fpl; **—s** traje m de ceremonia, traje m talar. **2** vt: **to — someone in something** vestir a uno de algo; **to appear —d in something** aparecer vestido de algo. **3** vi and vr: **to — oneself** vestirse.

Robert ['rɔbət] m Roberto.

robin[1] ['rɔbin] n (Orn) petirrojo m.

robin[2] ['rɔbin] n: **round —** petición f (or protesta f) firmada en rueda.

robot ['rəubɔt] n robot m, autómata m.

robust [rəu'bʌst] adj robusto; fuerte, vigoroso; **a — defence** una defensa vigorosa, una defensa enérgica; **a — sense of humour** un fuerte sentido del humor.

robustness [rəu'bʌstnis] n robustez f; fuerza f, vigor m, energía f.

rock[1] [rɔk] n roca f; (standing stone, —face) peña f, peñasco m; (Naut) escollo m; (sl) diamante m; **the R— (of Gibraltar)** el Peñón (de Gibraltar); **whisky on the —s** (fam) whisky m con cubitos de hielo; **to be on the —s** (broke) no tener un céntimo; **their marriage is on the —s** su matrimonio corre riesgo de fracasar; **to run on to the —s** (Naut) dar en un escollo, (fig) peligrar, estar en peligro.

rock[2] [rɔk] **1** vt (gently) mecer, balancear; (violently) sacudir; **to — a child to sleep** arrullar a un niño, adormecer a un niño meciéndole en la cuna (etc). **2** vi mecerse, balancearse; sacudirse; **the ship —ed gently on the waves** el buque se balanceaba en las olas; **the train —ed violently** el tren se sacudió violentamente; **we just —ed (with laughter)** nos morimos de risa; **the theatre —ed with laughter** las risas estremecieron el teatro.

rock-bottom ['rɔk'bɔtəm] **1** n fondo m, parte f más profunda; (fig) punto m más bajo; **prices are at —** los precios están por los suelos; **to reach** (or **touch) —** (fig) llegar a su punto más bajo.
2 attr price más bajo, mínimo.
rock carving ['rɔk,kɑːviŋ] n grabado m rupestre.
rock climber ['rɔk,klaimə*] n escalador m (de rocas).
rock climbing ['rɔk,klaimiŋ] n escalada f en rocas.
rock crystal ['rɔk,kristl] n cristal m de roca, cuarzo m.
rocker ['rɔkə*] n (Mech) balancín m, eje m de balancín; (sl) cabeza f; **he's off his —** (sl) le falta un tornillo; **you must be off your —!** (sl) ¡estás majareta! (sl).
rockery ['rɔkəri] n jardincito m rocoso, cuadro m alpino.
rocket[1] ['rɔkit] n (Bot) oruga f.
rocket[2] ['rɔkit] **1** n (a) cohete m; **distress —** cohete m de señales; **homing —** cohete m autodirigido buscador del blanco; **space —** cohete m espacial.
    (b) (sl) peluca f (fam); **to get a — from someone** recibir una peluca de uno; **to give someone a —** echar un rapapolvo a uno (for something por motivo de algo).
    2 vi: **to — upwards** subir como un cohete; **to — to the moon** ir en cohete a la luna; **to — to fame** hacerse famoso de la noche a la mañana, llegar repentinamente a ser conocidísimo; **prices have —ed** los precios se han puesto por las nubes.
rocket launcher ['rɔkit,lɔːntʃə*] n lanzacohetes m.
rocket plane ['rɔkitplein] n avión m cohete.
rocket-propelled ['rɔkitprə,peld] adj propulsado por cohete(s).
rocket propulsion ['rɔkitprə,pʌlʃən] n propulsión f a cohete.
rocketry ['rɔkitri] n cohetería f.
rocket ship ['rɔkitʃip] n aeronave f cohete.
rock face ['rɔkfeis] n pared f de roca.
rock fall ['rɔkfɔːl] n deslizamiento m de montaña.
rock garden ['rɔk,gɑːdn] n jardincito m rocoso, cuadro m alpino.
rocking chair ['rɔkintʃeə*] n mecedora f.
rocking horse ['rɔkiŋhɔːs] n caballo m de balancín.
rock painting ['rɔk,peintiŋ] n pintura f rupestre.
rock plant ['rɔkplɑːnt] n planta f alpestre.
rock rose ['rɔkrəuz] n heliantemo m.
rock salt ['rɔksɔːlt] n sal f gema.
rocky[1] ['rɔki] adj (of substance or roca, parecido a roca; slope etc rocoso; fragoso, escabroso.
rocky[2] ['rɔki] adj que se bambolea, inestable; government etc débil, flojo, nada firme.
Rocky Mountains ['rɔki'mauntinz] pl Montañas fpl Rocosas.
rococo [rəu'kəukəu] **1** adj rococó. **2** n rococó m.
rod [rɔd] n (Mech etc) vara f, varilla, f, barra f; (stick, of authority) vara f; (fishing —) caña f; (Surveying) jalón m; (curtain —) barra f; (connecting —) biela f; (measure) medida de longitud = 5,029 metros; (US sl) revólver m, pistola f; **to have a — in pickle for someone** tener en reserva un medio de ajustar cuentas con uno; **to make a — for one's own back** hacer algo que después resultará contraproducente; **to rule with a — of iron** gobernar con mano de hierro, ser un gobernador muy severo; **to spare the —** excusar la vara; **this is to spare the — and spoil the child** esto es excusar el castigo cuando conviene darlo.
rode [rəud] pret of **ride.**
rodent ['rəudənt] n roedor m.
rodeo ['rəudiəu] n (US) rodeo m.
Roderick ['rɔdərik] m Rodrigo; **—, the last of the Goths** Rodrigo el último godo.
rodomontade [,rɔdəmɔn'teid] n fanfarronada f.
roe[1] [rəu] n (Zool) corzo m, a f.
roe[2] [rəu] n (Fish): **hard —** hueva f; **soft —** lecha f.
roebuck ['rəubʌk] n corzo m.
roe deer ['rəudiə*] n corzo m, a f.
rogations [rəu'geiʃənz] npl (Eccl) rogativas fpl.
Roger ['rɔdʒə*] m Rogelio; **Jolly R—** pabellón m negro de los piratas.
rogue [rəug] n pícaro m, pillo m; (hum) picaruelo m; **you —!** ¡canalla!; **—s' gallery** fichero m de delincuentes.
roguery ['rəugəri] n picardía f, truhanería f; (mischief) travesuras fpl, diabluras fpl; **they're up to some —** están haciendo alguna diablura.
roguish ['rəugiʃ] adj picaresco; (mischievous) travieso; look, smile etc picaruelo, malicioso.
roguishly ['rəugiʃli] adv look, smile etc con malicia; **she looked at me —** me miró picaruela.
roil [rɔil] vt (US) = **rile.**
roister ['rɔistə*] vi jaranear.

roisterer ['rɔistərə*] n jaranero m.
Roland ['rəulənd] m Roldán, Rolando.
role [rəul] n (Theat and fig) papel m; **leading —** papel m principal; **supporting —** papel m secundario; **to play** (or **take) a —** (Theat) hacer un papel, (fig) desempeñar un papel.
roll [rəul] **1** n (a) (of paper, tobacco, film etc) rollo m; (of cloth) pieza f; (of fat on body) rodete m; (of banknotes: US) fajo m; (of bread) panecillo m, (breakfast —) suizo m.
    (b) (list) lista f; rol m, nómina f; **—s** (Hist) archivos mpl; **— of honour** lista f de honor; **electoral —** censo m, lista f electoral; **to call the —** pasar lista; **to have 500 pupils on —** tener inscritos 500 alumnos; **to strike someone off the —** tachar a uno de la lista.
    (c) (sound: of thunder) retumbo m; (of drum) redoble m.
    (d) (of gait) bamboleo m; (of ship) balanceo m; **to walk with a —** andar bamboleándose; **the ship gave a sudden —** el buque se balanceó de repente.
    2 vt vehicle, furniture etc hacer rodar; (move) mover; (push) empujar; soil allanar; lawn, pitch apisonar; pastry aplanar; metal laminar; cigarette liar, hacer; tongue vibrar; **to — letter R** pronunciar con énfasis, exagerar; **to — a car to the side of the road** empujar un coche al borde de la carretera; **to — a ball along the pavement** hacer rodar una pelota sobre la acera; **to — a stone downhill** hacer rodar una piedra cuesta abajo; **to — a stone over** remover una piedra, volver una piedra; **to — up** map, umbrella arrollar, enrollar; sleeves arremangar; **to — something up in paper** envolver algo en papel; **he was —ed up in the blankets** estaba envuelto en las mantas.
    3 vi (a) (go —ing) rodar, ir rodando, dar vueltas; (on ground, in pain etc) revolcarse; (land) ondular; **it —ed under the chair** desapareció debajo de la silla; **it went —ing downhill** fue rodando cuesta abajo; **to be —ing in plenty** nadar en la abundancia; **they're —ing in money**, **they're —ing in it** nadan en oro.
    (b) (sound: thunder) retumbar; (drum) redoblar; (organ) sonar.
    (c) (in walking) bambolearse; (Naut) balancearse; **he —ed from side to side as he walked** iba bamboleándose de un lado para otro.
    (d) (with adv or prep) **to — by** (cart, time) pasar; **to — down** rodar por, bajar rodando por; **tears —ed down her cheeks** las lágrimas le corrieron por las mejillas; **the waves came —ing in** llegaban grandes olas a la playa; **the money is —ing in** nos entra el dinero a raudales; **to — on** (vehicle) seguir su marcha; (river) correr, seguir su curso; (offensive, time) avanzar; **to — over** dar una vuelta, volverse al otro lado; **to — up** (car etc) llegar; (person) aparecer, presentarse, llegar (como si tal cosa); (hedgehog) enroscarse, arrollarse, hacerse un ovillo.
    4 vr: **to — oneself up into a ball** arrollarse, hacerse un ovillo; **to — oneself up in a blanket** envolverse en una manta.
rollaway ['rəulwei] n (US) (also **— bed**) cama f desmontable, cama f abatible.
roll call ['rəulkɔːl] n lista f, acto m de pasar lista.
rolled [rəuld] adj umbrella etc arrollado; metal laminado; **— oats** copos mpl de avena.
roller ['rəulə*] n (Agr, Tech) rodillo m; (castor) rueda f; (steam —) apisonadora f; (Naut) ola f larga, ola f grande.
roller bandage ['rəulə'bændidʒ] n venda f enrollada.
roller coaster ['rəulə'kəustə*] n montaña f rusa.
roller skate ['rəulə,skeit] n patín m de ruedas.
roller-skating ['rəulə,skeitiŋ] n patinaje m de ruedas.
roller towel ['rəulə'tauəl] n toalla f de rodillo.
roll film ['rəulfilm] n película f en rollo.
rollick ['rɔlik] vi jugar, divertirse; jaranear.
rollicking ['rɔlikiŋ] adj alegre, divertido; **we had a — time** nos divertimos una barbaridad; **it was a — party** fue una fiesta animadísima; **it's — nonsense** son disparates de los más divertidos; **it's a — farce** es una farsa de lo más divertido.
rolling ['rəuliŋ] **1** adj rodante; countryside ondulado. **2** n (Naut) balanceo m.
rolling mill ['rəuliŋmil] n tren m de laminación.
rolling pin ['rəuliŋpin] n rodillo m (de cocina).
rolling stock ['rəuliŋstɔk] n material m rodante, material m móvil.
roll-on ['rəulɔn] **1** n faja f elástica, tubular m. **2** adj elástico.
roll-top ['rəultɔp] adj: **— desk** buró m, escritorio m de tapa rodadera.

roly-poly ['rəuli'pəuli] **1** *n pudín en forma de rollo.* **2** *adj* regordete.

Roman ['rəumən] **1** *adj* romano. **2** *n* romano *m*, a *f*; **r—** (*Typ*) tipo *m* romano.

romance [rəu'mæns] **1** *n* (a) (*tale*) novela *f* (sentimental), cuento *m* (de amor); (*medieval*) libro *m* de caballerías, poema *m* caballeresco; (*Mus*) romanza *f*.
(b) (*love affair*) amores *mpl*, amorío *m*, aventura *f* sentimental; **their — lasted exactly 6 months** sus amores duraron exactamente 6 meses; **a young girl waiting for —** una joven que espera su primer amor; **I've finished with —** para mí no más amores.
(c) (*romantic character*) lo romántico, lo pintoresco, lo poético; **the — of the sea** el encanto del mar; **the — of travel** lo romántico del viajar; **the — of history** lo atractivo de la historia, lo poético de la historia.
(d) (*language*) romance *m*.
2 *adj language* romance, románico, neolatino.
3 *vi* soñar, inventar fábulas; exagerar; fantasear.

Romanesque [ˌrəumə'nesk] *adj*, **Romanic** [rəu'mænik] *adj* románico.

romanize ['rəumənaiz] *vt* romanizar.

romantic [rəu'mæntik] **1** *adj* romántico. **2** *n* romántico *m*, a *f*.

romantically [rəu'mæntikəli] *adv* románticamente, de modo romántico.

romanticism [rəu'mæntisizəm] *n* romanticismo *m*.

romanticize [rəu'mæntisaiz] **1** *vt* hacer romántico; añadir detalles románticos (*or* ambiente romántico) a. **2** *vi* hablar (*or* escribir *etc*) de modo romántico; soñar, fantasear.

Romany ['rɔməni] **1** *adj* gitano. **2** *n* gitano *m*, a *f*. **3** *n* (*language*) lengua *f* gitana, (*in Spain*) caló *m*.

Rome [rəum] (a) Roma; **— was not built in a day** no se ganó Zamora en una hora, Roma no se construyó en su solo día; **all roads lead to —** por todas partes se va a Roma; **when in —, do as the Romans do** allí donde fueres, haz lo que vieres.
(b) (*Eccl*) la Iglesia, el catolicismo; **Manning turned to —** Manning se convirtió al catolicismo.

Romish ['rəumiʃ] *adj* (*pej*) católico.

romp [rɔmp] **1** *n* retozo *m*, juego *m*; **to have a —** **in the hay** retozar en el heno; **the play was just a —** la obra era una farsa alegre nada más.
2 *vi* retozar, jugar, divertirse; (*lambs etc*) brincar, correr alegremente; **the horse —ed home to win by 19 lengths** el caballo ganó fácilmente por 19 cuerpos; **she —ed through the examination** encontró que el examen era muy fácil.

rompers ['rɔmpəz] *npl* pelele *m*, mono *m*.

Romulus ['rɔmjuləs] *m* Rómulo.

rondeau ['rɔndəu] *n* rondó *m*.

rondo ['rɔndəu] *n* (*Mus*) rondó *m*.

rood [ru:d] *n* cruz *f*, crucifijo *m*.

rood screen ['ru:dskri:n] *n* pantalla *f* de separación rematada por un crucifijo.

roof [ru:f] **1** *n*, *pl* **roofs** [ru:fs *or* ru:vz] techo *m*, tejado *m*; (*of car etc*) baca *f*, (*of coach*) imperial *f*; (*of heaven*) bóveda *f* celeste; **— of the mouth** paladar *m*, cielo *m* de la boca; **flat —** azotea *f*; **sliding —**, **sunshine —** techo *m* corredizo, techo *m* de corredera; **tiled —** tejado *m*; **they haven't a — over their heads** no tienen casa; **to raise the —** (*protest*) poner el grito en el cielo; (*sing etc*) cantar (*etc*) bastante fuerte como para hacer venir el techo abajo.
2 *vt* techar (*also* **to — in, to — over**), poner techo a; **it is —ed in wood** tiene techo de madera; **to — a hut in wood** (*or* **with wood**) poner techo de madera a una caseta.

roof garden ['ru:fˌgɑ:dn] *n* azotea *f* con flores y plantas.

roofing ['ru:fiŋ] **1** *n* techumbre *f*. **2** *attr* felt *etc* para techos.

rook[1] [ruk] **1** *n* (*Orn*) graja *f*.
2 *vt* engañar, estafar; **you've been —ed** te han cobrado demasiado, te han desollado; **they always — the customer in that shop** en esa tienda siempre le cobran un precio excesivo al cliente.

rook[2] [ruk] *n* (*Chess*) torre *f*.

rookery ['rukəri] *n* nidada *f* de grajas, colonia *f* de grajas.

rookie ['ruki] *n* (*Mil fam*) bisoño *m*.

room [rum] **1** *n* (a) (*in house*) cuarto *m*, habitación *f*; pieza *f*; (*large, public*) sala *f*; **—s** (*lodging*) alojamiento *m*, (*flat*) piso *m*; **double —** habitación *f* para dos personas; **single —** habitación *f* individual; **furnished —** cuarto *m* amueblado; **ladies' —** (*US: euph*) lavabo *m* de señoras; **men's —** (*US: euph*) lavabo *m* de caballeros; **in room 504** (*hotel*)

en la habitación número 504; **in the professor's —** en el cuarto del profesor; **he has —s in college** tiene un cuarto en el colegio; **they've always lived in —s** han vivido siempre en pisos alquilados.
(b) (*space*) sitio *m*, espacio *m*; cabida *f*; **is there —?** ¿hay sitio?; **is there — for this?** ¿cabe esto?; **there is no — for that** eso no cabe; **there's no — for anything else** no cabe más; **is there — for me?** ¿quepo yo?, ¿hay sitio para mí?; **there is plenty of —** queda mucho espacio libre; **there is still — on Tuesday** quedan todavía localidades para la función del martes; **to be cramped for —** tener poco espacio; **to make — for someone** hacer sitio para uno, hacer lugar; **make —!** ¡abran paso!
(c) (*fig*) **there is no — for doubt** no queda lugar a dudas; **there is — for improvement** esto se puede mejorar todavía; **to leave — for imponderables** dar cabida a un margen de imponderables.
2 *vi*: **to — with a landlady** alojarse en casa de una patrona; **to — with 3 other students** estar en una pensión con otros 3 estudiantes, compartir un piso con otros 3 estudiantes.

room divider ['rumdi'vaidə*] *n* biombo *m*; tabique *m*.

-roomed [rumd] *adj* de . . . piezas, *eg* **seven-roomed** de siete piezas.

roomer ['rumə*] *n* (*US*) (*subtenant*) subinquilino *m*, a *f*; (*lodger*) huésped *m*, a *f*.

roomful ['rumful] *n*: **a — of priests** un cuarto lleno de curas; **they have Picassos by the —** tienen salas enteras llenas de cuadros de Picasso.

roominess ['ruminis] *adj* espaciosidad *f*, amplitud *f*; holgura *f*.

rooming house ['ruminhaus] *n*, *pl* **— houses** [hauziz] (*US*) casa *f* donde se alquilan cuartos; pensión *f*.

roommate ['rummeit] *n* compañero *m* de cuarto, compañera *f* de cuarto.

room service ['rumˌsəːvis] *n* servicio *m* de restaurante en los cuartos de un hotel.

roomy ['rumi] *adj room* espacioso, amplio; *garment* holgado.

roost [ru:st] **1** *n* percha *f*; (*hen—*) gallinero *m*; **to rule the —** mandar.
2 *vi* dormir (*or* descansar) en una percha; (*fig*) pasar la noche; **the birds — in that tree** los pájaros pasan la noche en ese árbol; **now his policies have come home to —** ahora su política produce su fruto amargo, ahora se están viendo los malos resultados de su política.

rooster ['ru:stə*] *n* gallo *m*.

root [ru:t] **1** *n* raíz *f* (*also fig*); (*Gram*) radical *m*; **cube —** raíz *f* cúbica; **square —** raíz *f* cuadrada; **— and branch** completamente, del todo; **money is the — of all evil** el dinero es el origen de todos nuestros males; **the — of the problem is that . . .** lo fundamental del problema es que . . ., la esencia del problema es que . . .; **what lies at the — of his attitude?** ¿qué razón fundamental tiene su actitud?; **to put down one's —s in a country** radicarse en un país, establecerse de modo permanente en un país; **to strike** (*or* **take**) **—** echar raíces, arraigar; **to strike at the — of something** afectar la parte fundamental de algo, atacar la misma esencia de algo.
2 *adj*: **— idea** idea *f* fundamental, idea *f* esencial.
3 *vt* (a) (*plant*) hacer arraigar; **to — out** arrancar, desarraigar; (*fig*) desarraigar, extirpar; suprimir del todo.
(b) **to be —ed to the spot** quedar helado (de miedo *etc*), quedar inmovilizado, estar sin poderse mover; **it is firmly —ed in all minds that . . .** está grabado en la mente de todos que . . ., todos creen firmemente que . . .; **a —ed prejudice** un prejuicio muy arraigado.
4 *vi* (*Bot*) echar raíces, arraigar(se); **to — about** (*pig*) hozar, hocicar, (*fig*) andar buscando por todas partes (*for something algo*); **to — for** (*fig*) gritar por el éxito de; hacer propaganda por, apoyar a.

root beer ['ru:t'biə*] *n* (*US*) *bebida analcohólica hecha de extractos de diversas raíces.*

rootless ['ru:tlis] *adj person etc* desarraigado.

rootstock ['ru:tstɔk] *n* rizoma *m*.

root word ['ru:twəːd] *n* palabra *f* radical.

rope [rəup] **1** *n* cuerda *f*, soga *f*; (*Naut: hawser*) maroma *f*, cable *m*, (*in rigging*) cabo *m*; (*hangman's*) dogal *m*; (*of pearls*) collar *m*; (*of onions etc*) ristra *f*; **the —s** (*Boxing*) las cuerdas; **to give someone more —** dar a uno mayor libertad de acción; **if you give him enough — he'll hang himself** sin

ropemaker que tú hagas nada él se condenará a sí mismo; **to know the —s** conocer un negocio a fondo, saber cuántas son dos y dos; **there were 3 of us on the —** (*Mountaineering*) los tres estábamos encordados.
 2 *vt* (**a**) atar con una cuerda, amarrar con una cuerda; *animal* coger con lazo; **to — off a space** cercar un espacio con cuerdas; **to — two things together** atar dos cosas con una cuerda.
 (**b**) **to — someone in** persuadir a uno a tomar parte (*for something* en algo), entruchar a uno.
 3 *vr*: **they are roping themselves together** (*Mountaineering*) se están encordando; **there were 4 —d together** había 4 que iban encordados.
ropemaker ['rəupˌmeikə*] *n* cordelero *m*.
rope trick ['rəuptrik] *n* truco *m* de la cuerda.
ropewalk ['rəupwɔ:k] *n* (*Naut*) cordelería *f*.
ropy ['rəupi] *adj liquid* viscoso; (*fam*) deteriorado, desvencijado; inestable; *plan, argument etc* nada convincente, flojo.
rosary ['rəuzəri] *n* rosario *m*; **to say one's —** rezar el rosario.
Rose [rəuz] *f* Rosa.
rose[1] [rəuz] **1** *n* (*Bot*) rosa *f*; (*colour*) color *m* de rosa; (*of can*) roseta *f*; (*Archit*) rosetón *m*; **wild —** rosal *m* silvestre; **there's no — without a thorn** no hay rosa sin espina.
 2 *adj* color de rosa, rosado, rosáceo.
rose[2] [rəuz] *pret of* **rise**.
rosé ['rəuzei] **1** *adj* rosado. **2** *n* rosado *m*, clarete *m*.
roseate ['rəuziit] *adj* róseo, rosado.
rosebay ['rəuzbei] *n* adelfa *f*.
rosebed ['rəuzbed] *n* rosaleda *f*.
rosebud ['rəuzbʌd] *n* capullo *m* de rosa.
rosebush ['rəuzbuʃ] *n* rosal *m*.
rose-coloured, (*US*) **—-colored** ['rəuzˌkʌləd] *adj* color de rosa, rosado, rosáceo; **to see everything through — spectacles** verlo todo color de rosa.
rose garden ['rəuzˌgɑ:dn] *n* rosaleda *f*.
rose grower ['rəuzˌgrəuə*] *n* cultivador *m* de rosas, cultivadora *f* de rosas.
rose hip ['rəuzhip] *n* escaramujo *m*.
rosemary ['rəuzməri] *n* romero *m*.
Rosenkavalier ['rəuzənkævə'liə*] (*Mus*) el Caballero de la Rosa.
rose-red ['rəuz'red] *adj* color de rosa.
rose tree ['rəuztri:] *n* rosal *m*.
rosette [rəu'zet] *n* (*emblem, Archit*) rosetón *m*.
rose water ['rəuzˌwɔ:tə*] *n* agua *f* de rosas.
rose window ['rəuz'windəu] *n* rosetón *m*.
rosewood ['rəuzwud] *n* palo *m* de rosa.
rosin ['rɔzin] **1** *n* colofonia *f*. **2** *vt* aplicar colofonia a, frotar con colofonia.
roster ['rɔstə*] *n* lista *f*.
rostrum ['rɔstrəm] *n* (*speaker's*) tribuna *f*; (*Mus*) atril *m*.
rosy ['rəuzi] *adj* rosado, sonrosado; *future, prospect* prometedor, halagüeno; **with — cheeks** con mejillas sonrosadas.
rot [rɔt] **1** *n* (**a**) putrefacción *f*, podredumbre *f*; **it has — está** podrido.
 (**b**) (*fig*) decadencia *f*; **a — set in** comenzó un período de decadencia, todo empezó a decaer; **to stop the —** acabar con la decadencia, impedir que la situación vaya de mal en peor, reformarlo todo.
 (**c**) (*fam*) tonterías *fpl*, bobadas *fpl*; **oh —!, what —!** ¡tonterías!; **don't talk —!** ¡no digas bobadas!; **it is utter — to say that . . .** carece de sentido decir que . . .
 2 *vt* pudrir, corromper (*also fig*), descomponer.
 3 *vi* pudrirse, corromperse, descomponerse; **to — in jail** pudrirse en la cárcel; **it had —ted away with the passage of time** con el tiempo se había descompuesto; **it had quite —ted away** se había descompuesto y desaparecido del todo; **you can — for all I care!** ¡que te pudras!
rota ['rəutə] *n* lista *f* (de tandas *etc*).
Rotarian [rəu'tɛəriən] **1** *adj* rotario. **2** *n* rotario *m*.
rotary ['rəutəri] *adj* rotativo; giratorio.
Rotary Club ['rəutəri'klʌb] *n* Sociedad *f* Rotaria.
rotate [rəu'teit] **1** *vt* hacer girar; dar vueltas a; (*crops*) cultivar en rotación; (*vary*) alternar; **to — A and B** alternar A con B.
 2 *vi* girar; dar vueltas; alternarse.
rotating [rəu'teitiŋ] *adj* rotativo; giratorio.
rotation [rəu'teiʃən] *n* rotación *f* (*also Agr, Astron*); alternación *f*; **— of crops** rotación *f* de cultivos; **in —** por turno; **A and B in —** A y B alternadamente; **orders are dealt with in strict —** los pedidos se sirven por riguroso orden.
rotatory [rəu'teitəri] *adj* rotativo; giratorio.

rote [rəut] *n*: **to learn something by —** aprender algo maquinalmente, aprender a fuerza de repetirlo (en coro).
rotogravure [ˌrəutəugrə'vjuə*] *n* rotograbado *m*.
rotor ['rəutə*] *n* rotor *m*.
rotproof ['rɔtpru:f] *adj* a prueba de putrefacción.
rotten ['rɔtn] *adj* (**a**) podrido, putrefacto, corrompido; *tooth* cariado; *wood* carcomido; (*fig*) corrompido; **to smell —** oler a podredumbre.
 (**b**) (*fam: morally*) vil, despreciable; (*of bad quality*) malísimo, lamentable, fatal; (*Med*) malo; **what a — thing to do!** ¡qué cosa más vil!; **what a — thing to happen!** ¡que mala suerte!; **how — for you!** ¡cuánto te compadezco!, ¡lo que habrás sufrido!; **his English is —** tiene un inglés fatal; **it's a — novel** es una novela horrible, es una novela lamentable; **I feel —** estoy muy malo; **beer always makes me feel —** la cerveza siempre me pone malo; **to be — with money** (*fam*) estar podrido de dinero.
rottenness ['rɔtnnis] *n* podredumbre *f*, putrefacción *f*; (*fig*) corrupción *f*.
rotter ['rɔtə*] *n* caradura *m*, sinvergüenza *m*; **you —!** ¡canalla!
rotting ['rɔtiŋ] *adj* podrido, que se está pudriendo.
rotund [rəu'tʌnd] *adj* rotundo; (*fat*) gordo.
rotunda [rəu'tʌndə] *n* (*Archit*) rotonda *f*.
rotundity [rəu'tʌnditi] *n* rotundidad *f*; gordura *f*.
rouble ['ru:bl] *n* rublo *m*.
roué ['ru:ei] *n* libertino *m*.
Rouen ['ru:ɑ̃:ŋ] Ruán.
rouge [ru:ʒ] **1** *n* colorete *m*, carmín *m*. **2** *vr*: **to — oneself** ponerse colorete, ponerse carmín.
rough [rʌf] **1** *adj* (**a**) *surface, skin etc* áspero; *ground* quebrado, fragoso, escabroso; *road* desigual, lleno de baches; *cloth* basto; *hand* calloso; *hair* despeinado; *edge* desigual; **— to the touch** áspero al tacto.
 (**b**) *treatment, behaviour etc* brutal; *person* inculto, sin educación; *sea* bravo; encrespado, picado; *weather* borrascoso, tormentoso; *wind* violento; *play, sport* duro; **to be — with someone** tratar a uno de modo brutal; **to get — (sea)** embravecerse; **to get — with someone** empezar a pegar a uno; **he got a — handling in the press** le dieron una paliza en la prensa.
 (**c**) *manners* tosco, grosero; *voice* bronco, áspero; *speech* rudo; *style* tosco; *work* chapucero; *workman* torpe, desmañado; *material* crudo, bruto; *diamond etc* bruto.
 (**d**) *calculation, estimate* aproximado; *guess* aproximativo; *plan, sketch* a grandes rasgos; *draft* primero; *work* de preparación, preliminar; *translation* más o menos exacto; no completamente fiel.
 2 *adv*: **to cut up —** ofenderse, ponerse negro; **to live —** vivir sin comodidades, vivir como un vagabundo; **to play —** jugar duro; **to sleep —** pasar la noche al raso, echarse a dormir (en el suelo *etc*).
 3 *n* (*ground etc*) terreno *m* quebrado, superficie *f* áspera; (*person*) matón *m*; **in the —** en bruto, (*plan etc*) a grandes rasgos; **to take the — with the smooth** tomar las duras con las maduras, aceptar la vida como es.
 4 *vt*: **to — it** pasar apuros, luchar contra dificultades, vivir sin comodidades; **to — out a plan** esbozar un plan, bosquejar un plan, trazar un plan a grandes rasgos; **to — someone up** (*fam*) dar una paliza a uno.
roughage ['rʌfidʒ] *n* alimento *m* poco digerible.
rough-and-ready ['rʌfən'redi] *adj* tosco pero eficaz; improvisado; provisional; (*person*) inculto pero estimable.
rough-and-tumble ['rʌfən'tʌmbl] *n* (*quarrel, fight*) riña *f*, pendencia *f*; (*activity etc*) actividad *f* frenética; **the — of life** la confusión y violencia de la vida.
roughcast ['rʌfkɑ:st] *n* mezcla *f* gruesa.
roughen ['rʌfn] **1** *vt* poner áspero; hacer más tosco.
 2 *vi* ponerse áspero; hacerse más tosco; (*sea*) embravecerse.
rough-hewn ['rʌf'hju:n] *adj* toscamente labrado; desbastado; (*fig*) tosco, inculto.
roughhouse ['rʌfhaus] *n, pl* **—houses** [hauziz] (*fam*) trifulca *f*, riña *f* general.
roughly ['rʌfli] *adv* ásperamente; brutalmente, incultamente; violentamente; duramente; toscamente; groseramente; bruscamente; torpemente; aproximadamente, más o menos; de modo preliminar; **a — made table** una mesa toscamente hecha; **I put it at — 250** yo lo calculo en 250 aproximadamente.
roughneck ['rʌfnek] *n* (*sl*) matón *m*.
roughness ['rʌfnis] *n* aspereza *f*; lo quebrado, fragosidad *f*; desigualdad *f*; callosidad *f*; brutalidad

_f_; incultura _f_; falta _f_ de educación; braveza _f_; violencia _f_; dureza _f_; tosquedad _f_; rudeza _f_; lo chapucero; torpeza _f_, desmaña _f_.

roughrider ['rʌf,raidə*] _n_ domador _m_ de caballos.

roughshod ['rʌfʃɔd] _adv_: **to ride — over someone** tratar a uno sin miramientos, no hacer caso alguno de uno.

rough-spoken ['rʌf'spəukən] _adj_ inculto, de habla inculta.

roulette [ru:'let] _n_ ruleta _f_.

Roumania [ru:'meiniə] _etc see_ **Rumania** _etc_.

round [raund] **1** _adj_ redondo; _number, sum_ redondo; _denial etc_ rotundo, terminante; _trip_ de ida y vuelta, completo; _dance_ en ruedo; **a — dozen** una buena docena.

2 _adv_ alrededor; **all — por todos lados; all the year** — durante todo el año; **it has a fence all** — tiene una cerca que lo rodea completamente; **taking it all** — considerándolo en su totalidad, considerándolo desde todos los puntos de vista; **it is 200 metres** — tiene 200 metros en redondo; **for 5 miles — about** en 5 millas a la redonda, en 5 millas en torno; **it's a long way** — es el camino menos directo; **when you're — this way** cuando pases por aquí; **we were — at John's** estábamos en casa de Juan; **we shall be — at the pub** estaremos en el bar.

3 _prep_ alrededor de; _(fig)_ cerca de, cosa de; **a trip — the world** un viaje alrededor del mundo; **the wall — the town** la muralla que rodea la ciudad; **a walk — the town** un paseo por la ciudad; **it's just — the corner** está precisamente a la vuelta de la esquina; **we were sitting — the table** estábamos sentados alrededor de la mesa; **we were sitting — the fire** estábamos sentados junto a la lumbre; **it's written — the Suez episode** tiene por tema principal el episodio de Suez; **she's 36 inches — the bust** mide de pecho 36 pulgadas; **to sing hymns — the pubs** cantar himnos de bar en bar; **to deliver papers — the houses** llevar periódicos por las casas; **— 2 o'clock** a eso de las 2; **— about £50** cerca de 50 libras, cosa de 50 libras, 50 libras más o menos; **somewhere — that sum** esa cantidad más o menos.

4 _n_ (a) _(circle)_ círculo _m_; esfera _f_; _(slice)_ rodaja _f_; **a — of toast** una tostada.

(b) **the daily** — la rutina cotidiana, la rutina de siempre; **one long — of pleasures** una sucesión de placeres, una serie sin fin de placeres.

(c) _(beat: of watchman etc)_ ronda _f_, _(of postman, milkman etc)_ recorrido _m_; _(of golf etc)_ recorrido _m_, partido _m_; _(of doctor)_ visitas _fpl_; **a — of talks** una serie de conferencias; **the first — of negotiations** la primera ronda de negociaciones; **he's out on his — s** está fuera visitando sus enfermos; **to go the — s** _(watchman etc)_ estar de ronda, hacer su ronda de inspección; **the story is going the — s that . . .** se dice que . . ., se rumorea que . . .; **the story went the — s of the club** el chiste se contó en todos los corrillos del club.

(d) _(Boxing)_ asalto _m_; _(in tournament)_ vuelta _f_, rueda _f_; _(of election)_ vuelta _f_; _(lap)_ circuito _m_; _(in show jumping)_ recorrido _m_; **to have a clear —** hacer un recorrido sin penalizaciones.

(e) **— of drinks** ronda _f_ de bebidas; **— of applause** salva _f_ de aplausos; **— of ammunition** tiro _m_, cartucho _m_, bala _f_; **who bought the last —?** ¿quién pagó la última vez?; **whose — is it?** ¿a quién le toca (pagar)?

5 _vt_ (a) **to — a corner** doblar una esquina; **the ship — ed the headland** el buque dobló el promontorio.

(b) **to — off, to — out** redondear; acabar, perfeccionar; terminar; **to — the series off** para completar la serie; **to — up** acorralar, rodear (_SAm_); **we — ed up a few friends to help** logramos que nos ayudasen unos amigos.

6 _vi_: **to — on someone** volverse contra uno.

roundabout ['raundəbaut] **1** _adj_ indirecto; **by a — way** dando un rodeo, por una ruta indirecta; **to speak in a — way** ir con rodeos, hablar con circunloquios.

2 _n_ _(at fair)_ tiovivo _m_; _(Aut)_ cruce _m_ giratorio, glorieta _f_, redondel _m_.

rounded ['raundid] _adj end_ redondeado; esférico; _end of boat_ redondo; _style_ maduro, redondo.

roundelay ['raundilei] _n_ _(Hist)_ canción _f_ que se canta en rueda; baile _m_ en círculo.

round-eyed ['raund'aid] _adj, adv_: **to look at someone** — mirar a uno con los ojos desorbitados.

round-faced ['raund'feist] _adj_ de cara redonda.

roundhead ['raundhed] _n_ _(Hist)_ cabeza _f_ pelada.

roundhouse ['raundhaus] _n_, _pl_ **—houses** [hauziz] _(Rail)_ cocherón _m_ circular, rotonda _f_ para locomotoras; _(Naut)_ chupeta _f_.

roundly ['raundli] _adv_ _(fig)_ rotundamente, terminantemente.

roundness ['raundnis] _n_ redondez _f_.

round-shouldered ['raund'ʃəuldəd] _adj_ cargado de espaldas.

roundsman ['raundzmən] _n_, _pl_ **—men** [mən] repartidor _m_, proveedor _m_ casero.

roundup ['raundʌp] _n_ _(Agr)_ rodeo _m_; _(of suspects etc)_ detención _f_; _(by police)_ redada _f_; investigación _f_ en gran escala; **— of the latest news** vista _f_ de conjunto con las últimas noticias.

rouse [rauz] **1** _vt_ _(wake)_ despertar; _emotion_ excitar, suscitar, despertar; _(from torpor)_ animar, reanimar; _game_ levantar; **to — someone from sleep** despertar a uno; **to — someone to action** mover a uno a hacer algo; **to — someone to fury** provocar a uno a la furia; **it — ed the whole house** despertó a todo el mundo.

2 _vi_ despertar(se).

3 _vr_: **to — oneself** despertarse; _(to act etc)_ animarse a hacer algo.

rousing ['rauziŋ] _adj_ _welcome etc_ emocionado, entusiasta; _song etc_ vivo, lleno de vigor; _speech_ conmovedor.

Roussillon ['ru:sijɔ̃] Rosellón _m_.

rout¹ [raut] **1** _n_ _(defeat)_ derrota _f_ (completa); _(flight)_ fuga _f_ desordenada. **2** _vt_ derrotar (completamente).

rout² [raut] _vt_: **to — someone out** hacer salir a uno; **to — someone out of bed** hacer que uno se levante apresuradamente, hacer que uno abandone la cama.

route [ru:t] _n_ ruta _f_, camino _m_; itinerario _m_; _(Naut)_ rumbo _m_, derrota _f_; **to go by a new —** seguir una nueva ruta; **the — to the coast** el camino de la costa.

route map ['ru:tmæp] _n_ mapa _m_ de carreteras.

route march ['ru:tmɑ:tʃ] _n_ marcha _f_ de entrenamiento, marcha _f_ de maniobras.

routine [ru:'ti:n] **1** _n_ rutina _f_; **the daily —** la rutina de todos los días; **as a matter of —** por rutina.

2 _adj_ rutinario, de rutina; **a — inspection** una inspección rutinaria; **it's just — es** cosa de rutina.

rove [rəuv] **1** _vt_ vagar por, errar por, recorrer.

2 _vi_ vagar; **to — about** andar sin propósito fijo; **his eye — d over the room** registró rápidamente el cuarto con los ojos.

rover ['rəuvə*] _n_ vagabundo _m_, andariego _m_; _(Naut)_ pirata _m_; _(scout)_ escultista _m_.

roving ['rəuviŋ] _adj_ _(wandering)_ errante; _salesman etc_ ambulante; _ambassador_ volante; _disposition_ andariego; **to have a — commission** no tener puesto fijo, tener el cometido de hacer investigaciones _(etc)_ donde le parezca a uno; **he has a — eye** se le van los ojos tras las mujeres.

row¹ [rau] _n_ fila _f_, hilera _f_; _(Theat etc)_ fila _f_; _(of books, houses etc)_ hilera _f_; _(in knitting)_ pasada _f_; **in the front —** en primera fila; **in the fourth —** en la fila cuarta; **he killed four in a —** mató cuatro seguidos, mató cuatro uno tras otro; **for 5 days in a —** durante 5 días seguidos.

row² [rəu] **1** _n_ (a) _(trip)_ paseo _m_ en bote de remos; **to go for a —** pasearse en bote, hacer una excursión en bote.

(b) **it was a hard — to the shore** nos costó llegar a la playa remando; **you'll have a hard — upstream** les costará trabajo remar contra la corriente.

2 _vt boat_ conducir remando; **to — a race** tomar parte en una regata (de botes de remos); **you — ed a good race** habéis remado muy bien en la regata; **to — someone across a river** llevar a uno en bote a través de un río; **can you — me out to the yacht?** ¿me lleva Vd en bote al yate?

3 _vi_ remar, bogar; **to — hard** esforzarse remando, hacer fuerza de remos; **to — against someone** competir con uno en una regata a remo; **we — ed for the shore** remamos para llegar a la playa; **to — round an island** dar la vuelta a una isla en bote de remos.

row [rau] **1** _n_ (a) _(noise)_ ruido _m_, estrépito _m_, estruendo _m_; **hold your —!, stop your —!** ¡cállate!; **the — from the engine** el ruido del motor; **it makes a devil of a —** hace un ruido de todos los demonios.

(b) _(dispute)_ bronca _f_, pelea _f_; **the — about wages** la disputa acerca de los salarios; **now don't let's start a —** no riñamos.

(c) _(fuss, disturbance, incident)_ jaleo _m_, lío _m_, follón _m_; escándalo _m_; **what's the — about?** ¿a qué se debe el lío?; **there was a devil of a — about it** sobre esto se armó un tremendo follón; **to kick up**

a —, to make a — armar un jaleo, armar un follón; (*protest*) poner el grito en el cielo; **he makes a — about nothing** se queja por nada; **make a — with your member of parliament** quéjese a su diputado.

(d) (*scolding*) regaño *m*; **to get into a —** merecerse un regaño (*for something* por algo).

2 *vt*: **to — someone** echar un rapapolvo a uno.

3 *vi* reñir, refiirse; **they're always —ing** siempre están riñendo; **to — with someone** pelearse con uno.

rowan ['rauən] *n* serbal *m* (*also* — **tree**).

rowboat ['rəubəut] *n* bote *m* de remos.

rowdiness ['raudinis] *n* lo ruidoso, ruido *m*; carácter *m* pendenciero; alboroto *m*, desorden *m*.

rowdy ['raudi] **1** *adj person* (*noisy*) ruidoso; (*quarrelsome*) pendenciero, quimerista; *meeting etc* alborotado, desordenado. **2** *n* gamberro *mf*.

rowdyism ['raudiizəm] *n* disturbios *mpl*, pendencias *fpl*; gamberrismo *m*.

rower ['rəuə*] *n* remero *m*, a *f*.

rowing ['rəuiŋ] *n* remo *m*.

rowing boat ['rəuiŋbəut] *n* bote *m* de remos.

rowing club ['rəuiŋklʌb] *n* club *m* de remo.

rowlock ['rɔlək] *n* chumacera *f*, escalamera *f*.

royal ['rɔiəl] **1** *adj* (a) real; (*esp fig*) regio; — **palace** palacio *m* real; **R— Academy** Real Academia *f*.

(b) (*splendid*) magnífico, espléndido, suntuoso; **a — feast** un banquete suntuoso; **to have a right — time** pasarlo en grande.

2 *n* (*fam*) personaje *m* real, miembro *m* de la familia real; **the —s** la realeza.

royalism ['rɔiəlizəm] *n* sentimiento *m* monárquico, monarquismo *m*.

royalist ['rɔiəlist] **1** *adj* monárquico. **2** *n* monárquico *m*, a *f*.

royally ['rɔiəli] *adv* (*fig*) magníficamente, espléndidamente.

royalty ['rɔiəlti] *n* (a) realeza *f*; personajes *mpl* reales, familia *f* real; **in the presence of —** estando presente un miembro de la familia real; **a shop patronized by —** una tienda que visita la familia real, una tienda donde la familia real hace compras.

(b) (*payment*; *also* **royalties**) derechos *mpl* de autor; **the royalties on oil** los derechos del petróleo.

rozzer ['rɔzə*] *n* (*sl*) guili *m*, guindilla *m* (*sl*).

rub [rʌb] **1** *n* (a) frotamiento *m*; (*accidental friction*) roce *m*, rozadura *f*; **to give someone's back a —** frotar las espaldas de uno; **to give one's shoes a — (up)** limpiar los zapatos; **to give the silver a —** sacar brillo a la plata.

(b) **there's the —** ahí está el problema, ésa es la dificultad; **to come to the —** tropezar con la dificultad principal; **the — is that . . .** la dificultad es que . . .

2 *vt* (*apply friction*) frotar, (*Med etc*) friccionar; (*hard*) estregar, restregar; (*to clean*) limpiar frotando; (*polish*) sacar brillo a; **to — something dry** secar algo frotándolo; **to — a surface bare** alisar una superficie a fuerza de frotarla; **to — away** quitar frotando; **to — down** *body* secar frotando, *horse* almohazar, *wall etc* alisar frotando; **to — an ointment in** dar fricciones con un ungüento en la piel frotándola; **to — an idea in** reiterar una idea (desagradable), insistir en una idea; **the lesson has to be —bed in** que la lección se aprenda a fuerza de repetirla; **don't — it in !** ¡no machaques!, ¡no insistas!; **to — off** quitar frotando; **to — out** borrar; **to — someone out** (*sl*) cargarse a uno, despenar a uno; **to — one's hands together** frotarse las manos; **to — up** limpiar; pulir, sacar brillo a; (*fig*) refrescar; *see* **way 1 (h)**.

3 *vi*: **to — against something, to — on something** rozar algo; **to — along** (*fam*) ir tirando; **I can — along in Arabic** me defiendo en árabe; ¡**to — down** (*person*) secarse frotándose con una toalla; **to — off** borrarse debido al roce; **some of their opinions have —bed off on him** una parte de sus opiniones ha influido en él, él ha hecho suyas algunas de las opiniones de ellos; **to — out** borrarse; **it —s out easily** es fácil borrarlo.

rub-a-dub ['rʌbə'dʌb] *n* rataplán *m*.

rubber[1] ['rʌbə*] **1** *n* (*material*) caucho *m*, goma *f*; (*eraser*) goma *f* de borrar; (*Mech etc*) paño *m* de pulir; **synthetic —** caucho *m* artificial; **—s** (*shoes*) chanclos *mpl*, zapatos *mpl* de goma.

2 *adj*, *attr* de caucho, de goma; — **goods** artículos *mpl* de goma, (*euph*) gomas *fpl* higiénicas; — **industry** industria *f* gomera; *see* **band, cheque** *etc*.

rubber[2] ['rʌbə*] *n* (*Bridge etc*) juego *m*.

rubberized ['rʌbəraizd] *adj* engomado, cubierto de goma.

rubberneck ['rʌbənek] (*US fam*) **1** *n* mirón *m*, ona *f*. **2** *vi* curiosear.

rubber solution ['rʌbəsə'lu:ʃən] *n* disolución *f* de goma.

rubber stamp ['rʌbə'stæmp] **1** *n* estampilla *f* de goma, sello *m* de caucho.

2 **rubber-stamp** *vt* (*fig*) aprobar maquinalmente; aprobar con carácter oficial; poner su firma a.

rubber tree ['rʌbətri:] *n* árbol *m* gomero, árbol *m* de caucho.

rubbery ['rʌbəri] *adj* elástico, parecido a la goma.

rubbish ['rʌbiʃ] *n* (a) basura *f*; desperdicios *mpl*, desecho *m*, desechos *mpl*.

(b) (*fig*: *goods*) pacotilla *f*; (*production, work of art etc*) basura *f*, porquería *f*; (*spoken, written*) tonterías *fpl*, bobadas *fpl*; —!, **what** —! ¡tonterías!; **he talks a lot of —** no dice más que tonterías; **it's all —** todo son bobadas; **the novel is —** la novela es una basura.

rubbish bin ['rʌbiʃbin] *n* cubo *m* de la basura.

rubbish dump ['rʌbiʃdʌmp] *n*, **rubbish heap** ['rʌbiʃhi:p] *n* vertedero *m*, basurero *m*.

rubbishy ['rʌbiʃi] *adj goods* de pacotilla; *production, work of art etc* que no vale para nada, de bajísima calidad.

rubble ['rʌbl] *n* escombros *mpl*, cascote *m*; (*filling*) cascajo *m*.

rubdown ['rʌbdaun] *n* masaje *m*; acción *f* de secarse con una toalla (*etc*).

rube [ru:b] *n* (*US fam*) patán *m*, palurdo *m*.

Rubicon ['ru:bikən] Rubicón *m*; **to cross the —** pasar el Rubicón.

rubicund ['ru:bikənd] *adj* rubicundo.

rubric ['ru:brik] *n* rúbrica *f*.

ruby ['ru:bi] **1** *n* rubí *m*. **2** *adj necklace etc* de rubíes; *ring* de rubí, con un rubí; *colour* color de rubí.

ruck[1] [rʌk] *n* (*Racing*) grueso *m* del pelotón; (*Rugby*) mêlée *f*; (*fig*) gente *f* común, personas *fpl* corrientes; **to get out of the —** empezar a destacar, adelantarse a los demás.

ruck[2] [rʌk], **ruckle** ['rʌkl] (*esp* **to — up**) **1** *vt* arrugar. **2** *vi* arrugarse.

rucksack ['rʌksæk] *n* mochila *f*.

ruckus ['rʌkəs] *n* (*US*) = **ruction.**

ruction ['rʌkʃən] *n* (*fam*) lío *m*, jaleo *m*; **there will be —s** se va a armar la gorda.

rudder ['rʌdə*] *n* (*Naut*) timón *m*, gobernalle *m*; (*Aer*) timón *m* de dirección.

rudderless ['rʌdəlis] *adj* sin timón.

ruddiness ['rʌdinis] *n* rubicundez *f*; lo rojizo; frescote, frescura *f*.

ruddy[1] ['rʌdi] *adj* rubicundo; rojizo; *complexion* frescote.

ruddy[2] [rʌdi] *adj* (*euph*) condenado, puñetero.

rude [ru:d] *adj* (a) (*offensive*) grosero, descortés, ofensivo; **don't be —!** ¡Vd es un maleducado!, ¡Vd es un fresco!; **you were very — to me once** Vd estuvo muy descortés conmigo una vez; **it's — to eat noisily** es de mala educación hacer ruido al comer; **would it be — of me to ask if . . .?** ¿puedo sin ser descortés preguntar si . . .?; **how —!** ¡qué ordinario!

(b) (*indecent*) verde, indecente; **they sing — songs** cantan canciones verdes; **there's nothing — about that picture** ese cuadro no tiene nada de indecente.

(c) (*uncivilized etc*) rudo, grosero, tosco; inculto.

(d) (*sudden*) repentino; (*violent*) violento; **a — shock** un golpe inesperado; **a — awakening** una sorpresa desagradable.

(e) **to be in — health** estar muy bien de salud.

rudely ['ru:dli] *adv* groseramente, con descortesía, de modo ofensivo; toscamente; **a — made table** una mesa toscamente labrada; **to answer someone —** contestar a uno descortésmente.

rudeness ['ru:dnis] *n* grosería *f*, descortesía *f*; indecencia *f*; rudeza *f*, tosquedad *f*; violencia *f*.

rudiment ['ru:dimənt] *n* (*Bio*) rudimento *m*; —**s** rudimentos *mpl*, primeras nociones *fpl*.

rudimentary [,ru:di'mentəri] *adj* (*Bio*) rudimental; (*fig*) rudimentario; **he has — Latin** tiene las primeras nociones de latín, sabe un poquito de latín.

rue[1] [ru:] *vt* arrepentirse de, lamentar; **you shall — it** te arrepentirás de haberlo hecho; **I — the day when I did it** ojalá no lo hubiera hecho nunca; **he lived to — it** después se arrepintió de ello.

rue[2] [ru:] *n* (*Bot*) ruda *f*.

rueful ['ru:ful] *adj* triste; arrepentido; lamentable.

ruefully ['ru:fəli] *adv* tristemente.

ruefulness ['ru:fulnis] *n* tristeza *f*.

ruff[1] [rʌf] *n* gorguera *f*, gola *f*; (*Zool, Orn*) collarín *m*.

ruff[2] [rʌf] (*Cards*) **1** *n* fallada *f*. **2** *vt* fallar.

ruffian ['rʌfiən] *n* matón *m*, criminal *m*; **you —!** ¡canalla!

ruffianly ['rʌfiənli] *adj* brutal, criminal.
ruffle ['rʌfl] **1** *n* arruga *f*; (*Sew*) volante *m* fruncido; (*ripple*) rizo *m*.
　2 *vt* (*wrinkle*) arrugar; *surface* agitar, rizar; (*Sew*) fruncir; *hair* despeinar; *feathers* encrespar; *someone's composure* descomponer, perturbar; to — someone's feelings ofender a uno, herir los sentimientos de uno, irritar a uno; **nothing —s him** no se altera por nada.
　3 *vi* arrugarse; agitarse, rizarse.
rug [rʌg] *n* (*on floor*) alfombra *f*, alfombrilla *f*; (*travelling* —) manta *f* (de viaje).
rugby ['rʌgbi] *n* rugby *m*.
rugged ['rʌgid] *adj terrain* escabroso, áspero, accidentado, bravo; (*harsh*) duro, severo; *character* robusto; *features* fuerte, acentuado; *workmanship* tosco; *independence etc* vigoroso; *style* desigual.
ruggedness ['rʌgidnis] *n* escabrosidad *f*, aspereza *f*, lo accidentado; severidad *f*; robustez *f*; lo fuerte; tosquedad *f*; vigor *m*; desigualdad *f*.
rugger ['rʌgə*] *n* (*fam*) rugby *m*.
ruin ['ruːin] **1** *n* (a) ruina *f*; —s ruinas *fpl*; restos *mpl*; **to lay a town in** —s asolar una ciudad; **the city rose from the** —s la ciudad volvió a nacer sobre las ruinas.
　(b) (*act*) arruinamiento *m*.
　(c) (*fig*) ruina *f*; perdición *f*; **the** — **of someone's hopes** la destrucción de las esperanzas de uno; **it will be the** — **of him** será su ruina; **drink will be his** — el alcohol le perderá, el alcohol será su perdición; **to bring someone to** — arruinar a uno; — **stared us in the face** nos amenazó un desastre total.
　2 *vt* arruinar; (*spoil*) estropear; *taste etc* estragar; (*morally*) perder; **her extravagance** —**ed him** sus despilfarros le arruinaron; **what** —**ed him was gambling** fue el juego el que le perdió; **he** —**ed my new car** estropeó mi nuevo coche.
ruination [ˌruːiˈneiʃən] *n* arruinamiento *m*, perdición *f*.
ruinous ['ruːinəs] *adj* (*all senses*) ruinoso.
ruinously ['ruːinəsli] *adv* de modo ruinoso; — **expensive** carísimo, de lo más caro.
rule [ruːl] **1** *n* (a) (*ruling*) regla *f*; norma *f*; costumbre *f*; — **of the road** reglamento *m* del tráfico; — **of three** (*Math*) regla *f* de tres; — **of thumb** regla *f* empírica; **by** — **of thumb** por experiencia, por rutina; mediante una prueba práctica; **standing** — estatuto *m*; —**s and regulations** reglamento *m*; **the** — **es de regla**; **it's against the** —**s** eso infringe las reglas, eso no se permite; **our** — **is** ... nuestro principio es ...; **the golden** — **is** ... la regla principal es ...; **there is no hard-and-fast** — **about it** sobre eso no existe ninguna regla terminante; **to do everything by** — obrar siempre de acuerdo con las reglas; **to make it a** — **to** + *infin* hacerse una regla de + *infin*; **I make it a** — **never to drink** yo por sistema nunca bebo.
　(b) (*Law*) fallo *m*, decisión *f*.
　(c) (*dominion etc*) dominio *m*, imperio *m*; autoridad *f*; mando *m*; **home** — autonomía *f*; **under British** — bajo la autoridad británica; **under the** — **of Louis XV** bajo el reinado de Luis XV; **under the** — **of law** bajo el imperio de la justicia; **under the** — **of fear** bajo el imperio del miedo.
　(d) (*ruler*) metro *m*; **folding** — metro *m* plegable.
　(e) (*Eccl*) regla *f*; **the Benedictine** — la regla benedictina.
　2 *vt* (a) (*govern*) gobernar, mandar, regir (*also* **to** — **over**); **to** — **an empire** gobernar un imperio; **he** —**d the company for 40 years** durante 40 años rigió la compañía; **he's** —**d by his wife** le domina su mujer; **be** —**d by my advice** déjese guiar por mis consejos, guíese por mí.
　(b) (*Law*) decidir; (*of chairman etc*) disponer, determinar; **to** — **that** ... decidir que ..., decretar que ...; **to** — **something out of order** decidir que un asunto no se puede discutir.
　(c) (*draw*) line trazar, tirar; *paper* rayar, reglar.
　(d) **to** — **something out** excluir algo; **we can't** — **out the possibility that** ... no podemos excluir la posibilidad de que + *subj*; **you are not** —**d out because of that** Vd no queda excluido por eso.
　3 *vi* (a) (*govern*) gobernar; (*of monarch*) reinar.
　(b) **to** — **against something** fallar en contra de algo; **to** — **in favour of someone** decidir a favor de uno.
　(c) (*of price*) regir.
ruled [ruːld] *adj paper* rayado.
ruler ['ruːlə*] *n* (*person*) gobernante *mf*, gobernador *m*, ora *f*; soberano *m*, a *f*; (*rule*) regla *f*.
ruling ['ruːliŋ] **1** *adj passion* predominante; *price que*

rige; **the** — **classes** la clase que gobierna, la clase que manda.
　2 *n* fallo *m*, decisión *f*; **to give a** — fallar, decidir; **to give a** — **on a dispute** pronunciar un fallo sobre una disputa.
rum[1] [rʌm] *n* ron *m*; (*US*) aguardiente *m*, bebida *f* alcohólica.
rum[2] [rʌm] *adj* (*fam*) extraño, raro.
Rumania [ruːˈmeiniə] Rumania *f*.
Rumanian [ruːˈmeiniən] **1** *adj* rumano. **2** *n* rumano *m*, a *f*. **3** *n* (*language*) rumano *m*.
rumba ['rʌmbə] *n* rumba *f*.
rumble[1] ['rʌmbl] **1** *n* retumbo *m*, ruido *m* sordo, rumor *m*; (*of thunder etc*) redoble *m*; (*of tank etc*) rodar *m*.
　2 *vi* retumbar; hacer un ruido sordo; redoblar; rodar; (*stomach*) sonar; **the train** —**d past** el tren pasó con estruendo.
rumble[2] ['rʌmbl] *vt* (*fam*) calar (*fam*); **he's** —**d us** nos ha calado; **I soon** —**d what was going on** pronto descubrí lo que estaban haciendo.
rumble seat ['rʌmbl'siːt] *n* asiento *m* trasero descubierto.
rumbling ['rʌmbliŋ] *n see* **rumble**[1].
rumbustious [rʌmˈbʌstʃəs] *adj* bullicioso, ruidoso.
ruminant ['ruːminənt] **1** *adj* rumiante. **2** *n* rumiante *m*.
ruminate ['ruːmineit] *vti* rumiar (*also fig*).
rumination [ˌruːmiˈneiʃən] *n* (*act*) rumia *f*, rumiación *f*; (*thought*) meditación *f*, reflexión *f*.
ruminative ['ruːminətiv] *adj* (*Bio*) rumiante; (*fig*) pensativo, meditabundo.
ruminatively ['ruːminətivli] *adv* pensativamente; " —", **he said** — ", dijo pensativo.
rummage ['rʌmidʒ] *vi*: **to** — **about** revolverlo todo, buscar revolviéndolo todo; **to** — **about in a case** revolver en una maleta; **he** —**d in his pocket and produced a ticket** revolvió en el bolsillo y sacó un billete.
rummage sale ['rʌmidʒseil] *n* venta *f* de prendas usadas.
rummy[1] ['rʌmi] *adj* (*fam*) extraño, raro.
rummy[2] ['rʌmi] *n* (*Cards*) rummy *m*.
rumour, (*US*) **rumor** ['ruːmə*] **1** *n* rumor *m*; **as** — **has it según se dice**; **as it has that** ... se rumorea que ... **2** *vt*: **it is** —**ed that** ... se rumorea que ..., se dice que ...; **he is** —**ed to be rich** se dice que es rico.
rump [rʌmp] *n* (*Anat: of horse etc*) ancas *fpl*, grupa *f*; (*of bird*) rabadilla *f*; (*of person*) culo *m*, trasero *m*; (*Cook*) cuarto *m* trasero, cadera *f*.
rumple ['rʌmpl] *vt* ajar, arrugar, chafar.
rumpsteak ['rʌmp'steik] *n* filete *m* de lomo de vaca.
rumpus ['rʌmpəs] *n* (*fam*) lío *m*, jaleo *m*; batahála *f*, revuelo *m*; **to have a** — **with someone** pelearse con uno; **to kick up a** — armar un lío.
rumpus room ['rʌmpəsˌruːm] *n* (*US*) cuarto *m* de los niños, cuarto *m* de juegos.
rumrunner ['rʌmˌrʌnə*] *n* (*US*) contrabandista *m* de bebidas alcohólicas.
run [rʌn] **1** *n* (a) (*act of running*) corrida *f*, carrera *f*; (*Sport*) carrera *f*; (*in stocking*) carrera *f*; (*of fish*) migración *f*; **at a** — corriendo; **to go at a steady** — correr a un paso regular; **to break into a** — echar a correr, empezar a correr; **a prisoner on the** — un preso fugado, un preso evadido; **he's on the** — **from prison** escapó de la cárcel; **he was on the** — **for 6 weeks** estuvo libre durante 6 semanas; **he's on the** — **from his creditors** se está escapando de sus acreedores; **to keep someone on the** — hacer que uno corra de acá para allá; mantener a uno en constante actividad; **we soon had the enemy on the** — pronto pusimos al enemigo en fuga; **we've got them on the** — now ya están casi vencidos; **it came down with a** — bajó repentinamente, cayó todo junto; **prices came down with a** — los precios bajaron de golpe; **I had a** — **to catch it** tuve que correr bastante para cogerlo; **I have a** — **before breakfast** me entreno corriendo antes del desayuno; **to make a** — **for it** huir precipitadamente; **we shall have to make a** — **for it** tendremos que correr; **to give someone a** — **for his money** dar a uno alguna satisfacción por sus esfuerzos; hacer que uno se esfuerce para lograr lo que quiere; **to have a** — **for one's money** dar buena cuenta de sí, darse alguna satisfacción por sus esfuerzos.
　(b) (*outing, Aut etc*) paseo *m* (en coche), excursión *f* (en coche); **trial** — prueba *f*, viaje *m* de ensayo; **it was a very pleasant** — fue un viaje muy agradable; **to go for a** —, **to have a** — dar un paseo (en coche); **we'll have a** — **down to the coast** iremos de excursión a la costa.

(c) (*distance travelled*: Rail etc) trayecto *m*, recorrido *m*; day's — (*Naut*) singladura *f*.

(d) (*Typ*) tirada *f*; a — of 5,000 copies una tirada de 5.000 ejemplares.

(e) (*tendency*) tendencia *f*; the — of the market la tendencia del mercado; the — of the play was favourable to us el partido se desarrolló de modo favorable para nosotros; they scored against the — of play marcaron un gol durante el tiempo en el que dominaron los adversarios.

(f) (*series*) serie *f*; a — of four (*Cards*) una serie de cuatro; a — of luck una racha de suerte; a — of bad luck una temporada de mala suerte; to have a long — (*fashion*) estar en boga mucho tiempo, conservar su popularidad durante mucho tiempo; the play had a long — la obra se mantuvo mucho tiempo en la cartelera; when the London — was over al terminarse la serie de representaciones en Londres; in the long — a la larga.

(g) (*Comm*) — on a bank asedio *m* de un banco; there is a — on soap hay una gran demanda de jabón, el jabón tiene mucha demanda.

(h) the common — of people el común de las gentes; the common — of books la generalidad de los libros; it's above the common — es superior al nivel general.

(i) to have the — of someone's house poder entrar libremente en la casa de uno; to have the — of someone's library tener libre uso de la biblioteca de uno, poder usar a discreción la biblioteca de uno.

(j) (*Agr etc*) terreno *m* de pasto; (*hen*—) corral *m*, gallinero *m*; (*ski*—) pista *f* de esquí.

(k) (*Mus*) glisado *m*, fermata *f*.

2 (*irr*: *pret* ran, *ptp* run) vt (a) to — a race tomar parte en una carrera; you ran a good race corriste muy bien; they're not —ning the race this year este año no hay carrera; the race is — over 4 miles la distancia de la carrera es de 4 millas.

(b) to — a risk correr un riesgo.

(c) to — someone off his legs correr hasta cansar al compañero; to — someone close, to — someone hard casi alcanzar a uno, ir pisándole los talones a uno (*also fig*); to — it close, to — it fine llegar con muy poco tiempo, dejarse muy poco tiempo; see earth *etc*.

(d) to — sheep in a field pacer las ovejas en un campo.

(e) (*move etc*) to — a car into a garage poner un coche en un garaje; I'll — you up to town te llevo a la ciudad; to — a boat ashore varar una embarcación; to — guns across a frontier pasar fusiles de contrabando a través de una frontera; to — messages llevar recados; to — a new bus service establecer un nuevo servicio de autobuses; they're —ning an extra train ponen un tren suplementario; they don't — that bus on Sundays no ponen ese autobús los domingos.

(f) to — the blockade forzar el bloqueo, burlar el bloqueo.

(g) (*have, possess*) tener, poseer; he —s two mistresses tiene dos queridas; we don't — a car no tenemos coche; to — a (high) temperature tener fiebre; to — a temperature of 104° tener una temperatura de 104 grados.

(h) (*direct etc*) business dirigir; controlar, gobernar, regir; administrar; organizar; *machine* manejar; *campaign* dirigir, organizar; to — the house for someone llevar la casa a uno; a house which is easy to — (or easily —) una casa de fácil manejo; she's the one who really —s everything la que en realidad lo dirige todo es ella.

(i) to — a horse correr un caballo; he ran 3 horses last season en la última temporada corrió 3 caballos; to — a candidate proponer un candidato, apoyar un candidato; the liberals are not —ning anybody this time esta vez los liberales no tienen candidato.

(j) (*pass*) pasar; (*pierce*) traspasar; (*introduce*) introducir; to — one's hand over a chair pasar la mano por un sillón, recorrer un sillón con la mano; to — one's eye over a text examinar rápidamente un texto; — your eye over this mira esto un poco; to — a line round something trazar una línea alrededor de algo; we'll — a fence round it pondremos un cerco alrededor de él; to — a pipe through a wall pasar un tubo a través de una pared; to — someone through with a sword, to — a sword through someone traspasar a uno con una espada; I ran a thorn into my finger me clavé una espina en el dedo.

(k) (*with adv or prep*) to — down ship hundir, echar a pique; *pedestrian* atropellar; (*find*) encontrar; (*capture*) coger, cazar, acorralar; (*catch up*

with) alcanzar; (*denigrate*) hablar mal de, vilipendiar, desacreditar; to be — down (*battery*) estar descargado, (*clock*) estar parado, (*person, Med*) estar agotado, estar debilitado, no estar bien de salud; I ran that reference down encontré esa referencia; we ran him down in a café por fin lo encontramos en un café; the police will — him down la policía le cazará; to — someone in (*fam*) detener a uno, meter a uno en la cárcel; he got — in for being drunk le detuvieron por borracho; to — a car in rodar un coche; "running in" "en rodaje"; she ran the car into a lamppost dio con el coche contra un farol; this will — you into debt esto le hará contraer una deuda; to — off (*recite*) enumerar rápidamente; (*Typ*) imprimir, tirar; (*Sport*) *heat* decidir; *water etc* vaciar; dejar correr; the servant ran the water off la criada dejó salir el agua; to — on (*Typ*) continuar sin dejar espacio, unir al párrafo anterior; to — over *pedestrian* atropellar; to — up *debt* incurrir en, contraer; *flag* izar; *dress etc* hacer de prisa; *building* construir.

3 vi (a) (*general sense*) correr; (*hasten*) correr, darse prisa, apresurarse; (*in race*) competir, tomar parte; to — for all one is worth, to — like the devil correr a todo correr; to — downstairs bajar la escalera corriendo; to — down the garden correr por el jardín; to — for a bus correr para coger un autobús; to — to meet someone correr al encuentro de uno, acudir corriendo para recibir a uno; to — to help someone acudir corriendo a socorrer a uno.

(b) (*flee*) huir; we shall have to — for it tendremos que correr; — for your lives! ¡sálvese el que pueda!

(c) to — for office ser candidato para un puesto, presentarse como candidato para un puesto; are you —ning? ¿te vas a presentar?

(d) (*Naut*) to — before the wind navegar con viento a popa; to — aground encallar, embarrancar.

(e) (*function: engine etc*) funcionar, marchar, andar; estar en marcha; the lift isn't —ning el ascensor no funciona; the car —s smoothly el coche marcha bien; things did not — smoothly for them las cosas no les fueron bien; it —s on petrol funciona con gasolina, tiene motor de gasolina; it —s off the mains funciona con corriente de la red.

(f) (*function: of service etc*) circular, ir; the trains —ning between Madrid and Ávila los trenes que circulan entre Madrid y Ávila, los trenes que hacen el servicio entre Madrid y Ávila; there are no trains —ning to Toboso no hay servicio de trenes a Toboso; that train does not — on Sundays ese tren no circula los domingos; the buses — every 10 minutes los autobuses salen cada 10 minutos; steamers — daily between X and Y hay servicio diario de vapores entre X e Y.

(g) (*pass*) a rumour ran round the school un rumor corrió por la escuela; a ripple ran through the crowd la multitud se estremeció (de emoción *etc*); it —s through the whole history of art afecta toda la historia del arte, se observa en toda la historia del arte; it —s in the family viene de familia; the thought ran through my head that . . . se me ocurrió pensar que . . .; that tune keeps —ning in my head esa melodía la tengo metida en la cabeza; the conversation ran on wine el tema de la conversación era el vino; my thoughts ran on Mary mi pensamiento se concentró en María.

(h) (*go, continue*) seguir; the contract ran for 7 years el contrato fue válido durante 7 años; the play ran for 40 performances la obra tuvo 40 representaciones seguidas; the play — for 3 months la obra se mantuvo en la cartelera durante 3 meses; things must — their course las cosas han de desarrollarse normalmente; the affair has — its course el asunto ha terminado; where his writ does not — donde su autoridad no vale, donde él no tiene jurisdicción.

(i) to — to (*extend*) extenderse a; (*of amounts*) subir a, ascender a, sumar; the book has — into 20 editions el libro ha alcanzado 20 ediciones; the talk ran to 2 hours la charla se extendió a 2 horas; the book will — to 700 pages el libro tendrá 700 páginas en total; my salary won't — to a second car mi sueldo no me permite adquirir un segundo coche; we can't possibly — to a grand piano nos es imposible comprar un piano de cola.

(j) (*colour*) desteñirse; (*melt*) derretirse; (*Med: sore*) supurar; colours that will not — colores *mpl* sólidos, colores *mpl* inalterables; my ice is —ning mi helado se está derritiendo.

(k) (*flow*) correr, fluir; (*tears*) correr; (*drip*) gotear; the milk ran all over the floor la leche se derramó por todo el suelo; **tears ran down her cheeks** las lágrimas le corrían por las mejillas; **my pen** —s mi pluma gotea; **the streets were running with water** el agua corría por las calles; **we were running with sweat** chorreábamos de sudor; **a land** —ning **with milk and honey** una tierra que abunda en leche y miel; **to leave a tap** —ning dejar abierto un grifo; **the Tagus** —s **past Toledo** el Tajo pasa por Toledo; **the river** —s **for 300 miles** el río corre 300 millas; **it** —s **into the sea at Lisbon** desemboca en el mar en Lisboa; **the street** —s **into the square** la calle desemboca en la plaza; **blood ran from the wound** la sangre manaba de la herida, la herida manaba sangre; **the stream ran blood** el arroyo iba tinto de sangre; **a heavy sea was** —ning el mar estaba muy picado; había una fuerte corriente; **when the tide is** —ning **strongly** cuando sube la marea rápidamente; **to** — **dry** secarse.

(**l**) (*go, pass*) ir; **a balcony** —s **round the hall** una galería se extiende a lo largo del interior de toda la sala; **a fence** —s **round the field** el campo está rodeado por una cerca; **York has walls that** — **right round it** York tiene una muralla que la rodea completamente; **the road** —s **by our house** la carretera pasa junto a nuestra casa; **it** —s **north and south** va de norte a sur.

(**m**) **so the story** —s así dice el cuento; **the text** —s **like this** el texto dice así, el texto reza así.

(**n**) **to** — **to seed** granar; **to** — **to fat** engordar; tener tendencia a engordar; *see* **high, low** *etc*.

(**o**) (*with adv or prep*) **to** — **about** correr por todas partes; divertirse corriendo; **to** — **across the road** cruzar la calle corriendo; **to** — **across someone** toparse con uno; **to** — **across something** encontrar algo; **to** — **after a girl** correr detrás de una chica, dar caza a una chica, perseguir a una chica; **to** — **along** (*prep*) correr por; **the road** —s **along the river** la carretera sigue el río, la carretera va a lo largo del río; **a fence** —s **along that side** hay un cerco por ese lado; — **along!** ¡anda ya!; **to** — **at someone** lanzarse sobre uno, precipitarse sobre uno; **to** — **away** evadirse, huir, escaparse; (*horse*) dispararse; **to** — **away from home** huir de casa; **to** — **away from prison** evadirse de la cárcel; **to** — **away from the facts** no prestar atención a los hechos, no hacer caso de los hechos; **to** — **away from one's responsibilities** no cumplir con los deberes de uno; **to** — **away with someone** fugarse con uno; **to** — **away with the cash** alzarse con el dinero; **to** — **away with the race** ganar fácilmente la carrera; **don't** — **away with the idea that** . . . no te imagines que . . . , no te dejes arrastrar por la idea de que . . . ; **it simply** —s **away with the money** es que devora el dinero; **to** — **back** volver corriendo; **to** — **down** bajar corriendo; **the rain ran down the window pane** la lluvia corría por el cristal de la ventana; **to** — **down** (*adv: clock*) parar; **the spring has** — **down** se ha acabado la cuerda; **to** — **in** entrar corriendo; **to** — **into** (*collide with*) chocar con, dar contra; **the two cars ran into each other** chocaron los dos coches; **to** — **into someone** topar con uno, tropezar con uno; **to** — **into debt** contraer deudas; **to** — **into trouble** tropezar con dificultades; **to** — **off** huir corriendo, alejarse corriendo; **to** — **off with someone** fugarse con uno; **to** — **on** continuar, continuar sin interrupción; **it ran on for 4 hours** continuó durante 4 horas; **she does** — **on so** es tan habladora, no termina de hablar; **to** — **out** (*person etc*) salir corriendo; (*of liquid*) irse; (*of time*) acabarse; (*of lease, term*) expirar; (*of contract, permit etc*) vencer, caducar; (*of stock etc*) agotarse, acabarse; **when the money** —s **out** cuando se acabe el dinero; **the tide is** —ning **out** la marea está bajando; **the tide is** —ning **out** (*fig*), —ning **out** queda poco· tiempo; **we ran out of petrol** nos quedamos sin gasolina; **to** — **over** (*adv: water*) rebosar; **we're** —ning **over** hemos rebasado el límite; **the show ran over by 12 minutes** la función duró 12 minutos más de lo debido; **to** — **over** (*prep*) *text etc* repasar, leer por encima; (*rehearse*) volver a hacer, volver a ensayar; **shall we** — **over that bit again?** ¿hacemos ese trozo otra vez?; **to** — **through** *book* hojear, leer a la ligera; *instructions etc* repasar; *money* gastar; consumir; **to** — **up** (*adv*) acudir corriendo; *stairs etc* subir corriendo; **to** — **up** (*prep*) *plant etc* trepar por; **to** — **up against someone** tener que habérselas con uno; **to** — **up against difficulties** tropezar con dificultades.

runabout ['rʌnəbaut] *n* (*Aut*) coche *m* pequeño.
runaway ['rʌnəwei] 1 *adj* *prisoner, slave* fugitivo; *soldier* desertor; *horse* desbocado; *lorry* que está en movimiento sin conductor, con frenos inservibles;

victory fácil; *marriage* clandestino, no aprobado por los padres de los novios.

2 *n* (*person*) fugitivo *m*, a *f*; (*horse*) caballo *m* desbocado.
run-down ['rʌn'daun] *adj* en decadencia, debilitado.
rundown ['rʌndaun] *n* (*of industry etc*) cierre *m* gradual; (*of activity*) disminución *f*, reducción *f*.
rune [ru:n] *n* runa *f*.
rung[1] [rʌŋ] *n* escalón *m*, peldaño *m*.
rung[2] [rʌŋ] *ptp of* **ring**.
runic ['ru:nik] *adj* rúnico.
run-in ['rʌnin] *n* (*Typ*) palabras *fpl* insertadas en un párrafo.
runlet ['rʌnlit] *n*, **runnel** ['rʌnl] *n* arroyuelo *m*.
runner ['rʌnə*] *n* (*athlete*) corredor *m*, ora *f*, atleta *mf*; (*horse*) caballo *m*; (*messenger*) mensajero *m*, (*Mil*) ordenanza *m*; (*ring*) anillo *m* movible; (*wheel*) ruedecilla *f*; (*of sledge, aircraft*) patín *m*; (*table*—) tapete *m*; (*Bot*) tallo *m* rastrero, estolón *m*.
runner-up ['rʌnər'ʌp] *n* subcampeón *m*, ona *f*.
running ['rʌniŋ] 1 *adj* *water* corriente; *knot* corredizo; *writing* cursivo; *sore* supurante, purulento; *commentary* continuo; *start* lanzado; — **costs** gastos *mpl* corrientes; — **fight** acción *f* de retirada; *combate m* continuo; — **kick** puntapié *m* dado mientras corre el jugador (*etc*); **in** — **order** en buen estado; **5 days** — 5 días seguidos; **for the sixth time** — por sexta vez consecutiva.

2 *n* (*of business etc*) dirección *f*; control *m*; gobierno *m*; administración *f*; organización *f*; manejo *m*; (*of machine*) funcionamiento *m*, marcha *f*; **to be in the** — tener posibilidades de ganar; **to be in the** — **for a chair** tener posibilidades de ganar una cátedra; **to be out of the** — no tener posibilidad alguna de ganar; **to make (all) the** — ir a la cabeza, ir delante.
running board ['rʌniŋbɔ:d] *n* (*Aut etc*) estribo *m*.
running in ['rʌniŋ'in] *n* (*Aut*) rodaje *m*.
running mate ['rʌniŋ'meit] *n* (*US Pol*) candidato *m* a la vicepresidencia.
runny ['rʌni] *adj* líquido; derretido.
run-off ['rʌnɔf] *n* (*Sport*) carrera *f* final; carrera *f* de desempate.
run-of-the-mill ['rʌnəvðə'mil] *adj* corriente· y moliente.
runt [rʌnt] *n* redrojo *m*, enano *m*; (*fig*) enano *m*; **you little** — ! ¡canalla!
run-through ['rʌnθru:] *n* prueba *f* preliminar, ensayo *m*.
runway ['rʌnwei] *n* (*Aer*) pista *f* de aterrizaje.
rupee [ru:'pi:] *n* rupia *f*.
rupture ['rʌptʃə*] 1 *n* (*Med*) hernia *f*, quebradura *f*; (*fig*) ruptura *f*, rompimiento *m*.
2 *vt* causar una hernia en, quebrarse.
3 *vr*: **to** — **oneself** causarse una hernia, quebrarse.
rural ['ruərəl] *adj* rural.
ruse [ru:z] *n* ardid *m*, treta *f*, estratagema *f*.
rush[1] [rʌʃ] *n* (*Bot*) junco *m*.
rush[2] [rʌʃ] 1 *n* (**a**) (*act of* —*ing*) ímpetu *m*; (*Mil*) ataque *m*; acometida *f*; asalto *m*; **general** — desbandada *f* general; **the gold** — la carrera del oro; **there was a** — **to the door** se precipitaron todos hacia la puerta; **there was a** — **for safety** todos hicieron lo posible por ponerse a salvo; **to make a** — **at someone** arremeter contra uno, precipitarse sobre uno; **it got lost in the** — se perdió en la confusión; **2 were injured in the** — al precipitarse todos 2 resultaron heridos.

(**b**) (*haste*) prisa *f*, precipitación *f*; (*tumult*) bullicio *m*, ajetreo *m*; **the** — **of modern life** el ajetreo de la vida moderna; **the** — **of London** la prisa que tiene todo el mundo en Londres; **what's all the** — **about?** ¿por qué tanta prisa?; **is there any** — **for this?** ¿le corre prisa esto?; **we're in a** — tenemos prisa, llevamos prisa; **we're in a** — **to finish it** tenemos prisa por terminarlo; **I did it in a** — lo hice de prisa; **we had a** — **to get it ready** nos dimos prisa para tenerlo listo; **everything happened with a** — todo ocurrió de repente; **it came down with a** — cayó de repente.

(**c**) (*Comm*) demanda *f* (*for, on* de); **there has been a** — **on matches** ha habido una demanda extraordinaria de cerillas.

(**d**) (*current*) **a** — **of air** una fuerte corriente de aire, una ráfaga de aire; **a** — **of water** un torrente de agua; **a** — **of words** un torrente de palabras; **a** — **of people** un tropel; **we've had a** — **of orders** estamos inundados de pedidos; **he had a** — **of blood to the head** (*fig*) le pasó algo totalmente inesperado; tuvo un momento de locura.

2 *adj*: — **hours** horas *fpl* punta, horas *fpl* de máximo transito; **Barcelona in the** — **hour**

Barcelona a la hora punta; — **order** pedido *m* urgente; — **work** trabajo *m* hecho de prisa.

3 *vt* (**a**) (*person*) dar prisa a, apresurar; **I hate being** —**ed** no permito que me metan prisa, no aguanto a los que piden que vaya más de prisa.

(**b**) (*work*) hacer de prisa, ejecutar de prisa; **to** — **a bill through** hacer aprobar de prisa un proyecto de ley.

(**c**) (*carry etc*) llevar rápidamente; **to** — **medicine to someone** llevar con toda prisa medicina a uno; **he was** —**ed to hospital** le llevaron al hospital con la mayor urgencia.

(**d**) (*Mil*) *position etc* asaltar, tomar al asalto; *troops* atacar repentinamente; **the crowd** —**ed the barriers** el público asaltó las barreras.

(**e**) (*sl*) **how much did they** — **you?** ¿cuánto te cobraron?; **they** —**ed me £2** me hicieron pagar 2 libras.

4 *vi* precipitarse, lanzarse (*at* hacia, sobre); correr (*etc*) rápidamente, ir de prisa, ir a máxima velocidad; **to** — **across a road** cruzar una calle a toda prisa; **you mustn't** — **across roads like that** es peligroso cruzar las calles con tanta precipitación; **everyone** —**ed to the windows** se precipitaron todos hacia las ventanas; **the rocket was** —**ing through space** el cohete iba a gran velocidad por el espacio; **don't** — **!** ¡con calma!; **to** — **at someone** arremeter contra uno, abalanzarse sobre uno; **to** — **by, to** — **past** pasar como un rayo; **to** — **in** entrar precipitadamente; **to** — **into the fray** lanzarse a la batalla; **to** — **off** partir como un rayo; **to** — **out** salir precipitadamente; **I** —**ed to her side** me di prisa por ponerme a su lado; **I was** —**ing to finish** it me daba prisa por terminarlo.

rushlight ['rʌʃlait] *n* vela *f* de junco.
rushy ['rʌʃi] *adj* juncoso.
rusk [rʌsk] *n* bizcocho *m* tostado.
russet ['rʌsit] **1** *n* color *m* bermejo, color *m* rojizo. **2** *adj* bermejo, rojizo.
Russia ['rʌʃə] Rusia *f*.
Russian ['rʌʃən] **1** *adj* ruso. **2** *n* ruso *m*, rusa *f*. **3** *n* (*language*) ruso *m*.
rust [rʌst] **1** *n* (*action*) oxidación *f*, corrosión *f*; (*visible*) orín *m*, herrumbre *f*, moho *m*; (*colour*) color *m* de orín; (*Agr*) roya *f*.

2 *vt* oxidar, corroer; aherrumbrar.
3 *vi* oxidarse, corroerse; aherrumbrarse, tomarse de orín.
rustic ['rʌstik] **1** *adj* rústico; aldeano; (*pej*) rústico; (*person*) palurdo. **2** *n* rústico *m*, palurdo *m*.
rusticate ['rʌstikeit] **1** *vt* (*Univ*) suspender temporalmente. **2** *vi* rusticar.
rustication [ˌrʌsti'keiʃən] *n* (*Univ*) suspensión *f* temporal.
rusticity [rʌs'tisiti] *n* rusticidad *f*.
rustiness ['rʌstinis] *n* herrumbre *f*, lo aherrumbrado; (*fig*) falta *f* de práctica, torpeza *f*.
rustle[1] ['rʌsl] **1** *n* (*of leaves, wind*) susurro *m*; (*of paper*) crujido *m*; (*of silk, dress*) frufrú *m*.
2 *vt* hacer susurrar, mover ligeramente; hacer crujir.
3 *vi* susurrar; crujir; hacer frufrú.
rustle[2] ['rʌsl] *vt* (*US fam*) robar, hurtar.
rustless ['rʌstlis] *adj* inoxidable.
rustproof ['rʌstpruːf] *adj*, **rust-resistant** ['rʌstriˌzistənt] *adj* a prueba de herrumbre.
rusty ['rʌsti] *adj* oxidado, herrumbroso, aherrumbrado, mohoso; *colour* color de orín; (*fig*) falto de práctica, torpe; **my Catalan is pretty** — ya no hablo apenas catalán, mi catalán es bastante defectuoso.
rut[1] [rʌt] *n* rodera *f*, rodada *f*, carril *m*; bache *m*; (*fig*) rutina *f*, sendero *m* trillado; **to be in a** — estar sin poder salir de la rutina, ir encarrilado; **you've got into a** — te has hecho esclavo de la rutina; **to get out of the** — salir del bache.
rut[2] [rʌt] (*Bio*) **1** *n* celo *m*; **to be in** — estar en celo. **2** *vi* (*be*) estar en celo; (*begin to* —) caer en celo.
ruthless ['ruːθlis] *adj* despiadado; implacable, inexorable.
ruthlessly ['ruːθlisli] *adv* despiadadamente; implacablemente, inexorablemente.
ruthlessness ['ruːθlisnis] *n* crueldad *f*; implacabilidad *f*.
rutting ['rʌtiŋ] *adj* (*Bio*) en celo; — **season** época *f* de celo.
rutty ['rʌti] *adj* lleno de baches.
rye [rai] *n* centeno *m*.
rye bread ['rai'bred] *n* pan *m* de centeno.
ryegrass ['raigrɑːs] *n* cizaña *f*, joyo *m*.

S

Saar [zɑ:*] Sarre m.
sabbatarian [ˌsæbə'tɛəriən] **1** adj sabatario. **2** n sabatario m, a f, partidario m de guardar santamente el domingo.
sabbath ['sæbəθ] n (Christian) domingo m; (Jewish) sábado m.
sabbatical [sə'bætikəl] adj (Rel) sabático; dominical; — year (Univ) año m de licencia.
sable ['seibl] **1** n (animal, fur) cebellina f; (colour) negro m; (Her) sable m. **2** adj negro.
sabot ['sæbəu] n zueco m.
sabotage ['sæbətɑ:ʒ] **1** n sabotaje m. **2** vt sabotear (also fig).
saboteur [ˌsæbə'tə:*] n saboteador m.
sabre, (US) **saber** ['seibə*] **1** n sable m. **2** vt herir (or matar etc) a sablazos.
sabre rattler, (US) **saber** — ['seibəˌrætlə*] n patriotero m, jingoísta m.
sabre rattling, (US) **saber** — ['seibəˌrætliŋ] n patriotería f, jingoísmo m.
sac [sæk] n (Anat etc) saco m.
saccharin(e) ['sækərin] n sacarina f.
saccharine ['sækəri:n] adj sacarino; (fig) azucarado, empalagoso.
sacerdotal [ˌsæsə'dəutl] adj sacerdotal.
sachet ['sæʃei] n saquito m, bolsita f.
sack[1] [sæk] **1** n (a) saco m, costal m.
   (b) (fam) despido m; to get the — ser despedido; to give someone the — despedir a uno.
   2 vt (a) ensacar, meter en sacos.
   (b) (fam) despedir.
sack[2] [sæk] **1** n saqueo m. **2** vt saquear.
sackbut ['sækbʌt] n sacabuche m.
sackcloth ['sækkləθ] n (h)arpillera f; to wear — and ashes ponerse el hábito de penitencia, ponerse cenizas en la cabeza.
sackful ['sækful] n saco m, contenido m de un saco.
sacking[1] ['sækiŋ] n (material) (h)arpillera f.
sacking[2] ['sækiŋ] n (fam) despido m.
sack race ['sækreis] n carrera f de sacos.
sacrament ['sækrəmənt] n sacramento m; Eucaristía f; the Blessed S— el Santísimo Sacramento; to receive the Holy S— comulgar; to receive the last —s recibir los últimos sacramentos.
sacramental [ˌsækrə'mentl] adj sacramental.
sacred ['seikrid] adj sagrado; santo; consagrado; S— History Historia f Sagrada; — to the memory of . . . consagrado a la memoria de . . .; is —? ¿no hay nada sagrado para Vd?, ¿no respeta Vd nada?
sacrifice ['sækrifais] **1** n sacrificio m; (person etc) víctima f; the — of the mass el sacrificio de la misa; to make —s privarse de algo, renunciar a algo; to sell something at a — vender algo con pérdida.
   2 vt sacrificar; (Comm) vender con pérdida, vender a no importa qué precio.
   3 vr: to — oneself sacrificarse.
sacrificial [ˌsækri'fiʃəl] adj de sacrificio.
sacrilege ['sækrilidʒ] n sacrilegio m.
sacrilegious [ˌsækri'lidʒəs] adj sacrílego.
sacrist ['sækrist] n, **sacristan** ['sækristən] n sacristán m.
sacristy ['sækristi] n sacristía f.
sacrosanct ['sækrəusæŋkt] adj sacrosanto.
sacrum ['sækrəm] n (Anat) sacro m.
sad [sæd] adj (a) (sorrowful) triste; melancólico; how — ! ¡qué triste!; to be — at heart estar profundamente triste; 'to grow — entristecerse, ponerse triste; to make someone — entristecer a uno, poner triste a uno; he left a —der and a wiser man partió habiendo aprendido una dura lección.
   (b) (deplorable) lamentable; a — mistake un error lamentable; it's a — business es un asunto lamentable.

sadden ['sædn] vt entristecer; afligir.
saddle ['sædl] **1** n silla f (de montar); (cycle —) sillín m; (hill) collado m; (of meat) cuarto m trasero; to be in the — (fig) estar en el poder, mandar; to leap into the — saltar a la silla.
   2 vt horse (also to — up) ensillar; to — someone with something echar algo a cuestas a uno, echar a uno la responsabilidad de algo; now we're —d with it ahora tenemos que cargar con ello; to get —d with something cargar con algo.
   3 vr: to — oneself with something cargar con algo.
saddle-backed ['sædlbækt] adj ensillado.
saddlebag ['sædlbæg] n alforja f.
saddlebow ['sædlbəu] n arzón m delantero.
saddlecloth ['sædlkləθ] n sudadero m.
saddler ['sædlə*] n talabartero m, guarnicionero m.
saddlery ['sædləri] n talabartería f, guarnicionería f.
sadism ['seidizəm] n sadismo m.
sadist ['seidist] n sadista mf.
sadistic [sə'distik] adj sádico.
sadly ['sædli] adv (a) tristemente. (b) muy; — lacking in muy deficiente en; a — incompetent headmaster un director (de colegio) de lo más ineficaz.
sadness ['sædnis] n tristeza f, melancolía f.
safari [sə'fɑ:ri] n safari m; to be on — estar de safari.
safe [seif] **1** adj seguro; salvo, fuera de peligro; (from injury) ileso, incólume; bet etc seguro, cierto; person (trustworthy) digno de confianza, formal; (sound) prudente, sensato; — and sound sano y salvo; — from a salvo de, al abrigo de; as — as houses completamente seguro; the —st thing is to + infin lo más seguro es + infin; just to be — por precaución, para mayor seguridad; all the passengers are — todos los pasajeros están ilesos, no ha habido víctimas entre los pasajeros; these stairs are not very — esta escalera no es muy segura; it's a — beach es una playa sin peligro; no girl is — with him ninguna joven está sin peligro estando con él; is that dog — ? ¿es peligroso ese perro?; he's — with children es muy manso con los niños; your reputation is — su reputación está a salvo; the secret is — with me el secreto seguirá siéndolo conmigo; the book is — now ahora el libro está en buenas manos; you'll be perfectly — here aquí está Vd fuera de todo peligro; his life was not — no estaba seguro de su vida; is it — to go out? ¿se puede salir sin peligro?; it is — to say that . . . se puede decir con confianza que . . .; to come — home volver a casa sin novedad; to keep something — tener algo seguro; he plays a — game es un jugador prudente.
   2 n caja f de caudales; (for meat) fresquera f.
safe-blower ['seif,bləuə*] n ladrón m de cajas de caudales.
safe-conduct ['seif'kɔndəkt] n salvoconducto m.
safe deposit ['seifdi,pɔzit] n cámara f acorazada.
safeguard ['seifgɑ:d] **1** n protección f, garantía f; as a — por precaución; as a — against . . . como defensa contra . . ., para evitar . . .
   2 vt salvaguardar, proteger, defender.
safely ['seifli] adv seguramente, con seguridad; sin peligro; arrive, travel etc sin novedad, sin accidente; you may — do it now ahora puedes hacerlo sin peligro; to put something away — poner algo en un lugar seguro.
safeness ['seifnis] n seguridad f.
safety ['seifti] **1** n seguridad f; road — seguridad f en la carretera; in a place of — en un lugar seguro; for —'s sake por precaución, para mayor seguridad, en interés de la seguridad; with complete — con la mayor seguridad; to play for — obrar prudentemente; to reach — ponerse a salvo; to seek — in flight salvarse huyendo.
   2 attr de seguridad.

safety belt ['seiftibelt] n cinturón m de seguridad.
safety catch ['seiftikætʃ] n fiador m; dispositivo m de seguridad; (on gun) seguro m.
safety curtain ['seifti,kə:tn] n (Theat) telón m de seguridad.
safety first ['seifti'fə:st] attr: — **campaign** campaña f pro seguridad; **to believe in** — poner la seguridad en primer lugar, creer en la seguridad ante todo; "—" (as slogan) "¡precaución!", "¡prudencia!"
safety glass ['seiftiglɑ:s] n vidrio m inastillable.
safety lamp ['seiftilæmp] n lámpara f de seguridad.
safety measure ['seifti,meʒə*] n prevención f; **to take** —s tomar prevenciones.
safety net ['seiftinet] n red f de seguridad.
safety pin ['seiftipin] n imperdible m.
safety razor ['seifti,reizə*] n maquinilla f de afeitar.
safety valve ['seiftivalv] n válvula f de seguridad.
saffron ['sæfrən] 1 n azafrán m. 2 adj azafranado, color azafrán.
sag [sæg] 1 n comba f. 2 vi (bulge, warp) combarse, hundirse, pandear; (slacken) aflojarse, ceder; (price etc) bajar; (spirit) flaquear.
saga ['sɑːgə] n saga f; (fig) saga f, epopeya f.
sagacious [sə'geiʃəs] adj sagaz.
sagaciously [sə'geiʃəsli] adv sagazmente.
sagacity [sə'gæsiti] n sagacidad f.
sage[1] [seidʒ] n (Bot) salvia f.
sage[2] [seidʒ] 1 adj sabio. 2 n sabio m.
sagebrush ['seidʒbrʌʃ] n (Bot) artemisa f.
sagely ['seidʒli] adv sabiamente.
sago ['seigəu] n sagú m.
Sahara [sə'hɑːrə] Sahara m.
sahib ['sɑːhib] n (India) (a) señor m; **Smith S—** (el) señor Smith. (b) (hum) caballero m; **pukka —** caballero m de verdad.
said [sed] 1 pret and ptp of **say**. 2 adj dicho, antedicho; **the — animals** dichos animales, los cuales animales; **the — general** tal general.
sail [seil] 1 n (a) (cloth) vela f; **in full —, under full —, with all —s** set a toda vela, a vela llena; **to set —** hacerse a la vela, zarpar (for con rumbo a); **to lower the —s** arriar las velas; **to take in the —s** amainar.
  (b) (of mill) aspa f.
  (c) (trip) paseo m en barco (de vela), paseo m en balandro (etc); **it is 3 days' — from here** desde aquí es un viaje de 3 días en barco; **to go for a —** dar un paseo en barco (de vela), salir en balandro (etc).
  (d) (boat) barco m de vela, velero m; **20 — 20** barcos.
  2 vt (a) ship (steer) gobernar; **they —ed the ship to Cadiz** fueron con el barco a Cádiz, fueron en el barco a Cádiz.
  (b) **to — the seas** navegar los mares.
  3 vi (a) (Naut) navegar; **to — at 12 knots** navegar a 12 nudos, ir a 12 nudos; **we —ed into Lisbon** llegamos a Lisboa; **we —ed into harbour** entramos a puerto; **to — round the world** dar la vuelta al mundo; **to — round a headland** doblar un cabo; **to — up the Tagus** entrar en el Tajo, subir el Tajo.
  (b) (leave: Naut) hacerse a la vela, zarpar (for con rumbo a); (general sense) salir, partir; **she —s on Monday** sale el lunes; **we — for Australia** partimos para Australia, nos embarcamos para Australia.
  (c) (fig: swan etc) deslizarse; (cloud) flotar; (object) volar; **she —ed into the room** entró majestuosamente en la sala; **it —ed over my head** voló por encima de mi cabeza; **it —ed over into the next garden** voló por los aires y cayó en el jardín de al lado.
  (d) **to — into someone** (fam) arremeter contra uno, atacar a uno.
sailboat ['seilbəut] n (US) barco m de vela.
sailcloth ['seilklɔθ] n lona f.
sailfish ['seilfiʃ] n aguja f de mar, pez m vela.
sailing ['seiliŋ] n navegación f; (departure) salida f, partida f; **— date** fecha f de salida; **now it's all plain —** ahora es muy sencillo, ahora es cosa de coser y cantar; **it's not exactly plain —** no es sencillo que digamos.
sailing ship ['seiliŋʃip] n velero m, buque m de vela.
sail maker ['seil,meikə*] n velero m.
sailor ['seilə*] n marinero m, marino m; **to be a bad —** marearse fácilmente; **to be a good —** no marearse.
sailor suit ['seiləsu:t] n traje m de marinero (de niño).
sailplane ['seilplein] n velero m, planeador m.
sainfoin ['sænfɔin] n pipirigallo m.
saint [seint] n (a) santo m, a f.
  (b) before m names abbreviated to San, eg **St John** San Juan; except **St Dominic** Santo Domingo, **St Thomas** Santo Tomás.

  (c) (as name of church) at **St Mark's** en San Marcos, en la iglesia de San Marcos; **the church is dedicated to St Luke** la iglesia está bajo la advocación de San Lucas.
  (d) **St Andrew** (patrón de Escocia) San Andrés; **St Bernard** (dog) perro m de San Bernardo; **St George** (patrón de Inglaterra) San Jorge; **St James** (patrón de España) Santiago; **St John the Baptist** San Juan Bautista; **St Kitts** (W.I.) San Cristóbal; **St Patrick** (patrón de Irlanda) San Patricio; **St Theresa** Santa Teresa; **St Valentine's Day** día m de San Valentín (14 febrero, día de los enamorados); **St Vitus' dance** baile m de San Vito.
sainted ['seintid] adj santo; bendito; (of dead) que en santa gloria esté.
sainthood ['seinthud] n santidad f.
saintliness ['seintlinis] n santidad f.
saintly ['seintli] adj santo.
sake [seik] n: **for the — of** por; por motivo de; en consideración a, en atención a; **for God's —** por el amor de Dios; **for God's —!, for heaven's —!** ¡por Dios!; **for my —** por mí; **for your own —** por su propio bien, en interés propio; **for old times' —** por respeto al pasado, en atención a los recuerdos del pasado; **for the — of peace** por amor a la paz, en interés de la paz; para obtener la paz; **Art for Art's —** el arte por el arte; **to talk for talking's —** hablar por hablar.
salaam [sə'lɑːm] 1 n zalema f. 2 vt hacer zalema a. 3 vi hacer zalema.
salable ['seiləbl] adj (US) = **saleable**.
salacious [sə'leiʃəs] adj salaz.
salaciousness [sə'leiʃəsnis] n salacidad f.
salad ['sæləd] n ensalada f; **fruit —** macedonia f de frutas.
salad bowl ['sælədbəul] n ensaladera f.
salad days ['sælədeiz] npl juventud f; ingenuidad f juvenil.
salad dish ['sælədiʃ] n ensaladera f.
salad dressing ['sæləd,dresiŋ] n mayonesa f, aliño m.
salad oil ['sælədɔil] n aceite m para ensaladas.
salamander ['sælə,mændə*] n salamandra f.
salami [sə'lɑːmi] n salami m.
sal ammoniac [,sælə'məuniæk] n sal f amoníaca.
salaried ['sælərid] adj: — **post** puesto m retribuido; — **person** persona f que gana un sueldo, persona f que cobra cada mes; — **staff** personal m a sueldo, (freq) empleados mpl de oficina.
salary ['sæləri] n sueldo m.
salary earner ['sæləri,ə:nə*] n persona f que gana un sueldo, persona f que cobra cada mes.
sale [seil] 1 n venta f; (clearance —) liquidación f; (annual —, spring — etc) saldo m; (auction —, public —) subasta f; "—" (in shop window) "grandes rebajas"; **I bought it at a —** lo compré en un saldo, lo compré en una subasta; **"for —"** "se vende"; **"horse for —"** "se vende (un) caballo"; **is it for —?** ¿se vende?; **"not for —"** "no se vende"; **it's going cheap for a quick —** se ofrece a un precio módico para poder venderlo pronto; **to put a house up for —** ofrecer una casa en venta; **to be on —** estar en venta; **"on — at all fishmongers"** "de venta en todas las pescaderías"; **the —s are on** es la temporada de los saldos.
  2 attr: — **price** precio m de venta; — **value** valor m en el mercado.
saleable ['seiləbl] adj vendible.
saleroom ['seilrum] n sala f de subastas.
salesman ['seilzmən] n, pl —**men** [mən] (in shop) dependiente m, vendedor m; (traveller) viajante m; **"Death of a S—"** "La muerte de un viajante".
salesmanship ['seilzmənʃip] n arte m de vender.
sales resistance ['seilzri,zistəns] n resistencia f a comprar, resistencia f de parte del comprador.
sales tax ['seilztæks] n impuesto m sobre las ventas.
saleswoman ['seilzwumən] n, pl —**women** [wimin] dependienta f, vendedora f.
salient ['seiliənt] 1 adj saliente; (fig) sobresaliente, destacado, notable; **the most — feature** el aspecto más notable. 2 n saliente m.
saline ['seilain] adj salino.
salinity [sə'liniti] n salinidad f.
saliva [sə'laivə] n saliva f.
salivary ['sælivəri] adj salival.
salivate ['sæliveit] vi salivar.
salivation [,sæli'veiʃən] n salivación f.
sallow[1] ['sæləu] n (Bot) sauce m cabruno.
sallow[2] ['sæləu] adj cetrino, amarillento.
sallowness ['sæləunis] n lo cetrino, amarillez f.
Sallust ['sæləst] m Salustio.
Sally ['sæli] f nombre cariñoso de **Sarah**.

sally ['sæli] **1** *n* (*all senses*) salida *f*; **to make a —** hacer una salida. **2** *vi* hacer una salida; **to — forth, to — out** salir resueltamente.

salmon ['sæmən] **1** *n* salmón *m*; (*colour*) color *m* salmón. **2** *adj* color salmón.

salmon trout ['sæmən,traut] *n* trucha *f* asalmonada.

salon ['sælɔ:ŋ] *n* salón *m*.

saloon [sə'lu:n] *n* salón *m*; (*Naut*) cámara *f*, salón *m*; (*Aut*) turismo *m*; (*US*) bar *m*; taberna *f*; **billiard —** salón *m* de billar; **hairdressing —** salón *m* de peluquería.

saloon car [sə'lu:nka:*] *n* (*Rail*) coche-salón *m*.

salsify ['sælsifi] *n* (*Bot*) salsifí *m*.

salt [sɔ:lt] **1** *n* sal *f*; **—s** sales *fpl* medicinales; **kitchen —** sal *f* de cocina; **table —** sal *f* de mesa; **old —** lobo *m* de mar; **— of the earth** sal *f* de la tierra; **to be worth one's —** merecer el pan que se come; *see* **pinch**.

2 *adj meat, water etc* salado; *taste* salobre; **it's very —** está muy salado.

3 *vt* (*cure*) salar; (*flavour*) poner sal en, añadir sal a; **to — a dig** (*Archaeology*) poner objetos en una excavación para que se encuentren después; **to — away** (*fig*) ocultar para uso futuro.

saltcellar ['sɔ:lt,selə*] *n* salero *m*.

saltings ['sɔ:ltiŋz] *npl* saladar *m*.

salt lake ['sɔ:ltleik] *n* lago *m* de agua salada.

salt marsh ['sɔ:ltma:ʃ] *n* saladar *m*.

salt mine ['sɔ:ltmain] *n* mina *f* de sal.

saltness ['sɔ:ltnis] *n* salinidad *f*; sabor *m* de sal; salobridad *f*.

salt pan ['sɔ:ltpæn] *n* salina *f*.

saltpetre, (*US*) **saltpeter** ['sɔ:lt,pi:tə*] *n* salitre *m*.

salt spoon ['sɔ:ltspu:n] *n* cucharita *f* de sal.

saltwater ['sɔ:lt,wɔ:tə*] *attr fish etc* de mar, de agua salada.

saltworks ['sɔ:ltwə:ks] *n* salinas *fpl*.

salty ['sɔ:lti] *adj* salado (*also fig*); salobre.

salubrious [sə'lu:briəs] *adj* salubre, sano.

salubrity [sə'lu:briti] *n* salubridad *f*.

salutary ['sæljutəri] *adj* saludable.

salutation [,sælju'teiʃən] *n* salutación *f*, saludo *m*.

salutatory [,sælju'teitəri] *adj* de salutación.

salute [sə'lu:t] **1** *n* (*with hand etc*) saludo *m*; (*kiss*) beso *m*; (*of guns*) salva *f*; **to fire a — of 21 guns for someone** saludar a uno con una salva de 21 cañonazos; **to take the —** tomar el saludo.

2 *vti* saludar.

Salvadoran [,sælvə'dɔ:rən] **1** *adj* salvadoreño. **2** *n* salvadoreño *m*, a *f*.

salvage ['sælvidʒ] **1** *n* (*act*) salvamento *m*; recuperación *f*; (*objects*) objetos *mpl* salvados; (*material*) material *m* utilizable.

2 *vt* salvar; recuperar; **to — something from the wreckage** salvar algo de las ruinas.

salvation [sæl'veiʃən] *n* salvación *f*; **S— Army** Ejército *m* de Salvación.

salvationist [sæl'veiʃnist] *n* miembro *m* del Ejército de Salvación.

salve¹ [sælv] *vt* (*Naut etc*) salvar; recuperar.

salve² [sælv] **1** *n* (*fig*) ungüento *m*, bálsamo *m*. **2** *vt* curar (con ungüento); **to — one's conscience** tranquilizar la conciencia.

salver ['sælvə*] *n* bandeja *f*.

salvo¹ ['sælvəu] *n* salvedad *f*, reserva *f*.

salvo² ['sælvəu] *n* (*Mil*) salva *f*; **a — of applause** una salva de aplausos.

sal volatile [,sælvə'lætəli] *n* sal *f* volátil.

Sam [sæm] *m nombre cariñoso de* **Samuel.**

Samaritan [sə'mæritn] **1** *adj* samaritano. **2** *n* samaritano *m*, a *f*; **good —** buen samaritano *m*.

sambo ['sæmbəu] *n* (*pej*) mestizo *m*; negro *m*.

same [seim] *adj* mismo; igual; idéntico; **"Mr Jones" — "the —"** "¿Señor Jones?" . . . "el mismo"; **— here!** ¡yo también!; **it's the — with us** es igual para nosotros, nosotros tenemos lo mismo; **and I did the —** y yo hice lo mismo; **I'd do the — again** yo volvería a hacer lo mismo; **and the — to you!** ¡igualmente!; ¡a Vd!; **all the — con todo, de todas formas; a pesar de todo; it's all the —** es lo mismo, es todo uno; **it's all the — to me** me es igual, lo mismo me da; **if it's all the — to you** si a Vd le da lo mismo; **it's just the —** es exactamente igual; **things go on just the —** eso continúa como siempre; **they are much the —** son más o menos idénticos; **she's much about the —** sigue más o menos en el mismo estado; **it's the — old complaint** es lo de siempre; **I still feel the — about you** mis sentimientos respecto a ti siguen siendo los mismos; **the — as . . .** el mismo que . . .

sameness ['seimnis] *n* igualdad *f*; identidad *f*; (*pej*) monotonía *f*.

samovar [,sæməu'va:*] *n* samovar *m*.

sampan ['sæmpæn] *n* sampán *m*.

sample ['sa:mpl] **1** *n* (*all senses*) muestra *f*; **free —** muestra *f* gratuita. **2** *vt* probar; (*in blending*) catar; (*Math*) muestrear.

sample book ['sa:mplbuk] *n* muestrario *m*.

sampler ['sa:mplə*] *n* (*person*) catador *m*; (*Sew*) dechado *m*.

sampling ['sa:mpliŋ] *n* (*Math*) muestreo *m*; **— technique** método *m* de muestreo.

Samson ['sæmsn] *m* Sansón.

Samuel ['sæmjuəl] *m* Samuel.

sanatorium [,sænə'tɔ:riəm] *n*, *pl* **sanatoria** [,sænə'tɔ:riə] sanatorio *m*.

sanctification [,sæŋktifi'keiʃən] *n* santificación *f*.

sanctify ['sæŋktifai] *vt* santificar.

sanctimonious [,sæŋkti'məuniəs] *adj* mojigato, santurrón, beato.

sanctimoniously [,sæŋkti'məuniəsli] *adv* con mojigatería; **she said —** dijo mojigata.

sanctimoniousness [,sæŋkti'məuniəsnis] *n* mojigatería *f*, santurronería *f*, beatería *f*.

sanction ['sæŋkʃən] **1** *n* sanción *f*. **2** *vt* sancionar.

sanctity ['sæŋktiti] *n* santidad *f*; inviolabilidad *f*; **— of the mails** secreto *m* de correspondencia.

sanctuary ['sæŋktjuəri] *n* santuario *m*; (*high altar*) sagrario *m*; (*place of refuge: Hist*) sagrado ·*m*, (*modern*) refugio *m*, asilo *m*; **to seek —** acogerse a lo sagrado; **to seek — in** refugiarse en; **to seek — with** acogerse a.

sanctum ['sæŋktəm] *n* lugar *m* sagrado; (*fig, study*) despacho *m* particular.

sand [sænd] **1** *n* arena *f*; **—s** (*of desert*) arenas *fpl*, (*beach*) playa *f* (arenosa); **shifting —s** arenas *fpl* movedizas; **the —s are running out** queda poco tiempo.

2 *vt* enarenar.

sandal ['sændl] *n* sandalia *f*.

sandal(wood) ['sændl(wud)] *n* sándalo *m*.

sandbag ['sændbæg] **1** *n* saco *m* de arena. **2** *vt* proteger con sacos de arena.

sandbank ['sændbæŋk] *n* banco *m* de arena.

sand bar ['sændba:*] *n* barra *f* de arena, banco *m* de arena.

sandblast ['sændbla:st] *n* (*Tech*) chorro *m* de arena.

sandcastle ['sænd,ka:sl] *n* castillo *m* de arena.

sand dune ['sænddju:n] *n* duna *f*.

sand fly ['sændflai] *n* jijene *m*.

sandglass ['sændgla:s] *n* reloj *m* de arena.

sandlot ['sændlɒt] *n* (*US*) terreno en una ciudad que se usa para el béisbol (etc).

sandman ['sændmæn] *n* genio fabuloso que les trae el sueño a los niños.

sandpaper ['sænd,peipə*] **1** *n* papel *m* de lija. **2** *vt* lijar.

sandpiper ['sænd,paipə*] *n* (*Orn*) andarríos *m*, lavandera *f*.

sandpit ['sændpit] *n* arenal *m*; (*in garden*) cuadro *m* de arena.

sand shoes ['sændʃu:z] *npl* playeras *fpl*.

sandstone ['sændstəun] *n* piedra *f* arenisca.

sandstorm ['sændstɔ:m] *n* simún *m*, tempestad *f* de arena.

sandwich ['sænwidʒ] **1** *n* sándwich *m*, bocadillo *m*. **2** *vt* insertar; intercalar; (*Sport*) apretujar; **to — something between two things** poner algo (apretadamente) entre dos cosas; **the house is —ed between two big hotels** la casa se encuentra entre dos grandes hoteles, la casa ocupa un espacio estrecho entre dos grandes hoteles; **I was —ed between two fat ladies** me tocó estar apretujado entre dos señoras gordas.

sandwich board ['sænwidʒ,bɔ:d] *n* cartelón *m* (*que lleva el hombre-anuncio*).

sandwich man ['sænwidʒmæn] *n*, *pl* **— men** [men] hombre-anuncio *m*.

sandy ['sændi] *adj* arenoso; (*in colour*) rojizo, dorado; *hair* rojo.

sane [sein] *adj person* cuerdo, sensato, de juicio sano; *policy etc* prudente; **a very — person** una persona muy sensata.

Sanforize ['sænfəraiz]. (*Protected Trade Name*) *vt* sanforizar.

sang [sæŋ] *pret of* **sing.**

sangfroid ['sɑ:ŋ'frwa:] *n* sangre *f* fría.

sanguinary ['sæŋgwinəri] *adj* sanguinario; sangriento.

sanguine ['sæŋgwin] *adj* (*fig*) optimista.

sanguineous [sæŋ'gwiniəs] *adj* sanguíneo.

sanitarium [,sæni'teəriəm] *n* (*US*) sanatorio *m*.

sanitary ['sænitəri] *adj* sanitario; higiénico; **— inspector** inspector *m* de sanidad.

sanitary towel ['sænitəri,tauəl], (US) — **napkin** [,næpkin] n paño m higiénico, compresa f higiénica.
sanitation [,sæni'teiʃən] n sanidad f; higiene f; (domestic —) instalación f sanitaria, saneamiento m, (euph) servicios mpl.
sanity ['sæniti] n cordura f, sensatez f, juicio m sano; prudencia f; **to be restored to** — recobrar su juicio; — **demands that** . . . la razón exige que . . .; **to return to** — ponerse en razón, volver a la razón.
sank [sæŋk] pret of **sink**[1].
Sanskrit ['sænskrit] 1 adj sánscrito. 2 n sánscrito m.
Santa Claus [,sæntə'klɔːz] San Nicolás (que en los países del norte trae regalos para los niños, el día de Navidad; equivale a los Reyes Magos).
sap[1] [sæp] n (Bot) savia f; (fig) jugo m (vital), vitalidad f.
sap[2] [sæp] (Mil) 1 n zapa f. 2 vt zapar; socavar; strength etc minar, agotar.
sap[3] [sæp] n (sl) bobo m; you — ! ¡bobo!
sapling ['sæpliŋ] n pimpollo m, árbol m nuevo, arbolito m.
sapper ['sæpə*] n zapador m.
sapphire ['sæfaiə*] n zafiro m.
sappy[1] ['sæpi] adj (Bot) lleno de savia, jugoso.
sappy[2] ['sæpi] adj (sl) bobo.
saraband ['særəbænd] n zarabanda f.
Saracen ['særəsn] 1 adj sarraceno. 2 n sarraceno m, a f.
Saragossa [,særə'gɔsə] Zaragoza.
Sarah ['sɛərə] f Sara.
sarcasm ['sɑːkæzəm] n sarcasmo m.
sarcastic [sɑː'kæstik] adj sarcástico.
sarcastically [sɑː'kæstikəli] adv con sarcasmo, sarcásticamente.
sarcophagus [sɑː'kɔfəgəs] n, pl **sarcophagi** [sɑː-'kɔfəgai] sarcófago m.
sardine [sɑː'diːn] n sardina f.
Sardinia [sɑː'diniə] Cerdeña f.
Sardinian [sɑː'diniən] 1 adj sardo. 2 n sardo m, a f.
sardonic [sɑː'dɔnik] adj burlón, irónico, sarcástico.
sardonically [sɑː'dɔnikəli] adv con aire burlón, irónicamente, con sarcasmo.
sari ['sɑːri] n sari m.
sarsaparilla [,sɑːsəpə'rilə] n zarzaparrilla f.
sartorial [sɑː'tɔːriəl] adj relativo al vestido; — **elegance** elegancia f en el vestido; — **taste** gusto m en vestidos.
sash[1] [sæʃ] n faja f; (Mil: of order) fajín m.
sash[2] [sæʃ] n (window —) marco m corredizo de ventana.
sash cord ['sæʃkɔːd] n cuerda f de ventana (de guillotina).
sash window ['sæʃ,windəu] n ventana f de guillotina.
sass [sæs] (US) 1 n réplicas fpl. 2 vt: to — **someone** replicar a uno.
sassafras ['sæsəfræs] n sasafrás m.
Sassenach ['sæsənæx] n (Scot: pej) inglés m, esa f.
sassy ['sæsi] adj (US) fresco, descarado.
sat [sæt] pret and ptp of **sit**.
Satan ['seitn] m Satanás.
satanic [sə'tænik] adj satánico.
satchel ['sætʃəl] n bolsa f, cartera f; (schoolboy's) cabás m.
sate [seit] vt saciar, hartar.
sateen [sæ'tiːn] n satén m.
satellite ['sætəlait] 1 n satélite m. 2 attr: — **country** país m satélite; — **town** ciudad f satélite.
satiate ['seiʃieit] vt saciar, hartar.
satiation [,seiʃi'eiʃən] n, **satiety** [sə'taiəti] n saciedad f, hartura f; **to** — hasta la saciedad.
satin ['sætin] 1 n raso m. 2 adj (also **satiny** ['sætini]) terso, liso; lustroso.
satinwood ['sætinwud] n madera f satinada de las Indias.
satire ['sætaiə*] n sátira f.
satiric(al) [sə'tirik(əl)] adj satírico.
satirically [sə'tirikəli] adv satíricamente.
satirist ['sætərist] n escritor m satírico.
satirize ['sætəraiz] vt satirizar.
satisfaction [,sætis'fækʃən] n satisfacción f; (of debt) pago m, liquidación f; **to the general** — con la satisfacción de todos; **has it been done to your** —? ¿se ha hecho a su satisfacción? **to demand** — pedir satisfacción; **to express one's** — **at a result** expresar su satisfacción con un resultado, declararse satisfecho con un resultado; **it gives every** (or full) — es completamente satisfactorio; **it gives me much** — **to introduce** . . . es para mí un verdadero placer presentar a . . .
satisfactorily [,sætis'fæktərili] adv satisfactoriamente, de modo satisfactorio.
satisfactory [,sætis'fæktəri] adj satisfactorio.

satisfy ['sætisfai] 1 vt satisfacer; debt pagar, liquidar; (convince) convencer; **it completely satisfies me** me satisface completamente; **to** — **someone that** . . . convencer a uno de que . . .; **I am not satisfied that** . . . no estoy convencido de que . . .; **to** — **the requirements** llenar los requisitos; **you'll have to be satisfied with that** Vd tendrá que contentarse con eso; **we are very satisfied with it** estamos perfectamente satisfechos con él, nos satisface completamente.
2 vr: **to** — **oneself about something** satisfacerse con algo; **to** — **oneself that** . . . convencerse de que . . .
satisfying ['sætisfaiiŋ] adj satisfactorio, que satisface; food, meal bueno.
saturate ['sætʃəreit] 1 vt saturar, empapar (with de); **to be** —**d with** (fig) estar empapado de. 2 vr: **to** — **oneself in** (fig) empaparse en.
saturation [,sætʃə'reiʃən] n saturación f.
saturation point [,sætʃə'reiʃənpoint] n punto m de saturación.
Saturday ['sætədi] n sábado m.
Saturn ['sætən] m Saturno.
Saturnalia [,sætə'neiliə] npl saturnales fpl.
saturnine ['sætənain] adj saturnino.
satyr ['sætə*] n sátiro m.
sauce [sɔːs] n (a) salsa f; (sweet) crema f; (of fruit) compota f; **what's** — **for the goose is** — **for the gander** lo que es bueno para uno es bueno para el otro.
(b) (fig) frescura f; **what** — ! ¡qué fresco!; **none of your** — ! ¡Vd es un fresco!
sauceboat ['sɔːsbəut] n salsera f.
saucepan ['sɔːspən] n cacerola f, cazo m.
saucer ['sɔːsə*] n platillo m; **flying** — platillo m volante.
saucily ['sɔːsili] adv reply etc con frescura; con coquetería.
sauciness ['sɔːsinis] n frescura f, descaro m, desfachatez f; coquetería f.
saucy ['sɔːsi] adj fresco, descarado, desfachatado; girl coqueta; hat etc coquetón; **don't be** — ! ¡qué fresco!
Saudi Arabia ['saudiə'reibiə] Arabia f Saudita.
sauerkraut ['sauəkraut] n chucruta f.
Saul [sɔːl] m Saúl.
sauna ['sɔːnə] n sauna f.
saunter ['sɔːntə*] 1 n paseo m lento y tranquilo; **to have a** — **in the park** dar un paseo tranquilo en el parque.
2 vi pasearse despacio y tranquilamente; **to** — **up and down** deambular, pasearse despacio de acá para allá; **he** —**ed up to me** se acercó a mí con mucha calma.
saurian ['sɔːriən] n saurio m.
sausage ['sɔsidʒ] n (general term) embutido m; (small) salchicha f; **cocktail** — salchichita f de aperitivo; **pork** — salchicha f de cerdo.
sausage machine ['sɔsidʒmə,ʃiːn] n embutidora f.
sausage meat ['sɔsidʒmiːt] n masa f del embutido.
sausage roll ['sɔsidʒ'rəul] n pequeña empanada de salchicha (en forma cilíndrica).
sauté ['soutei] 1 adj salteado. 2 vt saltear.
savage ['sævidʒ] 1 adj salvaje; attack feroz, furioso, violento; **to be** — (fam) estar rabioso; **to get** — (fam) ponerse negro (fam).
2 n salvaje mf.
3 vt (of animal) embestir, atacar, morder.
savagely ['sævidʒli] adv de modo salvaje; ferozmente, furiosamente, violentamente; **he said** — dijo furioso.
savageness ['sævidʒnis] n, **savagery** ['sævidʒri] n salvajismo m, salvajería f; ferocidad f, furia f, violencia f.
savannah [sə'vænə] n sabana f.
savant ['sævənt] n sabio m, erudito m, intelectual m.
save[1] [seiv] 1 vt (a) (rescue) salvar; rescatar; **to** — **someone's life** salvar la vida a uno; **to** — **someone from death** salvar a uno de la muerte, rescatar a uno de la muerte; **to** — **someone from falling** impedir que caiga uno, agarrarse a uno para que no se caiga; **to** — **appearances** salvar las apariencias; **to** — **the situation** estar al nivel de las circunstancias; **to** — **one's soul** salvar su alma; **God** — **the Queen** Dios guarde a la Reina, Dios salve a la Reina; **God** — **us all**! ¡que Dios nos ayude!; **to** — **a building for posterity** lograr conservar un edificio para la posteridad; **to** — **one's eyes** cuidarse la vista; **to** — **something from the wreck** salvar algo de las ruinas.
(b) (put by) guardar, reservar; (preserve) conservar; money etc ahorrar; stamps etc coleccionar;

I —d this for you guardé esto para ti; — me a seat resérvame un asiento; she has £200 —d sus ahorros suman 200 libras.

(c) (avoid using up) time etc ahorrar; to — time . . . para ahorrar tiempo . . ., para ganar tiempo . . .; this way you — £8 por este sistema te ahorras 8 libras; this way you — 4 miles por esta ruta te ahorras 4 millas; it —s fuel economiza combustible; he's saving his strength for tomorrow se reserva para mañana.

(d) (prevent) evitar, impedir; to — a goal parar un tiro, impedir que se marque un gol; it —d a lot of trouble evitó muchas molestias, evitó muchos disgustos; to — someone trouble evitar molestias a uno.

2 vi ahorrar, economizar, hacer economías; to — up for a new bicycle ahorrar dinero para comprar una bicicleta.

3 vr: to — oneself for reservarse para.

save² [seiv] prep and conj (esp lit) salvo, excepto, con excepción de; all — one todos excepto uno, todos menos uno; — for excepto; si no fuera por; — that excepto que.

saveloy ['sævələi] n salchicha seca muy sazonada.

saving ['seiviŋ] 1 adj (a) económico; (pej) tacaño; she's not the — sort no es de las que economizan.

(b) see clause etc.

2 n (act: rescue) salvamento m, rescate m; (Eccl) salvación f; (of money etc) ahorro m; (of cost etc) economía f; —s ahorros mpl; she has —s of £300 sus ahorros suman 300 libras; we must make —s tenemos que economizar.

savings bank ['seiviŋzbæŋk] n caja f de ahorros; post office — caja f postal de ahorros.

saviour ['seivjə*] n salvador m, ora f; S— Salvador m.

savoir-faire ['sævwɑːˈfɛə*] n desparpajo m; habilidad f práctica; sentido m común.

savory ['seivəri] n (Bot) tomillo m salsero.

savour, (US) savor ['seivə*] 1 n sabor m, gusto m; (aftertaste) dejo m; (fig) sabor m (of a); it has lost its — ha perdido su sabor.

2 vt saborear, paladear; (fig) saborear.

3 vi: to — of saber a, oler a (also fig).

savouriness, (US) savoriness ['seivərinis] n sabor m, buen sabor m, lo sabroso; (fig) respetabilidad f.

savourless, (US) savorless ['seivəlis] adj soso, insípido.

savoury, (US) savory ['seivəri] 1 adj (appetizing) sabroso, apetitoso; (not sweet) no dulce; (salted) salado; not very — (fig) no muy respetable, poco decente; it's not a very — district es un barrio de mala fama.

2 n entremés m salado.

Savoy [sə'vɔi] Saboya f.

savoy [sə'vɔi] n berza f de Saboya.

savvy ['sævi] (sl) 1 n inteligencia f; desparpajo m.

2 vt comprender; —? ¿comprende?

saw¹ [sɔː] 1 n sierra f; circular — sierra f circular.

2 (irr: pret sawed, ptp sawed or sawn) vt serrar.

saw² [sɔː] n refrán m, dicho m.

saw³ [sɔː] pret of see.

sawbuck ['sɔːbʌk] n (US) caballete m para aserrar.

sawdust ['sɔːdʌst] n serrín m.

sawfish ['sɔːfiʃ] n pez m sierra.

sawhorse ['sɔːhɔːs] n caballete m para serrar.

sawmill ['sɔːmil] n aserradero m.

sawn [sɔːn] ptp of saw.

sawyer ['sɔːjə*] n aserrador m.

sax [sæks] n (fam) saxofón m, saxo m (fam).

saxifrage ['sæksifridʒ] n saxífraga f.

Saxon ['sæksn] 1 adj sajón. 2 n sajón m, ona f.

Saxony ['sæksəni] Sajonia f.

saxophone ['sæksəfəun] n saxofón m.

say [sei] 1 n: to have a (or some) — in something tener voz y voto; to have no — in something no tener voz en capítulo; I had no — in it no tuve nada que ver con ello, no pidieron mi parecer acerca de ello; if I had had a — in it si hubieran pedido mi parecer; I have had my — he dicho lo que quería; to let someone have his — dejar hablar a uno; let him have his —! ¡que hable él!

2 (irr: pret and ptp said) vt (a) decir; (text) decir, rezar; mass decir; prayer rezar; lesson recitar; to — yes decir que sí; to — no decir que no; to — yes to an invitation aceptar una invitación; to — no to a proposal rechazar una propuesta; to — good-bye to someone despedirse de uno; to — good morning to someone dar los buenos días a uno; my watch —s 3 o'clock mi reloj marca las 3; it —s 30 degrees marca 30 grados; they — se dice, dicen; I must — that . . . tengo que confesar que . . .; to — to

oneself decir para sí; who shall I —? ¿qué nombre digo?

(b) (idioms) that is to — es decir, esto es; to — nothing of the rest y no digamos de los demás; to — nothing of swearing sin mencionar lo de decir palabrotas (and see nothing 1 (d)); to — the least para no decir más; as one might — como si dijéramos; that's —ing a lot ya es decir; would you really — so? ¿lo cree Vd de veras?; what would you —? ¿qué dice Vd?; what would you — to that? ¿qué contesta Vd a eso?; what would you — to a cup of tea? ¿le apetece una taza de té?; she hasn't much to — for herself es muy reservada, no es nada habladora; that doesn't — much for her eso no dice mucho en su favor; it doesn't — much for his intelligence eso no dice mucho a favor de su inteligencia; it —s much for his courage that he stayed el que permaneciera allí demuestra su valor; it goes without —ing that . . . ni que decir tiene que . . .; that goes without —ing eso cae de su peso.

(c) (exclamatory idioms) —! (US), I —! (calling attention) ¡oiga!, (in surprise) ¡caramba!; you don't — (so)! ¡parece mentira!, ¿de veras?; I should — so!, you can — that again! ¡ya lo creo!; you've said it! ¡eso es!; so you —! ¡es Vd quien lo dice!; — no more! ¡basta!, ¡ni una palabra más!

(d) (phrases with ptp said) it is said that . . . se dice que . . .; he is said to be worth a million se dice que es millonario; there is something to be said for it hay algunas razones a favor de esa opinión (etc); there is a lot to be said for doing it now hay buenas razones por las que conviene hacerlo ahora; there is something to be said on both sides hay mucho que decir a favor de ambos; when all is said and done there's no money for it total que no hay dinero para ello, a fin de cuentas no hay dinero para ello; it's easier said than done es más fácil hablar de esto que hacerlo; no sooner said than done dicho y hecho; enough said! al buen entendedor pocas palabras le bastan.

(e) (suppose) — it is worth £20 pongamos por caso que vale 20 libras; we sell it at — £25 pongamos que lo vendemos por 25 libras; we were going at — 50 mph íbamos a 50 mph más o menos; shall we — £5? ¿convenimos en 5 libras?; shall we — Tuesday? ¿para el martes, pues?

saying ['seiiŋ] n dicho m, refrán m; as the — goes como dice el refrán; it's just a — es un refrán, es un decir.

say-so ['seisəu] n (a) (rumour) rumor m (infundado).

(b) (authority) autoridad f; aprobación f; decisión f; it depends on his — tiene que aprobarlo él.

scab [skæb] n (Med) costra f; (Vet) roña f; (fam) esquirol m.

scabbard ['skæbəd] n vaina f (de espada).

scabby ['skæbi] adj costroso; lleno de costras; (Vet) roñoso.

scabies ['skeibiːz] n sarna f.

scabious ['skeibiəs] n escabiosa f.

scabrous ['skeibrəs] adj escabroso.

scads [skædz] npl (fam) montones mpl; we have — of it lo tenemos a montones, tenemos montones de eso.

scaffold ['skæfəld] n (Archit) andamio m; (for execution) cadalso m, patíbulo m.

scaffolding ['skæfəldiŋ] n andamio m, andamiaje m.

scalawag ['skæləwæg] n (US) = scallywag.

scald [skɔːld] 1 n escaldadura f.

2 vt oneself, skin etc escaldar, quemar con agua caliente; milk calentar; instruments esterilizar con agua caliente; to — out a saucepan limpiar una cacerola con agua caliente.

scalding ['skɔːldiŋ] adj: — hot hirviendo.

scale¹ [skeil] 1 n (of fish etc) escama f; (flake) hojuela f; laminita f; (of skin) costra f.

2 vt fish escamar; (Tech) raspar; teeth quitar el sarro a.

3 vi (also to — off) descamarse; desconcharse.

scale² [skeil] 1 n (of balance) platillo m; —s balanza f, (for heavy weights) báscula f; the S— (Astron) Libra f; to turn (or tip) the —s (fig) inclinar la balanza, decidirlo; he turns the —s at 80 kilos pesa 80 kilos.

2 vi pesar; it —s 4 kilos pesa 4 kilos.

scale³ [skeil] 1 n escala f (also Math, Mus); (of salaries) escalafón m; — of charges tarifa f, lista f de precios; Fahrenheit — escala f de Fahrenheit; sliding — escala f móvil; the social — la escala social; on a — of 5 km to the centimetre a escala de 5 km al centímetro; on a big (or large) — a gran escala, a grande escala; on a small — a pequeña

escala; **on a national —** a escala nacional; **to draw something to —** dibujar algo a escala.
  2 *attr*: **— drawing** dibujo *m* a escala.
  3 *vt mountain etc* escalar; *tree etc* trepar a; **to — down** reducir a escala; **to — up** aumentar a escala.
scallion ['skæliən] *n* cebolleta *f*.
scallop ['skɔləp] **1** *n* (*Zool*) venera *f*; (*Sew*) festón *m*.
  2 *vt* (*Cook*) guisar en conchas; (*Sew*) festonear.
scallop shell ['skɔləpʃel] *n* venera *f*.
scallywag ['skæliwæg] *n see* **scamp**[1].
scalp [skælp] **1** *n* cuero *m* cabelludo, cabellera *f*; (*Anat*) pericráneo *m*; (*fig*) trofeo *m*. **2** *vt* escalpar, quitar el cuero cabelludo a.
scalpel ['skælpəl] *n* escalpelo *m*.
scaly ['skeili] *adj* escamoso.
scamp[1] [skæmp] *n* tunante *mf*, bribón *m*, ona *f*; (*child*) diablillo *m*; **you little —**! ¡pícaro!
scamp[2] [skæmp] *vt* chapucear, frangollar.
scamper ['skæmpə*] **1** *n* carrera *f* rápida; huida *f* precipitada.
  2 *vi* correr, darse prisa; **to — along** ir corriendo; **to — for the bus** correr para coger el autobús; **to — past** pasar corriendo; **to — away, to — off** escabullirse, escaparse corriendo.
scan [skæn] **1** *vt* (*examine*) escudriñar, examinar; (*glance at*) dar un vistazo a; *horizon etc* explorar con la vista; (*by radar etc*) explorar, registrar; *verse* medir, escandir.
  2 *vi* estar bien medido; **it does not —** no está bien medido.
scandal ['skændl] *n* (a) escándalo *m*; (*Law*) difamación *f*; **the groundnuts —** el escándalo de los cacahuetes; **to cause a —, to create a —** hacer un escándalo, armar un lío; **what a —**!, **it's a —**! ¡qué vergüenza!; **it is a — that ...** es una vergüenza que ...
  (b) (*gossip*) chismorreo *m*, murmuración *f*; (*pieces of gossip*) habladurías *fpl*, chismes *mpl*; **the local —** los chismes del pueblo (*or* del barrio *etc*); **have you heard the latest —**? ¿te han contado los chismes del momento?; **there's a lot of — going round about the vicar** se cuentan muchos chismes acerca del pastor; **to talk —** murmurar, contar chismes.
scandalize ['skændəlaiz] *vt* escandalizar; **she was —d** se escandalizó.
scandalmonger ['skændl,mʌŋgə*] *n* chismoso *m*, a *f*.
scandalous ['skændələs] *adj* escandaloso; (*libellous*) calumnioso; **— talk** habladurías *fpl*, chismes *mpl*; **it's simply —**! ¡es una vergüenza! ¡no hay derecho!
scandalously ['skændələsli] *adv* escandalosamente.
Scandinavia [,skændi'neiviə] Escandinavia *f*.
Scandinavian [,skændi'neiviən] **1** *adj* escandinavo. **2** *n* escandinavo *m*, a *f*.
scanner ['skænə*] *n* (*Radar*) antena *f* direccional giratoria; (*TV*) dispositivo *m* explorador.
scansion ['skænʃən] *n* escansión *f*; medida *f*.
scant [skænt] *adj* escaso.
scantily ['skæntili] *adv* insuficientemente; **— provided with ...** con escasa provisión de ...; **— dressed** ligeramente vestido.
scantiness ['skæntinis] *n* escasez *f*, cortedad *f*, insuficiencia *f*.
scanty ['skænti] *adj* escaso, corto, insuficiente; *clothing* ligero.
scapegoat ['skeipgəut] *n* cabeza *f* de turco, víctima *f* propiciatoria; **to be a —** for pagar el pato por.
scapegrace ['skeipgreis] *n* pícaro *m*, bribón *m*.
scapula ['skæpjulə] *n* (*Anat*) escápula *f*.
scar[1] [ska:*] **1** *n* (*Med*) cicatriz *f*, señal *f*; (*fig*) señal *f*; **it left a deep — on his mind** dejó una profunda señal en su espíritu.
  2 *vt* dejar una cicatriz en; marcar con una cicatriz, marcar con cicatrices; (*fig*) señalar, dejar señales en; **he was —red with many wounds** llevaba las cicatrices de muchas heridas; **the walls are —red with bullets** las balas han dejado señales en las paredes.
  3 *vi* (*also* **to — over**) cicatrizarse.
scar[2] [ska:*] *n* (*Geog*) paraje *m* rocoso, pendiente *f* rocosa.
scarab ['skærəb] *n* escarabajo *m*.
scarce ['skeəs] **1** *adj* escaso; poco común, poco frecuente; **money is —** hay poco dinero; **such people are —** tales personas son poco frecuentes; **the plant is — in the north** en el norte la planta es poco común; **to grow —** escasear; **to make oneself —** largarse, esfumarse.
  2 *adv see* **scarcely**.
scarcely ['skeəsli] *adv* apenas; **— 200** apenas 200; **— anybody** casi nadie; **— ever** casi nunca; **I could —**

stand up apenas pude levantarme; **I — know what to say** en realidad no sé qué decir.
scarceness ['skeəsnis] *n* escasez *f*; poca frecuencia *f*; **the — of the plant** la poca frecuencia de la planta.
scarcity ['skeəsiti] **1** *n* escasez *f*; poca frecuencia *f*; (*shortage*) carestía *f*; **in years of —** en años de carestía; **due to the — of money** debido a la escasez de dinero.
  2 *attr*: **— value** valor *m* excesivo debido a la poca frecuencia (de un artículo *etc*).
scare ['skeə*] **1** *n* susto *m*, sobresalto *m*; **the devaluation —** el pánico de la desvalorización; **to create** (*or* **raise**) **a —** infundir miedo a la gente, alarmar a las personas; **to give someone a —** dar un susto a uno; **what a — you gave me**! ¡qué susto me diste!
  2 *vt* asustar, espantar, infundir miedo a; **to — away, to — off** ahuyentar; **to be —d to death, to be —d stiff** estar muerto de miedo; **she was too —d to talk** estaba demasiado asustada para poder hablar.
  3 *vi*: **he doesn't — easily** no se asusta por poca cosa.
scarecrow ['skeəkrəu] *n* espantapájaros *m*; (*fig*) espantajo *m*.
scarehead ['skeəhed] *n* (*US Typ*) titulares *mpl* grandes y sensacionales.
scaremonger ['skeəmʌŋgə*] *n* alarmista *mf*.
scarf [ska:f] *n*, *pl* **scarves** [ska:vz] bufanda *f*; (*head—*) pañuelo *m*.
scarface ['ska:feis] *n* (*as nickname*) caracortada *mf*.
scarify ['skeərifai] *vt* (*Med, Agr*) escarificar; (*fig*) criticar severamente.
scarifying ['skeərifaiiŋ] *adj attack etc* mordaz, severo.
scarlatina [,ska:lə'ti:nə] *n* escarlatina *f*.
scarlet ['ska:lit] **1** *n* escarlata *f*. **2** *adj* color escarlata; **to turn —** enrojecer, ponerse escarlata; **he was — with rage** se puso escarlata de furia.
scarp [ska:p] *n* escarpa *f*, declive *m*.
scarves [ska:vz] *npl of* **scarf**.
scary ['skeəri] *adj* (*fam*) asustadizo.
scat [skæt] *interj* ¡zape!
scathing ['skeiðiŋ] *adj attack, criticism* mordaz, duro; **he was — about our trains** criticó duramente nuestros trenes; **he was pretty —** tuvo cosas bastante duras que decir.
scathingly ['skeiðiŋli] *adv* mordazmente, duramente; **he spoke — of ...** criticó duramente ...
scatter ['skætə*] **1** *n* (*Math, Tech*) dispersión *f*; **a — of houses** unas casas dispersas; **a — of raindrops** unas cuantas gotas de lluvia aquí y allá.
  2 *vt* (*dot about*) esparcir, desparramar; *benefits etc* derramar aquí y allá (*also* **to — about**); (*put to flight*) dispersar; *clouds etc* disipar; **the flowers were —ed about on the floor** las flores estaban desparramadas por el suelo; **the floor was —ed with flowers** el suelo estaba sembrado de flores dispersas.
  3 *vi* desparramarse; dispersarse; **the family —ed to distant parts** los miembros de la familia se desparramaron por sitios lejanos; **the crowd —ed** la multitud se dispersó.
scatterbrain ['skætəbrein] *n* cabeza *mf* de chorlito.
scatterbrained ['skætəbreind] *adj* ligero de cascos.
scattering ['skætəriŋ] *n*: **a — of books** unos cuantos libros aquí y allá.
scavenge ['skævindʒ] **1** *vt* limpiar las calles (*etc*), recoger la basura. **2** *vi*: **to — for food** andar buscando cosas que comer (entre la basura).
scavenger ['skævindʒə*] *n* basurero *m*, barrendero *m*; (*Zool*) animal *m* (*or* ave *f etc*) que se alimenta de carroña.
scenario [si'na:riəu] *n* guión *m*.
scenarist ['si:nərist] *n* guionista *mf*.
scene [si:n] *n* (a) (*Theat*) escena *f*; **the bedroom —** la escena del dormitorio; **the big — in the film** la principal escena de la película; **behind the —s** entre bastidores; **the — is set in a castle** la acción se desarrolla en un castillo, la escena es en un castillo; **to set the — for a love affair** (*fig*) crear el ambiente adecuado para una aventura sentimental; **now let our reporter set the — for you** ahora permitan que nuestro reportero les describa la escena; **there were unhappy —s at the meeting** en la reunión pasaron cosas nada agradables.
  (b) (*place in general*) escenario *m*, teatro *m*, lugar *m*; **the — of operations** el teatro de las operaciones; **the — of the disaster** el lugar de la catástrofe; **the — of the crime** el escenario del crimen; **the —s of one's early life** los lugares frecuentados por uno en su juventud; **the political — in Italy** el escenario político italiano; **to appear** (*or* **come** *etc*) **on the —** presentarse, llegar; **when I came on the —** cuando

yo llegué; **he appeared unexpectedly on the — se** presentó inesperadamente; **to disappear from the political —** desaparecer del escenario político.

(c) (*sight, vision*) vista *f*, perspectiva *f*, panorama *m*; (*landscape*) paisaje *m*; **the — from the top is marvellous** desde la cumbre se abarca un panorama maravilloso; **the — spread out before you el** panorama que se extiende delante de uno; **it was a — of utter destruction** fue una perspectiva de destrucción total; **it is a lonely —** es un paisaje solitario; **a change of — would do you good** le vendría bien un cambio de aire.

(d) (*fuss*) escándalo *m*, lío *m*, jaleo *m*; **try to avoid a —** procurar no armar un lío; **I hate —s** detesto los jaleos; **to make a —** armar un lío, armar un escándalo; **she had a — with her husband** riñó con su marido.

scene painter ['si:n,peintə*] *n* (*designer*) escenógrafo *m*, (*workman*) pintor *m* de decoraciones.

scenery ['si:nəri] *n* (*landscape*) paisaje *m*; (*Theat*) decoraciones *fpl*, decorado *m*.

scene shifter ['si:n,ʃiftə*] *n* tramoyista *mf*.

scenic ['si:nik] *adj* (*Theat*) escénico, dramático; (*picturesque*) pintoresco.

scenography [si:'nɔgrəfi] *n* escenografía *f*.

scent [sent] **1** *n* (*smell*) olor *m*; (*pleasant smell*) perfume *m*, aroma *m*, fragancia *f*; (*Hunting*) rastro *m*, pista *f*; (*sense of smell*) olfato *m*; **to be on the —** seguir la pista (*also fig*; *of* de); **to lose the —** perder la pista; **to throw someone off the —** despistar a uno.

2 *vt* (*add — to*) perfumar (*with* de); (*smell*) oler; *danger etc* percibir, sospechar; **to — something out** olfatear algo, husmear algo.

scent bottle ['sent,bɔtl] *n* frasco *m* de perfume.

scented ['sentid] *adj* perfumado.

scentless ['sentlis] *adj* inodoro.

scent spray ['sentsprei] *n* atomizador *m* (de perfume), pulverizador *m* (de perfume).

sceptic, (*US*) **skeptic** ['skeptik] *n* escéptico *m*, a *f*.

sceptical, (*US*) **skeptical** ['skeptikəl] *adj* escéptico; **he was — about it** se mostró escéptico acerca de ello, tenía dudas sobre ello.

scepticism, (*US*) **skepticism** ['skeptisizəm] *n* escepticismo *m*.

sceptre, (*US*) **scepter** ['septə*] *n* cetro *m*.

schedule ['ʃedju:l, *US* 'skedju:l] **1** *n* (*list*) lista *f*; (*timetable*) horario *m*; (*of events etc*) programa *m*; (*of questions*) cuestionario *m*; (*legal document*) inventario *m*, apéndice *m*; (*of work to be done etc*) plan *m*; **the train is behind —** el tren sufre un retraso; **the bus was on —** el autobús llegó a la hora debida, el autobús llegó sin retraso; **the work is up to —** los trabajos llevan el ritmo adecuado, los trabajos no sufren retraso; **we are working to a very tight —** trabajamos de acuerdo con un plan riguroso; **our — did not include the Prado** nuestro programa de visitas no incluía el Museo del Prado.

2 *vt* (*list*) poner en una lista, hacer una lista de; catalogar, inventariar; (*plan*) proyectar, redactar el plan de; *trains etc* establecer el horario de; *visit, lecture etc* fijar la hora de; **this stop is not —d** esta parada no es oficial; **the plane is —d for 2 o'clock, the plane is —d to land at 2 o'clock** el avión debe llegar a las 2; **you are —d to speak for 20 minutes** según el programa Vd hablará durante 20 minutos; **this building is —d for demolition** se prevé la demolición de este edificio.

Scheldt [ʃelt] Escalda *m*.

schema ['ski:mə] *n* (*Eccl etc*) esquema *m*.

schematic [ski'mætik] *adj* esquemático.

scheme [ski:m] **1** *n* (a) (*arrangement*) disposición *f*; combinación *f*; **colour —** combinación *f* de colores; **rhyme —** esquema *f* de la rima.

(b) (*systematic table*) plan *m*, esquema *m*; (*diagram*) diagrama *m*; (*summary*) resumen *m*.

(c) (*plan*) plan *m*, proyecto *m*; (*idea*) idea *f*; **the — for the new bridge** el proyecto del nuevo puente; **it's some crazy — of his** es una idea estrafalaria de las suyas; **it's not a bad —** no es mala idea.

(d) (*plot*) intriga *f*; (*ruse*) treta *f*, ardid *m*; **it's a — to get him out of the way** es un ardid para quitarle de su medio.

2 *vt* (*plan*) proyectar; (*pej*) tramar, urdir.

3 *vi* (*plan*) hacer proyectos, formar planes; (*pej*) intrigar; **they're scheming to get me out** están intrigando para expulsarme.

schemer ['ski:mə*] *n* intrigante *mf*.

scheming ['ski:miŋ] *adj* (*pej*) intrigante; astuto, mañoso.

schism ['sizəm] *n* cisma *m*.

schismatic [siz'mætik] **1** *adj* cismático. **2** *n* cismático *m*.

schismatical [siz'mætikəl] *adj* cismático.

schist [ʃist] *n* esquisto *m*.

schizo ['skitsəu] (*fam*) see **schizophrenic**.

schizoid ['skitsɔid] **1** *adj* esquizoide. **2** *n* esquizoide *mf*.

schizophrenia [,skitsəu'fri:niə] *n* esquizofrenia *f*.

schizophrenic [,skitsəu'frenik] **1** *adj* esquizofrénico. **2** *n* esquizofrénico *m*, a *f*.

schmaltz [ʃmɔ:lts] *n* (*US*) sentimentalismo *m*, sensiblería *f*.

scholar ['skɔlə*] *n* (*pupil*) colegial *m*, ala *f*, alumno *m*, a *f*, escolar *mf*; (*learned person*) erudito *m*, a *f*; sabio *m*, a *f*; (*scholarship holder*) becario *m*, a *f*; **he's a Tirso —** es especialista en Tirso; **the famous Cervantes —** el docto cervantista; **I'm no —** apenas sé nada, no soy nada intelectual.

scholarly ['skɔləli] *adj* erudito.

scholarship ['skɔləʃip] *n* erudición *f*; (*money award*) beca *f*.

scholarship holder ['skɔləʃip,həuldə*] *n* becario *m*, a *f*.

scholastic [skə'læstik] **1** *adj* (*relative to school*) escolar; (*relative to scholasticism*) escolástico; **— books** libros *mpl* escolares; **the — year** el año escolar; **the — profession** el magisterio.

2 *n* escolástico *m*.

scholasticism [skə'læstisizəm] *n* escolasticismo *m*.

school¹ [sku:l] **1** *n* (a) (*in general*) escuela *f*; (*primary, specialist, military etc*) escuela *f*; colegio *m*; academia *f*; **to be at —** estar en la escuela; **we have to be at — by 9** tenemos que estar en la clase para las 9; **you weren't at — yesterday** ayer faltaste a la clase; **which — were you at?** ¿dónde cursó Vd los estudios (del bachillerato)?; **we were at — together** fuimos al mismo instituto (*etc*); **to go to —** ir a la escuela; **to learn in a tough —** formarse en una escuela dura.

(b) **— of art** escuela *f* de bellas artes; **— of dancing** escuela *f* de baile, escuela *f* de ballet; **— of music** academia *f* de música, conservatorio *m*; **comprehensive —** instituto *m* integrado; **grammar — (state)** instituto *m*, (*private, independent, religious*) academia *f* (*or* colegio *m*) de segunda enseñanza; **high — (US, Scot)** instituto *m*; **infant —, infants' —** escuela *f* de párvulos; **junior high — (US)** colegio *m* de bachillerato elemental; **preparatory —** escuela *privada para los muchachos de 8 a 12 años (que pasan después a una* public school); **primary —** escuela *f* primaria; **private —** escuela *f* privada, escuela *f* particular; **public — (Brit, approx)** internado *m* privado, (*US, Scot*) escuela *f* pública; **secondary —** instituto *m* de segunda enseñanza; **Sunday —** escuela *en que se da instrucción religiosa los domingos*; **technical —, trade —** escuela *f* de artes y oficios, universidad *f* laboral; **upper —** cursos *mpl* superiores (de un instituto *etc*); *see* **driving —, night —, nursery —** *etc*.

(c) (*Univ*) departamento *m*, facultad *f*; **in the History —** en el departamento de Historia; **S— of Arabic Studies** Escuela *f* de Estudios Árabes.

(d) (*of thought etc*) escuela *f*; **Plato and his —** Platón y su escuela, Platón y sus discípulos; **the Dutch —** la escuela holandesa; **I am not of that —** yo no sigo esa opinión; **I am not of the — that . . .** yo no soy de los que . . .; **people of the old —** gente *f* de la vieja escuela, gente *f* chapada a la antigua.

2 *attr*: **— age** edad *f* escolar; **— book** libro *m* para uso escolar; **the — population is high** el porcentaje de escolaridad es elevado; **— year** año *m* escolar; *see* **fee** *etc*.

3 *vt* instruir, enseñar; disciplinar; **to — someone in a technique** instruir a uno en una técnica; **to — someone to do something** enseñar a uno a hacer algo; **he has been well —ed** ha sido bien instruido.

school² [sku:l] *n* (*Fish*) banco *m*, cardumen *m*.

schoolbook ['sku:lbuk] *n* libro *m* escolar.

schoolboy ['sku:lbɔi] *n* colegial *m*, escolar *m*.

schooldays ['sku:ldeiz] *npl* años *mpl* de colegio.

schoolfellow ['sku:l,feləu] *n* compañero *m* de clase, compañera *f* de clase.

schoolgirl ['sku:lgə:l] *n* colegiala *f*, escolar *f*.

schooling ['sku:liŋ] *n* (*teaching etc*) instrucción *f*, enseñanza *f*; disciplina *f*; **compulsory — up to 16** escolaridad *f* obligatoria hasta los 16 años; **— is free** la enseñanza es gratuita.

schoolman ['sku:lmən] *n*, *pl* **—men** [mən] escolástico *m*.

schoolmaster ['sku:l,mɑ:stə*] *n* (*grammar school*) profesor *m* (de instituto), (*other*) maestro *m*.

schoolmistress ['sku:l,mistris] n (*grammar school*) profesora f (de instituto); (*other*) maestra f.

schoolroom ['sku:lrum] n clase f.

schoolteacher ['sku:l,ti:tʃə*] n maestro m, a f.

schooner ['sku:nə*] n goleta f.

sciatic [sai'ætik] adj ciático.

sciatica [sai'ætikə] n ciática f.

science ['saiəns] n ciencia f; **domestic — ** ciencia f del hogar; **natural —s** ciencias fpl naturales; **physical —** ciencias fpl físicas; **social —** ciencia f social; **to blind someone with —** impresionar a uno citándole muchos datos científicos; lucir sus conocimientos para impresionar a uno.

science fiction ['saiəns,fikʃən] n ciencia-ficción f.

scientific [,saiən'tifik] adj científico.

scientifically [,saiən'tifikəli] adv científicamente.

scientist ['saiəntist] n científico m, científica f.

Scillies ['siliz] pl, **Scilly Isles** ['siliailz] pl Islas fpl Sorlingues.

scimitar ['simitə*] n cimitarra f.

scintillate ['sintileit] vi centellear, chispear; (*fig*) brillar.

scintillating ['sintileitiŋ] adj (*fig*) brillante; ingenioso; de lo más vivo, animadísimo.

scion ['saiən] n (*Bot, fig*) vástago m; **— of a noble family** vástago m de una familia noble.

Scipio ['skipiəu] n Escipión.

scissors ['sizəz] npl tijeras fpl; **a pair of —** unas tijeras.

sclerosis [skli'rəusis] n esclerosis f; **multiple —** esclerosis f múltiple.

scoff[1] [skɔf] vi mofarse, burlarse (*at* de).

scoff[2] [skɔf] (*fam*) **1** n comida f; **— up!** ¡la comida está servida! **2** vt zamparse, engullir; **she —ed the lot** se lo comió todo.

scoffer ['skɔfə*] n mofador m, ora f.

scoffing ['skɔfiŋ] n mofas fpl, burlas fpl.

scold [skəuld] **1** n virago f. **2** vt reprender, regañar (*for* por).

scolding ['skəuldiŋ] n reprensión f, regaño m; **to give someone a —** reprender a uno.

scollop ['skɔləp] see scallop.

sconce [skɔns] n candelabro m de pared.

scone [skɔn] n bollo m.

scoop [sku:p] **1** n (a) (*instrument*) pala f, paleta f, cuchara f; (*for bailing*) achicador m; (*carpenter's*) gubia f; (*of dredger*) cuchara f (de draga), cangilón m; (*Med*) espátula f.
(b) (*profit*) ganancia f grande; golpe m financiero; (*by newspaper*) primera publicación f de una noticia sensacional, exclusiva f, pisotón m; **it was a — for the paper** fue un gran éxito para el periódico; **we brought off the —** logramos un triunfo adelantándonos a los demás en la publicación de la noticia (*etc*).
2 vt (a) *grain, liquid etc* (*also* **to — out, to — up**) sacar con pala, sacar con cuchara; sacar con achicador; **to — up** *cards etc* recoger rápidamente.
(b) **to — out** (*hollow*) excavar, ahuecar; hacer.
(c) **to — the pool** llevar las diez de últimas; ganar todas las bazas; **we —ed the other papers** nos adelantamos a los demás periódicos publicando la noticia.

scoot [sku:t] vi (*fam*) escabullirse, largarse (*fam*); correr precipitadamente; **I must —** tengo que marcharme.

scooter ['sku:tə*] n (*child's*) patinete m; (*adult's*) motosilla f, escúter m, moto f.

scope [skəup] n alcance m; envergadura f; esfera f de acción; ámbito m; campo m, campo m de aplicación; **there is — for** hay campo para; **a programme of considerable —** un programa de gran alcance, un programa de ancha envergadura; **the — of the new measures must be defined** conviene delimitar el campo de aplicación de las nuevas medidas; **to give someone full —** dar carta blanca a uno; **this should give you plenty of — for your talents** esto ha de darle grandes posibilidades para explotar sus talentos; **it is outside my —** eso está fuera de mi alcance; **it is well within his —** está dentro de su alcance, está bien dentro de sus posibilidades.

scorbutic [skɔ:'bju:tik] adj escorbútico.

scorch [skɔ:tʃ] **1** vt chamuscar; (*of sun, wind*) abrasar; *plants etc* quemar, secar; **to — the earth** (*Mil*) quemar la tierra, destruir todo lo útil; arrasarlo todo.
2 vi chamuscarse; quemarse, secarse; (*fam*) ir volando, correr a gran velocidad.

scorcher ['skɔ:tʃə*] n día m de mucho calor.

scorching ['skɔ:tʃiŋ] adj *sun etc* abrasador; *day* de mucho calor; *speed* grande, excesivo; **it's — hot** hace un tremendo calor; **a few — remarks** algunas observaciones mordaces.

score [skɔ:*] **1** n (a) (*notch*) muesca f, entalladura f; señal f; (*line*) raya f, línea f.
(b) (*reckoning*) cuenta f; **to pay one's —** pagar la cuenta; **to pay off old —s** ajustar cuentas viejas; **to settle an old — with someone** desquitarse con uno; **I have a — to settle with him** tengo cuentas pendientes con él.
(c) (*in exam, test*) puntuación f; (*Sport*) tanteo m; tantos mpl, puntos mpl (*etc*); **what's the —?** ¿cómo estamos?, ¿cómo va esto?; **the — was Toboso 9, Barataria 1** el resultado fue Toboso 9, Barataria 1; **there was no — at half-time** en el primer tiempo no hubo goles; **to keep (the) —** tantear; **do you know the —?** ¿sabe Vd cuántos goles han marcado?; **he doesn't know the —** (*fig*) no está al tanto, (*pej*) es un despistado, es un pobre hombre; **to make a —** marcar un tanto, marcar un gol (*etc*).
(d) (*Mus*) partitura f; **full —** partitura f de orquesta.
(e) (20) veinte, veintena f; **a — of people** veinte personas, una veintena de personas; **3 — years and 10** 70 años; **there were —s of mistakes** había muchísimas erratas, había erratas a granel; **actresses by the —** muchísimas actrices.
(f) **on the — of illness** por enfermedad, con motivo de su enfermedad; **on that —** a ese respecto, por lo que se refiere a eso; **on what —?** ¿con qué motivo?
2 vt (a) (*notch*) hacer muescas en, hacer cortes en; señalar; (*line*) rayar; **the wall is heavily —d with lines** las paredes están profundamente rayadas; **the plane —d the runway as it landed** al aterrizar el avión hizo rayas en la pista; **to — something out, to — something through** tachar algo.
(b) **— it up to me** apúntelo en mi cuenta.
(c) (*in exam, test*) obtener una puntuación . . .; obtener una nota . . .; ser calificado de . . .; (*Sport*) *goal, points* ganar, *runs* hacer; **to — 70%** obtener una puntuación de 70 por ciento; **to — well in a test** obtener buena nota en un test; **to — a goal** marcar un gol; **they went 5 games without scoring a point in 5 partidos** no ganaron un solo punto; **they had 14 goals —d against them** sus adversarios metieron 14 goles a costa suya; **to — a great success** obtener un gran triunfo.
(d) (*Mus*) instrumentar, orquestar; **it is —d for 5 bassoons** está instrumentado para 5 bajones.
3 vi (a) (*Sport etc*) marcar un tanto, marcar un gol, ganar puntos (*etc*); **to fail to —** no marcar ningún gol; **that's where he —s** en eso es donde tiene más ventajas, es en ese aspecto donde sobresale; **to — off someone** triunfar a costa de uno, (*with witty remark*) hacer un chiste a costa de uno; **she's easy to — off** es fácil hacer chistes a costa suya.
(b) (*keep —*) tantear, llevar el tanteo.
(c) (*count*) puntuar; **that doesn't — ** eso no puntúa, eso no vale.

scoreboard ['skɔ:bɔ:d] n tanteador m, marcador m.

scorecard ['skɔ:ka:d] n tarjeta f en que se lleva el tanteo.

scorer ['skɔ:rə*] n (*player*) marcador m; (*recorder*) tanteador m; **he is top — in the league** es el principal goleador en la liga, ha marcado más goles que ningún otro en la liga; **the —s were A and B** marcaron los goles A y B.

scoring ['skɔ:riŋ] n tanteo m; **rules for —** reglas fpl para el tanteo; **a low — match** un partido en el que se marcan pocos goles (*etc*); **all the — was in the second half** todos los goles se marcaron en el segundo tiempo.

scorn ['skɔ:n] **1** n desprecio m, desdén m (*for* de); **to laugh something to —** hacer ver lo absurdo que es algo, tomar algo a broma.
2 vt despreciar, desdeñar; **to — to do something** desdeñarse de hacer algo, no dignarse hacer algo.

scornful ['skɔ:nful] adj desdeñoso; **to be — about something** desdeñar algo.

scornfully ['skɔ:nfəli] adv desdeñosamente, con desprecio.

Scorpio ['skɔ:piəu] n Escorpión m.

scorpion ['skɔ:piən] n escorpión m, alacrán m.

Scot [skɔt] n escocés m, esa f.

Scotch [skɔtʃ] **1** adj escocés. **2** n (*fam*) whisky m escocés; **the —** los escoceses.

scotch [skɔtʃ] **1** n calza f, cuña f. **2** vt *wheel* calzar, engalgar; *rumour* desmentir; *idea* hacer abandonar; *plan etc* frustrar.

Scotch broth ['skɔtʃ'brɔθ] n *caldo muy sustancioso con legumbres, cebada perlada, carne de cordero etc.*

scot-free ['skɔt'friː] adj impune; **to get off —** salir impune; quedar sin castigo.

Scotland ['skɔtlənd] Escocia f; **— Yard** oficina central de la policía de Londres.

Scots [skɔts] **1** adj escocés. **2** n (dialect) escocés m.

Scotsman ['skɔtsmən] n, pl **—men** [mən] escocés m.

Scotswoman ['skɔts,wumən] n, pl **—women** [,wimin] escocesa f.

scottie ['skɔti] n (fam) terrier m escocés.

Scottish ['skɔtiʃ] adj escocés.

scoundrel ['skaundrəl] n canalla m, sinvergüenza m.

scoundrelly ['skaundrəli] adj canallesco, vil.

scour[1] ['skauə*] vt pan etc fregar, estregar, limpiar fregando (also **— out**); channel limpiar; (Med) purgar; **the river had —ed out part of the bank** el río se había llevado una parte de la orilla.

scour[2] ['skauə*] **1** vt area recorrer, registrar; **we are —ing the countryside for him** recorremos el campo buscándole.
  2 vi: **to — about for something** buscar algo por todas partes.

scourer ['skauərə*] n estropajo m.

scourge [skəːdʒ] **1** n azote m (also fig); **the — of malaria** el azote del paludismo; **Attila, the — of God** Atila, azote de Dios; **it is the — of our times** es la calamidad de nuestros tiempos; **God sent it as a —** Dios lo envió como castigo.
  2 vt azotar, flagelar; (fig) hostigar.

scout[1] [skaut] **1** n **(a)** (person: Mil) explorador m, escucha m; (Univ) criado m; **boy —** muchacho m explorador, explorador m.
  (b) (reconnaissance) reconocimiento m; (search) búsqueda f; **to have a — round** reconocer el terreno; **we'll have a — for it** lo buscaremos.
  2 vi explorar; reconocer el terreno; **to — for something** buscar algo.

scout[2] [skaut] vt proposal rechazar con desdén; rumour etc desmentir.

scouting ['skautiŋ] n organización f de los exploradores; actividades fpl de los exploradores.

scoutmaster ['skaut,mɑːstə*] n jefe m de sección de exploradores.

scow [skau] n gabarra f.

scowl [skaul] **1** n ceño m; **he said with a —** dijo ceñudo. **2** vi fruncir el ceño, poner mal gesto; **to — at someone** mirar con ceño a uno.

scowling ['skauliŋ] adj ceñudo.

scrabble ['skræbl] vi (in writing) garrapatear; **to — about** escarbar; revolverlo todo al buscar algo; **she was scrabbling about in the coal** iba revolviendo el carbón mientras buscaba algo.

scrag [skræg] **1** n pescuezo m. **2** vt animal torcer el pescuezo a; person dar una paliza a.

scragginess ['skræginis] n flaqueza f.

scraggy ['skrægi] adj flaco, descarnado, escuálido.

scram [skræm] vi (sl) largarse (fam), dar un zarpazo (fam); **—!** ¡lárgate!

scramble ['skræmbl] **1** n **(a)** (climb) subida f; (outing) excursión f (de montaña, sobre terreno escabroso etc).
  (b) (fight etc) arrebatiña f, pelea f (for por).
  2 vt eggs revolver, hacer un revoltillo de; message cifrar, poner en cifra.
  3 vi **(a)** **to — out** salir de prisa, salir con dificultad, salir a gatas; **to — through the hedge** abrirse paso con dificultad a través de un seto; **to — up** trepar a, subir gateando a.
  (b) **to — for coins** andar a la rebatiña por unas monedas, disputarse unas monedas a gritos, luchar entre sí para recoger unas monedas.

scrap[1] [skræp] **1** n **(a)** (small piece) pedacito m, fragmento m; **a — of paper** (iro) un papel mojado.
  (b) (fig) pizca f; **a few —s of news** algunas noticias de escasa importancia; **it's a — of comfort** es una migaja de consolación; **I overheard a — of conversation** logré escuchar algunas palabras de la conversación; **there is not a — of truth in it** eso no tiene ni pizca de verdad; **not a —!** ¡ni pizca!, ¡en absoluto!
  (c) **—s** (left-overs) sobras fpl, desperdicios mpl; **the dog feeds on —s** el perro come las sobras de la mesa.
  (d) (—iron) chatarra f, hierro m viejo; **to sell a ship for —** vender un barco para chatarra; **what is it worth as —?** ¿cuánto vale como chatarra?
  2 attr iron etc viejo; **its — value is £30** como chatarra vale 30 libras.
  3 vt car, ship etc reducir a chatarra; vender para chatarra; plan etc desechar, descartar; **we had to — that idea** tuvimos que renunciar a esa idea.

scrap[2] [skræp] (fam) **1** n riña f, camorra f, bronca f; **to get into (or have) a — with someone** armar una bronca con uno; **there was a tremendous — over the steel bill** se armó una bronca fenomenal por cuestión del proyecto de ley del acero.
  2 vi reñir, armar una bronca, pelearse; **they were —ping in the street** se estaban peleando en la calle.

scrapbook ['skræpbuk] n álbum m de recortes.

scrap dealer ['skræp,diːlə*] n chatarrero m.

scrape [skreip] **1** n **(a)** (act) raspadura f; **to give something a —** raspar algo, limpiar algo raspándolo; **to give one's knee a —** rasguñarse la rodilla.
  (b) (fig) lío m; apuro m; **to get into a —** armarse un lío; **to get someone out of a —** ayudar a uno a salir de un apuro.
  2 vt raspar, raer; (flesh etc) rasguñar, raer; (— against) rozar; (Mus, hum) rascar; shoes restregar; **the lorry —d the wall** el camión rozó la pared; **the ship —d the bottom** el barco tocó el fondo; **to — one's boots** limpiarse las botas; **to — one's feet across the floor** arrastrar los pies por el suelo; **to — away, to — off** raspar, quitar raspando; **to — together, to — up** arañar, (fig) reunir poco a poco, rebañar.
  3 vi **(a)** **to — along** rozar; **to — past** pasar rozando; **we just managed to — through the gap** pudimos con dificultad pasar por la abertura sin tocar las paredes.
  (b) (fig) **to — along** ir tirando; **I can — along in Arabic** me defiendo en árabe; **to — through an exam** aprobar un examen por los pelos; **I just —d through** aprobé por los pelos.

scraper ['skreipə*] n (tool) rascador m, raspador m; (in roadmaking) niveladora f; (at door) limpiabarros m.

scrap heap ['skræphiːp] n montón m de desechos.

scrapings ['skreipiŋz] npl raspaduras fpl; **— of the gutter** (fig) hez f de la sociedad.

scrap iron ['skræp'aiən] n chatarra f, hierro m viejo.

scrap merchant ['skræp,məːtʃənt] n chatarrero m.

scrappy ['skræpi] adj meal etc pobre, escaso; text etc fragmentario; speech inconexo, descosido; knowledge superficial.

scratch [skrætʃ] **1** n **(a)** (from claw, on flesh etc) rasguño m, arañazo m; (on surface) raya f, marca f; **it's just a —** sólo es un rasguño; **the cat gave her a —** el gato la arañó; **he hadn't a — on him** no tuvo la más leve herida.
  (b) (Sport) línea f de salida; **to be (or come) up to —** (thing) estar en buen estado, llenar los requisitos, ser de buena calidad, (person) estar a la altura de las circunstancias; **to start from —** (with no resources) empezar sin nada, empezar sin ventaja alguna, (from beginning) empezar desde el principio; **we shall have to start from — again** tendremos que partir nuevamente de cero, tendremos que comenzar desde el principio otra vez.
  2 adj competitor sin ventaja; team improvisado, sin experiencia, reunido de prisa.
  3 vt (with claw etc) rasguñar, arañar; (to relieve itch) rascar; hard surface rayar, marcar; (of chicken etc) escarbar; **to — a hole in something** hacer un agujero en algo rascándolo; **she —ed the dog's ear** le rascó la oreja al perro; **he —ed his head se** rascó la cabeza; **the glass of this watch cannot be —ed** el cristal de este reloj no puede rayarse; **we —ed our names on the wood** grabamos nuestros nombres en la madera; **to — someone's eyes out** sacar los ojos a uno con las uñas; **to — someone off a list** tachar el nombre de uno de una lista.
  (b) (Sport) retirar (tachando el nombre de); **that horse has been —ed** ese caballo ha sido retirado; see **back, surface.**
  4 vi **(a)** rasguñar; (to relieve itch) rascarse; (of chicken etc) escarbar; (pen) raspear; **the dog —ed at the door** el perro arañó la puerta.
  (b) (Sport) retirarse.

scratch pad ['skrætʃpæd] n cuadernillo m de apuntes.

scratchy ['skrætʃi] adj pen que raspea; tone áspero; writing flojo, irregular.

scrawl [skrɔːl] **1** n garabatos mpl, garrapatos mpl; **the word finished in a —** la palabra terminó en un garabato; **I can't read her —** no soy capaz de leer su pésima escritura.
  2 vt: **to — a note to someone** escribir con mucha prisa una nota para uno; **a wall —ed all over with rude words** una pared llena de palabrotas mal escritas.
  3 vi garrapatear, hacer garabatos.

scrawny ['skrɔːni] adj descarnado, escuálido.

scream [skriːm] **1** n (a) chillido m, grito m (agudo); **there were —s of laughter** hubo grandes carcajadas; **to give a —** chillar, dar un grito.

(b) (fig) **it was a —** fue para morirse de risa; **he's a —** es célebre, es un chistoso.

2 vt abuse etc vociferar (at contra).

3 vi chillar, gritar, **to — with pain** lanzar gritos de dolor; **to — with laughter** reírse a carcajadas.

4 vr: **to — oneself hoarse** enronquecer a fuerza de gritar.

screamingly ['skriːmiŋli] adv: **a — funny joke** un chiste de lo más divertido; **it was — funny** fue para morirse de risa.

scree ['skriː] n ladera de montaña cubierta de cantos rodados.

screech [skriːtʃ] see **scream** (in most senses); vi (of brakes, wheels etc) chirriar.

screech owl ['skriːtʃaul] n lechuza f.

screed [skriːd] n escrito m largo y pesado, documento m aburrido.

screen [skriːn] **1** n (a) (protective) pantalla f; (folding) biombo m; (Mil etc) cortina f; (Phot) retícula f; (sieve) tamiz m, criba f; **focusing —** placa f esmerilada; **safety —** pantalla f de seguridad.

(b) (Cine, TV) pantalla f; **the small —** la pequeña pantalla; **stars of the —** estrellas fpl de la pantalla, estrellas fpl del cine; **to write for the —** escribir para el cine.

2 vt (hide) ocultar, esconder; (protect) proteger (con una pantalla), abrigar; (sift) tamizar, pasar por una criba; suspects etc investigar; novel etc adaptar para el cine, hacer una película de, hacer una versión cinematográfica de; film proyectar; **the house is —ed by trees** la casa se oculta detrás de unos árboles; **in order to — our movements from the enemy** para impedir que el enemigo observara nuestros movimientos; **the film will be —ed next year** la película se estrenará el año que viene.

screen test [skriːntest] n prueba f de pantalla (a que se somete el actor etc que quiere hacer cine).

screw [skruː] **1** n (Mech) tornillo m; (thread of —) rosca f; (Aer, Naut) hélice f; (sl) sueldo m; **he's got a — loose** (fam) le falta un tornillo (fam); **to put the —s on someone** (fam) apretar los tornillos a uno (fam).

2 vt screw atornillar; nut apretar; **to — something down** fijar algo con tornillos; **to — something on to a board** fijar algo en un tablón con tornillos; **to — money out of someone** arrancar dinero a uno; **to — the truth out of someone** arrancar la verdad a uno; **to — up** screw atornillar, nut apretar; paper arrugar; **to — up one's eyes** entornar los ojos; **to — up one's face** arrugar la cara, hacer visajes; see courage.

3 vi (of ball) torcerse; **it —s on here** se fija aquí con tornillos; **it will — up tighter than that** se puede apretar todavía más.

4 vr: **to — oneself up to do something** obligarse a hacer algo; cobrar bastante ánimo para hacer algo.

screwball ['skruːbɔːl] (US sl) **1** adj excéntrico, estrafalario. **2** n excéntrico m, tipo m estrafalario.

screwdriver ['skruːdraivə*] n destornillador m.

screwy ['skruːi] adj (sl) chiflado (fam).

scribble ['skribl] **1** n garabatos mpl; **I can't read her —** no soy capaz de leer su pésima escritura; **a wall covered in —s** una pared llena de garabatos.

2 vt: **to — one's signature** escribir con mucha prisa su firma; **a word —d on a wall** una palabra mal escrita en una pared; **a sheet of paper —d (over) with notes** una hoja de papel emborronada de notas.

3 vi garrapatear, hacer garabatos; escribir con mucha prisa; (pej, hum) ser escritor, ser periodista.

scribbler ['skriblə*] n (pej, hum) escritorzuelo m, periodista m de baja categoría.

scribbling pad ['skribliŋpæd] n borrador m.

scribe [skraib] n (professional letter-writer etc) escribiente m; amanuense m; (of MS) copista m; (Bible) escriba m; (pej, hum) escritorzuelo m, periodista m de baja categoría.

scrimmage ['skrimidʒ] n arrebatiña f, pelea f.

scrimp [skrimp] **1** vt escatimar. **2** vi economizar, hacer economías; **to — and save** hacer grandes economías, vivir muy justo.

scrimpy ['skrimpi] adj person tacaño; supply etc escaso.

scrimshank ['skrimʃæŋk] vi (Mil sl) racanear, hacer el rácano.

scrimshanker ['skrimʃæŋkə*] n (Mil sl) rácano m.

scrip [skrip] n (Fin) vale m, abonaré m.

script [skript] n (writing) escritura f, letra f (cursiva); (MS) manuscrito m; (School, Univ) examen m escrito; (Cine) guión m.

script girl ['skriptgəːl] n script-girl f, secretaria f de dirección, anotadora f (Acad).

scriptural ['skriptʃərəl] adj escrituario, bíblico.

Scripture ['skriptʃə*] n (also **Holy —**) Sagrada Escritura f; (as school subject, lesson) Historia f Sagrada.

scriptwriter ['skript,raitə*] n guionista mf.

scrofula ['skrɔfjulə] n escrófula f.

scrofulous ['skrɔfjuləs] adj escrofuloso.

scroll [skrəul] n rollo m; (ancient) rollo m de escritura; rollo m de pergamino; (Art, Archit) voluta f; **— of fame** lista f de la fama; **the Dead Sea —s** los pergaminos del Mar Muerto.

Scrooge [skruːdʒ] el avariento típico (personaje del "Christmas Carol", de Dickens).

scrotum ['skrəutəm] n escroto m.

scrounge [skraundʒ] (fam) **1** n: **to be on the —** ir de gorra (fam); tratar de adquirir cosas sin pagar; tratar de pedir algo prestado; **to have a — round for something** buscar algo.

2 vt obtener por medio de gorronería, obtener sin pagar, agenciarse; **I —d a ticket** me agencié una entrada.

3 vi ir de gorra, gorronear, sablear; **to — around for something** buscar algo.

scrounger ['skraundʒə*] n (fam) gorrón m (fam), sablista mf (fam).

scrub[1] [skrʌb] n (Bot) maleza f, monte m bajo, matas fpl.

scrub[2] [skrʌb] **1** n fregado m, fregadura f; **to give something a —** limpiar algo fregándolo; **it needs a hard —** hay que fregarlo con fuerza.

2 vt fregar, restregar; limpiar fregando.

3 vi: **let's — round it** (fam) pasemos la esponja, borrón y cuenta nueva.

scrubbing brush ['skrʌbiŋ,brʌʃ] n bruza f, estregadera f.

scrubby ['skrʌbi] adj achaparrado, enano.

scrubwoman ['skrʌb,wumən] n, pl **—women** [,wimin] (US) fregona f.

scruff [skrʌf] n: **— of the neck** pescuezo m; **to take someone by the — of the neck** agarrar a uno por el pescuezo.

scruffy ['skrʌfi] adj sucio, piojoso.

scrum [skrʌm] n, **scrummage** ['skrʌmidʒ] n (Rugby) mêlée f; **loose —** melée f abierta; **set —** melée f cerrada.

scrumptious ['skrʌmpʃəs] adj (fam) de rechupete (fam), riquísimo.

scrunch [skrʌntʃ] vt ronzar.

scruple ['skruːpl] **1** n (a) (weight) escrúpulo m (Pharm = 20 granos = 1,296 gramos).

(b) (fig) escrúpulo m; **a person of no —s** una persona sin escrúpulos; **he is entirely without —** no tiene conciencia en absoluto; **to have no —s about . . .** no tener escrúpulos acerca de . . .; **to make no — to + infin** no vacilar en + infin.

2 vi: **not to — to + infin** no vacilar en + infin.

scrupulous ['skruːpjuləs] adj escrupuloso (about en cuanto a).

scrupulously ['skruːpjuləsli] adv escrupulosamente; **a — fair decision** una decisión completamente justa; **a — clean room** un cuarto completamente limpio.

scrupulousness ['skruːpjuləsnis] n escrupulosidad f.

scrutineer [,skruːti'niə*] n escudriñador m.

scrutinize ['skruːtinaiz] vt escudriñar, examinar; votes escrutar.

scrutiny ['skruːtini] n escrutinio m, examen m; **it does not stand up to —** no resiste al examen; **to submit something to a close —** someter algo a un cuidadoso examen.

scud [skʌd] vi: **to — along** correr (llevado por el viento), deslizarse rápidamente; **the clouds were —ding across the sky** las nubes pasaron rápidamente a través del cielo; **the ship —ded before the wind** el barco iba viento en popa.

scuff [skʌf] **1** vt shoes desgastar, restregar; feet arrastrar. **2** vi andar arrastrando los pies.

scuffle ['skʌfl] **1** n refriega f, pelea f. **2** vi pelearse; **to — with the police** pelearse con la policía.

scull [skʌl] **1** n espadilla f. **2** vti remar (con espadilla).

scullery ['skʌləri] n trascocina f, fregadero m, office m, antecocina f (Acad).

scullery maid ['skʌlərimeid] n fregona f.

sculp [skʌlp] vt, **sculpt** [skʌlpt] vt esculpir.

sculptor ['skʌlptə*] n escultor m; (woman) escultora f.

sculptress ['skʌlptris] n escultora f.

sculptural ['skʌlptʃərəl] adj escultural.

sculpture ['skʌlptʃə*] **1** n (art, object) escultura f. **2** vt esculpir.

scum [skʌm] n (on liquid) espuma f, nata f; (on pond) verdín m; (on metal) escoria f; (fig) heces fpl; the — of the earth las heces de la sociedad; you —! ¡canalla!

scummy ['skʌmi] adj lleno de espuma; cubierto de verdín; (fig) canallesco, vil.

scupper ['skʌpə*] 1 n imbornal m. 2 vt (Naut) abrir los imbornales de, (loosely) hundir; (fig) arruinar, destruir, acabar con.

scurf [skəːf] n caspa f.

scurfy ['skəːfi] adj casposo.

scurrility [skʌ'riliti] n grosería f, procacidad f, chocarrería f; lo difamatorio.

scurrilous ['skʌriləs] adj grosero, procaz, chocarrero; difamatorio; a — journal una revista chocarrera; to make a — attack on someone atacar a uno de modo grosero.

scurrilously ['skʌriləsli] adv groseramente, con procacidad; de modo difamatorio.

scurry ['skʌri] vi correr, ir a toda prisa; to — along ir corriendo; to — away, to — off escabullirse; to — for shelter correr para ponerse al abrigo.

scurvy[1] ['skəːvi] adj vil, canallesco; ruin.

scurvy[2] ['skəːvi] n escorbuto m.

scut [skʌt] n rabito m (esp de conejo).

scutcheon ['skʌtʃən] n see escutcheon.

scuttle[1] ['skʌtl] n cubo m, carbonera f.

scuttle[2] ['skʌtl] 1 vt barrenar, poner un barreno a, echar a pique.
2 vi (fig) abandonar, renunciar; a policy of — una política de renunciar a todo.

scuttle[3] ['skʌtl] 1 n huida f precipitada, retirada f precipitada.
2 vi: to — along correr, ir a toda prisa; to — away, to — off escabullirse; we must — tenemos que marcharnos.

Scylla ['silə]: — and Charybdis Escila y Caribdis.

scythe [saið] 1 n guadaña f. 2 vt segar con guadaña.

sea [siː] 1 n (a) mar m or f; calm — mar f calma; rough — mar f alta; high —s alta mar f; on the high —s en alta mar; inland — mar m interior; open —s mar m abierto; the seven —s todos los mares del mundo; in Spanish —s en aguas españolas; at — en el mar; beyond the —s allende el mar; from beyond the —s desde allende el mar; by — por mar, por vía marítima; by the — a la orilla del mar, junto al mar; out at — en alta mar; to be all at — estar despistado, estar perplejo; to be all at — about something (or with something) no saber nada en absoluto de algo; to follow the —, to go to — hacerse marinero; to put to — hacerse a la mar; to remain 2 months at — estar navegando durante 2 meses, pasar 2 meses en el mar; to stand out to — apartarse de la costa.
(b) (state of the —) heavy —, strong — oleada f, marejada f; to ship a green (or heavy) — ser inundado por una ola grande.
(c) (fig) a — of faces una multitud de caras; a — of corn un mar de espigas; a — of flame una vasta extensión de llamas; —s of blood ríos mpl de sangre.
2 adj, attr de mar; marino, marítimo; — battle batalla f naval; — transport transporte m por mar, transporte m marítimo; — trip viaje m por mar; — air aire m de mar.

sea anemone ['siːə'neməni] n anémona f de mar.

sea bathing ['siːˌbeiðiŋ] n baños mpl de mar.

sea bird ['siːbəːd] n ave f marina.

seaboard ['siːbɔːd] n litoral m.

sea boots ['siːbuːts] npl botas fpl de marinero.

seaborne ['siːbɔːn] adj transportado por mar.

sea bream ['siːbriːm] n besugo m.

sea breeze ['siːˈbriːz] n brisa f de mar.

sea captain ['siːˈkæptin] n capitán m de mar.

sea coast ['siːkəust] n litoral m, costa f marítima, orilla f del mar.

sea cow ['siːˈkau] n manatí m.

sea dog ['siːdɔg] n lobo m de mar.

seafarer ['siːˌfɛərə*] n marinero m.

seafaring ['siːfɛəriŋ] 1 adj marinero. 2 n marinería f; vida f del marinero.

sea fight ['siːfait] n combate m naval.

sea fish ['siːfiʃ] n pez m de mar.

seafood ['siːfuːd] n mariscos mpl; — restaurant marisquería f.

sea front ['siːfrʌnt] n (beach) playa f; (promenade) paseo m marítimo; on Santander — en la playa de Santander.

seagirt ['siːgəːt] adj rodeado por el mar.

seagoing ['siːˌgəuiŋ] adj de alta mar, de altura.

sea-green ['siːgriːn] adj verdemar.

seagull ['siːgʌl] n gaviota f.

sea horse ['siːhɔːs] n caballito m de mar, hipocampo m.

sea kale ['siːkeil] n col f marina.

seal[1] [siːl] 1 n (Zool) foca f. 2 vi: to go —ing ir a cazar focas.

seal[2] [siːl] 1 n sello m; lead — sello m de plomo; wax — sello m de lacre; great — sello m real; official — sello m oficial; under the — of secrecy bajo promesa de guardar el secreto; under my hand and — firmado y sellado por mí; to set one's — to something sellar algo, poner su sello en algo.
2 vt sellar; cerrar, cerrar herméticamente; (with wax) lacrar; (with lead) emplomar; (fig) fate etc decidir; to — off obturar; separar, aislar; to — up cerrar; (Comm) packet precintar; to — a letter cerrar una carta; my lips are —ed he prometido no decir nada, me he resuelto a no decir nada; this —ed his fate esto acabó de perderle; the ship's fate is —ed la suerte del barco está decidida.

sea legs ['siːlegz] npl pie m marino; to get one's — acostumbrarse a la vida de a bordo.

sealer ['siːlə*] n (person) cazador m de focas; (boat) barco m en que se cazan focas.

sea level ['siːˌlevl] n nivel m del mar; 800 metres above — 800 metros sobre el nivel del mar.

sealing ['siːliŋ] n caza f de focas.

sealing wax ['siːliŋwæks] n lacre m.

sea lion ['siːlaiən] n león m marino.

sealskin ['siːlskin] n piel f de foca.

seam [siːm] 1 n (Sew) costura f; (Tech) juntura f; (line on skin) arruga f; (Anat) sutura f; (Naut) costura f de los tablones; (Geol) filón m, veta f; to burst (or come apart) at the —s descoserse; we're bursting at the —s in the office en la oficina ya no cabemos más.
2 vt (Sew) coser; (Tech) juntar; face arrugar.

seaman ['siːmən] n, pl —men [mən] marinero m; able-bodied — marinero de primera; ordinary — simple marinero m.

seamanlike ['siːmənlaik] adj de buen marinero.

seamanship ['siːmənʃip] n náutica f, marinería f.

sea mist ['siːmist] n bruma f.

seamless ['siːmlis] adj sin costura.

seamstress ['semstris] n costurera f.

seamy ['siːmi] adj miserable, vil; asqueroso; the — side (fig) el revés de la medalla.

séance ['seiɑːns] n sesión f de espiritismo.

sea piece ['siːpiːs] n (Art) marina f.

seaplane ['siːplein] n hidroavión m.

seaport ['siːpɔːt] n puerto m de mar.

sea power ['siːˌpauə*] n potencia f naval.

sear [siə*] vt (wither) secar, marchitar; (Med) cauterizar; (of pain etc) punzar; (of sun, wind) abrasar; (scorch) chamuscar, quemar.

search [səːtʃ] 1 n (quest) busca f, búsqueda f (for de); (of person, of house etc) registro m; (inspection) reconocimiento m; right of — derecho m de visita; in — of en busca de; en demanda de; to make a — in a house practicar un registro en una casa; a — is being made for the missing child se está buscando al niño desaparecido; I am having a — made in the archives estoy organizando un registro de los archivos.
2 vt (scan) examinar, escudriñar; place explorar, registrar; buscar en; conscience examinar; house, luggage etc registrar; person registrar, (for weapon) cachear; we have —ed the library for it lo hemos buscado en todas partes de la biblioteca, hemos registrado la biblioteca de arriba abajo; the police are —ing the woods la policía está explorando el bosque; — me! (fam) ¡yo qué sé!, ¡ni idea!; to — someone out buscar a uno, (and find) descubrir a uno tras una búsqueda; it —es out the weak spots identifica los puntos débiles.
3 vi buscar; (Med) tentar, sondar; to — after, to — for buscar; to — into investigar.

searcher ['səːtʃə*] n buscador m de focas.

searching ['səːtʃiŋ] adj look penetrante; question agudo, perspicaz.

searchingly ['səːtʃiŋli] adv con penetración; agudamente, con perspicacia.

searchlight ['səːtʃlait] n reflector m, proyector m.

search party ['səːtʃˌpɑːti] n pelotón m de salvamento.

search warrant ['səːtʃˌwɔrənt] n mandamiento m judicial de registro, auto m de registro domiciliario.

searing ['siəriŋ] adj heat etc abrasador; pain punzante.

sea room ['siːrum] n espacio m para hacer maniobras sin peligro.

seascape ['siːskeip] n marina f.

sea serpent ['siːˌsəːpənt] n serpiente f de mar.

sea shanty ['siːˌʃænti] n saloma f.

sea shell ['siː:ʃel] n concha f marina, caracol m marino.
seashore ['siː:ʃɔː*] n playa f; orilla f del mar.
seasick ['siː:sik] adj mareado; **to be** — estar mareado; **to get** — marearse.
seasickness ['siː:siknis] n mareo m.
seaside ['siː:said] 1 n playa f; orilla f del mar; **to go to the** — ir a una playa (a veranear); **to take the family to the** — **for a day** llevar a la familia a pasar un día junto al mar.
2 attr: — **resort** playa f, punto m marítimo de veraneo; **we like** — **holidays** nos gusta pasar las vacaciones en alguna playa, nos gusta veranear junto al mar.
season ['siːzn] 1 n (of the year) estación f; (indefinite) época f, período m; (eg social —, sporting —) temporada f; (opportune time) sazón f; **close** — veda f; **the dead** —, **the off** — la estación muerta, la parte muerta del año; **football** — temporada f de fútbol; **holiday** — época f de vacaciones; **hunting** — época f de caza; **mating** —, **rutting** — época f de celo; **monsoon** — época f de los monzones; **peak** — época f más popular del año; **rainy** — estación f de las lluvias; **silly** — época f de la serpiente de mar; **tourist** — temporada f de turismo; **at this** — en esta época del año; **at that** — a la sazón; **at the height of the** — en plena temporada; **for a** — durante una temporada; **in due** — a su tiempo; **a word in** — una palabra a propósito; **in** — **and out of** — a todo tiempo, en todo momento; **to be in** — (fruit) estar en sazón; **to be out of** — estar fuera de temporada; **the London** — la temporada social de Londres; **it was not the** — **for jokes** no era el momento oportuno para chistes; **we did a** — **at La Scala** representamos en la Scala durante una temporada; **did you have a good** — ? ¿qué tal la temporada?
2 vt food sazonar, condimentar; wood curar; (moderate) moderar, templar; person etc acostumbrar (to a); ejercitar (to en); **a speech** — **ed with wit** un discurso salpicado de agudezas.
seasonable ['siːznəbl] adj (suitable) oportuno; weather etc propio de la estación.
seasonal ['siːzənl] adj unemployment etc estacional; dress etc apropiado a la estación; **it's very** — varía mucho según la estación.
seasoned ['siːznd] adj food sazonado; timber curado, maduro; person experto, perito, (Mil) veterano, aguerrido; **highly** — muy picante, con muchas especias.
sea song ['siːsɔŋ] n saloma f.
seasoning ['siːzniŋ] n (Cook) condimento m; (of timber) cura f; (fig) salsa f, sal f; **with a** — **of jokes** con una salpicadura de chistes.
season ticket ['siːzn'tikit] n (Rail) billete m de abono; (Theat etc) abono m (de temporada); **season-ticket holder** abonado m, a f.
seat [siːt] 1 n (a) (chair) asiento m, silla f; (in counting numbers of —s in bus, plane etc) plaza f, asiento m; (Theat etc) localidad f, (as ticket) localidad f, entrada f; (of cycle) sillín m; **an aircraft with 250** —**s** un avión de 250 plazas; **are there any** —**s left?** ¿quedan entradas?; **driver's** —, **driving** — asiento m del conductor; **folding** — asiento m plegadizo; **front** — asiento m delantero; **reserved** — plaza f reservada; **sliding** — bancada f corrediza; **tip-up** — asiento m abatible; **to keep one's** — permanecer sentado; **to take a** — sentarse, tomar asiento; **please take your** —**s for supper** la cena está servida; **do take a** — siéntese por favor; see back—.
(b) (Parl) escaño m; **a majority of 50** —**s** una mayoría de 50 (miembros, votos etc); **to gain a** — **for the liberals** ganar un escaño para los liberales; **to keep one's** — retener su escaño; **to win 4** —**s from the nationalists** ganar 4 escaños a los nacionalistas; **to take one's** — prestar juramento como diputado.
(c) (of chair) fondo m; (of trousers) fondillos mpl; (Anat) culo m, trasero m; **to get a bump on one's** — darse un golpe en el trasero.
(d) (centre: of government etc) sede f; (of governor etc) residencia f; (of infection, fire, trouble) foco m; — **of learning** centro m de estudios; **country** — casa f solariega; finca f.
(e) (of rider) **to have a good** — montar bien, caer bien a caballo; **to keep one's** — seguir en la silla; **to lose one's** — caer del caballo.
2 vt (a) person etc sentar; **to be** —**ed** estar sentado; **please be** —**ed** siéntese por favor; **where shall we** — **the bishop?** ¿dónde ponemos al obispo?; **to remain** —**ed** permanecer sentado, no levantarse; **when you are comfortably** —**ed** cuando estén sentados cómodamente.

(b) (of capacity) tener asientos para; **the car** —**s 5** el coche tiene 5 asientos, el coche tiene asientos para 5; **the table** —**s 12** hay sitio para 12 en esta mesa; **the theatre** —**s 900** el teatro tiene un aforo de 900.
(c) **to** — **a valve** asentar una válvula, ajustar una válvula.
3 vr: **to** — **oneself** sentarse.
seat back ['siːtbæk] n respaldo m.
seat belt ['siːtbelt] n cinturón m de seguridad.
-seater ['siːtə*]: eg **a 10-seater plane** un avión de 10 plazas, un avión con capacidad para 10 plazas; see single- etc.
seating ['siːtiŋ] n asientos mpl; — **capacity** cabida f, número m de asientos.
sea trout ['siːtraut] n trucha f marina.
sea urchin ['siːˌəːtʃin] n erizo m de mar.
sea wall ['siːˈwɔːl] n dique m marítimo.
seaward ['siːwəd] adj de hacia el mar, de la parte del mar; **on the** — **side** en el lado del mar.
seaward(s) ['siːwəd(z)] adv hacia el mar; **to** — en la dirección del mar.
sea water ['siːˌwɔːtə*] n agua f de mar.
seaway ['siːwei] n vía f marítima.
seaweed ['siːwiːd] n alga f (marina).
seaworthy ['siːˌwəːði] adj marinero, en condiciones de navegar.
secant ['siːkənt] n secante f.
secateurs [ˌsekəˈtəːz] n podadera f; **a pair of** — una podadera.
secede [si'siːd] vi separarse (from de).
secession [si'seʃən] n secesión f, separación f.
secessionist [si'seʃnist] 1 adj secesionista, separatista.
2 n secesionista m, separatista m.
secluded [si'kluːdid] adj retirado, apartado.
seclusion [si'kluːʒən] n retiro m, apartamiento m; **to live in** — vivir en el retiro, vivir lejos del tumulto.
second ['sekənd] 1 adj segundo; otro; **a** — **Manolete** otro Manolete; **every** — **post** cada dos postes, un poste sí y otro no; **the** — **largest fish** el mayor pez después del primero; **to be** — **to none** no ser inferior a nadie; no ir a la zaga a nadie (in en); **to be** — **in command** ser el segundo después del jefe, (fig) ser el segundo de a bordo; **will you have a** — **cup?** ¿quieres otra taza?; **you won't get a** — **chance** no tendrás otra oportunidad; see fiddle etc.
2 adv en segundo lugar; **to come** — (in race) ocupar el segundo puesto; **to go** —, **to travel** — (Rail) viajar en segunda.
3 n (a) (time) segundo m; **just a** —! ¡un momento!; **it won't take a** — es cosa de unos momentos; **at that very** — en ese mismo instante; **in a split** — en un instante, en un abrir y cerrar de ojos; **the operation is timed to a split** — la operación está concebida con la mayor precisión en cuanto al tiempo.
(b) (Mus) segunda f.
(c) (Univ) segunda clase f.
(d) (Boxing) segundo m, cuidador m; (in duel) padrino m.
(e) **to come in** — llegar el segundo, ocupar el segundo puesto; **to come a poor** — resultar ser muy inferior al que gana.
(f) —s (Comm) artículos mpl de segunda calidad, artículos mpl con algún desperfecto.
4 vt secundar, apoyar; ayudar; motion apoyar.
second [si'kɔnd] vt trasladar temporalmente (to a).
secondary ['sekəndəri] adj secundario.
second-best ['sekənd'best] 1 adj segundo; (el) mejor después del primero; **our** — **car** nuestro coche número dos.
2 adv: **to come off** — quedarse en segundo lugar.
3 n expediente m; sustituto m; **it's a** — es un sustituto, no todos los que hubiéramos deseado, sabemos que es inferior.
second-class ['sekənd'klɑːs] adj de segunda clase; inferior, más bien mediocre; — **citizens** ciudadanos mpl de segunda clase.
seconder ['sekəndə*] n el (la) que apoya una moción; **there was no** — nadie apoyó la moción.
second hand ['sekəndhænd] n (of watch) segundero m.
secondhand ['sekənd'hænd] adj de segunda mano, de lance; usado, no nuevo; — **bookseller** librero m de viejo; — **bookshop** librería f de viejo; — **clothes** ropa f usada; — **car** coche m de segunda mano; — **information** información f que viene indirectamente.
secondly ['sekəndli] adv en segundo lugar.
second-rate ['sekənd'reit] adj de segunda categoría; inferior, más bien mediocre; **some** — **writer** algún escritor de segunda categoría.

secrecy ['si:krəsi] n secreto m; reserva f, discreción f; **in —** en secreto; **in strict —** en el mayor secreto; **to swear someone to —** hacer que uno jure no revelar algo.

secret ['si:krit] 1 adj secreto; *information etc* secreto, confidencial; (*secretive*) reservado; (*hidden*) oculto, encubierto; **— agent** agente m de la policía secreta; **— drawer** secreto m; **to keep something —** tener algo secreto, no revelar algo; **it's all highly —** todo es de lo más secreto.

2 n secreto m; **open —** secreto m a voces; **in — ** en secreto; clandestinamente; **to be in on the —** estar en el secreto; **there's no — about it** esto no tiene nada de secreto; **to keep a —** guardar un secreto, no revelar un secreto; **he can keep a —** es como una tumba; **to let someone into a —** revelar a uno un secreto; **shall I let you into a —?** ¿quieres que te revele un secreto?; **to make no — of something** no tratar de tener algo secreto; **he made no — that . . .** no trató de negar que . . .; **to tell someone something as a —** contar algo a uno como un secreto, decir algo a uno en confianza.

secretarial [ˌsekrə'tɛəriəl] adj de secretario; *college, course* de secretaria, comercial.

secretariat [ˌsekrə'tɛəriət] n secretaría f.

secretary ['sekrətri] n secretario m, a f; **private —** secretario m particular, secretaria f particular; **S— of State** (*Brit*) Ministro m (**for** de), (*US*) Ministro m de Asuntos Exteriores.

secretary-general ['sekrətri'dʒenərəl] n secretario m general.

secretaryship ['sekrətriʃip] n secretaría f, secretariado m.

secrete [si'kri:t] vt (*hide*) esconder, ocultar; (*Med*) secretar, segregar.

secretion [si'kri:ʃən] n escondimiento m, ocultación f; (*Med*) secreción f, segregación f.

secretive ['si:krətiv] adj reservado, callado; sigiloso; **to be — about something** hacer un secreto de algo, hacer algo con secreto.

secretively ['si:krətivli] adv calladamente; sigilosamente.

secretiveness ['si:krətivnis] n reserva f; sigilo m.

secretly ['si:kritli] adv secretamente, en secreto; a escondidas; **to be — pleased about something** alegrarse en el fondo de su corazón de algo.

sect [sekt] n secta f.

sectarian [sek'tɛəriən] 1 adj sectario. 2 n sectario m, a f.

sectarianism [sek'tɛəriənizəm] n sectarismo m.

section ['sekʃən] n sección f; parte f, porción f; (*of city*) barrio m; (*of country*) región f; (*of code, document, law etc*) artículo m; (*of pipeline, road etc*) tramo m; (*of opinion*) sector m; **conic —** sección f cónica; **longitudinal —** sección f longitudinal, corte m longitudinal; **vertical —** sección f vertical, corte m vertical; **passports —** sección f de pasaportes; **in all —s of the public** en todos los sectores del público.

sectional ['sekʃənl] adj seccional; relativo a una sección; regional, local; *furniture* combinado, desmontable, fabricado en secciones.

section mark ['sekʃənmɑ:k] n párrafo m.

sector ['sektə*] n sector m; **private — ** (*Comm*) sector m privado; **public — ** (*Comm*) sector m público.

secular ['sekjulə*] adj secular, seglar.

secularization ['sekjulərai'zeiʃən] n secularización f.

secularize ['sekjuləraiz] vt secularizar.

secure [si'kjuə*] 1 adj (*safe, certain*) seguro; (*firm*) firme, fijo, estable; **— in the knowledge that . . .** sabiendo perfectamente que . . .; **to be — against,** **to be — from** estar asegurado contra, estar protegido contra; **to feel — ** sentirse seguro; **to make a door —** cerrar firmemente una puerta; **to make a tile —** asegurar una teja.

2 vt (a) (*make firm*) asegurar, fijar, afianzar; cerrar.

(b) (*obtain*) obtener, conseguir; **to — the services of someone** obtener los servicios de uno; **I —d two fine specimens** obtuve dos bellos ejemplares; **he —d it for £900** lo adquirió por 900 libras.

securely [si'kjuəli] adv seguramente, firmemente, fijamente; **it is — fastened** está bien sujetado; **we are now — established** ahora estamos firmemente establecidos.

security [si'kjuəriti] 1 n (a) seguridad f; protección f; (*Fin: on loan*) fianza f; (*on small loan*) prenda f; (*person*) fiador m, ora f; **collective — ** seguridad f colectiva; **social — ** seguridad f social, seguro m social; **up to £100 without — ** hasta 100 libras sin fianza; **to lend money on —** prestar dinero sobre

fianza; **to stand — for someone** (*Fin*) salir fiador de uno, (*fig*) salir por uno.

(b) **securities** (*Fin*) títulos mpl, valores mpl, obligaciones fpl.

2 attr: **S— Council** Consejo m de Seguridad.

sedan [si'dæn] n (*also* **— chair**) silla f de manos; (*US Aut*) sedán m.

sedate [si'deit] adj tranquilo, sosegado; serio.

sedately [si'deitli] adv tranquilamente, sosegadamente; seriamente.

sedateness [si'deitnis] n tranquilidad f, sosiego m; seriedad f.

sedation [si'deiʃən] n tratamiento m con calmantes.

sedative ['sedətiv] 1 adj sedante, calmante. 2 n sedante m, calmante m.

sedentary ['sedntri] adj sedentario.

sedge [sedʒ] n junco m, juncia f.

sediment ['sedimənt] n sedimento m (*also Geol*); poso m.

sedimentary [ˌsedi'mentəri] adj sedimentario.

sedimentation [ˌsedimen'teiʃən] n sedimentación f.

sedition [sə'diʃən] n sedición f.

seditious [sə'diʃəs] adj sedicioso.

seduce [si'dju:s] vt seducir; **to — someone from his duty** apartar a uno de su deber.

seducer [si'dju:sə*] n seductor m.

seduction [si'dʌkʃən] n seducción f.

seductive [si'dʌktiv] adj seductor.

seductively [si'dʌktivli] adv de modo seductor; en tono seductor.

sedulous ['sedjuləs] adj asiduo, diligente.

sedulously ['sedjuləsli] adv asiduamente, diligentemente.

see[1] [si:] (*irr: pret* **saw**, *ptp* **seen**) 1 vt (a) (*general sense*) ver; **let me —,** let's —** a ver, vamos a ver; **I'll go and —** voy a ver; **"— page 8"** "véase la página 8"; **he's —n a lot of the world** ha visto mucho mundo; **she'll not — 40 again** no volverá a tener 40 años; **I can — to read** veo bastante bien para poder leerlo; **as far as the eye can —** hasta donde alcanza la vista; **to — someone do something** ver a uno hacer algo; **I saw him coming** lo vi venir; **he was —n to fall** se le vio caer; **I saw it done in 1968** lo vi hacer en 1968; **I'll — him damned first** antes le veré colgado; **there was not a house to be —n** no se veía ni una sola casa; **this dress is not fit to be —n** este vestido es indigno de que lo vea la gente; **he's not fit to be —n in public** no se le puede presentar a los ojos del público.

(b) (*accompany*) acompañar; **to — someone to the door** acompañar a uno a la puerta; **to — a girl home** acompañar a una chica a su casa; **may I — you home?** ¿quieres que te acompañe?; **he was so drunk we had to — him to bed** estaba tan borracho que tuvimos que llevarle a la cama.

(c) (*understand*) comprender, entender, ver; **I . . . lo veo . . .; I —!** ¡ya!, ¡ya comprendo!; **it's all over, —?** (*fam*) se acabó, ¿comprendes?; **he's dead, don't you —?** está muerto, ¿me entiendes?; **I don't — why** no veo por qué, no comprendo por qué; **I fail to — how** no comprendo cómo; **as far as I can —** según mi modo de entender las cosas; a mi ver; **this is how I —** it éste es mi modo de entenderlo, yo lo entiendo así; **the Russians — it differently** los rusos lo miran desde otro punto de vista, el criterio de los rusos es distinto; **I don't — you as a future minister** no puedo imaginarte como ministro; **I don't — it** (*fig*) no creo que sea posible; *see* **fit.**

(d) (*look, perceive*) mirar; observar; percibir; **now — here!** ¡mire!; **so I —** lo veo, lo estoy viendo; **I saw only too clearly that . . .** percibí con toda claridad que . . .; **— for yourself** véalo Vd; **I — in the paper that . . .** veo en el periódico que . . .; **did you — that Queen Anne is dead?** ¿has oído que ha muerto la reina Ana?; **I — nothing wrong in it** no le encuentro nada digno de represión; **I don't know what she —s in him** no sé lo que ella le encuentra.

(e) (*ensure*) **to — (to it) that . . .** procurar que + *subj*, asegurar que + *subj*; **— that he has all he needs** cuide que tenga todo lo que necesita; **— that it does not happen again** y que no vuelva a ocurrir; **— that you have it ready for Monday** procure tenerlo listo para el lunes; **to — that something is done** velar por que algo se haga.

(f) (*visit, frequent*) ver, visitar; **to — the doctor** consultar al médico; **I want to — you about my daughter** quiero hablar con Vd acerca de mi hija; **what did he want to — you about?** ¿qué asunto quería discutir con Vd?, ¿qué motivo tuvo su visita?; **we don't — much of them nowadays** ahora les vemos bastante poco; **we shall be** —**ing them for dinner** vamos a cenar con ellos; **to call** (*or* **go**) **and** — **someone** ir a visitar a uno; **the minister saw the Queen yesterday** el ministro se entrevistó con la Reina ayer; **I'm afraid I can't** — **you to-morrow** lamento no poder verle mañana; — **you soon!**, — **you later!** ¡hasta pronto!; — **you on Sunday!** ¡hasta el domingo!

(g) (*with adv or prep*) **to** — **the New Year in** celebrar el Año Nuevo; **to** — **someone off at the station** ir a despedirse de uno en la estación; **the policeman saw him off** el policía la acompañó a la puerta (*etc*), el policía le dijo que se fuera; **to** — **someone out** acompañar a uno a la puerta; **to** — **a play out** quedarse hasta el fin de una comedia, permanecer sentado hasta que termine una comedia; **to** — **someone through** ayudar a uno a salir de un apuro, ayudar a uno en un trance difícil; **to** — **a deal through** llevar a cabo un negocio; **don't worry, we'll** — **it through** no te preocupes, nosotros lo haremos todo.

2 *vi*: **to** — **about something** atender a algo; encargarse de algo; **I'll** — **about it** lo haré, me encargo de eso; (*non-committally*) lo pensaré; **he came to** — **about our television set** vino a ver nuestro televisor; vino a reparar nuestro televisor; **to** — **into something** investigar algo, examinar algo; **to** — **over a factory** visitar una fábrica; **to** — **through someone** calar a uno, conocer el juego de uno; **to** — **through a mystery** penetrar en un misterio; **that trick is easily** —**n through** ese truco se explica fácilmente; **to** — **to something** atender a algo; encargarse de algo; (*repair*) reparar, componer; **he** —**s to everything** se encarga de todo, lo hace todo; **the rats saw to that** las ratas se encargaron de eso; **it must be** —**n to at once** hay que investigar esto en seguida; **to** — **to it that . . .** procurar que + *subj*, asegurar que + *subj*.

see[2] [si:] *n* sede *f*; **Holy S**— Santa Sede *f*.
seed [si:d] 1 *n* (*Bot*; *for sowing*) semilla *f*, simiente *f*; (*within fruit*) pepita *f*; (*grain*) grano *m*; (*sperm*) simiente *f*; (*offspring*) descendencia *f*; (*fig, of idea etc*) germen *m*; **to go to** —, **to run to** — granar, dar en grana, (*fig*) echarse a perder; ir a menos; **to sow** —**s of doubt in someone's mind** hacer que uno empiece a tener dudas.
2 *vt land* sembrar (*with* de); (*extract* —**s from**) despepitar; (*Sport*) preseleccionar.
3 *vi* granar, dar en grana; dejar caer semillas.
seedbed ['si:dbed] *n* semillero *m*.
seedcake ['si:dkeik] *n* torta *f* de semillas aromáticas.
seed corn ['si:dkɔ:n] *n* trigo *m* de siembra.
seed drill ['si:ddril] *n* sembradora *f*.
seedling ['si:dliŋ] *n* planta *f* de semillero; planta *f* joven, plantón *m*.
seed pearl ['si:dpɜ:l] *n* aljófar *m*.
seed potato ['si:dpə,teitəu] *n* patata *f* de siembra.
seedsman ['si:dzmən] *n*, *pl* —**men** [mən] vendedor *m* de semillas.
seedtime ['si:dtaim] *n* siembra *f*.
seedy ['si:di] *adj* (*Med*) enfermo, indispuesto; ojeroso; *appearance* desaseado; *clothing* raído; *place* pobre, sórdido.
seeing ['si:iŋ] 1 *n* vista *f*, visión *f*; — **is believing** ver es creer; **a film worth** — una película que vale la pena de verse.
2 *conj*: — **that** visto que, puesto que.
seek [si:k] (*irr*: *pret and ptp* **sought**) 1 *vt* buscar; *post* pretender, solicitar; *honour* ambicionar; (*search*) registrar, recorrer buscando; **to** — **death** buscar la muerte; **to** — **shelter** buscar dónde cobijarse; **to** — **advice from someone** pedir consejos a uno; **it is much sought after** se le busca por todas partes; tiene mucha demanda; **the reason is not far to** — no es difícil indicar la causa; **he has been sought in many countries** se le ha buscado en muchos países.
2 *vi* buscar; **to** — **after**, **to** — **for** buscar; **to** — **to** + *infin* intentar + *infin*, procurar + *infin*; esforzarse por + *infin*.
seeker ['si:kə*] *n* buscador *m*, ora *f*.
seem [si:m] *vi* parecer; **so it** —**s** así parece; **how does it** — **to you?** ¿qué le parece?; **it** —**s that . . .** parece que . . .; **it does not** — **that . . .** no parece que + *subj*; **he** —**s honest** parece honrado; **he** —**ed absorbed in . . .** parecía estar absorto en . . .; **she** —**s not to want to go** parece que no quiere ir; **I** — **to have heard that before** me parece que ya me contaron eso antes; **what** —**s to be the trouble?** ¿pasa algo?
seeming ['si:miŋ] 1 *adj* aparente. 2 *n* apariencia *f*; **to all** — según todas las apariencias.

seemingly ['si:miŋli] *adv* aparentemente, según parece; **it is** — **finished** parece que está terminado.
seemliness ['si:mlinis] *n* decoro *m*, decencia *f*, corrección *f*.
seemly ['si:mli] *adj* decoroso, decente, correcto.
seen [si:n] *ptp of* **see**[1].
seep [si:p] *vi* filtrarse, rezumarse.
seepage ['si:pidʒ] *n* filtración *f*.
seer [siə*] *n* vidente *mf*, profeta *mf*.
seersucker ['siə,sʌkə*] *n* sirsaca *f*.
seesaw ['si:sɔ:] 1 *n* balancín *m*, columpio *m* de tabla; (*fig*) vaivén *m*. 2 *adj movement* de vaivén, oscilante. 3 *vi* columpiarse; (*fig*) oscilar.
seethe [si:ð] *vi* hervir; **to** — **with** hervir de; **he's seething** está furioso; **to** — **with anger** indignarse muchísimo, estar furioso.
see-through ['si:θru:] *adj dress* diáfano, transparente.
segment ['segmənt] *n* segmento *m*.
segregate ['segrigeit] *vt* segregar, separar (*from* de); **to be** —**d from** estar separado de.
segregation [,segri'geiʃən] *n* segregación *f*, separación *f*; (*esp*) separación *f* racial.
segregationist [,segri'geiʃnist] *n* segregacionista *mf*.
Seine [sein] Sena *m*.
seine [sein] *n* jábega *f*.
seismic ['saizmik] *adj* sísmico.
seismograph ['saizməgra:f] *n* sismógrafo *m*.
seismography [saiz'mɔgrəfi] *n* sismografía *f*.
seismology [saiz'mɔlədʒi] *n* sismología *f*.
seize [si:z] 1 *vt* (*clutch*) agarrar, asir, coger; (*Law*) *person* detener, prender, *property* embargar, secuestrar; *contraband etc* incautarse de; *territory etc* apoderarse de; *opportunity* aprovechar sin vacilar; **to** — **someone by the arm** asir a uno por el brazo; **to be** —**d with fear** sobrecogerse, ser preso del miedo; **he was** —**d with a desire to** + *infin* le entró un súbito deseo de + *infin*.
2 *vi*: **to** — **on** fijarse en; *pretext etc* valerse de; **to** — **up** (*Mech*) agarrotarse.
seizure ['si:ʒə*] *n* asimiento *m*; detención *f*; prendimiento *m*; embargo *m*, secuestro *m*; incautación *f*; (*Med*) ataque *m*; **the** — **of Slobodia** el acto de apoderarse de Eslobodia; **to have a** — (*Med*) sufrir un ataque (*esp* cardíaco).
seldom ['seldəm] *adv* rara vez, raramente.
select [si'lekt] 1 *vt* escoger, elegir; (*Sport*) seleccionar.
2 *adj* selecto, escogido; exclusivista; *tobacco etc* fino; **a very** — **neighbourhood** un barrio de muy buen tono; **a** — **group of people** un grupo selecto de personas.
selection [si'lekʃən] *n* selección *f*; elección *f*; (*Comm*) surtido *m*; **"**—**s from Rossini"** "selecciones *fpl* de Rossini"; **"**—**s from Cervantes"** "páginas *fpl* escogidas de Cervantes"; —**s for the big race** pronósticos *mpl* para la carrera principal; **natural** — selección *f* natural; **one has to make a** — hay que escoger, hay que tomar unos y dejar otros.
selective [si'lektiv] *adj* selectivo; **one has to be** — hay que escoger, hay que tomar unos y dejar otros.
selectivity [silek'tiviti] *n* selectividad *f*.
selector [si'lektə*] *n* (*Tech*) selector *m*; (*person*) seleccionador *m*.
self [self] 1 *reflexive pron* se (*etc*); (*after prep*) sí mismo (*etc*); (*Comm, hum, or fam*) = **myself** *etc*; **a room reserved for wife and** — una habitación reservada para mi esposa y yo.
2 *adj* (*esp Bot*) unicolor.
3 *n*, *pl* **selves** [selvz] uno mismo, una misma; **the** — el yo; **my better** — mi mejor parte; **my former** — mi ser anterior; **one's other** — su otro yo; **if your good** — **could possibly . . .** si Vd tuviera tanta amabilidad como para . . .; **my humble** — este servidor; **he's quite his old** — **again** se ha repuesto completamente; **he thinks of nothing but** — no piensa sino en sí mismo.
self- [self] *in compounds*: auto . . . ; — de sí mismo.
self-abasement ['selfə'beismənt] *n* rebajamiento *m* de sí mismo, autodegradación *f*.
self-abuse ['selfə'bju:s] *n* (*euph*) masturbación *f*.
self-acting ['self'æktiŋ] *adj* automático.
self-addressed ['selfə'drest] *adj*: — **envelope** sobre *m* con el nombre y dirección de uno mismo.
self-adhesive ['selfəd'hi:ziv] *adj* autoadhesivo.
self-advertisement ['selfəd'və:tismənt] *n* autobombo *m*.
self-apparent ['selfə'pærənt] *adj* evidente, patente.
self-appointed ['selfə'pɔintid] *adj* que se ha nombrado a sí mismo.
self-assertion ['selfə'sə:ʃən] *n* presunción *f*; agresividad *f*.
self-assertive ['selfə'sə:tiv] *adj* presumido; agresivo.

self-assurance ['selfə'ʃuərəns] n confianza f en sí mismo.

self-assured ['selfə'ʃuəd] adj seguro de sí mismo.

self-centred, (US) — **centered** ['self'sentəd] adj egocéntrico.

self-coloured, (US) — **colored** ['self'kʌləd] adj de color uniforme; de color natural.

self-command ['selfkə'mɑːnd] n dominio m sobre sí mismo.

self-complacent ['selfkəm'pleisənt] adj satisfecho de sí mismo.

self-composed ['selfkəm'pəuzd] adj ecuánime, sereno.

self-composure ['selfkəm'pəuzə*] n ecuanimidad f, serenidad f.

self-conceit ['selfkən'siːt] n presunción f, vanidad f, engreimiento m.

self-conceited ['selfkən'siːtid] adj presumido, vanidoso, engreído.

self-confidence ['self'kɔnfidəns] n confianza f en sí mismo.

self-confident ['self'kɔnfidənt] adj seguro de sí mismo, lleno de confianza en sí mismo.

self-conscious ['self'kɔnʃəs] adj cohibido, tímido.

self-consciousness ['self'kɔnʃəsnis] n timidez f.

self-contained ['selfkən'teind] adj independiente; que tiene sus propios recursos, que no necesita ayuda de afuera; flat, apartment completo en sí mismo, con entrada particular; person independiente; reservado, poco comunicativo.

self-contradiction ['self,kɔntrə'dikʃən] n proposición f que lleva implícita una contradicción.

self-contradictory ['self,kɔntrə'diktəri] adj que se contradice a sí mismo, que lleva implícita una contradicción.

self-control ['selfkən'trəul] n autodominio m, dominio m sobre sí mismo, control m de sí mismo; **to exercise one's** — contenerse, dominarse; **to lose one's** — perder la calma, ponerse nervioso.

self-controlled ['selfkən'trəuld] adj ecuánime, sereno.

self-criticism ['self'kritisizəm] n autocrítica f.

self-deception ['selfdi'sepʃən] n engaño m de sí mismo; **this is mere** — **son** ilusiones, esto es engañarse a sí mismo.

self-defeating ['selfdi'fiːtiŋ] adj contraproducente.

self-defence ['selfdi'fens] n defensa f propia; **to act in** — obrar en defensa propia.

self-denial ['selfdi'naiəl] n abnegación f.

self-denying ['selfdi'naiiŋ] adj abnegado.

self-destruction ['selfdis'trʌkʃən] n suicidio m.

self-determination ['selfdi,təːmi'neiʃən] n autodeterminación f.

self-discipline ['self'disiplin] n autodisciplina f.

self-educated ['self'edjukeitid] adj autodidacta.

self-effacement ['selfi'feismənt] n modestia f, humildad f.

self-effacing ['selfi'feisiŋ] adj modesto, humilde.

self-employed ['selfim'plɔid] adj que trabaja por cuenta propia.

self-esteem ['selfis'tiːm] n amor m propio.

self-evident ['self'evidənt] adj evidente, patente.

self-explanatory ['selfiks'plænitəri] adj que se explica por sí mismo.

self-expression ['selfiks'preʃən] n autoexpresión f.

self-filling ['self'filiŋ] adj de relleno automático.

self-fulfilling ['selfful'filiŋ] adj: — **prophecy** profecía f que por su propia naturaleza contribuye a cumplirse.

self-fulfilment ['selfful'filmənt] n realización f de los más íntimos deseos de uno, realización f completa de la potencialidad de uno.

self-governing ['self'gʌvəniŋ] adj autónomo.

self-government ['self'gʌvnmənt] n autonomía f, autogobierno m.

self-help ['self'help] n ayuda f propia.

self-importance ['selfim'pɔːtəns] n presunción f, vanidad f, engreimiento m.

self-important ['selfim'pɔːtənt] adj presumido, vanidoso, engreído.

self-imposed ['selfim'pəuzd] adj punishment etc que uno se impone a sí mismo.

self-incriminating ['selfin'krimineitiŋ] adj autoacusador, que se acusa a sí mismo.

self-indulgence ['selfin'dʌldʒəns] n falta f de moderación, excesos mpl (en el comer etc).

self-indulgent ['selfin'dʌldʒənt] adj inmoderado, que se permite excesos (en el comer etc).

self-inflicted ['selfin'fliktid] adj wound que uno se infiere a sí mismo.

self-interest ['self'intrist] n egoísmo m.

selfish ['selfiʃ] adj egoísta; interesado.

selfishly ['selfiʃli] adv con egoísmo, de modo egoísta.

selfishness ['selfiʃnis] n egoísmo m.

self-knowledge ['self'nɔlidʒ] n conocimiento m de sí mismo.

selfless ['selflis] adj desinteresado.

selflessly ['selflisli] adv desinteresadamente.

selflessness ['selflisnis] n desinterés m.

self-locking ['self'lɔkiŋ] adj de cierre automático.

self-love ['self'lʌv] n egoísmo m, egolatría f.

self-made ['self'meid] adj: — **man** hombre m que ha llegado a su posición actual por sus propios esfuerzos, hijo m de sus propias obras.

self-opinionated ['selfə'pinjəneitid] adj terco.

self-pity ['self'piti] n compasión f de sí mismo.

self-pollination ['self,pɔli'neiʃən] n autopolinización f.

self-portrait ['self'pɔːtrit] n autorretrato m.

self-possessed ['selfpə'zest] adj sereno, dueño de sí mismo.

self-possession ['selfpə'zeʃən] n serenidad f, dominio m sobre sí mismo.

self-praise ['self'preiz] n autoadulación f, autobombo m.

self-preservation ['self,prezə'veiʃən] n propia conservación f.

self-propelled ['selfprə'peld] adj autopropulsado, automotor (f: automotriz).

self-regulating ['self'regjuleitiŋ] adj de regulación automática.

self-reliance ['selfri'laiəns] n confianza f en sí mismo; independencia f.

self-reliant ['selfri'laiənt] adj seguro de sí mismo; independiente.

self-reproach ['selfri'prəutʃ] n remordimiento m.

self-respect ['selfris'pekt] n amor m propio, dignidad f.

self-respecting ['selfris'pektiŋ] adj que tiene amor propio, consciente de su dignidad personal.

self-restraint ['selfris'treint] n see self-control.

self-righteous ['self'raitʃəs] adj santurrón.

self-sacrifice ['self'sækrifais] n (act) sacrificio m de sí mismo; (spirit) abnegación f.

self-sacrificing ['self'sækrifaisiŋ] adj abnegado.

selfsame ['selfseim] adj mismo, mismísimo.

self-satisfaction ['self,sætis'fækʃən] n satisfacción f de sí mismo; suficiencia f.

self-satisfied ['self'sætisfaid] adj satisfecho de sí mismo, pagado de sí mismo; suficiente.

self-sealing ['self'siːliŋ] adj tank que tapa automáticamente cualquier abertura.

self-seeking ['self'siːkiŋ] 1 adj egoísta. 2 n egoísmo m.

self-service ['self'səːvis] adj: — **restaurant** autoservicio m.

self-starter ['self'stɑːtə*] n (Aut) arranque m automático.

self-styled ['self'staild] adj supuesto, sediciente.

self-sufficiency ['selfsə'fiʃənsi] n independencia f; (economic) autosuficiencia f; (of person) confianza f en sí mismo.

self-sufficient ['selfsə'fiʃənt] adj independiente; (economically) autosuficiente; person seguro de sí mismo.

self-supporting ['selfsə'pɔːtiŋ] adj independiente; que tiene sus propios recursos (económicos); que vive de su propio trabajo; **you can marry her when you are** — te puedes casar con ella cuando ganes un sueldo adecuado.

self-taught ['self'tɔːt] adj autodidacta.

self-willed ['self'wild] adj terco, voluntarioso.

self-winding ['self'waindiŋ] adj: — **watch** reloj m de cuerda automática.

sell [sel] (irr: pret and ptp sold) 1 vt (a) vender (at a, for por); "**car** —" "se vende coche"; "**to be sold**" "se vende"; **to** — **one's life dearly** vender cara la vida; **I was sold this in Valencia** esto me lo vendieron en Valencia; **to** — **something back to someone** revender algo a uno; **to** — **someone for a slave, to** — **someone into slavery** vender a uno como esclavo; **to** — **off, to** — **out** vender (todas las existencias de); liquidar, saldar; **we are sold out of bananas** hemos agotado las existencias de plátanos; **stocks of umbrellas are sold out** las existencias de paraguas están agotadas; see auction, loss etc.

(b) (fig: put over) comunicar, hacer aceptar; **if we can** — **coexistence to Ruritania** si podemos hacer aceptar en Ruritania la idea de la coexistencia; **he doesn't manage to** — **his personality** no consigue comunicar su personalidad.

(c) (fig: betray) vender, traicionar; **sold again!** ¡la estafa de siempre!; **you've been sold** le han dado gato por liebre.

(d) to be sold on estar cautivado por; **I'm not exactly sold on the idea** estoy lejos de dejarme cautivar por la idea.

2 *vi* **(a)** venderse (*at* a, *for* por); estar de venta; **it —s well** tiene buena venta, tiene una salida fácil, tiene mucha demanda; **that line doesn't —** ese género no tiene demanda; **to — out, to — up** venderlo todo, vender todas las existencias; realizar.

(b) (*fig*) ser aceptable; **the idea didn't —** la idea no resultó aceptable.

(c) to — out (*fig*) abandonar, renunciar; **to — out to the Russians** abandonar y dejar el paso libre a los rusos.

3 *vr:* **to — oneself** venderse; (*fig*) comunicar con el público, comunicar su personalidad.

4 *n* **(a)** (*fam*) decepción *f*; engaño *m*, estafa *f*; **what a —!** ¡cómo nos han decepcionado!; ¡todo ha sido engaño!

(b) (*Comm*) **to be a hard —** tener una salida difícil; **to be a soft —** tener una salida fácil.

seller ['selə*] *n* (*person who sells*) vendedor *m*, ora *f*; (*dealer*) comerciante *m* (*of* en); **good —** (*Comm*) artículo *m* que tiene mucha demanda; **—'s market** mercado *m* de signo favorable al vendedor.

selling price ['seliŋprais] *n* precio *m* de venta.

sellout ['selaut] *n* **(a)** (*betrayal*) traición *f*; abandono *m*, renuncia *f*. **(b)** (*Theat, Sport etc*) lleno *m*, función *f* para la que se venden todas las localidades.

seltzer (water) ['seltsə*(ˌwɔːtə*)] *n* agua *f* de seltz.

selvage, selvedge ['selvidʒ] *n* orillo *m*, borde *m*.

selves [selvz] *pl* of **self**.

semantic [si'mæntik] *adj* semántico.

semantics [si'mæntiks] *n* semántica *f*.

semaphore ['seməfɔː*] **1** *n* semáforo *m*. **2** *vt* comunicar por semáforo.

semblance ['sembləns] *n* apariencia *f*; **without a — of regret** sin mostrar remordimiento; **without a — of fear** sin dar señal alguna de miedo; **to put on a — of gaiety** procurar parecer alegre.

semen ['siːmən] *n* semen *m*.

semester [si'mestə*] *n* semestre *m*.

semi... ['semi] semi...; medio...

semibasement ['semi'beismənt] *n* semisótano *m*.

semibreve ['semibriːv] *n* semibreve *f*.

semicircle ['semiˌsəːkl] *n* semicírculo *m*.

semicircular ['semiˈsəːkjulə*] *adj* semicircular; *archway* de medio punto.

semicolon ['semiˈkəulən] *n* punto *m* y coma.

semiconscious ['semiˈkɔnʃəs] *adj* semiconsciente.

semiconsonant ['semiˈkɔnsənənt] *n* semiconsonante *f*.

semidarkness ['semiˈdɑːknis] *n:* **in the —** en la casi oscuridad.

semidetached ['semidiˈtætʃt] *adj* semiseparado; **a pair of — houses** una casa doble.

semifinal ['semiˈfainl] *n* semifinal *f*.

semifinalist ['semiˈfainəlist] *n* semifinalista *mf*.

seminal ['seminl] *adj* seminal.

seminar ['seminɑː*] *n* (*Univ: class*) seminario *m*, clase *f* de discusión; (*group*) grupo *m* de investigadores; (*conference*) congreso *m*; reunión *f*; (*institute*) instituto *m*.

seminarist ['seminərist] *n* seminarista *m*.

seminary ['seminəri] *n* seminario *m*.

semiofficial ['semiəˈfiʃəl] *adj* semioficial.

semiprecious ['semiˌpreʃəs] *adj* semiprecioso.

semiquaver ['semikweivə*] *n* semicorchea *f*.

semiskilled ['semiˈskild] *adj* semiexperto, semicualificado.

Semite ['siːmait] *n* semita *mf*.

Semitic [si'mitik] *adj* semítico.

semitone ['semitəun] *n* semitono *m*.

semivowel ['semiˈvauəl] *n* semivocal *f*.

semolina [ˌseməˈliːnə] *n* sémola *f*.

sempiternal [ˌsempiˈtəːnl] *adj* sempiterno.

sempstress ['sempstris] *n* costurera *f*.

senate ['senit] *n* senado *m*; (*Univ: approx*) claustro *m*; **the S—** (*US*) el Senado.

senator ['senitə*] *n* senador *m*.

senatorial [ˌsenəˈtɔːriəl] *adj* senatorial.

send [send] (*irr: pret and ptp* **sent**) **1** *vt* **(a)** (*general sense*) enviar, mandar; despachar; remitir; *telegram* poner; (*Radio*) *programme* transmitir; **the gods — it as a punishment** los dioses nos lo envían como castigo; **to — a child to school** poner a un niño en la escuela; **in Britain children are sent to school at 5** en Gran Bretaña los niños van a la escuela a los 5 años; **some children are sent to school without breakfast** hay niños que van a la escuela sin desayunar; **I wrote the letter but didn't — it** escribí la carta pero no la eché al correo;

to — someone for something enviar a uno a buscar algo; enviar a uno a comprar algo.

(b) (*propel*) *ball etc* lanzar; *arrow* enviar, lanzar, arrojar; **he sent everything flying** lo echó todo a rodar; **the blow sent him sprawling** el golpe le hizo caer redondo; *see* **shiver** *etc*.

(c) (*with adj*) hacer, volver, poner; **it —s the wool green** vuelve la lana verde; **it's enough to — you barmy** (*sl*) es para volverse loco.

(d) (*fam*) entusiasmar, llenar de emoción, embelesar; **that tune —s me** esa melodía me apasiona; **he —s me** me vuelve loca; **it doesn't — me** me trae sin cuidado.

(e) (*with adv or prep*) **to — away** despachar; (*by post etc*) enviar fuera; (*dismiss*) despedir; **to — back** devolver; *person* hacer volver; **to — down** hacer bajar; (*Univ*) expulsar; *criminal* encarcelar; **he was sent down for 6 months** le condenaron a 6 meses de prisión; **to — forth** *smoke etc* arrojar; *sparks* lanzar; **to — forth into the world** enviar a uno a vivir en el mundo; **to — in** *person* hacer entrar; hacer pasar; *bill, name, resignation* presentar; **— him in!** ¡que pase!; **to — off** *goods* despachar, expedir; (*by post*) enviar por correo, echar al correo; *player* expulsar; **to — on** *letter* hacer seguir; *application etc* dar curso a; *instructions* dar, transmitir; **to — out** *smoke etc* arrojar, despedir; *signal, programme* emitir; *invitations* mandar; *shoot* echar; **to — round** *letter etc* hacer circular; distribuir; **to — someone round to the pub** enviar a uno a la taberna; **I'll — the car round at 8** envío el coche a buscarle a las 8; **to — up** hacer subir; *one's name etc* enviar, presentar; *balloon* lanzar; *price, temperature* aumentar, hacer (*parody*) parodiar, satirizar; **— him up!** ¡que suba!; **please — up two cups of tea** por favor, que me suban dos tazas de té.

2 *vi:* **if you don't —** si no me lo dices, si no me lo haces saber; **she sent to say that ...** envió un recado diciendo que ...; **to — away for spares** encargar unos repuestos por correo; **we shall have to — away for it** tendremos que pedirlo por correo; **to — for someone** enviar por uno; enviar a uno a buscar algo; **to — for the doctor** llamar al médico; **a doctor was sent for** se llamó a un médico; **she sent for her glasses** requirió sus gafas.

sender ['sendə*] *n* remitente *mf*; (*Elec*) transmisor *m*.

send-off ['sendɔf] *n* (*farewell*) despedida *f*; (*start*) principio *m*; **to give a project a good —** inaugurar felizmente un proyecto, hacer que un proyecto comience felizmente.

send-up ['sendʌp] *n* parodia *f*, sátira *f*.

Seneca ['senikə] *m* Séneca.

Senegal [ˌseniˈgɔːl] el Senegal.

Senegalese [ˌseniɡəˈliːz] **1** *adj* senegalés. **2** *n* senegalés *m*, esa *f*.

senile ['siːnail] *adj* senil; **to get —** (*Med*) padecer debilidad senil.

senility [si'niliti] *n* senilidad *f*; (*Med*) debilidad *f* senil.

senior ['siːniə*] **1** *adj* (*in age*) mayor (de edad), más viejo; (*on a staff*) más antiguo (*to* que); *position, rank* superior, de categoría superior; *section* (*in competition etc*) para mayores; *partner* más antiguo, principal; **Joe Bloggs, S—** Joe Bloggs, padre; **he is — to me** (*in age*) tiene más años que yo, es más viejo quo yo, (*in rank*) tiene categoria superior a la mía.

2 *n* mayor *mf*; (*in group*) miembro *m* más antiguo; decano *m*; (*in company etc*) socio *m* más antiguo; (*Univ*) alumno *m* del último año, alumna *f* del último año; **he is my —** (*in age*) tiene más años que yo, es más viejo que yo, (*in rank*) tiene categoría superior a la mía; **he is 2 years my —**, he is my **— by 2 years** tiene 2 años más que yo, él me lleva 2 años.

seniority [ˌsiːniˈɔriti] *n* antigüedad *f*.

senna ['senə] *n* sena *f*.

sensation [sen'seifən] *n* sensación *f*; **to be a —, to cause a —, to create a —** causar sensación; **it was a — in New York** en Nueva York causó sensación; **it's a —!** ¡es formidable!

sensational [sen'seifənl] *adj* sensacional.

sensationalism [sen'seifnəlizəm] *n* sensacionalismo *m*.

sense [sens] **1** *n* **(a)** (*bodily*) sentido *m*; **the 5 —s** los 5 sentidos; **— of hearing** oído *m*; **— of sight** vista *f*; **— of smell** olfato *m*; **— of taste** gusto *m*; **— of touch** tacto *m*; **to have a keen — of smell** tener buen olfato; **sixth —** sexto sentido *m*.

(b) **—s** (*right mind*) juicio *m*; **any man in his —s** cualquier hombre sensato; **to be out of one's —s** haber perdido el juicio, no estar en sus cabales; **to bring someone to his —s** obligar a uno a sentar la cabeza, (*Med*) hacer a uno volver en sí; **to come**

to one's —s sentar la cabeza, (*Med*) volver en sí; to take leave of one's —s perder el juicio; have you taken leave of your —s? ¿estás loco?, ¿has perdido el juicio?

(c) (*good* —) buen sentido *m*, juicio *m*; inteligencia *f*; common —, good —, sound — sentido *m* común; a man of — un hombre sensato, un hombre juicioso; there is no — in that eso no sirve para nada, eso es inútil; there is no — in + *ger* es inútil + *infin*; what is the — of + *ger*? ¿de qué sirve + *infin*?; he had the — to call the doctor tuvo bastante inteligencia como para llamar al médico; didn't you have the — to shout? ¿no se te ocurrió gritar?; it doesn't make — no tiene sentido; it doesn't make — to me para mí no tiene sentido; can you make any — of it? ¿has logrado descifrar el misterio?; to make someone see — hacer que uno entre en razón; to talk — hablar con juicio, hablar razonablemente; now you're talking — esto es más razonable.

(d) (*feeling*) sensación *f*; a — of pleasure una sensación de placer; the picture conveys a — of occasion el cuadro comunica una sensación del gran acontecimiento; to labour under a — of injustice creer que uno ha sido tratado injustamente.

(e) (*instinct, insight*) sentido *m*; — of colour sentido *m* del color; — of humour sentido *m* del humor; she lacks all — of humour no tiene sentido del humor en absoluto; — of proportion sentido *m* de la medida; business — aptitud *f* para los negocios.

(f) (*sentiment*) opinión *f*; to take the — of the meeting interpretar la opinión colectiva de la reunión.

(g) (*meaning*) sentido *m*, significado *m*; acepción *f*; significación *f*; in a — hasta cierto punto; in the broad — en el sentido amplio; in the full — of that word en toda la extensión de la palabra; in the strict — en el sentido estricto; in what — do you use the word? ¿qué significado le das a la palabra?; it has various —s tiene diversas acepciones; there are —s in which that may be true desde algunos puntos de vista eso puede ser cierto; he's an amateur in the best — es un aficionado en el buen sentido de la palabra.

2 *vt* sentir, percibir; to — that... percibir que..., darse cuenta de que..., formarse la impresión de que...

senseless ['senslis] *adj* estúpido, insensato; (*Med*) sin sentido, sin conocimiento; to fall — caer sin sentido; to knock someone — derribar a uno y dejarle sin sentido.

senselessly ['senslisli] *adv* estúpidamente, insensatamente.

senselessness ['senslisnis] *n* insensatez *f*.

sense organ ['sens,ɔːgən] *n* órgano *m* sensorio.

sensibility [,sensi'biliti] *n* sensibilidad *f* (*to* a); sensibilities delicadeza *f*, sentimientos *mpl* delicados.

sensible ['sensəbl] *adj* (a) (*having good sense*) juicioso, sensato; prudente, discreto; inteligente; he's a — sort es una persona sensata, es una persona de buen criterio; try to be — about it procura ser razonable.

(b) (*reasonable*) act, decision etc prudente; razonable, lógico; reply, taste acertado; clothing etc práctico; that's a — thing to do eso me parece razonable; the — course would be to + *infin* lo más prudente sería + *infin*; that is very — of you en eso haces muy bien, me parece muy lógico.

(c) (*appreciable*) apreciable, perceptible.

(d) (*aware*) to be — of ser consciente de, darse cuenta de; I am — of the honour you do me agradezco el honor que se me hace.

sensibleness ['sensəblnis] *n* juicio *m*, sensatez *f*; prudencia *f*, discreción *f*; inteligencia *f*; lo razonable, lógica *f*; lo práctico.

sensibly ['sensəbli] *adv* sensatamente; prudentemente; discretamente; inteligentemente; razonablemente, lógicamente; acertadamente; she acted very — obró muy prudentemente; he — answered that... contestó acertadamente que...; try to behave — procura ser más formal.

sensitive ['sensitiv] *adj* (*impressionable*) impresionable, susceptible, sensible, delicado; (*touchy*) susceptible; (*Phot*: paper etc) sensibilizado; (*of instruments etc*) delicado; (*relating to the senses*) sensorio, sensorio; to be — ser sensible a; to be — about one's hair preocuparse mucho por su pelo, tener vergüenza de su pelo, no sentirse cómodo por lo del pelo; you're too — about your suit la gente no presta tanta atención a tu traje como tú te crees.

sensitiveness ['sensitivnis] *n*, **sensitivity** [,sensi'tiviti] *n* lo impresionable, susceptibilidad *f*; delicadeza *f*; sensibilidad *f* (*to* a).

sensitize ['sensitaiz] *vt* sensibilizar.

sensitized ['sensitaizd] *adj* sensibilizado.

sensory ['sensəri] *adj* sensorio.

sensual ['sensjuəl] *adj* sensual.

sensualism ['sensjuəlizəm] *n* sensualismo *m*.

sensualist ['sensjuəlist] *n* sensualista *mf*.

sensuality [,sensju'æliti] *n* sensualidad *f*.

sensuous ['sensjuəs] *adj* sensual, sensorio.

sensuousness ['sensjuəsnis] *n* sensualidad *f*.

sent [sent] *pret and ptp of* send.

sentence ['sentəns] 1 *n* (a) (*Gram*) frase *f*; oración *f*; compound — oración *f* compuesta; simple — oración *f* simple; he writes very long —s escribe frases larguísimas.

(b) (*Law*) sentencia *f*, fallo *m*; (*with expression of time etc*) condena *f*; death — condena *f* a la pena de muerte; to be under — of death estar condenado a muerte; life — condena *f* a perpetuidad, condena *f* de reclusión perpetua; the judge gave him a 6-month — el juez le condenó a 6 meses de prisión; he got a 5-year — se le condenó a 5 años de prisión; to pass — pronunciar sentencia, fallar (*on someone* en el proceso de uno); to serve one's — cumplir su condena.

2 *vt* condenar (*to* a).

sententious [sen'tenʃəs] *adj* sentencioso.

sententiously [sen'tenʃəsli] *adv* sentenciosamente.

sententiousness [sen'tenʃəsnis] *n* sentenciosidad *f*, estilo *m* sentencioso.

sentient ['sentiənt] *adj* sensitivo, sensible.

sentiment ['sentimənt] *n* sentimiento *m*; (*opinion*) opinión *f*, sentir *m*; (*sentimentality*) sentimentalismo *m*, sensiblería *f*; those are my —s too ése es mi criterio también, así lo pienso yo también; to wallow in — nadar en el sentimentalismo.

sentimental [,senti'mentl] *adj* sentimental; (*pej*) sentimental, sensiblero; romántico.

sentimentalism [,senti'mentəlizəm] *n* sentimentalismo *m*.

sentimentalist [,senti'mentəlist] *n* persona *f* sentimental, romántico *m*, a *f*.

sentimentality [,sentimen'tæliti] *n* sentimentalismo *m*, sensiblería *f*.

sentimentally [,senti'mentəli] *adv* de modo sentimental; say en tono sentimental.

sentinel ['sentinl] *n* centinela *m*.

sentry ['sentri] *n* centinela *m*, guardia *m*; to be on — duty estar de guardia.

sentry box ['sentriboks] *n* garita *f* de centinela.

sentry-go ['sentrigəu] *n* turno *m* de centinela; to be on — estar de guardia.

sepal ['sepəl] *n* sépalo *m*.

separable ['sepərəbl] *adj* separable.

separate ['seprit] *adj* separado (*from* de); distinto; suelto; independiente (*from* de); I wrote it on a — sheet lo escribí en otra hoja; take a — sheet for the next part tome una nueva hoja para lo que viene después; everybody has a — cup cada uno tiene su taza particular (*or* individual); to sign a — peace firmar un tratado de paz por separado; "with — toilet" "con inodoro aislado"; this is quite — from his profession esto no tiene nada que ver con su profesión.

separate ['sepəreit] 1 *vt* separar (*from* de); dividir, desunir; to — truth from error separar lo falso de lo verdadero, distinguir entre lo falso y lo verdadero; he is —d from his wife está separado de su mujer.

2 *vi* separarse; they —d in 1970 se separaron en 1970.

separately ['sepritli] *adv* separadamente; por separado.

separation [,sepə'reiʃən] *n* separación *f*.

separatism ['sepərətizəm] *n* separatismo *m*.

separatist ['sepərətist] 1 *adj* separatista. 2 *n* separatista *mf*.

separator ['sepəreitə*] *n* separador *m*.

Sephardic [se'fɑːdik] *adj* sefardí.

Sephardim [se'fɑːdim] *npl* sefardíes *mpl*.

sepia ['siːpiə] *n* (*colour, fish*) sepia *f*.

sepoy ['siːpoi] *n* cipayo *m*.

sepsis ['sepsis] *n* sepsis *f*.

September [sep'tembə*] *n* se(p)tiembre *m*.

septic ['septik] *adj* séptico.

septicaemia, (*US*) **septicemia** [,septi'siːmiə] *n* septicemia *f*.

septuagenarian [,septjuədʒi'neəriən] 1 *adj* septuagenario. 2 *n* septuagenario *m*, a *f*.

Septuagint ['septjuədʒint] *n* versión *f* de los setenta.

sepulchral [si'pʌlkrəl] *adj* sepulcral (*also fig*).

sepulchre, (US) **sepulcher** ['sepǝlkǝ*] n (lit) sepulcro m; **whited** — sepulcro m blanqueado.

sequel ['si:kwǝl] n consecuencia f, resultado m; (of story) continuación f; **in the** — como consecuencia; **it had a tragic** — tuvo un resultado trágico, la cosa terminó trágicamente.

sequence ['si:kwǝns] n sucesión f, orden m de sucesión; serie f; (Cards) serie f, escalera f; (Cine) secuencia f; — **of tenses** sucesión f de tiempos.

sequestered [si'kwestǝd] adj aislado, remoto.

sequestrate [si'kwestreit] vt secuestrar.

sequestration [,si:kwes'treiʃǝn] n secuestración f.

sequin ['si:kwin] n lentejuela f.

sequoia [si'kwoiǝ] n secoya f.

seraglio [se'rɑ:liǝu] n serallo m.

seraph ['serǝf] n, pl **seraphim** ['serǝfim] serafín m.

seraphic [sǝ'ræfik] adj seráfico.

Serb [sǝ:b] n servio m, a f.

Serbia ['sǝ:biǝ] n Servia f.

Serbian ['sǝ:biǝn] 1 adj servio. 2 n servio m, a f.

Serbo-Croat ['sǝ:bǝu'krǝuæt] n (language) servocroata m.

Serbo-Croatian ['sǝ:bǝukrǝu'eiʃǝn] 1 adj servocroata. 2 n servocroata mf.

sere [siǝ*] adj seco, marchito.

serenade [,serǝ'neid] 1 n serenata f. 2 vt dar serenata a.

serene [sǝ'ri:n] adj sereno, tranquilo; **all** —! ¡sin novedad!

serenely [sǝ'ri:nli] adv serenamente, tranquilamente; — **indifferent to the noise** sin molestarse en lo más mínimo por el ruido; **"No" he said** — "No" dijo con mucha tranquilidad.

serenity [si'reniti] n serenidad f, tranquilidad f.

serf [sǝ:f] n siervo m, a f (de la gleba).

serfdom ['sǝ:fdǝm] n servidumbre f (de la gleba); (fig) servidumbre f.

serge [sǝ:dʒ] n estameña f.

sergeant ['sɑ:dʒǝnt] n sargento m; — **at arms** oficial m de orden; — **first class, top** — (US) primer sargento m; **yes,** — sí, mi sargento.

sergeant-major ['sɑ:dʒǝnt'meidʒǝ*] n (approx) brigada m.

serial ['siǝriǝl] 1 adj consecutivo, en serie; **number** de serie; **story** por entregas. 2 n serial m, novela f por entregas; **radio** — serial m radiofónico.

serialize ['siǝriǝlaiz] vt publicar como serial, publicar por entregas; **it has been** —**d in the papers** ha aparecido en una serie de entregas en los periódicos.

serially ['siǝriǝli] adv en serie.

seriatim [,siǝri'eitim] adv en serie.

sericulture [,seri'kʌltʃǝ*] n sericultura f.

series ['siǝriz] n, pl **series** serie f; sucesión f; (Math) serie f, progresión f; (of lectures etc) ciclo m; **World S**— (US) Serie f Mundial; **to connect in** — (Elec) conectar en serie.

series-wound ['siǝriz'waund] adj arrollado en serie.

serious ['siǝriǝs] adj serio; condition, mistake, news etc grave; character serio, formal; **the injury is not** — la lesión no es de gravedad; **are you** — (about it)?, **you can't be** —! ¿lo dices en serio?; **gentlemen, let's be** — señores, un poco de formalidad; **he's** — **about her** está enamorado de verdad de ella; **when we're alone he gets** — cuando estamos a solas se pone muy serio; **things are getting** — las cosas están graves.

seriously ['siǝriǝsli] adv seriamente; en serio; gravemente; —, **though . . .** pero en serio . . .; — **wounded** herido de gravedad; **he is** — **ill** está grave; **do you say so** —? ¿me lo dices en serio?; **we are** — **worried** estamos gravemente preocupados; **I can't take Campoamor** — no puedo tomar a Campoamor en serio; **he takes himself** — se toma muy en serio.

seriousness ['siǝriǝsnis] n seriedad f; gravedad f; **in all** — en serio, seriamente; **the** — **of the situation** la gravedad de la situación.

sermon ['sǝ:mǝn] n sermón m (also fig); **the S**— **on the Mount** el Sermón de la Montaña.

sermonize ['sǝ:mǝnaiz] vti sermonear.

serous ['siǝrǝs] adj seroso.

serpent ['sǝ:pǝnt] n serpiente f, sierpe f; (fig) serpiente f.

serpentine ['sǝ:pǝntain] 1 adj serpentino. 2 n (Min) serpentina f.

serrated [se'reitid] adj serrado, dentellado.

serration [se'reiʃǝn] n endentadura f.

serried ['serid] adj apretado; **in** — **ranks** en filas apretadas.

serum ['siǝrǝm] n suero m.

servant ['sǝ:vǝnt] n (domestic) criado m, a f; (of company etc) empleado m, a f; (general fig sense)

servidor m, ora f; **civil** — funcionario m del Estado, funcionaria f del Estado; **your devoted** —, **your humble** — un servidor, servidor de Vd; **your obedient** — (in letters) suyo afmo, att. y s.s. (= atento y seguro servidor); **the** —**s** (collectively) la servidumbre; **the** — **problem** el problema del servicio.

serve [sǝ:v] 1 vt (a) (of person) servir; estar al servicio de; apprenticeship hacer; sentence cumplir; **to** — **the Queen** servir a la Reina; **he** —**d his country well** sirvió dignamente a la patria, prestó valiosos servicios a la patria.

(b) (of thing) servir; ser útil a; **if my memory** —**s me** si mi memoria no me falla, si tengo buena memoria; see **purpose**.

(c) (Rail etc) **in towns** —**d by this line** en las ciudades por donde pasa esta línea; **the villages used to be** —**d by buses** antes en estos pueblos había servicio de autobuses.

(d) (in shop) goods vender; despachar; customer servir, atender; food, meal servir; **to** — **someone with 5 kilos of potatoes** vender 5 kilos de patatas a uno; **to** — **someone with hors d'oeuvres** servir los entremeses a uno; **dinner is** —**d** la cena está servida; **are you being** —**d, madam?** ¿están despachando su pedido, señora?; **they** —**d cod as halibut** hicieron pasar bacalao por halibut, sirvieron bacalao e hicieron creer que era halibut.

(e) (Tennis etc) sacar.

(f) writ entregar; see **notice**.

(g) (treat) tratar; **he** —**d me very ill** me trató muy mal; **it** —**s you right!** ¡bien merecido lo tienes!; **it** —**d him right for being so greedy** lo mereció por ser tan glotón; **it would have** —**d them right if he had** bien merecido lo hubieran tenido ellos si lo hubiese hecho él.

(h) (of stallion etc) cubrir.

(i) (with adv or prep) **to** — **out** repartir, distribuir; food servir; **to** — **someone out** ajustar cuentas con uno; **I'll** — **you out for this!** ¡me las pagarás!; **to** — **up** food servir; **he** —**d that up as an excuse** eso lo ofreció como excusa.

2 vi (a) servir; **to** — **10 years in the army** servir 10 años en el ejército; **to** — **at table** servir a la mesa; **to** — **on the jury** formar parte del jurado, ser miembro del jurado; **to** — **in parliament** ser diputado; **he is not willing to** — no quiere servir, no está dispuesto a ofrecer sus servicios.

(b) **to** — **as, to** — **for** servir de; servir para; **it will** — servirá para el caso; **when the occasion** —**s** cuando se presente una ocasión propicia.

(c) (Tennis etc) sacar.

3 n (Tennis etc) saque m; **whose** — **is it?** ¿quién saca?

server ['sǝ:vǝ*] n (Tennis) saque mf; (for fish etc) pala f; (Eccl) acólito m.

service ['sǝ:vis] 1 n (a) (in general) servicio m; **active** — servicio m activo; **to be on active** — estar en activo; **to die on active** — morir en acto de servicio; **military** — servicio m militar; **to do one's military** — hacer el servicio militar; **he has 10 years'** — lleva 10 años en el servicio, sirve desde hace 10 años; **he saw long** — sirvió durante muchos años; **to see** — as prestar servicio de.

(b) (branch, department etc) servicio m; **after-sales** — servicio m de asistencia post-venta; **civil** — burocracia f oficial; **customs** — servicio m aduanero, aduana f; **diplomatic** — cuerpo m diplomático; **intelligence** — (Mil) servicio m de información; **"all main** —**s"** "todos servicios"; **medical** — servicio m médico; **postal** —**s** servicios mpl postales; **public** —**s** servicios mpl públicos; **secret** — servicio m secreto; servicio m de contraespionaje; **the Senior S**— (British) la marina; **social** —**s** servicios mpl sociales; **the S**— (Mil) el ejército, (Aer) la aviación, (Naut) la marina; **the (three) S**—**s** las fuerzas armadas; **the train** — **to Pamplona** el servicio de trenes a Pamplona; **the number 13 bus** — el servicio de autobuses número 13; **to be on government** — estar al servicio del gobierno; see **health** etc.

(c) (domestic) **to be in** — ser criado, ser criada; servir; **she was in** — **at Lord Copper's** era criada en la casa de Lord Copper; **to go into** — entrar a servir (with a).

(d) (act of serving etc) servicio m; **for** —**s to education** en premio a sus servicios a la educación; **his** —**s to industry** were most valuable prestó valiosísimos servicios a la industria; **the** — **is really poor in this hotel** en este hotel el servicio es francamente malo; **to dispense with someone's** —**s** despedir a uno; **to do someone a** — prestar un servicio a uno; **to do good** — servir bien, ser muy útil; **Tristram Shandy, at your** — Tristram Shandy, para servirle (*or* a su disposición): **I am at your** — estoy a su disposición; **Brand X is always at your** — la marca X está siempre lista para servirle; **to bring into** — empezar a usar, introducir; **to come into** — entrar en servicio; **to press into** — *thing* utilizar; echar mano de; *person* hacer trabajar, hacer prestar servicio; **to be of** — servir, ayudar; **can I be of** —? ¿puedo ayudarle?; **it's of no** — **in an emergency** en caso de urgencia no sirve para nada; **to be out of** — (*Mech*) no funcionar.

(e) (*Eccl: Catholic*) misa *f*; (*other*) culto *m*, oficio *m* divino.

(f) (*Tennis*) saque *m*.

(g) (*Law*) entrega *f*.

(h) (*set*) vajilla *f*, juego *m*, servicio *m* de mesa; **coffee** — juego *m* de café; **toilet** — juego *m* de tocador.

2 *vt* (*Mech*) atender, mantener; reparar; **to send a car to be** —d mandar un coche al garaje para engrase y mantenimiento.

serviceable ['səːvisəbl] *adj* servible, utilizable, útil; práctico; (*lasting*) duradero.

service flat ['səːvisflæt] *n* piso *m* con servicio de comida, criada *etc*.

service lift ['səːvislift], (*US*) — **elevator** [,eləveitə*] *n* montacargas *m*.

service line ['səːvislain] *n* (*Tennis etc*) línea *f* de saque.

serviceman ['səːvismən] *n*, *pl* —**men** [mən] militar *m*.

service station ['səːvis,steiʃən] *n* estación *f* de servicio.

service tree ['səːvistriː] *n* serbal *m*.

serviette [,səːvi'et] *n* servilleta *f*.

serviette ring [,səːvi'etriŋ] *n* servilletero *m*.

servile ['səːvail] *adj* servil.

servility [səː'viliti] *n* servilismo *m*.

servitude ['səːvitjuːd] *n* servidumbre *f*; **penal** — trabajos *mpl* forzados.

sesame ['sesəmi] *n* (*Bot*) sésamo *m*; **open** —! ¡sésamo ábrete!

sesquipedalian [,seskwipi'deiliən] *adj* sesquipedal; — **word** palabra *f* kilométrica.

sessile ['sesail] *adj* sésil.

session ['seʃən] *n* sesión *f*; (*School, Univ*) curso *m*; **petty** —s tribunal *m* de primera instancia; **to be in** — (*Parl*) estar celebrando sesión, sesionar; **to go into secret** — celebrar una sesión secreta.

sessional ['seʃənl] *adj* de una sesión; *exam* de fin de curso.

sestet [ses'tet] *n* sesteto *m*.

set [set] 1 *n* (a) (*group: of tools, cups, golf clubs etc*) juego *m*; (*of kitchen utensils*) batería *f*; (*of cutlery*) cubierto *m*; (*of turbines etc*) equipo *m*; (*of gears*) tren *m*; (*of stamps*) serie *f*; (*of rooms*) grupo *m*; (*of books, works*) colección *f*; — **of teeth** dentadura *f*; **coffee** — juego *m* de café; **dinner** — vajilla *f*, servicio *m* de mesa; **toilet** — juego *m* de tocador; **a complete** — **of Galdós novels** una colección completa de las novelas de Galdós, las obras completas de Galdós; **that one makes up the** — ése completa la serie; **it makes a** — **with those over there** hace juego con los que Vd ve allá; **I need two to make up the** — me faltan dos para completar la serie (*or* colección).

(b) (*Tennis*) set *m*.

(c) (*Elec etc*) aparato *m*; (*Radio*) aparato *m* de radio, radiorreceptor *m*; (*TV*) televisor *m*; **battery** — radio *f* de batería; **portable** — radio *f* portátil; **generating** — grupo *m* electrógeno.

(d) (*of persons*) grupo *m*; clase *f*; (*pej*) pandilla *f*, camarilla *f*; **the fast** — la gente de vida airada; **the literary** — los literatos, la gente literata; **the smart** — el mundo elegante, los elegantes; **they're a** — **of thieves** son unos ladrones; **they form a** — **by themselves** forman un grupo aparte.

(e) (*School*) clase *f*; **the mathematics** — la clase de matemáticas.

(f) **to make a dead** — **at someone** (*pick on*) emprenderla resueltamente con uno, escoger a uno como víctima; (*amorously*) proponerse conquistar a uno.

(g) (*hair*) **to have a shampoo and** — hacerse lavar y marcar el pelo.

(h) (*of fabric*) caída *f*; (*of dress*) corte *m*, ajuste *m*; (*of head*) porte *m*, manera *f* de llevar; (*of saw*) triscamiento *m*; (*of tide, wind*) dirección *f*; (*of person's mind etc*) inclinación *f*, sesgo *m*, tendencia *f*.

(i) (*Hort*) planta *f* de transplantar; esqueje *m*; **onion** —s cebollitas *fpl* de transplantar.

(j) (*Theat*) decorado *m*, decorados *mpl*; (*Cine*) plató *m*; **to be on the** — estar en plató.

2 *adj and ptp* (a) (*rigid*) rígido, inflexible; *face* rígido, sin expresión; *smile* forzado; permanente; (*in belief*) inflexible; **the fruit is** — el fruto está formado.

(b) (*ready*) listo; **all** —?, **are we all** —? ¿estamos?, ¿estamos listos?; **to be all** — **for** estar listo para; **with their cameras all** —, **to shoot** con las máquinas a punto para disparar.

(c) (*fixed, decided in advance*) fijo; decidido de antemano; *price, purpose* fijo; *phrase* hecho; *task* asignado; *subject* prescrito, establecido; *time* señalado; (*usual*) reglamentario; (*customary*) acostumbrado; **at a** — **time** a la hora señalada; **there is no** — **time for it** para eso no hay hora fija; — **books** autores *mpl* del programa; **with no** — **limits** sin límites determinados; **he gave us a** — **speech** pronunció un discurso preparado de antemano; **he has a** — **speech for these occasions** para estas ocasiones tiene un discurso invariable.

(d) (*resolved*) resuelto, decidido; **to be** — **in one's purpose** tener un propósito firme, mantenerse firme en su propósito; **to be** — **in one's ways** tener costumbres profundamente arraigadas; **to be** — **on something** estar empeñado en algo; **to be** — **on** + *ger* estar resuelto a + *infin*; **since you are so** — **on it** puesto que te empeñas en ello; **to be dead** — **against something** estar completamente opuesto a algo.

3 (*irr: pret and ptp* **set**) *vt* (a) (*place*) poner, colocar; situar; *jewel* engastar, montar; **bricks** — **in concrete** ladrillos puestos en hormigón; **to** — **places for 14** poner cubiertos para 14 personas; **to** — **the table** poner la mesa; — **the chairs by the window** ponga las sillas junto a la ventana; **to** — **a poem to music** poner música a un poema; **she** — **the dish before me** puso el plato delante de mí; **to** — **a plan before a committee** exponer un plan ante una comisión; **I** — **him above Greene** le creo superior a Greene, le antepongo a Greene; **what value do you** — **on it**? ¿en cuánto lo valoras?, (*fig*) ¿qué valor tiene para Vd?; **the ruins are** — **in a valley** las ruinas están enclavadas en un valle; **the scene is** — **in Rome** la escena tiene lugar en Roma, la acción pasa en Roma; **his stories,** — **in the society of 1890** . . . sus cuentos, ambientados en la sociedad de 1890 . . .

(b) (*adjust*) ajustar, arreglar; *clock* poner en hora; *alarm clock* regular; *bone* reducir, encasar, componer; *specimen* montar; *hair* marcar, fijar; *sail* desplegar; *saw* triscar; *trap* armar; *snare* tender (*also fig*); *type* componer; *cement etc* solidificar, endurecer; *jelly* cuajar; *teeth* apretar; **the alarm clock is** — **for 7** el despertador está puesto para las 7; **he** —**s his watch by Big Ben** pone su reloj por el Big Ben.

(c) (*fix*) fijar, señalar; **to** — **a time for a meeting** fijar una hora para una reunión; **to** — **limits to something** señalar límites a algo; **to** — **a period of 3 months** señalar un plazo de 3 meses; **to** — **the fashion** imponer la moda (*for* de); **to** — **a record of 10 seconds** establecer un récord de 10 segundos; **to** — **course for** hacer rumbo a.

(d) (*give*) *example* dar; *task* imponer, asignar; *problem* plantear, (*as test etc*) poner; **to** — **Lorca for 1980** poner una obra de Lorca en el programa de estudios para 1980; **Cela is not** — **this year** este año Cela no figura en el programa; **to** — **an exam paper in German** poner un examen en alemán.

(e) **to** — **a dog on someone** azuzar un perro contra uno; **I was** — **on by 3 dogs** me atacaron 3 perros; **we** — **the police on to him** le denunciamos a la policía; **what** — **the police on the trail?** ¿qué puso a la policía sobre la pista?

(f) **the noise** — **the dogs barking** el ruido hizo ladrar a los perros; **to** — **something going** poner algo en marcha; **to** — **someone laughing** hacer reír a uno; **to** — **everyone talking** dar que hablar a todos; **this** — **me thinking** esto me hizo meditar; **to** — **someone to work** poner a uno a trabajar.

(g) (*with adv or prep*) **to** — **someone against someone else** indisponer a uno con otra persona, enemistar a uno con otra persona; **one has to** — **A against B** hay que pesar A contra B, hay que contraponer A a B; **to** — **aside** poner aparte; reservar, guardar; *proposal* desechar, rechazar; *petition* desatender, desestimar; *law, will* anular; **to** — **back progress** detener, entorpecer; poner obstáculos a; *clock* retrasar; **the house is** — **back from the road** la casa está algo apartada de la carretera; **this has** — **us back some years** esto representa una pérdida de varios años, esto nos ha costado varios años de progreso; **the dinner** — **me** back £7 la cena me costó 7 libras; **to — down** (*put down*) poner en tierra, poner en el suelo, depositar; **the taxi — us down here** el taxi nos dejó aquí; **the train —s down passengers at . . .** los viajeros se apean en . . .; **to — down** (*in writing*) poner por escrito; apuntar, consignar, registrar; **it is not — down here** no consta aquí; **we — it down to . . .** lo atribuimos a . . ., lo achacamos a . . .; **I — him down as a liar** le tomé por un embustero, le juzgué de mentiroso; **to — forth** (*display*) mostrar, exhibir; *theory etc* exponer, explicar; **to — off** (*explode*) hacer estallar; **to — someone off** hacer reír a uno; dar a uno la oportunidad de hablar; **that really — him off** con eso sí se puso furioso; **to — off profits against losses** contraponer las ganancias a las pérdidas; **the black —s off the red** el negro hace resaltar el rojo, el negro pone de relieve el rojo; **her dress —s off her figure** su vestido le acentúa el tipo; **to — out** (*arrange*) arreglar; sacar y disponer; clasificar; (*state*) exponer, explicar; **it's very clearly — out here** aquí se explica con toda claridad; **the material is well — out on the page** el material está bien dispuesto en la página; **to — up** *monument* erigir, levantar; *institution, company etc* crear, fundar, establecer; *committee* constituir; *fund* crear; (*Typ*) componer; (*Tech*) armar, montar; *house* poner; *government* establecer, instaurar; *record* establecer; *precedent* sentar; *cry* levantar, lanzar, dar; *protest* levantar; **to — up a fashion for . . .** crear una moda de . . ., imponer la moda de . . .; **UNO was — up in 1945** se fundó la ONU en 1945; **he — her up in a flat** la instaló en un piso; **to — someone up in business** establecer a uno en un negocio, ayudar a uno a establecerse en un negocio; **to — someone up as a model** poner a uno como modelo; **to — someone up as a judge** erigir a uno como juez; **the medicine — me up again** la medicina me fortaleció; **now he's — up for life** ahora tiene una carrera (*or* recursos, renta *etc*) que le durará(n) toda la vida; **to be well — up for** estar bien provisto de, tener buena provisión de.

4 *vi* (**a**) (*of sun etc*) ponerse.

(**b**) (*of bone*) componerse.

(**c**) (*of jelly etc*) cuajarse; (*of blood*) coagularse; (*of cement*) fraguar; (*of gum, mud*) endurecerse, solidificarse.

(**d**) (*of dog*) estar de muestra; **the tide is — in our favour** la marea fluye para llevarnos adelante, (*fig*) la tendencia actual nos favorece, llevamos el viento en popa; **the wind is — strong from the north** el viento sopla recio del norte.

(**e**) **to — to work** ponerse a trabajar; poner manos a la obra.

(**f**) (*with adv or prep*) **to — about a job** emprender una tarea, comenzar una tarea; **to — about doing something** ponerse a hacer algo; **to — about someone** atacar a uno, agredir a uno; empezar a pegar a uno; **they — about each other** llegaron a las manos; **to — forth** partir, ponerse en camino; **to — in** (*begin*) comenzar; (*breakout*) declararse; (*of night, winter*) cerrar; (*of tide*) fluir; **reaction — in after the war** la reacción se afianzó después de la guerra; **the rain has — in for the night** parece que la lluvia continuará toda la noche; **the rain has really — in now** ahora está lloviendo de verdad; **to — off** partir, ponerse en camino; **to — out** partir, ponerse en camino; **to — out for** partir para, salir para; **to — out in search of someone** partir en busca de uno; **to — out to** + *infin* (*begin*) ponerse a + *infin*; **this book —s out to prove that . . .** este libro se propone demostrar que . . .; **we didn't — out to do that** no teníamos esa intención al principio; **to — to** (*start*) empezar; (*start work*) ponerse resueltamente a trabajar, aplicarse con vigor; (*start eating*) empezar a comer; **they — to with their fists** empezaron a pegarse con los puños; **— to!** ¡a ello!; **to — up as a judge** erigirse en juez, constituirse en juez; **to — up in business** establecerse en un negocio.

5 *vr*: **to — oneself against something** oponerse rotundamente a algo; **to — oneself up as a judge** erigirse en juez, constituirse en juez; **he —s himself up as a critic** se las da de crítico, hace creer que es crítico.

setback ['setbæk] *n* revés *m*, contratiempo *m*; **to suffer a —** sufrir un revés.

setscrew ['setskru:] *n* tornillo *m* de presión.

set square ['setskwɛə*] *n* cartabón *m*, escuadra *f*.

settee [se'ti:] *n* canapé *m*, sofá *m*.

settee-bed [se'ti:'bed] *n* sofá-cama *m*.

setter ['setə*] *n* (*of puzzle etc*) autor *m*, ora *f*; (*dog*) perro *m* de muestra inglés, setter *m*.

setting ['setiŋ] *n* (*of sun*) puesta *f*; (*act of placing*) colocación *f*; (*of jewel*) engaste *m*, montadura *f*, montura *f*; (*Theat etc*) escena *f*, escenario *m*; (*of action etc*) marco *m*; (*natural —, landscape etc*) marco *m*; alrededores *mpl*; (*of bone*) reducción *f*, composición *f*; (*of machine etc*) ajuste *m*; (*Typ*) composición *f*; (*Mus*) arreglo *m*, versión *f*; **a — for 2 violins** un arreglo para 2 violines.

setting lotion ['setiŋ.ləuʃən] *n* fijador *m* (para el pelo).

setting-up ['setiŋʌp] *n* (*of monument*) erección *f*; (*of institution, company*) creación *f*, fundación *f*, establecimiento *m*; (*Typ*) composición *f*.

settle[1] ['setl] *n* banco *m*.

settle[2] ['setl] **1** *vt* (**a**) (*place*) colocar; (*place firmly*) asentar; (*fix*) asegurar, fijar, afirmar; **to — one's feet in the stirrups** afirmarse en los estribos.

(**b**) *persons* establecer; *land* colonizar, poblar (*with* de); **it was first —d by the French** los primeros colonos fueron los franceses; **he —d her in a little flat** la instaló en un modesto piso.

(**c**) **to — an income on someone** asignar (*or* señalar) una renta a uno.

(**d**) **to — one's affairs** arreglar sus asuntos; **to — an invalid for the night** poner a un enfermo cómodamente para la noche.

(**e**) (*calm*) *nerves* calmar, sosegar; *doubts* disipar, desvanecer; *stomach* asentar.

(**f**) *account* ajustar, liquidar, saldar; *claim* satisfacer; *differences, quarrel* componer; *date etc* fijar, acordar; *deal* firmar; *problem* resolver, solucionar; **several points remain to be —d** quedan varios puntos por resolver; **the terms were —d by negotiation** se acordaron las condiciones mediante una negociación; **to — an affair out of court** arreglar una disputa de modo privado; **the result was —d in the first half** se decidió el resultado en el primer tiempo; **it's all —d** todo está resuelto; ya no hay problema; **so that's —d then** así que todo está arreglado; **that —s it!** ¡ya no hay más que decir!; **— it among yourselves!** ¡allá vosotros!

(**g**) (*fam*) **I'll soon — him** me lo cargaré; **that —d him** ya no hay problema con él, ya no volverá a molestarnos.

2 *vi* (*in many cases also* **to — down**) (**a**) (*establish oneself: in a house etc*) establecerse, instalarse; (*in a country*) arraigarse; (*of bird, insect*) posarse; **to — comfortably in an armchair** sentarse cómodamente en una butaca; **the snow is settling** la nieve no se derrite; **the wind —d in the east** el viento siguió soplando del este.

(**b**) **to — down** (*after wild period etc*) sentar la cabeza; **to marry and — down** casarse y empezar a tomar las cosas en serio; **to — down to a new life** adaptarse a una vida nueva; **he's settling down at school** se está acostumbrando a la escuela; **things are beginning to — down** las cosas empiezan a volver a la normalidad; **he —d down with two mistresses** se las arregló para vivir con dos queridas; **he can't — down anywhere** es un culo de mal asiento; **to — down to work** aplicarse al trabajo, dedicarse a trabajar (en serio).

(**c**) (*of building*) asentarse; (*of liquid*) clarificarse; (*of sediment*) depositarse, sedimentarse; (*of ship*) hundirse lentamente; **things are settling into shape** las cosas empiezan a adquirir una forma.

(**d**) (*of passion etc*) calmarse; (*of weather*) serenarse; (*of conditions*) normalizarse, volver a la normalidad.

(**e**) **to — on something** decidir algo, resolver algo; (*choose*) escoger algo, optar por algo; **to — on a date** fijar una fecha.

(**f**) **to — for £250** convenir en aceptar 250 libras; **will you — for a draw?** ¿quedamos en empate?; **to — out of court** arreglar una disputa de modo privado.

(**g**) **to — up** ajustar cuentas (*with someone* con uno; *also fig*).

3 *vr*: **to — oneself down in an armchair** sentarse cómodamente en una butaca; **to — oneself down for the night** arreglarse para pasar la noche.

settlement ['setlmənt] *n* (**a**) (*of account*) ajuste *m*, liquidación *f*; (*of claim*) satisfacción *f*; (*of difference, quarrel*) arreglo *m*; (*of problem*) solución *f*.

(**b**) (*agreement*) acuerdo *m*, convenio *m*; **marriage —** contrato *m* matrimonial, capitulaciones *fpl*; **to reach a —** llegar a un acuerdo.

(**c**) (*act of settling persons*) establecimiento *m*; (*of land*) colonización *f*.

(**d**) (*colony*) colonia *f*; (*village*) pueblo *m*; núcleo *m* rural; (*homestead*) caserío *m*.

settler ['setlə*] *n* colono *m*, a *f*; (*pioneer*) colonizador *m*.

set-to ['set'tu:] n (fam) bronca f, pelea f; **to have a —
with someone** pelearse con uno.
setup ['setʌp] n tinglado m, sistema m, organización
f; estructura f; plan m; **it's an odd — here** aquí
tienen un extraño sistema; **you have to know the —**
hay que conocer el tinglado.
seven ['sevn] **1** adj siete. **2** n siete m.
sevenfold ['sevnfəuld] **1** adj séptuplo. **2** adv siete veces.
seventeen ['sevn'ti:n] adj diecisiete; **she was sweet —**
estaba en la flor de sus 17 abriles.
seventeenth ['sevn'ti:nθ] adj decimoséptimo.
seventh ['sevnθ] **1** adj séptimo. **2** n séptimo m.
seventieth ['sevntiiθ] adj septuagésimo.
seventy ['sevnti] adj setenta; **the seventies** (eg 1970s)
los años setenta; **to be in one's seventies** tener más
de setenta años.
sever ['sevə*] vt cortar; separar, dividir; relations
romper.
several ['sevrəl] **1** adj (a) (of number) varios, algunos;
diversos; **— times already** varias veces ya; **I bought
— books** compré algunos libros.
   (b) (respective) respectivos, distintos; **they have
their — colours** tienen sus respectivos colores; **they
went their — ways** se fueron cada uno por su lado;
joint and — (Law**)** solidario.
   2 pron algunos; **— of them wore hats** algunos de
ellos llevaban sombrero; **— were dead** algunos
estaban muertos.
severally ['sevrəli] adv respectivamente; (one by one)
por separado, individualmente.
severance ['sevərəns] n corte m; separación f,
división f; (of relations) ruptura f; **— pay** cantidad
f que se paga a un empleado al despedirle.
severe [si'viə*] adj severo; riguroso, fuerte; duro;
weather, winter, critic, restriction etc riguroso; illness,
loss, wound grave; pain intenso, agudo; storm
violento; reprimand áspero; blow duro; style adusto,
austero; **to be — on someone** tratar a uno con rigor;
to be too — (on someone) cargar la mano.
severely [si'viəli] adv severamente; rigurosamente;
fuertemente; duramente; gravemente; intensamente;
agudamente; ásperamente; austeramente;
wounded herido de gravedad; **a — plain style** un
estilo de lo más austero; **to leave something —
alone** no tener nada en absoluto que ver con algo.
severity [si'veriti] n severidad f; rigor m; gravedad f;
intensidad f, agudeza f; aspereza f; austeridad f.
Seville [sə'vil] Sevilla.
Sevillian [sə'viliən] **1** adj sevillano. **2** n sevillano m,
a f.
sew [səu] (irr: pret **sewed**, ptp **sewn**) vti coser; **to —
on** coser, pegar; **to — up** coser, zurcir; **to get a
matter all —n up** arreglar un asunto de modo
definitivo; **we've got the game all —n up now** ya
estamos seguros de ganar este partido.
sewage ['sju:idʒ] n aguas fpl residuales.
sewage disposal ['sju:idʒdis‚pəuzəl] n depuración f
de aguas residuales.
sewage farm ['sju:idʒfɑ:m] n, **sewage works**
['sju:idʒwə:ks] n estación f depuradora (de aguas
residuales).
sewer ['sjuə*] n albañal m, alcantarilla f, cloaca f;
(fig) letrina f, sentina f.
sewerage ['sjuəridʒ] n alcantarillado m; (as service on
estate etc) saneamiento m.
sewing ['səuiŋ] **1** n costura f; labor f de costura. **2**
attr de coser.
sewing basket ['səuiŋ‚bɑ:skit] n cesta f de costura.
sewing machine ['səuiŋmə‚ʃi:n] n máquina f de coser.
sewing silk ['səuiŋsilk] n torzal m, seda f de coser.
sewn [səun] ptp of sew.
sex [seks] **1** n sexo m; **the female —** el sexo femenino;
the male — el sexo masculino; **the fair —** el bello
sexo; **the weaker —** el sexo débil; **of both —es** de
ambos sexos.
   2 attr sexual; **— act** coito m; **— education**
instrucción f sobre el sexo; **— hygiene** higiene f
sexual.
   3 vt chicks sexar, determinar el sexo de.
sexagenarian [‚seksədʒi'neəriən] **1** adj sexagenario.
2 n sexagenario m, a f.
sex appeal ['seksə‚pi:l] n atractivo m sexual, gancho
m (fam).
sexless ['sekslis] adj desprovisto de instinto sexual;
desprovisto de atractivo sexual; (Bio) sin sexo,
asexual.
sex-linked ['seks'liŋkt] adj (Bio) ligado al sexo.
sex maniac ['seks'meiniæk] n maníaco m sexual.
sexologist ['seks'ɔlədʒist] n sexólogo m.
sexology [sek'sɔlədʒi] n sexología f.
sextant ['sekstənt] n sextante m.
sextet(te) [seks'tet] n sexteto m.

sexton ['sekstən] n sacristán m; (gravedigger)
sepulturero m.
sexual ['seksjuəl] adj sexual.
sexuality [‚seksju'æliti] n sexualidad f.
sexually ['seksjuəli] adv sexualmente.
sexy ['seksi] adj person de gran atractivo sexual,
cachondo (fam); joke, film etc verde, escabroso;
dress etc que realza el atractivo sexual, provocativo.
sh [ʃ] interj ¡chitón!
shabbily ['ʃæbili] adv pobremente; injustamente;
a — dressed duke un duque pobremente vestido;
he was very — treated le trataron con suma
injusticia.
shabbiness ['ʃæbinis] n pobreza f, lo desharrapado;
lo raído, lo viejo; mal estado m; injusticia f; vileza f.
shabby ['ʃæbi] adj person pobremente vestido,
desharrapado; garment raído, gastado, viejo; area
pobre; building etc de aspecto pobre, en mal estado;
treatment injusto; trick vil, malo; **to feel —** creer ir
mal vestido; **to look —** tener aspecto pobre, tener
aspecto poco elegante.
shabby-looking ['ʃæbi‚lukiŋ] adj de aspecto pobre.
shack [ʃæk] **1** n chabola f, choza f. **2** vi: **to — up
with someone** (fam) ir a vivir con uno; **to — up
together** (fam) vivir juntos.
shackle ['ʃækl] vt encadenar; poner grilletes a; (fig)
poner trabas a, estorbar; **we are —d by tradition**
las trabas de la tradición nos tienen presos.
shackles ['ʃæklz] npl grillos mpl, grilletes mpl;
(fig) trabas fpl; **the — of convention** las trabas de la
convención.
shad [ʃæd] n sábalo m.
shade [ʃeid] **1** n (a) (shadow) sombra f; **—s of night**
tinieblas fpl, oscuridad f; **the —s of night were
falling fast** se hacía rápidamente de noche; **in the
— a la sombra** (of de); **temperature in the —**
temperatura f a la sombra; **35° in the —** 35 grados a
la sombra; **to put something in the —** (fig) oscurecer
(la fama de) algo, eclipsar algo, dejar algo chico.
   (b) (lamp-) pantalla f; (eye-) visera f; (window-,
US) persiana f.
   (c) (of colour) matiz m; tonalidad f, tono m;
(of meaning, opinion) matiz m, modalidad f; **a new
— of lipstick** una nueva tonalidad de lápiz labial;
have you a lighter —? ¿tiene una tonalidad más
clara?; **all —s of opinion are represented** todas las
modalidades de la opinión están representadas;
there is a further — of meaning here en el significado de esto hay todavía un matiz más.
   (d) (small quantity) poquito m; **just a — more**
un poquito más; **he's a — better** está un poquito
mejor; **it's a — awkward** es un tanto difícil.
   (e) (ghost) fantasma m; **the S—s** el infierno;
—s of Professor X! ¡qué diría el profesor X si
resucitara!
   2 vt (a) dar sombra a; face etc proteger contra el
sol (etc); resguardar de la luz; **to — one's eyes with
one's hand** llevar la mano a los ojos para protegerlos
contra el sol; **to — a light** poner pantalla a una
lámpara; **her face was —d by a big hat** un sombrero
ancho le daba sombra a la cara.
   (b) (Art) sombrear, esfumar; **to — away, to
— off** colours degradar; **to — one's eyes with
mascara** ponerse sombreador en los ojos.
   3 vi: **to — away, to — off** cambiar poco a poco (into
hasta hacerse), transformarse gradualmente (into
en); **blue that —s off into black** azul que se trans-
forma gradualmente en negro.
shadeless ['ʃeidlis] adj sin sombra, privado de
sombra.
shadiness ['ʃeidinis] n sombra f, lo umbroso.
shading ['ʃeidiŋ] n (for eyes) sombreado m; (of
colours) degradación f; transformación f gradual
(into en).
shadow ['ʃædəu] **1** n (a) sombra f; **the —s** la oscuridad,
las tinieblas; **the — of death** la sombra de la
muerte; **in the — of** dentro de la sombra de, (fig)
amenazado por; **under the — of serious charges**
amenazado por unas acusaciones graves; **without a
— of doubt** sin sombra de duda, sin la menor duda;
without a — of truth sin tener la más pequeña
parte de verdad; **he is but a — of his former self**
es apenas una sombra de lo que fue; **to cast a —**
proyectar una sombra; **to cast a — over the
festivities** ser una nota triste en la fiesta; **to wear
oneself to a —** adelgazar peligrosamente por exceso
de trabajo, debilitarse trabajando con exceso.
   (b) (person) policía m (or detective m etc) que
sigue a un sospechoso.
   2 adj: **— factory** fábrica f secreta; **— cabinet**
consejo de los diputados de la oposición que esperan

tener *carteras en un gobierno futuro;* **the — Foreign Secretary** *el portavoz de la oposición sobre asuntos exteriores, el diputado de la oposición que espera tener la cartera de asuntos exteriores en un gobierno futuro.*
  3 *vt* **(a)** *(darken)* oscurecer; *(Art)* sombrear; **to — forth** anunciar, indicar vagamente, simbolizar.
  (b) *(follow)* seguir y vigilar; **have that man —ed** que se vigile a ese hombre; **I was —ed all the way home** me siguieron todo el camino hasta mi casa.
shadow boxing [ˈʃædəu‚bɒksiŋ] *n* boxeo *m* con un adversario imaginario; *(fig)* disputa *f* con un adversario imaginario.
shadowy [ˈʃædəui] *adj* oscuro; *(fig)* oscuro; indistinto, indefinido; **a — form** un bulto, una forma indistinta; **the company leads a — existence** la compañía tiene una existencia misteriosa.
shady [ˈʃeidi] *adj* **(a)** *place* sombreado, umbroso, de sombra; **a la sombra; a — tree** un árbol que da sombra; **it's — here** aquí hay sombra.
  (b) *(fig)* *person* sospechoso; *deal* turbio; **the — side of politics** el aspecto turbio de la política; **to be on the — side of 40** tener más de 40 años.
shaft [ʃɑːft] *n* *(arrow etc)* flecha *f*, dardo *m*, saeta *f*; *(part of arrow)* astil *m*; *(of column)* caña *f*, fuste *m*; *(of tool, golf club etc)* mango *m*; *(of cart, carriage)* vara *f*; *(Mech)* eje *m*, árbol *m*; *(Min)* pozo *m*; *(of light)* rayo *m*; **the —s of Cupid** las flechas de Cupido; **— of wit** agudeza *f*; **driving —** *(Mech)* árbol *m* motor; **ventilating —** pozo *m* de ventilación.
shag¹ [ʃæg] *n* tabaco *m* picado.
shag² [ʃæg] *n* *(Orn)* cormorán *m* moñudo.
shaggy [ˈʃægi] *adj* velludo, peludo, lanudo; **— dog story** chiste *m* goma.
shagreen [ʃæˈgriːn] *n* chagrén *m*, zapa *f*.
Shah [ʃɑː] *n* cha *m*, chah *m*.
shake [ʃeik] **1** *n* **(a)** sacudida *f*, sacudimiento *m*; *(quiver)* temblor *m*; *(of vehicle etc)* vibración *f*; *(Mus)* trino *m*; *(of head)* movimiento *m*; **with a — in his voice** le tembló la voz al decir esto; **with a — of her head** moviendo la cabeza negativamente, con un movimiento negativo de la cabeza; **to be all of a —** estar todo tembloroso; **to give someone a good —** sacudir violentamente a uno; **to give a rug a good —** sacudir bien una alfombrilla.
  (b) *(milk —)* batido *m*.
  (c) **—s: he's no great —s at swimming** en natación es poco extraordinario; **he's no great —s as a swimmer** como nadador no vale mucho; **in a brace of —s**, **in two —s** en un decir Jesús, en un abrir y cerrar de ojos.
  2 *(irr: pret* **shook**, *ptp* **shaken)** *vt* **(a)** sacudir; *building etc* hacer temblar, hacer retemblar; *head* mover, menear; *hand* estrechar; *bottle* agitar; *cocktail etc* agitar, remover; **"— the bottle"** "agite la botella"; **"— well before using"** "agítese bien antes de usarlo"; **we had to — him to rouse him** tuvimos que sacudirle para despertarle; **to — one's finger at someone** negar con el dedo lo que dice *(etc)* uno; **to — one's fist at someone** amenazar a uno con el puño; **to — hands** estrecharse la mano, darse las manos; **to — hands with someone** estrechar la mano a uno; **to — one's head** negar algo con la cabeza, mover la cabeza negativamente.
  (b) *(fig)* *(weaken)* debilitar; hacer flaquear; *(impair)* perjudicar, afectar; **it has —n his health** ha afectado su salud; **nothing will — our resolve** nada hará flaquear nuestra resolución; **the firm's credit has been badly —n** ha sido perjudicada la reputación de la casa; **the prosecutor could not — his evidence** el fiscal no logró persuadirle a modificar su testimonio; el fiscal no pudo desacreditar su testimonio.
  (c) *(fig: alarm)* inquietar, perturbar; *(amaze)* sorprender, pasmar, dejar estupefacto; *(upset composure of)* desconcertar; *(shock)* dar una sacudida a; **the news shook me** la noticia me pasmó; **that shook him** eso le desconcertó; **7 days which shook the world** 7 días que estremecieron el mundo; **it shook me rigid** *(or* **solid**; *fam)* me sorprendió muchísimo, me chocó bastante; **he needs to be —n out of his smugness** hay que darle una sacudida para que deje de estar tan pagado de sí mismo.
  (d) *(with adv or prep)* **to — down** *fruit etc* hacer caer, sacudir; *bajar* sacudiendo; **to — someone down** *(fam: for money)* sacar dinero a uno por chantaje; **to — someone down for £50** exigir que uno pague 50 libras; **to — someone down (for arms)** palpar a uno (para comprobar si lleva armas); **to — off** *dust, yoke etc* sacudirse; *(get rid of)* quitarse de encima, deshacerse de, librarse de; *pursuer* zafarse de, dar esquinazo a; **I can't — off this cold** no logro quitarme este catarro; **to — out** *(unfurl)* desplegar;

blanket etc abrir y sacudir; **to — dust out** sacudir el polvo; **to — up** *liquid, bottle* agitar, remover; *(fig)* dar una sacudida a, dar un pinchazo a; reorganizar; estimular, reanimar; infundir nueva energía a.
  3 *vi* estremecerse; temblar, retemblar *(at, with* de); *(of voice)* temblar; *(Mus)* trinar; **to — like a leaf** temblar como un azogado; **to — with fear** temblar de miedo; **to — with laughter** desternillarse de risa; **the house shook with merry singing** la casa retemblaba con alegres canciones; **the walls shook at the sound** se estremecían las paredes con el ruido; **it shook in the wind** bamboleaba al viento; **his voice shook** le tembló la voz; **— !**, **— on it!** ¡chócala!; **to — down** acostarse, echarse a dormir; **I can — down anywhere** yo me duermo en cualquier sitio.
  4 *vr:* **to — oneself free** librarse de una sacudida.
shakedown [ˈʃeikdaun] *n* *(bed)* cama *f* improvisada; *(fam)* exacción *f* de dinero; chantaje *m*.
shaken [ˈʃeikən] *ptp of* **shake**.
shaker [ˈʃeikə*] *n* *(cocktail —)* coctelera *f*.
Shakespearian [ʃeiksˈpiəriən] *adj* shakespeariano.
shake-up [ˈʃeikʌp] *n* conmoción *f*; reorganización *f*; sacudida *f*, pinchazo *m*; infusión *f* de nueva energía; **the company needs a big —** la compañía necesita una reorganización completa.
shakily [ˈʃeikili] *adv* de modo inestable; con poca firmeza; **he said —** dijo en voz trémula; **to walk —** andar con paso vacilante.
shakiness [ˈʃeikinis] *n* inestabilidad *f*, falta *f* de firmeza; temblor *m*; debilidad *f*; *(of knowledge)* deficiencia *f*, mala calidad *f*.
shaking [ˈʃeikiŋ] **1** *adj:* **a — experience** una experiencia desconcertante.
  2 *n:* **to give someone a good —** sacudir violentamente a uno; **he needs a good —** *(fig)* hay que darle un pinchazo.
shako [ˈʃækəu] *n* chacó *m*.
shaky [ˈʃeiki] *adj* *(unstable)* inestable, poco firme, poco sólido; movedizo; *hands etc* tembloroso; *voice* trémula, débil; *writing* poco firme; **his Spanish is rather —** su español es algo defectuoso; **to be — on one's legs** tener las piernas débiles, andar con paso vacilante.
shale [ʃeil] *n* esquisto *m*.
shale oil [ˈʃeilɔil] *n* aceite *m* esquistoso.
shall [ʃæl] *(irr: see also* **should**) *v aux* **(a)** *(used to form future tense)* **I — go** iré; **no I — not, no I shan't** no, yo no; **it — be done** así se hará; **— I hear from you soon?** ¿me escribirás pronto?
  (b) *(emphatic)* **you — pay for this!** ¡me las pagarás!; **they — not pass!** ¡no pasarán!
  (c) *(in commands, of duty etc)* **passengers — not cross the line** se prohíbe a los señores viajeros cruzar la vía; **it — be done this way** ha de hacerse de este modo; **you — do it!** ¡sí lo harás!; **thou shalt not kill** no matarás.
  (d) *(in questions)* **— I go now?** ¿me voy ahora?, ¿quiere Vd que me vaya ahora?; **I'll buy 3, — I?** compro 3, ¿no te parece?; **let's go in, — we?** ¿entramos?; **— we let him?** ¿se lo permitimos?
shallot [ʃəˈlɒt] *n* chalote *m*.
shallow [ˈʃæləu] **1** *adj* **(a)** *water etc* poco profundo, no muy profundo, bajo; *dish etc* llano.
  (b) *person* superficial, frívolo, sin carácter; *knowledge etc* superficial, somero.
  2 —s *npl* bajos *mpl*, bajío *m*.
  3 *vi* hacerse menos profundo.
shallowness [ˈʃæləunis] *n* **(a)** poca profundidad *f*.
  (b) superficialidad *f*, frivolidad *f*, falta *f* de carácter.
shalt [ʃælt] *(arch) see* **shall**; **thou — not kill** no matarás.
sham [ʃæm] **1** *adj* falso, fingido, simulado; **— fight** simulacro *m* de combate; **she's terribly —** es la mar de afectada; **with — politeness** con fingida cortesía.
  2 *n* **(a)** *(imposture)* impostura *f*, fraude *m*, engaño *m*; imitación *f*; **it's all a —** todo es engaño; **the — of these elections** el fraude de estas elecciones; **the declaration was a mere —** la declaración no fue sino una impostura.
  (b) *(person)* impostor *m*; **he's just a big —** es un grandísimo farsante.
  3 *vt* fingir, simular; **to — illness** fingirse enfermo.
  4 *vi* fingir, fingirse; **he's just —ming** lo está fingiendo; **to — dead** fingir estar muerto; **to — ill** fingirse enfermo.
shamble [ˈʃæmbl] *vi* andar arrastrando los pies *(also* **to — along**); **he —d across to the window** fue arrastrando los pies a la ventana.
shambles [ˈʃæmblz] *n sing* *(scene of carnage)* lugar *m* de gran matanza; *(carnage)* matanza *f*, carnicería

f; (*ruined place*) ruina f, escombrera f; (*muddle*) confusión f; **the place was a — el sitio era todo escombros; this room is a —! ¡has visto qué desorden en este cuarto!; the game was a —** el partido fue una catástrofe.

shame [ʃeim] **1** n **(a)** (*feeling, humiliation*) vergüenza f; deshonra f; **the — of that defeat** la vergüenza de esa derrota; **the street is the — of the town** la calle es la vergüenza (*or* el baldón) de la ciudad; **—!, for —!, — on you!, — the — of it!** ¡qué vergüenza!; **to my eternal** (*or* **lasting**) **— I did nothing** me avergüenzo siempre de no haber hecho nada, siempre será para mí motivo de vergüenza el no haber hecho nada; **to be without —, to be lost to all sense of —** no tener vergüenza; **to bring — upon someone** deshonrar a uno; **have you no —?** ¡qué cinismo!; **to put someone to —** avergonzar a uno, (*fig*) superar con mucho a uno, dejar chico a uno.

(b) (*pity*) lástima f; **it's a — that . . .** es una lástima que + subj, es una pena que + subj; **it's a — to have to** + infin es una pena tener que + infin; **what a —!** ¡qué lástima!, ¡qué pena!

2 vt avergonzar; deshonrar; **to — someone into doing something** avergonzar a uno de tal modo que se vea obligado a hacer algo.

shamefaced [ˈʃeimfeist] adj avergonzado; vergonzoso; tímido.

shamefacedly [ˈʃeimfeisidli] adv con vergüenza, avergonzado; tímidamente.

shamefacedness [ˈʃeimfeistnis] n vergüenza f; timidez f.

shameful [ˈʃeimful] adj vergonzoso; **how —!** ¡qué vergüenza!

shamefully [ˈʃeimfəli] adv vergonzosamente; **— ignorant** tan ignorante que da vergüenza; **they are — underpaid** se les paga terriblemente mal.

shamefulness [ˈʃeimfulnis] n vergüenza f; ignominia f.

shameless [ˈʃeimlis] adj desvergonzado, descarado, descocado; impúdico; cínico; **— person** sinvergüenza mf; **are you completely —?** ¡qué cinismo!

shamelessly [ˈʃeimlisli] adv desvergonzadamente, descaradamente; impúdicamente; cínicamente.

shamelessness [ˈʃeimlisnis] n desvergüenza f, descaro m, descoco m; impudor m; cinismo m.

shaming [ˈʃeimiŋ] adj vergonzoso; **this is too —!** ¡qué vergüenza!

shammy [ˈʃæmi] n gamuza f.

shampoo [ʃæmˈpuː] **1** n champú m; **to give oneself a —** lavarse la cabeza.

2 vt person lavar la cabeza a; hair lavar; **to have one's hair —ed and set** hacerse lavar y marcar el pelo.

shamrock [ˈʃæmrok] n trébol m (*emblema nacional irlandés*).

shandy [ˈʃændi] n bebida mezclada de cerveza y limonada (*etc*).

shanghai [ʃæŋˈhai] vt (*Naut sl*): **to — someone** narcotizar (*or* emborrachar) a uno y embarcarle.

Shangri-la [ˈʃæŋriˈlaː] n jauja f, país m maravilloso.

shank [ʃæŋk] n (*part of leg*) caña f; (*bird's leg*) zanca f; (*Bot*) tallo m; (*handle*) mango m; **—s** (*fam*) piernas fpl; **to go on S—s' pony** ir en el coche de San Fernando, ir a golpe de calcetín.

shan't [ʃaːnt] = **shall not**.

shanty[1] [ˈʃænti] n choza f, chabola f.

shanty[2] [ˈʃænti] n (*Mus*) saloma f.

shantytown [ˈʃæntiˌtaun] n barrio m de chabolas, suburbio m.

shape [ʃeip] **1** n forma f; figura f; configuración f; (*of garment*) corte m; (*of person*) talle m, tipo m; (*for jelly etc*) molde m; (*thing dimly seen*) bulto m, forma f; **the — of things to come** la configuración del futuro; **not in any — or form** de ningún modo, en absoluto; **stamps of all —s** sellos mpl de todas las formas; **it is rectangular in —** es de forma rectangular, tiene forma rectangular; **what — is it?** ¿de qué forma es?; **to be in good —** estar en buenas condiciones, (*person*) estar bien de salud, estar en forma; **to be in bad —** estar en mal estado, (*person*) estar enfermo, estar en malas condiciones físicas; **to beat something into —** dar forma a algo a martillazos; **to knock** (*or* **lick**) **someone into —** desbastar a uno; disciplinar a uno; adiestrar a uno; **to lick a team into —** ir entrenando un equipo; **to put an essay into —** corregir un ensayo, preparar un ensayo para publicarlo (*etc*); **to get out of —,** **to lose —** perder la forma; **to take —** tomar forma, irse formando, (*fig*) irse perfilando.

2 vt formar, dar forma a; stone labrar; wood tallar; jug etc modelar, hacer; course etc determinar;

plasmar, amoldar; **Plato helped to — his ideas** Platón ayudó a formar sus ideas; **the factors which — one's life** los factores que determinan el desarrollo de la vida de uno; **he did not — the course of events** él no influyó en la marcha de los acontecimientos; **there is a destiny which —s our ends** hay un destino que gobierna nuestra vida.

3 vi formarse, tomar forma; **to — well** desarrollarse de modo esperanzador, prometer; **he is shaping nicely as a goalkeeper** como guardameta promete, es un guardameta que promete; **how are things shaping?** ¿cómo van las cosas?; **to — up to someone** adoptar una postura para defenderse contra uno.

-shaped [ˈʃeipt] adj en forma de, eg **heart-shaped** en forma de corazón; **U-shaped** en forma de U.

shapeless [ˈʃeiplis] adj informe, sin forma definida.

shapeliness [ˈʃeiplinis] n proporción f; elegancia f.

shapely [ˈʃeipli] adj bien formado, bien proporcionado; person de buen talle; **— columns** columnas fpl elegantes; **the — Miss Galicia** la atractiva Miss Galicia.

shard [ʃaːd] n tiesto m, casco m, fragmento m (de loza etc).

share[1] [ʃeə*] **1** n **(a)** (*thing received*) parte f, porción f; **— in the profits** participación f en los beneficios; **the lion's —** la parte del león; **fair —s for all** la equidad para todos, un trato equitativo para todos; **in equal —s** por partes iguales; **your — is £5** le tocan a Vd 5 libras; **how much will my — be?** ¿cuánto me corresponderá a mí?; **to come in for one's full — of work** tener que trabajar tanto como los otros o más; **the minister came in for a full — of criticism** se le criticó al ministro tanto como a cualquiera; **it fell to my —** me tocó a mí, me correspondió a mí; **to go —s** dividir lo recibido; **to go half —s with someone** dividir lo recibido con otro por partes iguales.

(b) (*contribution*) contribución f; cuota f; parte f; **to bear one's — of the cost** pagar la parte del coste que le corresponde a uno; **to do one's —** cumplir con su obligación; **he doesn't do his —** no hace todo lo que debiera, no hace todo lo que le cumple; **to have a — in something** participar en algo; **I had no — in that** yo no tuve nada que ver con eso; **to go —s** ir a escote, escotar cada uno lo suyo; **to pay one's —** pagar su cuota.

(c) (*Fin*) acción f; **ordinary —** acción f ordinaria; **paid-up —** acción f liberada; **preference —** acción f preferente; **to hold 1000 —s in a company** tener 1000 acciones en una compañía, poseer 1000 acciones de una compañía.

2 vt (*divide*) partir, dividir; (*have in common*) compartir, poseer en común; usar juntos de; **to — something with someone** partir algo con uno; **they — a room** comparten un cuarto; **to — certain characteristics** poseer en común ciertas características; **I do not — that view** no comparto ese criterio; **to — out** repartir, distribuir.

3 vi: **to — and — alike** participar por partes iguales; **children have to learn to —** los niños tienen que aprender a hacerse concesiones mutuas (*or* a ser tolerantes); **there were no rooms free so I had to —** no había habitación libre y por tanto tuve que compartir una con otra persona; **to — in** tener parte en, participar en, (*fig*) participar de; **to — in someone's success** contribuir al éxito de uno.

share[2] [ʃeə*] n (*Agr*) reja f.

share certificate [ˈʃeəˌtifikit] n acción f.

sharecropper [ˈʃeəˌkrɔpə*] n aparcero m.

sharecropping [ˈʃeəˌkrɔpiŋ] n aparcería f.

shareholder [ˈʃeəˌhəuldə*] n accionista mf.

share-out [ˈʃeəraut] n reparto m.

shark [ʃaːk] n (*Fish*) tiburón m; (*fam: swindler*) estafador m, (*expert*) perito m, as m (*fam*).

sharkskin [ˈʃaːkskin] n zapa f.

sharp [ʃaːp] **1** adj **(a)** (*cutting*) afilado, cortante; point puntiagudo; angle agudo; curve, bend cerrado, fuerte; turn by car repentino, brusco; feature bien marcado, anguloso; outline definido; photo nítido; contrast neto, marcado.

(b) (*of person*) mind listo, vivo, inteligente; hearing fino; sight agudo, penetrante; glance penetrante; **the child is quite —** el niño es bastante listo; **he's as — as they come** es de lo más avispado; **that was pretty — of you** en eso has estado muy perspicaz.

(c) (*of person: pej*) astuto, mañoso; poco escrupuloso; practice, trick poco honrado; **he's too — for me** es demasiado astuto para mi gusto, yo no aguanto sus malas mañas.

(d) (*fig*) shower, storm fuerte, repentino; frost

fuerte; *wind* penetrante; *pain* agudo, intenso; *fight* encarnizado; *pace* rápido, vivo; *walk* rápido; *fall in price etc* brusco; *temper* áspero, vivo; *retort* áspero; *tongue* mordaz; *rebuke* severo; *tone* acerbo, áspero, severo.

(e) *taste* acerbo, acre; *wine* ácido.

(f) *sound* agudo, penetrante; (*Mus*) sostenido.
2 *adv* (a) (*Mus*) desafinadamente.

(b) at 5 o'clock — a las 5 en punto; **and be** — about it y date prisa; **look** — ! ¡pronto!; **look** — about it! ¡menearse!; if you don't look — si no te meneas; **to pull up** — frenar en seco; **to turn** — left torcer repentinamente a la izquierda.

3 *n* (*Mus*) sostenido *m*; (*person*) estafador *m*, (*card*—) fullero *m*.
sharp-edged ['ʃɑːp'edʒd] *adj* afilado, de filo cortante.
sharpen ['ʃɑːpən] 1 *vt tool* afilar, aguzar; amolar; *pencil* sacar punta a; *appetite* abrir; *wits* despabilar; *conflict, emotion, sensation* agudizar.

2 *vi* (*fig*) agudizarse.
sharpener ['ʃɑːpnə*] *n* afilador *m*, máquina *f* de afilar.
sharpening ['ʃɑːpnɪŋ] *n* (*fig*) agudización *f*.
sharper ['ʃɑːpə*] *n* estafador *m*, (*card*—) fullero *m*.
sharp-eyed ['ʃɑːp'aid] *adj* de vista aguda, de ojos de lince.
sharp-faced ['ʃɑːp'feist] *adj* de facciones angulosas.
sharpness ['ʃɑːpnis] *n* (a) lo afilado, lo cortante; lo puntiagudo; lo cerrado; lo repentino, brusquedad *f*; definición *f*; nitidez *f*; lo marcado.

(b) viveza *f*, inteligencia *f*; finura *f*; agudeza *f*.

(c) fuerza *f*; lo fuerte, lo repentino; agudeza *f*, intensidad *f*; brusquedad *f*, aspereza *f*; mordacidad *f*; severidad *f*; **there was a note of** — **in his voice** se notaba cierta aspereza en su tono; **there is a** — **in the air** empieza a notarse el frío.
sharpshooter ['ʃɑːp,ʃuːtə*] *n* tirador *m* apostado.
sharp-sighted ['ʃɑːp'saitid] *adj* de vista aguda, de ojos de lince.
sharp-tongued ['ʃɑːp'tʌŋd] *adj* de lengua mordaz.
sharp-witted ['ʃɑːp'witid] *adj* listo, perspicaz.
shatter ['ʃætə*] 1 *vt* romper, hacer añicos, hacer pedazos; *health* quebrantar; *nerves* destrozar; *hopes etc* destruir, acabar con; **to** — **something against a wall** estrellar algo contra una pared; **I was** —**ed to hear it** al saberlo quedé estupefacto; **this will** — **you** tengo que decirte algo pasmoso; **she was** —**ed by his death** su muerte la anonadó.

2 *vi* romperse, hacerse añicos; hacerse pedazos; estrellarse (*against* contra); **the windscreen** —**ed** el parabrisas estalló en pedazos.
shattered ['ʃætəd] *adj street etc* destrozado.
shattering ['ʃætərɪŋ] *adj attack* demoledor; *news etc* pasmoso, fulgurante; *defeat* contundente; *experience* profundamente conmovedor.
shatterproof ['ʃætəpruːf] *adj* inastillable.
shave [ʃeiv] 1 *n* (a) afeitado *m*, rasurado *m*; **to have a** — afeitarse.

(b) (*fig*) **to have a close** (*or* **narrow**) — escaparse por un pelo; **that was a close** — eso fue cosa de milagro.

2 (*irr: pret* **shaved**, *ptp* **shaved** *or* **shaven**) *vt face* afeitar, rasurar; *wood* acepillar; (*skim*) casi tocar, pasar rozando; **to** — **one's legs** afeitarse las piernas, depilarse las piernas; **to** — **off one's beard** afeitarse la barba, quitar la barba.

3 *vi* (*person*) afeitarse, rasurarse; **that razor** —**s well** esa navaja afeita bien.
shaven ['ʃeivn] 1 *ptp of* **shave**. 2 *adj head etc* rapado.
shaver ['ʃeivə*] *n* (a) **electric** — máquina *f* de afeitar eléctrica, afeitadora *f* eléctrica. (b) **young** — (*fam*) muchacho *m*, rapaz *m*.
Shavian ['ʃeiviən] *adj* shaviano.
shaving ['ʃeiviŋ] 1 *n* (a) afeitado *m*, el afeitarse, rasurado *m*; — **is a nuisance** es una pesadez tener que afeitarse.

(b) —**s** virutas *pl*, acepilladuras *fpl*; **wood** —**s** virutas *fpl* de madera.

2 *attr* de afeitar.
shaving brush ['ʃeiviŋbrʌʃ] *n* brocha *f* (de afeitar).
shaving cream ['ʃeiviŋkriːm] *n* crema *f* de afeitar.
shaving lotion ['ʃeiviŋ,ləuʃən] *n* loción *f* para el afeitado.
shaving soap ['ʃeiviŋsəup] *n* jabón *m* de afeitar.
shaving stick ['ʃeiviŋstik] *n* barra *f* de jabón de afeitar.
shawl [ʃɔːl] *n* chal *m*.
she [ʃiː] 1 *pron* ella; — **who** la que, quien.

2 *n* hembra *f*.

3 *attr* hembra, *eg* **the she-hedgehog** el erizo hembra, la hembra del erizo; **she-bear** osa *f*; **she-cat** gata *f*.

sheaf [ʃiːf] *n*, *pl* **sheaves** [ʃiːvz] (*Agr*) gavilla *f*; (*of arrows etc*) haz *m*; (*of papers*) fajo *m*, lío *m*.
shear [ʃiə*] (*irr: pret* **sheared**, *ptp* **shorn**) 1 *vt sheep* esquilar, trasquilar; *cloth* tundir; **to** — **off** cortar, quitar cortando; **the machine** —**ed off two fingers** la máquina cercenó dos dedos; **the ship had its bows shorn off in the collision** en la colisión el buque quedó con la proa destrozada.

2 *vi*: **to** — **through** cortar, hender.
shearer ['ʃiərə*] *n* esquilador *m*.
shearing ['ʃiəriŋ] *n* esquileo *m*; —**s** lana *f* esquilada.
shearing machine ['ʃiəriŋmə,ʃiːn] *n* esquiladora *f*.
shears ['ʃiəz] *npl* tijeras *fpl* grandes; (*Hort*) tijeras *fpl* de jardín; (*for metals*) cizalla *f*.
shearwater ['ʃiəwɔːtə*] *n* pardela *f*.
sheath [ʃiːθ] *n* vaina *f*; funda *f*, cubierta *f*; (*Bot etc*) vaina *f*.
sheathe [ʃiːð] *vt sword* envainar; enfundar; **to** — **something in metal** revestir algo de metal, poner cubierta metálica a algo.
sheathing ['ʃiːðiŋ] *n* revestimiento *m*, cubierta *f*.
sheath knife ['ʃiːθnaif] *n*, *pl* — **knives** [naivz] cuchillo *m* de monte.
sheaves [ʃiːvz] *pl of* **sheaf**.
Sheba ['ʃiːbə] *n* Sabá; **Queen of** — reina *f* de Sabá.
shebang [ʃə'bæŋ] *n* (*sl*): **the whole** — todo ello, todo el negocio.
shebeen [ʃi'biːn] *n* (*Ir, Scot*) taberna *f* ilícita.
shed[1] [ʃed] (*irr: pret and ptp* **shed**) *vt clothes, leaves etc* despojarse de; *skin* mudar; *unwanted thing* deshacerse de; desprenderse de, quitarse; *tears* verter; *blood* verter, derramar; *light* dar, (*fig*) echar, arrojar; **the party tried to** — **its leader** el partido intentó deshacerse de su jefe; **I'm trying to** — **5 kilos** me esfuerzo por perder 5 kilos; **much blood has been** — se ha vertido mucha sangre; **that lamp doesn't** — **much light** esa lámpara no da mucha luz; **she** —**s happiness all around** ella irradia su felicidad por todas partes.
shed[2] [ʃed] *n* (*garden* — *etc*) cobertizo *m*, alpende *m*; (*workmen's*) barraca *f*; (*industrial*) nave *f*.
she'd [ʃiːd] = **she would**; **she had**.
sheen [ʃiːn] *n* lustre *m*; brillo *m*; **to take the** — **off something** deslustrar algo.
sheeny ['ʃiːni] *adj* lustroso, brillante.
sheep [ʃiːp] *n*, *pl* **sheep** (*plural*) oveja *f*; (*ram*) carnero *m*; (*pl, collectively*) ganado *m* lanar; **to be the black** — (**of the family**) ser la oveja negra, ser el garbanzo negro; **to count** — fingir contar ovejas (para dormirse); **to separate the** — **from the goats** (*fig*) apartar las ovejas de los cabritos.
sheep-dip ['ʃiːpdip] *n* desinfectante *m* para ovejas.
sheepdog ['ʃiːpdɔg] *n* perro *m* pastor; — **trials** concurso *m* de pastoreo.
sheep farmer ['ʃiːp,fɑːmə*] *n* dueño *m* de ganado lanar.
sheep farming ['ʃiːp,fɑːmiŋ] *n* pastoreo *m*, industria *f* del ganado lanar.
sheepfold ['ʃiːpfəuld] *n* redil *m*, aprisco *m*.
sheepish ['ʃiːpiʃ] *adj* tímido, vergonzoso.
sheepishly ['ʃiːpiʃli] *adv* tímidamente.
sheepishness ['ʃiːpiʃnis] *n* timidez *f*, vergüenza *f*.
sheep-run ['ʃiːprʌn] *n* pasto *m* de ovejas, dehesa *f* de ovejas.
sheepshearing ['ʃiːp,ʃiəriŋ] *n* esquileo *m*.
sheepskin ['ʃiːpskin] *n* piel *f* de carnero; zamarra *f*, badana *f*; — **jacket** zamarra *f*.
sheepwalk ['ʃiːpwɔːk] *n see* **sheep-run**.
sheer[1] [ʃiə*] 1 *adj* (a) (*absolute*) puro, completo, absoluto; **the** — **impossibility of . . .** la total imposibilidad de . . .; — **nonsense!** ¡puro disparate!; **this is** — **robbery** esto no puede llamarse sino robo.

(b) (*steep*) escarpado, cortado a pico; **perpendicular**; **there is a** — **fall of 200 metres** hay un descenso de 200 metros sin obstáculo alguno.

(c) (*of cloth etc*) diáfano.

2 *adv*: **it falls** — **to the sea** baja sin obstáculo alguno hacia el mar; **it rises** — **above the town** está cortado a pico por encima de la ciudad; **it rises** — **for 100 metres** se levanta verticalmente unos 100 metros.
sheer[2] [ʃiə*] *vi*: **to** — **off** (*Naut*) desviarse; (*fig*) largarse; **to** — **away from a topic** desviarse de un tema, evitar hablar de un tema.
sheet [ʃiːt] 1 *n* (*bed*—) sábana *f*; (*shroud*) mortaja *f*; (*of paper*) hoja *f*; (*newspaper*) periódico *m*, hoja *f*; (*of tin*) hoja *f*, (*of other metal*) chapa *f*, lámina *f*; (*of glass*) lámina *f*; (*of water etc*) extensión *f*; (*Naut*) escota *f*; (*cover*) cubierta *f*, (*tarpaulin*) alquitranado *m*.

2 *attr*: — **glass** vidrio *m* plano; — **steel** chapa

de acero; láminas *fpl* de acero, acero m en láminas.
3 *vt*: **to — something in, to — something over** cubrir algo con un alquitranado.
sheet anchor ['ʃi:t‚æŋkə*] n ancla *f* de la esperanza.
sheeting ['ʃi:tiŋ] n (*cloth*) lencería *f* para sábanas; (*metal*) placas *fpl* de metal, laminado m, cobertura *f* metálica.
sheet lightning ['ʃi:t'laitniŋ] n relámpago m difuso.
sheik(h) [ʃeik] n jeque m.
shekel ['ʃekl] n siclo m; **—s** (*fam*) pasta *f* (*sl*), parné m (*sl*).
shelf [ʃelf] n, *pl* **shelves** [ʃelvz] estante m, anaquel m; (*Naut*) banco m de arena, bajo m; (*on rock face*) repisa *f*; **continental —** (*Geog*) plataforma *f* submarina superior, schelf m; **shelves** (*collectively*) estantería *f*; **to be on the —** (*girl*) quedarse para vestir santos.
she'll [ʃi:l] = **she will, she shall.**
shell [ʃel] **1** n (**a**) (*Zool: of egg*) cáscara *f*, cascarón m; (*of nut*) cáscara *f*; (*of mollusc*) concha *f*; (*of tortoise, turtle*) caparazón m; (*of insect, lobster etc*) caparazón m, carapacho m; (*of pea*) vaina *f*; **to come out of one's —** salir del carapacho; **to retire into one's —** meterse en su carapacho.
(**b**) (*Tech: framework*) armazón *f*, esqueleto m; (*of house, after bombardment etc*) casco m; (*Naut*) casco m; (*outer covering*) cubierta *f*, exterior m.
(**c**) (*boat*) bote m de construcción lisa.
(**d**) (*Mil*) proyectil m, obús m, granada *f*; **dud —** obús m que no estalla; **live —** obús m con carga explosiva.
2 *vt* (**a**) *peas* desenvainar; *eggs, nuts* descascarar, quitar la cáscara a.
(**b**) **to — out** *money* (*sl*) desembolsar, pagar (de mala gana).
(**c**) (*Mil*) bombardear.
3 *vi* (*sl*) **to — out** desembolsar dinero (*for something para pagar algo*).
shellac [ʃə'læk] n laca *f*, goma *f* laca.
shelled [ʃeld] *adj*: **— nuts** nueces *fpl* sin cáscara.
shellfire ['ʃelfaiə*] n cañoneo m, fuego m de artillería, bombardeo m; **to be under —** sufrir un bombardeo; **the — lasted all night** el cañoneo duró toda la noche.
shellfish ['ʃelfiʃ] n (*Zool*) crustáceo m; (*as food*) mariscos *mpl*.
shell-hole ['ʃelhəul] n hoyo m que forma un obús al explotar.
shelling ['ʃeliŋ] n bombardeo m.
shellproof ['ʃelpru:f] *adj* a prueba de granadas.
shell shock ['ʃelʃɔk] n neurosis *f* de guerra.
shell-shocked ['ʃelʃɔkt] *adj* que padece neurosis de guerra.
shelter ['ʃeltə*] **1** n abrigo m, asilo m, refugio m; (*air-raid — etc*) refugio m; (*bus —*) refugio m (de espera); (*mountain —*) albergue m; (*fig*) protección *f*, resguardo m; **under —** al abrigo, **under the — of the mountain** al abrigo de la montaña; **to seek —** buscar dónde cobijarse; **to seek — for the night** buscar dónde pasar la noche; **to take —** ponerse al abrigo (*from de*), cobijarse (*from de*).
2 *vt* abrigar (*from de*); (*aid*) amparar, proteger (*from de*); (*hide*) esconder, ocultar; **to — a criminal** proteger a un criminal.
3 *vi* abrigarse, ponerse al abrigo, cobijarse (*from de*); refugiarse; **to — from the rain** ponerse al abrigo de la lluvia.
sheltered ['ʃeltəd] *adj* *place* abrigado; *industry* protegido contra la competencia extranjera; **she has led a very — life** se ha criado bajo las faldas de mamá, se ha criado en la inocencia; **a spot — from the wind** un sitio al abrigo del viento.
shelve[1] [ʃelv] *vt* (*fig*) dar carpetazo a, arrinconar, aplazar indefinidamente.
shelve[2] [ʃelv] *vi* formar declive, estar en declive; **the beach —s rapidly** el fondo está en fuerte declive; **it —s down to the sea** baja hacia el mar.
shelves [ʃelvz] *pl of* **shelf.**
shelving ['ʃelviŋ] n estantería *f*.
shemozzle [ʃə'mɔzl] n (*sl*) lío m; bronca *f*, follón m (*fam*).
shenanigans [ʃə'næniɡənz] *npl* (*sl*) embustes *mpl*.
shepherd ['ʃepəd] **1** n pastor m; **the Good S—** el Buen Pastor.
2 *vt* guiar, conducir; **to — children across a road** conducir niños a través de una calle.
shepherd boy ['ʃepədbɔi] n zagal m.
shepherdess ['ʃepədis] n pastora *f*, zagala *f*.
sherbet ['ʃə:bət] n sorbete m.
sherd [ʃɑ:d] *see* **shard.**

sheriff ['ʃerif] n sheriff m (*oficial de justicia inglés, escocés, o norteamericano*).
sherry ['ʃeri] n jerez m.
she's [ʃi:z] = **she is; she has.**
Shetland Islands ['ʃetlənd‚ailəndz] *pl*, **Shetlands** ['ʃetləndz] *pl* Islas *fpl* de Zetlandia.
shew [ʃəu] *vti* (*arch*) *see* **show.**
shewn [ʃəun] *ptp* (*arch*) *of* **show.**
shibboleth ['ʃibəleθ] n (*Bible*) lema m, santo m y seña; (*fig*) dogma m hoy desacreditado, doctrina *f* que ha quedado anticuada.
shield [ʃi:ld] **1** n escudo m (*also Her*); (*round*) rodela *f*; (*Tech*) blindaje m, capa *f* protectora; (*fig*) escudo m, defensa *f*.
2 *vt* proteger, resguardar, amparar; *criminal* proteger; (*Tech*) blindar, revestir de una capa protectora; **to — one's eyes from the sun** proteger los ojos contra el sol.
shieling ['ʃi:liŋ] n (*Scot*) (*pasture*) pasto m, prado m; (*hut*) choza *f*, cabaña *f*; albergue m; (*sheepfold*) aprisco m.
shift [ʃift] **1** n (**a**) (*change*) cambio m (*in, of* de); cambio m de sitio, traslado m, movimiento m; **— of wind** cambio m (de dirección) del viento; **consonant —** cambio m consonántico; **there has been a — in policy** ha habido un cambio de política; **one notes a — of emphasis** se nota un cambio de énfasis; **the — from north to south is increasing** el movimiento de norte a sur se acelera; **to make a —** cambiar de sitio, (*of person*) irse, largarse; **it's time we made a —** ya es hora de marcharnos.
(**b**) (*at work*) turno m; (*of workers*) tanda *f*; **an 8-hour —** un turno de 8 horas; **three-shift system** sistema m de tres turnos; **to work in —s** trabajar por turnos.
(**c**) (*expedient*) recurso m, expediente m; (*pej*) maña *f*, astucia *f*; **to make —** with ayudarse con, contentarse con; **to make — without** pasarse sin; **to make — to +** *infin* arreglárselas para + *infin*, ingeniarse por + *infin*.
(**d**) (*arch*) camisa *f* (de mujer).
2 *vt* cambiar; (*move*) cambiar de sitio, trasladar a otro sitio, mover; (*budge*) mover; (*get rid of*) quitarse de encima, librarse de; **to — scenery** cambiar el decorado; **— it over to the wall** póngalo contra la pared; **we could not — him from his opinion** no logramos hacerle cambiar de opinión; **I can't — this cold** no me quito este catarro; **they —ed him to Valencia** le trasladaron a Valencia; **we shall have to — 20 tons** hará falta mover 20 toneladas; **to — the blame on to someone else** echar la culpa a otro.
3 *vi* (**a**) (*move*) moverse; cambiar; cambiar de sitio; (*person*) cambiar de puesto, trasladarse a otro sitio, (*move house*) mudar; (*of ballast, cargo*) correrse; (*of wind*) cambiar; **to — about, to — around** cambiar (mucho) de sitio, (*in job*) cambiar de empleo; **the government has not —ed from its earlier position** el gobierno no ha modificado en lo más mínimo su actitud anterior; **to — into second gear** cambiar a segunda velocidad; **the scene —s to Burgos** la escena cambia a Burgos; **he —ed to Lima** se trasladó a Lima.
(**b**) (*fam: car etc*) ir a gran velocidad, correr; (*person*) darse prisa, menearse; **—!** ¡menearse!
(**c**) **to — for oneself** valerse por sí mismo, ayudarse a sí mismo.
shiftily ['ʃiftili] *adv* astutamente; furtivamente; **to behave —** comportarse de modo sospechoso.
shiftiness ['ʃiftinis] n lo tramposo, lo taimado, astucia *f*; lo sospechoso; lo furtivo.
shifting ['ʃiftiŋ] *adj* *sand etc* movedizo.
shift key ['ʃiftki:] n tecla *f* de mayúsculas.
shiftless ['ʃiftlis] *adj* (*lazy*) vago, holgazán; (*useless*) inútil; (*untrustworthy*) informal.
shiftlessness ['ʃiftlisnis] n holgazanería *f*; inutilidad *f*; informalidad *f*.
shift work ['ʃiftwə:k] n trabajo m por turno.
shifty ['ʃifti] *adj* tramposo, taimado, astuto; *conduct* sospechoso; *glance etc* furtivo.
shifty-eyed ['ʃifti'aid] *adj* de mirada furtiva.
shillelagh [ʃə'leilə] n (*Ir*) cachiporra *f*.
shilling ['ʃiliŋ] n chelín m; **6 —s in the pound** 6 chelines por libra; **to cut someone off with a —** desheredar a uno.
shilly-shally ['ʃili‚ʃæli] *vi* vacilar, no resolverse, no saber qué hacer; **you've shilly-shallied long enough** has estado bastante tiempo ya sin resolverte.
shimmer ['ʃimə*] **1** n reflejo m trémulo, resplandor m trémulo. **2** *vi* rielar, relucir.
shimmering ['ʃiməriŋ] *adj*, **shimmery** ['ʃiməri] *adj* reluciente; *light* trémulo.

shimmy ['ʃimi] n (fam) camisa f (de mujer).
shin [ʃin] 1 n espinilla f; (of meat) jarrete m, corvejón m. 2 vi: to — up trepar; to — up a tree trepar a un árbol.
shinbone ['ʃinbəun] n espinilla f.
shindig ['ʃindig] n (sl) fiesta f, juerga f.
shindy ['ʃindi] n (noise) ruido m grande, conmoción f; (dispute) lío m, bronca f; to kick up a — meter ruido; armar un lío.
shine [ʃain] 1 n (a) (brilliance) brillo m, lustre m; to give one's shoes a — sacar brillo a los zapatos, limpiar los zapatos; to take the — off something deslustrar algo, hacer que algo pierda su lustre; to take the — off something hacer que algo pierda su interés, hacer que algo resulte soso; to take a — to tomar simpatía por.
  (b) (Meteorol) buen tiempo m, tiempo m de sol; we'll go rain or — iremos no importa el tiempo que haga.
  2 (irr: pret and ptp shone) vt (a) shoes sacar brillo a, limpiar; silver etc pulir.
  (b) to — a light on something proyectar una luz sobre algo; — the torch this way dirige la linterna hacia este lado.
  3 vi (a) brillar; relucir, resplandecer; a lamp was shining brillaba una lámpara; the sun is shining hay sol; the metal shone in the sun el metal relucía al sol; her face shone with happiness su cara irradiaba felicidad; a certain quiet confidence —s through trasciende cierta serenidad.
  (b) (fig) brillar, lucirse, distinguirse; he doesn't exactly — at his work no brilla en sus estudios que digamos; he shone as a footballer se distinguió como futbolista.
shiner ['ʃainə*] n (person) limpiabotas m; (sl: eye) ojo m; (hum) ojo m morado; (Fin) moneda antigua (inglesa) de una libra.
shingle[1] ['ʃingl] 1 n (Archit) ripia f; (hair style) corte m a lo garçon. 2 vt hair cortar a lo garçon.
shingle[2] ['ʃingl] n (pebbles) guijos mpl, guijarral m; (beach) playa f guijarrosa.
shingles ['ʃinglz] npl (Med) herpes mpl or fpl.
shingly ['ʃingli] adj guijarroso.
shining ['ʃainin] adj brillante, lustroso; face etc radiante; example notable.
shin pad ['ʃinpæd] n, (US) — guard [gɑːd] n espinillera f.
Shintoism ['ʃintəuizəm] n sintoísmo m.
shinty ['ʃinti] n (Scot) especie de hockey sobre hierba.
shiny ['ʃaini] adj brillante, lustroso.
ship [ʃip] 1 n (a) buque m, barco m, navío m; capital — acorazado m; the good — Venus el buque Venus, el Venus; Her (or His) Majesty's S— (abbr HMS) buque m de guerra inglés; to serve on HMS Warspite servir en el Warspite; merchant — mercante m; the — of the desert el camello; — of the line buque m de línea; on board — a bordo; to abandon — abandonar el barco; to clear a — for action alistar un buque para el combate; when my — comes home cuando me haga rico, cuando la suerte me favorezca; to jump — desertar del buque; to take — for embarcarse para.
  (b) —'s boat lancha f, bote m salvavidas; —'s company tripulación f; —'s doctor médico m de a bordo; —'s papers documentación f del buque.
  2 vt (a) (put on board) goods embarcar; mast izar; oars desarmar; to — a sea embarcar agua.
  (b) (transport) transportar (por vía marítima), enviar, expedir; a new engine had to be —ped out to them hubo que enviarles un nuevo motor.
  3 vi embarcarse (on en).
shipboard ['ʃipbɔːd] n: on — a bordo.
shipbreaker ['ʃip,breikə*] n desguazador m.
shipbuilder ['ʃip,bildə*] n constructor m de buques, arquitecto m naval.
shipbuilding ['ʃip,bildin] n construcción f de buques, construcción f naval.
ship canal ['ʃipkə,næl] n canal m de navegación.
ship chandler ['ʃip,tʃɑːndlə*] n abastecedor m de buques.
shipload ['ʃipləud] n cargamento m (entero) de un buque; (loosely) envío m, cantidad f enviada; (fam) montón m; we have jam by the — tenemos mermelada a montones; the tourists are arriving by the — los turistas vienen en masa.
shipmate ['ʃipmeit] n camarada m de a bordo.
shipment ['ʃipmənt] n (act) embarque m; transporte m; (quantity) envío m, remesa f.
shipowner ['ʃip,əunə*] n naviero m.
shipper ['ʃipə*] n exportador m; (sender) remitente m.
shipping ['ʃipin] 1 n (act) embarque m; transporte

m (por vía marítima); (ships) buques mpl, barcos mpl; (ships of a country) flota f, marina f; dangerous to — peligroso para la navegación; — losses in 1942 cantidad f (or tonelaje m) de buques perdidos en 1942; the canal is closed to British — el canal está cerrado para la marina británica.
  2 attr agent marítimo; company naviero; office de compañía de navegación; — intelligence noticias fpl navieras.
shipshape ['ʃipʃeip] adv, adj en buen orden, en regla; to get everything — ponerlo todo en orden.
shipwreck ['ʃiprek] 1 n naufragio m (also fig). 2 vt: to be —ed naufragar.
shipwrecked ['ʃiprekt] adj: — person náufrago m, a f.
shipwright ['ʃiprait] n (worker) carpintero m de navío; (owner) naviero m.
shipyard ['ʃipjɑːd] n astillero m, varadero m.
shire ['ʃaiə*] n condado m; the S—s los condados centrales de Inglaterra.
-shire [ʃiə*] n in compounds: condado m.
shirk [ʃəːk] 1 vt eludir, esquivar; obligation faltar a; work no hacer, rehuir; difficulty, issue escamotear; to — doing something esquivar el deber de hacer algo.
  2 vi faltar al deber; escamotear; (not work) gandulear; you're —ing! ¡eres un gandul!
shirker ['ʃəːkə*] n gandul m.
shirr [ʃəː*] vt (Sew) fruncir.
shirt [ʃəːt] n camisa f; boiled — camisa f de pechera dura; soft — camisa f sin almidonar; to keep one's — on (fam) quedarse sereno; to put one's — on a horse apostar todo lo que tiene uno a un caballo.
shirt collar ['ʃəːt,kɔlə*] n cuello m de camisa.
shirt front ['ʃəːtfrʌnt] n pechera f.
shirtless ['ʃəːtlis] adj sin camisa, descamisado.
shirt sleeves ['ʃəːtsliːvz] npl: to be in — estar en mangas de camisa.
shirttail ['ʃəːtteil] n faldón m (de camisa).
shirtwaist ['ʃəːtweist] n (US) blusa f.
shirty ['ʃəːti] adj (sl): he was pretty — about it la cosa no le gustó en absoluto, la cosa no le cayó en gracia; to get — ponerse negro (fam).
shiver[1] ['ʃivə*] 1 n a — temblor m, estremecimiento m; (with cold) tiritón m; (of horror etc) escalofrío m; to give a — estremecerse; it sent —s down my back me dio escalofríos.
  (b) the —s (fig) dentera f, grima f; it gives me the —s (of fear) me da miedo, (of taste etc) me da dentera.
  2 vi temblar, estremecerse; vibrar; (with fear) temblar, dar diente con diente; (with cold) tiritar.
shiver[2] ['ʃivə*] 1 vt (break) romper, hacer añicos. 2 vi romperse, hacerse añicos.
shivery ['ʃivəri] adj estremecido; (sensitive to cold) friolento; to feel — tener frío, tener escalofríos.
shoal[1] [ʃəul] 1 n (sandbank etc) banco m de arena, bajío m, bajo m. 2 vi disminuir en profundidad, hacerse menos profundo.
shoal[2] [ʃəul] n (of fish) banco m, cardumen m; (of people etc) multitud f; muchedumbre f; to come in —s venir en tropel; we have —s of applications tenemos montones de solicitudes.
shock[1] [ʃɔk] 1 n (a) (Elec) descarga f (eléctrica); (collision) choque m, colisión f; (jolt) sacudida f; (of earthquake) seísmo m, temblor m de tierra; she got a — from the refrigerator la nevera le dio una descarga; the — of the explosion was felt 5 miles away se apreció el choque de la explosión a una distancia de 5 millas; the house collapsed at the first — al primer seísmo se hundió la casa.
  (b) (emotional) conmoción f (desagradable); (start) sobresalto m, susto m; our feeling is one of — lo que sentimos es un enorme disgusto; the — was too much for him la conmoción que le produjo la noticia le anonadó; the — killed him el disgusto le mató; it comes as a — to hear that . . . nos asombramos al saber que . . .; to give someone a — sobresaltar a uno; asombrar a uno; it gave me a nasty — me produjo una conmoción desagradable; the news gave me quite a — la noticia me afectó muchísimo, la noticia me disgustó bastante; what a — you gave me! ¡qué susto me diste!
  (c) (Med) shock m, postración f nerviosa; to be suffering from — padecer una postración nerviosa.
  2 adj, attr: — tactics táctica f de ataque repentino; — treatment (Med) tratamiento m de choque eléctrico; — troops tropas fpl de asalto; — worker trabajador m que se distingue superando la norma de producción.
  3 vt (startle) sobresaltar, dar un susto a; (affect

emotionally) dar un disgusto a, producir una conmoción desagradable a; (_make indignant_) indignar; (_because of impropriety_) escandalizar; ofender; **she is easily** —ed se ofende por cualquier cosa, se escandaliza por poca cosa; **I was** —ed **to hear the news** la noticia me dio un enorme disgusto, la noticia me asombró; **now don't be** —ed **at what I'm going to say** no se escandalice de lo que le voy a decir; **you can't** — **me** yo no me asombro de nada; **to** — **someone into doing something** dar una sacudida a uno para animarle a hacer algo; **to** — **someone out of his complacency** hacer que uno se dé cuenta de la necesidad de hacer algo, destruir el optimismo de uno.

shock² [ʃɔk] (_Agr_) **1** n tresnal m, garbera f. **2** vt poner en tresnales.

shock³ [ʃɔk] n: — **of hair** greña f; melena f.

shock absorber [ˈʃɔkəbˌzɔːbə*] n amortiguador m, parachoques m.

shocker [ˈʃɔkə*] n (a) (_Lit_) novelucha f. (b) **it's a** — es horrible; es de lo más vil; **he's a** — es un sinvergüenza, es un canalla; **you** —! (_hum_) ¡canalla!

shockheaded [ˈʃɔkˈhedid] adj greñudo; melenudo.

shocking [ˈʃɔkiŋ] **1** adj (_appalling_) espantoso, horrible; (_morally improper_) escandaloso, vergonzoso, ofensivo; **how** —! ¡qué horror!; **isn't it** —? ¿es espantoso, eh?; **it was a** — **sight** fue un espectáculo horrible; **she has a** — **taste** tiene un pésimo gusto; **the book is not all that** — el libro es menos escandaloso de lo que se dice.

2 adv (_fam_): **a** — **bad film** una película de bajísima calidad; **it was** — **awful** fue de lo más horrible.

shockingly [ˈʃɔkiŋli] adv horriblemente; escandalosamente; — **dear** terriblemente caro; **a** — **bad film** una película de bajísima calidad; **to behave** — comportarse de modo escandaloso.

shockproof [ˈʃɔkpruːf] adj a prueba de choques; _person_ imperturbable.

shock therapy [ˈʃɔkˌθerəpi] n shockterapia f.

shock wave [ˈʃɔkweiv] n onda f de choque.

shod [ʃɔd] pret and ptp of **shoe**; — **with** calzado de.

shoddiness [ˈʃɔdinis] n baja calidad f; mala hechura f; cursilería f.

shoddy [ˈʃɔdi] **1** adj de pacotilla, de bajísima calidad; muy mal hecho; cursi.

2 n (_cloth_) paño m burdo de lana; (_wool_) lana f regenerada; (_as waste, fertilizer_) desechos mpl de lana.

shoe [ʃuː] **1** n zapato m; (_horse_—) herradura f; (_brake_—) zapata f; **I wouldn't like to be in his** —**s** no quisiera estar en su pellejo; **to cast a** — (_horse_) perder una herradura; **to put on one's** —**s** calzarse; **to take off one's** —**s** quitarse los zapatos, descalzarse; **to step into someone's** —**s** pasar a ocupar el puesto de uno; **to be waiting for dead men's** —**s** esperar a que muera uno (para pasar luego a ocupar su puesto).

2 (_irr_: pret and ptp **shod**) vt calzar (_with_ de); _horse_ herrar.

shoeblack [ˈʃuːblæk] n limpiabotas m.

shoeblacking [ˈʃuːˌblækiŋ] n betún m.

shoebrush [ˈʃuːbrʌʃ] n cepillo m para zapatos.

shoehorn [ˈʃuːhɔːn] n calzador m.

shoelace [ˈʃuːleis] n cordón m.

shoe leather [ˈʃuːˌleðə*] n cuero m para zapatos; **to wear out one's** — gastarse el calzado (andando de acá para allá).

shoemaker [ˈʃuːˌmeikə*] n zapatero m; —**'s** (_shop_) zapatería f.

shoemender [ˈʃuːˌmendə*] n zapatero m remendón.

shoeshine [ˈʃuːʃain] n (_US_): **to have a** — hacerse limpiar los zapatos; — **boy** limpiabotas m.

shoeshop [ˈʃuːʃɔp] n zapatería f, tienda f de calzado.

shoestring [ˈʃuːstriŋ] n (_US_) cordón m; **to do something on a** — hacer algo con muy poco dinero; **to live on a** — vivir con escasos recursos.

shoetree [ˈʃuːtriː] n horma f.

shone [ʃɔn] pret and ptp of **shine**.

shoo [ʃuː] **1** interj ¡zape!, ¡ox!; (_to child_) ¡vete!, ¡fuera de aquí!

2 vt ahuyentar; **I had to** — **the children away** tuve que decirles a los niños que se fueran a otra parte; **somebody** —ed **us away** alguien nos mandó ir a otra parte.

shook [ʃuk] pret of **shake**.

shoot [ʃuːt] **1** n (a) (_Bot_) renuevo m, retoño m, vástago m.

(b) (_inclined plane_) conducto m inclinado; (_on ice_) resbaladero m; see **chute**.

(c) (_shooting party, hunt_) partida f de caza, cacería f; (_competition_) certamen m de tiro al blanco.

(d) (_preserve_) coto m, vedado m.

2 (_irr_: pret and ptp **shot**) vt (a) (_Mil etc_) _bullet_ disparar, tirar; _arrow etc_ disparar; _gun_ disparar, descargar.

(b) _person, animal_ matar con arma de fuego, herir con arma de fuego; (_execute_) fusilar; **to** — **someone dead, to** — **someone to death** matar a uno a tiros; **he was shot dead by a policeman** fue muerto a tiros por un policía; **he was shot in the leg** una bala le hirió en la pierna; **he had been shot through the heart** la bala le había atravesado el corazón; **I'll** — **you a rabbit** te cazaré un conejo; **he shot his wife** pegó un tiro a su mujer; **he was shot as a spy** le fusilaron por espía; **you'll get me shot** (_fig_) si hago esto para ti me despiden; **people have been shot for less** han fusilado a muchos por menos motivos.

(c) (_fig_) _film_ rodar; _film scene_ fotografiar, filmar; _subject of snapshot_ tomar, sacar una instantánea de; _goal_ marcar, meter; _bridge_ pasar por debajo de; _rapids_ salvar, atravesar; _coal, rubbish etc_ verter, vaciar; _dice_ echar; _net_ echar; _ray of light_ echar; _glance_ echar, lanzar; **"— no rubbish"** "prohibido verter basuras"; **to** — **the sun** tomar la altura del sol; **to** — **a question at someone** disparar una pregunta inesperada a uno.

(d) (_with adv or prep_) **to** — **away all one's ammunition** quemar todos sus cartuchos; **he had a leg shot away** un disparo le cercenó una pierna; **they shot the idea back to the committee** devolvieron la idea rápidamente al comité; **to** — **down** _aeroplane_ derribar, abatir; _person_ matar de un tiro; _argument_ rebatir; **he was shot down over Italy** fue derribado sobre Italia; **he had a finger shot off** una bala le cercenó un dedo; **to** — **out** _sparks etc_ arrojar; _hand_ extender rápidamente, extender inesperadamente; _tongue_ sacar rápidamente; **we were literally shot out of bed by the noise** nos vimos materialmente arrancados de nuestras camas por el estruendo; **they shot it out in the saloon** lo resolvieron a tiros en el bar; **to** — **up** _aerodrome_ destrozar a tiros, _town_ asaltar a tiros.

3 vi (a) (_with gun: as sport_) practicar el deporte del tiro al blanco, (_as hunter_) ser cazador de escopeta; **do you** —? ¿le gusta cazar con escopeta?; **I haven't shot for years** hace tiempo que no manejo la escopeta; **he** —s **for Oxford** forma parte del equipo de tiro de Oxford; **we can** — **over Lord Emsworth's ground** podemos cazar en la finca de Lord Emsworth; **if they attack you,** — si os atacan, disparad; — **to kill** tirad a matar; **don't** —! ¡ no dispare!; **to** — **at someone** tirar a uno, pegar un tiro a uno; **he shot at me but missed** disparó contra mí pero erró el tiro; **to** — **back** devolver el tiro; **to** — **wide of the mark** errar el tiro.

(b) —! (_in conversation: fam_) ¡adelante!, ¡bien, dígame!

(c) (_Football etc_) chutar, tirar; —! ¡chuta!; **to** — **at goal** tirar a gol.

(d) (_of pain_) punzar, dar punzadas.

(e) (_Bot_) brotar; **to** — **up** crecer, espigar (_also fig, of person_).

(f) (_move rapidly: of person_) lanzarse, precipitarse; **he shot to the door** se lanzó hacia la puerta; **to** — **ahead** adelantarse mucho (_of a_); **we were** —**ing along** íbamos a gran velocidad; **to** — **by, to** — **past** pasar como un meteoro; **to** — **in** entrar como una bala; **he shot into space** se lanzó al espacio; **to** — **off, to** — **out** (_person etc_) salir como una bala, salir disparado; **flames were** —**ing out of the window** las llamas salían de la ventana; **the car shot past us** el coche pasó como un rayo; **prices are** —**ing up** los precios suben vertiginosamente.

shooting [ˈʃuːtiŋ] **1** n (a) (_shots_) tiros mpl, disparos mpl; (_continuous_ —) tiroteo m; (_by artillery_) cañoneo m, bombardeo m.

(b) (_act: murder_) asesinato m; (_execution_) fusilamiento m; (_of film_) rodaje m.

(c) (_Hunting_) caza f con escopeta; **he comes each year for the** — viene cada año para la caza; **there is good** — **in Asturias** Asturias es buen terreno para la caza; **to go** — ir de caza, ir a cazar; **good** —! ¡buen tiro!; ¡bravo!

2 adj, attr de tiro; de caza; _pain_ punzante; — **war** guerra f a tiros; — **affray** refriega f con tiros.

shooting box [ˈʃuːtiŋbɔks] n, — **lodge** [lɔdʒ] n pabellón m de caza.

shooting brake [ˈʃuːtiŋbreik] n (_Aut_) rubia f, furgoneta f.

shooting gallery [ˈʃuːtiŋˌgæləri] n galería f de tiro al blanco.

shooting jacket [ˈʃuːtiŋˌdʒækit] n chaquetón m.

shooting match ['ʃuːtiŋˌmætʃ] n certamen m de tiro al blanco; **the whole —** (fam) el todo, todo el negocio.

shooting party ['ʃuːtiŋˌpɑːti] n partida f de caza.

shooting range ['ʃuːtiŋreindʒ] n campo m de tiro.

shooting star ['ʃuːtiŋˈstɑː*] n estrella f fugaz.

shooting stick ['ʃuːtiŋstik] n bastón m taburete.

shop [ʃɔp] 1 n (a) (Comm) tienda f; (large store) almacén m; —! ¿quién despacha?; **to keep a —** poseer un negocio; **to set up —** poner una tienda; **to shut up —** (fig) cerrar; dar por terminado un asunto; desistir de una empresa; **to talk —** hablar del propio trabajo, hablar de asuntos profesionales; **it's all over the —** (fam) está en el mayor desorden; **she leaves things all over the** (fam) — deja sus cosas de cualquier modo; **they're all over the** (fam) — no tienen ni idea, carecen de todo sentido del buen orden.

(b) (Tech) taller m; **closed —** coto m cerrado.

2 vt (fam): **to — someone** traicionar a uno, delatar a uno; denunciar a uno a la policía.

3 vi comprar, hacer compras; **to go —ping** ir de compras, ir de tiendas; **to send someone —ping** enviar a uno a hacer compras; **to — at Joe's** hacer sus compras en la tienda de Joe; **to — for fish** ir a buscar pescado en las tiendas.

shop front ['ʃɔpfrʌnt] n escaparate m.

shopgirl ['ʃɔpgəːl] n dependienta f.

shop hours ['ʃɔpauəz] npl horas fpl durante las que está abierta una tienda.

shopkeeper ['ʃɔpˌkiːpə*] n tendero m, a f.

shoplifter ['ʃɔpˌliftə*] n mechera f, ratero m de tiendas.

shoplifting ['ʃɔpˌliftiŋ] n ratería f de tiendas.

shopper ['ʃɔpə*] n comprador m, ora f.

shopping ['ʃɔpiŋ] n (act) el comprar en tiendas; (goods bought) compras fpl.

shopping bag [ʃɔpiŋbæg] n bolsa f de compras.

shopping centre, (US) **— center** ['ʃɔpiŋˌsentə*] n zona f de tiendas.

shop-soiled ['ʃɔpsɔild] adj deteriorado.

shop steward ['ʃɔp'stjuəd] n enlace m sindical.

shopwalker ['ʃɔpˌwɔːkə*] n vigilante m, a f.

shop window ['ʃɔp'windəu] n escaparate m.

shore[1] [ʃɔː*] 1 n playa f; orilla f, ribera f; **these —s** (fig) estas tierras, esta parte; **on —** en tierra. 2 attr: **— leave** licencia f para ir a tierra.

shore[2] [ʃɔː*] n puntal m; (Min) entibo m. 2 vt apuntalar; entibar; **to — up** (fig) apoyar, reforzar, sostener.

shoreline ['ʃɔːlain] n línea f de la playa.

shoreward(s) ['ʃɔːwəd(z)] adv hacia la playa.

shoring ['ʃɔːriŋ] n puntales mpl; entibos mpl.

shorn [ʃɔːn] ptp of **shear**; **— of** sin, desprovisto de; **— of its verbiage, this means . . .** quitando la palabrería, esto quiere decir . . .; **— of outside aid we cannot go on** sin la ayuda exterior no podemos continuar.

short [ʃɔːt] 1 adj (a) (in length, distance) corto; message etc corto, breve, sucinto; person bajo; radio wave corto; **the —est route** la ruta más corta; **a — way off** a poca distancia, no muy lejos; **by a — head** por una cabeza escasa; **to be — in the leg** tener las piernas cortas; **these trousers are a bit — in the leg** estos pantalones tienen la pierna algo pequeña; **the — answer is that . . .** en pocas palabras la razón es que . . .; **to take — steps** dar pequeños pasos; **to take a — walk** dar un paseíto.

(b) **"Pat" is — for "Patricia"** "Pat" es forma abreviada de "Patricia"; **"living" is — for "living room"** "living" es apócope de "living room".

(c) (in time) corto, breve; de poca duración; vowel breve; memory flaco, malo; **for a — time** por poco tiempo; **February is a — month** febrero es un mes corto; **the days are getting —er** los días se hacen más breves; **time is getting —er** nos queda poco tiempo.

(d) reply brusco, seco; manner brusco; temper vivo; **to be — with someone** tratar a uno con sequedad.

(e) (insufficient) insuficiente; **5 —** faltan 5, 5 de menos; **I'm £3 —** me faltan 3 libras; **it's 2 kilos —** faltan 2 kilos; **we were — last week** la semana pasada nos faltó algo; **to give — weight** vender algo con peso insuficiente; **to give someone — change** no devolver a uno toda la vuelta que se le debe; **to be on — time** trabajar en jornadas reducidas; **not far — of £100** poco menos de 100 libras; **nothing — of total surrender** nada menos que la rendición incondicional; **it's little — of madness** falta poco para que esto se llame una locura;

nothing — of a bomb would stop him fuera de una bomba nada le impediría.

(f) **to be — of** estar falto de, andar escaso de; **we are — of petrol** tenemos poca gasolina, casi no tenemos gasolina; **we're not — of volunteers** se han ofrecido muchos voluntarios, no andamos escasos de voluntarios; **I was — of clubs** (Cards) tenía poco trébol; **bananas are very —** escasean los plátanos, casi no hay plátanos; **to go — of** pasarse sin; **no one goes — in this house** en esta casa nadie padece hambre; **to run — escasear**; **we ran — of petrol** se nos acabó la gasolina, quedamos sin gasolina.

(g) pastry quebradizo.

2 adv (a) **to cut —** acortar, abreviar; interrumpir; terminar inesperadamente; **they had to cut — their holiday** tuvieron que interrumpir sus vacaciones; **to fall —** resultar ser insuficiente, no alcanzar el nivel previsto; **production has fallen — by 100 tons** la producción arroja un déficit de 100 toneladas; **to fall — of the target** no alcanzar el blanco, no llegar al blanco; **to fall — of expectations** no cumplir las esperanzas; **it falls far — of what we require** queda muy lejos de satisfacer nuestras exigencias; **to sell — (Fin)** vender al descubierto; **to sell someone — (fig)** engañar a uno en un negocio; **to stop —** parar en seco; parar de repente; **to stop — of** detenerse antes de llegar a; **to be taken —** necesitar urgentemente ir al wáter.

(b) **of blowing it up** a menos que lo volemos, a no ser que lo volemos; **— of murder I'll do anything** lo haré todo menos matar.

4 vt (Elec) poner en cortocircuito.

5 vi ponerse en cortocircuito.

shortage ['ʃɔːtidʒ] n escasez f, falta f; insuficiencia f; penuria f; **the housing —** la crisis de la vivienda; **— of staff** insuficiencia f de personal; **in times of —** en las épocas de penuria; **there is no — of advice** no es que falten los consejos.

shortbread ['ʃɔːtbred] n torta dulce seca y quebradiza.

shortcake ['ʃɔːtkeik] n torta f de frutas.

short-change ['ʃɔːt'tʃeindʒ] vt: **to — someone** no devolver a uno toda la vuelta que se le debe; (fig) estafar a uno, engañar a uno.

short-circuit ['ʃɔːt'səːkit] 1 n cortocircuito m. 2 vt poner en cortocircuito. 3 vi ponerse en cortocircuito.

shortcoming ['ʃɔːtkʌmiŋ] n defecto m, deficiencia f.

short-dated ['ʃɔːt'deitid] adj a corto plazo.

shorten ['ʃɔːtn] 1 vt acortar; abreviar; reducir; holiday, journey etc acortar.

2 vi acortarse; abreviarse; reducirse; **the odds have —ed** los puntos de ventaja se han reducido.

shortening ['ʃɔːtniŋ] n acortamiento m; abreviación f; reducción f.

shortfall ['ʃɔːtfɔːl] n déficit m.

short-haired ['ʃɔːt'heəd] adj pelicorto.

shorthand ['ʃɔːthænd] n taquigrafía f; **— note** nota f taquigráfica; **to take —** escribir al dictado; **to take something down in —** apuntar algo taquigráficamente.

short-handed ['ʃɔːt'hændid] adj falto de personal, falto de mano de obra.

shorthand typist ['ʃɔːthænd'taipist] n taquimeca f, taquimecanógrafa f.

shorthand writer ['ʃɔːthændˌraitə*] n taquígrafo m, a f.

shortish ['ʃɔːtiʃ] adj algo pequeño, más bien bajo.

short list ['ʃɔːt'list] 1 n lista f de candidatos escogidos.

2 vt: **to short-list someone** poner a uno en la lista de candidatos escogidos (quienes pasan después a otras pruebas para que se nombre a uno de ellos a un puesto); **he has not been —ed** no figura en la lista de los candidatos escogidos.

short-lived ['ʃɔːt'livd] adj efímero.

shortly ['ʃɔːtli] adv (a) en breve, dentro de poco; luego; **— after** poco después; **— before** this poco tiempo antes de esto; **you shall see it very —** lo va a ver muy pronto.

(b) (curtly) bruscamente, secamente.

shortness ['ʃɔːtnis] n (in length, distance) cortedad f; (of message etc) brevedad f; (of person) pequeñez f; (in time) brevedad f, poca duración f; (of manner) brusquedad f; **because of the — of my memory** debido a mi mala memoria; **— of sight** miopía f; **— of breath** falta f de aliento, respiración f difícil.

short-range ['ʃɔːt'reindʒ] adj gun de corto alcance; aircraft de autonomía limitada, de corto radio de acción.

short-sighted ['ʃɔːt'saitid] adj miope, corto de vista; (fig) person falto de previsión, imprevisor; measure etc imprudente, sin eficacia a la larga.

short-sightedly ['ʃɔːt'saitidli] *adv* con ojos de miope; *(fig)* imprudentemente.

short-sightedness ['ʃɔːt'saitidnis] *n* miopía *f*; cortedad *f* de vista; *(fig)* falta *f* de previsión, imprevisión *f*; imprudencia *f*, ineficacia *f* a la larga.

short-tempered ['ʃɔːt'tempəd] *adj* de genio vivo, enojadizo.

short-term ['ʃɔːttəːm] *adj* a plazo corto.

short-time ['ʃɔːt'taim] **1** *adj*: **— working** sistema *m* de jornadas reducidas, sistema *m* de jornada limitada; **to be on — working** trabajar en jornadas reducidas.

2 *adv*: **to work —** trabajar en jornadas reducidas.

shortwave ['ʃɔːt,weiv] *adj* de onda corta.

short-winded ['ʃɔːt'windid] *adj* corto de resuello.

shorty ['ʃɔːti] *n* *(fam)* persona *f* bajita.

shot [ʃɔt] **1** *n* **(a)** *(missile)* bala *f*; proyectil *m*; *(sound of —)* tiro *m*, disparo *m*; *(causing wound)* balazo *m*; *(pellets)* perdigones *mpl*; *(weight, Sport)* peso *m*; **— across the bows, warning —** cañonazo *m* de advertencia; **good —!** ¡muy bien!; **Parthian —** flecha *f* del parto; **parting —** última observación *f*; palabra *f* dicha al despedirse; **random —** disparo *m* hecho sin apuntar; **not by a long —** ni con mucho; **to fire a — at someone** disparar sobre uno, tirar a uno; **who fired that —?** ¿quién disparó?; **it surrendered without firing a —** *(or without a — being fired)* se rindió sin resistencia alguna; **we captured it without firing a —** lo tomamos sin disparar una sola vez; **to exchange —s** tirotearse; **to take a — at someone** tirar a uno.

(b) *(person)* tirador *m*, ora *f*; **big —** *(fam)* pez *m* gordo *(fam)*, personaje *m* importante; **to be a crack —** ser un tirador experto.

(c) *(of space exploration)* lanzamiento *m*; cohete *m*, vehículo *m* espacial; **moon —** lanzamiento *m* de un cohete hacia la luna; *see* **space —**.

(d) *(Sport: with club etc)* golpe *m*; *(throw)* tirada *f*, echada *f*; *(at goal)* tiro *m*.

(e) I'll do it like a — lo haré de muy buena gana; **he did it like a —** lo hizo de buena gana; **he was off like a —** partió como una bala.

(f) *(attempt)* tentativa *f*; *(guess)* conjetura *f*; **it's your —** te toca a ti; **to have a —** probar suerte; **to have a — at +** *ger* hacer una tentativa de + *infin*; **will you have a — at it?** ¿quieres probarlo?

(g) *(injection)* inyección *f*; *(dose)* dosis *f*; **a — of rum** un trago de ron; **a — in the arm for ...** es un estímulo para ..., es una ayuda a ...; **the industry needs a — in the arm** la industria necesita una ayuda económica.

(h) *(Phot)* foto *f*, instantánea *f*; *(in film)* fotograma *m*, toma *f*, plano *m*; **a series of —s of Venice** una serie de fotos de Venecia.

2 *pret and ptp of* **shoot**; **— silk** seda *f* tornasolada; **to get — of** *(fam)* deshacerse de, quitarse de encima.

-shot [ʃɔt]: *eg* **within ear—** al alcance del oído.

shot firer ['ʃɔtfaiərə*] *n* pegador *m*.

shotgun ['ʃɔtgʌn] *n* escopeta *f*; *see* **marriage**.

should [ʃud] *(irr: pret and conditional of* **shall**) *y aux* **(a)** *(used to form conditional tense)* **I — go if they sent for me** iría si me llamasen; **I — be out at the time** si estoy fuera en aquel momento; **I —n't be surprised if . . .** no me sorprendería si . . .; **I —n't if I were you** yo en tu lugar no lo haría; **he ordered that it — be done** mandó que se hiciera así; **thanks, I — like to** gracias, me gustaría; **I —n't like to say** prefiero no decirlo.

(b) *(statements of duty and command)* **all cars — carry lights** todos los coches han de llevar luces, conviene que todos los coches lleven luces; **you —n't do that** es aconsejable no hacer eso, es mejor no hacer eso; **all is as it —** be todo está en regla; **. . ., which is as it — be . . .**, como es razonable; **why — you want to know?** ¿por qué has de saberlo tú?; **he — know that . . .** debiera saber que . . .; **he — have paid it** debiera haberlo pagado.

(c) *(statements of probability)* **he — be there by now** ha de estar allí ya; **they — arrive tomorrow** han de llegar mañana; **this — be good** esto promete ser bueno.

shoulder ['ʃəuldə*] **1** *n* hombro *m*; espaldas *fpl*; *(of meat)* espalda *f*; *(of hill)* lomo *m*; *(of motorway)* andén *m*; **to carry something on one's —s** llevar algo a hombros; **he was carried out on their —s** le sacaron a hombros; **to give someone the cold —** volver la espalda a uno; **to give someone something straight from the —** decir algo a uno sin rodeos; **to put one's — to the wheel** arrimar el hombro; **to rub —s with someone** codearse con uno; **to stand — to —** estar hombro con hombro.

2 *vt* *(carry)* llevar al hombro; *(pick up)* poner al hombro; *(fig)* *responsibilities etc* cargar con; **— arms!** ¡armas al hombro!; **to — someone aside** apartar a uno con el hombro; abrirse paso empujando a uno con el hombro; *(fig)* dejar a uno al lado; **to — one's way through** abrirse paso empujando con el hombro.

shoulder blade ['ʃəuldəbleid] *n* omóplato *m*.

shoulder flash ['ʃəuldə,flæʃ] *n* *(Mil etc)* emblema *m* de hombrera, charretera *f*.

shoulder knot ['ʃəuldənɔt] *n* dragona *f*.

shoulder pad ['ʃəuldəpæd] *n* hombrera *f*.

shoulder strap ['ʃəuldəstræp] *n* *(Mil)* dragona *f*; *(of dress)* tirante *m*; *(of satchel etc)* correa *f*.

shouldn't ['ʃudnt] = **should not**.

shout [ʃaut] **1** *n* grito *m*, voz *f*; **a — of protest** un grito de protesta; **there were —s of applause** hubo grandes aplausos; **there were —s of laughter** hubo grandes carcajadas; **to give someone a —** llamar a uno.

2 *vt* gritar; **to — abuse at someone** lanzar improperios contra uno a voz en grito; **to — a protest** protestar en alta voz; **to — someone down** protestar hasta hacer callar a uno; **to — a play down** hundir una obra a gritos; **to — out** gritar, decir a voz en grito.

3 *vi* gritar; dar voces; *(talk loudly)* hablar a voz en grito; **to — for help** dar voces para pedir socorro, pedir socorro a voces; **to — with laughter** reírse a grandes carcajadas; **to — out** gritar, dar gritos.

4 *vr*: **to — oneself hoarse** enronquecer a fuerza de gritar.

shouting ['ʃautiŋ] *n* gritos *mpl*, vocerío *m*, clamoreo *m*.

shove [ʃʌv] **1** *n* empujón *m*; **to give someone a —** empujar a uno; **can you give me a —, please?** *(Aut)* ¿por favor, me ayuda a arrancar empujándolo?; **one more — and we're there** empujad una vez más y ya está.

2 *vt* empujar; **to — someone aside** apartar a uno empujándole, apartar a uno a codazos; **to — someone back** hacer retroceder a uno empujándole; **his friends —d him forward** sus amigos le empujaron hacia adelante; **to — a boat off** *(or out)* echar afuera un bote; **they —d him out** le empujaron fuera, *(fig)* le obligaron a salir de su puesto *(etc)*.

3 *vi* empujar, dar empujones; **stop shoving!** ¡dejen de empujar!; **to — off** *(Naut)* alejarse del muelle *(etc)*; *(fig, fam)* largarse *(fam)*, marcharse.

shovel ['ʃʌvl] **1** *n* pala *f*; *(mechanical)* excavadora *f* con pala.

2 *vt* traspalar, mover con pala; **to — earth into a pile** amontonar tierra con una pala; **he was —ling food into his mouth** iba llenando la boca con la mayor rapidez; **to — coal on to a fire** añadir carbón a la lumbre con pala; **they were —ling out the mud** estaban sacando el lodo con palas.

shovelboard ['ʃʌvlbɔːd] *n* juego *m* de tejo.

show [ʃəu] **1** *n* **(a)** *(showing)* demostración *f*; **— of hands** votación *f* por manos levantadas; **an impressive — of power** una impresionante exhibición de poder; **the garden is a splendid —** el jardín es un encanto; **the dahlias make a fine —** las dalias se muestran espléndidas.

(b) *(exhibition)* exposición *f*; **agricultural —** feria *f* de campo; **dog —** exposición *f* canina; **horticultural —** exposición *f* de horticultura; **trade —** feria *f* de muestras; **to be on —** estar expuesto; **he's holding his first London —** está organizando su primera exposición en Londres; *see* **horse —, motor —** *etc*.

(c) *(Theat etc)* función *f*, espectáculo *m*; **the last — starts at 11** la última función empieza a las 11; **there is no — on Sundays** el domingo no hay función; **to go to a —** ir a un teatro, ir a un espectáculo; **variety —** espectáculo *m* de variedades, revista *f*; **wild-beast —** espectáculo *m* de fieras; **Lord Mayor's S—** desfile *m* patrocinado por el alcalde de Londres el día de su inauguración.

(d) *(fam: undertaking, organization)* negocio *m*, empresa *f*, cosa *f*, organización *f*; **who's in charge of this —?** ¿quién manda aquí?; **he runs the —** manda él, él es el amo.

(e) *(fam)* **bad —!** ¡malo!; **good —!** ¡muy bien!, ¡bravo!; **to put up a good —** hacer un buen papel, dar buena cuenta de sí; **it's a pretty poor —, isn't it?** esto es un desastre, ¿no?; **to give the — away** tirar de la manta, *(involuntarily)* clararse.

(f) *(outward —)* apariencia *f*; *(pomp)* boato *m*, aparato *m*, pompa *f*; **it's just for —** es sólo para impresionar; **it's all — with him** todo lo hace para impresionar; es un farsante; **to do something for —** hacer algo para impresionar; **to make a — of resistance** aparentar resistir, fingir resistir; **to make a — of unwillingness** fingir no querer; **to make a great — of sympathy** desvivirse por mostrar compasión, llevar su compasión al exceso.

2 (irr: pret **showed,** ptp **shown;** (arch) **shewed, shewn**) vt **(a)** (manifest) mostrar, enseñar; film proyectar, poner; slides proyectar; picture exhibir; goods exponer; **to — someone something, to — something to someone** mostrar (or enseñar) algo a uno; **to — one's passport** mostrar su pasaporte, presentar su pasaporte; **what can I — you, madam?** ¿qué artículos quiere que le traiga, señora?; **to — a picture at the Academy** exhibir un cuadro en la Academia; **to — a film at Cannes** proyectar una película en Cannes; **the film was first —n in 1968** la película se estrenó en 1968; **to — someone a light** alumbrar a uno, dar luz a uno; **he had nothing to — for his trouble** se quedó sin nada después de tantos trabajos, no sacó provecho alguno de tantos trabajos.

(b) (indicate) indicar; (Comm) arrojar; **it —s 200°** indica 200°, marca 200°; **it —s a speed of . . .** indica una velocidad de . . .; **as —n in the illustration** según se indica en la lámina, como lo indica la lámina; **the roads are —n in red** las carreteras están marcadas en rojo; **to — a loss** dejar una pérdida; **to — a profit** arrojar un saldo positivo; **the figures — a rise** las cifras arrojan un aumento.

(c) (demonstrate) mostrar, manifestar; acusar; (prove) probar, demostrar; **to — intelligence** mostrar tener inteligencia, mostrar ser inteligente; **to — his disagreement, he . . .** para mostrar su disconformidad, él . . .; **she —ed no reaction** no acusó reacción alguna; **her face —ed her happiness** su felicidad se acusaba en la cara; **to — one's affection** demostrar su cariño; **a big crowd turned up to —** its feeling for him una gran multitud acudió para testimoniarle su simpatía; **the choice of dishes —s** excellent taste la selección de platos demuestra un gusto muy fino; **she's beginning to — her age** empiezan a verse en la cara las señales de su edad; **to — that . . .** demostrar que . . ., hacer ver que . . .; **I —ed him that this could not be true** le hice ver que esto no podía ser cierto.

(d) (reveal) revelar; **the gap —s her legs** el espacio deja ver sus piernas; **she likes to — her legs** le gusta hacer exhibición de sus piernas; **a dress which —s the figure** un vestido que deja ver la línea; **this —s him to be a swindler** esto le revela como estafador, esto demuestra que es estafador.

(e) (direct) **to — someone the way** enseñar a uno el camino; **let me — you** se lo voy a enseñar; **to — someone into a room** hacer que pase uno, hacer entrar a uno en un cuarto; **I was —n into a large hall** me hicieron pasar a un vestíbulo grande; **to — someone to his seat** enseñar a uno su asiento, acompañar a uno a su asiento.

(f) (with adv or prep) **to — someone in** hacer pasar a uno; **— him in at once, have him —n in at once** que pase ahora mismo; **to — off** (display) hacer gala de, lucir; beauty etc hacer resaltar, destacar; **to — someone out** acompañar a uno a la puerta; **to — up** work etc presentar; beauty etc hacer resaltar, destacar; fraud etc descubrir; person desenmascarar; defect etc revelar; **to — someone up** (upstairs) hacer subir a uno; **— him up!** ¡que suba!

3 vi **(a)** mostrarse, verse, revelarse; aparecer; (film) proyectarse; **your slip's —ing, madam** señora, se le ve la combinación; **it doesn't —** no se nota; **don't worry, it won't —** no te preocupes, no se notará; **the tulips are beginning to —** están apareciendo los tulipanes; **a little colour is beginning to —** now ahora se empieza a verles un poco de color; **it just goes to —!** ¡hay que ver!; **it all goes to — that . . .** todo sirve para demostrar que . . .

(b) (with adv) **to — off** lucirse; (pej) darse importancia, presumir; fachendear; **to — off in front of one's friends** presumir ante las amistades; **to — through** verse; transparentarse, trascender; **to — up** (stand out) destacar; (appear) acudir, presentarse; **he never —ed up** dejó de acudir a la cita.

4 vr: **to — oneself** presentarse; hacer acto de presencia; **to — oneself incompetent** descubrir su incompetencia, mostrarse incompetente; **it —s itself in his speech** se revela en su forma de hablar, se le nota en el habla.

show biz ['ʃəubiz] n (sl) see **show business.**

showboat ['ʃəubəut] n barco-teatro m.

show business ['ʃəubiznis] n los espectáculos, el mundo del espectáculo, el negocio del espectáculo; la vida de actor.

showcase ['ʃəukeis] n vitrina f (de exposición).

showdown ['ʃəudaun] n confrontación f; conflicto m; crisis f, momento m decisivo; **the Suez —** la crisis de Suez; **if it comes to a —** si llega a un conflicto, si llega el momento decisivo; **to have a — with someone** enfrentarse con uno, confrontarse con uno; **I'm going to have a — with the boss** le voy a decir cuatro verdades al jefe.

shower ['ʃauə*] **1** n **(a)** chaparrón m, chubasco m, aguacero m; **a day of sun and —s** un día en el cual los chubascos alternan con el sol.

(b) (fig: of arrows, stones etc) lluvia f.

(c) (fig, sl) gentuza f; **they were an —utter —** eran horribles, eran unos pesados; **what a —!** ¡qué pesados!

(d) (— bath) ducha f; **to take a —** ducharse, tomar una ducha.

2 vt (fig) llover, derramar (also **to — down**); **to — someone with honours, to — honours on someone** colmar a uno de honores; **he was —ed with invitations** le llovieron encima las invitaciones, le abrumaron de invitaciones.

3 vi llover, caer un chaparrón.

shower bath ['ʃauəba:θ] n, pl **— baths** [ba:ðz] ducha f; **to take a —** ducharse, tomar una ducha.

showerproof ['ʃauəpru:f] adj impermeable, a prueba de lluvia.

showery ['ʃauəri] adj day etc de chaparrones; weather lluvioso; **it will be — tomorrow** mañana habrá chaparrones.

show girl ['ʃəugə:l] n corista f.

showground ['ʃəugraund] n real m.

showily ['ʃəuili] adv vistosamente, llamativamente; aparatosamente; de modo espectacular; ostentosamente.

showiness ['ʃəuinis] n vistosidad f, lo llamativo; espectacularidad f, ostentación f; boato m.

showing ['ʃəuiŋ] n **(a)** (of pictures etc) exposición f; (of film) proyección f; **a second — of "The Blue Angel"** un reestreno de "El Ángel Azul".

(b) (performance) actuación f; **the team's — this season** la actuación del equipo durante la temporada actual; **the poor — of the team** la pobre actuación del equipo; **to make a good —** hacer un buen papel, dar buena cuenta de sí.

(c) on his own — según él mismo confiesa.

show jumping ['ʃəu,dʒʌmpiŋ] n concurso m de saltos y de hipismo.

showman ['ʃəumən] n, pl **—men** [mən] empresario m, director m de espectáculos; (fig) persona f ostentosa, persona f que hace gala de sus talentos, (pej) charlatán m; **the prime minister is a consummate —** el primer ministro es un brillante actor.

showmanship ['ʃəumənʃip] n instinto m del buen actor; teatralidad f; talento m para organizar grandes espectáculos.

shown [ʃəun] ptp of **show.**

show-off ['ʃəuɔf] n (fam) persona f ostentosa; presumido m, a f.

showpiece ['ʃəupi:s] n objeto m de valor (or interés etc) excepcional; **the — of the exhibition is . . .** el cuadro (etc) más interesante de la exposición es . . .; **this vase is a real —** este florero es realmente excepcional.

showplace ['ʃəupleis] n lugar m de gran atractivo, centro m turístico, monumento m; **Granada is a —** Granada es una ciudad de gran atractivo, Granada es un monumento artístico e histórico; **the new school is not typical but is a —** el nuevo colegio no es un colegio corriente, es más bien una cosa excepcional para mostrar a los visitantes.

showroom ['ʃəurum] n salón m de demostraciones; (Art) sala f de exposición.

show window ['ʃəu,windəu] n escaparate m.

showy ['ʃəui] adj vistoso, llamativo; aparatoso, espectacular; person ostentoso.

shrank [ʃræŋk] pret of **shrink.**

shrapnel ['ʃræpnl] n metralla f.

shred [ʃred] **1** n (bit) fragmento m, pedazo m; (of cloth) triza f, jirón m; (narrow strip) tira f; **there isn't a — of truth in it** eso no tiene ni pizca de verdad; **if you had a — of decency** si Vd tuviese una parte mínima de honradez; **without a — of clothing on** sin cubrirle el cuerpo vestido alguno; **to be in —s** estar roto, estar destrozado; **her dress hung in —s** su vestido estaba hecho jirones; **to tear something to —s** hacer algo trizas; **to tear an argument to —s** hacer un argumento pedazos.

2 *vt* hacer trizas, hacer tiras; *food etc* desmenuzar; *meat* deshilar.

shrew [ʃruː] *n* (*Zool*) musaraña *f*; (*fig*) arpía *f*, fiera *f*; **"The Taming of the S—"** "La fierecilla domada".

shrewd [ʃruːd] *adj person* sagaz, perspicaz; listo; *plan etc* prudente, astuto; **— reasoning** razonamiento *m* inteligente; **that is a — thing to do** eso es lo más prudente; **that is very —** of you en eso has sido muy perspicaz; **I have a — idea that . . .** se me ocurre pensar que . . ., me parece razonable suponer que . . .

shrewdly ['ʃruːdli] *adv* sagazmente, con perspicacia; prudentemente, astutamente.

shrewdness ['ʃruːdnis] *n* sagacidad *f*, perspicacia *f*; inteligencia *f*; prudencia *f*, astucia *f*.

shrewish ['ʃruːiʃ] *adj* regañón.

shriek [ʃriːk] **1** *n* chillido *m*, grito *m* agudo; **a — of pain** un grito de dolor; **with —s of laughter** con grandes carcajadas.

2 *vt* gritar; **to — abuse at someone** lanzar improperios contra uno a voz en grito.

3 *vi* chillar, gritar; **to — with pain** chillar de dolor; **to — with laughter** reírse a grandes carcajadas; **the colour simply —s at one** es un color de lo más chillón.

shrieking ['ʃriːkiŋ] **1** *adj child, colour* chillón. **2** *n* chillidos *mpl*, gritos *mpl*.

shrift [ʃrift] *n:* **to give someone short —** echar a uno con cajas destempladas; **he gave that idea short —** mostró su completa disconformidad con tal idea, desechó muy pronto tal posibilidad; **he got short — from the boss** el jefe se mostró poco compasivo con él; **he'll get short — from me!** ¡que no venga a mí a pedir compasión!

shrike [ʃraik] *n* alcaudón *m*.

shrill [ʃril] **1** *adj* chillón, agudo, estridente. **2** *vi* chillar.

shrillness ['ʃrilnis] *n* lo chillón, estridencia *f*.

shrilly ['ʃrili] *adv* agudamente, de modo estridente.

shrimp [ʃrimp] **1** *n* (*Zool*) camarón *m*; (*fig*) enano *m*, renacuajo *m*. **2** *vi* (*also* **to go —ing**) pescar camarones.

shrine [ʃrain] *n* (*tomb*) sepulcro *m* (de santo), santuario *m*; relicario *m*; (*chapel*) capilla *f*; (*altar*) altar *m*; (*fig*) lugar *m* sagrado.

shrink [ʃriŋk] (*irr: pret* **shrank**, *ptp* **shrunk**) **1** *vt* encoger; contraer; *quality* reducir, disminuir; **to — a part on** (*Tech*) montar una pieza en caliente.

2 *vi* (**a**) encogerse; contraerse; (*quantity*) reducirse, disminuir, mermar; **to — in the wash** encogerse al lavar; **"will not —"** "no se encoge", "inencogible"; **to — away to nothing** reducirse a nada, desaparecer.

(**b**) **to — away**, **to — back** retroceder (*from* ante); acobardarse, retirarse (*from, at* ante); **I — from doing it** no me atrevo a hacerlo, me repugna hacerlo.

shrinkage ['ʃriŋkidʒ] *n* encogimiento *m*; contracción *f*; reducción *f*, disminución *f*.

shrivel ['ʃrivl] **1** *vt* (*also* **to — up**) secar, marchitar; *skin* arrugar.

2 *vi* (*also* **to — up**) secarse, marchitarse; (*skin etc*) arrugarse, avellanarse, apergaminarse; consumirse.

shrivelled, (*US*) **shriveled** ['ʃrivld] *adj plant etc* seco, marchito; *skin* arrugado, apergaminado.

shroud [ʃraud] **1** *n* sudario *m*, mortaja *f*; (*fig*) velo *m*; **—s** (*Naut*) obenques *mpl*; **a — of mystery** un velo de misterio.

2 *vt* amortajar; (*fig*) velar, cubrir; **the castle was —ed in mist** el castillo estaba envuelto en niebla; **the whole thing is —ed in mystery** el asunto entero está envuelto en un velo de misterio.

Shrovetide ['ʃrəuvtaid] *n* carnestolendas *fpl*.

Shrove Tuesday ['ʃrəuv'tjuːzdi] *n* martes *m* de carnaval.

shrub [ʃrʌb] *n* arbusto *m*.

shrubbery ['ʃrʌbəri] *n* arbustos *mpl*, plantío *m* de arbustos.

shrug [ʃrʌg] **1** *n* encogimiento *m* de hombros; **he said with a —** dijo encogiéndose de hombros.

2 *vt:* **to — something off** negar importancia a algo, minimizar algo; **you can't just — that off** no puedes negar la importancia de eso; **to — one's shoulders = 3** *vi* encogerse de hombros.

shrunk [ʃrʌŋk] *ptp of* **shrink**.

shrunken ['ʃrʌŋkən] *adj* encogido; (*shrivelled*) seco; marchito; apergaminado; *head* reducido; *quantity* reducido, mermado.

shuck [ʃʌk] **1** *n* vaina *f*, hollejo *m*. **2** *vt* desenvainar.

shudder ['ʃʌdə*] **1** *n* estremecimiento *m*, escalofrío *m*; (*of vehicle etc*) vibración *f*, sacudida *f*; **a — ran through her** se estremeció; **she realized with a — that . . .** se estremeció al darse cuenta de que . . .

2 *vi* estremecerse (*with* de); vibrar, sacudirse.

shuffle ['ʃʌfl] **1** *n* (**a**) **to walk with a —** caminar arrastrando los pies.

(**b**) (*Cards*) barajadura *f*; **to give the cards a —** barajar las cartas; **whose — is it?** ¿a quién le toca barajar?

2 *vt* (**a**) *feet* arrastrar.

(**b**) (*mix up*) mezclar, revolver; *cards* barajar.

(**c**) **to — someone aside** apartar a uno, relegar a uno a un puesto menos importante; **to — something off** deshacerse de algo.

3 *vi* (**a**) (*walk*) arrastrar los pies; caminar (*or* bailar *etc*) arrastrando los pies; **he —d across to the door** fue hacia la puerta arrastrando los pies.

(**b**) (*Cards*) barajar.

shuffleboard ['ʃʌflbɔːd] *n* juego *m* de tejo.

shun [ʃʌn] *vt* evitar, esquivar, rehuir; volver la espalda a; **to — doing something** evitar hacer algo; **to feel —ned by the world** creer que la gente le vuelve la espalda a uno.

shunt [ʃʌnt] *vt* (*Rail*) maniobrar; **to — someone aside** apartar a uno, relegar a uno a un puesto menos importante; **to — someone off** apartar a uno de su propósito; **he was —ed into retirement** mediante una hábil maniobra entró en la vía muerta de la jubilación, lograron con maña que se jubilase; **to — someone to and fro** mandar a uno de acá para allá.

shunter ['ʃʌntə*] *n* guarda(a)gujas *m*, obrero *m* del servicio de maniobras.

shunting ['ʃʌntiŋ] *n* maniobras *fpl*.

shunting engine ['ʃʌntiŋ,endʒin] *n* locomotora *f* de maniobras.

shunting yard ['ʃʌntiŋjɑːd] *n* estación *f* de maniobras, playa *f* de clasificación *f*.

shush [ʃuʃ] *interj* ¡chitón!

shut [ʃʌt] (*irr: pret and ptp* **shut**) **1** *vt* (**a**) cerrar; **to find the door —** encontrar que la puerta está cerrada; **he had the door — in his face** le cerraron la puerta en sus narices; **to — one's fingers in the door** cogerse los dedos en la puerta.

(**b**) **to — down** *factory etc* cerrar; *machine* parar; **to — in** *person* encerrar; (*surround*) cercar, rodear; **to feel — in** sentirse muy encerrado; **to get — of** (*fam*) deshacerse de, quitarse de encima; **to — off** *supply* interrumpir, cortar; *water etc* cortar; *engine* parar; (*separate*) aislar, separar (*from* de); **to be — off from** estar aislado de; **to — out** excluir; *person* excluir, negar la entrada a; **the factory —s out the view** la fábrica impide ver el paisaje (*etc*); **to — up** (*close*) cerrar; (*enclose*) encerrar; (*block*) obturar; (*silence*) hacer callar, reducir al silencio; **to — someone up in prison** recluir a uno en la cárcel.

2 *vi* cerrarse; **the lid doesn't —** la tapa no cierra bien; **to — down** cerrar, cerrarse; **to — to** (*door*) cerrarse; **to — up** callarse; **— up!** ¡cállate!; **it's best to — up and get on with it** es aconsejable callarse y seguir trabajando.

3 *vr:* **to — oneself away** (*or* **up**) encerrarse; **he —s himself up all day in his study** permanece encerrado en su cuarto todo el día.

shutdown ['ʃʌtdaun] *n* cierre *m*.

shut-eye ['ʃʌtai] *n* (*sl*) sueño *m*; **to get some —** ir a dormir, acostarse.

shut-in ['ʃʌtin] *adj* encerrado.

shutoff ['ʃʌtɔf] *n* interruptor *m*.

shut-out ['ʃʌtaut] *n* cierre *m* (para impedir la entrada); (*Sport: US*) triunfo *m* en que el contrario no gana un solo tanto; **— bid** (*Cards*) declaración *f* aplastante.

shutter ['ʃʌtə*] *n* contraventana *f*; (*Phot*) obturador *m*; **to put up the —s** (*fig*) cerrar del todo, abandonar, (*Sport etc*) resolverse a no correr riesgo alguno.

shuttle ['ʃʌtl] **1** *n* lanzadera *f*.

2 *vt:* **to — someone about** mandar a uno de acá para allá; **the form was —d about between different departments** la solicitud fue enviada de departamento a departamento (sin que nadie la atendiese).

shuttlecock ['ʃʌtlkɔk] *n* volante *m*, zoquetillo *m*.

shuttle service ['ʃʌtl,sɜːvis] *n* servicio *m* de trenes (*etc*) que hacen viajes cortos entre dos puntos.

shy[1] [ʃai] **1** *adj* tímido, (*bashful*) vergonzoso; (*reserved*) reservado; (*unsociable*) huraño; *animal* huraño, asustadizo; **to be — of**, **to fight — of** procurar evitar; **to be — of +** *ger* procurar evitar **+** *infin*, no atreverse a **+** *infin*; **don't be — no** tengas miedo; **I'm £2 — (fam)** me faltan 2 libras, he perdido 2 libras; **he makes me —** él me hace sentirme miedoso.

2 *vi* (*of horse*) espantarse, respingar (*at something* al ver algo); **to — at a fence** negarse a saltar una valla; **to — away from something** alejarse asustado de algo; **they shied away from the idea** se asustaron de la idea; **to — away from** + ger asustarse y negarse a + infin.

shy[2] [ʃai] n (throw) tirada f; (fig) tentativa f; **to have a — at something** probar algo, intentar algo; **to have a — at** + ger hacer una tentativa de + infin; "**5 pesetas a —** " "5 pesetas la tirada".

shyly ['ʃaili] adv tímidamente; con vergüenza, vergonzosamente.

shyness ['ʃainis] n timidez f; vergüenza f; reserva f; lo huraño, lo asustadizo.

shyster ['ʃaistə*] n (US sl) abogado m trampista.

Siam [sai'æm] Siam m.

Siamese [,saiə'miːz] **1** adj siamés. **2** n siamés m, esa f. **3** n (language) siamés m.

Siberia [sai'biəriə] Siberia f.

Siberian [sai'biəriən] **1** adj siberiano. **2** n siberiano m, a f.

sibilant ['sibilənt] **1** adj sibilante. **2** n sibilante f.

sibling ['sibliŋ] n (Bio) hermano m, hermana f.

Sibyl ['sibil] f Sibila.

sibyl ['sibil] n sibila f.

sibylline ['sibilain] adj sibilino.

Sicilian [si'siliən] **1** adj siciliano. **2** n siciliano m, a f. **3** n (dialect) siciliano m.

Sicily ['sisili] Sicilia f.

sick [sik] **1** adj **(a)** (ill) enfermo; **the —** los enfermos; **to be (off)** — estar enfermo; **to go —** , **to take —** caer enfermo, enfermar; (be absent) ausentarse debido a enfermedad; **the cow took — and died** la vaca cayó enferma y murió; **to report —** darse de baja por enfermo.

(b) (dizzy, about to vomit) mareado; **to be —** vomitar; arrojar; **to feel —** estar mareado; **I get — in aeroplanes** me mareo en los aviones; **too much beer makes me —** un exceso de cerveza me da ganas de vomitar.

(c) (fig) **to be — at heart** tener la muerte en el alma; **to be — (and tired) of** estar harto de; **I get — of that** eso se me hace pesado, cojo asco a eso; **he just did look —!** ¡estaba la mar de abatido!; estaba furioso consigo mismo; **you make me —!** ¡me das asco!; **it makes me — to think that . . .** me da asco pensar que . . .

(d) humour negro, malsano.

2 vt (fam): **to — up** arrojar, devolver.

sick bay ['sikbei] n enfermería f.

sickbed ['sikbed] n lecho m de enfermo.

sick benefit ['sik,benifit] n subsidio m de enfermedad.

sicken ['sikn] **1** vt dar asco a (also fig); **it —s me** me da asco, me repugna.

2 vi caer enfermo, enfermar; **to — at something** sentir náuseas ante algo; **I — at the sight of blood** el ver sangre me da náuseas; **to — for, to be —ing for** (Med) mostrar síntomas de; **to — for want of something** añorar algo; enfermar debido a la falta de algo.

sickening ['sikniŋ] adj nauseabundo; (fig) asqueroso, repugnante.

sickeningly ['sikniŋli] adv (fig) asquerosamente; **— sentimental** tan sensiblero que da asco.

sickle ['sikl] n hoz f.

sick leave ['sikliːv] n permiso m de convalecencia.

sickliness ['siklinis] n lo enfermizo, lo achacoso; palidez f; lo nauseabundo; debilidad f; lo empalagoso.

sick list ['siklist] n lista f de enfermos; **to be on the —** estar enfermo.

sickly ['sikli] adj person enfermizo, achacoso; appearance pálido; smell nauseabundo; smile débil, forzado; taste empalagoso.

sick-making ['sikmeikiŋ] adj (fam) asqueroso.

sickness ['siknis] n (Med) enfermedad f, mal m; (fig) mal m, malestar m; mountain — mal m de montaña; **there is — on board** hay epidemia a bordo, hay una enfermedad contagiosa a bordo.

sick pay ['sikpei] n subsidio m de enfermedad.

sickroom ['sikrum] n cuarto m del enfermo.

side [said] **1** n **(a)** (Anat etc) costado m, lado m; (of animal) flanco m, ijada f; **— of bacon** hoja f de tocino; **by the — of** al lado de; **to sit by someone's —** estar sentado al lado de uno; **to sit — by — with someone** estar sentado al lado de uno; **to sleep on one's —** dormir de costado; **to split one's —s** desternillarse de risa.

(b) (flank etc, fig) lado m, flanco m; (of triangle) lado m; (of car, ship) costado m; (of hill) falda f, ladera f; (of lake) orilla f; (of small pond etc) borde m; (of wood) límite m, borde m; **weather —** costado m de barlovento: **near —** (Aut etc: Brit) lado m izquierdo, (US, Spain etc) lado m derecho; **off —**

(Aut etc: Brit) lado m derecho, (US, Spain etc) lado m izquierdo.

(c) (face, surface) lado m, superficie f; (of record, slice of bread, solid etc) cara f; **flip — (of record:** fam) cara f secundaria; **right — (of cloth)** derecho m, haz f; **to be right — out** estar bien puesto; **wrong — out** revés m, envés m; **to be wrong — out** estar al revés; **what's on the other —?** (of record) ¿qué hay a la vuelta?

(d) (part, region) lado m; **left-hand —** izquierda f; **right-hand —** derecha f; **to be on the left-hand —** estar a la izquierda; **on one — . . .**, **on the other . . .** por una parte . . ., por otra . . .; **on this —** por este lado; **on all —s** por todas partes, por todos lados; **on both —s** por ambos lados; **on the mother's —** por parte de madre; **to come up on the blind —** acercarse por el lado donde el conductor (etc) tiene la vista impedida; **on the — (as adv)** incidentalmente; de paso; (unofficially) de modo extraoficial; **to make a bit on the —** ganarse un poco de dinero con algún negocio extraoficial; **to be on the right —** of 40 no haber cumplido todavía los 40 años; **to put something on one —** poner algo aparte, guardarse algo; ahorrar; **I'll put it on one — for you** se lo guardaré; **to move to one —** apartarse, hacerse a un lado; **it's this — of Segovia** está más acá de Segovia; **it's the other — of Illescas** está más allá de Illescas.

(e) (aspect) aspecto m, lado m; **the other — (of the picture), the seamy —** el revés de la medalla; **to be on the safe —** . . . para mayor seguridad, por precaución . . .; **let's be on the safe —** atengámonos a lo más seguro; **to hear both —s of the question** escuchar los argumentos en pro y en contra; **to see only one — of the question** sólo ver un aspecto de la cuestión; **to get on the good — of someone** procurar congraciarse con uno; **to get on the wrong — of someone** ponerse a malas con uno; **to look on the bright —** ser optimista, ver el lado optimista de las cosas.

(f) **it's on the large —** es algo grande; **the results are on the poor —** los resultados son bastante mediocres; **the weather's on the cold —** el tiempo es algo frío.

(g) (superiority: fam) tono m, postín m; **there's no — about** (or to) **him** no presume, no se da aires de superioridad; **to put on —** darse tono.

(h) (party) partido m; (team) equipo m; (Bridge etc) bando m, campo m; **our —** nuestro campo (etc), los nuestros; **the home —** el equipo de casa, el equipo local; **the science — of the school** los estudios científicos del instituto; **he went on the science —** optó por estudiar ciencias; **to change —s** pasar al otro bando, cambiar de partido; cambiar de opinión; **to let the — down** hacer algo indigno de su colegio (etc), hacer algo que desmerece de su partido (etc); **to pick a —** seleccionar un equipo; **to take —s** tomar partido; **he's on our —** es de los nuestros, es partidario nuestro; **whose — are you on?** ¿a quiénes apoya Vd?; **you have tradition on your —** la tradición está de parte de los suyos, la tradición apoya su idea; **with a few concessions on the government —** con algunas concesiones por parte del gobierno.

2 adj, attr lateral, de lado; door, entrance accesorio; elevation lateral; glance de soslayo; issue etc secundario.

3 vi: **to — with someone** declararse por uno, tomar el partido de uno; **I'm siding with nobody** yo no tomo partido.

side arms ['saidɑːmz] npl armas fpl de cinto.

sideboard ['saidbɔːd] n aparador m.

sideboards ['saidbɔːdz] npl (fam: whiskers), **sideburns** ['saidbɜːnz] npl patillas fpl.

sidecar ['saidkɑː*] n sidecar m.

-sided ['saidid] adj de . . . lados, eg **six-sided** de seis lados.

side dish ['saiddiʃ] n entremés m.

side face ['saidfeis] **1** n perfil m. **2** attr, adv de perfil.

side glance ['saidglɑːns] n mirada f de soslayo.

sidekick ['saidkik] n compañero m (de trabajo etc), compinche m.

sidelight ['saidlait] n (Aut etc) luz f lateral; (fig) detalle m incidental, información f incidental (on relativo a).

sideline ['saidlain] n (Rail) apartadero m, vía f secundaria; (Sport, Football etc) línea f lateral, (Tennis etc) línea f de banda; (fig) empleo m suplementario, negocio m suplementario; **it's just a —** es solamente una cosa secundaria; **he breeds parrots as a —** como negocio suplementario se dedica a criar loros.

sidelong ['saidlɔŋ] **1** *adv* de lado, lateralmente; oblicuamente; *glance* de soslayo. **2** *adj* lateral; oblicuo; *glance* de soslayo.

sidereal [sai'di:riəl] *adj* sidéreo.

side road ['saidrəud] *n* calle *f* lateral; calle *f* secundaria.

sidesaddle ['said.sædl] **1** *n* silla *f* de mujer. **2** *adv*: **to ride** — montar a mujeriegas, montar a la inglesa.

side show ['saidʃəu] *n* (*at fair*) barraca *f*, caseta *f* (de feria); (*fig*) función *f* secundaria.

side slip ['saidslip] *n* (*Aer*) deslizamiento *m* lateral.

sidesman ['saidzmən] *n*, *pl* **-men** [mən] acólito *m*.

side-splitting ['said.splitiŋ] *adj joke* divertidísimo.

side-step ['saidstep] **1** *n* paso *m* hacia un lado; (*dodge*) esquivada *f* lateral. **2** *vt* evitar, esquivar; **he neatly —ped the question** esquivó hábilmente la pregunta.

side street ['saidstri:t] *n* calle *f* lateral; calle *f* secundaria.

sidestroke ['saidstrəuk] *n* natación *f* de costado.

sidetable ['said.teibl] *n* trinchero *m*.

sidetrack ['saidtræk] **1** *n* (*Rail*) apartadero *m*, vía *f* muerta; (*fig*) cuestión *f* secundaria. **2** *vt person* apartar de su propósito, desviar del asunto principal; *discussion* conducir por cuestiones de poca importancia; **I got —ed** me aparté del asunto principal, me despisté.

side view ['saidvju:] *n* perfil *m*.

sidewalk ['saidwɔ:k] *n* (*US*) acera *f*.

sidewards ['saidwədz] *adv*, **sideways** ['saidweiz] *adv* de lado; hacia un lado; oblicuamente; **it goes in —** se mete de lado.

side whiskers ['said.wiskəz] *npl* patillas *fpl*.

side wind ['saidwind] *n* viento *m* lateral.

siding ['saidiŋ] *n* (*Rail*) apartadero *m*, vía *f* muerta.

sidle ['saidl] *vi*: **to — up** acercarse cautelosamente (*or* sigilosamente, servilmente; **to** a).

siege [si:dʒ] *n* cerco *m*, sitio *m*; **to lay —** to poner sitio a, sitiar, cercar; *person* asediar; **to raise the —** levantar el cerco.

sienna [si'enə] *n* siena *f*.

Sierra Leone [si'erəli'əun] Sierra *f* Leona.

siesta [si'estə] *n* siesta *f*; **to have a —** dormir la siesta.

sieve [siv] **1** *n* tamiz *m*, cedazo *m*, criba *f*; (*Cook*) coladera *f*. **2** *vt see* **sift**.

sift [sift] *vt* tamizar, cerner, cribar; (*fig*) escudriñar, examinar.

sifter ['siftə*] *n* cedazo *m*, criba *f*.

sigh [sai] **1** *n* suspiro *m*; (*of wind*) susurro *m*; **to breathe a —** of relief suspirar, suspirar aliviado; **to heave a —** dar un suspiro. **2** *vi* suspirar; (*wind*) susurrar; **to — for** suspirar por.

sighing ['saiiŋ] *n* suspiros *mpl*; (*of wind*) susurro *m*.

sight [sait] **1** *n* **(a)** (*faculty, act of seeing*) vista *f*; visión *f*; **second —** doble vista *f*; **long —** presbicia *f*; **to have long —** ser présbita; **short —** miopía *f*; **to have short —** ser miope, ser corto de vista; **30 days' —** (*Comm*) (a) 30 días vista; **at —, at first —** a primera vista; **to hate someone at first —** detestar a uno desde el principio, odiar a uno desde el primer momento; **payable at —** (*Comm*) pagadero a la vista; **to shoot at —** disparar inmediatamente; **to translate at —** traducir sin preparación, traducir sin estudiar el texto (*etc*); **it was love at first —** fue un flechazo; **to know someone by —** conocer a uno de vista; **land in —** ! ¡tierra a la vista!; **to be in** (*or* within) — estar a la vista (*of* de); **our goal is in —** ya vemos la meta; **we are in — of victory** estamos a las puertas de la victoria; **to keep someone in —** no perder a uno de vista; **to find favour in someone's —** (*plan etc*) ser aceptable a uno, (*person*) merecerse la aprobación de uno; **to come into —** aparecer, asomarse; **to heave in(to) —** aparecer; **on — = at —**; **to be out of —** estar invisible, no estar a la vista, no poderse ver; **to drop out of —** desaparecer; **not to let someone out of one's —** no perder a uno de vista, vigilar constantemente a uno; **out of —, out of mind** ojos que no ven, corazón que no siente; **to be lost to —** desaparecer, perderse de vista; **I can't bear the — of blood** ver sangre me da asco; **I can't bear the — of him** no le puedo ver; **to catch — of** (*glimpse*) vislumbrar; (*happen to see*) ver por casualidad; (*on appearance of object*) alcanzar a ver; **to get a — of something** lograr ver algo; **I hate the — of him** no le puedo ver; **to lose —** of someone perder a uno de vista; **to lose — of the fact that . . .** no tener presente el hecho de que . . .; **to lose one's —** perder la vista, quedar ciego; **to regain one's —** recobrar la vista.

(b) (*on gun*) mira *f*, alza *f*, guión *m* de mira; **to set one's —s too high** (*fig*) ser demasiado ambicioso,

pedir demasiado; **to set one's —s on something** resolverse a adquirir (*or* obtener *etc*) algo.

(c) (*scene, spectacle*) vista *f*, escena *f*, espectáculo *m*; **it is a — to see** es cosa digna de verse; **it's a sad —** es una cosa triste; **it's not a pretty —** no es muy agradable para la vista; **it was a — for sore eyes** daba gusto verlo; **his face was a —** ! ¡había que ver la mueca que hizo!, (*after injury etc*) ¡había que ver el estado en que quedaba su cara!

(d) (*spectacle: of person*) **I must look a —** debo parecer horroroso, ¿no?; **doesn't she look a — in that hat!** ¡con ese sombrero parece un espantajo!; **what a — you are!** ¡qué adefesio!

(e) **—s** monumentos *npl*, cosas *fpl* de interés (turístico), curiosidades *fpl*; **the —s of Córdoba** los monumentos de Córdoba; **to see the —s** visitar los monumentos, visitar los puntos de interés.

2 *as adv* (*fam*): **it's a (long) — better than the other one** es muchísimo mejor que el otro; **it's a — dearer** es mucho más caro.

3 *vt* **(a)** (*see*) ver, divisar, avistar; **to — land** ver tierra; **we —ed him coming down the street** le vimos bajar la calle.

(b) **to — a gun** apuntar un cañón.

sighted ['saitid] *adj* que ve, de vista normal; **a blind man and a — companion** un ciego y su compañero de vista normal.

-sighted ['saitid] *adj*: *eg* **weak-sighted** corto de vista, miope.

sighting ['saitiŋ] *n* observación *f*.

sightless ['saitlis] *adj* ciego.

sightly ['saitli] *adj*: **not very —** no muy agradable para la vista.

sight-read ['saitri:d] (*irr: see* **read**) *vti* leer sin preparación; (*Mus*) ejecutar a la primera lectura.

sight-reading ['sait.ri:diŋ] *n* lectura *f* sin preparación; (*Mus*) ejecución *f* a la primera vista.

sightseeing ['sait.si:iŋ] *n* excursionismo *m*, turismo *m*, visita *f* de puntos de interés; **"S— in Ruritania"** "Monumentos *mpl* de Ruritania"; **to go —** visitar los monumentos.

sightseer ['sait.siə*] *n* excursionista *mf*, turista *mf*; visitante *mf*.

sight-singing ['sait.siŋiŋ] *n* (*Mus*) ejecución *f* a la primera lectura.

sign [sain] **1** *n* **(a)** (*with hand etc*) señal *f*, seña *f*; **— of recognition** señal *f* de reconocimiento *m*; **to communicate by —s** hablar por señas; **to make a —** to someone hacer una señal a uno; **to make a rude —** hacer una señal grosera; **to make the — of the Cross** hacer la señal de la cruz; **to make the — of the Cross over something** santiguar algo.

(b) (*indication*) señal *f*, indicio *m*; asomo *m*; (*Med*) síntoma *m*; **the —s of measles are . . .** los síntomas del sarampión son . . .; **at the slightest — of disagreement** ante cualquier asomo de discrepancia; **it's a — of rain** es indicio de lluvia; **it's a sure —** es un indicio inconfundible; **it's a — of the true expert** esto indica el verdadero experto; **it's a — of the times** así son los tiempos actuales; **it's a good —** es buena señal; **to show —s of** dar muestras de, dar indicios de; **as a — of, in — of** en señal de.

(c) (*trace*) huella *f*, vestigio *m*, rastro *m*; **there was no — of it** no quedaba rastro de él; **there was no — of him anywhere** no se le veía en ninguna parte; **there was no — of the former inhabitants** no quedaba huella de los antiguos habitantes; **there is no — of their agreeing** no hay indicio alguno de que se vayan a poner de acuerdo; **there was no — of life in the village** no había vestigio de ser viviente en el pueblo.

(d) (*road* —) señal *f* de carretera; indicador *m*; (*inn* —) letrero *m*; (*shop* —) rótulo *m*; **neon —** letrero *m* de neo; **there was a big — which said "Danger"** había un grande letrero que decía "Peligro de muerte".

(e) (*written symbol*) signo *m*; símbolo *m*; (*Astron, Math, Mus, Zodiac*) signo *m*; **plus —** signo *m* de más, signo de sumar; **positive —** señal *f* positiva, signo *m* positivo.

2 *vt* firmar; **—ed and sealed** firmado y lacrado, firmado y sellado; **to — away** firmar la cesión de, (*fig*) ceder, abandonar; **to — someone on, to — someone up** contratar a uno; **to — something over to someone** firmar el traspaso de algo a uno.

3 *vi* **(a)** **to — to someone to do something** hacer señas a uno para que haga algo, decir a uno por medio de señas que haga algo.

(b) (*with signature*) firmar, firmar su nombre; **to — off** terminar; (*Radio*) terminar el programa, terminar la transmisión; (*Bridge*) terminar la declaración; **to — on, to — up** contratarse, (*Sport etc*) fichar (*for* por); **to — on at an hotel** firmar el registro.

4 *vt*: **he —s himself Joe Soap** usa la firma Joe Soap, firma con el nombre Joe Soap.

signal ['signl] **1 n (a)** (*sign*) señal *f*, seña *f*; **calling —** (*Tel*) señal *f* de llamada; **engaged —, busy —** (*US*) señal *f* de ocupado; **at a pre-arranged —** al hacerse una señal predeterminada; **it was the — for revolt** fue la señal para la sublevación; **to give the — for** dar la señal de (*or* para); **to make a — to someone** hacer una señal a uno.

(b) (*apparatus*) señal *f*; **the — is at red** la señal está en rojo.

(c) S — s (*Mil*) transmisiones *fpl*, cuerpo *m* de transmisiones.

2 *adj* notable, señalado, insigne.

3 *vt*: **to — someone to do something** hacer señas a uno para que haga algo; **to — someone on** hacer señas a uno para que avance; **to — that . . .** comunicar por señales que . . . ; **to — a turn to the right** hacer una señal para hacer saber que uno va a torcer a la derecha; **to — a train** anunciar por señales la llegada de un tren; **the train is —led** la señal indica la llegada del tren.

4 *vi* hacer una señal, hacer señales; (*Aut*) señalizar; **to — before stopping** hacer una señal antes de parar.

signal box ['signlbɔks] *n* garita *f* de señales.
signal flag ['signlflæg] *n* bandera *f* de señales.
signalize ['signəlaiz] *vt* distinguir, señalar.
signal lamp ['signllæmp] *n* reflector *m* de señales, lámpara *f* de señales.
signally ['signəli] *adv* notablemente, señaladamente; **he has — failed to do it** ha sufrido un notable fracaso al tratar de hacerlo.
signalman ['signlmən] *n*, *pl* **—men** [mən] (*Rail*) guardavía *m*.
signatory ['signətəri] **1** *adj* firmante, signatario; **the — powers to an agreement** las potencias firmantes de un acuerdo. **2** *n* firmante *mf*, signatario *m*, a *f*.
signature ['signətʃə*] *n* firma *f*; (*Mus, Typ*) signatura *f*; **key —** (*Mus*) armadura *f*.
signature tune ['signətʃə,tjuːn] *n* sintonía *f*.
signboard ['sainbɔːd] *n* letrero *m*, muestra *f*.
signer ['sainə*] *n* firmante *mf*.
signet ['signit] *n* sello *m*.
signet ring ['signitriŋ] *n* anillo *m* de sello.
significance [sig'nifikəns] *n* significación *f*, significado *m*; trascendencia *f*.
significant [sig'nifikənt] *adj* significativo; trascendente, importante; *improvement etc* sensible; **look expresivo; it is — that . . .** es significativo que . . .
significantly [sig'nifikəntli] *adv* significativamente; expresivamente; **it has improved —** ha mejorado sensiblemente; **it is not — different** no hay diferencia importante; **she looked at me —** me lanzó una mirada expresiva.
signify ['signifai] **1** *vt* significar, querer decir; **it signifies that . . .** significa que . . . ; **what does it —?** ¿qué quiere decir?
2 *vi*: **it does not — no importa; in the wider context it does not —** en el contexto más amplio no tiene importancia.
sign language ['sain,læŋgwidʒ] *n* lenguaje *m* mímico, mímica *f*; **to talk in —** hablar por señas.
sign painter ['sain,peintə*] *n* rotulista *m*.
signpost ['sainpəust] **1** *n* poste *m* indicador, indicador *m* de dirección. **2** *vt* señalizar.
signposting ['sainpəustiŋ] *n* señalización *f*.
sign writer ['sain,raitə*] *n* rotulista *m*.
silage ['sailidʒ] *n* ensilaje *m*.
silence ['sailəns] **1** *n* silencio *m*; **—!** ¡silencio!; **in dead —** en el silencio más absoluto; **there was — hubo un silencio; — gives consent** quien calla otorga; **to keep radio —** mantener el silencio radiofónico; **to pass over something in —** silenciar algo; pasar algo por alto; **to reduce someone to —** hacer callar a uno; **to reduce guns to —** reducir los cañones al silencio.
2 *vt* hacer callar, acallar; *guns etc* reducir al silencio; (*Tech*) silenciar; *critic* imponer silencio a.
silencer ['sailənsə*] *n* silenciador *m*.
silent ['sailənt] *adj* silencioso; callado; *film, letter* mudo; **to be —, to keep —, to remain —** callarse, guardar silencio, permanecer silencioso; **to become —** callarse, enmudecer; **it was as — as the grave** había un silencio profundo.
silently ['sailəntli] *adv* silenciosamente, en silencio.

silhouette [,silu:'et] **1** *n* silueta *f*. **2** *vt* destacar, hacer aparecer en silueta; **to be —d against** destacarse contra, destacarse sobre.
silica ['silikə] *n* sílice *f*.
silicate ['silikit] *n* silicato *m*.
siliceous [si'liʃəs] *adj* silíceo.
silicon ['silikən] *n* silicio *m*.
silicosis [,sili'kəusis] *n* silicosis *f*.
silk [silk] **1** *n* seda *f*; **artificial —** seda *f* artificial; **raw —** seda *f* en rama; **to take —** (*approx*) tomar la toga, empezar a ejercer de abogado. **2** *adj*, *attr* de seda; **— industry** industria *f* sedera.
silken ['silkən] *adj* (*of silk*) de seda; (*like silk*) sedoso, sedeño; *manner, voice* suave, mimoso.
silkiness ['silkinis] *n* sedosidad *f*, lo sedoso; suavidad *f*, lo mimoso.
silk moth ['silkmɔθ] *n* mariposa *f* de seda.
silk raising ['silk,reiziŋ] *n* sericultura *f*.
silk-stocking ['silk'stɔkiŋ] *adj* (*US*) aristocrático.
silkworm ['silkwəːm] *n* gusano *m* de seda.
silky ['silki] *adj* sedoso.
sill [sil] *n* antepecho *m*; (*window—*) alféizar *m*; (*door—*) umbral *m*.
silliness ['silinis] *n* tontería *f*, estupidez *f*; insensatez *f*; lo absurdo.
silly ['sili] *adj* *person* tonto, bobo, estúpido; *act* tonto, insensato; *idea etc* absurdo; **you — child !, you big —!** ¡bobo!; **don't be —** no seas bobo; **that was — of you, that was a — thing to do** eso fue una estupidez; **I've done a — thing** he hecho una tontería, he sido un tonto; **I feel — in this hat** temo hacer el ridículo con este sombrero; **you look — carrying that fish** pareces un tonto llevando ese pez; **to knock someone —** (*fam: beat up*) dar una paliza a uno; **the blow knocked him —** el golpe le dejó sin sentido; **to make someone look —** poner a uno en ridículo.
silo ['sailəu] *n* silo *m*, ensiladora *f*.
silt [silt] **1** *n* sedimento *m*, aluvión *m*. **2** *vt* (*also to — up*) obstruir con sedimentos. **3** *vi* (*also to — up*) obstruirse con sedimentos.
silver ['silvə*] **1** *n* plata *f*. **2** *adj*, *attr* de plata, plateado. **3** *vt* *metal* platear (*also fig*); *mirror* azogar; *hair* blanquear.
silver birch ['silvə'bəːtʃ] *n* abedul *m* (plateado).
silver fir ['silvə'fəː*] *n* pinabete *m*.
silverfish ['silvəfiʃ] *n* pescadito *m* de plata, lepisma *f*.
silver foil ['silvə'fɔil] *n* hoja *f* de plata; (*paper*) papel *m* de plata.
silver fox ['silvə'fɔks] *n* zorro *m* plateado.
silver gilt ['silvə'gilt] *n* plata *f* dorada.
silver-grey ['silvə'grei] *adj* gris perla.
silver-haired ['silvə'heəd] *adj* de pelo entrecano.
silver paper ['silvə'peipə*] *n* papel *m* de plata.
silver-plate ['silvə'pleit] *vt* platear.
silver plating ['silvə'pleitiŋ] *n* plateado *m*.
silversmith ['silvəsmiθ] *n* platero *m*; **—'s (shop)** platería *f*.
silver-tongued ['silvə'tʌŋd] *adj* elocuente, con el pico de oro.
silverware ['silvəweə*] *n* plata *f*, vajilla *f* de plata.
silvery ['silvəri] *adj* plateado; *voice etc* argentino.
simian ['simiən] *adj* símico.
similar ['similə*] *adj* parecido, semejante; **A and B are —, A is — to B** A y B se parecen; **this is — to what happened before** esto es parecido a lo que pasó antes.
similarity [,simi'læriti] *n* parecido *m*, semejanza *f*; **there is a certain —** hay cierto parecido.
similarly ['similəli] *adv* de un modo parecido; **and —, . . .** y asimismo, . . .
simile ['simili] *n* símil *m*.
similitude [si'militjuːd] *n* similitud *f*.
simmer ['simə*] **1** *n*: **to be on the —, to keep on the —** hervir a fuego lento.
2 *vt* cocer a fuego lento.
3 *vi* hervir a fuego lento; (*fig*) estar hirviendo, estar a punto de estallar; **to — down** (*fig*) calmarse poco a poco, tranquilizarse lentamente; **— down!** ¡cálmate!; **to — over** irse, desbordarse, (*fig*) estallar.
Simon ['saimən] *m* Simón; **simple —** simple *m*, simplón *m*.
simony ['saiməni] *n* simonía *f*.
simp [simp] *n* (*US sl*) bobo *m*, a *f*.
simper ['simpə*] **1** *n* sonrisa *f* afectada, sonrisa *f* boba. **2** *vi* sonreírse afectadamente, sonreírse bobamente; **"Yes", she —ed** "Sí", dijo sonriendo afectada.
simpering ['simpəriŋ] *adj* afectado; bobo.
simperingly ['simpəriŋli] *adv* afectadamente; bobamente.
simple ['simpl] *adj* **(a)** (*uncomplicated, easy, plain*) sencillo; **it's as — as ABC** es de lo más sencillo;

the — **life** la vida sencilla; **I'm a — soul** soy un hombre sencillo; **it's very —** es muy sencillo; **it's — madness** es una locura ni más ni menos; **he's a — craftsman** es un simple artesano.

(**b**) (*not compound*) *interest, sentence etc* simple.

(**c**) (*foolish*) simple; imbécil; (*innocent*) ingenuo, inocente; crédulo; **he's a bit —** es muy bobo, está algo tocado; **I am not so — as to believe that . . .** yo no soy lo bastante ingenuo como para creer que . . .

simple-hearted ['simpl'hɑːtid] *adj* candoroso, ingenuo.

simple-minded ['simpl'maindid] *adj* candoroso, ingenuo; (*pej*) estúpido; **I am not so —** no soy tan ingenuo; **in their — way** en su modo ingenuo.

simple-mindedness ['simpl'maindidnis] *n* candor *m*, ingenuidad *f*; (*pej*) estupidez *f*.

simpleton ['simpltən] *n* inocentón *m*.

simplicity [sim'plisiti] *n* sencillez *f*; simpleza *f*, ingenuidad *f*, credulidad *f*; **it's — itself** es de lo más sencillo.

simplifiable ['simplifaiəbl] *adj* simplificable.

simplification [ˌsimplifi'keiʃən] *n* simplificación *f*.

simplify ['simplifai] *vt* simplificar.

simply ['simpli] *adv* sencillamente; simplemente; **a — furnished room** un cuarto amueblado sencillamente; **I — said that . . .** dije sencillamente que . . .; **it's — impossible!** ¡es sencillamente imposible!; **but you — must!** ¡pero no tienes más remedio que hacerlo!; **I was — amazed** me quedé completamente asombrado.

simulacrum [ˌsimju'leikrəm] *n* simulacro *m*.

simulate ['simjuleit] *vt* simular.

simulation [ˌsimju'leiʃən] *n* simulación *f*.

simultaneity [ˌsiməltə'niəti] *n* simultaneidad *f*.

simultaneous [ˌsiməl'teiniəs] *adj* simultáneo.

simultaneously [ˌsiməl'teiniəsli] *adv* simultáneamente.

sin [sin] **1** *n* pecado *m*; **the seven deadly —s** los siete pecados capitales; **mortal —** pecado *m* mortal; **original —** pecado *m* original; **like — con** vehemencia; **for my —s** por mis pecados; **his besetting — is . . .** su mayor defecto es . . ., tiene la manía de . . .; **it would be a — to +** *infin* sería un crimen + *infin*, sería lamentable que + *subj*; **to fall into —** caer en el pecado; **to live in —** vivir juntos, vivir como marido y mujer sin serlo.

2 *vi* pecar; **he was more —ned against than —ning** era más bien el ofendido y no el ofensor.

Sinbad ['sinbæd] *m* Simbad; **— the Sailor** Simbad el marinero.

since [sins] **1** *adv* desde entonces, después; **ever — desde** entonces; **a long time — hace** mucho (tiempo); **not long —, a short time — hace** poco.

2 *prep* desde; a partir de, después de; **— Monday** desde el lunes; **ever — 1900** siempre desde 1900; **todo** el tiempo de 1900 acá; **how long is it — the accident?** ¿cuánto tiempo ha pasado desde el accidente?; *see* **then.**

3 *conj* (**a**) (*time*) desde que; **— I arrived** desde que llegué; **it is a week — he left** hace una semana que salió, salió hace una semana.

(**b**) (*because*) ya que, puesto que; **— you can't come** puesto que Vd no puede venir; **— he is Spanish** como él es español, siendo él español.

sincere [sin'siə*] *adj* sincero.

sincerely [sin'siəli] *adv* sinceramente; **Yours — le** saluda afectuosamente.

sincerity [sin'seriti] *n* sinceridad *f*; **in all — con** toda sinceridad, con toda franqueza.

sine [sain] *n* (*Math*) seno *m*.

sinecure ['sainikjuə*] *n* sinecura *f*.

sinew ['sinju:] *n* tendón *m*; **—s of** (*fig*) nervio *m*, fibra *f*; recursos *mpl*; **the —s of war** los pertrechos de guerra.

sinewy ['sinju:i] *adj* nervudo, nervioso, vigoroso.

sinful ['sinful] *adj person* pecador; *act, thought* pecaminoso; *town etc* lleno de pecados, inmundo.

sinfully ['sinfəli] *adv* de modo pecaminoso.

sinfulness ['sinfulnis] *n* maldad *f*; lo pecaminoso.

sing [sin] (*irr: pret* **sang,** *ptp* **sung**) **1** *vt* cantar; **— us a song!** ¡cántanos algo!; **to — a child to sleep** arrullar a un niño, adormecer a un niño cantando.

2 *vi* contar; (*of bird*) trinar, gorjear; (*of ears*) zumbar; (*of wind*) susurrar; (*of kettle*) silbar (al hervir); **to — flat, to — out of tune** desafinar, cantar mal; **to — small** achantarse, ser más humilde; **to — out** cantar más fuerte; (*fig*) vocear, gritar; **if you want anything — out** si necesitas algo me llamas; **to — up** cantar más fuerte; **— up!** ¡más fuerte!

Singapore [ˌsingə'pɔː*] Singapur.

singe [sindʒ] *vt* chamuscar; *hair* quemar las puntas de.

singer ['siŋə*] *n* cantor *m*, ora *f*; (*professional*) cantante *mf*; (*in cabaret etc*) vocalista *mf*.

Singhalese [ˌsiŋgə'liːz] **1** *adj* cingalés. **2** *n* cingalés *m*, esa *f*.

singing ['siŋiŋ] *n* canto *m*; cantos *mpl*, canciones *fpl*; (*in the ears*) zumbido *m*.

single ['siŋgl] **1** *adj* único, solo; (*not double*) simple, sencillo; *bed, room* individual; *ticket, spacing* sencillo; *combat* singular; (*unmarried*) soltero; **every — day** todos los días sin excepción; **every — book I looked at** todos los libros que miré sin excepción; **not a — one spoke up** no habló ni uno solo; **there was a — rose in the garden** en el jardín había una rosa única; **she's a — woman** es soltera; **she remained —** siguió sin casarse.

2 —**s** *npl* (*Tennis*) juego *m* de individuales; **ladies' —s** individual *m* femenino; **men's —s** individual *m* masculino.

3 *vt*: **to — out** (*choose*) escoger; (*distinguish*) distinguir, singularizar; **he was —d out to lead the team** se le escogió para ser capitán del equipo; **to — (out) plants** entresacar plantas.

single-barrelled ['siŋgl'bærəld] *adj gun* de cañón único.

single-breasted ['siŋgl'brestid] *adj jacket* sin cruzar.

single-cell(ed) ['siŋgl'sel(d)] *adj* (*Bio*) unicelular.

single-chamber ['siŋgl'tʃeimbə*] *adj* (*Pol*) unicameral.

single-engined ['siŋgl'endʒind] *adj* monomotor.

single-entry ['siŋgl'entri] *n* partida *f* simple.

single-handed ['siŋgl'hændid] *adj, adv* sin ayuda (de nadie).

single-hearted ['siŋgl'hɑːtid] *adj* resuelto, firme.

single-masted ['siŋgl'mɑːstid] *adj* de palo único.

single-minded ['siŋgl'maindid] *adj* resuelto, firme.

singleness ['siŋglnis] *n*: **— of purpose** resolución *f*, firmeza *f*.

single-party ['siŋgl'pɑːti] *adj state etc* de partido único.

single-seater ['siŋgl'siːtə*] *n* (*Aer*) monoplaza *m*.

singlet ['siŋglit] *n* camiseta *f*.

singleton ['siŋgltən] *n* (*Bridge*): **to have a — tener** un semi-fallo (*in hearts* a corazones); **to play one's —** jugar la única carta que tiene uno de un palo.

single-track ['siŋgl'træk] *adj* (*Rail*) de vía única.

singly ['siŋgli] *adv* uno a uno, individualmente, separadamente.

singsong ['sin.sɔŋ] **1** *adj tone* monótono, cantarín.

2 *n* (*tone*) salmodia *f*, sonsonete *m*; (*songs*) concierto *m* improvisado; **to get together for a —** reunirse para cantar (canciones populares, folklóricas *etc*).

singular ['siŋgjulə*] **1** *adj* (**a**) (*Gram*) singular; **a — noun** un sustantivo en singular.

(**b**) (*odd*) raro, extraño, singular; **a most — occurrence** un acontecimiento muy extraño; **how very —!** ¡qué raro!

2 *n* singular; **in the —** en singular.

singularity [ˌsiŋgju'læriti] *n* singularidad *f*.

singularly ['siŋgjuləli] *adv* singularmente; **a — inappropriate remark** una observación de lo más inoportuno.

Sinhalese [ˌsinə'liːz] *see* **Singhalese.**

sinister ['sinistə*] *adj* siniestro.

sink[1] [sink] (*irr: pret* **sank,** *ptp* **sunk**) **1** *vt* (**a**) *ship* hundir, echar a pique; sumergir; (*fig*) *theory* destruir; acabar con; *person* acabar con.

(**b**) *mine* abrir, excavar; *hole* hacer, excavar; *well* perforar; *drink* beberse; **to — a post 2 metres in the ground** fijar un poste 2 metros bajo tierra; **to — one's teeth into something** hincar los dientes en algo; **he can — a glass of beer in 12 seconds** se bebe una caña de cerveza en 12 segundos.

(**c**) *differences* suprimir, olvidar; **to — one's identity in that of a group** olvidar su individualidad en la solidaridad de un grupo.

(**d**) **to — money in an enterprise** invertir dinero en una empresa.

(**e**) (*sunk*) **to be sunk in thought** estar absorto en la meditación, estar ensimismado; **to be sunk in depression** estar sumido en el abatimiento; **to be sunk in debt** estar agobiado por las deudas; **now we're sunk!** (*fam*) ¡estamos perdidos!

2 *vi* (**a**) (*of ship etc*) hundirse; irse a pique, naufragar; sumergirse; **to — by the bow** hundirse de proa; **to — to the bottom** ir al fondo; **it —s instead of floating** se hunde en lugar de flotar; **he was left to — or swim** (*fig*) dejaron de prestarle ayuda, dejaron de interesarse por su suerte.

(**b**) **to — in** (*fig*) penetrar, calar; **to let the paint — in** dejar que penetre la pintura; **the water —s in** in time con el tiempo va penetrando el agua; **his words seem to have sunk in** sus palabras parecen haber surtido efecto, parece que sus palabras han hecho mella.

(c) (*subside*) hundirse; (*building, land etc*) hundirse; (*fire*) estarse apagando, morir; (*person*) debilitarse, morirse; (*sun*) ponerse; **he sank in the mud up to his knees** se hundió en el lodo hasta las rodillas; **to — (down) into a chair** dejarse caer pesadamente en una silla; **to — into insignificance** perder su importancia; **to — deeper into degradation** hundirse cada vez más en la degradación, envilecerse más y más; **to — into poverty** caer en la miseria; **to — to one's knees** caer de rodillas; **his voice sank to a whisper** pasó a hablar en tono muy bajo; **my spirits sank, my heart sank** se me cayeron las alas del corazón; **to — out of sight** desaparecer.

(d) (*in quantity*) disminuir; (*in value*) perder su valor; (*decline*) declinar, menguar; **he has sunk in my estimation** ha perdido mi estima; **the shares have sunk to 3 dollars** las acciones han bajado a 3 dólares.

sink² [siŋk] n fregadero m, pila f; (*Tech*) sumidero m; (*fig*) sentina f; **— of iniquity** sentina f, lugar m de todos los vicios; *see kitchen* —.

sinker ['siŋkə*] n (*in fishing*) plomo m.

sinking ['siŋkiŋ] 1 adj: **that — feeling** esa sensación de que todo se está acabando, esa sensación del desastre inminente; **with — heart** con la muerte en el alma.
2 n hundimiento m.

sinking fund ['siŋkiŋfʌnd] n fondo m de amortización.

sink unit ['siŋk'juːnit] n lavadero m, fregadero m (de cocina).

sinner ['sinə*] n pecador m, ora f.

Sino... ['sainəu] adj sino..., chino...

sinuosity [ˌsinju'ɔsiti] n sinuosidad f.

sinuous ['sinjuəs] adj sinuoso.

sinus ['sainəs] n (*Anat*) seno m.

sinusitis [ˌsainə'saitis] n sinusitis f.

sip [sip] 1 n sorbo m. 2 vt sorber, beber a sorbitos.

siphon ['saifən] 1 n sifón m. 2 vt (*also to — off, to — out*) sacar con sifón; **to — off** (*fig*) quitar poco a poco, reducir gradualmente.

sir [sə:*] n (*in direct address*) señor m; (*as title*) sir m; **yes, —** (*Mil*) sí, mi capitán (*etc*); **S—** (*to editor of paper*) señor director; **Dear S—** muy señor mío; **my dear —!, my good —!** ¡pero amigo...!

sire ['saiə*] 1 n (*Zool*) padre m; (*stallion*) semental m, caballo m padre; **S—** (*to monarch: arch*) Señor m.
2 vt ser el padre de; engendrar; **he —d 49 children** tuvo 49 hijos; **the horse A, —d by B** el caballo A, cuyo padre fue B.

siren ['saiərən] n (*all senses*) sirena f.

Sirius ['siriəs] m Sirio.

sirloin ['sə:lbin] n solomillo m.

sirocco [si'rɔkəu] n siroco m.

sisal ['saisəl] n henequén m, fique m, pita f.

sissy ['sisi] n marica m, mariquita m.

sister ['sistə*] n hermana f; (*Eccl*) hermana f, (*before name*) Sor; (*Med*) enfermera f, hermana f enfermera, (*of higher rank*) enfermera f jefa.

sisterhood ['sistəhud] n hermandad f.

sister-in-law ['sistərinlɔ:] n cuñada f.

sisterly ['sistəli] adj de hermana, como hermana.

sister ship ['sistəʃip] n buque m gemelo; **X is the — of Z** X es hermano gemelo de Z.

Sisyphus ['sisifəs] m Sísifo.

sit [sit] (*irr: pret and ptp sat*) 1 vt (a) sentar; **to — someone in a chair** sentar a uno en una silla; **to — a child on one's knees** sentar a un niño sobre las rodillas; **to — an invalid up** ayudar a un enfermo a incorporarse en la cama.

(b) **to — a horse well** montar bien (a caballo).

(c) **to — an examination** presentarse a un examen; **to — an examination in French** examinarse de francés.

(d) **to — out a dance** no bailar; **let's — this one out** no nos bailemos esta vez; **to — a lecture out** aguantar hasta el fin de una conferencia, quedarse hasta el fin de una conferencia; **to — someone out** resistir durante más tiempo que uno, demostrar tener más aguante que uno.

2 vi (a) (*general sense: act*) sentarse, (*state*) estar sentado; **— here** siéntate aquí; **I was —ting there** estaba sentado allí; **— by me** siéntate a mi lado, siéntate conmigo; **to — at home all day** pasar todo el día en casa (sin hacer nada); **to — at table** sentarse a la mesa; **to — with someone** estar con uno; **to — still** permanecer sentado sin moverse;

— still! ¡quieto!; **to — tight** no moverse, (*fig*) no hacer nada.

(b) (*of assembly*) reunirse; celebrar junta, celebrar sesión; **the House sat all night** la sesión de la Cámara duró toda la noche; **the House sat for 22 hours** la Cámara tuvo una sesión de 22 horas.

(c) (*of bird, insect*) posarse; (*of hen*) empollar, incubar; **the hen is —ting on 12 eggs** la gallina empolla 12 huevos; **the pheasant —s pretty close** el faisán queda inmóvil y casi invisible.

(d) (*fig: of dress*) caer, sentar (*on someone* a uno); **that pie —s heavy on the stomach** la empanada esa no me sienta; **how —s the wind?** ¿de dónde sopla el viento?

(e) (*with adv or prep*) **to — back** sentarse cómodamente; **to — back (and do nothing)** cruzarse de brazos; **to — down** sentarse; **do — down!** ¡siéntese, por favor!; **to — down to table** sentarse a la mesa; **to — down to a big supper** sentarse a comer una cena fuerte; **to — down under an insult** aguantar un insulto; **to — for a painter** posar para un pintor, servir de modelo a un pintor; **she sat for Reynolds** se hizo retratar por Reynolds; **to — for one's portrait** hacerse retratar, hacerse un retrato; **to — for an examination** presentarse a un examen; **to — for Bury** (*Pol*) representar a Bury, ser diputado por Bury; **to — in Parliament** ser diputado (*in Spain*: a Cortes), ser miembro del parlamento; **to — in on talks** asistir a una conferencia (sin ser delegado oficial); **to — on** (*adv*) permanecer sentado; **to — on a committee** ser miembro de un comité, formar parte de un comité; **to — on a matter** dar carpetazo a un asunto; considerar un asunto; **to — on someone** (*fam: silence*) hacer callar a uno, (*suppress*) reprimir a uno, (*be hard on*) ser severo con uno; **to — over one's work** trabajar tenazmente; seguir trabajando sin descansar; **to — up** (*after lying*) incorporarse; **to — up in bed** incorporarse en la cama; **to — up with a start** incorporarse sobresaltado; **to — up** (*straighten oneself*) ponerse derecho, erguirse en la silla; **so I sat up and took notice** así que empecé a prestar atención; **to make someone — up** dar en qué pensar a uno; impresionar fuertemente a uno; sorprender a uno; **to — up to the table** sentarse a la mesa; **to — up** (*late*) velar, estar sin acostarse; **to — up for someone** esperar a que vuelva uno, estar sin acostarse hasta que vuelva uno; **to — up with a child** velar a un niño.

3 vr: **to — oneself down** sentarse.

sit-down ['sitdaun] n (*fam*) culo m, trasero m; **— strike** huelga f de brazos caídos.

site [sait] 1 n sitio m, local m; (*for building*) solar m; **the — of the battle** el lugar de la batalla; **a late Roman —** un lugar de ocupación romana tardía; **the only — for the plant in Spain** la única localidad de la planta en España.
2 vt situar; localizar; **a badly —d building** un edificio mal situado.

sit-in ['sitin] n (*fam*) manifestación f de brazos caídos.

siting ['saitiŋ] n situación f, localidad f; **the — of new industries** la localización de las nuevas industrias.

sitter ['sitə*] n (*Art*) modelo mf de pintor; (*sl*) cosa f fácil; **it was a —** (*Sport*) fue un gol (*etc*) que se canta; **you missed a —** erraste un tiro de lo más fácil.

sitting ['sitiŋ] 1 adj sentado; **a — bird** una ave que está posada, una ave que está inmóvil; **a — hen** una gallina clueca.
2 n (*Pol etc*) sesión f; (*of eggs*) nidada f; **— and standing room** sitio m para sentarse y para estar de pie; **at one —** en una sesión; de una vez, de un tirón; **second — for lunch** segundo turno m de comedor.

sitting room ['sitiŋrum] n sala f de estar.

situate ['sitjueit] vt situar.

situated ['sitjueitid] adj situado; **it is — in the High Street** está situado en la Calle Mayor; **how are you —?** ¿cuál es su situación actual?; **a pleasantly — house** una casa bien situada.

situation [ˌsitju'eiʃən] n situación f; (*job*) puesto m, colocación f, empleo m; **"S—s wanted"** "se busca trabajo"; **to save the —** estar a la altura de las circunstancias.

six [siks] 1 adj seis; **it's — of one and half-a-dozen of the other** lo mismo da; es tanto lo uno como lo otro.
2 n seis m; **to be at —es and sevens** (*things*) estar en confusión, estar en desorden, (*persons*) estar reñidos.

sixfold ['siksfəuld] **1** adj séxtuplo. **2** adv seis veces.

six-footer ['siks'futə*] n hombre m que mide 6 pies.

sixpence ['sikspəns] n 6 peniques mpl.

sixpenny ['sikspəni] adj de 6 peniques; (pej) insignificante, inútil.

six-shooter ['siks'ʃuːtə*] n revólver m de 6 tiros.

sixteen ['siks'tiːn] adj dieciséis.

sixteenth ['siks'tiːnθ] adj decimosexto.

sixth [siksθ] **1** adj sexto. **2** n sexto m, sexta parte f.

sixtieth ['sikstiiθ] adj sexagésimo.

sixty ['siksti] adj sesenta; the sixties (eg 1960s) los años sesenta; to be in one's sixties tener más de sesenta años.

sixtyish ['sikstiiʃ] adj sesentón.

size¹ [saiz] **1** n tamaño m; dimensiones fpl; extensión f; envergadura f, magnitud f; (of person) talla f, estatura f; (measurement: of gloves, shoes etc) número m; (of dress, shirt etc) talla f; a hall of immense — una sala de vastas dimensiones; the — of the problem daunted him la magnitud del problema le asombró; the great — of the operation la gran envergadura de la operación; it's the — of a brick es del tamaño de un ladrillo; what — is it? ¿de qué tamaño es?, ¿cómo es de grande?; it's quite a — es bastante grande; it's 2 —s too big yo lo quisiera 2 números más pequeño; he's about your — tiene más o menos la talla de Vd; that's about the — of it eso es lo que puedo decirle acerca del asunto, (as answer) así es; to be of a — ser del mismo tamaño, tener el mismo tamaño; they're all of a — tienen todos el mismo tamaño; to cut something to — cortar algo del tamaño preciso que se necesita; to cut someone down to — bajarle los humos a uno, hacer a uno darse cuenta de su escasa importancia; it is drawn to natural — está dibujado a tamaño natural; what — shoe do you take? ¿qué número calza Vd?; I take — 9 uso el número 9; what — shirt do you take? ¿qué talla de camisa es la de Vd?

2 vt clasificar según el tamaño; to — someone up medir a uno con la vista; to — up a problem formarse una idea de un problema, hacer un estudio preliminar de un problema; I can't quite — him up no le entiendo del todo.

size² [saiz] **1** n cola f, apresto m. **2** vt encolar, aprestar.

sizeable ['saizəbl] adj bastante grande, considerable, importante; a — sum una cantidad importante; it's quite a — house es una casa bastante grande.

sizzle ['sizl] vi chisporrotear, churruscar, crepitar; (in frying) crepitar al freírse.

sizzling ['sizliŋ] **1** adj attack, shot etc fulminante. **2** n chisporroteo m, crepitación f.

skate¹ [skeit] n (Fish) raya f.

skate² [skeit] **1** n patín m. **2** vi patinar; it went skating across the floor se deslizó velozmente sobre el suelo; I —d into a tree di contra un árbol.

skater ['skeitə*] n patinador m, ora f.

skating ['skeitiŋ] n patinaje m.

skating rink ['skeitiŋriŋk] n pista f de patinaje.

skedaddle [ski'dædl] vi (fam) largarse (fam), marcharse; they —d in all directions huyeron por todos lados.

skein [skein] n madeja f; a tangled — (fig) un asunto enmarañado.

skeletal ['skelitl] adj esquelético.

skeleton ['skelitn] **1** n (Anat) esqueleto m; (fig) esquema m, plan m; (Tech) armazón f, armadura f; the — at the feast el aguafiestas; — in the cupboard secreto m vergonzoso de la familia, parte f de la historia familiar que se oculta a los de fuera. **2** adj staff etc reducido; outline esquemático.

skeleton key ['skelitn.kiː] n llave f maestra, ganzúa f.

skeptic ['skeptik] (US) see sceptic.

sketch [sketʃ] **1** n (rough draft) esbozo m, boceto m, bosquejo m, croquis m (for de); (drawing) dibujo m, diseño m; (Theat) pieza f corta (esp satírica, jocosa); — for a costume diseño m de un traje. **2** vt (outline) esbozar, trazar a grandes líneas; (draw) bosquejar, dibujar; hacer un dibujo de; he —ed in the details for me me explicó los detalles.

sketchbook ['sketʃbuk] n libro m de dibujos.

sketchily ['sketʃili] adv incompletamente, superficialmente.

sketching ['sketʃiŋ] n dibujo m, arte m de dibujar.

sketching pad ['sketʃiŋ.pæd] n bloc m de dibujo.

sketchy ['sketʃi] adj incompleto, superficial.

skew [skjuː] **1** n: to be on the — estar desviado, estar sesgado; estar puesto mal.
2 adj sesgado, oblicuo, torcido.
3 vt sesgar, desviar; poner mal.
4 vi (also to — round) desviarse, ponerse al sesgo, torcerse.

skewer ['skjuə*] **1** n broqueta f, espetón m. **2** vt espetar; pasar una broqueta por.

skew-whiff [,skjuː'wif] adj (fam) sesgado, oblicuo, torcido; to be on — estar puesto mal.

ski [skiː] **1** n esquí m; (Aer) patín m. **2** vi esquiar.

ski boot ['skiːbuːt] n bota f de esquí.

skid [skid] **1** n (Aut etc) patinazo m, derrape m, deslizamiento m; (Aer) patín m; to put the —s under someone (fam) deshacerse de uno con maña, lograr con maña que uno abandone un puesto (etc).
2 vi (Aut etc) patinar, derrapar; (of person) resbalar; it went —ded across the floor se deslizó velozmente sobre el suelo; I —ded into a tree di contra un árbol.

skiddoo [ski'duː] vi (US sl) largarse (fam).

skidmark ['skidmaːk] n huella f del patinazo.

skidproof ['skidpruːf] adv a prueba de patinazos.

skid row ['skid'rəu] n (US) barrio m de mala vida; calles donde se refugian los borrachos, drogadictos incurables etc.

skier ['skiːə*] n esquiador m, ora f.

skiff [skif] n esquife m.

skiing ['skiːiŋ] n esquí m; to go — ir a esquiar.

skijump ['skiːdʒʌmp] n pista f para saltos de esquí.

skijumping ['skiː.dʒʌmpiŋ] n salto m de esquí.

skilift ['skiːlift] n telesquí m, telesilla m.

skilful ['skilful] adj hábil, diestro, experto (at, in en).

skilfully ['skilfəli] adv hábilmente, diestramente.

skilfulness ['skilfulnis] n habilidad f, destreza f.

skill [skil] n habilidad f, destreza f; pericia f; (technique) arte m, técnica f; his — at billiards su habilidad en el billar; he shows no small — muestra tener no poca habilidad; we could make good use of his — podríamos utilizar su pericia; it's a — that has to be acquired es una técnica que se aprende.

skilled [skild] adj (skilful) hábil, diestro; man cualificado, especializado; work especializado, que requiere técnicas especiales; to be — in a craft ser perito en una artesanía; a man — in diplomacy un hombre de gran habilidad diplomática.

skillet ['skilit] n sartén f; cacerola f de mango largo.

skim [skim] **1** vt espumar; milk desnatar, quitar la nata a; (graze) rozar, rasar, casi tocar al pasar.
2 vi: to — over pasar rasando, pasar casi tocando; to — through examinar superficialmente, hojear.

skimp [skimp] **1** vt escatimar; work chapucear, frangollar.
2 vi economizar, ahorrar lo que puede.

skimpy ['skimpi] adj allowance etc escaso, pequeño; skirt etc muy abreviado, muy corto; person tacaño.

skin [skin] **1** n (a) (of person) piel f; (with reference to texture etc) cutis m; by the — of one's teeth por los pelos; he's nothing but — and bone está en los huesos; to have a thick — ser bastante insensible, poderlo aguantar todo; to have a thin — ser muy susceptible; I've got you under my — el recuerdo de ti no se me quita de la cabeza; to save one's — salvar el pellejo; to wear wool next to one's — llevar prenda de lana sobre la piel.
  (b) (Zool) piel f, pellejo m; (as hide) piel f, cuero m; (for wine) odre m.
  (c) (Bot) piel f, pellejo m; corteza f.
  (d) (fig: on milk) capa f de nata; (for duplicating) clisé m; (Aer, Naut) revestimiento m.
2 attr de la piel; — disease enfermedad f cutánea, enfermedad f dérmica.
3 vt animal despellejar, desollar; fruit pelar, quitar la piel a; tree descortezar; to — someone (fam) despellejar a uno, esquilmar a uno; to — someone alive desollar vivo a uno; to — one's knee despellejarse la rodilla.
4 vi: to — over (Med) cicatrizarse.

skin-deep ['skin'diːp] adj superficial; beauty is only — la hermosura es cosa pasajera, la hermosura atañe a lo superficial.

skin diving ['skin.daiviŋ] n natación f submarina, exploración f submarina, pesca f submarina.

skinflint ['skinflint] n tacaño m, cicatero m.

skinful ['skinful] n (fam): to have had a — llevar una copa de más, haber bebido más de la cuenta.

skin game ['skingeim] n estafa f.

skin grafting ['skin.graːftiŋ] n injerto m de piel.

-skinned [skind] adj de piel . . ., eg dark-skinned de piel morena; rough-skinned de piel áspera.

skinner ['skinə*] n peletero m.

skinny ['skini] adj flaco, magro, escuálido, descarnado.

skint [skint] adj (sl): to be — no tener un céntimo.

skintight ['skintait] adj muy ajustado.

skip¹ [skip] **1** n brinco m, salto m (pequeño).
2 vt passage (in reading etc) omitir, pasar por alto; to — lunch saltarse el almuerzo, no almorzar;

— it! ¡déjalo!, ¡no te preocupes más de eso!; oh, — it! bueno, ¡no importa!

3 *vi* (a) brincar, saltar; (*with rope*) saltar a la comba; to — with joy brincar de alegría; to — from one subject to another saltar de un tema a otro; the book —s about a lot el libro da muchos saltos; to — over something saltar por encima de algo; (*omit*) omitir algo, pasar algo por alto.

(b) (*fam*) largarse (*fam*), escabullirse.

skip² [skip] *n* (*cage*) jaula *f*; (*bucket*) cuba *f*; (*basket*) cesta *f*, canasta *f*.

ski pants ['skiː'pænts] *npl* pantalones *mpl* de esquí.

skipper ['skipə*] *n* capitán *m* (*also Sport*); (*Naut*) patrón *m*; well, you're the — bueno, tú eres el jefe.

skipping rope ['skipiŋrəup] *n* cuerda *f* (de saltar), comba *f*.

skirl [skəːl] *n* (*Scot*): the — of the pipes el son de la gaita, la música de la gaita.

skirmish ['skəːmiʃ] **1** *n* escaramuza *f*. **2** *vi* escaramuzar.

skirmisher ['skəːmiʃə*] *n* escaramuzador *m*.

skirt [skəːt] **1** *n* falda *f*; (*of coat etc*) faldón *m*; (*sl*) falda *f*.

2 *vt* (*surround*) ceñir, rodear; (*go round*) orillar, ladear, seguir el borde (*or* la orilla) de; (*avoid*) evitar entrar en, mantenerse a distancia de; we —ed Seville to the north pasamos al norte de Sevilla.

skirting (board) ['skəːtiŋ(bɔːd)] *n* rodapié *m*.

ski run ['skiːrʌn] *n* pista *f* de esquí.

skit [skit] *n* sátira *f*, parodia *f* (*on* de); (*Theat*) número *m* corto satírico.

ski tow ['skiːtəu] *n* = **skilift**.

skittish ['skitiʃ] *adj* horse etc nervioso, asustadizo; *playful* juguetón; *girl* coqueta; caprichoso.

skittishly ['skitiʃli] *adv* nerviosamente; de modo juguetón; con coquetería; caprichosamente.

skittle ['skitl] *n* bolo *m*; —s juego *m* de bolos, boliche *m*.

skittle alley ['skitl,æli] *n* bolera *f*.

skive [skaiv] (*sl*) **1** *n*: to have a good — gandulear, no hacer nada. **2** *vi* gandulear, no hacer nada.

skivvy ['skivi] *n* (*fam*) fregona *f*.

skua ['skjuːə] *n* págalo *m*.

skulduggery [skʌl'dʌgəri] *n* (*fam*) trampas *fpl*, embustes *mpl*; piece of — trampa *f*, embuste *m*.

skulk [skʌlk] *vi* estar escondido, permanecer oculto; acechar sin ser visto, procurar no ser visto.

skull [skʌl] *n* calavera *f*; (*Anat*) cráneo *m*; — and crossbones calavera *f* y dos huesos cruzados (*bandera de los piratas*).

skullcap ['skʌlkæp] *n* casquete *m*.

skunk [skʌŋk] *n* (*Zool*) mofeta *f*; (*fam*) canalla *m*; you —! ¡canalla!

sky [skai] *n* cielo *m*; under blue skies bajo un cielo azul; the skies over England el cielo sobre Inglaterra; to praise someone to the skies poner a uno por las nubes.

sky blue ['skai'bluː] **1** *n* azul *m* celeste. **2 sky-blue** *adj* azul celeste.

sky-high ['skai'hai] *adv* hasta las nubes; por las nubes; the smoke rose — el humo se elevaba hasta las nubes; to blow something — destruir algo completamente con una carga explosiva; to blow a theory — refutar completamente una teoría.

skylark ['skailaːk] **1** *n* alondra *f*. **2** *vi* (*fam*) jaranear, juguetear.

skylarking ['skailaːkiŋ] *n* (*fam*) jarana *f*; bromas *fpl*; pelea *f* amistosa.

skylight ['skailait] *n* tragaluz *m*, claraboya *f*.

skyline ['skailain] *n* horizonte *m*, línea *f* del horizonte; (*of building*) silueta *f*, perfil *m*; (*of city*) perfil *m*.

sky pilot ['skai'pailət] *n* (*sl*) sacerdote *m*, cura *m*.

skyrocket ['skai,rɔkit] **1** *n* cohete *m*. **2** *vi* subir (como un cohete); (*fig, of price etc*) ponerse por las nubes, subir vertiginosamente.

skyscraper ['skai,skreipə*] *n* rascacielos *m*.

skyward(s) ['skaiwəd(z)] *adv* hacia el cielo.

skywriting ['skai,raitiŋ] *n* escritura *f* aérea, publicidad *f* aérea.

slab [slæb] *n* bloque *m*; (*of wood etc*) plancha *f*, tabla *f*; (*of stone*) bloque *m*, (*flat*) losa *f*; (*of meat etc*) tajada *f* (gruesa); (*of cake*) porción *f* gruesa; (*of chocolate*) tableta *f*.

slack [slæk] **1** *adj* (*not tight*) flojo; (*lax*) descuidado, negligente; (*lazy*) vago, perezoso; *student* desaplicado, inerte, poco serio; (*Comm*) *market* flojo, encalmado; *period* de inactividad; *season* muerto; to be — (*of student etc*) gandulear racanear (*fam*); business is — el mercado está flojo, hay poca

actividad en el mercado; to be — about one's work desatender su trabajo, ser negligente en su trabajo; to be — about (*or* in) doing something dejar de hacer algo por negligencia.

2 *n* (a) (*part of rope etc*) lo flojo, parte *f* floja; to take up the — quitar la parte floja, tensar la cuerda (*etc*); to take up the — in the economy utilizar toda la capacidad productiva de la economía.

(b) (*period*) período *m* de inactividad; (*season*) estación *f* muerta.

(c) (*Min*) cisco *m*.

(d) —s pantalones *mpl* (de mujer).

3 *vt* (a) see slacken. (b) see slake.

4 *vi* gandulear, racanear (*fam*); he's been —ing ha sido muy gandul.

slacken ['slækn] **1** *vt* (*also* to — off) aflojar; (*reduce*) disminuir; to — speed (*person*) aflojar el paso, ir más despacio, (*of car etc*) disminuir la velocidad, moderar la marcha.

2 *vi* aflojarse; disminuir, reducirse; (*of wind*) amainar; (*of activity etc*) hacerse menos intenso; (*Comm*) aflojarse; to — off dejar de trabajar (*etc*) tanto; to — up (*person*) aflojar el paso, ir más despacio.

slackening ['slækniŋ] *n* aflojamiento *m*; disminución *f*.

slacker ['slækə*] *n* vago *m*, a *f*, gandul *m*, rácano *m*.

slackness ['slæknis] *n* flojedad *f*, lo flojo; descuido *m*, negligencia *f*; vaguedad *f*, pereza *f*; desaplicación *f*, inercia *f*, falta *f* de seriedad; inactividad *f*; (*Comm*) flojedad *f*, inactividad *f*.

slag [slæg] *n* escoria *f*; basic — escoria *f* básica.

slag heap ['slæghiːp] *n* escorial *m*, escombrera *f*.

slain [slein] *ptp* of slay.

slake [sleik] *vt* lime, thirst apagar.

slam [slæm] **1** *n* (a) golpe *m*; (*of door*) portazo *m*; to close the door with a — dar un portazo, cerrar la puerta ruidosamente.

(b) (*Cards*) bola *f*, capote *m*; slam *m*; grand — gran slam *m*; small — pequeño slam *m*.

2 *vt* (*strike*) golpear; to — something down on the table arrojar violentamente algo sobre la mesa; to — the door dar un portazo, cerrar la puerta ruidosamente (*see also* door); Ruritania —s Slobodia Ruritania derrota fácilmente a Eslobodia (en un partido de fútbol etc); Ruritania —med in 5 goals Ruritania marcó 5 goles.

3 *vi* (*of door*) cerrarse de golpe; the door —med shut la puerta se cerró de golpe.

slander ['slaːndə*] **1** *n* calumnia *f*, difamación *f*; to sue someone for — demandar a uno por calumnia.

2 *vt* calumniar, difamar; decir mal de, hablar mal de.

slanderer ['slaːndərə*] *n* calumniador *m*, ora *f*.

slanderous ['slaːndərəs] *adj* calumnioso, difamatorio.

slanderously ['slaːndərəsli] *adv* calumniosamente.

slang [slæŋ] **1** *n* argot *m*; (*of a group, trade etc*) jerga *f*; (*thieves*) germanía *f*; (*gipsy*) caló *m*; that word is — esa palabra es del argot; to talk — hablar en argot.

2 *adj*: — word palabra *f* del argot, vulgarismo *m*.

3 *vt* (*insult*) llenar de insultos; (*criticize*) criticar duramente, poner como un trapo, emprenderla con.

slangily ['slæŋili] *adv*: to talk — hablar con mucho argot.

slangy ['slæŋi] *adj* person que emplea muchos vulgarismos, que habla en argot; style etc lleno de vulgarismos.

slant [slaːnt] **1** *n* (a) inclinación *f*, sesgo *m*; to be on the — estar inclinado, estar sesgado.

(b) (*fig*) punto *m* de vista; modo *m* de ver una cosa, modo *m* de enfocar un problema; what is your — on this? ¿cuál es su punto de vista en esto?; to get a — on a topic pedir pareceres sobre un asunto.

2 *vt* inclinar, sesgar; to — a report escribir un informe parcial, escribir un informe desde un punto de vista particular.

3 *vi* inclinarse, sesgarse; the light —ed in at the window la luz entraba oblicuamente por la ventana.

slant-eyed ['slaːnt'aid] *adj* de ojos almendrados.

slanting ['slaːntiŋ] *adj* inclinado, oblicuo, sesgado.

slantwise ['slaːntwaiz] *adj* oblicuamente, al sesgo.

slap [slæp] **1** *n* palmada *f*, manotada *f*; — in the face bofetada *f*, (*fig*) palmetazo *m*, golpe *m* rudo, desaire *m*; — on the back espaldarazo *m*.

2 *interj* ¡zas!

3 *adv* de lleno, de plano; directamente; it fell — in the middle cayó exactamente en el centro; he ran — into a tree dio de lleno contra un árbol.

4 *vt* (a) dar una palmada (*or* bofetada) a; pegar, golpear; **to — someone's face, to — someone on the face** dar una bofetada a uno, pegar un tortazo a uno; **to — someone on the back** dar un espaldarazo a uno; **to — one's knees** palmotearse las rodillas; **to — someone down** derribar a uno de una bofetada, (fig) aplastar a uno, apabullar a uno.

(b) he **—ped the book on the table** arrojó el libro violentamente sobre la mesa; **they've —ped another storey on the house** han añadido un piso a la casa (como si tal cosa); **the judge —ped £100 on the fine** el juez aumentó la multa en 100 libras; **— a coat of paint on it** dale una mano de pintura.

slap-bang ['slæp'bæŋ] *adv* ruidosamente, violentamente; directamente, exactamente.

slapdash ['slæpdæʃ] *adv person* descuidado; despreocupado; *work* de brocha gorda, descuidado, chapucero.

slap-happy ['slæp'hæpi] *adj* alegre y despreocupado; totalmente inconsciente.

slapstick ['slæpstik] *n* payasadas *fpl*; **— comedy** comedia *f* de payasadas, comedia *f* de golpe y porrazo.

slap-up ['slæpʌp] *adj* (*fam*): **— meal** banquetazo *m* (*fam*), comilona *f* (*fam*); **it was —** fue un banquetazo.

slash [slæʃ] 1 *n* cuchillada *f*; (*with whip*) latigazo *m*.
2 *vt* (*with knife etc*) acuchillar; rasgar; (*Sew*) acuchillar; (*with whip*) azotar; *price* machacar, quemar; *estimate etc* reducir radicalmente; *speech, text* abreviar sensiblemente; (*attack*) atacar, criticar severamente.
3 *vi*: **to — at someone** tirar tajos a uno, tratar de acuchillar a uno.

slashing ['slæʃiŋ] *adj attack etc* fulminante.

slat [slæt] *n* tablilla *f*, hoja *f*.

slate[1] [sleit] 1 *n* pizarra *f*; (*US Pol*) lista *f* de candidatos; **to wipe the — clean** borrar lo escrito y empezar de nuevo.
2 *adj* de pizarra; color pizarra; **— roof** empizarrado *m*.
3 *vt* (a) cubrir de pizarras.
(b) (*US*) **it is —d to start at 9** según el programa comienza a las 9, deberá comenzar a las 9.

slate[2] [sleit] *vt* (*fam*) censurar, criticar severamente; **it got —d in the press** tuvo unas reseñas muy desfavorables en la prensa.

slate-blue ['sleit'blu:] *adj* color azul pizarra.

slate-coloured ['sleit,kʌləd] *adj* color pizarra.

slate pencil ['sleit'pensl] *n* pizarrín *m*.

slate quarry ['sleit,kwɔri] *n* pizarral *m*.

slater ['sleitə*] *n* pizarrero *m*.

slattern ['slætən] *n* mujer *f* dejada, mujer *f* sucia.

slatternly ['slætənli] *adj* sucio, puerco, desaseado.

slaty ['sleiti] *adj* (*of material*) parecido a pizarra; (*in colour*) color pizarra.

slaughter ['slɔːtə*] 1 *n* (*of animals*) matanza *f*, sacrificio *m*; (*of persons*) carnicería *f*, mortandad *f*; **the — on the roads** la carnicería en las carreteras; **the S— of the Innocents** la Degollación de los Inocentes; **like a lamb to the —** como un cordero al sacrificio; **there was great —** hubo gran mortandad.
2 *vt animals* matar, sacrificar, carnear (*SAm*); *persons* matar (brutalmente), hacer una carnicería de.

slaughterer ['slɔːtərə*] *n* jifero *m*, matarife *m*.

slaughterhouse ['slɔːtəhaus] *n*, *pl* **—houses** [hauziz] matadero *m*.

slaughterman ['slɔːtəmən] *n*, *pl* **—men** [mən] jifero *m*, matarife *m*.

Slav [slɑːv] 1 *adj* eslavo. 2 *n* eslavo *m*, a *f*.

slave [sleiv] 1 *n* esclavo *m*, a *f*; **white — esclava** *f* blanca, prostituta *f*; **to be a — to tobacco** ser esclavo del tabaco; **to be a — to duty** ser esclavo del deber.
2 *vi* trabajar como un negro (*at* en), sudar tinta (*also* **to — away**).

slave driver ['sleiv,draivə*] *n* negrero *m*; (*fig*) amo *m* severo, jefe *m* despótico.

slave labour ['sleiv'leibə*] *n* (*work*) trabajo *m* de esclavos; (*persons*) trabajadores *mpl* forzados; **— camp** campamento *m* de trabajos forzados.

slaver ['sleivə*] *n* (*ship*) barco *m* negrero; (*person*) negrero *m*.

slaver ['slævə*] 1 *n* baba *f*. 2 *vi* babear.

slavery ['sleivəri] *n* esclavitud *f*; **his — to tobacco** la esclavitud en que el tabaco le tiene; **to sell someone into —** vender a uno como esclavo.

slave trade ['sleivtreid] *n* comercio *m* de esclavos, tráfico *m* de esclavos; **white —** trata *f* de blancas.

slave trader ['sleiv,treidə*] *n* traficante *m* en esclavos; negrero *m*.

slavey ['sleivi] *n* fregona *f*.

Slavic ['slævik] 1 *adj* eslavo. 2 *n* eslavo *m*.

slavish ['sleiviʃ] *adj* servil.

slavishly ['sleiviʃli] *adv* servilmente.

slavishness ['sleiviʃnis] *n* servilismo *m*.

Slavonic [slə'vɔnik] 1 *adj* eslavo. 2 *n* eslavo *m*.

slaw [slɔː] *n* (*US*) ensalada *f* de col.

slay [slei] (*irr*: *pret* **slew**, *ptp* **slain**) *vt* matar, asesinar; (*fam*) hacer morir de risa; **this will — you** esto os hará morir de risa; **you — me!** (*iro*) ¡qué divertido!

slayer ['sleiə*] *n* asesino *m*.

sleazy ['sliːzi] *adj person* desaseado, desaliñado; *place* asqueroso; de mala fama.

sled [sled], **sledge**[1] [sledʒ] 1 *n* trineo *m*. 2 *vt* transportar por trineo, llevar en trineo. 3 *vi* ir en trineo.

sledge[2] ['sledʒ] *n*, **sledgehammer** ['sledʒ,hæmə*] *n* macho *m*, acotillo *m*, mazo *m*.

sleek [sliːk] 1 *adj* liso y brillante, lustroso; (*of general appearance*) pulcro, muy aseado; *animal* gordo y de buen aspecto.
2 *vt* alisar, pulir; **to — one's hair down** alisar y arreglarse el pelo.

sleekness ['sliːknis] *n* lisura *f* y brillantez, lustre *m*; pulcritud *f*, aseo *m*; gordura *f*.

sleep [sliːp] 1 *n* sueño *m*; **deep —, heavy —** sueño *m* pesado, sueño *m* profundo; **winter —** (*Zool*) sueño *m* invernal, hibernación *f*; **to drop off to —**, **to go to —** dormirse, quedarse dormido; **to go to —**, (*limb*) dormirse; **to have a — dormir**, (*briefly*) descabezar un sueño; **to have a good night's —** dormir bien durante la noche; **to put someone to —** acostar a uno; dormir a uno, adormecer a uno; **to put an animal to —** sacrificar un animal; **to send someone to —** dormir a uno; **to sleep the — of the just** dormir con la conciencia tranquila; **to walk in one's —** ser sonámbulo, pasearse dormido; **she walked downstairs in her —** estando dormida bajó la escalera.
2 (*irr*: *pret and ptp* **slept**) *vt* (a) **to — the hours away** pasar las horas durmiendo; **to — something off** dormir algo; **to — it off, to — off a hangover** dormir la mona (*fam*); **she's —ing off the effects of the drug** duerme hasta que desaparezcan los efectos del fármaco.
(b) **we can — 4** tenemos camas para 4; **can you — all of us?** ¿hay camas para todos nosotros?
3 *vi* dormir; **to — like a log** (*or* top) dormir como un lirón; **to — heavily, to — soundly** dormir profundamente; **he was —ing soundly** estaba profundamente dormido; **to — around** acostarse con todo el mundo, acostarse con cualquiera; **to — in, to — on** (*late*) dormir tarde, seguir dormido; **to — in** (*in house*) dormir en casa; **to — on something** (*fig*) consultar algo con la almohada; **to — out** (*not at home*) dormir fuera de casa, (*in open air*) dormir al aire libre, pasar la noche al raso; **to — with someone** acostarse con uno; **to get to —** conciliar el sueño.

sleeper ['sliːpə*] *n* (a) (*person*) durmiente *mf*, persona *f* dormida; **to be a heavy —** tener el sueño pesado; **to be a light —** tener el sueño ligero.
(b) (*Rail*: *tie*) traviesa *f*; (*coach*) coche-cama *m*.

sleepily ['sliːpili] *adv* soñolientamente; **she said —** dijo soñolienta.

sleepiness ['sliːpinis] *n* somnolencia *f*; (*fig*) letargo *m*, carácter *m* soporífero.

sleeping ['sliːpiŋ] 1 *adj, attr* durmiente, dormido; *pill etc* para dormir; *partner* comanditario; **S— Beauty** la Bella Durmiente (del Bosque).
2 *n* sueño *m*, el dormir; **between — and waking** entre duerme y vela.

sleeping bag ['sliːpiŋbæg] *n* saco-manta *m*, saco *m* de dormir; (*baby's*) camiseta *f* de dormir.

sleeping car ['sliːpiŋkɑː*] *n* coche-cama *m*.

sleeping draught ['sliːpiŋdrɑːft] *n* soporífero *m*.

sleeping pill ['sliːpiŋpil] *n* comprimido *m* para dormir, somnífero *m*.

sleeping quarters ['sliːpiŋ,kwɔːtəz] *npl* dormitorio *m*; espacio *m* para dormir.

sleeping sickness ['sliːpiŋ,siknis] *n* enfermedad *f* del sueño, encefalitis *f* letárgica.

sleeping tablet ['sliːpiŋ,tæblit] *n* comprimido *m* para dormir, somnífero *m*.

sleepless ['sliːplis] *adj person* insomne, desvelado; *night* pasado en vela, sin dormir.

sleeplessness ['sliːplisnis] *n* insomnio *m*.

sleepwalker ['sliːp,wɔːkə*] *n* sonámbulo *m*, a *f*.

sleepwalking ['sliːp,wɔːkiŋ] *n* sonambulismo *m*.

sleepy ['sliːpi] *adj person, voice etc* soñoliento; *place* soporífero; *pear* fofo; **to be —** (*person*) tener sueño;

I feel very — **at midnight** a medianoche empiezo a tener mucho sueño.

sleepyhead ['sli:pihed] n dormilón m, ona f.

sleet [sli:t] 1 n nevisca f, nieve f granulada, aguanieve f. 2 vi: **it was —ing** caía aguanieve, neviscaba.

sleeve [sli:v] n manga f; (Mech) manguito m, enchufe m; **to have something up one's —** guardar algo como en secreto, tener algo en reserva; **to laugh up one's —** reírse con disimulo.

sleeved [sli:vd] adj con mangas.

-sleeved [sli:vd] adj con mangas . . ., eg **long-sleeved** con mangas largas.

sleeveless ['sli:vlis] adj sin mangas.

sleeve links ['sli:vliŋks] npl gemelos mpl.

sleigh [slei] see **sled**.

sleight [slait] n: **— of hand** escamoteo m, prestidigitación f; destreza f; **by — of hand** (fig) con maña, mañosamente.

slender ['slendə*] adj (not thick) delgado, tenue; hand, waist etc delgado; figure esbelto; resources etc escaso, limitado, reducido; chance pequeño, escaso; hope remoto; excuse poco convincente.

slenderize ['slendəraiz] vt (US) adelgazar.

slenderly ['slendəli] adv: **— built** (person) delgado; de talle esbelto; **— made** de construcción delicada.

slenderness ['slendənis] n delgadez f, tenuidad f; esbeltez f; escasez f, lo limitado; lo remoto.

slept [slept] pret and ptp of **sleep**.

sleuth [slu:θ] n detective m.

slew[1] [slu:] 1 vt torcer (also **to — round**); **to — something to the left** torcer algo a la izquierda. 2 vi torcerse (also **to — round**).

slew[2] [slu:] pret of **slay**.

slice [slais] 1 n (of meat etc) tajada f, lonja f; (of sausage) raja f; (of bread) rebanada f, trozo m; (of lemon, cucumber etc) rodaja f; (portion) parte f, porción f; (tool) estrelladera f, pala f; **a — of life** un trozo de la vida tal como es; **it took quite a — of our profits** nos quitó una buena parte de nuestras ganancias; **it affects a large — of the population** afecta a buena parte de la población.

2 vt cortar, tajar; cortar en rodajas; bread rebanar; ball cortar, torcer; **to — off** cercenar; **to — something in two** cortar algo en dos; **—d lemon** limón m en rodajas.

slicer ['slaisə*] n rebanadora f, máquina f de cortar.

slick [slik] 1 adj (skilful) hábil, diestro; (quick) rápido; (pej) person astuto, mañoso; meloso, zalamero; **he's the — sort** es un astuto; **he's too — for me** no me gusta por lo zalamero; **be — about it!** ¡date prisa!

2 n (of oil etc) extensión f; masa f flotante.

3 vt see **sleek**.

slicker ['slikə*] n (US) embaucador m, tramposo m; **city —** hombre m urbano y astuto procedente de la ciudad.

slickly ['slikli] adv hábilmente, diestramente; rápidamente; astutamente, mañosamente.

slickness ['sliknis] n habilidad f, destreza f; rapidez f; maña f; melosidad f, zalamería f.

slid [slid] pret and ptp of **slide**.

slide [slaid] 1 n (a) (on ice, mud etc) resbaladero m; (for logs etc) deslizadero m; (in playground, swimming pool) tobogán m.

(b) (Tech: part) corredera f, cursor m; (for hair) pasador m; (Mus) vara f, corredera f.

(c) (microscope —) platina f, portaobjeto m; (Phot) diapositiva f; colour — diapositiva f en color; **a lecture with —s** una conferencia con diapositivas, una conferencia con proyecciones.

(d) (act) resbalón m; (of land) desprendimiento m; **the — in share prices** la baja de las cotizaciones; **the — in temperature** el descenso de la temperatura.

2 (irr: pret and ptp **slid**) vt correr, pasar, deslizar; **to — furniture across the floor** deslizar un mueble sobre el suelo; **— the top on when you've finished** pon la tapa cuando termines.

3 vi (slip) resbalar; (glide) deslizarse; **they were sliding across the floor** se deslizaban sobre el suelo; **to — down the banisters** bajar deslizándose por la barandilla; **the ring —s down this rope** el anillo corre por esta cuerda; **it ought to — gently into place** debiera correr suavemente a su lugar; **to — into a habit** caer en un hábito (sin darse cuenta); **to let things —** no ocuparse de las cosas, no prestar atención a lo que pasa, dejar rodar la bola; **these last months he's let everything —** estos últimos meses se ha desatendido de todo.

slide holder ['slaid,həuldə*] n (Phot) portadiapositiva m.

slide projector ['slaidprə,dʒektə*] n (Phot) proyector m de diapositivas.

slide rule ['slaidru:l] n regla f de cálculo.

sliding ['slaidiŋ] adj part corredizo; seat corredizo; door, roof de corredera; scale móvil.

slight [slait] 1 adj (a) figure delgado, fino; stature pequeño, bajo; (of weak appearance) débil, frágil, delicado.

(b) (trivial) leve; insignificante, de poca importancia; **a — pain in the arm** un leve dolor de brazo; **the wound is only —** la herida es más bien leve, la herida no es de consideración; **of — importance** de escasa importancia.

(c) (small) leve; pequeño, escaso; **a — improvement** una pequeña mejora; **of — intelligence** de escasa inteligencia; **to a — extent** en un grado pequeño; **he showed some — optimism** mostró cierto optimismo; **the future does not justify the —est optimism** el futuro no autoriza el más leve optimismo; **there's not the —est possibility of that** de eso no existe la más remota posibilidad; **not in the —est** en absoluto, ni en lo más mínimo.

2 n desaire m, insulto m (on a, para); **this is a — on all of us** esto es un insulto para todos nosotros.

3 vt desairar, ofender, insultar.

slighting ['slaitiŋ] adj despreciativo, menospreciativo, despectivo.

slightingly ['slaitiŋli] adv con desprecio, despectivamente.

slightly ['slaitli] adv un poco; **yes, — sí**, un poco; **— better** un poco mejor; **— built** de talle delgado; **to know someone —** conocer a uno ligeramente, conocer a uno de vista.

slightness ['slaitnis] n delgadez f, finura f; pequeñez f; fragilidad f; insignificancia f, poca importancia f.

slim [slim] 1 adj (a) (of figure) delgado, esbelto; **to get —** adelgazar.

(b) resources etc escaso, insuficiente; **his chances are pretty —** tiene muy pocas posibilidades.

2 vi adelgazar.

slime [slaim] n limo m, légamo m, cieno m; (of snail) baba f; (fig) lodo m.

sliminess ['slaiminis] n lo limoso: lo baboso; viscosidad f; lo rastrero; zalamería f.

slimming ['slimiŋ] n adelgazamiento m; **to be on a — diet** seguir un régimen para adelgazar; **to eat only — foods** comer solamente cosas que no engordan a uno.

slimness ['slimnis] n delgadez f.

slimy ['slaimi] adj limoso, legamoso; snail baboso; viscoso; person rastrero; zalamero; odioso.

sling [sliŋ] 1 n (weapon) honda f; (Med) cabestrillo m; (for rifle etc) portafusil m; (Naut) eslinga f; tirador m; **to have one's arm in a —** llevar el brazo en cabestrillo.

2 (irr: pret and ptp **slung**) (throw) lanzar, tirar, arrojar; (hoist) colgar, suspender; alzar; (Naut) eslingar; **to — something away** tirar algo; **to — something over to someone** tirar algo a uno, pasar algo a uno.

slingshot ['sliŋʃɔt] n (weapon) honda f, tirador m; (shot) hondazo m.

slink [sliŋk] (irr: pret and ptp **slunk**) vi: **to — along** andar furtivamente; **to — away, to — off** largarse, irse cabizbajo.

slinky ['sliŋki] adj (fam) seductor, provocativo.

slip[1] [slip] 1 n (a) (slide) resbalón m; (trip) traspié m, tropezón m; (of earth) caída f, corriente m; (Geol) dislocación f.

(b) (mistake) falta f, error m, equivocación f; (moral) desliz m; (by neglect) descuido m; **— of the pen** lapsus m calami; **— of the tongue** lapsus m linguae; **it was a bad —** fue una grave equivocación; **there's many a — 'twixt cup and lip** del plato a la boca se pierde la sopa.

(c) (pillow—) funda f; (undergarment) combinación f; **gym —** túnica f de gimnasia.

(d) (Naut) **—s** grada f, gradas fpl.

2 vt (a) (slide) deslizar; **to — a coin into a slot** introducir una moneda en una ranura; **— that nut on here** pon esa tuerca aquí; **to — something across to someone** pasar algo (furtivamente) a uno; **would you — the salt across, please?** ¿me das la sal, por favor?; **to — an arm round someone's waist** pasar el brazo por la cintura de una; **to — one over on someone** jugar una mala pasada a uno; ganar por la mano a uno; **to — someone a fiver** pasar a uno un billete de 5 libras (como propina o para comprar su ayuda).

(b) (escape from) eludir, escaparse de; **to — a bone** dislocarse un hueso; **to — a cable** (Naut) soltar una amarra; **the dog —ped its chain el** perro soltó la cadena; **it —ped my memory** se me olvidó; **to — someone's notice** no ser advertido por uno, pasar inadvertido ante uno.

(c) (*with adv or prep*) **to — something in** introducir algo (suavemente, sin ruido *etc*); **I managed to — in a word about . . .** logré insinuar algunas palabras acerca de . . .; **to — off a dress** quitarse (rápidamente) un vestido; **to — on a jumper** ponerse (rápidamente) un jersey; **to — a dress over one's head** pasar un vestido por la cabeza.

3 *vi* **(a)** (*glide*) deslizarse (*along* por, sobre); (*stumble*) tropezar, resbalar; (*of bone etc*) dislocarse; (*of earth*) caer, correrse; **I —ped on the ice** resbalé en el hielo; **my foot —ed** se me fue el pie; **it —s easily along the wire** se desliza suavemente por el hilo; **the knot has —ped** el nudo se ha desatado; **it —ped from her hand** se le escapó de entre las manos; **the clutch —s** el embrague patina.

(b) (*move quickly*) ir (rápidamente); **I'll — round to the shop** voy a la tienda; **to — into bed** meterse en la cama; **she —ped into the room** entró (sin ser vista) en el cuarto, se introdujo (sin llamar la atención) en el cuarto; **the motorcycle —s through the traffic** la moto se cuela por entre la circulación.

(c) (*with let*) **to let it — that . . .** revelar inadvertidamente que . . .; **to let a secret —** revelar inadvertidamente un secreto; **to let a chance —** perder una oportunidad, no aprovechar una oportunidad.

(d) (*decline*) declinar, decaer; **you're —ping** no eres lo que eras antes; se te nota un ir a menos.

(e) (*with adv or prep*) **to — away, to — off** marcharse desapercibido; largarse, escabullirse; **time is —ping away** se nos escapa el tiempo, nos queda poco tiempo; **to — back** regresar con sigilo; **to — by** pasar inadvertido; **to — out for a moment** salir un instante; **it —ped out** se me escapó; lo dije sin querer; **to — through** colarse por; **to — up** (*fig*) equivocarse, cometer un error.

slip² [slip] *n* estaca *f*, plantón *m*; **— of paper** papeleta *f*, papelito *m*; (*in filing system etc*) ficha *f*; **a — of a girl** una jovenzuela.

slipcase ['slipkeis] *n* estuche *m*.

slipknot ['slipnɔt] *n* nudo *m* corredizo.

slip-on ['slipɔn] **1** *adj* que se pone por la cabeza; de quitaipón. **2** *n* prenda *f* (de vestir) que se pone por la cabeza; vestido *m* (*etc*) de estar por casa.

slipper ['slipə*] *n* zapatilla *f*; babucha *f*.

slippery ['slipəri] *adj surface* resbaladizo; *skin etc* viscoso; *person* astuto, escurridizo, evasivo, (*pej*) nada confiable, informal; **he's as — as they come** (*or* **as an eel**) es de lo más informal.

slippy ['slipi] *adv* (*fam*): **to be —, to look — about it** darse prisa, menearse; **look —!** ¡menearse! **we shall have to look —** tendremos que darnos prisa.

slipshod ['slipʃɔd] *adj* descuidado, poco correcto.

slipstream ['slipstri:m] *n* (*Aer*) viento *m* de la hélice.

slip-up ['slipʌp] *n* (*mistake*) falta *f*, error *m*, equivocación *f*; (*moral*) desliz *m*; (*by neglect*) descuido *m*.

slipway ['slipwei] *n* (*Naut*) grada *f*, gradas *fpl*.

slit [slit] **1** *n* hendedura *f*, raja *f*; resquicio *m*; corte *m* largo; **to make a — in something** hacer un corte en algo.

2 (*irr: pret and ptp* **slit**) *vt* hender, rajar; cortar; **to — a sack open** abrir un saco cortándolo con un cuchillo (*etc*); **to — someone's throat** degollar a uno.

slither ['sliðə*] *vi* deslizarse (*down a rope* por una cuerda); ir rodando (*down a slope* por una pendiente); **to — about on ice** ir resbalando sobre el hielo.

sliver ['slivə*] *n* raja *f*; (*of wood etc*) astilla *f*.

slob [slɔb] *n* (*sl*) tipo *m* odioso, sujeto *m* detestable; **you —!** ¡bestia!

slobber ['slɔbə*] **1** *n* baba *f*.

2 *vi* babear; **to — over something** extremar el sentimentalismo por algo, entusiasmarse de un modo ridículo por algo.

sloe [sləu] *n* (*fruit*) endrina *f*; (*tree*) endrino *m*.

slog [slɔg] **1** *n*: **it was a —** me costó trabajo; **it's a hard — to the top** cuesta mucho trabajo llegar a la cumbre.

2 *vt ball* golpear (sin arte).

3 *vi* **(a)** afanarse, sudar tinta; **to — away at something** afanarse por hacer algo, trabajar como un negro para terminar algo.

(b) (*walk etc*) caminar penosamente; **we —ged on for 8 kilometres** caminamos con dificultad 8 kilómetros más.

slogan ['sləugən] *n* slogan *m*.

sloop [slu:p] *n* balandra *f*; corbeta *f*.

slop [slɔp] **1** *vt* derramar, verter.

2 *vi* (*also* **to — over**) derramarse; desbordarse; **to — about in the mud** chapotear en el lodo; **the water was —ping about in the bucket** el agua chapoteaba en el cubo.

slop basin ['slɔp,beisn] *n* recipiente *m* para agua sucia; (*at table*) taza *f* para las hojas de té de desecho.

slope [sləup] **1** *n* inclinación *f*; (*up*) cuesta *f*, pendiente *f*; (*down*) declive *m*; (*of hill*) falda *f*; vertiente *f*, ladera *f*; **the —s of Mulacén** las laderas de Mulacén; **the southern — of the Guadarrama** la vertiente sur del Guadarrama; **the car got stuck on a —** el coche se quedó parado en una cuesta; **there is a — down to the town** la tierra está en declive hacia la ciudad.

2 *vt* inclinar; sesgar; **— arms!** ¡armas al hombro!

3 *vi* **(a)** inclinarse, estar inclinado; declinar, estar en declive; **to — down** estar en declive; **the garden —s down to the sea** el jardín baja hacia el mar; **to — forwards** estar inclinado hacia delante; **to — up** estar en pendiente.

(b) to — off (*fam*) largarse (*fam*).

sloping ['sləupiŋ] *adj* inclinado; (*up*) en pendiente, (*down*) en declive.

slop pail ['slɔppeil] *n* cubeta *f* para agua sucia.

sloppily ['slɔpili] *adv* descuidadamente, de modo poco sistemático; de modo sentimental, con sensiblería; **to dress —** vestir con poca elegancia.

sloppiness ['slɔpinis] *n* descuido *m*, lo descuidado, falta *f* de sistema; falta *f* de elegancia, desaseo *m*; sentimentalismo *m*, sensiblería *f*.

sloppy ['slɔpi] *adj* (*in consistency*) poco sólido, casi líquido; *road etc* lleno de charcos, lleno de barro; (*wet*) mojado; *work etc* descuidado, poco sistemático; *dress* desgalichado; *appearance* nada elegante, desaseado; (*sentimental*) sentimental, sensiblero.

slops [slɔps] *npl* (*food*) gachas *fpl*; (*waste*) agua *f* sucia, lavazas *fpl*.

slop shop ['slɔpʃɔp] *n* (*US sl*) bazar *m* de ropa barata, tienda *f* de pacotilla.

slosh [slɔʃ] (*fam*) **1** *vt person* pegar; **to — some water over something** echar agua sobre algo.

2 *vi*: **to — about in the puddles** chapotear en los charcos; **the water was —ing about in the pail** el agua chapoteaba en el cubo.

sloshed [slɔʃt] *adj* (*sl*): **to be —** estar ajumado (*fam*); **to get —** ajumarse.

slot [slɔt] **1** *n* muesca *f*, ranura *f*; **to put a coin in the — meter** una moneda en la ranura.

2 *vt*: **to — a part into another part** encajar una pieza en la ranura de otra pieza.

3 *vi*: **it —s in here** entra en esta ranura, encaja en esta ranura.

sloth [sləuθ] *n* pereza *f*; (*Zool*) perezoso *m*.

slothful ['sləuθful] *adj* perezoso.

slothfully ['sləuθfəli] *adv* perezosamente.

slot machine ['slɔtmə,ʃi:n] *n* aparato *m* vendedor automático; (*in fun fair etc*) máquina *f* tragaperras.

slouch [slautʃ] **1** *n*: **to walk with a —** andar con un aire gacho, caminar arrastrando los pies.

2 *vi*: **to — about, to — along** andar con un aire gacho, caminar arrastrando los pies; **to — about** (*fig*) gandulear, golfear; **to — off** irse cabizbajo, alejarse con un aire gacho; **to sit —ed in a chair** repanchigarse en un sillón; **he was —ed over his desk** estaba inclinado sobre su mesa de trabajo en postura desgarbada.

slouch hat ['slautʃ'hæt] *n* sombrero *m* gacho.

slough [slau] *n* fangal *m*, cenegal *m*; (*fig*) abismo *m*; **the S— of Despond** el abatimiento más profundo, el abismo de la desesperación.

slough [slʌf] **1** *n* (*Zool*) camisa *f*, piel *f* vieja (que muda la serpiente); (*Med*) escara *f*.

2 *vt* (*also* **to — off**) mudar, echar de sí; **to — off** (*fig*) deshacerse de, desechar.

3 *vi* (*also* **to — off**) desprenderse, caerse.

Slovak ['sləuvæk] **1** *adj* eslovaco. **2** *n* eslovaco *m*, *a f*.

Slovakian [sləu'vækiən] *adj* eslovaco.

sloven ['slʌvn] *n* (*in appearance*) persona *f* desgarbada, persona *f* desaseada; (*at work*) vago *m*, *a f*.

Slovene ['sləuvi:n] **1** *adj* esloveno. **2** *n* esloveno *m*, *a f*.

slovenliness ['slʌvnlinis] *n* desaseo *m*; despreocupación *f*, dejadez *f*; descuido *m*, chapucería *f*.

slovenly ['slʌvnli] *adj appearance* desgarbado, desaseado; *person* despreocupado, dejado, descuidado; *work* descuidado, chapucero.

slow [sləu] **1** *adj* **(a)** lento; pausado; **— but sure!** ¡despacio pero seguro!; **it's — work** es un trabajo lento; **he's a — worker** trabaja despacio; **this car is —er than my old one** este coche no es tan potente como el que tenía antes; **business is very —** el negocio está muy flojo; **life here is —** aquí se vive a un ritmo lento; *see* **train**.

(b) to be — to do something tardar en hacer algo; **they were — to act** tardaron en obrar; **he was not — to notice that . . .** no tardó en observar que . . .; **to be — to anger** ser ecuánime, tener mucho aguante.

(c) (*of clock*) atrasado; **my watch is —** mi reloj se atrasa; **my watch is 20 minutes —** mi reloj se atrasa 20 minutos, mi reloj lleva 20 minutos de atraso.

(d) (*of character*; *phlegmatic*) flemático, cachazudo; (*stupid*) torpe, lerdo.

(e) (*boring*) aburrido; **the game is very —** el partido es la mar de aburrido.

(f) *surface, pitch* poco elástico.

2 *adv* despacio, lentamente; **to go —** ir despacio, (*in industrial dispute*) trabajar a ritmo lento, hacer trabajo lento.

3 *vt* (*also to —* **down, to —** up) retardar; *engine, machine* reducir la velocidad de, moderar la marcha de; **that car —s up the traffic** ese coche entorpece la circulación.

4 *vi* (*also to —* **down, to —** up) ir más despacio; (*in walking etc*) aflojar el paso; (*Aut*) moderar la marcha, reducir la velocidad; **"S— down"** (*road sign*) "Disminuir velocidad"; **the car —ed to a stop** el coche moderó su marcha y paró; **production has —ed to almost nothing** la producción se ha reducido casi a cero.

slow-burning ['sləu'bə:niŋ] *adj* que se quema lentamente.

slowcoach ['sləukəutʃ] *n* (*fam*: *idler*) perezoso *m*, a *f*, vago *m*, a *f*; (*stupid person*) torpe *mf*.

slowly ['sləuli] *adv* despacio, lentamente; poco a poco.

slow match ['sləumætʃ] *n* mecha *f* tardía.

slow motion ['sləu'məuʃən] *adj*, *n*: **slow-motion film** película *f* a cámara lenta; **to show a film in —** pasar una película a cámara lenta.

slowness ['sləunis] *n* lentitud *f*; flema *f*; torpeza *f*; aburrimiento *m*; falta *f* de elasticidad.

slow-witted ['sləu'witid] *adj* torpe, lerdo.

slow worm ['sləuwə:m] *n* lución *m*.

sludge [slʌdʒ] *n* (*mud*) lodo *m*, fango *m*; (*sediment*) sedimento *m* fangoso; (*sewage*) aguas *fpl* de albañal.

slug[1] [slʌg] *n* (*Zool*) babosa *f*; (*bullet*) posta *f*; (*Typ*) lingote *m*.

slug[2] [slʌg] *vt* (*sl*) pegar, aporrear.

sluggard ['slʌgəd] *n* haragán *m*, ana *f*.

sluggish ['slʌgiʃ] *adj* (*indolent*) perezoso; (*slow-moving*) lento; *animal etc* inactivo, inerte, perezoso; *business, market* flojo; *person's temperament* flemático, cachazudo.

sluggishly ['slʌgiʃli] *adv* perezosamente; lentamente; inactivamente; flojamente; con flema.

sluggishness ['slʌgiʃnis] *n* pereza *f*; lentitud *f*; inactividad *f*, inercia *f*; flojedad *f*; flema *f*.

sluice [slu:s] **1** *n* **(a)** (*gate*) compuerta *f*, esclusa *f*; (*barrier*) dique *m* de contención; (*waterway*) canal *m*. **(b) to give something a — down** echar agua sobre algo (para lavarlo); **to — someone down** dar una ducha a uno.

2 *vt*: **to — something down** echar agua sobre algo (para lavarlo), regar algo con agua; **to — something with water** regar algo con agua.

3 *vi*: **to — out** salir a borbotones.

sluice gate ['slu:sgeit] *n* compuerta *f*.

sluiceway ['slu:swei] *n* canal *m*.

slum [slʌm] **1** *n* (*area*) barrio *m* bajo, barrio *m* pobre; (*house*) casucha *f*, tugurio *m*; **the —s** los barrios bajos, los tugurios; **they live in a —** viven en una casucha; **this house will be a — in 10 years** dentro de 10 años esta casa será una ruina; **—-clearance programme** programa *m* de reforma de viviendas en los barrios pobres.

2 *vi* **to —, to go —ming** visitar los barrios bajos; investigar los bajos fondos sociales, conocer los lugares de la baja vida.

slumber ['slʌmbə*] **1** *n* sueño *m* (*esp* tranquilo, profundo); (*fig*) inactividad *f*, inercia *f*; **—s** sueño *m* (*esp* tranquilo, profundo); **my —s were rudely interrupted** estando profundamente dormido me despertaron de modo brutal.

2 *vi* dormir; estar (profundamente) dormido; (*fig*) permanecer inactivo, estar inerte.

slumb(e)rous ['slʌmbərəs] *adj* soñoliento; (*fig*) inactivo, inerte.

slump [slʌmp] **1** *n* (*economic*) depresión *f*, declive *m* económico, retroceso *m*; **the 1929 —** la depresión de 1929, la crisis económica de 1929; **the — in the**

price of copper la baja repentina del precio del cobre; **— in morale** bajón *m* en la moral.

2 *vi* **(a)** (*price etc*) hundirse, bajar repentinamente; (*production*) bajar catastróficamente; (*morale etc*) sufrir un bajón, decaer gravemente.

(b) to — into a chair dejarse caer pesadamente en un sillón; **he was —ed over the wheel** se había desplomado sobre el volante; **he was —ed on the floor** estaba tumbado en el suelo.

slung [slʌŋ] *pret and ptp of* **sling**.

slunk [slʌŋk] *pret and ptp of* **slink**.

slur [slə:*] **1** *n* **(a)** (*stigma*) borrón *m*, mancha *f*, nota *f* infamante; calumnia *f*; **to cast a — on someone** calumniar a uno, hacer un reparo (injustificado) a uno; **it is no — on him to say that . . .** no es hacer un reparo a él decir que . . .

(b) (*Mus*) ligado *m*.

2 *vti* (*also to — over*) pasar por alto de, omitir, suprimir; (*hide*) ocultar; *word* pronunciar con poca corrección, *syllable* comerse; (*Mus*) ligar.

slurred [slə:d] *adj* *pronunciation* indistinto, poco correcto.

slush [slʌʃ] *n* (*watery snow*) nieve *f* a medio derretir; (*mud*) fango *m*, lodo *m* (líquido); (*fam*) sentimentalismo *m*, tonterías *fpl* sentimentales, cursilería *f*.

slushy ['slʌʃi] *adj* *snow* a medio derretir, casi líquido; *mud* casi líquido; *path etc* lleno de lodo, fangoso; (*fam*) tontamente sentimental, sensiblero, cursi.

slut [slʌt] *n* pazpuerca *f*, marrana *f*.

sluttish ['slʌtiʃ] *adj* puerco, desaliñado.

sly [slai] **1** *adj* (*wily*) astuto; (*hypocritical*) taimado; (*secretive*) furtivo, disimulado, sigiloso; (*arch*) malicioso; (*bantering*) guasón; (*insinuating*) intencionado.

2 *n*: **on the —** a hurtadillas; disimuladamente, sigilosamente.

slyly ['slaili] *adv* astutamente; furtivamente, disimuladamente, sigilosamente; maliciosamente; con intención.

slyness ['slainis] *n* astucia *f*; lo taimado, carácter *m* taimado; disimulo *m*, sigilo *m*; malicia *f*; guasa *f*; intención *f*.

smack[1] [smæk] **1** *n* (*taste*) sabor *m*, saborcillo *m*, dejo *m* (*of* a).

2 *vi* tener un saborcillo un poco raro; saber mal; **to — of** saber a, tener un saborcillo a; (*fig*, *pej*) tener resabios de; oler a; **the whole thing —s of bribery** el asunto entero huele a corrupción.

smack[2] [smæk] **1** *n* (*slap*) manotada *f*, palmada *f*; (*blow, stroke*) golpe *m*; (*sound*) ruido *m* de un golpe, chasquido *m*; **it hit the wall with a great —** dio contra la pared con mucho ruido; **to give a child a —** dar una manotada a un niño; **stop it or you'll get a —** déjalo o te pego.

2 *vt* (*slap*) dar una manotada a, pegar (con la mano); **he —ed it on to the table** lo arrojó ruidosamente sobre la mesa; **to — one's lips** relamerse, chuparse los dedos.

3 *adv*: **it fell — in the middle** cayó exactamente en el centro; **he went — into a tree** dio de golpe contra un árbol, dio de lleno contra un árbol.

4 *interj* ¡zas!

smack[3] [smæk] *n* (*Naut*) queche *m*, barco *m* de pesca.

smacker ['smækə*] *n* (*sl*: *kiss*) beso *m* sonado; (*blow*) golpe *m* ruidoso; (*US*) dólar *m*.

smacking ['smækiŋ] *n* zurra *f*, paliza *f*; **to give someone a —** dar una paliza a uno.

small [smɔ:l] **1** *adj* pequeño; chico; menudo; (*person*) pequeño, bajo (de estatura); *stock, supply etc* escaso, corto, exiguo; (*lesser*) menor; (*unimportant*) insignificante; *letter, print* menudo, minúsculo; *voice* humilde; (*the idea of — is often expressed by a diminutive, eg*) **a — house** una casita, **a — book** un librillo; **I'm sorry it's so —** siento que sea tan chiquito; **the fish here are very —** aquí los peces son chiquitines; **when we were —** cuando éramos pequeños; **to be a — eater** comer poco; **to feel —** sentirse humillado, tener vergüenza; **it made me feel pretty —** me dio vergüenza; **to make someone look —** humillar a uno, dar vergüenza a uno; **this house makes the other one look —** esta casa hace que la otra quede pequeña; **to make oneself —** hacerse chiquito, agacharse; **the —er of the two** el menor (de los dos); **the Earth is 75 times —er than Uranus** la Tierra es 75 veces menor que Urano; *see* **beer, letter** *etc*.

2 *n*: **— of the back** parte *f* más estrecha de la espalda; **—s** (*fam*) paños *mpl* menores.

small-arms ['smɔ:l'ɑ:mz] *npl* armas *fpl* cortas.

smallholding ['smɔ:l'həuldiŋ] *n* parcela *f*, granja *f* pequeña; minifundio *m*.

smallish ['smɔ:liʃ] *adj* más bien pequeño.

small-minded ['smɔːl'maindid] *adj* de miras estrechas; intolerante.

small-mindedness ['smɔːl'maindidnis] *n* estrechez *f* de miras; intolerancia *f*.

smallness ['smɔːlnis] *n* pequeñez *f*, pequeño tamaño *m*, tamaño *m* reducido; escasez *f*; insignificancia *f*.

smallpox ['smɔːlpɔks] *n* viruela *f*, viruelas *fpl*.

small-scale ['smɔːl'skeil] *adj* en pequeña escala.

small talk ['smɔːl'tɔːk] *n* vulgaridades *fpl*, banalidades *fpl*; cháchara *f*; **she has no** — es incapaz de charlar sobre las cosas corrientes de la vida; **to swap** — **with someone** intercambiar banalidades con uno.

small-time ['smɔːl'taim] *adj* (*fam*) de poca monta; de escasa importancia; en pequeña escala.

small-town ['smɔːl'taun] *adj* pueblerino.

smarm [smɑːm] *vt*: **to** — **one's hair down** alisarse y fijarse el pelo.

smarmy ['smɑːmi] *adj* (*fam*) cobista (*fam*); **he's a** — **sort** es un cobista.

smart {smɑːt} **1** *adj* (a) (*elegant*) elegante; pulcro, distinguido; (*not shabby*) aseado; *society* elegante, de buen tono; **that's a** — **car** qué coche más distinguido; **in a** — **shop on Serrano** en una tienda elegante de Serrano; **you're looking very** — I ¡qué elegante estás!, ¡qué guapo estás!

(b) (*bright*) listo, vivo, inteligente; (*pej*) ladino, astuto, cuco; **he's a** — **one** es un cuco; **he was too** — **for me** logró embaucarme; **that's a** — **trick** es un truco hábil; **he think's it's** — **to** + *infin* él se cree la mar de listo al + *infin*; **that was pretty** — **of you** en eso has mostrado ser muy inteligente.

(c) (*quick*) pronto, rápido, vivo; *pace* vivo; *attack etc* repentino; **that's** — **work** lo has hecho con toda rapidez; — **work by the police led to . . .** una pronta acción de parte de la policía condujo a . . .; **and look** — **about it!** ¡y dáte prisa!, ¡menéarse!

2 *n* escozor *m*; (*fig*) dolor *m*, resentimiento *m*.

3 *vi* (a) (*Med*) escocer, picar; **it makes my mouth** — escuece en la boca; **my eyes are** —**ing** me duelen los ojos; **it** —**s for a few minutes** escuece durante algunos minutos.

(b) (*fig*) **to** — **under, to** — **with** sufrir bajo, resentirse de; **to** — **under criticism** resentirse de una crítica; **you shall** — **for this!** ¡me las pagarás!

smart-aleck ['smɑːt,ælik] *n see* **Alec.**

smarten ['smɑːtn] **1** *vt* (*also* **to** — **up**) arreglar, mejorar el aspecto de; hermosear; **we'll** — **the house up for the summer** arreglaremos la casa para el verano.

2 *vi* (*also* **to** — **up**) = **3** *vr*: **to** — **oneself up** arreglarse; mejorarse de aspecto; **I must go and** — **myself up** tengo que ir a arreglarme un poco; **she has** —**ed herself up a lot in the last year** durante el año pasado ha mejorado mucho de aspecto.

smartly ['smɑːtli] *adv* (a) elegantemente; pulcramente, de modo distinguido; **she dresses very** — viste con mucha elegancia.

(b) inteligentemente; (*pej*) astutamente.

(c) pronto, rápidamente; a paso vivo; de repente, repentinamente; **they marched him** — **off to the police station** le llevaron con toda rapidez a la comisaría; **she snatched it** — **from me** me lo arrebató de repente.

smartness ['smɑːtnis] *n* (a) elegancia *f*; pulcritud *f*, distinción *f*; aseo *m*; buen tono *m*.

(b) viveza *f*, inteligencia *f*; (*pej*) astucia *f*, cuquería *f*.

(c) viveza *f*, rapidez *f*.

smarty ['smɑːti] *n* (*fam*) sabelotodo *m*.

smash [smæʃ] **1** *n* (*collision*) choque *m*, colisión *f*, encontronazo *m*; accidente *m*; (*breakage*) rotura *f*; (*Fin*) quiebra *f*; depresión *f*, crisis *f* económica; (*Tennis etc*) smash *m*, golpe *m* violento; (*noise of* —) estruendo *m*; **he died in a car** — murió en accidente de automóvil; **the 1969 rail** — el accidente de ferrocarril de 1969; **the 1929** — la crisis económica de 1929; **to go to** — destrozarse, quedar hecho pedazos.

2 *adj*: — **hit** éxito *m* fulminante, exitazo *m*; **the** — **hit of 1920** el mayor éxito de 1920.

3 *adv*: **to go** — **into something** dar de lleno contra algo, dar violentamente contra algo.

4 *vt* (*break*) romper; (*shatter*) hacer pedazos; (*annihilate*) destruir; *ball* golpear violentamente; *attack, opponent* aplastar; **when they** —**ed the atom** cuando desintegraron el átomo; **he** —**ed it against the wall** lo estrelló contra la pared; **the waves threatened to** — **the boat on the rocks** las olas amenazaban con estrellar el barco contra las rocas; **I've** —**ed my watch** he estropeado mi reloj;

we will — **this crime ring** acabaremos con esta confabulación; **A** —**ed his fist into B's face** A dio a B un puñetazo violento en la cara; **the gang** —**ed the place up** la pandilla destrozó el local; **he was all** —**ed up in the accident** sufrió grandes lesiones en el accidente.

5 *vi* (*break*) romperse; hacerse pedazos; estropearse; (*collide*) chocar (*against, into* con, contra), pearse; estrellarse (*against, into* contra); (*Fin*) quebrar.

smash-and-grab raid ['smæʃən'græb,reid] *n* robo *m* relámpago (en joyería *etc*).

smasher ['smæʃə*] *n* (*sl*) cosa *f* estupenda, (*esp girl*) bombón *m* (*fam*), guayabo *m* (*fam*); **it's a** — ! ¡es estupendo!

smashing ['smæʃiŋ] *adj* (*sl*) imponente, bárbaro (*fam*), pistonudo (*fam*); **a** — **dress** un vestido monísimo; **we had a** — **time** lo pasamos en grande; **isn't it** — ? ¿es estupendo, no?

smash-up ['smæʃʌp] *n* choque *m* violento, colisión *f* violenta, accidente *m*.

smattering ['smætəriŋ] *n* conocimientos *mpl* elementales, conocimiento *m* superficial, nociones *fpl*; **I have a** — **of Catalan** tengo algunas nociones de catalán.

smear [smiə*] **1** *n* mancha *f*; (*fig*) calumnia *f*, mancha *f*; (*Med*) frotis *m*.

2 *vt* (a) manchar (*with* de), untar (*with* de); **to** — **one's face with blood** untarse la cara de sangre; **to** — **wet paint** manchar la pintura fresca.

(b) (*fig*) calumniar, difamar; **to** — **someone as a traitor** calumniar a uno alegando que es traidor, tachar a uno de traidor; **to** — **someone because of his past** tachar a uno por su pasado.

smeary ['smiəri] *adj* manchado.

smell [smel] **1** *n* (a) (*sense of* —) olfato *m*; **to have a keen sense of** — tener buen olfato.

(b) (*odour*) olor *m* (*of* a); **bad** — mal olor *m*, hedor *m*; **it has a nice** — tiene un olor agradable.

(c) **let's have a** — déjame olerlo.

2 (*irr*: *pret and ptp* **smelled** *or* **smelt**) *vt* oler; (*of dog*) olfatear; **to** — **out** olfatear, husmear; **it's** —**ing the room out** hace oler mal todo el cuarto, apesta el cuarto.

3 *vi* oler (*of a*); **it** —**s good** huele bien; **it** —**s bad** huele mal, tiene mal olor; **that flower doesn't** — esa flor no tiene olor; **it's a gas which doesn't** — es un gas inodoro; **it's a damp in here** aquí dentro huele a húmedo; **the dog** —**ed at my shoes** el perro olió mis zapatos.

smelling bottle ['smeliŋ,bɔtl] *n* frasco *m* de sales.

smelling salts ['smeliŋsɔːlts] *npl* sales *fpl* (aromáticas).

smelly ['smeli] *adj* que huele mal, de mal olor, hediondo; **it's** — **in here** aquí dentro huele mal.

smelt¹ [smelt] *pret and ptp of* **smell.**

smelt² [smelt] *vt* fundir.

smelt³ [smelt] *n* (*Fish*) eperlano *m*.

smelting ['smeltiŋ] *n* fundición *f*.

smelting furnace ['smeltiŋ,fəːnis] *n* horno *m* de fundición.

smile [smail] **1** *n* sonrisa *f*; **with a** — **on one's lips** con una sonrisa en los labios; **a face wreathed in** —**s** una cara con una sonrisa radiante; **to give someone a** — sonreír a uno; **come on, give me a** — ! ¡vamos, una sonrisa!; **to knock the** — **off someone's face** hacer que uno deje de sonreír a fuerza de golpes; **to raise a** — forzar una sonrisa; **can't you even raise a** —? ¿no sonríes siquiera?

2 *vt emotion* expresar con una sonrisa; **she** —**d her thanks** dio las gracias con una sonrisa; **to** — **a bitter** — sonreír amargamente.

3 *vi* sonreír, sonreírse (*at* de); **to keep smiling** seguir con la sonrisa en los labios; **to** — **at danger** reírse del peligro; **fortune** —**d on him** le favoreció la fortuna; **if she** —**s on me** si me mira con buenos ojos.

smiling ['smailiŋ] *adj* sonriente, risueño.

smilingly ['smailiŋli] *adv* sonriendo, con cara risueña, con una sonrisa.

smirch [sməːtʃ] *vt* (*lit*) mancillar, desdorar.

smirk [sməːk] **1** *n* sonrisa *f* satisfecha; sonrisa *f* afectada. **2** *vi* sonreírse satisfecho; sonreírse afectadamente.

smirkingly ['sməːkiŋli] *adv* con una sonrisa satisfecha (*or* afectada).

smite [smait] (*irr*: *pret* **smote**, *ptp* **smitten**) *vt* (*strike*) golpear; (*punish*) castigar; (*pain*) doler, afligir; (*of light, sound etc*) herir; **an idea smote me** se me ocurrió una idea; **my conscience smote me** me remordió la conciencia; **he smote the ball hard** golpeó la pelota con violencia; *see also* **smitten.**

smith [smiθ] *n* herrero *m*.

smithereens ['smiðə'ri:nz] *npl*: **to smash something to — hacer algo añicos; it was in —** estaba hecho añicos.

smithy ['smiði] *n* herrería *f*.

smitten ['smitn] *ptp of* **smite**; **to be — with the plague** sufrir el azote de la peste, ser afligido por la peste; **to be — with an idea** entusiasmarse por una idea; **to be — with someone** estar chalado por uno; **I was — by the urge to +** *infin* me entraron deseos vehementes de + *infin*.

smock [smɔk] **1** *n* (*artist's, labourer's*) blusa *f*; (*child's*) delantal *m*; (*expectant mother's*) bata *f* corta, tontón *m*. **2** *vt* fruncir, adornar con frunces.

smocking ['smɔkiŋ] *n* adorno *m* de frunces.

smog [smɔg] *n* niebla *f* espesa con humo.

smoke [sməuk] **1** *n* (a) humo *m*; **holy —! ¡caramba!; there's no — without fire** cuando el río suena agua lleva, lo que hace humo es porque está ardiendo; **to go up in —** quedar destruido en un incendio, quemarse, (*person*: *fam*) subirse por las paredes.
(b) (*cigarette etc*) pitillo *m*, tabaco *m*; **to have a —** echar un pitillo, fumar un cigarrillo; **I like to have a — after meals** me gusta fumar después de comer; **will you have a —?** ¿quieres fumar?; **I've no —s** no tengo tabaco.
2 *vt* (a) *tobacco* fumar; *bacon, glass etc* ahumar; **he —s a pipe** fuma en pipa; **he's smoking his pipe** está fumando su pipa.
(b) (*insects*) **to — insects out** ahuyentar insectos con humo; **to — a gang out** hacer que salga una pandilla de su escondite pegándole fuego; **that lamp is smoking the room out** esa lámpara está llenando el cuarto de humo.
3 *vi* (a) (*of chimney etc*) humear, echar humo.
(b) (*of smoker*) fumar; **do you —?** ¿fuma Vd?; **will you —?** ¿quieres fumar?; **do you mind if I —?** ¿le molesta que fume?; **he —s like a chimney** fuma como un carretero.

smoke bomb ['sməukbɔm] *n* bomba *f* de humo.

smoked [sməukt] *adj bacon, glass etc* ahumado.

smoke-dried ['sməukdraid] *adj* ahumado, curado al humo.

smokeless ['sməuklis] *adj* sin humo; **— fuel** combustible *m* sin humo; **— zone** zona *f* libre de humo.

smoker ['sməukə*] *n* (a) (*person*) fumador *m*, ora *f*; **to be a heavy —** fumar mucho. (b) (*Rail*) coche *m* fumador.

smokeroom ['sməukrum] *n* salón *m* de fumar.

smoke screen ['sməukskri:n] *n* cortina *f* de humo; **to put up a — (***fig***)** entenebrecer un asunto, enmarañar un asunto (para despistar a la gente).

smoke signal ['sməuk,signl] *n* ahumada *f*.

smokestack ['sməukstæk] *n* chimenea *f*.

smoking ['sməukiŋ] **1** *adj* humeante, que humea.
2 *n* el fumar; **— is bad for you** el fumar te hace daño; **"no —" "se prohíbe fumar".
3** *attr* de (*or* para) fumador.

smoking compartment ['sməukiŋkəm,pɑːtmənt] *n*, (*US*) **— car** [,kɑː*] *n* (*Rail*) departamento *m* de fumadores, coche *m* fumador.

smoking jacket ['sməukiŋ,dʒækit] *n* chaqueta *f* casera, medio batín *m*.

smoking room ['sməukiŋ,rum] *n* salón *m* de fumar.

smoky ['sməuki] *adj chimney, fire* humeante, que humea; *room* lleno de humo; *flavour, surface etc* ahumado; **it's — in here** aquí hay mucho humo.

smolder ['sməuldə*] (*US*) *see* **smoulder**.

smooch [smuːtʃ] *vi* (*sl*) acariciarse, abrazarse amorosamente.

smooth [smuːð] **1** *adj* (a) *surface* liso, terso; suave; llano, igual, uniforme; *skin etc* liso, suave; *brow* sin arrugas; *sea* tranquilo, en calma.
(b) (*in consistency*) *paste etc* liso, sin grumos; *running of engine, take-off etc* suave; *voice* suave; *style* fluido, suave; *passage, trip* tranquilo, sin novedad; *person's manner* afable.
(c) *person* afable, culto; (*pej*) zalamero, meloso.
2 *vt* (*often* **to — out, to — down**) *hair etc* alisar; *surface* allanar, igualar; *dress etc* arreglar; *wood* desbastar; *style etc* suavizar; **to — the way for someone** allanar el camino para uno, preparar el terreno para uno; **to — away (***or* **over) difficulties** allanar dificultades, zanjar dificultades; **to — someone down** calmar a uno.

smooth-chinned ['smuːðtʃind] *adj*, **smooth-faced** ['smuːðfeist] *adj* barbilampiño; **bien afeitado; some — youth** algún joven imberbe.

smoothing iron ['smuːðiŋ,aiən] *n* plancha *f*.

smoothly ['smuːðli] *adv* lisamente; suavemente; de modo uniforme; tranquilamente; afablemente; **he said —** dijo sin alterarse; **everything went —** todo fue sobre ruedas, todo fue viento en popa.

smoothness ['smuːðnis] *n* lisura *f*, tersura *f*; suavidad *f*; igualdad *f*, uniformidad *f*; tranquilidad *f*, calma *f*; fluidez *f*; afabilidad *f*; (*pej*) zalamería *f*.

smooth-running ['smuːð'rʌniŋ] *adj engine etc* que funciona suavemente.

smooth-spoken ['smuːð'spəukən] *adj* afable, culto; (*pej*) zalamero, meloso.

smooth-tongued ['smuːð'tʌŋgd] *adj* (*pej*) zalamero, meloso.

smote [sməut] *pret of* **smite**.

smother ['smʌðə*] **1** *vt* (*stifle*) ahogar, sofocar; *fire* apagar; *yawn* contener; *criticism, doubt etc* ahogar, suprimir; **fruit —ed in cream** fruta *f* cubierta de crema; **a book —ed in dust** un libro cubierto de polvo; **the child was —ed in dirt** el niño estaba todo sucio. **2** *vi* ahogarse, sofocarse.

smoulder, US **smolder** ['sməuldə*] *vi* arder sin llama, arder lentamente; (*fig*) estar latente, estar sin apagarse.

smouldering, US **smoldering** ['sməuldəriŋ] *adj* que arde lentamente; (*fig*) latente; **she gave me a — look** me miró provocativa.

smudge [smʌdʒ] **1** *n* mancha *f*, tiznón *m*. **2** *vt* manchar; tiznar (*with de*). **3** *vi* mancharse.

smudgy ['smʌdʒi] *adj* manchado; lleno de manchas; *outline etc* borroso.

smug [smʌg] *adj* pagado de sí mismo, suficiente; presumido; **he said with — satisfaction** dijo muy pagado de sí; **don't be so —! ¡no presumas!

smuggle ['smʌgl] **1** *vt* pasar de contrabando; **to — goods in** introducir artículos de contrabando; **to — something past (***or* **through) the customs** pasar algo por la aduana sin declararlo; **to — someone out in disguise** hacer que uno pase inadvertido gracias a su disfraz.
2 *vi* hacer contrabando, dedicarse a pasar cosas de contrabando.

smuggled ['smʌgld] *adj goods* de contrabando.

smuggler ['smʌglə*] *n* contrabandista *mf*.

smuggling ['smʌgliŋ] *n* contrabando *m*.

smugly ['smʌgli] *adv* con un aire satisfecho, con aire de suficiencia; con presunción.

smugness ['smʌgnis] *n* satisfacción *f* de sí mismo, suficiencia *f*; presunción *f*.

smut [smʌt] *n* (*piece of dirt*) tizne *m*; (*in eye*) mota *f* de carbonilla; (*on paper*) tiznón *m*, mancha *f*; (*Bot*) tizón *m*; (*fig*) obscenidades *fpl*, cosas *fpl* verdes; **to talk —** contar cosas verdes.

smuttiness ['smʌtinis] *n* (*fig*) obscenidad *f*.

smutty ['smʌti] *adj* tiznado; (*Bot*) atizonado; (*fig*) obsceno, verde; **a lot of — talk** muchos cuentos verdes.

Smyrna ['smə:nə] Esmirna.

snack [snæk] *n* bocadillo *m*, tentempié *m*, piscolabis *m*; **to have a —** tomar un bocadillo, comer algo.

snack bar ['snækbɑ:*] *n* cafetería *f*, bar *m*.

snaffle[1] ['snæfl] *n* bridón *m*.

snaffle[2] ['snæfl] *vt* (*sl*) afanar (*fam*), guindar (*fam*).

snafu [snæ'fu:] (*US*) **1** *adj* confuso; complicadísimo; arruinado, estropeado.
2 *n* (*mistake*) equivocación *f* monumental; (*confusion*) confusionismo *m*; (*mess*) situación *f* confusa, situación *f* complicadísima; asunto *m* enmarañado; lío *m*.

snag [snæg] *n* (*in wood*) nudo *m*; (*of tree*) tocón *m*; (*of tooth*) raigón *m*; (*fig*) dificultad *f*, obstáculo *m*, estorbo *m*, pero *m*; **there's a —** hay una dificultad; **the — is that . . .** la dificultad es que . . .; **that's the — ahí** está el problema; **what's the —?** ¿qué obstáculo hay?; **to hit (***or* **run into) a — encontrar** un pero, tropezar con una dificultad.

snail [sneil] *n* caracol *m*; **— edible — caracol** *m* comestible; **at a —'s pace** a paso de tortuga.

snake [sneik] **1** *n* culebra *f*, serpiente *f*; **he's the — in the grass** él es el traidor, él es el enemigo oculto, él es el peligro oculto.
2 *vi*: **to — about, to — along** serpentear; **a hand —d out** se extendió de repente una mano.

snakebite ['sneikbait] *n* mordedura *f* de serpiente.

snake charmer ['sneik,tʃɑːmə*] *n* encantador *m* de serpientes.

snaky ['sneiki] *adj* serpentino, tortuoso.

snap [snæp] **1** *n* (a) (*sound: of fingers*) castañetazo *m*; (*of whip etc*) chasquido *m*; (*report*) estallido *m*; (*click*) golpe *m* seco, ruido *m* seco; **it shut with a —** se cerró de golpe, se cerró con un ruido seco.
(b) (*point of breakage*) rotura *f*.
(c) **cold — ola** *f* de frío, período *m* breve de frío.
(d) (*fam*) vigor *m*, energía *f*; **put some — into it! ¡menéarse!
(e)** (*fastener*) cierre *m*.
(f) (*Phot*) foto *f*, instantánea *f*; **to take a — of**

someone tomar una foto de uno; **these are our holiday—s** éstas son las fotos de nuestras vacaciones.

2 *adj* repentino; — **decision** decisión *f* tomada de repente; — **vote** votación *f* apenas discutida de antemano.

3 *adv*: —! ¡crac!; **to go** — hacer crac.

4 *vt* (a) *fingers* castañetear (*see also* **finger**); *whip* chasquear; **to** — **a box shut** cerrar una caja de golpe; **to** — **something into place** meter algo en su lugar con un golpe seco.

(b) (*break*) romper, quebrar, hacer saltar.

(c) **to** — **out an order** espetar una orden, dar una orden en tono brusco.

(d) **to** — **someone** (*Phot*) tomar una foto de uno.

(e) **to** — **off** romper, separar; (*of dog etc*) morder y separar, separar con los dientes; **to** — **someone's head off** echar un rapapolvo a uno; interrumpir bruscamente a uno; **to** — **up a bargain** comprar algo con avidez; **our stock was** —**ped up at once** nuestras existencias quedaron agotadas al instante.

5 *vi* (a) **to** — **at someone** (*of dog*) querer morder a uno, tratar de morder a uno; (*of person*) contestar (*or* hablar *etc*) bruscamente a uno; **don't** — **at me!** ¡habla con más educación!

(b) (*whip etc*) chasquear; (*fastener etc*) hacer un ruido seco; **it** —**ped shut** se cerró de golpe.

(c) (*break*) romperse, quebrarse; separarse, desprenderse; saltar; **it** —**ped off** se rompió y se separó.

(d) (*fig*) **to** — **into something** emprender algo con entusiasmo; **to** — **out of something** dejarse de algo, quitarse algo de encima; — **out of it!** ¡déjate de eso!, ¡ánimo!

snapdragon ['snæp,drægən] *n* (*Bot*) cabeza *f* de dragón.

snap fastener ['snæp'fɑːsnə*] *n* corchete *m* de presión.

snappish ['snæpiʃ] *adj* brusco, abrupto; irritable.

snappishness ['snæpiʃnis] *n* brusquedad *f*; irritabilidad *f*.

snappy ['snæpi] *adj* (*fam*) rápido; enérgico, vigoroso; **to be** — **about something** hacer algo con toda rapidez; **and be** — **about it!** ¡y date prisa!; **make it** —! ¡rápido!

snapshot ['snæpʃɔt] *n* (*Phot*) foto *f*, instantánea *f*.

snare [snɛə*] **1** *n* lazo *m*, trampa *f*; (*fig*) trampa *f*, engaño *m*; **it's a** — **and delusion** es una trampa.

2 *vt* coger con trampas; (*fig*) hacer caer en el lazo, engañar.

snarl[1] [snɑːl] **1** *n* gruñido *m*; **he said with a** — dijo gruñendo. **2** *vi* gruñir; **to** — **at someone** decir algo a uno gruñendo.

snarl[2] [snɑːl] **1** *vt* (*also* **to** — **up**) enmarañar, enredar; **it's got all** —**ed up** (*fig*) ha quedado en la mayor confusión.

2 *vi* (*also* **to** — **up**) enmarañarse, enredarse.

snatch [snætʃ] **1** *n* (a) (*act*) arrebatamiento *m*; **to make a** — **at something** tratar de arrebatar algo.

(b) (*fam: robbery*) robo *m*; (*kidnapping*) secuestro *m*; **jewellery** — robo *m* de joyas.

(c) (*Mus etc*) trocito *m*; **to whistle** —**es of Mozart** silbar trocitos de Mozart.

2 *vt* (a) (*pick up*) asir, coger, agarrar; (*from someone's hold*) arrebatar (*from* a); (*out of the air*) coger al vuelo; **to** — **a meal** comer algo a toda prisa; **to** — **an opportunity** aprovechar una oportunidad; **to** — **an hour of happiness** procurarse (a pesar de todo) una hora de felicidad; **to** — **something away** arrebatar algo (*from* a); **to** — **up a knife** asir un cuchillo; **to** — **up a child** coger a un niño en brazos.

(b) (*fam: steal*) robar, (*kidnap*) secuestrar.

3 *vi*: **don't** —! ¡no me arrebates las cosas de manera tan grosera!; **to** — **at something** tratar de arrebatar algo; tratar de coger algo al vuelo; **to** — **at an opportunity** aprovechar una oportunidad.

snazzy ['snæzi] *adj* (*sl*) de lo más elegante.

sneak [sniːk] **1** *n* soplón *m*, ona *f*.

2 *vt* robar a hurtadillas, afanar, biriar.

3 *vi* (a) **to** — **about** ir a hurtadillas, moverse furtivamente; **to** — **away, to** — **off** escabullirse; **to** — **in** entrar a hurtadillas, entrar sin ser visto; **to** — **off with something** alzarse con algo.

(b) **to** — **on someone** soplarse de uno.

sneakers ['sniːkəz] *npl* (*fam*) zapatos *mpl* ligeros de goma.

sneaking ['sniːkiŋ] *adj manner* furtivo, sigiloso; **to have a** — **regard for someone** respetar a uno a pesar de todo, respetar a uno sin querer confesarlo abiertamente.

sneak thief ['sniːkθiːf] *n* ratero *m*, garduño *m*.

sneaky ['sniːki] *adj manner* furtivo, sigiloso; (*of character*) soplón.

sneer [snɪə*] **1** *n* (*expression*) visaje *m* de burla y desprecio, sonrisa *f* de desprecio; (*remark*) burla *f*, mofa *f*; comentario *m* despreciativo; **he said with a** — dijo con desprecio; **the book is full of** —**s about** ... el libro se mofa constantemente de ...

2 *vi* hacer un visaje de burla y desprecio; **to** — **at someone** mofarse de uno, hablar con desprecio de uno.

sneerer ['snɪərə*] *n* mofador *m*, ora *f*.

sneering ['snɪəriŋ] *adj tone etc* burlador y despreciativo, lleno de desprecio.

sneeringly ['snɪəriŋli] *adv* en tono burlador y despreciativo; con una sonrisa de desprecio.

sneeze [sniːz] **1** *n* estornudo *m*. **2** *vi* estornudar; **an offer not to be** —**d at** una oferta que no es de despreciar.

snick [snik] **1** *n* corte *m*, tijeretada *f*.

2 *vt* (a) cortar (un poco), tijeretear; **to** — **something off** cortar algo con un movimiento rápido.

(b) *ball* desviar ligeramente.

snicker ['snikə*] = **snigger**.

snide [snaid] *adj* (*esp US*) despreciativo, sarcástico.

sniff [snif] **1** *n* sorbo *m* por las narices; (*of dog etc*) husmeo *m*; **to go out for a** — **of air** salir a tomar el fresco; **we never got a** — **of the vodka** no llegamos siquiera a oler el vodka.

2 *vt* sorber por las narices; (*of dog etc, also* **to** — **out**) husmear, olfatear; **just** — **these flowers** huele un poco estas flores; **you can** — **the sea air here** aquí se huele ese aire de mar; — **the gas deeply** aspire profundamente el gas.

3 *vi* (a) (*person*) sorber por las narices; **to** — **at** oler; **don't** —! ¡no hagas ese ruido con las narices!

(b) (*dog etc*) oler, husmear, olfatear; **the dog** —**ed at my shoes** el perro olió mis zapatos.

(c) **to** — **at something** (*fig*) despreciar algo, tratar algo con desdén; **an offer not to be** —**ed at** una oferta que no es de despreciar.

sniffle ['snifl] = **snuffle**.

sniffy ['snifi] *adj* (*fam*) estirado, desdeñoso; **he was pretty** — **about it** trató el asunto con bastante desdén.

snifter ['sniftə*] *n* (*sl*) trago *m* (*esp* de whiskey); **to have a** — echarse un trago.

snigger ['snigə*] **1** *n* risa *f* disimulada. **2** *vi* reírse con disimulo (*at* de).

snip [snip] **1** *n* (*cut*) tijeretada *f*, tijeretazo *m*; (*incision*) tijeretada *f*; (*piece of material etc*) recorte *m*; (*sl: bargain*) ganga *f*.

2 *vti* tijeretear; **to** — **off** recortar.

snipe [snaip] **1** *n* (*Orn*) agachadiza *f*.

2 *vi*: **to** — **at someone** tirar a uno desde un escondite; **to** — **from the shelter of** ... tirar desde la protección de ...; **to** — **at one's critics** contestar (con precaución) a los críticos de uno; **he was really sniping at the Minister** (*fig*) en realidad sus ataques iban dirigidos contra el Ministro.

sniper ['snaipə*] *n* tirador *m* escondido, francotirador *m*.

snippet ['snipit] *n* (*of cloth*) retazo *m*, retal *m*; (*of information etc*) retazo *m*; —**s** retazos *mpl*; "**S**—**s**" (*heading in press etc*) "Breverías".

snitch [snitʃ] (*sl*) **1** *n* (*nose*) napias *fpl* (*sl*). **2** *vi* soplarse (*on someone* de uno).

snivel ['snivl] *vi* lloriquear.

snivelling ['sniviŋ] **1** *adj* llorón. **2** *n* lloriqueo *m*.

snob [snɔb] *n* (e)snob *mf*.

snobbery ['snɔbəri] *n* (e)snobismo *m*.

snobbish ['snɔbiʃ] *adj* (e)snob.

snobbishness ['snɔbiʃnis] *n* (e)snobismo *m*.

snood [snuːd] *n* (*band*) cintillo *m*; (*net*) redecilla *f*.

snook [snuːk] *n* (*fam*): **to cock a** — **at someone** sacar la lengua a uno, hacer una señal grosera a uno; (*fig*) mofarse abiertamente de uno.

snooker ['snuːkə*] **1** *n* especie de billar.

2 *vt*: **to** — **someone** poner a uno en un aprieto; **now we're properly** —**ed** ahora no hay nada que hacer, en buen lío nos hemos metido.

snoop [snuːp] **1** *n* (a) (*person*) fisgón *m*, ona *f*.

(b) (*act*) **I'll have a** — **round** voy a reconocer el terreno, a ver si encuentro algo; **I had a** — **round the kitchen** registré la cocina (sin que nadie me viese).

2 *vi* (*also* **to** — **about, to** — **around**) curiosear, fisgonear; practicar un registro furtivo, hacer una investigación furtiva; **he comes** —**ing around here** viene aquí a fisgonear.

snooper ['snuːpə*] *n* investigador *m* encubierto, inspector *m* que no anuncia públicamente sus visitas.

snooty ['snu:ti] *adj* (*fam*) fachendoso, presumido; **people hereabouts are very —** por aquí la gente se da mucho tono; **there's no call to be — about it** Vd no tiene motivo para presumir.

snooze [snu:z] **1** *n* siestecita *f*, sueñecillo *m*; **to have a — = 2** *vi* dormitar, echar una siestecita.

snore [snɔ:*] **1** *n* ronquido *m*. **2** *vi* roncar.

snoring ['snɔ:riŋ] *n* ronquidos *mpl*.

snorkel ['snɔ:kl] *n* tubo *m* snorkel, tubo *m* de respiración.

snort [snɔ:t] **1** *n* bufido *m*; **with a — of rage** con un bufido de enojo. **2** *vi* bufar; **"No!" he —ed** "¡No!" dijo bufando.

snorter ['snɔ:tə*] *n* (*sl*): **a real — of a song** una canción estupenda; **it was a — of a game** fue un partido maravilloso.

snot [snɔt] *n* (*fam*) mocarro *m*.

snotty ['snɔti] *adj* (*fam*) mocoso; (*fig*: *snooty*) fachendoso, presumido; (*angry*) enojado.

snout [snaut] *n* hocico *m*, morro *m*.

snow [snəu] **1** *n* nieve *f*; (*sl*) cocaína *f*.
   2 *vi* nevar; **to be —ed in, to be —ed up** estar encerrado (*or* aprisionado) por la nieve; **to be —ed under** (*fig*) estar inundado (*by*, *with* por).

snowball ['snəubɔ:l] **1** *n* bola *f* de nieve.
   2 *vt* lanzar bolas de nieve a.
   3 *vi* (*fig*) aumentar progresivamente, aumentar rápidamente.

snow-blind ['snəublaind] *adj* cegado por los reflejos de la nieve.

snow blindness ['snəu͵blaindnis] *n* ceguera *f* causada por los reflejos de la nieve.

snowbound ['snəubaund] *adj* aprisionado por la nieve.

snow-capped ['snəukæpt] *adj* coronado de nieve.

snow-covered ['snəu͵kʌvəd] *adj* cubierto de nieve, nevado.

snowdrift ['snəudrift] *n* ventisquero *m*, montón *m* de nieve, nieve *f* amontonada.

snowdrop ['snəudrɔp] *n* campanilla *f* de febrero, campanilla *f* blanca.

snowfall ['snəufɔ:l] *n* nevada *f*.

snow fence ['snəufens] *n* valla *f* paranieves.

snowfield ['snəufi:ld] *n* campo *m* de nieve.

snowflake ['snəufleik] *n* copo *m* de nieve.

snow line ['snəulain] *n* límite *m* de las nieves perpetuas.

snowman ['snəumæn] *n*, *pl* **—men** [men] figura *f* de nieve; **the abominable —** el abominable hombre de las nieves.

snowplough, (US) **snow plow** ['snəuplau] *n* quitanieves *m*.

snowshoe ['snəuʃu:] *n* raqueta *f* de nieve.

snowslide ['snəuslaid] *n* (US) alud *m* de nieve, caída *f* de nieve.

snowstorm ['snəustɔ:m] *n* nevada *f*, nevasca *f*.

Snow White ['snəuwait] Blancanieves; **"— and the Seven Dwarfs"** "Blancanieves y los siete enanitos".

snow-white ['snəu'wait] *adj* blanco como la nieve; (*poet*) níveo, cándido.

snowy ['snəui] *adj* (a) (*Meteorol*) *climate*, *region* de mucha nieve, que tiene mucha nieve; *countryside etc* cubierto de nieve; **— day** día *m* de nieve; **— season** estación *f* de las nieves; **it was very — yesterday** ayer nevó mucho, ayer cayó mucha nieve.
   (b) (*fig*) blanco como la nieve, (*poet*) níveo, cándido.

snub [snʌb] **1** *n* desaire *m*; repulsa *f*. **2** *vt person* desairar, ofender; repulsar; *offer etc* rechazar con desdén.

snub-nosed ['snʌb'nəuzd] *adj* chato.

snuff [snʌf] **1** *n* rapé *m*, tabaco *m* en polvo; **to take —** tomar rapé.
   2 *vt* (*breathe in*) aspirar, sorber por la nariz; *candle* despabilar; **to — out** apagar; (*fig*) extinguir; **to — it** (*fam*) estirar la pata (*fam*).

snuffbox ['snʌfbɔks] *n* tabaquera *f*.

snuffers ['snʌfəz] *npl* despabiladeras *fpl*; **a pair of —** unas despabiladeras.

snuffle ['snʌfl] **1** *n* ruido *m* de la nariz; (*twang*) gangueo *m*.
   2 *vi* respirar con ruido, hacer ruido con la nariz; (*in speaking*) ganguear.

snug [snʌg] *adj* (*cosy*) cómodo y bien caliente; (*sheltered*) abrigado, al abrigo; (*of dress*) ajustado; *income etc* respetable, nada despreciable; **to be — in bed** estar cómodamente acostado.

snuggery ['snʌgəri] *n* cuarto *m* cómodo; despacho *m*, cuarto *m* particular.

snuggle ['snʌgl] *vi*: **to — down in bed** acomodarse en la cama; **they'll — down together** se las

arreglarán para estar juntos; **to — up to someone** arrimarse (amorosamente *etc*) a uno, apretarse contra uno; **— up to me arrímate a mí; I like to — up with a book** me gusta ponerme cómodamente y leer.

snugly ['snʌgli] *adv* cómodamente; al abrigo; **it fits —** se ajusta perfectamente.

so [səu] **1** *adv* (a) (*in comparisons: before adj and adv*) tan; **— quick** tan rápido, **— quickly** tan rápidamente; **it is — big that** . . . es tan grande que . . .; **it's not — very difficult** no es tan difícil, la dificultad no es tan grande; **he's not — silly as to do that** no es bastante tonto para hacer eso, no es tan tonto como para hacer eso; **— many flies** tantas moscas; **— much tea** tanto té (*and see* **many, much**); **we spent — much** gastamos tanto; **I love you —** te quiero tanto; **he who — loved Spain** él que amó tanto a España; *see* **kind, sure** *etc*.
   (b) (*thus*) así; (*in this way*) de este modo, de esta manera; **he does it —** él lo hace de este modo; **if —** si es así; **only more —** pero en mayor grado; **how —?** ¿cómo eso?; **why —?** ¿por qué?, ¿cómo?; **just —!** ¡eso es!, ¡perfectamente!, ¡precisamente!; **he likes things just —** quiere tener cada cosa en su lugar, le gusta una vida bien ordenada; **not —!** ¡nada de eso!; **— would I** yo también; **— do I** yo también, yo hago lo mismo; **he's wrong and — are you** él se equivoca y Vd también; **and — forth, and — on** y así sucesivamente, y así los demás; etcétera; **it is — es así; — it is!, — it does!** ¿es verdad!; **that's — eso es; is that —?** ¿de veras?, ¿es cierto eso?; **— be it** así sea; **— it was that** . . . así fue que . . .; **we — arranged things that** . . . lo arreglamos de modo que . . .; **and he did —** y lo hizo; **by — doing** haciéndolo así; **it — happens that** . . . da la casualidad que . . .; **I hope —** espero que sí; **— saying, he walked out** diciendo esto, se marchó; **— to speak** para decirlo así; **I think —** creo que sí, lo creo; **I told you —** te lo dije ya; **I tell you it is —** te digo que es así.
   (c) **— that** (*purpose*) para que + *subj*, a fin de que + *subj*; **I brought it — that you should see it** lo traje para que lo vieras.
   (d) **— that** (*result*) de modo que + *indic*; **he stood — that nobody could get past** estaba en tal posición que nadie podía pasar.
   (e) **— as to** + *infin* para + *infin*, a fin de + *infin*; **we hurried — as not to be late** nos dimos prisa para no llegar tarde.
   2 *conj* (a) **it rained and — we could not go out** llovió y por tanto (*or* por consiguiente) no pudimos salir.
   (b) **— you're Spanish?** ¿conque Vd es español?; **— you're not selling?** ¿de modo que Vd no lo vende?, ¿así que Vd no lo vende?; *see* **there** *etc*.

soak [səuk] **1** *vt* (a) **to — something in a liquid** remojar algo en un líquido, empapar algo en un líquido; **to be —ed (to the skin)** estar calado hasta los huesos; **to get —ed (to the skin)** calarse hasta los huesos.
   (b) **to — up** absorber, embeber.
   (c) **to — someone** (*fam*) desplumar a uno, clavar un precio excesivo a uno (*fam*); **to — someone for a loan** pedir prestado dinero a uno; **to — the rich** imponer contribuciones gravosas a los ricos.
   2 *vi* (a) remojarse, estar a remojo; **to leave something to —** dejar algo a remojo.
   (b) **to — in, to — through** calar, penetrar; **to — in** (*fig*) penetrar; hacer mella, tener efecto.
   (c) (*fam*) beber mucho; emborracharse.
   3 *vr*: **to — oneself** calarse hasta los huesos; **to — oneself in** (*fig*) empaparse en.
   4 *n* (*rain*) diluvio *m*; (*person: fam*) borrachín *m*.

soaking ['səukiŋ] **1** *adj*: **to be — wet** (*person*) estar hecho una sopa, (*object*) estar totalmente mojado; **a — wet day** un día de muchísima lluvia.
   2 *n* remojo *m*; **to get a —** calarse hasta los huesos.

so-and-so ['səuənsəu] *n* (a) **Mr —** don Fulano (de Tal); **old — up at the shop** fulano el de la tienda; **any — could pinch it** (*fam*) cualquiera pudiera guindarlo (*fam*).
   (b) **he's a —** es un tío.

soap [səup] **1** *n* jabón *m*; **soft —** (*sl*) coba *f* (*fam*).
   2 *vt* jabonar, enjabonar.

soapbox ['səupbɔks] *n* caja *f* vacía empleada como tribuna (en la calle); **— orator** orador *m* de barricada; **he has a — manner** habla como un orador de barricada.

soapdish ['səupdiʃ] *n* jabonera *f*.

soapflakes ['səupfleiks] *npl* escamas *fpl* de jabón.

soap opera ['səup,ɔpərə] n (US fam) serial m radiofónico de bajísima categoría.

soap powder ['səup,paudə*] n jabón m en polvo.

soapstone ['səupstəun] n esteatita f.

soapsuds ['səupsʌdz] npl jabonaduras fpl.

soapy ['səupi] adj jabonoso; cubierto de jabón; (like soap) parecido a jabón, jabonoso; (person: pej) zalamero, cobista.

soar [sɔ:*] vi (a) (rise) remontarse, encumbrarse, subir muy alto; (hover) cernerse.
(b) (fig: of tower etc) elevarse mucho sobre el suelo, elevarse hacia el cielo; (of price etc) subir vertiginosamente, ponerse por las nubes; after this his ambition —ed después de esto se extendió mucho más su ambición; our spirits —ed nos reanimamos de golpe; renació nuestra esperanza.

soaring ['sɔ:riŋ] adj flight encumbrado, por lo alto; building altísimo; ambition inmenso; price que va subiendo vertiginosamente.

sob [sɔb] 1 n sollozo m; she said with a — dijo sollozando.
2 attr: — stuff (fam) sentimentalismo m, sensiblería f.
3 vti sollozar; "No", she —bed "no", dijo sollozando; to — one's heart out llorar a mares.

sobbing ['sɔbiŋ] n sollozos mpl.

sober ['səubə*] 1 adj (a) (moderate, sedate) sobrio, serio, moderado; (sensible) sensato, juicioso; colour discreto; a — assessment of the facts una seria valoración de los hechos; a — statement una declaración razonada.
(b) (not drunk) no embriagado, que no ha bebido, sereno; to be as — as a judge, to be stone-cold — estar totalmente sereno; I'm perfectly — yo no he bebido en absoluto, tengo la cabeza perfectamente despejada; one has to be — to drive para conducir es necesario no haber bebido nada; tomorrow, when you're — mañana, cuando te hayas despejado de la borrachera.
2 vt: to — someone down calmar a uno; to — someone up quitar la sopa a uno; this will — you up esto te quitará la merluza.
3 vi: to — down calmarse; he's —ed down recently recientemente ha sentado la cabeza; to — up espabilar la borrachera.

soberly ['səubəli] adv sobriamente, seriamente, moderadamente; sensatamente; discretamente; — dressed discretamente vestido.

sober-minded ['səubə'maindid] adj serio, formal.

sobersides ['səubəsaidz] n (fam) persona f reservada.

sobriety [səu'braiəti] n (a) sobriedad f, seriedad f, moderación f; sensatez f, juicio m; discreción f. (b) serenidad f; moderación f en beber.

sobriquet ['səubrikei] n apodo m, mote m.

so-called ['səu'kɔ:ld] adj llamado, denominado; supuesto, presunto; in the — rush hours en las llamadas horas punta; all these — journalists todos estos presuntos periodistas.

soccer ['sɔkə*] n fútbol m.

sociability [,səuʃə'biliti] n sociabilidad f; afabilidad f.

sociable ['səuʃəbl] adj sociable; afable; amistoso; I'm not feeling very — no me siento con ganas de estar con las personas.

sociably ['səuʃəbli] adv sociablemente; afablemente; amistosamente; to live — together vivir juntos amistosamente.

social ['səuʃəl] 1 adj social; sociable; a — outcast una persona desterrada de la sociedad; the — column las notas de sociedad; man is a — animal el hombre es un animal sociable.
2 n velada f, tertulia f.

Social Democrat ['səuʃəl'demǝkræt] n socialdemócrata mf.

Social-Democratic ['səuʃəl,demǝ'krætik] adj social-democrático.

socialism ['səuʃəlizəm] n socialismo m.

socialist ['səuʃəlist] 1 adj socialista. 2 n socialista mf.

socialistic [,səuʃə'listik] adj socialista.

socialite ['səuʃəlait] n persona f mundana, persona f conocidísima en la buena sociedad.

socialization [,səuʃəlai'zeiʃən] n socialización f.

socialize ['səuʃəlaiz] vt socializar.

socially ['səuʃəli] adv socialmente; sociablemente; we meet — nos vemos en las reuniones de tipo social.

social worker ['səuʃəl,wǝ:kǝ*] n asistente m social, asistenta f social.

society [sə'saiəti] 1 n sociedad f; asociación f; (high —) buena sociedad f, mundo m elegante; charitable — asociación f benéfica; cooperative — cooperativa f;
friendly —, provident — sociedad f de socorro mutuo, mutualidad f, montepío m; the Great S— (US) la Gran Sociedad; high — buena sociedad f; learned — sociedad f científica, academia f; Royal S— Real Sociedad f; S— of Friends los cuáqueros; S— of Jesus Compañía f de Jesús; to try to get into — intentar penetrar en la buena sociedad; to go into — (girl) ponerse de largo.
2 attr: — news (in press) notas fpl de sociedad; — woman mujer f mundana, mujer f conocida en la buena sociedad.

socioeconomic ['səuʃiəu,i:kə'nɔmik] adj socioeconómico.

sociological [,səusiə'lɔdʒikəl] adj sociológico.

sociologist [,səusi'ɔlədʒist] n sociólogo m.

sociology [,səusi'ɔlədʒi] n sociología f.

sock[1] [sɔk] n calcetín m; (worn inside shoe) plantilla f; to pull one's —s up (fig) hacer un esfuerzo, procurar hacer mejor.

sock[2] [sɔk] (fam) 1 n tortazo m (fam); to give someone —s (defeat) cascar a uno (fam). 2 vt pegar; — him one! ¡pégale!

socket ['sɔkit] 1 n (of eye) cuenca f, órbita f; (of tooth) alvéolo m; (of joint) fosa f; (Elec) enchufe m; (Mech) encaje m, cubo m.

Socrates ['sɔkrəti:z] m Sócrates.

Socratic [sɔ'krætik] adj socrático.

sod[1] [sɔd] n césped m.

sod[2] [sɔd] n (of man) sodomita m; (as term of abuse) bestia f, bruto m; you —! ¡cabrón!

soda ['səudə] n (a) (Chem) sosa f, soda f; caustic — sosa f cáustica; common —, washing — sosa f; cooking — bicarbonato m sódico.
(b) (drink) agua f de seltz, gaseosa f; gin and — ginebra f con sifón; do you like — with it? ¿le echo un poco de sifón?

soda biscuit ['səudə,biskit] n (US), **soda cracker** ['səudə,krækə*] n (US) galletita f salada.

soda fountain ['səudə,fauntin] n sifón m.

sodality [səu'dæliti] n (Eccl) hermandad n, cofradía f.

soda water ['səudə,wɔ:tə*] n agua f de seltz, gaseosa f; ... with — ... con sifón.

sodden ['sɔdn] adj empapado, mojado, saturado; to be — with drink estar borracho; estar embrutecido por el alcohol.

sodium ['səudiəm] n sodio m; — carbonate carbonato m sódico.

sodomite ['sɔdəmait] n sodomita m.

sodomy ['sɔdəmi] n sodomía f.

sofa ['səufə] n sofá m.

sofa bed ['səufəbed] n sofá-cama n.

soft [sɔft] adj (a) (of material etc) blando; muelle; (flabby) flojo; skin suave, terso, fino; metal dúctil; hat flexible; fruit blando; — to the touch blando al tacto; as — as silk, as — as velvet tan suave como la seda; to go — ablandarse, ponerse blando; his muscles have gone — sus músculos han perdido su fuerza.
(b) (fig) air, sound suave; voice dulce; step suave; water blando; rain suave; landing suave; colour delicado; drink no alcohólico, analcohólico; heart, words tierno, compasivo; job fácil; character débil; muelle, afeminado; (lenient) indulgente, tolerante; to be — on someone tratar a uno con demasiada indulgencia; he's soft on communism es demasiado tolerante para con el comunismo.
(c) (foolish) estúpido, tonto; you must be —! ¿has perdido el juicio?; he's — (in the head) es un poco tocado; he's going — (in the head) está perdiendo el juicio.

softball ['sɔftbɔ:l] n (US) especie de béisbol sobre un terreno mas pequeño que el normal, con pelota grande y blanda.

soft-boiled ['sɔft,bɔild] adj egg pasado por agua.

soften ['sɔfn] 1 vt ablandar, reblandecer; (weaken) debilitar; (mitigate) mitigar, suavizar, templar; to — up resistance debilitar la resistencia.
2 vi ablandarse, reblandecerse; debilitarse, aflojarse; suavizarse, templarse; to — up on someone hacerse menos severo con uno, mitigar su severidad con uno; we must not — up on communism tenemos que seguir tan opuestos como siempre al comunismo.

softening ['sɔfniŋ] n reblandecimiento m; debilitación f; mitigación f, suavización f; — of the brain reblandecimiento m cerebral; there has been a — of his attitude se ha suavizado su actitud.

soft-footed ['sɔft'futid] adj (Anat) de pies blandos; (soundless) que pisa sin ruido, que anda sin hacer ruido.

soft-headed ['sɔft,hedid] adj bobo, tonto.

soft-hearted ['sɔft'hɑːtid] *adj* compasivo, bondadoso.
soft-heartedness ['sɔft'hɑːtidnis] *n* bondad *f*.
softly ['sɔftli] *adv* blandamente; suavemente; dulcemente; delicadamente; **she said** — dijo dulcemente; **to move** — moverse silenciosamente, moverse sin ruido.
softness ['sɔftnis] *n* blandura *f*; flojedad *f*; suavidad *f*, tersura *f*; ductilidad *f*; dulzura *f*; delicadeza *f*; ternura *f*; debilidad *f*; indulgencia *f*, tolerancia *f*; estupidez *f*.
soft-pedal ['sɔft'pedl] *vt* (*fig*) no dar tanto énfasis a, dejar de insistir en, conceder menos importancia a.
soft-spoken ['sɔft'spəukən] *adj* de voz suave, de tono sereno.
softy ['sɔfti] *n* (*fam*) mollejón *m*, ona *f*.
soggy ['sɔgi] *adj* empapado, saturado; esponjoso.
soi-disant ['swɑː'diːsɔːŋ] *adj* supuesto, presunto, sediciente.
soigné ['swɑːnjei] *adj* pulcro, acicalado.
soil[1] [sɔil] *n* tierra *f*, suelo *m*; **one's native** — su tierra, su patria.
soil[2] [sɔil] **1** *vt* ensuciar; manchar (*also fig*).
   2 *vi* ensuciarse.
   3 *vr*: **to** — **oneself** ensuciarse; **I would not** — **myself by contact with** ... no me rebajaría a tener contacto con ...
soiled [sɔild] *adj* sucio.
soil pipe ['sɔilpaip] *n* tubo *m* de desagüe sanitario.
soirée ['swɑːrei] *n* velada *f*.
sojourn ['sɔdʒəːn] **1** *n* permanencia *f*, estancia *f*. **2** *vi* permanecer, residir, morar; pasar una temporada.
solace ['sɔlis] **1** *n* consuelo *m*; **to seek** — **with** ... procurar consolarse con ...
   2 *vt* consolar.
   3 *vr*: **to** — **oneself** consolarse (*with* con).
solar ['səulə*] *adj* solar, del sol; — **plexus** plexo *m* solar; — **system** sistema *m* solar.
solarium [səu'lɛəriəm] *n*, *pl* **solaria** [səu'lɛəriə] solana *f*.
sold [səuld] *pret and ptp of* **sell**.
solder ['səuldə*] **1** *n* soldadura *f*. **2** *vt* soldar.
soldering iron ['səuldəriŋ‚aiən] *n* soldador *m*.
soldier ['səuldʒə*] **1** *n* soldado *m*; militar *m*; — **of fortune** aventurero *m* militar; **common** — soldado *m* raso; **old** — veterano *m*, excombatiente *m*; **to come the old** — **with someone** (*fam*) creerse superior a uno, darse aires de superioridad con respecto a uno; **private** — soldado *m* raso; **tin** — soldado *m* de plomo.
   2 *vi* militar, ser soldado; servir; **he** —**ed for 10 years in the East** sirvió durante 10 años en el Oriente; **to** — **on** continuar a pesar de todo.
soldierly ['səuldʒəli] *adj* militar.
soldiery ['səuldʒəri] *n* soldadesca *f*; **a brutal and licentious** — la soldadesca indisciplinada.
sole[1] [səul] **1** *n* (*Anat*) planta *f*; (*of shoe*) suela *f*, piso *m*. **2** *vt* poner suela a, poner piso a.
sole[2] [səul] *n* (*Fish*) lenguado *m*.
sole[3] [səul] *adj* único, solo; exclusivo; **the** — **reason is that** ... la única razón es que ...; *see* **agent, right.**
solecism ['sɔləsizəm] *n* solecismo *m*.
solely ['səulli] *adv* únicamente, solamente, sólo.
solemn ['sɔləm] *adj* solemne.
solemnity [sə'lemniti] *n* solemnidad *f*.
solemnization ['sɔləmnai'zeifən] *n* solemnización *f*.
solemnize ['sɔləmnaiz] *vt* solemnizar.
solemnly ['sɔləmli] *adv* solemnemente.
solenoid ['səulənɔid] *n* solenoide *m*.
solfa ['sɔl'fɑː] *n* solfa *f*.
solicit [sə'lisit] *vti* (*request*) solicitar; implorar, pedir insistentemente; (*importune*) importunar; (*of prostitute*) abordar, importunar; **to** — **someone for something, to** — **something of someone** solicitar algo a uno.
solicitation [sə‚lisi'teifən] *n* solicitación *f*.
solicitor [sə'lisitə*] *n* (a) (*US*) representante *mf*, agente *mf*.
   (b) (*Law*) procurador *m*, abogado *m*; (*for oaths, wills etc*) notario *m*; **S— General** (*British*) subfiscal *m* de la Corona, (*US*) procurador *m* general del Estado.
solicitous [sə'lisitəs] *adj* solícito (*about, for* por); preocupado, ansioso; atento.
solicitude [sə'lisitjuːd] *n* solicitud *f*; preocupación *f*, ansiedad *f*; atención *f*.
solid ['sɔlid] **1** *adj* sólido; *gold, silver, oak etc* macizo; *tyre* macizo, sin cámara; (*of consistency of soup etc*) sustancioso; *meal* fuerte; *crowd* denso, apretado; *vote* unánime; *person's character* enteramente serio, muy formal; **a** — **argument** un argumento sólido; **the** — **South** (*US Pol*) el bloque sólido constituido por los estados del Sur (que apoyan siempre al

Partido Democrático); **Slobodia is** — **for Smith** Eslobodia apoya unánimemente a Smith; **the house is** — **enough** la casa es perfectamente sólida; **the square was** — **with cars** la plaza estaba totalmente llena de coches, la plaza estaba repleta de coches; **to be frozen** — estar completamente helado; **it was cut into** — **rock** se excavó en peña viva; **to have** — **grounds for thinking that** ... tener buenos motivos para creer que ...; **it makes good** — **sense** hace muy buen sentido; **we walked 14** — **miles** anduvimos 14 millas largas; **we waited 2** — **hours** esperamos dos horas enteras.
   2 *n* sólido *m*.
solidarity [‚sɔli'dæriti] *n* solidaridad *f*; — **strike** huelga *f* por solidaridad; **out of** — **with the workers** por solidaridad con los obreros.
solidification [sə‚lidifi'keifən] *n* solidificación *f*.
solidify [sə'lidifai] **1** *vt* solidificar. **2** *vi* solidificarse.
solidity [sə'liditi] *n* solidez *f*; unanimidad *f*.
solidly ['sɔlidli] *adv* sólidamente; densamente, apretadamente; unánimemente; **a** — **reasoned argument** un argumento sólidamente razonado; **to vote** — **for someone** votar unánimemente por uno; **we were** — **for Smith** apoyamos unánimemente a Smith; **a** —**built house** una casa de sólida construcción.
solid-state ['sɔlid‚steit] *adj*: — **physics** física *f* del estado sólido.
soliloquize [sə'liləkwaiz] *vi* soliloquiar; "—", **he** —**d** "—" dijo para sí.
soliloquy [sə'liləkwi] *n* soliloquio *m*.
solipsism ['sɔulipsizəm] *n* solipsismo *m*.
solitaire [‚sɔli'tɛə*] *n* (*game, gem*) solitario *m*.
solitary ['sɔlitəri] **1** *adj* (*living alone*) solitario, solo; (*secluded*) retirado, apartado; (*sole*) único, solo; **not a** — **one** ni uno; **there has been one** — **case** ha habido un caso único; **there has not been one** — **case** no ha habido ni un solo caso; **to take a** — **walk** dar un paseo solo, pasearse sin compañía; **to feel rather** — sentirse solo, sentirse aislado; *see* **confinement.**
   2 *n* solitario *m*, a *f*.
solitude ['sɔlitjuːd] *n* soledad *f*.
solo ['səuləu] **1** *n*, *pl* **solos** ['səuləuz] (*Cards, Mus*) solo *m*; **to sing a** — cantar un solo; **a tenor solo** un solo para tenor.
   2 *adj*: — **flight** vuelo *m* a solas; **passage for** — **violin** pasaje *m* para violín solo.
   3 *adv*: **to fly** — volar a solas; **to sing** — cantar solo.
soloist ['səuləuist] *n* solista *mf*.
Solomon ['sɔləmən] *n* Salomón.
solstice ['sɔlstis] *n* solsticio *m*; **summer** — solsticio *m* de verano; **winter** — solsticio *m* de invierno.
solubility [‚sɔlju'biliti] *n* solubilidad *f*.
soluble ['sɔljubl] *adj* soluble; — **in water** soluble en agua.
solution [sə'luːfən] *n* (*all senses*) solución *f* (*to a problem* de un problema).
solvable ['sɔlvəbl] *adj* soluble, que se puede resolver.
solve [sɔlv] *vt* resolver, solucionar; *riddle* adivinar.
solvency ['sɔlvənsi] *n* solvencia *f*.
solvent ['sɔlvənt] **1** *adj* solvente. **2** *n* (*Chem*) solvente *m*.
solver ['sɔlvə*] *n* solucionista *mf*.
Somali [səu'mɑːli] **1** *adj* somalí. **2** *n* somalí *mf*.
Somalia [səu'mɑːliə] Somalia *f*.
sombre, (*US*) **somber** ['sɔmbə*] *adj* sombrío; pesimista; **in** — **hues** en colores sombríos; **a** — **prospect** una perspectiva sombría; **he was** — **about our chances** se mostró pesimista acerca de nuestras posibilidades.
sombrely ['sɔmbəli] *adv* sombríamente; con pesimismo, en tono pesimista.
sombreness ['sɔmbənis] *n* lo sombrío; pesimismo *m*.
some [sʌm] **1** *adj* (a) alguno, (*before m sing n*) algún, *eg* — **man** algún hombre; unos, unos cuantos; — **day** algún día; — **people** algunos, algunas personas; — **very big cars** algunos coches muy grandes, unos coches muy grandes; — **distance away** a cierta distancia; **after** — **time** después de cierto tiempo; — **books I could name** ciertos libros que pudiera mencionar; — **days ago** hace unos días; **in** — **form or other** en alguna que otra forma; **for** — **reason or other** por alguna que otra razón; — **politician or other** algún que otro político; — **other time** otro día; — **idiot of a driver** algún imbécil de conductor.
   (b) (*partitive*) un poco de, algo de; (*freq not translated, eg*) **have you** — **money?** ¿tienes dinero?, **will you have** — **tea?** ¿quieres té?; **all I have left is** — **chocolate** solamente me queda un poco de chocolate; **here is** — **water for you** te he traído un poco de agua; — **water, please** agua, por favor.

(c) (*intensive*) **that's — fish!** ¡eso es lo que se llama un pez!; ¡eso es un pez de verdad!; — **expert!** (*iro*) ¡valiente experto!; **that's — woman** es mucha mujer; **it was — party** ya lo creo que fue una fiesta divertida.

2 *pron* (a) algunos; — **went this way and — that** algunos fueron por aquí y otros por allá; — **say yes and — say no** algunos dicen que sí y otros que no; — **believe that . . .** algunos creen que . . ., hay quien cree que . . .

(b) algunos; algo, un poco; **do take —** (*pl*) toma algunos, (*sing*) toma algo, toma un poco; **thanks, I have —** gracias, ya tengo; **could I have — of that cheese?** ¿me puede servir un poco de ese queso?; — **of them are crazy** algunos de ellos están locos; **I like — of what you said in the speech** me gusta una parte de lo que Vd dijo en el discurso; — **of what you say is true** parte de lo que dice Vd es cierto.

(c) **and then —** (*fam*) y luego un poco más, y más todavía.

3 *adv* (a) — **20 people** unas 20 personas, aproximadamente 20 personas, una veintena de personas; — **£30** unas 30 libras, más o menos 30 libras; — **few difficulties** unas pocas dificultades.

(b) (*US fam*) mucho; **we laughed —** nos reímos mucho; **it sure bothered us —** ya lo creo que nos preocupó bastante; **he's travelling —** lleva gran velocidad.

—some [səm] *in compounds*: grupo *m* de . . ., *eg* **threesome** grupo *m* de tres personas; **we'll go in a threesome** iremos los tres, iremos como grupo de tres; **have we a foursome for bridge?** ¿tenemos cuatro para jugar al bridge?; **to make up a foursome** formar un grupo de cuatro.

somebody ['sʌmbədi] **1** *pron* alguien; — **else** algún otro, otra persona; — **told me so** alguien me lo dijo, me lo dijo alguno; — **or other must have taken it** alguien se lo habrá llevado.

2 *n*: **to be —** ser un personaje; **he thinks he's — now** ahora se cree un personaje.

someday ['sʌmdei] *adv* algún día.

somehow ['sʌmhau] *adv* (a) de algún modo, de un modo u otro; **it must be done — or other** de un modo u otro tiene que hacerse; — **or other I never liked him** por alguna que otra razón no me era simpático.

(b) **it seems — odd, it seems odd —** no sé por qué, pero me parece extraño.

someone ['sʌmwʌn] *pron see* **somebody.**

someplace ['sʌmpleis] *adv* (*US*) = **somewhere.**

somersault ['sʌməsɔːlt] **1** *n* (*by person*) salto *m* mortal; (*by car etc*) vuelco *m*, vuelta *f* de campana; **back —** salto *m* mortal hacia atrás; **to turn a —** dar un salto mortal; volcar; **to turn —s** dar saltos mortales; dar vueltas de campana.

2 *vi* dar un salto mortal; dar una vuelta de campana.

something ['sʌmθiŋ] **1** *n pron* (a) algo; alguna cosa; — **else** otra cosa; — **or other is bothering him** algo le trae preocupado; **there's — the matter** pasa algo; **did you say —?** ¿dijiste algo?; **there's — odd here** aquí hay algo raro; — **of the kind** algo por el estilo; **there's — in what you say** hay gran parte de verdad en lo que Vd dice; **well, that's — eso ya es algo; she has a certain —** tiene un no sé qué de atractivo; **that certain — that makes all the difference** ese no sé qué que importa tanto; **he's called John —** se llama Juan y no sé qué más; **there were 30 —** había treinta y algunos más; **will you have — to drink?** ¿quieres tomar algo?; **I need — to eat** necesito comer; **I gave him — for himself** le di una propina; **it gives her — to live for** le da un motivo para vivir; **do you want to make — of it?** ¿quién le mete a Vd en esto?; y a Vd ¿qué le importa?

(b) **it's — of a problem** es un problema bastante difícil; **he's — of a musician** es en cierto modo un músico, tiene cierto talento para la música; **let's see — of you soon** ven a vernos pronto.

2 *adv* (a) — **over 200** más de 200, 200 y más; **he left — over £10,000** dejó más de 10.000 libras; **he left — like £10,000** dejó algo así como 10.000 libras; **now that's — like a rose!** ¡eso es lo que se llama una rosa!

(b) (*fam*) **it's — chronic** es horrible; **the weather was — shocking** el tiempo fue asqueroso.

sometime ['sʌmtaim] **1** *adv* algún día; alguna vez; — **or other it will have to be done** tarde o temprano tendrá que hacerse; **write to me — soon** escríbeme pronto, escríbeme algún día de éstos; — **before tomorrow** antes de mañana; — **last century** durante el siglo pasado; — **next year** el año que viene (no se sabe exactamente cuándo).

2 *adj* **ex . . ., antiguo;** — **mayor of Wapping ex** alcalde de Wapping.

sometimes ['sʌmtaimz] *adv* algunas veces; a veces.

somewhat ['sʌmwɔt] *adv* algo, algún tanto; **we are — worried** estamos algo inquietos; **it was done — hastily** se hizo con demasiada prisa.

somewhere ['sʌmwɛə*] *adv* (*be*) en alguna parte; (*go*) a alguna parte; — **else** (*be*) en otra parte, (*go*) a otra parte; **I left it — or other** lo dejé en alguna parte, lo dejé por ahí; — **near Huesca** cerca de Huesca; **the temperature was — about 40°** la temperatura era de 40 grados más o menos; **he paid — about £12** pagó alrededor de 12 libras; — **in Aragón** en alguna parte de Aragón; **to broadcast from — in Europe** emitir de algún lugar de Europa.

somnambulism [sɔm'næmbjulizəm] *n* somnambulismo *m*.

somnambulist [sɔm'næmbjulist] *n* somnámbulo *m*, a *f*.

somniferous [sɔm'nifərəs] *adj* somnífero.

somnolence ['sɔmnələns] *n* somnolencia *f*.

somnolent ['sɔmnələnt] *adj* soñoliento.

son [sʌn] *n* hijo *m*; — **of a bitch** (*fam*) hijo *m* de puta; **S— of God** Hijo *m* de Dios; **S— of Man** Hijo *m* del Hombre.

sonata [sə'nɑːtə] *n* sonata *f*.

son et lumière [ˌsɔ̃elym'jɛːr] *n* (espectáculo *m* de) luz *f* y sonido.

song [sɔŋ] *n* canción *f*; (*art of singing*) canto *m*; (*epic*) cantar *m*; **festival of Spanish —** festival *m* de la canción española; **"A S— for Europe"** "Canción *f* para Europa"; **S— of Roland** Cantar *m* de Roldán; **S— of Solomon, S— of S—s** Cantar *m* de los Cantares; **to burst into —** romper a cantar; **give us a —!** ¡cántanos algo!; **to make a great — and dance about something** hacer algo a bombo y platillos; **he made a — and dance about the carpet** armó la gorda por lo de la alfombra; **there's no need to make a — and dance** no es para tanto; **to sell something for a (mere) —** vender algo medio regalado; **I got it for a —** lo adquirí muy barato; **to sing another —** (*fig*) bajar el tono, desdecirse.

songbird ['sɔŋbəːd] *n* pájaro *m* cantor.

songbook ['sɔŋbuk] *n* cancionero *m*.

song cycle ['sɔŋ'saikl] *n* ciclo *m* de canciones.

song hit ['sɔŋhit] *n* canción *f* de moda, canción *f* popular del momento.

songster ['sɔŋstə*] *n* pájaro *m* cantor.

song thrush ['sɔŋθrʌʃ] *n* tordo *m* cantor, tordo *m* melodioso.

song writer ['sɔŋˌraitə*] *n* compositor *m* de canciones.

sonic ['sɔnik] **1** *adj* sónico. **2 —s** sónica *f*.

son-in-law ['sʌninlɔː] *n* yerno *m*, hijo *m* político.

sonnet ['sɔnit] *n* soneto *m*.

sonny ['sʌni] *n* (*fam*) hijito *m*; (*in direct address*) hijo.

sonority [sə'nɔriti] *n* sonoridad *f*.

sonorous ['sɔnərəs] *adj* sonoro.

sonorousness ['sɔnərəsnis] *n* sonoridad *f*.

soon [suːn] *adv* (a) pronto, dentro de poco; (*early*) temprano; **come back —** vuelve pronto; — **afterwards** poco después; **how — can you come?** ¿cuándo puedes venir?; **how — can you be ready?** ¿para cuando estarás listo?; **we got there too —** llegamos demasiado pronto; **Friday is too —** el viernes es muy pronto; **all too — it was over** la función terminó muy pronto; **we were none too —** llegamos en el momento oportuno; menos mal que en ese momento llegamos nosotros.

(b) (*with as*) **as —** as en cuanto, tan pronto como, así que; **as — as you've seen him** en cuanto le veas, en cuanto le hayas visto; **as — as it was finished** en cuanto se terminó; **as — as possible** cuanto antes, lo antes posible, lo más pronto posible; **I would as — not go** igual me daría no ir, estaría tan contento de no ir; *see also* **sooner.**

sooner ['suːnə*] *adv* (a) (*of time*) más temprano; **we got there — nosotros** llegamos antes; — **or later** tarde o temprano; **the — the better** cuanto antes, mejor; **no — had we arrived, than . . .** apenas habíamos llegado, cuando . . ., no bien llegamos, cuando . . .; **no — said than done** dicho y hecho; **in 5 years or at his death, whichever is the —** al cabo de 5 años o a su muerte, lo que suceda antes; **the — we start the — we finish** cuanto más pronto empecemos, más pronto podremos concluir.

(b) (*of preference*) **I had — not do it, I would — not do it** preferiría no hacerlo; **which would you —?** ¿cuál prefieres?

soot [sut] *n* hollín *m*.

sooth [suːθ] *n*: **in —** en realidad.

soothe [suːð] *vt* tranquilizar, calmar; (*pain*) aliviar.

soothing ['suːðiŋ] *adj* tranquilizador, calmante; (*pain-killing*) quitadolores; **tone, words etc** dulce, consolador.

soothingly ['su:ðiŋli] adv speak etc dulcemente, con dulzura, en tono consolador.
soothsayer ['su:θ,seiə*] n adivino m, a f.
soothsaying ['su:θ,seiiŋ] n adivinación f.
sooty ['suti] adj hollinoso, cubierto de hollín; (fig) negro como el hollin.
sop [sɔp] 1 n (food) sopa f; (fig) regalo m, dádiva f; compensación f; (sl) tonto m, a f; as a — to his pride para ayudarle a salvar las apariencias, como compensación a su amor propio; this is a — to Cerberus esto es para comprar la benevolencia de ...
    2 vt: to — up absorber.
Sophia [sɔu'faiə] f Sofía.
sophism ['sɔfizəm] n sofisma m.
sophist ['sɔfist] n sofista m.
sophistical [sə'fistikəl] adj sofístico.
sophisticated [sə'fistikeitid] adj sofisticado.
sophistication [sə,fisti'keiʃən] n sofisticación f.
sophistry ['sɔfistri] n sofistería f.
Sophocles ['sɔfəkli:z] m Sófocles.
sophomore ['sɔfəmɔ:*] n (US) estudiante mf de segundo año.
soporific [,sɔpə'rifik] adj soporífero.
sopping ['sɔpiŋ] adj: it's — (wet) está totalmente mojado; he was — wet estaba hecho una sopa.
soppy ['sɔpi] adj (sl: foolish) bobo, tonto; (mushy) sentimental, sensiblero.
soprano [sə'pra:nəu] 1 n, pl sopranos [sə'pra:nəuz] n (person) soprano f, tiple f; (voice and part) soprano m. 2 adj part etc de soprano, para soprano; voice de soprano.
sorcerer ['sɔ:sərə*] n hechicero m, brujo m.
sorceress ['sɔ:sərəs] n hechicera f, bruja f.
sorcery ['sɔ:səri] n hechicería f, brujería f.
sordid ['sɔ:did] adj (squalid, dirty) asqueroso, sucio; place, room miserable; deal, motive etc vil; it's a pretty — business es un asunto de lo más desagradable.
sordidness ['sɔ:didnis] n lo asqueroso, suciedad f; lo miserable; vileza f.
sore [sɔ:*] 1 adj (a) (Med) inflamado, dolorido, que duele; — throat dolor m de garganta; my eyes are —, I have — eyes me duelen los ojos; I'm — all over me duele todo el cuerpo; where are you —? ¿dónde te duele?
    (b) (fig) to be — at heart tener la muerte en el alma; to be — about something estar resentido por algo; to be — about someone estar enojado con uno; what are you so — about? ¿por qué estás tan ofendido?; now don't get — no te vayas a ofender; it's a — point es un asunto delicado; see spot.
    2 n (Med) llaga f, úlcera f; (caused by harness etc) matadura f; (fig) llaga f, herida f; recuerdo m doloroso; running — úlcera f; (fig) llaga f; to open an old — (fig) renovar la herida.
sorehead ['sɔ:hed] n (US fam) persona f resentida, resentido m.
sorely ['sɔ:li] adv: — wounded herido de gravedad, gravemente herido; I am — tempted tengo grandes tentaciones; I am — tempted to + infin casi estoy por + infin; he has been — tried ha sufrido lo indecible.
soreness ['sɔ:nis] n (Med) inflamación f, dolor m.
sorghum ['sɔ:gəm] n sorgo m.
sorority [sə'rɔriti] n (US Univ) hermandad f de estudiantes.
sorrel[1] ['sɔrəl] n (Bot) acedera f.
sorrel[2] ['sɔrəl] 1 adj alazán. 2 n alazán m, caballo m alazán.
sorrow ['sɔrəu] 1 n pesar m, pena f, dolor m; tristeza f; more in — than in anger con más pesar que enojo; to my (great) — con gran pesar mío, con gran sentimiento mío; this was a great — to me esto me causó mucha pena; the —s of their race las aflicciones de su raza; to drown one's —s olvidar su tristeza emborrachándose, ahogar sus penas en alcohol.
    2 vi apenarse, afligirse (at, for, over de, por) dolerse (at, for, over de).
sorrowful ['sɔrəful] adj afligido, triste, pesaroso.
sorrowfully ['sɔrəfli] adv con pena, tristemente.
sorrowing ['sɔrəuiŋ] adj afligido.
sorry ['sɔri] adj (a) (regretful) arrepentido; (sad) triste, afligido, apenado; —! ¡perdón!, ¡perdone!; awfully —!, so —! lo siento mucho, lo siento en el alma, ¡cuánto lo siento!; to be — sentirlo; I am very — lo siento mucho; I can't say I'm — no es que me pese la noticia, el hecho no me causa ningún sentimiento; he wasn't in the least bit — no se arrepintió en lo más mínimo; no pidió perdón a nadie; to be — about something afligirse

por algo; I'm — about that vase te pido perdón por lo del florero; me da pena el florero ese; to be — for someone compadecer a uno, tener lástima a uno; I feel — for the child el niño me da lástima; there's no need to be — for him no hace falta compadecerle; you'll be — for this! ¡me las pagarás!; to be (or look) — for oneself estar muy abatido; to be — that ... sentir que + subj; to be — to + infin sentir + infin, lamentar + infin.
    (b) (bad) condition, plight lastimoso; sight triste; figure ridículo; excuse nada convincente; joke pobre; it was a — tale of defeat fue una triste narración de derrotas.
sort [sɔ:t] 1 n (a) clase f, género m, especie f; tipo m; what — do you want? ¿qué clase quiere Vd?; the — you gave me last time el mismo que Vd me dio la última vez; but not that — pero no de ese tipo, pero no como eso; I know his — ésos me los conozco, conozco el paño; he's the — who will cheat you es de los que te engañarán; books of all — s toda clase de libros, libros de toda clase; he's a painter of a —, he's a painter of —s es en cierto modo pintor; it's coffee of a — es café pero bastante inferior, es lo que apenas se puede llamar café; perfect of its — perfecto en su línea; something of the — algo por el estilo; nothing of the —! ¡nada de eso!, ¡ni hablar!; I shall do nothing of the — no haré eso bajo ningún concepto; in some — algo, en cierta medida; it takes all — s (to make a world) de todo hay en la viña del Señor.
    (b) (— of): what — of car? ¿qué clase de coche?; what — of man is he? ¿qué tipo de hombre es?; this — of house una casa de este tipo; an odd — of novel una novela rara, una novela de tipo extraño; all — s of dogs toda clase de perros, perros de toda clase; he's a — of agent es algo así como un agente; he's some — of painter es pintor pero no sé de qué género; I felt a — of shame sentí algo parecido a la vergüenza, en cierto modo sentí vergüenza; it's a — of dance una especie de baile; I have a — of idea that ... tengo cierta idea de que ...; that's the — of thing I need eso es lo que me hace falta; that's the — of thing I mean eso es precisamente lo que quiero decir; and all that — of thing y otras cosas por el estilo; that's the — of person I am yo soy así; he's not that — of person no es capaz de hacer eso, no es de los que hacen tales cosas; I'm not that — of girl yo no soy de ésas.
    (c) (— of, as adv: fam) it's — of awkward es bastante difícil; it's — of blue es más bien azul; it's — of finished está más o menos terminado; I — of feel that ... en cierto modo creo que ...; it — of made me laugh no sé por qué pero me hizo reír; aren't you pleased? ... — of ¿no te alegras? ... en cierto modo.
    (d) (person) he's a good — es buena persona, es un buen chico; she sounds a good — da la impresión de ser buena persona; he's an odd — es un tipo extraño; your — never did any good las personas como Vd nunca hicieron nada bueno.
    (e) to be out of —s (Med) estar indispuesto, no estar del todo bien; (in mood) estar molesto, sentirse incómodo.
    2 vt (a) (also to — out) clasificar; to — out the bad ones separar los malos, quitar los malos.
    (b) to — out (fig) problem etc arreglar; solucionar; we've got it —ed out now lo hemos arreglado ya; can you — this out for me? ¿puede Vd ayudarme con esto?; to — someone out (sl) ajustar cuentas con uno; I'll come down there and — you out! si bajo allá te pego una paliza.
sorter ['sɔ:tə*] n clasificador m, ora f; (Post) distribuidor m, oficial m de correos.
sortie ['sɔ:ti] n salida f; they flew 400 —s realizaron un total de 400 salidas; to make a — hacer una salida.
sorting office ['sɔ:tiŋ,ɔfis] n oficina f de distribución del correo.
so-so ['səu'səu] adv regular, así así.
sot [sɔt] n borrachín m.
sottish ['sɔtiʃ] adj embrutecido (por el alcohol).
sotto voce ['sɔtəu'vəutʃi] adv en voz baja.
Soudan [su'da:n] Sudán m.
Soudanese [,su:də'ni:z] 1 adj sudanés. 2 n sudanés m, esa f.
soufflé ['su:flei] n suflé m.
sough [sau] 1 n susurro m. 2 vi susurrar.
sought [sɔ:t] pret and pp of seek.
sought-after ['sɔ:t,a:ftə*] adj codiciado; solicitado; que tiene mucha demanda; this much — title este codiciado título.

soul [səul] n (a) alma f; **upon my —!, (God) bless my —!** ¡caramba!; ¡Dios me valga!; **with all one's —** con toda el alma; **God rest his —!** ¡Dios le acoja en su seno!; **to possess one's — in patience** tener muchísima paciencia.
(b) (fig: person) alma f; **3,000 —s** 3.000 almas; **poor —!** ¡pobrecito!; **the poor — had nowhere to sleep** el pobre no tenía dónde dormir; **he's a good —** es un bendito; **she's a simple —** es una alma de Dios; **without seeing a —** sin ver bicho viviente; **every living —** todo ser viviente; **the ship was lost with all —s** el buque se hundió con toda la tripulación (y pasajeros).
soul-destroying ['səuldis'trɔiiŋ] adj (fig) de lo más aburrido (or monótono etc); totalmente desprovisto de interés, de nulo interés intelectual (or estético etc).
soulful ['səulful] adj sentimental; conmovedor.
soulfully ['səulfəli] adv de modo sentimental; de modo conmovedor.
soulless ['səullis] adj person sin alma, desalmado; work etc mecánico, monótono, sin interés humano.
soul mate ['səulmeit] n perfecto compañero m espiritual, perfecta compañera f espiritual.
soul-stirring ['səul‚stəːriŋ] adj conmovedor, inspirador.
sound¹ [saund] 1 adj sano; firme, sólido; constitution robusto; (Comm) solvente; person formal, digno de confianza; argument, idea, opinion razonable, lógico, bien fundado; ortodoxo; policy prudente; investment bueno, seguro; move acertado, lógico; rule bueno; training etc sólido; sleep profundo; **in — condition** en buenas condiciones; **to be as — as a bell** estar en perfecta salud; **to be — in wind and limb** estar en buen estado físico; **to be — in mind and body** ser sano de cuerpo y de espíritu; **he's a very — man** es persona de la mayor confianza; **he's a — worker** es buen trabajador, trabaja con toda seriedad; **he is — enough on the theory** tiene una preparación sólida en cuanto a la teoría; tiene opiniones ortodoxas acerca de la teoría.
2 adv: **to be — asleep** estar profundamente dormido; **I shall sleep the —er for it** por eso dormiré más tranquilamente.
sound² [saund] 1 n sonido m, son m; ruido m; **to the —(s) of the national anthem** a los sones del himno nacional; **within — of** al alcance de; **not a — was heard** no hubo ruido alguno; **there came the — of breaking glass** se oyó el ruido de cristales que se rompían; **I don't like the — of it** esto no nos promete nada bueno, me inquieta la noticia, no me gusta la idea.
2 vt sonar; alarm, bell, horn, trumpet tocar; praises cantar, entonar; **to — the "d" in "hablado"** pronunciar la "d" en "hablado"; **to — the charge** tocar a carga; **to — the retreat** tocar a retirada.
3 vi (a) sonar, resonar; **the bell —ed** sonó el timbre; **it —s hollow** suena a hueco; **it —s like Dutch to me** me suena a holandés; **a gun —ed a long way off** se oyó un cañón a lo lejos.
(b) (seem) sonar, parecer; **that —s very odd** eso parece muy raro; **he —s like a good sort** parece que es buena persona, da la impresión de ser buena persona; **how does it — to you?** ¿a ti que te parece?
(c) **to — off** (fam) hablar en tono autoritario; (complain) quejarse; (protest) protestar, poner el grito en el cielo.
sound³ [saund] 1 n (Med) sonda f.
2 vt (Med, Naut) sondar; chest auscultar; **to — out** person, intentions, opinions sondear, tantear; **to — someone out about something** tratar de averiguar lo que piensa uno acerca de un asunto; **to — out one's conscience** consultar su conciencia.
sound⁴ [saund] n (Geog) estrecho m, brazo m de mar.
sound barrier ['saund‚bæriə*] n barrera f del sonido.
sound effects ['saundi‚fekts] npl efectos mpl sonoros.
sounding ['saundiŋ] n (Naut) sondeo m; —s (for oil etc) sondeos mpl; **to take —s** (fig) sondear la opinión, pulsar las opiniones.
sounding board ['saundiŋbɔːd] n (Mus) secreto m, caja f de resonancia; (fig) caja f de resonancia.
soundless ['saundlis] adj silencioso, sin ruido.
soundlessly ['saundlisli] adv silenciosamente, sin ruido.
soundly ['saundli] adv sólidamente, razonablemente, lógicamente, prudentemente; **to beat someone —** derrotar a uno completamente; **to thrash someone —** dar a uno una paliza de verdad; **to sleep —** dormir bien, dormir profundamente.
soundness ['saundnis] n firmeza f, solidez f; robustez f; solvencia f; formalidad f; lo razonable, lógica f, sólida fundación f; ortodoxia f; prudencia f;

seguridad f; **the — of someone's health** el buen estado físico de uno; **the — of a proposal** la solidez de una proposición.
soundproof ['saundpruːf] 1 adj insonorizado, a prueba de ruidos. 2 vt insonorizar.
soundproofing ['saundpruːfiŋ] n insonorización f.
sound recording ['saundri‚kɔːdiŋ] n grabación f sonora.
sound track ['saundtræk] n banda f sonora.
sound wave ['saundweiv] n onda f sonora.
soup¹ [suːp] n (clear, thin) caldo m, consomé m; (thick) puré m, sopa f; **fish —** sopa f de pescado; **vegetable —** sopa f de hortelano; **to be in the —** (fam) estar en apuros; **now we're properly in the —** (fam) ahora le hemos pringado de verdad.
soup² [suːp] vt (sl): **to — up** sobrealimentar.
soupçon ['suːpsɔ] n pizca f; **with a — of ginger** con una pizca de jengibre; **there is just a — of a rigged game** hay cierto olorcillo a tongo.
souped-up ['suːpt‚ʌp] adj (sl) sobrealimentado.
soup kitchen ['suːp‚kitʃin] n comedor m de beneficencia, comedor m gratuito para los pobres.
soup plate ['suːppleit] n plato m sopero.
soupspoon ['suːpspuːn] n cuchara f sopera.
soup tureen ['suːptə‚riːn] n sopera f.
soupy ['suːpi] adj liquid espeso, turbio; atmosphere pesado, espeso; viciado.
sour ['sauə*] 1 adj agrio, acre; milk cortado; land maleado; person agrio, desabrido, poco afable; **to go — (milk)** cortarse; **to turn —** agriarse, volverse agrio.
2 vt agriar; land malear; person agriar, amargar.
3 vi agriarse, volverse agrio; (land) malearse.
source [sɔːs] n (of river) fuente f, nacimiento m; (fig) fuente f, origen m; ¡procedencia f; (Lit etc) fuente f; (of infection) foco m; **what is the — of this information?** ¿de dónde proceden estos informes?; **I have it from a good — that...** sé de fuente fidedigna que...; **we have other —s of supply** tenemos otras fuentes de suministro.
sour-faced ['sauəfeist] adj con cara de pocos amigos.
sourish ['sauəriʃ] adj agrete.
sourly ['sauəli] adv (fig) agriamente; **to answer —** contestar en tono áspero.
sourness ['sauənis] n agrura f, acidez f; (fig) agrura f, aspereza f.
sourpuss ['sauəpus] n (US sl) persona f desabrida, persona f poco afable.
souse [saus] 1 n (pickle) escabeche m; **to have a —** (fam) lavarse, ducharse.
2 vt (pickle) escabechar; (plunge) zambullir (into en); (soak) mojar (with de); **to — someone with soup** mojar a uno derramando la sopa sobre él; **to be —ed** (sl) estar ajumado (fam); **to get —d** mojarse, calarse.
south [sauθ] 1 n sur m; mediodía m; **the Deep S—** el Profundo Sur. 2 adj del sur, meridional. 3 adv al sur, hacia el sur.
South Africa [sauθ'æfrikə] África f del Sur.
South African [sauθ'æfrikən] 1 adj sudafricano. 2 n sudafricano m, a f.
South America [‚sauθə'merikə] América f del Sur, Sudamérica f.
South American [‚sauθə'merikən] 1 adj sudamericano. 2 n sudamericano m, a f.
south-east ['sauθ'iːst] 1 n sudeste m. 2 adj point, direction sudeste; wind del sudeste.
south-easterly ['sauθ'iːstəli] adj point, direction sudeste; wind del sudeste.
south-eastern ['sauθ'iːstən] adj sudeste.
south-eastward(s) ['sauθ'iːstwəd(z)] adv hacia el sudeste.
southerly ['sʌðəli] adj point, direction sur; wind del sur; **the most — point in Europe** el punto más meridional de Europa.
southern ['sʌðən] adj del sur, meridional.
southerner ['sʌðənə*] n habitante mf del sur; meridional mf; **she's a —** es del Sur; **—s are shorter than northerners** los meridionales son menos altos que los septentrionales.
southernmost ['sʌðənməust] adj (el) más meridional, situado más al sur; **the — town in Europe** la ciudad más meridional de Europa.
South Korea ['sauθkə'riə] Corea f del Sur.
South Korean ['sauθkə'riən] 1 adj surcoreano. 2 n surcoreano m, a f.
southpaw ['sauθpɔː] n (esp US) jugador m zurdo, boxeador m zurdo.
South Seas ['sauθ'siːz] pl mares mpl del Sur.
South Vietnam ['sauθ‚vjet'næm] Vietnam m del Sur.
South Vietnamese ['sauθ‚vjetnə'miːz] 1 adj survietnamita. 2 n survietnamita mf.

southward(s) ['sauθwəd(z)] *adv* hacia el sur.
south-west ['sauθ'west] **1** *n* suroeste *m*. **2** *adj point, direction* suroeste; *wind* del suroeste.
south-wester [sauθ'westə*] *n* (*wind*) suroeste *m*; (*hat*) sueste *m*.
south-westerly [sauθ'westəli] *adj point, direction* suroeste; *wind* del suroeste.
south-western [sauθ'westən] *adj* suroeste.
south-westward(s) [sauθ'westwəd(z)] *adv* hacia el suroeste.
souvenir [,su:və'niə*] *n* recuerdo *m*.
sou'wester [sau'westə*] *n* sueste *m*.
sovereign ['sɔvrin] **1** *adj* soberano. **2** *n* soberano *m*, a *f*; (*coin*) soberano *m*.
sovereignty ['sɔvrənti] *n* soberanía *f*.
soviet ['səuviət] **1** *n* soviet *m*. **2** *adj, attr* soviético.
Soviet Russia ['səuviət'rʌʃə] la Rusia Soviética.
Soviet Union ['səuviət'ju:njən] Unión *f* Soviética.
sow [səu] (*irr: pret* **sowed**, *ptp* **sown**) *vt* sembrar (*with* de; *also fig*); esparcir; **to — mines in a strait, to — a strait with mines** plagar un estrecho de minas; **to — doubt in someone's mind** suscitar dudas en uno.
sow [sau] *n* cerda *f*, puerca *f*, marrana *f*; (*of wild boar*) jabalina *f*; (*of badger*) tejón *m* hembra; (*Tech*) galápago *m*.
sower ['səuə*] *n* sembrador *m*, ora *f*.
sowing ['səuiŋ] *n* siembra *f*.
sowing machine ['səuiŋmə,ʃi:n] *n* sembradora *f*.
sowing time ['səuiŋ,taim] *n* época *f* de la siembra, sementera *f*.
sown [səun] *ptp* of **sow**.
soya ['sɔiə] *n* soja *f*.
soya bean ['sɔiə'bi:n] *n* semilla *f* de soja.
sozzled ['sɔzld] *adj* (*sl*): **to be —** estar ajumado (*fam*); **to get —** ajumarse.
spa [spa:] *n* balneario *m*.
space [speis] **1** *n* espacio *m*; **blank —** espacio *m* en blanco; **outer —** espacio *m* exterior; **for a —** durante cierta distancia, durante cierto tiempo; **in a confined —** en un espacio restringido; **in the — of one hour** en el espacio de una hora; **in the — of 3 generations** en el espacio de 3 generaciones; **to clear a — for** hacer un sitio para; **to leave — for** dejar un sitio para; **leave a — for the name** deje un espacio para poner el nombre; **to stare into —** mirar al vacío; mirar distraído; **it takes up a lot of —** ocupa bastante espacio.
  2 *attr* espacial; **— research** investigaciones *fpl* espaciales; **— programme** programa *m* de investigaciones espaciales.
  3 *vt* (*also* **to — out**) espaciar (*also Typ*); **well —d out** bastante distanciados.
space capsule ['speis,kæpsju:l] *n* cápsula *f* espacial.
spacecraft ['speiskra:ft] *n* nave *f* espacial, astronave *f*.
space flight ['speisflait] *n* vuelo *m* espacial.
space helmet ['speis,helmit] *n* casco *m* espacial.
spaceman ['speismæn] *n*, *pl* **-men** [men] astronauta *m*, cosmonauta *m*.
spaceship ['speisʃip] *n* nave *f* espacial, astronave *f*.
space shot ['speisʃɔt] *n* (lanzamiento *m* de un) vehículo *m* espacial.
space station ['speis,steiʃən] *n* estación *f* espacial.
spacesuit ['speissu:t] *n* traje *m* espacial.
space vehicle ['speis,vi:ikl] *n* vehículo *m* espacial.
spacing ['speisiŋ] *n* espaciamiento *m*; **with double —** (*Typ*) a doble espacio.
spacing bar ['speisiŋba:*] *n* (*Typ*) barra *f* espaciadora.
spacious ['speiʃəs] *adj* espacioso, amplio; extenso; *living* holgado, lujoso.
spaciousness ['speiʃəsnis] *n* espaciosidad *f*, amplitud *f*; extensión *f*.
spade [speid] *n* (a) (*tool*) pala *f*, laya *f*; **to call a — a —** llamar al pan pan y al vino vino. (b) **-s** (*Cards*) picos *mpl*, (*in Spanish pack*) espadas *fpl*.
spadeful ['speidful] *n* pala *f*; **by the —** (*fig*) en grandes cantidades.
spadework ['speidwə:k] *n* (*fig*) trabajo *m* preliminar.
spaghetti [spə'geti] *n* espaguetis *mpl*; fideos *mpl*.
Spain [spein] España *f*.
spake [speik] *pret* (*arch*) of **speak**.
span¹ [spæn] **1** *n* (*of hand, as measure*) palmo *m*; (*of time*) lapso *m*, espacio *m*; duración *f*; (*of horses*) pareja *f*, (*of oxen*) yunta *f*; (*of wing*) envergadura *f*; (*of bridge: referring to space*) ojo *m*, luz *f*, (*referring to structure*) arcada *f*, entramado *m*; (*of roof*) vano *m*; **a — of 50 metres** (*bridge*) una luz de 50 metros; **a bridge with 7 —s** un puente de 7 arcadas, un puente de 7 ojos; **the longest single-span bridge in the world** el puente más largo del mundo de una sola arcada, el puente que tiene el entramado continuo más largo del mundo: **the average — of**

life la duración media de la vida; **for a brief —** durante una breve temporada; **the whole — of world affairs** toda la extensión de los asuntos mundiales, los asuntos mundiales en toda su amplitud.
  2 *vt* (*measure*) medir (a palmos); (*of bridge*) extenderse sobre, cruzar; (*of builder*) tender un puente sobre; (*in time etc*) abarcar; **his life —ned 4 reigns** su vida abarcó 4 reinados.
span² [spæn] *pret* of **spin**.
spangle ['spæŋgl] **1** *n* lentejuela *f*. **2** *vt* adornar con lentejuelas; **—d with** (*fig*) sembrado de.
Spaniard ['spænjəd] *n* español *m*, ola *f*.
spaniel ['spænjəl] *n* perro *m* de aguas.
Spanish ['spæniʃ] **1** *adj* español; **the —** los españoles.
  2 *n* (*language*) español *m*, castellano *m*; **Medieval —** español *m* medieval; **Modern —** español *m* moderno; **Old —** español *m* antiguo.
Spanish-American ['spæniʃə'merikən] **1** *adj* hispanoamericano. **2** *n* hispanoamericano *m*, a *f*.
Spanishness ['spæniʃnis] *n* españolidad *f*, españolismo *m*.
Spanish-speaking ['spæniʃ'spi:kiŋ] *adj* hispanohablante, de habla española.
spank [spæŋk] **1** *n* azote *m*, manotada *f* (en las nalgas); **to give someone a —** dar un azote a uno (en las nalgas).
  2 *vt* zurrar, manotear; **I'll — you!** ¡te voy a pegar!
  3 *vi*: **to — along** correr, ir volando.
spanker ['spæŋkə*] *n* (*Naut*) mesana *f*.
spanking ['spæŋkiŋ] **1** *adj* fuerte grande, rápido; *breeze* fuerte; **we had a — (good) time** lo pasamos en grande.
  2 *n* zurra *f*; **to give someone a —** zurrar a uno.
spanner ['spænə*] *n* llave *f* (inglesa), llave *f* de tuercas; **to throw a — in the works** meter un palo en la rueda.
spar¹ [spa:*] *n* (*Naut*) palo *m*, verga *f*.
spar² [spa:*] *vi* (*Boxing*) hacer fintas, fintar; entrenarse en el boxeo, hacer ejercicios de boxeo; **to — at someone** amagar a uno; **to — with someone about something** (*fig*) disputar algo amistosamente con uno; **he's only —ring with the problem** no intenta seriamente resolver el problema.
spar³ [spa:*] *n* (*Min*) espato *m*; **Iceland —** espato *m* de Islandia.
spare [speə*] **1** *adj* (a) (*left over*) sobrante, que sobra, de más; (*available*) disponible; *room* para convidados; *time* libre, desocupado; *part* (*Mech*) de repuesto, de recambio; **— collar** cuello *m* de repuesto; **in my — time** en mis ratos libres, en mis ratos de ocio; **if you have any — time** si Vd dispone de tiempo, si Vd tiene tiempo; **there are 2 going —** sobran 2, quedan 2; **if you have any — bottles** si Vd dispone de algunas botellas; **it's all the — cash I have** es todo el dinero contante que tengo.
  (b) (*of build etc*) enjuto.
  2 *n* pieza *f* de repuesto, repuesto *m*, recambio *m*; **we stock —s** tenemos existencia de repuestos.
  3 *vt* (a) (*be grudging with*) excusar; escatimar; **to — no expense** no escatimar dinero; **to — no pains to do something** no perdonar esfuerzos por hacer algo.
  (b) (*do without*) pasarse sin; ahorrar; economizar; **we can't — him now** ahora no podemos estar sin él, ahora no podemos permitir que se vaya; **can you — this for a moment?** ¿me puedo llevar esto un momento?, ¿me permite llevarme esto un momento?; **if you can — it** si Vd puede pasarse sin él, si Vd puede cedérmelo; **can you — the time?** ¿puede Vd dedicar su tiempo a esto?; **I can — you 5 minutes** estoy libre para verle durante 5 minutos, le puedo dedicar 5 minutos.
  (c) **to — de sobra; there is none to —** apenas queda nada; no tenemos nada de sobra, no nos sobra nada; **we have 9 bottles to —** no sobran 9 botellas; **there's enough and to —** no sólo hay bastante sino que sobra algo, hay más que suficiente para todos.
  (d) *life* perdonar; **the fire —d nothing** el incendio no perdonó nada; **he was —d another 3 years** tuvo otros 3 años de vida; **he —s nobody** hace trabajar a todos como demonios; es severo con todos sin excepción; **to — someone's feelings** procurar no herir los sentimientos de uno; **to — someone the trouble of doing something** evitar a uno la molestia de hacer algo; **— my blushes!** ¡considere mi modestia!, ¡qué cosas me dices!
sparerib ['speə'rib] *n* (*US*) costilla *f* de cerdo (con poca carne).
sparing ['speəriŋ] *adj* escaso; (*thrift*) económico; controlado, limitado; **his — use of colour** su

parquedad con los colores; **to be — of, to be — with** ser parco en, ser avaro de; **to be — of praise** escatimar los elogios; **to be — of words** ser persona de pocas palabras; ser parco en hablar.
sparingly ['spɛəriŋli] *adv* escasamente; económicamente; **we used water —** empleamos el agua bastante poco; **he uses colour —** es parco en el uso de los colores; **use it very —** úselo en pequeñas cantidades, úselo con moderación; **to eat —** comer poco, comer frugalmente.
sparingness ['spɛəriŋnis] *n* parquedad *f*; economía *f*, moderación *f*.
spark [spɑːk] **1** *n* chispa *f*; (*of wit*) chispazo *m*; **—s** (*Tel, fam*) telegrafista *m*; **bright —** (*fam*) tipo *m* muy listo; **there's not a — of life about it** no tiene ni un átomo de vida; **the book hasn't a — of interest** el libro no tiene ni pizca de interés.
  2 *vt*: **to — off** hacer estallar, (*fig*) hacer estallar, precipitar, provocar.
  3 *vi* chispear, echar chispas.
sparking plug ['spɑːkiŋplʌg] *n*, (*US*) **spark plug** ['spɑːkplʌg] *n* bujía *f*.
sparkle ['spɑːkl] **1** *n* centelleo *m*, destello *m*; (*fig*) brillo *m*, viveza *f*, vida *f*; **a person without —** una persona sin viveza.
  2 *vi* centellear, destellar, chispear; (*shine*) brillar, relucir; **she doesn't exactly —** no tiene mucha viveza que digamos; **the conversation —d** la conversación fue animadísima, en la conversación hubo muchas salidas ingeniosas.
sparkling ['spɑːkliŋ] *adj* centelleante; brillante, reluciente; *wine* espumoso; *eyes, wit, conversation* chispeante.
sparring partner ['spɑːriŋˌpɑːtnə*] *n* sparring *m*.
sparrow ['spærəu] *n* gorrión *m*.
sparrowhawk ['spærəuhɔːk] *n* gavilán *m*.
sparse [spɑːs] *adj* disperso, esparcido; poco denso; escaso; *hair* ralo; **— population** población *f* poco densa; **— furnishings** muebles *mpl* escasos.
sparsely ['spɑːsli] *adv* de modo poco denso; escasamente; **a — furnished room** un cuarto con pocos muebles; **a — inhabited area** una región de población poco densa.
Sparta ['spɑːtə] Esparta *f*.
Spartan ['spɑːtən] **1** *adj* espartano (*also fig*). **2** *n* espartano *m*, a *f*.
spasm ['spæzəm] *n* (*Med*) espasmo *m*; (*fig*) acceso *m*, arranque *m*; **in a — of fear** un acceso de miedo; **a sudden — of activity** un arranque repentino de actividad; **to work in —s** trabajar a rachas.
spasmodic [spæz'mɔdik] *adj* espasmódico; irregular, intermitente.
spasmodically [spæz'mɔdikəli] *adv* de modo espasmódico; de modo irregular, de modo intermitente; a rachas.
spastic ['spæstik] **1** *adj* espástico. **2** *n* espástico *m*, a *f*.
spasticity [spæs'tisiti] *n* espasticidad *f*.
spat¹ [spæt] *n* (*Fish*) freza *f*; (*of oysters*) masa *f* de ostras jóvenes.
spat² [spæt] *n* (*gaiter*) polaina *f* corta, botón *m*.
spat³ [spæt] *n* (*US fam*) riña *f*, disputa *f* (sin trascendencia).
spat⁴ [spæt] *pret and ptp of* **spit**.
spate [speit] *n* avenida *f*, crecida *f*; (*fig*) torrente *m*; **to be in —** estar crecido.
spatial ['speiʃəl] *adj* espacial.
spatter ['spætə*] *vt* salpicar, rociar (*with* de); **a dress —ed with mud** un vestido manchado de lodo; **a wall —ed with blood** una pared salpicada de sangre.
spatula ['spætjulə] *n* espátula *f*.
spavin ['spævin] *n* esparaván *m*.
spawn [spɔːn] **1** *n* (*Fish*) freza *f*, huevas *fpl*; (*of frog etc*) huevas *fpl*; (*of mushroom*) semillas *fpl*; (*fig*) prole *f*.
  2 *vt* (*pej*) engendrar, producir.
  3 *vi* desovar, frezar.
spawning ['spɔːniŋ] *n* desove *m*, freza *f*.
spay [spei] *vt animal* sacar los ovarios a.
speak [spiːk] (*irr: pret* **spoke**, *ptp* **spoken**) **1** *vt* (a) (*in general*) decir, hablar; **to — the truth** decir la verdad; **to — one's mind** hablar con franqueza, hablar claro; **nobody spoke a word** nadie habló, nadie dijo palabra.
  (b) *language* hablar; **do you — Arabic?** ¿hablas árabe?; "**English spoken here**" "se habla inglés".
  2 *vi* (a) (*general sense*) hablar; **did you —?** ¿dijiste algo?; **since they quarrelled they don't —** desde que riñeron no se hablan; **to — to someone** hablar con uno; **she never spoke to me again** no volvió a dirigirme la palabra; **I'll — to him about it** se lo diré; discutiré el asunto con él; **to — harshly to someone** hablar a uno en tono severo; **I don't**

know him to — to no le conozco bastante como para hablar con él; **I know him to — to** le conozco bastante bien para cambiar algunas palabras con él; **so to —** por decirlo así; **roughly —ing** más o menos, aproximadamente.
  (b) **to — for someone** hablar por uno; hablar en nombre de uno; interceder por uno; **he —s for the miners** habla por los mineros, representa a los mineros; **—ing for myself** en cuanto a mí, yo por mi parte; **it —s for itself** es evidente, habla por sí mismo; **the facts — for themselves** los datos hablan por sí solos; **that —s well for him** eso demuestra su mérito; eso es un punto a su favor; **that is already spoken for** eso está reservado ya.
  (c) (*of gun*) oírse, sonar; (*of dog*) ladrar; **the gun spoke** se oyó un tiro.
  (d) (*formally, in assembly*) hablar, pronunciar un discurso; intervenir (en un debate); (*begin to —*) tomar la palabra, hacer uso de la palabra; **are you —ing in the debate?** ¿interviene Vd en el debate?; **it's years since he spoke** hace años que no pronuncia ningún discurso; **the member rose to —** el diputado se levantó para tomar la palabra; **the speaker asked Mr X to —** el presidente le concedió la palabra al Sr X.
  (e) (*Tel*) **—ing!** ¡al habla!; **John —ing!** ¡soy Juan!; **who is that —ing?** ¿quién habla?
  (f) (*with adv or prep*) **to — of** hablar de; **—ing of tractors . . .** a propósito de los tractores . . .; **it's nothing to — of** no tiene importancia; no es nada; **there are no trees to — of** no hay árboles que digamos; **everything —s of hatred** por todas partes late el odio; **everything —s of luxury** todo indica el lujo; **to — well of someone** decir mil bienes de uno, poner a uno por las nubes; **to — out** hablar claro; hablar francamente; osar hablar; **— out!** ¡más fuerte!; **to — to the point** hablar acertadamente, hablar con tino; **to — up** hablar alto; **— up!** ¡más fuerte!; **to — up for someone** hablar en favor de uno.
speakeasy ['spiːkˌiːzi] *n* taberna *f* (clandestina).
speaker ['spiːkə*] *n* (*general sense*) el (*or* la) que habla; (*of language*) hablante *mf*; (*public —*) orador *m*, ora *f*; (*lecturer*) conferenciante *mf*; (*Parl*) presidente *m*; (*loud—*) altavoz *m*; **after-dinner —** orador *m* de sobremesa; **as the last — said** como dijo el señor que acaba de hablar; **he's a good —** es buen orador, habla bien; **are you a Welsh —?** ¿habla Vd galés?; **all —s of Spanish** todos los que hablan español, todos los hispanohablantes; **Catalan has several million —s** el catalán es hablado por varios millones.
speaking ['spiːkiŋ] *adj* hablante; *likeness* perfecto, expresivo; **to be within — distance** estar al habla; *see* **term**.
speaking trumpet ['spiːkiŋˌtrʌmpit] *n* bocina *f*.
speaking tube ['spiːkiŋtjuːb] *n* tubo *m* acústico.
spear [spiə*] **1** *n* lanza *f*; (*fishing —*) arpón *m*.
  2 *vt* alancear, herir (*or* matar) con lanza; *fish* arponear; (*fig*) pasar, atravesar, pinchar; **he —ed the paper on his fork** atravesó el papel en su tenedor.
spearhead ['spiəhed] *n* punta *f* de lanza (*also fig*).
spearmint ['spiəmint] *n* (*Bot etc*) menta *f* verde, menta *f* romana.
spear thrust ['spiəθrʌst] *n* lanzada *f*.
spec [spek] *n* (*Comm: fam*) **to buy something on —** comprar algo como especulación; **to go along on —** ir a ver lo que sale, ir a probar fortuna.
special ['speʃəl] **1** *adj* especial, particular; *correspondent, edition etc* extraordinario; *delivery* (*Post*) urgente; **my — friend** mi mejor amigo, uno de mis amigos más íntimos; **what happened? . . . nothing —** ¿qué tal? . . . sin novedad, nada de particular; **what's so — about this house?** ¿qué tiene de particular esta casa?; **what's so — about that?** y eso ¿qué importa?
  2 *n* (*constable*) guardia *m* auxiliar; (*edition*) número *m* extraordinario; (*train*) tren *m* extraordinario, tren *m* especial; (*US Comm*) oferta *f* extraordinaria, ganga *f*; (*US Cook*) plato *m* del día.
specialist ['speʃəlist] *n* especialista *mf*.
speciality [ˌspeʃi'æliti] *n*, **specialty** ['speʃəlti] *n* especialidad *f*; **it's a — of the house** es un plato especial de la casa; **to make a — of something** especializarse en algo, dedicarse a algo de modo especial.
specialization [ˌspeʃəlai'zeiʃən] *n* especialización *f*.
specialize ['speʃəlaiz] *vi* especializarse (*in, US on* en).
specially ['speʃəli] *adv* especialmente, particularmente; sobre todo, ante todo; **a — difficult task** un cometido especialmente difícil; **we asked for it —** lo pedimos especialmente; **— the yellow ones** sobre todo los amarillos.

specie ['spi:ʃi:] n metálico m, efectivo m; **in** — en metálico.

species ['spi:ʃi:z] n, pl **species** especie f.

specific [spə'sifik] **1** adj específico; expreso, explícito. **2** n específico m.

specifically [spə'sifikəli] adv específicamente; expresamente, explícitamente.

specification [ˌspesifi'keiʃən] n especificación f; —s (plan) presupuesto m, plan m detallado.

specify ['spesifai] vti especificar; designar (en un plan); mencionar de modo especial; **he did not** — no concretó, no mencionó nada concreto; **unless otherwise specified** a no ser que se especifique lo contrario.

specimen ['spesimin] n **1** ejemplar m, espécimen m; muestra f; **a fine** — **of trout** un bello ejemplar de trucha; **he's an odd** — es un tipo extraño; **you're a pretty poor** — Vd no vale para mucho.
2 attr: — **copy** ejemplar m de muestra; — **page** página f que sirve de muestra; — **signature** espécimen m de firma.

specious ['spi:ʃəs] adj especioso.

speciousness ['spi:ʃəsnis] n lo especioso.

speck [spek] **1** n (of dirt) pequeña mancha f, manchita f; (of dust) grano m; (smut) mota f (de carbonilla etc); (small portion) partícula f, pizca f; (dot, point) punto m; **just a** — **on the horizon** solamente un punto en el horizonte; **just a** —, **thanks** (of drink etc) un poquitín, gracias; **there's not a** — **of truth in it** no tiene ni pizca de verdad.
2 vt = **speckle**.

speckle ['spekl] **1** n punto m, mota f. **2** vt salpicar, motear (with de); salpicar de manchitas.

speckled ['spekld] adj con puntos, con manchas, moteado.

specs [speks] npl (fam) gafas fpl.

spectacle ['spektəkl] n (a) espectáculo m; **a sad** — un triste espectáculo.
(b) —s gafas fpl, anteojos mpl; **a pair of** —s unas gafas; **to see everything through rose-coloured** —s verlo todo color de rosa.

spectacle case ['spektəkl,keis] n estuche m de gafas.

spectacled ['spektəkld] adj con gafas.

spectacular [spek'tækjulə*] adj espectacular; fall etc aparatoso; success etc impresionante.

spectator [spek'teitə*] n espectador m, ora f; —s (collectively, at game etc) público m.

spectral ['spektrəl] adj espectral.

spectre, (US) **specter** ['spektə*] n espectro m, fantasma m.

spectroscope ['spektrəskəup] n espectroscopio m.

spectrum ['spektrəm] n espectro m.

speculate ['spekjuleit] vi especular (also Fin; in, on en); **to** — **about** especular sobre, hacer conjeturas acerca de, formular teorías acerca de.

speculation [ˌspekju'leiʃən] n especulación f; **it is the subject of much** — es tema de muchas conjeturas, sobre esto existen muchas teorías; **to buy something on** — comprar algo como especulación; **it's a good** — vale como especulación.

speculative ['spekjulətiv] adj especulativo.

speculator ['spekjuleitə*] n especulador m, ora f;

speculum ['spekjuləm] n (Med) espéculo m; (fig) espejo m.

sped [sped] pret and ptp of **speed**.

speech [spi:tʃ] n (a) (faculty of —) habla f; palabra f; **free** — libertad f de palabra; — **defect** defecto m de la palabra; **to be slow of** — hablar lentamente, ser torpe de palabra; **to lose the power of** — perder el habla; **to recover one's** — recobrar el habla.
(b) (words) palabras fpl; **fair** — palabras fpl afables; **without further** — sin decir más; **to have** — **with someone** hablar con uno.
(c) (language: national) idioma m, (of class etc) lenguaje m, (of region) dialecto m, habla f regional; **in dockers'** — en el lenguaje de los portuarios; **in the** — **of Leon** en el dialecto de León.
(d) (oration) discurso m, oración f; (Law, Theat) parlamento m; **closing** — discurso m de clausura; **keynote** — (US), **opening** — discurso m de apertura; **after-dinner** — discurso m de sobremesa; **set** — discurso m preparado de antemano; **to deliver a** —, **to make a** — pronunciar un discurso.
(e) (Gram) oración f; **direct** — oración f directa; **indirect** — oración f indirecta; see **figure**, **part**.

speech day ['spi:tʃdei] n distribución f de premios.

speechify ['spi:tʃifai] vi (pej) disertar prolijamente, dar un tostón.

speechifying ['spi:tʃifaiiŋ] n (pej) disertaciones fpl prolijas, rollos mpl, tostones mpl.

speechless ['spi:tʃlis] adj mudo, estupefacto; **everybody was** — **at this** con esto todos quedaron estupefactos; **to be** — **with rage** enmudecer de rabia.

speechmaking ['spi:tʃ,meikiŋ] n pronunciación f de discursos; (speeches collectively) discursos mpl; (pej) = **speechifying**.

speech therapy ['spi:tʃ'θerəpi] n terapia f de la palabra.

speed [spi:d] **1** n (a) velocidad f; rapidez f; (haste) prisa f; (promptness) prontitud f; **at** — a gran velocidad; **at full** —, **at top** — a máxima velocidad, a toda máquina, a todo correr; **full** — **ahead!** ¡adelante a toda máquina!; **with all possible** — con toda prontitud; **the maximum** — **is 90 mph** la velocidad máxima es de 90 mph; **what** — **were you doing?** ¿a qué velocidad ibas?; **to pick up** — acelerar, cobrar velocidad.
(b) (gear) velocidad f; **four forward** —s cuatro velocidades hacia adelante; **five-speed gearbox** caja f de cambios de cinco velocidades.
(c) **good** —! (arch) ¡buen viaje!
2 vt (regular) (a) **to** — **someone on his way** despedir a uno, desear un feliz viaje a uno; **God** — **you!** (arch) ¡vaya Vd con Dios!
(b) **to** — **up** engine acelerar; process acelerar, activar; fomentar; person dar prisa a.
3 vi (irr: pret and ptp **sped**) (a) (of person etc) darse prisa, apresurarse; **to** — **along** ir a gran velocidad, ir a toda rapidez; **he sped down the street** corrió a toda prisa por la calle; **to** — **off** irse a toda prisa.
(b) (Aut) exceder la velocidad permitida.

speedboat ['spi:d,bəut] n motora f, lancha f rápida.

speed cop ['spi:dkɔp] n (sl) policía m de tráfico.

speedily ['spi:dili] adv rápidamente; prontamente, con toda prontitud; **it** — **became obvious that . . .** pronto se hizo manifiesto que . . .; **as** — **as possible** lo más pronto posible.

speediness ['spi:dinis] n velocidad f, rapidez f; prontitud f.

speeding ['spi:diŋ] n (Aut) exceso m de velocidad; **he was fined for** — se le impuso una multa por exceso de velocidad.

speed limit ['spi:d,limit] n velocidad f máxima permitida, límite m de velocidad; **to exceed the** — exceder la velocidad permitida.

speedometer [spi'dɔmitə*] n velocímetro m, cuenta-kilómetros m.

speed-up ['spi:dʌp] n aceleración f.

speedway ['spi:dwei] n (track) pista f de ceniza, carretera f para carreras; (motor-cycle racing) carreras fpl de motocicleta; (US) autopista f.

speedwell ['spi:dwel] n (Bot) verónica f.

speedy ['spi:di] adj veloz, rápido; answer etc pronto; service etc rápido.

spelaeologist, (US) **speleologist** [ˌspi:li'ɔlədʒist] n espeleólogo m.

spelaeology, (US) **speleology** [ˌspi:li'ɔlədʒi] n espeleología f.

spell¹ [spel] n encanto m, hechizo m; ensalmo m; **to be under a** — estar hechizado; **to cast a** — **over someone, to put someone under a** — hechizar a uno (also fig); **Seville casts its** — **over the tourists** Sevilla hechiza a los turistas.

spell² [spel] (irr: pret and ptp **spelled** or **spelt**) vti (a) escribir; **she can't** — no sabe escribir correctamente las palabras, sabe poco de ortografía; **how do you** — **"onyx"?** ¿cómo se escribe "ónice"?; **what do these letters** —? ¿qué palabra se forma con estas letras?; **to** — **out** deletrear; **to** — **something out for someone** (fig) explicar algo a uno de un modo muy sencillo, explicar algo a uno detalladamente.
(b) (denote) anunciar, presagiar; significar; **it** —s **disaster for us** representa un desastre para nosotros; **it** —s **ruin** significa la ruina.

spell³ [spel] n (a) (at work) tanda f, turno m; **to take a** — **with the saw** trabajar su turno con la sierra.
(b) (period in general) rato m; temporada f, período m; **by** —s a rachas, a ratos; **cold** — período m de frío; **a prolonged** — **of bad weather** una larga temporada de mal tiempo; **we had a** — **in Chile** pasamos una temporada en Chile; **I had a** — **as a traveller** durante cierto tiempo trabajé como viajante; **they're going through a bad** — atraviesan un mal momento.

spellbinder ['spel,baində*] n orador m fascinante.

spellbound ['spelbaund] adj embelesado, hechizado; **to hold one's audience** — tener a sus oyentes embelesados.

speller ['spelə*] n: **to be a bad** — no saber escribir correctamente las palabras.

spelling ['speliŋ] n ortografía f; **the correct** — **is . . .** la buena ortografía es . . .; **reformed** — nueva ortografía f.

spelling bee ['spelɪŋˌbiː] n certamen m de ortografía.
spelling book ['spelɪŋˌbuk] n abecedario m.
spelt[1] [spelt] n (Bot) espelta f.
spelt[2] [spelt] pret and ptp of **spell**[2].
spend [spend] (irr: pret and ptp **spent**) 1 vt money, effort gastar; time pasar; time (on a journey, project etc) invertir (on en) dedicar (on a); anger, emotion etc agotar, consumir; **she spent 20 pesetas on sweets** gastó 20 pesetas en bombones; **where are you —ing your holiday?** ¿dónde pasa Vd sus vacaciones?; **the storm has spent its fury** la tempestad ha agotado su violencia.
  2 vi gastar dinero; **he —s freely** gasta muchísimo dinero.
spender ['spendə*] n gastador m, ora f; **to be a free — gastar libremente su dinero, ser derrochador.
spending money ['spendɪŋˌmʌni] n dinero m para gastos personales.
spending power ['spendɪŋˌpauə*] n poder m de compra, poder m adquisitivo.
spendthrift ['spendθrɪft] 1 adj derrochador, pródigo.
  2 n derrochador m, ora f, pródigo m, a f.
spent [spent] 1 pret and ptp of **spend**. 2 adj agotado; bullet frío; **he's a — force** es una vieja gloria, ya no vale lo que antes.
sperm [spəːm] n (Bio) esperma f.
spermaceti [ˌspəːmə'seti] n espermaceti m.
spermatozoon [ˌspəːmətəu'zəuɔn] n, pl **—zoa** ['zəuə] espermatozoo m.
sperm whale ['spəːmweil] n cachalote m.
spew [spjuː] vt vomitar; (fig) vomitar, arrojar, echar fuera (also **to — forth, to — out**); **it makes me —** (fig: fam) me da asco.
sphagnum ['sfægnəm] n esfágnea f.
sphere [sfɪə*] n esfera f; (fig) esfera f, campo m; competencia f; **— of influence** esfera f de influencia; **— of activity** campo m de actividad; **in the — of music** en la esfera de la música, en el mundo de la música; **that's outside my —** eso no es de mi competencia.
spherical ['sferikəl] adj esférico.
spheroid ['sfɪərɔid] n esferoide m.
sphincter ['sfɪŋktə*] n esfínter m.
sphinx [sfɪŋks] n esfinge f.
spice [spais] n especia f; (fig) sabor m, picante m; **the detail added — to the story** el detalle dio más sabor a la narración; **the papers like stories with some —** a los periódicos les gusta reportajes con cierto picante.
  2 vt especiar; condimentar; (fig) dar picante a; **gossip —d with scandal** unos chismes con el sabor adicional de detalles escandalosos; **a highly —d account** un relato de mucho picante.
spiciness ['spaisinis] n picante m, sabor m (also fig).
spick-and-span ['spikən'spæn] adj impecablemente limpio; house etc como una tacita de plata; person pulcro, aseado, acicalado.
spicy ['spaisi] adj especiado; condimentado, picante; (fig) picante, sabroso.
spider ['spaidə*] n araña f.
spiderman ['spaidəmæn] n, pl **—men** [men] obrero m que trabaja en la construcción de edificios altos.
spidery ['spaidəri] adj delgado; writing de patas de araña.
spiel [spiːl] n (sl) arenga f, discurso m; material m publicitario; relato m con que uno procura convencer a otro.
spigot ['spigət] n (of cask) espita f, grifo m; (Tech) espiga f.
spike [spaik] 1 n (point) punta f; (tool) escarpia f; (on shoes, for letters etc) clavo m; (Zool etc) pincho m, púa f; (Bot) espiga f.
  2 vt atravesar con un pincho; sujetar con un clavo (etc); gun clavar; (fig) inutilizar, hacer inútil; drink (US) echar licor a, fortalecer.
spiked [spaikt] adj shoe claveteado.
spikenard ['spaiknɑːd] n nardo m.
spiky ['spaiki] adj puntiagudo; armado de púas, cubierto de púas, erizado.
spill[1] [spil] 1 n caída f; vuelco m; **to have a —** sufrir una caída, tener un accidente.
  2 (irr: pret and ptp **spilled** or **spilt**) vt derramar, verter; rider hacer caer, desarzonar.
  3 vi derramarse, verterse; **to — over** irse, desbordarse, (fig) desbordarse.
spill[2] [spil] n alegrador m, pajuela f.
spillway ['spilwei] n derramadero m.
spilt [spilt] pret and ptp of **spill**.
spin [spin] 1 n (a) (revolution) vuelta f, revolución f; **to give a wheel a —** poner una rueda en movimiento, hacer que una rueda gire.

  (b) (trip) paseo m (en coche etc); **to go for a —** dar un paseo (en coche), salir de excursión en coche.
  (c) (Aer) barrena f; **to go into a —** entrar en barrena; **to be in a flat —** (fam) estar completamente confuso, estar totalmente despistado.
  (d) (on ball) torcimiento; **to put a — on a ball** dar efecto a una pelota, torcer una pelota.
  2 (irr: pret **spun** or **span**, ptp **spun**) vt (a) thread hilar; cocoon devanar, hacer.
  (b) (turn) girar, hacer girar; dar una vuelta a; top hacer bailar; ball dar efecto a, torcer; coin echar a cara o cruz.
  (c) **to — out** alargar, prolongar; see yarn.
  3 vi (resolve) girar, dar vueltas (also **to — round**); (top) bailar; (Aer) entrar en barrena; descender en barrena; **to — along** correr rápidamente, ir a buen tren; **my head is —ning** estoy mareado; **it makes my head —** me marea; **to send something —ning** echar algo a rodar; **the blow sent him —ning** el golpe le echó a rodar por los suelos.
spinach ['spinidʒ] n (plant) espinaca f; (dish) espinacas fpl.
spinal ['spainl] adj espinal; column vertebral.
spindle ['spindl] n (for spinning) huso m; (Mech) eje m.
spindleshanks ['spindlʃæŋks] n zanquivano m, a f.
spindly ['spindli] adj largo y delgado; leg zanquivano.
spin-drier ['spin'draiə*] n secador m centrífugo.
spindrift ['spindrift] n rocío m.
spine [spain] n (Anat) espinazo m, columna f vertebral; (Zool) púa f; (Bot) espina f; (of book) lomo m.
spineless ['spainlis] adj débil, flojo, falto de voluntad.
spinelessly ['spainlisli] adv débilmente, flojamente.
spinet [spi'net] n (Hist) espineta f.
spinnaker ['spinəkə*] n (Naut) balón m.
spinner ['spinə*] n hilandero m, a f.
spinneret [ˌspinə'ret] n (Zool) pezón m hilador.
spinney ['spini] n bosquecillo m.
spinning ['spinɪŋ] n (act) hilado m; (art) hilandería f; arte m de hilar.
spinning jenny ['spinɪŋ'dʒeni] n máquina f de hilar de husos múltiples.
spinning machine ['spinɪŋmə'ʃiːn] n máquina f de hilar.
spinning mill ['spinɪŋmil] n hilandería f.
spinning top ['spinɪŋtɔp] n peonza f.
spinning wheel ['spinɪŋwiːl] n torno m de hilar, rueca f.
spinster ['spinstə*] n soltera f; (pej) solterona f.
spiny ['spaini] adj con púas, erizado de púas; espinoso.
spiracle ['spirəkl] n espiráculo m.
spiral ['spaiərəl] 1 adj espiral, helicoidal; cn espiral; **— staircase** escalera f de caracol.
  2 n espiral f; hélice f; **the inflationary —** la espiral inflacionista.
  3 vi dar vueltas en espiral; **the plane —led down** el avión bajó en espiral; **the smoke —led up, the smoke went —ling up** el humo subió en espiral; **prices have —led up** los precios han subido vertiginosamente.
spirally ['spaiərəli] adv en espiral.
spire [spaiə*] n aguja f, chapitel m.
spirit ['spirit] 1 n (a) (soul) espíritu m, alma f; ánima f; **an unquiet —** un alma inquieta; **to be vexed in —** sentirlo en el alma.
  (b) (ghost) aparecido m, fantasma m; **evil —** espíritu m maligno; **Holy S—** Espíritu m Santo; **"Blithe S—"** "Un espíritu burlón"; **to believe in —s** creer en fantasmas
  (c) (person) alma f; **the leading (or moving) — in the party** el alma del partido, la figura más destacada del partido; **a few restless —s** algunas personas descontentadizas.
  (d) (humour, mood) espíritu m; temple m, humor m; **community —, public —** civismo m; **fighting —** espíritu m de lucha; **the — of the age** el espíritu de la época; **in a — of mischief** estando de humor para hacer alguna travesura; **everyone is in a party —** todo el mundo quiere divertirse; **it's in the — of the book** representa bien el espíritu del libro; **that's the —!** ¡muy bien!; **to enter into the — of something** dejarse emocionar por algo; empaparse en el ambiente de algo; **to take something in the wrong —** interpretar mal el espíritu con que se ha hecho algo; **it depends on the — in which it is done** depende del humor con que se hace.
  (e) (courage) valor m; (energy) energía f; (panache) brío m, ánimo m; **a man of some —** un

hombre de cierta energía; **to catch someone's —** ser influido por el valor de uno; **they lack —** carecen de energía, no tienen carácter; **to show some —** mostrar algún brío; **to sing with —** cantar con brío.

(f) —s ánimo *m*; humor *m*; **animal —s** vitalidad *f*; **high —s** optimismo *m*; alegría *f*; **to be in high —s** estar animadísimo, estar muy alegre; **low —s** pesimismo *m*, abatimiento *m*; **to be in low —s** estar abatido; **to keep up one's —s** no dejarse desanimar, no perder su optimismo; **we kept our —s up by singing** para no caer en el abatimiento nos dedicamos a cantar; **to raise someone's —s** dar aliento a uno, reanimar a uno; **to recover one's —s** volver a estar alegre, reanimarse; **my —s rose somewhat** me sentí algo más alegre, me sentí un poco más optimista.

(g) (*Chem*) alcohol *m*; (*Aut*) gasolina *f* (*also* **motor —s**); **raw —s** licores *mpl* de baja calidad; **—s of wine** espíritu *m* de vino; **I keep off —s** yo no bebo licores.

2 *vt*: **to — away, to — off** llevarse misteriosamente, volatilizar, hacer desaparecer.
spirited ['spiritid] *adj person* animoso, brioso; *attack etc* enérgico, vigoroso; *horse* fogoso; *other animal* bravo.
spirit lamp ['spiritlæmp] *n* lamparilla *f* de alcohol.
spiritless ['spiritlis] *adj* apocado, sin ánimo.
spirit level ['spirit,levl] *n* nivel *m* de aire.
spirit stove ['spiritstəuv] *n* infiernillo *m* de alcohol.
spiritual ['spiritjuəl] **1** *adj* espiritual. **2** *n* (*Mus*) canción *f* religiosa (*esp* de los negros de EE.UU.).
spiritualism ['spiritjuəlizəm] *n* espiritismo *m*.
spiritualist ['spiritjuəlist] *n* espiritista *mf*.
spirituality [,spiritju'æliti] *n* espiritualidad *f*.
spiritually ['spiritjuəli] *adv* espiritualmente.
spirituous ['spiritjuəs] *adj* espiritoso.
spirt [spə:t] **1** *n* chorro *m*, chorretada *f*.
2 *vt* hacer salir en chorro, arrojar un chorro de.
3 *vi* (*also* **to — out, to — up**) salir en chorro, salir a chorros; brotar a borbotones; *see also* **spurt**.
spit¹ [spit] **1** *n* (*Cook*) asador *m*, espetón *m*; (*of land*) lengua *f*; (*sandbank*) banco *m* de arena. **2** *vt* espetar.
spit² [spit] **1** *n* saliva *f*; esputo *m*; **to be the dead** (*or* **very**) **— of someone** (*fam*) ser la segunda edición de uno, ser la viva imagen de uno.
2 (*irr: pret and ptp* **spat**) *vt* escupir; **to — forth, to — out** escupir (*also fig*); **— it out!** ¡dilo!, ¡desembucha!
3 *vi* escupir (*at* a, *on* en); (*of cat*) bufar; **to — in someone's face** escupir a la cara a uno; **the fish is —ting in the pan** chisporrotea el pescado en la sartén; **it is —ting with rain** caen algunas gotas de lluvia, empieza a llover.
spit³ [spit] *n* (*Agr*) azadada *f*; **to dig 3 —s deep** excavar a una profundidad de 3 azadadas.
spite [spait] **1** *n* rencor *m*, ojeriza *f*, despecho *m*; **in — of** a pesar de, a despecho de; **in — of all he says** a pesar de todo lo que dice; **to do something out of** (*or* **from**) **—** hacer algo por despecho.
2 *vt* mortificar, herir, causar pena a; **she just does it to — me** lo hace solamente para causarme pena.
spiteful ['spaitful] *adj* rencoroso, malévolo; **to be — to someone** tratar a uno con malevolencia.
spitefully ['spaitfəli] *adv* con rencor, malévolamente; **por despecho; she said —** dijo malévola.
spitefulness ['spaitfulnis] *n* rencor *m*, malevolencia *f*.
spitfire ['spit,faiə*] *n* fierabrás *m*.
spittle ['spitl] *n* saliva *f*, baba *f*.
spittoon [spi'tu:n] *n* escupidera *f*.
spiv [spiv] *n* (*sl: approx*) chanchullero *m*, caballero *m* de industria; (*slacker*) gandul *m*; (*black marketeer*) estraperlista *m*.
splash [splæʃ] **1** *n* (*spray*) salpicadura *f*, rociada *f*; (*—ing noise*) chapoteo *m*; (*of colour*) mancha *f*; **whisky with a — of water** whisky *m* con un poquitín de agua; **it fell with a great — into the water** cayó ruidosamente al agua, cayó al agua levantando mucha espuma; **to make a —** causar una sensación, impresionar; hacer algo en grande.
2 *vt* salpicar (*with* de); **to — water about** hacer que el agua salpique; **to — one's money about** derrochar su dinero por todas partes.
3 *vi* (*of liquid*) esparcirse, rociarse; (*of person in water*; *also* **to — about**) chapotear; **to — about in the water** chapotear en el agua; **to — out** (*fam*) derrochar dinero; **so we —ed out and bought it** así que nos resolvimos de una vez a comprarlo.
splashboard ['splæʃbɔ:d] *n* guardabarros *m*, alero *m*.
splashdown ['splæʃdaun] *n* amerizaje *m*, chapuzón *m*.
splashy ['splæʃi] *adj* líquido; fangoso.

splay [splei] *vt* extender (sin gracia); (*Tech*) biselar, achaflanar.
splayfoot ['spleifut] *n* pie *m* aplastado y torcido.
splayfooted ['splei'futid] *adj* zancajoso.
spleen [spli:n] *n* (*Anat*) bazo *m*; (*fig*) spleen *m*, esplín *m*, rencor *m*; **to vent one's —** descargar la bilis (*on* contra).
splendid ['splendid] *adj* espléndido; **—!** ¡magnífico!; **that's simply —!** ¡pero qué bien!; **but how — for you!** ¡cuánto me alegro por ti!; **a — joke** un chiste excelente; **he has done — work** ha hecho una magnífica labor.
splendidly ['splendidli] *adv* espléndidamente; magníficamente; **a — dressed man** un hombre brillantemente vestido; **you did —** hiciste muy bien, lo has hecho rebién; **everything went —** todo fue a las mil maravillas; **we get along —** nos llevamos muy bien.
splendiferous [splen'difərəs] *adj* (*fam*) *see* **splendid**.
splendour, (*US*) **splendor** ['splendə*] *n* esplendor *m*; magnificencia *f*; (*of achievement etc*) brillo *m*, gloria *f*.
splenetic [spli'netik] *adj* (*Anat*) esplénico; (*fig*) enojadizo, de genio vivo; malhumorado.
splice [splais] **1** *n* empalme *m*, junta *f*. **2** *vt* empalmar, juntar; (*sl*) casar; **to get —d** (*sl*) casarse.
splint [splint] **1** *n* tablilla *f*; **to put someone's arm in —s** entablillar el brazo a uno. **2** *vt* entablillar.
splinter ['splintə*] **1** *n* astilla *f*; (*in finger*) espigón *m*.
2 *attr*: **— group** grupo *m* disidente, facción *f*; **— party** partido *m* nuevo formado a raíz de la escisión de otro.
3 *vt* astillar, hacer astillas.
4 *vi* astillarse, hacerse astillas; **to — off** separarse.
splinterbone ['splintəbəun] *n* peroné *m*.
splinterless ['splintəlis] *adj* inastillable.
split [split] **1** *n* (*crack*) hendedura *f*, raja *f*, grieta *f*; (*fig*) división *f*; cisma *m*; (*Pol*) escisión *f*; (*quarrel*) ruptura *f*; **a three-way —** una división en tres partes; **there are threats of a — in the progressive party** hay amenazas de escisión en el partido progresista; **to do the —s** esparrancarse.
2 *adj* partido, hendido; *pea* majado; *personality* desdoblado; *party etc* escindido, dividido; **the party was —** el partido estaba escindido; **the party is — 3 ways** el partido está escindido en 3 grupos; *see* **second**.
3 (*irr: pret and ptp* **split**) *vt* (*cleave*) partir, hender, rajar; dividir; **to — the atom** disgregar el átomo; **to — the difference** partir la diferencia; **the sea had — the ship in two** el mar había partido el barco en dos; **the blow — his head open** el golpe le abrió la cabeza; **the dispute — the party** la disputa escindió el partido; **to — off** separar; **to — up** partir, dividir; *estate* parcelar; **we'll — the work up among us** dividiremos el trabajo entre nosotros.
4 *vi* (**a**) partirse, henderse, rajarse; dividirse; (*of party*) escindirse; **the ship — on the rocks** el buque se estrelló contra las rocas; **my head is —ting** me duele terriblemente la cabeza; **to — off** separarse, desprenderse, (*Pol*) escindirse.
(b) (*of persons*) separarse; **let's — up for safety** separémonos para mayor seguridad; **they were married 14 years but then they — up** estuvieron casados durante 14 años pero por fin se separaron.
(c) (*fam*) soplar, chivatear (*on someone* contra uno); **don't — on me** de esto no digas ni pío.
split-level ['split,levl] *adj house* construido sobre dos niveles, con planta baja de dos niveles, a desnivel.
split pin ['split'pin] *n* pasador *m*.
splitting ['splitiŋ] *adj headache* terrible, enloquecedor.
splodge [splɔdʒ] *n*, **splotch** [splɔtʃ] *n* mancha *f*, borrón *m*.
splurge [splə:dʒ] *n* (*fam*) fachenda *f*, ostentación *f*.
splutter ['splʌtə*] **1** *n* chisporroteo *m*; (*of speech*) farfulla *f*. **2** *vi* chisporrotear; farfullar, balbucear; **"Yes", he —ed "Sí"**, balbuceó.
spoil [spoil] **1** *n* (*also* **—s**) despojo *m*, botín *m*; trofeo *m*; (*US Pol*) empleos *mpl* (*etc*) que se reparten los del partido victorioso; **the —s of war** el botín de la guerra, los trofeos de la guerra.
2 (*irr: pret and ptp* **spoiled** *or* **spoilt**) *vt* echar a perder, estropear, malograr, arruinar; deteriorar; *child* mimar, consentir; **to — someone's fun** aguar la fiesta a uno; **it quite —ed our holiday** arruinó completamente nuestras vacaciones; **the coast has been —ed by development** la costa ha sido arruinada por la urbanización; **to get —ed** echarse a perder, estropearse.
3 *vi* echarse a perder, estropearse; arruinarse; dañarse, deteriorarse; **if we leave it here it will —**

si lo dejamos aquí se estropeará; **to be —ing for a fight** querer de todos modos luchar, tener ganas de pelearse.

spoilsport ['spɔilspɔ:t] n aguafiestas m; **to be a —** aguar la fiesta.

spoilt [spɔilt] **1** pret and ptp of **spoil**. **2** adj estropeado; dañado, deteriorado; child consentido, muy mimado.

spoke[1] [spəuk] n rayo m, radio m; **to put a — in someone's wheel** estorbar a uno, poner obstáculos a uno.

spoke[2] [spəuk] pret of **speak**.

spoken ['spəukən] **1** ptp of **speak**. **2** adj hablado; **the — language** la lengua hablada, la lengua oral.

spokesman ['spəuksmən] n, pl **—men** [mən] portavoz m; **to act as —** hablar en nombre de; **they made him —** le eligieron para hablar en su nombre.

spokeshave ['spəuk,ʃeiv] n raedera f.

spoliation [,spəuli'eiʃən] n despojo m.

spondee ['spɔndi:] n espondeo m.

spondulicks [spɔn'dju:liks] npl (sl) parné m.

sponge [spʌndʒ] **1** n esponja f; (Cook) bizcocho m; **to throw up the —** darse por vencido, arriar velas.

2 vt (wash) lavar con esponja, limpiar con esponja (also **— down**); **to — a stain off** quitar una mancha con una esponja; **to — up** absorber.

3 vi (fam) dar sablazos, vivir de gorra; **to — on someone** vivir a costa de uno; **to — on someone for something** pedir algo a uno sin ofrecerse a pagar.

sponge bag ['spʌndʒbæg] n esponjera f.

sponge cake ['spʌndʒkeik] n bizcocho m.

sponger ['spʌndʒə*] n (fam) gorrón m, sablista mf.

sponginess ['spʌndʒinis] n esponjosidad f.

sponging ['spʌndʒiŋ] n (fam) gorronería f.

spongy ['spʌndʒi] adj esponjoso.

sponsor ['spɔnsə*] **1** n patrocinador m (also Radio, TV); (godparent) padrino m, madrina f; (of membership etc) padrino m; (Comm) fiador m, garante m.

2 vt patrocinar; (Radio, TV) patrocinar, costear, presentar; idea, plan etc fomentar, promover; (as godparent, for membership etc) apadrinar, actuar de padrino a.

sponsorship ['spɔnsəʃip] n patrocinio m; **under the — of** patrocinado por, bajo los auspicios de.

spontaneity [,spɔntə'neiiti] n espontaneidad f.

spontaneous [spɔn'teiniəs] adj espontáneo.

spontaneously [spɔn'teiniəsli] adv espontáneamente.

spoof [spu:f] (fam) **1** n trampa f, truco m, mistificación f. **2** vt engañar, burlar, mistificar. **3** vi bromear.

spook [spu:k] n (fam) espectro m.

spooky ['spu:ki] adj (fam) (like a ghost) fantasmal, espectral; (mysterious) misterioso; (frightening) horripilante; **a thoroughly — place** un sitio envuelto en misterio.

spool [spu:l] n (Sew, Phot) carrete m; (of sewing machine) canilla f; (fishing) cucharilla f.

spoon [spu:n] **1** n cuchara f; **to be born with a silver — in one's mouth** nacer en buena cuna, criarse en buenos pañales.

2 vt (also **to — out**) cucharear, sacar con cuchara; (fig) sacar como en cuchara; **to — up** recoger con cuchara.

3 vi (fam) acariciarse amorosamente, besuquearse.

spoonbill ['spu:nbil] n espátula f.

spoonerism ['spu:nərizəm] n juego de palabras (o error divertido) que consiste en trastrocar las letras iniciales de dos o más vocablos.

spoon-feed ['spu:nfi:d] (irr: see **feed**) vt dar de comer con cuchara a; (fig) tratar como a un niño a, ayudar hasta con las cosas más sencillas a.

spoon-fed ['spu:nfed] adj muy mimado.

spoonful ['spu:nful] n cucharada f.

spoony ['spu:ni] adj (fam) sobón; sentimental; **to be — on someone** estar tontamente enamorado de uno.

spoor [spuə*] n pista f, rastro m.

sporadic [spə'rædik] adj esporádico.

sporadically [spə'rædikəli] adv esporádicamente.

spore [spɔ:*] n espora f.

sporran ['spɔrən] n (Scot) escarcela f.

sport [spɔ:t] **1** n (a) (games in general) deporte m; (hunting) caza f; deporte m; (amusement) juego m, diversión f; (plaything) juguete m; **athletic —s** juegos mpl atléticos; **the — of kings** el deporte de los reyes (el hipismo); **in —** en broma; **to have some good —** tener éxito en la caza, lograr unas cuantas piezas hermosas; **the trout here give good —** aquí las truchas no se rinden fácilmente; **to make — with someone** burlarse de uno.

(b) (person) buen chico m; buen perdedor m; **be a —!** ¡como amigo!; **he's a real —** es una persona realmente buena.

(c) (Bio) mutación f.

2 vt llevar; gastar; lucir, ostentar; see **oak**.

3 vi divertirse; jugar, juguetear.

sporting ['spɔ:tiŋ] adj deportivo; conduct, spirit etc deportivo, caballeroso; chance, offer que da cierta posibilidad de éxito; dog, gun de caza; **I'm a — man** me gusta hacer apuestas arriesgadas.

sportive ['spɔ:tiv] adj juguetón.

sports car ['spɔ:tska:*] n coche m deportivo, deportivo m, coche m sport.

sports coat ['spɔ:tskəut] n chaqueta f sport.

sports commentator ['spɔ:ts,kɔmenteitə*] n comentarista m deportivo.

sports ground ['spɔ:tsgraund] n campo m de recreo, terreno m de deporte; pista f para juegos atléticos.

sports jacket ['spɔ:ts,dʒækit] n chaqueta f sport.

sportsman ['spɔ:tsmən] n, pl **—men** [mən] (player, hunter) deportista m; (honourable person) persona f honrada, caballero m; (betting man) persona f a quien le gusta hacer apuestas arriesgadas; **the — of the year** el mejor deportista del año.

sportsmanlike ['spɔ:tsmənlaik] adj deportivo; honrado, caballeroso.

sportsmanship ['spɔ:tsmənʃip] n deportividad f.

sports page ['spɔ:tspeidʒ] n página f deportiva.

sportswear ['spɔ:tswɛə*] n trajes mpl de deporte.

sportswoman ['spɔ:tswumən] n, pl **—women** [wimin] deportista f.

sporty ['spɔ:ti] adj (fam) (a) deportivo; aficionado a los deportes.

(b) (fig) alegre; guasón, jovial.

(c) (US) disipado, libertino; elegante, guapo.

spot [spɔt] **1** n (a) (place in general) sitio m, lugar m; **a pleasant —** un lugar agradable; **a good — for trout** un buen lugar para las truchas; **blind —** (Anat) punto m ciego, (fig) debilidad f, punto m flojo; **at the — where it happened** en el lugar donde ocurrió; **on this very —** en este mismo sitio; **to be in a (tight) —** estar en un aprieto; **to have a soft — for someone** tener una debilidad por uno; **to know someone's weak —s** saber de qué pie cojea uno; **to put one's finger on the weak —** poner el dedo en la llaga.

(b) (phrases with on) **our man on the —** nuestro hombre sobre el terreno; **the reporter was on the —** el reportero estaba allí mismo; **the firemen were on the — in 3 minutes** los bomberos llegaron al cabo de 3 minutos, acudieron los bomberos a los 3 minutos; **I always have to be on the —** yo estoy de servicio siempre; **to do something on the —** hacer algo en el acto, hacer algo acto seguido; hacer algo sin demora; **to put someone on the —** poner a uno en un aprieto; **now I'm really on the —** ahora me veo de verdad entre la espada y la pared.

(c) (Med etc) grano m, lunar m; (freckle) peca f; (stain) mancha f; **measles —s** manchas fpl de sarampión; **to break (or come) out in —s** salir a uno granos en la piel; **I have a — that itches** tengo un grano que me pica; **it made a — on the table** hizo una mancha en la mesa.

(d) (of colour) punto m; pinta f, mancha f; **a cloth with blue —s** un paño con puntos azules; **a dog with black —s** un perro con manchas negras; **black —** (fig) lunar m; **there are black —s in this prosperity** en esta prosperidad hay lunares; **it's a black — for accidents** es un sitio donde hay muchos accidentes; **there are black —s in his record** hay malas notas en su historial; **to knock —s off someone** vencer a uno fácilmente; **this can knock —s off yours any time** éste supera al tuyo en cualquier momento.

(e) (small quantity) poquito m, poquitín m; (of rain) gota f; **just a —, thanks** un poquitín, gracias; **we had a few —s** tuvimos algunas gotitas; **a — of bother** cierto disgusto, un poco de dificultad; **he had a — of bother with the police** se armó un lío con la policía; **we're in a — of trouble** tenemos cierta dificultad; **without a — of trouble** sin dificultad alguna.

(f) (Radio, TV) espacio m radiofónico (publicitario).

(g) **—s** (Comm) géneros mpl vendidos al contado; géneros mpl para entrega inmediata.

2 attr (a) **—goods** géneros mpl vendidos al contado; géneros mpl para entrega inmediata; **— cash** dinero m contante.

(b) **— check** comprobación f en el acto, reconocimiento m rápido; **— test** prueba f superficial.

3 vt (a) (speckle) manchar, motear, salpicar (with de); **to — someone with mud** salpicar a uno de lodo.

(b) (notice, see) notar, observar; encontrar; descubrir; (recognize) reconocer; (select) elegir, escoger; **I —ted him at once** le reconocí en seguida; **did you — the winner?** ¿escogiste el ganador?

4 vi: **to — (with rain)** chispear.

spotless ['spɔtlis] adj nítido; sin manchas, inmaculado; (clean) perfectamente limpio, como una tacita de plata.

spotlessly ['spɔtlisli] adv: **— clean** perfectamente limpio, como una tacita.

spotlessness ['spɔtlisnis] n nitidez f; perfecta limpieza f.

spotlight ['spɔtlait] **1** n (Theat lamp) foco m, reflector m, proyector m, (light) luz f del foco; (Aut) faro m auxiliar orientable; (fig) luz f concentrada; **to turn the — on someone** (fig) volver sobre uno la luz concentrada de la publicidad (or de la atención pública etc).

2 vt iluminar; destacar, subrayar.

spotted ['spɔtid] adj manchado; moteado; **a dress — with blue** un vestido con puntos azules; **a dress — with mud** un vestido manchado de lodo.

spotted fever ['spɔtid'fiːvə*] n tifus m exantemático.

spotter ['spɔtə*] n (Aer etc) observador m; (Rail) coleccionista m de números de locomotoras.

spotty ['spɔti] adj manchado, lleno de manchas; (Med: pimply) con granos, (of infection) con manchas; **to be all —** estar cubierto de manchas.

spouse [spauz] n cónyuge mf.

spout [spaut] **1** n (of jar) pico m; (of teapot, wine jug) pitón m, pitorro m; (of guttering) canalón m; (pipe) caño m, conducto m; (jet of water) chorro m; (column of water) surtidor m; **it's up the —** (fam) está empeñado, (fig) se acabó todo.

2 vt arrojar en chorro; levantar un surtidor de; (fig) declamar, recitar; **he can — figures about it** es capaz de recitar incansablemente las cifras referentes a ello.

3 vi chorrear; (fig) recitar, hablar incansablemente; **he was still —ing when we left** seguía hablando incansablemente cuando salimos.

sprain [sprein] **1** n torcedura f. **2** vt torcer; **to — one's wrist** torcerse la muñeca.

sprang [spræŋ] pret of **spring**.

sprat [spræt] n arenque m pequeño, sardineta f.

sprawl [sprɔːl] vi arrellanarse, repanchigarse; extenderse (en postura desgarbada), tumbarse (de modo poco elegante); (of plant, town) extenderse; **he was —ed in a chair** estaba tumbado de modo poco elegante en un sillón; **the body was —ed on the floor** el cadáver estaba tumbado en el suelo; **to send someone —ing (with a blow)** derribar a uno por el suelo; **the jolt sent him —ing** la sacudida le hizo ir rodando por el suelo.

spray[1] [sprei] n (Bot) ramita f.

spray[2] [sprei] **1** n (a) (liquid) rociada f; (of sea) espuma f; (as irrigation) riego m por aspersión; (of insecticide etc) pulverización f.

(b) (implement: scent—) atomizador m; (paint—) pistola f rociadora de pintura; (Med) rociador m; (insecticide —) pulverizador m.

2 vt rociar, regar (with de); atomizar, pulverizar; **to — the roses with insecticide** rociar las rosas de insecticida; **to — paint on to a car** pintar un coche con una pistola rociadora; **to — a house with bullets** rociar una casa de balas.

sprayer ['spreiə*] n see **spray 1** (b).

spray gun ['spreigʌn] n pistola f rociadora; pulverizador m.

spraying machine ['spreiiŋməˌʃiːn] n (Agr) pulverizador m.

spread [spred] **1** n (a) (act) extensión f; propagación f, diseminación f, difusión f; generalización f; proliferación f; **the — of education** la extensión de la educación; **the — of nuclear weapons** la proliferación de armas nucleares.

(b) (of wings) envergadura f; (of figures, marks etc) extensión f; gama f, escala f; **middle-aged —** gordura f de la mediana edad.

(c) (fam) comilona f, banquetazo m.

2 (irr: pret and ptp **spread**) vt extender, tender; intangible things propagar, diseminar, difundir; divulgar; generalizar; butter etc untar; banner, sails, wings desplegar; net tender; table poner; (scatter) esparcir, desparramar; **to — butter on one's bread** untar el pan con mantequilla, extender mantequilla sobre el pan; **to — cream on one's face** extender crema sobre el rostro; **to — oil on the sea** tender una capa de aceite sobre el mar; **to — the sea with oil** cubrir el mar con una capa de aceite; **meadows — with flowers** prados mpl cubiertos de flores; **the peacock —s its tail** el pavo real hace la rueda; **repayments will be — over 18 months** los pagos se efectuarán durante 18 meses; **to — news about** divulgar una noticia; **the book —s error** el libro disemina el error; **to — out** separar; abrir, extender, desplegar; **to — a map out on a table** extender un mapa sobre una mesa.

3 vi extenderse; propagarse, difundirse; divulgarse; generalizarse; desplegarse; (scatter) esparcirse, desparramarse; **the fire — rapidly** el incendio se extendió rápidamente; **a knowledge of this — widely** el conocimiento de esto se divulgó a muchas partes; **the disease —** la enfermedad se propagó; **to — out** (persons) separarse; desparramarse.

4 vr: **to — oneself** (a) (physically) arrellanarse; ponerse a sus anchas, tomar una postura cómoda; **I like to — myself** me gusta tener mucho espacio (para trabajar cómodamente etc).

(b) (in speech: fam) explayarse, hablar prolijamente.

spread-eagle ['spred'iːgl] vt extender (completamente), extender los miembros de.

spread-eagled ['spred'iːgld] adj con los miembros extendidos (sin poderse ayudar).

spree [spriː] n (fam) juerga f, parranda f; excursión f; spending — expedición f (or jira f etc) en la que se gasta mucho dinero; **to be (out) on a —** estar de juerga; **to go on a —** ir de juerga; **let's have a —** echemos una cana al aire.

sprig [sprig] n (Bot) ramita f; (of heather etc) espiga f; (Tech) puntilla f.

sprightliness ['spraitlinis] n viveza f, energía f, animación f.

sprightly ['spraitli] adj vivo, enérgico, animado.

spring [spriŋ] **1** n (a) (of water) fuente f, manantial f; **hot —** fuente f termal.

(b) (season) primavera f; **in —**, **in the —** en la primavera; **— is in the air** se nota la llegada de la primavera.

(c) (leap) salto m, brinco m; **in one —** de un salto; **to take a — into the air** dar un salto.

(d) (bounciness) elasticidad f.

(e) (Mech: of watch etc) resorte m, (of mattress, seat etc) muelle m; **—s** (Aut) ballestas fpl.

2 attr **water** de fuente; (of season) primaveral, de primavera.

3 (irr: pret **sprang**, ptp **sprung**) vt (a) (leap) saltar, saltar por encima de.

(b) (warp) torcer, combar.

(c) (mine) volar; trap hacer saltar; **to — a leak** abrirse una vía de agua; **to — a piece of news on someone** comunicar una noticia imprevista a uno; **to — a surprise on someone** coger a uno de improviso; **to — an idea on someone** espetar una idea a uno, sugerir una idea a uno de buenas a primeras.

4 vi (a) (of water etc) brotar, nacer; salir en chorro; (Bot) brotar; **to — into existence** nacer de la noche a la mañana, aparecer repentinamente; **to — from** (fig) nacer de, proceder de, provenir de; family ser de, nacer de; **a man sprung from the people** un hombre surgido de la plebe; **to — up** (plant) brotar; crecer rápidamente; (problem) surgir, presentarse; (friendship etc) nacer; **the weeds — up all over** las malas hierbas aparecen por todas partes.

(b) (leap) saltar, brincar; **the lid sprang open** la tapa se abrió de golpe; **to — aside** hacerse de prisa a un lado; **to — at someone** abalanzarse sobre uno; **to — back** dar un paso rápidamente hacia atrás, retroceder con toda prisa; **the branch sprang back** la rama volvió a su posición como un muelle; **where on earth did you — from?** ¿de dónde diablos ha salido Vd?; **to — into the air** dar un salto; **to — into the saddle** saltar a la silla; **to — out of bed** saltar de la cama; **to — to one's feet** levantarse de un salto; **to — to someone's aid** acudir con toda rapidez a ayudar a uno; **to — up** levantarse de un salto; (of breeze etc) levantarse de pronto.

(c) (warp) torcerse, combarse.

spring balance ['spriŋ'bæləns] n peso m de muelle.

springboard ['spriŋbɔːd] n trampolín m.

springbok ['spriŋbɔk] n especie de gacela (del sur de África).

spring bolt ['spriŋbəult] n pestillo m de golpe.

spring-clean ['spriŋ'kliːn] **1** vt limpiar completamente. **2** vi limpiarlo todo, limpiar toda la casa.

spring-cleaning ['spriŋ'kliːniŋ] n limpieza f general; **to do the —** limpiar toda la casa.

spring fever ['spriŋ'fiːvə*] n desasosiego m, sentimiento m de malestar (or intranquilidad etc);

deseo m fuerte de cambiar de estilo de vida; (hum) celo m amoroso.

springe [sprindʒ] n lazo m.

spring gun ['spriŋgʌn] n trampa f de alambre y escopeta.

springiness ['spriŋinis] n elasticidad f.

spring-like ['spriŋlaik] adj day, weather primaveral.

spring mattress ['spriŋ'mætris] n colchón m de muelles, somier m.

spring tide ['spriŋ'taid] n marea f viva.

springtime ['spriŋtaim] n primavera f.

springy ['spriŋi] adj elástico; turf etc muelle, muy molido.

sprinkle ['spriŋkl] 1 n rociada f; salpicadura f; a — of rain unas gotitas de lluvia; a — of salt un poquito de sal.

2 vt salpicar, rociar (with de); sembrar (with de); (with holy water) asperjar; esparcir; to — water on a plant, to — a plant with water rociar una planta de agua; a rose — with dew una rosa cubierta de rocío; they are —d about here and there están esparcidos aquí y allá.

3 vi (with rain) lloviznar.

sprinkler ['spriŋklə*] n (Agr) rociadera f, aparato m de lluvia artificial; (of watering can etc) regadera f; (in fire fighting) aparato m de rociadura automática; (Eccl) hisopo m.

sprinkling ['spriŋkliŋ] n rociada f, salpicadura f; aspersión f; a — of knowledge unos pocos conocimientos; there was a — of young people había unos cuantos jóvenes.

sprint [sprint] 1 n (in race) (e)sprint m; (dash) carrera f.

2 vi (in race) (e)sprintar; (dash) correr a todo correr, precipitarse; he —ed for the bus corrió a toda prisa para coger el autobús; we shall have to — tendremos que correr.

sprinter ['sprintə*] n (e)sprínter m, corredor m de cortas distancias.

sprit [sprit] n botavara f, verga f de abanico.

sprite [sprait] n duende m, trasgo m; hada f.

spritsail ['spritseil, Naut 'spritsl] n cebadera f, vela f de abanico.

sprocket wheel ['sprɔkitwi:l] n rueda f de cadena.

sprout [spraut] 1 n brote m, retoño m; —s col f de Bruselas.

2 vt echar, hacerse; to — new leaves echar nuevas hojas; the calf is —ing horns le salen los cuernos al ternero; the town is —ing new buildings en la ciudad surgen nuevos edificios.

3 vi brotar, retoñar, echar retoños; (shoot up) crecer rápidamente; skyscrapers are —ing up se levantan rápidamente los rascacielos.

spruce[1] [spru:s] 1 adj aseado, apuesto, pulcro. 2 vt: to — up arreglar, componer; all —d up muy acicalado. 3 vr: to — oneself up arreglarse; ataviarse; mejorar de aspecto, hacerse más elegante.

spruce[2] [spru:s] n (Bot) picea f (also — tree).

spruceness ['spru:snis] n aseo m, pulcritud f; elegancia f.

sprung [sprʌŋ] 1 ptp of **spring**. 2 adj: — bed cama f mullida; interior — mattress somier m, colchón m de muelles; — seat asiento m de ballesta.

spry [sprai] adj ágil, activo.

spud [spʌd] n (Agr) escarda f; (potato: fam) patata f.

spume [spju:m] n espuma f.

spun [spʌn] 1 pret and ptp of **spin**. 2 adj: — glass lana f de vidrio; — silk seda f hilada.

spunk [spʌŋk] n (fam) ánimo m, valor m, agallas fpl.

spur [spə:*] 1 n espuela f; (Zool) espolón m; (Geog) espolón m; (fig) estímulo m, aguijón m; (Rail) ramal m corto; the — of hunger el estímulo del hambre; it will be a — to further progress estimulará a progresos ulteriores; on the — of the moment sin reflexión, impulsivamente, de improviso; to win one's —s distinguirse, demostrar de modo concluyente lo que vale uno.

2 vt espolear, picar con las espuelas (also to — on); to — on (fig) estimular, incitar; to — someone on to do something incitar a uno a hacer algo, dar a uno aliento para que haga algo; this —red him on to greater efforts esto le incitó a hacer mayores esfuerzos; —red on by greed bajo el aguijón de la codicia, incitado a ello por la codicia.

3 vi: to — on picar el caballo con las espuelas; apretar el paso.

spurge [spə:dʒ] n euforbio m.

spur gear ['spə:giə*] n rueda f dentada recta.

spurge laurel ['spə:dʒ.lɔrəl] n lauréola f, torvisco m.

spurious ['spjuəriəs] adj falso.

spuriously ['spjuəriəsli] adv falsamente.

spuriousness ['spjuəriəsnis] n falsedad f.

spurn [spə:n] vt desdeñar, rechazar.

spurt [spə:t] 1 n esfuerzo m supremo; final — esfuerzo m final (para ganar una carrera); to put in (or on) a — hacer un esfuerzo supremo, acelerar.

2 vi hacer un esfuerzo supremo, acelerar.

sputnik ['sputnik] n satélite m artificial.

sputter ['spʌtə*] see **splutter**.

sputum ['spju:təm] n esputo m.

spy [spai] 1 n espía mf; — story novela f de espionaje.

2 vt divisar, columbrar; lograr ver; observar; descubrir; to — out the land reconocer el terreno; finally I spied him coming por fin le vi venir.

3 vi espiar, ser espía: he spied for Slobodia fue espía al servicio de Eslobodia; to — on someone espiar a uno, observar a uno clandestinamente; seguir los pasos a uno.

spyglass ['spaigla:s] n catalejo m.

spyhole ['spaihəul] n mirilla f.

spying ['spaiiŋ] n espionaje m.

squab [skwɔb] n (Orn) pichón m; pollito m, polluelo m; (fig) persona f regordeta. (b) (cushion) cojín m; (sofa) sofá m, canapé m.

squabble ['skwɔbl] 1 n riña f, disputa f. 2 vi reñir (about, over por cuestión de), disputar, pelearse.

squabbler ['skwɔblə*] n pendenciero m, a f.

squabbling ['skwɔbliŋ] n riñas fpl, disputas fpl.

squad [skwɔd] n (Mil) pelotón m; escuadra f; (of police) brigada f; flying — brigada f móvil.

squad car ['skwɔd.kɑ:*] n coche m patrulla.

squadron ['skwɔdrən] n (Mil) escuadrón m; (Naut) escuadra f; (Aer) escuadrilla f, escuadrón m.

squadron leader ['skwɔdrən'li:də*] n (Aer) comandante m (de aviación).

squalid ['skwɔlid] adj (dirty) miserable, vil, asqueroso; motive etc vil; affair asqueroso.

squall[1] [skwɔ:l] 1 n (cry) chillido m, grito m, berrido m. 2 vi chillar, gritar, berrear.

squall[2] [skwɔ:l] n (Naut: gust) ráfaga f; (brief storm) chubasco m, turbión m; (fig) tempestad f; there are —s ahead (fig) el futuro se anuncia no muy tranquilo.

squalling ['skwɔ:liŋ] adj child chillón; revoltoso.

squally ['skwɔ:li] adj wind que viene a ráfagas; day de chubascos; (fig) nada tranquilo, lleno de dificultades.

squalor ['skwɔlə*] n miseria f; suciedad f; to live in — vivir en la miseria, vivir en la suciedad.

squander ['skwɔndə*] vt money malgastar, derrochar, despilfarrar; dissipar (on en); opportunity desperdiciar; time, resources emplear mal.

square [skwɛə*] 1 adj (a) (in shape) cuadrado; corner en ángulo recto; edge escuadrado; build robusto, fornido; jaw, shoulder cuadrado; — brackets corchetes mpl, paréntesis mpl rectos.

(b) (Math) cuadrado; — kilometre kilómetro m cuadrado; 2 metres — 2 metros en cuadro.

(c) (fig) deal etc justo, equitativo; person honrado, formal; meal abundante, bueno; refusal rotundo; it's 3 days since I had a — meal hace 3 días que no tengo una comida decente; it met with a — refusal fue rechazado de plano.

(d) to be — with someone estar en paz con uno, no deber nada a uno; (Sport) ir iguales; now we're all — ahora vamos iguales; we can start again all — podemos volver a comenzar en pie de igualdad; if you pay me a pound we'll call it — si me pagas una libra diremos que no hay más deuda; to get — with someone ajustar cuentas con uno, desquitarse con uno; I'll get — with him yet! ¡me lo cargaré!

(e) (fam) idea, taste etc anticuado, pasado de moda; person de ideas anticuadas, que no se conforma con las tendencias actuales, que no comprende las actitudes de las nuevas generaciones; he's — es un carca.

2 adv: — to, — with en ángulo recto con; it fell — in the middle cayó de lleno en el centro, cayó exactamente en el centro.

3 n (a) (shape) cuadrado m; cuadro m (also Mil); (of chessboard, graph paper) casilla f; a 6-metre — un cuadrado de 6 metros de lado; to divide something into —s dividir algo en cuadrados.

(b) (of town) plaza f.

(c) (Math) cuadrado m; 4 is the — of 2 4 es el cuadrado de 2.

(d) (Archit, Tech) escuadra f.

(e) (Univ, fam) birrete m; (kerchief) pañuelo m.

(f) (fam) persona f de ideas anticuadas, persona f que no se conforma con las tendencias actuales, persona f que no comprende las actitudes de las nuevas generaciones; to be a — ser un carca.

3 vt (make —; also Math) cuadrar; (Archit, Tech) escuadrar; (arrange) arreglar; (reconcile) ajustar,

acomodar; (*bribe*) sobornar, comprar el silencio (*or* la ayuda *etc*) de; **can you — it with your conscience?** ¿lo puede acomodar con su conciencia?; **I'll — the porter, I'll — it with the porter** yo lo arreglaré con el conserje.

4 *vi* (a) cuadrar, conformarse (*with* con); **it doesn't — with what you said before** esto no cuadra con lo que dijiste antes; **it doesn't — with the facts** esto no cuadra con los hechos.

(b) **to — up to someone** ponerse en actitud para defenderse contra uno, mostrarse resuelto a defenderse contra uno.

(c) **to — up with someone** ajustar cuentas con uno, pagar a uno.

squared [skwɛəd] *adj paper* cuadriculado.

square dance ['skwɛə‚dɑːns] *n* danza *f* de figuras.

squarely ['skwɛəli] *adv* en cuadro; rotundamente; honradamente; de lleno, directamente; **we must face this —** tenemos que hacer frente a esto sin pestañear; **it hit — in the middle** dio de lleno en el centro.

squash[1] [skwɔʃ] **1** *n* (a) (*drink*) zumo *m*; **orange —** naranjada *f* natural, zumo *m* de naranja.

(b) (*crowd*) apiñamiento *m*, agolpamiento *m*; **there was such a — in the doorway** había tantísima gente en la puerta, se apiñaba tanto la gente en la puerta.

2 *vt* (*flatten*) aplastar; (*to — in, to — together*) apretar; apiñar; *argument* confutar; *person* apabullar, reducir a silencio; **can you — my shoes in?** ¿puedes poner mis zapatos? (aunque esté muy llena la maleta *etc*); **can you — 2 more in the car?** ¿caben 2 más en el coche?

3 *vi* aplastarse; **to — in** entrar (apretadamente, a pesar de la muchedumbre *etc*); **we all —ed in** entramos todos aunque con dificultad.

squash[2] [skwɔʃ] *n*, **squash rackets** ['skwɔʃ‚rækits] *n especie de tenis jugado contra frontón*.

squashy ['skwɔʃi] *adj* blando y algo líquido, muelle y húmedo.

squat [skwɔt] **1** *adj person* rechoncho, achaparrado; *building* desproporcionadamente bajo.

2 *vi* agacharse, sentarse en cuclillas (*also to — down*); (*fam*) sentarse; (*on property*) establecerse sin derecho, apropiarse sin derecho.

squatter ['skwɔtə*] *n* colono *m* usurpador, intruso *m*, persona *f* que se establece en un terreno público para crear un derecho.

squaw [skwɔː] *n* india *f* norteamericana, piel roja *f*.

squawk [skwɔːk] **1** *n* graznido *m*, chillido *m*. **2** *vi* graznar, chillar.

squeak [skwiːk] **1** *n* (*of hinge, wheel etc*) chirrido *m*, rechinamiento *m*; (*of shoe*) crujido *m*; (*of mouse etc*) chillido *m*, grito *m* agudo; (*of pen*) raspear *m*; **to have a narrow —** escaparse por un pelo; **we don't want a — out of you about this** de esto no digas ni pío.

2 *vi* chirriar, rechinar; crujir; chillar, dar chillidos, dar gritos agudos; raspear.

squeaky ['skwiːki] *adj* chirriador; que cruje; chillón; que raspea.

squeal [skwiːl] **1** *n* chillido *m*, grito *m* agudo; **with a — of pain** con un chillido de dolor.

2 *vi* chillar, dar gritos agudos; (*sl: inform*) cantar; (*complain*) quejarse; **someone —ed to the police** alguien cantó a la policía; **don't come —ing to me** no vengas a quejarte a mí; **to — for help** dar gritos agudos pidiendo socorro; **I'll make them —** (*suffer*) yo les haré sufrir, (*confess*) yo les haré cantar.

squeamish ['skwiːmiʃ] *adj* remilgado, delicado, susceptible; aprensivo; **I'm not —** yo no tengo esa delicadeza, eso me trae sin cuidado; **I'm — about spiders** tengo horror a las arañas; **don't be so —** no seas tan aprensivo, quítate esos remilgos.

squeamishness ['skwiːmiʃnis] *n* remilgos *mpl*, delicadeza *f*, susceptibilidad *f*; aprensión *f*; **to feel a certain —** sentir cierta repugnancia.

squeegee ['skwiː'dʒiː] *n* enjugador *m* de goma.

squeeze [skwiːz] **1** *n* estrujón *m*, estrujadura *f*; presión *f*; (*of hand*) apretón *m*; (*in bus etc*) apiñamiento *m*, apretura *f*; (*at Bridge*) tenaza *f* (*in diamonds* a diamantes); (*of credit*) restricción *f*; (*fig, difficulty*) aprieto *m*; **it was a tight — in the bus** íbamos muy apretados en el autobús; **it was a tight — to get through** había muy poco espacio para pasar; **the 1966 —** las restricciones económicas de 1966; **to give someone's hand a little —** apretar dulcemente la mano a uno.

2 *vt* (*painfully*) estrujar, apretar; *hand etc* apretar; presionar; **to — out** *juice* exprimir, *person* excluir; **3 were —d to death** 3 murieron estrujados; **I —d my finger in the door** me cogí el dedo en la puerta;

to — a lemon, to — the juice out of a lemon exprimir el zumo de un limón; **to — money out of someone** arrancar dinero a uno; **to — clothes into a case** meter ropa apretadamente en una maleta; **can you — 2 more in?** ¿caben 2 más?; **I'll see if we can — you in for Thursday** (*Theat etc*) veremos si quedan por casualidad entradas para el jueves, (*for appointment*) veremos si es posible ofrecerles una hora el jueves; **to — someone in hearts** (*Bridge*) atenazar a uno a corazones.

3 *vi*: **to — in** introducirse con dificultad en, deslizarse en; **to — through a crowd** abrirse paso a codazos por entre una multitud; **to — through a hole** pasar por un agujero a pesar del poco espacio que hay.

squeezer ['skwiːzə*] *n* exprimelimones *m*, exprimidor *m*.

squelch [skwɛltʃ] **1** *vt* aplastar, despachurrar; **to — one's way through mud** ir chapoteando por el lodo.

2 *vi* chapotear, ir chapoteando; **to — through the mud** ir chapoteando por el lodo.

squib [skwib] *n* buscapiés *m*.

squid [skwid] *n* calamar *m*.

squiffy ['skwifi] *adj* (*sl*): **to be —** estar achispado.

squint [skwint] **1** *n* (*Med*) estrabismo *m*; (*—ing look*) mirada *f* bizca; (*sidelong glance*) mirada *f* de soslayo, mirada *f* furtiva; (*fam*) vistazo *m*; **he has a terrible —** tiene un marcado estrabismo; **let's have a —** dame un vistazo, déjame verle.

2 *vi* (*Med*) bizquear, ser bizco; (*look sidelong*) mirar de soslayo, torcer la vista; (*narrow eyes*) cerrar casi los ojos; **to — at something** mirar algo de soslayo, (*fam*) mirar algo, echar un vistazo a algo; **he —ed in the sunlight** casi cerró los ojos en el sol.

squint-eyed ['skwint'aid] *adj* bizco.

squire ['skwaiə*] **1** *n* (*landowner*) propietario *m*, hacendado *m*; (*Hist*) escudero *m*; **the —** (*in relation to villagers etc*) el señor; **the — of Ambridge** el señor de Ambridge, el mayor terrateniente de Ambridge.

2 *vt lady* acompañar.

squirearchy ['skwaiəraːki] *n* aristocracia *f* rural.

squirm [skwəːm] *vi* retorcerse, revolverse; **to — with embarrassment** sentirse violento, avergonzarse mucho; **I'll make him —** yo le haré sufrir.

squirrel ['skwirəl] *n* ardilla *f*.

squirt [skwəːt] **1** *n* (*jet*) chorro *m*, jeringazo *m*; (*implement*) jeringa *f*; (*fam*) farolero *m*, farsante *m*.

2 *vt* arrojar un chorro de, arrojar a chorros; jeringar; **to — water at someone** lanzar un chorro de agua hacia uno.

3 *vi* salir a chorros; **the water —ed into my eye** salió un chorro de agua que me dio en los ojos.

stab [stæb] **1** *n* (a) (*with knife etc*) puñalada *f*; (*wound in general*) herida *f*; (*of pain*) pinchazo *m*, dolor *m* agudo; **— in the back** (*fig*) puñalada *f* por la espalda, puñalada *f* encubierta.

(b) (*fam*) tentativa *f*; **to have a — at something** intentar algo, probar a hacer algo.

2 *vt* apuñalar, dar de puñaladas a; **to — someone with a knife** herir a uno con un cuchillo; **to — someone in the back** (*fig*) apuñalar a uno por la espalda, apuñalar a uno encubiertamente; **to — someone to death** matar a uno a puñaladas.

3 *vi*: **to — at someone** tratar de apuñalar a uno; **he —bed at the picture with his finger** indicó el cuadro con un movimiento brusco del dedo.

stabbing ['stæbiŋ] *n* puñalada *f*, el apuñalar; muerte *f* a puñaladas.

stability [stə'biliti] *n* estabilidad *f*.

stabilization [‚steibəlai'zeiʃən] *n* estabilización *f*.

stabilize ['steibəlaiz] **1** *vt* estabilizar. **2** *vi* estabilizarse.

stabilizer ['steibəlaizə*] *n* (*Naut etc*) estabilizador *m*.

stable[1] ['steibl] *adj* estable, firme.

stable[2] ['steibl] **1** *n* cuadra *f*, caballeriza *f*; (*group of racehorses*) cuadra *f*; **to clean out the Augean —s** limpiar los establos de Augías.

2 *vt* poner en una cuadra, guardar en una cuadra.

stableboy ['steiblbɔi] *n* mozo *m* de cuadra.

stableman ['steiblmən] *n*, *pl* **—men** [mən] mozo *m* de cuadra.

stack [stæk] **1** *n* montón *m*, rimero *m*, pila *f*; (*Agr*) niara *f*, hacina *f*; (*Mil*) pabellón *m* de fusiles; (*chimney—*) cañón *m* de chimenea; fuste *m* de chimenea; (*book—*) estantería *f* de libros; (*fam*) montón *m*; **we have —s, thanks** gracias, tenemos montones; **we have —s of time** nos sobra tiempo; **I have —s of work to do** tengo un montón de trabajo que hacer.

2 *vt* amontonar, apilar; recoger en un montón, formar una pila de; (*Agr*) hacinar; **the cards are —ed against us** tenemos una gran desventaja.

stadium ['steidiəm] *n* estadio *m*.

staff [stɑːf] **1** n **(a)** (stick) palo m; (walking stick) bastón m, (pilgrim's) bordón m; (symbol of authority) bastón m de mando; (Eccl) báculo m; (of flag, lance etc) asta f; (fig) sostén m, apoyo m.

(b) (persons) personal m; (establishment) plantilla f de personal; (Mil) estado m mayor; **administrative** — personal m de administración; **domestic** — servidumbre f, criados mpl; **editorial** — redacción f; **teaching** — profesorado m, cuerpo m docente; **general** — estado m mayor general; **to be on the** — ser de plantilla; tener un puesto (permanente); **to join the** — entrar a formar parte del personal; **to leave the** — dimitir; **they keep a** — **of 5** (servants) tienen 5 criados.

(c) (Mus: pl staves) pentagrama m.

2 vt proveer de personal; **to be well** —**ed** tener un buen personal; **to be over** —**ed** tener un personal demasiado grande.

stag [stæg] n (Zool) ciervo m, venado m; (Fin) especulador m; (fam) soltero m.

stag beetle ['stæg,biːtl] n ciervo m volante.

stage [steidʒ] **1** n **(a)** (platform) plataforma f, estrado m, tablado m; (of microscope) portaobjeto m; (of rocket) escalón m, piso m; **a 4-stage rocket** un cohete de 4 pisos; **the second** — **fell away** se separó el segundo escalón.

(b) (Theat) escena f; (fig) escenario m, teatro m; **to go on the** — hacerse actor, hacerse actriz; **to put a play on the** — poner una obra; **to put a novel on the** — hacer una versión dramática de una novela; **don't put your daughter on the** — no permita que su hija se haga actriz; **to write for the** — escribir para el teatro.

(c) (of journey) etapa f, jornada f; (of road, pipeline etc) tramo m; (fig) fase f, etapa f; grado m; **in** —**s** por etapas; **in** (or **by**) **easy** — **s** en cortas etapas; gradualmente, poco a poco; **at this** — **in the negotiations** en esta fase de las negociaciones; **what** — **have we reached?** ¿a qué punto hemos llegado?; **to go through a difficult** — pasar por una fase difícil.

2 vt play representar, poner (en escena); (bring about) efectuar, lograr, llevar a cabo; (recovery) efectuar; (arrange) arreglar; organizar; **that was no accident, it was** —**d** eso no fue accidente, fue una cosa que se organizó; **to** — **a comeback** restablecerse, rehabilitarse; **to** — **a demonstration** organizar una manifestación.

stage box ['steidʒ,bɔks] n palco m de proscenio.

stagecoach ['steidʒkəutʃ] n diligencia f.

stagecraft ['steidʒkrɑːft] n arte m teatral.

stage direction ['steidʒdi,rekʃən] n acotación f.

stage door ['steidʒ'dɔː*] n entrada f de artistas.

stage fright ['steidʒfrait] n miedo m al público.

stagehand ['steidʒhænd] n tramoyista m.

stage manager ['steidʒ,mænidʒə*] n director m de escena.

stage name ['steidʒ,neim] n nombre m en el teatro, nombre m profesional.

stage-struck ['steidʒstrʌk] adj loco por el teatro.

stage whisper ['steidʒ'wispə*] n susurro m en voz bastante alta.

stagey ['steidʒi] adj teatral, dramático.

stagger ['stægə*] **1** n tambaleo m; —**s** (Vet) modorra f.

2 vt **(a)** (amaze) asombrar, sorprender; (cause to waver) hacer dudar, hacer vacilar; **you** — **me!** ¡me asombras!, ¡me asustas!

(b) hours, spokes etc escalonar.

3 vi tambalear, titubear, hacer eses; **he** —**ed to the door** fue tambaleando a la puerta; **he was** —**ing about** iba tambaleando.

staggered ['stægəd] adj **(a)** (amazed) asombrado; **I am** — **to hear that . . .** me asombra saber que . . .; **he seemed completely** — parecía estar totalmente asombrado.

(b) hours, spokes etc escalonado.

staggering ['stægəriŋ] adj asombroso, pasmoso.

staghound ['stæghaund] n perro m de caza, sabueso m.

staghunt ['stæghʌnt] n cacería f de venado.

staghunting ['stæg,hʌntiŋ] n caza f de venado.

stagnancy ['stægnənsi] n estancamiento m.

stagnant ['stægnənt] adj estancado; (fig) estancado, paralizado, inmóvil; (Fin) inactivo.

stagnate [stæg'neit] vi estancarse; estar estancado, quedar estancado (also fig); (fig) estar paralizado.

stagnation [stæg'neiʃən] n estancamiento m; (fig) estancamiento m, paralización f, inmovilismo m; inactividad f.

stag party ['stæg,pɑːti] n (fam) tertulia f (etc) de hombres solos (or de solteros).

stagy ['steidʒi] adj teatral, dramático.

staid [steid] adj serio, formal.

staidness ['steidnis] n seriedad f, formalidad f.

stain [stein] **1** n (mark) mancha f; (dye) tinte m, tintura f; (paint) pintura f; (fig) mancha f; **without a** — **on one's character** sin la menor nota infamante, sin que haya nada en contra de la buena fama de uno.

2 vt manchar; (dye) teñir, colorar; (paint) pintar; **her hands were** —**ed with blood** sus manos estaban manchadas de sangre.

3 vi mancharse.

stained glass ['steind'glɑːs] n vidrio m de color; **stained-glass window** vidriera f de colores.

stainless ['steinlis] adj inmanchable; steel inoxidable.

stain remover ['steinri,muːvə*] n quitamanchas m.

stair [steə*] n peldaño m, escalón m; (stairway) escalera f; —**s** escalera f; **flight of** —**s** tramo m de escalera.

stair carpet ['steə,kɑːpit] n alfombra f de escalera.

staircase ['steəkeis] n escalera f; caja f de escalera; **moving** — escalera f móvil, escalera f mecánica; **spiral** —, **winding** — escalera f de caracol.

stair rod ['steərɔd] n varilla f sujetadora (de alfombra de escalera).

stairway ['steəwei] n see **staircase**.

stairwell ['steəwel] n hueco m de escalera.

stake [steik] **1** n **(a)** (post) estaca f, poste m; (for plant) rodrigón m.

(b) (for execution) hoguera f; **to die at the** — morir en la hoguera; **to be condemned to the** — ser condenado a morir en la hoguera.

(c) (bet) puesta f, apuesta f, parada f; —**s** (prize) premio m, (race) carrera f; **the issue at** — la cuestión de que se trata; **to be at** — estar en juego, estar en litigio; estar en peligro; **there is a lot at** — here esto nos importa muchísimo, esto nos interesa muchísimo; **to have a** — in tener interés en; **Britain had a big** — in Rhodesia Gran Bretaña tuvo muchos intereses en Rodesia.

2 vt **(a)** (also **to** — **off, to** — **out**) estacar; cercar con estacas, señalar con estacas; plant rodrigar.

(b) (bet) apostar (on a); (Fin) aventurar, arriesgar; invertir (on en); **to** — **one's all** jugar el todo por el todo; aventurarlo todo; **to** — **one's reputation on something** afirmar que algo es lo que uno dice, jurar como hombre honrado que algo es así; **to** — **a claim** hacer una reclamación; **to** — **one's claim to a job** afirmar su derecho a ser considerado para un puesto.

stakeholder ['steik,həuldə*] n persona que guarda las apuestas hechas por otros (y paga al ganador).

stalactite ['stæləktait] n estalactita f.

stalagmite ['stæləgmait] n estalagmita f.

stale [steil] adj food no fresco, pasado, rancio; bread duro; air viciado; news viejo; joke viejo, mohoso; (old-fashioned) anticuado, pasado de moda; person cansado; **I'm getting** — me estoy cansando; ya no tengo la inventiva de antes.

stalemate ['steilmeit] **1** n (Chess) tablas fpl por ahogado; (fig) paralización f, estancamiento m; **the** — **is complete** la paralización es completa; **to reach** — llegar a un punto muerto; **there is** — **between the two powers** las relaciones entre las dos potencias están en un punto muerto.

2 vt (Chess) dar tablas por ahogado a; (fig) paralizar.

staleness ['steilnis] n rancidez f; dureza f; lo viciado; lo viejo, lo mohoso; lo anticuado; cansancio m, falta f de inventiva.

stalk[1] [stɔːk] **1** vt game cazar al acecho, acechar; person seguir los pasos a.

2 vi andar con paso majestuoso (also **to** — **along**); **to** — **away, to** — **off** irse con paso airado; **to** — **out** salir ofendido, salir con paso airado.

stalk[2] [stɔːk] n (Bot) tallo m, caña f; (cabbage —) troncho m; (of glass) pie m.

stalking-horse ['stɔːkiŋhɔːs] n pretexto m.

stall [stɔːl] **1** n **(a)** (Agr: stable) establo m, (part of stable) casilla f de establo, (manger) pesebre m; (in market etc) puesto m, caseta f; (Theat) butaca f; (Eccl) silla f de coro; **orchestra** — (Theat) butaca f de platea.

2 vt **(a)** (Agr) encerrar en establo, guardar en establo (para engordar).

(b) (Aut etc) parar, cortar accidentalmente, atascar.

(c) to — **someone off** deshacerse de uno mediante algún pretexto, tener a uno a raya.

3 vi **(a)** (Aut etc) pararse, atascarse; (Aer) perder velocidad; **we** —**ed on a steep hill** quedamos parados en una cuesta abrupta, se nos atascó el motor en una cuesta abrupta.

(b) (fig) buscar evasivas, evitar contestar

directamente, ir con rodeos; **stop** —**ing**! ¡déjese de evasivas!; **the minister** —**ed for 20 minutes** durante 20 minutos el ministro evitó contestar directamente.

stall-fed ['stɔːlfed] *adj* engordado en establo.

stallholder ['stɔːl‚həuldə*] *n* dueño *m* de un puesto (de mercado *etc*).

stallion ['stælian] *n* caballo *m* padre, semental *m*.

stalwart ['stɔːlwət] **1** *adj* (*in build*) fornido, robusto; (*in spirit*) leal; valiente; cien por cien, incondicional; **a** — **supporter of** . . . partidario incondicional de . . . **2** *n* partidario *m* leal.

stamen ['steimen] *n* estambre *m*.

stamina ['stæminə] *n* resistencia *f*, nervio *m*, vigor *m*; **intellectual** — dotes *fpl* intelectuales; **has he enough** — **for the job?** ¿tiene bastante resistencia para el puesto?; **you need** — hace falta tener carácter.

stammer ['stæmə*] **1** *n* tartamudeo *m*, balbuceo *m*; **he has a bad** — tartamudea terriblemente. **2** *vt* balbucir, decir tartamudeando (*also* **to** — **out**). **3** *vi* tartamudear; balbucir.

stammerer ['stæmərə*] *n* tartamudo *m*, a *f*.

stammering ['stæmərɪŋ] **1** *adj* tartamudo. **2** *n* tartamudeo *m*.

stammeringly ['stæmərɪŋli] *adv*: **he said** — dijo tartamudeando.

stamp [stæmp] **1** *n* **(a)** (*with foot*) patada *f*; **with a** — **of her foot** dando una patada. **(b)** (*rubber* —) estampilla *f*; (*die*) cuño *m*, troquel *m*. **(c)** (*mark*) marca *f*, huella *f*, impresión *f*; **a man of his** — un hombre de su temple, (*pej*) un hombre de esa calaña; **it bears the** — **of genius** lleva el sello de la genialidad. **(d)** (*postage* —) sello *m* (de correos), estampilla *f* (*SAm*); (*fiscal* —, *revenue* —) timbre *m*, póliza *f*; (*trading* —) cupón *m*; **airmail** — sello *m* para correo aéreo; **commemorative** — conmemorativo *m*; **mint** — sello *m* en nuevo; **unused** — sello *m* sin usar; **used** — sello *m* usado.

2 *vt* **(a) to** — **one's foot** patear, golpear con el pie; (*in dancing*) zapatear; (*of horse*) piafar; **they** —**ed out the rhythm** marcaron el ritmo con los pies; **to** — **something down** apisonar algo, comprimir algo con los pies. **(b)** (*impress mark etc on*) estampar, imprimir; (*fig*) marcar, señalar; sellar; **paper** —**ed with one's name** papel *m* con el nombre de uno impreso; **to** — **something on one's memory** grabar algo en la memoria de uno; **his manners** — **him a gentleman** sus modales aseguran que es un caballero. **(c)** (*mark with rubber* —) marcar con estampilla; (*mark with fiscal* —) timbrar; *letter* pegar un sello a, poner un sello en; franquear; **the letter is insufficiently** —**ed** la carta no lleva suficiente franqueo; **they** —**ed my passport at the frontier** sellaron mi pasaporte en la frontera. **(d) to** — **out** *fire* apagar pateando; (*fig*) extirpar, acabar con, desarraigar; **we must** — **out this abuse** tenemos que acabar con esta injusticia; **the doctors** —**ed out the epidemic** los médicos dominaron la epidemia.

3 *vi* patear, golpear con los pies; pisar muy fuerte; (*disapprovingly*) patalear; (*of horse*) piafar; **he** —**s about the house** anda por la casa pisando muy fuerte; **to** — **on** pisotear, hollar; **someone** —**ed on my foot** alguien me pisoteó el pie.

stamp album ['stæmp‚ælbəm] *n* álbum *m* para sellos.

stamp collecting ['stæmpkə‚lektɪŋ] *n* filatelia *f*.

stamp collector ['stæmpkə‚lektə*] *n* filatelista *mf*.

stamp dealer ['stæmp‚diːlə*] *n* comerciante *mf* en sellos (de correo).

stamped [stæmpt] *adj* *paper* sellado, timbrado; *envelope* con sello, que lleva sello.

stampede [stæm'piːd] **1** *n* estampida *f*; fuga *f* precipitada; movimiento *m* precipitado y unánime; **there was a sudden** — **for the door** de repente se precipitaron todos hacia la puerta; **the exodus turned into a** — el éxodo se transformó en una fuga precipitada. **2** *vt* hacer huir en desorden; infundir un terror pánico a, causar terror en; **to** — **someone into doing something** infundir terror a uno para que haga algo; hacer que uno haga algo sin la debida reflexión; **let's not be** —**d** no obremos precipitadamente. **3** *vi* huir en desorden, huir precipitadamente; **the horses suddenly** —**d** de repente los caballos se precipitaron hacia adelante presos de un terror pánico.

stamping ground ['stæmpɪŋ‚graund] *n* (*fam*) guarida *f*; **this is his private** — éste es terreno particular suyo, éste es coto cerrado de su propiedad; **to keep off someone's** — no invadir el territorio de uno.

stamp machine ['stæmpmə‚ʃiːn] *n* expendedor *m* automático de sellos (de correo).

stance [stæns] *n* postura *f*; **to take up a** — adoptar una postura.

stanch [stɑːntʃ] *vt* *blood* restañar.

stanchion ['stɑːnʃən] *n* puntal *m*, montante *m*.

stand [stænd] **1** *n* **(a)** (*position*) posición *f*, postura *f*; **to take up one's** — **by the door** ponerse cerca de la puerta; **to take one's** — **on a principle** aferrarse a un principio, sentar cátedra sobre un principio; **to take a firm** — adoptar una actitud firme. **(b)** (*Mil*) parada *f*, alto *m*; resistencia *f*; **the** — **of the Australians at Tobruk** la resistencia de los australianos en Tobruk; **they turned and made a** — hicieron alto para resistir de nuevo al enemigo; **to make a** — **against something** oponer resistencia a algo, hacer frente a algo. **(c)** (*for taxis*) punto *m*, parada *f*. **(d)** (*Theat*) función *f*, representación *f*; **one-night** — función *f* de una sola noche, representación *f* única. **(e)** (*for lamp etc*) sostén *m*; pie *m*, pedestal *m*; (*for display*) mesilla *f*; (*hall* —) perchero *m*; (*Mus*) atril *m*. **(f)** (*in market etc*) puesto *m*; barraca *f*, caseta *f*; (*news* —) quiosco *m*; (*band* —) quiosco *m*; (*at exhibition*) stand *m*; (*Sport*) tribuna *f*; **to take the** — (*Law*) subir a la tribuna de los testigos, (*fig*) prestar declaración.

2 (*irr*: *pret and ptp* **stood**) *vt* **(a)** (*place*) poner, colocar (de pie); **to** — **something (up) against a wall** poner algo contra una pared; **to** — **a vase on a table** poner un florero sobre una mesa. **(b) to** — **one's ground** mantenerse firme. **(c)** (*tolerate*) tolerar, aguantar, soportar; *examination* resistir a; *test* salir muy bien de; *cost* pagar, sufragar, correr con; **it won't** — **the cold** no resiste al frío; **it won't** — **serious examination** no resiste al examen cuidadoso; **his heart couldn't** — **the shock** su corazón no resistió al choque; **the company will have to** — **the loss** la compañía tendrá que encargarse de las pérdidas; **I can't** — **him** no le puedo ver; **I can't** — **Debussy** para mí Debussy es inaguantable; **I can** — **anything but that** lo aguanto todo menos eso; **I can't** — **it any longer!** ¡no aguanto más!, ¡no puedo más!; *see* **chance**. **(d) to** — **someone a drink** invitar a uno a beber, pagar la bebida de uno; **he stood beers all round** invitó a todos a tomar cerveza. **(e) to** — **workers off** suspender (temporalmente) a obreros (por falta de trabajo); **to** — **someone up** (*fam*) dar plantón a uno, dejar a uno plantado.

3 *vi* **(a)** (*be upright*) estar de pie; (*get up*) levantarse, ponerse de pie; **all** —! (*Law*) ¡levántense!; — **at ease!** en su lugar ¡descanso!; **he could hardly** — apenas podía estar de pie; **to** — **at the bar** estar junto al bar; **to** — **in the doorway** estar en la puerta; **to** — **talking** seguir hablando; quedarse a hablar; **we stood chatting for half an hour** charlamos durante media hora, pasamos media hora charlando; **he left everybody else** —**ing** (*fig*) dejó a todos muy atrás; superó fácilmente a los demás; *see* **end**, **leg** *etc*. **(b)** (*of measurement*) medir; **the tree** —**s 30 metres high** el árbol mide 30 metros, el árbol tiene 30 metros de alto; **he** —**s a good 6 feet** mide 6 pies largos; **the mountain** —**s 3000 metres high** la montaña tiene una altura de 3000 metros. **(c)** (*be*, *be placed*) estar, estar situado, encontrarse; **it** —**s beside the town hall** está junto al ayuntamiento; **to buy a house as it** —**s** comprar una casa tal como está; **to let something** — **in the sun** poner algo al sol, dejar algo al sol; **the car has been** —**ing in the sun** el coche ha estado expuesto al sol; **nothing now** —**s between us** ya no existe ningún estorbo entre nosotros. **(d)** (*remain*) quedar en pie, mantenerse en vigor; (*last*) perdurar, durar; **the record** —**s at 10 minutes** el record está en 10 minutos, el tiempo récord sigue siendo de 10 minutos; **the objection** —**s** la objeción es válida, la objeción vale; **the contract** —**s** el contrato sigue en vigor; **the theory** —**s or falls by this** con esto o se confirma o se destruye la teoría; **it has stood for 600 years** ha durado 600 años ya, lleva ya 600 años de vida; *see* **fast**, **firm** *etc*.

(e) (*of temporary conditions*) **as things —, as it —s** tal como están las cosas; **how do we —?** ¿cómo estamos?; **I like to know where I —** me gusta estar enterado de mi situación (con relación a otras personas); **where do you — with him?** ¿cuáles son sus relaciones con él?; **to — well with someone** llevarse bien con uno, ser tenido en mucho por uno.

(f) (*remain undisturbed*) estar; sedimentar; **to allow a liquid to —** dejar estar un líquido; **let it — for 3 days** dejarlo así durante 3 días; **don't let the tea —** no dejes que se pase el té.

(g) (*special cases*) **to — as a candidate** presentarse como candidato; **to — (as) security for someone** (*Fin*) salir fiador de uno, (*fig*) salir por uno; **the thermometer —s at 40°** el termómetro marca 40 grados; **there is £50 —ing to your credit** Vd tiene 50 libras en el haber; **sales — at 5% more than last year** las ventas han aumentado en un 5 por cien en relación con el año pasado; **we — to lose a lot** para nosotros supondría una pérdida importante, estamos en peligro de perder bastante; **what do we — to gain by it?** ¿qué posibilidades hay para nosotros de ganar algo?, ¿qué ventaja nos daría esto?; **he —s to win £5** tiene la posibilidad de ganar 5 libras; *see* **need** *etc*.

(h) (*with adv or prep*) **to — about** estar, esperar, seguir en un sitio sin propósito fijo; **they just — about all day** pasan todo el día por ahí sin hacer nada; **they kept us —ing about for hours** nos hicieron esperar de pie durante horas enteras; **to — aside** apartarse, quitarse de en medio, hacerse a un lado; **to — back** (*person*) retroceder, moverse hacia atrás; (*be placed further back*) estar algo apartado; **the house —s back from the road** la casa está algo apartada de la carretera; **— back, please!** ¡más atrás, por favor!; **to — by** (*adv*) estar cerca; estar presente (sin intervenir); (*Mil etc*) estar alerta, mantenerse listo, estar dispuesto para el combate (*etc*); estar a la expectativa; **— by for further news** estén listos para recibir más noticias; **the Navy is —ing by to help** unidades de la Flota están dispuestas a prestar ayuda; **to — by** (*prep*) *person* apoyar, sostener, defender; no abandonar; *promise* cumplir, atenerse a; **we — by what we said** nos atenemos a lo dicho; **the Minister stood by his decision** el Ministro reafirmó su decisión; **to — down** (*withdraw*) retirarse; **the candidate is —ing down to let a younger man in** el candidato se retira y cede su puesto a otro más joven; **someone has to — down** alguien tiene que ceder su puesto; **you may — down** (*to withdraw*) Vd puede retirarse; **to — for** (*defend*) apoyar; hablar por; creer en; afirmar su adhesión a; (*be instead of*) representar; (*mean*) significar; *post* proponerse para, presentarse como candidato a; (*permit, tolerate*) aguantar, permitir, consentir; **"A —s for apple"** "M es de manzana"; **here a dash —s for a word** aquí una raya representa una palabra; **I'll not — for that** eso no lo permito, eso no se ha de consentir; **I'll not — for your whims any longer** no aguanto tus caprichos un momento más; **he stood for Parliament in 1906** se presentó como candidato en las elecciones parlamentarias de 1906; **he stood for Bristol** fue uno de los candidatos de Bristol; **he stood for Labour** fue candidato laborista; **to — in to the shore** acercarse a la playa; **to — in for someone** suplir a uno; **to — in with someone** declararse por uno, apoyar a uno, (*financially*) contribuir lo mismo que uno; **to — off** (*Naut*) apartarse, alejarse; **to — on ceremony** hacer ceremonias, estar de cumplido; **let's not — on ceremony** dejémonos de cumplidos; **to — out** destacarse (*against* contra, sobre); (*fig*) destacarse, descollar, sobresalir; **to — out against something** oponerse a algo; **to — out for something** insistir en algo, no ceder hasta obtener algo; **to — out in relief** aparecer en relieve; **to — out to sea** hacerse a la mar; **to — over** (*adv*) quedar en suspenso; **to let an item — over** dejar un asunto para la próxima vez; **to — over someone to see that he studies** vigilar a uno para asegurarse de que estudie; **to — to** (*Mil*) estar alerta, estar sobre las armas; **to — up** levantarse, ponerse de pie; **a brew so strong that a spoon could — up in it** un brebaje en el cual se podría mantener de pie una cuchara; **to — up for someone** defender a uno; **to — up for oneself** defenderse a sí mismo; **to — up to someone** resistir resueltamente a uno, hacer frente a uno; **to — up to a test** salir muy bien de una prueba; **it —s up to hard wear** es muy resistente; **it won't — up to close examination** no resiste al examen cuidadoso.

standard ['stændəd] **1** *n* **(a)** (*flag*) estandarte *m*, bandera *f*; **to raise the — of revolt** encabezar una sublevación, sublevarse.

(b) (*measure etc used as norm*) patrón *m*; pauta *f*, norma *f*; (*fig*) modelo *m*, regla *f*; **gold —** patrón *m* oro; **bureau of —s** (*US*) oficina *f* de pesos y medidas.

(c) (*moral*) criterio *m*; **—s** valores *mpl* morales; **he has good —s** tiene buen criterio; **she has no —s** carece de valores morales; **to apply a double —** aplicar un doble criterio; **to judge by that — ...** si lo juzgamos desde ese criterio ...

(d) (*degree of excellence*) nivel *m*, grado *m*; **— of living** nivel *m* de vida; **— of culture** nivel *m* de cultura; **at first-year university —** al nivel del primer año universitario; **of low —** de baja calidad; inferior; **to be below —** estar por debajo del nivel correcto, ser inferior; **to be up to —** estar conforme con el debido nivel; **to set a good —** establecer un buen nivel.

(e) (*Bot*) árbol *m* (*etc*) de tronco derecho; (*of small lamp*) pie *m*; (*of street lamp*) poste *m*.

2 *adj, attr* normal, corriente; standard, estándar; uniforme, estereotipado; **— measure** medida *f* tipo; **— model** modelo *m* standard; **— work of reference** obra *f* clásica de consulta; **S— English** inglés *m* correcto, buen inglés *m*; **— nomenclature** nomenclatura *f* oficial; **— price** precio *m* oficial, precio *m* normal; **— weight** peso *m* legal; **that word is hardly —** esa palabra apenas pertenece al léxico oficial; **the practice became — in the 1940s** la práctica llegó a ser corriente en los años 40.

standard bearer ['stændəd͵bɛərə*] *n* abanderado *m*; (*fig*) jefe *m*, adalid *m*.

standard gauge ['stændəd'geidʒ] **1** *n* vía *f* normal. **2** *adj* **standard-gauge** de vía normal.

standardization [͵stændədai'zeiʃən] *n* normalización *f*, estandar(d)ización *f*.

standardize ['stændədaiz] *vt* normalizar, regularizar, estandar(d)izar, uniformar.

stand-by ['stændbai] *n* **(a)** (*person*) persona *f* de toda confianza, persona *f* siempre dispuesta a prestar su ayuda; paño *m* de lágrimas; (*thing*) recurso *m* seguro, artículo *m* de toda confianza.

(b) alerta *m*; aviso *m* (para partir); **to be on 24-hours —** estar listo para partir dentro de 24 horas; **to put someone on 3-day —** avisar a uno para que esté listo para partir dentro de 3 días.

standee ['stæn'di:] *n* (*US*) espectador *m* que asiste de pie.

stand-in ['stændin] *n* suplente *mf* (*for* de); (*Cine*) doble *mf* (*for* de).

standing ['stændiŋ] **1** *adj* **(a)** (*upright*) derecho; (*on foot*) de pie, en pie; *stone* derecho, vertical; *crop* que sigue creciendo, que está sin segar; *start* parado; *water* estancado, encharcado; **to leave someone —** dejar a uno muy atrás, (*fig*) aventajar a uno con mucho, resultar ser muy superior a uno.

(b) *army, committee, rule etc* permanente; *custom* arraigado; *grievance, joke* constante, eterno; *see* **order.**

2 *n* **(a)** (*position*) posición *f*, situación *f*; (*repute*) reputación *f*; categoría *f*; importancia *f*; **social —** posición *f* social; **of high —** de categoría; **the restaurant has a high —** el restaurante tiene una buena reputación; **a man of some —** un hombre de cierta categoría; **the relative — of these problems** la relativa importancia de estos problemas; **to be in good —** gozar de buen crédito; tener buena reputación; **what is his — locally?** ¿qué reputación tiene en la ciudad? (*etc*); **he has no — in this matter** no tiene voz ni voto en este asunto.

(b) (*duration*) duración *f*; existencia *f*; (*seniority*) antigüedad *f*; **of only 6 months'** — que existe desde hace 6 meses solamente; **a captain of only a month's —** un capitán que lleva solamente un mes en el puesto (*or* en tal graduación); **of long —** de mucho tiempo, existente desde hace mucho tiempo, viejo.

standing room ['stændiŋrum] *n* sitio *m* para estar de pie.

stand-offish ['stænd'ɔfiʃ] *adj* reservado, endiosado, que se da aires de superioridad; poco amable, frío.

stand-offishly ['stænd'ɔfiʃli] *adv* con poca amabilidad, fríamente.

stand-offishness ['stænd'ɔfiʃnis] *n* reserva *f*; endiosamiento *m*, superioridad *f*; falta *f* de amabilidad, frialdad *f*.

standpipe ['stændpaip] *n* columna *f* de alimentación; (*in street*) tubo *m* vertical.

standpoint ['stændpɔint] *n* punto *m* de vista; **from the — of ...** desde el punto de vista de ...

standstill ['stændstil] n parada f; paro m; alto m; paralización f; **to be at a** — estar parado; estar paralizado; **to bring a car to a** — parar un coche; **to bring an industry to a** — paralizar una industria; **to come to a** — (persons) pararse, hacer alto, (vehicle) pararse, (industry etc) quedar paralizado.

stand-up ['stændʌp] adj: — **buffet** cantina f donde se bebe y se come de pie; — **collar** cuello m alto; — **fight** pelea f violenta, riña f a puñetazos, (fig) altercado m violento.

stank [stæŋk] pret of **stink.**

stannic ['stænik] adj estánnico.

stanza ['stænzə] n estrofa f, estancia f.

staphylococcus [ˌstæfiləˈkɔkəs] n, pl —**cocci** [kɔkai] estafilococo m.

staple¹ ['steipl] **1** n (fastener) grapa f. **2** vt (also to — **together**) unir con grapa.

staple² ['steipl] **1** adj principal; establecido; corriente; **their** — **food** su comida corriente.

2 n (chief product) producto m principal; (raw material) materia f prima; (of wool) fibra f (textil); (of conversation etc) asunto m principal, elemento m esencial.

stapler ['steiplə*] n, **stapling machine** ['steipliŋməˌʃin] n máquina f cosepapeles, máquina f grapadora.

star [stɑ:*] **1** n (a) (Astron) estrella f, astro m; (Typ) asterisco m; **S—s and Stripes** (bandera f de) las barras y las estrellas; **evening** — estrella f vespertina; **fixed** — estrella f fija; **guiding** — estrella f de guía; **morning** — lucero m del alba; **north** — estrella f del norte; **polar** — estrella f polar; **to be born under a lucky** — nacer con estrella; **to believe in one's lucky** — creer en su buena estrella; **you can thank your lucky** —**s that** . . . puedes dar las gracias a Dios porque . . .; **to see** —**s** (fig) ver las estrellas.

(b) (person) figura f destacada, figura f más brillante; (Cine etc) astro m, estrella f, vedette f; **the** — **of the team was X** la figura más destacada del equipo fue X.

2 adj, attr principal; destacado, más brillante; **their** — **player** su jugador más destacado, su jugador más brillante; — **role** cargo m estelar; — **show** programa m estelar; — **turn** atracción f especial, número m más destacado.

3 vt (a) (adorn with —s) estrellar, adornar con estrellas, sembrar de estrellas; (mark with —) señalar con asterisco.

(b) (Cine etc) presentar como estrella; **a film** —**ring Greta Garbo** una película que presenta a Greta Garbo en el papel principal.

4 vi (Cine etc) ser el astro, ser la estrella; tener el papel principal; (be outstanding) destacar, descollar, actuar brillantemente; **the 3 films in which James Dean** —**red** las 3 películas que protagonizó James Dean; **he didn't exactly** — **in that game** no destacó no destacó que digamos.

starboard ['stɑ:bəd] **1** n estribor m; **on the** — **side** a estribor; **the sea to** — la mar a estribor; **land to** —! ¡tierra a estribor!

2 vt: **to** — **the helm** poner el timón a estribor, virar a estribor.

starch [stɑ:tʃ] **1** n almidón m; (in food) fécula f, cosas fpl feculentas. **2** vt almidonar.

starched [stɑ:tʃt] adj almidonado.

starchy ['stɑ:tʃi] adj feculento; (fig) estirado, entonado, etiquetero.

star-crossed ['stɑːˌkrɔst] adj malhadado, desventurado.

stardom ['stɑːdəm] n estrellato m; **to reach** — alcanzar el estrellato.

stare [stɛə*] **1** n mirada f fija; stony — mirada f dura; vacant — mirada f distraída; **to give someone a** — mirar fijamente a uno.

2 vt: **to** — **someone out of countenance** desconcertar a uno mirándole fijamente; **it's staring you in the face** salta a la vista.

3 vi mirar fijamente; **don't** —! ¡no mires tan fijo!; **it's rude to** — es de mala educación mostrar tanta curiosidad; **to** — **at someone** mirar fijamente a uno, clavar la vista en uno, (in surprise) mirar a uno con sorpresa; **to** — **into the distance, to** — **into space** mirar las telarañas.

starfish ['stɑːfiʃ] n estrella f de mar.

stargaze ['stɑːgeiz] vi mirar las estrellas; (fig) distraerse, mirar las telarañas.

stargazer ['stɑːˌgeizə*] n astrónomo m.

stargazing ['stɑːˌgeiziŋ] n estudio m de las estrellas; astronomía f; (fig) distracción f.

staring ['stɛəriŋ] adj que mira fijamente, curioso; eyes saltón, (in fear) lleno de espanto.

stark [stɑːk] **1** adj (stiff) rígido; (utter) completo,

puro; (unadorned) escueto, severo; cliff etc espantoso, ceñudo.

2 adv: — (staring) **mad** loco de atar; — **naked** en cueros, en pelota, como le parió su madre.

starless ['stɑːlis] adj sin estrellas.

starlet ['stɑːlit] n estrella f joven, estrella f en ciernes, aspirante f a estrella.

starlight ['stɑːlait] n luz f de las estrellas; **by** — a la luz de las estrellas.

starling ['stɑːliŋ] n estornino m.

starlit ['stɑːlit] adj iluminado por las estrellas.

starry ['stɑːri] adj estrellado, sembrado de estrellas.

starry-eyed ['stɑːri'aid] adj inocentón, ingenuo; idealista, poco práctico; lleno de amor (or entusiasmo etc) candoroso.

star shell ['stɑːʃel] n cohete m luminoso, bengala f iluminadora.

star-spangled ['stɑːˌspæŋgld] adj estrellado.

start [stɑːt] **1** n (a) (fright etc) susto m, sobresalto m; (of horse) respingo m; **to give a sudden** — sobresaltarse; **to give someone a** — asustar a uno, dar un susto a uno; **what a** — **you gave me!** ¡qué susto me diste!; **to wake with a** — despertarse sobresaltado; see fit.

(b) (beginning) principio m, comienzo m; (departure) salida f, partida f; (of race) salida f; **false** — falso comienzo m; **flying** —, **running** — salida f lanzada; **standing** — salida f parada; **at the** — al principio; **at the very** — muy al principio, en los mismos comienzos; **at the** — **of the century** a principios del siglo; **we are at the** — **of something big** estamos en los comienzos de algo grandioso; **for a** — en primer lugar, para empezar; **from the** — desde el principio; **from** — **to finish** desde el principio hasta el fin, de cabo a rabo; **to get off to a good** (or **flying**) — empezar bien, (fig) comenzar felizmente, entrar con buen pie; **to give someone a** — **in life** ayudar a uno a situarse en la vida; **the review gave the book a good** — la reseña ayudó al libro a venderse bien desde el principio; **to make a** — empezar; **to make an early** — ponerse en camino sin perder tiempo; **to make a fresh** (or **new**) — **in life** hacer vida nueva, empezar de nuevo; **to make a good** — (in life) emprender felizmente su carrera.

(c) (advantage) ventaja f; **to give someone a 5 minute** — dar a uno una ventaja de 5 minutos.

2 vt (a) (begin) comenzar, empezar; iniciar; principiar; discussion etc abrir, iniciar; (undertake) emprender; **to** — **negotiations** iniciar las negociaciones; **to** — **a new life** comenzar una vida nueva; **to** — **a novel** empezar a escribir (or leer) una novela; **don't** — **that again!** ¡no vuelvas a eso!

(b) **to** — **a race** dar la señal de salida para una carrera.

(c) **to** — **a partridge** levantar una perdiz.

(d) (cause) causar, provocar; **to** — **a fire** causar un incendio; **it** —**ed the collapse of the empire** causó el derrumbamiento del imperio.

(e) (found) fundar, crear; **to** — **an enterprise** fundar una empresa; **to** — **a newspaper** fundar un periódico.

(f) (Mech) poner en marcha, hacer funcionar; car, engine arrancar; clock poner en marcha.

(g) (with personal object) **to** — **someone reminiscing** hacer que uno empiece a contar sus recuerdos; **once you** — **him on that** en cuanto le pones a hablar de eso; **to** — **someone on a career** ayudar a uno a emprender una carrera.

(h) (with adv or prep) **to** — **off, to** — **up** see **2** (a) etc.

3 vi (a) (in fright) asustarse, sobresaltarse, sobrecogerse (at a, with de); **to** — **back** retroceder; **to** — **back in horror** retroceder horrorizado; **to** — **from one's chair** levantarse asustado de su silla; **to** — **out of one's sleep** despertarse sobresaltado; **his eyes were** —**ing out of his head** se le saltaban los ojos de la cabeza; **to** — **up** incorporarse bruscamente, ponerse de pie de un salto.

(b) (of timber etc) combarse, torcerse; (of rivets etc) soltarse.

(c) (begin) comenzar, empezar; principiar; iniciarse; (on journey) partir, ponerse en camino; (of bus, train) salir; (in race) salir; (car, engine etc) arrancar, ponerse en marcha; empezar a funcionar; —**ing from Tuesday** a partir del martes; **the route** —**s from here** la ruta sale de aquí; **to** — **afresh** volver a empezar, comenzar de nuevo; **to** — **at the beginning** empezar desde el principio; **to** — **with a prayer** empezar con una oración; **what shall we** — **with?** ¿con qué empezamos?; **to** — **with** (as adv phrase) en primer lugar, para empezar.

(d) (*with verb constructions*) **to — to + infin** comenzar (*or* empezar) a + *infin*; **to — talking** empezar a hablar; **to — by saying** comenzar diciendo.

(e) (*with adv or prep*) **to — after someone** ir en busca de uno; ir en pos de uno; **to — back** emprender el viaje de regreso; **to — off, to — out** (*begin*) comenzar; empezar; (*on journey*) partir, ponerse en camino, (*of bus, train*) salir; **it —s off with a murder** comienza con un asesinato; **it —ed out as a play** empezó como una obra dramática; **to — on a task** emprender una tarea; **to — on something new** emprender algo nuevo; **to — up** comenzar, empezar; **then the band —ed up** luego empezó a tocar la orquesta; **when I —ed up in business** cuando yo monté el negocio; cuando empecé mi carrera en los negocios.

starter ['stɑːtə*] n (a) (*person*) (*judge*) juez *m* de salida; (*competitor*) corredor *m*, ora *f*; caballo *m* (*etc*). (b) (*Aut etc: motor*) motor *m* de arranque; (*button*) botón *m* de arranque.

starting gate ['stɑːtiŋgeit] *n* barrera *f* que se levanta para dar la salida.

starting handle ['stɑːtiŋˌhændl] *n* manivela *f* de arranque.

starting line ['stɑːtiŋlain] *n* línea *f* de salida.

starting motor ['stɑːtiŋˌməutə*] *n* motor *m* de arranque.

starting point ['stɑːtiŋpoint] *n* punto *m* de partida, punto *m* de arranque.

starting post ['stɑːtiŋpəust] *n* poste *m* de salida.

starting price ['stɑːtiŋprais] *n* puntos *mpl* de ventaja al empezar la carrera.

starting switch ['stɑːtiŋswitʃ] *n* botón *m* de arranque.

startle ['stɑːtl] *vt* asustar, sobrecoger; alarmar; **to — someone out of his serenity** asustar tanto a uno que sale de su tranquilidad.

startling ['stɑːtliŋ] *adj* asombroso, sorprendente; alarmante; sobrecogedor; *colour etc* chillón; *dress etc* llamativo, exagerado.

starvation [stɑːˈveiʃən] **1** *n* hambre *f*, (*Med*) inanición *f*; (*fig*) privación *f*; **to die of —** morir de hambre.

2 *attr*: **— diet** régimen *m* de hambre; **— wages** sueldo *m* miserable.

starve [stɑːv] **1** *vt* (a) (*kill*) hacer morir de hambre; (*deprive of food*) privar de comida, hacer pasar hambre; **to — someone to death** hacer a uno morir de hambre; **to — a town into surrender** hacer que una ciudad se rinda por hambre; **to — a garrison out** hacer que una guarnición se rinda por hambre.

(b) (*fig*) **to — someone of something** privar a uno de algo; **to be —d of affection** estar privado de cariño (*paternal etc*).

2 *vi* (a) (*die*) morir de hambre; (*lack food*) pasar hambre, padecer hambre; **to — to death** morir de hambre.

(b) (*fig*) morir de hambre; **I'm simply starving!** ¡estoy muerto de hambre!, ¡qué hambre tengo!

starving ['stɑːviŋ] *adj* hambriento, famélico.

stash [stæʃ] *vt* (*fam*): **to — away** ir acumulando; ocultar para uso futuro.

state [steit] **1** *n* (a) (*condition*) estado *m*, condición *f*; **— of emergency** estado *m* de emergencia; **to declare a — of emergency** declarar el estado de emergencia; **— of health** salud *f*, estado *m* físico; **— of mind** estado *m* de ánimo; **— of siege** estado *m* de sitio; **— of war** estado *m* de guerra; **— of weightlessness** estado *m* de ingravidez; **the married —** el estado matrimonial; **the single —** el estado célibe; **in a comatose —** en estado comatoso; **races still in a savage —** razas *fpl* todavía en estado de salvajismo; **to be in a bad —** estar en mal estado; **to be in a good —** estar en buenas condiciones; **he's not in a (fit) — to do it** no está en condiciones para hacerlo; **he arrived home in a shocking —** llegó a casa en un estado espantoso.

(b) (*anxiety*) agitación *f*; estado *m* nervioso; **to be in a great —** estar muy agitado, estar aturrulado; **now don't get into a — about it** no te pongas nervioso.

(c) (*rank*) rango *m*, dignidad *f*; **he attained the — of bishop** llegó a la dignidad de obispo.

(d) (*pomp*) pompa *f*, fausto *m*; ceremonia *f*; **in —** con gran pompa; **to dine in —** cenar con mucha ceremonia; **to live in —** vivir lujosamente; **to travel in —** viajar con gran pompa; **to lie in —** estar de cuerpo presente, estar expuesto en capilla ardiente.

(e) (*Pol*) estado *m*; **the S— el Estado**; **the S—s** (*US*) Estados *mpl* Unidos; **a — within a —** un estado dentro del estado; **affairs of —** asuntos *mpl* de Estado; **Church and S— Iglesia y Estado**;

Secretary of S— (US) Ministro *m* de Asuntos Exteriores; **Secretary of S— for . . .** Ministro *m* de . . .

2 *adj*, *attr* (*Pol etc*) estatal, del Estado; público; **— control** control *m* público; **S— Department** (*US*) Ministerio *m* de Asuntos Exteriores; **— education** enseñanza *f* pública; **— papers** documentos *mpl* de Estado; **— secret** secreto *m* de Estado.

(b) *apartment, banquet, coach etc* de gala.

3 *vt* (a) declarar, afirmar, decir; manifestar; consignar, hacer constar; **as —d above** como se ha dicho arriba; **it is nowhere —d that . . .** no se dice en ninguna parte que . . .; **I have seen it —d that . . .** he visto afirmarse que . . .; **he is —d to have been there** se afirma que él estuvo allí; **— your name** escriba su nombre; **cheques must — the amount clearly** los cheques han de consignar claramente la cantidad; **it must be —d in the records** ha de hacerse constar en los archivos.

(b) *case* exponer, explicar; *law* formular; *problem* plantear, exponer; **to — the case for the prosecution** explicar los hechos en que se basa la acusación.

statecraft ['steitkrɑːft] *n* arte *m* de gobernar.

stated ['steitid] *adj* dicho; indicado; fijo, establecido; **the sum —** la cantidad dicha; **on the — date** en la fecha indicada; **within — limits** dentro de límites fijos.

statehood ['steithud] *n* categoría *f* de estado, dignidad *f* de estado; **when the country achieves —** cuando el país alcance la categoria de estado.

stateless ['steitlis] *adj* desnacionalizado, sin patria.

stateliness ['steitlinis] *n* majestad *f*, majestuosidad *f*.

stately ['steitli] *adj* majestuoso; imponente; augusto; **— home** casa *f* solariega.

statement ['steitmənt] *n* declaración *f*, afirmación *f*, manifestación *f*; informe *m*, relación *f*; exposición *f*; (*Law*) declaración *f*; **— of account** estado *m* de cuenta; **official —** informe *m* oficial, nota *f* oficial; **according to his own —** según su propia declaración; **to make a — (Law)** prestar declaración.

stateroom ['steitrum] *n* (*Naut*) camarote *m*.

statesman ['steitsmən] *n*, *pl* **—men** [mən] estadista *m*, hombre *m* de estado; **elder —** viejo estadista *m*; (*fig*) consejero *m* de máxima autoridad; figura *f* muy respetada.

statesmanlike ['steitsmənlaik] *adj* (digno) de estadista.

statesmanship ['steitsmənʃip] *n* arte *m* de gobernar; habilidad *f* de estadista; **that showed true —** eso demostró su verdadera capacidad de estadista; **— alone will not solve the problem** la habilidad de los estadistas no resolverá el problema por sí sola.

static ['stætik] *adj* inactivo, inmóvil, estancado; (*Phys*) estático.

statics ['stætiks] *npl* (*Phys*) estática *f*; (*Radio*) parásitos *mpl*.

station ['steiʃən] **1** *n* (a) (*place*) puesto *m*, sitio *m*; situación *f*; **Roman —** sitio *m* ocupado por los romanos; **the only — for this rare plant** el único sitio donde existe esta planta tan poco frecuente; **action —s!** ¡a los puestos de combate!; **from my — by the window** desde el sitio donde yo estaba junto a la ventana; **to take up one's —** colocarse, ir a su puesto.

(b) **(— in life)** posición *f* social; puesto *m* en la sociedad; **of humble —** de baja posición social, de condición humilde; **a man of exalted —** un hombre de rango elevado; **to marry below one's —** casarse con un hombre (*or* una mujer) de posición social inferior; **to get ideas above one's —** darse aires de superioridad, darse tono.

(c) (*specific*) estación *f*; (*Radio*) emisora *f*; (*Rail*) estación *f* (de ferrocarril); **coaling —** estación *f* carbonera; **frontier —** puesto *m* de frontera; **goods —** estación *f* de mercancías; **naval —** apostadero *m* naval; **pumping —** estación *f* de bombeo; **S—s of the Cross** Estaciones *fpl* del vía Crucis.

2 *vt* colocar, situar; (*Mil*) estacionar, apostar.

3 *vr*: **to — oneself** colocarse, situarse.

stationary ['steiʃənəri] *adj* estacionario; inmóvil; *engine etc* estacionario, fijo; **to remain — (*person*)** quedar inmóvil, estar sin moverse.

stationer ['steiʃənə*] *n* papelero *m*, a *f*; **—'s (shop)** papelería *f*.

stationery ['steiʃənəri] *n* papelería *f*, papel *m* de escribir, efectos *mpl* de escritorio.

station house ['steiʃənˌhaus] *n*, *pl* **— houses** [ˌhauziz] (*US*) *Rail* estación *f* de ferrocarril; (*police*) cuartel *m* de policía.

station master ['steiʃənˌmɑːstə*] *n* jefe *m* de estación.

station wagon ['steiʃən,wægən] *n* combinable *f*, rubia *f*.

statistic [stə'tistik] *n* estadística *f*, número *m*.

statistical [stə'tistikəl] *adj* estadístico.

statistically [stə'tistikəli] *adv*: **to prove something —** probar algo por medios estadísticos; **— that may be true** en cuanto a la estadística eso puede ser cierto.

statistician [,stætis'tiʃən] *n* estadístico *m*.

statistics [stə'tistiks] *n* (*subject*) estadística *f*; (*numbers*) estadísticas *fpl*; **vital —** estadísticas *fpl* demográficas, (*hum*) medidas *fpl* vitales.

stator ['steitə*] *n* (*Elec, Math*) estator *m*.

statuary ['stætjuəri] **1** *adj* estatuario. **2** *n* (*art*) estatuaria *f*; (*statues*) estatuas *fpl*; (*person*) estatuario *m*.

statue ['stætju:] *n* estatua *f*.

statuesque [,stætju'esk] *adj* estatuario, escultural.

statuette [,stætju'et] *n* figurilla *f*.

stature ['stætʃə*] *n* (**a**) estatura *f*, talla *f*; **to be of short —** ser de estatura baja, tener poca talla.
(**b**) (*fig*) talla *f*; valor *m*, carácter *m*; **to have sufficient — for a post** estar a la altura de un cargo; **he lacks moral —** le falta carácter.

status ['steitəs] *n* posición *f*, condición *f*; rango *m*, categoría *f*; prestigio *m*; reputación *f*; (*Law*) estado *m*; **civil —, marital —** estado *m* civil; **social —** posición *f* social; **the — of the Negro population** la posición social de la población negra; **what is his — in the profession?** ¿qué rango ocupa en la profesión?, ¿cómo se le considera en la profesión?; **he has not sufficient — for the job** no tiene categoría bastante alta para ocupar este cargo.

status quo ['steitəs'kwəu] *n* statu *m* quo.

status symbol ['steitəs,simbəl] *n* símbolo *m* de prestigio.

statute ['stætju:t] *n* ley *f*, estatuto *m*; **— law** ley *f* escrita; **by —** según la ley, de acuerdo con la ley.

statute book ['stætju:tbuk] *n* código *m* de leyes.

statutory ['stætjutəri] *adj* estatutario; legal.

staunch[1] [stɔːntʃ] *adj* leal, firme, incondicional.

staunch[2] [stɔːntʃ] *vt see* **stanch.**

staunchly ['stɔːntʃli] *adv* lealmente, firmemente, incondicionalmente.

staunchness ['stɔːntʃnis] *n* lealtad *f*, firmeza *f*.

stave [steiv] **1** *n* (*of barrel*) duela *f*; (*of ladder*) peldaño *m*; (*Mus*) pentagrama *m*; (*Lit*) estrofa *f*.
2 (*irr: pret and ptp* **stove** *or* **staved**) *vt*: **to — in** romper, quebrar (a golpes); abrir a golpes; desfondar; **to — off** *attack* rechazar; apartar, mantener a distancia; *threat etc* evitar, conjurar; (*delay*) diferir; aplazar.

staves [steivz] *npl of* **staff.**

stay[1] [stei] **1** *n* (**a**) estancia *f*, permanencia *f*; visita *f*; **a — of 10 days** una estancia de 10 días; **our second — in Murcia** nuestra segunda visita a Murcia; **come for a longer — next year** ven a estar más tiempo el año que viene.
(**b**) (*Law*) suspensión *f*, prórroga *f*; **— of execution** aplazamiento *m* de una sentencia; **— of proceedings** sobreseimiento *m*.
2 *vt* (**a**) detener; controlar; poner freno a; *epidemic etc* tener a raya; *hunger* matar, engañar; **to — one's hand** contenerse, detenerse; **to — someone's hand** parar la mano a uno.
(**b**) (*Law*) suspender, prorrogar; aplazar.
3 *vi* (**a**) (*wait*) esperar; **—!** ¡espera!
(**b**) (*remain*) quedar, quedarse, permanecer; (*as guest etc*) hospedarse, estar, vivir; **you — right there** tú te quedas ahí, no te muevas de ahí; **to — at home** quedarse en casa; **to — in bed** guardar cama; **how long can you —?** ¿hasta cuándo te puedes quedar?; **what? you —ed for the Debussy?** ¿cómo? ¿os quedasteis a escuchar lo de Debussy?; **to — for supper, to — to supper** quedarse a cenar; **to — at an hotel** hospedarse en un hotel; **to — with friends** hospedarse con unos amigos; **where are you —ing?** ¿dónde vives?; **she came for a weekend and —ed 3 years** vino a pasar el fin de semana y permaneció 3 años.
(**c**) (*remain, with adj*) **it —s red** sigue tan rojo como antes; **if it —s fine** si continúa el buen tiempo, si el tiempo sigue bueno; **it —s motionless for hours** sigue durante horas enteras sin moverse.
(**d**) (*last out*) resistir; **the horse doesn't — el** caballo no resiste esa distancia, el caballo no tiene bastante resistencia; **can he — 3 miles?** ¿aguanta 3 millas?; **to — the course** terminar la carrera, (*fig*) continuar hasta el final.
(**e**) (*with adv or prep*) **to — away** ausentarse (*from de*), no asistir (*from a*); **you — away from my daughter!** ¡no venga por aquí a molestar a mi hija!; **— away from that switch** no to acerques a

ese interruptor, no toques ese interruptor; **to — behind** quedarse; quedarse en casa, no salir; (*in race*) rezagarse; **to make someone — behind after school** hacer que uno se quede en la escuela después de las clases; **to — in** quedarse en casa, no salir; (*School*) quedarse después de las clases (como castigo); **the cork won't — in** el corcho no quiere entrar (en la botella *etc*); **to — on** quedarse; permanecer, continuar en su lugar; **he —ed on as manager** pasó a ser gerente en la misma compañía; **they —ed on after everyone else had left** se quedaron después de que todos los demás se habían marchado; **the lid won't — on** la tapa no quiere estar en su lugar; **to — out** quedarse fuera, no volver a casa; **to — out of something** no tomar parte en algo; **you — out of this!** ¡Vd no se meta en esto!; **she —s out till midnight** no vuelve a casa hasta medianoche; **to — over** pasar la noche, pernoctar; quedarse un poco; *see* put 1 (**h**); **to — up** velar, no acostarse, seguir sin acostarse; **Spanish children — up later than English ones** los niños españoles se acuestan más tarde que los ingleses; **they —ed up for me** estuvieron esperándome sin acostarse.

stay[2] [stei] **1** *n* (*Mech*) sostén *m*, soporte *m*, puntal *m*; (*Naut*) estay *m*; (*fig*) sostén *m*, apoyo *m*; **—s** corsé *m*; **the — of one's old age** el sostén de su vejez.
2 *vt* sostener, apoyar, apuntalar; **this will — you till lunchtime** esto te ayudará a resistir hasta la comida, esto engañará el hambre hasta la comida.

stay-at-home ['steiəthəum] **1** *adj* casero, hogareño. **2** *n* persona *f* casera, persona *f* que apenas tiene ganas de salir de su casa.

stayer ['steiə*] *n* (*horse*) caballo *m* apto para carreras de distancia; (*person*) persona *f* de carácter firme, persona *f* de mucho aguante.

staying power ['steiiŋ,pauə*] *n* resistencia *f*, aguante *m*.

staysail ['steiseil, *Naut* 'steisl] *n* vela *f* de estay.

stead [sted] *n*: **in his —** en su lugar; **to stand someone in good —** ser útil a uno, aprovechar a uno.

steadfast ['stedfɑst] *adj* firme, resuelto; constante; tenaz; *gaze* fijo; **— in adversity** firme en el infortunio; **— in danger** impertérrito; **— in love** constante en el amor.

steadfastly ['stedfɑstli] *adv* firmemente, resueltamente; con constancia; tenazmente; fijamente.

steadfastness ['stedfɑstnis] *n* firmeza *f*, resolución *f*; constancia *f*; tenacidad *f*; fijeza *f*.

steadily ['stedili] *adv* firmemente, fijamente; de modo estable; regularmente, constantemente, uniformemente; continuamente; sin parar, ininterrumpidamente; sensatamente; seriamente; diligentemente; tranquilamente; resueltamente; imperturbablemente; **it gets — worse** se hace cada vez peor; **the temperature goes — up** la temperatura sube constantemente, la temperatura no deja de subir; **to work —** trabajar ininterrumpidamente; **she looked at me —** me miró sin pestañear.

steadiness ['stedinis] *n* firmeza *f*, fijeza *f*; estabilidad *f*; regularidad *f*, constancia *f*, uniformidad *f*; sensatez *f*; juicio *m*; seriedad *f*, formalidad *f*; diligencia *f*; serenidad *f*, ecuanimidad *f*; sangre *f* fría; imperturbabilidad *f*.

steady ['stedi] **1** *adj* firme, fijo; estable; regular, constante, uniforme; continuo, ininterrumpido; (*in character*) sensato, juicioso; serio, formal; (*at work*) diligente, trabajador; aplicado; *boyfriend etc* formal; (*not nervous*) sereno, tranquilo, ecuánime; resuelto; imperturbable; **— demand** demanda *f* constante; **— temperature** temperatura *f* constante, temperatura *f* uniforme; **— progress** progreso *m* ininterrumpido; **— job** empleo *m* seguro, empleo *m* fijo; **with a — hand** con mano firme; **at a — pace** a paso regular; **the car is very — at corners** el coche es muy estable en las curvas; **there was a — downpour for 3 hours** llovió sin interrupción durante 3 horas; **we were going at a — 70 kph** íbamos a una velocidad uniforme de 70 kph; **he plays a very — game** juega muy sensatamente.
2 *adv*: **—!** ¡con calma!, despacio!; **they are going — now** (*fam*) son novios formales ya; **they've been going — for 6 months** (*fam*) llevan 6 meses de relaciones; **is he going — with her?** (*fam*) ¿es novio formal de ella?
3 *n* (*fam*) novio *m* formal, novia *f* formal.
4 *vt* (*hold*) mantener firme, sujetar en posición firme; (*stabilize*) estabilizar, hacer más estable; uniformar, regularizar; *nerves* calmar; *nervous person* tranquilizar, *wild person* hacer que siente la cabeza (*also* **to — down, to — up**).

5 *vi* estabilizarse, hacerse más estable; uniformarse, regularizarse; calmarse; tranquilizarse; sentar la cabeza (*also to — down, to — up*).

6 *vr*: **to — oneself** afirmarse, recobrar el equilibrio; **to — oneself against something** apoyarse en algo.

steak [steik] *n* biftec *m*; filete *m*; (*of meat other than beef*) tajada *f*; **underdone —** filete *m* poco hecho; **— and kidney pie** pastel *m* de biftec y riñones.

steakhouse ['steikhaus] *n, pl* **—houses** [ˌhauziz] *restaurante especializado en servir biftecs.*

steak knife ['steiknaif] *n, pl* **— knives**[naivz] cuchillo *m* para el biftec.

steal [stiːl] (*irr: pret* **stole**, *ptp* **stolen**) **1** *vt* robar, hurtar; (*fig*) robar; **to — a glance at someone** mirar de soslayo a uno, mirar rápidamente a uno.

2 *vi*: **to — away, to — off** marcharse sigilosamente, escabullirse; **to — into a room** deslizarse en un cuarto, entrar en un cuarto sin ruido; **to — up on someone** acercarse a uno sin ruido.

stealth ['stelθ] *n* cautela *f*, sigilo *m*; **by —** a escondidas, a hurtadillas, sigilosamente.

stealthily ['stelθili] *adv* clandestinamente, a hurtadillas.

stealthiness ['stelθinis] *n* cautela *f*, sigilo *m*; cáracter *m* furtivo.

stealthy ['stelθi] *adj* cauteloso, sigiloso, furtivo; clandestino.

steam [stiːm] **1** *n* vapor *m*; vaho *m*, humo *m*; **waste —** vapor *m* de escape; **wet —** vapor *m* húmedo; **full — ahead!** ¡todo avante!; **to get up —** acumular vapor, dar presión; **to let off —** descargar vapor, (*fig*) desahogarse; **the ship went on under its own —** el buque siguió adelante con sus propios motores.

2 *attr* de vapor.

3 *vt* (a) (*Cook*) cocer al vapor.

(b) (*window*) empañar (*also to — up*); **the windows quickly get —ed up** las ventanas se empañan pronto.

(c) **to — open an envelope** abrir un sobre por medio de vapor; **to — a stamp off** separar un sello por medio de vapor.

4 *vi* (a) (*give out —*) echar vapor; **the bowl was —ing on the table** la cacerola humeaba en la mesa.

(b) (*move etc, function*) **to — ahead** avanzar, (*fig*) adelantarse mucho; **to — along** ir, avanzar (echando vapor); **we were —ing at 12 knots** íbamos a 12 nudos; **the ship —ed into harbour** el buque entró al puerto (echando vapor); **the train —ed out** salió el tren (echando humo).

(c) **to — up** (*of window*) empañarse.

steamboat ['stiːmbəut] *n* vapor *m*, buque *m* de vapor.

steam-driven ['stiːmˌdrivn] *adj* impulsado por vapor, a vapor.

steam engine ['stiːmˌendʒin] *n* máquina *f* de vapor.

steam hammer ['stiːmˈhæmə*] *n* maza *f* de fragua.

steamer ['stiːmə*] *n* vapor *m*, buque *m* de vapor.

steamroller ['stiːmˌrəulə*] **1** *n* apisonadora *f*.

2 *vt* allanar con apisonadora; (*fig*) aplastar, arrollar; **to — a bill through parliament** hacer aprobar un proyecto de ley sin tener en cuenta los derechos de la oposición.

steamship ['stiːmʃip] *n* vapor *m*, buque *m* de vapor; **— company** compañía *f* naviera; **— line** línea *f* de vapores.

steam shovel ['stiːmˌʃʌvl] *n* pala *f* mecánica de vapor, excavadora *f*.

steam turbine ['stiːmˈtəːbain] *n* turbina *f* de vapor.

steamy ['stiːmi] *adj* vaporoso; *room etc* lleno de vapor; *atmosphere* húmedo y de mucho calor; *window* empañado.

steed [stiːd] *n* (*lit*) corcel *m*.

steel [stiːl] **1** *n* acero *m*; (*sharpener*) acero *m*, eslabón *m*; (*for striking spark*) eslabón *m*; **stainless —** acero *m* inoxidable; **to be made of —** (*fig*) ser de bronce; **to fight with cold —** luchar con armas blancas.

2 *adj, attr* de acero; acerado; **— industry** industria *f* siderúrgica.

3 *vt* acerar; revestir de acero; **to — one's heart** hacerse duro de corazón; **to — one's men** infundir valor a los suyos.

4 *vr*: **to — oneself** fortalecerse (*against* contra); **to — oneself to do something** cobrar bastante ánimo para hacer algo, persuadirse a hacer algo.

steel-clad ['stiːlklæd] *adj* revestido de acero, acorazado.

steel mill ['stiːlmil] *n* acería *f*, fábrica *f* de acero; fábrica *f* siderúrgica.

steel wool ['stiːl'wul] *n* virutillas *fpl* de acero.

steelworks ['stiːlwəːks] *n* acería *f*, fábrica *f* de acero, fábrica *f* siderúrgica.

steely ['stiːli] *adj* acerado, (*fig*) inflexible, duro; *gaze* duro.

steelyard ['stiːljɑːd] *n* romana *f*.

steep[1] [stiːp] *adj* (a) escarpado, abrupto; *cliff etc* cortado a pico, precipitoso; *stairs etc* empinado; **a — slope** una fuerte pendiente; **it's too — for the tractor** es demasiado fuerte para el tractor; **it's a — climb** la subida es difícil.

(b) (*fig*) *price etc* exorbitante, excesivo; *story etc* difícil de creer, increíble; **that's pretty —!** ¡eso es demasiado!, ¡no hay derecho!; **it seems a bit — that . . .** no parece razonable que + *subj*.

steep[2] [stiːp] **1** *vt* empapar, remojar (*in* en); **—ed in** (*fig*) saturado de, impregnado de, empapado en; **a town —ed in history** una ciudad saturada de historia.

2 *vi*: **to leave something to —** dejar algo en remojo.

steeple ['stiːpl] *n* aguja *f*, campanario *m*, torre *f*.

steeplechase ['stiːplˌtʃeis] *n* carrera *f* de obstáculos.

steeplechasing ['stiːplˌtʃeisiŋ] *n* deporte *m* de las carreras de obstáculos.

steeplejack ['stiːplˌdʒæk] *n* reparador *m* de chimeneas, torres *etc*.

steeply ['stiːpli] *adv*: **the mountain rises —** la montaña está cortada a pico; **the road climbs —** la carretera sube en fuerte pendiente; **prices have risen —** los precios han subido muchísimo.

steepness ['stiːpnis] *n* lo escarpado, lo abrupto; lo precipitoso; lo fuerte.

steer[1] [stiə*] **1** *vt* guiar, dirigir; *car etc* conducir; *ship* gobernar; **to — one's way through a crowd** abrirse paso por entre una multitud; **you nearly —ed us into that rock** por poco dimos con aquella roca; **I —ed her across to the bar** la llevé hacia el bar.

2 *vi* conducir; gobernar; **who's going to —?** ¿quién manejará el volante (*or* timón etc)?; **can you —?** ¿sabes gobernar el barco (*etc*)?; **to — for** dirigirse a, dirigirse hacia, ir con rumbo a; **to — clear of** evitar cualquier contacto con.

steer[2] [stiə*] *n* buey *m*; novillo *m*.

steerage ['stiəridʒ] *n* entrepuente *m*; **to go —** viajar en tercera clase.

steering ['stiəriŋ] *n* (*Aut etc*) dirección *f*, conducción *f*; (*Naut*) gobierno *m*.

steering arm ['stiəriŋɑːm] *n* brazo *m* de dirección.

steering column ['stiəriŋˌkɔləm] *n* columna *f* de dirección.

steering committee ['stiəriŋkə'miti] *n* comisión *f* de iniciativas, comisión *f* planificadora.

steering gear ['stiəriŋˌgiə*] *n* mecanismo *m* de dirección.

steering wheel ['stiəriŋwiːl] *n* volante *m* (de dirección).

steersman ['stiəzmən] *n, pl* **—men** [mən] timonero *m*.

stellar ['stelə*] *adj* estelar.

stem [stem] **1** *n* (*of plant*) tallo *m*, (*of tree*) tronco *m*, (*of leaf etc*) pedúnculo *m*; (*of glass*) pie *m*; (*of pipe*) cañón *m*, tubo *m*; (*Mech*) vástago *m*; (*of word*) tema *m*; (*Naut*) roda *f*, tajamar *m*; **from — to stern** de proa a popa.

2 *vt* (*check, stop*) refrenar, detener; *flood* represar; *attack* rechazar; *flow of blood* restañar.

3 *vi*: **to — from** provenir de, proceder de, resultar de.

stench [stentʃ] *n* hedor *m*.

stencil ['stensl] **1** *n* (*Tech*) patrón *m* picado, estarcido *m*; (*for lettering*) plantilla *f*; (*for typing*) cliché *m*, clisé *m*.

2 *vt* estarcir; (*in typing*) hacer un cliché de.

stenographer [ste'nɔgrəfə*] *n* taquígrafo *m*, a *f*.

stenography [ste'nɔgrəfi] *n* taquigrafía *f*.

stentorian [sten'tɔːriən] *adj* estentóreo.

step [step] **1** *n* (a) (*pace*) paso *m*; (*sound*) paso *m*, pisada *f*; (*footprint*) huella *f*; **at every —** a cada paso; **— by —** paso a paso, poco a poco; **it's a good —** es bastante camino, está algo lejos; **it's quite a — to the village** el pueblo queda algo lejos, hay mucho camino para ir al pueblo; **to be in — with** llevar el paso con, (*fig*) estar conforme a, estar de acuerdo con; **to be out of — with** no ir al paso de, no llevar el paso con, (*fig*) estar en desacuerdo con; estar desfasado de; **to break —** romper el paso; **to fall into —** empezar a llevar el paso, (*fig*) conformarse; **to keep in —** llevar el paso; **to retrace one's —s** desandar su camino, volver sobre sus pasos; **to take a —** dar un paso; **to turn one's —s towards** dirigirse hacia; **to watch one's —** ir con tiento.

(b) (*measure*) paso *m*; medida *f*, gestión *f*; **—s to deal with the problem** medidas *fpl* para resolver el problema; **the first — is to . . .** la primera medida a tomar es . . .; **it's a great — forward** esto significa un gran avance; **it's a — in the right direction** es una medida plausible; **to take —s to + infin** tomar medidas para + infin; **one can't take a single — without . . .** no se puede dar un solo paso sin . . .

(c) (stair) peldaño m, escalón m, grada f; (of vehicle) estribo m.

(d) **—s** (stairs) escalera f; (outside building) escalinata f; **folding —s, pair of —s** escalera f de tijera, escalera f doble.

2 vt (a) (place at intervals) escalonar, colocar de trecho en trecho.

(b) (also **to — out**) distance medir a pasos; **to — it out** apretar el paso, andar más rápidamente.

(c) **to — down** reducir, disminuir; **to — up** aumentar, elevar; **we shall have to — up our campaign** tendremos que reforzar nuestra campaña; **to — up production** aumentar la producción.

3 vi dar un paso; (walk) ir, andar, caminar; (with care, heavily etc) pisar; **— this way** haga el favor de pasar por aquí; **to — aside** hacerse a un lado, apartarse; **to — back** retroceder, dar un paso hacia atrás; **we — back into the 18th century** volvemos al siglo XVIII; **to — down** bajar (from de); (fig) ceder su puesto, retirarse, renunciar a sus pretensiones; **to — down for someone else** retirarse en favor de otro; **to — in** entrar; (fig) intervenir; **— in!** ¡adelante!; **— inside!** ¡pase!; **to — on something** pisar algo; **— on it!** ¡date prisa!; **to — on board** ir a bordo; **to — out** apretar el paso, andar más rápidamente; **just — outside a moment** pues salga un momento; **to — over something** evitar pisar algo, evitar chocar con algo; **he —ped carefully over the cable** miró con cuidado para no pisar el cable; **to — up** subir; **to — up to someone** acercarse a uno; **to — up to receive a prize** ir a recibir un premio.

stepbrother ['step,brʌðə*] n hermanastro m.
stepchild ['steptʃaild] n, pl **—children** [,tʃildrən] hijastro m, a f, alnado m, a f.
stepdaughter ['step,dɔːtə*] n hijastra f.
stepfather ['step,faːðə*] n padrastro m.
Stephen ['stiːvn] m Esteban.
stepladder ['step,lædə*] n escalera f de tijera, escalera f doble.
stepmother ['step,mʌðə*] n madrastra f.
steppe [step] n estepa f.
stepping stone ['stepiŋstəun] n pasadera f; (fig) escalón m (to para llegar a).
stepsister ['step,sistə*] n hermanastra f.
stepson ['stepsʌn] n hijastro m.
stepped-up ['stept'ʌp] adj elevado; aumentado.
step-up ['stepʌp] n elevación f; aumento m; aceleración f; refuerzo m; (promotion) ascenso m.
stereo . . . ['stiəriəu] estereo . . .
stereophonic [,stiəriə'fɔnik] adj estereofónico.
stereophony [steri'ɔfəni] n estereofonía f.
stereoscope ['stiəriəskəup] n estereoscopio m.
stereoscopic [,stiəriəs'kɔpik] adj estereoscópico; film tridimensional, en relieve; screen ancho.
stereotype ['stiəriətaip] 1 n clisé m, estereotipo m. 2 vt clisar, estereotipar; (fig) estereotipar.
sterile ['sterail] adj estéril.
sterility [ste'riliti] n esterilidad f.
sterilization [,sterilai'zeifən] n esterilización f.
sterilize ['sterilaiz] vt esterilizar.
sterling ['stəːliŋ] 1 adj (a) (fig) verdadero, excelente; **a — character** una persona de toda confianza; **a person of — worth** una persona de grandes méritos.
(b) **pound —** libra f esterlina; **— area** zona f de la libra esterlina.
2 n libras fpl esterlinas.
stern[1] [stəːn] adj severo; duro; austero; **a — glance** una mirada severa; **a — warning** un aviso terminante; **he was very — with me** fue muy duro conmigo; **but he was made of —er stuff** pero él tenía más carácter.
stern[2] [stəːn] n popa f.
sternly ['stəːnli] adv severamente; duramente; austeramente; terminantemente; **she looked at me —** me miró severamente.
sternness ['stəːnnis] n severidad f; dureza f; austeridad f; lo terminante.
sternum ['stəːnəm] n esternón m.
stertorous ['stəːtərəs] adj estertoroso.
stet [stet] vi (Typ) suprímase la cancelación, déjese tal como estaba en el original.
stethoscope ['steθəskəup] n estetoscopio m.
stevedore ['stiːvidɔː*] n estibador m.
Steven ['stiːvn] m Esteban.
stew[1] [stjuː] n (also **the —s**) lupanar m.

stew[2] [stjuː] 1 n (a) cocido m; estofado m; **Irish —** estofado m irlandés.
(b) (fig) **to be in a —** pasar apuros, sudar la gota gorda.
2 vt estofar; guisar; fruit cocer, hacer una compota de; **—ed fruit** compota f de frutas.
3 vi (of tea) pasarse; **to let someone — in his own juice** dejar a uno cocer en su propia salsa.
steward ['stjuəd] n (on estate etc) administrador m; (butler) mayordomo m; (Aer, Naut, in club etc) camarero m.
stewardess ['stjuədes] n (Naut) camarera f; (Aer) azafata f.
stewardship ['stjuədʃip] n administración f.
stewpan ['stjuːpæn] n, **stewpot** ['stjuːpɔt] n cazuela f, cacerola f, puchero m.
stick[1] [stik] 1 n (a) palo m, vara f; (as weapon) palo m, porra f; (walking —) bastón m; (Aer) palanca f de mando; (of wax, soap etc) barra f; (of celery) tallo m; **—s** (for the fire) astillas fpl, leña f; **— of furniture** mueble m; **policy of the big —** política f del palo grueso; **to use the big —** emplear la política del palo grueso; **to be in a cleft —** estar entre la espada y la pared; **to give someone the —, to take the — to someone** dar palo a uno.
(b) old — (fam) tío m; **he's a funny old —** es un tío raro (or divertido).
2 vt (Agr etc) apoyar con rodrigón.
stick[2] [stik] (irr: pret and ptp **stuck**) 1 vt (a) (gum) pegar, encolar; **to — a stamp on** pegar un sello; **to — something down** pegar algo; **to — two things together** pegar dos cosas, unir dos cosas con cola; **to — up a notice** fijar un anuncio.
(b) (thrust) clavar, hincar; **to — a knife into a table** clavar un cuchillo en una mesa; **to — out** asomar, sacar; **to — someone up** (sl) atracar a uno, encañonar a uno; **to — up a bank** (sl) asaltar un banco.
(c) (place, put) poner, meter; **— it on the shelf** ponlo en el estante; **— it in your case** mételo en la maleta; **to — one's hat on** ponerse el sombrero.
(d) (pierce) picar; **to — someone with a bayonet** herir a uno con bayoneta, clavar la bayoneta a uno; **a cork stuck all over with pins** un corcho lleno de alfileres, un corcho todo cubierto de alfileres.
(e) (tolerate) resistir, aguantar; **I can't — him at any price** no le puedo ver de ninguna manera; **I can't — it any longer** no aguanto más, no resisto más; **to — it out** aguantar hasta el final.
2 vi (a) (of gum etc) pegarse, adherirse; **this stamp won't —** este sello no se pega.
(b) (in mud) atascarse, quedar atascado; (of mechanism etc) bloquearse, trabarse, no poder moverse; (of pin etc) prender, estar prendido; **it stuck to the wall** quedó pegado a la pared; **to — fast in the mud** quedar clavado en el barro; **to get stuck in the snow** quedar sin poderse mover en la nieve; **the mechanism was stuck** el mecanismo estaba bloqueado; **the lift is stuck at the 9th floor** el ascensor está sin poderse mover en el piso 9; **the door —s in wet weather** en tiempo de lluvia la puerta no se mueve libremente.
(c) (remain) pararse, quedarse parado; (stay) quedarse, permanecer; **here I am and here I —** aquí estoy y aquí me quedo; **the name stuck to him** el apodo se le pegó; **the charge seems to have stuck** la acusación no ha sido olvidada nunca; **to make a charge —** hacer que una acusación tenga efecto; **to get stuck into something** (fam) emprender algo en serio, dedicarse seriamente a algo; **to be stuck with something** tener que cargar con algo; **and now we're stuck with it** y ahora no lo podemos quitar de encima, ahora no hay manera de deshacernos de él; **I was stuck with him for 2 hours** tuve que soportar su compañía durante 2 horas; **the problem had them all stuck** el problema les tenía a todos perplejos; **we're stuck at No. 13** no logramos pasar más allá del núm. 13.
(d) (with adv or prep) **to — around** esperar por ahí; **to — at something** (not give up) persistir en algo, no abandonar algo, seguir trabajando en algo; (have qualms) sentir escrúpulo por algo; **to — at nothing** no tener escrúpulos, no pararse en barras; **to — by someone** (follow) pisar los talones a uno; (support) apoyar a uno, defender a uno; ser fiel a uno; **to — out** (project) salir, sobresalir; asomarse; (fig) ser evidente; **it —s out a mile** es completamente obvio; se nota fácilmente; **to — out for something** insistir en algo, no ceder hasta obtener algo; **they're —ing out for an extra pound** porfían en reclamar una libra más; **to — to someone** = **to — by someone**; **to — to one's principles** seguir

fiel a sus principios, aferrarse a sus principios; **to —
to a promise** cumplir una promesa; **to — to it**
persistir, no cejar, seguir trabajando (*etc*); **— to it !**
¡ánimo!; **let's — to the matter in hand** ciñámonos
al asunto, no perdamos de vista el tema principal,
volvamos al grano; **to — together** mantenerse
unidos; no separarse; **to — up** salir, sobresalir (por
encima), asomarse por encima; (*hair etc*) estar de
punta; **to — up for someone** defender a uno,
sacar la cara por uno.

sticker ['stikə*] n (*person*) persona f aplicada,
persona f perseverante; (*label*) etiqueta f engomada,
letrero m engomado (con slogan publicitario,
político *etc*).

stickiness ['stikinis] n pegajosidad f; viscosidad f;
humedad f con calor; lo difícil.

sticking plaster ['stikiŋ,plɑːstə*] n esparadrapo m.

stick-in-the-mud ['stikinðəmʌd] n persona f
pesada; persona f rutinaria; reaccionario m, a f,
persona f chapada a la antigua, retrógrado m.

stickleback ['stiklbæk] n espinoso m.

stickler ['stiklə*] n rigorista mf (*for* en cuanto a),
persona f etiquetera; **he's a real — for correct
spelling** insiste terminantemente en la correcta
ortografía.

stick-up ['stikʌp] n (*sl*) atraco m, asalto m.

sticky ['stiki] adj pegajoso; viscoso; *label* engomado;
atmosphere húmedo y con mucho calor; (*fig*) *problem*,
person difícil; *situation* difícil, violento; **to come to
a — end** tener mal fin, ir a acabar mal.

stiff [stif] **1** adj (a) (*unbending*) rígido, inflexible,
tieso; *door, joint* duro, tieso; *collar, shirt front* duro,
(*starched*) almidonado; *brush* duro; *paste, soil*
espeso, consistente; **to be — in the legs** tener las
piernas entumecidas; **to be — with cold** estar
aterido; **you'll feel — tomorrow** mañana te van a
doler los músculos, mañana tendrás agujetas.
   (b) (*fig*) *breeze* fuerte; *climb, examination, task,
test etc* difícil; *resistance* tenaz; *price* exorbitante,
subido; *bow* frío; *person* etiquetero, ceremonioso;
manner estirado.
   2 n (*sl*) cadáver m.

stiffen ['stifn] **1** vt hacer más rígido, atiesar; endurecer;
hacer más espeso; *limb* entumecer; *morale, resistance
etc* fortalecer.
   2 vi hacerse más rígido, atiesarse; endurecerse;
hacerse más espeso, espesarse; entumecerse;
fortalecerse, robustecerse; hacerse más tenaz; **when
I said this she —ed** al decir yo esto, se volvió menos
cordial; **the breeze —ed** refrescó el viento; **resistance
to the idea seems to have —ed** parece que ha
aumentado la oposición a esta idea.

stiffly ['stifli] adv rígidamente, tiesamente; **to move
—** moverse con dificultad, moverse despacio con los
miembros entumecidos; **she said —** dijo fríamente,
dijo estirada; **this was — resisted** a esto opusieron
una tenaz resistencia.

stiff-necked ['stif'nekt] adj (*fig*) terco, obstinado;
estirado.

stiffness ['stifnis] n rigidez f, inflexibilidad f, tiesura
f; dureza f; espesura f, consistencia f; entumecimiento
m; fuerza f; dificultad f, lo difícil; tenacidad f; lo
exorbitante; frialdad f, carácter m etiquetero,
carácter m estirado.

stifle ['staifl] **1** vt ahogar, sofocar; (*fig*) suprimir; **to
— a yawn** ahogar un bostezo; **to — opposition**
suprimir la oposición.
   2 vi ahogarse, sofocarse.

stifling ['staifliŋ] adj sofocante (*also fig*), bochornoso;
it's — en here aquí dentro hay un calor sofocante;
the atmosphere in the company is — en la compañía
hay una atmósfera sofocante.

stigma ['stigmə] n, in some senses pl **stigmata**
[stig'mɑːtə] estigma m; (*moral stain*) estigma m,
tacha f, baldón m.

stigmatize ['stigmətaiz] vt estigmatizar; **to —
someone as** calificar a uno de, tachar a uno de.

stile [stail] n escalera f para pasar una cerca.

stiletto [sti'letəu] n estilete m; **— heel** tacón m de
aguja.

still[1] [stil] **1** adj (*motionless*) inmóvil; quieto; (*and
quiet*) tranquilo, silencioso; *wine* no espumoso; **be —!**
(*US*) ¡cállate!; **to keep —** estar inmóvil, no moverse;
keep —! ¡estáte quieto!; **he fell and lay —** cayó y
permaneció inmóvil; **to sit —** estarse quieto en su
silla; **to stand —** estarse quieto; **my heart stood —**
se me paró el corazón.
   2 n (a) silencio m, calma f; **in the — of the night**
en el silencio de la noche.
   (b) (*Cine*) vista f fija.
   3 adv todavía, aún; **— more** aun más, más aun;

there are **— 2 more** quedan 2 más; **he — hasn't
come** no ha venido todavía; **I can — recall it**
todavía lo recuerdo, lo recuerdo aún; **I — play a bit**
sigo jugando un poco; **do you — believe that ?**
¿sigues creyendo eso?
   4 conj sin embargo, con todo, a pesar de todo;
—, it was worth it sin embargo, valió la pena.
   5 vt calmar, tranquilizar; aquietar; (*silence*) acallar.

still[2] [stil] n alambique m.

stillbirth ['stil,bə:θ] n nacimiento m de un niño
muerto.

stillborn ['stil,bɔ:n] adj (a) nacido muerto; **the child
was —** el niño nació muerto. (b) (*fig*) fracasado,
malogrado.

still life ['stil'laif] n bodegón m, naturaleza f muerta.

stillness ['stilnis] n inmovilidad f; quietud f;
tranquilidad f, silencio m.

stilt [stilt] n zanco m; (*Archit*) pilar m, soporte m;
pilote m.

stilted ['stiltid] adj afectado, hinchado, artificial.

stimulant ['stimjulənt] **1** adj estimulante. **2** n
estimulante m, excitante m.

stimulate ['stimjuleit] vt estimular; **to — someone to
do something** estimular a uno a hacer algo, incitar
a uno a hacer algo.

stimulating ['stimjuleitiŋ] adj (*Med etc*) estimulador,
estimulante; *experience, book etc* sugestivo; alentador;
inspirador.

stimulation [,stimju'leiʃən] n (*stimulus*) estímulo m;
(*state*) excitación f.

stimulus ['stimjuləs] n, pl **stimuli** ['stimjulai]
estímulo m, incentivo m.

stimy ['staimi] vt (*fam*): **to — someone** poner obstáculos infranqueables delante de uno; **now we're
properly stimied !** ¡estamos jodidos!

sting [stiŋ] **1** n (*Zool, Bot: organ*) aguijón m; (*act,
wound*) picadura f; (*pain*) escozor m; picazón m;
(*pain, fig*) punzada f; **a — of remorse** un remordimiento; **the — of the rain in one's face** el azote de
la lluvia en la cara; **I felt the — of his irony** su
ironía me hirió en lo vivo.
   2 (*irr: pret and ptp* **stung**) (a) picar; punzar;
(*make smart*) picar, escocer en; (*of hot dishes*)
resquemar; (*of hail etc*) azotar; **the bee stung him**
la abeja le picó; **my conscience stung me** me
remordió la conciencia; **the reply stung him to the
quick** la respuesta le hirió en lo vivo.
   (b) **to — someone to do something** incitar a
uno a hacer algo, provocar a uno a hacer algo.
   (c) (*fam*) **they stung me for £4** me clavaron 4
libras; **how much did they — you (for)?** ¿cuánto te
clavaron?
   3 vi picar; escocer; **moths don't —** las mariposas
no pican; **my eyes —** me pican los ojos; **that
mouthful stung** me bocado me quemó la lengua;
that blow really stung ese golpe me dolió de verdad.

stingily ['stindʒili] adv con tacañería.

stinginess ['stindʒinis] n tacañería f.

stinging nettle ['stiŋiŋ,netl] n ortiga f.

stingray ['stiŋrei] n (*Fish*) pastinaca f.

stingy ['stindʒi] adj tacaño; **to be — with something**
ser tacaño con algo.

stink [stiŋk] **1** n hedor m, mal olor m; tufo m; **a —
of . . .** un hedor a . . . ; **the — of corruption** el olor a
corrupción.
   2 (*irr: pret* **stank**, *ptp* **stunk**) vt: **to — out** *room*
apestar, hacer oler mal; **to — someone out** ahuyen-
tar a uno con un mal olor.
   3 vi (a) heder, oler mal (*of* a); **it —s in here** aquí
huele muy mal.
   (b) (*fig*) **the idea —s** es una idea horrible; **I think
the plan —s** creo que es un proyecto abominable;
as a headmaster he —s como director es un asco;
they are —ing with money son unos ricachos,
tienen tanto dinero que da asco.

stink bomb ['stiŋk'bɔm] n bomba f de gas hediondo.

stinker ['stiŋkə*] n (*fam: person*) mal bicho m,
canalla m; **you —!** ¡bestia!; **this problem is a —**
este problema es terriblemente difícil.

stinking ['stiŋkiŋ] adj hediondo, fétido; (*fig*) horrible,
bestial, asqueroso.

stint [stint] **1** n (a) (*amount of work*) destajo m; tarea
f; **to do one's —** hacer la parte que le corresponde a
uno, trabajar (*etc*) como se debe, (*fig*) cumplir con
las obligaciones que uno tiene, hacer su contribución;
to finish one's — terminar el trabajo que le
corresponde a uno.
   (b) **without —** libremente, generosamente; sin
restricción.
   2 vt limitar, restringir; escatimar; **he did not —
his praises** no escatimó sus elogios, prodigó sus
elogios; **to — someone of something** privar a uno de

algo, dar a uno menor cantidad de algo de la que pide (*or* necesita).

3 *vr*: **to — oneself** estrecharse, privarse de cosas; **don't — yourself!** ¡no te prives de nada!, ¡sírvete (*etc*) cuanto quieras!; **to — oneself of something** privarse de algo, negarse algo, no permitirse algo.

stipend ['staipend] *n* estipendio *m*, sueldo *m*.

stipendiary [stai'pendiəri] **1** *adj* estipendiario. **2** *n* estipendiario *m*.

stipple ['stipl] *vt* puntear, granear.

stipulate ['stipjuleit] **1** *vt* estipular, poner como condición; especificar. **2** *vi*: **to — for something** estipular algo, poner algo como condición.

stipulation [,stipju'leiʃən] *n* estipulación *f*, condición *f*.

stir[1] [stə:*] **1** *n* **(a)** acto *m* de agitar (*etc*); hurgonada *f*; **to give one's tea a —** remover su té; **give the fire a —** remueve un poco la lumbre.

(b) (*fig*) conmoción *f*, revuelo *m*; sensación *f*; agitación *f*; **to cause a —** causar una sensación, armar gran revuelo; provocar mucho interés; **it didn't make much of a —** apenas despertó interés alguno; **there was a great — in parliament** hubo una gran conmoción en el parlamento.

2 *vt* **(a)** *liquid etc* (*also* **to — up**) remover, agitar, revolver, menear; *fire* atizar, hurgar; **to — sugar into coffee** añadir azúcar a su café y removerlo; **"— before using"** "agítese antes de usar".

(b) (*move*) mover, agitar; **a breeze —red the leaves** una brisa movió las hojas; **he never —ed a foot all day** no movió el pie en todo el día.

(c) (*fig*) *emotions* conmover, despertar; *imagination* estimular; **to — up** *passions* excitar; *revolt* fomentar; *trouble* armar; **to — up the past** remover el pasado; **to — someone to do something** incitar a uno a hacer algo; **to — someone to pity** provocar a uno a lástima, hacer que uno sienta compasión; **to feel deeply —red** conmoverse profundamente, estar muy emocionado; **we were all —red by the speech** el discurso nos conmovió a todos.

3 *vi* moverse, menearse; **she hasn't —red all day** no se ha movido en todo el día; **he never —red from the spot** no abandonó el sitio ni un solo momento; **don't you — from here** no te muevas de aquí; **nobody is —ring yet** están todavía en cama.

stir[2] [stə:*] *n* (*sl*) chirona *f*.

stirring ['stə:riŋ] *adj speech etc* emocionante, conmovedor; inspirador; *period etc* turbulento, agitado.

stirrup ['stirəp] *n* estribo *m*.

stirrup pump ['stirəppʌmp] *n* bomba *f* pequeña de mano.

stitch [stitʃ] **1** *n* (*Sew*) puntada *f*, punto *m*; (*Med: in surgery*) punto *m* de sutura, (*pain*) punzada *f*; **a — in time saves 9** es mejor hacerlo ahora para evitar mayores dificultades después; **she hadn't a — on** estaba en pelota; **he hadn't a dry — on him** estaba mojado hasta los huesos; **we were in —es** nos moríamos de risa; **to put —es in a wound** suturar una herida.

2 *vt* coser (*also* **to — together, to — up**); (*Med*) suturar.

stoat [stəut] *n* armiño *m*.

stock [stɔk] **1** *n* **(a)** (*of tree*) tronco *m*, (*of vine*) cepa *f*, (*for grafting*) patrón *m*.

(b) (*Bot: species*) alhelí *m*.

(c) (*family*) estirpe *f*, linaje *m*, raza *f*; **of good —** de buen linaje; **of good Castilian —** de buena cepa castellana.

(d) (*handle*) mango *m*, (*of gun*) caja *f*, culata *f*.

(e) —s (*punishment*) cepo *m*.

(f) —s (*Naut*) astillero *m*, grada *f* de construcción; **to be on the —s** (*ship*) estar en vía de construcción, (*book etc*) estar en preparación; **he has 3 plays on the —s** tiene 3 obras entre manos.

(g) (*supply*) provisión *f*, (*Comm*) surtido *m*, existencias *fpl*, stock *m*; **— of spares** stock *m* de recambios; **surplus —** artículos *mpl* sobrantes; **to be in —** estar en existencia, estar en almacén; **to be out of —** estar agotado; **we are out of — of umbrellas** no nos quedan paraguas, están agotados los paraguas; **to have something in —** tener algo en existencia; **to lay in a — of** proveerse de, hacer provisión de; **to take —** hacer inventario (*of* de); **to take — of** (*fig*) asesorarse de, considerar, calcular las posibilidades de.

(h) (*Agr: live —*) ganado *m*, ganadería *f*; **dead —** aperos *mpl*; *see* **rolling** *etc*.

(i) (*Cook*) caldo *m*.

(j) (*Fin: of company*) capital *m* (comercial); (*shares*) acciones *fpl*, valores *mpl*; **government —**

papel *m* del Estado; **joint —** fondo *m* social; **joint-stock company** sociedad *f* anónima; **his — is going up** su reputación crece, su crédito aumenta.

2 *adj, attr* (*Comm*) de surtido, en existencia; *size etc* corriente, normal; (*Theat*) de repertorio; *phrase* hecho; *remark* banal, vulgar; *response etc* que se espera, acostumbrado, consagrado.

3 *vt* (*supply*) surtir, proveer, abastecer (*with* de); (*of shop*) tener existencias de, tener en almacén; **to — up with** proveerse de, adquirir existencias de, (*fig*) ir acumulando; **to — a pond with fish** poblar un charco de peces; **we don't — that brand** no tenemos esa marca; **do you — bananas?** ¿vende Vd plátanos?

stockade [stɔ'keid] *n* estacada *f*.

stockbreeder ['stɔk,bri:də*] *n* ganadero *m*.

stockbreeding ['stɔk,bri:diŋ] *n* ganadería *f*.

stockbroker ['stɔk,brəukə*] *n* bolsista *m*, agente *m* de bolsa, corredor *m* de bolsa.

stockbroking ['stɔk,brəukiŋ] *n* correduría *f* de bolsa.

stock exchange ['stɔkiks,tʃeindʒ] **1** *n* bolsa *f*; **to be on the —** ser bolsista, ser miembro de la bolsa, dedicarse a negocios de bolsa; **prices on the —** cotizaciones *fpl* de bolsa.

2 *attr* bursátil.

stockholder ['stɔk,həuldə*] *n* accionista *mf*.

Stockholm ['stɔkhəum] Estocolmo.

stockinet [,stɔki'net] *n* tela *f* de punto.

stocking ['stɔkiŋ] *n* media *f*; (*knee-length*) calceta *f*; **a pair of —s** un par de medias; **nylon —s** medias *fpl* de nilón.

stock-in-trade ['stɔkin'treid] *n* (*Comm*) capital *m*; existencias *fpl*; (*fig*) repertorio *m*; **that joke is part of his —** es un chiste de su repertorio.

stockist ['stɔkist] *n* distribuidor *m*.

stockjobber ['stɔk,dʒɔbə*] *n* agiotista *m*.

stockjobbing ['stɔk,dʒɔbiŋ] *n* agiotaje *m*.

stock market ['stɔk,mɑ:kit] *n see* **stock exchange**.

stockpile ['stɔkpail] **1** *n* reserva *f* (de materias primas). **2** *vt* acumular, poner en reserva, formar una reserva de.

stock raising ['stɔk,reiziŋ] *n* ganadería *f*.

stockroom ['stɔkrum] *n* almacén *m*.

stock-still ['stɔk'stil] *adv*: **to be** (*or* **stand**) **—** estar completamente inmóvil.

stocktaking ['stɔk,teikiŋ] *n* inventario *m*, balance *m*; **— sale** venta *f* por balance.

stocky ['stɔki] *adj* rechoncho, bajo pero fuerte.

stockyard ['stɔkjɑ:d] *n* corral *m* de ganado.

stodge [stɔdʒ] *n* (*fam*) comida *f* indigesta, cosas *fpl* indigestas.

stodgy ['stɔdʒi] *adj food* indigesto, pesado; *book, style etc* pesado.

stoic ['stəuik] **1** *adj* estoico. **2** *n* estoico *m*.

stoical ['stəuikəl] *adj* estoico.

stoicism ['stəuisizəm] *n* estoicismo *m*.

stoke [stəuk] **1** *vt furnace* cargar, cebar; *fire* echar carbón a; (*fig*) cebar; (*hum*) comer.

2 *vi* (*also* **to — up**) cebar el hogar, echar carbón a la lumbre; (*hum*) comer.

stoker ['stəukə*] *n* fogonero *m*.

stokehold ['stəukhəuld] *n* (*Naut*) cuarto *m* de calderas.

stokehole ['stəukhəul] *n* boca *f* del horno.

stole[1] [stəul] *n* estola *f*.

stole[2] [stəul] *pret* of **steal**.

stolen ['stəulən] *ptp* of **steal**; **— goods** géneros *mpl* robados.

stolid ['stɔlid] *adj* impasible, imperturbable; flemático; (*pej*) terco.

stolidity [stɔ'liditi] *n* impasibilidad *f*, imperturbabilidad *f*; flema *f*; terquedad *f*.

stomach ['stʌmək] **1** *n* estómago *m*; vientre *m*; (*fig*) deseo *m*, apetito *m* (*for* de); **they have no — for the fight** no tienen ganas de pelear; **it turns my —** me da asco.

2 *attr* estomacal, del estómago; **— upset** trastorno *m* estomacal.

3 *vt* (*fig*) tragar, aguantar.

stomach ache ['stʌməkeik] *n* dolor *m* de estómago.

stomach pump ['stʌməkpʌmp] *n* bomba *f* estomacal.

stomach tube ['stʌməktju:b] *n* sonda *f* gástrica.

stomp [stɔmp] *vi* pisar muy fuerte.

stone [stəun] **1** *n* piedra *f*; (*of fruit*) hueso *m*; (*commemorative*) lápida *f*; (*Med*) cálculo *m*, piedra *f*, (*as complaint*) mal *m* de piedra; (*weight*) = 14 libras = 6,348 *kg*; **philosopher's —** piedra *f* filosofal; **precious —** piedra *f* preciosa; **within a —'s throw** a tiro de piedra, a dos pasos; **to cast the first —** lanzar la primera piedra; **which of you shall cast the first stone?** ¿quién se atreve a lanzar la primera piedra?; **to leave no — unturned** no

dejar piedra sin remover, revolver Roma con Santiago.
2 *adj* de piedra.
3 *vt* **(a)** apedrear, lapidar; *fruit* deshuesar.
(b) (*sl*) **to be —d** estar ajumado.
stone-blind ['stəun'blaind] *adj* completamente ciego.
stone-broke ['stəun'brəuk] *adj* (*US*) = **stony-broke**.
stonecrop ['stəunkrɔp] *n* pan *m* de cuco.
stone-dead ['stəun'ded] *adj* más muerto que una piedra.
stone-deaf ['stəun'def] *adj* completamente sordo.
stonemason ['stəun'meisn] *n* albañil *m*; (*in quarry*) cantero *m*.
stone pit ['stəunpit] *n*, **— quarry** [.kwɔri] *n* cantera *f*.
stonewall ['stəun'wɔ:l] *vi* (*Sport*) emplear la táctica de cerrojo; (*in answering questions*) evitar contestar directamente.
stonewalling ['stəun'wɔ:liŋ] *n* táctica *f* de cerrojo; el evitar contestar directamente.
stoneware ['stəunwɛə*] *n* gres *m*.
stonework ['stəunwə:k] *n* cantería *f*, obra *f* de sillería; piedras *fpl*.
stonily ['stəunili] *adv* (*fig*) glacialmente, fríamente.
stony ['stəuni] *adj* material pétreo; como piedra, parecido a piedra; *ground* pedregoso, cubierto de piedras; *glance* glacial, frío; *heart* empedernido.
stony-broke ['stəuni'brəuk] *adj* (*fam*): **to be —** no tener un céntimo.
stony-hearted ['stəuni'hɑ:tid] *adj* de corazón empedernido.
stood [stud] *pret and ptp of* **stand**.
stooge [stu:dʒ] *n* (*sl*) hombre *m* de paja; secuaz *m*, partidario *m*; paniaguado *m*; (*of comedian*) compañero *m*.
stook [stu:k] **1** *n* tresnal *m*, garbera *f*. **2** *vt* poner en tresnales.
stool [stu:l] *n* taburete *m*, escabel *m*; (*folding*) silla *f* de tijera; (*Bot*) planta *f* madre; (*Med*) cámaras *fpl*; **to fall between two —s** fracasar por no saber a qué carta quedarse, terminar sin conseguir ni lo uno ni lo otro.
stool pigeon ['stu:l,pidʒən] *n* (*fam*) soplón *m*, espía *m*.
stoop¹ [stu:p] **1** *n* inclinación *f*; (*defect*) cargazón *f* de espaldas; **to walk with a —** andar encorvado.
2 *vt* inclinar, bajar.
3 *vi* inclinarse, encorvarse; (*permanently, as defect*) ser cargado de espaldas, anda encorvado; **to — to pick something up** inclinarse para recoger algo; **to — to +** *infin* (*fig*) rebajarse a + *infin*.
stoop² [stu:p] *n* (*US*) escalinata *f* de entrada.
stooping ['stu:piŋ] *adj* inclinado, encorvado; cargado de espaldas.
stop [stɔp] **1** *n* **(a)** (*in general*) parada *f*; alto *m*; pausa *f*, interrupción *f*; **a 20-minute — for coffee** un alto de 20 minutos para tomar café; **to be at a —** estar parado; quedar paralizado; **to bring a car to a —** parar un coche; **to come to a —** venir a parar, pararse; **to come to a dead** (*or* **sudden**) **—** pararse en seco, detenerse repentinamente; **to come to a full —** quedar completamente parado; quedar paralizado; llegar a un punto muerto; **to go on for 2 hours without a —** continuar durante 2 horas sin parar (*or* sin interrupción); **to put a — to something** poner fin a algo, acabar con algo.
(b) (*stay*) estancia *f*; **a — of a few days** una estancia de unos días.
(c) (*of bus, tram etc*) parada *f*; (*Aer, Naut*) escala *f*; **intermediate —** escala *f*; **request —** parada *f* discrecional; **to make a — at Bordeaux** hacer escala en Burdeos.
(d) (*Typ: also* **full —**) punto *m*.
(e) (*Mus: of organ*) registro *m*; (*of other instrument*) llave *f*; **to pull out all the —s** (*fig*) desplegar todos sus recursos, emplear toda su fuerza.
(f) (*Mech*) tope *m*, retén *m*.
(g) (*Gram*) consonante *f* oclusiva.
2 *vt* **(a)** (*block: also* **to — up**) *leak, hole etc* tapar; cegar; *road etc* cerrar, obstruir, bloquear; *tooth* empastar; *flow of blood* restañar; **to — one's ears** taparse los oídos; **to — a gap** tapar un agujero, (*fig*) llenar un vacío; **"road —ped"** "cerrado por obras".
(b) (*arrest progress of*) parar, detener; *ball, bullet, engine, car, charge, traffic etc* parar; *blow* rechazar, parar; *aggression* rechazar, contener; *danger, threat* evitar, estorbar; *process* terminar; *abuse* poner fin a, acabar con; (*forbid*) prohibir, poner fin a; **— thief!** ¡al ladrón!; **and there is nothing to — him** y no hay nada que se lo impida; **the walls — some of the noise** las paredes suprimen una parte del ruido; **the curtains — the light** las cortinas impiden la entrada de la luz; **this should —**

any further trouble esto habrá de evitar cualquier dificultad en el futuro; **to — someone (from) doing something** (*prevent*) impedir a uno hacer algo, (*forbid*) prohibir a uno hacer algo; **to — something being done** impedir que algo se haga; **to — something happening** evitar que algo ocurra.
(c) (*cease*) terminar; **— it!** ¡basta!, ¡basta ya!; **— that noise!** ¡basta ya de ruido!; **— the nonsense!** ¡déjate de tonterías!
(d) (*suspend*) *payments etc* suspender; *supply* contar, interrumpir; **to — someone's electricity** cortar la electricidad de uno; **to — someone's wages** suspender el pago del sueldo de uno; **to — a pound of someone's wages** retener una libra del sueldo de uno; **all leave is —ped** han sido cancelados todos los permisos; **to — the milk for a fortnight** cancelar el encargo de la leche durante quince días.
3 *vi* **(a)** (*cease motion*) parar, pararse; detenerse; hacer alto; (*finish, run out*) terminarse, acabarse; (*of supply etc*) cortarse, interrumpirse; (*of process, rain etc*) cesar; **the car —ped** se paró el coche; **the clock has —ped** el reloj se ha parado; **—!** ¡pare!, ¡alto!; **when the programme —s** cuando termine el programa; **payments have —ped** (*temporarily*) se han suspendido los pagos, (*permanently*) han terminado los pagos; **the rain has —ped** la lluvia ha cesado, ha dejado de llover.
(b) (*stay*) hospedarse, alojarse (*at* en, *with* con); quedarse; **she's —ping with her aunt** se hospeda en casa de su tía; vive con su tía; **did you — till the end?** ¿te quedaste hasta el fin?
(c) (*with verb constructions*) **to — doing something** dejar de hacer algo; **she never —s talking** habla incansablemente, no termina de hablar; **it has —ped raining** ha dejado de llover, ya no llueve.
(d) (*with adv or prep*) **to — at nothing** no pararse en barras; **to — at nothing to +** *infin* emplear sin escrúpulo todos los medio; para + *infin*; **to — away** ausentarse (*from* de), no asistir (*from* a); **you — away from my sister!** ¡no venga más por aquí a molestar a mi hermana!; **to — behind** quedarse; quedarse en casa, no salir; **to make someone — behind after school** hacer que uno quede en la escuela después de las clases; **to — by** (*adv*) detenerse brevemente hacer una breve visita; **to — by** (*prep*) pasar por; **to — dead** pararse en seco; **to — in** quedarse en casa, no salir; **to — off** interrumpir el viaje (*at* en); **to — out** quedarse fuera; no volver a casa; **to — over** pasar la noche, pernoctar; quedarse un poco; **to — to do something** (*cease motion*) detenerse a hacer algo, (*stay*) quedarse a hacer algo; **to — up** velar, no acostarse, seguir sin acostarse; **don't — up for me** no os quedéis esperándome hasta muy tarde; *see* **short** *etc*.
4 *vr*: **I —ped myself in time** me detuve a tiempo: **to — oneself doing something** abstenerse de hacer algo, guardarse de hacer algo; **I can't seem to — myself doing it** parece que me es imposible no hacerlo.
stop-and-go ['stɔpən'gəu] *n* (*US*) *see* **stop-go**.
stopcock ['stɔpkɔk] *n* llave *f* de cierre.
stopgap ['stɔpgæp] *n* (*thing*) recurso *m* provisional, expediente *m*; (*person*) tapaagujeros *m*, sustituto *m*.
stop-go ['stɔp'gəu] *n*: **period of —** período *m* cuando una política de expansión económica alterna con otra de restricción.
stoplights ['stɔplaits] *npl* (*Aut*) luces *fpl* de detención.
stopover ['stɔpəuvə*] *n* parada *f* intermedia; interrupción *f* de un viaje.
stoppage ['stɔpidʒ] *n* parada *f*, cesación *f*, detención *f*; interrupción *f*; (*of work*) paro *m*, suspensión *f*; (*in game*) detención *f*; (*strike*) huelga *f*; (*blockage*) obstrucción *f*.
stopper ['stɔpə*] **1** *n* tapón *m*; (*Tech*) taco *m*, tarugo *m*. **2** *vt* tapar, taponar.
stopping ['stɔpiŋ] *n* parada *f*; suspensión *f*; (*of tooth*) empaste *m*.
stopping place ['stɔpiŋpleis] *n* paradero *m*; (*of bus etc*) parada *f*.
stop-press ['stɔp'pres] *n* (*also* **— news**) noticias *fpl* de última hora; **"—"** (*as heading*) "al cerrar la edición".
stopwatch ['stɔpwɔtʃ] *n* cronómetro *m*.
storage ['stɔ:ridʒ] *n* almacenaje *m*, depósito *m*; **— charges** derechos *mpl* de almacenaje; **to put something into —** poner algo en almacén; *see* **cold —**.
storage battery ['stɔ:ridʒ,bætəri] *n* acumulador *m*.
store [stɔ:*] **1** *n* **(a)** (*stock*) provisión *f*; (*reserve*) reserva *f*; repuesto *m*; (*storehouse*) almacén *m*, depósito *m*; **to be in —** estar en almacén, estar en depósito; **what is in — for someone** lo que le espera a uno, lo que la suerte tiene guardado para

uno; **what has the future in — for us?** ¿qué guarda
el futuro para nosotros?; **that is a treat in —** eso es
un placer que nos guarda el futuro; **to have** (*or*
keep) **something in —** tener algo en reserva; **to
lay in a — of** hacer provisión de, proveerse de; **to
put** (*or* **set**) **great — by something** conceder mucha
importancia a algo, estimar algo en mucho; **to set
little — by something** conceder poca importancia a
algo, estimar algo en poco.

　　(b) (*quantity*) abundancia *f*; tesoro *m*; **a great
— of expertise** gran pericia *f*; **he has a — of knowledge about . . .** tiene grandes conocimientos de . . .

　　(c) **—s** (*Mil etc: food*) víveres *mpl*, provisiones
fpl, (*equipment*) pertrechos *mpl*; **war —s material**
m bélico.

　　(d) (*shop: esp US*) tienda *f*; **—s** (*large shop*),
departmental —s almacén *m*, almacenes *mpl*;
multiple — cadena *f* de almacenes; **village —** tienda
f de pueblo; **Bloggs' S—s** Almacenes *mpl* Bloggs.

　　2 *vt* almacenar; poner en reserva, tener en reserva,
guardar (*also* **to — away**); *documents* archivar; **to —
up** acumular, ir acumulando, amontonar; **a hatred
—d up over centuries** un odio almacenado durante
siglos.

storehouse ['stɔːhaus] *n*, *pl* **—houses** [ˌhauziz]
almacén *m*, depósito *m*; (*fig*) mina *f*, tesoro *m*.

storekeeper ['stɔːˌkiːpə*] *n* almacenero *m*; (*US*)
tendero *m*; (*Naut*) pañolero *m*.

storeroom ['stɔːrum] *n* despensa *f*; (*Naut*) pañol *m*.

storey ['stɔːri] *n* piso *m*; **a 9-storey building** un
edificio de 9 pisos.

storeyed ['stɔːrid] *adj*: **an 8-storeyed building** un
edificio de 8 pisos.

stork [stɔːk] *n* cigüeña *f*.

storm [stɔːm] **1** *n* (a) (*Meteorol*) tormenta *f*, tempestad *f*, temporal *m*; (*Naut*) borrasca *f*; (*of wind*)
vendaval *m*, huracán *m*; **to brave the —** aguantar
la tempestad; **to ride out a —** capear un temporal,
hacer frente a un temporal.

　　(b) (*fig*) tempestad *f*, borrasca *f*; **a — in a
teacup** una tempestad en un vaso de agua; **— of
abuse** torrente *m* de injurias; **— of criticism**
vendaval *m* de críticas, nube *f* de críticas; **there
were —s of applause** sonaron fuertes aplausos,
hubo grandes aplausos; **there was a political —**
hubo un gran revuelo político; **it caused an international —** levantó una polvareda internacional; **to
bring a — about one's ears** atraer sobre sí una
lluvia de protestas.

　　(c) (*Mil*) **to take a town by —** tomar una
ciudad por asalto; **the play took Paris by —** la
obra cautivó a todo París, la obra obtuvo un
tremendo éxito en París.

　　2 *vt* (*Mil*) asaltar, tomar por asalto.

　　3 *vi* rabiar, bramar; **to — at someone** tronar contra
uno, enfurecerse con uno; **he came —ing into my
office** entró furioso en mi oficina; **he —ed on for an
hour about the government** pasó una hora lanzando
improperios contra el gobierno.

stormbound ['stɔːmbaund] *adj* inmovilizado por el
mal tiempo.

storm centre, (*US*) **— center** ['stɔːmˌsentə*] *n*
centro *m* de la tempestad; (*fig*) centro *m* de los
disturbios, centro *m* de la agitación.

storm cloud ['stɔːmklaud] *n* nubarrón *m*.

storm door ['stɔːmdɔː*] *n* contrapuerta *f*.

storm signal ['stɔːmˌsignl] *n* señal *f* de temporal.

storm-tossed ['stɔːmtɔst] *adj* sacudido por la
tempestad.

storm troops ['stɔːmtruːps] *npl* tropas *fpl* de asalto.

stormy ['stɔːmi] *adj* tempestuoso, borrascoso (*also* fig).

stormy petrel ['stɔːmi'petrəl] *n* (*Orn*) petrel *m* de la
tempestad; (*fig*) persona *f* pendenciera, persona *f*
de vida borrascosa.

story¹ ['stɔːri] *n* (a) (*account*) historia *f*, relación *f*,
relato *m*; (*Lit*) cuento *m*, historieta *f*; (*joke*) cuento
m, chiste *m*; **dirty —, rude —** chiste *m* verde;
funny — chiste *m*; **short —** cuento *m*; **tall —** cuento
m exagerado, cuento *m* increíble; **true —** historia *f*
verídica; **the — of her life** la historia de su vida;
the — of their travels la relación de sus viajes; **his
— is that . . .** según él dice . . ., según lo que él
cuenta . . .; **that's another —** eso es harina de otro
costal; **that's not the whole —** no te lo han contado
en su totalidad, hay una parte que no te han
contado; **it's the (same) old —** es lo de siempre;
it's a long — es muy largo de contar; **to cut a long
— short** para abreviar; **to tell a —** contar un cuento,
narrar una historia; **the marks tell their own —**
las señales hablan por sí solas, las señales no
necesitan interpretación; **the full — has still to be
told** todavía no se ha hecho pública toda la historia;

what a — this house could tell! ¡cuántas cosas nos
diría esta casa!

　　(b) (*plot*) argumento *m*, trama *f*.

　　(c) (*fig*) cuento *m*, mentira *f*; embuste *m*; **a likely
—!** ¡puro cuento!, ¡qué cuento más inverosímil!;
to tell stories contar embustes; **don't tell stories!**
¡no me vengas con tus embustes!

story² ['stɔːri] *n* (*Archit*) *see* **storey.**

storybook ['stɔːribuk] *n* libro *m* de cuentos.

storyteller ['stɔːriˌtelə*] *n* cuentista *mf*; (*fibber*)
cuentista *mf*, embustero *m*, a *f*.

stoup [stuːp] *n* copa *f*, frasco *m*; (*Eccl*) pila *f*.

stout [staut] **1** *adj* (*solid*) sólido, robusto, macizo,
fuerte; *person* gordo, corpulento; (*brave*) valiente;
(*sturdy*) fornido; (*resolute*) resuelto; *resistance etc*
terco, tenaz; **— fellow!** ¡muy bien!; **he's a — fellow**
es un buen chico; **with — hearts** resueltamente.

　　2 *n*: *especie de cerveza negra.*

stout-hearted ['staut'hɑːtid] *adj* valiente, resuelto.

stoutly ['stautli] *adv*: **— built** de construcción sólida,
fuerte; **to resist —** resistir tenazmente; **he —
maintains that . . .** sostiene resueltamente que . . .

stoutness ['stautnis] *n* gordura *f*, corpulencia *f*.

stove¹ [stəuv] *n* (*for heating*) estufa *f*; (*for cooking*)
hornillo *m*, cocina *f* (de gas *etc*); **electric —** cocina *f*
eléctrica.

stove² [stəuv] *pret and ptp of* **stave.**

stovepipe ['stəuvpaip] *n* tubo *m* de estufa.

stow [stəu] **1** *vt* (a) meter, poner, colocar; (*Naut*)
estibar, arrumar; (*and hide*) esconder (*also* **to —
away**); **where can I — this?** ¿esto dónde lo pongo?;
to — food away (*fam*) despachar rápidamente una
comida, zamparse una comida.

　　(b) (*sl*) **— it!** ¡déjate de eso!, ¡cállate!, ¡basta ya!

　　2 *vi*: **to — away** viajar de polizón (*on a ship* en un
buque), viajar sin pagar y clandestinamente.

stowage ['stəuidʒ] *n* (*act*) estiba *f*, arrumaje *m*;
(*place*) bodega *f*.

stowaway ['stəuəwei] *n* polizón *m*, llovido *m*, pasajero
m clandestino.

strabismus [strə'bizməs] *n* estrabismo *m*.

straddle ['strædl] *vt* esparrancarse encima de, estar
con una pierna a cada lado de; *horse* montar a
horcajadas; *target* cubrir, caer a ambos lados de.

strafe [strɑːf] *vt* bombardear, cañonear, atacar;
destrozar a tiros.

straggle ['strægl] *vi* (*lag*) rezagarse; (*get lost*) extraviarse; (*spread*) extenderse, estar esparcido;
(*wander*) vagar, vagar en desorden, (*Bot*) lozanear;
the village —s on for miles el pueblo se extiende
varios kilómetros (sin tener un plano fijo); **the
guests —d out into the night** los invitados salieron
poco a poco y desaparecieron en la noche; **her hair
—s over her face** el pelo le cae en desorden por la
cara.

straggler ['stræglə*] *n* rezagado *m*; (*Mil*) extraviado
m.

straggling ['strægliŋ] *adj* disperso; rezagado;
extendido; desordenado.

straight [streit] **1** *adj* (a) (*not bent*) derecho, recto;
line recto; *back* erguido; *hair* lacio; **as — as a die**
más derecho que una vela; **he carries himself as —
as a ramrod** se mantiene perfectamente erguido;
see **face.**

　　(b) (*honest*) honrado; *answer* franco, directo;
is he —? ¿es de fiar?; **let me be — with you** te digo
esto con toda franqueza, no hagamos confusiones;
he's always dealt very — with me en los negocios
siempre se ha comportado como hombre honrado,
siempre me ha tratado con justicia.

　　(c) (*plain, uncomplicated*) sencillo; *drink* sin
mezcla, puro; *fight* (*Pol*) sencillo, de dos candidatos
solamente; *part, play* (*Theat*) serio.

　　(d) (*in order*) en orden; **it's all — now** todo
está en regla ya; **your tie isn't —** tu corbata no
está bien; **let's get this —** no hagamos confusiones,
digámoslo claramente; **to put things —** arreglar
cosas, poner las cosas en orden; **are your affairs —
at last?** ¿por fin has arreglado tus cosas?

　　2 *adv* (a) (*in a — line*) derecho, directamente, en
línea recta; **to fly —** volar en línea recta; **— above
us** directamente encima de nosotros; **it's — across
the road from us** está exactamente enfrente de
nosotros; **— ahead, — on** todo seguido; **keep — on
for Toledo** vayan Vds todo seguido para Toledo;
I went — home fui derecho a mi casa; **I went — to
my room** fui derecho a mi cuarto, fui a mi cuarto
sin detenerme para nada; **to look someone — in the
eye** mirar directamente a los ojos de uno.

　　(b) (*immediately, without diversion*) directamente; inmediatamente; **— after this** inmediatamente después de esto; **— away** en seguida,

inmediatamente; — **off** sin parar, sin interrupción; de un tirón; sin vacilar; **for 3 days** — off durante 3 días seguidos; **he read the whole of Proust** — off leyó toda la obra de Proust de un tirón; **she just went** — off se fue sin vacilar; **he said** — off that ... dijo sin vacilar que ...; **to come** — **to the point** ir directamente al grano; **to drink** — **from the bottle** beber de la misma botella.

(c) (*frankly*) francamente, con franqueza; **I tell you** —, **I'll give it to you** — te lo digo con toda franqueza; — **out** francamente, sin rodeos.

(d) (*pure*) sin mezcla; **we drink it** — lo bebemos sin mezcla.

(e) **to go** — (*fam*) enmendarse, hacer nueva vida, vivir dentro de la ley; **he's been going** — **for a year now** lleva un año sin tener nada que ver con el crimen.

3 *n*: **the** — (*Racing, Rail*) la recta; **out of (the)** — fuera de la plomada, no vertical.

straightaway ['streitə'wei] *adv* en seguida, inmediatamente.

straightedge ['streitedʒ] *n* regla *f* de borde recto.

straighten ['streitn] **1** *vt* (*also to* — **out**) enderezar, poner derecho; (*fig*) arreglar, poner en orden; **problem** resolver; **confused situation** desenmarañar.

2 *vi* (*freq to* — **up**; *also vr to* — **oneself up**) enderezarse, ponerse derecho; (*person*) erguirse.

straight-faced ['streit'feist] **1** *adj* serio, grave, solemne; **a** — **attitude** una actitud seria.

2 *adv*: **he told the joke very** — contó el chiste con cara muy seria.

straightforward [ˌstreit'fɔːwəd] *adj* (*honest*) honrado; (*plain-spoken*) franco; (*simple*) sencillo.

straightforwardly [ˌstreit'fɔːwədli] *adv* honradamente; francamente; sencillamente.

straightforwardness [ˌstreit'fɔːwədnis] *n* honradez *f*; franqueza *f*; sencillez *f*.

strain¹ [strein] **1** *n* (a) (*Mech*) tensión *f*; esfuerzo *m*; (*damage*) deformación *f*; **the** — **on a rope** la tensión de una cuerda; **breaking** — esfuerzo *m* de ruptura; **to take the** — **off a beam** disminuir la presión sobre una viga; **can you take some of the** — ? ¿me puedes ayudar a sostener (*etc*) esto?

(b) (*fig*) tensión *f*, tirantez *f*; esfuerzo *m* (grande, excesivo); **mental** — agotamiento *m* nervioso, postración *f* nerviosa; **the** — **s of international politics** las tensiones de la política internacional; **the** — **s on the economy** las presiones sobre la economía; **the** — **s of modern life** las tensiones de la vida moderna; **the** — **of 6 hours at the wheel** el agotamiento nervioso que producen 6 horas al volante; **to write without** — escribir sin esfuerzo; **to put a great** — **on someone** someter a uno a gran esfuerzo; exigir un gran esfuerzo a uno.

(c) (*Med*) torcedura *f*.

(d) — **s** (*Mus*) son *m*, compases *mpl*; **the** — **s of a waltz** los compases de un vals; **the bride came in to the** — **s of the wedding march** la novia entró a los acordes (*or* compases) de la marcha nupcial.

(e) (*tenor*) tenor *m*, estilo *m*, sentido *m*; **there was a lot else in the same** — hubo mucho más a este tenor.

2 *vt* (a) (*stretch*) estirar, poner tirante, tender con fuerza.

(b) (*overtax: Med*) deformar, dañar por esfuerzo excesivo; **back, muscle** *etc* torcerse; **eyes** cansar; **heart** cansar (exigiendo un esfuerzo excesivo a); **patience** *etc* cansar, abusar de; **meaning, word** forzar, hacer violencia a; **friendship, relationship** pedir demasiado a; crear tensiones en, crear tirantez en; **to** — **one's ears to hear** esforzarse por oír; **to** — **the law to help someone** hacer violencia a una ley para ayudar a uno.

(c) **to** — **someone to one's breast** abrazar a uno estrechamente.

(d) (*filter*) filtrar; (*Cook*) colar; **to** — **the water off** separar el agua.

3 *vi*: **to** — **at something** esforzarse tirando de algo, tirar con fuerza de algo; **don't** — **at it** no te esfuerces tanto, no te hagas daño tirando tanto; **they** — **ed at the crate** manipulaban el cajón con gran esfuerzo; **to** — **after something** esforzarse por conseguir algo; **to** — **to do something** esforzarse por hacer algo, hacer grandes esfuerzos por hacer algo.

strain² [strein] *n* (*breed*) raza *f*, linaje *m*; (*tendency*) tendencia *f*; **a** — **of weakness** un rasgo de debilidad; **a** — **of madness** una vena de locura.

strained [streind] *adj* **muscle** *etc* torcido; **laugh, smile** *etc* forzado; **relations** tenso, tirante; **style** que muestra esfuerzo, afectado.

strainer ['streinə*] *n* (*Cook*) colador *m*; (*Tech*) filtro *m*, coladero *m*.

strait [streit] *n* (a) (*Geog*: also — **s**) estrecho *m*; **the S— of Gibraltar** el Estrecho de Gibraltar.

(b) — **s** (*fig*) estrecheces *fpl*; situación *f* apurada, apuro *m*; **to be in dire** — **s** estar muy apurado; **the economic** — **s we are in** la difícil situación económica en que nos encontramos.

straitened ['streitnd] *adj*: **in** — **circumstances** en apuro, en la necesidad.

strait jacket ['streit,dʒækit] *n* camisa *f* de fuerza.

strait-laced ['streit'leist] *adj* gazmoño; remilgado.

strand¹ [strænd] (*Naut*) **1** *n* (*lit*) playa *f*, ribera *f*.

2 *vt* **ship** varar, encallar; **to** — **someone without money in London** dejar a uno sin dinero ni recursos en Londres; **to be** — **ed** (*person*) quedar solo, estar sin poderse ayudar, estar abandonado, (*by missing train etc*) quedarse colgado; (*car etc*) quedar inmovilizado; **to leave someone** — **ed** dejar a uno desamparado, dejar a uno plantado.

3 *vi* varar, encallar.

strand² [strænd] *n* (*of rope*) ramal *m*; (*of thread*) hebra *f*, filamento *m*; (*of hair*) trenza *f*; (*of plant*) brizna *f*; **to tie up the loose** — **s** (*fig*) atar cabos.

strange [streindʒ] *adj* (*unknown*) desconocido (*to de*); (*new*) nuevo (*to para*), no acostumbrado; (*odd*) extraño, raro, curioso; (*exotic*) exótico, peregrino; **how** — ! ¡qué raro!; **it is** — **that** ... es raro que + *subj*; **I find it** — **that** ... me extraña que + *subj*, para mí resulta incomprensible que + *subj*; **I felt rather** — **at first** al principio no me sentí cómodo, me sentí algo molesto al principio; **I am** — **to the work** soy nuevo en el oficio, el trabajo es nuevo para mí; **to say** ... aunque parece mentira ...

strangely ['streindʒli] *adv* extrañamente; de un modo raro; **it was** — **familiar to me** me era extrañamente familiar; **she acts somewhat** — se comporta de un modo bastante raro.

strangeness ['streindʒnis] *n* novedad *f*; extrañeza *f*, rareza *f*; lo exótico.

stranger ['streindʒə*] *n* desconocido *m*, a *f*; (*from another area etc*) forastero *m*, a *f*; **he's a** — **to me** es nn desconocido para mí; **I'm a** — **here** yo no soy de aquí, yo soy nuevo aquí; **he is no** — **to vice** conoce bien los vicios.

strangle ['stræŋgl] *vt* estrangular; (*fig*) **abuse, sob** *etc* ahogar.

stranglehold ['stræŋglhəuld] *n* (*Sport*) collar *m* de fuerza; (*fig*) dominio *m* completo; **to have a** — **on something** (*fig*) dominar algo completamente.

strangler ['stræŋglə*] *n* estrangulador *m*.

strangling ['stræŋgliŋ] *n* estrangulación *f*.

strangulated ['stræŋgjuleitid] *adj* (*Med*) estrangulado.

strangulation [ˌstræŋgju'leiʃən] *n* estrangulación *f* (*also Med*).

strap [stræp] **1** *n* correa *f*; (*Sew etc*) tira *f*, banda *f*; (*shoulder* —) tirante *m*, hombrera *f*; **to give someone the** — azotar a uno con una correa (como castigo).

2 *vt* (*tie*) atar con correa; **to** — **someone down** sujetar a uno con correa; **to** — **someone** (*as punishment*) azotar a uno con una correa.

straphang ['stræphæŋ] *vi* (*fam*) viajar de pie (agarrado a la correa).

straphanger ['stræphæŋə*] *n* pasajero *m* que va de pie (agarrado a la correa).

strapless ['stræplis] *adj* **dress** sin tirantes.

strapping ['stræpiŋ] *adj* robusto, fornido.

Strasbourg ['stræzbəːg] Estrasburgo.

stratagem ['strætidʒəm] *n* estratagema *f*.

strategic(al) [strə'tiːdʒik(əl)] *adj* estratégico.

strategist ['strætidʒist] *n* estratega *m*.

strategy ['strætidʒi] *n* estrategia *f*.

stratification [ˌstrætifi'keiʃən] *n* estratificación *f*.

stratified ['strætifaid] *adj* estratificado.

stratify ['strætifai] **1** *vt* estratificar. **2** *vi* estratificarse.

stratocruiser ['strætəu,kruːzə*] *n* avión *m* estratosférico.

stratosphere ['strætəusfiə*] *n* estratosfera *f*.

stratospheric [ˌstrætəus'ferik] *adj* estratosférico.

stratum ['strɑːtəm] *n*, *pl* **strata** ['strɑːtə] estrato *m*; (*fig*) estrato *m*, capa *f*.

straw [strɔː] **1** *n* paja *f*; (*drinking* —) pajita *f*; **to drink through a** — sorber con una pajita; **it's a** — **the last** — ! ¡es el colmo!; **it's a** — **in the wind** es un indicio de cómo van las cosas; **to clutch at** — **s** echar mano de cualquier expediente.

2 *adj*, *attr* de paja; (*colour*) pajizo, color paja.

strawberry ['strɔːbəri] *n* (*fruit and plant*) fresa *f*; (*large, cultivated*) fresón *m*.

strawberry bed ['strɔːbəribed] *n* fresal *m*.

straw-coloured ['strɔːˌkʌləd] *adj* pajizo, color paja.

straw hat ['strɔː'hæt] *n* sombrero *m* de paja.

straw loft ['strɔːlɔft] *n* pajar *m*, pajera *f*.

straw vote ['strɔ:'vəut] n votación f de tanteo.
stray [strei] 1 adj animal etc extraviado; bullet perdido; (isolated) aislado; (scattered) disperso; (sporadic) esporádico; a — cat un gato extraviado, un gato errante; in a few — cases en algunos casos aislados; a few — thoughts unos cuantos pensamientos inconexos.
2 n (animal) animal m extraviado m; (child) niño m sin hogar, niño m desamparado, niña f sin hogar, niña f desamparada; —s (Radio) parásitos mpl.
3 vi (lose oneself) extraviarse, perderse; (wander) vagar, errar; to — from apartarse de (also fig); we had —ed 2 kilometres from the path nos habíamos desviado 2 kilómetros del camino; they —ed into the enemy camp erraron el camino y se encontraron en el campamento enemigo; if the gate is left open the cattle — si se deja abierta la puerta las vacas se escapan.
streak ['stri:k] 1 n raya f, lista f, línea f delgada; (of mineral) veta f, vena f; (fig: of madness etc) vena f; (of luck) racha f; — of lightning rayo m (also fig); there is a — of Spanish blood in her tiene una pequeña parte de sangre española; he had a yellow — era un tanto cobarde; he went past like a — (of lightning) pasó como un rayo.
2 vt rayar, listar (with de).
3 vi: to — along correr a gran velocidad; to — past pasar como un rayo.
streaky ['stri:ki] adj rayado, listado; bacon entreverado; shot con suerte, afortunado.
stream [stri:m] 1 n (brook) arroyo m, riachuelo m; (river) río m; (current) corriente f; (jet etc) chorro m, flujo m; (fig) torrente m; lluvia f, oleada f; (of cars etc) caravana f, riada f; —s of abuse torrente m de injurias; —s of people multitud f de gente; an unbroken — of cars una riada de coches; the B — (School) el grupo B; people were coming out in —s la gente salía en tropel; in one continuous — ininterrumpidamente; against the — contra la corriente; with the — con la corriente.
2 vt (a) water etc derramar, dejar correr; blood manar; his face —ed blood la sangre le corría por la cara.
(b) (School) clasificar, poner en grupos.
3 vi (liquid) correr, fluir; (blood) manar, correr; (in wind etc) ondear, flotar; her eyes were —ing lloraba a mares; the gas made my eyes — el gas me hizo lagrimear; her cheeks were —ing with tears las lágrimas le corrían por las mejillas, tenía las mejillas bañadas en lágrimas; to — out (of liquid) brotar, chorrear, salir a borbotones; people came —ing out la gente salía en tropel; the cars kept —ing past los coches pasaban ininterrumpidamente; her hair —ed in the wind su pelo le ondeaba al viento.
streamer ['stri:mə*] n flámula f; (Naut) gallardete m; (of paper, at parties etc) serpentina f.
streamline ['stri:mlain] vt aerodinamizar; (fig) coordinar, perfeccionar, hacer más eficiente.
streamlined ['stri:mlaind] adj aerodinámico.
street [stri:t] 1 n calle f; the back —s (quiet) las calles tranquilas, (poor) las calles de los barrios bajos; he came from the back —s of Seville salió de los barrios bajos de Sevilla; to be on easy — tener una vida fácil, vivir en el lujo; main — calle f mayor, calle f principal; one-way — calle f de dirección única; it's right up my — de eso sí sé algo; eso viene pintiparado para mí; to be —s ahead of someone llevar mucha ventaja a uno, haberse adelantado mucho a uno; we are —s ahead of them in design les somos muy superiores en el diseño; they're not in the same — as us no están a nuestra altura, quedan muy inferiores a nosotros.
2 attr callejero, de la calle; — accident accidente m de circulación; — incident incidente m callejero; — musician músico m ambulante; at — level en el nivel de la calle.
street arab ['stri:t.ærəb] n golfo m, chiquillo m de la calle.
streetcar ['stri:tkɑ:*] n (US) tranvía m.
street cleaner ['stri:t.kli:nə*] n barrendero m.
street cries ['stri:t.kraiz] npl pregones mpl, gritos mpl de los vendedores ambulantes.
street door ['stri:t'dɔ:*] n puerta f de la calle.
street fighting ['stri:t.faitiŋ] n luchas fpl en las calles.
street lamp ['stri:tlæmp] n farol m.
street lighting ['stri:t.laitiŋ] n alumbrado m público.
street sweeper ['stri:t.swi:pə*] n barrendero m.
street urchin ['stri:t.ə:tʃin] n golfo m, chiquillo m de la calle.
streetwalker ['stri:t.wɔ:kə*] n prostituta f callejera.

strength [streŋθ] n (a) fuerza f; (toughness) resistencia f; (of person) fuerzas fpl, vigor m; (of colour, feeling etc) intensidad f; (of drink) fuerza f; the — of the pound el valor de la libra; — of character carácter m, firmeza f de carácter; — of will resolución f; tensile — resistencia f a la tensión; on the — of fundándose en, confiando en; his — failed him se sintió desfallecer, le abandonaron sus fuerzas; give me —! ¡Dios me dé paciencia!; to save (or reserve) one's — reservarse.
(b) (Mil etc) número m; complemento m; efectivos mpl; fighting — número m de soldados (listos para el combate); to be at full — tener todo su complemento; to be on the — ser miembro del regimiento (etc); ser de plantilla; to come in — venir en gran número; to take someone on to the — dar a uno un puesto en el regimiento (etc).
strengthen ['streŋθən] 1 vt fortalecer, reforzar, hacer más fuerte; consolidar. 2 vi fortalecerse, reforzarse, hacerse más fuerte; consolidarse.
strengthening ['streŋθəniŋ] 1 adj (Med etc) fortificante, tonificante. 2 n fortalecimiento m, refuerzo m; consolidación f.
strenuous ['strenjuəs] adj (energetic) enérgico, vigoroso; (tough) arduo; (exhausting) agotador; opposition etc tenaz; exercise fuerte; to make — efforts to + infin esforzarse a más no poder por + infin.
strenuously ['strenjuəsli] adv enérgicamente, vigorosamente; tenazmente; to try — to + infin procurar por todos los medios + infin.
streptococcus [.streptəu'kɔkəs] n, pl —cocci ['kɔkai] estreptococo m.
streptomycin [.streptəu'maisin] n estreptomicina f.
stress [stres] 1 n (a) (constraining force) fuerza f, compulsión f; presión f; under — of bajo la compulsión de, impulsado por.
(b) (strain) tensión f; the —es and strains of modern life las presiones y tensiones de la vida moderna; mental —, nervous — tensión f nerviosa; times of — tiempos mpl difíciles; to be under — sufrir una tensión nerviosa; to subject someone to great — someter a uno a grandes tensiones.
(c) (emphasis) énfasis m; (accent) acento m; — system sistema m de acentos, acentuación f; the — is on the second syllable el acento cae en la segunda sílaba, la segunda sílaba está acentuada; to lay great — on something insistir mucho en algo, subrayar algo, recalcar la importancia de algo.
(d) (Mech) tensión f, carga f; esfuerzo m; tensile — esfuerzo m de tensión.
stressed [strest] adj acentuado.
stressful ['stresful] adj lleno de tensión (nerviosa), que produce tensión (nerviosa).
stretch [stretʃ] 1 n (a) (act of —ing) extensión f; estirón m; for hours at a — durante horas enteras; 3 days at a — 3 días seguidos; he read the lot at one — los leyó todos de un tirón; to be at full —, to go at full — esforzarse al máximo, emplear todas sus fuerzas (físicas etc); when the engine is at full — cuando el motor rinde su potencia máxima; with arms at full — con los brazos completamente extendidos; by a — of the imagination con un esfuerzo de imaginación.
(b) (amount of —) elasticidad f; capacidad f para ser estirado (or extendido).
(c) (distance) trecho m; extensión f; (of road etc) tramo m; (scope) alcance m; (of time) período m; home — recta f de llegada, (fig) última etapa f; in that — of the river en aquella parte del río; a splendid — of countryside un magnífico paisaje; for a long — it runs between . . . una extensión considerable corre entre . . .; for a long — of time durante mucho tiempo; to do a — (sl) cumplir una condena (en la cárcel).
2 vt (a) (also to — out) (pull out) extender, estirar, alargar; (widen) ensanchar, dilatar; arm extender; hand etc tender, alargar; (on ground etc) extender; to — one's legs estirar las piernas, (after stiffness) desentumecerse las piernas, (fig) dar un paseíto; the blow —ed him (out) cold on the floor el golpe le tumbó sin sentido en el suelo.
(b) money, resources estirar, hacer llegar.
(c) meaning forzar, violentar; to — a point hacer una excepción, hacer una concesión; that's —ing it too far eso va demasiado lejos.
(d) athlete, student etc exigir el máximo esfuerzo a; the course does not — the student enough el curso no exige bastante esfuerzo a los estudiantes.
3 vi (also to — out) extenderse, estirarse, alargarse; ensancharse, dilatarse; (after sleep etc) estirar los brazos (etc), desentumecerse las piernas; this cloth

won't — esta tela no se estira; **will it** —**?** (*ie reach*) ¿llega?; **how far will it** —**?** ¿hasta dónde llega?; ¿hasta dónde se extiende?; **it** —**es for miles along the river** se extiende varios kilómetros a lo largo del río; **he** —**ed out on the ground** se tendió en el suelo; **to** — **out to reach something** alargar el brazo (*etc*) para tomar algo.

4 *vr*: **to** — **oneself (a)** (*after sleep etc*) estirarse, estirarse los brazos.

(b) (*make effort*) esforzarse al máximo; **he doesn't** — **himself** no se esfuerza bastante, no se exige bastante esfuerzo a sí mismo.

stretcher ['stretʃə*] *n* (*Tech*) ensanchador *m*; (*for canvas*) bastidor *m*; (*Archit*) soga *f*; (*Med*) camilla *f*.

stretcher-bearer ['stretʃə‚beərə*] *n* camillero *m*.

stretcher case ['stretʃəkeis] *n* enfermo *m* (*or* herido *m*) que tiene que ser llevado en camilla.

stretcher party ['stretʃə‚pɑːti] *n* equipo *m* de camilleros.

strew [struː] (*irr*: *pret* **strewed**, *ptp* **strewed** *or* **strewn**) *vt* (*scatter*) derramar, esparcir; (*cover*) cubrir, sembrar (*with* de); **to** — **one's belongings about the room** dejar sus cosas en desorden por todo el cuarto; **there were fragments** —**n about everywhere** había fragmentos desparramados por todas partes; **to** — **sand on the floor** cubrir el suelo de arena, esparcir arena sobre el suelo; **the floors are** —**n with rushes** los suelos están cubiertos de juncos.

striated [strai'eitid] *adj* estriado.

stricken ['strikən] *adj* (*and in some senses ptp of* **strike**) (*wounded*) herido; (*doomed*) condenado; (*damaged*) destrozado; (*ill*) enfermo; **the** — **city** la ciudad condenada, la ciudad destrozada; **the** — **families** las familias afligidas; **to be** — **with** estar afligido por; **to be** — **with grief** estar agobiado por el dolor; **she was** — **with remorse** le remordió la conciencia.

strict [strikt] *adj* **(a)** (*precise*) estricto; exacto, preciso; riguroso; **in the** — **sense of the word** en el sentido estricto de la palabra; **we need** — **accuracy here** aquí es necesario emplear la más rigurosa exactitud; — **neutrality** neutralidad *f* rigurosa; **in** — **confidence** en la más absoluta confianza (*and see* **confidence**).

(b) *order, ban etc* terminante; *discipline* severo, riguroso.

(c) (*of person*) severo, riguroso; escrupuloso; **they're terribly** — **here** aquí son terriblemente rigurosos; **to be** — **with someone** ser severo con uno, tratar a uno con severidad.

strictly ['striktli] *adv* **(a)** estrictamente; exactamente; rigurosamente; — **speaking** en rigor; **not** — **true** no del todo verdad; — **between ourselves** . . . en confianza entre los dos . . .; **to be** — **accurate** . . . para decirlo con toda precisión . . .; **to remain** — **neutral** guardar la más rigurosa neutralidad.

(b) terminantemente; severamente; **it is** — **forbidden to** + *infin* se prohibe terminantemente + *infin*.

(c) severamente, rigurosamente; **to treat someone very** — tratar a uno con mucha severidad; **she was** — **brought up** se la educó estrictamente.

strictness ['striktnis] *n* exactitud *f*; rigor *m*, severidad *f*; lo terminante.

stricture ['striktʃə*] *n* **(a)** (*Med*) constricción *f*. **(b)** (*fig*) censura *f*, crítica *f*, reparo *m*; **to pass** —**s on someone** censurar a uno, poner reparos a uno.

stridden ['stridn] *ptp of* **stride**.

stride [straid] **1** *n* zancada *f*, tranco *m*, paso *m* largo; (*in measuring*) paso *m*; **he set off with big** —**s** partió a grandes zancadas; **to get into one's** — alcanzar el ritmo acostumbrado; **to make great** —**s** hacer grandes progresos; **to take it in one's** — sabérselo tomar bien, hacerlo sin esfuerzo, estar a la altura de las circunstancias.

2 (*irr*: *pret* **strode** *ptp* **stridden**) *vt horse* montar a horcajadas; poner una pierna a cada lado de; (*cross*) cruzar de un tranco.

3 *vi* (*also* **to** — **along**) andar a trancos, andar a pasos largos, dar zancadas; **to** — **away, to** — **off** alejarse a grandes zancadas; **to** — **up to someone** acercarse resueltamente a uno; **to** — **up and down** andar de aquí para allá a pasos largos.

stridency ['straidənsi] *n* estridencia *f*, estridor *m*; lo chillón; lo estrepitoso.

strident ['straidənt] *adj* estridente; *colour, person* chillón; *protest* fuerte, estrepitoso.

stridently ['straidəntli] *adv* ruidosamente, de modo estridente; estrepitosamente.

strife [straif] *n* lucha *f*; (*not armed*) lucha *f*, contienda *f*; disensión *f*; *party* — lucha *f* de partidos; **internal** — disensión *f* interna; **to cease from** — deponer las armas.

strike [straik] **1** *n* **(a)** (*of labour*) huelga *f*; **general** — huelga *f* general; **sympathy** — huelga *f* por solidaridad; **to be on** — estar en huelga; **to come out on** —, **to go on** — ponerse en huelga, declarar la huelga; *see* **hunger** *etc*.

(b) (*discovery*) descubrimiento *m* (repentino); **a big oil** — un descubrimiento de petróleo en gran cantidad; **to make a** — hacer un descubrimiento.

(c) (*Sport*) golpe *m*.

(d) (*Mil*) ataque *m*; **air** — ataque *m* aéreo, bombardeo *m*.

2 (*irr*: *pret* **struck**, *ptp* **struck** *and in some senses* **stricken**) *vt* **(a)** (*hit*) golpear; (*with fist etc*) pegar, dar una bofetada a; (*wound*) herir; (*Tech*) percutir; (*with bullet etc*) alcanzar; *ball* golpear; *blow* asestar (*at* a); *chord* tocar; *instrument* herir, pulsar; tocar; **never** — **a woman** no pegar nunca a una mujer; **to** — **one's fist on the table, to** — **the table with one's fist** golpear la mesa con el puño; **the president was struck by two bullets** el presidente fue alcanzado por dos balas; **the tower was struck by lightning** cayó un rayo en la torre; **a fisherman was struck by lightning** un rayo mató a un pescador; **the light** —**s the window** la luz hiere la ventana.

(b) (*produce, make*) *coin, medal* acuñar; *a light, match* frotar, encender; **to** — **sparks from something** hacer que algo eche chispas; **to** — **a cutting** hacer que un esqueje arranque; **to** — **root** echar raíces, arraigar; **to** — **someone blind** cegar a uno; **to** — **someone deaf** ensordecer a uno; **to** — **someone dumb** (*fig*) dejar a uno sin habla; **to** — **terror into someone** infundir terror a uno.

(c) (*collide with, meet*) dar con; *rocks etc* chocar contra, estrellarse contra; *mine* chocar con; *difficulty, obstacle* encontrar, topar con; **a sound struck my ear** un ruido hirió mi oído; **his head struck the beam** dio con la cabeza contra la viga.

(d) (*of thoughts, impressions*) **it** —**s me that** . . . , **the thought** —**s me that** . . . se me ocurre que . . .; **has it ever struck you that** . . .**?** ¿has pensado alguna vez que . . .?; **it** —**s me as being most unlikely** creo que es muy poco probable; **at least that's how it** —**s me** por lo menos eso es lo que pienso yo; **how does she** — **you?** ¿qué te parece (ella)?, ¿qué impresión te hace ella?; **I was much struck by his sincerity** su sinceridad me impresionó mucho; **I'm not much struck (with him)** no me hace buena impresión.

(e) (*find*) descubrir, encontrar; **to** — **oil** descubrir un yacimiento de petróleo; **he struck it rich** descubrió un buen filón, tuvo mucha suerte.

(f) to — **camp** levantar el campamento; **to** — **the flag** arriar la bandera.

(g) to — **work** abandonar el trabajo, declarar la huelga.

(h) *attitude* tomar, adoptar.

(i) to — **an average** calcular el promedio; **to** — **a balance** (*Comm*) hacer balance, (*fig*) establecer un equilibrio (*between* entre); **to** — **a bargain** cerrar un trato.

(j) (*with adv or prep*) **to** — **down** derribar; **he was struck down by paralysis** tuvo una parálisis, le acometió una parálisis; **he was struck down in his prime** se le llevó la muerte en la flor de la vida; **to** — **off** (*cut off*) cortar; cercenar, quitar de golpe; (*from list*) borrar, tachar; (*print*) tirar, imprimir; (*deduct*) rebajar; **to** — **out** borrar, tachar; **to** — **through** (*cross out*) tachar; (*penetrate*) penetrar; **to** — **up** *music* iniciar, empezar a tocar; *conversation* entablar; *friendship* trabar.

3 *vi* **(a)** (*attack, Mil etc*) atacar; **now is the time to** — éste es el momento en que conviene atacar; **to** — **against something** dar con algo, dar contra algo, chocar contra algo; **to** — **at someone** asestar un golpe a uno, tratar de golpear a uno; acometer a uno; (*Mil*) atacar a uno; **this** —**s at our very existence** esto amenaza con destruir nuestra misma existencia; **to** — **out** empezar a repartir golpes; **to** — **out wildly** dar golpes sin mirar a quién; *see* **home, iron** *etc*.

(b) (*of clock*) dar la hora; **the clock has struck** ha dado la hora ya; **when one's hour** —**s** cuando llega la hora de uno.

(c) (*of labour*) abandonar el trabajo, declarar la huelga; estar en huelga; **to** — **for higher wages** hacer una huelga para conseguir un aumento de los sueldos.

(d) (*of match*) encenderse.

(e) (*Naut*: *run aground*) encallar; tocar el fondo, dar contra las rocas.

(f) (*Naut*: *surrender*) arriar la bandera.

(g) (*Bot*) echar raíces, arraigar.

(h) to — on an idea ocurrírsele a uno una idea. **(i) the band struck up** la orquesta empezó a tocar.

(j) (of movement, with adv or prep) **to — across country** ir a campo traviesa; **to — into the woods** ir por el bosque, penetrar en el bosque; **the road —s off to the right** el camino se desvía hacia la derecha; **to — out for the shore** (empezar a) nadar (resueltamente) hacia la playa; **to — out for oneself, to — out on one's own** (fig) hacerse independiente, hacer rancho aparte, obrar por cuenta propia; **the sun —s through the mist** el sol penetra por entre la niebla.

strikebreaker ['straik,breikə*] n esquirol m.

strike fund ['straikfʌnd] n fondo m de huelga, caja f de resistencia.

strike pay ['straikpei] n subsidio m de huelga.

striker ['straikə*] n huelguista mf.

striking ['straikiŋ] adj notable, impresionante; chocante, sorprendente; contrast etc acusado, hiriente; colour etc llamativo; of — appearance de aspecto impresionante; **a — woman** una mujer imponente; **it is — that ...** es chocante que ...

strikingly ['straikiŋli] adv notablemente; de modo sorprendente; **a — beautiful woman** una mujer de notable hermosura, una mujer extraordinariamente hermosa.

string [striŋ] **1** n **(a)** (cord) cuerda f; cordel m, bramante m; guita f; (of beads) hilo m, sarta f, collar m; (of onions, garlic) ristra f; (of horses etc) reata f; (of lies) sarta f; (of curses) serie f, retahíla f; (row) fila f, hilera f; (of people) hilera f, desfile m; (of vehicles) caravana f; **to have someone on a —** dominar completamente la voluntad de uno, mover a uno como una marioneta; **to pull —s** tocar resortes, mover palancas.

(b) (Mus) cuerda f; **—s** instrumentos mpl de cuerda; **to have two —s to one's bow** tener dos cuerdas en su arco; **— instrument** instrumento m de cuerda; **— quartet** cuarteto m de cuerdas.

(c) (Bot) fibra f, nervio m.

(d) (fig) condición f; **without —s** sin condiciones; **there are no —s attached** no hay condiciones impuestas.

2 (irr: pret and ptp strung) vt **(a)** pearls etc ensartar (also **to — together**); bow, violin encordar; **to — sentences together** ir ensartando frases; **they are just stray thoughts strung together** son pensamientos aislados que se han ensartado sin propósito; **to — someone up** (fam) ahorcar a uno.

(b) beans etc quitar las fibras de.

3 vi: **to — along with someone** pegarse a uno, acompañar a uno; **to — out along a road** extenderse por una carretera; **they were strung out for miles** se extendían sobre varios kilómetros; **the posts are strung out across the desert** hay una serie de puestos aislados a través del desierto; **his plays are strung out from 1940 to 1965** aparecieron sus obras una a una desde 1940 hasta 1965; **they are too strung out to form a series** están demasiado aislados unos de otros para formar una serie.

4 vr: **to — oneself up to do something** resolverse a hacer algo, cobrar ánimo para hacer algo.

string bean ['striŋ'biːn] n (US) habichuela f, judía f.

stringed [striŋd] adj instrument de cuerda(s); **4-stringed** de 4 cuerdas.

stringency ['strindʒənsi] n **(a)** rigor m, severidad f. **(b)** tirantez f, dificultad f; **economic —** situación f económica apurada, estrechez f.

stringent ['strindʒənt] adj **(a)** riguroso, severo; **rules** reglas fpl rigurosas; **we shall have to be — about it** tendremos que obrar con rigor.

(b) (Comm etc) tirante, difícil.

stringently ['strindʒəntli] adv severamente, rigurosamente.

stringy ['striŋi] adj fibroso, lleno de fibras.

strip [strip] **1** n tira f; banda f, faja f; (of land) zona f, franja f; (of metal) cinta f, lámina f; **comic —** tira f cómica, banda f de dibujos.

2 vt **(a)** (denude) desnudar, quitar la ropa (etc) a; **to — someone naked** desnudar a uno completamente, dejar a uno en cueros; **to — off one's clothes** quitarse (rápidamente) la ropa, despojarse de la ropa; **the wind —ped the leaves off the trees** el viento arrancó las hojas de los árboles; **to — someone of something** despojar a uno de algo; **to — a house of its furniture** dejar una casa sin muebles; **—ped of all the verbiage, this means ...** sin palabrería, esto quiere decir ...; **to — someone to the skin** dejar a uno en cueros.

(b) (Tech) desmontar, desmantelar; gears estropear.

3 vi desnudarse, quitarse la ropa; **to — off** desnudarse; (of paint etc) desprenderse; separarse; **to — to the skin** quitarse toda la ropa; **to — to the waist** desnudarse hasta la cintura.

strip cartoon ['strɪpkɑː'tuːn] n tira f cómica, banda f de dibujos.

stripe [straip] **1** n raya f, lista f, banda f; (Mil) galón m; (lash) azote m, (weal) cardenal m. **2** vt rayar, listar (with de).

striped [straipt] adj listado, rayado; trousers etc a rayas.

strip lighting ['strip,laitiŋ] n alumbrado m de banda.

stripling ['stripliŋ] n mozuelo m, joven m imberbe.

stripper ['stripə*] n (fam) artista f de striptise.

striptease ['striptiːz] n estriptise f (espectáculo en el cual la artista se va despojando progresivamente de la ropa).

strive [straiv] (irr: pret strove, ptp striven) vi esforzarse, afanarse, luchar; **to — after something, to — for something** luchar por conseguir algo, afanarse por conseguir algo; **to — against something** luchar contra algo; **to — to do something** esforzarse por hacer algo, luchar por hacer algo.

striven ['strivn] ptp of strive.

strode [strəud] pret of stride.

stroke¹ [strəuk] **1** n **(a)** (blow) golpe m; **10`—s of the lash** 10 azotes; **— of lightning** rayo m; **at a —,** at one — de un golpe; **with one — of his knife** de un cuchillazo; **with one fell —** de un solo golpe fatal.

(b) (Sport etc: Cricket, Golf) golpe m; jugada f; (Billiards) tacada f; (Rowing) remada f, golpe m; (Swimming: movement) brazada f, (type of —) estilo m; **with a total of 281 —s** con un total de 281 golpes; **good —!** ¡muy bien!; **he went ahead at every —** se adelantaba con cada brazada; **they are rowing a fast —** reman a ritmo rápido; **he hasn't done a — of work** no ha hecho absolutamente nada; **he doesn't do a —** no da golpe; **— of diplomacy** éxito m diplomático; **— of genius** rasgo m de ingenio, genialidad f; **the idea was a — of genius** la idea ha sido genial; **— of luck** racha f de suerte; **by a — of luck** por suerte; **then we had a — of luck** luego nos favoreció la suerte; **a good — of business** un buen negocio; **his greatest — was to ...** su golpe maestro fue ...; see master —.

(c) (of bell, clock) campanada f; **on the — of 12** al acabar de dar las 12, a las 12 en punto; **to arrive on the — (of time)** llegar a la hora justa.

(d) (of piston) carrera f; **two-stroke engine** motor m de dos tiempos.

(e) (Med) ataque m fulminante, apoplejía f; **to have a —** tener una apoplejía; see heat—.

(f) (of pen) trazo m; rasgo m, plumada f, plumazo m; (of pencil) trazo m; (of brush) pincelada f; **at a — of the pen, with one — of the pen** de un plumazo; **with a thick — of the pen** con un trazo grueso de la pluma.

(g) (Rowing: person) primer remero m; **to row —** ser el primer remero, remar en el primer puesto.

2 vt: **to — a boat** ser el primer remero; **to — a boat to victory** ser el primer remero en el bote vencedor.

stroke² [strəuk] **1** n (caress) caricia f; **with a light — of the hand** con un suave movimiento de la mano.

2 vt acariciar; frotar suavemente; eg chin pasar la mano sobre, pasar la mano por.

stroll [strəul] **1** n paseo m, vuelta f; **to go for a —, to have a —, to take a —** dar un paseo.

2 vi pasear(se), dar un paseo, deambular, callejear; **to — up and down** pasearse de acá para allá; **to — up to someone** acercarse tranquilamente a uno.

stroller ['strəulə*] n paseante mf; (US) cochecito m.

strolling ['strəuliŋ] adj actor etc ambulante.

strong [strɔŋ] **1** adj fuerte; recio, robusto; enérgico; vigoroso; sólido; (Fin) firme; accent marcado; believer fervoroso; candidate que tiene buenas posibilidades, respetable; characteristic acusado; coffee fuerte, cargado; colour intenso; constitution robusto; conviction profundo, sincero; drink fuerte, alcohólico; emotion fuerte, intenso; evidence fehaciente; feature acusado; flavour fuerte; language fuerte, indecente; measure enérgico; personality acusado; protest enérgico; reason convincente; situation dramático, lleno de emoción; smell fuerte, penetrante, punzante; solution concentrado; suit (Cards) largo; supporter acérrimo; tea fuerte, cargado; terms enfático; verb irregular, fuerte; voice fuerte; wind fuerte, recio, violento; **to be as — as a horse** ser tan fuerte como un león; **to be — in the arm** tener los brazos fuertes; **to be — in chemistry** estar fuerte en química; **we are — in**

forwards tenemos una buena línea delantera; **the gallery is — in Goya** el museo tiene muchas obras de Goya; **he's getting —er every day** se va reponiendo poco a poco; **when you are — again** cuando te hayas repuesto del todo; **a group 20 —** un grupo de 20 (miembros *etc*); **they were 50 —** eran 50, contaban 50.

2 *adv*: **the market closed —** el mercado se cerró en situación firme; **he was going — still at the tape** al llegar a la cinta corría todavía con pleno vigor; **he pitches it pretty —** exagera mucho, es un exagerado.

strong-arm ['strɔŋɑːm] *adj policy, methods* de mano dura.

strong-armed ['strɔŋɑːmd] *adj* de brazos fuertes.

strongbox ['strɔŋbɔks] *n* caja *f* de caudales, caja *f* fuerte.

stronghold ['strɔŋhəuld] *n* fortaleza *f*, plaza *f* fuerte; *(fig)* baluarte *m*, centro *m*; **the last — of . . .** el último reducto de . . .

strongly ['strɔŋli] *adv* fuertemente; enérgicamente, vigorosamente; firmemente; fervorosamente; intensamente; **I — believe that . . .** creo firmemente que . . .; **he smelled — of beer** despedía fuerte olor a cerveza; **— marked** acusado, acentuado; **a — worded letter** una carta de tono enérgico.

strong-minded ['strɔŋ'maindid] *adj* resuelto; de carácter.

strong-mindedness ['strɔŋ'maindidnis] *n* resolución *f*; carácter *m*.

strongpoint ['strɔŋpɔint] *n* fuerte *m*, puesto *m* fortificado.

strongroom ['strɔŋrum] *n* cámara *f* acorazada.

strong-willed ['strɔŋ'wild] *adj* resuelto, de voluntad firme; *(pej)* obstinado.

strontium ['strɔntiəm] *n* estroncio *m*; **— 90** estroncio *m* 90.

strop [strɔp] **1** *n* suavizador *m*. **2** *vt* suavizar.

strophe ['strəufi] *n* estrofa *f*.

strove [strəuv] *pret of* **strive**.

struck [strʌk] *pret and ptp of* **strike**.

structural ['strʌktʃərəl] *adj* estructural.

structurally ['strʌktʃərəli] *adv* estructuralmente, desde el punto de vista de la estructura; **— sound** de estructura sólida.

structure ['strʌktʃə*] *n* estructura *f*; construcción *f*.

struggle ['strʌgl] **1** *n* lucha *f*, contienda *f*, conflicto *m*; *(effort)* esfuerzo *m*; **without a —** sin luchar, *(bloodlessly)* sin efusión de sangre; **the — for survival** la lucha por la vida; **the — to find a flat** la lucha por encontrarse un piso.

2 *vi* luchar; esforzarse; **to — to do something** luchar por hacer algo, esforzarse por hacer algo; **to — in vain** luchar en vano; **to — to one's feet** luchar por levantarse; levantarse con esfuerzo; **we —d on another kilometre** avanzamos con dificultad un kilómetro más; **he —d up the rock** subió penosamente por la roca; **the light tries to — through the panes** la luz se esfuerza por penetrar por los cristales.

strum [strʌm] **1** *vt guitar etc* rasguear; tocar distraídamente; tocar mal. **2** *vi* cencerrear.

strumpet ['strʌmpit] *n* ramera *f*.

strung [strʌŋ] *pret and ptp of* **string**; *see* **highly —**.

strut[1] [strʌt] *vi (also to — about, to — along)* pavonearse, contonearse; **to — into a room** entrar pavoneándose en un cuarto; **to — past someone** pasar delante de uno con paso majestuoso.

strut[2] [strʌt] *n* puntal *m*, riostra *f*, tornapunta *f*.

strychnine ['strikniːn] *n* estricnina *f*.

Stuart ['stjuːət] *m* Estuardo.

stub [stʌb] **1** *n (of tree)* tocón *m*; *(of cigarette)* colilla *f*; *(of candle, pencil etc)* cabo *m*; *(of cheque, receipt)* talón *m*.

2 *vt*: **to — one's toe** dar con el dedo del pie contra algo, dar un tropezón; **to — out** *cigarette* apagar; **to — up** *tree trunks* desarraigar, quitar.

stubble ['stʌbl] *n* rastrojo *m*; *(on chin)* barba *f* de tres días.

stubble field ['stʌblfiːld] *n* rastrojera *f*.

stubbly ['stʌbli] *adj chin* cerdoso, con barba de tres días; *beard* de tres días.

stubborn ['stʌbən] *adj* ' tenaz; *refusal* resuelto; inquebrantable; *(pej)* terco, testarudo, porfiado.

stubbornly ['stʌbənli] *adv* tenazmente; tercamente, con porfía; **he — refused to + infin** se negó resueltamente a + infin.

stubbornness ['stʌbənnis] *n* tenacidad *f*; terquedad *f*, testarudez *f*, porfía *f*.

stubby ['stʌbi] *adj* achaparrado.

stucco ['stʌkəu] **1** *n* estuco *m*. **2** *adj* de estuco. **3** *vt* estucar.

stuck [stʌk] *pret and ptp of* **stick**.

stuck-up ['stʌk'ʌp] *adj (fam)* engreído, presumido; **to be very — about something** presumir mucho a causa de algo.

stud[1] [stʌd] **1** *n (Mil)* tachón *m*; *(boot—)* taco *m*; *(decorative)* clavo *m* (de adorno); *(collar—, shirt—)* botón *m* de camisa.

2 *vt* tachonar; adornar con clavos; *(fig)* sembrar *(with* de).

stud[2] [stʌd] *n* caballeriza *f*, yeguada *f*.

studbook ['stʌdbuk] *n* registro *m* genealógico de caballos.

student ['stjuːdənt] **1** *n (pupil)* alumno *m*, a *f*; *(Univ)* estudiante *mf*; *(researcher)* investigador *m*, ora *f*; **French —** *(by nationality)* estudiante *m* francés, *(by subject)* estudiante *m* de francés; **medical —** estudiante *mf* de medicina; **old —s' association** asociación *f* de antiguos alumnos.

2 *attr* estudiantil.

studentship ['stjuːdəntʃip] *n* beca *f*.

stud farm ['stʌdfɑːm] *n* caballeriza *f*, yeguada *f*.

studhorse ['stʌdhɔːs] *n* caballo *m* padre.

studied ['stʌdid] *adj calm etc* calculado, deliberado; *insult* premeditado; *pose, style* afectado.

studio ['stjuːdiəu] *n (in most senses)* estudio *m*; *(sculptor's)* taller *m*; **television —** estudio *m* de televisión; **in our Barcelona —** en nuestro estudio de Barcelona.

studio couch ['stjuːdiəu‚kautʃ] *n* sofá-cama *m*.

studious ['stjuːdiəs] *adj* estudioso; aplicado, asiduo; *see* **studied**.

studiously ['stjuːdiəsli] *adv* con aplicación; **he — avoided mentioning the matter** evitó cuidadosamente aludir al asunto, se guardó de aludir al asunto.

studiousness ['stjuːdiəsnis] *n* aplicación *f*.

stud mare ['stʌd‚mɛə*] *n* yegua *f* de cría.

study ['stʌdi] **1** *n (in most senses)* estudio *m*; *(room)* despacho *m*, cuarto *m* de trabajo, estudio *m*; **to be in a brown —** estar absorto en la meditación, estar en Babia; **to make a — of something** estudiar algo, investigar algo; **my studies show that . . .** mis estudios demuestran que . . .

2 *vt* estudiar; investigar; examinar, mirar detenidamente; escudriñar.

3 *vi* estudiar; **to — under someone** estudiar con uno, trabajar bajo la dirección de uno; **to — for an exam** prepararse para un examen; **to — to be an agronomist** estudiar para agrónomo.

study group ['stʌdi'gruːp] *n grupo que se propone (o al que se le encarga) investigar un problema*.

stuff [stʌf] **1** *n* (a) *(material in general)* materia *f*; material *m*, sustancia *f*; **it's strange —** es una sustancia singular; **there is some good — in that book** ese libro tiene cosas buenas; **there's good — in him** tiene buenas cualidades; **it's poor —** no vale para nada; **do you call this — beer?** ¿llamas a esto cerveza?; **I can't read his —** no alcanzo a leer sus libros; **I can't listen to his —** no aguanto su música; **that's the —!** ¡muy bien!; **have you brought the —?** ¿lo has traído?, ¿has traído aquello?; **he is of the — that heroes are made of** tiene madera de héroe; **show him what — you are made of** demuéstrale tus cualidades, muéstrale si puedes o no.

(b) *(material, cloth)* tela *f*, paño *m*.

(c) *(possessions: fam)* cosas *fpl*, chismes *mpl*; **he leaves his — scattered about** deja sus cosas de cualquier modo; **is this your —?** ¿es tuyo esto?

(d) *(nonsense)* tonterías *fpl*; **all that — about Cervantes** todas esas tonterías acerca de Cervantes; **— and nonsense!** ¡ni hablar!, ¡narices!

(e) **hot —** *(sl)* cosa *f* maravillosa, persona *f* estupenda; **she's hot —** es cachonda, es de plan; **he's hot — at chess** es un hacha para el ajedrez.

(f) **to do one's —** *(fam)* actuar, trabajar *etc*; **you do your — next** tú eres el próximo; **he doesn't do his —** no trabaja *(etc)* como debiera; **he certainly knows his —** conoce perfectamente su oficio, domina su especialidad.

2 *vt (fill)* container llenar, hinchar, atiborrar *(with* de); *(stow)* contents meter sin orden, meter de prisa *(into* en); *hole, leak etc* tapar, atascar; *(Cook)* rellenar; *animal (for exhibition)* disecar; **to — away** *food* zampar, devorar; **he —ed it into his pocket** lo metió de prisa en el bolsillo; **can we — any more in?** ¿cabe más?; **her head is —ed with formulae** tiene la cabeza atiborrada de fórmulas; **two centuries —ed with history** dos siglos prietos *(or* llenos*)* de historia; **to be —ed up with (a) cold** estar fuertemente acatarrado; **get —ed!** *(sl)* ¡vete a la porra!

3 *vi* atracarse, comer a dos carrillos.

4 *vr*: **to — oneself with food** darse un atracón, atiborrarse de comida; **I have to — myself with sedatives** me veo obligado a embutirme de calmantes.

stuffed shirt ['stʌft'ʃə:t] *n* (*fam*) tragavirotes *m*.

stuffiness ['stʌfinis] *n* mala ventilación *f*, falta *f* de aire; (*fig*) estrechez *f* de miras; lo estirado; lo remilgado, pesadez *f*.

stuffing ['stʌfiŋ] *n* (*of furniture, animal*) relleno *m*, borra *f*; (*Cook*) relleno *m*; **he's got no —** no tiene carácter, no tiene agallas; **he had the — knocked out of him by the blow** el golpe le dejó sin fuerzas ni ánimo.

stuffy ['stʌfi] *adj* (**a**) *room* mal ventilado, donde falta el aire; *atmosphere* cargado, sofocante; **it's — in here** aquí falta el aire, aquí huele a encerrado.

(**b**) (*narrow-minded*) de miras estrechas; (*stiff*) estirado; (*prudish*) remilgado; (*of book etc*) pesado, poco interesante.

stultify ['stʌltifai] *vt* hacer inútil, quitar valor a, anular; hacer (parecer) ridículo.

stumble ['stʌmbl] **1** *n* tropezón *m*, traspié *m*.

2 *vi* tropezar, dar un traspié; **to — against** tropezar contra; **to — on** (*fig*) tropezar con, encontrar por casualidad; **to — on, to go stumbling on** avanzar dando traspiés; **to — through a speech** pronunciar muy mal un discurso.

stumbling block ['stʌmbliŋblɔk] *n* (*fig*) tropiezo *m*, obstáculo *m*.

stump [stʌmp] **1** *n* cabo *m*, fragmento *m*, último pedazo *m*; (*of tree etc*) tocón *m*; (*of limb*) muñón *m*; (*of tooth*) raigón *m*; (*Cricket*) palo *m*; (*Art*) esfumino *m*; (*fam*) pierna *f*; **to stir one's —s** (*fam*) menearse, moverse.

2 *vt* (**a**) desconcertar, dejar perplejo, dejar confuso; **I'm properly —ed** estoy totalmente perplejo; no sé qué hacer (*or* decir *etc*); no sé qué consejo darte; **he was —ed for an answer** no sabía qué contestar.

(**b**) **to — the country** (*Pol*) recorrer el país pronunciando discursos.

(**c**) (*fam*) **to — up £5** pagar 5 libras (de mala gana), desembolsar 5 libras (**for** para comprar algo, por algo).

3 *vi* (**a**) **to — about, to — along** andar pisando muy fuerte; (*lamely*) andar cojeando.

(**b**) **to — up** pagar (de mala gana; **for** something algo), soltar la guita.

stumpy ['stʌmpi] *adj person etc* achaparrado; *pencil etc* reducido a casi nada, muy gastado.

stun [stʌn] *vt* dejar sin sentido; aturdir de un golpe; (*fig*) aturdir, pasmar, dejar pasmado; **the news —ned everybody** la noticia aturdió a todos; **this will — you** esto será una gran sorpresa para ti; **the family were —ned by his death** la familia quedó anonadada a raíz de su muerte.

stung [stʌŋ] *pret and ptp of* **sting**.

stunk [stʌŋk] *ptp of* **stink**.

stunner ['stʌnə*] *n* (*fam*) persona *f* maravillosa, cosa *f* estupenda; **the picture is a —** el cuadro es maravilloso; **she's a real —** es francamente estupenda.

stunning ['stʌniŋ] *adj blow* que aturde; *news etc* pasmoso; *dress, girl etc* estupendo, maravilloso.

stunt¹ [stʌnt] *vt* atrofiar, impedir el desarrollo de.

stunt² [stʌnt] **1** *n* (*Aer*) vuelo *m* acrobático, ejercicio *m* acrobático; (*display*) proeza *f* excepcional; maniobra *f* sensacional; (*Comm*) truco *m* publicitario, treta *f* publicitaria; **it's just a — to get your money** es solamente un truco para sacarte dinero.

2 *vi* lucirse haciendo vuelos acrobáticos (*or* maniobras sensacionales *etc*).

stunted ['stʌntid] *adj* enano, achaparrado, mal desarrollado.

stuntman ['stʌntmæn] *n, pl* **—men** [men] *persona que se dedica a desempeñar los papeles peligrosos en el cine y otros espectáculos*.

stupefaction [,stju:pi'fækʃən] *n* estupefacción *f*.

stupefy ['stju:pifai] *vt* (**a**) (*Med*) causar estupor a, dejar sin conocimiento; **stupefied by drink** en estado de estupor después de haber bebido, (*permanently*) embrutecido por el alcohol.

(**b**) (*fig*) pasar, causar estupor a, dejar estupefacto.

stupefying ['stju:pifaiiŋ] *adj* (*fig*) pasmoso.

stupendous [stju(:)'rendəs] *adj* estupendo, asombroso.

stupendously [stju(:)'pendəsli] *adv* estupendamente.

stupid ['stju:pid] *adj* (*with sleep etc*) en estado de estupor, atontado; (*silly*) estúpido; **you — child!** ¡bobo!; **don't be — no** seas bobo; **that was — of you, that was a — thing to do** eso fue una estupidez;

I've done a — thing he hecho algo tonto; **to drink oneself —** beber tanto que uno queda en estado de estupor.

stupidly ['stju:pidli] *adv* estúpidamente.

stupor ['stju:pə*] *n* estupor *m* (*also fig*).

sturdily ['stə:dili] *adv* fuertemente; vigorosamente; enérgicamente; tenazmente; **— built** de construcción sólida, *person* robusto.

sturdiness ['stə:dinis] *n* robustez *f*, fuerza *f*; energía *f*; tenacidad *f*.

sturdy ['stə:di] *adj* robusto, fuerte; vigoroso; *opposition etc* enérgico; *resistance* tenaz; **— independence** espíritu *m* fuerte de independencia.

sturgeon ['stə:dʒən] *n* esturión *m*.

stutter ['stʌtə*] **1** *n* tartamudeo *m*; **he has a bad —** tartamudea terriblemente; **to say something with a —** decir algo tartamudeando. **2** *vt* balbucir, decir tartamudeando (*also* **to — out**). **3** *vi* tartamudear; balbucir.

stutterer ['stʌtərə*] *n* tartamudo *m*, a *f*.

stuttering ['stʌtəriŋ] **1** *adj* tartamudo. **2** *n* tartamudeo *m*.

stutteringly ['stʌtəriŋli] *adv*: **he said —** dijo tartamudeando.

sty [stai] *n* pocilga *f*, zahurda *f*.

stye [stai] *n* (*Med*) orzuelo *m*.

Stygian ['stidʒiən] *adj* estigio.

style [stail] **1** *n* (**a**) estilo *m*; (*Art, Lit etc*) estilo *m*; (*fashion*) estilo *m*; moda *f*; (*elegance*) elegancia *f*; **— of living** estilo *m* de vida; **the Norman —** el estilo románico; **in the Italian —** al estilo italiano, a la italiana; **that's the —!** ¡bravo!, ¡muy bien!; **there's no — about him** no tiene elegancia en absoluto; **she has —** tiene garbo, tiene aquél; lo hace todo con elegancia; **to cramp someone's —** cortar los vuelos a uno; **to be in —** estar de moda; **to do something in —** hacer algo lo mejor posible, hacer algo realmente bien; **to travel in —** viajar con todo confort; **to live in —** vivir en el lujo; **he won in fine —** ganó de modo concluyente.

(**b**) (*of address*) tratamiento *m*; título *m*.

2 *vt* (**a**) *dress* cortar a la moda, estilizar.

(**b**) (*entitle*) intitular, nombrar.

3 *vr*: **to — oneself** intitularse, darse el título de.

style sheet ['stail,ʃi:t] *n hoja en que se explican las normas de ortografía y sistema de referencias (etc) que han de seguirse en las colaboraciones a una revista*.

styling ['stailiŋ] *n* estilización *f*.

stylish ['stailiʃ] *adj* elegante; a la moda.

stylishly ['stailiʃli] *adv* elegantemente.

stylishness ['stailiʃnis] *n* elegancia *f*.

stylist ['stailist] *n* estilista *mf*.

stylistic [stai'listik] *adj* estilístico.

stylistics [stai'listiks] *n* estilística *f*.

stylized ['stailaizd] *adj* estilizado.

stylus ['stailəs] *n* (*pen*) estilo *m*; (*of gramophone*) aguja *f*.

stymie ['staimi] *vt see* **stimy**.

styptic ['stiptik] **1** *adj* estíptico. **2** *n* estíptico *m*.

suasion ['sweiʒən] *n* (*lit*) persuasión *f*.

suave [swɑːv] *adj* afable, cortés, fino; (*pej*) zalamero.

suavely ['swɑːvli] *adv* afablemente, cortésmente, con finura; con zalamería.

suavity ['swɑːviti] *n* afabilidad *f*, cortesía *f*, finura *f*; zalamería *f*.

sub [sʌb] *n abbr of* **subaltern**; **submarine**; **subordinate**; **subscription**; **substitute**.

sub . . . [sʌb] sub . . .

subalpine ['sʌb'ælpain] *adj* subalpino.

subaltern ['sʌbltən] *n* (*Mil*) alférez *m*.

subarctic ['sʌb'ɑːktik] *adj* subártico.

subcommittee ['sʌbkə,miti] *n* subcomisión *f*.

subconscious ['sʌb'kɔnʃəs] **1** *adj* subconsciente. **2** *n*: **the —** el subconsciente, la subconsciencia; **in one's —** en el subconsciente.

subconsciously ['sʌb'kɔnʃəsli] *adv* de modo subconsciente.

subcontinent ['sʌb'kɔntinənt] *n* subcontinente *m*.

subcontract ['sʌb'kɔntrækt] *n* subcontrato *m*.

subcontract [,sʌbkən'trækt] *vt* subcontratar.

subcontractor ['sʌbkən'træktə*] *n* subcontratista *mf*.

subcutaneous ['sʌbkju'teiniəs] *adj* subcutáneo.

subdivide ['sʌbdi'vaid] **1** *vt* subdividir. **2** *vi* subdividirse.

subdivision ['sʌbdi,viʒən] *n* subdivisión *f*.

subdue [səb'dju:] *vt* (*conquer*) sojuzgar, dominar, avasallar; (*diminish*) mitigar; *passions etc* dominar; *colour, voice etc* suavizar.

subdued [səb'dju:d] *adj emotion etc* templado, suave; *voice* bajo; *colour* suave, apagado; *light* tenue;

person (docile) sumiso, manso, *(depressed)* deprimido; **you were very — last night** anoche has mostrado poca animación, anoche estabas bastante callado; **he's very — these days** ahora es muy serio.

sub-edit ['sʌb'edit] *vt article* corregir, preparar para la prensa.

sub-editor ['sʌb'editə*] *n* redactor *m*.

subheading ['sʌb,hediŋ] *n* subtítulo *m*.

subhuman ['sʌb'hju:mən] *adj* infrahumano.

subject ['sʌbdʒikt] **1** *adj* (a) *people* subyugado, esclavizado.

(b) **to be — to** *(obedient to)* estar sujeto a; *(liable to)* estar propenso a, *(exposed to)* estar expuesto a; **to be — to natural laws** estar sujeto a las leyes naturales.

2 — to *as prep:* **— to anything he may say** esto depende de lo que diga él; **— to the approval of** sujeto a la aprobación de; **— to change without notice** sujeto a cambio sin previo aviso; **— to correction** bajo corrección.

3 *n* (a) *(Pol)* súbdito *m*, a *f*; **British — súbdito** *m* británico; **liberty of the — libertad** *f* del ciudadano; libertad *f* del individuo.

(b) *(Gram)* sujeto *m*.

(c) *(theme)* tema *m*, materia *f*; asunto *m*, cuestión *f*; *(School, Univ)* asignatura *f*; *(Art, Lit, Mus)* tema *m*; **on the — of . . .** a propósito de . . .; **it's a delicate —** es un asunto delicado; **to change the —** volver la hoja, cambiar de conversación; **to keep off a —** no aludir a un tema, no discutir una cuestión; **to raise the — of the war** *(in conversation)* introducir el tema de la guerra, empezar a hablar de la guerra; **this raises the whole — of money** esto plantea el problema general del dinero.

(d) *(Med etc)* caso *m*; **he's a nervous —** es un caso nervioso; **guinea pigs make excellent —s** los conejillos son materia excelente (para los experimentos etc).

subject [səb'dʒekt] *vt* (a) *(conquer)* sojuzgar, dominar.

(b) someter *(to* a); **to — someone to a test** poner a uno a prueba; **to — a book to criticism** someter un libro a la crítica; **to be —ed to inquiry** ser sometido a la investigación; **I will not be —ed to this questioning** no tolero esta interrogación; **she was —ed to much indignity** tuvo que aguantar muchas afrentas.

subjection [səb'dʒekʃən] *n* (a) sujeción *f*; sometimiento *m*; **to bring a people into —** subyugar a un pueblo; **to hold a people in —** tener subyugado a un pueblo; **to be in — to someone** estar sometido a uno; **to be in a state of complete —** estar completamente sumiso.

(b) *(act)* sometimiento *m*, el someter.

subjective [səb'dʒektiv] *adj* subjetivo.

subjectively [səb'dʒektivli] *adv* subjetivamente.

subjectivism [səb'dʒektivizəm] *n* subjetivismo *m*.

subjectivity [,sʌbdʒek'tiviti] *n* subjetividad *f*.

subject matter ['sʌbdʒikt,mætə*] *n* materia *f*; *(of letter etc)* contenido *m*.

subjoin ['sʌb'dʒɔin] *vt* adjuntar.

sub judice [sʌb'dju:disi] *adj:* **the matter is —** el asunto está en manos del tribunal (y por lo tanto hay que abstenerse de hacer comentarios sobre él); *(loosely)* el asunto está pendiente todavía, el asunto está siendo estudiado.

subjugate ['sʌbdʒugeit] *vt* subyugar.

subjugation [,sʌbdʒu'geiʃən] *n* subyugación *f*; **to live in —** vivir subyugado.

subjunctive [səb'dʒʌŋktiv] **1** *adj* subjuntivo. **2** *n* subjuntivo *m*.

sublease ['sʌb'li:s] *vt*, **sublet** ['sʌb'let] *(irr: see* let*)* *vt* realquilar, subarrendar.

sub-librarian ['sʌblai'breəriən] *n* subdirector *m* de biblioteca, subdirectora *f* de biblioteca.

sub-lieutenant ['sʌblef'tenənt] *n* *(Naut)* alférez *m* de fragata; *(Mil)* subteniente *m*.

sublimate ['sʌblimit] *n* *(Chem)* sublimado *m*.

sublimate ['sʌblimeit] *vt* *(all senses)* sublimar.

sublimation [,sʌbli'meiʃən] *n* sublimación *f*.

sublime [sə'blaim] **1** *adj* sublime; **the — lo** sublime. **2** *vt* sublimar.

sublimely [sə'blaimli] *adv* sublimemente; **— unaware of . . .** completamente inconsciente de . . ., demasiado exaltado para darse cuenta de . . .

subliminal [sʌb'liminl] *adj* subliminal.

sublimity [sə'blimiti] *n* sublimidad *f*.

submachine gun ['sʌbmə'ʃi:ngʌn] *n* pistola *f* ametralladora, metralleta *f*.

submarine [,sʌbmə'ri:n] **1** *adj* submarino. **2** *n* submarino *m*.

submarine chaser [,sʌbmə'ri:n,tʃeisə*] *n* cazasubmarinos *m*.

submariner [sʌb'mærinə*] *n* miembro *m* de la tripulación de un submarino, marinero *m* de submarino.

submerge [səb'mə:dʒ] **1** *vt* sumergir; *(flood)* inundar, cubrir. **2** *vi* sumergirse.

submerged [səb'mə:dʒd] *adj* sumergido.

submersible [səb'mə:səbl] *adj* sumergible.

submersion [səb'mə:ʃən] *n* sumersión *f*.

submicroscopic ['sʌb,maikrəs'kɔpik] *adj* submicroscópico.

submission [səb'miʃən] *n* sumisión *f*.

submissive [səb'misiv] *adj* sumiso.

submissively [səb'misivli] *adv* sumisamente.

submissiveness [səb'misivnis] *n* sumisión *f*.

submit [səb'mit] **1** *vt* someter; *evidence* presentar, aducir; *report* presentar, rendir; **to — that . . .** proponer que . . ., sugerir que . . .; **I — that . . .** me permito decir que . . .; **to — a play to the censor** someter una obra al censor; **to — a dispute to arbitration** someter una disputa a arbitraje.

2 *vi* someterse, rendirse; **to — to** someterse a; resignarse a, conformarse con; **he had to — to this indignity** tuvo que aguantar esta afrenta.

subnormal ['sʌb'nɔ:məl] *adj* anormal; *(educationally)* **— child** niño *m* retrasado.

subordinate [sə'bɔ:dnit] **1** *adj* subordinado *(also* Gram*)*; secundario, de importancia secundaria, menos importante; **A is — to B** A queda subordinado a B; **A no tiene tanta importancia como B; A depende de B.**

2 *n* subordinado *m*, a *f*.

subordinate [sə'bɔ:dineit] *vt* subordinar *(to* a).

subordination [sə,bɔ:di'neiʃən] *n* subordinación *f*.

suborn [sʌ'bɔ:n] *vt* sobornar.

subplot ['sʌb,plɔt] *n* intriga *f* secundaria.

subpoena [səb'pi:nə] **1** *n* comparendo *m*, citación *f*. **2** *vt* mandar comparecer, citar a uno para estrados.

sub rosa ['sʌb'rəuzə] **1** *adj* secreto, de confianza; **it's all very —** todo es de lo más secreto. **2** *adv* en secreto, en confianza.

subscribe [səb'skraib] **1** *vt money* suscribir, contribuir, dar; *signature* poner; *document etc* firmar, poner su firma en.

2 *vi* suscribir; **to — for something** contribuir dinero para algo; **to — to a paper** suscribirse a un periódico, abonarse a un periódico; **to — to an opinion** suscribir una opinión, aprobar una opinión.

subscriber [səb'skraibə*] *n* suscriptor *m*, ora *f*, abonado *m*, a *f*.

subscription [səb'skripʃən] *n* suscripción *f*, abono *m*; *(to club)* cuota *f*; **— rate** tarifa *f* de suscripción.

subsection ['sʌb,sekʃən] *n* subsección *f*, subdivisión *f*.

subsequent ['sʌbsikwənt] *adj* subsiguiente; posterior, ulterior; **— to** posterior a; **— to this** *(as prep)* después de esto, a raíz de esto.

subsequently ['sʌbsikwəntli] *adv* después, más tarde, con posterioridad.

subserve [səb'sə:v] *vt* ayudar, favorecer.

subservience [səb'sə:viəns] *n* subordinación *f (to* a); servilismo *m*.

subservient [səb'sə:viənt] *adj (secondary)* subordinado *(to* a); *(cringing)* servil.

subside [səb'said] *vi (water)* bajar; *(ground, pavement etc)* hundirse; *(foundations)* asentarse; *(wind)* amainar, hacerse menos violento; *(threat etc)* disminuir, alejarse; *(excitement etc)* calmarse; **to — into a chair** dejarse caer en una silla.

subsidence [səb'saidəns] *n* bajada *f*; hundimiento *m*, *(of pavement, road)* socavón *m*; asentamiento *m*; amaine *m*; disminución *f*; apaciguamiento *m*.

subsidiary [səb'sidiəri] **1** *adj* subsidiario; secundario; auxiliar; *(Fin)* afiliado, filial. **2** *n* *(Fin)* filial *f*, sucursal *f*.

subsidize ['sʌbsidaiz] *vt* subvencionar.

subsidy ['sʌbsidi] *n* subvención *f*, subsidio *m*; **state —** subvención *f* estatal; **export —** subsidio *m* de exportación; **agricultural subsidies** subvenciones *fpl* agrícolas.

subsist [səb'sist] *vi* subsistir; sustentarse *(on a food* con una comida).

subsistence [səb'sistəns] *n* subsistencia *f*; sustentación *f*; *(allowance)* dietas *fpl*.

subsoil ['sʌbsɔil] *n* subsuelo *m*.

subsonic ['sʌb'sɔnik] *adj* subsónico.

subspecies ['sʌb'spi:ʃiz] *n* subespecie *f*.

substance ['sʌbstəns] *n* sustancia *f*; esencia *f*, parte *f*, parte *f* esencial; **an argument of —** un argumento sólido; **man of —** hombre *m* acaudalado; **the — is good but the style poor** la materia es buena pero el estilo malo.

substandard ['sʌb'stændəd] *adj* inferior, inferior al nivel normal, no del todo satisfactorio.

substantial [səb'stænʃəl] adj sustancial, sustancioso; part, proportion importante; sum considerable; loss importante; build etc sólido, fuerte; person acomodado; acaudalado; **to be in — agreement** estar de acuerdo en sustancia.

substantially [səb'stænʃəli] adv sustancialmente; **— true** en gran parte verdadero; **— built** de construcción sólida; **it contributed — to our success** contribuyó materialmente a nuestro éxito.

substantiate [səb'stænʃieit] vt establecer, comprobar, justificar.

substantiation [səb‚stænʃi'eiʃən] n comprobación f, justificación f.

substantival [‚sʌbstən'taivəl] adj sustantivo.

substantive ['sʌbstəntiv] **1** adj sustantivo. **2** n sustantivo m.

substation ['sʌb‚steiʃən] n (Elec) subestación f.

substitute ['sʌbstitjuːt] **1** n (person) sustituto m, a f, suplente mf (for de); (thing) sustituto m, sucedáneo m; artículo m de reemplazo; **there is no — for petrol** la gasolina es insustituible.
2 adj sucedáneo; de reemplazo; person suplente. **3** vt sustituir (A for B B por A); reemplazar (A for B A por B).
4 vi: **to — for someone** suplir a uno, hacer las veces de uno.

substitution [‚sʌbsti'tjuːʃən] n sustitución f; reemplazo m.

substratum ['sʌb'strɑːtəm] n, pl **substrata** ['sʌb'strɑːtə] sustrato m.

substructure ['sʌb‚strʌktʃə*] n infraestructura f.

subsume [səb'sjuːm] vt subsumir.

subtenancy ['sʌb'tenənsi] n subarriendo m.

subtenant ['sʌb'tenənt] n subarrendador m, ora f.

subterfuge ['sʌbtəfjuːdʒ] n subterfugio m.

subterranean [‚sʌbtə'reiniən] adj subterráneo.

subtilize ['sʌtilaiz] vt sutilizar.

subtitle ['sʌb‚taitl] **1** n subtítulo m. **2** vt subtitular.

subtle ['sʌtl] adj sutil; fino, delicado; charm misterioso; perfume delicado, sutil, tenue; irony etc fino; (crafty) astuto.

subtlety ['sʌtlti] n sutileza f; finura f, delicadeza f; lo misterioso; astucia f.

subtly ['sʌtli] adv sutilmente; finamente, delicadamente; misteriosamente; astutamente.

subtract [səb'trækt] vt sustraer, restar; **to — 5 from 9** restar 5 a 9.

subtraction [səb'trækʃən] n sustracción f, resta f.

subtropical ['sʌb'trɒpikəl] adj subtropical.

suburb ['sʌbəːb] n barrio m, barrio m exterior; **new —** barrio m nuevo, ensanche m; **a London —** un barrio londinense, un distrito en las afueras de Londres; **the (outer) —s** los barrios exteriores, las afueras.

suburban [sə'bəːbən] adj suburbano; train de cercanías.

suburbanite [sə'bəːbənait] **1** adj surburbano. **2** n habitante mf de los barrios exteriores.

suburbia [sə'bəːbiə] n (freq pej) los barrios exteriores, las afueras; manera f de vivir de los barrios exteriores.

subvention [səb'venʃən] n subvención f.

subversion [səb'vəːʃən] n subversión f.

subversive [səb'vəːsiv] **1** adj subversivo. **2** n subversor m; elemento m subversivo, persona f de dudosa lealtad política.

subvert [sʌb'vəːt] vt subvertir, trastornar.

subway ['sʌbwei] n paso m subterráneo, paso m inferior; (US Rail) metro m.

sub-zero ['sʌb'ziərəu] adj: **in — temperatures** a una temperatura de varios grados bajo cero.

succeed [sək'siːd] vi **(a)** (be successful: of person) tener éxito, triunfar; (of plan etc) salir bien; **but he did not — (in this)** pero no tuvo éxito (con esto), pero no lo consiguió; **to — in life** triunfar en la vida; **to — in one's hopes** ver logradas sus esperanzas; **to — in one's plan** llevar a cabo su proyecto; **to — in doing something** lograr hacer algo, conseguir hacer algo.
(b) (follow) suceder; seguir; heredar; **who —s?** ¿quién hereda?; **to — to the crown** suceder a la corona, heredar la corona; **to — to the throne** subir al trono; **to — to an estate** heredar una finca; **to — someone in a post** suceder a uno en un puesto; **spring is —ed by summer** a la primavera le sigue el verano.

succeeding [sək'siːdiŋ] adj futuro; subsiguiente; sucesivo; **on 3 — Saturdays** tres sábados seguidos; **in the — chaos** en la confusión subsiguiente; **— generations will do better** las generaciones futuras harán mejor.

success [sək'ses] **1** n éxito m, buen éxito m; triunfo m; prosperidad f; **another — for our team** nuevo éxito m para nuestro equipo; **without —** sin éxito, sin resultado; **he was a great —** tuvo mucho éxito; **he was not a — as Segismundo** no estuvo bien en el papel de Segismundo; **the play was a — in New York** la obra obtuvo un éxito en Nueva York; **the new car is not a —** el nuevo coche no es satisfactorio; **the plan was a —** el proyecto salió muy bien; **she had no —** no tuvo éxito; **to make a — of something** tener éxito en algo; **to meet with —** tener éxito, prosperar.
2 attr: **— story** historia f de un triunfo.

successful [sək'sesful] adj person afortunado, feliz, que tiene éxito; attempt, plan etc logrado; business etc próspero; effort fructuoso; candidate elegido, afortunado; **to be — (person)** tener éxito, triunfar; (business etc) prosperar; **to be entirely —** tener un éxito completo; **to be — in doing something** lograr hacer algo; **he was not — last time** no lo logró la última vez.

successfully [sək'sesfəli] adv con éxito; afortunadamente; prósperamente.

succession [sək'seʃən] n **(a)** (series) sucesión f, serie f; **in —** sucesivamente; **4 times in —** 4 veces seguidas; **in quick —** en rápida sucesión; rápidamente uno tras otro; **after a — of disasters** después de una serie de catástrofes.
(b) (to post etc) sucesión f (to a); **in — to someone** sucediendo a uno; como sucesor de uno; **Princess Rebecca is 7th in — to the throne** la princesa Rebeca ocupa el 7º puesto en la línea de sucesión a la corona.
(c) (descendants) descendencia f.

successive [sək'sesiv] adj sucesivo; consecutivo; **4 — days** 4 días seguidos.

successively [sək'sesivli] adv sucesivamente.

successor [sək'sesə*] n sucesor m, ora f.

succinct [sək'siŋkt] adj sucinto.

succinctly [sək'siŋktli] adv sucintamente.

succour ['sʌkə*] **1** n socorro m. **2** vt socorrer.

succulence ['sʌkjuləns] n suculencia f.

succulent ['sʌkjulənt] adj suculento.

succumb [sə'kʌm] vi sucumbir (to a).

such [sʌtʃ] **1** adj **(a)** tal; semejante; parecido; tanto; **— a book** tal libro; **— books** tales libros; **in — cases** en tales casos, en semejantes casos; **we had — a case last year** tuvimos un caso parecido el año pasado; **on just — a day in June** un día exactamente parecido de junio; **no — thing!** ¡no hay tal!, ¡ni hablar!; **there's no — thing** no hay tal cosa; **did you ever see — a thing?** ¿se vio jamás tal cosa?; **some — idea** alguna idea de este tipo, alguna idea por el estilo; **— a plan is most unwise** un proyecto así es poco aconsejable, un proyecto de ese tipo no es aconsejable; **no — book exists** no existe tal libro; **X was — a one** X era así, el nuevo coche no es este tipo; **— is life** así es la vida; **— is not the case** esto no es así; **I am in — a hurry** tengo tanta prisa, estoy tan de prisa; **— an honour!** ¡tanto honor!; **it caused — trouble that...** dio lugar a tantos disgustos que...
(b) **— as** tal como; **— a man as Ganivet** un hombre tal como Ganivet; **— writers as Quevedo** los escritores tales como Quevedo; **there are no — things as giants** los gigantes no existen; **it is not — as to cause worry** no es tal que haya de causar inquietud; **it made — a stir as had not been known before** tuvo una repercusión como no se había conocido hasta entonces.
2 adv tan; **— good food** comida f tan buena; **— a clever girl** muchacha f tan inteligente; **it's — a long time ago** hace tanto tiempo ya.
3 pron los que, las que; **we took — as we wanted** tomamos los que queríamos; **I will send you — as I receive** te mandaré los que reciba; **and as — he was promoted** y como tal le ascendieron; **we know of no — no** tenemos noticias de ninguno así; **there are no — trees as —** no hay árboles propiamente dichos, no hay árboles que digamos, no hay árboles árboles; **rabbits and hares and —** conejos mpl y liebres y tal; **may all — perish!** ¡mueran cuantos hay como él!; **this is my car — as it is** éste es mi coche con todas sus imperfecciones.

such-and-such ['sʌtʃənsʌtʃ] adj: **she lives in — a street** vive en tal o cual calle; **on — a day in May** a tantos de mayo.

suchlike ['sʌtʃlaik] **1** adj tal, semejante; **sheep and — animals** ovejas fpl y otros tales animales, ovejas fpl y otros animales de la misma clase.
2 pron: **thieves and —** ladrones mpl y gente de esa calaña, ladrones mpl y otras tales personas; **buses and lorries and —** autobuses mpl y camiones y tal.

suck [sʌk] **1** n chupada f; sorbo m; (at breast) mamada f; **to give —** (to) amamantar.

2 vt chupar; sorber; breast mamar; **to — one's fingers** chuparse los dedos; **to — down** tragar; **to — in** liquid sorber; air, dust etc aspirar; **to — up** aspirar; absorber.

3 vi chupar; mamar; **to — at something** chupar algo; **to — up to someone** (fam) dar coba a uno, hacer la pelotilla a uno.

sucker ['sʌkə*] n (a) (Zool) ventosa f; (Bot) serpollo m, mamón m; (sl) dulce m, bombón m.

(b) (esp US sl) primo m, bobo m; **some —** algún pobre hombre; **to be a — for something** no poder resistir algo; sucumbir pronto a los encantos de algo.

sucking-pig ['sʌkiŋpig] n lechoncillo m.

suckle ['sʌkl] **1** vt amamantar, dar el pecho a; (fig) criar.

2 vi lactar.

suckling ['sʌkliŋ] n mamón m, ona f.

sucrose ['su:krəuz] n sucrosa f.

suction ['sʌkʃən] n succión f.

suction pump ['sʌkʃənpʌmp] n bomba f aspirante, bomba f de succión.

Sudan [su'dɑ:n] Sudán m.

Sudanese [,su:də'ni:z] **1** adj sudanés. **2** n sudanés m, esa f.

sudden ['sʌdn] adj (rapid, hurried) repentino, súbito; (unexpected) imprevisto, impensado; change of temperature, curve etc brusco; **all of a —** de repente.

suddenly ['sʌdnli] adv de repente, de pronto; inesperadamente; bruscamente.

suddenness ['sʌdnnis] n lo repentino; lo imprevisto; brusquedad f.

suds [sʌdz] npl jabonaduras fpl.

sue [su:] **1** vti: **to — someone** demandar a uno (for something por algo); **to — for damages** demandar a uno por daños y perjuicios; **to — for divorce** presentar demanda de divorcio, solicitar el divorcio; **to be —d for libel** ser demandado por calumnia.

2 vi: **to — for peace** pedir la paz.

suède [sweid] n suecia f, ante m; **— shoes** zapatos mpl de ante; **— gloves** guantes mpl de ante.

suet [suit] n sebo m.

Suetonius [swi:'təunias] m Suetonio.

suety ['suiti] adj seboso.

Suez Canal ['su:izkə'næl] Canal m de Suez.

suffer ['sʌfə*] **1** vt (a) (painfully) sufrir, padecer; (bear) aguantar, sufrir; (undergo) sufrir, experimentar; **I can't — it a moment longer** no lo aguanto un momento más; **it has —ed a sharp decline** ha experimentado un brusco descenso; **to — a defeat** sufrir una derrota; **to — death** morir, ser muerto.

(b) (allow) permitir, tolerar; **to — someone to do something** permitir a uno hacer algo; autorizar a uno para que haga algo; **to — something to be done** permitir que se haga algo.

2 vi (a) sufrir, padecer; **did you — much?** ¿sufriste mucho?; **how I —ed!** ¡lo que sufrí!; **the army —ed badly** el ejército tuvo pérdidas importantes; **the town —ed in the raids** la ciudad sufrió grandes daños en los bombardeos; **we will see that you do not — by the changes** aseguraremos que Vd no pierda nada a consecuencia de estos cambios.

(b) **to — for one's sins** sufrir las consecuencias de sus pecados; **you will — for it** lo pagarás después.

(c) **to — from** sufrir, padecer (de), estar afligido por; (fig) adolecer de; ser la víctima de; **to — from boils** tener diviesos; **to — from rheumatism** padecer reumatismo; **to — from the effects of something** resentirse de algo, estar resentido de algo; **she —s from her environment** es la víctima del medio ambiente; **the house is —ing from neglect** la casa padece abandono; **your style —s from overelaboration** su estilo adolece de una excesiva complicación.

sufferance ['sʌfərəns] n tolerancia f; **on —** por tolerancia.

sufferer ['sʌfərə*] n (Med) enfermo m, a f (from de); víctima f; **—s from diabetes** los enfermos de diabetes, los diabéticos; **the —s from the earthquake** las víctimas del terremoto; **fellow —** persona f que tiene la misma enfermedad que uno; compañero m en la desgracia.

suffering ['sʌfəriŋ] **1** adj que sufre; (Med) doliente, enfermo.

2 n sufrimiento m, padecimiento m; (grief etc) dolor m; **after months of —** después de sufrir durante varios meses; **the —s of the soldiers** los padecimientos de los soldados.

suffice [sə'fais] **1** vt satisfacer; ser bastante para. **2** vi bastar, ser suficiente.

sufficiency [sə'fiʃənsi] n (state) suficiencia f; (quantity) cantidad f suficiente; **to have a —** estar acomodado.

sufficient [sə'fiʃənt] adj suficiente, bastante; **to be —** ser suficiente, bastar.

sufficiently [sə'fiʃəntli] adv suficientemente, bastante; **— good** bastante bueno.

suffix ['sʌfiks] **1** n sufijo m. **2** vt añadir como sufijo (to a).

suffocate ['sʌfəkeit] **1** vt ahogar, asfixiar. **2** vi ahogarse, asfixiarse, quedar asfixiado.

suffocating ['sʌfəkeitiŋ] adj sofocante, asfixiante; **— heat** calor m sofocante.

suffocation [,sʌfə'keiʃən] n sofocación f, asfixia f.

suffragan ['sʌfrəgən] **1** adj sufragáneo. **2** n obispo m sufragáneo.

suffrage ['sʌfridʒ] n (a) sufragio m; derecho m de votar; **universal —** sufragio m universal; **to get the —** obtener el derecho de votar.

(b) voto m; aprobación f.

suffragette [,sʌfrə'dʒet] n sufragista f.

suffuse [sə'fju:z] vt bañar, cubrir (with de); difundirse por; **—d with light** inundado de luz, bañado de luz; **eyes —d with tears** ojos mpl bañados de lágrimas.

suffusion [sə'fju:ʒən] n difusión f.

sugar ['ʃugə*] **1** n azúcar m and f; **brown —** azúcar m negro; **cane —** azúcar m de caña; see castor —, lump —.

2 vt azucarar; echar azúcar a, añadir azúcar a.

sugar basin ['ʃugə,beisn] n azucarero m.

sugar beet ['ʃugəbi:t] n remolacha f azucarera.

sugar bowl ['ʃugəbəul] n azucarero m.

sugar candy ['ʃugə,kændi] n azúcar m candi.

sugar cane ['ʃugəkein] n caña f de azúcar.

sugar-coat ['ʃugəkəut] vt (Cook) azucarar, poner una capa de azúcar a.

sugar daddy ['ʃugə,dædi] n (US fam) viejo m adinerado amante de una joven, protector m (de una joven).

sugar loaf ['ʃugələuf] n pan m de azúcar.

sugarplum ['ʃugəplʌm] n confite m.

sugar plantation ['ʃugəplæn,teiʃən] n plantación f de caña de azúcar.

sugar refinery ['ʃugəri,fainəri] n refinería f de azúcar.

sugar tongs ['ʃugətɔŋz] npl tenacillas fpl para azúcar.

sugary ['ʃugəri] adj azucarado; (fig) style etc meloso, almibarado; (sentimental) sensiblero, sentimental; romántico.

suggest [sə'dʒest] **1** vt sugerir; (point to) indicar; (advise) aconsejar, indicar; (hint) insinuar; (evoke) evocar, hacer pensar en; **to — that . . .** (of person) sugerir que . . ., proponer que . . .; **this —s that . . .** esto hace pensar que . . ., esto lleva a pensar que . . .; **I — to you that . . .** (in law speeches) ¿no es cierto que . . .?; **it doesn't exactly — a careful man** no parece indicar un hombre prudente; **the coins — a Roman building** las monedas indican un edificio romano; **the symptoms — an operation** los síntomas aconsejan una operación; **prudence —s a retreat** la prudencia nos aconseja retirarnos; **what are you —ing?** ¿qué es lo que insinúa Vd?, ¿qué es lo que pretende Vd?

2 vr: **an idea —s itself** se me ocurre una idea; **nothing —s itself** no se me ocurre nada.

suggestible [sə'dʒestibl] adj (a) person sugestionable.

(b) thing sugerible, que se puede sugerir.

suggestion [sə'dʒestʃən] n (a) sugerencia f; indicación f; insinuación f; **if I may make** (or offer) **a —** si se me permite proponer algo; **my — is that . . .** yo propongo que . . .; **that is an immoral —** ésa es una idea inmoral; **following your — . . .** siguiendo sus indicaciones . . .

(b) (hypnotic) sugestión f.

(c) (trace) sombra f, traza f; **with just a — of garlic** con un poquitín de ajo; **with a — of irony in his voice** con un punto de ironía en la voz.

suggestive [sə'dʒestiv] adj sugestivo; (pej) indecente, sicalíptico; **— of** que evoca, que hace pensar en; que trasciende a.

suggestively [sə'dʒestivli] adj (pej) indecentemente.

suggestiveness [sə'dʒestivnis] n (pej) indecencia f, sicalipsis f.

suicidal [,sui'saidl] adj suicida; **to have a — tendency** tener tendencia al suicidio; **I feel — this morning** esta mañana estoy por desesperarme; **he drives in a — way** es un suicida conduciendo; **it would be —** sería peligrosísimo.

suicide ['suisaid] n (act) suicidio m; (person) suicida mf; **to commit —** suicidarse; **it would be — to say so** sería peligrosísimo decirlo.

suit [suːt] **1** n **(a)** traje m (also — of clothes); — of armour armadura f; ready-made — traje m hecho; two-piece — (woman's) conjunto m.

(b) (Law) pleito m, litigio m, proceso m; to bring a — poner pleito; to bring a — against someone entablar demanda contra uno (for something por algo).

(c) (request) petición f; at the — of a petición de.

(d) (in marriage) petición f de mano, oferta f de matrimonio; to press one's — hacer una oferta de matrimonio.

(e) (Cards) palo m; long —, strong — palo m largo; to have nothing in that — tener fallo a ese palo; to follow — servir del palo, (fig) hacer lo mismo.

2 vt **(a)** (adapt) adaptar, ajustar, acomodar (to a); to — one's style to one's audience adaptar su estilo al público; —ing the action to the word uniendo la acción a la palabra; the coat and hat are well —ed el abrigo y el sombrero van bien juntos; they are well —ed to each other están hechos el uno para el otro; he is not —ed for (or to be) a doctor no es apto para ser médico.

(b) (be suitable: of clothes) sentar a, ir bien a, caer bien a; (in general) convenir; gustar; the coat —s you el abrigo te sienta, el abrigo te va bien; the climate does not — me el clima no me sienta bien; the job —s me nicely el puesto me conviene perfectamente; does this — you? ¿te gusta esto?; come when it —s you ven cuando quieras, ven cuando te convenga; I know what —s me best sé lo que me conviene; I shall do it when it —s me lo haré cuando me dé la gana.

3 vr: he —s himself hace lo que le da la gana, hace lo que quiere; — yourself! ¡haz lo que quieras!, ¡como quieras!

suitability [ˌsuːtə'biliti] n conveniencia f; idoneidad f (for para).

suitable ['suːtəbl] adj conveniente, apropiado; adecuado, idóneo; indicado; the most — man for the job el hombre más indicado para el puesto; is this hat —? ¿me conviene este sombrero?; the film is not — for children la película no es apta para menores; we didn't find anything at all — no encontramos nada a propósito, no encontramos nada que nos conviniera; Tuesday is the most — day el martes no nos conviene más.

suitably ['suːtəbli] adv convenientemente; apropiadamente; — dressed for tennis convenientemente vestido para el tenis.

suitcase ['suːtkeis] n maleta f.

suite [swiːt] n (of retainers) séquito m, comitiva f; (of furniture) juego m, mobiliario m; (rooms) serie f de habitaciones, grupo m de habitaciones; (Mus) suite f; bedroom — (juego m de muebles para) alcoba f; dining-room — comedor m.

suited ['suːtid] adj: see suit 2 (a).

suiting ['suːtiŋ] n (Comm) tela f para trajes.

suitor ['suːtə*] n pretendiente m; (Law) demandante mf.

sulfa ['sʌlfə] etc: see sulpha etc.

sulk [sʌlk] vi estar mohino, estar amohinado, estar de mal humor.

sulkily ['sʌlkili] adv con mohino; answer etc con mal humor, de mala gana.

sulkiness ['sʌlkinis] n mohina f, murria f, mal humor m.

sulks [sʌlks] npl mohina f, murria f, mal humor m; to have the — estar mohino, estar de mal humor; to get the — amohinarse.

sulky ['sʌlki] adj mohino; malhumorado; resentido; to be — estar mohino, estar de mal humor.

sullen ['sʌlən] adj hosco, malhumorado; resentido; taciturno; countryside triste; sky plomizo.

sullenly ['sʌlənli] adv hoscamente; answer con mal humor; look con resentimiento.

sullenness ['sʌlənnis] n hosquedad f, mal humor m; resentimiento m; taciturnidad f.

sully ['sʌli] vt (lit) manchar.

sulpha drugs ['sʌlfə'drʌgz] npl fármacos mpl sulfa.

sulphate ['sʌlfeit] n sulfato m; copper — sulfato m de cobre.

sulphide ['sʌlfaid] n sulfuro m.

sulphonamide [sʌl'fɒnəmaid] n sulfonamida f.

sulphur ['sʌlfə*] n azufre m.

sulphureous [sʌl'fjuəriəs] adj sulfúrico.

sulphuric [sʌl'fjuərik] adj sulfúrico; — acid ácido m sulfúrico.

sulphurous ['sʌlfərəs] adj sulfuroso, sulfúreo.

sultan ['sʌltən] n sultán m.

sultana [sʌl'taːnə] (person) sultana f; (fruit) pasa f de Esmirna.

sultanate ['sʌltənit] n sultanato m.

sultriness ['sʌltrinis] n bochorno m; calor m sofocante.

sultry ['sʌltri] adj weather bochornoso; heat, atmosphere sofocante; (fig) apasionado; seductor, provocativo.

sum [sʌm] **1** n (total) suma f, total m; (quantity) suma f, cantidad f; (Math) problema m de aritmética; the — total of my ambitions is ... la meta de mis ambiciones es ..., lo único que ambiciono es ...; lump — suma f global; in — en suma, en resumen; to do —s hacer un cálculo mental; I was very bad at —s era muy malo en aritmética.

2 vt: to — up (tot up) sumar; (review) resumir; (evaluate rapidly) tomar las medidas a, evaluar (rápidamente), justipreciar; to — up an argument resumir un argumento, recapitular un argumento; to — up a debate recapitular los argumentos empleados en un debate; she —med me up at a glance me tomó las medidas con una sola mirada; he —med up the situation quickly se dio cuenta rápidamente de la situación.

3 vi: to — up recapitular, hacer un resumen; to — up ... en resumen ...

sumac(h) ['suːmæk] n zumaque m.

summarily ['sʌmərili] adv sumariamente.

summarize ['sʌməraiz] vt resumir.

summary ['sʌməri] **1** adj sumario. **2** n resumen m, sumario m.

summation [sʌ'meiʃən] n (act) adición f; recapitulación f, resumen m; (total) suma f, total m.

summer ['sʌmə*] **1** n verano m, estío m; Indian —, St Martin's — veranillo m de San Martín; a girl of 17 —s una joven de 17 abriles; a —'s day un día de verano; to spend the — veranear, pasar el verano.

2 attr day, clothing, residence de verano; season veraniego; resort de veraneo; weather, heat estival.

3 vi veranear, pasar el verano.

summerhouse ['sʌməhaus] n, pl —houses [ˌhauziz] cenador m, glorieta f.

summertime ['sʌmətaim] n (season) verano m; (hour) hora f de verano.

summery ['sʌməri] adj veraniego, estival.

summing-up ['sʌmiŋ'ʌp] n resumen m, recapitulación f.

summit ['sʌmit] **1** n cima f, cumbre f (also fig). **2** attr: — conference conferencia f cumbre, conferencia f en la cumbre.

summon ['sʌmən] vt servant etc llamar; meeting convocar; aid pedir, requerir; (Law) citar, emplazar; to — up courage cobrar; memory evocar; to be —ed to someone's presence ser llamado a la presencia de uno; they —ed me to advise them me llamaron para que les diera consejos; to — a town to surrender hacer una llamada a una ciudad para que se rinda.

summons ['sʌmənz] **1** n llamamiento m, llamada f; requerimiento m; (Law) citación f; to serve a — on someone entregar una citación a uno; to take out a — against someone entablar demanda contra uno, citar a uno para estrados.

2 vt citar, emplazar.

sump [sʌmp] n (Aut etc) cárter m, colector m de aceite; (Min etc) sumidero m; (fig) letrina f.

sumptuary ['sʌmptjuəri] adj suntuario.

sumptuous ['sʌmptjuəs] adj suntuoso.

sumptuously ['sʌmptjuəsli] adv suntuosamente.

sumptuousness ['sʌmptjuəsnis] n suntuosidad f.

sun [sʌn] **1** n sol m; in the July — bajo el sol de julio; to be out in the — estar al sol; the milk stood in the — all day la leche estuvo al sol todo el día; they have everything under the — tienen de todo como en botica; there's no reason under the — no hay razón alguna; to bask in the — tomar el sol, estar tumbado al sol; the sun is shining hace sol, el sol brilla.

2 attr de sol; solar.

3 vt asolear.

4 vr: to — oneself asolearse, tomar el sol.

sunbaked ['sʌnbeikt] adj endurecido al sol.

sunbath ['sʌnbaːθ] n, pl —baths [baːðz] baño m de sol.

sunbathe ['sʌnbeið] **1** n baño m de sol. **2** vi tomar el sol.

sunbather ['sʌnbeiðə*] n persona f que toma el sol.

sunbathing ['sʌnbeiðiŋ] n baños mpl de sol.

sunbeam ['sʌnbiːm] n rayo m de sol.

sunblind ['sʌnblaind] n toldo m, store m.

sunburn ['sʌnbəːn] n (tan) bronceado m; (painful) quemadura f del sol.

sunburnt ['sʌnbəːnt] adj (tanned) tostado por el sol, bronceado; (painfully) quemado por el sol; to get — broncearse; sufrir quemaduras del sol.

sunburst ['sʌnbəːst] n (US) resplandor m repentino del sol (entre las nubes).
sun deck ['sʌndek] n cubierta f de sol.
sundae ['sʌndei] n helado con frutas, nueces etc.
Sunday ['sʌndi] 1 n domingo m; **Easter** — Domingo m de Resurrección; **Palm** — Domingo m de Ramos. 2 attr paper, school, sermon etc dominical, de domingo; see best.
sunder ['sʌndə*] vt (lit) romper, dividir, hender; separar.
sundew ['sʌndjuː] n rocío m de sol, rosolí m.
sundial ['sʌndaiəl] n reloj m de sol.
sundown ['sʌndaun] n puesta f del sol; anochecer m; **at** — al anochecer; **before** — antes del anochecer.
sundowner ['sʌndaunə*] n (fam) trago de licor que se toma al anochecer.
sun-dried ['sʌndraid] adj secado al sol.
sundry ['sʌndri] 1 adj varios, diversos; **all and** — todos y cada uno. 2 **sundries** npl (Comm) géneros mpl diversos.
sunflower ['sʌnˌflauə*] n girasol m.
sung [sʌŋ] ptp of sing.
sunglasses ['sʌnˌglɑːsiz] npl gafas fpl de sol.
sun-god ['sʌngɔd] n dios m del sol, divinidad f solar.
sun hat ['sʌnhæt] n sombrero m ancho.
sunk [sʌŋk] ptp of sink.
sunken ['sʌŋkən] adj hundido.
sun lamp ['sʌnlæmp] n lámpara f solar ultravioleta.
sunless ['sʌnlis] adj sin sol.
sunlight ['sʌnlait] n sol m, luz f del sol, luz f solar; **in the** — al sol; **the** — **is strong** el sol es fuerte; **hours of** — (Meteorol) horas fpl de insolación.
sunlit ['sʌnlit] adj iluminado por el sol.
sun lounge ['sʌnlaundʒ] n solana f.
sunny ['sʌni] adj **(a)** place, room etc soleado; expuesto al sol; bañado de sol, iluminado por el sol; day de sol; **it is** — hace sol; **June is a** — **month** junio tiene mucho sol; **Málaga is sunnier than Manchester** Málaga tiene más sol que Manchester.
(b) (fig) face risueño; smile, disposition alegre; **to be on the** — **side of 40** tener menos de 40 años.
sunray ['sʌnrei] attr: — **lamp** lámpara f solar ultravioleta; — **treatment** helioterapia f, tratamiento m con lámpara solar ultravioleta.
sunrise ['sʌnraiz] n salida f del sol; **from** — **to sunset** de sol a sol.
sunset ['sʌnset] n puesta f del sol, ocaso m.
sunshade ['sʌnʃeid] n (portable) quitasol m; (over table) sombrilla f; (awning) toldo m.
sunshine ['sʌnʃain] n sol m, luz f del sol; **in the** — al sol; **hours of** — (Meteorol) horas fpl de insolación; **daily average** — insolación f media diaria.
sunspot ['sʌnspɔt] n mancha f solar.
sunstroke ['sʌnstrəuk] n insolación f; **to have** — sufrir una insolación.
sunsuit ['sʌnsuːt] n traje m de playa.
suntrap ['sʌntræp] n solana f, lugar m muy soleado.
sunup ['sʌnʌp] n salida f del sol.
sup [sʌp] 1 vt (also to — up) sorber, beber a sorbos. 2 vi cenar; **to** — **off something, to** — **on something** cenar algo.
super ['suːpə*] 1 adj (fam) estupendo, bárbaro; **how** — ! ¡qué bien!; **the new car is** — el nuevo coche es estupendo; **we had a** — **time** lo pasamos la mar de bien.
2 n (abbr: Theat, Cine) figurante m, a f; comparsa mf; (superintendent: Tech) superintendente m, (of police) subjefe m.
super... ['suːpə*] super..., sobre...; eg **super-salesman** supervendedor m.
superabound [ˌsuːpərə'baund] vi sobreabundar (in, with en).
superabundance [ˌsuːpərə'bʌndəns] n sobreabundancia f, superabundancia f.
superabundant [ˌsuːpərə'bʌndənt] adj sobreabundante, superabundante.
superannuate [ˌsuːpə'rænjueit] vt jubilar.
superannuated [ˌsuːpə'rænjueitid] adj jubilado; (fig) anticuado.
superannuation [ˌsuːpəˌrænjuː'eiʃən] n jubilación f; — **contribution** cuota f de jubilación.
superb [suː'pəːb] adj magnífico, espléndido.
superbly [suː'pəːbli] adv magníficamente; **a** — **painted picture** un cuadro de la mayor excelencia técnica; **a** — **fit man** un hombre en magnífico estado físico.
supercargo ['suːpəˌkɑːgəu] n sobrecargo m.
supercharged ['suːpətʃɑːdʒd] adj sobrealimentado.
supercharger ['suːpətʃɑːdʒə*] n sobrealimentador m.
supercilious [ˌsuːpə'siliəs] adj desdeñoso, arrogante; suficiente.

superciliously [ˌsuːpə'siliəsli] adv desdeñosamente, con desdén; con aire de suficiencia.
superciliousness [ˌsuːpə'siliəsnis] n desdén m, arrogancia f; suficiencia f.
supererogation [ˌsuːpərˌerə'geiʃən] n supererogación f.
superficial [ˌsuːpə'fiʃəl] adj superficial.
superficiality [ˌsuːpəˌfiʃi'æliti] n superficialidad f.
superficially [ˌsuːpə'fiʃəli] adv superficialmente; en la superficie; — **this may be true** a primera vista esto puede ser verdad.
superfine ['suːpəfain] adj (Comm) extrafino.
superfluity [ˌsuːpə'fluiti] n superfluidad f.
superfluous [suː'pəːfluəs] adj superfluo; sobrante, que sobra, que está de más.
superfluously [suː'pəːfluəsli] adv superfluamente; **he added** — añadió fuera de propósito.
superhighway ['suːpə'haiwei] n supercarretera f, autopista f.
superhuman [ˌsuːpə'hjuːmən] adj sobrehumano.
superimpose ['suːpərim'pəuz] vt sobreponer (on en).
superinduce ['suːpərin'djuːs] vt sobreañadir.
superintend [ˌsuːpərin'tend] vt vigilar; supervisar, dirigir.
superintendence [ˌsuːpərin'tendəns] n superintendencia f; supervisión f, dirección f.
superintendent [ˌsuːpərin'tendənt] n superintendente mf; inspector m; supervisor m; (eg in swimming pool) vigilante; — **of police** subjefe m de policía.
superior [suː'piəriə*] 1 adj superior (to a); (smug) desdeñoso; satisfecho, suficiente; **she thinks herself very** — se da aires de suficiencia; **he said in that** — **tone** dijo en ese tono suficiente.
2 n superior m; (Eccl) superior m, ora f; **Mother S** — (madre f) superiora f.
superiority [suːˌpiəri'ɔriti] n superioridad f (to a); desdén m; suficiencia f.
superlative [suː'pəːlətiv] 1 adj superlativo (also Gram), extremo. 2 n superlativo m.
superlatively [suː'pəːlətivli] adv en sumo grado, extremadamente; — **fit** en óptimo estado físico.
superman ['suːpəmæn] n, pl — **men** [men] superhombre m.
supermarket ['suːpəˌmɑːkit] n supermercado m.
supernatural [ˌsuːpə'nætʃərəl] adj sobrenatural; **the** — lo sobrenatural.
supernumerary [ˌsuːpə'njuːmərəri] 1 adj supernumerario. 2 n supernumerario m, a f; (Theat, Cine) figurante m, a f, comparsa mf.
superphosphate [ˌsuːpə'fɔsfeit] n superfosfato m.
superpose ['suːpəpəuz] vt sobreponer, superponer.
superposition ['suːpəpə'ziʃən] n superposición f.
superpower ['suːpəˌpauə*] n superpotencia f.
superscription ['suːpə'skripʃən] n sobrescrito m.
supersede [ˌsuːpə'siːd] vt reemplazar, sustituir; suplantar.
supersensitive ['suːpə'sensitiv] adj extremadamente sensible (to a).
supersonic ['suːpə'sɔnik] adj supersónico.
supersonically ['suːpə'sɔnikəli] adv fly etc a velocidad superior a la del sonido.
superstition [ˌsuːpə'stiʃən] n superstición f.
superstitious [ˌsuːpə'stiʃəs] adj supersticioso.
superstitiously [ˌsuːpə'stiʃəsli] adv supersticiosamente.
superstructure ['suːpəˌstrʌktʃə*] n superestructura f.
supertanker ['suːpəˌtæŋkə*] n superpetrolero m.
supertax ['suːpətæks] n impuesto m adicional (sobre los ingresos elevados de particulares).
supervene [ˌsuːpə'viːn] vi sobrevenir.
supervise ['suːpəvaiz] vt supervisar.
supervision [ˌsuːpə'viʒən] n supervisión f.
supervisor ['suːpəvaizə*] n supervisor m.
supervisory ['suːpəvaizəri] adj: **in a** — **post** en un cargo de supervisor; **in his** — **capacity** en su función de supervisor.
supine ['suːpain] 1 adj supino; (fig) flojo, sin carácter, débil. 2 n (Gram) supino m.
supper ['sʌpə*] n cena f; **the Last S** — la Última Cena; **to stay to** — quedarse a cenar; **to have** — cenar.
suppertime ['sʌpətaim] n hora f de cenar.
supplant [sə'plɑːnt] vt suplantar.
supple ['sʌpl] adj flexible.
supplement ['sʌplimənt] n suplemento m; apéndice m.
supplement [sʌpli'ment] vt suplir, complementar; **to** — **one's income by writing** aumentar sus ingresos escribiendo artículos (etc).
supplementary [ˌsʌpli'mentəri] adj suplementario; adicional; question (Parl) secundario.
suppleness ['sʌplnis] n flexibilidad f.

suppliant ['sʌpliənt] **1** *adj* suplicante. **2** *n* suplicante *mf*.

supplicant ['sʌplikənt] *n* suplicante *mf*.

supplicate ['sʌplikeit] *vti* suplicar.

supplication [,sʌpli'keiʃən] *n* súplica *f*.

supplier [sə'plaiə*] *n* suministrador *m*, ora *f*; (*Comm*) proveedor *m*, ora *f*; distribuidor *m*, ora *f*; **from your usual —** de su proveedor habitual.

supply [sə'plai] **1** *n* **(a)** suministro *m*, provisión *f*, abastecimiento *m*; (*stock*: *Comm*) surtido *m*, existencias *fpl*; **electricity —** suministro *m* de electricidad; **the — of fuel to the engine** el suministro de combustible al motor; **— and demand** oferta *f* y demanda; **new cars are in short —** hay pocos coches nuevos, hay escasez de coches nuevos; **we need a fresh — of something** hace falta proveernos de algo; **to lay in a — of** proveerse de, hacer provisión de.

(b) supplies (*food*) provisiones *fpl*, víveres *mpl*; (*Mil*) pertrechos *mpl*; **electrical supplies** artículos *mpl* eléctricos; **office supplies** material *m* para oficina; **supplies are running low** escasean las provisiones; se están agotando las existencias.

(c) (*Parl*) provisión *f* financiera; **Committee on S—** Comisión *f* del Presupuesto; **Ministry of S—** Ministerio *m* de Aprovisionamientos; **to vote supplies** votar créditos.

2 *vt material etc* suministrar, facilitar, proporcionar; (*Comm*) surtir; *army, city etc* aprovisionar; *want* suplir; **the tradesmen who — us** nuestros proveedores; **can you — this spare part?** ¿pueden facilitarme este repuesto?; **she supplied the vital clue** ella nos dio la pista esencial; **to — someone with something** (*of supplies*) abastecer a uno de algo, proveer a uno de algo; **he supplied us with some facts** nos facilitó (*or* proporcionó) varios datos; **this supplied me with the chance** esto me brindó la oportunidad; **we are not supplied with a radio** no estamos provistos de radio.

supply ship [sə'plaiʃip] *n* buque *m* de abastecimiento.

supply teacher [sə'plai'tiːtʃə*] *n* maestro *m* suplente, maestra *f* suplente.

support [sə'pɔːt] **1** *n* **(a)** (*Tech*) soporte *m*, apoyo *m*; pilar *m*.

(b) (*fig*) apoyo *m*; (*person*) sostén *m*; **moral —** apoyo *m* moral; **financial —** ayuda *f* económica; **in — of** en apoyo de; **documents in — of an allegation** documentos *mpl* que confirman una alegación; **to speak in — of a candidate** apoyar la candidatura de uno; **I will give you every —** le apoyaré todo lo que pueda; **the proposal got no —** la propuesta no recibió apoyo alguno; **to lean on someone for —** apoyarse en uno; **they depend on him for financial —** dependen de él para mantenerse, reciben ayuda económica de él; **our — comes from the workers** nos apoyan los obreros, los obreros son partidarios nuestros; **liberal — got him elected** los votos de los liberales aseguraron su elección.

2 *vt* **(a)** (*Tech*) apoyar, sostener; **it is —ed on 4 columns** descansa sobre 4 columnas, está apoyado en 4 columnas.

(b) (*fig*) apoyar; sostener, mantener; *campaign* apoyar, respaldar; (*financially*) mantener; *motion* aprobar, votar por; (*corroborate*) confirmar; **I cannot — what you are doing** no apruebo lo que Vd está haciendo; **the liberals will —** it los liberales votarán por esto.

3 *vr*: **to — oneself** (*physically*) apoyarse (*on* en); (*financially*) mantenerse; ganarse la vida.

supportable [sə'pɔːtəbl] *adj* soportable.

supporter [sə'pɔːtə*] *n* (*Tech*) soporte *m*, sostén *m*; (*Her*) tenante *m*, soporte *m*; (*person*) defensor *m*, ora *f*; (*Pol etc*) partidario *m*, a *f*; (*Sport*) seguidor *m*, hincha *mf*; **—s' club** peña *f* deportiva; **after the match —s flooded on to the pitch** al terminar el partido los hinchas invadieron el campo de juego.

supporting [sə'pɔːtiŋ] *adj film, programme, role* secundario.

suppose [sə'pəuz] *vti* **(a)** (*assume as hypothesis*) suponer; figurarse, imaginarse; **let us — that X equals 3** supongamos que X vale 3; **let us — that . . .** pongamos por caso que . . .; **let us — we are living in the 8th century** figurémonos que vivimos en el siglo VIII; **even supposing it were true** aun en el caso de que fuera verdad; **always supposing he comes** en el caso de que venga.

(b) (*imperative*, = *if*) **— he comes, supposing (that) he comes** y ¿si viene?; **— we have a go** ¿probamos?; **— we buy it?** ¿qué te parece si lo compramos?; **— you have a wash?** ¿no crees que conviene ir a lavarte?; **— they could see us now!** ¡si solamente pudieran vernos ahora!

(c) (*presuppose*) suponer, presuponer; **that —s unlimited resources** eso supone unos recursos ilimitados.

(d) (*take for granted, assume*) suponer, presumir; creer; **I — so** supongo que sí, creo que sí, (*unwillingly*) no hay más remedio, no cabe otra explicación; **it is not to be —d that . . .** no se ha de suponer que . . ., no se imagine nadie que . . .; **I — you are right** me parece que tienes razón; **I don't — he really means it** no creo que lo diga en serio; **do you — that . . .?** ¿crees en serio que . . .?; **he's rich, I —** me imagino que es rico; **I — you know that . . .** me imagino que sabes que . . .; **I don't — you could lend me a pound?** ¿podrías por casualidad prestarme una libra?; **he's —d to be coming** se cree que va a venir, se supone que va a venir; **and he's —d to be an expert!** ¡y él que tiene fama de experto!; **he's —d to be in Wales** dicen que está en Gales.

(e) (*of obligation*) deber; **he's the one who's —d to do it** él debe hacerlo, le toca a él hacerlo; **you're —d to be in bed** tú deberías estar en la cama.

supposed [sə'pəuzd] *adj* supuesto, pretendido.

supposedly [sə'pəuzidli] *adv* según cabe suponer; **he had — gone to Scotland** cabía suponer que había ido a Escocia; **the — brave James Bond** el James Bond que se suponía tan valiente; el supuesto valiente James Bond.

supposing [sə'pəuziŋ] *as conj* si, en el caso de que; *see* **suppose (a)** *and* **(b)**.

supposition [,sʌpə'ziʃən] *n* suposición *f*, hipótesis *f*; **that is pure —** eso es una hipótesis nada más.

supposititious [,sʌpə'ziʃəs] *adj* fingido, espurio.

suppository [sə'pɔzitəri] *n* supositorio *m*.

suppress [sə'pres] *vt* (*in most senses*) suprimir; *yawn etc* ahogar; *emotion* contener; *heckler etc* reprimir, hacer callar; *scandal etc* disimular.

suppressed [sə'prest] *adj book etc* suprimido; **with — emotion** con emoción contenida; **a half — laugh** una risa disimulada a medias.

suppression [sə'preʃən] *n* supresión *f*; represión *f*; disimulación *f*.

suppressive [sə'presiv] *adj* supresivo.

suppressor [sə'presə*] *n* (*Elec*) supresor *m*.

suppurate ['sʌpjuəreit] *vi* supurar.

suppuration [,sʌpjuə'reiʃən] *n* supuración *f*.

supra . . . ['suːprə] *supra — . .*, *eg* **supranormal** supranormal.

supranational ['suːprə'næʃənl] *adj* supranacional.

supremacy [su'preməsi] *n* supremacía *f*.

supreme [su'priːm] *adj* supremo; *court etc* supremo; sumo, *eg* **with — indifference** con suma indiferencia; **to reign —** ser el único soberano; (*fig*) estar en la cumbre (de su profesión *etc*), no tener rival alguno.

sura ['suərə] *n* sura *m*.

surcharge ['səːtʃaːdʒ] *n* sobrecarga *f*, sobretasa *f*; **import —** sobrecarga *f* de importación.

surcharge [səː'tʃaːdʒ] *vt* sobrecargar.

surd [səːd] *n* número *m* sordo.

sure [ʃuə*] **1** *adj* **(a)** seguro; cierto; *aim etc* certero; *hand, touch* firme; **as — as fate, as — as eggs** con toda seguridad.

(b) (*with to be*) **to be —!** ¡claro!; **and there he was, to be —** y ahí estaba, efectivamente; **are you quite —?** ¿estás seguro del todo? **; I'm perfectly —** estoy perfectamente seguro; **to be — about something** estar seguro de algo; **I'm not so — about that** no estoy del todo seguro, no diría yo tanto; **to be — of oneself** estar seguro de sí mismo; **to be — that . . .** estar seguro de que . . .; **it is — that he will come** es seguro que vendrá; **I'm — I don't know** que me maten si lo sé; **it is — to rain** seguramente lloverá; **he is — to come** seguramente vendrá; **be — to turn the gas off** ten cuidado de cortar el gas; **be — to go and see her** no dejes de ir a verla.

(c) I don't know for — no sé con seguridad, no sé a punto fijo; **that's for —** eso es seguro; **he'll come next time for —** vendrá la próxima vez sin falta.

(d) to make — of *facts* verificar, comprobar; **make — of someone** asegurarse del apoyo de uno, asegurarse de poder contar con uno; **(in order) to make quite —** para asegurarse del todo; **it's best to make —** vale más estar seguro.

2 *adv* **(a) —!** (*esp US*) sí; ¡claro!; ¡naturalmente! ¡ya lo creo!; **— enough** efectivamente, en efecto; **he'll come — enough** seguramente vendrá; **it's petrol — enough** en efecto es gasolina.

(b) (*US*) **he — was rich** ése sí que era rico; **that meat was — tough** la carne esa fue verdaderamente dura.

sure-fire ['ʃuə'faiə*] *adj* de éxito seguro, seguro.

sure-footed [ˈʃuəˈfutid] **1** *adj* de pie firme. **2** *adv* con pie firme.

surely [ˈʃuəli] *adv* seguramente; ciertamente; por supuesto; —! (*gladly*) con mucho gusto; — **you don't mean it?** ¿seguramente no lo dices en serio?; **it will — happen** seguramente pasará; — **he's come (hasn't he?)** ¿será posible que no haya venido?; — **he hasn't come (has he?)** ¿será posible que haya venido?

sureness [ˈʃuənis] *n* seguridad *f*; certeza *f*; lo certero; firmeza *f*.

surety [ˈʃuərəti] *n* (*sum*) garantía *f*; fianza *f*; (*person*) fiador *m*, ora *f*; garante *mf*; **to go** (*or* **stand**) — **for someone** ser fiador de uno, salir garante por uno; **in his own — of £50** bajo su propia fianza de 50 libras.

surf [səːf] *n* (*foam*) espuma *f*; (*waves*) olas *fpl*, rompientes *mpl*; (*swell*) oleaje m.

surface [ˈsəːfis] **1** *n* superficie *f*; exterior m; (*of road*) firme m; **temporary —** firme m provisional; **we haven't done more than scratch the —** yet todavía no hemos ido al fondo de este problema (*etc*); **on the — it seems that . . .** a primera vista parece que . . .
  2 *attr* de la superficie; **by — mail** por vía terrestre *or* por vía marítima; — **workers** (*Min*) personal m del exterior.
  3 *vt* poner superficie a; recubrir, revestir; (*smoothe*) alisar.
  4 *vi* (*submarine etc*) salir a la superficie, emerger; **he —s in London occasionally** de vez en cuando asoma la cara en Londres.

surface-air [ˈsəːfisˈeə*] *attr*: — **missile** proyectil m tierra-aire.

surface tension [ˈsəːfisˈtenʃən] *n* tensión *f* superficial.

surfboard [ˈsəːfbɔːd] *n* plancha *f* de deslizamiento, acuaplano m.

surfeit [ˈsəːfit] **1** *n* (*satiety*) hartura *f*, saciedad *f*; (*indigestion*) empacho m; (*excess*) exceso m; superabundancia *f*; **there is a — of** hay exceso de; **he died of a — of lampreys** murió después de hartarse de lampreas.
  2 *vt* hartar, saciar (*on, with* de).
  3 *vr*: **to — oneself** hartarse, saciarse (*on, with* de).

surfing [ˈsəːfiŋ] *n*, **surfriding** [ˈsəːfˌraidiŋ] *n* esquí m acuático, patinaje m sobre las olas.

surge [səːdʒ] **1** *n* (*Naut*) oleaje m, oleada *f*; (*fig*) oleada *f*, ola *f*; **a — of people** una oleada de gente; **there was a — of sympathy for him** hubo una oleada de compasión por él.
  2 *vi* (*water*) agitarse, hervir; **the crowd —d into the building** la multitud entró a tropel en el edificio; **people —d down the street** una oleada de gente avanzó por la calle; **blood —d into her face** se le subió la sangre a la cara; **they —d round him** se apiñaban en torno suyo.

surgeon [ˈsəːdʒən] *n* cirujano m; (*Mil, Naut*) médico m, oficial m médico; **dental —** dentista *mf*, odontólogo m; **house —** médico m interno (de hospital); **veterinary —** veterinario m.

surgery [ˈsəːdʒəri] *n* (*art, operation*) cirugía *f*; (*room*) consultorio m, gabinete m de consulta; — **hours** horas *fpl* de consulta; **plastic —** cirugía *f* estética, cirugía *f* plástica.

surgical [ˈsəːdʒikəl] *adj* quirúrgico; — **dressing** vendaje m quirúrgico.

surging [ˈsəːdʒiŋ] *adj* *water* agitado, bravo; *crowd* que se mueve en desorden, que avanza furioso (*or* indignado *etc*).

surliness [ˈsəːlinis] *n* hosquedad *f*, mal humor m; falta *f* de educación; aspereza *f*.

surly [ˈsəːli] *adj* hosco, malhumorado; maleducado; **of a — disposition** de genio áspero; **he gave me a — answer** contestó malhumorado.

surmise [səːˈmaiz] *n* conjetura *f*, suposición *f*; **my — is that . . .** yo supongo que . . .

surmise [səːˈmaiz] *vt* conjeturar, suponer; **I —d as much** ya lo suponía; **as one could — from his book** según cabía entender en su libro.

surmount [səːˈmaunt] *vt* (a) *difficulty* superar, vencer. (b) **—ed by** coronado de.

surmountable [səːˈmauntəbl] *adj* superable.

surname [ˈsəːneim] **1** *n* apellido m. **2** *vt* apellidar.

surpass [səːˈpɑːs] **1** *vt* superar, exceder; eclipsar; **it —es anything we have seen before** supera a cuanto hemos visto antes.
  2 *vr*: **to — oneself** excederse a sí mismo.

surpassing [səːˈpɑːsiŋ] *adj* incomparable, sin par; **of — beauty** de hermosura sin par.

surplice [ˈsəːpləs] *n* sobrepelliz *f*.

surplus [ˈsəːpləs] **1** *n* excedente m, sobrante m, exceso m; (*Fin, Comm*) superávit m; **the 1975 wheat —** el excedente de trigo de 1975.

2 *adj* excedente, sobrante; de sobra; **my — socks** los calcetines que me sobran, los calcetines que no necesito; **American — wheat** el excedente de trigo norteamericano; **sale of — stock** liquidación *f* de saldos; **have you any — sheets?** ¿tenéis sábanas que os sobren?

surprise [səˈpraiz] **1** *n* sorpresa *f*; asombro m, extrañeza *f*; **much to my —**, **to my great —** con gran sorpresa mía; **with a look of —** con un gesto de extrañeza; **it was a — to find that . . .** fue una sorpresa encontrar que . . .; **imagine my —** imaginaos cuál sería mi asombro; **it came as a — to us** nos cogió de nuevas; **to give someone a —** dar una sorpresa a uno; **to take someone by —** sorprender a uno, coger a uno desprevenido.
  2 *attr*: — **attack** sorpresa *f*; ataque m imprevisto; — **package** sorpresa *f*.
  3 *vt* sorprender; asombrar, extrañar; (*Mil*) coger por sorpresa; **to — someone in the act** coger a uno en el acto; **you — me!** ¡me asombras!; **it —s me to learn that . . .** me asombra saber que . . .; **to be —d** quedar asombrado; **to be —d to see someone** asombrarse de ver a uno; **I should not be —d if . . .** no me sorprendería que + *subj*; **to look —d** hacer un gesto de sorpresa.

surprising [səˈpraiziŋ] *adj* sorprendente, asombroso.

surprisingly [səˈpraiziŋli] *adv* de modo sorprendente; asombrosamente; **he is — young** se asombra uno de descubrir que es tan joven; **and then — he left** y luego con asombro de todos partió.

surrealism [səˈriəlizəm] *n* surrealismo m.

surrealist [səˈriəlist] **1** *adj* surrealista. **2** *n* surrealista *mf*.

surrealistic [səˌriəˈlistik] *adj* surrealista.

surrender [səˈrendə*] **1** *n* rendición *f*, capitulación *f*; entrega *f*; renuncia *f*; abandono m; **unconditional —** rendición *f* sin condiciones; **the — of Breda** la rendición de Breda; — **of property** (*Law*) cesión *f* de bienes; **no —!** ¡no nos rendimos!; **to make a — of one's principles** transigir con sus principios.
  2 *attr*: — **value** valor m de rescate.
  3 *vt* (*Mil*) rendir, entregar; *goods* entregar; *claim, right* renunciar a; *hope* renunciar a, abandonar.
  4 *vi* rendirse, entregarse; **to — to the police** entregarse a la policía; **I —!** ¡me rindo!
  5 *vr*: **to — oneself to remorse** abandonarse al remordimiento.

surreptitious [ˌsʌrəpˈtiʃəs] *adj* subrepticio, clandestino.

surreptitiously [ˌsʌrəpˈtiʃəsli] *adv* subrepticiamente, clandestinamente; a hurtadillas.

surrogate [ˈsʌrəgeit] *n* sustituto m, suplente m; (*Eccl*) vicario m.

surround [səˈraund] **1** *n* marco m; borde m.
  2 *vt* rodear, cercar, circundar; (*Mil*) copar, cercar; sitiar; **a town —ed by hills** una ciudad rodeada de colinas; **she was —ed by children** estaba rodeada de niños.

surrounding [səˈraundiŋ] *adj* circundante; **in the — hills** en las colinas vecinas, en las colinas de alrededor; **in the — darkness** en la oscuridad que le (*etc*) cercaba por todos lados.

surroundings [səˈraundiŋz] *npl* (*of place*) alrededores *mpl*, cercanías *fpl*, contornos *mpl*; (*environment*) ambiente m.

surtax [ˈsəːtæks] *n* impuesto m adicional (sobre los ingresos elevados de particulares).

surveillance [səːˈveiləns] *n* vigilancia *f*; **to be under —** estar vigilado, estar bajo vigilancia; **to keep someone under —** vigilar a uno.

survey [ˈsəːvei] *n* inspección *f*, examen m; estudio m; reconocimiento m; (*of land*) apeo m, medición *f*; (*general view*) vista *f* de conjunto; (*as published report*) informe m; **he gave a general — of the situation** hizo un informe general sobre la situación; **to make a — of housing in a town** estudiar la situación de la vivienda en una ciudad.

survey [səːˈvei] *vt* (*look at*) mirar, contemplar; (*inspect*) inspeccionar, examinar; (*study*) estudiar, hacer un estudio de; *ground before battle etc* reconocer; *land* apear, medir; *town etc* levantar el plano de; (*take general view of*) pasar en revista; obtener una vista de conjunto de; **he —ed the desolate scene** miró detenidamente la triste escena; **monarch of all he —s** monarca m de todo cuanto domina con la vista; **the report —s housing in Slobodia** el informe estudia la situación de la vivienda en Eslobodia; **the book —s events up to 1972** el libro pasa revista de los sucesos hasta 1972.

surveying [səːˈveiiŋ] *n* agrimensura *f*; planimetría *f*; topografía *f*.

surveyor [səːˈveiə*] *n* agrimensor m; topógrafo m.

survival [sə'vaivəl] n **(a)** (act) supervivencia f; — **of the fittest** supervivencia f de los mejor dotados. **(b)** (relic) supervivencia f; vestigio m, reliquia f.
survival kit [sə:'vaivəl'kit] n equipo m de emergencia.
survive [sə'vaiv] **1** vt (all senses) sobrevivir a. **2** vi sobrevivir; (remain, persist) durar, perdurar, subsistir.
survivor [sə'vaivə*] n superviviente mf.
Susan ['su:zn] f Susana.
susceptibility [sə,septə'biliti] n susceptibilidad f, sensibilidad f (to a); **to offend someone's susceptibilities** ofender las susceptibilidades (or la delicadeza) de uno.
susceptible [sə'septəbl] adj susceptible, sensible (to a); (easily moved) impresionable; (to women) enamoradizo; **to be — of** admitir, dar lugar a.
suspect ['sʌspekt] **1** adj sospechoso; **they are all —** todos están bajo sospecha; **his fitness is — es** sospechoso de no estar en buen estado físico, su estado físico deja lugar a dudas.
  2 n sospechoso m, a f; **the chief — is the butler** el más sospechoso es el mayordomo.
suspect [səs'pekt] **1** vt (accusingly) sospechar; (fear) recelar, recelarse de; (believe) imaginar, figurar, creer; **to — someone of a crime** hacer a uno sospechoso de un crimen, sospechar a uno de haber cometido un crimen; **I — her of having stolen it** sospecho que ella lo ha robado; **I — him of being the author** sospecho que él es el autor; **are you —ed?** ¿estás tú bajo sospecha?; **he never —ed her** él nunca sospechó de ella; **he —s nothing** no se recela de nada; **I — all Irishmen** me recelo de todos los irlandeses; **I — it may be true** tengo la sospecha de que puede ser verdad, creo que puede ser verdad; **it's not paid for, I —** sospecho que no está pagado; **I —ed as much** ya me lo figuraba.
  2 vi sospechar, tener sospechas.
suspend [səs'pend] vt (all senses) suspender; **he was —ed for 6 months** (Aut) le retiraron el carnet de conducir durante 6 meses.
suspender [səs'pendə*] n liga f; **—s** ligas fpl, (US) tirantes mpl.
suspender belt [səs'pendəbelt] n portaligas m.
suspense [səs'pens] n incertidumbre f, duda f; ansiedad f; (Lit, Theat, Cine etc) suspense m, suspensión f (Acad), tensión f; **it is in —** está en suspenso; **the question is in —** la cuestión está pendiente; **to keep someone in —** dejar a uno en la incertidumbre; **the — became unbearable** la tensión se hizo inaguantable.
suspension [səs'penʃən] n (most senses, also Tech) suspensión f; **independent —** (Aut) suspensión f independiente; **— of payments** suspensión f de pagos; **— of driving licence** privación f del carnet de conducir.
suspensory [səs'pensəri] **1** adj suspensorio. **2** n (also **— bandage**) suspensorio m.
suspicion [səs'piʃən] n **(a)** sospecha f; recelo m; **my — is that . . .** yo sospecho que . . .; **to be above —** estar por encima de toda sospecha; **to be under —** ser sospechoso, estar bajo sospecha; **to arouse —** despertar recelos; **to arouse someone's —s** despertar los recelos de uno; **to arrest someone on —** detener a uno como sospechoso; **to cast — on someone's honesty** hacer que se dude de la honradez de uno; **to have one's —s about something** tener sospechas acerca de algo; **I had no — that . . .** no sospechaba que . . .; **to lay oneself open to —** hacerse sospechoso: **I was right in my —s** resultaron ser ciertas mis sospechas; **— fell on him** se empezó a sospechar de él.
  (b) (trace) traza f ligera, sombra f, pizca f; (aftertaste) dejo m; **there is a — of corruption about it** esto tiene un dejo de corrupción, esto huele un poquito a corrupción.
suspicious [səs'piʃəs] adj **(a)** (feeling suspicion) receloso; **to be — about something** recelarse de algo, tener sospechas acerca de algo; **that made him —** eso le hizo sospechar.
  (b) (causing suspicion) sospechoso; **it's highly —** es sumamente sospechoso; **it looks very — to me** me parece muy sospechoso.
suspiciously [səs'piʃəsli] adv **(a)** look etc con recelo, desconfiadamente.
  (b) behave etc de modo sospechoso; **it looks — like measles to me** para mí tiene toda la apariencia de ser sarampión.
suspiciousness [səs'piʃəsnis] n **(a)** recelo m. **(b)** lo sospechoso, carácter m sospechoso.
sustain [səs'tein] vt **(a)** (bear weight of) sostener, apoyar; body, life sustentar; (Mus) sostener; part (Theat) estar al nivel de; hacer dignamente; pretence

continuar; effort sostener, continuar; assertion sostener; objection (Law) confirmar la validez de; charge, theory confirmar, corroborar.
  (b) (receive) attack sufrir (y rechazar); damage sufrir; injury sufrir, tener, recibir; loss sufrir, tener.
sustained [səs'teind] adj effort etc sostenido, ininterrumpido, continuo; note sostenido; applause prolongado.
sustenance ['sʌstinəns] n sustento m; **they depend for their — on, they get their — from** se sustentan de, se alimentan de.
suture ['su:tʃə*] **1** n sutura f. **2** vt suturar, coser.
suzerain ['su:zərein] n soberano m, a f.
suzerainty ['su:zəreinti] n soberanía f.
svelte [svelt] adj esbelto.
swab [swɔb] **1** n (cloth, mop) estropajo m, trapo m, (Naut) lampazo m; (Mil) escobillón m; (Med) algodón m, torunda f.
  2 vt (also **to — down**) limpiar (con estropajo etc), fregar.
swaddle ['swɔdl] vt envolver (in en); baby empañar, fajar; **he came out —d in bandages** salió envuelto en vendas.
swaddling clothes ['swɔdliŋkləuðz] npl pañales mpl; **to be still in —** (fig) estar todavía en mantillas.
swag [swæg] n (fam) botín m.
swagger ['swægə*] **1** n contoneo m, pavoneo m; **to walk with a —** andar contoneándose, andar con paso jactancioso.
  2 adj (fam) muy elegante, muy pera.
  3 vi (also **to — about, to — along**) contonearse, pavonearse, andar pavoneándose; **he —ed over to our table** se acercó a nuestra mesa con aire fanfarrón; **with that he —ed out** con eso salió con paso jactancioso.
swagger cane ['swægəkein] n bastón m ligero de paseo.
swaggering ['swægəriŋ] adj person fanfarrón, jactancioso; gait importante, jactancioso.
swain [swein] n (arch or hum: lad) zagal m; (suitor) pretendiente m, amante m.
swallow¹ ['swɔləu] **1** n trago m; **at one —, with one — de un trago.**
  2 vt **(a)** tragar; engullir, deglutir; bait tragarse; **he —ed the lot** se lo tragó todo; **just — this pill** tómate esta píldora; **to — up** tragar; acabar de comer.
  (b) (fig) tragar; **to — an insult** tragar un insulto; **to — one's pride** humillarse, olvidarse de su amor propio; **he —ed the story** se tragó la bola; **to — one's words** desdecirse, retractarse; **to — up** savings etc agotar, consumir; (of the sea) tragar; **the mist —ed them up** la niebla les envolvió; **they were soon —ed up in the darkness** desaparecieron pronto en la oscuridad.
  3 vi: **to —, to — hard** (fig) tragar saliva.
swallow² ['swɔləu] n (Orn) golondrina f; **one doesn't make a summer** una golondrina no hace verano.
swallowtail ['swɔləuteil] n (butterfly) macaón m.
swallow-tailed ['swɔləuteild] adj: **— coat** frac m.
swam [swæm] pret of **swim.**
swamp [swɔmp] **1** n pantano m, marisma f, ciénaga f.
  2 vt **(a)** (submerge) sumergir, cubrir de agua (etc); (flood) inundar, llenar de agua; (sink) hundir.
  (b) abrumar (with de), agobiar (with de); **towards the end of the game they —ed us** hacia el fin del partido nos arrollaron completamente; **they have —ed us with applications** nos han abrumado de solicitudes; **we are —ed with work** estamos agobiados de trabajo, tenemos trabajo hasta encima de las cejas.
  3 vi (of field etc) inundarse, quedar inundado, empantanarse.
swampy ['swɔmpi] adj pantanoso; **to become —** empantanarse.
swan [swɔn] **1** n cisne m; **the Swan of Avon** el Cisne del Avon (Shakespeare). **2** vi (fam) pavonearse; darse mucho tono.
swank [swæŋk] (fam) **1** n **(a)** (vanity, boastfulness) fachenda f; ostentación f; **it's just a lot of —** no es sino fachenda; **he does it for —** lo hace para darse tono.
  (b) (person) currutaco m; fachendón m, ona f; **he's a terrible —** es terriblemente fachendón.
  2 vi darse tono, darse humos, fachendear; **to — about** (adv) pavonearse; **to — about something** fachendear a causa de algo, darse humos con motivo de algo.
swanky ['swæŋki] adj (fam) person ostentoso, fachendoso, fachendón; car etc la mar de elegante, muy pera.

swannery ['swɔnəri] n colonia f de cisnes.
swan song ['swɔnsɔŋ] n canto m del cisne.
swan-upping ['swɔn‚ʌpiŋ] n censo m anual de los cisnes (del Támesis).
swap [swɔp] **1** n intercambio m, canje m; —s (stamps) duplicados mpl; **it's a fair** — es un trato equitativo.
2 vt intercambiar, canjear; **to — stories (with someone)** contarse chistes; **we sat —ing reminiscences** estábamos contando nuestros recuerdos; **will you — your hat for my jacket?** ¿quieres cambiar tu sombrero por mi chaqueta?; **to — places with someone** cambiar de silla (etc) con uno.
3 vi hacer un intercambio; cambiar con uno; **I wouldn't — with anyone** no cambio lo que tengo con nadie; **shall we —?** ¿cambiamos?
sward [swɔːd] n césped m.
swarm[1] [swɔːm] **1** n (of bees etc) enjambre m; (fig) multitud f, muchedumbre f; **a — of mosquitoes** un enjambre de mosquitos; **a — of creditors** un enjambre de acreedores; **they came in —s** vinieron en tropel; **there were —s of women** hubo una multitud de mujeres, hubo millares de mujeres.
2 vi (of bees) enjambrar; (of other insects, people etc) hormiguear, pulular; **to — with** (of place) hervir de, pulular de, estar plagado de; **the tourists — everywhere** en todas partes pululan los turistas; **Stratford —s with Americans** Stratford hierve de americanos; **children —ed all over the car** los niños subían y bajaban por todas partes del coche.
swarm[2] [swɔːm] vi: **to — up a tree** trepar (rápidamente) a un árbol.
swarthiness ['swɔːðinis] n tez f morena, color m moreno; lo atezado.
swarthy ['swɔːði] adj moreno, atezado.
swashbuckler ['swɔʃ‚bʌklə*] n espadachín m, matón m.
swashbuckling ['swɔʃ‚bʌkliŋ] adj valentón, fanfarrón.
swastika ['swɔstikə] n esvástica f, cruz f gamada.
swat [swɔt] **1** vt fly aplastar, matar. **2** vi: **to — at a fly** tratar de aplastar una mosca (con palmeta).
swath [swɔːθ] n, pl **swaths** [swɔːðs] guadaña f, ringlera f (de heno segado etc); **to cut corn in —s** segar el trigo y dejarlo en ringleras; **to cut —s through something** avanzar por algo a guadañadas.
swathe [sweið] vt envolver; fajar; (with bandage) vendar; **—d in sheets** envuelto en sábanas.
swatter ['swɔtə*] m palmeta f matamoscas.
sway [swei] **1** n **(a)** (movement) balanceo m, oscilación f; (violent jerk) sacudimiento m; vaivén m.
(b) (rule) imperio m, dominio m; (influence) influencia f, ascendiente m; (power) poder m; **his — over the party** su influencia con el partido, su dominio del partido; **to bring a people under one's —** sojuzgar un pueblo, hacer que un pueblo reconozca el dominio de uno; **to hold — over a nation** gobernar una nación, dominar una nación.
2 vt **(a)** (move) balancear, hacer oscilar; sacudir; hacer tambalear.
(b) (influence) mover, influir en; inclinar; **these factors finally —ed me** estos factores terminaron de convencerme; **he is not —ed by any such considerations** tales cosas no influyen en él en absoluto; **I allowed myself to be —ed** me dejé persuadir.
3 vi balancearse, oscilar (in the wind al viento); mecerse; bambolearse; tambalearse; **she —s as she walks** se cimbrea al andar; **he was —ing with drink** estaba tan borracho que se tambaleaba; **the train —ed from side to side** el tren se bamboleaba de un lado para otro.
swear [sweə*] (irr: pret **swore**, ptp **sworn**) **1** vt **(a)** oath prestar, jurar; fidelity jurar; **I — it!** ¡lo juro!; **I — (that) I did not steal it** juro que no lo robé; **I could have sworn that was Lulu** juraría que ésa fue Lulú, que me maten si aquélla no fue Lulú; **to — something on the Bible** jurar algo sobre la Biblia.
(b) to — someone in tomar juramento a uno, juramentar a uno, hacer prestar juramento a uno; **to be sworn in** prestar juramento; **to — someone to secrecy** hacer que uno jure no revelar algo.
(c) to — one's fortune away hacer voto de renunciar a su fortuna.
2 vi **(a)** (solemnly) jurar; (with swearwords) jurar, decir tacos, soltar palabrotas, (blasphemously) blasfemar; **don't — in front of the children** no digas palabrotas estando los pequeños delante; **to — black and blue** echar sapos y culebras; **to — like a trooper** jurar como un carretero; **he swore most horribly** soltó unos tremendos tacos; **it's enough to make a bishop —** esto bastaría para hacer blasfemar a un obispo; **to — to do something** jurar hacer algo.

(b) (with adv or prep) **to — at someone** maldecir a uno, echar pestes de uno; **to — by something** (solemnly) jurar por algo; (fig) tener entera confianza en algo, creer ciegamente en algo; **to — off alcohol** jurar renunciar al alcohol; **to — to something** declarar algo bajo juramento; **I would — to it** juraría que fue así; **I can't — to it** no lo sé a punto fijo, no puedo afirmarlo con entera confianza.
3 n (fam): **to have a good —** desahogarse soltando palabrotas.
swearword ['sweəwəːd] n taco m, palabrota f.
sweat [swet] **1** n **(a)** sudor m; **by the — of one's brow** con el sudor de su frente, a pulso sudando; **to be in a —** estar sudando, estar todo sudoroso, (fig) estar en un apuro, apurarse; **to be in a — about something** estar muy preocupado por algo; **to get into a — empezar a sudar; **to get into a — about something** apurarse por algo.
(b) (piece of work etc) trabajo m difícil, trabajo m pesado; **what a — that was!** eso ¡como nos hizo sudar!; **we had such a — to do it** nos costó hacerlo.
(c) old — (fam) veterano m.
2 vt **(a)** sudar; **to — blood** (fig) sudar la gota gorda.
(b) workers explotar.
3 vi sudar; **to — a lot, to — like a bull** (or pig etc) sudar la gota gorda.
sweatband ['swetbænd] n badana f del forro del sombrero, tafilete m.
sweated ['swetid] adj: **— labour** trabajo m muy mal pagado.
sweater ['swetə*] n suéter m.
sweater girl ['swetə'gəːl] n muchacha f vestida de suéter.
sweat gland ['swetglænd] n glándula f sudorípara.
sweating ['swetiŋ] **1** adj sudoroso. **2** n transpiración f; (of workers) explotación f.
sweat shirt ['swetʃəːt] n camisa f floja (de deporte etc).
sweat shop ['swetʃɔp] n fábrica f donde se explota al obrero.
sweaty ['sweti] adj sudoroso; cubierto de sudor, mojado de sudor; **to be all —** estar todo sudoroso.
Swede [swiːd] n sueco m, a f.
swede [swiːd] n (Bot) nabo m sueco.
Sweden ['swiːdn] n Suecia f.
Swedish ['swiːdiʃ] **1** adj sueco. **2** n sueco m.
sweep [swiːp] **1** n **(a)** (act of —ing) barredura f, escobada f; (of scythe) golpe m, guadañada f; (of net) redada f; (of arm) gesto m, movimiento m; **at one — de un solo golpe; **with a wide — of his arm** con un ancho movimiento del brazo; **this room could do with a —** hace falta limpiar esta habitación; **we gave it a —** lo limpiamos, lo barrimos; **to make a clean — (Sport) ganar todos los puntos, (Cards) copar, ganar todas las bazas; **to make a clean — of** cambiar completamente, hacer tabla rasa de.
(b) (by police etc) redada f; **they made a — for hidden arms** hicieron una redada buscando armas clandestinas.
(c) (person) deshollinador m.
(d) (area) extensión f; (of wings) envergadura f; (range) alcance m; (curve) curva f; **the whole — of the Thames at Putney** toda la extensión del Támesis en Putney; **a wide — of country** una ancha extensión de paisaje, un paisaje extenso; **the — of her lines** (Naut etc) su línea, su perfil (aerodinámico etc).
(e) see **sweepstake**.
2 (irr: pret and ptp **swept**) vt **(a)** room, surface barrer; chimney deshollinar; channel etc dragar; **to — a room clean** limpiar un cuarto barriéndolo; **to — a channel clear of mines** hacer navegable un canal barriendo las minas de él; **the beach was swept by great waves** la playa fue barrida (or azotada) por olas gigantescas; **to — a road with bullets** barrer una carretera con balas; **to — the horizon with a telescope** examinar toda la extensión del horizonte con un telescopio; see **board** etc.
(b) dust barrer, quitar barriendo; mines rastrear, barrer; person, obstacle etc arrastrar, llevarse; **a wave swept him overboard** fue arrastrado por una ola y cayó al mar; **he was swept off his feet by the water** fue arrastrado por la corriente; **to — a girl off her feet** enamorar a una chica; **they swept him off to lunch** se lo llevaron con toda prisa a comer.
(c) (with adv or prep) **the crowd swept him along** le arrastró la multitud, desapareció arrastrado por la multitud; **to — aside** apartar bruscamente con la mano; protest desatender, no hacer caso alguno de; suggestion desechar bruscamente; **to — away**

barrer; (snatch) arrebatar, arrastrar; (remove) quitar, eliminar, suprimir; vestiges etc borrar; **the current —s logs down with it** la corriente arrastra (or lleva) consigo los troncos; **to — out room** barrer; **to — up** barrer, recoger.

3 vi **(a)** (with broom) barrer; **to — up after someone** recoger la basura que ha dejado uno; **to — up after a party** recoger la basura que ha resultado de un guateque.

(b) (extend) extenderse (along, down etc por); **the river —s away to the east** el río hace una gran curva hacia el este; **the hills — down to the sea** las colinas bajan (majestuosamente) hacia el mar; **the road —s up to the house** la carretera llega hasta la casa (de modo impresionante).

(c) (of movement) **to — into a room** entrar en una sala con paso majestuoso; **she swept past me angrily** pasó enfadada delante de mí; **the car swept along** el coche avanzó a gran velocidad; **it swept round the corner** dobló velozmente la esquina.

(d) (with adv or prep) **to — by** pasar rápidamente; pasar majestuosamente; (nearly touch) rozar; **they swept down the slope** se lanzaron cuesta abajo; descendieron precipitadamente por la cuesta; **to — down on someone** abalanzarse sobre uno; **to — on** seguir su avance inexorable (to hasta); **to — past = to — by.**

sweeper ['swi:pə*] n (person) barrendero m, a f; (machine) barredera f.

sweeping ['swi:piŋ] adj **(a)** gesture dramático; bow profundo; flight majestuoso.

(b) statement etc comprensivo pero infundado, comprensivo pero que no tiene en cuenta las excepciones; change radical, fundamental; **that's pretty —** eso es mucho decir.

sweepings ['swi:piŋz] npl barreduras fpl; (fig, of society etc) heces fpl.

sweepstake ['swi:psteik] n lotería en la cual una persona gana todas las apuestas.

sweet [swi:t] **1** adj **(a)** (of taste) dulce; azucarado; **this coffee is too —** este café tiene demasiado azúcar; **is it — enough for you?** ¿le he puesto bastante azúcar?

(b) (fresh, pleasant) food fresco, nuevo; smell fragante, agradable, bueno; breath sano; land fértil; **en buen estado; to smell —** tener buen olor, oler bien.

(c) (of sounds) dulce, melodioso.

(d) (of person's character) dulce, amable, simpático; **isn't he —?** ¡es un ángel!; **that's very — of you** eres muy amable; **to be — on someone** estar un poco enamorado de uno; **to keep someone —** asegurarse de la amistad de uno, asegurarse de la buena voluntad de uno (mediante un regalo, propina etc).

(e) (generally agreeable, charming) memory, revenge etc dulce; face lindo; dress etc mono, majo, precioso; **it is — to be able to...** es agradable poder...; **you look so — in that hat** con ese sombrero eres un encanto; **what a — little hat!** ¡qué sombrerito más mono!

(f) (of running of car, machine etc) suave.

2 n **(a)** dulce m, caramelo m; **—s** dulces mpl, bombones mpl, golosinas fpl; **the —s of solitude** las dulzuras de la soledad; **the —s of office** (Pol) las ventajas materiales de estar en el poder, los premios que brinda el triunfo político.

(b) (course) postre m.

(c) yes, my **—** sí, mi amor.

sweet-and-sour ['swi:tən'sauə*] n (Cook) plato agridulce (especialmente en la comida china).

sweetbreads ['swi:tbredz] npl lechecillas fpl.

sweet corn ['swi:tkɔ:n] n (US) maíz m tierno.

sweeten ['swi:tn] vt endulzar (also fig); azucarar, poner azúcar a.

sweetening ['swi:tniŋ] n (Cook) dulcificante m.

sweetheart ['swi:thɑ:t] n novio m, a f; yes, **—** sí, mi amor.

sweetie ['swi:ti] n (fam) chica f, gachí f (sl); novia f; **she's a —** es un encanto, es muy mona; **isn't she a —?** ¡qué chica más mona!

sweetish ['swi:tiʃ] adj algo dulce.

sweetly ['swi:tli] adv dulcemente; amablemente; suavemente.

sweetmeats ['swi:tmi:ts] npl dulces mpl, confites mpl.

sweetness ['swi:tnis] n dulzura f; lo dulce f; azucarado; fragancia f; buen olor m; fertilidad f; amabilidad f; suavidad f; **now all is — and light** reina ahora la más perfecta armonía; **to go around spreading — and light** ir por el mundo con una sonrisa amable para todos.

sweet-scented ['swi:t'sentid] adj perfumado, fragante, de olor agradable.

sweetshop ['swi:tʃɔp] n bombonería f, confitería f.

sweet-smelling ['swi:t'smeliŋ] adj see **sweet-scented.**

sweet-tempered ['swi:t'tempəd] adj de carácter dulce, amable; **she's always —** es siempre tan amable, no se altera nunca.

sweet-toothed ['swi:t'tu:θd] adj goloso.

sweet william ['swi:t'wiliəm] n minutisa f.

swell [swel] **1** n **(a)** (Naut) mar m de fondo, marejada f, oleaje m.

(b) (fam: toff) guapo m, majo m; (important person) pez m gordo, espadón m; **the —s** la gente bien, la gente de buen tono.

2 adj (fam: in dress etc) elegantísimo; (fine, good) estupendo, bárbaro, de órdago; (esp US) **we had a — time** lo pasamos en grande; **it's a — place** es un sitio estupendo; **that's mighty — of you** es Vd muy amable.

3 (irr: pret **swelled**, ptp **swollen**) vt **(a)** (physically) hinchar; abultar; inflar; (Med) hinchar; **to have a swollen hand** tener la mano hinchada; **eyes swollen with tears** ojos mpl hinchados de lágrimas; **the rains had swollen the river** las lluvias habían hecho crecer el río; **the river is swollen** el río está crecido.

(b) numbers etc aumentar; engrosar; **this will go to — the numbers of...** esto vendrá a aumentar el número de...

4 vi **(a)** (physically: also **to — up**) hincharse; abultarse; inflarse; (in size, numbers) crecer, aumentar(se); (of river etc) crecer; **her arm —ed up** se le hinchó el brazo; **to — with pride** envanecerse, (justifiably) sentirse lleno de orgullo; **numbers have swollen greatly** el número se ha aumentado muchísimo; **the debt had swollen to...** la deuda había aumentado mucho hasta alcanzar la cifra de...

swellhead ['swelhed] n (US) vanidoso m, a f.

swellheaded ['swel'hedid] adj (US) vanidoso, engreído.

swelling ['sweliŋ] n hinchazón f; protuberancia f; (Med) tumefacción f; (bruise) chichón m, bulto m; (of gland etc) ganglio m.

swelter ['sweltə*] vi abrasarse, sofocarse de calor; chorrear de sudor; **we —ed in 40°** nos sofocábamos a una temperatura de 40 grados.

sweltering ['sweltəriŋ] adj day de muchísimo calor; heat sofocante, abrasador; **it's — in here** aquí se sofoca uno de calor.

swept [swept] pret and ptp of **sweep.**

sweptback ['swept'bæk] adj wing en flecha.

swerve [swə:v] **1** n **(a)** (dodge, turn) desvío m brusco, viraje m repentino; (of body, in sport etc) esguince m, regate m.

(b) (spin on ball) efecto m; **to put a — on a ball** lanzar una pelota con efecto.

2 vt **(a)** desviar bruscamente, torcer (a un lado).

(b) dar efecto a, lanzar con efecto, cortar.

3 vi **(a)** desviarse bruscamente; hurtar el cuerpo; **to — to the right** torcer repentinamente a la derecha.

(b) torcerse.

swift [swift] **1** adj rápido, veloz; repentino; pronto; **— of foot** de pies ligeros; **to be — to anger** tener prontos enojos; **we must be — to act** hemos de obrar con toda prontitud.

2 n vencejo m.

swift-flowing ['swift'fləuiŋ] adj current rápido; river de corriente rápida.

swift-footed ['swift'futid] adj de pies ligeros, veloz.

swiftly ['swiftli] adv rápidamente, velozmente; repentinamente; pronto.

swiftness ['swiftnis] n rapidez f, velocidad f; lo repentino; prontitud f.

swig [swig] (fam) **1** n trago m, tragantada f; **have a — of this** bébete un poco de esto; **he took a — at his flask** se echó un trago de la botella.

2 vt beber; beber a grandes tragos.

swill [swil] **1** n **(a)** bazofia f; (pej) bazofia f, aguachirle f; **how can you drink this —?** ¿cómo te es posible beber esta basura?

(b) **to give something a — (out)** limpiar algo con agua.

2 vt **(a)** (clean: also **to — out**) lavar, limpiar con agua.

(b) (drink) beber (a grandes tragos).

3 vi emborracharse.

swim [swim] **1** n **(a)** nadada f (SAm); **after a 2-kilometre —** después de cubrir 2 kilómetros nadando; **it's a long — back to the shore** nos costará llegar nadando a la playa; **that was a**

long — for a child eso fue mucho nadar para un niño; **that was a nice** —! ¡cuánto me gusta nadar así!; **I like a** — me gusta nadar, me gusta la natación; **to go for a** —, **to have a** — ir a nadar.

(b) **to be in the** — estar al corriente; **to keep in the** — mantenerse al día.

2 (*irr: pret* **swam**, *ptp* **swum**) *vt* (a) *river etc* pasar a nado, cruzar a nado; **it was first swum in 1900** un hombre lo cruzó a nado por primera vez en 1900; **it has not been swum before** hasta ahora nadie lo ha cruzado a nado.

(b) **she can't** — **a stroke** no sabe nadar en absoluto; **before I had swum 10 strokes** antes de haber dado 10 brazadas.

3 *vi* (a) nadar; **to** — **across a river** pasar un río a nado; **to** — **out to sea** alejarse nadando de la playa; **to** — **under water** nadar debajo del agua, bucear; **then we swam back** luego volvimos (nadando); **we shall have to** — **for it** tendremos que echarnos al agua, tendremos que salvarnos nadando; **to go** —**ming** ir a nadar, ir a bañarse.

(b) **the meat was** —**ing in gravy** la carne estaba inundada de salsa, la carne flotaba en salsa.

(c) (*of head*) dar vueltas; **everything swam before my eyes** todo parecía estar girando alrededor de mí, todo parecía bailar ante mis ojos.

swimmer ['swimə*] *n* nadador *m*, ora *f*.
swimming ['swimiŋ] *n* natación *f*.
swimming bath ['swimiŋbɑ:θ] *n*, *pl* — **baths** [bɑ:ðz] piscina *f*; **indoor** — piscina *f* cubierta.
swimming cap ['swimiŋkæp] *n* gorro *m* de baño.
swimming costume ['swimiŋ‚kɔstju:m] *n* traje *m* de baño.
swimmingly ['swimiŋli] *adv*: **to go** — ir a las mil maravillas.
swimming pool ['swimiŋpu:l] *n see* **swimming bath**.
swimsuit ['swimsu:t] *n* traje *m* de baño.
swindle ['swindl] 1 *n* estafa *f*, timo *m*; **it's a** —! ¡nos han robado!

2 *vt* estafar, timar; **to** — **someone out of something** estafar algo a uno, quitar algo a uno por estafa.
swindler ['swindlə*] *n* estafador *m*, timador *m*.
swine [swain] *n* (a) *pl* (*Zool*) cerdos *mpl*, puercos *mpl*.

(b) *sing* (*fig*) canalla *m*, cochino *m*; **you** —! ¡canalla!; **what a** — **he is**! ¡es un canalla!; **they're a lot of** — son unos cochinos.
swineherd ['swainhə:d] *n* (*arch*) porquero *m*.
swing [swiŋ] 1 *n* (a) (*movement*) balanceo *m*, oscilación *f*, vaivén *m*; (*of pendulum*) oscilación *f*; (*Boxing*) golpe *m* lateral, balanceado *m*; **it has a** — **of 2 metres** tiene un recorrido de 2 metros; **to give the starting handle a** — girar la manivela; **to give a hammock a** — empujar una hamaca; **to give a child a** — empujar a un niño en un columpio; **balancear a un niño colgado de los brazos** (*etc*); **he took a** — **at me** me asestó un golpe (lateral); **he took a** — **at me with the axe** trató de golpearme con el hacha.

(b) (*Pol*, *in votes etc*) movimiento *m*, desplazamiento *m*, viraje *m*; **a sudden** — **in opinion** un viraje repentino de la opinión; **the** — **of the pendulum** (*fig*) el flujo y reflujo de la popularidad de los partidos; **there was a strong** — **in the election** en las elecciones se registró un fuerte viraje; **a** — **of 5%** **would give the opposition the majority** un 5 por 100 de desplazamiento de los votos daría a la oposición la mayoría.

(c) (*seat*) columpio *m*.

(d) (*rhythm*) ritmo *m* (fuerte, agradable); (*kind of music*) swing *m*; **a tune that goes with a** — una melodía que tiene un ritmo agradable; **it all went with a** — todo fue sobre ruedas; **to walk with a** — andar rítmicamente; **to be in full** — estar en plena marcha, estar en plena actividad; **to get with the** — **of things** acostumbrarse al ritmo de las cosas.

2 (*irr: pret and ptp* **swung**) *vt* (a) (*to and fro*) balancear; hacer oscilar; (*on a swing*) columpiar; (*brandish*) blandir, menear; *arms* menear; *propeller* girar; **to** — **a child** empujar a un niño en un columpio; **balancear a un niño colgado de los brazos** (*etc*); **he sat on the table** —**ing his legs** estaba sentado sobre la mesa balanceando las piernas; **to** — **one's fist at someone** asestar un golpe (lateral) a uno con el puño; **he swung the case up on to his shoulders** haciendo un esfuerzo se echó la maleta sobre los hombros.

(b) **he swung the car round** hizo un viraje brusco; **they swung the gun barrel round** hicieron girar el cañón.

(c) (*sl*) **to** — **it** fingirse enfermo, racanear, hacer el rácano; **to** — **it on someone** embaucar a uno.

3 *vi* (a) (*to and fro*) balancearse; oscilar; (*on a swing*) columpiarse; (*hang*) colgar, pender; (*door etc*) girar; **to** — **at anchor** estar anclado; **the door** —**s on its hinges** la puerta gira sobre sus goznes; **it swung open** de pronto se abrió; **it** —**s in the wind** se balancea al viento; **a revolver swung from his belt** un revólver colgaba de su cinturón; **he'll** — **for it** le ahorcarán por ello.

(b) (*change direction*) cambiar de dirección; **he swung round** giró sobre los talones, se volvió bruscamente; **the car swung into the square** el coche viró y entró en la plaza; **it swung right round** dio una vuelta completa; **to** — **into action** ponerse en marcha; empezar a ponerse por obra; **the country has swung to the right** el país ha virado a la derecha.

4 *vr*: **to** — **oneself into the saddle** subir a la silla con un solo movimiento enérgico; **to** — **oneself round** girar sobre los talones.
swing bridge ['swiŋ'bridʒ] *n* puente *m* giratorio.
swing door ['swiŋ'dɔ:*] *n* puerta *f* giratoria.
swingeing ['swindʒiŋ] *adj* abrumador.
swinging ['swiŋiŋ] *adj* (*fam*) *city etc* alegre, de vida alegre, lleno de diversiones.
swinish ['swainiʃ] *adj* (*fig*) cochino, canallesco; brutal.
swipe [swaip] 1 *n* golpe *m* fuerte; **to take a** — **at someone** asestar un golpe a uno.

2 *vt* (a) golpear fuertemente; pegar; **he** —**s her** la pega.

(b) (*sl*) apandar, guindar.

3 *vi*: **to** — **at someone** asestar un golpe a uno.
swirl [swə:l] 1 *n* remolino *m*, torbellino *m*; **it disappeared in a** — **of water** desapareció en el agua arremolinada; **the** — **of the dancers' skirts** el girar de las faldas de las bailadoras.

2 *vi* arremolinarse; girar, girar confusamente.
swish [swiʃ] 1 *n* silbar; (*of dress etc*) crujir.

2 *adj* (*sl: smart*) elegantísimo; (*posh*) de buen tono.

3 *vt cane* agitar (*or* blandir) produciendo un silbido; *tail* agitar, menear; (*thrash*) azotar.

4 *vi* silbar; sonar, crujir.
Swiss [swis] 1 *adj* suizo. 2 *n* suizo *m*, a *f*.
switch [switʃ] 1 *n* (a) (*stick*) vara *f*, varilla *f*; (*whip*) látigo *m*.

(b) (*of hair*) trenza *f* postiza, trenza *f*, postizo *m*.

(c) (*Rail: points*) aguja *f*; (*change of line*) desviación *f*.

(d) (*Elec etc*) interruptor *m*, conmutador *m*, llave *f*, botón *m*.

(e) (*change*) cambio *m*; **a rapid** — **of plan** un cambio repentino de idea; **to do a** —, **to make a** — hacer un cambio.

2 *vt* (a) *tail* agitar, menear.

(b) (*Rail*) desviar, cambiar de vía; **to** — **a train to another line** cambiar un tren a otra vía.

(c) (*change*) *position etc* cambiar; *policy etc* cambiar de; **so we** —**ed hats** así que cambiamos los sombreros; **to** — **over A and B** cambiar A con B.

(d) (*Elec etc*) **to** — **on** (*Elec*) encender, conectar, poner; (*Aut etc*) arrancar, poner en marcha; **please** — **the radio on** por favor, encienda la radio; **to leave the television** —**ed on** dejar puesta la televisión; **to** — **off** (*Elec*) desconectar, quitar; *light* apagar; *engine* parar.

3 *vi* (a) (*change*) cambiar; **to** — **(over) from Y to Z** cambiar de Y a Z, dejar Y para tomar Z; **to** — **over to another station** cambiar a otra emisora; **we've** —**ed over altogether to gas** lo hemos cambiado todo a gas; **to** — **round** cambiar de sitio; cambiar de idea.

(b) **to** — **on** encender la radio, poner la televisión (*etc*); arrancar el motor; **to** — **off** desconectar la televisión (*etc*).
switchback ['switʃbæk] *n* (*at fair etc*) montaña *f* rusa, tobogán *m*; (*road*) camino *m* muy desigual, carretera *f* llena de baches.
switchboard ['switʃbɔ:d] *n* (*Tech*) cuadro *m* de mandos; (*Elec*) tablero *m* de conmutadores, cuadro *m* de distribución; (*Tel: at exchange*) cuadro *m* de conexión manual, (*in office etc*) centralita *f*.
switchman ['switʃmən] *n*, *pl* —**men** [mən] (*Rail*) guardagujas *m*.
switchyard ['switʃjɑ:d] *n* (*US Rail*) patio *m* de maniobras.
Switzerland ['switsələnd] Suiza *f*.
swivel ['swivl] 1 *n* eslabón *m* giratorio; pivote *m*.

2 *attr* giratorio, movil.

3 *vt* (*also* **to** — **round**) girar.

4 vi (*also* **to — round**) girar; (*of person*) volverse, girar sobre los talones.
swivel seat ['swivlsi:t] n silla f giratoria.
swizz [swiz] n, **swizzle** ['swizl] n (*fam*) *see* **swindle**.
swollen ['swəulən] ptp of **swell**.
swoon [swu:n] **1** n desmayo m, desvanecimiento m; **to fall in a —** desmayarse.
   2 vi desmayarse, desvanecerse (*also* **to — away**); **she —ed at the news** al saber la noticia se desmayó.
swoop [swu:p] **1** n calada f, descenso m súbito; arremetida f; (*by police*) redada f; visita f de inspección; **at one fell —, in one —** de un solo golpe.
   2 vi (*also* **to — down**; *of bird*) calarse; precipitarse, lanzarse (*on* sobre); **the plane —ed low over the village** el avión picó y voló muy bajo sobre el pueblo; **the police —ed on 8 suspects** la policía detuvo a 8 sospechosos; **he —ed on this mistake** saltó sobre este error.
swoosh [swu(:)ʃ] = **swish**.
swop [swɔp] *see* **swap**.
sword [sɔ:d] n espada f; **to cross —s with someone** habérselas con uno; reñir con uno; **to measure —s with someone** cruzar espadas con uno; **to put people to the —** pasar a cuchillo a unas gentes; **those that live by the — die by the —** el que a hierro mata a hierro muere.
sword dance ['sɔ:ddɑ:ns] n danza f de espadas.
swordfish ['sɔ:dfiʃ] n pez m espada.
swordplay ['sɔ:dplei] n esgrima f; manejo m de la espada; **the film has 5 minutes of —** en la película se combate a espada durante 5 minutos.
swordsman ['sɔ:dzmən] n, pl **-men** [mən] espadachín m; (*fencer*) esgrimidor m.
swordsmanship ['sɔ:dzmənʃip] n esgrima f, manejo m de la espada.
swordstick ['sɔ:dstik] n bastón m de estoque.
sword-swallower ['sɔ:d,swɔləuə*] n tragasables m.
sword thrust ['sɔ:dθrʌst] n estocada f.
swore [swɔ:*] pret of **swear**.
sworn [swɔ:n] **1** ptp of **swear**. **2** adj *enemy* implacable; *evidence* dado bajo juramento.
swot [swɔt] (*fam*) **1** n empollón m, ona f. **2** vt empollar; **to — up one's maths** empollar matemáticas. **3** vi empollar; **to — at something** empollar algo.
swum [swʌm] ptp of **swim**.
swung [swʌŋ] pret *and* ptp of **swing**.
sybarite ['sibərait] n sibarita mf.
sybaritic [,sibə'ritik] adj sibarita, sibarítico.
sycamore ['sikəmɔ:*] n sicomoro m (*also* **— tree**).
sycophancy ['sikəfənsi] n adulación f; servilismo m.
sycophant ['sikəfənt] n sicofante m, adulador m; persona f servil; sobón m.
sycophantic [,sikə'fæntik] adj *person* servil, sobón; *speech etc* adulatorio; *manner* servil.
syllabic [si'læbik] adj silábico.
syllabicate [si'læbikeit] vt silabear, dividir en sílabas.
syllabication [si,læbi'keiʃən] n silabeo m, división f en sílabas.
syllable ['siləbl] n sílaba f.
syllabus ['siləbəs] n programa m (*esp* de estudios).
syllogism ['silədʒizəm] n silogismo m.
syllogistic [,silə'dʒistik] adj silogístico.
sylph [silf] n (*Myth*) silfo m, silfide f; (*woman*) silfide f.
sylphlike ['silflaik] adj figure etc de sílfide.
sylvan ['silvən] adj selvático, silvestre; rústico.
symbiosis [,simbi'əusis] n simbiosis f.
symbol ['simbəl] n símbolo m.
symbolic(al) [sim'bɔlik(əl)] adj simbólico.
symbolically [sim'bɔlikəli] adv simbólicamente.
symbolism ['simbəlizəm] n simbolismo m.
symbolist ['simbəlist] **1** adj simbolista. **2** n simbolista mf.
symbolize ['simbəlaiz] vt simbolizar.
symmetrical [si'metrikəl] adj simétrico.
symmetrically [si'metrikəli] adv simétricamente.
symmetry ['simitri] n simetría f.
sympathetic [,simpə'θetik] adj (a) (*showing pity*) compasivo (*to* con), compadecido; (*kind*) amable, benévolo; **we found a — policeman** encontramos a un policía que amablemente nos ayudó (*etc*); **they were — but could not help** se compadecieron de nosotros pero no podían hacer nada para ayudarnos; **they are — to actors** están bien dispuestos hacia los actores.
   (b) (*understanding*) comprensivo; **with a — smile** con una sonrisa comprensiva.
   (c) *ink, nerve, pain etc* simpático.
sympathetically [,simpə'θetikəli] adv con compasión; amablemente, benévolamente; con comprensión; **she looked at me —** me miró compasiva.
sympathize ['simpəθaiz] vi (a) (*in sorrow etc*) compadecerse, condolerse; **I really do —** lo siento de verdad; **to — with someone** compadecerse de uno, condolerse de uno; **to — with someone in his bereavement** dar el pésame a uno por la muerte de . . .; **they called to —** vinieron a dar el pésame.
   (b) (*understand*) comprender; **I — with what you say, but . . .** comprendo el punto de vista de Vd, pero . . .
sympathizer ['simpəθaizə*] n simpatizante mf, partidario m, a f (*with* de).
sympathy ['simpəθi] **1** n (a) (*fellow feeling*) simpatía f; solidaridad f; **I am not in — with him** yo no comparto su criterio, yo no lo entiendo así; **the sympathies of the crowd were with him** la multitud estaba de lado de él, la multitud le apoyaba; **to strike in — with someone** declararse en huelga por solidaridad con uno.
   (b) (*pity*) compasión f, condolencia f; sentimiento m; (*kindness*) amabilidad f, benevolencia f; **he has my —** yo le compadezco; **my sympathies are with her family** yo lo siento por la familia de ella; **have you no —?** ¿no tiene compasión?; **to express one's —** dar el pésame (*on the death of* por la muerte de); **his — for the underdog** su compasión por los desvalidos.
   2 attr: **— strike** huelga f por solidaridad.
symphonic [sim'fɔnik] adj sinfónico.
symphony ['simfəni] n sinfonía f; **— orchestra** orquesta f sinfónica.
symposium [sim'pəuziəm] n, pl **symposia** [sim'pəuziə] simposio m.
symptom ['simptəm] n síntoma m; indicio m.
symptomatic [,simptə'mætik] adj sintomático (*of* de).
synagogue ['sinəgɔg] n sinagoga f.
synchromesh ['siŋkrəumeʃ] n (*also* **— gear**) cambio m de velocidades sincronizado.
synchronism ['siŋkrənizəm] n sincronismo m.
synchronization [,siŋkrənai'zeiʃən] n sincronización f.
synchronize ['siŋkrənaiz] **1** vt sincronizar (*with* con).
   2 vi sincronizarse, ser sincrónico (*with* con); coincidir (*with* con).
synchronous ['siŋkrənəs] adj sincrónico, síncrono.
syncopate ['siŋkəpeit] vt sincopar.
syncopation [,siŋkə'peiʃən] n síncopa f.
syncope ['siŋkəpi] n (*Mus*) síncopa f; (*Ling, Med*) síncope m.
syndicalism ['sindikəlizəm] n sindicalismo m.
syndicalist ['sindikəlist] **1** adj sindicalista. **2** n sindicalista mf.
syndicate ['sindikit] n sindicato m.
syndicate ['sindikeit] vt sindicar.
syndrome ['sindrəum] n síndrome m.
synecdoche [si'nekdəki] n sinécdoque f.
synod ['sinəd] n sínodo m.
synonym ['sinənim] n sinónimo m.
synonymous [si'nɔniməs] adj sinónimo (*with* con).
synonymy [si'nɔnəmi] n sinonimia f.
synopsis [si'nɔpsis] n, pl **synopses** [si'nɔpsi:z] sinopsis f.
synoptic(al) [si'nɔptik(əl)] adj sinóptico.
syntactic(al) [sin'tæktik(əl)] adj sintáctico.
syntax ['sintæks] n sintaxis f.
synthesis ['sinθəsis] n, pl **syntheses** ['sinθəsi:z] síntesis f.
synthesize ['sinθəsaiz] vt sintetizar.
synthetic [sin'θetik] adj sintético.
synthetically [sin'θetikəli] adv sintéticamente.
syphilis ['sifilis] n sífilis f.
syphilitic [,sifi'litik] **1** adj sifilítico. **2** n sifilítico m, a f.
syphon ['saifən] *see* **siphon**.
Syracuse ['saiərəkju:z] Siracusa.
Syria ['siriə] Siria f.
Syrian ['siriən] **1** adj sirio. **2** n sirio m, a f.
syringe [si'rindʒ] **1** n jeringa f. **2** vt jeringar.
syrup ['sirəp] n jarabe m; almíbar m.
syrupy ['sirəpi] adj parecido a jarabe, espeso como jarabe.
system ['sistəm] n sistema m; método m; (*Med*) organismo m, constitución f; (*Elec*) circuito m, instalación f; **feudal —** feudalismo m; **metric —** sistema m métrico; **nervous —** sistema m nervioso; **a shock to the —** una sacudida para el organismo; **to get something out of one's —** (*fig*) quitarse algo de encima.
systematic [,sistə'mætik] adj sistemático, metódico.
systematically [,sistə'mætikəli] adv sistemáticamente, metódicamente.
systematize ['sistəmətaiz] vt sistematizar.
systematization ['sistəmətai'zeiʃən] n sistematización f.

T

T [tiː]: **to a —** (fam) de perlas, de maravilla, al pelo; **it fits you to a —** te sienta perfectamente; **it suits me to a —** me va de perlas.

ta [tɑː] interj (fam) ¡gracias!; **— very much!** ¡muchas gracias!

tab [tæb] n oreja f, lengüeta f; (label) etiqueta f; (Theat) cortina f; **to keep —s on someone** echar un ojo sobre uno, vigilar a uno; **to keep —s on something** tener algo a la vista, tener cuenta de algo.

tabard ['tæbəd] n tabardo m.

tabby ['tæbi] **1** adj atigrado. **2** n (also **— cat**) gato m atigrado, gata f atigrada.

tabernacle ['tæbənækl] n tabernáculo m.

table ['teibl] **1** n **(a)** (furniture) mesa f; (Archit) tablero m; (of land) meseta f; **bedside —** mesita f de noche; **occasional —, small —** mesita f; **operating —** mesa f de operaciones; **round —** mesa f redonda; **round-— conference** conferencia f de mesa redonda; **water —** (Geog) nivel m de agua freática; **to keep a good —** tener buena mesa; **to clear the —** levantar la mesa; **to lay the —,** **to set the —** poner la mesa; **to rise from the —** levantarse de la mesa; **to sit down to —** sentarse a la mesa; **to turn the —s on someone** devolver la pelota a uno, vencer a uno empleando sus propias armas.

(b) (Math etc) tabla f; (statistical etc) tabla f, cuadro m; (of prices) lista f, tarifa f; (league —) liga f; clasificación f, escalafón m; **— of contents** índice m de materias; **multiplication —** tabla f de multiplicar; **log —s** tablas fpl de logaritmos; **we are in fourth place in the —** ocupamos el cuarto lugar en la clasificación.

2 vt (Parl etc) motion presentar, poner sobre la mesa; (set out) poner en una tabla, disponer en un cuadro; ordenar sistemáticamente; (US) bill dar carpetazo a.

tableau ['tæbləu] n cuadro m (vivo).

tablecloth ['teiblklɔθ] n, pl **—cloths** [klɔθs] mantel m.

table d'hôte ['tɑːbl'dəut] n mesa f redonda.

table lamp ['teibllæmp] n lámpara f de mesa.

tableland ['teibllænd] n meseta f.

table leg ['teiblleg] n pata f de mesa.

table linen ['teibl,linin] n mantelería f.

tablemat ['teiblmæt] n salvaplatos m, salvamanteles m.

Table Mountain ['teibl'mauntin] Monte m de la Mesa.

table napkin ['teibl,næpkin] n servilleta f.

table runner ['teibl,rʌnə*] n mantelillo m, camino m de mesa.

tablespoon ['teiblspuːn] n cuchara f grande, cuchara f para servir.

tablespoonful ['teibl,spuːnful] n cucharada f.

tablet ['tæblit] n tabla f; tableta f; (Med) tableta f, comprimido m; (of soap etc) pastilla f; (stone, inscribed) lápida f; (writing —) bloc m, taco m (de papel).

table talk ['teibltɔːk] n conversación f de sobremesa.

table tennis ['teibl,tenis] n tenis m de mesa.

tableware ['teiblweə*] n artículos mpl de mesa.

table water ['teibl,wɔːtə*] n agua f mineral.

table wine ['teiblwain] n vino m de mesa.

tabloid ['tæblɔid] n (Med) tableta f, comprimido m; (newspaper) periódico m de formato reducido, tabloide m.

taboo [tə'buː] **1** adj tabú, prohibido. **2** tabú m; **all kinds of —s** toda clase de tabúes. **3** vt declarar tabú, prohibir.

tabular ['tæbjulə*] adj tabular.

tabulate ['tæbjuleit] vt disponer en tablas, exponer en forma de tabla; resumir en tablas.

tabulation [,tæbju'leiʃən] n disposición f en tablas, exposición f en forma de tabla.

tachometer [tæ'kɔmitə*] n tacómetro m.

tachymeter [tæ'kimitə*] n taquímetro m.

tacit ['tæsit] adj tácito.

tacitly ['tæsitli] adv tácitamente.

taciturn ['tæsitəːn] adj taciturno.

taciturnity [,tæsi'təːniti] n taciturnidad f.

Tacitus ['tæsitəs] m Tácito.

tack [tæk] **1** n **(a)** (nail) tachuela f; **to get down to brass —s** ir al grano.

(b) (Sew) hilván m.

(c) (Naut: rope) amura f; (course) virada f, bordada f; (fig) rumbo m, dirección f; línea f de conducta, política f; **to be on the right —** (fig) ir por buen camino; **to be on the wrong —** estar equivocado; **to try another —** abordar un problema desde otro punto de partida; cambiar de política.

2 vt **(a)** (nail) clavar con tachuelas; **to — something down** afirmar algo con tachuelas, sujetar algo con tachuelas.

(b) (Sew) hilvanar; **to — something on to a letter** añadir algo a una carta; **somehow it got —ed on** de algún modo u otro quedó unido a lo principal, de algún modo u otro llegó a ser añadido a la parte principal.

3 vi **(a)** (Naut) virar, cambiar de bordada; **the ship —ed this way and that** el buque cambió constantemente de bordada.

(b) **to — on to someone** (fig) unirse a uno, pegarse a uno.

tackle ['tækl] **1** n **(a)** (esp Naut: pulley) aparejo m; polea f; (ropes) jarcia f; cordaje m.

(b) (gear, equipment) equipo m, avíos mpl, aperos mpl; (fig) cosas fpl, enseres mpl; (fishing —) aparejo m de pescar.

(c) (Sport) carga f, atajo m, blocaje m; **rough —** atajo m duro.

2 vt (grapple with) agarrar, asir; atacar; (Sport) atajar, blocar; problem abordar, atacar; task emprender; **he had to — 3 intruders** tuvo que hacer frente a 3 intrusos; **he —d Greek on his own** emprendió el estudio del griego sin ayuda de nadie; **did you ever — Mulacén?** ¿os atrevisteis alguna vez a escalar el Mulacén?; **can you — another helping?** ¿puedes comerte otra porción?; **I'll — him about it at once** lo discutiré con él en seguida (quiera o no quiera).

tacky ['tæki] adj pegajoso.

tact [tækt] n tacto m, discreción f.

tactful ['tæktful] adj discreto, diplomático; **be as — as you can** use la mayor discreción; **that was not very — of you** pudieras haberlo hecho con más tacto.

tactfully ['tæktfəli] adv discretamente, diplomáticamente.

tactfulness ['tæktfulnis] n tacto m, discreción f.

tactic ['tæktik] n **(a)** táctica f; maniobra f. **(b)** **—s** (collectively) táctica f.

tactical ['tæktikəl] adj táctico.

tactically ['tæktikəli] adv tácticamente.

tactician [tæk'tiʃən] n táctico m.

tactile ['tæktail] adj táctil.

tactless ['tæktlis] adj indiscreto, falto de tacto, poco diplomático.

tactlessly ['tæktlisli] adv indiscretamente, de modo poco diplomático.

tadpole ['tædpəul] n renacuajo m.

taffeta ['tæfitə] n tafetán m.

taffrail ['tæfreil] n coronamiento m, pasamano m de la borda.

taffy ['tæfi] n (US) **(a)** = **toffee**. **(b)** (fam) coba f (fam).

Taffy ['tæfi] (= **David**) el galés típico.

tag¹ [tæg] n (loose end) cabo m, rabito m; (rag) pingajo m; (metal tip) herrete m; (label) etiqueta f, marbete m; (commonplace) dicho m, lugar m común;

tag (*quotation*) cita *f*; **identification** — chapa *f* de identificación; **price** — etiqueta *f* que lleva el precio.

2 *vt* (*follow*) seguir de cerca, pisar los talones a; (*label*) poner una etiqueta a, pegar una etiqueta a; **to — something on to an article** pegar algo a un artículo; **can we — this on?** ¿podemos añadir esto?

3 *vi*: **to — along** (*jog along*) seguir despacio su camino; proceder con calma; (*accompany*) ir también, venir después; **to — on to someone** unirse a uno, (insistir en) acompañar a uno.

tag² [tæg] *n*: **to play —** dar la despedida, jugar al tócame tú.

Tagus ['teigəs] Tajo *m*.

Tahiti [tɑː'hiːti] Tahití *m*.

tail [teil] **1** *n* (*Anat*) cola *f*, rabo *m*; (*loose end*) cabo *m*; (*of hair*) trenza *f*; (*of comet*) cabellera *f*; (*Aer*) cola *f*; (*of procession etc*) cola *f*, parte *f* final; (*of coat*) faldón *m*, faldillas *fpl*; (*of shirt*) faldón *m*; **—s** (*coat*) frac *m*; (*of coin*) cruz *f*; **with its — between its legs** con el rabo entre las patas; **—s you lose** cruz y pierde Vd; **but there's a sting in the —** pero lo malo viene al final; **to turn —** volver la espalda, huir.

2 *vt* (**a**) (*follow*) seguir de cerca, pisar los talones a; vigilar.

(**b**) *animal* descolar; *fruit* quitar el tallo a.

3 *vi* (**a**) **to — away, to — off** ir disminuyendo (*into* hasta, hasta no ser más que), desaparecer poco a poco; **his voice —ed away** su voz se fue debilitando; **after that the book —s away** después de eso el libro ya no es tan bueno, después de eso el libro no tiene tantas cosas buenas.

(**b**) **to — after someone** seguir a uno (de mala gana).

tailboard ['teilbɔːd] *n* escalera *f*, tablero *m* posterior.

tail coat ['teilkəut] *n* frac *m*.

-tailed [teild] *adj* con rabo..., *eg* **long-tailed** con rabo largo, rabilargo.

tail end ['teil'end] *n* cola *f*; extremo *m*; parte *f* de atrás, parte *f* posterior; (*fig*) parte *f* que queda, porción *f* inservible.

tail gunner ['teil,gʌnə*] *n* (*Aer*) artillero *m* de cola.

tail lamp ['teillæmp] *n* faro *m* trasero.

tailless ['teillis] *adj* sin rabo.

taillight ['teillait] *n* faro *m* trasero.

tailor ['teilə*] **1** *n* sastre *m*; **—'s** (*shop*) sastrería *f*. **2** *vt suit* hacer, confeccionar; (*fig*) adaptar.

tailored ['teiləd] *adj*: **— dress** vestido *m* sastre; **a well-— suit** un traje bien hecho, un traje que entalla bien.

tailoring ['teiləriŋ] *n* (*craft*) sastrería *f*; (*cut*) corte *m*, hechura *f*.

tailor-made ['teiləmeid] *adj* (**a**) hecho por sastre, de sastre; **— costume** traje *m* hechura sastre.

(**b**) (*fig*) **— for you** especial para Vd, creado especialmente para Vd.

tailpiece ['teilpiːs] *n* (*Typ*) florón *m*; (*addition*) apéndice *m*, añadidura *f*.

tailpipe ['teilpaip] *n* (*US: Aut*) tubo *m* de escape.

tailplane ['teilplein] *n* (*Aer*) cola *f*, plano *m* de cola.

tail skid ['teilskid] *n* (*Aer*) patín *m* de cola.

tailspin ['teilspin] *n* (*Aer*) barrena *f* picada.

tail unit ['teil,juːnit] *n* conjunto *m* de cola.

tail wheel ['teil'wiːl] *n* rueda *f* de cola.

tailwind ['teilwind] *n* viento *m* de cola.

taint [teint] **1** *n* infección *f*; (*fig*) mancha *f*, tacha *f*; olor *m* (*of* a); **the — of sin** la mancha del pecado; **not free from the — of corruption** no sin cierto olor a corrupción.

2 *vt* corromper, inficionar, viciar.

3 *vi* corromperse, inficionarse, viciarse.

tainted ['teintid] *adj* viciado, corrompido; *meat etc* pasado; **a belief — with heresy** una creencia no exenta de herejía.

take [teik] (*irr: pret* **took**, *ptp* **taken**) **1** *vt* (**a**) (*general sense*) tomar; (*by force*) coger, asir, arrebatar; (*steal*) robar; (*keep*) quedarse con; **to — something from someone** tomar algo a uno; **who took my beer?** ¿quién se ha llevado mi cerveza?; **to — a book from a shelf** sacar un libro de un estante; **to — a passage from an author** tomar un pasaje de un autor; **to — someone's arm** tomar del brazo a uno; **to — someone in one's arms** abrazar a uno, rodear a uno con los brazos.

(**b**) (*capture*) *city etc* tomar, conquistar; *specimen, fish etc* coger; (*Chess*) comer; *prisoner* hacer; *suspect, wanted man* coger, detener; **to — someone alive or dead** coger a uno vivo o muerto; **the devil — it!** ¡maldición!, ¡que se lo lleve el diablo!; **to be —n ill** ponerse enfermo, enfermar; **we were very —n with him** le encontramos simpatiquísimo; **I'm not at all —n with the idea** la idea no me gusta nada, la idea no me hace gracia.

(**c**) (*win*) *prize* ganar; *trick* ganar, hacer; **to — one's degree** recibir un título; **to — a degree in** licenciarse en; **to — £30 a day** cobrar 30 libras al día; **last year we took £30,000** el año pasado los ingresos sumaron 30.000 libras.

(**d**) (*rent*) alquilar; **we shall — a house for the summer** alquilaremos una casa para el verano; **we took rooms at Torquay** alquilamos un piso en Torquay.

(**e**) (*occupy*) ocupar; **is that seat —n?** ¿está ocupada esa plaza?; **please — your seats!** ¡siéntense, por favor!

(**f**) (*go by*) *bus, train etc* coger; *road* tomar, ir por; *fence* saltar, saltar por encima de; **— the first on the right** vaya por la primera calle a la derecha; **we took the wrong road** nos equivocamos de camino; **we — the golden road to Samarkand** vamos por el camino dorado de Samarkand.

(**g**) (*ingest*) *drink, food* tomar; **to — a meal** comer; **he took no food for 4 days** durante 4 días no comió; **how much alcohol had he —n?** ¿cuánto alcohol había ingerido?; **"not to be —n"** (*Med*) "para uso externo"; **will you — something before you go?** ¿quieres tomar algo antes de irte?

(**h**) (*have, make, undertake etc*) *bath, bend, breath, decision, exercise, holiday, liberty, possession* tomar; *step, walk,* dar; *photo* sacar, tomar; *ticket* sacar; *trip* hacer; *oath* prestar; *census* levantar, efectuar; *examination* presentarse para, sufrir; *opportunity* aprovechar; *see* **effect, stock** *etc*.

(**i**) (*receive*) recibir, tomar; *advice* seguir; *bet* aceptar, hacer; *responsibility* asumir; *guests* recibir; *pupils* tomar; *course of study* seguir, cursar; *subject* estudiar; *newspaper etc* leer, abonarse a; **— that!** ¡toma!; **— it from me!** ¡escucha lo que te digo!; **you can — it from me that...** puedes tener la seguridad de que...; **to — the service** (*Tennis*) restar la pelota, ser restador; **he took the ball full in the chest** el balón le dio de lleno en el pecho; **what will you — for it?** ¿cuánto pides por él?; **to — a wife** casarse; **to — someone into partnership** tomar a uno como socio; **to — (holy) orders** ordenarse de sacerdote; *see* **badly, ill** *etc*.

(**j**) (*tolerate*) aguantar, sufrir; **we can — it** lo aguantamos todo; **he took a lot of punishment** sufrió mucho, sufrió un duro castigo; **London took a battering in 1941** Londres recibió una paliza en 1941, Londres sufrió terriblemente en 1941; **I won't — no for an answer** no permito que digas no, no permito que me des una respuesta negativa; **I won't — that from you** no permito que digas eso; no tolero semejante cosa de Vd.

(**k**) (*consider*) tomar, considerar; **now — Ireland** consideren el caso de Irlanda, pongamos por caso Irlanda; **taking one thing with another...** considerándolo todo junto..., considerándolo en conjunto...; **taking one year with another...** tomando un año con otro...

(**l**) (*contain*) tener cabida para; **a car that —s 6 passengers** un coche con cabida para 6 personas, un coche donde caben 6 personas; **can you — 2 more?** ¿puedes llevar 2 más?, ¿caben otros 2?; **it won't — any more** no cabe(n) más; **it —s weights up to 8 tons** soporta pesos hasta de 8 toneladas.

(**m**) (*experience*) experimentar; *illness* coger; **to — cold** tomar frío; coger un resfriado, resfriarse; **to — fright** asustarse (*at* de); **to — a dislike to someone** coger antipatía a uno, tomar hincha a uno (*fam*); *see* **liking** *etc*.

(**n**) (*suppose*) suponer; **I — it that...** supongo que..., imagino que...; **I — her to be about 30** supongo que tiene unos 30 años; **I took him for a foreigner** creí que era extranjero, le tomé por extranjero; **what do you — me for?** ¿por quién me ha tomado Vd?, ¿crees que soy un tonto?; **we took A for B** equivocamos A con B.

(**o**) (*require*) necesitar; hacer falta; **a recipe that —s 10 eggs** una receta en la que hacen falta 10 huevos; **it —s a lot of courage** exige gran valor; **it —s a brave man to do that** hace falta que un hombre tenga mucho valor para hacer eso; **he's got what it —s** tiene las cualidades precisas; **it —s 4 days** es cosa de 4 días; **it —s 4 days to get there** tarda 4 días en llegar allá; **it won't — long** no exige mucho tiempo; no tarda mucho; **it took 3 policemen to hold him down** se necesitó de 3 policías para sujetarle; **that verb —s the dative** ese verbo rige el dativo; *see* **size** *etc*.

(**p**) (*lead, transport*) llevar; **to — something to someone** llevar algo a uno; **to — someone some-**

where llevar a uno a un sitio; **we took her to the doctor** la llevamos al médico; **an ambulance took him to hospital** una ambulancia le llevó al hospital; **they took me over the factory** me mostraron la fábrica, me acompañaron en una visita a la fábrica; **to — someone for a walk** llevar a uno de paseo; **it took us out of our way** nos hizo desviarnos de nuestra ruta; **whatever took you to Miami?** ¿con qué propósito fuiste a Miami?, ¿qué propósito tuvo su viaje a Miami?

(**q**) (with adv or prep) **to — aback** see **aback**; **to — along** llevar, traer; person llevar; **to — apart** desmontar; **to — away** quitar; llevarse; person llevarse; (Math) restar; **7 — away 4 is 3** 7 menos 4 son 3; **to — back** (return) devolver; (receive back) object recibir devuelto, person recibir otra vez (como amigo or novio etc); words retractar, promise desdecirse de; **they gave it to me but then they took it back again** me lo dieron pero volvieron luego a quitármelo; **the company took him back** la compañía volvió a emplearle, la compañía le restituyó a su puesto; **to — down** (get down) bajar; descolgar; (Tech) desmontar, desarmar; note apuntar; poner por escrito; **to — someone down** quitar los humos a uno; **to — in** work aceptar, admitir; person acoger, recibir (en su casa); food tomar, ingerir; (include) abarcar; clothes achicar, belt apretarse; sail desmontar; paper abonarse a, leer; (understand) entender, comprender; **to — someone in** (fam) embaucar a uno, estafar a uno, dar a uno gato por liebre; **I was properly —n in by the disguise** el disfraz me despistó completamente; **don't let yourself be —n in by appearances** no te dejes engañar por las apariencias; **to — off** clothes, hat quitarse; limb amputar; lid, wrapping, etc quitar; (unstick) despegar; discount descontar, rebajar; (imitate) imitar; contrahacer, parodiar; **they took him off to lunch** se le llevaron a comer; **to — on** (assume) asumir, tomar; work emprender; aceptar; duties tomar sobre sí, cargar con, encargarse de; workmen contratar; cargo cargar, tomar; **to — someone on** (as challenge) desafiar a uno, atreverse a competir con uno; (Sport) jugar contra uno, luchar contra uno; **he's —n on more than he bargained for** le está resultando peor de lo que él se creía, él no contaba con tener que esforzarse tanto; **to — out** (from pocket etc) sacar; (extract) extraer, sacar; (remove) quitar; stain quitar; (outside house etc) llevar fuera; children, dog llevar de paseo; girl invitar; escoltar; salir con; pretender; patent obtener; **to — it out of someone** cansar a uno, rendir a uno; **to — it out on someone** desahogarse riñendo a uno; vengarse de uno; **to — over** responsibility asumir, encargarse de; leadership, office etc asumir; tomar posesión de; **the army has —n over power** el ejército se ha hecho cargo del poder, el ejército ha ocupado el poder; **the tourists have —n over the museums** los turistas han acaparado los museos; **to — up** (carry up) subir; (pick up) coger, recoger; arms empuñar; water etc absorber; dress etc acortar; carpet quitar; passengers tomar; case emprender investigaciones acerca de; post tomar posesión de; residence establecer, fijar; room, time ocupar, llenar; story empezar a contar, (after break) continuar, reanudar; study empezar, dedicarse a; challenge, offer aceptar; **the bus —s up and sets down passengers** el autobús toma y deja pasajeros; **it —s up a lot of my time** me quita mucho tiempo; **to — someone up on something** censurar algo or expresar dudas acerca de algo que ha dicho uno; **I feel I must — you up on that** creo que es mi deber criticar esto que ha dicho Vd; **to — something upon oneself** tomar algo sobre sí, encargarse de algo; **to — it upon oneself to** + infin atreverse a + infin, (pej) tener bastante caradura como para + infin.

2 vi (**a**) (stick) pegar; (set) cuajar; (of vaccination) prender; (of plant) arraigar; (succeed) tener éxito; resultar ser eficaz.

(**b**) (Phot) **he —s well** saca buen retrato, saca buenas fotos.

(**c**) (with adv or prep) **to — after** (in looks) salir a, parecerse a; (in conduct) seguir el ejemplo de; **to — off** (for para); (Aer) despegar (for con rumbo a); **to — on** (fam) apurarse, excitarse, ponerse nervioso; quejarse; **don't — on so!** ¡no te apures!, ¡cálmate!; **to — over** tomar posesión; entrar en funciones; **to — to someone** coger simpatía a uno, tomar cariño a uno; **to — to something** aficionarse a algo, cobrar afición a algo; **to — to** + ger empezar a + ger; dedicarse a + infin, aficionarse a + infin; **to — up with someone**

relacionarse con uno, estrechar amistad con uno; **he took up with the wrong set** empezó a alternar con gente que no valía para nada.

3 n (Phot) toma f, vista f.

taken ['teikən] ptp of **take**.

takeoff ['teikɒf] n (**a**) (Aer) despegue m. (**b**) (imitation) imitación f; parodia f; sátira f; (**c**) (Mech) power — toma f de fuerza.

takeover ['teik,əuvə*] n toma f de posesión; entrada f en funciones; **the — of company A by company Z** la absorción de la compañía A por la compañía Z, la compra de la compañía A en su totalidad por la compañía Z; — **bid** oferta f para comprar la totalidad (de una compañía etc).

taker ['teikə*] n: —s of snuff los que acostumbran tomar rapé; —s of drink in moderation los que beben con moderación; **at £5 there were no** —s a un precio de 5 libras nadie se ofreció a comprarlo; **this challenge found no** —s no hubo nadie que quisiera aceptar este desafío.

taking ['teikiŋ] **1** adj atractivo, encantador.

2 n toma f, conquista f; —s (Fin) ingresos mpl; (at show etc) taquilla f, entrada f, recaudación f; **this year's —s were only half last year's** este año se ha embolsado la mitad de la recaudación del año pasado.

talc [tælk] n talco m.

talcum powder ['tælkəm,paudə*] n (polvo m de) talco m.

tale [teil] n cuento m; historia f, relación f; (pej) cuento m, patraña f; "**T—s of King Arthur**" "Leyendas fpl del Rey Artús"; **old wives'** — cuento m de viejas, patraña f; **I hear —s about you** me cuentan cosas acerca de Vd; **to tell —s (out of school)** soplar, chismear, contar cuentos; **he told the — of his life** contó la historia de su vida; **he had quite a — to tell** tuvo cosas bastante interesantes que contar.

talebearer ['teil,bɛərə*] n soplón m, ona f, chismoso m, a f.

talent ['tælənt] n talento m (for para); **man of** — hombre m de talento; **all the local** — toda la gente de talento de la comarca; **he watches for — at away matches** busca jugadores de talento en los partidos fuera de casa.

talented ['tæləntid] adj talentoso, de talento.

talent scout ['tælənt,skaut] n, **talent spotter** ['tælənt,spɒtə*] n cazatalentos m.

talisman ['tælizmən] n talismán m.

talk [tɔːk] **1** n (conversation) conversación f, (chat) charla f; (informal lecture) charla f; (gossip) chismes mpl, habladurías fpl; **idle** — charla f insustancial; **it's just** — son cosas que se dicen, son rumores; **with him it's all** — no hace más que hablar; **she's the — of the town** todos hablan de ella, es la comidilla de la ciudad; **there is (some)** — of se habla de; **there has been some** — of his going se ha hablado de que va él; **to give a** — dar una charla (about sobre); **to have a — to (or with) someone** hablar con uno; **we must have a — sometime** tenemos que citarnos un día para hablar.

2 vt (**a**) hablar; **to — Arabic** hablar árabe; — **some Arabic to me** díme algo en árabe, díme unas palabras de árabe; **to — business** hablar de negocios; **to — nonsense** no decir más que tonterías; **to — sense** hablar con juicio, hablar razonablemente; see **shop** etc.

(**b**) (with adv or prep) **to — away an hour** pasar una hora charlando; **to — someone down** no dejar meter baza a uno; **to — a plane down** controlar el aterrizaje de un avión desde tierra; **to — someone into something** persuadir a uno para que haga algo, convencer a uno de la conveniencia de hacer algo; **to — someone out of something** disuadir a uno de algo; **to — something over** hablar de algo, discutir algo; pasar revista a algo; **to — someone round** convencer a uno.

3 vi hablar; (about, of de; to con, a); charlar; **now you're —ing!** ¡eso es más razonable!; **to keep someone —ing** entretener a uno en conversación; **to — through one's hat** decir tonterías; — **about fleas!** ¡y las pulgas!; ¡Dios mío, qué pulgas!; **what shall we — about?** ¿de qué vamos a hablar?; **it is much —ed about** se habla mucho de ello; **to get oneself —ed about** in the papers lograr que los periódicos hablen de uno; **he knows what he's —ing about** habla con conocimiento de causa; **he doesn't know what he's —ing about** no tiene la menor idea; **to — away** seguir hablando; seguir hablando más que siete; **to — back to someone** contestar con frescura a uno; **to — down to someone** darse aires de superioridad con uno; —**ing of bats, we . . .** a propósito de los murciélagos, nosotros ...; to — to oneself hablar consigo mismo; see big.

4 *vr*: to — oneself hoarse enronquecer a fuerza de hablar; he —ed himself into it se autosugestionó, se convenció a sí mismo; he —ed himself out of the job hizo tan mala impresión hablando que no le dieron el puesto.

talkative ['tɔːkətiv] *adj* locuaz, hablador.

talkativeness ['tɔːkətivnis] *n* locuacidad *f*.

talked-of ['tɔːktɔv] *adj*: a much — event un suceso muy sonado.

talker ['tɔːkə*] *n* hablador *m*, ora *f*; to be a good — hablar bien; tener una conversación amena; he's just a — habla mucho pero no hace nada.

talkie ['tɔːki] *n* (*Cine*) película *f* sonora.

talking ['tɔːkiŋ] **1** *adj* parlante; *film etc* sonoro, hablado; *bird* parlero.

2 *n* .conversación *f*; palabras *fpl*; "no —" "prohibido hablar"; no —, please, ¡silencio, por favor!; she does all the — ella es quien habla.

talking point ['tɔːkiŋpɔint] *n* tema *m* de conversación.

talking-to ['tɔːkiŋtuː] *n*: to give someone a — echar un rapapolvo a uno.

tall [tɔːl] *adj* alto; grande; *story* exagerado, increíble; that's pretty —! ¡eso no puede ser!; ¡es increíble! a building 30 metres — un edificio que tiene 30 metros de alto; how — you've got! ¡qué grande estás!; ¡cómo has crecido!; how — are you? ¿cuánto mides?; I'm 6 feet — mido 6 pies.

tallboy ['tɔːlbɔi] *n* cómoda *f* alta.

tallness ['tɔːlnis] *n* altura *f*; talla *f*.

tallow ['tæləu] *n* sebo *m*.

tallowy ['tæləui] *adj* seboso.

tally ['tæli] **1** *n* (*stick*) tarja *f*; (*account*) cuenta *f*; (*fig*) número *m*, total *m*; to keep a — of llevar la cuenta de.

2 *vi* concordar, corresponder, cuadrar (*with* con).

tally clerk ['tæliklaːk] *n* medidor *m*.

tallyho ['tæli'həu] *interj*, *n* grito del *cazador*. (de zorras).

Talmud ['tælmud] *n* Talmud *m*.

Talmudic [tæl'mudik] *adj* talmúdico.

talon ['tælən] *n* garra *f*.

tamable ['teiməbl] *adj* domable, domesticable.

tamarind ['tæmərind] *n* tamarindo *m*.

tamarisk ['tæmərisk] *n* tamarisco *m*.

Tamberlane ['tæmbəlein] *m* Tamerlán.

tambour ['tæmbuə*] *n* (*Archit*, *Mus etc*) tambor *m*.

tambourine [ˌtæmbə'riːn] *n* pandereta *f*.

tame [teim] **1** *adj* (*tamed*) domesticado; (*by nature*) manso, dócil; (*spiritless*) insípido, soso; inocuo;. (*boring*, *flat*) soso, aburrido; we have a — rabbit tenemos un conejo doméstico; the birds grow — los pájaros se acostumbran a la presencia de personas, los pájaros pierden su temor a las personas.

2 *vt* *animal* domar, domesticar; amansar; *passion etc* reprimir, contener.

tameness ['teimnis] *n* mansedumbre *f*; insipidez *f*, sosería *f*; falta *f* de temor.

tamer ['teimə*] *n* domador *m*, ora *f*.

taming ['teimiŋ] *n* domadura *f*; "The T— of the Shrew" "La fierecilla domada".

tam o' shanter [ˌtæmə'ʃæntə*] *n* boina *f* escocesa.

tamp [tæmp] *vt* (*also* to — down, to — in) apisonar, afirmar; (*Min*) atacar.

tamper ['tæmpə*] *vi*: to — with (*mess up*) estropear, descomponer; ajar; *lock* tratar de forzar; *document* falsificar; interpolar; *witness* sobornar; (*meddle in*) entrometerse en; my car had been —ed with alguien había tratado de forzar la puerta de mi coche; they are —ing with our plans están estropeando nuestros planes.

tampon ['tæmpən] *n* tapón *m*; (*Med*) tampón *m*.

tan [tæn] **1** *n* (*sun*) bronceado *m*, tostado *m*; (*bark*) casca *f*; (*colour*) color *m* café claro, color *m* canela; to acquire a —, to get a — broncearse.

2 *adj* color café claro, color canela; color marrón; *shoes* de color.

3 *vt* (*of sun*) broncear, tostar; *leather* curtir, adobar; to — someone, to — the hide off someone (*fam*) zurrar a uno.

4 *vi* broncearse, tostarse.

tandem ['tændəm] **1** *n* tándem *m*. **2** *adj*, *adv* en tándem.

tang [tæŋ] *n* (*of knife*) espiga *f*; (*taste*) sabor *m*, sabor *m* fuerte y picante; it has the — of the soil tiene fuerte sabor a tierra.

tangent ['tændʒənt] *n* tangente *f*; to fly off at a —, to go off at a — (*fig*) salirse por la tangente.

tangential [tæn'dʒenʃəl] *adj* tangencial.

tangerine [ˌtændʒə'riːn] *n* mandarina *f*.

tangibility [ˌtændʒi'biliti] *n* tangibilidad *f*.

tangible ['tændʒəbl] *adj* tangible; (*fig*) palpable, concreto, sensible.

tangibly ['tændʒəbli] *adv* de modo palpable, concretamente.

Tangier(s) [tæn'dʒiə(z)] Tánger.

tangle ['tæŋgl] **1** *n* nudo *m*; enredo *m*, maraña *f*; (*of streets etc*) laberinto *m*; (*fig*) enredo *m*, lío *m*; confusión *f*; to be in a — estar enmarañado, haberse formado un nudo; (*fig*) estar en confusión; I'm in a — with the accounts me he hecho un lío con las cuentas; to get into a — hacerse un nudo, anudarse; (*fig*) enredarse, enmarañarse; I got into a — with the police me hice un lío con la policía.

2 *vt* enredar, enmarañar (*also* to — up).

3 *vi* enredarse, enmarañarse (*also* to — up); to — with someone pelearse con uno, meterse con uno; habérselas con uno.

tango ['tæŋgəu] **1** *n*, *pl* tangos ['tæŋgəuz] tango *m*; **2** *vi* bailar el tango.

tank [tæŋk] **1** *n* tanque *m*, depósito *m*; (*large*, *water*) cisterna *f*, aljibe *m*; (*Mil*) tanque *m*, carro *m* (de combate).

2 *vt*: to get —ed up (*sl*) emborracharse (*on beer* bebiendo cerveza).

tankard ['tæŋkəd] *n* bock *m*, pichel *m*.

tank car ['tæŋkkaː*] *n* (*Rail*) vagón *m* cisterna.

tank engine ['tæŋk,endʒin] *n* (*Rail*) locomotora *f* ténder.

tanker ['tæŋkə*] *n* (*Naut*) petrolero *m*; (*Aut*) camión-tanque *m*.

tankful ['tæŋkful] *n* contenido *m* (or capacidad *f*) de un depósito (*esp* de gasolina); to get a — of petrol llenar el depósito de gasolina; a — is 25 litres la capacidad del depósito es de 25 litros.

tank wagon ['tæŋk,wægən] *n* (*Rail*) vagón *m* cisterna; (*Aut*) carro *m* cuba.

tanned [tænd] *adj* bronceado.

tanner[1] ['tænə*] *n* curtidor *m*.

tanner[2] ['tænə*] *n* (*sl*) seis peniques *mpl*, moneda *f* de seis peniques.

tannery ['tænəri] *n* curtiduría *f*.

tannic ['tænik] *adj*: — acid ácido *m* tánico.

tannin ['tænin] *n* tanino *m*.

tanning ['tæniŋ] *n* curtido *m*; (*fam*) zurra *f* (*fam*); to give someone a — (*fam*) zurrar a uno (*fam*).

tansy ['tænzi] *n* tanaceto *m*, atanasia *f*.

tantalize ['tæntəlaiz] *vti* atormentar (mostrando or prometiendo lo que no se puede conseguir), tentar (con cosas imposibles).

tantalizing ['tæntəlaiziŋ] *adj* atormentador, tentador; it is — to think that ... es tentador pensar que ...; with — slowness con desesperante lentitud; a most — offer una oferta de lo más tentador.

tantalizingly ['tæntəlaiziŋli] *adv* de modo atormentador, de modo tentador.

tantamount ['tæntəmaunt] *adj*: — to equivalente a; this is — to esto equivale a.

tantrum ['tæntrəm] *n* (*fam*) rabieta *f*.

Tanzania [ˌtænzə'niə] Tanzanía *f*.

tap[1] [tæp] **1** *n* (*water—*) grifo *m*; (*gas—*) llave *f*; (*of barrel*) espita *f*; (*tool*) macho *m* de terraja; (*Elec*) derivación *f*; beer on — cerveza *f* (sacada) de barril, cerveza *f* servida al grifo; to be on — (*fig*) estar a mano, estar disponible, estar listo.

2 *vt* *barrel* espitar; *tree* sangrar; (*Med*) hacer una puntura en; *wire* (*Elec*) hacer una derivación en, (*Tel*) intervenir, escuchar clandestinamente; *resources* explotar, utilizar.

tap[2] [tæp] **1** *n* palmadita *f*; golpecito *m*, golpe *m* ligero; (*on typewriter etc*) pulsación *f*; there was a — on the door llamaron suavemente a la puerta; I felt a — on my shoulder sentí que alguien me daba una palmadita en el hombro.

2 *vt* dar una palmadita a (or en); golpear suavemente, golpear ligeramente; *typewriter etc* pulsar; to — in a nail hacer que entre un clavo golpeándolo ligeramente; to — out a message enviar un mensaje en · Morse; to — out one's pipe vaciar la pipa golpeándola ligeramente.

3 *vi* dar golpecitos; to — at a door llamar suavemente a una puerta; he —ped on the table several times dio varios golpecitos en la mesa.

tap-dance ['tæpdaːns] **1** *n* zapateado *m*. **2** *vi* zapatear.

tap-dancer ['tæp,daːnsə*] *n* bailarín *m* de zapateado, bailarina *f* de zapateado.

tape [teip] **1** *n* (*Sew etc*) cinta *f*; (*Sport*) cinta *f*; (*ceremonial*) cinta *f* simbólica; (*sticking —*) cinta *f* adhesiva, (*Med*) esparadrapo *m*; (*recording —*) cinta *f* de grabación, cinta *f* magnetofónica; (— *measure*) cinta *f* métrica; red — (*fig*) (*rules*)

reglas *fpl*; (*formalities*) formulismo *m*, formalidades *fpl* burocráticas; trámites *mpl*; papeleo *m*.
 2 *vt* (*seal*) poner una cinta a, cerrar con una cinta; (*record*) grabar en cinta, registrar en un magnetofón; **I've got him —d** (*fam*) le tengo calado; **we've got it all —d** (*fam*) lo tenemos todo organizado, todo funciona perfectamente; **we have the game —d** (*fam*) hemos hecho nuestros preparativos para dominar el partido.
tape measure ['teip,meʒə*] *n* cinta *f* métrica.
taper ['teipə*] 1 *n* bujía *f*, cerilla *f*; (*Eccl*) cirio *m*. 2 *vt* afilar, ahusar. 3 *vi* ahusarse, rematar en punta; **to — away, to — off** (*fig*) ir disminuyendo.
tape-record ['teipri,kɔ:d] *vt* grabar en cinta, registrar en un magnetofón.
tape recorder ['teipri,kɔ:də*] *n* magnetofón *m*, magnetófono *m*.
tape recording ['teipri,kɔ:diŋ] *n* grabación *f* en cinta.
tapered ['teipəd] *adj*, **tapering** ['teipəriŋ] *adj* ahusado, que termina en punta; (*Mech*) cónico; **finger** afilado.
tapestry ['tæpistri] *n* (*object*) tapiz *m*; (*art*) tapicería *f*.
tapeworm ['teipwə:m] *n* tenia *f*, solitaria *f*.
tapioca [,tæpi'əukə] *n* tapioca *f*.
tapir ['teipə*] *n* tapir *m*.
tapper ['tæpə*] *n* (*Elec*, *Tel*) manipulador *m*.
tappet ['tæpit] *n* alzaválvulas *m*.
taproom ['tæprum] *n* bodegón *m*.
taproot ['tæpru:t] *n* raíz *f* central.
tapster ['tæpstə*] *n* mozo *m* de taberna.
tap water ['tæp,wɔ:tə*] *n* agua *f* corriente, agua *f* de grifo.
tar[1] [ta:*] 1 *n* alquitrán *m*, brea *f*.
 2 *vt* alquitranar, embrear; **to — and feather someone** embrear y emplumar a uno; **a newly —red road** una carretera recién alquitranada; **he's —red with the same brush** él es otro que tal, él es un ídem de lienzo.
tar[2] [ta:*] *n* (*also* **Jack T—**) marinero *m*.
tarantella [,tærən'telə] *n* tarantela *f*.
tarantula [tə'ræntjulə] *n* tarántula *f*.
tardily ['ta:dili] *adv* tardíamente; lentamente.
tardiness ['ta:dinis] *n* tardanza *f*; lentitud *f*.
tardy ['ta:di] *adj* (*late*) tardío; (*slow*) lento.
tare[1] [tɛə*] *n* (*Bot*; *also* **—s**) arveja *f*; (*Bib*) cizaña *f*.
tare[2] [tɛə*] *n* (*Comm*) tara *f*.
target ['ta:git] *n* (*Mil*) blanco *m*; (*fig*) blanco *m*, objetivo *m*; **the — vehicle** (*space research*) el vehículo blanco; **our — is £10** nuestro objetivo es reunir (*etc*) 10 libras, nos proponemos reunir (*etc*) 10 libras; **the —s for production in 1980** los objetivos previstos para la producción en 1980; **to be the — for criticism** ser el blanco de la crítica; **to be on —** (*rocket etc*) llevar la dirección que se había previsto, ir hacia el blanco.
target practice ['ta:git,præktis] *n* tiro *m* al blanco.
tariff ['tærif] 1 *n* tarifa *f*, arancel *m*. 2 *attr* arancelario; **— reform** reforma *f* arancelaria.
tarmac ['ta:mæk] *n* alquitranado *m*.
tarn [ta:n] *n* lago *m* pequeño de montaña.
tarnish ['ta:niʃ] 1 *vt* deslustrar, quitar el brillo a; (*fig*) deslustrar, empañar. 2 *vi* deslustrarse, perder su brillo, empañarse.
tarot ['tærəu] *n* *naipe de dibujos alegóricos*.
tarpaulin [ta:'pɔ:lin] *n* alquitranado *m*, encerado *m*.
tarpon ['ta:pɔn] *n* tarpón *m*.
tarragon ['tærəgən] *n* (*Bot*) dragoncillo *m*, estragón *m*.
tarry ['ta:ri] *adj* alquitranado, embreado; cubierto (*or* manchado *etc*) de alquitrán; **to taste —** saber a alquitrán.
tarry ['tæri] *vi* (*lit*) (*stay*) quedarse; (*dally*) entretenerse, quedarse atrás; (*be late*) tardar (en venir).
tarsus ['ta:səs] *n*, *pl* **tarsi** ['ta:sai] tarso *m*.
tart[1] [ta:t] *adj* ácido, agrio; (*fig*) áspero.
tart[2] [ta:t] *n* tarta *f*; pastelillo *m* de fruta, pastelillo *m* de mermelada; (*sl*) furcia *f* (*sl*), fulana *f* (*sl*).
tartan ['ta:tən] *n* tartán *m*.
tartar ['ta:tə*] *n* (*Chem*) tártaro *m*; sarro *m*.
tartar(e) ['ta:tə*] *attr*: **— sauce** salsa *f* tártara; **— steak** biftec *crudo*, *picado y condimentado con sal*, *pimiento*, *cebolla etc*.
Tartar ['ta:tə*] 1 *adj* tártaro. 2 *n* tártaro *m*, a *f*; (*fig*) arpía *f*, fiera *f*; **to catch a —** meterse con uno que resulta tener fuerzas superiores.
tartaric [ta:'tærik] *adj*: **— acid** ácido *m* tártarico.
Tartary ['ta:təri] Tartaria *f*.
tartly ['ta:tli] *adv* (*fig*) ásperamente.
tartness ['ta:tnis] *n* acidez *f*, agrura *f*; (*fig*) aspereza *f*.

task [ta:sk] *n* tarea *f*, labor *f*; empresa *f*, cometido *m*, deber *m*; **it's an uphill —** es una labor difícil; **to set someone the — of doing something** dar a uno el encargo de hacer algo; **to take someone to —** reprender a uno (*for something* algo), llamar a uno a capítulo.
task force ['ta:skfɔ:s] *n* (*Mil*) agrupación *f* de fuerzas (para una operación especial).
taskmaster ['ta:sk,ma:stə*] *n* amo *m*; capataz *m*; **he's a hard —** es un amo severo.
Tasmania [tæz'meiniə] Tasmania *f*.
Tasmanian [tæz'meiniən] 1 *adj* tasmanio. 2 *n* tasmanio *m*, a *f*.
tassel ['tæsəl] *n* borla *f*.
taste [teist] 1 *n* (a) (*flavour*) sabor *m* (*of* a); dejo *m* (*of* de); **it has an odd —** tiene un sabor raro, sabe algo raro; **it has no —** no sabe a nada, es insípido.
 (b) (*sample*) muestra *f*; (*sip*) sorbo *m*, trago *m*; **just a —, then** pues un sorbito nada más, pues sólo un poquitín; **add a — of salt** añadir una pizca de sal; **may I have a —?** ¿me permites probarlo?; **we got a — of what was to come** tuvimos una muestra de lo que había de venir después, se nos proporcionó un anticipo de lo que se estaba preparando; **we had a — of his bad temper** tuvimos una muestra de su mal humor.
 (c) (*liking*) afición *f*, inclinación *f*, gusto *m*; **one's —s in music** las inclinaciones de uno en asuntos de música; **to acquire** (*or* **develop**) **a — for** tomar gusto a, cobrar afición a; **to have a — for** gustar de, ser aficionado a; **with sugar to —** con azúcar al gusto, con azúcar a discreción; **it is to my —** me gusta; **Wagner is not to my —** no me gusta Wagner; **—s differ, each to his own —** entre gustos no hay disputa.
 (d) (*good — etc*) **good —** buen gusto *m*; **people of —** gente *f* de buen gusto; **they certainly have —** es cierto que tienen buen gusto; **to be in bad —**, **to be in poor —** ser de mal gusto.
 2 *vt* (a) (*sample*) probar; probar un bocado de, tomarse un trago de; (*professionally*) catar; **just — this** prueba un poco de esto; **I haven't —ed salmon for years** hace años que no como salmón; **he hadn't —ed food for 3 days** desde hacía 3 días no comía.
 (b) (*perceive flavour of*) percibir un sabor de; **I fancy I — garlic** creo notar un sabor a ajos; **I can't — anything when I have a cold** cuando estoy resfriado no noto sabor alguno.
 (c) (*experience*) experimentar, conocer; **at last we —ed happiness** por fin conocimos la felicidad; **when he first —ed power** cuando conoció por primera vez las delicias del poder.
 3 *vi*: **it doesn't — at all** no se nota sabor alguno; **it —s good** es muy sabroso, está sabrosísimo, está muy rico; **it — s all right to me** para mi gusto está bien; **to — of** saber a, tener sabor a; **it doesn't — of anything in particular** no sabe a nada en particular.
taste bud ['teistbʌd] *n* papila *f* del gusto.
tasteful ['teistful] *adj* elegante, de buen gusto.
tastefully ['teistfəli] *adv* elegantemente, con buen gusto; **a — furnished flat** un piso amueblado con buen gusto, un piso con muebles elegantes.
tastefulness ['teistfulnis] *n* elegancia *f*, buen gusto *m*.
tasteless ['teistlis] *adj* (*flat*) insípido, soso, insulso; (*in bad taste*) de mal gusto.
tastelessly ['teistlisli] *adv* insípidamente; con mal gusto.
tastelessness ['teistlisnis] *n* insipidez *f*; mal gusto *m*.
taster ['teistə*] *n* catador *m*.
tastily ['teistili] *adv* sabrosamente, apetitosamente.
tastiness ['teistinis] *n* sabor *m*, lo sabroso, lo apetitoso.
tasty ['teisti] *adj* sabroso, apetitoso.
tat [tæt] *vi* (*Sew*) hacer frivolité.
tata ['tæ'ta:] *interj* (*fam*) adiós, adiosito (*fam*).
tattered ['tætəd] *adj* *person* andrajoso, harapiento; *dress*, *flag etc* en jirones.
tatters ['tætəz] *npl* andrajos *mpl*; jirones *mpl*; **a tramp in —** un vagabundo andrajoso; **his jacket hung in —** su chaqueta estaba hecha jirones.
tatting ['tætiŋ] *n* (*Sew*) trabajo *m* de frivolité.
tattle ['tætl] 1 *n* (*chat*) charla *f*; (*gossip*) chismes *mpl*, habladurías *fpl*. 2 *vi* (*chat*) charlar, parlotear; (*gossip*) chismear, contar chismes.
tattler ['tætlə*] *n* charlatán *m*, ana *f*; chismoso *m*, a *f*.
tattoo[1] [tə'tu:] *n* (*Mil*) retreta *f*; (*pageant*) gran espectáculo *m* militar, exhibición *f* del arte militar; **to beat a — with one's fingers** tamborilear con los dedos.
tattoo[2] [tə'tu:] 1 *n* tatuaje *m*. 2 *vt* tatuar.

tatty ['tæti] *adj* (*fam*) raído, desaseado; poco elegante; en mal estado.

taught [tɔːt] *pret and ptp of* teach.

taunt [tɔːnt] **1** *n* mofa *f*, pulla *f*, dicterio *m*; sarcasmo *m*, dicho *m* sarcástico.

2 *vt* mofarse de; insultar, reprochar con insultos; **to — someone with something** reprochar algo a uno en tono de mofa, echar algo en cara a uno.

taunting ['tɔːntiŋ] *adj* insultante, mofador, burlón.

tauntingly ['tɔːntiŋli] *adv* burlonamente, en son de burla.

tauromachy ['tɔːrəmæki] *n* tauromaquia *f*.

taut [tɔːt] *adj* tieso, tenso, tirante; (*fig*) tirante.

tauten ['tɔːtn] **1** *vt* tesar, tensar. **2** *vi* tensarse, ponerse tieso.

tautness ['tɔːtnis] *n* tiesura *f*, tirantez *f*.

tautological [ˌtɔːtə'lɔdʒikəl] *adj* tautológico.

tautology [tɔː'tɔlədʒi] *n* tautología *f*.

tavern ['tævən] *n* taberna *f*.

tawdriness ['tɔːdrinis] *n* lo charro; lo cursi; lo indigno.

tawdry ['tɔːdri] *adj* charro; de oropel, de relumbrón, cursi; *motive etc* indigno, vergonzoso.

tawny ['tɔːni] *adj* leonado.

tax [tæks] **1** *n* (a) impuesto *m* (*on* sobre), contribución *f*; tributo *m*; derechos *mpl*; **betting** — impuesto *m* sobre apuestas; **capital gains** — impuesto *m* de plusvalía; **direct** — contribucion *f* directa; **indirect** — contribución *f* indirecta; **petrol** — impuesto *m* sobre gasolina; **free of** — exento de contribuciones, no imponible; **to collect a** — recaudar contribuciones; **to levy a** — **on something** imponer contribución sobre algo.

(b) (*fig*) carga *f* (*on* sobre), esfuerzo *m* (*on* para); **it is a** — **on his energies** exige un esfuerzo de él.

2 *attr*: — **matters** asuntos *mpl* tributarios; — **system** sistema *m* tributario, tributación *f*; — **privileges** privilegios *mpl* tributarios; — **evasion** evasión *f* fiscal; **to declare something for** — **purposes** declarar algo al fisco.

3 *vt* (a) (*Fin*) *person* imponer contribuciones a, *thing* imponer contribución sobre, gravar con un impuesto; **they are heavily —ed** pagan unas fuertes contribuciones; **the rich are being —ed out of existence** los ricos pagan tantas contribuciones que dejarán pronto de existir.

(b) (*Law*) *costs* tasar.

(c) (*fig*) cargar, abrumar (*with* de); *resources etc* exigir un esfuerzo excesivo a, someter a un esfuerzo excesivo; *patience* agotar; *tolerance* abusar de.

(d) (*fig*: *accuse*) acusar (*with* de); interrogar (*with* acerca de); **to — someone with a fault** censurar una falta a uno.

taxable ['tæksəbl] *adj* imponible, sujeto a impuesto; — **income** renta *f* imponible.

taxation [tæk'seifən] **1** *n* impuestos *mpl*, contribuciones *fpl*; (*system*) sistema *m* tributario, tributación *f*; **direct** — contribuciones *fpl* directas; **indirect** — contribuciones *fpl* indirectas; — **is too heavy** las contribuciones son demasiado fuertes.

2 *attr* tributario; — **system** sistema *m* tributario, tributación *f*.

tax-collecting ['tækskə,lektiŋ] *n* recaudación *f* de contribuciones.

tax collector ['tækskə,lektə*] *n* recaudador *m* de contribuciones.

tax-exempt ['tæksig'zempt] *adj* (*US*) exento de contribuciones; exento de impuesto.

tax-free ['tæks'friː] **1** *adj* exento de contribuciones, no imponible. **2** *adv*: **to live** — vivir sin pagar contribuciones.

taxi ['tæksi] **1** *n* taxi *m*. **2** *vi* (*Aut*) ir en taxi; (*Aer*) carretear, rodar de suelo.

taxicab ['tæksikæb] *n* taxi *m*.

taxidermist ['tæksidəːmist] *n* taxidermista *mf*.

taxidermy ['tæksidəːmi] *n* taxidermia *f*.

taxi driver ['tæksi,draivə*] *n* taxista *mf*.

taxi man ['tæksimæn] *n*, *pl* —**men** [men] taxista *mf*.

taximeter ['tæksi,miːtə*] *n* taxímetro *m*, contador *m* de taxi.

taxi rank ['tæksiræŋk] *n*, **taxi stand** ['tæksistænd] *n* parada *f* de taxis.

taxonomist [tæk'sɔnəmist] *n* taxonomista *mf*.

taxonomy [tæk'sɔnəmi] *n* taxonomía *f*.

taxpayer ['tæks,peiə*] *n* contribuyente *mf*.

tax return ['tæksri'təːn] *n* declaración *f* de ingresos.

tea [tiː] *n* (a) (*drink*) té *m*; **not for all the** — **in China** por nada del mundo. (b) (*meal*) merienda *f*; **high** — merienda-cena *f*; **to have** — merendar.

tea bag ['tiːbæg] *n* sobre *m* de té.

tea break ['tiːbreik] *n* descanso *m* para el té.

tea caddy ['tiː,kædi] *n* bote *m* para té.

teacake ['tiːkeik] *n* bollo pequeño con trocitos de frutas que se toma tostado en la merienda.

teach [tiːtʃ] (*irr*: *pret and ptp* **taught**) **1** *vt* enseñar; **to — someone how to do something** enseñar a uno a hacer algo; **to — someone a language** enseñar una lengua a uno, instruir a uno en una lengua; **to — someone a lesson** (*fig*) hacer que uno vaya aprendiendo; **that will — him!** ¡así irá aprendiendo!; **he taught me a thing or two** él me enseñó cosas de gran utilidad; **I'll — you to leave the gas on!** ¡así aprenderás a no dejar encendido el gas!

2 *vi* enseñar; ser profesor(a), dedicarse a la enseñanaza.

teachability [ˌtiːtʃə'biliti] *n* capacidad *f* para aprender.

teachable ['tiːtʃəbl] *adj* educable.

teacher ['tiːtʃə*] *n* (*in general*) preceptor *m*, profesor *m*, ora *f*; (*grammar school*) profesor *m* (de instituto), profesora *f* (de instituto); (*in other school*) maestro *m*, a *f*; **our French** — nuestro profesor de francés.

teacher training ['tiːtʃə'treiniŋ] *n* formación *f* pedagógica.

tea chest ['tiːtʃest] *n* caja *f* para té.

teach-in ['tiːtʃ,in] *n* reunión *f* general en la que se escuchan conferencias y se organizan discusiones sobre un tema concreto.

teaching ['tiːtʃiŋ] **1** *n* (*act*) enseñanza *f*; (*belief*) enseñanza *f*, doctrina.

2 *attr* docente; — **centre** centro *m* docente; — **hospital** hospital *m* utilizado para la enseñanza de la medicina; — **profession** magisterio *m*; — **staff** personal *m* docente, profesorado *m*.

teaching machine ['tiːtʃiŋmə,ʃiːn] *n* autoprofesor *m*, profesor *m* robot.

teacloth ['tiːklɔθ] *n*, *pl* —**cloths** [klɔθs] paño *m* de cocina.

tea cosy ['tiː,kəuzi] *n* cubretetera *f*, guardacalor *m* de la tetera.

teacup ['tiːkʌp] *n* taza *f* para té.

tea dance ['tiːdɑːns] *n* té *m* bailable, té-baile *m*.

tea garden ['tiː,gɑːdn] *n* café *m* al aire libre; (*Agr*) plantación *f* de té.

teahouse ['tiːhaus] *n*, *pl* —**houses** [hauziz] salón *m* de té.

teak [tiːk] *n* teca *f*, madera *f* de teca.

teakettle ['tiː,ketl] *n* (*US*) tetera *f*.

teal [tiːl] *n* cerceta *f*.

tea leaf ['tiːliːf] *n*, *pl* — **leaves** [liːvz] hoja *f* de té.

team [tiːm] **1** *n* (*of persons*) equipo *m*, grupo *m*; (*Sport*) equipo *m*; (*of horses*) tiro *m*; (*of oxen*) yunta *f*; **away** — equipo *m* de fuera; **home** — equipo *m* de casa; **our research** — nuestro equipo de investigadores.

2 *attr*: — **tournament** torneo *m* por equipos.

3 *vt*: **a film which** —**s A with Z** una película que asocia A con Z, una película que ofrece juntamente A y Z.

4 *vi*: **to — up** asociarse, formar un equipo (*with* con).

team mate ['tiːmmeit] *n* compañero *m* de equipo.

team spirit ['tiːm'spirit] *n* compañerismo *m*, espíritu *m* de equipo.

teamster ['tiːmstə*] *n* (*US*) camionero *m*, camionista *m*.

teamwork ['tiːmwəːk] *n* labor *f* de equipo, trabajo *m* en equipo; cooperación *f*, colaboración *f*.

tea party ['tiː,pɑːti] *n* tertulia *f* donde se toma el té.

teapot ['tiːpɔt] *n* tetera *f*.

tear [teə*] **1** *n* rasgón *m*, desgarrón *m*; **it has a** — **in it** está roto.

2 (*irr*: *pret* **tore**, *ptp* **torn**) *vt* (a) (*rip*) rasgar, desgarrar; *flesh* lacerar, romper; (*to pieces*) romper, despedazar, hacer pedazos; **to — a hole in a cloth** rasgar un paño; **to — one's hair** arrancarse los pelos, mesarse los pelos; **to — a muscle** desgarrarse un músculo.

(b) (*snatch*) arrancar; **to — something from someone** arrancar algo a uno, quitar algo a uno violentamente.

(c) **the country was torn by civil war** el país fue desgarrado por una guerra civil; **she was torn by conflicting emotions** estaba atormentada por dos emociones opuestas, le desgarraban dos emociones opuestas; **I am very much torn** sigo sin saber a qué carta quedarme.

(d) **to — away** arrancar, quitar violentamente; **the wind tore the flag away** el viento arrancó la bandera; **we tore him away from the party** le sacamos del guateque; **to — down** *flag, hangings etc* quitar (arrancando), arrancar (de las paredes etc); *building* derribar, echar abajo; **to — off** arrancar; **to — open** abrir apresuradamente, abrir violentamente; **to — out** arrancar; **to — up** *paper etc* romper; (*by roots*) desarraigar (violentamente), arrancar.

3 *vi* (a) rasgarse, romperse; **it —s easily** se rasga fácilmente.

(b) **to — at the earth with one's hands** tratar frenéticamente de remover la tierra con las manos; **she tore at my eyes** trató de arrancarme los ojos; **he tore at the paper wrapping** luchó violentamente por quitar la envoltura.

(c) **to — along** correr precipitadamente, precipitarse; ir a máxima velocidad; **to — along the street** correr a todo correr por la calle; **to — away** marcharse apresuradamente; **to — into a room** entrar precipitadamente en un cuarto; **to — off** irse apresuradamente; **to — past** pasar como un rayo; **he tore up in a car** llegó a toda prisa en un automóvil.

4 *vr:* **to — oneself away** irse de mala gana; **I could not — myself away** fui incapaz de moverme de allí, me fue imposible partir; **if you can — yourself away from that book** si puedes dejar ese libro de las manos un momento.

tear [tiə*] *n* lágrima *f*; **to be in —s** estar llorando; **to burst into —s, to dissolve** (*or* **melt**) **into —s** deshacerse en lágrimas; **to shed bitter —s** llorar amargamente; **to wipe away one's —s** secarse las lágrimas.

teardrop ['tiədrɔp] *n* lágrima *f*.

tearful ['tiəful] *adj* lloroso, llorón; lacrimoso; **to say in a — voice** decir llorando.

tearfully ['tiəfəli] *adv:* **to say —** decir lloroso, decir llorando.

teargas ['tiəgæs] *n* gas *m* lacrimógeno; **— bomb** bomba *f* lagrimógena.

tearing ['tɛəriŋ] *adj* (a) **with a — noise** con un ruido de tela que se rasga. (b) **at a — speed** a una velocidad vertiginosa, a una velocidad peligrosa.

tear-jerker ['tiə‚dʒəːkə*] *n* (*song*) canción *f* lacrimógena; (*play*) obra *f* lacrimógena, comedia *f* muy sentimental; **a real —** una cosa realmente lacrimógena.

tear-jerking ['tiə‚dʒəːkiŋ] *adj* lagrimógeno, muy sentimental.

tear-off ['tɛərɔf] *adj:* **— calendar** calendario *m* de taco.

tearoom ['tiːrum] *n* salón *m* de té.

tear-stained ['tiəsteind] *adj* manchado de lágrimas.

tease [tiːz] **1** *n* (a) (*person*) embromador *m*, ora *f*, guasón *m*, ona *f*; **he's a dreadful —** es terriblemente guasón, le gusta atormentar a las personas.

(b) **to do something for a —** hacer algo para divertirse.

2 *vt* (a) (*annoy*) jorobar, fastidiar, molestar; (*banter*) embromar, tomar el pelo a, guasearse con, (*cruelly*) atormentar; **they tease her about her hair** la molestan con chistes acerca de su pelo, la atormentan por lo de su pelo; **I don't like being —d** no me gusta que se me tome el pelo.

(b) (*Tech*) cardar.

teasel ['tiːzl] *n* (*Bot*) cardencha *f*; (*Tech*) carda *f*.

teaser ['tiːzə*] *n* rompecabezas *m*.

tea service ['tiː‚səːvis] *n*, **tea set** ['tiːset] *n* servicio *m* de té.

teashop ['tiːʃɔp] *n* café *m*, cafetería *f*, (*strictly*) salón *m* de té.

teasing ['tiːziŋ] **1** *adj* guasón, burlón. **2** *n* guasa *f*, burlas *fpl*.

teaspoon ['tiːspuːn] *n* cucharilla *f*, cucharita *f*.

teaspoonful ['tiːspunful] *n* cucharadita *f*.

tea strainer ['tiː‚streinə*] *n* colador *m* de té.

teat [tiːt] *n* (*of human*) pezón *m*; (*of animal*) teta *f*; (*of bottle*) chupador *m*, tetilla *f*, pezón *m* de goma.

tea table ['tiː‚teibl] *n* mesita *f* de té.

teatime ['tiːtaim] *n* hora *f* del té, hora *f* de la merienda.

tea towel ['tiː‚tauəl] *n* paño *m* de cocina.

tea tray ['tiːtrei] *n* bandeja *f* en que se sirve el té.

tea trolley ['tiː‚trɔli] *n* carrito *m* para servir el té.

tea urn ['tiːəːn] *n* tetera *f* grande.

tea waggon ['tiː‚wægən] *n* carrito *m* para servir el té (*en fábricas, oficinas etc*).

technical ['teknikəl] *adj* técnico; *college, school* de artes y oficios; laboral; **— offence** (*Law*) cuasidelito *m*.

technicality [‚tekni'kæliti] *n* tecnicidad *f*, carácter *m* técnico; cosa *f* técnica; (*word*) tecnicismo *m*; **I don't understand all the technicalities** no entiendo todos los detalles técnicos; **it failed because of a —** fracasó debido a una dificultad técnica.

technically ['teknikəli] *adv* técnicamente.

technician [tek'niʃən] *n* técnico *m*; (*Univ etc*) ayudante *m* de laboratorio.

Technicolor ['tekni‚kalə*] (*Protected Trade Name*) **1** *n* tecnicolor *m*; **in —** en tecnicolor. **2** *adj* en tecnicolor; de tecnicolor.

technique [tek'niːk] *n* técnica *f*.

technological [‚teknə'lɔdʒikəl] *adj* tecnológico.

technologist [tek'nɔlədʒist] *n* tecnólogo *m*.

technology [tek'nɔlədʒi] *n* tecnología *f*.

techy ['tetʃi] *adj* enojadizo, malhumorado.

Ted [ted] *nombre cariñoso de* **Edward**.

tedder ['tedə*] *n* heneador *m*.

Teddy ['tedi] *nombre cariñoso de* **Edward**.

teddy (bear) ['tedi(bɛə*)] *n* osito *m* de felpa.

teddy-boy ['tedibɔi] *n* joven *m* de atuendo ultra-moderno; (*pej*) gamberro *m*.

tedious ['tiːdiəs] *adj* aburrido, pesado.

tediously ['tiːdiəsli] *n* aburridamente, de modo pesado.

tediousness ['tiːdiəsnis] *n*, **tedium** ['tiːdiəm] *n* tedio *m*, aburrimiento *m*, pesadez *f*.

tee [tiː] **1** *n* tee *m*. **2** *vti* golpear desde el tee.

tee-hee ['tiː'hiː] **1** *n* risita *f* (tonta); **—!** ¡ja, ja! **2** *vi* reírse con una risita tonta, reírse un poquito.

teem [tiːm] *vi* abundar, pulular; **to — with** abundar en, hervir de; **the book —s with errors** el libro está plagado de errores; **to — with rain** diluviar.

teeming ['tiːmiŋ] *adj* numerosísimo; **the — millions** los muchos millones; **a lake — with fish** un lago donde abundan los peces; **through streets — with people** por calles llenas de gente.

teenage ['tiːneidʒ] *adj*, *attr fashion etc* de los jóvenes (de 13 a 19 años); **he has — daughters already** tiene hijas ya de más de 13 años.

teenager ['tiːn‚eidʒə*] *n* joven *mf* de 13 a 19 años; **a club for —s** un club para jóvenes (de 13 a 19 años).

teens [tiːnz] *npl* edad *f* de 13 a 19 años; **to be in one's —** tener de 13 a 19 años; **to be still in one's —** no haber cumplido aún los 20.

teeny(weeny) ['tiːni'wiːni] *adj* (*fam*) chiquito, chiquitín.

teeter ['tiːtə*] *vi* balancearse, oscilar; **to — on the edge of something** balancearse en el borde de algo, (*fig*) estar sin resolverse sobre algo.

teeth [tiːθ] *npl of* **tooth**.

teethe [tiːð] *vi* endentecer, echar los dientes.

teething ['tiːðiŋ] *n* dentición *f*.

teething ring ['tiːðiŋriŋ] *n* chupador *m*.

teetotal ['tiː'təutl] *adj* abstemio; *propaganda etc* antialcohólico.

teetotalism ['tiː'təutəlizəm] *n* abstinencia *f* (de bebidas alcohólicas).

teetotaller, (US) teetotaler ['tiː'təutlə*] *n* abstemio *m*, a *f*, persona *f* que no bebe alcohol.

tegument ['tegjumənt] *n* tegumento *m*.

telecast ['telikɑːst] *n* teledifusión *f*.

telecommunication ['telikə‚mjuːni'keiʃən] *n* tele-comunicación *f*.

telefilm ['telifilm] *n* telefilm *m*, telefilme *n* (*Acad*).

telegram ['teligræm] *n* telegrama *m*; **to send someone a —** poner un telegrama a uno.

telegraph ['teligrɑːf] **1** *n* telégrafo *m*. **2** *attr* tele-gráfico. **3** *vti* telegrafiar.

telegraphic [‚teli'græfik] *adj* telegráfico.

telegraphese ['teligrɑː'fiːz] *n* estilo *m* telegráfico.

telegraphist [ti'legrəfist] *n* telegrafista *mf*.

telegraph pole ['teligrɑːfpəul] *n* poste *m* telegráfico.

telegraph wire ['teligrɑːfwaiə*] *n* hilo *m* telegráfico.

telegraphy [ti'legrəfi] *n* telegrafía *f*.

teleology [‚teli'ɔlədʒi] *n* teleología *f*.

telepathic [‚teli'pæθik] *adj* telepático.

telepathist [ti'lepəθist] *n* telépata *mf*.

telepathy [ti'lepəθi] *n* telepatía *f*.

telephone ['telifəun] **1** *n* teléfono *m*; **to be on the —** (*subscriber*) tener teléfono, (*be speaking*) estar hablando por teléfono; **you're wanted on the —** quieren hablar con Vd por teléfono, le llaman al teléfono.

2 *attr* telefónico.

3 *vti* llamar por teléfono, llamar al teléfono, telefonear.

telephone booth ['telifəunbuːð] *n*, **telephone box** ['telifəunbɔks] *n* locutorio *m*, cabina *f* de teléfono.

telephone call ['telifəunkɔːl] *n* llamada *f* (telefónica).

telephone directory ['telifəundi‚rektəri] *n* guía *f* telefónica.

telephone exchange ['telifəuniks‚tʃeindʒ] *n* central *f* telefónica.

telephone kiosk ['telifəun‚kiɔsk] *n* locutorio *m*, cabina *f* de teléfono.

telephone number ['telifəun,nʌmbə*] n número m de teléfono.
telephone operator ['telifəun,ɔpəreitə*] n telefonista mf.
telephonic [,teli'fɔnik] adj telefónico.
telephonist [ti'lefənist] n telefonista mf.
telephony [ti'lefəni] n telefonía f.
telephoto ['teli'fəutəu] adj telefotográfico; — lens objetivo m telefotográfico, teleobjetivo m.
teleprinter ['teli,printə*] n teletipo m.
telescope ['teliskəup] 1 n telescopio m. 2 vt telescopar; enchufar; to — something into something else meter algo dentro de otra cosa. 3 vi telescoparse; enchufarse; A —s into B A se mete dentro de B.
telescopic [,telis'kɔpik] adj telescópico; enchufable, de enchufe.
teletype ['telitaip] n teletipo m.
teletypist ['teli,taipist] n teletipista mf.
televiewer ['teli,vju:ə*] n televidente mf, telespectador m, ora f.
televise ['telivaiz] vt televisar.
television ['teli,viʒən] 1 n televisión f; colour — televisión f en colores; to be on — estar en la televisión; to watch — mirar la televisión. 2 attr de televisión.
television screen ['teli,viʒənskri:n] n pantalla f de televisión.
television set ['teli,viʒən'set] n televisor m, aparato m de televisión.
tell [tel] (irr: pret and ptp **told**) 1 vt (a) (general sense) decir; adventure, story etc contar; (formally) comunicar, informar; to — a lie mentir; to — someone the news comunicar las noticias a uno, contar novedades a uno; to — the truth decir la verdad (see also **truth**); to — someone something decir algo a uno; I have been told that . . . me han dicho que . . ., se me ha dicho que . . .; I hear — that . . . dicen que . . .; I am glad to — you that . . . (formal letter) me es grato comunicarle que . . .; — me all about it cuéntame todo; I'll — you all about it te diré todo; I told him about the missing money le informé acerca del dinero perdido, le dije lo del dinero desaparecido; I cannot — you how pleased I am no encuentro palabras para expresar mi contento; so much happened that I can't begin to — you pasaron tantas cosas que no sé cómo empezar a contarlas; I — you no !, I — you it isn't ! ¡te digo que no!; I told you so !, didn't I — you so ? ¿no te lo dije ya?

(b) (general sense: idiomatic uses) — me another ! ¡vaya!; — that to the marines ! ¡a otro perro con ese hueso!; you're —ing me ! ¡a quién se lo cuentas!; he's no saint, let me — you ! ¡no es ningún santo, se lo aseguro!; he won't like it, I can — you esto seguramente no le va a caer en gracia; I could — you a thing or two about him hay cosas de él que yo me sé; I — you what ! ¡se me ocurre una idea!; it hurt more than words can — dolió una barbaridad, dolió lo indecible.

(c) (announce) decir, anunciar; (of clock, dial etc) indicar, marcar; the sign —s us which way to go la señal nos dice qué ruta conviene seguir; the clock —s the quarter hours el reloj da los cuartos de hora; to — somebody's fortune decir a uno la buenaventura.

(d) (order) to — someone to do something decir a uno que haga algo, mandar a uno hacer algo; I told you not to te dije que no lo hicieras; do as you are told ! ¡haz lo que te digo!; he won't be told no acepta las órdenes de nadie; no quiere hacer caso de ningún consejo; to — someone off to do something mandar a uno hacer algo.

(e) (distinguish) distinguir; (recognize) conocer, reconocer; to — A from B distinguir A de B; to — right from wrong (saber) distinguir el bien del mal; one can — he's a German se conoce que es alemán; you can — him in any disguise se le reconoce bajo cualquier disfraz; can you — the time ? ¿sabes decir la hora?; see **apart**.

(f) (know) saber; decidir, determinar; how can I — ? ¿yo qué sé?; who can — ? ¿quién sabe?; we cannot — nos es imposible saberlo; it's impossible for anyone to — es imposible que nadie lo sepa; you can't — much from this de esto no es posible deducir gran cosa; you never can — no se puede saber con certeza; podría pasar cualquier cosa; podría ser tanto lo uno como lo otro.

(g) (count) contar; to — one's beads rezar el rosario; 30 pigs all told en total 30 cerdos.

(h) (reprimand) to — someone off reñir a uno, echar un rapapolvo a uno.

2 vi (a) to — of hablar de; I hear — of a disaster oigo hablar de una catástrofe, tengo noticias de una catástrofe; I have never heard — of it no he oído nunca hablar de eso; the ruins told of a sad history las ruinas hablaban de una triste historia.

(b) to — on someone (fam) soplarse de uno, chivatear contra uno; don't — on us de esto no digas ni pío.

(c) (have an effect) tener efecto, hacer mella; blood will — los lazos de parentesco resultan ser bastante fuertes; words that — palabras fpl que hacen mella, palabras fpl que impresionan; every blow told cada golpe tuvo su efecto; it told on his health afectó su salud, se dejó ver en su salud; the effort was beginning to — (on him) el esfuerzo empezaba a afectarle de mala manera; everything —s against him todo obra en contra de él; stamina —s in the long run a la larga importa más la resistencia, a la larga vale más la resistencia.

teller ['telə*] n (of story) narrador m, ora f; (Parl) escrutador m; (in bank) cajero m.
telling ['teliŋ] 1 adj eficaz; fuerte, enérgico; a — argument un argumento eficaz.
2 n narración f; there is no — no se sabe, es imposible saberlo; there is no — what he will do es imposible saber qué va a hacer; the story did not lose in the — el cuento no perdió en la narración.
telltale ['telteil] 1 adj revelador; indicador. 2 n (person) soplón m, ona f; (Naut) aciómetro m.
telly ['teli] n (fam) tele f.
temblor ['temblə*] n (US) temblor m de tierra.
temerity [ti'meriti] n temeridad f; to have the — to + infin ser bastante atrevido como para + infin; and you have the — to say . . . ! ¡y Vd se atreve a decir que . . . !, ¡y Vd me dice tan fresco que . . . !
temper ['tempə*] 1 n (a) disposición f, natural m; humor m, genio m; (bad) genio m, mal genio m; — ! ¡qué mal genio!; bad —, hot —, quick — genio m, mal genio m, genio m vivo; good — buen humor m; to be in a good — estar de buen humor; he has a — tiene genio; he has a foul (or vile etc) — es un hombre de malas pulgas; to have a quick — tener genio, tener prontos de enojo; to keep one's — contenerse, no alterarse; to lose one's — perder la paciencia, enojarse (with con); to try someone's — provocar a uno.

(b) (of metal) temple m.
2 vt metal templar; (fig) templar, moderar, mitigar; to — justice with mercy templar la justicia con la compasión.
tempera ['tempərə] n (Art) pintura f al temple.
temperament ['tempərəmənt] n temperamento m, disposición f; (moodiness, difficult —) excitabilidad f, tendencia f a cambiar repentinamente de humor; genio m; he has a — tiene genio, tiene sus caprichos.
temperamental [,tempərə'mentl] adj (relating to temperament) complexional, relativo al temperamento; (moody, difficult) excitable, caprichoso, sujeto a impulsos repentinos, con tendencia a cambiar repentinamente de humor.
temperance ['tempərəns] 1 n templanza f; moderación f; abstinencia f (del alcohol).
2 attr: — movement campaña f antialcohólica; — hotel hotel m donde no se sirven bebidas alcohólicas.
temperate ['tempərit] adj templado; moderado; (in drinking) abstemio; climate, zone templado; to be — in one's demands ser moderado en sus exigencias.
temperature ['tempritʃə*] n temperatura f; (Med: high —) calentura f, fiebre f; to have a —, to run a — tener calentura.
temperature chart ['tempritʃətʃɑ:t] n gráfica f de temperaturas.
tempered ['tempəd] adj templado.
tempest ['tempist] n tempestad f; "The T—" (Shakespeare) "La Tempestad".
tempestuous [tem'pestjuəs] adj tempestuoso; (fig) tempestuoso, borrascoso.
Templar ['templə*] n templario m.
template, (US) **templet** ['templit] n plantilla f.
temple¹ ['templ] n templo m; the T— (London) Colegio m de Abogados.
temple² ['templ] n (Anat) sien f.
tempo ['tempəu] n, pl **tempi** ['tempi:] (Mus) tempo m, tiempo m; (fig) ritmo m.
temporal ['tempərəl] adj temporal.
temporarily ['tempərərili] adv temporalmente.
temporary ['tempərəri] adj temporáneo, provisional; transitorio, poco duradero, de poca duración; official interino; worker temporero; these arrangements are purely — este arreglo es provisional

nada más; **there was a — improvement** durante cierto tiempo las cosas mejoraron.

temporize ['tempəraiz] *vi* contemporizar.

tempt [tempt] *vt* (a) tentar; atraer; seducir; **to — someone to do something** tentar a uno a hacer algo, inducir a uno a hacer algo; **to be —ed to do something** (*fig*) estar tentado de hacer algo; **there was a time when he was —ed to resign** hubo un momento en que estuvo tentado de dimitir; **to allow oneself to be —ed** ceder a la tentación; **I am greatly —ed** es una oferta atractiva, es una perspectiva agradable; **doesn't the idea — you at all?** ¿la idea no te interesa siquiera un poquitín?; **can I — you to another cup?** ¿quieres otra taza?

(b) (*Bib etc*) poner a prueba; tentar; **one must not — fate** no hay que tentar a la suerte.

temptation [temp'teiʃən] *n* tentación *f*; atractivo *m*, aliciente *m*; **there is a — to** + *infin* es tentador + *infin*; hay tendencia a + *infin*; **to give way** (*or* **yield**) **to —** ceder a la tentación; **to lead someone into —** hacer que uno caiga en el pecado; **lead us not into —** guárdanos del pecado; **to resist —** resistir (a) la tentación (*of* + *ger* de + *infin*); **to put — in someone's way** exponer a uno a la tentación.

tempter ['temptə*] *n* tentador *m*.

tempting ['temptiŋ] *adj* tentador; atractivo; *meal* apetitoso, rico; *theory etc* seductor; **a — offer** una oferta tentadora; **it is — to think so** estamos tentados de considerarlo así; es fácil asentir a ello.

temptingly ['temptiŋli] *adv* de modo tentador; de modo seductor; apetitosamente.

temptress ['temptris] *n* tentadora *f*.

ten [ten] **1** *adj* diez. **2** *n* diez *m*; (*as round number*) decena *f*; **some — people** una decena de personas; **—s of thousands of Spaniards** decenas de miles de españoles.

tenable ['tenəbl] *adj* defendible, sostenible.

tenacious [ti'neiʃəs] *adj* tenaz; porfiado; **to be — of life** estar muy apegado a la vida.

tenaciously [ti'neiʃəsli] *adv* tenazmente; porfiadamente.

tenacity [ti'næsiti] *n* tenacidad *f*; porfía *f*.

tenancy ['tenənsi] *n* tenencia *f*; (*of house*) inquilinato *m*, ocupación *f*; (*lease*) arriendo *m*.

tenant ['tenənt] **1** *adj*: **— farmer** agricultor *m* que tiene sus tierras en arriendo.

2 *n* (*inhabitant*) habitante *mf*, morador *m*, ora *f*; (*paying rent*) inquilino *m*, a *f*, arrendatario *m*, a *f*.

tenantry ['tenəntri] *n* inquilinos *mpl*; (*Agr*) agricultores *mpl* que tienen sus tierras en arriendo.

tench [tentʃ] *n* tenca *f*.

tend¹ [tend] *vi* tender; **to — to, to — towards** tender a, inclinarse a, tener tendencia a; **we — to think that . . .** nos inclinamos a pensar que . . .; **I rather — to agree with you** casi estoy por compartir ese criterio; **anything that —s to help solve the problem** cualquier cosa que contribuya a resolver el problema, todo lo que conduzca a resolver el problema; **it is a blue —ing to green** es un azul que tira a verde; **these clothes — to shrink** estas prendas tienen tendencia a encogerse; **which way is it —ing?** ¿hacia qué lado se inclina?

tend² [tend] *vt* *sick etc* cuidar, atender; *cattle* guardar; *machine* manejar, operar, servir; mantener.

tendency ['tendənsi] *n* tendencia *f*, inclinación *f*, propensión *f*; proclividad *f*; **he has a — to say too much** tiene tendencia a decir demasiado; **there is a — for the ponds to dry up** los estanques tienen tendencia a secarse; **the present — to the left** la actual tendencia hacia la izquierda.

tendentious [ten'denʃəs] *adj* tendencioso.

tendentiously [ten'denʃəsli] *adv* de modo tendencioso.

tendentiousness [ten'denʃəsnis] *n* tendenciosidad *f*.

tender¹ ['tendə*] *n* (*Rail*) ténder *m*; (*Naut*) gabarra *f*, embarcación *f* auxiliar.

tender² ['tendə*] **1** *n* (a) (*Comm*) oferta *f*, proposición *f*; **to make a —, to put in a —** hacer una oferta (*for* para la construcción *etc*) de), ofertar; **to put something out to —** solicitar ofertas para hacer algo.

(b) **legal —** moneda *f* corriente, moneda *f* de curso legal.

2 *vt* ofrecer; *resignation etc* presentar; *thanks* dar. **3** *vi* (*Comm*) ofertar, hacer una oferta (*for* para).

tender³ ['tendə*] *adj* (*soft*) tierno, blando; *spot* delicado, sensible; (*painful*) dolorido; *age etc* tierno; *conscience* escrupuloso; *problem, subject* espinoso, delicado, difícil; (*affectionate*) tierno, afectuoso; compasivo; **I still feel — there** ese sitio me duele todavía; **it is — to the touch** es sensible al tacto; **I have — memories of her** la recuerdo con mucha ternura; **those of — years** los de tierna edad.

tenderfoot ['tendəfut] *n* (*esp US*) recién llegado *m*; principiante *m*, novato *m*.

tender-hearted ['tendə'hɑːtid] *adj* compasivo, tierno de corazón.

tender-heartedness ['tendə'hɑːtidnis] *n* compasión *f*, ternura *f*.

tenderize ['tendəraiz] *vt* ablandar.

tenderloin ['tendəlɔin] *n* (*meat*) filete *m*.

tenderly ['tendəli] *adj* tiernamente, con ternura.

tenderness ['tendənis] *n* ternura *f*; delicadez *f*, sensibilidad *f*.

tendon ['tendən] *n* tendón *m*.

tendril ['tendril] *n* zarcillo *m*.

tenement ['tenimənt] *n* vivienda *f*; habitación *f*; **— house, —s** casa *f* de pisos, casa *f* de vecindad.

tenet ['tenət] *n* principio *m*, dogma *m*.

tenfold ['tenfauld] **1** *adj* décuplo, diez veces mayor. **2** *adv* diez veces.

tenner ['tenə*] *n* (*fam*) billete *m* de diez libras.

tennis ['tenis] *n* tenis *m*.

tennis ball ['tenisbɔːl] *n* pelota *f* de tenis.

tennis court ['teniskɔːt] *n* pista *f* de tenis, cancha *f* de tenis (*SAm*).

tennis elbow ['tenis'elbəu] *n* sinovitis *f* del codo.

tennis player ['tenis,pleiə*] *n* tenista *mf*.

tennis racquet ['tenis,rækit] *n* raqueta *f* de tenis.

tennis shoe ['tenisʃuː] *n* zapatilla *f* de tenis.

tenon ['tenən] *n* espiga *f*, almilla *f*.

tenon saw ['tenənsɔː] *n* serrucho *m*, sierra *f* de espigas.

tenor ['tenə*] **1** *adj* *instrument*, *part*, *voice* de tenor; *aria* para tenor. **2** *n* (*Mus*) tenor *m*; (*purport*) tenor *m*, tendencia *f*; curso *m*.

tenpin bowling ['tenpin'bauliŋ] *n* juego *m* de los bolos.

tense¹ [tens] *n* (*Gram*) tiempo *m*; **present —** tiempo *m* presente; **in the perfect —** en tiempo perfecto.

tense² [tens] **1** *adj* (*stretched*) tirante, estirado, tieso; (*stiff*) rígido, tieso; *moment, nerves, situation etc* tenso; **it has been a — day** la jornada ha sido muy tensa; **we waited with — expectancy** aguardamos con tensa expectación; **he looked rather —** parecía estar algo tenso; **in a — voice** en tono entrecortado.

2 *vt* tensar, tesar; estirar.

tensely ['tensli] *adv* tensamente, con tensión.

tenseness ['tensnis] *n* tirantez *f*; tensión *f*.

tensile ['tensail] *adj* tensor; extensible; de tensión, relativo a la tensión.

tension ['tenʃən] *n* tirantez *f*; tensión *f*; **there is a great racial —** existe gran tensión racial; **— is being relaxed** la tensión está disminuyendo.

tent [tent] *n* tienda *f* (de campaña).

tentacle ['tentəkl] *n* tentáculo *m*.

tentative ['tentətiv] *adj* provisional; experimental; de prueba, de ensayo; **these are — conclusions** son conclusiones provisionales; **everything is very — at the moment** por el momento todo está en vía de prueba; **she's a rather — person** es una persona que no tiene confianza en sí misma.

tentatively ['tentətivli] *adv* provisionalmente; en vía de prueba, como tanteo; **"yes", he said — "sí"**, dijo sin gran confianza.

tenterhooks ['tentəhuks] *npl*: **to be on —** estar sobre ascuas; **to keep someone on —** tener a uno sobre ascuas.

tenth [tenθ] **1** *adj* décimo. **2** *n* décimo *m*; (*part*) décima parte *f*, décima *f*.

tent peg ['tent,peg] *n* estaquilla *f* (de tienda).

tent pole ['tentpəul] *n* mástil *m* de tienda, poste *m* de tienda.

tenuity [te'njuiti] *n* tenuidad *f*; raridad *f*.

tenuous ['tenjuəs] *adj* tenue; sutil; *connection* poco fuerte; *argument* poco sólido; *air* raro.

tenure ['tenjuə*] *n* posesión *f*, tenencia *f*, ocupación *f*.

tepee ['tiːpiː] *n* (*US*) tipi *m*.

tepid ['tepid] *adj* tibio.

tepidity [te'piditi] *n*, **tepidness** ['tepidnis] *n* tibieza *f*.

tercentenary [,təːsen'tiːnəri] *n* tricentenario *m*.

tercet ['təːsit] *n* terceto *m*.

Terence ['terəns] *m* Terencio *m*.

term [təːm] **1** *n* (a) (*limit*) término *m*, límite *m*, fin *m*; (*Comm*) plazo *m*; **to put** (*or* **set**) **a — to** señalar un límite a; fijar un plazo para.

(b) (*period*) período *m*; duración *f*; plazo *m*; (*of president etc*) mandato *m*; **during his — of office** durante su posesión del puesto, durante su mandato; **for a — of 6 years** durante un período de 6 años; **in the long —** a la larga; **in the short —** en el futuro próximo.

(c) (*School, Univ*) trimestre *m*; **during —, in —** durante el curso; **out of —** fuera del curso; **to keep —s** residir, estar de interno, cumplir su período de residencia.

(d) (*Math, Logic*) término m; **A expressed in —s of B** A expresado en términos de B; **in —s of production we are doing well** por lo que se refiere a la producción vamos bien; **he sees novels in —s of sociology** considera la novela en su función sociológica, se explica la novela desde el punto de vista sociológico.

(e) (*word*) término m; vocablo m, voz f, expresión f; **in plain —s, in simple —s** en términos sencillos, en lenguaje sencillo; **to choose one's —s carefully** elegir sus palabras con cuidado.

(f) **—s** (*conditions*) condiciones fpl; **—s of reference** puntos mpl de consulta; **—s of sale** condiciones fpl de venta; **—s of surrender** capitulaciones fpl, condiciones fpl de la rendición; **—s of trade** relación f real de intercambio; **according to the —s of the contract** según las condiciones del contrato, conforme a lo estipulado en el contrato; **not on any —s** bajo ningún concepto; **what are your —s?** ¿cuáles son sus condiciones?; **to accept someone on his own —s** aceptar a uno sabiendo lo que es, aceptar a uno sin esperar cambiar su naturaleza; **to come to —s** llegar a un acuerdo, ponerse de acuerdo; **to come to —s with a situation** adaptarse a una situación, conformarse con una situación; **to dictate —s** dictar las condiciones; **you may name your own —s** Vd puede estipular todo lo que quiera.

(g) **—s** (*Comm, Fin*) precio m, tarifa f; **our —s for full board** nuestro precio para la pensión completa; **"inclusive —s: £12"** "12 libras todo incluido", "pensión completa: 12 libras"; **we bought it on advantageous —s** lo compramos a buen precio; **we offer easy —s** ofrecemos facilidades de pago.

(h) **—s** (*relationship*) relaciones fpl; **to be on easy** (*or* **familiar**) **—s with someone** tener confianza con uno; **to be on bad —s with someone** llevarse mal con uno, estar en malas relaciones con uno; **to be on good —s with someone** estar en buenas relaciones con uno; **we are on the best of —s** somos muy amigos; **we're not on speaking —s** no nos hablamos; **what —s are they on?** ¿cuáles son sus relaciones?; **to fight someone on equal —s** luchar con uno en iguales condiciones.

2 vt llamar; nombrar, denominar; calificar de; **he —s himself a businessman** se llama hombre de negocios; **I — it a disgrace** yo lo llamo una vergüenza, yo digo que es una vergüenza.

termagant ['tə:məgənt] n arpía f, fiera f.

terminal ['tə:minl] **1** adj terminal, final; (*School, Univ*) trimestral.
2 n (*Elec*) borne m; polo m; (*Aer, Naut*) terminal f; (*Rail*) estación f terminal, término m.

terminate ['tə:mineit] **1** vt terminar. **2** vi terminar(se).

termination [,tə:mi'neiʃən] n terminación f (*also Gram*).

terminological [,tə:minə'bdʒikəl] adj terminológico.

terminology [,tə:mi'nɔlədʒi] n terminología f.

terminus ['tə:minəs] n, pl **termini** ['tə:mini:] término m; (*Rail*) estación f terminal término m.

termite ['tə:mait] n termita f, termite m, comején m.

tern [tə:n] n golondrina f de mar; **common —** charrán m común.

ternary ['tə:nəri] adj ternario.

Terpsichore [tə:p'sikəri] f Terpsícore.

terpsichorean [,tə:psikə'riən] adj de Terpsícore.

terrace ['terəs] **1** n (*Agr*) terraza f; (*raised bank*) terraplén m; (*of houses*) hilera f de casas sin división entre sí; (*roof*) azotea f; **—s** (*Sport*) gradas fpl.
2 vt formar terrazas en; terraplenar.

terraced ['terəst] adj en terrazas; terraplenado.

terracotta ['terə'kɔtə] n terracota f.

terrain [te'rein] n terreno m.

terrapin ['terəpin] n tortuga f de agua dulce.

terrazzo [te'rætsəu] n (*US*) piso m veneciano.

terrestrial [ti'restriəl] adj terrestre.

terrible ['terəbl] adj terrible; (*fam*) horrible (*fam*), malísimo, fatal (*fam*); **it was just —** fue sencillamente horrible; **his Spanish is —** su español es fatal.

terribly ['terəbli] adv terriblemente, espantosamente; (*fam*) terriblemente; **it's — dangerous es** tremendamente peligroso; **I think he's — nice** para mi gusto es simpatiquísimo; **she plays —** toca malísimamente.

terrier ['teriə*] n terrier m.

terrific [tə'rifik] adj tremendo (*fam*), bárbaro (*fam*), fabuloso (*fam*); **what — news!** ¡qué noticia más estupenda!; **isn't he —?** ¿es fabuloso, no?

terrifically [tə'rifikəli] adv tremendamente; (*fam*) tremendamente, fabulosamente.

terrify ['terifai] vt aterrar, aterrorizar.

terrifying ['terifaiiŋ] adj aterrador, espantoso.

terrifyingly ['terifaiiŋli] adv espantosamente.

territorial [,teri'tɔ:riəl] **1** adj territorial; *see* **water. 2** n (*Mil*) reservista m.

territoriality [,teri'tɔ:ri'æliti] n territorialidad f.

territory ['teritəri] n territorio m; **mandated —** territorio m bajo mandato.

terror ['terə*] n terror m, espanto m.

terrorism ['terərizəm] n terrorismo m.

terrorist ['terərist] **1** adj terrorista. **2** n terrorista m.

terrorize ['terəraiz] vt aterrorizar.

terror-stricken ['terə,strikən] adj espantado, preso de un terror pánico.

Terry ['teri] nombre cariñoso de **Terence, Theresa.**

terry cloth ['teri,klɔθ] n (*US*) albornoz m.

terse [tə:s] adj breve, conciso, lacónico; brusco.

tersely ['tə:sli] adv concisamente, lacónicamente; bruscamente.

terseness ['tə:snis] n brevedad f, concisión f, laconismo m; brusquedad f.

tertiary ['tə:ʃəri] adj terciario.

Tertullian [tə:'tʌliən] m Tertuliano.

Terylene ['terəli:n] n (*Protected Trade Name*) terylene m.

tesselated ['tesileitid] adj formado con teselas; **— pavement** mosaico m.

tesselation [,tesi'leiʃən] n mosaico m.

test [test] **1** n prueba f; ensayo m; (*School, Univ etc*) examen m, test m; (*Chem*) prueba f, análisis m; (*standard of judgement*) criterio m; **a weekly French —** un examen semanal de francés; **acid —** (*fig*) prueba f de fuego; piedra f de toque; **endurance —** prueba f de resistencia; **eye —** examen m para graduar la vista; **intelligence —** test m de inteligencia, prueba f de inteligencia; **nuclear —** prueba f nuclear; **oral —** examen m oral; **structural —** prueba f estructural; **Wasserman —** (*Med*) prueba f de Wasserman; **if we apply the — of visual appeal to it** si lo sometemos a la prueba de la atracción visual; **to put something to the —** poner algo a prueba, someter algo a prueba; **to stand the —** soportar la prueba; **it has stood the — of time** ha resistido el paso del tiempo; *see* **blood —, driving —, high —.**
2 attr de prueba(s).
3 vt probar, poner a prueba, someter a prueba; examinar; **sight graduar;** (*Chem etc*) ensayar; *new drug etc* experimentar; **it severely —ed our nerves** puso nuestros nervios a toda prueba; **the new weapon is being —ed** se está sometiendo a prueba la nueva arma.

testament ['testəmənt] n testamento m; **New T— Nuevo Testamento m; Old T— Antiguo** Testamento m.

testamentary [,testə'mentəri] adj testamentario.

testator [tes'teitə*] n testador m.

testatrix [tes'teitriks] n testadora f.

test bench ['testbentʃ] n banco m de pruebas.

test card ['testka:d] n (*TV*) carta f de ajuste.

test case ['testkeis] n (*Law*) pleito m de ensayo (*para determinar la interpretación de una nueva ley*).

tester[1] ['testə*] n (*person*) ensayador m, ora f.

tester[2] ['testə*] n (*arch*) baldaquín m.

testes ['testi:z] npl testes mpl.

test flight ['testflait] n vuelo m de ensayo.

testicle ['testikl] n testículo m.

testification [,testifi'keiʃən] n testificación f.

testify ['testifai] **1** vt atestiguar, dar fe de; **to — that . . .** testificar que . . .; declarar que . . .
2 vi **(a)** (*Law*) prestar declaración, declarar.
(b) to — to something atestiguar algo, atestar algo; (*fig*) atestiguar algo, dar fe de algo.

testily ['testili] adv *answer etc* con enojo, malhumoradamente.

testimonial [,testi'məuniəl] n **(a)** certificado m; (*reference about person*) recomendación f, carta f de recomendación; **as a — to** como testimonio a, en homenaje a.
(b) (*gift*) regalo m, obsequio m (*de jubilación etc*).

testimony ['testiməni] n testimonio m, declaración f; **in — whereof . . .** en fe de lo cual . . .; **to bear — to something** atestar algo.

testing ground ['testiŋgraund] n zona f de pruebas.

test match ['testmætʃ] n partido m internacional.

test paper ['test,peipə*] n (*School etc*) test m, examen m; (*Chem*) papel m reactivo.

test piece ['testpi:s] n (*Mus*) obra f elegida para un certamen de piano (*etc*).

test pilot ['test,pailət] n piloto m de pruebas.
test print ['testprint] n (Phot) copia f de prueba.
test tube ['testtju:b] n probeta f.
testy ['testi] adj enojadizo, malhumorado.
tetanus ['tetənəs] n tétanos m.
tetchy ['tetʃi] adj = **testy**.
tête-à-tête ['teitɑː'teit] n conversación f íntima.
tether ['teðə*] **1** n atadura f, traba f, cuerda f; see **end**.
　　2 vt atar, atar con una cuerda (to a).
tetragon ['tetrəgən] n tetrágono m.
tetrahedron [,tetrə'hi:drən] n tetraedro m.
tetrameter [te'træmitə*] n tetrámetro m.
Teuton ['tju:tən] n teutón m, ona f.
Teutonic [tju'tɔnik] adj teutónico.
Texan ['teksən] **1** adj tejano. **2** n tejano m, a f.
Texas ['teksəs] Tejas m.
text [tekst] n texto m; (subject) tema m; **to stick to one's —** no apartarse de su tema; **to preach on a —** predicar un sermón valiéndose de un pasaje de la Sagrada Escritura.
textbook ['tekstbuk] n libro m de texto.
textile ['tekstail] adj textil; **— industry** industria f textil.
textiles ['tekstailz] npl textiles mpl, tejidos mpl.
textual ['tekstjuəl] adj textual; **— criticism** crítica f textual.
textually ['tekstjuəli] adv textualmente.
texture ['tekstʃə*] n textura f (also fig).
Thai [tai] **1** adj tailandés. **2** n tailandés m, esa f.
Thailand ['tailænd] Tailandia f.
thalidomide [θə'lidəmaid] n talidomida m.
Thames [temz] Támesis m; **it won't set the — on fire** no llamará la atención, no tiene nada de particular.
than [ðæn] conj **(a)** que; **I have more — you** yo tengo más que tú; **he swears less — her** él jura menos que ella; **nobody is more sorry — I (am)** nadie lo siente más que yo; **he has more money — brains** tiene más dinero que inteligencia; **clothes come out whiter — white** sale la ropa más que blanca; **it is better to phone — to write** más vale telefonear que escribir; **I'll do anything rather — that** haré cualquier cosa no sea ésa, lo haré todo menos eso.
　　(b) (with numerals) de; **more — 90** más de 90; **— than half** más de la mitad; **not less — 8** no menos de 8; **more — once** más de una vez; **it doesn't happen more — once** no ocurre más que una sola vez.
　　(c) (with following clause) **they have more money — we have** tienen más dinero del que nosotros tenemos; **we have more chips — you have** nosotros tenemos más patatas fritas de las que Vds tienen; **it was an even sillier play — we had thought** la obra fue aun más estúpida de lo que habíamos pensado; **the car went faster — we had expected** el coche fue más rápidamente de lo que habíamos esperado.
thank [θæŋk] vt **(a) to — someone** dar las gracias a uno; **— you** gracias; **— you!** (emphatic, reciprocating thanks) ¡a usted!; **no — you** no gracias; **I cannot — you enough!** ¡cuánto se lo agradezco!; see **goodness** etc.
　　(b) to — someone for something agradecer algo a uno; **— you for the present** muchas gracias por el regalo; **did you — him for the flowers?** ¿le diste las gracias por las flores?; **you have him to — for that** eso tienes que agradecérselo a él, ese favor se lo debes a él; **he has himself to — for that** él mismo tiene la culpa de eso; **which he could never properly — you for** que él no agradecería nunca lo bastante.
　　(c) I'll — you not to do it agradecería que no lo hiciera; **I'll — you to be more polite!** ¡conviene hablar con más educación!
　　(d) without so much as a "— you" sin la menor señal de agradecimiento.
thankful ['θæŋkful] adj agradecido; **to be — to + infin** alegrarse de + infin; **let us be — that . . .** agradezcamos que + subj; **how — we were for that umbrella!** ¡cuánto nos ayudó ese paraguas!, ¡cómo bendecimos ese paraguas!
thankfully ['θæŋkfəli] adv con gratitud, con agradecimiento; **he said —** dijo agradecido; dijo con alivio.
thankfulness ['θæŋkfulnis] n gratitud f, agradecimiento m.
thankless ['θæŋklis] adj person ingrato; task ímprobo, ingrato.
thanks [θæŋks] npl gracias fpl; **many —!** ¡muchas gracias!, ¡muchísimas gracias!; **my warmest —**

for your help mis gracias más efusivas por su ayuda; **vote of —** voto m de gracias; **that's all the — I get!** ¡cómo se me agradece!; **— to you** gracias a ti; **it's all — to brand X** todo es gracias a la marca X, todo lo debo a la marca X; **— be to God** gracias a Dios; **no — to you** no le debo nada a Vd.
thanksgiving ['θæŋks,giviŋ] n acción f de gracias; **T— Day** (US) día m de Acción de Gracias.
that [ðæt] **1** dem adj (pl those) m: ese, (more remote) aquel; f: esa, (more remote) aquella; **— book** ese libro; **— hill over there** aquella colina; **— one** ése, aquél; **— lad of yours** ese chico suyo; **what about — cheque?** ¿y el cheque ese?
　　2 dem pron (pl those) m: ése, (more remote) aquél; f: ésa, (more remote) aquélla; "neuter": eso, aquello; **this car is new but —** is old este coche es nuevo pero ése es viejo; **— is true** eso es verdad; **— is all I can tell you** eso es todo lo que puedo decirle; **—'s what I say** eso digo yo, lo mismo digo yo; **they all say —** todos dicen lo mismo; **what is —?** ¿qué es?, ¿eso qué es?; **who is —?** ¿quién es?; **— is Joe** es Pepe; **— is . . . esto es . . .,** es decir . . .; **and —'s —!** y eso es todo; **you can't go and —'s —** no puedes ir y no hay más qué decir; **so — was —** y no había más que hacer, y ahí terminó la cosa; **—'s odd!** ¡qué raro!, ¡qué cosa más rara!; **will he come? . . . — he will!** ¿si vendrá? . . . ¡ya lo creo!; **after —** después de eso; **at — acto** seguido, sin más; con eso, con lo cual; **and it was broken at —** y además estaba roto; **do it like —** hazlo de esa manera, hazlo de la manera que ves; **with —** con eso; **if it comes to —** en tal caso; si vamos a eso; **how do you like —?** ¿qué te parece?, (iro) ¡vaya!; see **all 1, 2**; as **(f)**; it **(e)**.
　　3 rel pron **(a)** que; **the book — I read** el libro que leí; **the houses — I painted** las casas que pinté; **all — I have** todo lo que tengo.
　　(b) (with prep) que, el cual, la cual etc; **the box — I put it in** la caja en la cual lo puse, la caja donde lo puse; **the house — we're speaking of** la casa de que hablamos; **not — I know of** no que yo sepa.
　　4 adv tan; **— far** tan lejos; **— high** tan alto, así de alto; **— many frogs** tantas ranas; **— much money** tanto dinero; **it is — much better** es tanto mejor; **he can't be — clever** no puede ser tan inteligente como tú dices; **nobody can be — rich** nadie puede ser tan rico como eso; **I didn't know he was — ill** no sabía que estuviera tan enfermo; **he was — wild** (fam) estaba tan furioso.
　　5 conj **(a)** que; **I believe — he exists** creo que existe; **— he should behave like this!** ¡que se comporte así!; **— he should behave like this is incredible** que se comporte así es increíble; **— he refuses is natural** el que rehuse es natural; **oh — we could!** ¡ojalá pudiéramos!, ¡ojalá!; see **would** etc.
　　(b) (in order that) para que + subj, eg **it was done (so) — he might sleep** se hizo para que él pudiera dormir; see **so**.
　　(c) in **— en** que, por cuanto.
thatch [θætʃ] **1** n (straw) paja f; (roof) techo m de paja; (over wall etc) barda f. **2** vt poner techo de paja a; bardar.
thatched [θætʃt] adj: **— roof** techo m de paja; **the roof is —** el techo es de paja.
thaw [θɔː] **1** n deshielo m.
　　2 vt deshelar, derretir; (fig) ablandar, hacer menos severo; **to — out** meat etc deshelar.
　　3 vi deshelarse, derretirse; (fig) ablandarse, hacerse menos severo; (of person) hacerse más afable, ir perdiendo su reserva; **to — out** (meat, frozen fingers etc) deshelarse; **it is —ing** deshiela.
the [ðiː, ðə] **1** def art **(a)** el, la, (pl) los, las (masculine singular a + el = al, eg **to — man** al hombre; masculine singular **de** + el = del, eg **of — cat** del gato).
　　(b) ("neuter") lo; **— good and — beautiful** lo bueno y lo bello; **within the realms of — possible** dentro de lo posible; **it is — unusual which counts** es lo insólito lo que importa.
　　(c) (special uses) **Charles — Fifth** Carlos Quinto; **Philip — Second** Felipe Segundo; **— Browns** los Brown; **— cheek of it!** ¡qué frescura!; **oh — pain!** ¡ay qué dolor!; **he hasn't — sense to understand** no tiene bastante inteligencia para comprender; **the child has — measles** el niño tiene sarampión; **2 dollars — pound** 2 dólares la libra.
　　(d) (emphatic) **he's — man for the job** es él hombre más indicado para el puesto; **you don't mean —**

Professor Bloggs? ¿quieres decir el célebre profesor Bloggs?, ¿quieres decir el profesor Bloggs de que se habla tanto?; **it was — colour of 1971** fue el color que estaba tan de moda en 1971.

2 adv: **— more he works the more he earns** cuanto más trabaja (tanto) más gana; **— sooner — better** cuanto antes mejor; **it will be all — better** será tanto mejor.

theatre, (US) **theater** ['θiətə*] n teatro m (also fig, Mil etc); (lecture —) aula f; **variety —** teatro m de variedades; **to go to the —** ir al teatro.

theatregoer, (US) **theatergoer** ['θiətə,gəuə*] n aficionado m al teatro, aficionada f al teatro.

theatrical [θi'ætrikəl] adj teatral; company etc de teatro; person's manner exagerado.

theatrically [θi'ætrikəli] adv teatralmente, de modo teatral; de modo exagerado.

theatricals [θi'ætrikəlz] npl funciones fpl teatrales; **amateur —** teatro m de aficionados.

Thebes [θi:bz] Tebas.

thee [ði:] pron (arch or poet) te; (after prep) ti; **with —** contigo.

theft [θeft] n hurto m, robo m.

their [ðeə*] poss adj su(s).

theirs [ðeəz] poss pron (el) suyo, (la) suya etc.

theism ['θi:izəm] n teísmo m.

theist ['θi:ist] n teísta mf.

theistic [θi'istik] adj teísta.

them [ðem, ðəm] pron (acc) los, las; (dat) les; (after prep) ellos, ellas.

thematic [θi'mætik] adj temático.

theme [θi:m] n tema m.

theme song ['θi:msɔŋ] n motivo m principal.

themselves [ðəm'selvz] pron (subject) ellos mismos, ellas mismas; (acc, dat) se; (after prep) sí (mismos, mismas); see oneself.

then [ðen] **1** adv (at that time) entonces; por entonces; en ese momento; a la sazón, en aquella época; (afterwards, next) luego, después; **it was — 8 o'clock** eran las 8, eran las 8 ya; **— we went to Madrid** luego fuimos a Madrid; **he was — a little-known writer** en aquella época era un escritor poco conocido; **and — again he's a red** y además es un rojo; **first this — that** primero esto y luego aquello; **by —** para entonces, antes de eso; **from — on, since —** desde entonces, desde aquel momento, a partir de entonces; **until —** hasta entonces; **what —?** ¿qué pasó después?; (so what) ¿y qué?, ¿qué más?; see now 1 (a).

2 conj pues, en ese caso; por tanto; entonces; **what do you want me to do —?** ¿pues qué quieres que haga yo?; **— you don't want it?** ¿así que no lo quieres?, ¿con qué no lo quieres?; **well —** ahora bien, pues; see now 1 (a).

3 adv entonces, de entonces; **the — King of Slobodia** el entonces rey de Eslobodia, el rey de Eslobodia de entonces; **the — existing government** el gobierno que existía en esa época, el gobierno de entonces.

thence [ðens] adv (lit) (a) (from that place) de allí, desde allí. (b) (therefore) por eso, por consiguiente.

thenceforth ['ðens'fɔ:θ] adv, **thenceforward** [,ðens-'fɔ:wəd] adv (lit) desde entonces, de allí en adelante, a partir de entonces.

theocracy [θi'ɔkrəsi] n teocracia f.

theocratic [θiə'krætik] adj teocrático.

theodolite [θi'ɔdəlait] n teodolito m.

theologian [θiə'ləudʒiən] n teólogo m.

theological [θiə'lɔdʒikəl] adj teológico.

theologist [θi'ɔlədʒist] n teólogo m.

theology [θi'ɔlədʒi] n teología f.

theorem ['θiərəm] m teorema m.

theoretic(al) [θiə'retik(əl)] adj teórico.

theoretically [θiə'retikəli] adv teóricamente, en teoría.

theoretician [,θiərə'tiʃən] n, **theorist** ['θiərist] n teórico m, teorizante m.

theorize ['θiəraiz] vi teorizar.

theorizer ['θiəraizə*] n teorizante m.

theory ['θiəri] n teoría f; **in —** teóricamente, en teoría.

theosophical [θiə'sɔfikəl] adj teosófico.

theosophist [θi'ɔsəfist] n teósofo m.

theosophy [θi'ɔsəfi] n teosofía f.

therapeutic(al) [,θerə'pju:tik(əl)] adj terapéutico.

therapeutics [,θerə'pju:tiks] n terapéutica f.

therapist ['θerəpist] n terapeuta mf.

therapy ['θerəpi] n terapia f, terapéutica f; **occupational —** terapia f laboral.

there [ðeə*] **1** adv (a) allí; allá; **(— near you)** ahí; **back —, down —, over —** allá; **12 kilometres — and back** 12 kilómetros ida y vuelta; **it's in —**

está allí dentro; **when we left —** cuando partimos de allí.

(b) (less precisely) **mind out —!** ¡ojo!, ¡cuidado!; **make way —!** ¡abran paso!, ¡atención!; **hurry up —!** ¡despabílense!; ¡menearse!; **you —!** ¡eh, usted!; **— we differ** en ese punto discrepamos; **— you are wrong** en eso te equivocas; **—'s the bus** ya viene el autobús; **— she comes** ya viene; **— we were, stuck** así que nos encontramos allí sin podernos mover.

(c) **— is, — are** hay; **— will be** habrá; **— were 10** había 10, hubo 10; **how many are —?** ¿cuántos hay?; **— was laughter at this** en esto hubo risas; **— was singing and dancing** se cantó y se bailó; **— is a pound missing** falta una libra; **— is no wine left** no hay vino, no queda vino; **are — any bananas?** ¿hay plátanos?

(d) **he's all —** es la mar de listo; **he's not all —** le falta un tornillo.

2 interj ¡vaya!; **—, —** (comforting) ¡cálmate!, ¡no es nada!, ¡no te preocupes!; **—, drink this** bebe esto; **but —, what's the use?** pero ¡vamos!, es inútil.

thereabouts ['ðeərəbauts] adv por ahí, allí cerca; **12 or —** 12 más o menos, alrededor de 12; **£5 or —** 5 libras o así.

thereafter [ðeər'ɑ:ftə*] adv después, después de eso.

thereat [ðeər'æt] adv (thereupon) con eso, acto seguido; (for that reason) por eso, por esa razón.

thereby ['ðeə'bai] adv por eso, de ese modo; por esa razón; **it does not — become easier** no por eso se hace más fácil; **— hangs a tale** sobre eso hay mucho que decir.

therefore ['ðeəfɔ:*] adv por tanto, por lo tanto, por consiguiente; por esta razón.

therefrom [ðeə'frɔm] adv de ahí, de allí.

therein [ðeər'in] adv (inside) allí dentro; (in this regard) en eso, en esto, en este respecto; **— lies the danger** en eso consiste el peligro.

thereof [ðeər'ɔv] adv de eso, de esto; de lo mismo.

thereon [ðeər'ɔn] adv = thereupon.

there's [ðeəz] = there is; there has.

Theresa [ti'ri:zə] f Teresa.

thereto [ðeə'tu:] adv a eso, a ello.

thereupon ['ðeərə'pɔn] adv (at that point) en eso, con eso; acto seguido, en seguida; (consequently) por tanto; por consiguiente.

therewith [ðeə'wiθ] adv con eso, con lo mismo.

therm [θə:m] n unidad f térmica.

thermal ['θə:məl] adj termal.

thermic ['θə:mik] adj térmico.

thermionic [,θə:mi'ɔnik] adj termoiónico; **— valve** lámpara f termoiónica.

thermocouple ['θə:məu,kʌpl] n termopar m, par m térmico.

thermodynamic ['θə:məudai'næmik] adj termodinámico.

thermodynamics ['θə:məudai'næmiks] n termodinámica f.

thermoelectric ['θə:məui'lektrik] adj termoeléctrico; **— couple** par m termoeléctrico.

thermometer [θə'mɔmitə*] n termómetro m; **clinical —** termómetro m clínico.

thermonuclear ['θə:məu'nju:kliə*] adj termonuclear.

thermopile ['θə:məupail] n termopila f.

Thermopylae [θə:'mɔpili] Termópilas fpl.

Thermos ['θə:məs] n (Protected Trade Name) (also — bottle, — flask) termos m, termo m.

thermostat ['θə:məstæt] n termostato m.

thermostatic [,θə:məs'tætik] adj termostático.

thesaurus [θi'sɔ:rəs] n tesoro m.

these [ði:z] (pl of this) **1** dem adj m: estos; f: estas. **2** dem pron m: éstos; f: éstas; see also this.

Theseus ['θi:sju:s] m Teseo.

thesis ['θi:sis] n, pl theses ['θi:si:z] tesis f.

Thespian ['θespiən] **1** adj de Tespis; (fig) dramático, trágico. **2** n actor m, actriz f.

Thespis ['θespis] m Tespis.

Thessaly ['θesəli] Tesalia f.

Thetis ['θi:tis] f Tetis.

they [ðei] pron ellos, ellas; **— who** los que, quienes.

they'd [ðeid] = they would; they had.

they'll [ðeil] = they will, they shall.

they're [ðeə*] = they are.

they've [ðeiv] = they have.

thiamine ['θaiəmi:n] n tiamina f.

thick [θik] **1** adj (a) (of solid) espeso; book, thread, stroke etc grueso; **it is 2 metres —** tiene 2 metros de espesor; **on ice only 4 centimetres —** sobre hielo de solamente 4 centímetros de espesor.

(b) (dense) forest, vegetation etc espeso, denso; growth tupido; eyebrows, beard poblado; **the leaves** were — on the ground había una capa espesa de hojas en el suelo; **bodies lay — on the road** había cadáveres por toda la carretera; **the field is — with strawberries** el campo abunda en fresas; **the place will be — with tourists** el sitio estará atestado de turistas.

(c) (*of liquid: cloudy*) turbio, (*stiff*) viscoso; *cream, gravy etc* espeso; *fog, smoke* denso, espeso; *air* viciado; *voice* velado, apagado, poco distinto; *accent* cerrado; **the air is pretty — in here** aquí huele a encerrado, aquí se respira con dificultad; **the air was — with insults** el aire estaba lleno de insultos.

(d) (*stupid*) estúpido, lerdo.

(e) (*of relationship*) íntimo; **they're very —** son íntimos amigos; **intiman mucho; they're as — as thieves** son uña y carne; **A is — with B** A tiene mucha intimidad con B.

(f) (*fam*) **it's a bit —! ** ¡no hay derecho!, ¡esto es injusto!; **it's a bit — to have to** + *infin* es injusto tener que + *infin*.

2 *adv:* **to spread butter —** poner mucha mantequilla; **put the paint on —** ponga una buena capa de pintura; **they cut the bread very —** sirven el pan en trozos muy gruesos; **the blows fell — and fast upon him** le llovieron los golpes encima.

3 *n* (a) **in the — of battle** en lo más reñido de la batalla; **he likes to be in the — of things** le gusta tener una vida muy activa, le gusta estar en el centro de las actividades, le gusta estar muy metido en todo.

(b) **to stick to someone through — and thin** seguir completamente fiel a uno, apoyar a uno incondicionalmente.

thicken ['θikən] **1** *vt* espesar, hacer más espeso.

2 *vi* espesarse, hacerse más espeso; hacerse más denso; (*Cook*) espesarse; (*of plot*) complicarse, enmarañarse más.

thicket ['θikit] *n* matorral *m*, espesura *f*.

thickheaded ['θik'hedid] *adj* estúpido, lerdo; terco.

thickheadedness ['θik'hedidnis] *n* estupidez *f*; terquedad *f*.

thick-lipped ['θik'lipt] *adj* de labios gruesos, bezudo.

thickly ['θikli] *adv* espesamente; gruesamente; *speak* con voz apagada, indistintamente; **— populated areas** regiones *fpl* densamente pobladas; **bread — spread with butter** pan *m* con mucha mantequilla, pan *m* con una buena capa de mantequilla; **the snow was falling —** nevaba muchísimo.

thickness ['θiknis] *n* espesura *f*; densidad *f*; grueso *m*; (*in measuring*) espesor *m*; grosor *m*; **what is the — of the snow?** ¿cuánta nieve hay?; **boards of the same —** tablas *fpl* del mismo espesor.

thickset ['θik'set] *adj* rechoncho, grueso.

thickskinned ['θik'skind] *adj* (*fig*) insensible, duro.

thief [θi:f] *n, pl* **thieves** [θi:vz] ladrón *m*, ona *f*; **stop — !** ¡al ladrón!; **to set a — to catch a —** poner al ladrón de ladrón y medio.

thieve [θi:v] *vti* hurtar, robar.

thievery ['θi:vəri] *n* robo *m*, latrocinio *m*.

thieving ['θi:viŋ] **1** *adj* ladrón, largo de uñas. **2** *n* robo *m*, latrocinio *m*.

thievish ['θi:viʃ] *adj* ladrón; **to have — tendencies** ser largo de uñas.

thievishness ['θi:viʃnis] *n* propensión *f* a ser ladrón.

thigh [θai] *n* muslo *m*.

thighbone ['θaibəun] *n* fémur *m*.

thimble ['θimbl] *n* dedal *m*; (*Naut*) guardacabo *m*.

thimbleful ['θimblful] *n* dedada *f*; **just a —** unas gotas nada más.

thin [θin] **1** *adj* (a) (*of materials*) delgado; *clothing, covering* ligero; *veil etc* transparente; diáfano; *layer* tenue, fino, delgado; *person* flaco; **with — legs** con piernas flacas; **to be as — as a rake** (*or lath*) estar en los huesos; **to get —ner, to grow —ner** enflaquecer.

(b) *hair* ralo, escaso; *crop, crowd, population* poco denso, escaso; *doctors* **are — on the ground** hay pocos médicos, escasean los médicos; **the wheat is — this year** este año hay poco trigo; **he's getting — on top** le escasea el pelo por encima.

(c) *liquid* poco denso; *soup, wine* aguado; que más bien parece ser agua; *scent, sound* tenue; *air, light* tenue, sutil; *voice* delgado; **at 20,000 metres the air is —** a los 20.000 metros el aire está enrarecido.

(d) *excuse etc* poco convincente, flojo; **to have a — time** pasarlo mal, pasar por un período difícil; **they gave him a — time of it** hicieron sufrir al pobre, le hicieron sudar la gota gorda.

2 *adv:* **to spread butter —** poner poca mantequilla; **they cut the bread very —** sirven el pan en trozos muy delgados.

3 *vt:* **to — someone down** adelgazar a uno, hacer que uno enflaquezca; **to — paint (down)** desleír la pintura, diluir la pintura; **to — soup (down)** aguar la sopa; **to — out** *plants etc* entresacar, aclarar; *crowd, number, army etc* reducir, mermar.

4 *vi* adelgazar(se), (*and weaken*) enflaquecer; (*of crowd etc*) hacerse menos denso, aclararse; (*of number etc*) reducirse; **the forest starts to — out here** aquí el bosque empieza a ser menos denso.

thine [ðain] *poss pron* (*arch*) (el) tuyo, (la) tuya *etc*; **mine and —** lo mío y lo tuyo; **for thee and —** para ti y los tuyos; **what is mine is —** lo que es mío también es tuyo.

thing [θiŋ] *n* (a) (*object*) cosa *f*; objeto *m*; artículo *m*; **—s** (*belongings*) cosas *fpl*, efectos *mpl*; (*equipment*) avíos *mpl*, equipo *m*; (*clothes*) ropa *f*, trapos *mpl*; (*luggage*) equipaje *m*; **—s of value** objetos *mpl* de valor; **a — of beauty** una cosa estética, una cosa bella; **my painting —s** mis avíos de pintar; **tea —s** servicio *m* de té; **to wash up the tea —s** lavar la vajilla; **where shall I put my —s?** ¿dónde pongo mis cosas?; **to pack up one's —s** hacer las maletas; **to take off one's —s** desnudarse, quitarse la ropa.

(b) (*person*) ser *m*, criatura *f*; (*pej*) sujeto *m*; **you poor —!, poor old —!** ¡pobrecito!; **he's a poor old — now** ahora no vale para nada; **you beastly** (*or* **horrid, rotten etc**) **—!** ¡canalla!; **how are you, old —?** ¿qué tal, hijo?

(c) (*matter, circumstance etc*) cosa *f*; asunto *m*; **the main —** lo más importante, lo esencial; **above all —s** ante todo, sobre todo; **for one —** en primer lugar; **and for another — . . .** y además . . ., y por otra parte . . .; **no such —!** ¡no hay tal!; ¡ni hablar!; **what with one — and another** entre unas cosas y otras; **one — or the other . . .** una de dos . . .; **it's neither one — nor the other** no es ni lo uno ni lo otro; **first — (in the morning)** a primera hora (de la mañana); **last — (at night)** a última hora (de la noche); **the first — to do is . . .** lo primero que hay que hacer es . . .; **that's the last — we want** eso es lo que queremos menos; **the best — would be to** + *infin* lo mejor sería + *infin*; **the next best —** lo mejor después de eso; **it's a good — that . . .** menos mal que . . .; **the good — about it is that . . .** lo bueno es que . . .; **it's finished and a good — too** se acabó y me alegro de ello; **it was a close —,** it was a near — escapé (*etc*) por un pelo; **this is the real — at last** por fin lo tenemos sin trampa ni cartón; **it's the very —!, it's just the —!** ¡es exactamente lo que necesitábamos!; **that's the — for me** eso es lo que me hace falta; **the — is . . .** el caso es que . . ., es que . . .; **the — is this . . .** la dificultad es que . . .; se trata de saber si . . .; **the — is to sell your car first** conviene vender primero tu coche; **the only — is to paint it** no hay más remedio que pintarlo; **the play's the —** lo que importa es la representación; **this is too much of a good —** esto es demasiado; **as —s are** tal como están las cosas; **how are —s?** ¿qué tal?; **how are —s with you?** ¿qué tal te va?; ¿cómo te va eso?; **—s are going badly** las cosas van mal; **that's how —s are** así están las cosas; **I've done a silly —** he hecho algo tonto; **we had hoped for better —s** habíamos esperado algo mejor; **I don't know a — about cars** no sé nada en absoluto de coches; **I didn't know a — for that exam** para ese examen yo estaba pez; **he knows a — or two** él sabe cuántos son cinco; **he makes a good — out of it** sabe sacar provecho de ello, con eso tiene un buen negocio; **to make a mess of —s** hacerlo todo mal; **did you ever see such a —?** ¿se vio jamás tal cosa?

(d) (*fashion*) **the latest — in hats** la última moda del sombrero, el sombrero según la moda actual; **it's quite the —** está muy de moda.

(e) (*socially acceptable —*) **it's not the (done) —** eso no se hace, eso no está bien visto; **to do the right —** obrar bien, obrar honradamente.

(f) (*obsession*) obsesión *f*; manía *f*; **she has a — about snakes** está obsesionada por las culebras, le obsesionan las culebras; **he's got a — about me** me tiene manía.

thingumabob ['θiŋəmibɔb] *n*, **thingamajig** ['θiŋəmidʒig] *n*, **thingummy** ['θiŋəmi] *n* (*fam*) cosa *f*, chisme *m*.

think [θiŋk] (*irr: pret and ptp* **thought**) **1** *vt* (a) pensar; **to — great thoughts** pensar cosas profundas, tener pensamientos profundos.

(b) to — out *plan etc* imaginar, idear; *answer* descubrir (después de pensarlo mucho); *problem* resolver (después de pensarlo mucho); **this wants —ing out** hay que pensar esto mucho; hay que estudiar esto detenidamente; **a well thought out answer** una respuesta estudiada; una contestación razonada; **he —s things out for himself** piensa por sí mismo.

(c) to — something over considerar algo detenidamente; reflexionar sobre algo; consultar algo con la almohada; **I'll — it over** lo pensaré; **you — it over!** ¡medítelo!

(d) to — up imaginar, idear; *excuse* inventar; **who thought this one up?** ¿quién ideó esto?, ¿a quién se le ocurrió esto?

2 *vti* **(a)** (*general sense, absolute sense*) pensar; meditar; **to — hard** pensar mucho; **he says little but —s a lot** dice poco pero piensa mucho, la procesión le va por dentro; **to act without —ing** obrar sin reflexionar; **— before you reply** reflexione antes de contestar; **give me time to —** déme tiempo para reflexionar; **now let me —** déjame pensarlo; **to — again** volver a pensarlo, reflexionar; **— again!** ¡medítelo!; **to — twice** pensar dos veces, reflexionar; **to — aloud** pensar en alta voz, expresar lo que uno piensa; **to — about something** pensar algo bien, considerar algo detenidamente, reflexionar sobre algo; consultar algo con la almohada; **I'll — about it** lo pensaré; **you — about it!** ¡medítelo!; **you — about money too much** le das demasiada importancia al dinero; **to — for oneself** pensar por sí mismo.

(b) (*imagine*) pensar, creer, imaginar; **who do you — you are?** ¿quién se cree Vd que es?; **who do you — you are to come marching in?** y usted ¿qué derecho cree tener para entrar aquí tan fresco?; **— of me in a bathing costume!** ¡imaginadme en traje de baño!; **just —!** ¡fíjate!, ¡imagínate!; **to — that . . .!** ¡y pensar que . . .!; **to — she once slept here!** ¡pensar que ella durmió aquí una vez!; **I can't — what you mean** no entiendo lo que Vd quiere decir; **I can't — what he can want** no llego a comprender su motivo; **I would have thought that . . .** hubiera creído que . . .; **I never thought that . . .** nunca pensé que . . .; **one might — that . . .** podría creerse que . . .; **anyone would — he was dying** cualquiera diría que se estaba muriendo; **who'd have thought it!** ¿quién lo diría?

(c) (*of ideas occurring*) **I was —ing that . . .** se me ocurrió pensar que . . .; **to — of doing something** pensar hacer algo, ocurrírsele a uno hacer algo; **don't you ever — of washing?** ¿no se te ocurre alguna vez lavarte?; **had you ever thought of going to Spain?** ¿has pensado alguna vez ir a España?

(d) (*intend*) pensar; **to — to + infin** pensar + *infin*; **I came here —ing to find you** vine aquí con la intención de buscarte.

(e) (*expect*) esperar; **I never thought to hear that from you** no esperaba nunca escuchar tales cosas de boca de Vd; **I thought as much** ya me lo figuraba, lo había previsto ya; **we little thought that . . .** estábamos lejos de pensar que . . .

(f) (*believe, consider*) creer, pensar; considerar; opinar; **I — so** creo que sí; **I shouldn't — so** no creo; **I — not** creo que no; **I should — so too!** ¡haces muy bien!; ¡ya era hora!; ¡buena falta te hacía!; **and it was free, I don't —!** ¡ya lo creo que me lo dieron gratis!; **I — (that) it is true** creo que es verdad, me parece que es verdad; **I don't — it can be done** no creo que se pueda hacer, no creo que sea factible; **so you — that . . .?** ¿así que Vd cree que . . .?; **what do you — I should do?** ¿qué crees tú que debiera hacer?, ¿qué me aconsejas hacer?; **to — oneself very clever** creerse la mar de listo, creerse muy astuto; *see* **better 1, 2** *etc*.

(g) (*believe, consider: with pred adj*) creer; **I — it very difficult** lo creo muy difícil, lo veo muy difícil, creo que es muy difícil; **I don't — it at all likely** lo creo muy poco probable; **everyone thought him mad** todos le tenían por loco; **they are thought to be poor** se cree que son pobres, t_nen fama de ser pobres; *see* **fit, proper**.

(h) (*opine*) pensar; **she didn't know what to —** no sabía a qué carta quedarse; le fue imposible decidir; **now I don't know what to —** ahora tengo dudas, ahora estoy en duda; **what do you — ?** ¿qué te parece?; **what do you — about it?** ¿qué te parece (de esto)?; **see what you — about it and let me know** estúdielo y dígame luego su opinión; **what do you — of him?** ¿qué piensas de él?, ¿qué

te parece él?, ¿qué concepto tienes de él?; **to — highly of someone** tener en mucho a uno; **to — well of someone** tener un buen concepto de uno; **he is well thought of here** aquí se le estima mucho; **we don't — much of X** tenemos un concepto más bien bajo de X; **I don't — much of that cheese** no me gusta nada ese queso; **I told him what I thought of him** le dije la opinión que tenía de él; le dije un par de cosas; *see* **nothing (d)** *etc*.

(i) (*devote thought to, bear in mind, remember*) **to —** of pensar en; **I — of you always, I am always —ing of you** pienso constantemente en ti; **— of me tomorrow in the exam** ayúdame mañana en el examen con tus pensamientos; **one can't — of everything** es imposible atender a todo, es imposible preverlo todo; **I couldn't — of the right word** no pude recordar la palabra exacta; **what can you have been —ing of?** ¿qué demonios pensabas hacer?; ¿cómo se te ocurrió hacer (*etc*) eso?; **his style makes me — of Baroja** su estilo me hace pensar en Baroja, su estilo me recuerda el de Baroja; **that is worth —ing about** eso vale la pena de pensarlo un poco; **there is so much to — about** hay tantas cosas que tener en cuenta; **you've given us a lot to — about** nos ha dado Vd muchas cosas en que pensar; **— what you have done** recapacite lo que ha hecho.

(j) (*be sympathetic to, take into account*) considerar, tener en cuenta; **to — of other people's feelings** tener en cuenta los sentimientos de los demás; **one has to — of the expense** hay que considerar lo que se gasta; **he —s of nobody but himself** no piensa más que en sí mismo.

3 *n*: **I'll have a — about it** lo pensaré; **to have a good — about something** meditar algo, pensar mucho acerca de algo; **you'd better have another —** conviene volver a pensarlo, conviene reconsiderarlo; **I was having a quiet —** meditaba tranquilamente.

thinkable ['θiŋkəbl] *adj* concebible; **is it — that . . .?** ¿es concebible que + *subj*?, ¿se concibe que + *subj*?

thinker ['θiŋkə*] *n* pensador *m*.

thinking ['θiŋkiŋ] **1** *adj* pensante, que piensa; inteligente, racional; serio; **to any — person** para cualquier persona seria.
2 *n* pensamiento *m*; (*thoughts collectively*) pensamientos *mpl*; **wishful —** espejismo *m*, ilusionismo *m*; **his way of —** su modo de pensar; **to my way of —** a mi juicio, en mi opinión.

thin-lipped ['θin'lipt] *adj* de labios apretados.

thinly ['θinli] *adv*: **— disguised as . . .** ligeramente disfrazado de . . .; **with — spread butter** con una capa delgada de mantequilla.

thinness ['θinnis] *n* delgadez *f*; flaqueza *f*; tenuidad *f*.

thin-skinned ['θin'skind] *adj* de piel fina; (*fig*) sensible, demasiado sensible.

third [θəːd] **1** *adj* tercero.
2 *n* tercio *m*, tercera parte *f*; (*Mus*) tercera *f*; **two-thirds of the votes** dos tercios de los votos; **two-thirds of those present** las dos terceras partes de los asistentes.
3 *adv*: **to travel —** viajar en tercera clase.

third-class ['θəː'dklɑːs] **1** *adj* de tercera clase; (*pej*) de tercera clase, de baja categoría. **2** *adv*: **to travel —** viajar en tercera.

thirdly ['θəːdli] *adv* en tercer lugar.

third-party ['θəːd'pɑːti] *attr*: **— insurance** seguro *m* contra tercera persona.

third-rate ['θəː'dreit] *adj* de baja categoría.

thirst [θəːst] **1** *n* sed *f*; **the — for** (*fig*) la sed de, el ansia de, el afán de; **to quench one's —** apagar la sed. **2** *vi*: **to — for** (*fig*) tener sed de.

thirsty ['θəːsti] *adj* sediento; *land* árido, que necesita regarse mucho; **to be —** tener sed; **how — I am!** ¡qué sed tengo!; **it's — work** es un trabajo que hace sudar.

thirteen ['θəː'tiːn] *adj* trece.

thirteenth ['θəː'tiːnθ] *adj* decimotercio, decimotercero.

thirtieth ['θəːtiiθ] *adj* trigésimo.

thirty ['θəːti] *adj* treinta; **the thirties** (*eg* 1930s) los años treinta; **to be in one's thirties** tener más de treinta años.

this [ðis] (*pl* **these**) **1** *dem adj m*: este; *f*: esta; **— evening** esta tarde; **this coming week** esta semana que viene; **— day last year** hoy hace un año; **— day fortnight** hoy a quince días.
2 *dem pron m*: éste; *f*: ésta; "*neuter*": esto; **— is new** esto es nuevo; **like —** así, de este modo; **it was like —** le contaré la cosa como pasó; le diré lo que pasó; **what's all —?** ¿qué pasa?; **who's —?** ¿quién es?; **— is Joe** (*on telephone etc*) soy

Pepe; — **is Joe Soap** (*introduction*) quiero presentarle al señor Joe Soap; — **is Tuesday** hoy es martes; **but** — **is May** pero estamos en mayo.

3 *adv*: — **far** tan lejos; — **high** tan alto, así de alto (*and see that* 4).

thistle ['θisl] *n* cardo *m*.

thistledown ['θisldaun] *n* borrilla *f* de cardo.

thistly ['θisli] *adj* (*prickly*) espinoso; (*full of thistles*) lleno de cardos; *problem etc* espinoso, erizado de dificultades.

thither ['ðiðə*] *adv* (*arch*) allá.

thole [θəul] *n* escálamo *m*.

Thomas ['tɔməs] *m* Tomás; **Saint** — Santo Tomás; — **More** Tomás Moro.

Thomism ['tɔmizəm] *n* tomismo *m*.

Thomist ['tɔmist] **1** *adj* tomista. **2** *n* tomista *mf*.

thong [θɔŋ] *n* correa *f*.

thoracic [θɔːˈræsik] *adj* torácico.

thorax ['θɔːræks] *n* tórax *m*.

thorium ['θɔːriəm] *n* torio *m*.

thorn [θɔːn] *n* espina *f* (*also fig*); **to be a** — **in the flesh of someone** ser una espina en el costado de uno.

thorn bush ['θɔːnbuʃ] *n* espino *m*.

thornless ['θɔːnlis] *adj* sin espinas.

thorn tree ['θɔːntriː] *n* espino *m*.

thorny ['θɔːni] *adj* espinoso; (*fig*) espinoso, erizado de dificultades.

thorough ['θʌrə] *adj* (*complete*) completo, cabal; acabado; (*not superficial*) minucioso, concienzudo, meticuloso; **he's very** — es muy cuidadoso, es muy concienzudo; **to have a** — **knowledge of a region** conocer una región a fondo; **we made a** — **search** lo registramos minuciosamente; **there will be a** — **investigation into the charges** las acusaciones serán investigadas a fondo.

thoroughbred ['θʌrəbred] **1** *adj* de pura sangre. **2** *n* pura sangre *mf*.

thoroughfare ['θʌrəfeə*] *n* vía *f* pública; carretera *f*, calle *f*; **"no** — **"** "prohibido el paso".

thoroughgoing ['θʌrəgəuiŋ] *adj* *person* cien por cien, totalista, de cuerpo entero; *examination etc* minucioso, a fondo.

thoroughly ['θʌrəli] *adv*: **to know something** — conocer algo a fondo; **to investigate something** — investigar algo a fondo; **he works** — trabaja cuidadosamente, trabaja concienzudamente; **a** — **bad influence** una influencia totalmente mala; **a** — **stupid thing to do** una acción completamente estúpida.

thoroughness ['θʌrənis] *n* minuciosidad *f*, meticulosidad *f*; perfección *f*; **with great** — con el mayor cuidado, con todo cuidado.

those [ðəuz] (*pl of that*) **1** *dem adj m*: esos, (*more remote*) aquellos, *f*: esas, (*more remote*) aquellas.

2 *dem pron m*: ésos, (*more remote*) aquéllos, *f*: ésas, (*more remote*) aquéllas; — **of** los de, las de; — **which** los que, las que; — **who** los que, las que, quienes; *see also* **that**.

thou [ðau] *pron* (*arch*) tú.

though [ðəu] **1** *conj* aunque; si bien; — **it was raining at the time** aunque llovía entonces; (*even*) — **he doesn't want to** aunque no quiera; **as** — como si + *subj*; — **small it's good** aunque es pequeño es bueno; **strange** — **it may appear** aunque parezca extraño, por extraño que parezca; **what** — **there is no money?** ¿qué importa que no hay dinero?

2 *adv* sin embargo; **it's not so easy,** — sin embargo no es tán fácil; **did he** — **?** ¿de veras?

thought [θɔːt] **1** *pret and ptp of* **think**.

2 *n* (**a**) pensamiento *m*; idea *f*, concepto *m*; reflexión *f*, meditación *f*; consideración *f*; (*thoughtfulness*) solicitud *f*; **the** — **of Sartre** el pensamiento de Sartre; **happy** — **idea** *f* luminosa; **that's a** — **!** eso hay que tenerlo en cuenta; **after much** —, **on second** —**s** después de pensarlo bien, después de mucho pensar; **my** —**s were elsewhere** pensaba en otra cosa; **his one** — **is to** + *infin* su único propósito es de + *infin*; **the very** — **frightens me** sólo pensar en ello me da miedo; **to collect one's** —**s** orientarse, concentrarse; **let me collect my** —**s** déjame pensar; **to give** — **to something** pensar algo, meditar algo; considerar algo detenidamente; **we must give some** — **to the others** hay que tener en cuenta a los demás, conviene tener presentes a los demás; **I didn't give it another** — no volví a pensar en ello; **I had no** — **of offending you** no tenía la intención de ofenderle; **then I had second** —**s** luego tuve otra idea, mudé luego de parecer; **to be lost in** — estar absorto en meditación; **perish the** —**!** ¡ni por pensamiento!; **to read somebody's** —**s** adivinar el pensamiento de uno; **to**

take — **how to do something** pensar cómo hacer algo; **to take no** — **for the morrow** no pensar en mañana.

(**b**) (*fig*) pizca *f*, poquito *m*; **it's a** — **too bright** es un poquito claro.

thoughtful ['θɔːtful] *adj* (*pensive*) pensativo, meditabundo; (*in character*) serio; (*kind*) atento, solícito, considerado; (*far-sighted*) clarividente, previsor; **how** — **of you!**, **that's very** — **of you!** ¡qué detalle!, ¡es Vd muy amable!; **he's a** — **boy** es un chico serio.

thoughtfully ['θɔːtfəli] *adv* pensativamente; seriamente; atentamente, solícitamente, con consideración; con clarividencia, con previsión; **"Yes"**, **he said** — **"Sí"**, dijo pensativo; **someone had** — **provided a cup** alguien había puesto amablemente una taza.

thoughtfulness ['θɔːtfulnis] *n* seriedad *f*; carácter *m* reflexivo; atención *f*, solicitud *f*, consideración *f*; clarividencia *f*, previsión *f*.

thoughtless ['θɔːtlis] *adj act* irreflexivo, descuidado; *person* inconsiderado, desconsiderado, inconsciente.

thoughtlessly ['θɔːtlisli] *adv* sin pensar, irreflexivamente; inconscientemente; **to act** — obrar con poca consideración, obrar sin pensar.

thoughtlessness ['θɔːtlisnis] *n* irreflexión *f*, descuido *m*; inconsideración *f*, inconsciencia *f*.

thought reading ['θɔːt,riːdiŋ] *n* adivinación *f* de pensamientos.

thousand ['θauzənd] **1** *adj* mil; **a** —, **one** — mil; **4** — **specimens** cuatro mil ejemplares.

2 *n* mil *m*; (*more loosely*) millar *m*; **they sell them by the** — los venden a millares; **they were there in** —**s** los había a millares.

thousandfold ['θauzəndfəuld] **1** *adj* multiplicado por mil; **a** — **veces. 2** *adv* mil veces.

thousandth ['θauzəntθ] **1** *adj* milésimo. **2** milésimo *m*.

thraldom ['θrɔːldəm] *n* esclavitud *f*.

thrall [θrɔːl] *n* (*person*) esclavo *m*, *a f*; (*state*) esclavitud *f*; **to be in** — **to** ser esclavo de; **to hold someone in** — retener a uno en la esclavitud.

thrash [θræʃ] **1** *vt* golpear; *person* apalear, (*as punishment*) azotar, zurrar; (*Sport etc*) derrotar, cascar; **to** — **out** resolver mediante larga discusión, discutir largamente.

2 *vi*: **to** — **about** sacudirse, dar vueltas; revolcarse; debatirse; **he** —**ed about with his stick** daba golpes por todos lados con su bastón; **they were** —**ing about in the water** se estaban debatiendo en el agua; *see also* **thresh**.

thrashing ['θræʃiŋ] *n* zurra *f*, paliza *f*; **to give someone a** — zurrar a uno; **to give a team a** — dar una paliza a un equipo.

thread [θred] **1** *n* (*Sew etc*) hilo *m*; (*fibre*) hebra *f*, fibra *f*; (*of silkworm, spider etc*) hebra *f*; (*of screw*) filete *m*, rosca *f*; **to hang by a** — pender de un hilo; **to lose the** — (*of what one is saying*) perder el hilo (de su discurso); **to pick** (*or* **take**) **up the** — **again** coger el hilo, reanudar lo que uno estaba diciendo (*or* haciendo *etc*).

2 *vt* *needle* enhebrar; *beads etc* ensartar; **to** — **one's way through** colarse a través de, abrirse paso por, lograr pasar por.

threadbare ['θredbeə*] *adj* raído, gastado; *tyre* poco cubierto; *excuse etc* flojo, poco convincente.

threat [θret] *n* amenaza *f*; **it is a grave** — **to . . .** constituye una grave amenaza para . . .

threaten ['θretn] *vti* amenazar; proferir amenazas contra; **to** — **violence** amenazar violencia, amenazar con ponerse violento; **to** — **someone with something** amenazar a uno con algo; **a species** —**ed with extinction** una especie amenazada de extinción; **to** — **to** + *infin* amenazar con + *infin*; **to** — **to kill someone** amenazar con matar a uno; **it is** —**ing to rain** amenaza llover.

threatening ['θretniŋ] *adj* amenazador, amenazante.

threateningly ['θretniŋli] *adv* de modo amenazador; *say etc* en tono amenazador.

three [θriː] **1** *adj* tres. **2** *n* tres *m*.

three-act ['θriːˈækt] *adj* *play* de tres actos, en tres actos.

three-colour(ed), (*US*) **-color(ed)** ['θriːˈkʌləd] *adj attr* de tres colores.

three-cornered ['θriːˈkɔːnəd] *adj* triangular; — **hat** tricornio *m*, sombrero *m* de tres picos.

three-decker ['θriːˈdekə*] *n* (*also* — **novel**) novelón *m*, novela *f* larga.

three-dimensional ['θriːdiˈmenʃənl] *adj* tridimensional.

threefold ['θriːfəuld] **1** *adj* triple. **2** *adv* tres veces.

three-legged ['θriːˈlegid] *adj* de tres piernas; *stool* de tres patas.

three-masted ['θriː'mɑːstid] adj de tres palos.
threepence ['θrepəns] n 3 peniques mpl.
threepenny ['θrepəni] adj de 3 peniques; (fig) de poca monta, despreciable; — bit, — piece moneda f de 3 peniques.
three-phase ['θriːfeiz] adj (Elec) trifásico.
three-piece ['θriːpiːs] adj: — suite tresillo m.
three-ply ['θriːplai] adj wood de tres capas; wool triple.
three-quarter [.θriː'kwɔːtə*] adj: — length sleeves mangas fpl tres cuartos.
threescore ['θriːskɔː*] n sesenta; — years and ten setenta años.
three-sided ['θriː'saidid] adj trilátero.
threesome ['θriːsəm] n grupo m de tres, conjunto m de tres.
three-wheeler ['θriː'wiːlə*] n (Aut) coche-cabina m triciclo.
threnody ['θrenədi] n lamento m; canto m fúnebre.
thresh [θreʃ] vt (Agr) trillar; see also **thrash.**
thresher ['θreʃə*] n trilladora f.
threshing ['θreʃiŋ] n trilla f.
threshing floor ['θreʃiŋflɔː*] n era f.
threshing machine ['θreʃiŋmə.ʃiːn] n trilladora f.
threshold ['θreʃhəuld] n umbral m; to be on the — of (fig) estar en los umbrales de, estar en la antesala de, estar al borde de; to cross someone's — traspasar el umbral de uno.
threw [θruː] pret of **throw.**
thrice [θrais] adv (arch) tres veces.
thrift [θrift] n, **thriftiness** ['θriftinis] n economía f, frugalidad f.
thriftless ['θriftlis] adj malgastador, pródigo.
thriftlessness ['θriftlisnis] n prodigalidad f.
thrifty ['θrifti] adj económico, frugal, ahorrativo.
thrill [θril] 1 n emoción f; sensación f; estremecimiento m; with a — of excitement, he . . . estremecido de emoción, él . . .; what a —! ¡qué emoción!; it's the — of the year es la sensación del año; he just does it for the — lo hace simplemente porque ello le emociona; to get a — out of something emocionarse con algo; it gives me a — me emociona; me hace mucha ilusión.
2 vt emocionar, conmover, estremecer; hacer ilusión a; the film —ed me la película me emocionó; I was —ed to get your letter tu carta me hizo mucha ilusión; we were —ed with (or about, at) your news tu noticia nos emocionó muchísimo.
3 vi emocionarse, conmoverse, estremecerse; to — to someone's touch estremecerse al ser tocado por uno.
thriller ['θrilə*] n novela f (or obra f, película f) escalofriante, novela f de suspense, novela f de misterio.
thrilling ['θriliŋ] adj emocionante, conmovedor; apasionante; sensacional; an absolutely — journey un viaje de lo más interesante; a — play una obra muy emocionante; how —! ¡qué emoción!; how — for you! ¡qué bien!
thrillingly ['θriliŋli] adv de modo emocionante; de modo sensacional.
thrive [θraiv] (irr: pret **throve,** ptp **thriven**) vi (do well) prosperar, medrar; florecer; (grow) crecer mucho, desarrollarse bien; he —s on hard work le gusta estar muy ocupado, se encuentra perfectamente bien con un trabajo agotador; the plant —s here la planta crece muy bien aquí; children — on milk a los niños les aprovecha la leche.
thriven ['θrivn] ptp of **thrive.**
thriving ['θraiviŋ] adj próspero, floreciente.
throat [θrəut] n garganta f; (from exterior) cuello m; to clear one's — carraspear, aclarar la voz; to cut one's — cortarse la garganta; to have a sore — tener anginas; to moisten one's — remojar el gaznate; to thrust something down someone's — (fig) hacer que uno trague algo a la fuerza, imponer algo a uno.
throaty ['θrəuti] adj gutural; ronco.
throb [θrɔb] 1 n (of heart etc) latido m, pulsación f; palpitación f; (of engine) vibración f; (of emotion) estremecimiento m.
2 vi latir; palpitar; vibrar; estremecerse; the crowd —bed with excitement la multitud se estremeció emocionada.
throbbing ['θrɔbiŋ] 1 adj palpitante; vibrante; pain pungente; rhythm marcado, fuerte.
2 n latido m, pulsación f; palpitación f; vibración f; estremecimiento m.
throes [θrəuz] npl (of death) agonía f; (of childbirth etc) dolores mpl; (fig) angustia f, agonía f; to be in the — of estar en medio de; estar sufriendo todas las molestias de.

thrombosis [θrɔm'bəusis] n trombosis f.
throne [θrəun] n trono m; (fig freq) corona f, poder m real; to ascend the —, to come to the — subir al trono.
throne room ['θrəunrum] n sala f del trono.
throng [θrɔŋ] 1 n multitud f, tropel m, muchedumbre f; great —s of tourists multitudes fpl de turistas; to come in a — venir en tropel.
2 vt atestar, llenar de bote en bote.
3 vi: to come —ing venir en tropel, venir en masa; to — round someone apiñarse en torno a uno; to — to hear someone venir en tropel a escuchar a uno; to — together reunirse en tropel.
thronged [θrɔŋd] adj atestado, lleno de bote en bote; the streets are — with tourists las calles están llenas de turistas; everywhere is — todo está lleno, no queda espacio libre en ninguna parte.
thronging ['θrɔŋiŋ] adj crowd etc grande, apretado, nutrido.
throttle ['θrɔtl] 1 n (Anat) gaznate m; (Mech) regulador m, válvula f reguladora, estrangulador m; (Aut, loosely) acelerador m; to give an engine full — acelerar un motor al máximo.
2 vt ahogar, estrangular; (Mech) estrangular.
3 vi: to — down moderar la marcha.
through [θruː] 1 adv (a) (of place) de parte a parte, completamente; the nail went right — el clavo penetró de parte a parte; the wood has rotted — la madera se ha podrido completamente.
(b) (of time, process) desde el principio hasta el fin; hasta el fin; did you stay right —? ¿te quedaste hasta el final?; we're staying — till Tuesday nos quedamos hasta el martes; to sleep the whole night — dormir la noche entera; he knew it right — lo sabía todo, lo sabía de corrido.
(c) (with to be) you're —! (Tel) ¡puede hablar!, ¡hable!; are you —? ¿has terminado?; we'll be — at 7 terminaremos a las 7; when I'm — with him cuando haya terminado con él; I'm not — with you yet todavía no he terminado de decir (etc) lo que tenía pensado; I'm — with bridge renuncio al bridge, ya no vuelvo a jugar al bridge; I'm — with her he roto con ella.
(d) a Catalan — and — catalán hasta los tuétanos, catalán por los cuatro costados; see carry, fall etc.
2 prep (a) (of place) por; a través de; de un lado a otro de; to look — a telescope mirar por un telescopio; to walk — the woods dar un paseo por el bosque; the bullet went — 3 layers la bala penetró 3 capas; it went right — the wall atravesó la pared y salió al otro lado.
(b) (of time) (US) hasta, hasta e incluso; (from) Monday — Friday desde el lunes hasta el viernes, de lunes a viernes; all — our stay durante toda nuestra estancia; right — the year durante el año entero.
(c) he's — the exam ha aprobado el examen.
(d) (of means) mediante, por medio de; por, por causa de; debido a; gracias a; — him I found out that . . . por él supe que . . .; — not knowing the way por no saber el camino; he got it — friends lo consiguió gracias a los amigos; it was — you that we were late fue por vosotros por lo que llegamos tarde; to act — fear obrar movido por el miedo.
3 adj carriage, traffic, train directo.
throughout [θruː'aut] 1 adv (a) (of place) en todas partes, por todas partes; the hull is welded — el casco esta totalmente soldado; the room has been cleaned — el cuarto ha sido limpiado completamente; the house has electric light — la casa tiene luz eléctrica en todos los cuartos.
(b) (of time, process) todo el tiempo, desde el principio hasta el fin; the weather was good — hizo buen tiempo todos los días; it's a boring journey — es un viaje pesado en todo el recorrido, todo el viaje es monótono.
2 prep (a) (of place) por todo, por todas partes de; — the country por todo el país, en todo el país.
(b) (of time, process) durante todo, en todo.
throughput ['θruːput] n cantidad f invertida, cantidad f de materias primas.
throve [θrəuv] pret of **thrive.**
throw [θrəu] 1 n echada f, tirada f, tiro m; (move, at games) jugada f; (in wrestling) derribo m; (at dice) lance m; within a stone's — a tiro de piedra.
2 (irr: pret **threw,** ptp **thrown**) vt (a) (general sense) echar, tirar, lanzar, arrojar; dice echar; glance lanzar, dirigir; kiss echar, tirar; to — a coat over someone cubrir a uno con un abrigo, envolver a uno en un abrigo; to — a ball 200 metres lanzar

una pelota 200 metros; **to — a bridge over a river** tender (or construir) un puente sobre un río; **to — a door open** abrir una puerta de golpe, abrir una puerta de par en par; **to — two rooms into one** hacer un solo cuarto de dos que había; **to — the blame on someone** echar la culpa a uno; **to — temptation in someone's path** exponer a uno a la tentación; **to be —n on one's own resources** tener que depender de sí mismo, no tener más que los propios recursos.

(b) light, shadow, slides etc proyectar; **to — light on** (fig) aclarar, arrojar luz sobre.

(c) rider desmontar, desarzonar; opponent derribar; skin mudar, quitarse; **to be —n** (of rider) ser desarzonado.

(d) (disconcert) confundir, desconcertar, dejar perplejo; **this answer seemed to — him** esta respuesta parecía desconcertarle.

(e) (Tech) pot formar, dar forma a, hacer; silk torcer.

(f) (fam phrases) **to — a fight** perder deliberadamente un encuentro; **to — a fit** (Med) sufrir un ataque (epiléptico); sufrir una crisis nerviosa; desmayarse; (fig) subirse por las paredes (fam); **to — a party** ofrecer una fiesta, organizar una fiesta (for someone en honor de uno).

(g) (with adv or prep) **to — about** tirar por aquí y por allá, esparcir; **to — money about** derrochar dinero; **to — one's arms about** agitar mucho los brazos; **to — aside** tirar, tirar a un lado; apartar, desechar; **to — away** tirar, echar; desechar; money malgastar, derrochar; one's life sacrificar inútilmente; chance desperdiciar; **it's old and can be —n away** es viejo y se puede tirar; **to — back** ball devolver; enemy rechazar, arrollar; hair, head echar hacia atrás; offer rechazar (con desprecio); **to — down** ball etc echar a tierra; hair hacia abajo; building, defences derribar, echar abajo; arms, tools dejar, abandonar; challenge lanzar; glove (fig) arrojar; **it's —ing it down** (of rain) está lloviendo a cántaros; **to — in** ball (Sport) sacar; remark hacer, insertar, lanzar (de improviso); cards arrojar sobre la mesa (en señal de abandono); (as addition) añadir; dar de más; ofrecer de más; **with an extra meal —n in** con una comida de más, con una comida gratis; **to — off** burden, yoke sacudirse, deshacerse de, quitarse de encima; clothes quitarse (de prisa); disguise abandonar; habit renunciar a; idea, suggestion ofrecer (de improviso); composition hacer rápidamente; improvisar; (emit) emitir, despedir; arrojar; **to — the dogs off the scent** despistar los perros; **in order to — the police off the trail** para despistar a la policía; **to — on** clothes ponerse (de prisa); **to — out** rubbish tirar; defective articles desechar, tirar; person expulsar, echar; poner de patitas en la calle; (Parl) bill rechazar; (emit) emitir, despedir, arrojar; hint proferir; idea, suggestion hacer (de improviso); **to — out one's chest** sacar el pecho, abultar el pecho; **it has —n many men out of work** ha privado de trabajo a muchos hombres; **to — over** (abandon) dejar, abandonar; friend romper con, sweetheart dar calabazas a; **to — together** reunir de prisa; **they where —n together by chance** se conocieron por casualidad; **to — up** (cast upwards) lanzar al aire; lanzar hacia arriba; work, project abandonar; claim, post renunciar a; defences levantar rápidamente, construir de prisa; (vomit) devolver, vomitar; see sponge etc.

3 vi: **to — up** vomitar; **it makes me — up** me da asco, me repugna.

4 vr: **to — oneself about** agitar mucho el cuerpo; **to — oneself at someone's feet** echarse a los pies de uno; **to — oneself at someone** (or at someone's head) proponerse conquistar a uno (como novio); **to — oneself backwards** echarse hacia atrás; **to — oneself down from a building** arrojarse desde un edificio; **to — oneself into the fray** lanzarse a la batalla; **to — oneself on someone** lanzarse sobre uno, precipitarse sobre uno; **to — oneself to the ground** tirarse al suelo; see mercy etc.

throwaway ['θrəuəwei] adj: **— wrapping** envase m desechable, envase m a tirar.

throwback ['θrəubæk] n (Bio) reversión f (to a).

thrower ['θrəuə*] n lanzador m, ora f.

throw-in ['θrəuin] n (Sport) saque m (de banda).

thrown [θrəun] ptp of **throw**.

throw-out ['θrəuaut] n cosa f desechada, cosa f inútil.

thru [θru:] (US) see **through**.

thrum [θrʌm] 1 vt piano teclear en; guitar rasguear, rasguear las cuerdas de. 2 vi teclear; rasguear las cuerdas.

thrush[1] [θrʌʃ] n (Orn) zorzal m.

thrush[2] [θrʌʃ] n (Med) ubrera f; (Vet) higo m.

thrust [θrʌst] 1 n (push) empuje m (also Mech etc); (Mil) avance m, ataque m; (of sword) estocada f; (of dagger) puñalada f; (of knife) cuchillada f; (thrustfulness) empuje m; **a shrewd —** un golpe certero, un golpe bien dado; **that was a — at you** eso lo dijo por ti, esa observación iba dirigida contra ti.

2 (irr: pret and ptp **thrust**) vt (push) empujar; (drive) impeler, impulsar; (insert) introducir, meter (into en); (insert piercingly) clavar, hincar (into en); **to — a dagger into someone's back** clavar un puñal en la espalda de uno; **to — a stick into the ground** hincar un palo en el suelo; **to — one's hands into one's pockets** meter las manos en los bolsillos; **to — someone through with a sword** atravesar a uno (de parte a parte) con una espada; **with an arrow — through his hat** con una flecha que le atravesaba el sombrero; **to — one's way to the front** abrirse paso (empujando) hasta la parte delantera; **to — aside** person apartar bruscamente, plan rechazar; **to — back** crowd hacer retroceder, enemy arrollar, rechazar, thought rechazar; **to — forward** empujar hacia adelante; **to — something on someone** imponer algo a uno; obligar a uno a aceptar algo; **Spain had greatness — upon her** España recibió su grandeza sin buscarla, se le impuso la grandeza a España sin quererlo ella; **to — out** sacar, sacar fuera; hand tender, (Aut etc) sacar; tongue sacar; head asomar; **to — someone out of a door** expulsar a uno por una puerta.

3 vi: **to — at someone** asestar un golpe a uno; **to — forward** seguir adelante, proseguir su marcha (etc), (Mil) avanzar; **to — past someone** cruzar (empujando) delante de uno; **to — through** abrirse paso por la fuerza.

4 vr: **to — oneself forward** (fig) ponerse delante de otros, darse importancia; ofrecerse para hacer algo (con poca modestia); **to — oneself in** introducirse a la fuerza; (fig) entrometerse.

thrustful ['θrʌstful] adj, **thrusting** ['θrʌstiŋ] adj emprendedor, vigoroso, enérgico; ambicioso; (pej) agresivo.

thrustfulness ['θrʌstfulnis] n empuje m, pujanza f, espíritu m emprendedor; ambición f; (pej) espíritu m agresivo.

thruway ['θru:wei] n (US) supercarretera f directa.

thud [θʌd] 1 n ruido m sordo, golpe m sordo.

2 vi hacer un ruido sordo, caer (etc) con un ruido sordo; **to — across the floor** andar con pasos pesados; **he was —ding about upstairs all night** pasó la noche andando con pasos pesados por el piso de arriba; **a shell —ded into the hillside** una granada estalló con ruido sordo en la ladera del monte.

thug [θʌg] n asesino m, ladrón m, criminal m (brutal); (fig, as term of abuse etc) bruto m, bestia f, desalmado m.

thumb [θʌm] 1 n pulgar m; **I'm all —s today** hoy no hago nada bien, hoy estoy terriblemente desmañado; **to be under someone's —** estar dominado por uno; **to twiddle one's —s** voltear los pulgares, (fig) no tener nada que hacer.

2 vt (a) manosear; **to — through a book** hojear un libro; **a well —ed book** un libro muy manoseado.

(b) **to — a lift, to — a ride** hacer autostop; **to — a lift to London** viajar gratis en coche (etc) ajeno a Londres.

thumb index ['θʌm'indeks] n índice m recortado.

thumbnail ['θʌmneil] n uña f del pulgar; **— sketch** dibujo m en miniatura.

thumbprint ['θʌmprint] n impresión f del pulgar.

thumbscrew ['θʌmskru:] n empulgueras fpl.

thumbtack ['θʌmtæk] n (US) chinche f.

thump [θʌmp] 1 n (blow) golpazo m, porrazo m; (noise of fall etc) ruido m sordo; **it came down with a —** cayó con un ruido sordo.

2 vt golpear, aporrear; **to — the table** golpear la mesa, dar golpes en la mesa; **to — out a tune on the piano** tocar una melodía al piano golpeando las teclas.

3 vi (of heart) latir con golpes pesados; (of machine) funcionar con ruido sordo, vibrar con violencia; **it came —ing down** cayó con un ruido sordo; **he —ed across the floor** anduvo con pasos pesados.

thumping ['θʌmpiŋ] adj (fam) enorme, enorme de grande; **a — great book** un enorme libro, un librote (fam).

thunder ['θʌndə*] 1 n trueno m; (loud report) tronido m; (of passing vehicle etc) rodar m pesado, estruendo m; (of applause) estruendo m; (of hooves) estampido m; **there is — about, there is — in the air** amenaza tronar; **to steal someone's —** adelantarse a uno robándole una idea (or un chiste, una observación etc).

2 vt: **to — threats against someone** fulminar amenazas contra uno; **to — out an order** dar una orden en tono muy fuerte; **"yes", he —ed "sí"**, rugió.

3 vi tronar; **the guns —ed in the distance** los cañones retumbaban a lo lejos; **the train —ed past** el tren pasó con gran estruendo.

thunderbolt ['θʌndəbəult] n rayo m (also fig).

thunderclap ['θʌndəklæp] n tronido m.

thundercloud ['θʌndəklaud] n nubarrón m.

thunderer ['θʌndərə*] n: **the T—** el Fulminador; (Jupiter) Júpiter tonante.

thunderflash ['θʌndəflæʃ] n petardo m.

thundering ['θʌndəriŋ] adj (fam) enorme, imponente; **a — great row** un ruido de todos los demonios; **it's a — nuisance** es una tremenda lata (fam); **it was a — success** obtuvo un tremendo éxito.

thunderous ['θʌndərəs] adj applause etc atronador, ensordecedor.

thunderstorm ['θʌndəstɔːm] n tronada f, tempestad f de truenos.

thunderstruck ['θʌndəstrʌk] adj (fig) pasmado, estupefacto.

thundery ['θʌndəri] adj weather tormentoso, bochornoso.

Thursday ['θəːzdi] n jueves m; **Holy T—** Jueves m Santo.

thus [ðʌs] adv así; de este modo; **— far** hasta aquí; **— it is that . . .** así es que . . .; **—, when he got home . . .** así que, cuando llegó a casa . . .

thwack [θwæk] see **whack**.

thwart [θwɔːt] **1** n (Naut) bancada f. **2** vt frustrar; impedir, estorbar; plan etc frustrar, desbaratar; **to be —ed at every turn** verse frustrado en todo.

thy [ðai] poss adj (arch) tu(s).

thyme [taim] n tomillo m.

thyroid ['θairɔid] **1** adj tiroideo. **2** n (also — gland) tiroides m.

thyself [ðai'self] pron (arch) (subject) tú mismo, tú misma; (acc, dat) te; (after prep) ti (mismo, misma).

tiara [ti'ɑːrə] n diadema f.

Tiber ['taibə*] Tíber m.

Tiberius [tai'biəriəs] m Tiberio.

Tibet [ti'bet] el Tibet.

Tibetan [ti'betən] **1** adj tibetano. **2** n tibetano m, a f. **3** n (language) tibetano m.

tibia ['tibiə] n tibia f.

tic [tik] n (Med) tic m.

tick¹ [tik] **1** n **(a)** (of clock) tictac m.

(b) (moment) momento m, instante m; **at 6 o'clock on the —** a las 6 en punto; **to arrive at** (or **on**) **the —** llegar puntualmente; **half a —!**, **just a —!** ¡un momentito!; **I shan't be a —** tardo dos minutos nada más, termino en seguida; **he won't take two —s to do it** lo hará en menos de nada.

(c) (mark) señal f, marca f (de aprobación); palomita f; **to put a — against someone's name** poner una señal contra el nombre de uno.

2 vt (also **to — off**) poner una señal contra; **to — someone off** echar a uno como un trapo (fam), echar un rapapolvo a uno (fam).

3 vi hacer tictac; **to — over** (Aut, Mech) marchar en vacío.

tick² [tik] n (Zool) garrapata f.

tick³ [tik] n (cover) funda f.

tick⁴ [tik] n (fam): **to buy something on —** comprar algo de fiado; **to live on —** vivir de compras hechas de fiado.

ticker ['tikə*] n (fam) (watch) reloj m; (heart) corazón m.

ticker-tape ['tikəteip] n cinta f de cotizaciones.

ticket ['tikit] **1** n (bus **—**, Rail etc) billete m; boleto m (SAm); (Cine, Theat) entrada f; localidad f; (label) etiqueta f, rótulo m; (counterfoil) talón m; (Aut: fam) multa f (por infracción del código etc); (US Pol) lista f de candidatos, candidatura f; programa m político; **complimentary —** entrada f de favor; **return —, round-trip —** (US) billete m de ida y vuelta; **runabout —** billete m kilométrico; **single —** billete m sencillo; **that's the —!** ¡muy bien!, ¡eso es!; ¡así me gustas!; see **season —**.

2 vt rotular, poner etiqueta a.

ticket agency ['tikit,eidʒənsi] n (Rail etc) agencia f de viajes; (Theat) agencia f de teatros.

ticket collector ['tikitkə,lektə*] n, **ticket inspector** ['tikitin,spektə*] n revisor m.

ticket holder ['tikit,həuldə*] n tenedor m de billete; (season **—**) abonado m, a f.

ticket office ['tikit,ɔfis] n (Rail) despacho m de billetes; (Theat etc) taquilla f.

ticket-of-leave ['tikitəv'liːv] n cédula f de libertad condicional; **— man** hombre m bajo libertad condicional.

ticket window ['tikit,windəu] n (Rail) despacho m de billetes; (Theat etc) taquilla f.

ticking ['tikiŋ] n cutí m, terliz m.

ticking-off ['tikiŋ'ɔf] n bronca f; **to give someone a —** echar una bronca a uno.

tickle ['tikl] **1** n: **to have a — behind one's ear** sentir cosquillas detrás de la oreja; **to have a — in one's throat** tener picor de garganta, tener anginas; **he never got a — all day** (Fishing) no picó pez alguno en todo el día; **at £5 he never got a —** a 5 libras nadie le echó un tiento.

2 vt **(a)** cosquillear, hacer cosquillas a.

(b) (amuse) divertir; hacer gracia a; **it —d us no end** nos divirtió mucho, nos hizo mucha gracia; **we were —d to death about it, we were —d pink about it** nos moríamos de risa con eso; see **fancy**.

3 vi: **my ear —s** siento cosquillas en la oreja, siento hormiguillo en la oreja; **don't, it —s!** ¡por Dios, que me hace cosquillas!

tickling ['tikliŋ] n cosquillas fpl.

ticklish ['tikliʃ] adj **(a)** cosquilloso; **to be — tener** cosquillas, ser cosquilloso.

(b) (problem etc) peliagudo, espinoso; delicado; **it's a — business** es un asunto delicado.

tick tock ['tik'tɔk] n tictac m.

tidal ['taidl] adj de marea; **— wave** maremoto m, ola f de marea; (fig) ola f gigantesca; **— basin** dique m de marea; **the river is — up to here** la marea sube hasta aquí; **the Mediterranean is not —** en el Mediterráneo no hay mareas.

tidbit ['tidbit] (US) see **titbit**.

tiddler ['tidlə*] n (fam) espinoso m; pececillo m.

tiddly ['tidli] adj (fam) achispado (fam).

tiddlywinks ['tidliwiŋks] n juego m de la pulga.

tide [taid] **1** n marea f; (fig) corriente m; marcha f, progreso m; tendencia f; **high —** pleamar f, (fig) cumbre f, apogeo m; **low —** bajamar f, (fig) punto m más bajo; **slack —** repunte m de la marea; **the — of battle turned** cambió la suerte de la batalla; **the — of events** la marcha de los sucesos; **to go against the —** ir contra la corriente; **to go with the —** seguir la corriente.

2 vt: **to — someone over** ayudar a uno a salvar el bache, ayudar a uno a salir de un apuro.

tideland ['taidlænd] n terreno m inundado por la marea.

tideless ['taidlis] adj sin mareas.

tidemark ['taidmɑːk] n lengua f del agua.

tiderace ['taidreis] n aguaje m, marejada f.

tidewater ['taid,wɔːtə*] n agua f de marea.

tideway ['taidwei] n canal m de marea.

tidily ['taidili] adv bien, en orden; aseadamente, pulcramente; metódicamente; **to be — dressed ir** bien vestido; **to arrange things —** poner las cosas en orden.

tidiness ['taidinis] n buen orden m; limpieza f; aseo m, pulcritud f; carácter m metódico.

tidings ['taidiŋz] npl noticias fpl.

tidy ['taidi] **1** adj **(a)** objects etc en orden, ordenado; room, desk limpio; bien arreglado; appearance, dress aseado, pulcro; person metódico; **to get a room —** limpiar un cuarto, arreglar un cuarto; **he has a — mind** tiene una mentalidad lógica, tiene una inteligencia metódica.

(b) (fam) pace bastante rápido; sum considerable; **it cost a — bit** costó bastante; **he's a pretty — player** es un jugador bastante estimable.

2 vt (also **to — up**) arreglar, poner en orden, limpiar; **to — one's hair** arreglarse el pelo; **to — books away** devolver los libros a su lugar; **to — the dishes away** quitar los platos.

3 vi: **to — up** arreglar las cosas, ponerlo todo en orden.

4 vr: **to — oneself up** asearse, arreglarse.

tie [tai] **1** n **(a)** (bond) lazo m, vínculo m; **the —s of friendship** los lazos de la amistad; **the —s of blood** los lazos del parentesco.

(b) (hindrance) estorbo m; **the children are a — in the evenings** los pequeños son un estorbo para poder salir por las tardes; **he has no —s here** no tiene nada que le retenga aquí, no tiene nada que le impida irse de aquí.

(c) (cord etc) atadura f, ligazón f; (neck—) corbata f; (Archit) tirante m; (US Rail) traviesa f; (Mus) ligado m; **black —** corbata f de lazo,

corbata *f* de smoking; **white — corbatín** *m* blanco.
 (d) (*Sport: match*) encuentro *m*, partido *m*.
 (e) (*draw*) empate *m*; **it ended in a — at 3-all** terminó en empate a 3; **there was a — in the voting** en la votación resultó un empate.
 2 *vt* (a) atar, liar; enlazar, unir; (*Mus*) ligar; *bow, knot, necktie* hacer; (*fig, with bond*) liar, ligar, vincular; **to — two things together** atar dos cosas; **to — a dog to a post** atar un perro a un poste; **to — someone's hands** atar las manos a uno (*also fig*); **his hands are —d** tiene las manos atadas (*also fig*); **to be —d hand and foot** (*fig*) verse atado de pies y manos.
 (b) (*hinder*) estorbar; (*limit*) limitar, restringir (*to* a); **we are very —d in the evenings** por las tardes nos vemos estorbados para salir; **are we —d to this plan?** ¿estamos restringidos a este plan?; **the house is —d to her husband's job** la casa está ligada al puesto que tiene su marido, la casa pertenece a la compañía en que trabaja su marido.
 (c) (*with adv or prep*) **to — down** atar; sujetar, afianzar (con cuerdas *etc*); inmovilizar; **to — someone down to a task** obligar a uno a hacer una tarea (sin pensar en otra cosa); **to — someone down to a contract** obligar a uno a cumplir (*or* respetar) un contrato; **we can't — him down to a date** no podemos conseguir que fije una fecha; **we're —d down for months to come** no podemos aceptar otro compromiso hasta que hayan pasado muchos meses; **I refuse to be —d down** me niego a aceptar compromisos molestos; **to — a label on** atar una etiqueta, pegar una etiqueta; **to — up** atar; envolver; (*Naut*) atracar (*to* a); *traffic etc* obstruir, bloquear; *deal, business* concluir, despachar, arreglar; *capital* invertir (sin poder retirarlo); **he's —d up with the manager at the moment** ahora está conferenciando con el gerente, de momento está ocupado en un asunto con el gerente; **he's —d up with a girl in Lima** tiene un lío con una chica en Lima; **the fog —d up all shipping** la niebla inmovilizó toda la navegación; **he has a fortune —d up in property** tiene una fortuna invertida en bienes raíces.
 3 *vi* (a) **to — up** (*Naut*) atracar; **to — up to a post** atracar a un poste; **to — up at a wharf** atracar en un muelle.
 (b) (*draw*) empatar; **we —d with them 4-all** empatamos con ellos a 4.
tie-in ['taiin] *n* (*fig*) unión *f*; relación *f* estrecha (*between* entre).
tieless ['tailis] *adj* sin corbata.
tiepin ['taipin] *n* alfiler *m* de corbata.
tier [tiə*] *n* grada *f*, fila *f*; piso *m*; nivel *m*; **to arrange in —s** disponer en gradas.
tiered ['tiəd] *adj* con gradas, en una serie de gradas; **steeply —** con gradas en pendiente; **a three-tiered cake** un pastel de tres pisos.
tie-up ['taiʌp] *n* (*link*) enlace *m*; (*by strike etc*) paralización *f*; (*of traffic*) bloqueo *m*; embotellamiento *m*.
tiff [tif] *n* disgusto *m*, fregado *m*.
tiffin ['tifin] *n* (*Indian*) almuerzo *m*.
tig [tig] *n*: **to play —** dar la despedida.
tiger ['taigə*] *n* tigre *mf*.
tigerish ['taigəriʃ] *adj* (*fig*) salvaje, feroz.
tiger lily ['taigə,lili] *n* tigridia *f*.
tight [tait] **1** *adj* (a) (*not leaky*) impermeable; a prueba de ...; *container* estanco; *joint* hermético.
 (b) (*taut*) tieso, tirante; (*stretched*) estirado; *nut etc* apretado; *clothing* ajustado, ceñido, (*too —*) apretado, estrecho; *embrace* estrecho; *box* bien cerrado; *curve* cerrado; **as — as a drum** muy tirante; **to be in a — corner** (*or situation*) estar en un aprieto; **to keep — hold of something** seguir fuertemente agarrado a algo.
 (c) *money* escaso; *credit* difícil.
 (d) (*close-fisted*) agarrado, tacaño.
 (e) (*drunk*) borracho; **to be —** estar borracho; **to get —** emborracharse (*on gin* bebiendo ginebra).
 2 *adv* herméticamente; de modo tirante; apretadamente, estrechamente; **the door was shut —** la puerta estaba bien cerrada; **shut the box —** cierra bien la caja; **screw the nut up —** aprieta la tuerca a fondo, apriete bien la tuerca; **to hold something —** agarrar algo fuertemente; **to hold someone —** abrazar a uno estrechamente; **hold —!** ¡agárrense bien!; **to sit —** estarse quieto, no moverse, seguir en su lugar; seguir sin hacer nada; **to squeeze someone's hand —** apretar mucho la mano a uno.
tighten ['taitn] **1** *vt* (*also* **to — up**; *tauten*) atiesar, estirar; estrechar; *nut etc* apretar; *regulations etc* hacer más severo; hacer observar, velar por la

observancia de; *restrictions* reforzar, aplicar en forma más rigurosa; *see* belt.
 2 *vi* atiesarse, estirarse; estrecharse; apretarse; **to — up on** *see vt*.
tight-fisted ['tait'fistid] *adj* agarrado, tacaño.
tight-fitting ['tait'fitiŋ] *adj* muy ajustado, muy ceñido.
tightknit ['tait'nit] *adj* estrechamente unidos entre sí; *family etc* muy unido.
tight-lipped ['tait'lipt] *adj* (*fig*) callado; hermético; **to maintain a — silence** mantener un silencio absoluto; **he's being very — about it** sobre eso no dice nada en absoluto.
tightly ['taitli] *adv* *see* **tight 2.**
tightness ['taitnis] *n* impermeabilidad *f*; lo estanco; lo hermético; tensión *f*, tirantez *f*; lo apretado; estrechez *f*; escasez *f*; tacañería *f*; **to have a — in the chest** sentir opresión en el pecho.
tightrope ['taitrəup] *n* alambre *m* (de circo *etc*).
tightrope walker ['taitrəup,wɔ:kə*] *n* funámbulo *m*, a *f*, volatinero *m*, a *f*.
tights [taits] *npl* pantalón *m* ajustado; (*Theat etc*) traje *m* de malla.
tightwad ['taitwɔd] *n* (*US fam*) cicatero *m* (*fam*).
tigress ['taigris] *n* tigresa *f*.
Tigris ['taigris] Tigris *m*.
tilde ['tildi] *n* tilde *f*.
tile [tail] **1** *n* (*roof —*) teja *f*; (*floor —*) baldosa *f*; (*wall —, coloured, glazed*) azulejo *m*; (*sl*) sombrero *m*; **he's got a — loose** le falta un tornillo; **to spend a night on the —s** estar fuera toda la noche, pasar la noche de juerga.
 2 *vt* *roof* tejar; cubrir de tejas; *floor* embaldosar; *wall* adornar con azulejos.
tiler ['tailə*] *n* tejero *m*.
tiling ['tailiŋ] *n* tejas *fpl*, tejado *m*; baldosas *fpl*, embaldosado *m*; azulejos *mpl*.
till[1] [til] *vt* (*Agr*) cultivar, labrar.
till[2] [til] **1** *prep* hasta. **2** *conj* hasta que; (*for usage, see* **until**).
till[3] [til] *n* (*drawer*) cajón *m*; (*machine*) caja *f* registradora.
tillage ['tilidʒ] *n* cultivo *m*, labranza *f*.
tiller[1] ['tilə*] *n* (*Agr*) labrador *m*.
tiller[2] ['tilə*] *n* caña *f* del timón.
tilt [tilt] **1** *n* (a) (*sloping*) inclinación *f*; ladeo *m*; **it is on the —, it has a — to it** está ladeado; **to give something a —** inclinar algo, ladear algo.
 (b) (*Hist*) torneo *m*, justa *f*; (**at**) **full —** a toda velocidad; **to run full — into a wall** dar de lleno contra una pared; **to have a — at** arremeter contra.
 2 *vt* inclinar, ladear; **— it this way** inclínelo hacia este lado; **— it back** inclínelo hacia atrás; **to — something out of a container** verter algo de un recipiente (inclinando éste); **to — over a table** volcar una mesa.
 3 *vi* (a) inclinarse, ladearse; **to — over** (*lean*) inclinarse, (*fall*) volcarse, caer; **lorry that —s up** camión *m* que bascula, camión *m* basculante; **seat that —s up** asiento *m* abatible.
 (b) (*Hist*) justar; **to — against** arremeter contra.
tilth [tilθ] *n* cultivo *m*, labranza *f*; condición *f* (cultivable) de la tierra.
Tim [tim] *nombre cariñoso de* **Timothy.**
timber ['timbə*] **1** *n* (*material*) madera *f* (de construcción); (*growing trees*) árboles *mpl*, árboles *mpl* de monte; bosque *m*; (*beam*) madero *m*, viga *f*, (*Naut*) cuaderna *f*; **—!** ¡ojo, que cae!, ¡agua va!
 2 *vt* enmaderar.
timbered ['timbəd] *adj* *house etc* enmaderado; *land* arbolado; **the land is well —** el terreno tiene mucho bosque.
timbering ['timbəriŋ] *n* maderamen *m*.
timberland ['timbəlænd] *n* (*US*) tierras *fpl* maderables.
timber line ['timbəlain] *n* límite *m* forestal.
timber merchant ['timbə,mə:tʃənt] *n* maderero *m*.
timberyard ['timbəja:d] *n* almacén *m* de madera.
timbre [tɛ̃:mbr] *n* timbre *m*.
time [taim] **1** *n* (a) (*general sense*) tiempo *m*; (**Father**) **T—** el Tiempo; **— flies** el tiempo vuela; **— presses** el tiempo apremia; **— will show, — will tell** el tiempo lo dirá; **race against —** carrera *f* contra reloj; **in (good) —, in process of —, as —** goes on andando el tiempo, con el tiempo; **all in good —** todo a su tiempo; **all in good —!** ¡despacio!; **— and motion study** estudios *mpl* de tiempo y movimiento; **—!** ¡es la hora!, ¡la hora!; **— gentlemen please!** ¡se cierra!; **my — is my own** dispongo libremente de mi tiempo; **to find — for** tener tiempo para; **to gain —** ganar tiempo; **we have —, we have plenty of —** tenemos tiempo de

sobra; **to have no — to read** no tener tiempo para leer; **I've no — for him** (*fig*) no le estimo, tengo un concepto más bien bajo de él; **I've no — for sport** (*fig*) desprecio los deportes, no apruebo los deportes; **to have — on one's hands** estar ocioso; no saber cómo ocuparse; tener tiempo libre; **to kill —** entretener el tiempo, pasar el rato; **to lose —** atrasarse; **to lose no — in +** *ger* no tardar en + *infin*; **to make up for lost —** recuperar el tiempo perdido; **to play for —** tratar de ganar tiempo; **to be pressed for —** tener poco tiempo; **it takes —** es una cosa lenta, en esto se tarda bastante; **it takes — to +** *infin* se tarda bastante en + *infin*; **it took him all his — to find it** sólo encontrarlo le ocupó bastante tiempo; **to take one's —** hacer las cosas con calma; ir despacio, no darse prisa; **he's certainly taking his —** es cierto que tarda bastante ya; **take your —!** ¡hágalo con calma!, ¡no hay prisa!; **to take — by the forelock** aprovechar la ocasión.

(b) (*period*) período *m*, tiempo *m*; plazo *m*; **extra —** (*Sport*) prórroga *f*; **spare —** ratos *mpl* libres, horas *fpl* libres; ratos *mpl* de ocio; **a long — ** mucho tiempo; **a long — ago** hace mucho tiempo; **a short —** poco tiempo, un rato; **a short — ago** hace poco; **a short — after** poco tiempo después, al poco tiempo; **for a —** durante un rato, durante una temporada; **for a long — to come** hasta que haya transcurrido mucho tiempo; **for some — past** de algún tiempo a esta parte; **for the — being** por ahora; **he hasn't been seen for a long —** hace mucho tiempo que no se le ve; **in (good) —** (*early*) a tiempo, con tiempo; **to arrive in good —** llegar con bastante anticipación; **let me know in good —** avíseme con anticipación; **he'll come in his own good —** vendrá cuando le parezca conveniente; **in a short —** en breve; con la mayor brevedad; **in a short — they were all gone** muy pronto habían desaparecido todos; **in 2 weeks' —** en 2 semanas; al cabo de 2 semanas; **in no — at all** en muy poco tiempo; **within the agreed —** antes del plazo convenido; dentro del límite de tiempo que se había fijado; **to do —** (*fam*) cumplir una condena; **it will last our —** durará lo que nosotros; **to serve one's —** hacer su aprendizaje; servir; **to take a long — to +** *infin* tardar mucho en + *infin*.

(c) (*at work*) horas *fpl* de trabajo; jornada *f*; he did the draft in his own — preparó el borrador fuera de las horas normales de trabajo; **to be on** (*or* **to work**) **short —** trabajar en jornadas reducidas; see also **full-—**, **short-—** etc.

(d) (*epoch, period; often* **—s**) época *f*, tiempos *mpl*; **a sign of the —s** un indicio de cómo cambian los tiempos; **the good old —s** los buenos tiempos pasados; **the —s we live in** los tiempos en que vivimos; **these naughty —s** estos tiempos tan escandalosos; **in my —(s)** en mis tiempos; **in Victoria's —(s)** en los tiempos de Victoria, en la época victoriana, bajo el reinado de Victoria; **in our —** en nuestra época; **in —s past**, **in former** (*or* **olden, older**) **—s** en otro tiempo, antiguamente; **in —s to come** en los siglos venideros; **—s are somewhat hard** atravesamos un período bastante difícil; **those were tough —s** fue un período de grandes dificultades; **what —s they were!, what —s we had!** ¡qué tiempos aquellos!; **the —s are out of joint** los tiempos actuales están revueltos; **— was when . . .** hubo un tiempo en que . . .; **to be behind the —s** (*person*) ser un atrasado; estar atrasado de noticias; (*thing*) estar fuera de moda, haber quedado anticuado; **to fall on hard —s** estar en el tiempo de las vacas flacas; **to keep abreast of** (*or* **up with**) **the —s** ir con los tiempos, mantenerse al día.

(e) (*moment, point of —*) momento *m*; **any —** en cualquier momento; **come (at) any —** (**you like**) ven cuando quieras; **it might happen (at) any —** podría ocurrir de un momento a otro; **at the —**, **at that —** por entonces; en aquella época, en aquel entonces; a la sazón; **at this particular —** en este preciso momento; **at the present —** en la actualidad, actualmente; **at one —** en cierto momento, en cierta época; **había momentos en que . . .; at one —. . ., at another —** ora . . ., ora . . .; **Rodriguez, at one — minister of . . .** Rodríguez, ministro que fue de . . .; **at no —** jamás, nunca; **at a given —** en un momento convenido; **at a convenient —** en un momento oportuno; **at the proper —** en el momento oportuno; **at the same —** al mismo tiempo; a la vez; **at —s** a veces; **at all —s** en todo momento, siempre; **at odd —s** de vez en cuando; **at various —s in the past** en

determinados momentos del pasado; **between —s** en los intervalos; **by this —** ya, antes de esto; **(by) this — next year** para estas fechas del año que viene; **by the — we got there** antes de que llegásemos, antes de nuestra llegada, antes de llegar nosotros; **cuando llegamos; from — to —** de vez en cuando; **from that — (on)** a partir de entonces; **until such — as he agrees** hasta que consienta; **now is the — to do it** éste es el momento en que conviene hacerlo; **now is the — to plant roses** ésta es la época para plantar las rosas; **the proper — to do it is . . .** el momento más indicado para hacerlo es . . .; **when the — comes** cuando llegue el momento; **the — has come to +** *infin* ha llegado el momento de + *infin*; **to choose one's — carefully** elegir con cuidado el momento más propicio; **this is no — for superstition** éste no es el momento para mostrarse supersticioso, tal momento no es para tomar en serio las supersticiones.

(f) (*as marked on clock*) hora *f*; **closing —** hora *f* de cerrar; **opening —** hora *f* de abrir; **Greenwich mean —** hora *f* media de Greenwich; **standard —** hora *f* normal; **summer —** hora *f* de verano; **what's the —?** ¿qué hora es?; **what — do you make it?**, **what do you make the —?** ¿qué hora tienes?; **have you the right —?** ¿tiene Vd la hora exacta?; **the — is 2.30** son las 2 y media; **a watch that keeps good —** un reloj muy exacto; **to look at the —** mirar su reloj.

(g) (*as marked on clock: phrases with prep etc*) **(and) about — too!** ¡ya era hora!; **it is about —** he was there ya era hora que estuviera allí; **to be 23 minutes ahead of —** llevar 23 minutos de adelanto; **to arrive ahead of —** llegar temprano; **to die before one's —** morir temprano; **to be behind —** atrasarse, retrasarse; **the train is 8 minutes behind —** el tren lleva 8 minutos de retraso; **to come in (good) — for lunch** venir con bastante anticipación a comer; **we were just in — to see it** llegamos justo a tiempo para verlo; **to start in good —** partir temprano, partir pronto; **to be on —** ser puntual, llegar (*etc*) puntualmente; llegar a la hora exacta; **to be up to —** llegar con retraso; **at any — of the day or night** en cualquier momento del día o de la noche; **at this — of day** a esta hora; **to pass the — of day with someone** detenerse a charlar un rato con uno; **it's — for tea** es la hora del té; **ha llegado la hora de servir el té; it's coffee —** es la hora del café; **it's — to go** ya es hora de marcharse; **it's high —** ya era hora; **there's a — and a place for everything** todo tiene su hora y su lugar debidos; **éste no es ni el momento ni el lugar** indicado.

(h) (*as marked by calendar*) época *f*; temporada *f*; estación *f*; **at my — of life** a mi edad, con los años que yo tengo; **at this — of year** en esta época del año; **it's a lovely — of year** es una estación encantadora; **my favourite — is autumn** mi estación predilecta es el otoño.

(i) (*good — etc*) **to have a good — (of it)** pasarlo bien; **have a good —!** ¡que lo pases bien!; **to give someone a good —** hacer que uno se divierta; hacer que uno lo pase bien; **she's out for a good —** se propone divertirse; **all they want to do is have a good —** no quieren más que divertirse; **we have a lovely —** lo pasamos la mar de bien; **I hope you have a lovely —!** ¡que os divertáis!; **to have a rough** (*or* **bad, thin** *etc*) **— of it** pasarlo mal, pasarlas negras; **what a — we'll have with the girls!** ¡vaya juergazo que nos vamos a correr con las chicas!

(j) (*occasion*) vez *f*; **3 —s** 3 veces; **this —** esta vez; **last —** la última vez; **next —** la próxima vez; **the first — I did it** la primera vez que lo hice; **for the first —** por primera vez; **for the last —** por última vez; **after —, — and again** repetidas veces; **each —, every —** cada vez; **each — that . . .** cada vez que . . .; **he won every —** ganó todas las veces; **it's the best, every —!** ¡es el mejor, no hay duda!; **many —s** muchas veces; **many a — I saw him act, many's the — I saw him act** muchas veces le vi representar; **several — s** varias veces; **third — lucky!** ¡a la tercera va la vencida!; **I remember the — when . . .** me acuerdo de cuando . . .; **to bide one's —** esperar la hora propicia; **for weeks at a —** durante semanas enteras, durante varias semanas seguidas; **to do 2 things at a —** hacer 2 cosas a la vez; hacer 2 cosas al mismo tiempo; **to eat biscuits 4 at a —** comer 4 galletas a la vez; **he ran upstairs 3 at a —** subió la escalera de 3 en 3 escalones.

(k) (*Math*) 4 —s 3 4 por 3; it's 4 —s as fast as yours es 4 veces más rápido que el tuyo.

(l) (*adv phrase*) **at the same — you must remember that . . .** de todas formas conviene recordar que . . .; **at the same — as** (*fig*) al mismo tiempo que, al igual que, a la par que.

(m) (*Mus*) tiempo *m*; compás *m*; **in 3/4 —** al compás de 3 por 4; **in — to the music** de acuerdo a la música; **to beat** (*or* **keep**) **—** llevar el compás; **to get out of —** perder el ritmo, dejar de llevar el compás; **to mark —** (*Mil*) llevar el paso; (*fig*) esperar, hacer tiempo.

(n) (*Mech*) **the ignition is out of —** el encendido está fuera de fase, el encendido funciona mal.

2 *vt* **(a)** (*reckon* — *of*) medir el tiempo de, calcular la duración de; *race* cronometrar.

(b) (*regulate*) *watch* regular, poner en hora; **it is —d to go off at midnight** debe estallar a medianoche, la espoleta está graduada para que haga explosión a medianoche; **the train is —d for 6** el tren debe llegar a las 6.

(c) (*do at right* —) hacer en el momento oportuno; **you —d that perfectly** elegiste a la perfección el momento para hacerlo (*etc*).

time bomb ['taimbɔm] *n* bomba *f* de relojería.

time clock ['taim'klɔk] *n* reloj *m* registrador.

time-consuming ['taimkən,sju:miŋ] *adj* que exige mucho tiempo.

time exposure ['taimik,spəuʒə*] *n* (*Phot*) pose *f*.

time fuse ['taimfju:z] *n* espoleta *f* de tiempo, espoleta *f* graduada.

time-honoured, (*US*) **time-honored** ['taim,ɔnəd] *adj* sacramental, consagrado, clásico.

timekeeper ['taim,ki:pə*] *n* (*watch*) reloj *m*, cronómetro *m*; (*person*) cronometrador *m*, apuntador *m* del tiempo.

time-lag ['taimlæg] *n* intervalo *m*; retraso *m*, pérdida *f* de tiempo.

timeless ['taimlis] *adj* eterno; *race etc* sin limitación de tiempo.

time limit ['taim,limit] *n* limitación *f* de tiempo; (*esp Comm*) plazo *m*; (*closing date*) fecha *f* tope; **without a —** sin limitación de tiempo; **to fix a — for something** fijar un plazo para algo, señalar un plazo a algo.

timeliness ['taimlinis] *n* oportunidad *f*.

timely ['taimli] *adj* oportuno.

timepiece ['taimpi:s] *n* reloj *m*.

timer ['taimə*] *n* (*egg* — *etc*) reloj *m* de arena; (*Mech*) reloj *m* automático; (*Aut etc*) distribuidor *m* de encendido.

time-saving ['taim,seiviŋ] *adj* que ahorra tiempo.

timeserver ['taim,sɜ:və*] *n* contemporizador *m*.

time signature ['taim'signitʃə*] *n* (*Mus*) signatura *f*.

time sheet ['taimʃi:t] *n* tarjeta *f* registradora (de horas trabajadas), hoja *f* de presencia.

time signal ['taim,signl] *n* (*Radio*) señal *f* horaria.

time switch ['taimswitʃ] *n* interruptor *m* horario.

timetable ['taim,teibl] *n* horario *m*; (*programme of classes etc*) programa *m*.

timework ['taimwɜ:k] *n* trabajo *m* a jornal; trabajo *m* por horas.

timeworn ['taimwɔ:n] *adj* deteriorado por el tiempo.

timid ['timid] *adj* tímido.

timidity [ti'miditi] *n* timidez *f*.

timidness ['timidnis] *n* timidez *f*.

timing ['taimiŋ] **1** *n* (*reckoning of time*) medida *f* del tiempo, medida *f* de la duración; (*Sport etc*) cronometraje *m*; **the — of this is important** importa hacer esto en el momento exacto, importa elegir el momento más propicio para hacer esto.

2 *attr* (*Mech*) de distribución, de encendido; **— gear** engranaje *m* de distribución; **it has a — mechanism** tiene un dispositivo para medir el tiempo.

timorous ['timərəs] *adj* temeroso, tímido; *animal* huraño, asustadizo.

Timothy ['timəθi] *m* Timoteo.

timpani ['timpəni] *npl* (*Mus*) tímpanos *mpl*, atabales *mpl*.

tin [tin] **1** *n* **(a)** (*element, metal*) estaño *m*; (*—plate*) hojalata *f*.

(b) (*container*) lata *f*; **meat in —s** carne *f* en lata, carne *f* enlatada.

(c) (*sl*) parné *m* (*sl*).

2 *adj*, *attr* de estaño; de hojalata; *hat* de acero; *soldier* de plomo; (*fam, pej*) inferior, de poco valor, de pacotilla.

3 *vt* **(a)** (*cover with* —) estañar.

(b) (*can*) envasar en lata, conservar en lata, enlatar; *see also* **tinned**.

tin can ['tin'kæn] *n* lata *f*.

tincture ['tiŋktʃə*] **1** *n* tintura *f* (*also fig*); (*Pharm*) tintura *f*. **2** *vt* tinturar, teñir (*with* de).

tinder ['tində*] *n* yesca *f* (*also fig*); **to burn like —** arder como la yesca.

tinderbox ['tindəbɔks] *n* yescas *fpl*.

tine [tain] *n* púa *f*.

tinfoil ['tinfɔil] *n* papel *m* de estaño.

ting [tiŋ] *see* **tinkle**.

ting-a-ling ['tiŋə'liŋ] *n* tilín *m*; **to go —** hacer tilín.

tinge [tindʒ] **1** *n* tinte *m*; (*fig*) dejo *m*; matiz *m*; **not without a — of regret** no sin cierto sentimiento.

2 *vt* teñir (*with* de); (*fig*) matizar (*with* de); **pleasure —d with sadness** placer *m* matizado de tristeza, placer *m* no exento de tristeza.

tingle ['tiŋgl] **1** *n* comezón *f*; hormigueo *m* (de la piel); (*thrill*) estremecimiento *m*.

2 *vi* sentir comezón, sentir hormigueo; (*ears*) zumbar; (*thrill*) estremecerse (*with* de).

tingly ['tiŋgli] *adj*: **— feeling** sensación *f* de hormigueo; **my arm feels —** siento hormigueo en el brazo; **I feel — all over** se me estremece todo el cuerpo.

tin hat ['tin'hæt] *n* casco *m* de acero.

tinker ['tiŋkə*] **1** *n* calderero *m* hojalatero; (*gipsy*) gitano *m*; (*fam: child*) pícaro *m*, tunante *m*; **you —!** ¡tunante!

2 *vt* (*also to — up*) remendar; (*pej*) remendar mal, remendar chapuceramente.

3 *vi*: **to — with** (*mend*) tratar de reparar; (*play*) jugar con, manosear; (*and damage*) estropear; **they're only —ing with the problem** no se esfuerzan seriamente por resolver el problema; **he's been —ing with the car all day** ha pasado todo el día tratando de reparar el coche.

tinkle ['tiŋkl] **1** *n* tilín *m*, retintín *m*; campanilleo *m*, cencerreo *m*; **"A resounding —"** "Un sonoro retintín".

2 *vt* hacer retiñir; hacer tintinar; hacer campanillear.

3 *vi* retiñir, tintinar; campanillear.

tinkling ['tiŋkliŋ] **1** *adj* que hace tilín (*etc*); **a — sound** un tilín (*etc*); **a — stream** un arroyo cantarín.

2 *n* tilín *m*, retintín *m*; campanilleo *m*, cencerreo *m*; **the — of the telephone** el campanilleo del teléfono.

tin mine ['tinmain] *n* mina *f* de estaño.

tin miner ['tin,mainə*] *n* minero *m* de estaño.

tinned [tind] *adj* en lata, de lata.

tinny ['tini] *adj* *taste* que sabe a lata; *sound* cascado, que suena a lata; (*fam*) inferior, de poco valor, de pacotilla; desvencijado.

tin opener ['tin,əupnə*] *n* abrelatas *m*.

tinplate ['tinpleit] *n* hojalata *f*.

tinsel ['tinsəl] **1** *n* oropel *m* (*also fig*); (*cloth*) lama *f* de oro (*or* de plata).

2 *adj* de oropel; (*fig*) de oropel, de relumbrón.

3 *vt* oropelar.

tinsmith ['tinsmiθ] *n* hojalatero *m*.

tin soldier ['tin'səuldʒə*] *n* soldado *m* de plomo.

tint [tint] **1** *n* tinte *m*, matiz *m*, color *m*; media tinta *f*.

2 *vt* teñir, matizar (*blue* de azul); **it's yellow —ed with red** es amarillo matizado de rojo; **to — one's hair** teñirse el pelo.

tintack ['tintæk] *n* tachuela *f*.

tintinnabulation ['tinti,næbju'leiʃən] *n* campanilleo *m*.

tintype ['tintaip] *n* (*Phot*) ferrotipo *m*.

tiny ['taini] *adj* pequeñito, chiquitín, diminuto, minúsculo.

tip¹ [tip] **1** *n* **(a)** (*end*) punta *f*, cabo *m*, extremidad *f*; (*of stick etc*) regatón *m*, casquillo *m*; (*of cigarette*) boquilla *f*, embocadura *f*; **from — to toe** de pies a cabeza; **I had it on the — of my tongue** lo tenía en la punta de la lengua.

2 *vt* poner regatón a; **—ped with steel** con punta de acero.

tip² [tip] **1** *n* **(a)** (*tap*) golpecito *m*.

(b) (*gratuity*) propina *f*; **to give** (*or* **leave**) **someone a —** dar una propina a uno.

(c) (*hint*) aviso *m*, advertencia *f*; consejo *m*, indicación *f*; (*to police etc*) soplo *m*; (*Racing*) confidencia *f*; pronóstico *m* confidencial; **let me give you a —** permítame darle un consejo; **if you take my —** si sigues mi consejo; **the horse is a hot — for the 2.30** se pronostica con seguridad que el caballo ganará la carrera de las 2 y media.

(d) (*rubbish —*) vertedero *m*, basurero *m*; escombrera *f*.

2 *vt* **(a)** (*tap, strike*) golpear ligeramente, tocar ligeramente (*al pasar*), chocar ligeramente con; **to — one's hat to someone** tocarse el sombrero para saludar a uno.

(b) (*incline*) inclinar, ladear; *drinking vessel* empinar; *seat* abatir, levantar; **to — away** *liquid* vaciar, verter, echar; **to — forward** inclinar hacia adelante; **to — someone off his seat** hacer que uno caiga de su asiento; **to — out the contents of a box** verter el contenido de una caja; **all the passengers were —ped out** todos los pasajeros cayeron fuera; **to — over** volcar; **to — up** (*incline*) inclinar, ladear; *container* volcar; *person* hacer perder el equilibrio; hacer caer, volcar; derribar; **to — someone into the water** hacer caer a uno al agua (empujándole); **he —s the scales at 100 kg** pesa 100 kg justos.

(c) (*reward*) dar una propina a, dejar una propina para; **to — someone a pound** dar a uno una libra de propina; **to — someone generously** dar a uno una propina generosa.

(d) to — someone off advertir a uno clandestinamente; **the police had been —ped off** la policía había recibido una confidencia.

(e) *winner* pronosticar, recomendar, elegir; **I — that horse to win** pronostico que ganará ese caballo; **he is being freely —ped for the job** muchos creen que le darán el puesto; **he is strongly —ped as prime minister** se pronostica con confianza que será primer ministro.

3 *vi* (*incline*) inclinarse, ladearse; (*topple*) tambalearse; **he —ped off into the sea** perdió el equilibrio y cayó al mar; **to — over** volcarse; caer; **to — up** volcarse; (*seat*) abatirse, levantarse; (*lorry etc*) bascular.

tip-cart ['tipkɑːt] *n* volquete *m*.

tip-off ['tipɔf] *n* advertencia *f* (clandestina), aviso *m*; soplo *m*, confidencia *f*.

tipped [tipt] *adj cigarette* emboquillado.

tipple ['tipl] **1** *n* bebida *f* (alcohólica); **his — is Cointreau** él bebe Cointreau; **what's your —?** ¿qué quieres tomar?

2 *vi* beber más de la cuenta; envasar, empinar el codo.

tippler ['tiplə*] *n* bebedor *m*, borracho *m*.

tipsily ['tipsili] *adv* como borracho; **to walk —** andar con pasos de borracho.

tipsiness ['tipsinis] *n* borrachera *f*.

tipster ['tipstə*] *n* pronosticador *m*.

tipsy ['tipsi] *adj* achispado, algo borracho.

tiptoe ['tiptəu] **1** *n*: **to walk on —** caminar de puntillas; **to stand on —** ponerse de puntillas.

2 *vi*: **to — across the floor** atravesar el suelo de puntillas; **to — to the window** ir de puntillas a la ventana.

tiptop ['tip'tɔp] *adj* de primera, excelente; **in — condition** en excelentes condiciones; **a — show** un espectáculo de primerísima calidad.

tip-up ['tipʌp] *attr lorry* basculante; *seat* abatible.

tirade [tai'reid] *n* invectiva *f*, diatriba *f*.

tire[1] ['taiə*] **1** *vt* cansar, fatigar; (*bore*) aburrir; **to — someone out** cansar a uno, rendir a uno de cansancio, agotar las fuerzas de uno.

2 *vi* cansarse, fatigarse; aburrirse; **to — of** cansarse de; aburrirse con; **she —s easily** se cansa pronto.

tire[2] ['taiə*] *n* (US) see **tyre**.

tired ['taiəd] *adj* **a**) cansado; **in a — voice** con voz cansada; **the — old clichés** los lugares comunes de siempre, los tópicos trillados.

(b) *person* cansado, fatigado; **to be — estar** cansado; **to be — out** estar rendido, estar agotado; **I'm — of all that** estoy harto de todo eso; **to get (or grow) — of doing something** cansarse de hacer algo; **I get — of telling you** estoy harto de decírtelo; **you make me —** me fastidias terriblemente.

tiredly ['taiədli] *adv walk etc* como cansado; *say* con voz cansada.

tiredness ['taiədnis] *n* cansancio *m*, fatiga *f*.

tireless ['taiəlis] *adj* infatigable, incansable.

tirelessly ['taiəlisli] *adv* infatigablemente, incansablemente.

tiresome ['taiəsəm] *adj* molesto, fastidioso; *person* pesado; **how very —!** ¡qué lata!; **he's a — sort** es un pesado; **he can be —** a veces es un pesado.

tiresomeness ['taiəsəmnis] *n* molestia *f*, fastidio *m*, lo fastidioso; pesadez *f*.

tiring ['taiərin] *adj* molesto, fatigoso, que cansa, agotador; **after a — journey** después de un viaje cansado; **it's — work** es un trabajo agotador.

tiro ['taiərəu] *n* novicio *m*, principiante *m*.

tisane [ti'zæn] *n* tisana *f*.

tissue ['tiʃu] *n* (*cloth*) tisú *m*, lama *f*; (*Anat etc*) tejido *m*; **a — of lies** una sarta de mentiras.

tissue paper ['tiʃuː,peipə*] *n* papel *m* de seda.

tit[1] [tit] *n* (*blue—*) herrerillo *m* común; (*coal—*) carbonero *m* garrapinos; (*long-tailed —*) mito *m*.

tit[2] [tit] *n*: **— for tat** ¡donde las dan las toman!; **so that was — for tat** así que ajustamos cuentas, así que le pagué en la misma moneda.

tit[3] [tit] *n* (*fam*) pecho *m*, seno *m*.

Titan ['taitən] *n* titán *m*.

titanic [tai'tænik] *adj* titánico; inmenso, gigantesco.

titanium [ti'teiniəm] *n* titanio *m*.

titbit ['titbit] *n*, (US) **tidbit** *n* golosina *f* (*also fig*).

tithe [taið] *n* (*Eccl*) diezmo *m*.

Titian ['tiʃiən] *m* Ticiano.

titillate ['titileit] *vt* estimular, excitar.

titillation [,titi'leiʃən] *n* estimulación *f*, excitación *f*.

titivate ['titiveit] **1** *vt* emperejilar, ataviar, adornar.

2 *vi* emperejilarse, ataviarse; arreglarse.

title ['taitl] **1** *n* (**a**) (*appellation, heading*) título *m*; (*Sport*) título *m*, campeonato *m*; **noble —, — of nobility** título *m* de nobleza; **what — are you giving the book?** ¿qué título vas a dar al libro?, ¿cómo vas a titular el libro?; **what — should I give him?** ¿qué tratamiento debo darle?; **George V gave him a —** Jorge V le ennobleció.

(b) (*Law*) título *m*, derecho *m*; **his — to the property** su derecho a la propiedad.

2 *vt* titular, intitular.

titled ['taitld] *adj* con título de nobleza, noble.

title deed ['taitldiːd] *n* título *m* de propiedad.

title holder ['taitl,həuldə*] *n* (*Sport*) titular *mf*, campeón *m*, ona *f*.

title page ['taitlpeidʒ] *n* portada *f*.

title rôle ['taitl'rəul] *n* papel *m* principal.

titmouse ['titmaus] *n*, *pl* **—mice** [mais] *see* **tit**[1].

titrate ['taitreit] *vt* valorar.

titration [tai'treiʃən] *n* valoración *f*.

titter ['titə*] **1** *n* risa *f* disimulada. **2** *vi* reírse disimuladamente.

tittle ['titl] *n* pizca *f*, ápice *m*; **there's not a — of truth in it** eso no tiene ni pizca de verdad.

tittle-tattle ['titl,tætl] **1** *n* chismes *m*, chismografía *f*. **2** *vi* chismear.

titular ['titjulə*] *adj* titular; nominal.

tizzy ['tizi] *n* (*fam*): **to get into a —** ponerse nervioso, aturdirse, armarse un lío.

to [tuː, tə] *prep* (**a**) (*dat*) a; **to give something — someone** dar algo a uno; **I gave it — my friend** se lo di a mi amigo; **the person I sold it — la persona a quien lo vendí; **it belongs — me** me pertenece a mí, es mío; **it's new — me** es nuevo para mí; **I said — myself** dije para mí; **what is that — me?** y eso ¿qué me importa?; **they were kind — me** me fueron amables conmigo.

(b) (*of movement, direction*) a; hacia; **to go — the town** ir a la ciudad; **to go — school** ir a la escuela; **to go — Italy** ir a Italia; **to go — Rome** ir a Roma; **to go — Peru** ir al Perú; **to go — the doctor** ir a ver al médico; **let's go — John's** vamos a casa de Juan; **she went back — her husband** volvió a estar con su marido, volvió a vivir con su marido; **from door — door** de puerta en puerta; **the road — Zaragoza** la carretera de Zaragoza; **it's 90 kilometres — Lima** de aquí a Lima hay 90 kilómetros; **— the left** a la izquierda; **— the west** al oeste, hacia el oeste.

(c) (*as far as, right up to*) hasta; **to count up — 20** contar hasta 20; **— this day** hasta hoy, hasta el día de hoy; **I'll see you — the door** te acompaño hasta la puerta; **funds — the value of . . .** fondos *mpl* por valor de . . .; **— some degree** hasta cierto punto; **it's accurate — a millimetre** es exacto hasta el milímetro; **to be wet — the skin** estar mojado hasta los huesos; **they perished — a man** perecieron todos (sin excepción); **everybody down — the youngest** todos hasta el más joven.

(d) (*against*) a, contra; **to stand back — back** estar espalda con espalda; **to talk to someone man — man** hablar con uno de hombre a hombre; **to turn a picture — the wall** volver un cuadro contra la pared; **to clasp someone — one's breast** estrechar a uno contra su pecho.

(e) (*of time*) a, hasta; **from morning — night** de la mañana a la noche, desde la mañana hasta la noche; **8 years ago — the day** hoy hace exactamente 8 años; **at 8 minutes — 10** a las 10 menos 8; **a quarter — 5** las 5 menos cuarto.

(f) (*of*) de; **wife — Mr Milton** mujer *f* del Sr Milton; **secretary — the manager** secretaria *f* del gerente; **ambassador — King Cole** embajador *m* cerca del rey Cole; **he is heir — the duke** es heredero del duque; **he was heir — a million** heredó un millón de libras; **he has been a good friend — us** ha sido buen amigo nuestro.

(g) (of dedications) a; **greetings — all our friends!** ¡saludos a todos los amigos!; **welcome — you all!** ¡bienvenida a todos!, ¡bienvenidos todos!; **to build a monument — someone** erigir un monumento en honor de uno; **here's — you!** ¡vaya por Vd!, ¡por Vd!; **to drink — someone** brindar por uno, beber a la salud de uno.

(h) (in comparisons) a; **inferior —** inferior a; **that's nothing — what is —** come eso no es nada en comparación con lo que está todavía por venir.

(i) (of proportion) a; **A is — B as C is — D** A es a B como C es a D; **by a majority of 12 — 10** por una mayoría de 12 a 10; **Slobodia won by 4 goals —** 2 ganó Eslobodia por 4 goles a 2; **the odds are 8 — 1** los puntos de ventaja son de 8 a 1; **200 people — the square mile** 200 personas por milla cuadrada.

(j) (concerning) a; **what do you say — this?** ¿qué contestación me das a esto?, ¿cómo contestas a esta pregunta?; **that's all there is —** it no hay nada más; no hay ningún misterio; todo queda tan sencillo como ves; **"— repairing pipes: . . ."** (bill) "Reparación de los tubos: . . ."; **"— services rendered: . . ."** "Por los servicios que se han prestado: . . ."

(k) (according to) según; **— all appearances** al parecer, según todos los indicios; **— my way of thinking** según mi modo de pensar; **it is not — my taste** no me gusta; **to write — someone's dictation** escribir al dictado de uno; **— the best of my recollection** que yo recuerde; **it is sung — the tune of "Tipperary"** se canta con la melodía de "Tipperary"; **they came out — the strains of the national anthem** salieron a los compases del himno nacional.

(l) (of purpose, result) **— this end** con este propósito; **to come — someone's aid** acudir en ayuda de uno; **to sentence someone — death** condenar a uno a muerte; **— my great surprise** con gran sorpresa mía; **— my lasting shame** I did nothing me avergüenzo siempre de no haber hecho nada; **to put an army —** flight poner en fuga a un ejército; **to go — ruin** arruinarse, echarse a perder; **to run — seed** granar, dar en grana (and see **seed**).

2 prep (before infin) (a) (with simple infin, not translated) — **know** saber, conocer; **"— be or not — be"** "ser o no ser"; (following another verb a variety of constructions appears, for which see the verb in each case, eg) **to forbid someone — do something** prohibir a uno hacer algo; **to begin — do something** comenzar a hacer algo, empezar a hacer algo; **to try — do something** tratar de hacer algo, procurar hacer algo; **I want you — do it** quiero que tú lo hagas; **I wanted you — do it** quería que tú lo hicieras; **they asked me — do it** me rogaron hacerlo.

(b) (purpose) para; **I did it — help you** lo hice para ayudarte.

(c) (purpose, with verbs of motion) a, para; **I came — see you** vine a verte; **I came specially — see you** vine expresamente para verte.

(d) (result) **I have done nothing — deserve** this no he hecho nada que mereciera esto.

(e) (equivalent to **on** + ger) **— see him now** one would never think that . . . al verle (or viéndole) ahora no creería nadie que . . .

(f) (expressing subsequent fact) para; **I arrived — find she had gone** llegué para descubrir que ella se había ido; **it disappeared never — be found again** desapareció para no volver a encontrarse jamás.

(g) (with ellipsis of verb) **I don't want — no** quiero; **you ought — debieras** hacerlo (etc); **I should love —!** ¡ojalá!, ¡cuánto me gustaría hacerlo (etc)!; **we didn't want to sell it but we had to** no queríamos venderlo pero tuvimos que hacerlo, no queríamos venderlo pero no había más remedio.

(h) **I have things — do** tengo cosas que hacer; **there is much — be done** hay mucho que hacer; **that book is still — be written** ese libro está todavía por escribir; **there was no-one for me — consult** no había nadie a quien yo pudiese consultar; **he is not — be trusted** no hay que fiarse de él; **he's not the sort — do** that no es capaz de hacer eso, tal cosa no cabe en él; **this is the time — do it** éste es el momento de hacerlo; **and who is the Academy — protest?** ¿y quién es la Academia para protestar?

(i) (construction after adjs etc) **to be ready — go** estar listo para partir; **it's hard — get hold of es** difícil de obtener; **he's slow — learn** es lento en aprender, aprende lentamente; **you are foolish —**

try it eres un tonto si lo emprendes; **is it good — eat?** ¿es bueno de comer?, ¿se puede comer?; **to be the first — do something** ser el primero en hacer algo; **who was the last — see her?** ¿quién la vio por última vez?; **he's a big boy — be still in short trousers** es mayorcito ya para llevar todavía pantalón corto; **it's too heavy — lift** es demasiado pesado para poder levantarlo; **it's too hot — touch** no se puede tocar por el mucho calor; **he's too old — manage it** es demasiado viejo para poder hacerlo.

3 adv: **to come —** (Naut) fachear; (Med) volver en sí; **to lie —** (Naut) ponerse a la capa; see **fro**.

toad [təud] n sapo m.

toadflax ['təudflæks] n linaria f, pajarita f.

toadstool ['təudstuːl] n hongo m (venenoso).

toady ['təudi] 1 n pelotillero m, lameculos m. 2 vi: **to — to someone** hacer la pelotilla a uno, adular servilmente a uno.

toadying ['təudiiŋ] n, **toadyism** ['təudiizəm] n adulación f servil.

toast [təust] 1 n (a) (Cook) pan m tostado, tostada f; **a piece of —** un trozo de pan tostado.

(b) (drink) brindis m (to por); **to drink a — to someone** brindar por uno; **here's a — to all who . . .** brindemos por todos los que . . .; **A will propose a — to B** A pronunciará algunas palabras al brindar por B.

(c) **she was the — of the town** la celebraron mucho en toda la ciudad, en todas partes de la ciudad se brindó por ella.

2 vt (a) (Cook) tostar.

(b) (drink to) brindar por, beber a la salud de; **we —ed the victory in champagne** celebramos la victoria bebiendo champán.

toaster ['təustə*] n tostador m, tostadora f.

toasting fork ['təustiŋfɔːk] n tostadera f.

toast list ['təustlist] n lista f de brindis.

toastmaster ['təust,mɑːstə*] n oficial m que anuncia a los oradores en un banquete.

toast rack ['təustræk] n portatostadas m.

tobacco [tə'bækəu] n tabaco m; **cut —** picadura f (de tabaco); **leaf —** tabaco m en rama; **pipe —** tabaco m de pipa; **Turkish —** tabaco m turco; **Virginian —** tabaco m rubio.

tobacco jar [tə'bækəudʒɑ:*] n tabaquera f.

tobacconist [tə'bækənist] n estanquero m, tabaquero m; **—'s (shop)** estanco m, tabaquería f.

tobacco plantation [tə'bækəuplæn,teiʃən] n tabacal m, plantación f de tabaco.

tobacco pouch [tə'bækəupautʃ] n petaca f.

toboggan [tə'bɔgən] 1 n tobogán m. 2 vi ir en tobogán, deslizarse en tobogán; (fig) deslizarse, correr.

toboggan run [tə'bɔgənrʌn] n pista f de tobogán.

tocsin ['tɔksin] n campana f de alarma; campanada f de alarma; (fig) voz f de alarma; **to sound the —** (fig) dar la voz de alarma.

today [tə'dei] adv hoy; (at the present time) hoy día, hoy en día; **— week, a week —** de hoy en ocho días; **a fortnight —** de hoy en quince (días); **what day is it —?** ¿qué día es hoy?; ¿a cuántos estamos?; **— is the 4th** estamos a 4; **a year ago —** hoy hace un año; **from —** desde hoy, a partir de hoy.

toddle ['tɔdl] vi (begin to walk) empezar a andar, dar los primeros pasos; (walk unsteadily) caminar sin seguridad; (fam: go) ir; (stroll) dar un paseo; (depart) irse, marcharse (also to — off); **we must be toddling** es hora de irnos; **so I —d round to see him** así que fui a visitarle.

toddler ['tɔdlə*] n pequeñito m, a f (que aprende a andar, que da sus primeros pasos).

toddy ['tɔdi] n ponche m.

to-do [tə'duː] n (fam) lío m (fam), follón m (fam); **there was a great —** hubo un tremendo follón; **what's all the — about?** ¿qué pasa?; **she made a great —** armó un lío imponente.

toe [təu] 1 n (Anat) dedo m del pie; punta f del pie; (of shoe) puntera f; (of sock) puntera f; **big —** dedo m gordo del pie, dedo m grande del pie; **little —** dedo m pequeño del pie; **he put the cigarette out with his —** apagó el cigarrillo con la punta del pie; **to keep someone on his —s** mantener a uno en estado de vigilancia, hacer que uno siga estando alerta; **you have to keep on your —s** hay que estar alerta, hay que mantenerse bien despierto; **to turn up one's —s** (fam) estirar la pata (fam).

2 vt tocar con la punta del pie; **to — the line** conformarse, someterse.

toecap ['təukæp] n puntera f.

-toed [təud] adj de . . . dedos del pie, eg **four-toed** de cuatros dedos del pie.

toenail ['təuneil] n uña f del dedo del pie; **ingrowing** — uñero m (del pie).

toff [tɔf] n (fam) currutaco m, chuleta m (fam).

toffee ['tɔfi] n caramelo m; **he can't do it for** — (fam) no tiene la menor idea de cómo hay que hacerlo.

toffee apple ['tɔfi,æpl] n piruli m.

toffee-nosed ['tɔfi'nəuzd] adj presumido, engreído.

tog [tɔg] **1** vt: **to** — **someone up** ataviar a uno (in de), vestir a uno (in de) de modo impresionante (or ridículo etc); **to get** —**ged up** ataviarse, vestirse.
  2 vr: **to** — **oneself up** ataviarse, vestirse (in de), emperejilarse.

toga ['təugə] n toga f.

together [tə'geðə*] adv (a) (in company) junto, juntos; juntamente; (in concert) juntos, a la vez, a un tiempo; (uninterruptedly) sin interrupción; (consecutively) seguido; **all** — **now!** (pulling) ¡todos a la vez!; ¡bien, ahora!; **for weeks** — durante varias semanas seguidas; **now we're** — ahora estamos juntos; **they were all** — **in the bar** todos estaban reunidos en el bar; **we're in this** — en esto tenemos igual responsabilidad los dos; nos une la misma suerte; **they were both in it** — resultó que los dos se habían confabulado, los dos estaban metidos en el asunto; **you can't all get in** — no podéis entrar todos a la vez; **we'll do parts A and B** — haremos juntamente las partes A y B; — **they managed it** entre los dos lo lograron; **they belong** — están bien juntos, forman una pareja; **they work** — trabajan juntos; see **bring, call** etc.
  (b) — **with** junto con; conjuntamente con; — **with A, B is important** junto con A es importante B.

togetherness [tə'geðənis] n sentimiento m de estar todos estrechamente unidos; compañerismo m; espíritu m de familia (or de grupo etc).

toggle ['tɔgl] n cazonete m de aparejo; fiador m.

Togoland ['təugəulænd] Togolandia f.

togs [tɔgz] npl (fam) ropa f.

toil [tɔil] **1** n labor f, trabajo m; fatiga f; afán m, esfuerzo m; **after months of** — después de varios meses de trabajo (agotador).
  2 vi (a) trabajar; fatigarse; apurarse, afanarse; **to** — **to do something** esforzarse por hacer algo, afanarse por hacer algo; **we** —**ed at it for hours** trabajamos en ello durante muchas horas (sin éxito); **they** —**ed on into the night** siguieron trabajando hasta muy entrada la noche.
  (b) **to** — **along** caminar con dificultad, avanzar penosamente; **to** — **up a hill** subir penosamente una colina; **the engine is beginning to** — el motor empieza a funcionar con dificultad.

toilet ['tɔilit] **1** n (process of dressing) tocado m; atavío m; (dress) vestido m; (euph: lavatory) inodoro m, lavabo m, wáter m; (dressing table) tocador m.
  2 attr de tocador; — **requisites** artículos mpl de limpieza; — **set** juego m de tocador.

toilet bag ['tɔilitbæg] n, **toilet case** ['tɔilitkeis] n neceser m, estuche m de aseo.

toilet paper ['tɔilit,peipə*] n papel m higiénico.

toiletries ['tɔilitriz] npl artículos mpl de tocador, artículos mpl de limpieza.

toilet roll ['tɔilit,rəul] n rollo m de papel higiénico.

toilet soap ['tɔilit,səup] n jabón m de tocador.

toilet water ['tɔilit'wɔːtə*] n agua f de tocador.

toilette [twaː'let] n = **toilet.**

toils [tɔilz] npl red f, lazo m.

toilsome ['tɔilsəm] adj penoso, fatigoso.

toilworn ['tɔilwɔːn] adj completamente cansado, rendido.

token ['təukən] **1** n (a) (sign, symbol) señal f, muestra f, indicio m; (remembrance) prenda f, recuerdo m; (of one's appreciation etc) detalle m, señal f de agradecimiento; **as a** — **of, in** — **of** en señal de; como recuerdo de; **by the same** — igualmente; del mismo modo; **love** — prenda f de amor.
  (b) (disc etc) ficha f, disco m (metálico).
  2 adj, attr simbólico; — **payment** pago m nominal, pago m simbólico; **to put up a** — **resistance** oponer una resistencia simbólica, resistirse por pura fórmula.

told [təuld] pret and ptp of **tell.**

tolerable ['tɔlərəbl] adj (bearable) tolerable, soportable; (fair) regular, pasable.

tolerably ['tɔlərəbli] adv bastante; pasablemente; **a** — **good player** un jugador bastante bueno, un jugador pasable; **it is** — **certain that...** es casi seguro que...

tolerance ['tɔlərəns] n tolerancia f; paciencia f, indulgencia f.

tolerant ['tɔlərənt] adj tolerante; indulgente.

tolerantly ['tɔlərəntli] adv con tolerancia; con indulgencia.

tolerate ['tɔləreit] vt tolerar, soportar, aguantar; **are we to** — **this?** ¿hemos de soportar esto sin protestar?; **I can't** — **any more** no aguanto más; **it is not to be** —**d** es intolerable, es insoportable.

toleration [,tɔlə'reifən] n tolerancia f; **religious** — tolerancia f religiosa; libertad f de cultos.

toll¹ [təul] n (a) (on road) peaje m, portazgo m; (on bridge) pontazgo m; **to pay** — pagar el peaje.
  (b) (losses, casualties) mortalidad f, número m de víctimas, número m de pérdidas; **the** — **on the roads** el número de víctimas en accidentes de circulación; **there is a heavy** — hay muchas víctimas, son muchos los muertos; **the disease takes a heavy** — **each year** cada año la enfermedad se lleva a muchas víctimas, cada año la enfermedad causa gran número de muertes; **to take** — **of** causar bajas en, tener su efecto en.

toll² [təul] **1** vt bell tañer, tocar, doblar (a muerto); **to** — **the hour** dar la hora.
  2 vi doblar (a muerto); **the bells were** —**ing in mourning for...** doblaron las campanas en señal de duelo por...

tollbar ['təulbaː*] n barrera f de peaje.

tollbridge ['təulbridʒ] n puente m de peaje.

toll call ['təulkɔːl] n (US Tel) conferencia f interurbana.

tollgate ['təulgeit] n barrera f de peaje.

tolling ['təuliŋ] n tañido m, doblar m.

tollkeeper ['təul,kiːpə*] n peajero m, portazguero m.

tollway ['təulwei] n (Aut) autopista f de peaje.

Tom [tɔm] nombre cariñoso de **Thomas; — Dick and Harry** el hombre medio, el hombre de la calle; **you shan't marry any** — **Dick or Harry** no te casarás con un cualquiera; — **Thumb** Pulgarcito; **peeping** — curioso m.

tom [tɔm] n gato m (macho).

tomahawk ['tɔməhɔːk] n tomahawk m.

tomato [tə'maːtəu, US tə'meitəu] n, pl **tomatoes** [tə'maːtəuz] (fruit) tomate m; (plant) tomatera f.

tomato plant [tə'maːtəuplaːnt] n tomatera f.

tomb [tuːm] n tumba f, sepulcro m.

tombola [tɔm'bəulə] n tómbola f.

tomboy ['tɔmbɔi] n muchacha f hombruna, muchacha f, chica f poco femenina.

tombstone ['tuːmstəun] n lápida f sepulcral.

tomcat ['tɔmkæt] n gato m (macho).

tome [təum] n (hum) librote m.

tomfool ['tɔm'fuːl] **1** adj tonto, estúpido. **2** n tonto m, imbécil m.

tomfoolery [tɔm'fuːləri] n pataratas fpl, payasadas fpl.

Tommy ['tɔmi] nombre cariñoso de **Thomas; — Atkins** el soldado raso inglés.

tommy gun ['tɔmigʌn] n metralleta f, pistola f ametralladora.

tommyrot ['tɔmirɔt] n tonterías fpl.

tomorrow [tə'mɔrəu] **1** adv mañana; **a week** — de mañana en ocho días; — **morning** mañana por la mañana; — **evening** mañana por la tarde.
  2 n mañana f; **the day after** — pasado mañana; — **is Sunday** mañana es domingo; — **is another day** mañana es otro día; **will** — **do?** ¿lo puedo dejar para mañana?, ¿le conviene mañana?

tomtit ['tɔmtit] n carbonero m común.

tomtom ['tɔmtɔm] n tantán m.

ton [tʌn] n (a) tonelada f; **metric** — tonelada f métrica; **register** — tonelada f de registro; **a ship of 60,000 gross register** —**s** un buque de 60.000 toneladas de registro bruto.
  (b) —**s** (fam) montones mpl; **we have** —**s of it at home** tenemos montones de eso en casa; **we have** —**s of time** nos sobra tiempo, tenemos tiempo de sobra.
  (c) (sl) velocidad f de 100 millas por hora; **to do a** — ir a 100 millas por hora (en moto).

tonal ['təunl] adj tonal.

tonality [təu'næliti] n tonalidad f.

tone [təun] **1** n (a) (in most senses) tono m; (of colour) tono m, tonalidad f; matiz m; **in low** —**s** en tono bajo; **in an angry** — en tono de enojo.
  (b) (class) distinción f, buen tono m, elegancia f; **the place has** — el sitio tiene buen tono, es un sitio elegante; **the clientèle gives the restaurant** — la clientela da distinción al restaurante.
  (c) (tendency) tendencia f; **the prevailing** — la tendencia actual, la tendencia predominante; **the** — **of the market** la tendencia general del mercado.

2 vt (Mus) entonar; (Phot) virar; **to — down** amortiguar, suavizar el tono de; (fig) suavizar, modificar; **to — up** (Med) tonificar, entonar; (fig) elevar el tono de.
3 vi armonizar, ir bien juntos; **to — down** moderarse, hablar (etc) con más calma; **to — in with** armonizar con, ir bien con.
tone control ['təʊnkən,trəʊl] n (Radio etc) control m de tonalidad.
tone-deaf ['təʊn'def] adj falto de sentido musical.
toneless ['təʊnlis] adj soso, flojo; voice monótono.
tonelessly ['təʊnlisli] adv monótonamente.
tone poem ['təʊn,pəʊim] n poema m sinfónico.
tongs [tɔŋz] npl (for coal etc) tenazas fpl; (for sweets, sugar etc) tenacillas fpl; **a pair of —** unas tenazas, unas tenacillas.
tongue [tʌŋ] n (Anat) lengua f; (language) lengua f. idioma m; (of shoe etc) lengüeta f; (of bell) badajo m; (of flame, land) lengua f; **mother —, native —** lengua f materna; **in the vulgar —** en la lengua vulgar, en la lengua vernácula; **with one's — in one's cheek** irónicamente, burla burlando; **to give —** empezar a ladrar; **to give a ready —** no morderse la lengua; **to hold one's —** callarse; **hold your —!** ¡a callarse!; **to loosen someone's —** hacer hablar a uno; **wine loosens the —** el vino hace soltar la lengua.
tongue-lashing ['tʌŋ'læʃiŋ] n latigazo m, represión f; **to give someone a —** poner a uno como un trapo.
tongue-tied ['tʌŋtaid] adj que tiene dificultad al hablar, que tiene defecto del habla; (fig) tímido, premioso, confuso.
tongue twister ['tʌŋ,twistə*] n trabalenguas m.
tonic ['tɔnik] **1** adj tónico.
2 n **(a)** (Mus) tónica f.
(b) (Med) tónico m; (as drink, with gin etc) tónica f; (fig) tónico m; **this news will be a — for the market** esta noticia será un tónico para la bolsa.
tonicity [tɔ'nisiti] n tonicidad f.
tonight [tə'nait] adv esta noche.
toning solution ['təʊniŋsə'luːʃən] n solución f entonadora.
tonnage ['tʌnidʒ] n tonelaje m; **gross register —** toneladas fpl de registro bruto; **the — lost in 1942** la cantidad de buques hundidos en 1942 (expresada en toneladas).
-tonner ['tʌnə*] n de . . . toneladas, eg **a 1,000—** un barco de 1.000 toneladas.
tonsil ['tɔnsl] n amígdala f.
tonsillectomy [,tɔnsi'lektəmi] n amigdalotomía f.
tonsillitis [,tɔnsi'laitis] n amigdalitis f.
tonsorial [tɔn'sɔːriəl] adj (esp hum) barberil; relativo a la barba.
tonsure ['tɔnʃə*] **1** n tonsura f. **2** vt tonsurar.
tonsured ['tɔnʃəd] adj tonsurado.
Tony ['təʊni] nombre cariñoso de **Anthony**.
too [tuː] adv **(a)** (excessively) demasiado; muy; **it's — hard** es demasiado duro, es muy duro; **it's — easy** es muy fácil, es muy sencillo; **it's — heavy for me to lift** es demasiado pesado para que yo lo levante; **— often** con demasiada frecuencia, muy a menudo; **it's — early for that** es (muy) temprano para eso; see **many, much, well**.
(b) (also) también; además, por otra parte; **I went —** yo fui también; **and it's broken —** y además está roto.
took [tuk] pret of **take**.
tool [tuːl] **1** n **(a)** herramienta f; utensilio m; (set of) **—s** útiles mpl, utillaje m; **garden —s** útiles mpl de jardinería; **plumber's —s** útiles mpl de fontanero; **to down —s** suspender el trabajo; (strike) declararse en huelga; **give us the —s and we will finish the job** dadnos las herramientas y nosotros terminaremos la obra.
(b) (fig: person, book etc) instrumento m; **the book is an essential —** el libro es indispensable, el libro es instrumento imprescindible; **he was an unwilling — of the gang** sin quererlo fue un instrumento de la pandilla; **he is just the — of the minister** es la criatura del ministro nada más.
2 vt labrar con herramienta; book estampar en seco; filetear.
toolbag ['tuːlbæg] n bolsa f de herramientas.
toolbox ['tuːlbɔks] n, **tool chest** ['tuːltʃest] n caja f de herramientas.
tooling ['tuːliŋ] n estampación f en seco; fileteado m.
toolkit ['tuːlkit] n juego m de herramientas.
toolshed ['tuːlʃed] n cobertizo m para herramientas.
toot [tuːt] **1** n sonido m breve (de claxon etc); **he went off with a — on the horn** partió con un breve toque de bocina.
2 vt sonar, tocar.

3 vi sonar (la bocina etc); (of person, Aut) tocar la bocina, dar un bocinazo.
tooth [tuːθ] n, pl **teeth** [tiːθ] **(a)** (Anat) diente m; (esp molar) muela f; **back —** muela f; **false teeth** dentadura f postiza; **front —** incisivo m; **wisdom —** muela f del juicio; **in the teeth of the wind** contra un viento violento; **in the teeth of great opposition** contra una resistencia de lo más terco; **to be armed to the teeth** estar armado hasta los dientes; **to cast something in someone's teeth** echar algo en cara a uno; **to cut one's teeth** endentecer, echar los dientes; **to be fed up to the (back) teeth with** estar hasta la coronilla de; **to fight — and nail** luchar encarnizadamente; **to get one's teeth into** hincar el diente a (also fig); **to be getting long in the —** ser bastante viejo ya; **to have a — out** hacerse sacar una muela; **she has a sweet —** le gustan las cosas dulces; es golosa; **to show one's teeth** enseñar los dientes.
(b) (of saw, wheel) diente m; (of comb) púa f.
toothache ['tuːθeik] n dolor m de muelas.
toothbrush ['tuːθbrʌʃ] n cepillo m de dientes; **— moustache** bigote m de cepillo.
toothcomb ['tuːθkəʊm] n: **to go through something with a fine —** registrar algo minuciosamente.
toothed ['tuːθt] adj wheel etc dentado; **de dientes . . ., eg big-toothed** de dientes grandes.
toothing ['tuːθiŋ] n (Archit) adaraja f.
toothless ['tuːθlis] adj desdentado.
toothpaste ['tuːθpeist] n pasta f dentífrica, pasta f de dientes, crema f dental.
toothpick ['tuːθpik] n palillo m mondadientes.
tooth powder ['tuːθ,paudə*] n polvos mpl dentífricos.
toothsome ['tuːθsəm] adj sabroso.
toothy ['tuːθi] adj dentón; **to give someone a — smile** sonreír a uno mostrando mucho los dientes.
tootle ['tuːtl] **1** n sonido m breve (de flauta, trompeta etc); serie f de notas breves; **give us a — on your trumpet** tócanos algo a la trompeta; see also **toot**.
2 vt flute etc tocar.
3 vi **(a)** tocar la flauta (etc); see also **toot**.
(b) (Aut: fam) **we —d down to Brighton** hicimos una escapada a Brighton, fuimos de excursión a Brighton; **we were tootling along at 60** íbamos a 60 millas por hora.
too-too ['tuː'tuː] adj (fam): **she's terribly —** es la mar de afectada (fam), es una persona muy exagerada; **isn't it just —?** ¡qué monada! (fam), ¡qué precioso!
toots(y) ['tuːts(i)] n (US fam) chica f, gachí f (sl); **hey —!** ¡oye, guapa!
top[1] [tɔp] **1** n **(a)** (topmost point) cumbre f, cima f; ápice m; (of tree) copa f; (of head) coronilla f; (of building) remate m; (of wall) coronamiento m; (of wave) cresta f; (of stairs etc) lo alto, parte f alta; (of list, page, table, classification) cabeza f; primer puesto m, primera posición f; (of plant) hojas fpl, parte f superior; **at the — of the hill** en la cumbre de la colina; **at the — of the tree** en lo alto del árbol; **at the — of the list** a la cabeza de la lista, en la primera posición de la lista; **executives who are at the — of their companies** ejecutivos que están en la cumbre de sus empresas; **Toboso is at the — of the league** Toboso encabeza la liga, Toboso va en posición primera de la liga; **he lives at the — of the house** ocupa el piso más alto de la casa; **from — to bottom** de arriba abajo, de cabo a rabo; **the system is rotten from — to bottom** el sistema entero está podrido; **from — to toe** de pies a cabeza; **on —** encima; **to be on —** estar encima; estar en la parte superior; (fig) llevar ventaja, estar ganando; **to come out on —** salir ganando, salir ganancioso; **it's just one thing on — of another** es una cosa tras otra; **and then on — of all that . . .** y luego por añadidura . . .; y luego para colmo de desgracias; **to go over the —** lanzarse al ataque (saliendo de las trincheras).
(b) (surface) superficie f; **on —** de sobre, encima de; **it floats on —** of the water flota sobre el agua; **oil comes to the —** el aceite sale a la superficie; **the table — is damaged** la superficie de la mesa está deteriorada.
(c) (further part) otro extremo m, parte f más lejana; **I saw him at the — of the street** le vi al otro extremo de la calle; **he sits at the — of the table** se sienta a la cabecera de la mesa.
(d) (Naut) cofa f.
(e) (cap of bottle) cápsula f, tapa f; (of pen) capuchón m; (lid) tapa f, tapadera f; (of carriage) baca f; (of bus) piso m superior, imperial f; (Aut, US) capota f; **with a sliding —, with a sunshine —**

descapotable, con techo corredizo; **to blow one's —** (*fam*) subirse por las paredes (*fam*).

(**f**) (*best*) lo mejor; **the — of the flood** (*or* **tide**) la pleamar; **the — of the morning to you!** ¡buenos días!; **to be at the — of one's form** estar en plena forma; **to shout at the — of one's voice** llamar a voz en grito; **it's the —s** (*fam*) es tremendo (*fam*), es fabuloso (*fam*), es la flor de la canela.

2 *adj* (*highest*) más alto, el más alto; cimero; *part* superior, más alto; *floor, stair etc* más alto, último; (*first*) primero; (*greatest*) máximo; (*highest in rank*) principal, primero; *price* máximo, tope; **at — speed** a máxima velocidad; **the — 20** (*records*) los primeros 20 discos en la clasificación nacional; **the — men in the party** los líderes del partido, los jerarcas del partido; **he was — boy** se clasificó primero (entre los muchachos); **to come —** ganar, ganar el primer puesto, clasificarse primero; **he came — in maths** tuvo la mejor nota en matemáticas; *see* **dog, people** etc.

3 *vt* (**a**) *tree* desmochar; *plant* descabezar; *fruit etc* quitar las hojas (*etc*) de; *person* (*hang: sl*) colgar, (*murder: sl*) apiolar (*fam*), cargarse a (*fam*).

(**b**) (*complete upper part of*) coronar, rematar; **the wall is —ped with stone** el muro tiene un coronamiento de piedras; **and to — it all . . .** y por añadidura . . .; y para colmo de desgracias; **he —ped this off by saying that . . .** esto lo remató diciendo que . . .; **he —ped off the 8th course with a cup of coffee** para completar el octavo plato se bebió una taza de café; **to — up someone's glass** acabar de llenar (*or* volver a llenar) el vaso de uno; **to — up a battery** llenar una pila hasta el nivel indicado.

(**c**) (*exceed*) exceder, aventajar; salir por encima de; **to — someone in height** ser más alto que uno; **to — someone by a head** sacar a uno una cabeza; **this —s everything** esto supera a todo lo demás; **we have —ped last year's takings by £20** hemos recaudado 20 libras más que el año pasado, los ingresos exceden a los del año pasado en 20 libras.

(**d**) (*reach summit of*) llegar a la cumbre de; *class, list* encabezar, estar a la cabeza de; llegar a ocupar la primera posición de; **the team —ped the league all season** el equipo iba en cabeza de la liga toda la temporada.

top² [tɔp] *n* (*spinning —*) peonza *f*, peón *m*; (*humming —, musical —*) trompa *f*.

topaz ['təupæz] *n* topacio *m*.

top boots ['tɔpbuːts] *npl* botas *fpl* de campaña.

topcoat ['tɔpkəut] *n* sobretodo *m*.

tope [təup] *vi* beber (más de la cuenta), emborracharse.

topee ['təupiː] *n* casco *m* colonial.

toper ['təupə*] *n* borrachín *m*.

topflight ['tɔpflait] *adj* sobresaliente, de primera clase.

topgallant [tɔp'gælənt, *Naut* tə'gælənt] *n* (*also — sail*) juanete *m*.

top hat ['tɔp'hæt] *n* chistera *f*, sombrero *m* de copa.

top-hatted ['tɔp'hætid] *adj* en chistera, enchisterado.

top-heavy ['tɔp'hevi] *adj* demasiado pesado por arriba; (*fig*) falto de equilibrio, mal equilibrado.

top-hole ['tɔp'həul] *adj* (*sl*) de primera; **—!** ¡estupendo!, ¡pipudo! (*sl*).

topic ['tɔpik] *n* asunto *m*, tema *m*.

topical ['tɔpikəl] *adj* actual, de interés actual, corriente; **— talk** charla *f* sobre cuestiones del día, charla *f* sobre actualidades; **a highly — question** una cuestión de palpitante actualidad.

topicality [ˌtɔpi'kæliti] *n* actualidad *f*; importancia *f* actual, interés *m* actual.

topknot ['tɔpnɔt] *n* moño *m* (*also* Orn); (*fam*) cabeza *f*.

topless ['tɔplis] *adj* *dress* que deja el pecho al descubierto, que no cubre el pecho.

top-level ['tɔp'levl] *adj*: **— conference** conferencia *f* al más alto nivel.

topmast ['tɔpmɑːst] *n* mastelero *m*.

topmost ['tɔpməust] *adj* más alto, el más alto.

topnotch ['tɔp'nɔtʃ] *adj* (*fam*) de rango muy alto; de primera, estupendo.

topographer [tə'pɔgrəfə*] *n* topógrafo *m*.

topographic(al) [ˌtɔpə'græfik] *adj* topográfico.

topography [tə'pɔgrəfi] *n* topografía *f*.

topper ['tɔpə*] *n* (*fam*) chistera *f*, sombrero *m* de copa.

topping ['tɔpiŋ] *adj* (*fam*) bárbaro (*fam*), pistonudo (*fam*).

topple ['tɔpl] **1** *vt* (*also* **to — over**) derribar, derrocar; hacer caer; volcar.

2 *vi* (*also* **to — down**) caerse, venirse abajo; (*also* **to — over**) volcarse; (*lose balance*) perder el equilibrio; (*totter*) tambalearse; **he —d over a cliff** cayó por un precipicio; **after the crash the bus —d over** después del choque el autobús se volcó.

top-rank ['tɔp'ræŋk] *adj* de primera categoría; *officer* de alta graduación.

topsail ['tɔpsl] *n* gavia *f*.

top-secret ['tɔp'siːkrit] *adj* de lo más secreto, de reserva absoluta.

topsoil ['tɔpsɔil] *n* capa *f* superficial del suelo.

topsy-turvy ['tɔpsi'təːvi] **1** *adv* en desorden, patas arriba; **everything is —** todo está patas arriba. **2** *adj* confuso, desordenado.

toque [təuk] *n* toca *f*.

tor [tɔː*] *n* colina *f* abrupta y rocosa, pico *m* pequeño (*en el suroeste de Inglaterra*).

torch [tɔːtʃ] *n* (*flaming*) antorcha *f*, tea *f*, hacha *f*; (*electric*) linterna *f* eléctrica, lámpara *f* de bolsillo; **Olympic —** antorcha *f* olímpica; **to carry a — for someone** (*fig*) seguir enamorado de uno a pesar de no ser correspondido por él.

torchbearer ['tɔːtʃˌbɛərə*] *n* portahachón *m*.

torchlight ['tɔːtʃlait] *n* luz *f* de antorcha; **— procession** desfile *m* de portahachones.

tore ['tɔː*] *pret* of **tear**.

toreador ['tɔriədɔ*] *n* torero *m*.

torment ['tɔːment] *n* tormento *m*; angustia *f*; suplicio *m*; **the —s of jealousy** los tormentos de los celos; **to be in —** estar sufriendo, sufrir mucho.

torment [tɔː'ment] *vt* atormentar, martirizar; (*torture*) torturar; **we were —ed by thirst** sufrimos los tormentos de la sed; **she was —ed by doubts** la atormentaron las dudas; **don't — the cat** no le des guerra al gato.

tormentor [tɔː'mentə*] *n* atormentador *m*, ora *f*.

torn [tɔːn] *pt ptp* of **tear**.

tornado [tɔː'neidəu] *n*, *pl* **tornadoes** [tɔː'neidəuz] tornado *m*.

torpedo [tɔː'piːdəu] **1** *n*, *pl* **torpedoes** [tɔː'piːdəuz] torpedo *m*. **2** *vt* torpedear (*also fig*).

torpedo boat [tɔː'piːdəubəut] *n* torpedero *m*, lancha *f* torpedera.

torpedo tube [tɔː'piːdəutjuːb] *n* tubo *m* lanzatorpedos.

torpid ['tɔːpid] *adj* aletargado, inactivo; (*fig*) torpe, apático; aburrido.

torpidity [tɔː'piditi] *n*, **torpor** ['tɔːpə*] *n* letargo *m*, inactividad *f*; (*fig*) torpeza *f*, apatía *f*; aburrimiento *m*.

torque [tɔːk] *n* par *m* de torsión.

torrent ['tɔrənt] *n* torrente *m* (*also fig*); **to rain in —s** llover a cántaros, diluviar.

torrential [tɔ'renʃəl] *adj* torrencial.

torrid ['tɔrid] *adj* tórrido.

torsion ['tɔːʃən] *n* torsión *f*.

torsional ['tɔːʃənl] *adj* torsional.

torso ['tɔːsəu] *n*, *pl* **torsos** ['tɔːsəuz] torso *m*.

tort [tɔːt] *n* agravio *m*, tuerto *m*.

tortoise ['tɔːtəs] *n* tortuga *f*.

tortoiseshell ['tɔːtəʃel] *n* carey *m*; **— glasses** gafas *fpl* de carey.

tortuous ['tɔːtjuəs] *adj* tortuoso.

torture ['tɔːtʃə*] **1** *n* tortura *f*; (*fig*) tormento *m*; **it was —!** ¡lo que sufrí!; **to put someone to the —** torturar a uno.

2 *vt* torturar; (*fig*) atormentar; *sense etc* torcer, violentar; **to be —d by doubts** ser atormentado por las dudas.

torturer ['tɔːtʃərə*] *n* verdugo *m*.

torturing ['tɔːtʃəriŋ] *adj* torturador, atormentador.

Tory ['tɔːri] **1** *adj* conservador; **the T— Party** el Partido Conservador. **2** *n* conservador *m*, ora *f*.

Toryism ['tɔːriizəm] *n* conservatismo *m*, conservadurismo *m*.

tosh [tɔʃ] *n* (*fam*) música *f* celestial; **—!** ¡tonterías!

toss [tɔs] **1** *n* (**a**) (*movement: of head etc*) movimiento *m* brusco; sacudida *f*, meneo *m*; (*throw*) echada *f*, tirada *f*; (*by bull*) cogida *f*; (*fall from horse*) caída *f*; **the ball came to him full —** la pelota llegó a sus manos sin tocar la tierra; **he took a bad —** sufrió una violenta caída.

(**b**) (*of coin*) echada *f*; sorteo *m* (*para la elección de lado etc*); **to argue the —** andar en dimes y diretes, discutir; **to win the —** ganar el sorteo; **it's a — up** puede ser lo uno tanto como lo otro; **it's a — up whether I go or stay** no decido si irme o quedarme.

2 *vt head etc* mover bruscamente, hacer un movimiento brusco de; sacudir, menear; (*throw*) echar, tirar; (*of bull*) coger (y lanzar al aire); *coin* echar a cara o cruz; **to — someone in a blanket** mantear a uno; **the currents —ed the boat about**

las corrientes zarandeaban la embarcación; **the horse —ed its head** el caballo levantó airosamente la cabeza; **to — aside** echar a un lado, apartar bruscamente, abandonar; **to — off a drink** beberse algo de un trago, beberse algo rápidamente; **to — a book over to someone** tirar un libro a uno; **— it over!** ¡dámelo!; **to — up** *coin* echar a cara o cruz.

3 *vi* (a) agitarse, sacudirse; (*of plumes etc*) ondear; (*in a boat: gently*) balancearse sobre las ondas, (*violently*) ser sacudido por las ondas; **to — (in one's sleep), to — and turn** revolverse (en la cama).

(b) (*also* **to — up**) jugar a cara o cruz (*for something* algo); (*Sport*) sortear (*for something* algo); **we'll — up to see who does it** jugaremos a cara o cruz para decidir quién lo hará.

tot[1] [tɔt] *n* (a) (*drink*) trago *m*, copita *f*; **just a —** unas gotitas nada más; **let's go in here for a —** entremos aquí a tomar algo. (b) (*child*) nene *m*, a *f*.

tot[2] [tɔt] *vi*: **to — up** sumar. **2** *vi*: **it —s up to £5** suma 5 libras, viene a ser 5 libras; **what does it — up to?** ¿cuánto suma?

total ['təutl] **1** *adj* (*Math etc*) total; (*complete, utter*) total, completo, entero; **the — losses amount to . . .** las pérdidas suman un total de . . .; **what is the — amount?** ¿cuánto es el importe total?; **— failure** fracaso *m* completo, fracaso *m* rotundo; **— war** guerra *f* total; **we were in — ignorance** lo ignorábamos por completo; **the disagreement is —** el desacuerdo es total.

2 *n* total *m*; suma *f*; cantidad *f* global; **grand —** importe *m* total; **it comes to a — of . . .** suma en total . . ., asciende a . . .; **the sum — of people** la colectividad de las personas.

3 *vt* sumar (*also* **to — up**).

4 *vi* ascender a, sumar, totalizar.

totalitarian [ˌtəutælɪ'tɛərɪən] *adj* totalitario.

totalitarianism [ˌtəutælɪ'tɛərɪənɪzəm] *n* totalitarismo *m*.

totality [təu'tælɪti] *n* totalidad *f*.

totalizator ['təutəlaɪzeɪtə*] *n* totalizador *m*.

totalize ['təutəlaɪz] *vt* totalizar.

totally ['təutəli] *adv* totalmente, completamente.

tote[1] [təut] *n* (*fam*) totalizador *m*.

tote[2] [təut] *vt* (*fam*) acarrear, llevar (con dificultad); **I —d it around all day** lo llevé de acá para allá todo el día.

totem ['təutəm] *n* tótem *m*.

totemic [təu'temik] *adj* totémico.

totem pole ['təutəmpəul] *n* poste *m* totémico.

totter ['tɔtə*] *vi* (*stagger*) bambolearse, tambalearse; (*be about to fall*) tambalearse, estar para desplomarse.

tottering ['tɔtərɪŋ] *adj*, **tottery** ['tɔtəri] *adj* tambaleante; nada seguro; ruinoso; **he's getting tottery** empieza a andar con poca seguridad; **with tottering steps** con pasos inseguros, con pasos vacilantes.

toucan ['tu:kən] *n* tucán *m*.

touch [tʌtʃ] **1** *n* (a) (*sense of —*) tacto *m*; **it feels rough to the —** es áspero al tacto.

(b) (*act of —ing, contact*) toque *m*; contacto *m*; (*light brushing*) roce *m*; (*Mus, of typist*) pulsación *f*; (*Art*) pincelada *f*, toque *m*; **final —**, **finishing —** última mano *f*, último toque *m*; **to give something a finishing —**, **to put the finishing — to something** dar el último toque a algo; **human —**, **personal —** (*in person's character*) don *m* de gentes, (*in contacts etc*) nota *f* personal, nota *f* humana; **the master's —** la mano del maestro; **it has the — of genius** lleva el sello de la genialidad; **it's the Nelson —** es el genio de Nelson; **the cold — of a dead fish** el contacto glacial con un pez muerto; **at a — of her hand, I . . .** al tocarme la mano de ella, yo . . .; **with the barest — of a finger** con una ligerísima presión del dedo; **by — a tiento, tentándolo; I felt a — on my neck** sentí que alguien me tocaba el cuello; **to give someone a — on the arm** tocar el brazo de uno.

(c) (*contact, fit*) contacto *m*; **to be in — with someone** estar en contacto (*or* comunicación) con uno; **to be in — with new inventions** estar al tanto de los inventos; **to be out of — with someone** haber perdido contacto con uno; **he's completely out of —** sus ideas están completamente postergadas, está quedando anticuado; **we're very much out of — here** aquí no recibimos noticias de lo que pasa; **to get into — with someone** ponerse en contacto con uno; **you can get into — with me at No. 7** si me quiere para algo llame al número 7; **you ought to get into — with the police** conviene informar a la policía; **to keep in — with someone** mantener relaciones con uno; **well, keep in —!** ¡bueno, téngame al corriente!; **to lose — with someone**

perder contacto con uno; **to put someone into — with another person** ayudar a uno a establecer contacto con otra persona.

(d) (*sl*) **he's good for a —** seguramente nos dará (*or* prestará) algo; **to make a —** lograr sacar dinero de uno, lograr dar un sablazo a uno.

(e) (*small quantity*) pizca *f*; poquito *m*; (*Med*) ataque *m* leve; **a — of the sun** una insolación; **with a — of irony** con un dejo de ironía, con un punto de ironía; **add a — of salt** agregue un poquitín de sal; **to have a — of 'flu** tener un ataque leve de gripe.

(f) (*Sport*) touche *f*, parte *f* fuera de juego; **to be in —** estar fuera de juego; **to kick for —, to kick the ball into —** poner el balón fuera de juego.

2 *vt* (a) (*come into contact with*) tocar; (*and explore*) palpar; (*brush against*) rozar; (*reach*) alcanzar; **to — something with one's finger** tocar algo con el dedo; **someone —ed me on the arm** alguien me tocó el brazo; **don't —!** ¡no tocar!, ¡fuera las manos!; **his property —es ours** su propiedad linda con la nuestra, su finca es contigua a la nuestra; **and the police can't — him** y la policía no tiene motivo para detenerle, la policía no tiene autoridad para detenerle; **I never —ed her!** ¡no la toqué siquiera!; **I wouldn't — it** (*with a barge pole*) no lo quiero ver ni de lejos; **to — ground** (*Aer*) tocar tierra, tomar tierra; *see* **bottom**, **wood**.

(b) (*eat, drink*) tomar, probar; **I haven't —ed a mouthful** no he probado un solo bocado; **I never — onion** no pruebo la cebolla; **I never — gin** no bebo nunca ginebra.

(c) (*equal*) compararse con, igualar; **there's no violinist to — him, no one can — him as a violinist** no hay violinista que se le iguale, no hay violinista que pueda compararse con él.

(d) (*make an impression on*) hacer efecto en, hacer mella en; **this saw won't —** it esta sierra no le hace mella, esta sierra es inútil para esto; **I couldn't — the third question** quedé muy lejos de poder contestar la tercera pregunta.

(e) (*move*) conmover, enternecer; **I was deeply —ed** me conmoví mucho, me emocioné profundamente; **it —ed our hearts** enterneció nuestros corazones; **no one can see it without being —ed** nadie lo ve sin conmoverse.

(f) (*concern*) afectar, tocar; **it —es us all closely** nos toca de cerca a todos; **if it —es the national interest** si afecta al interés nacional.

(g) (*sl*) **to — someone for a loan** dar un sablazo a uno, lograr sacar dinero de uno; **to — someone for £5** lograr que uno preste 5 libras.

(h) **to — down** (*Sport*) poner en tierra; **to — off** *explosion* hacer estallar; *revolt* hacer estallar, provocar; **it —ed off a series of ideas** dio origen a una serie de ideas; **it —ed off a fierce argument** causó una violenta discusión; **to — up** retocar (*also Art, Phot*).

3 *vi* (a) (*come into contact*) tocarse; encontrarse; tocar al pasar, rozar pasando; (*collide*) chocar ligeramente; (*be adjacent*) lindar, estar contiguo; **our hands —ed** se encontraron nuestras manos; **the subjects — at several points** los temas tienen varios aspectos en común.

(b) **to — at** (*Naut*) tocar en, hacer escala en; **to — down** (*Aer*) tocar tierra, aterrizar; (*of space capsule*) amerizar; (*Sport*) tocar en tierra; **to — on, to — upon** tocar, aludir (brevemente) a.

touch-and-go ['tʌtʃən'gəu] **1** *adj* decision difícil, dudoso. **2** *n*: **it's — whether . . .** está en vilo si . . ., es difícil decidir si . . .

touchdown ['tʌtʃdaun] *n* (*Aer*) aterrizaje *m*; (*of space capsule*) amerizaje *m*; (*Sport*) tocado *m* en tierra.

touched [tʌtʃt] *adj* (*fam*) chiflado, tocado.

touchiness ['tʌtʃinis] *n* susceptibilidad *f*.

touching ['tʌtʃiŋ] **1** *adj* conmovedor, patético. **2** *prep* tocante a.

touchingly ['tʌtʃiŋli] *adv* de modo conmovedor, patéticamente.

touchline ['tʌtʃlain] *n* línea *f* de banda, línea *f* de toque, línea *f* lateral.

touchstone ['tʌtʃstaun] *n* piedra *f* de toque (*also fig*).

touch-typing ['tʌtʃˌtaipiŋ] *n* mecanografía *f* al tacto.

touchy ['tʌtʃi] *adj* susceptible, quisquilloso; **to be —** ofenderse por poca cosa, tener prontos enojos; **he's — about his weight** no le hacen gracia las referencias a su gordura, no le gusta que se le tome el pelo con motivo de su gordura.

tough [tʌf] **1** *adj* (a) (*of materials*) duro, fuerte, resistente; *meat* duro, estropajoso; (*leathery*) correoso.

(b) (*hardy*) resistente, fuerte, vigoroso; **the — sports** los deportes violentos; **he's pretty —** tiene mucha resistencia.

(c) (*unyielding, stubborn*) tenaz, terco; *person* (*pej*) duro, malvado; **we can expect — resistance** hemos de contar con una resistencia tensa.

(d) (*difficult*) difícil, penoso; *problem* espinoso; *journey, work* arduo; **there's a — road ahead** el camino a recorrer es arduo; **to have a — time of it** pasar las de Caín.

(e) (*of luck etc*) malo; **— luck!** ¡mala suerte!; **that's pretty —** eso me parece muy injusto; **but it was — on the others** pero perjudicó a los demás, pero fue muy desagradable para los demás.

2 *n* (*fam*) machote *m*; (*pej*) gorila *m*, forzudo *m*; caradura *m*; **a gang of —s** una pandilla de forzudos.

toughen ['tʌfn] **1** *vt* endurecer. **2** *vi* endurecerse.

toughly ['tʌfli] *adv* vigorosamente; tenazmente, tercamente.

toughness ['tʌfnis] *n* dureza *f*, resistencia *f*; lo correoso; vigor *m*; tenacidad *f*, terquedad *f*; lo difícil, lo penoso; lo arduo; **the job needs a certain —** el trabajo exige cierta resistencia.

Toulon ['tu:'lɔ̃:ŋ] Tolón.

Toulouse ['tu:'lu:z] Tolosa (de Francia).

toupée ['tu:pei] *n* casquete *m*, peluca *f*.

tour ['tuə*] **1** *n* (*journey*) viaje *m* (largo), excursión *f* (larga); (*by team, actors, musicians etc*) gira *f*; (*of building, exhibition*) visita *f*; inspección *f*; (*of duty* período *m* de servicio; **— of inspection** visita *f*; recorrido *m* de inspección; **circular —** viaje *m* redondo; **conducted —** excursión *f* con guía; visita *f* en grupo, visita *f* de inspección; **package —** viaje *m* (de turismo) con todo incluido; **walking —** excursión *f* (larga) a pie; **the Australian — of 1972** la gira australiana de 1972; **the — includes a week in Venice** el programa del viaje incluye una semana en Venecia; **to be on —** estar de viaje; (*of team etc*) estar gira; **to go on —** partir de viaje, (*of team etc*) partir de gira; **to take a company on —** (*Theat*) llevar a una compañía de gira; **to take a play on —** llevar una obra a una serie de teatros (de provincia *etc*).

2 *vt country etc* viajar por, recorrer (como turista); *building, exhibition* visitar, recorrer.

3 *vi* viajar; estar de viaje, hacer viaje de turista; **we're just —ing around** hacemos viajes de turismo aquí y allá.

Touraine [tu'rein] Turena *f*.

tour de force ['tuədə'fɔ:s] *n* juego *m* de destreza; demostración *f* de genialidad.

tourer ['tuərə*] *n* (coche *m* de) turismo *m*.

touring ['tuəriŋ] **1** *n* turismo *m*; viajes *mpl* turísticos.

2 *attr company* (*Theat*) que hace una gira; ambulante.

touring car ['tuəriŋka:*] *n* (coche *m* de) turismo *m*.

tourism ['tuərizəm] *n* turismo *m*.

tourist ['tuərist] **1** *n* turista *mf*.

2 *attr* turista, turístico; para turistas; de viajes; **— of — interest** de interés turístico; **the — trade** la industria del turismo; *see* **agency, class** etc.

tournament ['tuənəmənt] *n* torneo *m*; concurso *m*, certamen *m*; **chess —** torneo *m* de ajedrez; **tennis —** torneo *m* de tenis.

tourney ['tuəni] *n* (*Hist*) torneo *m*.

tourniquet ['tuənikei] *n* torniquete *m*.

touse [tauz] *vt* dar una paliza a (*also fig*).

tousing ['tauziŋ] *n* paliza *f* (*also fig*).

tousle ['tauzl] *vt* ajar, desarreglar; *hair* despeinar.

tousled ['tauzld] *adj* ajado, desarreglado, en desorden; *hair* despeinado.

tout [taut] **1** *n* (*seller*) pregonero *m*; (*agent*) gancho *m*; (*ticket—*) revendedor *m*; (*Racing*) pronosticador *m*.

2 *vt wares* ofrecer, pregonar; *tickets* revender.

3 *vi*: **to — for custom** solicitar clientes; tratar de hacer un negocio.

tout court ['tu:'kuə*] *adv*: **his name is Rodríguez —** se llama Rodríguez a secas.

tow¹ [təu] **1** (*act*) remolque *m*; (*rope*) remolque *m*, cable *m* de remolque; (*thing towed*) vehículo *m* (*etc*) remolcado; **to be on —** ser remolcado, ser llevado a remolque; **to have a car in —** dar remolque a un coche; **he had 3 girls in —** iba acompañado de 3 chicas, (*fig*) andaba en relaciones con 3 chicas, tenía 3 chicas al retortero; **to take in —** dar remolque a.

2 *vt* remolcar, llevar a remolque; **to — something about** (*fig*) llevar algo consigo.

tow² [təu] *n* estopa *f*.

towage ['təuidʒ] *n* (*act*) remolque *m*; (*fee*) derechos *mpl* de remolque.

toward(s) [tə'wɔ:d(z)] *prep* (*of direction*) hacia; (*of time*) hacia, cerca de; (*of attitude*) con, para con; **his feelings — the church** sus sentimientos para con la iglesia; **— noon** hacia mediodía; **— 6 o'clock** hacia las 6, a eso de las 6; **we're saving — our holiday** ahorramos dinero para nuestras vacaciones; **it helps — a solution** contribuye a la solución, ayuda en el esfuerzo por encontrar una solución.

towboat ['təubəut] *n* (*US*) remolcador *m*.

tow car ['təuka:*] *n* (*US*) coche *m* que remolca otro.

towel ['tauəl] **1** *n* toalla *f*. **2** *vt* secar con toalla; frotar con toalla.

towel rail ['tauəlreil] *n* toallero *m*.

tower ['tauə*] **1** *n* torre *f*; (*bell—*) campanario *m*; **ivory —** (*fig*) torre *f* de marfil; **to be a — of strength to someone** ayudar muchísimo a uno.

2 *vi* elevarse; encumbrarse; **to — above, to — over** dominar, destacarse sobre, (*fig*) descollar entre; **it —s to over 300 metres** se eleva a más de 300 metros; **he —s above his contemporaries** descuella fuertemente entre sus coetáneos.

towering ['tauəriŋ] *adj mountain* encumbrado; elevado, elevadísimo; *building* muy alto, imponente por su altura; *figure* destacado, dominante; *rage* muy violento.

towline ['təulain] *n* sirga *f*.

town [taun] **1** *n* ciudad *f*; (*smaller, country —*) pueblo *m*, población *f*; **— and gown** ciudadanos *mpl* y universitarios, ciudad *f* y universidad; **model —** ciudad *f* modelo; **new —** poblado *m* de absorción; **satellite —** ciudad *f* satélite; **to be on the —** estar en plan de juerga; **to go on the —** salir de juerga; **to live in —** vivir en la capital (*esp* Londres); **to go up to —** ir a la capital (*esp* Londres); **to go to —** ir a la ciudad; **to go to — on** (*fam*) dedicarse con entusiasmo a, entregarse de lleno a; **he certainly went to — on that mistake** cierto que aprovechó todas las posibilidades de ese error; **he's out of —** está fuera, está de viaje; **to paint the — red** echar una cana al aire.

2 *attr* urbano; urbanístico; de (la) ciudad, municipal; **— house** casa *f* de ciudad; **— life** vida *f* urbana; *see* **clerk, crier** etc.

town plan ['taun'plæn] *n* plan *m* de desarrollo urbano.

town planner ['taun'plænə*] *n* urbanista *mf*.

town planning ['taun'plæniŋ] *n* urbanismo *m*.

townsfolk ['taunzfəuk] *n* ciudadanos *mpl*.

township ['taunʃip] *n* municipio *m*, término *m* municipal; pueblo *m*.

townsman ['taunzmən] *n*, *pl* **—men** [mən] ciudadano *m*; (*as opposed to countryman*) hombre *m* de la ciudad, habitante *m* de la ciudad.

townspeople ['taunz,pi:pl] *npl* ciudadanos *mpl*.

towpath ['təupɑ:θ] *n* camino *m* de sirga.

towrope ['təurəup] *n* remolque *m*, cable *m* de remolque; (*on canal*) sirga *f*.

toxic ['tɔksik] *adj* tóxico.

toxicological [,tɔksikə'lɔdʒikəl] *adj* toxicológico.

toxicology [,tɔksi'kɔlədʒi] *n* toxicología *f*.

toxin ['tɔksin] *n* toxina *f*.

toy [tɔi] **1** *n* juguete *m*; (*pej, iro*) juguete *m*, chuchería *f*.

2 *adj, attr railway etc* de juguete, de jugar; *dog etc* de raza muy pequeña, miniatura; **— car** coche *m* de juguete; **— soldier** soldadito *m* de plomo; **— theatre** teatro *m* de títeres.

3 *vi*: **to — with** *object* jugar con, divertirse jugando con; *food* comer melindrosamente; *idea* acariciar; *someone's affections* divertirse con.

toybox ['tɔibɔks] *n* caja *f* de juguetes.

toy maker ['tɔi,meikə*] *n* fabricante *m* de juguetes.

toyshop ['tɔiʃɔp] *n* juguetería *f*.

trace¹ [treis] **1** *n* rastro *m*, huella *f*; vestigio *m*; señal *f*, indicio *m*; (*small amount*) pequeñísima cantidad *f*, pizca *f*; (*remaining taste etc*) dejo *m*; **without a — of ill feeling** sin asomo de rencor; **sunk without —** desaparecido sin dejar el menor indicio; **to vanish without —** desaparecer sin dejar rastro; **there is no — of it now** no queda vestigio alguno de ello ahora; **we looked all over but couldn't find a single —** buscamos por todas partes pero sin encontrar el menor indicio.

2 *vt curve, line etc* trazar; (*with tracing paper*) calcar; (*follow trail of*) seguir, seguir la pista de; rastrear; (*find, locate*) encontrar; averiguar el paradero de; **I cannot — any reference to it** no he logrado encontrar ninguna referencia a ello; **she was finally —d to a house in Soho** por fin la encontraron en una casa del Soho; **to — an idea for someone** exponer una idea a uno; **to — one's ancestry back to Ferdinand III** hacer remontar su ascendencia hasta Fernando III; **to — a rumour back to its source** averiguar dónde se originó un rumor, seguir la pista de un rumor hasta llegar a su punto de partida.

trace[2] [treis] *n* tirante *m*, correa *f*; **to kick over the —s** (*fig*) sacar los pies del plato, mostrar las herraduras.

traceable ['treisəbl] *adj*: **a person not now** — una persona cuyo paradero actual es imposible de encontrar; **an easily — reference** una referencia fácil de encontrar.

tracer ['treisə*] *n*, **tracer bullet** ['treisə,bulit] *n* bala *f* trazadora.

tracer element ['treisər,elimənt] *n* (*Phys*) elemento *m* trazador.

tracery ['treisəri] *n* tracería *f*.

trachea [trə'kiə] *n* tráquea *f*.

trachoma [træ'kəumə] *n* tracoma *m*.

tracing ['treisiŋ] *n* calco *m*.

tracing paper ['treisiŋ,peipə*] *n* papel *m* de calco, papel *m* transparente.

track [træk] **1** *n* (a) (*mark: of animal*) huella *f*; pista *f*, rastro *m*; (*of person*) pista *f*; (*of vehicle*) huella *f*; (*of wheel*) rodada *f*; (*of boat*) estela *f*; (*of hurricane*) rastro *m*, marcha *f*; (*of bullet, rocket etc*) trayectoria *f*; **to be on someone's — (s)** seguir la pista de uno, andar a los alcances de uno; **he had the police on his —** le buscaba la policía, le estaba cazando la policía; **they got on to his —** very quickly se pusieron sobre la pista sin pérdida de tiempo; **to cover up one's —s** borrar sus huellas, procurar no dejar rastro de sí; **to follow in someone's —** seguir el camino que ha marcado uno; **to keep — of someone** no perder de vista a uno; seguir la suerte a uno; **to keep — of new inventions** mantenerse al tanto de los nuevos inventos; **to lose — of someone** perder a uno de vista; **to lose — of what someone is saying** perder el hilo de lo que está diciendo uno; **to make —s** (*fam*) irse, largarse; **we must be making —s** tenemos que marcharnos; **to throw someone off the —** despistar a uno.

(b) (*path*) senda *f*, camino *m*; **beaten —** camino *m* trillado (*also fig*); **a village off the beaten —** un pueblo poco conocido, un pueblo apartado de las carreteras principales; **to get off the beaten —** apartarse del camino trillado, explorar un terreno menos conocido; **forest —** camino *m* forestal; **mule —** camino *m* carretero; **sheep —** cañada *f*; **to be on the right —** ir por buen camino; **to be on the wrong —** (*fig*) haberse equivocado, estar equivocado; **to be way off the —** estar totalmente despistado; **to put someone on the right —** mostrar a uno el camino que le conviene seguir.

(c) (*Sport*) pista *f*; **dog-racing —** canódromo *m*; **motor-racing —** pista *f* de automovilismo.

(d) (*Rail*) vía *f*; **double —** vía *f* doble; **single —** vía *f* única; **he has a one-** mind no tiene más que un solo pensamiento; **to cross the —s** cruzar la vía; **to run off the —(s)** descarrilar.

(e) (*Mech: also* **caterpillar —s**) llanta *f* de oruga.

2 *attr*: **— athletics** atletismo *m* en pista; **— events** pruebas *fpl* en pista; **— maintenance** (*Rail*) conservación *f* de la vía.

3 *vt animal* rastrear, seguir la pista de; *satellite etc* rastrear, seguir la trayectoria de; **to — down** averiguar el paradero (*or* origen) de, buscar y encontrar; **finally we —ed it down in the library** por fin lo encontramos en la biblioteca.

4 *vi*: **to — along** avanzar por, ir por, seguir.

tracker ['trækə*] *n* rastreador *m*.

tracker dog ['trækədɔg] *n* perro *m* rastreador.

tracking ['trækiŋ] *n* rastreo *m*.

tracking station ['trækiŋ,steiʃən] *n* centro *m* de rastreo, estación *f* de rastreo.

trackless ['træklis] *adj* sin caminos, impenetrable.

track meet ['træk'mi:t] *n* (US) concurso *m* de carreras y saltos.

track race ['trækreis] *n* carrera *f* en pista.

track racing ['træk,reisiŋ] *n* carreras *fpl* en pista, ciclismo *m* (*etc*) en pista.

tract[1] [trækt] *n* región *f*, zona *f*; extensión *f*; (*Anat*) región *f*; **digestive —** canal *m* digestivo; **respiratory —** vías *fpl* respiratorias, sistema *m* respiratorio.

tract[2] [trækt] *n* (*pamphlet*) folleto *m*; (*treatise*) tratado *m*.

tractable ['træktəbl] *adj person* tratable, dócil; *problem* soluble; *material* dúctil, maleable.

traction ['trækʃən] *n* tracción *f*.

traction engine ['trækʃən,endʒin] *n* locomóvil *f*, máquina *f* de tracción.

tractive ['træktiv] *adj* tractivo.

tractor ['træktə*] *n* tractor *m*; **agricultural —, farm —** tractor *m* agrícola.

tractor-drawn ['træktədrɔ:n] *adj* arrastrado por tractor.

tractor driver ['træktə,draivə*] *n* tractorista *mf*.

trade [treid] **1** *n* (a) (*commerce*) comercio *m*; negocio *m*; tráfico *m* (*in* en); industria *f*; **the wool —** la industria de la lana; **the — in drugs, the drug —** el tráfico en narcóticos, el comercio de narcóticos; **Board of T—** Ministerio *m* de Comercio; **coasting —** cabotaje *m*; **foreign —** comercio *m* exterior; **to be in —** ser comerciante, tener un negocio, (*esp*) tener una tienda; **to do a good** (*or* **brisk, roaring**) **—** hacer un buen negocio (*in* con); *see* **fair, retail** *etc*.

(b) (*calling*) oficio *m*, profesión *f*; empleo *m*; oficio *m* manual; **a butcher by —** de oficio carnicero; **a lawyer by —** (*hum*) de profesión abogado; **to carry on a —** ejercer un oficio; **to put someone to a —** hacer que uno aprenda un oficio; **known in the — as . . .** conocido por los que son del oficio como . . .

(c) (*persons collectively*) comerciantes *mpl*.

(d) **—s** (*Geog*) vientos *mpl* alisios.

2 *attr* (a) de comercio, comercial; **— discount** descuento *m* comercial; **— secret** secreto *m* comercial; **the — returns for March** las estadísticas del balance del comercio (exterior) de marzo.

(b) **— allowance** descuento *m*, rebaja *f* (del precio al por menor); **— price** precio *m* al comerciante, precio *m* al por mayor.

3 *vt* (*fig*) vender; **to — A for B** cambiar A por B, trocar A por B; **to — a car in** ofrecer un coche como parte del pago, devolver un coche usado al comprar otro nuevo.

4 *vi* comerciar (*in* en, *with* con); **we do not — with Ruritania** no tenemos relaciones comerciales con Ruritania; **to — on an advantage** aprovecharse de una ventaja, explotar una ventaja.

trade-in ['treidin] *attr*: **— arrangements** sistema *m* de devolver un artículo usado al comprar otro nuevo; **— price, — value** valor *m* de un artículo usado que se descuenta del precio de otro nuevo.

trademark ['treidmɑ:k] *n* marca *f* registrada, marca *f* de fábrica; (*fig*) marca *f*, sello *m*.

trade name ['treidneim] *n* nombre *m* comercial, nombre *m* de fábrica.

trader ['treidə*] *n* comerciante *m*; traficante *m*; (*street* **—**) vendedor *m* ambulante; (*Hist*) mercader *m*.

trade school ['treidsku:l] *n* universidad *f* laboral, escuela *f* de artes y oficios.

tradesman ['treidzmən] *n*, *pl* **—men** [mən] (*shopkeeper*) tendero *m*; (*roundsman*) repartidor *m*, proveedor *m*; (*artisan*) artesano *m*; **—'s entrance** puerta *f* de servicio.

tradespeople ['treidz,pi:pl] *npl* tenderos *mpl*.

trade union ['treid'ju:njən] **1** *n* sindicato *m*, gremio *m* (obrero); **to form a —** formar un sindicato, agremiarse.

2 trade-union *attr* sindical, gremial; **— labour** mano *f* de obra agremiada; **— shop** taller *m* donde todos los obreros son miembros de un sindicato.

trade unionism ['treid'ju:njənizəm] *n* sindicalismo *m*, sistema *m* de sindicatos.

trade unionist ['treid'ju:njənist] *n* sindicalista *mf*, miembro *m* de un sindicato.

trade winds ['treidwindz] *npl* vientos *mpl* alisios.

trading ['treidiŋ] **1** *adj*, *attr* comercial, mercantil; **— nation** nación *f* con importante comercio exterior; **— profits for 1975** beneficios *mpl* obtenidos en el ejercicio de 1975.

2 *n* comercio *m*; tráfico *m*.

trading estate ['treidiŋis,teit] *n* zona *f* industrial.

trading post ['treidiŋpəust] *n* factoría *f*.

trading stamp ['treidiŋstæmp] *n* cupón *m*.

tradition [trə'diʃən] *n* tradición *f*.

traditional [trə'diʃənl] *adj* tradicional; clásico, consagrado.

traditionalism [trə'diʃnəlizəm] *n* tradicionalismo *m*.

traditionalist [trə'diʃnəlist] **1** *adj* tradicionalista. **2** *n* tradicionalista *mf*.

traditionally [trə'diʃnəli] *adv* tradicionalmente; según tradición, de acuerdo con la tradición.

traduce [trə'dju:s] *vt* calumniar, denigrar.

traffic [træfik] **1** *n* (a) (*Aut etc*) circulación *f*, tráfico *m*; movimiento *m*; **holiday —** (*Aut*) movimiento *m* de coches que llevan a las familias a veranear, (*Aer etc*) tránsito *m* de pasajeros que van de vacaciones; **peak —** movimiento *m* máximo; **rail —** tráfico *m* por ferrocarril; **road —** circulación *f* por carretera; **tourist —** tránsito *m* de turistas, movimiento *m* de turistas; turismo *m*; **vehicular —** circulación *f* rodada; **the — is heavy this morning**

esta mañana hay muchos coches; — **was quite light** había poco movimiento de coches, circulaban poco los coches; — **was blocked for some hours** la circulación quedó interrumpida durante varias horas.
　　(b) *(trade)* tráfico *m*, comercio *m* (**in** en); *(pej)* trata *f* (**in** de); **the drug** — el tráfico en narcóticos.
　　2 *attr* de la circulación, del tráfico; — **problems in Buenos Aires** los problemas de la circulación en Buenos Aires.
　　3 *vi* traficar, comerciar (**in** en); *(pej)* tratar (**in** en).
trafficator ['træfikeitə*] *n* indicador *m* de dirección, flecha *f* de dirección.
traffic circle ['træfik'sə:kl] *n (US)* cruce *m* giratorio, glorieta *f*, redondel *m*.
traffic island ['træfik'ailənd] *n (Aut)* refugio *m*.
traffic jam ['træfikdʒæm] *n* embotellamiento *m*, aglomeración *f*; **a 5-mile** — una cola de coches que se extiende hasta 5 millas; **there are always** —**s here** aquí siempre se embotella el tráfico.
trafficker ['træfikə*] *n* traficante *m* (**in** en), tratante *m* (**in** en).
traffic lights ['træfiklaits] *npl* luces *fpl* de tráfico, señales *fpl* luminosas, semáforo *m*.
traffic police ['træfikpə‚li:s] *n* policía *f* de tráfico.
traffic sign ['træfiksain] *n* señal *f* de tráfico.
tragedian [trə'dʒi:diən] *n* trágico *m*.
tragedienne [trədʒi:di'en] *n* trágica *f*, actriz *f* trágica.
tragedy ['trædʒidi] *n* tragedia *f*; **it is a** — **that**... es trágico que...; **what a** —! ¡qué trágico!; **the** — **of it is that**... lo trágico es que...
tragic ['trædʒik] *adj* trágico.
tragically ['trædʒikəli] *adv* trágicamente; **don't take it too** — no seas tan pesimista.
tragicomedy ['trædʒi'kɔmidi] *n* tragicomedia *f*.
tragicomic ['trædʒi'kɔmik] *adj* tragicómico.
trail [treil] 1 *n* (a) *(wake)* estela *f*; *(of comet, rocket)* cola *f*; — **of fire** estela *f* de fuego; **vapour** — estela *f* de humo; **the speech left a long** — **of comments** el discurso ha dejado larga estela de comentarios; **the hurricane left a** — **of destruction** el huracán dejó una estela de estragos.
　　(b) *(track of animal)* rastro *m*, pista *f*; **false** — pista *f* falsa; **to be on the** — **of, to follow the** — of seguir la pista de; **to pick up the** — encontrar la pista.
　　(c) *(path)* camino *m*, sendero *m*; **forest** — camino *m* forestal.
　　2 *vt* (a) *(drag)* arrastrar; **arms** bajar.
　　(b) *(track)* rastrear, seguir la pista de; seguir de cerca; *(of detective etc)* vigilar; **have that man** —**ed** que vigilen a ese hombre.
　　3 *vi* (a) *(be drawn along)* arrastrarse; **he walked with his coat** —**ing on the ground** andaba arrastrando su abrigo por los suelos; **with a small boat** —**ing behind** con un bote remolcado.
　　(b) *(of person)* **to** — **along** arrastrarse; caminar penosamente, ir con aire desanimado; **to** — **far behind** quedar muy a la zaga, rezagarse mucho; **El Toboso is** —**ing at the foot of the league** El Toboso va en última posición de la liga; **the children** —**ed home in the rain** los niños se fueron muy tristes a su casa bajo la lluvia.
　　(c) *(of plant)* arrastrarse; trepar.
　　(d) **to** — **away, to** — **off** ir desapareciendo (hasta perderse completamente), desvanecerse poco a poco.
trailer ['treilə*] *n (Aut etc)* remolque *m*; *(Cine)* trailer *m*, avance *m* *(Acad)*.
trailing ['treiliŋ] *adj* colgado; *plant* rastrero, trepador; **edge** posterior.
train [trein] 1 *n* (a) *(Rail)* tren *m*; **accommodation** — *(US)* tren *m* ómnibus; **down** — tren *m* descendente; **excursion** — tren *m* de excursión, tren *m* de recreo; **express** — rápido *m*; **freight** —, **goods** — (tren *m* de) mercancías *m*; **passenger** — tren *m* de pasajeros; **relief** — tren *m* suplementario; **slow** —, **stopping** — tren *m* correo, tren *m* ómnibus; **through** — tren *m* directo; **up** — tren *m* ascendente; **by** — (go) en tren, (send) por ferrocarril; **to catch a** — coger un tren, tomar un tren; **to change** —**s** cambiar de tren, hacer transbordo.
　　(b) *(Mech)* tren *m*; — **of gears** tren *m* de engranajes.
　　(c) *(series)* serie *f*, sucesión *f*; **a** — **of cars** una serie de coches; — **of powder** reguero *m* de pólvora; — **of events** serie *f* de sucesos; — **of thought** hilo *m* del pensamiento; **he began another** — **of thought** dejó discurrir el pensamiento en otra cosa, dirigió el pensamiento a otra cosa; **in an unbroken** — en una serie ininterrumpida; **sin solución de**

continuidad; it is in — está en preparación; **to set something in** — poner algo en movimiento, empezar a poner algo en obra.
　　(d) *(of dress)* cola *f*; **to carry someone's** — llevar la cola del vestido de una.
　　(e) *(entourage)* séquito *m*, comitiva *f*; *(of mules)* recua *f*, reata *f*; **baggage** — tren *m* de equipajes; **it brought ruin in its** — acarreó la ruina, trajo consigo la ruina.
　　2 *vt* (a) *(instruct etc)* adiestrar; preparar, formar; *(Mil)* adiestrar, ejercitar; disciplinar; *child* enseñar; *(Sport)* entrenar, preparar; *animal* amaestrar; *voice* educar; **they** — **boys for the Navy** preparan a los muchachos para la Marina; **to** — **someone in firearms** enseñar a uno el manejo de las armas de fuego; **where were you** —**ed?** ¿dónde cursó Vd sus estudios?; **he was** —**ed at Salamanca** tuvo su formación profesional en Salamanca; **to** — **someone to do something** enseñar a uno a hacer algo, enseñar a uno el arte *(or* la técnica *etc)* de hacer algo; habituar a uno a hacer algo, acostumbrar a uno a hacer algo; **to** — **someone up** preparar a uno, formar a uno.
　　(b) *(direct)* *gun* apuntar (**on** a); *camera, telescope* enfocar (**on** a); *plant* guiar (**up**, **along** por).
　　3 *vi* *(instruct oneself)* adiestrarse; prepararse, formarse; educarse; *(Mil)* adiestrarse, ejercitarse; *(Sport etc)* entrenarse; **I** — **for 6 hours a day** me entreno 6 horas diarias, hago prácticas durante 6 horas cada día; **to** — **as a teacher, to** — **to become a teacher** seguir un curso de formación pedagógica; **we're** —**ing for the cup game** nos entrenamos para el partido de copa; **where did you** —? ¿dónde cursó Vd sus estudios?, ¿dónde se formó Vd?
　　(b) *(Rail)* ir en tren; **then we** —**ed to Seville** luego fuimos en tren a Sevilla.
　　4 *vr*: **to** — **oneself in a craft** enseñarse un arte, adiestrarse en un arte; **to** — **oneself to do something** enseñarse a hacer algo; habituarse a hacer algo, formarse la costumbre de hacer algo.
trained [treind] *adj teacher etc* graduado, diplomado; *worker* cualificado, capacitado, especializado; *animal* amaestrado; **a well-** **child** un niño (bien) educado, un niño bien enseñado; **a well-** **horse** un caballo bien preparado; **a well-** **army** un ejército disciplinado; **a fully-** **nurse** una enfermera diplomada.
trainee [trei'ni:] *n* aprendiz *m* (profesional), aprendiza *f* (profesional); **business** — aprendiz *m* de comercio, joven *m* que sigue un curso de formación comercial; **management** — aspirante *m* a un puesto en la dirección (de una compañía).
trainer ['treinə*] *n* (a) *(Sport: person)* entrenador *m*, preparador *m* físico; *(of horses)* preparador *m*, cuidador *m*; *(of circus animals)* domador *m*.
　　(b) *(plane)* entrenador *m*.
training ['treiniŋ] 1 *n* adiestramiento *m*; preparación *f*, formación *f* (profesional); orientación *f*; instrucción *f*; *(Mil)* instrucción *f*, ejercicios *mpl*; *(Sport)* entrenamiento *m*, preparación *f* (física); *(of staff for new job)* capacitación *f*; **military** — instrucción *f* militar, *(loosely)* servicio *m* militar; **physical** — gimnasia *f*, cultura *f* física; **to be in** — estar entrenado, estar en forma; **to be out of** — estar desentrenado.
　　2 *adj, attr*: — **camp** campamento *m* de instrucción; — **centre** centro *m* de instrucción; centro *m* de formación laboral; — **manual** manual *m* de instrucción; — **plane** entrenador *m*.
training college ['treiniŋ‚kɔlidʒ] *n* escuela *f* normal.
training ship ['treiniŋʃip] *n* buque-escuela *m*.
trainman ['trainmæn] *n, pl* —**men** [men] ferroviario *m*; guardafrenos *m*.
train oil ['treinɔil] *n* aceite *m* de ballena.
traipse [treips] *vi see* **trapes.**
trait [treit] *n* rasgo *m*.
traitor ['treitə*] *n* traidor *m*; **to be a** — **to one's country** traicionar a la patria; **to turn** — volverse traidor, volver la casaca.
traitorous ['treitərəs] *adj* traidor; traicionero.
traitorously ['treitərəsli] *adv* traidoramente, con traición.
traitress ['treitris] *n* traidora *f*.
Trajan ['treidʒən] *m* Trajano.
trajectory [trə'dʒektəri] *n* trayectoria *f*.
tram [træm] *n*, **tramcar** ['træmka:*] *n* tranvía *m*.
tramlines ['træmlainz] *npl* carriles *mpl* de tranvía.
trammel ['træməl] *vt* poner trabas a, trabar, impedir.
trammels ['træməlz] *npl* trabas *fpl*.
tramp [træmp] 1 *n* (a) *(sound of feet)* marcha *f* pesada, pasos *mpl* pesados.

(b) (*hike*) paseo m largo, caminata f, excursión f a pie; **to go for a — in the hills** hacer una excursión a pie por la montaña; **after a — of many miles** después de recorrer muchos kilómetros a pie; **it's a long —** es mucho camino.

(c) (*person: man*) vago m, vagabundo m; (*woman*) puta f, fulana f; **you (little) —!** ¡lagarta!

(d) (*Naut*) vapor m volandero, mercante m (*also —* **steamer**).

2 *vt* (*stamp on*) pisar con fuerza; (*walk across*) recorrer a pie, hacer una excursión por; **to — the streets** andar (penosamente) por las calles, recorrer (de muy mala gana) las calles; **they had to — it** tuvieron que ir a pie.

3 *vi* marchar pesadamente, andar con pasos pesados; ir a pie; **someone —ed up to the door** alguien se acercó con pasos pesados a la puerta.

trample ['træmpl] **1** *vt* pisar, pisotear, hollar (*also* **to —** **underfoot**).

2 *vi* pisar fuerte, andar con pasos pesados (*also* **to — about, to — along**); **to — on something** pisar algo, pisotear algo, hollar algo; **to — on someone** (*fig*) tratar a uno sin miramientos; **to — on someone's feelings** herir los sentimientos de uno.

trampoline ['træmpəlin] *n* trampolín m.

tramway ['træmwei] *n* tranvía m.

trance [trɑːns] *n* rapto m, arrobamiento m, éxtasis m; (*Med*) catalepsia f; (*spiritualistic*) trance m; **estado m hipnótico; to go into a —** entrar en un estado hipnótico, (*fig*) extasiarse.

tranquil ['træŋkwil] *adj* tranquilo.

tranquility [træŋ'kwiliti] *n* tranquilidad f.

tranquillize, (US) tranquilize ['træŋkwilaiz] *vt* tranquilizar.

tranquillizer, (US) tranquilizer ['træŋkwilaizə*] *n* (*Med*) tranquilizante m.

trans . . . [træns] trans . . .

transact [træn'zækt] *vt* hacer, despachar; tramitar.

transaction [træn'zækʃən] *n* (*deal*) negocio m, transacción f, operación f; (*act*) negociación f, tramitación f; **—s** (*of society*) actas fpl, memorias fpl.

transatlantic ['trænzət'læntik] *adj* transatlántico.

transcend [træn'send] *vt* exceder, superar, rebasar.

transcendence [træn'sendəns] *n*, **transcendency** [træn'sendənsi] *n* superioridad f; lo sobresaliente; (*Philos*) trascendencia f.

transcendent [træn'sendənt] *adj* superior; sobresaliente.

transcendental [.trænsen'dentl] *adj* (*Philos*) trascendental.

transcontinental ['trænz.kɔnti'nentl] *adj* transcontinental.

transcribe [træn'skraib] *vt* transcribir, copiar.

transcript ['trænskript] *n* trasunto m, copia f.

transcription [træn'skripʃən] *n* (*act*) transcripción f; (*copy*) transcripción f, trasunto m, copia f; **phonetic —** pronunciación f figurada.

transept ['trænsept] *n* (*Archit*) crucero m.

transfer ['trænsfə*] *n* **(a)** (*act*) transferencia f, traspaso m; (*Law*) transferencia f, cesión f; enajenación f; transbordo m; (*Sport*) traspaso m; traslado m; **— of ownership** cesión f de propiedad.

(b) (*picture*) cromo m, calcomanía f.

transfer [træns'fə:*] **1** *vt* property etc transferir, traspasar, pasar (*to* a); (*Law*) transferir, ceder; enajenar; passenger etc transbordar; (*Sport*) traspasar; (*to new post, place etc*) trasladar; (*in banking, accounting etc*) transferir; **to — one's affections to another** dar su amor a otro.

2 *vi* (*to a post etc*) trasladarse (*to* a); (*Rail etc*) cambiar, hacer transbordo (*to* a); **to — to a new course** (*Univ*) cambiar a otra asignatura; **the firm is —ring to Quito** la compañía se traslada a Quito.

transferable [træns'fə:rəbl] *adj* transferible; **not — inalienable.**

transference ['trænsfərəns] *n* transferencia f; traspaso m; traslado m.

transfiguration [.trænsfigə'reiʃən] *n* transfiguración f.

transfigure [træns'figə*] *vt* transfigurar, transformar (*into* en).

transfix [træns'fiks] *vt* traspasar, pasar de parte a parte; **to be —ed, to stand —ed** (*fig*) estar totalmente pasmado (*with* de), estar completamente paralizado (*with* de).

transform [træns'fɔ:m] *vt* transformar (*into* en), convertir; metamorfosear (*into* en).

transformation [.trænsfə'meiʃən] *n* transformación f, conversión f; metamorfosis f.

transformer [træns'fɔ:mə*] *n* (*Elec*) transformador m.

transformer station [træns'fɔ:mə.steiʃən] *n* estación f transformadora.

transfuse [træns'fju:z] *vt* transfundir; **blood** hacer una transfusión de.

transfusion [træns'fju:ʒən] *n* transfusión f; **to give someone a blood —** hacer a uno una transfusión de sangre.

transgress [træns'gres] **1** *vt* (*go beyond*) traspasar, exceder, ir más allá de; (*violate*) violar, infringir; (*sin against*) pecar contra.

2 *vi* pecar, cometer una transgresión.

transgression [træns'greʃən] *n* pecado m, transgresión f; infracción f.

transgressor [træns'gresə*] *n* transgresor m, ora f; pecador m, ora f; infractor m, ora f.

tranship [træn'ʃip] *vt* transbordar.

transhipment [træn'ʃipmənt] *n* transbordo m.

transience ['trænziəns] *n* lo pasajero, transitoriedad f.

transient ['trænziənt] **1** *adj* pasajero, transitorio, fugaz. **2** *n* (*US*) transeúnte mf.

transistor [træn'zistə*] *n* transistor m.

transistorized [træn'zistəraizd] *adj* transistorizado.

transit ['trænzit] *n* tránsito m, paso m; **in — de** tránsito, de paso; **— visa** visado m de tránsito.

transition [træn'ziʃən] *n* transición f, paso m (*from* de, *to* a); transformación f, evolución f (*to* en).

transitional [træn'ziʃənəl] *adj* transicional, de transición.

transitive ['trænzitiv] *adj* transitivo.

transitively ['trænzitivli] *adv* transitivamente.

transitory ['trænzitəri] *adj* transitorio.

translatable [trænz'leitəbl] *adj* traducible.

translate [trænz'leit] *vt* **(a)** traducir (*from* de, *into* a); (*fig*) interpretar; **to — words into deeds** dar efecto a palabras, poner por obra lo que sólo son palabras; **how do you — "posh"?** ¿cómo se traduce "posh"?

(b) (*change place or post of*) trasladar (*from* de, *to* a).

translation [trænz'leiʃən] *n* **(a)** traducción f; versión f. **(b)** traslado m.

translator [trænz'leitə*] *n* traductor m, ora f.

transliterate [trænz'litəreit] *vt* transcribir.

translucence [trænz'lu:sns] *n* translucidez f.

translucent [trænz'lu:snt] *adj* translúcido.

transmigrate ['trænzmai'greit] *vi* transmigrar.

transmigration [.trænzmai'greiʃən] *n* transmigración f.

transmissible [trænz'misəbl] *adj* transmisible.

transmission [trænz'miʃən] *n* (*all senses*) transmisión f.

transmit [trænz'mit] *vt* (*all senses*) transmitir (*to* a).

transmitter [trænz'mitə*] *n* (*apparatus*) transmisor m; (*station*) estación f transmisora, emisora f.

transmitting station [trænz'mitiŋ.steiʃən] *n* estación f transmisora, emisora f.

transmogrify [trænz'mɔgrifai] *vt* transformar (como por encanto; *into* en), metamorfosear (extrañamente; *into* en).

transmutable [trænz'mju:təbl] *adj* transmutable.

transmutation [.trænzmju:'teiʃən] *n* transmutación f; (*Bio*) transformismo m.

transmute [trænz'mju:t] *vt* transmutar (*into* en).

transom ['trænsəm] *n* travesaño m.

transparency [træns'peərənsi] *n* (*quality*) transparencia f; (*Phot*) diapositiva f, proyección f.

transparent [træns'peərənt] *adj* transparente, diáfano; (*fig*) claro, limpio; **excuse etc** transparente, clarísimo.

transpiration [.trænspi'reiʃən] *n* transpiración f.

transpire [træns'paiə*] **1** *vt* transpirar.

2 *vi* **(a)** (*of fluid, odour*) transpirar.

(b) (*become known*) revelarse, divulgarse, saberse; **finally it —d that . . .** por fin se supo que . . . , por fin se desprendió que . . .

(c) (*happen*) tener lugar, pasar, ocurrir; **his report on what —d** su informe acerca de lo que pasó.

transplant [træns'plɑ:nt] *vt* trasplantar (*also Med*).

transplantation [.trænsplɑ:n'teiʃən] *n* trasplante m (*also Med.*)

transport ['trænspɔ:t] **1** *n* **(a)** (*general sense*) transporte m; acarreo m; **road —** transportes mpl por carretera; **rail —** transportes mpl por ferrocarril; **Ministry of T—** Ministerio m de Transportes.

(b) (*ship*) navío m de transporte; (*Aer*) avión m de transporte.

(c) (*fig*) transporte m, éxtasis m; **to be in a — of delight** estar extasiado, extasiarse; **to be in a — of rage** estar fuera de sí (de rabia).

2 *attr:* **— costs** gastos mpl de transporte, gastos mpl de acarreo.

transport [træns'pɔːt] vt (a) transportar; llevar, acarrear; (Hist) convict deportar.
(b) (fig) transportar, embelesar; **to be —ed with joy** estar extasiado, extasiarse.
transportable [træns'pɔːtəbl] adj transportable.
transportation [ˌtrænspɔː'teiʃən] n transporte m, transportación f; transportes mpl; (Hist: Law) deportación f; **the — system** el sistema de transportes.
transpose [træns'pəuz] vt transponer, cambiar (into a); (Mus) transportar.
transposition [ˌtrænspə'ziʃən] n transposición f (also Mus), cambio m.
transship [træns'ʃip] vt transbordar.
transshipment [træns'ʃipmənt] n transbordo m.
trans-Siberian [trænzsai'biəriən] adj transiberiano.
transubstantiate [ˌtrænsəb'stænʃieit] vt transustanciar.
transubstantiation ['trænsəbˌstænʃi'eiʃən] n transustanciación f.
transversal [trænz'vəːsəl] adj transversal.
transverse ['trænzvəːs] adj transverso, trasversal.
transversely [trænz'vəːsli] adv transversalmente.
transvestism ['trænzˌvestizəm] n transvestismo m.
transvestite [trænz'vestait] **1** adj transvestido. **2** n transvestido m, a f.
trap [træp] **1** n (a) (general sense) trampa f; (fig) trampa f, lazo m; **it's a —** aquí hay trampa; **to catch an animal in a —** capturar un animal con una trampa; **he was caught in his own —** cayó en su misma trampa; **we were caught like rats in a —** estábamos como ratas en ratonera; **to lure someone into a —** hacer que uno caiga en una trampa; **to set a — for someone** tender un lazo a uno.
(b) (sl) boca f; **to keep one's — shut** callarse; **you keep your — shut about this** de esto no digas ni pío; **shut your —!** ¡callarse!
(c) (Tech) sifón m; bombillo m.
(d) (—door) escotilla f, trampa f; (Theat) escotillón m.
(e) (carriage) coche m ligero de dos ruedas.
2 vt (a) animal coger en una trampa, entrampar, atrapar; coger con trampas.
(b) person atrapar, aprisionar; vehicle, ship etc aprisionar, bloquear; **the miners are —ped** los mineros están aprisionados, los mineros están sepultados; **we were —ped in the snow** estábamos aprisionados por la nieve; **the climbers were —ped** los escaladores estaban atrapados, los escaladores no podían moverse en ninguna dirección.
(c) **to — a ball** (Sport) parar el balón (con los pies); **to — one's foot in the door** cogerse el pie en la puerta.
(d) (fig) hacer caer en el lazo, entrampar; **to — someone into an admission** lograr mediante un ardid que uno haga una confesión; **she —ped him into marriage** logró mañosamente que él se casara con ella; **to — someone into saying something** lograr mañosamente que uno diga algo.
trap door ['træpdɔː*] n escotilla f, trampa f; (Theat) escotillón m.
trapes [treips] vi (fam) ir (a desgana), andar (penosamente); andar sin propósito fijo; **I had to — over to see him** tuve que tomarme la molestia de ir a verle; **we —ed about all morning** pasamos la mañana yendo de acá para allá.
trapeze [trə'piːz] n trapecio m (de circo, de gimnasia).
trapeze artist [trə'piːzˌɑːtist] n trapecista mf.
trapezium [trə'piːziəm] n (Math) trapecio m.
trapezoid ['træpizɔid] n trapezoide m.
trapper ['træpə*] n cazador m (esp de animales de piel), trampero m.
trappings ['træpiŋz] npl arreos mpl; jaeces mpl; (fig) adornos mpl, galas fpl; **shorn of all its —** sin ninguno de sus adornos, desprovisto de adorno; **that statement, shorn of its — ...** esa declaración, en términos sencillos ...; **with all the — of kingship** con todo el boato de la monarquía.
Trappist ['træpist] **1** adj trapense. **2** n trapense m.
traps [træps] npl (fam) cosas fpl, chismes mpl, cachivaches mpl; **to pack up one's —s** hacer las maletas, (fig) liar el petate (fam).
trash [træʃ] n pacotilla f, hojarasca f; trastos mpl viejos; **the book is —** el libro es una basura, el libro no vale para nada; **he talks a lot of —** no dice más que tonterías; **human —** gente f inútil, personas fpl inútiles; **—!** ¡tonterías!
trash can ['træʃˌkæn] n (US) cubo m de la basura.
trashy ['træʃi] adj inútil, baladí.
trauma ['trɔːmə] n trauma m.
traumatic [trɔː'mætik] adj traumático.
traumatism ['trɔːmætizəm] n traumatismo m.
travail ['træveil] n (arch or hum: Med) dolores mpl

del parto; **to be in —** afanarse, azacanarse; (Med) estar de parto.
travel ['trævl] **1** n (a) viajes mpl, el viajar; **—s** viajes mpl; **to be on one's —s** estar de viaje.
(b) (Mech) recorrido m.
2 attr agency etc de viajes, de turismo.
3 vt (a) country etc viajar por (todas partes de), recorrer.
(b) distance recorrer, hacer, cubrir; **we —led 50 miles that day** ese día cubrimos 50 millas.
4 vi (a) (make a journey) viajar; **to — by car** viajar en coche, ir en coche; **he —s into the centre to work** se desplaza al centro a trabajar; **they have —led a lot** han viajado mucho, han visto mucho mundo; **to — round the world** dar la vuelta al mundo; **to — over** viajar por, recorrer; **we've —led a lot since then** (fig) hemos recorrido mucho terreno desde entonces, mucho ha llovido desde entonces.
(b) (go at a speed etc) ir; **it —s at 600 mph** tiene una velocidad de 600 mph; **we were —ling at 30 mph** íbamos a 30 mph; **you were —ling too fast** Vd iba a la velocidad excesiva, Vd iba demasiado de prisa; **he was certainly —ling** es cierto que iba a buen tren; **light —s at a speed of ...** la luz viaja a una velocidad de ...; **news —s fast** las noticias se propagan con una rapidez extraordinaria.
(c) (move, pass) correr; moverse, desplazarse; **it —s along this wire** corre por este hilo; **it doesn't — freely on its rod** no corre lisamente por la varilla; **it —s 3 centimetres** (Mech) tiene un recorrido de 3 centímetros; **his eye —led slowly over the scene** examinó detenidamente la escena.
(d) (reach) llegar, extenderse; **will it — that far?** ¿llega hasta allí?, ¿se puede estirar hasta allí?
(e) (of wine etc) poderse transportar; **it's a nice wine but it won't —** es un buen vino pero pierde calidad cuando se le transporta.
(f) (Comm) ser viajante; **he —s for Pérez** es viajante de la compañía Pérez; **he —s in underwear** es viajante de una compañía que fabrica ropa interior; **he —s in soap** es viajante en jabones.
travelled, (US) **traveled** ['trævld] adj que ha viajado; **much —, widely —** que ha viajado mucho, que ha visto mucho mundo.
traveller, (US) **traveler** ['trævlə*] n viajero m, a f; (Comm) viajante m (also commercial —); **a — in soap** un viajante en jabones.
traveller's joy, (US) **traveler's joy** ['trævləz'dʒɔi] n (Bot) clemátide f.
travelling, (US) **traveling** ['trævliŋ] **1** adj, attr salesman, exhibition etc ambulante; expenses de viaje; crane etc corredero, corredizo; bag, rug de viaje.
2 n el viajar, viajes mpl.
travelogue ['trævlɔg] n película f de viajes; documental m de interés turístico.
travel sickness ['trævlˌsikniss] n propensión f a marearse en un coche (or avión etc).
travel-worn ['trævlwɔːn] adj fatigado por el viaje, rendido después de tanto viajar.
traverse ['trævəs] **1** n (Tech) travesaño m; (Mil) través m; (Mountaineering) escalada f oblicua, camino m oblicuo.
2 vt atravesar, cruzar; recorrer; pasar por; **we are traversing a difficult period** atravesamos un momento difícil.
3 vi (Mountaineering) hacer una escalada oblicua.
travesty ['trævisti] **1** n parodia f (also fig). **2** vt parodiar.
trawl [trɔːl] **1** n red f barredera.
2 vt rastrear; dragar; **to — up** pescar, sacar a la superficie.
3 vi pescar al arrastre, rastrear.
trawler ['trɔːlə*] n barco m rastreador, barco m de pesca a la rastra.
trawling ['trɔːliŋ] n pesca f a la rastra.
tray [trei] n bandeja f; (of balance) platillo m; (drawer) cajón m, batea f; (Phot, Tech) cubeta f.
traycloth ['treiklɔθ] n cubrebandeja m.
treacherous ['tretʃərəs] adj traidor, traicionero; falso; (fig) engañoso, incierto, nada seguro; memory infiel; ground movedizo; ice etc peligroso, poco firme.
treacherously ['tretʃərəsli] adv traidoramente, a traición; falsamente; engañosamente; peligrosamente.
treachery ['tretʃəri] n traición f, perfidia f; falsedad f; **an act of —** una traición.
treacle ['triːkl] n melado m, melaza f.

treacly ['tri:kli] *adj* parecido a melado; cubierto de melado.

tread [tred] **1** *n* (a) (*step*) paso *m*, pisada *f*; (*gait*) andar *m*, modo *m* de andar; **with heavy —** con pasos pesados, pisando fuertemente; **with measured —** con pasos rítmicos.

(b) (*of stair*) huella *f*; (*of shoe*) suela *f*; (*of tyre*) huella *f*, (banda *f* de) rodamiento *m*.

2 (*irr: pret* **trod**, *ptp* **trodden**) *vt* (*also* **to — down, to — underfoot**) pisar, pisotear, hollar; *path* batir, (*fig*) abrir; *grapes* pisar; *dance* bailar; **to — water** pedalear en agua; **a place never trodden by human féet** un sitio no hollado por pie humano; **he trod his cigarette end into the mud** apagó la colilla pisándola en el lodo.

3 *vi* pisar; poner el pie; **to — on** pisar; **to — on someone's heels** pisar los talones a uno; **careful you don't — on it!** ¡ojo, que lo vas a pisar!; **to — carefully, to — warily** (*fig*) andar con pies de plomo; **we must — very carefully in this matter** en este asunto conviene andar con pies de plomo; **to — softly** pisar dulcemente, no hacer ruido al andar.

treadle ['tredl] **1** *n* pedal *m*. **2** *vi* pedalear.

treadmill ['tredmil] *n* rueda *f* de andar; (*fig*) rutina *f*, monotonía *f*; tráfago *m*; **back to the —!** ¡volvamos al trabajo!

treason ['tri:zn] *n* traición *f*; **high —** alta traición *f*.

treasonable ['tri:zənəbl] *adj* traidor, desleal.

treasure ['treʒə*] **1** *n* tesoro *m*; (*fig*) tesoro *m*; joya *f*, preciosidad *f*; **yes, my —** sí, mi tesoro; **—s of Spanish art** joyas *fpl* del arte español; **our charlady is a real —** nuestra asistenta es una verdadera joya.

2 *vt* (a) **to — up** atesorar; guardar, acumular.

(b) (*fig*) guardar como un tesoro; apreciar muchísimo; *memory etc* guardar.

treasure-house ['treʒəhaus] *n*, *pl* **—houses** [,hauziz] tesoro *m* (*also fig*).

treasure hunt ['treʒəhʌnt] *n* (*game*) caza *f* al tesoro.

treasurer ['treʒərə*] *n* tesorero *m*.

treasure-trove ['treʒətrəuv] *n* tesoro *m* hallado; (*fig*) tesoro *m*.

treasury ['treʒəri] **1** *n* (a) tesoro *m*, tesorería *f*, erario *m*, hacienda *f*; **T— (*Brit*), T— Department (*US*)** Ministerio *m* de Hacienda.

(b) (*anthology*) tesoro *m*, antología *f*, florilegio *m*.

2 *attr*: **T— Bench (*Brit Pol*)** banco *m* azul, banco *m* del gobierno; **— bill** vale *m* de la Hacienda.

treat [tri:t] **1** *n* (a) (*entertainment*) convite *m*, extraordinario *m*; (*present*) regalo *m*; (*outing*) visita *f*; **it's my —** invito yo; **to have a Dutch —** pagar cada uno su cuota, ir a escote; **to stand someone a —** invitar a uno a un extraordinario.

(b) (*pleasure*) placer *m*, gusto *m*; recompensa *f* (especial); **a — in store** un placer futuro, un placer guardado para el futuro; **it is a — to hear you** da gusto escucharte, es un placer escucharte; **it's no sort of — for me** para mí no es ningún placer; **just to give them all a —** sólo para darles placer a todos; **to give oneself a —** permitirse un lujo, permitirse hacer algo no acostumbrado.

2 *vt* (a) (*behave towards*) tratar; **to — someone well** tratar bien a uno; **to — someone as if he were a child** tratar a uno como a un niño; **to — something as a joke** tomar algo en broma, tomar algo en chunga.

(b) (*invite*) invitar, convidar (*to* a); **I'm —ing you** invito yo; **they —ed him to a dinner** le obsequiaron con un banquete; **let me — you to a drink** permítame invitarle a tomar algo.

(c) (*Med*) tratar, curar; atender, asistir; **to — someone for a broken leg** curar la pierna rota de uno; **to — someone with X-rays** dar a uno un tratamiento de rayos X; **which doctor is —ing you?** ¿qué médico le atiende?

(d) (*Tech*) tratar; **to — a substance with acid** tratar una sustancia con ácido.

(e) *subject, theme* tratar, discutir; **he —s the subject objectively** trata el asunto con objetividad.

3 *vi* (a) (*negotiate*) **to — for peace** pedir la paz; **to — with someone** tratar con uno, negociar con uno.

(b) (*discuss*) **to — of** tratar de, discutir; versar sobre.

4 *vr*: **to — oneself to something** permitirse el lujo, permitirse hacer algo no acostumbrado.

treatise ['tri:tiz] *n* tratado *m*.

treatment ['tri:tmənt] *n* tratamiento *m*; (*Med*) tratamiento *m*, cura *f*, medicación *f*; **good —** buen tratamiento *m*, buenos tratos *mpl*; **medical —** tratamiento *m* médico; asistencia *f* médica; **preferential — (*Comm*)** trato *m* preferente; **his —**

of his parents su conducta con sus padres; **our — of foreigners** el trato que damos a los extranjeros; **to give someone the — (*fam*)** hacer sufrir a uno; **to respond to —** responder al tratamiento.

treaty ['tri:ti] *n* tratado *m*.

treble ['trebl] **1** *adj* triple; (*Mus*) de tiple; **— clef** clave *f* de sol.

2 *n* (*Mus*) tiple *mf*; voz *f* de tiple.

3 *vt* triplicar.

4 *vi* triplicarse.

trebly ['trebli] *adv* tres veces; **it is — dangerous to ...** es tres veces más peligroso ...

tree [tri:] **1** *n* árbol *m*; (*for shoes*) horma *f*; (*of saddle*) arzón *m*; **family —** árbol *m* genealógico; **— of knowledge** árbol *m* de la ciencia; **to be at the top of the —** estar en la cumbre de su profesión; **to be up a — (*fam*)** estar en un aprieto; **to be barking up the wrong —** tomar el rábano por las hojas.

2 *vt* *animal etc* ahuyentar por un árbol, hacer refugiarse en un árbol.

tree-covered ['tri:,kʌvəd] *adj* arbolado.

tree creeper ['tri:,kri:pə*] *n* agateador *m*.

tree frog ['tri:frɔg] *n* rana *f* de San Antonio, rana *f* arbórea.

treeless ['tri:lis] *adj* pelado, sin árboles.

tree-lined ['tri:laind] *adj*: **— street** calle *f* con árboles en las aceras, alameda *f*.

treetop ['tri:tɔp] *n* copa *f*, cima *f* de árbol.

tree trunk ['tri:trʌnk] *n* tronco *m* de árbol.

trefoil ['trefɔil] *n* trébol *m*.

trek [trek] **1** *n* migración *f*; (*day's march*) jornada *f*; (*fam*) viaje *m* largo y aburrido; caminata *f*; excursión *f*.

2 *vi* emigrar; viajar; (*fam*) ir (de mala gana), caminar (penosamente); **we —ked for days on end** caminamos día tras día; **I had to — up to the top floor** tuve que darme la molestia de subir al último piso.

trellis ['trelis] *n* enrejado *m*; (*Bot*) espaldera *f*, espaldar *m*.

trelliswork ['treliswə:k] *n* enrejado *m*.

tremble ['trembl] **1** *n* temblor *m*, estremecimiento *m*; **to be all of a —** estar todo tembloroso; **she said with a —** dijo temblando.

2 *vi* temblar, estremecerse (*at* ante, *with* de); vibrar; agitarse; **to — all over** estar todo tembloroso.

trembling ['tremblin] **1** *adj* tembloroso. **2** *n* temblar *m*, temblor *m*, estremecimiento *m*; vibración *f*; agitación *f*.

tremendous [trə'mendəs] *adj* tremendo, inmenso, formidable; (*fam*) tremendo, estupendo; **that's —!** ¡qué estupendo!; **there was a — crowd** había una inmensa multitud.

tremendously [trə'mendəsli] *adv* tremendamente; **— good** tremendamente bueno.

tremor ['tremə*] *n* temblor *m*; estremecimiento *m*; vibración *f*; **earth —** temblor *m* de tierra; **he said without a —** dijo sin inmutarse.

tremulous ['tremjuləs] *adj* trémulo, tembloroso; tímido.

tremulously ['tremjuləsli] *adv* trémulamente; tímidamente.

trench [trentʃ] **1** *n* zanja *f*, foso *m*; (*Mil*) trinchera *f*; (*shelter*) refugio *m* antiaéreo.

2 *vt* hacer zanjas (*or* fosos) en; (*Mil*) hacer trincheras en, atrincherar; (*Agr*) excavar, remover.

trenchant ['trentʃənt] *adj* mordaz, incisivo.

trenchantly ['trentʃəntli] *adv* mordazmente.

trench coat ['trentʃkəut] *n* trinchera *f*.

trencher ['trentʃə*] *n* tajadero *m*.

trencherman ['trentʃəmæn] *n*, *pl* **—men** [mən]: **to be a good —** comer bien, tener siempre buen apetito.

trend [trend] **1** *n* tendencia *f*; curso *m*, dirección *f*, marcha *f*; (*fashion*) boga *f*, moda *f*; **now there is a — towards ...** ahora hay tendencia hacia ...; **—s in popular music** tendencias *fpl* de la música popular.

2 *vi* tender.

trendy ['trendi] *adj* (*sl*) según la última moda, elegante; de acuerdo con las tendencias actuales, modernísimo.

Trent [trent] Trento.

trepan [tri'pæn] *vt* trepanar.

trephine [tre'fi:n] *vt* trefinar.

trepidation [,trepi'deiʃən] *n* turbación *f*, agitación *f*; **in some —** algo turbado, agitado.

trespass ['trespəs] **1** *n* (*illegal entry*) intrusión *f*, entrada *f* ilegal; entrada *f* sin derecho, penetración *f* en finca ajena; (*transgression*) infracción *f*, violación *f*, ofensa *f*; (*Eccl*) pecado *m*; **forgive us our —es** perdónanos nuestras deudas.

2 *vi* entrar sin derecho (*on* en), entrar ilegalmente (*on* en); penetración *f* en finca ajena; **to — against** infringir, violar, (*Eccl*) pecar contra; **to — upon** (*fig*) abusar de; **to — upon someone's privacy** invadir la vida íntima de uno; **may I — upon your kindness to ask that...** permítame molestarle pidiendo que...; perdone Vd que le moleste pidiendo que...

trespasser ['trespəsə*] *n* intruso *m*, a *f*; "**T—s will be prosecuted**" "Se procesará a los intrusos", (*loosely*) "Prohibida la entrada".

tress [tres] *n* trenza *f*; **—es** cabellera *f*, pelo *m*.

trestle ['tresl] *n* caballete *m*.

trestle bridge ['tresl'bridʒ] *n* puente *m* de caballetes.

trestle table ['tresl'teibl] *n* mesa *f* de caballete.

trews [truːz] *npl* (*Scot*) pantalón *m*.

tri... [trai] tri...

triad ['traiəd] *n* tríada *f*.

trial ['traiəl] **1** *n* (**a**) (*Law*) proceso *m*, juicio *m*, vista *f* de una causa; **— by jury** juicio *m* por jurado; **new —** revisión *f*; **to be on —** estar en juicio; **to be on — for one's part in a crime** ser procesado por su complicidad en un crimen; **to be on — for one's life** ser acusado de un crimen que pudiera castigarse con pena de muerte; **to bring someone to —** procesar a uno; **to commit someone for —** remitir a uno al tribunal; **to go on —, to stand one's —** ser procesado.
(**b**) (*test*) prueba *f*, ensayo *m*; tentativa *f*; (*of sheepdogs etc*) concurso *m*; **—s** (*Sport, Tech*) pruebas *fpl*; **— of strength** lucha *f*; **by a system of — and error** por un sistema de prueba y desacierto, por un método de tanteos; **to be on —** estar a prueba; **to give someone a —** poner a uno a prueba.
(**c**) (*hardship*) aflicción *f*, adversidad *f*; desgracia *f*; (*nuisance*) molestia *f*; **the —s of old age** las aflicciones de la vejez; **the child is a great — to them** el niño les amarga la vida, el niño es terrible.
2 *attr* (**a**) (*Law*) procesal; relativo al proceso.
(**b**) de prueba, de ensayo; **— flight** vuelo *m* de prueba; **— run, — trip** viaje *m* de ensayo.

triangle ['traiæŋgl] *n* triángulo *m* (*also Mus*).

triangular [trai'æŋgjulə*] *adj* triangular.

triangulate [trai'æŋgjuleit] *vt* triangular.

triangulation [trai.æŋgju'leiʃən] *n* triangulación *f*.

tribal ['traibəl] *adj* tribal, tribual.

tribalism ['traibəlizəm] *n* organización *f* en tribus; sistema *m* de tribus; mentalidad *f* de la tribu.

tribe [traib] *n* tribu *f* (*also Zool*); (*fig*) tropel *f*, masa *f*; ralea *f*.

tribesman ['traibzmən] *n*, *pl* **—men** [mən] miembro *m* de una tribu; **to stir up the tribesmen** sublevar las tribus; **the tribesmen are friendly** las tribus no son peligrosas.

tribulation [.tribju'leiʃən] *n* tribulación *f*; **—s** aflicciones *fpl*, dificultades *fpl*, sufrimientos *mpl*.

tribunal [trai'bjuːnl] *n* tribunal *m*.

tribune ['tribjuːn] *n* (*stand*) tribuna *f*; (*person*) tribuno *m*.

tributary ['tribjutəri] **1** *adj* tributario. **2** *n* (*person*) tributario *m*; (*Geog*) afluente *m*.

tribute ['tribjuːt] *n* (*payment, tax*) tributo *m*; (*fig*) homenaje *m*; elogio *m*; **floral —** ofrenda *f* floral; **that is a — to his loyalty** eso acredita su lealtad, eso hace honor a su lealtad; **to pay — to** rendir homenaje a, elogiar, pronunciar elogios de.

trice [trais] *n*: **in a —** en un santiamén.

trichina [tri'kainə] *n* triquina *f*.

trichinosis [.triki'nəusis] *n* triquinosis *f*.

trick [trik] **1** *n* (**a**) (*deceit*) engaño *m*, truco *m*; (*swindle*) estafa *f*; (*ruse*) trampa *f*, ardid *f*, estratagema *f*; (*harmless deception*) travesura *f*; (*hoax*) trastada *f*, primada *f*, burla *f*; **dirty —, low —,** **shabby —** mala pasada *f*, faena *f*; **—s of the trade** trucos *mpl* del oficio, triquiñuelas *fpl* del oficio; **there must be a — in it** aquí debe haber trampa; **he's up to all the —s, he knows a — or two** se lo sabe todo; **he's up to his old —s again** ha vuelto a hacer de las suyas; **I know a — worth two of that** yo me sé algo mucho mejor; **to play a — on someone** hacer una mala pasada a uno, hacer una faena a uno; (*practical joke*) gastar una broma a uno; **his memory played him a —** le falló la memoria; **unless my eyes are playing me —s** a menos que me engañen mis ojos.
(**b**) (*peculiarity*) peculiaridad *f* (*personal*); (*custom*) hábito *m*, manía *f*; **— of style** ciertas peculiaridades estilísticas, ciertos rasgos del estilo; **it's just a —** he has es una manía suya; **it's a — of the light** es una ilusión de la luz; **history has a — of repeating itself** la historia tiene tendencia a repetirse.

(**c**) (*card —*) juego *m* de naipes, truco *m* de naipes; (*conjuring —*) juego *m* de manos; **the whole bag of —s** todo el negocio; todo ello; **that should do the —** eso seguramente será satisfactorio, eso habrá de bastar.
(**d**) (*Cards*) baza *f*; **to take all the —s** ganar (*or* hacer) todas las bazas; **he doesn't miss a —** (*fig*) es la mar de listo; no pierde detalle por pequeño que sea.
(**e**) (*knack*) tino *m*, truco *m*; **to get the — of it** coger el tino, aprender el modo de hacer algo.
2 *attr*: **— photography** trucaje *m*; **— question** pregunta *f* de pega; **— riding** acrobacia *f* ecuestre.
3 *vt* (**a**) (*deceive*) engañar; trampear; burlar; (*swindle*) estafar, timar; **we were —d** nos engañaron, nos dejamos engañar; **to — someone into doing something** lograr mañosamente que uno haga algo, inducir fraudulentamente a uno a hacer algo; **to — someone out of something** quitar mañosamente algo a uno, estafar algo a uno.
(**b**) **to — out** (*decorate*) ataviar, adornar (*with* de).

trickery ['trikəri] *n* astucia *f*, superchería *f*, mañas *fpl*; (*Law*) fraude *m*; **to obtain something by —** obtener algo fraudulentamente.

trickle ['trikl] **1** *n* hilo *m*, chorro *m* delgado, goteo *m*; (*fig*) pequeña cantidad *f*; **a — of people** unas pocas personas; **we received a — of news** nos llegaba alguna noticia de vez en cuando; **what was a — is now a flood** lo que era un goteo es ya un torrente.
2 *vt* dejar caer gota a gota, dejar salir en un chorro delgado; **you're trickling blood** estás sangrando un poquito.
3 *vi* (**a**) gotear, salir gota a gota, salir en un chorro delgado; (*fig*) salir poco a poco; **blood —d down his cheek** la sangre le corría gota a gota por la mejilla; **our money is trickling away** nuestro dinero se consume poco a poco.
(**b**) (*of persons*) salir (*etc*) poco a poco; **people kept trickling in** iban llegando unas cuantas personas; **shall we — over to the café?** (*fam*) ¿nos trasladamos al café?

trickster ['trikstə*] *n* estafador *m*, embustero *m*.

tricky ['triki] *adj person* astuto; mañoso, tramposo; *situation etc* delicado, difícil; *problem* espinoso; **it's all rather —** es un poco complicado, es un tanto difícil.

tricolour ['trikələ*] *n* tricolor *f*, bandera *f* tricolor.

tricot ['trikəu] *n* tejido *m* de punto.

tricycle ['traisikl] *n* triciclo *m*.

trident ['traidənt] *n* tridente *m*.

tried [traid] *adj* probado, de toda garantía.

triennial [trai'eniəl] *adj* trienal.

triennially [trai'eniəli] *adv* trienalmente, cada tres años.

trier ['traiə*] *n* persona *f* que se esfuerza mucho.

trifle ['traifl] **1** *n* (**a**) (*unimportant thing*) friolera *f*, bagatela *f*, fruslería *f*; **£5 is a mere —** 5 libras son una bagatela; **he worries about —s** se preocupa por pequeñeces; **any — can distract her** le distrae cualquier tontería; **you could have bought it for a —** hubieras podido comprarlo por muy poco dinero.
(**b**) **a —** (*as adv*) un poquito, un poquitín; **it's a — difficult** es un tantico difícil; **it's a — too much** es un poquito demasiado; **we were a — put out** quedamos un poquito desconcertados.
(**c**) (*Cook*) dulce *m* de bizcocho borracho.
2 *vt*: **to — away** malgastar, desperdiciar; *money* despilfarrar.
3 *vi*: **to — with one's food** comer melindrosamente, hacer melindres al comer; **to — with someone** jugar con uno, tratar a uno con poca seriedad; **he's not a person to be —d with** es persona que hay que tratar con la mayor seriedad; **to — with a girl's affections** divertirse fingiendo querer a una joven.

trifler ['traiflə*] *n* persona *f* frívola, persona *f* informal.

trifling ['traiflin] *adj* insignificante, sin importancia, de poca monta.

triforium [trai'fɔːriəm] *n* triforio *m*.

trigger ['trigə*] **1** *n* (*Mil*) gatillo *m*; (*Tech*) disparador *m*, tirador *m*.
2 *vt*: **to — off** hacer estallar; (*fig*) provocar, hacer estallar, desencadenar.

trigger finger ['trigə.fiŋgə*] *n* índice *m* de la mano derecha (empleado para apretar el gatillo).

trigger-happy ['trigə.hæpi] *adj* que está dispuesto a apretar el gatillo por cualquier motivo.

trigonometric(al) ['trigənə'metrik(əl)] *adj* trigonométrico.
trigonometry [,trigə'nɔmitri] *n* trigonometría *f.*
trike [traik] *n (fam)* triciclo *m.*
trilateral ['trai'lætərəl] *adj* trilátero.
trilby ['trilbi] *n* sombrero *m* flexible.
trilingual ['trai'liŋgwəl] *adj* trilingüe.
trill [tril] 1 *n (of bird)* trino *m*, gorjeo *m; (Mus)* trino *m*, quiebro *m; (of R)* vibración *f.* 2 *vt* pronunciar con vibración. 3 *vi* trinar, gorjear.
trillion ['triliən] *n (Brit)* trillón *m; (US)* billón *m.*
trilogy ['trilədʒi] *n* trilogía *f.*
trim [trim] 1 *adj* aseado, arreglado; elegante; en buen estado; she has a — figure tiene buen tipo.
　2 *n* (a) *(condition)* estado *m*, condición *f;* buen estado *m; (of boat)* asiento *m; (of sails)* orientación *f;* in good — en buen estado, en buenas condiciones, *person* en forma; in fighting — listo para el combate, listo para entrar en acción; to get things into — arreglar las cosas; hacer sus preparativos.
　(b) *(cut)* recorte *m;* to give one's hair a — recortarse el pelo.
　3 *vt* (a) *(tidy)* arreglar, ordenar; disponer; ajustar, componer; *boat* equilibrar; *sails* orientar; to — up arreglar, componer.
　(b) *(Sewing) dress* adornar, guarnecer *(with* de); sleeves —med with lace mangas *fpl* guarnecidas de encaje.
　(c) *(cut)* cortar; *hair, hedge* recortar; *bush etc* podar; *lamp, wick* despabilar; *wood* desbastar, alisar.
　4 *vr:* to — oneself up arreglarse.
trimming ['trimiŋ] *n* adorno *m*, guarnición *f;* orla *f;* —s *(cuttings)* recortes *mpl; (adornments)* adornos *mpl;* accesorios *mpl; (pej)* arrequives *mpl;* without all the —s sin todos aquellos adornos.
trimness ['trimnis] *n* aseo *m;* elegancia *f;* buen estado *m.*
Trinidad ['trinidæd] Trinidad *f.*
trinitrotoluene [trai'naitrəu'tɔljuːiːn] *n* trinitrotolueno *m.*
Trinity ['triniti] *n* Trinidad *f.*
trinket ['triŋkit] *n* dije *m*, chuchería *f; (pej)* baratijas *fpl*, chucherías *fpl.*
trinomial [trai'nəumiəl] 1 *adj* trinomio. 2 *n* trinomio *m.*
trio ['triəu] *n* trío *m.*
trip [trip] 1 *n* (a) *(journey)* viaje *m; (excursion)* excursión *f;* business — viaje *m* de negocios; cheap —s to Majorca viajes *mpl* en plan económico a Mallorca; pleasure — viaje *m* de recreo; excursión *f;* round — viaje *m* de ida y vuelta; tourist — viaje *m* turístico; excursión *f* turística ; he's away on a — está de viaje; to take a — hacer un viaje; salir de excursión; I must take a — into town tengo que ir a la ciudad.
　(b) *(stumble)* tropiezo *m*, traspié *m; (in wrestling etc)* zancadilla *f; (fig)* desliz *m*, tropiezo *m.*
　(c) *(Mech)* trinquete *m*, disparo *m.*
　2 *vt (also* to — up) hacer tropezar, hacer caer, *(deliberately)* echar la zancadilla a; to — someone up *(fig)* coger a uno en una falta; the fourth question —ped him up la cuarta pregunta le confundió, la cuarta pregunta le desconcertó.
　3 *vi* (a) to — along, to go —ing along andar *(or* ir, correr *etc)* con paso ligero, andar airosamente.
　(b) *(also* to — up) tropezar *(against, on, over* en), caer, dar un tropezón; *(fig)* tropezar, equivocarse.
tripartite ['trai'paːtait] *adj* tripartito.
tripe [traip] *n* (a) *(Cook)* callos *mpl;* —s *(Anat, hum)* tripas *fpl.*
　(b) *(fam)* tonterías *fpl*, bobadas *fpl;* what utter —! ¡tonterías!; he talks a lot of — no habla más que bobadas.
triphase ['traifeiz] *adj (Elec)* trifásico.
triphthong ['trifθɔŋ] *n* triptongo *m.*
triple ['tripl] 1 *adj* triple; — the sum el triple; T— Alliance Triple Alianza *f.*
　2 *n* triple *m.*
　3 *vt* triplicar.
　4 *vi* triplicarse.
triplet ['triplit] *n (Mus)* tresillo *m; (Poet)* terceto *m;* —s *(persons)* trillizos *mpl*, as *fpl.*
triplicate ['triplikit] 1 *adj* triplicado. 2 *n:* in — por triplicado.
triplicate ['triplikeit] *vt* triplicar.
triply ['tripli] *adv* tres veces; — dangerous tres veces más peligroso.
tripod ['traipɔd] *n* trípode *m.*
tripper ['tripə*] *n* excursionista *mf;* turista *mf* (que hace una visita de un día).

tripping ['tripiŋ] *adj* ligero, airoso.
trippingly ['tripiŋli] *adv* ligeramente, airosamente.
triptych ['triptik] *n* tríptico *m.*
trireme ['trairiːm] *n* trirreme *m.*
trisect [trai'sekt], *vt* trisecar.
Tristram ['tristrəm] *n* Tristán.
trisyllabic ['traisi'læbik] *adj* trisilábico.
trisyllable ['trai'siləbl] *n* trisílabo *m.*
trite [trait] *adj* vulgar, trivial; gastado, trillado y llevado.
triteness ['traitnis] *n* vulgaridad *f*, trivialidad *f;* lo gastado.
Triton ['traitn] *m* Tritón.
triturate ['tritʃəreit] *vt* triturar.
trituration [,tritʃə'reiʃən] *n* trituración *f.*
triumph ['traiʌmf] 1 *n* triunfo *m;* éxito *m;* a new — for Slobodian industry nuevo éxito de la industria eslobodia; to achieve a great — obtener un gran éxito; it is a — of man over nature en esto el hombre triunfa de la naturaleza; to come home in — volver a casa triunfalmente.
　2 *vi* triunfar; to — over triunfar de, vencer.
triumphal [trai'ʌmfəl] *adj* triunfal.
triumphant [trai'ʌmfənt] *adj* triunfante; victorioso; he was — estaba jubiloso, estaba lleno de júbilo.
triumphantly [trai'ʌmfəntli] *adv* triunfalmente, de modo triunfal; he said — dijo en tono triunfal.
triumvirate [trai'ʌmvirit] *n* triunvirato *m.*
trivia ['triviə] *npl* trivialidades *fpl.*
trivial ['triviəl] *adj* trivial, insignificante; banal; superficial; *excuse, pretext etc* frívolo, poco serio.
triviality [,trivi'æliti] *n* trivialidad *f*, insignificancia *f;* banalidad *f;* superficialidad *f;* frivolidad *f*, falta *f* de seriedad; trivialidades *fpl.*
triweekly ['trai'wiːkli] 1 *adj* trisemanal. 2 *adv* trisemanalmente, tres veces por semana.
trochaic [trə'keiik] *adj* trocaico.
trochee ['trɔkiː] *n* troqueo *m.*
trod [trɔd] *pret of* **tread.**
trodden ['trɔdn] *ptp of* **tread.**
troglodyte ['trɔglədait] *n* troglodita *m.*
troika ['trɔikə] *n* troica *f.*
Trojan ['trəudʒən] 1 *adj* troyano; — horse caballo *m* de Troya; — War Guerra *f* de Troya. 2 *n* troyano *m*, a *f.*
troll [trəul] *n* gnomo *m*, duende *m.*
trolley ['trɔli] *n (hand —)* carretilla *f; (tea —)* mesita *f* de ruedas; *(child's)* carretón *m; (Tech)* corredera *f* elevada; *(Elec)* trole *m*, arco *m* de trole; *(US)* tranvía *m.*
trolley bus ['trɔlibʌs] *n* trolebús *m.*
trolley car ['trɔlika:*] *n (US)* tranvía *m.*
trolley pole ['trɔlipəul] *n* trole *m.*
trollop ['trɔləp] *n* marrana *f;* puta *f.*
trombone [trɔm'bəun] *n* trombón *m.*
trombonist [trɔm'bəunist] *n* trombón *m.*
troop [truːp] 1 *n* (a) banda *f*, grupo *m*, compañía *f; (Mil)* tropa *f*, *(of cavalry)* escuadrón *m; (Theat) see* troupe; —s *(Mil)* tropas *fpl;* to come in a — venir en tropel, venir en masa.
　(b) the steady — of feet el ruido rítmico de pasos.
　2 *vt:* to — the colour presentar la bandera, desfilar con la bandera.
　3 *vi:* to — along marchar (todos juntos); to — away, to — off marcharse en tropel; to — out salir todos juntos, salir en masa; to — past desfilar (ante); to — together reunirse en masa.
troop carrier ['truːp,kæriə*] *n (Naut)* transporte *m; (Aut)* camión *m* blindado.
trooper ['truːpə*] *n* soldado *m* de caballería; state — *(US)* soldado *m* de reserva.
troopship ['truːpʃip] *n* transporte *m.*
troop train ['truːptrein] *n* tren *m* militar.
trope [trəup] *n* tropo *m.*
trophy ['trəufi] *n* trofeo *m.*
tropic ['trɔpik] *n* trópico *m;* —s trópicos *mpl*, zona *f* tropical; T— of Cancer trópico *m* de Cáncer; T— of Capricorn trópico *m* de Capricornio.
tropic(al) ['trɔpik(əl)] *adj* tropical.
trot[1] [trɔt] 1 trote *m;* at an easy —, at a slow — a trote corto; to break into a — empezar a trotar; for 5 days on the — durante 5 días seguidos; to be always on the — estar ocupado siempre; tener una vida ajetreada; to keep someone on the — no dejar a uno descansar.
　2 *vt* (a) *horse* hacer trotar.
　(b) to — out *excuses etc* ensartar; *arguments* sacar a relucir, presentar otra vez; *erudition* hacer alarde de.
　3 *vi* (a) trotar, ir al trote.

(b) (fam: of person) ir; irse, marcharse; **he —s round to the shop** va a la tienda; **we must be —ting** es hora de marcharnos.
trot² [trɔt] n (US sl) chuleta f.
troth [trəυθ] n (arch or hum) see **plight**.
trotter ['trɔtə*] n (horse) trotón m, caballo m trotón; (Cook) pie m de cerdo, manita f de cerdo.
troubadour ['tru:bədɔ:*] n trovador m.
rouble ['trʌbl] **1** n **(a)** (grief, affliction) aflicción f; pena f, angustia f; (misfortune) desgracia f, desventura f; (worry) inquietud f, preocupación f; (jam) apuro m, aprieto m; **to be in** — estar en un apuro; **to be in great** — estar muy apurado; **now your —s are over** ya no tendrás de que preocuparte, se acabaron las preocupaciones; **life is full of —s** la vida está llena de aflicciones; **then this — came upon them** luego sufrieron esta aflicción; **to drown one's —s** beber para olvidar sus aflicciones; **to lay up — for oneself** hacer algo que causará pena en el futuro; **to tell someone one's —s** contar sus desventuras a uno.
(b) (difficulty) dificultad f; disgusto m; (hindrance) estorbo m, inconveniente m; **family —s** dificultades fpl con la familia; **money —s** dificultades fpl económicas; **the — is that...** la dificultad es que..., lo malo es que..., el inconveniente es que...; **what's the —?**, what seems to be the —? ¿pasa algo?; **their aunt is a great — to them** su tía constituye un gran estorbo para ellos; **it's just asking for** — eso es buscar tres pies al gato; **to get into** — meterse en un lío; **Peter got into — for saying that** Pedro se mereció una bronca diciendo eso; **he got into — with the police** tuvo una dificultad con la policía; **to get someone into** — comprometer a uno, crear un lío a uno; **to get a girl into** — (euph) dejar encinta a una joven; **to get out of** — salir del apuro; **to get someone out of** — ayudar a uno a salir del apuro; echar un cable a uno; **you'll have — with it** tendrás dificultades con eso; **did you have any** —? ¿tuviste alguna dificultad?; **to make — for someone** crear un lío a uno; amargar la vida a uno.
(c) (bother) molestia f; dificultad f; (effort) esfuerzo m; **with no little** — con bastante dificultad, con no poca dificultad; **it's no** — no es molestia; **it's no — to do it properly** no cuesta nada hacerlo bien; **it's not worth the** — no vale la pena; **nothing is too much — for her** pone el máximo cuidado en todo lo que hace, se presta a todo sin reparar en las molestias que pudiera suponer para ella; **to give someone** — causar molestia a uno; **to go to the — of +** ger darse la molestia de + infin; **we had — getting here in time** nos costó trabajo llegar aquí a tiempo; **we had all our — for nothing** todo aquello fue trabajo perdido; **to put someone to the — of doing something** molestar a uno pidiéndole que haga algo; **I fear I am putting you to a lot of** — me temo que esto le vaya a molestar bastante; **to save oneself the** — ahorrarse el trabajo; **to spare no — in order to +** infin no regatear medio para + infin; **to take the — to +** infin tomarse la molestia de + infin; **he didn't even take the — to say thank you** ni se dignó siquiera darme las gracias; **to take a lot of** — esmerarse, trabajar (etc) con el mayor cuidado.
(d) (upset: Med) enfermedad f, mal m; **chest** — enfermedad f del pecho; **heart** — enfermedad f cardíaca.
(e) (upset: Mech) avería f; fallo m; **engine** — avería f del motor; **a mechanic put the — right** un mecánico reparó las piezas averiadas; **we drove 5,000 miles without — of any kind** cubrimos 5.000 millas sin la menor avería.
(f) (upset: between persons) disgusto m, desavenencia f, sinsabor m; **the Parnell** — el caso Parnell; **there is constant — between them** riñen constantemente; **X caused — between Y and Z** X provocó un disgusto entre Y y Z.
(g) (unrest, Pol etc) conflicto m; trastorno m, disturbio m; **the Irish —s** los conflictos de los irlandeses, la guerra civil irlandesa; **labour —s** conflictos mpl laborales; **there's — at t'mill** hay un disturbio en la fábrica, hay huelga en la fábrica; **there's — brewing** soplan vientos de fronda; **to stir up** — meter cizaña, revolver el ajo.
2 vt **(a)** (afflict, grieve) afligir; (worry) inquietar, preocupar; (disturb) agitar, turbar; **the thought —d him** el pensamiento le afligió; **the heat —d us** nos molestó el calor; **his eyes — him** le duelen los ojos; **I am deeply —d** estoy sumamente inquieto; **it's not that that —s me** no me inquieto por eso, eso me trae sin cuidado.

(b) (bother) molestar, incomodar; (badger) importunar; **I'm sorry to — you** lamento tener que molestarle; **may I — you for a match?** ¿tiene fuego por favor?, ¿me hace el favor de darme fuego?; **may I — you to hold this?** ¿le molestaría tener esto?; **does it — you if I smoke?** ¿le molesta que fume?; **I shan't — you with all the details** no les molesto citando todos los detalles; **maths never —d me at all** las matemáticas no me costaron trabajo en absoluto.
3 vi preocuparse, molestarse; **please don't —!** ¡no se moleste!, ¡no se preocupe!; **don't — to write** no se moleste en escribir; **he didn't — to shut the door** no se tomó la molestia de cerrar la puerta; **if you had —d to find out** si se hubiera tomado la molestia de averiguarlo.
4 vr: **to — oneself about something** preocuparse por algo; **to — oneself to do something** tomarse la molestia de hacer algo; **don't — yourself!** ¡no se moleste!, ¡no se preocupe!
troubled ['trʌbld] adj person inquieto, preocupado; expression preocupado; period turbulento, agitado; life, story accidentado; waters revuelto, turbio; **to look —** parecer estar preocupado.
trouble-free ['trʌblfri:] adj libre de inquietudes, totalmente tranquilo; (Pol etc) libre de disturbios; (Aut, Mech) exento de averías; **a thousand miles** mil millas sin avería alguna.
troublemaker ['trʌbl,meikə*] n alborotador m, buscarruidos m, elemento m perturbador.
troubleshooter ['trʌbl,ʃu:tə*] n investigador m de conflictos laborales, árbitro m de conflictos laborales.
troublesome ['trʌblsəm] adj molesto, fastidioso; importuno; dificultoso; **it's very —** es terriblemente molesto; **now don't be —** no seas difícil, no te pongas así.
trouble spot ['trʌblspɔt] n (Pol) centro m de fricción, lugar m turbulento.
troublous ['trʌbləs] adj **times** turbulento, agitado, revuelto.
trough [trɔf] n **(a)** (depression) depresión f, hoyo m; (between waves) seno m; (channel) canal m; (Meteorol) mínimo m de presión; (fig) parte f baja, punto m más bajo.
(b) (drinking —) abrevadero m; (feeding —) comedero m; (kneading —) artesa f; (of stone) pila f.
trounce [trauns] vt (thrash) pegar, zurrar, dar una paliza a; (defeat) derrotar, cascar; (castigate) fustigar.
troupe [tru:p] n (Theat etc) compañía f, grupo m, conjunto m.
trouper ['tru:pə*] n (Theat) miembro m de una compañía de actores; **old —** actor m veterano, actriz f veterana.
trouser press ['trauzəpres] n prensa f para pantalones.
trousers ['trauzəz] npl pantalones mpl, pantalón m; **a pair of —** un pantalón, unos pantalones; **to wear the —s** (fig) llevar los pantalones.
trousseau ['tru:səu] n ajuar m, equipo m (de novia).
trout [traut] n trucha f.
trout fisherman ['traut,fiʃəmən] n, pl **-men** [mən] pescador m de truchas.
trout fishing ['traut,fiʃiŋ] n pesca f de truchas.
trowel ['trauəl] n (Agr) desplantador m, transplantador m; (builder's) paleta f, llana f.
Troy [trɔi] Troya f.
troy (weight) ['trɔi('weit] n peso m troy.
truancy ['truənsi] n ausencia f sin permiso.
truant ['truənt] **1** adj (slack) gandul, haragán, vago; (absent) ausente, desparecido.
2 n (slacker) gandul m, vago m; (absentee) novillero m; **to play —** ausentarse, (School) hacer novillos.
truce [tru:s] n (Mil) tregua f; (fig) suspensión f, cesación f; **to call a — to something** suspender algo.
truck¹ [trʌk] **1** n: **to have no — with someone** no tratar con uno, no tener relaciones con uno; **we want no — with that** no queremos tener nada que ver con eso.
2 attr: **— system** pago m de salarios en especie.
truck² [trʌk] n (waggon) carro m; (hand—) carretilla f; (Rail) vagón m (de mercancías); (lorry) camión m.
truckage ['trʌkidʒ] n (US) acarreo m.
truckdriver ['trʌk,draivə*] n camionero m, camionista m, conductor m de camión.
trucker ['trʌkə*] n (US) camionero m, camionista m.
truck farm ['trʌk'fɑ:m] n (US), **truck garden** ['trʌk'gɑ:dn] n (US) huerto m de hortalizas.
trucking ['trʌkiŋ] n acarreo m, transporte m.
truckle ['trʌkl] vi: **to — to someone** someterse servilmente a uno.
truckle bed ['trʌkl'bed] n carriola f.

truckload ['trʌkləud] *n* carretada *f*; vagón *m* (lleno); **—s of soldiers** camiones *mpl* llenos de soldados; **by the —** (*fig*) a carretadas, a montones.

truckman ['trʌkmən] *n, pl* **—men** [mən] (*US*) camionero *m*, camionista *m*.

truculence ['trʌkjuləns] *n* agresividad *f*; mal humor *m*, aspereza *f*.

truculent ['trʌkjulənt] *adj* agresivo; malhumorado, áspero.

truculently ['trʌkjuləntli] *adv* **behave** de modo agresivo; **answer** malhumorado, ásperamente.

trudge [trʌdʒ] **1** *n* caminata *f* (difícil, larga, penosa).
  2 *vt* recorrer a pie (penosamente); **we —d the streets looking for him** nos cansamos buscándole por las calles.
  3 *vi* (*also to —* **along**) caminar penosamente, andar con dificultad.

true [truː] **1** *adj* (a) (*not false*) verdadero; **—!, too —!** ¡es verdad!; **it is — that...** es verdad que...; **can this be —?** ¿es cierto esto?; **so — is this that...** tan es así que...; **to come —** realizarse, cumplirse, verificarse; **to hold something to be —** creer que algo es verdad; **it holds — of...** también es cierto por lo que se refiere a...
  (b) (*genuine*) auténtico, verdadero, genuino; **account** verídico; **copy** fiel, exacto; **what is the — situation?** ¿cuál es la verdadera situación?; **it is not a — account of what happened** no es un informe verdadero de lo que pasó; **in a — spirit of service** en un auténtico espíritu de servicio; **like a — Englishman** como un inglés auténtico.
  (c) (*of measures etc*) exacto; **surface, join** uniforme, a nivel; **upright** a plomo; **the walls are not —** las paredes no están a plomo.
  (d) (*faithful*) fiel, leal; **a — friend** un fiel amigo; **all good men and —** todos los buenos y leales; **to be — to someone** ser fiel a uno; **to be — to one's word** cumplir su promesa, cumplir lo prometido.
  (e) **voice etc** puro.
  (f) (*Bio etc*) **— to life** conforme con la realidad; **— to type** conforme con el tipo.
  2 *adv:* **to aim —** apuntar bien, acertar en la puntería; **to breed —** reproducirse conforme con el tipo; **to run — to type** estar conforme con el tipo; **now tell me —** dime la verdad.
  3 *n:* **to be out of —** (*of things joining*) no estar a nivel, estar mal alineado, estar desalineado; (*of things vertical*) no estar a plomo; (*of wheel*) estar descentrado.

true-blue ['truː'bluː] **1** *adj* de lo más leal, acérrimo. **2** *n* partidario *m* de lo más leal, partidario *m* acérrimo.

true-born ['truː'bɔːn] *adj* auténtico, verdadero.

true-bred ['truː'bred] *adj* de casta legítima, de pura sangre.

true-hearted ['truː'hɑːtid] *adj* fiel, leal; sincero.

true-life ['truː'laif] *adj* verdadero, conforme con la realidad.

truelove ['truːlʌv] *n* novio *m*, a *f*, fiel amante *mf*.

truffle ['trʌfl] *n* trufa *f*.

truism ['truːizəm] *n* perogrullada *f*, tópico *m*; **it is a — to say that...** es un tópico decir que...

truly ['truːli] *adv* verdaderamente; auténticamente; exactamente; fielmente; **and — it was tough** y efectivamente fue difícil; **a — great painting** un cuadro verdaderamente grande; **really and —?** ¿de veras?; **yours —** le saluda atentamente; **nobody knows it better than yours —** nadie lo sabe mejor que este pobre hombre.

trump [trʌmp] **1** *n* triunfo *m*; **hearts are —s** triunfan corazones, pintan corazones; **what's —s?** ¿a qué pinta?; **he always turns up —s** no nos falla nunca, es persona de la mayor confianza.
  2 *vt* (a) (*Cards*) fallar.
  (b) **to — up charge** forjar, falsificar, inventar.
  3 *vi* triunfar, poner un triunfo.

trumped-up ['trʌmpt'ʌp] *adj* **accusation etc** forjado, inventado.

trumpery ['trʌmpəri] **1** *adj* frívolo; (*valueless*) inútil, sin valor; (*insignificant*) sin importancia; (*trashy*) de relumbrón. **2** *n* oropel *m*.

trumpet ['trʌmpit] **1** *n* trompeta *f*. **2** *vt* trompetear; (*fig: also to — forth*) pregonar, anunciar (a son de trompeta). **3** *vi* (*elephant*) barritar.

trumpet blast ['trʌmpitblɑːst] *n*, **trumpet call** ['trʌmpitkɔːl] *n* trompetazo *m*; (*fig*) clarinazo *m*.

trumpeter ['trʌmpitə*] *n* trompetero *m*, trompeta *m*.

truncate [trʌŋ'keit] *vt* truncar.

truncated [trʌŋ'keitid] *adj* truncado, trunco.

truncation [trʌŋ'keiʃən] *n* truncamiento *m*.

truncheon ['trʌntʃən] *n* porra *f*.

trundle ['trʌndl] **1** *vt* hacer rodar, hacer correr (sobre ruedas); (*fig*) llevar, arrastrar (con dificultad).

2 *vi* rodar (con mucho ruido, pesadamente).

trunk [trʌŋk] **1** *n* (*Anat, Bot*) tronco *m*; (*case*) baúl *m*; (*US Aut*) portaequipaje *m*; (*elephant's*) trompa *f*.
  2 *attr:* **— line** (*Rail*) línea *f* troncal; (*Tel*) línea *f* principal; **see call, road.**

trunks [trʌŋks] *npl* taparrabo *m*.

trunnion ['trʌniən] *n* muñón *m*.

truss [trʌs] **1** *n* (*bundle*) lío *m*, paquete *m*; (*of hay etc*) haz *m*, lío *m*; (*of fruit*) racimo *m*; (*Archit*) entramado *m*; (*Med*) braguero *m*.
  2 *vt* (*tie*) liar, atar; **fowl** espetar; (*Archit*) apuntalar, apoyar con entramado; **to — someone up** atar a uno con cuerdas (*etc*).

trust [trʌst] **1** *n* (a) (*belief, faith*) confianza *f* (**in** en); **breach of —** abuso *m* de confianza; **to put one's — in** confiar en; **to take something on —** aceptar algo a ojos cerrados, creer algo sin tener (*or* pedir) pruebas de ello.
  (b) (*Comm*) **to supply goods on —** suministrar artículos al fiado, proveer artículos a crédito.
  (c) (*charge*) cargo *m*, deber *m*, obligación *f*; responsabilidad *f*; **our sacred —** nuestra sagrada obligación; **position of —** puesto *m* de responsabilidad, puesto *m* de confianza; **to commit something to someone's —** hacer que uno se encargue de algo; **to desert one's —** faltar a su deber.
  (d) (*Law*) fideicomiso *m*; **to hold money in — for someone** tener dinero en administración a nombre de uno.
  (e) (*Comm, Fin*) trust *m*; (*pej*) monopolio *m*, cartel *m*; **investment —** compañía *f* inversionista.
  2 *attr:* **— company** banco *m* fideicomisario.
  3 *vt* (a) (*believe in, rely on*) confiar en, fiarse de; tener confianza en; creer; **don't you — me?** ¿no te fías de mí?; **she is not to be —ed** ella no es de fiar; **you can't — a word he says** es imposible creer ninguna palabra suya; **to — someone with something** confiar algo a uno; **to — someone with a task** confiar un cometido a uno; **will you — me with your bike?** ¿me permites usar tu bicicleta?; **to — someone to do something** confiar en que uno haga algo; **— you!** ¡siempre igual!, ¡lo mismo que siempre!; **— him to make a mess of it** no es sorprendente que lo haya hecho mal; **mother wouldn't — us out of her sight** mamá no permitía que nos alejásemos de ella, mamá nos tenía cosidos a sus faldas.
  (b) (*Comm*) dar al fiado.
  (c) (*hope*) esperar; **I — not** espero que no; **I — that all will go well** espero que todo vaya bien.
  3 *vi* confiar; esperar; **to — in God** confiar en Dios; **to — to chance, to — to luck** confiar en tener suerte; hacer algo a la ventura.

trusted ['trʌstid] *adj* leal, de confianza.

trustee [trʌs'tiː] *n* (*in bankruptcy*) síndico *m*; (*holder of property for another*) fideicomisario *m*, depositario *m*; administrador *m*; (*of college*) regente *m*.

trusteeship [trʌs'tiːʃip] *n* cargo *m* de síndico, cargo *m* de fideicomiso (*etc*); administración *f* fiduciaria.

trustful ['trʌstful] *adj*, **trusting** ['trʌstiŋ] *adj* confiado.

trustingly ['trʌstiŋli] *adv* confiadamente.

trustworthiness ['trʌst,wəðinis] *n* formalidad *f*, honradez *f*, confiabilidad *f*; carácter *m* fidedigno; exactitud *f*.

trustworthy ['trʌst,wəði] *adj* **person** formal, honrado, confiable, de confianza; **news, source etc** fidedigno; **statistics etc** exacto.

trusty ['trʌsti] **1** *adj* **servant etc** fiel, leal; **weapon** seguro, bueno. **2** *n* (*fam*) preso *m* que ha dado pruebas de buena conducta.

truth [truːθ] *n, pl* **truths** [truːðz] verdad *f*; realidad *f*; verosimilitud *f*; **the plain —** la pura verdad, la verdad lisa y llana; **the whole —** toda la verdad; **the — of the matter is that...,** **— to tell...** la verdad del caso es que..., a decir verdad...; **there is some — in this** hay una parte de verdad en esto; **— will out** no hay mentira que no salga; **to tell the — to** decir la verdad; **to tell someone a few home —s** decir a uno cuatro verdades; **in —** en verdad.

truthful ['truːθful] *adj* **account** verídico, exacto; **person** veraz; **are you being —?** ¿es esto la verdad?

truthfully ['truːθfəli] *adv* con verdad; **now tell me —** ahora bien, dime la verdad.

truthfulness ['truːθfulnis] *n* veracidad *f*; verdad *f*, exactitud *f*.

try [trai] **1** *n* (a) (*attempt*) tentativa *f*; **to have a —** hacer una tentativa, probar suerte; **to have a — for a job** presentarse como candidato a un puesto, solicitar un puesto; **have another —!** ¡a probar otra vez!; **it's worth a —** vale la pena probarlo.

(**b**) (*Rugby*) ensayo *m*; **to score a —** marcar un ensayo.

2 *vt* (**a**) (*attempt*) intentar, probar; **shall we — it?** ¿lo probamos?; **you tried only 3 questions** Vd intentó 3 preguntas nada más.

(**b**) (*test*) probar, poner a prueba, ensayar; **to — one's strength** ensayar sus fuerzas; **to — one's strength against someone** ensayarse para determinar cuál de los dos es más fuerte; **he was tried and found wanting** fue sometido a prueba y resultó ser deficiente.

(**c**) (*expose to suffering*) hacer sufrir; afligir; **his much-tried relations** sus familiares que tanto habían sufrido; **they have been sorely tried** han sufrido mucho.

(**d**) (*tire*) *eyes* cansar; *person* irritar; **to — one's eyes by reading too much** cansarse los ojos leyendo demasiado; **you — my patience** me haces perder la paciencia.

(**e**) (*taste, sample*) probar; **have you tried these olives?** ¿has probado estas aceitunas?

(**f**) (*Law*) *case* ver; *person* procesar (*for* por), juzgar; **to be tried for murder** ser procesado por asesino; **to be tried by one's peers** ser juzgado por sus iguales.

(**g**) (*with adv or prep*) **to — on** *clothes* probarse; **to — it on with someone** (*fam*) tratar de embaucar a uno; **he's just —ing it on** lo hace nada más para ver si tragamos el anzuelo; **to — out** probar, poner a prueba, someter a prueba, ensayar; **— it out on the dog first** dáselo primero al perro para ver qué pasa, pruébalo dandóselo de comer al perro; **to — over** (*Mus etc*) ensayar, ensayar a tocar (*etc*).

3 *vi* probar; esforzarse; **to — one's best, to — one's hardest** esforzarse mucho, poner todo su esfuerzo; **— as he would . . .** por más que se esforzase . . .; **to — again** volver a probar; **you had better not —** más vale no probarlo; le aconsejo no hacerlo; **to — for something** tratar de obtener algo; **to — for a post** presentarse como candidato a un puesto, solicitar un puesto; **to — to do something, to — and do something** tratar de hacer algo, intentar hacer algo; procurar hacer algo; querer hacer algo; **it's —ing to rain** empieza a llover, quiere llover; **— not to cough** procura no toser, procura contener la tos; **do — to understand** trata de comprender; **it's no use —ing to persuade him** no vale la pena tratar de convencerle.

trying ['traiiŋ] *adj* molesto; cansado; difícil.

try-on ['traiɔn] (*fam*) trampa *f*, tentativa *f* de engañar.

tryout ['traiaut] *n* prueba *f*; **to give a car a —** someter un coche a prueba.

tryst [trist] *n* (*lit, hum*) cita *f*; lugar *m* de una cita.

tsar [zɑ:*] *n* zar *m*.

tsarina [zɑ:'ri:nə] *n* zarina *f*.

tsetse fly ['tsetsiflai] *n* mosca *f* tsetsé.

T-shirt ['ti:ʃə:t] *n* camiseta *f*.

T-square ['ti:skweə*] *n* regla *f* T, té *f*.

tub [tʌb] **1** *n* tina *f*; cubo *m*, cuba *f*; artesón *m*; (*bath—*) baño *m*, bañera *f*; (*Naut*) carcamán *m*; **to have a —** (*bath*) tomar un baño.

2 *vi* tomar un baño.

tuba ['tju:bə] *n* tuba *f*, bombardón *m*.

tubby ['tʌbi] *adj* rechoncho.

tube [tju:b] *n* tubo *m*; (*TV*) tubo *m*; (*US Radio*) lámpara *f*; (*Aut*) cámara *f* de aire; (*Rail*) metro *m*; **Eustachian —** trompa *f* de Eustaquio; **Fallopian —** trompa *f* de Falopio; **inner —** cámara *f* de aire; **to go by —** ir en el metro, viajar por metro.

tubeless ['tju:blis] *adj* tyre sin cámara.

tuber ['tju:bə*] *n* tubérculo *m*.

tubercle ['tju:bə:kl] *n* (*all senses*) tubérculo *m*.

tubercular [tju'bə:kjulə*] *adj* tubercular; (*Med*) tuberculoso.

tuberculosis [tju,bə:kju'ləusis] *n* tuberculosis *f*.

tuberculous [tju'bə:kjuləs] *adj* tuberculoso.

tube station ['tju:b,steiʃən] *n* estación *f* de metro.

tubing ['tju:biŋ] *n* tubería *f*; tubos *mpl*; **a piece of —** un trozo de tubo.

tub-thumper ['tʌb,θʌmpə*] *n* orador *m* demagógico.

tub-thumping ['tʌb,θʌmpiŋ] **1** *adj* demagógico.

2 *n* oratoria *f* demagógica.

tubular ['tju:bjulə*] *adj* tubular, en forma de tubo; *furniture* de tubo.

tuck [tʌk] **1** *n* (**a**) (*Sew*) alforza *f*; pliegue *m*; **to take a — in a dress** hacer una alforza en un vestido.

(**b**) (*fam: food*) provisiones *fpl*, comestibles *mpl*, (*sweets*) dulces *mpl*, golosinas *fpl*.

2 *vt* (*Sew*) alforzar; plegar; **to — away** (*hide*) ocultar, esconder; *food* (*fam*) devorar, zampar; **he**

can certainly **— it away** ése sí sabe comer; **I can't think where he —s it all away** no llego a comprender dónde lo almacena; **— it away out of sight** ocúltalo para que no se vea; **the village is —ed away among the woods** la aldea se esconde en el bosque; **he —ed it away in his pocket** lo guardó en el bolsillo; **to — in a flap** meter una solapa para dentro; **to — bedclothes in** guarnecer una cama con su ropa; **to — A under B** poner A debajo de B; esconder A debajo de B; **to — up** *skirt, sleeves* arremangar; **to — someone up in bed** arropar a uno en la cama; (*fig*) acostar a uno; **you'll soon be nicely —ed up** pronto te verás instalado cómodamente en la cama.

3 *vi*: **to — in** (*fam*) comer con apetito, comer vorazmente; **— in!** ¡a comer!, ¡a ello!; **to — into something** comer algo vorazmente, zamparse algo.

tucker ['tʌkə*] *vt* (*US fam*) cansar, agotar (*also* **to — out**).

tuck-in ['tʌk'in] *n* (*fam*) banquetazo *m*, comilona *f*; **to have a good —** darse un atracón.

tuck-shop ['tʌkʃɔp] *n* (*School*) bombonería *f*, confitería *f*.

Tuesday ['tju:zdi] *n* martes *m*.

tufa ['tju:fə] *n* toba *f*.

tuft [tʌft] *n* (*of hair*) copete *m*; (*of hairs, wool*) mechón *m*; (*of feathers*) cresta *f*, copete *m*; (*on helmet etc*) penacho *m*; (*of grass etc*) manojo *m*.

tufted ['tʌftid] *adj* copetudo.

tug [tʌg] **1** *n* (**a**) (*action*) tirón *m*; estirón *m*; **to give something a —** tirar de algo, dar un estirón a algo.

(**b**) (*Naut*) remolcador *m*; **ocean-going —** remolcador *m* de alta mar.

2 *vt* (**a**) tirar de; dar un estirón a; **to — something along** arrastrar algo, llevar algo arrastrándolo.

(**b**) (*Naut*) remolcar; **eventually they —ged the boat clear** por fin sacaron el barco a flote.

3 *vi*: **to — at something** tirar de algo; **someone was —ging at my sleeve** alguien me tiraba de la manga; **they —ged their hardest** se esforzaron muchísimo tirando de él.

tugboat ['tʌgbəut] *n* remolcador *m*.

tug-of-war ['tʌgə(v)'wɔ:*] *n* lucha *f* de la cuerda; (*fig*) lucha *f*; tira *m* y afloja; **the — between rival interests** el tira y afloja de intereses opuestos; **then comes the —** luego es el momento crítico, luego se inicia la lucha decisiva.

tuition [tju'iʃən] *n* enseñanza *f*, instrucción *f*; **private —** clases *fpl* particulares (*in* de).

tulip ['tju:lip] *n* tulipán *m*.

tulip tree ['tju:liptri:] *n* tulipanero *m*, tulipero *m*.

tulle [tju:l] *n* tul *m*.

tumble ['tʌmbl] **1** *n* caída *f*; (*somersault*) voltereta *f*; **to have a —, to take a —** caerse; **to have a — in the hay** retozar, hacer el amor (en el pajar); **to take a —** (*fig*) bajar de golpe, dar un bajón.

2 *vt* (*knock down*) derribar, abatir, tumbar; (*fig*) derrocar; (*upset: also* **to — over**) derramar, hacer caer; (*disarrange*) desarreglar; **to — someone in the hay** tumbar a uno (en el pajar); **to — out** echar en desorden.

3 *vi* (*fall*) caer; (*stumble*) tropezar; **to toss and —** (*in bed*) agitarse, revolverse mucho; **to — down** caer; desplomarse, hundirse, venirse abajo; **to — in, to — into bed** acostarse; acostarse del modo que sea; **to — out** salir en desorden; **to — out of a car** caerse de un coche; **to — out of bed** levantarse de prisa; **to go tumbling over and over** ir rodando, ir dando tumbos; **to — to something** caer en la cuenta de algo, comprender algo.

tumbledown ['tʌmbldaun] *adj* destartalado, ruinoso.

tumbler ['tʌmblə*] *n* (*glass*) vaso *m*; (*of lock*) seguro *m*, fiador *m*; (*person*) volteador *m*, ora *f*; (*Orn*) pichón *m* volteador.

tumbrel ['tʌmbrəl], **tumbril** ['tʌmbril] *n* chirrión *m*, carreta *f*.

tumefaction [,tju:mi'fækʃən] *n* tumefacción *f*.

tumescent [tju:'mesnt] *adj* tumescente.

tumid ['tju:mid] *adj* túmido.

tummy ['tʌmi] *n* (*fam*) estómago *m*, vientre *m*.

tumour ['tju:mə*] *n* tumor *m*.

tumult ['tju:mʌlt] *n* tumulto *m*.

tumultuous [tju:'mʌltjuəs] *adj* tumultuoso.

tumultuously [tju:'mʌltjuəsli] *adv* tumultuosamente.

tumulus ['tju:mjuləs] *n*, *pl* **tumuli** ['tju:mjulai] túmulo *m*.

tun [tʌn] *n* tonel *m*.

tuna ['tju:nə] *n* atún *m*.

tundra ['tʌndrə] *n* tundra *f*.

tune [tju:n] **1** *n* aire *m*, melodía *f*, tonada *f*; (*fig*) tono *m*; **to be in —** (*Mus*) estar templado, estar afinado; **to sing in —** cantar afinadamente, cantar bien; **to be in — with** (*fig*) armonizar con, concordar con; **to be out of —** (*Mus*) estar destemplado, estar desafinado; **to sing out of —** cantar desafinadamente, cantar mal; **to be out of — with** (*fig*) desentonar con, estar en desacuerdo con; **to go out of —** desafinar; **to change one's —,** to sing **another —** mudar de tono; **to the — of** (*fig*) por la suma de, por la cantidad de.

2 *vti* afinar, acordar, templar (*also* **to — up**); **to — up** (*in practice*) tocar algunas notas (para afinar los instrumentos); **to — up** (*fig*) prepararse, ejercitarse; (*Aut*) poner a punto, reglar.

3 *vi*: **to — in** (*Radio*) sintonizar; (*loosely*) escuchar, escuchar un programa; **to — in to a station** sintonizar una emisora.

tuneful ['tjuːnful] *adj* melodioso, armonioso.
tunefully ['tjuːnfəli] *adv* melodiosamente, armoniosamente.
tunefulness ['tjuːnfulnis] *n* lo melodioso, lo armonioso.
tuneless ['tjuːnlis] *adj* disonante, discordante.
tunelessly ['tjuːnlisli] *adv* de modo disonante.
tuner ['tjuːnə*] *n* (*person*) afinador *m*; (*Radio*: knob) botón *m* sintonizador.
tune-up ['tjuːnʌp] *n* (*Mus*) afinación *f*; (*Aut*) puesta *f* a punto, reglaje *m*.
tungsten ['tʌŋstən] *n* tungsteno *m*.
tunic ['tjuːnik] *n* túnica *f*.
tuning ['tjuːniŋ] *n* (*Mus*) afinación *f*; (*Radio*) sintonización *f*.
tuning coil ['tjuːniŋkɔil] *n* bobina *f* sintonizadora.
tuning fork ['tjuːniŋfɔːk] *n* diapasón *m*.
tuning knob ['tjuːniŋnɔb] *n* botón *m* sintonizador.
Tunis ['tjuːnis] Túnez (*ciudad*).
Tunisia [tjuːˈniziə] Túnez *m* (*país*).
Tunisian [tjuːˈniziən] **1** *adj* tunecino. **2** *n* tunecino *m*, a *f*.
tunnel ['tʌnl] **1** *n* túnel *m*; (*Min*) galería *f*.
2 *vt* construir un túnel bajo, construir un túnel a través de; **a mound—led by rabbits** un montículo lleno de madrigueras de conejo; **wood—led by beetles** madera *f* carcomida, madera *f* agujereada por coleópteros; **shelters — led out in the hillsides** refugios *mpl* horadados en las colinas.
3 *vi* construir un túnel (*or* galería); (*of animal*) excavar una madriguera; **they — into the hill** construyen un túnel bajo la colina; **to — down into the earth** perforar un túnel en la tierra; **the rabbits — under the fence** los conejos hacen madrigueras que pasan debajo de la valla.
tunny ['tʌni] *n* atún *m*; **striped —** bonito *m*.
tunny fishery ['tʌni,fiʃəri] *n* almadraba *f*.
tuppence ['tʌpəns] *n* see **twopence**.
tuppenny ['tʌpəni] *adj* see **twopenny**.
turban ['təːbən] *n* turbante *m*.
turbid ['təːbid] *adj* túrbido.
turbine ['təːbain] *n* turbina *f*; **gas —** turbina *f* de gas.
turbojet ['təːbəuˈdʒet] **1** *n* turborreactor *m*. **2** *adj*, *attr* turborreactor.
turboprop ['təːbəuˈprɔp] **1** *n* turbohélice *m*. **2** *adj*, *attr* turbohélice.
turbot ['təːbət] *n* rodaballo *m*.
turbulence ['təːbjuləns] *n* turbulencia *f*; desorden *m*, disturbios *mpl*; (*Meteorol*) turbulencia *f*.
turbulent ['təːbjulənt] *adj* turbulento; revoltoso.
tureen [təˈriːn] *n* sopera *f*.
turf [təːf] **1** *n* (*sward*) césped *m*; (*clod*) tepe *m*, césped *m*; (*peat*) turba *f*; **the T— (***Sport***)** el turf, las carreras de caballos.
2 *vt* encespedar, cubrir con céspedes (*also* **to — over**); **to — someone out** (*fam*) echar a uno, expulsar a uno.
turgid ['təːdʒid] *adj* turgente; (*fig*) hinchado; pesado, indigesto.
turgidity [təːˈdʒiditi] *n* turgencia *f*; (*fig*) hinchazón *f*; pesadez *f*.
Turk [təːk] *n* turco *m*, a *f*; **little —, young — tunante** *m*.
Turkey ['təːki] Turquía *f*.
turkey ['təːki] *n* pavo *m*, a *f*; **to talk — (***fam***)** no tener pelos en la lengua.
turkey cock ['təːkikɔk] *n* pavo *m* (*also fig*).
Turkish ['təːkiʃ] **1** *adj* turco. **2** *n* turco *m*.
turmeric ['təːmərik] *n* (*Bot*) cúrcuma *f*.
turmoil ['təːmɔil] *n* confusión *f*, desorden *m*; alboroto *m*; tumulto *m*; **everything is in a — todo** está en confusión, todo está revuelto; **we had complete — for a week** durante una semana reinó la confusión.
turn [təːn] **1** *n* (a) (*revolution*) vuelta *f*, revolución *f*; (*of spiral*) espira *f*; **with a quick — of the hand** con un movimiento rápido de la mano; **he never does a hand's —** no da golpe; **the meat is done to**

a — la carne está en su punto; **to give a screw another —** apretar un tornillo una vuelta más.
(b) (*change of direction*) cambio *m* de dirección; (*Aut*) giro *m*, vuelta *f*; (*Naut*) viraje *m*; **reverse —** vuelta *f* al revés; **"no left —"** (*Aut*) "prohibido girar a la izquierda"; **— of the tide** cambio *m* de la marea, vuelta *f* de la marea (*also fig*); **at every —** a cada paso, a cada momento; **the tide is on the —** la marea está cambiando; **the milk is on the —** la leche está cortándose; **to make a — to the left** girar a la izquierda; **to make a — to port** virar a babor; **things took a new —** las cosas cambiaron de aspecto; **events took a tragic —** los acontecimientos tomaron un cariz trágico; **events are taking a sensational —** los acontecimientos vienen tomando un rumbo sensacional; **then things took a — for the better** luego las cosas empezaron a mejorar.
(c) (*Med: fainting fit etc*) vahído *m*, desmayo *m*; (*crisis*) crisis *f*, ataque *m*; (*fright*) susto *m*; **it gave me quite a —** me dio un susto; **he had another — last night** anoche le dio otro ataque.
(d) (*short walk*) vuelta *f*; **to take a — in the park** dar una vuelta por el parque.
(e) (*successive opportunity*) turno *m*, vez *f*; oportunidad *f*; **— and — about** cada uno por turno; **ahora esto y luego aquello; by —s, in —** por turnos, sucesivamente; **I felt hot and cold by —s** tuve calor y luego frío en momentos sucesivos; **it's my — me toca a mí; then it was my — to protest** luego protesté a mi vez; **it's her — next** le toca a ella después, ella es la primera en turno; **your — will come** Vd tendrá su oportunidad; **to give up one's —** ceder la vez; **to go out of — jugar** (*etc*) fuera de orden; **to miss one's — perder** la vez; perder la ocasión; **the player shall miss two —s** el jugador deberá perder dos jugadas; **to take one's — esperar** su turno; turnar, alternar; **to take —s at the controls** alternar a los mandos; **to take a — at the wheel** conducir por su turno; **to take —s at doing something,** **to take it in —s to do something** turnar para hacer algo.
(f) (*Theat etc*) número *m*; **the star — of the evening** la atracción principal del programa; **she was the star —** ella fue la atracción principal; **he came on and did a funny —** salió a escena y presentó un número cómico.
(g) (*service*) **bad —** mala jugada *f*, mala pasada *f*; **good —** favor *m*, servicio *m*; **to do someone a bad —** hacer una mala pasada a uno; **a scout does a good — each day** el explorador presta un servicio cada día; **one good — deserves another** una buena acción merece recompensa; **it will serve my —** servirá para lo que yo quiero.
(h) (*inclination*) propensión *f* (*to* a); (*of mind*) disposición *f*, sesgo *m*; (*talent*) talento *m*, aptitud *f*; **to have a — for business** tener aptitud para los negocios; **it showed an odd — of mind** demostró una disposición de ánimo algo rara.
(i) (*form*) forma *f*; **the — of her arm** la configuración de su brazo, el contorno de su brazo; **— of phrase** giro *m*, expresión *f*; **that's a French —** of style eso es un modismo francés; **the car has a good — of speed** el coche tiene buena capacidad para acelerar.
(j) (*bend*) curva *f*, recodo *m*; **sharp —, sudden —** curva *f* cerrada, curva *f* brusca; **the road is full of twists and —s** la carretera tiene muchísimas curvas.
2 *vt* (a) (*revolve*) girar, hacer girar; *handle* dar vueltas a, torcer; *key* dar vuelta a; *screw* atornillar, destornillar; **the belt —s the wheel** la correa hace girar la rueda; **— it to the left** dale una vuelta hacia la izquierda; **you can — it through 90°** se puede girarlo hasta 90 grados.
(b) (*— to the other side*) volver; *ankle* torcer; *brain* trastornar; *stomach, soil etc* revolver; *hay etc* volver al revés; **to — a page** volver una hoja; **to — a dress inside out** volver un vestido del revés; **the plough —s the soil** el arado revuelve la tierra.
(c) (*direct*) volver, dirigir; *blow* desviar; **to — one's head** volver la cabeza; **to — one's steps homeward** dirigirse a casa, volver los pasos hacia casa; **to — one's eyes in someone's direction** volver la mirada hacia donde está uno; **to — a gun on someone** apuntar un revólver a uno; **to — someone's argument against himself** volver el arma contra el que la empleó; **to — A against B** predisponer a A en contra de B; **they —ed him against his parents** le enemistaron con sus padres; **to — someone from doing something** disuadir a uno de hacer algo; **we must — our thoughts to . . .** hemos de concentrar nuestro pensamiento en . . .; **if you will — your**

attention to ... tengan la bondad de fijar la atención en ...

(d) (*pass*) *corner* doblar; **he has —ed 50** ha cumplido los 50, ya tiene lo menos 50 años; **it's —ed 11 o'clock** son las 11 ya, ya dieron las 11.

(e) (*transform*) cambiar, mudar (*into*, *to* en); convertir, transformar (*into*, *to* en); *milk* agriar, volver agrio; **to — iron into gold** transformar el hierro en oro; **his admiration was —ed to scorn** su admiración se transformó en desprecio; **to — verse into prose** hacer una versión en prosa de un poema; **to — a play into a film** hacer una versión cinematográfica de una obra dramática; **to — English into Spanish** traducir el inglés al español, verter el inglés en español; **to — colour** cambiar de color; **the heat —ed the walls black** el calor volvió negras las paredes, el calor ennegreció las paredes.

(f) (*Tech*) tornear; **to — wood on a lathe** labrar la madera en un torno; **a well —ed leg** una pierna bien formada, una pierna bien torneada; **a well —ed sentence** una frase elegante.

(g) (*with adv or prep*) **to — about** see to round; **to — aside** desviar, apartar; **to — away** desviar, apartar; *head* volver; *person* despedir; *business, offer etc* rechazar, desechar; **to — back** (*fold*) doblar; *clock* retrasar; *person* hacer retroceder; hacer volver; **they were —ed back at the frontier** en la frontera les hicieron volver; **to — down** (*bend, fold*) doblar (hacia abajo); *glass etc* poner boca abajo; *thumb* volver hacia abajo; *gas, radio etc* bajar; *offer* rechazar; *suitor, candidate* no aceptar; **to — in** doblar hacia adentro; *wanted man etc* entregar (a la policía); **to — off** *light* apagar; (*Elec*) desconectar, quitar; *engine* parar; *tap* cerrar; *gas* cortar, cerrar la llave de; **to — on** (*Elec*) encender, conectar; poner; *tap* abrir; *gas* abrir la llave de; **to leave the radio —ed on** dejar encendida la radio; **to — out** *light* apagar; *gas* cortar, cerrar la llave de; *person* echar, expulsar; poner en la calle; *pocket* vaciar; *product* producir, fabricar; **to — out the guard** (*Mil*) formar la guardia; **to be well —ed out** ir bien trajeado, ir bien vestido; **the college —s out good secretaries** la escuela produce secretarias con buena formación profesional; **to — over** *page etc* volver; *container, vehicle etc* volcar; (**— upside down**) volver, poner al revés; *engine* hacer girar; *matter in mind* revolver, meditar; (*hand over*) entregar; ceder, traspasar (*to* a); **to — round** volver, poner al revés; **to — up** (*bend*) doblar hacia arriba; *gas* abrir, abrir más; *radio etc* poner más fuerte; *earth* revolver; *buried object* desenterrar, hacer salir a la superficie; (*fig*) encontrar; tropezar con; *reference* buscar, consultar; *see* upside.

3 *vi* (a) (*revolve*) girar, dar vueltas; (*of person*) volverse; girar sobre los talones; **my head is —ing** mi cabeza está dando vueltas; **to toss and —** in bed revolverse en la cama; **everything —s on whether** ... todo depende de si ...; **the conversation —ed on newts** la conversación versaba sobre los tritones, el tema de la conversación era los tritones.

(b) (*change direction*) volver, volverse; (*Aer, Naut*) virar; (*Aut*) girar, torcer; (*of tide*) repuntar; (*of weather etc*) cambiar; **to — left** torcer a la izquierda; **right —!** (*Mil*) ¡media vuelta a la derecha!; **to — to port** virar a babor; **to — for home** ir hacia casa; **the wind has —ed** el viento ha cambiado de dirección; **to wait for the weather to —** esperar a que cambie el tiempo; **then our luck —ed** luego mejoramos de suerte; **he —ed to me and smiled** se volvió hacia mí y sonrió; **to — to someone for help** acudir a uno a pedir ayuda; **he —ed to politics** se dedicó a la política; **he —ed to mysticism** recurrió al misticismo; empezó a estudiar el misticismo; **our thoughts — to those who** ... concentramos el pensamiento en los que ...; pensamos ahora en los que ...; **I don't know which way to —** estoy para volverme loco; **I don't know where to — for money** no sé en qué parte ir a buscar dinero; **to — against someone, to — on someone** volverse contra uno; **to — against something** coger aversión a algo.

(c) (*change*) cambiar, cambiarse; convertirse, transformarse (*into*, *to* en); (+ *adj*) ponerse, volverse; (+ *n*) hacerse; (*of leaves*) descolorarse; dorarse; (*of milk*) agriarse, cortarse; **it —s red** se pone colorado; **matters are —ing serious** las cosas se ponen graves; **then he began to — awkward** luego empezó a ponerse difícil; **the princess —ed into a toad** la princesa se transformó en sapo, la princesa quedó transformada en sapo; **it —ed to stone** se convirtió en piedra; **to — soldier**

hacerse soldado; **to — communist** hacerse comunista.

(d) (*with adv or prep*) **to — about** dar una vuelta completa; (*Pol etc*) cambiar completamente de política; **about —!** (*Mil*) media vuelta — ¡ar!; **to — aside** desviarse (*from* de); apartarse del camino; **I —ed aside in disgust** me aparté lleno de asco; **to — away** volver la cara, volver la cabeza; (*coldly*) volver la espalda; **to — away from** apartarse de; renunciar a; **to — back** volverse (atrás); retroceder; volverse sobre sus pasos; **to — from** apartarse de; **to — in** doblarse hacia adentro; (*go to bed*) acostarse; **to — off** desviarse; **to — off the path** desviarse del camino; **to — out** (*from bed*) levantarse, abandonar la cama; (*from house*) salir de casa, salir a la calle; (*of guard etc*) formarse, presentarse para servicio; **how are things —ing out?** ¿cómo van tus cosas?; **it all —ed out well** todo salió bien; **it —s out to be harder than we thought** resulta ser más difícil de lo que pensábamos; **it —s out that he's a vegetarian** resulta que él es vegetariano; **as it —ed out nobody went** resultó que no fue nadie; **that depends how it —s out** eso depende del éxito que tenga, eso depende de los resultados; **he has feet that — out** sus pies están vueltos hacia fuera; **to — over** revolverse; (*Aut etc*) capotar, dar una vuelta de campana; **it —ed over and over** fue dando tumbos; **my stomach —ed over** se me revolvió el estómago; **it's enough to make your stomach — over** es para revolver a uno el estómago; **to — round** (*revolve*) girar; dar vueltas; (*person*) volverse; girar sobre los talones; **I could hardly — round** apenas pude revolverme; **as soon as I —ed round they were quarrelling again** en cuanto les volví la espalda se pusieron otra vez a reñir; **the government has —ed right round** el gobierno ha cambiado completamente de política; **to — round and round** seguir dando vueltas; **to — to** (*adv*) empezar; empezar a trabajar (en serio); **to — up** (*point upwards*) doblarse hacia arriba, apuntar hacia arriba; (*appear*) aparecer, surgir; (*of card etc*) salir; (*arrive, show up*) llegar, acudir; presentarse; asomar la cara; (*be found again*) volver a aparecer, reaparecer; **we'll see if anyone —s up** veremos si viene alguien; **he —ed up 2 hours late** llegó con 2 horas de retraso; **he never —s up at class** no asiste nunca a la clase; **something is sure to — up** es seguro que surgirá alguna solución.

turnabout ['tə:nəbaut] *n* (*US*), **turnaround** ['tə:nəraund] *n* (*US*) = turn-round.

turncoat ['tə:nkəut] *n* renegado *m*, a *f*; **to become a —** volver la chaqueta.

turned-down ['tə:nd'daun] *adj* doblado hacia abajo.

turned-up ['tə:nd'ʌp] *adj* doblado hacia arriba; *nose* respingona.

turner ['tə:nə*] *n* tornero *m*.

turnery ['tə:nəri] *n* tornería *f*.

turning ['tə:niŋ] *n* vuelta *f*; ángulo *m*; recodo *m*; **the first — on the left** la primera bocacalle a la izquierda; **we parked in a side —** aparcamos el coche en una calle que salía de la carretera.

turning lathe ['tə:niŋleið] *n* torno *m* (de tornero).

turning point ['tə:niŋpoint] *n* (*fig*) punto *m* decisivo, coyuntura *f* crítica; **that was the —** eso fue la vuelta de la marea, eso marcó el cambio decisivo.

turning radius ['tə:niŋˌreidiəs] *n* (*Aut*) diámetro *m* de giro.

turnip ['tə:nip] *n* nabo *m*.

turnkey ['tə:nki:] *n* (*Hist*) llavero *m* (de una cárcel), carcelero *m*.

turnout ['tə:naut] *n* (*attendance*) concurrencia *f*; número *m* de asistentes; (*paying spectators*) entrada *f*, público *m*; (*production*) producción *f*; (*dress*) atuendo *m*; **there was a poor —** había poca gente, asistieron pocos; **we hope for a good — at the dance** esperamos que el baile sea muy concurrido.

turnover ['tə:nˌəuvə*] *n* (a) (*Comm*) volumen *m* de negocios, volumen *m* de ventas; número *m* de transacciones; movimiento *m* de mercancías; rotación *f* de existencias; **there is a rapid — in staff** hay mucho movimiento de personal; **our difficulty is labour —** tenemos problema con la rotación de la mano de obra.

(b) (*Cook*) pastel *m* con repulgo.

turnpike ['tə:npaik] *n* (*Hist*) barrera *f* de portazgo; (*US Aut*) autopista *f* de peaje.

turn-round ['tə:nraund] *n* (*Naut*) período *m* de descarga y carga (de un buque).

turnspit ['tə:nspit] *n* mecanismo *m* que da vueltas al asador.

turnstile ['tə:nstail] *n* torniquete *m*.

turntable ['tə:n,teibl] *n* (*Rail*) placa *f* giratoria; (*of gramophone*) plato *m* giratorio.

turn-up ['tə:nʌp] *n* (*of trousers*) vuelta *f*; (*fam: quarrel*) riña *f*, trifulca *f*; **that was a — for him** (*fam*) en eso tuvo mucha suerte.

turpentine ['tə:pəntain] *n* trementina *f*.

turpitude ['tə:pitju:d] *n* (*lit*) infamia *f*, vileza *f*; **to be dismissed for gross moral —** ser despedido por su inmoralidad manifiesta, ser expulsado por su conducta infame.

turps [tə:ps] *n* (*fam*) *see* **turpentine**.

turquoise ['tə:kwɔiz] *n* turquesa *f*.

turret ['tʌrit] *n* (*Archit*) torreón *m*; (*Mil*, *Hist*) torre *f*, torrecilla *f*; (*of tank, warship, aircraft*) torreta *f*; (*US, Tech*) cabrestante *m*.

turreted ['tʌritid] *adj* con torres, con torretas.

turret lathe ['tʌritleið] *n* torno *m* revolver.

turtle ['tə:tl] *n* tortuga *f* marina; **to turn —** volverse patas arriba, (*Naut*) zozobrar, (*Aut etc*) volcarse, dar una vuelta de campana.

turtledove ['tə:tldʌv] *n* tórtola *f*.

Tuscan ['tʌskən] **1** *adj* toscano. **2** *n* toscano *m*, a *f*. **3** *n* (*dialect*) toscano *m*.

Tuscany ['tʌskəni] la Toscana.

tush [tʌʃ] *n* = **tosh**.

tusk [tʌsk] *n* colmillo *m*.

tussle ['tʌsl] **1** *n* (*struggle*) lucha *f* (*for* por); (*scuffle*) pelea *f*, agarrada *f*.
2 *vi* luchar (*with* con); pelearse, reñir (*about*, *over* por causa de); **they —d with the police** se pelearon con la policía.

tussock ['tʌsək] *n* montecillo *m* de hierbas.

tut [tʌt] (*also* **tut-tut**) **1** *interj* ¡vamos!, ¡eso no!, ¡qué horror! **2** *vi* hacer un gesto de desaprobación, hacer un gesto de horror.

tutelage ['tju:tilidʒ] *n* tutela *f*; **under the — of** bajo la tutela de.

tutelary ['tju:tiləri] *adj* tutelar.

tutor ['tju:tə*] **1** *n* (*Hist*) ayo *m*; (*private teacher*) preceptor *m*; profesor *m* particular; (*Univ, approx*) profesor *m* que tiene a su cargo un pequeño grupo de estudiantes; (*moral —*) profesor *m* consejero moral; (*Law*) tutor *m*.
2 *vt* enseñar, instruir; dar clase particular a; **to — a boy in French** dar a un muchacho clases particulares de francés.

tutorial [tju:'tɔ:riəl] **1** *adj* preceptoral; (*Law*) tutelar. **2** *n* (*Univ*) clase *f* particular, clase *f* que consiste en un grupo pequeño de estudiantes.

tutu ['tu:tu:] *n* tutú *m*.

tuxedo [tʌk'si:dəu] *n* (*US*) smoking *m*, esmoquin *m* (*Acad*).

twaddle ['twɔdl] *n* tonterías *fpl*, bobadas *fpl*.

twain [twein] (*arch*) *n*: **the —** los dos; **to split something in —** partir algo en dos; **and ne'er the — shall meet** sin que el uno se acerque al otro jamás; sin que tengan nada en común.

twang [twæŋ] **1** *n* (*Mus etc*) tañido *m*, punteado *m*; (*of bow etc*) ruido *m*, sonido *m* (de cuerda que se estira y se suelta); **nasal —** gangueo *m*, timbre *m* nasal; **with an American —** con voz gangosa americana.
2 *vt* (*Mus*) puntear; *bowstring* estirar y soltar repentinamente.

twangy ['twæŋi] *adj string etc* elástico, muy estirado; *accent* nasal, gangoso.

'twas [twɔz] (*arch*) = **it was**.

tweak [twi:k] **1** *n* pellizco *m*; **to give someone a —** dar un pellizco a uno. **2** *vt* pellizcar (*retorciendo*); **to — something off** quitar algo pellizcándolo.

tweed [twi:d] *n* tweed *m*, mezcla *f* de lana; **—s** (*suit*) traje *m* de tweed.

'tween [twi:n] *prep* = **between**.

tweeter ['twi:tə*] *n* altavoz *m* para altas audiofrecuencias.

tweezers ['twi:zəz] *npl* bruselas *fpl*, pinzas *fpl*; **a pair of —** unas bruselas, unas pinzas.

twelfth [twelfθ] **1** *adj* duodécimo. **2** *n* duodécimo *m*; dozavo *m*, duodécima parte *f*.

Twelfth Night ['twelfθ'nait] *n* Día *m* de Reyes, Epifanía *f*.

twelve [twelv] **1** *adj* doce. **2** *n* doce *m*.

twelvemonth ['twelvmʌnθ] *n* año *m*; **this day —** de hoy en un año; **we've not seen him for a —** hace un año que no le vemos.

twentieth ['twentiiθ] **1** *adj* vigésimo. **2** *n* vigésimo *m*, vigésima parte *f*.

twenty ['twenti] *adj* veinte; **the twenties** (*eg 1920s*) los años veinte; **to be in one's twenties** tener más de veinte años.

twentyfold ['twentifəuld] **1** *adv* veinte veces. **2** *adj* veinte veces mayor.

twerp [twə:p] *n* (*sl*) tío *m* (*fam*); **you —!** ¡imbécil!

twice [twais] *adv* dos veces; **— as much** dos veces más; **A is — as big as B** A es dos veces más grande que B; **I am — as old as you are** tengo dos veces la edad de Vd, tengo el doble de la edad de Vd; **— the sum, — the quantity** el doble; **at a speed — that of sound** a una velocidad dos veces superior a la del sonido; **to do something —** over hacer algo dos veces, volver a hacer algo; **to go to a meeting — weekly** ir a una reunión dos veces cada semana; **he didn't have to be asked —** no se hizo de rogar; *see* **think 2 (a)**.

twiddle ['twidl] **1** *n* vuelta *f* (ligera); **to give a knob a —** girar un botón.
2 *vt* girar, hacer girar; jugar con; revolver ociosamente; **to — one's thumbs** voltear los pulgares, (*fig*) no tener nada que hacer.

twig[1] [twig] *n* ramita *f*; **—s** (*for fire*) leña *f* menuda.

twig[2] [twig] (*fam*) **1** *vt* comprender, caer en la cuenta de. **2** *vi* comprender, caer en la cuenta.

twilight ['twailait] **1** *n* crepúsculo *m*; (*fig*) crepúsculo *m*, ocaso *m*; **at —** al anochecer; **in the —** en el crepúsculo; **in the — of his room** en la media luz de su habitación.
2 *adj* crepuscular; **— sleep** (*Med*) sueño *m* crepuscular.

twill [twil] *n* tela *f* cruzada.

'twill[twil] = **it will**.

twin [twin] **1** *adj* gemelo; **— brother** hermano *m* gemelo; **— sister** hermana *f* gemela; **— beds** camas *fpl* gemelas; **— town** ciudad *f* gemela.
2 *n* gemelo *m*, a *f*; **John and his —** Juan y su hermano gemelo; **identical —s** gemelos *mpl* idénticos; **Siamese —s** hermanos *mpl* siameses.
3 *vt*: **the town with which Wigan is —ned** la ciudad que tiene a Wigan como gemela.

twin-cylinder ['twin'silində*] *adj* de dos cilindros.

twine [twain] **1** *n* guita *f*, hilo *m*, bramante *m*.
2 *vt* (*weave*) tejer; (*encircle*) ceñir, rodear; (*roll up*) enrollar; **she —d the string round her finger** enrolló la cuerda sobre el dedo; **she —d her arms about his neck** le rodeó el cuello con los brazos.
3 *vi* (*of spiral movement*) enroscarse; (*of plant*) trepar, entrelazarse; (*of road*) serpentear.

twin-engined ['twin'endʒind] *adj* bimotor.

twinge [twindʒ] *n* punzada *f*, dolor *m* agudo; (*fig*) remordimiento *m*; **I've been having —s of conscience** me ha estado remordiendo la conciencia.

twining ['twainiŋ] *adj plant* sarmentoso, trepador.

twin-jet ['twin'dʒet] **1** *adj* birreactor. **2** *n* birreactor *m*.

twinkle ['twiŋkl] **1** *n* centelleo *m*, parpadeo *m*; **in a —** en un instante; **"No", he said with a —** "No", dijo maliciosamente, "No" dijo medio riendo; **he had a — in his eye** tenía los ojos risueños.
2 *vi* (*of light*) centellear, parpadear, titilar; (*of eyes*) brillar; (*of feet*) moverse rápidamente.

twinkling ['twiŋkliŋ] **1** *adj light* centelleante, titilante; *eye* brillante, risueño; *feet* rápido, ligero.
2 *n* centelleo *m*, parpadeo *m*; **in the — of an eye** en un abrir y cerrar de ojos.

twinset ['twinset] *n* (*Sew*) conjunto *m*.

twirl [twə:l] **1** *n* vuelta *f* (rápida), giro *m*; (*of pen etc*) rasgo *m*; (*of body*) pirueta *f*.
2 *vt* girar rápidamente, dar vueltas rápidas a; voltear; (*twist*) torcer.
3 *vi* girar rápidamente, dar vueltas rápidas; piruetear.

twist [twist] **1** *n* (**a**) (*of yarn*) torzal *m*; (*of hair*) mecha *f*; trenza *f*; (*of tobacco*) rollo *m*; (*of paper*) barquillo *m*.
(**b**) (*twisting action*) torsión *f*, torcimiento *m*; (*Med*) torcedura *f*; (*on ball*) efecto *m*; **to give one's ankle a —** torcerse el tobillo; **to give a knob a —** girar un botón; **with a quick — of the hand** torciendo rápidamente la mano.
(**c**) (*of mind*) rasgo *m* peculiar, sesgo *m*, peculiaridad *f*.
(**d**) (*coil*) vuelta *f*; (*spiral shape*) enroscadura *f*; (*in road etc*) vuelta *f*, recodo *m*; **—s and turns** vueltas *fpl*; **to take a — round a post with a rope** atar una cuerda alrededor de un poste; **the plot has an unexpected —** la trama tiene un esguince inesperado, la trama tiene un giro imprevisto.
(**e**) (*Mus*) twist *m*.
(**f**) (*fam*) trampa *f*; **it's a —!** ¡aquí hay trampa!; ¡me han robado!
2 *vt* (*wrench out of shape*) torcer, retorcer; *ball* dar efecto a, lanzar con efecto; (*turn*) dar vueltas a, girar; (*give spiral form to*) enroscar, formar en espiral; (*interweave*) trenzar, entrelazar; (*fam*) estafar; (*fig*) *sense, words, argument* forzar, retorcer,

torcer; **to — someone's arm** torcer el brazo a uno; **to — one's arm** torcerse el brazo; **to — a piece off** separar un trozo torciéndolo; **to — something out of shape** deformar algo torciéndolo; **to — paper up into a ball** retorcer un papel en forma de pelota; **I've been —ed!** (*fam*) ¡me han robado!

3 *vi* torcerse, retorcerse; (*coil up*) enroscarse, ensortijarse; (*of road etc*) serpentear, dar vueltas; (*writhe*) retorcerse, revolcarse; (*dance*) bailar el twist.

twister ['twistə*] *n* (*fam*) tramposo *m*, estafador *m*.

twit[1] [twit] *n* (*fam*) imbécil *m*, tonto *m*.

twit[2] [twit] *vt* embromar, tomar el pelo a, guasearse con; **to — someone about something** tomar el pelo a uno con motivo de algo.

twitch [twitʃ] **1** *n* sacudida *f* repentina, tirón *m*; (*nervous*) tic *m*, contracción *f* nerviosa; movimiento *m* espasmódico.

2 *vt* tirar bruscamente de, tirar ligeramente de; *hands* crispar, retorcer; *ears*, *nose etc* mover nerviosamente; **to — something away from someone** quitar algo a uno con un movimiento rápido.

3 *vi* crisparse; moverse nerviosamente.

twitter ['twitə*] **1** *n* (*of bird*) gorjeo *m*; (*fig*) agitación *f*, inquietud *f*, nerviosismo *m*; **to be all of a —, to be in a —** (*fam*) estar nerviosísimo, estar muy agitado.

2 *vi* gorjear; (*fig*) agitarse, estar inquieto, estar nervioso.

'twixt [twikst] *prep* = **betwixt**, *see* **between**.

two [tu:] **1** *adj* dos.

2 *n* dos *m*; **— by —, in —s** de dos en dos; **to break something in —** romper algo en dos, partir algo por la mitad; **they're — of a kind** son idénticos, son dos ejemplares del mismo fenómeno; **to put — and — together** atar cabos.

two-chamber ['tu:'tʃeimbə*] *adj* *parliament* bicamaral, de dos cámaras.

two-decker ['tu:'dekə*] *n* autobús *m* de dos pisos.

two-door ['tu:'dɔ:*] *adj* *car* de dos puertas.

two-edged ['tu:'edʒd] *adj* de doble filo.

two-engined ['tu:'endʒind] *adj* bimotor.

two-faced ['tu:'feist] *adj* (*fig*) doble, falso.

twofold ['tu:fəuld] **1** *adv* dos veces. **2** *adj* doble.

two-handed ['tu:'hændid] *adj* de dos manos; *tool etc* para dos manos.

two-legged ['tu:'legid] *adj* de dos piernas, bípedo.

two-masted ['tu:'ma:stid] *adj* de dos palos.

two-party ['tu:'pɑ:ti] *adj* *state etc* de dos partidos.

twopence ['tʌpəns] *npl* 2 peniques *mpl*; *see* **care**.

twopenny ['tʌpəni] *adj* de 2 peniques, que vale 2 peniques; (*fig*) insignificante, miserable, despreciable.

two-phase ['tu:'feiz] *adj* (*Elec*) bifásico.

two-piece ['tu:'pi:s] **1** *adj* de dos piezas. **2** *n* dos piezas *m*.

two-ply ['tu:'plai] *adj* *wood* de dos capas; *wool* doble.

two-seater ['tu:'si:tə*] **1** *attr* biplaza, de dos plazas. **2** *n* coche *m* (*or* avión *m etc*) biplaza.

twosome ['tu:səm] *n* pareja *f*; grupo *m* de dos, partido *m* de dos.

two-step ['tu:step] *n* paso *m* doble.

two-storey ['tu:'stɔ:ri] *adj* *house* de dos pisos.

two-stroke ['tu:'strəuk] *adj* *engine* de dos tiempos.

two-time ['tu:'taim] *vt* (*US fam*) engañar; hacer una mala jugada a; traicionar.

two-tone ['tu:'təun] *adj* *car* bicolor.

two-way ['tu:'wei] *adj*: **— switch** conmutador *m* de dos direcciones; **— traffic** circulación *f* en ambas direcciones.

'twould [twud] = **it would**.

tycoon [tai'ku:n] *n* magnate *m*.

tyke [taik] *n* (a) (*fam: dog*) perro *m* de la calle; (*child*) chiquillo *m*; **you little —!** ¡tunante! (b) (*prov*) hombre *m* de Yorkshire.

tympanum ['timpənəm] *n* (*Anat, Archit*) tímpano *m*.

type [taip] **1** *n* (a) (*characteristic specimen*) tipo *m*; **to deviate from the —** apartarse del tipo; **to revert to**

— saltar atrás en la cadena natural; **she was the very — of Spanish beauty** era el tipo exacto de la belleza española.

(b) (*person: fam*) tipo *m*, sujeto *m*; **he's an odd —** es un tipo raro; **a — I know** un tío que yo conozco.

(c) (*class*) tipo *m*, género *m*; **people of that —** la gente de ese tipo; **he's not my —** ese tipo de hombre no me gusta, no me gustan los hombres así; **what — of car is it?** ¿qué modelo de coche es?

(d) (*Typ*) tipo *m*, letra *f*, carácter *m*; (*collectively*) tipos *mpl*; **Gothic —** letras *fpl* góticas; **bold —**, **heavy —** negrita *f*; **in heavy —** en negrita.

2 *vt* escribir a máquina, hacer a máquina, mecanografiar.

3 *vi* escribir a máquina; **"secretary ... must be able to —"** "secretaria ... sabiendo mecanografía".

type-cast ['taipkɑ:st] (*irr: see* **cast**) **1** *vt*: **to — an actor** dar a un actor papeles de la misma clase siempre. **2** *ptp, adj actor* encasillado.

typeface ['taipfeis] *n* = **type 1** (d); área *f* de texto impreso, (*loosely*) tipografía *f*.

typescript ['taipskript] **1** *adj* mecanografiado. **2** *n* mecanografiado *m*.

typesetter ['taip.setə*] *n* (*person*) cajista *m*; (*machine*) máquina *f* de componer.

typesetting ['taip.setiŋ] *n* composición *f* (tipográfica).

typewrite ['taiprait] (*irr: see* **write**) *vt see* **type 2**.

typewriter ['taip.raitə*] *n* máquina *f* de escribir.

typewriting ['taip.raitiŋ] *n* mecanografía *f*.

typewritten ['taip.ritn] *adj* mecanografiado, hecho a máquina.

typhoid ['taifɔid] *n* tifoidea *f*, fiebre *f* tifoidea.

typhoon [tai'fu:n] *n* tifón *m*.

typhus ['taifəs] *n* tifus *m*.

typical ['tipikəl] *adj* típico; característico; clásico; **the — Spaniard** el español típico; **wearing the — beret** con la clásica boina; **it is — of him that ...** es característico de él que ...; **isn't that just —!** ¡eso es muy de él!

typically ['tipikəli] *adv* típicamente; **all that is — Spanish** todo lo que es típico de España; **a — smug person** una persona típicamente satisfecha.

typify ['tipifai] *vt* tipificar; simbolizar; representar, ser ejemplo de.

typing ['taipiŋ] *n* mecanografía *f*.

typing paper ['taipiŋ.peipə*] *n* papel *m* para máquina de escribir.

typist ['taipist] *n* mecanógrafo *m*, a *f*.

typographer [tai'pɔgrəfə*] *n* tipógrafo *m*.

typographic(al) [.taipə'græfik(əl)] *adj* tipográfico.

typography [tai'pɔgrəfi] *n* tipografía *f*.

tyrannic(al) [ti'rænik(əl)] *adj* tiránico.

tyrannically [ti'rænikəli] *adv* tiránicamente.

tyrannicide [ti'rænisaid] *n* (*act*) tiranicidio *m*; (*person*) tiranicida *mf*.

tyrannize ['tirənaiz] **1** *vt* tiranizar. **2** *vi*: **to — over a people** tiranizar un pueblo.

tyranny ['tirəni] *n* tiranía *f*.

tyrant ['tairənt] *n* tirano *m*, a *f*.

Tyre ['taiə*] Tiro.

tyre ['taiə*] *n* (*Aut etc*) neumático *m*, llanta *f* (*SAm*); (*outer cover*) cubierta *f*; (*inner tube*) cámara *f* (de aire); (*of cart*) llanta *f*, calce *m*; (*of pram etc*) rueda *f* de goma; **non-skid —** neumático *m* antideslizante; **pneumatic —** neumático *m*; **solid —** neumático *m* macizo; **spare —** neumático *m* de recambio.

tyre-burst ['taiəbə:st] *n* pinchazo *m*, reventón *m*.

tyre valve ['taiəvælv] *n* válvula *m* de neumático.

tyro ['taiərəu] *n see* **tiro**.

Tyrol [ti'rəul] el Tirol.

Tyrolean [.tirə'li(:)ən], **Tyrolese** ['tirə'li:z] **1** *adj* tirolés. **2** *n* tirolés *m*, esa *f*.

tzar [zɑ:*] *n* zar *m*.

tzarina [zɑ:'ri:nə] *n* zarina *f*.

U

ubiquitous [juː'bikwitəs] *adj* ubicuo, omnipresente, que se encuentra en todas partes: **it is — in Spain** se encuentra en toda España; **the secretary has to be** — el secretario tiene que estar constantemente en todas partes.
ubiquity [juː'bikwiti] *n* ubicuidad *f*, omnipresencia *f*.
U-boat ['juːbəut] *n* submarino *m* alemán.
udder ['ʌdə*] *n* ubre *f*.
ugh [əːh] *interj* ¡puf!
uglify ['ʌglifai] *vt* (*fam*) afear.
ugliness ['ʌglinis] *n* fealdad *f*, lo feo; lo peligroso; lo repugnante.
ugly ['ʌgli] *adj appearance, person* feo; *custom, vice etc* feo, repugnante, asqueroso; *situation, wound* peligroso; *rumour etc* nada grato, inquietante; *mood* peligroso, violento; **to be as — as sin** ser feísimo: **to cut up —, to turn —** (*fam*) ponerse violento, amenazar violencia.
Ukraine [juː'krein] Ucrania *f*.
Ukrainian [juː'kreiniən] **1** *adj* ucraniano. **2** *n* ucraniano *m*, a *f*.
ukulele [ˌjuːkə'leili] *n* guitarra *f* hawaiana.
ulcer ['ʌlsə*] *n* úlcera *f*; (*fig*) llaga *f*.
ulcerate ['ʌlsəreit] **1** *vt* ulcerar. **2** *vi* ulcerarse.
ulceration [ˌʌlsə'reiʃən] *n* ulceración *f*.
ulcerous ['ʌlsərəs] *adj* ulceroso.
ulna ['ʌlnə] *n, pl* **ulnae** ['ʌlniː] cúbito *m*.
ulster ['ʌlstə*] *n* úlster *m*.
ulterior [ʌl'tiəriə*] *adj* ulterior; (*motive*) oculto.
ultimate ['ʌltimit] *adj* (*furthest*) más remoto, extremo; (*final*) último, final; *destination etc* definitivo; *purpose, reason, truth etc* fundamental, esencial.
ultimately ['ʌltimitli] *adv* (*in the end*) por último, al final; (*in the long run*) a la larga; (*fundamentally*) en el fondo, fundamentalmente.
ultimatum [ˌʌlti'meitəm] *n, pl* **ultimata** [ˌʌlti'meitə] ultimátum *m*.
ultimo ['ʌltiməu] *adv* (Comm): **the 5th** — el 5 del mes pasado.
ultra... ['ʌltrə] ultra...
ultra-fashionable ['ʌltrə'fæʃnəbl] *adj* muy de moda, elegantísimo.
ultramarine [ˌʌltrəmə'riːn] **1** *adj* ultramarino. **2** *n* azul *m* de ultramar.
ultramodern ['ʌltrə'mɔdən] *adj* ultramoderno.
ultramontane [ˌʌltrə'mɔntein] **1** *adj* ultramontano. **2** *n* ultramontano *m*.
ultramontanism [ˌʌltrə'mɔntinizəm] *n* ultramontanismo *m*.
ultra-red [ˌʌltrə'red] *adj* infrarrojo.
ultra-short wave ['ʌltrə,ʃɔːt'weiv] **1** *n* onda *f* extracorta. **2** *attr* de onda extracorta.
ultrasonic ['ʌltrə'sɔnik] *adj* ultrasónico.
ultraviolet ['ʌltrə'vaiəlit] *adj* ultravioleta; **— rays** rayos *mpl* ultravioleta; **— treatment** tratamiento *m* de onda ultravioleta.
ululate ['juːljuleit] *vi* ulular.
ululation [ˌjuːlju'leiʃən] *n* ululato *m*.
Ulysses [juː'lisiːz] *m* Ulises.
umber ['ʌmbə*] **1** *n* tierra *f* de sombra. **2** *adj* color ocre oscuro, pardo oscuro.
umbilical [ˌʌmbi'laikəl] *adj* umbilical.
umbilicus [ˌʌmbi'laikəs] *n* ombligo *m*.
umbrage ['ʌmbridʒ] *n* resentimiento *m*; **to take —** ofenderse (*at por*), resentirse (*at de*).
umbrella [ʌm'brelə] *n* paraguas *m*; (*Mil: of fire*) cortina *f* de fuego antiaéreo; (*of aircraft*) sombrilla *f* protectora.
umbrella stand [ʌm'breləstænd] *n* paragüero *m*.
umpire ['ʌmpaiə*] **1** *n* árbitro *m*. **2** *vt* arbitrar.
umpteen ['ʌmptiːn] *adj* (*fam*) tantísimos, muchísimos.
umpteenth ['ʌmptiːnθ] *adj* (*fam*) enésimo; **for the — time** por enésima vez.

un... [ʌn] in...; des...; no...; nada...; poco...; sin...; anti...
unabashed ['ʌnə'bæʃt] *adj* descarado, desvergonzado; desenfadado; **"Yes", he said quite —** "Sí", dijo sin alterarse.
unabated ['ʌnə'beitid] *adj* sin disminución, no disminuido.
unable ['ʌn'eibl] *adj*: **to be — to do something** no poder hacer algo; ser incapaz de hacer algo; verse imposibilitado de hacer algo; **I am —** to see why no veo por qué, no comprendo cómo; **those — to go** los que no pueden ir.
unabridged ['ʌnə'bridʒd] *adj* íntegro; **the — text** la versión íntegra.
unaccented ['ʌnæk'sentid] *adj* inacentuado, átono.
unacceptable ['ʌnək'septəbl] *adj* inaceptable.
unaccommodating ['ʌnə'kɔmədeitiŋ] *adj* poco amable, poco servicial.
unaccompanied ['ʌnə'kʌmpənid] *adj* (Mus) sin acompañamiento, no acompañado; **to go somewhere —** ir a un sitio sin compañía, ir solo a un sitio.
unaccountable ['ʌnə'kauntəbl] *adj* inexplicable.
unaccountably ['ʌnə'kauntəbli] *adv* inexplicablemente; **— annoyed** extrañamente enfadado, enfadado sin motivo.
unaccounted ['ʌnə'kauntid] *adj*: **two passengers are — for** no hay noticias de dos de los pasajeros, se ignora la suerte de dos de los pasajeros.
unaccustomed ['ʌnə'kʌstəmd] *adj* (a) **to be — to something** no estar acostumbrado a algo; **to be — to doing something** no acostumbrar hacer algo, no tener la costumbre de hacer algo.
(b) **with — zeal** con un entusiasmo insólito.
unacknowledged ['ʌnək'nɔlidʒd] *adj* no reconocido; (*letter etc*) no contestado, sin contestar.
unacquainted ['ʌnə'kweintid] *adj*: **to be — with something** desconocer algo, ignorar algo.
unadaptable ['ʌnə'dæptəbl] *adj* inadaptable.
unaddressed ['ʌnə'drest] *adj letter* sin señas.
unadorned ['ʌnə'dɔːnd] *adj* sin adorno, sencillo; **beauty —** la hermosura sin adorno.
unadulterated ['ʌnə'dʌltəreitid] *adj* sin mezcla, puro.
unadvisable ['ʌnəd'vaizəbl] *adj* poco aconsejable; **it is — to + infin** es poco aconsejable + *infin*.
unaesthetic [ˌʌniːs'θetik] *adj* antiestético.
unaffected ['ʌnə'fektid] *adj* (a) *person etc* sin afectación. (b) **to be — by** no ser afectado por.
unaffectedly ['ʌnə'fektidli] *adv* sin afectación; sinceramente, hondamente.
unafraid ['ʌnə'freid] *adj* sin temor, impertérrito.
unaided ['ʌn'eidid] **1** *adv* sin ayuda, por sí solo. **2** *adj*: **by his own — efforts** por sí solo, sin ayuda de nadie.
unalloyed ['ʌnə'lɔid] *adj* sin mezcla, puro.
unalterable [ʌn'ɔltərəbl] *adj* inalterable.
unalterably [ʌn'ɔltərəbli] *adv* de modo inalterable; **we are — opposed to it** nos oponemos rotundamente a ello.
unaltered ['ʌn'ɔltəd] *adj* inalterado, sin cambiar, sin alteración.
unambiguous ['ʌnæm'bigjuəs] *adj* inequívoco.
unambiguously ['ʌnæm'bigjuəsli] *adv* de modo inequívoco.
unambitious ['ʌnæm'biʃəs] *adj* poco ambicioso, poco emprendedor.
un-American ['ʌnə'merikən] *adj* antiamericano.
unamiable ['ʌn'eimiəbl] *adj* poco simpático.
unanimity [ˌjuːnə'nimiti] *n* unanimidad *f*.
unanimous [juː'næniməs] *adj* unánime.
unanimously [juː'næniməsli] *adv* unánimemente; por unanimidad; **the motion was passed —** la moción fue aprobada por unanimidad.
unanswerable [ʌn'ɑːnsərəbl] *adj* (*question*) incontestable; (*attack etc*) irrebatible, irrefutable.

unanswered ['ʌn'ɑ:nsəd] *adj question* incontestado, sin contestar; *letter* no contestado, sin contestar.

unappealable ['ʌnə'pi:ləbl] *adj* inapelable.

unappetizing ['ʌn'æpitaiziŋ] *adj* poco apetitoso; *(fig)* repugnante, nada atractivo.

unappreciative ['ʌnə'pri:ʃiətiv] *adj* desagradecido; **to be — of something** no agradecer algo debidamente.

unapproachable ['ʌnə'prəutʃəbl] *adj* inaccesible; *person* intratable, inabordable.

unappropriated ['ʌnə'prəuprieitid] *adj* no asignado.

unarmed ['ʌn'ɑ:md] *adj* que no lleva armas, desarmado; *(defenceless)* inerme.

unascertained ['ʌnæsə'teind] *adj* no averiguado, que queda por averiguar.

unashamed ['ʌnə'ʃeimd] *adj* desvergonzado, descarado; **he was quite — about it** no tuvo remordimiento alguno por esto, no sintió el menor remordimiento.

unashamedly ['ʌnə'ʃeimidli] *adv* desvergonzadamente; **to be — proud of something** enorgullecerse sin remordimiento de algo.

unasked ['ʌn'ɑ:skt] *adj*: **to do something — hacer** algo sin ser rogado; **they came to the party —** vinieron al guateque sin ser invitados.

unassailable ['ʌnə'seiləbl] *adj fortress* inexpugnable; *position* inatacable; *argument* irrebatible; **he is quite — on that score** ne se le puede atacar por ese lado.

unassisted ['ʌnə'sistid] *adj* sin ayuda, por sí solo.

unassuming ['ʌnə'sju:miŋ] *adj* modesto, sin pretensiones.

unassumingly ['ʌnə'sju:miŋli] *adv* modestamente.

unattached ['ʌnə'tætʃt] *adj part etc* suelto, separable; *person* libre, no prometido, que no tiene novio *(or novia)*; *(Mil)* de reemplazo; *(Law)* no embargado.

unattainable ['ʌnə'teinəbl] *adj* inasequible; *record etc* inalcanzable.

unattended ['ʌnə'tendid] *adj* sin guardia, sin personal; **to leave something — dejar algo sin** personal.

unattractive ['ʌnə'træktiv] *adj* poco atractivo.

unattractiveness ['ʌnə'træktivnis] *n* falta *f* de atractivo.

unauthorized ['ʌn'ɔ:θəraizd] *adj* desautorizado.

unavailable ['ʌnə'veiləbl] *adj* indisponible, inasequible; *person* que no puede atender a uno, que no está libre.

unavailing ['ʌnə'veiliŋ] *adj* inútil, vano, infructuoso.

unavailingly ['ʌnə'veiliŋli] *adv* inútilmente, en vano.

unavoidable [,ʌnə'vɔidəbl] *adj* inevitable, ineludible; **it is — that . . .** es inevitable que . . .

unavoidably [,ʌnə'vɔidəbli] *adv* inevitablemente; **he is — detained** tiene un retraso inevitable.

unaware ['ʌnə'wɛə*] *adj*: **to be — that** ignorar que; **I am not — that** no ignoro que; **to be — of something** ignorar algo, no darse cuenta de algo.

unawares ['ʌnə'wɛəz] *adv* de improviso, inopinadamente; **to catch someone — coger a uno desprevenido.**

unbacked ['ʌn'bækt] *adj (Fin)* a descubierto.

unbalance ['ʌn'bæləns] *n* desequilibrio *m*.

unbalanced ['ʌn'bælənst] *adj* desequilibrado; *(mentally)* trastornado, desequilibrado.

unbandage ['ʌn'bændidʒ] *vt* desvendar, quitar las vendas a.

unbaptized ['ʌnbæp'taizd] *adj* sin bautizar.

unbar ['ʌn'bɑ:*] *vt door etc* desatrancar; *(fig)* abrir, franquear.

unbearable [ʌn'bɛərəbl] *adj* inaguantable, insufrible, intolerable.

unbearably [ʌn'bɛərəbli] *adv* insoportablemente; **it is — hot** hace un calor inaguantable; **she is — vain** es vanidosa en un grado inaguantable.

unbeatable ['ʌn'bi:təbl] *adj team etc* imbatible; *price, offer* inmejorable.

unbeaten ['ʌn'bi:tn] *adj team* imbatido; *army* invicto; *price* no mejorado.

unbecoming ['ʌnbi'kʌmiŋ] *adj* indecoroso, impropio; *dress etc* que sienta mal a uno; **it is — to + infin** no es elegante + *infin*.

unbeknown ['ʌnbi'nəun] *adj*: **— to me** sin saberlo yo.

unbelief ['ʌnbi'li:f] *n (Rel: in general)* descreimiento *m, (of person)* falta *f* de fe; *(astonishment)* incredulidad *f*.

unbelievable [,ʌnbi'li:vəbl] *adj* increíble; **it is — that . . .** es increíble que + *subj*.

unbelievably [,ʌnbi'li:vəbli] *adv* increíblemente.

unbeliever ['ʌnbi'li:və*] *n* no creyente *mf*, descreído *m*, a *f*.

unbelieving ['ʌnbi'li:viŋ] *adj* incrédulo.

unbend ['ʌn'bend] *(irr: see* bend*)* **1** *vt* desencorvar, enderezar. **2** *vi (fig)* suavizarse; *(person)* hacerse más afable.

unbending ['ʌn'bendiŋ] *adj* inflexible, rígido; *(person)* inflexible; poco afable.

unbias(s)ed ['ʌn'baiəst] *adj* imparcial.

unbidden ['ʌn'bidn] *adj*: **to do something — hacer** algo sin ser rogado; **they came to the party —** vinieron al guateque sin ser invitados.

unbind ['ʌn'baind] *(irr: see* bind*)* *vt* desatar; *(unbandage)* desvendar.

unbleached ['ʌn'bli:tʃt] *adj* sin blanquear.

unblemished [ʌn'blemiʃt] *adj* sin tacha, intachable.

unblinking [ʌn'bliŋkiŋ] *adj* imperturbable; *(pej)* desvergonzado.

unblock ['ʌn'blɔk] *vt pipe etc* desatascar, desobstruir; *road etc* abrir, franquear.

unblushing [ʌn'blʌʃiŋ] *adj* desvergonzado, fresco.

unblushingly [ʌn'blʌʃiŋli] *adv* desvergonzadamente; **he said —** dijo tan fresco.

unbolt ['ʌn'bəult] *vt* desatrancar.

unborn ['ʌn'bɔ:n] *adj* no nacido aún, nonato; **generations yet — generaciones** *fpl* que están todavía por nacer.

unbosom [ʌn'buzəm] *vr*: **to — oneself of something** desahogarse de algo, confesar algo abiertamente; **to — oneself to someone** abrir su pecho a uno.

unbound ['ʌn'baund] *adj* en hojas sueltas, sin encuadernar.

unbounded [ʌn'baundid] *adj* ilimitado, infinito.

unbowed ['ʌn'baud] *adj*: **with head — con la cabeza** erguida, orgullosamente.

unbreakable ['ʌn'breikəbl] *adj* irrompible.

unbribable ['ʌn'braibəbl] *adj* insobornable.

unbridled [ʌn'braidld] *adj (fig)* desenfrenado.

unbroken ['ʌn'brəukən] *adj crockery etc* entero, intacto; *seal* intacto; *time, silence* no interrumpido; *series* continuo, sin solución de continuidad; *sheet of ice etc* continuo; *record* imbatido; *horse* no domado; *spirit* indómito.

unbuckle ['ʌn'bʌkl] *vt* deshebillar.

unburden [ʌn'bɔ:dn] **1** *vt person* aliviar; **to — someone of a load** aliviar a uno quitándole un peso; **to — one's heart** abrir su pecho.

2 *vr*: **to — oneself** abrir su pecho *(to someone a* uno*)*; **to — oneself of something** desahogarse de algo, confesar algo abiertamente.

unburied ['ʌn'berid] *adj* insepulto.

unbusinesslike [ʌn'biznislaik] *adj* poco práctico, poco metódico; *informal*; que carece de instinto comercial.

unbutton ['ʌn'bʌtn] **1** *vt* desabotonar, desabrochar. **2** *vi (fam)* hacerse más afable.

uncalled-for [ʌn'kɔ:ldfɔ:*] *adj* gratuito, inmerecido; impertinente.

uncannily [ʌn'kænili] *adv* misteriosamente; **it is — like the other one** tiene un extraño parecido con el otro, se parece extraordinariamente al otro.

uncanny [ʌn'kæni] *adj* misterioso, extraño, extraordinario; **it's quite — es extraordinario; it's — how he does it** no llego a comprender cómo lo hace.

uncap ['ʌn'kæp] *vt* destapar.

uncared-for ['ʌn'kɛədfɔ:*] *adj person* abandonado, desamparado; *appearance* desaseado, de abandono; *building etc* abandonado.

unceasing [ʌn'si:siŋ] *adj* incesante.

unceasingly [ʌn'si:siŋli] *adv* incesantemente, sin cesar.

uncensored ['ʌn'sensəd] *adj* no censurado.

unceremonious ['ʌn,seri'məuniəs] *adj* descortés, brusco, poco formal.

unceremoniously ['ʌn,seri'məuniəsli] *adv* sin miramientos.

uncertain [ʌn'sə:tn] *adj* incierto, dudoso; *person (of character)* indeciso, vacilante; *temper* vivo; **to be — of** no estar seguro de; **I am — whether . . .** no estoy seguro si . . .

uncertainly [ʌn'sə:tnli] *adv* inciertamente; **he said —** dijo indeciso.

uncertainty [ʌn'sə:tnti] *n* incertidumbre *f*, duda *f*; indecisión *f*, irresolución *f*; **in view of this — . . .** teniendo en cuenta estas dudas . . .; **in order to remove any — para disipar estas dudas.**

uncertificated ['ʌnsə'tifikeitid] *adj teacher etc* sin título.

unchain [ʌn'tʃein] *vt* desencadenar.

unchallengeable [ʌn'tʃælindʒəbl] *adj* incontestable, incuestionable.

unchallenged [ʌn'tʃælindʒd] *adj* incontestado; **we cannot let that go — eso no lo podemos dejar pasar** sin protesta.

unchangeable [ʌn'tʃeindʒəbl] *adj* inalterable, inmutable.
unchanged [ʌn'tʃeindʒd] *adj* sin alterar.
unchanging [ʌn'tʃeindʒiŋ] *adj* inalterable, inmutable.
uncharitable [ʌn'tʃæritəbl] *adj* poco caritativo, duro.
uncharted ['ʌn'tʃɑːtid] *adj* inexplorado, desconocido.
unchaste ['ʌn'tʃeist] *adj* impúdico; *wife* infiel.
unchecked ['ʌn'tʃekt] 1 *adv* libremente, sin estorbo, sin restricción. 2 *adj abuse etc* desenfrenado; *fact etc* no comprobado.
unchivalrous ['ʌn'ʃivəlrəs] *adj* poco caballeroso.
unchristian ['ʌn'kristiən] *adj* poco cristiano, indigno de un cristiano.
uncial ['ʌnsiəl] 1 *adj* uncial. 2 *n* uncial *f*.
uncircumcised ['ʌn'səːkəmsaizd] *adj* incircunciso.
uncivil ['ʌn'sivil] *adj* descortés, grosero, incivil; **to be — to someone** ser grosero con uno.
uncivilized ['ʌn'sivilaizd] *adj* incivilizado, inculto.
unclad ['ʌn'klæd] *adj* desnudo.
unclaimed ['ʌn'kleimd] *adj* sin reclamar, sin dueño.
unclasp ['ʌn'klɑːsp] *vt dress etc* desabrochar; *hands* soltar, separar.
unclassified ['ʌn'klæsifaid] *adj* sin clasificar.
uncle ['ʌŋkl] *n* tío *m*; (*sl*) prestamista *m*; prendero *m*; **my — and aunt** mis tíos; **to talk to someone like a Dutch —** decir a uno cuatro verdades; **U— Sam** el tío Sam (*personificación de EE.UU.*).
unclean ['ʌn'kliːn] *adj* sucio, inmundo; (*fig*) deshonesto; (*ritually*) poluto.
uncleanliness ['ʌn'klenlinis] *n* suciedad *f*; (*fig*) deshonestidad *f*.
unclench ['ʌn'klentʃ] *vt* desapretar, soltar.
uncloak ['ʌn'kləuk] *vt* desencapotar.
unclog ['ʌn'klɔg] *vt* desobstruir, desatrancar.
unclothe ['ʌn'kləuð] *vt* desnudar.
unclothed ['ʌn'kləuðd] *adj* desnudo.
unclouded ['ʌn'klaudid] *adj* despejado.
uncoil ['ʌn'kɔil] 1 *vt* desenrollar. 2 *vi* desenrollarse; desovillarse; (*snake*) desanillarse.
uncollected [ʌnkə'lektid] *adj fare etc* sin cobrar.
uncoloured ['ʌn'kʌləd] *adj* en blanco; *account etc* objetivo.
uncombed ['ʌn'kəumd] *adj* despeinado, sin peinar.
uncomely ['ʌn'kʌmli] *adj* desgarbado.
uncomfortable [ʌn'kʌmfətəbl] *adj* (*physically*) incómodo; *feeling* molesto; **to be —** (*chair etc*) ser incómodo; *person* (*ill at ease*) estar inquieto, sentirse molesto; **to feel — about something** preocuparse por algo, inquietarse por algo, no estar del todo satisfecho acerca de algo; remorderle a uno la conciencia por algo; **we had an — few minutes** pasamos un mal rato; **to make life — for someone** amargar la vida a uno, crear dificultades a uno.
uncomfortably [ʌn'kʌmfətəbli] *adv* incómodamente; **he thought —** pensaba con cierto remordimiento, pensaba algo inquieto; **the shell fell — close** cayó el proyectil inquietantemente cerca.
uncommitted ['ʌnkə'mitid] *adj nation* no comprometido, no alineado.
uncommon [ʌn'kɔmən] 1 *adj* poco común, nada frecuente; extraño, insólito. 2 *adv* (*fam*) sumamente, extraordinariamente.
uncommonly [ʌn'kɔmənli] *adv* raramente, rara vez; extraordinariamente; **that's — kind of you** ha sido Vd amabilísimo; **not —** con cierta frecuencia.
uncommunicative ['ʌnkə'mjuːnikətiv] *adj* poco comunicativo, reservado.
uncomplaining ['ʌnkəm'pleiniŋ] *adj* resignado, sumiso.
uncomplainingly ['ʌnkəm'pleiniŋli] *adv* con resignación, sumisamente.
uncomplicated [ʌn'kɔmplikeitid] *adj person etc* sin complicaciones, sencillo.
uncomplimentary ['ʌn,kɔmpli'mentəri] *adj* nada lisonjero, poco halagüeño.
uncompromising [ʌn'kɔmprəmaiziŋ] *adj* intransigente.
unconcealed ['ʌnkən'siːld] *adj* abierto, no disimulado; **with — glee** con abierta satisfacción.
unconcern ['ʌnkən'səːn] *n* (*calm*) calma *f*, tranquilidad *f*, (*in face of danger*) sangre *f* fría; (*lack of interest*) indiferencia *f*, despreocupación *f*.
unconcerned ['ʌnkən'səːnd] *adj* tranquilo; indiferente, despreocupado; **he went on speaking —** siguió hablando sin inmutarse; **to be — about something** no inquietarse por algo.
unconcernedly ['ʌnkən'səːnidli] *adv* con calma, tranquilamente; con sangre fría; con indiferencia; sin preocuparse, sin inquietarse.
unconditional ['ʌnkən'diʃənl] *adj* incondicional, sin condiciones.

unconditionally ['ʌnkən'diʃnəli] *adv* incondicionalmente.
unconfessed ['ʌnkən'fest] *adj* inconfeso.
unconfined ['ʌnkən'faind] *adj* ilimitado, no restringido, libre; **let joy be —** que se regocijen todos.
unconfirmed ['ʌnkən'fəːmd] *adj* no confirmado, inconfirmado.
uncongenial ['ʌnkən'dʒiːniəl] *adj* antipático; desagradable.
unconnected ['ʌnkə'nektid] *adj* inconexo; **— with** no relacionado con.
unconquerable [ʌn'kɔŋkərəbl] *adj* inconquistable, invencible.
unconquered [ʌn'kɔŋkəd] *adj* invicto.
unconscionable [ʌn'kɔnʃnəbl] *adj* desmedido, desrazonable.
unconscious [ʌn'kɔnʃəs] 1 *adj* (a) inconsciente, no intencional; **to be — of** estar inconsciente de, ignorar, no darse cuenta de; **to remain blissfully — of the danger** continuar tranquilamente sin darse cuenta del peligro.
(b) (*Med*) sin sentido, desmayado, inconsciente; **to be —** estar sin sentido, estar desmayado; **to be — for 3 hours** pasar 3 horas antes de volver en sí; **to become —** perder el sentido, perder el conocimiento, desmayarse; **to fall —** caer sin sentido; **they found him —** le encontraron inconsciente. 2 *n*: **the —** lo inconsciente.
unconsciously [ʌn'kɔnʃəsli] *adv* inconscientemente; **an — funny remark** una observación que no quería ser humorística, una observación hecha sin intención humorística.
unconsciousness [ʌn'kɔnʃəsnis] *n* (*Med*) insensibilidad *f*, pérdida *f* de conocimiento, falta *f* de sentido.
unconsidered ['ʌnkən'sidəd] *adj* desatendido; **— trifles** pequeñeces *fpl* a las que nadie ha prestado atención.
unconstitutional ['ʌn,kɔnsti'tjuːʃənl] *adj* inconstitucional.
unconstitutionally [ʌn,kɔnsti'tjuːʃnəli] *adv* inconstitucionalmente.
unconstrained ['ʌnkən'streined] *adj* libre, no franco.
uncontested ['ʌnkən'testid] *adj* incontestado; (*Parl*) *seat* ganado sin oposición.
uncontrollable ['ʌnkən'trəuləbl] *adj* incontrolable; *temper* ingobernable; *laughter* incontenible; *terror etc* irrefrenable.
uncontrolled ['ʌnkən'trəuld] *adj* incontrolado, libre, desenfrenado.
unconventional ['ʌnkən'venʃənl] *adj* poco convencional; *person* poco formalista, extravagante, original, despreocupado.
unconversant [ʌnkən'vəːsənt] *adj*: **to be — with** estar poco versado en.
unconverted ['ʌnkən'vəːtid] *adj* no convertido (*also Fin*).
unconvinced ['ʌnkən'vinst] *adj*: **to remain —** seguir sin convencerse.
unconvincing ['ʌnkən'vinsiŋ] *adj* poco convincente.
unconvincingly ['ʌnkən'vinsiŋli] *adv* (*argue etc*) sin convencer a nadie.
uncooked ['ʌn'kukt] *adj* sin cocer, crudo.
uncork ['ʌn'kɔːk] *vt* descorchar, destapar.
uncorrected ['ʌnkə'rektid] *adj* sin corregir.
uncorroborated ['ʌnkə'rɔbəreitid] *adj* no confirmado.
uncorrupted ['ʌnkə'rʌptid] *adj* incorrupto; **— by** no corrompido por.
uncountable ['ʌn'kauntəbl] *adj* incontable.
uncounted ['ʌn'kauntid] *adj* sin cuenta.
uncouple ['ʌn'kʌpl] *vt* desacoplar, desenganchar.
uncouth [ʌn'kuːθ] *adj* grosero, ineducado, inculto.
uncover [ʌn'kʌvə*] *vt* descubrir; (*remove lid of*) destapar; (*remove coverings of*) dejar al descubierto; (*disclose*) descubrir, dejar al descubierto, dejar patente.
uncovered [ʌn'kʌvəd] *adj* descubierto, sin cubierta.
uncritical ['ʌn'kritikəl] *adj* falto de sentido crítico.
uncrossed ['ʌn'krɔst] *adj cheque* sin cruzar.
uncrowned ['ʌn'kraund] *adj* sin corona; **the — king of Slobodia** el rey sin corona de Eslobodia.
unction ['ʌŋkʃən] *n* (*unguent*) unción *f*, ungüento *m*; (*fig*) unción *f*; celo *m*, fervor *m*; (*pej*) efusión *f*, celo *m* fingido, fervor *m* afectado; zalamería *f*; **extreme —** (*Eccl*) extremaunción *f*; **he said with —** dijo efusivo.
unctuous ['ʌŋktjuəs] *adj* (*fig*) afectadamente fervoroso; sobón, zalamero; **in an — voice** en tono efusivo, en tono meloso.
unctuousness ['ʌŋktjuəsnis] *n* (*fig*) efusión *f*, celo *m* fingido, fervor *m* afectado; zalamería *f*.
uncultivable ['ʌn'kʌltivəbl] *adj* incultivable.
uncultivated ['ʌn'kʌltiveitid] *adj* inculto (*also fig*).

uncultured ['ʌn'kʌltʃəd] *adj* inculto, iletrado.
uncurl ['ʌn'kəːl] **1** *vt* desrizar, desenrollar, abrir. **2** *vi* desrizarse, desenrollarse, abrirse; desovillarse.
uncut ['ʌn'kʌt] *adj* sin cortar; *stone* sin labrar; *diamond* en bruto, sin tallar; *book* intonso.
undamaged [ʌn'dæmidʒd] *adj* indemne, intacto; sin sufrir desperfectos.
undamped ['ʌn'dæmpt] *adj* (*fig*) no disminuido.
undated ['ʌn'deitid] *adj* sin fecha.
undaunted ['ʌn'dɔːntid] *adj* impávido, impertérrito; **he carried on quite** — siguió sin inmutarse; **with** — **bravery** con valor intrépido; **to be** — **by** no dejarse desanimar por.
undeceive ['ʌndi'siːv] *vt* desengañar, desilusionar.
undecided ['ʌndi'saidid] *adj* *question* pendiente, no resuelto; *person's character* indeciso; **we are still** — **whether to** + *infin* no hemos decidido todavía si + *infin*; **that is still** — eso queda por resolver.
undecipherable ['ʌndi'saifərəbl] *adj* indescifrable.
undeclinable ['ʌndi'klainəbl] *adj* (*Gram*) indeclinable.
undefeated ['ʌndi'fiːtid] *adj* invicto, imbatido; **he was** — **at the end** siguió invicto al final.
undefended ['ʌndi'fendid] *adj* indefenso; (*Law*) *suit* ganado por incomparecencia del demandado.
undefiled ['ʌndi'faild] *adj* puro, inmaculado; — **by any contact with** ... no corrompido por contacto alguno con ...
undefined [,ʌndi'faind] *adj* indefinido.
undemonstrative ['ʌndi'mɔnstrətiv] *adj* reservado, cohibido, poco expresivo.
undeniable [,ʌndi'naiəbl] *adj* innegable; **it is** — **that** ... es innegable que ...
undeniably [,ʌndi'naiəbli] *adv* indudablemente; **it is** — **true that** ... es innegable que ...; **an** — **successful trip** un viaje de éxito innegable.
undenominational ['ʌndi,nɔmi'neiʃənl] *adj* no sectario.
undependable ['ʌndi'pendəbl] *adj* poco formal, poco confiable.
under ['ʌndə*] **1** *adv* debajo; abajo; *see* **down** *etc.*
 2 *prep* **(a)** (*place: precise*) debajo de, *eg* — **the table** debajo de la mesa; (*less precise*) bajo, *eg* — **the sky** bajo el cielo, — **the water** bajo el agua.
 (b) (*place, fig*) — **the Romans** bajo los romanos; — **Ferdinand VII** bajo Fernando VII, bajo el reinado de Fernando VII; — **the command of** bajo el mando de; — **lock and key** bajo llave; — **oath** bajo juramento; — **full sail** a todo trapo, a vela llena; a toda vela; **the field is** — **wheat** el campo está sembrado de trigo.
 (c) (*number etc*) — **50** menos de 50; **any number** — **90** cualquier número inferior a 90; **in** — **2 hours** en menos de 2 horas; **aged** — **21** que tiene menos de 21 años; **it sells at** — **£5** se vende a menos de 5 libras.
 (d) (*according to, by*) con arreglo a, de acuerdo con, conforme a, según; — **Article 25 of the Code** conforme al Artículo 25 del Código; **his rights** — **the contract** sus derechos según el contrato.
under- ['ʌndə*] *in compounds*: **(a)** *adv* insuficientemente, *eg* **under-prepared** insuficientemente preparado.
 (b) *prep*: **an under-15** un menor de 15 años, una persona que tiene menos de 15 años.
 (c) *adj part etc* bajo, inferior; *clothing* inferior; (*in rank*) subalterno, segundo, *eg* **the under-cook** la cocinera segunda; **the under-gardener** el mozo de huerto.
underact ['ʌndər'ækt] *vi* no dar de sí, hacer un papel sin el debido brío.
underarm ['ʌndərɑːm] **1** *adj* (*Anat*) sobacal, del sobaco; *service etc* hecho con la mano debajo del hombro.
 2 *adv*: **to serve** — sacar con la mano debajo del hombro.
underbelly ['ʌndə,beli] *n* (*fig*) parte *f* indefensa, parte *f* más expuesta al ataque.
underbid ['ʌndə'bid] (*irr: see* **bid**) **1** *vt* ofrecer precio más bajo que. **2** *vi* (*Bridge*) declarar menos de lo que tiene uno.
underbrush ['ʌndəbrʌʃ] *n* maleza *f*, monte *m* bajo.
undercarriage ['ʌndə,kæridʒ] *n*, **undercart** ['ʌndəkɑːt] *n* (*fam*) tren *m* de aterrizaje.
undercharge ['ʌndə'tʃɑːdʒ] *vt* cobrar menos del precio justo a.
underclothes ['ʌndəkləuðz] *npl*, **underclothing** ['ʌndə,kləuðiŋ] *n* ropa *f* interior.
undercoat ['ʌndəkəut] *n* (*of paint*) primera capa *f*.
undercover ['ʌndə,kʌvə*] *adj* secreto, clandestino.
undercurrent ['ʌndə,kʌrənt] *n* corriente *f* submarina, contracorriente *f*; (*fig*) nota *f* callada; tendencia *f*

oculta; **an** — **of criticism** una serie de críticas calladas.
undercut ['ʌndəkʌt] (*irr: see* **cut**) *vt* *competitor* rebajar los precios para competir con.
underdeveloped ['ʌndədi'veləpt] *adj* subdesarrollado.
underdevelopment ['ʌndədi'veləpmənt] *n* subdesarrollo *m*.
underdog ['ʌndədɔg] *n* (*socially*) desvalido *m*; (*in game*) perdidoso *m*, el que está perdiendo; **the** —**s** los de abajo, los débiles, los desamparados.
underdone ['ʌndə'dʌn] *adj* poco hecho, medio asado.
underdrawers ['ʌndə'drɔːəz] *npl* (*US*) calzoncillos *mpl*.
underdress ['ʌndə'dres] *vi* vestirse sin la debida elegancia.
underemployed ['ʌndərim'plɔid] *adj*: — **person** persona *f* a la que no se exige todo el trabajo de que es capaz, persona *f* de una capacidad que no se utiliza debidamente; **the factory is** — la fábrica tiene capacidad no utilizada, la fábrica tiene menos trabajo del que quisiera.
underestimate ['ʌndər'estimit] *n* estimación *f* demasiado baja.
underestimate ['ʌndər'estimeit] *vt* subestimar; *person etc* tener en menos de lo que merece; **to** — **one's opponent** menospreciar a su adversario.
underexpose ['ʌndəriks'pəuz] *vt* (*Phot*) exponer insuficientemente.
underexposed ['ʌndəriks'pəuzd] *adj* (*Phot*) subexpuesto.
underexposure ['ʌndəriks'pəuʒə*] *n* (*Phot*) exposición *f* insuficiente.
underfed ['ʌndə'fed] *adj* subalimentado.
underfeed ['ʌndə'fiːd] (*irr: see* **feed**) *vt* alimentar insuficientemente.
underfeeding ['ʌndə'fiːdiŋ] *n* subalimentación *f*.
underfoot ['ʌndə'fut] *adv* debajo de los pies; **it's very wet** — el suelo está mojado.
undergarment ['ʌndə,gɑːmənt] *n* prenda *f* de ropa interior; —**s** ropa *f* interior.
undergo ['ʌndə'gəu] (*irr: see* **go**) *vt* sufrir, experimentar; *operation* someterse a; *treatment* recibir; **to** — **repairs** ser reparado.
undergraduate ['ʌndə'grædjuit] **1** *n* estudiante *mf* (*no graduado*).
 2 *adj*, *attr* *student* no graduado; *study* de licenciatura, para estudiantes no graduados; **70** — **rooms** 70 habitaciones para estudiantes.
underground ['ʌndəgraund] **1** *adj* subterráneo; (*fig*) clandestino, secreto.
 2 *adv* bajo tierra; **it's 6 feet** — está a 6 pies bajo tierra.
 3 *n* (*Rail*) metro *m*; (*Mil, Pol*) resistencia *f*; movimiento *m* clandestino.
undergrowth ['ʌndəgrəuθ] *n* maleza *f*, monte *m* bajo.
underhand ['ʌndəhænd] **1** *adj* *service etc* hecho con la mano debajo del hombro; (*fig*) *method* turbio, poco limpio; *trick* malo; *attack* solapado.
 2 *adv*: **to serve** — sacar con la mano debajo del hombro.
underlie [,ʌndə'lai] (*irr: see* **lie**) *vt* estar debajo de, extenderse debajo de; servir de base a; (*fig*) estar a la base de, ser la razón fundamental de.
underline [,ʌndə'lain] *vt* subrayar (*also fig*).
underling ['ʌndəliŋ] *n* subordinado *m*, inferior *m*; (*follower*) secuaz *m*.
underlining [,ʌndə'lainiŋ] *n* subrayado *m*.
underlying ['ʌndə'laiiŋ] *adj* subyacente; (*fig*) fundamental, esencial.
undermanned ['ʌndə'mænd] *adj*: **to be** — estar sin la debida tripulación, no tener el debido personal.
undermentioned ['ʌndə'menʃənd] *adj* abajo citado.
undermine [,ʌndə'main] *vt* socavar, minar (*also fig*); **his health is being** —**d by** ... su salud está siendo arruinada por ...
undermost ['ʌndəməust] *adj* (el) más bajo.
underneath ['ʌndə'niːθ] **1** *adv* debajo. **2** *prep* bajo, debajo de. **3** *adj* inferior, de abajo; **the** — **one** el de abajo. **4** *n* superficie *f* inferior.
undernourished ['ʌndə'nʌriʃt] *adj* desnutrido.
undernourishment ['ʌndə'nʌriʃmənt] *n* desnutrición *f*.
underpaid ['ʌndə'peid] *adj* insuficientemente retribuido, mal pagado.
underpants ['ʌndəpænts] *npl* calzoncillos *mpl*.
underpass ['ʌndəpɑːs] *n* paso *m* inferior.
underpay ['ʌndə'pei] (*irr: see* **pay**) *vt* pagar mal, pagar un sueldo insuficiente a.
underpin [,ʌndə'pin] *vt* apuntalar.
underpinning [,ʌndə'piniŋ] *n* apuntalamiento *m*.

underplay ['ʌndə'plei] **1** vt (a) to — **a card** poner una carta de menos valor que otra.

(b) (Theat) to — **a part** hacer flojamente un papel.

2 vi (Theat) hacer flojamente su papel, estar muy flojo en su papel.

underpopulated ['ʌndə'pɔpjuleitid] adj poco poblado, con baja densidad de poblacion.

underpraise ['ʌndə'preiz] vt no alabar debidamente, no tributar el debido elogio a.

underprice ['ʌndə'prais] vt señalar un precio demasiado bajo a; **at 5 dollars it is —d** el precio de 5 dólares es más bien bajo.

underprivileged ['ʌndə'privilidʒd] adj desvalido, desamparado.

underproduction ['ʌndəprə'dʌkʃən] n producción f deficiente.

underrate [,ʌndə'reit] vt opponent etc menospreciar, tener en menos de lo que merece; danger etc subestimar, juzgar mal.

underripe ['ʌndə'raip] adj poco maduro, verde.

underscore [,ʌndə'skɔ:*] vt subrayar.

undersea ['ʌndəsi:] **1** adj submarino. **2** adv bajo la superficie del mar.

undersecretary ['ʌndə'sekrətəri] n subsecretario m, a f.

undersecretaryship ['ʌndə'sekrətəriʃip] n subsecretaría f.

undersell ['ʌndə'sel] (irr: see **sell**) vt person vender a precio más bajo que; article malvender; **Burnley has been undersold as a tourist centre** no se ha hecho la debida publicidad de Burnley como centro turístico.

undershirt ['ʌndəfə:t] n (US) camiseta f.

undershorts ['ʌndə,fɔ:ts] npl (US) calzoncillos mpl.

underside ['ʌndəsaid] n superficie f inferior; (of small object) envés m, cara f inferior.

undersigned ['ʌndəsaind] adj: **the —** el abajo firmante, (pl) los abajo firmantes.

undersized ['ʌndə'saizd] adj pequeño, no bastante grande, de tamaño insuficiente; person (pej) sietemesino.

underskirt ['ʌndəskə:t] n enaguas fpl.

underslung ['ʌndəslʌŋ] adj con bajo centro de gravedad; colocado debajo del eje.

understaffed ['ʌndə'sta:ft] adj: **to be —** no tener el debido personal.

understand [,ʌndə'stænd] (irr: see **stand**) vti (a) comprender, entender; **I —** lo comprendo; **I quite —** lo comprendo perfectamente; **do you —?** ¿me entiende?, ¿comprende?; **I don't — Arabic** no entiendo el árabe; **I don't — you** no te entiendo; **I don't — why** no entiendo por qué; **we — each other** nos entendemos, nos comprendemos; **to give someone to — that ...** dar a uno a entender que ...; **I was given to — that ...** me dieron a entender que ..., me hicieron creer que ...; **I — you have been absent** tengo entendido que Vd ha estado ausente.

(b) (assume) sobreentender; **one has to — 3 words here** aquí se sobreentienden 3 palabras; see also **understood**.

understandable [,ʌndə'stændəbl] adj comprensible; **it is — that ...** se comprende que ...; **it is very — that ...** se comprende perfectamente que ...

understanding [,ʌndə'stændiŋ] **1** adj comprensivo, compasivo; **they were very — about it** se mostraron muy comprensivos; **he gave me an — look** me miró compasivo.

2 n (a) (intelligence) entendimiento m, inteligencia f; (grasp) comprensión f; **he has good —** tiene una inteligencia fina; **his — of these problems** su comprensión de estos problemas, su capacidad para comprender estos problemas; **she has reached the age of —** ha llegado a la edad de discreción.

(b) (agreement) acuerdo m, arreglo m; **to come to an — with someone** ponerse de acuerdo con uno, llegar a un acuerdo con uno; **to have an — with someone** tener un acuerdo (esp verbal) con uno; **I have an — with the milkman** tengo un arreglo con el lechero, nos entendemos el lechero y yo.

(c) (sympathy) comprensión f mutua, inteligencia f; **this will encourage good — between peoples** esto ha de fomentar la buena inteligencia entre los pueblos.

(d) **on the — that ...** con tal que + subj, bien entendido que + subj.

understandingly [,ʌndə'stændiŋli] adv con comprensión, compasivamente; **he looked at me —** me miró compasivamente.

understate ['ʌndə'steit] vt situation exponer incompletamente, describir sin el debido énfasis; needs subestimar; (Gram) atenuar.

understatement ['ʌndə,steitmənt] n exposición f incompleta, descripción f insuficiente; (Gram) atenuación f; (quality) moderación f, modestia f excesiva; **the — of the year** la declaración más modesta del año.

understood [,ʌndə'stud] adj and ptp (a) **it is — that** (believed) se cree que, tenemos entendido que; (understandable) se comprende que; **that is —** eso se entiende; **it being — that ...** con tal que + subj; **I wish it to be — that ...** entiéndase que ..., quiero decir bien claro que ...; **to make oneself —** hacerse entender.

(b) **with 3 words —** con 3 palabras que se sobreentienden.

(c) **it is an — thing that ...** se entiende que ..., se acepta el que ...

understudy ['ʌndə,stʌdi] **1** n suplente mf, sobresaliente mf. **2** vt doblar a, aprender un papel para poder suplir a.

undertake [,ʌndə'teik] (irr: see **take**) vt task etc emprender; acometer; duty etc encargarse de; **to — to do something** comprometerse a hacer algo, prometer hacer algo; **to — that ...** comprometerse a que ..., prometer que ...

undertaker ['ʌndə,teikə*] n director m de pompas fúnebres; **—'s** funeraria f.

undertaking [,ʌndə'teikiŋ] n (Comm) empresa f; (task) empresa f, tarea f; (pledge) garantía f, compromiso m, promesa f; **it's quite an —** es una tarea bastante grande; **to give an — that ...** prometer que ..., asegurar que ...; **I can give no such —** no puedo comprometerme a eso, no puedo dar esa promesa.

undertone ['ʌndətəun] n (sound) voz f baja, sonido m suave; (Art) matiz m suave; (of criticism etc) nota f callada, trasfondo m; **in an —** en voz baja; **there are —s of protest here** aquí hay notas calladas de protesta.

undertow ['ʌndətəu] n resaca f.

undervalue ['ʌndə'vælju:] vt valorizar incompletamente, apreciar en menos de su justo valor; (fig) subestimar; menospreciar; **he has been —d as a writer** como escritor no se le ha apreciado debidamente.

underwater ['ʌndə'wɔ:tə*] adj submarino; **— fisherman** submarinista mf; **— fishing** pesca f submarina.

underwear ['ʌndəwɛə*] n ropa f interior.

underweight [,ʌndə'weit] adj de peso insuficiente; **to be —** (person) no pesar bastante.

underworld ['ʌndəwə:ld] n (hell) infiernom; (criminal) hampa f, inframundo m; bajos fondos mpl.

underwrite ['ʌndərait] (irr: see **write**) vt asegurar, asegurar contra riesgos; (on 2nd insurance) reasegurar; (fig) apoyar, respaldar, aprobar, garantizar.

underwriter ['ʌndə,raitə*] n asegurador m, reasegurador m.

undeserved ['ʌndi'zə:vd] adj inmerecido.

undeservedly ['ʌndi'zə:vidli] adv inmerecidamente.

undeserving ['ʌndi'zə:viŋ] adj indigno.

undesirable ['ʌndi'zaiərəbl] **1** adj indeseable; **it is — that ...** no es recomendable que + subj, es poco aconsejable que + subj. **2** n indeseable mf.

undetected ['ʌndi'tektid] adj no descubierto; **to go —** pasar inadvertido.

undeterred ['ʌndi'tə:d] adj: **he was — by ...** no se dejó intimidar por ...; **he carried on —** siguió sin inmutarse.

undeveloped ['ʌndi'veləpt] adj subdesarrollado; fruit etc verde, inmaturo; film sin revelar; land sin cultivar; resources sin explotar.

undeviating [ʌn'di:vieitiŋ] adj directo, constante; **to follow an — path** seguir un curso recto.

undeviatingly [ʌn'di:vieitiŋli] adv directamente, constantemente; **to hold — to one's course** seguir su curso sin apartarse para nada de él.

undies ['ʌndiz] npl (fam) paños mpl menores.

undigested ['ʌndai'dʒestid] adj indigesto.

undignified [ʌn'dignifaid] adj act, position etc indecoroso; person sin dignidad, informal, poco serio.

undiluted ['ʌndai'lu:tid] adj sin diluir, puro; (fig) puro.

undiminished ['ʌndi'miniʃt] adj no disminuido.

undimmed ['ʌn'dimd] adj tan brillante como antes.

undiplomatic ['ʌn,diplə'mætik] adj impolítico, indiscreto.

undiscernible ['ʌndi'sə:nəbl] adj imperceptible.

undiscerning ['ʌndi'sə:niŋ] adj sin discernimiento, poco discernidor.

undischarged ['ʌndis'tʃa:dʒd] adj debt impagado, por pagar; promise no cumplido; **— bankrupt** persona f que sigue en estado de quiebra.

undisciplined [ʌn'disiplind] *adj* indisciplinado.
undisclosed ['ʌndis'kləuzd] *adj* no revelado.
undiscovered ['ʌndis'kʌvəd] *adj* no descubierto; **he remained — for 3 days** siguió durante 3 días sin que averiguasen su paradero.
undiscriminating ['ʌndis'krimineitiŋ] *adj* sin discernimiento, poco discernidor.
undisguised ['ʌndis'gaizd] *adj* sin disfraz; (*fig*) franco, abierto; **with — satisfaction** con abierta satisfacción.
undismayed ['ʌndis'meid] *adj* impávido; **he was — by this** no se dejó desanimar por esto; **he said —** dijo sin inmutarse.
undisposed-of ['ʌndis'pəuzdɔv] *adj* (*Comm*) no vendido.
undisputed ['ʌndis'pju:tid] *adj* incontestable.
undistinguished ['ʌndis'tiŋgwiʃt] *adj* más bien mediocre.
undisturbed ['ʌndis'tə:bd] *adj*: **to leave things —** dejar las cosas como están, dejar las cosas sin tocar; **he was — by this** no se perturbó con esto; **to go on with one's work —** continuar su trabajo en paz; **he likes to be left —** no quiere que le interrumpan las visitas (*or* llamadas *etc*).
undivided ['ʌndi'vaidid] *adj* indiviso, íntegro, entero; **I want your — attention** quiero que me presten toda su atención.
undo ['ʌn'du:] (*irr: see* **do**) *vt arrangement etc* anular; *work* deshacer; *knot* desatar; *clasp* desabrochar; *box* abrir; *mischief* reparar; *see also* **undone**.
undoing ['ʌn'du:iŋ] *n* ruina *f*, perdición *f*; **that was his —** aquello fue su ruina.
undomesticated ['ʌndə'mestikeitid] *adj* indomado, no domesticado.
undone ['ʌn'dʌn] *adj*: **I am —!** ¡estoy perdido!, ¡es mi ruina!; **to come —** desatarse; **to leave something —** dejar algo sin hacer.
undoubted [ʌn'dautid] *adj* indudable.
undoubtedly [ʌn'dautidli] *adv* indudablemente, sin duda.
undreamt-of [ʌn'dremtɔv] *adj* no soñado, nunca pensado.
undress ['ʌn'dres] **1** *n* traje *m* de casa, desabillé *m*; (*Mil*) traje *m* de cuartel; **in a state of —** desnudo. **2** *vt* desnudar. **3** *vi* desnudarse.
undrinkable ['ʌn'driŋkəbl] *adj* no potable, que no se puede beber.
undue ['ʌn'dju:] *adj* indebido, excesivo.
undulate ['ʌndjuleit] *vi* ondular, ondear.
undulating ['ʌndjuleitiŋ] *adj* ondulante, ondeante; *land* ondulado.
undulation [ˌʌndju'leiʃən] *n* ondulación *f*.
undulatory ['ʌndjulətəri] *adj* ondulatorio.
unduly ['ʌn'dju:li] *adv* indebidamente, excesivamente, con exceso; **we are not — worried** no estamos demasiado preocupados.
undying [ʌn'daiiŋ] *adj* (*fig*) imperecedero, inmarcesible.
unearned ['ʌn'ə:nd] *adj* no ganado.
unearth ['ʌn'ə:θ] *vt* desenterrar; (*fig*) desenterrar, descubrir.
unearthly [ʌn'ə:θli] *adj* sobrenatural; *light etc* misterioso, fantástico; *hour etc* inverosímil.
uneasily [ʌn'i:zili] *adv* inquietamente, con inquietud; **I noted — that . . .** me inquieté al observar que . . .
uneasiness [ʌn'i:zinis] *n* inquietud *f*; desasosiego *m*, intranquilidad *f*.
uneasy [ʌn'i:zi] *adj* calm, peace, etc inseguro; *sleep* poco tranquilo; *conscience* desasosegado, intranquilo; **to be —** estar inquieto (*about* por), sentirse mal a gusto; **to become —** empezar a inquietarse (*about* por); **I have an — feeling that . . .** me inquieta la posibilidad de que + *subj*; **to make someone —** intranquilizar a uno, turbar a uno.
uneatable ['ʌn'i:təbl] *adj* incomible, que no se puede comer.
uneaten ['ʌn'i:tn] *adj* no comido, sin comer.
uneconomic(al) ['ʌnˌi:kə'nɔmik(əl)] *adj* antieconómico.
unedifying ['ʌn'edifaiiŋ] *adj* indecoroso, poco edificante.
uneducated ['ʌn'edjukeitid] *adj* ineducado, ignorante.
unemotional ['ʌni'məuʃənl] *adj* character impasible, reservado; *person* que no se deja emocionar; *account etc* objetivo.
unemotionally ['ʌni'məuʃnəli] *adv*: **to look on —** mirar impasible, mirar sin dejarse emocionar.
unemployable ['ʌnim'plɔiəbl] *adj* inútil para el trabajo.
unemployed ['ʌnim'plɔid] **1** *adj* parado, sin empleo, desempleado. **2** *n*: **the —** los parados, los sin trabajo, los desempleados.

unemployment ['ʌnim'plɔimənt] *n* paro *m* (forzoso), desempleo *m*, desocupación *f*; **seasonal —** paro *m* estacional.
unencumbered ['ʌnin'kʌmbəd] *adj* suelto, sin trabas; (*estate etc*) libre de gravamen; **— by** no impedido por, sin el estorbo de.
unending [ʌn'endiŋ] *adj* interminable, sin fin.
unendurable ['ʌnin'djuərəbl] *adj* inaguantable, insufrible.
unengaged ['ʌnin'geidʒd] *adj* libre; sin compromiso.
un-English ['ʌn'iŋgliʃ] *adj* (*unworthy*) indigno de un inglés; (*unlike*) nada típico de un inglés.
unenlightened ['ʌnin'laitnd] *adj* person, age ignorante, poco instruido; *policy etc* estúpido.
unenterprising ['ʌn'entəpraiziŋ] *adj* person falto de iniciativa, poco emprendedor; *policy etc* tímido.
unenthusiastic ['ʌnin,θu:zi'æstik] *adj* poco entusiasta; **everybody seemed rather — about it** nadie mostró gran entusiasmo por la idea.
unenviable ['ʌn'enviəbl] *adj* poco envidiable.
unequal ['ʌn'i:kwəl] *adj* desigual; desproporcionado; **to be — to a task** no estar a la altura de una tarea, no tener fuerzas para una tarea.
unequalled ['ʌn'i:kwəld] *adj* inigualado, sin par; **a record — by anybody** un historial mejor que el de nadie.
unequally ['ʌn'i:kwəli] *adv* desigualmente; desproporcionadamente.
unequivocal ['ʌni'kwivəkəl] *adj* inequívoco.
unequivocally ['ʌni'kwivəkəli] *adv* de modo inequívoco, sin dejar lugar a dudas.
unerring ['ʌn'ə:riŋ] *adj* infalible.
unerringly ['ʌn'ə:riŋli] *adv* infaliblemente.
unessential ['ʌni'senʃəl] *adj* no esencial.
unesthetic [ˌʌni:s'θetik] *adj* antiestético.
unethical ['ʌn'eθikəl] *adj* inmoral; injusto.
uneven ['ʌn'i:vən] *adj* desigual; *road etc* escabroso, quebrado, ondulado.
unevenly ['ʌn'i:vənli] *adv* desigualmente.
unevenness ['ʌn'i:vənnis] *n* desigualdad *f*; escabrosidad *f*.
uneventful ['ʌni'ventful] *adj* sin incidentes notables, sin accidentes, tranquilo.
unexampled ['ʌnig'zɑ:mpld] *adj* sin igual.
unexceptionable [ˌʌnik'sepʃnəbl] *adj* intachable, impecable.
unexceptional [ˌʌnik'sepʃənl] *adj* usual, corriente, normal.
unexciting ['ʌnik'saitiŋ] *adj* poco emocionante, de poco interés.
unexpected ['ʌniks'pektid] *adj* inesperado, inopinado.
unexpectedly ['ʌniks'pektidli] *adv* inesperadamente, inopinadamente.
unexpendable ['ʌniks'pendəbl] *adj* que no se puede gastar.
unexpended ['ʌniks'pendid] *adj* no gastado.
unexpired ['ʌniks'paiəd] *adj* bill no vencido; *lease, ticket* no caducado.
unexplained ['ʌniks'pleind] *adj* inexplicado.
unexploded ['ʌniks'pləudid] *adj* sin explotar.
unexploited ['ʌniks'plɔitid] *adj* inexplotado, sin explotar.
unexplored ['ʌniks'plɔ:d] *adj* inexplorado.
unexposed ['ʌniks'pəuzd] *adj* (*Phot*) inexpuesto.
unexpressed ['ʌniks'prest] *adj* no expresado; tácito.
unexpressive ['ʌniks'presiv] *adj* inexpresivo.
unexpurgated ['ʌn'ekspə:geitid] *adj* sin expurgar, íntegro.
unfading [ʌn'feidiŋ] *adj* (*fig*) inmarcesible.
unfailing [ʌn'feiliŋ] *adj* indefectible; *zeal* infalible; *supply* inagotable.
unfailingly [ʌn'feiliŋli] *adv* indefectiblemente; infaliblemente; inagotablemente; **to be — courteous** ser siempre cortés, no faltar en ningún momento a la cortesía.
unfair ['ʌn'feə*] *adj* comment etc injusto; *practice* sin equidad; *competition* desleal; *play* sucio; *tactics* no aprobado, no permitido por las reglas; **that's very —** eso es muy injusto; **how —!** ¡no hay derecho!; **it was — of him to** + *infin* era injusto que él + *subj*.
unfairly ['ʌn'feəli] *adv* injustamente; deslealmente; de modo contrario a las reglas; **he was — condemned** se le condenó injustamente.
unfairness ['ʌn'feənis] *n* injusticia *f*; deslealtad *f*; suciedad *f*.
unfaithful ['ʌn'feiθful] *adj* infiel; **to be — to someone** ser infiel a uno.
unfaithfulness ['ʌn'feiθfulnis] *n* infidelidad *f*.
unfaltering [ʌn'fɔ:ltəriŋ] *adj* resuelto, firme.
unfamiliar ['ʌnfə'miliə*] *adj* subject etc desconocido, nuevo; **to be — with** desconocer, ignorar.

unfashionable ['ʌn'fæʃnəbl] *adj* pasado de moda, fuera de moda; poco elegante; **it is now — to talk of** ... no está de moda ahora hablar de ...

unfasten ['ʌn'fɑːsn] *vt* (*untie*) desatar; *dress* desabrochar; *door* abrir; (*get free*) soltar; (*loosen*) aflojar.

unfathomable ['ʌn'fæðəməbl] *adj* insondable.

unfathomed ['ʌn'fæðəmd] *adj* no sondado.

unfavourable, (*US*) **unfavorable** ['ʌn'feivərəbl] *adj* desfavorable, adverso; *outlook etc* poco propicio; *weather* malo.

unfavourably, (*US*) **unfavorably** ['ʌn'feivərəbli] *adv* desfavorablemente; **to be — impressed** formarse una impresión desfavorable.

unfeeling [ʌn'fiːliŋ] *adj* insensible.

unfeelingly [ʌn'fiːliŋli] *adv* insensiblemente.

unfeigned [ʌn'feind] *adj* no fingido, verdadero.

unfeignedly [ʌn'feinidli] *adv* sin fingimiento, verdaderamente.

unfermented ['ʌnfə'mentid] *adj* no fermentado.

unfettered ['ʌn'fetəd] *adj* sin trabas.

unfinished ['ʌn'finiʃt] *adj* incompleto, inacabado, sin terminar; **I have 3 — letters** tengo 3 cartas por terminar; **we have — business** tenemos asuntos pendientes.

unfit ['ʌn'fit] *adj* (*incompetent*) incapaz, incompetente; (*unsuitable*) no apto (*for* para); (*useless*) inservible, inadecuado (*for* para); (*unworthy*) indigno (*to* de); (*ill*) enfermo, indispuesto, (*injured*) lesionado; **— to eat** impropio para el consumo humano; **— for publication** indigno de publicarse; **— for military service** no apto para el servicio militar; **he is quite — to hold office** es totalmente incapaz de ocupar ningún cargo; **the road is — for lorries** el camino es intransitable para los camiones.

unfit [ʌn'fit] *vt*: **to — someone for something** inhabilitar a uno para algo, incapacitar a uno para algo; **he is —ted for such a career** no es apto para tal carrera.

unfitness ['ʌn'fitnis] *n* incapacidad *f*, incompetencia *f*; falta *f* de aptitud; inadecuación *f*; (*Med*) mala salud *f*, falta *f* de salud.

unflagging [ʌn'flægiŋ] *adj* incansable.

unflaggingly [ʌn'flægiŋli] *adv* incansablemente.

unflappable ['ʌn'flæpəbl] *adj* imperturbable.

unflattering ['ʌn'flætəriŋ] *adj* poco lisonjero, poco grato.

unflatteringly ['ʌn'flætəriŋli] *adv* de modo poco lisonjero.

unfledged ['ʌn'fledʒd] *adj* implume.

unflinching ['ʌn'flintʃiŋ] *adj* impávido, resuelto.

unflinchingly ['ʌn'flintʃiŋli] *adv* impávidamente, resueltamente.

unflyable ['ʌn'flaiəbl] *adj*: **— weather** tiempo *m* que imposibilita el despegue de aviones.

unfold [ʌn'fəuld] **1** *vt* desplegar, desdoblar, abrir; *idea, plan* exponer; *secret* revelar; **to — a map on a table** extender un mapa sobre una mesa. **2** *vi* desplegarse, desdoblarse, abrirse; (*view etc*) revelarse, extenderse.

unforeseeable ['ʌnfɔː'siːəbl] *adj* imprevisible.

unforeseen ['ʌnfɔː'siːn] *adj* imprevisto.

unforgettable ['ʌnfə'getəbl] *adj* inolvidable.

unforgivable ['ʌnfə'givəbl] *adj* imperdonable, indisculpable.

unforgiving ['ʌnfə'giviŋ] *adj* implacable.

unformed ['ʌn'fɔːmd] *adj* informe, sin formar aún.

unfortified ['ʌn'fɔːtifaid] *adj* no fortificado; *town* abierto.

unfortunate [ʌn'fɔːtʃnit] **1** *adj* *person* desgraciado, desdichado, desventurado; (*lately dead*) malogrado; *event* funesto, desgraciado; *manner, remark* infeliz, inoportuno; **how very —!** ¡qué mala suerte!, ¡qué desgracia!; **it is most — that** ... es muy de lamentar que + *subj*; **you have been most —** ha tenido muy mala suerte. **2** *n* desgraciado *m*, a *f*.

unfortunately [ʌn'fɔːtʃnitli] *adv* por desgracia, desgraciadamente, desafortunadamente; **it is — true that** ... desgraciadamente es verdad que ...; **an — phrased statement** una declaración expresada en términos infelices.

unfounded ['ʌn'faundid] *adj* infundado, que carece de fundamento.

unframed ['ʌn'freimd] *adj* sin marco.

unfrequented ['ʌnfri'kwentid] *adj* poco frecuentado.

unfriendliness ['ʌn'frendlinis] *n* hostilidad *f*.

unfriendly ['ʌn'frendli] *adj* poco amistoso.

unfrock ['ʌn'frɔk] *vt* degradar, expulsar; **an —ed priest** un sacerdote a quien han quitado las órdenes.

unfruitful ['ʌn'fruːtful] *adj* infructuoso.

unfulfilled ['ʌnful'fild] *adj* incumplido.

unfurl [ʌn'fəːl] *vt* desplegar.

unfurnished ['ʌn'fəːniʃt] *adj* desamueblado, sin muebles.

ungainliness [ʌn'geinlinis] *n* desgarbo *m*, torpeza *f*.

ungainly [ʌn'geinli] *adj* desgarbado, torpe.

ungallant ['ʌn'gælənt] *adj* falto de cortesía, descortés.

ungenerous ['ʌn'dʒenərəs] *adj* poco generoso.

ungentlemanly ['ʌn'dʒentlmənli] *adj* poco caballeroso, indigno de un caballero.

un-get-at-able ['ʌnget'ætəbl] *adj* inaccesible.

ungird ['ʌn'gəːd] (*irr: see* **gird**) *vt* desceñir.

unglazed ['ʌn'gleizd] *adj* no vidriado.

ungodliness ['ʌn'gɔdlinis] *n* impiedad *f*.

ungodly [ʌn'gɔdli] *adj* impío, irreligioso; (*fam*) atroz; **at this — hour** a hora tan inverosímil.

ungovernable ['ʌn'gʌvənəbl] *adj* ingobernable; *temper* incontrolable, irrefrenable.

ungracious ['ʌn'greiʃəs] *adj* descortés, grosero; **it would be — to refuse** sería descortés no aceptarlo.

ungrammatical ['ʌngrə'mætikəl] *adj* incorrecto.

ungrammatically ['ʌngrə'mætikəli] *adv* incorrectamente; **to talk Spanish —** hablar español con poca corrección.

ungrateful [ʌn'greitful] *adj* desagradecido, ingrato.

ungratefully [ʌn'greitfəli] *adv* desagradecidamente.

ungrudging ['ʌn'grʌdʒiŋ] *adj* liberal, generoso; *support etc* incondicional.

ungrudgingly [ʌn'grʌdʒiŋli] *adv* liberalmente, generosamente; de buena gana, incondicionalmente.

unguarded ['ʌn'gɑːid] *adj* (*Mil*) indefenso, no defendido, sin protección; *remark etc* imprudente; **in an — moment** en un momento de descuido.

unguent ['ʌngwənt] *n* ungüento *m*.

ungulate ['ʌngjuleit] **1** *adj* ungulado. **2** *n* ungulado *m*.

unhallowed [ʌn'hæləud] *adj* no consagrado; (*fig*) profano.

unhampered ['ʌn'hæmpəd] *adj* libre, sin estorbos; **— by** no estorbado por.

unhand [ʌn'hænd] *vt* soltar; **— me, sir!** ¡suélteme, señor!

unhandsome [ʌn'hænsəm] *adj* feo, nada atractivo.

unhandy [ʌn'hændi] *adj* *person* desmañado; *thing* incómodo; **to be — with something** ser desmañado en el manejo de algo.

unhappily [ʌn'hæpili] *adv* (*miserably*) infelizmente; (*unfortunately*) desgraciadamente.

unhappiness [ʌn'hæpinis] *n* desdicha *f*, tristeza *f*; desgracia *f*.

unhappy [ʌn'hæpi] *adj* *person* infeliz, desdichado; *childhood etc* desgraciado; (*ill-fated*) malhadado; *remark etc* infeliz, inoportuno; **that — time** aquella triste época; **to be — about something** inquietarse por algo, no aceptar algo de buena gana; **we are — about the decision** no nos gusta la decisión; **to make someone —** poner triste a uno, amargar la vida a uno; **she was — in her marriage** era desgraciada en su matrimonio.

unharmed ['ʌn'hɑːmd] *adj* *person* ileso, incólume; *thing* indemne; **to escape —** salir ileso.

unharness ['ʌn'hɑːnis] *vt* desguarnecer.

unhealthy [ʌn'helθi] *adj* *person* enfermizo; *place* malsano, insalubre; *complexion* de aspecto poco sano; *curiosity* morboso.

unheard ['ʌn'həːd] *adj*: **to condemn someone —** condenar a uno sin escuchar su defensa.

unheard-of [ʌn'həːdɔv] *adj* inaudito; **it's quite —** es totalmente inaudito.

unheeded ['ʌn'hiːdid] *adj* desatendido; **the warning went —** nadie prestó atención a la advertencia, nadie hizo caso de la advertencia.

unheeding ['ʌn'hiːdiŋ] *adj* desatento, sordo; **they passed by —** pasaron sin prestar atención.

unhelpful ['ʌn'helpful] *adj* *person* poco servicial; *advice etc* inútil.

unhesitating ['ʌn'heziteitiŋ] *adj* *person etc* resuelto; *reply etc* pronto.

unhesitatingly [ʌn'heziteitiŋli] *adv*: **he said —** dijo sin vacilar, dijo decidido.

unhindered ['ʌn'hindəd] *adj* libre, sin estorbos; **— by** no estorbado por.

unhinge [ʌn'hindʒ] *vt* desquiciar; (*fig*) *mind* trastornar; *person* trastornar el juicio de.

unhistorical ['ʌnhis'tɔrikəl] *adj* antihistórico, que no tiene nada de histórico.

unhitch ['ʌn'hitʃ] *vt* desenganchar.

unholy [ʌn'həuli] *adj* impío; (*fam*) atroz.

unhook ['ʌn'huk] *vt* desenganchar; (*from wall etc*) descolgar; *dress* desabrochar.

unhoped-for [ʌn'həuptfɔː*] *adj* inesperado.

unhopeful [ʌn'həupful] *adj* *prospect* poco prometedor; *person* pesimista.
unhorse [ʌn'hɔːs] *vt* desarzonar.
unhurried [ʌn'hʌrid] *adj* lento, pausado, parsimonioso.
unhurriedly [ʌn'hʌridli] *adv* lentamente, pausadamente, con parsimonia.
unhurt [ʌn'həːt] *adj* ileso, incólume; **to escape —** salir ileso.
unhygienic [ʌnhai'dʒiːnik] *adj* antihigiénico.
unicameral [juːni'kæmərəl] *adj* unicameral.
unicellular [juːni'seljuləʳ] *adj* unicelular.
unicorn ['juːnikɔːn] *n* unicornio *m*.
unidentified [ʌnai'dentifaid] *adj* sin identificar, no identificado aún.
unification [juːnifi'keiʃən] *n* unificación *f*.
uniform ['juːnifɔːm] **1** *adj* uniforme; igual, constante; **to make something —** hacer algo uniforme, uniformar algo.
2 *n* uniforme *m*; **in full —** de gran uniforme.
uniformed ['juːnifɔːmd] *adj* uniformado.
uniformity [juːni'fɔːmiti] *n* uniformidad *f*.
uniformly ['juːnifɔːmli] *adv* uniformemente, de modo uniforme.
unify ['juːnifai] *vt* unificar, unir.
unilateral [juːni'lætərəl] *adj* unilateral.
unilaterally [juːni'lætərəli] *adv* unilateralmente.
unimaginable [ʌni'mædʒinəbl] *adj* inimaginable.
unimaginative ['ʌni'mædʒinətiv] *adj* poco imaginativo.
unimpaired ['ʌnim'pɛəd] *adj* no disminuido; no afectado; intacto, entero.
unimpeachable [ʌnim'piːtʃəbl] *adj* irrecusable, intachable; **from an — source** de fuente fidedigna.
unimpeded ['ʌnim'piːdid] *adj* sin estorbo.
unimportant [ʌnim'pɔːtənt] *adj* sin importancia, insignificante.
unimposing ['ʌnim'pəuziŋ] *adj* poco impresionante.
unimpressed ['ʌnim'prest] *adj*: **he remained —** no se convenció; **I remain —** no se convenció; **the new building el nuevo edificio** no me hace buena impresión.
unimpressive ['ʌnim'presiv] *adj* poco impresionante, poco convincente; *person* soso, insignificante.
unimproved ['ʌnim'pruːvd] *adj* no mejorado, sin mejora; tan malo (*or* defectuoso *etc*) como antes.
unincorporated [ʌnin'kɔːpəreitid] *adj* no incorporado.
uninfluenced ['ʌn'influənst] *adj*: **— by any argument** no afectado por ningún argumento; **a style — by any other** un estilo no influido por ningún otro.
uninformed ['ʌnin'fɔːmd] *adj* *character* poco instruido, ignorante; **to be — about something** no estar enterado de algo, desconocer algo.
uninhabitable ['ʌnin'hæbitəbl] *adj* inhabitable.
uninhabited ['ʌnin'hæbitid] *adj* deshabitado, inhabitado; desierto.
uninhibited ['ʌnin'hibitid] *adj* nada cohibido, totalmente libre.
uninitiated [ʌni'niʃieitid] **1** *adj* no iniciado. **2** *n*: **the —** los no iniciados.
uninjured [ʌn'indʒəd] *adj* ileso; **to escape —** salir ileso.
uninspired [ʌnin'spaiəd] *adj* sin inspiración, soso, mediocre.
uninsured [ʌnin'ʃuəd] *adj* no asegurado.
unintelligent [ʌnin'telidʒənt] *adj* ininteligente.
unintelligibility [ʌnin,telidʒə'biliti] *n* ininteligibilidad *f*, incomprensibilidad *f*.
unintelligible [ʌnin'telidʒəbl] *adj* ininteligible, incomprensible.
unintelligibly [ʌnin'telidʒəbli] *adv* de modo ininteligible, de modo incomprensible.
unintended [ʌnin'tendid] *adj*, **unintentional** [ʌnin'tenʃənl] *adj* involuntario, no intencional; **it was —** fue sin querer.
unintentionally [ʌnin'tenʃnəli] *adv* sin querer.
uninterested [ʌn'intristid] *adj* sin interés; **to be — in a subject** no tener interés alguno en un asunto.
uninteresting [ʌn'intristiŋ] *adj* poco interesante, falto de interés.
uninterrupted [ʌn,intə'rʌptid] *adj* ininterrumpido.
uninterruptedly [ʌn,intə'rʌptidli] *adv* ininterrumpidamente.
uninvited ['ʌnin'vaitid] *adj* *guest* no invitado; *comment* gratuito; **to do something —** hacer algo sin ser rogado; **they came to the party —** vinieron al guateque sin ser invitados.
uninviting ['ʌnin'vaitiŋ] *adj* poco atractivo.
union ['juːnjən] **1** *n* unión *f*; (*marriage*) enlace *m*; (*Pol*) sindicato *m*, gremio *m* obrero; (*Mech*) unión *f*, manguito *m* de unión; **customs — unión *f*

aduanera; **Universal Postal U—** Unión *f* Postal Universal; **the U—** (*USA*) la Unión.
2 *attr* sindical, de los sindicatos, gremial; **— shop** taller *m* de obreros agremiados.
unionism ['juːnjənizəm] *n* *see* **trade unionism**; **U—** (*British Pol*) conservatismo *m*, Partido *m* Conservador.
unionist ['juːnjənist] *n* *see* **trade unionist**; **U—** (*British Pol*) conservador *m*, ora *f*.
unionize ['juːnjənaiz] **1** *vt* agremiar. **2** *vi* agremiarse.
Union Jack ['juːnjən'dʒæk] *n* *bandera del Reino Unido*.
Union of South Africa ['juːnjənəv,sauθ'æfrikə] Unión *f* Sudafricana.
Union of Soviet Socialist Republics ['juːnjənəv'səuviət'səuʃəlistri'pʌbliks] Unión *f* de Repúblicas Socialistas Soviéticas.
union suit ['juːnjənsuːt] *n* (*US*) traje *m* interior de una sola pieza.
unique [juː'niːk] *adj* único.
uniquely [juː'niːkli] *adv* especialmente.
uniqueness [juː'niːknis] *n* unicidad *f*; lo singular, lo incomparable; **because of its —** por su carácter incomparable.
unison ['juːnizn] *n* armonía *f*; (*Mus*) unisonancia *f*; **to sing in —** cantar al unísono; **to act in — with someone** obrar de acuerdo con uno.
unit ['juːnit] **1** *n* unidad *f* (*also Math, Mil*); (*Elec: measurement*) unidad *f*; (*Mech, Elec*) grupo *m*; **compressor —** grupo *m* compresor; **generating —** grupo *m* electrógeno; **mobile —** (*TV*) unidad *f* móvil; **monetary —** unidad *f* monetaria.
2 *attr*: **— furniture** muebles *mpl* de elementos adicionables, muebles *mpl* combinados.
Unitarian [juːni'tɛəriən] **1** *adj* unitario. **2** *n* unitario *m*, a *f*.
Unitarianism [juːni'tɛəriənizəm] *n* unitarismo *m*.
unitary ['juːnitəri] *adj* unitario.
unite [juː'nait] **1** *vt* unir, juntar; (*marry*) casar; **parts of country** unificar.
2 *vi* unirse, juntarse; **to — against someone** unirse para hacer frente a uno; **to — in doing something** unirse para hacer algo, concertarse para hacer algo.
united [juː'naitid] *adj* unido.
United Arab Republic [juː'naitid'ærəbri'pʌblik] República *f* Árabe Unida.
United Kingdom [juː'naitid'kiŋdəm] Reino *m* Unido (*Inglaterra, Gales, Escocia, Irlanda del Norte*).
United Nations [juː'naitid'neiʃənz] *pl* Naciones *fpl* Unidas.
United States (of America) [juː'naitid'steits-(əvə'merikə)] *pl* (Los) Estados *mpl* Unidos (de América).
unity ['juːniti] *n* unidad *f*; unión *f*; armonía *f*; **— is strength** la unión hace la fuerza; **— of place** unidad *f* de lugar; **— of time** unidad *f* de tiempo.
univalent ['juːni'veilənt] *adj* univalente.
univalve ['juːnivælv] **1** *adj* univalvo. **2** *n* molusco *m* univalvo.
universal [juːni'vəːsəl] *adj* universal; *joint, suffrage, union etc* universal; **a — favourite** una cosa querida de todos; **its use has been — since 1900** desde 1900 tiene un empleo general; **soap is now —** el jabón se emplea ahora en todas partes; **to become —** universalizarse, generalizarse; **to make — universalizar, generalizar**.
universality [juːnivəː'sæliti] *n* universalidad *f*.
universalize [juːni'vəːsəlaiz] *vt* universalizar.
universally [juːni'vəːsəli] *adj* universalmente; generalmente, comúnmente; **— known** mundialmente conocido.
universe ['juːnivəːs] *n* universo *m*.
university [juːni'vəːsiti] **1** *n* universidad *f*; **to be at —** estar en la universidad; **to go to —** ir a la universidad.
2 *adj, attr* *degree, year etc* universitario; *professor, student* de universidad.
unjust ['ʌn'dʒʌst] *adj* injusto.
unjustifiable [ʌn'dʒʌstifaiəbl] *adj* injustificable.
unjustifiably [ʌn'dʒʌstifaiəbli] *adv* injustificadamente.
unjustified ['ʌn'dʒʌstifaid] *adj* injustificado.
unjustly ['ʌn'dʒʌstli] *adv* injustamente.
unkempt ['ʌn'kempt] *adj* *appearance* desaseado, descuidado; *hair* despeinado.
unkind [ʌn'kaind] *adj* (*of person etc*) poco amable, nada amistoso, poco compasivo; cruel, despiadado; *remark, word, blow* cruel; *climate* riguroso; **that was very — of him** en eso no se mostró nada amable; **he was — enough to + *infin* fue lo bastante cruel como para + *infin*.

unkindly [ʌn'kaindli] *adv* cruelmente; **don't take it** — **if** . . . no lo tome a mal si . . .

unkindness [ʌn'kaindnis] *n* falta *f* de amabilidad; crueldad *f*, rigor *m*, severidad *f*; (*act*) acto *m* de crueldad.

unknowable ['ʌn'nəuəbl] *adj* inconocible; insondable, impenetrable; **the** — lo inconocible.

unknowingly ['ʌn'nəuiŋli] *adv* sin querer; sin saberlo; **he did it all** — lo hizo sin darse cuenta en absoluto de ello.

unknown ['ʌn'nəun] **1** *adj* desconocido, ignorado; ignoto, incógnito; **the** — **soldier** el soldado desconocido; **towards** — **regions** hacia regiones desconocidas; **a substance** — **to science** una sustancia ignorada por la ciencia.

2 *adv*: — **to me** sin saberlo yo.

3 *n* (*person*) desconocido *m*, a *f*; (*Math, also fig*) incógnita *f*; **the** — lo desconocido; **to go out into the** — salir a explorar tierras incógnitas.

unlace [ʌn'leis] *vt* desenlazar.

unladen ['ʌn'leidn] *adj* vacío, sin cargamento.

unladylike ['ʌn'leidilaik] *adj* vulgar, ordinario, impropio de una señora.

unlamented ['ʌnlə'mentid] *adj* no llorado, no lamentado.

unlatch ['ʌn'lætʃ] *vt* alzar el pestillo de, abrir levantando el picaporte de.

unlawful ['ʌn'lɔ:ful] *adj* ilegal, ilícito.

unlawfully ['ʌn'lɔ:fəli] *adv* ilegalmente, ilícitamente.

unlearn [ʌn'lə:n] *vt* desaprender, olvidar.

unlearned ['ʌn'lə:nid] *adj* indocto, ignorante.

unleash ['ʌn'li:ʃ] *vt dog* destraillar, soltar; (*fig*) desencadenar, desatar.

unleavened ['ʌn'levnd] *adj* ázimo, sin levadura.

unless [ən'les] *conj* a menos que + *subj*; a no ser que + *subj*; — **you can find another one** a menos que pueda encontrar otro; — **I am mistaken** si no me equivoco; — **I hear to the contrary** a menos que me digan lo contrario.

unlettered ['ʌn'letəd] *adj* indocto.

unlicensed ['ʌn'laisənst] *adj* sin permiso, sin licencia, no autorizado.

unlike ['ʌn'laik] **1** *adj* desemejante, distinto; (*Math*) de signo contrario; **they are quite** — son muy distintos, no se parecen en nada.

2 *prep* a diferencia de; **it's quite** — **him** no es nada característico de él; **the photo is quite** — **him** la foto no le representa en absoluto; **I,** — **others,** . . . yo, a diferencia de otros . . .

unlikelihood [ʌn'laiklihud] *n*, **unlikeliness** [ʌn-'laiklinis] *n* improbabilidad *f*.

unlikely [ʌn'laikli] *adj* improbable, poco probable; (*odd*) inverosímil; **it is most** — no es nada probable; **it is** — **that he will come, he is** — **to come** no es probable que venga; **wearing a most** — **hat** con un sombrero inverosímil.

unlimited [ʌn'limitid] *adj* ilimitado, sin límite.

unlined ['ʌn'laind] *adj coat* sin forro; *face* sin arrugas; *paper* sin rayar.

unlisted ['ʌn'listid] *adj* que no figura en una lista.

unlit ['ʌn'lit] *adj* oscuro, sin luz; *street* sin alumbrado, sin faroles.

unload ['ʌn'ləud] **1** *vt* descargar; (*get rid of*) deshacerse. **2** *vi* descargar.

unlock ['ʌn'lɔk] *vt* abrir (con llave); *mystery etc* resolver.

unlooked-for [ʌn'luktfɔ:*] *adj* inesperado, inopinado.

unloose ['ʌn'lu:s], **unloosen** [ʌn'lu:sn] *vt* aflojar, soltar.

unlovable ['ʌn'lʌvəbl] *adj* poco apetecible, repugnante; *person* antipático.

unlovely ['ʌn'lʌvli] *adj* feo, desgarbado.

unloving ['ʌn'lʌviŋ] *adj* nada cariñoso.

unluckily [ʌn'lʌkili] *adv*: — **I couldn't go** desgraciadamente no pude ir; **it was** — **left at the station** por desgracia quedó olvidado en la estación.

unluckiness [ʌn'lʌkinis] *n* mala suerte *f*; lo nefasto.

unlucky [ʌn'lʌki] *adj person, stroke etc* desgraciado; (*ill-omened*) funesto, nefasto; **a very** — **day** un día de los menos propicios; **to be** — (*person*) tener mala suerte; **I've been** — **all my life** toda la vida he sido desgraciado; **how very** — **!** ¡qué mala suerte!; **it's** — **to go under ladders** pasar por debajo de las escaleras trae mala suerte.

unmake ['ʌn'meik] (*irr: see* **make**) *vt* deshacer.

unman ['ʌn'mæn] *vt* acobardar.

unmanageable [ʌn'mænidʒəbl] *adj* (*unwieldy*) inmanejable, difícil de manejar; *person* indócil, ingobernable.

unmanly ['ʌn'mænli] *adj* afeminado; cobarde.

unmannerly [ʌn'mænəli] *adj* descortés, mal educado.

unmarked ['ʌn'mɑːkt] *adj* sin marcar; (*uninjured*) ileso; (*Sport*) desmarcado.

unmarketable ['ʌn'mɑːkitəbl] *adj* invendible.

unmarriageable ['ʌn'mæridʒəbl] *adj* incasable.

unmarried ['ʌn'mærid] *adj* soltero; **the** — **state** el estado de soltero.

unmask ['ʌn'mɑːsk] **1** *vt* desenmascarar (*also fig*). **2** *vi* quitarse la máscara, descubrirse.

unmast ['ʌn'mɑːst] *vt* desarbolar.

unmatched ['ʌn'mætʃt] *adj* incomparable, sin par.

unmentionable ['ʌn'menʃnəbl] **1** *adj* que no se puede mencionar; indescriptible, indecible. **2** —**s** *npl* (*hum*) prendas *fpl* íntimas, pantalones *mpl*.

unmerciful [ʌn'mɔːsiful] *adj* despiadado.

unmercifully [ʌn'mɔːsifəli] *adv* despiadadamente.

unmerited ['ʌn'meritid] *adj* inmerecido.

unmethodical ['ʌnmi'θɔdikəl] *adj* poco metódico, desordenado.

unmindful [ʌn'maindful] *adj*: **to be** — **of** no pensar en; **he,** — **of the danger** él, sin pensar en el peligro.

unmistakable ['ʌnmis'teikəbl] *adj* inconfundible, inequívoco.

unmistakably ['ʌnmis'teikəbli] *adv* de modo inconfundible; **it is** — **mine** sin duda alguna es mío.

unmitigated [ʌn'mitigeitid] *adj* no mitigado, absoluto; *rogue etc* redomado.

unmixed ['ʌn'mikst] *adj* sin mezcla, puro.

unmolested ['ʌnmə'lestid] *adj* indemne.

unmortgaged ['ʌn'mɔːgidʒd] *adj* libre de hipoteca.

unmotivated ['ʌn'məutiveitid] *adj* inmotivado, sin motivo.

unmounted ['ʌn'mauntid] *adj rider* desmontado; *stone* sin engastar; *photo, stamp* sin pegar.

unmourned ['ʌn'mɔːnd] *adj* no llorado.

unmoved ['ʌn'muːvd] *adj* impasible; **to remain** — **by** no dejarse conmover por, seguir siendo insensible a; **it leaves me** — me trae sin cuidado.

unmoving ['ʌn'muːviŋ] *adj* inmóvil.

unmusical ['ʌn'mjuːzikəl] *adj* (*Mus*) inarmónico; *person* sin instinto musical, sin oído para la música.

unnamed ['ʌn'neimd] *adj* sin nombre.

unnatural [ʌn'nætʃrəl] *adj* antinatural, no natural; contrario a la naturaleza; anormal; *habit, vice* perverso; *person's manner* afectado.

unnavigable ['ʌn'nævigəbl] *adj* innavegable.

unnecessarily [ʌn'nesisərili] *adv* innecesariamente, sin necesidad.

unnecessary [ʌn'nesisəri] *adj* innecesario, inútil; **it is** — **to add that** . . . apenas hace falta añadir que . . .

unneighbourly, (US) unneighborly ['ʌn'neibəli] *adj* poco amistoso, impropio de un buen vecino.

unnerve ['ʌn'nəːv] *vt* acobardar.

unnoticed ['ʌn'nəutist] *adj* inadvertido, desapercibido; **to go** —, **to pass** — pasar inadvertido.

unnumbered ['ʌn'nʌmbəd] *adj* sin numerar; (*countless*) innumerable.

unobjectionable ['ʌnəb'dʒekʃnəbl] *adj* intachable, impecable; aceptable; *person etc* inofensivo; **it seems perfectly** — **to me** me parece perfectamente aceptable.

unobservant ['ʌnəb'zəːvənt] *adj* distraído, que no se fija.

unobserved ['ʌnəb'zəːvd] *adj* desapercibido; **to get away** — lograr escapar inadvertido.

unobstructed ['ʌnəb'strʌktid] *adj* libre, sin obstáculos, despejado.

unobtainable ['ʌnəb'teinəbl] *adj* inasequible.

unobtrusive ['ʌnəb'truːsiv] *adj* discreto, modesto, no demasiado visible.

unobtrusively ['ʌnəb'truːsivli] *adv* discretamente, modestamente.

unoccupied ['ʌn'ɔkjupaid] *adj house* deshabitado; *territory* despoblado, sin habitantes, (*Pol*) sin colonizar; *seat, place* libre; *post* vacante; *person* desocupado, ocioso.

unofficial ['ʌnə'fiʃəl] *adj* extraoficial, no oficial.

unofficially ['ʌnə'fiʃəli] *adv* de modo extraoficial.

unopened ['ʌn'əupənd] *adj* sin abrir.

unopposed ['ʌnə'pəuzd] *adj* sin oposición; (*Mil*) sin encontrar resistencia; **to be returned** — (*Parl*) ganar un escaño por ser el único candidato que se presenta.

unorganized ['ʌn'ɔːgənaizd] *adj* no organizado.

unoriginal ['ʌnə'ridʒinəl] *adj* poco original.

unorthodox ['ʌn'ɔːθədɔks] *adj* poco ortodoxo, nada convencional; (*Eccl*) heterodoxo.

unostentatious ['ʌn‚ɔsten'teiʃəs] *adj* modesto, sin ostentación.

unpack ['ʌn'pæk] **1** *vt* desembalar, desempaquetar; *suitcase* vaciar, deshacer. **2** *vi* deshacer las maletas.

unpaid ['ʌn'peid] *adj bill* por pagar, no pagado; *debt* no liquidado; *work, person* no retribuido.

unpalatable [ʌn'pælitəbl] *adj food* incomible, de mal sabor; (*fig*) desagradable, intragable, nada grato; **the — truth** la verdad lisa y llana.

unparalleled [ʌn'pærəleld] *adj* incomparable, sin par; sin precedentes; **this is — in our history** esto no tiene precedentes en nuestra historia.

unpardonable [ʌn'pɑ:dnəbl] *adj* imperdonable, indisculpable.

unparliamentary ['ʌn,pɑ:lə'mentəri] *adj* antiparlamentario.

unpatented ['ʌn'peitntid] *adj* sin patentar.

unpatriotic ['ʌn,pætri'ɔtik] *adj* antipatriótico.

unpatriotically ['ʌn,pætri'ɔtikəli] *adv* de modo antipatriótico.

unpaved ['ʌn'peivd] *adj* sin pavimentar.

unperceived ['ʌnpə'si:vd] *adj* inadvertido, desapercibido.

unperturbed ['ʌnpə:'tə:bd] *adj* impertérrito; **he carried on —** continuó sin alterarse, siguió sin inmutarse; **— by this disaster ...** sin dejarse desanimar por esta catástrofe . . .

unpick ['ʌn'pik] *vt seam* descoser.

unpin ['ʌn'pin] *vt* desprender; quitar los alfileres de.

unplaced ['ʌn'pleist] *adj* (*Sport*) no colocado.

unpleasant [ʌn'pleznt] *adj* desagradable; repugnante; *person* (*by character*) antipático, (*in words etc*) grosero, mal educado; **he was — to her** se portó groseramente con ella; **he had some very — things to say** hizo unas observaciones de las más desagradables; **it was a most — hour** fue una hora muy desagradable.

unpleasantly [ʌn'plezntli] *adv* desagradablemente; **"No", he said — "**No", dijo en tono nada amistoso; **the bomb fell — close** cayó la bomba lo bastante cerca como para inquietarnos.

unpleasantness [ʌn'plezntnis] *n* lo desagradable; lo repugnante; antipatía *f*; (*quarrel*) desavenencia *f*, disgusto *m*; **that — with the conductor** aquel disgusto con el cobrador; **there has been a lot of —** ha habido muchos disgustos.

unpleasing [ʌn'pli:ziŋ] *adj* poco atractivo, antiestético.

unplug ['ʌn'plʌg] *vt* desenchufar, desconectar.

unplumbed ['ʌn'plʌmd] *adj* no sondado.

unpoetic(al) ['ʌnpəu'etik(əl)] *adj* poco poético.

unpolished ['ʌn'pɔliʃt] *adj* sin pulir; *diamond* en bruto; (*fig*) grosero, tosco, inculto.

unpolluted ['ʌnpə'lu:tid] *adj* impoluto.

unpopular ['ʌn'pɔpjulə*] *adj* impopular, poco popular; **it is — with the miners** los mineros no lo quieren; **the decision is —** la decisión resulta inaceptable; **to make oneself —** hacerse detestar; **you will be very — with me** no se lo agradeceré.

unpopularity ['ʌn,pɔpju'læriti] *n* impopularidad *f*.

unpractical ['ʌn'præktikəl] *adj* falto de sentido práctico, poco práctico, desmañado.

unpractised, (*US*) **unpracticed** [ʌn'præktist] *adj* inexperto.

unprecedented [ʌn'presidəntid] *adj* sin precedentes, inaudito.

unpredictable ['ʌnpri'diktəbl] *adj thing* impredictible, incierto; *person* imprevisible, voluble, de reacciones imprevisibles, desconcertante.

unprejudiced [ʌn'predʒudist] *adj* imparcial.

unpremeditated ['ʌnpri'mediteitid] *adj* impremeditado.

unprepared ['ʌnpri'pɛəd] *adj* no preparado; *speech etc* improvisado; **to be — for something** no contar con algo, no esperar algo; **to catch someone —** coger a uno desprevenido.

unpreparedness ['ʌnpri'pɛəridnis] *n* desapercibimiento *m*, desprevención *f*.

unprepossessing ['ʌn,pri:pə'zesiŋ] *adj* poco atractivo.

unpresentable ['ʌnpri'zentəbl] *adj* mal apersonado.

unpretentious ['ʌnpri'tenʃəs] *adj* modesto, sin pretensiones.

unprincipled [ʌn'prinsipld] *adj* poco escrupuloso, cínico, sin conciencia.

unprintable ['ʌn'printəbl] *adj* intranscribible.

unproductive ['ʌnprə'dʌktiv] *adj soil etc* improductivo; *meeting etc* infructuoso.

unprofessional ['ʌnprə'feʃənl] *adj* (*ethically*) indigno de su profesión; contrario a la ética profesional; (*unskilled*) inexperto.

unprofitable [ʌn'prɔfitəbl] *adj enterprise* improductivo; *meeting etc* infructuoso; (*useless*) inútil; (*financially*) poco provechoso, nada lucrativo.

unpromising ['ʌn'prɔmisiŋ] *adj* poco prometedor; **it looks —** no promete mucho.

unpronounceable ['ʌnprə'naunsəbl] *adj* impronunciable.

unpropitious ['ʌnprə'piʃəs] *adj* impropicio, poco propicio.

unprotected ['ʌnprə'tektid] *adj* sin protección, indefenso.

unproved ['ʌn'pru:vd] *adj* no probado.

unprovided ['ʌnprə'vaidid] *adj*: **— for** (*unforeseen*) imprevisto; (*person*) desamparado, desvalido; **— with** desprovisto de.

unprovoked ['ʌnprə'vəukt] *adj* no provocado, sin provocación.

unpublished ['ʌn'pʌbliʃt] *adj* inédito.

unpunctual ['ʌn'pʌŋktjuəl] *adj* impuntual, poco puntual; **this train is always —** este tren siempre llega con retraso.

unpunctuality ['ʌn,pʌŋktju'æliti] *n* impuntualidad *f*.

unpunished ['ʌn'pʌniʃt] *adj* impune; **to go —** (*crime*) quedar sin castigo; (*person*) escapar sin castigo, salir impune.

unqualified ['ʌn'kwɔlifaid] *adj person* incompetente; *teacher* sin título; *workman* no cualificado; *success, assertion* incondicional; *praise* grande; **to be — to do something** no reunir las condiciones para hacer algo.

unquenchable [ʌn'kwentʃəbl] *adj* (*fig*) inextinguible; *thirst* inapagable; *desire etc* insaciable.

unquestionable [ʌn'kwestʃənəbl] *adj* incuestionable, indiscutible.

unquestionably [ʌn'kwestʃənəbli] *adv* indudablemente.

unquestioned [ʌn'kwestʃənd] *adj* incontestable.

unquestioning [ʌn'kwestʃəniŋ] *adj* incondicional; *faith etc* ciego.

unquiet ['ʌn'kwaiət] *adj* inquieto.

unquote ['ʌn'kwəut] *n*: **"—"** "fin *m* de la cita".

unquoted ['ʌn'kwəutid] *adj* (*Fin*) no cotizado.

unravel [ʌn'rævəl] *vt* desenmarañar (*also fig*).

unread ['ʌn'red] *adj* no leído; **to leave something —** dejar algo sin leer.

unreadable ['ʌn'ri:dəbl] *adj* ilegible; (*fig*) imposible de leer, de lectura muy pesada; **I found the book —** el libro me resultó pesadísimo.

unreadiness ['ʌn'redinis] *n* desapercibimiento *m*; desprevención *f*.

unready ['ʌn'redi] *adj* desapercibido, desprevenido.

unreal ['ʌn'riəl] *adj* irreal; imaginario, ilusorio.

unrealistic ['ʌnriə'listik] *adj* ilusorio, fantástico; *estimate etc* no basado en los hechos, que no tiene que ver con la realidad; *scheme* impracticable; *person* poco realista.

unreality ['ʌnri'æliti] *n* irrealidad *f*.

unrealizable ['ʌnriə'laizəbl] *adj* irrealizable.

unrealized ['ʌn'ri:əlaizd] *adj* no realizado, que ha quedado sin realizar; *objective* no logrado.

unreason ['ʌn'ri:zn] *n* insensatez *f*.

unreasonable [ʌn'ri:znəbl] *adj* irrazonable, poco razonable; *demand etc* excesivo; **he was most — about it** se negó a considerarlo razonablemente; **don't be so —!** ¡no seas tan porfiado!; ¡no te pongas así!

unreasonableness [ʌn'ri:znəblnis] *n* irracionalidad *f*; exorbitancia *f*, lo excesivo; (*of person*) porfía *f*.

unreasonably [ʌn'ri:znəbli] *adv*: **to be — difficult about something** porfiar estúpidamente en algo.

unreclaimed ['ʌnri'kleimd] *adj land* no rescatado, no utilizado.

unrecognizable ['ʌn'rekəgnaizəbl] *adj* irreconocible.

unrecognized ['ʌn'rekəgnaizd] *adj* no reconocido; **he went — through the market** atravesó el mercado sin que nadie le conociese.

unrecorded ['ʌnri'kɔ:did] *adj* no registrado, de que no hay constancia.

unredeemed ['ʌnri'di:md] *adj* no redimido; *promise* sin cumplir, incumplido; *pledge* no desempeñado; **— by** no mitigado por.

unreel [ʌn'riəl] *vt* desenrollar.

unrefined ['ʌnri'faind] *adj material* no refinado; (*fig*) inculto.

unreflecting ['ʌnri'flektiŋ] *adj* irreflexivo.

unreformed ['ʌnri'fɔ:md] *adj* no reformado.

unregarded ['ʌnri'gɑ:did] *adj* desatendido, no estimado; **those — aspects** aquellos aspectos de los que nadie hace caso.

unregenerate ['ʌnri'dʒenərit] *adj* empedernido.

unregistered ['ʌn'redʒistəd] *adj* no registrado; *letter* sin certificar.

unregretted ['ʌnri'gretid] *adj* no llorado, no lamentado.

unrehearsed ['ʌnri'hə:st] *adj speech etc* improvisado; *incident* imprevisto.

unrelated ['ʌnri'leitid] *adj* inconexo.
unrelenting ['ʌnri'lentiŋ] *adj* inexorable, implacable.
unreliable ['ʌnri'laiəbl] *adj person* informal, de poca confianza; *news* nada fidedigno; *machine, service etc* en lo que no se puede confiar del todo.
unrelieved ['ʌnri'li:vd] *adj* absoluto, monótono, total; — **by** no aliviado por, no mitigado por; **3 hours of — boredom** 3 horas de aburrimiento total.
unremitting ['ʌnri'mitiŋ] *adj* infatigable, incansable.
unremittingly ['ʌnri'mitiŋli] *adv* incansablemente.
unremunerative ['ʌnri'mju:nərətiv] *adj* poco provechoso, infructuoso; *(financially)* poco lucrativo.
unrepealed ['ʌnri'pi:ld] *adj* no revocado.
unrepeatable ['ʌnri'pi:təbl] *adj* que no puede repetirse; **what he said is quite** — no me atrevo a repetir lo que me dijo.
unrepentant ['ʌnri'pentənt] *adj* impenitente.
unrepresentative ['ʌn,repri'zentətiv] *adj assembly etc* poco representativo; *(untypical)* poco típico, nada característico.
unrepresented ['ʌn,repri'zentid] *adj* sin representación; **they are — in the House** no tienen representación en la Cámara.
unrequited ['ʌnri'kwaitid] *adj* no correspondido.
unreserved ['ʌnri'zə:vd] *adj* no reservado, libre.
unreservedly ['ʌnri'zə:vidli] *adv* sin reserva, incondicionalmente.
unresisting ['ʌnri'zistiŋ] *adj* sumiso.
unresolved ['ʌnri'zɔlvd] *adj problem* no resuelto, pendiente.
unresponsive ['ʌnris'pɔnsiv] *adj* insensible, sordo *(to* a).
unrest [ʌn'rest] *n* malestar *m*, inquietud *f*; *(Pol)* desasosiego *m*, *(active)* desorden *m*; **the — in the Congo** los disturbios del Congo.
unrestrained ['ʌnri'streind] *adj* desenfrenado, desembarazado (de trabas); *language, remarks* libre.
unrestricted ['ʌnri'striktid] *adj* sin restricción, libre.
unrevealed ['ʌnri'vi:ld] *adj* no revelado.
unrewarded ['ʌnri'wɔ:did] *adj* sin recompensa, sin premio; **his work went** — su labor quedó sin recompensa.
unrewarding ['ʌnri'wɔ:diŋ] *adj* sin provecho, infructuoso, inútil.
unrighteous [ʌn'raitʃəs] *adj* malo, perverso.
unripe ['ʌn'raip] *adj* verde, inmaturo.
unrivalled [ʌn'raivəld] *adj* sin par, incomparable; **Bilbao is — for food** la cocina bilbaína es incomparable.
unroll ['ʌn'rəul] 1 *vt* desenrollar. 2 *vi* desenrollarse.
unromantic ['ʌnrə'mæntik] *adj* poco romántico.
unroof ['ʌn'ru:f] *vt* destechar, quitar el techo de.
unrope ['ʌn'rəup] 1 *vt* desatar. 2 *vi* desatarse.
unruffled ['ʌn'rʌfld] *adj person* imperturbable, ecuánime; *hair, surface* liso; **he carried on quite** — siguió sin inmutarse.
unruled ['ʌn'ru:ld] *adj paper* sin rayar.
unruly [ʌn'ru:li] *adj* revoltoso, ingobernable; *hair* despeinado.
unsaddle ['ʌn'sædl] *vt rider* desarzonar; *horse* desensillar, quitar la silla a.
unsafe [ʌn'seif] *adj machine, car etc* inseguro; *policy, journey* peligroso, arriesgado; — **to eat** malo para comer; — **to drink** malo para beber; **it is — to rely on it** no se puede contar con eso; **it is — to let him have a gun** es peligroso permitirle llevar escopeta.
unsaid [ʌn'sed] *adj* sin decir, sin expresar; **to leave something** — callar algo, dejar de decir algo; **much was left** — se dejaron de decir muchas cosas.
unsalaried ['ʌn'sælərid] *adj* sin sueldo, no remunerado.
unsal(e)able [ʌn'seiləbl] *adj* invendible.
unsatisfactory ['ʌn,sætis'fæktəri] *adj* insatisfactorio.
unsatisfied ['ʌn'sætisfaid] *adj* insatisfecho.
unsatisfying ['ʌn'sætisfaiiŋ] *adj* que no satisface, insuficiente.
unsavoury, *(US)* **unsavory** ['ʌn'seivəri] *adj* desagradable, repugnante; *person* indeseable.
unsay ['ʌn'sei] *(irr: see* say) *vt* desdecirse de.
unscathed ['ʌn'skeiðd] *adj* ileso; **to get out** — salir ileso.
unscholarly ['ʌn'skɔləli] *adj person* nada erudito; poco metódico; *work* indigno de un erudito.
unschooled ['ʌn'sku:ld] *adj* indocto; no instruido, sin instrucción; **to be — in a technique** no haber aprendido nada de una técnica.
unscientific ['ʌn,saiən'tifik] *adj* poco científico.
unscramble ['ʌn'skræmbl] *vt message* descifrar.
unscrew ['ʌn'skru:] *vt* destornillar.

unscrupulous [ʌn'skru:pjuləs] *adj* poco escrupuloso, sin escrúpulos, desaprensivo.
unscrupulously [ʌn'skru:pjuləsli] *adv* de modo poco escrupuloso.
unscrupulousness [ʌn'skru:pjuləsnis] *n* falta *f* de escrúpulos, desaprensión *f*.
unseal ['ʌn'si:l] *vt* desellar, abrir.
unseaworthy ['ʌn'si:,wə:ði] *adj* innavegable.
unseemliness [ʌn'si:mlinis] *n* lo indecoroso, falta *f* de decoro.
unseemly [ʌn'si:mli] *adj* indecoroso.
unseen ['ʌn'si:n] 1 *adj* invisible; secreto, oculto; inadvertido; *translation* hecho a primera vista; **he managed to get through** — logró pasar inadvertido.
   2 *n* traducción *f* hecha a primera vista; **the** — lo invisible, lo oculto.
unselfish ['ʌn'selfiʃ] *adj* desinteresado; abnegado; altruista.
unselfishly ['ʌn'selfiʃli] *adv* desinteresadamente; abnegadamente; de modo altruista, con altruismo.
unselfishness ['ʌn'selfiʃnis] *n* desinterés *m*; abnegación *f*; altruismo *m*.
unserviceable ['ʌn'sə:visəbl] *adj* inservible, inútil.
unsettle ['ʌn'setl] *vt* perturbar, agitar, inquietar.
unsettled ['ʌn'setld] *adj person* inquieto, intranquilo; *weather* variable; *state, market* inestable; *land* inhabitado, despoblado, no colonizado; *question* pendiente; *account* por pagar; **he's feeling — in his job** no está del todo contento en su puesto, se siente algo molesto en su puesto.
unsettling ['ʌn'setliŋ] *adj influence etc* perturbador.
unsex ['ʌn'seks] *vt* privar de la sexualidad, suprimir el instinto sexual de.
unshackle ['ʌn'ʃækl] *vt* desencadenar, quitar los grillos a.
unshakeable ['ʌn'ʃeikəbl] *adj resolve* inquebrantable; **he was — in his resolve** se mostró totalmente resuelto; **after 3 hours he was still** — después de 3 horas siguió tan resuelto como antes.
unshaken ['ʌn'ʃeikən] *adj* impertérrito; **he was — by what had happened** no se dejó amedrentar por lo que había pasado.
unshaven ['ʌn'ʃeivn] *adj* sin afeitar.
unsheathe ['ʌn'ʃi:ð] *vt* desenvainar.
unship ['ʌn'ʃip] *vt goods* desembarcar; *rudder, mast etc* desmontar.
unshod [ʌn'ʃɔd] *adj* descalzo; *horse* desherrado.
unshrinkable [ʌn'ʃriŋkəbl] *adj* inencogible.
unshrinking [ʌn'ʃriŋkiŋ] *adj* impávido.
unsighted ['ʌn'saitid] *adj:* **I was — for a moment** por un momento no pude ver, por un momento tuve la vista impedida.
unsightly ['ʌn'saitli] *adj* feo, repugnante.
unsigned ['ʌn'saind] *adj* sin firmar.
unsinkable ['ʌn'siŋkəbl] *adj* insumergible.
unskilled ['ʌn'skild] *adj worker* no cualificado.
unskil(l)ful ['ʌn'skilful] *adj* inexperto, desmañado.
unskimmed ['ʌn'skimd] *adj* sin desnatar.
unsociability ['ʌn,səusə'biliti] *n* insociabilidad *f*.
unsociable [ʌn'səuʃəbl] *adj* insociable.
unsold ['ʌn'səuld] *adj* sin vender; **to remain** — quedar sin vender.
unsoldierly ['ʌn'səuldʒəli] *adj* indigno de un militar.
unsolicited ['ʌnsə'lisitid] *adj* no solicitado.
unsolvable ['ʌn'sɔlvəbl] *adj* irresoluble.
unsolved ['ʌn'sɔlvd] *adj* no resuelto.
unsophisticated ['ʌnsə'fistikeitid] *adj* sencillo, cándido.
unsought ['ʌn'sɔ:t] *adj* no solicitado; no buscado; **the offer came quite** — se hizo la oferta sin que se hubiera pedido nada.
unsound ['ʌn'saund] *adj (in construction)* defectuoso; *fruit* podrido; *argument, opinion* falso, erróneo; **of — mind** mentalmente incapacitado; **the book is — on some points** no hay que fiarse del libro en ciertos aspectos, el libro tiene algunas cosas erróneas.
unsoundness ['ʌn'saundnis] *n* lo defectuoso; falsedad *f*, lo erróneo.
unsparing [ʌn'spɛəriŋ] *adj (generous)* generoso, pródigo; *effort* incansable; *(cruel)* despiadado; **to be — of praises** no escatimar las alabanzas; **to be — in one's efforts to** + *infin* no regatear ningún esfuerzo por + *infin*.
unsparingly [ʌn'spɛəriŋli] *adv* generosamente, pródigamente; incansablemente.
unspeakable [ʌn'spi:kəbl] *adj* indecible; *(very bad)* horrible.
unspeakably [ʌn'spi:kəbli] *adv:* **to suffer** — sufrir lo indecible; **it was — bad** fue horroroso.
unspecified [ʌn'spesifaid] *adj* no especificado.

unspent ['ʌn'spent] *adj* no gastado.
unsplinterable ['ʌn'splintərəbl] *adj* inastillable.
unspoiled, unspoilt ['ʌn'spɔilt] *adj* intacto; no estropeado; *child* natural, no mimado; *countryside* que conserva sus encantos, que sigue en su estado natural.
unspoken ['ʌn'spəukən] *adj* no expresado, tácito.
unsporting ['ʌn'spɔ:tiŋ] *adj*, **unsportsmanlike** ['ʌn'spɔ:tsmənlaik] *adj* antideportivo.
unspotted ['ʌn'spɔtid] *adj* sin manchas, inmaculado.
unstable ['ʌn'steibl] *adj* inestable.
unstamped ['ʌn'stæmpt] *adj* sin sello, sin franquear.
unstatesmanlike ['ʌn'steitsmənlaik] *adj* indigno de un estadista.
unsteadiness ['ʌn'stedinis] *n* inestabilidad *f*, inseguridad *f*; inconstancia *f*; lo movedizo, falta *f* de firmeza.
unsteady ['ʌn'stedi] *adj* inestable, inseguro; inconstante; (*shaky*) movedizo, poco firme; **to be —** **on one's feet** no poder estar de pie sin tambalearse.
unstick ['ʌn'stik] *vt* despegar.
unstinted [ʌn'stintid] *adj praise etc* generoso; *effort* incansable.
unstinting [ʌn'stintiŋ] *adj*: **to be — in one's praise** no escatimar sus alabanzas; **to be — in one's efforts to** + *infin* no regatear ningún esfuerzo por + *infin*.
unstitch ['ʌn'stitʃ] *vt* descoser; **to come —ed** descoserse.
unstop ['ʌn'stɔp] *vt* desobstruir, desatascar.
unstoppable ['ʌn'stɔpəbl] *adj* incontenible, irrefrenable; (*Sport*) *shot etc* imparable.
unstressed ['ʌn'strest] *adj* átono, inacentuado.
unstring ['ʌn'striŋ] (*irr: see* **string**) *vt* (*Mus*) desencordar; *nerves* trastornar; *pearls* desensartar.
unstuck ['ʌn'stʌk] *adj*: **to come —** despegarse, desprenderse, soltarse; (*fig*) fracasar; sufrir un revés.
unstudied ['ʌn'stʌdid] *adj* natural, sin afectación.
unsubdued ['ʌnsəb'dju:d] *adj* indomado.
unsubmissive ['ʌnsəb'misiv] *adj* insumiso.
unsubstantial ['ʌnsəb'stænʃəl] *adj* insustancial.
unsuccessful ['ʌnsək'sesful] *adj person, negotiation etc* fracasado; *effort etc* infructuoso, inútil, ineficaz; **to be —** fracasar, malograrse, no tener éxito; **to be — in doing something** no lograr hacer algo, fracasar en sus esfuerzos por hacer algo.
unsuccessfully ['ʌnsək'sesfəli] *adv* en vano, sin éxito, inútilmente.
unsuitability ['ʌn,su:tə'biliti] *n* impropiedad *f*; inconveniencia *f*; lo inadecuado; lo inoportuno; incompetencia *f*; **his — for the post** su incompetencia para el puesto.
unsuitable ['ʌn'su:təbl] *adj* inapropiado; inconveniente; inadecuado; inoportuno; (*in a post etc*) incompetente; **a most — word** una palabra sumamente impropia; **he married a most — girl** se casó con una chica nada conveniente; **the film is — for children** la película no es apta para menores.
unsuited ['ʌn'su:tid] *adj*: **— for** inapto para; **to do something** inapto para hacer algo; **they are — to each other** no están hechos el uno para el otro.
unsullied ['ʌn'sʌlid] *adj* inmaculado, no corrompido; **— by** no corrompido por.
unsung ['ʌn'sʌŋ] *adj* desconocido, que no recibe los elogios que merece.
unsupported ['ʌnsə'pɔ:tid] *adj statement etc* que carece de base firme, no apoyado por datos; *candidate* sin apoyo, no respaldado por nadie.
unsure ['ʌn'ʃuə*] *adj* poco seguro; **he seemed very — about it** no parecía estar muy seguro de ello.
unsurmountable ['ʌnsə'mauntəbl] *adj* insuperable.
unsurpassable ['ʌnsə'pɑ:səbl] *adj* inmejorable, insuperable.
unsurpassed ['ʌnsə'pɑ:st] *adj* insuperado, sin par; **— in quality** de calidad inmejorable; **— by anybody** no superado por nadie.
unsuspected ['ʌnsəs'pektid] *adj* insospechado.
unsuspecting ['ʌnsəs'pektiŋ] *adj* nada suspicaz, sin recelo, confiado, inocente.
unsweetened ['ʌn'swi:tnd] *adj* sin azucarar.
unswerving [ʌn'swə:viŋ] *adv resolve* inquebrantable; *loyalty* inquebrantable, firme; *course* sin vacilar.
unswervingly [ʌn'swə:viŋli] *adv*: **to be — loyal to someone** seguir totalmente leal a uno; **to hold — to one's course** seguir sin vacilar.
unsympathetic ['ʌn,simpə'θetik] *adj* incompasivo, poco compasivo; falto de comprensión; **he was totally —** no mostró la más mínima comprensión; **they were — to my plea** no hicieron caso de mi ruego; **I am not — to your request** no veo con malos ojos su petición.

unsystematic ['ʌn,sisti'mætik] *adj* poco metódico.
unsystematically ['ʌn,sisti'mætikəli] *adv* de modo poco metódico.
untainted ['ʌn'teintid] *adj* inmaculado, no corrompido; **— by** no corrompido por.
untam(e)able ['ʌn'teiməbl] *adj* indomable.
untamed ['ʌn'teimd] *adj* indomado.
untangle ['ʌn'tæŋgl] *vt* desenmarañar.
untanned ['ʌn'tænd] *adj* sin curtir.
untapped ['ʌn'tæpt] *adj resources* sin explotar.
untarnished ['ʌn'tɑ:niʃt] *adj reputation etc* sin tacha.
untasted ['ʌn'teistid] *adj* sin probar.
untaught ['ʌn'tɔ:t] *adj* no enseñado.
untaxed ['ʌn'tækst] *adj* libre de impuestos, no sujeto a contribuciones.
unteachable ['ʌn'ti:tʃəbl] *adj* demasiado estúpido para aprender nada.
untempered ['ʌn'tempəd] *adj steel etc* sin templar.
untenable ['ʌn'tenəbl] *adj* insostenible.
untenanted ['ʌn'tenəntid] *adj* desocupado.
untested ['ʌn'testid] *adj* no probado.
unthinkable [ʌn'θiŋkəbl] *adj* inconcebible, impensable; **it is — that . . .** es inconcebible que + *subj*.
unthinking ['ʌn'θiŋkiŋ] *adj* irreflexivo.
unthinkingly ['ʌn'θiŋkiŋli] *adv* irreflexivamente, sin pensar.
unthread ['ʌn'θred] *vt cloth* deshebrar, descoser; *needle* desenhebrar; *pearls* desensartar.
unthrifty ['ʌn'θrifti] *adj* manirroto, derrochador.
untidily [ʌn'taidili] *adv* desaliñadamente; sin método; en desorden; **she does everything —** todo lo hace de cualquier modo.
untidiness [ʌn'taidinis] *n* desaliño *m*; falta *f* de método; desorden *m*.
untidy [ʌn'taidi] *adj* (*in dress, appearance*) desaliñado, desaseado; *work* poco metódico; *room* en desorden; **she's a very — person** es una persona que vive sin método, es una persona que hace las cosas (*or* deja sus cosas) de cualquier modo, es una persona desordenada.
untie ['ʌn'tai] *vt* desatar.
until [ən'til] **1** *prep* hasta; **— 10** hasta las 10; **— his arrival** hasta su llegada.
2 *conj* **(a)** (*of future time*) hasta que + *subj, eg* **wait — I get back** espera hasta que yo vuelva.
(b) (*of past time*) hasta que + *indic, eg* **he did nothing — I told him** no hizo nada hasta que yo se lo dije.
untilled ['ʌn'tild] *adj* sin cultivar.
untimely [ʌn'taimli] *adj* intempestivo, inoportuno; prematuro.
untiring [ʌn'taiəriŋ] *adj* incansable.
untiringly [ʌn'taiəriŋli] *adv* incansablemente.
unto ['ʌntu] *prep* (*arch*) *see* **to; towards.**
untold ['ʌn'təuld] *adj story* nunca contado, inédito; *secret* nunca revelado; *loss, wealth etc* incalculable; *suffering* indecible.
untouchable [ʌn'tʌtʃəbl] (*India*) **1** *adj* intocable. **2** *n* intocable *mf*.
untouched ['ʌn'tʌtʃt] *adj* intacto; (*safe*) incólume, indemne; **a product — by human hand** un producto que ninguna mano humana ha tocado; **he is — by any plea** es insensible a todas las súplicas; **to leave one's food —** dejar su comida sin probar; **those peoples — by civilization** esos pueblos no influidos por la civilización.
untoward [,ʌntə'wɔ:d] *adj* desfavorable; adverso; *event etc* fatal, funesto.
untrained ['ʌn'treind] *adj person* inexperto; (*unskilled*) no cualificado; *teacher etc* sin título, que no tiene título; (*Sport*) no entrenado; *animal* sin amaestrar, no adiestrado.
untransferable ['ʌntræns'fə:rəbl] *adj* intransferible.
untranslatable ['ʌntræns'leitəbl] *adj* intraducible.
untravelled ['ʌn'trævld] *adj place* inexplorado; *road etc* no trillado, poco frecuentado; *person* que no ha viajado.
untried ['ʌn'traid] *adj* **(a)** *method etc* no probado; *person* novicio, no puesto a prueba; *soldier* bisoño. **(b)** (*Law*) *person* no procesado, *case* no visto.
untrodden ['ʌn'trɔdn] *adj* no trillado.
untroubled ['ʌn'trʌbld] *adj* tranquilo; **— by thoughts of her** sin pensar en ella para nada, no afectado por ningún recuerdo de ella.
untrue ['ʌn'tru:] *adj statement* falso; *world etc* ficticio, imaginario; *person* infiel, desleal; **that is wholly —** eso es completamente falso.
untrustworthy ['ʌn'trʌst,wə:ði] *adj person* informal, indigno de confianza; *source etc* no fidedigno; *book etc* de dudosa autoridad; *machine, car* inseguro.
untruth ['ʌn'tru:θ] *n, pl* **—truths** [tru:ðz] mentira *f*.

untruthful ['ʌn'truːθful] adj mentiroso, falso.
untruthfully ['ʌn'truːθfəli] adv falsamente.
untruthfulness ['ʌn'truːθfulnis] n falsedad f.
untutored ['ʌn'tjuːtəd] adj indocto, poco instruido.
untwine ['ʌn'twain] vt, **untwist** ['ʌn'twist] vt destorcer.
unusable ['ʌn'juːzəbl] adj inservible, inútil.
unused ['ʌn'juːzd] adj stamp etc nuevo, sin usar; sin estrenar.
unused ['ʌn'juːst] adj: **to be — to** no estar acostumbrado a.
unusual [ʌn'juːʒuəl] adj insólito, poco común, extraordinario.
unusually [ʌn'juːʒuəli] adv: **an — awkward matter** un asunto extraordinariamente difícil; **an — gifted man** un hombre de talentos poco comunes.
unutterable [ʌn'ʌtərəbl] adj indecible.
unutterably [ʌn'ʌtərəbli] adv indeciblemente.
unvaried [ʌn'vɛərid] adj sin variación, constante; (pej) monótono.
unvarnished ['ʌn'vɑːniʃt] adj sin barnizar; (fig) sencillo, llano, sin adornos; **the — truth** la verdad lisa y llana.
unvarying [ʌn'vɛəriiŋ] adj invariable, constante.
unveil [ʌn'veil] vt quitar el velo a; statue etc descubrir.
unventilated ['ʌn'ventileitid] adj sin ventilación, sin aire.
unverifiable ['ʌn'verifaiəbl] adj que no puede verificarse.
unverified ['ʌn'verifaid] adj sin verificar.
unversed ['ʌn'vəːst] adj: **— in** poco ducho en.
unvisited ['ʌn'vizitid] adj no visitado, no frecuentado.
unvoiced ['ʌn'vɔist] adj no expresado; (Gram) sordo.
unvouched-for ['ʌn'vautʃfɔː*] adj no garantizado.
unwanted ['ʌn'wɔntid] adj superfluo; child no deseado.
unwarily [ʌn'wɛərili] adv imprudentemente, incautamente.
unwariness [ʌn'wɛərinis] n imprudencia f.
unwarlike ['ʌn'wɔːlaik] adj pacífico, poco belicoso.
unwarranted [ʌn'wɔrəntid] adj injustificado.
unwary [ʌn'wɛəri] adj imprudente, incauto.
unwashed ['ʌn'wɔʃt] adj sin lavar, sucio; **the Great U— la plebe.**
unwavering [ʌn'weivəriŋ] adj loyalty, resolve inquebrantable, firme; course constante; gaze fijo.
unwaveringly [ʌn'weivəriŋli] adv firmemente; constantemente; **to hold — to one's course** seguir su curso sin apartarse para nada de él.
unwearying [ʌn'wiəriiŋ] adj incansable.
unwelcome [ʌn'welkəm] adj importuno, molesto, inoportuno; desagradable; **a most — piece of news** una noticia nada grata (to para); **the change is not —** el cambio no es del todo molesto para nosotros.
unwell ['ʌn'wel] adj: **to be —** estar indispuesto; **to feel —** sentirse mal; **I felt — on the ship** me mareé en el barco.
unwholesome ['ʌn'həulsəm] adj insalubre, nocivo; (morally) indeseable.
unwieldy [ʌn'wiːldi] adj pesado, abultado, difícil de manejar.
unwilling ['ʌn'wiliŋ] adj desinclinado; **to be — to do something** estar poco dispuesto a hacer algo; **to be — for someone to do something** estar poco dispuesto a permitir que uno haga algo.
unwillingly ['ʌn'wiliŋli] adv de mala gana.
unwillingness ['ʌn'wiliŋnis] n falta f de inclinación, desgana f; **his — to help us** su desgana para ayudarnos, su renuencia a ayudarnos.
unwind ['ʌn'waind] (irr: see **wind**) 1 vt desenvolver; thread desovillar. 2 vi desenvolverse; desovillarse; (fig: relax) esparcirse, calmar los nervios.
unwisdom ['ʌn'wizdəm] n imprudencia f.
unwise ['ʌn'waiz] adj imprudente; poco aconsejable; **it would be — to + infin** sería poco aconsejable + infin; **that was most — of you** en eso has sido muy imprudente.
unwisely ['ʌn'waizli] adv imprudentemente.
unwitting [ʌn'witiŋ] adj inconsciente.
unwittingly [ʌn'witiŋli] adv inconscientemente; sin saber, sin darse cuenta.
unwomanly [ʌn'wumənli] adj poco femenino.
unwonted [ʌn'wəuntid] adj insólito, inusitado.
unworkable ['ʌn'wəːkəbl] adj impracticable.
unwordly ['ʌn'wəːldli] adj poco mundano, poco realista.
unworn ['ʌn'wɔːn] adj nuevo, sin estrenar.
unworthiness [ʌn'wəːðinis] n indignidad f.
unworthy [ʌn'wəːði] adj indigno (of de); **to be — to do something** ser indigno de hacer algo; **it is —**

of attention no merece que se la preste atención.
unwounded ['ʌn'wuːndid] adj ileso.
unwrap ['ʌn'ræp] vt desenvolver; parcel deshacer.
unwritten ['ʌn'ritn] adj no escrito.
unyielding [ʌn'jiːldiŋ] adj inflexible.
unyoke ['ʌn'jəuk] vt desuncir.
unzip ['ʌn'zip] vt abrir la cremallera de.
up [ʌp] 1 adv (a) (general sense) hacia arriba; arriba, para arriba; en el aire, en lo alto; **—!** ¡arriba!, (from bed) ¡levántate!; **all the way —** durante toda la subida, en todo el recorrido; en toda su extensión; **halfway — a mitad** de camino; **"this side —"** "este lado hacia arriba"; **"road —"** "cerrado por obras"; **— above** allí arriba; **to be — above** something estar por encima de algo; **— in London** allá en Londres; **my office is 5 floors —** mi oficina está en el quinto piso; **we're — for the day** hemos venido a pasar el día; **when I was — (Univ)** cuando yo estaba en la universidad, cuando yo era estudiante; **to throw something — (in the air)** lanzar algo al aire, lanzar algo por alto; **to walk — and down** pasearse, andar de un lado para otro, andar de acá para allá.
(b) **to be — (out of bed)** estar levantado; **we were — at 7** nos levantamos a las 7; **to be — and about again** estar levantado y salir (después de una enfermedad), estar mucho mejor; **to be — and doing** estar activo; **to be — all night** no acostarse en toda la noche; **we were still — at midnight** a medianoche seguíamos sin acostarnos.
(c) **when the sun is —** después de la salida del sol; cuando brilla el sol; **the river is — el** río ha subido; **the tide is —** la marea está alta.
(d) (of price, quantity etc) potatoes are **—** han subido las patatas; **the thermometer is — 2 degrees** ha subido el termómetro 2 grados; **Ceuta was 3 goals — Ceuta** tenía 3 goles de ventaja; **we were 20 points — on them** les llevábamos una ventaja de 20 puntos.
(e) (and upwards) **from £2 —** de 2 libras para arriba; **from the age of 13 —** desde los 13 años para arriba; a partir de los 13 años.
(f) (on a level) **put it — beside the other one** ponlo junto al otro; **to be — with someone** estar a la altura de uno, haber alcanzado el nivel de uno; **is he — to advanced work?** ¿tiene capacidad para estudios superiores?; **to be — to a task** estar a la altura de un cometido; **I don't feel — to it** no me siento con fuerzas para ello; **it's not — to much** no vale gran cosa; **to be well — in maths** estar fuerte en matemáticas.
(g) **to be — against difficulties** tener dificultades, haber tropezado con dificultades; **to be — against it** estar en un aprieto; **now we're really — against it!** ¡con la iglesia hemos topado!; **to be — against someone** tener que habérselas con uno; see **hard** etc.
(h) **what's —?** ¿qué pasa?; **what's — with John?** ¿qué le pasa a Juan?; **there's something —** pasa algo malo, (of a plot) están tramando algo.
(i) (finished) **time is —** se ha terminado el tiempo permitido, es la hora; **when the period is —** cuando termine el plazo; **his holiday is —** han terminado ya sus vacaciones; **our time here is —** no podemos estar más tiempo aquí, se ha acabado nuestra estancia aquí; see **all**.
(j) **— to** hasta; **— to now** hasta ahora; **— to here** hasta aquí; **— to this week** hasta esta semana; **— to £10** hasta 10 libras; **to count — to 100** contar hasta 100; **they advanced — to the wood** avanzaron hasta el bosque.
(k) **they're — to something** están tramando algo; **what are you — to?** ¿qué haces ahí?; **what are you — to with that knife?** ¿qué haces con ese cuchillo?; **what does he think he's — to?** ¿qué diablos piensa hacer?
(l) **it is — to you to decide** te toca a Vd decidir; **I feel it is — to me to tell him** creo que me incumbe a mí decírselo; **if it was — to me** si yo tuviera que decidirlo.
2 prep en lo alto de; encima de; **— a tree** en lo alto de un árbol; **halfway — the stairs** a mitad de la escalera; **halfway — the mountain** a mitad de la subida del monte; **they live further — the road** viven en esta calle pero más arriba; **he went off — the road** se fue calle arriba; **— (the) river** río arriba.
3 adj: **the — train** el tren ascendente.
4 n (a) **—s and downs** vicisitudes fpl, alternativas fpl, altibajos mpl, peripecias fpl; **after many —s and downs** después de mil peripecias; **the —s and downs that every politician has** las alternativas a que está sometido todo político.

(b) to be on the — and — ir cada vez mejor.
5 *vi* (*fam*): **to — and +** *inf* ponerse de repente a + *infin*; **he —ped and hit her** sin más la pegó.

up-and-coming ['ʌpənd'kʌmiŋ] *adj* joven y prometedor, nuevo y emprendedor.

up-and-down ['ʌpən'daun] *adj movement* vertical, perpendicular; *business, progress etc* poco uniforme, variable; *eventful* accidentado.

upbraid [ʌp'breid] *vt* reprender, censurar; **to — someone with something** censurar algo a uno.

upbringing ['ʌp͵briŋiŋ] *n* educación *f*, crianza *f*.

upcast ['ʌpkɑ:st] *n* (*Min*; *also* **— shaft**) pozo *m* de ventilación.

upcountry ['ʌp'kʌntri] **1** *adv*: **to be —** estar tierra adentro, estar en el interior; **to go —** ir hacia el interior, penetrar en el interior.
2 *adj* del interior.

up-current ['ʌp'kʌrənt] *n* (*Aer*) viento *m* ascendente.

update [ʌp'deit] *vt* modernizar, actualizar; **to — someone on a matter** poner a uno al tanto de un asunto, dar a uno los últimos detalles de un asunto.

upend [ʌp'end] *vt* volver de arriba abajo, poner al revés; *person* volcar.

upgrade ['ʌpgreid] *n* cuesta *f*, pendiente *f*; **to be on the —** ir cuesta arriba, prosperar, estar en auge; (*Med*) estar mejor, estar reponiéndose.

upgrade [ʌp'greid] *vt person* ascender; *job* asignar a un grado más alto; valorar en más.

upheaval [ʌp'hi:vəl] *n* (*Geol*) solevantamiento *m*; (*fig*) cataclismo *m*, sacudida *f*, trastorno *m*.

uphill ['ʌp'hil] **1** *adv* cuesta arriba; **to go —** ir cuesta arriba; **the road goes — for 2 miles** la carretera sube durante 2 millas.
2 *adj task* arduo, penoso.

uphold [ʌp'həuld] (*irr*: *see* **hold**) *vt* (*hold up*) sostener, apoyar; (*maintain*) sostener, defender; (*Law*) confirmar.

upholder [ʌp'həuldə*] *n* defensor *m*, ora *f*.

upholster [ʌp'həulstə*] *vt* tapizar, entapizar (*with* de).

upholsterer [ʌp'həulstərə*] *n* tapicero *m*.

upholstery [ʌp'həulstəri] *n* tapicería *f*, tapizado *m*; (*cushioning etc*) almohadillado *m*.

upkeep ['ʌpki:p] *n* conservación *f*; (*of car, house etc*) mantenimiento *m*; (*cost*) gastos *mpl* de mantenimiento.

upland ['ʌplənd] **1** *n* tierra *f* alta, meseta *f*; **—s** tierras *fpl* altas. **2** *adj* de la meseta.

uplift ['ʌplift] *n* sustentación *f*; (*fig*) inspiración *f*, edificación *f*; **moral —** edificación *f*.

uplift [ʌp'lift] *vt* (*fig*) inspirar, edificar.

upon [ə'pɒn] *prep see* **on**.

upper ['ʌpə*] *adj* superior, más alto; de arriba; *class, house* (*Pol*) alto; (*in Geog names*) alto, *eg* **U— Egypt** Alto Egipto *m*; *deck, floor etc* superior, de arriba.

upper-class ['ʌpə'klɑ:s] *adj* de la clase alta.

upper-crust ['ʌpə'krʌst] *adj* de categoría (social) superior, de buen tono.

uppercut ['ʌpəkʌt] *n* (*Boxing*) golpe *m* de abajo arriba.

uppermost ['ʌpəməust] *adj* **(a)** (el) más alto; **to put something face —** poner algo con la cara hacia arriba.
(b) (*fig*) principal, predominante; **what is — in someone's mind** lo que ocupa el primer lugar en el pensamiento de uno; **it was — in my mind** pensé en eso antes que en otra cosa.

uppers ['ʌpəz] *npl* (*of shoe*) pala *f*; **to be on one's —** no tener un céntimo.

uppish ['ʌpiʃ] *adj*, **uppity** ['ʌpiti] *adj* (*fam*) engreído; fresco; **to get —** enfurecerse.

upraise [ʌp'reiz] *vt* levantar.

upright ['ʌprait] **1** *adj* vertical; derecho; *piano* vertical, recto; (*fig*) honrado, recto, probo.
2 *adv*: **to hold oneself —** mantenerse erguido; **to sit bolt —** ponerse derecho en su silla.
3 *n* montante *m*; (*of goalpost*) poste *m*.

uprightly ['ʌp͵raitli] *adv* (*fig*) honradamente, rectamente.

uprightness ['ʌp͵raitnis] *n* (*fig*) honradez *f*, rectitud *f*.

uprising [ʌp'raiziŋ] *n* alzamiento *m*, sublevación *f*.

up-river ['ʌp'rivə*] *adv* = **upstream**.

uproar ['ʌprɔ:*] *n* alboroto *m*, tumulto *m*; escándalo *m*; **at this there was —** en esto estallaron ruidosas las protestas, en esto se armó un escándalo; **the whole place was in —** la sala estaba alborotada.

uproarious [ʌp'rɔ:riəs] *adj* tumultuoso, estrepitoso; *laughter* tumultuoso, escandaloso; *joke etc* divertidísimo; *success* clamoroso.

uproariously [ʌp'rɔ:riəsli] *adv* tumultuosamente, con estrépito; **to laugh —** estar para morirse de risa.

uproot [ʌp'ru:t] *vt* desarraigar, arrancar; (*destroy*) extirpar; **whole families have been —ed** se han desplazado familias enteras.

upset ['ʌpset] *n* (*accident*) vuelco *m*; (*in plans etc*) revés *m*, contratiempo *m*; (*Med*) trastorno *m*, desarreglo *m*; **to have a stomach —** tener un trastorno estomacal, tener el estómago trastornado.

upset [ʌp'set] **1** (*irr*: *see* **set**) *vt* (*overturn*) volcar, trastornar; (*spill*) derramar; *stomach* trastornar, hacer daño a; *plans etc* dar al traste con; *person* (*emotionally*) desconcertar, alterar, perturbar; **garlic —s me** el ajo no me sienta bien; **the news — her a lot** la noticia le causó gran pesar; **I didn't intend to — her** no tenía la intención de alterarla.
2 *vr*: **to — oneself** acongojarse, apurarse; **don't — yourself!** ¡no te acongojes!
3 *adj*: **to be —** estar perturbado, estar acongojado, estar preocupado; sentirse molesto; **to get —** alterarse, perturbarse; **she looked terribly —** parecía estar apuradísima; **she is easily —** se apura por cualquier cosa; **what are you so — about?** ¿qué motivo tienes para emocionarte tanto?, ¿a qué se debe tanto sentimiento?; **I have an — stomach** tengo el estómago trastornado.
4 *attr*: **— price** precio m mínimo.

upsetting [ʌp'setiŋ] *adj* inquietante, desconcertante; **it's very —** es para volverse loco.

upshot ['ʌpʃɒt] *n* resultado *m*; **in the —** al fin y al cabo; **the — of it all was . . .** resultó por fin que . . .

upside ['ʌpsaid] *n*: **to be — down** estar al revés, tener lo de arriba abajo; **to turn a box — down** volver una caja al revés, invertir una caja; **the room was — down** reinaba la mayor confusión en el cuarto, en el cuarto todo estaba patas arriba; **to turn a room — down** introducir el desorden en un cuarto; **we turned everything — down looking for it** al buscarlo lo revolvimos todo, en la búsqueda lo registramos todo de arriba abajo.

upstage ['ʌp'steidʒ] **1** *adv*: **to be —** estar en el fondo de la escena; **to go —** ir hacia el fondo de la escena.
2 *adj* (*fam*) engreído.
3 *vt*: **to — someone** lograr captar la atención del público a costa de otro.

upstairs ['ʌp'steəz] **1** *adv* arriba; **to go —** ir arriba, subir al piso superior; **to walk slowly —** subir lentamente la escalera.
2 *adj* de arriba; **we looked out of an — window** nos asomamos a una ventana del piso superior.

upstanding [ʌp'stændiŋ] *adj* **(a) a fine — young man** un buen mozo gallardo. **(b) to be —** levantarse, ponerse de pie.

upstart ['ʌpstɑ:t] **1** *adj* arribista; advenedizo; **some — youth** algún joven presuntuoso. **2** *n* arribista *mf*; advenedizo *m*, a *f*; insolente *mf*.

upstate [ʌp'steit] *adj* (*US, esp of New York*) interior, septentrional.

upstream ['ʌp'stri:m] *adv* aguas arriba, río arriba (*from* de); **to go —** ir río arriba; **to swim —** nadar contra la corriente; **a town — from Windsor** una ciudad más arriba de Windsor; **about 3 miles — from Seville** unas 3 millas más arriba de Sevilla.

upstretched ['ʌpstretʃt] *adj* extendido hacia arriba.

upstroke ['ʌpstrəuk] *n* (*with pen*) plumada *f* ascendente; (*Mech*) carrera *f* ascendente.

upsurge ['ʌpsɜ:dʒ] *n* acceso *m*, aumento *m* grande; **a great — of interest in Góngora** un gran renacimiento del interés por Góngora; **there has been an — of feeling about this question** ha aumentado de pronto la preocupación por esta cuestión.

upswept ['ʌpswept] *adj wing* elevado, inclinado hacia arriba; **with — hair** con peinado alto.

upswing ['ʌpswiŋ] *n* movimiento *m* hacia arriba; (*fig*) curva *f* ascensional, mejora *f* notable (*in, of* de).

uptake ['ʌpteik] *n*: **to be quick on the —** ser muy listo; **to be a bit slow on the —** ser algo torpe.

upthrust ['ʌp'θrʌst] **1** *adj* empujado hacia arriba, dirigido hacia arriba; (*Geol*) solevantado. **2** *n* empuje *m* hacia arriba; (*Geol*) solevantamiento *m*.

up-to-date ['ʌptə'deit] *adj* moderno, actual; *see also* **date**.

uptown [ʌp'taun] **1** *adv* **go** hacia la parte alta de la ciudad; **be** en la parte alta de la ciudad. **2** *adj* de la parte alta de la ciudad.

upturn ['ʌptɜ:n] *n* mejora *f*, aumento *m* (*in* de).

upturn [ʌp'tɜ:n] *vt* volver hacia arriba; (*overturn*) volcar.

upturned ['ʌptɜ:nd] *adj* vuelto hacia arriba; *nose* respingona.

upward ['ʌpwəd] *adj curve, movement etc* ascendente, ascensional; *slope* en pendiente; *tendency* al alza.

upward(s) ['ʌpwəd(z)] *adv* hacia arriba; **to lay something face** — poner algo con la cara hacia arriba; **to look** — mirar hacia arriba; £50 **and** — de 50 libras para arriba; **from the age of 13** — desde los 13 años para arriba; a partir de los 13 años; — **of 200 más de** 200.

upwind ['ʌp'wind] *adv*: **to stay** — quedarse en la parte de donde sopla el viento.

Urals ['juərəlz] *pl* Urales *mpl*, Montes *mpl* Urales.

uranium [juə'reiniəm] *n* uranio *m*.

Uranus [juə'reinəs] Urano *m*.

urban ['ə:bən] *adj* urbano.

urbane [ə:'bein] *adj* urbano, cortés, fino.

urbanity [ə:'bæniti] *n* urbanidad *f*, cortesía *f*, fineza *f*.

urbanization [,ə:bənai'zeiʃən] *n* urbanización *f*.

urbanize ['ə:bənaiz] *vt* urbanizar.

urchin ['ə:tʃin] *n* galopín *m*, pilluelo *m*, golfillo *m*.

Urdu ['uədu:] *n* urdu *m*.

urea ['juəriə] *n* urea *f*.

ureter [juə'ri:tə*] *n* uréter *m*.

urethra [juə'ri:θrə] *n* uretra *f*.

urge [ə:dʒ] **1** *n* impulso *m*; instinto *m*, deseo *m*; ambición *f*; **the** — **to win** el afán de victoria; **the** — **to write** el deseo apremiante de escribir algo, la ambición de hacerse escritor; **to feel an** — **to do something** sentir un deseo apremiante de hacer algo, sentirse impulsado a hacer algo; **to get the** —, **to have the** — desear algo con vehemencia.

2 *vt* **(a) to** — **someone** on animar a uno, instar a uno a ir adelante; **to** — **someone to do something** instar a uno a hacer algo, incitar a uno a hacer algo, recomendar a uno encarecidamente que haga algo; **to** — **that something should be done** recomendar encarecidamente que se haga algo.

(b) to — **something on someone** incitar a uno a algo, recomendar encarecidamente algo a uno; **to** — **a policy on the government** hacer presión en el gobierno para que adopte una política.

urgency ['ə:dʒənsi] *n* urgencia *f*; **with a note of** — **in his voice** en tono algo perentorio, con una nota de perentoriedad; **is there much** — **about this?** ¿corre prisa esto?; **it is a matter of** — es un asunto urgente.

urgent ['ə:dʒənt] *adj* urgente; *tone etc* apremiante, perentorio; *entreaty etc* insistente, apremiante; **it is** — **that . . .** urge que + *subj*; **is this** — **?** ¿corre prisa esto?

urgently ['ə:dʒəntli] *adv* urgentemente; de modo apremiante, con insistencia.

uric ['juərik] *adj* úrico; — **acid** ácido *m* úrico.

urinal ['juərinl] *n* (*building*) urinario *m*; (*vessel*) orinal *m*.

urinary ['juərinəri] *adj* urinario.

urinate ['juərineit] **1** *vt* orinar. **2** *vi* orinar(se).

urine ['juərin] *n* orina *f*, orines *mpl*.

urn [ə:n] *n* urna *f*; (*for tea*) tetera *f*.

urogenital [juərəu'dʒenitl] *adj* urogenital.

urologist [juə'rɔlədʒist] *n* urólogo *m*.

urology [juə'rɔlədʒi] *n* urología *f*.

Ursa Major ['ə:sə'meidʒə*] Osa *f* Mayor.

Ursa Minor ['ə:sə'mainə*] Osa *f* Menor.

Uruguay ['juərəgwai] el Uruguay.

Uruguayan [,juərə'gwaiən] **1** *adj* uruguayo. **2** *n* uruguayo *m*, a *f*.

us [ʌs] *pron* nos; (*after prep*) nosotros, nosotras.

usable ['ju:zəbl] *adj* utilizable, aprovechable; **it is no longer** — ya no sirve.

usage ['ju:zidʒ] *n* **(a)** (*custom*) uso *m*, costumbre *f*; **in the** — **of railwaymen** en el lenguaje de los ferroviarios, en el uso ferroviario; **an ancient** — **of the Celts** una antigua costumbre de los celtas.

(b) (*treatment*) tratamiento *m*; (*handling*) manejo *m*; **kind** — buenos tratos *mpl*, buen tratamiento *m*; **it's had some rough** — ha sido manejado con bastante dureza.

use [ju:s] *n* **(a)** uso *m*, empleo *m*; manejo *m*; **a new** — **for old tyres** nuevo método *m* para utilizar los neumáticos viejos; "**directions for** —" "modo *m* de empleo"; **for the** — **of the blind** para uso de los ciegos, para los ciegos; **fit for** — servible, en buen estado; **ready for** — listo para ser usado; **care in the** — **of guns** cuidado *m* en el manejo de las armas de fuego; **word in** — en uso, palabra *f* que se usa; **it is not now in** — ya no se usa; **it has not been in** — **for 5 years** hace 5 años que no se usa; **an article of everyday** — un artículo de uso corriente; **it is now out of** — ya no se usa; eso ha quedado anticuado, eso está fuera de moda ya; **to find a** — **for something** utilizar algo, aprovechar algo; **it improves with** — parece mejor a medida que se va usando; **to make** — **of** servirse de; utilizar, aprovechar; explotar; (*right etc*) valerse de, ejercer; **to make good** — **of** aprovecharse debidamente de; **to put something to good** — servirse de algo, sacar partido de algo; hacer que algo trabaje (*or* rinda *etc*); **to put something into** — poner en servicio.

(b) to have the — **of a garage** poder usar un garaje; **I have the** — **of it on Sundays** me permiten usarlo los domingos; **I should like to have the** — **of it** quisiera poderlo usar; **he lost the** — **of his arm** se le quedó inútil el brazo.

(c) (*usefulness*) utilidad *f*; **to be of** — servir (*for* para); **to be of no** — no servir; **can I be of any** —? ¿puedo ayudar?; **it's (of) no** — es inútil; **it's no** — **your protesting** de nada sirve quejarse, es inútil quejarse; **it's no** — **discussing it further** no vale la pena discutirlo más; **he's no** — no vale para nada; **he's no** — **as a goalkeeper** no vale para portero; **what's the** — **of all this?** ¿de qué sirve todo esto?, ¿qué utilidad tiene todo esto?, ¿qué finalidad tiene todo esto?; **to have no** — **for something** no necesitar algo; **to have no** — **for someone** despreciar a uno; **I've no** — **for those who . . .** detesto a los que . . .; **to have no further** — **for something** no poder usar algo más.

(d) (*custom*) uso *m*, costumbre *f*.

use [ju:z] *vt* **(a)** usar, emplear; servirse de, utilizar; *tool etc* manejar; **he** —**d a knife** empleó un cuchillo; **are you using this book?** ¿te hace falta este libro?, ¿estás trabajando con este libro?; **which book did you** — **?** ¿qué libro consultaste?; **I could** — **a drink!** (*fam*) ¡qué sed tengo!; **this room could** — **some paint** (*fam*) no le vendría mal a este cuarto una mano de pintura; **careful how you** — **that razor!** ¡cuidado con la navaja esa!; **have you** —**d a gun before?** ¿has manejado alguna vez una escopeta?; **the money is** —**d for the poor** el dinero se dedica a los pobres, el dinero se emplea en los pobres; **the word is no longer** —**d** la palabra ya no se usa; **may I** — **your name?** ¿puedo dar su nombre?; **to** — **something as a hammer** emplear algo como martillo; **to** — **something for a purpose** servirse de algo con un propósito.

(b) (*of abstract things*) emplear; **to** — **force** emplear la fuerza; **to** — **every means** emplear todos los medios; no perdonar esfuerzo (*to* + *infin* por + *infin*); **to** — **one's influence** valerse de su influencia.

(c) (*treat*) tratar; **to** — **someone well** tratar bien a uno; **to** — **someone roughly** tratar a uno brutalmente; **she had been cruelly** —**d by . . .** había sido tratada con crueldad por . . .

(d) to — **something (up)** consumir algo, agotar algo; **it's all** —**d up** todo está agotado; **when we've** —**d up all our money** cuando hayamos gastado todo nuestro dinero; **please** — **up all the coffee** que no quede café sin beber.

(e) (*v/aux*) [ju:st] **I** —**d to go** iba, solía ir, acostumbraba ir, tenía la costumbre de ir; **but I** —**d not to** pero antes no; **things aren't what they** —**d to be** las cosas ya no son lo que eran.

used [ju:zd] *adj* usado; gastado, viejo; *stamp* usado.

used [ju:st] *ptp of* use: **to be** — **to** estar acostumbrado a; **to be** — **to** + *gen* estar acostumbrado a + *infin*; **to get** — **to** acostumbrarse a; **I still haven't got** — **to the lifts** todavía no me he acostumbrado a los ascensores.

useful ['ju:sful] *adj* útil; provechoso; **a** — **player** un buen jugador, un jugador que vale; **it is very** — **to be able to . . .** es muy útil poder . . .; **he's** — **with his fists** sabe defenderse con los puños; **he's** — **with a gun** sabe manejar un fusil; **to come in** — servir, ser útil; venir a propósito; **to make oneself** — ayudar, trabajar (*etc*); **come on, make yourself** — **!** ¡vamos, a trabajar!; **we had a** — **time in Spain** nuestra estancia en España fue muy provechosa.

usefully ['ju:sfəli] *adv* útilmente; provechosamente, con provecho.

usefulness ['ju:sfulnis] *n* utilidad *f*; valor *m*; provecho *m*; **it has outlived its** — ha dejado de tener utilidad.

useless ['ju:slis] *adj* inútil; inservible; *person* inepto, incompetente; **he's** — no vale para nada; **he's** — **as a forward** no vale para delantero; **it is** — **to shout** de nada sirve gritar, es inútil gritar; **to make (*or* render) something** — inutilizar algo.

uselessly ['ju:slisli] *adv* inútilmente, en vano.

uselessness ['ju:slisnis] *n* inutilidad *f*.

user ['ju:zə*] *n* usuario *m*, a *f*.

U-shaped ['ju:ʃeipt] *adj* en forma de U.

usher ['ʌʃə*] **1** *n* ujier *m*, portero *m*; (*Theat*) acomodador *m*; (*at public meeting etc*) guardia *m* de sala, encargado *m* del orden.

2 *vt* **(a) to** — **someone in** (*Theat etc*) acomodar a uno; **to** — **someone into a room** hacer pasar a uno

a un cuarto, hacer entrar a uno en un cuarto; **I was —ed in by the butler** el mayordomo me hizo pasar, el mayordomo acudió a la puerta para recibirme; **to — someone out** acompañar a uno a la puerta.
  (b) it —ed in a new reign anunció un nuevo reinado, marcó el comienzo del reinado nuevo; **summer was —ed in by storms** el verano empezó con tormentas.

usherette [ˌʌʃə'ret] n acomodadora f.

usual ['juːʒuəl] adj usual; acostumbrado, habitual; corriente; normal; **as —** como de costumbre, como siempre; **as per —!** (fam) ¡lo de siempre!; **more than —** más que de costumbre, más que lo normal; **his — restaurant** su restaurante habitual; **to come earlier than —** venir antes de la hora (or fecha etc) acostumbrada; **it's not —** no es normal; **it's not — for people to leave so soon** no es normal que la gente se marche tan pronto.

usually ['juːʒuəli] adv por lo general, por regla general; **we — wash it ourselves** acostumbramos a lavarlo nosotros mismos; **what do you do —?** ¿qué hacen Vds normalmente?

usufruct ['juːzjufrʌkt] n usufructo m.

usufructuary [ˌjuːzju'frʌktəri] n usufructuario m.

usurer ['juːʒərə*] n usurero m.

usurious [juː'zjuəriəs] adj usurario.

usurp [juː'zəːp] vt usurpar.

usurpation [ˌjuːzəː'peiʃən] n usurpación f.

usurper [juː'zəːpə*] n usurpador m, ora f.

usurping [juː'zəːpiŋ] adj usurpador.

usury ['juːʒuri] n usura f.

utensil [juː'tensl] n utensilio m; **kitchen —s** batería f de cocina.

uterine ['juːtərain] adj uterino.

uterus ['juːtərəs] n útero m.

utilitarian [ˌjuːtili'tɛəriən] **1** adj utilitario. **2** n utilitarista mf.

utilitarianism [ˌjuːtili'tɛəriənizəm] n utilitarismo m

utility [juː'tiliti] **1** n utilidad f; **public —** empresa f de servicio público. **2** attr car, clothing etc utilitario.

utility room ['juːtiliti‚rum] n trascocina f.

utilization [ˌjuːtilai'zeiʃən] n utilización f.

utilize ['juːtilaiz] vt utilizar.

utmost ['ʌtməust] **1** adj mayor; supremo; **of the — importance** de primerísima importancia; **with the — ease** con suma facilidad.
  2 n: **the —** that one can do todo lo que puede hacer uno; **to do one's —** hacer todo lo posible (to + infin por + infin); **200 at the —** 200 a lo más, 200 a lo sumo; **to the —** al máximo, hasta más no poder; **to the — of one's ability** lo mejor que sepa uno.

Utopia [juː'təupiə] n Utopía f.

Utopian [juː'təupiən] **1** adj dream etc utópico; person utopista. **2** n utopista mf.

utricle ['juːtrikl] n utrículo m.

utter[1] ['ʌtə*] adj completo, total, absoluto; fool, madness etc puro; **— nonsense!** ¡tonterías!; **it was an — disaster** fue un desastre total; **he was in a state of — depression** estaba completamente abatido.

utter[2] ['ʌtə*] vt **(a)** words pronunciar; cry etc dar; threat, insult etc proferir; libel publicar; **she never —ed a word** no dijo ni pío; **don't — a word about it** de esto no digas ni pío.
  (b) counterfeit money poner en circulación, expender.

utterance ['ʌtərəns] n pronunciación f; palabras fpl; declaración f; **to give — to** manifestar, declarar.

utterly ['ʌtəli] adv completamente, totalmente, del todo.

uttermost ['ʌtəməust] adj más remoto, más lejano; extremo; see utmost.

U-turn ['juː'təːn] n viraje m en U.

uvula ['juːvjələ] n úvula f.

uvular ['juːvjələ*] adj uvular.

uxorious [ʌk'sɔːriəs] adj gurrumino.

V

vac [væk] n (fam) = **vacation**.
vacancy ['veikənsi] n (a) (emptiness) lo vacío; (of mind etc) vaciedad f, vacuidad f.
(b) (in boarding house etc) cuarto m vacante; **have you any vacancies?** ¿hay algún cuarto libre?, ¿tiene algo disponible?; **we have no vacancies for August** para agosto no hay nada disponible, en agosto todo está lleno.
(c) (in post) vacante f; **"vacancies"** "se ofrece trabajo", "se necesita mano de obra"; **"vacancy for keen young man"** "búscase joven enérgico"; **to fill a** — proveer una vacante.
vacant ['veikənt] adj (a) seat, room etc libre, desocupado; disponible; space vacío, desocupado; **is this seat** —? ¿está libre este asiento?; **have you a room** —? ¿tienen algo disponible?; **to become** —, **to fall** — vaciar.
(b) look etc distraído, vago, (stupid) de bobo.
vacantly ['veikəntli] adv look etc distraídamente, vagamente, (stupidly) sin comprender, boquiabierto.
vacate [və'keit] vt house desocupar; post dejar, dejar vacante, salir de; throne etc renunciar a.
vacation [və'keiʃən] **1** n vacación f, vacaciones fpl; **long** — (Univ) vacación f de verano; **to be on** — estar de vacaciones.
2 attr: — **course** curso m de vacaciones, (esp) curso m de verano.
3 vi (US) estar de vacaciones; tomarse unas vacaciones; pasar las vacaciones; see also **holiday**.
vacationist [və'keiʃənist] n (US) vacacionista mf.
vaccinate ['væksineit] vt vacunar.
vaccination [,væksi'neiʃən] n vacunación f.
vaccine ['væksi:n] n vacuna f.
vacillate ['væsileit] vi (sway, vary) oscilar (between entre); (hesitate) vacilar, dudar; **to** — **about a course of action** no resolverse a seguir una política determinada.
vacillating ['væsileitiŋ] adj vacilante, irresoluto.
vacillation [,væsi'leiʃən] n vacilación f.
vacuity [væ'kju:iti] n vacuidad f.
vacuous ['vækjuəs] adj bobo, necio.
vacuum ['vækjum] **1** n vacío m. **2** attr de vacío; al vacío.
vacuum bottle ['vækjum,bɒtl] n (US) termo(s) m.
vacuum brake ['vækjum'breik] n freno m de vacío.
vacuum cleaner ['vækjum,kli:nə*] n aspirador m.
vacuum flask ['vækjumfla:sk] n termo(s) m.
vacuum pump ['vækjum'pʌmp] n bomba f al vacío.
vacuum tube ['vækjumtju:b] n tubo m al vacío.
vade mecum ['va:di'meikum] n vademécum m.
vagabond ['vægəbɒnd] **1** adj vagabundo. **2** n vagabundo m, a f.
vagary ['veigəri] n (whim) capricho m, extravagancia f; (of thermometer etc) irregularidad f, variación f; (of the mind) divagación f; **the vagaries of taste** lo caprichoso del gusto, la inconstancia de la moda.
vagina [və'dʒainə] n vagina f.
vaginal [və'dʒainəl] adj vaginal.
vagrancy ['veigrənsi] n vagancia f, vagabundaje m; — **in 16th century Spain** los vagabundos (or el vagabundeo) en España en el siglo XVI.
vagrant ['veigrənt] **1** adj vagabundo, vagante; (fig) errante. **2** n vagabundo m, a f.
vague [veig] n (a) vago; indistinto, borroso; incierto; impreciso; **the** — **outline of a ship** el perfil indistinto de un buque; **the outlook is somewhat** — la perspectiva es algo incierta; **it is a** — **concept** es un concepto impreciso; **he made some** — **promises** hizo varias promesas imprecisas; **I haven't the** —st no tengo la más remota idea.
(b) (of person: in giving details etc) impreciso, equívoco; (absent-minded) despistado, distraído; **he was** — **about the date** no quiso precisar la fecha, no dijo concretamente cuál era la fecha; **he's**

terribly — tiene un tremendo despiste, es un despistado; **you mustn't be so** — hay que decir las cosas con claridad, hay que concretar; **I am** — **on the subject of ants** sé muy poca cosa en concreto de las hormigas.
vaguely ['veigli] adv vagamente; indistintamente; imprecisamente; distraídamente; **a picture** — **resembling another** un cuadro que tiene cierto parecido vago con otro; **he talks very** — habla en términos muy vagos; **she looked at me** — me miró distraída, me miró sin comprender.
vagueness ['veignis] n vaguedad f; lo indistinto, lo borroso; incertidumbre f, imprecisión f; despiste m, distracción f.
vain [vein] adj (a) (useless) vano, inútil; **in** — en vano; **it is** — **to try** es inútil intentarlo; **all our efforts were in** — todos nuestros esfuerzos resultaron ser infructuosos; **to take someone's name in** — hablar con poco respeto de uno.
(b) (conceited) vanidoso; presumido, engreído; **she is very** — **about her hair** es muy orgullosa de su cabello, se enorgullece de su cabello.
vainglorious [vein'glɔ:riəs] adj vanaglorioso.
vainglory [vein'glɔ:ri] n vanagloria f.
vainly ['veinli] adv (a) vanamente, inútilmente; infructuosamente; sin éxito. (b) vanidosamente.
valance ['væləns] n cenefa f, doselera f.
vale [veil] n valle m; — **of tears** valle m de lágrimas.
valediction [,væli'dikʃən] n despedida f.
valedictory [,væli'diktəri] adj address etc de despedida.
valence ['veiləns] n valencia f.
Valencian [və'lensiən] **1** adj valenciano. **2** n valenciano m, a f. **3** n (dialect) valenciano m.
valency ['veiləns] n valencia f.
valentine ['væləntain] n tarjeta f del día de San Valentín (enviada por jóvenes, sin firmar, de tono amoroso o jocoso); (person) novio m, a f (escogido el día de San Valentín).
valerian [və'liəriən] n valeriana f.
valet ['vælei] n ayuda m de cámara.
valetudinarian ['væli,tjudi'nəariən] **1** adj valetudinario. **2** n valetudinario m, a f.
Valhalla [væl'hælə] Valhala m.
valiant ['væliənt] adj (lit) esforzado, denodado.
valiantly ['væliəntli] adv esforzadamente, denodadamente, con denuedo.
valid ['vælid] adj válido; ticket etc valedero; law vigente; **a ticket** — **for 3 months** un billete valedero para 3 meses; **that ticket is no longer** — ese billete ya no vale, ese billete ha caducado ya; **that argument is not** — ese argumento no vale, ese argumento no es válido.
validate ['vælideit] vt validar.
validation [,væli'deiʃən] n validación f.
validity [və'liditi] n validez f; vigencia f.
valise [və'li:z] n portamantas m.
Valkyrie ['vælkiri] n Valquiria f.
valley ['væli] n valle m.
valorous ['vælərəs] adj (lit) esforzado, denodado.
valour, (US) **valor** ['vælə*] n valor m, valentía f.
valuable ['væljuəbl] **1** adj valioso; estimable; costoso; **a** — **contribution** una valiosa aportación; **is it** —? ¿vale mucho?
2 —**s** npl objetos mpl de valor.
valuation [,vælju'eiʃən] n valuación f, valorización f; tasación f; **to take someone at his own** — aceptar todo lo que dice uno acerca de sí mismo.
value ['vælju:] **1** n (a) (general sense) valor m; estimación f; importancia f; (Gram, Mus etc) valor m; **aggregate** — valor m total, valor m global; **sentimental** — valor m sentimental; **things of** — cosas fpl de valor; **of great** — de gran valor, muy valioso (to para); **of no** — sin valor; **to be of** —

to someone ser de valor para uno, ser útil a uno; **to be of little — to someone** ser de poco valor para uno, servir poco a uno; **of what — is Greek nowadays?** ¿qué valor tiene el griego hoy?, ¿qué utilidad tiene el griego hoy?; **to the — of** por valor de; **this dress is good —** este vestido bien vale lo que pagué por él; **to get good — for one's money** estar satisfecho de una compra; **to set a — of £20 on something** tasar algo en 20 libras; **to set a high — on someone** estimar a uno en mucho, tener un concepto muy bueno de uno; **to attach no — to** no conceder importancia a.

(b) (moral) —s valores mpl morales, principios mpl; **sense of —s** sentido m de los valores morales; **— judgement** juicio m de valor.

2 vt (financially) valorar, valorizar, tasar (at en); (morally etc) estimar, apreciar; (— highly) tener en mucho, tener un buen concepto de, apreciar; **it is —d at £8** está valorado en 8 libras; **I — my leisure** para mí son muy importantes mis ratos de ocio; **he doesn't — his life** desprecia su vida, no hace estimación de su vida; **she sent her rings to be —d** envió sus joyas para que se las tasaran.

valued ['vælju:d] adj estimado, apreciado; **my — colleague** mi estimado colega.

valueless ['væljulis] adj sin valor.

valuer ['valjuə*] n tasador m.

valve [vælv] n (Anat, Mech) válvula f; (Radio) lámpara f, válvula f; (Bot, Zool) valva f; **inlet —** válvula f de admisión.

valve tester ['vælv,testə*] n comprobador m de válvulas.

vamoose [və'mu:s] vi (sl) largarse; desaparecer.

vamp¹ [væmp] 1 n (of shoe) empella f; (patch) remiendo m.

2 vt shoe poner empella a; remendar; (Mus) improvisar, improvisar un acompañamiento para; **to — up an engine** (repair) componer un motor, (supercharge) sobrealimentar un motor.

3 vi improvisar.

vamp² [væmp] 1 n vampiresa f.

2 vt coquetear con, flirtear con; **to — someone into doing something** engatusar a uno para que haga algo, fascinar a uno lo bastante para que consienta en hacer algo.

vampire ['væmpaiə*] n (a) (also Zool) vampiro m. (b) (fig: extortioner) desollador m; (woman) vampiresa f.

van¹ [væn] n (Mil, fig) vanguardia f; **to be in the —** ir a la vanguardia; **to be in the — of progress** estar en la vanguardia del progreso.

van² [væn] n (Aut) camioneta f, furgoneta f; (for removals) camión m de mudanzas; (Rail) furgón m de equipajes.

Vandal ['vændəl] 1 adj vándalo, vandálico. 2 n vándalo m, a f.

Vandalic [væn'dælik] adj vándalo, vandálico.

vandalism ['vændəlizəm] n vandalismo m; **piece of —** acto m de vandalismo.

vandalize ['vændəlaiz] vt destruir, estropear, arruinar.

vane [vein] n (weathercock) veleta f; (of mill) aspa f; (of propeller) paleta f; (of feather) barba f.

vanguard ['vænga:d] n vanguardia f; **to be in the —** ir a la vanguardia; **to be in the — of progress** estar en la vanguardia del progreso.

vanilla [və'nilə] n vainilla f.

vanillin ['vænilin] n vainillina f.

vanish ['væniʃ] vi desaparecer, desvanecerse; **to — without trace** desaparecer sin dejar rastro.

vanishing cream ['væniʃiŋ,kri:m] n crema f de belleza.

vanishing point ['væniʃiŋ,point] n punto m de fuga.

vanity ['væniti] n vanidad f; **all is —** todo es vanidad; **to do something out of —** hacer algo por vanidad.

vanity case ['væniti,keis] n neceser m de belleza, polvera f (de bolsillo).

vanquish ['væŋkwiʃ] vt (lit) vencer, derrotar.

vantage ['va:ntidʒ] n (Tennis) ventaja f.

vantage point ['va:ntidʒ,point] n posición f ventajosa, lugar m estrátegico; (for views) punto m panorámico; **from our modern — we can see that . . .** desde nuestra atalaya moderna vemos que . . .

vapid ['væpid] adj insípido, soso.

vapidity [væ'piditi] n insipidez f, sosería f.

vapour, (US) **vapor** ['veipə*] 1 n vapor m; vaho m, exhalación f; **the —s** (Med) los vapores.

2 vi (boast) fanfarronear; **to — about** decir disparates acerca de.

vapourization, (US) **vaporization** [,veipərai'zeiʃən] n vaporización f.

vapourize, (US) **vaporize** ['veipəraiz] 1 vt vaporizar, volatilizar. 2 vi vaporizarse, volatilizarse.

vapourizer, (US) **vaporizer** ['veipəraizə*] n vaporizador m.

vaporous ['veipərəs] adj vaporoso.

variability [,veəri'biliti] n variabilidad f.

variable ['veəriəbl] 1 adj variable. 2 n variable f.

variance ['veəriəns] n: **to be at —** estar en desacuerdo (with con), desentonar (with con), estar reñidos (with con).

variant ['veəriənt] 1 adj variante. 2 n variante f.

variation [,veəri'eiʃən] n variación f (also Mus); (variant form) variedad f.

varicoloured adj, (US) **varicolored** ['væri'kʌləd] adj abigarrado, multicolor.

varicose ['værikəus] adj varicoso; **— veins** varices fpl.

varied ['veərid] adj variado.

variegated ['veərigeitid] adj abigarrado; jaspeado.

variegation [,veəri'geiʃən] n abigarramiento m.

variety [və'raiəti] n variedad f (also Bio); diversidad f; (Comm: of stock) surtido m; **in a — of colours** en muchos colores, de diversos colores, (Comm) en gran surtido de colores; **in a — of ways** de diversas maneras; **a — of opinions was expressed** se expresaron diversas opiniones; **for —** por variar; **to lend — to something** servir para variar algo, dar diversidad a algo; see **artist** etc.

variety store [və'raiəti'stɔ:*] n (US) tienda f barata que vende de todo.

variola [və'raiələ] n viruela f.

various ['veəriəs] adj vario, diverso; **for — reasons** por diversas razones; **in — ways** de diversos modos; **at — times in the past** en determinados momentos del pasado.

variously ['veəriəsli] adv diversamente, de diversos modos; **she stated her age —** declaraba su edad de diversos modos.

varmint ['va:mint] n (Hunting) bicho m; (fam) golfo m, bribón m.

varnish ['va:niʃ] 1 n barniz m; (for nails) esmalte m para las uñas, laca f para las uñas; (fig) barniz m, capa f, apariencia f.

2 vt barnizar; nails laquear, esmaltar; (fig: also **to — over**) dar apariencia respetable a, disimular, paliar.

varsity ['va:siti] n (fam) universidad f.

vary ['veəri] 1 vt variar; decision etc cambiar, modificar.

2 vi variar; (disagree) estar en desacuerdo; discrepar (from de); (deviate) desviarse (from de); **it varies** depende; **it varies from 2 to 10** varía de 2 a 10; **it varies a lot from the norm** se desvía mucho de la norma; **authors — about the date** los autores discrepan acerca de la fecha; **it varies in price** varía de precio; **they — in price** los hay de diversos precios; **it varies inversely with . . .** varía en razón inversa según . . .

varying ['veəriiŋ] adj cambiante; diverso; **with — results** con resultados diversos.

vascular ['væskjulə*] adj vascular.

vase [va:z] n florero m, jarrón m.

Vaseline ['væsili:n] (Protected Trade Name) n vaselina f.

vassal ['væsəl] n vasallo m.

vassalage ['væsəlidʒ] n vasallaje m.

vast [va:st] adj vasto; inmenso, enorme; **majority** abrumador.

vastly ['va:stli] adv enormemente; **— improved** muy mejorado; **— superior to** con mucho superior a; **we were — amused** nos reímos muchísimo con eso; **— different** muy distinto.

vastness ['va:stnis] n inmensidad f.

vat [væt] n tina f, tinaja f.

Vatican ['vætikən] 1 n Vaticano m. 2 adj vaticano, del Vaticano.

vaudeville ['vəudəvil] n vaudeville m.

vault¹ [vɔ:lt] 1 n (Archit) bóveda f; (for wine) bodega f; (of bank) sótano m, cámara f acorazada; (tomb) tumba f; (of church) cripta f; **barrel —** bóveda f de cañón; **family —** panteón m familiar; **— of heaven** bóveda f celeste.

2 vt abovedar.

vault² [vɔ:lt] 1 n salto m; **at one —, with one —** de un salto.

2 vti saltar; **to — into the saddle** colocarse de un salto en la silla; **to — over a stream** cruzar un arroyo de un salto.

vaulted ['vɔ:ltid] adj abovedado.

vaulting ['vɔ:ltiŋ] n abovedado m.

vaulting horse ['vɔ:ltiŋ,hɔ:s] n potro m de madera, caballo m de aros.

vaunt [vɔ:nt] 1 vt jactarse de, hacer alarde de; lucir, ostentar. 2 vi jactarse.

vaunted ['vɔ:ntid] *adj* cacareado, alardeado; **much — tan** cacareado.

vaunting ['vɔ:ntiŋ] **1** *adj* jactancioso. **2** *n* jactancia *f.*

V-Day ['vi:dei] *n* día *m* de la victoria (*esp de los aliados en Europa, 8 mayo de 1945*).

veal [vi:l] *n* ternera *f.*

vector ['vektə*] *n* vector *m.*

Veda ['veidə] Veda *m.*

Vedic ['veidik] *adj* védico.

veep [vi:p] *n* (*US fam*) vicepresidente *m.*

veer [viə*] *vi* (*also to — round*) (*ship, also fig*) virar; (*wind*) girar, cambiar; **the country has —ed to the left** el país ha virado hacia la izquierda; **it —s from one extreme to the other** oscila. desde un extremo al otro; **people are —ing round to our point of view** la gente está empezando a aceptar nuestro criterio.

vegetable ['vedʒitəbl] **1** *adj* vegetal; **— kingdom** reino *m* vegetal.
  2 *n* (*Bot*) vegetal *f*; (*edible plant*) legumbre *f*, hortaliza *f*; **—s** (*on sale as food, as item of diet*) legumbres *fpl*, hortalizas *fpl*, (*cooked, greens*) verduras *fpl.*

vegetable dish ['vedʒitəbldiʃ] *n* fuente *f* de legumbres.

vegetable garden ['vedʒitəbl,ga:dn] *n* huerto *m.*

vegetarian [,vedʒi'tɛəriən] **1** *adj* vegetariano. **2** *n* vegetariano *m*, a *f.*

vegetarianism [,vedʒi'tɛəriənizəm] *n* vegetarianismo *m.*

vegetate ['vedʒiteit] *vi* vegetar (*also fig*).

vegetation [,vedʒi'teiʃən] *n* vegetación *f.*

vegetative ['vedʒitətiv] *adj* vegetativo.

vehemence ['vi:iməns] *n* vehemencia *f*; violencia *f*, pasión *f.*

vehement ['vi:imənt] *adj* vehemente; violento, aspasionado; **a — speech** un discurso apasionado; **there was — opposition** hubo una resistencia violenta.

vehemently ['vi:iməntli] *adv* con vehemencia; violentamente, apasionadamente; **we are — opposed to it** nos oponemos totalmente a ello, estamos cien por cien en contra.

vehicle ['vi:ikl] *n* vehículo *m*; (*means*) vehículo *m*, medio *m*, instrumento *m* (*for* de).

vehicular [vi'hikjulə*] *adj* road etc de vehículos, para coches; *traffic* rodado.

veil [veil] **1** *n* velo *m* (*also Phot and fig*); **under a — of secrecy** en el mayor secreto; **to draw a — over something** correr un velo sobre algo, encubrir algo; **we had better draw a — over that** es mejor no hablar de eso; **to take the —** tomar el hábito, meterse monja.
  2 *vt* velar (*also fig*); **eyes —ed by tears** ojos *mpl* velados por lágrimas; **the town was —ed by mist** la ciudad estaba cubierta por un velo de niebla.

veiled [veild] *adj* velado; **with — irony** con velada ironía; **that was a — reference to the bishop** fue una referencia velada al obispo.

veiling ['veiliŋ] *n* (*Phot*) velo *m.*

vein [vein] *n* (*Anat, Bot*) vena *f*; (*Min: of ore etc*) filón *m*, veta *f*; (*in stone*) vena *f*; (*in wood*) fibra *f*; hebra *f*, veta *f*; (*fig*) vena *f*, rasgo *m*; **a — of madness** una vena de loco, un rasgo de locura; **to be in the — estar** en vena; **to be in the — for** estar de humor para.

veined [veind] *adj* veteado.

velar ['vi:lə*] *adj* velar.

Velasquez [vi'læskwiz] *m* Velázquez.

vellum ['veləm] *n* vitela *f.*

velocipede [və'lɒsipi:d] *n* velocípedo *m.*

velocity [vi'lɒsiti] *n* velocidad *f.*

velour [və'luə*] *n* terciopelo *m.*

velum ['vi:ləm] *n* (*Anat*) velo *m* del paladar.

velvet ['velvit] **1** *n* terciopelo *m*; (*Anat*) piel *f* velluda, vello *m*; **to be on —** (*fam*) estar en situación muy ventajosa; **a skin like —** una piel aterciopelada.
  2 *adj, attr* (*velvety*) aterciopelado; (*of —*) de terciopelo.

velveteen [velvi'ti:n] *n* pana *f.*

velvety ['velviti] *adj* aterciopelado.

venal ['vi:nl] *adj* venal.

venality [vi:'næliti] *n* venalidad *f.*

vend [vend] *n* (*Comm*) vender.

vendetta [ven'detə] *n* enemistad *f*; odio *m* de sangre; disputa *f*; **to carry on a — against someone** hacer una campaña contra uno; hostigar a uno, perseguir a uno.

vending ['vendiŋ] *n* (*Comm*) venta *f*, distribución *f.*

vending machine ['vendiŋmə,ʃi:n] *n* distribuidor *m* automático.

vendor ['vendɔ:*] *n* vendedor *m*, ora *f*; (*pedlar*) buhonero *m.*

veneer [və'niə*] **1** *n* chapa *f*, enchapado *m*; (*fig*) barniz *m*, apariencia *f*; **with a — of culture** con un barniz de cultura; **it's just a —** es un barniz superficial nada más.
  2 *vt* chapear.

venerable ['venərəbl] *adj* venerable.

venerate ['venəreit] *vt* venerar, reverenciar.

veneration [,venə'reiʃən] *n* veneración *f*; **his — for ... la** veneración que sentía por ...; **to hold someone in —** reverenciar a uno.

venereal [vi'niəriəl] *adj* venéreo.

Venetian [vi'ni:ʃən] **1** *adj* veneciano. **2** *n* veneciano *m*, a *f.*

Venezuela [,vene'zweilə] Venezuela *f.*

Venezuelan [,vene'zweilən] **1** *adj* venezolano. **2** *n* venezolano *m*, a *f.*

vengeance ['vendʒəns] *n* venganza *f*; **with a —** con creces; de verdad; **it's raining with a —** está lloviendo de verdad; **to take — on someone** tomar venganza en uno.

vengeful ['vendʒful] *adj* (*lit*) vengativo.

venial ['vi:niəl] *adj* venial.

veniality [,vi:ni'æliti] *n* venialidad *f.*

Venice ['venis] Venecia.

venison ['venizn] *n* carne *f* de venado.

venom ['venəm] *n* veneno *m*; (*fig*) virulencia *f*, malignidad *f*; **he spoke with real — in his voice** habló en tono de verdadero odio.

venomous ['venəməs] *adj* venenoso; (*fig*) virulento, maligno.

venomously ['venəməsli] *adv* (*fig*) con malignidad, con odio.

venous ['vi:nəs] *adj* venoso.

vent [vent] **1** *n* (*opening*) abertura *f*; válvula *f*; (*Mech*) válvula *f* de purga, orificio *m*, lumbrera *f*; (*airhole*) respiradero *m*; (*in pipe*) ventosa *f*; (*Orn*) cloaca *f*; **to give — to** dar salida a, desahogar, expresar; **to give — to one's feelings** desahogarse; **to give — to a sigh** exhalar un suspiro.
  2 *vt* (*Mech*) purgar; (*discharge*) descargar, emitir, dejar escapar; (*pierce*) agujerear; *feelings etc* desahogar, descargar; **to — one's anger** desahogar su cólera, desahogarse; **to — one's spleen** descargar la bilis (*on* contra).

ventilate ['ventileit] *vt* ventilar (*also fig*).

ventilation [,venti'leiʃən] *n* ventilación *f.*

ventilator ['ventileitə*] *n* ventilador *m.*

ventral ['ventrəl] *adj* ventral.

ventricle ['ventrikl] *n* ventrículo *m.*

ventriloquism [ven'triləkwizəm] *n* ventriloquia *f.*

ventriloquist [ven'triləkwist] *n* ventrílocuo *m*, a *f.*

venture ['ventʃə*] **1** *n* aventura *f*, empresa *f* (arriesgada); **at a —** a la ventura; **his — into business** su aventura en el mundo de los negocios; **it seemed a stupid — at the time** en aquel momento parecía ser una empresa descabellada; **a new — in publishing** un nuevo rumbo en la edición de libros, una nueva empresa editorial.
  2 *vt* aventurar; (*stake*) jugar; *opinion etc* osar expresar; **they —d everything** lo jugaron todo; **if I may — an opinion** si se me permite expresar mi opinión; **may I — a guess?** ¿puedo hacer una conjetura? **he —d to remark that ...** se permitió observar que ...; **nothing —d nothing gain** quien no se arriesga no pasa la mar.
  3 *vi* (**a**) **to — on something** arriesgarse en algo, osar emprender algo, lanzarse a algo; **when we —d on this** cuando emprendimos esto; **to — into a wood** (osar) penetrar en un bosque; **to — out of doors** osar salir fuera, arriesgarse fuera.
    (**b**) **to — to** + *infin* osar + *infin*, atreverse a + *infin*; permitirse + *infin*; **I — to add that ... me** permito agregar que ...; **I — to write to you** me tomo la libertad de dirigirme a Vd; **but he did not — to speak** pero no osó hablar.

venturesome ['ventʃəsəm] *adj* person atrevido, audaz; *enterprise* arriesgado, azaroso.

venue ['venju:] *n* punto *m* de reunión, lugar *m* en que se han de reunir dos (*etc*) personas; **the — for the next match** el campo para el próximo partido; **the — has been changed** se ha cambiado de lugar.

Venus ['vi:nəs] (*Myth*) Venus *f*; (*Astron*) Venus *m.*

Venusian [və'nu:ziən] **1** *adj* venusiano. **2** *n* venusiano *m*, a *f.*

veracious [və'reiʃəs] *adj* veraz.

veracity [və'ræsiti] *n* veracidad *f.*

veranda(h) [və'rændə] *n* veranda *f*, terraza *f*, galería *f.*

verb [və:b] *n* verbo *m*; **auxiliary — verbo** *m* auxiliar; **defective — verbo** *m* defectivo; **deponent — verbo**

m deponente; **finite** — verbo *m* finito; **intransitive** — verbo *m* intransitivo, verbo *m* neutro; **reflexive** — verbo *m* reflexivo; **transitive** — verbo *m* transitivo.

verbal ['vəːbəl] *adj* verbal.

verbalize ['vəːbəlaiz] **1** *vt* expresar en palabras; exteriorizar hablando. **2** *vi* expresarse en palabras; **he does not** — **easily** no se expresa con facilidad.

verbally ['vəːbəli] *adv* verbalmente; de palabra, por boca.

verbatim [vəː'beitim] *adv, adj* palabra por palabra.

verbena [vəː'biːnə] *n* verbena *f*.

verbiage ['vəːbiidʒ] *n* verbosidad *f*, palabrería *f*.

verbose [vəː'bəus] *adj* verboso, prolijo.

verbosely [vəː'bəusli] *adv* prolijamente.

verbosity [vəː'bɔsiti] *n* verbosidad *f*.

verdant ['vəːdənt] *adj* verde.

verdict ['vəːdikt] *n* (*Law*) veredicto *m*, fallo *m*, sentencia *f*, juicio *m*; (*fig*) opinión *f*, juicio *m*; **a** — **of guilty** una sentencia de culpabilidad; **open** — juicio *m* en el que se determina el crimen sin designar el culpable; **what's your** —? ¿qué opinas de esto?, ¿qué juicio te has formado sobre esto?; **his** — **on the wine was unfavourable** hizo un juicio desfavorable acerca del vino; **to bring in a** —, **to return a** — pronunciar una sentencia, dar un fallo; **to bring in a** — **of guilty** pronunciar una sentencia de culpabilidad.

verdigris ['vəːdigriːs] *n* verdete *m*, cardenillo *m*.

verdure ['vəːdjuə*] *n* verdura *f*.

verge [vəːdʒ] **1** *n* borde *m*, margen *m*; **to be on the** — **of disaster** estar a dos dedos del desastre, estar en el mismo borde de la catástrofe; **to be on the** — **of a nervous breakdown** estar al borde de una crisis nerviosa; **to be on the** — **of a great discovery** estar en la antesala de un gran descubrimiento; **we are on the** — **of war** estamos al borde de la guerra; **she was on the** — **of tears** estaba para deshacerse en lágrimas; **to be on the** — **of** + *ger* estar a punto de + *infin*.

2 *vi*: **to** — **on** acercarse a, rayar en; estar a un paso mínimo de; **a state verging on madness** un estado que raya en la locura.

verger ['vəːdʒə*] *n* sacristán *m*.

Vergil ['vəːdʒil] *m* Virgilio.

Vergilian [vəː'dʒiliən] *adj* virgiliano.

verifiable ['verifaiəbl] *adj* comprobable, verificable.

verification [,verifi'keiʃən] *n* comprobación *f*, verificación *f*.

verify ['verifai] *vt* comprobar, verificar.

verisimilitude [,verisi'militjuːd] *n* verosimilitud *f*.

veritable ['veritəbl] *adj* verdadero; **a** — **monster** un verdadero monstruo.

veritably ['veritəbli] *adv* verdaderamente.

verity ['veriti] *n* verdad *f*; **the eternal verities** las verdades eternas.

vermicelli [,vəːmi'seli] *n* fideos *mpl*.

vermicide ['vəːmisaid] *n* vermicida *m*.

vermifuge ['vəːmifjuːdʒ] *n* vermífugo *m*.

vermilion [vəː'miliən] **1** *n* bermellón *m*. **2** *adj* bermejo.

vermin ['vəːmin] *n* bichos *mpl*, sabandijas *fpl*; parásitos *mpl*; (*fig*) sabandijas *pl*.

verminous ['vəːminəs] *adj* verminoso, piojoso; (*fig*) vil.

vermouth ['vəːməθ] *n* vermut *m*.

vernacular [vəː'nækjulə*] **1** *adj* vernáculo, vulgar; **in** — **Persian** en persa vulgar, en la lengua vernácula de Persia.

2 *n* lengua *f* vernácula; (*fig*) lenguaje *m* corriente, lenguaje *m* vulgar.

veronica [vəː'rɔnikə] *n* (*Bot*) verónica *f*.

Veronica [vəː'rɔnikə] *f* Verónica.

Versailles [vəː'sai] Versalles.

versatile ['vəːsətail] *adj* *person* versátil, hábil para muchas cosas, de talentos variados, polifacético, de genio multiforme; *mind* adaptable, flexible; universal; *writer etc* que domina varios géneros.

versatility [,vəːsə'tiliti] *n* versatilidad *f*; talentos *mpl* variados, aptitudes *fpl* diversas; adaptabilidad *f*, flexibilidad *f*; universalidad *f*.

verse [vəːs] *n* (*stanza*) estrofa *f*; (*of Bible*) versículo *m*; (*genre*) verso *m*; (*poetry*) poesías *fpl*, versos *mpl*; **comic** —, **light** — poesías *fpl* jocosas; **is it in** —? ¿está en verso?; — **drama** teatro *m* en verso, drama *m* poético; **a** — **version of the "Celestina"** una versión en verso de la "Celestina".

versed [vəːst] *adj*: **to be well** — **in** estar versado en, conocer, ser conocedor de.

versification [,vəːsifi'keiʃən] *n* versificación *f*.

versifier ['vəːsifaiə*] *n* versificador *m*, ora *f*.

versify ['vəːsifai] **1** *vt* versificar. **2** *vi* versificar, escribir versos.

version ['vəːʃən] *n* versión *f*; **in Lope's** — **of the story** en la versión que hizo Lope de la historia;

my — **of events is as follows . . .** yo veo los sucesos del siguiente modo . . .; **according to his** — según su interpretación; **that's a different** — **again** ése es otro modo distinto de contarlo.

versus ['vəːsəs] *prep* contra; **Ceuta** — **Alcoy** Ceuta contra Alcoy.

vertebra ['vəːtibrə] *n*, *pl* **vertebrae** ['vəːtibriː] vértebra *f*.

vertebral ['vəːtibrəl] *adj* vertebral.

vertebrate ['vəːtibrit] **1** *adj* vertebrado. **2** *n* vertebrado *m*.

vertex ['vəːteks] *n*, *pl* **vertices** [vəːtisiːz] vértice *m*.

vertical ['vəːtikəl] **1** *adj* vertical. **2** *n* vertical *f*.

vertically ['vəːtikəli] *adv* verticalmente.

vertiginous [vəː'tidʒinəs] *adj* vertiginoso.

vertigo ['vəːtigəu] *n* vértigo *m*.

verve [vəːv] *n* energía *f*, empuje *m*; brío *m*; entusiasmo *m*.

very ['veri] **1** *adv* (a) muy; — **good** muy bueno, — **well** muy bien; — **much** mucho, muchísimo; **she felt** — **much better** se encontró muchísimo mejor; **I was** — (**much**) **surprised** me sorprendió mucho, para mí era una gran sorpresa; **it's not so** — **difficult** no es tan difícil, la dificultad no es tan grande; **that's** — **kind of you** es Vd muy amable; **you're not being** — **helpful** realmente no nos ayudas nada.

(b) **it is** — **cold** (*object*) está muy frío, (*weather*) hace mucho frío.

(c) **the** — **first** el primero, el primero de todos; **the** — **best** el mejor, el mejor que haya; **we did our** — **hardest** esfuércese al máximo; **at the** — **most** a lo más, a lo sumo, todo lo más; **the** — **most we can offer** el límite de lo que podemos ofrecer; **the** — **next day** precisamente el día siguiente; **the** — **same hat** el idéntico sombrero.

(d) (*alone, in reply to question*) mucho; **are you tired?** . . . — ¿estás cansado? . . . mucho.

(e) (*emotional use*) **they are so** — **poor** son pobrísimos; **it is a** — **good wine** es un vino rebueno, es un vino requetebueno.

2 *adj* (a) mismo; **in this** — **house** en esta misma casa; **at that** — **moment** en ese mismo momento; **to the** — **bone** hasta el mismo hueso; **he's the** — **man we want** es precisamente el hombre que buscamos; **it's the** — **thing!** ¡es exactamente lo que necesitamos!; **at the** — **beginning** ya en los comienzos; **the** — **bishop himself was there** el mismísimo obispo estaba allí, hasta el propio obispo estaba allí; **the** — **idea!** ¡ni hablar!, ¡qué cosas dices!; **the** — **thought frightens me** sólo pensar en ello me da miedo.

(b) **the veriest rascal** el mayor bribón.

vesicle ['vesikl] *n* vesícula *f*.

vespers ['vespəz] *npl* vísperas *fpl*.

vessel ['vesl] *n* (a) (*Anat, Bot*) vaso *m*; (*receptacle*) vasija *f*, recipiente *m*; **he's a weak** — es una persona sin carácter.

(b) (*Naut*) buque *m*, barco *m*.

vest[1] [vest] *n* camiseta *f*; (*US*) chaleco *m*.

vest[2] [vest] *vt* (a) **to** — **someone with something** investir a uno de algo.

(b) **to** — **rights in someone** conferir derechos a uno, conceder derechos a uno, revestir a uno de derechos; **by the authority** — **ed in me** en virtud de la autoridad que se me ha concedido; **to** — **property in someone** ceder una propiedad a uno, hacer a uno titular de una propiedad.

vesta ['vestə] *n* cerilla *f*.

vestal ['vestl] **1** *adj* vestal. **2** *n* vestal *f*.

vested ['vestid] *adj* *right* inalienable; *interest* creado.

vestibule ['vestibjuːl] *n* vestíbulo *m*; (*hall of house*) zaguán *m*; (*anteroom*) antecámara *f*.

vestige ['vestidʒ] *n* vestigio *m*, rastro *m*; (*Bio*) rudimento *m*; **not a** — **of it remains** no queda rastro de ello, de ello no queda ni el menor vestigio; **without a** — **of decency** sin la menor decencia; **if there is a** — **of doubt** si hay una sombra de duda.

vestigial [ves'tidʒiəl] *adj* vestigial; rudimentario.

vestment ['vestmənt] *n* vestidura *f*.

vest-pocket ['vest'pɔkit] *adj* (*US*) en miniatura.

vestry ['vestri] *n* sacristía *f*.

vesture ['vestʃə*] *n* (*lit*) vestidura *f*.

Vesuvius [vi'suːviəs] Vesubio.

vet [vet] (*fam*) **1** *n* veterinario.

2 *vt* repasar, revisar; examinar, investigar; aprobar; **he's** — **ting the proofs** está corrigiendo las pruebas; **we'll have it** — **ted by the boss** haremos que el jefe lo repase; **he was** — **ted by Security** fue sometido a investigación por la Seguridad.

vetch [vetʃ] *n* arveja *f*.

veteran ['vetərən] **1** *adj* veterano. **2** *n* veterano *m*; ex combatiente *m*.

veterinarian [,vetəri'neəriən] *n* (*US*) veterinario *m*.

veterinary ['vetərinəri] *adj* veterinario; **— medicine, — science** medicina *f* veterinaria, veterinaria *f*; **— surgeon** veterinario *m*.

veto ['vi:təu] **1** *n*, *pl* **vetoes** ['vi:təuz] veto *m*; **to have a —** tener veto; **to put a — on something** poner su veto a algo.
  2 *vt* vedar, vetar, prohibir; **he —ed it** él lo prohibió, él lo vedó; **the president —ed it** el presidente le puso su veto.

vex [veks] *vt* (*anger*) fastidiar, irritar, contrariar; (*make impatient*) impacientar, sacar de quicio; (*afflict*) afligir; **the problems that are —ing the country** los problemas que afligen el país, los problemas que alteran el país.

vexation [vek'seiʃən] *n* irritación *f*, contrariedad *f*; impaciencia *f*; aflicción *f*; **he had to put up with numerous —s** tuvo que soportar muchos disgustos.

vexatious [vek'seiʃəs] *adj* fastidioso, molesto, engorroso.

vexed [vekst] *adj* (a) **to be — about something** estar enfadado de algo, estar enfadado por algo; **to be — with someone** estar enfadado con uno; **to be very —** estar muy enfadado; **to get —** enfadarse, impacientarse.
  (b) **in a — tone** en tono ofendido, en tono de enojo.
  (c) *question* batallón.

vexing ['veksiŋ] *adj* fastidioso, molesto, engorroso; **it's very —** es una lata.

via ['vaiə] *prep* por, por vía de; **we came — London** pasamos por Londres.

viability [,vaiə'biliti] *n* viabilidad *f*.

viable ['vaiəbl] *adj* viable.

viaduct ['vaiədʌkt] *n* viaducto *m*.

vial ['vaiəl] *n see* **phial**.

viands ['vaiəndz] *npl* (*lit*) manjares *mpl* (exquisitos).

viaticum [vai'ætikəm] *n* viático *m*.

vibrant ['vaibrənt] **1** *n* vibrante (*also* fig; *with* de). **2** *n* vibrante *f*.

vibrate [vai'breit] *vti* vibrar.

vibration [vai'breiʃən] *n* vibración *f*.

vibrator [vai'breitə*] *n* vibrador *m*.

vibratory ['vaibrətəri] *adj* vibratorio.

viburnum [vai'bə:nəm] *n* viburno *m*.

vicar ['vikə*] *n* vicario *m*; (*parish priest*) párroco *m*, cura *m*.

vicarage ['vikəridʒ] *n* casa *f* del párroco.

vicar-general ['vikə'dʒenərəl] *n* vicario *m* general.

vicarious [vi'keəriəs] *adj* experimentado por otro; **to get — pleasure out of something** sentir placer por lo que está haciendo otro; **I got a — thrill** me emocioné mucho sin tener nada que ver con lo que pasaba.

vicariously [vi'keəriəsli] *adv*: **to feel excitement —** emocionarse por lo que está haciendo otro, emocionarse a través de la emoción de otro.

vice¹ [vais] *n* vicio *m*.

vice² [vais] *n* (*Mech*) torno *m* de banco, tornillo *m* de banco.

vice³ ['vaisi] *prep* en lugar de, sustituyendo a.

vice . . . [vais] in compounds: vice-.

vice-admiral ['vais'ædmərəl] *n* vicealmirante *m*.

vice-chairman ['vais'tʃeəmən] *n*, *pl* **-men** [mən] vicepresidente *m*.

vice-chairmanship ['vais,tʃeəmənʃip] *n* vicepresidencia *f*.

vice-chancellor ['vais'tʃɑ:nsələ*] *n* (*Univ*, *approx*) rector *m*.

vice-consul ['vais'kɔnsəl] *n* vicecónsul *m*.

vice-presidency ['vais'prezidənsi] *n* vicepresidencia *f*.

vice-president ['vais'prezidənt] *n* vicepresidente *m*.

viceroy ['vaisrɔi] *n* virrey *m*.

viceroyalty ['vais'rɔiəlti] *n* virreinato *m*.

vice squad ['vaisskwɔd] *n* brigada *f* contra el vicio.

vice versa ['vaisi'və:sə] *adv* viceversa, a la inversa; **and —** y a la inversa.

vicinity [vi'siniti] *n* (*area*) vecindad *f*, región *f*; (*nearness*) proximidad *f* (*to* de); **and other towns in the —** y otras ciudades de la región, y otras ciudades cercanas; **we are in the — of Wigan** estamos en la región de Wigan, estamos cerca de Wigan; **in the — of 90** unos 90, alrededor de 90.

vicious ['viʃəs] *adj* (*related to vice*) vicioso; *person* depravado, perverso; cruel; *dog* bravo; *horse* resabiado, arisco; *blow* cruel, sañudo; *crime* atroz; *criticism* virulento, cruel, rencoroso; **with — intent** con mala intención, con intención criminal.

viciously ['viʃəsli] *adv* viciosamente; perversamente; cruelmente; con virulencia, con rencor, rencorosamente.

viciousness ['viʃəsnis] *n* viciosidad *f*; perversidad *f*, crueldad *f*; bravura *f*, resabios *mpl*; atrocidad *f*; virulencia *f*, rencor *m*.

vicissitudes [vi'sisitju:dz] *npl* vicisitudes *fpl*; altibajos *mpl*, peripecias *fpl*.

vicissitudinous [vi,sisi'tju:dinəs] *adj* accidentado.

victim ['viktim] *n* víctima *f*; **to be the — of an accident** ser víctima de un accidente, morir (*etc*) en un accidente; **to be the — of a swindle** ser víctima de una estafa; **to fall a — to flu** enfermar con la gripe; **to fall a — to someone's charms** rendirse (*or* sucumbir) a los encantos de uno.

victimization [,viktimai'zeiʃən] *n* sacrificio *m*; persecución *f*; (*of striker etc*) castigo *m*, represalias *fpl*.

victimize ['viktimaiz] *vt* hacer víctima de; escoger y castigar, tomar represalias contra; **the strikers should not be —d** no hay por qué castigar a los huelguistas; **she feels she has been —d** ella cree que ha sido escogida como víctima.

victor ['viktə*] *n* vencedor *m*, ora *f*.

Victoria [vik'tɔ:riə] *f* Victoria.

Victoria Falls [vik'tɔ:riə'fɔ:lz] *pl* Cataratas *fpl* de Victoria.

Victorian [vik'tɔ:riən] **1** *adj* victoriano. **2** *n* victoriano *m*, a *f*.

victorious [vik'tɔ:riəs] *adj* victorioso; **the — team** el equipo vencedor, los vencedores; **to be —** triunfar (*over* sobre), salir victorioso, vencer.

victoriously [vik'tɔ:riəsli] *adv* victoriosamente, triunfalmente.

victory ['viktəri] *n* victoria *f*; triunfo *m*; **moral —** victoria *f* moral; **Pyrrhic —** victoria *f* pírrica; **to win a famous —** obtener un triunfo señalado.

victual ['vitl] **1** *vt* abastecer, avituallar. **2** *vi* abastecerse, avituallarse, tomar provisiones.

victualler ['vitlə*] *n*: **licensed —** vendedor *m* de bebidas alcohólicas.

victuals ['vitlz] *npl* víveres *mpl*, provisiones *fpl*, vitualla *f*.

vicuna [vi'kju:nə] *n* vicuña *f*.

vide ['videi] (*vt*) vea, véase.

videlicet [vi'di:liset] *adv* a saber.

video ['videiəu] **1** *n* vídeo *m*. **2** *attr* de vídeo.

vie [vai] *vi* competir, ser rivales; **to — for something** disputarse algo; **to — with someone for something** disputar algo a alguien, luchar contra uno para conseguir algo; **to — with someone** competir con uno, rivalizar con uno.

Vienna [vi'enə] Viena.

Viennese [,viə'ni:z] **1** *adj* vienés. **2** *n* vienés *m*, esa *f*.

Vietnam ['vjet'næm] Vietnam *m*.

Vietnamese [,vjetnə'mi:z] **1** *adj* vietnamita. **2** *n* vietnamita *mf*. **3** *n* (*language*) vietnamita *m*.

vieux jeu ['vjə:'ʒə:] *adj* anticuado, fuera de moda.

view [vju:] **1** *n* (a) (*general sense*) vista *f*; panorama *m*; perspectiva *f*; (*Art*, *Phot*) panorama *m*; (*landscape*) paisaje *m*; **private —** inauguración *f* privada; **it's a beautiful —** es un bello panorama; **there is a fine — from the top** desde la cumbre se ofrece un magnífico panorama; **50 —s of Venice** 50 vistas de Venecia; **a — of Toledo from the north** Toledo en su aspecto norte, Toledo visto desde el norte; **to be in —** ser visible; **to be in full —** ser totalmente visible; **he did it in full — of hundreds of people** lo hizo estando delante centenares de personas, lo hizo a plena vista de centenares de personas; **to have (or keep) someone in —** no perder a uno de vista; **to be on —** estar expuesto; **the house will be on — to the public on Saturdays** la casa estará abierta al público los sábados.
  (b) (*opinion etc*) opinión *f*, parecer *m*; criterio *m*; actitud *f*; **in my —** en mi opinión; **in — of this** en vista de esto; **with a — to doing something** con miras a hacer algo, con el propósito de hacer algo; **our — of the problem** nuestro modo de enfocar el problema; **what is the government's —?** ¿cuál es la actitud del gobierno?; **it is not easy to form a —** no es fácil llegar a una conclusión; **to have (or keep) something in —** tener algo en cuenta, tener algo presente; **I do not share that —** no comparto ese criterio; **to take the — that . . .** opinar que . . .; **we take a different —** nosotros pensamos de otro modo; **to take a dim (or poor) — of someone** tener un concepto desfavorable de uno, tener a uno en poco; **I should take a dim — if . . .** no me agradaría que + subj.
  2 *vt* mirar; ver, contemplar; examinar, inspeccionar; considerar; **we went to — the house** fuimos a ver la casa; **Cadiz —ed from the sea** Cádiz visto desde el mar; **we — it with some alarm** para nosotros se motivo de cierta alarma; **how does the government — it?** ¿cuál es la actitud del gobierno?

viewer ['vjuːə*] n (onlooker) espectador m, ora f; (TV) televidente mf, telespectador m, ora f.

viewfinder ['vjuːˌfaində*] n (Phot) visor m de imagen.

viewpoint ['vjuːpɔint] n (a) (Geog) mirador m, punto m panorámico.

(b) (fig) punto m de vista; criterio m; from the — of the economy desde el punto de vista de la economía.

vigil ['vidʒil] n vigilia f; to keep — velar.

vigilance ['vidʒiləns] n vigilancia f; to escape someone's —burlar la vigilancia de uno.

vigilant ['vidʒilənt] adj vigilante; desvelado, alerta.

vigilante [ˌvidʒi'lænti] n vigilante m.

vigilantly ['vidʒiləntli] adv vigilantemente.

vignette [vi'njet] n (Phot, Typ) viñeta f.

vigorous ['vigərəs] adj vigoroso, enérgico.

vigorously ['vigərəsli] adv vigorosamente, con vigor, enérgicamente.

vigour, (US) vigor ['vigə*] n vigor m, energía f; in the full — of manhood en la flor de la edad viril.

Viking ['vaikiŋ] n vikingo m.

vile [vail] adj vil; infame, detestable; (very bad) horrible, asqueroso; the weather was — el tiempo fue horrible; it's a — play es una obra malísima; he has a — temper tiene un genio muy vivo, es un hombre de malas pulgas; that was a — thing to say eso fue infame.

vilely ['vailli] adv vilmente; de modo infame, de modo detestable; malísimamente, horriblemente; he treated her — la trató de modo infame.

vileness ['vailnis] n vileza f; infamia f; lo horrible, lo asqueroso; the — of the weather el tiempo tan horrible que hace.

vilification [ˌvilifi'keiʃən] n vilipendio m.

vilify ['vilifai] vt vilipendiar.

villa ['vilə] n (Roman etc) villa f; (seaside) chalet m; (country house) casa f de campo, quinta f.

village ['vilidʒ] 1 n (small) aldea f, pueblecito m; lugar m; (large) pueblo m. 2 attr aldeano; pueblerino; de aldea, de la aldea.

villager ['vilidʒə*] n aldeano m, a f.

villain ['vilən] n malvado m; (Lit) malo m, traidor m; (criminal) ladrón m, criminal m; (hum) tunante m, bribón m; you — ! ¡ladrón!; the — of the piece is X el que debiera cargar con la culpa de esto es X, el verdadero responsable es X.

villainous ['vilənəs] adj malvado, vil, infame; (very bad) malísimo, horrible; and other — characters y otros personajes infames.

villainously ['vilənəsli] adv vilmente; — ugly feísimo.

villainy ['viləni] n maldad f, vileza f; they must be up to some — estarán tramando algo malo.

villein ['vilin] n (Hist) villano m, a f.

vim [vim] n energía f, empuje m, vigor m.

Vincent ['vinsənt] m Vicente.

vindicate ['vindikeit] 1 vt vindicar, justificar. 2 vr: to — oneself justificarse.

vindication [ˌvindi'keiʃən] n vindicación f, justificación f.

vindictive [vin'diktiv] adj vengativo; rencoroso; to feel — about something guardar rencor por motivo de algo; to feel — towards someone guardar rencor a uno.

vindictively [vin'diktivli] adv rencorosamente, con rencor.

vindictiveness [vin'diktivnis] n deseo m de venganza espíritu m de venganza; rencor m.

vine [vain] n vid f; (climbing, trained) parra f.

vine arbour, (US) — arbor ['vain,ɑːbə*] n emparrado m.

vinedresser ['vain,dresə*] n viñador m.

vinegar ['vinigə*] n vinagre m.

vinegary ['vinigəri] adj vinagroso.

vine grower ['vain,grəuə*] n viticultor m, viñador m.

vine growing ['vain,grəuiŋ] n viticultura f.

vine leaf ['vainliːf] n, pl — leaves [liːvz] hoja f de parra, hoja f de vid, pámpana f.

vineyard ['vinjəd] n viña f, viñedo m.

vinous ['vainəs] adj vinoso.

vintage ['vintidʒ] 1 n (season, harvest) vendimia f; (with reference to quality or year) cosecha f; the 1970 — la cosecha de 1970; it will be a good — la cosecha promete ser buena.

2 adj: — wine vino m añejo, vino m de calidad; — car coche m de época, coche m antiguo, coche m clásico; it was a — year fue un año famoso, fue un año clásico; it has been a — year for plays en el teatro ha sido una temporada excelente.

vintner ['vintnə*] n vinatero m.

vinyl ['vainl] n vinilo m.

viol ['vaiəl] n viola f.

viola ['vaiələ] n (Bot) viola f.

viola [vi'əulə] n (Mus) viola f.

violate ['vaiəleit] vt (all senses) violar.

violation [ˌvaiə'leiʃən] n violación f; in — of a law violando así una ley; in — of someone's privacy invadiendo la vida privada de uno.

violator ['vaiəleitə*] n violador m, ora f.

violence ['vaiələns] n violencia f; there was — se recurrió a la fuerza; there has been — on the streets ha estallado la violencia en las calles; to die by — morir violentamente; to do someone a — agredir a uno, herir a uno; to do — to a theory torcer una teoría; to offer — mostrarse violento; to resort to — recurrir a la fuerza, venirse a las manos; tomar medidas violentas; to rob someone with — robar algo a uno a mano airada.

violent ['vaiələnt] adj violento; feeling etc intenso, acerbo; colour chillón; to become — mostrarse violento; apelar a la fuerza; to lay — hands on someone agredir a uno; to take a — dislike to someone tomar un odio intenso a uno.

violently ['vaiələntli] adv violentamente, con violencia; to die — morir violentamente; to fall — in love with someone enamorarse perdidamente de uno; he expresses himself rather — se expresa en términos algo violentos.

violet ['vaiəlit] 1 n (Bot) violeta f; (colour) violado m. 2 adj violado.

violin [ˌvaiə'lin] n violín m; first — (person) primer violín m.

violinist [ˌvaiə'linist] n violinista mf.

violoncellist [ˌvaiələn'tʃelist] n violoncelista mf.

violoncello [ˌvaiələn'tʃeləu] n violoncelo m.

viper ['vaipə*] n víbora f.

viperish ['vaipəriʃ] adj (fig) viperino.

virago [vi'rɑːgəu] n fiera f, arpía f.

Virgil ['vəːdʒil] m Virgilio.

Virgilian [vəː'dʒiliən] adj virgiliano.

virgin ['vəːdʒin] 1 adj virgen; cork, forest, soil etc virgen. 2 n virgen f; the V— la Virgen; the Blessed V— la Santísima Virgen.

virginal ['vəːdʒinl] adj virginal.

Virginian [və'dʒiniən] n (also — tobacco) tabaco m rubio.

Virgin Isles ['vəːdʒin,ailz] pl Islas fpl Vírgenes.

virginity [vəː'dʒiniti] n virginidad f.

virile ['virail] adj viril.

virility [vi'riliti] n virilidad f.

virologist [ˌvaiə'rɔlədʒist] n virólogo m.

virology [ˌvaiə'rɔlədʒi] n virología f.

virtual ['vəːtjuəl] adj virtual; the — dictator of the country el que es en efecto el dictador del país; it was a — defeat era casi una derrota; he made a — admission of guilt en efecto se confesó culpable.

virtually ['vəːtjuəli] adv virtualmente; it is — impossible to do anything es prácticamente imposible hacer nada, es casi imposible hacer nada; it — destroyed the building destruyó virtualmente el edificio.

virtue ['vəːtjuː] n virtud f; a woman of easy — una mujer de vida alegre, una mujer de moralidad laxa; by — of, in — of en virtud de; to make a — of necessity poner a mal tiempo buena cara, lograr sacar provecho de lo inevitable; I see no — in that no encuentro ninguna ventaja en eso; I see no — in trams no comprendo el porqué de los tranvías.

virtuosity [ˌvəːtjuˈɔsiti] n virtuosismo m.

virtuoso [ˌvəːtjuˈəuzəu] n virtuoso m.

virtuous ['vəːtjuəs] adj virtuoso.

virtuously ['vəːtjuəsli] adv virtuosamente.

virulence ['viruləns] n virulencia f.

virulent ['virulənt] adj virulento.

virulently ['viruləntli] adv con virulencia.

virus ['vaiərəs] n virus m.

visa ['viːzə] 1 n visado m. 2 vt visar.

visage ['vizidʒ] n (lit) semblante m.

vis-à-vis ['viːzəviː] prep respecto de, con relación a.

viscera ['visərə] npl vísceras fpl.

viscid ['visid] adj viscoso.

viscose ['viskəus] 1 adj viscoso. 2 n viscosa f.

viscosity [vis'kɔsiti] n viscosidad f.

viscount ['vaikaunt] n vizconde m.

viscountcy ['vaikauntsi] n vizcondado m.

viscountess ['vaikauntis] n vizcondesa f.

viscous ['viskəs] adj viscoso.

vise [vais] n (US) = vice².

visé ['viːzei] see visa.

visibility [ˌvizi'biliti] n visibilidad f (also Aer etc); **in good —** en buenas condiciones de visibilidad; **there was a — of 500 metres** la visibilidad era de 500 metros; **— is down to nil** la visibilidad queda reducida a cero.

visible ['vizəbl] adj visible.

visibly ['vizəbli] adv visiblemente; **he had got — thinner** había adelgazado visiblemente; **she was — moved** patentizó su emoción, acusó una fuerte conmoción.

Visigoth ['vizigɔθ] n visigodo m, a f.

Visigothic [ˌvizi'gɔθik] **1** adj visigodo, visigótico. **2** n lengua f visigótica.

vision ['viʒən] **(a)** visión f (also Eccl); (eyesight) vista f; **to have normal —** tener la vista normal.
  (b) (farsightedness) clarividencia f; **a man of —** un hombre clarividente; **he had the — to see that ...** era lo bastante clarividente como para ver que ...
  (c) (dream) sueño m; **my — of the future** mi sueño del porvenir, mi manera de imaginar el futuro; **to have —s of wealth** soñar con ser rico; **I had —s of having to walk home** me estaba viendo en el caso de tener que llegar a casa andando.

visionary ['viʒənəri] **1** adj visionario. **2** n visionario m, a f.

visit ['vizit] **1** n visita f; **to be on a — to ...** estar de visita en ...; **to pay someone a —** hacer una visita a uno; **to return a —** devolver una visita.
  2 vt **(a)** visitar, hacer una visita a; ir a; conocer; **when we first —ed the town** cuando conocimos la ciudad por primera vez; **to — the sick** visitar a los enfermos.
  (b) to — a punishment on someone castigar a uno con algo, mandar un castigo a uno; **they were —ed with the plague** sufrieron el azote de la peste.
  3 vi hacer visitas (also **to go —ing**); (US fam) visitarse.

visitation [ˌvizi'teiʃən] n (Eccl) visitación f; (inspection) inspección f; (fam) visita f larga y molesta; (punishment) castigo m.

visiting ['vizitiŋ] adj card etc de visita; team visitante, de fuera; **to be on — terms with someone** conocerse bastante para visitarse.

visiting card ['vizitiŋkɑːd] n tarjeta f de visita.

visitor ['vizitə*] n visitante mf; (to one's home) visita f; (tourist) turista mf, visitante mf; (tripper) excursionista mf; (stranger) forastero m, a f; **the museum had 900 —s** el museo recibió a 900 visitantes; **we can't invite you because we have —s** no podemos invitarte pues tenemos visita; **sorry, we're just —s here** lo siento, estamos aquí de visita nada más; **the summer —s bring a lot of money** los veraneantes aportan mucho dinero.

visitors' book ['vizitəzbuk] n libro m de visitas, libro m de honor.

visor ['vaizə*] n visera f.

vista ['vistə] n vista f, panorama m; (fig) perspectiva f; **there are new —s** hay perspectivas nuevas; **it opened up —s of wealth** ofreció perspectivas de riqueza.

visual ['vizjuəl] adj visual.

visualize ['vizjuəlaiz] vt **(a)** (form a picture of) representarse (en la mente), imaginarse.
  (b) (foresee) prever; **the government —s that ...** el gobierno prevé que ...; **we do not — any great change** no prevemos ningún cambio de importancia; **that is not how we —d it** eso no corresponde a lo que nosotros preveíamos.

visually ['vizjuəli] adv visualmente.

vital ['vaitl] **1** adj **(a)** (essential) esencial; imprescindible; de suma importancia, trascendental; **of — importance** de primerísima importancia, de importancia primordial (to para); **the book is —** el libro es esencial; **it is — that ...** es esencial que + subj, importa muchísimo que + subj.
  (b) (critical) decisivo, crítico; **at the — moment** en el momento decisivo.
  (c) person (of character) enérgico, vivo, lleno de vida; **she's a very — person** es una persona que rebosa de energía.
  (d) (relating to life) vital; **— parts** partes fpl vitales; see **statistics**.
  2 —s npl partes fpl vitales.

vitality [vai'tæliti] n vitalidad f, energía f.

vitalize ['vaitəlaiz] vt vitalizar, vivificar, infundir nueva vida a.

vitally ['vaitəli] adv: **— important** de primerísima importancia; **it is — important that ...** es esencial que + subj.

vitamin ['vitəmin] **1** n vitamina f. **2** attr content etc vitamínico.

vitaminize ['vitəminaiz] vt vitaminar.

vitaminized ['vitəminaizd] adj vitaminado, reforzado con vitaminas.

vitiate ['viʃieit] vt viciar (also Law); estropear, destruir; quitar valor a.

viticulture ['vitikʌltʃə*] n viticultura f.

vitreous ['vitriəs] adj vítreo.

vitrifaction [ˌvitri'fækʃən] n vitrificación f.

vitrify ['vitrifai] **1** vt vitrificar. **2** vi vitrificarse.

vitriol ['vitriəl] n vitriolo m.

vitriolic [ˌvitri'ɔlik] adj (fig) mordaz.

vituperate [vi'tjuːpəreit] vt vituperar, llenar de injurias.

vituperation [viˌtjuːpə'reiʃən] n vituperio m, injurias fpl.

vituperative [vi'tjuːpərətiv] adj vituperioso, injurioso.

viva ['vaivə] see **viva voce**.

vivacious [vi'veiʃəs] adj animado, vivaz, alegre, lleno de vida.

vivaciously [vi'veiʃəsli] adj animadamente, alegremente.

vivacity [vi'væsiti] n animación f, vivacidad f, vida f, alegría f.

vivarium [vi'vɛəriəm] n vivero m.

viva voce ['vaivə'vəusi] **1** adv de viva voz. **2** adj exam oral. **3** n examen m oral.

vivid ['vivid] adj colour, light intenso; flash súbito; impression, memory etc vivo; description gráfico, enérgico, pintoresco

vividly ['vividli] adv intensamente; súbitamente; vivamente; enérgicamente, con rasgos enérgicos, de modo pintoresco.

vividness ['vividnis] n intensidad f; vivacidad f; energía f.

vivify ['vivifai] vt vivificar.

viviparous [vi'vipərəs] adj vivíparo.

vivisection [ˌvivi'sekʃən] n vivisección f.

vixen ['viksn] n zorra f, raposa f; (fig) arpía f.

vizier [vi'ziə*] n visir m; **grand —** gran visir m.

vocable ['vəukəbl] n vocablo m.

vocabulary [vəu'kæbjuləri] n vocabulario m, léxico m.

vocal ['vəukəl] adj vocal (also Mus); (noisy) ruidoso; chillón, gritón; **they're getting rather — about it** están empezando a protestar; **there was some — opposition** algunos manifestaron su disconformidad con protestas ruidosas.

vocalic [vəu'kælik] adj vocálico.

vocalist ['vəukəlist] n cantante mf; (in cabaret etc) vocalista mf.

vocalize ['vəukəlaiz] **1** vt vocalizar. **2** vi vocalizarse.

vocally ['vəukəli] adv vocalmente; ruidosamente.

vocation [vəu'keiʃən] n vocación f; **to have a — for art** tener vocación por el arte; **he has missed his —** se ha equivocado de carrera.

vocational [vəu'keiʃənl] adj vocacional, profesional.

vocative ['vɔkətiv] n vocativo m.

vociferate [vəu'sifəreit] vti vociferar, gritar.

vociferation [vəuˌsifə'reiʃən] n vociferación f.

vociferous [vəu'sifərəs] adj vocinglero, clamoroso; (noisy) ruidoso; **there were — protests** hubo protestas ruidosas, se protestó ruidosamente.

vociferously [vəu'sifərəsli] adv a gritos, clamorosamente; ruidosamente.

vodka ['vɔdkə] n vodka f.

vogue [vəug] n boga f, moda f; **the — for short skirts** la moda de la falda corta; **to be in —** estar de moda, estar en boga.

voice [vɔis] **1** n voz f; active **— voz** f activa; passive **— voz** f pasiva; **in a gentle —** en tono dulce; **in a loud —** en voz alta; **in a low —** en voz baja; **with one —** a una voz, al unísono; **to be in (good) —** estar en voz; **to give — to** expresar, hacerse eco de; **to have no — in a matter** no tener voz en capítulo; **to raise one's —** levantar el tono, (protest) protestar; see top etc.
  2 vt expresar, hacerse eco de; (Gram) sonorizar.
  3 vi sonorizarse.

voiced [vɔist] adj (Gram) sonoro.

voiceless ['vɔislis] adj (Gram) sordo.

void [vɔid] **1** adj (empty) vacío; desocupado; post vacante; (Law) nulo, inválido; **to be — of** estar falto de, estar desprovisto de; **to make a contract —** anular un contrato, invalidar un contrato; **to make someone's efforts —** hacer inútiles los esfuerzos de uno; see **null**.
  2 n **(a)** vacío m; hueco m, espacio m; **the — la** nada; **to fill the —** llenar el hueco; **to have an aching —** tener mucha hambre.
  (b) (Cards) fallo m; **to have a — in hearts** tener fallo a corazones.
  3 vt evacuar, vaciar; (Law) anular, invalidar.

volatile ['vɔlətail] *adj* volátil (*also fig*).
volatility [ˌvɔlə'tılıtı] *n* volatilidad *f* (*also fig*).
volatilize [vɔ'lætəlaiz] **1** *vt* volatilizar. **2** *vi* volatilizarse.
volcanic [vɔl'kænik] *adj* volcánico.
volcano [vɔl'keinəu] *n*, *pl* **volcanoes** [vɔl'keinəuz] volcán *m*.
vole [vəul] *n* campañol *m*.
volition [və'liʃən] *n* volición *f*; **of one's own** — por voluntad propia.
volley ['vɔli] **1** *n* (*of shots*) descarga *f*, descarga *f* cerrada; (*of stones etc*) lluvia *f*; (*of applause*) salva *f*; (*of abuse etc*) torrente *m*, retahíla *f*; (*Tennis*) voleo *m*. **2** *vt* (*Tennis*) volear; *abuse etc* dirigir (*at* a). **3** *vi* (*Mil*) lanzar una descarga.
volleyball ['vɔlibɔːl] *n* balón *m* volea.
volt [vəult] *n* voltio *m*.
voltage ['vəultidʒ] *n* voltaje *m*.
voltaic [vɔl'teiik] *adj* voltaico.
volte-face ['vɔlt'faːs] *n* viraje *m*, cambio *m* súbito de opinión, tergiversación *f*.
voltmeter ['vəultˌmiːtə*] *n* voltímetro *m*.
volubility [ˌvɔlju'biliti] *n* locuacidad *f*.
voluble ['vɔljubl] *adj person* locuaz, hablador; **in** — **French** en francés elocuente y rápido; **a** — **protest** una protesta larga y enérgica.
volubly ['vɔljubli] *adv* de modo locuaz, con locuacidad; con soltura, rápidamente; larga y enérgicamente.
volume ['vɔljuːm] *n* volumen *m*; (*book, number in series*) tomo *m*; (*total*) cantidad *f*, masa *f*; (*of sound*) volumen *m* sonoro; (*of water*) cantidad *f* de agua; caudal *m* (de río *etc*); (*in the third* — en el tercer tomo; **an edition in 4** —**s** una edición en 4 tomos; **it speaks** —**s** es sumamente significativo; **it speaks** —**s for it** lo evidencia de modo inconfundible; **it speaks** —**s for him** es un testimonio muy significativo acerca de él.
volume control ['vɔljuːmkənˌtrəul] *n* (*Radio etc*) control *m* del volumen sonoro.
volumetric [ˌvɔlju'metrik] *adj* volumétrico.
voluminous [və'luːminəs] *adj* voluminoso.
voluntarily ['vɔləntərili] *adv* voluntariamente, sin ser forzado, libremente.
voluntary ['vɔləntəri] **1** *adj* voluntario; espontáneo; libre. **2** *n* solo *m* de órgano; **trumpet** — solo *m* de trompeta.
volunteer [ˌvɔlən'tiə*] **1** *n* voluntario *m*. **2** *adj, attr force etc* de voluntarios. **3** *vt services* ofrecer; *remark* hacer. **4** *vi* ofrecerse; (*Mil*) alistarse como voluntario; **to** — **for service overseas** ofrecerse para servir en ultramar; **to** — **to do a job** ofrecerse a hacer un trabajo; **he wasn't forced to, he** —**ed** nadie le obligó a ello, se ofreció libremente.
voluptuary [və'lʌptjuəri] *n* voluptuoso *m*, a *f*.
voluptuous [və'lʌptjuəs] *adj* voluptuoso.
voluptuously [və'lʌptjuəsli] *adv* voluptuosamente.
voluptuousness [və'lʌptjuəsnis] *n* voluptuosidad *f*.
volute [və'luːt] *n* voluta *f*.
vomit ['vɔmit] **1** *n* vómito *m*. **2** *vt* vomitar, arrojar. **3** *vi* vomitar, tener vómitos.
voodoo ['vuːduː] *n* vudú *m*.
voracious [və'reiʃəs] *adj* voraz.
voraciously [və'reiʃəsli] *adv* vorazmente.
voracity [vɔ'ræsiti] *n* voracidad *f*.
vortex ['vɔːteks] *n*, *pl* **vortices** ['vɔːtisiːz] vórtice *m*.
Vosges [vəuʒ] *pl* **Vosges** *mpl*.
votary ['vəutəri] *n* (*Rel*) devoto *m*, a *f*; (*fig*) partidario *m*, a *f*.
vote [vəut] **1** *n* (a) voto *m*; sufragio *m*; **casting** — voto *m* de calidad, voto *m* decisivo; **in the case of a tie the chairman shall have a casting** — el voto del presidente será dirimente en caso de empate; **by a majority** — por la mayoría de los votos; **to cast one's** —, **to give one's** — dar su voto (*for, to* a); **how many** —**s did he get?** ¿cuántos votos obtuvo?; **he won by 89** —**s** ganó por 89 votos.
(b) (*voting*) votación *f*; (*election*) elección *f*, elecciones *fpl*; — **of censure** voto *m* de censura; — **of confidence** voto *m* de confianza; — **of thanks** voto *m* de gracia; **by popular** — por votación popular, (*fig*) en la opinión de muchos; **by secret** — por votación secreta; **as the 1931** — **showed** según demostraron las elecciones de 1931; **to put a motion to the** —, **to take a** — **on a motion** someter una moción a votación; **let's take a** — **on it** (*fig*) veamos qué opiniones hay sobre esto.
(c) (*right to* —) derecho *m* de votar; **when women got the** — cuando se concedió a las mujeres

el derecho de votar; **to have the** — tener el derecho de votar.
2 *vt*: **to** — **a sum for defence** votar una cantidad para la defensa, aprobar por votación el presupuesto de la defensa; **she was** —**d Miss Granada 1970** fue elegida como Miss Granada 1970; **we** —**d it a failure** opinamos que fue un fracaso; **the team** —**d it a hit** el equipo pronosticó que tendría éxito; **to** — **a proposal down** rechazar una propuesta por votación; **we** —**d that idea down** (*fig*) rechazamos esa idea; **to** — **a government in** elegir un gobierno; **to** — **someone into office** elegir a uno para ocupar un puesto.
3 *vi* votar; (*go to polls*) ir a votar, acudir a las urnas; **to** — **for someone** votar por uno; **to** — **that . . .** resolver por votación que . . .; **I** — **that . . .** (*fam*) yo propongo que . . ., yo sugiero que . . .
voter ['vəutə*] *n* votante *mf*.
voting ['vəutiŋ] *n* votación *f*.
voting booth ['vəutiŋˌbuːð] *n* caseta *f* de votar, cabina *f* de votación.
voting machine ['vəutiŋməˌʃiːn] *n* (*US*) máquina *f* de votar.
voting paper ['vəutiŋˌpeipə*] *n* papeleta *f* (de votación).
voting power ['vəutiŋˌpauə*] *n* potencia *f* electoral.
votive ['vəutiv] *adj* votivo.
vouch [vautʃ] **1** *vt* garantizar, atestiguar; confirmar; **to** — **that . . .** afirmar que . . ., asegurar que . . . **2** *vi*: **to** — **for something** garantizar algo; confirmar algo; responder de algo; **I cannot** — **for its authenticity** no puedo responder de su autenticidad; **to** — **for someone** responder por uno.
voucher ['vautʃə*] *n* documento *m* justificativo; (*Comm*) comprobante *m*; **cash** — vale *m* que representa una cantidad en metálico; **luncheon** — vale *m* de comida.
vouchsafe [vautʃ'seif] *vt* conceder, otorgar; *reply etc* servirse hacer, dignarse hacer; **to** — **to** + *infin* dignarse + *infin*.
vow [vau] **1** *n* voto *m* (*also Eccl*); promesa *f* solemne; **lovers'** —**s** promesas *fpl* solemnes de los amantes; **monastic** —**s** votos *mpl* monásticos; **the** — **of poverty** el voto de pobreza; **to be under a** — **to do something** haber hecho voto de hacer algo, haber prometido solemnemente hacer algo; **to take a** — **to** + *infin* hacer voto de *infin*, jurar + *infin*.
2 *vt*: **to** — **vengeance against someone** jurar vengarse (de uno); **to** — **that . . .** jurar que . . ., prometer solemnemente que . . .
3 *vi*: **to** — **to** + *infin* hacer voto de + *infin*, jurar + *infin*.
vowel [vauəl] **1** *n* vocal *f*. **2** *adj, attr* vocálico; — **sound** sonido *m* vocálico; — **system** sistema *m* vocálico.
voyage ['vɔiidʒ] **1** *n* viaje *m* (por mar, en barco); (*crossing*) travesía *f*; **the** — **out** el viaje de ida; **the** — **home** el viaje de regreso.
2 *vi* viajar (por mar); navegar; **to** — **across unknown seas** viajar por mares desconocidos.
voyager ['vɔiidʒə*] *n* viajero *m*, a *f* (por mar).
Vulcan ['vʌlkən] *m* Vulcano.
vulcanite ['vʌlkənait] *n* vulcanita *f*, ebonita *f*.
vulcanization [ˌvʌlkənai'zeiʃən] *n* vulcanización *f*.
vulcanize ['vʌlkənaiz] *vt* vulcanizar.
vulgar ['vʌlgə*] **1** *adj* (a) (*of the people*) vulgar; **in the** — **tongue** en la lengua vulgar, en la lengua vernácula; **that is a** — **error** eso es un error vulgar. (b) (*indecent*) ordinario, grosero; (*in bad taste*) de mal gusto, cursi; *joke, song* verde; *person* ordinario.
2 *n*: **the** — el vulgo.
vulgarian [vʌl'gɛəriən] *n* persona *f* ordinaria; (*wealthy*) ricacho *m*.
vulgarism ['vʌlgərizəm] *n* vulgarismo *m*.
vulgarity [vʌl'gæriti] *n* vulgaridad *f*; ordinariez *f*, grosería *f*; mal gusto *m*, cursilería *f*; lo verde, indecencia *f*.
vulgarize ['vʌlgəraiz] *vt* vulgarizar.
vulgarly ['vʌlgəli] *adv* vulgarmente; de modo ordinario; groseramente; con mal gusto, de modo cursi; indecentemente; **X,** — **known as Y** X, vulgarmente llamado Y.
Vulgate ['vʌlgit] *n* Vulgata *f*.
vulnerability [ˌvʌlnərə'biliti] *n* vulnerabilidad *f*.
vulnerable ['vʌlnərəbl] *adj* vulnerable (*to* a).
vulpine ['vʌlpain] *adj* vulpino.
vulture ['vʌltʃə*] *n* buitre *m*.
vulva ['vʌlvə] *n* vulva *f*.
vying ['vaiiŋ] *ger of* **vie**.

W

wacky ['wæki] *adj* (*US sl*) *person* chiflado; *thing* absurdo.

wad [wɔd] **1** *n* (*used to stuff something*) taco *m*, tapón *m*; (*in gun, cartridge*) taco *m*; (*of cotton wool etc*) bolita *f* de algodón; (*of papers*) lío *m*; (*of notes: US*) fajo *m*; (*sl: cake*) pastel *m*.
2 *vt* (*stuff*) rellenar; (*Sew*) acolchar.

wadding ['wɔdiŋ] *n* taco *m*, tapón *m*; relleno *m*; (*lining*) entretela *f*, forro *m*; (*Med*) algodón *m* absorbente.

waddle ['wɔdl] **1** *n* anadeo *m*; **to walk with a —** anadear. **2** *vi* anadear; **she —d over to the window** fue anadeando a la ventana.

wade [weid] **1** *vt* vadear.
2 *vi* (*also* **to —— along**) caminar por el agua (*or* nieve, lodo *etc*), caminar con el agua hasta la cintura (*etc*); **we shall have to —** tendremos que meternos en el agua; **to —— ashore** llegar a tierra vadeando; **to —— in** entrar en el agua; **to —— into someone** (*fig*) emprenderla con uno, arremeter contra uno; **to —— through the water** caminar por el agua; **to —— through a book** leer un libro a pesar de lo aburrido (*or* lo difícil *etc*); **it took me an hour to —— through your essay** tardé una hora en leer su ensayo tan largo.

wader ['weidə*] *n* (*Orn*) ave *f* zancuda; **—s** botas *fpl* altas.

wafer ['weifə*] *n* (*biscuit*) galleta *f*; (*with ice cream*) barquillo *m*; (*for sealing*) oblea *f*; (*Eccl*) hostia *f*.

wafer-thin ['weifə'θin] *adj* delgadísimo, finísimo.

wafery ['weifəri] *adj* delgado, ligero.

waffle ['wɔfl] **1** *n* (*approx*) buñuelo *m*; (*fam*) palabras *fpl* inútiles, palabrería *f*; (*in essay etc*) paja *f*.
2 *vi* (*fam*) hablar mucho sin decir gran cosa, ser muy charlatán; (*in essay etc*) poner mucha paja.

waft [wɑːft] **1** *n* soplo *m*, ráfaga *f* de olor.
2 *vt* llevar por el aire; hacer flotar; (*stir*) mecer, mover.
3 *vi* moverse (de un sitio a otro); ser llevado por el aire; flotar.

wag[1] [wæg] **1** *n* meneo *m*, movimiento *m*; (*of tail*) coleada *f*.
2 *vt* mover, menear, agitar; **the dog —ged its tail** el perro meneó la cola.
3 *vi* moverse, menearse, agitarse.

wag[2] [wæg] *n* (*joker*) bromista *m*, zumbón *m*.

wage [weidʒ] **1** *n* (*also* **—s**) salario *m*; (*esp day* **—**) jornal *m*; (*fig*) pago *m*, premio *m*; **living —** jornal *m* suficiente para vivir; **minimum —** salario *m* mínimo.
2 *vt war* hacer; *battle* librar, dar; *campaign* proseguir.

wage earner ['weidʒ,ə:nə*] *n* asalariado *m*, a *f*.

wage freeze ['weidʒfri:z] *n* congelación *f* de los salarios.

wager ['weidʒə*] **1** *n* apuesta *f*; **to lay a —** hacer una apuesta; **to lay a —— on a horse** apostar dinero a un caballo.
2 *vti* apostar; **to —— £2 on a horse** apostar 2 libras a un caballo; **to —— that . . .** apostar a que . . .; **he won't do it, I ——!** ¡a que no lo hace!

wages ['weidʒiz] *npl see* **wage.**

wages clerk ['weidʒiklɑ:k] *n* pagador *m*, ora *f*.

waggish ['wægiʃ] *adj* zumbón.

waggishly ['wægiʃli] *adv*: **he said —** dijo zumbón.

waggle ['wægl] = **wag**[1].

wag(g)on ['wægən] *n* carro *m*; (*Rail*) vagón *m*; **to be on the —** (*fam*) no beber; **to go on the —** (*fam*) resolverse a no beber.

wag(g)onette [,wægə'net] *n* break *m*.

wag(g)onload ['wægənləud] *n* carretada *f*, carga *f* de un carro (*etc*); **50 —s of coal** 50 vagones de carbón.

Wagnerian [vɑːg'niəriən] *adj* wagneriano.

wagtail ['wægteil] *n* lavandera *f*.

waif [weif] *n* niño *m* abandonado, niña *f* abandonada; **—s and strays** niños *mpl* desamparados.

wail [weil] **1** *n* lamento *m*, gemido *m*; (*baby's*) vagido *m*; (*complaint*) queja *f*, protesta *f*; **a great —— went up** pusieron el grito en el cielo.
2 *vi* lamentarse, gemir; (*child*) gimotear; llorar; (*complain*) quejarse, protestar.

wailing ['weiliŋ] *n* lamentación *f*, lamentaciones *fpl*, gemidos *mpl*; vagidos *mpl*; quejas *fpl*, protestas *fpl*.

wain [wein] *n* carro *m*; **the W—** (*Astron*) el Carro.

wainscot ['weinskət] *n* friso *m*; entablado *m*, revestimiento *m* (de la pared).

waist [weist] *n* (*Anat etc*) cintura *f*, talle *m*; (*fig, narrow part*) cuello *m*; (*Naut*) combés *m*.

waistband ['weistbænd] *n* pretina *f*, cinturilla *f*.

waistcoat ['weiskəut] *n* chaleco *m*.

waist-deep ['weist'di:p] *adv* hasta la cintura.

-waisted ['weistid] *adj* de cintura . . ., de talle . . ., *eg* **slim-waisted** de cintura delgada.

waist-high ['weist'hai] **1** *adv* hasta la cintura; al nivel de la cintura. **2** *adj*: **—— vegetation** vegetación *f* que crece hasta la altura de la cintura.

waistline ['weistlain] *n* talle *m*.

wait [weit] **1** *n* (a) espera *f*; (*pause*) pausa *f*, intervalo *m*; **there was a —— of 10 minutes** tuvimos que esperar 10 minutos; **to have a long ——** tener que esperar mucho tiempo; **to be** (*or* **lie**) **in ——** acechar (*for someone* a uno).
(b) **—s** murga *f* (de Nochebuena).
2 *vt* esperar; aplazar; guardar para después; **to —— one's chance** esperar su ocasión; **we'll —— dinner for you** no empezaremos a cenar hasta que vengas.
3 *vi* (a) esperar; aguardar; **—— a moment!** ¡un momento!, (*fig, querying*) ¡oiga!; **—— and see!** espera y verás; **"repairs while you ——"** "reparaciones en el acto", "reparaciones instantáneas"; **—— till you're asked** espera hasta que te inviten; **—— till you're older** eso es para cuando seas algo mayor; **to keep someone ——ing** hacer que uno espere, hacer esperar a uno; **to —— about** esperar, perder el tiempo; **to —— for someone** esperar a uno, (*in ambush*) acechar a uno; **to —— for someone to do something** esperar hasta que uno haga algo; **we are ——ing for you to decide** estamos pendientes de la decisión de Vd; **to —— up** velar, no acostarse, seguir sin acostarse; **don't —— up for me!** ¡idos a la cama sin esperar hasta que yo vuelva!
(b) (*as servant etc*) servir; **to —— at table** servir a la mesa; **to —— on someone** servir a uno; **to —— on someone hand and foot** atender a los menores gustos de uno, mimar a uno; **to —— upon someone** cumplimentar a uno, presentar sus respetos a uno.

waiter ['weitə*] *n* camarero *m*.

waiting ['weitiŋ] *n* (a) espera *f*; **all this ——!** ¡tanto esperar! (b) servicio *m*.

waiting list ['weitiŋ'list] *n* lista *f* de solicitudes no atendidas, lista *f* de aspirantes; **there is a long —— for housing** hay muchas solicitudes de vivienda (que no hemos podido atender).

waiting room ['weitiŋrum] *n* sala *f* de espera.

waitress ['weitris] *n* camarera *f*; **——!** ¡señorita!

waive [weiv] *vt* renunciar a.

waiver ['weivə*] *n* renuncia *f*.

wake[1] [weik] *n* (*Naut*) estela *f*; **in the —— of** (*fig*) como consecuencia de, tras, a raíz de; **wars bring misery in their ——** las guerras acarrean la miseria; **they came in the —— of the invaders** siguieron a los invasores.

wake[2] [weik] **1** *n* (*over corpse*) vela *f*, velatorio *m*.
2 (*irr: pret* **woke**, *ptp* **woken**, **waked**) *vt* despertar (*also* **to —— up**); *corpse* velar; **a noise which would —— the dead** un ruido que despertaría a un muerto.

3 *vi* despertar, despertarse *(also to — up):* — up! ¡despierta!; **she woke up with a start** despertó sobresaltada; **he woke up (to find himself) in prison** amaneció en la cárcel; **he woke up to find himself rich** a la mañana siguiente encontró que era rico; **to — up to reality** despertar a la realidad; **to — up to the truth** darse cuenta de la verdad.

wakeful ['weikful] *adj (awake)* despierto; *(alert)* vigilante; desvelado; *(unable to sleep)* insomne; **to have a — night** pasar la noche sin dormir.

wakefulness ['weikfulnis] *n* vigilancia *f*, desvelo *m*; insomnia *f*.

waken ['weikən] **1** *vt* despertar. **2** *vi* despertar, despertarse.

waker ['weikə*] *n*: **to be an early —** despertar temprano por costumbre.

waking ['weikiŋ] **1** *adj*: **in one's — hours** en las horas en que uno está despierto. **2** *n* despertar *m*; **on —** al despertar.

Wales [weilz] Gales *f*; **South — Gales** *f* del Sur.

walk [wɔːk] **1** *n* **(a)** *(spell of —ing: stroll)* paseo *m*; *(hike)* caminata *f*, excursión *f* a pie; **it's only a 10-minute — from here** ir desde aquí a pie es solo cosa de 10 minutos; **from there you have a short — to his house** desde allí a su casa se va a pie en muy poco tiempo; **to go for (or have, take) a —** dar un paseo, dar una vuelta; **to take someone for a —** llevar a uno de paseo.

(b) *(gait)* andar *m*, paso *m*; **he has an odd sort of —** tiene un modo de andar algo raro; **to know someone by (or from) his —** conocer a uno por su modo de andar; **he went at a quick —** caminó a un paso rápido.

(c) *(route)* **there's a nice — by the river** se pasea muy bien a lo largo del río, es encantador pasearse a lo largo del río; **this is my favourite —** ésta es mi ruta favorita para dar un paseo.

(d) — of life profesión *f*; esfera *f*; clase *f* social; **people from every — of life** gente *f* de toda condición.

(e) *(avenue)* paseo *m*, alameda *f*.

2 *vt* **(a)** *person* llevar a paseo, pasear; **to — someone off his legs** dejar a uno rendido tras una larguísima caminata.

(b) to — a horse llevar un caballo al paso.

(c) *(distance)* cubrir, recorrer a pie, andar; **we —ed 40 kilometres yesterday** ayer recorrimos 40 kilómetros a pie.

(d) to — the streets andar por las calles, *(aimlessly)* vagar por las calles; **to — the boards** *(Theat)* salir a escena; **to — the wards** *(Med)* hacer prácticas de clínica.

(e) to — off a headache quitarse de un dolor de cabeza a fuerza de andar; **dar una vuelta para quitarse de un dolor de cabeza**; **to — off one's lunch** bajar la comida dando un paseo.

3 *vi* **(a)** *(general sense)* andar; **can the boy — yet?** ¿sabe andar el niño ya?; **— a little with me** ven a acompañarme un poco; **to — in one's sleep** ser sonámbulo, pasearse dormido; **to — slowly** andar despacio.

(b) *(not ride)* andar, ir a pie; *(stroll)* pasearse; **we had to —** tuvimos que ir andando; **to — home** ir andando hasta casa; **you can — there in 5 minutes** en 5 minutos se va allá andando; **we were out —ing** nos estábamos paseando.

(c) *(of ghost)* andar, aparecer.

(d) *(with adv or prep)* **to — about** pasearse; ir y venir; **to — away** irse, alejarse; **to — away from someone** alejarse de uno; **to — back** volverse; volver a pie, regresar a pie; **to — down** bajar (a pie); **to — downstairs** bajar la escalera; **to — in** entrar; **"please — in" "entren sin llamar"; to — into food** *(fam)* devorar la comida, zampar la comida; **to — into a room** entrar en un cuarto; **to — into someone** *(fam)* atacar a uno, arremeter contra uno; **who should — in but John!** y fíjate, ¡aparece Juan!; **to — off** irse; **he —ed off angrily** se fue enfadado; **to — off with something** llevarse algo; **they —ed off with the first three prizes** coparon los tres primeros premios; **to — on** *(step on)* pisar; **to — out** *(from conference)* salir, retirarse *(of* de); *(on strike)* declararse en huelga; **you can't — out now!** ¡no podéis abandonar ahora!; **to — out on a girl** dejar plantada a una chica, plantar a una chica; **to — out with a boy** salir con un chico; **to — over** *(Sport)* ganar la carrera por ser el único caballo *(etc)* que participa; **to — all over someone** *(fig)* tratar a uno con el mayor desprecio; **she lets him — all over her** permite que él la trate malísimamente sin protestar; **to — up** subir (a pie); **to — upstairs** subir la escalera; **to — up to someone** acercarse a

uno, abordar a uno; **to — up and down** pasearse de acá para allá.

walker ['wɔːkə*] *n (stroller)* paseante *mf*; *(not rider)* peatón *m*; *(Sport)* andarín *m*; *(baby —)* pollera *f*; **to be a great —** ser gran andarín; ser aficionado a las excursiones a pie.

walker-on ['wɔːkər'ɒn] *n (Theat)* figurante *m*, a *f*.

walkie-talkie ['wɔːki'tɔːki] *n* transmisor-receptor *m* portátil.

walking ['wɔːkiŋ] **1** *adj* ambulante; *race* pedestre; **at a — pace** a paso de andadura; **— tour** viaje *m* a pie, excursión *f* a pie; **it's within — distance** se puede ir allí andando; **he's a — encyclopaedia** es una enciclopedia ambulante.

walking stick ['wɔːkiŋstik] *n* bastón *m*.

walk-on ['wɔːkɒn] *adj (Theat etc):* **— part** papel *m* de figurante.

walkout ['wɔːkaut] *n (from conference)* salida *f*, retirada *f*; *(strike)* huelga *f*.

walkover ['wɔːk,əuvə*] *n (Sport)* walkover *m*; *(fig)* triunfo *m* fácil.

walk-ups ['wɔːkʌps] *npl* pisos *mpl* sin ascensor.

wall [wɔːl] **1** *n* muro *m*; *(interior, Anat etc)* pared *f*; *(city —)* muralla *f*; *(garden —)* tapia *f*; **containing — muro** *m* de contención; **partition — tabique** *m*; **party — pared** *f* medianera; **a high tariff — una alta barrera arancelaria; the Great W— of China la Gran Muralla China; the north — of the Eiger** la pared norte del Eiger; **to come up against a blank — (fig)** tener por delante una barrera infranqueable; **it drives me up the — (fam)** me vuelve loco, me hace subir por las paredes; **to go to the — ser** desechado por inútil; **— have ears** las paredes oyen.

2 *attr map etc* de pared, mural.

3 *vt* murar; cerrar con muro *(also to — in)*; *city* amurallar; *garden* tapiar, cercar con tapia; **to — up person** emparedar; *opening* cerrar con muro, tabicar.

wallaby ['wɒləbi] *n* ualabí *m*.

wallah ['wɒlə] *n (fam)* hombre *m*; *(pej)* tío *m*, sujeto *m*; **the ice-cream —** el hombre de los helados; **the — with the beard** él de la barba.

wallboard ['wɔːlbɔːd] *n (US)* cartón *m* de yeso.

wall clock ['wɔːlklɒk] *n* reloj *m* de pared.

walled [wɔːld] *adj city* amurallado; *garden* con tapia.

wallet ['wɒlit] *n* cartera *f*.

wall-eyed ['wɔːl'aid] *adj* de ojos incoloros; de ojos desviados hacia fuera.

wallflower ['wɔːl,flauə*] *n* alhelí *m*; **to be a — (fig)** comer pavo.

wall fruit ['wɔːlfruːt] *n* fruta *f* de espalera.

wall map ['wɔːlmæp] *n* mapa *m* mural.

Walloon [wɒ'luːn] **1** *adj* valón. **2** *n* valón *m*, ona *f*.

wallop ['wɒləp] **1** *n* **(a)** *(blow: fam)* golpe *m*, golpazo *m*; **—! ¡zas!; to give someone a —** pegar a uno.

(b) *(speed: fam)* velocidad *f*; **to go at a fair —** correr rápidamente.

(c) *(beer: sl)* cerveza *f*.

2 *vt (fam)* golpear fuertemente; *(punish)* zurrar.

walloping ['wɒləpiŋ] **1** *adj (fam)* colosal, grandote. **2** *n* zurra *f*, paliza *f*; **to give someone a —** dar una paliza a uno *(also fig)*.

wallow ['wɒləu] *vi* revolcarse *(in* en); **to — in money** nadar en la opulencia; **to — in vices** revolcarse en los vicios.

wall painting ['wɔːl,peintiŋ] *n* pintura *f* mural.

wallpaper ['wɔːl,peipə*] *n* papel *m* pintado, papel *m* de paredes.

wall socket ['wɔːl,sɒkit] *n* enchufe *m* de pared.

walnut ['wɔːlnʌt] *n (nut)* nuez *f*; *(tree, wood)* nogal *m*.

walnut tree ['wɔːlnʌttriː] *n* nogal *m*.

walrus ['wɔːlrəs] *n* morsa *f*.

Walter ['wɔːltə*] *m* Gualterio.

waltz [wɔːlts] **1** *n* vals *m*. **2** *vi* valsar.

wan [wɒn] *adj* pálido, macilento; *(sad)* triste.

wand [wɒnd] *n (of office)* vara *f*; **magic — varilla** *f* de virtudes.

wander ['wɒndə*] **1** *vt* vagar por, recorrer; **to — the streets** vagar por las calles, pasearse por las calles; **to — the world** ir por el mundo.

2 *vi* vagar, errar; pasearse sin propósito fijo; *(get lost)* extraviarse; **to — about, to — aimlessly** deambular; **to — (in one's mind)** divagar, delirar; **to — from the path** desviarse (sin darse cuenta) del camino; **to — from the point** salirse del tema; **to — off** irse (distraído); **the children —ed off into the woods** los niños se alejaron y entraron casi sin darse cuenta en el bosque; **his speech —ed on and on** continuó incansable su discurso tan confuso; **to — round a shop** curiosear en una tienda; **to let one's mind —** dejar que la imaginación fantasee.

wanderer ['wɒndərə*] *n* hombre *m* errante, mujer *f* errante; *(traveller)* viajero *m*, a *f*; *(pej)* vagabundo m, a f; (tribesman etc) nómada mf; **I've always been a** — nunca he querido establecerme de fijo en un sitio.

wandering ['wɔndəriŋ] adj errante, errabundo; salesman etc ambulante; tribesman nómada; mind, thoughts distraído.

wanderings ['wɔndəriŋz] npl viajes mpl; errabundeo m; (pej) vagabundeo m; (Med) delirio m.

wanderlust ['wɔndəlʌst] n pasión f de viajar, ansia f de ver mundo.

wane [wein] 1 n: **to be on the** — menguar, estar menguando; (fig) decaer, menguar, disminuir; declinar, estar en decadencia. 2 vi = **to be on the** —.

wangle ['wæŋgl] (fam) 1 n chanchullo m, trampa f, truco m; **it's a** — aquí hay trampa; **he got in by a** — fue admitido gracias a un truco.

2 vt job etc mamarse, agenciarse; **he** —**d his way in** logró entrar gracias a un truco; **he'll** — **it for you** él te lo procurará por el sistema que él se sabe; **can you** — **me a free ticket?** ¿puedes procurarme una entrada de favor?

wangler ['wæŋglə*] n (fam) chanchullero m, trapisondista m.

wangling ['wæŋgliŋ] n chanchullos mpl, trampas fpl; **there's a lot of** — **goes on** hay muchas trampas.

waning ['weiniŋ] 1 adj moon ¦menguante; (fig) decadente. 2 n (of moon) menguante f; (fig) mengua f; disminución f; decadencia f.

wanly ['wɔnli] adv pálidamente; (sadly) tristemente.

wanness ['wɔnnis] n palidez f.

want [wɔnt] 1 n (a) (lack) falta f; ausencia f; (shortage) carencia f, escasez f; — **of judgement** falta f de juicio; **for** — **of** por falta de; **for** — **of anything better** por falta de algo mejor; **for** — **of something to do** por no tener nada que hacer; **to feel the** — **of** sentir la falta de.

(b) (poverty) miseria f, pobreza f, indigencia f; **to be in** — estar necesitado.

(c) (need) necesidad f; **my** —**s are few** necesito poco; **to be in** — **of** necesitar; **to attend to someone's** —**s** atender a las necesidades de uno; **it fills a long-felt** — viene a llenar un vacío hace tiempo sentido; — **ad** (US fam) anuncio m clasificado.

2 vt (a) (need: of person) necesitar; **all I** — **is sleep** lo único que necesito es dormirme; **children** — **lots of sleep** es necesario que los niños duerman mucho tiempo; **we have all we** — tenemos todo lo que necesitamos; **you** — **to be careful** (fam) hay que tener cuidado, conviene proceder con cuidado; **what you** — **is a good hiding** (fam) no te vendría mal una paliza de las buenas; **those** —**ing a job** los que buscan trabajo; "—**ed**" (police notice) "se busca"; **the** —**ed man** el hombre buscado; "—**ed: general maid**" (advert) "necesítase criada para todo"; **he is** —**ed for murder** se le busca por asesino.

(b) (need: of thing) exigir, requerir; **it** —**s some doing** exige mucho esfuerzo (etc) hacerlo; **that work** —**s a lot of time** ese trabajo exige mucho tiempo; **does my hair** — **cutting?** ¿me hace falta cortar el pelo?; **the house will** — **painting next year** el año que viene será necesario pintar la casa.

(c) (wish) querer, desear; **she knows what she** —**s** sabe lo que quiere; **I** — **to see the manager!** ¡quiero ver al gerente!; **to** — **someone to do something** querer que uno haga algo; **I** — **him sent away at once** quiero que se le despida en seguida; **I was** —**ing to leave** estaba deseando marcharme; **what does he** — **with me?** ¿qué quiere decirme?, ¿qué tiene que ver conmigo?; **he** —**s £20 for the picture** pide 20 libras por el cuadro; **you don't** — **much** (iro) ¡eso no es mucho pedir!; **you're** —**ed on the 'phone** le llaman al teléfono.

(d) (lack) carecer de; **he** —**s talent** carece de talento; **he** —**s enterprise** le falta iniciativa; **it** —**s 2 for a complete set** faltan 2 para hacer una serie completa.

3 vi: **to** — **for** necesitar, carecer de; **they** — **for nothing** no carecen de nada, lo tienen todo; **it** —**ed only this last step to** + infin sólo hacía falta que se diese este último paso para + infin.

wanting ['wɔntiŋ] adj defectuoso; deficiente (in en), falto (in de); **charity is** — **in the novel** a la novela le falta caridad, la novela es deficiente en caridad; **there is something** — falta algo; **he is** —**ing in enterprise** le falta iniciativa, está falto de iniciativa; **he was tried and found** — se le sometió a la prueba y resultó que le faltaban las cualidades indispensables.

wanton ['wɔntən] 1 adj (a) (playful) juguetón; (wayward) travieso; caprichoso; (unrestrained) desenfrenado; (licentious) lascivo.

(b) (motiveless) sin motivo, inmotivado; destruction sin propósito, sin sentido; cruelty gratuito.

2 n libertino m, a f.

3 vi jugar, retozar.

wantonly ['wɔntəli] adv (a) caprichosamente; desenfrenadamente; lascivamente. (b) sin motivo; sin propósito; gratuitamente.

wantonness ['wɔntənnis] n (a) lo caprichoso; desenfreno m; lascivia f. (b) falta f de motivo; lo gratuito.

war [wɔ:*] 1 n guerra f; **cold** — guerra f fría; **hot** —, **shooting** — guerra f a tiros; — **of nerves** guerra f de nervios; — **of words** guerra f de propaganda; — **to the knife** guerra f a muerte; **Great W**— (1914-18) Primera Guerra f Mundial; **Second World W**— (1939-45) Segunda Guerra f Mundial; **the period between the** —**s** (1918-39) el período de entreguerras; **to be at** — estar en guerra (with con); **to declare** — declarar la guerra (on a); **to go to** — emprender la guerra; hacer la guerra; **we shall not go to** — **over the Slobodian question** no emprenderemos la guerra por la cuestión de Eslobodia; **they went to** — **singing** fueron a la guerra cantando; **to make** — hacer la guerra (on a).

2 attr (in most senses) de guerra; effort, material bélico; memorial a los caídos; **W**— **Office** (Brit), **W**— **Department** (US) Ministerio m de Guerra.

3 vi (lit) guerrear (on con).

warble ['wɔ:bl] 1 n trino m, gorjeo m. 2 vt song etc cantar en voz atiplada. 3 vi trinar, gorjear.

warbler ['wɔ:blə*] n mosquitero m, curruca f.

war correspondent ['wɔ:ˌkɔris'pɔndənt] n corresponsal m de guerra.

war crime ['wɔ:kraim] n crimen m de guerra.

war cry ['wɔ:krai] n grito m de guerra.

ward ['wɔ:d] 1 n (a) (—ship) tutela f, custodia f; **in** — bajo tutela.

(b) (person) pupilo m, a f; — **of court** persona f bajo la protección del tribunal.

(c) (Pol) distrito m electoral.

(d) (of hospital) sala f, crujía f; "**W**— **7**" "Sala 7"; **to walk the** —**s** hacer práctica de clínica; **casual** — asilo m para pobres, asilo m para vagabundos.

(e) (of key) guarda f.

2 vt: **to** — **off** blow desviar, parar; danger evitar; attack rechazar, defenderse contra.

-**ward(s)** [wəd(z)] in compounds hacia, eg **townward(s)** hacia la ciudad; **pubward(s)** hacia la taberna.

war dance ['wɔ:dɑ:ns] n danza f guerrera.

war debt ['wɔ:det] n deuda f de guerra.

warden ['wɔ:dn] n guardián m; (Univ etc) director m; (of castle etc) alcaide m.

warder ['wɔ:də*] n guardián m, vigilante m, carcelero m.

ward heeler ['wɔ:d'hi:lə*] n (US Pol) muñidor m.

wardress ['wɔ:dris] n guardiana f.

wardrobe ['wɔ:drəub] n (clothes) vestidos mpl, trajes mpl; (Theat) vestuario m; (cupboard) guardarropa m, armario m (ropero).

wardrobe dealer ['wɔ:drəub,di:lə*] n ropavejero m.

wardrobe mistress ['wɔ:drəub,mistris] n encargada f de vestuario.

wardrobe trunk ['wɔ:drəubtrʌŋk] n baúl m ropero.

wardroom ['wɔ:drum] n (Naut) cuarto m de oficiales.

wardship ['wɔ:dʃip] n tutela f.

-**ware** [wɛə*] n loza f; eg **kitchenware** batería f de cocina.

warehouse ['wɛəhaus] n, pl —**houses** [ˌhauziz] almacén m, depósito m.

warehouse ['wɛəhauz] vt almacenar.

warehouseman ['wɛəhausmən] n, pl —**men** [mən] almacenista m.

wares [wɛəz] npl mercancías fpl; **to cry one's** — pregonar sus mercancías.

warfare ['wɔ:fɛə*] n guerra f; (as study) arte m militar, arte m de la guerra; **chemical** — guerra f química; **naval** — guerra f naval; **siege** — guerra f de sitio; **trench** — guerra f de trincheras.

war fever ['wɔ:ˌfi:və*] n psicosis f de guerra.

war game ['wɔ:geim] n simulacro m de guerra; juego m en que se simula la guerra, juego m de carácter militar.

war guilt ['wɔ:gilt] n responsabilidad f de la guerra.

warhead ['wɔ:hed] n (of torpedo) punta f de combate; (of rocket) cabeza f de guerra; **atomic** — cabeza f atómica.

warhorse ['wɔ:hɔ:s] n caballo m de guerra; (fig) veterano m.

warily ['wɛərili] adj con cautela, cautelosamente; **to tread** — andar con pies de plomo (also fig).

wariness ['wɛərinis] n cautela f, precaución f; recelo m.

warlike ['wɔːlaik] adj guerrero, belicoso.

war loan ['wɔːləun] n empréstito m de guerra.

war lord ['wɔːlɔːd] n jefe m militar.

warm [wɔːm] 1 adj (a) caliente (pero no con exceso); climate cálido; day, summer caluroso, de calor; blanket, clothing etc cálido; **to be** — (person) tener calor, (thing) estar caliente, (weather) hacer calor; **to be very** — (person) tener mucho calor, (thing) estar muy caliente, (weather) hacer mucho calor; **to get** — (thing) calentarse, (weather) empezar a hacer calor; **to get** — (person) entrar en calor; **I still haven't got** — todavía no he entrado en calor; **you're getting** —! (in games) ¡te quemas!; **to keep oneself** — mantener el calor del cuerpo; **to keep something** — tener algo caliente, mantener el calor de algo; **to be as** — **as toast** disfrutar de un calor agradable.

(b) (fig) scent fresco; tint cálido; thanks efusivo; heart, temperament afectuoso; dispute acalorado; greeting, welcome caluroso; applause cálido, entusiasta; supporter entusiasta; **it's** — **work** es un trabajo que hace sudar; **the book is rather** — (fam) el libro es algo verde.

2 vt calentar; heart etc alegrar, regocijar; (fam) zurrar (fam); **to** — **up** food recalentar; atmosphere etc avivar, reanimar.

3 vi (a) **to** — **up** calentarse; (Sport) hacer ejercicios (para entrar en calor); (argument) acalorarse; **things are** —**ing up** hay más actividad, hay más animación; **the game is** —**ing up** el partido se está animando.

(b) **I** (or **my heart**) —**ed to him** le fui cobrando afición; **to** — **to one's subject** entusiasmarse con su tema.

2 vr: **to** — **oneself at the fire** calentarse junto a la lumbre.

warm-blooded ['wɔːm'blʌdid] adj de sangre caliente; (fig) ardiente, apasionado.

warmed-up ['wɔːmd'ʌp] adj recalentado.

warm-hearted ['wɔːm'hɑːtid] adj bondadoso, afectuoso.

warming ['wɔːmiŋ] n (fam) zurra f (fam).

warming pan ['wɔːmiŋpæn] n calentador m (de cama).

warmly ['wɔːmli] adv (a) **the sun shone** — brillaba el sol y hacía calor.

(b) (fig) efusivamente, con efusión; afectuosamente; calurosamente; con entusiasmo; **he thanked me most** — me dio las gracias con efusión; **we welcome it** nosotros lo acogemos con entusiasmo.

warmonger ['wɔːˌmʌŋgə*] n belicista m, incendiario m de la guerra.

warmongering ['wɔːˌmʌŋgəriŋ] 1 adj belicista. 2 n belicismo m.

warmth [wɔːmθ] n (a) calor m; lo cálido, lo caluroso.

(b) (fig) efusión f; afecto m; lo caluroso; entusiasmo m; **the** — **of their greeting** su acogida calurosa; **he replied with some** — contestó bastante indignado.

warm-up ['wɔːmʌp] n (Sport) ejercicios mpl (para entrar en calor); actividad f preliminar, preparativos mpl.

warn [wɔːn] vt avisar, advertir; amonestar; prevenir; **to** — **the police** avisar a la policía; **the bell is to** — **the workmen** el timbre es para dar aviso a los obreros; — **me before you blow it up** avísame antes de volarlo; **you have been** —**ed!** Vd no podrá decir que no se le haya avisado; **to** — **someone not to do something** advertir a uno que no haga algo; **to** — **someone about something** amonestar a uno acerca de algo; **to** — **someone against someone else** prevenir a uno contra otra persona; **to** — **someone of a danger** prevenir a uno contra un peligro; **to** — **someone off** expulsar a uno; **to** — **someone off a subject** advertir a uno que no se meta en un asunto; **I** —**ed him off Espronceda** le dije que no le convenía estudiar a Espronceda.

warning ['wɔːniŋ] 1 n aviso m, advertencia f; **without** — sin dar aviso, sin previo aviso; **it fell without** — cayó de repente, cayó inesperadamente; **they came without** — vinieron sin avisarnos; **let this be a** — **to you** que esto le sirva de escarmiento; **thank you for the** — gracias por la advertencia; **the bell gives** — el timbre da la alarma; **to give someone a week's** — avisar a uno con ocho días de anticipación; **to give someone due** — avisar a uno con mucha antelación; **you were given due** — le avisamos a Vd debidamente; **I give you due** — **that** . . . le advierto en serio que . . .; **to send a** — **to the police** avisar a la policía; **to take** — **from** aprender la lección de, escarmentar en.

2 adj: — **device** dispositivo m de alarma; — **light** luz f de advertencia; — **notice** aviso m; — **shot** disparo m de aviso; — **sign** señal f admonitoria; **in a** — **tone** en tono amonestador; — **voices** voces fpl admonitorias.

warp [wɔːp] 1 n (in weaving) urdimbre f; (of wood) deformación f, alabeo m, comba f; (fig) sesgo m. 2 vt wood deformar, alabear, torcer; mind pervertir, torcer, afectar. 3 vi deformarse, alabearse, torcerse.

war paint ['wɔːpeint] n pintura f de guerra.

warpath ['wɔːpɑːθ] n: **to be on the** — estar en pie de guerra, estar preparado para la guerra; (fig) estar dispuesto a armar un lío; estar buscando pendencia.

warped [wɔːpt] adj wood deformado, torcido; character, sense of humour etc pervertido.

warping ['wɔːpiŋ] n (of wood) deformación f, alabeo m; (Aer) torsión f.

warplane ['wɔːplein] n avión m militar.

warrant ['wɔrənt] 1 n autorización f, justificación f; (certificate) cédula f, certificado m; (Comm) garantía f; (Law) mandamiento m judicial; mandato m, orden f; — **of arrest** orden f de prisión; **there is a** — **out for his arrest** se ha ordenado su detención. 2 vt autorizar, justificar; (Comm etc) garantizar; **I** —, **I** — **you** se lo aseguro; **nothing** —**s such an assumption** no hay nada que autorice tal suposición; **the facts do not** — **it** los hechos no lo justifican.

warrantable ['wɔrəntəbl] adj justificable.

warranted ['wɔrəntid] adj justificado; (Comm) garantizado.

warrant officer ['wɔrənt,ɔfisə*] n (Mil) suboficial m; (Naut) contramaestre m.

warranty ['wɔrənti] n (Comm) garantía f.

warren ['wɔrən] n madriguera f (de conejos); (fig) (house etc) conejera f, casa f con muchísimos inquilinos; casa f laberíntica; (area of town) barrio m densamente poblado; **it is a** — **of little streets** el barrio tiene muchas callejuelas estrechas, el barrio consiste en callejuelas sin ningún plano lógico.

warring ['wɔriŋ] adj interests, nations etc opuesto, en lucha abierta entre sí.

warrior ['wɔriə*] n guerrero m; **the Unknown W—** el Soldado Desconocido.

Warsaw ['wɔːsɔː] Varsovia.

warship ['wɔːʃip] n buque m de guerra, barco m de guerra.

wart [wɔːt] n (Med, Bot) verruga f.

wart hog ['wɔːthɔg] n jabalí m de verrugas.

wartime ['wɔːtaim] 1 n tiempo m de guerra; **in** — en tiempos de guerra, en la guerra. 2 attr de tiempos de guerra, de guerra.

warty ['wɔːti] adj verrugoso.

war-weary ['wɔːˌwiəri] adj cansado de la guerra.

wary ['wɛəri] adj cauteloso, cauto; **it's best to be** — **here** aquí conviene andar con pies de plomo; **I was** — **about it** tuve mis dudas acerca de ello, me recelé, desconfié de ello; **to keep a** — **eye on someone** vigilar a uno con recelo, observar a uno con recelo.

war zone ['wɔːzəun] n zona f de guerra.

was [wɔz, wəz] see **be**.

wash [wɔʃ] 1 n (a) (act of —ing) lavado m; baño m; **to give something a** — lavar algo; **to have a** — lavarse; **to have a** — **and brush-up** lavarse y arreglarse; **my shirt is at the** — mi camisa está siendo lavada, mi camisa está en la lavandería; **to send sheets to the** — mandar sábanas a la lavandería; **it will all come out in the** — todo se arreglará, no será un estorbo permanente.

(b) (clothes: dirty) ropa f sucia, ropa f para lavar; (hung to dry) tendido m, colada f; **the Monday** — la ropa para lavar el lunes.

(c) (of ship) estela f, remolinos mpl; (Aer) disturbio m aerodinámico; **the** — **of the water** (sound) el movimiento del agua, el chapoteo del agua.

(d) (liquid: hair—) champú m; (mouth—) enjuague m; (of distemper, paint) capa f; pintura f; (of insecticide etc) baño m; (liquid remains) lavazas fpl, despojos mpl líquidos; (pej) aguachirle f; **a coat of blue** — una capa de pintura azul.

2 vt (a) (clean with water etc) lavar; dishes fregar; clothes lavar; **to** — **one's hair** lavarse el pelo; **to** — **one's hands** lavarse las manos; **to** — **something clean** limpiar algo lavándolo, lavar algo hasta dejarlo limpio; **the sea** —**ed it clean of oil** el mar quitó todo el aceite y lo dejó limpio.

(b) **to** — **the walls with distemper** dar una capa de pintura (al temple) a las paredes; **to** —

a metal with gold dar una capa de oro a un metal, bañar un metal en oro.
   (c) **an island —ed by a blue sea** una isla bañada por el mar azul.
   (d) (*of river, sea; carry*) llevar, llevarse; **the house was —ed downstream** la casa fue llevada aguas abajo; **the sea —ed it ashore** el mar lo echó a la playa; **he was —ed overboard** fue arrastrado por las olas.
   (e) (*with adv or prep*) **to — dirt away** quitar la suciedad lavando; **the boat was —ed away** el bote fue arrastrado por la corriente; **the river —ed away part of the bank** el río se llevó una parte de la orilla; **to — a car down** limpiar un coche lavándolo; **to — one's dinner down with wine** regar la cena con vino; **to — off** quitar lavando, hacer desaparecer lavando; **to — out a saucepan** limpiar una cacerola lavándola; **to — out an insult** lavar un insulto; **to feel —ed out** no estar bien de salud; **to look —ed out** estar ojeroso; **the game was —ed out** el partido tuvo que ser cancelado por la lluvia; **let's — it all out** abandonémoslo todo, renunciemos a la empresa; **you can — that out for a start** conviene renunciar a esa idea desde el principio; **to — up the dishes** fregar los platos; **it was —ed up on the shore** apareció echado en la playa; **that's all —ed up** eso es un fracaso total, eso ya se acabó.
   3 *vi* (a) (*have a —*) lavarse; (*do the —ing*) lavar la ropa.
   (b) **a cloth that —es well** una tela que puede lavarse; **it's nice but it won't —** es atractivo pero no se puede lavar; **that excuse won't —!** ¡esa razón es inaceptable!
   (c) (*of sea etc*) moverse; chapotear; **the river was —ing against the top of the bridge** el río estaba a la altura de la parte alta del puente; **the sea —ed over the promenade** el mar inundó el paseo marítimo.
   (d) (*with adv or prep*) **it —es off** (*or out*) **easily** es fácil quitarlo lavando; **the colour —es out** el color se destiñe; **to — up** fregar los platos.
washable ['wɔʃəbl] *adj* lavable.
wash-and-wear ['wɔʃən'wɛə*] *adj clothing* de lava y pon.
washbasin ['wɔʃ,beisn] *n*, **washbowl** *n* ['wɔʃbəul] palangana *f*, jofaina *f*.
washboard ['wɔʃbɔːd] *n* tabla *f* de lavar.
washcloth ['wɔʃklθ] *n*, *pl* **—cloths** [klθs, klθz] (US) paño *m* para lavarse, manopla *f*.
washday ['wɔʃdei] *n* día *m* de colada.
washer ['wɔʃə*] *n* (a) (*Tech*) arandela *f*, (*on tap*) arandela *f*, zapatilla *f*. (b) (*washing machine*) lavadora *f*.
washerwoman ['wɔʃə,wumən] *n*, *pl* **—women** [,wimin] lavandera *f*.
wash house ['wɔʃhaus] *n*, *pl* **— houses** [,hauziz] lavadero *m*.
washing ['wɔʃiŋ] *n* (*act*) lavado *m*, el lavar; (*clothes: dirty*) ropa *f* sucia, ropa *f* para lavar; (*hung to dry*) tendido *m*, colada *f*; **—s** lavazas *fpl*, lavadura *f*; **to take in —** ser lavandera.
washing day ['wɔʃiŋdei] *n* día *m* de colada.
washing machine ['wɔʃiŋmə,ʃiːn] *n* lavadora *f*.
washing powder ['wɔʃiŋ,paudə*] *n* jabón *m* en polvo.
washing soda ['wɔʃiŋ,səudə] *n* carbonato *m* sódico.
washing-up ['wɔʃiŋ'ʌp] *n* (*act*) fregado *m*, el fregar (los platos); (*dishes*) platos *mpl* para lavar; platos *mpl* lavados; **he did all the —** fregó todos los platos.
wash leather ['wɔʃ,leðə*] *n* gamuza *f*.
wash-out ['wɔʃaut] *n* (*fam*): **it was a —** fue un fracaso total; **he's a —** es una calamidad (*fam*).
washrag ['wɔʃræg] *n* (US) paño *m* de cocina; = **washcloth.**
washroom ['wɔʃrum] *n* (*euph*) aseos *mpl*; urinario *m* público.
washstand ['wɔʃstænd] *n* lavabo *m*, lavamanos *m*.
washtub ['wɔʃtʌb] *n* tina *f* de lavar; (*bath*) bañera *f*.
washy ['wɔʃi] *adj* aguado, diluido; débil; (*fig*) flojo, soso.
wasn't ['wɔznt] = **was not.**
wasp [wɔsp] *n* avispa *f*.
waspish ['wɔspiʃ] *adj character* irascible; *person* de prontos enojos, fácil de enojar; *comment* mordaz, punzante.
waspishly ['wɔspiʃli] *adv* mordazmente.
wasp's nest ['wɔspsnest] *n* avispero *m*.
wasp waist ['wɔsp'weist] *n* (*fig*) talle *m* de avispa.
wasp-waisted ['wɔsp'weistid] *adj* (*fig*) con talle de avispa.

wastage ['weistidʒ] *n* desgaste *m*, desperdicio *m*; pérdida *f*; (*from container*) merma *f*; **the — of our resources** el desperdicio de nuestros recursos; **the — rate among students** la proporción de estudiantes que no obtienen su licenciatura (*etc*); **the — rate among entrants to the profession** el porcentaje de los que abandonan la profesión poco tiempo después de ingresar en ella.
waste [weist] 1 *adj* (*rejected*) desechado, de desecho; (*left over*) sobrante, superfluo; (*useless*) inútil; *land* baldío; yermo; *paper* viejo, usado; **"The W— Land"** "Tierra *f* baldía"; **to lay —** asolar, devastar; **to lie —** quedar sin cultivar; quedar sin utilizar; *see* **product** etc.
   2 *n* (a) (*act*) despilfarro *m*, derroche *m*; (*of time etc*) pérdida *f*; (*wastage*) desgaste *m*, desperdicio *m*; merma *f*; **it's a — of time** es tiempo perdido; **it's a — of effort** es un esfuerzo inútil; **there's a lot of — here** hay mucho desperdicio aquí, aquí despilfarran todo; **to go to —**, **to run to —** echarse a perder, perderse.
   (b) (*— material*) desperdicios *mpl*, desechos *mpl*; (*rubbish*) basura *f*; **cotton —** borra *f*; **metal —** metales *mpl* de desecho.
   (c) (*land*) yermo *m*, tierra *f* baldía; desierto *m*; **lost in the —s of Siberia** perdido en la inmensidad de Siberia; **to plough the —s of Siberia** cultivar la tierra baldía de Siberia.
   3 *vt* (*squander*) despilfarrar, derrochar; malgastar; *time etc* perder; (*not use*) desperdiciar; *opportunity etc* desaprovechar, desperdiciar; (*use up*) agotar, consumir; **a —d life** una vida desperdiciada; **nothing is —d** no queda nada sin aprovechar; **we —d 3 litres of petrol** usamos inútilmente 3 litros de gasolina; **you're wasting your time talking to him** es tiempo perdido hablar con él; **don't — your efforts on him** no te canses tratando de hacer cosas por él.
   4 *vi* gastarse, perderse; **to — away** consumirse, mermar; (*person*) consumirse; **you're not exactly wasting away** (*iro*) no pareces haber enflaquecido de modo peligroso, que digamos.
wastebasket ['weist,baskit] *n* (US) cesto *m* de los papeles, papelera *f*.
wasteful ['weistful] *adj person etc* pródigo, despilfarrado, derrochador; *process* antieconómico; *expenditure* pródigo, excesivo; **it is — of effort** no utiliza debidamente el esfuerzo.
wastefully ['weistfəli] *adv* pródigamente; antieconómicamente; excesivamente.
wastefulness ['weistfulnis] *n* prodigalidad *f*, despilfarro *m*; falta *f* de economía, lo antieconómico; lo excesivo.
wasteland ['weistlænd] *n* tierra *f* baldía, yermo *m*.
wastepaper basket [weist'peipə,baːskit] *n* cesto *m* de los papeles, papelera *f*.
waste pipe ['weistpaip] *n* tubo *m* de desagüe.
waster ['weistə*] *n* artículo *m* defectuoso, desecho *m*; (*person*) derrochador *m*, perdido *m*.
wastrel ['weistrəl] *n* derrochador *m*, perdido *m*.
watch [wɔtʃ] 1 *n* (a) (*vigilance*) vigilancia *f*; (*act of —ing*) vigilia *f*, vela *f*; **to be on the —** estar a la mira (*for* de), velar, vigilar; **they're on the — for smugglers** están a la mira de contrabandistas; **to keep —** estar de guardia; **to keep — all night** velar toda la noche; **to keep a close —** on something vigilar algo con mucho cuidado; **to keep — over** *person* velar, vigilar; *thing* velar por; **to set a — on** someone ordenar que se vigile a uno.
   (b) (*period of duty*) guardia *f*; **middle —**, **dog —** media guardia *f*; **to have a 4-hour —** estar de guardia durante 4 horas.
   (c) (*persons: Hist*) ronda *f*; (*Mil: persons*) guardia *f*, (1 *man*) guardia *m*, centinela *m*; (*Naut: persons*) guardia *f*, vigía *f*, (1 *man*) vigía *m*; **officer of the —** oficial *m* de guardia.
   (d) (*timepiece*) reloj *m* (de bolsillo, de pulsera); **what does your — say?** ¿qué hora tienes?
   2 *vt* (a) (*guard*) guardar, vigilar; proteger.
   (b) (*observe*) observar, mirar; (*at length*) contemplar; (*spy on*) espiar, acechar; *TV etc* ver; **did you — the programme?** ¿viste el programa?; **to — someone doing something** mirar a uno hacer algo, observar a uno hacer algo; **now — this closely** ahora observen esto con mucho cuidado; **we are being —ed** nos están observando; **have you ever —ed an operation?** ¿ha visto Vd alguna vez una operación?
   (c) (*be careful with*) ser cuidadoso con, prestar atención a, tener ojo a; **— it!** ¡ojo!, ¡cuidado!; **you'd better — it** conviene tener más cuidado; **we shall have to — the expenses** tendremos que

estudiar cuidadosamente los gastos, convendrá tener ojo a los gastos; — **how you go!** ¡anda con cuidado!; see **step** etc.
  (d) chance etc esperar, aguardar; **he —ed his chance and slipped out** esperó el momento propicio y se escabulló.
  3 vi ver, mirar; observar; (watchfully) vigilar; **to — for someone** esperar a uno, aguardar a uno; **to — for something to happen** esperar a que pase algo; **to — out** tener ojo, tener cuidado; **— out!** ¡ojo!; **— out for thieves** cuidado con los ladrones; **to — out for trouble** estar dispuesto a aguantar cualquier disturbio; **then you'd better — out!** ¡pues aténgase a las consecuencias!; **to — over someone** velar a uno; **to — over the safety of the country** velar por la seguridad de la patria; **to — over a property** vigilar una propiedad.
watchband ['wɒtʃbænd] n (US) pulsera f de reloj.
watchcase ['wɒtʃkeis] n caja f de reloj.
watchdog ['wɒtʃdɔg] n perro m guardián.
watcher ['wɒtʃə*] n observador m, ora f; espectador m, ora f; (pej) mirón m, ona f.
watchful ['wɒtʃful] adj vigilante; observador; (esp fig) desvelado.
watchfully ['wɒtʃfəli] adv vigilantemente.
watchfulness ['wɒtʃfulnis] n vigilancia f; desvelo m.
watch glass ['wɒtʃglɑːs] n cristal m de reloj.
watchmaker ['wɒtʃ,meikə*] n relojero m; **—'s (shop)** relojería f.
watchman ['wɒtʃmən] n, pl **—men** [mən] guardián m; (night —: in street, flats) sereno m, (in factory etc) vigilante m, nocturno.
watch strap ['wɒtʃstræp] n pulsera f de reloj.
watchtower ['wɒtʃ,tauə*] n atalaya f, vigía f.
watchword ['wɒtʃwəːd] n (Mil etc) santo m y seña; (motto) lema m, consigna f.
water ['wɔːtə*] **1** n (a) agua f; **boiling —** agua f hirviendo; **cold —** agua f fría; **distilled —** agua f destilada; **fresh —** agua f dulce; **hard —** agua f dura; **heavy —** agua f pesada; **holy —** agua f bendita; **hot —** agua f caliente; **running —** agua f corriente; **salt —** agua f salada; **soft —** agua f blanda; **like — (fig)** como agua, pródigamente, en abundancia; **the square is under —** la plaza está inundada; **much — has flowed under the bridges** ya ha llovido desde entonces; **to get into hot —** cargársela (for, over en el asunto de); **to hold —** retener el agua, (fig) estar bien fundado, ser lógico; **that excuse won't hold —** esa excusa no vale; **to pour cold — on an idea** echar un jarro de agua fría a una idea; **to take on — (Rail)** tomar agua; **to turn on the —** hacer correr el agua; (from tap) abrir el grifo; **still —s run deep** la procesión va por dentro.
  (b) (urine) orina f, orines mpl; **to make —** hacer aguas, mear.
  (c) **—s** (Med) aguas fpl; **to drink (or take) the —s at Harrogate** tomar las aguas en Harrogate.
  (d) (of sea etc) agua f; **the —s of the Ebro** las aguas del Ebro; **high —** pleamar f, marea f alta; **low —** bajamar f, marea f baja; **slack —** repunte m de la marea; **home —s** aguas fpl cerca de la patria; **territorial —s** aguas fpl jurisdiccionales, aguas fpl territoriales; **by —** por mar; **on land and —** por tierra y por mar; **to back —** (Naut) ciar; **to fish in troubled —s** pescar en río revuelto; **to get into deep —(s)** meterse en honduras; **to tread —** mantenerse a flote pataleando en el agua.
  (e) (Med) **— on the brain** hidrocefalía f; **— on the knee** derrame m sinovial.
  (f) **of the first —** de lo mejor, de primerísima calidad.
  2 adj, attr acuático; de agua; para agua; **— supply** abastecimiento m de agua; **— plants** plantas fpl acuáticas.
  3 vt garden, plant regar; horses abrevar; wine aguar; diluir; (moisten) mojar, humedecer; **to — a plant with an insecticide** regar (or rociar) una planta con insecticida; **the river —s the provinces of . . .** el río riega las provincias de . . .; **to — capital** (Fin) emitir un número excesivo de acciones; **to — down** aguar; diluir; (fig) mitigar; suavizar; **I should — the abuse down a bit** conviene suavizar un poco las injurias.
  4 vi (of eyes) hacerse agua, lagrimear, llorar; **my mouth —ed** se me hizo la boca agua; **it's enough to make your mouth —** se hace la boca agua.
water bird ['wɔːtəbəːd] n ave f acuática.
waterborne ['wɔːtəbɔːn] adj llevado por barco (etc).
water bottle ['wɔːtə,bɒtl] n cantimplora f.
water carrier ['wɔːtə,kæriə*] n aguador m.
water cart ['wɔːtəkɑːt] n cuba f de riego, carro m aljibe; (motorized) camión m de agua.

water closet ['wɔːtə,klɒzit] n (freq abbreviated WC) wáter m, inodoro m.
watercolour, (US) **watercolor** ['wɔːtə,kʌlə*] n acuarela f.
watercolourist, (US) **—colorist** ['wɔːtə,kʌlərist] n acuarelista mf.
water-cooled ['wɔːtəkuːld] adj refrigerado por agua.
water-cooling ['wɔːtəkuːliŋ] n refrigeración f por agua.
watercourse ['wɔːtəkɔːs] n (stream) arroyo m; (bed) lecho m, cauce m; (dried) torrentera f.
watercress ['wɔːtəkres] n berro m, mastuerzo m.
water diviner ['wɔːtədi,vainə*] n zahorí m.
water divining ['wɔːtədi,vainiŋ] n arte m del zahorí.
waterfall ['wɔːtəfɔːl] n cascada f, salto m de agua.
water fountain ['wɔːtə'fauntin] n (US) surtidor m de agua, fuente f.
waterfowl ['wɔːtəfaul] npl aves fpl acuáticas.
waterfront ['wɔːtəfrʌnt] n (esp US) terreno m ribereño; (harbour area) puerto m, muelles mpl, dársenas fpl.
water hole ['wɔːtəhəul] n charco m.
water ice ['wɔːtərais] n sorbete m, helado m.
watering ['wɔːtəriŋ] n riego m; **frequent — is needed** hay que regar con frecuencia.
watering can ['wɔːtəriŋkæn] n regadera f.
watering place ['wɔːtəriŋpleis] n (spa) balneario m; (seaside resort) playa f, ciudad f marítima de veraneo; (Agr) abrevadero m.
water jacket ['wɔːtə,dʒækit] n camisa f de agua.
waterless ['wɔːtəlis] adj sin agua, árido.
water level ['wɔːtə,levl] n nivel m del agua; (Naut) línea f de agua.
water lily ['wɔːtə,lili] n nenúfar m.
waterline ['wɔːtəlain] n línea f de flotación.
waterlogged ['wɔːtəlɒgd] adj ground etc anegado, inundado; wood etc empapado; **to get —** anegarse; empaparse.
Waterloo [,wɔːtə'luː] Waterloo (1815); **to meet one's —** llegar hasta el desastre.
waterman ['wɔːtəmən] n, pl **—men** [mən] barquero m.
watermark ['wɔːtəmɑːk] n filigrana f.
water meadow ['wɔːtə,medəu] n vega f.
watermelon ['wɔːtə,melən] n sandía f.
water mill ['wɔːtəmil] n molino m de agua.
water pipe ['wɔːtəpaip] n caño m de agua.
water polo ['wɔːtə'pəuləu] n polo m acuático, water-polo m.
water power ['wɔːtə,pauə*] n fuerza f hidráulica.
waterproof ['wɔːtəpruːf] **1** adj impermeable. **2** n impermeable m. **3** vt impermeabilizar.
water pump ['wɔːtəpʌmp] n bomba f de agua.
water rat ['wɔːtəræt] n rata f de agua.
water rate ['wɔːtəreit] n tarifa f de agua.
watershed ['wɔːtəʃed] n (Geog) línea f divisoria de las aguas; cuenca f; (fig) división f, línea f divisoria; **the — of the Duero** la cuenca del Duero.
waterside ['wɔːtəsaid] **1** n orilla f del agua, ribera f. **2** attr ribereño; situado en la orilla.
water-ski ['wɔːtəski] vi practicar el esquí acuático.
water-skiing ['wɔːtə,skiːiŋ] n esquí m acuático.
waterspout ['wɔːtəspaut] n tromba f marina.
water table ['wɔːtə,teibl] n nivel m del subsuelo acuífero.
water tank ['wɔːtətæŋk] n cisterna f, depósito m de agua; aljibe m.
watertight ['wɔːtətait] adj compartment etc estanco; hermético; (fig) irrecusable, completamente lógico.
water tower ['wɔːtə,tauə*] n arca f de agua, alcubilla f.
water vapour ['wɔːtə,veipə*] n vapor m de agua.
waterway ['wɔːtəwei] n vía f fluvial; (inland —) canal m, canal m navegable.
waterwheel ['wɔːtəwiːl] n rueda f hidráulica; (Agr) noria f.
water wings ['wɔːtəwiŋz] npl nadaderas fpl, flotadores mpl.
waterworks ['wɔːtəwəːks] n central f depuradora.
watery ['wɔːtəri] adj substance acuoso; (wet) húmedo, mojado; eye lagrimoso; sky que amenaza lluvia, lluvioso; soup, wine débil, flojo.
watt [wɒt] n vatio m.
wattage ['wɒtidʒ] n vatiaje m.
wattle[1] ['wɒtl] n zarzo m.
wattle[2] ['wɒtl] n (Orn) barba f.
wave [weiv] **1** n (a) (of water) ola f.
  (b) (Phys, Radio) onda f; **long —** onda f larga; **medium —** onda f media; **short —** onda f corta.
  (c) (in hair, on surface) ondulación f; **permanent —** ondulación f permanente.
  (d) (fig) oleada f; **— of enthusiasm** oleada f de entusiasmo; **— of panic** oleada f de pánico; **— of**

strikes oleada *f* de huelgas; **cold —** oleada *f* de frío; **the first — of the attack** la primera oleada de asalto; **the attackers came in —s** las tropas atacaron en oleadas.

(e) (*movement of hand*) movimiento *m*, ademán *m* (de la mano), señal *f* (hecha con la mano); **with a — of his hand** con un movimiento de la mano, haciendo una señal con la mano; **with a — he was gone** hizo una señal con la mano y desapareció.

2 *vt* **(a)** (*brandish*) agitar, (*threateningly*) blandir; *flag etc* ondear, agitar; **don't — it about!** ¡no lo agites!; **he —d the ticket under my nose** agitó el billete en mis narices; **to — one's hand to someone** hacer una señal a uno con la mano; **to — one's arms about** agitar mucho los brazos; **to — someone goodbye** decir adiós a uno con la mano; **to — a handkerchief to someone** agitar el pañuelo para dar una señal a uno; **he —ed a greeting to the crowd** saludó a la multitud con un movimiento de la mano; **to — an offer aside** rechazar una oferta; **to — someone aside** hacer una señal a uno para que se aparte; **he —d my help aside** indicó con un movimiento de la mano que no necesitaba mi ayuda; **to — a car down** hacer señales a un coche para que se detenga; **to — someone on** hacer señales a uno para que avance.

(b) *hair etc* ondular; **to have one's hair —d** hacerse ondular el pelo, hacerse una permanente.

3 *vi* **(a)** (*person*) hacer señales con la mano, agitar el brazo; **to — to someone** hacer señales con la mano a uno; **we —d as the train drew out** cuando partió el tren nos dijimos adiós con la mano.

(b) (*of flag etc*) ondear; flotar; (*of arm etc*) agitarse.

waveband ['weivbænd] *n* banda *f* de ondas; **long —** banda *f* de onda larga.

wavelength ['weivleŋθ] *n* longitud *f* de onda.

wavelet ['weivlit] *n* pequeña ola *f*, rizo *m*.

waver ['weivə*] *vi* (*oscillate*) oscilar (*between* entre); (*hesitate*) vacilar; (*weaken*) flaquear; **I —ed for some days** durante varios días no me resolví; **he's beginning to —** está empezando a vacilar.

wave range ['weivreindʒ] *n* (*Radio*) gama *f* de ondas.

waverer ['weivərə*] *n* irresoluto *m*, a *f*.

wavering ['weivəriŋ] **1** *adj* irresoluto, vacilante. **2** *n* oscilación *f*; vacilación *f*, irresolución *f*.

wavy ['weivi] *adj* *hair, surface* ondulado; *motion* ondulante.

wax¹ [wæks] **1** *n* cera *f*; (*in ear*) cerilla *f*. **2** *adj* de cera. **3** *vt* encerar.

wax² [wæks] *vi* (*moon*) crecer; (*with adj*) ponerse, hacerse; **to — enthusiastic** entusiasmarse; **to — talkative** empezar a hablar mucho.

waxed [wækst] *adj* *paper etc* encerado.

wax(ed) paper ['wæks(t)'peipə*] *n* papel *m* encerado.

waxen ['wæksən] *adj* (*of wax*) de cera; (*like wax*) ceroso, parecido a cera; como cera; de color de cera.

waxing ['wæksiŋ] **1** *adj* *moon* creciente. **2** *n* crecimiento *m*.

waxwork ['wækswə:k] *n* figura *f* de cera; **—s** museo *m* de (figuras de) cera.

waxy ['wæksi] *adj* = **waxen**.

way [wei] **1** *n* **(a)** (*road*) camino *m*, vía *f*; carretera *f*; calle *f*; **W— of the Cross** Vía *f* Crucis; **permanent — ** (*Rail*) vía *f*; **the public —** la vía pública; **across the —,** **over the —** enfrente (*from* de); **by — of** vía, por vía de; pasando por.

(b) (*route*) camino *m*, ruta *f* (*to* de); **the — to the station** el camino de la estación; **which is the — to the town hall, please?** por favor, ¿qué camino tomo para ir al Ayuntamiento?; **this isn't the — to Lugo!** ¡por aquí no se va a Lugo!; **the — is hard** el camino es duro; **the — of virtue** el camino de la virtud; **to go the shortest —** ir por el camino más corto; **to go the — of all things** padecer la suerte de todas las cosas; **to lead the —** ir primero, (*fig*) dar el ejemplo, mostrar el camino; **to prepare the —** preparar el terreno (*for* a, para); **on the —** en el camino; durante el viaje; **on the — here** mientras veníamos aquí; **on the — to Aranjuez** camino de Aranjuez; **it's on the — to Murcia** está en la carretera de Murcia; **you pass it on your — home** al ir a casa pasas delante de él; **an out-of-the-— place** un lugar apartado, un lugar remoto; **an out-of-the-— subject** un tema insólito, un tema poco conocido, un tema original; **her painting is nothing out of the —** su pintura no tiene nada de particular; **to go out of one's —** desviarse del camino; **to go out of one's — to +** *infin* (*fig*) tomarse la molestia de + *infin*; desvivirse por + *infin*.

(c) (*route, with adv*) — **down** ruta *f* para bajar; **— in** entrada *f*; **"— in"** "entrada"; **Spain's — into the United Nations** el camino que siguió España para ingresar en las Naciones Unidas; **to find a —** in encontrar un modo de entrar; — **out** salida *f*; **"— out"** "salida"; **you'll find it on the — out** lo encontrarás cerca de la salida; **it's on its — out** está en camino de desaparecer, ya está pasando de moda; **there's no — out** (*fig*) no hay solución, esto no tiene solución; **there's no other — out** (*fig*) no hay más remedio; — **through** paso *m*; **"no — through"** "cerrado el paso"; — **up** ruta *f* para subir.

(d) (*route, with personal associations*) **to ask one's —** preguntar por el camino; **to feel one's —** andar a tientas, (*fig*) proceder con tiento; **to find one's — into a building** encontrarse un modo de entrar en un edificio; **the cat found the — into the pantry** el gato logró introducirse en la despensa; **can you find your — home?** ¿sabes por dónde ir a tu casa?; **to go the wrong —** equivocarse de camino; **to go one's own —** (*fig*) ir a la suya; hacer rancho aparte; **I know my — about town** conozco el plano de la ciudad; **she knows her — about** (*fig*) tiene bastante experiencia; no es que sea una inocente; **to lose one's —** extraviarse, errar el camino; **to make one's — to** dirigirse a; **to make one's — home** ir a casa, volver a casa; **to make one's — through a crowd** abrirse camino entre una multitud; **to make one's — in the world** hacer progresos en su profesión, hacerse una carrera; valerse por sí mismo; **he had to make his own — in the art world** tuvo que introducirse por sus propios medios en el mundo del arte; **to pay one's —** (*as fare*) pagar su billete; (*in restaurant*) pagar su parte; (*Fin*) ser solvente; **the company isn't paying its —** la compañía tiene un saldo negativo; **Britain must pay her —** Gran Bretaña ha de lograr la solvencia; **to see one's — to +** *ger or infin* ver la forma de + *infin*; **could you possibly see your — to +** *infin*? ¿sería Vd tan amable como para + *infin*?; **to start on one's —** ponerse en camino; **to work one's — up a rock** escalar a duras penas una roca, escalar poco a poco una roca; **to work one's — to the front** abrirse camino hacia la primera fila (*etc*); **he worked his — up in the company** a fuerza de trabajar llegó a ocupar un alto puesto en la sociedad; logró ser ascendido en la sociedad gracias a sus esfuerzos personales; **he worked his — up from nothing** empezó sin nada y fue muy lejos por sus méritos personales.

(e) (*path*) camino *m*, vía *f*; **the middle —** el camino de en medio; **to be in someone's —** estorbar a uno; **am I in the —?** ¿estorbo?; **to get in the —** estorbar; **to get in one another's —** estorbarse uno a otro; **to put difficulties in someone's —** crear dificultades a uno; **to stand in someone's —** estorbar; **now nothing stands in our —** ahora no hay obstáculo alguno; **his age stands in his —** su edad es una desventaja para él; **to stand in the — of progress** estorbar el progreso, ser un estorbo para el progreso; **out of my —!** ¡quítese allá!; **it's out of the — of the wind** está al abrigo del viento; **to get out of the —** quitarse de en medio; **to get something out of the —** quitar algo de en medio; **to get someone out of the —** (*fig*) quitar a uno de en medio; **as soon as I've got my exams out of the —** en cuanto esté libre de exámenes; **one should keep matches out of the — of children** conviene no poner las cerillas al alcance de los niños; **I kept well out of the —** me mantuve muy lejos; **I try to keep out of his —** procuro evitar cualquier contacto con él; **he wants his wife out of the —** quiere deshacerse de su mujer; **to bar the —,** **to block the —** cerrar el paso; **to clear a — for** abrir camino para; **to clear the —** despejar el camino; **to fight one's — out** lograr salir luchando; **to fight one's — to the sea** abrirse paso luchando hacia el mar; **to force one's — through** abrirse paso luchando; **to force one's — in** introducirse a la fuerza; **to hack one's — through something** abrirse paso por algo a fuerza de tajos; **to leave the — open for further talks** dejar la vía libre para otra conferencia; **to leave the — open to abuse** dejar vía libre al desafuero; **make —!** ¡calle!; **to make —** hacer lugar (*for* para).

(f) (*distance*) distancia *f*; trayecto *m*, recorrido *m*; **there are flowers all the —** por todo el recorrido hay flores; **it rained all the —** there durante todo el viaje llovió; **I was sick part of the —** me mareé durante una parte del viaje; **a little — away,** **a little — off** no muy lejos, a poca distancia; **a long**

— away, a long — off muy lejos, a gran distancia; a lo lejos; it's a long (or good) — es mucho camino; it's a long — from here está muy lejos de aquí; you're a long — out Vd se ha extraviado bastante, (fig) Vd está muy lejos de acertar; to go the long — round ir por rodeos; he'll go a long — irá lejos; we have a long — to go tenemos mucho camino por delante; it should go a long — towards + ger ha de contribuir mucho a + infin; a little help goes a long — un poco de ayuda puede ser muy valioso; better by a long — mejor con mucho; not by a long — ni con mucho; a short — off no muy lejos, a poca distancia.

(g) (direction) dirección f, sentido m; this — por aquí; "this — for the lions" "a los leones"; this — and that por aquí y por allá, en todas direcciones; down our — en nuestro barrio; en nuestra región; allí donde vivimos nosotros; it's out Windsor — está en la región de Windsor, está cerca de Windsor; está en la carretera de Windsor; which — are you going? ¿adónde vas?; which — did it go? ¿hacia dónde fue?; which — do we go from here? ¿en qué dirección continuamos desde aquí?; which — is the wind blowing? ¿de dónde sopla el viento?; she didn't know which — to look no sabía adónde poner los ojos; to look the other — (fig) hacer la vista gorda; no darse por aludido; it doesn't matter to me one — or the other me es igual, no me importa que sea lo uno o lo otro; it doesn't often come my — para mí es una oportunidad poco frecuente; if the chance comes your — si tienes la oportunidad, si la suerte te favorece; are you going my —? ¿vas por donde voy yo?

(h) (of position) it's the wrong — up está al revés, lo de abajo está arriba; put it right — up póngalo en su posición correcta; to rub an animal up the wrong — frotar a un animal a contrapelo; to rub someone up the wrong — irritar a uno, sacar a uno de quicio; they seem to rub each other up the wrong — parecen irritarse mutuamente; we'll split it 3 —s lo dividiremos en 3 partes iguales.

(i) (means) medio m; —s and means medios mpl; that's not the right — no es ése el método correcto; we'll find a — of doing it buscaremos el método de hacerlo; love will find a — el amor lo arreglará, el amor triunfará a la larga.

(j) (manner) manera f, modo m; forma f; método m, sistema m; — of life estilo m de vida; each — (Racing) ganador y colocado; this —, in this — de este modo; an odd — of talking un extraño modo de hablar; the only — of doing it la única forma de hacerlo; there are many —s of . . . hay muchas maneras de . . .; her — of looking at things su modo de ver las cosas; my — is to + infin mi sistema consiste en + infin; he has his own — of doing it tiene su sistema particular para hacerlo; that's the —! ¡así!; ¡eso es!; that's the — money goes así se gasta el dinero; the — things are tal como están las cosas; to leave things the — they are dejar las cosas donde están; the — things are going we shall have nothing left si esto continúa así nos vamos a quedar sin nada; it was this — . . . lo que pasó fue esto . . .; that's always the — with him siempre le pasa igual; there are no two —s about it no cabe otra posibilidad, no le encuentro otra posibilidad; yo lo veo perfectamente claro.

(k) (manner: phrases with in) in this — de este modo; in one — or another de algún que otro modo; in a general — this is true en general esto es verdad; without in any — wishing to + infin sin querer en lo más mínimo + infin, sin tener intención alguna de + infin; I'll do it in my own — lo haré según mi método particular; he's a good sort in his — tiene sus rarezas pero es buena persona; a pesar de todo es buena persona; they interpret it each in his own — lo interpretan cada uno a su modo; he said in his rough — dijo en ese tono suyo un poco brusco; to go on in the same old — continuar como siempre, seguir empleando los viejos métodos; to be in a small — of business tener un negocio modesto; to be in the family — estar en estado de buena esperanza; to get someone in the family — dejar a una encinta; to get oneself in the family — empreñar, hacerse una criatura.

(l) (custom) costumbre f; the —s of the Spaniards las costumbres de los españoles; the —s of good society los modales de la buena sociedad; la etiqueta de la buena sociedad; that is our — with traitors así tratamos a los traidores; he has a — with him tiene atractivo personal, es simpático; tiene mucha persuasiva; he has his little —s

tiene sus manías, tiene sus rarezas; he has a — with children maneja bien los niños, los niños le creen muy simpático; he has a — with people tiene don de gentes; the child has some pretty —s el niño hace las cosas de un modo que encanta; to mend one's —s enmendarse, reformarse; to be out of the — of + ger haber perdido la costumbre de + infin; to get out of the — of + ger perder la costumbre de + infin; to get into the — of + ger (by habit) adquirir la costumbre de + infin, (by learning) aprender el modo de + infin.

(m) (of will) to get one's (own) — salirse con la suya; hacer aceptar su opinión; they had it all their own — in the second half en el segundo tiempo hicieron lo que les dio la gana; they didn't have things all their own — no dominaron el partido (etc) completamente, su dominio no fue completo; he wants his own — all the time todo el tiempo insiste en su punto de vista, todo el tiempo insiste en hacer únicamente lo que él mismo quiere.

(n) (respect) respecto m; in a — en cierto modo, hasta cierto punto; in no — de ningún modo; in every possible — en todos los respectos; desde todos los puntos de vista; I will help in every possible — ayudaré por todos los medios a mi disposición; in many —s en muchos respectos, por muchas cosas; in some —s en ciertos modos; in a big — en grande, en gran escala; we lost in a really big — perdimos de modo realmente espectacular; in a small — en pequeña escala; we help in a small — ayudamos un poco, prestamos una modesta ayuda; he's not a plumber in the ordinary — no es de esos fontaneros corrientes; no es un fontanero de profesión; in the ordinary — we go out once a week en general salimos una vez por semana.

(o) (Naut etc) to be under — estar en marcha, (fig) estar en curso; to gather — empezar a moverse; acelerar, ir más rápidamente; to get under — (Naut) zarpar, hacerse a la vela; (Aut etc) ponerse en marcha; (of person) partir, ponerse en camino; things are getting under — at last por fin las cosas están haciendo progresos; to get a ship under — hacer navegar un barco; to give — (break) romperse; (Aut etc) ceder el paso; "give —" "ceda el paso"; to give — to the left ceder el paso a los coches que vienen de la izquierda; the radio gave — to a television set la radio cedió el paso a un televisor; you gave — too easily abandonaste demasiado pronto, te dejaste vencer demasiado fácilmente; she gave — to tears se deshizo en lágrimas; he never gives — to despair no se deja ganar en ningún momento por la desesperación.

(p) (state) estado m; things are in a bad — las cosas van mal; the car is in a bad — el coche está en mal estado; he's in a very bad — (Med) está grave, está de cuidado; he's in a fair — to succeed tiene buenas posibilades de lograrlo.

(q) (with by) by the — a propósito; entre paréntesis, de paso; by the —! ¡eh!; ¡oiga!; oh, and by the — . . . hay otra cosa . . ., antes que se me olvide . . .; all this is by the — todo esto está un poco al margen, todo esto está entre paréntesis; by — of an answer a título de respuesta; by — of a warning a modo de advertencia; he's by — of being a painter es algo a modo de pintor, tiene sus ribetes de pintor.

2 adv (fam): — back in 1900 allá en 1900; that was — back eso fue hace mucho tiempo ya.

waybill ['weibil] n hoja f de ruta.

wayfarer ['wei,fɛərə*] n caminante mf; viajero m, a f.

wayfaring tree ['weifɛəriŋ,tri:] n viburno m.

waylay [wei'lei] (irr: see lay) vt acechar; salir al paso a; detener; they were waylaid by thieves les atacaron unos ladrones; I was waylaid by the manager me detuvo el gerente.

way-out ['wei'aut] 1 adv: it's — in Nevada está muy lejos en Nevada, está en una región remota de Nevada. 2 adj (fam) ultramoderno, revolucionario, nueva ola.

wayside ['weisaid] 1 n borde m del camino, borde m de la carretera; by the — al borde de la carretera. 2 attr del borde del camino; inn etc de camino, de carretera; flower silvestre.

wayward ['weiwəd] adj (self-willed) voluntarioso; (naughty) travieso; rebelde; (capricious) caprichoso; (freakish) caprichoso, variable, inexplicable.

waywardness ['weiwədnis] n voluntariedad f; travesura f; rebeldía f; lo caprichoso; variabilidad f.

we [wi:] pron nosotros, nosotras.

weak [wi:k] adj débil; flojo; argument etc flojo, poco convincente; market etc flojo; sound débil, tenue;

character débil; *tea etc* claro, no muy cargado; **to grow** — debilitarse; **to have** — **eyes** ser corto de vista; **to have a** — **stomach** tener el estómago débil; **her maths is** —, **she is** — **at maths** es floja en matemáticas.

weaken ['wi:kən] **1** *vt* debilitar; (*lessen*) disminuir, reducir; (*mitigate*) atenuar, mitigar; **this fact** —**s your case** este dato quita fuerza a su argumento; **his resignation** —**ed the party** su dimisión debilitó el partido.

2 *vi* debilitarse; flaquear, desfallecer; (*give way*) ceder, abandonar; **his influence is** —**ing** su influencia flaquea; **we must not** — **now** ahora tenemos que ser más firmes que nunca; **prices have** —**ed** las cotizaciones han aflojado.

weak-kneed ['wi:k'ni:d] *adj* (*fig*) sin voluntad, débil.

weakling ['wi:kliŋ] *n* ser *m* delicado, persona *f* débil; cobarde *m*; (*of litter etc*) redrojo *m*; (*in health*) persona *f* enfermiza; **he's no** — no es ningún alfeñique.

weakly ['wi:kli] **1** *adj* enclenque, achacoso, enfermizo.
2 *adv* débilmente; flojamente; tenuemente.

weak-minded ['wi:k'maindid] *adj* vacilante, sin voluntad, sin carácter; (*Med*) imbécil.

weakness ['wi:knis] *n* (*quality*) debilidad *f*; flojedad *f*; tenuidad *f*; (*weak point*) flaco *m*, lado *m* débil; desventaja *f*; (*of character*) falta *f* de voluntad; falta *f* de carácter; **to have a** — **for** tener gusto por, ser muy aficionado a; **to make allowances for human** — tener en cuenta la flaqueza humana.

weak-willed ['wi:k'wild] *adj* de voluntad débil, indeciso.

weal[1] [wi:l] *n* (*arch*) bienestar *m*; **the common** — el bien público.

weal[2] [wi:l] *n* (*Med*) verdugón *m*.

wealth [welθ] *n* riqueza *f*; abundancia *f*; "**The W**— **of Nations**" "La riqueza de las naciones"; **for all his** — a pesar de su riqueza; por rico que sea; **with a** — **of details** con abundantes detalles, con acopio de datos.

wealthy ['welθi] *adj* rico; acaudalado, pudiente; **the** — los ricos.

wean [wi:n] *vt* destetar; **to** — **someone from something** (*fig*) apartar a uno gradualmente de algo, hacer que uno abandone algo poco a poco.

weaning ['wi:niŋ] *n* destete *m*, ablactación *f*.

weapon ['wepən] *n* arma *f*; **nuclear** — arma *f* nuclear.

weaponry ['wepənri] *n* armas *fpl*.

wear [wɛə*] **1** *n* (a) (*use*) uso *m*; **for evening** — para la noche, para llevar de noche; **for everyday** — para todos los días, para todo trote (*fam*); **for hard** — resistente, duradero; **he got 4 years'** — **out of it** la prenda le duró 4 años; **you will get plenty of** — **out of this** esto le ha de durar muchos años, esto tiene gran durabilidad.

(b) (— **and tear**) deterioro *m*, desgaste *m*, uso *m*; **the** — **on the engine** el desgaste del motor; **one has to allow for** — **and tear** hay que tener en cuenta el desgaste natural; **to look the worse for** —, **to show signs of** — mostrarse deteriorado, dar indicios de deterioro; **she looks the worse for** — parece algo desmejorada.

(c) (*clothing*) ropa *f*; prenda *f*; **children's** — ropa *f* para niños; **summer** — ropa *f* para verano; **light** — **for hot countries** ropa *f* ligera para países cálidos; **it is compulsory** — **for schoolboys** la prenda es obligatoria para los colegiales.

2 (*irr*: *pret* **wore**, *ptp* **worn**) *vt* (a) *objects in general* llevar, usar, gastar; *clothing* llevar; traer, traer puesto; vestir; *shoes* calzar; *look, smile etc* tener; (*put on*) ponerse; **she wore her blue dress** llevaba el vestido azul; **she wore blue** se vestía de azul, vestía un vestido azul; **what shall I** —? ¿qué vestido me pongo?; **I have nothing to** — **to the dinner** no tengo qué ponerme para ir a la cena; **I haven't worn that for ages** hace mucho tiempo que no me pongo eso; **were you** — **a watch?** ¿llevabas el reloj?; **my uncle wore a beard** mi tío gastaba barba; **Eskimos don't** — **bikinis** los esquimales no usan bikini; **what size do you** —? ¿qué número usa Vd?; **to** — **one's hair long** llevar el pelo largo, dejarse el pelo largo; **he wore a big smile** sonreía alegremente; **he wore a serious look** parecía grave, tenía el gesto grave.

(b) (— *out*) desgastar, deteriorar; **to** — **something into holes**, **to** — **holes in something** hacer agujeros en algo (rayéndolo *etc*); **to** — **something to a threadbare state** dejar algo raído.

(c) (*tolerate*: *fam*) aguantar; consentir, permitir; **he won't** — **that** eso no lo permitirá; **we'll see if he'll** — **it** veremos si consiente en ello.

(d) (*with adv or prep*) **to** — **away** gastar, desgastar; raer; consumir; **he's worn away to a shadow** está hecho una sombra; **the water has worn away the rock** el agua ha desgastado la roca; **to** — **down** gastar, desgastar; *resistance* agotar; rendir; *patience* agotar, cansar; *enemy* cansar hasta rendir; **the heels are very worn down** los tacones están muy desgastados; **to** — **out** *clothes* usar, desgastar; romper con el uso; (*exhaust, tire*) agotar, rendir; **children** — **shoes out so quickly** los niños rompen tan pronto los zapatos; **you can** — **them out next winter** el invierno que viene te los volverás a poner hasta que se rompan, los acabarás el invierno que viene.

3 *vi* (a) (*last*) durar; **they will** — **for years** le durarán muchos años; **that dress has worn well** ese vestido ha sido muy duradero; **she's worn well** se ha conservado muy bien, no representa su edad; **the theory has worn well** la teoría ha resistido muy bien, la teoría ha sido muy duradera.

(b) **the cloth has worn into holes** al paño le han salido agujeros con el uso; **the rock has worn smooth** la roca se ha alisado.

(c) (*of time*) pasar, transcurrir; **the year is** —**ing on** pasan los meses; **as the evening wore on** a medida que pasaban las horas de la tarde.

(d) (*with adv or prep*) **to** — **away** gastarse, desgastarse; consumirse; **the metal has almost worn away** el metal se ha desgastado casi completamente; **to** — **off** quitarse; pasar, desaparecer; **the pain is** —**ing off** está desapareciendo el dolor, ya duele menos; **it soon wore off** pronto desapareció; **to** — **out** usarse, romperse con el uso, quedar inservible; consumirse.

4 *vr*: **to** — **oneself to death** matarse (trabajando *etc*); **to** — **oneself out** agotarse, matarse.

wearable ['wɛərəbl] *adj* que se puede llevar; **it's still** — todavía se puede llevar.

wearer ['wɛərə*] *n* el (*or* la) que lleva puesto algo; —**s of bowler hats** los que llevan hongo; **straight from maker to** — directamente del fabricante al cliente.

wearily ['wiərili] *adv* cansadamente, fatigadamente; **he said** — dijo cansado, dijo en tono de hastío.

weariness ['wiərinis] *n* cansancio *m*, fatiga *f*; abatimiento *m*, hastío *m*; aburrimiento *m*.

wearing ['wɛəriŋ] *adj* cansado, pesado, molesto.

wearisome ['wiərisəm] *adj* cansado, pesado; fatigoso, agotador.

weary ['wiəri] **1** *adj* (*tired*) cansado, fatigado; (*dispirited*) abatido, hastiado; (*tiring*) aburrido, pesado; (*annoying*) fastidioso; **to be** — **of** estar cansado de, estar harto de; **to grow** — **of** cansarse de; **three** — **hours** tres horas aburridas; **five** — **miles** cinco millas pesadas.

2 *vt* cansar, fatigar; aburrir.

3 *vi* cansarse, fatigarse; **to** — **of** cansarse de; aburrirse de; **to** — **of** + *ger* cansarse de + *infin*.

weasel ['wi:zl] *n* comadreja *f*.

weather ['weðə*] **1** *n* tiempo *m*; (*harsh* —) intemperie *f*; — **permitting** si el tiempo no lo impide; **in the hot** — en tiempo de calor, cuando el calor; **in this** — con el tiempo que hace; **it is fine** — hace buen tiempo, el tiempo es bueno; **what's the** — **like?** ¿qué tiempo hace?; **he has to go out in all** —**s** tiene que salir en todo tiempo; **it gets left outside in all** —**s** está fuera a la intemperie; **to be under the** — (*Med*) estar mal, estar indispuesto, (*with drink*) estar con la turca (*fam*); **to make heavy** — **of something** encontrar algo difícil; crearse dificultades al tratar de hacer algo.

2 *adj, attr* meteorológico, del tiempo; (*Naut*) de barlovento; — **report** boletín *m* meteorológico; — **side** costado *m* de barlovento.

3 *vt* (a) *storm etc* (*also* **to** — **out**) aguantar, hacer frente a; **the government has** —**ed many storms** el gobierno ha aguantado muchas tempestades.

(b) (*Naut*) *cape* doblar; **to** — **a barlovento.**

(c) (*Geol etc*) desgastar; *wood* curar; *skin* curtir.

4 *vi* (*Geol*) desgastarse; (*skin etc*) curtirse a la intemperie.

weather-beaten ['weðə,bi:tn] *adj* curtido por la intemperie.

weatherboard ['weðəbɔ:d] *n* tabla *f* de chilla.

weather-bound ['weðəbaund] *adj* bloqueado por el mal tiempo.

weather bureau ['weðə,bjuərəu] *n* oficina *f* meteorológica, servicio *m* meteorológico.

weather chart ['weðətʃɑ:t] *n* mapa *m* meteorológico.

weather cock ['weðəkɔk] *n* veleta *f*.

weathered ['weðəd] *adj* *oak etc* maduro, curado.

weather forecast ['weðə'fɔːkɑːst] n parte m (or boletín m, pronóstico m) meteorológico.

weatherman ['weðəmæn] n, pl —**men** [men] hombre m del tiempo, meteorólogo m.

weather map ['weðəmæp] n mapa m meteorológico.

weatherproof ['weðəpruːf] adj a prueba de la intemperie.

weather ship ['weðəʃip] n barco m del servicio meteorológico.

weather station ['weðə,steiʃən] n estación f meteorológica.

weather strip ['weðəstrip] n burlete m.

weather vane ['weðəvein] n veleta f.

weave [wiːv] **1** n tejido m; textura f.

  2 (irr: pret **wove**, ptp **woven**) vt tejer; trenzar; entretejer, entrelazar; (fig) plot urdir, tramar; to — **details into a story** insertar detalles en un cuento; to — **episodes into a plot** ir entretejiendo episodios para formar un argumento.

  3 vi tejer; to — **in and out** (boxer etc) evadirse torciendo rápidamente a derecha e izquierda; the plane was **weaving in and out among the clouds** el avión cambiaba constantemente de dirección entre las nubes; to — **in and out among traffic** aprovecharse de cualquier espacio entre los vehículos para adelantarse a toda prisa; the **road —s about a lot** el camino serpentea mucho.

weaver ['wiːvə*] n tejedor m, -ora f.

weaving ['wiːviŋ] **1** n tejeduría f. **2** attr de tejer; para tejer; de tejidos.

weaving machine ['wiːviŋmə,ʃiːn] n telar m.

weaving mill ['wiːviŋmil] n tejeduría f.

web [web] n (fabric) tela f, tejido m; (spider's) telaraña f; (membrane) membrana f; (fig) red f.

webbed [webd] adj palmeado.

webbing ['webiŋ] n cincha f, (Tech) pretina f de reps.

webfooted ['web'futid] adj palmípedo.

wed [wed] **1** vt casarse con; (of priest etc, also fig) casar. **2** vi casarse.

we'd [wiːd] = **we would; we had.**

wedded ['wedid] adj **(a)** (person) casado; bliss, life etc conyugal; his — **wife** su legítima esposa.

  (b) to be — to estar casado con; (fig: connected) estar relacionado con, estar unido a; **to be — to an opinion** aferrarse a una opinión, estar aferrado a una opinión; **to be — to a pursuit** ser aficionado a una actividad, ser entusiasta de un pasatiempo.

wedding ['wediŋ] **1** n boda f; casamiento m; bodas fpl; (fig) unión f, enlace m; **diamond** — bodas fpl de diamante; **golden** — bodas fpl de oro; **silver** — bodas fpl de plata; **civil** — matrimonio m civil; **to have a civil** — casarse por lo civil; **to have a church** — casarse por la iglesia; **to have a quiet** — casarse en la intimidad, casarse en privado.

  2 attr de boda, de bodas; nupcial.

wedding breakfast ['wediŋ'brekfəst] n banquete m de boda.

wedding cake ['wediŋkeik] n tarta f de boda, pastel m de boda.

wedding day ['wediŋdei] n día m de boda.

wedding dress ['wediŋdres] n traje m de novia.

wedding march ['wediŋmɑːtʃ] n marcha f nupcial.

wedding night ['wediŋnait] n noche f de boda.

wedding present ['wediŋ,preznt] n regalo m de boda.

wedding ring ['wediŋriŋ] n anillo m de boda.

wedge [wedʒ] **1** n cuña f; calce m, calza f; (Typ) cuña f de fijación; (of cake etc) porción f, pedazo m (grande); **it's the thin end of the** — éste es el primer paso hacia el desastre, esto puede ser el principio de muchos males; **to drive a** — **between two people** romper el vínculo que une a dos personas, enemistar a dos personas, separar a dos personas.

  2 vt acuñar, calzar; **to — a door open** hacer que una puerta quede abierta introduciendo una calza debajo de ella; **it's —d** está sin poderse mover, se ha agarrado; **I was —d between two bishops** me encontré apretado entre dos obispos, estuve entre dos obispos sin poderme mover; **can we — a few more in?** ¿podemos introducir algunos más? (por apretados que estén).

  3 vr: **to — oneself in** introducirse con dificultad.

wedge-shaped ['wedʒʃeipt] adj de forma de cuña.

wedlock ['wedlɔk] n matrimonio m; **to be born out of** — nacer fuera del matrimonio.

Wednesday ['wenzdei] n miércoles m.

wee [wiː] adj (Scot, fam) pequeñito, diminuto; **a — bit** un poquitín; **I'm a — bit worried** estoy un poco inquieto.

weed [wiːd] **1** n mala hierba f; (person, fam) madeja f (fam); **the** — (hum) el tabaco.

  2 vt ground escardar, desherbar, sachar; **to — out** plant arrancar; (fig) suprimir, quitar, eliminar.

weeding ['wiːdiŋ] n desherbaje m.

weed-killer ['wiːd,kilə*] n herbicida m; **selective** — herbicida m selectivo.

weeds [wiːdz] npl: **widow's** — ropa f de luto.

weedy ['wiːdi] adj ground lleno de malas hierbas; person (fam) flaco, desmirriado; — **youth** mozalbete m.

week [wiːk] n semana f; **Holy W**— Semana f Santa; **working** — semana f laborable; — **in,** — **out** semana tras semana; **twice a** — dos veces a la semana; **this day** —, **a]** — **today** de hoy en ocho días; **to-morrow** — de mañana en ocho días; **Tuesday** — del martes en ocho días; **in a** — **or so** en una semana o poco más; **in the middle of the** — a mitad de semana; **to knock someone into the middle of next** — (fam) dar una tremenda paliza a uno.

weekday ['wiːkdei] n día m laborable.

weekend ['wiːk'end] **1** n fin m de semana, weekend m; **a** — **trip** una excursión de fin de semana; — **case** neceser m de fin de semana; **to stay over the** — pasar el fin de semana; **to take a long** — hacer puente.

  2 vi pasar el fin de semana.

weekender ['wiːk'endə*] n persona f que va a pasar solamente el fin de semana (en una casa de campo etc).

weekly ['wiːkli] **1** adj semanal; de cada semana. **2** adv semanalmente, cada semana; £15 — 15 libras por semana. **3** n semanario m.

weep [wiːp] (irr: pret and ptp **wept**) **1** vt tears llorar, derramar; **to** — **one's eyes out** llorar a mares.

  2 vi llorar; **I could have wept** era para desesperarse; **to** — **for someone** llorar a uno; **to** — **for joy** llorar de alegría; **to** — **for what has happened** llorar por lo que ha pasado; **to** — **to see something** llorar al ver algo.

  3 n: **to have a good** — llorar a mares; aliviarse llorando.

weeping ['wiːpiŋ] **1** adj lloroso. **2** n llanto m, lágrimas fpl.

weepy ['wiːpi] adj lloroso; que llora por poca cosa.

weevil ['wiːvl] n gorgojo m.

weewee ['wiːwiː] (fam) **1** n pipí m (fam). **2** vi hacer pipí (fam).

weft [weft] n trama f; (fig) red f.

weigh [wei] **1** vt **(a)** pesar; **to** — **something in one's hand** pesar algo en la mano.

  (b) (fig) pesar, ponderar; **to** — **something in one's mind** ponderar algo, meditar algo; **to** — **A against B** contraponer A y B, considerar A con relación a B; **to** — **the pros and cons** pesar las ventajas y las desventajas.

  (c) to — **anchor** levar anclas.

  (d) to — **down** sobrecargar; (fig) abrumar, agobiar (with de); **she was —ed down with parcels** iba muy cargada de paquetes; **a branch —ed down with fruit** una rama doblada bajo el peso del fruto; **to be —ed down with sorrow** estar agobiado de dolor; **to** — **out, to** — **up** pesar.

  2 vi **(a)** pesar; **it —s 4 kilos** pesa 4 kilos; **how much does it —?** ¿cuánto pesa?; **it —s heavy** pesa mucho.

  (b) it —s on his mind pesa sobre su mente, le preocupa, le inquieta; **these factors do not** — **with him** estos factores no tienen importancia para él, estos factores no influyen en él.

  (c) to — **in** (jockey) pesarse; **to** — **in with an argument** intervenir afirmando que . . .

weighbridge ['weibridʒ] n báscula-puente f, báscula f de puente.

weighing machine ['weiiŋmə,ʃiːn] n báscula f.

weight [weit] n **(a)** peso m; (heaviness) peso m, pesadez f; **atomic** — peso m atómico; **gross** — peso m bruto; **live** — peso m en vivo; **net** — peso m neto; **specific** — peso m específico; **3 kilos in** — que pesa 3 kilos, de 3 kilos; **it is worth its** — **in gold** vale su peso en oro; **to feel the** — **of. to test** (or try) **the** — **of something** sopesar algo; **to gain** —, **to put on** — engordar, hacerse más gordo; **to lose** —, adelgazar.

  (b) (of clock; disc etc used on scales) pesa f; **system of —s and measures** sistema m de pesos y medidas; **to put the** — lanzar el peso; **putting the** — lanzamiento m del peso.

  (c) (fig: of worries etc) peso, m, carga f; (of blow) fuerza f; (importance) peso m, autoridad f, importancia f; **the** — **of the years** la carga de los años; **a blow without much** — **behind it** un golpe de poca fuerza; **a person of no** — una persona de poca monta, una persona de escasa importancia; **these are arguments of some** — son argumentos de cierto peso; that's a — off my mind es un gran alivio para mí; he carries no — no tiene autoridad; those arguments carry great — with the minister esos argumentos influyen poderosamente en el ministro; to chuck (or throw) one's — about darse importancia; hablar (etc) en tono autoritario; to give due — to an argument conceder la debida importancia a un argumento; he doesn't pull his — in the section no trabaja en la sección tanto como debiera.

2 vt cargar (with de), añadir peso a; (hold down) sujetar con un peso; (statistically) ponderar; this is —ed in your favour esto se inclina del lado de Vd, esto le favorece a Vd.

weightiness ['weitinis] n peso m; (fig) peso m, importancia f; influencia f.

weightless ['weitlis] adj ingrávido.

weightlessness ['weitlisnis] n ingravidez f.

weight lifter ['weit,liftə*] n levantador m de pesos.

weight lifting ['weit,liftiŋ] n levantamiento m de pesos.

weighty ['weiti] adj pesado; (fig) importante, de peso, influyente.

weir [wiə*] n vertedero m, vertedor m; (fish trap) presa f, pesquera f.

weird [wiəd] adj misterioso, fantástico, sobrenatural; (odd) raro, extraño; how —! ¡qué raro!

weirdly ['wiədli] adv misteriosamente, fantásticamente; extrañamente; — dressed vestido de un modo raro.

weirdness ['wiədnis] n misterio m, lo fantástico, lo sobrenatural; rareza f.

weirdy ['wiədi] n (fam) persona f rara.

welch [welʃ] vi (fam) dejar de cumplir una obligación (on someone contraída con uno); (in gambling) dejar de pagar una apuesta (on someone a uno).

welcome ['welkəm] 1 adj (a) bienvenido; —! ¡bienvenido!; — on board! (Aer) ¡bienvenidos a bordo!; — to Spain! ¡bienvenido a España!; to make someone — recibir a uno afectuosamente, dar una buena acogida a uno; I didn't feel very — there no creía que mi presencia allí les fuera muy grata.

(b) (pleasing) grato, agradable; that is — news es una noticia grata; it's a — change es un cambio beneficioso; a glass of sherry is always — siempre se agradece una copita de jerez, una copita de jerez siempre viene bien.

(c) you're —! (answer to thanks) ¡de nada!, ¡no hay de qué!; (iro) ¡buen provecho le haga!; you are — to it está a su disposición; you are — to try Vd es muy dueño de probarlo, Vd tiene permiso para probarlo; you will always be — here está Vd en su casa.

2 n bienvenida f; (buena) acogida f, recepción f; to bid someone — dar la bienvenida a uno; to give someone a hearty — acoger a uno con entusiasmo; the crowd gave him an enthusiastic — el público le dispensó una calurosa acogida; to meet with a cold — ser recibido fríamente; what sort of a — will this product get? ¿qué aceptación tendrá este artículo?; see outstay.

3 vt dar la bienvenida a; acoger, recibir; aprobar; they went to the airport to — him fueron a recibirle al aeropuerto; we should — this tendency deberíamos dar la bienvenida a esta tendencia; we — this step aprobamos esta medida.

welcoming ['welkəmiŋ] adj acogedor, cordial.

weld [weld] 1 vt (a) (Tech) soldar; to — parts together soldar unas piezas; the hull is —ed throughout el casco es totalmente soldado.

(b) (fig) to — together soldar, unir, unificar; we must — them together into a new body hemos de soldarlos para formar un nuevo organismo.

2 vi soldarse.

welder ['weldə*] n soldador m.

welding ['weldiŋ] 1 n soldadura f. 2 attr de soldar, de soldadura, soldador; — torch soplete m soldador.

welfare ['welfeə*] 1 n (a) bienestar m, bien m; prosperidad f; child — bienestar m de los niños; to work for the nation's — trabajar en bien de la nación.

(b) (social aid etc) asistencia f social; to live on — vivir a cargo de la asistencia social.

2 attr: — centre centro m de asistencia social; — state estado m benefactor; — work trabajos mpl de asistencia social; — worker empleado m de asistencia social.

well¹ [wel] 1 n pozo m; (fig) fuente f, manantial m; (of stairs) hueco m, caja f; to sink a — perforar un pozo.

2 vi (also to — out, to — up) brotar, manar.

well² [wel] 1 adv (a) bien; the child speaks — el niño habla bien; it's — painted está bien pintado.

(b) (intensive) — and good bien está; we got — and truly wet nos mojamos de verdad; — over a thousand mucho más de mil; it was — worth the trouble realmente valió la pena; we were — beaten nos derrotaron fácilmente.

(c) (with qualifying adv) very — muy bien; very —, I'll do it bueno, lo haré; that's all very —, but . . . todo eso está muy bien, pero . . .; all too —, only too — de sobra, sobradamente.

(d) as — también; she cried, as — she might lloró, y con razón; it is as — to remember that . . . conviene recordar que . . .; in cars as — as on bikes en coches así como en bicicletas; she swims as — as she walks nada tan bien como anda; A as — as B A además de B, tanto A como B.

(e) (concessive) pues; — now ahora bien; —, it was like this bueno, se lo diré; bueno, pasó lo siguiente; —? ¿y entonces?; — then pues bien; — then? ¿y qué?

(f) (exclamatory) —! ¡vaya!, ¡caramba!; —, —! ¡vaya, vaya!; —, that's that! ¡bueno, asunto concluido!

2 adj bien, bien de salud; are you —? ¿qué tal estás?; I'm very —, thanks estoy muy bien, gracias; I'm fairly — estoy regular; she's not been — lately recientemente ha estado algo indispuesta; I don't feel at all — no me siento bien del todo; to get — reponerse (after de); to make someone — curar a uno, devolver la salud a uno.

well- [wel] adv in compounds: bien . . ., eg well-preserved bien conservado.

we'll [wi:l] = we will, we shall.

well-aimed ['wel'eimd] adj certero.

well-appointed ['welə'pɔintid] adj bien amueblado, bien equipado.

well-attended ['welə'tendid] adj muy concurrido.

well-balanced ['wel'bælənsd] adj bien equilibrado.

well-behaved ['welbi'heivd] adj bien educado, formal; animal manso.

well-being ['wel,bi:iŋ] n bienestar m.

wellborn ['wel'bɔ:n] adj bien nacido.

well-bred ['wel'bred] adj bien educado, culto, cortés; accent etc culto; animal de pura raza.

well-built ['wel'bilt] adj sólidamente construido, de construcción sólida; person fornido.

well-chosen ['wel'tʃəuzn] adj elegido con cuidado; remarks, words etc acertado.

well-defined ['weldi'faind] adj bien definido.

well-deserved ['weldi'zə:vd] adj merecido.

well-developed ['weldi'veləpt] adj arm, muscle etc bien desarrollado; sense agudo, fino.

well-disposed ['weldis'pəuzd] adj favorable, benévolo; to be — towards something estar bien dispuesto hacia algo.

well-dressed ['wel'drest] adj bien vestido, elegantemente vestido.

well-earned ['wel'ə:nd] adj merecido.

well-educated ['wel'edjukeitid] adj instruido, culto.

well-equipped ['weli'kwipt] adj bien equipado.

well-favoured ['wel'feivəd] adj bien parecido.

well-fed ['wel'fed] adj bien alimentado, que come bien; (in appearance) regordete.

well-founded ['wel'faundid] adj bien fundado.

well-grown ['wel'grəun] adj grande, maduro, adulto.

wellhead ['welhed] n fuente f, manantial m.

well-informed ['welin'fɔ:md] adj (in general) enterado, instruido; to be — about something estar enterado de algo, estar al corriente de algo.

wellingtons ['weliŋtənz] npl botas fpl de goma.

well-intentioned ['welin'tenʃnd] adj bienintencionado; lie piadoso.

well-judged ['wel'dʒʌdʒd] adj bien calculado.

well-kept ['wel'kept] adj bien cuidado, bien conservado, en buen orden; a — secret un secreto bien guardado.

well-knit ['wel'nit] adj bien ensamblado; (fig) body robusto, recio; scheme etc lógico, bien razonado; speech etc bien pensado, de estructura lógica.

well-known ['wel'nəun] adj conocido.

well-made ['wel'meid] adj bien hecho, fuerte.

well-mannered ['wel'mænəd] adj educado, culto, cortés.

well-marked ['wel'ma:kt] adj bien marcado.

well-meaning ['wel'mi:niŋ] adj bienintencionado.

well-meant ['wel'ment] adj bienintencionado.

well-nigh ['welnai] adv casi; poco menos que; it's — finished está casi terminado; this is — impossible esto es punto menos que imposible.

well-off ['wel'ɔf] adj acomodado, pudiente; (with pej sense) adinerado; the less — las gentes menos

pudientes; **he spoke with a — accent** habló con acento culto, (pej) habló con acento afectado.
well-oiled ['wel'ɔild] adj bien lubricado.
well-preserved ['welpri'zə:vd] adj = **well-kept**; person de buen aspecto (a pesar de su edad).
well-proportioned ['welprə'pɔ:ʃnd] adj bien proporcionado, de forma elegante; person de talle elegante.
well-read ['wel'red] adj leído, instruido; culto; **to be — in history** haber leído mucha historia, estar muy documentado en historia.
well-rounded ['wel'raundid] adj redondeado, acabado.
well-spent ['wel'spent] adj bien empleado, fructuoso.
well-spoken ['wel'spəukən] adj bienhablado, con acento culto.
well-stocked ['wel'stɔkt] adj bien provisto, bien surtido; **— shelves** estantes mpl llenos.
well-timed ['wel'taimd] adj oportuno.
well-to-do ['weltə'du:] adj acomodado, pudiente; **the —** la gente pudiente, (pej) la gente bien.
well-trodden ['wel'trɔdn] adj trillado.
well-turned ['wel'tə:nd] adj elegante.
well-wisher ['wel.wiʃə*] n amigo m, a f.
well-worn ['wel'wɔ:n] adj garment raído; path trillado; cliché traído y llevado, trillado, manoseado.
Welsh [welʃ] **1** adj galés, de Gales; **the —** los galeses. **2** n (language) galés m.
welsh [welʃ] vi see **welch**.
Welshman ['welʃmən] n, pl **—men** [mən] galés m.
Welshwoman ['welʃ.wumən] n, pl **—women** [.wimin] galesa f.
welt [welt] **1** n (of shoe) vira f; (weal) verdugón m. **2** vt poner vira a; pegar, zurrar, hacer verdugones a.
welter ['weltə*] **1** n confusión f, mezcla f confusa; **in a — of blood** en un mar de sangre. **2** vi revolcarse; **to — in** estar bañado en, bañarse en.
welterweight ['weltəweit] n wélter m.
wen [wen] n lobanillo m, quiste m sebáceo; **the Great W—** el gran basurero (Londres).
wench [wentʃ] **1** n mozuela f, muchacha f; (pej) moza f; (whore) puta f. **2** vi (also **to go —ing**) putañear.
wend [wend] vt: **to — one's way** to dirigirse a.
went [went] pret of **go**.
wept [wept] pret and ptp of **weep**.
were [wə:*] pret of **be**.
we're [wiə*] = **we are**.
weren't [wə:nt] = **were not**.
werewolf ['wiəwulf] n, pl **—wolves** [wulvz] ser m humano transformado en lobo.
wert [wə:t] (arch) see **be**.
Wesleyan ['wezliən] **1** adj metodista. **2** n metodista mf.
Wesleyanism ['wezliənizəm] n metodismo m.
west [west] **1** n oeste m, occidente m; **the W—** el Oeste, el Occidente; **tales of the American W—** cuentos mpl del Oeste americano.
2 adj del oeste, occidental; wind del oeste; **to go —** (fam: object, machine) romperse, estropearse; (plan etc) fracasar; (person) estirar la pata (fam).
westerly ['westəli] adj point, direction oeste; wind del oeste.
western ['westən] **1** adj occidental, del oeste. **2** n película f de cowboys, película f que se desarrolla en el Oeste de EE.UU.
westerner ['westənə*] n habitante mf del Oeste; (Pol etc) occidental mf.
westernization ['westənai'zeiʃən] n occidentalización f.
westernize ['westənaiz] vt occidentalizar, convertir al estilo de vida del Occidente.
westernized ['westənaizd] adj occidentalizado, influido por el Occidente; **to become —** occidentalizarse, adoptar el estilo de vida del Occidente.
westernmost ['westənməust] adj (el) más occidental, situado más al oeste.
West Indian ['west'indiən] **1** adj antillano. **2** n antillano m, a f.
West Indies ['west'indi:z] pl Antillas fpl.
westward(s) ['westwəd(z)] adv hacia el oeste.
wet [wet] **1** adj (a) (naturally) húmedo; (accidentally, temporarily) mojado; (US fam) no prohibicionista; paint etc fresco; **in — clothes** en ropa mojada; **to be — through, to be — to the skin, to be wringing —** estar mojado hasta los huesos; **the ink is still —** la tinta no se ha secado todavía; **to get —** mojarse; **to get one's feet —** mojarse los pies; **it grows in — places** se encuentra en lugares húmedos.
(b) (of weather) lluvioso; **a — day** un día de lluvia; **a — climate** un clima lluvioso; **the — season**

la estación de las lluvias; **in — weather** cuando llueve; **it was — in the night** llovió durante la noche; **it was too — for us to go out** llovió tanto que no pudimos salir.
(c) (fam) soso, bobo; **don't be so —** ¡no seas bobo!
2 n humedad f; (rain) lluvia f; **it's out in the —** está fuera a la intemperie.
3 vt mojar, humedecer; tea hacer; echar agua hirviente a; bargain (fam) cerrar con un brindis; **to — the baby's head** (fam) celebrar un nacimiento bebiendo a la salud del niño; **to — the bed** orinarse en la cama; **to — one's pants** orinarse en las bragas.
wether ['weðə*] n carnero m castrado.
wetness ['wetnis] n humedad f; (raininess) lo lluvioso.
wet-nurse ['wetnə:s] n nodriza f, ama f de cría.
wetting ['wetiŋ] n mojada f; **to get a —** mojarse; **to give someone a —** mojar a uno.
we've [wi:v] = **we have**.
whack [wæk] n **(a)** (blow) golpe m grande, golpe m ruidoso; **to give something a —** golpear algo ruidosamente.
(b) (fam: attempt) tentativa f; **to have a — at something** intentar algo, probar algo; **let's have a — probemos.**
(c) (fam: share) parte f, porción f; **you should get your —** seguramente recibirás lo que te corresponde.
whacking ['wækiŋ] **1** (fam) adj grandote, enorme, imponente.
2 (fam) adv: **a — big book** un libro enorme de grande.
3 n zurra f; **to give someone a —** zurrar a uno, pegar a uno.
whale [weil] n ballena f; **a — of a difference** una enorme diferencia; **to have a — of a time** divertirse en grande, pasarlo bomba (fam).
whalebone ['weilbəun] n ballena f (lámina, material).
whale oil ['weiloil] n aceite m de ballena.
whaler ['weilə*] n (person, ship) ballenero m.
whaling ['weiliŋ] n pesca f de ballenas.
whaling ship ['weiliŋʃip] n ballenero m.
whaling station ['weiliŋ.steiʃən] n estación f ballenera.
wham [wæm] = **whang; interj —! ¡zas!**
whang [wæŋ] **1** n golpe m resonante.
2 vt golpear de modo resonante.
3 vi: **to — against something, to — into something** chocar ruidosamente con algo.
wharf [wɔ:f] n, pl **wharfs** or **wharves** [wɔ:vz] muelle m.
wharfage ['wɔ:fidʒ] n muellaje m.
what [wɔt] **1** adj **(a)** (rel) que; **— little I had** lo poco que tenía; **with — money I have** con el dinero que tengo; **buy — food you like** compra la comida que quieras.
(b) (interrog) qué; cuál de . . .; **— book do you want?** ¿qué libro quieres?, ¿cuál de los libros quieres?; **— news did he bring?** ¿qué noticias trajo?
(c) (interj) qué; **— a man!** ¡qué hombre!; **— luck!** ¡qué suerte!; **— a fool I've been!** ¡qué tonto he sido!; **— an ugly dog!** ¡qué perro más (or tan) feo!
(d) (interj, iro) lindo, valiente, bueno; **— a general!** ¡valiente general!; **— an excuse!** ¡buen pretexto!
2 pron **(a)** (rel, = that which) el que, la que, lo que (etc); **— I like is tea** lo que me gusta de verdad es el té; **that is not — I asked for** eso no es lo que pedí; **— is done is done** lo que está hecho no se puede cambiar; **and — not** y qué sé yo qué más; **and — is more . . .** y además . . .; **— with the weather and the crisis** entre el mal tiempo y la crisis; **— with one thing and another** entre una cosa y otra; **come what may** venga lo que viniere; **say — he will** diga lo que quiere; **not a day but — it rains** no hay día que no llueva; **to give someone — for** cargarse a uno.
(b) (interrog) ¿qué?; (please repeat) ¿cómo?; **— is it?** ¿qué es?; **—'s that?** ¿y eso qué es?; **— is that to you?** ¿y eso qué te importa?; **— is the reason?** ¿cuál es la razón?; **— is the formula for . . . ?** ¿cuál es la fórmula de . . . ?; **— is this called?** ¿cómo se llama esto?; **— can we do?** ¿qué podemos hacer?; **— do 4 and 3 make?** ¿cuánto suman 4 y 3?; **so — ?** ¿y qué?; **— if . . . ?** ¿y si . . . ?, ¿qué será si . . . ?; **— of it?**, **— of that?** y eso ¿qué importa?; **I know — you're after** yo sé lo que buscas; **I don't know — to do** no sé qué hacer; **I'll tell you —** se me ocurre una idea, tengo una idea; **he knows —'s —** sabe cuántas son cinco; see **about**, **for** etc.
(c) (interj) ¡cómo!; **—! you sold it!** ¡cómo! ¡lo has vendido!; **—! a man in your room?** ¡qué

horror! ¿un hombre en tu cuarto?; **shameful, —?** vergonzoso, ¿no?

what-d'ye-call-him ['wɔtdʒu,kɔ:lim] *pron* fulano; **old — with the red nose** ése que tiene la nariz tan coloradota.

what-d'ye-call-it ['wɔtdʒu,kɔ:lit] *pron* cosa *f*, chisme *m*; **he does it with the —** lo hace con el chisme ese; **that green — on the front** esa cosa verde en la parte delantera.

whatever [wɔt'evə*] **1** *pron* lo que; todo lo que; **— you like** lo que quieras; **— you find** cualquier cosa que encuentres; **— I have is yours** todo lo que tengo es tuyo; **— it may be** sea lo que sea; **— he says** diga lo que diga; **— happens** pase lo que pase; **or — they're called** o como quiera que se llamen; **— do you mean?** ¿qué quiere Vd decir?; **or —** o lo que sea.

2 *adj* (a) **— book you choose** cualquier libro que elija Vd; **— books you choose** cualesquier libros que elija Vd; **every book of — size** todo libro de no importa qué tamaño.

(b) **no man —** ningún hombre sea quien sea; **nothing —** nada en absoluto; **he said nothing — of interest** no dijo nada en absoluto que tuviera interés; **it's of no use —** no sirve para nada en absoluto.

what-ho ['wɔt'həu] *interj* (*surprise*) ¡caramba!, ¡vaya!; (*greeting*) ¡hola!, ¡oye!

whatnot ['wɔtnɔt] *n* estantería *f*, mueble *m* de estantes.

whatsoever [,wɔtsəu'evə*] *pron, adj* = **whatever**.

wheat [wi:t] **1** *n* trigo *m*. **2** *attr* de trigo, triguero; **— loaf** pan *m* de trigo.

wheatear ['wi:tiə*] *n* (*Orn*) collalba *f*.

wheaten ['wi:tn] *adj* de trigo; de color de trigo.

wheat field ['wi:tfi:ld] *n* trigal *m*.

wheat sheaf ['wi:tʃi:f] *n* haz *f* de trigo.

wheedle ['wi:dl] *vt* engatusar; **to — someone into doing something** engatusar a uno para que haga algo, conseguir por medio de halagos que uno haga algo; **to — something out of someone** sonsacar algo a alguien.

wheedling ['wi:dliŋ] **1** *adj* mimoso. **2** *n* mimos *mpl*, halagos *mpl*.

wheel [wi:l] **1** *n* (a) rueda *f*; (*steering —*) volante *m*; (*Naut*) timón *m*; **— of fortune** rueda *f* de fortuna; **the —s of government** el mecanismo del gobierno; **back —** rueda *f* trasera; **big —** (*at fair*) noria *f*, (*person: fam*) personaje *m*, pez *m* gordo (*fam*); **fixed —** rueda *f* fija; **front —** rueda *f* delantera; **potter's —** torno *m* de alfarero; **there are —s within —s** esto es más complicado de lo que parece, esto tiene su miga.

(b) (*Mil*) vuelta *f*, conversión *f*; **a — to the right** una vuelta hacia la derecha.

2 *vt* (*turn*) hacer girar; hacer rodar; *bicycle, pram* empujar; *child* pasear en cochecito; **we —ed it over to the window** lo empujamos hasta la ventana; **when it broke down I had to — it** cuando se averió tuve que empujarlo.

3 *vi* (*turn*) girar; rodar; dar vueltas; (*of birds*) revolotear; (*Mil*) dar un vuelta, cambiar de frente; **to — left** dar una vuelta hacia la izquierda; **to — round** (*person*) girar sobre los talones; (*fig*) cambiar de rumbo, cambiar de opinión.

wheelbarrow ['wi:l,bærəu] *n* carretilla *f*.

wheelbase ['wi:lbeis] *n* batalla *f*, distancia *f* entre ejes.

wheelchair ['wi:ltʃeə*] *n* silla *f* de ruedas.

wheeled [wi:ld] *adj*: **— traffic** tránsito *m* rodado; **— transport** transporte *m* rodado.

-wheeled [wi:ld] *adj eg* **four-wheeled** de cuatro ruedas.

wheelhouse ['wi:lhaus] *n*, *pl* **—houses** [,hauziz] timonera *f*, cámara *f* del timonel.

wheel spider ['wi:l,spaidə*] *n* estrella *f* de rueda.

wheelwright ['wi:lrait] *n* ruedero *m*, carretero *m*.

wheeze [wi:z] **1** *n* (a) resuelto *m* (ruidoso), respiración *f* sibilante.

(b) (*fam*) truco *m*, treta *f*; idea *f*; **that's a good —** es buena idea; **to think up a —** idear una treta.

2 *vti* resollar (con ruido), jadear; ser asmático; **"Yes," he —ed** "Sí", dijo resollando con ruido (*or* respirando con dificultad).

wheezing ['wi:ziŋ] *adj*, **wheezy** ['wi:zi] *adv breath* ruidoso, difícil; *pronunciation* sibilante.

whelk [welk] *n* buccino *m*.

whelp [welp] **1** *n* cachorro *m*. **2** *vi* parir (*la perra etc*).

when [wen] **1** *adv* cuándo; **— did it happen?** ¿cuándo ocurrió?; **I know — it happened** yo sé cuándo

ocurrió; **— is the interview?** ¿cuándo es la interviú?; **since —?** ¿desde cuándo?; **since — do you have a car?** ¿de cuándo acá tienes tú coche?

2 *conj* (a) cuando; **— I came in** cuando yo entré; al entrar (yo); **— I was young** cuando era joven; en mi juventud; **you can go — I have finished** puedes irte en cuanto yo termine; **— the bridge is built** cuando se construya el puente; **he's only happy — drunk** es feliz únicamente cuando está borracho; **he did it — a child** lo hizo de niño, lo hizo siendo niño.

(b) (*rel*) cuando; **this is — it always rains** esto es cuando llueve siempre; **at the very moment — . . .** en el mismo momento cuando . . .; **one day — the tide is out** un día cuando la marea esté baja.

whence [wens] *adv* (*lit*) (a) (*of place*) ¿de dónde?; **— comes it that . . .?** ¿cómo es que . . .?

(b) (*fig*) por lo cual, y por consiguiente; **— I conclude that . . .** por lo cual concluyo que . . .

whenever [wen'evə*] *adv* (a) (*rel*) siempre que, cuando quiera que; cuando, todas las veces que; **come — you like** ven cuando quieras; **I go — I can** voy todas las veces que puedo; **— you see one of those, stop** cuando quiera que vea uno de ésos, pare.

(b) (*interrog*) **— can he have done it?** ¿cuándo demonios ha podido hacerlo?; **— do I have the time for such things?** ¿cuándo cree Vd que tengo tiempo para estas cosas?

where [wɛə*] *adv* (a) (*interrog*) ¿dónde?; **— am I?** ¿dónde estoy?; **I know — he is** yo sé dónde está; **— are you going?** ¿adónde vas?; **— are you from?** ¿de dónde eres?; **— should we be if . . .?** ¿dónde estaríamos nosotros si . . .?; **— is the sense of it?** ¿qué sentido tiene esto?

(b) (*rel*) donde; **go — you like** ve donde quieras; **this is — we got to** éste es el punto al que habíamos llegado; **this is — we got out** nos apeamos aquí; **the house — I was born** la casa donde nací, la casa en la que nací; **from — I'm sitting** desde aquí; **that's just — you're wrong** en eso se equivoca Vd.

whereabouts ['wɛərə'bauts] *adv* ¿dónde?

whereabouts ['wɛərəbauts] *n* paradero *m*; **nobody knows his —** se desconoce su paradero actual.

whereas [wɛər'æz] *conj* visto que, por cuanto, mientras; (*in legal parlance*) considerando que.

whereat [wɛər'æt] *adv* con lo cual.

whereby [wɛə'bai] *adv* por lo cual, por donde; **the rule — it is not allowed to + *infin*** la regla según la cual no se permite + *infin*.

wherefore ['wɛəfɔ:*] **1** *adv* (*why*) por qué; (*and for this reason*) y por tanto, por lo cual.

2 *n*: **the whys and —s** las razones, el por qué; **los detalles**, la explicación detallada.

wherein [wɛər'in] *adv* en donde.

whereof [wɛər'ɔv] *adv* de que.

whereon [wɛər'ɔn] *adv* en que.

wheresoever [,wɛəsəu'evə*] *adv* dondequiera que.

whereupon ['wɛərəpɔn] *adv* con lo cual, después de lo cual.

wherever [wɛər'evə*] *adv* (a) (*rel*) dondequiera que; **— you go I'll go too** dondequiera que vayas yo te acompañaré; **— they went they were cheered** por dondequiera que fueron se les aplaudió; **sit — you like** siéntate donde te parezca bien; **I'll buy them — they come from** los compraré no importa su procedencia.

(b) (*interrog*) **— did you put it?** ¿dónde demonios lo pusiste?; **— can they have got to?** ¿dónde demonios se habrán metido?

wherewith [wɛə'wiθ] *adv* con lo cual.

wherewithal ['wɛəwiðɔ:l] *n* medios *mpl*, recursos *mpl*, cónquibus *m*; **they haven't got the —** no tienen los medios.

wherry ['weri] *n* chalana *f*.

whet [wet] *vt tool* afilar, amolar; *appetite, curiosity* estimular, despertar, aguzar.

whether ['weðə*] *conj* si; **I am not certain — . . .** no sé si . . .; **I doubt —** dudo que + *subj*; **— he is here or in Madrid** que esté aquí o en Madrid; **— she sings or dances** que cante o que baile; **— they come or not** vengan o no (vengan).

whetstone ['wetstəun] *n* piedra *f* de amolar, afiladera *f*.

whew [hwju:] *interj* ¡vaya!

whey [wei] *n* suero *m*.

which [witʃ] **1** *adj* (a) (*interrog*) ¿qué?; ¿cuál?; **— picture do you prefer?** ¿qué cuadro prefieres?, ¿cuál de los cuadros prefieres?; **I don't know — tie he wants** yo no sé qué corbata quiere; **— way**

did she go? ¿por dónde se fue?; — one? ¿cuál?; — one of us? ¿cuál de nosotros?; — house do you live in? ¿cuál es la casa en que vive Vd?

(b) (rel) he used "peradventure", — word is now archaic dijo "peradventure", palabra que ha quedado anticuada; look — way you will ... miren por donde quieran ...

2 pron (a) (interrog) ¿cuál?; — do you want? ¿cuál quieres?; — of you did it? ¿cuál de vosotros lo hizo?; I don't mind — no me importa cuál; I can't tell — is — no sé cuál es cuál.

(b) (rel) que; lo que; the bear — I saw el oso que vi; two forms — are to be filled in dos formularios que han de llenarse; the meeting — we attended la reunión a que asistimos; it rained hard — upset her llovió mucho, lo que la desconcertó; ... God forbid ... lo que Dios no quiera.

(c) (rel governed by prep) el que (etc), el cual (etc); lo cual; the hotel at — we stayed the hotel en el que nos hospedamos; the cities to — we are going las ciudades a las que vamos; the bull — I'm talking about el toro del que hablo; at — con lo cual, sobre lo cual; from — we deduce that ... de lo cual deducimos que ...; after — we went to bed después de lo cual nos acostamos.

whichever [witʃ'evə*] 1 adj cualquier; — possibility you choose cualquier posibilidad que elija Vd; you can choose — system you want Vd puede elegir el sistema que quiera; — system you have there are difficulties hay dificultades no importa el sistema que tenga Vd.

2 pron cualquiera; el que, la que; — of the methods you choose cualquiera de los métodos que elija Vd, no importa el método que elija Vd; — can he mean? ¿cuál quiere decir?

whiff [wif] 1 n soplo m, soplo m fugaz; vaharada f; bocanada f; (smell) olorcillo m; a — of grapeshot un poco de metralla; not a — of wind ni el menor soplo de viento; to catch a — of something percibir un olorcillo de algo, oler algo brevemente; to go out for a — of air salir a tomar el fresco.

2 vt soplar.

3 vi (fam) oler (mal); to — of oler a.

while [wail] n (a) rato m, tiempo m; after a — poco tiempo después, al poco tiempo; for a — durante algún tiempo; a good —, a great —, a long — largo rato, mucho tiempo; a long — ago hace mucho; it will be a good — before he gets here tardará bastante en llegar; it will be a good — before they finish tardarán bastante en terminarlo; a little — ago hace poco; it takes quite a — es cosa de bastante tiempo, exige mucho tiempo; in a short — dentro de poco; stay a — with us quédate un rato con nosotros.

(b) the — entretanto, mientras tanto; he looked at me the — mientras tanto me estaba mirando.

(c) it is worth — to ask whether ... vale la pena preguntar si ...; it's not worth my — desde mi punto de vista no vale la pena; we'll make it worth your — le pagaremos bien, le compensaremos generosamente.

2 conj (a) (time) mientras; — this was happening mientras pasaba esto; — you are away mientras estés fuera; she fell asleep — reading mientras leía quedó dormida; se durmió mientras leía; to drink — on duty beber estando de servicio.

(b) (concessive) aunque, bien que; — I admit it is awkward aunque confieso que es difícil.

(c) (whereas) mientras; I have a blue car — you have a red one yo tengo un coche azul mientras Vd tiene uno rojo.

3 vt: to — away the time pasar el rato, entretener los ocios.

whilst [wailst] conj = while.

whim [wim] n capricho m, antojo m; manía f; a passing — un capricho; her every — todos sus antojos y fantasías; it's just a — of hers es un capricho suyo; as the — takes me según se me antoja.

whimper ['wimpə*] 1 n quejido m, gemido m; without a — sin quejarse. 2 vi lloriquear; quejarse, gemir; "Yes", she —ed "Sí", dijo lloriqueando.

whimpering ['wimpəriŋ] 1 adj que lloriquea. 2 n lloriqueo m, gimoteo m.

whimsical ['wimzikəl] adj person caprichoso; idea caprichoso, fantástico; to be in a — mood estar de humor para dejar volar la fantasía.

whimsicality [wimzi'kæliti] n capricho m; fantasía f; a novel of a pleasing — una novela de agradable fantasía.

whimsically ['wimzikəli] adv caprichosamente; fantásticamente.

whimsy ['wimzi] n (whim) capricho m, antojo m; (whimsicality) fantasía f, extravagancia f.

whin [win] n tojo m.

whine [wain] 1 n (complaining cry) quejido m, gimoteo m; (of dog) gañido m; (of bullet) silbido m.

2 vi quejarse, gimotear; gañir; silbar; "Yes", he —d "Sí", dijo gimoteando; don't come whining to me about it no venga a mí a quejarse; the dog was whining to be let in el perro estaba gañiendo para que le abrieran.

whining ['wainiŋ] 1 adj quejumbroso; que gimotea. 2 n quejidos mpl, gimoteo m; el silbar.

whinny ['wini] 1 n relincho m. 2 vi relinchar.

whip [wip] 1 n (a) (riding —) látigo m; (used in punishment) azote m, zurriago m.

(b) (Parl: call) llamada f; three-line — llamada f apremiante (para que un diputado acuda a votar en un debate importante).

(c) (Parl: person) oficial m disciplinario de partido.

2 vt (a) azotar; dar con un látigo; (Cook) batir; (defeat) batir, cascar; (criticize etc) fustigar; (Sew) sobrecoser; rope ligar, envolver con cuerda.

(b) to — something away from someone arrebatar algo a uno; to — in (Parl) member llamar (para que vote); (Parl) electors hacer que acudan a las urnas; the conductor was —ping the orchestra into a frenzy el director exigía el máximo esfuerzo a los músicos; to — off lid quitar con un movimiento brusco; dress quitarse con toda rapidez; to — someone off to a meeting llevar a uno con toda prisa a una reunión; to — on lid poner con un movimiento brusco; dress ponerse con toda rapidez; to — out sacar de repente; to — up (pick up) coger de repente; feeling etc avivar, estimular; support procurar, obtener.

3 vi moverse rápidamente; ir con toda prisa; the car —ped past el coche pasó como un rayo; to — round (person) volverse de repente; I'll — round to the shop voy corriendo a la tienda; the car —ped round the corner el coche dobló la esquina a gran velocidad; to — round for someone (fam) hacer una colecta a beneficio de uno.

whipcord ['wipkɔːd] n tralla f.

whip hand ['wip'hænd] n: to have the — llevar la ventaja (over someone a uno); mandar.

whiplash ['wiplæʃ] n tralla f.

whipped [wipt] adj cream etc batido.

whipper-in ['wipər'in] n (Hunting) piqueur m, montero m que cuida los perros de caza.

whippersnapper ['wipə,snæpə*] n (also young —) mequetrefe m.

whippet ['wipit] n perro m lebrel.

whipping ['wipiŋ] n azotamiento m; flagelación f; (defeat) derrota f; (criticism etc) paliza f; to give someone a — azotar a uno, (fig) dar una paliza a uno.

whipping boy ['wipiŋbɔi] n cabeza f de turco.

whipping top ['wipiŋtɔp] n peonza f, trompo m.

whip-round ['wipraund] n (fam) colecta f; to have a — for someone hacer una colecta a beneficio de uno.

whipsaw ['wipsɔː] n sierra f cabrilla.

whirl [wəːl] 1 n (turn) giro m, vuelta f; (turning) rotación f; el girar; (of dust, water etc) remolino m; a — of pleasures una serie vertiginosa de placeres; my head is in a — mi cabeza está dando vueltas; he disappeared in a — of dust desapareció en una nube de polvo.

2 vt (make turn) hacer girar, hacer dar vueltas; (wave, shake) agitar; (transport) llevar con toda rapidez; he —ed his hat round his head agitaba el sombrero alrededor de la cabeza; he —ed her off to the dance la llevó con toda rapidez al baile; the train —ed us up to Paris el tren nos llevó muy rápidamente a París.

3 vi (spin: also to — round) girar rápidamente, dar vueltas; (of dust, water) arremolinarse; my head —s mi cabeza está dando vueltas; they —ed past us in the dance pasaron delante de nosotros girando alegremente en el baile.

whirligig ['wəːligig] n (toy) molinete m; (roundabout) tiovivo m; (Ent) girino m; (fig) vicisitudes fpl; movimiento m confuso.

whirlpool ['wəːlpuːl] n torbellino m, remolino m; (fig) vorágine f.

whirlwind ['wəːlwind] n torbellino m, manga f de viento; like a — como un torbellino, como una tromba; to reap the — segar lo que ha sembrado.

whirlybird ['wəːlibəːd] n (US fam) helicóptero m.

whirr [wəː*] 1 n (of bird's wings) ruído m, batir m, (of insect's wings) zumbido m; (of machine:

quiet) zumbido *m*, runrún *m*, (*louder*) rechino *m*.

2 *vi* hacer ruido, batir; zumbar, runrunear; rechinar; **the cameras —ed** runruneaban las cámaras.

whisk [wisk] **1** *n* (a) (*brush*) escobilla *f*; (*fly—*) mosqueador *m*; (*Cook*) batidor *m*, (*electric etc*) batidora *f*.

(b) (*movement*) movimiento *m* brusco; movimiento *m* rápido.

2 *vt* (*Cook*) batir; **to — away, to — off** *dust etc* quitar con un movimiento brusco; **the horse —ed the flies away with its tail** el caballo ahuyentó las moscas con un movimiento brusco de la cola; **she —ed it away from me** me lo arrebató; me lo quitó de repente; **the waiter —ed the dishes away** el camarero se llevó de repente los platos; **they —ed him off to a meeting** le llevaron con toda prisa a una reunión; **we were —ed up in the lift to the 9th floor** el ascensor nos llevó con toda rapidez al piso 9.

3 *vi* moverse rápidamente; **to — away** desaparecer de repente.

whisker ['wiskə*] *n* pelo *m* (de la barba); **—s** barbas *fpl*; (*moustache*) bigotes *mpl*; (*side —s*) patillas *fpl*; (*Zool*) bigotes *mpl*.

whiskered ['wiskəd] *adj* bigotudo.

whisk(e)y ['wiski] *n* whisk(e)y *m*; **— and soda** whisky *m* con sifón.

whisper ['wispə*] **1** *n* (a) (*low tone*) cuchicheo *m*; (*of leaves*) susurro *m*; **at the least —** of scandal al menor indicio del escándalo; **to say something in a —** decir algo en tono muy bajo; **to speak in a —** hablar muy bajo; **her voice scarcely rose above a —** apenas pudo hablar sino en tono muy bajo.

(b) (*rumour*) rumor *m*, voz *f*; **there is a — that . . .** corre la voz de que . . ., se rumorea que . . .

2 *vt* (a) decir en tono muy bajo; **to — something to someone, to — a word in someone's ear** decir algo al oído de uno.

(b) **it is —ed that . . .** corre la voz de que . . ., se rumorea que . . .

3 *vi* cuchichear, hablar muy bajo; (*of leaves*) susurrar; **to — to someone** cuchichear a uno, decir algo al oído de uno; **just — to me** dímelo al oído; **stop —ing!** ¡silencio!; **it's rude to — in company** es de mala educación hablar entre sí en tono bajo estando otras personas delante.

whispering ['wispəriŋ] *n* cuchicheo *m*; (*of leaves*) susurro *m*; (*gossip*) chismes *mpl*, chismografía *f*; (*rumours*) rumores *mpl*; **— campaign** campaña *f* de rumores; campaña *f* de difamación; **— gallery** galería *f* de los murmullos.

whist [wist] *n* whist *m*.

whist drive ['wistdraiv] *n* certamen *m* de whist.

whistle ['wisl] **1** *n* (*sound*) silbido *m*, silbo *m*; (*instrument*) silbato *m*, pito *m*; **blast on the —** pitido *m*; **the referee blew his —** el árbitro pitó; **to wet one's —** (*fam*) remojar el gaznate, beber un trago.

2 *vt* silbar; **to — a tune** silbar una melodía; **to — up one's dog** llamar a su perro con un silbido.

3 *vi* silbar; (*Sport etc*) pitar; **it —d past my ear** pasó (silbando) muy cerca de mi oreja, me rozó casi la oreja al pasar; **the car —d past us** el coche pasó como una bala; **the boys — at the girls** los chicos silban a las chicas; **the crowd —d at the referee** el público silbó al árbitro; **he —d for a taxi** llamó un taxi con un silbido; **the referee —d for a foul** el árbitro pitó para señalar una falta; **he can — for it** lo pedirá en vano, que siga esperando hasta siempre.

whistle stop ['wislstɔp] *n* (*US*) población *f* pequeña.

Whit [wit] **1** *n* Pentecostés *m*. **2** *attr* de Pentecostés.

whit [wit] *n*: **never a —, not a —** ni pizca; **without a —** of sin pizca de; **every — as good as** de ningún modo inferior a.

white [wait] **1** *adj* blanco; *bread, hair, meat, wine etc* blanco; *face* (*of complexion*) blanco, (*with fear*) pálido; (*fig*) honorable, decente; *lie* piadoso; **a — man** un blanco, **a — woman** una blanca; **to be as — as a sheet** estar pálido como la muerte; **to go —, to turn —** (*thing*) blanquear, (*person*) palidecer, ponerse pálido.

2 *n* (*colour*) blanco *m*, color *m* blanco; (*whiteness*) blancura *f*; (*person*) blanco *m*, a *f*; (*of egg*) clara *f* del huevo; **the — of the eye** el blanco del ojo.

whitebait ['waitbeit] *n* salmonetes *mpl*.

whitebeam ['waitbiːm] *n* mojera *f*.

white-collar ['wait.kɔlə*] *adj worker* profesional, de oficina; *work* oficinesco.

whitefish ['waitfiʃ] *n* (*species*) corégono *m*; (*col-*

lectively) peces *mpl* de mar (*excepto el arenque y el salmón*).

white-haired ['wait'hɛəd] *adj*, **white-headed** ['wait'hedid] *adj* de cabeza blanca, de pelo blanco; (*fam*) favorito, protegido.

white-hot ['wait'hɔt] *adj* candente, calentado al blanco.

White House ['waithaus] *n*: **the —** la Casa Blanca.

whiten ['waitn] **1** *vt* blanquear. **2** *vi* blanquear; (*person*) palidecer, ponerse pálido.

whiteness ['waitnis] *n* blancura *f*.

whitening ['waitniŋ] *n* tiza *f*; blanco *m* para zapatos; (*whitewash*) jalbegue *m*.

White Paper ['wait'peipə*] *n* Libro *m* Rojo.

whitesmith ['waitsmiθ] *n* hojalatero *m*.

whitethorn ['waitθɔːn] *n* espino *m*.

whitethroat ['waitθrəut] *n* curruca *f* zarcera.

whitewash ['waitwɔʃ] **1** *n* jalbegue *m*; (*fig*) excusas *fpl*, argumentos *mpl* con que se intenta encubrir una falta.

2 *vt* enjalbegar, encalar, blanquear; (*fig*) *fault* encubrir, intentar justificar; *person* disculpar, absolver (injustamente).

whither ['wiðə*] *adv* (*lit*) ¿adónde?

whiting[1] ['waitiŋ] *n* (*colouring*) tiza *f*; blanco *m* para zapatos.

whiting[2] ['waitiŋ] *n* (*Fish*) pescadilla *f*.

whitish ['waitiʃ] *adj* blanquecino.

whitlow ['witləu] *n* panadizo *m*.

Whitsun ['witsn] **1** *n* Pentecostés *m*. **2** *attr* de Pentecostés.

Whitsunday ['wit'sʌndei] *n* domingo *m* de Pentecostés.

Whitsuntide ['witsntaid] **1** *n* Pentecostés *m*. **2** *attr* de Pentecostés.

whittle ['witl] *vt* cortar pedazos a (con un cuchillo); **to — away, to — down** (*fig*) reducir poco a poco, rebajar gradualmente.

whizz [wiz] **1** *n* silbido *m*, zumbido *m*.

2 *vi* silbar, zumbar; (*arrow*) rehilar; **to — along, to go —ing along** ir como una bala; **it —ed past my head** pasó (silbando) muy cerca de mi cabeza; me rozó casi la cabeza al pasar; **the sledge —ed down the slope** el trineo bajó la cuesta a gran velocidad.

whizz kid ['wizkid] *n* (*sl*) joven *m* prometedor, promesa *f*; persona *f* muy activa, persona *f* emprendedora.

who [hu:] *pron* (a) (*interrog*) quién; **— is it?** ¿quién es?; **— are they?** ¿quiénes son?; **I know — it was** yo sé quién fue; **— do you think you are?** ¿quién le mete a Vd en esto?; **— does she think she is?** ¿qué derecho se cree tener para hacer (*etc*) eso?; **"W—'s W—"** "Quién es Quién"; **you'll soon get to know —'s — in the office** pronto aprenderás los nombres y los cargos del personal de la oficina.

(b) (=*whom*) **— are you looking for?** ¿a quién buscas?; **— should it be but Jaimito?** y henos aquí a Jaimito, y como por milagro aparece Jaimito.

(c) (*rel*) que; el (*etc*) que, quien; **my cousin — plays the accordion** mi primo que toca el acordeón; **he — wishes to . . .** el que quiera . . .; **those — swim** los que nadan; **deny it — may** aunque habrá quien lo niegue.

whoa [wəu] *interj* ¡so!

whodunit [hu:'dʌnit] *n* (*sl*) novela *f* policíaca.

whoever [hu:'evə*] *pron* (a) (*rel*) quienquiera que, cualquiera que; **— finds it can keep it** quienquiera que lo encuentre puede quedarse con él; **— said that was an idiot** el que dijo eso fue un imbécil; **ask — you like** pregúntaselo a cualquiera, pregúntaselo a quien te parezca bien.

(b) (*interrog*) ¿quién?; **— can have told you that?** ¿quién diablos te dijo eso?

whole [həul] **1** *adj* (a) (*entire*) todo, entero; total; íntegro; **the — world** el mundo entero; **she swallowed it —** se lo tragó entero; **a pig roasted —** un cerdo asado entero; **along its — length** por todo el largo; **is that the — truth?** ¿me has contado toda la verdad?; **but the — man eludes us** pero el hombre en su totalidad se nos escapa; **but the — purpose was to . . .** pero la única finalidad era de . . .; **a — lot of people will be glad** muchísimas personas se alegrarán.

(b) (*unbroken*) sano; ileso, intacto; **not a cup was left —** after the party después de la fiesta no quedó copa sana; **to our surprise he came back —** nos asombramos al verle volver ileso.

2 *n* todo *m*; total *m*; conjunto *m*, totalidad *f*; **nearly the — of our production** casi toda nuestra producción; **the — of Madrid** todo Madrid; **the**

— of his works todas sus obras, la totalidad de sus obras; **the — and its parts** el todo y sus partes; **as a —** en su totalidad, en conjunto; **on the —** en general, por regla general.

wholehearted ['həul'hɑːtid] *adj* entusiasta, incondicional, cien por cien.

wholeheartedly ['həul'hɑːtidli] *adv* con entusiasmo, incondicionalmente, cien por cien.

wholeheartedness ['həul'hɑːtidnis] *n* entusiasmo *m*.

wholemeal ['həulmiːl] **1** *adj* íntegro, de harina integral. **2** *n* harina *f* integral.

wholesale ['həulseil] **1** *n* venta *f* al por mayor.
2 *attr, adj* **(a) — dealer, — trader** comerciante *mf* al por mayor, mayorista *mf*; **— price** precio *m* al por mayor; **— trade** comercio *m* al por mayor.
(b) *(fig)* en masa; general; **— destruction** destrucción *f* general.
3 *adv* **(a) to sell something —** vender algo al por mayor.
(b) *(fig)* en masa; sin hacer distinción de personas *(etc)*; **the books were burnt —** los libros fueron quemados en masa.

wholesaler ['həul,seilə*] *n* comerciante *mf* al por mayor, mayorista *mf*.

wholesome ['həulsəm] *adj* sano, saludable.

wholesomeness ['həulsəmnis] *n* lo sano, lo saludable.

whole-wheat ['həulwiːt] *adj* de trigo integral, hecho con trigo entero.

wholly ['həuli] *adv* enteramente, completamente.

whom [huːm] *pron* **(a)** *(interrog)* a quién; **— did you see?** ¿a quién viste?; **of — are you talking?** ¿de quién hablas?; **I know of — you are talking** yo sé de quién hablas; **from — did you receive it?** ¿de quién lo recibiste?
(b) *(rel)* que, a quien; **the lady — I saw** la señora a quien vi; **the lady with — I was talking** la señora con quien hablaba; **three policemen, all of — were drunk** tres policías, todos ellos borrachos; **three policemen, none of — wore a helmet** tres policías, ninguno de los cuales llevaba casco.

whomever [huːm'evə*] *pron see* **whoever.**

whoop [huːp] **1** *n* alarido *m*, grito *m*; **with a — of joy** con un grito de alegría.
2 *vt*: **to — it up** *(fam)* divertirse ruidosamente; echar una cana al aire.
3 *vi* gritar, dar alaridos.

whoopee [wuˈpiː] *n*: **to make —** *(fam)* divertirse una barbaridad *(fam)*.

whooping cough ['huːpiŋ,kɔf] *n* tos *f* ferina, coqueluche *f*.

whoosh [wu(ː)ʃ] *n* ruido del agua etc que sale bajo presión, o del viento fuerte; **it came out with a —** salió con mucho ruido.

whop [wɔp] *vt* *(sl)* pegar.

whopper ['wɔpə*] *n* *(sl: big thing)* cosa *f* muy grande; *(lie)* mentirón *m*; **that fish is a —** ese pez es enorme; **what a —!** ¡qué grande es!

whopping ['wɔpiŋ] *adj* *(sl)* enorme, muy grande, grandísimo.

whore ['hɔː*] **1** *n* puta *f*. **2** *vi* *(also* **to go whoring)** putañear, putear.

whorehouse ['hɔːhaus] *n*, *pl* **—houses** [,hauziz] *(US)* casa *f* de putas.

whorl [wəːl] *n* *(of shell)* espira *f*; *(Bot)* verticilo *m*; *(Tech)* espiral *f*.

whortleberry ['wəːtl,bəri] *n* arándano *m*.

whose [huːz] *pron* **(a)** *(interrog)* ¿de quién?; **— is this?** ¿de quién es esto?; **¿a quién pertenece esto?;** **— car did you go in?** ¿en qué coche fuiste?; **— fault was it?** ¿quién tuvo la culpa?; **— umbrella did you take?** ¿qué paraguas tomaste?; **I know — it was** yo sé de quién era.
(b) *(rel)* cuyo; **the man — hat I took** el hombre cuyo sombrero tomé; **the man — seat I sat in** el hombre en cuya silla me senté; **those — passports I have** aquellas personas cuyos pasaportes tengo.

whosoever [,huːsəu'evə*] *see* **whoever.**

why [wai] **1** *adv* ¿por qué?, ¿para qué?; ¿por qué razón?; ¿con qué objeto?; **— not?** ¿por qué no?, ¿cómo no?; **— did you do it?** ¿por qué lo hiciste?; **— on earth didn't you tell me?** ¿por qué demonios no me lo dijiste?; **I know — you did it yo** sé por qué lo hiciste; **— he did it we shall never know** no sabremos nunca por qué razón lo hizo; **that's — I couldn't come** por eso no pude venir, ésa es la razón por la que no pude venir.
2 *interj* ¡cómo!, ¡toma!; **—, what's the matter?** bueno, ¿qué pasa?; **—, it's you!** ¡toma, eres tú!; **—, there are 8 of us!** ¡si somos 8!

3 *n* por qué *m*; causa *f*, razón *f*; **I don't know — or wherefore** no sé por qué ni cómo; *see* **wherefore.**

wick [wik] *n* mecha *f*.

wicked ['wikid] *adj* **(a)** *(iniquitous)* malo, malvado; perverso; inicuo; **you're a — man** eres muy malo; **that was a — thing to do** eso fue inicuo.
(b) *(fig)* satire etc muy mordaz, cruel; *temper* muy vivo; *(fam)* horroroso, horrible, malísimo.

wickedly ['wikidli] *adv* mal; perversamente; inicuamente; cruelmente; *(fam)* horriblemente.

wickedness ['wikidnis] *n* maldad *f*; perversidad *f*; iniquidad *f*; crueldad *f*; **all manner of —** toda clase de maldades.

wicker ['wikə*] **1** *n* mimbre *m or f*. **2** *adj, attr* de mimbre.

wickerwork ['wikəwəːk] **1** *n* artículos *mpl* de mimbre; cestería *f*; *(of chair etc)* rejilla *f*. **2** *adj, attr* de mimbre.

wicket ['wikit] *n* *(gate)* postigo *m*, portillo *m*; *(Cricket: stumps)* rastrillo *m*, palos *mpl*, *(pitch)* terreno *m*; **to be on a sticky —** estar en una situación difícil.

wide [waid] **1** *adj* ancho; extenso, vasto; *gap* grande, muy abierto; *difference* grande, considerable; *understanding etc* amplio; **it is 3 metres —** tiene 3 metros de ancho; **how — is it?** ¿cuánto tiene de ancho?; **the — plains of Castile** las extensas llanuras de Castilla; **his — knowledge of the subject** sus amplios conocimientos del tema.
2 *adv* lejos; extensamente; **far and —** por todas partes; **to be — open** estar muy abierto, *(door etc)* estar abierto de par en par; **to be — open to criticism** estar expuesto a ser criticado desde muchos puntos de vista; **to fling the door — open** abrir la puerta de par en par; **they are set — apart** están puestos muy lejos uno de otro, están muy apartados.

-wide [waid] *eg* **nation-wide** por toda la nación, a escala nacional; **de toda la nación; a country-wide inquiry** una investigación a escala nacional.

wide-angle ['waid,æŋgl] *adj lens etc* granangular, de ángulo ancho, de gran diámetro.

wide-awake ['waidə'weik] *adj* muy despierto; *(fig)* despabilado; vigilante, alerta.

wide-eyed ['waid'aid] *adj* con los ojos desorbitados, con los ojos desmesuradamente abiertos.

widely ['waidli] *adv* extensamente; generalmente; **to travel —** viajar extensamente; viajar por muchos países *(etc)*; **it is — believed that . . .** existe una creencia general de que . . .; **the opinion is — held** es una creencia general; **a —-known author** un autor generalmente conocido; **a —-read student** un estudiante que ha leído mucho.

widen ['waidn] **1** *vt* ensanchar. **2** *vi* *(also* **to — out)** ensancharse; **the passage —s out into a cave** el pasillo se ensancha para formar una caverna.

wideness ['waidnis] *n* anchura *f*; extensión *f*, amplitud *f*.

wide-ranging ['waid,reindʒiŋ] *adj survey etc* de gran alcance, de amplia extensión; *interests* múltiples, muy diversos.

wide-screen ['waidskriːn] *adj film* para pantalla ancha.

widespread ['waidspred] *adj* **(a)** extendido; **with arms —** con los brazos extendidos, con los brazos abiertos.
(b) *(fig)* extenso, amplio; muy difundido, general; **to become —** extenderse, generalizarse; **there is — fear that . . .** muchos temen que . . .; **knowledge of this is now —** el conocimiento de esto está muy difundido ahora.

widow ['widəu] **1** *n* viuda *f*; **W— Twankey** la viuda de Twankey; **I'm a golf —** paso mucho tiempo sola mientras mi marido juega al golf; **all the cricket —s got together for tea** las mujeres cuyos maridos estaban jugando al críquet se reunieron para tomar el té; **to be left a —** enviudar, quedar viuda; *see* **grass.**
2 *vt* dejar viuda; **she was twice —ed** quedó viuda dos veces.

widowed ['widəud] *adj* viudo.

widower ['widəuə*] *n* viudo *m*.

widowhood ['widəuhud] *n* viudez *f*.

width [widθ] *n* anchura *f*; extensión *f*, amplitud *f*; *(of cloth)* ancho *m*; **to be 6 centimetres in —** tener 6 centímetros de ancho.

wield [wiːld] *vt pen, sword etc* manejar; *sceptre* empuñar; *power* ejercer, poseer; **to — a pen in the service of . . .** menear cálamo al servicio de . . .

wife [waif] *n, pl* **wives** [waivz] mujer *f*, esposa *f*; **the —** *(fam)* la parienta *(fam)*; **"The Merry Wives**

of Windsor" "Las alegres comadres de Windsor"; **this is my** — ésta es mi mujer; **my boss and his** — mi jefe y su esposa; **to take a** — casarse; **to take someone to** — casarse con una, contraer matrimonio con una.

wifely ['waifli] *adj* de esposa, de mujer casada.
wig [wig] *n* peluca *f*.
wigeon ['widʒən] *n* ánade *m* silbón.
wigging ['wigiŋ] *n* (*fam*) peluca *f* (*fam*); **to give someone a** — echar una peluca a uno.
wiggle ['wigl] **1** *n* meneo *m* rápido, movimiento *m* rápido.
   2 *vt* menear rápidamente; *hips etc* mover rítmicamente, mover mucho.
   3 *vi* menearse rápidamente; moverse rítmicamente, moverse mucho.
wiggly ['wigli] *adj* que se menea rápidamente, que se mueve mucho.
wight [wait] *n* (*arch or hum*) criatura *f*, pobre hombre *m*.
wigmaker ['wig,meikə*] *n* peluquero *m*.
wigwam ['wigwæm] *n* tienda *f* de pieles rojas, tipi *m*.
wild [waild] **1** *adj* (a) (*not domesticated*) *animal, man* salvaje; *plant* silvestre; campestre, de los campos; *country* agreste, difícil, bravo; **to grow** — crecer libre, crecer sin cultivo; **to run** — (*plant*) volver al estado silvestre.
   (b) (*of cruel disposition*) feroz, fiero, bravo; *horse* sin domar, arisco.
   (c) (*rough*) *wind etc* furioso, violento; *weather* tormentoso; *sea* bravo; **it was a** — **night** fue una noche de tormenta.
   (d) (*unrestrained, disordered*) *child* desmandado, desgobernado; **he was** — **in his youth, he had a** — **youth** tuvo una juventud desordenada; **to lead a** — **life** vivir desenfrenadamente; **the room was in** — **disorder** el cuarto estaba en el mayor desorden; **they were** — **times** fue un período turbulento, fueron años alborotados; **to run** — (*children*) vivir como salvajes.
   (e) (*of person*) loco, insensato, frenético; **to be** — **about someone** andar loco por uno; **to be** — **with joy** estar loco de alegría; **to be** — **with someone** estar furioso contra uno; **it drives me** —, **it makes me** — me saca de quicio, me hace rabiar; **to get** — ponerse furioso, ponerse negro; **he has** — **eyes** tiene ojos de loco; **there were moments of** — **enthusiasm** hubo momentos de loco entusiasmo.
   (f) (*rash, ill-judged*) extravagante, estrafalario; disparatado, descabellado; fantástico; **there was some** — **talk** se propusieron unas ideas estrafalarias, se dijeron cosas insensatas; **it's a** — **exaggeration** es una enorme exageración; **to make a** — **guess** hacer una conjetura poco lógica; **he had some** — **scheme for . . .** tuvo algún proyecto disparatado de . . .
   2 *n* tierra *f* virgen, tierra *f* poco poblada (*or* poco conocida); soledad *f*, yermo *m*; **the call of the** — la atracción de la soledad, el encanto de las tierras vírgenes; **to go out into the** —**s** ir a vivir en tierras poco conocidas; **they live out in the** —**s of Berkshire** viven en las soledades de Berkshire.
wildcat ['waild'kæt] **1** *n* gato *m* montés.
   2 *adj*: — **strike** huelga *f* espontánea, huelga *f* no sancionada por el sindicato; — **scheme** proyecto *m* descabellado, proyecto *m* arriesgado.
wildebeest ['wildibi:st] *n* ñu *m*.
wilderness ['wildənis] *n* desierto *m*, yermo *m*, soledad *f*; **a** — **of ruins** un desierto de ruinas, una infinidad de ruinas.
wildfire ['waild,faiə*] *n*: **to spread like** — propagarse como la pólvora.
wildfowl ['waildfaul] *n* ánades *mpl*.
wildfowler ['waild,faulə*] *n* cazador *m* de ánades.
wildfowling ['waild,fauliŋ] *n* caza *f* de ánades.
wild-goose chase [,waild'gu:stʃeis] *n* empresa *f* desatinada, búsqueda *f* inútil.
wildlife ['waildlaif] *n* fauna *f*.
wildly ['waildli] *adv* *blow etc* (*of wind*) furiosamente, violentamente; *live* desordenadamente, de modo alborotado; *behave* de modo indisciplinado; (*madly*) locamente, insensatamente; frenéticamente; *act* sin reflexión; **to be** — **happy** estar loco de contento; **to shoot** — disparar sin apuntar; **to hit out** — repartir golpes a tontas y a locas; **to talk** — (*loosely*) hablar sin ton ni son, hablar incoherentemente, (*extravagantly*) hablar como un loco; **she looked** — **from one to another** miró con ojos espantados a uno y a otro; **you're guessing** — haces conjeturas sin pensar lógicamente; **to clap** — aplaudir con el

mayor entusiasmo; **to dash about** — correr de un lado para otro sin mirar dónde.
wildness ['waildnis] *n* (a) lo salvaje; selvatiquez *f*, estado *m* silvestre; lo agreste, lo difícil; braveza *f*.
   (b) ferocidad *f*, fiereza *f*.
   (c) furia *f*, violencia *f*.
   (d) desgobierno *m*, desenfreno *m*; turbulencia *f*, lo alborotado.
   (e) locura *f*, insensatez *f*; frenesí *m*.
   (f) extravagancia *f*, lo estrafalario; lo disparatado; lo fantástico.
wiles [wailz] *npl* engaños *mpl*, tretas *fpl*, ardides *mpl*.
wilful ['wilful] *adj* *person* voluntarioso; testarudo; *child* travieso; *act* intencionado, deliberado; *murder etc* premeditado; **you have been** — **about it** has sido testarudo en esto.
wilfully ['wilfəli] *adv* voluntariosamente; intencionadamente; deliberadamente; con premeditación; **you have** — **ignored . . .** te has obstinado en no hacer caso de . . .
wilfulness ['wilfulnis] *n* voluntariedad *f*; testarudez *f*; lo travieso; lo intencionado; lo premeditado.
wiliness ['wailinis] *n* astucia *f*.
Will [wil] *nombre cariñoso de* **William**.
will[1] [wil] *v aux* **1** (a) (*forming fut tense*) **he** — **come** vendrá; **no, he won't** no, no quiere; **you won't lose it,** — **you?** ¿no lo vas a perder, eh?; **you** — **come to see us, won't you?** ¿vendrás a vernos, no?
   (b) (*fut emphatic*) **I** — **do it!** ¡sí lo haré!; **no he won't!** ¡no lo hará!; **I** — (*marriage service*) sí quiero.
   2 (a) (*wish*) querer; **come when you** — venga cuando quiera; **do as you** — haga lo que quiera, haga lo que le parezca bien; **look where you** — mire dondequiera que sea; dondequiera que mire . . .
   (b) (*consent*) **the engine won't start** el motor no arranca, el motor no quiere arrancar; **wait a moment,** — **you?** espera un momento, ¿quieres?; **won't you sit down?** ¿quiere sentarse?, siéntese, por favor; **I** — **not have it!** ¡no lo permito!; **he** — **have none of it** no lo aprueba de ningún modo, no quiere siquiera pensarlo; **I** — **not have it that . . .** no permito que se diga que + *subj*; *see also* **have 1** (i).
   (c) (*habit, potentiality*) **the car** — **do up to 120 kph** el coche hará hasta 120 kph; **accidents** — **happen** ocurren inevitablemente accidentes; **boys** — **be boys** eso es muy de chicos.
will[2] [wil] **1** *n* (a) (*faculty*) voluntad *f*; (*free* —) albedrío *m*; (*wish*) voluntad *f*, placer *m*, deseo *m*; **iron** —, — **of iron** voluntad *f* de hierro; **the** — **to win** el afán de triunfar; **the** — **of God** la voluntad de Dios; **against one's** — contra su voluntad; **a pesar suyo, a desgana; at** — **a voluntad; of one's own free** — por voluntad propia; **what is your** —? ¿qué manda?; **it is my** — **that you should do it** quiero que lo hagas; **where there's a** — **there's a way** querer es poder; **to do someone's** — cumplir la voluntad de uno; **Thy W** — **be done** hágase tu voluntad; **she has a** — **of her own** tiene voluntad propia; **to set to work with a** — empezar a trabajar con ilusión (*or* con entusiasmo), emprender resueltamente una tarea.
   (b) *see* **good**—, **ill**—.
   (c) (*testament*) testamento *m*; **the last** — **and testament of . . .** la última disposición de . . .; **to make one's** — hacer su testamento, otorgar testamento.
   2 *vt* (a) (*dispose*) querer; ordenar, disponer; **God has so** —**ed it** Dios lo ha ordenado así; **if God** —**s** si lo quiere Dios.
   (b) (*urge by willpower*) lograr por fuerza de voluntad; sugestionar; **to** — **someone to do something** sugestionar a uno para que haga algo; **having** —**ed the end we must** — **the means** habiendo creado el fin a fuerza de voluntad también hemos de crear los medios por la misma; **I was** —**ing you to win** estaba deseando tanto que ganaras, te estaba ayudando a ganar con la fuerza de mi voluntad.
   (c) (*by testament*) legar, dejar en testamento; **he** —**ed his pictures to the nation** legó sus cuadros a la nación.
William ['wiljəm] *m* Guillermo; — **the Conqueror** Guillermo el Conquistador.
willies ['wiliz] *npl* (*sl*): **to get the** — pegarse un susto (*fam*), pasar horrores (*fam*); **I get the** — **whenever I think about it** me horroriza pensar en ello; **it gives me the** — me da horror.
willing ['wiliŋ] (a) (*helpful*) servicial; complaciente; de buena voluntad, de buen corazón; **a** — **boy** un chico de buen corazón, un chico que trabaja

(etc) de buena gana; **we need — helpers** necesitamos personas dispuestas a ayudarnos; **there were plenty of — hands** hubo muchos que nos ayudaron espontáneamente.

(b) **to be —** querer, querer hacerlo (etc); **are you —?** ¿quieres?; **God —** si Dios quiere; **I asked her and she was —** se lo pedí y ella asintió gustosa; **to be — to do something** estar dispuesto a hacer algo, hacer algo de buena gana; **he was — for me to take it** me permitió llevarlo, consintió en que yo me lo llevase; **to be — that . . .** consentir en que + subj, permitir que + subj.

willingly ['wiliŋli] adv de buena gana, con gusto; **they — helped us** nos ayudaron de buena gana; **did he come — or by force?** ¿vino libremente o a la fuerza?; **yes, —** sí, con mucho gusto.

willingness ['wiliŋnis] n buena voluntad f, complacencia f; deseo m de servir (or ayudar etc); consentimiento m; **in spite of his — to buy it** a pesar de que estaba dispuesto a comprarlo.

will-o'-the-wisp ['wiləðə'wisp] n fuego m fatuo; (fig) quimera f, ilusión f, sueño m imposible.

willow ['wiləu] n sauce m (also **willow tree**); **weeping —** sauce m llorón.

willowherb ['wiləuhə:b] n adelfa f.

willow pattern ['wiləu,pætən] adj: **— plate** plato m de estilo chino.

willow warbler ['wiləu,wɔ:blə*] n mosquitero m musical.

willowy ['wiləui] adj (fig) esbelto, cimbreño.

willy-nilly ['wili'nili] adv de grado o por fuerza, quiera o no quiera.

wilt[1] [wilt] (arch) see **will 1**.

wilt[2] [wilt] **1** vt marchitar; (fig) debilitar, hacer decaer.

2 vi marchitarse; (fig) debilitarse, decaer; (lose courage) perder el ánimo; (of effort etc) languidecer.

wily ['waili] adj astuto, mañoso.

wimple ['wimpl] n (arch) griñón m.

win [win] **1** n victoria f, triunfo m; éxito m; **another — for Real Madrid** nueva victoria del Real Madrid; **their fifth — in a row** su quinta victoria consecutiva; **to back a horse for a —** apostar dinero a un caballo para el primer puesto; **to have a —** ganar, vencer; **to play for a —** jugar para ganar.

2 (irr: pret and ptp **won**) vt race, cup, prize etc ganar; victory llevarse; (obtain) lograr, conseguir, (Mil sl) agenciarse (fam); sympathy, support atraerse, captar; metal arrancar (from a); **how to — friends and influence people** cómo hacer amistades y ejercer influencia sobre las personas; **to — someone's esteem** llegar a ser estimado por uno; **to — someone's favour** alcanzar el favor de uno; **to — someone's love** enamorar a uno; **to — glory** laurearse; **to — a reputation for honesty** hacerse una reputación de honrado; **it won him the first prize** le valió el primer premio; **to — back** land volver a conquistar; gaming loss etc recobrar; **to — over, to — round** support, supporters atraerse, conquistar; **we won him round eventually** por fin le convencimos; **we won him round to our point of view** le persuadimos a adoptar nuestro punto de vista.

3 vi ganar; triunfar; tener éxito; **to — by a head** ganar por una cabeza; **to — out** ganar, tener éxito; **to — through** triunfar por fin, tener al fin el éxito deseado; **to — through to a place** alcanzar un sitio, llegar por fin a un sitio.

wince [wins] **1** n mueca f de dolor; **he said with a —** dijo con una mueca de dolor.

2 vi hacer una mueca de dolor, estremecerse; (flinch) retroceder, asustarse; **without wincing** sin quejarse.

winch [wintʃ] **1** n cabrestante m, torno m. **2** vt: **to — up** levantar con un torno (etc).

wind [wind] **1** n (a) (in general) viento m; **high —** viento m fuerte; **west —** viento m del oeste; **—s of change** aires mpl de cambio; **where is the —?**, **which way is the —?** ¿de dónde sopla el viento?; **it's an ill — that blows nobody any good** no hay mal que por bien no venga; a río revuelto, ganancia de pescadores; **to be in the —** (fig) estar en el aire, estar en preparación; **there's something in the —** están tramando algo; **to get — of something** llegar a saber algo, husmear algo; **to get (or have) the — up** encogérsele a uno el ombligo; **to put the — up someone** meter a uno el ombligo para dentro; **it properly put the — up me** me asustó de verdad; **to raise the —** dar un sablazo; **to see which way the — blows** esperar antes de resolverse, ver qué pasa antes de tomar partido.

(b) (Naut) viento m; **following —** viento m en popa; **between — and water** cerca de la línea de flotación; **in the teeth of the —** contra el viento; **to run before the —** navegar viento en popa; **to sail close to the —** (fig) decir (etc) cosas algo peligrosas, correr riesgo de provocar un escándalo; **to take the — out of someone's sails** bajar los humos a uno.

(c) (Med) flatulencia f; (from bowel) pedo m, (from stomach) eructo m; **to break —** ventosear, soltar un pedo; **to bring up —** eructar.

(d) (breath) aliento m, resuello m; **to be short of —** respirar con dificultad, estar corto de aliento; **to get one's second —** volver a respirar normalmente, cobrar el aliento.

(e) (Mus) **the —** los instrumentos de viento.

2 vt: **to — someone** dejar a uno sin aliento; **to be —ed by a ball** quedar sin aliento después de ser golpeado por un balón; **to be —ed after a race** quedar sin aliento después de una carrera.

wind [waind] (irr: pret and ptp **wound**) **1** vt (a) (wrap etc) enrollar, envolver; wool etc devanar, ovillar; **to — one's arms round someone** rodear a uno con los brazos, abrazar a uno estrechamente; **to — in a fishing line** ir cobrando sedal; **to — wool into a ball** ovillar lana, hacer un ovillo de lana; **to — off** devanar; desenrollar; **— this round your head** envuélvete la cabeza con esto, líate esto a la cabeza; **with a rope wound tightly round his waist** con una cuerda que le ceñía estrechamente la cintura; **to — something up with a winch** levantar algo con cabrestante.

(b) handle (also **to — round, to — up**) dar vueltas a, girar; clock, watch, clockwork toy etc dar cuerda a remontar.

(c) **the road —s its way through the valley** la carretera serpentea por el valle.

(d) **to — up** (end) terminar, concluir; (Comm) liquidar; **he wound up his speech by saying that . . .** terminó su discurso diciendo que . . .; **the company was ordered to be wound up** se ordenó la liquidación de la sociedad.

(e) **to — up** (nervously) agitar, emocionar con exceso; **she's dreadfully wound up** está nerviosísima; **it gets me all wound up (inside)** con esto me pongo nervioso, esto me emociona terriblemente.

2 vi (a) (also **to — along, to — round** (of road etc) serpentear; **the road —s up the valley** el camino serpentea por el valle; **to — round** (of snakes etc) enroscarse; **the procession wound round the town** el desfile serpenteaba por la ciudad; **the car wound slowly up the hill** el coche subió lentamente la colina (torciéndose a la izquierda y a la derecha).

(b) **to — up** terminar, acabar; **how does the play — up?** ¿cómo termina la obra?; **we wound up in Santander** fuimos a parar a Santander; **he —s up for the government** cierra el debate hablando como representante del gobierno.

windbag ['windbæg] n saco m de aire; (person) charlatán m.

windblown ['windbləun] adj leaf etc llevado por el viento, arrancado por el viento; hair despeinado por el viento.

windbreak ['windbreik] n abrigada f, mampara f; protección f contra el viento.

windcheater ['wind,tʃi:tə*] n chaqueta f forrada.

wind cone ['windkəun] n (Aer) manga f, indicador m cónico de la dirección del viento.

winder ['waində*] n devanadera f; carrete m, bobina f.

windfall ['windfɔ:l] n fruta f caída; (fig) ganancia f inesperada, golpe m de suerte inesperado, cosa f llovida del cielo.

wind gauge ['windgeidʒ] n (Aer) anemómetro m, manga f.

winding ['waindiŋ] **1** adj tortuoso, sinuoso, serpentino; staircase de caracol.

2 n (of watch) cuerda f; (of road) tortuosidad f; (Elec) bobinado m, devanado m; **the —s of a river** las vueltas de un río, los meandros de un río.

winding gear ['waindiŋgiə*] n manubrio m, cabrestante m.

winding sheet ['waindiŋʃi:t] n mortaja f.

winding-up ['waindiŋ'ʌp] n conclusión f; (Comm) liquidación f.

wind instrument ['wind,instrumənt] n instrumento m de viento.

windjammer ['wind,dʒæmə*] n buque m de vela (grande y veloz).

windlass ['windləs] n torno m, maquinilla f; cabrestante m.

windless ['windlis] adj sin viento.

windmill ['windmil] *n* molino *m* (de viento); (*toy*) molinete *m*.

window ['windəu] *n* ventana *f*; (*shop* —) escaparate *m*; (*of vehicle, of booking office etc, of envelope*) ventanilla *f*; **French** — puerta *f* ventana; **stained-glass** — vidriera *f*; **to lean out of the** — asomarse a la ventana; **to look out of the** — mirar por la ventana.

window box ['windəubɔks] *n* jardinera *f* de ventana.

window cleaner ['windəu,kli:nə*] *n* limpiacristales *m*.

window dresser ['windəu,dresə*] *n* escaparatista *mf*.

window dressing ['windəu,dresiŋ] *n* decoración *f* de escaparates; (*fig*) camuflaje *m*; (esfuerzo *m* por salvar las) apariencias *fpl*.

window frame ['windəufreim] *n* marco *m* de ventana.

window ledge ['windəuledʒ] *n* antepecho *m*, alféizar *m*.

window pane ['windəupein] *n* cristal *m*.

window seat ['windəusi:t] *n* asiento *m* junto a una ventana, (*Rail etc*) asiento *m* junto a una ventanilla.

window-shop ['windəuʃɔp] *vi* mirar los escaparates de las tiendas (sin tener intención de comprar), curiosear por las tiendas.

windowsill ['windəusil] *n* alféizar *m*.

windpipe ['windpaip] *n* tráquea *f*.

windproof ['windpru:f] *adj* a prueba de viento.

windscreen ['windskri:n] *n*, (US) **windshield** ['windʃi:ld] *n* parabrisas *m*.

windscreen wiper ['windskri:n,waipə*] *n*, (US) **windshield** — ['windʃi:ld] *n* limpiaparabrisas *m*.

windsleeve ['windsli:v] *n*, **windsock** ['windsɔk] *n* (*Aer*) manga *f*.

windstorm ['windstɔ:m] *n* ventarrón *m*, huracán *m*.

windswept ['windswept] *adj* azotado por el viento, barrido por el viento; *person* despeinado.

wind tunnel ['wind,tʌnl] *n* túnel *m* aerodinámico, túnel *m* de pruebas aerodinámicas.

windward ['windwəd] **1** *adj* de barlovento. **2** *n* barlovento *m*; **to** — **a** barlovento.

Windward Isles ['windwəd,ailz] *pl* Islas *fpl* de Barlovento.

windy ['windi] *adj* (a) *day* de mucho viento; *place* expuesto al viento; **it is** — **today** hoy hace viento; **it's** — **out here** aquí fuera el viento sopla fuerte.

(b) *speech, style etc* pomposo, hinchado.

(c) (*sl*) **to be** — pasar miedo; **to get** — encogérsele a uno el ombligo; **are you** —? ¿tienes miedo?

wine [wain] **1** *n* vino *m*; **heavy** — vino *m* fuerte; **light** — vino *m* ligero; **local** — vino *m* del país; **red** — vino *m* tinto; **sparkling** — vino *m* espumoso; **white** — vino *m* blanco; **good** — **needs no bush** el buen paño en el arca se vende.

2 *vt*: **to** — **and dine someone** dar a uno muy bien de comer y de beber, hacer grandes agasajos a uno.

winebibber ['wain,bibə*] *n* bebedor *m* de vino.

wine bottle ['wain,bɔtl] *n* botella *f* para vino.

wine cask ['wainkɑ:sk] *n* tonel *m* para vino, barril *m* para vino.

wine cellar ['wain,selə*] *n* bodega *f*.

wineglass ['waingla:s] *n* copa *f* para vino, vaso *m* para vino.

wine grower ['wain,grəuə*] *n* viñador *m*, vinicultor *m*.

wine growing ['wain,grəuiŋ] **1** *adj* vinícola. **2** *n* viticultura *f*.

wine list ['wainlist] *n* lista *f* de vinos.

wine merchant ['wain,mə:tʃənt] *n* vinatero *m*.

wine press ['wainpres] *n* prensa *f* de uvas, lagar *m*.

winery ['wainəri] *n* lagar *m*.

wineskin ['wainskin] *n* pellejo *m*, odre *m*.

wine taster ['wain,teistə*] *n* probador *m* de vinos, catador *m* de vinos.

wine waiter ['wain,weitə*] *n* escanciador *m*.

wing [wiŋ] **1** *n* ala *f*; (*Archit*) ala *f*; (*Aut*) aleta *f*, guardabarros *m*; (*of chair*) cabecera *f*, oreja *f*; (*Sport: position*) ala *f*, exterior *m*, (*player*) extremo *m*; (*Aer: section*) escuadrilla *f*; —**s** (*Theat*) bastidores *mpl*; **left** — (*Pol*) ala *f* izquierda; **right** — (*Pol*) ala *f* derecha; **on the** —**s of fantasy** en alas de la fantasía; **to be on the** — estar volando; **to be on the left** —, **to belong to the left** — (*Pol*) ser de izquierdas; **to clip someone's** —**s** cortar las alas a uno; **to shoot a bird on the** — matar un pájaro mientras está volando; **to take** — irse volando, alzar el vuelo; **to take someone under one's** — tomar a uno bajo su protección.

2 *vt bird* tocar, herir en el ala; *person* herir en el brazo; **to** — **one's way** volar, ir volando.

3 *vi* volar.

wing case ['wiŋkeis] *n* (*Zool*) élitro *m*.

wing chair ['wiŋtʃeə*] *n* butaca *f* de orejas.

wing commander ['wiŋkə,mɑ:ndə*] *n* teniente *m* coronel de aviación.

winged [wiŋd] *adj* (*Zool*) alado; *seed* con alas; **de alas** . . ., *eg* **brown-winged** de alas pardas; **four-winged** de cuatro alas.

winger ['wiŋə*] *n* (*Sport*) extremo *m*.

wingless ['wiŋlis] *adj* sin alas.

wing nut ['wiŋnʌt] *n* tuerca *f* mariposa.

wingspan ['wiŋspæn] *n*, **wingspread** ['wiŋspred] *n* envergadura *f* (de alas).

wing tip ['wiŋtip] *n* punta *f* del ala.

wink [wiŋk] **1** *n* (*blink*) pestañeo *m*; (*meaningful*) guiño *m*; **I didn't get a** — **of sleep** no pegué los ojos; **to give someone a** — guiñar el ojo a uno; **to have 40** —**s** descabezar un sueño, echarse una siestecita; **he said with a** — dijo guiñándome el ojo; **I didn't sleep a** — no pegué los ojos; **to tip someone the** — (*fam*) avisar a uno clandestinamente.

2 *vt eye* guiñar.

3 *vi* (*blink*) pestañear; (*meaningfully*) guiñar el ojo; (*of light, star etc*) titilar, parpadear; **to** — **at someone** guiñar el ojo a uno; **to** — **at something** (*fig*) hacer la vista gorda a algo.

winkle ['wiŋkl] **1** *n* bígaro *m*.

2 *vt*: **to** — **someone out** hacer salir a uno; **to** — **a secret out of someone** hacer que uno revele un secreto; **to** — **something out of a crevice** sacar algo con dificultad de una grieta.

winner ['winə*] *n* (*person, horse etc*) ganador *m*, ora *f*, vencedor *m*, ora *f*; (*book, entry etc*) obra *f* premiada; (*Tennis: ball*) pelota *f* imposible de restar; **this disc is a** —! (*fam*) ¡este disco es fabuloso! (*fam*); **the tune is bound to be a** — (*fam*) la melodía obtendrá seguramente un éxito.

winning ['winiŋ] **1** *adj* *person, horse, team etc* vencedor, victorioso; *book, entry etc* premiado; *hit, shot* decisivo; *smile, ways etc* atractivo, encantador.

2 —**s** *npl* ganancias *fpl*.

winning post ['winiŋpəust] *n* poste *m* de llegada, meta *f*.

winnow ['winəu] *vt* aventar.

winnower ['winəuə*] *n*, **winnowing machine** ['winəuiŋmə,ʃi:n] *n* aventadora *f*.

winsome ['winsəm] *adj* atractivo, encantador.

winter ['wintə*] **1** *n* invierno *m*; **"W**—**'s Tale"** "Cuento *m* de invierno".

2 *adj, attr* de invierno, invernal; — **quarters** cuarteles *mpl* de invierno; — **solstice** solsticio *m* invernal; — **sports** deportes *mpl* de invierno.

3 *vi* invernar.

wintergreen ['wintəgri:n] *n* aceite *m* de gualteria.

winterize ['wintəraiz] *vt* (US) adaptar para el invierno, proteger contra el rigor del invierno.

wintertime ['wintətaim] *n* (*season*) invierno *m*; (*hour*) hora *f* de invierno.

wintry ['wintri] *adj* frío, glacial; (*fig*) glacial.

wipe [waip] **1** *n* limpión *m*, limpiadura *f*; (*sl*) cate *m* (*sl*), lapo *m* (*sl*); **to give something a** — (**down** *etc*) limpiar algo, pasar un trapo (*etc*) sobre algo.

2 *vt* limpiar; enjugar; **to** — **a table dry** secar una mesa con un trapo, enjugar una mesa; **to** — **one's brow** enjugarse la frente; **to** — **one's eyes** enjugarse las lágrimas; **to** — **a child's eyes** enjugar las lágrimas a un niño; **to** — **one's nose** sonarse (las narices); **to** — **away, to** — **off** quitar con un trapo, quitar frotando; **to** — **out** (*erase*) borrar; (*suppress*) borrar, cancelar; suprimir; *debt* liquidar; *memory* borrar; (*destroy*) destruir, extirpar; (*kill off completely*) aniquilar.

wiper ['waipə*] *n* paño *m*, trapo *m*.

wire ['waiə*] **1** *n* alambre *m*; (*Tel*) telegrama *m*; **live** — alambre *m* cargado, alambre *m* con corriente, (*fig*) polvorilla *mf*; **to pull** —**s** tocar resortes; **he can pull** —**s** tiene muchos enchufes, tiene buenas agarraderas; **to send someone a** — poner un telegrama a uno.

2 *vt* (a) *house* instalar el alambrado de; *fence* alambrar; **to** — **up** instalar el alambrado de, completar la instalación eléctrica de; **it's all** —**d up for television** se ha completado la instalación eléctrica para la televisión.

(b) **to** — **someone** poner un telegrama a uno; **to** — **information to someone** enviar información a uno por telegrama.

3 *vi* poner un telegrama (*for something* pidiendo algo, *to someone* a uno).

wire cutters ['waiə,kʌtəz] *npl* cizalla *f*, cortaalambres *m*; **a pair of** — una cizalla, un cortaalambres.

wire gauge ['waiəgeidʒ] *n* calibre *m* para alambres.

wire gauze ['waɪə'gɔːz] n tela f metálica.
wire-haired ['waɪəheəd] adj de pelo áspero.
wireless ['waɪəlɪs] **1** n (as science etc) radio f, radiofonía f; (set) radio f, receptor m de radio, radiorreceptor m; **by —**, **on the —**, **over the —** por radio; **to talk on the —** hablar por radio.
  2 attr de radio, radiofónica; **— message** radiograma m.
  3 vt radiar, transmitir por radio.
  4 vi: **to — to someone** enviar un mensaje a uno por radio.
wireless cabin ['waɪəlɪs,kæbɪn] n cabina f de radio.
wireless operator ['waɪəlɪs,ɔpəreɪtə*] n radiotelegrafista mf.
wireless set ['waɪəlɪsset] n radio f, receptor m de radio, radiorreceptor m.
wireless station ['waɪəlɪs,steɪʃən] n emisora f.
wire netting ['waɪə'netɪŋ] n red f de alambre, alambrada f de tela metálica.
wirepuller ['waɪə,pulə*] n (fam) enchufista mf (fam).
wirepulling ['waɪə,pulɪŋ] n (fam) empleo m de resortes (fam), uso m de enchufes (fam).
wiretap ['waɪətæp] vi intervenir las conexiones telefónicas.
wiretapper ['waɪə,tæpə*] n persona f que interviene las conexiones telefónicas.
wiretapping ['waɪə,tæpɪŋ] n intervención f de las conexiones telefónicas.
wireworm ['waɪəwəːm] n gusano m de elatérido.
wiring ['waɪərɪŋ] n alambrado m, instalación f de alambres; **— diagram** esquema m del alambrado.
wiry ['waɪərɪ] adj person, build delgado pero fuerte; hand nervudo, nervioso.
wisdom ['wɪzdəm] n sabiduría f; saber m; prudencia f, juicio m; lo acertado, acierto m.
wise¹ [waɪz] adj **(a)** (learned) sabio; (prudent) prudente, juicioso; move, step etc acertado; **a — man** un sabio; **the (Three) Wise Men (of the East)** los Reyes Magos; **it does not seem — to + infin** no parece aconsejable + infin; **the —st thing to do is . . .** lo más prudente es . . . ; **I'm none the —r** sigo sin entenderlo, ahora lo entiendo menos que antes; **nobody will be any the —r** nadie sabrá de esto, nadie se dará cuenta.
  (b) (fam) **to be — to someone** conocer el juego de uno, calar a uno (fam); **to get — to something** caer en la cuenta de algo; **to put someone — to something** poner a uno al tanto de algo, informar a uno acerca de algo.
wise² [waɪz] (arch) guisa f, modo m; **in this —** de esta guisa; **in no —** de ningún modo.
-wise [waɪz] suffix con respecto a, en cuanto a, relativo a, por lo que se refiere a, eg **profitwise** en cuanto a las ganancias; **how are you off moneywise?** ¿cómo te va el dinero?
wiseacre ['waɪz,eɪkə*] n sabihondo m.
wisecrack ['waɪzkræk] **1** n cuchufleta f, chiste m.
  2 vi cuchufletear; **"—", he —ed "—"** dijo bromeando.
wisely ['waɪzlɪ] adv sabiamente; prudentemente, con prudencia; acertadamente.
wish [wɪʃ] **1** n **(a)** deseo m (for de); ruego m; **according to one's —es** según los deseos de uno; **her — to do it** su deseo de hacerlo; **your — is my command** sus deseos son órdenes para mí; **it has long been my — to + infin** desde hace mucho tiempo vengo deseando + infin; desde hace mucho tengo la intención de + infin; **to go against someone's —es** oponerse a los deseos de uno; **the fairy granted her 3 —es** el hada le concedió 3 deseos; **you shall have your —** se hará lo que Vd pide, se cumplirá tu deseo; **I have no great — to go** me apetece poco ir, realmente no tengo ganas de ir; **to make a —** pensar en algo que uno quiere.
  (b) **with best —es** (in letter) saludos de tu amigo . . . , un abrazo de . . . ; **with best —es for the future** con mis augurios para el porvenir; **I went to give him my best —es** fui a darle la enhorabuena; **please give him my best —es** por favor dale recuerdos míos, salúdale de mi parte; **we sent a message of good —es on Slobodian independence day** enviamos un mensaje de buenos augurios el día de independencia de Eslobodia.
  2 vt **(a)** desear, querer; **I do not — it** no lo quiero, no quiero que se haga; **to — something on someone** lograr que uno acepte algo que no desea; **it was —ed on me** apareció sin que yo lo pidiera; **the job was —ed on to me** me dieron el cometido sin quererlo yo.
  (b) **to — someone good luck, to — someone well** desear a uno mucha suerte; **I — you all possible happiness** os deseo muchísima felicidad; **I don't — her ill, I don't — her any harm** no le deseo ningún mal; **to — someone good morning** dar los buenos días a uno; **to — someone goodbye** despedirse de uno; **to — someone a happy Christmas** desear a uno unas Pascuas muy felices.
  (c) (with verb complement) **to — to do something** querer hacer algo, desear hacer algo; **to — someone to do something** querer que uno haga algo; **what do you — me to do?** ¿qué quieres que haga yo?; **I do — you'd let me help me** gustaría muchísimo que me dejaras ayudar; **I — she'd come** estoy deseando que venga ella; **I —ed after that I had stayed till the end** después de eso sentí no haberme quedado hasta el fin; **I — I could!** ¡ojalá!, ¡ojalá pudiera!; **I — it were not so** ojalá no fuera así; **I — I could be there!** ¡ojalá estuviera allí!
  3 vi: **to — for something** desear algo, anhelar algo; **what more could you — for?** ¿qué más pudieras desear?; **she has everything she could — for** tiene todo cuanto pudiera desear.
wishbone ['wɪʃbəun] n espoleta f.
wishful ['wɪʃful] adj deseoso (to + infin de + infin); ilusionado; see **thinking**.
wishing bone ['wɪʃɪŋbəun] n espoleta f.
wish-wash ['wɪʃwɔʃ] n (fam) aguachirle f.
wishy-washy ['wɪʃɪ,wɔʃɪ] adj (fam) soso, flojo, insípido.
wisp [wɪsp] n (fragment) trozo m ligero, pedazo m menudo; (trace) vestigio m; (of grass) manojito m; brizna f; (of hair) mechón m; (of cloud) jirón m; **— of smoke** columna f delgada, espiral f ligera.
wispy ['wɪspɪ] adj delgado, sutil, tenue.
wistaria [wɪs'tɛərɪə] n vistaria f.
wistful ['wɪstful] adj triste, melancólico; pensativo; ansioso.
wistfully ['wɪstfəlɪ] adv tristemente, con melancolía; pensativamente; con ansia; **she looked at me —** me miró pensativa.
wistfulness ['wɪstfulnɪs] n tristeza f, melancolía f; lo pensativo; ansia f.
wit¹ [wɪt] n: **to — a saber**, esto es.
wit² [wɪt] n **(a)** (understanding) inteligencia f, entendimiento m, juicio m; talento m; **mother —**, **native —** sentido m común; **a battle of —s** una contienda entre dos inteligencias; **to be at one's —'s end** estar para volverse loco (wondering what to do pensando qué hacer); **to be out of one's —s** estar fuera de sí; **to collect one's —s** reconcentrarse; **to frighten someone out of his —s** dar a uno un susto mortal; **to have (or keep) one's —s about one** tener mucho ojo; conservar su presencia de ánimo; **he hadn't the — to see that . . .** no tenía bastante inteligencia para comprender que . . . ; **to live by one's —s** vivir del cuento, ser caballero de industria; **to sharpen one's —s** despabilarse; **to use one's —s** usar su sentido común; valerse de su ingenio.
  (b) (humour, wittiness) ingenio m, agudeza f; sal f; gracia f; **to have a ready (or pretty) —** ser ingenioso, tener chispa; **there's a lot of — in the book** el libro tiene mucha sal; **a story told without —** un cuento narrado sin gracia; **in a flash of —** he said . . . con un rasgo de ingenio dijo . . .
  (c) (person) chistoso m, a f, persona f de mucha sal; (Hist) ingenio m; **an Elizabethan —** un ingenio de la época isabelina.
witch [wɪtʃ] n bruja f, hechicera f.
witchcraft ['wɪtʃkrɑːft] n brujería f.
witch doctor ['wɪtʃ,dɔktə*] n hechicero m.
witchery ['wɪtʃərɪ] n brujería f; (fig) encanto m, magia f.
witch hunt ['wɪtʃhʌnt] n lucha f contra la subversión; (pej) persecución f de personas subversivas, persecución f (política).
with [wɪð, wɪθ] prep **(a)** (general sense) con; en compañía de; **I was — him** yo estaba con él; **she stayed with friends** se hospedó con unos amigos; **I'll be — you in a moment** un momento y estoy con vosotros; **to leave something — someone** dejar algo en manos de uno; **to leave a child — someone** dejar a un niño al cuidado de uno; **that problem is always — us** ese problema sigue afectándonos, ese problema no se resuelve; **the fashion ended — the century** la moda terminó al terminar el siglo, la moda terminó cuando el siglo; **— the Alcántara it is the biggest ship of its class** junto con el Alcántara es el mayor buque de su tipo; **she's good — children** sabe manejar a los niños, se adapta perfectamente al mundo infantil; **I am — you there** en eso estoy de acuerdo con Vd; **he took**

it away — **him** se lo llevó consigo; — **no** sin, *eg* — **no trouble at all** sin dificultad alguna.

(b) (*descriptive*) de, con; **a house** — **big windows** una casa con grandes ventanas; **the fellow** — **the big beard** él de la barba grande; **you can't speak to the queen** — **your hat on** no se puede hablar con la reina llevando puesto el sombrero.

(c) (*in spite of*) con; — **all his faults** con todos sus defectos.

(d) (*according to*) según, de acuerdo con; **it varies** — **the season** varía según la estación.

(e) (*manner*) con; — **all his might** con todas sus fuerzas; — **all speed** a toda prisa; — **one blow** de un solo golpe; **to cut wood** — **a knife** cortar madera con un cuchillo; **to welcome someone** — **open arms** recibir a uno con los brazos abiertos; **to walk** — **a stick** andar apoyándose en un bastón.

(f) (*cause*) de; **to jump** — **joy** saltar de alegría; **to shake** — **fear** temblar de miedo; **to shiver** — **cold** tiritar de frío; **the hills are white** — **snow** las colinas están cubiertas de nieve; **to be ill** — **measles** tener sarampión; **it's pouring** — **rain** está lloviendo a cántaros; **to fill a glass** — **wine** llenar un vaso de vino.

(g) (*construction with certain verbs*) **the trouble** — **Harry** la dificultad con Enrique; el disgusto que hubo con Enrique; **it's a habit** — **him** es una costumbre que él tiene, es cosa de él; **be honest** — **me** cuéntamelo con toda franqueza; **be honest** — **yourself** no te forjes ilusiones; **you must be patient** — **her** hay que tener paciencia con ella; **we agree** — **you** estamos de acuerdo con Vd; **to fill someone** — **fear** infundir miedo a uno; llenar a uno de miedo.

(h) — **it** (*fam: also* **with-it**); **to be** — **it** estar al tanto, estar al día; tener ideas modernas; comprender el mundo actual, estar de acuerdo con las tendencias actuales; (*of dress etc*) estar de moda; **to get** — **it** ponerse al día, (*in dress etc*) ponerse a la moda; **a with-it dress** un vestido a la moda.

withal [wi'ðɔːl] *adv* (*arch*) además, también; por añadidura.

withdraw [wiθ'drɔː] (*irr: see* **draw**) **1** *vt object* retirar, sacar, quitar (*from* de); *troops, money, stamps, ambassador etc* retirar (*from* de); *words* retractar; *charge* (*Law*) apartar.

2 *vi* (*Mil etc*) retirarse (*from* de, *to* a), replegarse; (*Sport*) abandonar; (*move away*) apartarse, alejarse, irse; **he withdrew a few paces** se retiró unos pasos, se apartó un poco; **then they all withdrew** luego se retiraron todos; **to** — **from business** retirarse de los negocios; **to** — **from a contest** abandonar, renunciar a tomar parte en una contienda; **to** — **in favour of someone else** renunciar en favor de otro; **to** — **into oneself** ensimismarse; **you can't** — **now** Vd no puede abandonar ahora.

withdrawal [wiθ'drɔːəl] *n* retirada *f*; retiro *m*; abandono *m*; retractación *f*; renuncia *f*; **to make a** — **of funds from a bank** efectuar una retirada de fondos de un banco; **they made a rapid** — se retiraron rápidamente.

withdrawn [wiθ'drɔːn] **1** *ptp of* **withdraw**. **2** *adj* reservado, encerrado en sí mismo, introvertido.

withe [wiθ] *n* mimbre *m or f*.

wither ['wiðə*] **1** *vt* marchitar, secar; (*fig*) aplastar; **to** — **someone with a look** aplastar a uno con una mirada, hacer callar a uno mirándole severo.

2 *vi* marchitarse, secarse.

withered ['wiðəd] *adj* marchito, seco.

withering ['wiðəriŋ] *adj heat* abrasador; *gunfire etc* arrollador; *look, tone* lleno de desprecio, desdeñoso; *criticism* mordaz.

withers ['wiðəz] *npl* cruz *f*.

withhold [wiθ'həuld] (*irr: see* **hold**) *vt* (*keep back*) retener; (*refuse*) negar; (*refuse to reveal*) ocultar; no revelar; **to** — **a pound of someone's pay** retener una libra del pago a uno; **to** — **one's help** negarse a ayudar a uno; **to** — **the truth from someone** no revelar la verdad a uno.

withholding tax [wiθ'həuldiŋˌtæks] *n* (*US*) descuento *m* anticipado de las contribuciones.

within [wið'in] **1** *adv* dentro; **from** — desde dentro, desde el interior.

2 *prep* (*inside*) dentro de; (— *range of*) al alcance de; **here** — **the town** aquí dentro de la ciudad; — **a radius of 10 kilometres** en un radio de 10 kilómetros; **we were** — **100 metres of the summit** estábamos a 100 metros nada más de la cumbre, nos faltaron sólo 100 metros para llegar a la cumbre; **the village is** — **a mile of the river** el pueblo dista poco menos de una milla del pueblo; **to be** — **an inch of** estar a dos dedos de; **to be** — **call** estar al

alcance de la voz; — **the week** antes de terminar la semana; — **a year of her death** menos de un año después de su muerte; — **the stipulated time** dentro del plazo señalado; **to keep** — **the law** obrar dentro de los límites que impone la ley; **to live** — **one's income** vivir con arreglo a los ingresos; **a voice** — **me said . . .** una voz interior me dijo . . .

without [wið'aut] **1** *adv* (*lit*) fuera; por fuera; **from** — desde fuera.

2 *prep* sin; a falta de, en ausencia de; — **a tie** sin corbata; **3 days** — **food** 3 días sin comer; — **speaking** sin hablar, sin decir nada; — **my noticing it** sin verlo yo, sin que yo lo notase; **not** — **some difficulty** no sin alguna dificultad.

withstand [wiθ'stænd] (*irr: see* **stand**) *vt* resistir a; oponerse a; aguantar.

withy ['wiði] *n* mimbre *m or f*.

witless ['witlis] *adj* estúpido, tonto.

witness ['witnis] **1** *n* **(a)** (*evidence*) testimonio *m*; **in** — **of** en fe de; **in** — **whereof** en fe de lo cual; **to bear** — **to** dar fe de, atestiguar; **to bear false** — perjurarse.

(b) (*person*) testigo *mf*; espectador *m*, ora *f*; — **for the defence** testigo *mf* de descargo; — **for the prosecution** testigo *mf* de cargo; **there were no** —**es** no hubo testigos; **we want no** —**es to this** no queremos que nadie vea esto, que nadie sepa de esto; **to call someone as** — citar a uno como testigo.

2 *vt* **(a)** (*see*) asistir a, presenciar, ser espectador de; ver; **the accident was** —**ed by two people** hay dos testigos del accidente, dos personas vieron el accidente; **I have never** —**ed such scenes before** no he visto nunca tales escenas; **to** — **someone doing something** ver a uno que hace algo, ver como uno hace algo.

(b) — **what happened when . . .** ved lo que pasó cuando . . ., consideren lo que pasó cuando . . .; — **the case of X** según quedó demostrado en el caso de X; — **my hand** en fe de lo cual firmo.

(c) to — **a document** firmar un documento como testigo.

witness box ['witnisbɔks] *n*, (*US*) **witness stand** ['witnisstænd] *n* barra *f* de los testigos, puesto *m* de los testigos, tribuna *f* de los testigos.

witticism ['witisizəm] *n* agudeza *f*, chiste *m*, dicho *m* gracioso.

wittily ['witili] *adv* ingeniosamente; con gracia, de modo divertido.

wittiness ['witinis] *n* agudeza *f*, viveza *f* de ingenio; gracia *f*, lo divertido.

wittingly ['witiŋli] *adv* a sabiendas.

witty ['witi] *adj person* ingenioso, chistoso, salado; *remark, speech etc* gracioso, divertido; **he's very** — tiene mucha gracia, es un tipo muy salado.

wives [waivz] *npl of* **wife**.

wizard ['wizəd] **1** *n* hechicero *m*, brujo *m*; (*fam*) as *m* (*fam*), genio *m*; experto *m*. **2** *adj* (*sl*) estupendo, maravilloso.

wizardry ['wizədri] *n* hechicería *f*, brujería *f*.

wizened ['wiznd] *adj* seco, marchito; *person, skin etc* arrugado, apergaminado.

wo [wəu] *interj*, **woa** [wəu] *interj* ¡so!

woad [wəud] *n* hierba *f* pastel.

wobble ['wɔbl] **1** *n* bamboleo *m*, tambaleo *m*; **to walk with a** — tambalearse al andar, andar tambaleándose; **this chair has a** — esta silla no es nada firme, esta silla baila.

2 *vi* bambolear, tambalearse; vacilar, oscilar; (*rock*) balancearse; (*of chair etc*) bailar, ser poco firme; (*be indecisive*) vacilar.

wobbly ['wɔbli] *adj* inseguro, poco firme.

woe [wəu] *n* (*lit*) aflicción *f*, dolor *m*; mal *m*, infortunio *m*; — **is me!** ¡ay de mí!; — **betide him who . . .!** ¡ay del que . . .!; **to tell someone one's** —**s** contar a uno sus males; **it was such a tale of** — fue una historia tan triste, fue una historia tan llena de desgracias.

woebegone ['wəubiˌgɔn] *adj* desconsolado, angustiado.

woeful ['wəuful] *adj person etc* triste, afligido, desconsolado; *sight, story etc* triste, lamentable.

woefully ['wəufəli] *adv* tristemente; lamentablemente.

woke [wəuk] *pret and ptp of* **wake**.

wold [wəuld] *n* (*approx*) rasa *f* ondulada.

wolf [wulf] **1** *n*, *pl* **wolves** [wulvz] lobo *m*, a *f*; (*fam*) tenorio *m*; **lone** — (*fig*) caballero *m* solitario; — **in sheep's clothing** lobo *m* en piel de cordero; **to cry** — gritar el lobo; **to keep the** — **from the door** guardarse del hambre, evitar caer en la miseria;

to throw someone to the wolves arrojar a uno a los lobos.
 2 vt food zampar, comer vorazmente.
wolf cub ['wulfkʌb] n lobezno m.
wolfhound ['wulfhaund] n perro m lobo.
wolfish ['wulfiʃ] adj lobuno.
wolf pack ['wulfpæk] n manada f de lobos.
wolfram ['wulfrəm] n wolfram m, volframio m.
wolverine ['wulvəri:n] n carcayú m, glotón m de América.
wolves [wulvz] npl of **wolf**.
woman ['wumən] 1 n, pl **women** ['wimin] mujer f; (servant) criada f; young — joven f; old — vieja f; my old — (fam) la parienta (fam); he's rather an old — es una persona bastante sosa; se queja por poca cosa; se inquieta sin motivo; — of the town prostituta f; — of the world mujer f mundana; X and all his women X y todas sus queridas; Z and his kept — Z y su querida; to make an honest — of someone casarse con una (a causa de haberla dejado encinta); he runs after women se dedica a la caza de mujeres.
 2 as adj: — doctor médica f; — pilot mujer f piloto; — writer escritora f.
woman-hater ['wumən,heitə*] n misógino m.
womanhood ['wumənhud] n (women in general) mujeres fpl, sexo m femenino; (age) edad f adulta (de mujer); (womanliness) feminidad f; to reach — llegar a la edad adulta (de mujer).
womanish ['wuməniʃ] adj mujeril, propio de mujer; man afeminado.
womankind ['wumən'kaind] n mujeres fpl, sexo m femenino.
womanlike ['wumənlaik] adj mujeril.
womanliness ['wumənlinis] n feminidad f.
womanly ['wumənli] adj femenino.
womb [wu:m] n matriz f, útero m; (fig) seno m.
women ['wimin] npl of **woman**; —'s rights derechos mpl de la mujer; —'s page sección f para la mujer; —'s team equipo m femenino.
womenfolk ['wiminfəuk] npl las mujeres.
won [wʌn] pret and ptp of **win**.
wonder ['wʌndə*] 1 n (a) (object) maravilla f; prodigio m; portento m, milagro m; the — of electricity el milagro de la electricidad; —s of science maravillas fpl de la ciencia; the 7 —s of the world las 7 maravillas del mundo; a nine-days' — un prodigio que deja pronto de serlo; and no — y con razón, como era lógico, como era de esperar; he paid cash, for a — pagó al contado, lo cual asombró a todos; the — of it was that . . . lo asombroso fue que . . .; it is a — that . . . es un milagro que . . .; it is no (or little, small) — that . . . no es sorprendente que + subj, no es mucho que + subj; to do —s with something hacer maravillas con algo; to work —s hacer milagros.
 (b) (sense of —) admiración f, asombro m; to be lost in — quedar asombrado.
 2 as adj: — drug fármaco m milagroso.
 3 vti (a) desear saber, preguntarse; I —! ¡quizá!, ¡quién sabe!; I — what he'll do now me pregunto qué hará ahora; I — if she'll come me pregunto si viene, ¿si vendrá?; I — who first said that ¿quién habrá dicho eso por primera vez?; I — if you really love me a veces me pregunto si me quieres de verdad.
 (b) admirarse, asombrarse, maravillarse (at de); I — at your rashness me admiro de su temeridad, me asombra su temeridad; that's hardly to be —ed at eso no tiene nada de extraño, no hay que asombrarse de eso; it set me —ing me hizo pensar; she's married by now, I shouldn't — se habrá casado ya cómo sería lógico, cabe presumir que está casada ya.
wonderful ['wʌndəful] adj maravilloso; estupendo; —! ¡estupendo!
wonderfully ['wʌndəfəli] adv maravillosamente.
wondering ['wʌndəriŋ] adj tone, look etc perplejo, sorprendido.
wonderingly ['wʌndəriŋli] adv: to look — at someone mirar a uno perplejo, mirar a uno sorprendido.
wonderland ['wʌndəlænd] n admiración f, asombro m.
wonderment ['wʌndəmənt] n = **wonder** 1 (b).
wonderstruck ['wʌndəstrʌk] adj asombrado, pasmado.
wonder-worker ['wʌndə,wə:kə*] n (Med etc) droga f (etc) que efectúa curas al parecer milagrosas.
wondrous ['wʌndrəs] adj maravilloso.
wondrously ['wʌndrəsli] adv maravillosamente;

— beautiful extraordinariamente hermoso, hermoso en extremo.
wonky ['wɔŋki] adj (fam) poco firme, poco seguro; flojo; to put something on — poner algo mal, colocar algo incorrectamente.
won't [wəunt] = **will not**.
wont [wəunt] 1 adj: to be — to + infin soler + infin, acostumbrar + infin; as he was — (to) como solía (hacer).
 2 n costumbre f; it is his — to + infin suele + infin, acostumbra + infin.
wonted ['wəuntid] adj acostumbrado.
woo [wu:] vt (lit) pretender, cortejar; (fig) procurar ganarse la amistad de, solicitar el apoyo de.
wood [wud] 1 n (a) (forest) bosque m; —s bosque m, bosques mpl, monte m; we're not out of the — yet no estamos todavía a salvo, todavía queda algún peligro (or dificultad etc); he can't see the — for the trees se anda por las ramas, está obsesionado por los detalles sin ver el problema en conjunto; to take to the —s echarse al monte.
 (b) (material) madera f; (fire—) leña f; dead — ramas fpl muertas; leña f seca; (fig) material m inútil, personas fpl inútiles; to knock on —, to touch — tocar madera; touch —! ¡toca madera!; we shall manage it, touch — lo lograremos si Dios quiere (or Dios mediante).
 (c) (in winemaking etc) barril m; drawn from the — de barril.
 (d) (Mus) instrumento m de viento de madera.
 (e) (Bowls) bola f.
 2 adj, attr (a) de los bosques, selvático.
 (b) de madera.
wood alcohol ['wud'ælkəhɔl] n alcohol m metálico.
wood anemone ['wudən'eməni] n nemorosa f, anémona f de los bosques.
woodbine ['wudbain] n madreselva f.
wood block ['wudblɔk] n bloque m de madera; (in paving) adoquín m de madera.
wood carving ['wud,kɑ:viŋ] n escultura f en madera.
woodchuck ['wudtʃʌk] n marmota f de América.
woodcock ['wudkɔk] n chocha f perdiz.
woodcraft ['wudkrɑ:ft] n conocimiento m de la vida del bosque; destreza f en la montería.
woodcut ['wudkʌt] n grabado m en madera.
woodcutter ['wud,kʌtə*] n leñador m.
wooded ['wudid] adj arbolado, enselvado.
wooden ['wudn] adj (a) de madera; de palo.
 (b) (fig) face etc sin expresión, inexpresivo; personality soso, poco imaginativo, sin animación; response etc inflexible.
wood engraving ['wudin'greiviŋ] n grabado m en madera.
woodland ['wudlənd] 1 n bosque m, monte m, arbolado m. 2 adj, attr de los bosques, selvático.
woodlark ['wudlɑ:k] n totovía f.
woodlouse ['wudlaus] n, pl —lice [lais] cochinilla f.
woodman ['wudmən] n, pl —men [mən] leñador m; trabajador m forestal.
woodpecker ['wud,pekə*] n pito m, pico m; green — pito m real; lesser spotted — pico m menor.
woodpigeon ['wud,pidʒən] n paloma f torcaz.
woodpile ['wudpail] n montón m de leña.
wood pulp ['wudpʌlp] n pulpa f de madera, lignocelulosa f, pasta f celulosa.
wood shavings ['wud,ʃeiviŋz] npl virutas fpl.
woodshed ['wudʃed] n leñera f.
woodsy ['wudzi] adj (US) densamente poblado de árboles, cubierto (or rodeado etc) de bosques; selvático.
woodwind ['wudwind] n (also — instruments) instrumentos mpl de viento de madera.
woodwork ['wudwə:k] n (wood) maderaje m; molduras fpl; (craft) carpintería f, ebanistería f.
woodworm ['wudwə:m] n carcoma f.
woody ['wudi] adj tissue etc leñoso.
wooer ['wu:ə*] n pretendiente m.
woof [wu:f] n trama f.
wooing ['wu:iŋ] n galanteo m.
wool [wul] 1 n lana f; (fam) pelo m; a dyed in the — supporter un partidario fanático, un partidario acérrimo; to pull the — over someone's eyes dar a uno gato por liebre.
 2 adj, attr de lana; lanar; — trade comercio m de lana.
wool gathering ['wul,gæðəriŋ] n: to go — estar en la luna de Valencia, estar en Babia.
woollen, (US) **woolen** ['wulən] 1 adj de lana; lanar, lanero; — industry industria f de la lana.
 2 —s npl ropa f (esp interior) de lana; (Comm) géneros mpl de lana.

woollies, (US) **woolies** ['wuliz] npl ropa f (esp interior) de lana.

woolliness, (US) **wooliness** ['wulinis] n lanosidad f; (fig) lo borroso; confusión f.

woolly, (US) **wooly** ['wuli] adj lanudo, lanoso; de lana; outline etc borroso; idea confuso.

woolman ['wulmæn] n, pl —men [men] comerciante m en lanas; dueño m de una fábrica textil, lanero m.

wool merchant ['wul,mə:tʃənt] n comerciante m en lanas, lanero m.

woolsack ['wulsæk] n saco m de lana (silla del Gran Canciller en la Cámara de los Lores).

woozy ['wu:zi] adj (fam) aturdido, confuso; (Med) ligeramente indispuesto.

wop [wɔp] n (sl) italiano m.

word [wə:d] **1** n (a) (general sense) palabra f; vocablo m; voz f, término m; —s (of song) letra f; — for — palabra por palabra; — of honour palabra f, palabra f de honor; **high** —s palabras fpl airadas, palabras fpl mayores; **fine** —s palabras fpl elocuentes (pero quizá poco sinceras); **a man of few** —s un hombre nada locuaz; **never a** — ni una palabra; **by** — **of mouth** de palabra; **too funny for** —s tremendamente divertido; **too stupid for** —s de lo más estúpido; **in a** — en una palabra; **in other** —s en otros términos, es decir . . ., esto es; **in the** —s **of Calderón** con palabras de Calderón, como dice Calderón; **with these** —s **he finished** diciendo esto terminó; **without a** — sin decir palabra; **a** — **to the wise is sufficient** al buen entendedor pocas palabras le bastan; **that's not the** — I would have chosen yo no me hubiera expresado así; **his** — **is law** su palabra es ley; **it's his** — **against mine** se trata de contraponer su testimonio al mío; **it's the last** — **in luxury** es la última palabra en lujo; **rough isn't the** — **for it** no hay que llamarlo brutal sino algo más fuerte; —s **fail me** no encuentro palabras para expresarme; —s **passed between them** cambiaron algunas palabras injuriosas; **not to breathe a** — no decir palabra, no decir ni pío; **to eat one's** —s desdecirse, retractarse; **I can't get a** — **out of him** no logro sacarle una palabra; **not to let someone get a** — **in edgeways** no dejar a uno meter baza; **to have a** — **with someone** cambiar unas palabras con uno; **I'll have a** — **with him about it** hablaré con él, lo discutiré con él, se lo mencionaré; **could I have a** — **with you?** ¿me hace el favor de escucharme un momento?; **to have** —s **with someone** reñir con uno; **to have the last** — **in an argument** salir victorioso de una discusión; **I won't hear a** — **against him** no permito que se le critique; **not to mince one's** —s no tener pelos en la lengua, no morderse la lengua; **to put in a** — **for someone** defender a uno, hablar por uno; **she didn't say so in so many** —s no lo dijo exactamente así, no lo dijo así concretamente; **he never said a** — no dijo una sola palabra; **don't say a** — **about this** de esto no digas ni pío; **nobody had a good** — **to say for him** nadie quería defenderle, nadie habló en su favor; **I now call on Mr X to say a few** —s ahora le cedo la palabra al Señor X; **you took the** —s **right out of my mouth** me quitaste la palabra de la boca.

(b) (message) aviso m, recado m; noticia f; — **came that . . .** llegó noticia de que . . ., se supo que . . .; **to bring** — **of something to someone** llevar a uno la noticia de algo; **to leave** — dejar recado; **to leave** — **that . . .** dejar dicho que . . .; **to send** — mandar recado; **to send someone** — **of something** avisar a uno de algo.

(c) (promise) palabra f; (upon) **my** —! ¡caramba!; **he is a man of his** — es hombre de entera confianza; **his** — **is as good as his bond** su palabra merece entera confianza; **to be as good as one's** — cumplir lo prometido; **to break one's** — faltar a la palabra; **to give someone one's** — **that . . .** prometer que . . .; **to go back on one's** — faltar a la palabra; **to keep one's** — cumplir su promesa, cumplir lo prometido; **take my** — **for it** se lo aseguro; **I take your** — **for it** acepto lo que Vd me dice, lo creo; **to take someone at his** — coger a uno la palabra.

(d) (order) orden f; (pass—) santo m y seña; — **of command** voz f de mando; **the** — **has gone round that . . .** se ha transmitido la orden de que . . .; **to give the** — dar la orden; **you have only to say the** — solamente hace falta que Vd dé la orden.

(e) (Rel) Verbo m; **the W**— **of God** el Verbo de Dios.

2 vt redactar; expresar; **a well**—**ed declaration** una declaración bien expresada; **how shall we** — **it?** ¿cómo lo expresamos?

wordbook ['wə:dbuk] n vocabulario m.

word count ['wə:dkaunt] n recuento m de vocabulario.

word game ['wə:dgeim] n juego m de formación (or adivinación etc) de palabras.

wordiness ['wə:dinis] n verbosidad f, prolijidad f.

wording ['wə:diŋ] n fraseología f, estilo m; términos mpl.

word list ['wə:dlist] n lista f de palabras, vocabulario m.

word-of-mouth ['wə:dəv'mauθ] adj verbal, oral; see also **word 1** (a).

word perfect ['wə:d'pə:fikt] adj: **to be** — saber perfectamente su papel.

wordplay ['wə:dplei] n juego m de palabras.

wordy ['wə:di] adj verboso, prolijo.

wore [wɔ:*] pret of wear.

work [wə:k] **1** n (a) (in general) trabajo m; empleo m, ocupación f; **to be at** — estar trabajando; estar en la fábrica, estar en la oficina (etc); tener trabajo; **there are forces at** — hay fuerzas en movimiento; **to be in** — tener trabajo, tener un empleo; **to be out of** — estar desempleado; estar parado, no tener trabajo; see off **3** (d); **to put** (or **throw**) **someone out of** — privar a uno de trabajo; **to make short** — **of something** concluir algo con toda rapidez, (fig) comerse algo rápidamente; **to go the right way to** — empezar correctamente; **to set to** — ponerse a trabajar, (fig) poner manos a la obra; **to set someone to** — poner a uno a trabajar.

(b) (task, — to be done) trabajo m; labor f; **a piece of** — un trabajo, una labor; **domestic** — trabajo m de casa, labor f doméstica; **social** — asistencia f social; **day's** — jornal m; **it's all in a day's** —, **it's warm** — es un trabajo que hace sudar; **it was grim** — (fig) fue una cosa repugnante; **there's been dirty** — (at the crossroads) en esto no se ha jugado limpio, han pasado cosas asquerosas; **it's nice** — **if you can get it** (fig) es muy agradable para los que tienen esa suerte; — **has been begun on the new dam** se han comenzado las obras del nuevo embalse; **it's closed for** — **on the steeple** está cerrado debido a las obras del campanario; **I have my** — **cut out as it is** ya tengo trabajo hasta por encima de las cejas; **I had my** — **cut out to stop it** tuve que hacer grandes esfuerzos para detenerlo; **you'll have your** — **cut out trying to stop him** le costará muchísimo trabajo impedirle; **to do one's** — hacer su trabajo; **the medicine had done its** — la medicina había tenido efecto; **to do someone's dirty** — for him sacar a uno las castañas del fuego.

(c) (product: Art, Lit etc) obra f; **the** —s **of God** las obras de Dios; **good** —s buenas obras fpl; **a literary** — una obra literaria; — **of art** obra f de arte; **the** —s **of Cervantes** las obras de Cervantes; **collected** —s, **complete** —s obras fpl completas; — **of reference** libro m de consulta; **standard** — obra f clásica.

(d) —s (Mil) obras fpl, fortificaciones fpl; **defensive** —s fortificaciones fpl; **public** —s obras fpl públicas; **road** —s obras fpl de carretera; **Ministry of W**—s Ministerio m de Obras Públicas.

(e) —s (Mech) mecanismo m; motor m.

(f) —s (factory) fábrica f; taller m; eg **gasworks** fábrica f de gas.

2 vt (a) (cause to —) men hacer trabajar; **they** —**ed us from 8 till 6** nos hicieron trabajar de 8 a 6.

(b) (Mech etc) machine hacer funcionar; manejar, operar; brake accionar; moving part mover; **it is** —**ed by electricity** funciona con electricidad, es accionado por electricidad; **can you** — **it?** ¿sabes manejarlo?; **can we** — **that scheme again?** ¿podemos volver a emplear ese sistema?; **he** —**ed the lever up and down** movió la palanca hacia arriba y hacia abajo.

(c) (bring out) change producir, motivar; miracle, cure etc hacer, efectuar, operar; mischief hacer; **to** — **it** lograrlo, conseguirlo, manejar las cosas; **they** —**ed it so that she could come** se las arreglaron para que ella pudiese venir; **they** —**ed his promotion** agenciaron su ascenso, hicieron diligencias para asegurar su ascenso.

(d) (Sew) bordar; —**ed with blue thread** bordado de hilo azul.

(e) wood etc tallar; metal trabajar.

(f) mine explotar; land cultivar; **he** —s **the eastern part of the province** él trabaja en la parte este de la provincia; él se dedica a cubrir la parte este de la provincia; **we** —**ed the river bank looking for the plant** recorrimos la orilla del río buscando la planta; **this land has not been —ed for many years** estas tierras hace mucho tiempo que no se cultivan.

(g) **to — one's passage on a boat** pagar el precio del viaje en un barco haciendo trabajos de marinero (etc), viajar gratis en un barco a cambio de trabajar como marinero.

(h) (manoeuvre etc) ship maniobrar; **to — an incident into a book** introducir un episodio en un libro; **we'll try to — in a reference somewhere** trataremos de insinuar una referencia en alguna parte; **can't you — me into your plans?** ¿no sería posible dejarme entrar a formar parte de tus proyectos?; **to — one's hands free** lograr soltar las manos; **to — one's way to the top of the company** llegar a ocupar un alto puesto en la sociedad a fuerza de trabajar; **to — one's way up a cliff** escalar a duras penas un precipicio, escalar poco a poco un precipicio (and see way (d)).

(i) (with adv or prep) **to — something in** introducir algo poco a poco; **to — off one's feelings** desahogarse, aliviarse; **to — off one's surplus fat** quitarse sus grasas excesivas trabajando; **don't — your bad temper off on me!** ¡no desahogue Vd su mal humor en mí!; **to — out** problem resolver; sum calcular, hacer; idea desarrollar; plan trazar, elaborar; mine etc agotar; **to — out one's salvation** determinar su suerte; **to — out one's time** servir el plazo de su aprendizaje; **who —ed all this out?** ¿quién ideó todo esto?; **the mine is —ed out** la mina está agotada; **to — up** business desarrollar, fomentar; theme desarrollar, elaborar; feelings excitar; **the speaker was —ing them up into a frenzy** el orador excitaba los ánimos hasta el frenesí; **it gets me properly —ed up** me emociona mucho, con esto me emociono mucho; **to get —ed up** exaltarse, sofocarse; **now don't get —ed up!** ¡no te exaltes!; ¡cálmate!; **together they —ed the business up from nothing** entre los dos crearon el negocio de la nada.

3 vi (a) (general sense) trabajar (at, on en); (be in a job) tener trabajo, tener un empleo; **to — hard** trabajar mucho; **to — like a maniac** (or a Trojan etc) trabajar como un negro, trabajar como un demonio; **what are you —ing at now?** ¿en qué trabajas ahora?, (more generally) ¿a qué te dedicas ahora?

(b) (Mech etc) funcionar, marchar; **it won't —** no funciona; **"not —ing"** (lift etc) "no funciona"; **to get something —ing** hacer funcionar algo; reparar algo para que funcione; **it —s off the mains** funciona con electricidad de la red, se conecta con la red; **the motor —s with gas** el motor funciona con gas.

(c) (of medicine etc) ser eficaz, surtir efecto, obrar; **how long does it take to —?** ¿cuánto tiempo hace falta para que empiece a surtir efecto?; **this can — both ways** esto puede ser un arma de dos filos, esto puede ser contraproducente; **the scheme won't —** el proyecto no es práctico, esto no será factible, el proyecto no tendrá resultados útiles; **it won't —, I tell you!** ¡te digo que no se puede (hacer)!

(d) (of yeast) fermentar.

(e) (of mouth, face) torcerse, moverse.

(f) **to — loose** see loose.

(g) (with adv or prep) **to — in** penetrar poco a poco, calarse; **to — off** separarse, soltarse (con el uso); **to — on** (adv) seguir trabajando; **what are you —ing on?** ¿a qué se dedica Vd?, ¿qué trae Vd entre manos?; **they —ed on the car for 2 days** durante 2 días trabajaron en la reparación del coche; **they will get —ing on it at once** empezarán la reparación (etc) en seguida; **the police are —ing on it** la policía lo está investigando; **have you any clue to — on?** ¿tienen alguna pista que seguir?; **there are few facts to — on** apenas hay datos en que basarse; **we — on the principle that …** nos atenemos al principio de que …, nos guiamos por el principio de que …; **they —ed on him for 3 hours** durante 3 horas se esforzaron por persuadirle; **to — out** resolver; resolverse; **it doesn't — out** (of sum) parece que no hay solución; **it —s out at £8** llega a 8 libras, asciende a 8 libras, viene a sumar 8 libras; **how much does it — out at?** ¿cuánto suma?; **everything —ed out extremely well** todo resultó ser perfecto, la cosa salió perfectamente; **how did it — out?** ¿qué tal salió?, ¿qué resultados tuvo?; **what are you —ing up to?** ¿qué propósito tiene todo esto?; **I thought he was —ing up to a proposal** creía que estaba preparando el terreno para hacerme una declaración.

4 vr: **to — oneself to death** matarse trabajando, matarse con exceso de trabajo; **to — oneself into a frenzy** excitarse hasta el frenesí, exaltarse en grado extremo; **to — oneself up** exaltarse, sofocarse.

workable ['wə:kəbl] adj práctico, factible.

workaday ['wə:kədei] adj de cada día; (fig) rutinario, prosaico.

workbasket ['wə:k‚baːskit] n (Sew) neceser m de costura.

workbench ['wə:kbentʃ] n obrador m, banco m de trabajo.

workbook ['wə:kbuk] n libro m de trabajo; (School) cuaderno m.

workbox ['wə:kbɔks] n neceser m de costura.

workday ['wə:kdei] n día m laborable.

worker ['wə:kə*] n trabajador m, ora f; obrero m, a f (also Pol); operario m, a f; (ant) obrera f; **research —** investigador m, ora f; **skilled —** obrero m cualificado, obrera f cualificada; **all the —s in the industry** todos los trabajadores de la industria; **what about the —s?** ¿y los obreros?, ¡justicia para los obreros!; **he's a fast —** trabaja con toda prisa; (fig) obra con mucha prontitud.

worker ant ['wə:kərænt] n hormiga f obrera.

worker bee ['wə:kəbiː] n abeja f obrera.

worker priest ['wə:kəpriːst] n sacerdote m obrero.

workhouse ['wə:khaus] n, pl **—houses** [‚hauziz] asilo m de pobres; asilo m de ancianos; asilo m para desamparados.

working ['wə:kiŋ] **1** adj, attr model que funciona; capital, expenses de explotación; day laborable; class obrero; face etc (Min) de trabajo; population, partner etc activo; majority suficiente; hypothesis de guía; see day, order etc.

2 n trabajo m, el trabajar; funcionamiento m; explotación f; manejo m, operación f; labra f, laboreo m; **—s** (Min etc) labores fpl.

working-class ['wə:kiŋklɑːs] adj de la clase obrera.

working clothes ['wə:kiŋkləuðz] npl ropa f de trabajo.

working man ['wə:kiŋmæn] n, pl **— men** [men] obrero m.

working party ['wə:kiŋ‚paːti] n comisión f de investigación.

workman ['wə:kmən] n, pl **—men** [mən] obrero m; trabajador m; **to be a good —** ser buen trabajador, trabajar bien.

workmanlike ['wə:kmənlaik] adj competente, hábil (pero no brillante).

workmanship ['wə:kmənʃip] n hechura f; arte m, artificio m; destreza f, habilidad f; **of fine —** esmerado, exquisito.

workout ['wə:kaut] n (Sport) (período m de) entrenamiento m, ejercicios mpl.

workpeople ['wə:k‚piːpl] n obreros mpl; personal m, mano f de obra.

workroom ['wə:krum] n taller m, sala f de trabajo.

work sharing ['wə:k‚ʃeəriŋ] n repartimiento m del trabajo (entre los obreros de una fábrica, para evitar el desempleo).

workshop ['wə:kʃɔp] n taller m.

workshy ['wə:kʃai] adj gandul, holgazán.

world [wə:ld] **1** n (a) (general sense, Geog) mundo m, tierra f; **all the — over** en todas partes del mundo; **are there —s other than ours?** ¿existen otros mundos aparte de éste nuestro?; **it's a small —** el mundo es un pañuelo; **to feel on top of the —** estar como un reloj; **to go round the —** dar la vuelta al mundo; **to have the best of both —s** salir ganando cualquiera que sea el resultado; **to knock about the —,** to see the — ver mundo; **he lives in a — of his own** habita un pequeño mundo suyo, queda absorto en sus cosas sin prestar atención a otros.

(b) **New W—** Nuevo Mundo m; **Old W—** Viejo Mundo m.

(c) (realm) mundo m; **the — of sport, the sporting —** el mundo deportivo, el mundo de los deportes; **the business —** el mundo comercial, los negocios; **the animal —** el reino animal; **the Roman —** el mundo romano; **the — of dreams** el mundo de la fantasía, el mundo de los sueños.

(d) **man of the —** hombre m de mundo; **to come down in the —** venir a menos; **to go up in the —** ir adelante; hacer progresos en su carrera, ser ascendido; **to have the — at one's feet** triunfar, estar en la cumbre de la fama (etc); **to take the — as it is** adaptarse a la realidad, aceptar la vida como es; see lead, rise etc.

(e) (this life, Rel etc) mundo m; siglo m; **the other —,** the next —, the — to come el otro mundo; **without end** por los siglos de los siglos; **in the —** (Eccl) en el siglo; **in this —** en esta vida; **it's out of**

this — es tremendo, es increíble; he's not long for
this — le queda poco tiempo de vida; to bring into
the — echar al mundo; to come into the — nacer;
to go to a better — pasar a mejor vida.

(f) (emphatic idioms etc) not for all the — por
nada del mundo; nothing in the — would make me
do it, I wouldn't do it for the — no lo haría por
nada del mundo; what in the — can I do about it?
¿qué demonios puedo hacer?; it's what she most
wants in the — es lo que ella más desea sobre todas
las cosas; to be alone in the — estar totalmente
solo, estar completamente desamparado; it was for
all the — as if ... fue exactamente como si +
subj; I'm the —'s worst cook yo soy el peor cocinero
del mundo; she's all the — to me para mí ella
importa más que cualquier otra persona; since the
— began desde que el mundo es mundo; to be dead
to the — (asleep) estar profundamente dormido,
(drunk) estar completamente borracho; to think
the — of someone tener un altísimo concepto de
uno.

2 attr mundial; universal; — champion campeón
m mundial; — fair feria f mundial; — language
lengua f universal; on a — scale a escala mundial.
World Bank ['wəːld'bæŋk] n Banco m Mundial.
world-famous ['wəːld'feiməs] adj mundialmente
conocido, famosísimo.
worldliness ['wəːldlinis] n mundanería f.
worldly ['wəːldli] adj mundano.
worldly-wisdom ['wəːldli'wizdəm] n mundología f;
astucia f.
worldly-wise ['wəːldli'waiz] adj que tiene mucho
mundo; astuto.
world-weariness ['wəːld'wiərinis] n hastío m.
world-weary ['wəːld'wiəri] adj hastiado, cansado de
la vida.
world-wide ['wəːld'waid] adj mundial, universal.
worm [wəːm] 1 n (a) (grub) gusano m; (earth-)
lombriz f; (person) canalla m, persona f de lo más
vil; —s (Med) lombrices fpl; the — will turn un
día se acabará la paciencia del más sufrido.

(b) (Mech) tornillo m sin fin.

2 vt: to — one's way along arrastrarse como un
gusano; to — one's way into a group insinuarse en
un grupo, introducirse astutamente en un grupo;
to — a secret out of someone arrancar (or sonsacar)
un secreto a uno.

3 vr: to — oneself along arrastrarse como un
gusano; to — oneself through something atravesar
algo serpenteando.
worm drive ['wəːmdraiv] n (Mech) transmisión f
por tornillo sin fin.
worm-eaten ['wəːm,iːtn] adj wood carcomido; cloth
apolillado.
worm gear ['wəːmgiə*] n engranaje m de tornillo
sin fin.
wormhole ['wəːmhəul] n agujero m de gusano,
picadura f de polilla.
wormwood ['wəːmwud] n ajenjo m; (fig) hiel f,
amargura f.
wormy ['wəːmi] adj gusanoso, agusanado, lleno de
gusanos; carcomido: apolillado.
worn [wɔːn] ptp of wear.
worn-out ['wɔːn'aut] adj gastado; estropeado; inservible; inútil; anticuado; to be — (person) estar
rendido.
worried ['wʌrid] adj tone, look etc inquieto, preocupado; to be — about something inquietarse por
algo, estar preocupado por algo; to look — tener
aire preocupado, parecer estar inquieto.
worrier ['wʌriə*] n aprensivo m, a f; he's a terrible
— es muy aprensivo, se inquieta por cualquier
cosa.
worrisome ['wʌrisəm] adj inquietante; aprensivo.
worry ['wʌri] 1 n inquietud f, preocupación f; cuidado
m; problema m; financial worries preocupaciones
fpl de tipo financiero; he had business worries
tenía problemas con sus negocios: it's a great —
to us all nos trae a todos muy preocupados; what's
your —? ¿qué mosca te ha picado?, ¿qué problema
es éste?; the — of having to + infin el problema
de tener que + infin; to settle someone's —s
resolver los problemas de uno.

2 vt (a) inquietar, intranquilizar, preocupar;
molestar; that photo worries me esa foto me
inquieta; no estoy satisfecho con esa foto; what
worries me is not that at all no es eso lo que
me preocupa; it worries me terribly me tiene
preocupadísimo; that doesn't — me in the least
eso me tiene absolutamente sin cuidado.

(b) (of dog etc) prey pillar, sacudir y morder,
morder sacudiendo; that dog worries sheep el

perro ese ataca las ovejas; is this man worrying
you, madam? ¿le molesta este hombre, señora?

(c) to — out a problem esforzarse por resolver
un problema, devanarse los sesos para resolver un
problema; finally we worried it out por fin lo
resolvimos a costa de mucho trabajo.

3 vi inquietarse, preocuparse (about, over por);
apurarse; molestarse; he worries a lot se apura por
cualquier cosa; don't —! ¡no se preocupe!; ¡descuida!;
it's all right, don't — está bien, no se moleste;
don't — about me no te preocupes por mí; I
should —! y a mí ¿qué?
worrying ['wʌriiŋ] adj inquietante.
worse [wəːs] 1 adj comp of bad; peor; inferior; A is
— than B A es peor que B, A es inferior a B; —
and —! ¡peor todavía!; it gets — and — va de
mal en peor; it's — than ever es peor que nunca;
it could have been —! ¡menos mal!; it would have
been — if . . . hubiera sido más grave si . . . ; it
will be the — for you será peor para Vd; so much the
— for him tanto peor para él; to be the — for
drink estar algo borracho; to be the — for wear
estar deteriorado (and see wear); he is none the
— for it no se ha hecho daño; la experiencia no
le ha hecho mal (and see none); to get —, to grow
— empeorar, hacerse peor, (Med) ponerse peor;
to make a situation — hacer una situación más
difícil; to make matters — para colmo de desgracias;
I don't think any the — of you esto no afecta la
opinión que tengo de Vd.

2 adv comp of badly; it hurts — me duele más;
she behaves — than ever se comporta peor que
nunca; you might do — hay cosas peores; you
might do — than to + infin sería quizá posible +
infin, quizá sea aconsejable + infin; he is now —
off than before ahora está en peores circunstancias
que antes, ahora está en una situación más apurada
que antes; we are — off than them for books en
cuanto a libros nosotros estamos peores que ellos.

3 n el peor, lo peor; there is — to come hay más,
todavía no te he dicho (etc) lo peor; it's changed
for the — ha cambiado y está peor; see bad.
worsen ['wəːsn] 1 vt agravar, hacer peor; hacer más
difícil.

2 vi empeorar, hacerse peor; agravarse; hacerse
más difícil; (Med) ponerse peor.
worship ['wəːʃip] 1 n (a) (adoration) adoración f,
veneración f; (organized —) culto m (of a); (church
service) culto m, oficio m; with a look of — con una
mirada llena de adoración; place of — edificio m
de culto. (b) (in titles) His W— the Mayor of X el
señor alcalde de X; Your W— (to judge) señor
juez, (to mayor) señor alcalde; if your w— wishes
(iro) si el caballero lo desea. 2 vt adorar (also fig),
venerar.
worshipful ['wəːʃipful] adj (in titles) excelentísimo.
worshipper ['wəːʃipə*] n adorador m, ora f, devoto
m, a f; —s (collectively) fieles mpl.
worst [wəːst] 1 adj superl of bad; (el) peor; the —
film of the three la peor película de las tres.

2 adv superl of badly; peor; I did it — yo lo
hice peor.

3 n lo peor; in the — of the winter en lo más
recio del invierno; in the — of the storm en el
peor momento de la tormenta; when the crisis
was at its — en el momento más grave de la crisis;
at (the) — en el peor de los casos; that's the — of
it ésa es la peor parte; the — of it is that ... lo
peor del caso es que ... ; if the — comes to the
— si pasa lo peor; do your —! ¡haga todo lo que
quiera!; to get the — of it salir perdiendo, llevar
la peor parte, sufrir más que su contrincante;
to give someone the — of it derrotar a uno; we're
over (or past) the — of it now hemos vencido la
cuesta ya; once you get the — over en cuanto salves
el bache.
worsted ['wustid] n estambre m.
worth [wəːθ] 1 adj (a) (in monetary senses) equivalente
a, que vale, del valor de; it's — £5 vale 5 libras;
what's this —? ¿cuánto vale esto?; it's not —
much no vale mucho; apenas tiene valor; he was
— a million when he died murió millonario, murió
dejando una fortuna de un millón; one Ruritanian
is — 3 Slobodians un ruritano vale por (or
equivale a) 3 eslobodios; I tell you this for what
it's — te digo esto sin poder afirmar que sea cierto,
te digo esto por si acaso el dato te interesa; to run for
all one is — correr a todo correr; to sing for all
one is — cantar con toda el alma.

(b) (deserving) digno de, que merece; it's not —
it, it's not — the trouble no vale la pena; a thing
— having una cosa digna de ser poseída, una cosa

que vale la pena adquirir; **is the book — buying?** ¿me vale la pena comprar el libro?; **it's — thinking about** merece que se considere, merece consideración; *see* **while.**

2 *n* (*monetary*) valor *m*; (*fig*) valía *f*, mérito *m*; **£10's — of books** libros *mpl* por valor de 10 libras; **5 pesetas' — of sweets** 5 pesetas de bombones; **he had no chance to show his true** — no tuvo ocasión de demostrar su verdadera valía; **his moral — is not in question** no se trata de su valor moral; **what's the — of this table?** ¿cuánto vale esta mesa?; *see* **money's-worth.**

worthily ['wəːðili] *adv* dignamente; **to respond — to an occasion** estar a la altura de las circunstancias.

worthiness ['wəːðinis] *n* mérito *m*, merecimiento *m*.

worthless ['wəːθlis] *adj* sin valor; inútil, que no vale para nada; **a — individual** una persona despreciable, una persona sin carácter; **he's not completely —** no es que carezca absolutamente de buenas cualidades.

worthlessness ['wəːθlisnis] *n* falta *f* de valor; inutilidad *f*; lo despreciable, falta *f* de carácter.

worthwhile ['wəːθ'wail] *adj* valioso, útil; digno de consideración; que vale la pena; **a — film** una película seria, una película que merece atención; *see also* **while.**

worthy ['wəːði] **1** *adj* (**a**) meritorio; benemérito; respetable; loable, plausible; *motive etc* honesto, honrado; **a — person** una persona respetable; **your — newspaper** (*letter to editor*) su estimado periódico.

(**b**) **— of** digno de; **— of remark** notable, digno de notar; **— of respect** digno de respeto, respetable; **to be — of something** ser digno de algo, merecer algo; **it is — of note that . . .** vale observar que . . . ; **es notable que . . .** ; **that comment was not — of you** esa observación fue indigna de Vd; **the car is — of a better driver** el coche merece tener mejor conductor.

2 *n* personaje *m*; dignatario *m*.

would [wud] *v aux* **1** (**a**) (*used to form conditional tense*) **she — come** vendría; **if you asked him he — do it** si se lo pidieras lo haría; **if you had asked him he — have done it** si se lo hubieras pedido lo habría hecho (*or* lo hubiera hecho); **I thought you — want to know** se me figuraba que desearías enterarte.

(**b**) (*conditional, emphatic*) **you — be the one to forget** desde luego eres tú el que se olvida.

(**c**) (*conditional, probability*) **it — seem so** así parece ser; **it — be about 8 o'clock** serían las 8.

(**d**) (*conjecture*) **what — this be?** ¿esto qué será?

2 (**a**) (*wish*) querer; **what — you have me do?** ¿qué quieres que haga?; **try as he —** por mucho que se esforzara, por más que intentase; **the place where I — be** el lugar donde me gustaría estar; **— (that) it were not so!** ¡ojalá no fuera así!; **— to God!, — to heaven!** ¡ojalá!

(**b**) (*consent*) querer; **— you care for some tea?** ¿quieres una taza de té?; **— you tell me your name?** ¿me hace el favor de darme su nombre?; **he — not do it** no quería hacerlo, se negó a hacerlo.

(**c**) (*habit*) **he — paint it each year** solía pintarlo cada año, lo pintaba cada año.

would-be ['wudbiː] *adj*: **a — poet** un aspirante a poeta, uno que presume de poeta, uno que quiere ser poeta.

wouldn't ['wudnt] = **would not.**

wound [wuːnd] **1** *n* herida *f*; **deep —** herida *f* profunda; **skin —** herida *f* superficial; **to lick one's —s** lamer sus heridas.

2 *vt* herir (*also fig*); **the —ed** los heridos; **to — someone's feelings** herir los sentimientos de uno.

wound [waund] *pret and ptp of* **wind.**

wounding ['wuːndiŋ] *adj remark, tone* hiriente, mordaz.

wove [wəuv] *pret of* **weave.**

woven ['wəuvən] *ptp of* **weave.**

wow [wau] *n* (*sl*): **it's a —!** ¡es tremendo!

wrack¹ [ræk] *n* (*Bot*) fuco *m*.

wrack² [ræk] *see* **rack¹** *and* **rack².**

wraith [reiθ] *n* fantasma *m*.

wrangle ['ræŋgl] **1** *n* altercado *m*, riña *f* (indecorosa).

2 *vi* reñir (indecorosamente) (*about, over* a causa de, *with* con); (*in bargaining*) regatear.

wrap [ræp] **1** *n* (*indoor*) bata *f*, (*outdoor*) abrigo *m*.

2 *vt* (*also* **to — up**) envolver; (*for warmth*) arropar; (*cover*) cubrir; **shall I — it (up) for you?** ¿quiere que se lo envuelva?; **he does so — it up** (*fig*) lo dice con tal exceso de palabras, lo expone de manera tan enmarañada; **to be —ped up in** estar envuelto en; (*fig*) estar absorto en, estar completamente dedicado a; **he is —ped up in her** no quiere pensar en nada

sino en ella, le dedica todas sus atenciones a ella; **they are —ped up in each other** están absortos el uno en el otro.

3 *vi*: **to — up** arroparse, arrebujarse; **— up!** (*sl*) ¡cállate!; **see that you — up warm** cuida de arroparte bien.

wrapper ['ræpə*] *n* envoltura *f*, envase *m*; (*of book*) sobrecubierta *f*, camisa *f*; (*postal*) faja *f*.

wrapping ['ræpiŋ] *n* envoltura *f*, envase *m*.

wrapping paper ['ræpiŋ,peipə*] *n* papel *m* de envolver.

wrath [rɔθ] *n* (*lit*) cólera *f*, ira *f*; (*fig*) ira *f*.

wrathful ['rɔθful] *adj* (*lit*) colérico, airado.

wrathfully ['rɔθfəli] *adv* coléricamente, airadamente.

wreak [riːk] *vt* (*lit*) ejecutar; *destruction etc* hacer, causar; *vengeance* tomar (*on* en); *anger* descargar (*on* en); *punishment* infligir (*on* en); **to — havoc** hacer estragos.

wreath [riːθ] *n*, *pl* **wreaths** [riːðz] (*of flowers etc*) guirnalda *f*, (*funeral —*) corona *f*; (*of smoke*) espiral *f*; **laurel —** corona *f* de laurel.

wreathe [riːð] **1** *vt* (*encircle*) ceñir, rodear (*with* de); (*plait*) trenzar; entrelazar; (*garland*) enguirnaldar (*with* con); **to — flowers into one's hair** ponerse flores en el pelo; **a face —d in smiles** una cara muy sonriente, una cara muy risueña; **trees —d in mist** árboles *mpl* envueltos en niebla.

2 *vi* (*of smoke etc*; *also* **to — upwards**) enroscarse, formar espirales, elevarse en espirales.

wreck [rek] **1** *n* (**a**) (*Naut act*) naufragio *m*; (*ship*) buque *m* naufragado, buque *m* hundido; **the ship was a total —** el buque se consideró como totalmente perdido, fue imposible salvar el buque.

(**b**) (*Rail etc*) colisión *f*, accidente *m*.

(**c**) (*fig*) ruina *f*, destrucción *f*; **the — of one's hopes** la ruina de las esperanzas de uno; **he's a —** es un carcamal; **I'm a —, I feel a —** estoy hecho polvo; **she's a nervous —** tiene una tremenda tensión nerviosa; **I'm a nervous —** tengo los nervios de punta; **if this goes on I shall be a nervous —** si las cosas siguen así acabaré con los nervios destrozados; **she looks a —** está hecha una pena.

2 *vt* (**a**) (*ship*) hacer naufragar, hundir, destruir; *train* descarrilar; *car, plane, mechanism etc* estropear, destrozar; **you've —ed my gears** Vd ha estropeado la caja de cambios; **to be —ed** (*Naut*) naufragar, irse a pique, ser hundido; **the ship was —ed on those rocks** el buque naufragó en aquellas rocas.

(**b**) (*fig*) *hopes etc* arruinar, destruir, acabar con.

wreckage ['rekidʒ] *n* (**a**) (*act*) naufragio *m*; (*fig*) naufragio *m*, ruina *f*, destrucción *f*.

(**b**) (*remains: Naut*) pecios *mpl*, restos *mpl* de un buque naufragado; (*of car etc*) restos *mpl*; (*of house etc*) escombros *mpl*, ruinas *fpl*.

wrecked [rekt] *adj ship* naufragado, hundido; *car etc* estropeado, averiado.

wrecker ['rekə*] *n* (*Naut*) raquero *m*; (*Rail*) descarrilador *m*; (*fig*) destructor *m*, ora *f*.

wrecking service ['rekiŋ,səːvis] *n* (*Aut*) servicio *m* de auxilio (para coches averiados).

wren [ren] *n* chochín *m*.

wrench [rentʃ] **1** *n* (**a**) (*tug*) arranque *m*, tirón *m*; (*Med*) torcedura *f*; **to give something a —** tirar violentamente de algo, torcer algo violentamente; **to give one's arm a —** torcerse el brazo.

(**b**) (*tool*) llave *f* inglesa.

(**c**) (*fig*) dolor *m*; sacudida *f*; choque *m*; **the — of parting** el dolor de la separación, la angustia de la separación; **it was a — to have to leave** me causó pena tener que partir.

2 *vt* arrancar, tirar violentamente de; **to — one's arm** torcerse el brazo, dislocarse el brazo; **to — something (away) from someone** arrebatar algo violentamente a uno; **to — something off** quitar algo torciéndolo violentamente; **to — a door open** abrir una puerta tirando violentamente de ella; **to — a bulb out** sacar una bombilla torciéndola violentamente.

wrest [rest] **1** *vt*: **to — something from someone** arrebatar algo a uno, arrancar algo a uno; **to — gold from the rocks** extraer a duras penas oro de las rocas; **to — a living from the soil** ganarse la vida cultivando con mucha dificultad el suelo.

2 *vr*: **to — oneself free** (*lograr*) libertarse tras grandes esfuerzos; **try to — yourself free** procura soltarte haciendo un esfuerzo.

wrestle ['resl] **1** *n* lucha *f*; partido *m* de lucha; **to have a — with someone** luchar con uno.

2 *vt* luchar con, luchar contra.

3 *vi* luchar (*with* con, *contra*); **to — with** (*fig*) luchar con; **we are wrestling with the problem** estamos luchando con el problema, nos esforzamos

por resolver el problema; **the pilot —d with the controls** el piloto luchaba con los mandos.
wrestler ['reslə*] n luchador m (de lucha libre).
wrestling ['reslɪŋ] n lucha f libre.
wrestling match ['reslɪŋmætʃ] n partido m de lucha.
wretch [retʃ] n desgraciado m, a f, infeliz mf; **little —** (often hum) tunante m, pícaro m, a f; **some poor —** algún desgraciado, algún pobre diablo; **you — !** (hum) ¡canalla!
wretched ['retʃid] adj (unfortunate) desgraciado, desdichado; (contemptible) miserable, despreciable; pobre, lamentable; (very bad) horrible; (ill) malo, enfermo; **that — dog** ese maldito perro; **where's that — stick?** ¿dónde está el condenado bastón ese?; **it's — weather** hace un tiempo horrible; **what — luck!** ¡qué mala suerte!; **I'm a — player** juego malísimamente; **to feel —** (Med) sentirse muy mal; (depressed) estar deprimido, estar abatido; **I felt — about it** me daba grandes remordimientos.
wretchedly ['retʃidli] adv lamentablemente; horriblemente; muy mal; **to be — unlucky** tener malísima suerte; **she plays —** toca horriblemente mal; **they treated her —** la trataron de modo infame.
wretchedness ['retʃidnis] n desgracia f, desdicha f; lo despreciable; lo lamentable; lo horrible; infamia f; depresión f, abatimiento m.
wrick [rik] **1** n torcedura f. **2** vt torcer; **to — one's neck** darse un tortícolis.
wriggle ['rigl] **1** n meneo m; serpenteo m, culebreo m.
    2 vt menear; ears, hips etc mover; **to — one's way into** deslizarse en, introducirse (con dificultad) en; **to — one's way through** lograr pasar (con dificultad) por.
    3 vi menearse; (also — along) culebrear, moverse culebreando, avanzar serpenteando; **to — away** escaparse culebreando; **to — out of a difficulty** escaparse mañosamente de un apuro; **to — through a hole** pasar (culebreando, con dificultad) por un agujero; **to — with pain** retorcerse de dolor.
wriggly ['rigli] adj sinuoso, tortuoso.
wring [riŋ] (irr: pret and ptp **wrung**) **1** vt (a) torcer, retorcer; clothes exprimir el agua de, escurrir; hands retorcer; animal's neck torcer; **to — clothes out** escurrir la ropa; **to — water out of clothes** exprimir el agua de la ropa.
    (b) (fig) heart etc acongojar, apenar; **to — money out of someone** sacar dinero por la fuerza a uno; **to — a concession out of someone** persuadir a uno (tras muchos esfuerzos) a hacer una concesión, lograr (con dificultad) que uno haga una concesión; **eventually we wrung the truth out of them** por fin logramos que nos dijeran la verdad.
    2 n: **to give clothes a —** exprimir el agua de la ropa.
wringer ['riŋə*] n escurridor m, máquina f de exprimir.
wringing ['riŋiŋ] adj: **to be — (wet)** estar completamente mojado, (person) estar mojado hasta los huesos.
wrinkle¹ ['riŋkl] **1** n arruga f; pliegue m. **2** vt arrugar; brow fruncir. **3** vi arrugarse; plegarse, ajarse.
wrinkle² ['riŋkl] n (fam) idea f, noción f; (tip) sugerencia f, indicación f; (dodge) truco m, estratagema f.
wrinkled ['riŋkld] adj, **wrinkly** ['riŋkli] adj arrugado, lleno de arrugas.
wrist [rist] n muñeca f.
wristband ['ristbænd] n puño m (de camisa).
wristlet ['ristlit] n pulsera f, muñequera f, brazalete m.
wrist watch ['ristwɔtʃ] n reloj m de pulsera.
writ [rit] n escritura f; (Law) orden f, mandato m, decreto m judicial; (fig) autoridad f; **Holy W—** Sagrada Escritura f; **— for an election** autorización f para celebrar elecciones; **— of attachment** orden f de detención; **— of execution** auto m de ejecución; **— of restraint** inhibitoria f; **to issue a —** dar orden, hacer un decreto judicial; **to issue a — against someone** demandar a uno en juicio; **to issue a — for slander against someone** demandar a uno por calumnia; **to serve a — on someone** entregar una orden (etc) a uno; **his — does not run here** aquí el no tiene autoridad, su autoridad no se extiende hasta aquí.
write [rait] (irr: pret **wrote**, ptp **written**) **1** vt (a) (general sense) escribir; redactar; poner por escrito; **did I — that?** ¿lo escribí yo así?; ¿fui capaz de escribir eso?; **how is that written?** ¿cómo se escribe eso?; **she —s a good hand** tiene buena letra.
    (b) (compose) escribir; componer.
    (c) (fig) **his guilt was written all over him** tenía aspecto de culpable, todo en él daba indicios

de su culpabilidad; **he had "policeman" written all over him** su aspecto entero revelaba que era policía, daba indicios inconfundibles de ser policía.
    (d) (+ adv or prep) **to — down** (note) apuntar, anotar; (put in writing) poner por escrito; (record) hacer constar; (Comm) rebajar, bajar el precio de; reducir el valor nominal de; **we wrote him down as useless** decidimos que era inútil; **to — in** escribir, insertar; **name of candidate** (US) añadir a la lista oficial; **to — off** (quickly) escribir rápidamente, (at once) escribir en seguida; (Comm) debt borrar (como incobrable), (fig) cancelar, anular; **to — something off as a total loss** considerar algo como totalmente perdido; **to — £100 off for depreciation** quitar 100 libras al valor nominal de algo debido a la depreciación; **to — out** cheque escribir, extender; (transcribe) copiar, transcribir; (in full) escribir en su forma completa, escribir sin abreviar; **to — up** report etc escribir; event escribir una crónica de, hacer un reportaje de; diary, ledger poner al día; **to — someone up (in a big way)** dar bombo a uno (en un artículo etc), describir a uno en términos elogiosos; **to — something up (in a big way)** describir algo exageradamente.
    2 vi (a) escribir; **as I —** mientras escribo estas líneas; **we — to each other** nos escribimos, nos carteamos; **will you — to me?** ¿me escribirás?; **I wrote to him to come** le escribí diciéndole que viniera; **that's nothing to — home about** eso no tiene nada de particular; **I'll — for it at once** lo pediré por escrito en seguida, escribiré para pedirlo en seguida.
    (b) (as profession) escribir, ser escritor; **he —s for a living** se gana la vida escribiendo, es escritor de profesión; **he —s as a hobby** escribe como distracción; **to — for a paper** colaborar en un periódico, escribir en un periódico.
    (c) (with adv) **to — back** contestar; **to — in** escribir (for something pidiendo algo); **to — off** escribir (con prontitud; for something pidiendo algo).
write-off ['raitɔf] n (Comm) depreciación f; (fig) pérdida f total.
writer-['raitə*] n escritor m, ora f; autor m, ora f; **the (present) —** el que esto escribe; **— to the signet** (Scot) notario m; **a — of detective stories** un autor de novelas policíacas; **to be a poor —** (in handwriting) tener mala letra.
write-up ['raitʌp] n (report) crónica f, reportaje m; (pej) bombo m, descripción f exagerada, descripción f muy elogiosa.
writhe [raið] vi retorcerse, contorcerse; debatirse; **to — with pain, to — in pain** retorcerse de dolor; **to make someone —** (painfully) hacer sufrir a uno, (with disgust) dar asco a uno; **it made me — with embarrassment** con eso me sentí terriblemente molesto.
writing ['raitiŋ] **1** n (a) (art in general) el escribir, escritura f; **in —** por escrito; **evidence in —** declaración f escrita, testimonio m por escrito; **at the time of —** en el momento de escribir esto; **to commit something to —, to put something in —** poner algo por escrito.
    (b) (hand-) escritura f, letra f; **in one's own —** de su propia letra; **in Góngora's own —** de puño y letra de Góngora; **the — on the wall** advertencias fpl graves, profecías fpl terribles; **the — is on the wall for them** es una advertencia muy clara para ellos; **he had seen the — on the wall** se había dado cuenta de lo grave de su situación.
    (c) (thing written) escrito m; obra f; **the —s of Cela** las obras de Cela.
    (d) (profession) profesión f de autor; trabajo m literario; **he earns a bit from his —** gana algo con su trabajo literario.
    2 attr de escribir.
writing case ['raitiŋkeis] n cartera f (or cartapacio m) para papeles de escribir.
writing desk ['raitiŋdesk] n escritorio m.
writing pad ['raitiŋpæd] n taco m de papel, bloc m.
writing paper ['raitiŋpeipə*] n papel m de escribir.
written ['ritn] **1** ptp of **write**. **2** adj escrito.
wrong [rɔŋ] **1** adj (a) (morally: wicked) malo, inicuo; (unfair) injusto; **it's — to steal** robar es un crimen; **that was very —** of you en eso has hecho muy mal; **you were — to** + infin hiciste mal en + infin; **what's — with a drink now and again?** ¿será pecado tomar algo de vez en cuando?; **what's — in cuddling?** ¿por qué no nos podemos abrazar?, ¿es que es un pecado abrazarse?
    (b) (incorrect) erróneo, incorrecto, inexacto, equivocado; **the — use of drugs** el uso impropio

de las drogas; **to be —** (*person*) no tener razón; equivocarse, estar equivocado; **that is —** eso no es exacto, eso no es cierto; **the answer is —** la respuesta es inexacta; **is that still —?** ¿eso está mal todavía?; **that clock is —** ese reloj anda mal, ese reloj no marcha bien.

(c) (*improper, not sought, not wanted*) impropio, inoportuno; **it's the — one** no es el que buscaba (*or* quería), no es el que hacía falta; **on the — side of the road** en el lado contrario de la carretera, (*Brit*) en el lado derecho de la carretera, (*US*) en el lado izquierdo de la carretera; **at the — time** inoportunamente; **it's in the — place** está mal situado, está mal colocado; **I'm in the — job** tengo un puesto que no me conviene, soy miembro de una profesión que no me conviene; me he equivocado de profesión; **we were on the — train** nos habíamos equivocado de tren; **is this the — road?** ¿nos habremos equivocado de camino?; **to play a — note** equivocarse al tocar una nota; **to say the — thing** decir algo inoportuno; **you have the — number** (*Tel*) Vd se ha confundido de número; *see* **way** etc.

(d) (*amiss*) **something is —** hay algo que no está bien; **is anything —?, is something— ?** ¿pasa algo?; **what's — with you?** ¿qué te pasa?; **I hope there's nothing — at home** espero que no pasa nada malo en casa; **something's — with my watch** le pasa algo a mi reloj, mi reloj no anda bien; **there is something — with my lights** los faros tienen una avería, los faros están averiados.

2 *adv* mal; sin razón; injustamente; incorrectamente, equivocadamente; al revés; **to answer —** contestar mal, contestar incorrectamente; **you did — hiciste mal; you're doing it all —** no se hace así, no comprendes el modo de hacerlo; **to get it — (misunderstand)** comprender mal; no acertar; (*Math etc*) calcular mal, equivocarse en el cálculo; **to go —** (*on route*) equivocarse de camino; extraviarse; (*in calculation*) equivocarse; (*morally*) extraviarse, caer en el vicio; (*of affair*) ir mal, salir mal; (*Mech*) fallar; estropearse, averiarse; dejar de funcionar; **something went — with the gears** se averió la caja de cambios; **something went — with their plans** algo falló en sus planes, fracasaron sus planes; **something is seriously —** pasa algo grave; **you can't go —!** ¡es imposible perder!

3 *n* **(a)** (**the —**) mal *m*; **to know right from —** saber distinguir el bien del mal; **two —s do not make a right** no se subsana un error cometiendo otro.

(b) (*injustice*) injusticia *f*; agravio *m*, entuerto *m*; **to do someone a great —** ser muy injusto con uno, agraviar gravemente a uno; **to labour under a sense of —** sentirse agraviado, creer que uno ha sido tratado injustamente; **to right a —** deshacer un agravio, acabar con un abuso.

(c) to be in the — no tener razón, estar equivocado; tener la culpa; **to put someone in the —** quitar la razón a uno; hacer que otro cargue con la culpa.

4 *vt* agraviar; ser injusto con; **you — me** eso no es justo; **to feel that one has been —ed** sentirse agraviado, creer que uno ha sido tratado injustamente.

wrongdoer ['rɔŋˌduːə*] *n* malhechor *m*, ora *f*; pecador *m*, ora *f*.

wrongdoing ['rɔŋˌduːɪŋ] *n* maldad *f*; pecados *mpl*; perversidad *f*; crímenes *mpl*.

wrongful ['rɔŋful] *adj* injusto; ilegal.

wrongfully ['rɔŋfəli] *adv* injustamente; ilegalmente.

wrong-headed ['rɔŋ'hedid] *adj* obstinado, terco, perversamente equivocado; **to be — about something** obstinarse perversamente en sostener (*etc*) algo.

wrong-headedly ['rɔŋ'hedidli] *adv* obstinadamente, perversamente.

wrong-headedness ['rɔŋ'hedidnis] *n* obstinación *f*, terquedad *f*; error *m* perverso.

wrongly ['rɔŋli] *adv* mal; injustamente; incorrectamente; equivocadamente; al revés; **he — maintains that...** él sostiene equivocadamente que...; **to put a screw in —** poner un tornillo mal; **she had been very — treated** la habían tratado muy injustamente.

wrongness ['rɔŋnis] *n* iniquidad *f*; injusticia *f*; inexactitud *f*, error *m*, falsedad *f*; impropiedad *f*, inoportunidad *f*.

wrote [rəut] *pret of* **write**.

wrought [rɔːt] **1** (*arch*) *pret and ptp of* **work**; **he — valiantly** luchó denodadamente, trabajó con esfuerzo; **great changes have been —** se han efectuado grandes cambios.

2 *adj* **(a)** *iron etc* forjado; *silver etc* labrado.

(b) to be — (up) (*person*) estar muy agitado, estar muy nervioso.

wrought-up ['rɔːt'ʌp] *adj* agitado, nervioso.

wrung [rʌŋ] *pret and ptp of* **wring**.

wry [rai] *adj* torcido; *sense of humour, joke etc* pervertido, raro; *speech etc* irónico, lleno de ironía; **to make a — face** hacer una mueca, torcer el gesto.

wryly ['raili] *adv* irónicamente, con ironía.

wryneck ['rainek] *n* (*Orn*) torcecuello *m*.

wych-elm ['witʃ'elm] *n* olmo *m* escocés.

X

x [eks] *n* (*Math; fig*) x *f*; incógnita *f*; — **marks the spot** el sitio está señalado con una X; **if you have** — **pesetas a year** si se tiene equis pesetas al año.

Xavier ['zeiviə*] *m* Javier.

xenon ['zenɒn] *n* xeno *m*, xenón *m*.

xenophobe ['zenəfəub] *n* xenófobo *m*.

xenophobia [ˌzenə'fəubiə] *n* xenofobia *f*.

Xenophon ['zenəfən] *m* Jenofonte.

Xmas ['eksməs] *n* (*fam*) *abbr of* **Christmas**.

X-ray ['eks'rei] **1** *n* radiografía *f*; —**s** rayos *mpl* X. **2** *adj, attr* radiográfico; — **examination** examen *m* con rayos X; — **photograph** radiografía *f*. **3** *vt* radiografiar.

xylograph [ˈzailəgrɑːf] *n* xilografía *f*, grabado *m* en madera.

xylographic [zailə'græfik] *adj* xilográfico.

xylography [zai'lɒgrəfi] *n* xilografía *f*.

xylophone ['zailəfəun] *n* xilófono *m*.

Y

yacht [jɔt] **1** n (esp large, seagoing) yate m; (small, model) balandro m.
2 vi pasear en yate, navegar en yate; tomar parte en regatas de balandros; dedicarse al balandrismo.
yacht club ['jɔtklʌb] n club m náutico.
yachting ['jɔtiŋ] **1** n deporte m de la vela, balandrismo m; pasear m en yate, navegar m en yate; regatas fpl de balandros.
2 attr de yates, de balandros; de balandristas; **in — circles** entre los aficionados al deporte de la vela, entre balandristas; **it's not a — coast** en esa costa no se practica el deporte de la vela.
yacht race ['jɔtreis] n regata f de yates, regata f de balandros.
yachtsman ['jɔtsmən] n, pl **—men** [mən] deportista m náutico; balandrista m.
yachtsmanship ['jɔtsmənʃip] n arte m de navegar en yate (or balandro).
yackety-yak ['jækiti'jæk] n (chatter) palabreo m, cháchara f; (argument) dimes mpl y diretes; (insistence) machaqueo m.
yah [jɑː] interj ¡bah!
yahoo [jɑː'huː] n patán m.
yak [jæk] n yac m, yak m.
yam [jæm] n batata f, ñame m.
yank [jæŋk] **1** n tirón m; **to give a rope a —** tirar de una cuerda. **2** vt tirar de; **to — a nail out** sacar un clavo de un tirón.
Yank [jæŋk] n (fam) yanqui mf (fam).
Yankee ['jæŋki] (fam) **1** adj yanqui (fam). **2** n yanqui mf (fam).
yap [jæp] **1** n ladrido m agudo. **2** vi dar ladridos agudos; (fam: chat) charlar; (protest) quejarse, protestar (sin razón).
yapping ['jæpiŋ] n ladridos mpl agudos.
yard[1] [jɑːd] n **(a)** yarda f (= 91,44 cm); **an essay —s long** un ensayo larguísimo; **he pulled out —s of handkerchief** sacó un enorme pañuelo; **with a face a — long** muy cariacontecido, tristísimo; **a few —s off** a varios metros, a poca distancia.
(b) (Naut) verga f.
yard[2] [jɑːd] n (of house) patio m; (of farm etc) corral m; (School) patio m de recreo; **the Y—, Scotland Y —** oficina central de la policía de Londres.
yardarm ['jɑːdɑːm] n verga f, penol m.
yardstick ['jɑːdstik] n (fig) criterio m, norma f.
yarn [jɑːn] **1** n **(a)** hilo m, hilaza f.
(b) (tale) cuento m, historia f; **to spin a —** contar una historia; contar cosas inverosímiles; **to spin someone a —** disculparse con un pretexto inverosímil.
2 vi contar historias; contar cosas inverosímiles; contar chistes.
yarrow ['jærəu] n milenrama f.
yashmak ['jæʃmæk] n velo m (de musulmana).
yaw [jɔː] (Naut) **1** n guiñada f. **2** vi guiñar, hacer una guiñada.
yawl [jɔːl] n yol m, yola f.
yawn [jɔːn] **1** n bostezo m; **it was a — from start to finish** fue aburridísimo; **to say something with a —** decir algo bostezando.
2 vt decir bostezando (also to — out); **to — one's head off** bostezar mucho; bostezar abriendo muchísimo la boca.
3 vi bostezar.
yawning ['jɔːniŋ] adj (fig) muy abierto, grande.
yaws [jɔːz] n (Med) frambesia f.
ye [jiː] pron (arch) vosotros, vosotras.
yea [jei] (arch) **1** adv (yes) sí; (indeed) sin duda, ciertamente; (moreover) además. **2** n sí m; **the —s and the nays** los votos afirmativos y los negativos.
yeah [jɛə] adv (fam) = yes.
year ['jiə*] n **(a)** año m; **— of grace** año m de gracia; **in the — of our Lord . . .** en el año del Señor . . .; **all the — round** durante todo el año; **— in, — out**

año tras año; todos los años sin falta; **3 times a —** 3 veces al año; **100 dollars a —** 100 dólares al año; **to reckon by the —** calcular por años; **in after —s** en los años siguientes, años después; **in my early —s** en mi infancia, en mi tierna edad, en mi juventud; **in his later —s** en sus últimos años; **of late —s** en estos últimos años; **last —** el año pasado; **the — before last** el año antepasado; **next —** (looking to future) el año que viene, (in past time) el año siguiente; **he looks old for his —s** parece más viejo de lo que es en realidad; **he's getting on in —s** es bastante viejo, va para viejo; **he got 10 —s** le condenaron a 10 años de prisión; **it takes —s** es cosa de años y años, se tarda años y años; **we waited —s** esperamos una eternidad.
(b) calendar — año m civil; **financial —** año m económico; **school —** año m escolar; **New Y—** Año m Nuevo; **New Y—'s Day** día m de Año Nuevo; **New Y—'s Eve** noche f vieja; **happy new —!** ¡feliz año nuevo!; **to see the old — out** festejar el año nuevo.
(c) (school, Univ) curso m; **he's in (the) second —** está en el segundo curso; **the fellows in my —** los chicos de mi curso; **he's in fourth — Law** estudia cuarto de Derecho.
yearbook ['jiəbuk] n anuario m.
yearling ['jiəliŋ] **1** adj primal. **2** n primal m, ala f.
yearlong ['jiə'lɒŋ] adj que dura un año (entero).
yearly ['jiəli] **1** adj anual. **2** adv anualmente, cada año; (once) — una vez al año.
yearn [jəːn] vi suspirar; **to — for** anhelar, añorar, ansiar, suspirar por; **person** suspirar por; **to — to +** infin anhelar + infin, suspirar por + infin.
yearning ['jəːniŋ] **1** adj ansioso, anhelante; look, tone etc tierno, amoroso. **2** n ansia f, anhelo m, añoranza f (for de).
yearningly ['jəːniŋli] adv ansiosamente, con ansia; tiernamente, amorosamente.
yeast [jiːst] n levadura f.
yeasty ['jiːsti] adj (fig) frívolo, superficial.
yell [jel] **1** n grito m, alarido m, chillido m; **to give a —, to let out a —** dar un alarido. **2** vt gritar, decir a gritos, vociferar. **3** vi gritar, dar un alarido.
yelling ['jeliŋ] n gritos mpl, alaridos mpl, chillidos mpl.
yellow ['jeləu] **1** adj amarillo; hair rubio; (cowardly) cobarde; paper, press sensacionalista; **— novel** novelucha f; **to go —, to turn —** amarillear, amarillecer.
2 n amarillo m.
3 vt volver amarillo.
4 vi amarillecer, amarillear, ponerse amarillo.
yellowback ['jeləubæk] n novelucha f.
yellowhammer ['jeləu.hæmə*] n escribano m cerillo.
yellowish ['jeləuiʃ] adj amarillento.
yellowness ['jeləunis] n amarillez f.
yellowy ['jeləui] adj amarillento, que tira a amarillo.
yelp [jelp] **1** n gañido m. **2** vi gañir; (of person) gritar, dar un grito.
yelping ['jelpiŋ] n gañidos mpl.
yen [jen] n (fam) deseo m vivo; **to have a — to +** infin desear vivamente + infin, anhelar + infin.
yeoman ['jəumən] n, pl **—men** [mən] (Brit) **(a)** labrador m rico, pequeño propietario m rural, pequeño terrateniente m.
(b) (Mil) soldado m (voluntario) de caballería; **— of the guard** alabardero m de la Casa Real.
yeomanry ['jəumənri] n **(a)** clase f de los labradores ricos, pequeños propietarios mpl rurales. **(b)** (Mil) caballería f voluntaria.
yep [jep] adv (fam, esp US) sí.
yes [jes] **1** adv sí; **—?** (doubtfully) ¿es cierto eso?, ¿ah sí?; **—?** (awaiting further reply) ¿y qué más?; **—?** (answering knock at door) ¿quién es?, ¡adelante!;

to say — decir que sí, (*to marriage proposal*) dar el sí; **he says** — **to everything** se allana a todo, se conforma con cualquier cosa.

2 *n* sí *m*; **he gave a reluctant** — asintió pero de mala gana.

yes man ['jesmæn] *n*, *pl* — **men** [men] (*sl*) pelotillero *m*.

yesterday ['jestədei] **1** *adv* ayer; — **afternoon** ayer por la tarde; — **morning** ayer por la mañana; **late** — ayer a última hora; **no later than** — no más lejos que ayer.

2 *n* ayer *m*; **the day before** — anteayer; — **was Monday** ayer era lunes; **all our** —**s** todos nuestros recuerdos de antaño.

yesteryear ['jestə'jiə*] *adv* (*poet*) antaño.

yet [jet] **1** *adv* (**a**) (*time*) todavía, aún; **as** — hasta ahora, todavía; **not** —, **not just** — todavía no; **I hear it** — lo oigo todavía; **need you go** — ? ¿no te puedes quedar un poco más?; **I don't have to go** — me puedo quedar todavía un poco; **it is** — **to be settled** eso queda por resolver; **half is** — **to be built** la mitad queda todavía por construir; **it hasn't happened** — todavía no ha ocurrido; no ha ocurrido aún; **it's not time** — todavía no ha llegado la hora.

(**b**) (*emphatic*) todavía; — **again** otra vez (más); — **more** todavía más, más todavía, más aun.

2 *conj* con todo, a pesar de todo; **and** — y sin embargo, pero con todo; **we'll do it** — a pesar de todo lo lograremos.

yeti ['jeti] *n* yeti *m*.

yew [ju:] *n* tejo *m* (*also* **yew tree**).

Yid [jid] *n* (*fam*, *pej*) judío *m*, a *f*.

Yiddish ['jidiʃ] **1** *adj* judío. **2** *n* lengua *f* (*alemánhebreo*) que emplean varios sectores de los judíos.

yield [ji:ld] **1** *n* producción *f*; (*Agr*) cosecha *f*; (*Fin*, *Comm*) rendimiento *m*, (*on capital*) rédito *m*; **net** — rédito *m* neto; **a** — **of** 5% un rédito de 5 por cien; **what is the** — **on the shares**? ¿cuánto rinden las acciones?

2 *vt crop*, *result* producir, dar; *profit* rendir; *opportunity etc* ofrecer, dar, deparar; (*give up*) entregar, ceder (*also* **to** — **up**); **the shares** — 5% las acciones rinden el 5 por cien, las acciones dan un rédito de 5 por cien.

3 *vi* (*submit*) rendirse, someterse; (*give way*) ceder; (*US Aut*) ceder el paso; **to** — **to a plea** ceder a un ruego; **to** — **to temptation** ceder a la tentación; **I** — **to nobody in my admiration for** . . . yo admiro como todos a . . . , no me quedo corto en mi admiración por . . . ; **finally the door** — **ed** por fin cedió la puerta; **the ice began to** — el hielo empezó a ceder; el hielo empezó a romperse; **we shall never** — no nos rendiremos nunca.

yielding ['ji:ldiŋ] *adj* flexible, blando; (*fig*) dócil, complaciente; tierno, amoroso.

yippee [ji'pi:] *interj* (*fam*) ¡estupendo!

yod [jɔd] *n* yod *f*.

yodel, **yodle** ['jəudl] **1** *n* canto *m* a la tirolesa. **2** *vti* cantar a la tirolesa.

yoga ['jəugə] *n* yoga *f*.

yogi ['jəugi] *n* yogui *m*.

yogourt ['jɔugət] *n* yogur *m*.

yo-heave-ho ['jəu'hi:v'həu] *interj* see **heave-ho**.

yoke [jəuk] **1** *n* (*of oxen*) yunta *f*; (*carried on shoulder*) balancín *m*, percha *f*; (*Mech*) horquilla *f*; (*Sew*) canesú *m*; (*fig*) yugo *m*; **under the** — **of the Nazis** bajo el yugo de los nazis, bajo la férula de los nazis; **to throw off the** — sacudir el yugo.

2 *vt* (*also* **to** — **together**) uncir, acoplar; (*fig*) unir.

yokel ['jəukəl] *n* palurdo *m*, patán *m*.

yolk [jəuk] *n* yema *f* (de huevo).

yon [jɔn] *adv* (*arch*, *prov*) aquel.

yonder ['jɔndə*] (*arch*) **1** *adj* aquel. **2** *adv* allá, a lo lejos.

yore [jɔ:*] *n* (*arch*): **of** — (*lit*) de antaño, de otro tiempo, de hace siglos.

you [ju:] *pron* **1** *in familiar use*, *with second person verb*: (subject: *sing*) tú, (*pl*) vosotros, vosotras; (acc, dat: *sing*) te, (*pl*) os; (after prep: *sing*) ti, (*pl*) vosotros, vosotras; **with** — (*sing*, *reflexive*) contigo, (*pl*, *reflexive*) con vosotros, con vosotras.

2 *in formal use*, *with third person verb*: (subject: *sing*) usted, (*pl*) ustedes; (acc, dat: *sing*) le, la, (*pl*) les; (after prep: *sing*) usted, (*pl*) ustedes; **with** — (*sing and pl*, *reflexive*) consigo.

3 *when impersonal or general*, *often translated by* (**a**) *reflexive*: — **can't do that** eso no se hace, eso no se permite; — **can't smoke here** no se puede fumar aquí, no se permite fumar aquí, se prohíbe fumar aquí; **when** — **need one it's not here** cuando se necesita uno, no está aquí.

(**b**) *uno*: — **never know whether** . . . uno nunca sabe si . . .

(**c**) *impersonal constructions*: — **need to check it every day** hay que comprobarlo cada día, conviene comprobarlo cada día; — **must paint it** hace falta pintarlo.

4 *phrases and special uses*: — **rogue**! ¡canalla!; — **there**! ¡eh! ¡usted!; — **doctors** vosotros los médicos; — **Spaniards** vosotros los españoles; **poor** —! , **poor old** —!, — **poor old thing**! ¡pobrecito!; **away with** —! ¡vete!, ¡fuera de aquí!; **between** — **and me** entre tú y yo; **if I were** — yo que tú, yo en tu lugar; **there's a pretty girl for** —! ¡mira que chica más guapa!

you'd [ju:d] = **you would**; **you had**.

you'll [ju:l] = **you will**, **you shall**.

young [jʌŋ] **1** *adj* joven; nuevo, reciente; *brother etc* menor; **a** — **man** un joven; **a** — **woman** una joven; **the** — los jóvenes, la juventud; **old and** — grandes y pequeños; **the** —**er son** el hijo menor; **Pitt the Y**—**er** Pitt el Joven, Pitt hijo; **the** — **idea, Y**—**England** las nuevas generaciones, la juventud de hoy; **in my** — **days** en mi juventud; **if I were 10 years** —**er** si tuviera 10 años menos; **you're only** — **once** no se es joven más que una vez en la vida, hay que aprovechar la juventud mientras dure; **I'm not so** — **as I was** empiezo a notar los efectos de la edad, ya no soy lo que fui en mis veinte; **the night is** — la noche es joven; **the pile is like a** — **mountain** el montón se parece a una montaña menor de edad; **to marry** — casarse joven.

2 *npl* (*Zool*) cría *f*, hijuelos *mpl*.

youngish ['jʌŋiʃ] *adj* bastante joven, más bien joven.

young-looking ['jʌŋ,lukiŋ] *adj* de aspecto joven.

youngster ['jʌŋstə*] *n* joven *mf*, jovencito *m*, a *f*.

your ['juə*] *poss adj* **1** *in familiar use*, *second person*: tu(s); vuestro(s), vuestra(s).

2 *in formal use*, *third person*: su(s).

you're ['juə*] = **you are**.

yours ['juəz] *poss pron* **1** *in familiar use*, *second person*: (el) tuyo, (la) tuya etc; (el) vuestro, (la) vuestra etc.

2 *in formal use*, *third person*: (el) suyo, (la) suya etc; **you and** — Vd y los suyos.

3 *in ending letters*: — **faithfully** le saluda atentamente; *see sincerely etc*.

yourself [jə'self] *pron* **1** *in familiar use*, *second person*: (subject) tú mismo, tú misma; (acc, dat) te; (after prep) ti (mismo, misma).

2 *in formal use*, *third person*: (subject) usted mismo, usted misma; (acc, dat) se; (after prep) sí (mismo, misma); *see oneself*.

yourselves [jə'selvz] *pron pl* **1** *in familiar use*, *second person*: (subject) vosotros mismos, vosotras mismas; (acc, dat) os; (after prep) vosotros (mismos), vosotras (mismas).

2 *in formal use*, *third person*: (subject) ustedes mismos, ustedes mismas; (acc, dat) se; (after prep) sí (mismos, mismas); *see oneself*.

youth [ju:θ] *n*, *pl* **youths** [ju:ðz] (*in general*) juventud *f*; (*person*) joven *m*; (*persons collectively*) jóvenes *mpl*, juventud *f*; **present-day British** — la juventud actual inglesa; **Hitler Y**— Juventudes *fpl* Hitlerianas.

youthful ['ju:θful] *adj* juvenil; joven; **to look** — tener aspecto joven, parecer joven.

youthfulness ['ju:θfulnis] *n* juventud *f*.

youth hostel ['ju:θ,hɔstl] *n* albergue *m* para jóvenes.

you've [ju:v] = **you have**.

yowl [jaul] **1** *n* aullido *m*, alarido *m*. **2** *vi* aullar, dar alaridos.

yucca ['jʌkə] *n* yuca *f*.

Yugoslav ['ju:gəu'sla:v] **1** *adj* yugo(e)slavo. **2** *n* yugo(e)slavo *m*, yugo(e)slava *f*.

Yugoslavia ['ju:gəu'sla:viə] Yugo(e)slavia *f*.

Yule(tide) ['ju:l(taid)] *n* (*lit*) Navidad; **at** — por Navidades; — **log** leño *m* de Navidad.

yummy ['jʌmi] *adj* (*fam*) de rechupete.

Z

Zambesi [zæm'biːzi] Zambeze m.
Zambia ['zæmbiə] Zambia f.
zany ['zeini] **1** adj tonto; *humour etc* estrafalario, surrealista. **2** n bufón m, tonto m.
Zanzibar ['zænzibɑː*] Zanzíbar m.
zeal [ziːl] n celo m, estusiasmo m (*for por*), ardor m.
zealot ['zelət] n fanático m.
zealotry ['zelətri] n fanatismo m.
zealous ['zeləs] adj celoso (*for* de), entusiasta (*for* de); apasionado (*for por*).
zealously ['zeləsli] adv con entusiasmo.
zebra ['ziːbrə] n cebra f.
zebra crossing ['ziːbrə'krɔsiŋ] n paso m de peatones.
zebu ['ziːbuː] n cebú m.
zenana [ze'nɑːnə] n harén m indio.
zenith ['zeniθ] n cenit m; (*fig*) cenit m, apogeo m, punto m culminante; **to be at the — of one's power** estar en el apogeo de su poder.
Zeno ['ziːnəu] m Zenón.
zephyr ['zefə*] n céfiro m.
zeppelin ['zeplin] n zepelín m.
zero ['ziərəu] **1** adj cero, nulo. **2** n cero m; **absolute — cero** m absoluto; **it is 5° below —** hace cinco grados bajo cero.
zero hour ['ziərəu,auə*] n (*Mil*) hora f de ataque; (*fig*) momento m decisivo, momento m crítico.
zest [zest] n gusto m, entusiasmo m; **to do something with —** hacer algo con entusiasmo; **to eat with —** comer con gusto.
zestful ['zestful] adj entusiasta.
zestfully ['zestfəli] adv con entusiasmo.
zigzag ['zigzæg] **1** n zigzag m. **2** adj en zigzag. **3** vi zigzaguear, moverse en zigzag; (*person*) hacer eses.
zinc [ziŋk] n cinc m.
zinnia ['ziniə] n (*Bot*) rascamoño m.
Zion ['zaiən] Sión m.

Zionism ['zaiənizəm] n sionismo m.
Zionist ['zaiənist] **1** adj sionista. **2** n sionista mf.
zip [zip] **1** n **(a)** (*sound*) silbido m, zumbido m.
   (b) (— *fastener*) cremallera f, cierre m de cremallera.
   (c) (*fig*) energía f, vigor m.
   2 vt: **to — up** cerrar (la cremallera de).
   3 vi: **to — past** pasar silbando; (*fig*) pasar como un rayo.
zip code ['zipkəud] n (*US Post*) número cifrado para facilitar la distribución del correo.
zip fastener ['zip,fɑːsnə*] n, **zipper** ['zipə*] n cremallera f, cierre m de cremallera.
zippy ['zipi] adj enérgico, vigoroso; pronto, rápido.
zircon ['zəːkən] n circón m.
zither ['ziðə*] n cítara f.
zodiac ['zəudiæk] n zodíaco m.
zombie ['zɔmbi] n cadáver m resucitado por arte mágico.
zonal ['zəunl] adj zonal.
zone [zəun] n zona f.
zoo [zuː] n zoo m, jardín m zoológico, parque m zoológico; (*small, private*) colección f de fieras.
zoological [,zəuə'lɔdʒikəl] adj zoológico; **— gardens** see zoo.
zoologist [zəu'ɔlədʒist] n zoólogo m.
zoology [zəu'ɔlədʒi] n zoología f.
zoom [zuːm] **1** n (*sound*) zumbido m; (*Aer*) empinadura f. **2** vi zumbar; (*Aer*) empinarse; **it —ed past my ear** pasó zumbando cerca de mi oído.
zoomorphic [,zəuəu'mɔːfik] adj zoomórfico.
Zoroaster [,zɔrəu'æstə*] m Zoroastro.
Zulu ['zuːluː] **1** adj zulú. **2** n zulú mf.
Zululand ['zuːlulænd] Zululandia f.
zygote ['zaigəut] n cigoto m.

Abbreviations commonly used in Spanish and English

Abreviaturas más usadas en español e inglés

Spanish Abbreviations
Abreviaturas españolas

A

A	bomba A: bomba f atómica.
a.	área*.
AA	Aerolíneas *fpl* Argentinas.
ab.¹, abr.	abril *m* (*Ap., Apr.*: *April*).
A.C.	**1** año *m* de Cristo (*A.D.: Anno Domini, in the year of our Lord*). **2** (*Rel*) Acción *f* Católica.
a.c.	año *m* corriente (*current year*).
a/c	**1** al cuidado de (*c/o: care of*). **2** (*Fin*) a cuenta (*on account*).
acr.	acreedor *m* (*Cr.: creditor*).
A. de C.	= A.C. 1.
a. de C.	antes de Cristo (*A.C.: ante Christum, before Christ*).
a. de J.C.	antes de Jesucristo (*B.C.: before Christ*).
a D.g.	a Dios gracias (*thanks be to God*).
adj.	adjunto (*encl.: enclosure(s); enclosed*).
admón.	administración *f* (*admin.: administration*).
A.E.C.E.	Asociación *f* Española de Cooperación Europea.

a/f.	a favor (*in favour*).
afma., afmo., affma., affmo.	afectísima, afectísimo*.
ag., ag.°	agosto *m* (*Aug.: August*).
A.H.N.	Archivo *m* Histórico Nacional.
A.L.A.L.C.	Asociación *f* Latinoamericana de Libre Comercio.
a L.R.P.	a los reales pies (*courtesy formula*).
a.m.	(*S Am*) ante meridiem.
A.P.D.	Asistencia *f* Pública Domiciliara (*social welfare organization*).
apdo.	apartado *m* (de correos) (*P.O.B.: post-office box*).
A.P.E.	Asociaciones *fpl* Profesionales de Estudiantes.
A.P.R.A.	Alianza *f* Popular Revolucionaria Americana.
A.R.	Alteza *f* Real (*R.H.: Royal Highness*).
Arz.	Arzobispo *m* (*Abp: Archbishop*).
A.T.	Antiguo Testamento *m* (*O.T.: Old Testament*).
atta., atto.	atenta, atento* (*used in courtesy formulae in letters, with servidor etc*).
Av., Avda.	Avenida *f* (*Av., Ave: Avenue*).
a /v.	a vista (*at sight*).
AVIANCA	Aerovías *fpl* Nacionales de Colombia.

A.Y.C.	Aviación *f* y Comercio (*Spanish airline*).

B

B.	**1** Barcelona. **2** (*Eccl*) Beata, Beato (*B.: Beatus, Blessed*).
B.A.E.	Biblioteca *f* de Autores Españoles.
Barna.	Barcelona.
Bib.	Biblioteca *f* (*Lib.: Library*).
B.I.C.	Brigada *f* de Investigación Criminal (*equivalent to CID, (US) FBI*).
B.I.D.	Banco *m* Interamericano de Desarrollo.
b.l.m	besa las manos (*courtesy formula*).
b.l.p.	besa los pies (*courtesy formula*).
B.N.	Biblioteca *f* Nacional (*Madrid*).
B.O.	Boletín *m* Oficial.
B.°	banco *m* (*bk: bank*).
B.O.E.	Boletín *m* Oficial del Estado.
Bol.	Boletín *m* (*bulletin, journal*).
Bs.As.	Buenos Aires (*B.A.*).
Bta., Bto.	Beata, Beato (*B.: Beatus, Blessed*).

C

C.	(*Comm, Fin*) compañía *f* (*Co.: company*).

C/ Calle f (Rd: Road; St: Street).

c. = cap.

c³ centímetro(s) m(pl) cúbico(s) (c.c.: cubic centimetre(s)).

c/ cuenta f (a /c: account).

C.A. 1 (Elec) corriente f alterna (A.C.: alternating current). 2 (Sport) Club m Atlético (A.C.: Athletic Club).

C.A.E. cóbrese al entregar (C.O.D.: cash on delivery).

CAMPSA Compañía f Arrendataria del Monopolio de Petróleos, Sociedad Anónima.

cap., cap.º capítulo m (cap., ch.: chapter).

C.A.T. Comisaría f de Abastecimientos y Transportes.

c/c cuenta f corriente (C/A: current account).

C.D. 1 (Pol) Cuerpo m Diplomático (C.D.: Corps Diplomatique). 2 (Elec) corriente f directa (D.C.: direct current). 3 (Sport) Club m Deportivo (S.C.: Sports Club).

c/d 1 en casa de (c /o: care of). 2 (Comm, Fin) con descuento (with discount).

C. de J. Compañía de Jesús (S.J.: Society of Jesus).

CECA Comunidad f Europea del Carbón y del Acero (ECSC: European Coal and Steel Community).

C.E.D.A. Confederación f Española de Derechas Autónomas.

CEE Comunidad f Económica Europea (EEC: European Economic Community).

cént(s). céntimo(s) m(pl) (c.: centime(s)).

CEPSA Compañía f Española de Petróleos, Sociedad Anónima.

C.F. Club m de Fútbol.

c.f. caballo m de fuerza, caballos mpl de fuerza (H.P.: horsepower).

cfr. confróntese, compárese (cf.: confer, compare).

Cía. Compañía f (Co.: Company).

C.I.D. Centro m Internacional para el Desarrollo.

cje. corretaje m (brokerage).

cm² centímetro(s) m(pl) cuadrado(s) (sq. cm.: square centimetre(s)).

cm³ centímetro m cúbico, centímetros mpl cúbicos (c.c.: cubic centimetre(s)).

c.m.b. cuya mano beso (courtesy formula).

C.N.S. Confederación f Nacional de Sindicatos.

C.N.T. Confederación f Nacional del Trabajo.

col., col.ª columna f (col.: column).

comp. compárese (cp.: compare).

CONDESA Consorcio m de Diarios Españoles, Sociedad Anónima(press agency).

C.P. contestación f pagada (R.P.: reply paid).

c.p.b. cuyos pies beso (courtesy formula).

cs. 1 centavos mpl (c.: cents). 2 céntimos mpl (c.: cents).

c.s.f. coste, seguro y flete (c.i.f.: cost, insurance and freight).

cta., c.ta cuenta f (a /c: account).

cte. corriente, de los corrientes (inst.: instant, of the present month).

c /u cada uno (ea.: each).

C.V. caballos mpl de vapor (H.P.: horsepower).

CH

ch. cheque m (ch.: cheque).

D

D. 1 debe (debit side). 2 Don* (Esq.: Esquire).

Da., D.ª Doña*.

D.A. duración f ampliada (E.P.: extended play).

dcha. derecha (r.h.: right hand).

d. de J.C. después de Jesucristo (A.D.: Anno Domini, in the year of our Lord).

der., der.º derecho (r.: right).

D.F. (Mex) Distrito m Federal (Federal District).

D.G.T. Dirección f General de Turismo.

dha., dho. dicha, dicho (aforesaid).

dic., dic.e diciembre m (Dec.: December).

D.m. Dios mediante (D.V.: Deo volente).

D.ⁿ Don* (Esq.: Esquire).

D.N.D. Delegación f Nacional de Deportes.

D.N.S. Delegación f Nacional de Sindicatos.

do. descuento m (discount).

doc. 1 docena f (doz.: dozen). 2 documento m (doc.: document).

dom.º domingo m (Sun.: Sunday).

D.R.A.E. Diccionario m de la Real Academia Española.

D.R.C. Departamento m de Relaciones Culturales.

d.to descuento m (discount).

dup., dup.do duplicado (duplicated).

E

E. este m, adj (E.: east).

e/ envío m (consignment).

EE.UU. Estados mpl Unidos (US, USA: United States (of America)).

ej. ejemplo m (ex.: example).

E.M. Estado m Mayor (G.S.: General Staff).

Em.ª Eminencia (Eminence).

ENE. estenordeste (E.N.E.: east-north-east).

ene., en.º enero m (Jan.: January).

ENESA Empresa f Nacional de Electricidad, Sociedad Anónima.

ENSIDESA Empresa f Nacional Siderúrgica, Sociedad Anónima.

entlo. entresuelo*.

E.P.D. en paz descanse (R.I.P.: requiescat in pace).

ESE. estesudeste (E.S.E.: east-south-east).

esp. español m (also adj) (Sp., Span.: Spanish).

Exc.ª Excelencia (Excellency).

Excmo. Excelentísimo (courtesy title).

F

f.ª factura f (bill, account).

f.a.b. franco a bordo (f.o.b.: free on board).

F.C., f.c. ferrocarril m (Rly: Railway).

feb.º febrero m (Feb.: February).

F.E.C.I.T. Federación f Española de Centros de Iniciativas y Turismo.

F.E.F. Federación f Española de Fútbol.

F.E.T. Falange f Española Tradicionalista.

fha. fecha f (d.: date).

F.M.I. Fondo m Monetario Internacional (IMF: International Monetary Fund).

F.N.A.S. Fondo m Nacional de Asistencia Social.

F.N.P.T. Fondo m Nacional de Protección del Trabajo.

f.º, fol. folio m (Fo., fol.: folio).

F.P.A. Formación f Profesional Acelerada.

Fr. Fray m (Fr: Friar).

fr(s). franco(s) m(pl) (fr.: franc(s)).

fra. factura f (bill, account).

G

g / giro m (draft, money order).

gob.no gobierno m (govt: government).

g.p. giro m postal (money order).

gr. gramo(s) m(pl) (g., gm.: gram(s), gramme(s)).

Gral. General m (Gen.: General).

H

H. 1 (Fin) haber m (Cr.: credit). 2 bomba H: bomba f de hidrógeno. 3 hectárea(s) f(pl) (hectare(s)). 4 (Eccl) Hermano m (Br.: Brother).

h. 1 hacia (c.: circa). 2 hora(s) f(pl) (h., hr: hour(s)). 3 habitantes mpl (pop.: population).

Ha(s). = H. 3.

hect. = H. 3.

Hg. hectogramo(s) m(pl) (hg.: hectogram(s), hectogramme(s)).

Hm. hectómetro m, hectómetros mpl (hm.: hectometre(s)).

Hnos. Hermanos mpl (Bros: Brothers).

I

I.C.H. Instituto m de Cultura Hispánica.

íd. idem, lo mismo (do.: ditto).

I.L.A.R.I. Instituto m Latinoamericano de Relaciones Internacionales.

Ilmo. Ilustrísimo (courtesy title).

Imp. Imprenta f (printers, printing works).

I.N.C. Instituto m Nacional de Colonización (land settlement institute).

I.N.E. Instituto m Nacional de Estadística.

I.N.E.F. Instituto m Nacional de Educación Física.

I.N.I. Instituto m Nacional de Industria.

I.N.L.E. Instituto m Nacional del Libro Español.

I.N.P. Instituto m Nacional de Previsión.

I.N.T.A. Instituto m Nacional de Técnicas Aéreas.

izq., izq.ª izquierda f (l.h.: left hand).

izq., izq.º izquierdo (l.: left).

J

J.C. Jesucristo (J.C.: Jesus Christ).

J.E.N. Junta f de Energía Nuclear.

J.O.C.I. Juventud f Obrera Católica Internacional.

J.O.N.S. Juntas fpl de Ofensiva Nacional-Sindicalista.

jul. julio m (July).

jun. junio m (June).

K

k/c. kilociclos mpl (k/c.: kilocycles).

km/h. kilómetros mpl por hora (in Britain and US reckoned in m.p.h.: miles per hour).

kv. kilovatio m, kilovatios mpl (kw.: kilowatt(s)).

kv/h. kilovatios-hora mpl (kw/h.: kilowatt-hours).

L

l. 1 libro m (bk: book). 2 (Law) ley f (law). 3 litro m, litros mpl (l.: litre(s)).

L/ letra f (letter).

Lda., Ldo. = Lic.

lib. libro m (bk: book).

Lic. Licenciado m, Licenciada f; Lic. en Fil. y Let. = Licenciado m en Filosofía y Letras (B.A.: Bachelor of Arts).

M

M. Madrid.

m. 1 metro(s) m(pl) (m.: metre(s)). 2 minuto(s) m(pl) (m., min.: minute(s)).

m² metro(s) m(pl) cuadrado(s) (sq. m.: square metre(s)).

m³ metro(s) m(pl) cúbicos (cu. m.: cubic metre(s)).

mar. marzo m (Mar.: March).

M.C. Mercado m Común (C.M.: Common Market).

m/c 1 mi cuenta (my account). 2 mi casa (my firm).

M.F. modulación f de frecuencia (FM: frequency modulation).

miérc. miércoles m (Wed., Weds.: Wednesday).

M.I.J.A.R.C. Movimiento m Internacional de la Juventad Agrícola y Rural Católica.

M.I.T. Ministerio m de Información y Turismo.

M.º 1 Ministerio m (Ministry). 2 Maestro m (Master).

m/n. moneda f nacional (national currency).

m/o. mi orden (my order).

Mons. Monseñor m (Mgr, Mons.: Monsignor).

N

N. norte m, adj (N.: north).

n. nacido (b.: born).

n/ nuestro (our).

N.ª S.ra Nuestra Señora (Our Lady, The Virgin).

N.B.A.E. Nueva Biblioteca de Autores Españoles.

n/cta. nuestra cuenta (our account).

N. de la R. nota f de la redacción (editor's note).

NE. nor(d)este m, adj (N.E.: north-east).

n/f. nuestro favor (our favour).

n/g. nuestro giro (our money order).

n/L. nuestra letra (our letter).

NNE. nornordeste (N.N.E.: north-north-east).

NNO. nornoroeste (N.N.W.: north-north-west).

NN.UU. Naciones fpl Unidas (UN: United Nations).

NO. noroeste m, adj (N.W.: north-west).

n.º número m (No.: number).

n/o. nuestra orden (our order).

NODO Noticiario m y Documentales Cinematográficos (Spanish newsreel and documentary films).

nov. noviembre m (Nov.: November).

nra., nro. nuestra, nuestro (our).

N.R.F.H. Nueva Revista f de Filología Hispánica.

N.S. Nuestro Señor (Our Lord).

N.T. Nuevo Testamento m (N.T.: New Testament).

N.U. Naciones fpl Unidas (UN: United Nations).

núm. número m (No.: number).

O

O. oeste m, adj (W.: west).

o/ orden m (order).

OACI Organización f de Aviación Civil Internacional (ICAO: International Civil Aviation Organization).

Ob.po Obispo m (Bp: Bishop).

obr. cit. obra f citada (op. cit.: opere citato).

O.C.A.S.E.I. Obra f Católica de Asistencia a Estudiantes Iberoamericanos.

O.C.A.S.H.A. Obra f de Cooperación Apostólica Seglar Hispanoamericana.

O.C.A.U. Obra f Católica de Asistencia Universitaria.

O.C.E.D. Organización f de Cooperación Económica y Desarrollo (OECD: Organization for European Cooperation and Development).

O.C.I.C. Oficina f Católica Internacional del Cine.

oct. octubre m (Oct.: October).

O.E.A. Organización f de Estados Americanos (OAS: Organization of American States).

O.E.C.E. Organización f Europea de Cooperación Económica (OEEC: Organization for European Economic Cooperation).

O.E.I. Oficina f de Educación Iberoamericana.

O.I.S.S. Organización f Iberoamericana de Seguridad Social.

O.I.T. Organización f (or Oficina f) Internacional del Trabajo (ILO: International Labour Organization).

O.J.E. Organización f Juvenil Española.

O.M. 1 Orden f Ministerial (ministry order). 2 Orden f de la Merced.

O.M.S. Organización f Mundial de la Salud (WHO: World Health Organization).

ONO. oesnoroeste (W.N.W.: west-north-west).

ONU Organización f de las Naciones Unidas (UNO: United Nations Organization).

O.P. 1 Obras fpl Públicas. 2 (Eccl) Orden f de Predicadores (O.S.D.: Order of St Dominic).

Op.D. Opus m Dei (Catholic lay order).

OSO. oessudoeste (W.S.W.: west-south-west).

OTAN Organización f del Tratado del Atlántico Norte (NATO: North Atlantic Treaty Organization).

OTASE Organización f del Tratado del Sudeste Asiático (SEATO: South-East Asia Treaty Organization).

OVNI objeto m volante no identificado (UFO: unidentified flying object).

P

P. 1 Padre m (F., Fr: Father). 2 Papa m (Pope).

p.ª para*.

p.a. 1 por autorización (as authorized, by authority). 2 por ausencia (owing to absence).

pág(s). página(s) f(pl) (p(p).: page(s)).

pat. patente f (pat.: patent).

P.C. Partido m Comunista (C.P.: Communist Party).

p.c. por cien, por ciento (p.c., %: per cent).

P.D. posdata f (P.S.: postscript).

pdo. pasado (ult.: ultimo).

P.e =P. 1

p.ej. por ejemplo (e.g.: exempli gratia, for example).

p.m. (SAm) post meridiem (p.m.: post meridiem).

pmo. próximo (prox.: proximo).

P.N.A. Patronato m Nacional Antituberculoso.

P.º Paseo m (Av., Ave: Avenue).

p.o. por orden = p.p.

p.º n.º peso m neto (nt wt: net weight).

port. portugués m (Port.: Portuguese).

PP. Padres mpl (Frs: Fathers).

P.P. porte m pagado (C.P.: carriage paid).

p.p. por poder (p.p.: per procurationem, by proxy).

p.pdo.	próximo pasado (*ult.*: *ultimo*).	**R.P.**	Reverendo Padre *m* (*Reverend Father*).	**SS**	Santos, Santas (*SS*: *Saints*).
P.P.M.	Patronato *m* de Protección a la Mujer.	**rte.**	remite, remitente *mf* (*sender*).	**s.s.**	seguro servidor (*courtesy formula*).
P.R.	Puerto *m* Rico (*P.R.*: *Puerto Rico*).		**S**	**SSE.**	sudsudeste (*S.S.E.*: *south-south-east*).
pr.fr.	próximo futuro (*proximo*).	**S.**	1 sur *m*, *adj* (*S.*: *south*). 2 (*Rel*) San, Santa (*St*: *Saint*).	**SSO.**	sudsudoeste (*S.S.W.*: *south-south-west*).
prom.	promedio *m* (*av.*: *average*).	**s.**	1 siglo *m* (*c.*: *century*). 2 siguiente (*foll.*: *following*).	**s.s.s.**	su seguro servidor (*courtesy formula*).
Pta.	(*Geog*) Punta *f* (*Point*).			**Sta.**	Santa (*St*: *Saint*).
pta., ptas.	peseta *f*, pesetas *fpl* (*peseta(s)*).	**s/**	su, sus (*your*).	**Sto.**	San (*St*: *Saint*).
P.V.P.	precio *m* de venta al público (*sale price to the public*).	**S.ª**	Sierra *f* (*Mts*: *Mountains*).		**T**
PYRESA	Prensa y Radio Españolas, Sociedad Anónima (*press agency*).	**S.A.**	1 (*Comm, Fin*) Sociedad *f* Anónima (*Ltd*: *Limited*; *Corp.*: *Corporation*; *Inc.*: *Incorporated*).	**t.**	tomo(s) *m*(*pl*) (*vol*(*s*): *volume(s)*).
				T /año	toneladas *fpl* por año.
			2 Su Alteza (*H.H.*: *His Highness, Her Highness*).	**tel., teléf.**	teléfono *m* (*Tel.*: *telephone*).
	Q			**tít.**	título *m* (*title*).
q.b.s.m.	que besa sus manos (*courtesy formula*).	**sáb.**	sábado *m* (*Sat.*: *Saturday*).	**Tm.**	tonelada *f* métrica, toneladas *fpl* métricas (*metric ton(s)*).
q.b.s.p.	que besa sus pies (*courtesy formula*).	**S.A.R.**	Su Alteza Real (*H.R.H.*: *His Royal Highness, Her Royal Highness*).	**trad.**	traducido (*trans.*: *translated*).
q.D.g.	que Dios guarde (*whom God protect*).			**T.R.B.**	toneladas *fpl* de registro bruto (*G.R.T.*: *gross register tons*).
q.e.g.e.	que en gloria esté (*equivalent to R.I.P.*).	**s /c.**	1 su casa (*your firm*). 2 su cuenta (*your account*).	**TVE**	Televisión *f* Española.
q.e.p.d.	que en paz descanse (*R.I.P.*).	**SE.**	sudeste *m*, *adj* (*S.E.*: *south-east*).		**U**
q.e.s.m.	que estrecha su mano (*courtesy formula*).	**S.E.**	Su Excelencia (*H.E.*: *His Excellency*).	**Ud.**	usted (*you*).
quil., qts.	quilates *mpl* (*carats*).	**S.Em.ª**	Su Eminencia (*H.E.*: *His Eminence*).	**Uds.**	ustedes (*you*).
qm.	quintale(s)* *m*(*pl*) métrico(s).	**sep., sept.**	se(p)tiembre *m* (*Sept.*: *September*).	**U.E.P.**	Unión *f* Europea de Pagos (*EPU*: *European Payments Union*).
q.s.g.h.	que santa gloria haya (*equivalent to R.I.P.*).	**SEU**	Sindicato *m* Español Universitario.	**U.G.T.**	Unión *f* General de Trabajadores.
	R	**s.e.u.o.**	salvo error u omisión (*E. & O.E.*: *errors and omissions excepted.*)	**U.P.A.**	Unión *f* Panamericana (*PAU*: *Pan-American Union*).
R.	1 Real (*royal*). 2 (*Eccl*) Reverendo (*Rev.*: *Reverend*).	**s.f.**	sin fecha (*n.d.*: *no date*).	**U.P.A.E.**	Unión *f* Postal de las Américas y de España.
R.A.C.E.	Real Automóvil Club *m* de España.	**s /f.**	su favor (*your favour*).	**U.R.S.S.**	Unión *f* de Repúblicas Socialistas Soviéticas (*USSR*: *Union of Socialist Soviet Republics*).
R.A.E.	Real Academia *f* Española.	**sgte(s).**	siguiente(s) (*f.*, *ff.*, *foll.*: *following*).		
R.A.H.	Real Academia *f* de la Historia.	**S.M.**	Su Majestad (*H.M.*: *His (Her) Majesty*).		**V**
R.A.U.	República *f* Árabe Unida (*U.A.R.*: *United Arab Republic*).	**S.M.N.**	Servicio *m* Meteorológico Nacional.	**V.**	usted (*you*)
		SO.	suroeste *m*, *adj* (*S.W.*: *south-west*).	**v.**	1 (*Elec*) voltio(s) *m*(*pl*) (*v.*: *volt(s)*). 2 véase (*v.*: *vide, see*).
Rdo.	Reverendo (*Rev.*: *Reverend*).	**s /o.**	su orden (*your order*).	**V.A.**	Vuestra Alteza (*Your Highness*).
RENFE	Red Nacional de los Ferrocarriles Españoles.	**S.O.E.**	Seguro *m* Obligatorio de Enfermedad.	**Vd.**	usted (*you*).
R.F.E.	Revista *f* de Filología Española.	**Sr.**	Señor *m* (*Mr*: *Mister*).	**Vda. de**	viuda *f* de (*widow of*).
		Sra.	Señora *f* (*Mrs*: *Mistress*).	**Vds.**	ustedes (*you*).
R.M.	Reverenda Madre *f* (*Reverend Mother*).	**S.R.C.**	se ruega contestación (*RSVP*).	**vers.º**	(*Bib*) versículo *m* (*v.*: *verse*).
Rmo.	Reverendísimo (*Rt Rev.*: *Right Reverend*).	**Sres., Srs.**	Señores *mpl* (*Messrs*: *Messieurs*).	**v.g., v.gr.**	verbigracia (*viz.*: *videlicet, namely*).
R.N.E.	Radio *f* Nacional de España.	**Srta.**	Señorita *f* (*Miss*).	**vier.**	viernes *m* (*Fri.*: *Friday*).
R.O.	real orden *f* (*royal decree*).	**S.S.**	Su Santidad (*H.H.*: *His Holiness*).	**V.M.**	Vuestra Majestad (*Your Majesty*).
				V.º B.º	visto bueno*.
				vra., vro.	vuestra, vuestro (*your*).
				VV.	ustedes (*you*).

English Abbreviations
Abreviaturas inglesas

A
A 1 answer (respuesta f). 2 (Cine: Brit) adults (película f apta para mayores).

AA 1 (Aut) Automobile Association. 2 Alcoholics Anonymous (sociedad de los alcohólicos reformados). 3 (Cine: Brit) Restricted (película f más apta para mayores).

AAA 1 (Sport) Amateur Athletic Association. 2 (US) American Automobile Association.

AAU (US) Amateur Athletic Union.

A.A.U.P. American Association of University Professors.

AB 1 (Naut) able-bodied seaman (marinero m de primera). 2 (US: Univ) = B.A.

ABA Amateur Boxing Association.

A-bomb atomic bomb (bomba A. bomba f atómica).

Abp Archbishop (Arz.: arzobispo m).

abr. abridged (abreviado, resumido).

abs., absol. absolutely (absolutamente).

abs., abstr. abstract (abstracto).

A/C account current (c/c: cuenta f corriente).

a/c account (c.ta: cuenta f).

AC 1 (Elec) alternating current. 2 (Aer) aircraftman (soldado raso de las fuerzas aéreas).

acc. (Fin) account (c.ta: cuenta f).

ACGB Arts Council of Great Britain (organización para el fomento de las artes).

A.D. Anno Domini, in the year of our Lord (A. C.: año m de Cristo).

ad advertisement (anuncio m).

ADC aide-de-camp (edecán m).

Adjt adjutant (ayudante m).

ad lib.* ad libitum, at pleasure.

admin. administration (admón.).

advt advertisement (anuncio m).

AEC (US) Atomic Energy Commission.

AEF 1 Amalgamated Union of Engineering and Foundry Workers. 2 (US) American Expeditionary Forces.

AEU Amalgamated Engineering Union (sindicato de ingenieros).

A.F.C. (US) Air Force Cross (condecoración).

AFL-CIO American Federation of Labor and Congress of Industrial Organizations.

A.F.M. (US) Air Force Medal (condecoración).

AFN (US) American Forces Network (Red f de Radiodifusión de las Fuerzas Armadas de EE. UU.).

AGM Annual General Meeting (Junta f Anual).

A 1* first class.

A.I.D. artificial insemination by donor.

Ala. (US) Alabama.

Alas. (US) Alaska.

A-level Advanced level (grado superior del General Certificate of Education (a los 17–18 años); = bachillerato m superior).

Alta. Alberta (provincia canadiense).

Am. 1 America (América f). 2 American (americano).

A.M. (US: Univ) = M.A.

a.m. ante meridiem, before noon (antes del mediodía, de la mañana).

A.M.A. American Medical Association.

anon. anonymous (anónimo).

AOB Any Other Business (ruegos mpl y preguntas).

AP Associated Press.

Ap., Apr. April (abr.: abril m).

A.P.O. (US) Army Post Office.

app. appendix (apéndice m).

appro.* approval.

apt. (US) apartment (apartamento m).

A.R.A.M. Associate of the Royal Academy of Music.

A.R.C.M. Associate of the Royal College of Music.

A.R.I.B.A. Associate of the Royal Institute of British Architects.

Ariz. (US) Arizona.

Ark. (US) Arkansas.

ARP air-raid precautions (servicios de defensa civil contra los bombardeos aéreos).

arr. arrives (llega).

A/S account sales (cuenta f de ventas).

A.S.P.C.A. American Society for the Prevention of Cruelty to Animals (sociedad f protectora de animales).

assn association (asociación f).

asst assistant (ayudante mf).

ASTMS Association of Scientific, Technical and Managerial Staffs.

ATS Auxiliary Territorial Service (reserva de la sección femenina del ejército).

Att., Atty Attorney (abogado m).

Atty. Gen. Attorney-General.

Aug. August (ag.: agosto m).

AUT Association of University Teachers.

A.V. Authorized Version (of the Bible) (versión oficial de la Biblia en lengua inglesa).

av. average (prom.: promedio m).

Av., Ave Avenue (Av., Avda.: avenida f).

avdp. avoirdupois*.

a.w. atomic weight (peso m atómico).

AWOL (Mil) absent without leave (ausente sin permiso).

B
B black (negro: mina del lápiz).

b. born (n.: nacido).

b. & b. bed and breakfast (cama f con desayuno, en los hoteles, pensiones etc).

B.A. 1 (Univ) Bachelor of Arts (Lic. en Fil. y Let.). 2 British Academy (academia literaria). 3 British Association (for the Advancement of Science). 4 (Geog) Buenos Aires (Bs. As.).

BAOR British Army of the Rhine (ejército británico en Alemania).

Bart Baronet (título de la nobleza británica).

Battn battalion (Bón.: batallón m).

BB Boy's Brigade.

BBC British Broadcasting Corporation (Radio Nacional de Gran Bretaña).

B.C. 1 before Christ (a. de J.C.: antes de Jesucristo). 2 British Columbia.

BCG Bacillus Calmette-Guérin (bacilo antituberculosis).

B.D. Bachelor of Divinity (Licenciado m en Teología).

b.e. bill of exchange (letra f de cambio).

BEA British European Airways.

Beds. Bedfordshire (condado inglés).

BEF British Expeditionary Force.

B.E.M. British Empire Medal (condecoración británica).

Benelux Belgium, Netherlands, Luxembourg.

Berks. Berkshire (condado inglés).

B.F. (euph) bloody fool (idiota m).

b/f brought forward (suma f del anterior).

BFI British Film Institute.

B.F.P.O. British Forces Post Office.

b/fwd brought forward (suma f del anterior).

B'ham Birmingham.

b.h.p. brake horsepower (potencia f al freno).

BIF British Industries Fair (Feria f de Muestras de la Industria Británica).

biog. 1 biography (biografía f). 2 biographical (biográfico).

bk 1 book (l.: libro m). 2 (Fin) bank (B.º: banco m).

B.L. Bachelor of Law.

B/L bill of lading (conocimiento m de embarque).

bldg building (edificio m).

B. Litt. Bachelor of Letters.

Blvd Boulevard (bulevar m).

B.M. 1 Bachelor of Medicine. 2 British Museum.

BMA British Medical Association.

B.Mus. Bachelor of Music.

B.O. (euph) body odour (olor m a sudor).

BOAC British Overseas Airways Corporation.

B. of E. Bank of England.

bor. borough (municipio m).

bot. bought (comprado).

BOT Board of Trade (Ministerio m de Comercio).

Bp Bishop (*ob.ᵖᵒ: obispo m*).

BP British Petroleum (*compañía de petróleo*).

Br Brother (*hermano m*).

BR British Rail (*ferrocarriles británicos*).

B/R bills receivable (*obligaciones fpl por cobrar*).

Brecon. Breconshire (*condado galés*).

Brig. Brigadier (*general de brigada*).

Brit. 1 Britain (*Gran Bretaña f*). 2 British (*británico*).

Bro. Brother (*hermano m*).

Bros Brothers (*Hnos.: Hermanos*).

B/S bill of sale (*hipoteca f de bienes*).

B.Sc. Bachelor of Science.

B.Sc.Econ. Bachelor of Economic Science.

BSI British Standards Institution (*instituto de normas británico*).

BST 1 British Summer Time (*hora de verano*). 2 British Standard Time.

Bucks. Buckinghamshire (*condado inglés*).

BUP British United Press (*agencia de noticias*).

B.V.M. Blessed Virgin Mary (*B.M.V.*).

B.W.I. British West Indies (*Antillas fpl Británicas*).

C

C. 1 (*Lit*) chapter (*c., cap., cap.ᵒ: capítulo m*). 2 (*Geog*) Cape (*Cabo m*). 3 central (*central*). 4 centigrade (*termómetro m centígrado*). 5 Conservative (*conservador m*: also adj).

c. 1 (*Fin: US*) cent (*centavo m*). 2 (*Fin: France*) centime (*céntimo m*). 3 century (*s.: siglo m*). 4 (*Hist*) circa, about (*h.: hacia; eg c. 1490 = hacia 1490*). 5 (*Math*) cubic (*cúbico*).

C.A. Chartered Accountant (*contable m diplomado*).

C/A current account (*c/c: cuenta f corriente*).

Caer. Caernarvonshire (*condado galés*).

Cal., Calif. (*US*) California.

Cambs. Cambridgeshire (*condado inglés*).

Can. 1 Canada (*El Canadá*). 2 Canadian (*canadiense*).

Cantab. Cantabrigiensis, of Cambridge (*de la Universidad de Cambridge*).

cap. (*Typ*) capital letter (*mayúscula f*).

Capt. Captain (*capitán m*).

Card. Cardiganshire (*condado galés*).

Carm. Carmarthenshire (*condado galés*).

carr. carriage (*porte m*).

cat. catalogue (*catálogo m*).

CAT College of Advanced Technology (*equivalent to universidad laboral*).

C.B. 1 Companion of the Bath (*título honorífico británico*). 2 (*Mil*) confined to barracks ((men) *arresto m menor en ⁑ cuartel*, (officers) *arresto m en banderas*). 3 cash book (*libro m de caja*).

CBC Canadian Broadcasting Corporation (*radio nacional del Canadá*).

C.B.E. Commander of the Order of the British Empire (*título honorífico británico*).

CBI Confederation of British Industries (*organización patronal*).

CC 1 Chamber of Commerce (*cámara f de comercio*). 2 County Council (*concejo m del condado*). 3 Cricket Club; Cycling Club.

Cent. centigrade (*termómetro m centígrado*).

CENTO Central Treaty Organization.

cert. certificate (*certificado m*).

CEWC Council for Education in World Citizenship.

cf. confer, compare (*cfr.: confróntese, compárese*).

c/f, c/fwd carried forward (*suma y sigue*).

ch. 1 (*Lit*) chapter (*c., cap., cap.ᵒ: capítulo m*). 2 (*Fin*) cheque (*ch.: cheque m*).

Ch.B Chirurgiae Baccalaureus, Bachelor of Surgery.

Ches. Cheshire (*condado inglés*).

chq. cheque (*ch.: cheque m*).

C.I. Channel Islands (*Islas fpl Normandas*).

c/i certificate of insurance (*certificado m de seguro*).

CIA (*US*) Central Intelligence Agency (*servicio secreto y de contraespionaje*).

CID Criminal Investigation Department (*equivalent to Brigada f de Investigación Criminal*).

c.i.f. cost, insurance and freight (*c.i.f., c.s.f.: coste, seguro y flete*).

C.(I.)G.S. Chief of (Imperial) General Staff.

C.-in-C. Commander-in-Chief.

CIO (*US*) Congress of Industrial Organizations.

C.M. Common Market (*M.C.: Mercado m Común*).

C.M.S. Church Missionary Society (*sociedad misionera de la Iglesia Anglicana*).

CND Campaign for Nuclear Disarmament.

Co. 1 (*Comm*) company (*C., Cía.: compañía f*). 2 county (*condado m*).

C.O. 1 (*Mil*) Commanding Officer. 2 conscientious objector (*objetor m de conciencia*).

c/o care of (*c/d: en casa de; a/c: al cuidado de*).

C.O.D. 1 (*Comm*) cash on delivery (*pagar contra recepción, cóbrese a la entrega*). 2 Concise Oxford Dictionary.

C. of E. Church of England.

COI Central Office of Information.

Col. (*Mil*) Colonel (*Cnel.: coronel m*).

col. column (*col.: columna f*).

coll. college (*colegio m*).

Colo. (*US*) Colorado.

Com. Communist (*comunista mf*: also adj).

conj. conjugation (*conjugación f*).

Conn. (*US*) Connecticut.

Cons. Conservative (*conservador m*: also adj).

cont., cont'd continued (*continuación. f*).

Co-op Co-operative (Society).

Corn. Cornwall (*Cornualles, condado inglés*).

Corp. 1 (*Comm, Fin*) Corporation (*S.A.: sociedad f anónima*). 2 (*Pol*) Corporation (*ayuntamiento m; municipio m*). 3 (*Mil*) Corporal (*cabo m*).

Coy company (*C., Cía.: compañía f*).

C. P. 1 (*Pol*) Communist Party (*P.C.: Partido m Comunista*). 2 (*Comm*) carriage paid (*P.P.: porte m pagado*).

cp. compare (*comp.: compárese*).

c.p. candlepower (*potencia f lumínica*).

C.P.A. (*US*) Certified Public Accountant (*contable m diplomado*).

Cpl Corporal (*cabo m*).

Cr. 1 (*Comm*) credit (*haber m*). 2 (*Comm*) creditor (*acreedor m*). 3 (*Pol*) councillor (*concejal m*).

C.R.T. cathode-ray tube (*tubo m de rayos catódicos*).

C.S.M. Company Sergeant-Major (*approx: brigada m de compañía*).

C.U. Cambridge University.

cu. cubic (*cúbico*).

cu. ft. cubic foot, cubic feet (*pie m cúbico, pies mpl cúbicos*).

cu. in. cubic inch(es) (*pulgada f cúbica, pulgadas fpl cúbicas*).

Cumb. Cumberland (*condado inglés*).

CUP Cambridge University Press.

c.w.o. cash with order (*pago m al contado*).

CWS Cooperative Wholesale Society (*cooperativo de consumidores*).

cwt hundredweight(s)*.

C.Z. Canal Zone (*Zona f del Canal de Panamá*).

D

d. 1 date (*fecha f*). 2 daughter (*hija f*). 3 died (*m.: murió*). 4 (*Rail etc*) departs (*sale*). 5 (*Fin*) denarius, penny (*penique m*).

D.A. 1 (*Fin*) deposit account (*approx: cuenta f de ahorros*). 2 (*US*) District Attorney (*fiscal m de distrito*).

DAB (*US*) Dictionary of American Biography.

dag. decagram(s), decagramme(s) (*Dg.: decagramo m, decagramos mpl*).

dal. decalitre(s) (*Dl.: decalitro m, decalitros mpl*).

dam. decametre(s) (*Dm.*: decámetro m, decámetros mpl).

D.B.E. Dame Commander of the Order of the British Empire (*título honorífico británico*).

D.C. 1 (*Elec*) direct current. 2 (*US*) District of Columbia (*Washington, capital de Estados Unidos, y sus alrededores*).

D.C.M. Distinguished Conduct Medal (*condecoración británica*).

D.D. Doctor of Divinity (*Doctor m en Teología*).

D.D.S. Doctor of Dental Surgery.

Dec. December (*dic.*: diciembre m).

dec. deceased (*m.*: murió; *fallecido*).

Del. (*US*) Delaware.

del. delete (*táchese, a suprimir*).

Dem. Democrat (*demócrata mf*; also adj).

Denb. Denbighshire (*condado galés*).

dep. departs (*sale*).

dept department (*departamento m*).

Derbys. Derbyshire (*condado inglés*).

DES Department of Education and Science.

D.F.C. Distinguished Flying Cross (*condecoración británica*).

D.F.M. Distinguished Flying Medal (*condecoración británica*).

diam. diameter (*diámetro m*).

Dip. Diploma (*diploma m*).

dist. district (*distrito m*).

div. dividend (*dividendo m*).

DJ 1 dinner jacket (*smoking m*). 2 (*Radio*) disc jockey (*presentador m de discos*).

D.Lit. Doctor of Letters.

DM Deutschmark (*marco m alemán*).

D.M. Doctor of Medicine.

D.N.B. Dictionary of National Biography.

do. ditto (*íd.*: ídem, lo mismo).

D.O.A. (*US*) dead on arrival (e.g. at hospital).

dol. dollar(s) (*dólar m, dólares mpl*).

doz. dozen (*d.ᵃ*: docena f).

D.P. displaced person (*desplazado m, desplazada f*).

D.Phil. Doctor of Philosophy.

D.P.P. Director of Public Prosecutions.

dpt department (*departamento m*).

Dr 1 Doctor (*Dr.*: doctor m). 2 (*Comm*) debtor (*deudor m*).

dr. drachm, dram (*US*) (*dracma f*).

d/s. days after sight (*d/v*: a . . . días vista).

D.S.C. Distinguished Service Cross (*condecoración británica*).

D.Sc. Doctor of Science.

D.S.M. Distinguished Service Medal (*condecoración británica*).

D.S.O. Distinguished Service Order (*condecoración británica*).

DTs delirium tremens*.

D.V. Deo volente, God willing (*D.m.*: Dios mediante).

E

E. east (*E.*: este m, adj).

E. & O.E. errors and omissions excepted (*s.e.u.o.*: salvo error u omisión).

ea. each (*c/u*: cada uno).

ECG electrocardiogram*.

ECOSOC Economic and Social Council (*Consejo m Económico y Social (de las Naciones Unidas)*).

ECSC European Coal and Steel Community (*CECA: Comunidad f Europea del Carbón y del Acero*).

ed. 1 edition (*ed.*: edición f). 2 editor*. 3 edited*.

E/E. errors excepted (*salvo error*).

EEC European Economic Community (*CEE: Comunidad f Económica Europea*).

EFTA European Free Trade Association (*EFTA: Asociación f Europea de Libre Comercio*).

e.g. exempli gratia, for example (*p.ej.*: por ejemplo).

encl. enclosure(s) (*adjunto*).

E.N.E. east-north-east (*ENE.*: estenordeste).

Eng. 1 England (*Inglaterra f*). 2 English (*inglés m*; also adj).

E.P. 1 electroplate*. 2 (*Mus*) extended play (*duración f ampliada*).

EPU European Payments Union (*Unión f Europea de Pagos*).

E.R. Elizabeth Regina, Queen Elizabeth.

ERNIE Electronic Random Number Indicator Equipment (*máquina electrónica que elige los números premiados entre los Premium Bonds (bonos de la Caja de Ahorros británica)*).

E.S.E. east-south-east (*ESE.*: estesudeste).

E.S.N. (*euph*) educationally subnormal (*de inteligencia inferior a la normal*).

E.S.P. extrasensory perception (*percepción f extrasensorial*).

Esq. Esquire*.

est. established (*eg est. 1899 = se fundó en 1899*).

et al. et alii, and others (*y otros*).

et seq. et sequentia, and the following (*y sigs.*: y siguientes).

ETU Electrical Trades Union.

Eur. 1 Europe (*Europa f*). 2 European (*europeo*).

ex. example (*ej.*: ejemplo m).

ex div. ex dividend, without dividend (*sin dividendo*).

ex int. ex interest, without interest (*sin interés*).

ext. (*Tel*) extension*.

F

F. 1 Fahrenheit (*termómetro m Fahrenheit*).
2 (*Eccl*) Father (*P., P.ᵉ*: padre m). 3 French (*fr.*: francés m).

f. 1 (*Naut*) fathom (*braza f*). 2 (*Math*) foot, feet (*pie m, pies mpl*). 3 following (sig.: siguiente). 4 female (*hembra f*).

FA Football Association.

FAA (*US*) Federal Aviation Agency.

fac(s). facsimile (*facsímil m*).

FAO Food and Agriculture Organization (*FAO: Organización f para la Alimentación y la Agricultura*).

FBI (*US*) Federal Bureau of Investigation (equivalent to Brigada f de Investigación Criminal).

F.C. Football Club (*C.F.*: club m de fútbol).

FCC (*US*) Federal Communications Commission.

F.D. Fidei Defensor, Defender of the Faith (*uno de los títulos del monarca británico*).

FDA (*US*) Food and Drug Administration.

Feb. February (*feb.º*: febrero m).

ff. following (sigs.: siguientes).

FHA (*US*) Federal Housing Administration.

F'hold freehold*.

Fla. (*US*) Florida.

Flint. Flintshire (*condado galés*).

F/Lt Flight Lieutenant (*teniente m de aviación*).

F.M. 1 (*Mil*) Field Marshal*. 2 (*Radio*) frequency modulation.

fm fathom (*braza f*).

F.O. 1 (*Brit Pol*) Foreign Office (*Ministerio m de Asuntos Exteriores*). 2 (*Aer*) Flying Officer (*subteniente m de aviación*).

Fo., fol. folio (*fol.*: folio m).

f.o.b. free on board (*f.a.b.*: franco a bordo*).

foll. following (*sig., sigs.*: siguiente, siguientes).

f.o.r. free on rail (*el precio de la mercancía incluye el transporte por ferrocarril*).

F.P. 1 fire plug (*boca f de agua*). 2 freezing point (*punto m de congelación*).

Fr 1 Father (*P., P.ᵉ*: padre m). 2 Friar (*Fr.*: fray m).

fr. 1 (*Fin*) franc(s) (*fr., frs.*: franco m, francos mpl). 2 from (*de; de parte de*).

Fri. Friday (*vier.*: viernes m).

F.R.I.B.A. Fellow of the Royal Institute of British Architects.

F.R.S. Fellow of the Royal Society.

ft foot, feet (*pie m, pies mpl*).

FTC (*US*) Federal Trade Commission.

G

G (*Cine*: US) General (*película apta para todos los públicos*).

g. 1 (*Fin*) guinea(s)*. 2 gram(s), gramme(s) (*gr.: gramo* m, *gramos* mpl).

Ga. (*US*) Georgia.

gal. gallon(s)*.

GATT General Agreement on Tariffs and Trade (GATT: *Acuerdo* m *General Sobre Aranceles Aduaneros y Comercio*).

G.B. Great Britain (*Gran Bretaña* f).

G.C. George Cross (*condecoración británica*).

G.C.E. General Certificate of Education (equivalent to *bachillerato elemental y superior*).

G.C.F. greatest common factor (*máximo común divisor* m).

Gdns Gardens (*jardines* mpl).

Gen. General (*Genl.: general* m).

gen. genitive (*gen.: genitivo*).

Ger. 1 Germany (*Alemania* f). 2 German (*alemán* m; also adj).

GHQ General Headquarters (*cuartel* m *general*).

G.I. (*US*) government issue (*propiedad* f *del Estado; por extensión, se le llama así al soldado raso norteamericano*).

Gib. Gibraltar.

Gk Greek (*griego* m; also adj).

Glam. Glamorgan (*condado galés*).

GLC Greater London Council (*ayuntamiento de Londres*).

Glos. Gloucestershire (*condado inglés*).

G.M. George Medal (*condecoración británica*).

gm, gms gram(s), gramme(s) (*gr.: gramo* m, *gramos* mpl).

GMC General Medical Council (*consejo regidor de la medicina*).

GMT Greenwich Mean Time.

GMWU General and Municipal Workers' Union.

gn., gns guinea(s)*.

GNP gross national product (*producto* m *nacional bruto*).

G.O.C. General Officer Commanding (*general* m, *jefe* m).

G.O.M. grand old man (*viejo* m *distinguido, antiguo jefe* m (*del partido etc*) *muy respetado*).

G.O.P. (*US*) Grand Old Party (*Partido* m *Republicano*).

Gov. Governor (*gobernador* m).

Govt Government (*gob.ⁿᵒ: gobierno* m).

G.P. general practitioner (*médico* m *general, médica* f *general*).

GP (*Cine: US*) for mature audiences (*película* f *más apta para los mayores*).

GPO General Post Office (*Administración* f *General de Correos*).

G.R. Georgius Rex, King George.

gr. 1 gross (*bruto*). 2 gross (*gruesa* f; = 12 *docenas*, = 144).

G.R.T. gross register tons (*T.R.B.: toneladas* fpl *de registro bruto*).

G.S. General Staff (*E.M.: estado* m *mayor*).

Gt Br. Great Britain (*Gran Bretaña* f).

guar. guaranteed (*garantizado*).

H

H hard (*duro: mina del lápiz*).

h. hour(s) (*h:. hora* f, *horas* fpl).

h. & c. hot and cold (water) (*con agua corriente caliente y fría*).

Hants. Hampshire (*condado inglés*).

HB hard black (*negro duro: mina del lápiz*).

H-bomb hydrogen bomb (*bomba* H: *bomba* f *de hidrógeno*).

H.C. House of Commons (*Cámara* f *de los Comunes*).

H.C.F. highest common factor (*máximo común divisor* m).

H.E. 1 high explosive*. 2 His Excellency (*S.E.: Su Excelencia*). 3 (*Eccl*) His Eminence (*S.Em.ᵃ: Su Eminencia*).

Herts. Hertfordshire (*condado inglés*).

HEW (*US*) Department of Health, Education and Welfare.

H.F. high frequency ((*de*) *alta frecuencia*).

H.G. Home Guard (*cuerpo de voluntarios para la defensa de la patria* (1940)).

hg. hectogram(s), hectogramme(s) (*Hg.: hectogramo* m, *hectogramos* mpl).

H.H. 1 His Highness, Her Highness (*S.A.: Su Alteza*). 2 (*Eccl*) His Holiness (*S.S.: Su Santidad*).

hl. hectolitre(s) (*H.: hectolitro* m, *hectolitros* mpl).

hm. hectometre(s) (*Hm.: hectómetro* m, *hectómetros* mpl.

H.M. His (Her) Majesty (*S.M.: Su Majestad*).

H.M.I. His (Her) Majesty's Inspector.

HMS His (Her) Majesty's Ship (*buque de guerra británico*).

ho. house (*casa* f).

Hon. 1 Honorary*. 2 Honourable (*título de la nobleza británica*).

H.P., h.p. 1 (*Comm*) hire purchase (*compra* f *a plazos*). 2 (*Mech*) horsepower (*caballos* mpl *de vapor*). 3 (*Tech*) high-pressure (*de alta presión*).

HQ Headquarters (*cuartel* m *general*).

hr(s) hour(s) (*h.: hora* f, *horas* fpl).

H.R.H. His (Her) Royal Highness (*S.A.R.: Su Alteza Real*).

ht height (*alt.: altura* f).

HT high-tension (*de alta tensión*).

Hunts. Huntingdonshire (*condado inglés*).

HV high-voltage (*de alto voltaje*).

I

I. (*Geog*) Island, Isle (*isla* f).

Ia. (*US*) Iowa.

IAAF International Amateur Athletic Federation.

I.B. 1 (*Comm*) invoice book (*libro* m *de facturas*). 2 (*Pol*) International Brigade (*Brigadas* fpl *Internacionales*).

I.C. Intelligence Corps (equivalent to *S.I.M.: Servicio* m *de Información Militar*).

i/c in charge (of) (*encargado de*).

I.C.A. 1 Institute of Chartered Accountants. 2 Institute of Contemporary Arts.

ICAO International Civil Aviation Organization (*OACI: Organización* f *de Aviación Civil Internacional*).

ICBM intercontinental ballistic missile*.

ICFTU International Confederation of Free Trade Unions (*Confederación* f *Internacional de Sindicatos Libres*).

Ida. (*US*) Idaho.

i.e. id est, that is, namely (*esto es, a saber*).

I.L.G.W.U. (*US*) International Ladies' Garment Workers' Union.

Ill. (*US*) Illinois.

ill. 1 illustrated (*con grabados, con láminas*). 2 illustration (*grabado* m, *lámina* f).

ILO International Labour Organization (*O.I.T.: Organización* f *Internacional del Trabajo*).

ILP Independent Labour Party (*partido laborista independiente*).

IMF International Monetary Fund (*F.M.I.: Fondo* m *Monetario Internacional*).

in., ins inch(es) (*pulgada* f, *pulgadas* fpl).

Inc. (*US*) Incorporated (*S.A.: sociedad* f *anónima*).

incl. 1 including (*incluso*). 2 inclusive*.

incog. incognito*.

Ind. 1 (*US*) Indiana. 2 (*Pol*) Independent (*independiente* m; also adj).

I.N.S. International News Service (*agencia de noticias*).

ins. insurance (*seguro* m).

Inst. Institute (*instituto* m).

inst. instant, of the present month (*cte.: corriente, de los corrientes*).

intro. introduction (*introducción* f).

I.O.M. Isle of Man.

IOU I owe you (*pagaré* m).

I.O.W. Isle of Wight.

IPA 1 International Phonetic Association. 2 International Phonetic Alphabet.

IQ intelligence quotient (*cociente* m *intelectual*).

I.R.A. Irish Republican Army.

IRS (US) Internal Revenue Service.

Is. Isle(s), Island(s) (isla(s) f(pl)).

It. 1 Italy (*Italia* f). 2 Italian (*italiano* m; also adj).

ITA Independent Television Authority (*comisión regidora de la TV independiente*).

ital. italics*.

ITN Independent Television Network (*red transmisora de la TV independiente*).

ITV Independent Television (*televisión independiente*).

IUS International Union of Students.

J

Jan. January (*ene., en.º: enero* m).

J.C. Jesus Christ (*J.C.: Jesucristo*).

Jn junction (*estación f de empalme*).

J.P. Justice of the Peace (*juez m de paz*).

Jr, Jun., Junr junior*.

Jul. July (*jul.: julio* m).

Jun. June (*jun.: junio* m).

K

Kan. (US) Kansas.

K.B.E. Knight of the British Empire (*título honorífico británico*).

K.C. King's Counsel (*abogado m de categoría superior*).

Ken. (US) Kentucky.

K.G. Knight of the Garter (*título honorífico británico*).

KKK (US) Ku Klux Klan (*organización secreta del Sur de Estados Unidos*).

K.O. knock-out*.

Kt Knight (*título de la nobleza británica*).

kw. kilowatt(s) (*kv.: kilovatio* m, *kilovatios* mpl).

kw/h. kilowatt-hours (*kv/h.: kilovatios-hora* mpl).

Ky. (US) Kentucky.

L

L. 1 (Ling) Latin (*latín* m). 2 (Pol) Liberal (*liberal* m; also adj). 3 (Aut) learner (*aprendiz m de conductor, aprendiza f de conductora*). 4 Lake (*lago* m).

l. 1 left (*izq., izq.º: izquierdo*). 2 litre(s) (*l.: litro* m, *litros* mpl).

La. (US) Louisiana.

Lab. 1 (Pol) Labour (*laborista* m; also adj). 2 (Canada) Labrador.

Lancs. Lancashire (*condado inglés*).

Lat. Latin (*latín* m).

lat. latitude (*latitud* f).

lb. libra, pound* (*libra* f).

L.C. 1 Lord Chancellor (*presidente de la Cámara de los Lores etc*). 2 (Comm) letter of credit (*carta f de crédito*).

l.c. lower case (*minúscula* f).

LCC London County Council.

L.C.D. lowest common denominator (*mínimo común denominador* m).

L.C.F. lowest common factor (*mínimo común factor* m).

L.C.M. lowest common multiple (*mínimo común múltiplo* m).

L-Cpl Lance-Corporal (*soldado m primera*).

Ld Lord (*título de la nobleza británica*).

LEA Local Education Authority (*comisión municipal etc de educación*).

Leics. Leicestershire (*condado inglés*).

l.h. left hand (*izq., izq.ª: izquierda* f).

L.I. Long Island (*Estados Unidos*).

Lib. 1 Library (*Bib.: biblioteca* f). 2 (Pol) Liberal (*liberal* m; also adj).

Lieut. Lieutenant (*ten.ᵗᵉ: teniente* m).

Lieut.-Col. Lieutenant-Colonel (*teniente coronel* m).

Lincs. Lincolnshire (*condado inglés*).

Litt.D. Litterarum Doctor, Doctor of Letters.

ll. lines (*líneas* fpl).

Ll.B. Legum Baccalaureus, Bachelor of Laws.

Ll.D. Legum Doctor, Doctor of Laws.

Lon. London (*Londres*).

long. longitude (*longitud* f).

L.P. 1 (Pol) Labour Party (*Partido m Laborista*). 2 (Mus etc) long-playing (*microsurco, de larga duración*).

L.P., l.p. low-pressure (*de baja presión*).

L'pl, L'pool Liverpool.

L.R.A.M. Licenciate of the Royal Academy of Music.

L.s.d. Librae, solidi, denarii; pounds, shillings and pence (*libras, chelines y peniques:* (fam) *pasta f* (sl), *dinero* m).

LSD (Chem) lysergic acid diethylomide (*droga*).

LSE London School of Economics (*colegio de la Universidad de Londres*).

Lt Lieutenant (*ten.ᵗᵉ: teniente* m).

LT 1 low-tension (*de baja tensión*). 2 London Transport.

Lt-Col. Lieutenant-Colonel (*teniente coronel* m).

Ltd Limited (*S.A.: sociedad f anónima*).

Lt-Gen. Lieutenant-General (*teniente general* m).

LV luncheon voucher (*vale para la comida de mediodía, entregado al empleado como plus de sueldo*).

M

M (Cine: US: old) = GP

m. 1 married (*se casó con*). 2 metre(s) (*m.: metro m, metros* mpl). 3 mile(s) (*milla f, millas* fpl). 4 male (*macho* m). 5 minute(s) (*m.: minuto m, minutos* mpl). 6 (Math) million (*millón m, millones* mpl).

M.A. Master of Arts.

Maj. Major (*comandante* m).

Maj.-Gen. Major-General (*general m de división*).

Man., Manit. Manitoba (*provincia canadiense*).

Mar. March (*mar.: marzo* m).

Mass. (US) Massachusetts.

max. maximum (*máximo m, máximum* m).

M.B. Medicinae Baccalaureus, Bachelor of Medicine.

M.B.E. Member of the Order of the British Empire (*título honorífico británico*).

M.C. 1 Master of Ceremonies. 2 (US) Member of Congress. 3 (Mil) Military Cross (*condecoración británica*).

MCC Marylebone Cricket Club.

M.D. 1 Medicinae Doctor, Doctor of Medicine. 2 (euph) mentally deficient (*de inteligencia inferior a la normal*).

Md. (US) Maryland.

Mddx Middlesex (*condado inglés*).

Me. (US) Maine.

Med. 1 medieval (*medieval*). 2 (Med) medical (*médico*).

Medit. Mediterranean (*Mediterráneo* m).

memo. memorandum*.

Mer. Merionethshire (*condado galés*).

Messrs Messieurs (*Sres.: Señores* mpl).

Met. Metropolitan (*metropolitano*).

met. meterological (*meteorológico*).

mfd manufactured (*fabricado* adj).

mfg manufacturing (*fabricación f, manufacturero* adj).

mfr manufacturer (*fabricante* m).

mfs manufacturers (*fabricante* m).

Mgr Monsignor (*Mons.: Monseñor* m).

M.I.5 Military Intelligence (5) (*servicio secreto y de contraespionaje*).

Mich. (US) Michigan.

Min. 1 Minister (*ministro* m). 2 Ministry (*ministerio* m).

min. 1 minute(s) (*m.: minuto m, minutos* mpl). 2 minimum (*mínimo m, mínimum* m).

Minn. (US) Minnesota.

misc. miscellaneous (*vario, diverso*).

Miss. (US) Mississippi.

M.I.T. Massachusetts Institute of Technology.

MLA Modern Language Association.

M.M. Military Medal (*condecoración británica*).

MM Messieurs (*Sres.: Señores* mpl).

M.N. Merchant Navy (*marina f mercante*).

Mo. (US) Missouri.

M.O. 1 (Fin) money order (*giro m postal*). 2 medical officer (*médico* m).

M.O.H. 1 Medical Officer of Health (*jefe de los servicios de sanidad (de* una ciudad etc)). **2** Ministry of Health (*Ministerio m de Sanidad*, equivalent to (Spain) *Dirección f General de Sanidad*).

mol. wt molecular weight (*peso m molecular*).

Mon. **1** Monday (*lunes m*). **2** Monmouthshire (*condado anglo-galés*).

Mont. **1** Montgomeryshire (*condado galés*). **2** (*US*) Montana.

MOT Ministry of Transport.

M.P. **1** (*Pol*) Member of Parliament. **2** (*Mil*) Military Police. **3** Metropolitan Police (*policía de Londres*).

M.P.B.W. Ministry of Public Building and Works (*Ministerio m de Obras Públicas*).

m.p.g. miles per gallon (in Spain reckoned in *kilómetros por litro*).

m.p.h. miles per hour (in Spain reckoned in *km./h.: kilómetros por hora*).

M.P.S. Member of the Pharmaceutical Society.

Mr Mister*.

MRC Medical Research Council.

Mrs Mistress*.

M.S. motorship (*motonave f*).

M.Sc. Master of Science.

M.S.L. mean sea-level (*nivel m medio del mar*).

Mt Mount (*monte m, montaña f*).

MTB motor torpedo-boat (*torpedero m*).

Mus.B. Musicae Baccalaureus, Bachelor of Music.

Mus.D. Musicae Doctor, Doctor of Music.

Mx Middlesex (*condado inglés*).

N

N. north (*N.: norte m, adj*).

n. **1** neuter (*neutro*). **2** name (*nombre m*). **3** natus, born (*n.: nacido*).

NAACP (*US*) National Association for the Advancement of Colored People (*asociación para el fomento del progreso de la gente de color*).

NAAFI Navy, Army and Air Force Institutes (*servicio de cantinas etc para las fuerzas armadas*).

NALGO National Association of Local Government Officers.

NAS **1** National Association of Schoolmasters. **2** (*US*) National Academy of Science.

NASA (*US*) National Astronautics and Space Administration.

Nat. **1** National (*nacional*). **2** (*Pol*) Nationalist (*nacionalista m*).

Nat. Hist. Natural History (*historia f natural*).

NATO North Atlantic Treaty Organization (*NATO, OTAN: Organización f del Tratado del Atlántico Norte*).

N.B. **1** nota bene, note well (*N.B.: nótese bien*). **2** New Brunswick (*provincia canadiense*).

N.C. (*US*) North Carolina.

NCB National Coal Board (*junta nacional del carbón*).

N.C.O. non-commissioned officer*.

N.D., N.Dak. (*US*) North Dakota.

n.d. no date (*s.f.: sin fecha*).

N.E. **1** (*US*) New England (*región de EE.UU.*). **2** north-east (*NE.: nor(d)este m, adj*).

N.E.B. New English Bible.

Neb., Nebr. (*US*) Nebraska.

N.E.D. New English Dictionary.

NEDC (*fam: Neddy*) National Economic Development Council.

Neth. Netherlands (*Países mpl Bajos*).

Nev. (*US*) Nevada.

N.F. Newfoundland (*Terranova f*).

NFS National Fire Service (*servicio de bomberos*).

NFU National Farmers' Union (*asociación de agricultores*).

N.H. (*US*) New Hampshire.

N.H.(I.) National Health (Insurance) (*Seguro m Social Nacional*, equivalent to (Spain) *Seguro m de Enfermedad*).

N.H.S. National Health Service (*Servicio m Nacional de Sanidad*).

NIBMAR no independence before majority rule (*fórmula que resume la política del gobierno del Reino Unido en el asunto de Rodesia (1965 etc)*).

N.J. (*US*) New Jersey.

NLI National Lifeboat Institution (*servicio de lanchas de socorro*).

N.M., N.Mex. (*US*) New Mexico (*Nuevo Méjico*).

N.N.E. north - north - east (*NNE.: nornordeste*).

N.N.W. north - north - west (*NNO.: nornoroeste*).

No. **1** numero, number (*n.º, núm.: número m*). **2 = N.**

non seq. non sequitur, it does not follow (*no sigue*).

Northants. Northamptonshire (*condado inglés*).

Northumb. Northumberland (*condado inglés*).

Nos. numbers (*n.º, núm.: números mpl*).

Notts. Nottinghamshire (*condado inglés*).

Nov. November (*nov.: noviembre m*).

n.p. new paragraph (*(punto y) aparte*).

n.p. or d. no place or date (*s.l. ni f.: sin lugar ni fecha*).

nr near (*cerca de*).

N.S. Nova Scotia (*Nueva Escocia, provincia canadiense*).

NSPCC National Society for the Prevention of Cruelty to Children (*sociedad protectora de los niños*).

N.S.W. New South Wales (*Nueva Gales f del Sur, estado australiano*).

nt wt net weight (*p.º n.º: peso m neto*).

N.U.I. National University of Ireland.

NUJ National Union of Journalists.

NUM National Union of Mineworkers.

NUR National Union of Railwaymen.

NUS National Union of Students.

NUT National Union of Teachers.

N.W. north-west (*NO.: noroeste m, adj*).

N.W.T. North West Territory (*parte del Canadá*).

N.Y. New York (*Nueva York, estado norteamericano*).

N.Y.C. New York City (*Ciudad de Nueva York*).

N.Z. New Zealand (*Nueva Zelanda f*).

O

O. **1** (*US*) Ohio. **2** (*Canada*) Ontario (*provincia canadiense*).

O. & M. Organization and Methods (*estudio de la organización y de los métodos (en las empresas comerciales etc)*).

OAS Organization of American States (*O.E.A.: Organización f de Estados Americanos*).

ob. obiit, died (*m.: murió*).

O.B.E. Officer of the Order of the British Empire (*título honorífico británico*).

O.C. Officer Commanding (*jefe m*).

Oct. October (*oct.: octubre m*).

OECD Organization for European Cooperation and Development (*O.C.E.D.*).

O.E.D. Oxford English Dictionary.

OEEC Organization for European Economic Co-operation (*O.E.C.E.*).

O.H.M.S. On His (Her) Majesty's Service.

O.K.* (*US*) Oklahoma.

Oklá.

O-level Ordinary level (*grado inferior del General Certificate of Education (a los 15–16 años); = bachillerato m elemental*).

O.M. Order of Merit (*título honorífico británico*).

o.n.o. or near offer (*en los anuncios: se admitirán ofertas un poco más bajas que el precio mencionado*).

Ont. Ontario (*provincia canadiense*).

op. cit. opere citato, in the work cited (*obr. cit.: obra f citada*).

opp. opposite (*en frente de*).

O.R. operational research (*estudio de las operaciones de las compañías y organizaciones*).

o.r. (at) owner's risk (*bajo la responsabilidad del cliente (or usuario)*).

ord. ordinary (*corriente, común, normal*).

Ore. (*US*) Oregon.

O.S. **1** (*Naut*) ordinary seaman (*marinero m*). **2**

620

(Geog) Ordnance Survey (servicio oficial de topografía). 3 (Sew) outsize (de tamaño extraordinario). 4 (Hist) old style (según el calendario juliano).

O.T. Old Testament (A.T.: Antiguo Testamento m).

OUP Oxford University Press.

Oxon. 1 Oxfordshire (condado inglés). 2 (Univ) Oxoniensis, of Oxford (de la Universidad de Oxford).

oz. ounce(s)* (onza f, onzas fpl).

P

p. page (pág: página f).

p (Fin) penny, pence pl (nuevo penique m británico).

P.A. Press Association (agencia de noticias).

Pa. (US) Pennsylvania (Pensilvania).

p.a. per annum, yearly (por año, al año).

par., para. paragraph (párrafo m).

pat. patent (pat.: patente f).

PAU Pan-American Union (U.P.A.).

P.A.Y.E. Pay as you earn (sistema de calcular el impuesto sobre la renta).

P.C. 1 police constable (policía m). 2 Privy Council (Consejo m Privado (de Su Majestad)). 3 Privy Councillor (miembro m del Consejo Privado). 4 Parish Council (consejo de parroquia).

p.c. 1 (Post) postcard (tarjeta f postal). 2 (Math) per cent (p.c.: por cien, por ciento).

p. & p. postage and packing (gastos mpl de embalaje y envío).

pd paid (pagado).

P.E. physical education (cultura f física).

P.E.I. Prince Edward Island (parte del Canadá).

Pemb. Pembrokeshire (condado galés).

P.E.N. Club (International Association of) Poets, Playwrights, Editors, Essayists and Novelists.

Penn. (US) Pennsylvania (Pensilvania).

per pro. per procurationem, by proxy (p.p.: por poder)

Pfc. (US: Mil) private first class (soldado m de primera).

Ph.D. Doctor of Philosophy.

PIB Price and Incomes Board (junta regidora de precios y rentas).

Pl. Place (plaza f).

P/L. profit and loss (ganancias fpl y pérdidas).

P.M. Prime Minister (primer ministro m).

p.m. post meridiem, after noon, in the afternoon (después del mediodía, de la tarde).

P.M.G. Postmaster General (Director m General de Correos).

P.O. 1 (Post) post office (oficina f de correos).

2 (Aer) Pilot Officer (oficial m piloto).

p.o. postal order (giro m postal).

P.O.B. post-office box (apartado m de correos).

pop. population (h.: habitantes mpl).

poss. 1 possible (posible). 2 possibly (posiblemente).

P.O.W. prisoner of war (prisionero m).

p.p. per procurationem, by proxy (p.p.: por poder).

pp. pages (págs.: páginas fpl).

PPE philosophy, politics and economics (grupo de asignaturas de la Universidad de Oxford).

PPS 1 (Pol) Parliamentary Private Secretary. 2 (Post) post-postscriptum (posdata f adicional).

P.R. 1 (Pol) proportional representation. 2 (Comm) public relations. 3 Puerto Rico (P.R.: Puerto m Rico).

pr pair (par m).

Pres. 1 president (presidente m). 2 (Eccl) Presbyterian (presbiteriano m).

P.R.O. 1 Public Record Office (archivo m nacional). 2 (Comm etc) public relations officer (encargado m de relaciones públicas).

prop. proprietor (propietario m).

Prot. Protestant (protestante m; also adj).

pro tem. pro tempore, for the time being (en el interín).

prox. proximo, in the next month (pr. fr.: próximo futuro).

P.S. postscript (P.D.: posdata f).

P.T. physical training (gimnasia f, cultura f física).

pt 1 part (parte f). 2 (Fin) payment (pago m). 3 pint(s)*. 4 point (punto m).

PTA Parent-Teacher Association (asociación de padres y profesores, en un colegio).

Pte Private (soldado m raso).

PTO please turn over (véase al dorso).

PVC polyvinyl chloride (sustancia plástica).

Pvt. (US: Mil) Private (soldado m raso).

PX (US) Post Exchange (organización de tiendas etc especiales para las fuerzas armadas).

Q

Q. 1 Queen (reina f). 2 (Canada) Quebec (provincia canadiense). 3 question (pregunta f).

q. 1 query (pregunta f; duda f). 2 quart(s)*.

Q.C. Queen's Counsel (abogado m (de catogoría superior)).

Q.E.D. quod erat demonstrandum, which was to be proved (que es lo que había de probar).

Q.E.F. quod erat faciendum, which was to be done (que es lo que había de hacer).

Q.M. Quartermaster*.

qr 1 quarter(s)*. 2 quire(s)*.

qt quart(s)*.

qto quarto (in-4º: en cuarto).

Qu. Queen (reina f).

Que. Quebec (provincia canadiense).

quot. quotation (cotización f).

q.v. quod vide, which see (véase).

R

R. 1 Rex, King (rey m). 2 Regina, Queen (reina f). 3 (Geog) river (río m). 4 (Rail) railway (ferrocarril m). 5 Réaumur (termómetro m Réaumur).

R (Cine: US) Restricted (película f más apta para mayores).

r. right (der., der.º: derecho).

R.A. 1 (Art) Royal Academy (Real Academia f de Bellas Artes). 2 (Art) Royal Academician (miembro m de la Real Academia de Bellas Artes). 3 (Mil) Royal Artillery.

RAC 1 (Aut) Royal Automobile Club. 2 (Mil) Royal Armoured Corps.

Rad. Radnorshire (condado galés).

RADA Royal Academy of Dramatic Art (escuela de actores etc).

RAF Royal Air Force (fuerzas aéreas británicas).

R.C. Roman Catholic (católico m; also adj).

R.C.M. Royal College of Music.

R.C.P. Royal College of Physicians.

R.C.S. Royal College of Surgeons.

Rd Road (calle f).

R/D refer to drawer (protestar este cheque por falta de fondos).

RDC Rural District Council.

R.E. Royal Engineers.

recd received (recibido).

ref. 1 reference (referencia f). 2 (as prep) with reference to (en cuanto a, respecto de).

regd 1 (Comm etc) registered (registrado). 2 (Post) registered (certificado).

regt regiment (regimiento m).

REME Royal Electrical and Mechanical Engineers.

Rep. 1 Republic (república f). 2 (Pol) Republican (republicano m; also adj).

ret. retired (jubilado, (Mil) retirado).

Rev. Reverend (R., Rdo.: Reverendo).

Rgt regiment (regimiento m).

r.h. right hand (der., der.ª: derecha f).

R.H.S. 1 Royal Horticultural Society. 2 Royal Humane Society. 3 Royal Historical Society.

R.I. (US) Rhode Island.

R.I.B.A. Royal Institute of British Architects.

R.I.P. requiescat in pace, may he (etc) rest in peace (E.P.D.: en paz descanse).

Rly Railway (f.c.: ferrocarril m).

R.M. Royal Marines.

R.M.S. Royal Mail Steamer.

RN 1 Royal Navy. 2 (US) Registered Nurse (enfermera f diplomada).

RNIB Royal National Institute for the Blind.

RNLI Royal National Lifeboat Institution.

RNR Royal Naval Reserve.

RNVR Royal Naval Volunteer Reserve.

R.P. reply paid (C.P.: contestación f pagada).

R.P.M. resale price maintenance.

R.R. (US) Railroad (f.c.: ferrocarril m).

R.S. Royal Society.

R.S.A. 1 Royal Scottish Academy. 2 Royal Scottish Academician. 3 Royal Society of Arts. 4 Royal Society of Antiquaries.

R.S.M. Regimental Sergeant-Major (approx = brigada m de regimiento).

RSPCA Royal Society for the Prevention of Cruelty to Animals (sociedad protectora de animales).

RSVP répondez s'il vous plaît, please reply (S.R.C.: se ruega contestación).

Rt Hon. Right Honourable (título honorífico británico).

Rt Rev. Right Reverend (Rmo.: Reverendísimo).

RU Rugby Union.

Rutl. Rutland (condado inglés)

R.V. Revised Version (of the Bible).

r.v. rateable value*.

Ry Rail (f.c.: ferrocarril m).

S

S. 1 south (S.: sur m, adj). 2 (Rel) Saint (S.: San, Santa).

s. 1 second (segundo m). 2 son (hijo m). 3 (Fin) shilling(s) (chelín m, chelines mpl).

S.A. 1 South Africa (África f del Sur). 2 South America (América f del Sur, Sudamérica f). 3 South Australia (estado australiano). 4 Salvation Army (Ejército m de Salvación).

s.a.e. stamped addressed envelope (sobre m con las propias señas de uno y con sello).

Salop Shropshire (condado inglés).

Sask. Saskatchewan (provincia canadiense).

Sat. Saturday (sáb.: sábado m).

S.C. (US) South Carolina.

Sc.D. Scientiae Doctor, Doctor of Science.

S.C.E. Scottish Certificate of Education.

Sch. School (escuela f).

S.D., S.Dak. (US) South Dakota.

S.E. south-east (SE.: sudeste m, adj).

SEATO South-East Asia Treaty Organization (SEATO, OTASE: Organización f del Tratado de la Asia Sudeste).

sec. 1 secondary (segundo, secundario). 2 section (sección f). 3 second(s) (segundo m, segundos mpl).

Sec., Secy Secretary (Srio.: Secretario m).

S.E.D. Scottish Education Department.

Sen., Senr senior*.

Sept. September (sep.: septiembre m).

Serg., Sergt Sergeant (sargento m).

S.E.T. Selective Employment Tax (impuesto que paga el patrono por cada empleado).

SF science fiction (ciencia-ficción f).

s.g. specific gravity (peso m específico).

Sgt Sergeant (sargento m).

sh. shilling(s) (chelín m, chelines mpl).

SHAPE Supreme Headquarters Allied Powers in Europe.

S.M. Sergeant-Major (approx = brigado m).

So. = S. 1

Soc. 1 Society (sociedad f). 2 (Pol) Socialist (socialista mf; also adj).

S.O.E.D. Shorter Oxford English Dictionary.

Som. Somerset (condado inglés).

sov. sovereign (soberano m (moneda de oro de 1 libra)).

Sp., Span. Spanish (esp.: español m, adj).

S.P. starting price (en las carreras de caballos, puntos de ventaja ofrecidos a la salida).

sp. gr. specific gravity (peso m específico).

Sq. Square (plaza f).

sq. (Math) square (cuadrado).

sq. ft square foot, square feet (pie m cuadrado, pies mpl cuadrados).

Sr senior*.

S.R.N. state registered nurse (enfermera f diplomada).

SS Saints (SS: santos mpl, santas fpl).

S.S. steamship (vapor m).

S.S.E. south - south - east (SSE.: sudsudeste).

S.S.W. south - south - west (SSO.: sudsudoeste).

St 1 (Eccl) Saint (S.: San, Santa). 2 (Geog) Strait (estrecho m). 3 Street (calle f).

St. (Rail etc) Station (estación f).

st. stone(s)*.

Sta. = St.

Staffs. Staffordshire (condado inglés).

STD (Tel) subscriber trunk dialling.

stg sterling (moneda f esterlina, libras fpl esterlinas).

Stn Station (estación f).

Sun. Sunday (dom.º: domingo m).

supp. supplement (suplemento m).

Supt Superintendent (subjefe m de policía).

S.W. south-west (SO.: suroeste m, adj).

Sx Sussex (condado inglés).

syn. 1 synonym (sinónimo m). 2 synonymous (sinónimo).

T

t. ton(s) (tonelada f, toneladas fpl).

T.A. Territorial Army (reserva f del ejército).

TB tuberculosis (tuberculosis f).

TCD Trinity College, Dublin (universidad irlandesa).

T.D. 1 Territorial Decoration (condecoración británica). 2 (US) Treasury Department (Ministerio m de Hacienda).

Tel. telephone (tel.: teléfono m).

temp. temperature (temperatura f).

Tenn. (US) Tennessee.

Tex. (US) Texas (Tejas).

TGWU Transport and General Workers' Union.

Thurs. Thursday (jueves m).

T.O. Telegraph Office.

trans. 1 translation (traducción f). 2 translated (trad.: traducido). 3 transactions (actas fpl, memorias fpl).

Trs. Treasurer (tesorero m).

TT 1 teetotal, teetotaller*. 2 (Aut) Tourist Trophy. 3 (Agr) tuberculin-tested (a prueba de tuberculinas).

TU trade union.

TUC Trades Union Congress (confederación de los sindicatos (británicos)).

Tues. Tuesday (martes m).

TVA Tennessee Valley Authority (comisión para el fomento del desarrollo económico del Tennessee Valley, EE.UU.).

U

U (Cine) Universal (película f apta para todos los públicos).

U.A.R. United Arab Republic (R.A.U.: República f Árabe Unida).

UDC Urban District Council (ayuntamiento de distrito urbano).

UDI Unilateral Declaration of Independence (Rodesia: 1965).

UFO unidentified flying object (OVNI: objeto m volante no identificado).

UHF ultra-high frequency (frecuencia f extra alta).

U.K. United Kingdom (Reino m Unido (Inglaterra, Escocia, Gales e Irlanda del Norte)).

ult. ultimo, last month (p.pdo.: próximo pasado).

UMW (US) United Mineworkers.

UN United Nations (N.U., NN.UU.: Naciones fpl Unidas).

UNA United Nations Association.

UNESCO United Nations Educational, Scientific and Cultural Organization (UNESCO: Organización f de las Naciones Unidas para la Educación, la Ciencia y la Cultura).

UNICEF United Nations International Children's Emergency Fund (UNICEF: Fondo m Internacional de las Naciones Unidas de Socorro a la Infancia).

Univ. University (universidad f).

UNO United Nations Organization (ONU: Organización f de las Naciones Unidas).

U.P. United Press (agencia de noticias).

US United States (EE.UU.: Estados mpl Unidos).

USA 1 United States of America (EE.UU.: Estados mpl Unidos). 2 United States Army.

USAF United States Air Force.

U.S.C.G. United States Coast Guard.

USDA United States Department of Agriculture.

U.S.M. 1 (Post) United States Mail. 2 (Mil) United States Marines. 3 (Fin) United States Mint.

USN United States Navy.

USNG United States National Guard.

U.S.N.R. United States Naval Reserve.

USS 1 (Pol) United States Senate. 2 (Naut) United States Ship. 3 United States Service.

USSR Union of Soviet Socialist Republics (U.R.S.S.: Unión f de Repúblicas Socialistas Soviéticas).

U.S.T.C. United States Tariff Commission.

Ut. (US) Utah.

V

V 1 flying bomb (bomba f volante (1944–45)).

V 2 rocket bomb (bomba f cohete (1944–45)).

v. 1 (Lit) verse (estrofa f). 2 (Bib) verse (vers.º: versículo m). 3 (Sport, Law etc) versus, against (contra). 4 (Elec) volt(s) (v.: voltio m, voltios mpl). 5 vide, see (v.: véase; vid.: vide).

Va. (US) Virginia.

V.C. 1 (Mil) Victoria Cross (condecoración británica). 2 (Univ) Vice-Chancellor*. 3 Vice-Chairman (vicepresidente m).

V.D. venereal disease (enfermedad f venérea).

V.E. Day Victory in Europe Day (día m de la victoria en Europa (8 mayo 1945).

Ven. Venerable (venerable).

v.g. very good (muy bueno).

VHF very high frequency (frecuencia f muy alta).

VIP very important person (often hum) (persona f importante, personaje m).

viz. videlicet, namely (v.gr.: verbigracia).

V.J. Day Victory over Japan Day (día m de la victoria sobre el Japón (Brit: 15 agosto 1945; US: 2 setiembre 1945)).

vol., vols volume(s) (t.: tomo m, tomos mpl).

V.P., V.Pres. Vice President (vicepresidente m).

V.R. Victoria Regina, Queen Victoria.

vs versus, against (contra).

VSO Voluntary Service Overseas.

Vt. (US) Vermont.

VTO(L) vertical takeoff (and landing) (despegue m (y aterrizaje) vertical).

vv. verses (see v. 1 and 2).

v.v. vice versa (viceversa).

W

W. west (O.: oeste m, adj).

w. watt(s) (w.: vatio m, vatios mpl).

WAAC Women's Auxiliary Army Corps.

WAAF Women's Auxiliary Air Force.

WAC (US) Women's Army Corps.

War., Warwicks. Warwickshire (condado inglés).

Wash. (US) Washington.

WAVES (US) Women's Appointed Volunteer Emergency Service.

W.C. water closet (W.C.: wáter m, inodoro m).

W.D. War Department (Ministerio m de Guerra).

WEA Worker's Educational Association.

Wed(s). Wednesday (miérc.: miércoles m).

WFTU World Federation of Trade Unions (Federación f Mundial de Sindicatos).

WHO World Health Organization (O.M.S.: Organización f Mundial de la Salud).

W.I. 1 Women's Institute. 2 West Indies (Antillas fpl).

Wilts. Wiltshire (condado inglés).

Wis(c). (US) Wisconsin.

wk week (semana f).

W/L wavelength (longitud f de onda).

W.N.W. west - north - west (ONO.: oesnoroeste).

W.O. 1 (Mil) War Office (Ministerio m de Guerra). 2 (Mil) Warrant Officer (suboficial m). 3 (Naut) Warrant Officer (contramaestre m).

Worcs. Worcestershire (condado inglés).

W.P. weather permitting (si lo permite el tiempo).

WRAC Women's Royal Army Corps.

WRAF Women's Royal Air Force.

WRNS Women's Royal Naval Service.

W.S.W. west - south - west (OSO.: oessudoeste).

wt weight (peso m).

W/T wireless telegraphy (radiotelegrafía f).

WUS World University Service (organización benéfica de las universidades del mundo).

W.Va. (US) West Virginia.

W.V.S. Women's Voluntary Service.

Wyo. (US) Wyoming.

X

X (Cine) adults only (película f únicamente para mayores).

Xmas Christmas*.

X-ray*

Y

yd. yard(s)*.

YHA Youth Hostels Association.

YMCA Young Men's Christian Association.

YMHA Young Men's Hebrew Association.

Yorks. Yorkshire (condado inglés).

yr 1 year(s) (año m, años pl). 2 your (su).

yrs 1 years (años mpl). 2 yours (suyo).

YWCA Young Women's Christian Association.

YWHA Young Women's Hebrew Association.

The Spanish Verb   *El verbo español*

EACH VERB ENTRY IN THE SPANISH-English section of the Dictionary includes a reference by number and letter to the tables below, in which the simple tenses and parts of the three conjugations and of irregular verbs are set out. For verbs having only a slight irregularity the indication of it is given in the main text of the dictionary (*eg* escribir [3a; *ptp* escrito]) and is not repeated here. Certain other verbs have been marked in the main text as *defective* and in some cases indications of usage have been given there, but for further information it is best to consult a full grammar of the language.

Certain general points may be summarized here:

The **imperfect** is regular for all verbs except *ser* (*era* etc), *ir* (*iba* etc) and *ver* (*veía* etc).

The **conditional** is formed by adding to the stem of the future tense (in most cases the infinitive) the endings of the imperfect tense of *haber*: *contaría* etc. If the stem of the future tense is irregular, the conditional will have the same irregularity: *decir* — *diré, diría*; *poder* — *podré, podría*.

Compound tenses are formed with the auxiliary *haber* and the past participle:

perfect:	he cantado (*subj*: haya cantado)
pluperfect:	había cantado (*subj*: hubiera cantado, hubiese cantado)
future perfect:	habré cantado
conditional perfect:	había cantado
perfect infinitive:	haber cantado
perfect gerund:	habiendo cantado

The **imperfect subjunctives** I and II can be seen as being formed from the 3rd person plural of the preterite using as a stem what remains after removing the final -*ron* syllable and adding to it -*ra* (I) or -*se* (II), *eg:*

cantar: canta/ron — cantara, cantase
perder: perdie/ron — perdiera, perdiese
reducir: reduje/ron — redujera, redujese

The form of the **imperative** depends not only on number but also on whether the person(s) addressed are treated in familiar or in formal terms. The "true" imperative is used only in familiar address in the affirmative:

cantar: canta (tú), cantad (vosotros)
vender: vende (tú), vended (vosotros)
partir: parte (tú), partid (vosotros)

(There are a few irregular imperatives in the singular — *salir* — *sal*, *hacer* — *haz*, etc, but all the plurals are regular.) The imperative affirmative in formal address requires the subjunctive: *envíemelo, háganlo, conduzca Vd con más cuidado, ¡oiga!* The imperative negative in both familiar and formal address also requires the subjunctive: *no me digas, no os preocupéis, no grite tanto Vd, no se desanimen Vds.*

Continuous tenses are formed with *estar* and the gerund: *está leyendo, estaba lloviendo, estábamos hablando de eso.* Other auxiliary verbs may occasionally replace *estar* in certain senses: *según voy viendo, va mejorando, iba cogiendo flores, lo venía estudiando desde hacía muchos años.* Usage of the continuous tenses does not exactly coincide with that of English.

The **passive** is formed with tenses of *ser* and the past participle, which agrees in number and gender with the subject: *las casas fueron construidas, será firmado mañana el tratado, después de haber sido vencido.* The passive is much less used in Spanish than in English, its function often being taken over by a reflexive construction, by *uno*, etc.

First Conjugation

[1a] cantar

INFINITIVE: cantar   GERUND: cantando

PAST PARTICIPLE: cantado

INDICATIVE

	PRESENT	IMPERFECT	PRETERITE	FUTURE	CONDITIONAL
	canto	cantaba	canté	cantaré	cantaría
	cantas	cantabas	cantaste	cantarás	cantarías
	canta	cantaba	cantó	cantará	cantaría
	cantamos	cantábamos	cantamos	cantaremos	cantaríamos
	cantáis	cantabais	cantasteis	cantaréis	cantaríais
	cantan	cantaban	cantaron	cantarán	cantarían

SUBJUNCTIVE

	PRESENT	IMPERFECT I	IMPERFECT II
	cante	cantara	cantase
	cantes	cantaras	cantases
	cante	cantara	cantase
	cantemos	cantáramos	cantásemos
	cantéis	cantarais	cantaseis
	canten	cantaran	cantasen

IMPERATIVE

canta (tú)   cantad (vosotros)

[1b] cambiar
The i of the stem is not stressed and the verb is regular

INFINITIVE	PRESENT INDICATIVE	PRESENT SUBJUNCTIVE	PRETERITE
	cambio	cambie	cambié
	cambias	cambies	cambiaste
	cambia	cambie	cambió
	cambiamos	cambiemos	cambiaron
	cambiáis	cambiéis	cambiasteis
	cambian	cambien	cambiaron

INFINITIVE	PRESENT INDICATIVE	PRESENT SUBJUNCTIVE	PRETERITE
[1c] enviar The i of the stem is stressed in parts of the present tenses	envío	envíe	envié
	envías	envíes	enviaste
	envía	envíe	envió
	enviamos	enviemos	enviamos
	enviáis	enviéis	enviasteis
	envían	envíen	enviaron
[1d] evacuar The u of the stem is not stressed and the verb is regular	evacuo	evacue	evacué
	evacuas	evacues	evacuaste
	evacua	evacue	evacuó
	evacuamos	evacuemos	evacuamos
	evacuáis	evacuéis	evacuasteis
	evacuan	evacuen	evacuaron
[1e] situar The u of the stem is stressed in parts of the present tenses	sitúo	sitúe	situé
	sitúas	sitúes	situaste
	sitúa	sitúe	situó
	situamos	situemos	situamos
	situáis	situéis	situasteis
	sitúan	sitúen	situaron
[1f] cruzar The stem consonant z is written c before e	cruzo	cruce	crucé
	cruzas	cruces	cruzaste
	cruza	cruce	cruzó
	cruzamos	crucemos	cruzamos
	cruzáis	crucéis	cruzasteis
	cruzan	crucen	cruzaron
[1g] picar The stem consonant c is written qu before e	pico	pique	piqué
	picas	piques	picaste
	pica	pique	picó
	picamos	piquemos	picamos
	picáis	piquéis	picasteis
	pican	piquen	picaron
[1h] pagar The stem consonant g is written gu (with u silent) before e	pago	pague	pagué
	pagas	pagues	pagaste
	paga	pague	pagó
	pagamos	paguemos	pagamos
	pagáis	paguéis	pagasteis
	pagan	paguen	pagaron
[1i] averiguar The u of the stem is written ü (so that it should be pronounced) before e	averiguo	averigüe	averigüé
	averiguas	averigües	averiguaste
	averigua	averigüe	averiguó
	averiguamos	averigüemos	averiguamos
	averiguáis	averigüéis	averiguasteis
	averiguan	averigüen	averiguaron

[2b] vencer
The stem consonant **c** is written **z** before **a** and **o**

INFINITIVE	PRESENT INDICATIVE	PRESENT SUBJUNCTIVE	PRETERITE
	venzo	venza	vencí
	vences	venzas	venciste
	vence	venza	venció
	vencemos	venzamos	vencimos
	vencéis	venzáis	vencisteis
	vencen	venzan	vencieron

[2c] coger
The stem consonant **g** is written **j** before **a** and **o**

INFINITIVE	PRESENT INDICATIVE	PRESENT SUBJUNCTIVE	PRETERITE
	cojo	coja	cogí
	coges	cojas	cogiste
	coge	coja	cogió
	cogemos	cojamos	cogimos
	cogéis	cojáis	cogisteis
	cogen	cojan	cogieron

[2d] conocer
The stem consonant **c** becomes **zc** before **a** and **o**

INFINITIVE	PRESENT INDICATIVE	PRESENT SUBJUNCTIVE	PRETERITE
	conozco	conozca	conocí
	conoces	conozcas	conociste
	conoce	conozca	conoció
	conocemos	conozcamos	conocimos
	conocéis	conozcáis	conocisteis
	conocen	conozcan	conocieron

[2e] leer
Unstressed **i** between vowels is written **y**.
Past Participle: *leído*.
Gerund: *leyendo*

INFINITIVE	PRESENT INDICATIVE	PRESENT SUBJUNCTIVE	PRETERITE
	leo	lea	leí
	lees	leas	leíste
	lee	lea	leyó
	leemos	leamos	leímos
	leéis	leáis	leísteis
	leen	lean	leyeron

[2f] tañer
Unstressed **i** after **ñ** (and also after **ll**) is omitted

INFINITIVE	PRESENT INDICATIVE	PRESENT SUBJUNCTIVE	PRETERITE
	taño	taña	tañí
	tañes	tañas	tañiste
	tañe	taña	tañó
	tañemos	tañamos	tañimos
	tañéis	tañáis	tañisteis
	tañen	taña	tañeron

[2g] perder
The stem vowel **e** becomes **ie** when stressed

INFINITIVE	PRESENT INDICATIVE	PRESENT SUBJUNCTIVE	PRETERITE
	pierdo	pierda	perdí
	pierdes	pierdas	perdiste
	pierde	pierda	perdió
	perdemos	perdamos	perdimos
	perdéis	perdáis	perdisteis
	pierden	pierdan	perdieron

[2h] mover
The stem vowel **o** becomes **ue** when stressed

INFINITIVE	PRESENT INDICATIVE	PRESENT SUBJUNCTIVE	PRETERITE
	muevo	mueva	moví
	mueves	muevas	moviste
	mueve	mueva	movió
	movemos	movamos	movimos
	movéis	mováis	movisteis
	mueven	muevan	movieron

[1k] cerrar
The stem vowel **e** becomes **ie** when stressed

INFINITIVE	PRESENT INDICATIVE	PRESENT SUBJUNCTIVE	PRETERITE
	cierro	cierre	cerré
	cierras	cierres	cerraste
	cierra	cierre	cerró
	cerramos	cerremos	cerramos
	cerráis	cerréis	cerrasteis
	cierran	cierren	cerraron

[1l] errar
As [1k], but the diphthong is written **ye-** at the start of the word

INFINITIVE	PRESENT INDICATIVE	PRESENT SUBJUNCTIVE	PRETERITE
	yerro	yerre	erré
	yerras	yerres	erraste
	yerra	yerre	erró
	erramos	erremos	erramos
	erráis	erréis	errasteis
	yerran	yerren	erraron

[1m] contar
The stem vowel **o** becomes **ue** when stressed

INFINITIVE	PRESENT INDICATIVE	PRESENT SUBJUNCTIVE	PRETERITE
	cuento	cuente	conté
	cuentas	cuentes	contaste
	cuenta	cuente	contó
	contamos	contemos	contamos
	contáis	contéis	contasteis
	cuentan	cuenten	contaron

[1n] agorar
As [1m], but the diphthong is written **üe** (so that the **u** should be pronounced)

INFINITIVE	PRESENT INDICATIVE	PRESENT SUBJUNCTIVE	PRETERITE
	agüero	agüere	agoré
	agüeras	agüeres	agoraste
	agüera	agüere	agoró
	agoramos	agoremos	agoramos
	agoráis	agoréis	agorasteis
	agüeran	agüeren	agoraron

[1o] jugar
The stem vowel **u** becomes **ue** when stressed; the stem consonant **g** is written **gu** (with **u** silent) before **e**

INFINITIVE	PRESENT INDICATIVE	PRESENT SUBJUNCTIVE	PRETERITE
	juego	juegue	jugué
	juegas	juegues	jugaste
	juega	juegue	jugó
	jugamos	juguemos	jugamos
	jugáis	juguéis	jugasteis
	juegan	jueguen	jugaron

[1p] estar
Irregular.
Imperative: *está (tú)*

INFINITIVE	PRESENT INDICATIVE	PRESENT SUBJUNCTIVE	PRETERITE
	estoy	esté	estuve
	estás	estés	estuviste
	está	esté	estuvo
	estamos	estemos	estuvimos
	estáis	estéis	estuvisteis
	están	estén	estuvieron

[1q] andar
Irregular

INFINITIVE	PRESENT INDICATIVE	PRESENT SUBJUNCTIVE	PRETERITE
	ando	ande	anduve
	andas	andes	anduviste
	anda	ande	anduvo
	andamos	andemos	anduvimos
	andáis	andéis	anduvisteis
	andan	anden	anduvieron

doy	di	dé
das	diste	des
da	dio	dé
damos	dimos	demos
dais	disteis	deis
dan	dieron	den

Second Conjugation

[2a] temer

INFINITIVE: temer GERUND: temiendo
PAST PARTICIPLE: temido

INDICATIVE

PRESENT	IMPERFECT	PRETERITE
temo	temía	temí
temes	temías	temiste
teme	temía	temió
tememos	temíamos	temimos
teméis	temíais	temisteis
temen	temían	temieron

FUTURE	CONDITIONAL
temeré	temería
temerás	temerías
temerá	temería
temeremos	temeríamos
temeréis	temeríais
temerán	temerían

SUBJUNCTIVE

PRESENT	IMPERFECT I	IMPERFECT II
tema	temiera	temiese
temas	temieras	temieses
tema	temiera	temiese
temamos	temiéramos	temiésemos
temáis	temierais	temieseis
teman	temieran	temiesen

IMPERATIVE

teme (tú) temed (vosotros)

[2j] oler

As [2h], but the diphthong is written **hue-** at the start of the word

huelo	huela	olí
hueles	huelas	oliste
huele	huela	olió
olemos	olamos	olimos
oléis	oláis	olisteis
huelen	huelan	olieron

[2k] haber
Irregular.
Future: *habré*

he	haya	hube
has	hayas	hubiste
ha	haya	hubo
hemos	hayamos	hubimos
habéis	hayáis	hubisteis
han	hayan	hubieron

[2l] tener
Irregular.
Future: *tendré*
Imperative: *ten (tú)*

tengo	tenga	tuve
tienes	tengas	tuviste
tiene	tenga	tuvo
tenemos	tengamos	tuvimos
tenéis	tengáis	tuvisteis
tienen	tengan	tuvieron

[2m] caber
Irregular.
Future: *cabré*

quepo	quepa	cupe
cabes	quepas	cupiste
cabe	quepa	cupo
cabemos	quepamos	cupimos
cabéis	quepáis	cupisteis
caben	quepan	cupieron

[2n] saber
Irregular.
Future: *sabré*

sé	sepa	supe
sabes	sepas	supiste
sabe	sepa	supo
sabemos	sepamos	supimos
sabéis	sepáis	supisteis
saben	sepan	supieron

[2o] caer
Irregular.
Unstressed i between vowels is written y, as [2e].
Past Participle: *caído*
Gerund: *cayendo*

caigo	caiga	caí
caes	caigas	caíste
cae	caiga	cayó
caemos	caigamos	caímos
caéis	caigáis	caísteis
caen	caigan	cayeron

[2p] traer
Irregular.
Past Participle: *traído*
Gerund: *trayendo*

traigo	traiga	traje
traes	traigas	trajiste
trae	traiga	trajo
traemos	traigamos	trajimos
traéis	traigáis	trajisteis
traen	traigan	trajeron

INFINITIVE	PRESENT INDICATIVE	PRESENT SUBJUNCTIVE	PRETERITE
[2q] valer Irregular. Future: *valdré*	valgo vales vale valemos valéis valen	valga valgas valga valgamos valgáis valgan	valí valiste valió valimos valisteis valieron
[2r] poner Irregular. Future: *pondré* Past Participle: *puesto* Imperative: *pon (tú)*	pongo pones pone ponemos ponéis ponen	ponga pongas ponga pongamos pongáis pongan	puse pusiste puso pusimos pusisteis pusieron
[2s] hacer Irregular. Future: *haré* Past Participle: *hecho* Imperative: *haz (tú)*	hago haces hace hacemos hacéis hacen	haga hagas haga hagamos hagáis hagan	hice hiciste hizo hicimos hicisteis hicieron
[2t] poder Irregular. In present tenses like [2h]. Future: *podré* Gerund: *pudiendo*	puedo puedes puede podemos podéis pueden	pueda puedas pueda podamos podáis puedan	pude pudiste pudo pudimos pudisteis pudieron
[2u] querer Irregular. In present tenses like [2g]. Future: *querré*	quiero quieres quiere queremos queréis quieren	quiera quieras quiera queramos queráis quieran	quise quisiste quiso quisimos quisisteis quisieron
[2v] ver Irregular. Imperfect: *vela* Past Participle: *visto*	veo ves ve vemos veis ven	vea veas vea veamos veáis vean	vi viste vio vimos visteis vieron
[2w] ser Irregular. Imperfect: *era* Future: *seré* Part Participle: *sido* Gerund: *siendo* Imperative: *sé (tú), sed (vosotros)*	soy eres es somos sois son	sea seas sea seamos seáis sean	fui fuiste fue fuimos fuisteis fueron

INFINITIVE	PRESENT INDICATIVE	PRESENT SUBJUNCTIVE	PRETERITE
[3b] esparcir The stem consonant **c** is written **z** before **a** and **o**	esparzo esparces esparce esparcimos esparcís esparcen	esparza esparzas esparza esparzamos esparzáis esparzan	esparcí esparciste esparció esparcimos esparcisteis esparcieron
[3c] dirigir The stem consonant **g** is written **j** before **a** and **o**	dirijo diriges dirige dirigimos dirigís dirigen	dirija dirijas dirija dirijamos dirijáis dirijan	dirigí dirigiste dirigió dirigimos dirigisteis dirigieron
[3d] distinguir The **u** after the stem consonant **g** is omitted before **a** and **o**	distingo distingues distingue distinguimos distinguís distinguen	distinga distingas distinga distingamos distingáis distingan	distinguí distinguiste distinguió distinguimos distinguisteis distinguieron
[3e] delinquir The stem consonant **qu** is written **c** before **a** and **o**	delinco delinques delinque delinquimos delinquís delinquen	delinca delincas delinca delincamos delincáis delincan	delinquí delinquiste delinquió delinquimos delinquisteis delinquieron
[3f] lucir The stem consonant **c** becomes **zc** before **a** and **o**	luzco luces luce lucimos lucís lucen	luzca luzcas luzca luzcamos luzcáis luzcan	lucí luciste lució lucimos lucisteis lucieron
[3g] huir The **i** of **-ió** and **-ie-** becomes **y**; a **y** is inserted before endings not beginning with **i**. Gerund: *huyendo*	huyo huyes huye huimos huis huyen	huya huyas huya huyamos huyáis huyan	huí huiste huyó huimos huisteis huyeron
[3h] gruñir Unstressed **i** after **ñ** (and also after **ch** and **ll**) is omitted	gruño gruñes gruñe gruñimos gruñís gruñen	gruña gruñas gruña gruñamos gruñáis gruñan	gruñí gruñiste gruñó gruñimos gruñisteis gruñeron

[2x] **placer.** Now used exclusively in 3rd person singular. Irregular forms: Present subj. *plazca* (less commonly *plega* or *plegue*); Preterite *plugo* (less commonly *plació*); Imperfect subj. I *pluguiera*, II *pluguiese* (less commonly *placiera*, *placiese*).

[2y] **yacer.** Now rather archaic. Irregular forms: Present indic. *yazco* (less commonly *yazgo* or *yago*), *yaces* etc; Present subj. *yazca* (less commonly *yazga* or *yaga*), *yazcas* etc; Imperative *yace* (*tú*) (less commonly *yaz*).

[2z] **raer.** The Present indic. is usually *raigo*, *raes* etc (like *caer* [2o]), but *rayo* is occasionally found; Present subj. usually *raiga*, *raigas* etc (also like *caer*), but *raya*, *rayas* etc is occasionally found.

[2za] **roer.** Alternative forms in present tenses: Indicative, *roo*, *roigo* or *royo*; *roes*, *roe* etc. Subjunctive, *roa*, *roiga* or *roya*. The first persons are usually avoided because of the uncertainty. The gerund is *royendo*.

Third Conjugation

(3a) partir

INFINITIVE: **partir**   GERUND: **partiendo**

PAST PARTICIPLE: **partido**

INDICATIVE

PRESENT	IMPERFECT	PRETERITE
parto	partía	partí
partes	partías	partiste
parte	partía	partió
partimos	partíamos	partimos
partís	partíais	partisteis
parten	partían	partieron

SUBJUNCTIVE

PRESENT	IMPERFECT I	IMPERFECT II
parta	partiera	partiese
partas	partieras	partieses
parta	partiera	partiese
partamos	partiéramos	partiésemos
partáis	partierais	partieseis
partan	partieran	partiesen

IMPERATIVE

parte (tú)	partid (vosotros)

[3i] **sentir**

Present indic.	Present subj.	Preterite
siento	sienta	sentí
sientes	sientas	sentiste
siente	sienta	sintió
sentimos	sintamos	sentimos
sentís	sintáis	sentisteis
sienten	sientan	sintieron

The stem vowel **e** becomes **ie** when stressed; unstressed **e** becomes **i** in 3rd persons of Preterite, 1st and 2nd persons pl. of Present Subjunctive.
Gerund: *sintiendo*.
In *adquirir* the stem vowel **i** becomes **ie** when stressed

[3k] **dormir**

Present indic.	Present subj.	Preterite
duermo	duerma	dormí
duermes	duermas	dormiste
duerme	duerma	durmió
dormimos	durmamos	dormimos
dormís	durmáis	dormisteis
duermen	duerman	durmieron

The stem vowel **o** becomes **ue** when stressed; unstressed **o** becomes **u** in 3rd persons of Preterite, 1st and 2nd persons pl. of Present Subjunctive.
Gerund: *durmiendo*

[3l] **pedir**

Present indic.	Present subj.	Preterite
pido	pida	pedí
pides	pidas	pediste
pide	pida	pidió
pedimos	pidamos	pedimos
pedís	pidáis	pedisteis
piden	pidan	pidieron

The stem vowel **e** becomes **i** when stressed, and also when unstressed in 3rd persons of Preterite, 1st and 2nd persons pl. of Present Subjunctive.
Gerund: *pidiendo*

[3m] **reír**

Present indic.	Present subj.	Preterite
río	ría	reí
ríes	rías	reíste
ríe	ría	rio
reímos	riamos	reímos
reís	riáis	reísteis
ríen	rían	rieron

Irregular.
Past Participle: *reído*
Gerund: *riendo*
Imperative: *ríe* (*tú*)

[3n] **erguir**

Present indic.	Present subj.	Preterite
yergo	yerga	erguí
yergues	yergas	erguiste
yergue	yerga	irguió
erguimos	yergamos	erguimos
erguís	yergáis	erguisteis
yerguen	yergan	irguieron

Irregular.
Gerund: *irguiendo*
Imperative: *yergue* (*tú*) and less commonly *irgue* (*tú*)

(also, less commonly)

Present indic.	Present subj.
irgo	irga
irgues	irgas
irgue	irga
erguimos	irgamos
erguís	irgáis
irguen	irgan

[3o] **reducir**

Present indic.	Present subj.	Preterite
reduzco	reduzca	reduje
reduces	reduzcas	redujiste
reduce	reduzca	redujo
reducimos	reduzcamos	redujimos
reducís	reduzcáis	redujisteis
reducen	reduzcan	redujeron

The stem consonant **c** becomes **zc** before **a** and **o** as [3f]; but there is an irregular preterite in **-uje**

INFINITIVE	PRESENT INDICATIVE	PRESENT SUBJUNCTIVE	PRETERITE
[3p] decir Irregular. Future: *diré* Past Participle: *dicho* Gerund: *diciendo* Imperative: *di (tú)*	digo dices dice decimos decís dicen	diga digas diga digamos digáis digan	dije dijiste dijo dijimos dijisteis dijeron
[3q] oír Irregular. Unstressed i between vowels becomes y. Part Participle: *oído* Gerund: *oyendo*	oigo oyes oye oímos oís oyen	oiga oigas oiga oigamos oigáis oigan	oí oíste oyó oímos oísteis oyeron
[3r] salir Irregular. Future: *saldré* Imperative: *sal (tú)*	salgo sales sale salimos salís salen	salga salgas salga salgamos salgáis salgan	salí saliste salió salimos salisteis salieron
[3s] venir Irregular. Future: *vendré* Gerund: *viniendo* Imperaitve: *ven (tú)*	vengo vienes viene venimos venís vienen	venga vengas venga vengamos vengáis vengan	vine viniste vino vinimos vinisteis vinieron
[3t] ir Irregular. Imperfect: *iba* Gerund: *yendo* Imperative: *ve (tú), id (vosotros)*	voy vas va vamos vais van	vaya vayas vaya vayamos vayáis vayan	fui fuiste fue fuimos fuisteis fueron

The English Verb   El verbo inglés

EL VERBO INGLÉS ES BASTANTE MÁS sencillo que el español, a lo menos en cuanto a su forma. Hay muchos verbos fuertes o irregulares (damos una lista de ellos a continuación) y varias clases de irregularidad ortográfica (véanse las notas al final); pero hay una sola conjugación, y dentro de cada tiempo no hay variación para las seis personas excepto en el presente (tercera persona de singular). Por tanto, no es necesario ofrecer para el verbo inglés los cuadros y paradigmas con que se suele explicar el verbo español; la estructura general y las formas del verbo inglés se resumen en las siguientes notas.

1 Indicativo

(a) **Presente:** tiene la misma forma que el infinitivo en todas las personas menos la tercera del singular; en ésta, se añade una -s al infinitivo, p.ej. *he sells*, o se añade *-es* si el infinitivo termina en sibilante (los sonidos [s], [z], [ʃ] y [tʃ]; en la escritura -ss, -zz, -sh y -ch, etc). Esta -s añadida tiene dos pronunciaciones: tras consonante sorda se pronuncia sorda [s], p.ej. *scoffs* [skəfs], *likes* [laiks], *taps* [tæps], *waits* [weits], *baths* [bɑːθs]; tras consonante sonora se pronuncia sonora, p.ej. *robs* [rəbz], *bends* [bendz], *seems* [siːmz], *gives* [givz], *bathes* ['beiðz]; *-es* se pronuncia también sonora tras sibilante o consonante sonora, *-es* o letra final del infinitivo, p.ej. *races* ['reisiz], *urges* ['əːdʒiz], *lashes* ['læʃiz], *passes* ['pɑːsiz].

Los verbos que terminan en -y la cambian en *-ies* en la tercera persona del singular, p.ej. *tries, pities, satisfies*; pero son regulares los verbos que en el infinitivo tienen una vocal delante de la -y, p.ej. *pray—he prays, annoy—she annoys*.

El verbo *be* es irregular en todas las personas:

I am	we are
you are	you are
he is	they are

Cuatro verbos más tienen forma irregular en la tercera persona del singular:

| do—he does [dʌz] | go—he goes [gəuz] |
| have—he has [hæz] | say—he says [sez] |

(b) **Pretérito (o pasado simple) y participio de pasado:** tienen la misma forma en inglés; se forman añadiendo *-ed* al infinitivo, p.ej. *paint—I painted—painted*, o bien añadiendo *-d* a los infinitivos terminados en *-e* muda, p.ej. *bare—I bared—bared*, *move—I moved—moved, revise—I revised—revised*. (Para los muchos verbos irregulares, véase la lista abajo.) Esta *-d* o *-ed* se pronuncia por lo general [t]: *raced* [reist], *passed* [pɑːst]; pero cuando se añade a un infinitivo terminado en consonante sonora o en *r*, se pronuncia [d], p.ej. *bared* [bɛəd], *moved* [muːvd], *seemed* [siːmd], *buzzed* [bʌzd]. Si el infinitivo termina en *-d* o *-t*, la desinencia *-ed* se pronuncia como una sílaba más, [id], p.ej. *raided* ['reidid], *dented* ['dentid]. Para los verbos cuyo infinitivo termina en *-y*, véase 7 (e) abajo.

(c) **Tiempos compuestos del pasado:** se forman como en español con el verbo auxiliar *to have* y el participio de pasado: perfecto *I have painted*, pluscuamperfecto *I had painted*.

(d) **Futuro y condicional (o potencial):** se forma el futuro con el auxiliar *will* o *shall* y el infinitivo, p.ej. *I will do it, they shall not pass*; se forma el condicional (o potencial) con el auxiliar *would* o *should* y el infinitivo, p.ej. *I would go, if she should come*. Como en español y de igual formación existen los tiempos compuestos llamados futuro perfecto, p.ej. *I shall have finished*, y potencial compuesto, p.ej. *I would have paid*.

(e) Para cada tiempo del indicativo existe una forma continua que se forma con el tiempo apropiado del verbo *to be* (equivalente en este caso al español *estar*) y el participio de presente (véase abajo): *I am waiting, we were hoping, they will be buying it, they would have been waiting still, I had been painting all day.* Conviene subrayar que el modo de emplear estas formas continuas no corresponde siempre al sistema español.

2 Subjuntivo

Este modo tiene muy poco uso en inglés. En el presente tiene la misma forma que el infinitivo en todas las personas, (*that*) *I go*, (*that*) *she go* etc. En el pasado simple el único verbo que tiene forma especial es *to be*, que es *were* en todas las personas, (*that*) *I were*, (*that*) *we were* etc. En los demás casos donde la lógica de los tiempos en español pudiera parecer exigir una forma de subjuntivo en pasado, el inglés emplea el presente, p.ej. *he had urged that we do it at once.* El subjuntivo se emplea obligatoriamente en inglés en *if I were you, if he were to do it, were I to attempt it* (el indicativo *was* es tenido por vulgar en estas frases y análogas); se encuentra también en la frase fosilizada *so be it*, y en el lenguaje oficial de las actas, etc, p.ej. *it is agreed that nothing be done, it was resolved that the pier be painted* (pero son igualmente correctos *should be done, should be painted*).

3 Gerundio y participio de presente

Tienen la misma forma en inglés; se añade al infinitivo la desinencia *-ing*, p.ej. *washing, sending, passing.* Para las muchas irregularidades ortográficas de esta desinencia, véase la sección 7.

4 Voz pasiva

Se forma exactamente como en español, con el tiempo apropiado del verbo *to be* (equivalente en este caso a *ser*) y el participio de pasado: *we are forced to, he was killed, they had been injured, the company will be taken over, it ought to have been rebuilt, were it to be agreed.*

5 Imperativo

Hay solamente una forma, que es la del infinitivo: *tell me, come here, don't do that.*

6 Verbos fuertes (o irregulares)

Infinitivo	Pretérito	Participio de pasado	Infinitivo	Pretérito	Participio de pasado
abide	abode *or* abided	abode *or* abided	heave	heaved, (*Naut*) hove	heaved, (*Naut*) hove
arise	arose	arisen	hew	hewed	hewed *or* hewn
awake	awoke	awaked	hide	hid	hidden
be	was, were	been	hit	hit	hit
bear	bore	(*llevado*) borne, (*nacido*) born	hold	held	held
beat	beat	beaten	hurt	hurt	hurt
become	became	become	keep	kept	kept
beget	begot, (*arch*) begat	begotten	kneel	knelt	knelt
begin	began	begun	know	knew	known
bend	bent	bent	lade	laded	laden
beseech	besought	besought	lay	laid	laid
bet	bet *or* betted	bet *or* betted	lead	led	led
bid (*ordenar*)	bade	bidden	lean	leaned *or* leant	leaned *or* leant
(*licitar etc*)	bid	bid	leap	leaped *or* leapt	leaped *or* leapt
bind	bound	bound	learn	learned *or* learnt	learned *or* learnt
bite	bit	bitten	leave	left	left
bleed	bled	bled	lend	lent	lent
blow	blew	blown	let	let	let
break	broke	broken	lie	lay	lain
breed	bred	bred	light	lit *or* lighted	lit *or* lighted
bring	brought	brought	lose	lost	lost
build	built	built	make	made	made
burn	burned *or* burnt	burned *or* burnt	may	might	—
burst	burst	burst	mean	meant	meant
buy	bought	bought	meet	met	met
can	could	—	mow	mowed	mown *or* mowed
cast	cast	cast	pay	paid	paid
catch	caught	caught	put	put	put
chide	chid	chidden *or* chid	quit	quit *or* quitted	quit *or* quitted
choose	chose	chosen	read [ri:d]	read [red]	read [red]
cleave[1] (*vt*)	clove *or* cleft	cloven *or* cleft	rend	rent	rent
cleave[2] (*vi*)	cleaved	cleaved	rid	rid	rid
cling	clung	clung	ride	rode	ridden
come	came	come	ring[2]	rang	rung
cost (*vt*)	costed	costed	rise	rose	risen
(*vi*)	cost	cost	run	ran	run
creep	crept	crept	saw	sawed	sawed *or* sawn
cut	cut	cut	say	said	said
deal	dealt	dealt	see	saw	seen
dig	dug	dug	seek	sought	sought
do	did	done	sell	sold	sold
draw	drew	drawn	send	sent	sent
dream	dreamed *or* dreamt	dreamed *or* dreamt	set	set	set
			sew	sewed	sewn
drink	drank	drunk	shake	shook	shaken
drive	drove	driven	shave	shaved	shaved *or* shaven
dwell	dwelt	dwelt	shear	sheared	shorn
eat	ate	eaten	shed	shed	shed
fall	fell	fallen	shine	shone	shone
feed	fed	fed	shoe	shod	shod
feel	felt	felt	shoot	shot	shot
fight	fought	fought	show	showed	shown
find	found	found	shrink	shrank	shrunk
flee	fled	fled	shut	shut	shut
fling	flung	flung	sing	sang	sung
fly	flew	flown	sink	sank	sunk
forbid	forbad(e)	forbidden	sit	sat	sat
forget	forgot	forgotten	slay	slew	slain
forsake	forsook	forsaken	sleep	slept	slept
freeze	froze	frozen	slide	slid	slid
get	got	got, (*US*) gotten	sling	slung	slung
gild	gilded	gilded *or* gilt	slink	slunk	slunk
gird	girded *or* girt	girded *or* girt	slit	slit	slit
give	gave	given	smell	smelled *or* smelt	smelled *or* smelt
go	went	gone	smite	smote	smitten
grind	ground	ground	sow	sowed	sown
grow	grew	grown	speak	spoke	spoken
hang	hung, (*Law*) hanged	hung, (*Law*) hanged	speed (*vt*)	speeded	speeded
			(*vi*)	sped	sped
have	had	had	spell	spelled *or* spelt	spelled *or* spelt
hear	heard	heard	spend	spent	spent
			spill	spilled *or* spilt	spilled *or* spilt

Infinitivo	Pretérito	Participio de pasado	Infinitivo	Pretérito	Participio de pasado
spin	spun *or* span	spun	swell	swelled	swollen
spit	spat	spat	swim	swam	swum
split	split	split	swing	swung	swung
spoil	spoiled *or* spoilt	spoiled *or* spoilt	take	took	taken
spread	spread	spread	teach	taught	taught
spring	sprang	sprung	tear	tore	torn
stand	stood	stood	tell	told	told
stave	stove *or* staved	stove *or* staved	think	thought	thought
steal	stole	stolen	thrive	throve	thriven
stick	stuck	stuck	throw	threw	thrown
sting	stung	stung	thrust	thrust	thrust
stink	stank	stunk	tread	trod	trodden
strew	strewed	strewed *or* strewn	wake	woke	woken *or* waked
			wear	wore	worn
stride	strode	stridden	weave	wove	woven
strike	struck	struck	weep	wept	wept
string	strung	strung	win	won	won
strive	strove	striven	wind	wound	wound
swear	swore	sworn	wring	wrung	wrung
sweep	swept	swept	write	wrote	written

N.B.—No constan en esta lista los verbos compuestos con prefijo etc; para ellos véase el verbo básico, p.ej. para *forbear* véase *bear*, para *understand* véase *stand*.

7 Verbos débiles con irregularidad ortográfica

(a) Hay muchos verbos cuya ortografía varía ligeramente en el participio de pasado y en el gerundio. Son los que terminan en consonante simple precedida de vocal simple acentuada; antes de añadirles la desinencia -*ed* o -*ing*, se dobla la consonante:

Infinitivo	Participio de pasado	Gerundio
sob	sobbed	sobbing
wed	wedded	wedding
lag	lagged	lagging
control	controlled	controlling
dim	dimmed	dimming
tan	tanned	tanning
tap	tapped	tapping
prefer	preferred	preferring
pat	patted	patting

(pero *cook-cooked-cooking*, *fear-feared-fearing*, *roar-roared-roaring*, donde la vocal no es simple y por tanto no se dobla la consonante).

(b) Los verbos que terminan en -*c* la cambian en -*ck* al añadirse las desinencias -*ed*, -*ing*:

frolic	frolicked	frolicking
traffic	trafficked	trafficking

(c) Los verbos terminados en -*l*, -*p*, aunque precedida de vocal átona, tienen doblada la consonante en el participio de pasado y en el gerundio en el inglés británico, pero simple en el de Estados Unidos:

grovel	(*Brit*) grovelled	(*Brit*) grovelling
	(*US*) groveled	(*US*) groveling
travel	(*Brit*) travelled	(*Brit*) travelling
	(*US*) traveled	(*US*) traveling
worship	(*Brit*) worshipped	(*Brit*) worshipping
	(*US*) worshiped	(*US*) worshiping

Nota — existe la misma diferencia en los sustantivos formados sobre tales verbos: *Brit* traveller = *US* traveler, *Brit* worshipper = *US* worshiper.

(d) Si el verbo termina en -*e* muda, se suprime ésta al añadir las desinencias -*ed*, -*ing*:

rake	raked	raking
care	cared	caring
smile	smiled	smiling
move	moved	moving
invite	invited	inviting

(Pero se conserva esta -*e* muda delante de -*ing* en los verbos *dye*, *singe* y otros, y en los pocos que terminan en -*oe*: *dyeing*, *singeing*, *hoeing*.)

(e) Si el verbo termina en -*y* (con las dos pronunciaciones de [i] y [ai]) se cambia ésta en -*ied* (con las pronunciaciones respectivas de [id] y [aid]) para formar el pretérito y el participio de pasado: *worry-worried-worried; pity-pitied-pitied; falsify-falsified-falsified; try-tried-tried*. El gerundio de tales verbos es regular: *worrying*, *trying* etc. Pero el gerundio de los verbos monosílabos *die*, *lie*, *vie* se escribe *dying*, *lying*, *vying*.

Numerals, Weights and Measures

Los números, pesos y medidas

I NUMERALS—LOS NÚMEROS

1 Cardinal numbers—Números cardinales

nought	0	cero
one	1	(m) uno, (f) una
two	2	dos
three	3	tres
four	4	cuatro
five	5	cinco
six	6	seis
seven	7	siete
eight	8	ocho
nine	9	nueve
ten	10	diez
eleven	11	once
twelve	12	doce
thirteen	13	trece
fourteen	14	catorce
fifteen	15	quince
sixteen	16	dieciséis
seventeen	17	diecisiete
eighteen	18	dieciocho
nineteen	19	diecinueve
twenty	20	veinte
twenty-one	21	veintiuno (see note b)
twenty-two	22	veintidós
twenty-three	23	veintitrés
thirty	30	treinta
thirty-one	31	treinta y uno
thirty-two	32	treinta y dos
forty	40	cuarenta
fifty	50	cincuenta
sixty	60	sesenta
seventy	70	setenta
eighty	80	ochenta
ninety	90	noventa
ninety-nine	99	noventa y nueve
a (or one) hundred	100	cien, ciento (see note c)
a hundred and one	101	ciento uno
a hundred and two	102	ciento dos
a hundred and ten	110	ciento diez

a hundred and eighty-two	182	ciento ochenta y dos
two hundred	200	(m) doscientos, (f) —as
three hundred	300	(m) trescientos, (f) —as
four hundred	400	(m) cuatrocientos, (f) —as
five hundred	500	(m) quinientos, (f) —as
six hundred	600	(m) seiscientos, (f) —as
seven hundred	700	(m) setecientos, (f) —as
eight hundred	800	(m) ochocientos, (f) —as
nine hundred	900	(m) novecientos, (f) —as
a (or one) thousand	1000	mil
a thousand and two	1002	mil dos
two thousand	2000	dos mil
ten thousand	10000	diez mil
a (or one) hundred thousand	100000	cien mil
a (or one) million	1000000	un millón (see note d)
two million	2000000	dos millones (see note d)

Notes on usage of the cardinal numbers

(a) **One,** and the other numbers ending in one, agree in Spanish with the noun (stated or implied): *una casa, un coche, si se trata de pagar en libras ello viene a sumar treinta y una, había ciento una personas.*

(b) **21:** In Spanish there is some uncertainty when the number is accompanied by a feminine noun. In the spoken language both *veintiuna peseta* and *veintiuna pesetas* are heard; in "correct" literary language only *veintiuna pesetas* is found. With a masculine noun the numeral is shortened in the usual way: *veintiún perros rabiosos.* These remarks apply also to 31, 41 *etc.*

(c) 100: When the number is spoken alone or in counting a series of numbers both *cien* and *ciento* are heard. When there is an accompanying noun the form is always *cien: cien hombres, cien chicas.* In the compound numbers note 101 = *ciento uno,* 110 = *ciento diez,* but 100000 = *cien mil.*

(d) 1000000: In Spanish the word *millón* is a noun, so the numeral takes *de* when there is a following noun: *un millón de fichas, tres millones de árboles quemados.*

(e) In Spanish the cardinal numbers may be used as nouns, as in English; they are always masculine: *jugó el siete de corazones, el once nacional de Ruritania, éste es el trece y nosotros buscamos el quince.*

(f) To divide the larger numbers clearly a point is used in Spanish where English places a comma: English 1,000 = Spanish 1.000, English 2,304,770 = Spanish 2.304.770. (This does not apply to dates: see below.)

2 Ordinal numbers—Números ordinales

first	1	primero (*see note* **b**)
second	2	segundo
third	3	tercero (*see note* **b**)
fourth	4	cuarto
fifth	5	quinto
sixth	6	sexto
seventh	7	séptimo
eighth	8	octavo
ninth	9	noveno, nono
tenth	10	décimo
eleventh	11	undécimo
twelfth	12	duodécimo
thirteenth	13	decimotercio, decimotercero
fourteenth	14	decimocuarto
fifteenth	15	decimoquinto
sixteenth	16	decimosexto
seventeenth	17	decimoséptimo
eighteenth	18	decimoctavo
nineteenth	19	decimonoveno, decimonono
twentieth	20	vigésimo
twenty-first	21	vigésimo primero, vigésimo primo
twenty-second	22	vigésimo segundo
thirtieth	30	trigésimo
thirty-first	31	trigésimo primero, trigésimo primo
fortieth	40	cuadragésimo

fiftieth	50	quincuagésimo
sixtieth	60	sexagésimo
seventieth	70	septuagésimo
eightieth	80	octogésimo
ninetieth	90	nonagésimo
hundredth	100	centésimo
hundred and first	101	centésimo primero
hundred and tenth	110	centésimo décimo
two hundredth	200	ducentésimo
three hundredth	300	trecentésimo
four hundredth	400	cuadringentésimo
five hundredth	500	quingentésimo
six hundredth	600	sexcentésimo
seven hundredth	700	septingentésimo
eight hundredth	800	octingentésimo
nine hundredth	900	noningentésimo
thousandth	1000	milésimo
two thousandth	2000	dos milésimo
millionth	1000000	millonésimo
two millionth	2000000	dos millonésimo

Notes on usage of the ordinal numbers

(a) All these numbers are adjectives in *-o,* and therefore agree with the noun in number and gender: *la quinta vez, en segundas nupcias, en octavo lugar.*

(b) *primero* and *tercero* are shortened to *primer, tercer* when they directly precede a masculine singular noun: *en el primer capítulo, el tercer hombre* (but *los primeros coches en llegar, el primero y más importante hecho*).

(c) In Spanish the ordinal numbers from 1 to 10 are commonly used; from 11 to 20 rather less; above 21 they are rarely written and almost never heard in speech (except for *milésimo,* which is frequent). The custom is to replace the forms for 21 and above by the cardinal number: *en el capítulo treinta y seis, celebran el setenta aniversario* (or *el aniversario setenta*), *en el poste ciento cinco contando desde la esquina.*

(d) Kings, popes and centuries. The ordinal numbers from 1 to 9 are employed for these in Spanish as in English: *en el siglo cuarto, Eduardo octavo, Pío nono, Enrique primero.* For 10 either the cardinal or the ordinal may be used: *siglo diez* or *siglo décimo, Alfonso diez* or *Alfonso décimo.* For 11 and above it is now customary to use only the cardinal number: *Alfonso once* (but *onceno* in the Middle Ages), *Juan veintitrés, en el siglo dieciocho.*

(e) Abbreviations. English 1st, 2nd, 3rd, 4th, 5th *etc* = Spanish 1º *or* 1ᵉʳ, 2º, 3º *or* 3ᵉʳ, 4º, 5º and so on (*f*: 1ᵉʳᵃ, 2ª).

(f) See also the notes on Dates, below.

3 Fractions—números quebrados

$\frac{1}{2}$: one half, a half/(m) *medio*, (f) *media*

$1\frac{1}{2}$: one and a half helpings/(*una*) *porción y media*

$2\frac{1}{2}$: two and a half kilos/*dos kilos y medio*

$\frac{1}{3}$: one third, a third/*un tercio, la tercera parte*

$\frac{2}{3}$: two thirds/*dos tercios, las dos terceras partes*

$\frac{1}{4}$: one quarter, a quarter/*un cuarto, la cuarta parte*

$\frac{3}{4}$: three quarters/*tres cuartos, las tres cuartas partes*

$\frac{1}{6}$: one sixth, a sixth/*un sexto, la sexta parte*

$5\frac{5}{6}$: five and five sixths/*cinco y cinco sextos*

$\frac{1}{12}$: one twelfth, a twelfth/*un duodécimo; un dozavo, la duodécima parte*

$\frac{7}{12}$: seven twelfths/*siete dozavos*

$\frac{1}{100}$: one hundredth, a hundredth/*un centésimo, una centésima parte*

$\frac{1}{1000}$: one thousandth, a thousandth/*un milésimo*

4 Decimals—las decimales

In Spanish a comma is written where English writes a point: English 3·56 (three point five six) = Spanish 3,56 (*tres coma cinco seis*); English ·07 (point nought seven) = Spanish ,07 (*coma cero siete*). The recurring decimal 3·3333 may be written in English as 3·3̇ and in Spanish as 3,3̄.

5 Nomenclature—nomenclatura

3,684 is a four-digit number/*3.684 es un número de cuatro dígitos* (or *guarismos*). It contains 4 units, 8 tens, 6 hundreds and 3 thousands/*Contiene 4 unidades, 8 decenas, 6 centenas y 3 unidades de millar.* The decimal ·234 contains 2 tenths, 3 hundredths and 4 thousandths/*la fracción decimal ,234 contiene 2 décimas, 3 centésimas y 4 milésimas.*

6 Percentages—los porcentajes

$2\frac{1}{2}\%$ two and a half per cent/*2½ por 100*, (less frequently) $2\frac{1}{2}\%$; *dos y medio por cien, dos y medio por ciento* (in spoken usage and among the authorities there is disagreement about *cien/ciento* here).

18% of the people here are over 65/*el dieciocho por cien de la gente aquí tienen más de 65 años.* Production has risen by 8%/*la producción ha aumentado en un 8 por 100.*

(*See also* per, hundred *in the main text.*)

7 Signs—los signos

English

$+$ addition sign

$+$ plus sign (*eg* $+ 7$ = plus seven)

$-$ subtraction sign

$-$ minus sign (*eg* $- 3$ = minus three)

$\times$ multiplication sign

$\div$ division sign

$\sqrt{}$ square root sign

∞ infinity

$\equiv$ sign of identity, is exactly equal to

$=$ sign of equality, equals

$\simeq$ is approximately equal to

$\neq$ sign of inequality, is not equal to

$>$ is greater than

$<$ is less than

Spanish

$+$ signo de adición

$+$ signo de más (*p.ej.* $+ 7 = 7$ de más)

$-$ signo de sustracción

$-$ signo de menos (*p.ej.* $- 3 = 3$ de menos)

$\times$ signo de multiplicación

$:$ signo de división

$\sqrt{}$ signo de raíz cuadrada

∞ infinito

$\equiv$ signo de identidad, es exactamente igual a

$=$ signo de igualdad, es igual a

$\approx$ es aproximadamente igual a

$\neq$ signo de no identidad, no es igual a

$>$ es mayor que

$<$ es menor que

8 Calculations—el cálculo

$8 + 6 = 14$ eight and (*or* plus) six are (*or* make) fourteen/*ocho y* (or *más*) *seis son catorce*

$15 - 3 = 12$ fifteen take away three are (*or* equals) twelve, three from fifteen leaves twelve/*quince menos tres resta doce, de tres a quince van doce*

$3 \times 3 = 9$ three threes are nine, three times three is nine/*tres por tres son nueve*

$32 \div 8 = 4$ thirty-two divided by eight is (*or* equals) four/*32 : 8 = 4 treinta y dos dividido por ocho es cuatro*

$3^2 = 9$ three squared is nine/*tres al cuadrado son nueve*

$2^5 = 32$ two to the fifth (*or* to the power of five) is (*or* equals) thirty-two/*dos a la quinta potencia son treinta y dos*

$\sqrt{16} = 4$ the square root of sixteen is four/*la raíz cuadrada de dieciséis es cuatro.*

9 Time—la hora

2 hours 33 minutes and 14 seconds/*2 horas 33 minutos y 14 segundos*

half an hour/*media hora*

a quarter of an hour/*un cuarto de hora*

three quarters of an hour/*tres cuartos de hora*

what's the time?/*¿qué hora es?*

what do you make the time?/*¿qué hora tienes?*

have you the right time?/*¿tiene Vd la hora exacta?*

I make it 2.20/*yo tengo las dos veinte*

my watch says 3.37/*mi reloj marca las tres treinta y siete*

it's 1 o'clock/*es la una*

it's 2 o'clock/*son las dos*

it's 5 past 4/*son las cuatro y cinco*

it's 10 to 6/*son las seis menos diez*

it's half-past 8/*son las ocho y media*

it's a quarter past 9/*son las nueve y cuarto*

it's a quarter to 2/*son las dos menos cuarto*

at 10 a.m./*a las diez de la mañana*

at 4 p.m./*a las cuatro de la tarde*

at 11 p.m./*a las once de la noche*

at exactly 3 o'clock, at 3 sharp, at 3 on the dot/*a las tres en punto*

the train leaves at 19.32/*el tren sale a las diecinueve treinta y dos*

(at) what time does it start?/*¿a qué hora comienza?*

it is just after 3/*son un poco más de las tres*

it is nearly 9/*son casi las nueve*

about 8 o'clock/*cerca de las ocho, hacia las ocho, a eso de las ocho*

at (*or* by) 6 o'clock at the latest/*a las seis a más tardar*

have it ready for 5 o'clock/*téngalo listo para las cinco*

it is full each night from 7 to 9/*está lleno todas las noches de siete a nueve*

"closed from 1.30 to 4.30"/"*cerrado de 1.30 a 4.30*"

until 8 o'clock/*hasta las ocho*

it would be about 11/*serán las once*

it would have been about 10/*serían las diez*

at midnight/*a medianoche*

before midday, before noon/*antes del mediodía*

10 Dates—las fechas

N.B. The days of the week and the months are written with small letters in Spanish: *lunes, martes, febrero, mayo.*

the 1st of July, July 1st/*el 1º de julio, el primero de julio*

the 2nd of May, May 2nd/*el 2 de mayo, el dos de mayo* (the cardinal numbers are used in Spanish for dates from 2nd to 31st)

on the 21st (of) June/*el 21 de junio, el día veintiuno de junio*

on Monday/*el lunes*

he comes on Mondays/*viene los lunes*

"closed on Fridays"/"*cerrado los viernes*"

he lends it to me from Monday to Friday/*me lo presta de lunes a viernes*

from the 14th to the 18th/*desde el 14 hasta el 18, desde el catorce hasta el dieciocho*

what's the date?, what date is it today?/*¿qué día es hoy?*

today's the 12th/*hoy es el doce, estamos a doce*

one Thursday in October/*un jueves en octubre*

about the 4th of July/*hacia el cuatro de julio*

Heading of letters: 19th May 1984/*19 de mayo de 1984*

1975, nineteen (hundred and) seventy-five/*mil novecientos setenta y cinco*

4 B.C., B.C. 4/*4 a. de J.C.* (*see* Abbreviations)

70 A.D., A.D. 70/*70 d. de J.C.* (*see* Abbreviations)

in the 13th Century/*en el siglo XIII, en el siglo trece*

in (*or* during) the 1930s/*en el decenio de 1930 a 40, durante los años treinta*

in 1940 something/*en el año 1940 y tantos*

(*See* also in the main text of the dictionary week, year *etc.*)

II WEIGHTS AND MEASURES—PESOS Y MEDIDAS

1 Metric system—sistema métrico

(Measures formed with the following prefixes are mostly omitted/*se omiten la mayor parte de las medidas formadas con los siguientes prefijos:*

deca-	10 times,	10 veces
hecto-	100 times,	100 veces
kilo-	1000 times,	1000 veces
deci-	one tenth,	una décima
centi-	one hundredth,	une centésima
mil(l)i-	one thousandth,	una milésima)

Linear measures—medidas de longitud

1 millimetre (milímetro)	= 0·03937 inch (pulgada)
1 centimetre (centímetro)	= 0·3937 inch (pulgada)
1 metre (metro)	= 39·37 inches (pulgadas)
	= 1·094 yards (yardas)
1 kilometre (kilómetro)	= 0·6214 mile (milla) *or* almost exactly five-eighths of a mile

Square measures—medidas cuadradas o de superficie

1 square centimetre (centímetro cuadrado)	= 0·155 square inch (pulgada cuadrada)
1 square metre (metro cuadrado)	= 10·764 square feet (pies cuadrados)
	= 1·196 square yards (yardas cuadradas)
1 square kilometre (kilómetro cuadrado)	= 0·3861 square mile (milla cuadrada)
	= 247·1 acres (acres)
1 are = 100 square metres (área)	= 119·6 square yards (yardas cuadradas)
1 hectare = 100 ares (hectárea)	= 2·471 acres (acres)

Cubic measures—medidas cúbicas

1 cubic centimetre (centímetro cúbico)	= 0·061 cubic inch (pulgada cúbica)
1 cubic metre (metro cúbico)	= 35·315 cubic feet (pies cúbicos)
	= 1·308 cubic yards (yardas cúbicas)

Measure of capacity—medida de capacidad

1 litre (litro) = 1000 cubic centimetres	= 1·76 pints (pintas)
	= 0·22 gallon (galón)

Weights—pesos

1 gramme (gramo)	= 15·4 grains (granos)
1 kilogramme (kilogramo)	= 2·2046 pounds (libras)
1 quintal (quintal métrico) = 100 kilogrammes	= 220·46 pounds (libras)
1 metric ton (tonelada métrica) = 1000 kilogrammes	= 0·9842 ton (tonelada)

2 British system—sistema británico

Linear measures—medidas de longitud

1 inch (pulgada)	= 2,54 centímetros
1 foot (pie) = 12 inches	= 30,48 centímetros
1 yard (yarda) = 3 feet	= 91,44 centímetros
1 furlong (estadio) = 220 yards	= 201,17 metros
1 mile (milla) = 1760 yards	= 1609,33 metros = 1,609 kilómetros

Surveyors' measures—medidas de agrimensura

1 link = 7·92 inches	= 20,12 centímetros
1 rod (*or* pole, perch) = 25 links	= 5,029 metros
1 chain = 22 yards = 4 rods	= 20,12 metros

Square measures—medidas cuadradas o de superficie

1 square inch (pulgada cuadrada)	= 6,45 cm^2
1 square foot (pie cuadrado) = 144 square inches	= 929,03 cm^2
1 square yard (yarda cuadrada) = 9 square feet	= 0,836 m^2
1 square rod = 30·25 square yards	= 25,29 m^2
1 acre = 4840 square yards	= 40,47 áreas
1 square mile (milla cuadrada) = 640 acres	= 2,59 km^2

Cubic measures—medidas cúbicas

1 cubic inch (pulgada cúbica)	= 16,387 cm^3
1 cubic foot (pie cúbico) = 1728 cubic inches	= 0,028 m^3
1 cubic yard (yarda cúbica) = 27 cubic feet	= 0,765 m^3
1 register ton (tonelada de registro) = 100 cubic feet	= 2,832 m^3

Measures of capacity—medidas de capacidad

(a) Liquid—para líquidos

1 gill	= 0,142 litro
1 pint (pinta) = 4 gills	= 0,57 litro
1 quart = 2 pints	= 1,136 litros
1 gallon (galón) = 4 quarts	= 4,546 litros

(b) Dry—para áridos

1 peck = 2 gallons	= 9,087 litros
1 bushel = 4 pecks	= 36,36 litros
1 quarter = 8 bushels	= 290,94 litros

Weights—pesos (Avoirdupois system—sistema avoirdupois)

1 grain (grano)	= 0,0648 gramo
1 drachm or dram	= 1,77 gramos
= 27,34 grains	
1 ounce (onza)	= 28,35 gramos
= 16 dra(ch)ms	
1 pound (libra)	= 453,6 gramos
= 16 ounces	= 0,453 kilogramo
1 stone = 14 pounds	= 6,348 kilogramos
1 quarter = 28 pounds	= 12,7 kilogramos
1 hundredweight	= 50,8 kilogramos
= 112 pounds	
1 ton (tonelada)	= 1,016 kilogramos
= 2240 pounds	
= 20 hundredweight	

3 US Measures—medidas norteamericanas

In the US the same system as that which applies in Great Britain is used for the most part; the main differences are mentioned below/*En EE.UU. se emplea en general el mismo sistema que en Gran Bretaña; las principales diferencias son las siguientes:*

Measures of capacity—medidas de capacidad

(a) Liquid—para líquidos

1 US liquid gill	= 0,118 litro
1 US liquid pint = 4 gills	= 0,473 litro
1 US liquid quart = 2 pints	= 0,946 litro
1 US gallon = 4 quarts	= 3,785 litros

(b) Dry—para áridos

1 US dry pint	= 0,550 litro
1 US dry quart = 2 dry pints	= 1,1 litros
1 US peck = 8 dry quarts	= 8,81 litros
1 US bushel = 4 pecks	= 35,24 litros

Weights—pesos

1 hundredweight	= 45,36 kilogramos
(or short hundredweight)	
= 100 pounds	
1 ton (or short ton)	= 907,18 kilogramos
= 2000 pounds = 20 short hundredweights	

4 Traditional Spanish weights and measures—pesos y medidas españoles tradicionales

(These are the measures which were standard until the introduction of the metric system in Spain in 1871, and they are still in use in some provinces and in agriculture/*Son éstas las medidas que se emplearon hasta la introducción del sistema métrico en España en 1871. Se emplean todavía en algunas provincias y en la agricultura*)

Linear measures—medidas de longitud

1 vara	= 0·836 metre
1 braza	= 1·67 metres
1 milla	= 1·852 kilometres
1 legua	= 5·5727 kilometres

Square measure—medida cuadrada o de superficie

1 fanega = 6460 square metres = 1·59 acres

Measures of capacity—medidas de capacidad

(a) Liquid—para líquidos

1 cuartillo	= 0·504 litre
1 azumbre	= 2·016 litres
= 4 cuartillos	
1 cántara	= 16·128 litres
= 8 azumbres	

(b) Dry—para áridos

1 celemín	= 4·625 litres
1 fanega	= 55·5 litres = 1·58 bushels
= 12 celemines	

Weights—pesos

1 onza	= 28·7 grammes
1 libra	= 460 grammes
= 16 onzas	
1 arroba	= 11·502 kilogrammes
= 25 libras	= 25 pounds
1 quintal	= 46 kilogrammes
= 4 arrobas	

Abbreviations and Field labels

Abreviaturas e Indicaciones semánticas

abbreviated	abbr	abreviado
Academy	Acad	Academia
accusative	acc	acusativo
adjective	adj	adjetivo
adverb	adv	adverbio
Aeronautics	Aer	Aeronáutica
Agriculture	Agr	Agricultura
Anatomy	Anat	Anatomía
anglicism	angl	anglicismo
Antilles, West Indies	Ant	Antillas
approximately	approx	aproximadamente
archaic	arch	arcaico
Architecture	Archit	Arquitectura
Argentina	Arg	
article	art	artículo
	Art	Arte
Astronomy	Astron	Astronomía
attributive	attr	atributivo
Automobiles	Aut	Automóviles
Bible	Bib	Biblia
Biology	Bio	Biología
Bolivia	Bol	
Botany	Bot	Botánica
	Boxing	Boxeo
	Bridge	
British	Brit	británico
Central America	CAm	Centroamérica
	Cards	Naipes
	Carpentry	Carpintería
Chemistry	Chem	Química
	Chess	Ajedrez
Chile	Chi	
Cinematography	Cine	Cinematografía
Colombia	Col	
Commerce	Comm	Comercio
comparative	comp	comparativo
conjunction	conj	conjunción
Cooking	Cook	Cocina
Costa Rica	CR	
Cuba	Cu	
	Dancing	Baile
dative	dat	dativo
definite	def	definido
demonstrative	dem	demostrativo
direct	dir	directo
Ecuador	Ec	
Ecclesiastical	Eccl	eclesiástico
Economics	Econ	Economía
(exempli gratia) for example	eg	por ejemplo
Electricity	Elec	Electricidad
Entomology	Ent	Entomología
especially	esp	especialmente
et cetera	etc	etcétera
euphemism	euph	eufemismo
exclamation	excl	exclamación
feminine	f	femenino
familiar	fam	familiar
	Fencing	Esgrima
figurative	fig	figurado
Finance	Fin	Finanzas
	Fish	Peces
	Football	Fútbol
feminine plural	fpl	femenino plural
frequently	freq	frecuentemente
gallicism	gall	galicismo
generally	gen	generalmente
Geography	Geog	Geografía
Geology	Geol	Geología
gerund	ger	gerundio
	Golf	
Grammar	Gram	Gramática
Guatemala	Guat	
Heraldry	Her	Heráldica
History	Hist	Historia
Honduras	Hond	
Horticulture	Hort	Horticultura
humorous	hum	humorístico
	Hunting	Caza
(id est) that is	ie	esto es, es decir
impersonal	impers	impersonal
indefinite	indef	indefinido
indicative	indic	indicativo
infinitive	infin	infinitivo
interjection	interj	interjección